Chambers
English
Dictionary

The editors wish to express their indebtedness to
previous editors of the dictionary who laid the
foundations on which this edition has been built.
These include the Rev. Thomas Davidson, William
Geddie, John Dickie, Miss A M Macdonald O.B.E.,
and Elizabeth M Kirkpatrick.

The editors would like to acknowledge with thanks the
contributions of the many members of the public who
send suggestions and comments. Such contributions are
always welcome, and will be acknowledged. They should
be sent to Catherine Schwarz, W & R Chambers Ltd,
43-45 Annandale Street, Edinburgh EH7 4AZ.

Chambers
English
Dictionary

Consultant editors:
USA
Sidney I Landau

Australia and New Zealand
W S Ramson, MA(NZ), PhD(Syd)

Editors
Catherine Schwarz, George Davidson,
Anne Seaton, Virginia Tebbit

Assistant Editors
Pandora Kerr Frost, Rachel Sherrard,
Mary Jane Kelly, Fergus McGauran

CHAMBERS
CAMBRIDGE

CAMBRIDGE   EDINBURGH
NEW YORK   NEW ROCHELLE   MELBOURNE   SYDNEY

Published jointly by W & R Chambers Limited
43–45 Annandale Street, Edinburgh EH7 4AZ, and
The Press Syndicate of the University of Cambridge
The Pitt Building, Trumpington Street, Cambridge CB2 1RP
32 East 57th Street, New York, NY 10022, USA
10 Stamford Road, Oakleigh, Melbourne 3166, Australia.

© W & R Chambers Ltd and Cambridge University Press 1988
This book first published as
Chambers's Twentieth Century Dictionary in 1901
and first published as
Chambers English Dictionary in 1988

Reprinted 1988, 1989

British Library Cataloguing in Publication Data

Chambers English dictionary—7th ed.
   1. English language—Dictionaries
   I. Chambers 20th century dictionary
   423

ISBN 1-85296-000-0, Standard
ISBN 1-85296-001-9, Thumb index
ISBN 1-85296-002-7, Presentation
ISBN 1-85296-003-5, Half Leather
ISBN 1-85296-005-1, Full Leather handbound

Typeset by Rand Services Ltd, Cambridge, UK
Printed in Great Britain by Richard Clay Ltd, Bungay, Suffolk

Contents

Using the dictionary

(See also inside covers)

The arrangement of entries

Dictionaries are all about words, and this particular dictionary contains a great many words for its size. The exceptionally large number of references has been achieved by the method of organising the entries. Words which are derived from the same root have often been grouped together under one headword as a space-saving device. This applies not only to words which simply add a suffix to the headword, e.g. **coolness**, which is under **cool**, but also to words which are more radically different from the root word. Thus, for example, **bronchitis** is entered under **bronchus, conclusion** under **conclude**, and **laborious** under **labour**.

These words are still quite easy to find, although they are not main entries, since their position in the dictionary is frequently very close alphabetically to what it would have been had they appeared as separate entries, e.g. **curvature**.

Cross-references have been given in many cases to make the entries easier to find, whilst still preserving the etymological 'nesting' system; e.g. **invasion** see **invade, donor** see **donation, liar** see **lie, zoon** see **zoo-**. This edition of the dictionary includes many cross-references of this nature.

The derivatives given under a headword are arranged alphabetically in three categories. The direct derivatives of the headword, i.e. those words which are formed by adding a suffix or ending to the headword or root word, are given immediately after the various meanings of the headword. After these come the compounds, some of which are hyphenated, some of which are one word and some of which are two words; where no grammatical label has been given at compounds they are to be assumed to be nouns. Those compounds which do not begin with the headword or derivative of the headword are listed under the third category, the phrases.

Order of definitions

Many words have more than one definition—some have a great many. There are at least two possible ways of ordering these definitions. One way is to give the most modern meaning first and the oldest last. The other is the way selected for this dictionary, historical order. In this method the original or oldest meaning of the word is given first and the most modern or up-to-date last.

Both methods are equally easy to use but historical order is perhaps more logical since it shows at a glance the historical development of the word, each entry providing a potted history of the word.

Labels

A label relating to grammatical form, e.g. *n., v.t., adj.,* appears before the word or meaning(s) to which it applies. A label relating to the classification (e.g. *coll., slang, obs., chem., elect., psych.*) precedes the list of meanings where it applies to all the meanings given. Where a label applies to only one meaning of a word it immediately follows that meaning.

Foreign words

Words in the text which are still regarded as foreign words, rather than as naturalised English words, have been labelled accordingly, e.g. (Fr.), (Ger.) etc.

German nouns have been spelt with a capital letter, as they are in their country of origin.

Etymologies

The etymology is given in square brackets at the end of each entry. The sign − indicates 'derived from'. The semicolon in etymologies is often used to separate words which are from the same source.

Hyphenation

Where the hyphen separating the elements of a hyphenated compound word in bold type occurs at the end of a line this has been shown by the symbol = to distinguish it from the ordinary hyphen which indicates a line-break.

Foreword

Chambers English Dictionary: An American View

Sidney I. Landau

author of *Dictionaries: The Art and Craft of Lexicography*

A strange thing has happened to the word 'English' in the last decade. It has become capable of being counted: one English, two Englishes, three Englishes—like peas or peppercorns. 'Let us now use the term "other Englishes",' writes Braj B. Kachru in *Language in the USA*, 'for those varieties of English which were spread and developed in areas other than the British Isles.'*

Once upon a time, the only recognized varieties of English were those found within Britain, and they were seldom accorded the status of English spoken in the few privileged public schools and at the universities of Oxford and Cambridge. As the years passed, the Englishes of the United States, Canada, Australia, New Zealand, India, the Caribbean and Africa developed new lexical forms and distinctive ranges of pronunciation that further distanced their speech from any recognizable variety of English used in the British Isles. These varieties of English have developed their own standard forms and can no longer be usefully identified as offshoots of the English of Britain. Of course, this is an old story in America; Noah Webster in the 19th century and H. L. Mencken in the 20th century made the case for viewing American English as a separate language.

The words we use to describe things count in establishing status. It is not mere variety that disposes people to care very much about what their languages are called; it most directly and materially affects how others perceive them. American English is not a mere variation of a true and proper English; it has its own standard forms derived from the distinctive character of the United States, its political history, its customs and conventions, and the values and character of its people.

This difference goes far deeper than the trivial dualities so often cited in discussions of US/British differences (gas/petrol; elevator/lift; mail/post, etc). Perhaps more fundamental are those differences that suggest different types of humor, different processes for forming metaphor and slang, and the particular path of deviations from each national standard to forms considered incorrect. Why do Americans tend to use 'lay' for 'lie' or 'like' for 'as' or fall into the trap of hypercorrection and say, 'He told James and I not to be late'?

Chambers dictionaries have long reflected an interest in American English. *Chambers's English Dictionary* of 1872 included an eight-page appendix of Americanisms printed in small type, three columns to the page. The appendix includes such familiar American expressions as 'cotton to', 'enthuse', 'human' (for human being), 'like' (= as), 'lay' (= lie), 'potwalloper', 'sockdolager', and 'reckon' (to think, imagine, believe, conjecture).

It must be acknowledged, however, that *Chambers* has not consistently maintained a full record of English as it is used in the United States. The current edition, retitled *Chambers English Dictionary* and thus restoring the original 1872 title, marks the beginning of the process of enlarging coverage of American English, while at the same time recognizing that this is essentially a dictionary of British English. American readers will find *Chambers* especially valuable in guiding them from the American form of a word to the form used in Britain and elsewhere in the English-speaking world. Those who already own an American dictionary can profit from owning this dictionary in addition; they will find that it covers much ground that no American dictionary touches.

*Ferguson, Charles A. and Shirley Brice Heath, eds. *Language in the USA* (Cambridge: Cambridge University Press 1981), p. 26.

The Chambers Tradition

Tom McArthur

editor of *English Today* and author of *Worlds of Reference*

Chambers English Dictionary not only spans nine decades of the present century, but is the product of a tradition that dates back to 1832, the year of the Reform Act, when Gladstone entered British politics, Andrew Jackson was the President of the United States, Lewis Carroll was born, and both Sir Walter Scott and Johann von Goethe died. The copy in your hand serves strictly contemporary ends, but it has 156 years of continuous experience behind it, from the days when popular educational publishing took root in Britain.

In 1832, William and Robert Chambers brought out in the city of Edinburgh *Chambers's Journal*, a weekly whose circulation grew to many thousands, with every copy having numerous readers. In the Galloway hills of Scotland, for example, shepherds passed it round. When the first had read the latest issue, he put it under a stone at the edge of the next reader's territory. So it circulated, helping the Chambers brothers fulfil their claim to be 'publishers for the people'.

In 1844, they brought out a *Cyclopaedia of English Literature*; in 1859, the first edition of *Chambers's Encyclopaedia*, a *Dictionary of Universal Knowledge for the People*; and in 1867, James Donald's *Chambers's Etymological Dictionary*. Donald's larger *Chambers's English Dictionary* came out in 1872, 'at a moderate price . . . for the general use'. It was the prototypical Chambers wordbook—a cornucopia of classical, vernacular, obsolete, rare, literary, biblical, scientific, technical, simple, compound, and derived words.

In 1898, a new edition of *Chambers's English Dictionary* appeared. Its editor, the Rev. Thomas Davidson, included 'the obsolete words imperishable in Spenser, Shakespeare, the Authorized Version of the Bible, and Milton; the Scotch words of Burns and Scott; the slang words of Dickens and the man in the street; the honest Americanisms of Lowell and Mark Twain; the coinages of wordmasters like Carlyle, Browning and Meredith; [and] provincial and dialect words that have attained to immortality in the pages of the Brontes and George Eliot'. The 1914 edition added 'words and phrases characteristic of the British dominions'.

In 1901, a compact version of Davidson's dictionary incorporated the phrase 'twentieth century' into its title, and over the decades grew into the flagship of the Chambers fleet. Now, looking ahead to a new century, the *20th Century Dictionary* has been retitled *Chambers English Dictionary*, a return to the name in use for the leading Chambers dictionary a hundred years ago.

This most recent edition is both cumulative and contemporary, an endearing and enticing blend of information, education and entertainment. Cacolets and coistrels rub shoulders with cokernuts, colleens, colporteurs and commots (which are of course sub-divisions of cantreds). They also co-occur with word-sets like companion, companionable, companionate, companionate marriage, and the companion star (of astronomy).

Chambers is the canonical reference book of the United Kingdom Scrabble® Championships, the recommended dictionary for the crossword puzzles of the *Listener*, the *Observer* Magazine, and the *Spectator*; it is the touchstone for word games and puzzle magazines of all kinds. It therefore serves both the general inquirer/enquirer and the dedicated aficionado ('an ardent follower', from Spanish). The shepherds of old Galloway would have approved.

SCRABBLE® is the trademark of J. W. Spears & Sons PLC

Preface

Chambers English Dictionary is a direct descendant of *Chambers Twentieth Century Dictionary*, which became, over the decades, an international institution. In common with all the best institutions, *Chambers* has evolved and altered with the times and this latest edition has been meticulously prepared with the demands of the modern era in mind.

Language, being the very substance of communication, is ever-changing as people develop and widen their interests and capabilities. Dictionaries, which must be faithful recorders of the language, need to reflect changes. Dramatic events in science, medicine and technology, politics, business, industry, sport and international relations all make their mark on the words we employ. The editors of *Chambers English Dictionary* always try to do justice to these developments when selecting words to include.

The chief concern of modern lexicographers in compiling or updating a dictionary, therefore, is to take account of contemporary English by including new words and new meanings of old words. At the same time, Chambers lexicographers never overlook the importance of words that have been with us for some time. The dictionary is, for its size, unparalleled in its comprehensiveness.

Generations of users of *Chambers* have numbered not only students of language and literature but also people who love language and like to see how English has evolved historically. *Chambers* has long played its full part in recording and encouraging the development of modern English.

The unusual and archaic words in *Chambers* represent a treasure-house for the word-game fan. Crossword compilers and solvers hunger for such words, whilst Scrabble® players use them as deadly ammunition with which to confound their opponents. *Chambers* is a familiar sight to Scrabble players, being the reference dictionary for the National Scrabble Championship and the National Scrabble Club Tournament. Many dedicated players can state offhand, without looking, on which page and column of the dictionary a particular word appears.

Word-puzzlers remind us that language should contain an element of fun and entertainment. Regular users of *Chambers* appreciate the place of humour and know that wryly amusing definitions lurk within its pages.

Chambers has a large and loyal readership of people who not only use it for finding the meaning of a word, for checking a spelling or for solving word-puzzles, but who read it simply for pleasure, as though the dictionary were a novel or biography. The wealth of pleasure to be derived from dictionaries is being ever more widely appreciated.

Thanks to newspapers, radio and television, people nowadays are much more aware of language and its power and effect. The result, happily, is that love and appreciation of language is less the exclusive preserve of a particular section of society. Whether coming to *Chambers English Dictionary* as new acquaintances or as old friends, users will not be disappointed.

Detailed chart of pronunciation

Respelling is a rough method of showing pronunciation compared with the use of phonetic symbols, but it has two merits — it is intelligible to a large number of people who do not know phonetic symbols, and it allows for more than one interpretation so that each user of the dictionary may choose a pronunciation in keeping with his speech.

Vowels and diphthongs in accented syllables

Symbol	Examples	Pronunciation
ā	as in name, aid, rein, tare, wear, hair, heir, fairy	*nām, ād, rān, tār, wār, hār, ār, fār'i*
ä	„ grass, path, palm, harm, heart	*gräs, päth, päm, härm, härt*
a	„ sat, bad, have, marry	*sat, bad, hav, mar'i*
ē	„ lean, keel, dene, chief, seize, gear, sheer, here, bier, query	*lēn, kēl, dēn, chēf, sēz, gēr, shēr, hēr, bēr, kwe'ri*
e	„ red, thread, said, bury	*red, thred, sed, ber'i*
ī	„ side, shy, dye, height, hire, byre, fiery	*sīd, shī, dī, hīt, hīr, bīr, fīr'i*
i	„ pin, busy, hymn	*pin, biz'i, him*
ō	„ bone, road, foe, low, dough, more, soar, floor, port, Tory	*bōn, rōd, fō, lō, dō, mōr, sōr, flōr, pōrt, tō'ri*
	(For alternative pronunciation of port, more, etc., see ö)	
ö	„ haul, lawn, fall, bought, swarm, more, soar, floor, port, Tory	*höl, lön, föl, böt. swörm, mör, sör, flör, pört, tö'ri*
	(For alternative pronunciation of port, more, etc., see ō)	
o	„ got, shot, shone	*got, shot, shon*
o͞o	„ fool, sou, boor, tour	*fo͞ol, so͞o, bo͞or, to͞or*
o͝o	„ good, full, would	*go͝od, fo͝ol, wo͝od*
ū	„ tune, due, newt, view, endure, fury	*tūn, dū, nūt, vū, in-dūr', fū'ri*
u	„ bud, run, love	*bud, run, luv*
û	„ heard, bird, word, absurd, bury	*hûrd, bûrd, wûrld, ab-sûrd', bûr'i*
ow	„ mount, frown, sour	*mownt, frown, sowr*
oi	„ toy, buoy, soil	*toi, boi, soil*

Stress

In words of more than one syllable, the syllable with the main accent is shown by a stress mark ' following that syllable, both in the respellings (e.g. *äf'tər, bi-gin'*) and in entries in bold-faced type (e.g. **af'ters, beginn'er**).

Note the difference in pronunciation, as shown by the position of the stress mark, between **blessed'** (*blest*) and **bless'ed** (*bles'id*), **refined'** (*ri-fīnd'*) and **refin'edly** (*ri-fīn'id-li*).

Vowels in unaccented syllables

Neutral vowels in unaccented syllables are usually shown by ə (schwa)
   e.g. *el'ə-mənt, in'fənt, ran'dəm, pre'shəs* (precious), *nā'chər* (nature).

In certain cases, they are more exactly represented by *i*
   e.g. *ē'vil, bi-hōld', bles'id, man'ij, di-ment'.*

Vowels followed by *r*

In certain accents, for example in Scots, Irish, General American, **r** is pronounced wherever it occurs in the spelling and this is the form adopted in the dictionary.

In certain other accents, for example Received Pronunciation or what is sometimes called the BBC accent, it is pronounced only when it occurs before a vowel. Elsewhere the following rules apply:

ār	is pronounced as		eə	ör	is pronounced as		ö or öə
är	„	„ „	ä	o͞or	„	„ „	o͞oə
ēr	„	„ „	iə	ūr	„	„ „	ūə
er	„	„ „	eə	ûr	„	„ „	û
ir	„	„ „	īə	owr	„	„ „	owə

Consonants

Symbol		Examples	Pronunciation
b	as in	hob, rabbit	*hob, rab'it*
ch	,,	church, much, match	*chûrch, much, mach*
d	,,	ado, dew	*ə-dōō', dū*
dh	,,	then, father	*dhen, fä'dhər*
f	,,	faint, phase, rough	*fānt, fāz, ruf*
g	,,	gold, guard, ghastly	*gōld, gärd, gäst'li*
gz	,,	exact	*igz-akt'*
h	,,	happy, home	*hap'i, hōm*
hh	,,	loch, leprechaun	*lohh, lep're-hhön*
hl	,,	pennill, (*W.*) llan	*pen'ihl, hlan*
(h)w	,,	whale, which	*(h)wāl, (h)wich*
j	,,	jack, gentle, ledge, region	*jak, jen'tl, lej, rē'jən*
k	,,	keep, cat, chorus	*kēp, kat, kōr'əs (kör')*
ks	,,	lax, vex	*laks, veks*
kw	,,	quite, coiffeur	*kwit, kwä-fœr'*
l	,,	lamp, collar	*lamp, kol'ər*
m	,,	meat, palm, stammer	*mēt, päm, stam'ər*
n	,,	net, gnome, knee, dinner	*net, nōm, nē, din'ər*
ng	,,	fling, longing	*fling, long'ing*
ngg	,,	single, longer, languor	*sing'gl, long'gər, lang'gər*
ngk	,,	monkey, precinct	*mungk'i, prē'singkt*
p	,,	peat, apple	*pēt, ap'l*
r	,,	rest, wreck, arrive	*rest, rek, ə-riv'*
s	,,	sad, city, circuit, scene, mass, psalm	*sad, sit'i, sûr'kit, sēn, mas, säm*
sh	,,	shine, machine, sure, militia, acacia	*shin, mə-shēn, shōōr, mi-lish'ə, ə-kā'sh(y)ə*
t	,,	tape, nettle, thyme	*tāp, net'l, tim*
th	,,	thin, three	*thin, thrē*
v	,,	valid, river	*val'id, riv'ər*
w	,,	was, one, twig	*woz, wun, twig*
y	,,	young, bastion	*yung, bast'yən*
z	,,	zoo, was, roads	*zōō, woz, rōdz*
zh	,,	azure, measure, congé, lesion	*azh'ər (or ā'zhūr), mezh'ər, kɔ̃-zhā, lē'zhən*

Additional sounds in foreign and dialect words

Symbol		Examples	Pronunciation
ø	as in *Fr.*	deux, feu, peu	*dø, fø, pø*
œ	,, *Fr.*	fleur, leur, cœur	*floer, loer, koer*
ü	,,	(1) *Fr* sur, luminaire	*sür, lä-mē-ner*
		(2) *Ger.* über, Führer	*üb'ər, fü'rər*
		(3) *Scots* bluid, buik	*blüd, bük*

Nasalised vowels

ã	as in *Fr.*	sang, temps, dent	*sã, tã, dã*
ɛ̃	,, *Fr.*	faim, vin, plein	*fɛ̃, vɛ̃, plɛ̃*
ɔ̃	,, *Fr.*	tomber, long, sonde	*tɔ̃-ba, lɔ̃, sɔ̃d*
õe	,, *Fr.*	lundi, humble, un	*lõe-dē, õebl', õe*
ə̃	,, *Port.* são	*sə̃ōō*

An apostrophe is used to mark such pronunciations as *t'h* (representing the sound of two separate consonants, *t* followed by *h*) to distinguish this from the sound *th* (as in *thin*). It is also used in words such as timbre (*tɛ̃br'*), maître (*metr'*) and humble (*õebl'*) in the pronunciation of which a final *ə* (e.g. *tɛ̃-brə*) is possible.

Vowels in bold-faced entries

A breve, ‿, is used to show the pronunciation of certain short vowels in bold-faced entries. These vowels are to be pronounced as follows:

Symbol	Pronunciation	Symbol	Pronunciation
ắ	*a, e*	**ĭ, y̆**	*i*
ĕ	*e*	**ŏ**	*o*

The long vowels **ā, ē, i, ō, ū** have the values *ā, ē, i, ō, ū*; **ȳ** is to be pronounced *i*.

American English

Despite increased contact and communication between Britain and America there are still major differences in the forms of English spoken and written in the two countries.

Spelling differences in a number of individual words (e.g. *maneuver, defense*, and *practice* as a verb) have been noted in the dictionary. Groups of words in which the spelling is different are as follows:

Brit.	U.S.	
our	*or*	American spellings such as *color, humor,* have often been noted in the text.
re	*er*	*center, meter, reconnoiter, saltpeter, theater,* etc.
		But, to show the hard sound of *c* or *g*: *acre, lucre, massacre, ogre,* etc.
ll	*l*	Americans have single *l* in all derivatives in *-ed, -ing, -er* (or *-or*) of words ending in an *l*: *canceled, -ing, caroled, -ing, chiseled, -ing, counseled, -ing, -or, disheveled, -ing, equaled, -ing, imperiled, -ing, jeweled, -ing, -er, libeled, -ing, -er, reveled, -ing, -er, traveled, -ing, -er, victualed, -ing, -er,* etc. Also *woolen, marvelous.*
l or *ll*	*ll*	*enroll, enthrall, instill, thralldom.*
l	*ll*	In *fulfill, skillful, willful.*
		In nouns in *-ment: enrollment, enthrallment, fulfillment, installment.*
pp	*p*	*kidnaped, -ing, -er, worshiped, -ing, -er.*
tt	*t*	*carbureted, -or, sulfureted.*
ae, oe or *e*	*e*	The tendency to replace *ae* and *oe* in words from Greek or Latin by *e* is more strongly developed in the United States than in Britain: e.g. *etiology, hemoglobin, esophagus.*
ise or *ize*	*ize*	In verbs and their derivatives that may be spelt *-ise* or *-ize*, Americans prefer *-ize*.

American pronunciation is naturally not the same in all areas and in all classes, but generally speaking it shows differences from British English pronunciation in the following respects (not specifically noted in the dictionary):

Brit.	U.S.
ä	Various shorter forms of the vowel are common in place of English *ä*.
i	Where British English has *i* in final position, as in *happy*, Americans tend to pronounce the vowel *ē*.
ö	Alternative form *ä* is common in words such as *haunt, launch, saunter, taunt, vaunt*.
o	A longer vowel than the normal British one is heard in *coffee, long, officer, soft*, etc., (mostly words in which the vowel is followed by *f, th, s, r, g, ng*); *ä* also is widely used in these words. *Block, pond, probable, top*, etc. always have *ä*.
ū	In British English this is a diphthong; in American English it often loses its diphthongal character when preceded by *t, d, n, l,* or *s*, becoming ōō.
-il	In the commoner words Americans pronounce *-il*, as *agile* (aj'il), *fertile, fragile, futile, hostile, versatile*. In *infantile* and *juvenile*, both *-il* and *-il* are heard; *gentile* is always pronounced *-il; mercantile* is usually pronounced *-ēl*.
t	In words such as *batter, butter, writing*, the *-tt-/-t-* is pronounced with a sound similar or identical to that of the *-dd-/-d-* of *madder, shudder, riding*.

Vowels and diphthongs before *r*

Brit.	U.S.
ā	In America, this is commonly pronounced as a diphthong, the first element of which approaches a lengthened form of *e*. Sometimes the second element, *ə*, is not pronounced when the diphthong occurs in initial or medial position in a word; for example, the usual pronunciation of *Maryland* is mer'i-lənd.
a	Some Americans tend to make a sound approaching *e*, so that *marry*, for instance, approximates to *merry*.
i	The sound heard in *squirrel, stirrup*, and commonly also in *syrup*, approaches *û*.
u	In English speech, when *ur* is followed by a vowel, the sound of the *u* is not *û*, but Americans tend to pronounce the same vowel in *her* and *hurry*. Other examples are *occurring, worry*, and *courage*.
är spelt *er*	In words such as *clerk* and *Derby* where English speech preserves an older pronunciation *är*, American speech follows the spelling, pronouncing the words klûrk, dûr'bi, etc.
-ə-ri	Americans tend to give words in *-ary* and *-ory* a stronger secondary accent and to pronounce *-er'ē* and *-ōr'ē*. Examples are *necessary, monetary, secondary, temporary, obligatory, peremptory, respiratory.*

Some individual differences in the sounds of certain words and prefixes are noted in the dictionary, e.g. *tomato, schedule, simultaneous, anti-*.

Some variations in vocabulary and meaning between British English and American English are indicated in the dictionary, e.g. *bonnet, hood; braces, suspenders*. A few words used only in the U.S. are likewise indicated, e.g. *sidewalk*.

Some other varieties of English

British English and American English are only two of the many varieties of English which exist in the world today. Other forms of English exist elsewhere, notably in Canada, South Africa, India and Pakistan, Australia and New Zealand. These differ to a greater or lesser extent from the English of Britain and America with regard to vocabulary, grammar, pronunciation and sometimes spelling. Many words or meanings of words unique to these regional forms are noted in the dictionary, e.g. *baas, billabong, coloured, hartal, joey*. Some guidance on the pronunciation and spelling is given in the following notes. The grammatical differences are for the most part beyond the scope of a dictionary.

Canadian English

In spelling, Canadian usage stands midway between American English and British English. The usage is however far from uniform and varies from province to province and even from person to person. Hence such spellings as *color, traveler,* and *center,* which reflect American usage, and *colour, traveller,* and *centre,* which reflect the British, are to be found alongside each other.

In pronunciation, Canadian English exhibits features found in both American and British English although it more commonly follows American English, e.g. speakers of Canadian English pronounce *tomato* with an *ä* as do speakers of American English.

Brit.   Can.

r   Like American English, Canadian English pronounces *r* in word-final position and before a consonant.

t   In the pronunciation of many Canadians, words such as *matter* and *madder* rhyme, as in American English.

i   The sound heard in *squirrel,* etc. approaches *û.*

-il   Of the words which end in *-il* in British English, some e.g. *docile, textile, fragile,* end in *-il* as in British English, while others such as *missile* and *fertile* end in *-il* as in American English.

i, ow   Canadian English differs from both American and British English in its treatment of the vowels *ow* and *i,* in that the vowels in for example *loud* and *ride* do not rhyme with those of *lout* and *write.*

English in Australia and New Zealand

Although there are differences between the English spoken in Australia and that of New Zealand, some of which will be commented on below, the two varieties are sufficiently similar to each other to be treated together here.

The spelling of Australian English traditionally follows that of British English but American spelling is now sometimes also found.

Among the features of pronunciation that can be noted are:

Brit.   Austr., N.Z.

r   As in British English, *r* is not pronounced before a consonant or at the end of a word, except by speakers in the southern part of the South Island of New Zealand.

i   Like American English, Australian and New Zealand English has *ē* in words such as *happy, very,* where British English has *i.* In closed unstressed syllables, where British English has *i,* Australian and New Zealand English have *e,* as for example in *mistake, defeat, ticket,* etc.

ōōr   The pronunciation *ōōe* of words like *sure, pure,* etc. has been almost entirely superseded by either *ö* or *ōōa.*

ä   In many words in which British English has *ä,* Australian and New Zealand English have *a.* In words ending in *-ance,* New Zealand English has *ä* where Australian English has *a* or *ä.* In Australian English *lather* is pronounced with *a,* but in New Zealand with *ä.*

ō   Before *l,* this tends to be pronounced as *o.*

English in South Africa

In spelling, South Africa follows British English. In pronunciation, the following features are notable:

Brit.   S. Africa

r   The S. African English treatment of *r* word-finally and before consonants is the same as that of British English.

i   As in American, Australian and New Zealand English, S. African English has *ē* where British English has *i* in *very, secretary,* etc. In other positions, *i* is pronounced more centrally than in British English, with a vowel close to *ə.*

a, e, ä. etc.   There is a tendency to raise these vowels to values approaching *e, i, o/ö,* etc. so giving *de'dē* for *daddy, kit'l* for *kettle,* and so on.

är   This is normally pronounced as a long *e* or *ä* sound in words like *bear, fair,* etc.

English in the Indian Subcontinent

English in India, Pakistan and Bangladesh is normally not the mother tongue of its users, but learned as a second language. There is often a great deal of influence from the speakers' first language on the English used in India. The result is that there is no homogeneous Indian English which can be described here but only a number of features about which one may make some general remarks.

Two common features of Indian English are the use of retroflex *t, d,* etc. for British English *t, d,* etc., and the substitution of *p, t, d* for *f, th, dh.* Speakers whose native language is Hindi or Urdu tend to insert an *i* before the initial consonant clusters in words such as *speech, school,* because these consonant groups do not occur in initial positions in Hindi or Urdu.

Indian English pronounces word-final *r* and pre-consonantal *r.*

Vowels in unstressed syllables are often pronounced in the way they would be in stressed syllables, where British English has *ə* or *i.*

Characters used in etymologies

A brief guide to the pronunciation of some of the non-English characters which appear most frequently in etymologies is given below. The pronunciations given are necessarily approximate as it is not always possible to convey the exact phonetic values intended by means of respelling symbols or verbal explanations.

Vowels

Symbol	Sound
ā, ē, ī, ū	In etymologies, these are long vowels with the sounds (or approximately the sounds) represented by the respelling symbols *a* or *ä*, *ā* or *e*, *ē*, and *oo* respectively.
ō	This represents a long *o* or *ö* sound or a monophthongal pronunciation of the respelling character *ō*.
ȳ	A long *ü* sound.
ǣ	A long vowel similar in sound to the RP pronunciation of respelling symbol *a*.
a, e, etc., ă, ĕ, etc.	Short vowels corresponding to ā, ē, etc., with values, varying from language to language, similar to those of the corresponding long vowels or those of the short vowels of English.
â, ê, î, ô, û	In some languages, e.g. Middle High German, these symbols are used for long vowels with the values *ä*, *ā*, *ē*, *ō*, *oo* respectively.
ä, ö	These have the values of respelling symbols *e/ā and ø/œ* respectively.
ĩ etc.	The diacritic ˜ is used, as in the respelling, to show nasalisation of vowels.

Consonants

Symbol	Sound
ḍ, ṭ, ṇ, ṣ, ẓ,	These are retroflex counterparts of *t, d,* etc.
ṛ	In Sanskrit, a vowel rather than a consonant; in Hindi, etc., a consonant formed by the tongue moving from a retroflex position to strike against the teeth-ridge.
ḥ	The normal *h*-sound of English.
ṁ	This marks nasalisation of the preceding vowel or the following consonant in Sanskrit.
ñ	A sound similar to *ny*, as in Sp. *cañon*.
ṅ	The sound written *ng* in the respelling and in English orthography.
ś	In Sanskrit, etc., a sound similar to *sh*.
c	In Sanskrit, etc., a sound midway between *k* and *ch*; in Turkish, the sound of *j* as in *judge*.
ç	In French, Arabic and Portuguese, this represents the sound *s*; in Turkish, *ch*.
ş	In Turkish, the sound *sh*.
q	A sound similar to *k* but pronounced slightly farther back in the mouth.
ğ	This marks a lengthening of the preceding vowel in Turkish.
gg	In Gothic, the sound *ng*.
ˌ	In Russian words, this represents a 'soft sign', marking a *y*-like palatalisation of the preceding consonant; in Chinese words, it is a mark of strong aspiration; in Arabic, Hebrew and Hawaiian, a glottal stop.
ˌ	In Arabic and Hebrew, a sound like *hh* but produced rather deeper in the throat.

Abbreviations used in the dictionary

abbrev.	abbreviation
abl.	ablative
acc.	according
accus.	accusative
adj(s).	adjective(s)
adv(s).	adverb(s)
Aen.	Aeneid
aero.	aeronautics
agri.	agriculture
alch.	alchemy
alg.	algebra
anat.	anatomy
anc.	ancient(ly)
ant.	antiquities
anthrop.	anthropology
aor.	aorist
app.	apparently
approx.	approximately
arch.	archaic
archaeol.	archaeology
archit.	architecture
arith.	arithmetic
astrol.	astrology
astron.	astronomy
at. numb.	atomic number
attrib.	attributive(ly)
augm.	augmentative
A.V.	Authorised Version
B.	Bible (A.V.)
biol.	biology
book-k.	bookkeeping
bot.	botany
Bucks.	Buckinghamshire
c.	(L. circa) about
cap.	capital
cent.	century
cf.	(L. confer) compare
chem.	chemistry, chemical
Ch. of Eng.	Church of England
cog.	cognate
coll.	colloquial(ly)
collec.	collectively
comp.	composition
compar.	comparative
comput.	computers, computing
conj(s).	conjunction(s)
conn.	connected, connection
contr.	contracted, contraction
cook.	cookery
corr.	corruption, corresponding
crystal.	crystallography
dat.	dative
demons.	demonstrative
der.	derived, derivation
deriv.	derivative
derog.	derogatory, derogatorily
dial.	dialect(al)
Dict.	Dictionary
dim.	diminutive
dub.	doubtful
E.	East
eccles.	ecclesiastical
econ.	economics
e.g.	(L. exempli gratia) for example
elect.	electricity, electrical
electron.	electronic(s)
entom.	entomology
erron.	erroneous(ly)
esp.	especially
ety.	etymology
euph.	euphemistic(ally), euphemism
exc.	except
f.	feminine
facet.	facetiously
fam.	familiar, family
fem.	feminine
ff.	following
fig.	figurative(ly)
fl.	floruit
fol.	followed, following
form.	formerly
fort.	fortification
freq.	frequentative
F.Q.	Faerie Queene
fut.	future
gen.	genitive
gener.	generally
geog.	geography
geol.	geology
geom.	geometry
ger.	gerundive
gram.	grammar
Gr. Ch.	Greek Church
her.	heraldry
hist.	history
hort.	horticulture
hyperb.	hyperbolically
i.e.	(L. id est) that is
illit.	illiterate
imit.	imitative
imper.	imperative
impers.	impersonal(ly)
incl.	including
indic.	indicative
infin.	infinitive
infl.	influenced
intens.	intensive
interj(s).	interjection(s)
interrog.	interrogative(ly)
intrans.	intransitive
iron.	ironic
irreg.	irregular(ly)
lit.	literal(ly)
Linc.	Lincolnshire
log.	logic
m.	masculine
mach.	machinery
masc.	masculine
math.	mathematics
mech.	mechanics
med.	medicine
metaph.	metaphysics
meteor.	meteorology
mil.	military
Milt.	Milton
min.	mineralogy
mod.	modern
mus.	music
myth.	mythology
N.	North
n(s).	noun(s)
nat. hist.	natural history
naut.	nautical
N.E. Bible	New English Bible
neg.	negative
neut.	neuter
nom.	nominative
North.	Northern
n.pl.	noun plural
n.sing.	noun singular
N.T.	New Testament (A.V.)
nuc.	nucleonics, nuclear
obs.	obsolete
opp.	opposed, opposite
opt.	optics
org.	organic
orig.	original(ly), origin
O.S.	Old Style
O.T.	Old Testament (A.V.)
p.	participle
p.adj.	participial adjective
paint.	painting
palaeog.	palaeography
pa.p.	past participle
part.	participle
pass.	passive
pa.t.	past tense
path.	pathology
perf.	perfect
perh.	perhaps
pers.	person(al)
petr.	petrology
pfx.	prefix
philol.	philology
philos.	philosophy
phon.	phonetics
phot.	photography
phys.	physics
physiol.	physiology
pl.	plural
poet.	poetical
pol.	politics, political
pol. econ.	political economy
pop.	popular(ly)
poss.	possessive, possibly
Pr. Bk.	Book of Common Prayer
pr.p.	present participle
prep(s).	preposition(s)
pres.	present

pret.	preterite	*Shak.*	Shakespeare	*trig.*	trigonometry
print.	printing	*sig.*	signifying	*TV*	television
priv.	privative	*sing.*	singular		
prob.	probably	*South.*	Southern		
pron(s).	pronoun(s)	*specif.*	specifically	*ult.*	ultimately
pron.	pronunciation	*Spens.*	Spenser	*usu.*	usually
prop.	properly	*subj.*	subjective		
pros.	prosody	*suff.*	suffix		
psych.	psychology	*superl(s).*	superlative(s)	*vb(s).*	verb(s)
		surg.	surgery	*v(s).i.*	verb(s)
q.v., qq.v.(pl.) which see		*s.v.*	(L. *sub verbo*)		intransitive
			under the word	*voc.*	vocative
®	registered	*symb.*	symbol	*v(s).t.*	verb(s) transitive
	trademark			*vulg.*	vulgar
R.C.	Roman Catholic	*telecomm.*	telecommunica-		
redup.	reduplication		tions		
refl.	reflexive(ly)	*teleg.*	telegraphy	*W.*	West
rel.	related, relative	*Tenn.*	Tennyson		
rhet.	rhetoric	*term.*	termination		
R V	Revised Version	*theat.*	theatre,	*Yorks.*	Yorkshire
			theatrical		
		theol.	theology		
S.	South	*trans.*	transitive		
sculp.	sculpture		translation	*zool.*	zoology

A.Fr.	Anglo-French	*Heb.*	Hebrew	*O.H.G.*	Old High
Afrik.	Afrikaans	*Hind.*	Hindustani		German
Amer.	American	*Hung.*	Hungarian	*O.Ir.*	Old Irish
Angl.	Anglian			*O.N.,*	Old Norse
Ar.	Arabic	*Icel.*	Icelandic	*O.N.Fr.*	Old Northern
Assyr.	Assyrian		(Modern)		French
Austr.	Australian	*Ind.*	Indian	*O.Sax.*	Old Saxon
		Ir.	Irish	*Pers.*	Persian
Bav.	Bavarian	*It.*	Italian	*Peruv.*	Peruvian
Beng.	Bengali			*Pol.*	Polish
Bohem.	Bohemian	*Jap.*	Japanese	*Port.*	Portuguese
Braz.	Brazilian	*Jav.*	Javanese	*Prov.*	Provençal
Brit.	British				
		L.	Latin	*Rom.*	Roman
Can.	Canadian	*L.G(er).*	Low German	*Rum.*	Rumanian
Celt.	Celtic	*Lith.*	Lithuanian	*Russ.*	Russian
Chin.	Chinese	*L.L.*	Low or Late		
Copt.	Coptic		Latin	*S.Afr.*	South African
Corn.	Cornish			*Sans.*	Sanskrit
				Scand.	Scandinavian
Dan.	Danish	*M.Du.*	Middle Dutch	*Scot.*	Scottish
Du.	Dutch	*M.E.*	Middle English		(Broad Scots)
		Mex.	Mexican	*Serb.*	Serbian
Egypt.	Egyptian	*M.Flem.*	Middle Flemish	*Sinh.*	Sinhalese
Eng.	English	*M.Fr.*	Middle French	*Slav.*	Slavonic
		M.H.G.	Middle High	*Sp.*	Spanish
Finn.	Finnish		German	*Sw.*	Swedish
Flem.	Flemish	*M.L.G.*	Middle Low		
Fr.	French		German	*Turk.*	Turkish
Fris.	Frisian				
		Norm.	Norman	*U.K.*	United Kingdom
Gael.	Gaelic	*Norw.*	Norwegian	*U.S.*	United States
Ger.	German	*N.Z.*	New Zealand		(often includes
Gmc.	Germanic				Canadian)
Goth.	Gothic	*O.E.*	Old English	*Viet.*	Vietnamese
Gr.	Greek	*O.Fr.*	Old French	*W.*	Welsh
		O.Fris.	Old Frisian	*W.S.*	West Saxon

A

A¹, a *ā, n.* the first letter in our alphabet, as in the Roman, etc. (see **aleph, alpha**): in music, the major sixth of the scale of C: one of first class or order, or of a class arbitrarily designated A: see **blood-group:** the designation of the principal series of paper sizes, ranging from A0 (841 × 1189 mm.) to A10 (26 × 37 mm.): in road-classification, followed by a number, the designation of a major, or trunk, road, as *A68*: as a mediaeval Roman numeral A = 50 or 500; Ā = 5000. — **A1** (*ā wun*) the symbol for a first-class vessel in Lloyd's Register: hence first-rate; **A′-bomb** atomic bomb; **A′-effect** see under **alien; A level, Advanced level** esp. in England and Wales, (a pass in) an examination generally taken after seven years of secondary education. — Also *adjs.* (often with *hyphen*); also **advanced level**); **A′-road** a trunk or a principal road. — **from A to B** from one point or place to another; **from A to Z** from beginning to end: right through.

A² *ä, ə,* (*dial.*) *pron.* a monophthongised form of **I.**

a¹ *ə,* also (esp. emphatic) *ā, adj.* the indefinite article, a broken down form of **an¹** used before a consonant sound. [O.E. *ān,* one.]

a² *ä, ə,* (*dial.*) *pron.* he: she: it: they. [O.E. *hē,* he, *hēo,* she, *hīe,* they.]

a³ *ə,* a reduced form of the O.E. prep. *an, on,* on, in, at, chiefly used in composition as a prefix, as *a*broad, *a*fire, *a*float, *a*sleep, *a*-begging, *a*-hunting, occasionally used separately as a preposition, as *once a year.*

a′ *ö, ä,* Scots and Northern form of **all.** — *pron.* **a′′body** everybody. — *adv.* **a′′gate** every way. — *pron.* **a′′thing** everything. — *adv.* **a′′where** everywhere.

à *ə,* a form of the Latin prep. *ab,* from, of, as in Thomas à Kempis (Thomas from Kempen).

aa *ä′ä, n.* a type of scoriaceous lava with a rough surface and many jagged fragments. [Hawaiian.]

aardvark *ärt′färk′* (S.Afr.), *ärd′värk, n.* the ant-bear, a South African edentate. [Du. *aarde,* earth, *vark* (now *varken*), pig.]

aardwolf *ärt′volf′* (S.Afr.), *ärd′woolf, n.* the earthwolf, a hyena-like South African carnivore. [Du. *aarde,* earth, *wolf,* wolf.]

Aaronic, -al *ā-ron′ik, -l, adjs.* pertaining to Aaron, the Jewish high-priest: pontifical. — **Aaron's beard** a saxifrage, grown dangling from pots: the great St John's wort: ivy-leaved toadflax, or other plant; **Aaron's rod** mullein, golden-rod, or other plant, with tall straight flowering stem.

aasvogel *äs′fool* (S.Afr.), *äs′fō-gəl, n.* a South African vulture. [Du. *aas,* carrion, *vogel,* bird.]

Ab *ab, n.* the eleventh civil, fifth ecclesiastical month of the Jewish Calendar (parts of July and August). — Also **Av.** [Syriac.]

ab- *ab-, pfx.* used to indicate a centimetre-gram-second electromagnetic unit (e.g. **abam′pere, ab′volt** equivalent respectively to 10 amperes, 10^{-8} volts). [**absolute.**]

aba, abba *a′bə,* or **abaya** *a-bā′yə, ns.* a Syrian cloth, of goat's or camel's hair, usually striped: an outer garment made of it. [Ar. *'abā, 'abāya.*]

abac *ā′bak, n.* a nomogram. [Fr. *abaque* — L. *abacus.*]

abaca *ä-bä-kä′, n.* a plantain grown in the Philippine Islands: its fibre, called Manila hemp. [Tagálog.]

abaci. See **abacus.**

aback *ə-bak′, adv.* backwards: said of sails pressed backward against the mast by the wind (*naut.*) — hence (*fig.*) **taken aback** taken by surprise. [O.E. *on bæc,* on back; see **a³.**]

abactinal *ab-ak-tī′nəl, ab-ak′ti-nəl,* (*zool.*) *adj.* remote from the actinal area: without rays. — *adv.* **abactinally.**

abactor *ab-ak′tər, n.* a cattle thief. [L.L.]

abacus *ab′ə-kəs, n.* a counting-frame: a level tablet on the capital of a column, supporting the entablature (*archit.*): — *pl.* **ab′aci** (*-sī*), **ab′acuses.** [L. *abacus* — Gr. *abax, -akos.*]

Abaddon *ə-bad′ən, n.* Apollyon: hell (*Milt.*). [Heb. *ābaddōn,* from *ābad,* to be lost.]

ahaft *ə-bäft′,* (*naut.*) *adv.* and *prep.* behind. [**a³** and O.E. *bæftan,* after — pfx. *be-, æftan.* See **aft.**]

abalone *ab-a-lō′nä, n.* an edible shellfish, the sea-ear, especially a richly coloured kind found on the Pacific coast of North America, a source of mother-of-pearl. [Amer. Sp. *abulón.* Origin uncertain.]

abampere. See **ab-.**

abandon *ə-ban′dən, v.t.* to give up: to desert: to yield (oneself) without restraint: to give up all claims to: to banish (*Shak.*). — *n.* (sometimes as Fr. *ä-bā-dō*) the condition of letting oneself go: careless freedom of action. — *v.t.* (*Spens.*) **aband′** to abandon. — *adj.* **aban′doned** completely deserted: given up, as to a vice: profligate: very wicked. — *adv.* **aban′donedly.** — *ns.* **abandonee′** (*law*) an insurer to whom a wreck has been abandoned; **aban′donment.** [O.Fr. *abandoner,* to put at one's disposal or in one's control (*à bandon*), or to the ban; see **ban.**]

à bas *a bä,* (Fr.) *interj.* down, down with!

abase *ə-bās′, v.t.* to lower: to cast down: to humble: to degrade. — *adj.* **abased′** lowered. — *n.* **abase′ment.** [O.Fr. *abaissier,* to bring low — L. *ad,* to, L.L. *bassus,* low.]

abash *ə-bash′, v.t.* to strike with shame: to put out of countenance: to astound: to confound. — *adjs.* **abashed′; abash′less** shameless: unabashed. — *n.* **abash′ment.** [O.Fr. *esbahir* — pfx. *es-* (L. *ex,* out), *bahir,* to astound — interj. *bah.*]

abask *ə-bäsk′, adv.* in genial warmth. [**a³** and **bask.**]

abate¹ *ə-bāt′, v.t.* to demolish (*obs.*): to put an end to (*law*): to nullify, to bring down (*law*): to lessen: to deduct (with *of*): to mitigate: to blunt: to curtail (*Shak.*): to except (*Shak.*). — *v.i.* to grow less: to subside: to be abated (*law*). — *adjs.* **abāt′able; abāt′ed** blunted: diminished: lowered: subdued: beaten down or cut away, as the background of relief. — *n.* **abate′-ment** the act or process of abating: the sum or quantity abated: the state of being abated: the abandonment of an action, or the reduction of a legacy (*law*): a supposed mark of dishonour on a coat of arms (*her.*) — apparently never actually used. [O.Fr. *abatre,* to beat down — L. *ab,* from, and L.L. *batĕre,* for L. *batuĕre,* to beat.]

abate² *ə-bāt′, v.i.* and *v.t.* (*refl.*) to intrude on a freehold and take possession before the heir. — *ns.* **abate′ment; abāt′or.** [O.Fr. *enbatre,* to thrust in.]

abatis, abattis *ab′ə-tis, ə-bat′ē, -is,* (*fort.*) *n.* a rampart of felled trees, branches outward: — *pl.* **abat(t)is** (*-ēz*) [Fr.; see **abate¹.**]

abat-jour *a-ba-zhoor,* (Fr.) *n.* a skylight: a screen or shutter.

abattoir *ab′ə-twär, n.* a public slaughterhouse. [Fr.; see **abate¹.**]

abattu *a-bat-ü,* (Fr.) *adj.* cast down, dejected.

abature *ab′ə-chər, n.* the trail through underwood beaten down by a stag. [Fr.; see **abate¹.**]

abat-voix *a-ba-vwä,* (Fr.) *n.* a sounding-board.

abaxial *ab-ak′si-əl,* (*bot.*) *adj.* away from the axis. [Pfx. *ab-* and **axis¹.**]

abaya. See **aba.**

abb *ab, n.* properly woof- or weft-yarn, but sometimes warp-yarn. [O.E. *āb, āweb* — pfx. *ā,* out, *webb,* web.]

abba[1] *ab'ə, n.* father (applied to God) (*N.T.*): a Syriac or Coptic bishop. [Aramaic word *abbā* retained in the Greek N.T. and its translations.]

abba[2]. See **aba.**

abbacy *ab'ə-si, n.* the office or jurisdiction of abbot: the time during which one is abbot: an abbey. — *adj.* **abbatial** (*ab-ā'shl*) pertaining to an abbey, abbot or abbess. [App. orig. Scot.: L.L. *abbātia*, abbey.]

Abbasid(e) *a-bas'id, -īd, ab'ə-sid, -sīd, n.* any member of the later (750–1543) of the two great dynasties of caliphs, descendants of *Abbas*, uncle of Mohammed.

abbé *ab'ā, n.* a courtesy title for a priest, an ecclesiastic in minor orders, or for a tutor or holder of a benefice, even if a layman. [Fr., orig. abbot.]

abbess *ab'es, n.* a woman who is head of an abbey. [L.L. *abbātissa,* fem. of *abbās,* abbot.]

abbey *ab'i, n.* a convent under an abbot or abbess, or (*loosely*) a prior or prioress: the church now or formerly attached to it: a name often retained by an abbatial building that has become a private house: — *pl.* **abb'eys.** — **abb'ey-counter, -piece** a pilgrim's token, evidence of a visit to an abbey; **abb'ey-laird** (*hist.*) a debtor in sanctuary in the precincts of Holyrood Abbey; **abb'ey-lubber** a lazy monk — a term much used by the Reformers. [O.Fr. *abaïe* (Fr. *abbaye*) — L.L. *abbātia*; see **abba**[1], **abbacy.**]

abbot *ab'ət, n.* a male head of an abbey: — *fem.* **abb'ess.** — *n.* **abb'otship.** — **abbot of unreason** a lord of misrule or mock abbot in mediaeval revels. [L.L. *abbās, abbātis* — Aramaic *abbā*; see **abba**[1].]

abbreviate *ə-brē'vi-āt, v.t.* to shorten: to contract: to abridge. — *adj.* shortened. — *ns.* **abbrēviā'tion** an act of shortening: a shortened form: part of a word written or printed for the whole; **abbrē'viātor.** — *adj.* **abbrē'viatory** (*-ə-tor-i*). — *n.* **abbrē'viāture** (*obs.*) an abbreviation: an abridgment. [L. *abbreviāre, -ātum* — *ab,* intens., *brevis,* short.]

ABC *ā-bē-sē', also* (*obs.*) **abcee, absey** *ab'si, n.* the alphabet, from its first letters: a first reading-book: hence first rudiments: anything arranged alphabetically, as an acrostic, a railway guide. — **absey book** (*Shak.*) a primer or hornbook.

abdabs. See **habdabs.**

Abderian *ab-dē'ri-ən, adj.* of *Abdera,* a town in Thrace, the Gotham of the ancients, and birthplace of Democritus, 'the laughing philosopher'. — Also *n.* — *n.* **Abderite** (*ab'dər-īt*) a native or citizen of Abdera: a simpleton, Gothamite.

abdicate *ab'di-kāt, v.t. and v.i.* formally to renounce or give up (office or dignity). — *adjs.* **ab'dicable; ab'dicant.** — *n.* **abdicā'tion.** [L. *ab,* from or off, *dicāre, -ātum,* to proclaim.]

abdomen *ab'də-mən, ab-dō'mən, n.* the belly: in mammals, the part between diaphragm and pelvis: in arthropods, the hind-body. — *adj.* **abdominal** (*-dom'*). — *adv.* **abdom'inally.** — *adj.* **abdom'inous** pot-bellied. [L. *abdōmen, -inis.*]

abduce *ab-dūs', v.t.* an earlier form of **abduct.** — *adj.* **abdūc'ent** drawing back: separating. — *v.t.* **abduct** (*-dukt'*) to take away by fraud or violence: to kidnap: of a muscle, to cause abduction in (a part of the body). — *ns.* **abductee'** one who is abducted; **abduction** (*-duk'shən*) the carrying away, esp. of a person by fraud or force: separation of parts of the body after a wound or fracture (*surg.*): muscular action drawing one part of the body (such as an arm or finger) away from another or away from the median axis of the body: a syllogism whose minor premise is only probable (*log.*); **abduc'tor** one who abducts: a muscle that draws away. [L. *abdūcēre* — *ab,* from, *dūcēre, ductum,* to draw, lead.]

abeam *ə-bēm', (naut.) adv.* on the beam, or in a line at right angles to a vessel's length. [a[3] and **beam.**]

abear *ə-bār', v.t.* to bear, comport, behave (*obs.*): (only as *infinitive*) to endure or tolerate (*dial.*): — *pa.t.* **abore';** *pa.p.* **aborne'.** [O.E. *āberan.*]

abecedarian *ā-bi-sē-dā'ri-ən, adj.* pertaining to the ABC:

rudimentary: arranged in the manner of an acrostic. — *n.* a learner of the ABC, a beginner: a teacher of the ABC: an Anabaptist of a sect that rejected all learning. [ABC.]

abed *ə-bed', adv.* in bed. [a[3] and **bed**[1].]

abeigh *ə-bēhh', (Scot.) adv.* aloof. [Origin obscure.]

abele *ə-bēl', ā'bl, n.* the white poplar-tree. [Du. *abeel* — O.Fr. *abel, aubel* — L.L. *albellus* — L. *albus,* white.]

Abelia *ə-bēl'i-ə, n.* a genus of shrubs of the honeysuckle family with pink or white flowers: (without *cap.*) a plant of this genus. [Clarke *Abel,* 1780–1826, English physician and botanist.]

Aberdeen *ab-ər-dēn', sometimes ab', adj.* of or originating in *Aberdeen* or Aberdeenshire. — *n.* (in full **Aberdeen terrier**) a coarse-haired kind of Scottish terrier. — *adj.* **Aberdō'nian** of Aberdeen: (*traditionally*) parsimonious. — Also *n.* — **Aberdeen Angus** (*ang'gəs*) a breed of polled cattle descended from Aberdeenshire humlies and Angus doddies.

aberdevine *ab-ər-di-vīn', n.* a bird-fancier's name for the siskin. [Ety. uncertain.]

Aberdonian. See **Aberdeen.**

Aberglaube *ab-ər-glow'bə,* (Ger.) *n.* superstition.

Abernethy biscuit *ab-ər-neth'i, -nēth'i, or ab', bis'kit* a hard biscuit, apparently originally with caraway seeds. [Poss. after Dr John *Abernethy* (1764–1831), who was interested in diet.]

aberrate *ab'ər-āt, v.i.* to wander or deviate from the right way. — *ns.* **aberrance** (*-er'*), **aberr'ancy.** — *adj.* **aberr'ant** wandering: having characteristics not strictly in accordance with type (*bot., zool.*). — *n.* **aberrā'tion** (*-ər-*) a deviation from the usual, normal, or right: a wandering of the intellect, mental lapse: a non-convergence of rays, owing to difference in refrangibility of different colours (*chromatic aberration*) or to difference of focus of the marginal and central parts of a lens or mirror (*spherical aberration*): an apparent displacement of a star, owing to the finite ratio of the velocity of light to that of the earth (*aberration of light*). [L. *aberrāre, -ātum* — *ab,* from, *errāre,* to wander.]

abessive *ab-es'iv, (gram.) adj.* denoting absence or lack. — *n.* the abessive case. [L. *abesse,* to be absent.]

abet *ə-bet', v.t.* to incite by encouragement or aid (used chiefly in a bad sense; see also **aid and abet** under **aid**): to back up (*Spens.*): to make good: — *pr.p.* **abett'ing;** *pa.p.* **abett'ed.** — *n.* (*Spens.*) abetting. — *ns.* **abet'ment; abett'er,** (esp. *legal*) **abett'or.** [O.Fr. *abeter* — *à* (L. *ad,* to), and *beter,* to bait; see **bait.**]

ab extra *ab eks'tra,* (L.), from the outside.

abeyance *ə-bā'əns, n.* a state of suspension or temporary inactivity: the state of being without a claimant (as a peerage). — Also **abey'ancy.** — *adj.* **abey'ant.** [O.Fr. *abeance* — *à* (L. *ad,* to), and *beer, baer,* to gape, open wide; origin uncertain.]

abhominable. See **abominable.**

abhor *ab-hör', v.t.* to shrink from with horror: to detest: to loathe: to protest against, to reject (*Shak.*): to fill with horror (*Shak.*): — *pr.p.* **abhorr'ing;** *pa.t. and pa.p.* **abhorred'.** — *ns.* **abhorr'ence** (*-hor'*) extreme hatred: a thing abhorred; **abhorr'ency** (*obs.*). — *adj.* **abhorr'ent** detesting: repugnant: strongly opposed: out of keeping: detestable: detested. — *adv.* **abhorr'ently.** — *ns.* **abhorr'er** one who abhors: (with *cap.; hist.*) a member of the court party in England in 1679, who abhorred the Petitioners, a Tory; **abhorr'ing** repugnance: an object of abhorrence. [L. *abhorrēre* — *ab,* from, and *horrēre,* to bristle, shudder.]

Abib *ā'bib, n.* earlier name for **Nisan.** [Heb. *ābīb,* lit. an ear of corn.]

abide[1] *ə-bīd', v.t.* to bide or wait for: to meet, face, sustain: to endure: to tolerate. — *v.i.* to remain: to dwell or stay: to conform to, adhere to, comply with, obey (with *by*): — *pa.t.* **abōde',** *also* **abīd'ed,** *Spens.* **abīd';** *pa.p.* **abōde', abīd'ed,** *also* **abīdd'en.** — *n.* **abīd'ance.** — *adj.* **abīd'ing** continual, permanent. — *n.* a continuance (*arch.*). — *adv.* **abīd'ingly.** [O.E. *ābīdan* — pfx. *ā-,* and *bīdan,* to wait.]

abide[2] *ə-bīd'*, (*Shak.*; *Milt.*) *v.t.* to aby. [**aby**, confounded with **abide**[1].]

à bientôt *a byě-tō*, (Fr.) see you again soon.

Abies *āb'i-ēz*, *n.* the genus of the true firs: (without *cap.*) a tree of the genus.

abigail *ab'i-gāl*, *n.* a lady's-maid. [From *Abigail*, in Beaumont and Fletcher's *Scornful Lady*, or 1 Sam. xxv.]

ability *ə-bil'i-ti*, *n.* the quality or fact of being able (to): power (physical and mental): strength: skill. [O.Fr. *ableté* (Fr. *habileté*), remodelled on its source, L. *habilitās, -ātis — habēre*, to have, hold; see **able**.]

ab initio *ab in-ish'i-ō, -it'i-ō*, (L.) from the beginning.

ab intra *ab in'tra*, (L.) from the inside.

abiogenesis *ab-i-ō-jen'is-is*, or *ā-bī-*, *n.* the origination of living by non-living matter, spontaneous generation. — *adj.* **abiogenetic** (*-ji-net'ik*). — *adv.* **abiogenet'ically.** — *n.* **abiogenist** (*-oj'ə-nist*) a believer in abiogenesis. [Coined by T. H. Huxley in 1870; Gr. *a-*, neg., *bios*, life, *genesis*, birth.]

abiosis *ā-bī-ō'sis, n.* absence of life. — *adj.* **ābiot'ic** without life: inanimate. [Gr. *a-*, neg., *biotikos — bios*, life.]

abiturient *ab-it-ū'ri-ənt*, *n.* in Germany, a pupil leaving school for a university. [Mod. L. *abituriēns, -entis*, pr.p. of *abiturīre*, desiderative of L. *abīre*, to go away — *ab*, from, *īre*, to go.]

abject *ab-jekt'*, *v.t.* to throw or cast down or away (*obs.*). — *adj.* **ab'ject** cast away: mean: worthless: grovelling: base. — *n.* an outcast: a base slave: one in more servile subjection than a subject. — *n.* **abjec'tion** abjectness: casting forth: forcible expulsion of spores (*bot.*). — *adv.* **ab'jectly.** — *n.* **ab'jectness.** [L. *abjicěre, abjectum — ab*, from, *jacěre*, to throw.]

abjoint *ab-joint'*, (*bot.*) *v.t.* to cut off by forming a septum. — *n.* **abjunction** (*-jungk'shən*). [L. *ab*, from, **joint**, **junction.**]

abjure *ab-jōōr'*, *v.t.* to renounce on oath or solemnly: to recant: to repudiate. — *ns.* **abjurā'tion; abjur'er.** [L. *ab*, from, *jurāre, -ātum*, to swear.]

ablactation *ab-lak-tā'shən*, *n.* a weaning: grafting by inarching. [L. *ab*, from, *lactāre*, to suckle — *lac*, milk.]

ablation *ab-lā'shən*, *n.* removal: decrease by melting, evaporation, weathering. — *v.t.* **ablate** (*ab-lāt'*) to remove or decrease by ablation. — *adjs.* **ablatitious** (*-lə-tish'əs*); **ab'lative** (*-lə-tiv*) pertaining to ablation: in or belonging to a case which in Indo-European languages originally expressed *direction from*, or *time when*, later extended to other functions (*gram.*). — *n.* the ablative case: a word in the ablative. — *adj.* **ablatī'val.** — *n.* **ablā'tor** a substance or material undergoing ablation, esp. the heat shield of a spacecraft. — **ablative absolute** in Latin a phrase generally comprising a noun or pronoun coupled with another noun, an adjective or a participle, both in the ablative case and usu. indicating the time or cause of an event. [L. *ab*, from, *lātum*, used as supine of *ferre*, to take.]

ablaut *äp'lowt, ab'lowt*, (*philol.*) *n.* a variation in root vowel as in sing, sang, song, sung, explained by former accentuation — also called gradation. [Ger., *ab*, off, *Laut*, sound.]

ablaze *ə-blāz'*, *adv.* and *adj.* in a blaze, on fire: gleaming brightly. [**a**[3] and **blaze**[1].]

able *ā'bl, adj.* having enough strength, power or means (to do a thing): skilful. — *v.t.* to enable (*obs.*): to warrant (*Shak.*). — *adj.* **a'ble-bod'ied** of a strong body: free from disability, etc.: robust. — *advs.* **a'bly; a(i)blins** (*ā'blinz*) or **yibbles** (*yib'lz*) perhaps (*Scot.*). — **able seaman, able-bodied seaman, rating** (abbrev. **A.B.**) one able to perform all the duties of seamanship and having a higher rating than the ordinary sailor. [See **ability**.]

-able *-ə-bl, adj. suff.* combining with verbs to convey any of various passive senses (now the chief use of **-able** as a living suffix), such as 'capable of being', 'able to be', 'worthy of being', 'likely to be', 'that must be': combining with verbs to convey any of various active senses, as 'capable of', 'able to', 'worthy of', 'suitable to', 'likely to': combining with nouns to convey such meanings as 'worthy of', suitable for', 'in accordance with', 'causing'. — *n. suff.* **-ability.** — *adv. suff.* **-ably.** — See also **-ible.** [O.Fr., — L. *-ābilis — -bilis* as used with a 1st-conjugation verb.]

ablet *ab'lit*, *n.* the bleak. [Fr. *ablette* — L.L. *a(l)bula*, dim. of *alba*, white.]

abloom *ə-blōōm'*, *adv.* and *adj.* in a blooming state. [**a**[3] and **bloom**[1].]

ablow *ə-blō'*, *adv.* and *adj.* in a blowing state. [**a**[3] and **blow**[2,3].]

ablush *ə-blush'*, *adv.* and *adj.* in a blushing state. [**a**[3] and **blush.**]

ablution *ə-blōō'shən*, *n.* (*often in pl.*) the act of washing, esp. the body: ceremonial washing: (*sing.*) the wine and water used to rinse the chalice, drunk by the officiating priest. — *adj.* **ablu'tionary.** — *n.* **ablutomane** (*ə-blōō'tō-mān*; Fr. *-mane* — Gr., see **mania**) one who is obsessed with cleanliness. [L. *ablūtiō, -ōnis — ab*, away, *luěre*, to wash.]

abnegate *ab'ni-gāt*, *v.t.* to deny: to renounce. — *ns.* **abnegā'tion; ab'negātor.** [L. *ab*, away, *negāre*, to deny.]

abnormal *ab-nör'ml, adj.* not normal. — *ns.* **abnor'malism; abnormality** (*-nör-mal'i-ti*). — *adv.* **abnor'mally.** — *n.* **abnor'mity.** — *adj.* **abnor'mous** (*rare*). — **abnormal load** (usu. of road transport) a larger or heavier load than is generally carried. [Fr. *anormal* — L.L. *anormalus* — Gr. *anōmalos* (see **anomaly**); influenced by L. *norma*, rule, and *ab*, from.]

abo. See **aborigine.**

aboard *ə-bōrd', -börd', adv.* or *prep.* on board: in or into a ship, railway train, etc.: alongside. [**a**[3] and **board.**]

abode[1] *ə-bōd'*, *n.* a dwelling-place: a stay. — *v.t.* and *v.i., pa.t.* and *pa.p.* of **abide**. — **of no fixed abode** (*legal*) having no permanent address.

abode[2] *ə-bōd'*, *n.* a presage. — *v.t.* (*Shak.*) to presage. — *n.* **abode'ment** (*obs.*) a foreboding: an omen. [O.E. *ābodian*, to proclaim; cf. **bode**[1], **forebode**.]

a'body. See **a'.**

ab officio et beneficio *ab o-fish'i-ō (-fik') et ben-e-fish'i-ō (-fik')*, (L.L.) from office and benefice — of a clergyman suspended.

aboideau, aboiteau *ä-bwä-dō, -tō, ns.* a tide-gate. [Canadian Fr.]

aboil *ə-boil'*, *adv.* and *adj.* in a boiling state. [**a**[3] and **boil**[1].]

abolish *ə-bol'ish*, *v.t.* to put an end to. — *adj.* **abol'ishable.** — *ns.* **abol'ishment** (*rare*); **aboli'tion.** — *adjs.* **aboli'tional, aboli'tionary.** — *ns.* **aboli'tionism; aboli'tionist** one who seeks to abolish anything, e.g. slavery, capital punishment. [L. *abolēre, -itum*, partly through Fr. *abolir*.]

abolla *ab-ol'ä*, *n.* a Roman military cloak. [L.]

abomasum *ab-ō-mā'səm*, *n.* the fourth or true stomach of ruminants, lying close to the omasum. — Also **abomā'sus.** [L. *ab*, away from, *om āsum*, tripe, paunch (a Gallic word).]

abominate *ə-bom'in-āt*, *v.t.* to abhor: to detest. — *adj.* **abom'inable** hateful: detestable. —An old spelling is **abhom'inable** to agree with a fancied derivation from Lat. *ab homine*. — *n.* **abom'inableness.** — *adv.* **abom'inably.** — *ns.* **abominā'tion** extreme aversion: an object of detestation; **abom'inator.** — **abominable snowman** a mythical hairy manlike creature supposed to live in the snows of Tibet — also **yeti.** [L. *abōminārī, -ātus*, to turn from as of bad omen; see **omen**.]

abundance. See **abundance.**

à bon droit *a bɔ̃ drwä*, (Fr.) with justice.

à bon marché *a bɔ̃ mar-shä*, (Fr.) at a good bargain, cheap.

abonnement *a-bon-mã*, (Fr.) *n.* a subscription.

aboral *ab-ō'rəl, -ö'*, (*zool.*) *adj.* away from the mouth. [L. *ab*, from, and **oral**.]

abord[1] *ə-bōrd', -börd'*, (*arch.*) *v.t.* to accost. — *n.* approach. [Fr. *aborder — à bord*, to the side.]

abord[2] *ə-bōrd', -börd'*, (*Spens.*) *adv.* astray. [Perh. for **abroad**.]

ab origine *ab ō-rij'in-ē, -rēg'in-e,* (L.) from the very first, from the source.

aborigine *ab-ə-rij'i-nē, -ni, n.* an original or native inhabitant of a country, esp. (often, in Australia always, with *cap.*) Australia. — Also (*rare*) **aborigin, -en** (*a-bor'i-jin*). — *offensive abbrev.* **abo** (*ab'ō*): — *pl.* **ab'os.** — *adj.* **aborig'inal** (often with *cap.*) earliest, primitive, indigenous. — *n.* (often with *cap.*) an aborigine: (with *cap.*) an Australian Aboriginal language. — *ns.* **aborig'inalism** due recognition of native peoples; **aboriginality** (*-al'i-ti*) the fact of being aboriginal. — *adv.* **aborig'inally.** [L. (pl.) *aborīginēs* — *ab,* from, *orīgō,* *-inis* beginning; in English, **aborigines** originally had no singular form.]

abort *ə-bört', v.i.* to miscarry in birth: to be arrested in development at an early stage: to come to nothing. — *v.t.* to cause to abort: to check or call off (an attack, mission, etc.) at an early stage: to stop (e.g. flight of rocket) in emergency before completion of mission. — *n.* an instance of abortion (esp. of rocket). — *adj.* **abortifacient** (*-i-fā'shənt, -shi-ənt*) causing abortion. — *n.* means of causing abortion. — *ns.* **abor'ticide** (*-i-sīd*) foeticide; **abor'tion** the premature expulsion of an embryo or a foetus, or the procuring of this, esp. in the first three months of pregnancy: arrest of development: the product of such arrest: anything that fails in course of coming into being: a misshapen being or monster; **abor'tionist** one who procures abortion. — *adj.* **abor'tive** born untimely: unsuccessful: brought forth in an imperfect condition: checked in development. — *adv.* **abort'ively.** — *n.* **abort'iveness.** — **contagious abortion** contagious bacterial infections of cattle and of horses, causing abortion. [L. *aborīrī, abortus* — pfx. *ab-,* reversing the meaning, *orīrī,* to rise.]

abought *ə-böt', pa.t.* and *pa.p.* of **aby.**

aboulia, abulia *a-boō'li-ə, -bow', -bū', n.* loss of willpower: inability to make decisions. [Gr. *a-,* priv., *boulē,* will.]

abound *ə-bownd', v.i.* to be in great plenty: to be rich (with *in*): to be filled (with *with*). — *adj.* **abound'ing.** [O.Fr. *abunder* — L. *abundāre,* to overflow — *ab,* from, *unda,* a wave.]

about *ə-bowt', prep.* round on the outside of: around: here and there in: near in place, time, size, etc.: on the person of: connected with: concerning: engaged in. — *adv.* around: halfway round, in the opposite direction (e.g. *to face about*): nearly: here and there: on the opposite tack: in motion or activity. — *prep.* **abouts'** (*Spens.*) about. — **about'-face** (orig. used in U.S. as command) the act of turning to face in the opposite direction: a complete change of opinion, attitude, etc. — Also *v.i.* — Also **about'-turn.** — *v.t.* and *v.i.* **about'-ship'** to put (the ship) on the opposite tack. — **about'-sledge** a blacksmith's heavy hammer. — **about** **to** on the point of (doing etc.; also **just about to**): (in *neg.*) not likely or keen (to do something) (*coll.*); **be about** to be astir; **bring about** to cause to take place; **come about** to happen in the course of time; **go about** to prepare to do; **put about** see **put**[1]; **turn about** alternately: in rotation. [O.E. *onbūtan* — *on,* in (compare **a**[3]), *būtan,* without — *be,* by, *ūtan,* orig. a locative — *ūt,* out.]

above *ə-buv', prep.* over: in or to a position higher than that of: beyond in degree, amount, number, importance, etc.: too magnanimous or proud for. — *adv.* overhead: in a higher position, order, or power: in an earlier passage: in heaven. — *adj.* mentioned, stated, or given in an earlier passage. — *adjs.* **above'-board** open, without deception; **above'-ground** alive: not buried; **above'-mentioned; above'-named; above'-the=line** of or pertaining to the Government's expenditure and revenue allowed for in its original estimates and provided for by taxation: of or pertaining to the expenditure and revenue detailed in a company's profit and loss account. — **above oneself** elated: conceited. [Late O.E. *ābufan* — O.E. *ā-,* on (compare **a**[3]), *bufan,*

above — *be,* by, *ufan,* above.]

ab ovo *ab ō'vō, -wō,* (L.; 'from the egg') from the beginning. See *Quotations from Latin.*

abracadabra *ab-rə-kə-dab'rə, n.* a magic word, written in amulets: a spell or conjuring word: gibberish. [Found in a 2nd-cent. poem by Q. Serenus Sammonicus.]

abrade[1] *ə-brād', v.t.* to wear down or off. — *adj.* and *n.* **abrā'dant** abrasive. [L. *ab,* from, *rādĕre, rāsum,* to scrape.]

abrade[2]. See **abraid.**

Abraham-man *ā'brə-həm-man', **Abram-man** ā'brəm-man', ns.* originally a Bedlam inmate let out to beg: a sturdy beggar, esp. one shamming insanity (*arch.*). — **sham Abraham** to feign sickness. [Said to be from an Abraham Ward in old Bedlam, London.]

abraid, abrade *ə-brād',* or (*Spens.*) **abray** *ə-brā', (obs.) v.t.* to awake, rouse. — *v.i.* to start: to awake. [O.E. *ābregdan* — intens. pfx. *ā-,* and *bregdan;* see **braid**[1].]

abram *ā'brəm,* (*Shak.*) *adj.* an obs. form of **auburn.**

abranchiate *ə-brang'ki-āt, adj.* without gills. [Gr. *a-,* priv., *branchia,* gills.]

abrasion *ə-brā'zhən, n.* a wearing away: a worn-down or grazed place. — *adj.* **abrā'sive** (*-ziv, -siv*) tending to abrade: harsh: of a person, tending to irritate or annoy. — *n.* a substance used to remove matter by scratching and grinding. [See **abrade**[1].]

à bras ouverts *a brä-zoō-ver,* (Fr.) with open arms.

abraxas *ə-braks'əs, n.* a mystic word, or a gem engraved therewith, often bearing a mystical figure of combined human and animal form, used as a charm: (with *cap.*) the genus of the gooseberry or magpie moth. [Said to have been coined by the 2nd-cent. Egyptian Gnostic Basilides to express 365 by addition of the numerical values of the Greek letters.]

abray. See **abraid.**

abrazo *ə-brä'sō, n.* in Central and South America, an embrace, esp. in greeting: — *pl.* **abra'zos.** [Sp.]

abreaction *ab-rē-ak'shən,* (*psych.*) *n.* the resolution of a neurosis by reviving forgotten or repressed ideas of the event first causing it. — *v.i.* **abreact'.** [L. *ab,* from, and **reaction.**]

abreast *ə-brest', adv.* with fronts in line: side by side: keeping pace with (with *of*), e.g. *abreast of the other car, the times.* [**a**[3] and **breast.**]

abrégé *a-brā-zhā,* (Fr.) *n.* an abridgment.

abricock *ab'ri-kok,* an obs. form of **apricot.**

abridge *ə-brij', v.t.* to shorten: to epitomise: to curtail. — *ns.* **abridg'er; abridg'ment** (sometimes **abridge'ment**) contraction: shortening: a compendium of a larger work: an epitome or synopsis: (prob.) a pastime (*Shak.*). [O.Fr. *abregier* (Fr. *abréger*) — L. *abbreviāre.*]

abrim *ə-brim', adv.* and *adj.* in a brimming state, up to the brim. [**a**[3] and **brim.**]

abrin *ə-brim'.* See **Abrus.**

abroach *ə-brōch', adv.* and *adj.* in a condition to let the liquor run out: in a state to be diffused, afloat, astir. [**a**[3] and **broach.**]

abroad *ə-bröd', adv.* over a wide area: in full breadth: out of doors: at large: in the field: current: in or to another country: wide of the mark: astray. — *n.* anywhere foreign, foreign places. [**a**[3] and **broad.**]

abrogate *ab'rō-gāt, v.t.* to annul. — *n.* **abroga'tion.** — *adj.* **ab'rogative.** — *n.* **ab'rogator.** [L. *ab,* away, *rogāre, -ātum,* to ask, or to propose a law.]

Abroma *a-brō'mə, n.* a genus of East Indian sterculiaceous fibre-yielding trees. [Gr. *a-,* priv., *brōma,* food.]

abrooke *ə-broōk',* (*Shak.*) *v.t.* to brook, bear, or endure. [Pfx. *a-,* intens., and **brook**[2].]

abrupt *ə-brupt', adj.* truncated: as if broken off: sudden: unexpected: precipitous: passing with sudden transitions: (of manners) short, rude. — *n.* (*Milt.*) an abyss. — *n.* **abrup'tion** (*-shən*) a breaking off. — *adv.* **abrupt'ly.** — *n.* **abrupt'ness.** [L. *abruptus* — *ab,* from, *rumpĕre, ruptum,* to break.]

Abrus *a'brəs*, or *ā'*, *n.* a tropical genus akin to the bean, to which crab's-eyes belong. — *n.* **ā'brin** a poisonous protein contained in its seeds. [Gr. *habros*, graceful.]
abscess *ab'ses*, *-sis*, *n.* a collection of pus in a cavity. [L. *abscessus* — *abs*, from, *cēdĕre*, *cēssum*, to go, retreat.]
abscind *ab-sind'*, *v.t.* to cut off. — *n.* **abscissa** (*-sis'ə*), also **absciss, abscisse** (*ab'sis*) the intercept between a fixed point and the foot of an ordinate: the *x*-co-ordinate in analytical geometry: — *pl.* **abscissae** (*ab-sis'ē*, *-sis'ī*), **absciss'as, ab'scisses**. — *ns.* **absciss'in** same as **abscisin** (see under **abscise**); **abscission** (*-sizh'ən*) an act of cutting off, or state of being cut off: a figure of speech in which words demanded by the sense are left unsaid, the speaker stopping short suddenly (*rhet.*): organised shedding of a part (e.g. a leaf or fruit) by means of an absciss layer (*bot.*): liberation of a fungal spore by breakdown of part of its stalk (*bot.*). — **absciss(ion) layer** (*bot.*) a layer of parenchymatous cells through which a leaf, branch, or bark scale separates off. [L. *abscindĕre*, *abscissum*, to cut off — *ab*, from, *scindĕre*, to cut.]
abscise *ab-sīz'*, *v.i.* to fall off by abscission. — *v.t.* to cause to separate by abscission. — *n.* **abscisin** (*-sis'in*) any of a number of plant hormones which promote abscission. — **abscisic acid** an abscisin that promotes abscission in leaves and dormancy in buds and seeds. [L. *abscīsus*, pa.p. of *abscīdĕre* — *abs*, away, *caedĕre*, to cut.]
abscond *ab-skond'*, *v.i.* to hide, or get out of the way, esp. to escape a legal process. — *ns.* **abscond'ence; abscond'er.** [L. *abscondĕre* — *abs*, from or away, *condĕre*, to hide.]
abseil *ap'zīl*, *ab-sīl'*, *v.i.* to let oneself down a rock face using a double rope. — *n.* **abseiling.** [Ger. *ab*, down, *Seil*, rope.]
absent *ab'sənt*, *adj.* being away: not present: inattentive. — *v.t.* (*ab-sent'*; usu. *refl.*) to keep away. — *ns.* **ab'sence** the state of being away or not present: want: non-existence: abstraction, inattention; **absentee'** one who is absent on any occasion: one who makes a habit of living away from his estate or his office; **absentee'ism** the practice of absenting oneself from duty, station, or estate. — *adv.* **ab'sently.** — *adj.* **ab'sent-mind'ed** inattentive to surroundings: preoccupied. — *adv.* **ab'sent-mind'edly.** — *n.* **ab'sent-mind'edness.** [L. *absēns*, *-sentis*, pr.p. of *abesse* — *ab*, away from, *esse*, to be.]
absente reo *ab-sent'ē rē'ō*, *-te rā'ō*, (L.) in absence of the accused.
absey, absey book. See **ABC.**
absinth(e) *ab'sinth*, *n.* wormwood or other species of Artemisia: a liqueur containing (orig. at all events) extract of wormwood. — *adj.* **absinth'iated** impregnated with absinth. [Fr. *absinthe* — L. *absinthium* — Gr. *apsinthion*, wormwood.]
absit *ab'sit*, *n.* leave to pass one night away from college. — **absit invidia** (*ab'sit invid'i-a*, *-wid'*) may there be no ill will: no offence; **absit omen** (*ab'sit ō'mən*) may there be no (ill) omen (as in a word just used). [L., let him be absent, — *abesse*, — *ab*, away from, *esse*, to be.]
absolute *ab'səl-ōōt*, *-ūt*, *adj.* free from limits, restrictions, or conditions: certain, positive: complete: unlimited: free from mixture: independent of relation to other things: peremptory: unrestricted by constitutional checks: out of ordinary syntactic relation, standing as an independent construction, as the Latin *ablative absolute* and Greek *genitive absolute* (*gram.*): existing in and by itself without necessary relation to anything else (*philos.*): capable of being conceived independently of anything else. — *n.* (with *the*; often *cap.*) that which is absolute, self-existent, uncaused. — *adv.* **ab'solutely** separately, by itself: unconditionally: positively: completely — as a colourless but emphatic affirmative (*-lōōt'li*, *-lūt'*). — *ns.* **ab'soluteness; absolu'tion** release from punishment: acquittal: remission of sins, declared officially by a priest, or the formula by which it is expressed; **ab'solutism** government, or

theory of government, by a ruler without restriction: adherence to the doctrine of the Absolute; **ab'solutist** a supporter of absolute government, or of a philosophy of the Absolute. — Also *adj.* — *adj.* **absolutory** (*ab-sol'ū-tər-i*) of, or giving, absolution. — **absolute alcohol** water-free alcohol; **absolute humidity** humidity expressed as grams of water per cubic metre of air; **absolute magnitude** the magnitude that a star would have at a standard distance of 10 parsecs; **absolute majority** a majority, in an election, etc., which is greater than the total number of votes for all other candidates; **absolute music** music which does not attempt to illustrate or describe — opp. to *programme music*; **absolute pitch** the pitch of a note as determined by the number of vibrations per second: a sense of or memory for absolute pitch; **absolute privilege** (*law*) a privilege that protects members of a lawmaking body, in making (even malicious) statements from the floor, from possible charges under the laws of slander; **absolute temperature** temperature measured on the Kelvin scale or Rankine scale; **absolute units** those derived directly from fundamental units and not based on arbitrary numerical definitions; **absolute zero** the zero of the absolute scale of temperature (approx. – 273°C). [L. *absolūtus*, pa.p. of *absolvĕre*; see **absolve.**]
absolve *əb-zolv'*, *-solv'*, *v.t.* to loose or set free (from): to pardon: to give absolution to or for: to acquit: to discharge (from): to accomplish, finish off (*Milt.*). — *ns.* **absolv'er; absolv'itor** (L. *3rd pers. imper. passive*, let him be absolved; *Scots law*) a decision favourable to a defender. [L. *absolvĕre* — *ab*, from, *solvĕre*, to loose.]
absonant *ab'sən-ənt*, *adj.* discordant: abhorrent: unnatural: contrary to reason (with *to* or *from*) — opp. to *consonant.* [L. *ab*, from, *sonāns*, *-antis*, pr.p. of *sonāre*, to sound.]
absorb *ab-sörb'*, *-zörb'*, *v.t.* to suck in: to swallow up: to imbibe: to take in: to incorporate: to take up and transform (energy) instead of transmitting or reflecting: to engage wholly. — *n.* **absorbabil'ity.** — *adj.* **absorb'able.** — *n.* **absorb'ate** an absorbed substance. — *adj.* **absorbed'** swallowed up: entirely occupied. — *adv.* **absorb'edly.** — *adj.* **absorbefacient** (*-i-fā'shənt*, *-shi-ənt*) causing or promoting absorption. — *n.* a medicine, etc., which causes or promotes absorption. — *n.* **absorb'ency.** — *adj.* **absorb'ent** absorbing: able to absorb. — *n.* that which absorbs. — *n.* **absorb'er** that which absorbs: material for capturing neutrons without generating more neutrons (*nuc.*). — *adj.* **absorb'ing** engrossing the attention. — *adv.* **absorb'ingly.** — *ns.* **absorptiometer** (*-sörp-shi-om'i-tər*) an apparatus for determining the solubility of gases in liquids; **absorp'tion** the act of absorbing: entire occupation of mind. — *adj.* **absorp'tive** having power to absorb. — *ns.* **absorp'tiveness, absorptiv'ity.** — **absorption bands, lines** dark bands, lines, interrupting a spectrum, due to absorption of light in the medium traversed; **absorption spectrum** a system of such lines and bands. [L. *ab*, from, *sorbēre*, *sorptum*, to suck in.]
absquatulate *ab-skwot'ū-lāt*, (*facet.*; *U.S.*) *v.i.* to decamp: to squat.
abstain *ab-stān'*, *v.i.* to hold or refrain (from). — *v.t.* (*Spens.*) to restrain — *ns.* **abstain'er** one who abstains, esp. from alcoholic drinks; **absten'tion.** [Fr. *abstenir* — L. *abs*, from, *tenēre*, to hold.]
abstemious *ab-stē'mi-əs*, *adj.* temperate: sparing in food, drink, or enjoyments. — *adv.* **abstē'miously.** — *n.* **abstē'miousness.** [L. *abstēmius* — *abs*, from, *tēmētum*, strong wine.]
absterge *ab-stûrj'*, *v.t.* to wipe: to cleanse: to purge. — *adj.* **absterg'ent** serving to cleanse. — *n.* a cleansing agent. — *n.* **abster'sion.** — *adj.* **abster'sive** having the quality of cleansing: purgative. — Also *n.* [L. *abstergēre*, *-tersum*, to wipe away — *abs*, from, *tergēre*, to wipe.]
abstinent *ab'stin-ənt*, *adj.* abstaining: temperate. — *ns.* **ab'stinence** an abstaining or refraining, especially from

some indulgence (with *from*); **ab'stinency** the quality of being abstinent. — *adv.* **ab'stinently.** [L. *abstinēns, -entis,* pr.p. of *abstinēre;* see **abstain.**]

abstract *ab-strakt'*, *v.t.* to draw away: to separate: to remove quietly: to purloin: to summarise: to separate by the operation of the mind, as in forming a general concept from consideration of particular instances. — *n.* (*ab'strakt*) a summary, abridgment: in Shak. *Ant. and Cleo.* III. vi., explained by some as an abridgment of time of separation — others conjecture *obstruct*: that which represents the essence: an abstraction: an abstract painting or sculpture. — *adj.* (*ab'strakt*) abstracted: apart from actual material instances, existing only as a mental concept — opp. to *concrete:* away from practice, theoretical: (of terms) denoting a quality of a thing apart from the thing, as 'redness': representing ideas in geometric and other designs, not the forms of nature (*paint.* and *sculp.*): (of verse) employing words primarily for their auditory and rhythmic qualities. — *adj.* **abstract'ed** drawn off (with *from*): removed: absent in mind. — *adv.* **abstract'edly.** — *ns.* **abstract'edness; abstrac'ter, abstrac'tor** one who makes abstracts (with -**or** for a grade of Civil Service clerks); **abstrac'tion** the act of abstracting: the state of being abstracted: abstract quality or character: withdrawal from worldly things: absence of mind: a purloining: the process of abstracting by the mind: a thing existing only in idea: a theory, visionary notion: an abstract term: an abstract composition (*paint.* and *sculp.*). — *adj.* **abstrac'tional.** — *n.* **abstrac'tionist** one dealing in abstractions or unrealities. — *adj.* **abstrac'tive** able or tending to abstract: formed by or pertaining to abstraction. — *n.* anything abstractive: an abstract. — *adv.* **ab'stractly.** — *n.* **ab'stractness.** — **abstract expressionism** a development in art that began in America in the 1940's in which the expression of the artist's feelings informs his abstract representations. — **abstract of title** (*law*) a summary of facts concerning ownership; **in the abstract** as an abstraction: in theory. [L. *abs,* away from, *trahĕre, tractum,* to draw.]

abstrict *ab-strikt'*, (*biol.*) *v.t.* to set free (spores, etc.), esp. by constriction of the stalk. — *n.* **abstric'tion.** [L. *ab,* from, *stringĕre, strictum,* to tie.]

abstruse *ab-strōōs'*, *adj.* hidden (*arch.*): remote from apprehension: difficult to understand. — *adv.* **abstruse'ly.** — *n.* **abstruse'ness.** [L. *abstrūsus,* thrust away — *abs,* away, *trūdĕre, trūsum,* to thrust.]

absurd *ab-sûrd'*, *adj.* opposed to reason: ridiculous. — *ns.* **absurd'ity, absurd'ness.** — *adv.* **absurd'ly.** [L. *absurdus* — *ab,* from, *surdus,* deaf, inaudible, indistinct, harsh, out of fashion, not to the purpose.]

abthane *ab'thān, n.* a monastic territory of the Columban church. [L.L. *abthania* — Gael. *abdhaine,* abbacy.]

abulia. See **aboulia.**

abuna *ä-bōō'nə, n.* an Ethiopian patriarch. [Ethiopian, — Ar., our father.]

abundance *ə-bund'əns, n.* ample sufficiency: great plenty: a call of nine tricks (*solo whist;* also **abondance** (-*bund'*)). — *n.* **abund'ancy.** — *adj.* **abund'ant.** — *adv.* **abund'antly** enough: fully. [See **abound.**]

abune *ə-bün'.* A Scots form of **above.**

ab urbe condita *ab ŭr'be kon'di-ta, ōōr'bä kon'di-tä,* from the founding of the city (of Rome) 753 B.C. — Abbrev. **A.U.C.**

aburst *ə-bûrst'*, *adv.* and *adj.* in a bursting condition. [**a³** and **burst.**]

abuse *ə-būz'*, *v.t.* to make a bad use of: to take undue advantage of: to betray (as confidence): to misrepresent: to deceive: to revile: to maltreat: to violate. — *ns.* **abusage** (*ə-bū'sij*) wrong use, esp. of words or grammar; **abuse** (*ə-būs'*) wrong use: an evil or corrupt practice: deceit: hurt: undue advantage: betrayal (of confidence): ill usage: violation: reviling; **abuser** (*ə-bū'zər*); **abū'sion** (-*zhən; Spens.* also -*zi-ən;* now rare) misuse: deception: wrong: outrage: reviling. — *adj.* **abū'sive** (-*siv*) wrong: containing, giving, of the nature

of, abuse: coarsely reviling: catachrestical (*arch.*). — *adv.* **abū'sively.** — *n.* **abū'siveness.** [L. *ab,* from, *ūti, ūsus,* to use.]

abut *ə-but'*, *v.i.* to end or lean (on, upon, against). — *v.t.* to border: — *pr.p.* **abutt'ing;** *pa.t.* and *pa.p.* **abutt'ed.** — *ns.* **abut'ment** an endwise meeting or junction: that which a limb of an arch ends or rests against (*archit.*): a place of abutting; **abutt'al** abutment: (in *pl.*) boundaries; **abutt'er** one whose property abuts. — *adj.* **abutt'ing** confronting. [O.Fr. *abouter,* to touch by an end, and O.Fr. *abuter,* to touch at the end; cf. also Fr. *aboutir,* to end at — *à,* to, *bout, but,* end; see **butt⁴.**]

Abutilon *a-bū'ti-lon, n.* a showy-flowered genus of the mallow family, some species yielding fibres: (without *cap.*) a member of the genus. [Ar. *aubūtilūn.*]

abuzz *ə-buz'*, *adv.* and *adj.* in a buzz. [**a³** and **buzz¹.**]

abvolt. See **ab-.**

aby, abye *ə-bī'*, (*arch.*) *v.t.* to pay the penalty for: to pay as a penalty. — *v.t.* to atone: to endure, continue: — *pa.t.* and *pa.p.* **abought** (*ə-böt'*). [Pfx. *a-,* back, and O.E. *bycgan,* to buy; merging and confused with **abide¹.**]

abysm *ə-bizm'*, (*arch.* and poet.) *n.* an abyss. — *adj.* **abys'mal** bottomless: unfathomable: very deep: abyssal: very bad (*coll.*). — *adv.* **abys'mally.** [O.Fr. *abisme,* from a L.L. superl. of *abyssus;* see **abyss.**]

abyss *ə-bis'*, *n.* a bottomless gulf: primal chaos: the supposed water-filled cavity under the earth: hell: anything very deep: the depths of the sea: a measureless or apparently measureless chasm. — *adj.* **abyss'al** abysmal — esp. of ocean depths. [Gr. *abyssos,* bottomless — *a-,* priv., *byssos,* depth, bottom.]

Abyssinian cat *ab-i-sin'i-ən, -sin'yən, kat* a small domestic cat, of African origin, greyish or brownish ticked with darker colour.

acacia *ə-kā'sh(y)ə, n.* a wattle, any plant of the genus *Acacia,* akin to the sensitive plants: also applied to the *false acacia* (of the genus Robinia). [L. — Gr. *akakiā.*]

academy *ə-kad'ə-mi, n.* (*orig.*) Plato's school of philosophy: a higher, would-be higher, or specialised school, or a university: a riding-school: a society for the promotion of science or art: the annual exhibition of the Royal Academy or of the Royal Scottish Academy. — *n.* **academe** (*ak-ə-dēm'*) an academic, esp. if pedantic: an academy (*poet.*): the world of scholars: academic life. — *n.* **academ'ia** the academic world. — *adj.* **academic** (-*dem'*) of the philosophical school of Plato: of an academy or university: sceptical: scholarly: formal: theoretical only, of no practical importance or consequence. — *n.* a Platonic philosopher: one studying or teaching at a university, esp. one who has scholarly tastes (sometimes *derog.*): (*pl.*) purely theoretical arguments. — *adj.* **academ'ical** academic. — *n.* (in *pl.*) university garb. — *n.* **academ'icalism** close adherence to formal academic teaching. — *adv.* **academ'ically.** — *ns.* **academician** (*ə-kad-ə-mish'ən*) a member of an academy esp. of the French Academy or the R.A. or R.S.A.; **academ'icism, academ'icalism; acad'emist** an academic: an academician. [Gr. *Akadēmeiā,* the garden, orig. outside Athens, where Plato taught.]

Acadian *ə-kā'di-ən, adj.* and *n.* Nova Scotian. [Fr. *Acadie,* Nova Scotia — Micmac Ind. *ākāde,* abundance.]

acajou *ak'ə-zhōō, -zhōō', n.* the cashew tree or its fruit or gum: a kind of mahogany. [See **cashew.**]

acaleph(e) *ak'ə-lef, -lēf,* **acalepha** -*le'fə, ns.* old names for a jellyfish — applied to a group of varying extension of Coelenterata. — *n.* and *adj.* **acale'phan.** [Gr. *akalēphē,* a nettle, sea-anemone.]

acanaceous *ak-ə-nā'shəs,* (*bot.*) *adj.* prickly. [L. *acanos,* a kind of thistle — Gr. *akanos* — *akē,* a point.]

acanth *ə-kanth', n.* acanthus. — *n.* **acanth'a** a thorn, prickle: a spinous process. — *n.pl.* **Acantha'ceae** (*ak-*) the acanthus family, akin to the figworts. — *adj.* **acantha'ceous** prickly: of the Acanthaceae. — *n.* **acanth'in** strontium sulphate in skeletons of Radiolaria. —

adj. **acanth'ine** of, like, ornamented with, acanthus. — *n.pl.* **Acanthoceph'ala** a division of parasitic worms with spiny proboscis and no mouth or alimentary canal (Gr. *kephalē*, head). — *adjs.* **acanth'oid** like acanthus; **acanthopterygian** (*ak-an-thop-tər-ij'yən*) spiny-finned (Gr. *pteryx, -ygos*, wing, fin); **acanth'ous** spiny. — *n.* **acanth'us** any plant of the prickly-leaved genus **Acanthus**, esp. *A. spinosus* or *A. mollis*: a conventionalised representation of an acanthus leaf, as in Corinthian capitals. [Gr. *akantha*, prickle, *akanthos*, acanthus — *akē*, point.]

acapnia *ə-kap'ni-ə, n.* deficiency of carbon dioxide. [Gr. *a-*, priv., *kapnos*, smoke.]

a cappella *a ka-pel'ə, ä käp-pel'lä* (*mus.*), 'in (early) church style', *i.e.* sung without accompaniment or with accompaniment merely doubling the voice parts: alla breve. — Also **al'la cappel'la.** [It.]

acarpous *a-kär'pəs, ā-*, (*bot.*) *adj.* sterile, not bearing fruit. [Gr. *a-*, priv., *karpos*, fruit.]

acarus *ak'ə-rəs, n.* a mite: — *pl.* **ac'arī.** — *adj.* **acā'rian.** — *ns.* **acarī'asis** disease due to mites; **acaricide** (*akar'i-sīd*), a mite killer; **ac'arid** one of the Acarida. — *n.pl.* **Acar'ida** the order of Arachnida to which mites and ticks belong. — *adjs.* and *ns.* **acar'idan, acarid'ean, acarid'ian.** — *n.pl.* **Acarī'na** Acarida. — *adj.* **ac'arine.** — *n.* **acarodomatium, acaridomatium** (*-dō-mā'shyəm*), a dwelling for mites provided by certain plants that benefit from their presence: — *pl.* **-ā'tia.** — *adj.* **ac'aroid** mite-like. — *ns.* **acarol'ogist; acarol'ogy; acaroph'ily** symbiotic association of plants with mites. — **acarine disease** a disease of bees due to mites in the spiracles. [Gr. *akari*, a mite — *akarēs*, too short to cut — *a-*, priv., *keirein*, to cut.]

acatalectic *a-kat-ə-lek'tik,* (*pros.*) *adj.* having the full number of syllables. — *n.* an acatalectic verse. [Gr. *akatalēktos* — *a-*, priv.; see **catalectic.**]

acatalepsy *a-kat-ə-lep'si,* (*Sceptic philos.*) *n.* the unknowableness to a certainty of all things. — *adj.* and *n.* **acatalep'tic.** [Gr. *akatalēpsiā* — *a-*, priv., *kata*, thoroughly, *lēpsis*, a seizing.]

acatamathesia *a-kat-ə-mə-thē'zi-ə, -zhə,* (*psych.*) *n.* the inability to comprehend data (objects, language, etc.) presented to the senses. [Gr. *a-*, priv., *katamanthanein*, to observe, understand — *kata*, intens., *manthanein*, to learn.]

acates *ə-kāts',* (*obs.*) *n.pl.* bought provisions. — *n.* **acāt'er, -our** (*obs.*) an officer who bought provisions, a caterer. [O.Fr. *acat* — L.L. *accaptāre*, to acquire — L. *ad*, to, *captāre*, to seize; see **cate, cater**[1].]

acaudal *ā-kö'dl, adj.* tailless. — Also **acau'date.** [Gr. *a-*, priv., and **caudal.**]

acaulescent *ak-ö-les'ənt, adj.* having a very short stem. — *adjs.* **acaul'ine** (*-līn, -lin*), **acaulose'** (*-lōs'*) stemless. [Gr. *a-*, priv., L. *caulis*, stem, and suffs. *-escent, -ine, -ose.*]

accablé *ak-a-blä,* (Fr.), *adj.* depressed, overwhelmed.

Accadian. Same as **Akkadian.**

accede *ək-sēd', v.i.* to come forward: to arrive (with *to*): to come to office or dignity: to join up, become a party, hence agree or assent (with *to*). — *ns.* **accēd'ence; accēd'er.** [L. *accēdĕre, accēssum*, to go near — *ad*, to, *cēdĕre*, to go; see **cede.**]

accelerando *ak-sel-ər-an'dō,* It. *ät-chel-er-än'dō,* (*mus.*) *adj.* and *adv.* with increasing speed. [It.]

accelerate *ək-sel'ər-āt, v.t.* to increase the speed of: to hasten the progress or occurrence of. — *v.i.* to become faster. — *ns.* **accel'erant** an accelerating agent (also *adj.*); **accelerā'tion** increase of speed: rate of change of velocity: a cumulative advance ahead of the normal or theoretical: the power or means of accelerating. — *adj.* **accel'erative** quickening. — *n.* **accel'erātor** any person or thing that accelerates, esp. a substance that accelerates chemical action, a nerve or muscle that increases rate of action, an apparatus for changing the speed of a machine, or one for imparting high energies to atomic particles. Devices for accelerating charged particles include the **cyclotron** type (for accelerating

the heavier particles, as protons; used in the treatment of cancer), modifications of this, as the **synchrocyclotron** type and the **synchrotron** type (for accelerating electrons). Other types of accelerators are the **proton synchrotron** (of which examples are the **cosmotron** and the **bevatron**), the **betatron** (for accelerating electrons; used in medicine and industry), **linear accelerators** and **electron ring accelerators.** — *adj.* **accel'cratory.** — *n.* **accelerom'eter** an instrument for measuring acceleration of aircraft, etc. [L. *accelerāre, -ātum* — *ad*, to, *celer*, swift.]

accend *ək-send',* (*obs.*) *v.t.* to kindle. — *n.* **accen'sion.** [L. *accendĕre, accēnsum*, to kindle.]

accent *ak'sənt, n.* modulation of the voice: tone of voice: stress on a syllable, word, or note: a mark used to direct this stress: a mark over a letter to indicate differences of stress, pitch, length, or quality of sound, or for other purpose: intensity: any mode of utterance characteristic of a region, a class, or an individual: a distinguishing mark: distinctive mode of expression, as of an artist: a significant word, or words generally (*poet.*): a touch bringing out some particular effect (*paint.*): (*pl.*) speech, language. — *v.t.* (*ək-sent'*) to express or mark the accent of: to utter: to accentuate. — *adj.* **accent'ual** according to, characterised by, accent. — *n.* **accentual'ity.** — *adv.* **accent'ually.** — *v.t.* **accent'uate** to mark, play, or pronounce with accent: to make prominent, emphasise. — *n.* **accentuā'tion.** [L. *accentus* — *ad*, to, *cantus*, song.]

Accentor *ak-sent'ör, -ər, n.* the former name of the hedge-sparrow genus, now superseded by Prunella: (without *cap.*) a general term for a member of the genus. [L., one who sings with another — *ad*, to, *cantor*, singer.]

accept *ək-sept', v.t.* (old-fashioned or formal, *v.i.* with *of*) to take (something offered): to receive (with approbation, favour, consent, resignation, or passivity): to reply to, engaging more or less to comply: to reply to in the affirmative, say yes to: to promise to pay (a bill of exchange): to understand, take, in respect of meaning. — *adj.* **accept'able** worth accepting: welcome, pleasing: capable of being accepted: satisfactory, adequate. — *n.* **accept'ableness.** — *adv.* **accept'ably.** — *ns.* **acceptabil'ity; accept'ance** accepting: favourable reception: favour: acceptableness: an agreeing to terms: an accepted bill: acceptation; **accept'ancy; accept'ant** one who accepts. — *adj.* ready to receive. — *ns.* **accepta'tion** a kind reception: sense in which a word, etc., is understood; **accept'er.** — *adj.* **accept'ive** ready to receive. — *ns.* **acceptiv'ity; accept'or** one who accepts, esp. a bill of exchange: an impurity in semiconductor material which increases the conductivity of the material: a horse which has its entry for a race confirmed. — **accepting house** a financial institution, such as a merchant bank, which accepts bills of exchange. [L. *acceptāre* — *accipĕre, acceptum* — *ad*, to, *capĕre*, to take.]

acceptilation *ək-sept-il-ā'shən, n.* the remission of a debt by fictitious payment (*Roman* and *Scots law*); Christ's atonement on the theory that only God's acceptance made his sacrifice sufficient (*theol.*). [L. *acceptilātiō*, lit. 'bringing of receipt', verbal release from debt.]

access *ak'ses, n.* approach: admittance: a way of opportunity, of approach or entrance: addition, accession: onset or attack of illness: a fit (of illness or passion). — *v.t.* (*comput.*) to locate or retrieve information: to retrieve information from (a computer), or from a computer in (a particular location). — *n.* and *adj.* **access'ary** accessory (esp. in legal senses). — *n.* **accessibil'ity.** — *adj.* **access'ible** within reach: approachable: easily comprehensible. — *adv.* **access'ibly.** — *n.* **accession** (*ak-sesh'ən*) the act or event of acceding: a coming, esp. to office or dignity, or as an addition or new member: that which is added: addition by nature or industry to existing property (*law*): acquisition of such addition by the owner of the existing property (*law*): assent: an access, fit (*obs.*). — *v.t.* to enter in a book as an accession to a library. — *v.t.* **access′orise, -ize** to add accessories to. — *adj.* **access′ory** additional: subsidiary, present along with something more important: adventitious: contributing: aiding, participating in, a crime (*law*) or misdeed, but not as principal. — *n.* anything, esp. an item of equipment, that is secondary, additional, or non-essential: one who aids or gives countenance to a crime. — *adj.* **accessor′ial.** — *adv.* **access′orily.** — **accessary before** or **after the fact** one who helps a criminal before or after the committing of a crime; **access broadcasting, access television** radio or television programmes put out independently by groups of people, not professionally involved in broadcasting, who want to bring their points of view to public notice; **Access®** **card** a credit card issued by a group of banks; **accessory minerals** those whose presence or absence is not regarded in naming a rock; **access road** a minor road built to give access to a house, locality, etc.; **access television** see **access broadcasting**; **access time** the time needed for information stored in a computer to be retrieved; **deed of accession** (*Scots law*) one by which a bankrupt's creditors accede to a settlement privately, *i.e.* by trust-deed. [See **accede.**]

acciaccatura *ät-chäk-a-tōō′rə,* (*mus.*) *n.* a short appoggiatura. [It. *acciaccare,* to crush.]

accidence *ak′sid-əns, n.* the part of grammar treating of the 'accidents', *i.e.* inflexions of words. — *n.* **ac′cident** that which happens: an unforeseen or unexpected event: a chance: a mishap: an unessential quality or property: unevenness of surface. — *adj.* **accidental** (*-dent′*) happening by chance: not essential. — *n.* a sharp, flat, or natural not in the key-signature (*mus.*): (in *pl.*) strong chance effects of light (*paint.*). — *ns.* **accident′alism** the state or quality of being accidental: chance manner: a system based on symptoms rather than on causes (*med.*): use of accidentals (*paint.*): the theory that events happen without a cause (*philos.*); **accidental′ity.** — *adv.* **accident′ally.** — *adj.* **accident′ed** uneven: varied. — *adj.* **ac′cident-prone** (usu. predicatively) more than normally liable to have accidents. — **a chapter of accidents** an unforeseen course of events: a series of accidents. [L. *accidēns, -entis,* pr.p. of *accidĕre,* to happen — *ad,* to, *cadĕre,* to fall.]

accidie *ak′si-di, n.* acedia. [O.Fr. *accide* — L.L. *acēdia;* see **acedia.**]

accinge *ak-sinj′,* (*fig.*) *v.t.* to gird. [L. *ad,* to, *cingĕre,* to gird.]

accipitrine *ak-sip′i-trīn, -trin, adj.* pertaining to hawks. [L. *accipiter,* a hawk.]

accite *ak-sīt′, v.t.* to cite: to summon: to excite (*Shak.*). [L.L. *accitāre* — *ad,* to, *citāre,* to cite, call.]

acclamation *ak-lə-mā′shən, n.* a shout of applause or assent. — *v.t.* **acclaim** (*ə-klām′*) to hail or declare by acclamation. — *n.* acclamation. — *adj.* **acclamatory** (*əklam′ə-tər-i*). [L. *acclāmāre* — *ad,* to, *clāmāre, -ātum,* to shout; see **claim.**]

acclimatise, -ize *ə-klī′mə-tīz, v.t.* to inure to a new climate. — Also **accli′mate** (or *ak′līt, -li-*), **cli′matise, -ize.** — *n.* **acclimatīsā′tion, -z-.** — Also **acclimatā′tion, acclimā′tion** (*ak-lī-, -li-*). [Fr. *acclimater* — *à,* to, *climat,* climate.]

acclivity *ə-kliv′i-ti, n.* an upward slope. — *adjs.* **accliv′itous, accli′vous.** [L. *ad,* to, *clīvus,* a slope.]

accloy *ə-kloi′,* (*obs.*) *v.t.* to prick or lame with a horseshoe nail: to clog, choke or encumber (*Spens.*): to sate, cloy (*Spens.*). [See **cloy.**]

accoast *ə-kōst′.* An older form of **accost.**

accoied. See **accoy.**

accoil *ə-koil′,* (*rare*) *n.* reception. — *v.i. pa.t.* (*Spens.*) **accoyld′** assembled. [O.Fr. *acoil* (Fr. *accueil*).]

accolade *ak′əl-ād, -ād′, ak-ol-äd′, n.* an embrace: the action used in conferring knighthood, formerly an embrace, a kiss, now a tap on each shoulder with the flat of a sword: high award, honour, or praise publicly given: a brace or other line connecting staves (*mus.*; *rare*): a brace-like ornament (*archit.*). [Fr., — L. *ad,* to, *collum,* neck.]

accommodate *ə-kom′ə-dāt, v.t.* to adapt: to make suitable: to adjust: to harmonise or force into consistency: to furnish or supply (with): to find or afford room, etc., for: to provide with a loan: to oblige. — *v.i.* to come to terms: to make adjustment. — *adjs.* **accomm′odable; accomm′odating** ready to make adjustment: obliging: pliable: easily corrupted. — *n.* **accommodā′tion** adaptation: adjustment, esp. of the eye to change of distance: wresting of language to a sense not intended: obligingness: settlement or compromise: supplying of wants (esp. housing or refreshment): a help towards satisfaction of a want: a convenience: lodgings, quarters (formerly sometimes *pl.*): space for what is required: adaptation of revelation by way of compromise with human ignorance or weakness (*theol.*): a loan of money. — *adj.* **accomm′odātive.** — *ns.* **accomm′odātiveness; accomm′odātor.** — **accommodation address** an address to which mail may be sent but which is not that of the addressee's home or office; **accommodation bill** a bill drawn, accepted, or endorsed by one or more persons as security for a sum advanced to another by a third party, as a banker; **accommodation ladder** a stairway outside of a ship for entering and leaving boats; **accommodation land** land to be used for the building of dwelling-houses; **accommodation road** a road giving access to buildings, etc., off the public road; **accommodation train** (*U.S.*) one stopping at all or most stations on the way. [L. *accommodāre, -ātum* — *ad,* to, *commodus,* fitting.]

accompany *ə-kum′pə-ni, v.t.* to go or be in company with: to attend: to go along with: to perform an accompaniment to or for: to associate, join, or couple. — *ns.* **accom′panier; accom′paniment** that which accompanies: a subsidiary part or parts supporting a solo (*mus.*); **accom′panist** (also **accom′panyist**) a player of accompaniments. [Fr. *accompagner;* see **company.**]

accomplice *ə-kom′plis,* or *-kum′, n.* an associate in crime (*of* or *with* a person, *in* or *of* the crime): an associate (*Shak.*). [L. *complex, -icis,* joined; pfx. unexplained.]

accomplish *ə-kom′plish,* or *-kum′, v.t.* to complete: to fulfil: to achieve: to equip: to finish off, complete, in culture and acquirements. — *adjs.* **accom′plishable; accom′plished** complete, finished, or highly skilled in acquirements, esp. graceful acquirements: polished. — *ns.* **accom′plisher; accom′plishment** completion: an achievement: rendering accomplished: a skilled acquirement in matters of culture or social grace, sometimes superficial or merely ornamental. [O.Fr. *acomplir* — L. *ad,* to, *complēre,* to fill up; see **complete.**]

accompt, accomptable, accomptant. Obsolescent spellings of **account, accountable, accountant,** with the same pronunciation.

accorage. See **accourage.**

accord *ə-körd′, v.i.* to agree: to be in correspondence (with). — *v.t.* to cause to agree: to reconcile: to grant (to a person). — *n.* agreement: harmony: the set of notes to which an instrument is tuned: grant: assent. — *adj.* **accord′able.** — *ns.* **accord′ance, accord′ancy** agreement: conformity: a granting. — *adj.* **accord′ant** agreeing: corresponding. — *adv.* **accord′antly.** — *n.* **accord′er.** — *adj.* **accord′ing** in accordance: agreeing: harmonious. — *adv.* **accord′ingly** agreeably (*obs.*): suitably: in agreement (with what precedes): therefore. — **according as** in proportion as: depending on whether; **according to** in accordance with, or agreeably to: as asserted by; **as accords** (*formal*) as may be appropriate; **of one's own accord** of one's own spontaneous motion; **with one accord** with spontaneous unanimity. [O.Fr. *acorder* — L. *ad,* to, *cor, cordis,* the heart.]

accordion *ə-kör′di-ən, n.* a musical instrument consisting of folding bellows, keyboard, and free metal reeds. — *n.* **accord′ionist.** — **accord′ion-pleating, accordion pleats** pleating with very narrow folds like the bellows of an accordion. [**accord.**]

accost *ə-kost′,* earlier **accoast** *-kōst′, v.t.* to approach and address: to speak first to: to solicit as a prostitute. —

v.i. (*Spens.*) to lie alongside, border: to fly along near the ground. — *n.* address: greeting. — *adj.* **accost'able.** [O.Fr. *acoster* — L.L. *accostāre*, to be side by side — L. *ad*, to, *costa*, a rib, a side.]

accouchement *a-kōōsh'mã, -mənt, n.* delivery in childbed. — *ns.* **accoucheur** (*-shær'*) a man who assists women in childbirth; **accoucheuse** (*-shæz'*) a midwife. [Fr.]

account *ə-kownt', v.t.* to reckon: to judge, value: to recount (*obs.*). — *v.i.* to count: to reckon: to keep accounts: to give a reason or explanation: to give a statement of money dealings: to answer as one responsible: to have the responsibility or credit (of killing or otherwise disposing of anything or anybody; with *for*). — *n.* counting: reckoning: a reckoning of money or other responsibilities: a statement of money owing: a business relationship involving the provision of goods or services in return for money: advantage: value: estimation: consideration: sake: a descriptive report: a statement: a narrative: a performance. — *n.* **accountabil'ity.** — *adj.* **account'able** liable to account, responsible: explicable. — *n.* **account'ableness.** — *adv.* **account'ably.** — *ns.* **account'ancy** the office, work, or profession of an accountant; **account'ant** one who keeps, or is skilled in, accounts; **account'antship.** — *n.* and *adj.* **account'ing.** — **account'-book** a book for keeping accounts in; **account day** a designated day on which accounts are settled on the London Stock Exchange. — **bring, call, to account** to demand of someone an explanation or justification of what they have done: to reprimand; **by all accounts** according to general opinion; **find one's account** to derive advantage; **for account of** on behalf of; **for the account** for settlement on the regular settling-day; **give a good account of oneself** to give a good performance: to do well; **go to one's (long) account** to go to the last judgment, die; **hold to account** to hold responsible; **in account with** in business relations requiring the keeping of an account with; **make account of** to set value upon; **on** or **to account** as an instalment or interim payment; **on account of** because of; **on no account** not for any reason or consideration; **on one's own account** for one's own sake: on one's own responsibility; **take into account** to take into consideration; **take no account of** to overlook; **turn to (good) account** to turn to advantage. [O.Fr. *acconter* — L. *ad*, to, *computāre*, to reckon; see **compute, counts²**.]

accourage *a-kur'ij*, **accorage** *ak-or-āj', (Spens.) vs.t.* to encourage. [O.Fr. *acorager* — *à*, to, and *corage*, courage.]

accourt *ə-kōrt', -kört', v.t.* to entertain. [An invention of Spenser's — **court.**]

accoutre *ə-kōō'tər, v.t.* to dress or equip (esp. a warrior): — *pr.p.* **accoutring** (*ə-kōō'tər-ing*); *pa.p.* **accou'tred** (*-tərd*). — *n.* **accou'trement** (*-tər-* or *-trə-*), also obs. **accustrement, accoustrement** equipping: (usu. in *pl.*) dress: military equipments. [Fr. *accoutrer*, earlier *accoustrer*; origin doubtful.]

accoy *ə-koi', (Spens.) v.t.* to still: to soothe: to subdue: — *pa.p.* **accoied', accoyed'.** [O.Fr. *acoyer* — *à*, to, and *coi*, quiet — L. *quiētus*; see **coy.**]

accoyld. See **accoil.**

accredit *ə-kred'it, v.t.* to bring into credit, show to be true or correct: to accept as true: to furnish or send with credentials: to certify as meeting official requirements: to attribute (to): to ascribe to (*with* the thing attributed): to accept (a student) for University entrance on the basis of work done in school as opposed to an examination (*N.Z.*). — *n.* **accreditā'tion.** — *adj.* **accred'ited** furnished with credentials: certified officially: accepted as valid: (of livestock) certified free from a particular disease, e.g. brucellosis. [Fr. *accréditer* — *à*, to, *crédit*, credit.]

accrescent *ə-kres'ənt, adj.* growing: ever-increasing: enlarged and persistent (*bot.*). — *n.* **accresc'ence.** — *v.i.* **accrēte'** grow together: to become attached. — *v.t.* to unite: to form or gather round itself. — *n.* **accrē'tion** continued growth: the growing together of parts ex-

ternally, or continuous coherence: that which has grown in such a way: an extraneous addition. — *adj.* **accrē'tive.** [L. *accrēscěre, accrētum* — *ad*, to, *crēscěre*, to grow.]

accrue (*Spens.* **accrew**), *ə-krōō', v.i.* to come as an accession, increment, or product: to fall (to one) by way of advantage: to fall due: to increase (*Spens.*). — *v.t.* (*Spens.*) to accumulate. — *n.* **accru'al.** [O.Fr. *ucrewe*, what grows up to the profit of the owner — *acreistre* — L. *accrēscěre.*]

accubation *ak-ū-bā'shən, n.* a lying or reclining on a couch. [L. *ad*, to, and *cubāre*, to lie down.]

acculturation *ə-kul-chər-ā'shən, n.* the process, or result, of assimilating, through continuous contact, features (customs, beliefs, etc.) of another culture. — *adj.* **accul'tural** — *v.t.* and *v.i.* **accul'turate.** [L. *ad*, and **culture.**]

accumbent *ə-kumb'ənt, adj.* lying down or reclining on a couch: having the radicle lying along the edges of the cotyledons (*bot.*). [L. *ad*, to, *cumběre*, to lie.]

accumulate *ə-kūm'ūl-āt, v.t.* to heap or pile up: to amass. — *v.i.* to increase greatly: to go on increasing: to take university, etc. degrees by accumulation, to take a higher degree at the same time with a lower, or at a shorter interval than usual (also *v.t.*). — *adj.* heaped up: amassed. — *n.* **accūmū'lātion** heaping up: a heap or mass. — *adj.* **accūm'ūlātive** heaping up or growing by progressive addition: cumulative. — *n.* **accūm'ūlātor** a thing or person that accumulates: a means of storing energy, esp. an electric battery that can be recharged by sending a reverse current through it: in a computer, etc., a device that performs arithmetical operations and stores the results. — **accumulator (bet)** a bet on four or more races, original stake and winnings from each race being, by previous arrangement, laid on the next race, so that the gambler either wins much or loses all. [L. *ad*, to, *cumulus*, a heap.]

accurate *ak'ū-rit, adj.* exact. — *n.* **acc'ūracy** (*-ə-si*) correctness: exactness. — *adv.* **acc'ūrately.** — *n.* **acc'ūrateness.** [L. *accūrātus*, performed with care — *ad*, to, *cūra*, care.]

accurse *ə-kûrs', v.t.* to curse: to devote to misery or destruction. — *adj.* **accurs'ed** (or *-kûrst'*), (*poet.*) **accurst'** subjected to a curse: doomed: worthy of a curse. [O.E. pfx. *ā-*, and *cursian*, to curse.]

accuse *ə-kūz', v.t.* to bring a charge against (with *of*). — *n.* (*Shak.*) accusation. — *adj.* **accūs'able.** — *ns.* **accūs'al** accusation; **accūsā'tion** the act of accusing: a charge brought. — *adj.* **accūs'ative** accusing: in or belonging to a grammatical case which expresses the direct object of transitive verbs — primarily expressing destination or the goal of motion. — *n.* the accusative case: a word in the accusative. — *adjs.* **accūsatī'val; accūsatō'rial** of an accuser: of a trial, in which the judge is not the same person as the prosecutor; **accūs'atory** containing accusation; **accused'.** — *n.* (*sing.* or *pl.*) the person or persons accused. — *ns.* **accuse'ment** (*Spens.*), a charge; **accūs'er.** [L. *accūsāre, -ātum* — *ad*, to, *causa*, cause, partly through O.Fr. *accuser.* Accusative case (L. *casus accūsātīvus* is a mistranslation of Gr. *ptōsis aitiātikē*, the case indicating what is caused or effected — *aitiā*, cause (also accusation).]

accustom *ə-kus'təm, v.t.* to make familiar by custom (with *to*): to habituate. — *adj.* **accus'tomary.** — *adj.* **accus'tomed** usual: frequent: habituated: in the habit. — *n.* **accus'tomedness.** [O.Fr. *acostumer* (Fr. *accoutumer*) — *à*, to, *costume, coustume*; see **custom.**]

accustrement. See **accoutre.**

AC/DC *ā'sē-dē'sē*, (*slang*) *adj.* bi-sexual.

ace *ās, n.* a unit: the one in dice, cards, dominoes, etc.: a single point: a hole in one (see under **hole¹**; *golf*): a winning serve, esp. one which the opponent fails to touch (*tennis*): a jot: one of the highest character (*Burns*): an airman or other of distinguished achievement (*coll.*). — *adj.* of highest quality: outstanding. — *v.t.* to serve an ace against (an opponent) (*tennis*): to play (a hole) in one stroke (*golf*). — **an ace up one's**

sleeve, **an ace in the hole** a decisive but hidden advantage; **play one's ace** to use one's best weapon, resource, etc.; **within an ace of** within a hair's-breadth of. [Fr. *as* — L. *as*, unity — *as*, Tarentine Doric form of Gr. *heis*, one.]

-acea *-ā-sē-ə, n.pl. suff.* used in names of zoological divisions, esp. orders, classes.

-aceae *-ā-sē-ē, n.pl. suff.* used in names of plant families.

acedia *ə-sē'di-ə, n.* listlessness: torpor: sloth. [Gr. *akēdiā, akēdeia* — *a-*, priv., *kēdos*, care. See **accidie.**]

acellular *ā-sel'ū-lər, (biol.) adj.* not containing cells: not made up of cells. [Gr. *a-*, priv., **cell.**]

acephalous *a-, ä-, ə-sef'ə-ləs, adj.* headless. [Gr. *akephalos* — *a-*, priv., *kephalē*, head.]

Acer *ā'sər, äk'ər, n.* the maple genus, giving name to the family **Acerā'ceae** (*as-*). — *adj.* **acerā'ceous.** [L. *acer*, maple.]

acerb *a-sûrb'*, **acerbic** *ə-sûr'bik, adjs.* bitter and sour. — *v.t.* **acerbate** (*as'ər-bāt*) to embitter: to irritate. — *n.* **acerb'ity.** [L. *acerbus*.]

acerose *as'ər-ōs, adj.* chaffy: needle-pointed (*bot.*). [L. *acerosus* — *acus, -eris*, chaff, confused with *acus, -ūs*, needle, or *acer*, sharp.]

acerous *ə-sē'rəs, adj.* without horns, antennae, tentacles. [Gr. *a-*, priv. *keras*, horn.]

acervate *ə-sûr'vāt, adj.* heaped. — *n.* **acervā'tion.** [L. *acervāre, -ātum*, to heap.]

acescence *as-es'əns*, **acesc'ency** *-i, ns.* souring: turning (of milk). — *adj.* **acesc'ent.** [L. *acēscĕre*, to sour — *acēre*, to be sour.]

acesulfame K *a-si-sul'fām kā*, an artificial sweetener, 130 times sweeter than sugar. [*K* for *potassium*, and *sulfamic acid*.]

acet-, aceto- *as'it-(ō-), a-, ə-set'-(ō-), a-sēt'-(ō-), in composition, vinegar. — *ns.* **ac'etal** a liquid formed by oxidation of alcohol, etc.: any of a class of compounds of which this is the type; **acetal'dehyde** a liquid of characteristic smell, acetic aldehyde; **acet'amide** the amide of acetic acid; **ac'etate** a salt of acetic acid (**acetate rayon** a rayon made from cellulose acetate). — *adj.* **acetic** (*-sēt', -set'*) of, of the nature of, producing, vinegar (**acetic acid** the sour principle in vinegar, CH_3COOH). — *n.* **acetificā'tion** (*-set-*). — *v.t.* and *v.i.* **acet'ify** to turn into vinegar. — *n.* **ac'etone** the simplest of the ketones: any ketone. — *adjs.* **ac'etose** acetous; **acē'tous** like, or producing, vinegar: sour. — *ns.* **acetyl** (*as'i-til, -til*, or *a-sē'*) the radical (CH_3CO) of acetic acid (**acetyl-salicylic acid** aspirin, got by heating salicylic acid with acetyl chloride); **ac'etylchō'line** (*-kō'len; also -sē, -tīl, -ko'-, -lin, -lin*) a substance secreted at the ends of nerve fibres when they activate muscles; **acetylene** (*-set'*) a gas (C_2H_2), produced from calcium carbide and water, used in welding, synthesising acetic acid, illumination, etc. [L. *acētum*, vinegar.]

acetabulum *as-et-ab'ū-ləm, -ēt-, n.* the hollow that receives the head of the thigh-bone: one of the cotyledons of the placenta of ruminants: the cavity that receives a leg in the body of insects: in various animals, a sucker: — *pl.* **acetab'ula.** — *adj.* **acetab'ular.** [L. *acētābulum*, a vinegar cup.]

Achaean *ə-kē'ən*, **Achaian** *-kī', -kā', adj.* belonging to *Achaiā*, in the Peloponnese, or to Greece generally. — Also *n.*

achaenium, etc. See **achene.**

acharné *a-shär-nā*, (Fr.) *adj.* furious, desperate (esp. of battles). — **avec acharnement** (*a-vek a-shär-nə-mã*) obstinately, furiously, rancorously, with gusto.

acharya *ä-chär'yə, n.* a Hindu teacher or learned man. [Hind. *āchārya*, — Sans.]

Achates *ə-kā'tēz, n.* an intimate and trusty comrade, from Aeneas's friend the 'fidus Achates' of the Aeneid.

achates *ə-chāts', (Spens.).* Same as **acates.**

ache¹ *āk, n.* a continued pain. — *v.i.* to be in or be the site of continued pain: to long (for). — *ns.* **ach'age** (*Tennyson*); **ach'ing.** — *adj.* **ach'y.** [The verb was properly *ake*, the noun *ache*, as in *speak, speech*. — O.E. *acan* (*vb.*), *æce* (*n.*).]

ache² *āch.* Same as **aitch.**

achene *a-kēn'*, **achaenium, achenium** *a-kē'ni-əm, n.* a dry, indehiscent, one-seeded fruit, formed of one carpel, the seed separate from the fruit wall, as in the buttercup. — *adj.* **achē'nial.** — *n.* **achae'nocarp** any dry, indehiscent fruit, esp. an achene. [From Gr. *a-*, priv., and *chainein*, to gape.]

Achernar *ā'kər-när, n.* a first-magnitude star in the constellation Eridanus. [Ar. *ākhir al nahr*, end of the river (Eridanus).]

Acheron *ak'ər-on,* (Gr. myth.) *n.* one of the rivers of the infernal regions. — *adj.* **Acheron'tic.** [Gr. *Acherōn*.]

Acheulean, Acheulian *ə-shoō'li-ən, adj.* belonging to an early Palaeolithic culture above the Chellean and below the Mousterian. [Saint *Acheul*, near Amiens, France, where implements of this period are found in river deposits.]

achieve (*obs.* **atchieve**), *ə-chēv', v.t.* to bring to a successful issue: to end (*obs.*): to perform: to accomplish: to win. — *adj.* **achiev'able.** — *ns.* **achieve'ment** achieving: something achieved: an exploit: an escutcheon or armorial shield granted in memory of some achievement: escutcheon, armour, etc., hung over a tomb: a hatchment; **achiev'er.** — **achievement age** level of individual's educational achievement as determined by comparing his score in a test with the average score of others of the same age; **achievement quotient** ratio of achievement age to chronological age (usu. × 10). [Fr. *achever*, from *à chief* (*venir*) — L.L. *ad caput*, to a head; see **chief, hatchment.**]

Achillea *a-kil'i-ə n.* the yarrow genus of perennial plants (fam. Compositae). [L. *achillea, achilleos*, — Gr. *achilleios*, — *Achilleus*, Achilles.]

Achillean *ak-il-ē'ən, adj.* like *Achilles*, the great Greek hero in the Trojan war, invulnerable except in the heel, by which his mother held him when she dipped him in the Styx. — **Achilles' heel, heel of Achilles** a person's weak or most vulnerable point; **Achilles' tendon** the attachment of the soleus and gastrocnemius muscles of the calf of the leg to the heel-bone.

Achimenes *a-kim'in-ēz, -men', n.* a genus of herbaceous perennial plants (fam. Gesneriaceae) of tropical S. America: (without *cap.*) a plant of the genus: — *pl.* **-nes.** [L.]

Achitophel, Ahithophel *ə-kit', or -hit'ō-fel, ns.* a cautious person (*Shak.*): (after Dryden's application to Shaftesbury) an able but unprincipled counsellor. [From David's counsellor who abetted the rebellion of Absalom.]

achkan *äch'kən, n.* in India, a knee-length coat with a high collar, buttoned all the way down. [Hind. *ackan*.]

achlamydeous *ak-lə-mid'i-əs,* (*bot.*) *adj.* without perianth. [Gr. *a-*, priv., *chlamys, -ydos*, a mantle.]

achondroplasia *ā-kon-drō-plā'zhi-ə, n.* dwarfism characterised by shortness of the arms and legs. — *adj.* **achondroplastic** (*-plas'tik*). [Gr. *a-*, priv., *chondros*, cartilage, *plassein*, to make.]

achromatic *ak-rō-mat'ik, adj.* transmitting light without much chromatic aberration: without colour. — *n.* **a'chromat** an achromatic lens. — *adv.* **achromat'ically.** — *n.* **achrō'matin** the part of a cell nucleus that does not stain with basic dyes. — *v.t.* **achrō'matise, -ize** to render achromatic. — *ns.* **achrō'matism** the state of being achromatic; **achromatopsia** (*ə-krō-mə-top'si-ə*; Gr. *ops*, eye) total colour blindness. [Gr. *a-*, priv., *chrōma, -atos*, colour.]

achy. See **ache¹.**

acicular *as-ik'ū-lər, adj.* needle-shaped: slender and sharp-pointed. — *adj.* **acic'ulate** marked as if with needle-scratches. [L. *acicula*, dim. of *acus*, a needle.]

acid *as'id, adj.* sharp: sour: of acid, having an acid reaction: biting, keen (*fig.*): ill-natured, morose (*fig.*): pertaining to, of the nature of, having the properties of, an acid (*chem.*): containing a large proportion of silica (*geol.*). — *n.* a substance with a sour taste: in chemistry, variously considered as: —any of a class of substances which turn vegetable blues (e.g. litmus) red, and combine with bases, certain metals, etc., to form salts; any of a class of substances that dissolve in water with the formation of hydrogen ions; any of a class of substances that can transfer a proton to another substance, etc.: something harsh, biting, sarcastic (*fig.*): LSD or other hallucinogenic drug (*slang*). — *adjs.* **acid'ic; acidifi'able.** — *n.* **acidificātion.** — *v.t.* **acid'ify** to make acid: to convert into an acid. — *v.i.* to become acid: — *pr.p.* **acid'ifying;** *pa.t.* and *pa.p.* **acid'ified.** — *ns.* **acidim'eter** an apparatus for performing acidimetry; **acidim'etry** measurement of the concentration of acids by titration with a standard solution of alkali; **acid'ity** the quality of being acid or sour: the extent to which a solution is acid (see **pH-value**); **acidō'sis** (*med.*) the presence of acids in the blood beyond normal limits. — *v.t.* **acid'ūlate** to make slightly acid. — *adj.* **acid'ūlous** slightly sour: subacid: containing carbonic acid, as mineral waters: caustic, sharp (*fig.*). — **acid drop** a sweet flavoured with tartaric acid; **acid dye** a dyestuff with acid properties; **ac'idfreak, ac'id-head** (*drug-taking slang*) a head (q.v.); **acid rain** precipitation containing sulphur and nitrogen compounds and other pollutants released by the combustion of fossil fuels in industrial processes; **acid rock** a type of rock music featuring bizarre electronic and instrumental effects supposedly influenced by, or suggestive of the effects of, hallucinogenic drugs; **acid salt** a salt in which only part of the replaceable hydrogen is replaced by a metal; **acid test** a test for gold by acid: a searching test (*fig.*). — **put the acid on** (*coll.; Austr.* and *N.Z.*) to apply pressure (on a person). [L. *acidus*, sour — *acēre*, to be sour.]

Acidanthera *as-id-an'thi-rə, ak-id-, n.* a genus of white-flowered plants of N.E. Africa (fam. Iridaceae): (without *cap.*) a plant of the genus. [Gr. *akis*, pointed object, *anthēra* (see **anther**.)]

acierate *as'i-ər-āt, v.t.,* to turn into steel. — *n.* **ac'ierage** the covering of a metal plate with a film of iron. [Fr. *aciérer* — *acier*, steel. — L.L. *aciārium* (*ferrum*), lit. edging (iron) — L. *aciēs*, edge.]

aciform *as'i-förm, adj.* needle-shaped. [L. *acus*, needle, suff. **-form.**]

acinaciform *as-in-as'i-förm,* (*bot.*) *adj.* scimitar-shaped. [Gr. *akīnakēs*, a short sword (a Persian word), suff. **-form.**]

acinus *as'i-nəs, n.* one of the small fruits that compose an aggregate fruit, as in the raspberry: an aggregate fruit: a pip: a racemose gland: — *pl.* **ac'ini.** — *adjs.* **acinā'ceous** full of pips: berry-like: like a cluster of grapes; **acin'iform** berry-like. — *adjs.* **ac'inous, ac'inose** (or *-ōs*) consisting of acini: like a cluster of berries. [L. *acinus*, berry, pip.]

ack-ack *ak'-ak', adj.* anti-aircraft. — *adv.* **ack-emm'a** ante meridiem. [Formerly signallers' names for the letters AA, AM.]

ackee. Same as **akee.**

ackers *ak'əz,* (*slang*) *n.pl.* money. — Also **akk'as.** [Origin uncertain.]

acknow *ak-nō',* (*obs.*) *v.t.* to recognise: to acknowledge: — *pa. t.* **acknew;** *pa. p.* **acknown(e)'.** — *adj.* **acknowne'** (*Shak.*) confessedly cognisant. [O.E. *on*, in, on, *cnāwan*, to know.]

acknowledge *ək-nol'ij, v.t.* to own a knowledge of: to own as true, or genuine, or valid, or one's own: to confess: to own with gratitude or thanks: to admit or intimate receipt of. — *adj.* **acknowl'edgeable.** — *adv.* **acknowl'-edgeably.** — *n.* **acknowl'edgment** (sometimes **acknowl'-edgement**) recognition: admission: confession: thanks: an intimation of receipt. [From **acknow;** see **knowledge.**]

aclinic *ak-lin'ik, adj.* without inclination, or magnetic dip. [Gr. *aklīnēs*, horizontal — *a-*, priv., *klīnein*, to tilt.]

acme *ak'mi, n.* the top or highest point: the culmination or perfection in the career of anything: the crisis, as of a disease (*arch.*). — *n.* **ac'mite** a soda pyroxene

whose crystals often show a steep pyramid. [Gr. *akmē* — *akē*, a point.]

acne *ak'ni, n.* inflammation of the sebaceous follicles, as on the nose. — **acne rosacea** see **rosacea** under **Rosa.** [Perh. Gr. *akmē*, a point.]

acock *a-kok', adv.* in a cocked manner: defiantly. — *adv.* **acock'-bill** (*naut.*) having the end pointing upward, as an anchor ready for dropping, or yards topped up (a sign of mourning). [a³ and **cock**¹.]

acoemeti *a-sem'i-tī, n.pl.* an Eastern order of monks (5th–6th cent.), who by alternating choirs kept divine service going on day and night. [Latinised pl. of Gr. *akoimētos*, sleepless — *a-*, priv., and *koimaein*, to put to sleep.]

acold *ə-kōld',* (*Shak.*) *adj.* chilled. [Prob. O.E. *ācōlod*, pa.p. of *ācōlian* pfx. *ā-*, intens., and *cōlian*, to cool.]

acolouthos *ak-ə-lōō'thos,* (*hist.*) *n.* the head of the Varangian guard of the Byzantine emperors. — *n.* **acolou'thite** (*obs.*) an acolyte. — *adj.* **acol(o)u'thic** pertaining to an after-image or sensation following upon the immediate effect of a stimulus. — *ns.* **acolyte** (*ak'ə-līt*), **ac'olyth** (*-lith*) one in minor orders, next below subdeacon (*R.C. Church*): an inferior church officer: an attendant or assistant: a faithful follower. [Gr. *akolouthos*, an attendant — *akoloutheein*, to follow.]

acolyte. See **acolouthos.**

à compte *a kɔ̃t,* (Fr.) on account: in part payment.

aconite *ak'ə-nīt, n.* wolf's-bane or monk's-hood (*Aconitum*): poison got from it, or (*poet.*) deadly poison in general (often **aconī'tum**). — *adj.* **aconit'ic.** — *n.* **aconitine** (*-kon'*) a poisonous alkaloid from aconite. — **winter aconite** an early-flowering ranunculaceous plant (*Eranthis hyemalis*). [L. *aconītum* — Gr. *akonīton*.]

à contre cœur *a kɔ̃-tr' kœr,* (Fr.) reluctantly.

acorn *ā'körn, n.* the fruit of the oak. — *adj.* **ā'corned.** — **ā'corn-cup'** the woody cup-shaped involucre of an acorn; **ā'corn-shell** a cirripede of the genus Balanus (L., acorn); **acorn worm** any of various worm-like sea-animals (enteropneusts) of the Hemichordata which have a proboscis and collar somewhat like an acorn in shape. [O.E. *æcern;* form influenced by confusion with **corn**¹ and perh. **oak** (Northern *aik*, O.E. *āc*).]

à corps perdu *a kor per-dü,* (Fr.) desperately, with might and main.

Acorus *ak'ə-rəs, n.* the sweet-flag genus of the arum family. [Latinised from Gr. *akoros.*]

acosmism *ə-koz'mizm, n.* disbelief in the existence of an eternal world, or of a world distinct from God. — *n.* **acos'mist.** [Gr. *a-*, priv., and *kosmos*, the world.]

acotyledon *a-kot-i-lē'dən, n.* a cryptogam. — *adj.* **acotylē'-donous.** [Gr. *a-*, priv., and **cotyledon.**]

acouchy *ə-kōō'shē, n.* a kind of agouti. [Tupí *acuchy.*]

à coup sûr *a kōō sür,* (Fr.) to a certainty.

acoustic, -al *ə-kōōs'tik, -əl,* (esp. formerly) *-kows',* *adjs.* pertaining to the sense of hearing or to the theory of sounds: used in hearing, auditory: operated by sound vibrations, as an *acoustic mine*: (of musical instruments) not electric, as an *acoustic guitar, piano*. — *n.* **acous'tic** acoustic properties. — *adv.* **acous'tically.** — *ns.* **acoustician** (*-ti'shən*) one who studies or has studied the science of acoustics: one who makes or repairs acoustic instruments, etc.; **acous'tics** (*sing.*) the science of sound: (as *pl.*) acoustic properties. [Gr. *akoustikos* — *akouein*, to hear.]

à couvert *a kōō-ver,* (Fr.) under cover, protected.

acquaint *ə-kwānt', v.t.* to let or make to know: to inform. — *adj.* (*Scot.* and *North.*) acquainted. — *ns.* **acquaint'-ance** knowledge, esp. falling short of intimacy: a person (sometimes persons) known slightly; **acquaint'anceship** slight knowledge. — *adj.* **acquaint'ed** personally known: having personal knowledge of (usu. with *with*). [O.Fr. *acointer* — L.L. *accognitāre* — L. *ad*, to, *cognitus*, known.]

acquest *ə-kwest', n.* acquisition: a thing acquired. [O.Fr.; see **acquire.**]

acquiesce *ak-wi-es'*, *v.i.* to rest satisfied or without making opposition: to assent (with *in*). — *n.* acquiesc'ence quiet assent or submission. — *adj.* acquiesc'ent acquiescing. — *n.* one who acquiesces. — *advs.* acquiesc'ently, acquiesc'ingly. [L. *acquiēscĕre* — *ad*, to, *quiēs*, rest.]

acquight. See acquit.

acquire *ə-kwīr'*, *v.t.* to gain: to attain to. — *n.* acquirabil'ity. — *adj.* acquīr'able that may be acquired. — *n.* acquīr'al. — *adj.* acquired'. — *ns.* acquire'ment acquisition: something learned or got by effort, not a gift of nature; acquisition (*ak-wi-zish'ən*) the act of acquiring: that which is acquired. — *adj.* acquisitive (*ə-kwiz'*) able, desiring or ready to acquire. — *ns.* acquis'itiveness propensity to acquire; acquist (*ə-kwist'*; *Milt.*) acquisition. — acquired character a character originating in the actual life of an organism, not inherited; acquired taste a liking that comes after some experience: a thing so liked (often ironically). — Acquired Immune Deficiency Syndrome (also known as AIDS *ādz*) a condition brought about by a virus which causes the body's immune system to become deficient, leaving the sufferer very vulnerable to infection; target acquisition a fighter or bomber pilot's sighting of his target, either visually or by radar. [L. *acquīrĕre*, *-quīsītum* — *ad*, to, *quaerĕre*, to seek.]

acquit *ə-kwit'*, (*obs.*) acquite, acquight *ə-kwīt'*, *v.t.* to free: to release: to discharge, as a debt: to discharge (oneself of a duty): hence to behave, conduct (oneself): to prove (oneself): to release from an accusation: — *pr.p.* acquitt'ing; *pa.t.* and *pa.p.* acquitt'ed, *obs.* acquit'. — *ns.* acquit'ment (*obs.*); acquitt'al a judicial discharge from an accusation; acquitt'ance a discharge from an obligation or debt: a receipt in evidence of such a discharge. — *v.t.* (*Shak.*) to acquit, clear. [O.Fr. *aquiter* — L. *ad*, to, *quiētāre*, to quiet, settle; see quit.]

acrawl *ə-kröl'*, *adv.* crawling (with *with*). [a³ and crawl¹.]

acre *ā'kər*, *n.* a measure of 4840 sq. yards: (Scottish acre) 6150·4 sq. yards, (Irish) 7840 sq. yards — both obsolete: (in *pl.*) lands, estates. — *n.* acreage (*ā'kər-ij*) area in acres. — *adj.* acred (*ā'kərd*) landed. — a'cre('s)=breadth 22 yards; a'cre('s)-length 220 yards. [O.E. *æcer*, field; Ger. *Acker*, L. *ager*, Gr. *agros*, Sans. *ajra*, a plain.]

acrid *ak'rid*, *adj.* biting: pungent. — *n.* acrid'ity. [L. *ācer*, *ācris*, sharp, keen; noun suffix perh. in imitation of *acid*.]

acridin(e) *ak'ri-dēn*, *-din*, *n.* a compound found in coal-tar, a parent substance of dyes and anti-bacterial drugs. — *n.* acriflavin(e) *-flā'vēn*, *-vin*; *acri*dine and *flavin(e)*) an antiseptic. [acrid, and n. suff. *-ine*.]

Acrilan® *ak'ri-lan*, *n.* a type of acrylic fibre (somewhat resembling wool).

acrimony *ak'ri-mən-i*, *n.* bitterness of feeling or language. — *adj.* acrimō'nious. — *adv.* acrimō'niously. [L. *ācrimōnia* — *ācer*, sharp.]

acro- *ak-rō-*, in composition, tip, point, summit. [Gr. *akron*, tip, end, *akros*, highest, outermost.]

acroamatic, -al *ak-rō-ə-mat'ik*, *-əl*, *adjs.* oral (not published): esoteric. [Gr. *akroāmatikos* — *akroāma*, anything to be listened to — *akroaesthai*, to listen.]

acrobat *ak'rō-bat*, *n.* a rope-dancer: a tumbler: a performer of gymnastic feats. — *adj.* acrobat'ic. — *n.pl.* acrobat'ics acrobatic performances (often *fig.*); — *n.sing* the art of the acrobat. — *n.* ac'robatism the art of the acrobat. [Gr. *akrobatēs*, acrobat, *akrobatos*, walking on tiptoe — *akron*, point, and the root of *bainein*, to go.]

acrogen *ak'rō-jən*, *n.* a cryptogam with growing-point at the tip — a fern or moss. — *adj.* acrogenous (*ə-kroj'i-nəs*). [Gr. *akron*, *-genēs*, born.]

acrolein *a-krō'li-in*, (*chem.*) *n.* the aldehyde of allyl alcohol, a pungent-smelling colourless liquid. [L. *ācer*, *ācris*, sharp, *olēre*, to smell.]

acrolith *ak'rō-lith*, *n.* a wooden statue with stone extremities. [Gr. *akrolithos* — *akron*, point, *lithos*, stone.]

acromegaly *ak-rō-meg'ə-li*, *n.* a disease characterised by overgrowth, esp. of the face and extremities. — *adj.* acromegal'ic suffering from acromegaly. [Gr. *akron*, point, *megas*, *megalos*, great.]

acromion *ə-krō'mi-on*, *n.* a process of the spine of the scapula (also acromion process). — *adj.* acro'mial. [Gr. *akros*, outermost, *ōmos*, shoulder.]

acronychal *ə-kron'ik-əl*, *adj.* at nightfall (of the rising or setting of stars). — *adv.* acron'ychally. [Gr. *akronychos*, at nightfall — *akron*, point, *nychos*, *-eos*, night.]

acronym *ak'rō-nim*, *n.* a word formed from, or based on, the initial letters or syllables of other words, as *radar*. — *n.* acronymā'nia a craze for forming acronyms. — *adjs.* acronym'ic, acron'ymous. [acro-, and Gr. *onyma* = *onoma*, name.]

acropetal *ə-krop'i-tl*, (*bot.*) *adj.* in the direction of the tip of the plant. — *adv.* acrop'etally. [Gr. *akron*, petal, L. *petĕre*, to seek.]

acrophobia *ak-rō-fō'bi-ə*, *n.* fear of heights. [Gr. *akron*, tip, *akros*, highest, *phobos*, fear.]

acrophony *ə-krof'ən-i*, *n.* the use of a symbol (derived from an ideogram) to represent the initial sound only of the name of the object for which the ideogram stood. — *adjs.* acrophonet'ic, acrophon'ic (*-fon'*). [acro-, Gr. *phōnē*, sound.]

acropolis *a-krop'ol-is*, *ə-krop'ə-lis*, *n.* a citadel, esp. that of Athens. [Gr. *akropolis* — *akros*, highest, *polis*, a city.]

acrospire *ak'rō-spīr*, (*bot.*) *n.* the first leaf that sprouts from a germinating seed. [M.E. *akerspire* — O.E. *æhher* (see icker), ear, spire¹.]

across *ə-kros'*, *prep.* from side to side of: on or to the other side of: crosswise. — Also *adv.* — *adj.* across'=the-board' of wage increases, etc., applying in all cases (*adverbially* across the board). — come across to alight upon, meet: to hand over information, confession, money, etc., in answer to demand or inducement (*coll.*); get or come across to take effect (on the audience across the footlights, and so generally); get it across to make acceptable, to bring to a successful issue; put it across (someone), to deceive (him). [a³ and cross.]

acrostic *ə-kros'tik*, *n.* a poem or puzzle in which the first (or last) letters of each line spell a word or sentence: an acronym. [Gr. *akros*, extreme, *stichos*, a line.]

acroterion *ak-rō-tē'ri-on*, (*archit.*) *n.* a pedestal or ornament at the top or side angle of a pediment: — *pl.* acrotē'ria. — Also acroterium, acrō'ter (or *ak'*). — *adj.* acrotē'rial. [Gr. *akrōtērion*, extremity — *akros*.]

acrotism *ak'rot-izm*, (*med.*) *n.* absence of pulsation. [Gr. *a-*, priv., *krotos*, sound by striking.]

acrylic *ə-kril'ik*, *n.* a synthetic fibre. — Also *adj.* — acrylic acid a very reactive acid belonging to the series of oleic acids, obtainable from acrolein by oxidation; acrylic resins thermoplastic resins formed by the polymerisation of esters, amides, etc., derived from acrylic acid. [acrolein, Gr. *hylē*, matter.]

acrylonitrile *ə-kril-ō-nī'trīl*, *n.* vinyl cyanide, used in making by polymerisation synthetic fibres for carpets, etc., and synthetic rubbers.

act *akt*, *v.i.* to exert force or influence: to produce an effect: to behave oneself: to perform, as on the stage: to feign: to be suitable for performance. — *v.t.* to perform: to imitate or play the part of. — *n.* something done or doing: an exploit: the very process (of doing something): a decree: a legislative enactment: a written instrument in verification: a short prayer (*R.C. Church*): a distinct main section of a play: an individual performance, as in variety: a public disputation or lecture maintained for a degree. — *ns.* actabil'ity; act'ing action: the act or art of performing an assumed or a dramatic part: feigning. — *adj.* performing some duty temporarily, or for another. — *ns.* act'or one who acts: a stage-player: — *fem.* act'ress; act'ure (*Shak.*, *Lover's Complaint*) action, performance. — act curtain, act drop a curtain for closing the proscenium arch between acts or scenes. — act as to perform the duties of; act of God a result of natural forces, unexpected and not preventable by human foresight; act of grace a favour, esp. a pardon granted by a sovereign; **act of parliament** see **parliament; act on** to exert an influence on: to act in accordance with; **act out** to play as an actor; **act up** (*coll.*) to behave badly; **act up to** to come in practice up to the standard of: to fulfil; **get in on, get into the act** (*coll.*) to start participating in something apparently profitable already taking place in order to share in the benefits; **get one's act together** to get oneself organised; **put on an act** to make a pretence: to show off.   [L. *āctus, -ūs,* an action, doing, *āctum,* a thing done, *āctor,* a doer, actor; *agĕre, āctum,* to do, drive.]

acta *ak'tə, n.pl.* official minutes of proceedings: official proceedings or acts. — **acta sanctorum** (*ak'ta sangktō'rəm, -tö', -rōom;* L.) deeds of the saints.   [L., records.]

Actaeon *ak-tē'ən, n.* a hunter transformed into a stag by Artemis: hence one with horns implanted upon him, a cuckold. — *v.t.* to cuckold.   [L. *Actaeōn* — Gr. *Aktaiōn.*]

acte gratuit *akt gra-twē,* (Fr.) an impulsive act lacking motive.

actin *ak'tin, n.* a protein found in muscle, active in muscular contraction.   [act.]

actin(o)- *ak-tin-(o-),* in composition, ray. — *adj.* **actinal** (*ak-tī'nəl,* or *ak'ti-nəl*) belonging to the radiating bands on the body of an echinoderm where the tube-like feet are, or to the region of the mouth and tentacles in Anthozoa. — *n.* **actinia** (*-tin'*) a sea-anemone (properly (with *cap.*) a particular genus): — *pl.* **actin'iae** or **actin'ias.** — *n.* and *adj.* **actin'ian.** — *adj.* **actin'ic** of or showing actinism. — *ns.* **ac'tinide, actinoid** any element of a group from atomic number 89 (actinium) upwards; **ac'tinism** the chemical action of radiant energy; **actin'ium** a radioactive metal (atomic number 89; symbol Ac) found in pitchblende; **Actinobacillus** (*-bə-sil'əs*) a genus of bacteria, one of which causes **actinobacillō'sis,** woody-tongue (q.v.): (without *cap.*) a bacillus of this genus: — *pl.* **actinobacill'i; actin'olite** (Gr. *lithos,* a stone) a green amphibole; **actinom'eter** an instrument for measuring the heat-intensity or the actinic effect of light rays. — *adj.* **actinomor'phic** (Gr. *morphē,* form; *biol.*) radially symmetrical. — *ns.* **Actinomyces** (*-mī'sēz;* Gr. *mykēs,* fungus) the ray-fungus, a genus of minute fungi or filamentous bacteria with radiating mycelium; **actinomycosis** (*-kō'sis*) lumpy-jaw in cattle, etc., or other disease caused by Actinomyces; **ac'tinon** actinium emanation, an isotope of radon; **actinother'apy** the treatment of disease by exposure to rays, esp. ultraviolet rays. — *n.pl.* **Actinozo'a** the Anthozoa. — **actinic glass** glass that impedes actinic rays; **actinic rays** those rays that have a marked chemical action, esp. the ultraviolet.   [Gr. *aktīs, aktīnos,* ray.]

action *ak'shən, n.* acting: activity: behaviour: a deed: an operation: a gesture: fighting: a battle: a lawsuit, or proceedings in a court: a mode of moving the legs: the movement of events in a drama, novel, etc.: the mechanism, esp. of a keyboard instrument. — *adj.* **ac'tionable** giving ground for a lawsuit. — *n.* **ac'tionist** an activist. — **action committee** or **group** members of an organisation who are chosen to take active measures; **action painting** an American version of tachism in which paint is dripped, spattered, smeared, etc. onto the canvas; **action radius** the distance a ship or aircraft can go without running out of fuel before reaching its base or starting-point again; **action replay** on television, the repeating of a piece of film, e.g. the scoring of a goal in football, usu. in slow motion; **action stations** posts to be manned during or preparatory to battle (often *fig.*); **ac'tion-taking** (*Shak.*), resorting to law instead of resorting to fighting. — **a piece of the action** (*coll.*) participation in an enterprise, etc., often including a share in the profits.   [Fr., — L. *āctiō, -ōnis.*]

active *ak'tiv, adj.* acting: in actual operation: given to action: brisk: busy: nimble: practical, as opp. to spec-ulative: effective: (of a volcano) liable to erupt, not extinct: (of bacteria, etc.) potent: radioactive: of that voice in which the subject of the verb represents the doer of the action (*gram.*). — *v.t.* **ac'tivate** to make active: to increase the energy of: to increase the capacity for adsorption in (carbon): to increase the biological activity of (sewage, etc.) by aeration: to stimulate: to make radioactive. — *ns.* **activā'tion; ac'tivātor** a person or usu. thing, substance, etc. that activates. — *adv.* **ac'tively.** — *ns.* **ac'tiveness; ac'tivism** a philosophy of creative will, esp. the practical idealism of Rudolf Eucken (1846–1926): a policy of direct vigorous action; **ac'tivist** a believer in the philosophy of activism: one who supports a policy of vigorous action: one who plays a special part in advancing a project or in strengthening the hold of political ideas; **activ'ity** quality, state, or fact of being active: a training exercise designed to teach through practical experiment, research, and discussion: (esp. in *pl.*) doings. — **activated** or **active carbon** carbon in a highly adsorbent condition, obtained from vegetable matter by carbonisation in the absence of air; **active immunity** immunity due to the making of antibodies within the organism; **active life** (*theol.*) life devoted to good works as opposed to contemplation; **active list** a list of full-pay officers engaged in or available for service; **active service** service in the battle area, or (orig. *U.S.*) in army, navy or air force even in time of peace.   [L. *āctīvus.*]

acton *ak'tən,* **ha(c)queton** *hak'(i)tən, ns.* a stuffed jacket worn under a coat of mail.   [O.Fr. *auqueton* — Sp. — Ar. *al qūtun,* the cotton.]

actor, actress. See under **act.**

actual *ak'tū-əl, ak'chōo-əl, adj.* of the nature of an action (*Shak.*): real: existing in fact: at the time being. — *v.t.* **ac'tualise, -ize** to make actual: to realise in action. — *ns.* **actuali'sā'tion, -z-; ac'tualist** one who looks to actual facts; **actuality** (*-al'i-ti*) the fact or state of being actual: realism: something that really is: a newsreel or current affairs programme (also **actualités** *aktū-al-ē-tā, Fr.*). — *adv.* **ac'tually** as a matter of fact: truly, however little one might expect it.   [Fr. *actuel* — L.L. *āctuālis.*]

actuary *ak'tū-ər-i, n.* a registrar or clerk (still in the Convocation of Canterbury): one who makes the calculations connected with insurance. — *adj.* **actuarial** (*-ā'ri-əl*). — *adv.* **actuā'rially.**   [L. *āctuārius* (*scriba*), an amanuensis, a clerk.]

actuate *ak'tū-āt, v.t.* to put into, or incite to, action. — *v.i.* to act. — *ns.* **actūā'tion; ac'tūātor.**   [L. *āctus,* action; see **act.**]

acture. See **act.**

actus reus *ak'təs rē'əs, ak'tōos rā'ōos,* (law) the act which is necessary for the crime to be constituted: — *pl.* **actus** (*-tōos*) **rei** (*-ī, -ē*).   [Modern L., guilty act.]

acuity *ə-kū'i-ti, n.* sharpness.   [L.L. *acuitās, -ātis* — L. *acus,* needle.]

aculeate(d) *ə-kū'li-āt(-id), adjs.* pointed: prickly: having a sting: stinging.   [L. *aculeātus* — *aculeus,* a sting, goad, dim. of *acus,* needle.]

acumen *ə-kū'men, ak'ū-mən, n.* sharpness: quickness of perception: penetration. — *v.t.* **acū'minate** to sharpen: to give a point to. — *v.i.* (*rare*) to taper. — *adj.* (*bot.*) tapering in long hollow curves to a point (also **acū'-minated**). — *n.* **acūmina'tion.**   [L. *acūmen, -inis,* a point.]

acupressure *ak-ū-presh'ər, n.* arrest of haemorrhage by a needle pressing across the artery: in acupuncture or related treatments, pressure (as opposed to a needle) applied to an acupoint (q.v. under **acupuncture**).   [L. *acus,* needle, **pressure.**]

acupuncture *ak'ū-pungk-chər, n.* the science (orig. Chinese) of puncturing the skin with needles at specified points (**acupoints**) in order to cure illness, relieve symptoms, or effect anaesthesia.   [L. *acus,* needle, **point, puncture.**]

acushla *ə-kōōsh'lə,* (*Anglo-Irish*) *n.* darling.   [Ir. *a chuisle,* voc. of *cuisle,* vein.]

acute *ə-kūt, adj.* sharp: sharp-pointed: ending in an acute angle (*bot.*): keen: mentally penetrating: piercing: finely discriminating: keenly perceptive: shrewd: urgently pressing: of a disease, coming to a crisis, as opp. to *chronic*. — *n.* an acute accent. — *adv.* acute'ly. — *n.* acute'ness. — acute accent a mark (') in ancient Greek indicating a rising pitch, now used for various purposes; acute angle one less than a right angle. [L. *acūtus*, pa.p. of *acuĕre*, to sharpen.]

acyclic *ā-, a-sī'klik, adj.* not periodic: not whorled (*bot.*): with open-chain structure, aliphatic (*chem.*). — *n.* acy'clovir (*-klō-vīr*) a drug used in the treatment of forms of herpes. [Gr. *a-*, priv., *kyklos*, a wheel.]

acyl *ā'sil, as', as'il*, (*chem.*) *n., adj.* (denoting) the carboxylic acid RCO-. [*A*cid and *-yl*.]

ad *ad, n.* coll. for advertisement.

-ad¹ *ad*, a suffixal element found in (1) names for nymphs, etc. (*naiad, dryad, hamadryad*); (2) titles of poems, etc. (*Iliad, Dunciad*); (3) words for numerical groups (*triad, decad*(e), *myriad, Olympiad* (q.v.)). [Gr. *-as, -ados*.]

-ad² *ad*, (*biol.*) *suff.* denoting 'towards', as in *caudad, cephalad*, towards the tail, head. [L. *ad*, to, towards.]

Ada *ā'də, n.* a computer-programming language orig. devised for military use., one of its applications being simultaneous control of diverse operations. [Named after *Ada* Lovelace (1816-52), daughter of Byron and assistant to C. Babbage.]

ad absurdum. See reductio ad absurdum.

adage *ad'ij, n.* an old saying: a proverb. [Fr., — L. *adagium* — *ad*, to, and root of *āiō*, I say.]

adagio *ə-dä'j*(*y*)*ō*, (*mus.*) *adv.* slowly. — *adj.* slow. — *n.* a slow movement: a piece in adagio time: — *pl.* ada'gios. [It., — *ad agio*, at ease.]

Adam *ad'əm, n.* the first man, according to Genesis: unregenerate human nature: a gaoler (perh. as wearing buff) (*Shak.*). — *adjs.* Adam applied to a style of architecture, interior decoration and furniture, designed by Robert and James Adam in the 18th century; Adamic, -al (*ə-dam'ik, -əl*) of or like Adam: naked. — *n.* Ad'amite a descendant of Adam: one who goes naked, esp. a member of a 2nd-century sect in North Africa. — *adjs.* Adamit'ic, -al. — *n.* Ad'amitism. — Adam's ale or wine water; Adam's apple the projection of the thyroid cartilage in front of the throat, fabled to be part of the forbidden fruit stuck in Adam's throat: forbidden fruit (see forbid); Adam's flannel mullein; Adam's needle a species of Yucca. — not know someone from Adam (*coll.*) not to know someone, or who someone is. [Heb. *Ādām*.]

adamant *ad'əm-ənt, -ant, n.* a name applied by the ancients to various hard substances, e.g. steel: an imagined rock with fabulous properties: diamond (*obs.*): lodestone (*obs.*). — *adj.* unyielding. — *adjs.* adamantē'an (*Milt.*) hard as adamant; adaman'tine unbreakable: impregnable: impenetrable: magnetically attractive (*obs.*). — adamantine lustre (*min.*) a lustre approaching the metallic but without opacity. [Gr. *adamas, -antos*, prob. orig. steel, also diamond — *a-*, priv., and *damaein*, to tame, overcome.]

Adansonia *ad-ən-sō'ni-ə, n.* the baobab genus. [Michel *Adanson*, French botanist (1727-1806).]

ad aperturam libri *ad ap-er-tūr'am lib'rī, -tōor'am lib'rē*, (L.) as the book opens.

adapt *ə-dapt', v.t.* to make fit or suitable. — *n.* adaptabil'ity. — *adj.* adapt'able. — *n.* adaptation (*ad-əp-tā'shən*) the fact, act, process, or result of adapting: a character by which anything is adapted to conditions: adjustment. — *adjs.* adapt'ative; adapt'ed modified to suit: suitable. — *ns.* adapt'er, -or, one who, or that which, adapts: an attachment or accessory enabling a piece of apparatus to be used for a purpose, or in conditions, other than that, or those, for which it was orig. intended; adap'tion adaptation. — *adj.* adapt'ive. — *adv.* adapt'ively. — *n.* adapt'iveness. [Fr. *adapter* — L. *adaptāre* — *ad*, to, and *aptāre*, to fit.]

Adar *ä'där*, or *ā'där, n.* the twelfth month of the Jewish ecclesiastical, the sixth of the civil, year (part of February and March). — Adar Sheni *shä'nē*; 'Adar

the second'), Veadar. [Heb. *adār*.]

ad arbitrium *ad är-bit'ri-əm, -ōom*, (L.) at pleasure.

ad astra *ad as'tra*, (L.) to the stars.

ad avizandum *ad a-viz-an'dəm, a-vēz-än'dōom*, (*Scottish law*; L.) for further consideration; see avizandum.

adaw *ə-dö', (Spens.), v.t.* to daunt: to subdue. — *v.i.* to subside. [App. a 16th-cent. misunderstanding of the M.E. adv. *adaw*, out of life — O.E. *of dagum*, from days (dat. pl.).]

adaxial *ad-aks'i-əl*, (*bot.*) *adj.* next to or towards the axis. [L. *ad*, to.]

adays *ə-dāz', (obs.) adv.* by day: daily (*Spens.*). [O.E. *dæges*, gen. of *dæg*, day, with prep. *a* (see **a³**) added later.]

ad captandum (vulgus) *ad kap-tan'dəm* (*vul'gəs*), *-dōom* (*wōol'gōos*), (L.) (used as *adv.* or *adj.*) with the intention of appealing to the emotions of, or pleasing, the crowd.

ad clerum *ad kler'əm, klā'rōom*, (L.) to the clergy.

ad crumenam *ad krōō'mə-nam, krōō-mā'nam*, (L.) to the purse.

add *ad, v.t.* to put, join, or annex (to something else): to sum up, compute the sum of: to say further. — *v.i.* to make an addition: to increase (with *to*): to find the total of numbers, etc. — *ns.* add'er one who adds: a machine for adding; additament (*ə-dit'ə-mənt*, or *ad'*) something added: in heraldry, an additional ornament external to the shield, e.g. supporters or symbols of office; addi'tion the act of adding: a thing added: the part of arithmetic or algebra that deals with adding: title, designation (*Shak.*). — *adj.* addi'tional added. — *adv.* addi'tionally. — *adjs.* additi'tious increasing; add'itive of the nature of an addition: characterised by addition: to be added. — *n.* a substance added to foodstuffs or other commodities for a special purpose. — adding machine an apparatus, electrically or manually operated, for performing basic arithmetical calculations; addition compound, product (*chem.*) one formed by the direct union of two or more substances; add'-on (esp. *comput.*) an additional unit, a peripheral: — *pl.* add'-ons; add-to system a hire-purchase arrangement by which a customer obtains a series of articles, making a down payment on the first only; add up to amount on adding: to be consistent, satisfactory to the mind: to point to as result or conclusion; add up to to come to as result or conclusion. [L. *addĕre, additum* — *ad*, to, *dăre*, to put.]

addax *ad'aks, n.* a large African antelope with long slightly twisted horns. [L., from an African word.]

addeem *ə-dēm', (obs.) v.t.* to adjudge: to award. [Pfx. *ad-*, and deem.]

addend *ad'end, ə-dend', n.* a number or quantity added. [addendum.]

addendum *ə-den'dəm, n.* a thing to be added, as supplementary material to a book, etc.: the distance between the centre and the outer edge of a tooth on a gear or of the thread of a screw (*eng*): — *pl.* adden'da. [L. gerundive of *addĕre*; see add.]

adder¹ *ad'ər, n.* the only venomous British snake, a viper (q.v.). — add'erstone a prehistoric spindle-whorl or bead, popularly attributed to the agency of adders; ad'der's-tongue a genus (Ophioglossum) of ferns whose spores grow on a spike resembling a snake's tongue; ad'der's-wort, add'erwort the bistort, or snakeweed, supposed to cure snake-bite. [O.E. *nædre* (*an adder* for *a nadder*; cf. obs. Ger. *Atter* for *Natter*).]

adder². See add.

addict *ə-dikt', v.t.* to give up (to), devote, apply habitually (to). — *adj.* (*obs.*) addicted. — *n.* (*ad'ikt*) a slave to a habit or vice, esp. drugs. — *adj.* addict'ed inclined or given up (to). — *ns.* addict'edness; addic'tion the state of being addicted: a habit that has become impossible to break. — *adj.* addict'ive tending to cause addiction: habit-forming. — drug of addiction a habit-forming drug. [L. *addīcĕre, addictum* — *ad*, to, *dīcĕre*, to declare.]

addio *ad-ē'o*, (It.) *interj.* good-bye (**a Dio** to God): — *pl.* **addi'os.**

Addison's disease *ad'i-sənz diz-ēz'*, a disease in which there is progressive destruction of the suprarenal cortex, accompanied by wasting, weakness, low blood-pressure, and pigmentation of the skin (bronzed skin). [Dr Thomas *Addison* (1793–1860), who investigated it.]

additament, addition, etc., **additive.** See **add.**

addle *ad'l, n.* liquid filth (now *dial.*). — *adj.* putrid: bad (as an egg): barren, empty: muddled. — *v.t.* and *v.i.* to make or become addle. — *adj.* **add'led.** — *n.* **add'lement.** — *adjs.* **add'le-brained, -headed, -pated** muddleheaded. [O.E. *adela*, mud.]

adduom *ə-dōōm', (Spens.) v.t.* to adjudge, award. [Pfx. *ad-*, and **doom.**]

addorsed *ə-dörst', (her.) adj.* turned back to back. [L. *ad*, to, *dorsum*, back.]

address *ə-dres', v.t.* to arrange (*obs.*): to prepare (*obs.*): to dress (*obs.*): to don (*arch.*): to apply or devote (oneself; with *to*): to apply oneself to: to direct: to aim: to direct one's words to, speak directly to: to send: to put a written or printed direction or indication of destination upon: to woo (*arch.*). — *v.i.* to direct one's words (towards) (*Shak.*): to prepare oneself (*Shak.*). — *n.* act or mode of addressing: deportment: adroitness: preparation, a move, incipient act (*Milt.*): a formal communication in writing: a speech: a direction, as of a letter: a place to which letters may be directed: a place where one may be found: a name, label or number that identifies the location of a stored item of data, etc. (*comput.*): (in *pl.*) attentions of the nature of courtship. — *adj.* **addressed', addrest'** set up (*Spens.*): ready, prepared (*Shak.*): arrayed (*obs.*): equipped (*obs.*): aimed: directed. — *ns.* **addressee'** the person to whom a missive or communication is addressed; **address'er, -or.** — *n.* **Addressograph®** (*ə-dres'ō-gräf*) a machine for printing addresses automatically, on envelopes, etc. — **address book** a notebook, usu. with alphabetical thumb-index, in which names and addresses can be entered. [Fr. *adresser* — L.L. *addirectiare* — L. *ad*, to, *directum*, straight; see **dress, direct.**]

adduce *ə-dūs', v.t.* to bring forward in discussion, to cite or quote. — *adj.* **addūc'ent** drawing inward or together, as a muscle. — *n.* **addūc'er.** — *adj.* **addūc'ible.** — *v.t.* **adduct** (*ə-dukt'*) to draw inward or together. — *n.* **adduc'tion** the act of adducing or of adducting. — *adj.* **adduc'tive** tending to bring forward. — *n.* **adduc'tor** an adducent muscle. [L. *addūcĕre, adductum* — *ad*, to, and *dūcĕre*, to lead.]

adeem *ə-dēm', (law) v.t.* to cancel (a bequest) by destruction or sale of the thing bequeathed, or otherwise. — *n.* **ademption** (*-dem'shən*). [L. *ad*, to, and *emĕre, emptum*, to take.]

adelantado *a-de-lan-tä'dō, n.* a grandee: a provincial governor: — *pl.* **adelanta'dos.** [Sp.]

à demi *a də-mē*, (Fr.) by halves, half.

aden- *ad'ən*, in composition, gland. — *ns.* **adenec'tomy** surgical removal of a gland; **adenine** (*ad'ən-ēn*) a substance found in all glandular tissues, one of the four bases in deoxyribonucleic acids, in close association with thymine; **adenitis** (*ad-ən-ī'tis*) inflammation of glands. — *ns.* **adenocarcinoma** (*-ō-kär-si-nō'mə*) a malignant tumour of glandular origin or gland-like structure: — *pl.* **adenocarcinō'mata** or **-mas; adenohypophosis** (*-ō-hī-poph'i-sis*) the anterior lobe of the pituitary gland: — *pl.* **adenohypoph'yses** (*-sēz*). — *adj.* **ad'enoid** glandlike: glandular. — *n.* (usu. in *pl.*) enlargement of glandular tissue at the back of the nose. — *adj.* **adenoid'al** of adenoids: affected by, or as if by, adenoids (as a voice). — *ns.* **adenoidec'tomy** surgical removal of adenoids; **adenō'ma** a benign tumour like, or originating in, a gland: — *pl.* **adenō'mata** or **-mas.** — *adj.* **adenō'matous.** — *ns.* **adenosine** (*ad'ə-nō-sin, ə-den'*) a nucleoside made up of adenine and ribose, one of its compounds being **adenosine triphosphate**

(abbrev. **ATP**), which is present in all cells and stores energy for muscle contraction; **adenovi'rus** any of a group of viruses that attack the upper respiratory tract, and may produce malignancy. [Gr. *adēn*, gland.]

Adeni *ā'di-ni, n.* and *adj.* (a citizen) of Aden.

adept *ad'ept, ə-dept', a-dept', adj.* completely skilled (at, in). — *n.* (*ad'ept, ə-dept', a-dept'*) a proficient: one who has attained the great secret (e.g. of the philosopher's stone). — *n.* **adept'ness.** [L. *adeptus* (*artem*), having attained (an art), pa.p. of *adipīscī*, to attain.]

adequate *ad'i-kwit, -kwāt, adj.* sufficient: competent. — *adv.* **ad'equately.** — *ns.* **ad'equateness, ad'equacy** (*-kwə-si*). — *adj.* **ad'equative.** [L. *adaequātus*, made equal — *ad*, to, and *aequus*, equal.]

adermin *ə-dûr'min, n.* former name of pyridoxine. [Gr. *a-*, privative, *derma*, skin, because deprivation of this vitamin was shown to cause dermatitis in rats.]

Ades *ā'dēz, (Milt.) n.* variant of **Hades.**

adespota *ə-des'pot-a, n.pl.* anonymous works. [Gr. *a-*, priv., and *despotēs*, master.]

à dessein *a des-ẽ*, (Fr.) on purpose.

adessive *ad-es'iv, (gram.) adj.* denoting, as in Finnish, place 'where'. — *n.* the adessive case. [L. *adesse*, to be at a place, to be present.]

ad eundem gradum *ad ē-un'dəm grād'əm, ā-ōōn'dem grād'ōōm*, (L.) to the same degree (at another university).

à deux *a dø*, (Fr.) of two, between two, two-handed; **à deux mains** (*mẽ*) with both hands: for two hands.

ad finem *ad fīn'əm, fēn'em*, (L.) to the end: toward the end.

adharma *ə-där'mä, ə-dûr'mə, n.* unrighteousness — opposite of **dharma.** [Sans.]

adhere *əd-, ad-hēr', v.i.* to stick (to): to remain fixed or attached (to): to cleave (as to a party, a leader, a doctrine): to be consistent (*Shak.*): to agree: to affirm a judgment (*Scots law*). — *n.* **adhēr'ence** state of adhering: concrescence of unlike parts (*bot.*). — *adj.* **adhēr'ent** sticking: concrescent and unlike. — *n.* one who adheres: a follower: a partisan: one who is loosely associated with a body without being a member. — *n.* **adhēr'er.** [L. *ad*, to, *haerēre, haesum*, to stick.]

adhesion *əd-hē'zhən, n.* the act of adhering or sticking: strong, firm contact: steady attachment: concrescence of unlike parts (*bot.*): reunion of separated surfaces (*surg.*): abnormal union of parts that have been inflamed (*path.*): (often in *pl.*) a band of fibrous tissue joining such parts. — *adj.* **adhē'sive** (*-siv, -ziv*) sticky: apt to adhere. — *n.* a substance used for sticking things together. — *adv.* **adhē'sively.** — *n.* **adhē'siveness.** [See **adhere.**]

adhibit *əd-hib'it, v.t.* to apply: to attach: to admit: to administer. — *n.* **adhibi'tion.** [L. *adhibēre, -itum* — *ad*, to, *habēre*, to hold.]

ad hoc *ad hok*, (L.) for this special purpose (used as *adj.*). — **ad hocery** (*hok'ə-ri; facet.*) the use of ad hoc measures — improvisation or pragmatism.

ad hominem *ad hom'in-em*, (L.) to the man, addressed to the feelings or prejudices of the hearer or reader: dealing with an opponent by attacking his character instead of answering his argument.

adiabatic *ad-i-ə-bat'ik, adj.* without transference of heat. — *adv.* **adiabat'ically.** [Gr. *a-*, priv., *dia*, through, *batos*, passable.]

Adiantum *ad-i-an'təm, n.* the maidenhair genus of ferns. [Gr. *adiantos* — *a-*, priv., and *diantos*, capable of being wetted.]

adiaphoron *ad-i-af'ə-ron, n.* in theology and ethics, a thing indifferent — any tenet or usage considered non-essential: — *pl.* **adiaph'ora.** — *ns.* **adiaph'orism** tolerance or indifference in regard to non-essential points in theology: latitudinarianism; **adiaph'orist.** — *adj.* **adiaph'orous.** [Gr., from *a-*, priv., *diaphoros*, differing — *dia*, apart, *pherein*, to carry.]

adiathermic *ad-i-ə-thûr'mik, adj.* impervious to radiant heat. [Gr. *a-*, priv., *dia*, through, *thermē*, heat.]

adieu *ə-dū, interj.* (I commend you) to God: farewell. —

n. a farewell: — *pl.* **adieus** or **adieux** (*ə-dūz'*). [Fr. *à Dieu*, to God.]

Adi-Granth *u-dhē'grunt'*, *n.* another name for the **Granth (Sahib).** [Hindi, the first scripture.]

ad infinitum *ad in-fin-īt'əm, -ēt'ōōm*, (L.) to infinity.

ad inquirendum *ad in-kwīr-en'dəm, in-kwēr-en'dōōm*, (L.L.) for making inquiry — name of a writ.

ad interim *ad in'tər-im*, (L.L.) for the meantime.

adiós *ad-ē-os'*, (Sp.; lit. 'to God') *interj.* good-bye.

adipic *ə-dip'ik, adj.* of fat (**adipic acid** $C_6H_{10}O_4$, an acid got by treating fat with nitric acid). — *adj.* **adipose** (*ad'i-pōs*) fatty. — *n.* **adiposity** (*-pos'i-ti*). — **adipose tissue** the vesicular structure in the animal body which contains the fat. [L. *adeps, adipis*, soft fat.]

adipocere *ad'i-pō-sēr*, or *-sēr'*, *n.* a fatty, waxy substance resulting from the decomposition of animal bodies in moist places or under water, but not exposed to air. [L. *adeps, adipis*, soft fat, and *cēra*, wax.]

adipose, etc. See **adipic.**

adit *ad'it*, *n.* an opening or passage, esp. into a mine. [L. *aditus* — *ad*, to, *ire, ĭtum*, to go.]

adjacent *ə-jā'sənt, adj.* lying near or next (to). — *n.* **adjā'cency.** — *adv.* **adjā'cently.** [L. *ad*, to, *jacēns, -entis*, pr.p. of *jacēre*, to lie.]

adjective *aj'ik-tiv, adj.* added: dependent: subsidiary: (of dyes) requiring a mordant. — *n.* a word added to a noun to qualify it, or limit its denotation by reference to quality, number, or position. — *adj.* **adjectival** (*-tīv'l*) of an adjective: using many adjectives: used facetiously as a euphemism (e.g. *What adjectival nonsense!*). — *advs.* **adjectī'vally; ad'jectively.** [L. *adjectīvum* (*nōmen*), added (word) — *adjicěre, -jectum*, to add — *ad*, to, *jacěre*, to throw.]

adjoin *ə-join', v.t.* to join on: to lie next to. — *v.i.* to be in contact. — *adj.* **adjoin'ing.** — *n.* **adjoint** (*aj'oint*, Fr. *ad-zhwã*) a civil officer who assists a French maire: an assistant professor in a French college. [Through Fr. *adjoign-*, pr.p. stem, and *adjoint*, pa.p., of *adjoindre* — L. *adjungěre* — *ad*, to, *jungěre*, to join.]

adjourn *ə-jûrn', v.t.* to put off to another day: to postpone: to discontinue (a meeting) in order to reconstitute it at another time or place. — *v.i.* to suspend proceedings and disperse for any time specified, or (*sine diē*) without such time being specified. — *n.* **adjourn'ment.** — **adjournment debate** a brief parliamentary debate, immediately before the adjournment of the House, allowing members to raise issues which would otherwise not be discussed; **Acts of Adjournal** (*Scots law*) procedural rules of the High Court. [O.Fr. *ajorner* — L.L. *adiurnāre* — L. *ad*, to, L.L. *jurnus*, L. *diurnus*, daily; cf. **journal**[1].]

adjudge *ə-juj', v.t.* to decide: to assign: to award. — *n.* **adjudg'ment** (sometimes **adjudge'ment**) the act of adjudging: sentence. [O.Fr. *ajuger* — L. *adjūdicāre*; cf. **judge.**]

adjudicate *ə-jōō'di-kāt, v.t.* to determine judicially: to pronounce: to award. — *v.i.* to pronounce judgment: to act as judge in a competition between amateurs in one of the arts, e.g. music. — *ns.* **adjudi'cā'tion** act or process of adjudicating: an order of the Bankruptcy Court, adjudging a debtor to be a bankrupt, and transferring his property to a trustee (*Eng. law*); **adju'dicātor.** [L. *adjūdicāre, -ātum.*]

adjunct *aj'ung(k)t, adj.* joined or added. — *n.* a thing joined or added, but subordinate or not essentially a part: a person (usually subordinate) joined to another in office or service: any word or clause enlarging the subject or predicate (*gram.*): any accompanying quality or non-essential attribute (*logic*). — *n.* **adjunction** (*ə-jungk'shən*). — *adj.* **adjunct'ive** forming an adjunct. — *advs.* **adjunct'ively; ad'junct'ly.** [L. *adjunctus* pa.p. of *adjungěre*, to join.]

adjure *ə-jōōr', v.t.* to cause to swear (*obs.*): to charge on oath or solemnly. — *n.* **adjurā'tion** (*aj-*). — *adjs.* **adjur'atory; adjur'ing.** [L. *adjūrāre* — *ad*, to, *jūrāre, -ātum*, to swear.]

adjust *ə-just', v.t.* to put in due relation: to regulate: to

settle. — *v.i.* to adapt oneself (to). — *adj.* **adjust'able.** — *ns.* **adjust'er** one who adjusts: see **average, loss; adjust'ment; adjust'or** an organ or faculty that determines behaviour in response to stimuli. [Obs. Fr. *adjuster* — L.L. *adjuxtāre*, to put side by side — L. *juxtā*, near; confused by association with *jūstus*, right.]

adjutage, ajutage *aj'ōō-tij*, *n.* a nozzle as for a fountain. [Fr. *ajutage*; cf. **adjust.**]

adjutant *aj'ōō-tənt*, *n.* an officer specially appointed to assist a commanding officer: a large Indian stork or crane (from its stalking gait). — *n.* **ad'jutancy** the office of an adjutant: assistance. — **ad'jutant-gen'eral** head of a department of the general staff: the executive officer of a general: — *pl.* **ad'jutants-gen'eral.** [L. *adjūtāns, -antis*, pr.p. of *adjūtāre*, freq. of *adjŭvāre* — *ad*, to, *jŭvāre*, to assist.]

adjuvant *aj'ōō-vənt, adj.* helping. — *n.* a help: a substance added e.g. to a medicine, vaccine, etc. to increase its effectiveness (*med.*). — *n.* **ad'juvancy.** [Fr. — L. *ad*, to, *jŭvāre*, to help.]

ad lib. See **ad libitum.**

ad libitum *ad lib'i-təm, -tōōm*, (L.) at pleasure: extempore, impromptu. — Shortened to **ad lib.** — *adj.* **ad-lib** (*ad-lib'*) impromptu, extemporised. — *v.t.* and *v.i.* to extemporise, esp. to fill up time. — *ns.* **ad-lib'ber; ad-libb'ing.**

ad litem *ad līt'əm, lē'tem*, (L.) (of a guardian, etc.) appointed for a lawsuit.

ad-man. See under **advertise.**

ad manum *ad mān'əm, mān'ōōm*, (L.) at hand, ready.

ad-mass, admass. See under **advertise.**

admeasure *ad-mezh'ər, v.t.* to measure: to apportion. — *n.* **admeas'urement.** [O.Fr. *amesurer* — L.L. *admēnsūrāre* — L. *ad*, to, *mēnsūra*, measure.]

admin. See under **administer.**

adminicle *əd-min'i-kl*, *n.* anything that aids or supports: an auxiliary: any corroboratory evidence (*law*). — *adj.* **adminic'ūlar.** — *v.t.* and *v.i.* **adminic'ūlate.** [L. *adminiculum*, a support — *ad*, to, *manus*, hand.]

administer *əd-min'is-tər, v.t.* to govern: to manage as a steward, substitute, or executor: to dispense (justice, rites): to tender (an oath, medicine). — *v.i.* to minister. — *adj.* **admin'istrable.** — *adj.* and *n.* **admin'istrant.** — *v.t.* **admin'istrate** to administer. — *n.* **administrā'tion** (*coll.* shortening **ad'min**) the act of administering: management: dispensation of sacraments: the government. — *adj.* **admin'istrative** concerned with administration. — *n.* **admin'istrātor** one who manages or directs: the person to whom is committed, under a commission entitled **letters of administration,** the administration or distribution of the personal estate of a deceased person, in default of an executor: one empowered to act for a person legally incapable of acting for himself (*Scots law*): — *fem.* **admin'istrātrix.** — *n.* **admin'istrātorship.** [L. *administrāre, -ātum* — *ad*, to, *ministrāre*, to minister.]

admirable, etc. See **admire.**

admiral *ad'mər-əl*, *n.* the chief commander of a navy: a naval officer ranking with a general in the army (**admiral of the fleet** with field-marshal): an admiral's flagship: the chief ship in a fleet of merchantmen or fishing boats: a cone-shell: a butterfly of certain kinds (see **red, white**). — *ns.* **ad'miralship** the office or art of an admiral; **Ad'miralty** the board administering navy (since 1964 under Ministry of Defence): the building where it transacts business. — **Lord High Admiral** an office dating from 15th century, William IV (when Duke of Clarence) being last holder until office was taken over by the Queen in 1964. [O.Fr. *a(d)miral* — Ar. *amīr-al-bahr*, a lord of the sea, confused with L. *admīrābilis* (see **admire**).]

admire *əd-mīr', v.t.* to have (or express) a high opinion of: to wonder at (*arch.*). — *v.i.* (*obs.*) to wonder. — *adj.* **ad'mirable** worthy of being admired. — *n.* **ad'mirableness.** — *adv.* **ad'mirably.** — *ns.* **admīr'a(u)nce** (*Spens.*) admiration; **admīrā'tion** the act of admiring: wonder, together with esteem, love, or veneration:

astonishment (*B.*, *Shak.*, and *Milt.*): admirableness (*Shak.*): an object of admiration (*Shak.*): a wonder (*Shak.*). — *adj.* **ad'mīrātive.** — *n.* **admīr'er** one who admires: a lover. — *adv.* **admīr'ingly.** — **Admirable Crichton** (*krī͞'tən*) one who excels in many things, from James Crichton (1560–82), Scottish athlete, Latin poet, polymath. [Fr. *admirer* — L. *ad*, at, *mīrāri*, to wonder.]

ad misericordiam *ad mi-zer-i-kŏr'di-am*, (L.) (appealing) to pity — of an argument, etc.

admissible, etc. See **admit.**

admit *əd-mit'*, *v.t.* to allow to enter (with *into* or *to*): to let in: to concede: to acknowledge: to be capable of (also *v.i.* with *of*): — *pr.p.* **admitt'ing;** *pa.p.* **admitt'ed** — *n.* **admissibil'ity.** — *adj.* **admiss'ible** that may be admitted or allowed (generally, or specially as legal proof). — *n.* **admission** (*-mish'ən*) the act of admitting: anything admitted or conceded: leave to enter. — *adjs.* **admiss'ive; admitt'able** that may be admitted. — *n.* **admitt'ance** admission: acceptability, acceptance (*Shak.*): the property of an electric circuit by virtue of which a current flows under the action of a potential difference (*elect.*). — *adj.* **admitt'ed** acknowledged, conceded: (of a law clerk) qualified to practise as a solicitor, having been admitted to the Law Society's roll of solicitors. — *adv.* **admitt'edly.** [Partly through Fr., — L. *admittĕre, -missum* — *ad*, to, *mittĕre, missum*, to send.]

admix *əd-*, *ad-miks'*, *v.t.* to mix with something else. — *n.* **admix'ture** the action of mixing: what is added to the chief ingredient of a mixture. [L. *ad*, to, and **mix.**]

ad modum *ad mōd'əm*, *mod'ŏom*, (L.) after the manner (of).

admonish *əd-mon'ish*, *v.t.* to warn: to reprove mildly. — *n.* **admon'ishment** admonition. [O.Fr. *amonester* — L.L. *admonestāre* — L. *admonere* — *ad*, to, *monēre*, to warn.]

admonition *ad-mon-ish'ən*, or *-mən-*, *n.* reproof: counsel: advice: ecclesiastical censure. — *adjs.* **admonitive** (*-mon'*), **admon'itory** containing admonition. — *n.* **admon'itor.** [L. *admonitiō, -ōnis;* cf. **admonish.**]

adnascent *ad-nas'ənt*, *adj.* growing together with or upon something else. [L. *adnāscens, -entis*, pr.p. of *adnāsci* — *ad*, to, *nāscī*, to be born.]

adnate *ad'nāt*, *ad-nāt'*, (*bot.*) *adj.* attached (esp. by the whole length) to another organ. — *n.* **adnation** (*-nā'shən*). [L. *adnātus*, usu. *agnātus* — *ad*, to, (*g*)*nātus*, born.]

ad nauseam *ad nŏ'zi-am*, *-shi-*, *now'si-*, (L.) to the pitch of producing disgust.

ado *ə-do͞o'*, *n.* a to-do: bustle: trouble: difficulty: stir or fuss: — *pl.* **ados'.** [**at do**, Northern English infin. with **at** instead of **to**, borrowed from Scand.]

adobe *ə-dō'bi*, *n.* a sun-dried brick: a house made of such bricks: (also **adobe clay**) a name for any kind of mud which, when mixed with straw, can be sun-dried into bricks. — Also *adj.* [Sp., — *adobar*, to plaster.]

adolescent *ad-ō-les'ənt*, *adj.* passing from childhood to maturity: belonging to, typical of, this state. — Also *n.* — *n.* **adolesc'ence** the state or time of being adolescent. [L. *adolēscēns, -entis*, pr.p. of *adolēscĕre*, to grow up.]

Adonai *ə-dōn'ī*, *ə-don-ā'ī*, *n.* a name of the Deity in the O.T., usu. translated 'Lord'. — See also **Jehovah.** [Heb. *adōnāi*, my lord.]

Adonis *ə-dō'nis*, *n.* a youth beloved by Aphrodite: a beautiful youth: a beau or dandy: the ranunculaceous pheasant's-eye genus. — *n.pl.* **Adō'nia** the festival of mourning for Adonis. — *n.* **Adonic** (*ə-don'ik*) a verse of a dactyl and a spondee (or a trochee), said to have been used in the Adonia. — Also *adj.* — *v.t.* and *v.i.* **ad'onise, -ize** to adorn (oneself). [Gr. *Adōnis* — Phoenician *adōn*, lord.]

adoors *ə-dōrz'*, *-dŏrz'*, (*obs.*) *adv.* at doors: at the door. [Prep. **a³**, at, and **door.**]

adopt *ə-dopt'*, *v.t.* to take voluntarily as one's own child,

with the rights of a child: to take into any relationship: to take as one's own: to take up: to take over: to take (a precaution, etc.): to choose formally (e.g. a candidate): to endorse, approve (e.g. a resolution, minutes). — *adj.* **adopt'ed** taken by adoption. — *ns.* **adopt'er; Adoptianism, Adoptionism** (*ə-dop'shən-izm;* often **adoptianism**) the doctrine that Christ, as man, is the adopted son of God; **adop'tianist, adop'tionist; adop'tion.** — *adjs.* **adop'tious** (*-shəs; Shak.*) adopted; **adopt'ive** that adopts or is adopted. [L. *adoptāre* — *ad*, to, *optāre*, to choose.]

adore *ə-dōr'*, *-dör'*, *v.t.* to worship: to love or reverence intensely: to adorn (*Spens.*). — *adj.* **ador'able.** — *n.* **ador'ableness.** — *adv.* **ador'ably.** — *ns.* **adorā'tion; ador'er.** — *adv.* **ador'ingly.** [L. *ad*, to, *ōrāre*, to pray.]

adorn *ə-dörn'*, *v.t.* to deck or dress: to embellish. — *n.* (*Spens.*) adornment. — *adj.* (*Milt.*) adorned, ornate. — *n.* **adorn'ment** ornament: decoration. [O.Fr. *äorner, adorner* — L. *adōrnāre* — *ad*, to, *ōrnāre*, to furnish.]

adown *ə-down'*, (*arch.*, *poet.*) *adv.* and *prep.* same as **down³.** [**a³** and **down.**]

ad patres *ad pāt'rēz, pat'rās*, (L.) (gathered) to his fathers, dead.

adpress *ad-pres'*, *v.t.* to press together. — *adj.* **adpressed'** (*bot.*) closely pressed together but not united. — Also **appress'.** [L. *ad*, to, *premĕre, pressum*, to press.]

adrad *ə-drad'*, **adred** *ə-dred'*, (*Spens.*) *adj.* afraid. [O.E. *ofdrǣd* — pfx. *of-*, *drǣdan*, to dread.]

adread *ə-dred'*, (*obs.*) *v.t.* to fear. — *pa.t.* **adrad'** (*Spens.*). [O.E. *ondrǣdan* — pfx. *on-*, on, *and-*, to, and *drǣdan*, to dread.]

ad referendum *ad ref-er-en'dum*, *-dŏom*, (L.) to be further considered.

ad rem *ad rem* (L.) to the point: to the purpose.

adren(-o)- *ə-dren(-ō-)*, *-drēn(-ō-)*, in composition, adrenal, adrenal glands, adrenalin. — *adj.* **adrenal** (*ə-drē'nəl*) beside the kidneys: of, relating to the adrenal glands. — *n.* an adrenal gland. — *n.* **adrenaline** (*ə-dren'ə-lin*, *-lēn*) a hormone secreted by the adrenal glands that causes constriction of the arteries, so increasing blood pressure and stimulating the heart muscle; also produced synthetically (as **Adrenalin®**) for this property. — *adjs.* **adrener'gic** (of the sympathetic nerve fibres) releasing (a substance resembling) adrenaline: activated by adrenline: (of an agent) having the same effect as adrenaline; **adre'nocorticotrop(h)ic** (*-kŏr'tik-ō-trop'-ik*, *-trof'ik*; **cortex** and Gr. *trophē*, food) stimulating the activity of the adrenal cortex. — *ns.* **adrenocorticotrop(h)ic hormone**, also **adrenocorticotrop(h)in** (*-trof'in*, *-trop'in*, *-trō'*) a hormone having this action, secreted by the pituitary gland, also produced synthetically e.g. as a treatment for rheumatoid arthritis: —abbrev. **ACTH.** — **adrenal glands** the suprarenal capsules, two small ductless glands over the kidneys, the medulla of which secretes adrenaline, and the cortex steroids. [L. *ad*, to, *rēnēs*, kidneys.]

Adriamycin®, adriamycin® *ā-dri-ə-mī'sin*, *n.* an antibiotic used in the treatment of cancer.

adrift *ə-drift'*, *adj.* or *adv.* in a drifting condition: loose from moorings: left to one's own resources, without help, guidance, or contacts: cut loose. [**a³** and **drift.**]

adroit *ə-droit'*, *adj.* dexterous: skilful: ingenious. — *adv.* **adroit'ly.** — *n.* **adroit'ness.** [Fr. *à droit*, according to right — L. *directus*, straight; see **direct.**]

à droite *a drwät*, (Fr.) to the right.

adry *ə-drī'*, (*arch.* or *poet.*) *adj.* and *adv.* in a state of thirst or dryness. [After **athirst, acold,** etc.]

adscititious *ad-sit-ish'əs*, *adj.* added or assumed: additional. [L. *adscīscĕre, -scītum*, to take or assume — *ad*, to, *scīscĕre*, to inquire — *scīre*, to know.]

adscript *ad'skript*, *adj.* attached to the soil. — *n.* a feudal serf so attached. — *n.* **adscrip'tion.** [L. *adscrīptus* — *ad*, to, *scrībĕre*, to write.]

adsorb *ad-sörb'*, *v.t.* of a solid or a liquid, to accumulate on its surface a thin film of the molecules of a gas or liquid that is in contact with it (cf. **absorb**). — *ns.*

adsorb′ate the vapour adsorbed; **adsorb′ent** a solid (as charcoal) that adsorbs a gas, etc. in contact with it; **adsorp′tion.** [L. *ad*, to, *sorbēre*, to suck in.]

adsuki bean. Same as **adzuki bean.**

adsum *ad′sum, -sŏŏm*, (L.) I am present: here.

ad summum *ad sum′um, sŏŏm′ŏŏm*, (L.) to the highest point.

aduki bean. Same as **adzuki bean.**

adularia *ad-ū-lā′ri-ə, n.* a transparent orthoclase feldspar. [From the *Adula* group in the Alps.]

adulate *ad′ū-lāt, v.t.* to fawn upon, to flatter: to praise excessively. — *ns.* **adūlā′tion; ad′ūlātor.** — *adj.* **ad′ūlatory.** [L. *adūlārī, adūlātus*, to fawn upon.]

Adullamite *ə-dul′əm-īt, n.* John Bright's name for a Whig seceder from the Liberal party (1866). [From the cave of *Adullam*, 1 Sam. xxii. 1, 2.]

adult *ad′ult, ə-dult′, adj.* grown-up: mature: of or for adults: suitable for the mature person only, esp. pornographic. — *n.* a grown-up person. — *n.* **ad′ulthood.** [L. *adultus*, pa.p. of *adolēscĕre*, to grow up; see **adolescent.**]

adulterate *ə-dult′ər-āt, v.t.* to debase, falsify, by mixing with something inferior or spurious: to commit adultery with (*obs.*). — *v.i.* (*Shak.*) to commit adultery. — *adj.* defiled by adultery: spurious: corrupted by base elements. — *ns.* **adult′erant** that with which anything is adulterated; **adulterā′tion** the act of adulterating: the state of being adulterated; **adult′erātor** one who adulterates a commodity; **adult′erer** one guilty of adultery: — *fem.* **adult′eress.** — *adj.* **adult′erine** resulting from adultery: spurious: illegal (*hist.*). — *n.* the offspring of adultery. — *v.i.* **adult′erise, -ize** (*arch.*) to commit adultery. — *adj.* **adult′erous** pertaining to, of the nature of, guilty of, adultery. — *adv.* **adult′erously.** — *n.* **adult′ery** violation of the marriage-bed, whether one's own or another's: unchastity generally (*B.*): applied opprobriously, esp. by theologians to marriages disapproved of: image-worship: adulteration, falsification (*obs.*). [L. *adulterāre, -ātum*, prob. from *ad*, to, and *alter*, another. Some forms come from Fr., remodelled later on Latin.]

adumbrate *ad′um-brāt*, or *-um′, v.t.* to give a faint shadow of: to shadow forth: to foreshadow: to overshadow. — *n.* **adumbrā′tion.** [L. *adumbrāre, -ātus* — *ad*, to, *umbra*, a shadow.]

adunc *ə-dungk′, adj.* hooked. — Also **adunc′ate, -d, adunc′ous.** — *n.* **aduncity** (*ə-dun′si-ti*). [L. *aduncus, aduncātus* — *ad*, to, *uncus*, a hook.]

ad unguem *ad ung′gwem, ōŏng′*, (L.) to the nail: to a nicety.

ad unum omnes *ad ūn′əm om′nēz, ōŏn′ŏŏm om′nās*, (L.) all to a man.

adust *ə-dust′, v.t.* (*Milt.*) to scorch. — *adj.* burnt up or scorched (*obs.*): browned with the sun (*obs.*): sallow and atrabilious (from the old notions of dryness of body) (*arch.*). [L. *adūstus*, pa.p. of *adūrĕre*, to burn up.]

ad valorem *ad val-ör′əm, -ör′, wal-ör′-em*, (L.) according, in proportion, to value.

advance *əd-väns, v.t.* to put forward: to promote: to further: to raise (*Shak.*): to extol (*obs.*): to raise in price: to supply beforehand: to pay before due time: to lend, esp. on security. — *v.i.* to move or go forward: to approach esp. aggressively (with *on*): to make progress: to rise in rank or in value. — *n.* a forward move: progress: an increase: a rise in price, value, wages: payment beforehand: a loan: an approach, overture, move towards agreement, favour, etc. — *adj.* before in place: made, given, etc., ahead of time. — *adj.* **advanced′** at, appropriate to, a far-on stage (of education, thought, emancipation, life, etc.). — *n.* **advance′ment** promotion: furthering: payment in advance. — **advance copy, proof** one sent in advance of publication; **advance factory** one built to encourage development, in the belief that a firm will take it over; **advance(d) guard** a guard or party in front of the main body; **advanced level** see **A level; advance note** an order for

(generally) a month's wage given to a sailor on engaging. — **advanced gas-cooled reactor** (abbrev. **AGR**) a nuclear reactor in which carbon dioxide is used as a coolant; — **advanced passenger train** a lightweight type of train, electrically powered, designed to run at 250 km h (156 m hour) and to tilt at curves. abbrev. **APT; in advance** beforehand: in front. [O.Fr. *avancer* — L.L. *abante* (Fr. *avant*) — L. *ab ante*, from before; the prefix refashioned later as if from *ad*.]

advantage *əd-vänt′ij, n.* superiority over another: a favouring condition or circumstance: gain or benefit: the first point after deuce (*tennis, lawn-tennis*). — *v.t.* and *v.i.* to benefit or profit. — *adjs.* **advan′tageable** (*rare*) profitable: convenient; **advantageous** (*ad-vənt-ā′jəs*) of advantage: useful (with *to* and *for*). — *adv.* **advantā′geously.** — *n.* **advantā′geousness.** — **advantage rule** in games, a rule under which an infringement and its penalty are overlooked when this is to the advantage of the non-offending side. — **advantage server, striker** the server, the striker has gained the first point after deuce; **have the advantage of** to recognise without being recognised; **take advantage of** to avail oneself of: to make undue use of an advantage over; **take at advantage** to use favourable conditions against: to take by surprise; **to advantage** so that the merits are readily perceived. [Fr. *avantage* — *avant*, before; see **advance.**]

advection *ad-vek′shən*, (*meteor.*) *n.* movement horizontally of air or atmospheric conditions. [L. *advectio* — *ad, vehĕre*, to carry.]

advene *ad-vēn′, v.i.* to be superadded. — *n.* **advent** (*ad′vənt, -vent*) a coming or arrival: (with *cap.*) the first or the second coming of Christ: the period immediately before the festival of the Nativity, including four Sundays. — *n.* **Ad′ventist** one who expects a second coming of Christ: a millenarian. — *adj.* **adventitious** (*advən-tish′əs*; L. *adventicius*, extraneous) accidental: additional: foreign: appearing casually: developed out of the usual order or place. — *adv.* **adventi′tiously.** — *adj.* **adventive** (*-vent′*) adventitious: not permanently established (*bot.*). — *n.* a thing or person coming from without. [L. *advenire, adventum*, to approach, happen — *ad*, to, *venire*, to come; *adventus*, arrival.]

adventure *əd-ven′chər, n.* a chance: a remarkable incident: an enterprise: trial of the issue: risk: a commercial speculation: an exciting experience: the spirit of enterprise. — *v.t.* to risk: to dare: to venture: to put forward as a venture: to venture to say or utter. — *v.i.* to risk oneself: to take a risk. — *n.* **adven′turer** one who engages in hazardous enterprises: a soldier of fortune, or speculator: one who pushes his fortune, esp. by unscrupulous means: — *fem.* **adven′turess** (chiefly in bad sense). — *adj.* **adven′turesome** adventurous. — *n.* **adven′turism** the practice of engaging in hazardous and ill-considered enterprises: in foreign policy, opportunism employed in the service of expansionism. — *n.* and *adj.* **adven′turist.** — *adjs.* **adventuris′tic; adven′turous** enterprising: ready to incur risk. — *adv.* **adven′turously.** — *n.* **adven′turousness.** — **adventure playground** a playground with objects that can be used by children for building, to climb on, etc. [L. *adventūrus*, fut. p. of *advenire*, to approach, happen — *ad*, to, *venire*, to come; partly through Fr.]

adverb *ad′vûrb, n.* a word added to a verb, adjective, or other adverb to express some modification of the meaning or an accompanying circumstance. — *adj.* **adverb′ial** (*əd-*). — *v.t.* **adverb′ialise, -ize** to give the character of adverb to. — *adv.* **adverb′ially.** [L. *adverbium* — *ad*, to, *verbum*, a word (a trans. of Gr. *epirrēma*, lit. that which is said afterwards).]

ad verbum *ad vûr′bəm, wer′bŏŏm*, (L.) to a word: word for word.

adversaria *ad-vər-sā′ri-ə, n.pl.* miscellaneous notes: a commonplace book. [L. *adversāria.*]

adversary *ad′vər-sər-i, n.* an opponent. — *adjs.* **adversative** (*əd-vûrs′*) denoting opposition, contrariety, or variety; **ad′verse** (*-vûrs*) contrary (with *to*): opposed: un-

favourable: facing the main axis (*bot.*). — *adv.*
ad′versely. — *ns.* **ad′verseness; advers′ity** adverse circumstances: misfortune: perversity (*Shak.*). — **the Adversary** Satan. [L. *adversus* — *ad*, to, and *vertĕre*, *versum*, to turn.]
advert¹ *ad-vûrt′*, *v.i.* (with *to*) to turn one's attention: to refer. — *ns.* **advert′ence, advert′ency** attention: heedfulness: regard. — *adj.* **advert′ent** attentive: heedful. — *adv.* **advert′ently.** [L. *advertĕre* — *ad*, to, *vertĕre*, to turn.]
advert². See **advertise.**
advertise *ad′vər-tīz, -tīz′*, formerly (as *Shak.*) *-vûrt′iz*, *v.t.* to inform, give notice to (*arch.*): to give notice of: to give public information about merits claimed for: to draw attention to: to offer for sale by public notice, printed or broadcast. — *v.i.* to issue advertisements: to ask (for) by means of public notice, e.g. in a newspaper. — *ns.* **advertisement** (*əd-vûr′tis-mənt, -tiz-*), or (esp. U.S.) **advertizement** (*-tiz,-tiz′*) the act of advertising: a public notice (*coll.*): short forms **ad, ad′vert:** any device for obtaining public favour or notoriety: news (*obs.*); **advertiser** (*ad′*, or *-tīz′*) one who advertises: often part of a newspaper's title; **ad′vertīsing.** — *adj.* (*Shak.*) attentive. — **ad-man** (*ad′-man*) one who takes part in advertising, esp. advertising addressed to the admass; **ad′-mass, ad′mass** advertising intended to appeal to a mass public: the mass aimed at by such advertising. [Fr. *avertir*, *avertis-* — L. *advertĕre*; see **advert¹.**]
advew *ad-vū′*, (*Spens.*) *v.t.* to view. [L. *ad*, to, and **view.**]
advice *əd-vis′*, *n.* counsel: information (usu. in *pl.*): formal official intelligence about anything: specially skilled opinion, as of a physician or lawyer. — *adjs.* **advice′ful** (*obs.*) (*Spens.*, avize′full), watchful: attentive: skilled in advising. — **advice′-boat** (*obs.*) a swift vessel employed in conveying despatches. [O.Fr. *advis* (Fr. *avis*) — L. *ad visum*, according to what is seen or seems best.]
advise *əd-vīz′*, *v.t.* to view (*obs.*): to take thought of, consider (*obs.*)· to take to avizandum (*Scots law*): to bethink: to counsel: to recommend: to inform: to announce. — *v.i.* to reflect, deliberate (*obs.*): to consult (with). — *n.* **advīsabil′ity.** — *adj.* **advīs′able** to be recommended: expedient: open to advice. — *n.* **advīs′-ableness.** — *adv.* **advīs′ably.** — *adjs.* **advīs′atory** (*rare*) advisory; **advīsed′** having duly considered: considered: deliberate: apprised: amenable to advice. — *adv.* **advīs′edly** (*-id-li*) after consideration: intentionally: wisely, prudently. — *ns.* **advīs′edness** deliberate consideration: prudent procedure; **advīse′ment** (*obs.* or *arch.*) counsel, deliberation; **advīs′er, advīs′or** one who advises: a teacher appointed by an education authority to advise on the teaching and development of his subject; **advīs′ership; advīs′ing** (*Shak.*) counsel, advice. — *n.* **advīs′orate** the body of advisers appointed by an education authority. — *adj.* **advīs′ory** having the attribute or function of advising. [O.Fr. *aviser*, and L.L. *advisāre*; cf. **advice.**]
ad vivum *ad vī′vum, wē′wōōm*, (L.) to the life, lifelike.
advocaat *ad′vō-kät*, *n.* a liqueur containing eggs and flavourings: a medicinal drink of eggs, rum, and lemon-juice. [Du. *advokaatenborrel*, advocate's dram, as a clearer of the throat.]
advocate *ad′və-kit, ad′və-kāt*, *n.* an intercessor or defender: one who pleads the cause of another: one who is qualified to plead before the higher courts of law — the ordinary name in Scotland and some other countries, corresponding to barrister in England: one who recommends or urges something e.g. a certain reform, method, etc.: (with *cap.*; New English Bible) the Holy Spirit. — *v.t.* (*ad′və-kāt*) to plead in favour of: to recommend. — Also *v.i.* (with *for*). — *ns.* **ad′vocacy** (*-kə-si*) the function of an advocate: a pleading for: defence; **advocā′tion; ad′vocātor.** — *adj.* **ad′vocātory.** — **advocate in Aberdeen** a solicitor (in Aberdeen); **Lord Advocate** the first law-officer of the crown and public prosecutor of crimes for Scotland. [O.Fr. *avocat* and

L. *advocātus* — *advocāre, -ātum*, to call in — *ad*, to, *vocāre*, to call.]
advocatus diaboli *ad-və-kä′təs dī-ab′ə-lī, ad-wō-kä′tōos dē-ab′o-lē*, (L.) the devil's advocate (q.v.).
advoutrer *əd-vow′trər*, **advou′try.** Obs. forms intermediate between **avoutrer** and **adulterer**, etc.
advowson *əd-vow′zən, n.* the right of presentation to a church benefice. [O.Fr. *avoeson* — L.L. *advocātiō, -ōnis* — L. *advocātus.*]
adward (*Spens.*). Same as **award.**
adynamia *a-di-nā′mi-ə, n.* helplessness, want of power accompanying a disease. — *adj.* **adynamic** (*-am′*) without strength: characterised by the absence of force (*phys.*). [Gr. *a-*, priv., and *dynamis*, strength.]
adytum *ad′i-təm, n.* the most sacred part of a temple: the chancel of a church: — *pl.* **ad′yta.** [Latinised from Gr. *adyton* — *a-*, priv., *dyein*, to enter.]
adze *adz, n.* a cutting tool with an arched blade which is set at right angles to the handle. [O.E. *adesa.*]
adzuki bean *ad-zōō′ki bēn*, a type of kidney bean grown esp. in China and Japan. — Also **adsuki bean** (*ad-sōō′-ki*), **aduki bean** (*a-dōō′ki*). [Jap. *azuki.*]
ae *ā, yā, ye, adj.* (Scots form of O.E. *ān*, one; used attributively) one: very, same. — *adj.* **aefa(u)ld, ā′fald, -fawld** one-fold, single: single-minded: faithful: simple: sincere: honest.
aecidium *ə-sid′i-əm, n.* a cup-shaped fructification in rust fungi. — Also **aecium** (*ē′si-əm*): — *pls.* **aecid′ia, aec′ia.** — *ns.* **aecid′iospore, aec′iospore** spore produced in it. [Gr. (dim. of) *aikiā*, injury.]
Aedes *ā-ē′dēz, n.* a genus of mosquitoes including *Aedes aegypti*, the species that carries yellow fever and dengue fever. [Gr. *aedes*, distasteful.]
aedile *ē′dīl, n.* a magistrate in ancient Rome who had the charge of public buildings, games, markets, police, etc. — *n.* **ae′dileship.** [L. *aedīlis* — *aedēs, -is*, a building.]
aegirine *ē′jir-ēn*, **ae′girite** *-īt, ns.* a green pleochroic pyroxene. [*Ægir*, Norse sea-god or giant.]
aegis *ē′jis, n.* orig. a shield belonging to Zeus, or to Pallas: protection: patronage. [Gr. *aigis.*]
acglogue *ēg′log, n.* arch. for **eclogue.** [From the mistaken belief that the word meant goat-herd discourse — Gr. *aix, aigos*, goat, *logos*, discourse.]
aegrotat *ē-grō′tat*, or *ē′, n.* in universities, a medical certificate of illness, or a degree granted on it. [L. *aegrōtat*, is sick, 3rd pers. sing. pres. indic. of *aegrōtāre* — *aeger*, sick.]
Aegypt. An archaic spelling for **Egypt.**
aeluro-. See **ail(o)ur(o)-.**
aemule *ē′mūl*, (*Spens.*) *v.t.* to emulate. [L. *aemulārī.*]
Aeneid *ē′ni-id, ə-nē′id, n.* an epic poem written by Virgil, the hero of which is Aeneas. [L. *Aenēis, -idos.*]
Aeneolithic *ā-ē-ni-ō-lith′ik, adj.* belonging to a transitional stage at the end of the Neolithic age, when copper was already in use. [L. *aēneus*, brazen, and Gr. *lithos*, stone.]
aeolian *ē-ō′li-ən, adj.* pertaining to, acted on by, or due to the agency of, the wind: aerial. — **aeolian** (or with *cap.*) **harp** a sound-box with strings tuned in unison, sounding harmonics in a current of air; **aeolian rocks** (*geol.*) those deposited by wind, as desert sands. [L. *Aeolus* — Gr. *Aiolos*, god of the winds.]
Aeolian *ē-ō′li-ən, adj.* of Aeolis or Aeolia, in north-west Asia Minor, or its Greek colonists. — *n.* an Aeolian Greek. — *adj.* **Aeolic** (*-ol′ik*) the Greek dialect of the Aeolians. — **Aeolian mode** in ancient Greek music, the same as the Hypodorian or Hyperphrygian: in old church music, the authentic mode with A for its final.
aeolipile, aeolipyle *ē′əl-i-pīl*, or *ē-ol′i-pīl, n.* a hollow ball turned by tangential escape of steam. [L. *Aeolus*, god of the winds, and *pila*, ball; or Gr. *Aiolou pylai*, Gates of Aeolus.]
aeolotropy *ē-əl-ot′rə-pi, n.* variation in physical properties according to direction. — *adj.* **aeolotrop′ic.** [Gr. *aiolos*, changeful, *tropē*, a turn.]
aeon, eon *ē′on, n.* a vast age: eternity: the largest, or a very large division of geological time: a power ema-

nating from the supreme deity, with its share in the creation and government of the universe. — *adj.* **aeō′nian** eternal. [L. *aeon* — Gr. *aiōn*.]

Aepyornis *ē-pi-ör′nis, n.* a gigantic Recent fossil wingless bird of Madagascar. [Gr. *aipys*, tall, *ornis*, bird.]

aequo animo *ē-, ī-kwō an′i-mō,* (L.) with an equable mind.

aerate *ā′ər-āt, v.t.* to put air into: to charge with air or with carbon dioxide or other gas (as **aerated waters**): to excite, perturb (*coll.*). — *ns.* **aerā′tion** exposure to the action of air: mixing or saturating with air or other gas: oxygenation of the blood by respiration; **ā′erātor** an apparatus for the purpose. — **aerated concrete** lightweight concrete made by a process which traps gas bubbles in the mix; **aerating root** a root that rises erect into the air, a breathing organ in mud plants. [L. *āēr*, air.]

aerenchyma *ā-(ə)r-eng′ki-mə,* (*bot.*) *n.* respiratory tissue. — *adj.* **aerenchymatous** (*-kī′*). [Gr. *āēr*, air, *en*, in, *chyma*, that which is poured.]

aerial *ā-ē′ri-əl,* also *-er′, adj.* of, in, belonging to, the air: airy: unreal: lofty: (for the following meanings usu. *ā′(ə)ri-əl*) atmospheric: elevated: performed high above the ground, as *aerial acrobatics*: connected with aircraft, e.g. used in, against, aircraft: using aircraft (as *aerial support, reconnaissance, warfare*): carried out from aircraft: growing in air (*biol.*). — *n.* (all *ā′(ə-)ri-əl*) a wire, rod, etc. exposed to receive or emit electromagnetic waves: an antenna. — *ns.* **aer′ialist** one who performs on the high wire or trapeze; **aeriality** (*-al′i-ti*). — *adv.* **aer′ially.** — **aerial railway, ropeway** one for overhead conveyance. [L. *āērius* — *āēr*, air.]

aerie[1]. Same as **eyrie**.

aerie[2]. See **aery[1]**.

aeriform *ā′(ə)r-i-förm, adj.* gaseous: unreal. [L. *āēr*, air, and *förma*, form.]

aero- *ā′(ə)r-ō-,* in combination, air. — *n. sing.* **aerobat′ics** (Gr. *bateein*, to tread) the art of performing stunts in the air: — *n.pl.* aerial acrobatics. — *n.* **a′erobe** (Gr. *bios*, life) an organism that requires free oxygen for respiration. — *adjs.* **aerobic** (*-ōb′, -ob′*) requiring free oxygen for respiration: effected by aerobes, as a biochemical change: involving the activity of aerobes: of, relating to, aerobics. — *adv.* **aerob′ically.** — *n. sing.* **aerob′ics** exercising by means of such rhythmic activities as walking, swimming, cycling, etc., in order to improve physical fitness through increased oxygen consumption: a system intended to increase fitness and improve body-shape, consisting of fast, repeated and strenuous gymnastic exercises (also **Aerobics®**). — *adj.* **aerobiological** (*-bī-ō-loj′*). — *ns.* **aerobiol′ogy** the study of airborne micro-organisms; **aerobī′ont** an aerobe; **aerobī′osis** life in the presence of oxygen. — *adj.* **aerobiotic** (*-ot′ik*). — *adv.* **aerobiot′ically.** — *ns.* **a′erobomb** a bomb for dropping from aircraft; **a′erobus** an airbus: a passenger helicopter; **a′erodart** an arrowheaded missile of steel dropped from aircraft in warfare; **a′erodrome** an area, with its buildings, etc., used for the take-off and landing of aircraft: an early flying machine (*hist.*; Gr. *dromos*, running). — *adjs.* **aerodynam′ic, -al.** — *adv.* **aerodynam′ically.** — *n.* **aerodynam′icist** one concerned with the movement of bodies in a flow of air or gas. — *n. sing.* **aerodynam′ics** the dynamics of gases. — *n.* **a′erodyne** (*-dīn;* Gr. *dynamis*, power) a heavier-than-air aircraft. — *adj.* **aeroelas′tic** able to be deformed by aerodynamic forces. — *ns.* **aeroelastic′ian** one who studies flutter and vibration in high-speed aircraft; **aeroem′bolism** an airman's condition similar to caisson disease, caused by rapid ascent to high altitudes; **a′ero-engine** an aircraft engine; **a′erofoil** a body (e.g. wing, tail plane) shaped so as to produce an aerodynamic reaction (lift) normal to its direction of motion, for a small resistance (drag) in that plane; **aerogen′erator** a generator driven by wind; **a′erogram** a message by wireless telegraphy: a message sent by telegram (or telephone) and aeroplane: an aerogramme: an aerograph record; **a′erogramme, aérogramme** an air letter: a sheet of thin paper, with postage

stamp imprinted, to be folded and sent by airmail at a special low rate; **a′erograph** a meteorograph: an airborne automatic recording instrument; **aerog′raphy** meteorology; **aerohy′droplane** a winged hydroplane or flying-boat; **a′erolite, a′erolith** a meteoric stone or meteorite (Gr. *lithos*, a stone); **aerolithol′ogy** the science of aerolites. — *adjs.* **aerolit′ic; aerolog′ical.** — *ns.* **aerol′ogist; aerol′ogy** the branch of science that treats of the atmosphere; **a′eromancy** divination by atmospheric phenomena: weather forecasting (Gr. *manteiā*, divination); **aerom′eter** an instrument for measuring the weight or density of air and gases. — *adj.* **aeromet′ric.** — *ns.* **aerom′etry** pneumatics; **a′eromotor** an engine for aircraft; **a′eronaut** (Gr. *nautēs*, a sailor) a balloonist or airman. — *adjs.* **aeronaut′ic, -al.** — *n. sing.* **aeronaut′ics** the science or art of aerial navigation. — *ns.* **a′eroneuros′is** flight fatigue, a nervous disorder of airmen, with emotional and physical symptoms; **aeron′omist; aeron′omy** the science of the earth's atmosphere; **aerophō′bia** morbid fear of draughts: (*loosely*) morbid fear of flying (Gr. *phobos*, fear). — *adj.* **aerophöb′ic** (or *-föb′*). — *ns.* **a′erophone** any wind-instrument; **a′erophyte** an epiphyte (Gr. *phyton*, a plant); **a′eroplane** any heavier-than-air power-driven flying-machine, with fixed wings: a small plane for aerostatic experiments (see **plane[2]**); **aeroplank′ton** minute organisms carried in the air; **a′eroshell** a form of parachute enabling a spacecraft to make a soft landing; **aerosid′erite** (Gr. *sidēros*, iron) an iron meteorite; **a′erosol** a colloidal system, such as a mist or a fog, in which the dispersion medium is a gas: a liquid, e.g. insecticide, in a container under pressure: the container; **a′erospace** the earth's atmosphere together with space beyond: the branch of technology or of industry concerned with the flight of spacecraft through this (as *adj.* pertaining to, or capable of operating in, air and/or space); **a′erostat** a balloon or other aircraft lighter than air: a balloonist: an air sac (*zool.*; Gr. *statos*, standing). — *adj.* **aerostat′ic.** — *n. sing.* **aerostat′ics** the science of the equilibrium and pressure of air and other gases: the science or art of ballooning. — *n.* **aerostation** (*-stā′shən*) ballooning. — *adj.* **aerotac′tic** pertaining to or showing aerotaxis. — *ns.* **aerotax′is** (*biol.*) movement towards or from oxygen (Gr. *taxis*, arrangement; adj. *taktikos*); **a′erotrain** a train driven by an aircraft engine, riding on a cushion of air. — *adj.* **aerotrop′ic** (Gr. *tropē*, turning). — *n.* **aerot′ropism** (*bot.*) curvature in response to concentration of oxygen. [Gr. *āēr*, air.]

aeruginous *ē-roo′ji-nəs, i-roo′jə-, adj.* pertaining to or like copper-rust or verdigris. [L. *aerūginōsus* — *aerūgō*, rust of copper — *aes, aeris*, brass, copper.]

aery[1], aerie *ā′(ə-)ri,* (*poet.*) *adj.* aerial: incorporeal: spiritual: visionary. — **aerie light** (*Milt.*) light as air. [L. *āērius;* see **aerial**.]

aery[2]. Same as **eyrie**.

aes alienum *ēz al-i-ēn′əm, īs al-i-ān′ŏom,* (L.) debt, lit. another's copper or brass.

æsc *ash, n.* the rune (Ϝ) for a, used in O.E. for æ: the ligature æ used in O.E. for the same sound (that of *a* in Mod. Eng. *cat*). [O.E. *æsc*, ashtree, the name of the rune.]

Aeschna *esk′nə, n.* a genus of large usu. colourful dragonflies.

Aesculapian *ēs-kū-lā′pi-ən,* or *es-, adj.* pertaining to Aesculapius, and so to the art of healing. — Also **Escūla′-pian.** [L. *Aesculāpius*, Gr. *Asklēpios*, god of healing.]

Aesculus *ēs′kū-ləs, n.* the horse-chestnut genus of Hippocastanaceae. — *n.* **aes′cūlin** a glucoside in horsechestnut bark. [L. *aesculus*, a species of oak.]

aesir. See **as[2]**.

aesthesia, in *U.S.* **es-,** *es-thēz′i-ə, ēs-,* **aesthēsis** *ns.* feeling: sensitivity. — *n.* **aesthēs′iogen** something producing sensation, esp. a stimulus or suggestion producing a sensory effect on a subject under hypnosis. — *adj.* **aesthēsiogen′ic.** — *n.* **aes′thete** (*-thēt*) a professed disciple of aestheticism: one who affects an extravagant love of art. — *adjs.* **aesthetic** (*es-thet′ik, is-, ēs-*) orig.

love of art. — *adjs.* **aesthetic** (*es-thet'ik, is-, ēs-*) orig. relating to perception by the senses: generally relating to possessing, or pretending to, a sense of beauty; artistic or affecting to be artistic; **aesthet'ical** pertaining to aesthetics. — *adv.* **aesthet'ically.** — *n.* **aesthetician** (*-tish'ən*) one devoted to or versed in aesthetics: a beauty therapist (*U.S.*). — *v.t.* **aesthet'icise, -ize** (*-sīz*) to render aesthetic. — *ns.* **aesthet'icism** the principles of aesthetics: the cult of the beautiful, applied esp. to a late 19th-century movement to bring art into life, which developed into affectation: **aesthet'icist.** — *n. sing.* **aesthet'ics** the principles of taste and art: the philosophy of the fine arts. [Gr. *aisthētikos*, perceptive — *aisthanesthai*, to feel or perceive.]

aestival, in *U.S.* **es-, ēs-tī'vəl,** or *es-, adj.* of summer. — *v.i.* **aes'tivate** (*-ti-vāt*) to pass the summer, esp. (usu. of animals and insects) in a state of torpor. — *n.* **aestivā'tion** a spending of the summer: manner of folding in the flower-bud (*bot.*): arrangement of foliage leaves relative to one another in the bud (*bot.*): dormancy during the dry season (*zool.* and *bot.*). [L. *aestīvus, aestīvālis*, relating to summer, *aestīvāre*, to pass the summer — *aestās*, summer.]

aes triplex *ēz trī'pleks, īs trip'leks,* (L.) triple brass, a strong defence.

aetatis suae *ē-tat'is sū'ē, ī-tät'is sōō'ī,* (L.) of his (or her) age.

aether *ē'thər, n.* Same as **ether** (but not generally used in the chemical sense).

Aethiopian. See **Ethiopian.**

aethrioscope *ē'thri-ō-skōp, n.* an instrument for measuring the minute variations of temperature due to the condition of the sky. [Gr. *aithriā*, the open sky, *skopeein*, to look at.]

aetiology, in U.S. **et-,** *ē-ti-ol'ə-ji, n.* the science or philosophy of causation: an inquiry into the origin or causes of anything, esp. a disease. — *adj.* **aetiolog'ical.** [Gr. *aitiologiā* — *aitiā*, cause, *logos*, discourse.]

Aetnean. See **etna.**

afa(w)ld. See **ae.**

afar *ə-fär', adv.* from a far distance (usually *from afar*): at or to a distance (usually *afar off*). [of and on, **far.**]

afara *ə-fär'ə, n.* a type of West African tree having a light-coloured, straight-grained wood. [Yoruba.]

afear, affear(e) *ə-fēr', (Spens.) v.t.* to frighten. — *adj.* **afeard', affeard'** (*Shak.*) afraid. [Pfx. *a-*, intens., O.E. *fǣran*, to frighten.]

affable *af'ə-bl, adj.* easy to speak to: courteous, esp. towards inferiors: pleasant, friendly. — *n.* **affabil'ity.** — *adv.* **aff'ably.** [Fr., — L. *affābilis* — *affārī*, to speak to — *ad*, to, and *fārī*, to speak.]

affair *ə-fär', n.* that which is to be done: business: any matter, occurrence, etc.: a minor battle: a matter of intimate personal concern: a thing (*coll.*): a romantic intrigue, a love affair: (*pl.*) transactions in general: public concerns. [O.Fr. *afaire* (Fr. *affaire*) — *à* and *faire* — L. *ad*, to, *facĕre*, to do; cf. **ado.**]

affaire *a-fer,* (Fr.) *n.* liaison, intrigue: (usu. with name of chief person involved following or preceding) an episode, involving speculation and scandal. — **affaire (d'amour)** *a-fer* (*dam-ōōr*), a love affair; **affaire de cœur** *a-fer də kœr,* affair of the heart; **affaire d'honneur** *a-fer do-nœr,* affair of honour (a duel).

affear(e), affeard, affear'd. See **afear, affeer.**

affect[1] *ə-fekt', v.t.* to act upon: to infect or attack as disease: to influence: to move the feelings of: (in *pass.* only) to assign, allot. — *n.* disposition of body or mind (*obs.*): affection, love (*obs.*): (*af'ekt*) the emotion that lies behind action (*psych.*): pleasantness or unpleasantness of, or complex of ideas involved in, an emotional state (*psych.*). — *adjs.* **affect'ed; affect'ing** having power to move the emotions. — *adv.* **affect'ingly.** — *adj.* **affect'ive** of, arising from, or influencing, emotion. — *adv.* **affect'ively.** — *n.* **affectivity** (*af-ek-tiv'i-ti*). [L. *afficĕre, affectum* — *ad*, to, *facĕre*, to do.]

affect[2] *ə-fekt', v.t.* to aim at, aspire to (*obs.*): to have a

liking for (*arch.*): to make a show of preferring: to do, wear, inhabit, by preference: to assume: to assume the character of: to make a show or pretence of. — *v.i.* to incline, tend. — *n.* **affectā'tion** (*af-ik-*) assumption of or striving after an appearance of what is not natural or real: pretence. — *adj.* **affect'ed** full of affectation: feigned. — *adv.* **affect'edly.** — *ns.* **affect'edness; affect'er.** [L. *affectāre, -ātum,* freq. of *afficĕre*; see **affect**[1] above.]

affection *ə-fek'shən, n.* the act of influencing: emotion: disposition: inclination: love: attachment: affectation (*Shak.*): an attribute or property: a disease. — *v.t.* (*rare*) to love. — *adjs.* **affec'tional; affec'tionate** full of affection: loving: eager, passionate, well inclined (*obs.*). — *adv.* **affec'tionately.** — *n.* **affec'tionateness.** — *adj.* **affec'tioned** disposed (*B.*): full of affectation (*Shak.*). [L. *affectiō, -ōnis.*]

affeer *ə-fēr', v.t.* to assess: to reduce to a certain fixed sum. — *adj.* **affeered'** (*Shak.* **affear'd'**) confirmed. — *n.* **affeer'ment.** [O.Fr. *affeurer* — L.L. *afforāre* — L. *ad*, to, *forum*, a market.]

affenpinscher *af'en-pinsh-ər, n.* a small dog related to the Brussels griffon, having tufts of hair on the face. [Ger., — *Affe*, monkey, *Pinscher*, terrier.]

afferent *af'ər-ənt, adj.* bringing inwards, as the nerves that convey impulses to the central nervous system. [L. *afferēns, -entis* — *ad*, to, and *ferre*, to carry.]

affettuoso *äf-fet-tōō-ō'sō,* (*mus.*) *adj.* tender. — *adv.* tenderly. — Also *n.* [It.]

affiance *ə-fī'əns, v.t.* to betroth. — *n.* faith pledged: contract of marriage: trust: affinity (*obs.*). — *adj.* **affi'anced** betrothed. [O.Fr. *afiance*; see **affy.**]

affiche *af-ēsh,* (Fr.) *n.* notice, placard.

affidavit *af-i-dā'vit, n.* a written declaration on oath. [L.L. *affīdāvit*, 3rd pers. sing. perf. of *affīdāre*, to pledge one's faith; see **affy.**]

affied. See **affy.**

affiliate *ə-fil'i-āt, v.t.* to adopt or attach as a member or branch: to impute paternity of: to assign the origin of. — *v.i.* to become closely connected, to associate: to fraternise. — *n.* (*-ət*) an affiliated person, an associate: a branch, unit, or subsidiary of an organisation. — *n.* **affilia'tion.** — *adj.* **affil'iable.** — **affiliation order** a court order requiring that the putative father of an illegitimate child should contribute to its support. [L. *affīliātus*, adopted — *ad*, to, *fīlius*, a son.]

affine *a-fīn', a', n.* a relation, esp. by marriage. — *adj.* related: preserving finiteness (**affine geometry** the geometry associated with affine transformations; **affine transformation** the composition of a reversible linear mapping followed by a translation). — *adj.* **affined'** related: bound by some tie. — *n.* **affinity** (*ə-fin'i-ti*) nearness (*obs.*): relationship by marriage: relation of sponsor and godchild: natural or fundamental relationship, esp. common origin: attraction, esp. chemical attraction: a spiritual attraction between two persons: a person whose attraction for another is supposed to be of this kind. — *adj.* **affin'itive.** [O.Fr. *affin* — L. *affīnis*, neighbouring — *ad*, to, at, *fīnis*, a boundary.]

affirm *ə-fûrm', v.t.* to assert confidently or positively: to ratify (a judgment): to confirm or stand by (one's own statement): to declare one's commitment to: to state in the affirmative (*log.*): to declare formally, without an oath (*law*). — *v.i.* to make an affirmation. — *adj.* **affirm'able.** — *n.* **affirm'ance** affirmation: assertion: confirmation. — *adj.* and *n.* **affirm'ant.** — *n.* **affirmation** (*af-ər-mā'shən, -ûr-*) assertion: that which is affirmed: a positive judgment or proposition: a solemn declaration in lieu of an oath. — *adj.* **affirm'ative** affirming or asserting: positive, not negative: (of an answer, etc.) agreeing, saying 'yes': dogmatic. — *n.* the affirmative mode: an affirmative word, proposition or utterance. — *adv.* **affirm'atively.** — *adj.* **affirm'atory.** — *n.* **affirm'er.** — *adv.* **affirm'ingly.** — **affirmative action** (chiefly *U.S.*) positive steps taken to ensure that minority groups and women are not discriminated against, esp. as regards employment. [O.Fr. *afermer*

— L. *affirmāre* — *ad*, to, *firmus*, firm.]
affix *ə-fiks'*, *v.t.* to fix to something: to subjoin: to attach: to append: to add (to something). — *n.* (*af'iks*) an addition to a root, stem, or word, whether *prefix*, *suffix* or *infix*, to produce a derivative or an inflected form: any appendage or addition. [L. *affīgere*, *-fīxum* — *ad*, to, *fīgere*, to fix.]
afflated *ə-flā'tid*, *adj.* inspired. — *ns.* **afflā'tion, afflā'tus** inspiration (often divine). [L. *afflāre*, *-flātum* (vb.), *afflātus*, *-ūs* (n.) — *ad*, to, *flāre*, to breathe.]
afflict *ə-flikt'*, *v.t.* to humble (*B.*): to distress grievously: to harass: to vex. — *adj.* **afflict'ed** overthrown (*Milt.*): humble (*Spens.*): harassed by disease of body or mind (with *with*): suffering. — *n.* and *adj.* **afflict'ing** distressing. — *n.* **afflic'tion** state or cause of grievous distress. — *adj.* **afflict'ive** causing distress. [L. *afflīgere*, *-flīctum*, to overthrow, cast down — *ad*, to, *flīgere*, to dash to the ground.]
affluent *af'lŏŏ-ənt*, *adj.* inflowing: abounding: wealthy. — *n.* an inflowing stream. — *n.* **aff'luence** inflow: abundance: wealth. — *adv.* **aff'luently.** — *ns.* **aff'luentness; aff'lux, affluxion** (*ə-fluk'shən*) an inflow, an accession. — **affluent society** a society in which the ordinary person can afford many things once regarded as luxuries. [L. *affluĕre* — *ad*, to, *fluĕre*, *fluxum*, to flow.]
afforce *ə-fōrs'*, *ə-förs'*, (*law*) *v.t.* to strengthen (e.g. a jury by addition of skilled persons). — *n.* **afforce'ment.** [O.Fr. *aforcer* — L.L. *exfortiāre* — L. *ex*, out, *fortis*, strong.]
afford *ə-fōrd'*, *ə-förd'*, *v.t.* to yield, give, provide: to bear the expense, or disadvantage, of (having the necessary money or other resources or security of position): (*Spens.* **affoord**) to consent. [M.E. *aforthen* — O.E. *geforthian*, to further or cause to come forth.]
afforest *a-*, *ə-for'ist*, *v.t.* to convert into hunting ground: to cover with forest. — *adj.* **affor'estable.** — *n.* **afforestā'tion.** [L.L. *afforestāre* — L. *ad*, to, and L.L. *forēsta*, forest.]
affranchise *a-*, *ə-fran'chīz*, *-shīz*, *v.t.* to free from slavery, or from some obligation. — *n.* **affran'chisement** (*-chiz-*, *-shiz-*). [O.Fr. *afranchir*, *afranchiss-* — *à*, to, *franchir*, to free, *franc*, free.]
affrap *a-frap'*, (*Spens.*) *v.t.* and *v.i.* to strike. [It. *affrappare* — pfx. *af-* (L. *ad*, to), and *frappare*, to strike; or directly from **frap.**]
affray *ə-frā'*, *n.* a disturbance, breach of the peace: a brawl, fight, fray: fear (*Spens.*). — *v.t.* to disturb, startle: to frighten: to scare away. — *adj.* **affrayed'** alarmed (now **afraid'**). [O.Fr. *afrayer*, *esfreer* (Fr. *effrayer*) — L.L. *exfrīdāre*, to break the king's peace — L. *ex*, out of, O.H.G. *fridu* (Ger. *Friede*), peace.]
affreightment *ə-frāt'mənt*, *n.* the hiring of a vessel. [Fr. *affrétement* (*affrètement*), remodelled upon *freight.*]
affrended *a-frend'id*, (*Spens.*) *adj.* reconciled. [**friend.**]
affret *a-fret'*, (*Spens.*) *n.* a furious onset. [Prob. from It. *affrettare*, to hasten.]
affricate *af'ri-kət*, *-kāt* *n.* consonant sound beginning as a plosive and passing into the corresponding fricative (*phon.*). — *adjs.* **affric'ative; aff'ricated.** — *n.* **affricā'tion.** [L. *affricāre*, *-ātum*, to rub against — *ad*, to, *fricāre*, to rub.]
affright *ə-frīt'*, *v.t.* to frighten. — *n.* sudden terror. — *adj.* **affright'ed.** — *adv.* **affright'edly.** — *v.t.* **affright'en.** — *adj.* **affright'ened.** — *adj.* **affright'ful** (*arch.*) frightful. — *n.* **affright'ment** sudden fear. [O.E. *āfyrhtan* — *ā-*, intens., *fyrhtan*, to frighten.]
affront *ə-frunt'*, *v.t.* to meet face to face: to face: to confront: to throw oneself in the way of (*Shak.*): to insult to one's face. — *n.* a contemptuous treatment: an open insult: indignity. — *adj.* **affronté, affrontée,** **affrontee** (*ä-fron'tā*, *ə-frun'tē*) facing each other; also looking frontwise, or towards the beholder (*her.*). — *adj.* **affront'ed** insulted or offended, esp. in public. — *n.* and *adj.* **affront'ing.** — *adv.* **affront'ingly.** — *adj.* **affront'ive.** [O.Fr. *afronter*, to slap on the forehead — L.L. *affrontāre* — L. *ad*, to, *frōns*, *frontis*, forehead.]

affusion *ə-fū'zhən*, *n.* pouring on (esp. in baptism). [L. *affūsiō*, *-ōnis* — *affundĕre* — *ad*, to, *fundĕre*, *fūsum*, to pour.]
affy *ə-fī'*, (*obs.*) *v.t.* to trust: to assure on one's faith: to betroth: to repose or put (trust). — *v.i.* to trust or confide: — *pr.p.* **affy'ing;** *pa.t.* and *pa.p* **affied'** (*Spens.* **affyde'**). [O.Fr. *afier* — L.L. *affīdāre* — L. *ad*, to, *fidēs*, faith; cf. **affiance.**]
Afghan *af'gan*, *n.* a native or citizen, or the language, of Afghanistan: (without *cap.*) a heavy knitted or crocheted woollen blanket or shawl. — **Afghan hound** an ancient hunting and sheep dog of Afghanistan and northern India, kept as a pet in the West.
aficionado *a-fish-yo-nä'dō*, *a-fē-thyō-nä'dhō*, *n.* an amateur: an ardent follower, fan: — *pl.* **aficiona'dos.** [Sp.]
afield *ə-fēld'*, *adv.* to, in, or on the field; to or at a distance. [a[3], **field.**]
afire *ə-fīr'*, *adj.* and *adv.* on fire: in a state of inflammation. [a[3], **fire.**]
aflame *ə-flām'*, *adj.* and *adv.* in a flaming or glowing state. [a[3], **flame.**]
aflatoxin *af-lə-toks'in*, *n.* a (possibly carcinogenic) toxin produced in foodstuffs by species of the mould Aspergillus. [*Aspergillus flavus* and **toxin** — L. *aspergĕre*, to sprinkle, *flavus*, yellow.]
afloat *ə-flōt*, *adv.* and *adj.* in a floating state: at sea: unfixed: in circulation. [a[3], **float.**]
à fond *a fõ*, (Fr.) fundamentally: thoroughly.
afoot *ə-fŏŏt'*, *adv.* and *adj.* on foot: astir: actively in being. [a[3], **foot.**]
afore *ə-fōr'*, *-för'*, *prep.* in front of, before. — *adv.* beforehand, previously. — *adv.* **afore'hand** beforehand: before the regular time for accomplishment: in advance. — *adjs.* **afore'mentioned** previously mentioned, aforesaid; **afore'said** said or named before; **afore'thought** thought of or meditated before: premeditated. — *n.* premeditation. — *adv.* **afore'time** in former or past times. [O.E. *onforan* — *on*, *foran*; see **before.**]
a fortiori *ā för-ti* (or *-shi*)-*ör'ī*, *ä för-ti-ör'ē*, (L.) with stronger reason.
afoul *ə-fowl'*, *adj.* and *adv.* in entanglement: in collision (with *of*). [a[3], **foul.**]
afraid *ə-frād'*, *adj.* struck with fear, fearful (with *of*): timid: reluctantly inclined to think (that): regretfully admitting. [Pa.p. of **affray.**]
afreet. See **afrit.**
afresh *ə-fresh'*, *adv.* anew. [Pfx. *a-*, of, and **fresh.**]
African *af'rik-ən*, *adj.* of Africa. — *n.* a native of Africa: a Negro or other person of black race, esp. one whose people live now, or lived recently, in Africa. — *n.* **Af'ric** (*poet.*) Africa. — *adj.* African. — *ns.* **African'der** a South African breed of cattle; **Africanisā'tion, -z-.** — *v.t.* **Af'ricanise, -ize** to make African: to exclude people of other races from, replacing them with Africans. — Also *v.i.* — *ns.* **Af'ricanism** an African characteristic; **Af'ricanist** one learned in matters relating to Africa. — *adj.* **Af'ricanoid** of African type. — *ns.* **Afrikaans** (*af-ri-käns'*) one of two official languages of S. Africa; it developed from 17th cent. Dutch; **Afrikan'er** (formerly **African'er, African'der, Afrikan'der**) one born in South Africa of white parents (esp. of Dutch descent). — Also *adj.* — *n.* **Afrika'nerdom** the nationalistic feeling, or the political ascendancy, of the Afrikaners in South Africa. — **African coast fever** see **East Coast fever; African violet** a plant from tropical Africa (*Saintpaulia ionantha*), commonly with violet-coloured flowers but not related to the violet; **Afrikander Bond** a South African nationalist league (1881–1911). [L. *Africānus*.]
afrit, afreet *ä-frēt'*, *af'rēt*, *n.* an evil demon in Arabian mythology. [Ar.'*ifrīt*, a demon.]
Afro *af'rō*, (*coll.*, sometimes without *cap.*) *adj.* a shortening for African: (of a hairstyle) characterised by thick, bushy curls standing out from the head, as worn by some negroes (also *n.*). — **Afro-** in composition, African (and). — *adj.* **Afro-Amer'ican** pertaining to American(s) of African descent. — Also *n.* — *adjs.*

Afro-Asian (-*āzh'yən*) of, consisting of, Africans and Asians: of Asian origin but African citizenship: of mixed Asian and African blood: (of language) belonging to a group spoken in southwest Asia and north Africa; **Afro-Caribbē'an** of, relating to (the culture, music, dance, etc. of) people of African descent in or from the Caribbean area.

afront *ə-frunt'*, *adv.* in front (*obs.*): abreast (*Shak.*). [a³, **front.**]

afrormosia *af-rör-mō'zi-ə*, *n.* a very durable West African wood used as an alternative to teak.

aft *äft*, *adj.* or *adv.* behind: near or towards the stern of a vessel. [O.E. *æftan.*]

after *äf'tər*, *prep.* and *adv.* behind in place: later in time than: following in search of: in imitation of: in proportion to, or in agreement with: concerning: subsequent to, or subsequently, afterwards: in the manner of, or in imitation of: according to: in honour of: with the name, or a name derived from the name, of. — *adj.* behind in place: later in time: more towards the stern (in this sense as if the *comp.* of **aft**). — *conj.* later than the time when. — *ns. pl.* **af'terings** (*arch.* or *dial.*) the last milk drawn in milking a cow; **af'ters** (*coll.*) dessert or other course following a main course. — *advs.* **af'terward** (chiefly *U.S.*), **af'terwards** at a later time: subsequently. — **af'terbirth** the placenta and membranes expelled from the uterus after a birth: a posthumous birth; **af'terburner** the device used in afterburning; **af'terburning** reheat; **af'tercare** care subsequent to a period of treatment, corrective training, etc. — Also *adj.* — **af'ter-clap** an unexpected sequel, after an affair is supposed to be at an end; **af'ter-crop** a second crop from the same land in the same year; **af'ter-damp** choke-damp, arising in coal-mines after an explosion of fire-damp; **after-dinn'er** the time following dinner. — *adj.* belonging to that time, esp. before leaving the table. — **af'ter-effect** an effect that comes after an interval. — *v.t.* **aftereye'** (*Shak.*) to gaze after. — **af'tergame** a second game played in the hope of reversing the issue of the first: means employed after the first turn of affairs; **af'terglow** a glow remaining after a light source has faded, esp. that in the sky after sunset; **af'tergrass** the grass that springs after mowing or reaping; **af'tergrowth** a later growth: an aftermath; **af'ter-guard** the men on the quarter-deck and poop who work the after sails, many of them unskilled: hence a drudge or person in a mean capacity: a merchant ship's officers; **af'ter-image** an image that persists for a time after one looks at an object. — **af'ter-life** a future life: later life: a life after death; **af'ter-light** the light of later knowledge; **af'termath** a second mowing of grass in the same season: later consequences, esp. if bad (*fig.*). — *adj.* **af'ter-mentioned** mentioned subsequently. — **afternoon'** the time between noon and evening. — Also *adj.* **af'ternoon.** — **af'terpains** the pains after childbirth; **af'terpiece** minor piece after a play; **af'tershaft** a second shaft arising from the quill of a feather; **af'tershave** a lotion for men, for use after shaving; **af'tershock** one of several minor shocks following the main shock of an earthquake. — **af'tersupper** time between supper and bedtime (*obs.*): prob. a dessert at the end of a supper, poss. a reresupper (*Shak.*). — *adj.* in the time after supper. — **af'terswarm** a second swarm or cast (q.v.) of bees; **af'tertaste** a taste that remains or comes after eating or drinking. — *adj.* **af'ter-tax'** (of profit) remaining after (esp. income) tax has been paid. — **af'terthought** a thought or thing thought of after the occasion: a later thought or reflection or modification; **af'tertime** later time; **af'terword** an epilogue; **af'terworld** the world inhabited by the souls of the dead. — **after a fashion** see **fashion**; **after all** when everything is taken into account: in spite of everything. [O.E. *æfter*, in origin a comparative from *af* (*æf*), off, of which **aft** is orig. a superlative, but itself compared *æfter*, *æfterra*, *æftemest*, and tending to be regarded as comparative of **aft**; see **of, off.**]

aftermost *äf'tər-mōst*, -*məst*, **aftmost** *äft'*, *adjs.* superl. of **aft**, nearest the stern: hindmost. [O.E. *æftemest*, a double superlative.]

afterward(s). See under **after**.

aga, agha *ä'gə*, *ä-gä'*, *n.* a Turkish commander or chief officer. — **Aga Khan** (*kän*) the head of the Ismaili Muslims. [Turk. *aga*, *aghā*.]

agaçant *a-ga-sã*, *fem.* **agaçante** -*sãt*, (Fr.) *adj.* provoking, alluring. — *n.* **agacerie** -*s(ə)rē*, allurement, coquetry.

Agadah. See **Haggada.**

again, *ə-gen'*, also *ə-gān'*, *adv.* once more: in return: in response or consequence: back: further: on the other hand: to the same amount in addition: at some future time (*dial.*). — *prep.* (*dial.*). against. — **again and again** repeatedly. [O.E. *ongēan*, *ongegn*; Ger. *entgegen*.]

against *ə-genst'*, also *ə-gānst'*, *prep.* opposite to: in opposition or resistance to: in protection from: in or into contact or collision with or pressure upon: towards the time of (*obs.*): in anticipation of: in contrast or comparison with: in exchange for: instead of. — *conj.* in readiness for the time that. [**again**, with gen. ending -*es*, and -*t* as in **whilst, betwixt, amongst.**]

agalactia *ag-ə-lak'shi-ə*, *n.* failure to secrete milk. [Gr. *a-*, priv., *gala*, *galaktos*, milk.]

agalloch *ə-gal'ək*, *n.* eaglewood. [Gr. *agallochon*, a word of Eastern origin; see **eaglewood.**]

agalmatolite *ag-al-mat'ə-līt*, *n.* material of various kinds (steatite, pyrophyllite, etc.) from which the Chinese cut figures. [Gr. *agalma*, -*atos*, a statue (of a god), *lithos*, stone.]

Agama *ag'ə-mə*, *n.* an Old World genus of thick-tongued lizards giving name to the family **Agamidae** (*a-gam'i-dē*). — *adjs.* and *ns.* **ag'amid** (a lizard) of this family; **ag'amoid** (a lizard) having the features of an agamid. [Carib name of another lizard.]

Agamemnon *a-ga-mem'non*, (Gr.) *n.* the leader of the Greeks in the Trojan war, king of Mycenae: generic name for a king.

agami *ag'ə-mi*, *n.* the golden-breasted trumpeter, a cranelike bird of South America. [Carib name.]

agamic *a-gam'ik*, **agamous** *ag'ə-məs*, *adjs.* asexual: parthenogenetic: cryptogamous (*obs.*). — *n.* **agamogenesis** (-*jen'*) reproduction without sex, as in lower animals and in plants. [Gr. *a-*, priv., *gamos*, marriage.]

agamid, agamoid. See **Agama.**

agamous. See **agamic.**

Aganippe *ag-ə-nip'ē*, *n.* a fountain on Mt Helicon, sacred to the Muses: poetic inspiration. [Gr. *Aganippē.*]

Agapanthus *a-gə-pan'thəs*, *n.* a genus of lily native to South Africa: (without *cap.*). any of several plants of the genus, with clusters of blue flowers. [Gr. *agape*, love, *anthos*, flower.]

agape¹ *ag'ə-pē*, *n.* a love-feast, held by the early Christians at communion time, when contributions were made for the poor: selfless Christian brotherly love: the love of God for man: — *pl.* **ag'apae** (-*pē*). — *n.* **Agapemone** (-*pēm'* or -*pem'ə-nē*) a religious community of men and women whose 'spiritual marriages' were in some cases not strictly spiritual, founded in 1849 at Spaxton, near Bridgwater: any similar community, esp. with reference to its delinquencies. [Gr. *agapē*, love, *monē*, tarrying, abode.]

agape² *ə-gāp'*, *adj.* or *adv.* with gaping mouth. [Prep. **a**, and **gape.**]

agar-agar *ä'gär-ä'gär*, *ä'gär-ä'gär*, *n.* a jelly prepared from seaweeds of various kinds used in bacteria-culture, medicine, glue-making, silk-dressing, and cooking: any of the seaweeds concerned. — Also **a'gar.** [Malay.]

agaric *ag'ər-ik*, or *ə-gar'ik*, *n.* a fungus, properly one of the mushroom family, but loosely applied. — *adj.* **agar'ic.** [Gr. *agarikon.*]

agast. See **aghast.**

agate¹ *ag'it*, -*āt*, *n.* a banded variegated chalcedony: a marble used in games, made of this material or of variegated glass: a dwarfish person (as if a figure cut in agate) (*Shak.*): ruby type. [Fr., — Gr. *achātēs*, said to be so called because first found near the river *Achates* in Sicily.]

agate² *ə-gāt'*, (*arch.* or *dial.*) *adv.* agoing, on the way: astir: afoot: astray. [a³, and **gate²**; a Northern word.]

a'gate. See **a'**.

agathodaimon *a'ga-thō-dī'mon*, (Gr.) *n.* one's good genius.

à gauche *a gōsh*, (Fr.) to the left: on the left.

Agave *a-gā'vē*, *n.* an aloe-like American genus of amaryllids, in Mexico usually flowering about the seventh year, in hothouse conditions requiring 40–60 (popularly a hundred) years: (without *cap.*) a plant of this genus. — Also called *American aloe, maguey, century plant*. [L. *Agāvē*, Gr. *Agauē*, daughter of Cadmus, fem. of *agauos*, illustrious.]

agaze *ə-gāz'*, (*arch.*) *adj.* and *adv.* at gaze, gazing. [a³, and **gaze.**]

agazed *ə-gāzd'*, (*Shak.*) *adj.* struck with amazement. [Prob. a variant of **aghast.**]

age *āj*, *n.* duration of life: the time during which a person or thing has lived or existed: time of life reached: mature years: legal maturity: the time of being old: equivalence in development to the average of an actual age: a period of time: any great division of world, human, or individual history: a generation: a century: (often *pl.*) a long time, however short (*coll.*). — *v.i.* to grow old: to develop the characteristics of old age. — *v.t.* to make to seem old or to be like the old: to mature: — *pr.p.* **aging** or **ageing** (*āj'ing*); *pa.t.* and *pa.p.* **aged** (*ājd*). — *adj.* **aged** (*āj'id*) advanced in age: (*ājd*) of the age of. — *n. pl.* (*āj'id*; usu. with *the*) old people. — *ns.* **agedness** (*āj'id-nis*) the condition of being aged; **ag(e)'- ing** the process of growing old or developing qualities of the old: maturing: change in properties that occurs in certain metals at atmospheric temperature after heat treatment or cold working; **age'ism** discrimination on grounds of age. — *n.* and *adj.* **age'ist**. — *adjs.* **age'less** never growing old, perpetually young: timeless; **age'- long** lasting an age. — **age'-bracket** the people between particular ages, taken as a group; **age group** a group of people of a similar age. — **be, act your age!** don't be childish; **be ages with** (*Scot.*) to be the same age as; **of age** old enough to be deemed legally mature (with respect to voting, crime, contracts, marriage, etc.); **over age** too old; **under age** too young: not yet of age. [O.Fr. *aäge* (Fr. *âge*) — L. *aetās, -ātis*, for *aevitās* — L. *aevum*, age.]

agee. See **ajee.**

agelast *aj'i-last n.* a person who never laughs. — *adj.* **agelas'tic.** [Gr. *a*, not, *gelaein*, to laugh.]

agen (*poet.*). Same as **again.**

agency. See **agent.**

agenda *ə-* or *a-jen'də*, *n.pl.* things to be done: programme of business for a meeting (often treated as a *sing.*). [L. neuter pl. of *agendus*, to be done, gerundive of *agĕre*, to do.]

agene (Ⓡ in U.S.) *ā'jēn*, *n.* nitrogen trichloride, formerly widely used as a whitening agent in flour.

agent *ā'jənt*, *n.* a person or thing that acts or exerts power: any natural force acting on matter: one authorised or delegated to transact business for another: formerly a bank manager: formerly the representative of the government in a group of Indian states: a paid political party worker: a secret agent, spy. — *v.t.* to conduct as a law agent (*Scot.*): to act as an agent to. — *adj.* acting: of an agent. — *n.* **agency** (*ā'jən-si*) the operation or action of an agent: instrumentality: the office or business of an agent: such a business putting employers and those requiring employment in contact with each other: formerly a group of Indian states assigned to an agent. — *adj.* **agen'tial** (*-shəl*) pertaining to an agent or agency. — **agency shop** a shop in which the union usu. by agreement with the management represents all workers whether they are members of it or not; **ag'ent-gen'eral** a representative in England of an Australian state or Canadian province: — *pl.* **ag'ents-**

gen'eral; Agent Orange a defoliant containing dioxin. — **law agent** (*Scot.*) a solicitor — any qualified legal practitioner other than an advocate. [L. *agēns, -entis*, pr.p. of *agĕre*, to do.]

agent provocateur *a-zhä prō-vo-ka-tœr*, (Fr.) one employed to lead others, by pretended sympathy, into acts incurring penalties.

agger *aj'ər, ag'*, (*Rom. hist.*) *n.* a mound, esp. one of wood or earth for protection or other military purpose: any elevation, esp. artificial. [L.]

aggiornamento *a-jör-na-men'tō*, (It.) *n.* modernising.

agglomerate *ə-glom'ər-āt*, *v.t.* to make into a ball: to collect into a mass. — *v.i.* to grow into a mass. — *adj.* (*-rət, -rāt*) agglomerated: clustered: gathered in a head (*bot.*). — *n.* (*-rət, -rāt*) a volcanic rock consisting of irregular fragments. — *adj.* **agglom'erated.** — *n.* **agglomerā'tion.** — *adj.* **agglom'crative.** [L. *agglomerāre, -ātum* — *ad*, to, *glomus, glomeris*, a ball.]

agglutinate *ə-glōōt'in-āt*, *v.t.* to glue together: to cause to cohere or clump. — *v.i.* to cohere as if glued: to clump. — *adj.* (*-nət, -nāt*) agglutinated. — *adjs.* **agglut'inable; agglut'inant.** — *n.* an agglutinating agent. — *n.* **agglutinā'tion** the act of agglutinating: an agglutinated mass: the clumping of bacteria, blood corpuscles, protozoa, etc. (*biol.*): a type of word-formation process in which words are inflected by the addition of one or more meaningful elements to a stem, each of which elements expresses one single element of meaning (*linguistics*). — *adj.* **agglut'inative** tending, or having power, to agglutinate. — *ns.* **agglut'inin** an antibody causing agglutination of bacteria, blood-corpuscles, etc.; **agglut'inogen** the substance in bacteria or in blood cells that stimulates the formation of, and unites with, agglutinin. — **agglutinating, agglutinative languages** languages in which words are inflected by agglutination. [L. *agglūtināre* — *ad*, to, *glūten, -inis*, glue.]

aggrace *ə-grās'* (*Spens.*) *v.t.* to grace: to favour: — *pa.t.* **aggraced', agraste'.** — *n.* kindness: favour. [**grace**, after It. *aggratiare* (now *aggraziare*).]

aggrade *ə-grād'*, (*geol.*) *v.t.* to raise the level of (a surface) through the deposition of detritus. — *v.i.* to build up in this way. — *n.* **aggradation** (*ag-rəd-ā'shən*). [L. *ad*, to, *gradus*, a step, in imitation of **degrade.**]

aggrandise, -ize *ə-gran'dīz, ag'rən-*, *v.t.* to make greater. — *n.* **aggrandisement, -z-** (*əg-ran'diz-mənt*). [Fr. *agrandir, agrandiss-* — L. *ad*, to, *grandis*, large.]

aggrate *ə-grāt'*, (*obs.*) *v.t.* to gratify or please: to thank. [It. *aggratare* — L. *ad*, to, *grātus*, pleasing.]

aggravate *ag'rə-vāt*, *v.t.* to make more grievous or worse: to irritate (*coll.*). — *adjs.* **agg'ravated** (*law*) of an offence, rendered more serious (e.g. by violence); **agg'ravating.** — *adv.* **agg'ravatingly.** — *n.* **aggravā'tion.** [L. *aggravāre, -ātus* — *ad*, to, *gravis*, heavy.]

aggregate *ag'ri-gāt*, *v.t.* to collect into a mass or whole: to assemble: to add as a member to a society: to amount to (*coll.*). — *v.i.* to accumulate. — *adj.* (*-gət, -gāt*) formed of parts that combine to make a whole: gathered in a mass or whole: united in a colonial organism: formed from an apocarpous gynaeceum (*bot.*). — *n.* (*-gət, -gāt*) an assemblage: a mass: a total: any material mixed with cement to form concrete: a collection of elements having a common property that identifies the collection (*math.*). — *adv.* **agg'regately.** — *n.* **aggregā'tion.** — *adj.* **agg'regātive.** [L. *aggregāre, -ātum* — *ad*, to, *grex, gregis*, a flock.]

aggress *ə-gres'*, *v.i.* to make a first attack: to begin a quarrel: to intrude. — *n.* **aggression** (*-gresh'ən*) a first act of hostility or injury: the use of armed force by a state against the sovereignty, territorial integrity or political independence of another state: self-assertiveness, either as a good characteristic or as a sign of emotional instability. — *adj.* **aggress'ive** making the first attack, or prone to do so: discourteously hostile or self-assertive: offensive as opposed to defensive: showing energy and initiative. — *adv.* **aggress'ively.** — *ns.* **aggress'iveness; aggress'or** one who attacks first.

[L. *aggredī*, *-gressus* — *ad*, to, *gradī*, to step.]
aggri, aggry *ag'ri, adj.* applied to ancient West African variegated glass beads. [Origin unknown.]
aggrieve *ə-grēv', v.t.* to press heavily upon: to pain or injure. — *adj.* **aggrieved'** injured: having a grievance. [O.Fr. *agrever* — L. *ad*, to, *gravis*, heavy.]
aggro *ag'rō, n.* slang short form of **aggravation**, also associated with **aggression**, meaning aggressive behaviour or trouble-making, esp. between gangs, racial groups, etc.
aggry. See **aggri**.
agha. See **aga**.
aghast *ə-gäst'*, earlier (as *Milt.*) **agast,** *adj.* stupefied with horror. [Pa.p. of obs. *agast* — O.E. intens. pfx. *ā-*, and *gæstan*, to terrify.]
agila *ag'i-lä, n.* eaglewood. [Port. *águila*, eaglewood, or Sp. *águila*, eagle; see **eaglewood**.]
agile *aj'īl*, in U.S. *-əl, adj.* nimble. — *adv.* **ag'ilely.** — *n.* **agility** *(ə-jil'i-ti)* nimbleness. [Fr., — L. *agilis* — *agere*, to do or act.]
agin *ə-gin', prep. (dial.* or *facet.)* against. — *n.* **aginn'er** *(coll.)* an opponent (e.g. of change): a rebel, a malcontent. [**again**.]
agio *aj'(i)ō, āj', n.* the sum payable for the convenience of exchanging one kind of money for another, as silver for gold, paper for metal: the difference in exchange between worn or debased coinage and coinage of full value: the amount of deviation from the fixed par of exchange between the currencies of two countries: the discount on a foreign bill of exchange: money-changing: — *pl.* **ag'ios.** — *n.* **agiotage** *(aj'ə-tij)* agio: money-changing: stock-jobbing: speculative manoeuvres in stocks. [The word used in It. is *aggio*, a variant of *agio*, convenience.]
agist *ə-jist', v.t.* to take in to graze for payment: to charge with a public burden. — *ns.* **agist'ment** the action of agisting: the price paid for cattle pasturing on the land: a burden or tax; **agist'or, agist'er** an officer in charge of cattle agisted. [O.Fr. *agister* — *à* (L. *ad*) to, *giste, resting place* — *gésir*, from a freq. of L. *jacēre*, to lie.]
agitate *aj'i-tāt, v.t.* to keep moving: to stir violently: to disturb: to perturb: to excite: to discuss, or keep up the discussion of. — *v.i.* to stir up public feeling. — *adj.* **ag'itāted.** — *adv.* **ag'itātedly.** — *n.* **agitā'tion.** — *adj.* **ag'itātive.** — *n.* **ag'itātor** an agent, esp. for the private soldiers in the Parliamentary army (*hist.*): one who excites or keeps up a social or political agitation: an apparatus for stirring. [L. *agitāre*, freq. of *agere*, to put in motion.]
agitato *äj-it-ä'tō, (mus.) adj.* agitated. — *adv.* agitatedly. [It., — L. *agitāre*, to agitate.]
agitprop *aj'it-prop', n.* (often *cap.*) pro-communist agitation and propaganda. — Also *adj.* [Russ. *Agitpropbyuro*, office of *agitatsiya*, agitation, and *propaganda*.]
Aglaia *ä-glī'a, n.* one of the Graces. [Gr. *aglaiā*, splendour, triumph.]
aglee. See **agley**.
aglet, aiglet, aiguillette *ag'lit, āg'lit, ā-gwi-let', ns.* the metal tag of a lace or string: an ornamental tag or other metal appendage: anything dangling: (usu. **aiguillette**) a tagged point of braid hanging from the shoulder in some uniforms. — **aglet babie** (*Shak.*) prob. a small figure forming the tag of a lace. [Fr. *aiguillette*, dim. of *aiguille*, a needle — from L. *acūcula*, dim. of *acus*, a needle.]
agley, aglee *ə-glī', ə-glē', (Scot.) adv.* askew: awry. [**a³**, and Scot. *gley*, squint.]
aglimmer *ə-glim'ər, adj.* and *adv.* in a glimmering state. [**a³**, and **glimmer¹**.]
aglitter *ə-glit'ər, adj.* and *adv.* in a glitter. [**a³**, and **glitter.**]
aglow *ə-glō', adj.* and *adv.* in a glow. [**a³**, and **glow.**]
agma *ag'mə, n.* (the phonetic symbol ŋ for) a velar nasal consonant, as the *ng* in *thing* or the *n* in *think*. — See also **eng.** [Gr., fragment, nasalised g.]
agnail *ag'nāl, n.* a torn shred of skin beside the nail. —

Also **hangnail** *(hang')*. [O.E. *angnægl*, corn — *ange, enge*, compressed, painful, *nægl*, nail (for driving in), confused with *hang, anger*, and (finger-) *nail*.]
agname *ag'nām, n.* a name over and above the ordinary name and surname. — *adj.* **ag'named.** [**name;** after L.L. *agnōmen.*]
agnate *ag'nāt, adj.* related on the father's side or (*Roman law*) through males only: allied. — *n.* a person so related. — *adjs.* **agnatic** *(-nat'),* **-al.** — *adv.* **agnat'ically.** — *n.* **agnā'tion.** [L. *agnātus* — *ad*, to, *(g)nāscī*, to be born. See **cognate.**]
agnise, -ize *ag-, əg-nīz', (arch.) v.t.* to acknowledge, to confess. [L. *agnōscĕre* — *ad*, to, *(g)nōscĕre*, to know; on the model of **cognise,** etc.]
agnomen *ag-, əg-nō'mən, n.* a name added to the family name, generally on account of some great exploit, as *Africanus* to Publius Cornelius Scipio. [L., — *ad*, to, and *(g)nōmen*, a name.]
agnostic *ag-, əg-nos'tik, n.* one who holds that we know nothing of things beyond material phenomena — that a First Cause and an unseen world are things unknown and (some would add) apparently unknowable. — Also *adj.* — *n.* **agnos'ticism.** [Coined by T. H. Huxley in 1869 from Gr. *agnostos*, unknown, unknowable — *a-*, priv., *gnostos*, known, knowable, and *-ic.*]
agnus castus *ag'nəs kas'təs*, a species of Vitex, a verbenaceous tree. [Gr. *agnos*, the name of the tree, and L. *castus*, a translation of Gr. *hagnos*, chaste, with which *agnos* was confused.]
agnus dei *ag'nəs dē'ī, äg'nōōs dā'ē*, a part of the mass beginning with these words: music for it: a figure of a lamb emblematic of Christ, bearing the banner of the cross: a cake of wax stamped with such a figure, and blessed by the Pope. [L. *agnus Dēī*, lamb of God.]
ago *ə-gō', (arch.)* **agone** *ə-gon', adv.* gone: past: since. [O.E. *āgān*, pa.p. of *āgān*, to pass away — intens. pfx. *ā-*, and *gān*, to go.]
agog *ə-gog', adj.* and *adv.* in excited eagerness. [Perh. connected with O.Fr. *en gogues*, frolicsome, of unknown origin.]
agoge *a-gō'jē, n.* in ancient Greek music, tempo: sequence in melody. — *adj.* **agogic** *(a-goj'ik)* giving the effect of accent by slightly dwelling on a note. — *n. sing.* **agog'ics.** [Gr. *agōgē*, leading.]
à gogo, à go-go *a gō-gō*, (Fr.) in abundance, to one's heart's content; used in names of discothèques, etc. — See also **go-go.**
agoing *ə-gō'ing, adj.* and *adv.* in motion. [**a³**, and **going².**]
agon. See **agony**.
agone. See **ago**.
agonic *ə-gon'ik, adj.* making no angle. — **agonic line** the line of no magnetic variation, along which the magnetic needle points directly north and south. [Gr. *agōnos* — *a-*, priv., *gōniā*, angle.]
agonise, etc. See **agony**.
agonothetes *ə-gō-nə-thē'tēz, a-gō'no-thet-ās*, (Gr.) *n.* a judge or director of public games.
agony *ag'ə-ni, n.* conflict in games: a violent struggle: extreme suffering: the death struggle: Christ's anguish in Gethsemane. — *v.i.* **ag'onise, -ize** to struggle, contend: to suffer agony: to worry (*coll.*). — *v.t.* to subject to agony. — *adj.* **ag'onised, -z-** suffering or expressing anguish. — *adv.* **ag'onisedly, -z-** *(-īz-id-li).* — *adj.* **ag'onising, -z-** causing agony. — *adv.* **ag'onisingly, -z-.** — *ns.* **ag'on** a conflict between two protagonists: a struggle; **ag'onist** a competitor in public games: one engaged in a struggle, whether physical or spiritual: a chief character in a literary work: (in the following senses, a back-formation from **antagonist**) a muscle whose action is opposed by another action (the *antagonist*): a chemical substance (e.g. a drug) which produces an observable inhibitory or excitatory response in a body tissue (e.g. a muscle or nerve); **agonistes** *(a-gon-is'tēz)* one in the grip of inner conflict. — *adjs.* **agonist'ic, -al** relating to athletic contests: combative: (**agonistic**) pertaining to a chemical ago-

nist: pertaining to a broad class of behaviour patterns including attack, threat, appeasement, and flight. — *adv.* **agonist'ically**. — *n. sing.* **agonist'ics** the art and theory of games and prize-fighting. — **agony aunt** (sometimes with *caps.*) a person, usu. a woman, who gives advice in an agony column; **agony column** the part of a newspaper containing special advertisements, as for missing friends and the like: the part of a newspaper or magazine in which readers submit, and receive advice about, personal problems. [Gr. *agōniā*, contest, agony, *agōnistēs*, competitor — *agōn*, meeting, contest.]

agood *ə-gŏŏd'*, (*Shak.*) *adv.* in good earnest, heartily. [**a³**, and **good.**]

agora¹ *ag'ə-rə, n.* an assembly, place of assembly, market-place. — *n.* **agoraphō'bia** morbid fear of (crossing) open places. — *adj.* and *n.* **agoraphō'bic** (or *-fob'*). [Gr. *agorā*, assembly, market-place, *phobos*, fear.]

agora² *ag-ə-rä', n.* a monetary unit of Israel, worth 1/100 of an Israeli pound: — *pl.* **agorot** (*-rot'*). [Heb. *agōrāh* — *āgōr*, to collect.]

agouta *ə-gŏŏ'tə, n.* a rat-like insectivore (*Solenodon*) of Haiti. [Taino *aguta*.]

agouti, agouty, aguti *ə-gŏŏ'tē, n.* a small South American rodent allied to the guinea-pig. [Fr., — Sp. *aguti* — Guaraní *acuti*.]

agraffe *ə-graf', n.* a hooked clasp. [Fr. *agrafe* — *à*, to, *grappe* — L.L. *grappa* — O.H.G. *chrapfo* (Ger. *krappen*), hook.]

à grands frais *a grā fre,* (Fr.) at great expense.

agranulocytosis *a-gran-ū-lō-sī-tō'sis, n.* a blood disorder in which there is a marked decrease in granulocytes, with lesions of the mucous membrane and skin. — Also **agranulō'sis**. [Gr. *ā*, priv., **granule, granulocycte**, and **-osis.**]

agrapha. See **agraphon.**

agraphia *a-graf'i-ə, n.* loss of power of writing, from brain disease or injury. — *adj.* **agraph'ic**. [Gr. *a-*, priv., *graphein*, to write.]

agraphon *a'gra-fon, n.* a traditional utterance ascribed to Jesus, not in the canonical Gospels: — *pl.* **a'grapha** (*-fa*). [Gr., unwritten.]

agrarian *ə-rā'ri-ən, adj.* relating to land, or its management or distribution. — *n.* **agrā'rianism** equitable division of lands: a political movement in favour of change in conditions of property in land. [L. *agrārius* — *ager*, a field.]

agraste (*Spens.*), *pa.t. of* **aggrace.**

agravic *ə-grav'ik, ā-grav', adj.* pertaining to a condition or place where the effect of gravity is zero.

agree *ə-grē', v.i.* to be, or come to be, of one mind (with): to make friends again (*obs.* or *dial.*): to suit, do well (with): to concur (with *with* and *in, on* or *about*): to accede, assent (to): to be consistent (with): to harmonise: to get on together: to be in grammatical concord, take the same gender, number, case, or person (with *with*). — *v.t.* to please, satisfy (*obs.*): to reconcile (persons; *obs.*): to settle (a dispute or a difference; *obs.*): to arrange with consent of all (*obs.* for a time, but in recent use): to concede (that): to decide jointly (to do, that): to consent (to do): — *pr.p.* **agree'ing**; *pa.t.* and *pa.p.* **agreed'**. — *n.* **agreeabil'ity**. — *adj.* **agree'able** suitable: pleasant: in harmony: conformable: willing, consenting (*coll.*). — *adv.* in accordance. — *n.* **agree'ableness**. — *adv.* **agree'ably**. — *n.* **agree'ment** concord: conformity: harmony: a compact, contract, treaty: an embellishment (*obs.*). [O. Fr. *agréer*, to accept kindly — L. *ad*, to, and *grātus*, pleasing.]

agrégé *a-grā-zhā,* (Fr.) *n.* a successful candidate in a competitive university examination for teaching posts. — *n.* **agrégation** (*a-grā-ga-sjō*) the examination.

agrément *a-grā-mā,* (Fr.) *n.* approval by state of diplomatic representative sent to it. — *n.pl.* **agréments** amenities (also **agrémens**): courtesies, charms, blandishments: embellishments, as grace notes and trills (*mus.*).

agrestal, agrestial. See **agrestic.**

agrestic *ə-gres'tik, adj.* of the fields: rural: unpolished. — *adj.* **agrestial** (*ə-gres'ti-əl*) growing, etc. in the open country: wild: growing wild in cultivated ground, as weeds (*bot.*). — Also **agres'tal**. [L. *agrestis* — *ager*, a field.]

agri-, agribusiness, etc. See under **agriculture.**

agriculture *ag'ri-kul-chər, n.* the art or practice of cultivating the land. — *adj.* **agricult'ural**. — *n.* **agricult'urist** one skilled in agriculture: a farmer. — Also **agricult'uralist**. — **agri-, agro-** (*-rō-*) in composition, pertaining to fields, land use, or agriculture. — *ns.* **ag'ribusiness, ag'robusiness** all the operations of supplying the market with farm produce taken together, including growing, provision of farm machinery, distribution, etc.; **ag'riproduct** a commodity for the use of farmers, e.g. fertiliser, animal feed; **agrobiol'ogy** the study of plant nutrition and soil yields. — *adj.* **agrobiolog'ical**. — *ns.* **agrobiol'ogist; agrochem'ical** a chemical intended for agricultural use. — Also *adj.* — *ns.* **agrofor'estry** any system of land use which integrates the cultivation of trees and shrubs and the raising of agricultural crops and/or animals on the same land, whether at the same time or sequentially, taking economic, ecological and cultural factors into account; **agroind'ustry** the area of production that serves the needs of both agriculture and industry. — *adj.* **agroindust'rial**. — *n.* **agrol'ogy** the study of the structure, history, etc. of soils, esp. as they affect agriculture. — *adj.* **agrolog'ical**. — *ns.* **agrol'ogist; agron'omy** (Gr. *nemein*, to administer, dispense) rural economy. — *adjs.* **agronō'mial; agronōm'ic**. — *n.sing.* **agronom'ics** the science dealing with the management and productivity of land. [L. *ager*, (Gr. *agros*) field, *cultūra*, cultivation.]

agrimony *ag'ri-mən-i, n.* a perennial herb of a genus (*Agrimonia*) of the rose family, with small yellow flowers and bitter taste and a rootstock which provides a yellow dye: extended to other plants, especially **hemp-agrimony** (*Eupatorium cannabinum*), a composite. [L. *agrimōnia* (a blunder or misreading) — Gr. *argemōnē*, long prickly-headed poppy.]

agrin *ə-grin',* (*arch.*) *adv.* in the act of grinning. [**a³**, and **grin.**]

agriology *ag-ri-ol'ə-ji, n.* the comparative study of the customs found among primitive peoples. [Gr. *agrios*, wild — *agros*, field, and *logos*, a discourse.]

agrise, agrize, agryze *a-grīz',* (*obs.*) *v.t.* to terrify (*Spens.*): to horrify: to disfigure. — *adj.* **agrised'**. [O.E. *āgrīsan*, to dread.]

agro-, agrobiology, etc. See under **agriculture.**

agrostology *ag-ros-tol'ə-ji, n.* the study of grasses. — *adj.* **agrostological** (*-tə-loj'i-kl*). — *n.* **agrostol'ogist**. [Gr. *agrōstis*, dog's-tooth grass.]

aground *ə-grownd', adv.* in or to a stranded condition: on the ground. [**a³**, and **ground.**]

aguacate *ä-gwä-kä'tä, n.* the avocado pear. [Sp., — Nahuatl *ahuacatl*.]

aguardiente *ä-gwär-dyen'tä, n.* a brandy made in Spain and Portugal: any spirituous liquor. [Sp., from *agua ardiente*, burning water — L. *aqua*, water, *ardēns, -entis* — *ardēre*, to burn.]

ague *ā'gū, n.* a burning fever (*B.*): a fever with hot and cold fits: malaria: a shivering fit. — *adjs.* **agued** (*ā'gūd*) struck with ague: shivering: cold; **ā'guish**. — *adv.* **ā'guishly**. — **a'gue-cake** a swelling on the spleen, caused by ague; **ā'gue-fit'**. — *adj.* **ā'gue-proof**. [O.Fr. (*fièvre*) *ague* — L. (*febris*) *acūta*, sharp (fever).]

aguise, aguize *a-gīz',* (*obs.*) *v.t.* to dress, equip (*Spens.*): to adorn: to fashion. [Pfx. **a-**, and **guise.**]

aguti. See **agouti.**

ah *ä, interj.* expressing surprise, joy, pity, complaint, objection, etc. [Perh. O.Fr. *ah.*]

aha *ə-hä', interj.* of exultation, pleasure, surprise, or contempt. [**ah**, and **ha.**]

à haute voix *a ōt vwä,* (Fr.) aloud.

ahead *ə-hed', adv.* further on: in advance: forward: headlong. [**a³**, and **head.**]

aheap ǝ-hēp', (obs.) adv. in a heap. [a³, and **heap**.]
aheight ǝ-hīt', (arch.) adv. on high, aloft. [a³, and **height**.]
ahem ǝ-h(e)m', interj. a lengthened form of **hem**².
ahigh ǝ-hī', (obs.) adv. on high. [a³, and **high**.]
ahimsa ǝ-him'sǝ, n. duty of sparing animal life: nonviolence. [Sans. ahimsā.]
ahint ǝ-hint', **ahind** ǝ-hin(d)', (Scot., etc.) adv. and prep. behind. [O.E. æthindan.]
ahistorical ā-his-tor'i-kǝl, adj. not historical: taking no account of, or not related to, history. [Gr. a-, priv., and **historical**.]
Ahithophel. See **Achitophel.**
ahold ǝ-hōld', adv. at or to grips, or a condition of holding: near the wind (i.e. so as to hold there) (obs. naut.; Shak.). [a³, and **hold**¹.]
-aholic, -oholic -ǝ-hol'ik, (facet.) suffix having an addiction to (something) as in workaholic, clothesoholic. **-ahol'ism, -ohol'ism** (-izm) noun suffix. [By analogy, from alcoholic, alcoholism.]
ahorse, ahorseback ǝ-hörs' (-bak), (arch.) advs. on horseback. [Prep. **a**.]
ahoy ǝ-hoi', (naut.) interj. used in hailing. [ah and **hoy**².]
Ahriman ä'ri-män, n. in Zoroastrianism, the evil spirit, opposed to Ormuzd. [Pers. Ahrīman, Zend anro mainyus, dark spirit.]
à huis clos a wē klō, (Fr.) with closed doors.
ahull ǝ-hul', (naut.) adv. with sails furled, and helm lashed to the lee-side. [a³, and **hull**².]
ahungered ǝ-hung'gǝrd, **ahungry** -gri, (both arch.) adjs. oppressed with hunger. Also, from confusion of prefixes, **anhung'(e)red**, **an-hung'ry** (or **an hungry**). [Prob. O.E. of-hyngred.]
Ahura Mazda ä'hŏŏr-ä maz'dä, the chief god of the ancient Persians, the creator and lord of the whole universe. [See **Ormuzd**.]
ai¹ ä'ē, n. the three-toed sloth. [Tupí ai, representing the animal's cry.]
ai². See **ayu**.
aia. Same as **ayah.**
aiblins. See **able.**
aichmophobia āk-mō-phō'bi-ǝ, n. abnormal fear of sharp or pointed objects. [Gr. aichmē, point of a spear, phobos, fear.]
aid ād, v.t. to help. — n. help: succour: assistance, as in defending an action: that which helps: an auxiliary: a helper: an apparatus, etc., that gives help, e.g. hearing-aid, navigational aid: a feudal tax for certain purposes paying the lord's ransom, the expense of knighting his son, his daughter's marriage: subsidy or money grant to the king: money, etc., donated to relieve poor or disaster-stricken countries. — n. **aid'ance** aid, help, support. — adj. **aid'ant** (arch.) aiding, helping. — adj. **aid'ed**. — n. **aid'er**. — adjs. **aid'ful; aid'ing; aid'less**. — **aid and abet** (law) to assist and encourage usu. the commission of a crime; **in aid of** (coll.) intended to achieve: in support of. [O.Fr. aider — L. adjūtāre, freq. of adjuvāre — jūvāre, jūtum, to help.]
aide ād, n. a confidential assistant to a person of senior rank e.g. an ambassador or president: an aide-de-camp. — **aide-de-camp** (ed-, ād'-dǝ-kä) an officer who carries the orders of a general and acts as secretary: an officer attending a king, governor, etc.: — pl. **aides-de-camp** (ed-, ād'-). [Fr., assistant, assistant on the field.]
aide-mémoire ed-mā-mwär, (Fr.) n. an aid to the memory: a reminder: a memorandum-book: a written summary of a diplomatic document.
aidos, ī'dŏs, (Gr.) n. shame, modesty.
AIDS. See under **acquire.**
aiery. A variant of **eyrie.**
aiglet. Same as **aglet.**
aigre-doux egr'-dŏō (fem. **-douce** -dŏōs), (Fr.) adj. bitter-sweet, sourish.
aigrette ā'gret, ā-gret', n. an egret: an egret plume: a plume: a tuft: a pappus: a spray of jewels: a savoury cooked in deep fat. [Fr.]

aiguille ā-gwēl', n. a sharp, needle-like peak of rock: a slender boring-tool. — n. **aiguillette'** see **aglet**. [Fr.]
aikido ī-kē'dō, n. a Japanese combative sport using locks and pressure against joints. [Jap., — ai, harmonise, ki, breath, spirit, dō, way, doctrine.]
aikona ī'kon'ǝ, (Bantu) interj. it is not: no.
ail āl, v.t. (impers.) to trouble, afflict, be the matter with: to have the matter with one. — v.i. to be sickly, indisposed. — n. trouble: indisposition. — adj. **ail'ing** unwell: in poor health. — n. **ail'ment** pain: indisposition: disease, esp. if not very serious. — **what ails him at?** (Scot.) what is his objection to? [O.E. eglan, to trouble.]
ailanto ā-lan'tō, n. the tree of heaven (genus Ailantus; family Simarubaceae), a lofty and beautiful Asiatic tree: — pl. **-s.** — Also **ailan'thus**. [Amboyna (Moluccas) name aylanto, tree of the gods.]
aileron āl', el'ǝ-rɔ̄, -ron, n. a flap on an aeroplane wingtip for lateral balancing: a half-gable, as on a penthouse. — n. **ailette** (ā-let') a plate of armour for the shoulder. [Fr. dims. of aile — L. āla, a wing.]
ailes de pigeon el dǝ pē-zhɔ̄, (Fr.) pigeon's wings — powdered side-curls of hair.
ailette. See **aileron.**
ailour(o)-, ailur(o)- ī-lŏōr'(ǝ)-, **aelur(o)-** ē-lŏōr', i-, in composition, cat. — ns. **ail(o)ur'ophile** (-fīl) a cat lover or fancier; **ail(o)urophilia** (-fil'i-ǝ) love of cats. — adj. **ail(o)ur'ophilic**. — **ail(o)ur'ophobe** (-fōb) a cat hater: one with an abnormal fear of cats; **ail(o)urophō'bia**. — adj. **ail(o)uropho'bic**. [Gr. ailouros, cat.]
aim ām, v.t. to estimate, guess (obs.): to place: to point, level, direct, with (or as if with) a view to hitting an object: to purpose or try (to do). — v.i. (with at) to conjecture (obs.): to direct a course: to level a weapon: to direct a blow or missile: to direct an utterance with personal or special application: to direct one's intention and endeavours with a view to attainment. — n. a guess or estimate (Shak.): an act or manner of aiming: a shot (Shak.): an object or purpose aimed at: design: intention. — adj. **aim'less** without fixed aim. — adv. **aim'lessly**. — n. **aim'lessness**. — **aim off** to aim slightly off the target to allow for wind or other factor: to allow for the possible bias, exaggeration or eccentricity inherent in a statement, opinion, etc.; **cry aim** (arch.) to encourage by calling out 'aim', hence, to applaud; **give aim** (arch.) to guide by reporting result of previous shots; **take aim** to aim deliberately. [Prob. partly O.Fr. esmer (Picardian amer) — L. aestimāre, partly O.Fr. aesmer — L. adaestimāre; cf. **esteem, estimate**.]
ain ān, (Scot.) adj. own. [O.N. eiginn or O.E. ægen, a variant of āgen.]
aîné (fem. **aînée**), e-nā, (Fr.) adj. elder, senior.
ain't änt, (coll.) contracted form of are not, used also for am or is not: also of have not.
Ainu ī'nŏō, n. a people of Japan whose abundant body hair has been the subject of remark: their language.
aioli, aïoli ī-ō'lē, n. a garlic-flavoured mayonnaise. [Prov. ai, garlic, — L. allium, and oli, oil, — L. oleum.]
air ār, n. the gaseous mixture (chiefly nitrogen and oxygen) of which the atmosphere is composed: the medium through which sound-waves travel (radio): the medium in which aircraft operate: any gas (obs.): a light breeze: breath (obs.): effluvium: the aura or atmosphere that invests anything: bearing, outward appearance, manner, look: an assumed or affected manner: (in pl.) affectation of superiority: exposure, noising abroad: melody, tune (see also **ayre**): the chief, usually upper, part or tune. — adj. of, pertaining to, the air: affecting, regulating, (the) air: by means of (the) air: operated by air: of aircraft: carried out, or conveyed, by aircraft. — v.t. to expose to the air: to ventilate: to warm and dry: to give an airing to: to wear openly, display: to publish abroad. — v.i. to take an airing: to become aired. — n. **air'er** one who airs: a frame on which clothes are dried. — adv. **air'ily** in an airy manner: jauntily. — ns. **air'iness; air'ing** exposure to air or heat or to general notice: a short

excursion in the open air. — *adj.* **air'less** without air: without free communication with the outer air: without wind: stuffy. — *advs.* **air'ward, air'wards** up into the air. — *adj.* **air'y** consisting of or relating to air: open to the air: having sufficient (fresh) air: like air: unsubstantial: sprightly: offhand. — **air'-am'bulance** an aircraft used to take patients from remote places to hospital; **air'-arm** the branch of the fighting services that uses aircraft; **air bag** a safety device in a motor-car, etc. consisting of a bag that inflates to protect the occupants in a collision: an air-filled bag for another purpose, e.g. raising sunken craft; **air'-base** a base of operations for aircraft; **air'-bath** exposure of the body to air: apparatus for therapeutic application of compressed or rarefied air, or for drying substances in air; **air'-bed** an inflated mattress; **air'-bell** an air-bubble; **air'-bends** aeroembolism; **air'-bladder** a sac containing gas, as those that buoy up certain seaweeds: a fish's swim bladder, serving to regulate buoyancy and in some cases acting as a lung. — *adj.* **air'borne** carried by air: borne up in the air. — **air'-brake** a brake worked by compressed air: a means of checking the speed of an aircraft. — *adj.* **air'-breathing** (of a means of propulsion) which needs to take in air for combustion. — **air'-brick** a block for ventilation; **air'-bridge** a link by air transport between two points; **air'-brush** a device for spraying paint by compressed air. — *adj.* **air'-brushed.** — **air'-bubble** a bubble of air, specif. one causing a spot on a photograph. — *adj.* **air'-built** built in air; having no solid foundation. — **air'burst** the explosion of a bomb, etc. in the air. — *adj.* designed to explode in the air. — **air'-bus** a very large passenger jet aircraft used for short flights; **air'-car** one made to ride on a cushion of air; **air'-cavity, air'-cell** (*bot.*) an intercellular space containing air; **air'-chief-mar'shal** an airforce officer ranking with an admiral or general; **air'-comm'odore** an air-force officer ranking with a commodore or brigadier; **air'-compress'or** a machine which draws in air at atmospheric pressure, compresses it, and delivers it at higher pressure. — *v.t.* **air'-condi'tion** to equip, e.g. a building, with devices for air-conditioning. — *adj.* **air'-condi'tioned.** — **air'-condi'tioning** the bringing of air to the desired state of purity, temperature and humidity; **air'-cooling** cooling by means of air. — *adj.* **air'-cooled.** — **air'-corr'idor** in an area where flying is restricted, a narrow strip along which flying is allowed; **air'-cov'er** protection given by fighter aircraft to other forces during a military operation: the protecting aircraft; **aircraft** *sing.* (also *pl.*) any structure or machine for navigating the air; **air'-craft-carrier** a vessel from which aircraft can take off and on which they may alight; **air'craftman** an air-force member of lowest rank. — Also **air'craftsman; air'-craft(s)woman** lowest rank in the W.R.A.F.; **air'-crew'** the crew of an aircraft; **air'-cushion** a cushion that can be inflated: protective barrier, e.g. between a hovercraft and land or water, formed by down-driven air: **air'-drain** a cavity in the external walls of a building to prevent damp from getting through to the interior. — *adj.* **air'drawn** drawn in air: visionary: imaginary (*Shak.*). — **air'drome** (chiefly *U.S.*) aerodrome; **air'-drop** (*mil.*) a landing of men or supplies by parachute; **air'-engine** an engine driven by heated or compressed air; **air'field** an open expanse where aircraft may land and take off; **air force** a force organised for warfare in the air; **air'frame** the body of an aircraft as opposed to its engines; **air'gap** a gap in the magnetic circuit of a piece of electrical apparatus, e.g. the gap between the rotor and stator of an electric machine; **air'-gas** producer gas; **air'graph** a letter photographically reduced for sending by air; **air'-grating** a grating admitting air for ventilation; **air'-gun** a gun that discharges missiles by means of compressed air: **air'hole** a hole for the passage of air: a hole in ice where animals come up to breathe: an airpocket; **air-hostess** see **host**[1]; **air'-house** an inflatable building of nylon or Terylene coated with polyvinyl chloride which can be used by

industrial firms for storage, etc.; **air'-jacket** a casing containing air to reduce loss or gain of heat: a garment with airtight cavities to buoy up in water; **air'-lane'** a route normally taken by aircraft because of steady winds; **air layering** the layering of shoots, not by bending them down to root in the soil but by enclosing in compost or the like; **air letter** a letter sent by air mail; **air lieutenant** a rank in the Zimbabwean Air Force equivalent to a flying officer in the Royal Air Force; **air'lift** a transport operation carried out by air: transportation by air. — Also *v.t.* — **air'line** a route or system of traffic by aircraft: a company operating such a system: — Also *adj.* — **air'liner** a large passenger aircraft: an aircraft plying in an airline; **air loadmaster** one of a team of usu. three men in charge of winching operations on a helicopter; **air'-lock** a small chamber in which pressure of air can be raised or lowered, through which communication is made between a caisson where the air is compressed and the outer air: a bubble in a pipe obstructing flow of liquid; **air'mail** mail conveyed by air. — *v.t.* to send by airmail. — Also *adj.* — **air'man** an aviator: — *fem.* **air'woman; air'manship** the art of handling aircraft; **air'-mar'shal** an air-force officer ranked with a vice-admiral or a lieutenant-general; **air'-mechan'ic** one who tends and repairs aircraft. — *adj.* **air'-minded** having thought habitually and favourably directed towards flying. — **air'-miss** a near collision between aircraft; **air'-officer** an air-force officer of general rank; **air'-passage** the passage by which air enters and leaves the lungs; **air-pir'acy** the hijacking of an aircraft; **air'plane** (chiefly *U.S.*) an aeroplane; **air'-plant** an epiphyte; **air play** the broadcasting of a song, singer, record, etc.; **air'-pocket** a region of rarefied or down-flowing air, in which aircraft drop; **air'port** an opening for the passage of air: an aerodrome with a custom-house, used as a station for international transport of passengers and cargo; **air'-power** military power in respect of aircraft; **air'-pump** an instrument for pumping air out or in; **air'-raid** an attack on a place by aircraft; **air'-rail** a rail on which a road vehicle is carried overhead for part of its course; **air rifle** one discharging missiles by means of compressed air; **air'-sac** an alveolus, or the cluster of alveoli, at the termination of a bronchiole in the lungs: an outgrowth of the lung in birds, helping respiration or lightening the body: in insects, a dilatation of the trachea; **air'screw** the propeller of an aircraft; **Air Scout** a member of a branch of the Scouts with special interest in air activities; **air'shaft** a passage for air into a mine, building, etc.; **air'ship** a mechanically driven dirigible aircraft, lighter than air; **air'-sickness** nausea affecting travellers by air. — *adj.* **air'sick.** — **air'space** cubic contents available for respirable air: an air-cell: the part of the atmosphere above a particular territory, state, etc.: the space used, or required by, an aircraft in manoeuvring; **air'-splint'** a contrivance zipped up and inflated for giving temporary support to an injured limb; **air'stop** a stopping-place for helicopters; **air'stream** a flow of air; **air'-strike'** an attack with aircraft; **air'strip** a temporary or emergency landing-place for aircraft: a runway; **air terminal** a terminus to or from which passengers are conveyed from or to an airport. — *adj.* **air'tight** impermeable to air: impenetrable (*fig.*). — **air'time** the amount of broadcasting time on radio or television allotted to a particular topic, type of material, commercial advertisement, etc.: the time at which the broadcasting of a programme, etc. is due to begin. — *adj.* **air'-to-air'** from one aircraft to another. — **air'-trap** a device to prevent escape of foul air; **air'-umbrella** strong air-cover; **air'-vice-mar'shal** an air-force officer ranking with a rear-admiral or major-general; **air'wave** a channel for broadcasting; **air'way** a passage for air: a channel for broadcasting: a radio channel: an organised route for air travel: used in *pl.* to form names of airline companies; **air'worthiness.** — *adjs.* **air'worthy** in fit condition for safe flying; **air'y-fair'y** fanciful: delicate. — **air-sea rescue** combined use of aircraft and high-speed launches in sea rescue; **airstream mechanism** the part(s) of the body, e.g. the lungs, which can produce a flow of air on which speech-sounds, etc. may be produced; **air-traffic control** system of regional centres and airport units which instruct aircraft exactly about route to follow, height at which to fly, etc.; **give oneself airs** to affect superiority; **give the air** to dismiss; **(go) up in the air** (to become) excited or angry; **in the air** prevalent in an indefinite form; **off the air** not broadcasting, or being broadcast, for a period of time; **on the air** broadcast by radio: in the act of broadcasting; **take air** to get wind, become known; **take the air** to have an airing.   [O.Fr. (and Fr.) *air* - L. *āēr, āēris* — Gr. *āēr, āeros*, air.]

Airedale *ār'dāl, n.* (*in full* **Airedale terrier**) a large terrier of a breed from *Airedale* in Yorkshire.

airn *ārn*, a Scots form of **iron.**

airt *ārt*, (*Scot.*) *n.* direction, quarter. — *v.t.* to direct. [Perh. Gael. *aird*, point (of compass).]

aisle *īl, n.* a side division of the nave or other part of a church or similar building, generally separated off by pillars: (*loosely*) any division of a church, or a small building attached: (*loosely*) a passage between rows of seats e.g. in an aircraft: a passageway (*U.S.*): the corridor of a railway train or aircraft (*U.S.*). — *adj.* **aisled** (*īld*) having aisles.   [O.Fr. *ele* (Fr. *aile*) — L. *āla*, a wing; confused with **isle** and **alley.**]

aisling *īsh'ling, ash', n.* (a poetic description of) a vision or dream.   [Ir.]

ait[1], **eyot** *āt, n.* a small island.   [Cf. O.E. *ēgath, īgeoth,* app. conn. with *īeg*, island; the phonology is obscured.]

ait[2] *āt*, Scots form of **oat.**

aitch *āch, n.* the eighth letter of the alphabet (H, h). — **drop one's aitches** to fail to pronounce initial aitches, formerly considered a sign of lack of education. [O.Fr. *ache*, from which L.L. *ahha* is inferred.]

aitchbone *āch'bōn, n.* the bone of the rump: the cut of beef over it.   [An *aitchbone* is for a *nachebone* — O.Fr. *nache* — L. *natis*, buttock; and **bone.**]

aitu *ī'tōō, n.* in Polynesia, a demigod.

aizle. See **easle.**

Aizoon *ā-ī-zō'on, n.* an African genus of plants giving name to the family **Aizoā'ceae,** akin to the goosefoots. [App. Gr. *āei*, ever, *zōos*, living.]

à jamais *a zha-me*, (Fr.) for ever.

ajar *ə-jär', adv.* and *adj.* partly open.   [O.E. *on*, on, *cerr*, a turn.]

Ajax *ā'jaks*, (L., — Gr. *Aiās*) *n.* the Greek hero next to Achilles in the Trojan war: a privy, by a pun on *a jakes* (*obs.*).

ajee, agee *ə-jē', (Scot.* and *dial.) adv.* off the straight: ajar.   [Prep. **a,** and **gee**[3], **jee**[1].]

ajowan *aj'ō-wən,* or **ajwan** *aj'wən, ns.* a plant of the caraway genus yielding ajowan oil and thymol.   [Origin uncertain.]

ajutage. See **adjutage.**

ake *āk.* Old spelling of the verb **ache.**

akedah *ə-kā'dä, ə-kā-dä* (Heb.) *n.* the binding of Isaac in Genesis xxii.

akee *a-kē', n.* a small African sapindaceous tree, now common in the West Indies: its edible fruit.   [Kru *ā-kee.*]

akene *a-kēn', n.* Same as **achene.**

akimbo *ə-kim'bō, adj.* and *adv.* with hand on hip and elbow out.   [M.E. *in kenebow*; poss. in a keen (sharp) bow or bend; other suggestions are *can-bow* (i.e. canhandle), and O.N. *kengboginn*, bent into a crook — *kengr*, kink, *boginn*, bowed.]

akin *ə-kin', adv.* by kin: of nature. — *adj.* related by blood: of like nature.   [**a**[3], and **kin**[1].]

akinesia *ā-kin-ē'zi-ə, -ē'shə,* (*path.*) *n.* the lack, loss, or impairment of the power of voluntary movement. — Also **akinesis** (*-ē'sis*).   [Gr. *akinesia*, lack of motion; *a-*, priv., *kinein*, to move.]

Akkadian *ə-kād'i-ən, n.* the Semitic language of the ancient Middle-Eastern kingdom of Akkad: a native

of this kingdom. — Also *adj.*   [City of *Agade.*]

akkas. See **ackers.**

akol(o)uthos, etc. Same as **acolouthos,** etc.

akvavit. Same as **aquavit.**

à la *a la, prep.* in the manner of, e.g. *à la James Joyce*; in cooking, prepared with, in the manner of (a person or place), e.g. *à la Dubarry*, with cauliflower, *à la Florentine*, with spinach, etc.   [Fr. — contraction of *à la mode de.*]

ala *ā'lə, n.* a membranous outgrowth on a fruit (*bot.*): a side petal in the pea family (*bot.*): a large side sepal in the milkworts (*bot.*): a leafy expansion running down the stem from a leaf (*bot.*): any flat winglike process, esp. of bone (*zool.*): — *pl.* **alae** (*ā'lē*). — *adjs.* **ā'lar, ā'lary** pertaining to a wing; **ā'late, -d** winged, having an ala.   [L. *āla*, wing.]

alaap. See **alap.**

alabamine *al-ə-bäm'ēn, n.* a name proposed for element no. 85; now called **astatine.**   [*Alabama*, where its discovery in nature was claimed.]

alabandine. See **almandine.** — *n.* **aluband'ite** a cubic mineral, manganese sulphide.

à l'abandon *a la-bä-dō,* (Fr.) neglected, uncared for: (in *Eng.*) carelessly, recklessly.

alabaster *al'ə-bäs-tər,* or *bäs',* (*Spens., Shak., Milt.,* etc. **alablaster**) *n.* a semi-transparent massive gypsum. — *adj.* of or like alabaster. — **oriental alabaster** stalactitic calcite.   [Gr. *alabastros*, said to be from *Alabastron*, a town in Egypt.]

à la belle étoile *a la be-lā-twäl,* (Fr.) in the open air.

à la bonne heure! *a la bo-nœr,* (Fr.) well done! that is right.

à l'abri *a la-brē,* (Fr.) under shelter.

à la campagne *a la kã-pan-y',* (Fr.) in the country.

à la carte *a la kärt, ä lä kärt,* (Fr.) according to the bill of fare: with each dish charged individually at the price shown on the menu.

alack *ə-lak', arch. interj.* denoting regret. — *interj.* **alack'=a-day** woe be to the day: alas.   [Prob. **ah,** and **lack**[1].]

alacrity *ə-lak'ri-ti, n.* briskness: cheerful readiness: promptitude.   [L. *alacritās, -ātis* — *alacer, alacris,* brisk.]

Aladdin's cave *ə-lad'inz kāv,* a place of immense treasure. — **Aladdin's lamp** a charmed object able to grant all one's desires.   [*Aladdin,* a character in *Arabian Nights.*]

à la dérobée *a la dā-ro-bā,* (Fr.) by stealth.

alae. See **ala.**

à la hauteur de *a la ō-tœr də,* (Fr.) on a level with, abreast of: able to understand, or to deal with.

alaiment. Old spelling of **allayment** (see **allay**[1]).

alalagmos *a-la-lag'mos,* (Gr.) *n.* a war-cry, cry of *alalai.*

à la lanterne *a la lã-tern,* (Fr.) to the lamp(-chain) — away with them and hang them (as in the French Revolution).

alalia *ə-lā'li-ə, n.* loss of speech.   [Gr. *a-,* priv., and *laleein,* to talk.]

à la main *a la mē,* (Fr.) in hand, ready: by hand.

à la maître d'hôtel *a la metr' dō-tel,* (Fr.) in the style of a house-steward, of a hotel-keeper: in major-domo fashion: in cooking, served plain with a parsley garnish.

alameda *a-la-mā'dä, n.* a public walk, esp. between rows of poplars.   [Sp. *álamo,* poplar.]

à la mode *a la mod(ə),* **alamode** *a-lə-mōd', advs.* and *adjs.* according to the fashion, fashionable; in cooking, of beef, larded and stewed with vegetables: of desserts, served with ice-cream (*U.S.*). — *n.* **alamode** a light glossy silk.   [Fr. *à la mode.*]

alamort *a-lə-mort', adj.* half-dead: dejected.   [Fr. *à la mort,* to the death; see also **amort.**]

aland *ə-land', (arch.) adv.* ashore.   [**a**[3], and **land**[1].]

alang *ä'läng,* or **a'lang-a'lang.** Same as **lalang.**

alannah *ə-län'ə, n.* in endearment, my child.   [Ir. *a,* O, *leanbh,* child.]

alap *ə-läp', n.* in Indian music, the introductory section of a raga. — Also **alaap', alap'a.**   [Sans.]

à la page *a la päzh,* (Fr.) up to date, au courant.

For other sounds see detailed chart of pronunciation.

à la Portugaise. See **Portugaise.**

à la poupée *a la pōō-pā*, (Fr.) of the printing of an engraving or etching, with inks of different colours being spread on the plate with paper or cloth pads (*poupées*) before the impression is taken.

alar, alary. See **ala.**

alarm *ə-lärm', n.* a call to arms: notice of danger: a mechanical contrivance for arousing, warning, or giving notice: the noise made by it: a din (*obs.*): a fear-stricken state: apprehension of danger. — *v.t.* to call to arms (*obs.*): to give notice of danger: to arouse: to strike with fear. — *adj.* **alarmed'.** — *adv.* **alarm'edly.** — *adj.* **alarm'ing.** — *adv.* **alarm'ingly.** — *ns.* **alarm'ism; alarm'ist** *a la clock* radio. — *n.* and *v.t.* **alarum** (*ala'rəm, -lä', -lā')* alarm (now *arch.* except of a warning mechanism or sound). — **alarm'-bell; alarm'-clock'** a clock that can be set to ring an alarm at a chosen time; **alarm'-radio** a clock radio. — **alar(u)ms and excursions** a stage direction for a sketchy conventionalised representation of skirmishing or the outskirts of a battle: hence, vague hostilities or confused activity; **sound the alarm** to give the signal to prepare for an emergency. [O.Fr. (Fr.) *alarme* — It. *all'arme*, to (the) arms.]

alarum. See under **alarm.**

alas *ə-läs', interj.* expressive of grief. — **alas the day, alas the while** ah! unhappy day, time. [O.Fr. *ha las, a las* (mod. Fr. *hélas*); *ha*, ah, and *las, lasse*, wretched, weary — L. *lassus*, wearied.]

alastrim *ə-las'trim, n.* a mild form of smallpox or a similar disease. [Port.]

alate¹ *ə-lāt', adv. (arch.)* lately. [**of** and **late.**]

alate². See **ala.**

a latere *ā la'tə-rē, ä la'tə-rā*, (L.) lit. from the side: confidential (of legate sent by the Pope).

à la volée *a la vo-lā*, (Fr.) on the flight (said of any quick return).

alay. Old spelling of **allay¹.**

alb *alb, n.* a long white tight-sleeved vestment. [O.E. *albe* — L.L. *alba* — L. *albus*, white.]

albacore *al'bə-kōr, -kör, n.* a large tunny: a species of mackerel (*S.Afr.*). — Also written **al'bicore.** [Port. *albacor* — Ar. *al*, the, *bukr*, young camel.]

Alban *al'bən*, **Albany** *-i*, **Albion** *-i-ən*, *ns.* ancient names for the island of Great Britain, now used poetically for Britain, England, or esp. Scotland. — **Alban** the ancient kingdom of the Picts and (Celtic) Scots, which the addition of Lothian and Strathclyde transformed into Scotland; **Albany** a Scottish dukedom first conferred in 1398. — **Albany herald** one of the Scottish heralds. [Celtic.]

Albanian *al-bā'ni-ən, adj.* of or pertaining to the S.E. European Republic of *Albania.* — *n.* a native or citizen thereof: the language thereof.

albarello *al-bə-rel'ō, al-bar-el'lō, n.* a majolica jar used for dry drugs. — *pl.* **albarell'os, albarel'li** (*-lē*). [It.]

albata *al-bā'tə, n.* a variety of German silver. [L. *albāta* (*fem.*), whitened — *albus*, white.]

albatross *al'bə-tros, n.* a large, long-winged sea-bird of remarkable powers of flight: a hole in three below par (*golf*): used symbolically to mean an oppressive and inescapable fact, influence, etc. (from the dead bird hung round the neck of the sailor in Coleridge's *Ancient Mariner*). [See **alcatras**; perh. influenced by L. *albus*, white.]

albe, albee, all-be *öl-bē', öl'bē, conj. (arch.)* albeit. [**all** and **be.**]

albedo *al-bē'dō, n.* whiteness: the proportion of incident light reflected, as by a planet: — *pl.* **albe'dos.** [L. *albēdō*, whiteness — *albus*, white.]

albeit *öl-bē'it, conj.* although it be (that): even if, although. [**all be it.**]

albergo *al-ber'gō* (It.) *n.* an inn, auberge: — *pl.* **alber'ghi.**

albert *al'bərt, n.* a short kind of watch-chain. [After Queen Victoria's husband.]

Alberti bass *al-bûr'ti bäs, -ber'*, a type of bass accompaniment consisting of broken chords. [Domenico *Alberti* (1710-40), an exponent of this.]

albertite *al'bər-tīt, n.* a pitch-black solid bitumen. [Discovered at the *Albert* mine, New Brunswick, Canada.]

albescent *al-bes'ənt, adj.* becoming white: whitish. — *n.* **albesc'ence.** [L. *albēscēns, -entis*, pr.p. of *albēscĕre*, to grow white — *albus*, white.]

albespyne, albespine *al'bə-spīn, (arch.) n.* hawthorn. [O.Fr. *albespine* (Fr. *aubépine*) — L. *alba spīna*, white thorn.]

albicore. See **albacore.**

Albigensian *al-bi-jen'si-ən, adj.* of the town of *Albi* or its district (the Albigeois), in the S. of France: of a Catharist or Manichaean sect or of the 13th-century crusade (beginning in the Albigeois) by which, with the Inquisition, the Catholic Church stamped it out in blood. — Also *n.* — *n.pl.* **Albigen'sēs.** — *n.* **Albigen'sianism.** [L.L. *Albigēnsēs.*]

albino *al-bē'nō*, in U.S. *-bī', n.* a person or other animal with abnormally white skin and hair and pink irises: a plant lacking in pigment: — *pl.* **albi'nos:** — *fem.* **albiness** (*al'bin-es*). — *ns.* **al'binism** (*-bin-*), **albinoism** (*-bē'*). — *adj.* **albinotic** (*al-bin-ot'ik*). [Port. *albino*, white Negro or albino — L. *albus*, white.]

Albion. See **Alban.**

albite *al'bīt, n.* a white plagioclase felspar, sodium and aluminium silicate. — *v.t.* **al'bītise, -ize** to turn into albite. [L. *albus*, white.]

albricias *al-brē-thē'as*, (Sp.) *n.* a reward to the bearer of good news.

albugo *al-bū'gō, n.* leucoma: — *pl.* **-s.** — *adj.* **albugineous** (*-jin'i-əs*) like the white of an egg or of the eye. [L. *albūgō, -inis*, whiteness — *albus*, white.]

album *al'bəm, n.* among the Romans, a white tablet or register on which the praetor's edicts and such public notices were recorded: a blank book for the insertion of photographs, autographs, poetical extracts, scraps, postage-stamps, or the like: a printed book of selections, esp. of music: a book-like container for gramophone records: a long-playing gramophone record: a visitors' book (*U.S.*): — *pl.* **al'bums.** — **al'bum-leaf** (trans. of Ger. *Albumblatt*) a short musical composition. [L. neut. of *albus*, white.]

albumen *al-bū'mən, -min*, or *al', n.* white of egg: the nutritive material surrounding the yolk in the eggs of higher animals, a mixture of proteins (*zool.*): any tissue within the seed-coat other than the embryo itself — endosperm and perisperm, a store of food for the young plant, no matter what its chemical nature (*bot.*): an albumin (*obs.*). — *v.t.* **albū'menise, albū'minise, -ize** (*phot.*) to cover or impregnate with albumen or an albuminous solution. — *ns.* **albū'min** (or *al'*) a protein of various kinds soluble in pure water, the solution coagulable by heat; **albū'minate** an alkali compound of an albumin. — *adj.* **albū'minoid** like albumen. — *n.* an old name for a protein in general: any one of a class of substances including keratin and chondrin. — *adj.* **albū'minous** like or containing albumen or albumin: insipid. — *n.* **albūminūr'ia** presence of albumin in the urine. [L. *albūmen, -inis* — *albus*, white.]

album Graecum *al'bum grē'kum, al'bōōm grī'kōōm*, (L.L.) the dried dung of dogs, once used for inflammation of the throat.

albumin albuminise, etc. See **albumen.**

alburnum *al-bûrn'əm, n.* sapwood, the soft wood between inner bark and heartwood. — *adj.* **alburn'ous.** [L. *albus*, white.]

alcahest. See **alkahest.**

Alcaic *al-kā'ik, adj.* of or pertaining to the Greek lyric poet *Alcaeus* (*Alkaios*, fl. 600 B.C.), or of the kind of verse invented by him. — *n.* (esp. in *pl.*) Alcaic verses. — **Alcaic strophe** a form much used by Horace, consisting of two eleven-syllable Alcaics: ⌣–⌣–/ –⌣⌣–⌣, a nine-syllable: ⌣–⌣–⌣–⌣–⌣, and a ten-syllable: –⌣⌣–⌣⌣–⌣–⌣; imitated by Tennyson in 'O mighty-mouth'd inventor of harmonies'.

alcaicería *al-kī-the-rē'a*, (Sp.) *n.* a bazaar.

alcaide, alcayde *al-kād', äl-kī'dhä, -dā*, (Sp.) *n.* governor of a fortress: a gaoler. [Sp. *alcaide* — Ar. *al-qā'īd* — *al*, the, *qā'īd*, leader — *qāda*, to lead.]

alcalde *äl-käl'dä*, (Sp.) *n.* (formerly) a judge, magistrate: a mayor. [Sp., — Ar. *al-qādī* — *qada*, to judge.]

alcarraza *al-ka-ra'tha*, (Sp.) *n.* a porous vessel for cooling water.

alcatras *al'kə-tras*, *n.* a name applied to several large water birds, as the pelican, gannet, frigate bird, albatross. [Sp. *alcatraz*, pelican.]

alcayde. See **alcaide.**

alcázar *al-ka-zär'*, *-kä'thär*, (Sp.) *n.* a palace, fortress, bazaar.

Alcelaphus *al-sel'ə-fəs.* Same as **Bubalis.**

alchemy, alchymy *al'ki-mi*, *kə-*, *n.* the infant stage of chemistry, its chief pursuits the transmutation of other metals into gold, and the elixir of life: transmuting potency (*fig.*): a gold-like substance (e.g. brass) (*obs.*): a trumpet made of it (*obs.*). — *adjs.* **alchemic** (*-kem'ik*), **-al.** — *n.* **al'chemist.** [Ar. *al-kīmīā* — *al*, the, and *kīmīā* — late Gr. *chēmeiā, chỹmeiā*, variously explained as the Egyptian art (*Khēmiā*, 'black-land', Egypt, from the Egyptian name), the art of *Chymēs* (its supposed inventor), or the art of pouring (*chỹma*, fluid; cf. *cheein*, to pour).]

alcheringa *al-chə-ring'gə*, **alchera** *al'chə-rə*, *ns.* dreamtime. [Australian Aboriginal words.]

Alcides *al-sī'dēz*, (L., — Gr.) a patronymic of Hercules, from Alcaeus, father of Amphitryon.

alcohol *al'kə-hol*, *n.* a fine powder, esp. a sublimate (*obs.*): hence (*obs.*) an essence, a distillate: a liquid generated by the fermentation of sugar or other saccharine matter and forming the intoxicating element of fermented liquors: a general term for a class of hydrocarbon compounds analogous to common (or ethyl) alcohol, in which a hydroxyl group is substituted for an atom of hydrogen. — *adj.* **alcohol'ic** of, like, containing, or due to alcohol. — *n.* one addicted to excessive drinking of alcohol. — *n.* **alcholīsā'tion, -z-.** — *v.t.* **al'coholīse, -ize** to convert into or saturate with alcohol. — *ns.* **al'coholism** alcoholic poisoning: condition suffered by an alcoholic; **alcoholom'eter** an instrument for measuring the proportion of alcohol in solutions; **alcoholom'etry.** [Ar. *al-koh'l* — *al*, the, *koh'l*, antimony powder used in the East to stain the eyelids.]

al conto *al kon'tō*, (It.) à la carte.

al contrario *al kon-trä'ri-ō*, (Sp.) on the contrary.

Alcoran *al-ko-rän'*, (*arch.*) *n.* the Koran. [Fr., — Arab. *al*, the, **Koran.**]

alcorza *al-kör'tha*, (Sp.) *n.* a kind of sweetmeat: icing.

alcove *al'kōv*, *n.* a recess in a room: any recess: a shady retreat. [Sp. *alcoba*, a place in a room railed off to hold a bed — Ar. *al*, the, *qobbah*, a vault.]

Alcyonium *al-si-ō'ni-əm*, *n.* a genus of Anthozoa growing in masses of polyps called dead men's fingers. — *n.pl.* **Alcyonā'ria** the order to which belong Alcyonium, sea-pens, red coral and organ-pipe coral. — *n.* and *adj.* **alcyonā'rian.** [Gr. *alkyoneion*, an organism said to resemble a halcyon's nest — *alkyōn*, halcyon, kingfisher.]

aldea *al-dā'a*, (Sp.) *n.* a village, hamlet.

Aldebaran *al-deb'ə-ran*, *n.* a first-magnitude red star of the Hyades. [Ar. *al-dabarān*, the follower (of the Pleiades).]

aldehyde *al'di-hīd*, *n.* a volatile fluid with a suffocating smell, obtained by the oxidation of alcohol: a compound differing from an alcohol in having two atoms fewer of hydrogen. [Contr. for *alcohol dēhydrogenātum*, alcohol deprived of hydrogen.]

al dente *al den'tā*, (It.) of pasta, firm to the teeth.

alder *öl'dər*, *n.* any tree of the genus Alnus, related to the birches, usually growing in moist ground: extended to various other trees or shrubs: an artificial fishing fly. — *adj.* **al'dern** made of alder. — **al'der-buck'thorn** a species of buckthorn (*Rhamnus frangula*); **al'der-fly** a riverside neuropterous insect. — *adj.* **al'der-leaved.** [O.E. *alor*; Ger. *Erle*; L. *alnus*.]

alder-liefest *öl-dər-lēf'ist*, (*Shak.*) *adj.* most beloved of all. [O.E. *alra* (W.S. *ealra*), gen. pl. of *al* (*eal*), all, and superl. of **lief.**]

alderman *öl'dər-mən*, *n.* in O.E. times a nobleman of highest rank, a governor of a shire or district, a high official: later, head of a guild: in English boroughs, a civic dignitary next in rank to the mayor, elected by fellow councillors (chiefly *hist.*): a superior member of an English county council (chiefly *hist.*): a member of the governing body of a borough or of its upper house, elected by popular vote (*U.S.*): — *pl.* **al'dermen.** — *adj.* **aldermanic** (*-man'ik*). — *n.* **alderman'ity.** — *adjs.* **al'dermanlike, al'dermanly** pompous and portly. — *ns.* **al'dermanry; al'dermanship.** [O.E. *aldorman* (W.S. *ealdorman*) — *aldor* (*ealdor*), a chief — *ald* (*eald*) old, and noun-forming suffix *-or*.]

Alderney *öl'dər-ni*, *n.* a small dairy-cow, formerly of a breed kept in *Alderney*, now loosely including Jersey and Guernsey. — Also *adj.*

Aldine *öl'dīn*, *adj.* from the press, or named in honour, of *Aldus* Manutius of Venice and his family (15th–16th cent.).

aldose *al'dōs*, *n.* any of a class of monosaccharide sugars which contain an aldehyde group. — **aldō-** denoting a sugar which belongs to this class, such as glucose (an **aldohex'ose**) or ribose (an **aldopen'tose**). [*ald*ehyde.]

aldrin *al'drin*, *n.* a chlorinated hydrocarbon, used as a contact insecticide. [From K. *Alder*, German chemist (1902–58).]

ale *āl*, *n.* a beverage made from an infusion of malt by fermentation name applied to beers in brewing of which yeast ferments on the top of the liquid: a festival, from the liquor drunk (*arch.*). — **ale'bench** a bench in or before an alehouse; **ale'-berry** a beverage made from ale and bread sops with flavouring; **ale'-bush, ale'-pole,** **ale'-stake** a bush, pole, or stake used as an alehouse sign; **ale'-conner** a civic officer appointed to test the quality of the ale brewed (*hist.*); **ale'cost** costmary (used in flavouring ale); **ale'-draper** (*obs.*) a tavernkeeper; **ale'-hoof** ground-ivy (O.E. *hōfe*); **ale'-house** a house in which ale is sold. — *adj.* (*Shak.*) **ale'washed.** — **ale'wife** a woman who sells ale: a fish akin to the herring, common off the N.E. of America (perhaps from its corpulent shape, but perhaps a different word): — *pl.* **ale'wives.** [O.E. (Anglian) *alu* (W.S. *ealu*); O.N. *öl*.]

aleatory *ā'li-ə-tər-i*, *adj.* depending on contingencies: used of the element of chance in poetic composition, etc: of music, aleatoric. — *n.* aleatoric music. — *adj.* **aleatoric** (*ā-li-ə-tör'ik*) in which chance influences choice of notes (*mus.*): aleatory. [L. *āleātōrius* — *āleātor*, a dicer — *ālea*, a die.]

alecost. See **ale.**

Alecto *a-lek'tō*, *n.* one of the Furies. [Gr. *Alēktō*, lit. unceasing.]

alectryon *a-lek'tri-ōn*, (Gr.) *n.* a cock.

alee *ə-lē'*, *adv.* on or toward the lee-side. [O.N. *ā*, on, *hlē*, lee.]

aleft *ə-left'*, *adv.* on or to the left hand. [*a³*, and **left².**]

alegar *al'* or *äl'i-gər*, *n.* sour ale, or vinegar made from it. [**ale**, with termination as **vinegar.**]

alegge, aleggeaunce. See **allege¹.**

Alemaine. See **Almain.**

Alemannic *al-ə-man'ik*, *adj.* of the Alemannen (L. *Alamanni, Alemanni*), an ancient people of S.W. Germany, or their dialect. — *n.* the High German dialect of Switzerland, Alsace, etc.

alembic *ə-lem'bik*, *n.* old distilling apparatus. — *adj.* **alem'bicated** over-refined. [Ar. *al*, the, *anbīq* — Gr. *ambix*, cap of a still.]

alembroth *ə-lem'broth.* Same as **sal alembroth.**

alength *ə-length'*, *adv.* at full length. [*a³* and **length.**]

à l'envi *a lä-vē*, (Fr.) emulously: in emulation.

aleph *ä'lef, ā'lef*, *n.* the first letter of the Phoenician and Hebrew alphabets, resembling an ox's head, representing a glottal stop, but adopted by the Greeks for a

vowel sound. See **A, alpha.** [Heb. *āleph*, ox.]
alepine *al'i-pēn, n.* a mixed fabric of wool and silk or mohair and cotton. [Perh. *Aleppo.*]
à l'époque *a lā-pok,* (Fr.) at the time.
alerce *ə-lûrs', ä-ler'thā, n.* the wood of the sandarach-tree: the Chilean arbor vitae. [Sp., larch — L. *larix, -īcis,* larch, perhaps confused with Ar. *al'arza,* the cedar.]
alerion, allerion *a-lē'ri-ən (her.) n.* an eagle displayed, without feet or beak. [Fr.]
alert *ə-lûrt', adj.* watchful: wide-awake: brisk. — *n.* a sudden attack or surprise: a danger warning: the time for which it lasts: condition of preparedness. — *v.t.* to make alert. — *adv.* **alert'ly.** — *n.* **alert'ness.** — **on, upon the alert** upon the watch: wakefully attentive. [Fr. *alerte* — It. *all'erta,* on the erect — *erto* — L. *ērēctus,* erect.]
Aleuritis *al-ū-rī'tēz, n.* a genus of plants of the spurge family, yielding tung-oil and candle-nut. [Gr. *aleuron,* flour.]
aleurone *a-lū'rōn, n.* a protein found in some seeds. — Also **aleu'ron** (*-on, -ən*). [Gr. *aleuron,* flour.]
alevin *al'i-vin, n.* a young fish, esp. a salmonid. [Fr., — O.Fr. *alever,* to rear — L. *ad,* to, *levāre,* to raise.]
alew *ə-lōō', -lū', (Spens.) n.* Same as **halloo.**
alewashed, alewife. See **ale.**
alexanders *al-ig-zän'dərz, n.* an umbelliferous plant (genus *Smyrnium*) formerly used as celery is. [O.E. *alexandre;* L. *olus atrum, olusatrum,* lit. 'black herb, vegetable', has been suggested as source.]
Alexandrian *al-ig-zän'dri-ən, adj.* relating to *Alexandria* in Egypt, its school of philosophy, its poetry, or the general character of its culture and taste, erudite and critical rather than original in inspiration sometimes with a suggestion of decadence: relating to *Alexander* the Great or other of the name. — Also *n.* — *n.* and *adj.* **Alexan'drine** Alexandrian. — *n.* **alexan'drine** a verse of six iambs (as in English), or in French of 12 and 13 syllables in alternate couplets (perhaps from a poem on *Alexander* the Great by *Alexandre* Paris). — Also *adj.* — *n.* **alexan'drite** a dark green chrysoberyl discovered on the day of majority of the Cesarevich later *Alexander* II.
alexia *a-lek'si-ə, n.* loss of power to read: word-blindness. — *adj.* **alex'ic.** [Gr. *a-,* priv., *legein,* to speak, confused with L. *legĕre,* to read.]
alexin *a-lek'sin, n.* a body present in the blood serum, which uniting with an anti-serum gives protection against disease. — *adj.* **alexipharmic** (*-si-fär'mik*) acting against poison. — *ns.* **alexiphar'mic, alexiphar'-makon** an antidote to poison. [Gr. *alexein,* to ward off, *alexipharmakos* — *pharmakon,* poison.]
aleye. See **allay[1].**
alfa. See **halfa.**
alfalfa *al-fal'fə, n.* a variety of, or (esp. *U.S.*) another name for, lucerne. [Sp. *alfalfa* — Ar. *alfaçfaçah.*]
alfaquí *al-fa-kē', (Sp.) n.* a Muslim expounder of the law.
alférez *al-fā'rāth, (Sp.) n.* a standard-bearer.
alforja *al-för'hha, (Sp.) n.* a saddle-bag: a baboon's cheek-pouch.
alfresco *al-fresk'ō, adv.* and *adj.* on fresh or moist plaster: in the fresh or cool air. [It.; see **fresco, fresh.**]
alga *al'gə, n.* a seaweed: any member of the Algae: *pl.* **algae** (*al'jē* or *-gē*). — *n.pl.* **Algae** (*bot.*) a great group of Thallophytes, the seaweeds and allied forms. — *adj.* **al'gal** (*-gəl*). — *ns.* **al'gicide** (*-ji-sīd*) a substance used to destroy algae; **al'gin** (*-jin*) sodium alginate, a gummy nitrogenous organic compound got from seaweeds; **al'ginate** a salt of alginic acid. — *adjs.* **algin'ic** (as **alginic acid,** an acid obtained from certain seaweeds, used in plastics, medicine, as a food-thickening agent, etc.); **al'goid** (*-goid*) of the nature of, resembling, an alga; **algolog'ical.** — *ns.* **algol'ogist; algol'ogy** phycology. [L. *alga,* seaweed.]
algarroba *al-ga-rō'bə, n.* the carob: the mesquite: the fruit of either. — Also **algarō'ba, algarrō'bŏ** (*pl. -os*). [Sp. *algarroba, -o.* — Ar. *al kharrūbah;* cf. **carob.**]
algate, -s *öl'gāt(s), advs.* always, at all events, nevertheless

(*obs.*): altogether (*Spens.*). [**all** and **gate**[2]; orig. *dat.,* with *-s* on analogy of *always,* etc.]
algebra *al'ji-brə, n.* a method of calculating by symbols by means of letters employed to represent quantities, and signs to represent their relations, thus forming a kind of generalised arithmetic: in modern mathematics, any of a number of systems using symbols and involving reasoning about relationships and operations. — *adjs.* **algebraic** (*-brā'ik*), **-al.** — *adv.* **algebraically.** — *n.* **algebrā'ist** one skilled in algebra. [It. and Sp., — Ar. *al-jebr,* resetting (of anything broken): hence combination — *jabara,* to reunite.]
Algerian *al-jē'ri-ən, adj.* of Algeria or Algiers. — *n.* a native of Algeria. — *n.* **Algerine** (*al'jə-rēn*) an Algerian: (without *cap.*) a pirate (*hist.*).
algesia *al-jē'zi-ə,* or *-si-, n.* sensitiveness to pain. — *n.* **algē'sis** sensation of pain. [Mod. I. — Gr. *algēsis* — *ulgein,* to suffer.]
-algia *al'ji-ə,* in composition, denoting pain (in a particular part or because of a particular thing). [Gr. *algos,* pain.]
algicide. See **alga.**
algid *al'jid, adj.* cold, chill esp. applied to a cold fit in disease. — *n.* **algid'ity.** [L. *algidus,* cold.]
alginate, algology, etc. See **alga.**
Algol[1] *al'gol, n.* a variable star in the constellation Perseus. [Ar. *al ghūl,* the ghoul.]
Algol[2] *al'gol, n.* a type of computer language. [Algo(rithmic) l(anguage).]
algolagnia *al-gō-lag'ni-ə, n.* sexual pleasure got from the inflicting or suffering pain. [Gr. *algos,* pain, *lagneiā,* lust.]
Algonkian *al-gong'ki-ən,* **Algonquian** also *-kwi-, n.* a family of North American Indian languages, including Natick, Shawnee, Ojibwa, Cheyenne, etc., spoken over a wide area: a member of a tribe speaking one of these languages. — Also *adj.* [Amer. Eng. — **Algonquin.**]
Algonquin *al-gong'kwin,* **Algonkin** *-kin, n.* a leading group of Indian tribes in the valley of the Ottawa and around the northern tributaries of the St Lawrence: a member of this group: their language. — Also *adj.* [Micmac Indian *algoomaking,* at the place of spearing fish.]
algophobia *al-gō-fō'bi-ə, n.* obsessive fear of pain. [Gr. *algos,* pain, and **phobia.**]
algorism *al'gə-rizm, n.* the Arabic system of numeration: arithmetic. — Also **al'gorithm** (*-ridhm*). [L.L. *algorismus* — Ar. *al-Khwārazmi,* the native of Khwārazm (Khiva), i.e. the 9th-cent. mathematician Abu Ja'far Mohammed ben Musa.]
algorithm *al'gə-ridhm, n.* a rule for solving a mathematical problem in a finite number of steps: a set of prescribed computational procedures for solving a problem or achieving a result (*comput.*): a step-by-step method for solving a problem. — *adj.* **algorith'mic.** — **algorithmic language** see **Algol**[2]. [**algorism.**]
alguazil *al-gwa-zil',* **alguacil** *äl-gwä-thēl', n.* in Spain, an officer who makes arrests, etc. [Sp. (now) *alguacil* — Ar. *al-wazīr.* See **vizier.**]
algum *al'gəm, (B.) n.* a wood imported into ancient Palestine, prob. red sandalwood. — Also **al'mug.** [Heb. *algūm.*]
Alhagi *al-hā'jī, -hä'jē, n.* a papilionaceous manna-yielding genus of desert shrubs. [Ar. *al-hāj.*]
Alhambra *al-ham'brə, n.* the palace of the Moorish kings of Granada in Spain. — *adj.* **Alhambresque** (*-bresk'*). [Ar. *al-hamrā',* the red (house).]
alias *ā'li-əs,* (L. *ä'li-äs*) *adv.* otherwise. — *n.* an assumed name: — *pl.* **a'liases.** [L. *aliās,* at another time, otherwise — *alius,* other.]
alibi *al'i-bī,* (L. *äl'-i-bē*) *n.* the plea in a criminal charge of having been elsewhere at the material time: the fact of being elsewhere: an excuse for failure (*coll.*). [L. *alibī,* elsewhere, orig. locative — *alius,* other.]
alicant *al-i-kant', n.* wine made near *Alicante,* in Spain.
Alice *al'is, n.* the main character in the children's fantasies *Alice's Adventures in Wonderland* (1865) and *Through the Looking-glass* (1872) by Lewis Carroll. — **Alice**

band a wide hair-band of coloured ribbon (as worn by Alice in Tenniel's illustrations to *Through the Looking-glass*). — *adj.* **Al'ice-in-Won'derland** as if happening in a dream or fantasy: unreal.

alicyclic *al-i-sīk'lik, adj.* having properties of aliphatic organic compounds but containing a ring of carbon atoms instead of an open chain. [**aliphatic, cyclic.**]

alidad *al'i-dad*, or *-dad'*, **alidade** *-dād, ns.* a revolving index for reading the graduations of an astrolabe, quadrant, or similar instrument, or for taking the direction of objects. [Ar. *al 'idādah*, the revolving radius — *'adid*, humerus.]

alien *ā'li-ən, -lyən, adj.* belonging to something else: foreign: from elsewhere: extraneous: repugnant: inconsistent (with *to*): incompatible: estranged. — *n.* a foreigner: a resident neither native-born nor naturalised: an outsider: a plant introduced by man but maintaining itself. — *v.t.* to alienate: to transfer: to estrange. — *n.* **alienabil'ity.** — *adj.* **a'lienable** capable of being transferred to another. — *n.* **a'lienage** state of being an alien. — *v.t.* **a'lienate** to transfer: to estrange. — *adj.* withdrawn: estranged. — *ns.* **alienā'tion** estrangement: insanity: the state of not being involved: the critical detachment with which, according to Bertolt Brecht, audience and actors should regard a play, considering action and dialogue and the ideas in the drama without emotional involvement; **a'lienātor.** — *adj.* **al'iened** made alien: estranged. — *ns.* **alienee'** one to whom property is transferred; **al'ienism** the position of being a foreigner: study and treatment of mental diseases; **a'lienist** one who specially studies or treats mental diseases; **a'lienor** (*law*) one who transfers property. — **alienation effect, A-effect** the effect sought or produced in accordance with Brecht's theory. [L. *aliēnus* — *alius*, other.]

aliform *ā'li-förm, al', adj.* wing-shaped. [L. *āla*, wing, *forma*, shape.]

aligarta. See **alligator.**

alight[1] *ə-līt', v.i.* to dismount, descend: to perch, settle: to land: to come to rest: to come by chance (upon something): to fall, strike: — *pa.t.* and *pa.p.* **alight'ed** (or **alit'**). [O.E. *ālīhtan.* See **light**[2].]

alight[2] *ə-līt, adj.* on fire: lighted up. [**a**[3] and **light**[1].]

align *ə-līn', v.t.* to regulate by a line: to arrange in line. — Rarely **aline'.** — *n.* **align'ment** a laying out by a line: setting in a line or lines: the ground-plan of a railway or road: a row, as of standing-stones; taking of side, or side taken, politically, etc. — Rarely **aline'ment.** — **alignment chart** a nomogram, esp. one comprising three scales in which a line joining values on two determines a value on the third. [Fr. *aligner* — L. *ad*, to, *līneāre*, to line.]

alike *ə-līk', adj.* the same in appearance or character. — *adv.* equally. [O.E. *gelīc*, combined with O.N. *ālīkr*, O.E. *onlīc*; see **like**[1].]

aliment *al'i-mənt, n.* nourishment: food: provision for maintenance, alimony. — *v.t.* to support, sustain: to provide aliment for. — *adjs.* **alimental** (*-ment'l*) supplying food; **aliment'ary** pertaining to aliment: nutritive. — *n.* **alimentā'tion.** — *adj.* **aliment'ative.** — *n.* **aliment'iveness** a phrenologist's word for the instinct to seek food or drink. — **alimentary canal** the passage from mouth to anus. [L. *alimentum* — *alĕre*, to nourish.]

alimony *al'i-mən-i, n.* an allowance for support made by one spouse to the other pending or after their divorce or legal separation. [L. *alimōnia* — *alĕre*, to nourish.]

à l'improviste *a lē-prō-vēst*, (Fr.) on a sudden: unexpectedly: unawares.

aline, alinement. See **align.**

alineation. See **allineation.**

aliped *al'i-ped, adj.* (*zool.*) having winged feet, used e.g. of the bat, whose toes are connected by a wing-like membrane. — *n.* an animal with winged feet. [L. *ālipes, -pedis* — *āla*, wing, *pēs, pedis*, foot.]

aliphatic *al-i-fat'ik*, (*chem.*) *adj.* fatty: belonging to the open-chain class of organic compounds, or methane

derivatives (opp. to *aromatic*). [Gr. *aleiphar, aleiphatos*, oil.]

aliquant *al'i-kwənt, adj.* such as will not divide a number without a remainder, thus 5 is an aliquant part of 12. [L. *aliquantum*, somewhat.]

aliquot *al'i-kwot, adj.* such as will divide a number without a remainder. [L. *aliquot*, some, several.]

Alisma *a-liz'mə, n.* the water-plantain genus of monocotyledons, giving name to the family **Alismā'ceae:** (without *cap.*) a plant of this genus. — *adj.* **alismā'ceous.** [Gr. *alisma*, water-plantain.]

alit. See **alight**[1].

aliunde *ā-li-un'de,* (*law*) *adv.* from another source. — Also *adj.* [L., from elsewhere.]

alive *ə-līv', adj.* in life: in vigour: in being: lively: of a wire, etc., live: sensitive, cognisant (with *to*). — **alive and kicking** strong and active: full of vigour; **alive with** swarming with; **look alive** be brisk: hurry up. [O.E. *on līfe* (dat. of *līf*, life), in life.]

alizare *al-i-zä'rē, n.* levantine madder. — *n.* **alizarin(e)** (*a-liz'ə-rin, -rēn*) the colouring matter of madder root (C₁₄H₈O₄), now made synthetically. [Sp. and Fr., prob. — Ar. *al*, the, *'açārah*, juice pressed out.]

alkahest, alcahest *al'kə-hest, n.* the universal solvent of the alchemists. [App. a sham Ar. coinage of Paracelsus.]

alkali *al'kə-li*, or *-lī*, (*chem.*) *n.* a substance which in aqueous solution has more hydroxyl ions than hydrogen ions, and has strong basic properties: — *pl.* **al'kali(e)s.** — *adj.* of, pertaining to, containing, forming, an alkali. — *ns.* **alkalesc'ence, alkalesc'ency.** — *adj.* **alkalesc'ent** tending to become alkaline: slightly alkaline. — *v.t.* and *v.i.* **al'kalify.** — *ns.* **alkalim'eter** an instrument for measuring the concentration of alkalies; **alkalim'etry.** — *adj.* **al'kaline** (*-līn, -lin*) having the properties of an alkali: containing much alkali. — *n.* **alkalinity** (*-lin'*) quality of being alkaline: extent to which a solution is alkaline. — *v.t.* **al'kalise, -ize** to render alkaline. — *n.* **al'kaloid** any of various nitrogenous organic bases found in plants, having specific physiological action. — *adj.* pertaining to, resembling, alkali. — *ns.* **alkalosis** (*al-kə-lō'sis*) an illness in which the blood or tissues of the body become too alkaline; **al'kyl** (*-kil*) general name for monovalent hydrocarbon radicals of formula C$_n$H$_{2n+1}$, often denoted R: a compound with one or more such radicals in it, as *lead alkyl.* — **alkali metals** the univalent metals of first group of periodic system, lithium, sodium, potassium, rubidium, caesium, francium, forming strong basic hydroxides; **alkaline earth** an oxide of any of the alkaline earth metals: an alkaline earth metal; **alkaline earth metals** the bivalent metals of the second group, calcium, strontium, barium, and sometimes magnesium and radium. [Ar. *alqalīy*, the calcined ashes.]

alkane *al'kān, n.* the general name of a hydrocarbon of the methane series, of general formula C$_n$H$_{2n+2}$. [*alk*yd + meth*ane*.]

alkanet *al'kə-net, n.* a Mediterranean boraginaceous plant (genus *Alkanna*): a red dye got from its root: extended to various kindred plants (*Anchusa*, etc.). [Sp. *alcaneta*, dim. — Ar. *al-hennā*, the henna.]

alkene *al'kēn, n.* the general name for an unsaturated hydrocarbon of the ethylene series, of general formula C$_n$H$_{2n}$. [*alk*yl + eth*ene*.]

Alkoran *n.* Same as **Alcoran.**

alkyd *al'kid, n.* any of a group of synthetic resins used in paints and protective coatings and in adhesives. — Also **alkyd resin** (*rez'in*). [*alk*yl and acid.]

alkyl. See **alkali.**

alkyne *al'kīn, n.* the general name for a hydrocarbon of the acetylene series, of general formula C$_n$H$_{2n-2}$. [*alk*yd and eth*yne*.]

all *öl, adj.* comprising every individual one (e.g. *all men, all roads, all instances*): comprising the whole extent, etc., of (e.g. *all winter*): any whatever: (preceding 'the') as many as there are, or as much as there is (e.g. *all the men, all the cheese*): also used following *pl. pers.*

pron., or sometimes pl. n. (e.g. *we all laughed, the guests all came*): the greatest possible (e.g. *with all haste, in all sincerity*): every. — *n.* the whole: everybody: everything: the totality of things the universe: one's whole possessions (formerly often in *pl.*). — *adv.* wholly: entirely: quite: without limit, infinitely: on all sides: on each side, apiece: even, just (passing into a mere intensive, as in *all on a summer's day*, or almost into a conjunction by omission of *if* or *though*). — In composition, infinite, infinitely: universal: completely: wholly: by all: having all for object. — *n.* **all′ness** the condition of being all. — Possible compounds are without limit and only a selection can be given. — *adj.* **all′-Amer′ican** representative of the whole of America, esp. in some admirable quality: typically American (in behaviour, appearance, etc.): chosen to represent the United States: consisting entirely of U.S. or American members. — **All Blacks** the New Zealand international rugby team. — *adj.* **all′-building** (*Shak.*) possibly, on which all is built, but prob. a misprint. — **all-chang′ing-word** a spell that transforms everything. — *adj.* **all-cheer′ing** giving cheerfulness to all. — **all′-clear′** a signal that the reason for sheltering, or (*fig.*) for inactivity, is past. — *adjs.* **all′-day** lasting all day; **all-dread′ed** dreaded by all; **all′-elec′tric** using only electricity for heating and lighting; **all-end′ing.** — **All′-father** Woden: Zeus: God. — *adj.* **all′-fired** (*coll.* orig. *U.S.*) infernal (perh. for hell-fired). — *adv.* **all′-firedly.** — **all-fives′** a game of dominoes in which it is sought to make the end pips sum a multiple of five; **all-fours′** a card game in which there are four chances that score a point (see also **four**); **all-giv′er** (*Milt.*) the giver of all — God; **all′-good** the plant good-King-Henry. — *adj.* **all-good′** infinitely good. — *interj.* **all-hail** a greeting, *lit.* all health. — *n.* a salutation of 'All hail'. — *v.t.* to greet with 'All hail'. — *adj.* (orig. gen. pl. of n.; *obs.*) **all′hall′own, -hall′owen, -hollo′wn, -hall′ond** (*Shak.*). **al-hallown summer** a spell of fine weather about All Hallows). — **All-hall′owmass** the feast of All Saints; **All-Hall′ows** All Saints' Day; **All-hall′owtide** the season of All-Hallows; **all′heal** a panacea (*obs.*): the great valerian or other plant thought to have healing properties, e.g. self-heal; **all-hid′** hide-and-seek. — *adjs.* **all′-import′ant** essential: crucial; **all′-in′** including everything: of a school, etc., comprehensive; **all′night** lasting, open, etc. all night; **all-obey′ing** (*Shak.*) obeyed by all; **all′-or-noth′ing** that must be gained, accepted, etc. completely or not at all; **all′-out** using maximum effort: of a strike, with everyone participating; **all′-ov′er** over the entire surface, body, etc.; **all-ō′verish** having an indefinite sense of indisposition, discomfort, or malaise. — *n.* **all-ō′verishness.** — *adjs.* **all′-play-all′** of a competition, in which every competitor plays against every other in turn; **all-pow′erful** supremely powerful: omnipotent; **all′-pur′pose** that can be used for any purpose, in any circumstances, etc.; **all′-red′** (*obs.*) exclusively on British territory (from the conventional colouring of maps); **all′-risks′** (of insurance) covering all risks except a number specifically excluded (as e.g. war risks, damage due to depreciation, etc.); **all′-round′** including, applying to, all: adequate, complete, or competent on all sides. — **all′-round′er** one who shows ability in many sports or many aspects of a particular sport, esp. cricket: one who shows an ability in or who has an involvement in many kinds of work, etc. (also *adj.*); **all′-round′ness.** — *adj.* **all-rul′ing.** — **all′seed** a weed (genus *Radiola*) of the flax family, or other many-seeded plant. — *adj.* **all-see′ing.** — **all-sē′er** (*Shak.*) one who sees all — God; **all′spice** pimento or Jamaica pepper, supposed to combine the flavours of cinnamon, nutmeg, and cloves (see also **Calycanthus**). — *adjs.* **all′-star′** having a cast or team all of whom are stars; **all-tell′ing** (*Shak.*). — *adv.* **all′-thing** (*Shak.*) every way. — *adj.* **all′-time** of all time to date. — *n.*, *adj.* **all′-up** (of loaded aircraft) total (weight). — **all′-work** all kinds of work (esp. domestic). — **after all** when

everything has been considered: in spite of all that: nevertheless; **all along** everywhere along: all the time; **all and some** (*obs.*) one and all; **all at once** suddenly; **all but** everything short of, almost; **All Fools' Day** the day of making April fools, 1st April; **all for** (*coll.*) in favour of; **all found** (usu. of a price) all in, with everything included; **All Hallows' Day** All Saints' Day; **all in** exhausted; everything included; **all in all** all things in all respects, all or everything together: that which one is wholly wrapped up in; **all-in wrestling** wrestling with almost no holds barred as against the rules; **all of** (*coll.*) as long, far, etc. as: the whole distance, time, etc. of; **all out** at full power or speed: completely exhausted; **all over** everywhere: over the whole of: covered with (*coll.*): thoroughly, entirely: very characteristically; **all over with** finished, done with, completely at an end with; **all right** a coll. phrase expressing assent or approbation; **all-round camera** a camera able to make a strip picture of the whole periphery of an object revolved before it; **All Saints' Day** 1st November, a festival in honour of the saints collectively; **all's one** it is just the same; **All Souls' Day** 2nd November, a R.C. day of prayer for souls in Purgatory; **all systems go** everything (is) in working order, starting up, etc. (also *fig.*); **all that** (usu. after a negative or a question) so, that, as... as all that; **all the best** phrase used to wish someone good luck, etc.; **all there** completely sane: alert; **all the same** see **same**; **all-time high, low** a high, low, level never before reached; **all-time record** a record exceeding all others in all times; **all told** including every person, thing, etc.: taking everything into account; **all to one** (*obs.*) altogether; **all up with** at an end with: beyond any hope for; **all-wing aeroplane** an aeroplane with no fuselage, the cabin being in the wings; **and all** as well as the rest; **and all that** and all the rest of it, *et cetera*; **as all that** to that extent; **at all** in the least degree: in any way: in any circumstances: used also merely to give emphasis; **be all over someone** to irk someone, or treat someone, with too much show of friendliness; **for all** notwithstanding; **for good and all** finally; **in all** all told: in total; **once (and) for all** once and once only, finally; **when all is said and done** after all: all things considered. [O.E. (Anglian) *all*, (W.S. *eall*); Ger. *all*.]

alla breve *a′lə, äl′lä brā′vä*, (*mus.*) in quick common time. [It., according to the breve, there being orig. a breve to the bar.]

alla cappella *a′lə ka-pel′ə, äl′lä käp-pel′lä.* See **a cappella**.

alla Franca *a′lə frang′kə, äl′lä frängk′ä*, (It.) in the French style.

Allah *al′ä, n.* among Muslims, God. [Ar. *allāh — alilāh*, the God.]

alla marcia *a′lə mär′chə, äl′lä mär′chä*, (*mus.*) in the manner of a march. [It.]

allantois *a-lan′tō-is, n.* a membranous sac-like appendage for effecting oxygenation in the embryos of mammals, birds, and reptiles. — *adjs.* **allanto′ic; allan′toid** (*-toid*) sausage-shaped: pertaining to the allantois. — *n.* the allantois. [Irregularly formed from Gr. *allās, -āntos*, a sausage, *eidos*, form.]

alla prima *a′lə prē′mə, äl′lä prē′mä*, (It.) a technique of painting in which only one layer of pigment is applied to the surface to complete the canvas.

alla stoccata *a′lə sto-kat′ə, äl′lä sto-kä′tä*, (It.) thrusting with a pointed weapon.

alla Tedesca *a′lə te-des′kə, äl′lä te-des′kä*, (It.) in the German style.

allative *al′ə-tiv*, (*gram.*) *adj.* describing a case denoting movement to or towards. — *n.* (a word in) the allative case. [L. *allatum*, supine of *afferre — ad*, to, *ferre*, to bear.]

alla vostra salute *äl′lä vōs′trä sa-lōō′tä*, (It.) to your health.

allay[1], earlier **aleye, alay**, etc., *ə-lā′, v.t.* to put down: to quell: to calm: to alleviate: to abate: to reduce: to alloy. — *v.i.* to abate. — *ns.* **allay′er; allay′ing; allay′ment.** [O.E. *ālecgan* — pfx. *ā-*, intens., *lecgan*, to lay. This vb. in M.E. became indistinguishable in form in some of its parts from allay² or alloy, and from allege¹, and the meanings also overlapped.]

allay² *ə-lā'*, *v.t.* to alloy: to mix with something inferior: to dilute: to debase: to abate or detract from the goodness of. — *n.* alloy: alloying: dilution: abatement: impairment. [See alloy and the etymological note to allay¹.]

all-be. See albe.

alledge. Old spelling of allege¹,².

allée *a-lā*, (Fr.) *n.* an avenue, a walk or garden path.

allege¹ (Spens. allegge, alegge) *ə-lej'*, *v.t.* to alleviate: to allay. — *n.* allege'ance (*ə-lej'əns*; Spens. aleggeaunce *alej'i-ans*) alleviation. [O.Fr. aleger — L. alleviāre (see alleviate) fused with O.E. ālecgan (see allay¹).]

allege² *ə-lej'*, *v.t.* to declare in court upon oath (obs.): to assert with a view to subsequent proof, hence without proof: to bring forward in argument or plea: to adduce: to cite (arch.). — *n.* allegation (al-i-gā'shən) the act of alleging: that which is alleged: an unproved or unaccepted assertion: citation. — adj. alleged (ə-lejd'). adv. allegedly (-lej'əd-li). — *n.* alleg'er. [O.Fr. esligier, to clear at law — L. ex, from, lītigāre, to sue.]

allegiance *ə-lē'jəns*, *n.* the relation or obligation of liegeman to liege-lord or of subject to sovereign or state: loyalty (to a person or cause). — adj. (Shak.) alle'giant. [L. ad, to, and liege.]

allegory *al'i-gər-i*, *n.* a narrative to be understood symbolically: symbolical narration. — adjs. allegoric (-gor'ik), -al. — adv. allegor'ically. — *v.t.* all'egorise, -ize to put in form of an allegory: to treat as allegory. — *v.t.* to use allegory. — *ns.* allegorīsā'tion, -z-; all'egoriser, -z-; all'egorist. [Gr. allēgoriā — allos, other, agoreuein, to speak.]

allegro *a-lā'grō* (It. äl-lā'grō), (mus.) adv., adj. with brisk movement. — *n.* an allegro piece or movement: — pl. alle'gros. — adv. and adj. allegret'to somewhat brisk. — Also *n.* (pl. allegret'tos). [It., — L. alacer, brisk.]

allele, allel *al-ēl'*, *n.* shortened forms of allelomorph (al-ēl'ō-mörf) any one of the two or more possible forms of a gene: a gene considered as the means of transmission of an allele. — adj. allelomor'phic. — *n.* allelomor'phism. [Gr. allēlōn, of one another, morphē, form.]

alleluia, alleluiah *al-i-lōō'yä.* Same as hallelujah.

allemande *al'(i-)mand, al-măd*, *n.* a smooth-running suite movement of moderate tempo, in common time, coming after the prelude (of German origin): a Swabian dance in triple time: a German dance in 2–4 time: a movement affecting change of order in a dance. [Fr. allemande (fem.), German.]

allenarly *al-en'ər-li* (obs. except in Scots law) adv. solely, only. [all, anerly.]

allergy *al'ər-ji*, *n.* an altered or acquired state of sensitivity: abnormal reaction of the body to substances normally harmless: hypersensitivity to certain antigens or other exciting substances: (coll.) antipathy. — *n.* all'ergen any substance that induces an allergic reaction. — adjs. allergen'ic causing an allergic reaction; allergic (ə-lûr'jik) (of the body) reacting in an abnormally sensitive manner: suffering from an allergy (to). — *n.* an allergic person. [Gr. allos, other, ergon, work.]

allerion. See alerion.

alleviate *ə-lēv'i-āt*, *v.t.* to make light: to mitigate. — *ns.* allēviā'tion; allēv'iātor. — adjs. allēv'iative; allēviā'tory. [L.L. alleviāre, -ātum — L. ad, to, levis, light.]

alley¹ *al'i*, *n.* a walk in a garden or shrubbery: a passage: a narrow lane: a back lane: a long narrow enclosure, or rink, for bowls or skittles: — pl. all'eys. — adj. alleyed (al'id) having alleys or the form of an alley. — all'eyway a narrow passage: a corridor. [O.Fr. alee (Fr. allée), a passage, from aller, to go.]

alley², ally *al'i*, *n.* a choice taw or large marble. — *n.* all'(e)-taw', -tor'. [Prob. originally made of alabaster.]

allez-vous-en *a-lā-vōō-zä*, (Fr.) away with you: begone.

allheal. See all.

alliaceous *al-i-ā'shəs, adj.* garlic-like. [L. allium, garlic.]

alliance. See ally.

allice, allis *al'is*, *n.* a species of shad. — Also allis shad. [L. alōsa, alausa, shad.]

allicholy, allycholly *al'i-kol-i*, (Shak.) *n.* and adj. jocularly, for melancholy.

alligarta. See alligator.

alligate *al'i-gāt*, *v.t.* to conjoin: to perform alligation. — *n.* alligation (-gā'shən) binding together: conjunction: calculation of values or properties of a mixture (arith.). [L. alligāre, -ātum — ad, to, and ligāre, to bind.]

alligator *al'i-gā-tər*, earlier al(l)igarta *-gär'tə, ns.* a reptile of a mainly American family differing from crocodiles in the broader snout and other characteristics. — alligator apple a fruit and tree of the custard-apple genus; alligator pear see avocado. [Sp. el, (the (L. ille), lagarto, lizard (L. lacertus).]

allineation, alineation *a-lin-i-ā'shən*, *n.* position in a straight line: alignment. [L. ad, to, līneāre, -ātum, to draw a line — līnea, line.]

allis. See allice.

alliteration *ə-* or *a-lit-ər-ā'shən*, *n.* the recurrence of the same initial sound (not necessarily letter) in words in close succession, as 'Sing a Song of Sixpence': headrhyme — the characteristic structure of versification of O.E. and other old Gmc. languages, each line having three accented syllables (two in the first half) with the same initial consonant, or with different initial vowels. — *v.i.* allit'erate to begin with the same sound: to constitute alliteration: to practise alliteration. — adj. allit'erative. [L. ad, to, and lītera, littera, a letter.]

Allium *al'i-əm*, *n.* the plant genus to which onions, leeks, garlic, etc. belong. [L., garlic.]

allo- *a'lō-, a'lə-*, in composition, other: denoting one of a group constituting a structural unit: different: from outside. — *ns.* all'ocarpy (bot.; Gr. karpos, fruit) fruiting after cross-fertilisation; alloch(e)iria (-kī'ri-ə, -ki'; Gr. cheir, hand) attribution of a sensation to the wrong part of the body, e.g. to the other hand when one is painful. — adj. allog'amous. — *ns.* allog'amy (bot.; Gr. gamos, marriage) cross-fertilisation; all'-ograph (Gr. graphē, writing) a writing made by one person on behalf of another. — adj. allomet'ric. — *ns.* allom'etry (Gr. metron, measure) (the study of) the growth of a part of the body relative to that of other parts or of the whole body, in one organism or comparatively in a number of different organisms; all'omorph (-mörf; Gr. morphē, form) one of two or more forms of the same morpheme; all'ophone (-fōn; Gr. phōnē, sound) one of two or more forms of the same phoneme. — adj. allophonic (-fon'). — *n.* all'-oplasm protoplasm differentiated to perform a special function. — adj. alloplas'tic (Gr. plastikos, see plastic) affected by, or affecting, external factors. — *n.* allopurinol (-pūr'in-ol; purin, and -ol — L. oleum, oil) a drug, $C_5H_4N_4O$, used in the the treatment of gout, reducing the formation of uric acid; all'osaur (-sör; Gr. sauros, lizard) a member of the genus Allosaur'us, large, lizard-hipped, carnivorous dinosaurs. — adj. allosteric (-ster' or -stēr'; see steric) pertaining to an enzyme the activity of which may be influenced by a combination with another substance, or to the inhibition or stimulation of activity thus caused. — *ns.* allos'tery; all'otheism (Gr. theos, god) the worship of gods or other people's gods; allotrope (al'ə-trōp; Gr. tropos, turn, habit) an allotropic form. — adj. allotrop'ic. — *n.* allot'ropism. — adj. allot'ropous having nectar accessible to all kinds of insects (bot.): of insects, short-tongued, as visiting allotropous flowers. — *n.* allot'ropy the property (esp. in chemical elements, as carbon) of existing in more than one form. [Gr. allos, other.]

allocarpy. See allo-.

allocate *al'ō-kāt, al'ə-kāt*, *v.t.* to place: to locate: to apportion. — adjs. all'ocable, allocāt'able. — *n.* allocā'-

tion act of allocating: a share allocated: allotment: apportionment: an allowance made upon an account. [L. *allocāre* — *ad*, to, *locāre*, *-ātum*, to place — *locus*, a place.]

alloch(e)iria. See **allo-**.

allocution *al-ō-kū'shǝn, n.* an exhortation, esp. (*Roman hist.*) of a general to his troops: a formal address, esp. of the Pope to the cardinals. [L. *allocūtiō, -ōnis* — *ad*, to, and *loquī, locūtus*, to speak.]

al(l)odium *a-lō'di-ǝm, n.* an estate not subject to a feudal superior. — Also **a(l)lod** (*al'od*). — *adj.* **al(l)ō'dial** (opp. to *feudal*). [L.L. *allōdium*, from a Gmc. word meaning complete ownership; cf. **all** and O.E. *ēad*, wealth, prosperity.]

allogamous, allogamy, allograph. See **allo-**.

alloiostrophos *a-loi-os'tro-fos,* (Gr.) *adj.* irregularly divided, not in alternate strophe and antistrophe.

allometric, allometry, allomorph. See **allo-**.

allonge *ul-ʒzh, n.* a piece of paper attached to a bill of exchange for further endorsement. [Fr.]

allons *a-lɔ̃,* (Fr.) *interj.* let us go: come on: come.

allonym *al'ō-nim, n.* another person's name adopted as a pseudonym by a writer. [Fr. — Gr. *allos*, other, *onyma = onoma*, name.]

allopathy *al-op'ǝ-thi, n.* orthodox medical practice, treatment of diseases by drugs, etc., whose effect on the body is the opposite of that of the disease, distinguished from *homoeopathy*. — *n.* **all'ōpath**. — *adj.* **allopathic** (*al-ō-path'ik*). — *n.* **allōp'athist** [Ger. *Allopathie*, coined by Hahnemann (1755–1843) — Gr. *allos*, other, *pathos*, suffering.]

allophone...to...allostery. See **allo-**.

allot *ǝ-lot', v.t.* to divide as by lot: to distribute in portions: to parcel out: to assign: — *pr.p.* **allott'ing**; *pa.t.* and *pa.p.* **allott'ed**. — *ns.* **allot'ment** the act of allotting: a part or share allotted: a portion of a field assigned to a cottager to labour for himself: a piece of ground let out for spare-time cultivation under a public scheme; **allottee'** one to whom something is allotted; **allott'ery** (*Shak.*) a share allotted. [O.Fr. *aloter* — *à*, to, and the Gmc. root of **lot**.]

allotheism. See **allo-**.

allotriomorphic *a-lot-ri-ō-mör'fik, adj.* crystalline in internal structure but not in outward form. [Gr. *allotrios*, alien, *morphē*, form.]

allotrope, allotropy, etc. See **allo-**.

allow *ǝ-low', v.t.* to praise (*obs.*): to pass, sanction, accept (*arch.*): to concede: to conclude, hence to assert (*U.S.*): to permit: to indulge (*Shak.*): to accord as due: to assign: to grant or give, esp. periodically: to abate: to assume as an element in calculation or as something to be taken into account. — *v.i.* to admit of: to make allowance for. — *adj.* **allow'able** that may be allowed: permissible: excusable. — *n.* **allow'ableness.** — *adv.* **allow'ably.** — *n.* **allow'ance** that which is allowed: approbation (*arch.*): admission, acknowledgment, permission (*Shak.*): a limited portion or amount allowed, allotted, granted: a ration or stint: money allowed to meet expenses or in consideration of special conditions: abatement: a sum periodically granted: a taking into account in calculation or excuse, as, e.g., in *make allowances for.* — *v.t.* to put upon an allowance: to supply in limited quantities. — *adj.* **allowed'** permitted: licensed: acknowledged. — *adv.* **allow'edly.** [O.Fr. *alouer*, to praise, bestow, of double origin: (1) L. *allaudāre* — *ad*, to, *laudāre*, to praise; (2) L. *ad, locāre*, to place.]

alloy *al'oi, ǝ-loi', n.* a mixture of metals: extended to a mixture of metal with non-metal: the baser ingredient in such a mixture (esp. in gold or silver): any admixture that impairs or debases: fineness, standard, of gold or silver. — *v.t.* to mix (metal): to mix with a less valuable metal: to impair or debase by being present: to temper, qualify. — *v.i.* to become alloyed. [Fr. *aloi* (n.), *aloyer* (vb.) — O.Fr. *alei, aleier* — L. *alligāre* — *ad*, to, *ligāre*, to bind; **allay²** is from the corresponding Norm. Fr. *alai*, confused with **allay¹**.]

allseed, allspice. See under **all**.

all-to, alto, also **all to,** *öl'tōō,* a spurious *adv.* and *pfx.* arising from the wrong division of **all** and a word with the pfx. *to-*, asunder, as **allto brake, all to brake** for **all tobrake:** hence, altogether, as **altoruffled** (*Milt.* **all to ruffl'd**).

allude *ǝ-lōōd', -lūd', v.i.* (with *to*) to convey an indirect reference in passing: to refer without explicit mention, or with suggestion of further associations: to refer. — *n.* **allu'sion** (*-zhǝn*) indirect reference. — *adj.* **allu'sive** (*-siv*) alluding: hinting: referring indirectly: canting (*her.*). — *adv.* **allu'sively.** — *n.* **allu'siveness.** [L. *allūdere* — *ad*, at, *lūdere, lūsum*, to play.]

allure¹ *ǝ-lūr', -lōōr', v.t.* to draw on as by a lure (*old*): to entice. — *ns.* **allure', allure'ment, allur'er.** — *adj.* **allur'ing.** — *adv.* **allur'ingly.** [O.Fr. *alurer* — *à*, to, *lurer*, to lure.]

allure² *a-lür,* (Fr.) *n.* mien, gait, air.

allusion, etc. See **allude**.

alluvion *ǝ-lōō'vi-ǝn, -lū', n.* land gradually gained from a river or the sea by the washing up of sand and earth: the formation of such land: a flood: alluvium. [L. *alluviō, -ōnis*; see **alluvium**.]

alluvium *ǝ-lōō'vi-ǝm, -lū', n.* matter transported in suspension and deposited by rivers or floods: — *pl.* **allu'via.** — *adj.* **allu'vial.** [L. neut. of *alluvius*, washed up — *ad*, to, *luěre*, to wash.]

ally¹ *ǝ-lī', v.t.* to join in relation of marriage, friendship, treaty, co-operation, or assimilation: — *pr.p.* **ally'ing**; *pa.t.* and *pa.p.* **allied'.** — *n.* **a'lly** (formerly, and still by some, *ǝ-lī'*) a member of or party to an alliance: a state or sovereign joined in league for co-operation in a common purpose: anything that co-operates or helps: a kinsman (*Shak.*): anything near to another in classification or nature: — *pl.* **a'llies** (or *-liz'*). — *n.* **alli'ance** the state of being allied: union, or combination by marriage, treaty, etc.: kinship: a group of allies or kindred: a subclass or group of families (*bot.*). — *adj.* **a'llied** (or *-līd'*). [O.Fr. *alier* — L. *alligāre*; see **alligate**.]

ally², ally-taw. See **alley²**.

allycholly. See **allicholy**.

allyl *al'il,* (*chem.*) *n.* an organic radical (C_3H_5) whose sulphide is found in oil of garlic. [L. *allium*, garlic, and Gr. *hȳlē*, matter.]

alma¹, almah *al'ma, n.* an Egyptian dancing-girl. — Also **al'me, al'meh** (*-me*). [Ar. *'almah*, learned (in dancing and music) — *'alama*, to know.]

alma² *äl'mä,* (It.) *n.* soul, essence.

almacantar, almucantar *al-mǝ-kan'tǝr, -mū-, ns.* a circle of altitude, parallel to the horizon: an instrument for determining a star's passage across an almacantar. [Ar. *almuqantarāt*, the sundials — *al*, the, *qantarah*, bridge.]

Almagest *al'mǝ-jest, n.* a great treatise by the Alexandrian astronomer Ptolemy (*c.* A.D. 150): extended to other great works. [Ar. *al-majistē* — *al*, the, Gr. *megistē* (*syntaxis*), greatest (systematic treatise).]

Almain *al'mān,* (*obs.*) *n.* and *adj.* German. — *ns.* **al'main** the allemande (suite movement, or leaping dance); **Al'maine, Al'many, Al'emaine** Germany. [Fr. *allemand*, German, *Allemagne*, Germany — L. *Alamanni*, a people of South-west Germany.]

alma mater *al'mǝ mā'tǝr, al'mä mä'ter,* (L.) benign mother applied by alumni to their university.

almanac *öl'mǝ-nak, n.* a register of the days, weeks, and months of the year, with astronomical events, anniversaries, etc. [App. from an Ar. word *al-manākh*.]

almandine *al'man-dīn, -dēn,* earlier **alaban'dine**, *n.* precious (red iron-alumina) garnet. [L.L. *alabandīna* — *Alabanda*, a town in Caria, where it was found.]

alme, almeh. See **alma¹**.

almery. See **ambry**.

almighty *öl-mīt'i, adj.* omnipotent: irresistible: invincible: mighty. — Also *adv.* — **the Almighty** God; **the almighty dollar** (*Washington Irving*) money, esp. as all-powerful. [O.E. *ælmihtig*.]

almirah *al-mīr'ə, n.* a cupboard, wardrobe, cabinet. [Hindi *almārī* — Port. *almario* — L. *armārium*; see **ambry.**]

almond *ä'mənd, n.* the fruit, and esp. the kernel, of a tree akin to the peach, with a dry husk instead of flesh: anything of the shape of an almond (an ellipse pointed at one end), as a tonsil, a rock-crystal ornament. — **al'mond-bloss'om.** — *adj.* **al'mond-eyed'** with apparently almond-shaped eyes. — **al'mond-oil'; al'mond-tree.** [O.Fr. *almande* (Fr. *amande*) — L. *amygdala* — Gr. *amygdalē.*]

almoner *ä'mən-ər, al'mən-ər, n.* a distributor or (*arch.*) giver of alms: a medical social worker attached to a hospital (no longer official title). — *n.* **al'monry** a place of distribution of alms. [O.Fr. *aumoner, aumonier* (Fr. *aumônier*) — L.L. *eleēmosynārius* (adj.); see **alms.**]

almost *öl'mōst, -məst, adv.* very nearly. [**all, most** (in sense of nearly).]

almous *ä'məs, (obs.* or *dial.) adj.* same as **awmous.**

alms *ämz, n. sing.* and *pl.* relief given out of pity to the poor: a good or charitable deed (*obs.*). — **alms'-deed** a charitable deed; **alms'-dish** a dish for receiving alms; **alms'-drink** leavings of drink (*Shak.*); **alms'-fee** Peter's pence; **alms'-folk** people supported by alms; **alms'-house** a house endowed for the support and lodging of the poor; **alms'-man** a man who lives by alms; **alms'-woman.** [O.E. *ælmysse,* through L.L. from Gr. *eleēmosynē* — *eleos,* compassion; see also **awmous.**]

almucantar. See **almacantar.**

almug *al'mug, (B.) n.* algum. [Heb. *almūg,* prob. for *algūm.*]

alnage *öl'nij, n.* measurement by the ell: inspection of cloth. — *n.* **al'nager** an official inspector of cloth. [O.Fr. *aulnage — aulne,* ell.]

Alnus. See **alder.**

alodium, alod, alodial. Same as **allodium, allod, allodial.**

Aloe *al'ō-ē, n.* a liliaceous genus, mainly South African, mostly trees and shrubs: (without *cap.; al'ō*) any member of the genus, extended to the so-called **American aloe** (see **Agave**), also (often *pl.*) to aloes-wood or its resin: (without *cap.;* usu. in *pl.* form but treated as *sing.*) a bitter purgative drug, the inspissated juice of the leaves of various species of Aloe. — *adjs.* **aloed** (*al'ōd*) planted, shaded, mixed, flavoured, with aloes; **aloet'ic.** — *n.* a medicine containing a great proportion of aloes. — **al'oes-wood** the heartwood of eaglewood. [Directly and through O.E. *aluwan, alewan* (pl.) — L. *aloē* — Gr. *aloē*; the application to eaglewood comes from the Septuagint translation of Heb. *ahālīm, ahālōth,* agalloch.]

aloft *ə-loft', -löft', adv.* on high: overhead: above: on the top: high up: up the mast: in or to heaven. — *prep.* (*Shak.*) on the top of. [O.N. *ā lopt* (pron. *loft*), of motion; *ā lopti,* of position — *ā,* on, in, to, *lopt* (see **loft**).]

alogia *ə-lōj'ē-ə, n.* inability to speak, due to brain lesion. [Gr. *a-,* priv., and *logos,* speech.]

alogical *a-loj'i-kl,* or *ā-, adj.* outside the domain of logic. [Gr. *a-,* priv., and **logical.**]

aloha *ä-lō'ə, -lō'hä, n.* love: kindness. — *interj.* greetings: farewell. [Hawaiian.]

alone *ə-lōn', adj.* single: solitary: unaccompanied: without any other: by oneself: unique. — *adv.* singly. — *adv.* **alone'ly** (*obs.* or *arch.*). — *n.* **alone'ness. — go it alone** (*coll.*) to act on one's own, without help. [**all** and **one.**]

along[1] *ə-long', adv.* by or through the length: lengthwise: at full length: throughout: onward: together, in company or conjunction. — *prep.* lengthwise by, through, or over: by the side of. — *adj.* **alongshore'** see **longshore.** — *n.* **alongshore'man.** — *prep.* and *adv.* **along'side** beside: side by side (with): close to the side (of). [O.E. *andlang* — pfx. *and-,* against, and *lang,* long[1].]

along[2] *ə-long', (arch.* and *dial.) adj.* on account (of, on). [O.E. *gelang;* see **long.**]

alongst *ə-longst, (obs.* and *dial.) adv.* and *prep.* along: by the length (of). [O.E. *andlanges — andlang,* along,

with *adv. gen.* ending *-es* and *-t* as in **amidst, betwixt,** etc.]

aloof *ə-lōōf', adv.* to windward (*obs.*): some way off (from): apart: with avoidance or detachment: without participation: with reserve suggesting consciousness of superiority. — *adj.* distant, withdrawn. — *prep.* (*Milt.*) aloof from. — *adv.* **aloof'ly.** — *n.* **aloof'ness.** [a³ and **loof**[1].]

alopecia *al-ō-pē'si-ə, -shə, n.* baldness. — *adj.* **alopecoid** (*al-ō-pē'koid, al-op'i-koid*) fox-like. — **alopecia areata** (*ar-ē-ā'tə, ar-ē-ā'tə*) baldness occurring in patches on the scalp, possibly caused by a nervous disturbance. [Gr. *alōpekiā,* fox-mange, a bald spot, *alōpekoeidēs,* fox-like — *alōpēx,* fox.]

aloud *ə-lowd', adv.* loudly: audibly. [a³ and **loud.**]

à l'outrance *a lōō-träs,* erroneously for **à outrance** (Fr.).

alow *ə-lō', (naut.) adv.* to a lower position: in the lower part of a ship. [a³ and **low**[2].]

alow(e) *ə-low', (Scot.) adv.* ablaze. [a³ and **low**[4].]

alp *alp, n.* a high mountain: a mountain pasture: (*pl.;* with *cap.*) specially applied to the lofty ranges of Switzerland and neighbouring countries. — *adj.* **Alp'ine, alp'ine** (*-īn*) of the Alps or other mountains: growing on mountain tops. — *n.* an alpine plant: a member of the Alpine race. — *ns.* **alp'inism** (*-in-*) the art or practice of mountain-climbing; **alp'inist.** — **alp'enhorn, alp'horn** a long powerful horn, of wood and bark, used chiefly by Alpine cowherds; **alp'enstock** a mountain traveller's long spiked staff. — **Alpine race** one of the principal races of white men, characterised by broad head, sallow skin, moderate stature. [L. *Alpēs,* the Alps; perh. Celtic.]

alpaca *al-pak'ə, n.* a domesticated animal akin to the llama: cloth made of its long silken wool. [Sp., prob. from Quechua.]

alpargata *äl-pär-gä'tä, n.* a light sandal with rope or hemp sole. [Sp.]

al pasto *äl päs'tō,* (It.) according to a fixed rate (said of meals in a restaurant).

alpeen *al'pēn, n.* a cudgel. [Ir. *ailpin.*]

alpenhorn, alpenstock. See **alp.**

alpha *al'fə, n.* the first letter of the Greek alphabet (A, α): the first or brightest star of a constellation: the beginning: in classification, the first or one of the first grade: as an ancient Greek numeral α′ = 1, ͵α = 1000. — *adj.* short for **alphabetical** (*coll.* or *comput.*): in chemical classification, designating one of two or several isomeric forms of a compound. — *n.* **alphafētōprō'tein** a protein whose presence in excessive quantities in amniotic fluid has been found to correlate with certain foetal abnormalities, e.g. those leading to spina bifida. — *adjs.* **alpha(nū)mer'ic, -al** consisting of, or (of a machine) using, both letters and numbers. — *adv.* **alpha(nū)mer'ically.** — *n.* **alphamet'ic** a popular mathematical puzzle in which numbers are replaced by letters forming words. — **al'pha-block'er** a drug used to produce vasodilatation, esp. in muscle; **alpha particle** a helium nucleus given off by radioactive substances; **alpha rays** streams of alpha particles. — *v.t.* **al'phasort** to sort into esp. alphabetical order (*comput.*). — **alpha and omega** beginning and end. [Gr. *alpha* — Heb. *āleph.* See **aleph, A.**]

alphabet *al'fə-bit, -bet, n.* a system of letters, esp. arranged in conventional order: first elements: an index (*obs.*). — *v.t.* (*U.S.*) to arrange alphabetically. — *n.* **alphabetā'rian** one learning his alphabet, a beginner: a student of alphabets. — *adjs.* **alphabet'ic, -al** relating to or in the order of an alphabet. — *adv.* **alphabet'ically.** — *adj.* **alphabet'iform** shaped like letters. — *v.t.* **al'phabetise, -ize** to arrange alphabetically. — **alphabet soup** a confusing or off-putting series or mass of strings of letters, esp. the abbreviations of names of official bodies (*fig.,* after a type of soup with letter-shaped noodles in it). [Gr. *alphabētos — alpha, bēta,* the first two Greek letters.]

Alphonsine *al-fon'sīn, -zin, adj.* of Alphonso X (the Wise), king of Castile, or his planetary tables, completed in 1252.

alpine, etc. See **alp**.

Alpini *äl-pē'nē, n.pl.* Italian troops for mountain warfare: — *sing.* **Alpi'no.** [It., Alpine.]

al più *äl pū*, (It.) at most.

already *öl-red'i, adv.* previously, or by the time in question. [**all, ready**.]

alright *öl-rīt'.* An alternative, less acceptable, spelling of **all right.**

als *äls, öls.* An obs. form of **also, as**[1].

Alsatia *al-sā'sh(y)ə, n.* a district long disputed by Germany and France — Alsace or Elsass: cant name for the sanctuary (till 1697) for debtors and criminals at Whitefriars, London. — *adj.* **Alsa'tian** of Alsatia in either sense: officially chosen to apply to a German sheep-dog of wolf-like breed, often used by police and security officers because of its strength and fierceness (in U.S. **German Shepherd dog, German Police dog**). — Also *n.*

alsike *al'sik, n.* a white or pink-flowered clover. [From *Alsike*, near Uppsala, a habitat.]

also *öl'sō, adv.* likewise: further. — **al'so-ran** a horse that *also ran* in a race but did not get a 'place': a person of like degree of importance. [O.E. *all* (W.S. *eall*) *swā*, all so.]

alsoon(e) *al-sōōn', (Spens.) adv.* as soon. [**as**[1], **soon**.]

Alstroemeria *al-strə-mē'ri-ə, n.* a South American genus of amaryllids with inverted leaves: (without *cap.*) a plant of the genus. [C. *Alströmer*, 18th-cent. Swedish botanist.]

alt[1] *alt, n.* a high tone, in voice or instrument. — **in alt** in the octave above the treble stave beginning with G: in an exalted and high-flown mood. [L. *altus*, high.]

alt[2] *alt, (Milt.) n.* halt, rest. [Fr. *alte* or Sp. *alto* — Ger. *Halt*.]

Altaic *al-tā'ik, n.* a family of languages, forming one branch of Ural-Altaic, and consisting of Turkic, Mongolic and Tungusic. — Also *adj.*

Altair *al-tä'ir, al-tār', n.* a first-magnitude star in the constellation Aquila. [Ar. *al ta'ir*, the bird.]

altaltissimo *alt-al-tis'i-mō, n.* the very highest summit. [Reduplicated compound of It. *alto*, high, and *altissimo*, highest.]

alta moda *äl'tä mo'dä*, (It.) high fashion, the art of designing and making exclusive, fashionable clothes.

altar *ölt'ər, n.* a block or table for making sacrifices on: a table used for mass or the eucharist (by those who regard it as a sacrifice): sometimes, without such implication, the communion table: a scene of worship or marriage ceremony (*fig.*): a ledge on a dry-dock wall. — *n.* **alt'arage** offerings made upon the altar during the offertory, provided for the maintenance of the priest. — *adv.* **alt'arwise** in the position of an altar north and south, at the upper end of the chancel. — **alt'ar-cloth** the covering of the altar, often used as including the frontal and the superfrontal; **al'tarpiece** a work of art placed above and behind an altar; **alt'ar-rails** rails separating the sacrarium from the rest of the chancel; **alt'ar-stone** a stone serving as an altar: a consecrated slab forming, or inserted in, the top of an altar; **al'tar-tomb** a monumental memorial, in form like an altar, often with a canopy. — **family altar** the symbol or place of family worship; **high altar** the principal altar; **lead to the altar** to marry (a woman). [L. *altāre* — *altus*, high.]

altazimuth *alt-az'i-məth, n.* an instrument devised by Airy for determining *al*titude and *azimuth*.

alter[1] *öl'tər, v.t.* to make different: to modify: to castrate. — *v.i.* to become different. — *n.* **alterabil'ity.** — *adjs.* **al'terable; al'terant** altering: having the power of producing changes. — *n.* an alternative. — *n.* **alterä'tion.** — *adj.* **al'terātive** having power to alter. — *n.* a medicine that makes a change in the vital functions. — *p.adj.* **al'tered** (of a rock) changed in mineral composition by natural forces. — *n.* **alterity** (*öl-, al-ter'i-ti*) otherness. [L. *alter*, one of two, the other

of two, from the root of *alius*, other, and the old comp. suff. *-ter*.]

alter[2] *al'tər, adj. (psych.)* other, distinct from oneself — used of people or things seen in contrast with the ego. — **alter ego** (*al'tər eg'ō, ē'gō, al'ter eg'ō*) one's second self (see **second**): a trusted, intimate friend, a confidant: — *pl.* **alter egos.** [L., other.]

altercate *öl'tər-kāt, v.i.* to bandy words, wrangle. — *n.* **altercā'tion.** — *adj.* **al'tercātive.** [L. *altercārī, -ātus* — *alter*, other.]

altern *öl-, al-tûrn', (arch.) adj.* alternate. — *adv.* alternately. [L. *alternus*.]

alternat *al-ter-na, (Fr.) n.* the diplomatic practice of determining precedence among powers of equal rank by lot or of otherwise avoiding the difficulty.

alternate *öl'tər-nāt, also al', formerly (as Milt.) -tûr', v.t.* to cause to follow by turns or one after the other (prop. of two things). — *v.i.* to follow or interchange (with each other: prop. of two things): to happen by turns, change by turns. — *n.* a deputy, substitute: an alternative. — *adj.* **alter'nate** (*-tûr'*; in the U.S. *öl'*) arranged or coming one after the other by turns: every other or second: sometimes used with the sense 'alternative': of leaves, placed singly with change of side at each node: of floral whorls, each occupying, in ground plan, the spaces of the next: of angles, placed one after the other on either side of a line (*geom.*). — *n.* **alter'nance** (or *al'-*) alternation, interchange, variation. — *adj.* **alter'nant** (or *al'-*) alternating. — *n.* a spelling or sound variant that does not affect meaning (allomorph or allophone): a type of determinant (*math.*): an alternative proposition, e.g. one of the components in an alternation (*log.*). — *adj.* **al'ternating.** — *ns.* **alternā'tion** the act of alternating: alternate succession: interchange: the type of disjunction in which 'or' is used inclusively (*log.*): reading or singing antiphonally; **alter'native** (*-nə-tiv*) either of a pair, or any of a set, of possiblities, esp. of choice: a choice between them: one of them, esp. other than the one in question. — *adj.* possible as an alternative: disjunctive: alternate (*obs.*): considered by some as preferable to the existing state or form of something, very often with the connotation of being less conventional, less materialistic, more in harmony with the environment and the natural order of things, etc., as *alternative society, alternative technology, alternative energy, alternative medicine*, etc. — *adv.* **alter'natively** with an alternative: by way of alternative. — *n.* **alt'ernātor** a generator of alternating current. — **alternating current** an electric current that periodically reverses its direction; **alternative vote** a system of voting whereby, if an elector's favourite candidate is out of the running, his vote is transferred to the candidate he has marked next in order of preference. — **alternation of generations** (*biol.*) the occurrence in a life-cycle of two or more different forms in successive generations, the offspring being unlike the parents, and commonly reproducing by a different method. [L. *alternāre, -ātum* — *alter*, one or other of two.]

alternatim *öl-tər-nā'təm, (mus.) adv.* alternately. [L. *alternātim*.]

alterne *al-tûrn', n.* one of two or more plant communities adjoining but differing greatly. [Fr. *alterne*, alternate — L. *alternus*.]

alternis vicibus *al'tûr'nis vi'si-bus, al-ter'nēs vē'ki-bōōs, wē', (L.)* alternately.

alterum tantum *al'tə-rum tan'tum, al'te-rōōm tan'tōōm, (L.)* as much more.

altesse *al-tes, (Fr.), alteza al-tā'tha, (Sp.), altezza al-tet'sa*, (It.) *ns.* highness.

Althaea *al-thē'ə, n.* the marsh-mallow and hollyhock genus: (without *cap.*) a plant of this genus: sometimes extended to the hibiscus genus and applied (without *cap.*) esp. to the Rose of Sharon. [Gr. *althaiā*, marsh-mallow.]

Althing *öl'thing, n.* the Icelandic parliament. [O.N. and Icel.]

althorn *alt'hörn, n.* a tenor saxhorn. [alt¹.]
although *öl-dhö', conj.* though (esp., but not necessarily, in stating matter of fact). [**all, though**.]
altimeter *al-tim'i-tər, al'ti-mē-tər, öl', n.* an instrument for measuring heights, by means of differences in atmospheric pressure, or (*radio altimeter*) by means of time taken for radio wave from an aircraft to be reflected back. [L. *altus*, high, and **meter¹**.]
Altiplano *al-ti-plä'nō, n.* a plateau in the Bolivian and Peruvian part of the Andes, containing Lake Titicaca. [Sp., plateau.]
altisonant *al-tis'ən-ənt, adj.* high-sounding. [L. *altus*, high, *sonāns, -antis*, pr.p. *sonāre*, sound.]
altissimo *al-tis'(s)i-mō,* (*mus.*) *adj.* very high. — **in altissimo** in second octave above treble stave, beginning with G. [It., superl. of *alto*, high.]
altitonant *al-tit'ən-ənt, adj.* thundering on high or loudly. [L. *altus*, high, *tonāns, -antis*, pr.p. of *tonāre*, to thunder.]
altitude *al'ti-tūd, n.* height: angle of elevation above the horizon: perpendicular from vertex upon base: high rank or eminence: a high point or position: (in *pl.*) exalted mood, passion, or manner. — *adj.* **altitūd'inal** pertaining to altitude: found at high level. — *n.* **altitūdinā'rian** one given to loftiness in doctrine or belief. — Also *adj.* — *adj.* **altitūd'inous** high. [L. *altitūdō, -inis,* — *altus*, high.]
alto¹ *al'tō,* (*mus*) *n.* properly counter-tenor, the highest male voice: extended to contralto, the lowest female voice; the part sung by a counter-tenor or contralto: an instrument of corresponding compass: the possessor of a counter-tenor or contralto voice: a viola: — *pl.* **al'tos.** — Also *adj.* [It., — L. *altus*, high.]
alto² See **all-to**.
altogether *öl-tōō-gedh'ər,* or *-tə-, adv.* all together (*obs.* or by confusion): wholly: completely: without exception: in total: all things considered. — **for altogether** for all time, for good and all; **the altogether** (*coll.*) the nude. [**all** and **together**.]
alto-rilievo *äl'tō-rēl-yä'vō, n.* high relief: figures projected by at least half their thickness from the background on which they are sculptured. — Partly anglicised as **al'to-relic'vo** (*al-tō-ri-lē'vō*). [It. See **relief**.]
altrices *al-trī'sēz, n.pl.* birds whose young are hatched very immature and have to be fed in the nest by the parents. — *adj.* **altricial** (*-trish'l*). [L. *altrīcēs* (pl. of *altrix*), feeders, nurses.]
altruism *al'trōō-izm, n.* the principle of living and acting for the interest of others. — *n.* **al'truist.** — *adj.* **altruist'ic.** — *adv.* **altruist'ically.** [Fr. *altruisme,* formed by Comte from It. *altrui*, someone else — L. *alterī huīc*, to this other.]
altum silentium *al'tum si-len'sh(y)um, al'tōōm si-len'-ti-ōōm,* (L.) profound silence.
aludel *al'ōō-dəl, -ū-, n.* a pear-shaped pot used in sublimation. [Sp., — Ar. *al-uthāl*.]
alula *al'ū-lə, n.* the bastard-wing. [L. dim. of *āla*, wing.]
alum *al'əm, n.* double sulphate of aluminium and potassium, with 24 molecules of water, crystallising in transparent octahedra: any like compound of a trivalent metal (especially aluminium) and a univalent metal or radical. — *ns.* **alumina** (*ə-lū'* or *ə-lōō'mi-nə*) oxide of aluminium; **alu'minate** a salt whose acid is aluminium hydroxide. — *adj.* **aluminif'erous** alum-bearing. — *v.t.* **alum'inise, -ize** to treat (a metal) so as to form an aluminium alloy on its surface: to coat (e.g. glass) with aluminium. — *n.* **alumin'ium** (*al-ū-* or *al-ōō-*) an element (symbol Al; at. numb. 13), a remarkably light silvery metal first named (though not then isolated) by Sir Humphry Davy **alu'mium,** then (as still *U.S.*) **alu'inum.** — *adjs.* **alu'minous** of the nature of, or containing, alum or alumina; **al'umish** having the character or taste of alum. — **aluminium bronze** an alloy of aluminium and copper, of lighter weight than gold, but like it in colour; **alu'mino= sil'icates** compounds of alumina, silica and bases; **al'um-root** an American plant of the saxifrage family

with astringent root; **al'um-shale, -slate** a slate consisting mainly of clay, iron pyrites, and coaly matter, from which alum is obtained: **al'um-stone** alunite. [L. *alūmen, -inis,* alum.]
alumnus *al-um'nəs, n.* a former pupil or student: — *pl.* **alum'nī:** — *fem.* **alum'na** (*pl.* **alum'nae** *-nē*). [L., foster-son, pupil — *alĕre*, to nourish.]
alunite *al'ū-nīt, -ōō-, n.* alum-stone, a hydrous sulphate of aluminium and potassium. [Fr. *alun,* alum.]
alure *al'yər,* (*obs.*) *n.* a walk behind battlements: a gallery: a passage. [O.Fr. *aleure* — *aller*, to go.]
alveary *al'vi-ər-i, n.* a beehive: a name given to an early dictionary of English, French, Greek and Latin: a hollow of the external ear, where wax collects (*anat.*). — *adj.* **al'veated** vaulted, like a beehive. [L. *alveār-ium*, beehive — *alveus*, a hollow.]
alveolus *al-vē'ə-ləs, al'vi-, n.* a pit, small depression or dilatation: a tooth socket: one of the clustered cells at the termination of a bronchiole in the lungs: —*pl.* **alveoli.** — *adjs.* **alve'olar** (or *-öl'*, or *al'*) of an alveolus: produced with the tongue against the roots of the upper teeth (*phon.*): pitted; **alvē'olate** (or *al'vi-*) pitted: honeycombed: inserted in an alveolus. — *n.* **al'veole** an alveolus. — **alveolar arch** the part of the jaw in which the teeth are inserted. [L. *alveolus,* dim. of *alveus*, a hollow.]
alvine *al'vīn, adj.* of the belly. [L. *alvīnus* — *alvus,* belly.]
alway *öl'wä,* (*arch.*) *adv.* through all time: always. — *adv.* **al'ways** every time: ever: continually: in any case: still (*Scot.*) [**all** and **way²** — O.E. *ealne weg* (accus.) and M.E. *alles weis* (gen.).]
alycompaine. Same as **elecampane.**
Alyssum *al'is-əm, ə-lis', n.* a genus of cruciferous plants with white or yellow flowers, grown in rock-gardens: (without *cap.*) a plant of this genus: (without *cap.*) a mass of such plants. — **sweet alyssum** a white scented perennial of a related genus. [Gr. *alysson,* a plant reputed to cure madness — *a-,* priv., and *lyssa,* madness.]
Alzheimer's disease *alts'hī-mərz diz-ēz',* an illness affecting the brain and causing premature senile dementia.
am *am, əm,* used as 1st person sing. of the verb *to be.* [O.E. (Anglian) *am, eam* (W.S. *eom*), a relic of the verbs in *-mi,* from the root *es-;* cf. Gr. *eimi* (for *esmi*), L. *sum,* Sans. *asmi.*]
amabile *a-mä'bi-lā,* (It.) *adj.* of wines, etc., sweet.
amadavat *am-ə-də-vat', n.* an Indian songbird akin to the weaver-birds. — Now usu. **avadavat'.** [From Ahmadabad, whence they were sent to Europe.]
amadou *am'ə-dōō, n.* tinder made from fungi (genus *Polyporus*) growing on trees, used also as a styptic. [Fr., of doubtful origin.]
amah *ä'mə,* (*Oriental*) *n.* a native maidservant or child's nurse, esp. wet-nurse. [Port.]
amain *ə-mān', adv.* with main force: violently: at full speed: exceedingly. [a³ and main¹.]
à main armée *a mē-när-mā,* (Fr.) by force of arms, with mailed fist.
a majori (ad minus) *ä mə-jö'rī (ad mī'nus), ä mī-ör'ē (ad mi'nōōs),* (L.) from the greater (to the less).
amalgam *ə-mal'gəm, n.* a mixture of mercury with other metal: any soft mixture: an intimate mixture: an ingredient. — *v.t.* **amal'gamate** to mix with mercury: to merge. — *v.i.* to unite in an amalgam: to come together as one: to blend. — *n.* **amalgamā'tion** a blending or merging: a union of diverse elements. — *adj.* **amal'gamātive.** [L.L. *amalgama,* perh. — Gr. *malagma,* an emollient.]
amandine *am-an'din, -dīn, -dēn,* or *am', n.* a protein in sweet almonds: a candle or a cosmetic which is prepared from them. [Fr. *amande,* almond.]
Amanita *am-ə-nī'tə, n.* a genus of toadstools, near akin to the mushroom, including the fly agaric (q.v.) and other poisonous kinds: (without *cap.*) a toadstool of this genus. [Gr. *amānītai* (pl.), a kind of fungus.]
amanuensis *ə-man-ū-en'sis, n.* one who writes to dictation:

a copying secretary: — *pl.* **amanuen'sēs.** [L. *āmanuēnsis* — *ā,* from, *manus,* hand.]

amaracus *ə-mar'ə-kəs, n.* marjoram. [L. *amāracus* — Gr. *amārakos.*]

amarant(h) *am'ər-ant(h), ns.* a fabled never-fading flower, emblem of immortality: any species of **Amarant(h)'us,** the love-lies-bleeding genus, with richly coloured spikes, long in withering, giving name to the family **Amarant(h)ā'ceae,** akin to the goosefoots: **(amaranth)** a type of dye used for colouring foodstuffs. — *adjs.* **amarant(h)ā'ceous; amarant(h)'ine** (*-īn*); **amarant'in** (*Milt.*) of or like amaranth: fadeless: immortal: purple. [Gr. *amarantos* — *a-,* priv., *marainein,* to wither; the *th* forms from confusion with *anthos,* flower.]

amaryllis *am-ə-ril'is, n.* the belladonna lily, forming the genus *Amaryllis,* which gives name to the narcissus and snowdrop family **Amaryllidā'ceae,** differing from lilies in the inferior ovary. — *n.* **amaryll'id** any member of the family. — *adj.* **amaryllidā'ceous.** [*Amaryllis,* a girl's name, in the Gr. and L. poets, and others.]

amass *ə-mas', v.t.* and *v.i.* to gather in great quantity: to accumulate. — *adj.* **amass'able.** — *n.* **amass'ment.** [Fr. *amasser* — L. *ad,* to, and *massa,* a mass.]

amate¹ *ə-māt', (Spens.) v.t.* to match. [Pfx. **a-,** intens., and **mate¹.**]

amate² *ə-māt', (arch.) v.t.* to daunt: to dismay. [O.Fr. *amatir,* to subdue; cf. **checkmate, mat², mate².**]

amateur *am'ə-tər, -tūr, -tûr', n.* an enthusiast, admirer: one who cultivates a study or art for the love of it, not as a profession: one whose understanding of, or ability in, a particular art, etc. is superficial, trifling, dilettantish, or inexpert: one who engages in sport for pleasure (opp. to *professional*). — Also *adj.* — *adj.* **amateur'ish** imperfect and defective, as the work of an amateur rather than a professional hand. — *adv.* **amateur'ishly.** — *ns.* **amateur'ishness; am'ateurism; am'ateurship.** [Fr., — L. *amātor, -ōris,* a lover — *amāre,* to love.]

Amati *ə-mä'tē, n.* a violin or cello made by the *Amati* family (c. 1550–1700) of Cremona.

amation *a-mā'shən, (rare) n.* love-making. [L. *amatio, amationis* — *amāre,* to love.],

amative *am'ə-tiv, adj.* inclined towards love. — *n.* **am'ativeness** propensity to love or to sexuality. [L. *amāre, -ātum,* to love.]

amatol *am'ə-tol, n.* a high explosive composed of ammonium nitrate and trinitro*tol*uene.

amatory *am'ə-tər-i, adj.* relating to or causing love: amorous. — *adj.* **amatō'rial** (or *tö'*). — *adv.* **amatō'rially.** — *adjs.* **amatō'rian; amatō'rious.** [L. *amātōrius.*]

amaurosis *am-ö-rō'sis, n.* blindness without outward change in the eye. — *adj.* **amaurotic** (*-rot'ik*). [Gr. *amaurōsis* — *amauros,* dark.]

amaze *ə-māz', v.t.* to daze (*obs.*): to bewilder (*obs.*): to stun (*obs.*): to strike with fear (*obs.*): to confound with astonishment or wonder. — *n.* **bewilderment** (*obs.*): panic (*obs.*): extreme astonishment. — *adv.* **amaz'edly.** — *ns.* **amaz'edness** (*rare*), stupefaction (*obs.*): bewilderment (*obs.*): panic, terror (*obs.*): astonishment mingled with wonder. — *adj.* **amaz'ing.** — *adv.* **amaz'ingly** (often hyperbolically). [O.E. *āmasian* (found in the pa.p. *āmasod*).]

Amazon *am'ə-zon, -zən,* formerly *a-mā'zon, n.* in Greek story, one of a nation of women warriors, located in Asia or Scythia: the great river of South America (Port. *Amazonas,* Amazons, perh. based on a misunderstood Tupí-Guaraní word *amassona, amaçunu,* tidal bore, connected with records of Amazons living on its banks): an Indian of the Amazons: (the following usu. without *cap.*) a female soldier: a warlike, manlike, strong, or vigorous woman: a tropical American green parrot: an amazon-ant. — Also *adj.* **Amazō'nian** (also without *cap.*). — *n.* **am'azonite** amazon-stone. — *adj.* and *adv.* **Ama'zon-like.** — **am'azon-ant'** a European and American ant (genus *Polyergus*) helpless in everything except slave-raiding; **am'azon-stone** a green microline, said to be given by the Brazilian Amazons

to the men who visited them. [Gr. *Amāzōn, -onos,* in folk-etymology referred to *a-,* priv., *māzos,* breast, with the explanation that Amazons cut off the right breast lest it should get in the way of the bowstring.]

ambages *am-bā'jēz, n.pl.* windings: roundabout ways: delays. — Also *n.sing.* — **ambage** (*am'bij*) with *pl.* **am'bages.** — *adjs.* **ambagious** (*-bā'jəs*) tortuous: circumlocutory; **ambagitory** (*-baj'i-tər-i; Scott*). [L. *ambāgēs* (pl.) — *ambi-,* about, *agĕre,* to drive, lead.]

amban *am'ban, n.* a Chinese resident official in a dependency. [Manchu, minister.]

Ambarvalia *amb-är-vā'li-ə, n.pl.* an ancient Roman festival with processions round the cornfields. [L. *Ambarvālia* — *ambi,* around, *arvum,* field.]

ambassador *am-bas'ə-dər, n.* a diplomatic minister of the highest order: a messenger or agent: — *fem.* **ambass'adress.** — *adj.* **ambassadorial** (*dö'ri-əl, -dō'*). — *ns.* **ambass'adorship; am'bassage** (*-bəs-ij*), **am'bassy** forms of **embassage, embassy.** — **ambass'ador-at-large'** an ambassador not accredited to any particular foreign government; **ambassador extraordinary** an ambassador sent on a special occasion, as distinguished from the ordinary or resident ambassador. [Fr. *ambassadeur* — L. *ambactus,* a slave or servant, gener. thought to be of Celtic origin.]

ambatch *am'bach, n.* a pith-tree. [Apparently native name.]

amber *am'bər, n.* ambergris (*obs.*): a yellowish fossil resin: the orange traffic-light, which acts as a cautionary signal between red (stop) and green (go). — *adj.* made of amber: amber-hued — clear brownish yellow. — *adj.* **am'bered** (*obs.*) embedded in amber: flavoured with ambergris. — *n.* **am'berite** an amberlike smokeless powder. — *adjs.* **am'berous; am'bery.** — *n.* **am'broid** or **am'beroid** pressed amber, a synthetic amber formed by heating and compressing pieces of natural amber too small to be of value in themselves, sometimes along with other resins. — **am'ber-fish** a golden or greenish fish (genus *Seriola*) of the horse-mackerels (Carangidae), abundant in warm seas; **am'berjack** (the species *Seriola dumerili* of) the amber-fish. [Fr. *ambre* — Ar. *'anbar,* ambergris.]

ambergris *am'bər-grēs, n.* an ash-grey strongly-scented substance, found floating or cast up, and in the intestines of the spermaceti whale, where it originates. [Fr. *ambre gris,* grey amber.]

ambi- *am'bi-, pfx.* meaning round, both, on both sides. [L., — *ambo,* both.]

ambiance. See ambient.

ambidext(e)rous *am-bi-deks'trəs, -tər-əs, (arch.)* **ambidexter** *-deks'tər, adjs.* able to use both hands alike: on both sides: double-dealing. — *ns.* **ambidex'ter** (*arch.*) one who is ambidexterous; **ambidexterity** (*-ter'i-ti*). [**ambi-,** and L. *dexter,* right.]

ambient *am'bi-ənt, adj.* going round: (of e.g. air temperature) surrounding: investing. — *n.* that which encompasses: the air or sky. — *n.* **ambience** (*am'bi-əns*) environment: surrounding influence: atmosphere: (also **ambiance** (*ä-bē-äs*) the use or disposition of accessories in art. [L. *ambiēns, -entis,* pr.p. of *ambīre* — pfx. *ambi-,* about, *īre,* to go.]

ambiguous *am-big'ū-əs, adj.* doubtful: undetermined: of intermediate or doubtful nature: indistinct: wavering: admitting of more than one meaning: equivocal. — *n.* **ambigū'ity** doubtful or double meaning: an equivocal expression. — *adv.* **ambig'uously.** — *n.* **ambig'uousness.** [L. *ambiguus* — *ambigĕre,* to go about, waver — pfx. *ambi-,* both ways, *agĕre,* to drive.]

ambilateral *am-bi-lat'ə-rəl, adj.* relating to, involving, both sides. [**ambi-,** and L. *latus, lateris,* side.]

ambisexual *am-bi-seks'ū-əl, adj.* (esp. of sexual characteristics, e.g. pubic hair) common to both sexes. [**ambi-,** and **sexual.**]

ambisonics *am-bi-son'iks, n. sing.* a system of high-fidelity sound reproduction which electronically reproduces the natural ambience of the sound. [**ambi-,** and **sonics.**]

ambit *am'bit, n.* circuit: scope: compass: precincts: confines. [L. *ambitus*, a going round — pfx. *ambi*-, round, *itus*, going — *īre*, *itum*, to go.]

ambition *am-bish'ən, n.* aspiration after success or advancement: the object of aspiration. — *adjs.* **ambi'-tionless; ambitious** (*am-bish'əs*), full of ambition: strongly desirous (of, to do): aspiring: indicating ambition: pretentious. — *adv.* **ambi'tiously.** — *n.* **ambi'-tiousness.** [L. *ambitiō, -ōnis*, canvassing — pfx. *ambi*, about, and *īre*, *itum*, to go.]

ambitty *am-bit'i, adj.* devitrified. [Fr. *ambité*, of obscure origin.]

ambivalence *am-biv'ə-ləns*, **ambivalency** *-i, ns.* co-existence in one person of opposing emotional attitudes towards the same object. — *adj.* **ambiv'alent.** [ambi-, and L. *valēns, -entis*, pr.p. of *valēre*, to be strong.]

ambivert *am'bi-vûrt, n.* one neither an extravert nor an introvert. — *n.* **ambiver'sion** (*-shən*). [ambi-, and L. *vertĕre*, to turn.]

amble *am'bl, v.i.* to move, as a horse, by lifting together both legs on one side alternately with those on the other side: to move at an easy pace: to go like an ambling horse: to ride an ambling animal. — *n.* an ambling pace. — *n.* **am'bler.** — *n.* and *adj.* **am'bling.** [Fr. *ambler* — L. *ambulāre*, to walk about.]

amblyopia *am-bli-ō'pi-ə, n.* (partial) blindness or dullness of sight without any apparent damage to the eye. [Gr. *amblyōpiā* — *amblys*, dull, *ops*, eye.]

Amblyopsis *am-bli-op'sis, n.* the blindfish of the Mammoth Cave in Kentucky. [Gr. *amblys*, dull, *opsis*, sight.]

Amblystoma *am-blis'to-mə, n.* a genus of tailed amphibians in the gill-less or salamandroid suborder, in the larval stage called axolotl. [Gr. *amblys*, blunt, *stoma*, mouth.]

ambo *am'bō, n.* an early Christian raised reading-desk or pulpit: — *pl.* **am'bos, ambō'nes** (*-nēz*). [L.L. *ambō* — Gr. *ambōn, -ōnos*, crest of a hill, pulpit.]

Amboyna-wood (now usu. **Amboina-**), *am-boi'nə-wŏŏd, n.* the finely coloured knotty wood of *Pterocarpus indicus*, a papilionaceous tree. — **Ambolna pine** a tree (*Agathis alba*), a source of resin. [Island of *Amboina* in the Moluccas, Indonesia.]

ambroid. See **amber.**

ambrosia *am-brō'z(h)i-ə, -z(h)ə, n.* the food (later, the drink) of the Greek gods, which conferred everlasting youth and beauty: the anointing oil of the gods: any finely flavoured beverage: something sweet and pleasing: bee-bread: fungi cultivated for food by certain bark-beetles (**ambrosia beetles**) of the Scolytidae: (with *cap.*) a genus of Compositae called in America ragweeds. — *adj.* **ambro'sial** fragrant: delicious: immortal: heavenly. — *adv.* **ambrōs'ially.** — *adj.* **ambrō'sian.** [Gr. *ambrosiā* — *ambrotos*, immortal — *a*-, priv., and *brotos*, for *mbrotos*, mortal; cf. Sans. *amr̥ta*, immortal.]

Ambrosian *am-brō'z(h)ən, -z(h)yən, adj.* pertaining to St *Ambrose*, 4th-cent. bishop of Milan, to his liturgy, to the form of plainsong introduced by him, to various religious orders and to the public library at Milan (founded 1602–9 by Cardinal Federigo Borromeo) named in his honour. — *n.* a member of any of these orders.

ambrotype *am'brō-tīp, n.* an early kind of photograph made by backing a glass negative with black varnish or paper so that it appears as a positive. [Gr. *ambrotos*, immortal, and **type.**]

ambry, aumbry, almery, *Scot.* **awmry, awmrie** *am', ŏm'(b)ri, ns.* a recess for church vessels: a cupboard: a pantry: a dresser: a safe. [O.Fr. *almerie* — L. *armārium*, a chest, safe — *arma*, arms, tools.]

ambs-ace, ames-ace *amz'ās, āmz'ās, ns.* double ace, the lowest possible throw at dice: ill-luck: worthlessness. [O.Fr. *ambes as* — L. *ambōs assēs*, both aces.]

ambulacrum *am-bū-lā'krəm, -la', n.* a radial band in the shell of an echinoderm, bearing rows of pores through which protrude the tube-feet: — *pl.* **ambulā'cra.** — *adj.*

ambulā'cral. [L. *ambulācrum*, a walk — *ambulāre*, to walk.]

ambulance *am'bū-ləns, n.* a vehicle or (**air ambulance**) helicopter, etc., for conveying sick or injured: a movable field hospital. — *adj.* **am'bulant** walking: moving from place to place: unfixed (*rare*): allowing or calling for walking. — *n.* a walking patient. —*v.i.* **am'bulate** to walk. — *ns.* **ambulā'tion; am'bulātor** a walker: a wheel for road-measuring. — *adj.* **am'bulatory** (*-ə-tər-i*) of or for walking: moving from place to place, not stationary: mutable. — *n.* a covered walk, as an aisle, cloister, portico, corridor. — **am'bulance-chaser** a lawyer on the look-out for accidents in order to instigate actions for damages (*U.S.*): a person, firm, offering to pursue a claim on behalf of an accident-victim in return for a percentage of the sum obtained; **am'bulanceman, am'bulancewoman** a member of the crew of an ambulance. [L. *ambulāre, -ātum*, to walk about.]

ambuscade *am-bəs-kād', n.* an ambush. — *v.t.* and *v.i.* to ambush. — *n.* **ambuscā'do** (esp. 16th–17th cent.; would-be *Sp.*) an ambuscade: — *pl.* **ambuscā'do(e)s.** [Fr. *embuscade* or Sp. *emboscada*; see **ambush.**]

ambush *am'bŏŏsh, n.* a lying, or laying, in wait to attack by surprise: a place of lying in wait: a body (or person) lying in wait. — *v.t.* to lay in wait: to waylay. — *v.i.* to lie in wait. — *n.* **am'bushment** ambush. — **ambush bug** (*U.S.*) any of several insects of the *Phymatidae* that prey on other insects from a place of concealment, e.g. within a flower. [O.Fr. *embusche* (Fr. *embûche*) — *embuscher* — L.L. *imboscāre* — *im*, in, *boscus* (see **bush¹**).]

amearst (*Spens.*) for **amerced.**

ameba, amebic, etc. *U.S.* spelling of **amoeba, amoebic,** etc.

âme damnée *äm da-nā*, (Fr.) lit. damned soul, a tool or agent blindly devoted to one's will; **âme de boue** (*də bōō*) lit. a soul of mud, a low-minded person; **âme perdue** (*per-dü*) lit. lost soul, a desperate character.

ameer. See **amir.**

Amelanchier *am-ə-lang'ki-ər, n.* the shadbush genus of the rose family. [Fr. *amélanchier*.]

amelcorn *am'əl-körn, n.* emmer. [Ger. *Amelkorn*, Du. *amelkorn*; cf. **amylum, corn¹**.]

amelia *a-mēl'i-ə, -mel', -yə, n.* a congenital condition in which one or more limbs are completely absent. [Gr. *a*-, priv., and *melos*, limb.]

ameliorate *ə-mē'lyə-rāt, v.t.* to make better: to improve. — *v.i.* to grow better. — *n.* **amēliorā'tion.** — *adj.* **amē'liorātive.** [Fr. *améliorer* — L. *ad*, to, *melior*, better.]

amen *ä-men', ā-men', interj.* so let it be. — *n.* an expression of assent, as by saying 'amen': the last word. — *v.t.* to say amen to: to ratify solemnly: to approve: to conclude. — **Amen glass** a type of drinking-glass engraved with a Jacobite inscription, esp. 'God save the king. Amen'. [Heb. *āmēn*, true, truly, retained in Gr. and English translations.]

amenable *ə-mēn'ə-bl, adj.* ready to be led or won over: liable or subject. — *ns.* **amenabil'ity, amen'ableness.** — *adv.* **amen'ably.** [Fr. *amener*, to lead — *à* — L. *ad*, to, and *mener*, to lead — L.L. *mināre*, to lead, to drive (as cattle) — L. *minārī*, to threaten.]

amenage *am'e-nāj*, (*Spens.*) *v.t.* to tame. [O.Fr. *ame(s)nager* — *à*, to, *mesnage*, household.]

amenaunce *am'ə-nŏns*, (*Spens.*) *n.* bearing. [O.Fr. *amenance*; see **amenable.**]

amend *ə-mend', v.t.* to free from fault or error: to correct: to improve: to alter in detail, with a view to improvement, as a bill before parliament: to rectify: to cure: to mend. — *v.i.* to grow or become better: to reform: to recover. — *adjs.* **amend'able; amend'atory** corrective. — *ns.* **amend'er; amend'ment** correction: improvement: an alteration proposed on a bill under consideration: a counter-proposal put before a meeting: a counter-motion. — **make amends** to supply a loss: to compensate (for). [Fr. *amender* — L. *ēmendāre* —

ē, out of, and *mendum*, a fault.]

amende *am-ād*, (Fr.) *n.* a fine, penalty. — **amende honorable** (*o-nor-äbl'*) orig. an ignominious public confession: now a frank admission of wrong satisfying the honour of the injured.

amene *ə-mēn'*, *adj.* (now *rare*) pleasant. — *n.* **amenity** (*-mēn'*, *-men'*) pleasantness, as in situation, climate, manners, disposition: a pleasing feature, object, characteristic: a facility (usu. *pl.*): civility. [L. *amoenus*, pleasant.]

amenorrhoea *a-, ā-men-ō-rē'ə*, *n.* failure of menstruation. [Gr. *a-*, priv., *mēn*, month, *rhoiā*, a flowing.]

ament *ā'mənt*, *ə-ment'*, *n.* one who is mentally defective by failure to develop: a sufferer from amentia. — *n.* **amentia** (*a-, ā-men'shi-ə*) mental deficiency. [L. *āmēns, -entis* — *ā*, from, *mēns, mentis*, mind.]

amentum *a-men'təm*, *n.* a catkin: — *pl.* **amen'ta.** — Also **a'ment.** — *adjs.* **amentā'ceous, amen'tal; amentif'erous** catkin-bearing. [L., thong.]

amerce *ə-mûrs'*, *v.t.* to fine (esp. at discretion): to deprive: to punish. — *ns.* **amerce'ment, amerc'iament** infliction of a fine: a fine. — *adj.* **amerc'iable.** [A.Fr. *amercier* — *à merci*, at mercy.]

American *ə-mer'i-kən*, *adj.* pertaining to America, esp. to the United States. — *n.* a native or citizen of America: the English language as spoken in America. — *n.pl.* **Americana** (*ə-mer-i-kä'nə*) things characteristic of America, esp. old books, paintings, furniture, etc. — *v.t.* **Amer'icanise, -ize** to render American. — *ns.* **Amer'icanism** a custom, characteristic, word, phrase, or idiom characteristic of Americans: condition of being an American citizen: (advocacy of) American policies, political attitudes, etc.: devotion to American institutions; **Amer'icanist** a student of American biology, archaeology, and the like. — **American aloe** Agave; **American blight** a plant-louse pest of apple-trees; **American bowls** tenpins, a game like skittles; **American cloth** cloth with a glazed coating; **American Express®** **card** a type of credit card issued by a commercial company; **American football** an American game of football, somewhat resembling British rugby football, played with an elliptical ball between teams of eleven players (unlimited substitution being allowed), scoring being by points won for touch-downs and goals; **American Indian** a member of the native race of America, thought on discovery to be Indian; **American organ** an instrument resembling the harmonium, in which air is sucked inwards to the reeds; **American plan** in a hotel, etc., the system of including meals in the charge for a room (see also **European plan**); **American tiger** a jaguar. [From *America*, perh. so called from Richard *Ameryk*, Sheriff of Bristol, who financed John Cabot's voyage; also said to be from Amerigo (L. *Americus*) Vespucci.]

americium *am-ər-ish'i-əm*, *n.* a radioactive metallic element (at. numb. 95; symbol Am), obtained artificially in *America*.

Amerind *am'ər-ind*, *n.* and *adj. Amer*ican *Ind*ian. — Also **Amerind'ian.**

à merveille *a mer-vāy'*, (Fr.) wonderfully, perfectly.

ames-ace. See **ambs-ace.**

Ameslan *a'məs-lən*, *n. Amer*ican *s*ign *lan*guage, a means of communication by specified symbols and gestures.

Ametabola *am-et-ab'ə-lə*, *n.pl.* in some classifications the lowest insects, with little or no metamorphosis. — *n.* **ametab'olism.** — *adjs.* **ametabol'ic** (*-bol'ik*), **ametab'-olous.** [Gr. *a-*, priv., and *metabolē*, change.]

amethyst *am'ə-thist*, *n.* a bluish violet quartz anciently supposed to prevent drunkenness: its colour. — *adj.* of, or coloured like, amethyst. — *adj.* **amethyst'ine** (*-īn*). — **oriental amethyst** a purple corundum. [Gr. *amethystos* — *a-*, priv., and *methyein*, to be drunken — *methy*, wine; cf. **mead**[1], Sans. *madhu*, sweet.]

Amharic *am-har'ik*, *n.* an Ethiopic language, the official language of Ethiopia. — Also *adj.* [*Amhara* district.]

ami *a-mē*, (Fr.) *n.* a friend: — *fem.* **amie** (*a-mē*) a friend: a mistress. — **ami de cour** (*də kōōr*) a court friend —

an untrustworthy friend; **ami du peuple** (*dü pøpl'*) friend of the people (esp. Marat, French revolutionist).

amiable *ām'i-ə-bl*, *adj.* friendly (*Shak.*): love-inspiring (*Shak.*): lovable: of sweet and friendly disposition. — *ns.* **āmiabil'ity, ām'iableness.** — *adv.* **ām'iably.** [O.Fr. *amiable*, friendly — L. *amīcābilis* — *amīcus*, friend; confused in meaning with O.Fr. *amable* (Fr. *aimable*) — L. *amābilis* — *amāre*, to love.]

amianthus *am-i-anth'əs*, more correctly **amiantus** (*-ant'-əs*), *n.* the finest fibrous asbestos, which can be made into cloth readily cleansed by fire. [Gr. *amiantos* (*lithos*), undefiled (stone) — *a-*, priv., and *miainein*, to soil.]

amicable *am'ik-ə-bl*, *adj.* in friendly spirit. — *ns.* **amicabil'ity, am'icableness.** — *adv.* **am'icably.** [L. *amīcābilis* — *amīcus*, a friend — *amāre*, to love.]

amice[1], *am'is*, *n.* a strip of fine linen, worn formerly on the head, now on the shoulders, by a priest at mass: a cloak, wrap. [O.Fr. *amit* — L. *amictus*, cloak — *amb-*, about, and *jacēre*, to throw.]

amice[2], *am'is*, *n.* a furred hood with long ends hanging down in front, originally a cap or covering for the head, afterwards a hood, or cape with a hood, later a mere college hood. [O.Fr. *aumuce*, of doubtful origin.]

amicus curiae *a-mī'kus kū'ri-ē, a-mē'kōōs kōō'ri-ī*, (L.) a friend of the law-court: formerly, in Scots law, a disinterested adviser, not a party to the case: in Eng. law, counsel acting for a person who is interested in the outcome of a case he is not personally involved in: (wrongly) a friend in high quarters: — *pl.* **ami'cī** (or *-mē'kē*).

amid *ə-mid'*, *prep.* in the midst of: among. — *adv.* (*arch.*) in the midst. — *adv.* and *prep.* **amid'most** in the very middle (of). — *adv.* **amid'ships** in, near, towards, the middle of a ship lengthwise (from gen. of **ship**). — *adv.* and *prep.* **amidst'** amid. [O.E. *on middan* (dat. of *adj.*), in middle; the *s* is a later adverbial genitive ending, the *t* as in **amongst, betwixt**, etc.]

amide *am'īd*, *n.* a derivative of ammonia in which an acid radical takes the place of one or more of the three hydrogen atoms. — *n.* **amido-group** (*ə-mē'dō*) the group NH_2 in such combination. [From **ammonia.**]

Amidol® *am'i-dol*, *n.* a colourless chemical ($C_6H_3(NH_2)_2(OH).2HCl$) used as a photographic developer.

amie. See **ami.**

amigo *a-mē'gō*, (Sp.) *n.* a friend: — *pl.* **ami'gos.**

amildar *am'il-där*, *n.* a factor or manager in India: a collector of revenue amongst the Mahrattas. [Hind. '*amaldār* — Ar. '*amal*, work, Pers. *dār*, holder.]

amine *am'īn, -ēn*, *n.* a derivative of ammonia (NH_2) in which one or more hydrocarbon radicals take the place of one or more of the three hydrogen atoms. — *ns.* **amino-a'cid** (*a-mē'nō-*) a fatty acid (e.g. **ami'no-acet'ic acid**, glycine) in which the amino-group takes the place of a hydrogen atom of the hydrocarbon radical; **ami'no-group'** the group NH_2 in such combination. [From **ammonia.**]

aminobutene *a-mē'nō-bū'tēn*, *n.* a pain-relieving drug, less addiction-forming than morphine. [**amine** and **butene.**]

a minori (ad majus) *ā min-ōr'ī (ad māj'us), ä min-ōr'ē (ad mī'ūs)* (L.) from the less (to the greater).

amir, ameer *a-mēr', ə-mēr'*, *n.* the title borne by certain Muslim princes. [Ar. *amīr*; see **admiral, emir.**]

amis (*Spens.*). Same as **amice**[1].

Amish *ä'mish, am'*, *adj.* of or belonging to a strict U.S. Mennonite sect. — Also *n.pl.* [Ger. *amisch*, after 17th-cent. Swiss bishop, J. *Amman* or *Amen*.

amiss *ə-mis'*, *adv.* astray: wrongly: improperly: faultily. — *adj.* out of order: wrong: unsuitable: to be objected to. — *n.* an evil: a misdeed. — **come amiss** to be unwelcome, untoward; **take amiss** to take offence at (strictly, by misinterpretation). [**a**[3], and **miss**[1].]

amissible *ə-mis'i-bl*, *adj.* liable to be lost. — *n.* **amissibil'-**

ity. [L. *āmittĕre, āmissum*, to lose — *ā*, from, *mittĕre*, to send.]

amissing *ə-mis'ing*, (*Scot.*) *adj.* wanting: lost. [a³, and **missing.**]

amitosis *am-i-tō'sis*, (*biol.*) *n.* cell-division without mitosis. — *adj.* **amitotic** (*-tot'ik*). — *adv.* **amitot'ically.** [Gr. *a-*, priv., and *mitos*, thread.]

amitryptyline *am-i-trip'tə-lēn, n.* an antidepressant drug, also used for enuresis. [From *amino, tryp*tamine (a hallucinogenic substance), meth*yl*, with ending *-ine.*]

amity *am'i-ti, n.* friendship: goodwill: friendly relations. [Fr. *amitié* — L. *amicus*, a friend.]

amla *äm'lə, n.* an emblic.

amman. See **amtman.**

ammeter *am'i-tər, n.* an instrument for measuring electric current. [From **ampere,** and Gr. *metron*, measure.]

ammiral. An old form (*Milt.*) of **admiral.**

ammo *am'ō, n.* a familiar contraction of **ammunition.**

Ammon *am'on, n.* the ancient Egyptian ram-headed god *Amûn, Amen,* identified by the Greeks with Zeus, famous for his temple and oracle in the Libyan oasis of Siwa: (without *cap.*) the argali (from its gigantic horns). — *n.* **ammonia** (*a-, ə-mō'ni-ə*) a pungent compound of nitrogen and hydrogen (NH₃) first obtained in gaseous form from *sal-ammoniac:* its solution in water, strictly ammonium hydroxide (*liquid ammonia,* long known as spirits of hartshorn). — *adjs.* **ammō'niac** of the region of the temple of Ammon (applied only to gum-ammoniac, and to sal-ammoniac, which is said to have been first made in that district from cameldung): ammoniacal; **ammoni'acal** of ammonia. — *n.* **ammoniacum** (*am-ə-nī'ə-kəm*) gum-ammoniac (see **gum**). — *adj.* **ammō'niated** combined, impregnated, with ammonia. — *ns.* **amm'onite** a fossil cephalopod of many kinds, with coiled chambered shell like Ammon's horn; **ammō'nium** a univalent radical, NH₄, resembling the alkali metals in chemical behaviour; **amm'onoid** a member of the order *Ammonoidea,* to which the ammonites and related cephalopods belong. [Gr. *Ammōn, -ōnos.*]

ammonal *am'ən-al, n.* a high explosive made from *am*monium nitrate and *al*uminium.

ammonia, ammoniacum, ammonite, ammonium. See under **Ammon.**

ammophilous *am-of'i-ləs, adj.* sand-loving. [Gr. *ammos,* sand, *phileein,* to love.]

ammunition *am-ū-nish'ən, n.* orig. military stores generally: things used for charging fire-arms — missiles, propellants (*coll.* **am'mo**): explosive military devices: anything that can be used in fighting (*lit.* and *fig.*). — *adj.* for ammunition: supplied from army stores. — *v.t.* to supply with ammunition. [Obs. Fr. *amunition,* app. from *l'amunition* for *la munition;* see **munition.**]

amnesia *am-nē'zh(y)ə, n.* the loss of memory. — *n.* **amne'siac** one who suffers from amnesia. — Also *adj.* — *adj.* and *n.* **amne'sic.** [Gr. *amnēsiā.*]

amnesty *am'nəs-ti, n.* a general pardon: an act of oblivion. — *v.t.* to give amnesty to. [Gr. *amnēstiā,* forgetfulness.]

amnion *am'ni-ən, n.* the innermost membrane enveloping the embryo of reptiles, birds, and mammals: — *pl.* **am'nia.** — *amnio-* in composition, amnion: amniotic. — *n.* **amniocentesis** (*am-ni-ō-sin-tē'sis*) the insertion of a hollow needle into the uterus of a pregnant woman to withdraw a sample of the amniotic fluid to test for foetal abnormalities, etc. — *adj.* **amniot'ic.** — *n.* **amniot'omy** surgical rupture of the amnion during, or in order to induce, labour. — **amniotic fluid** the fluid within the amnion in which the embryo is suspended. [Gr.]

amoeba *ə-mē'bə, n.* a protozoon of ever-changing shape: — *pl.* **amoe'bae** (*-bē, -bī*), **amoe'bas.** — *n.* **amoebī'asis** infection (esp. of the colon) by amoebae. — *adjs.* **amoe'bic; amoe'biform; amoe'boid.** [Gr. *amoibē,* change.]

amoebaean *a-mē-bē'ən, adj.* answering alternately, responsive, as often in pastoral poetry. [L. *amoebaeus*

— Gr. *amoibaios* — *amoibē,* alternation.]

à moitié *a mwa-tyā,* (Fr.) half: by halves.

amok *ə-mok', ***amuck** *ə-muk', adjs.* and *advs.* in a frenzy, esp. in phrase **run amok,** to run forth murderously assailing all who come in the way (also *fig.*). [Malay *amoq,* frenzied.]

Amomum *a-mō'məm, n.* a genus of the ginger family including cardamoms and grains of paradise: (without *cap.*) a plant of this genus. [Latinised from Gr. *amōmon,* prob. cardamom.]

à mon avis *a mo-na-vē,* (Fr.) in my opinion.

among *ə-mung', ***amongst** *ə-mungst', preps.* of the number of: amidst. — *adv.* **among** (*arch.*) meanwhile: all the time: betweenwhiles: here and there. [O.E. *on-ge-mang,* lit. in mixture, crowd — *gemengan,* to mingle: for *-st* see **against.**]

amontillado *ä-mon-til-(y)ä'dō, n.* a slightly sweet sherry of light colour and body, orig. from *Montilla:* — *pl.* **amontilla'dos.** [Sp.]

amoove (*Spens.*). Same as **amove**¹.

amoral *ā-mor'əl,* also *a-, adj.* non-moral, outside the domain of morality. — *ns.* **amor'alism** refusal to recognise the validity of any system of morality; **amor'alist.** [Gr. *a-,* priv., and **moral.**]

amorce *ə-mörs', n.* a percussion cap for a toy pistol. [Fr., priming.]

amoret *am'ər-et, n.* a sweetheart (*obs.*): a love-glance: a love-knot: a love sonnet or song. — *ns.* **amoret'to** a lover: a cupid; — *pl.* **amoret'ti** (*-tē*); **amorino** (*-ē'nō*) a cupid: — *pl.* **amori'ni** (*-nē*). [O.Fr. *amorete* and It. *amoretto, amorino,* dims. from L. *amor,* love.]

amorist *am'ər-ist, n.* a lover: a gallant: one who writes of love: a seeker of sexual adventures or experiences. — *n.* **am'orism.** [L. *amor,* love.]

amornings *ə-mörn'ingz,* (*obs.*) *adv.* of a morning. [a³, and **morning,** with gen. ending added.]

amoroso *am-or-ō'sō,* (*mus.*) *adj.* tender. — Also *adv.* — *n.* a lover: a gallant: — *pl.* **amoro'sos:** — *fem.* **amoro'sa.** [It.]

amorous *am'ər-əs, adj.* inclined to love: in love: fond: amatory: relating to love. — *n.* **amorosity** (*-os'i-ti; rare*). — *adv.* **am'orously.** — *n.* **am'orousness.** [O.Fr. *amorous* (Fr. *amoureux*) — L.L. *amōrōsus* — *amor,* love.]

amor patriae *ä'mör pä'tri-ē, ä'mor pa'tri-ī,* (L.) love of country.

amorphous *ə-mör'fəs, adj.* without definite shape or structure: shapeless: without crystalline structure. — *n.* **amor'phism.** [Gr. *amorphos,* shapeless — *a-,* priv., *morphē,* form.]

amort *ə-mört',* (*obs.* or *arch.*) *adj.* spiritless, dejected. [Fr. *à, mort,* death; but partly from **alamort** wrongly understood as *all amort.*]

amortise, -ize *ə-mör'tīz, -tiz, v.t.* to alienate in mortmain or convey to a corporation: to wipe out esp. through a sinking-fund. — *n.* **amortisa'tion, -z-.** [L.L. *a(d)mortizāre* — Fr. *à,* to, *mort,* death.]

amosite *am'ə-sīt, n.* brown asbestos, a form of asbestos mined only in S. Africa. [*A*sbestos *M*ines *of South Africa,* and *-ite.*]

amount *ə-mownt', v.i.* to go up (*Spens.*): to come in total: to come in meaning or substance (with *to*). — *n.* the whole sum: principal and interest together: quantity: value, import, equivalence. [O.Fr. *amonter,* to ascend — L. *ad,* to, *mōns, montis* a mountain.]

amour *ə-mōōr', n.* love, friendship (*obs.*): love-making (usu. in *pl.;* *arch.*): a love affair (now usu. discreditable): a loved one. — *n.* **amourette** (*a-mōō-ret'*) a petty amour: an amoretto. [Fr., — L. *amor, amōris,* love.]

amour courtois *a-mōōr kōōr-twä,* (Fr.) courtly love.

amour-propre *a-mōōr-propr',* (Fr.) *n.* self-esteem: sometimes in exaggerated form, shown in readiness to take offence at slights.

amove¹ *ə-mōōv', v.t.* to stir up (*obs.*): to affect (*obs.*): to rouse (*Spens.*). [O.Fr. *amover* — L. *admovēre* — *ad,* to, *movēre,* to move.]

amove² ə-mōōv', (law) v.t. to remove.   [L. āmovēre —
ā, from, movēre, to move.]
amp amp, n. short for ampere.
ampassy. See ampersand.
ampelo-, ampeli- in composition, of the vine, vine-like.
— n. ampelography (am-pel-og'rə-fi) the botany of the
vine.   [Gr. ampelos, vine.]
ampelopsis am-pi-lop'sis, n. a plant of the genus Ampelopsis: (form. and rarely) any of certain related plants
such as the Virginia creeper: — pl. ampelop'ses (-sēz).
[Gr. ampelos, vine, opsis, appearance.]
ampere, ampère am'per, -pēr', ā-per, (elect.) n. the SI and
MKSA unit of current, defined as that which, flowing
in two parallel conductors, each infinitely thin and
long, one metre apart in a vacuum, will produce a
force between the conductors of 2×10^{-7} newtons
per metre length (international ampere a unit formerly
defined by means of the rate of deposition of silver
from a solution of silver nitrate and slightly less than
the practical unit in use; now the same as the unit just
defined). — n. am'perage current in amperes.   [From
A. M. Ampère (1775–1836), French physicist.]
ampersand am'pərs-and, n. the character (&; originally
ligatured E and T, for L. et) representing and. — Also
am'perzand, am'pussy-and, am'passy (amp'ə-si).   [and
per se, and — that is, &, by itself, means 'and': cf.
a-per-se.]
Ampex ® am'peks, n. a system of magnetic recording of
television signals. — v.t. to record by Ampex.
amphetamine am-fet'ə-mēn, n. $C_9H_{13}N$, or its sulphate or
phosphate, a synthetic drug used to relieve nasal
congestion or taken internally to stimulate the central
nervous system.   [alpha methyl phenethyl + amine.]
amphi- am'fi-, pfx. indicating both, on both sides (or
ends) or around.   [Gr.]
amphibious am-fib'i-əs, adj. leading two lives: living, or
adapted to life, or use, on land and in or on water: of
military operations, in which troops are conveyed
across the sea or other water in landing barges,
assault-craft, etc., and land on enemy-held territory:
of double, doubtful, or ambiguous nature. — n.pl.
Amphib'ia a class of vertebrates typically gill-breathing
in the larval state and lung-breathing or skin-breathing
as adults — frogs, toads, newts, salamanders, caecil-
ians. — adj. amphib'ian amphibious: of the Amphibia.
— n. a member of the Amphibia: an aeroplane designed to alight on land or water: a vehicle for use on
land or water.   [Gr. amphibios — amphi, on both
sides, bios, life.]
amphibole am'fi-bōl, n. any mineral of a group differing
from the pyroxenes in cleavage angle (about 56°
instead of about 87°), silicates of calcium, magnesium,
and other metals, including hornblende, actinolite,
tremolite, etc. — n. amphib'olite a rock composed
essentially of amphibole.   [Gr. amphibolos, ambiguous, on account of the resemblance between hornblende and tourmaline.]
amphibology am-fi-bol'ə-ji, n. a phrase or sentence ambiguous not in its individual words but in its construction: the use of such ambiguities. — adjs. amphibol'ic;
amphibological (-bə-loj'); amphib'olous (-ə-ləs). — n.
amphib'oly amphibology.   [Gr. amphibolos — amphi,
on both sides, ballein, to throw.]
amphibrach am'fi-brak, n. in prosody, a foot of three
syllables, a long between two short, or stressed between
two unstressed. — adj. amphibrach'ic.   [Gr. amphi-
brachus, short at both ends — amphi, on both sides,
brachys, short.]
amphictyon am-fik'ti-on, (Gr. hist.) n. a delegate to a
council of an amphic'tyony, a league of neighbouring
communities connected with a temple and cult, esp.
of Delphi. — adj. amphictyon'ic.   [Gr. amphiktyones,
app. for amphiktiones, dwellers around — amphi,
around, ktizein, to dwell.]
amphigastrium am-fi-gas'tri-əm, n. a scale-like leaf on the
ventral side of some liverworts: — pl. amphigas'tria.
[amphi-, gastēr, belly.]

amphigory am'fi-gə-ri, n. nonsense verse.   [Fr. am-
phigouri: origin unknown.]
amphimacer am-fim'ə-sər, n. in prosody, a foot of three
syllables, short between two long.   [Gr. amphimakros
— amphi, on both sides, makros, long.]
amphimixis am-fi-mik'sis, n. fusion of gametes: sexual
reproduction: combination of characters from both
parents. — adj. amphimic'tic.   [Gr. amphi, on both
sides, mīxis, intercourse, mixing.]
Amphineura am-fi-nū'rə, n.pl. a class of molluscs with two
ventral and two lateral nerve-cords, including Chiton.
[amphi-, neuron, nerve.]
amphioxus am-fi-oks'əs, n. a lancelet of the genus Amphioxus or Branchiostoma.   [amphi-, and oxys, sharp.]
amphipod am'fi-pod, n. one of the Amphip'oda, an order
of small sessile-eyed crustaceans with swimming feet
and jumping feet — sand-hoppers, etc. — adj. amphip'-
odous.   [amphi-, pous, podos, a foot.]
amphisbaena am-fis-bē'nə, n. a fabulous two-headed
snake: (cap.) a genus of snake-like lizards, chiefly
tropical American, whose rounded tails give the appearance of a head at each end. — adj. amphisbae'nic.
[Gr. amphisbaina — amphis, both ways, bainein, to go.]
amphiscian am-fish'i-ən, n. an inhabitant of the torrid
zone, whose shadow is thrown both ways — that is,
to the north one part of the year, and to the south the
other part. — Also adj.   [Gr. amphiskios — amphi,
both ways, skiā, a shadow.]
amphistomous am-fis'tə-məs, adj. having a sucker at either
end, as some worms.   [Gr. amphistomos, with double
mouth — amphi, on both sides, stoma, mouth.]
amphitheatre am'fi-thē-ə-tər, n. a building with rows of
seats one above another, around an open space: a
similar configuration of hill slopes: one of the galleries
in a theatre. — adjs. amphithe'atral; amphitheatrical
(-at'ri-kl). — adv. amphitheat'rically.   [Gr. am-
phitheātron — amphi, theātron, theatre.]
amphitropous am-fit'rə-pəs, adj. (of an ovule) placed
T-wise on the funicle.   [amphi-, tropos, a turning.]
Amphitryon am-fit'ri-ən, n. in Gr. myth. husband of
Alcmene; on Alcmene Zeus, in Amphitryon's semblance, begot Herakles: a hospitable entertainer, esp.
of doubtful identity (in allusion to the line in Molière's
play, 'Le véritable Amphitryon est l'Amphitryon où
l'on dîne').   [Gr. Amphitryōn.]
ampholyte am'fō-līt, n. an amphoteric electrolyte.
amphora am'fə-rə, n. a two-handled jar used by the
Greeks and Romans for holding liquids: — pl.
am'phorae (-rē; -rī). — adj. amphor'ic (-for'; med.) like
the sound produced by speaking into a bottle.   [L.
amphora — Gr. amphoreus, amphiphoreus — amphi,
on both sides, and phoreus, a bearer.]
amphoteric am-fō-ter'ik, adj. of both kinds: acting both
ways, e.g. as acid and base, electropositive and electronegative.   [Gr. amphoteros, both.]
Ampicillin® am-pi-sil'in, n. an antibiotic drug, a type of
penicillin.
ample am'pl, adj. spacious: wide: large enough: abundant: liberal: copious: full or somewhat bulky in form.
— ns. am'pleness; am'pliā'tion enlarging: an enlargement. — adj. am'pliātive (rare). — ns. amplificā'tion
enlargement; am'plifier one who amplifies: a lens that
enlarges the field of vision: a device for giving greater
loudness. — v.t. am'plify (-fi) to make more copious
in expression: to add to: to increase loudness of
(sound), strength of (current), etc.: — pr.p. am'plifying;
pa.p. and pa.t. am'plified. — n. am'plitude largeness:
abundance: width: range: extent of vibratory movement (from extreme to extreme, or from mean to
extreme): the angular distance from the east point of
the horizon at which a heavenly body rises, or from
the west point at which it sets. — adv. am'ply (-pli)
— amplitude modulation (telecomm.) modulation in
radio transmission by varying the amplitude of the
carrier wave — cf. frequency modulation.   [Fr. ample,
amplifier, amplitude — L. amplus, amplificāre, ampli-
tūdō.]

amplexicaul *am-pleks'i-köl*, (*bot.*) *adj.* clasping the stem by a dilated base. [L. *amplexus, -ūs*, embrace, *caulis*, stem.]

ampliation, amplification, etc. See **ample.**

amplosome *am'plǝ-sōm, n.* the short, or stocky, type of human figure. [L. *amplus*, large, Gr. *sōma*, body.]

ampollosity. See **ampulla.**

ampoule *am'pōōl* (also *-pōōl'*), *n.* a small glass etc. container for a hypodermic dose, etc. — Also **am'pul, am'pule** (*-pūl*). [Fr.; see **ampulla.**]

ampulla *am-pōōl'ǝ, n.* a small two-handled flask: a pilgrim's bottle: a vessel for holy oil, as at coronations: cruet for the wine and water used at the altar: any small membranous vesicle (*biol.*): the dilated end of a semicircular canal in the ear; — *pl.* **ampull'ae** (*-ē*). — See also **ampoule.** — *n.* **ampollos'ity** (*Browning*) turgidity, bombast. [L. irregular dim. of *amphora*, a flagon; partly directly from L., partly through O.E. *ampulle*, O.Fr. *ampo(u)le*, and It. *ampolla.*]

ampussy-and. See **ampersand.**

amputate *am'pūt-āt, v.t.* to cut off, as a limb. — *ns.* **amputā'tion; am'putātor; amputee'.** [L. *amputāre, -ātum* — *amb-*, around, and *putāre, -ātum*, to lop.]

amrit *am'rǝt, n.* a sacred sweetened water used in the Sikh baptismal ceremony: the ceremony itself. [Punjabi, — Sans. *amṛta*, immortal.]

amrita *am-rē'tä, n.* the drink of the Hindu gods. — *n.* **amritattva** (*am-rē-tät'vä*) immortality. [Sans. *amṛta*, immortal; cf. Gr. *ambrotos.*]

amtman *ämt'män*, **amman** *am'an, n.* in Germany, Switzerland, the Netherlands, Scandinavia, a district magistrate. [Ger. *Amtmann, Amman*, Dan. and Norw. *amtmand* — *amt*, office, administration (from the root of **ambassador**) and Ger. *Mann*, Dan. *mand*, man.]

amtrack *am'trak, n.* an amphibious tracked military motor landing-vehicle. [**am** for *am*phibious, and **track**[1].]

Amtrak *am'trak, n.* a U.S. corporation (the National Railroad Passenger Corporation) managing passenger rail-travel between major U.S. cities. [*American Travel* and *Track*.]

amuck *ǝ-muk'*. See **amok.**

amulet *am'ū-let, -lit, n.* a charm carried about the person: a medicine supposed to have occult operation. — *adj.* **amulet'ic.** [L. *amulētum.*]

amuse *ǝ-mūz', v.t.* to put in a muse (*obs.*): to beguile with expectation: to occupy the attention of: to beguile (*arch.*): to occupy pleasantly: to entertain, divert: to excite mirth in. — *adjs.* **amus'able; amused'.** — *adv.* **amus'edly.** — *ns.* **amuse'ment** distraction of attention: beguiling: trifling: a pleasant feeling of the ludicrous: that which amuses: recreation: pastime; **amus'er; amusette** (*am-ū-zet'*) a light field gun invented by Marshal Saxe. — *adj.* **amus'ing** affording amusement: entertaining. — *adv.* **amus'ingly.** — *adj.* **amus'ive** deceptive (*obs.*): recreational (*obs.*): interesting: entertaining: amusing. — *n.* **amus'iveness.** — **amusement arcade** a public hall, etc. with mechanical gambling machines, etc. [Fr. *amuser* — *à*, to, *muser*, to stare; see **muse**[1].]

amygdal *ǝ-mig'dǝl, n.* (*obs.*) an almond. — *n.* **amyg'dala** (*zool.*) a lobe of the cerebellum: one of the palatal tonsils. — *adj.* **amygdalā'ceous** akin to the almond. — *ns.* **amyg'dale** (*-dāl*) an amygdule; **amyg'dalin** a glucoside found in cherry kernels, bitter almonds, etc. at one time thought useful in treating cancer. — *adj.* **amyg'daloid** almond-shaped: having amygdules. — *n.* an igneous rock in which almond-shaped steam-cavities have been filled with minerals. — *adj.* **amygdaloid'al** having amygdules. — *ns.* **Amyg'dalus** the almond genus, or section of Prunus; **amyg'dule** a mineral-filled steam-cavity in a lava. [L. *amygdala* — Gr. *amygdalē*, almond.]

amyl *am'il, n.* an alcohol radical, C_5H_{11}. — *ns.* **am'ylase** (*-ās*) any of the enzymes that play a part in hydrolysis of starch and similar substances; **am'ylene** a hydrocarbon of composition C_5H_{10}. — **amyl nitrate** a liquid

added to diesel fuel to improve its ignition quality, also inhaled to heighten sexual pleasure; **amyl nitrite** a fruity-smelling, amber-coloured liquid, inhaled medicinally as a vasodilator. [From the first syllable of Gr. *amylon*, starch, fine meal, and *hȳlē*, matter, from having been first got from fusel-oil made from starch.]

amylum *am'il-ǝm*, (*chem.*) *n.* starch. — *adjs.* **amylā'ceous; am'yloid.** — *n.* in any of several pathological conditions, an intercellular deposit of starch-like material in the tissues. — *adj.* **amyloid'al** — *ns.* **amyloidō'sis** the condition of the body in which amyloid is deposited in the tissues; **amylop'sin** an enzyme in pancreatic juice that converts starch into sugar. [Gr. *amylon*, the finest flour, starch; literally unmilled — *a-*, priv., *mylē*, a mill.]

amyotrophy *a-mi-ot'rǝ-fi, n.* atrophy of the muscles. [Gr. *a-*, not, *mys*, muscle, *trophē*, nourishment.]

an[1] *an, ǝn, adj.* one: the indefinite article, used before a vowel sound, and by some (now rarely) before an unstressed syllable beginning with a sounded *h.* [O.E. *ān*; see **one.**]

an[2] *an, ǝn*, (*arch.*) *conj.* if. — **an'** and. [A form of **and**[1].]

an[3] *an, ǝn*, (*obs.*) *prep.* a form of **on.**

-ana *-ä'nǝ, -ā'nǝ*, also **-iana** *-i-ä'nǝ, -ā'nǝ suff.* things belonging to, or typical of, such as sayings, anecdotes, small objects, etc., e.g. Johnson*iana*, Victor*iana* (gener. used in reference to the time of Queen Victoria rather than to Victoria herself). — **a'na** *n.pl.* or *collective sing.* (with *pl.* **a'na's, a'nas**) a collection of someone's table-talk or of gossip, literary anecdotes or possessions. [L. neut. pl. ending of adjs. in *-anus.*]

ana *ä'nǝ*, written **āā, ā** (L.L. — Gr.) lit. throughout: (in recipes and prescriptions) in equal quantities.

anabaptist *an-ǝ-bap'tist, n.* a name given by opponents to one holding that baptism should be of adults only and therefore that those baptised in infancy must be baptised again: (with *cap.*) one of a Protestant sect of German origin (1521) rejecting infant baptism and seeking establishment of a Christian communism. — *v.t.* **anabaptise', -ize'** to baptise anew: to rename. — *n.* **anabapt'ism.** — *adj.* **anabaptist'ic.** [Gr. *ana-*, again, and *baptizein*, to dip.]

Anabas *an'a-bas, n.* the genus to which belongs the climbing perch, an East Indian fish that often leaves the water: (without *cap.*) a fish of this genus. [Gr. *anabās*, aor. part. of *anabainein*, to climb — *ana*, up, *bainein*, to go.]

anabasis *an-ab'ǝ-sis, n.* a going up: a military advance up-country, such as that of Cyrus the younger (401 B.C.) related (with the subsequent katabasis or retreat of the 10,000) by Xenophon in his *Anabasis.* — *adj.* **anabatic** (*-bat'ik*) upward-moving. [Gr., — *ana*, up, *basis*, going.]

anabiosis *an-ǝ-bī-ō'sis, n.* (the power of) returning to life after apparent death: a state of suspended animation. — *adj.* **anabiot'ic.** [Gr. *anabiōsis* — *ana*, up, back, *bios*, life.]

Anableps *an'ǝ-bleps, n.* a genus of bony fishes with open air-bladders, and projecting eyes divided in two for vision in air and water: (without *cap.*) a fish of this genus. [Gr. *ana*, up, *blepein*, to look.]

anabolism *an-ab'ǝl-izm, n.* chemical upbuilding of complex substances in living matter (opp. to *katabolism*). — *adj.* **anabolic** (*an-ǝ-bol'ik*). — **anabolic steroids** steroids used to increase the build-up of body tissue, esp. muscle; illegally used by some athletes. [Gr. *anabolē*, a heaping up — *ana*, up, *bolē*, a throw.]

anabranch *an'ǝ-bränch*, (esp. *Austr.*) *n.* a stream that leaves a river and re-enters lower. [For *ana*stomosing *branch*.]

Anacardium *an-ǝ-kär'di-ǝm, n.* the cashew-nut genus, giving name to a family **Anacardiä'ceae** akin to the hollies and maples: (without *cap.*) a plant of this genus. — *adj.* **anacardiā'ceous.** [Gr. *ana*, according to, *kardiā*, heart (from the shape of the fruit).]

anacatharsis *an-ǝ-ka-thär'sis, n.* vomiting. — *n.* and *adj.* **anacathar'tic.** [Gr. *anakatharsis*, clearing up — *ana*, up, throughout, *katharsis* (see **catharsis**).]

Anacharis *ən-ak'ə-ris, n.* a genus of water-plants including *Anacharis helodea* or *Elodea canadensis*, a North American weed found in Britain in 1842, soon clogging canals and rivers by vegetative growth: (without *cap.*) a plant of this genus. [Gr. *ana*, up, and *charis*, grace.]

anachronism *ə-nak'rə-nizm, n.* an error assigning a thing to an earlier or (less strictly) to a later age than it belongs to: anything out of keeping with chronology. — *adjs.* **anachron'ic, anachronist'ic, anach'ronous.** — *advs.* **anachron'ically, anachronist'ically, anach'ronously.** [Gr. *ana-*, backwards, *chronos*, time.]

anaclastic *an-ə-klas'tik, adj.* refractive. [Gr. *anaklastos*, bent back — *ana-*, back, *klaein*, break.]

anacoluthia *an-ə-ko-lōō'thi-ə, -lū-, n.* want of syntactical sequence, when the latter part of a sentence does not grammatically fit the earlier. — *n.* **anacolu'thon** an instance of anacoluthia: anacoluthia: — *pl.* **anacolu'tha.** [Gr. *anakolouthiā, anakolouthon* — an-, priv., *akolouthos,* following.]

anaconda *an-ə-kon'də, n.* a gigantic South American water-boa, *Eunectes murinus.* [Perhaps from a Sinhalese name for another snake in Sri Lanka.]

anacoustic zone *an-ə-kōōst'ik zōn,* a zone of absolute silence in space. [Gr. *an-,* priv.; **acoustic.**]

Anacreontic *an-ak-ri-ont'ik, adj.* after the manner of the Greek poet Anacreon (*Anakreōn*; 6th cent. B.C.) — free, convivial, erotic. — *n.* a poem in this vein. — *adv.* **anacreont'ically.**

anacrusis *an-ə-krōō'sis,* (*pros.*) *n.* one or more short syllables introductory to the normal rhythm of a line: — *pl.* **anacru'ses** (*-sēz*). — *adj.* **anacrustic** (*-krus'tik*). [Gr. *anakrousis,* a pushing back, striking up a tune — *ana,* up, back, *krouein,* to strike.]

anadem *an'ə-dem, n.* a fillet, chaplet, or wreath. [Gr. *anadēma* — *ana,* up, and *deein,* to bind.]

anadiplosis *an-ə-di-plō'sis, n.* rhetorical repetition of an important word (or sometimes phrase). [Gr. *anadiplōsis* — *ana,* back, *diploein,* to double.]

anadromous *an-ad'rə-məs, adj.* of fish, ascending rivers to spawn (opp. to *catadromous*). [Gr. *anadromos,* running up — *ana,* up, *dromos,* a run.]

anadyomene *a-na-dī-o'mə-nē, adj.* coming up, emerging (esp. of Aphrodite from the sea). [Gr. *anadyomenē.*]

anaemia, in U.S. **anemia,** *an-ēm'i-ə, n.* bloodlessness: lack of red blood corpuscles or of haemoglobin — a condition marked by paleness and languor. — *adj.* **anaem'ic** suffering from anaemia: sickly, spiritless, washed-out, lacking in body (*fig.*). — **pernicious anaemia** a severe form of anaemia characterised by abnormalities in the red blood corpuscles, etc. [Gr. *anaimiā* — *an-,* priv., *haima,* blood.]

anaerobe *an'ā(ə)r-ōb, n.* an organism that lives in absence of free oxygen. — Also **anaero'biont.** — *adjs.* **anaerobic** (*-ob'ik, -ōb'ik*), **anaerobiotic** (*-ō-bī-ot'ik*) living in the absence of free oxygen: of a process, etc., requiring the absence, or not requiring the presence, of free oxygen: effected by anaerobes, as a biochemical change: involving the activity of anaerobes. — *advs.* **anaerob'ically, anaerobiot'ically.** — *n.* **anaerobio'sis** life in the absence of oxygen. [Gr. *an-,* priv., *āēr,* air, *bios,* life.]

anaesthesia, in U.S. **anesthesia,** *an-əs-thē'zi-ə, -zyə* or *-ēs', **anaesthe'sis** *-sis, ns.* loss of feeling: insensibility, general or local. — *adj.* **anaesthetic** (*-thet'ik, -thēt'ik*) producing or connected with insensibility. — *n.* an anaesthetic agent. — *adv.* **anaesthet'ically.** — *n.sing.* **anaesthet'ics** the science of anaesthesia. — *n.* **anaesthetisā'tion, -z-.** — *v.t.* **anaes'thetise, -ize.** — *ns.* **anaesthetist** (*-ēs'thə-tist,* or *-es'*) one who administers anaesthetics; **anaesthesiol'ogy** the science of administering anaesthetics; **anaesthesiol'ogist.** — **general anaesthetic** one which produces insensibility in the whole body, usually causing unconsciousness; **local anaesthetic** one producing insensibility in only the relevant part of the body. [Gr. *anaisthēsiā,* insensibility, *anaisthētos,* insensible — *an-,* priv., *aisthanesthai,* to perceive.]

anaglyph *an'ə-glif, n.* an ornament in low relief: a picture composed of two prints, in complementary colours, seen stereoscopically through spectacles of these colours. — *adj.* **anaglyph'ic.** — *n.* **Anaglypta®** (*anaglip'tə*) a type of plain white wallpaper that has a heavily embossed pattern. — Also *adj.* — *adj.* **anaglyp'tic.** [Gr. *anaglyphos, anaglyptos,* in low relief — *ana,* up, back, *glyphein,* to engrave, carve.]

anagnorisis *an-ag-nō'ri-sis, -nō', n.* recognition leading to dénouement. [Gr. *anagnōrisis.*]

anagoge *an-ə-gō'ji, n.* mystical interpretation. — Also **an'agogy.** — *adjs.* **anagogic** (*-goj'ik*) pertaining to mystical interpretation: of the strivings in the unconscious towards morally high ideals; **anagog'ical.** — *adv.* **anagog'ically.** [Gr. *anagōgē,* leading up, elevation — *ana,* up, *agein,* to lead.]

anagram *an'ə-gram, n.* word or phrase formed by the letters of another in different order. — *v.t.* and *v.i.* to anagrammatise. — *adjs.* **anagrammat'ic; anagrammat'ical.** — *adv.* **anagrammat'ically.** — *v.t.* and *v.i.* **anagramm'atise, -ize** to transpose so as to form an anagram. — *ns.* **anagramm'atism** the practice of making anagrams; **anagramm'atist** a maker of anagrams. [Gr. *ana-,* back, *gramma,* letter.]

anal, anally. See **anus.**

analcime *an-al'sim,* **analcite** *an-al'sīt, ns.* a cubic zeolite, a hydrated sodium aluminium silicate. [Gr. *an-,* priv., *alkimos, alkis,* strong, because weakly electrified by friction.]

analects *an'ə-lekts,* **analecta** *-lek'tə, ns.pl.* collected literary fragments. — *adj.* **analec'tic.** [Gr. (*pl.*) *analekta* — *ana,* up, *legein,* to gather.]

analeptic *an-ə-lep'tik, adj.* restorative: comforting. [Gr. *analēptikos,* restorative — *ana,* up, and the root *lab* of *lambanein,* to take.]

analgesia *an-al-jē'zi-ə, n.* painlessness: insensibility to pain. — *n.* **analgesic** (*-jē'sik*) an anodyne. — *adj.* producing analgesia. [Gr. *analgēsiā* — *an-,* priv., and *algein,* to feel pain.]

analogy *an-al'ə-ji, n.* an agreement or correspondence between things otherwise different: a resemblance of relations: parallelism: relation in general: a likeness: proportion, or the equality of ratios (*math.*): agreement in function, as distinguished from *homology* or agreement in origin (*biol.*): a resemblance by virtue of which a word may be altered on the model of another class of words, as *strove, striven,* remodelled upon *drove, driven, throve, thriven,* etc. (*philol.*). — *adjs.* **analogic** (*an-ə-loj'ik; rare*); **analog'ical.** — *adv.* **analog'ically.** — *v.t.* **anal'ogise, -ize** to explain or consider by analogy. — *ns.* **anal'ogist** one who sees, follows, or uses analogies; **anal'ogon** (*-gon;* Gr.) analogue. — *adj.* **anal'ogous** (*-gəs*) having analogy: bearing some correspondence or resemblance: similar in certain circumstances or relations (with *to*): positively electrified by heating. — *adv.* **anal'ogously.** — *ns.* **anal'ogousness; an'alogue** (*-log;* in U.S. also **an'alog**) that which is analogous to something else, e.g. protein substances prepared to resemble meat: that which is of like function (distinguished from a *homologue*) (*biol.*): a variable physical quantity which is similar to some other variable in that variations in the former are in the same proportional relationship as variations in the latter, often being used to record or represent such changes (also *adj.*): a watch with the traditional face and hands (also *adj.*; opp. to *digital*). — **analogue computer** a type of computer in which varying electrical currents or voltages, etc., are used to represent proportionally other quantities (e.g. forces, speeds) in working out problems about these qualities; **analogue transmission** (*telecomm.*) the transmission of signals and messages by means of radio waves, without first converting them to a computerised form as in *digital transmission.* [Gr. *analogiā* — *ana,* according to, and *logos,* ratio.]

analphabet(e) *an-al'fə-bet, -bēt, adjs.* ignorant of the alphabet. — Also *ns.* — *adj.* **analphabet'ic** totally illiterate: not alphabetic. [Gr. *analphabētos* — *an-*, priv.; see **alphabet.**]

analysis *ən-al'is-is*, *n.* a resolving or separating of a thing into its elements or component parts: ascertainment of those parts: a table or statement of the results of this: the tracing of things to their source, and so discovering the general principles underlying individual phenomena: resolution of a sentence into its syntactic elements (*gram.*): formerly, proof by assuming the result and reasoning back to principles (*math.*): use of algebraical methods: psychoanalysis: — *pl.* **anal'yses** (*-sēz*). — Opp. to *synthesis.* — Spellings with *-z-* in following words are chiefly U.S. — *adj.* **analysable, -zable** (*an-ə-līz'ə-bl*). — *n.* **analysand** (*ən-al'i-zand*) a person undergoing psychoanalysis. — *v.t.* **an'alyse, -yze** (*-līz*) to subject to analysis. — *ns.* **analys'er, -yz'er** one who analyses: in a polariscope the nicol (or substitute) through which the polarised light passes: a device that analyses; **an'alyst** (*-list*) one skilled in or practising analysis, esp. chemical or economic: a psychoanalyst. — *adj.* **analytic** (*-lit'ik*) pertaining to, performing, or inclined to analysis: resolving into first principles. — *n.* (often *pl.* in form) analytical logic: analytical geometry. — *adj.* **analyt'ical.** — *adv.* **analyt'ically.** — *n.* **analytic'ity.** — **analysis situs** (*sīt'əs; math.*) older name for topology (*math.* meanings 1 and 2); **analytical chemistry** (*loosely* **analysis**) chemistry concerned with determination of the constituents of chemical compounds, or mixtures of compounds; **analytical geometry** co-ordinate geometry; **analytical languages** those that use separate words instead of inflexions; **analytical logic** logic which is concerned with analysis. — **in the last analysis** when all inessentials are excluded from the problem, or the situation. [Gr. *analȳsis* — *analȳein*, to unloose, *ana*, up, *lȳein*, to loose.]

anamnesis *an-am-nēs'is*, *n.* the recalling to memory of things past: the recollection of the Platonic pre-existence: a patient's medical history: — *pl.* **anamnē'ses** (*-sēz*). — *adj.* **anamnēs'tic.** — *adv.* **anamnes'tically.** [Gr. *anamnēsis* — *ana*, up, back, *mimnēskein*, to remind, recall to memory.]

anamorphosis *an-ə-mör'fə-sis*, or *-fō'*, *n.* a deformed figure appearing in proportion when rightly viewed, e.g. in a curved mirror, or in a particular direction: — *pl.* **anamorphoses** (*-fə-sēz* or *fō'sēz*) — *adjs.* **anamor'phic, anamor'phous.** [Gr. *anamorphōsis*, a forming anew — *ana*, back, anew, and *morphōsis*, a shaping — *morphē*, shape, form.]

anan *ə-nan'*, (*obs.* or *dial.*) *interj.* expressing failure to understand. [**anon.**]

ananas *ə-nä'nas*, *n.* the pineapple (*Ananas sativus*): the pinguin (*Bromelia pinguin*), or its fruit. — Also **an'ana.** [From an American Indian language.]

anandrous *an-an'drəs*, (*bot.*) *adj.* lacking stamens. [Gr. *anandros*, lacking men — *an-*, priv., *anēr*, *andros*, a man.]

Ananias *an-ə-nī'əs*, *n.* a liar. [*Acts of the Apostles*, v. 1–5.]

ananke *a-nangk'ē*, (Gr. *anankē*) *n.* necessity.

ananthous *an-an'thəs*, (*bot.*) *adj.* lacking flowers. [Gr. *ananthēs* — *an-*, priv., *anthos*, a flower.]

anapaest, in U.S. **anapest**, *an'ə-pēst*, (*pros.*) *n.* a foot of two short (or unstressed) syllables followed by a long (or stressed) syllable — a dactyl reversed. — *adjs.* **anapaes'tic, -al.** [Gr. *anapaistos*, struck back — *ana*, back, *paiein*, to strike.]

anaphase *an'ə-fāz*, *n.* the stage of mitosis at which the daughter-chromosomes move towards the poles of the spindle. [Gr. *ana*, up, back, and **phase.**]

anaphora *ən-af'ə-rə*, *n.* the rhetorical device of beginning successive sentences, lines, etc., with the same word or phrase: the use of a word (such as *it*, *do*) to avoid repetition of a preceding word or group of words: the offering of the Eucharistic elements. — *adjs.* **anaphoric** (*anə-for'ik*), **-al** referring to a preceding word or group of words. — *adv.* **anaphor'ically.** [Gr. *anaphorā*, a carrying back, reference — *ana*, back, *pherein*, to bear.]

anaphrodisiac *an-af-rō-diz'i-ak*, *adj.* tending to diminish sexual desire. — *n.* an anaphrodisiac agent. [Gr. *an-*, priv., *aphrodīsiakos*, sexual.]

anaphylaxis *an-ə-fil-aks'is*, *n.* an increased susceptibility to injected foreign material, protein or non-protein, brought about by a previous introduction of it. — Also **anaphylax'y.** — *adjs.* **anaphylac'tic; anaphylac'toid** having a resemblance to anaphylaxis. [Gr. *ana*, back, *phylaxis*, protection.]

anaplasty *an'ə-pläs-ti*, *n.* the reparation of superficial lesions by the use of adjacent healthy tissue, as by transplanting a portion of skin. — *adj.* **anaplas'tic.** [Gr. *ana*, again, *plassein*, to form.]

anaplerosis *an-ə-plē-rō'sis*, *n.* the filling up of a deficiency. — *adj.* **anaplerŏt'ic.** [Gr. *anaplērōsis* — *ana*, up, and *plēroein*, to fill.]

anaptyxis *an-əp-tik'sis*, (*phon.*) *n.* the development of a vowel between consonants. — *adj.* **anaptyc'tic.** [Gr. *anaptyxis*, gape — *ana*, back, *ptyssein*, to fold.]

anarak. See **anorak.**

anarchy *an'ər-ki*, *n.* complete absence of law or government: a harmonious condition of society in which government is abolished as unnecessary: utter lawlessness: chaos: complete disorder. — *n.* **anarch** (*an'ärk*) an author, promoter, or personification of lawlessness. — *adjs.* **anarchal** *an-ärk'l*; *rare*); **anarch'ial** (*rare*); **anarch'ic, -al.** — *adv.* **anarch'ically.** — *v.t.* **anarchise, -ize** (*an'ər-kīz*) to render anarchic. — *ns.* **an'archism** the teaching of the anarchists; **an'archist** one whose ideal of society is one without government of any kind: one who seeks to advance such a condition by terrorism. — Also *adj.* — *adj.* **anarchist'ic** — *ns.* **anarch'o= syn'dicalism** syndicalism (q.v.); **anarch'o-syn'dicalist.** [Gr. *anarchiā*, leaderlessness, lawlessness — *an-*, priv., *archē*, government.]

anarthrous *an-är'thrəs*, *adj.* used without the article (of Greek nouns): without distinct joints. — *adv.* **anar'-thrously.** [Gr. *an-*, priv., *arthron*, a joint, article.]

anasarca *an-ə-sär'kə*, *n.* diffused dropsy in the skin and subcutaneous tissue. [Gr. phrase *ana sarka*, throughout the flesh.]

anastasis *an-as'tə-sis*, *n.* in Byzantine art, the Harrowing of Hell: convalescence: resurrection. — *adj.* **anastatic** (*anə-stat'ik*) of anastasis: with characters raised in relief. [Gr. *anastasis*, rising or raising up, or again — *ana*, up, again, *stasis*, a setting, standing.]

anastigmat *an-as'tig-mat*, or *-stig'*, *n.* an anastigmatic lens. — *adj.* **anastigmat'ic** (*an-ə-*) not astigmatic. — *n.* **anastig'matism.** [Gr. *an-*, priv., and **astigmatic.**]

anastomosis *an-as-tə-mō'sis*, *n.* communication by cross-connections to form a network: — *pl.* **anastomō'ses** (*-sēz*). — *v.i.* **anas'tomose** to intercommunicate in such a way. — *adj.* **anastomŏt'ic.** [Gr. *anastomōsis*, outlet — *ana*, back, *stoma*, mouth.]

anastrophe *a-* or *ə-nas'trə-fi*, (*rhet.*) *n.* inversion. [Gr. *anastrophē* — *ana*, back, and *strephein*, to turn.]

anatase *an'ə-tās*, *n.* a mineral consisting of titanium oxide. [Gr. *anatasis*, a stretching, from its long crystals.]

anathema *a-* or *ə-nath'i-mə*, *n.* a solemn ecclesiastical curse or denunciation involving excommunication: a curse, execration: a person or thing cursed ecclesiastically or generally: an object of abhorrence: — *pl.* **anath'emas.** — *adj.* **anathematical** (*-mat'i-kl*). — *n.* **anathematisation, -z-** (*-mə-tī-zā'shən*). — *v.t.* and *v.i.* **anath'ematise, -ize.** — **anathema maranatha** (*marə-na'thə*; Syriac *māran athā*, the Lord cometh, or Lord come) words happening to occur together in 1 Cor. xvi. 22, wrongly understood as an intensified curse. [Gr. *anathĕma*, a thing dedicated or accursed, for *anathēma*, a votive offering. — *ana*, up, and the root of *tithenai*, to place.]

Anatolian *an-ə-tōl'i-ən*, *adj.* of *Anatolia*, now the major part of Turkey: of or denoting any or all of an extinct family of languages belonging to, or closely related to, the Indo-European family. — *n.* a native or inhabitant of Anatolia: the Anatolian family of languages.

anatomy *ə-nat'ə-mi, n.* the art of dissecting any organised body: the science of the structure of the body learned by dissection: a subject for dissection (*obs.*): a skeleton, shrivelled and shrunken body, alive or dead, or mummy (*arch.*): bodily frame or structure: dissection: analysis. — *adjs.* **anatomic** (*an-ə-tom'ik*), **-al.** — *adv.* **anatom'ically.** — *v.t.* **anat'omise, -ize** to dissect: to lay open minutely (*fig.*). — *n.* **anat'omist** one skilled in anatomy. [Gr. *anatomē*, dissection — *ana*, up, *tomē*, a cutting.]

anatropous *a-* or *ə-nat'rə-pəs,* (*bot.*) *adj.* of an ovule, turned back and attached at the side of the funicle, which thus becomes a ridge on the ovule. — *n.* **anat'ropy.** [Gr. *ana,* back, up, *tropē,* a turning.]

anatta, anatto. See **annatto.**

a natura rei *ä na-tū'rə rē'ī, na-tōō'rä rā'ē,* (L.) from the nature of the case.

anax andron *a'naks and'rōn,* (Gr. *andrōn*) lord of men (esp. Agamemnon).

anbury *an'bər-i, n.* a soft bloody wart on horses, etc.: a disease in turnips, cabbages, etc., due to a slime-fungus. [Perh. for *angberry* — O.E. *ange*, narrow, painful, and **berry.**]

ance *äns.* Northern form of **once.**

ance-errand. See **errand.**

ancestor *an'sis-tər, n.* one from whom a person is descended: a forefather: — *fem.* **an'cestress.** — *adjs.* **ances'tral** (*-ses'*); **ancestorial** (*-sis-tō'ri-əl, -tö'*). — *n.* **an'cestry** a line of ancestors: lineage. — **an'cestor=wor'ship.** [O.Fr. *ancestre* — L. *antecēssor* — *ante,* before, *cēdere, cēssum,* to go.]

anchor¹ *ang'kər, n.* an implement for retaining a ship by chaining it to the bottom, or for holding a balloon to the ground, or the like: anything that gives stability or security (*fig.*). — *v.t.* to fix by an anchor: to fasten. — *v.i.* to cast anchor: to stop, or rest. — *n.* **anch'orage** the act of anchoring: a place of or for anchoring: a set of anchors (*Shak.*): rest or support to the mind (*fig.*): duty imposed for anchoring. — *adj.* **anch'orless.** — **anchor boys** the most junior section of the Boys' Brigade; **anchor escapement** or **recoil escapement** in a clock escapement in which the pallets push the escape-wheel slightly backwards at the end of each swing, causing a recoil of the pendulum; **anch'or-hold** the hold of an anchor upon the ground: security (*fig.*); **anch'or-ice'** ground ice; **anchor (man)** the man at the back of a team in a tug-of-war: the man who runs the last stage of a relay-race: (or **anch'or-man**) a person on whom the success of an activity depends, esp., on television, the person responsible for smooth running of a dialogue or discussion between or among others; **anch'or-ring** a solid generated by the revolution of a circle about an axis in its plane but not cutting it and not passing through its centre; **anch'or-stock** the cross-bar of an anchor, which causes one or other of the flukes to turn to the bottom. — **at anchor** anchored; **cast anchor** to let down the anchor; **weigh anchor** to take up the anchor. [O.E. *ancor* — L. *ancŏra;* cf. Gr. *ankȳra* — *ankos,* a bend; conn. with **angle¹.**]

anchor² *ang'kər* (*Shak.*), **anchoret** *-et,* **anchorite** *-īt, ns.* a man or woman who has withdrawn from the world, especially for religious reasons: a recluse. — *ns.* **anch'-orage** a recluse's cell; **anch'oress, anc'ress** a female anchorite. — *adjs.* **anchoret'ic, -al, anchorīt'ic, -al.** [Gr. *anachōrētēs* — *ana,* apart, *chōreein,* to withdraw.]

anchovy *an'chə-vi,* or *-chō-, an-chō'vi, n.* a small Mediterranean fish (*Engraulis encrasicholus*) of the herring family, used for pickling, and making sauce, paste, etc. — *n.* **anchoveta** (*-vet'ə; Sp.*) a small Pacific anchovy, used for bait. — **an'chovy-pear** the fruit of a W. Indian lecythidaceous tree (*Grias cauliflora*), often pickled. [Sp. and Port. *anchova*; of doubtful etymology.]

anchylose, etc. See **ankylose,** etc.

ancien régime *ã-syẽ rā-zhēm,* (Fr.) the old order (esp. before the French Revolution); **ancienne noblesse** (*ã-syen nob-les*) the old nobility: the nobility of the ancien régime.

ancient¹ *ān'shənt, adj.* very old: of former times: of long standing: belonging or relating to times long past, esp. before the downfall of the Western Roman Empire (A.D. 476). — *n.* an aged man: an elder or senior: one who lived in ancient times — usu. in *pl.* and applied esp. to the Greeks and Romans. — *adv.* **an'ciently.** — *ns.* **an'cientness; an'cientry** (*arch.*) antiquity: seniority: ancestry: dignity of birth: old people (*Shak.*). — **ancient history** (*coll. fig.*) information, news or gossip which, contrary to the expectations of the teller, one is already well aware of: something no longer of importance; **ancient lights** the legal right to receive in perpetuity, by certain windows, a reasonable amount of daylight; **Ancient Monument** a building of historical interest scheduled for preservation, in many cases under the care of a government department; **the Ancient of days** (*B.*) the Almighty. [Fr. *ancien* — L.L. *antiānus,* former, old — L. *ante,* before.]

ancient² *ān'shənt,* (*obs.*) *n.* a flag: a standard-bearer: an ensign. [See **ensign.**]

ancile *an-sī'lē, an-kē'lā,* (L.) *n.* the shield that fell from heaven in the reign of Numa Pompilius, on the safety of which the prosperity of Rome depended.

ancillary *an-sil'ər-i, an'sil-ər-i, adj.* subserving: ministering: auxiliary: supplementary: subsidiary: subordinate: (of computer equipment) additional in any way, not necessarily connected to the central processing unit. — Also *n.* [L. *ancilla,* a maid-servant.]

ancipitous *an-sip'i-təs,* (*bot.*) *adj.* two-edged and flattened. — Also **ancip'ital.** [L. *anceps, -cipitis,* two-edged, double — *ambi-,* on both sides, *caput, capitis,* head.]

ancle. An archaic spelling of **ankle.**

ancome *an'kəm,* (*obs.* or *dial.*) *n.* a sudden inflammation: a whitlow. [Cf. **oncome, income.**]

ancon *ang'kon, n.* the elbow: a console to support a door cornice: a breed of sheep with very short legs: — *pl.* **ancones** (*-kō'nēz*). [Latinised from Gr. *ankōn,* a bend, elbow.]

Ancona *ang-kō'nə, n.* a speckled variety of laying poultry of Mediterranean family. — Also *adj.* [*Ancona* in Italy.]

ancora *ang-kō'rä, -kō', adv.* encore. [It.]

ancress. See **anchor².**

and¹ *and, ənd, ən, n, conj.* indicating addition: also: also of another kind: used to introduce a consequence or aim: used to introduce a question expressive of surprise, realisation, wonder, incredulity, etc.: sometimes app. meaningless ('When that I was and a little tiny boy'): as a conditional conjunction (from M.E. times only; often in *Shak.*; now *arch.* — also **an, an if**) if: even if, although: as if. — **and all** not without; **and how** (*coll.*) I should think so indeed; **but and** (*obs.*) and also. [O.E. *and, ond;* cf. Ger. *und,* and L. *ante,* before, Gr. *anti,* against.]

and² *and, n.* the sign ampersand: a use of the word 'and': something added.

and³ *ən,* (*dial.* and *Shak.*) *conj.* than. [Perh. O.N. *an, en, enn,* than.]

AND *and,* (*comput.*) *n.* a logic circuit that has two or more inputs and one output, the output signal being 1 if all its inputs are 1, and 0 if any of its inputs is 0. [**and.**]

Andalusian *an-də-lōō'* (or *-lū'z(h)yən, -s(h)yən, n.* a native of *Andalusia* (Sp. *Andalucía*), in Spain: a blue variety of laying poultry, of Mediterranean family. — Also *adj.* — *n.* **andalu'site** (*-sīt*) a silicate of aluminium, first found in Andalusia.

andante *an-dan'tā,* (*mus.*) *adv.* and *adj.* moving with moderately slow, even expression. — *n.* a movement or piece composed in andante time. — *adj., adv.* and *n.* **andantino** (*mus.; an-dan-tē'nō*) (a movement, etc.) somewhat slower than andante: now more usu. intended for somewhat quicker: — *pl.* **-nos.** [It., pr.p. of *andare,* to go.]

Andean *an-dē'ən,* **Andine** *an'dīn, adjs.* of, or like, the Andes Mountains. — *ns.* **andesine** (*an'diz-ēn, -in*) a

feldspar intermediate between albite and anorthite; **an'desite** a volcanic rock with plagioclase and some ferromagnesian mineral as phenocrysts in a microlithic ground-mass (both found in the Andes). — *adj.* **andesitic** (*-it'ik*).

Anderson shelter *and'ǝr-sǝn shel'tǝr*, a small air-raid shelter consisting of an arch of corrugated iron, built partially under ground, used in Britain during World War II. — Also **And'erson**. [Sir John *Anderson*, Home Secretary 1939–1940.]

andiron *and'ī-ǝrn*, *n.* an iron bar to support the end of a log in a fire: a fire-dog. [O.Fr. *andier* (Fr. *landier* = *l'andier*); origin unknown; early confused with **iron**.]

andouillette *ā-dōō-yet*, *n.* a small chitterling sausage. [Fr.]

Andrew *an'drōō*, *n.* one of the twelve Apostles, patron saint of Scotland. — **St Andrew's cross** a saltire, or cross of equal shafts crossed diagonally: the saltire of Scotland, white on a blue ground.

Andrew Ferrara *an'drōō fi-rä'rä*, a make of sword-blade highly esteemed in Scotland from *c.* 1600. — Also **An'dro** or **Andrea** (*-drä'ä*, or *an'*) **Ferrara**. [According to some from *Andrea dei Ferrari* of Belluno, to others *Andrew Ferrars* or *Ferrier* of Arbroath, poss. as a native of Ferrara, or — L. *ferrārius, smith.]

andro-, andr- *an-dr*(ō)-, *an-dro'*, in composition, man: male. — *adjs.* **androcentric** (*an-drō-sent'rik*) male-centred, centering on the man; **androcephalous** (*-sef'ǝ-lǝs*) man-headed (Gr. *kephalē*, head); **androdioecious** (*-dī-ē'shǝs*) having hermaphrodite and male flowers on separate plants (see **dioecious**). — *ns.* **androdioe'cism; androecium** (*an-drē'shi-ǝm*, or *-si-ǝm*) stamens collectively (Gr. *oikion*, house); **androgen** (*an'drō-jǝn*) any one of the male sex hormones: a synthetic compound with similar effect. — *adjs.* **androgen'ic** pertaining to an androgen. — *n.*, *adj.* **an'drogyne** (*-jīn*) (a) hermaphrodite. — *adj.* **androgynous** (*an-droj'i-nǝs*, or *-drog'*) having the characteristics of both male and female in one individual: hermaphrodite: having an inflorescence of both male and female flowers (*bot.*). — *ns.* **androg'yny** hermaphroditism (Gr. *gynē*, woman); **an'droid** a robot in human form; **androl'ogy** the branch of medicine which deals with the functions and diseases peculiar to men. — *adj.* **andromonoecious** (*an-drō-mon-ē'shǝs*) having hermaphrodite and male flowers on the same plant (see **monoecious**). — *ns.* **andromonoe'cism; an'drophore** (*-fōr, -för*) a prolongation of the receptacle carrying the stamens (Gr. *phoros*, a bearing); **androsterone** (*ǝn-dros'tǝ-rōn, an-dro-stē'-rōn*; from *sterol*) a male sex-hormone, found in the testes and in urine. [Gr. *anēr, andros*, man, male.]

Andromeda *an-drom'i-dǝ, n.* a genus of shrubs of the heath family: (without *cap.*) a plant of this genus: a northern constellation. — *n.* **andromedotoxin** (*androm'i-dō-tok'-sin*) a vegetable drug got from Andromeda, used in relief of high blood pressure. [*Andromeda*, in Greek myth, a maiden delivered by Perseus from a sea-monster.]

andvile (*Spens.*). Same as **anvil**.

ane *yin, ān* (*Scot.* and *obs.*) *adj., n.* and *pron.* one: an, a. [O.E. *ān*.]

anear *ǝ-nēr', adv.* nearly: near. — *prep.* near. — *v.t.* to approach, to come near to. [**of**, and **near**.]

aneath *ǝ-nēth', (Scot. ǝ-neth', ǝ-nāth'), (chiefly Scot.) adv.* and *prep.* beneath. [a³ and the root of **beneath**.]

anecdote *an'ik-dōt, n.* a short narrative of an incident of private life: such narratives. — *ns.* **an'ecdotage** anecdotes collectively: garrulous old age (with pun on *dotage*); **an'ecdotist.** — *adj.* **anecdōt'al.** — *adv.* **anecdot'ally.** — *adj.* **anecdōt'ical.** [Gr. *an-*, priv., *ekdotos*, published — *ek*, out, *didonai*, to give.]

anechoic *an-ǝk-ō'ik, adj.* echoless. [Gr. *an-*, priv., and **echoic**.]

anelace. See **anlace**.

anele *ǝ-nēl', v.t.* to anoint (*arch.*): to administer extreme unction to. [O.E. *an*, on, *ele*, oil; used in reminiscence of Shakespeare; see **unaneled**.]

anemia, anemic. *U.S.* spellings of **anaemia, anaemic.**

anemo- *ǝ-nem'ō-, an-i-mo'-*, in composition, wind. — *ns.* **anemogram** (*ǝ-nem'o-gram*) an anemographic record; **anem'ograph** (*-gräf*) an instrument for measuring and recording the pressure and velocity of the wind. — *adj.* **anemographic** (*-graf'ik*). — *ns.* **anemology** (*ani-mol'ǝ-ji*) the science of the winds; **anemometer** (*-mom'i-tǝr*) a wind-gauge. — *adj.* **anemometric** (*-mōmet'rik*). — *ns.* **anemom'etry; anemone** (*ǝ-nem'ǝ-ni*) windflower — any member of the genus *Anemone* of the crowfoot family: a sea-anemone (Gr. *anemōnē.*). — *adj.* **anemoph'ilous** wind-pollinated. — *ns.* **anemoph'ily; anemophō'bia** fear of wind or draughts. [Gr. *anemos*, wind; cf. L. *animus, anima.*]

anencephaly *an-ǝn-sef'ǝ-li, -kef', n.* congenital absence of all or part of the brain. — Also **anencephal'ia** (*-āl'yǝ*). — *adj.* **anencephal'ic.** [Gr. *an-*, priv.; see **encephalon**.]

an-end *ǝn-end', adv.* to the end, continuously (*Shak.*): upright (*Shak.*): straight ahead (*naut.*). — **most an end** (*obs.*) almost always. [**an³** and **end**.]

anent *ǝ-nent', (mainly Scot.) prep.* in a line with: against: towards: in regard to, concerning, about. [O.E. *on efen*, on even.]

anerly *an'ǝr-li, (arch. Scot.) adv.* only. [**ane**; *r* perh. on analogy of some other word.]

aneroid *an'ǝ-roid, adj.* dispensing with the use of liquid. — *n.* an aneroid barometer. [Fr. *anéroïde* — Gr. *a-*, priv., *nēros*, wet, *eidos*, form.]

anesthesia, etc. *U.S.* spelling of **anaesthesia**, etc.

anestrum, etc. U.S. spelling of **anoestrum**, etc..

anetic *a-net'ik, (med.) adj.* soothing. [L. *aneticus* — Gr. *anetikos*, abating sickness.]

aneurin *an'ū-rin, ǝ-nū'rin, n.* vitamin B₁, deficiency of which affects the nervous system. — Also called **thiamine.** [Gr. *a-*, priv., *neuron*, nerve.]

aneurysm *an'ūr-izm, n.* dilatation of an artery (*path.*): any abnormal enlargement. — *adj.* **aneurys'mal.** — Also **aneurism, -al.** [Gr. *aneurysma* — *ana*, up, *eurys*, wide.]

anew *ǝ-nū', in U.S. -nōō', adv.* afresh: again. [**of** and **new.**]

anfractuous *an-frakt'ū-ǝs, adj.* winding, involved, circuitous. — *n.* **anfractü'osity** (*-os'i-ti*). [L. *anfractuōsus* — *ambi-*, about, *frangěre*, to break.]

Angaraland *ang-gä-rä'land, (geol.) n.* the primitive nucleus of N.E. Asia. [*Angara* River.]

angary *ang'gǝr-i, n.* a belligerent's right to seize and use neutral or other property (subject to compensation). [Gr. *angareiā*, forced service — *angaros*, a courier — a Persian word — Assyrian *agarru*, hired labourer.]

angek(k)ok *ang'gi-kok, n.* an Eskimo sorcerer or shaman. [Eskimo.]

angel *ān'jl, n.* a divine messenger: a ministering spirit: an attendant or guardian spirit: a person possessing the qualities attributed to these — gentleness, purity, etc.: a dead person regarded as received into heaven: one supposed to have a special commission, as the head of the Church in Rev. ii and iii: in the Catholic Apostolic Church, one who corresponds in a limited sense to a bishop: a messenger generally (*poet.*): an old Eng. coin bearing the figure of an angel: a radar echo of unknown origin: a financial backer or adviser (*coll.*): a rich man who is an easy victim for those in search of money (*coll.*). — *n.* **ān'gelhood.** — *adjs.* **angelic** (*an-jel'ik*), **-al.** — *adv.* **angel'ically.** — *ns.* **Angel'ica** a genus of umbelliferous plants with large leaves and double-winged fruit, once highly reputed as a defence against poison and pestilence: (without *cap.*) a garden plant by some included in the genus as *A. archangelica*, by others called *Archangelica officinalis*: its candied leaf-stalks and midribs; **āngelol'atry** angel-worship; **āngelol'ogy** doctrine regarding angels; **ān'geloph'any** the manifestation of an angel to a man. — **an'gel-cake, an'gel-food** a cake made of flour, sugar, and white of egg; **angel dust** (*coll.*) the drug phencyclidine, a hallucinogen; **an'gel-fish** a kind of shark (*Squatina*, or *Rhina*), with large wing-like pectoral fins:

For other sounds see detailed chart of pronunciation.

a tropical American river-rish (*Pterophyllum*) of the family Cichlidae, much compressed, almost circular in body but crescent-shaped owing to the long fin filaments, the whole banded with changing black vertical stripes: applied also to *Pomacanthus* and several other fishes of the Chaetodontidae; **angel′ica-tree** an American aralia; **ang′els-on-horse′back** oysters and bacon on toast; **an′gel-water** a perfumed liquid, at first made largely from angelica, then from ambergris, rosewater, orange-flower water, etc. — **on the side of the angels** basically in sympathy with traditional virtues and virtuous aims.   [Gr. *angelos*, a messenger.]

angelus *an′ji-ləs, n.* a short devotional exercise in honour of the Incarnation, repeated three times daily: the bell rung in Roman Catholic countries at morning, noon, and sunset, to invite the faithful to recite it.   [From the introductory words, '*Angelus domini nuntiavit Mariae*'.]

anger *ang′gər, n.* hot displeasure, often involving a desire for retaliation: wrath: inflammation (now *dial.*). — *v.t.* to make angry: to irritate. — *adj.* **an′gerless.** — *advs.* **an′gerly** (*arch.*), **ang′rily.** — *n.* **ang′riness.** — *adj.* **ang′ry** excited with anger: inflamed: of threatening or lowering aspect. — *n.* an angry young man. — **angry young man** a young man loud in disgust at what his elders have made of society (from *Look Back in Anger*, play, 1956, by John Osborne, one of a group of writers of the period to whom the term was applied).   [O.N. *angr*; cf. **agnail, anbury, angina, anguish.**]

Angevin *an′ji-vin, adj.* of *Anjou*, in France: relating to the Plantagenet house that reigned in England from 1154 to 1485, descended from Geoffrey V, Count of Anjou. — *n.* a native of Anjou: a member of the house of Anjou — by some reckoned only down to loss of Anjou (1204), by others, till the deposition of Richard II in 1399.

angico *an′ji-kō, n.* a S. American mimosaceous tree (*Piptadenia*): its gum: — *pl.* **an′gicos.**   [Port. — Tupi.]

angina *an-jī′nə, (rare* but etymologically better *an′ji-nə), n.* any inflammatory affection of the throat, as quinsy, croup, etc. — *adj.* **anginal** (*an-jī′nl, an′ji-nl).* — **angina pec′toris** a disease of the heart marked by paroxysms of intense pain, radiating from the breastbone mainly towards the left shoulder and arm.   [L. *angīna*; see **anguish.**]

angiocarpous *an-ji-ō-kär′pəs, adj.* having the fruit, or in fungi the hymenium, within a special covering.   [Gr. *angeion*, a case, *karpos*, fruit.]

angiogram *an′ji-ō-gram, n.* a photograph made by angiography. — *ns.* **angiogen′esis** the development of blood vessels and heart tissue in the embryo; **angiog′raphy** the art or process of making X-ray photographs of blood-vessels by injecting the vessels with a substance opaque to the rays; **angioma** (*an-ji-ō′mə*) a benign tumour composed of blood or lymph vessels: — *pl.* **angiō′mas, angiō′mata; angioplas′ty** surgery of the blood vessels; **angiosarcō′ma** a malignant tumour of the vascular endothelia, occurring in the liver and other sites.   [Gr. *angeion*, a case, vessel.]

angiosperm *an′ji-ō-spûrm, n.* a plant of the **Angiosperm′ae,** one of the main divisions of flowering plants, in which the seeds are in a closed ovary, not naked as in gymnosperms. — *adjs.* **angiosperm′al; angiosperm′ous.**   [Gr. *angeion*, case, *sperma*, seed.]

angiostomous *an-ji-os′təm-əs,* **angiostomatous** *an-ji-ō-sto′-mə-təs, adjs.* narrow-mouthed: with a mouth that is not distensible.   [Gr. *angeion*, a vessel, case, confused with L. *angĕre*, to compress; Gr. *stŏma, stomatos,* mouth.]

angle¹ *ang′gl, n.* a corner: the point from which lines or surfaces diverge: the inclination of two straight lines, or of two curves measured by that of their tangents, or of two planes measured by that of perpendiculars to their intersection (*geom.*): the spread of a cone, a number of meeting planes or the like, measured by the area on the surface of a sphere subtending it at the centre (*geom.*): an outlying corner or nook: a point of

view: a frame (*snooker,* etc.): an angle shot (*squash).* — *v.t.* to put in a corner: to corner: to put in the jaws of a billiard pocket: to move, drive, direct, turn, adjust, present, at an angle: to present (news, etc.) in such a way as to serve a particular end. — *v.i.* to proceed at an angle or by an angular course. — *adj.* **angled** having angles: biased. — *adv.* **ang′lewise.**   *adj.* **ang′ular** (*ang′gū-lər*) having an angle or corner: measured by an angle: stiff in manner, the opposite of easy or graceful (*fig.*): bony and lean in figure. — *n.* **angūlarity** (*-lar′i-ti*). — *adjs.* **ang′ūlate(d)** formed with angles. — *n.* **angūlā′tion** the action of making angulate(d): an angular formation, angle: the measurement of angles. — **ang′ledozer** a bulldozer whose blade may be angled or tilted to the left or right; **angle iron** an L-shaped piece of iron or steel used in structural work; **angle shot** in cinematography, a shot taken with a camera tilted above or below the horizontal: in squash, a shot which hits first the side wall, then the front wall, without touching the floor; **angular velocity** the rate at which an object rotates round a fixed point or axis, measured as the rate of change in the angle turned through by the line between the object and the point or axis.   [Fr., — L. *angulus,* cog. with Gr. *ankylos*; both from root *ank,* to bend, seen also in **anchor¹, ankle.**]

angle² *ang′gl, n.* a fish-hook or fishing-tackle (*obs*): an act of angling (esp. *fig.*). — *v.i.* to fish with rod and line (for): to try to gain by some artifice (with *for*). — *v.t.* to angle for. — *ns.* **ang′ler** one who fishes with rod and line, esp. for sport: the devil-fish or fishing-frog, a wide-mouthed voracious fish (*Lophius piscatorius*) that attracts its prey by waving filaments attached to its head: extended to related kinds, some of them remarkable for the dwarf males parasitic on the female; **ang′ling.** — **ang′le-worm** any worm used as bait by anglers.   [O.E. *angul,* hook.]

Angle *ang′gl, n.* a member or descendant of the German tribe (O.E. *Engle*) from Schleswig that settled in Northumbria, Mercia, and East Anglia. — *adj.* **Ang′-lian** of the Angles. — *n.* an Angle: the English dialect of the Angles. — *adj.* **Ang′lican** of or characteristic of the Church of England and churches in communion with it: English (esp. *U.S.*). — Also *n.* — *n.* **Ang′-licanism** the principles of the Church of England: attachment to English institutions, esp. the English Church. — *adv.* **Anglice** *ang′gli-sē;* L. *ang′gli-kā;* also without *cap.*) in English. — *n.* **anglicisa′tion, -z-.** — *v.t.* **ang′licise, -ize** (*-sīz*) to make English. — *v.i.* to assume or conform to English ways. — *ns.* **ang′licism** (*-sizm*) an English idiom or peculiarity: English principles; **ang′licist, ang′list** one who has a scholarly knowledge of the English language, literature, and culture. — *n.sing.* **anglist′ics** the study of these subjects. — *v.t.* **ang′lify** to make English. — *adj.* **Anglo** (*ang′glō*) of British extraction: (esp. *U.S.*) Anglo-American. — Also *n.:* — *pl.* **Ang′los.**   **Anglo-** in composition, English: British: esp. conjointly English or British and something else. — *adj.* **Anglo-Amer′ican** English in origin or birth, American by settlement or citizenship: (esp. *U.S.*) having English as one's mother tongue and sharing a cultural outlook of British origin: (esp. *U.S.*) non-Latin: (of England or Britain and America. — *n.* an Anglo-American person. — *n.* **Anglo-Cath′olic** one who regards himself as a Catholic of Anglican pattern: a High-Churchman. — Also *adj.* — *n.* **Anglo-Cathol′icism.** — *adjs.* **Anglocen′tric** taking English or British affairs, institutions, culture, etc. as a norm, focus, etc. in one's outlook or behaviour; **Anglo-French′** of England or Britain and France. — *n.* the form of the French language formerly spoken in England. — *adj.* **Anglo-In′dian** of England or Britain and India: of India under the British: of the English or British in India: of British birth but (formerly or presently) long resident in India: of English as spoken in India: Eurasian. — *n.* a person of British birth long resident (formerly or presently) in India: an Indian Eurasian. — *n.*

Anglo-I'rish the English language as spoken in Ireland: Irish people of English descent: people of mixed English and Irish descent. — *adj.* of England or Britain and Ireland: of the Anglo-Irish people or speech. — *n.* **Anglo-Is'raelite** one who believes that the British are descendants of the Jewish 'lost tribes' carried off by the Assyrians 721 B.C. — Also *adj.* — *ns.* **angloma'nia** (also with *cap.*) a craze, or indiscriminate admiration, for what is English; **angloma'niac** (also with *cap.*); **Anglo-Nor'man** the French dialect of the Normans in England. — Also *adj.* (All the following also with *cap.*) *n.* **ang'lophil** (*-fil*), also **-phile** (*-fīl*) a friend and admirer of England and things English (Gr. *philos*, friend). — Also *adj.* — *n.* **anglophil'ia.** — *adj.* **anglophil'ic.** — *n.* **ang'lophobe** one who fears or dislikes England and things English (Gr. *phobos*, fear). — Also *adj.* — *n.* **anglophō'bia.** — *adjs.* **anglophō'biac, -phobic** (*-fob', -fob'*); **Ang'lophone** (sometimes without *cap.*) of a state, person, etc., speaking or using English, esp. as opp. to French, in everyday affairs. — *n.* an English-speaking, esp. as opp. to French-speaking, person, esp. in a state, etc. where English is not the only language spoken. — *adj.* **Anglophŏn'ic** (sometimes without *cap.*) — *n.* **Anglo-Sax'on** Old English (q.v.): one of the Germanic settlers in England and Scotland, including Angles, Saxons, and Jutes, or of their descendants: a Saxon of England, distinguished from the Old Saxons of the Continent: anybody of English speech. — Also *adj.* — *n.* **Anglo-Sax'ondom.** [L. *Anglus*.]

anglesite *ang'gli-sīt, n.* orthorhombic lead sulphate, first found in *Anglesey*.

Anglican, etc., **Anglo-,** etc. See **Angle.**

Angola *ang-gō'lə, adj.* Angora: pertaining to *Angola* in Africa. — *n.* and *adj.* **Ango'lan** (a native or inhabitant) of Angola.

Angora *ang-gō'rə, -gö', adj.* of *Ang'ŏra* (Gr. *Ankȳra*; in later times *Angora, Ankara*) a town of ancient Galatia, now capital of Turkey: (sometimes without *cap.*) of an Angora breed, yarn, etc. — *n.* (in all meanings sometimes without *cap.*) an Anatolian goat: its long silky wool (the true mohair): cloth made from it: a silky-haired rabbit: an Angora cat: yarn or material partly or wholly of Angora rabbit hair. — **Angora cat** a silky-haired kind of cat similar to the Persian and possibly no longer existing as a pure breed, the term now being treated by some as an obsolete term for Persian cat.

Angostura *ang-gos-tū'rə, n.* a town (now Ciudad Bolivar) on the narrows (Sp. *angostura*) of the Orinoco in Venezuela, giving name to an aromatic bitter bark from certain trees of the family Rutaceae, esp. *Cusparia,* formerly used in medicine. — **Angostura bitters®** a brand of aromatic bitters first made in Angostura.

angry. See **anger.**

Angst, angst *ängst, n.* anxiety, esp. a general feeling of anxiety produced by awareness of the uncertainties and paradoxes inherent in the state of being human. — *adj.* **Angst'-, angst'-ridden.** [Ger. *Angst*, Dan. *angst*, fear, anxiety.]

Ångström, angstrom *ang'* or *ong'strəm, n.* a unit (10⁻¹⁰ metres) used in expressing wavelengths of light, ultraviolet rays, X-rays, molecular and atomic distances. — Formerly, but not now usu., **Ång-, angstrom unit.** [Anders J. *Ångström* (1814–74), Swedish physicist.]

Anguis *ang'gwis, n.* the generic name not of a snake but of the blindworm. — *n.* **ang'uifauna** fauna of snakes. — *adj.* **ang'uiform** snake-shaped. — *n.* **Anguill'a** the common eel genus. — *adj.* **anguill'iform** eel-like. — *n.* **Anguill'üla** the paste-eel genus of nematode worms. — *adjs.* **anguine** (*ang'gwin*) of or like a snake; **ang'uiped(e)** (*-ped, -pēd*) having feet or legs in the form of snakes. [L. *anguis,* snake; *adj. anguinus*; *dim. anguīlla,* eel.]

anguish *ang'gwish, n.* excessive pain of body or mind: agony. — *v.t.* to afflict with anguish. — *v.i.* to suffer anguish. — *adj.* **ang'uished.** [O.Fr. *angoisse*, choking — L. *angustia*, tightness, narrowness.]

angular, angulated, etc. See under **angle¹.**

angusti- *ang-gus'ti-,* in composition, narrow. — *adjs.* **angustifo'liate** narrow-leaved; **angustiros'trate** narrow-beaked. [L. *angustus*, narrow.]

angwantibo *ang-wăn'ti-bō, n.* a small W. African lemur: — *pl.* **angwan'tibos.** [W. African word.]

anharmonic *an-här-mon'ik, adj.* not harmonic. — **anharmonic ratio** cross-ratio (harmonic when = −1). [Gr. *an-*, priv., *harmonikos,* harmonic.]

anhedonia *an-hi-dō'ni-ə, (psych.) n.* the inability to feel pleasure: the loss of interest in formerly pleasurable pursuits. [Gr. *an-,* priv., *hēdonē*, pleasure.]

anhedral *an-hē'drəl, adj.* allotriomorphic (*chem.*).

an-heires (*Shak.*), an obscure word in *Merry Wives* II, i. 227, variously conjectured to be an error for **on here,** for **mynheers,** or for **ameers.**

anhelation *an-hi-lā'shən, n.* shortness of breath. [L. *anhēlātiō, -ōnis* — *anhēlāre*, to gasp.]

anhungered. See **ahungered.**

anhydride *an-hī'drīd, n.* a compound representing in its composition an acid *minus* water. — *n.* **anhy'drite** a mineral, anhydrous calcium sulphate. — *adj.* **anhy'drous** free from water. [Gr. *an-*, priv., *hydōr*, water.]

aniconic *an-ī-kon'ik, adj.* symbolising without aiming at resemblance: pertaining to aniconism. — *ns.* **ani'conism** (*-kən-izm*) worship or veneration of an object that represents a god without being an image of him; **ani'conist.** [Gr. *an-*, priv., *eikōn*, image.]

anicut, annicut *an'i-kut, n.* a dam. [Tamil *anaikattu*.]

anigh *ə-nī', prep.* and *adv.* nigh. [*a-* as in *anear, afar,* and **nigh;** a modern formation.]

anight *ə-nīt', (Shak.) adv.* of nights, at night. [*of* and **night.**]

anil *an'il, n.* indigo, plant or dye. [Port. *anil* — Ar. *an-nil,* the indigo plant — Sans. *nīlī*, indigo.]

anile *an'īl, ān'īl, adj.* old-womanish: imbecile. — *n.* **anility** (*a-* or *ə-nil'i-ti*) old-womanishness: imbecile dotage. [L. *ănus, -ūs,* an old woman.]

aniline *an'il-ēn, -in,* or *-īn, n.* a product of coal tar extensively used in dyeing and other industrial arts, first obtained from *anil.* — Also *adj.* (as in *aniline dye*).

anima *an'i-mə, n.* the soul, the innermost part of the personality: in Jungian psychology, the female component of the male personality. — **anima mundi** (*mun'di, mŏŏn'dē*) the soul of the world. [L.]

animadvert *an-im-ad-vûrt', v.i.* to take cognisance (*law*; usu. with *on, upon*): to take note: to comment critically (on): to express censure. — *v.t.* to consider, to observe (*obs.*). — *ns.* **animadver'sion; animadvert'er.** [L. *animus,* the mind, *ad,* to, and *vertĕre,* to turn.]

animal *an'i-məl, n.* an organised being having life, sensation, and voluntary motion — typically distinguished from a plant, which is organised and has life, but apparently not sensation or voluntary motion: often, a lower animal — one below man: a mammal: a brutish or sensual man: loosely or colloquially, a person, thing, organisation, etc. — *adj.* of, of the nature of, derived from, or belonging to an animal or animals: brutal, sensual. — *adj.* **animal'ic** of or pertaining to animals. — *n.* **animalisā'tion, -z-.** — *v.t.* **an'imalise, -ize** to represent or conceive in animal form: to endow with animal life or the properties of animal matter: to convert into animal matter: to brutalise, sensualise. — *ns.* **an'imalism** exercise or enjoyment of animal life, as distinct from intellectual: the state of being actuated by mere animal appetites: brutishness, sensuality: the theory that man is a mere animal being; **an'imalist** one who practises or believes in animalism: one who paints, carves, or writes stories about, animals; **animality** (*-al'i-ti*) animal nature or life: status of an animal or of a lower animal. — *adv.* **an'imally** physically. — **animal liberationalist** a member or supporter of any body dedicated to ending the exploitation of animals by man; — **animal magnetism** see under **magnet; animal spirits** (orig. *spirit*) formerly, a supposed principle formed in the brain out of vital spirits and conveyed to all parts of the body through the nerves: nervous force: exuberance of health and life: cheerful buoyancy of temper: the spirit or principle of volition and sensation (*Milt.*); **an'imal-worship; an'imal-worshipper.** — **there is, ain't, no such animal** (*coll.*) there is no such person, creature or thing. [L. *animal* — *anima*, air, breath, life, soul.]

animal bipes *an'i-mal bī'pēz, bi'pās,* (L.) a two-footed animal, man; **animal implume** *im-plōō'mē, -me,* a featherless animal; **animal rationale** *rā-shi-ō-nā'lē, ra-ti-ō-nā'le,* a reasoning animal; **animal risibile** *rī-si'bi-lē, rē-si'bi-le,* an animal able to laugh.

animalcule *an-im-al'kūl, n.* a small animal: (now) one that cannot be seen by the naked eye: — *pl.* **animal'cules, animal'cula.** — *adj.* **animal'cular.** — *n.* **animal'culist** one who believes that the spermatozoon contains all future generations in germ. [L. *animalculum,* dim. of *animal.*]

animate *an'im-āt, v.t.* to give life to: to enliven: to inspirit: to actuate. — *adj.* (*-mit*) living: having animal life. — *adj.* **an'imated** lively: full of spirit: endowed with life: moving as if alive. — *adv.* **an'imatedly.** — *adj.* **an'imating.** — *adv.* **an'imatingly.** — *ns.* **anima'tion** the act of animating: the state of being alive: liveliness: vigour; **an'imatism** primitive attribution of life to natural phenomena and natural objects, but not, as in *animism,* belief that spirits reside in them; **an'imātor** one who enlivens or animates something: an artist who makes drawings for animated cartoons. — **animated cartoon** a motion picture produced from drawings, each successive drawing showing a very slight change of position so that a series of them gives the effect of a definite movement. [L. *animāre, -ātum* — *anima,* air, breath, life.]

animé, anime *an'i-mā, -mē, n.* the resin of the W. Indian locust-tree: extended to other gums and resins. [Said to be Fr. *animé,* living, from the number of insects in it; but perhaps a native name.]

animism *an'im-izm, n.* the attribution of a soul to natural objects and phenomena: G. E. Stahl's theory that the soul is the vital principle. — *n.* **an'imist.** — *adj.* **animis'tic.** [L. *anima,* the soul.]

animo et fide *an'i-mō et fī'dē, fi'dā,* (L.) by courage and faith.

animosity *an-im-os'i-ti, n.* strong dislike: enmity. [L. *animōsitās,* fullness of spirit.]

animus *an'im-əs, n.* intention: actuating spirit: hostility: in Jungian psychology, the male component of the female personality. [L. *animus,* spirit, soul.]

anion *an'ī-ən, n.* an ion that seeks the anode: an electronegative ion. — *adj.* **anion'ic.** [Gr. *ana,* up, *iŏn,* going, pr.p. neut. of *ienai,* to go.]

anise *an'is, n.* an umbelliferous plant (*Pimpinella*) whose aromatic seeds, of a flavour similar to liquorice, are used in making cordials: in Matt. xxiii. 23 (Gr. *an ēthon*) believed to be dill. — *ns.* **an'iseed** the seed of anise: anisette; **anisette** (*an-i-zet'*) a cordial or liqueur prepared from anise seed. — **star-anise** see **star**[1]. [Gr. *anīson,* anise.]

aniso- *an-ī'sō-,* or *-so',* in composition, unequal. — *adjs.* **anisocercal** (*-sûr'kl*) with unequal tail-lobes; **anisodac'tylous** (of birds) with three toes turned forward, one backward; **anisom'erous** with unequal numbers of parts in the floral whorls; **anisophyll'ous** with differently formed leaves on different sides of the shoot; **anisotrop'ic** not isotropic, showing differences of property or of effect in different directions. — *n.* **anisot'ropy.** [Gr. *anisos,* unequal — *an-,* priv., *isos,* equal.]

anker *angk'ər, n.* an old measure for wines and spirits used in Northern Europe, varying considerably — that of Rotterdam 8½ imperial gallons. [Du.]

ankerite *ang'kər-īt, n.* a rhombohedral carbonate of calcium, iron, magnesium, and manganese. [After Professor M. J. Anker (1772–1843), Austrian mineralogist.]

ankh *angk, n.* an ansate cross — T-shaped with a loop above the horizontal bar — the symbol of life. [Egypt., life.]

ankle *or* (*arch.*) **ancle** *angk'l, n.* the joint connecting the foot and leg. — *adj.* **ank'led** having ankles. — *n.* **ank'let** (*-lit*) an ornamental or supporting ring or chain for the ankle. — **ank'le-boot, ank'le-jack** a boot reaching above the ankle; **ank'le-chain** a chain worn as decoration round the ankle; **ankle sock** a sock reaching to and covering the ankle; **ankle strap** (a shoe with) a strap which fastens round the ankle. [O.E. *anclēow*; cf. Ger. *Enkel,* and **angle**[1].]

Ankole *ang-kō'lē, n.* a breed of large cattle with long horns. — Also *adj.* [*Ankole,* plateau region in Uganda.]

ankus *ang'kəs, n.* an elephant goad. [Hind.]

ankylosaur *ang'kə-lə-sör, n.* any of the **Ankylosauria** (*-sör'i-ə*), a suborder of bird-hipped plant-eating dinosaurs of the Cretaceous period, with short legs and flattened heavily-armoured bodies, including **Ankylosaur'us** which gave name to the suborder. [Mod. L. — Gr. *ankylos,* crooked, *sauros,* lizard.]

ankylosis, anchylosis *ang-ki-lō'sis, n.* the fusion of bones or skeletal parts: the fixation of a joint by fibrous bands or union of bones. — *v.t.* and *v.i.* **ank'ylose, anch'ylose** to stiffen or fuse, as a joint or bones. — *adj.* **ank'ylosed, anch'ylosed.** — **ankylosing spondylitis** rheumatoid arthritis of the spine. [Gr. *ankylōsis,* stiffening of a joint — *ankyloein,* to crook.]

ankylostomiasis, anchylostomiasis *ang-ki-lō-sto-mī'ə-sis, n.* hookworm disease or miner's anaemia, caused by a parasitic nematode (*Ankylostomum duodenale* or other). [Gr. *ankylos,* crooked, *stoma,* mouth.]

anlace, anelace *an'las, -ləs, n.* a short two-edged tapering dagger. [Ety. unknown.]

anlage *än'lä-gə, (biol.) n.* the primordium or first rudiment of an organ. [Ger.]

ann *an, (Scot.) n.* see **annat.**

anna *an'ə, n.* a former coin of India, Pakistan, and Bangladesh, the sixteenth part of a rupee. (Decimal coinage introduced India, 1957, Pakistan, 1961.) [Hind. *ānā.*]

annabergite *an'ə-bûrg-īt, n.* an apple-green mineral, hydrous nickel arsenate. [*Annaberg* in Saxony in E. Germany.]

annal *an'əl, n.* a year's entry in a chronicle: (in *pl.*) records of events under the years in which they happened: historical records generally: year-books. — *v.t.* **ann'alise, -ize** to record. — *n.* **ann'alist** a writer of annals. — *adj.* **annalist'ic.** [L. *annālis,* yearly — *annus,* a year.]

annat *an'ət, n.,* **annates** *an'āts, n.pl.,* the first-fruits, or one year's income of a benefice, paid to the Pope (in England from 1535 to the crown, from 1703 to Queen Anne's bounty; extinguished or made redeemable 1926): **annat** or **ann** (*Scots law*) from 1672 to 1925 the half-year's stipend payable after a parish minister's death to his widow or next of kin. [L.L. *annāta* — L. *annus,* a year.]

an(n)atto *a-* or *ə-nat'ō,* **an(n)atta** *-ə,* **arnotto** *är-not'ō, ns.* a bright orange colouring matter got from the fruit pulp of a tropical American tree, *Bixa orellana* (fam. *Bixaceae*): — *pl.* **-s.** [Supposed to be of Carib origin.]

anneal *ə-nēl', v.t.* to heat and cool gradually (glass, metals), usu. in order to soften: to heat in order to fix colours on, as glass. — Also *v.i.* — *ns.* **anneal'er; anneal'ing.** [Pfx. *an-,* on, and O.E. *ǣlan,* to burn.]

annectent *ə-nek'tənt, (biol.) adj.* connecting, linking, having characteristics that are intermediate between those of two other species, genera, etc. [L. *annectĕre* — *ad,* to, *nectĕre,* to tie.]

annelid *an'ə-lid, n.* a member of the **Annelida** (*ə-nel'i-də*) a class comprising the red-blooded worms, having a long body composed of numerous rings. [L. *annellus, ānellus,* dim. of *ānulus,* a ring.]

annex *ə-neks', v.t.* to add to the end: to join or attach: to take permanent possession of: to purloin, appropriate (*coll.*): to affix: to append. — *n.* (*an'eks*) something added: a supplementary building — sometimes (as Fr.) **annexe** (*a-neks', an'eks*). — *n.* **annexā'tion** (*an-*). — *n.* and *adj.* **annexā'tionist.** — *ns.* **annexion**

(ə-nek'shən) the act of annexing: something annexed (*Shak.*); **annex'ment** addition (*Shak.*): the thing annexed; **annexure** (*a-nek'shər*) something added, esp. an addition to a public document. [L. *annectĕre*, *annexum* — *ad*, to, *nectĕre*, to tie.]

annicut. See **anicut.**

annihilate ə-nī'(h)il-āt, *v.t.* to reduce to nothing: to put out of existence: to crush or wither by look or word (*fig.*): to defeat completely (*coll. fig.*): to cause to annihilate (*phys.*). — *v.i.* to undergo annihilation (*phys.*). — *ns.* **annīhilā'tion** reduction to nothing: the destruction of soul as well as body (*theol.*): the process by which a particle and its corresponding antiparticle, e.g. an electron and a positron, combine and are spontaneously transformed into radiation (**annihilation radiation**) (*phys.*); **annīhilā'tionism** the belief that the soul (esp. of the unrepentant wicked) dies with the body. — *adj.* **annī'hilātive.** — *n.* **annī'hilātor.** [L. *annihilāre*, *-ātum* — *ad*, to, *nihil*, nothing.]

anniversary an-i-vûrs'ə-ri, *adj.* returning, happening or commemorated about the same date every year: pertaining to annual recurrence or celebration. — *n.* the day of the year on which an event happened or is celebrated as having happened in a previous year: the celebration proper to recurrence, esp. a mass or religious service. [L. *anniversārius* — *annus*, a year, and *vertĕre*, *versum*, to turn.]

anno an'ō, (L.) in the year; **anno Christi** kris'tī, *-tē*, in the year of Christ; **anno Domini** dom'in-ī, *-ē*, in the year of our Lord (used as *n.* for 'advancing old age'); **anno mundi** mun'dī, mōōn'dē, in the year of the world (used in reckoning dates from the supposed time of creation); **anno regni** reg'nī, *-nē*, in the year of the reign; **anno salutis** sal-ū'tis, *-ōō'*, in the year of redemption; **anno urbis conditae** ûr'bis kon'dit-ē, ōōr'bis kon'dit-ī, in the year of the founding of the city (i.e. Rome, 753 B.C.).

Annona. See **Anona.**

annotate an'ō-tāt, *v.t.* to make notes upon. — *v.i.* to append notes. — *ns.* **annōtā'tion** the making of notes: a note of explanation: comment; **ann'ōtātor.** [L. *annotāre* — *ad*, to, *notāre*, *-ātum*, to mark.]

announce ə-nowns', *v.t.* to declare: to give public notice of: to make known. — *ns.* **announce'ment; announc'er** one who announces: in radio and television, one who reads the news and announces other items in the programme. [O.Fr. *anoncer* — L. *annuntiāre* — *ad*, to, *nuntiāre*, to report.]

annoy ə-noi', *v.t.* and *v.i.* to trouble: to vex: to tease: to harm, esp. in military sense. — *ns.* **annoy'** (now poetic), **annoy'ance** that which annoys: the act of annoying: the state of being annoyed. — *adjs.* **annoyed'** (with *at*, *with*); **annoy'ing.** — *adv.* **annoy'ingly.** [O.Fr. *anoier* (noun *anoi*, mod. *ennui*) — L. L. *inodiāre* — L. phrase, *in odiō*, as in 'est mihi *in odiō*' = it is to me hateful; It. *annoiare*.]

annual an'ū-əl, *adj.* yearly: coming every year: lasting or living for a year: requiring to be renewed every year: performed in a year: being, or calculated as, the total for one year. — *n.* a plant that lives for one year only: a publication appearing yearly, esp. an illustrated gift-book: a year-book. — *v.t.* **annualise, -ize** to convert to a yearly rate, amount, etc. — *adv.* **ann'ually.** — **annual rings** rings, as seen in cross-section, in a branch or trunk, representing generally a year's growth of wood. [L.L. *annuālis* — *annus*, a year.]

annuity ə-nū'i-ti, *n.* a payment (generally of uniform amount) falling due in each year during a given term, such as a period of years or the life of an individual, the capital sum not being returnable. — *n.* **annū'itant** one who receives an annuity. — **annuity due** one whose first payment is due in advance; **certain annuity** one for a fixed term of years, subject to no contingency whatever; **complete annuity** one of which a proportion is payable up to the day of death; **contingent annuity** one that depends on the continuance of some status, as the life of a person; **curtate annuity** one payable only at the end of each year survived; **deferred** or **reversion-**

ary annuity one whose first payment is not to be made until the expiry of a certain number of years. [Fr. *annuité* — L.L. *annuitās*, *-ātis* — L. *annus*, year.]

annul ə-nul', *v.t.* to make null: to reduce to nothing: to abolish: — *pr.p.* **annull'ing;** *pa.t.* and *pa.p.* **annulled'.** — *n.* **annul'ment.** [Fr. *annuler* — L.L. *annūllāre* — L. *ad*, to, *nūllus*, none.]

annular an'ū-lər, *adj.* ring-shaped: cutting in a ring: ring-bearing. — *n.* the ring-finger. — *n.* **annūlarity** (*-lar'i-ti*). — *n.pl.* **Annūlā'ta** (*obs.*) the Annelida. — *n.* **ann'ūlate** (*obs.*) an annelid. — *adjs.* **ann'ūlate, -d** ringed. — *ns.* **annūlā'tion** a ring or belt: a circular formation; **ann'ūlet** a little ring: a small flat fillet encircling a column, etc. (*archit.*): a little circle borne as a charge (*her.*). — *adj.* **ann'ūlose** ringed. — *n.* **ann'ūlus** (*biol.*) any ring-shaped structure, esp. a ring of cells that brings about dehiscence of a moss sporogonium or a fern capsule: — *pl.* **ann'ūlī.** — **annular eclipse** one in which a ring-shaped part of the sun remains visible. [L. *annulāris*, for *ānulāris* — *ānulus*, a ring — dim. of *ānus*, a rounding or ring.]

annunciate, annuntiate ə-nun's(h)i-āt, *v.t.* to proclaim. — *ns.* **annunciā'tion** (*-si-*) proclamation: esp. (*cap.*) that of the angel to the Virgin Mary, or its anniversary, 25th March (**Annunciā'tion-day** Lady-day). — *adj.* **annun'ciātive.** — *n.* **annun'ciātor** a device giving audible or visual information, e.g. indicating where a bell or telephone is being rung, now often operated by closed-circuit television: an announcer. — **Annunciation lily** the white lily (*Lilium candidum*) often seen in pictures of the Annunciation. [L. *annuntiāre*, *-ātum* — *ad*, to, *nuntiāre* — *nuntius*, a messenger; *c* from mediaeval spelling of Latin; cf. **announce.**]

annus mirabilis an'əs mir-ab'il-is, an'ōōs mēr-äb'il-is, (L.) year of wonders — applied to 1666 (year of plague and fire of London), etc.

anoa a-nō'ə, *n.* the sapi-utan, or wild ox of Celebes, like a small buffalo. [Native name.]

Anobium a-nō'bi-əm, *n.* a genus of small beetles of the family **Anobiidae** (*a-nō-bī'i-dē*), a number of species of which bore in dry wood. [Mod. L. — Gr. *ano*, upwards, *bios*, life.]

anode an'ōd, *n.* the electrode by which an electric current enters an electrolyte or gas (opp. to *cathode*): in high vacuum, the electrode to which electrons flow. — *v.t.* **an'odise, -ize** to give a protective or decorative coat to (a metal) by using it as an anode in electrolysis. — *adjs.* **anōd'al** (or *an'od-əl*), **anodic** (*an-od'ik*) of an anode: upwards on the genetic spiral (*bot.*). [Gr. *anodos*, way up — *ana*, up, *hodos*, way.]

anodyne an'ō-dīn, *n.* a medicine that allays pain: something that relieves mental distress: something that prevents, soothes, or avoids argument, criticism, or controversy. — *adj.* allaying pain or mental distress: preventing, soothing, or avoiding argument, criticism, or controversy: harmless, innocent. [Gr. *anōdynos* — *an-*, priv., and *ŏdynē*, pain.]

anoesis a-nō-ē'sis, *n.* sensation or emotion not accompanied by understanding of it. — *adj.* **anoĕt'ic.** [Gr. *anoia*, lack of understanding.]

anoestrus, in U.S. **anestrus**, *an-ēs'trəs*, *n.* a (sometimes prolonged) period of sexual inactivity between periods of oestrus. — Also **anoes'trum.** — *adj.* **anoes'trous.** [Gr. *an-*, priv., and **oestrus.**]

anoint ə-noint', *v.t.* to smear with ointment or oil: to consecrate with oil: (ironically) to drub. — *n.* **anoint'-ment. — the Anointed** the Messiah; **the Lord's anointed** in royalist theory, king by divine right. [Fr. *enoint*, pa.p. of *enoindre* — L. *inungĕre*, *inunctum* — *in*, on, *ung(u)ĕre*, to smear.]

anomaly ə-nom'ə-li, *n.* irregularity: deviation from rule: the angle measured at the sun between a planet in any point of its orbit and the last perihelion (*astron.*). — *adjs.* **anomalis'tic, -al** anomalous: departing from established rules: irregular. — *adv.* **anomalis'tically.** — *adj.* **anom'alous** irregular: deviating from rule: of vision, relatively insensitive to one or more colours.

— **anomalistic month, year** see **month, year; anomalous water** polywater. [Gr. *anōmalos* — *an-*, priv., and *homalos*, even — *homos*, same.]

anomie *an'ə-mē*, *n.* in society or in an individual, a condition of hopelessness caused by or characterised by breakdown of rules of conduct and loss of belief and sense of purpose. — Also **an'omy**. — *adj.* **anomic** (*ə-nom'ik*). [Fr., — Gr. *anomia*, or *-iē*, lawlessness — *ā-*, priv., *nomos*, law.]

anon *ə-non'*, *adv.* in one (instant): immediately: soon: at another time: coming (in reply to a call). — *interj.* expressing failure to hear or understand. [O.E. *on*, in, *ān*, one.]

Anona, Annona *ä-nō'nə*, *n.* a tropical genus of dicotyledons, including custard-apple, sweet-sop, and other edible fruits, giving name to the family **Anonā'ceae**, akin to the magnolias. — *adj.* **anonā'ceous**. [Latinised from Sp. *anón*, from Taino.]

anonyma *ə-non'i-mə*, (*obs.*) *n.* a showy woman of easy morals. [Latinised Gr.]

anonymous *ə-non'i-məs*, *adj.* wanting a name: without name of author, real or feigned: lacking distinctive features or individuality. — *ns.* **anonym** (*an'*) a person whose name is not given: a pseudonym; **anonym'ity**. — *adv.* **anon'ymously**. [Gr. *anōnymos* — *an-*, priv., and *onyma* = *onoma*, name.]

Anopheles *an-of'əl-ēz*, *n.* a genus of germ-carrying mosquitoes: (without *cap.*) a mosquito of this genus. — *adj.* **anoph'eline** relating to Anopheles. — *n.* a mosquito of this genus. [Gr. *anōphelēs*, hurtful — *an-*, priv., *ophelos*, help.]

Anoplura *an-o-plōō'rə*, *n.pl.* an order or suborder of insects, the bugs. [Gr. *anoplos*, unarmed, *ourā*, tail.]

anorak, anarak *an'ə-rak*, *n.* a Greenlander's fur coat: a usu. hooded waterproof outer jacket. [Greenland Eskimo word.]

anorexia *an-or-ek'si-ə*, **anorexy** *an'or-ek-si* (or *-ek'*), *ns.* lack of appetite: anorexia nervosa. — *adj.* **anorec'tic** causing a lack of appetite: relating to, or suffering from, anorexia (nervosa). — *n.* an anorectic substance. — Also *n.* and *adj.* **anoret'ic**. — *adj.* **anorex'ic** relating to, or suffering from, anorexia (nervosa): relating to anorexics. — *n.* a person suffering from anorexia (nervosa). — **anorexia nervosa** (*nər-vō'sə, -zə; psych.* or *med.*) a condition characterised by loss of appetite and aversion to food due to emotional disturbance, normally leading to marked emaciation, etc. [Gr. *an-*, priv., *orexis*, longing — *oregein*, to reach out.]

anorthic *an-ör'thik*, (*crystal.*) *adj.* triclinic, referable to three unequal oblique axes. — *n.* **anor'thite** a plagioclase feldspar, calcium aluminium silicate (from the oblique angles between the prism faces). [Gr. *an-*, priv., *orthos*, right.]

anorthosite *an-ör'thō-sīt*, *n.* a coarse-grained rock consisting almost entirely of plagioclase feldspar. [Fr. *anorthose* (— Gr. *an-*, priv., *orthos*, right) and *-ite*.]

anosmia *an-oz'mi-ə*, *n.* the loss of sense of smell. [Gr. *an-*, priv., *osmē*, smell, *-ia*.]

another *ə-nudh'ər*, *adj.* and *pron.* a different or distinct (thing or person): one more: a second: one more of the same kind: any other. — *adj.* **anoth'erguess** see **othergates**. — **one another** a compound reciprocal pronoun usu. regarded as interchangeable with 'each other', but by some restricted to cases where more than two individuals are involved; **one with another** taken all together, taken on an average. [Orig. **an other**.]

anough (*Milt.*). Same as **enough** (*sing.*).

anourous. Same as **anurous**.

anow (*Milt.*). Same as **enow**[1], **enough** (*pl.*).

anoxia *an-ok'si-ə*, *n.* deficient supply of oxygen to the tissues. — *adj.* **anox'ic**. [Gr. *an-*, priv., *oxygen*, *-ia*.]

Ansafone® *an'sə-fōn*, *n.* a telephone-answering machine.

ansate, -d *an'sāt, -id*, *adjs.* having a handle. — **ansate cross** see **ankh**. [L. *ansātus* — *ansa*, handle.]

Anschauung *an-show'ŏong*, *n.* direct perception through the senses (*psych.* or *philos.*): an attitude or point of view. [Ger. *Anschauung*, perception, intuition, view.]

Anschluss *an'shlŏos*, (Ger.) *n.* union, esp. the political union of Germany and Austria in 1938.

anserine *an'sər-īn*, *adj.* of the goose or the goose family: stupid. [L. *anserīnus* — *anser*, goose.]

answer *än'sər*, *n.* that which is said, written, or done in meeting a charge, combating an argument, objection, or attack: that which is called for by a question or questioning state of mind: the solution of a problem: an acknowledgment: a return in kind: anything given, sent or said in return: an immediate result or outcome in definite relation to the act it follows: a repetition or echo of a sound: restatement of a theme by another voice or instrument (*mus.*). — *v.t.* to speak, write, or act in answer to or against: to say or write as an answer: to give, send, afford, or be an answer to: to behave in due accordance with: to be in proportion to or in balance with: to give a conclusive or satisfactory answer to: to serve the purpose of: to fulfil: to recompense satisfactorily: to be punished for. — *v.i.* to give an answer: to behave in answer: to be responsible: to suffer the consequences: to be in conformity: to serve the purpose: to succeed: to react. — *adj.* **an'swerable** able to be answered: accountable: suitable: equivalent: in due proportion. — *n.* **an'swerabil'ity**. — *adv.* **an'swerably**. — *n.* **an'swerer**. — *adj.* **an'swerless**. — **answer back** (*coll.*) to answer one who expects silent submission: to answer pertly; **answering service** a commercial service which answers telephone calls, takes messages, etc. for its clients when they are not available. — **answer to (the name of)** to show sign of accepting as one's name: to have as one's name (*coll.*); **know all the answers** to be in complete command of the situation with no chance of being caught out — statement usu. made with reference to another person who is too self-confident. [O.E. *andswaru* (n.), *andswarian* (vb.) — *and-*, against, *swerian*, to swear.]

ant *ant*, *n.* a small hymenopterous insect (of the Formicidae), of proverbial industry, the emmet or pismire: loosely, a termite. — *n.* **ant'ing** the introduction by birds of live ants or other stimulants into their plumage, possibly as a pleasurable means of cleaning it and their skin. — **ant'bear** the great ant-eater, the largest species of ant-eaters, found in swampy regions in S. America: the aardvark of S. Africa; **ant'-bird** a S. American ant-thrush; **ant'-cow** an aphis kept and tended by ants for its honey-dew; **ant'-eater** any one of a S. American family of edentates, feeding chiefly on ants: a pangolin: an aardvark: an echidna. — *n.pl.* **ant(s')'-eggs** pupae of ants. — **ant'-hill** hillock raised as nest by ants or by termites: anything like an ant-hill in terms of crowdedness, bustle, etc. (*fig.*); **ant'-lion** a neuropterous insect (*Myrmeleon*) whose larva traps ants in a funnel-shaped sand-hole; **ant'-thrush** any bird of the northern S. American family Formicariidae which feed on insects disturbed by travelling ants, or of the long-legged thrush-like Oriental and Australian family *Pittidae*. — **have ants in one's pants** (*coll.*) to be restless, impatient, needlessly hurrying. [O.E. *æmete*; cf. **emmet**.]

an't *änt*, a contr. of **are not, am not, has not**, (*ant*) **on it, and it** (= if it).

anta *an'tə*, *n.* a square pilaster at either side of a doorway or the corner of a flank wall: — *pl.* **an'tae** (*-tē*). [L.]

antacid *ant-as'id*, *adj.* counteracting acidity of the stomach. — *n.* a medicine that counteracts acidity. [Gr. *anti*, against, and **acid**.]

antagonist *an-tag'ə-nist*, *n.* one who contends or struggles with another: an opponent: a muscle that opposes the action of another: in an organism, something that has an opposite effect: a drug acting against another drug or other chemical. — Also *adj.* — *n.* **antagonīsā'tion**, **-z-**. — *v.t.* **antagonise, -ize** to struggle violently against: to counteract the action of: to arouse opposition in. — *n.* **antag'onism** opposition: hostility: production of opposing effects, e.g. in a living body: interference with the growth of another organism, as by using up the food supply or producing an antibiotic substance. —

adj. **antagonist'ic.** — adv. **antagonis'tically.** [Gr. *antagōnistēs* — *anti*, against, *agōn*, contest. See **agony.**]
antaphrodisiac *ant-af-rō-diz'i-ak, -rə-,* adj. counteracting sexual desire. — n. an antaphrodisiac agent. [Gr. *anti*, against, and **aphrodisiac.**]
antar *an'tər,* (*Shak.*) n. a cave. [Fr. *antre* — L. *antrum* — Gr. *antron.*]
Antarctic *ant-ärk'tik,* adj. opposite the Arctic: of, near, or relating to the south pole. — n. the south polar regions. — **Antarctic Circle** the parallel of latitude 66°32′ S, bounding the region of the earth surrounding the south terrestial pole. [Gr. *antarktikos* — *anti,* opposite, and *arktikos;* see **Arctic.**]
Antares *an-tā'rēz,* or *-tä',* n. a first magnitude red star in the Scorpion. [Gr. *Antarēs* — pfx. *anti-,* like, *Arēs,* Mars.]
antarthritic *ant-är-thrit'ik,* adj. counteracting gout. [Gr. *anti,* against, and **arthritic.**]
antasthmatic *ant-as(th)-mat'ik,* adj. counteracting asthma. [Gr. *anti,* against, and **asthmatic.**]
ante- *ant'i-, pfx.* before. [L. *ante,* old form *anti;* conn. with Gr. **anti-.**]
ante *an'ti,* n. a fixed stake put down by a poker player, usu. before the deal: advance payment. — v.t. to stake: to pay. — **up, raise, the ante** (*coll. fig.*) to increase the costs or risks involved in, or the demands requiring to be met before, some action. [L., before.]
ante-bellum *an'ti-bel'əm,* n. and adj. (happening in) the time before the war (whichever is in mind). [L. phrase.]
antecedent *an-ti-sē'dənt,* adj. going before in time: prior. — n. that which precedes in time: an ancestor: the noun or its equivalent to which a relative pronoun refers (*gram.*): the conditional part of a hypothetical proposition (*logic*): the numerator term of a ratio (*math.*): (in *pl.*) previous principles, conduct, history, etc. — v.t. **antecēde'** to go before in time, rank, etc. — n. **antecē'dence.** — adv. **antecē'dently.** [L. *antecēdēns, -entis* — *ante,* before, *cēdĕre,* to go.]
antecessor *an'ti-ses-ər,* or *-ses',* n. a predecessor (*rare*): an ancestor (*obs.*). [L. *antecessor;* cf. preceding word and **ancestor.**]
antechamber *an'ti-chām-bər,* n. a chamber or room leading to a more important apartment. [Fr. *antichambre* — L. *ante,* before, and *camera,* a vault.]
antechapel *an'ti-chap-l,* n. the outer part of the west end of a college chapel. [L. *ante,* before, and **chapel.**]
antechoir *an'ti-kwīr,* n. the space in front of the choir in a church. [L. *ante,* before, and **choir.**]
antedate *an'ti-dāt,* n. a date assigned which is earlier than the actual date. — v.t. to date before the true time: to assign to an earlier date: to bring about at an earlier date: to be of previous date to: to accelerate: to anticipate. [L. *ante,* before, and **date**[1].]
antediluvian *an-ti-di-lōō'vi-ən, -lū',* adj. existing or happening before Noah's Flood: resembling the state of things before the Flood: very old-fashioned, primitive. — n. one who lived before the Flood: one who lives to be very old. — adj. **antedilu'vial.** — adv. **antedilu'vially.** [L. *ante,* before, *dīlūvium,* flood.]
antefix *an'ti-fiks,* n. (usu. in *pl.*) an ornament concealing the ends of roofing tiles: — pl. **an'tefixes, antefix'a** (L.). — adj. **antefix'al.** [L. *ante,* before, in front, *figĕre, fixum,* to fix.]
antelope *an'ti-lōp,* n. a fabulous fierce horned beast (*Spens.*): since the 17th cent., any one of a group of hollow-horned ruminants closely related to goats. [O.Fr. *antelop* — mediaeval L. *antalopus* — Late Gr. *antholops,* of unknown origin.]
antelucan *an-ti-lū'kən, -lōō'* adj. before dawn or daylight (of e.g. worship). [L. *antelūcānus* — *ante,* before, *lūx,* light.]
ante lucem *an'te lū'səm, lōō'kəm,* (L.) before light.
antemeridian *an-ti-mə-rid'i-ən,* adj. before midday. [L. *antemerīdiānus* — *ante merīdiem,* before noon.]
ante meridiem *an-te mer-id'i-em, mer-ēd',* (L.) before noon.

antemundane *an-ti-mun'dān,* adj. before the existence of the world. [L. *ante,* before, *mundānus* — *mundus,* world.]
antenatal *an-ti-nā'tl,* adj. before birth. — n.pl. **antenā'tī** (L. *-nā'tē*) those born before a certain time, as opposed to *post-nati,* born after it — of Scotsmen born before 1603, and Americans before the Declaration of Independence (1776). — **antenatal clinic** a clinic for the purpose of treating and giving advice to pregnant women. [L. *ante,* before, *nātālis,* natal, *nātus,* born.]
ante-Nicene *an-ti-nī'sēn,* adj. before the first council of Nicaea in Bithynia, A.D. 325.
antenna *an-ten'ə,* n. a feeler or horn in insects, crustaceans, and myriapods: in wireless communication, a structure for sending out or receiving electric waves: an aerial: pl. **antenn'ae** (*-ē*), **antenn'as** (*radio*). — adjs. **antenn'al, antenn'ary; antennif'erous; antenn'-iform.** — n. **antenn'ūle** one of first or smaller pair of antennae in crustaceans. [L. *antemna, antenna,* yard (of a mast).]
antenuptial *an-ti-nup'shəl,* adj. before marriage. [L. *ante,* before, and **nuptial.**]
anteorbital *an-ti-ör'bit-l,* adj. situated in front of the eyes. [L. *ante,* before, and **orbit.**]
antepast *an'ti-päst,* (*obs.*) n. something to whet the appetite: a foretaste. [L. *ante,* before, and *pāscĕre, pāstum,* to feed.]
antependium *an-ti-pend'i-əm,* n. a frontlet, or forecloth, for an altar: a frontal. [L. *ante,* before, and *pendĕre,* to hang.]
antepenult *an-ti-pen-ult',* n. the last syllable but two. — adj. **antepenult'imate** last but two. [L. *ante,* before, and **penult.**]
ante-post *an'ti-pōst,* adj. of betting, beginning before the runners' numbers are posted. [L. *ante,* before, and **post.**]
anteprandial *an-ti-prand'i-əl,* adj. before dinner. [L. *ante,* before, and *prandium,* dinner.]
anterior *an-tē'ri-ər,* adj. before, in time or place: in front: towards the bract or away from the axis (*bot.*). — n. **anteriority** (*-or'i-ti*). — adv. **antē'riorly.** [L. *antĕrior* (compar.) — *ante,* before.]
anteroom *an'ti-rōōm,* n. a room leading into another larger room: a waiting-room: an officers' mess sitting-room. [L. *ante,* before, and **room.**]
anteversion *an-ti-vûr'shən,* (*med.*) n. the tipping forward of a bodily organ. — v.t. **antevert'.** [L. *ante,* before, and *vertĕre, versum,* to turn.]
anthelion *an-thē'li-ən, -lyən,* n. a luminous coloured ring seen on a cloud or fog-bank opposite the sun: — pl. **anthe'lia.** [Gr. *ant(h)ēlios, -on,* — *anti,* opposite, *hēlios,* the sun.]
anthelix. See antihelix.
anthelminthic, anthelmintic *an-thel-min'thik, -tik,* adj. destroying or expelling worms. — n. a drug used for that purpose. [Gr. *anti,* against, and *helmins, helminthos,* a worm.]
anthem *an'thəm,* n. an antiphon (*obs.*): a composition for a church choir, commonly with solo passages, usually set to a passage from the Bible: any song of praise or gladness: loosely applied to an officially recognised national hymn or song (as *national anthem*). — v.t. to praise in an anthem. — adv. **an'themwise** (*Bacon*) in the manner of an antiphonal anthem. [O.E. *antefn* — Gr. *antiphōna* (*pl.*) sounding in answer — *anti,* in return, *phōnē,* voice. See **antiphon.**]
anthemion *an-thē'mi-ən,* n. the so-called honeysuckle ornament in ancient art, a conventionalised plant-form more like a palmetto: — pl. **anthe'mia.** [Gr. *anthĕmion,* dim. of *anthos,* a flower.]
anther *an'thər,* n. that part of a stamen that contains the pollen. — ns. **antherid'ium** (*bot.*) the gametangium in which male gametes are produced: — pl. **antherid'ia; antherozō'oid, antherozō'id** a motile male gamete produced in an antheridium (Gr. *zōoeidēs,* like an animal — *zōion,* animal, and *eidos,* shape). [Gr. *anthēra, a*

medicine made from flowers, esp. their inner parts — *anthos,* flower.]

anthesis *an-thē′sis, n.* the opening of a flower-bud: the lifetime of a flower from opening to setting of seed. [Gr. *anthēsis,* flowering — *anthos,* flower.]

Anthesteria *an-thes-tē′ri-ə, n.pl.* the Athenian spring festival of Dionysos, held in the month of *Anthestē′rion* (February–March). [Gr. *ta Anthestēria* (Feast of Flowers), *Anthestēriōn* (the month) — *anthos,* flower.]

antho- *an′tho-, an′thə-,* in composition, flower. — *n.* **anthocarp** (*an′thō-kärp;* Gr. *karpos,* fruit) a fruit resulting from many flowers, as the pineapple: a fruit of which the perianth or the torus forms part. — *adj.* **anthocarp′ous.** — *ns.* **an′thochlore** (*-klōr, -klōr;* Gr. *chlōros,* green, yellow) a yellow pigment in flowers; **anthocyan** (*-sī′ən*), **-cy′anin** (Gr. *kyanos,* blue) a glucoside plant pigment, violet in neutral, red in acid, blue in alkaline cell-sap. — *adj.* **an′thoid** (Gr. *eidos,* shape) flower-like. — *v.t.* and *v.i.* **anthologise, -ize** (*an-thol′ə-jīz*). — *ns.* **anthol′ogist; anthol′ogy** a flower-gathering (*lit.*): a choice collection of writings, songs, paintings, etc. (orig. of Greek epigrams); **anthomā′nia** (Gr. *maniā,* madness) a craze for flowers; **anthomā′niac; Anthonomus** (*an-thon′ə-məs;* Gr. *nomos,* herbage, food) the genus of the cotton-boll weevil. — *adj.* **anthophilous** (*an-thof′i-ləs*) loving, frequenting, or feeding on flowers. — *ns.* **an′thophore** (*-thō-fōr, -för*) an elongation of the receptacle between calyx and corolla; **anthophyllite** (*an-thō-fil′īt, -thə-, -thof′;* Mod.L. *anthophyllum,* clove — Gr. *phyllon,* leaf) an orthorhombic amphibole, usually clove-brown; **anthoxan′thin** (Gr. *xanthos,* yellow) a yellow pigment in plants. — *n.pl.* **Anthozō′a** (Gr. *zōia,* animals) the Actinozoa, a class of coelenterates including sea-anemones, corals, etc. [Gr. *anthos,* flower.]

anthologise, etc., **anthology.** See **antho-.**

Anthony *an′tən-i, n.* a 4th-century saint who has a pig and a bell among his symbols and who was believed to have stayed an epidemic (perhaps raphania, but commonly supposed to be erysipelas) in 1089: (also **tantony** *tan′,* **St Anthony pig, tantony pig**) the smallest pig in a litter: an obsequious follower. — **St Anthony's cross** a tau-cross; **St Anthony's fire** (*pop.*) erysipelas; **St Anthony's nut** earthnut or pignut; **tantony bell** a small bell.

anthophilous, etc. See **antho-.**

anthrax *an′thraks, n.* a carbuncle, malignant boil: malignant pustule, woolsorter's disease, a deadly disease due to a bacillus, most common in sheep and cattle but communicable to men. — *adj.* **anthracic** (*an-thras′-ik*). — *ns.* **anthracene** (*an′thrə-sēn*) a product of coal-tar distillation ($C_{14}H_{10}$), a source of dye-stuffs; **an′thracite** (*an′thrə-sīt*) hard lustrous coal that burns nearly without flame or smoke, consisting almost entirely of carbon. — *adj.* **anthracitic** (*-thrə-sit′ik*) of, of the nature of, anthracite. — *n.* **anthrac′nose** (Gr. *nosos,* disease) any of several plant diseases caused by fungus and characterised by the appearance of dark sunken spots. — *adj.* **anthracoid** (*an′thrə-koid*) like anthrax. — *n.* **anthracosis** (*-kō′sis*) a diseased state of the lung due to breathing coal-dust. [Gr. *anthrax, -akos,* charcoal, coal, carbuncle (stone or boil).]

anthrop-, anthropo- in composition, man, human. — *adjs.* **anthropic** (*an-throp′ik*), **-al** human. — *n.* **anthropobiol′ogy** human biology. — *adj.* **anthropocentric** (*an-thrō-pō-sent′rik;* Gr. *kentron,* centre) centring the universe in man. — *n.* **anthropogenesis** (*-jen′*). — *adj.* **anthropogen′ic.** — *ns.* **anthropogeny** (*-poj′ən-i;* Gr. *genos,* race, birth) the study of man's origin; **anthrōpogeog′raphy** the geography of the races of man; **anthropogony** (*-pog′ə-ni;* Gr. *gonē, gonos,* birth, begetting) the study, or an account, of the origin of man; **anthropography** (*-pog′rə-fi*) study of the geographical distribution of human races. — *adj.* **an′thropoid** (or *-thrōp′;* Gr. *eidos,* form) manlike: applied esp. to the highest apes — gorilla, chimpanzee, orang-utan, gibbon, but also to the higher Primates generally — man, apes, monkeys,

but not lemurs. — *n.* an anthropoid ape. — *adj.* **anthropoid′al.** — *n.* **anthropol′atry** (Gr. *latreiā,* worship) man-worship, the giving of divine honours to a human being. — *adj.* **anthrōpological** (*-loj′*). — *adv.* **anthrōpolog′ically.** — *ns.* **anthropol′ogist; anthropol′ogy** the science of man in its widest sense. — *adj.* **anthropomet′ric.** — *ns.* **anthropometry** (*-pom′i-tri;* Gr. *metreein,* to measure) measurement of the human body; **anthrō′pomorph** (Gr. *morphē,* shape) a representation, esp. conventionalised, of the human form in art. — *adj.* **anthropomorph′ic.** — *v.t.* **anthropomor′phise, -ize** to regard as or render anthropomorphic. — *n.* **anthropomorph′ism** conception or representation of a god as having the form, personality, or attributes of man: ascription of human characteristics to what is not human; **anthropomorph′ist; anthropomorph′ite.** — *adj.* **anthropomorphit′ic.** — *ns.* **anthropomorph′itism; anthropomorphō′sis** (or *-mörf′ə-sis*) transformation into human shape. — *adjs.* **anthropomorph′ous** formed like or resembling man; **anthropopathic** (*-path′ik*). — *adv.* **anthropopath′ically.** — *ns.* **anthropopathism** (*-pop′ə-thizm*), **anthropop′athy** (Gr. *pathos,* suffering, passion) ascription of human passions and affections (to God, nature, etc.). — *n.pl.* **anthropophagi** (*-pof′ə-jī, -gē;* Gr. *phagein,* to eat) man-eaters, cannibals. — *ns.* **anthropophaginian** (*-jin′i-ən; Shak.*) a cannibal; **anthropoph′agite** (*-ə-jīt*). — *adj.* **anthropoph′agous** (*-ə-gəs*). — *ns.* **anthropoph′agy** (*-ə-ji*) cannibalism; **anthropophō′bia** a morbid fear of people; **anthropoph′üism** (Gr. *phyē,* nature) the ascription of a human nature to the gods; **Anthropopithē′cus** the chimpanzee (Gr. *pithekos,* ape); **anthropos′ophist; anthropos′ophy** (Gr. *sophiā,* wisdom) the knowledge of the nature of men: human wisdom: esp. the spiritualistic doctrine of Rudolf Steiner (1861–1925). — *adj.* **anthroposy′chic** (*-sī′kik, -psī′kik*). — *adv.* **anthroposy′chically.** — *ns.* **anthroposy′chism** (Gr. *psychē,* soul) ascription to nature or God of a soul or mind like man's; **anthropot′omy** (Gr. *tomē,* a cut) human anatomy. [Gr. *anthrōpos,* man (in general sense).]

Anthurium *an-thū′ri-əm, n.* a genus of tropical American plants with showy leaves and flowers: (without *cap.*) a member of the genus. [Gr. *anthos,* flower, *oura,* tail.]

anti *an′ti,* in U.S. also *an′tī, prep.* opposed to, against. — *n.* and *adj.* (one who is) opposed to anything. [Gr. *anti,* against, instead of, etc.]

anti- *an′ti,* in U.S. also *an′tī, pfx.* (1) acting against, counteracting, resisting, resistant to; (2) opposed to; (3) opposite or reverse. [Gr. *anti,* against.]

antiaditis *an-ti-ə-dī′tis, n.* tonsillitis. [Gr. *antias, -ados,* tonsil.]

anti-aircraft *an′ti-ār′kräft, adj.* intended for use against hostile aircraft. [Pfx. **anti-** (1).]

antiar *an′chär, an′ti-är, n.* the upas-tree: its poisonous latex. [Jav. *antjar.*]

antibacchius *an-ti-bə-kī′əs,* (*pros.*) *n.* a foot of two long (stressed) syllables followed by a short (unstressed). [Pfx. **anti-** (3); see under **bacchanal.**]

antiballistic *an-ti-bə-lis′tik, adj.* (of a missile, etc.) designed to destroy a ballistic missile. — Also **A.B.M.** [Pfx. **anti-** (1).]

antibarbarus *an′ti-bär′bär-us,* (L.L.) *n.* a list of words and locutions to be avoided in the classical usage of a language.

antibiosis *an-ti-bī-ō′sis, n.* antagonistic relation between associated organisms: inhibition of growth by a substance produced by another organism. — *adj.* **antibiotic** (*-ot′ik*) inimical to life: inhibiting the growth of another organism, used esp. of a substance produced by micro-organisms which, in dilute solution, has the capacity to inhibit the growth of, or to destroy, micro-organisms causing infectious diseases: pertaining to antibiosis. — *n.* an antibiotic substance. [Pfx. **anti-** (1), Gr. *biosis,* way of life; adj. *biōtikos* — *bios,* life.]

antibody *an′ti-bod-i, n.* a defensive substance produced in an organism in response to the action of a foreign body such as the toxin of a parasite. [Pfx. **anti-** (1).]

Antiburgher *an-ti-bûrg'ər, n.* a member of that section of the Scottish Secession Church which parted from the main body (the *Burghers*) in 1747, interpreting the reference in the oath administered to burgesses in Edinburgh, Glasgow and Perth, to 'the true religion presently professed within this realm' to mean the Established Church. — Also *adj.* [Pfx. **anti-** (2).]

antic *ant'ik, adj.* grotesque. — *n.* a fantastic figure or ornament: a grotesque pageant (*Shak.*): a buffoon, clown, mountebank (*arch.*): (usu. in *pl.*) a fantastic action or trick: a caper. — *v.t.* (*Shak.*) to make grotesque. — *v.i.* to cut capers: — *pr.p.* **ant'icking;** *pa.t.* and *pa.p.* **ant'icked.** — Obsolete forms **ant'icke** or sometimes **ant'ique.** — *v.i.* **anticize** (*ant'i-sīz; Browning*) to play antics. — See also **antique.** [It. *antico*, ancient — L. *antīquus*; orig. used of the fantastic decorations found in the remains of ancient Rome.]

anticathode *an-ti-kath'ōd, n.* the target of an X-ray tube, on which the cathode rays are focused and from which X-rays are emitted. [Pfx. **anti-** (3).]

anticatholic *an-ti-kath'ə-lik, adj.* opposed to the Catholic or the Roman Catholic Church, to Catholics, or to what is catholic. [Pfx. **anti-** (2).]

antichlor *an'ti-klōr, -klör, n.* any substance used in paper-making to free the pulp from the last traces of free chlorine. [Pfx. **anti-** (1).]

anticholinergic *an-ti-kō-lin-ûr'jik, adj.* blocking parasympathetic nerve impulses. — *n.* a drug which blocks these impulses. [Pfx. **anti-** (1).]

Antichrist *an'ti-krīst, n.* an opponent of Christ: the great opposer of Christ and Christianity expected by the early Church, applied by some to the Pope and others. — *adj.* **antichristian** (*-kris'*) relating to Antichrist: opposed to Christianity. — *n.* **antichris'tianism.** — *adv.* **antichris'tianly.** [Gr. *Antichristos* — *anti-*, against, *Christos*, Christ.]

Antichthon *an-tik'thon, n.* the second earth placed by Pythagoreans on the other side of the sun: the southern hemisphere. — *n.pl.* **antich'thones** (*-thon-ēz*) the antipodeans. [Gr. *anti*, opposite to, *chthōn*, earth.]

anticipate *an-tis'ip-āt, v.t.* to forestall (a person or thing): to preoccupy: to use, spend, deal with in advance or before the due time: to realise beforehand: to foresee or count upon as certain: to expect: to precede: to advance to an earlier time, bring on sooner. — *v.i.* to be before the normal time: to do anything before the appropriate time. — *adj.* **antic'ipant** anticipating, anticipative. — Also *n.* — *n.* **anticipā'tion** act of anticipating: assignment to too early a time: introduction of a tone or tones of a chord before the whole chord (*mus.*): intuition: foretaste: previous notion: presentiment: prejudice: imagining beforehand: expectation. — *adjs.* **antic'ipative, antic'ipatory.** — *advs.* **antic'ipatively, anti'cipatorily.** — *n.* **antic'ipātor.** [L. *anticipāre, -ātum* — *ante*, before, *capĕre*, to take.]

anticivic *an-ti-siv'ik, adj.* opposed to citizenship, esp. the conception of it engendered by the French Revolution. — *n.* **anticiv'ism.** [Pfx. **anti-** (2).]

antick, anticke. Obsolete forms of **antic, antique.**

anticlerical *an-ti-kler'i-kl, adj.* opposed to the clergy or their power. — *n.* a member of an anticlerical party. — *n.* **anticler'icalism.** [Pfx. **anti-** (2).]

anticlimax *an-ti-klī'maks, n.* the opposite of climax: a ludicrous drop in impressiveness after a progressive rise. — *adj.* **anticlimac'tic.** — *adv.* **anticlimac'tically.** [Pfx. **anti-** (3).]

anticline *an'ti-klīn, (geol.) n.* an arch-like fold dipping outwards from the fold-axis. — *adj.* **anticlin'al** sloping in opposite directions: perpendicular to the surface near the growing-point (*bot.*). — *n.* an anticline. — *n.* **anticlinō'rium** (*-klin-* or *-klīn-*) a series of folds which as a whole is anticlinal. [Pfx. **anti-** (1), Gr. *klinein,*

to lean; *oros,* a mountain.]

anticlockwise *an-ti-klok'wīz, adv.* in the opposite direction to that of the hands of a clock. [Pfx. **anti-** (3).]

anticoagulant *an-ti-kō-ag'ū-lənt, n.* a drug that hinders clotting of blood. — Also *adj.* [Pfx. **anti-** (1).]

anticonvulsant *an-ti-kən-vul'sənt, n.* a drug used to control epilepsy, etc. — Also *adj.* [Pfx. **anti-** (1).]

anticous *an-tī'kəs,* (*bot.*) *adj.* on the anterior side, or away from the axis. [L. *antīcus,* in front — *ante,* before.]

anticyclone *an-ti-sī'klōn, n.* a rotatory outflow of air from an area of high pressure. — *adj.* **anticyclonic** (*-klon'ik*). [Pfx. **anti-** (3).]

antidepressant *an-ti-di-pres'ənt, n.* a drug used to counteract depression. — Also *adj.* [Pfx. **anti-** (1).]

antidesiccant *an-ti-des'i-kənt, n.* a chemical which prevents or inhibits the drying-out of a plant, etc. [Pfx. **anti-** (1).]

anti-devolutionist *an-ti-dē-vəl-ōō'shən-ist, -dev-, -ū', n.* one who is opposed to devolution. [Pfx. **anti-** (1).]

antidisestablishmentarianism *an-ti-dis-es-tab-lish-mən-tār'i-ən-izm, n.* a movement against the removing of state recognition of an established church, esp. the Anglican church in the nineteenth century. — *adj.* **antidisestablishmenta'rian.** [Pfx. **anti-** (1).]

antidote *an'ti-dōt, n.* that which counteracts poison: anything that prevents an evil (with *against, for, to*) (*fig.*). — *adj.* **antido'tal.** [Gr. *antidotos* — *didonai,* to give.]

antidromic *an-ti-drom'ik,* (*med.*) *adj.* (of nerve fibres) conducting or able to conduct impulses in the opposite direction to normal. [Pfx. **anti-** (1), Gr. *dromos,* a course, run.]

antient. An obsolete spelling of **ancient.**

anti-establishment *an-ti-es-tab'lish-mənt, adj.* opposed to the opinions and values of the establishment in society. — *n.* the people who are opposed to such opinions, etc. [Pfx. **anti-** (1).]

anti-fade *an-ti-fād', adj.* resistant to fading. [Pfx. **anti-** (1).]

anti-federal *an'ti-fed'ər-əl, adj.* opposed to federalism: applied to the U.S. party afterwards called Democratic. — *ns.* **anti-fed'eralism; anti-fed'eralist.** [Pfx. **anti-** (2).]

anti-feedant *an-ti-fēd'ənt, n.* any of a number of substances present in some species of plants which make the plants resistant to insect pests. [Pfx. **anti-** (1).]

anti-flash *an-ti-flash', adj.* protecting against the flash of explosions, etc. [Pfx. **anti-** (1).]

antifouling *an-ti-fowl'ing, adj.* intended to prevent fouling of ships' bottoms. [Pfx. **anti-** (1).]

antifreeze *an'ti-frēz, n.* a substance, as ethylene glycol, with low freezing point put into the radiator of an internal-combustion engine to prevent freezing up. [Pfx. **anti-** (1).]

antigen *an'ti-jen, n.* any substance that stimulates the production of an antibody. — *adj.* **antigen'ic.** — *adv.* **antigen'ically.** [Pfx. **anti-** (1), Gr. *gennaein,* to engender.]

antigropelo(e)s *an-ti-grop'ə-lōz,* (*old*) *n.pl.* waterproof leggings. [Said to be from Gr. *anti,* against, *hygros,* wet, and *pēlos,* mud.]

antihalation *an-ti-ha-lā'shən,* (*phot.*) *n.* the prevention of halation by placing a layer of dye usu. on the back of the film to absorb light which has passed through the emulsion on the film. [Pfx. **anti-** (1).]

antihelix *an-ti-hē'liks,* **anthelix** *an'thi-liks, an-thē'liks, ns.* the inner curved ridge of the external ear: — *pls.* **antihelices** (*-li-sēz*), **anthel'ices.** [Gr. *anthĕlix* — *hĕlix,* a coil.]

anti-hero *an'ti-hē'rō, n.* a principal character who lacks noble qualities and whose experiences are without tragic dignity: — *fem.* **anti-heroine** (*her'ō-in*). — *adj.* **anti-heroic** (*hi-rō'ik*). [Pfx. **anti-** (3).]

antihistamine *an-ti-his'tə-mēn, n.* any of a group of drugs

---

antibil'ious *adj.* anti- (1).
antifric'tion *adj.* anti- (1).

anti-Gall'ican *adj.* and *n.*
anti- (2).

anti-Gall'icanism *n.* anti- (2).
anti-inflamm'atory *adj.* anti- (1).

that prevents the action of histamines in allergic conditions. [Pfx. **anti-** (1).]

antihypertensive *an-ti-hī-pər-ten'siv, adj.* (of a drug or other measure) used to lower the blood pressure. — *n.* an antihypertensive drug. [Pfx. **anti-** (1).]

anti-Jacobin, antijacobin *an'ti-jak'ə-bin, adj.* opposed to the Jacobins and to the French Revolution or to democratic principles. — *n.* one opposed to the Jacobins: (with *cap.*) a weekly paper started in England in 1797 by Canning and others to refute the principles of the French Revolution. — *n.* **anti-Jac'obinism.** [Pfx. **anti-** (2).]

antiknock *an-ti-nok', n.* a substance that prevents knock or detonation in internal-combustion engines. [Pfx. **anti-** (1).]

antilegomena *an-ti-leg-om'i-nə, n.pl.* those books of the New Testament not at first universally accepted but ultimately admitted into the Canon — 2 Peter, James, Jude, Hebrews, 2 and 3 John, and the Apocalypse: — opp. to *homologoumena.* [Gr., spoken against.]

antilogarithm *an-ti-log'ə-ridhm, -rithm, n.* a number of which a particular number is the logarithm: — *contr.* **an'tilog.** [Pfx. **anti-** (3).]

antilogy *an-til'ə-ji, n.* a contradiction. — *adj.* **antil'ogous** (*-gəs*) of the contrary kind: negatively electrified by heating. [Gr. *antilogiā,* contradiction.]

Antilope *an-til'ō-pē, n.* the Indian antelope genus. — *adj.* **antil'opine** (*-pīn*) of antelopes. [Form of **antelope,** adopted by P. S. Pallas, naturalist.]

antilymphocyte serum *an-ti-lim'fə-sīt sē'rəm,* serum used to prevent defensive action of lymphocytes, e.g. in cases where they would reject an organ transplanted into the body. [Pfx. **anti-** (1).]

antimacassar *an-ti-mə-kas'ər, n.* a covering for chair-backs, etc., to protect them from macassar oil or other grease in the hair, or for ornament. [Pfx. **anti-** (1).]

anti-marketeer *an-ti-mär-ki-tēr', n.* a person who opposes Britain's entry into or membership of the European Common Market. [Pfx. **anti-** (1).]

antimask, antimasque *an'ti-mäsk, n.* a farcical interlude dividing the parts of, or preceding, the more serious mask. [Pfx. **anti-** (3).]

antimatter *an'ti-mat'ər, n.* extra-terrestrial matter (not as yet discovered) that would consist of particles similar to those of terrestrial matter but of opposite electrical charge or, in the case of the neutron, reversed magnetic polarity. [Pfx. **anti-** (3).]

antimetabole *an-ti-mə-tab'ol-i, (rhet.) n.* a figure in which the same words or ideas are repeated in inverse order, as Quarles's 'Be wisely worldly, but not worldly wise'. [Gr.]

antimetathesis *an-ti-mə-tath'ə-sis, n.* inversion of the members of an antithesis, as in Crabbe's 'A poem is a speaking picture; a picture, a mute poem'. [Gr.]

antimnemonic *an-ti-ni-mon'ik, adj.* tending to weaken the memory. — Also *n.* [Pfx. **anti-** (1).]

antimony *an'ti-mən-i, n.* a brittle, bluish-white element (at. numb. 51; symbol Sb, for stibium) of metallic appearance: type (*printers' slang*). — *ns.* **an'timonate** (*-mən-*) **antimō'niate** a salt of any antimonic acid. — *adj.* **antimonial** (*-mō'ni-əl*) pertaining to, or containing, antimony. — *n.* a drug containing antimony. — *adj.* **antimonic** (*-mon'ik*) containing pentavalent antimony; **antimō'nious** containing trivalent antimony. — *ns.* **an'timonide** a binary compound with antimony as one of its constituents; **an'timonite** a salt of antimonious acid: the mineral stibnite (not chemically an antimonite). [L.L. *antimōnium,* of unknown origin, prob. from some Arabic word.]

antinephritic *an-ti-ne-frit'ik, adj.* acting against diseases of the kidney. [Pfx. **anti-** (1).]

antineutrino *an-ti-nū-trē'nō, n.* the antiparticle of the neutrino. — *n.* **antineu'tron** (*-tron*) an uncharged particle that combines with the neutron with mutual

annihilation and emission of energy. [Pfx. **anti-** (3).]

anting. See **ant.**

antinode *an'ti-nōd, (phys.) n.* a point of maximum disturbance midway between nodes. — *adj.* **antinōd'al.** [Pfx. **anti-** (3).]

antinomian *an-ti-nō'mi-ən, n.* one who denies the obligatoriness of moral law: one who believes that Christians are emancipated by the gospel from the obligation to keep the moral law, faith alone being necessary. — Also *adj.* — *n.* **antino'mianism.** — *adjs.* **antinomic** (*-nom'ik*), **-al** pertaining to, of the nature of, or involving, antinomy. — *n.* **antinomy** (*an-tin'ə-mi*) a contradiction in a law: a conflict of authority: conclusions discrepant though apparently logical. [Pfx. **anti-** (1), Gr. *nomos,* law.]

anti-novel *an'ti-nov'l, -nuv'l, n.* a type of novel of the mid-twentieth century which largely discards plot and character and concerns itself with tiny inner dramas on the border of consciousness. [Pfx. **anti-** (3).]

Antiochian *an-ti-ō'ki-ən,* **Antiochene** *an-tī'ō-kēn, adjs.* of the city of *Antioch*: of the eclectic philosophy of *Antiochus* of Ascalon: of any of the Seleucid kings of the name. — *n.* **Antio'chianism** a school of theology in the 4th and 5th centuries in revolt against allegorising of Scripture by the Alexandrian school.

antiodontalgic *an-ti-o-dont-alj'ik, adj.* of use against toothache. — Also *n.* [Pfx. **anti-** (1), Gr. *odous, odontos,* tooth, and *algeein,* to suffer pain.]

antipapal *an-ti-pā'pəl, adj.* opposed to the pope or the papal system. — See also **antipope.** [Pfx. **anti-** (2).]

antiparallel *an-ti-par'ə-lel, adj.* making with a transverse line an internal angle equal to the external angle made by another line. — Also *n.* [Pfx. **anti-** (3).]

antiparticle *an'ti-pär'ti-kl, n.* the 'pair' of an elementary particle, particle and antiparticle being mutually destructive. [Pfx. **anti-** (3).]

antipasto *an'ti-päs'tō,* (It.) *n.* an hors d'œuvre, a whet. [Cf. **antepast.**]

antipathy *an-tip'əth-i, n.* opposition in feeling: aversion: repugnance: incompatibility: mutual opposition: an object of antipathy. — *adjs.* **antipathet'ic, -al** — *adv.* **antipathet'ically.** — *adj.* **antipathic** (*an-ti-path'ik*) belonging to antipathy: opposite: contrary. — *n.* **antip'athist** one possessed by an antipathy. [Pfx. **anti-** (1), Gr. *pathos,* feeling.]

antiperiodic *an-ti-pē-ri-od'ik, adj.* destroying the periodicity of diseases. — *n.* a drug with such an effect. [Pfx. **anti-** (1).]

antiperistasis *an-ti-pər-ist'ə-sis, n.* opposition of circumstances: resistance or reaction. [Gr., surrounding, interchange — *anti,* against, *peristasis,* a circumstance — *peri,* around, *stasis,* a setting, stand.]

anti-personnel *an'ti-pûr-sən-el', adj.* intended to destroy military personnel and other persons. [Pfx. **anti-** (1).]

antiperspirant *an-ti-pûr'spi-rənt, n.* a substance helping to stop perspiration. — Also *adj.* [Pfx. **anti-** (1).]

antipetalous *an-ti-pet'ə-ləs, adj.* opposite a petal. [Pfx. **anti-** (3).]

antiphiloprogenitive *an-ti-fil-ō-prō-jen'i-tiv, adj.* intended to prevent the production of offspring. [Pfx. **anti-** (1).]

antiphlogistic *an-ti-flə-jist'ik, adj.* acting against heat, or inflammation. — *n.* a medicine to allay inflammation. [Pfx. **anti-** (1).]

antiphon *an'ti-fon, n.* alternate chanting or singing: a species of church music sung by two parties each responding to the other — also **antiph'ony** (*-ən-i*). — *adj.* **antiph'onal.** — *n.* a book of antiphons or of anthems. — Also **antiph'onary** and **antiph'oner.** — *adv.* **antiph'onally.** — *adjs.* **antiphonic** (*-fon'*), **-al** mutually responsive. — *adv.* **antiphon'ically.** [Gr. *anti,* in return, and *phōnē,* voice: a doublet of **anthem.**]

antiphrasis *an-tif'rə-sis, (rhet.) n.* the use of words in a sense opposite to the literal one. — *adjs.* **antiphrastic**

---

antimalā'rial *adj.* **anti-** (1). **antimonarch'ical** *adj.* **anti-** (2). **anti-na'tional** *adj.* **anti-** (2).

antimicrō'bial *adj.* **anti-** (1). **antimon'archist** *n.* **anti-** (2). **antiperistal'tic** *adj.* **anti-** (3).

(*an-ti-fras'tik*), **-al** involving antiphrasis: ironical. — *adv.* **antiphras'tically.** [Gr., — *anti*, against, *phrasis*, speech.]

antipodes *an-tip'ə-dēz, n.pl.* (also *sing.*) those who live on the other side of the globe, or on opposite sides, standing feet to feet: a point or place diametrically opposite to another on the surface of the earth or of any globular body or sphere: a pair of points or places so related to each other: (sometimes with *cap.*) Australia and New Zealand, as being so related to Great Britain or Europe: the exact opposite of a person or a thing: — *sing.* (*rare*) **antipode** (*an'ti-pōd*). — *adjs.* **antip'ōdal,** (esp. of the Antipodes) **antipōdē'an.** — **antipodal cells** (*bot.*) in flowering plants, three cells in the embryo-sac at the end remote from the micropyle, representing the prothallus. [Gr. *antipŏdēs*, pl. of *antipous*, with feet opposite — *pous, podos*, a foot.]

antipole *an'ti-pōl, n.* the opposite pole: direct opposite. [Pfx. **anti-** (3).]

antipope *an'ti-pōp, n.* a pontiff set up in opposition to one asserted to be canonically chosen, as those who resided at Avignon in the 13th and 14th centuries. — See also **antipapal.** [**anti-** (3).]

antiproton *an-ti-prō'ton, n.* a particle comparable to the proton but negatively charged. [Pfx. **anti-** (3).]

antipruritic *an-ti-proō-rit'ik, n.* a substance that reduces itchiness. — Also *adj.* [Pfx. **anti-** (1).]

antipsychotic *an-ti-sī-kot'ik, adj.* (of a drug) alleviating psychosis. — *n.* an antipsychotic drug. [Pfx. **anti-** (1).]

antipyretic *an-ti-pī-ret'ik, adj.* counteracting fever. — *n.* an antipyretic agent. [Gr. *anti-*, against, *pyretos*, fever — *pȳr*, fire.]

antiquark *an'ti-kwärk, n.* the antiparticle (not as yet discovered) corresponding to the quark. [Pfx. **anti-** (3)]

antiquary *an'ti-kwər-i, n.* one who studies, collects, or deals in relics of the past, but not usually very ancient things — curiosities rather than objects of serious archaeological interest. — *adj.* (*Shak.*) ancient. — *adj.* **antiquarian** (*-kwā'ri-ən*) connected with the study of antiquities. — *n.* an antiquary: before metrication a size of drawing-paper, 53 × 31 inches. — *n.* **antiquā'rianism.** [L. *antīquārius* — *antiquus*, old.]

antique *an-tēk',* formerly *an'tik* (and sometimes written **antick,** now an *obs.* form), *adj.* ancient: of a good old age, olden (now generally rhetorical in a good sense): old-fashioned: savouring of bygone times: after the manner of the ancients. — *n.* anything very old: an old relic: a piece of old furniture or other object sought by collectors: a type of thick and bold face with lines of equal thickness (*print.*). — *v.t.* to alter the appearance of (wood, leather, etc.) so that it seems very old. — *v.t.* **antiquate** (*an'ti-kwāt*) to make antique, old, or obsolete: to put out of use. — *adj.* **an'tiquated.** — *n.* **antiquā'tion.** — *adv.* **antique'ly.** — *n.* **antique'ness.** — *ns.* **antiquitarian** (*an-tik-wi-tā'ri-ən*) one attached to old ways or beliefs; **antiq'uity** ancient times, esp. the times of the ancient Greeks and Romans: great age: old age, seniority (*Shak.*): ancient style: the people of old time: a relic of the past: (*pl.*) manners, customs, etc., of ancient times. — **the antique** ancient work in art: the style of ancient art. — See also **antic.** [L. *antīquus*, old, ancient — *ante*, before; influenced by Fr. *antique*.]

antirachitic *an-ti-ra-kit'ik, adj.* tending to prevent or cure rickets. — Also *n.* [Pfx. **anti-** (1).]

Antirrhinum *an-ti-rī'nəm, n.* the snapdragon genus: (without *cap.*) a plant of the genus. [Latinised from Gr. *antirrhīnon,* snapdragon — *anti,* like, mimicking, *rhīs, rhīnos,* nose.]

antiscian *an-tish'i-ən, n.* a dweller on the same meridian on the other side of the equator, whose shadow at noon falls in the opposite direction. — Also *adj.* [Pfx. **anti-** (3), Gr. *skiā,* shadow.]

antiscorbutic *an-ti-skör-būt'ik, adj.* acting against scurvy. — *n.* a remedy or preventive for scurvy. [Pfx. **anti-** (1).]

antiscriptural *an-ti-skrip'chər-əl, adj.* opposed to the authority of the Bible. [Pfx. **anti-** (2).]

anti-Semite *an'ti-sem'īt, -sēm', n.* a hater of Semites, esp. Jews, or of their influence. — *adj.* **anti-Semitic** (*-simit'*). — *n.* **anti-Semitism** (*-sem', -sēm'*). [Pfx. **anti-** (2).]

antisepalous *an-ti-sep'ə-ləs, adj.* opposite a sepal. [Pfx. **anti-** (3).]

antisepsis *an-ti-sep'sis, n.* destruction, or inhibition of growth, of bacteria. — *adj.* **antisep'tic.** — *n.* an antiseptic agent. — *n.* **antisep'ticism** (*-sizm*) antiseptic treatment. — *adv.* **antisept'ically.** — *v.t.* **antisep'ticise, -ize** (*-sīz*). [Gr. *anti-*, against, *sēpsis*, putrefaction.]

antiserum *an'ti-sēr-əm, n.* a serum which contains antibodies: — *pl.* **antiser'ums, antiser'a.** [*anti*body and serum.]

antisocial *an-ti-sō'shl, adj.* opposed to the good of society, or the principles of society: disinclined to mix in society: without social instincts. — *adv.* **antiso'cially.** — *ns.* **antiso'cialism; antiso'cialist** (formerly) unsociable person: now opponent of socialism; **antisociality** (*-shi-al'i-ti*) unsociableness: opposition to the principles of society. [Pfx. **anti-** (2).]

antispasmodic *an-ti-spaz-mod'ik, adj.* preventing or causing spasms or convulsions. — *n.* a remedy for spasms. [Pfx. **anti-** (1).]

antispast *an'ti-spast,* (*pros.*) *n.* a foot composed of an iambus and a trochee. — *adj.* **antispast'ic.** [Gr. *antispastos* — *antispaein,* to draw back — *spaein,* to draw.]

antistatic *an-ti-stat'ik, adj.* having the property of counteracting static electricity. — Also **antistat** (*an'* or *-stat'*). — Also *n.* [Pfx. **anti-** (1).]

antistrophe *an-tis'trə-fi, n.* the returning dance in Greek choruses, reversing the movement of the strophe: the stanza answering the strophe in the same metre: repetition in reverse order: retortion of an argument: an inverse relation. — *adj.* **antistrophic** (*an-ti-strof'ik*). — *adv.* **antistroph'ically.** — *n.* **antis'trophon** an argument retorted on an opponent. [Gr. *antistrophē* — *strophē,* a turning.]

antisyzygy *an-ti-si'zi-ji, n.* union of opposites. [Gr. *antisyzygiā* — *anti-*, against, opposite, *syzygiā*, union, coupling (— *sy-, syn-*, with, together, *zygon*, a yoke).]

antithalian *an-ti-thə-lī'ən, adj.* opposed to mirth. [Pfx. **anti-** (1), Gr. *Thaleia,* the comic muse.]

antitheism *an-ti-thē'izm, n.* doctrine antagonistic to theism: denial of the existence of a God: opposition to God. — *n.* **antithē'ist.** — *adj.* **antithēist'ic.** [Pfx. **anti-** (1), Gr. *theos,* a god.]

antithesis *an-tith'i-sis, n.* a figure in which thoughts or words are balanced in contrast: a thesis or proposition opposing another: opposition: the direct opposite: — *pl.* **antith'eses** (*-sēz*). — *n.* **an'tithet** (*-thet; rare*) an instance of antithesis. — *adjs.* **antithet'ic, -al.** — *adv.* **antithet'ically.** [Gr. *antithesis* — *thesis*, placing.]

antithrombin *an-ti-throm'bin, n.* a substance produced by the liver which prevents clotting of the blood in the veins. [Pfx. **anti-** (1), Gr. *thrombos*, a clot.]

antitoxin *an-ti-tok'sin, n.* a substance that neutralises toxin formed in the body. — *adj.* **antitox'ic.** [Pfx. **anti-** (1).]

antitrade *an'ti-trād, n.* a wind that blows in the opposite direction to the trade wind — that is, in the northern hemisphere from south-west, and in the southern hemisphere from north-west. [Pfx. **anti-** (3).]

antitragus *an-ti-trā'gəs, n.* a prominence of the external ear, opposite the tragus: — *pl.* **antitrā'gī.** [Pfx. **anti-** (3).]

anti-trust *an-ti-trust', adj.* of legislation, etc., directed

---

anti-ra'cist *adj.* **anti-** (2).   **antitrinitā'rian** *adj.* and *n.*   **antitrinitā'rianism** *n.* **anti-** (2).
antiship' *adj.* **anti-** (1).   **anti-** (2).   **antivī'ral** *adj.* **anti-** (1).

against the adverse effects of monopolies on commerce. [Pfx. **anti-** (1).]

antitussive *an-ti-tus'iv, adj.* tending to alleviate or suppress coughing. — *n.* an antitussive agent. [Pfx. **anti-** (1), L. *tussis*, a cough.]

antitype *an'ti-tīp, n.* that which corresponds to the type: that which is prefigured by the type. — *adjs.* **antityp'al, -typic** (*-tip'ik*), **-al.** [Pfx. **anti-** (3).]

antivaccinationist *an-ti-vak-si-nā'shən-ist, n.* an opponent of vaccination. — *n.* **antivaccinā'tionism.** [Pfx. **anti-** (2).]

antivenin *an-ti-ven'in,* **antivenene** *-ēn', ns.* an antitoxin counteracting esp. snake venom. [Pfx. **anti-** (1).]

anti-vitamin *an'ti-vit'ə-min, -vīt', n.* a substance with a chemical structure very similar to a vitamin, which prevents that vitamin from having its effect. [Pfx. **anti-** (1).]

antivivisection *an'ti-viv-i-sek'shən, n.* opposition to vivisection. — *ns.* **antivivisec'tionism; antivivisec'tionist.** [Pfx. **anti-** (2).]

antler *ant'lər, n.* a bony outgrowth from the frontal bone of a deer: orig. the lowest branch of a stag's horn, then any branch, then the whole. — *adj.* **ant'lered.** — **ant'ler-moth** a noctuid moth (*Charaeas graminis*), with antler-like markings on the wings, its larvae very destructive to pastures. [O.Fr. *antoillier;* assumed derivation from L.L. *ant(e)oculāris,* in front of the eyes, is unlikely.]

antlia *ant'li-ə, n.* the suctorial proboscis of Lepidoptera (*pl.* **ant'liae** *-ē*): (with *cap.*) the Air Pump, a small southern constellation. — *adj.* **ant'liate.** [L. *antlia,* a pump — Gr. *antliā,* bilge-water.]

antoninianus *an-tə-nin-i-ā'nəs, n.* a Roman coin equal to two denarii in value. [From 3rd-cent. emperor *Antoninus.*]

antonomasia *ant-on-o-mā'zi-ə, n.* use of an epithet, or the name of an office or attributive, for a person's proper name, e.g. his lordship for an earl; and conversely, e.g. a Napoleon for a great conqueror. [Gr. *antonomasiā* — *onomazein,* to name, *onoma,* a name.]

antonym *ant'ə-nim, n.* a word opposite in meaning to another. [Gr. *onyma = onoma,* a name.]

antre *an'tər, n.* a cave. — Also **an'tar** (*Shak.*). [Fr.; L. *antrum* — Gr. *antron,* a cave.]

antrorse *an-trörs', adj.* turned up or forward. [From *anterus,* hypothetical positive of L. *anterior,* front, and L. *versus,* turned.]

antrum *an'trəm, n.* a cavity. [L., cave.]

Antrycide® *an'tri-sīd, n.* a drug useful for cure and prevention of trypanosome diseases.

Anubis *a-nū'bis, n.* the ancient Egyptian jackal-headed god of the dead. [L., — Gr. *Anoubis* — Egypt. *Anup.*]

anucleate *ā-nū'kli-āt,* **anucleated** *ā-nū-kli-āt'id, adjs.* without a nucleus. [Gr. *a-,* priv., and **nucleate.**]

anuria *an-ū'ri-ə, n.* failure in secretion of urine. [Gr. *an-,* priv., *ouron,* urine.]

anurous *an-ū'rəs,* **anourous** *an-ōō'rəs, adj.* tailless. — *n.pl.* **Anu'ra, Anou'ra** the Salientia or tailless amphibians, frogs and toads. [Gr. *an-,* priv., *ourā,* tail.]

anus *ā'nəs, n.* the opening of the alimentary canal by which undigested residues are voided. — *adj.* **ā'nal.** — *adv.* **ā'nally.** [L. *ānus, -ī,* a ring.]

anvil *an'vil, n.* an iron block on which smiths hammer metal into shape: the incus of the ear. — **on** or **upon the anvil** in preparation, under discussion. [O.E. *anfilte, onfilti.*]

anxious *ang(k)'shəs, adj.* uneasy with fear and desire regarding something doubtful: solicitous: eager (for something, to do something). — *n.* **anxiety** (*ang(g)-zī'i-ti*) state of being anxious: a state of chronic apprehension as a symptom of mental disorder. — *adj.* **anxiolytic** (*angk-si-ō-lit'ik*) of a drug, reducing anxiety and tension. — Also *n.* — *adv.* **an'xiously.** — *n.* **an'xiousness.** — **the age of anxiety** the present time (W. H. Auden, 1947). [L. *anxius* — *angĕre,* to press tightly. See **anger, anguish.**]

any *en'i, adj.* and *pron.* one indefinitely: some: whichever,

no matter which. — *adv.* at all, to an appreciable extent. — *n.* and *pron.* **an'ybody** any single person: a person of any account. — *adv.* **an'yhow** in any way whatever: in any case, at least: indifferently, carelessly. — *n.* and *pron.* **an'yone** (or **any one**) anybody at all: anybody whatever. — *adv.* **an'yroad** (*dial.*) anyway. — *n.* and *pron.* **an'ything** a thing indefinitely, as opposed to nothing. — *adv.* any whit, to any extent. — *ns.* **anythinga'rian** one with no beliefs in particular; **any-thinga'rianism.** — *advs.* **an'ytime** at any time; **an'yway, an'yways** in any manner: anyhow: in any case; **an'ywhen** (*rare*); **an'ywhere** in or to any place; **an'ywhither** (*rare*); **an'ywise** in any manner, to any degree. — **any amount** a lot (*coll.*); **any day** in any circumstances; **any more** any longer; **any old** any, with connotations of indifference, lack of thought, etc. (**any old how** without any special care; **any old thing** anything at all); **anyone else** any other person; **at any rate** whatever may happen: at all events; **like anything** very much: with great vigour. [O.E. *ænig — ān,* one.]

Anzac *an'zak, n.* a member of the Australian and New Zealand Army Corps (1914 *et seq.*): any Australian or New Zealand soldier. — Also *adj.* — **Anzac Day** April 25, a public holiday in Australia and New Zealand in memory of the Anzac landing in Gallipoli (1915).

anziani *ant-sē-än'ē,* (It.) *n.pl.* councillors, senators.

Anzus *an'zəs, n.* an alliance between Australia, New Zealand, and the United States.

Aonian *ā-ō'ni-ən, adj.* pertaining to *Aonia* in Greece, or to the Muses supposed to dwell there. — **Aonian fount** the fountain Aganippe, on a slope of Mount Helicon — **the Aonian mount.**

aorist *ā'ər-ist, n.* a tense, esp. in Greek, expressing simple past time, with no implications of continuance, repetition, or the like. — *adj.* **aorist'ic.** [Gr. *aoristos,* indefinite — *a-,* priv., and *horistos,* limited.]

aorta *ā-ör'tə, n.* the great arterial trunk that carries blood from the heart. — *adjs.* **aor'tal, aor'tic.** — *n.* **aorti'tis** inflammation of the aorta. [Gr. *aortē — aeirein,* to raise up.]

aoudad *ä'ōō-dad, n.* a North African wild sheep. [Native name in French spelling.]

à outrance *a ōō-trãs,* (Fr.) to the utmost: to the death: to the bitter end.

apace *ə-pās', adv.* at a quick pace: swiftly. [a[3], and **pace**[1].]

Apache *ə-pa'chi, n.* a Red Indian of a group of tribes in Arizona, New Mexico, etc.: (**apache,** *ə-pash'*) a lawless ruffian or hooligan in Paris or elsewhere. [Perh. Zuñi *āpachu,* enemy.]

apage (Satanas) *ap'ə-jē, ap-a-ge* (*sat'an-as*), (Gr.) away, avaunt (Satan).

apagoge *ap-ə-gō'jē, n.* reduction to absurdity, indirect proof by showing the falsehood of the opposite. — *adjs.* **apagogic** (*-goj'ik*), **-al.** — *adv.* **apagog'ically.** [Gr. *apagōgē,* leading away, *apagein,* to lead off.]

apaid. See **apay.**

apanage. See **appanage.**

apart *ə-pärt', adv.* separately: aside: asunder, parted: separate: out of consideration. — *n.* **apart'ness.** — **set apart** to separate: to devote; **take apart** (*slang*) to reprimand severely; **tell apart** to distinguish, see the difference between. [Fr. *à part* — L. *ad partem,* to the side.]

apartheid *a-pärt'hāt, -pär'tīd, n.* segregation and separate development (of races) (also *fig.,* of e.g. segregation of the sexes). [Afrikaans.]

apartment *ə-pärt'mənt, n.* a separate room in a house occupied by a particular person or party: a suite or set of such rooms (*arch.* and *U.S.*) — now in this sense in the *pl.*: a compartment (*obs.*). — *adj.* **apartmental** (*-ment'əl*). [Fr. *appartement,* a suite of rooms forming a complete dwelling — L. *ad,* to, and *partīre, partīrī,* to divide — *pars, partis,* part.]

à pas de géant *a pa də zhä-ã,* (Fr.) with a giant's stride.

apatetic *ap-ə-tet'ik, adj.* of an animal's coloration or marking which closely resembles that of another species or of its surroundings. [Gr. *apatētikos*, deceitful.]

apathaton *ə-path'i-tən, n.* (*Shak.*) for **epitheton.**

apathy *ap'əth-i, n.* want of feeling, passion, or interest: indifference. — *adjs.* **apathet'ic, -al.** — *adv.* **apathet'ically.** [Gr. *apatheia* — *a-*, priv., *pathos*, feeling.]

apatite *ap'ə-tīt, n.* a mineral consisting of calcium phosphate and fluoride (or chloride). [Gr. *apatē*, deceit, from its having been confused with other minerals.]

Apatosaurus *ə-pat-ə-sör'əs, n.* the scientific name for Brontosaurus. [Gr. *apatē*, deceit, *sauros*, lizard.]

apay, appay *ə-pā', v.t.* to satisfy (*arch.*): to repay (*obs.*): — *pa.p.* and *pa.t.* **ap(p)aid', ap(p)ayd'.** [O.Fr. *apayer* — L. *ad*, and *pācāre* — *pāx*, peace.]

ape *āp, n.* a monkey: a large monkey without a tail or with a very short one: a mimic: an imitator. — *v.t.* to mimic: to imitate. — *ns.* **ape'dom; ape'hood; ap'ery** conduct of one who apes: any ape-like action: a colony of apes. — *adj.* **ap'ish** like an ape: imitative: foppish. — *adv.* **ap'ishly.** — *ns.* **ap'ishness, ap'ism** (*Carlyle*). — **ape'man** any of several extinct primates thought to have been intermediate in development between man and the higher apes. — **go ape** (*U.S. slang*) to go crazy (with *over* or *for*); **God's ape** a born fool; **lead apes in hell** feigned to be the lot of old maids in after life; **make someone one's ape, put an ape in someone's hood** (*obs.*) to make a fool of someone. [O.E. *apa*; Ger. *Affe*.]

apeak, apeek *ə-pēk*, (*naut.*) *adv.* vertical. [a³, and **peak.**]

apepsy *a-pep'si,* **apepsia** *a-pep'si-ə, ns.* weakness of digestion. [Gr. *apepsiā*, indigestion; *a-*, priv., *peptein*, to digest.]

aperçu *a-per-sü, n.* a summary exposition: a brief outline: a glimpse: an immediate intuitive insight. [Fr. *aperçu*, survey, sketch — lit. (pa.p. of *apercevoir*) perceived.]

aperient *ə-pē'ri-ənt, n.* and *adj.* laxative. — *adj.* **aperitive** (*ə-per'i-tiv*) laxative. — *n.* same as **apéritif:** an aperitive medicine. [L. *aperīre, apertum,* to open.]

aperiodic *ā-pē-ri-od'ik, adj.* not periodic: coming to rest without oscillation. — *n.* **aperiodicity** (*-ə-dis'i-ti*). [Gr. *a-*, priv., and **periodic.**]

apéritif *ə-per-i-tēf', -per',* (Fr.) *a-pā-rē-tēf, n.* a drink taken as an appetiser. [Fr., — L.L. *aperitīvus* — *aperīre*, to open.]

a-per-se *ā-pər-sē, n.* the letter **a** spelling a word by itself (*arch.*): anything unique in excellence (*fig.*). [L. *a per sē*, **a** by itself; cf. **ampersand.**]

apert *ə-pûrt',* (*arch.*) *adj.* open, public. — *n.* **apert'ness.** [O.Fr., — L. *apertus*, open.]

aperture *ap'ər-chər, n.* an opening: a hole: the diameter of the opening through which light passes in an optical instrument. [L. *apertūra* — *aperīre*, to open.]

apery. See **ape.**

apetalous *ə-pet'əl-əs, adj.* (*bot.*) without petals. — *n.* **apet'aly.** [Gr. *a-*, priv., and *petalon*, a leaf.]

à peu près *ä pø pre,* (Fr.) nearly.

apex *ā'peks, n.* summit, tip, or point: a vertex (*geom.*): the culminating point, climax of anything: — *pl.* **ā'pexes, apices** (*āp',* or *ap'i-sēz*). [L. *āpex, ăpĭcis*, a tip.]

apfelstrudel *ap-fəl-s(h)trōō'dəl, n.* a sweet pastry containing apples, spices, etc. [Ger.]

aphaeresis, apheresis *a-fē'ri-sis,* (*gram.*) *n.* the taking away of a sound or syllable at the beginning of a word. [Gr. *aphairesis*, a taking away, *apo*, away, and *haireein*, to take.]

aphagia *ə-fā'j(i)-ə, n.* inability to swallow: (of imago of certain insects) inability to feed. [Gr. *a-*, priv., *phagia* — *phagein*, to eat.]

Aphaniptera *af-an-ip'tər-ə, n.pl.* the flea order (or suborder) of insects. — *adj.* **aphanip'terous.** [Gr. *aphanes*, invisible, *pteron*, wing.]

aphanite *af'ə-nīt, n.* any rock of such close texture that separate minerals contained within cannot be distinguished by the naked eye. [Gr. *aphanes*, invisible.]

aphasia *a-fā'z(h)i-ə, n.* inability to express thought in words, or inability to understand thought as expressed

in the spoken or written words of others, by reason of some brain disease. — *n.* and *adj.* **aphā'siac.** — *adj.* **aphasic** (*a-fā'zik, a-faz'ik*). [Gr. *a-*, priv., *phasis*, speech — *phanai*, to speak.]

aphelion *a-fē'li-ən, n.* a planet's furthest point in its orbit from the sun: — *pl.* **aphē'lia.** — *adjs.* **aphē'lian, aphē'lic.** [Gr. *apo*, from, *hēlios*, sun.]

apheliotropic *a-fē-li-ə-trop'ik, adj.* turning away from the sun. — *n.* **apheliot'ropism.** [Gr. *apo*, from, *hēlios*, sun, and *tropikos*, pertaining to turning.]

apheresis. Same as **aphaeresis.**

aphesis *af'i-sis, n.* the gradual and unintentional loss of an unaccented vowel at the beginning of a word, as in *squire* from *esquire* — a special form of aphaeresis. — *adj.* **aphetic** (*ə-fet'ik*). — *v.t.* **aph'etise, -ize.** [Gr. *aphesis*, letting go — *apo*, from, *hienai*, to send.]

aphis *af'is, āf'is,* **aphid** *af'id, ns.* a plant-louse or greenfly, a small homopterous insect that sucks plant juices: — *pl.* **aph'ides** (*-i-dēz*), **aph'ids.** — *adj.* and *n.* **aphid'ian.** — *adj.* **aphid'ical.** — *ns.* **aph'icide, aphid'icide** (*-sīd*) an aphis killer. [Ety. unknown.]

aphonia *a-fō'ni-ə,* **aphony** *af'ə-ni, ns.* loss of voice from hysteria, disease of larynx or vocal cords, etc. — *adjs.* **aphonic** (*-fon'*), **aphonous** (*af'ə-nəs*) voiceless. [Gr. *a-*, priv., *phōnē*, voice.]

aphorism *af'ər-izm, n.* a concise statement of a principle in any science: a brief, pithy saying: an adage. — *v.i.* **aph'orise, -ize.** — *ns.* **aph'oriser, -z-; aph'orist.** — *adj.* **aphoris'tic.** — *adv.* **aphorist'ically.** [Gr. *aphorizein,* to define — *apo*, from, *horos*, a limit.]

aphotic *a-fō'tik, adj.* lightless. [Gr. *a-*, priv., *phōs, phōtos*, light.]

aphrodisiac *af-rō-diz'i-ak, -rə-, adj.* exciting sexually. — *n.* that which so excites. — *n.* **aphrodis'ia** sexual desire, esp. violent. — *adj.* **Aphrodis'ian** belonging to Aphrodite. [Gr. *aphrodīsiakos* — *Aphrodītē*, the goddess of love.]

aphtha *af'thə, n.* the disease thrush: a small whitish ulcer on the surface of a mucous membrane: — *pl.* **aph'thae** (*-thē*). — *adj.* **aph'thous.** [Gr. *aphtha,* mostly in pl. *aphthai.*]

aphyllous *a-fil'əs,* (*bot.*) *adj.* without foliage, leaves. — *n.* **aphyll'y.** [Gr. *a-*, priv., *phyllon*, a leaf.]

a piacere *ä pē-a-chā'rā,* (It.) at pleasure.

apian *ā'pi-ən, adj.* relating to bees. — *adj.* **āpiarian** (*-ā'ri-ən*) relating to beehives or beekeeping. — *ns.* **ā'piarist** a beekeeper; **ā'piary** (*-ər-i*) a place where bees are kept; **ā'piculture** beekeeping; **āpicul'turist.** — *adj.* **āpiv'orous** feeding on bees. [L. *ăpis*, a bee, *ăpiārium,* a bee-house.]

apical *ap', or āp'ik-l, adj.* of or at the apex: denoting a sound articulated with the tip of the tongue (*phon.*). — *adv.* **ap'ically.** — *n.pl.* **ap'ices** see **apex.** — *adj.* **apiculate** (*ap-ik'; bot.*) with a short sharp point on an otherwise blunt end. [See **apex.**]

Apician *ə-pish'(y)ən, adj.* relating to *Apīcius,* the Roman epicure in the time of Tiberius: luxurious and expensive in diet.

apiculture. See **apian.**

apiece *ə-pēs', adv.* for each piece, thing, or person: to each individually. [a¹, **piece.**]

apiezon oils *a-pī'zən oilz,* the residue of almost zero vapour pressure left by vacuum distillation of petroleum products. [Gr. *a-*, neg., *piezein*, press.]

apiol *ā'pi-ol, ap', n.* an organic substance got from parsley seeds, used (esp. formerly) as an emmenagogue and abortifacient. [L. *apium*, parsley, and *-ol* — L. *oleum.*]

apish, etc. See **ape.**

apivorous. See **apian.**

aplacental *a-plə-sen'tl, adj.* without placenta. [Gr. *a-*, priv., and **placental.**]

aplanatic *ap-lə-nat'ik, adj.* free from spherical aberration. — *ns.* **a'planat** an aplanatic lens or instrument; **aplanatism** (*ə-plan'ə-tizm*); **aplan'ogamete, aplan'ospore** a non-motile gamete, spore. [Gr. *a-*, priv., *planaein*, to wander.]

aplasia *a-plā'z(h)i-ə*, *n.* imperfect development or absence of an organ or part. — *adj.* **aplastic** (*-plas'*). — **aplastic anaemia** a form of anaemia caused by malfunctioning of the bone marrow. [Gr. *a-*, priv., and Mod. L. *-plasia* — Gr. *plasis*, moulding.]

aplenty *ə-plen'ti*, (*dial.*) *adv.* in plenty. [**a³**, plenty.]

aplite *ap'līt*, *n.* a fine-grained, light-coloured igneous rock containing mainly quartz and feldspar. [Ger. *Aplit* — Gr. *haploos*, simple.]

aplomb *ə-plom'*, Fr. *a-plɔ̃*, *n.* perpendicularity: self-possession, coolness. [Fr. *aplomb* — *à plomb*, according to plummet.]

aplustre *a-plus'tər*, *n.* the stern ornament of an ancient ship. [L. *āplustre*, *ǎplustre* — Gr. *aphlaston*.]

apnoea, apnea *ap-nē'ə*, *n.* a cessation of breathing. [Gr. *apnoia* — *a-*, priv., *pno(i)ē*, breath.]

Apocalypse *a-pok'əl-ips*, *n.* the last book of the New Testament, otherwise the Revelation of St John: (without *cap.*) any book purporting to reveal the future or last things: a revelation or disclosure. — *adjs.* **apocalypt'ic** pertaining to the Apocalypse: prophetic of disaster or of the end of the world; **apocalypt'ical.** — *adv.* **apocalypt'ically.** — **apocalyptic number** the number of the Beast, the mystical number 666, spoken of in the Apocalypse (xiii. 18), supposed to be the sum of the numerical values of the Greek and Hebrew letters of a name, for which many solutions have been offered. [Gr. *apokalypsis*, an uncovering — *apo*, from, *kalyptein*, to cover.]

apocarpous *ap-ō-kär'pəs*, (*bot.*) *adj.* having the carpels separate. [Gr. *apo*, from, *karpos*, fruit.]

apocatastasis *ap'ō-kə-tas'tə-sis*, (*theol.*) *n.* the final restitution of all things at the appearance of the Messiah — an idea extended by Origen (185–254) to the final conversion and salvation of all created beings, the devil and his angels not excepted. [Gr. *apokatastasis* — *apo-*, again, back, *katastasis*, establishment; cf. **catastasis.**]

apochromatic *ap-ə-krō-mat'ik*, *adj.* relatively free from chromatic and spherical aberration. — *ns.* **ap'ochromat** an apochromatic lens or instrument; **apochro'matism.** [Gr. *apo*, from, *chrōma*, *-atos*, colour.]

apocope *ə-pok'ə-pē*, *n.* the cutting off of the last sound or syllable of a word. — *v.t.* **apoc'opate.** — *n.* **apocopā'tion.** [Gr. *apokopē* — *apo*, off, *koptein*, to cut.]

apocrine *ap'ə-krīn*, *adj.* (of a gland) whose product is formed by the breakdown of part of its active cells. [Gr. *apo*, off, *krīnein*, to separate.]

apocrypha *ə-pok'rif-ə*, *n.pl.* hidden or secret things: applied specially to certain books or parts of books included in the Septuagint and Vulgate translations of the Old Testament but not accepted as canonical by Jews or Protestants, and to later books (Apocrypha of the New Testament) never accepted as canonical or authoritative by any considerable part of the Christian Church: — *sing.* **apoc'ryphon.** — *adj.* **apoc'ryphal** of the Apocrypha: of doubtful authority: spurious: fabulous. [Gr., things hidden — *apo*, from, *kryptein*, to hide.]

Apocynum *a-pos'i-nəm*, *n.* the dogbane genus, giving name to the periwinkle family **Apocyna'ceae**, closely related to the asclepiads. — *adj.* **apocyna'ceous.** [Gr. *apokÿnon*, an asclepiad poisonous to dogs — *apo*, off, *kyōn*, *kynos*, a dog.]

apod *ap'od*, **apode** *ap'ōd*, *ns.* an animal without feet or ventral fins. — *adjs.* **ap'od, ap'odal, ap'ode, ap'odous.** [Gr. *a-*, priv., *pous, podos, podos*, a foot.]

apodictic *ap-ə-dik'tik*, **apodeictic** *-dīk'*, *adjs.* necessarily true: demonstrative without demonstration: beyond contradiction. — *adj.* **apod(e)ic'tical.** — *adv.* **apod(e)ic'tically.** [Gr. *apodeiktikos* — *apodeiknynai* (*apo* and *deiknynai*), to demonstrate.]

apodosis *ə-pod'ə-sis*, (*gram.*) *n.* the consequent clause in a conditional sentence: — opp. *protasis*. [Gr. *apodosis* — *apo*, back, *didonai*, to give.]

apodous. See **apod.**

apodyterium *ap-ə-di-tēr'i-əm*, *n.* an undressing-room at an ancient bath. [Gr. *apodytērion* — *apodyein*, to undress — *apo*, from, *dyein*, to get into, put on.]

apoenzyme *ap-ō-en'zīm*, *n.* a protein component which combines with a coenzyme (q.v.) to form an enzyme. [Gr. *apo*, from, and **enzyme.**]

apogaeic. See **apogee.**

apogamy *ə-pog'ə-mi*, (*bot.*) *n.* omission of the sexual process in the life-history — the sporophyte developing either from an unfertilised egg-cell or some other cell. — *adj.* **apog'amous.** — *adv.* **apog'amously.** [Gr. *apo*, from, *gamos*, marriage.]

apogee *ap'ō-jē*, *n.* a heavenly body's point of greatest distance from the earth: the sun's greatest meridional altitude (*obs.*): culmination (*fig.*). — opp. to *perigee.* — *adjs.* **apogaeic** (*-jē'ik*), **apogē'al, apogē'an; apogeotrop'ic** (*biol.*) turning against the direction of gravity. — *adv.* **apogeotrop'ically.** — *n.* **apogeotropism** (*-ot'*). [Gr *apogaion* — *apo*, from, *gaia*, or *gē*, the earth.]

apograph *ap'ə-gräf*, *n.* an exact copy. [Gr. *apographon*, a copy — *apo*, from, and *graphein*, to write.]

à point *a pwɛ̃*, (Fr.) to a nicety.

apolaustic *ap-ə-lö'stik*, *adj.* devoted to the search of enjoyment. — *n.* the philosophy of the pleasurable. [Gr. *apolaustikos* — *apolauein*, to enjoy.]

apolitical *a-pəl-it'ik-əl*, also *ā-*, *adj.* indifferent to political affairs: uninvolved in politics. — *adv.* **apolit'ically.** — *ns.* **apolitical'ity, apolit'icism.** [Gr. *a-*, priv., and **political.**]

Apollo *ə-pol'ō*, *n.* the Greek sun-god, patron of poetry and music, medicine, archery, etc: (sometimes without *cap.*) an extremely handsome young man: — *pl.* **apol'l'os.** — *adj.* **Apollinarian** (*-i-nā'ri-ən*) sacred to Apollo: of Apollinaris, (d. *c.* A.D. 390) Bishop of Laodicea in Syria, or of his doctrine that in Christ the Logos took the place of a soul: of any other Apollinaris. — *n.* a follower of Apollinaris. — *ns.* **Apollinā'rianism; Apollina'ris (water)** a mineral water rich in sodium bicarbonate and carbon dioxide, from the Apollinaris spring in the Ahr valley. — *adj.* **apoll'ine** (*-īn*) of Apollo. — *adjs.* **Apollōnian** (*ap-ə-lō'ni-ən*) of Apollo: having the characteristics of Apollo (often opposed to *Dionysian*): of the mathematician Apollonius of Perga (3rd century B.C.), or other Apollonius. — *n.* **apolloni-con** (*-on'i-kən*) a gigantic organ, partly automatic (*mus.*). [Gr. *Apollōn, -ōnos*, L. *Apollō, -inis.*]

Apollyon *a-pol'yən*, *n.* the destroyer or devil (Rev. ix. 11). [Gr. *apollyōn*, pr.p. of *apollyein*, to destroy utterly — *apo-*, indicating completeness, *ollyein*, or *ollynai*, to destroy.]

apologetic *ə-pol-ə-jet'ik*, *adj.* (primarily) vindicatory, defensive: (now usu.) regretfully acknowledging fault. — *n.* a defence, vindication. — *adj.* **apologet'ical.** — *adv.* **apologet'ically.** — *n. sing.* **apologet'ics** the defensive argument or method, esp. the defence of Christianity. — *n.* **apologia** (*ap-ə-lō'ji-ə*) a written defence or vindication. — *v.i.* **apologise, -ize** (*ə-pol'ə-jīz*) to put forward a defence: (now usu.) to express regret for a fault. — *ns.* **apol'ogist** (*-jist*) a defender by argument; **apologue** (*ap'ə-log*) a fable: esp. a beast fable; **apology** (*ə-pol'ə-ji*) a defence, justification, apologia: an explanation with expression of regret: a regretful acknowledgment of a fault: a poor specimen hardly worthy of its name: an apologue (*obs.*). [Gr. *apologia*, defence, *apologos*, a tale — *apo*, off, *logos*, speaking.]

apomixis *ap-ə-miks'is*, *n.* omission of sexual fusion in reproduction, as in parthenogenesis, or in apogamy. — *adjs.* **apomictic** (*-mik'tik*), **-al.** — *adv.* **apomic'tically.** [Gr. *apo*, from, *mixis*, mingling, intercourse.]

apomorphine *ap-ə-mör'fēn*, **apomorphia** *-fi-ə*, *ns.* an alkaloid prepared by dehydrating morphine (morphia) — a rapid and powerful emetic and expectorant. [Gr. *apo*, from, and **morphine, morphia.**]

aponeurosis *ap-ō-nū-rō'sis*, *n.* a flat thin tendon. — *adj.* **aponeurotic** (*-rot'ik*). [Gr. *aponeurōsis* — *apo*, off, *neuron*, tendon.]

apoop *ə-pōōp'*, *adv.* on the poop, astern. [**a³**, and **poop.**]

apopemptic *ap-ə-pemp'tik, adj.* valedictory. [Gr. *apopemptikos* — *apo,* away from, *pempein,* to send.]

apophatic *a-pə-fat'ik, (theol.) adj.* (of a description of God) using negatives, i.e., saying what God is not.

apophlegmatic *ap-ə-fleg-mat'ik, adj.* promoting the discharge of mucus. — *n.* an apophlegmatic agent. [Gr. *apophlegmatikos* — *apo,* off; see **phlegm.**]

apophthegm, apothegm *ap'ə-them, n.* a pithy saying, more short, pointed, and practical than the aphorism need be. — *adjs.* **apo(ph)thegmat'ic, -al** *(-theg-).* — *adv.* **apo(ph)thegmat'ically.** — *v.i.* **apo(ph)theg'matise, -ize** to speak in apophthegms. — *n.* **apo(ph)theg'matist.** [Gr. *apophthegma* — *apo,* forth, and *phthengesthai,* to utter.]

apophyge *a-pof'i-jē, n.* the curve where a column merges in its base or capital. [Gr. *apophygē,* escape.]

apophyllite *a-pof'i-līt, ap-ə-fil'īt, n.* a mineral, hydrated calcium potassium silicate, that exfoliates on heating. [Gr. *apo,* off, *phyllon,* leaf.]

apophysis *a-pof'i-sis, -zis, n.* an outgrowth or protuberance, esp. on a bone, on the end of a pine-cone scale, on a moss stalk below the capsule (*biol.*): a branch from a mass of igneous rock (*geol.*): — *pl.* **apoph'yses** *(-sēz).* [Gr., offshoot — *apo,* off, *phyein,* to grow.]

apoplectic, etc. See **apoplexy.**

apoplexy *ap'ə-pleks-i, n.* sudden loss of sensation and motion, generally the result of haemorrhage or thrombosis in the brain. — *adjs.* **apoplec'tic, -al.** — *adv.* **apoplec'tically.** — *n.* **ap'oplex** (*arch.*) apoplexy. — *v.t.* (*Shak.*) to affect with apoplexy. [Gr. *apoplēxiā* — *apo-,* expressing completeness, *plēssein,* to strike.]

aporia *a-pōr'i-a, -pōr', (Gr.) n.* in rhetoric, a professed doubt of what to say or to choose: a difficulty.

aport *ə-pōrt', -pört, adv.* on or towards the port side. [**a³,** and **port¹.**]

à portée *a por-tā, (Fr.)* within reach or range.

aposematic *ap-ə-sē-mat'ik, adj.* (of animal coloration) warning. [Gr. *apo,* away from, *sēma, sēmatos,* sign.]

aposiopesis *ə-pos-i-ō-pē'sis, ap-ō-sī-, n.* a sudden breaking off in the midst of a sentence, e.g. Virgil, *Aeneid,* i. 135, 'Quos ego — '. — *adj.* **aposiopetic** *(-pet').* [Gr. *aposiōpēsis* — *apo,* off, and *siōpē,* silence.]

apositia *ap-ō-sish'i-ə, n.* an aversion to food. [Gr. *apo,* away from, *sītos,* bread, food.]

apospory *ə-pos'pə-ri, (bot.) n.* omission of spore-formation in the life-history — the gametophyte developing vegetatively from the sporophyte. — *adj.* **apos'porous.** [Gr. *apo,* away from, and **spore.**]

apostasy *ə-post'ə-si, n.* abandonment of one's religion, principles, or party: a revolt from ecclesiastical obedience, from a religious profession, or from holy orders: defection. — *n.* **apost'ate** *(-āt, -it)* one who has apostatised: a renegade. — Also *adj.* — *adjs.* **apostatic** *(ap-ō-stat'ik),* **-al.** — *v.i.* **apostatise, -ize** *(ə-pos'tə-tīz).* [Gr. *apostasiā,* a standing away — *apo,* from, *stasis,* a standing.]

a posteriori *ā pos-tē-ri-ō'rī, -ō'rī, ä pos-ter-i-ō'rē, adj.* applied to reasoning from experience, from effect to cause: inductive: empirical: gained from experience: — opp. to *a priori.* — Also *adv.* [L. *ā,* from, *posteriōrī,* abl. of *posterior,* coming after.]

apostil, -ille *ə-pos'til, n.* a marginal note. [Fr. *apostille.* See **postil;** origin of *a-* doubtful.]

apostle *ə-pos'l, n.* one sent to preach the gospel: esp. one of Christ's twelve: a first introducer of Christianity in a country, e.g. Augustine, the apostle of the English: a principal champion or supporter of a new system, or of a cause: the highest in the fourfold ministry of the Catholic Apostolic Church: one of the twelve officials forming a presiding high council in the Mormon Church. — *ns.* **apos'tleship; apost'olate** *(ə-post'ə-lāt)* the office of an apostle: leadership in a propaganda (q.v.). — *adjs.* **apostolic** *(ap-əs-tol'ik),* **-al.** — *adv.* **apostol'ically.** — *ns.* **apostol'icism** *(-i-sizm),* **apostolicity** *(ə-post-ə-lis'i-ti)* the quality of being apostolic. — **Apostles' Creed** the oldest form of Christian creed that exists, early ascribed to the apostles; **apostle spoons**

silver spoons with handles ending in figures of the apostles, once a common baptismal present; **apostolical succession** the derivation of holy orders by unbroken chain of transmission from the apostles through bishops — the theory of the Catholic Church: the assumed succession of a ministry so ordained to apostolic powers and privileges; **apostolic fathers** the immediate disciples and fellow-labourers of the apostles, more especially those who have left writings (Barnabas, Clement of Rome, Ignatius, Hermas, Polycarp); **apostolic see** the see of Rome; **apostolic vicar** the cardinal representing the Pope in extraordinary missions. [Gr. *apostolos,* one sent away, *apo,* away, *stellein,* to send.]

apostrophe¹ *ə-pos'trə-fi, n.* (in *rhet.*) a sudden turning away from the ordinary course of a speech to address some person or object present or absent, explained by Quintilian as addressed to a person present, but extended by modern use to the absent or inanimate: the ranging of chloroplasts along the side walls of the cell in intense light (*bot.*). — *adj.* **apostrophic** *(ap-ə-strof'ik).* — *v.t.* **apos'trophise, -ize** to address by apostrophe. [Gr. *apo,* from, and *strophē,* a turning.]

apostrophe² *ə-pos'trə-fi, n.* a mark (') showing (among other uses) the omission of a letter or letters in a word: a sign of the modern Eng. genitive or possessive case — orig. marking the dropping of *e.* [Gr. *apostrophos,* turning away, elision; confused with foregoing.]

apostrophus *ə-pos'trə-fəs, n.* the symbol Ɔ, used in Roman numerals — IƆ = 500, IƆƆ = 5000, IƆƆƆ = 500 000.

apothecary *ə-poth'i-kər-i, n.* a druggist or pharmacist (*arch.*) — still a legal description for licentiates of the Society of Apothecaries: a medical practitioner of an inferior branch, who often kept a shop for drugs (*obs.*). — **apothecaries' measure** liquid units of capacity (fluid ounce, etc.) used by pharmacists before 1969; **apothecaries' weight** a pre-1969 system based on the troy ounce. [L.L. *apothēcarius* — Gr. *apothēkē,* a storehouse — *apo,* away, and *tithenai,* to place.]

apothecium *ap-ə-thē's(h)i-əm, (bot.) n.* an open fructification in Discomycetes and lichens: — *pl.* **apothe'cia.** — *adj.* **apothe'cial.** [Latinised dim. of Gr. *apothēkē,* a storehouse.]

apothegm, etc. See **apophthegm.**

apothem *ap'ə-them, n.* the perpendicular from the centre to any of the sides of a regular polygon. [Gr. *apo,* away from, *thema,* that which is placed.]

apotheosis *ə-poth-i-ō'sis, n.* a deification: glorification: — *pl.* **apotheo'ses** *(-sēz).* — *v.i.* **apoth'eosise, -ize** (or *a-pə-thē'ə-sīz).* [Gr. *apotheōsis* — *apo-,* expressing completion, *theos,* a god.]

apotropaic *ə-pot-rō-pā'ik,* or *ap'ō-trō-, adj.* turning aside (or intended to turn aside) evil. — *adj.* **apot'ropous** (*bot.*) anatropous with ventral raphe. [Gr. *apo,* from, *tropē,* turning.]

apozem *ap'ə-zem, n.* a decoction. [Gr. *apozema* — *apo,* off, and *zeein,* to boil.]

appaid. See **apay.**

appair *ə-pār'.* An obs. form of **impair¹.**

appal *ə-pöl', v.i.* to wax pale, flat or flavourless (*obs.*): to wax faint (*Spens.*). — *v.t.* to abate (*Spens.*): to horrify, dismay: — *pr.p.* **appall'ing;** *pa.t.* and *pa.p.* **appalled'.** — *adj.* **appall'ing.** — *adv.* **appall'ingly.** [Perh. from O.Fr. *apalir, apallir,* to wax pale, make pale. See **pall²** and **pale².**]

Appaloosa *a-pə-lōō'sə, n.* a North American breed of horse, usu. white or grey with dark spots. [Prob. the *Palouse* Indians.]

appalto *a-päl'tō, (It.) n.* a contract or monopoly: — *pl.* **appal'ti** *(-tē).*

appanage, apanage *ap'ən-ij, n.* a provision for maintenance, esp. of a king's younger child: dependent territory: a perquisite: an adjunct or attribute. — *adj.* **ap(p)'anaged** endowed with an appanage. [Fr. *apanage* — L. *ad,* and *panis,* bread.]

apparat *ä'pə-rät, n.* the political machine of the Communist party. — *n.* **apparatchik** (*ä-pə-räch'ik*) a member of the Soviet bureaucracy or Communist party machine elsewhere: a Communist agent: a party official in any political party. [Russ., apparatus.]

apparatus *ap-ə-rā'təs, -ra'təs, n.* things prepared or provided, material: set of instruments, tools, natural organs, etc: materials (as various readings) for the critical study of a document (**apparatus criticus** *ap-ə-rā'təs krit'i-kəs, ap-a-rä'tōōs krit'i-kōōs*): — *pl.* **appara'-tuses** or **appara'tus** (L. *appārātūs*). [L. *appārātus, -ūs* — *ad,* to, *pārāre, -ātum,* to prepare.]

apparel *ə-par'əl, v.t.* to equip (*obs.*): to dress, clothe: to adorn: — *pr.p.* **appar'elling;** *pa.t.* and *pa.p.* **appar'elled.** — *n.* equipment (*obs.*): rigging (*arch.*): attire, dress: ecclesiastical embroidery (*arch.*). — *n.* **appar'elment.** [O.Fr. *apareiller* — L. *ad,* to, *pār,* equal.]

apparent *ə-par'ənt,* or *-pār',* *adj.* that may be seen: obvious: conspicuous: seeming: obtained by observation without correction, distinguished from *true* or from *mean.* — *n.* (*Shak.*) heir-apparent. — *n.* **appar'ency** apparentness: position of being heir-apparent. — *adv.* **appar'ently.** — *n.* **appar'entness.** — **apparent (solar) time** true time, as shown e.g. on a sundial, as opposed to mean (solar) time. [L. *appārens, -entis,* pr.p. of *appārēre;* see **appear.**]

apparition *ap-ə-rish'ən, n.* an appearing: an appearance: reappearance after occultation: that which appears: a phantom: a ghost. — *adj.* **appari'tional.** [See **appear.**]

apparitor *ə-par'i-tər, n.* an officer in attendance on a court, to execute orders (*obs.*): still, such an officer of an ecclesiastical court: a university beadle: one who appears (*rare*). [L. *appāritor.* See **appear.**]

appartement *a-par-t(ə)-mã,* (Fr.) *n.* a set of rooms in a house for an individual or a family.

appay, appayd. See **apay.**

appeach *ə-pēch',* (*Shak.*) *v.t.* to accuse, censure, or impeach. — *n.* **appeach'ment.** [O.Fr. *empechier;* see **impeach.**]

appeal *ə-pēl', v.i.* to call upon, have recourse to (with *to*): to refer (to a witness or superior authority): to make supplication or earnest request (to a person for a thing): to resort for verification or proof (to some principle or person): to make a demand on the feelings that comes home: to attract one's interest or enjoyment: to demand another judgment by a higher court: to remove to another court: to ask for the umpire's decision esp. as to whether a player is out (*cricket*). — *v.t.* to remove to a higher court (*arch.* except in U.S.): to accuse (*Spens., Shak.*): to offer up (prayers) (*Spens.*). — *n.* an impeachment (*Shak.*): a challenge (*obs.*): recourse: an act of appealing: a supplication: removal of a cause to a higher tribunal: an evocation of sympathetic feeling. — *adjs.* **appeal'able** (of a decision) that can be appealed against or referred to a superior tribunal; **appeal'ing** making an appeal: imploring: calling forth sympathy: attractive. — *adv.* **appeal'ingly.** — *n.* **appeal'ingness.** — **appeal to the country** to seek approval by a general election; **Court of Appeal** a section of the English High Court of Justice; **Court of Criminal Appeal** an English Court created in 1907 for appeal in criminal cases. [O.Fr. *apeler* — L. *appellāre, -ātum,* to address, call by name; also to appeal to, impeach.]

appear *ə-pēr', v.i.* to become visible: to present oneself formally before an authority or tribunal, hence to act as the representative or counsel for another: to come into view, to come before the public, be published: to be manifest: to seem. — *ns.* **appear'ance** the act of appearing, e.g in court to prosecute or answer a charge: the publication of a book: the effect of appearing conspicuously, show, parade: the condition of that which appears, form, aspect: outward look or show: a natural phenomenon: an apparition; **appear'er.** — **keep up appearances** to keep up an outward show, often with intent to conceal absence of the inward reality; **put in an appearance** to appear in person; **to all appearance(s)** so far as appears to any one. [O.Fr.

apareir — L. *appārēre — ad,* to, *pārēre, pāritum,* to come forth.]

appease *ə-pēz', v.t.* to pacify: to propitiate by concessions: to satisfy: to quiet: to allay. — *adj.* **appeas'able.** — *n.* **appease'ment** the action of appeasing: the state of being appeased. — *adv.* **appeas'ingly.** [O.Fr. *apeser,* to bring peace — L. *ad,* to, *pāx, pācis,* peace.]

appel au peuple *a-pel ō pœpl',* (Fr.) a plebiscite.

appellant *ə-pel'ənt, n.* one who appeals: one who impeaches: a challenger to single combat (*obs.*): one who in the Jansenist controversy appealed against the bull Unigenitus (1713) to a pope 'better informed', or to general council. — *adj.* **appell'ate** relating to appeals. — *n.* **appellation** (*ap-ə-lā'shən*) that by which anything is called: name, esp. one attached to a particular person. — *adj.* **appellā'tional.** — *n.* **appell'ative** (*ə-pel'ə-tiv*) a common as distinguished from a proper name: a designation. — *adj.* common (as distinguished from proper): of or pertaining to the giving of names. — *adv.* **appell'atively.** [L. *appellāre, -ātum,* to call.]

appellation (d'origine) contrôlée *a-pel-a-syō (dor-ē-zhēn) cō-trō-lā,* (Fr.) in the labelling of French wines a guarantee that the wine conforms to certain specified conditions of origin, strength, etc.

append *ə-pend', v.t.* to hang on (to something): to add. — *n.* **append'age** something appended: esp. one of the paired jointed structures of arthropods — antennae, jaws, legs. — *adj.* **append'ant** attached, annexed, consequent. — *n.* an adjunct, quality. — *ns.* **appendec'tomy,** more commonly **appendicec'tomy** (*-dis-*), removal of the vermiform appendix (Gr. *ektomē,* cutting out); **appendici'tis** inflammation of the vermiform appendix. — *adj.* **appendicular** (*ap-en-dik'ū-lər*) of the nature of, or belonging to, an appendix. — *n.* **Appendiculā'ria** a genus of Ascidians that retains the larval vertebrate characters which are lost in the more or less degenerate sea-squirts. — *adj.* **appendic'ūlate** furnished with appendages. — *n.* **appendix** (*ə-pen'diks*) something appended or added: a supplement: an addition to a book or document, containing matter explanatory, but not essential to its completeness: a process, prolongation, or projection, esp. the vermiform appendix (*anat.*): — *pl.* **append'ixes, append'ices** (*-sēz, -siz*). — **appendix vermiformis** or **vermiform appendix** a blind process terminating the caecum. [L. *ad,* to, *pendēre,* to hang.]

apperception *ap-ər-sep'shən, n.* the mind's perception of itself as a conscious agent: an act of voluntary consciousness, accompanied with self-consciousness: the assimilation of a new sense-experience to a mass already in the mind. — *adjs.* **appercep'tive; appercipient** (*-sip'i-ənt*). — *v.t.* **apperceive** (*-sēv'*). [L. *ad,* to, and **perception, perceive.**]

apperil(l) *ə-per'il,* (*Shak.*) *n.* peril. [L. *ad,* and **peril.**]

appertain *ap-ər-tān', v.i.* to belong, as a possession, a right, or attribute. — *n.* **appertain'ance** appurtenance. — *adj.* **appertain'ing** proper, appropriate (with *to*). — *n.* **appertain'ment** (*Shak.*) appurtenance. — *adj.* **apper'-tinent** appertaining. — *n.* (*Shak.*) appurtenance. [O.Fr. *apartenir, apertenir* — L. *ad,* to, *pertinēre,* to belong.]

appestat *ap'i-stat, n.* a neural centre in the hypothalamus believed to control (food) appetite. [**appetite,** and **-stat.**]

appetent *ap'i-tənt, adj.* eagerly desirous: craving: longing. — *ns.* **app'etence, app'etency.** [L. *appetēns, -entis,* pr.p. of *appetēre — ad,* to, *petēre,* to seek.]

appetite *ap'i-tīt, n.* physical craving, accompanied with uneasy sensation (hunger, thirst, sex): natural desire: inclination: desire for food: hunger (with *for*). — *adjs.* **app'etible** attractive, desirable. — *v.t.* **app'etise, -ize** to create or whet appetite in. — *ns.* **appetise'ment** (*Scott* **appeteeze'ment**); **app'etiser, -z-** something, esp. food or drink, to whet the appetite. — *adj.* **appetis'ing, -z-.** — *adv.* **appetis'ingly, -z-.** — *n.* **appetition** (*-tish'ən*) direction of desire. — *adj.* **app'etitive** (or *a-pet'i-tiv*) having or giving an appetite. [O.F. *apetit* — L.

appetitus — appetĕre; see foregoing.]

applaud *ə-plöd', v.t.* to express approbation of by clapping the hands or otherwise: to extol: to commend. — *v.i.* to clap the hands or otherwise express approval. — *n.* **applaud'er**. — *adj.* **applaud'ing**. — *adv.* **applaud'ingly**. — *n.* **applause** (*-plöz'*) clapping of hands or other sign of approval: general approbation: loud praise: acclamation. — *adj.* **applausive** (*ə-plös'iv*). — *adv.* **applaus'ively**. [L. *applaudĕre, -plausum — ad*, to, *plaudĕre*, to clap; cf. **explode**.]

apple *ap'l, n.* the fruit of the apple-tree: extended to other fruits (as pineapple, custard-apple) or even galls (oak-apple): the fruit of the forbidden tree in the Garden of Eden. — **ap'ple-blight** American blight, a woolly plant-louse that infests apple-trees; **app'le-blossom; apple butter** a kind of spread made from stewed apples, sugar and spices; **app'le-cart; app'le-jack** (*U.S.*) brandy, distilled from fermented apple juice; **app'le=John** (*Shak.*) a variety of apple considered to be in perfection when shrivelled and withered — also **John=app'le; app'le-pie** a pie made with apples; **app'le-squire** a prostitute's attendant: a man kept by a woman as concubine; **apple-tart** a tart made with apples; **app'le=tree** a tree (*Pyrus malus*) of the rose family, closely related to the pear-tree; **app'le-wife, app'le-woman** a woman who sells apples at a stall. — **apple of discord** any cause of envy and contention, from the golden apple inscribed 'for the fairest', thrown among the gods by Eris, goddess of discord, and claimed by Aphrodite, Pallas, and Hera; **apple of Sodom** or **Dead Sea apple** a fruit described by the ancients as fair to look upon but turning when touched to ashes, variously thought to be a gall, or the fruit of an asclepiad *Calotropis procera*: by botanists applied to the poisonous green-pulped fruit of *Solanum sodomaeum*: any fair but disappointing thing; **apple of the eye** the pupil of the eye: something especially dear; **apple-pie bed** a bed prepared playfully, e.g. with sheets doubled up, so as to be impossible or painful to get into; **apple-pie order** perfect order; **apples and pears** (*rhyming slang*; often shortened to **apples**) stairs; **she's apples** (*Austr. coll.*) everything is all right, the **Big Apple** see **big**; **upset the apple-cart** to throw plans into confusion. [O.E. *æppel*, cf. Ger. *Apfel*; O.N. *epli*; Ir. *abhal*; W. *Afal*.]

appleringie *ap-əl-ring'i*, (*Scot.*) *n.* southernwood (*Artemisia abrotanum*). [Anglo-Fr. *averoine* — L. *abrotanum* — Gr. *abrotanon*.]

Appleton layer *ap'əl-tən lā'ər*, an ionised region in the atmosphere, about 150 miles up, that acts as a reflector of radio waves. [From the physicist Sir Edward *Appleton*.]

appliqué *a-plē'kā, -kā'*, Fr. *ä-plē-kā*, *n.* work applied to, or laid on, another material, either of metal-work or of lace or the like. — Also *adj.* [Pa.p. of Fr. *appliquer*, to apply.]

apply *ə-plī', v.t.* to lay or put in contact: to administer: to bring to bear: to put to use: to show the reference or relevance of: to assign: to ascribe (*obs.*): to wield or ply: to direct: to devote (to a pursuit): to adapt (*obs.*): to lay on as appliqué: to cover with appliqué. — *v.i.* to suit or agree: to have recourse: to offer oneself as a candidate: to make or lodge a request: to be relevant: to hold good: to give close attention: to betake oneself (*obs.*): — *pr.p.* **apply'ing;** *pa.t.* and *pa.p.* **applied'.** — *adj.* **applī'able** applicable: compliant (*obs.*). — *ns.* **applī'ance** compliance (*Shak.*): application: apparatus; **applicability** (*ap-li-kə-bil'i-ti*). — *adj.* **app'licable** (now also *-plik'* in *adj.* and *adv.*) that may be applied: suitable. — *adv.* **app'licably.** — *n.* **app'licant** one who applies: a petitioner: a candidate for a post. — *adj.* **app'licate** put to practical use, applied. — *n.* **applicā'tion** the act of applying, administering, or using: a thing applied: a formal request for a post, etc.: an appeal or petition: diligence: close thought or attention: employment, use of anything in special regard to something else: a particular type of problem or process (*comput.*): a bringing to bear: the lesson or moral of

a fable: employment of a word with assignment of meaning: a kind of needlework, appliqué: compliance (*obs.*). — *adj.* **app'licātive** put into actual use in regard to anything: practical. — *n.* **app'licator** a device or tool for applying something. — *adj.* **app'licatory** (*-kə-tər-i*) having the property of applying. — *adj.* **applied** (*ə-plīd'*) placed with a flat surface against or close to something: turned to use. — **application(s) package, program** (*comput.*) a package, program, designed to cope with a particular job, as payroll-processing, vehicle-scheduling, warehouse control, etc.; **applied mathematics** mathematics applied to observed facts of nature, or to practical life; **applied science** science put to use for a purpose, generally utilitarian, other than its own end (opposed to *pure*). [O.Fr. *aplier*, and its source, L. *applicāre, -ātum — ad*, to, *plicāre*, to fold.]

appoggiatura *äp-pod-jä-tōō'rä, n.* a leaning note — a grace-note written in smaller size taking its time at the expense of the following note: a similar note with a stroke through the tail, played very quickly — an acciaccatura. [It. — *appoggiare*, to lean upon; same root as **appui**.]

appoint *ə-point', v.t.* to fix: to settle: to assign, grant: to fix the time of: to engage to meet: to name to an office: to ordain: to prescribe: to destine, devote: to equip (*obs.* except in *pa.p.*): to blame, arraign (*Milt.*). — *adj.* **appoint'ed** fixed: furnished. — *n.* **appointee'** a person appointed to a job, position or office. — *adj.* **appoint'ive** (*U.S.*) filled by appointment. — *ns.* **appoint'ment** engagement, esp. for a meeting, consultation, etc.: direction: nomination: an office to which one is or may be nominated: (now usu. in *pl.*) equipment: article of equipment: allowance paid to a public officer (*obs.*); **appoint'or** one to whom is willed the power to nominate persons to take property (*law*). [O.Fr. *apointer — à point*, to (the) point.]

apport *ə-pōrt', -pört', n.* in psychical research, the (supposed) transport of material objects without material agency: an object brought on the scene at a spiritualistic séance by no visible agency. [Fr., — L. *apportāre*, to bring.]

apportion *ə-pōr'shən, -pör', v.t.* to portion out: to divide in just shares: to adjust in due proportion. — *n.* **appor'tionment**. [L. *ad*, to, and **portion.**]

appose[1] *ə-pōz', v.t.* to apply, e.g. a seal to a document: to place side by side. [Fr. *apposer* — L. *ad*, to, *pausāre*, to cease, rest; confused and blended in meaning with words from *pōnĕre, pŏsitum*, to put.]

appose[2] *ə-pōz', v.t.* to confront: to examine, question (*Spens.*). — *ns.* **appos'er; apposition** (*ap-ə-zish'ən*) a public examination, a disputation, as on Speech Day at St Paul's School, London. [Variant of **oppose.**]

apposite *ap'ə-zit, adj.* apt: to the purpose. — *adv.* **app'ositely.** — *ns.* **app'ositeness; apposition** (*-zish'ən*) application: juxtaposition: the position of a word parallel to another in syntactic relation (*gram.*): growth by deposition on the surface (*bot.*). — *adjs.* **apposi'tional; appositive** (*ə-poz'*) placed in apposition. [L. *appŏsitus*, pa.p. of *appōnĕre*, to put to — *ad*, to, *pōnĕre*, to put.]

appraise *ə-prāz', v.t.* to set a price on: to value with a view to sale or (in U.S.) payment of customs duty: to estimate the worth of. — *adj.* **apprais'able.** — *ns.* **apprais'al** appraisement; **apprais'ment** a valuation: estimation of quality; **apprais'er** one who values property: one who estimates quality. — *adj.* **apprais'ive.** — *adv.* **apprais'ively.** [Later form of **apprize.**]

appreciate *ə-prē'shi-āt, v.t.* to estimate justly: to be fully sensible of all the good qualities in: to estimate highly: to perceive: to raise in value, to advance the quotation or price of, as opposed to *depreciate*. — *v.i.* to rise in value. — *adj.* **apprē'ciable** capable of being estimated: perceptible. — *adv.* **apprē'ciably.** — *n.* **apprēciā'tion** the act of setting a value, especially on a work of literature or art: just — and also favourable — estimation: a sympathetic critical essay: increase in value. — *adj.* **apprē'ciative** characterised by, implying appreciation. — *adv.* **apprē′ciatively.** — *n.* **apprē′ciātor** one who appreciates, or estimates justly. — *adj.* **apprē′ciatory** (*-shyƏ-tƏr-i*). [L.L. *appretiāre, -ātum* — *ad,* to, and *pretium,* price.]

apprehend *ap-ri-hend′, v.t.* to lay hold of: to arrest: to be conscious of by the senses: to lay hold of by the intellect: to catch the meaning of: to understand: to recognise: to consider: to look forward to, esp. with fear. — *n.* **apprehensibil′ity.** — *adj.* **apprehens′ible.** — *n.* **apprehen′sion** act of apprehending or seizing: arrest: conscious perception: conception: ability to understand: fear. — *adj.* **apprehens′ive** pertaining to the laying hold of sensuous and mental impressions: intelligent, clever: having an apprehension or notion: fearful: anticipative of something adverse. — *adv.* **apprehens′ively.** — *n.* **apprehens′iveness.** [L. *apprae-hendēre* — *ad,* to, *praehendēre, -hēnsum,* to lay hold of.]

apprentice *Ə-prent′is, n.* one bound to another to learn a craft: a mere novice. — Also *adj.* — *v.t.* to bind as an apprentice. — *ns.* **apprent′icehood** (*Shak.*) apprenticeship; **apprent′icement; apprent′iceship** the state of an apprentice: a time of training for a trade, or for any activity: hence, (*Hood*) a period of seven years. — **serve an apprenticeship** to undergo the training of an apprentice. [O.Fr. *aprentis* — *aprendre,* to learn — L. *appraehendēre;* see **apprehend**.]

appress. See **adress.**

apprise *Ə-prīz′, v.t.* to give notice to: to inform. [Fr. *apprendre,* pa.p. *appris;* see **apprehend**.]

apprize, -ise *Ə-prīz, v.t.* to put a selling price on (*Scots law*): to value, appreciate: to have sold for payment of debt (*Scots law*). — *ns.* **appriz′er** a creditor for whom property is apprized (*Scots law*); **appriz′ing** the sheriff's sentence directing property to be apprized (*Scott*). [O.Fr. *appriser, aprisier* — *à,* to, and *prisier,* to price, prize. See **appraise**.]

appro. See **approbation, approve¹.**

approach *Ə-prōch′, v.t.* to bring near: to come near to in any sense: to come into personal relations or seek communication with: to resemble — *v.i.* to come near. — *n.* a drawing near: in golf, play on drawing near the putting-green (also **approach′-stroke, -shot,** etc.): access: an avenue or means of access: approximation: attitude towards, way of dealing with: (usu. *pl.*) advances towards personal relations: (*pl.*) trenches, etc., by which besiegers strive to reach a fortress, or routes into any area of military importance. — *n.* **approach-abil′ity.** — *adj.* **approach′able.** [O.Fr. *aprochier,* L.L. *adpropiāre* — L. *ad,* to, *prope,* near.]

approbation *ap-rƏ-bā′shƏn, n.* a formal sanction: approval: confirmation (*Shak.*): probation (*Shak.*). — *v.t.* **app′robate** to approve authoritatively (chiefly *U.S.*): to accept as valid (*Scots law*). — *adjs.* **app′robātive, approbatory** (*ap′rƏ-bƏ-tƏr-i,* or *Ə-prō′*). — **approbate and reprobate** at once to accept and reject the same deed or instrument — forbidden by Scots law; **on approbation** (*coll.* **appro** *ap′rō*) on approval [L. *approbāre, -ātum;* see **approve¹**.]

approof *Ə-prōōf′, n.* trial, proof: sanction, approval. [O.Fr. *approve;* see **approve¹**.]

appropinque *ap-rō-pingk′,* **appropinquate** *-wāt,* (*arch.*) *vs.t.* and *vs.i.* to approach. — *ns.* **appropinquā′tion** approach; **appropinq′uity** nearness. [L. *appropinquāre,* to approach — *ad,* to, *propinquus* — *prope,* near.]

appropriate *Ə-prō′pri-āt, v.t.* to make to be the private property of any one: to take to oneself as one's own: to filch: to set apart for a purpose, assign: to suit (with *to*). — *adj.* set apart for a purpose: peculiar (with *to*): suitable (with *to* or *for*). — *adv.* **apprō′priately.** — *ns.* **apprō′priateness; apprōpriā′tion** the act of appropriating: the making over of a benefice to a monastery or other corporation: the assigning of supplies granted by parliament to particular specified objects: sometimes used loosely for *impropriation.* — *adj.* **apprō′priative.** — *ns.* **apprō′priativeness; apprō′priātor.** — **appropriate technology** (the development, adaption or

upgrading of) local or locally appropriate industries (e.g. spinning, weaving, pottery, etc. in developing countries) as an alternative to expensive and inappropriate imported technologies; **appropriation bill** a bill stating in some detail how the revenue is to be spent. [L. *appropriāre, -ātum* — *ad,* to, *proprius,* one's own; see **proper**.]

approve¹ *Ə-prōōv′, v.t.* to show, demonstrate (esp. *refl.*): to confirm: to sanction or ratify: to think well of, to be pleased with: to commend: to test (*Shak.*): to convict (*Shak.*). — *v.i.* to judge favourably, to be pleased (with *of*). — *adj.* **approv′able** deserving approval. — *ns.* **approv′al,** (*rare*) **approv′ance** approbation; **approv′er** one who approves: an accomplice in crime admitted to give evidence against a prisoner (*law*): an informer. — *adv.* **approv′ingly.** — **approved school** (1933 (Scotland 1937) to 1969) a state boarding school for young people who have broken the law or who are pronounced to be in need of care and protection. — **on approval** (*coll.* **appro** (*ap′rō*)) subject to approval: without obligation to buy. [O.Fr. *aprover* — L. *approbāre* — *ad,* to, and *probāre,* to test or try — *probus,* good.]

approve² *Ə-prōōv′,* (*law*) *v.t.* to turn to one's profit, increase the value of. [O.Fr. *aproer, aprouer* — *à,* to (L. *ad*), and *pro, prou,* advantage; see **prowess;** confused with **approve¹**.]

approximate *Ə-proks′im-it, adj.* close together: nearest or next: approaching correctness (**very approximate** very nearly exact; but by some used to mean very rough). — *v.t.* (*-āt*) to bring near: to come or be near to. — *v.i.* to come near (to), approach. — *adj.* **approx′imal** close together: next to. — *adv.* **approx′imately** (abbrev. **approx′**). — *n.* **approximā′tion** an approach: an imprecise account, calculation, etc.: a result in mathematics not rigorously exact, but so near the truth as to be sufficient for a given purpose. — *adj.* **approx′imative** (*-i-mā-tiv,-i-mƏ-tiv*) approaching closely. [L. *approx-imāre, -ātum* — *ad,* to, *proximus,* nearest, superl. adj. — *prope,* near.]

appui *a-pwē′, n.* support: the reciprocal action between horse's mouth and rider's hand. — *v.t.* **appui, appuy** to support: to place beside a *point d'appui:* — *pr.p.* **appuy′ing;** *pa.t.* and *pa.p.* **appuied′, appuyed′.** — **point d'appui** (*pwē da-pwē*) a position of strength or support in a line of defences: a prop: a fulcrum. [Fr., — O.Fr. *apuyer* — assumed L.L. *appodiāre* — L. *ad,* to, *podium,* support.]

appulse *Ə-puls′, n.* a striking against something: a coming to conjunction or to the meridian (*astron.;* *obs.*). [L. *appulsus, -ūs* — *appellēre* — *ad,* towards, *pellēre,* to drive.]

appurtenance *Ə-pûr′tƏn-Əns, n.* that which appertains: an appendage or accessory: a right belonging to a property (*law*). — *adj.* and *n.* **appur′tenant.** [A.Fr. *apurtenance* — O.Fr. *apertenance* — *apertenir.* See **appertain**.]

appuy. See **appui.**

apraxia *a-praks′i-Ə, n.* an inability, not due to paralysis, to perform voluntary purposeful movements of parts of the body, caused by brain lesion. [Gr., inaction.]

après *a-pre,* (Fr.) *prep.* after. — **après-goût** (*-gōō*) an after-taste. — **après coup** (*kōō*) too late. **après-ski, apres-** *a-pre-ske, -prä-, n.* (evening period of, or clothes, etc. suitable for) amusements after skiing. — Also *adj.* [Fr.]

apricate *ap′ri-kāt, v.i.* to bask in the sun. — *v.t.* to expose to sunlight. — *n.* **apricā′tion.** [L. *aprīcārī,* to bask in the sun, *aprīcus,* open to the sun.]

apricot *ā′pri-kot, -kƏt,* or *a′,* formerly **apricock** *-kok, n.* a fruit of the plum genus, roundish, pubescent, orange-coloured, of a rich aromatic flavour: its colour: the tree that bears it. [Port. *albricoque* — Ar. *al-birqūq* — *al,* the, Late Gr. *praikokion* — L. *praecoquum* or *praecox,* early ripe; the form is perh. due to a fancied connection with L. *aprīcus,* sunny; assimilated to Fr. *abricot;* see **precocious**.]

April ā'pril, -prəl, n. the fourth month of the year. — adjs. April'ian, A'prilish. — A'pril-fish an April fool's hoax, deception, or errand (Fr. poisson d'Avril); April fool one hoaxed, deceived, or sent upon a bootless errand on the first of April (in Scotland also a gowk, as in the phrase hunt-the-gowk (q.v. under hunt)). [L. Aprīlis.]

a prima vista a prē'ma vēs'ta, (It.) at first sight.

a priori ā prī-ō'rī, -ō', L. ä prē-ōr'ē, the term applied to reasoning from what is prior, logically or chronologically, e.g. reasoning from cause to effect; from a general principle to its consequences; even from observed fact to another fact or principle not observed, or to arguing from pre-existing knowledge, or even cherished prejudices; from the forms of cognition independent of experience (Kant). — ns. apriŏ'rism; apriŏ'rist one who believes in Kant's view of a priori cognition; apriority (-or'i-ti). [L. ā, from, priōrī (abl.), preceding.]

apron ā'prən, n. a cloth or piece of leather or the like worn in front: an English bishop's short cassock: anything resembling an apron in shape or use, as a leg-covering in an open vehicle: a timber behind the stem of a ship: a stage or part of stage in front of the proscenium arch, projecting to greater or less extent into the auditorium (also a'pron-stage): a rim, border, etc.: ground surface at entrance to a hangar, lock, etc.: an extent of e.g. gravel, sand, spread outward from a source (geol.). — v.t. to cover with, or as with, an apron. — n. ā'pronful an amount capable of being carried in one's upturned apron. — a'pron-man (Shak.) a man who wears an apron, a mechanic; a'pron-string a string by which an apron is tied. — tied to a woman's apron-strings bound as a child to its mother. [M.E. napron — O.Fr. naperon — nappe, cloth, table-cloth — L. mappa, a napkin (an apron from a napron; cf. adder).]

apropos a-prō-pō', -prə-, adv. to the purpose: appropriately: in reference to (with of): by the way, incidentally. — adj. to the purpose. [Fr. à propos. See propose, purpose.]

à propos de rien a prō-pō də ryē, (Fr.) apropos of nothing; à propos de bottes (bot) apropos of boots — i.e. without real relevancy: by the way.

apse aps, n. a semicircular or polygonal recess, esp. at the east end of a church choir — where, in the Roman basilica, stood the praetor's chair: an apsis. — adj. ap'sidal of an apse or apsis. — ns. apsid'iole a subsidiary apse; aps'is in an orbit, the point of greatest or least distance from the central body: an apse: — pl. aps'ides (-dēz; or əp-sī'dēz). [L. apsis, -īdis — Gr. hapsis (apsis), -īdos (a felly, wheel, arch, loop — haptein, to fit, connect. See apt.]

apso. See lhasa apso.

apt apt, adj. fitting: fit: suitable: apposite: tending (to): liable: ready or prone: open to impressions, ready to learn (often with at): likely (to). — v.t. to fit (obs.). — n. ap'titude fitness: tendency (with to): natural ability, readiness to learn (with for). — adv. apt'ly. — n. apt'ness. [L. aptus, fit, suitable.]

apterous ap'tər-əs, adj. wingless. — adj. ap'teral wingless: without side columns. — n. apterium (ap-tē'ri-əm) a bare patch on a bird's skin: — pl. apte'ria. [Gr. a-, priv., pteron, feather, wing, side-wall.]

Apteryx ap'tər-iks, n. a flightless genus of birds, the kiwis, found in New Zealand, having vestigial wings, no tail, reddish-brown feathers that lack aftershafts, and being about the size of a large hen: (without cap.) a member of the genus: — pl. ap'teryxes. — adj. apterygial (-tər-ij'i-əl) lacking paired fins or other limbs. — n.pl. Apterygota (ap-ter-i-gō'tə) a class of primitive insects, wingless, without metamorphosis (bristle-tails, springtails — but see Collembola). [Gr. a-, priv., pteryx, -ygos, wing.]

aptote ap'tōt, n. an indeclinable noun. — adj. aptotic (-tot'ik) uninflected. [Gr. aptōtos — a-, priv., ptōsis, case.]

apyrexia ap-i-reks'i-ə, n. intermission of fever. — adj. apyret'ic. [Gr. apyrexiā — a-, priv., pyressein, to be feverish.]

aqua ak'wə, (L.) n. water. — aqua caelestis (sē-les'tis, kī-) rain water: rectified spirits: cordial (L. caelestis, coming from heaven); aqua fontana (fon-tän'ə) spring water (L. fontānus, -a, -um, of a spring); aqua fortis, aquafor'tis nitric acid: etching with nitric acid (L. fortis, strong); aquafor'tist an etcher or engraver who uses aqua-fortis; aqua mirabilis a preparation distilled from cloves, nutmeg, ginger, and spirit of wine (L. mīrābilis, wonderful); aqua regia (rē'jyə, L. rā'gi-a) a mixture of nitric and hydrochloric acids, which dissolves the royal (L. rēgius, -a, -um) metal, gold; aqua Tofana (tō-fä'nə) a secret poison (probably arsenical) made by a 17th-cent. Sicilian woman Tofana; aqua vitae (vī'tē; wē'ti of life) alcohol: brandy, whisky, etc. [L. aqua, water.]

aqua- ak'wə-, ak'wa-, in composition, water. — adj. aquabat'ic. — n.sing or n.pl. aquabat'ics spectacular feats and evolutions in water. — ns. a'quaboard a board for riding on the surface of water; a'quacade an exhibition of swimming, diving, etc., usu. accompanied by music; a'quaculture, a'quiculture the practice of using the sea, lakes, rivers, etc. for fish-farming, shellfish cultivation, the growing of plants, etc.; a'quadrome a centre with facilities for water-skiing competitions; a'quafer aquifer; a'qualung a lightweight, self-contained diving apparatus with compressed-air supply carried on the back; a'quanaut a skin-diver: one who explores and/or lives in the sea at considerable depth. — n.sing. or n.pl. aquanaut'ics. — n. a'quaplane a board on which one stands and is towed behind a motor-boat. — v.i. to ride on an aquaplane: (of a car, etc.) to travel or skid on a film of water which has built up between the tyres and the road surface. — ns. a'quaplaner; a'quaplaning; aquifer (ak'wi-fer), aquafer (geol.) any formation containing water sufficient to supply wells, etc. [L. aqua, water.]

aquamanile ak-wə-mə-nī'lē, -nē'lā, aquamanale -nä'lē, ns. a mediaeval ewer: a basin in which the priest washes his hands during the celebration of mass. [Through L.L. — L. aquae, of water, mānālis, flowing, or manus, hand.]

aquamarine ak-wə-mə-rēn', n. a pale green beryl. — adj. bluish-green. [L. aqua marīna, sea water — mare, the sea.]

aquanaut, aquaplane, etc. See aqua-.

aquarelle ak-wə-rel', n. water-colour painting: a painting in (transparent) water-colours. — n. aquarell'ist. [Fr., — It. acquerella, acquarella — acqua — L. aqua.]

aquarium ə-kwā'ri-əm, n. a tank or (a building containing) a series of tanks for keeping aquatic animals or plants: — pl. aquā'riums, aquā'ria. — adj. aquā'rian. — n. one who keeps an aquarium. — ns. aquā'riist, aquā'rist (or ak'wə-) an aquarian. — n. Aquā'rius the Water-bearer, a sign of the zodiac, and a constellation once coincident with it: one born under this sign. [L. aquārius, -a, -um, adj. — aqua, water.]

aquatic ə-kwat'ik, -kwot', adj. living, growing, practising sports, taking place, in or on water. — n. an aquatic plant, animal, or sportsman. — ns. or n.pl. aquat'ics water sports. [L. aquāticus — aqua, water.]

aquatint ak'wə-tint, n. a mode of etching on copper with resin and nitric acid. — Also aquatint'a. — v.t. and v.i. a'quatint to engrave in aquatint. [It. acqua tinta, dyed water — L. aqua, water, and tingĕre, tinctum, to dye.]

à quatre a katr', (Fr.) of or between four: four together; à quatre mains (mẽ) for four hands.

a quattr' occhi a kwat-ro'kē, (It.) face to face, tête-à-tête.

aquavit ak'wə-vēt, ak', n. a Scandinavian spirit flavoured with caraway seeds. — Also ak'vavit. [Dan., Sw., Norw. akvavit — Mediaeval L. aqua vītae.]

aqueduct ak'wi-dukt, n. an artificial channel or pipe for conveying water, most commonly understood to mean a bridge across a valley: a bridge carrying a canal: a small passage in an animal body. [L. *aqua*, water, *dūcĕre, ductum*, to lead.]

aqueous *ā'kwi-əs, adj.* of water: watery: deposited by water. — **aqueous humour** the watery fluid between the cornea and the lens in the eye. [L. *aqua*, water.]

aquiculture, aquifer. See **aqua-.**

Aquifoliaceae *ak-wi-fō-li-ā'si-ē, n.pl.* the holly family. — *adj.* **aquifoliā'ceous** (*-shəs*). [L. *aquifolium*, holly — *acus, -ūs*, needle, *folium*, leaf.]

Aquila *ak'wi-lə, n.* the golden eagle genus: the Eagle, a constellation north of Sagittarius. — *adj.* **aq'uiline** (*-līn*) of the eagle: hooked like an eagle's beak. [L. *aquila*, eagle.]

Aquilegia *ak-wi-lē'jyə, n.* the columbine genus: (without *cap.*) a member of the genus. [Prob. L. *aquila*, eagle.]

Aquilon *ak'wi-lon,* (*Shak.*) *n.* the north wind. [L. *aquilō, -ōnis.*]

aquiver *ə-kwiv'ər, adv.* or predicative *adj.* in a quivering state. [a³, and **quiver.**]

a quoi bon? *a kwa bõ,* (Fr.) what's the good of it?

ar *är, n.* the eighteenth letter of the alphabet (R, r).

Arab *ar'əb, n.* one of the Semitic people inhabiting Arabia and neighbouring countries: an Arabian horse: a neglected or homeless boy or girl (usu. **street** or **city Arab**). — *adj.* **Arabian.** — *adj.* **Arabian** (*ə-rā'bi-ən, -byən*) of or belonging to Arabia or the Arabs. — *n.* a native of Arabia. — *adj.* **Arabic** (*ar'əb-ik*) relating to Arabia, or to its language. — *n.* the language of the Arabs: see also **gum.** — *v.t.* **ar'abise, -ize** to make Arab. — *n.* **arabisā'tion, -z-.** — *ns.* **Ar'abism** an Arabic idiom; **Ar'abist** one learned in, or studying, Arabic culture, history, language, etc.; **Ar'aby** a poetical form of *Arabia.* — **Arabian camel** a one-humped camel; **Arabian** or **Arabic numerals** the numerals in ordinary use in arithmetic, transmitted from India to Europe by the Arabs. [L. *Arabs, Arabis* — Gr. *Araps, Arabos.*]

araba *är-ä'bä, n.* a heavy screened wagon used by the Tatars and others. — Also **ar'ba, arō'ba.** [Ar. and Pers. *'arābah.*]

arabesque *ar-ə-besk', adj.* after the manner of Arabian designs. — *n.* a fantastic painted or sculptured ornament among the Spanish Moors, consisting of foliage and other forms curiously intertwined: a musical composition with analogous continuity: a posture in ballet dancing in which one leg is stretched out backwards parallel with the ground and the body is bent forward from the hips. — *adj.* **arabesqued'** ornamented with arabesques. [Fr., — It. *arabesco; -esco* corresponding to Eng. *-ish.*]

arabica *ə-rab'i-kə, n.* coffee produced from the shrub *Coffea arabica,* grown esp. in Brazil and other S. American countries.

arabin *ar'əb-in, n.* the essential principle of gum arabic (see **gum**). — **ar'abinose** (or *-ab'*) a sugar got from arabin. [See **Arab.**]

Arabis *ar'ə-bis, n.* a large genus of trailing plants (fam. Cruciferae), including rockcress, wall-cress, etc. [L.L. *Arabis,* Arabian, perhaps from its dry habitats.]

arabise, Arabism, etc. See **Arab.**

arable *ar'ə-bl, adj.* fit for ploughing or tillage. [L. *arābilis* — *arāre,* cog. with Gr. *aroein,* to plough, O.E. *erian,* Eng. **ear** (v.t.), Ir. *araim.*]

Araby. See **Arab.**

Araceae, araceous. See **Arum.**

Arachis *ar'ə-kis, n.* a Brazilian genus of the pea family, including the monkey-nut, ground-nut, or peanut, which ripens its pods underground: (without *cap.*) a member of the genus. [Gr. *arachos* and *arakis,* names of leguminous plants.]

Arachnida *a-rak'ni-də, n.pl.* a class of Arthropoda, embracing spiders, scorpions, mites, etc. — *n.* **arach'nid** any member of the class. — *n.* and *adj.* **arach'nidan.** — *adj.* **arach'noid** like a cobweb. — *n.* the arachnoid membrane. — *adjs.* **arachnoi'dal; arachnolog'ical.** — *ns.* **arachnol'ogist** one who studies the Arachnida; **arachnol'ogy; arachnophō'bia** fear of spiders; **arach'-nophobe.** — **arachnoid membrane** one of the three

coverings of the brain and spinal cord, between the dura-mater and pia-mater, non-vascular, transparent, thin. [Gr. *arachnē,* spider.]

araeometer, areometer *ar-i-om'i-tər, n.* an instrument for determining specific gravity, a hydrometer. — *adjs.* **araeometric, -al** (*-met'*). — *n.* **araeom'etry** the measuring of specific gravity. [Gr. *araios,* thin, *metron,* measure.]

araeostyle, areostyle *a-rē'ō-stīl, adj.* having columns four diameters or more apart. — *n.* a building or colonnade so built. — *adj.* **araeosystyle, areosystile** (*-sis'tīl*) alternately araeostyle and systyle. — Also *n.* [Gr. *araios,* thin, sparse, *stylos,* column.]

aragonite *ar'ə-gə-nīt, ə-rag'ə-nīt, n.* an orthorhombic mineral composed of calcium carbonate. [*Aragon,* in Spain.]

araise, arayse *ə-rāz',* (*Shak.*) *v.t.* to raise from the dead. [Pfx. *a-,* intensive, and **raise.**]

arak. Once *obs.,* now more usu., spelling of **arrack.**

Araldite® *a'rəl-dīt, n.* an epoxy resin used as a strong glue.

Aralia *ə-rā'li-ə, n.* a genus of the ivy family, **Araliā'ceae,** much grown as decorative plants: (without *cap.*) a plant of the genus. — *adj.* **araliā'ceous.** [Perh. American Indian origin.]

Aramaic *ar-ə-mā'ik, adj.* relating to Aramaea, or Aram (roughly, modern Syria), or to its language — also **Aramaean** (*-mē'ən*). — *n.* any of a group of Semitic languages (including that spoken by Christ) once used in this and neighbouring areas in commerce and government. — *n.* **Aramā'ism** an Aramaic idiom. [Gr. *Aramaios.*]

arame *ə-rä'mi, n.* a type of edible seaweed, looking like black bootlaces. [Jap.]

Aran *a'rən, adj.* (of knitwear) made in a style or with a pattern that originated in the *Aran* Islands, off the south-west of Ireland.

Aranea *a-rā'ni-ə, n.* the garden-spider genus (otherwise Epeira): — *ns.pl.* **Arā'neae** (*-ē*), **Araneida** (*ar-ə-nē'i-də*), **-idae** (*-dē*) spiders as a class or order. — *n.* **arā'neid** (*-ni-id*) a spider. — *adj.* **arā'neous** cobwebby. [L. *arānea,* spider.]

arapaima *ar-ə-pī'mə, n.* the pirarucu (*Arapaima,* or *Sudis, gigas;* fam. Osteoglossidae), a gigantic South American river-fish, chief food-fish of the Amazon, reaching sometimes 4 cwt. [Tupí origin.]

arapunga *ar-ə-pung'gə,* **araponga** *-pong'gə, ns.* the campanero or South American bell-bird. [Tupí *araponga.*]

arar *är'är, n.* the sandarac tree. [Moroccan name.]

araroba *ä-rä-rō'bə, n.* Goa powder, a bitter yellow powder got from cavities in a papilionaceous Brazilian tree (*Andira,* or *Vataireopsis, araroba*), and introduced to Goa from Brazil, yielding chrysarobin. [Prob. Tupí.]

Araucaria *a-rö-kā'ri-ə, n.* the monkey-puzzle genus, coniferous trees of S. America and Australasia: (without *cap.*) a tree of the genus. [*Arauco,* in S. Chile.]

à ravir *a ra-vēr,* (Fr.) ravishingly.

arayse. See **araise.**

arba. See **araba.**

arbalest *är'bəl-est, n.* a crossbow: a cross-staff. — Also **ar'balist, ar'blast, ar'cubalist.** — *ns.* **ar'balester, ar'balister, ar'blaster** a crossbowman. [L. *arcubalista* — *arcus,* bow, *ballista* (see **ballista**); partly through O.E. *arblast* — O.Fr. *arbaleste.*]

arbiter *är'bi-tər, n.* a judge: an umpire: one chosen by parties to decide between them: one who has absolute control: — *fem.* **ar'bitress.** — *adj.* **ar'bitrable.** — *ns.* **ar'bitrage** (*-trij*) arbitration: traffic in bills of exchange or stocks to profit by different prices in different markets (also *v.i.*); **ar'bitrager, arbitrageur** (*-tra-zhœr'*) a person who carries out arbitrage. — *adj.* **ar'bitral** (*Scots law*). — *n.* **arbit'rament** (now less usu. **arbit'-rement**) the decision of an arbiter: determination: power of decision. — *v.i.* and *v.t.* **ar'bitrate** to decide, determine: to refer to arbitration: to judge as arbiter. — *ns.* **arbitrā'tion** (submission to) the decision of an arbiter; **ar'bitrātor** arbiter: — *fem.* **ar'bitrātrix.** —

Arbitration Court (*Austr.* and *N.Z.*) a tribunal for the settlement of industrial disputes. [L.]

arbiter elegantiarum *ar'bit-er el-e-gan-shi-ār'əm, el-e-gan-ti-är'ōōm*, (L.) judge of taste.

arbitrary *är'bi-trər-i, adj.* not bound by rules: despotic, absolute: capricious: arising from accident rather than from rule. — *adv.* **ar'bitrarily.** — *n.* **ar'bitrariness.** [L. *arbitrārius* — *arbiter.*]

arbitrate, arbitration, etc. See **arbiter.**

arbitrium *ar-bit'ri-əm, -ōōm,* (L.) *n.* power of decision.

arblast. See **arbalest.**

arbor *är'bər, n.* a tree: a shaft or beam: a spindle or axis. — *adjs.* **arborā'ceous** tree-like: wooded; **arboreal** (*är-bō'ri-əl, -bö'*) of, of the nature of, trees: tree-dwelling; **arbo'reous** of or belonging to trees: tree-like: in the form of a tree: wooded. — *n.* **arboresc'ence,** a tree-like growth: a tree-like crystalline formation. — *adj.* **arboresc'ent** growing, formed, branched, like a tree: approaching the character of a tree. — *ns.* **ar'boret** shrubbery (*obs.*): arboretum (*obs.*): a little tree, shrub (*Milt.*); **arborē'tum** (L. *är-bor-ā'tōōm*) a botanic garden of trees: — *pl.* **arborē'ta.** — *adj.* **arboricul'tural.** — *ns.* **ar'boriculture** forestry, the culture of trees, esp. timber-trees; **arboricul'turist; arborīsā'tion, -z-** an arborescence; **ar'borist** one who studies trees. — *adj.* **ar'borous** of, or formed by, trees. — **Arbor Day** in some countries a day yearly set apart for the general planting of trees; **arbor vitae** (L., tree of life; *vī'tē, wē'tī*) a coniferous tree of the genus Thuja, akin to cypress: a tree-like appearance seen when the human cerebellum is cut vertically. [L. *arbor,* tree.]

arbour *är'bər, n.* a grass-plot, garden, herb-garden, or orchard (*obs.*): a grassy seat (*obs.*): hence, a retreat or bower of trees or climbing plants: a shaded walk (*Milt.*). — *adj.* **ar'boured.** [A.F. *herber* — L. *herbārium* — *herba,* grass, herb; meaning changed through confusion with L. *arbor,* tree.]

Arbutus *är-bū'təs, är', n.* the strawberry-tree genus: (without *cap.*) a tree of this genus. — *n.* **ar'bute** the strawberry-tree or other arbutus. [L. *arbŭtus.*]

arc *ärk, n.* a part of the circumference of a circle or other curve: an arch (*Milt.*): a luminous discharge of electricity across a gap between two conductors or terminals. — *adj.* (*math.*) denoting an inverse hyberbolic or trigonometrical function (as in **arc sine** (or **arcsin**), **arc cosine** (or **arccos**), **arc tangent** (or **arctan**)). — *v.i.* to form an arc: — *pr.p.* **arc(k)'ing;** *pa.t.* and *pa.p.* **arc(k)ed'.** — *n.* **arc(k)'ing.** — *ns.* **arc'-lamp, arc'-light** a lamp whose source of light is an electric arc between carbon electrodes; **arc'second** (*astron.*) a unit of angle measurement, $^1/_{3600}$ of a degree; **arc-welding** see **weld².** [L. *arcus,* a bow.]

arcade *är-kād', n.* a row of arches, open or closed, on columns or pilasters: a walk arched over: a covered passageway lined with shops. — *adj.* **arcād'ed.** — *n.* **arcād'ing.** [Fr., — L.L. *arcāta,* arched; see **arch¹.**]

Arcadian *är-kād'i-ən, adj.* of *Arcadia* (*poet.* **Arcady** *är'kə-di*), a district in Greece whose people were primitive in manners and given to music and dancing: pastoral: simple, innocent. — Also *n.* — *n.* **Arcād'ianism.**

arcanum *är-kā'nəm, n.* a secret: a mystery: a secret remedy or elixir: — *pl.* **arca'na.** — *adj.* **arcane'** secret: mysterious. — *adv.* **arcane'ly.** — *ns.* **arcane'ness; arcan'ist** (*-kān'*) one having knowledge of a secret ceramic process. [L., neut. of *arcānus* — *arca,* a chest.]

arccos. See **arc.**

arc de triomphe *ärk də trē-ɔ̄f,* (Fr.) triumphal arch.

arc-en-ciel *ärk-ã-syel,* (Fr.) *n.* a rainbow.

arch¹ *ärch, n.* a structure of wedge-shaped stones or other pieces supporting each other by mutual pressure and able to sustain a superincumbent weight: anything of like form: an archway: the part from heel to toes of the bony structure of the foot, normally having an upward curve: (in *pl.*) with various adjs. (grey, dark, silvery, etc.), collectors' names for moths of different kinds, with markings like arcading. — *v.t.* to cover or furnish with an arch. — *v.t.* and *v.i.* to bend in the

form of an arch. — *adj.* **arched** having the form of an arch: covered with an arch. — **arch'let** a little arch. — *adv.* **arch'wise** in the manner of an arch. — **arch'way** an arched or vaulted passage. — **(Court of) Arches** the ecclesiastical court of appeal for the province of Canterbury, formerly held at the church of St Mary-le-Bow (or **of the Arches;** from the arches that support its steeple). — **dropped** or **fallen arch** a flattened foot arch. [O.Fr. *arche* — L. *arcus,* bow (as if *arca*).]

arch² *ärch, adj.* chief, principal (*Shak.*): finished, accomplished, pre-eminent, esp. in evil (*Bunyan*): cunning: waggish: roguish: shrewd. — *n.* (*Shak.*) chief. — *adv.* **arch'ly.** — *n.* **arch'ness.** [From the prefix *arch-,* in words such as *arch-*rogue, etc.]

arch- *ärch- (ärk-* in direct borrowings from Greek), *pfx.* first or chief: often an intensive in an odious sense. — *ns.* **arch'-druid** a chief or presiding druid; **arch'-en'emy** a chief enemy: Satan — also **arch'-fel'on, arch'-fiend', arch'-foe'; arch'-flā'men** a chief flamen or priest; **arch'=her'etic** a leader of heresy; **arch'-mock'** (*Shak.*) the height of mockery; **arch'-pi'rate** a chief pirate; **arch'=pō'et** a chief poet: a poet-laureate (*obs.*); **arch'-prel'ate** a chief prelate; **arch'-priest'** a chief priest: in early times, a kind of vicar to the bishop — later, a rural dean: a superior appointed by the Pope to govern the secular priests sent into England from the foreign seminaries during the period 1598–1621: in the Eastern Orthodox Church, the highest title among the secular clergy; **arch-stone** see **voussoir; arch'-trait'or** a chief traitor, greatest of traitors, sometimes applied esp. to the devil, or to Judas; **arch'-vill'ain** one supremely villainous. [O.E. *arce-, ærce-,* through L. from Gr. *archi- — archos,* chief.]

-arch *-ärk, -ərk,* in composition, chief, ruler, as *matriarch, monarch.* [Gr. *archē,* rule.]

Archaean *är-kē'ən,* (*geol.*) *adj.* and *n.* (of or relating to) the oldest geological period, early Pre-Cambrian. [Gr. *archaios,* ancient — *archē,* beginning.]

arch(a)e(o)- *är-ki(-o)-, (-ō)-,* in composition, ancient, primitive: pertaining to archaeology. — *ns.* **archaeoas-tron'omy** the study of prehistoric (e.g. megalithic) monuments with a view to establishing their possible astronomical significance; **archaeol'ogy** the study of human antiquities, usu. as discovered by excavation. — *adj.* **archaeolog'ical.** — *adv.* **archaeolog'ically.** — *ns.* **archaeol'ogist; archaeomag'netism** the process of ascertaining magnetic intensity and direction in a prehistoric object (the date at which there was a corresponding intensity and direction in the earth's magnetic field being the date also of the object); **archaeometall'urgy** the study of archaeological metal objects and methods of metal production, etc.; **archaeom'etry** the use of scientific methods in archaeology; **archaeopteryx** (*-op'tə-riks;* Gr. *pteryx,* wing) a Jurassic fossil bird of the **Archaeopteryx** genus, with a long bony tail. — *n.pl.* **Archaeornithes** (*-ör-nī'thēz;* Gr. *ornithes,* pl. of *ornīs, ornĭs,* bird) the Saururae, or primitive reptile-like birds, the archaeopteryx and its kin. — *n.* **archaeozool'ogy** the study of zoological remains in archaeology. [Gr. *archaios,* ancient — *archē,* beginning.]

Archaeus. See **Archeus.**

archaic *är-kā'ik, adj.* ancient: savouring of the past: not absolutely obsolete but no longer in general use: old-fashioned. — *adv.* **archā'ically.** — *n.* **archā'icism.** — *v.i.* **ar'chāise, -ize** to imitate the archaic. — *ns.* **ar'chāiser, -z-; ar'chāism** inclination to archaise: an archaic word or phrase; **ar'chāist.** — *adj.* **archāist'ic** affectedly or imitatively archaic. [Gr. *archaikos* — *archaios,* ancient — *archē,* beginning.]

archangel *ärk'ān-jl,* or *-ān', n.* an angel of the highest order: garden angelica: dead-nettle: a kind of pigeon. — *adj.* **archangelic** (*-an-jel'*). [Gr. *archangelos* — *archos,* chief, *angelos,* messenger.]

archbishop *ärch-bish'əp,* or *ärch', n.* a metropolitan bishop who superintends the bishops in his province, and also exercises episcopal authority in his own diocese. — *n.*

archbish′opric the office or jurisdiction of, or area governed by, an archbishop. [O.E. *ærcebiscop*; see **arch-**, and **bishop**[1].]

arch-chimic *ärch-kim′ik*, (*Milt.*) *adj.* supreme in alchemy. [See **arch-**, and **chemic**.]

archdeacon *ärch-dē′kən*, or *ärch′*, *n.* a chief deacon: the ecclesiastical dignitary having the chief supervision of a diocese or part of it, next under the bishop — the 'bishop's eye'. — *n.* **archdeac′onry** the office, jurisdiction, or residence of an archdeacon. [O.E. *ærcedīacon*; see **arch-**, and **deacon**.]

archdiocese *ärch-dī′ə-sis, -sēs, n.* an archbishop's diocese. [**arch-**, chief, and **diocese**.]

archduke *ärch′dūk, ärch′dūk′*, (*hist.*) *n.* the title of certain early reigning dukes of importance, and of princes of the imperial house of Austria: — *fem.* **archduchess** (*ärch′duch′is*). — *adj.* **arch′dū′cal.** — *ns.* **arch′duch′y, arch′duke′dom.** [**arch-**, chief, and **duke**.]

archegonium *ärk-i-gō′ni-əm, n.* the flask-shaped female reproductive organ of mosses and ferns, and (in a reduced form) of flowering plants: — *pl.* **archego′nia.** — *adjs.* **archego′nial; archego′niate** having archegonia. — *n.pl.* **Archegoniā′tae** a main division of the vegetable kingdom, bryophytes and pteridophytes. [Gr. *archegonos*, founder of a race.]

archenteron *ärk-en′tər-on, n.* in the embryo, the primitive gut. [Gr. pfx. *arch-*, *enteron*, gut.]

archeology. See **arch(a)(e)o**.

archer *ärch′ər, n.* one who shoots with a bow and arrows: (with *cap.*; with *the*) the constellation and sign of the zodiac Sagittarius: — *fem.* **arch′eress.** — *n.* **arch′ery** the art or sport of shooting with the bow: a company of archers. — **arch′er-fish** an acanthopterygian fish of India that catches insects by shooting water at them from its mouth. [O.Fr. *archier* — L. *arcārius* — *arcus*, a bow.]

archetype *ärk′i-tīp, n.* the original pattern or model, prototype. — *adjs.* **archetȳp′al, archetȳp′ical.** [Gr. *archetypon, arche-, archi-,* and *typos,* a model.]

Archeus, Archaeus *är-kē′əs,* (also without *cap.*) *n.* personification by Paracelsus of a supposed spirit dwelling in and controlling all living things and processes. [Mod. L. *archaeus* — Gr. *archaios*, original.]

archgenethliac *ärch′je-neth′li-ak,* (*Browning*; in derogatory sense) *n.* greatest of genethliacs or astrologers. [**arch-**, chief.]

Archibald *är′chi-bəld,* **Archie,** *är′chi,* (*mil. slang*) *ns.* an anti-aircraft gun. [Arbitrary name.]

Archichlamydeae *är-ki-klə-mid′i-ē,* (*bot.*) *n.pl.* one of the main divisions of the Dicotyledons, in which the petals, if present, are in general not united. — *adj.* **archichlamyd′eous.** [Gr. pfx. *archi-* denoting primitiveness, *chlamys, -ydos,* mantle.]

archidiaconal *är-ki-dī-ak′ə-nəl, adj.* of an archdeacon. [Gr. *archidiākonos*; see **deacon**.]

archiepiscopal *är-ki-i-pis′kə-pəl, adj.* of an archbishop. — *ns.* **archiepis′copacy, archiepis′copate** dignity or province of an archbishop. — **archiepiscopal cross** a patriarchal cross. [Gr. *archiepiskopos,* archbishop.]

archil *är′chil, -kil, n.* a red or violet dye made from various lichens: a lichen yielding it, esp. species of Roccella. — Also **orchel** (*ör′chəl*), **orchella** (*-chel′ə*), **or′chil, orchill′a.** — **orchill′a-weed** an archil lichen. [O.Fr. *orchel, orseil* (Fr. *orseille*) — It. *orcello,* origin undetermined.]

Archilochian *är-ki-lō′ki-ən, adj.* of *Archilŏchus* (Gr. *Archilŏchos*) of Paros (*c.* 714–676 B.C.), Greek lyric poet and lampooner, reputed originator of iambic metre, proverbially bitter. — *n.* an Archilochian verse — dactylic tetrameter catalectic, dactylic trimeter catalectic (*lesser Archilochian*), or dactylic tetrameter combined with trochaic tripody (*greater Archilochian*).

archilowe *är′hhi-lō,* (*obs. Scot.*) *n.* a treat in return. [Origin unknown.]

archimage *är′ki-māj, n.* a chief magician or enchanter. [Gr. *archi-,* chief, *magos,* a magician; older than Spenser's Archimago.]

archimandrite *är-ki-man′drīt, n.* in the Greek Church, an abbot. [Late Gr. *archimandrītēs* — pfx. *archi-,* first, and *mandrā,* an enclosure, a monastery.]

Archimedean *ärk-i-mē-dē′ən,* or *-mē′di-ən, adj.* pertaining to *Archimedes,* a celebrated Greek mathematician of Syracuse (*c.* 287–212 B.C.). — **Archimedean screw** a machine for raising water, etc., in simplest form a tube bent spirally turning on its axis; **Archimedean spiral** the curve described by a point moving uniformly along a uniformly revolving radius vector, its polar equation being $r = a\theta$; **principle of Archimedes** that a body weighed when immersed wholly or partly in a fluid shows a loss of weight equal to the weight of fluid it displaces.

Archipelago *ärk-i-pel′ə-gō, n.* the Aegean Sea: (without *cap.*) a sea abounding in islands, hence a group of islands: — *pl.* **archipel′ago(e)s.** — *adj.* **archipelagic** (*-pi-laj′ik*). [An Italian compound *arcipelago* from Gr. *archi-,* chief, *pelagos,* sea, with pfx. restored to Gr. form.]

architect *ärk′i-tekt, n.* a designer of buildings: a designer of ships (*naval architect*): a maker: a contriver. — *v.t.* to plan or design as an architect. — *adj.* **architecton′ic** pertaining to architecture: constructive: controlling, directing: pertaining to the arrangement of knowledge. — *n.* (often in *pl.* form) the science of architecture: the systematic arrangement of knowledge. — *adj.* **architec′tural** (*-chər-əl*). — *n.* **arch′itecture** the art or science of building: structure: in specific sense, one of the fine arts, the art of designing buildings: style of building: the overall design of the hardware and software of a computer, particularly of the former. [Gr. *architektōn,* master-builder — *archi-,* chief, and *tektōn,* a builder.]

architrave *ärk′i-trāv,* (*archit.*) *n.* the lowest division of the entablature resting immediately on the abacus of the column: collective name for the various parts, jambs, lintels, etc., that surround a door or window: moulding round an arch. — *adj.* **arch′itraved.** [It. *architrave* — Gr. *archi-,* chief, and L. *trabs, trabis,* a beam.]

archive *ärk′īv, n.* (usu. in *pl.*) a repository of public records or of records and monuments generally: public records: (rare in *sing.*) a document, monument. — *adj.* **archīv′al** (or *ärk′i-vəl*). — *n.* **archivist** (*ärk′i-vist*) a keeper of archives or records. [Fr., — L.L. *archī(v)um* — Gr. *archeion,* magisterial residence — *archē,* government.]

archivolt *är′ki-vōlt, n.* the under-curve of an arch: moulding on it. [It. *archivolto* — *arco* (L. *arcus,* an arch) and *volta,* vault.]

archlute *ärch′lōōt, -lūt, n.* a large double-necked bass lute. [Pfx. **arch-**, and **lute**[1].]

archology *ärk-ol′ə-ji,* (*rare*) *n.* doctrine of the origin of things: the science of government. [Gr. *archē,* beginning, rule, *logos,* discourse.]

archon *är′kon, -ōn, -ən, n.* one of nine chief magistrates of ancient Athens. — *ns.* **arch′onship** the office of an archon; **arch′ontate** the archon's tenure of office. — *adj.* **archontic** (*-ont′ik*). [Gr. *archōn, -ontos,* pr.p. of *archein,* to be first, to rule.]

-archy *-ärk-i, -ərk-i,* in composition, denoting government of a particular type, as *oligarchy, monarchy.* [Gr. *archē,* rule.]

arco saltando *är′kō säl-tän′dō,* (*mus.*) with rebounding bow. — *n.* a quick staccato. — **(coll′) arco** (*mus.*) with the bow, a direction marking the end of a pizzicato passage. [It.]

arcsin, arctan. See **arc**.

Arctic, arctic *ärk′tik, adj.* relating to the Great Bear, or to the north: extremely cold. — *n.* (without *cap.*) a waterproof overshoe (*U.S.*): (usu. *cap.* and with **the**) the area lying north of the Arctic Circle or north of the timber line. — *n.pl.* **Arctiidae** (*-tī′i-dē*) the tiger-moth family, whose caterpillars are called woolly-bears. — *adj.* **arc′toid** bear-like. — **Arctic Circle** the parallel of latitude 66°32′N, bounding the region of the earth surrounding the north terrestrial pole. [Gr. *arktos*, a bear.]

Arctogaea *ärk-tō-jē'ə, n.* a zoological region including all lands outside of Notogaea and Neogaea. — *adjs.* **Arctogae'an, Arctogae'ic.** [Gr. *arktos*, bear, *gaia*, earth.]

arctophile *ärk'tə-fīl, n.* a lover or collector of teddy-bears (also **arc'tophil**). — *ns.* **arctoph'ilist; arctophil'ia; arctoph'ily.** [Gr. *arktos*, bear, and **-phile**.]

Arctostaphylos. See **bear-berry.**

Arcturus *ärk-tū'rəs, -tōō', n.* the Bear-ward, a yellow star in Boötes, fourth in order of brightness in the entire heavens. [Gr. *Arktouros* — *arktos*, bear, and *ouros*, guard.]

arcuate *är'kū-āt,* **arcuated** *-id, adjs.* arched. — *n.* **arcuā'tion.** — **arcus (senilis)** *är'kəs (sə-nī'lis, -nē')* a bow-shaped or ring-shaped greyish fatty deposit in the cornea (esp. in the aged). [L. *arcuātus,* pa.p. of *arcuāre,* to bend like a bow — *arcus,* a bow.]

arcubalist *är'kū-bə-list.* See **arbalest.**

arcus. See **arcuate.**

Ardas *ur-das' n.* in the Sikh religion, a short direct prayer to God, similar in status to the Lord's Prayer. [Punjabi, supplication.]

Ardea *är'di-ə, n.* the heron and bittern genus. [L. *ardea,* heron.]

ardeb *är'deb, n.* an Egyptian dry measure of 5½ bushels. [Ar. *irdab*.]

ardent *ärd'ənt, adj.* burning: fiery: fervid: combustible, inflammable (*obs.* except in **ardent spirits,** distilled alcoholic liquors, whisky, brandy, etc.). — *n.* **ard'ency.** — *adv.* **ard'ently.** — *n.* **ard'our** warmth of passion or feeling: eagerness: enthusiasm (with *for*). [L. *ardēns, -entis,* pr.p. of *ardēre,* to burn.]

ardentia verba *ar-den'shi-ə, -ti-a, vûr'bə, wer'ba,* (L.) words that burn, glowing language.

ardour. See **ardent.**

ard-ri(gh), ardri(gh) *örd'rē,* or *-rē', n.* a head king. [Ir. *ārd,* noble, *rī,* king.]

arduous *ärd'ū-əs, adj.* steep, difficult to climb: difficult to accomplish: laborious. — *adv.* **ard'uously.** — *n.* **ard'-uousness.** [L. *arduus,* steep, high.]

are[1] *är, n.* the unit of the metric land measure, 100 sq. metres. [Fr., — L. *ūrea,* a site, space, court.]

are[2] *är,* used as plural of the present indicative of the verb *to be.* [Old Northumbrian *aron,* which ousted the usual O.E. *sind, sindon*; both from the root *es-*.]

area *ā'ri-ə, n.* a space or piece of ground: a portion of surface: a region (*lit.* and *fig.*): the floor of a theatre, etc.: a sunken space alongside the basement of a building: superficial extent. — *adj.* **ā'real.** — **area code** (*U.S.*) a three-digit number used before the local telephone number when dialling long-distance telephone calls; **ā'rea-sneak**' a thief who sneaks in by area doors. [L. *ārea,* an open empty place, etc.]

areach *a-rēch', (obs.) v.t.* to reach, get at: to seize. — *pa.t.* (*Spens.*) **arraught** (*a-röt'*). [O.E. *ārǣcan* — *ā-,* intens., *rǣcan,* to reach.]

aread, arede, arreede *a-rēd', v.t.* to declare (*obs.*): to utter (*obs.*): to guess (*arch.*): to interpret, explain (*arch.*): to adjudge (*obs.*): to decide (*obs.*): to counsel (*Milt.* and *Spens.*). — *pa.t.* and *pa.p.* **ared(d)'.** [O.E. *ārǣdan:* see **read.**]

areal. See **area.**

arear, arere. Spenserian spellings of **arrear** (*adv.*).

à rebours *a rə-bōōr, (*Fr.*) against the grain.

Areca *ar'i-kə, ə-rē', n.* the betel-nut genus of palms: (without *cap.*) a tree of the genus. — **areca-nut** betel-nut, the nut of *Areca catechu,* chewed by the Malays, southern Indians, etc., with lime in a betel-pepper leaf. [Port., — Malayalam *adekka*.]

ared(d), arede. See **aread.**

arefaction *ar-i-fak'shən, (obs.) n.* drying. — *v.t.* and *v.i.* **ar'efy** to dry up, wither. [L. *ārefacēre,* to make dry — *ārēre,* to dry, *facēre,* to make.]

arena *ə-rē'nə, n.* part of the ancient amphitheatre strewed with sand for combats: any place of public contest:

any sphere of action. — *adj.* **arenaceous** (*ar-i-nā'shəs*) sandy: composed of sand or quartz grains: with shell of agglutinated sand-grains: sand-growing. — *ns.* **Arenā'ria** the sandwort genus, akin to chickweed: a genus of birds, the turnstones; **arenā'tion** remedial application of sand. — *adj.* **arenic'olous** sand-dwelling. — **arena stage** a stage which can have audience all round it (see **theatre-in-the-round** under **theatre**). [L. *arēna,* sand.]

aren't *ärnt.* Contraction of **are not.**

areography *ar-i-og'rə-fi, n.* description of the physical features of the planet Mars. [Gr. *Arēs,* Mars, *graphein,* to write.]

areola *a-rē'ō-lə, n.* a small area: a small space marked off by lines, or a slightly sunken spot (*biol.*): an interstice in a tissue (*physiol.*): any circular spot such as that around the nipple (*physiol.*): the part of the iris of the eye bordering on the pupil (*physiol.*): — *pl.* **arē'olae** (*-lē*). — *adjs.* **arē'olar; arē'olate, arē'olated** divided into small areas. — *ns.* **areolā'tion** division into areolae; **areole** (*ar'i-ōl*) an areola: a spiny or hairy spot on a cactus. [L. *āreola,* dim. of *ārea*.]

areometer. See **araeometer.**

Areopagus *ar-i-op'əg-əs, n.* the Hill of Arēs, on which the supreme court of ancient Athens was held: the court itself: any important tribunal. — *n.* **Areop'agite** (*-gīt, -jīt*) a member of the Areopagus. — *adj.* **Areopagitic** (*-git',* or *-jit'*) pertaining to the Areopagus. [Latinised from Gr. *Areios pagos,* hill of Arēs (identified with Roman Mars).]

areostyle, areosystile. See **araeostyle.**

aret, arett *a-ret', v.t.* to entrust, commit (*Spens.*): to assign, allot (*obs.*): to adjudge, award (*obs.*). [O.Fr. *areter, a-,* to, *reter* — L. *reputāre,* to reckon.]

arête *a-ret', n.* a sharp ridge: esp. in French Switzerland, a rocky edge on a mountain. [Fr., — L. *arista,* an ear of corn, fish-bone, spine.]

Aretinian *ar-i-tin'i-ən, adj.* pertaining to Guido of Arezzo (d. 1050). — **Aretinian syllables** the initial syllables of the half-lines of a hymn to John the Baptist, which, falling on successive notes of the diatonic scale, were used (apparently by Guido) as names for the notes: — *Ut* queant laxis *resonare* fibris *Mi*ra gestorum *fa*muli tuorum, *Sol*ve polluti *la*bii reatum, Sancte Ioannes. Thus C in the bass is C *fa ut,* being the fourth note (fa) of the first hexachord (on G) and the first note (ut) of the second hexachord (on C). See **gamut.** [L. *Arētīnus, Arrētinus,* of Arrētium or Arezzo.]

arett. See **aret.**

arew *a-rōō', (Spens.) adv.* arow, in a row.

arfvedsonite *är'ved-sən-īt, n.* a soda amphibole. [After J. A. *Arfvedson* (1792–1841), Swedish mineralogist.]

argal *är'gl, adv.* Shakespeare's gravedigger's attempt at L. *ergō,* therefore.

argala *är'gə-lə, n.* the adjutant stork. [Hind. *hargīla*.]

argali *är'gə-li, n.* the great wild sheep (*Ovis ammon*) of Asia. [Mongol.]

argan *är'gan, n.* a Moroccan timber-tree of the family Sapotaceae: its oil-bearing seed. [N. African pron. of Ar. *arjān*.]

argand *är'gand, n.* a burner admitting air within a cylindrical flame. — Also *adj.* [Invented by Aimé *Argand* (1755–1803).]

Argathelian *är-gə-thē'li-ən, adj.* of the party in Scotland in the 18th century that approved of the political influence of the house of Argyle. [L.L. *Argathelia,* Argyle.]

argemone *är-jem-ō'nē, n.* the prickly poppy. [Gr. *arge-mōnē,* a kind of poppy.]

argent *ärj'ənt, adj.* and *n.* silver: silvery-white (*her.*). — *adjs.* **argentif'erous** silver-bearing; **ar'gentine** (*-īn*) of or like silver: sounding like silver: (with *cap.*) of, or belonging to, Argentina or its people. — *n.* white metal coated with silver: spongy tin: a small smelt with silvery sides: (with *cap.*) a native or citizen of Argentina (also **Argentino** *-tē'nō,* Sp. *är-hhen-tē'nō*). — *n.* **ar'gentite** silver-glance, native sulphide of silver. [Fr., —

L. *argentum*, silver; the republic is named from the Rio de la Plata (silver river).]

argent comptant *ar-zhã kõ-tã*, (Fr.) ready money.

Argestes *är-jes'tēz*, (*Milt.*) *n.* the north-west wind personified. [Gr. *Argestēs*.]

arghan *är'gan*, *n.* pita fibre, or the plant yielding it. [Origin unknown.]

argie-bargie. See under **argue**.

argil *är'jil*, *n.* potter's clay: pure clay or alumina. — *adj.* **argillā'ceous** clayey. — *n.* **ar'gillite** an indurated clay rock. [L. *argilla*, Gr. *argillos*, white clay — *argēs*, white.]

arginine *ar'ji-nīn*, *n.* one of the essential amino-acids. [Origin obscure.]

Argive *är'gīv*, *-jīv*, *adj.* belonging to *Argos*: Greek. — Also *n.*

argle-bargle. See under **argue**.

Argo *är'gō*, *n.* a large southern constellation consisting of four separate constellations.

argol[1] *är'gol*, *n.* dried dung used as fuel. [Mongolian.]

argol[2] *är'gol*, *n.* a hard crust formed on the sides of wine-vessels, from which cream of tartar and tartaric acid are obtainable — generally reddish. [Prob. conn. with Gr. *argos*, white.]

argon *är'gon*, *n.* a colourless, odourless inert gas (at. numb. 18; symbol Ar) discovered in the atmosphere in 1894 by Rayleigh and Ramsay. It constitutes about 1% by volume of the atmosphere from which it is obtained by fractionation of liquid air. It is used in gas-filled electric lamps, radiation counters and fluorescent tubes. [Gr. *ārgon* (neut.) inactive — *a-*, priv., *ergon*, work.]

Argonaut *är'gō-nöt*, *n.* one of those who sailed in the ship *Argo* in search of the golden fleece: (without *cap.*) the paper nautilus (*Argonauta*). — *adj.* **argonaut'ic.** [Gr. *Argō*, and *nautēs*, a sailor.]

argosy *är'gə-si*, *n.* a great merchant ship, esp. of Ragusa (modern Dubrovnik) or Venice. [It. *Ragusea*, Ragusan (ship).]

argot *är'gō*, *n.* slang, originally that of thieves and vagabonds: cant. [Fr.; of unknown origin.]

argue *ärg'ū*, *v.t.* to prove or indicate: to give reason to believe: to seek to show by reasoning: to discuss with reasoning: to persuade or bring by reasoning (into or out of course of action): to accurse (*obs.*). — *v.i.* to offer reasons: to contend with reasoning: to contradict. — *adj.* **arg'uable** capable of being maintained: capable of being disputed. — *adv.* **ar'guably.** — *n.* **arg'uer.** — *v.i.* **ar'gufy** (*coll.*) to bandy arguments: to wrangle. — *v.t.* to beset with wrangling. — *ns.* **ar'gument** proof: evidence: a reason or series of reasons offered or possible towards proof or inducement (with *for* or *against*): exchange of such reasons: debate: matter of debate or contention: a summary of subject-matter: hence contents (*Shak.*): a quantity upon which another depends, or under which it is to be sought in a table (*math.*): the angle between a vector and its axis of reference (*math.*); **argūmentā'tion** reasoning: sequence or exchange of arguments. — *adj.* **argūment'ative** controversial: addicted to arguing. — *adv.* **argūment'atively.** — *n.* **argūment'ativeness.** — *v.i.* **ar'gy-bar'gy, ar'gie-bar'gie, ar'gle-bar'gle** (*orig. Scot.*) to argue tediously or vexatiously. — *n.* a bandying of argument. [Fr. *arguer* — L. *argūtāre*, freq. of *argūĕre*, to show, accuse; *argūmentum*, proof, accusation, summary of contents.]

Argulus *är'gū-ləs*, *n.* a genus of fish lice extremely destructive to fish life: (without *cap.*) a louse of this genus: — *pl.* **ar'gulī.** [Dim. of **Argus** (q.v.).]

argument, etc. See **argue**.

argumentum *är-gū-men'tum*, *är-gōō-men'tōōm*, (L.) *n.* argument. — **argumentum ad crumenam** (*ad krōō'mən-əm*, *-mān-am*) argument addressed to the purse (i.e. to cupidity); **argumentum ad hominem** (*hom'-in-em*) an appeal to the known prepossessions or previous admissions of an opponent; **argumentum ad ignorantiam** (*ig-nör-an'shi-əm*, *ig-nōr-an'ti-am*) one

founded on the ignorance of an opponent; **argumentum ad invidiam** (*in-vid'i-am*, *-wid'*) an appeal to prejudices; **argumentum ad judicium** (*jōō-dish'i-əm*, *ū-dik'-i-ōōm*) an appeal to the commonsense of mankind; **argumentum ad rem** (*rem*) argument to the purpose; **argumentum ad verecundiam** (*ve-re-kun'di-am*, *-kōōn'*) an appeal to awe; **argumentum baculinum** (*ba-kūl-īn'um*, *ba-kōōl-ēn'ōōm*) the argument of the stick — most forcible of arguments; **argumentum per impossibile** (*per im-po-sib'il-ē*, *-ā*) the proof from the absurdity of a contradictory supposition; **argumenti causa** (*är-gū-men'tī kö'zə*, *ar-gōō-men'tē kow'za*) for the sake of argument.

Argus *är'gəs*, *n.* in Greek mythology, Io's guardian, whose hundred eyes Hera transferred to the peacock's tail: a vigilant watcher: (without *cap.*) an East Indian pheasant (**argus pheasant**) of the genus *Argusianus*: (without *cap.*) a butterfly with many eye-spots on the wings (as some *Lycaenidae* and *Satyridae*): (without *cap.*) an ophiuroid with much-divided coiling arms. — *adj.* **Ar'gus-eyed'.** — **argus tortoise beetle** a black-spotted, reddish, tortoise-shaped beetle that feeds on plants of the convolvulus family. [Gr. *Argos*, lit., bright.]

argute *är-gūt'*, *adj.* shrill: keen: shrewd. — *adv.* **argute'ly.** — *n.* **argute'ness.** [L. *argūtus*.]

argy-bargy. See under **argue**.

argyle, Argyll *är-gīl'*, *n.* a vessel for containing gravy and keeping it hot, designed by John, 4th Duke of *Argyll*, in early 1770s: (a sock knitted in) a lozenge pattern adapted from Campbell of Argyll tartan (also *adj.*).

argyria *är-jir'i-ə*, *n.* skin pigmentation caused by taking preparations of silver. — *ns.* **ar'gyrite** same as **argentite; ar'gyrodite** a mineral composed of silver, germanium, and sulphur. [Gr. *argyros*, silver.]

arhythmia, arhythmic. See **arrhythmic**.

aria *ä'ri-ə*, (*mus.*) *n.* an air or melody, esp. an accompanied vocal solo in a cantata, oratorio, or opera: a regular strain of melody followed by another in contrast and complement, and then repeated *da capo.* [It., from root of **air**.]

Arian *ä'ri-ən*, *adj.* pertaining to, or following, *Arius* of Alexandria (d. 336). — *n.* one who adheres to the doctrines of Arius: a Unitarian. — *v.t.* and *v.i.* **A'rianise, -ize.** — *n.* **A'rianism.**

arid *ar'id*, *adj.* dry: parched: barren: jejune. — *ns.* **arid'ity, ar'idness.** — *adv.* **ar'idly.** [L. *aridus*.]

Ariel *ä'ri-əl*, *n.* a man's name in the Old Testament: in later demonology, a water-spirit: an angel: a spirit of the air (as Shakespeare's Ariel, a sylph in Pope): (without *cap.*) species of swallow, petrel, and toucan. [Heb. *Ariel*, with meaning influenced by air.]

ariel *ä'ri-əl*, *n.* a kind of gazelle. [Ar. *aryil*.]

Aries *ä'ri-ēz*, *n.* the Ram, a constellation giving name to, and formerly coinciding with, a sign of the zodiac: one born under this sign. — **first point of Aries** the intersection of equator and ecliptic passed by the sun in (the northern) spring, now actually in Pisces. [L. *ariēs*, *-etis*, ram.]

arietta *ar-i-et'ə*, (*mus.*) *n.* a little aria or air. — Also (Fr.) **ariette** (*-et'*). [It. *arietta*, dim. of *aria*.]

aright *ə-rīt'*, *adv.* in a right way: rightly: on or to the right. — **a-rights'** (*Spens.*) rightly. [a[3] and **right**[1].]

aril *är'il*, *n.* a covering or appendage of some seeds, an outgrowth of the funicle: sometimes, a caruncle (*false aril*). — Also **arill'us:** — *pl.* **arill'ī.** — *adjs.* **ar'illary, ar'illate, ar'illated** having an aril. — *n.* **ar'illode** a caruncle or false aril, from near the micropyle. [L.L. *arillus*, raisin.]

Arimaspian *ar-i-mas'pi-ən*, *adj.* pertaining to the *Arimaspi*, described by Herodotus as a one-eyed people of the extreme north, warring perpetually with griffins for gold hoards. — Also *n.* — Also **Ar'imasp** *adj.* and *n.*

arioso *a-ri-ō'sō*, *adj.* and *adv.* in the melodious manner of an aria, or between aria and recitative. — Also *n.*: — *pl.* **ario'sos, -si** (*-sē*). [It. *aria*.]

ariot *ə-rī'ət, adv.* in riot, riotously. [a³ and **riot.**]

aripple *ə-rip'l, adv.* in a ripple. [a³ and **ripple.**]

aris *ar'is,* (*Cockney slang*) *n.* arse. [Short for 'Aristotle', rhyming slang for 'bottle', which is in turn short for 'bottle and glass', rhyming slang for 'arse'.]

arise *ə-rīz', v.i.* to rise up: to take rise, originate (with *from, out of*): to come into being, view, or activity: — *pa.t.* **arose** (*ə-rōz'*); *pa.p.* **arisen** (*ə-riz'n*). [Pfx. *a-*, up, out, and **rise.**]

arish. See **arrish.**

arista *ə-ris'tə, n.* an awn: a bristle-like appendage on some insects' antennae. — *adj.* **aris'tate** (or *ar'*) awned. [L. *arista,* an awn.]

Aristarch *ar'is-tärk, n.* a severe critic. [*Aristarchus,* Alexandrian grammarian (*c.* 160 B.C.).]

aristate. See **arista.**

Aristides *ar-is-tī'dēz,* (L., — Gr. *Aristeidēs*) *n.* an embodiment of justice, from the Athenian statesman (5th cent. B.C.).

Aristippus *ar-is-tip'əs,* (L., — Gr. *Aristippos*) *n.* an embodiment of self-indulgence, from the founder of the Cyrenaic school of philosophy.

aristocracy *ar-is-tok'rə-si, n.* government by, or political power of, a privileged order: a state so governed: a nobility or privileged class: an analogous class in respect of any quality. — *n.* **aristocrat** (*ar'is-tə-krat,* or *ə-ris'*; sometimes (*coll.*) shortened to **aristo** (*a'ris-tō* or *ə-ris'tō*: — *pl.* **aristos**)) a member of an aristocracy: one who has the characteristics of or attributed to an aristocracy: a haughty person: one of the, or the, best of its kind. — *adjs.* **aristocrat'ic, -al** belonging to aristocracy: having the character that belongs to, or is thought to befit, aristocracy. — *adv.* **aristocrat'ically.** — *n.* **aristocratism** (*-tok'rə-tizm*) the spirit of, or belief in, aristocracy. [Gr. *aristokratiā* — *aristos,* best, and *kratos,* power.]

Aristolochia *ar-is-tō-lō'ki-ə, n.* the birthwort genus, herbs and climbers, specially abundant in tropical South America, giving name to the family **Aristolochiā'ceae.** [Gr. *aristolocheia* — *aristos,* best, *locheiā,* child-birth, from the former repute of birthwort.]

aristology *ar-is-tol'ə-ji, n.* the science or art of dining. [Gr. *ariston,* breakfast, luncheon, *logos,* discourse.]

ariston metron *ar-is'ton met'ron,* (Gr.) the middle course is the best: the golden mean.

Aristophanic *ar-is-to-fan'ik, adj.* relating to or characteristic of the Greek comic dramatist *Aristophanes.*

Aristotelian *ar-is-to-tē'li-ən,* **Aristotelean** *ar-is-tot-i-lē'ən, adj.* relating to Aristotle (Gr. *Aristotelēs*) or to his philosophy. — *n.* a follower of Aristotle. — *ns.* **Aristotē'lianism, Aristot'elism.** — **Aristotle's lantern** a chewing apparatus in sea-urchins, compared by Aristotle to a ship's lantern.

Arita *a-rē'tə, n.* a Japanese porcelain manufactured from the early 17th century at *Arita* near Nagasaki.

arithmetic *ə-rith'mə-tik, n.* the science of numbers: the art of reckoning by figures: a treatise on reckoning. — *adjs.* **arithmetic** (*ar-ith-met'ik*), **-al.** — *adv.* **arithmet'ically.** — *n.* **arithmetician** (*-mə-tish'n,* or *ar'*) one skilled in arithmetic. — **arithmetical progression** a series increasing or diminishing by a common difference, as 7, 10, 13, 16, 19, 22; or 12, 10½, 9, 7½, 6; **arithmetic(al) mean** see **mean².** [Gr. *arithmētikē* (*technē,* art), of numbers — *arithmos,* number.]

arithmo- *ar-ith-mo-,* in composition, number. — *ns.* **arithmomā'nia** an obsessive preoccupation with numbers, characterised by a compulsion to count people or objects; **arithmom'eter** a calculating machine; **arithmophō'bia** fear of numbers. [Gr. *arithmos,* number.]

ark *ärk, n.* a chest or coffer: in Jewish history, the wooden coffer in which the Tables of the Law were kept: a large floating vessel, as Noah's in the Deluge (Gen. vi-viii): a toy representing Noah's ark. — *v.t.* to put in an ark. — *adj.* and *n.* **ark'ite.** — **ark'-shell** a boxlike bivalve shell (*Arca*). [O.E. *arc* (*earc*) — L. *arca,* a chest — *arcēre,* to guard.]

arkose *är-kōs', n.* a sandstone rich in feldspar grains,

formed from granite, etc. [Fr.]

arles *ärlz,* also *ārlz,* (*arch.*) *n.pl.* earnest, esp. in confirmation of a bargain, or an engagement of a servant. — *v.t.* to give earnest-money to or for. — **arle'-penny, arles'-penny.** [Scot. and Northern; M.E. *erles* — app. through O.Fr. from a dim. of L. *arrha.*]

arm¹ *ärm, n.* the forelimb from shoulder to hand, esp. when used for purposes other than locomotion: a tentacle: a narrow projecting part: an inlet: a branch: a rail or support for the arm as on a chair: power (*fig.*). — *v.t.* to take in the arms: to conduct arm-in-arm. — *adj.* **armed** (usu. in composition) having an arm or arms, as *one-armed.* — *n.* **arm'ful.** — *adj.* **arm'less.** — *n.* **arm'let** a little arm: a ring or band round the arm. — **arm'band** a band of cloth worn round the sleeve; **arm'chair'** a chair with arms. — *adj.* **arm'chair** amateur: stay-at-home: doctrinaire. — **arm'hole** the hole in a garment through which the arm is put. — *adv.* **arm'-in-arm'** with arms interlinked. — **arm'lock** in wrestling, etc. a hold by the arms; **arm'pit** the hollow under the shoulder. — **at arm's length** at a distance (*lit., fig.*), not showing friendliness or familiarity: (of negotiations, etc.) in which each party preserves its independent ability to bargain (*adj.* **arms'-length,** e.g. in shareholding, having broad and ultimate control, without involvement in policy decisions, etc.); **in arms** carried as a child: young enough for this; **right arm** the main support or assistant; **secular arm** the civil authority, opp. to the spiritual or ecclesiastical; **the long arm of the law** the far-reaching power and influence of the law — esp. the police force; **(with)in arm's reach** able to be reached easily, i.e. from where one is sitting; **with open arms** with hearty welcome. [O.E. *arm* (*earm*); cog. with L. *armus,* the shoulder-joint and with Gr. *harmos,* a joint.]

arm² *ärm, n.* a weapon: a branch of the fighting forces. — *in pl.* weapons of offence and defence: hostilities: fighting: soldiering: heraldic devices. — *v.t.* to furnish with weapons, means of protection, armature, or (*fig.*) equipment: to make (a bomb, etc.) ready to explode: to strengthen with a plate or otherwise. — *v.i.* to take arms. — *ns.* **ar'mament** a force equipped for war: total means of making war: munitions, esp. for warships: act of arming or equipping for war: defensive equipment; **armamentā'rium** (L., arsenal, armoury) the equipment, medicines, etc. available to a doctor, etc.; **ar'mature** armour: any apparatus for defence: a wooden or wire support around which a sculpture, model, etc., is constructed: a piece of iron set across the poles of a magnet: a moving part in a magnetic circuit to indicate the presence of electric current: a rotor, the metal part (wound with current-carrying wire) that, in a generator, turns to produce a current, and in a motor, provides the current that produces torque. — *adj.* **armed** furnished with arms: provided with means of defence: thorny: with beak, claws, etc., of such and such a tincture (*her.*). — **armed eye** the aided eye (opp. to *naked eye*); **arms race** competition among nations in building up armaments. — **bear arms** to serve as a soldier: (also **give arms**) to show armorial bearings; **in arms** armed: quartered (*her.*); **lay down one's arms** to surrender, submit; **of all arms** of every kind of troops; **take (up) arms** to resort to fighting; **under arms** armed; **up in arms** in readiness to resist: protesting hotly. [Fr. *armes,* from L. *arma* (*pl.*); L. *armāmenta,* tackle, equipment; *armātūra,* armour.]

armada *är-mä'də,* (sometimes *mā'*), *n.* a fleet of armed ships, esp. that sent by Philip II of Spain against England in 1588. [Sp., fem. pa.p. of *armar* — L. *armāre,* to arm.]

armadillo *ärm-ə-dil'ō, n.* an American edentate armed with bands of bony plates: — *pl.* **armadill'os.** [Sp., dim. of *armado,* armed; see foregoing.]

Armageddon *är-mə-ged'n, n.* the great symbolical battlefield of the Apocalypse, scene of the final struggle between the powers of good and evil: a great war or battle of nations. [*Harmagedōn* or *Armageddōn* given as Heb. name in Rev. xvi. 16; perh. suggested by the famous battlefield of *Megiddo*, in the plain of Esdraelon.]

Armagnac *är-mä-nyak, n.* a dry brandy distilled in S.W. France. [Name of district.]

Armalite ® *ar'mə-līt, n.* a low-calibre, high-velocity assault rifle with an automatic and semi-automatic facility.

armament, armature. See under **arm²**.

Armenian *är-mē'nyən, adj.* belonging to *Armenia*, in Western Asia, or its people or language, or their branch of the Christian Church. — *n.* native of Armenia: one of the Armenian people: the language of the Armenians. — *adj.* **Armē'noid** of the eastern branch of the Alpine race. — Also *n.*

armes parlantes *ärm par-lät,* (Fr.) lit. talking arms, arms that indicate the name of the family that bears them, as a press and a tun for Preston.

armet *är'mit, n.* a helmet introduced about 1450 in place of the basinet, consisting of an iron cap, spreading over the back of the neck, having in front the visor, beaver, and gorget. [Fr.]

armgaunt *ärm'gönt,* (Shak., *Ant. and Cleo.,* I, v. 48) *adj.* perh. with gaunt limbs, or perh. worn with armour, but probably an error.

armiger *är'mi-jər, n.* one entitled to a coat-of-arms: an esquire. — Also **armi'gero** (*Shak.*; Slender's blunder in *Merry Wives*). — *adjs.* **armi'geral, armi'gerous.** [L., an armour-bearer — *arma,* arms, *gerĕre,* to bear.]

armilla *är-mil'ə, n.* bracelet (*archaeol.*; also **ar'mil**): frill on a mushroom stalk (*bot.*). — *adj.* **armill'ary** (or *är'*). — **armillary sphere** a skeleton sphere made up of hoops to show the motions of the heavenly bodies. [L. *armilla,* an armlet, dim. of *armus,* the upper arm, the shoulder.]

Arminian *är-min'i-ən, n.* a follower of *Arminius* (1560–1609), who denied the Calvinistic doctrine of absolute predestination, as well as irresistible grace. — Also *adj.* — *n.* **Armin'ianism.**

armipotent *är-mip'ə-tənt, adj.* powerful in arms. [L. *arma,* arms, *potēns, -entis,* powerful.]

armistice *är'mi-stis, n.* a suspension of hostilities: a truce. — **Armistice Day** 11th Nov. 1918, the day fighting ended in the 1st World War, kept since as an anniversary, from 1946 as Remembrance Sunday (q.v.). [Fr., — L.L. *armistitium* — L. *arma,* arms, *sistĕre,* to stop.]

armlet. See **arm¹**.

armoire *är-mwär', n.* an ambry or cupboard. [Fr.]

armorial. See **armour**.

Armoric *är-mor'ik, adj.* of *Armorica,* or Brittany. — *n.* the Breton language. — *n., adj.* **Armor'ican.** [L. *Armoricus* — Gallic *are-morici,* dwellers by the sea.]

armour, (*U.S.* **armor**), *är'mər, n.* defensive dress: protective covering: armoured vehicles: heraldic insignia. — *adj.* **armō'rial** of heraldic arms. — *n.* a book of coats-of-arms. — *ns.* **ar'morist** one skilled in heraldry; **ar'mory** heraldry: armoury (*U.S.*): drill hall and headquarters of an army unit (*U.S.*): arsenal (*U.S.*). — *adj.* **ar'moured** protected by armour. — *n.* **ar'mourer** a maker, repairer or custodian of arms and armour. — *adj.* **ar'mourless.** — *n.* **ar'moury** a collection of arms and armour: a place where arms are kept: armour collectively. — **ar'mour-bearer** one carrying another's armour, a squire. — *adj.* **ar'mour-clad'** clad in armour. — **ar'mour-clad** an armoured ship; **ar'moured-car', -crui'ser, -train';** **ar'mour-plate** a defensive plate for a ship, tank, etc. — *adj.* **ar'mour-plat'ed.** — **armorial bearings** the design in a coat of arms. [O.Fr. *armure* — L. *armātūra* — *arma,* arms.]

armozeen, armozine *är-mō-zēn', n.* a kind of taffeta or plain silk, usu. black, used for clerical gowns. [Fr. *armoisin.*]

armure *är'mūr, n.* a type of fabric with a pebbled surface. [Fr.]

army *ärm'i, n.* a large body of people armed for war and under military command: a body of people banded together in a special cause, whether mimicking military

methods as the 'Salvation Army', or not, as the 'Blue Ribbon Army': a host: a great number. — **army ant** any of several kinds of stinging ants which move about in vast numbers; **army corps** (*kōr, kör*) a miniature army comprising all arms of the service; **army list** a list of all commissioned officers; **army worm** the larva of a small fly (*Sciara*) that collects in vast armies: that can move in multitudes from field to field destroying crops. the larva of any of several (esp. N. American and E. African) types of moth that can move in multitudes from field to field destroying crops. [Fr. *armée,* pa.p. fem. of *armer* — L. *armāre, -ātum* to arm.]

arna *är'nä, n.* the Indian water-buffalo, *Bubalus bubalis.* [Hindi.]

Arnaut, Arnaout *är-nowt', n.* an Albanian, esp. one in the Turkish army. [Turk.]

arnica *är'ni-kə, n.* a tincture of the flowers of a composite plant, *Arnica montana,* or mountain tobacco, applied to sprains and bruises (but not to open wounds). [Origin unknown.]

arnotto *är-not'ō.* See **annatto**.

arnut *är'nət.* Same as **earth-nut**.

aroba. See **araba**.

aroid. See **Arum**.

aroint, aroynt *ə-roint',* apparently *v.t.,* used twice by Shakespeare in the phrase, '*Aroint* thee, witch', meaning away, begone: to drive or frighten away (*Browning*). [Origin unknown.]

arolla *a-rol'ə, n.* the Swiss stone-pine or Siberian cedar (*Pinus cembra*). [Fr. *arolle.*]

aroma *ə-rō'mə, n.* a spicy fragrance: flavour or peculiar charm (*fig.*). — *n.* **aromather'apy** a method of treating bodily ailments using essential plant oils. — *adj.* **aromatic** (*ar-ō-mat'ik*) fragrant: spicy: in chemistry, belonging to the closed-chain class of organic compounds, or benzene derivatives — opp. to *fatty* or *aliphatic.* — Also *n.* — *v.t.* **arō'matise, -ize** to render aromatic: to perfume. [L., from Gr. *arōma, -atos,* spice.]

arose. See **arise**.

around *ə-rownd', prep.* on all sides of: round, round about: somewhere near: in existence or circulation. — *adv.* on every side: in a circle: round about, astir. — **get around to** (*coll.*) to reach the point of (doing something); **have been around** (*coll.*) to be experienced, sophisticated. [**a³** and **round²**.]

arouse *ə-rowz', v.t.* and *v.i.* to rouse: to stimulate. — *n.* an arousing, alarm. — *ns.* **arous'al; arous'er.** [Pfx. *a-,* intensive, and **rouse¹**.]

arow *ə-rō', adv.* in a row: one following the other. [**a³** and **row¹**.]

aroynt. Same as **aroint.**

arpeggio *är-ped'j(y)ō,* (*mus.*) *n.* a chord of which the notes are performed, not simultaneously, but in rapid (normally upward) succession: the notes of a chord played or sung, esp. as an exercise, in rapid ascending or descending progression, according to a set pattern: — *pl.* **arpegg'ios.** — *v.t.* **arpegg'iate** (*-ji-āt*) to perform or write in arpeggios. — *ns.* **arpeggia'tion; arpeggione** (*är-pej-i-ōn'ā*) an early 19th century bowed stringed instrument. [It. *arpeggiare,* to play the harp — *arpa,* harp.]

arpent *är'pənt, är-pä, n.* an old French measure for land still used in Quebec and Louisiana varying from about 50 to 35 ares (1¼ acres to ⅚ of an acre). [Fr., — L. *arepennis,* said to be a Gallic word.]

arquebus(e), harquebus (*h*)*är'kwi-bus, ns.* an oldfashioned handgun. — *ns.* **arquebusade'** a lotion for shot-wounds; **arquebusier** (*-bus-ēr'*) a soldier armed with an arquebus. [Fr. *arquebuse* — Du. *haakbus* — *haak,* hook, and *bus,* box, barrel of a gun; Ger. *Hakenbüchse.*]

arracacha *ar-a-käch'ə, n.* an umbelliferous plant (*Arracacia*) of northern South America, with edible tubers. [Quechua *aracacha.*]

arrack *ar'ək, n.* an ardent spirit used in the East, procured from toddy, or the fermented juice of the coco and

fāte; fär; hûr; mīne; mōte; för; mūte; mōōn; fŏŏt; dhen (then); *el'ə-mənt* (element)

other palms, as well as from rice and jaggery sugar. [Ar. *'araq*, juice.]

arragonite. Another spelling of **aragonite**.

arrah *ar'ə, interj.* Anglo-Irish expression of emotion, wonder, mild expostulation, etc.

arraign *ə-rān', v.t.* to call to account: to put upon trial: to accuse publicly. — *ns.* **arraign'er; arralgn'ing; arraign'ment.** [O.Fr. *aresnier* — L.L. *arrationāre* — L. *ad*, to, *ratiō, -ōnis*, reason.]

arrange *ə-rānj', v.t.* to set in a rank or row: to put in order: to settle: to adapt for other instruments or voices (*mus.*). — *v.i.* to come to an agreement (with *to*): to make plans (with *for*). — *ns.* **arrange'ment, arranger.** [O.Fr. *arangier* — *à* (L. *ad*, to), and *rangier, rengier*; see **range**.]

arrant *ar'ənt, adj.* downright, unmitigated, out-and-out: notorious: rascally. — *adv.* **arr'antly.** [A variant of **errant**.]

arras *ar'əs, n.* tapestry (made at *Arras* in France): a hanging screen of tapestry for a wall. — *adj.* **arr'ased** covered with arras. — *n.* **arr'asene** an embroidery material, of wool and silk.

arraught. See **areach**.

array *ə-rā', n.* order: dress: equipage: an imposing, purposeful, or significant arrangement: an arrangement of terms in rows and columns, (esp. if square) a matrix (*math.*). — *v.t.* to put in order: to arrange: to empanel (jurors) (*law*): to dress, adorn, or equip. — *n.* **array'ment** act of arraying: clothing (*obs.*). [A.Fr. *arai*, O.Fr. *arei*, array, equipage — L. *ad*, and the Gmc. root found in Eng. **ready**, Ger. *bereit*.]

arrear *ə-rēr', n.* that which is in the rear or behind: (usu. in *pl.*) that which remains unpaid or undone: (in *sing.* or *pl.*) condition of being behind-hand. — *adv.* (*obs.*) aback, backward, behind. — *n.* **arrear'age** arrear, arrears. — **in arrears** behind-hand, esp. in the payment of rent, etc. [O.Fr. *arere, ariere* (Fr. *arrière*) — L. *ad*, to, *retrō*, back, behind.]

arrect *a-rekt', adj.* upright: pricked up: on the alert. [L. *arrēctus*.]

arrectis auribus *ar-ek'tēs ow'ri-bŏŏs*, (L.) with ears pricked up.

arreede. See **aread**.

arrest *ə-rest', v.t.* to bring to a standstill, check: to seize: to catch, fix (as the attention): to apprehend by legal authority: to seize by warrant: to take in security (*Shak.*). — *n.* stoppage: seizure by warrant. — *adj.* **arrest'able** (of an offence) such that the offender may be arrested without warrant: liable to arrest. — *ns.* **arrestation** (*ar-es-tā'shən*) the act of arresting: arrest; **arrestee'** a person prevented by arrestment from making payment or delivery to another until the arrester's claim upon that other is secured or satisfied; **arrest'er** one who, or that which, arrests: a lightning-arrester: one who makes an arrestment (also **arrest'or**). — *adj.* **arrest'ive** tending to arrest. — *n.* **arrest'ment** a checking: detention of a person arrested till liberated on bail, or by security (*law*): process which prohibits a debtor from handing over to his creditor money or property until a debt due by that creditor to a third party, the arrester, is paid or secured (*Scots law*). — **arrester gear** shock-absorbing transverse cables on an aircraft-carrier's deck for the arrester hook of an alighting aircraft to catch on; **arrester hook** a hook put out from an aircraft alighting on an aircraft-carrier, to catch on the arrester gear. — **arrest of judgment** a delay between conviction and sentence because of possible error; **cardiac arrest** a heart attack: heart failure; **under arrest** having been apprehended by legal authority. [O.Fr. *arester* — L. *ad*, to, *restāre*, to stand still.]

arrêt *a-ret', ä're', ä-rā', n.* decision: judgment of a tribunal. [Fr. See **arrest**.]

arrhenotoky *ar-ən-ot'ə-ki, n.* parthenogenetic production of males alone. [Gr. *arrēn*, male, *tokos*, offspring.]

arrhythmic, arhythmic *ā-rith'mik, -ridh', adj.* having an irregular or interrupted rhythm. — *n.* **arrhyth'mia,**

arhyth'mia (*med.*) irregularity of the heart-beat. [Gr. *a-*, priv.]

arriage *ar'ij, n.* a former feudal service in Scotland, said to have been rendered by the tenant with his beasts of burden, later indefinite. [See **average** and **aver²**.]

arride *ə-rīd', (Lamb) v.t.* to please, gratify. [L. *arrīdēre*.]

arriéré *ar-ē-ār-ā,* (Fr.) *adj.* backward, old-fashioned.

arrière-ban *ar'ē-er-ban, -bä, n.* a feudal sovereign's summons to all freemen to take the field: the army thus collected. [O.Fr. *ariereban* — O.H.G. *hari*, army, and *ban*, public proclamation; confused with Fr. *arrière*.]

arrière-garde *ar-ē-er-gärd,* (Fr.) *n.* rear-guard.

arrière-pensée *ar-ē-er-pä-sā,* (Fr.) *n.* a mental reservation: a subsidiary aim.

arriero *ar-i-ā'rō, n.* a muleteer: — *pl.* **arrie'ros.** [Sp.].

arris *ar'is, n.* a sharp edge on stone, metal, etc. at the meeting of two surfaces. — **arris rail** a wooden, etc. rail of triangular section. [See **arête**.]

arrish, arish *är'ish, (dial.) n.* a stubble field. [O.E. *ersc* (in compounds).]

arrive *ə-rīv', v.i.* to reach shore or port (*obs.*): to reach any place: to attain to any object (with *at*): to achieve success or recognition: to happen. — *v.t.* (*obs.*) to reach. — *ns.* **arriv'al** the act of arriving: a person or thing that arrives; **arriv'ance, -ancy** (*Shak.*) company arriving. [O.Fr. *ariver* — L.L. *adrīpāre* — L. *ad*, to, *rīpa*, shore.]

arrivederci, a rivederci *är-ē-vəd-er'chē,* (It.) goodbye until we meet again.

arriviste *a'rē-vēst, n.* a person 'on the make': a parvenu: a self-seeker. — *n.* **a'rrivisme.** [Fr.].

arroba *a-rō'bə, ä-ro'bä, n.* a weight of 25 pounds (11·35kg) or more, used in Spanish and Portuguese regions. [Sp. and Port., — Ar. *ar-rub'*, the quarter.]

arrogate *ar'ə-gāt, v.t.* to claim as one's own: to claim proudly or unduly: to ascribe, attribute, or assign (to another). — *ns.* **arr'ogance, arr'ogancy** undue assumption of importance. — *adj.* **arr'ogant** claiming too much: overbearing. — *adv.* **arr'ogantly.** — *n.* **arrogā'tion** act of arrogating: undue assumption. [L. *arrogāre* — *ad*, to, *rogāre, -ātum*, to ask, to claim.]

arrondissement *ä-rɔ̃-dēs'mä, n.* a subdivision of a French department. [Fr., — *arrondir*, to make round.]

arrow¹ *ar'ō, n.* a straight, pointed missile, made to be shot from a bow or blowpipe: any arrow-shaped mark or object: the chief shoot of a plant, esp. the flowering stem of the sugar-cane: (in *pl.*) darts (*coll.*). — *v.t.* to indicate, show the position of, by an arrow. — *adj.* **arr'owy** of or like arrows. — **arr'ow-grass** a genus of marsh plants (*Triglochin*) whose burst capsule is like an arrow-head; **arr'ow-head** the head or pointed part of an arrow: an aquatic plant (*Sagittaria sagittifolia*) of the Alismaceae, with arrow-shaped leaves. — *adj.* **arr'ow-headed** shaped like the head of an arrow. — **arr'ow-poi'son** poison smeared on arrow-heads; **arr'owroot** a West Indian plant, *Maranta arundinacea* or other species: its rhizome, esteemed in S. America as an antidote to arrow-poison: a nutritious starch from the rhizome: extended to other plants and their starch (see **Portland**); **arr'ow-shot** the range of an arrow; **arr'owwood** species of Viburnum, esp. *V. dentatum*, or other shrubs, or trees formerly used by American Indians to make arrows. [O.E. *arwe*; prob. cog. with L. *arcus*, bow.]

arrow². See **ary**.

arroyo *ə-roi'ō, n.* a rocky ravine: dry watercourse: — *pl.* **arroy'os.** [Sp.]

'Arry *ar'i, n.* a jovial vulgar Cockney: — *fem.* **'Arr'iet.** — *adj.* **'Arr'yish.** [Cockney pronunciation of *Harry, Harriet*.]

arse *ärs* (*U.S.* **ass** *as*), (now *vulg.*) *n.* the buttocks: impudence, cheek (*Austr.*). — *n.* **arse'hole** (U.S. **ass'-hole**) the anus (*vulg.*): a worthless, contemptible, etc. person (*vulg. slang*). — *adv.* and *adj.* **ars'y-vers'y** (*slang*) backside foremost, contrary. — **arse licker, arse'-licker** (*vulg. slang*) an extremely obsequious person; **arse'=**

licking. — **arse around, about** (*vulg. slang*) to mess around, do nothing in particular. [O.E. *ærs* (*ears*); Ger. *Arsch*, Sw. *ars*; cog. with Gr. *orros* (for *orsos*).]

arsenal ärs′(i-)*nl*, *n.* a dockyard (*hist.*): a magazine or manufactory for naval and military weapons and ammunition: a storehouse (*fig.*). [It. *arzenale, arsenale* (Sp., Fr. *arsenal*) — Ar. *dār açčinā'ah*, workshop — (*dār,* house), *al,* the, *çinā'ah,* art.]

arsenic ärs′(ə-)*nik*, *n.* the chemical element (As) of at. number 33: a poison, the trioxide of the element (As₂O₃; white arsenic). — *ns.* **ar′senate, arseniate** (*-sē′ni-āt*) a salt of arsenic acid. — *adjs.* **arsenic** (*-sen′ik*), **-al**, **arsē′nious** composed of or containing arsenic. — In chemistry **arsen′ic** is applied to compounds in which arsenic is pentavalent, **arsē′nious** to those in which it is trivalent. — *ns.* **ar′senide** a compound of arsenic with a metal; **ar′senite** a salt of arsenious acid; **arseno=pyrī′tes** mispickel, a mineral composed of iron, arsenic and sulphur; **arsine** (*är′sēn, -sin, -sīn*) the poisonous gas, hydride of arsenic (AsH₃): a compound in which one or more hydrogen atoms of AsH₃ are replaced by an alkyl radical, etc.; **arsphen′amine** (*-min* or *-mēn*; from *arsenic, phen*e and *amine*) salvarsan. [Gr. *arsenikon,* yellow orpiment, fancifully associated with Gr. *arsēn,* male, and the alchemists' notion that metals have sex.]

arses. See **arsis.**

arshin, arshine, arsheen *är-shēn′, n.* an old measure of length, about 28 in. in Russia, about 30 inches (legally a metre) in Turkey. [Turkish.]

arsine. See **arsenic.**

arsis *är′sis,* (Gr. *pros.* and *mus.*) *n.* lit. a lift, an up-beat: hence the weak position in a bar or foot: understood by the Romans as the strong position: used in English in both senses: elevation of the voice to higher pitch: — *pl.* **ar′sēs:** — opp. to *thesis.* [L., — Gr. *arsis* — *airein,* to lift.]

arsmetrick *ärz-met′rik, n.* an obs. form of **arithmetic** founded on the false etymology L. *ars metrica,* art of measuring.

arson¹ *är′sn, n.* the crime of feloniously burning houses, haystacks, ships, forests, or similar property. — *ns.* **ar′sonist,** (*rare*) **ar′sonite.** [O.Fr. *arson* — L. *arsiō, -ōnis* — *ardēre, arsum,* to burn.]

arson² *är′sn,* (*obs.*) *n.* a saddlebow. [O.Fr. *arçun* — L. *arcus,* a bow.]

arsphenamine. See under **arsenic.**

arsy-versy. See **arse.**

art¹ *ärt,* (*arch.* and *poet.*) used as 2nd pers. sing. pres. indic. of the verb *to be.* [O.E. (W.S.) *eart,* (Mercian) *earth,* (Northumbrian) *arth*; from the root *es-* seen in *is, are.*]

art² *ärt, n.* practical skill, or its application, guided by principles: human skill and agency (opp. to *nature*): application of skill to production of beauty (esp. visible beauty) and works of creative imagination, as in the fine arts: a branch of learning, esp. one of the *liberal* arts (see **trivium, quadrivium**), as in *faculty of arts, master of arts*: skill or knowledge in a particular department: a skilled profession or trade, craft, or branch of activity: magic or occult knowledge or influence: a method of doing a thing: a knack: contrivance: address: cunning: artifice: crafty conduct: a wile. — *adj.* of, for, concerned with, painting, sculpture, etc. (as *art gallery, art historian*): intended to be decorative: produced with studied artistry, not arising spontaneously by chance. — *adj.* **art′ful** dexterous, clever (*arch.*): cunning: produced by art. — *adv.* **art′fully.** — *n.* **art′fulness.** — *adj.* **art′less** simple: inartistic (*rare*): guileless, unaffected. — *adv.* **art′lessly.** — *n.* **art′lessness.** — *adj.* **art′y** (*coll.*), less commonly **art′sy**, artistic, or aspiring to be. — **art autre** (*är-tō-tr'*) a post World War II movement in painting, including tachisme; **art deco** (*är dek′ō*) the style of decorative art characteristic of the 1920s and 1930s, developing the curvilinearity of art nouveau into more streamlined geometrical forms; **art form** a set form or arrangement in poetry or music: an accepted medium of artistic expression; **art nouveau** (*är nōō-vō*) a decorative form of art (*c.* 1890–1910) in which curvilinear forms are important and fundamentally unrelated images are often combined in a single design; **art paper** paper for illustrations, coated with a composition containing china clay; **arts′man** a craftsman (*obs.*): a scholar (*obs.*); **art′-song** a song whose words and music are the product of conscious art, the music reflecting every turn of meaning — distinguished from a *folk-song*; **arts student** a student in the faculty of arts; **art student** a student of painting, sculpture, etc.; **art union** (*Austr.* and *N.Z.*) a lottery; **art′work** the illustrations and other decorative material in a publication. — *adjs.* **art′y=craft′y** self-consciously artistic; **art′y-fart′y** (*derog. coll.*) arty, arty-crafty. — **art and part** originally (*law*) concerned in either by *art* in contriving or by *part* in actual execution, now loosely used in the sense of participating, sharing; **be a fine art** to be an operation or practice requiring nicety of craftsmanship; **get something down to a fine art** to become very skilled at something through practice; **term of art** a technical word; **the fine arts** painting, poetry, music, etc. [L. *ars, artis.*]

artal. See **rotl.**

artefact, artifact *är′ti-fakt, n.* (esp. *archaeol.*) a thing made by human workmanship. [L. *arte,* by art (abl. of *ars*), *factum,* made.]

artel *är-tel′, n.* a Russian workers' guild. [Russ.]

Artemisia *är-te-miz′i-ə, n.* a genus of composites including wormwood, southernwood, mugwort, sagebrush, etc: (without *cap.*) a member of the genus. [Gr. *artemisiā.*]

artery *är′tər-i, n.* a tube or vessel that conveys blood from the heart: any main channel of communication or movement. — *adj.* **arterial** (*-tē′ri-əl*). — *n.* **artērialisā′-tion, -z-.** — *v.t.* **artēr′ialise, -ize** to make arterial. — *ns.* **artē′riole** a very small artery; **artēriosclerō′sis** (Gr. *sklērōsis,* hardening) hardening of the arteries. — *adj.* **artēriosclerotic** (*-ot′ik*). — *ns.* **artēriot′omy** (Gr. *tomē,* a cut) the cutting or opening of an artery, to let blood; **arterī′tis** inflammation of an artery. [L. *artēria* — Gr. *artēriā,* windpipe, artery.]

Artesian *är-tē′zyən, -zh(y)ən, adj.* of Artois (L.L. *Artesium*), in the north of France, or (often without *cap.*) a type of well in early use there, in which water rises in a borehole by hydrostatic pressure from a basin whose outcrop is at a higher level.

artful. See **art².**

arthralgia *är-thral′j(i-)ə, n.* pain in a joint. — *adj.* **arthral′-gic.** — *n.* **arthritis** (*är-thrī′tis*) inflammation of a joint: gout. — *adj.* **arthritic** (*-thrit′ik*) of or near a joint: of, of the nature of, arthritis. — *n.* a gouty person: a person suffering from arthritis. [Gr. *arthron,* a joint, *algos,* pain.]

arthrodesis *är-thrō-dē′sis n.* the immobilising of a joint in the body by the surgical fusion of the bones. [Gr. *arthron,* joint, *desis,* binding together.]

arthromere *är′thrō-mēr, n.* a body segment of an articulated animal — a somite. [Gr. *arthron,* a joint, *meros,* part.]

arthroplasty *är′thrō-plas-ti, n.* surgical repair of a joint: replacement of a joint by an artificial joint: the artificial joint itself. [Gr. *arthron,* joint, *plastos,* moulded.]

arthropod *är′thrō-pod, n.* any member of the **Arthropoda** (*är-throp′od-ə*), a great division of the animal kingdom, with segmented bodies and jointed appendages — crustacea, arachnids, peripatuses, millipedes, centipedes, insects, tardigrades, etc. — *adj.* **arthrop′odal.** [Gr. *arthron,* joint, and *pous, podos,* a foot.]

arthroscopy *är-thros′ko-pi, n.* examination of a joint with an endoscope. [Gr. *arthron,* joint, *skopeein,* to look.]

arthrosis *är-thrōs′is, n.* connection by a joint, articulation. [Gr. *arthrōsis* — *arthron,* a joint.]

arthrospore *är′thrō-spōr, -spör, n.* a conidium: (inappropriately) a vegetative cell that has passed into a resting state. [Gr. *arthron,* joint, *sporā,* seed.]

Arthurian är-thū´ri-ən, adj. relating to King *Arthur*, a ruler of the Britons, whose court is the centre of many legends, but who himself had perhaps real existence: pertaining to the legends. — *n.* **Arthurian´a** stories, etc., connected with the court of King Arthur.

artic. See **articulated lorry** under **article**.

artichoke är´ti-chōk, *n.* a thistle-like perennial plant (*Cynara scolymus*) with large scaly heads and edible receptacles. — **Jerusalem artichoke** a totally different plant, a species of sunflower with edible tubers like potatoes, Jerusalem being a corr. of It. *girasole* (turnsun), sunflower. [North It. *articiocco* (It. *carciofo*) — Old Sp. *alcarchofa* — Ar. *al-kharshōfa, al-kharshūf.*]

article är´ti-kl, *n.* a joint, segment (*obs.*): a juncture, critical moment, nick of time (*obs.*): a separate element, member, or part of anything: a particular object or commodity: an item: a single clause or term: a distinct point in an agreement, or (in *pl.*) an agreement looked at as so made up, as in *articles of apprenticeship*, etc.: (in *pl.*) rules or conditions generally: a section, paragraph, or head: a literary composition in a newspaper, periodical, encyclopaedia, etc., treating of a subject distinctly and independently: the adjective *the* (*definite article*), *a* or *an* (*indefinite article*) or the equivalent in another language (*gram.*) — *v.t.* to arrange by agreement, etc. (*obs.*): to bind by articles of apprenticeship: to set forth as a charge (that): to stipulate (*obs.*). — *v.i.* to bring specific charges (against; *obs.*). — *adjs.* **ar´ticled** bound as apprentice; **artic´ūlable** that can be articulated; **artic´ūlar** belonging to the joints: at or near a joint. — *n.pl.* **Articūlā´ta** in Cuvier's classification, the arthropods and higher worms. — *adj.* **artic´ūlate** jointed: composed of distinct parts: composed of recognisably distinct sounds, as human speech: clear: able to express one's thoughts with ease. — *v.t.* to attach by a joint: to connect by joints: to form into distinct sounds, syllables, or words. — *v.i.* to form a joint (with; *lit.* and *fig.*): to come to terms (*Shak.*): to speak distinctly. — *adj.* **artic´ūlated.** — *adv.* **artic´ūlately.** — *ns.* **artic´ūlateness; articūlā´tion** jointing: a joint: a segment: distinctness, or distinct utterance: a consonant; **artic´ūlātor** one who articulates or speaks: one who articulates bones and mounts skeletons. — *adj.* **artic´ūlatory.** — **articulated lorry,** etc. a lorry, etc. made easier to manœuvre by having its (sometimes detachable) front section flexibly attached to the rear section so that it can move at an angle to it (*coll.* shortening **artic´** (or **är´**)). — **articles of association** regulations for the business of a joint-stock company registered under the Companies Acts; **articles of faith** binding statement of points of belief of a Church, etc.; **articles of war** code of regulations for the government and discipline of armed services; **in the article of death** (L. *in articulō mortis*) at the point of death; **Lords of the Articles** a standing committee of the Scottish parliament who drafted the measures to be submitted; **of great article** (*Shak.*) of great importance; **Thirty-nine Articles** the articles of religious belief finally agreed upon by the bishops and clergy of the Church of England in 1562. [L. *articulus*, a little joint, *articulāre, -ātum*, to furnish with joints, to utter distinctly — *artus*, joint.]

artifact. See **artefact.**

artifice är´ti-fis, *n.* handicraft (*Milt.*): workmanship (*obs.*): skill: contrivance, or trickery: an ingenious expedient: a crafty trick. — *n.* **artif´icer** a mechanic (esp. *mil.*, navy): one who creates skilfully: a craftsman: a contriver: (*cap.*) the creator: a trickster (*obs.*). — *adj.* **artificial** (-fish´l, or *är´*) contrived (opp. to *spontaneous*): made by man: synthetic (opp. to *natural*): fictitious, factitious, feigned, made in imitation (opp. to *real*): affected in manners: ingenious (*obs.*): perh. creative, playing the artificer, or perh. merely skilful (*Shak.*): technical (*obs.*): of classifications, based on superficial structural features rather than on natural relationships (*biol.*). — *v.t.* **artific´ialise, -ize** to render artificial. — *n.* **artificiality** (-fish-i-al´i-ti). — *adv.* **arti-**

fic´ially. — *n.* **artific´ialness.** — **artificial horizon** a gyroscopic device indicating an aircraft's altitude in relation to the horizontal; **artificial insemination** the injection of semen into the uterus otherwise than by sexual union; **artificial intelligence** the use of computers in such a way that they perform functions normally associated with human intelligence, such as learning, adapting, self-correction and decision-taking; **artificial kidney** a kidney machine; **artificial language** an invented language functioning not as the native speech of its users but as a computer language or means of international communication; **artificial porcelain** softpaste porcelain; **artificial respiration** stimulation of respiration manually or mechanically by forcing air in and out of the lungs; **artificial silk** see **silk; artificial sunlight** light from lamps rich in ultraviolet rays. [L. *artificium* — *artifex, -ficis*, an artificer — *ars, artis*, and *facĕre*, to make.]

artillery är-til´ər-i, *n.* offensive weapons of war, formerly in general, now the heavier kinds — ancient ballistas, catapults, modern cannon, etc.: a branch of the military service using these: missiles (*obs.*): gunnery. — *n.* **artill´erist** one skilled in artillery: a gunner. — **artill´ery-man** a soldier of the artillery; **artill´ery-plant** a tropical American plant (*Pilea*) of the nettle family that ejects its pollen in puffs. [O.Fr. *artillerie* — *artiller*, to arm, of doubtful origin.]

artiodactyl är-ti-ō-dak´til, *adj.* even-toed. — *n.* a member of the **Artiodac´tyla** or even-toed ungulates, in which the third and fourth digit form a symmetrical pair and the hind-foot bears an even number of digits — cf. **perissodactyl.** [Gr. *artios*, even in number, and *daktylos*, finger or toe.]

artisan ärt-i-zan´, or *ärt´*, *n.* a handicraftsman or mechanic, a skilled workman. — *adj.* **artis´anal** (or *ärt´*). [Fr. *artisan* — It. *artigiano*, ult. from L. *artitus*, skilled — *ars, artis*, art.]

artist ärt´ist, *n.* one who practises or is skilled in an art, now esp. a fine art: one who has the qualities of imagination and taste required in art: a painter or draughtsman: a learned man (*obs.*): one who professes magic, astrology, alchemy, etc., or chemistry (*obs.*): a performer, esp. in music: a person good at, or given to, a particular activity, as *booze artist* (esp. *Austr.* and *U.S. slang*). — *adjs.* **artist´ic, -al.** — *adv.* **artist´ically.** — *n.* **art´istry** artistic pursuits: artistic workmanship, quality, or ability. — **artistic temperament** the emotional and capricious temperament ascribed to artists. [Fr. *artiste* — L. *ars, artis*, art.]

artiste är-tēst´, *n.* a public performer: an adept in a manual art. [Fr.]

Artium Baccalaureus är´shi-um (or -ti-ōōm) bak-a-lö´rē-us (or *-low´rā-ōōs*) (L.) Bachelor of Arts; **Artium Magister** (*ma-jis´tər* or *-gis´ter*) or **Magister Artium** Master of Arts.

artless. See **art²**.

Artocarpus är-tō-kär´pəs, *n.* a genus of the mulberry family including breadfruit and jack: (without *cap.*) a plant of the genus. [Gr. *artos*, bread, *karpos*, fruit.]

artsy, arty, arty-farty. See **art²**.

Arum ā´rəm, *n.* the cuckoo-pint or wake-robin genus: (without *cap.*) any kindred plant. — *n.pl.* **Arā´ceae** (*a-*) the family of spadicifloral monocotyledons to which it belongs. — *adjs.* **araceous** (*a-rā´shəs*), **aroid** (*ā´roid*) of the Araceae: like an arum. — *n.* **ā´roid** any plant of the family. — **arum lily** Zantedeschia. [L. *arum* — Gr. *aron*.]

arundinaceous ə-run-di-nā´shəs, *adj.* of or like a reed. [L. *arundināceus* — *arundō, -inis*, a reed.]

arval är´vəl, *adj.* pertaining to ploughed land. — **Arval Brethren** in ancient Rome, a college of priests who sacrificed to the field deities. [L. *arvālis* — *arāre*, to plough.]

Arvicola är-vik´ō-lə, *n.* the water-rat genus of voles. — *adj.* **arvic´oline.** [L. *arvum*, a field, *colĕre*, to inhabit.]

arvo är´vō, (*Austr. coll.*) *n.* afternoon: — *pl.* **ar´vos.**

For other sounds see detailed chart of pronunciation.

ary ä'ri, e'ri, **arrow** ar'ō, (*dial.*) *adjs.* any. [From **e'er a, ever a**; cf. **nary**.]

Aryan ä'ri-ən or ä', *adj.* Indo-Germanic, Indo-European: now generally of the Indian, or Indian and Iranian, branch of the Indo-European languages: speaking one of these languages: in Nazi politics, Caucasian, esp. of northern European type and esp. as opp. to Jewish. — *n.* the parent Indo-European language: a speaker of an Aryan language. — *v.t.* **Ar'yanise, -ize.** [Sans. *ārya*, noble.]

Arya Samaj är'yä sä-mäj', a reformed Hindu religious body or school, founded by Dayananda Saraswati (1824–83), based on the Vedas, opposing idolatry, caste, child-marriage, and other evils. [Hind. *ārya samāj*, noble association.]

aryballos ar-i-bal'os, *n.* a globular oil-flask with a neck. — *adj.* **aryball'oid.** [Gr.]

aryl ar'il, *n.* any aromatic univalent hydrocarbon radical. [**aromatic**, and Gr. *hȳlē*, matter.]

arytaenoid, arytenoid ar-i-tē'noid, *adj.* pitcher-shaped. — *n.* a cartilage or a muscle of the larynx. [Gr. *arytainoeidēs* — *arytaina*, a cup, *eidos*, form.]

as¹ az, əz, *adv.* in whatever degree, proportion, manner: to whatever extent: in that degree: to that extent: so far: however: specifically: passing into *conj.* or almost *prep.*, for instance: in the manner, character, part, aspect, of: in so far as: whereas. — *conj.* because, since: while, when: as if: that (consequence) (*Milt.*): than (*illiterate* or *dial.*). — *pron.* who, which, that (after *such, so, same*, or where a statement is treated as antecedent: in *Shak.* after a demons. pron.: otherwise *dial.* or *illiterate*). — **as also** likewise; **as concerning, as for, as regards, as to,** for the matter of; **as from, as of** from (a specified time); **as how** that (with noun clause) (*illit.* or *dial.*): introducing a question (similarly **as why**) (*obs.*); **as if, as though** as it would be if; **as it were** so to speak: in some sort; **as many as** all who; **as much** the same: just that; **as now, as then** just as at this, that, time; **as was** formerly: in a former state; **as well** also: in addition: equally well, suitably, happily, etc.; **as yet** up to the moment; **as you were** a military order to return to the former position; **so as to** with the purpose or consequence specified; **when as** at what time (*arch.*). [O.E. *all-swā* (*eall-swā*), all so, wholly so.]

as² äs, *n.* a Norse god, inhabitant of Asgard: — *pl.* **aesir** (*es'ir*). [O.N. *āss*, a god (pl. *æsir*); cf. O.E. *ōs*, seen in such proper names as *Os*wald, *Os*ric.]

as³ as, *n.* a Roman unit of weight, a pound of 12 ounces: a copper coin, originally a pound in weight, ultimately half an ounce: — *pl.* **ass'es.** [L. *ās, assis*, a unit.]

ås ōs, (*geol.*) *n.* a kame or esker: — *pl.* **åsar** (*ōs'är*). [Sw.]

asafoetida as-ə-fet'i-də, or -*fēt'*, *n.* an ill-smelling medicinal gum resin, got from the root latex of some species of *Ferula* — also **asafetida, assafoetida, assafetida.** [Pers. *azā*, mastic, and L. *fētida* (*fem.*) stinking.]

a salti ä säl'tē, (It.) by fits and starts.

asana ä'sə-nə, *n.* any of the positions taught in yoga. [Sans. *āsana*.]

åsar. See **ås.**

asarum as'ə-rəm, *n.* the dried root of the wild ginger (*Asarum canadense*). — *n.* **asarabacca** (as-ə-rə-bak'ə; L. *bacca*, berry) a plant (*Asarum europaeum*), of the birthwort family, formerly used in medicine. [L. *asarum* (— Gr. *asaron*), hazelwort.]

asbestos az-bes'tos, *n.* a fine fibrous amphibole capable of being woven into incombustible cloth: (commercially) chrysotile, a fibrous serpentine. — *adjs.* **asbes'tic, asbes'tiform, asbes'tine, asbes'tous** of or like asbestos. — *n.* **asbestō'sis** a lung disease caused by inhaling asbestos dust. — **asbestos cement** cement containing asbestos fibres, used to make thin slabs for various purposes in building. [Gr., (*lit.*) unquenchable — *a-*, priv., *sbestos*, extinguished.]

asbestos gelōs (Gr.). See Appendices.

ascarid as'kə-rid, *n.* any nematode worm of the parasitic genus **As'caris** (family **Ascar'idae**), infesting the small intestines. — Also **ascaris** (-kə-ris): — *pl.* **ascarides**

(-*kar'i-dēz*). — *n.* **ascariasis** (as-kə-rī'ə-sis) infestation with, or disease caused by, ascarids, esp. *Ascaris lumbricoides.* [Gr. *askaris*, pl. *askarides*.]

ascaunt. See **askance.**

ascend ə-*send'*, *a-send'*, *v.i.* to go up, mount, rise: to go back in time or ancestry. — *v.t.* to go up, mount, climb: to go up to (*Shak.*). — *ns.* **ascend'ance, -ence** (both *rare*), **ascend'ancy, -ency** dominating influence; **ascend'ant**, less commonly **ascend'ent**, (*astrol.*) the part of the ecliptic just risen or about to rise at any instant (a planet in this was supposed to influence a person born at the time): (from the phrase **in the ascendant**) a position of pre-eminence: an ancestor or relative in the ascending line: one who rises or mounts: a rise, up-slope. — *adj.* rising: just risen above the horizon: predominant. — *n.* **ascend'er** one who ascends: (the upper part of) a letter such as b, d, h, k (*print.*, etc.). — *adjs.* **ascend'ible** (also -**able**) scalable; **ascend'ing** rising: curving up from a prostrate to an erect position (*bot.*). — *n.* **ascension** (-sen'shən) ascent (a Gallicism when used of a mountain ascent): an ascent to heaven, esp. Christ's. — *adjs.* **ascen'sional; ascen'sive** moving or tending upwards. — *n.* **ascent'** a going up: advancement: a going back in time or ancestry: a way up: an up-slope. — **Ascen'sion-day** (or **Ascension Day**) Holy Thursday, ten days before Whitsunday, commemorating Christ's Ascension; **Ascen'siontide** Ascension-day to Whitsunday. — **ascend the throne** to become king or queen; **right ascension** (*astron.*) a co-ordinate of the position of a heavenly body measured (usually in terms of time) eastwards along the celestial equator from the First Point of Aries, the other co-ordinate being the declination. [L. *ascendĕre, ascēnsum* — *ad*, to, *scandĕre*, to climb.]

ascertain as-ər-tān', *v.t.* to apprise (*obs.*): to assure (*obs.*): to make certain, prove (*arch.*): to find out for certain: to insure, prove. — *adj.* **ascertain'able.** — *n.* **ascertain'ment.** [O.Fr. *acertener* — *à*, to, *certain*, certain.]

ascesis ə-sē'sis, *n.* the practice of disciplining oneself: asceticism. [Gr. *askēsis*, exercise, training.]

ascetic a- or ə-set'ik, *n.* one who rigidly denies himself ordinary bodily gratifications for conscience's sake: one who aims to compass holiness through mortification of the flesh: a strict hermit: one who lives a life of austerity. — *adjs.* **ascet'ic, -al** rigorous in mortifying the flesh: of asceticism: recluse. — *adv.* **ascet'ically.** — *n.* **ascet'icism** (-sizm). [Gr. *askētikos* — *askētēs*, one who is in training — *askeein*, to work, exercise, train.]

asci *pl.* of **ascus.**

ascian ash'i-ən, *n.* an inhabitant of the torrid zone, shadowless when the sun is right overhead. [Gr. *askios*, shadowless — *a-*, priv., *skiā*, a shadow.]

ascidium a-sid'i-əm, *n.* a pitcher-shaped leaf or part of a leaf, as the pitcher of the pitcher-plants, the bladder of the bladderwort: — *pl.* **ascid'ia.** — *n.* **ascid'ian** a seasquirt, or tunicate, a degenerate survivor of the ancestors of the vertebrates, shaped like a double-mouthed flask. [Gr. *askidion*, dim. of *askos*, a leather bag, wine-skin.]

ascites a-sī'tēz, *n.* dropsy of the abdomen. — *adjs.* **ascit'ic** (-sit'ik), **ascit'ical.** [Gr. *askītēs* — *askos*, belly.]

ascititious. Same as **adscititious.**

Asclepias, Asclepios as-klē'pi-əs, *n.* the Greek god of healing (L. *Aesculapius*). — *n.* **asclē'piad** a plant of the genus Asclepias: (with *cap.*) a son of Asclepius, a physician: a verse used by the Greek poet *Asclepiades* (*Asklēpiadēs*; 3rd cent. B.C.) — a spondee, two (in the *Greater Asclepiad* three) choriambi, and an iambus (—/ —⌣⌣/ —⌣⌣/ ⌣-). — *n.pl.* **Asclepiadā'ceae** the milk-weed and swallow-wort family, closely related to the periwinkle family. — *adj.* **asclepiadaceous** (-ā'shəs; *bot.*). — *ns.* and *adjs.* **Asclepiadē'an, Asclepiad'ic** (*pros.*). — *n.* **Asclē'pias** a chiefly American genus of the swallow-wort family, milk-weed: (without *cap.*) a plant of this genus. [Gr. *Asklēpios*, the god, *Asklēpiadēs*, the poet, *asklēpias, -ados*, swallow-wort.]

ascomycete, ascospore. See **ascus.**

asconce. Obs. form of **askance** (in *Shak.* **a sconce**).

ascorbic *ə-skör'bik, adj.* antiscorbutic — only in **ascorbic acid** vitamin C ($C_6H_8O_6$). — *n.* **ascor'bate** a salt of ascorbic acid.   [Gr. *a-*, priv., and **scorbutic**.]

ascot *as'kot, n.* a type of necktie with broad ends that are tied to lie one across the other.   [The race-course at *Ascot*, England, well-known for the fashionable wear of spectators.]

ascribe *ə-* or *a-skrīb', v.t.* to attribute, impute, or assign. — *adj.* **ascrīb'able.** — *n.* **ascription** (*-skrip'shən*) act, expression, formula of ascribing or imputing, e.g. that ascribing glory to God at the end of a sermon.   [L. *ascrībēre — ad,* to, *scrībēre, scrīptum,* to write.]

ascus *as'kəs, (bot.) n.* an enlarged cell, commonly elongated, in which usually eight spores are formed: — *pl.* **asci** (*as'ī*). — *ns.* **as'comycete** (*as'kō-mī-sēt*) any one of the **Ascomycetes** (*-sē'tēz*), one of the main divisions of the fungi, characterised by formation of asci; **as'cospore** a spore formed in an ascus.   [Gr. *askos,* bag.]

Asdic *as'dik, n.* an apparatus for detecting and locating a submarine or other underwater object by means of ultrasonic waves echoed back from the submarine, etc.   [*A*llied (or *A*nti-) *S*ubmarine *D*etection *I*nvestigation *C*ommittee.[

aseismic *a-, ā-,* or *ə-sīz'mik, adj.* free from earthquakes.   [Gr. *a-*, priv., and **seismic**.]

aseity *a-* or *ā-sē'i-ti, (philos.) n.* self-origination.   [L. *ā,* from, *sē* (*abl.*), oneself.]

asepalous *a-, ā-,* or *ə-sep'ə-ləs, adj.* without sepals.   [Gr. *a-*, priv., and **sepal**.]

aseptate *a-, ā-,* or *ə-sep'tāt, adj.* not partitioned by septa.   [Gr. *a-*, priv., and **septum**.]

aseptic *a-, ā-,* or *ə-sep'tik, adj.* not liable to, or preventing, decay or putrefaction: involving or accompanied by measures to exclude micro-organisms. — *n.* an aseptic substance. — *ns.* **asep'ticism** (*-sizm*) aseptic treatment; **asep'sis** freedom from sepsis or blood-poisoning: the process of rendering, or condition of being, aseptic: exclusion of micro-organisms: — *pl.* **asep'ses.** — *v.t.* **asep'ticise, -ize** (*-ti-sīz*) to make aseptic: to treat with aseptics.   [Gr. *asēptos — a-*, priv., *sēpein,* to cause to decay.]

asexual *a-, ā-,* or *ə-seks'ū-əl, adj.* without sex: not involving sexual activity: vegetative. — *n.* **asexuality** (*-al'i-ti*). — *adv.* **asex'ūally.**   [Gr. *a-*, priv., and **sexual**.]

Asgard *äs'gärd, n.* the heaven of Norse mythology, abode of the twelve gods and twenty-six goddesses, and of heroes slain in battle.   [O.N. *Āsgarthr — āss,* a god, *garthr,* an enclosure.]

ash[1] *ash, n.* a well-known timber tree (*Fraxinus excelsior,* or other species) of the olive family: its wood, white, tough, and hard: an ashen spear-shaft or spear (*obs.*). — *adj.* **ash'en.** — **ash'-key** the winged fruit of the ash; **ash'-plant** an ash sapling.   [O.E. *æsc;* Ger. *Esche,* O.N. *askr.*]

ash[2] *ash, n.* (often in *pl.*) the dust or remains of anything burnt: (also **volcanic ash(es)**) volcanic dust, or a rock composed of it: (in *pl.*) remains of human body when burnt: (in *pl.*) a dead body (*fig.*). — *adj.* **ash'en** of the colour of ash: (of the face) very pale. — *n.* **ash'ery** a place where potash or pearl-ash is made. — *adj.* **ash'y.** — **ash'-bin, -bucket, -can** a receptacle for ashes and other household refuse. — *adjs.* **ash-blond'** (of hair) of a pale, silvery blond colour: having hair of this colour: — *fem.* (also *n.*) **ash-blonde';** **ash'en-grey** of the colour of wood ashes. — **ash'-heap** a heap of ashes and household refuse; **ash'-hole, -pit** a hollow, esp. under a fireplace, to receive ashes; **ash'-leach** a tub in which alkaline salts are dissolved from woodashes; **ash'-pan** a tray fitted underneath a grate to receive the ashes; **ash'-stand, ash'-tray** a small tray or saucer for tobacco ash; **Ash Wednesday** the first day of Lent, from the custom of sprinkling ashes on the head. — *adj.* **ash'y-grey.** — **the ashes** a term applied by the *Sporting Times* (in a mock 'In Memoriam' notice) to the loss of prestige in English cricket after the Australians' suc-

cessful visit in 1882, after which English teams strove to 'bring back the ashes', or mortal remains.   [O.E. *asce;* O.N. *aska.*]

ashake *ə-shāk', (arch.) adv.* or predicative *adj.* in a shaking state.   [**a[3]** and **shake**.]

ashamed *ə-shāmd', adj.* affected with shame (with *of* action, person; *for,* meaning on behalf of, person; *to do; that*). — *v.i.* **ashame'** (*obs.*) to feel shame. — *v.t.* (*arch.*) to put to shame. — *adv.* **ashamed'ly** (or *-id-li*). — *n.* **ashamed'ness** (or *-id-nes*). — *adj.* **asham'ing.**   [Pfx. *a-*, intensive, and O.E. *sc(e)amian,* to shame.]

ashen, etc. See **ash[1,2].**

ashet *ash'it,* (now only *Scot.*) *n.* a large meat-plate.   [Fr. *assiette.*]

ashine *ə-shīn', adv.* (*arch.*) or predicative *adj.* in a shining state.   [**a[3]** and **shine**.]

ashiver *ə-shiv'ər, adv.* or predicative *adj.* in a shivering or quivering state.   [**a[3]** and **shiver[2].**]

Ashkenazim *äsh-kə-näz'im, n.pl.* the Polish and German Jews, as distinguished from the *Sephardim,* the Spanish and Portuguese Jews.   [Heb. *Ashkenaz,* a northern people (Gen. x.) by later Jews identified with Germany.]

ashlar, ashler *ash'lər, n.* a squared stone used in building or facing a wall: masonry of such stones. — Also *adj.* — *v.t.* to face with ashlar. — *ns.* **ash'laring, ash'lering** ashlar masonry or facing: a vertical timber between floor-joist and rafter. — **ash'lar-work** ashlar masonry.   [O.Fr. *aiseler* — L. *axillāris — axilla,* dim. of *axis,* axle, plank.]

ashore *ə-shōr', -shör', adv.* on, or on to, the shore or land (from the sea).   [**a[3]** and **shore[1].**]

ashram(a) *äsh'rəm(-ə) n.* usu. in India, a hermitage, or a place of retreat for a religious group.   [Sans. *āśrama.*]

Ashtaroth, Ashtoreth. See **Astarte.**

Asian *ā'sh(i)ən, ā'shyən, -zh-,* **Asiatic** *-i-at'ik, adjs.* belonging to *Asia* (esp. Asia Minor): (formerly) in literature or art, florid. — *n.* a native of Asia. — *adj.* **Asianic** (*-an'ik*) Asian, esp. of a group of non-Indo-European languages of Asia and Europe. — *n.* **Asiat'icism** (*-i-sizm*) imitation of Asiatic or Eastern manners.

aside *ə-sīd', adv.* on or to one side: privately: apart. — *n.* words spoken in an undertone, so as not to be heard by some person present, words spoken by an actor which the other persons on the stage are supposed not to hear: an indirect effort of any kind. — *adj.* (*U.S.*) private, apart. — *prep.* (now only *Scot.*) beside. — **aside from** apart from; **set aside** to quash (a judgment).   [Prep. **a**, and **side[1].**]

asinico *as-i-nē'kō,* (*Shak.*) *n.* a stupid fellow.   [Sp. *asnico* — dim. of *asno* — L. *asinus,* ass.]

asinine *as'in-īn, adj.* of or like an ass. — *n.* **asininity** (*-in'i-ti*).   [L. *asinīnus — asinus,* ass.]

ask[1] *äsk, v.t.* to seek: to beg, request: to make a request of: to inquire: to inquire of: to invite: to proclaim. — *v.i.* to make a request (for): to inquire (*after* a person, his welfare, etc.; *about* a matter, etc.). — *n.* **ask'er.** — **asking price** price set by the seller of an article before bargaining has begun. — **ask for it** (*coll.*) to behave in a way likely to bring trouble on oneself; **I ask you!** would you believe it, don't you agree — usu. expressing criticism; **if you ask me** in my opinion.   [O.E. *ascian, acsian;* Ger. *heischen,* O.N. *æskja.*]

ask[2] *ask,* (*dial.*) *n.* a newt. — Also **ask'er.**   [Apparently O.E. *āthexe;* cf. Ger. *Eidechse,* lizard.]

askance *ə-skans',* **askant** *ə-skant', adv.* sideways: awry: obliquely. — *v.t.* (*Shak.*) to turn aside. — *prep.* (*Shak.*) **ascaunt'** (folio reading *aslant*) slantwise across. — **eye, look** or **view askance** to look (at) with disdain, disapprobation, envy, or (now usually) suspicion.   [Ety. very obscure.]

askari *äs'kä-rē, äs-kä'rē, n.* an East African soldier or policeman.   [Ar. *'askarī,* soldier.]

asker. See **ask[1,2].**

askesis. Same as **ascesis.**

askew *ə-skū', adv.* or *adj.* at or to an oblique angle: awry.   [App. **a[3]**, and **skew[1].**]

asklent. See aslant.

aslake *ə-slāk'*, *v.t.* to slake (*obs.*): to mitigate (*arch.*): to appease (*obs.*).   [O.E. *āslacian*; see slake¹.]

aslant *ə-slänt'*, *adv.* or *adj.* on the slant, slantwise. — *prep.* slantwise across, athwart. — Also asklent' (*Scot.*). [a³ and slant¹.]

asleep *ə-slēp'*, *adv.* or *adj.* in or to a sleeping state: dead: (of limbs) numbed, sometimes with tingling or prickly feeling.   [a³ and sleep.]

aslope *ə-slōp'*, (*arch.*) *adv.* or *adj.* on the slope.   [O.E. *āslopen*, pa.p. of *āslūpan*, to slip away.]

-asm. See -ism.

asmear *ə-smēr'*, (*arch.*) *adj.* smeared over.   [a³ and smear.]

Asmodeus *as-*, *az-mə-dē'əs*, Asmoday *-dā'*, *ns.* an evil spirit of Semitic mythology.   [L., — Gr. *Asmodaios* — Heb. *Ashmadai*.]

asmoulder *ə-smōl'dər*, (*arch.*) *adv.* in a smouldering state. [a³ and smoulder.]

asocial *a-*, *ā-sō'shl*, *adj.* not social: antisocial.   [Gr. *a-*, priv., and social.]

asp¹ *asp*, *äsp*, *n.* an aspen.

asp² *asp*, *äsp*, aspic(k), *asp'ik*, *ns.* a venomous snake of various kinds — *Vipera aspis* of Southern Europe, Cleopatra's asp (prob. the horned viper), the biblical asp (prob. the Egyptian juggler's snake, *Naja haje*), the cobra de capello.   [L., — Gr. *aspis*.]

Asparagus *əs-par'ə-gəs*, *n.* a genus of Liliaceae, with leaves reduced to scales: (without *cap.*) any of the members of this genus, some cultivated as ornamental plants, and one species (*A. officinalis*) for its young shoots as a table delicacy. — *ns.* asparag'inase (*-aj'*) an enzyme that causes asparagine to hydrolyse to aspartic acid and ammonia; aspar'agine (*-jin*, *-jēn*) an amide found in asparagus and other vegetables; aspar'tame (*əs-pär'tām*) an artificial sweetener, 200 hundred times sweeter than sucrose derived from aspartic acid and phenylalanine. — aspar'agus-stone a pale yellowish green apatite; aspartic acid an amino-acid found in young sugar-cane, etc.   [L., — Gr. *asp(h)aragos*.]

Aspasia *as-pā'zyə*, *as-pä'zi-a*, *n.* a gifted Athenian courtesan, mistress of Pericles: any charming and accomplished woman of easy morals.

aspect *as'pekt* (in *Spens.*, *Shak.*, *Milt.*, etc., *as-pekt'*), *n.* a look, a glance: a view: direction of facing: appearance presented: way of viewing: face: the situation of one planet with respect to another, as seen from the earth (*astron.*): in some languages, a verbal form expressing simple action, repetition, beginning, duration, etc. (*gram.*): attitude (*aircraft*). — *v.t.* aspect' (*obs.*) to look at or for. — *adjs.* as'pectable visible: worth looking at; aspec'tual (*gram.* and *astron.*) of, relating to, aspect. — aspect ratio ratio of the width to the height of a reproduced image (*TV*; also picture ratio): ratio of the span of an aerofoil to its mean chord.   [L. *aspectus*.]

aspen *asp'ən*, *äsp'*, *-in* (*Spens.* aspine) *n.* the trembling poplar. — *adj.* made of, or like, the aspen: tremulous: timorous. — *adj.* as'pen-like.   [O.E. *æspe*; Ger. *Espe*.]

asper¹ *as'pər*, *n.* a Turkish monetary unit, worth 1/120 of a piastre, formerly a silver coin.   [Gr. *aspron*, rough, later white.]

asper² *as'pər*, *adj.* (*obs.*) rough, harsh. — *n.* the Greek rough breathing (*spīritus asper*). — *v.t.* as'perate to roughen. — *n.* asperity (*-per'*) roughness: harshness: bitter coldness: (in *pl.*) excrescences, rough places. — *adj.* as'perous rough with short hairs.   [L. *asper*.]

asperge *as-pûrj'*, *v.t.* to sprinkle. — *n.* an aspergillum for holy water. — *ns.* aspergation (*-gā'*); asper'ger (*-jər*); asper'ges a short service introductory to the mass, so called from the words *Asperges me, Domine, hyssopo et mundabor* (Ps. li); aspergill (*as'pər-jil*) a holy-water sprinkler. — Also aspergillum (*-jil'əm*): — *pl.* aspergill'a, -ums; aspergillō'sis a disease, fatal to birds and also occurring in domestic animals and man, caused by any of various moulds, esp. species of Aspergillus; Aspergill'um a genus of boring Lamellibranchs in which the shell forms an elongated cone,

ending in a disc pierced with numerous small tubular holes; Aspergill'us a genus of minute moulds occurring on decaying substances.   [L. *aspergĕre* — *ad*, to, *spargĕre*, to sprinkle.]

asperity, asperous. See asper².

asperse *as-pûrs'*, *v.t.* to slander or calumniate: to bespatter. — *n.* asper'sion calumny: slander: a shower or spray (*Shak.*): sprinkling with holy water (*R.C.*). — *adjs.* aspers'ive; aspers'ory tending to asperse: defamatory. — *n.* an aspergillum: an aspersorium. — *ns.* aspersoir (*äs-per-swär*; Fr.) an aspergillum; aspersō'rium (*-ri-əm*) (L.) a holy-water vessel.   [L. *aspergĕre*, *aspersum* — *ad*, to, *spargĕre*, to sprinkle.]

asphalt *as'falt*, asphaltum *as-falt'əm*, *ns.* a black or dark-brown, hard, bituminous substance, found native, and got as a residue in petroleum distillation, etc., anciently used as a cement: a mixture of this with rock chips or other material, used for paving, roofing, etc. — *v.t.* as'-phalt to lay, cover, or impregnate with asphalt. — *adj.* asphalt'ic.   [Gr. *asphaltos*, from an Eastern word.]

aspheterism *as-fet'ər-izm*, (*Southey*) *n.* denial of the right of private property. — *v.i.* asphet'erise, -ize.   [Gr. *a-*, priv., and *spheteros*, one's own.]

asphodel *as'fə-del*, *-fo-*, *n.* a plant of the lily family — in Greek mythology, the peculiar plant of the dead: applied to other plants, esp. bog-asphodel.   [Gr. *asphodelos*; cf. daffodil.]

asphyxia *as-fik'si-ə*, *n.* lit. stoppage of the pulse: cessation of the vital functions or suspended animation owing to any cause interfering with respiration. — Also asphyx'y. — *n.* and *adj.* asphyx'iant (a chemical substance) producing asphyxia. — *v.t.* asphyx'iate to produce asphyxia in. — *adj.* asphyx'iāted. — *ns.* asphyxiā'tion action of asphyxiating or condition of being asphyxiated; asphyx'iātor.   [Gr. *asphyxiā* — *a-*, priv., *sphyxis*, pulse.]

aspic¹, aspick. See asp².

aspic² *as'pik*, *n.* a savoury meat-jelly containing fish, game, hard-boiled eggs, etc.   [Perh. from *aspic*, asp, because it is 'cold as an aspic' (French proverb).]

aspic³ *as'pik*, *n.* the broad-leaved lavender.   [Fr., — L. *spīca*, spike.]

Aspidistra *as-pid-ist'rə*, *n.* a genus of plants of the asparagus group of Liliaceae — often grown indoors: (without *cap.*) a plant of this genus.   [Perh. Gr. *aspis*, a shield.]

Aspidium *as-pid'i-əm*, the shield-fern genus of ferns (including those usu. divided between the genera *Dryopteris*, *Polystichum* and *Tectaria*) — from the shield-shaped or kidney-shaped indusium: (without *cap.*) a fern of one of these genera: — *pl.* aspid'ia. — *adj.* aspid'ioid.   [Gr. *aspidion*, dim. of *aspis*, shield.]

aspine. See aspen.

aspire *əs-* or *as-pīr'*, *v.i.* (with *to*, *after*, or an infinitive) to desire eagerly: to aim at, or strive for, high things: to tower up. — *n.* aspīr'ant (or *as'pir-*) one who aspires (with *after*, *for*): a candidate. — *adj.* ambitious: mounting up (*rare* in both senses). — *v.t.* aspirate (*as'pir-āt*) to pronounce with a full breathing, i.e. the sound of *h*, as in *house* (*phon.*): to follow (a stop) by an audible breath (*phon.*): to replace (a consonant) by another sound, normally a fricative, when there is a combination with the sound *h* or the letter *h* (*gram.*, *phon.*, etc.): to draw (gas, fluid, etc.) out of a cavity by suction: to inhale (*med.*). — Also *v.i.* — *n.* (*-it*, *-ət*) the sound represented by the letter *h*: a consonant sound, a stop followed by an audible breath, as that of *bh* in Sanskrit: sometimes extended to a fricative: a mark of aspiration, the rough breathing (') in Greek: a letter representing an aspirate sound. — Also *adj.* — In French '*h* aspirate', no longer sounded, still affects the junction with the preceding word. — *ns.* aspirā'tion eager desire: (usu. in *pl.*) lofty hopes or aims: breathing (*obs.*): pronunciation of a sound with a full breathing: an aspirated sound: drawing a gas, liquid or solid, in, out, or through; as'pirātor an apparatus for drawing air or other gases through bottles or other vessels: an instrument for removing fluids or solids from cavities of the body (*med.*). — *adjs.* **aspir'atory** (-ə-tə-ri or as'pir-) relating to breathing; **aspir'ing** desiring, aiming at, etc. — *adv.* **aspir'ingly.** — *n.* **aspir'ingness.** — **drop one's aspirates** to omit to pronounce the sound of *h*. [L. *aspīrāre, -ātum* — *ad*, to, *spīrāre*, to breathe.]

aspirin as'pər-in, *n.* a drug (acetyl-salicylic acid) used for relieving rheumatic pains, neuralgia, etc.

Asplenium as-plē'ni-əm, *n.* spleenwort, a widely-distributed genus of ferns, with long or linear sori, with indusium arising from a vein — including wall-rue. [Gr. *asplēnon*, lit. spleenless — *a-* priv., and *splēn*, spleen: reputed a cure for spleen.]

asport as-pōrt', -pört', (*rare*) *v.t.* to carry away, esp. wrongfully. — *n.* **asportā'tion.** [L. *asportāre* — *abs*, away, and *portāre*, to carry.]

aspout ə-spowt', (*arch.*) *adv.* spoutingly. [a³.]

asprawl ə-spröl', (*arch.*) *adv.* in a sprawl. [a³.]

aspread ə-spred', (*arch.*) *adv.* in or into a spreading state. [a³.]

asprout ə-sprowt', (*arch.*) *adv.* in a sprouting state. [a³.]

asquat ə-skwot', (*arch.*) *adv.* squattingly. [a³.]

asquint ə-skwint', *adv.* and *adj.* towards the corner of the eye: obliquely. [App. **a³**, and some such word as Du. *schuinte*, slant.]

ass¹ as, äs, *n.* a small, usually grey, long-eared animal of the horse genus: a dull, stupid fellow (*fig.*). — **asses' bridge** the *pons asinorum*, or fifth proposition in the first book of Euclid, for some an impassable barrier to further progress. [O.E. *assa* — L. *asinus*; cf. Gr. *onos*, ass.]

ass². See **arse.**

assafetida. Same as **asafoetida.**

assagai. Same as **assegai.**

assai¹ äs-sä'ē, (*mus.*) *adv.* very. [It., — L. *ad*, to, *satis*, enough.]

assai² ä-sä'ē, *n.* a S. American palm (*Euterpe edulis*): its fruit: a drink made from its fruit. [Tupí.]

assail ə-sāl', *v.t.* to attack. — *adj.* **assail'able.** — *ns.* **assail'ant** one who attacks; **assail'ment.** [O.Fr. *asaillir* — L. *assilīre* — *ad*, upon, and *salīre*, to leap.]

assart as-ärt', (*hist.*) *v.t.* to reclaim for agriculture by grubbing. — *n.* a forest clearing: assarted land. grubbing up of trees and bushes. [A.Fr. *assarter* — L.L. *exsartāre* — L. *ex*, out, *sar(r)īre*, to hoe, weed.]

assassin ə- or a-sas'in, *n.* a follower of the Old Man of the Mountains, a member of his military and religious order in Persia and Syria (11th–13th cent.), notorious for secret murders: one who, usually for a reward, or for political reasons, kills by surprise or secretly. — *v.t.* **assass'inate** to murder by surprise or secret assault: to murder (especially a prominent person) violently, often publicly: to maltreat (*Milt.*): to destroy by treacherous means, as a reputation (*fig.*). — *n.* (*obs.*) one who assassinates. — *ns.* **assassinā'tion; assass'-inātor.** [Through Fr. or It. from Ar. *hashshāshīn*, hashish-eaters.]

assault ə-sölt', *n.* a sudden attack: a storming, as of a town: in Eng. law, unlawful attempt to apply force to the person of another — when force is actually applied, the act amounts to *battery*: an attack of any sort by arguments, appeals, etc. — *v.t.* to make an assault or attack upon. — *adj.* used in attack: preparing, or prepared, for attack. — *n.* **assault'er.** — **assault boat** a portable boat for landing on beaches or crossing rivers; **assault course** a course laid out with obstacles that must be negotiated, used for training soldiers, etc. — **assault at** or **of arms** a display of attack and defence in fencing. [O.Fr. *asaut* — L. *ad*, upon, *saltus*, a leap, *salīre*, to leap. See **assail.**]

assay a- or ə-sā', *v.t.* to put to the proof: to make trial of: to test: to determine the proportion of a metal, or other component, in: to give as result: to test fatness of (a killed stag) by a trial cut (*obs.*): to taste before presenting (as guarantee against poison) (*obs.*): to put to proof in action: to afflict (*Spens.*): to tempt (*obs.*):

to affect (*Spens.*): to experience (*Shak.*): to endeavour (now usu. **essay**): to assail (*Spens., Shak.*): to challenge (*Shak.*): to accost (*Shak.*). — *v.i.* to adventure, make an attempt: to practise assaying (of ores, etc.). — *n.* (by some *as'ā*) a test, trial: a determination of proportion of metal: a specimen used for the purpose: determination of the fatness of a stag (*obs.*): experiment: experience: endeavour, attempt, tentative effort (usu. **essay**): assault (*Spens., Shak.*): proof, temper, quality, standard, such as might be found by assaying (*Spens., Shak.*). — *adj.* **assay'able.** — *ns.* **assay'er** one who assays metals; **assay'ing.** — **assay'-master** an officer who determines the amount of gold or silver in coin or bullion; **assay office** (often with *caps.*) a (government) department in which gold and silver articles are assayed and hallmarks assigned; **assay'-piece** a sample chosen for assay: an example of excellence. — **cup of assay** a small cup for trial tasting before offering. [O.Fr. *assayer*, n. *assai*; see **essay.**]

assegai, assagai (*Afrik.* **assegaai**) as'ə-gī, *n.* a slender spear of hard wood tipped with iron, some for hurling, some for thrusting with — used in South Africa. —*v.t.* to kill or wound with an assegai. [Through Fr. or Port. from Ar. *azzaghāyah* — *az* = *al*, the, *zaghāyah*, a Berber word.]

assemble ə-sem'bl, *v.t.* to call or bring together: to collect: to put together the parts of. — *v.i.* to meet together. — *ns.* **assem'blage** a collection of persons or things: the whole collection of remains found on an archaeological site: all the flora and fauna of one type in an ecosystem (*biol.*): (also *a-sä-bläzh*), (putting together) a sculptural or other work of art consisting in whole or in part of selected objects, usu. objects made for another purpose; **assem'bla(u)nce** an assembling (*Spens.*): semblance (*Shak.*); **assem'bler** one who or that which assembles: a program that converts a program in assembly language into one in machine-code (*comput.*); **assembly** the act of assembling: the putting together of parts: a company assembled: a formal ball or meeting for dancing and social intercourse: a reception or at-home: a meeting for religious worship or the like: a deliberative or legislative body, esp. in some legislatures a lower house: a drumbeat, esp. a signal for striking tents (*mil.*). — **assembly hall** a hall, e.g in a school, in which assemblies are held; **assembly language** a program language more like a natural language than is machine-code (*comput.*); **assembly line** a serial arrangement of workers and apparatus for passing on work from stage to stage in assembling a product; **assem'blyman** a member of an assembly or lower house; **assembly room** a public ballroom. — **General Assembly** in Scotland, Ireland and the United States, the highest court of the Presbyterian Church: in England and Wales, the highest court of the United Reformed Church; **Legislative Assembly, House of Assembly** the lower or only house of some legislatures; **National Assembly** (also **Constituent Assembly**) the first of the revolutionary assemblies in France (1789–91): a body set up in 1920 'to deliberate on all matters concerning the Church of England and to make provision in respect thereof', consisting of houses of Bishops, Clergy, and Laity — also **Church Assembly,** superseded in 1970 by the **General Synod** (see **synod**). [Fr. *assembler* — L.L. *assimulāre*, to bring together — *ad*, to, *similis*, like. See **assimilate.**]

assemblé ä-sä-blā, *n.* a ballet dancer's leap with extended leg followed by crossing of legs. [Fr. *assembler*, to bring together.]

assembly. See **assemble.**

assent a- or ə-sent', *v.i.* to express agreement or acquiescence (with *to*). — *n.* an agreeing or acquiescence: compliance. — *adj.* **assentaneous** (as-ən-tā'ni-əs) ready to agree. — *ns.* **assentā'tion** obsequious assent, adulation; **ass'entātor** (*obs.*); **assent'er.** — *adjs.* **assentient** (ə-sen'shənt), **assent'ive.** — *adv.* **assent'ingly.** — *ns.* **assent'iveness; assent'or** one who subscribes a candidate's nomination paper in addition to proposer and seconder. — **royal assent** the sovereign's formal acquiescence in a measure which has passed the Houses of Parliament.   [L. *assentārī*, to flatter, freq. of *assentīrī*, to assent, agree.]

assert *ə-sûrt', v.t.* to vindicate or defend by arguments or measures (now used only with cause as object, or reflexively): to declare positively: to lay claim to: to insist upon: to affirm: to bear evidence of (*rare*). — *adj.* **assert'able.** — *ns.* **assert'er, assert'or** a champion: one who makes a positive statement; **asser'tion** (*-shən*) vindication of championship (*arch.*): the act of claiming one's rights: affirmation, averment: a positive statement or declaration: that which is averred or declared. — *adj.* **assert'ive** asserting or confirming confidently: positive: dogmatic. — *adv.* **assert'ively.** — *n.* **assert'iveness.** — *adj.* **assert'ory** affirmative. — **assert oneself** to defend one's rights or opinions, sometimes with unnecessary zeal: to thrust oneself forward.   [L. *asserĕre, assertum*, to lay hands on, claim — *ad*, to, and *serĕre*, to join.]

assess *ə-ses', v.t.* to fix the amount of, as a tax: to tax or fine: to fix the value or profits of, for taxation (with *at*): to estimate, judge. — *adj.* **assess'able.** — *ns.* **assess'ment** act of assessing: a valuation for the purpose of taxation: a tax; **assess'or** one who assesses: a legal adviser who sits beside a magistrate: one appointed as an associate in office with another: one who assesses taxes, or value of property, income, etc., for taxation: one who shares another's dignity. — *adj.* **assessō'rial** (*as-*). — *n.* **assess'orship.** — **assessment centre** a place where young offenders are detained so that their individual needs can be assessed and recommendations formulated about their future.   [L. *assidēre, assessum*, to sit by, esp. of judges in a court, from *ad*, to, at, *sedēre*, to sit.]

assets *as'ets, n.pl.* (*orig. sing.*) the property of a deceased or insolvent person, considered as chargeable for all debts, etc.: the entire property of all sorts belonging to a merchant or to a trading association. — *false sing.* **ass'et** an item of property: something advantageous or well worth having. — **ass'et-stripping** (now usu. *derog.*) the practice of acquiring control of a company and selling off its assets; **ass'et-stripper.**   [From the Anglo-Fr. law phrase *aver assetz*, to have enough, O.Fr. *asez*, enough — L. *ad*, to, *satis*, enough.]

asseverate *ə-, a-sev'ər-āt, v.t.* to declare solemnly — earlier **assev'er.** — *adj.* **assev'erating.** — *adv.* **assev'eratingly.** — *n.* **asseverā'tion.**   [L. *assevērāre, -ātum* — *ad*, to, *sevērus*, serious; see **severe.**]

assez bien *a-sā byē,* (Fr.) pretty well.

assibilate *a-* or *ə-sib'i-lāt, v.t.* to sound as a sibilant. — *n.* **assibilā'tion.**   [L. *ad*, to, *sībilāre*, to hiss.]

assiduity *as-id-ū'i-ti, n.* persistent application or diligence: (in *pl.*) constant attentions. — *adj.* **assiduous** (*ə-sid'ū-əs*) constant or unwearied in application. — *adv.* **assid'ūously** unremittingly. — *n.* **assid'ūousness.**   [L. *assiduus* — *ad*, to, at, *sedēre*, to sit.]

assiege *ə-sēj', (Spens.) v.t.* to besiege.   [See **siege.**]

assiento *as-ē-en'tō, (hist.) n.* a treaty (esp. that between Spain and Britain, 1713) for the supply of African slaves for Spanish American possessions: — *pl.* **assien'tos.**   [Sp. (now *asiento*), seat, seat in a court, treaty.]

assign *ə-sīn', v.t.* to allot: to designate, appoint: to put forward, adduce: to make over, transfer: to ascribe, refer: to specify: to fix, determine. — *n.* one to whom any property or right is made over: (in *pl., Shak.*) appendages. — *adj.* **assign'able** that may be assigned. — *ns.* **assignation** (*as-ig-nā'shən*) an appointment to meet, used chiefly of love trysts, and mostly in a bad sense: the making over of any right to another (*Scots law*); **assignee** (*as-īn-ē'*) one to whom any right or property is assigned: a trustee of a sequestrated estate; **assignment** (*-sīn'*) act of assigning: anything assigned: the writing by which a transfer is made: a task allotted: (*Spens.* altered in 1596 to **dessignment**) design, enterprise; **assignor** (*as-i-nör'*) one who makes over (*law*).

[Fr. *assigner* — L. *assignāre*, to mark out — *ad*, to, *signum*, a mark or sign.]

assignat *as'ig-nat, a-sēn-yä', n.* one of the notes first issued in 1790 by the French government as bonds on the security of the appropriated church lands.   [Fr.]

assignation, assignee, assignment, assignor. See **assign.**

assimilate *ə-sim'il-āt, v.t.* to make similar or like (with *to, with*): to convert into a like substance, as food in the body: to take fully into the mind, experience effects of (e.g. knowledge): to receive and accept fully within a group, absorb: to modify (a speech sound), making it more like a neighbouring sound in a word or sentence. — *v.i.* to become like (with *to*): to be incorporated or absorbed (into). — *adj.* **assim'ilable.** — *ns.* **assimilā'tion; assimilā'tionist** one who advocates a policy of assimilation, esp. of racial groups (also *adj.*). — *adj.* **assim'ilātive** having the power or tendency to assimilate.   [L. *assimilāre, -ātum* — *ad*, to, *similis*, like.]

assist *ə-sist', v.t.* to help (*with* work, etc.; *in* a matter, etc.): to accompany (*Shak.*). — *v.i.* to help (with *with, in*): to be present (now a Gallicism). — *n.* **assis'tance** help: relief. — *adj.* **assis'tant** helping. — *n.* one who assists: a helper. — *adj.* **assis'ted** for which help (e.g. financial aid, additional power) is supplied.   [Fr. *assister* — L. *assistĕre*, to stand by — *ad*, to, *sistĕre*, to set, take one's stand.]

assize *ə-sīz', v.t.* to assess (*obs.*): to set or fix the quantity or price of. — *n.* a statute settling the weight, measure, or price of anything (*hist.*): a trial by jury (*Scot.*): a jury (*Scot.*): judgment, sentence: (in *pl.*) periodical sittings of judges on circuit through the English counties, with a jury (till 1972). — *n.* **assiz'er** an officer with oversight of weights and measures: a juror (*Scots law*).   [O.Fr. *assise*, assembly of judges, set rate — *asseoir* — L. *assidēre* — *ad*, to, *sedēre*, to sit.]

associate *ə-sō'shi-āt, -si-, v.t.* to join, connect, link: to connect in one's mind: to make a colleague or partner: to accompany (*Shak.*). — *v.i.* to consort, keep company (with *with*): to combine or unite. — *adj.* (*-ət, -āt*) associated: connected: confederate: joined as colleague or junior colleague. — *n.* (*-ət, -āt*) one joined or connected with another: a colleague, companion, friend, partner, or ally: a person admitted to a society without full membership. — *n.* **associabil'ity.** — *adj.* **asso'ciable** (*-shi-ə-bl,* or *-shə-bl*) capable of being associated. — *ns.* **assō'ciateship; associā'tion** (*-si-,* or *-shi-*) act of associating: union or combination: a society of persons joined to promote some object: a set of species of plants or animals characteristic of a certain habitat (*biol.*): loose aggregation of molecules (*chem.*): (*football*; also **association football,** *coll.* **soccer**) the game as formulated by the Football Association (formed 1863), with eleven players a side, opp. to *Rugby*: connection of thoughts, of feelings: (usu. in *pl.*) thought, feeling, memory, more or less permanently connected with e.g. a place, an occurrence, something said: a relationship between the EEC and certain other countries, e.g. in Africa and the Caribbean, being more than just a trade agreement but with the associated members not enjoying membership of the EEC; **associa'tionism** (*psych.*) the theory which considers association of ideas to be the basis of all mental activity. — *adj.* **assō'ciātive** tending to association: such that (*a*b*)**c* = *a*(b*c*) — where * denotes a binary operation (*math.*). — *n.* **associativity** (*-ə-tiv'*). — **associate professor** in U.S., Australia and New Zealand, a university or college teacher immediately below professor in rank; **association copy** a copy of a book deriving additional interest from some association, e.g. a copy inscribed as given to or by some person of note. — **association of ideas** mental linkage that facilitates recollection — by similarity, contiguity, repetition.   [L. *associāre, -ātum* — *ad*, to, *socius*, a companion.]

assoil[1] *ə-soil', (arch.) v.t.* to absolve: to acquit: to discharge: to release: to solve: to dispel: to determine. —

n. **assoil'ment.** — *v.t.* **assoilzie** (*ə-soil'i*, *-yi*) to absolve (*Scot.*): to free (defender or accused) of a claim or charge (*Scots law*). [A.Fr. *assoilier* — L. *ab*, from, *solvēre*, to loose.]

assoil² *ə-soil'*, (*arch.*) *v.t.* to soil, sully, dirty. [L. *ad*, and **soil².**]

assonance *as'ən-əns*, *n.* a correspondence in sound: vowel-rhyme, coincidence of vowels without regard to consonants, as in *mate* and *shape*, *feel* and *need*: extended to correspondence of consonants with different vowels: resemblance, correspondence. — *adjs.* **ass'onant; assonantal** (*-ant'əl*). — *v.i.* **ass'onate** to correspond in vowel sound: to practise assonance. [L. *assonāre*, *-ātum* — *ad*, to, *sonāre*, to sound.]

assort *ə-sört'*, *v.t.* to distribute in classes, classify: to class. — *v.i.* to agree or be in accordance: to suit well: to keep company (*arch.*). — *adjs.* **assort'ative** (*-ə-tiv*); **assort'ed** classified, arranged in sorts: made up of various sorts. — *ns.* **assort'edness; assort'er; assort'ment** act of assorting: a quantity or number of things assorted: variety. [Fr. *assortir* — L. *ad*, to, *sors*, *sortis*, a lot.]

assot *ə-sot'*, (*obs.*) *v.t.* to befool, to besot. — *p.adj.* **assott'** or **assott'ed** (*Spens.*) infatuated. [O.Fr. *asoter* — *à*, to, *sot*, fool; see **sot¹.**]

assuage *ə-swāj'*, *v.t.* to soften, mitigate, or allay. — *v.i.* (*arch.*) to abate or subside: to diminish. — *n.* **assuage'-ment.** — *n.* and *adj.* **assuag'ing.** — *adj.* **assuā'sive** (*-siv*) soothing: mitigating. [O.Fr. *assouager* — L. *ad*, to, *suāvis*, mild.]

assubjugate *a-sub'jŏŏ-gāt*, (*Shak.*) *v.t.* to reduce to subjection. [Pfx. *a-*, intensive, **subjugate.**]

assuefaction *as-wi-fak'shən*, *n.* habituation. [L. *as-suēfacěre* — *assuētus*, accustomed, and *facěre*, to make.]

assuetude *as'wi-tūd*, *n.* accustomedness: habit. [L. *as-suētus.*]

assume *ə-sūm'*, *-sōōm'*, *v.t.* to adopt, take in: to take up, take upon oneself: to take for granted: to arrogate: to pretend to possess. — *v.i.* to make undue claims: to be arrogant. — *adj.* **assum'able.** — *adv.* **assum'ably.** — *adj.* **assumed'** appropriated, usurped: pretended: taken as the basis of argument. — *adv.* **assum'edly.** — *adj.* **assum'ing** haughty: arrogant. — *n.* assumption: arrogance: presumption. — *conj.* (often with *that*) if it can be taken for granted that. — *adv.* **assum'ingly.** — *ns.* **assumpsit** (*ə-sump'sit*) an action at law, wherein the plaintiff asserts that the defendant undertook (L. *assūmpsit*) to do a certain act and failed to fulfil his promise; **assumption** (*-sum'*, *-sump'*) an act of assuming: reception (*arch.*): taking upon oneself: arrogance: taking for granted: supposition: that which is taken for granted or supposed: the minor premise in a syllogism (*logic*): a taking up bodily into heaven, especially the **Assumption of the Virgin,** celebrated on the 15th of August (declared a dogma of the Roman Catholic Church on the 1st of November 1950). — *n.* **Assump'tionist** a member of the Roman Catholic congregation (*Augustinians of the Assumption*) founded at Nîmes in 1843. — Also *adj.* — *adj.* **assump'-tive** of the nature of an assumption: gratuitously assumed: apt, or too apt, to assume. — **deed of assumption** (*Scots law*) a deed executed by trustees under a trust-deed assuming a new trustee or settlement. [L. *assūměre*, *assūmptum* — *ad*, to, *sūměre*, to take.]

assure *ə-shŏŏr'*, *v.t.* to make sure or secure: to give confidence: to betroth (*obs.*): to tell positively: to insure. — *adj.* **assur'able.** — *n.* **assur'ance** confidence: feeling of certainty: subjective certainty of one's salvation (*theol.*): self-confidence: unabashedness: audacity: positive declaration: insurance, now esp. life-insurance: security: the securing of a title to property: a promise: a surety, warrant: a betrothal (*obs.*). — *adj.* **assured'** secured: pledged: betrothed (*obs.*): certain: confident: beyond doubt: insured: self-confident: over-bold: brazen-faced. — *n.* a person whose life or

property is insured: the beneficiary of an insurance policy. — *adv.* **assur'edly** confidently (*arch.*): certainly, in truth, undoubtedly (also *interj.*). — *ns.* **assur'edness; assur'er** one who gives assurance: an insurer or under-writer: one who insures his life. [O.Fr. *aseürer* (Fr. *assurer*) — L.L. *adsēcūrāre* — *ad*, to, *sēcūrus*, safe; see **sure¹.**]

assurgent *ə-sûr'jənt*, *adj.* rising, ascending: rising in a curve to an erect position (*bot.*): depicted as rising from the sea (*her.*). — *n.* **assur'gency** the tendency to rise. [L. *ad*, to, *surgěre*, to rise.]

asswage. An old spelling of **assuage.**

Assyrian *a-*, or *ə-sir'i-ən*, *adj.* of Assyria. — *n.* an inhabitant or native of Assyria: the Semitic language of ancient Assyria. — *ns.* **Assyriol'ogist; Assyriol'ogy** the science of Assyrian antiquities. [Gr. *Assyrios* — *Assyriā.*]

assythment *ə-sīth'mənt*, (*Scots law*; *obsolescent*) *n.* indemnification by one who has caused a death, etc. [M.E. *aseth*, amends — O.Fr. *aset*, adv. mistaken for objective of nom. *asez*; see **assets.**]

astable *ā-stā'bl*, *adj.* not stable: oscillating between two states (*elect.*). [Gr. *a-*, priv. and **stable¹.**]

astacology *as-tə-kol'ə-ji*, *n.* the science of the crayfish or of breeding it. — *adj.* **astacological** (*-loj'*). — *n.* **asta-col'ogist.** [Gr. *astakos*, lobster, crayfish, *logos*, discourse.]

astarboard *ə-stär'börd*, *-börd*, *adv.* on or towards the starboard. [a³ and **starboard.**]

astare *ə-stār'*, (*arch.*) *adv.* in a state of staring. [a³ and **stare¹.**]

astart *ə-stärt'*, (*Spens.*) *v.i.* to start up: to befall. — *adv.* with a start, suddenly. [Pfx. *a-*, up, and **start.**]

Astarte *as-tär'ti*, *n.* the Greek and Roman form of the name of a Semitic goddess whose attributes symbolise the notion of productive power. — Also **Ashtaroth** (*ash'tar-oth*), **Ash'toreth** (*B.*).

astatic *a-stat'ik*, *adj.* having no tendency to stand in a fixed position: without polarity, as a pair of magnetic needles set in opposite directions. — *n.* **astatine** (*as'tə-tēn*) a radioactive chemical element (at. numb. 85; symbol At) of the halogen series. [Gr. *astatos*, unstable — *a-*, priv., *statos*, verb. adj. of *histanai*, to make to stand.]

astatki *as-tat'kē*, *n.* the residue of petroleum-distillation, used as fuel. [Russ. *ostatki*, *pl.* of *ostatok*, residue.]

asteism *as'tē-izm*, *n.* refined irony. [Gr. *asty*, *-eōs*, a town; seen as a place of refinement.]

astely *a-stē'li*, (*bot.*) *n.* absence of a central cylinder or stele. — *adj.* **astē'lic.** [Gr. *a-*, priv., *stēlē*, column.]

aster *as'tər*, *n.* a star (*obs.*): a starlike figure, as in mitotic cell-division: (with *cap.*) a genus of Compositae, with showy radiated heads, white to lilac-blue or purple, flowering in late summer and autumn, hence often called Michaelmas daisies: a plant of this genus or a related form: extended to the kindred **China aster** (*Callistephus hortensis*) brought from China to France by a missionary in the 18th century. — *ns.* **asteria** (*as-tē'ri-ə*) a precious stone that shows asterism when cut *en cabochon* — star-sapphire, star-ruby; **Astē'rias** the common crossfish or five-fingers genus of sea-urchins. — *adj.* **astē'riated** (*min.*) showing asterism. — *ns.* **as'terid** a starfish; **as'terisk** a star-shaped mark (*) used as a reference to a note, as a mark of omission, as a mark of a word or root inferred to have existed but not recorded, and for other purposes. — *v.t.* to mark with an asterisk. — *adj.* **as'terisked.** — *ns.* **as'terism** a group of stars: three asterisks placed to direct attention to a passage: in some minerals the property of showing by reflected or transmitted light a star-shaped luminous figure due to inclusions or tubular cavities; **as'teroid** a minor planet: a starfish. — *adj.* resembling a star, starfish, or aster. — *adj.* **asteroid'al.** — *n.pl.* **Asteroid'ea** a class of echinoderms, the starfishes. [Gr. *astēr*, star.]

-aster in combination, a poor imitation of: one who has pretensions to being, as in *criticaster*, *poetaster*. [L.]

astern *ə-stûrn'*, *adv.* in or towards the stern: behind. [a³ and **stern.**]

astert *ə-stûrt'*, *v.i.* same as **astart.**

asthenia *as-thē'ni-ə*, *-thi-nī'ə*, *n.* debility. — *adj.* **asthenic** (*-then'ik*) of, relating to, asthenia: lacking strength: of a slender type, narrow-chested, with slight muscular development (*anthrop.*): belonging to a type thought prone to schizophrenia, having a small, light trunk and disproportionately long limbs (*psych.*). — *n.* a person of asthenic type. — *n.* **asthenosphere** (*-then'ə-sfēr; geol.*) a hypothetical sphere lying between the crust and the solid nucleus of the earth, supposed to yield more readily than either to persistent stresses. [Gr. *astheneia* — *a-*, priv., *sthenos*, strength.]

asthma *as'mə*, also *asth', ast'*, in U.S. usu. *az', n.* a chronic disorder of the organs of respiration, characterised by difficulty of breathing, wheezing, and a tightness in the chest. — *adjs.* **asthmatic** (*-mat'*), (*old*) **-al.** — *adv.* **asthmat'ically.** [Gr. *asthma, -atos* — *aazein*, to breathe with open mouth.]

asthore *as-thōr'*, (*Anglo-Irish*) *n.* darling. [Ir. *a stóir*, voc. of *stór*, treasure.]

Asti *as'tē*, *n.* an Italian white wine made round about *Asti* in the Monferrato hills in Piedmont.

astichous *as'ti-kəs*, (*bot.*) *adj.* not in rows. [Gr. *a-*, priv., *stichos*, a row.]

astigmatism *ə-stig'mə-tizm*, *n.* a defect in an eye, lens, or mirror, by which rays from one point are not focused at one point. — Also **astig'mia** (*-mi-ə*). — *adj.* **astigmatic** (*a-stig-mat'ik*). — *adv.* **astigmat'ically.** [Gr. *a-*, priv., and *stigma, -atos*, a point.]

Astilbe *as-til'bi*, *n.* a genus of perennial plants of the family Saxifragaceae, with clusters of red or white flowers: (without *cap.*) a plant of this genus. [Gr. *a-*, priv., *stilbos*, glittering.]

astir *ə-stûr'*, *adv.* on the move: out of bed: in motion or excitement. [a³ and **stir¹.**]

astomatous *a-stom'ə-təs*, or *-stōm'*, (*bot., zool.*) *adj.* mouthless, or without a mouthlike opening. — Also **astomous** (*as'tə-məs*). [Gr. *a-*, priv., *stoma, -atos*, mouth.]

astonish *əs-ton'ish*, *v.t.* to impress with sudden surprise or wonder: to amaze: to daze, to stun (*Shak.*). — Earlier forms **astone** (*ə-stun'*), **astun', astony** (*-ston'i*). — *adjs.* **aston'ied** (*obs.*); **aston'ished** amazed: dazed, stunned (*obs.*). — *adj.* **aston'ishing** very wonderful, amazing. — *adv.* **aston'ishingly.** — *n.* **aston'ishment** amazement: wonder: a cause for astonishment. [Ultimately from L. *ex*, out, *tonāre*, to thunder.]

astoop *ə-stōōp'*, *adv.* in a stooping position. [a³ and **stoop¹.**]

astound *əs-townd'*, *v.t.* to amaze, to strike dumb with astonishment. — *adjs.* **astound'** (*arch.*), **astound'ed** stunned: dazed: amazed; **astound'ing.** — *adv.* **astound'ingly.** — *n.* **astound'ment.** [From the pa.p. *astoned*; see **astonish.**]

astraddle *ə-strad'l*, *adv.* with legs wide apart. [a³ and **straddle.**]

astragal *as'trə-gəl*, *n.* a small semicircular moulding round a column or elsewhere (*archit.*): a round moulding near the mouth of a cannon: one of the bars that hold the panes of a window (*archit.*): (in *pl.*) dice. — *n.* **astragalus** (*as-trag'əl-əs*) the ankle-bone: (with *cap.*) the tragacanth and milk-vetch genus. [Gr. *astragalos*, a vertebra, ankle-bone, moulding, milk-vetch, in *pl.* (knucklebones used as) dice.]

astrakhan *as-trə-kan'*, *n.* lambskin with a curled wool from the Middle East: a rough fabric made in imitation of it. [*Astrakhan* on the Caspian Sea.]

astral *as'trəl*, *adj.* belonging to the stars: starry: belonging to a mitotic aster: in theosophy, of a supersensible substance supposed to pervade all space and enter into all bodies. — **astral body** an astral counterpart of the physical body: a ghost or wraith; **astral spirits** spirits supposed to animate the heavenly bodies, forming, as it were, their souls. [L. *astrālis* — *astrum*, a star.]

astrand *ə-strand'*, *adv.* on the strand. [a³ and **strand¹.**]

Astrantia *as-tran'shi-ə*, *n.* a genus of umbelliferous plants with showy petal-like bracts. [Gr. *astron*, star.]

astraphobia, astrapophobia *as-trə-fō'bi-ə, -tra-pə-fō'bi-ə*, *ns.* a morbid fear of thunder and lightning. [Gr. *astrapē*, lightning, *phobos*, fear.]

astray *ə-strā'*, *adv.* out of the right way: out of one's reckoning: in a lost state. [a³ and **stray.**]

Astrex (rabbit). See **Rex.**

astrict *ə-strikt'*, *v.t.* to bind, to compress: to constipate: to restrict. — *n.* **astric'tion** (*-shən*). — *adj.* **astric'tive** astringent. — *v.t.* **astringe** (*-strinj', -strinzh'*) to bind: to draw together: to draw tight: to compress: to constipate. — *n.* **astrin'gency** (*-jən-si*). — *adj.* **astrin'gent** (*ə-strin'jənt*) binding: contracting: drawing together: having power to contract organic tissues: styptic: (of e.g. manner) sharp, austere, severe. — *n.* an astringent agent. — *adv.* **astrin'gently** [L. *astringĕre, astrictum* — *ad*, to, *stringĕre*, to draw tight.]

astride *ə-strīd'*, *adv.* in a striding position: with a leg on each side. — *prep.* astride of: on either side of. [a³ and **stride.**]

astringency, etc. See under **astrict.**

astringer. A Shakespearian form of **austringer.**

astro- *as'trō-, -tro'*, in composition, star. — *n.* **as'trodome** a small transparent observation dome on the top of the fuselage of an aeroplane: a sports centre covered by a huge translucent plastic dome, orig. one at Houston, Texas. — *n.sing.* **astrodynam'ics** the science of the motion of bodies in outer space and the forces that act on them. — *ns.* **astrodynam'icist; astrogeol'ogist; astrogeol'ogy** study of the geology of the moon, etc.; **astroid** (*math.*) a hypocycloid with four cusps; **as'trolabe** (*-lāb*) an old instrument for taking altitudes (from *lab-*, root of Gr. *lambanein*, to take); **astrol'atry** star-worship (Gr. *latreiā*, worship); **astrol'oger.** — *adjs.* **astrolog'ic, -al.** — *adv.* **astrolog'ically.** — *ns.* **astrol'ogy** orig. practical astronomy: now almost confined to the once-supposed art or science of the influence of the stars on human and terrestrial affairs (*judicial astrology*; Gr. *logos*, discourse); **astrometereol'ogy** the study of the influence, or supposed influence, of the stars, planets, etc. on climate and weather; **astronaut** (*as'trō-nöt*; Gr. *nautes*, a sailor) one engaged in space travel. — *n.sing.* **astronaut'ics** the science of travel in space. — *ns.* **astronaviga'tion** the navigation of aircraft, spacecraft or sailing craft by means of observation of the stars; **astron'omer.** — *adjs.* **astronom'ic, -al** relating to astronomy: prodigiously great, like the distance of the stars — (**astronomical unit** the earth's mean distance from the sun, about 92.9 million miles, used as a measure of distance within the solar system; **astronomical year** see **year**). — *adv.* **astronom'ically.** — *v.i.* **astron'omise, -ize** to study astronomy. — *n.* **astron'omy** the science of the heavenly bodies (Gr. *nomos*, law). — *adj.* **astrophys'ical.** — *n.* **astrophys'icist.** — *n.sing.* **astrophys'ics** the science of the chemical and physical condition of the heavenly bodies. [Gr. *astron*, star.]

astrophel, astrofell *as'trō-fel*, *n.* an unidentified bitter starlike plant into which Spenser feigns Astrophel and Stella (Sir Philip Sidney and Penelope Devereux) to have been transformed — the seaside aster has been suggested. [Poss. Gr. *astron*, star, *phyllon*, leaf.]

Astroturf® *as'trō-tûrf*, *n.* an artificial surface for sports pitches, etc., having a woven, grass-like pile on a rubber base (used esp. for American or Association football). — Also *adj.*

astrut *ə-strut'*, *adv.* protrudingly: distendedly. — *adj.* protruding: distended. [a³ and **strut¹.**]

astucious, astucity. See **astute.**

astun. See **astonish.**

astute *as-, əs-tūt'*, in U.S. *-tōōt'*, *adj.* shrewd: sagacious: wily. — Also **astucious** (*-tū'shəs*). — *adv.* **astu'ciously.** — *n.* **astucity** (*-tū'si-ti*). — *adv.* **astute'ly.** — *n.* **astute'ness.** [L. *astūtus* — *astus* (found in abl. *astū*), craft.]

astylar *a-stī'lər*, *adj.* without columns. [Gr. *a-*, priv., *stȳlos*, a column.]

asudden ə-sud'ən, (arch.) adv. suddenly. [**a³**.]
asunder ə-sun'dər, adv. apart: into parts: separately. [**a³**.]
aswarm ə-swörm', adv. in swarms. [**a³**, and **swarm¹**.]
asway ə-swā', adv. swayingly: in a sway. [**a³**.]
aswim ə-swim', adv. afloat. [**a³**.]
aswing ə-swing', adv. swingingly: in a swing. [**a³**.]
aswirl ə-swûrl', adv. in a swirl. [**a³**.]
aswoon ə-swoon', (arch.) adv. in a swoon. [Poss. for *on* or *in* swoon; or orig. a pa.p., M.E. *iswowen* — O.E. *geswōgen*, swooned (not known in other parts of speech).]
asylum ə-sī'ləm, n. a place of refuge for debtors and for those accused of crime: an institution for the care or relief of the unfortunate as the blind or (*old-fashioned*) mentally ill: (any place of) refuge or protection: — pl. **asy'lums**. — **political asylum** protection given to a person by one country from arrest in another: refuge provided by a country to a person leaving his own without the permission of its government. [L. *asylum* — Gr. *asỹlon* (neut.) inviolate — *a-*, priv., *sỹlon, sỹlē*, right of seizure.]
asymmetry a-sim'ə-tri, ā-, n. want of symmetry. — adjs. **asymmetric** (-*et'rik*), **-al**. — adv. **asymmet'rically**. — n. **Asymmetron** (-*sim'ə-tron*) one of the genera making up the lancelets. [Gr. *asymmetriā* — *a-*, priv., *symmetriā*, symmetry.]
asymptote a'sim-tōt, (*math*.) n. a line that continually approaches a curve but never meets it. — adjs. **asymptotic** (-*tot'ik*), **-al**. — adv. **asymptot'ically**. [Gr. *asymptōtos* — *a-*, priv., *syn*, together, *ptōtos*, apt to fall, *piptein*, to fall.]
asynartete, a-sin'är-tēt, (*pros*.) adj. not connected, consisting of two members having different rhythms. — n. a verse of such a kind. — Also **asynartetic** (-*tet'ik*). [Gr. *asynartētos* — *a-*, priv., *syn*, together, *artaein*, to knit.]
asynchronism a-sing'krə-nizm, ā-, n. want of synchronism or correspondence in time. — Also **asyn'chrony**. — adj. **asyn'chronous**. [Gr. *a-*, priv., *syn*, together, *chronos*, time.]
asyndeton a-sin'də-ton, (*rhet*.) n. a figure in which the conjunctions are omitted. — adj. **asyndet'ic**. [Gr. *asyndeton* — *a-*, priv., *syndetos*, bound together — *syn*, together, *deein*, to bind.]
asynergia a-sin-ûr'ji-ə, ā-, n. lack of coordination in action, as of muscles. [Gr. *a-*, priv., *syn*, together, *ergon*, work.]
asyntactic a-sin-tak'tik, ā-, adj. loosely put together, irregular, ungrammatical. [Gr. *asyntaktikos* — *a-*, priv., *syntaktos* — *syntassein*, to put in order together.]
asystole a-sis'to-lē, ā-, (*med*.) n. inability of the heart to empty itself. — Also **asys'tolism**. [Gr. *a-*, priv., *systolē*, contraction.]
at at, ət, prep. denoting (precise) position in space or time, or some kindred relation, as amount, response, occupation, aim, activity. — **at it** occupied in a particular way, doing a particular thing; **at that** see **that**; **where it's at** see **where**. [O.E. *æt*; cf. Goth. and O.N. *at*, L. *ad*, Sans. *adhi*.]
atabal at'ə-bal, ä-tä-bäl', n. a Moorish kettledrum. [Sp., — Ar. *at-tabl*, the drum.]
atabeg, atabek ät-ä-beg', -bek', ns. a ruler or high official. [Turk. *atabeg* — *ata*, father, *beg*, prince.]
atabrin, atebrin at'ə-brin, n. mepacrine.
atacamite a-tak'ə-mīt, n. a mineral, a basic chloride of copper. [*Atacama*, in Chile.]
atactic. See **ataxia**.
ataghan. Same as **yataghan**.
Atalanta a-tə-lan'tə, n. a fleet-footed Arcadian (or Boeotian) maiden who raced against her suitors — defeated by Milanion (or Hippomenes), who dropped golden apples on the course to delay her.
atalaya ä-tä-lä'yä, (Sp., — Ar.) n. a watch-tower.
ataman at'a-man, n. a Cossack headman or general — a hetman: — pl. **at'amans**. [Russ., — Ger. *Hauptmann* — *Haupt*, head, *Mann*, man.]

atap, attap at'ap, n. the nipa palm: its leaves used for thatching. [Malay.]
ataraxia at-ə-rak'si-ə, **ataraxy** at'ə-rak-si, ns. calmness, the indifference aimed at by the Stoics. — adjs. and ns. **atarac'tic, atarax'ic** tranquillising (drug). [Gr. *ataraxiā* — *a-*, priv., *tarassein*, to disturb.]
à tâtons a tä-tõ, (Fr.) gropingly.
atavism at'əv-izm, n. appearance of ancestral, but not parental, characteristics: reversion to an ancestral, or to a primitive, type. — adj. **atavist'ic**. [L. *atavus*, a great-great-great-grandfather, an ancestor — *avus*, a grandfather.]
ataxia a-tak'si-ə, **ataxy** a-tak'si, at'aks-i, ns. inability to co-ordinate voluntary movements (*med*.; see **locomotor ataxy** under **locomotive**): lack of order. — adjs. **atact'ic, atax'ic**. [Gr. *ataxiā*, disorder — *a-*, priv., *taxis*, order.]
atchieve. See **achieve**.
Ate ä'tē, ä'tē, ä'tā, n. the Greek goddess of mischief and of all rash actions and their results. [Gr. *Ātē*.]
ate et, or ät, pa.t. of **eat**.
atebrin. See **atabrin**.
atelectasis a-tel-ek'tə-sis, n. incomplete inflation of a lung at birth: the collapse of a lung in an adult. — adj. **atelectatic** (-*tat'ik*). [Gr. *atelēs*, incomplete, *ektasis*, stretching out.]
ateleiosis a-tel-ī-ō'sis, -i-, a-tēl-, n. dwarfism without disproportion. [Gr. *ateleiōtos*, insufficient — *a-*, priv., *telos*, an end.]
atelier at'əl-yā, n. a workshop, esp. an artist's studio. [Fr.]
a tempo ä tem'pō, (*mus*.) in time, i.e. revert to the previous or original tempo. [It.]
à terre a ter, (Fr.) on the ground: with the foot (usu. both feet) flat on the ground (*ballet*).
Athanasian ath-ə-nā'sh(y)ən, -z(h)yən, adj. relating to *Athanasius* (c. 296–373), or to the creed erroneously attributed to him.
athanasy ə-than'ə-si, n. deathlessness. [Gr. *athanasiā* — *a-*, priv., *thanatos*, death.]
athanor ath'ə-nör, n. an alchemist's self-feeding digesting furnace. [Ar. *at-tannūr* — *al*, the, *tannūr*, furnace — *nūr*, fire.]
Atharvaveda ä-tär'vä-vä'dä, n. one of the Vedas. [Sans. — *atharvan*, fire-priest, and *veda*, knowledge.]
atheism ä'thi-izm, n. disbelief in the existence of a god. — v.i. **a'theise, -ize** to talk or write as an atheist. — v.t. to render godless: to make an atheist of. — n. **a'theist**. — adjs. **atheist'ic, -al**. — adv. **atheist'ically**. — adj. **a'theous** (*Milt*.) atheistic: godless. [Gr. *atheos* — *a-*, priv., and *theos*, god.]
atheling ath'əl-ing, (*hist*.) n. a member of a noble family: later, a prince of the blood royal, or the heir-apparent. [O.E. *ætheling* — *æthele*, noble; cf. Ger. *Adel*.]
athematic ath-i-mat'ik, adj. without a thematic vowel (*gram., linguistics*): not using themes as a basis (*mus*.). — adv. **athemat'ically**. [Gr. *a-*, priv., and **thematic**.]
Athene a-thē'nē, **Athena** -nə, n. Greek goddess of wisdom, born from the head of Zeus, tutelary goddess of Athens, identified by the Romans with Minerva. — n. **Athenaeum** (*ath-ə-nē'əm*) a temple of Athene: an ancient institution of learning, or literary university: a name sometimes taken by a literary institution, library, or periodical. — adj. **Athenian** (*a-thē'ni-ən*) of Athens. — n. a native or citizen of Athens or Attica.
atheology ä-thi-ol'ə-ji, n. opposition to theology. — adj. **atheological** (-ə-loj'i-kl). [Gr. *a-*, priv., and **theology**.]
atherine ath'ər-īn, adj. of a genus (**Atheri'na**) of small fishes of a family (**Atherinidae**; -*in'i-dē*) akin to the grey mullets, sometimes sold as smelt. — n. an atherine fish. [Gr. *atherinē*, atherine.]
athermancy ath-ûr'mən-si, n. impermeability to radiant heat. — adj. **ather'manous**. [Gr. *a-*, priv., *thermainein*, to heat.]
atheroma ath-ər-ō'mə, n. a cyst with porridge-like contents: a thickening of the inner coat of arteries. — adj. **atherōm'atous**. — n. **atherosclero'sis** (-ō'sis) arterioscle-

rosis, or a form or stage of it. — *n.* and *adj.* **atherosclerotic** (*-ot'ik*). [Gr. *athērōma* — *athērē* or *athărē*, porridge.]
athetesis *ath-i-tē'sis*, *n.* rejection as spurious. — *v.t.* **ath'etise**, **-ize** to reject. — *n.* **athetō'sis** involuntary movement of fingers and toes due to a lesion of the brain. — *adj.* **ath'etoid.** — *n.* a spastic who has involuntary movements. [Gr. *athetos*, without position, set aside, *athetēsis*, rejection — *a-*, priv., and the root of *tithenai*, to set.]
a'thing. See **a'**.
athirst *ə-thûrst'*, *adj.* thirsty: eager. [O.E. *ofthyrst*; see **thirst**.]
athlete *ath'lēt*, *n.* a contender for victory in feats of strength, speed, endurance, or agility: one vigorous in body or mind. — Also **athlē'ta** (*obs.*). — *adj.* **athletic** (*-let'ik*) of a long-limbed, large-chested, muscular type of body (*anthrop.*): relating to athletics: strong, vigorous. — *adv.* **athlet'ically.** — *n.* **athlet'icism** (*-i-sizm*) practice of, training in, or devotion to, athletics. — *n.pl.* or *n. sing.* **athlet'ics** athletic sports. — *n. sing.* the practice of athletic sports. — **athlete's foot** a contagious disease of the foot, caused by a fungus; **sexual athlete** see under **sex**. [Gr. *athlētēs* — *athlos*, contest.]
at-home. See **home**.
athrill *ə-thril'*, (*arch.*) *adv.* in a thrill. [**a³**.]
athrob *ə-throb'*, *adj.* and *adv.* with throbs, throbbing. [**a³**.]
athrocyte *ath'ro-sīt*, *n.* a cell having the ability to absorb and store foreign matter. [Gr. *athroos*, in a group, crowded, and **cyte**.]
athwart *ə-thwört'*, *prep.* across. — *adv.* sidewise: transversely: awry: wrongly: perplexingly. [**a³**.]
atilt *ə-tilt'*, *adv.* on tilt: as a tilter. [**a³** and **tilt²**.]
atimy *at'i-mi*, *n.* loss of honour: in ancient Athens, loss of civil rights, public disgrace. [Gr. *atimiā* — *a-*, priv., and *timē*, honour.]
atingle *ə-ting'gl*, *adj.* and *adv.* in a tingle. [**a³** and **tingle¹**.]
Atkins. See **Tommy Atkins**.
Atlantic, etc. See **Atlas**.
Atlas *at'ləs*, *n.* the Titan who bore the heavens on his shoulders, and whose figure used to appear on title-pages of atlases: the African mountain range into which he was transformed: (*pl.* **Atlantes** *at-lan'tēz*) a figure of a man serving as a column in a building: (for the following definitions, without *cap.*; *pl.* **at'lases**) the vertebra supporting the skull: a book of maps, plates, or the like: before metrication a size of drawing-paper. — *adjs.* **Atlantē'an** of Atlas: gigantic: of Atlantis; **Atlan'tic** of Atlas: of the Atlantic Ocean. — *n.* the Atlantic Ocean, separating Europe and Africa from America. — *ns.* **Atlan'ticism** (*-sizm*) the policy of close cooperation between North America and Western Europe; **Atlan'ticist**; **Atlan'tis** a traditional vanished island in the Atlantic Ocean; **Atlantosaurus** (*-ō-sö'rəs*; Gr. *sauros*, lizard) a gigantic lizard-hipped, four-footed, herbivorous Jurassic dinosaur of Colorado and Wyoming. — **Atlantic Charter** an Anglo-American declaration during the Second World War of eight common principles of right in future peace; **Atlantic Time** the standard time used in the easternmost part of Canada. [Gr. *Atlas*, *Atlantos*.]
atlas¹. See under **Atlas**.
atlas² *at'ləs*, *n.* a satin manufactured in the East. [Ar.]
atman *ät'mən*, *n.* in Hinduism, the divine within the self. [Sans. *ātman*, self, soul.]
atmology *at-mol'ə-ji*, *n.* the science of the phenomena of aqueous vapour. — *n.* **atmol'ogist.** [Gr. *atmos*, vapour, and *logos*, discourse.]
atmolysis *at-mol'i-sis*, *n.* a method of separating mixed gases by their different rates of passage through a porous septum. — *v.t.* **at'molyse**, **-yze** (*-līz*). [Gr. *atmos*, vapour, *lysis*, loosing — *lyein*, to loose.]
atmometer *at-mom'i-tər*, *n.* an instrument for measuring the rate of evaporation from a moist surface. [Gr. *atmos*, vapour, *metron*, measure.]
atmosphere *at'məs-fēr*, *n.* the gaseous envelope that sur-

rounds the earth or any of the heavenly bodies: any gaseous medium: a unit of atmospheric pressure equal to the pressure exerted by a column of mercury 760 millimetres in height at 0°C, practically the same as standard atmosphere (see **standard**): a feeling of space and distance in a picture: any surrounding influence or pervading feeling (*fig.*). — *adjs.* **atmospher'ic** (*-fer'-ik*), **-al** of or depending on the atmosphere. — *adv.* **atmospher'ically.** — *n.pl.* **atmospher'ics** noises interfering with radio reception, due to electric disturbances in the ether. — **atmospheric engine** a variety of steam-engine in which the steam is admitted only to the underside of the piston; **atmospheric hammer** a hammer driven by compressed air. [Gr. *atmos*, vapour, *sphairā*, a sphere.]
atoc. See **atok**.
atocia *a-tō'shi-ə*, *n.* sterility in a female. — *n.* **atoke** (*at'ōk*) the sexless part in certain polychaete worms. — *adjs.* **atokous** (*at'ək-əs*), **at'okal** without offspring. [Gr. *atokiā* — *a-*, priv., *tokos*, birth, offspring.]
atok, atoc *a-tok'*, *n.* a species of skunk. [Peruvian.]
atoke, etc. See **atocia**.
atoll *at'ol*, or *ə-tol'*, *n.* a coral island consisting of a circular belt of coral enclosing a central lagoon. [Name in Maldive Islands.]
atom *at'əm*, *n.* a particle of matter so small that, so far as the older chemistry goes, it cannot be cut or divided: anything very small. — *adjs.* **atomic** (*ə-tom'ik*) pertaining to atoms: obtained by means of atomic fission, as **atomic power**: driven by atomic power, as **atomic aircraft-carrier, icebreaker, merchantman, submarine**, etc.: heated by atomic power, as **atomic radiator**; **atom'ical.** — *ns.* **atomicity** (*at-əm-is'i-ti*) state or fact of being composed of atoms: number of atoms in a molecule: valency; **atomisā'tion**, **-z-** the reduction of liquids to the form of spray. — *v.t.* **at'omise**, **-ize** to reduce to atoms: to reduce (a liquid or solid) to a fine spray or minute particles: to destroy by bombing. — *ns.* **atomī'ser**, **-z-** an instrument for discharging liquids in a fine spray; **at'omism** the doctrine that atoms arranged themselves into the universe: the atomic theory: a theory that mental processes and psychological states can be analysed into simple elements (*psych.*); **at'omist** one who believes in atomism. — *adj.* **atomis'tic.** — *adv.* **atomist'ically.** — *n.* **at'omy** an atom, or mote: a pygmy (*Shak.*). — **atom(ic) bomb** a bomb in which the nuclei of uranium or plutonium atoms bombarded by neutrons split with explosive transformation of part of their mass into energy; **atomic clock** a clock in which, to achieve greater accuracy, the oscillations of a quartz crystal (see **quartz clock**) are regulated by the vibration of certain atoms as a caesium atom; **atomic energy** nuclear energy; **atomic mass unit** 1/12 of the mass of an atom of C-12; **atomic number** the number of units of charge of positive electricity on the nucleus of an atom of an element; **atomic philosophy** a system of philosophy enunciated by Democritus, which taught that the ultimate constituents of all things are indivisible particles, differing in form and in their relations to each other; **atomic pile** a device for the controlled release of nuclear energy, e.g. a lattice of small rods of natural uranium embedded in a mass of pure graphite which serves to slow down neutrons; **atomic second** a time interval whose measurement uses the frequency of radiation emitted or absorbed during transition from one energy state to another of a chosen atom; **atomic theory** the hypothesis that all atoms of the same element are alike and that a compound is formed by union of atoms of different elements in some simple ratio; **atomic time** time whose unit is the atomic second; **atomic warfare** warfare using atomic bombs; **atomic weight** relative atomic mass (q.v.); **a'tom-smasher** (*coll.*) an apparatus for breaking up the atom, an accelerator. — **Atomic Energy Authority** and **Atomic Energy Commission** the respective bodies in Britain and the U.S.A. responsible for the development and control of atomic energy;

primeval atom a hypothetical dense conglomerate from whose explosion 60 thousand million years ago the universe was (according to one theory) gradually formed. [Gr. *atomos* — *a-*, priv., and *tomos*, verbal adj. of *temnein*, to cut.]

atomy *at'əm-i*, (*Shak.*) *n.* a skeleton, walking skeleton: see also under **atom**. [Formerly also *atamy* and *natomy*, for **anatomy**, mistakingly divided *an atomy*.]

atonal, etc. See **atony**.

atone (*Spens.* **attone**) *ə-tōn'*, *adv.* at one, at once, together. — *v.i.* originally to make *at one*, to reconcile: to give satisfaction or make reparation (with *for*): to make up for deficiencies: to agree, be in accordance (*Shak.*). — *v.t.* to appease, to expiate: to harmonise, or reconcile (*arch.*). — *ns.* **atone'ment** the act of atoning: reconciliation: expiation: reparations: in Christian theology, the reconciliation of God and man by means of the incarnation and death of Christ; **aton'er**. — *advs.* **aton'ingly; attonce** (*ə-tons'*), **attones** (*ə-tōnz'*; both *Spens.*) at once: together.

atony *at'ən-i*, *n.* want of tone or energy or of stress: debility: relaxation. — *adj.* **atonal** (*ā-tō'nl*, *a-*; *mus.*) not referred to any scale or tonic. — *ns.* **atonality** (*at-ə-nal'i-ti*); **atō'nalism.** — *adj.* **atonic** (*a-ton'ik*) without tone (*pros.*): unaccented (*pros.*): debilitated. — *n.* **atonic'ity** (*-is'*) debility, weakness. [Gr. *atoniā* — *a-*, priv., *tonos*, tone, strength.]

atop *ə-top'*, *adv.* on or at the top. — *prep.* on top of. [**a**[3] and **top**[1].]

atopy *at'ə-pi*, *ā'*, (*med.*) *n.* hypersensitivity where the tendency to allergy is inherited, without predisposition to any particular type of allergic reaction. — *adj.* **atopic** (*-top'*). [Gr. *atopia*, strangeness — *a-*, priv., *topos*, place.]

à tort et à travers *a tor ā a tra-ver*, (Fr.) at random; **à toute force** *a tōōt fors*, (Fr.) by all means, absolutely; **à toute hasard** *a tōō-ta-zār*, (Fr.) at all hazards; **à tout prix** *a tōō prē*, (Fr.) at any price; **à tout propos** *a tōō prō-pō*, (Fr.) on every occasion.

atrabilious *at-rə-bil'yəs*, (*arch.*) *adj.* of a melancholy temperament: hypochondriac: splenetic, acrimonious. [L. *āter*, *ātra*, black, *bīlis*, gall, bile.]

atrament *a'trə-mənt*, (*arch.*) *n.* blacking: ink: any black fluid, as that emitted by the octopus. — *adjs.* **atramen- t'al, atrament'ous.** [From L. *ātramentum*, ink — *āter*, black.]

à travers *a tra-ver*, (Fr.) across, through.

atremble *ə-trem'bl*, *adv.* in a tremble. [**a**[3].]

atresia *ə-trēzh'(y)ə*, *n.* absence of, or closure of, a passage in the body. [Formed from Gr. *trēsis*, perforation.]

atrip *ə-trip'*, *adv.* (of an anchor when it is just drawn out of the ground), in a perpendicular position: (of a sail) when it is hoisted from the cap, sheeted home and ready for trimming. [**a**[3].]

atrium *ā'*, *ā'tri-əm*, L. *āt'ri-ōom*, *n.* the entrance hall or chief apartment of a Roman house: a cavity or entrance (*zool.*): either of the two upper cavities of the heart into which blood passes from the veins: — *pl.* **a'tria.** — *adj.* **a'trial.** [L. *ātrium*.]

atrocious *ə-trō'shəs*, *adj.* extremely cruel or wicked: heinous: very grievous: execrable. — *adv.* **atrō'ciously.** — *ns.* **atrō'ciousness; atrocity** (*ə-tros'i-ti*) atrociousness: an atrocious act. [L. *ātrōx*, *ătrōx*, *-ōcis*, cruel.]

atrophy *at'rəf-i*, *n.* wasting away: degeneration: diminution of size and functional activity by disuse: emaciation. — *v.t.* and *v.i.* to (cause to) suffer atrophy: to starve, to waste away. — *adj.* **at'rophied.** [Gr. *a-*, priv., and *trophē*, nourishment.]

Atropos *at'rō-pos*, *n.* the Fate that cuts the thread of life. — *ns.* **At'ropa** the deadly nightshade genus of the potato family; **at'ropin, atropine** (*-pēn*, *-pin*, *-pīn*) a poisonous alkaloid in deadly nightshade (also **atropia** *ə-trō'pi-ə*); **at'ropism** atropin poisoning. [Gr. *Atropos*.]

atropous *at'rō-pəs*, (*bot.*) *adj.* of an ovule, orthotropous. [Gr. *a-*, priv., *tropos*, turning.]

Ats *ats*, *n.pl.* women of the Auxiliary Territorial Service.

[From the initial letters; see under *Abbreviations*.]

attaboy *at'ə-boi*, (*coll.*) *interj.* expressing encouragement or approval. [Poss. corr. of *that's the boy!*]

attach *ə-tach'*, *v.t.* to bind or fasten: to seize: to gain over: to connect, associate: to join in action, function, or affection: to arrest. — *v.i.* to adhere, to be fastened: to be attributable, incident (to): to come into effect (*rare*). — *adjs.* **attach'able; attached'.** — *n.* **attach'ment** act or means of fastening: a bond of fidelity or affection: seizure of goods or person by virtue of a legal process: a piece, etc. that is to be attached. [O.Fr. *atachier*, from *a* (— L. *ad*), and perhaps the root of **tack**[1].]

attaché *ə-tash'ā*, *n.* a junior member of an ambassador's suite: an attaché-case. — **atta'ché-case** a small rigid rectangular leather receptacle for documents, etc. [Fr., attached.]

attack *ə-tak'*, *v.t.* to fall upon violently: to assault: to assail: to begin to affect or act destructively upon. — *v.i.* to take the initiative in attempting to score (*sport*). — *v.t.* and *v.i.* (*mus.*) to begin (a phrase or piece). — *n.* an assault or onset: the offensive part in any contest: the beginning of active operations on anything, even dinner: severe criticism or calumny: an access of illness: a performer's approach to a piece, dance, etc. or mode of beginning with respect to crispness, verve, and precision (*mus.*, ballet, etc.): used collectively to designate the players in a team who are in attacking positions, e.g. the forwards in football or hockey: in lacrosse, the name of certain positions between centre and the opponents' goal. — *adj.* **attack'able.** — *n.* **attack'er.** [Fr. *attaquer*; a doublet of **attach**.]

attain *ə-tān'*, *v.t.* to reach or gain by effort: to arrive at. — *v.i.* to come or arrive. — *adj.* **attain'able** that may be reached. — *ns.* **attainabil'ity, attain'ableness; attain'- ment** act of attaining: the thing attained: acquisition (*pl.*) acquirements in learning. [O.Fr. *ataindre* — L. *attingĕre* — *ad*, to, *tangĕre*, to touch.]

attainder *ə-tān'dər*, *n.* act of attainting: loss of civil rights through conviction for high treason (*law*). — *v.t.* **attaint'** to convict: to deprive of rights by conviction for treason (*law*): to accuse: to disgrace, stain (from a fancied connection with *taint*). — *n.* the act of touching (*arch.*): a hit (in tilting): infection (*Shak.*): attainder: a stain, disgrace. — Older *pa.p.* **attaint'** (*Shak.*), corrupted, tainted. — *ns.* **attaint'ment, attaint'ure.** [O.Fr. *ataindre* — see **attain**.]

attaint. See **attainder**.

attap. See **atap**.

attar *at'ər*, *n.* a very fragrant essential oil made in Bulgaria and elsewhere, chiefly from the damask rose. — Also **ott'o, ott'ar.** [Pers. *atar*.]

attask *ə-täsk'*, *v.t.* to take to task (only in the *pa.p.* **attaskt'** a doubtful reading in Shak. *King Lear*). [Pfx. *a-*, intensive, and **task**.]

attemper *ə-tem'pər*, *v.t.* to mix in due proportion: to modify or moderate: to adapt. — *adj.* **attem'pered.** [L. *attemperāre* — *ad*, to, *temperāre*, to regulate.]

attempt *ə-temt'*, *v.t.* to try, endeavour (to do, or with *n.* of action): to try to obtain (*obs.*): to tempt, entice (*arch.*): to make an attack upon (*arch.* or *obs.*). — *v.i.* to make an attempt or trial. — *n.* an effort: a personal assault: temptation (*Milt.*): any act that can fairly be described as one of a series which, if uninterrupted and successful, would constitute a crime (*law*). — *n.* **attemptabil'ity.** — *adj.* **attempt'able** that may be attempted. — *n.* **attempt'er** (*Milt.*) a tempter. [O.Fr. *atempter* — L. *attentāre* — *ad*, and *temptāre*, *tentāre*, to try — *tendĕre*, to stretch.]

attend *ə-tend'*, *v.t.* to wait on: to accompany (*arch.*): to be present at: to go regularly to (a school, etc.): to wait for (*arch.*): to give attention to (*arch.*). — *v.i.* to listen (to): to apply oneself, direct one's mind and efforts (with *to*): to act as an attendant or companion (with *on*, *upon*; *arch.*): to wait, be consequent (with *on*, *upon*; *arch.*). — *ns.* **attend'ance** the act of attending: attention, careful regard (*B.*): presence: gathering of persons attending; **attend'ancy** attendance, a retinue (*obs.*): relative position (*obs.*). — *adj.* **attend'ant** giving attendance: accompanying. — *n.* one who attends or accompanies: a servant: what accompanies or follows: one who owes a duty or service to another (*law*). — *ns.* **attendee'** used in the sense of 'attender', of a person attending a conference, attendance centre, etc.; **atten-d'er** one who gives heed: a companion: one who attends. — **attend'ment** (*rare*) accompaniments: (*Spens.* **atten'dement**) intention. — *adj.* **attent'** (*Spens., Shak.*) giving attention. — *n.* (*Spens.*) attention. — *n.* **atten'tion** (*-shən*) act of attending: steady application of the mind: heed: civility, courtesy: (in *pl.*) courtship: position of standing rigidly erect with hands by the sides and heels together. — *interj.* (*mil.*) a cautionary word calling for an attitude of readiness to execute a command. — *adjs.* **atten'tional** (*psych.*, etc.) relating to attention or concentration; **attent'ive** full of attention: courteous, mindful. — *adv.* **attent'ively.** — *n.* **attent'iveness.** — **attendance allowance** a grant paid to an invalid who requires the constant attendance of a nurse; **attendance centre** a centre where a young offender may be required to attend regularly, instead of serving a prison sentence. — **draw (someone's) attention to** to direct (someone's) notice towards.   [L. *attendēre, attentum; attentiō, -ōnis.*]

attentat *a-tä-tä*, (*Fr.*) *n.* an (esp. unsuccessful) attempt at an (esp. political) crime of violence.

attenuate *ə-ten'ū-āt, v.t.* to make thin or lean: to break down into finer parts: to reduce in density: to reduce in strength or value. — *v.i.* to become thin or fine: to grow less. — *n.* **atten'uant** anything that attenuates. — Also *adj.* — *adjs.* **atten'uate, atten'uated** thin: thinned: dilute, rarefied: tapering. — *n.* **attenuā'tion** process of making slender: reduction of intensity, density, force, or (of bacteria) virulence: in homoeopathy, the reduction of the active principles of medicines to minute doses: reduction in magnitude, amplitude, or intensity, arising from absorption or scattering (*nuc., telecomm.*); **atten'uator.**   [L. *attenuāre, -ātum* — *ad,* to, *tenuis,* thin.]

attercop *at'ər-kop,* (*obs.* or *dial*) *n.* a spider: an ill-natured person.   [O.E. *attorcoppa* — *attor, ātor,* poison, and perh. *cop,* head, or *copp,* cup.]

attest *ə-test', v.t.* to testify or bear witness to: to affirm by signature or oath: to give proof of, to manifest: to call to witness (*obs.*). — *v.t.* and *v.i.* to enrol for military service. — *v.i.* to bear witness (to). — *n.* (*Shak.*) witness, testimony. — *adjs.* **attest'able, attest'ative.** — *n.* **attestā'tion** (*at-*) act of attesting: administration of an oath. — *adj.* **attest'ed** certified free from the tubercle bacillus. — *ns.* **attest'er, attest'or.**   [L. *attestārī* — *ad,* to, *testis,* a witness.]

Attic *at'ik, adj.* of Attica or Athens: chaste, refined, classical, in taste, language, etc., like the Athenians. — *v.t.* **Atticise, -ize** (*at'i-sīz*) to make conformable to the language or idiom of Attica. — *v.i.* to use the idioms of the Athenians: to side with the Athenians: to affect Attic or Greek style or manners. — *n.* **Att'icism** (*-sizm*). — **Attic salt** wit of a dry, delicate, and refined quality.   [Gr. *Attikos* — *Attikē,* Attica.]

attic *at'ik, n.* in archit., a low storey or structure above the cornice of the main part of an elevation, usually of the so-called **Attic order,** i.e. with square columns or pilasters instead of pillars: a room in the roof of a house.   [The structure was supposed to be in the Athenian manner; see foregoing.]

attire *ə-tīr', v.t.* to dress, array or adorn: to prepare. — *n.* dress: any kind of covering. — *ns.* **attire'ment; attir'ing.**   [O.Fr. *atirer,* put in order — *à tire,* in a row — *à* (L. *ad*), to, and *tire, tiere,* order, dress; see **tier.**]

attitude *at'i-tūd, n.* posture, or position: a studied or affected posture: a position on one leg with the other leg extended behind, modelled on the position of the *Flying Mercury* of Giovanni Bologna (1524–1608) (*ballet*): of an aircraft in flight, or on the ground, the

angles made by its axes with the relative airflow, or with the ground, respectively: the tilt of a vehicle measured in relation to the surface of the earth as horizontal plane (*space flight*): any condition of things or relation of persons viewed as expressing some thought, feeling, etc. — *adj.* **attitud'inal.** — *n.* **attitu-dinā'rian** one who studies attitudes. — *v.i.* **attitud'inise, -ize** to assume affected attitudes. — *ns.* **attitud'iniser, -z-; attitud'inising, -z-.** — **attitude angle** in a cornering motor vehicle, the slight angle between the track of the vehicle and the direction in which the tyres are pointing. — **strike an attitude** to assume a position or figure indicative of a feeling or emotion not really felt.   [Fr. *attitude* or It. *attitudine* — L. *aptitūdō, -inis* — *aptus,* fit.]

atto- *pfx.* one million million millionth, 10^{-18}.   [Dan., Norw. *atten,* eighteen.]

attollent *ə-tol'ənt, adj.* lifting up, raising. — *n.* a muscle that raises.   [L. *attollēns, -entis,* pr.p. of *attollēre,* to lift up — *ad,* to, *tollēre,* to lift.]

attonce, attone. See **atone.**

attorn *ə-tûrn', (law) v.t.* to transfer to another. — *v.i.* to accept tenancy under a new landlord. — *n.* **attorn'ey** (O.Fr. pa.p. *atorné*) one legally authorised to act for another: one legally qualified to manage cases in a court of law: a solicitor: — *pl.* **attor'neys.** — *v.t.* (*Shak.*) to perform by proxy: to employ as a proxy. — *ns.* **attor'neydom; attor'neyism; attor'neyship; attorn'ment** acknowledgment of a new landlord. — *n.* **Attor'ney= Gen'eral** the chief law-officer for England, the Republic of Ireland, a dominion, colony, etc.: the king's attorney in the duchies of Lancaster and Cornwall, and the county palatine of Durham: in the United States, one of the seven officials who constitute the president's cabinet, the head of the Department of Justice: also the legal adviser of a State governor. — **attorney at law** or **public attorney** a professional and duly qualified legal agent; **attorney in fact** or **private attorney** one duly appointed by power of attorney to act for another in matters of contract, money payments, and the like; **letter, warrant,** or **power of attorney** a formal instrument by which one person authorises another to perform certain acts for him.   [L.L. *attornāre,* to assign; see **turn.**]

attract *ə-trakt', v.t.* to cause to approach otherwise than by material bonds: to draw (a crowd, attention, financial investment, etc.): to entice: to be liable to (tax) (*legal,* etc.). — *adj.* **attract'able** that may be attracted. — *n.* **attract'ant** something that attracts, esp. that effects communication in insects and animals. — *adv.* **attract'ingly.** — *n.* **attrac'tion** act of attracting: an attracting force: that which attracts. — *adj.* **attract'ive** having the power of attracting: alluring. — *adv.* **attract'ively.** — *ns.* **attract'iveness; attract'or.**   [L. *attrahēre, attractum* — *ad,* to, *trahēre,* to draw.]

attrahent *at'rə-hənt, ə-trā'ənt, adj.* attracting or drawing. — *n.* that which attracts.   [L. *attrahēns, -entis,* pr.p. of *attrahēre;* see **attract.**]

attrap *ə-trap', (Spens.) v.t.* to adorn with trappings: to dress or array.   [L. *ad,* to, **trap**[4].]

attribute *ə-trib'ūt (Milt. at'ri-būt), v.t.* to ascribe, assign, or consider as belonging. — *n.* (*at'*) that which is attributed: that which is inherent in, or inseparable from, anything: that which can be predicated of anything: a quality or property: a virtue: an accessory: a conventional symbol: a word added to another to denote an attribute (*gram.*). — *adj.* **attrib'utable.** — *n.* **attribution** (*at-ri-bū'shən*) act of attributing: that which is attributed. — *adj.* **attrib'utive** expressing an attribute: (of an adjective) placed immediately before or immediately after the noun it qualifies (*gram.*). — *n.* a word added to another to denote an attribute (*gram.*). — *adv.* **attrib'utively.**   [L. *attribuēre, -tribūtum* — *ad,* to, *tribuēre,* to give.]

attrist *ə-trist', (obs.) v.t.* to sadden.   [Fr. *attrister* — L. *ad,* to, *tristis,* sad.]

attrite *ə-trīt', adj.* worn by rubbing or friction: repentant through fear of punishment, not yet from the love of God (*theol.*). — *n.* **attrition** (*a-* or *ə-trish'ən*) rubbing together: wearing down: a defective or imperfect sorrow for sin (*theol.*): the wearing down of an adversary, resistance, resources, etc. (*fig.*). — *adj.* **attrit'ional**. [L. *attrītus* — *atterĕre* — *ad*, to, and *terĕre*, *trītum*, to rub.]

attuition *at-ū-ish'ən*, *n.* a mental operation intermediate between sensation and perception. — *adjs.* **attui'tional**; **att'uent** performing the function of attuition. — *v.t.* **att'uite** (*-īt*) to be conscious of by attuition. — *adj.* **attu'itive.** — *adv.* **attu'itively.** [L. *ad*, to, *tuērī*, to attend to.]

attune *ə-tūn'*, in U.S. *-tōōn*, *v.t.* to put in tune: to make tuneful (one's voice, song, etc.): to make to harmonise or accord: to accustom or acclimatise. — *n.* **attune'-ment.** [L. *ad*, to, and **tune.**]

atwain *ə-twān'*, (*arch.*) *adv.* in twain: asunder. [a³ and **twain.**]

atweel *ə-twēl'*, (*Scot.*) *adv.* or *interj.* well: indeed. [**wat weel,** i.e. wot well.]

atween *ə-twēn'*, (*Spens.*) *adv.* betweenwhiles. — *prep.* between. — *adv.* and *prep.* **atwixt'** (*Spens.*) betwixt.

atypical *a-*, *ā-tip'i-kl*, *adj.* not typical. [Gr. *a-*, priv. and **typical.**]

aubade *ō-bäd'*, *n.* a musical announcement of dawn: a sunrise song. [Fr., — *aube*, dawn — Prov. *alba*, dawn.]

auberge *ō-berzh'*, *n.* an inn. — *n.* **aubergiste** (*ō-ber-zhēst'*) an innkeeper. [Fr., of Gmc. origin; see **harbour.**]

aubergine *ō'ber-jēn*, *-zhēn*, *n.* the fruit of the egg-plant, the brinjal: its purple colour. — *adj.* of this colour. [Fr. dim. of *auberge*, a kind of peach — Sp. *alberchigo* — Ar. *al*, the Sp. *pérsigo* — L. *persicum*, a peach.]

Aubrey holes *ō'bri hōlz*, the 56 circular pits surrounding the stone circle of Stonehenge in Wiltshire. [John *Aubrey*, 1626–97, who discovered them.]

Aubrietia *ö-brē'*, *ö-bri-ē'sh(y)ə*, *n.* a purple-flowered Mediterranean genus of trailing cruciferous plants, much grown in rock-gardens, etc.: (without *cap.*) a plant of this genus. [After Claude *Aubriet* (*c.* 1665–1742), naturalist-painter.]

auburn *ö'bûrn*, *adj.* orig. light yellow: reddish brown. [L.L. *alburnus*, whitish — L. *albus*, white.]

auceps *ö'seps*, (*Walton*) *n.* a hawker. [L., bird-catcher, fowler — *avis*, bird, *capĕre*, to catch.]

au contraire *ō kɔ̃-trer*, (Fr.) on the contrary.

au courant *ō kōō-rä*, (Fr.) in the stream: well-informed: well up in the facts or situation.

auction *ök'shən*, *n.* a public sale at which goods are sold to the highest bidder: auction bridge. — *v.t.* to sell by auction. — *adj.* **auc'tionary.** — *n.* **auctioneer'** one who sells or is licensed to sell by auction. — *v.t.* to sell by auction. — **auction bridge** a development of the game of bridge in which the players bid for the privilege of choosing trump suit or no-trumps and the declarer of trumps plays his partner's hand as a dummy. — **Dutch auction** a kind of auction at which the salesman starts at a high price, and comes down till he meets a bidder: any of several other unconventional or informal types of auction. [L. *auctiō*, *-ōnis*, an increasing — *augēre*, *auctum*, to increase.]

auctorial *ök-tō'ri-əl*, *-tö'*, *adj.* of an author or his trade. [L. *auctor*, *-ōris*, author.]

Aucuba *ö'kū-bə*, *n.* the Japan laurel genus: (without *cap.*) a plant of this genus. [Jap.]

audacious *ö-dā'shəs*, *adj.* daring: bold: impudent. — *adv.* **audā'ciously.** — *ns.* **audā'ciousness,** **audacity** (*ö-das'i-ti*). [Fr. *audacieux* — L. *audāx* — *audēre*, to dare.]

audax et cautus *ö'daks et kö'təs*, *ow'daks et kow'tōōs*, (L.) bold and cautious.

au désespoir *ō dā-zes-pwär*, (Fr.) in despair.

audible *öd'i-bl*, *adj.* able to be heard. — *ns.* **audibil'ity,** **aud'ibleness.** — *adv.* **aud'ibly.** — *n.* **aud'ience** the act of hearing: a judicial hearing: admittance to a hearing: a ceremonial interview: an assembly of hearers or spectators: the listeners to a radio programme, viewers

of a television programme, or even readers of a book, magazine, author, etc.: a court of government or justice in Spanish America: the territory administered by it. — *adj.* **aud'ient** listening: paying attention. — *n.* a hearer. — *adj.* **audile** (*ö'dīl*, *-dīl*) pertaining to hearing. — *n.* one inclined to think in terms of sound. **audio-** (*ö'di-ō*) in composition, pertaining to sound, esp. broadcast sound: pertaining to, using, or involving, audio-frequencies. — *n.* **aud'io** reproduction of recorded or broadcast sounds (also *adj.*): an acoustic device by which an airman returning to an aircraft-carrier knows when he is at a proper speed for landing: short for **audiotypist** or **audiotyping:** — *pl.* **aud'ios.** — *ns.* **aud'io-engineer'** one concerned with the transmission and reception of broadcast sound; **audio-frequency** (*ö'di-ō-frē'kwən-si*) a frequency of oscillation which, when the oscillatory power is converted into a sound pressure, is perceptible by the ear; **aud'iogram** a tracing produced by an audiograph; **aud'iograph** a machine used to test a patient's hearing by transmitting soundwaves directly to his inner ear; **audio-loca'tion** echo location. — *adj.* **audiolog'ical.** — *ns.* **audiol'ogist; audiol'ogy** the science of hearing esp. with reference to the diagnosis and treatment of hearing defects.; **audiom'eter** instrument for measuring differences in hearing: one for measuring minimum intensities of sounds which, for specified frequencies, are perceivable by the ear. — *adj.* **audiomet'ric.** — *ns.* **audiometrician** (*-mi-trish'ən*); **aud'iophil(e)** (*-fīl*, *-fīl*) an enthusiast for the true reproduction of recorded or broadcast sound; **aud'iotyping; aud'iotyp'ist** a typist able to type directly material reproduced by a Dictaphone. — *adj.* **audio-vis'ual** concerned simultaneously with seeing and hearing. — *ns.* **aud'iphone** an instrument which, pressed against the teeth, communicates sounds through the bones to the ears; **aud'it** an examination of accounts by an authorised person or persons: a calling to account generally: a statement of account: a check or examination: a periodical settlement of accounts (*obs.*): audience, hearing (*obs.*). — *v.t.* to examine and verify by reference to vouchers, etc.: to attend (a class) without intending to take any examination (*U.S.*). — *ns.* **audi'tion** (*ö-dish'ən*) the sense, or an act, of hearing; a trial performance by an applicant for an acting, etc., position (also *v.t.* and *v.t.* with *for*): mode of hearing: something heard (*rare*). — *adj.* **aud'itive** of, or related to, hearing. — *ns.* **aud'itor** a hearer: one who audits accounts: — *fem.* **aud'itress; auditō'rium** in a theatre, or the like, the space allotted to the hearers: the reception-room of a monastery: hall (*U.S.*): — *pl.* **audito'riums** or **-ia; aud'itorship.** — *adj.* **aud'itory** relating to the sense of hearing. — *n.* an audience: a place where lectures, etc., are heard. — **audience participation** drawing audience into a theatrical performance by direct appeals to its members; **audio-visual aids** material such as pictures, closed-circuit TV, teaching machines, used in the classroom; **audit ale** an ale of special quality brewed for some Oxford and Cambridge colleges — orig. for use on the day of audit. [L. *audīre*, to hear.]

audio(-), audit, etc. See **audible.**

audita querela *ö-dī'tə kwə-rē'lə*, *ow-dē'tä kwe-rā'lä*, (L.) the suit having been heard — name of a writ giving leave to appeal.

audition, auditor, etc. See **audible.**

auf *öf*, *n.* an elf's child, an oaf. [O.N. *ālfr*, elf.]

au fait *ō fe*, (Fr.) well-acquainted with a matter: well-informed, expert (with *with*).

aufgabe *owf'gä-bə*, *n.* (*psych.*) a task set as an experiment, etc. [Ger.]

Aufklärung *owf-kle'rōong*, (Ger.) *n.* enlightenment, esp. the 18th-century intellectual movement.

au fond *ō fɔ̃*, (Fr.) at bottom.

au fromage *ō fro-mäzh*, (Fr.) with cheese.

auf Wiedersehen *owf vē'dər-zā-ən*, (Ger.) goodbye till we meet again.

Augean *ö-*, *ow-jē'ən*, *adj.* filthy: difficult. [From *Augeas*, king of Elis into whose uncleansed oxstalls Herakles turned the river Alpheus.]

auger ö′gər, *n.* a carpenter's boring tool: an instrument for boring holes in the ground. — **au′ger-bit** an auger that fits into a carpenter's brace; **au′ger-hole; au′ger-shell** Terebra; **au′ger-worm** the goat-moth larva, which bores trees. [From *nauger* (*an auger* for *a nauger*) — O.E. *nafugār* — *nafu*, a nave of a wheel, *gār*, a piercer; see **nave²**, **gore²**.]

Auger effect ō-zhā i-fekt′, non-radiative transition of an atom from an excited state to one of lower energy with emission of an electron (**Auger electron**). [Pierre *Auger*, physicist.]

aught öt, *n.* a whit: ought: anything: a part. [O.E. *ā-wiht* contr. to *āht* (whence **ought**), and shortened to *aht* (whence **aught**); *ā-wiht* is from *ā, ō,* ever, and *wiht,* creature, whit, wight.]

augite ö-jīt, -gīt, *n.* one of the pyroxene group of minerals, closely allied to hornblende, usu. greenish, an essential component of many igneous rocks. — *adj.* **augitic** (-jit′, -git′). [Gr. *augē,* brightness.]

augment ög-ment′, *v.t.* to increase: to make larger. — *v.i.* to grow larger. — *n.* **aug′ment** (-mənt) increase: the prefixed vowel or initial vowel-lengthening in some past tenses of the verb in Sanskrit and Greek: sometimes applied also to such inflectional prefixes as the *ge-* of the German perfect participle. — *adjs.* **augment′able; augment′ative** having the quality or power of augmenting: (of an affix or derivative) increasing the force of the original word (*gram.*; also *n.*). — *ns.* **augmentā′tion** increase: addition: an additional charge in a coat-of-arms bestowed as a mark of honour (*her.*): the repetition of a melody in notes of greater length than the original (*mus.*): in Scots law an increase of stipend obtained by a parish minister by an action raised in the Court of Teinds against the titular and heritors. — *adj.* **augment′ed.** — *ns.* **augment′er; augment′or** a nerve that increases the rate of activity of an organ. — **augmented interval** (*mus.*) one increased by a semitone. — **Augmented Roman Alphabet** earlier name for Initial Teaching Alphabet. [L. *augēre,* increase.]

Augmentin® ög-men′tin, *n.* a drug administered along with an antibiotic such as Ampicillin® that prevents the antibiotic from being metabolised, and thus ensures its potency.

au grand sérieux ō grã sā-ryø, (Fr.; now **très au sérieux** tre-zō) in all seriousness.

au gratin ō gra-tɛ̃, (Fr.) cooked covered with breadcrumbs or grated cheese, or with both.

augur ö′gər, *n.* among the Romans, one who sought knowledge of secret or future things by observing the flight and the cries of birds: a diviner: a soothsayer: an augury or portent (*Shak.,* app.). — *v.t.* to foretell from signs. — *v.i.* to guess or conjecture: to forebode. — *adj.* **au′gural** (-ū-rəl; -yər-əl). — *ns.* **au′gurer** (*Shak.*) an augur; **au′gurship; au′gury** the art or practice of auguring; an omen. — **augur well, ill, for** to be an encouraging, discouraging, sign with respect to. [L.; prob. from *avis,* bird.]

august¹ ö-gust′, *adj.* venerable: imposing: sublime: majestic. — *adv.* **august′ly.** — *n.* **august′ness.** [L. *augustus* — *augēre,* to increase, honour.]

august², **auguste** ow-gōōst′, *n.* a circus clown of the maladroit type. [Ger., Augustus.]

August ö′gəst, *n.* the eighth month of the year. [After the Roman emperor *Augustus.*]

Augustan ö-gust′ən, *adj.* pertaining to the Emperor *Augustus,* or to the time in which he reigned (31 B.C. — A.D. 14) — the most brilliant age in Roman literature: hence pertaining to any similar age, as the reign of Anne in English, and that of Louis XIV in French, literature: classic: refined.

auguste. See **august².**

Augustine ö′gəst-in, ö-gust′in, **Augustinian** -tin′i-ən, *ns.* one of any order of monks or nuns whose rule is based on the writings of St. Augustine: one who holds the

opinions of St Augustine, esp. on predestination and irresistible grace (*theol.*). — *adj.* **Augustin′ian** of or relating to St. Augustine. — *n.* **Augustin′ianism.** — **Augustinian canons** or **Austin canons** see **canon; Augustinian** or **Austin friars** or **hermits** the fourth order of mendicant friars, wearing a black habit, but not to be confused with the Black Friars or Dominicans.

Aujeszky's disease ow-yes′kis dizēz, a disease of pigs, with symptoms similar to those of rabies. [*Aujeszky,* a Hungarian scientist (died 1933), who identified it.]

au jour le jour ō zhōōr lə zhōōr, (Fr.) from day to day, from hand to mouth.

auk ök, *n.* a short-winged, heavy-bodied bird of the family *Alcidae.* — *n.* **auk′let** one of the smaller birds of the family. — **great auk** garefowl, extinct *c.* 1844; **little auk** an auk (*Plautus alle*) of the North Atlantic and Arctic Oceans, the rotche or dovekie. [O.N. *ālka.*]

aula ö′lə, *n.* a hall. — *adj.* **aulā′rian** relating to a hall. — *n.* at Oxford, a member of a hall, as distinguished from a collegian. — *adj.* **au′lic** of, or relating to a royal court: courtly. — **Aula Regis,** or **Curia Regis,** (*hist.*) a feudal assembly of tenants-in-chief: the Privy Council: the Court of King's Bench; **Aulic Council** (Ger. *Reichshofrat*) a court or personal council of the Holy Roman Empire, established in 1501 by Maximilian I, and co-ordinate with the Imperial Chamber (*Reichskammergericht*). [L. *aula,* Gr. *aulē,* court, courtyard, hall.]

auld öld, (*Scot.*) *adj.* old. — *adjs.* **auld′-farr′ant** (i.e. old-favouring) old-fashioned: precocious; **auld′-warld** old-world, ancient. — **the Auld Kirk** the Church of Scotland: whisky; **auld lang syne** lit. old long since, long ago; **Auld Reekie** old smoky, i.e. Edinburgh. [O.E. *ald.*]

aulic. See **aula.**

aulnage, aulnager. Variant spellings of **alnage, alnager.**

aulos ö′los, ow′los *n.* an ancient Greek wind instrument, a double pipe with double reeds: — *pl.* **aul′oi** (-*oi,* -*e*). [Gr.]

aumail ö-māl′, *v.t.* to enamel: to figure or variegate (*Spens.*). [See **enamel.**]

aumbry öm′bri, *n.* Same as **ambry.**

au mieux ō myø, (Fr.) on the best of terms.

aumil ö′mil, ä′mil, *n.* an amildar.

au naturel ō na-tü-rel, (Fr.) in the natural state: cooked plainly.

aunt änt, *n.* a father's or mother's sister, or an uncle's wife or a great-aunt (used with *cap.* as a title either before a woman's first name or independently): an old woman (*obs.*): a gossip (*obs.*): a procuress (*obs.*): a woman to whom one can turn for advice, sympathy, practical help, etc. (*fig.*): —(usu. in dim., with *cap.*) a title sometimes used by children for female friends of their parents: (in dim., with *cap.*) a facetious name for the British Broadcasting Corporation: **auntie, aunty.** — **Auntie** a facetious name for the British Broadcasting Corporation; **Aunt Sally** a pastime at fairs, in which sticks or balls are thrown to smash a pipe in the mouth of a wooden figure: a target for abuse (*fig.*). [O.Fr. *ante* — L. *amita,* a father's sister.]

aunter ön′tər, *n.* an old form of **adventure.** [O.Fr. *aventure.*]

au pair ō per, (Fr.) *adj.* orig. by mutual service without payment: used of arrangement whereby girls perform light domestic duties in exchange for board and lodging and pocket-money. — *n.* an au pair girl.

au pied de la lettre ō pyä də la letr′, (Fr.) literally.

au pis aller ō pē-za-lā, (Fr.) at the worst.

au poids de l'or ō pwa də lor, (Fr.) at its weight in gold, very dear.

au premier ō prə-myä, (Fr.) on the first (floor).

aura ö′rə, *n.* a supposed subtle emanation, esp. that essence which is claimed to emanate from all living things and to afford an atmosphere for occult phenomena: air, distinctive character (*fig.*): peculiar sensations that precede an attack in epilepsy, hysteria, and certain other ailments (*path*.): — *pl.* **aur′ae** (-*ē*), **aur′as.** — *adj.* **aur′al** pertaining to the air, or to a subtle vapour or exhalation arising from a body. [L. *aura*, a breeze.]

aural *ō′rəl, adj.* pertaining to the ear. — *adv.* **aur′ally.** — *adj.* **aur′iform** ear-shaped. — *ns.* **aur′iscope** an instrument for examining the ear; **aur′ist** a specialist in diseases of the ear. [L. *auris*, ear.]

aura popularis *ō′rə po-pū-la′ris,* ow-ra *po-poō-lä′ris*), (L.) the breeze of popular favour.

aurate *ō′rāt, n.* a salt of auric acid. — *adjs.* **au′rated** gold-coloured: compounded with auric acid; **aureate** (*ō′ri-ət*) gilded: golden: floridly rhetorical. — *ns.* **aurē′ity** the peculiar properties of gold; **Aurē′lia** a common genus of jelly-fishes: (without *cap*.) a jellyfish of this or a related genus: (without *cap*.) formerly, a chrysalis, from its golden colour. — *adj.* **aurē′lian** golden: of an aurelia. — Also *n.* (*obs*.) a lepidopterist. — *ns.* **aurē′ola**, **aureole** (*ō′ri-ōl*) a crown, or an increment to the ordinary blessedness of heaven, gained by virgins, martyrs, and doctors (*theol*.): the gold or coloured disc or ring round the head in a picture, symbolising glory: a glorifying halo (*fig*.): a halo or corona around the sun or moon, or the clear space within it (*meteor*.): the coloured rings around the spectre of the Brocken (*meteor*.): (apparently erroneously) a halo surrounding the whole figure (e.g. a *vesica piscis*): any halo-like appearance. — *adj.* **au′reoled** encircled with an aureole. — *ns.* **aureomycin** (-*mī′sin*) an antibiotic used against typhus and other diseases, got from Strepto*myces aureo*faciens; **au′reus** *ō′ri-əs,* ow′rā-ōōs a gold coin of the Roman empire: — *pl.* **au′rei** (-*ī*, -*ē*). — *adjs.* **au′ric** pertaining to gold: containing trivalent gold (*chem*.); **aurous** (*ō′rəs*) containing univalent gold. — **auric acid** a hypothetic acid of composition HAuO₂ — usually applied to auric hydroxide, Au(OH)₃, or auric oxide, Au₂O₃. [L. *aurum*, gold.]

aurea mediocritas *ō′rē-a mē-dē-ō′kri-tas,* ow′rā-a me-di-o′kri-täs, (L.) the golden or happy mean.

aureate, aurelia, etc., **Aurelia,** etc., **aureola,** etc. See **aurate.**

au reste *ō rest,* (Fr.) as for the rest: besides.

au revoir *ō rə-vwär,* (Fr.) goodbye until we meet again.

auric. See **aurate.**

auricle *ör′i-kl, n.* the external ear: an ear-like appendage to an atrium in the heart, or the atrium itself: an earlike lobe of a leaf, etc. — *adj.* **aur′icled** having appendages like ears. — *n.* **auric′ula** a species of primula (bear's ear, or dusty-miller): (with *cap*.) a genus of gasteropod molluscs. — *adj.* **auric′ular** pertaining to the ear: known by hearing, or by report: told privately. — *adv.* **auric′ularly.** — *adjs.* **auric′ulate** (-*lət*), **auric′ulated** ear-shaped. — **auricular confession** confession to a priest. [L. *auricula*, dim. of *auris*, the ear.]

auriferous *ör-if′ər-əs, adj.* bearing or yielding gold. — *v.t.* and *v.i.* **au′rify** to turn into gold. [L. *aurifer* — *aurum*, gold, *ferre,* to bear; *facĕre,* to make.]

auriform. See under **aural.**

aurify. See **auriferous.**

Auriga *ō-rī′gə, n.* a northern constellation. [L. *auriga*, charioteer.]

Aurignacian *ō-rig-nā′sh(y)en, adj.* belonging to an upper Palaeolithic culture that succeeded the Mousterian and preceded the Solutrean. [*Aurignac*, in Haute-Garonne, where objects of this culture have been found.]

auriscope, aurist. See under **aural.**

aurochs *ör′, owr′oks, n.* the extinct urus or wild ox: (erroneously) the European bison. [O.H.G. *ûr-ohso* — *ûr* (adopted into L. as *ūrus*, into Gr. as *ouros*), and *ohso,* ox.]

Aurora *ō-rō′rə, -rö′, n.* the dawn: the goddess of dawn: (without *cap*.) a rich orange colour: a luminous meteoric phenomenon of electrical character seen in and towards the Polar regions, with a tremulous motion, and streamers of light: — *pl.* **auro′ras, -rae.** — *adjs.* **auro′ral, auro′rean** pertaining to the dawn or the aurora: rosy: fresh and beautiful. — *adv.* **auro′rally.**

— **aurora borealis** (*bō-ri-ā′lis,* -*ä′lis* or *bö-*) or **septentrionalis** (*sep-ten-tri-on-ā′lis*) the northern aurora or northern lights; **aurora australis** (*ōs-trā′lis*) the southern lights, a similar phenomenon in the southern hemisphere. [L. *Aurōra*.]

aurous. See **aurate.**

aurum potabile *ō′rum po-tab′i-lē,* ow′rōōm *pō-täb′i-le,* (L.) lit. potable gold, a former medicine or cordial containing a small quantity of gold.

auscultation *ōs-kəl-tā′shən, n.* the art of discovering the condition of the lungs and heart by applying the ear or the stethoscope. — *v.t.* and *v.i.* **aus′cultate** to examine by auscultation. — *n.* **aus′cultător** one who practises auscultation: an instrument for the purpose: in Germany, formerly one who had passed his first public examination in law, and who was merely retained, not yet employed or paid by government. — *adj.* **auscultatory** (-*kul′tə-tə-ri*). [L. *auscultāre,* to listen.]

au second *ō sə-gŏ,* (Fr.) on the second (floor).

au secours *ō sə-kŏŏr,* (Fr.) help!

au sérieux *ō sā-ryø,* (Fr.) seriously.

Ausgleich *ows′glīhh,* (Ger.) *n.* a settlement: an arrangement: the agreement between Austria and Hungary in 1867.

Ausländer *ows′len-dər,* (Ger.) *n.* a foreigner.

Auslese *ows′lā-zə,* (Ger.) *n.* choice, selection: wine made from selected bunches of grapes.

Ausonian *ö-sō′ni-ən, adj.* Italian. [L. *Ausonia,* a poetical name for Italy.]

auspice *ös′pis, n.* an omen drawn from observing birds: augury: prognostic: (in *pl*.) patronage. — *v.t.* **auspicate** (*ös′pi-kāt*) to foreshow: to initiate or inaugurate with hopes of good luck. — *adj.* **auspicious** (-*pish′əs*) having good auspices or omens of success: favourable: fortunate: propitious. — *adv.* **auspi′ciously.** — *n.* **auspi′ciousness.** [Fr., — L. *auspicium* — *auspex, auspicis,* a bird-seer, from *avis,* bird, and *specĕre,* to look, to observe.]

Aussichtspunkt *ows′zihhts-pŏŏngkt,* (Ger.) *n.* a selected position for admiring scenery, a vantage point: — *pl.* **Aussichtspunkte** (-*tə*).

Aussie *oz′i, os′i,* (slang) *n.* and *adj.* Australian.

austenite *ös′tə-nīt, n.* a solid solution of carbon or other substance in one of the forms of iron. — **austenitic** (-*it′*) **stainless steels** stainless steels composed chiefly of austenite. [W. C. Roberts-Austen (1843–1902), English metallurgist.]

Auster *ös′tər, n.* the south wind. [L.]

austere *ös-tēr′, adj.* sour and astringent: harsh: severe: stern: grave: severe in self-discipline: severely simple, without luxury. — *adv.* **austere′ly.** — *ns.* **austere′ness, austerity** (-*ter′*) quality of being austere: severity of manners or life: harshness: asceticism: severe simplicity of style, dress, or habits. — *adj.* evincing or adopted in austerity. [L. *austērus* — Gr. *austēros* — *auein,* to dry.]

Austin. See **Augustine.**

Austral *ös′trəl, adj.* (also with *cap*.) southern. — *adj.* **Australasian** (-*ā′zhən*) pertaining to Australasia, or the lands that lie south-east of Asia. — *n.* a native or colonist of one of these. — *n.* **Australopithecus** (-*pith′ə-kəs* or -*pi-thē′kəs*) a genus of extinct primates, represented by skulls, etc., found in southern Africa, belonging to the subfamily **Aus′tralopithecinae** (-*sī′nē*). — *adj.* and *n.* **australopithecine** (-*pith′ə-sīn*). [L. *australis* — *Auster,* the south wind.]

Australian *ös-trā′li-ən, adj.* of, or pertaining to, Australia, the largest island in the world and the smallest continent, an independent member of the Commonwealth (formerly a British colony). — *n.* a person native to or resident in Australia. — *ns.* **Austrā′lianism** an Australian idiom: feeling for Australia; **aus′tralite** tektite found in the interior of Australia; **Aus′tralorp** an Australian breed of hen (*Austra*lian and *Orp*ington). — **Australia Day** (a public holiday celebrating) the anniversary of the founding of the colony of

New South Wales on 26 January 1788; **Australian crane** see **brolga; Australian rules (football)** an Australian code of football played by eighteen a side with an oval ball (familiarly **rules**).   [L. *austrālis*, southern — *Auster*, south wind.]

Austrian *ös'tri-ən, adj.* of or pertaining to *Austria.* — *n.* a native or citizen of Austria.

Austric *ös'trik, adj.* belonging to a family of languages divided into **Austrōāsiat'ic** (in eastern India and Indo-China, including the Munda or Kolarian, Mon-Khmer and Khasi groups, and the languages of the Semang and Sakai) and **Austrōnē'sian** (including the Indonesian, or Malay, Polynesian, Micronesian, and Melanesian groups).   [L. *Auster*, south wind, **Asiatic**, and Gr. *nēsos*, island.]

austringer *ö'strin-jər, n.* a keeper of goshawks. — Also **a'stringer, ostreger** (*os'tri-jər; Shak.*).   [O.Fr. *ostruchier*.]

Austroasiatic, Austronesian. See **Austric.**

aut-. See **auto-.**

autacoid *ö'tə-koid, n.* an internal secretion that excites or inhibits action in various tissues: a hormone or chalone.   [Gr. *autos*, self, *akos*, drug.]

autarchy *öt'är-ki, n.* absolute power. — *adjs.* **autar'-chic(al).** — *n.* **aut'archist.**   [Gr. *autos*, self, and *archein*, to rule.]

autarky *öt'är-ki, n.* self-sufficiency. — *adjs.* **autar'kic, -al.** — *n.* **aut'arkist.**   [Gr. *autarkeiā* — *autos*, self, *arkeein*, to suffice.]

autecology *ö-tek-ol'ə-ji, n.* (study of) the ecology of an individual organism or species. — *adjs.* **autecolog'ic, -al.**   [**aut-** (1) and **ecology.**]

auteur *ō-tœr,* (Fr.) *n.* a film-director, esp. thought of as the creator of a particular genre.

authentic, -al *ö-then'tik, -əl, adjs.* genuine: authoritative: true, entitled to acceptance, of established credibility: (of writing) trustworthy, as setting forth real facts: own, proper (*Milt.*): applied in music to old modes having their sounds within the octave above the final — opp. to *plagal*: in existentialism, used to describe the way of living of one who takes full cognisance of the meaninglessness of the world yet deliberately follows a consistent course of action. — *adv.* **authent'-ically.** — *v.t.* **authen'ticate** to make authentic: to prove genuine: to give legal validity to: to certify the authorship of. — *ns.* **authenticā'tion; authen'ticātor; authenticity** (*ö-thən-tis'i-ti*) quality of being authentic: state of being true or in accordance with fact: genuineness. — **authentic cadence** (*mus.*) a perfect cadence.   [Gr. *authentikos*, warranted — *autos*, self.]

author *öth'ər, n.* one who brings anything into being: a beginner of any action or state of things: the original writer of a book, article, etc. (*fem.* **auth'oress**): elliptically, an author's writings: one's authority for something (*arch.*). — Also *v.t.* — *n.* **auth'orcraft.** — *adjs.* **authorial** (*-thō', -thö'*); **auth'orish.** — *v.t.* **auth'orise, -ize** to give authority to: to sanction: to justify: to establish by authority. — *adj.* **authoris'able, -z.** — *n.* **authorisā'tion, -z.** — *adj.* **auth'orless** anonymous. — *ns.* **auth'oring; auth'orism** state or quality of being an author; **auth'orship.** — **Authorised Version** the English translation of the Bible completed in 1611.   [Through Fr. from L. *auctor* — *augēre, auctum,* to increase, to produce.]

authority *ö-thor'it-i, n.* legal power or right: power derived from office or character or prestige: weight of testimony: permission: a person or body holding power: an expert: a passage or book referred to in witness of a statement: the original bestower of a name (*biol.*). — *adj.* **authoritā'rian** setting authority above liberty. — Also *n.* — *n.* **authoritā'rianism.** — *adj.* **authoritative** (*ö-thor'it-āt-iv, ö-thor'it-ət-iv*) having the sanction or weight of authority: dictatorial. — *adv.* **author'itatively.** — *n.* **author'itativeness.**   [L. *auctōritas, -ātis* — *auctor*.]

autism *öt'izm, n.* absorption in imaginative activity directed by the thinker's wishes, with loss of contact with reality: an abnormality of childhood development affecting language and social communication. — *adj.* **autis'tic.** — *adv.* **autis'tically.**   [Gr. *autos*, self.]

auto-, aut- *ö-t(ō)-,* in composition, (1) self; (2) same; (3) self-caused; (4) automobile; (5) automatic.   [Gr. *autos*, self.]

auto¹ *ö'tō, n.* (chiefly *U.S.*) short for **automobile:** — *pl.* **au'tos.**

auto² *ä'ōō-tō,* (*Sp. and Port.*) *n.* an act: a drama, esp. a short religious one: an auto-da-fé: — *pl.* **au'tos.**

autoantibody *ö-tō-an'ti-bod-i,* (*med.*) *n.* an antibody produced in reaction to an antigenic constituent of the body's own tissues.   [**auto-** (1).]

Autobahn, autobahn *ow'tō-bän, ö'tə-,* (Ger.) *n.* a highway with dual carriageway for motor traffic only, a motorway.

autobiography *ö-tō-bi-og'rə-fi, n.* a person's life written by himself. — *n.* **autobiog'rapher.** — *adjs.* **autobiographic** (*-ō-graf'ik*), **-al.** — *adv.* **autobiograph'ically.**   [Gr. *autos*, self, *bios*, life, *graphein*, to write.]

autobus *ö'tō-bus, n.* a motor-bus.   [**auto-** (4), and **bus.**]

autocade. Same as **motorcade.**

autocar *ö'tō-kär, n.* a motor-car.   [**auto-** (4), and **car.**]

autocarp *ö'tō-kärp, n.* a fruit produced by self-fertilisation.   [Gr. *autos*, self, *karpos*, fruit.]

autocatalysis *ö-tō-kə-tal'is-is, n.* the catalysis of a reaction by a product of that reaction (*chem.*): reaction or disintegration of a cell or tissue due to the influence of one of its own products (*zool.*). — *v.t.* **autocatalyse, -yze** (*-kat'ə-līz*). — *adj.* **autocatalytic** (*-lit'ik*).   [**auto-** (2).]

autocephalous *ö-tō-sef'ə-ləs, adj.* having its own head: independent. — *n.* **autoceph'aly** condition of being autocephalous.   [Gr. *autos*, self, *kephalē*, head.]

autochanger *ö'tō-chān-jər, n.* (a record-player having) a device by means of which records are dropped from a stack one at a time on to the turntable.   [**auto-** (5).]

autochthon *ö-tok'thon, n.* one of the primitive inhabitants of a country: an aboriginal: — *pl.* **autoch'thons** and **autoch'thonēs.** — *adj.* **autoch'thonous** (of flora, fauna) indigenous: formed in the region where found (*geol.*): found in the place of origin: pertaining to ideas unrelated to a person's train of thought which come into the mind (*psych.*). — *ns.* **autoch'thonism, autoch'-thony** the condition of being autochthonous.   [Gr. *autochthōn*, sprung from the soil — *autos*, self, *chthōn, chthonos,* soil: the Athenians claiming to have actually sprung from the soil.]

autoclave *ö'tō-klāv, n.* a strong, sealed vessel for carrying out chemical reactions under pressure and at high temperatures, or one in which super-heated steam under pressure is used for sterilising or cooking.   [Fr., self-fastening apparatus — Gr. *autos*, self, perhaps L. *clāvis*, key or *clāvus*, nail.]

autocrat *ö'tō-krat, n.* one who rules by his own power: an absolute sovereign. — *n.* **autocracy** (*-tok'rə-si*) an absolute government by one man: despotism. — *adj.* **autocrat'ic.** — *adv.* **autocrat'ically.**   [Gr. *autokratēs* — *autos*, self, *kratos*, power.]

autocritique *ö-tō-krē-tēk,* (Fr.) *n.* self-criticism, esp. political.

autocross *ö'tō-kros, n.* a motor race round a grass field.   [**auto-** (4).]

autocue *ö'tō-kū, n.* a device showing a television speaker the text of what he has arranged to say.   [**auto-** (5).]

autocycle *ö'tō-sī'kl, n.* a motor-cycle.   [**auto-** (4), and **cycle.**]

auto-da-fé *ö'tō-da-fā', n.* the public declaration of the judgment passed on heretics in Spain and Portugal by the Inquisition: the infliction of the punishment that immediately followed thereupon, *esp.* the public burning of the victims: — *pl.* **autos-da-fé.**   [Port. *auto da fé* (Sp. *auto de fe*); *auto* — L. *actum,* act; *da,* of the — L. *de,* of; and *fé* — L. *fidēs,* faith.]

autodestruct *ö-tō-di-strukt', adj.* (of a craft, missile, etc.) capable of destroying itself: pertaining to the function of self-destruction. — *v.i.* to destroy itself. [**auto-** (1).]

autodidact *ö'-tō-ī'dakt, n.* a self-taught person. — *adj.* **autodidact'ic.** [Gr. *autodidaktos — autos,* self, *didaktos,* taught.]

auto-digestion. Same as **autolysis.**

autodyne *ö'tō-dīn, adj.* in radio, of an electrical circuit in which the same elements and valves are used both as oscillator and detector. [**auto-** (2), **(hetero)dyne.**]

autoerotic *ö-tō-ə-rot'ik, adj.* relating to sexual excitement or gratification gained from one's own body, with or without external stimulation. — *ns.* **autoerot'icism, autoer'otism.** [**auto-** (1), and Gr. *erōtikos,* amorous — *erōtaein,* to love.]

autoflare *ö'tō-flār, n.* an aircraft automatic landing system operating from an altitude of 50 feet and dependent on a very accurate radio altimeter. [**auto-** (5).]

autogamy *ö-tog'ə-mi, n.* self-fertilisation. — *adjs.* **autog'-amous, autogamic** *(ö-tō-gam'ik).* [Gr. *autogamos,* breeding alone — *autos,* self, *gamos,* marriage.]

autogenous *ö-toj'ə-nəs, adj.* self-generated: independent: of a graft, vaccine, produced from tissue, bacteria, from the patient's own body: of a joint, made without flux, etc., by melting edges together *(metal-working).* — *n.* **autogen'esis** spontaneous generation. — *adj.* **autogen'ic** self-generated or produced from the subject's own body, autogenous. — *n.sing.* **autogen'ics** (also **autogenic training**) a system of relaxation teaching voluntary control of bodily tension, etc. — *n.* **autog'eny** autogenesis. [Gr. *autogenēs — genos,* offspring.]

autogiro, autogyro *ö-tō-jī'rō, n.* a rotating-wing aircraft whose chief support in flight is derived from the reaction of the air upon freely-revolving rotors: — *pl.* **autogi'ros, -gy'ros.** [Orig. trademark; invented by Juan de la Cierva; Sp., — Gr. *autos,* self, *gyros,* circle.]

autograft *ö'tō-gräft, n.* a graft from one part to another of the same body. — Also *v.t.* [**auto-** (2) and **graft¹**.]

autograph *ö'tō-gräf, n.* one's own handwriting: a signature: an original manuscript. — *v.t.* to write with one's hand: to write one's signature in or on, to sign. — *adj.* of painting, sculpture, etc., done by the artist himself, not a pupil or follower. — *adj.* **autographic** *(-graf').* — *adv.* **autograph'ically.** — *n.* **autography** *(ö-tog'rəfi)* act of writing with one's own hand: reproduction of the outline of a writing or drawing by facsimile. — **autograph album, book** one in which to collect signatures, etc. [Gr. *autographos,* written with one's own hand — *autos,* self, *graphein,* to write.]

autogravure *ö-tō-grav-ūr', or ö', n.* a process of photo-engraving akin to autotype. [**auto-** (2).]

autoharp *ö'tō-härp, n.* a kind of zither, with button-controlled dampers, which produces chords. [**auto-** (5).]

autohypnosis *ö-tō-hip-nō'sis, n.* a self-induced hypnotic state, or the process of bringing it on. [**auto-** (1).]

auto-immunisation, -z-, *ö'tō-im-ū-nī-zā'shən, n.* production by a living body of antibodies which attack constituents of its own tissues, perhaps the cause of certain serious diseases **(auto-immune diseases).** — *n.* **auto-immun'ity.** [**auto-** (1).]

auto-intoxication *ö'tō-in-toks-i-kā'shən, n.* poisoning by substances produced within the body. — *n.* and *adj.* **au'to-intox'icant.** [**auto-** (1).]

autokinesis *ö-tō-kin-ē'sis, n.* spontaneous motion, esp. the apparent movement of a stationary object. — *adj.* **autokinet'ic.** [Gr. *autokinesis,* self-motion.]

autolatry *ö-tol'ə-tri, n.* worship of oneself. [Gr. *autos,* self, *latreiā,* worship.]

autology *ö-tol'ə-ji, n.* scientific study of oneself. [Gr. *autos,* self, *logos,* discourse.]

Autolycus *ö-tol'i-kəs, n.* a thief: a plagiarist: a snapper-up of unconsidered trifles. [From the character in Shakespeare's *Winter's Tale,* or in Greek mythology.]

autolysis *ö-tol'is-is, n.* the breaking down of dead tissue by the organism's own ferments. — *v.t.* and *v.i.* **aut'olyse, -yze** *(-līz)* to (cause to) undergo autolysis. —

adj. **autolyt'ic.** [Gr. *autos,* self, *lysis,* loosening.]

automaton *ö-tom'ə-tən, n.* a self-moving machine, or one that moves by concealed machinery: a living being regarded as without consciousness: one who acts by routine, without intelligence: — *pl.* **autom'atons, autom'ata.** — *n.* **aut'omat** (or *-mat'*) a restaurant where dishes, hot or cold, are obtained from slot machines: a slot machine of this kind: an automaton. — *v.t.* **automate** *(ö'tō-māt)* to apply automation to. — *adj.* **automatic** *(-tə-mat'ik)* working by itself without direct and continuing human operation: (of a firearm) reloading itself from an internal magazine, or able to continue firing as long as there is pressure on the trigger: of (the gears of) a motor vehicle, operated by automatic transmission: (of a telephone system) worked by automatic switches: (of behaviour, reactions, etc.) done, etc. without thinking, mechanical: occurring as a matter of course. — *n.* an automatic firearm, machine, etc.: the position of the switches, etc. on a machine, etc. that allows it to operate automatically. — *adj.* **automat'ical** *(arch.).* — *adv.* **automat'ically.** — *ns.* **automaticity** *(-tis'i-ti);* **automā'-tion** a high degree of mechanisation in manufacture, the handling of material between processes being automatic, and the whole automatically controlled; **autom'atism** automatic or involuntary action: power of self-moving: power of initiating vital processes from within the cell, organ, or organism, independently of any direct or immediate stimulus from without: the self-acting power of the muscular and nervous systems, by which movement is effected without intelligent determination: action without conscious volition: the doctrine that animals are automata, their movements, etc., being the result of mechanical laws: suspension of control by the conscious mind, so that ideas may be released from the unconscious — a technique of surrealism *(art);* **autom'atist** one who holds the doctrine of automatism: one who acts automatically. — **automatic drive** automatic transmission; **automatic pilot** also **autopilot** a device which can be set to steer an aircraft or a ship on a chosen course: used *(fig.)* of an automatism that takes over one's actions or behaviour in fatigue, abstraction, etc.; **automatic transmission** in a motor vehicle, power transmission by fluid drive, allowing gears to change automatically; **automatic writing** writing performed without the volition of the writer. — **automatic teller machine** (abbrev. **ATM**) an electronic panel set into the exterior wall of a bank from which (on the insertion of one's cash card and the keying of one's personal identification number) to obtain cash or information about one's bank account. [Gr. *automatos,* self-moving — *autos,* self.]

automobile *ö-tō-mō-bēl', or ö', or -mō', adj.* self-moving. — *n.* a motor-car. — *n.pl.* **automobil'ia** collector's items of motoring interest. — *ns.* **automō'bilism, automō'-bilist.** [Gr. *autos,* self; L. *mōbilis,* mobile.]

automorphism *ö-tō-mör'fizm, n.* ascription to others of one's own characteristics: isomorphism of an algebraic system with itself *(math.).* — *adj.* **automor'phic** marked by automorphism: idiomorphic. — *adv.* **automor'-phically.** [Gr. *autos,* self, *morphē,* form.]

automotive *ö-tō-mō'tiv, adj.* self-propelling: pertaining to automobiles: pertaining to the motor-car trade. [Gr. *autos,* self, L.L. *motivus,* causing to move.]

autonomy *ö-ton'əm-i, n.* the power or right of self-government, esp. partial self-government: the doctrine that the human will carries its guiding principle within itself (Kant's *philos.*). — *adjs.* **autonomic** *ö-tō-nom'ik,* self-governing: pertaining to the autonomic nervous system: spontaneous *(bot., zool.);* **autonom'ical.** — *n.sing.* **autonom'ics** the study of self-regulating systems for process control. — *n.* **auton'omist.** — *adj.* **auton'-omous** (of a country, etc.) (partially) self-governing: independent: (of the will) guided by its own principles *(philos.);* autonomic *(bot., zool.).* — **autonomic nervous system** system of nerve fibres, innervating muscles, glands, etc., whose actions are automatic. [Gr.

autonomos — nomos, law.]

autonym *ö'to-nim*, or *-tə-, n*. a writing published under the author's real name: an author's real name. — Also *adj*. [Gr. *autos*, self, *onyma* (*onoma*), name.]

autophagous *ö-tof'ə-gəs, adj*. self-devouring: of a bird, capable of feeding itself from the moment of hatching. — *n*. **autophagy** (*-ə-ji*) sustenance by self-absorption of the tissues of the body: eating or biting of part of one's own body. [Gr. *autos*, self, *phagein*, to eat.]

autophanous *ö-tof'ə-nəs, adj*. self-luminous. [Gr. *autos*, self, *phānos*, bright.]

autophoby *ö-tof'əb-i, n*. a shrinking from making any reference to oneself. [Gr. *autos*, self, *phobos*, fear.]

autophony *ö-tof'ən-i, n*. in the diagnosis of thoracic disease, observation of the resonance of one's own voice by speaking with the ear on the patient's chest. [Gr. *autos*, self, *phōnē*, sound.]

autopilot. See **automatic pilot** under **automaton**.

autopista *ow'tö-pēs-ta*, (Sp.) *n*. a highway for motor traffic only: a motorway.

autoplasty *ö'tö-plas-ti, n*. grafting of healthy tissue from another part of the same body. — *adj*. **autoplas'tic**. [Gr. *autos*, self, *plastos*, formed.]

autopoint *ö'tö-point, n*. a point-to-point over rough country in motor vehicles. [auto- (4).]

autopsy *ö'top-si*, or *-top', n*. **autop'sia**, *ns*. personal inspection: a post-mortem examination. — *v.t*. **autopsy**. — *adjs*. **autopt'ic, -al**. — *adv*. **autopt'ically**. [Gr. *autos*, self, *opsis*, sight.]

autoradiograph *ö-tö-rā'di-ö-gräf, n*. in tracer work, the record of a treated specimen on a photographic plate caused by radiations from the radioisotope used. — *adj*. **autoradiograph'ic**. — *n*. **autoradiog'raphy** (*-og'raf-i*) the production of autoradiographs. [auto- (1).]

autorickshaw *ö-tö-rik'shö, n*. a light, three-wheeled vehicle powered by a motor-cycle engine, used in India, etc. [auto- (4).]

autoroute *ö-tö-rōōt*, (Fr.) *n*. a highway for motor traffic only: a motorway.

autoschediasm *ö-tö-sked'i-azm*, or *-skēd', n*. anything extemporised. — *v.t*. **autosched'iaze** (*-āz*) — *adj*. **autoschedias'tic**. [Gr. *autoschediasma*, improvisation, *autoschediazein*, to extemporize — *autoschedon*, on the spot — *autos*, self, *schedios*, off-hand.]

autoscopy *ö-tos'kə-pi*, (*psych*.) *n*. hallucination of an image of one's body. — *adj*. **autoscop'ic**. [Gr. *autos*, self, *skopeein*, to see.]

autosome *ö'tö-sōm, n*. a chromosome other than a sexchromosome. — *adj*. **autosom'al**. [Gr. *autos*, self, *sōma*, body.]

autostrada *ä'ōōtö-strä-da*, (It.) *n*. a highway for motor traffic only, a motorway.

auto-suggestion *ö'tö-sə-jes'chən, n*. a mental process similar to suggestion, but originating in a belief in the subject's own mind. [auto- (3).]

autotelic *ö-tö-tel'ik, adj*. being an end in itself, or its own justification. [Gr. *autotelēs — autos*, self, *telos*, end.]

autotheism *ö-tö-thē'izm, n*. assumption of divine powers: the doctrine of the self-subsistence of God, esp. of the second person in the Trinity. — *n*. **autothe'ist**. [Gr. *autos*, self, *theos*, a god.]

autotimer *ö'tö-tīm-ər, n*. a device on a cooker, etc. that can be adjusted in advance to turn the apparatus on or off at a desired time. [auto- (5).]

autotomy *ö-tot'ə-mi, n*. reflex separation of part of the body. [Gr. *autos*, self, *tomē*, cut.]

autotoxin *ö-tö-tok'sin, n*. a poisonous substance formed within the organism against which it acts. [Gr. *autos*, self, and **toxin**.]

autotrophic *ö-tö-trof'ik, adj*. capable of building up food materials from inorganic matter. — *n*. **au'totroph** an autotrophic organism. [Gr. *autos*, self, *trophē*, food.]

autotype *ö'tö-tīp, n*. a true impress or copy of the original: a process of printing from a photographic negative in a permanent pigment. — *v.t*. to reproduce by such a process. — *n*. **autotypog'raphy** a process by which

drawings made on gelatine are transferred to a plate from which impressions may be taken. [auto- (2).]

autovac *ö'tö-vak, n*. a vacuum mechanism in a motor-car for raising petrol to a higher tank so that it may flow by gravity to the carburettor. [auto- (4).]

autrefois acquit, attaint, convict *ōt-rə-fwä a-kē, a-tē, kö-vē*, (*law*) three defence pleas, arguing that a defendant cannot be charged a second time with an offence of which he has been acquitted, or a (capital) offence of which he has been found guilty. [Fr.]

autumn *ö'təm, n*. the third season of the year, when fruits are gathered in, generally (in the northern hemisphere) from August or September to October or November: astronomically, from the autumnal equinox to the winter solstice: a period of harvest or of maturity. — *adj*. **autum'nal** (*ö-tum'nəl*) pertaining to autumn: blooming in autumn: beyond the prime: withering or withered. — *adv*. **autum'nally**. — *adj*. **au'tumny** (*-tə-mi*; *coll*.) autumn-like. — **autumn crocus** a species of *Colchicum*, meadow-saffron. [L. *autumnus*.]

autunite *ö'tun-īt, n*. a mineral composed of a hydrous phosphate of uranium and calcium. [*Autun* in France, one of its localities.]

au voleur *ö vo-lœr*, (Fr.) stop thief!

auxanometer *öks-ən-om'it-ər, n*. an instrument for measuring plant-growth. [Gr. *auxanein*, to grow, *metron*, measure.]

aux armes *ö-zärm*, (Fr.) to arms.

auxesis *ök-sē'sis, n*. increase in size: hyperbole: growth of cell, etc. — *adj*. **auxet'ic**. — *n*. something that promotes auxesis. [Gr. *auxēsis*, increase.]

auxiliary *ög-zil'yər-i, adj*. helping: subsidiary: peripheral (*comput*.). — *n*. a helper: a subordinate or assistant person or thing: an auxiliary verb (*gram*.): (esp. in *pl*.) a soldier serving with another nation: a naval vessel not used for combat. — *n*. and *adj*. **auxil'iar** (*arch*.) (an) auxiliary. — **auxiliary verb** (*gram*.) a verb that helps to form the mood, tense or voice of another verb. [L. *auxiliāris — auxilium*, help — *augēre*, to increase.]

auxin *öks'in, n*. any of a number of growth-promoting substances present in minute quantities in plants. [Gr. *auxein*, to increase.]

auxometer *öks-om'it-ər*, (*opt*.) *n*. an instrument for measuring magnifying power. [Gr. *auxein*, to increase, *metron*, measure.]

Av *av, n*. a variant spelling of **Ab**.

ava[1], ava' *ə-vö'*, (*Scot*.) *adv*. at all. [For **of all**.]

ava[2] *ä'vä*. Same as **kava**.

avadavat. Same as **amadavat**.

avail[1], *ə-vāl', v.t*. to be of value or service to: to benefit (used reflexively with *of* in the sense of make use, take advantage): to give (someone) the benefit (of), inform (someone of) (*U.S.*; *arch*.). — *v.i*. to be of use: to answer the purpose: to draw advantage, be the better (*Shak*.). — *n*. effectual advantage (esp. in phrases such as *of, to no avail, of any avail*): (in *pl*.) profit proceeds (*obs*.). — *n*. **availabil'ity** quality of being available: power of effecting or promoting an end: the possession of qualities, other than merit, which predispose a candidate to success in an election (esp. *U.S. politics*; *arch*.). — *adj*. **avail'able** that one may avail oneself of: accessible: within reach: obtainable: to be had or drawn upon: valid (*law*): profitable (*obs*.). — *n*. **avail'ableness**. — *adv*. **avail'ably**. — *adjs*. **avail'ful** (*obs*.) of avail: serviceable; **avail'ing**. — *adv*. **avail'ingly**. [L. *ad*, to, *valēre*, to be worth, to be strong; app. modelled on **vail[3]**.]

avail[2], **availe**. Same as **avale**.

aval *āv'əl, adj*. pertaining to a grandparent. [L. *avus*, grandfather.]

avalanche *av'ə-länsh, -länch, -ö-, n*. a hurtling mass of snow, with ice and rock, descending a mountain side: a snow-slip, as from a roof: an overwhelming influx: a shower of particles resulting from the collision of a high-energy particle with matter (*nuc*.). — *v.t*. and *v.i*. to carry or come down as or like an avalanche. [Fr. dial. — *avaler*; see next word.]

avale, avail, availe, *ə-vāl', v.t.* to lower (*Spens.*): to doff (*obs.*). — *v.i.* (*Spens.*) to come down: to alight. [Fr. *avaler,* to descend — *à* (L. *ad*), to, *val* (L. *vallis*), valley.]

avant *a-vä,* (Fr.) before. — *ns.* **avant-goût** (*gōō*) a foretaste; **avant-propos** (*prō-pō*) preliminary matter: preface.

avant-courier *av-ä-kōōr'i-ər, -kōō-ryä, n.* one sent before: (in *pl.*) scouts or advance guard. [Fr. *avant-coureur,* forerunner, scout; *avant-courrier,* forerunner.]

avant-garde *av-ä-gärd', n.* those who create or support the newest ideas and techniques in an art, etc. — Also *adj.* — *ns.* **avant-gard'ism** avant-garde theory or practice, or support of these; **avant-gard'ist(e)** a member of the avant-garde. [Fr. *avant-garde,* vanguard.]

avanti *a-vän'tē,* (It.) *interj.* forward!

avanturine. See **aventurine.**

avarice *av'ər-is, n.* eager desire for wealth: covetousness. — *adj.* **avaricious** (*-ish'əs*) extremely covetous: greedy of gain. — *adv.* **avari'ciously.** — *n.* **avari'ciousness.** [Fr., — L. *avāritia* — *avārus,* greedy — *avēre,* to pant after.]

avast *ə-väst',* (*naut.*) *interj.* hold fast! stop! [Prob. Du. *houd vast,* hold fast.]

avatar *a-və-tär', n.* the descent of a Hindu deity in a visible form: incarnation: supreme glorification of any principle (*fig.*). [Sans. *ava,* away, down, and root *tar-,* to pass over.]

avaunt¹ *ə-vönt', interj.* move on: begone. — *n.* (*Shak.*) dismissal. — *v.i.* to advance (*Spens.*): to depart (*obs.*). [Fr. *avant,* before — L. *ab,* from, *ante,* before.]

avaunt² *ə-vönt',* (*obs.*) *v.t.* and *v.i.* to boast. — *n.* a boast. [O.Fr. *avanter* — L.L. *vānitāre,* to boast — L. *vānus,* vain.]

ave *ā'vē, ä'vi,* or *ä'vä, interj.* be well and happy: hail. — *n.* an address or prayer to the Virgin Mary, in full, **ave Maria** (*ä'vä mə-rē'ə*) or **ave Mary,** the Hail Mary, or angelic salutation (Luke i. 28). [Imper. of L. *avēre,* to be well. See **angelus.**]

ave atque vale *ā'vē at'kwi vä'lē, ä'vä(-wä) at'kwe vä'lä* (*-wä'*), (L.) hail and farewell.

avec plaisir *a-vek ple-zēr,* (Fr.) with pleasure

Avena *a-vē'nə, n.* the oat genus of grasses. — *adj.* **avenaceous** (*av-i-nā'shəs*) of the nature of oats. [L. *avēna,* oats.]

avenge *ə-venj', -venzh', v.t.* to vindicate: to take vengeance on someone on account of. — *n.* (*obs.*) revenge. — *adjs.* **avenge'ful; avenge'ing.** — *ns.* **avenge'ment; aveng'er:** — *fem.* **aveng'eress.** [O.Fr. *avengier* — L. *ad,* to, *vindicāre,* to claim. See **vengeance.**]

avenir *av-ə-nēr,* (Fr.) *n.* future.

avens *av'ənz, n.* any plant of the rosaceous genus *Geum* (**water avens** *Geum rivale*; **wood avens** herb-bennet): also the related sub-alpine **mountain avens** (*Dryas octopetala*). [O.Fr. *avence.*]

aventail, aventaile *av'ən-tāl, n.* the flap or movable part of a helmet in front, for admitting air. [O.Fr. *esventail,* air-hole — L. *ex,* out, *ventus,* wind.]

aventre *a-ven'tr,* (*Spens.*) *v.t.* apparently, to thrust, direct. [Origin unknown.]

aventure *ə-ven'chər.* Obsolete form of **adventure.**

aventurine *a-ven'chə-rin,* **avanturine** *van', ns.* a brown, spangled kind of Venetian glass: a kind of quartz enclosing spangles of mica or haematite (also **gold'-stone**). — *adj.* shimmering or spangled, as kinds of feldspar or sealing-wax. [It. *avventura,* chance — because of the accidental discovery of the glass.]

avenue *av'ən-ū,* in U.S. *-ōō, n.* the principal approach to a country-house, usually bordered by trees: a double row of trees, with or without a road: a wide and handsome street, with or without trees: any passage or entrance into a place: means of access or attainment (*fig.*). [Fr., — L. *ad,* to, *venīre,* to come.]

aver¹ *ə-vûr', v.t.* to declare to be true: to affirm or declare positively: to prove or justify (*law*): — *pr.p.* **averr'ing;** *pa.p.* **averred'.** — *n.* **aver'ment** positive assertion: a formal offer to prove a plea (*law*): the proof offered (*law*). [Fr. *avérer* — L. *ad,* and *vērus,* true.]

aver² *ā'vər, n.* possessions (*obs.*): cattle (*obs.*): a draught animal, esp. an old or worthless cart-horse (*Scot.*). [O.Fr. *aveir, aver* (Fr. *avoir*), possessions, stock — L. *habēre,* to have.]

average *av'ər-ij, n.* orig. a customs duty or similar charge: any expense other than freight payable by the owner of shipped goods: expense or loss by damage of ship or cargo: equitable distribution of expense or loss: assessment of compensation in the same proportion as amount insured bears to actual worth: arithmetical mean value of any quantities: estimation of such a mean: loosely, ordinary or prevailing value, common run. — *adj.* mean: prevailing, ordinary. — *v.t.* to obtain the average of: to amount to on an average: to do on an average. — *v.t.* and *v.i.* to even out to an average. — **average adjuster** an assessor employed by an insurance company in marine claims. — **law of averages** pop., a proposition stating that the mean of a situation is maintained by the averaging of its extremes. [Cf. Fr. *avarie,* It. *avaria,* duty on goods; poss. conn. with foregoing.]

Avernus *a-vûr'nəs, a-ver'nōōs, -wer', n.* the infernal regions: any abyss — from Lake Avernus in Campania. [L., — Gr. *aornos* (*limnē*), birdless (lake), from the tradition that birds were killed by the lake's poisonous exhalations.]

Averr(h)oism *av-ər-ō'izm, n.* the doctrine of the Arab philosopher *Averrhoës* (1126–98), that the soul is perishable, the only immortal soul being the world-soul from which individual souls went forth, and to which they return. — *n.* **Averr(h)ō'ist.**

averruncate *av'ər-ung-kāt,* (*rare*) *v.t.* to ward off: (wrongly) to uproot. — *ns.* **averruncā'tion; av'erruncātor** an instrument for cutting off branches of trees. [L. *āverruncāre,* to avert, perh. confused with *ēruncāre,* to weed out.]

averse *ə-vûrs', adj.* disinclined (with *to*; but some prefer *from*): reluctant: turned away or backward. — *adv.* **averse'ly.** — *ns.* **averse'ness; aver'sion** turning aside: dislike: hatred: the object of dislike. — *adj.* **aver'sive** showing aversion: with purpose, or result, of averting. — *v.t.* **avert'** to turn aside: to prevent: to ward off. — *adj.* **avert'ed.** — *adv.* **avert'edly.** — *adj.* **avert'ible,** *rarely* **avert'able,** capable of being averted. — **aversion therapy** treatment of a person suffering from a perversion or a compulsive form of behaviour by associating his or her thoughts about it with something unpleasant such as the administration of an electric shock. [L. *āvertēre, āversus* — *ab,* from, *vertēre,* to turn.]

avert. See **averse.**

avertiment *a-vûr'ti-ment,* (*Milt.*) *n.* advertisement.

Avertin® *a-vûr'tin, n.* tradename of the anaesthetic *tribromoethanol.*

Aves *ā'vēz,* L. *ä'vās, -wās, n.pl.* birds as a class of vertebrates. — *adjs.* **ā'vian, avine** (*ā'vīn*) of birds. — *ns.* **ā'viarist** one who keeps an aviary; **ā'viary** a large cage or the like for keeping birds; **Avicula** (*av-ik'ū-lə*; from the winglike shape) a genus of pearl oysters, giving name to the family **Avicū'lidae** (*-dē*) and **Avicūlā'ria** the bird-catching spider genus, giving name to the family **Avicūlariidae** (*-lar'i-i-dē*); **ā'viculture** bird-rearing: bird-fancying; **āvifau'na** the assemblage of birds found in a region. — *adj.* **ā'viform** bird-like in form or structure; **avine** avian. [L. *avis,* bird, *avicula,* little bird, *aviculārius,* bird-keeper.]

Avesta *ə-ves'tä, n.* the Zoroastrian holy Scriptures. — *adjs.* **Aves'tan, Aves'tic** of the Avesta or its East Iranian language. — *ns.* the language of the Avesta, also called Zend. [Pehlevi *Avîstâk,* lore.]

avgas *av'gas,* (*U.S.*) *n.* any kind of aviation *gasoline.*

avian, aviary, Avicula, etc. See **Aves.**

aviate *ā'vi-āt, v.i.* to fly mechanically, navigate the air, a back-formation from **aviation.** — *ns.* **āviā'tion** the art or practice of mechanical flight; **ā'viātor** an airman, flying man; **aviatrix** (*ā-vi-ā'triks*) a female pilot; **aviette** (*av-yet', ā-vi-et'*) an aeroplane driven by man-power. — *adj.* **āvion'ic.** — *n. sing.* **āvion'ics** the science concerned with development and use of electronic and electrical devices for aircraft (*avi*ation electr*onics*). — **aviation spirit** a motor fuel with a low initial boiling-point and complying with a certain specification, for use in aeroplanes. [L. *avis*, a bird.]

avid *av'id*, *adj*. greedy: eagerly desirous. — *n.* **avid'ity.** — *adv.* **av'idly.** [L. *avidus*.]

aviette. See **aviate.**

aviform, avine. See **Aves.**

avion *av-yɔ̃*, (Fr.) *n*. aeroplane. — **par avion** (*par av-yɔ̃*) by air: by airmail.

avionic(s). See **aviate.**

avisandum. See **avizandum.**

avis au lecteur *a-vē ō lek-tœr*, (Fr.) *n*. notice to the reader.

avise, avize, avyze *a-vīz'*, obs. forms (*Spens.*, etc.) of **advise.** — *n.* **avise'ment.** — *adj.* **avize'full** (*Spens.*) watchful. — *n.* **avī'so** a notification: an advice-boat: — *pl.* **avi'sos.**

avised. See **black-a-vised** under **black.**

avital *ə-vī'tl*, *av'i-tl*, *adj*. of a grandfather: ancestral. [L. *avītus — avus*, a grandfather.]

avitaminosis *ā-vit-ə-min-ōs'is*, *n*. lack of vitamins or a condition due to this. [Gr. *a-*, priv.]

avizandum *av-iz-an'dəm*, (*Scots law*) *n*. private consideration of a case by a judge before giving judgment. — Also **avisan'dum.** [Gerund of L.L. *avizāre*, *avisāre*, to advise.]

avize. See **avise.**

avocado *a-və-kä'dō*, *n*. a tropical lauraceous tree: (also **avocado pear** (*pār*)) its pear-shaped fruit (also **alligator pear**): the colour of the skin of the fruit, blackish-green: the colour of the flesh of the fruit, yellowish-green: — *pl.* **avoca'dos.** — Also *adj*. [Sp. *aguacate* — Aztec *ahuacatl*.]

avocat consultant *a-vō-kä kɔ̃-sül-tā*, (Fr.) consulting lawyer, chamber counsel.

avocation *av-ə-kā'shən*, *n*. properly, a diversion or distraction from one's regular employment: improperly used for **vocation,** business which calls for one's time and attention: diversion of the thoughts from any employment (*arch.*): the calling of a case to a higher court (*law*). [L. *āvocātiō, -ōnis*, a calling away — *ab*, from, *vocāre*, to call.]

avocet, avoset *av'ə-set*, *n*. a wading bird (genus *Recurvirostra*) with webbed feet and long, slender, curved, elastic bill. [Fr. *avocette*, It. *avosetta*.]

Avogadro's constant, number *a-və-gä'drōz kon'stant, num'bər*, the number of specified elementary units (e.g. molecules) in a mole of any substance; **Avogadro's law, rule, hypothesis** the law that at equal temperature and pressure equal volumes of gases contain the same number of molecules. [A. *Avogadro* (1776–1856), Italian physicist.]

avoid *ə-void'*, *v.t.* to evade: to shun: to empty (*obs.*): to invalidate (*law*): to leave, to quit (*Shak.*): to dismount from. — *v.i.* (*obs.*) to take oneself off. — *adj.* **avoid'able.** — *n.* **avoid'ance** the act of avoiding or shunning: act of annulling: the shunning of certain relatives among primitive peoples (*anthrop.*). [A.Fr. *avoider*, O.Fr. *esvuidier* — L. *ex*, out, and root of **void.**]

avoirdupois *av-ər-də-poiz'*, or *av'*, or *av-wär-dü-pwä'*, *n*. a system of weights in which the lb. equals 16 oz.: (esp. *facet.*) weight: heaviness or stoutness. — *adj*. of the system of weights. [O.Fr. *aveir de pes*, to have weight — L. *habēre*, to have, *dē*, from, *pēnsum*, that which is weighed.]

avoision *ə-voi'zhən*, *n*. a portmanteau-word coined by the Institution of Economic Affairs in 1979 to represent a compromise, and blurring of the moral distinction between, tax *avoi*dance (legal) and tax eva*sion* (illegal).

à volonté *a vo-lɔ̃-tā*, (Fr.) at pleasure.

avoset. See **avocet.**

a vostro beneplacito *a vos'trō bā-nā-plä'chē-tō*, (It.) at your pleasure, at your will.

à votre santé *a votr' sä-tā*, (Fr.) to your health.

avouch *ə-vowch'*, *v.t.* to avow: to acknowledge: to vouch for: to assert positively: to maintain: to guarantee: to own to: to appeal to. — *v.i.* to give assurance. — *n.* (Shak.) evidence. — *adj.* **avouch'able.** — *n.* **avouch'ment.** [O. Fr. *avochier* — L. *advocāre*, to call to one's aid. See **vouch, advocate.**]

avoué *a-voo̅-ā*, (Fr.) *n*. attorney, solicitor.

avoure *a-vowr'*, (*Spens.*) *n*. avowal. [See **avow.**]

avouterer *a-voo̅'tər-ər*, **avoutrer** *-trər*, **avoutry** *-tri*. Obs. forms of **adulterer, adultery.**

avow *ə-vow'*, *v.t.* to declare: to acknowledge: to maintain. — *v.i.* (*law*) to justify an act done. — *n.* a solemn promise: a vow. — *adj.* **avow'able.** — *ns.* **avow'ableness; avow'al** a positive declaration: an acknowledgment: a frank confession. — *adj.* **avowed'.** — *adv.* **avow'edly.** — *n.* **avow'ry** the act of avowing and justifying in one's own right the distraining of goods (*law*): advocacy considered as personified in a patron saint (*obs.*). [O.Fr. *avouer*, orig. to swear fealty to — I_ *ad*, to, and L.L. *vōtāre* — L. *vōtum*, a vow: with sense affected by L. *advocāre*. See **vow, avouch.**]

avoyer *a-vwa-yā*, (Fr.) *n*. formerly the chief magistrate in some Swiss cantons.

a vuestra salud *a voo̅-äs'tra sä-loo̅dh'*, (Sp.) to your health.

avulse *ə-vuls'*, *v.t.* to pluck or tear away. — *n.* **avul'sion** forcible separation: sudden removal of land by change of a river's course, whereby it remains the property of the original owner (opp. to **alluvion**). [L. *āvellĕre, āvulsum*.]

avuncular *ə-vung'kū-lər*, *adj*. of or suitable to an uncle: benign, kindly. [L. *avunculus*, an uncle.]

avvogadore *a-vō-ga-dō'rä*, (It.) *n*. an official criminal prosecutor in Venice.

avyze. See **avise.**

aw *ö*, *interj*. expressing disappointment, sympathy, disgust, etc.

awa, awa' *ə-wo'*, *-wä'*, (*Scot.*) *adj*. away.

await *ə-wāt'*, *v.t.* to wait or look for: to be in store for: to attend: to lie in wait for, to watch (*obs.*). — *n.* (*Spens.*) an ambush, watch. [O.N.Fr. *awaitier — à*, to; see **wait**[1].]

awake *ə-wāk'*, *v.t.* to rouse from sleep: to rouse from inaction. — *v.i.* to cease sleeping: to rouse oneself from sleep or indifference: — *pa.t.* **awoke', awaked'; pa.p. awaked', awoke'** or **awōk'en.** — *adj.* not asleep: vigilant: aware, cognisant (with *to*). — *v.t.* **awak'en** to awake: to rouse into interest or attention: to call to a sense of sin (*theol.*). — *v.i.* to awake: to spring into being. — *adj.* **awak'ening** becoming awake: rousing: revivifying, reanimating. — *n.* a becoming awake, aware, active: a throwing off of indifference or ignorance: a rousing. — *n.* and *adj.* **awak'ing.** — **be awake to** to be fully aware of. [O.E. *āwæcnan* (pa.t. *āwōc*, pa.p. *āwacen*), confused with *āwacian* (pa.t. *āwacode*). See **wake**[1], **watch.**]

awanting *ə-wont'ing*, (chiefly *Scot.*) *adj*. wanting: missing. [**a**[3], and the gerund of **want.**]

award *ə-wörd'*, *v.t.* to adjudge: to determine: to grant. — *n.* judgment: final decision, esp. of arbitrators: that which is awarded: a prize. [O.Fr. *ewarder, eswarder* — L. *ex*, in sense of thoroughly, and the root of **ward, guard.**]

aware *ə-wār'*, *adj*. wary: informed, conscious (with *of*). — *n.* **aware'ness** state of being aware: consciousness, esp. a dim form. [O.E. *gewær — wær*, cautious. See **ware**[3].]

awarn *a-wörn'*, (*Spens.*) *v.t.* to warn. [Pfx. *a-*, intensive, and **warn**[1].]

awash *ə-wosh'*, *adv*. on a level with the surface of the water: afloat at the mercy of the waves. — *adj.* having the surface covered with water: full of (with *with*). [**a**[3], and **wash.**]

awatch *ə-woch'*, *adv*. on the watch. [**a**[3], and **watch.**]

awave *ə-wāv'*, *adv*. in a wave: in waves. [**a**[3], and **wave.**]

away *ə-wā'*, *adv*. onward: continuously: without hesitation, stop, or delay: forthwith: out of the place in question: not at home: on the opponents' ground (*sport*; also *adj.*), at or to a distance: off: in or into an averted direction: out of existence, life, or consciousness: with effect of removal or elimination: far: about (with *here*, *there*, *where*; now *dial.*): with omission of verb = go or (with *with*) take away (usu. *imper.*), to endure (with *with*). — *n.* in football pools, a match won by a team playing on the opponents' ground. — *interj.* begone: get out. — *adv.* **aways′** (*obs.*, *Spens.* **awayes′**) away. — **away from it all** in or into a place which is remote from the bustle of life; **do away with** to abolish; **explain away** to explain so as to make the thing explained seem not to exist; **fall away** to dwindle: to waste away: to lose zeal and drop off, as followers; **fire away** go on, proceed now without further delay; **make away with** to destroy: to murder: to steal; **once and away** (now usu. **once in a way**) on occasion. [O.E. *aweg*, *onweg* — *on*, on, *weg*, way.]

awdl *owdl*, (*W.*) *n.* a Welsh ode conforming to the strict metrical, alliterative and internal rhyming conventions of traditional bardic verse.

awe *ö*, *n.* reverential wonder or fear: dread: power to inspire awe (*arch.*). — *v.t.* to strike with or influence by awe or fear. — *adjs.* **awed** (*öd*) awe-stricken: expressive of awe; **awe′less** without awe: fearless: regarded without awe (*Shak.*). — *n.* **awe′lessness.** — *adj.* **awe′some, aw′some** awed: awe-inspiring (*Scot.*): dreadful. — *adv.* **awe′somely.** — *n.* **awe′someness.** — *adj.* **aw′ful** inspiring awe: filled with awe: very bad, tiresomely great, etc. (*coll.*). — *adv.* very (*coll.*). — *adv.* **aw′fully** in an awe-inspiring or awe-stricken manner: with awe: very (*coll.*). — *n.* **aw′fulness.** — **awe′-inspiring; awe′-stricken, awe′-struck** struck with awe (*v.t.* **awe′-strike**). [O.N. *agi*; cf. O.E. *ege*, fear; Gr. *achos*, distress.]

aweary *ə-wē′ri*, *adj.* weary. — *adj.* **awea′ried** weary. [Pfx. *a-*, intensive, and **weary**[1].]

a-weather *ə-wedh′ər*, (*naut.*) *adv.* towards the weather or windward side — opp. to *alee*. [a[3].]

a-week′ *ə-wēk′*, *adv.* in the week. [a[3].]

aweel *ə-wēl′*, (*Scot.*) *interj.* well: well then. [**ah well.**]

a-weigh *ə-wā′*, *adv.* in the process of being weighed, as an anchor just raised from the bottom. [a[3], and **weigh**[1].]

aweto *ä-wā′tō*, (*Maori*) *ä-fe′tō*, *n.* the so-called vegetable caterpillar, the body of the caterpillar filled with a parasitic fungus: — *pl.* **awe′tos.** [Maori *awheto*.]

awhape *ə-(h)wāp′*, (*Spens.*) *v.t.* to confound, amaze. [Cf. Goth. *af-hwapjan*, to choke.]

awheel *ə-(h)wēl′*, (*obs.* **awheels**), *adv.* on wheels, esp. on a bicycle. [a[3], and **wheel**.]

a′where. See **a′.**

awhile *ə-(h)wīl′*, *adv.* for some time: for a short time. [O.E. *āne hwīle*, a while (dat.): combined as early as 13th century.]

a-wing *ə-wing′*, *adv.* on the wing. [a[3], and **wing**[1].]

awkward *ök′wərd*, *adj.* oblique, inverted, backhanded (*obs.*): froward (*obs.*): clumsy: ungraceful: embarrassed: difficult to deal with: adverse (*Shak.*): embarrassing. — *adj.* **awk′wardish.** — *adv.* **awk′wardly.** — *n.* **awk′wardness** clumsiness: embarrassing or inharmonious quality or condition. [Prob. O.N. *afug*, turned the wrong way, and suff. -*ward*.]

awl *öl*, *n.* a pointed instrument for boring small holes. — **awl′bird** the green woodpecker: the avocet (*dial.*). [O.E. *æl*; O.N. *alr*, Ger. *Ahle*.]

awmous *ö′məs*, (*Scot.*) *n.* alms. [O.N. *almusa*; cf. O.E. *ælmysse*, alms.]

awmrie, awmry. See **ambry.**

awn *ön*, *n.* the beard of barley, or similar bristly process. — *adj.* **awned** — *n.* **awn′er** a machine for removing the awns from grain. — *adjs.* **awn′less; awn′y.** [O.N. *ögn* or a lost O.E. cognate; Ger. *Ahne*.]

awning *ön′ing*, *n.* a covering to shelter from the sun or weather. — *v.t.* **awn** to shelter with an awning. [Origin unknown; Fr. *auvent*, window-shade, may be connected.]

awny. See **awn.**

awoke *ə-wōk′*, *pa.t.* of **awake.**

awork *ə-wûrk′*, *adv.* at work. [a[3], and **work**]

awrack *ə-rak′*, *adv.* in a state of wreck. [a[3], and **wrack**[1,2].]

awrong *ə-rong′*, *adv.* wrongly. [a[3], and **wrong.**]

awry *ə-rī′*, *adj.* twisted to one side: distorted, crooked: wrong: perverse. — *adv.* askew: unevenly: perversely: erroneously. — **look awry** to look askance at anything; **walk awry** to go wrong. [a[3], and **wry.**]

axe, ax *aks*, *n.* a tool for hewing or chopping, with edge and handle in the same plane: a stone-dressing hammer: ruthless cutting down of expenditure (*fig.*): — *pl.* **ax′es** (see also **axis**). — *v.t.* to hew or strike with an axe: to dismiss as superfluous: to cut down, reduce (*fig.*): to dispense with (*fig.*). — **axe′-breaker** (*Austr.*) any of several kinds of hard-wooded tree; **axe′-stone** a kind of jade used for making axes. — **axe to grind** a private purpose to serve. [O.E. *æx*; cf. Gr. *axīnē*.]

axel *aks′l*, *n.* in figure skating, a jump from one skate to the other, incorporating one and a half turns in the air. [*Axel* Paulsen (1855–1938), a Norwegian skater.]

axerophthol *aks-ər-of′thol*, *n.* vitamin A, a pale yellow crystalline substance, defect of which causes xerophthalmia. [Gr. *a-*, priv., and *xerophthalmia*.]

axial, axile. See under **axis**[1].

axilla *ak-sil′ə*, *n.* the armpit (*anat.*): axil (*bot.*): — *pl.* **axillae** (-*ē*). — *n.* **ax′il** the angle between leaf and stem. — *adjs.* **ax′illar, ax′illary.** [L. *āxilla*, the armpit.]

axinite *aks′in-īt*, *n.* a brilliant brown mineral with axe-shaped crystals, containing calcium, aluminium, boron, silicon, etc. — *n.* **axin′omancy** (Gr. *manteiā*, divination) divination from the motions of an axe poised upon a stake, or of an agate placed upon a red-hot axe. [Gr. *axīnē*, an axe.]

axiology *aks-i-ol′ə-ji*, *n.* the science of the ultimate nature, reality, and significance of values. — *adj.* **axiological** (-*ə-loj′i-kl*). — *n.* **axiologist** (-*ol′ə-jist*). [Gr. *axios*, worthy, *logos*, discourse.]

axiom *aks′i-əm*, *n.* a self-evident truth: a universally received principle: a postulate, assumption. — *adjs.* **axiomat′ic, axiomat′ical.** — *adv.* **axiomat′ically.** — *n.sing.* **axiomat′ics** the study of axioms and axiom systems. [Gr. *axiōma*, -*atos* — *axioein*, to think worth, to take for granted *axios*, worthy]

axioma medium *ak-si-ōm′a mē′di-əm, me′di-ōōm*, (L.) a generalisation from experience.

axis[1] *ak′sis*, *n.* an axle (*obs.*): a line about which a body rotates, or about which a figure is conceived to revolve: a straight line about which the parts of a figure, body or system are symmetrically or systematically arranged: a fixed line adopted for reference in co-ordinate geometry, curve-plotting, crystallography, etc.: the second vertebra of the neck (*zool.*): the main stem or root, or a branch in relation to its own branches and appendages (*bot.*): an alliance of powers, as if forming together an axis of rotation — esp. of Germany and Italy (1936): — *pl.* **axes** (*ak′sēz*). — *adj.* **ax′ial** relating to, or of the nature of, an axis. — *adv.* **ax′ially.** — *adj.* **ax′ile** (*ak′sīl*) coinciding with an axis. — *ns.* **ax′oid** a curve generated by the revolution of a point round an advancing axis; **ax′on** a process of the nerve cell or neuron which in most cases transmits impulses away from the cell. — *adj.* **axonomet′ric** pertaining to a method of projection in which a drawing of a three-dimensional object has all lines to exact scale and appears distorted. — *n.* **ax′oplasm** cytoplasm of an axon. — **axis cylinder** the excitable core of a medullated nerve-fibre. — **axis of incidence** the line passing through the point of incidence of a ray perpendicular to the refracting surface; **axis of refraction** the continuation of the same line through the refracting medium; **axis of the equator** the polar diameter of the earth which is also the axis of rotation. [L. *axis*; cf. Gr. *axōn*, Sans. *aksa*, O.E. *eax*.]

axis[2] *ak′sis*, *n.* a white-spotted deer of India. [L. *axis*, Pliny's name for an Indian animal.]

axle *aks′l*, **axle-tree** *aks′l-trē*, *ns.* the pin or rod in the nave of a wheel on which the wheel turns: a pivot or support of any kind: an axis (*arch.*). — **ax′le-box** the box in which the axle end turns; **ax'le-guard** a pedestal or pillow-block. [More prob. O.N. *öxull* than a dim. from O.E. *eax*.]

Axminster *aks'min-stər, n.* a variety of cut-pile carpet, the tufts of pile each being inserted separately into the backing during its weaving. — Also *adj.* [*Axminster* in Devon, where it originated.]

axolotl *aks'ə-lot-l, n.* the larval form of Amblystoma, commonly retaining its larval character in life, though capable of breeding. [Aztec.]

axon, axonometric, axoplasm. See **axis**[1].

ay[1] *ā, interj.* ah: oh: alas: esp. in *ay me*. [M.E. *ey, ei,* perh. from Fr. *ahi, ai*; cf. Sp. *ay de mi*.]

ay[2]**, aye** *ī, adv.* yea: yes: indeed. — *n.* **aye** (*ī*) a vote in the affirmative: one who votes in the affirmative. [Perh. a dial. form of **aye,** ever; perh. a variant of **yea.**]

ay[3]. See **aye**[1].

ayah *ī'ə, n.* an Indian or South African waiting-maid or nursemaid. — Also **aia.** [Hind *āyā*; from Port. *aia,* nurse.]

ayahuasco *a-yə-(h)was'kō, n.* a S. American vine of the family Malpighiaceae: a drink made from the roots of the vine, having hallucinatory effects: — *pl.* **ayahuas'- cos.** [Amer. Sp. *ayahuasca* — Quechua *ayawáskha*.]

ayatollah *a-yə-tol'ə, -tō', n.* (sometimes with *cap.*) a Muslim religious leader of the Shiah sect. [Ar. *ayatollah,* sign of God — *āya,* sign, *ollāh,* God.]

aye[1]**, ay** *ā, adv.* ever: always: for ever. — **for aye, for ever and aye** for ever, to all eternity. — In combination, with sense of ever, as in Shakespeare's **aye'-remain'ing,** etc. [O.N. *ei,* ever; O.E. *ā*; conn. with **age, ever.**]

aye[2]. See **ay**[2].

aye-aye *ī'ī, n.* an aberrant squirrel-like lemur of Madagascar. [Malagasy *aiay*.]

ayelp *ə-yelp', adv.* in a state of yelping. [Prep. **a**[3].]

ayenbite *ä-yen'bīt, (obs.) n.* remorse, as in the book-title *Ayenbite of Inwyt* (remorse of conscience). [M.E. *ayen,* again, and **bite.**]

aygre *ā'gər, (Shak.).* Same as **eager.**

Aylesbury *ālz'bər-i, n.* a breed of ducks much valued for the table. — Also *adj.* [*Aylesbury,* a market town in Bucks.]

ayont *ə-yont', (Scot.) adv.* and *prep.* beyond. [Pfx. **a-,** and **yond.**]

ayre *ār, n.* an old spelling of **air,** esp. as a tune or song, in particular an Elizabethan or Jacobean song for solo voice.

ayrie. Same as **eyrie.**

Ayrshire *ār'shər, n.* a breed of reddish-brown and white cattle. — Also *adj.* [*Ayrshire,* a former Scottish county, where they originated.]

ayu *ä'ū, ī'(y)ōō,* **ai** *ī, ns.* a small edible Japanese fish (*Plecoglossus altevis*). — Also **sweet'fish.** [Jap].

ayuntamiento *a-yōōn-ta-mē-än'tō, (Sp.) n.* municipal council: — *pl.* **ayuntamien'tos.**

Ayurveda *ä-yōōr-vā'də, n.* the body of classical Indian medical teaching. — *adj.* **ayurve'dic.** [Sanskrit, knowledge of long life.]

ayword *ā'wûrd, (Shak.) n.* a byword, proverbial reproach. [Origin obscure; Rowe proposed to read **nayword.**]

Azalea *a-zā'li-ə, n.* a genus close akin to, or subgenus of, *Rhododendron,* shrubby plants, with five stamens and annual leaves: (without *cap.*) a plant of the genus. [Gr. *azaleos,* dry; reason for name uncertain.]

azan *ä-zän', n.* the Muslim call to public prayer made five times a day by a muezzin. [Ar. *'adhan,* invitation.]

azeotrope *ə-zē'ə-trōp, n.* any liquid mixture which distils over without decomposition in a certain ratio, the boiling-point of the mixture differing from that of any constituent. — *adj.* **azeotrop'ic** (*-trop'*). [Gr. *a-,* priv., *zeein,* to boil, *tropos,* a turn.]

azide *ā'zīd, a', n.* a salt or an ester derived from hydrazoic acid. [az(o)-, and *-ide*.]

Azilian *a-zil'i-ən, adj.* belonging to a transition between Palaeolithic and Neolithic. [Mas d'*Azil,* Ariège, where objects of this culture have been found in a cave.]

azimuth *az'im-əth, n.* the arc of the horizon between the meridian of a place and a vertical circle passing through any celestial body. — *adj.* **az'imuthal** (or -*mūdh', -mūth'*) pertaining to the azimuth. [Ar. *as-sumūt, as = al,* the, *sumūt,* pl. of *samt,* direction. See **zenith.**]

azione (sacra) *a-tsi-ö'nā* (*sak'ra*), (*mus.*) *n.* a composition, in form like an oratorio, but performed as a drama. [It.]

az(o)- *āz(-ō)-, az-,* in combination, nitrogen. — *ns.* **az'o-com'pound** a compound in which two nitrogen atoms are each attached to (usually) a carbon atom, as **az'oben'zene** $C_6H_5N{:}NC_6H_5$; **az'o-dye'** a dye of such composition. [**azote.**]

azoic *a-zō'ik, adj.* without life: before the existence of animal life: formed when there was no animal life on the globe, as rocks. [Gr. *a-,* priv., and *zoē,* life.]

Azolla *a-zol'ə, n.* a genus of tiny water ferns: (without *cap.*) a fern of this genus. [Modern L., apparently formed from Gr. *azein,* to dry, *ollynai,* to destroy.]

azonal *a-zōn'əl, ā-, adj.* not arranged in zones or regions. — *adj.* **azonic** (*a-zon'ik*) not limited to a zone, not local. [Gr. *a-,* priv., *zōnē,* a belt.]

azote *a-zōt', n.* an old name for nitrogen, so called because it does not sustain animal life. — *adjs.* **azot'ic** (*a-zot'ik*) nitric; **azō'tous** nitrous. — *v.t.* **az'otise, -ize** to combine with nitrogen. — *n.* **Azōtobac'ter** a genus of nitrogen-fixing bacteria. [Gr. *a-,* priv., *zaein,* to live.]

azoth *äz'oth, n.* the alchemist's name for mercury: Paracelsus's universal remedy. [From Ar. *az-zāūg* — *al,* the, *zāūg,* from Pers. *zhīwah,* quicksilver.]

Azrael *az'rā-el, n.* in Muslim mythology, the angel of death.

Aztec *az'tek, n.* one of a people dominant in Mexico before the Spanish conquest: Nahuatl. — Also *adj.*

azulejo *a-thōō-lā'hhō, (Sp.) n.* a glazed tile: — *pl.* **azule'jos.**

azure *azh'ər, āzh'ər,* or *ā'zhūr, adj.* of a faint blue: sky-coloured: blue (represented in engraving, etc., by horizontal lines) (*her.*). — *n.* a delicate blue colour: the sky. — *adjs.* **azurē'an, az'urine** (*-īn*) azure. — *ns.* **az'urine** a blue-black aniline dye: a fresh-water fish, the blue roach; **az'urite** blue basic carbonate of copper, chessylite. — *adjs.* **az'urn** (*Milt.*) azure; **az'ury** bluish. [O.Fr. *azur* — L.L. *azura* — Ar. (*al*) *lazward,* Pers. *lājward,* lapis lazuli, blue colour.]

azygous *az'i-gəs, adj.* not yoked or joined with another: unpaired (*anat.*). — *n.* **azygy** (*az'i-ji*). [Gr. *azygos* — *a-,* priv., and *zygon,* a yoke.]

azymous *az'i-məs, adj.* unfermented: unleavened. — *ns.* **az'ym** (*-im*), **az'yme** (*-īm, -im*) unleavened bread; **az'ymite** a member of any church using unleavened bread in the Eucharist. [Gr. *azymos* — *a-,* priv., *zȳmē,* leaven.]

B

B, b *bē, n.* the second letter of our alphabet, called by the Phoenicians *beth*, the house, corresponding to the Greek β, beta: in music, the seventh note of the scale of C major (H in German notation, B being used for B flat): the subsidiary series of paper sizes, ranging from B0 (1000 × 1414 mm.) to B10 (31 × 44 mm.): one of second class or order (as a road of secondary importance), or of a class arbitrarily designated B; see **blood-group**: a designation indicating lesser importance (as the *B-side* of a record, a *B-movie*); as a mediaeval Roman numeral B = 300; B̄ = 3000. — **B or B flat** a 19th-cent. euphemism for domestic bedbug; in old music **B quadratum, quadrate B, square B** is B natural, **B rotundum, round B** is B flat. — **not know a B from a battledore, broomstick, bull's foot** (*old slang*) to be very ignorant; **the three B's** Bach, Beethoven, Brahms.

ba *bä, n.* in ancient Egyptian religion, the soul, represented as a bird with a human head. [Egypt.]

ba' *bö, n.* Scots form of ball[1,2]. —*ns.* **ba'ing, ba'spiel** see under **ball**[1].

baa *bä, n.* the cry of a sheep. — *v.i.* to bleat. — *n.* **baa'ing.** [Imit.]

Baal *bä'əl, n.* a god of the Phoenicians, originally probably a fusion of many local gods: a false god generally: — *pl.* **Bā'alim.** — *ns.* **Bā'alism; Bā'alite.** [Heb.]

baas *bäs, (S. Afr.) n.* master, overseer, sir. — *n.* **baas'skap** condition in which one section of the population is treated as a master race: the theory used to justify this. [Afrik. — Du.]

Baathist, Ba'athist *bä'thist, n.* a member of the socialist or reformist party of various Arab countries, esp. Syria and Iraq. — Also *adj.* — *n.* **Baa'thism, Ba'a'thism.** [Ar. *baath*, renaissance.]

baba *bä'bä, n.* a small cake, leavened with yeast, with or without fruit, soaked in a rum syrup. — Also **rum baba** or **baba au rhum** (*ō rom*). [Fr. — Pol. *baba*, 'old woman'.]

babacoote *bab'ə-kōōt, n.* a large lemur, the indri or a closely related species. [Malagasy *babakoto.*]

babassu *bab-ə-sōō', n.* a Brazilian palm (Attalea) or its oil-yielding nut. [Prob. Tupí.]

Babbitt *bab'it, n.* a conventional middle-class businessman (or other person) who esteems success and has no use for art or intellectual pursuits. — *ns.* **Babb'it(t)ry; Babb'ittism.** [Eponymous hero of novel (1922) by Sinclair Lewis.]

babbitt *bab'it, v.t.* to fit with **Babbit(t's) metal,** a soft anti-friction alloy (tin, with copper antimony, and usu. lead). [Isaac *Babbitt* (1799–1862), the Massachusetts inventor.]

babble *bab'l, v.i.* to speak like a baby: to make a continuous murmuring sound like a brook, etc.: to talk incessantly: to tell secrets: to prate. — *v.t.* to utter confusedly or by rote: to divulge by foolish talk. — *n.* idle senseless talk: prattle: confused murmur, as of a stream. — *adj.* **babb'lative.** — *ns.* **babb'lement; babb'ler** one who babbles: a bird of an ill-defined family somewhat akin to the thrushes (also **babbling thrush**). — *n. and adj.* **babb'ling.** — *adj.* **babb'ly.** [Prob. imit., from the repeated syllable *ba*; cf. Du. *babbelen*, Ger. *pappelen*, Fr. *babiller*, perh. influenced by *Babel*.]

babe *bāb, n.* a form of **baby.**

Babee. See **Babi.**

Babel *bā'bl, n.* a foolishly conceived lofty structure: (also without *cap.*) a confused sound of voices: (also without *cap.*) a scene of confusion. — *ns.* **bā'beldom; bā'belism.** — *adj.* **bā'belish.** [Heb. *Bābel*, prob. Assyr. *bāb-ili*, gate of God, associated in Gen. xi. 9, with confusion.]

babesiasis *bab-i-zī-'ə-sis,* **babesiosis** *ba-bē-zē-ō'sis, ns.* redwater, a cattle infection caused by the parasite **Babesia** (*ba-bē'zh(y)a*). [Victor *Babes* (died 1926), Romanian bacteriologist.]

Babi, Babee *bä'bē, n.* a member of a Persian sect, followers of *Bab*-ed-Din 'the Gate of Righteousness' (Mirza Ali Mohammed, 1821–50), who claimed to be a prophet bringing a new revelation from God. — Also **Ba'bist.** — *ns.* **Ba'bism, Ba'bIism, Ba'beeism.**

babiche *ba-bēsh', n.* thongs or laces made of rawhide. [Fr.-Can., from Algonquian.]

babingtonite *bab'ing-tən-īt, n.* a pyroxene, ferrous silicate with admixtures, sometimes worked as an iron ore. [After William *Babington* (1756–1833), mineralogist.]

babiroussa, -russa *bä-bi-rōō'sə, n.* a wild hog found in Celebes, etc., with great upturned tusks in the male, hence called the horned or deer hog. [Malay *bäbi*, hog, and *rūsa*, deer.]

bablah *bab'lə,* **babul** *bä'bōōl, -bōōl', ns.* a species of acacia (*A. arabica*) from which gum arabic is obtained: the pods of that and other species, used for tanning. [Hind. and Pers. *babūl.*]

baboo. See **babu.**

baboon *bə-bōōn', n.* large monkey of various species, with long face, dog-like tusks, large lips, a tail, and buttock-callosities: a clumsy, brutish person of low intelligence. — *n.* **baboon'cry.** — *adj.* **baboon'ish.** [M.E. *babewyn,* grotesque figure, baboon — O.Fr. *babuin,* poss. — *baboue,* grimace.]

babouche, babuche, baboosh *bə-bōōsh', n.* an Oriental heelless slipper. [Fr., — Ar. *bābūsh* — Pers. *pā,* foot, *pūsh,* covering.]

babu, baboo *bä'bōō, n.* a title for Hindus in some parts of India corresponding to Mr: an Indian clerk: an Indian with a superficial English education (esp. *hist.*). — Also *adj.* — *ns.* **ba'budom; ba'buism.** [Hind. *bābū.*]

babuche. See **babouche.**

babul. See **bablah.**

babushka *bə-bōōsh'kə, n.* a triangular headscarf tied under the chin: a grandmother, granny. [Russ. *bábushka,* grandmother, dim. of *baba,* old woman.]

baby *bā'bi, n.* an infant, young child: a doll (*obs.*): the reflection of oneself in the pupil of another's eye (*obs.*): a young animal: a babyish person: a thing small of its kind, as varieties of grand piano, aeroplane, etc.: a girl (*coll.*): an inexperienced person: one's pet project, invention, machine, etc.: one's own responsibility. — *v.t.* to treat as a baby. — Also *adj.* — *n.* **ba'byhood.** — *adj.* **ba'byish.** — **ba'by-batt'erer** one who indulges in **ba'by-batt'ering** in instances of the **battered baby syndrome** (q.v. under **batter**); **baby beef** beef from calves which are fattened for slaughter on a diet of roughage and high protein concentrates; **baby bonus** (*Can. coll.*) family allowance; **baby boom** (*coll.*) an increase in the birth-rate; **ba'by-boun'cer, -jump'er** a harness or seat suspended from springs, elastic straps, etc. in which a young baby can disport itself; **Baby Buggy®** a light, collapsible push-chair for a baby or toddler; **ba'by-farm'er, -mind'er** a person who takes in infants to nurse for pay; **ba'byfood** any of various foods specially prepared, e.g. by straining, blending, etc., for babies; **baby grand** a small grand piano, about 2 metres in length; **Ba'bygro®** an all-in-one stretch-fabric suit for a baby: — *pl.* **Ba'bygros; baby house** a doll's-house; **ba'by-ribb'on** a very narrow ribbon. — *v.i.* **ba'by-sit** to act as baby-sitter. — **ba'by-sitter** one who mounts guard over a baby to relieve the usual attendant; **ba'by-sitting; ba'by-snatcher** a person marrying or having as a lover someone who is much younger (usu.

derog.: also **cradle-snatcher**): a person who steals a baby, e.g. from its pram; **ba′by-snatching; ba′by-talk** the speech of babies learning to talk, or an adult's imitation of it; **ba′by-walker** a wheeled frame with a canvas, etc. seat for supporting a baby learning to walk. — **be left holding the baby** to be left in the lurch with an irksome responsibility; **throw out the baby with the bathwater** to allow over-enthusiasm to lead one into getting rid of the essential along with the superfluous. [Prob. imitative. See **babble**.]

Babylon *bab′i-lon, n.* a place of sorrowful exile: a place, etc. of luxury and decadence, used (*derog.*) formerly by protestants in reference to the Roman Catholic Church, more recently by Rastafarians of western culture. — *adj.* **Babylō′nian** of Babylon: hence huge, gigantic: Romish, popish (*obs.*; from the identification with Rome of the scarlet woman of Rev. xvii.): Babel-like, confused in language: luxurious, decadent. — *n.* an inhabitant of Babylon: the ancient language of Babylonia, Akkadian. — *adj.* **Babylon′ish**. — **Babylonian** or **Babylonish captivity** the exile of the Jews deported to Babylon in 597 and 586 B.C., lasting till *c.* 538: the exile of the popes at Avignon, 1309–77. [*Babylon,* city of ancient Mesopotamia.]

bacca *bak′ə,* (*bot.*) *n.* a berry. — *adjs.* **bacc′ate** having berries: berry-like: pulpy; **bacciferous** (*bak-sif′ər-əs*) bearing berries; **bac′ciform** of the shape of a berry; **bacciv′orous** living on berries. [L. *bacca,* a berry.]

baccalaureate *bak-ə-lö′ri-āt, n.* the university degree of bachelor or a diploma of lesser status awarded by a college, etc. — *adj.* **baccalau′rean.** [L.L. *baccalaureus,* altered from *baccalārius.* See **bachelor**.]

baccarat, baccara *bak′ə-rä, n.* a French card game played by betters and a banker: a type of crystal made at *Baccarat,* France. [Fr.]

baccare. See **backare.**

baccate. See **bacca.**

Bacchus *bak′əs, n.* the god of wine. — *n.* **bacchanal** (*bak′ə-nəl*) a worshipper, priest or priestess, of Bacchus: a drunken reveller: a dance, song, or revel in honour of Bacchus. — *adj.* relating to drinking or drunken revels. — *ns.pl.* **bacchanā′lia, bacch′anals** originally feasts in honour of Bacchus: hence, drunken revels. — *n.* **bacchanalian** (*-nā′li-ən*) a drunken reveller. — *adj.* bacchanal. — *n.* **bacchanā′lianism.** — *n.* and *adj.* **bacchant** (*bak′ant*) a priest or votary of Bacchus: a reveller: a drunkard. — *n.* **bacchante** (*bə-kant′, bak′ant,* or after Italian *baccante, ba-kant′i*) a priestess of Bacchus: a female bacchanal. — *adjs.* **bacchiac** (*bak-ī′ək*) relating to the bacchius; **Bacch′ian, Bacchic** (*bak′ik*) relating to Bacchus: jovial: drunken. — *n.* **bacchī′us** (Gr. and Lat. *pros.*) a foot of two long syllables preceded by one short: — *pl.* **bacchī′ī.** [L. *Bacchus,* Gr. *Bakchos.*]

bacciferous, etc. See **bacca.**

baccy, bacco *bak′i, -ō,* short forms of **tobacco.**

bach. See **bachelor.**

bacharach *bak′ər-ak, bähh′ə-rähh, n.* an excellent wine named from *Bacharach,* on the Rhine.

bachelor *bach′əl-ər, n.* a young knight following the banner of another, as too young to display his own (*hist.*): an unmarried man: one who has taken his or her first degree at a university: a young unmated bull-seal or other male animal. — *n.* **bach** (*coll.*) a bachelor. — *v.i.* to live as a bachelor: to do for oneself. — Also *v.t.* with *it.* — *ns.* **bach′elordom; bach′elorhood; bach′elorism** habit or condition of a bachelor; **bach′-elorship** the degree of bachelor. — **bachelor flat,** (*slang*) **pad** a flat or other dwelling-place for an unmarried person; **bach′elor-girl** a girl with a latch-key (*obs.*): a young unmarried woman who supports herself; **bach′-elor's-butt′ons** a double-flowered yellow or white buttercup: also applied to double feverfew, species of Centaurea, and many other plants; **bachelor's wife** an ideal woman with none of the shortcomings of married men's wives. — **knight-bachelor** see **knight.** [O.Fr. *bacheler* — L.L. *baccalārius;* of doubtful origin.]

bacillus *bə-sil′əs, n.* (*cap.*) a genus of Schizomycetes (fam. Bacillaceae), aerobic rod-shaped bacteria: a member of the genus: loosely, any rod-shaped bacterium: popularly, any disease-causing bacterium: — *pl.* **bacill′ī.** — *n.pl.* **Bacillā′ceae** a family (order Eubacteriales) of endospore-producing bacteria. — *adjs.* **bacill′ar, bacill′ary** (or *bas′*) of the shape or nature of a bacillus, rodlike. — *n.* **bacill′icide** that which destroys bacilli. — *adj.* **bacill′iform.** [L.L. *bacillus,* dim. of *baculus,* a rod.]

bacitracin *bas-i-trā′sin, n.* an antibiotic obtained from a certain bacterium and used against Gram-positive bacteria, esp. in skin infections. [L.L. *bacillus,* and Margaret *Tracy,* an American child in whom the substance was found.]

back[1] *bak, n.* the hinder part of the body in man, and the upper part in beasts, extending from the neck and shoulders to the extremity of the backbone: put for the whole body in speaking of clothes: the hinder part, or the side remote from that presented or that habitually seen or contemplated (opposite to the front): the under side of a leaf or of a violin: part of the upper surface of the tongue opposite the soft palate; the convex side of a book, opposite to the opening of the leaves: the thick edge of a knife or the like: the upright hind part of a chair, bench, etc.: something added to the hinder side: the surface of the sea, or of a river: the keel and keelson of a ship: in football, etc., one of the players behind the forwards — *full back* (who guards the goal), *half* and *three-quarter backs*: in mining, that side of an inclined mineral lode which is nearest the surface of the ground — the *back* of a level is the ground between it and the level above. — *adj.* rearward: remote: reversed: made by raising the back of the tongue (*phon.*): belonging to the past. — *adv.* to or towards the back: to or towards the place from which one came: to a former state or condition: behind: behind in time: in return: again: ago. — *v.t.* to mount or ride: to help or support, as if standing at someone's back: to support (an opinion, etc.) by a wager or bet on: to countersign or endorse: to write or print at the back of (a parliamentary bill or the like): to furnish with a back: to lie at the back of: to form the back of: to cause to move backward, as a horse: to put or propel backward, or in the opposite direction, by reversing the action, as an engine or a boat. — *v.i.* to move or go back or backwards: (of the wind) to change counterclockwise. — *adj.* **backed** having a back. — *ns.* **back′er** one who backs or supports another in a contest or venture: one who places a bet, e.g. on a horse; **back′ing** support at the back: mounting of a horse: the action of putting or going back: a body of helpers: anything used to form a back or line the back: counter-clockwise change of wind: support for an enterprise: musical accompaniment, esp. of a popular song. — *adj.* **back′-most** farthest to the back. — *adj.* and *adv.* **backward** (*bak′wərd*) towards the back: on the back: towards the past: from a better to a worse state: in a direction opposite to the normal. — *adj.* keeping back: shy, bashful: unwilling: slow in development: late: dull or stupid. — *n.* the past portion of time (*poet.*). — *n.* **backwardā′tion** percentage paid by a seller of stock for keeping back its delivery till the following account. — *adv.* **back′wardly.** — *n.* **back′wardness.** — *adv.* **back′-wards** backward. — **back′ache** pain in the back; **back′-band** a rope, strap, or chain passing over a cart saddle and holding up the shafts of a vehicle (also **back′-chain, back′-rope**). — *adj.* **back′-bench** of or sitting on the back benches, the seats in parliament occupied by members who do not hold office. — **back′bench′er.** — *v.t.* **back′bite** to speak evil of in absence (also *v.i.*). — **back′biter; back′biting** (also *adj.*). — *adj.* **back′-block** of the back-blocks. — **back′-blocker.** — *n.pl.* **back=blocks** (*Austr.* and *N.Z.*) remote, sparsely populated country: the back part of a station, far from water. — **back′-board** a board at the back of a cart, boat, etc.: a board fastened across the back to straighten the body; **back′bond** a deed attaching a qualification or condition to the terms of a conveyance or other instrument (*Scots law*); **back′bone** the spinal column: a main support or axis: mainstay: firmness of character. — *adjs.* **back′boned; back′-boneless.** — **back′-breaker** a very heavy job. — *adj.* **back′breaking.** — *v.i.* and *v.t.* **back′-cal′culate** to make a calculation as to an earlier condition, situation, etc. (esp. as to the level of person's intoxication) based on data recorded at a later time. — **back′-calcula′tion; back-chain** see **backband; back′chat** answering back, retorting: impertinence, repartee: informal talk, gossip. — Also *v.i.* — **back′= cloth, back′drop** the painted cloth at the back of the stage: the background to any situation, activity, etc. — *v.i.* and *v.t.* **back′-comb** to give (the hair) a puffed-out appearance by combing the underlying hairs towards the roots and smoothing the outer hairs over them. — **back′-country** remote, thinly-populated districts (also *adj.*); **back′court** in lawn tennis, that part of the court lying behind the service-line (also *adj.*); **back′-crawl** a swimming stroke similar to the crawl, performed on the back; **back′-cross** a cross between a hybrid and a parent race or strain. — *v.t.* **back′-date′** to put an earlier date on: to count as valid retrospectively from a certain date. — **back door** a door in the back part of a building. — *adj.* **back′-door** unworthily secret: clandestine. — **backdown** see **back down** below; **back′-draught** a backward current; **backdrop** see **back= cloth; back′-end′** the rear end: the later part of a season (*dial.*): the late autumn (*dial.*); **back′fall** an obsolete ornament like an appoggiatura (*mus.*): a fall on the back as in wrestling (often *fig.*): a lever in the coupler of an organ; **back′fill** the material used in backfilling. — *v.t.* and *v.i.* to refill (e.g. foundations or an excavation) with earth or other material. — **back′fire** ignition of gas in an internal-combustion engine's cylinder at the wrong time, or within a bunsen-burner or the like instead of at the outlet. — *v.i.* (*bak-fīr′*) to have a backfire: to go wrong (*coll.*). — **back′-formā′tion** the making of a word from one that is, in error or jocularity, taken to be a derivative, as the verb *sidle* from the adverb *sidelng* treated as if it were a participle; **back′-friend** a pretended friend (*obs.*): a backer, a friend who stands at one's back. — *adj.* **back′-ganging** (*Scot.*) in arrears. — **back garden, back green** a garden, green, at the back of a house; **back′ground** ground at the back: a place of obscurity: the space behind the principal figures of a picture: that against which anything is, or ought to be, seen (*fig.*): upbringing and previous history: environment. — *adj.* in the background (*lit.* or *fig.*). (**background radiation** low-level radiation from substances present in the environment). — **back′-hair** the hair at the back of the head; **back′-hand** the hand turned backwards in making a stroke: handwriting with the letters sloping backwards: the part of the court to the left of a right-handed player, or the right of a left-handed (*tennis*): a stroke made with the hand turned backwards. — Also *adj.* — *adj.* **back′-hand′ed** backhand: (of a compliment, etc.) indirect, dubious, sarcastic, insincere. — **back′-hand′er** a blow with the back of the hand: a bribe (*coll.*): an extra glass of wine out of turn, the bottle being passed back. — *v.t.* **back′-heel′** in football, to kick (the ball) backwards with the heel. — Also *n.* — **back′hoe** (also **backhoe loader**) (a tractor equipped with) a shovel at the end of a mechanical arm, for making minor excavations; **back′ing-down** shirking; **backing store** (*comput.*) a large-capacity computer store supplementary to a computer's main memory; **back lane, back street** a lane or street to the rear of a building or buildings; **back′lash** the jarring or play of ill-fitting machinery in recoil: reaction or consequence, esp. if violent; **back′-lill** the left-hand thumb-hole at the back of a bagpipe chanter (*Scott*; sometimes *erron.* -**lilt**); **back′list** books previously published which a publisher keeps in print, as opposed to newly published books; **back′-load** a load taken on by a lorry for a return

journey. — *v.i.* to obtain a back-load. — **back′-loading; back′log** a log at the back of a fire: a reserve or accumulation of business, stock, work, etc., that will keep one going for some time (*coll.*); **back′marker** a person who starts a race at scratch or with the least advantageous handicap; **back′-numb′er** a copy or issue of a newspaper or magazine of a bygone date: a person or thing out of date or past the useful stage (*fig.*); **back′pack** a pack carried on the back. — *v.i.* to carry a pack on the back esp. as a hiker. — **back′packer; back′packing; back′pay** pay that is overdue. — *v.i.* **back′-ped′al** to press the pedals back, as in slowing a fixed-wheel bicycle: to hold back: to reverse one's course of action: to retreat from an opponent while still facing him (*boxing*). — **back′-ped′alling; back′-piece, back′-plate** a piece or plate of armour for the back. — *adj.* **back′room** (of persons) doing important work behind the scenes, esp. in secret (*coll.*). — **back-rope** see **backband; back′saw** a saw stiffened by a thickened back; **back′scatter** the scattering of rays or particles backwards by deflection (*phys.*). — *v.t.* to scatter in this way. — *v.i.* **back′scratch.** — **back′-scratcher** a clawed instrument for scratching the back: one who practises backscratching; **back′scratching** doing favours in return for favours, for advantage of both parties: servile flattery; **back′set** a setting back, reverse: an eddy or counter-current; **back′sey′** (-*sī*; *Scot.*) sirloin; **back′-shift** a group of workers whose time of working overlaps or comes between the day-shift and the night-shift: the time this group is on duty; **back′side** the back or hinder side or part of anything: the hinder part of an animal: the premises at the rear of a house (*Scot.*); **back′sight** in surveying, a sight taken backwards: the sight of a rifle nearer the stock; **back′= slang** slang in which every word is pronounced as if spelt backwards. — *v.i.* **back′slide** to slide or fall back in faith or morals. — **back′slider; back′sliding.** — *v.i.* **back′space** (or -*spās′*) to move the carriage of a typewriter one or more spaces back by means of a particular key. — *n.* the key used for backspacing (also **back′spacer, backspace key**): the act of backspacing. — **back′-spaul(d)** (*Scot.*) the back of the shoulder: the hindleg. — *v.t.* and *v.i.* **backspeir′, -speer′** (*Scot.*) to cross-question. — **back′spin** a rotary movement against the direction of travel of a ball (in golf, billiards, etc.) imparted to reduce its momentum on impact. — *adj.* and *adv.* **back′stage′** (*lit.* and *fig.*) behind the scenes, unobserved by the public. — **back′-stairs** servants′ or private stairs of a house. — *adj.* secret or underhand. — **back′stall** a garrotter's confederate on the look-out behind. — *v.i.*: — *pr. p.* only, **backstart′ing** (*Spens.*) starting back. — **back′stays** ropes or stays extending from the topmast-heads to the sides of a ship, and slanting a little backward: any stay or support at the back; **back′stitch** a method of sewing in which, for every new stitch, the needle enters behind, and comes out in front of, the end of the previous one; **back′stop** a screen, wall, etc. acting as a barrier in various sports or games, e.g. shooting, baseball, etc.: (the position of) a player, e.g. in baseball who stops the ball: something providing additional support, protection, etc.; **back street** see **back lane; back streets** the less fashionable and usu. poorer streets of a town; **back′-stroke** back-crawl: a swimming-stroke with circular movements of the arms and legs, performed on the back; **back′sword** a sword with a back or with only one edge: a stick with a basket-handle, singlestick; **backsword′man.** — *v.i.* **back′track** to go back on one's course. — *n.* a return track to starting point: a retracing of steps. — **back′tracking; back-up** see **back up** below; **back′veld** (-*felt*; *S. Afr.*) country remote from towns. — *adj.* remote, rustic, primitive. — **backvel′der** (-*dər*); **back′wash** a receding wave: a backward current: a reaction, repercussion or aftermath. — *v.t.* to affect with backwash: to clean the oil from (wool) after combing. — **back′water** water held back by a dam: a pool or belt of water connected with a river but not in the line of its present course or current: water thrown back by the turning of a water-wheel: a place unaffected by the movements of the day (*fig.*): a backward current of water: swell of the sea caused by a passing ship; **back′woods** the forest beyond the cleared country; **backwoods′man** a dweller in the backwoods: a person of uncouth manners (*fig.*): a peer who seldom attends the House of Lords (*fig.*); **back′-word** a withdrawal of a promise, etc.: a retort; **back′-work** in coal-mining, work done underground but not at the coal-face; **back′worker.** — *adj.* **back′-wounding** (*Shak.*) backbiting. — **back′yard′** a yard behind a house. — *adj.* of one operating a small business from domestic premises, as *backyard mechanic*, or practising unofficially, illegally. — **back and fill** to trim sails so that the wind alternately presses them back and fills them: to vacillate; **back down** to abandon one's opinion or position (*n.* **back′down**); **back of** (*U.S.*) behind; **back out** to move out backwards: to evade an obligation or undertaking; **back-seat driver** one free of responsibility but full of advice: one controlling from a position from which he ought not to control; **back-street abortion** an abortion performed by an unqualified person operating illicitly; **back-to-back′** with backs facing each other: (of houses) built thus (also *n.*): following in close sequence (*coll.*); **back up** to give support to (*n.* and *adj.* **back′-up**); **backward and forward** to and fro; **back water** to ply the oars or turn the paddle-wheels backward; **bend, fall, lean over backwards** (*coll.*) to go even to the point of personal discomfort (to be accommodating or to please); **break the back of** to overburden: to accomplish the hardest part of; **get off someone's back** to stop pestering or bothering someone; **give** or **make a back** to take up position for leap-frog; **know backwards** to have a thorough knowledge of; **on the back of** close behind: just after (*Scot.*); **put one's back into** to do with might and main; **ring bells backward** to begin with the bass bell, in order to give tidings of dismay; **set** or **put one's, someone's, back up** to show resentment, arouse resentment in someone; **take a back seat** to withdraw into obscurity or subordination; **talk through the back of one's neck** see **neck; to the backbone** through and through. [O.E. *bæc*; Sw. *bak*, Dan. *bag.*]

back² *bak, n.* a trough for carrying fuel: a tub. — *n.* **back′et** (*Scot.*) a shallow wooden trough for carrying ashes, coals, etc. [Fr. *bac*, trough, dim. *baquet*, perh. partly through Du. *bak.*]

backare, baccare *bak′ār*, or *bak′ā′ri,* (*Shak.*) *interj.* back: stand back. [Perh. for *back there*; or sham Latin.]

backfisch *bäk′fish, n.* a young girl, a flapper. [Ger. *Backfisch*, fish for frying, perhaps in allusion to immaturity.]

backgammon *bak-gam′ən,* or *bak′, n.* a game played by two persons on a board with dice and fifteen men or pieces each: a triple game scored by bearing all one's men before the other has brought all to his own table. — *v.t.* to defeat in such a way. [*back,* because the pieces are sometimes taken up and obliged to go *back* — that is, re-enter at the table, and M.E. *gamen,* play.]

backsheesh, backshish. See **baksheesh.**
backward(s), etc. See **back¹.**
baclava. See **baklava.**
bacon *bā′kn, n.* pig's flesh (now the back and sides) salted or pickled and dried: a rustic, a chaw-bacon (*Shak.*). — **bring home the bacon** (*coll.*) to achieve an object, successfully accomplish a task: to provide material support; **save (some)one's bacon** (to enable someone) to come off scatheless with difficulty. [O.Fr. *bacon,* of Gmc. origin; cf. O.H.G. *bahho, bacho;* Ger. *Bache.*]
Baconian *bā-kō′ni-ən, adj.* pertaining to Francis *Bacon* (1561–1626), or to his inductive philosophy, or to Roger *Bacon* (d. *c.* 1292) or his teaching, or to the theory that Francis Bacon wrote Shakespeare's plays. — Also *n.* — *n.* **Baco′nianism.**
bacteria *bak-tē′ri-ə, n.pl.* the Schizomycetes, a class of microscopic unicellular or filamentous plants, saprophytic, parasitic or autotrophic, agents in putrefac-

tion, nitrogen fixation, etc., and the cause of many diseases: — *sing.* **bactē′rium** any member of the class, esp. a rod-shaped schizomycete. — *n.* **bacteraemia,** U.S. **bacteremia** (*-ē′mi-ə*) the presence of bacteria in the blood. — *adjs.* **bactē′rial; bactē′rian, bacteric** (*-ter′-ik*); **bactēricī′dal.** — *ns.* **bactē′ricide** a substance that destroys bacteria; **bacteriochlorophyll** (*-klor′, -klōr′ō-fil*) in some bacteria, a substance related to the chlorophyll of green plants; **bactē′rioid, bac′tēroid** a swollen bacterium living symbiotically in the root-nodules of beans and other plants. — *adj.* **bactēriolog′ical.** — *ns.* **bactēriol′ogist; bactēriol′ogy** the scientific study of bacteria; **bactērioly′sin** (or *-ol′i-*) an antibody that destroys bacteria; **bactēriol′ysis** destruction of bacteria by an antibody (Gr. *lysis,* dissolution). — *adj.* **bactēriolyt′ic.** — *ns.* **bacteriophage** (*bak-tē′ri-ō-fāj, -fäzh*) any of a large number of virus-like agents, present in the atmosphere, soil, water, living things, etc., whose function is to destroy bacteria (Gr. *phagein,* to eat); **bactērio′sis** any bacterial plant-disease; **bactērios′tasis** inhibition of the growth of bacteria (Gr. *stasis,* standing); **bactē′riostat** an agent that inhibits their growth. — *adj.* **bactēriostat′ic.** — *v.t.* **bac′tērise, -ize** to treat with bacteria. — **bacterial leaching** see **leaching.** [Gr. *baktērion,* dim. of *baktron,* a stick.]

Bactrian *bak′tri-ən, adj.* belonging to *Bactria* (now nearly corresponding to Balkh, a district of N. Afghanistan), esp. applied to a two-humped camel. — *n.* a two-humped camel.
baculine *bak′ū-līn, adj.* pertaining to the stick or cane — in flogging. [L. *baculum.*]
baculite *bak′ū-līt, n.* a fossil of the genus **Baculites** (*-īt′ēz*), allied to the ammonites, with a straight, tapering shell. [L. *baculum,* a stick.]
bad *bad, adj.* ill or evil: wicked: hurtful: incorrect, faulty: poor: unskilful: worthless: unfavourable: painful: unwell: spurious: severe: having serious effects: good, attractive (*slang,* orig. *U.S.*): — *compar.* **worse;** *superl.* **worst.** — *n.* **badd′ie, badd′y** (*coll.*) a criminal person or villain, esp. as portrayed in films, television or radio shows. — *adj.* **badd′ish** somewhat bad: not very good. — *adv.* **bad′ly** in a faulty or unskilful way: unfavourably: severely: to a marked extent: very much. — *n.* **bad′ness.** — **bad blood** angry feeling; **bad debt** a debt that cannot be recovered; **bad lands** wastes of much eroded soft strata in South Dakota: (usu. **bad′-lands**) any similar eroded region; **bad language** profane language, swearing. — *adj.* **bad′ly-off** poorly provided esp. with money. — **bad′man** (*U.S.*) an outlaw. — *v.t.* **bad′mouth** (*coll.*) to criticise, malign. — **bad shot** a wrong guess. — *adj.* **bad-tem′pered.** — **bad trip** (*coll.*) an episode of terrifying hallucinations and physical discomfort resulting from taking a drug, esp. LSD. — **go bad** to decay; **go to the bad** to go to moral ruin; **in someone's bad books** in disfavour with someone; **to the bad** in a bad condition: in deficit; **with a bad grace** ungraciously. [Ety. very obscure. The M.E. *badde* is perh. from O.E. *bæddel,* a hermaphrodite, *bædling,* an effeminate fellow.]
baddeleyite *bad′li-īt, n.* a mineral yielding zirconium, consisting of 90% zirconium dioxide; found in beach sands, in Sri Lanka and Brazil. [Joseph *Baddeley,* who brought specimens to Europe in 19th cent.]
badderlock *bad′ər-lok,* (*Scot.*) *n.* an edible seaweed (*Alaria*) resembling tangle. — Also **balderlocks** (*böl′-dər-loks*). [Poss. for *Balder's locks.*]
bade *bad* (*poet. bād*), *pa.t.* of **bid** (both verbs).
badge *baj, n.* a mark or emblem showing rank, membership of a society, etc.: any distinguishing mark or symbol. [M.E. *bage.* Origin obscure.]
badger *baj′ər, n.* a burrowing, nocturnal, hibernating animal of the otter and weasel family; extending to other animals — hyrax, wombat, ratel: a painting, or other, brush made of badger's hair. — *v.t.* to pursue with eagerness, as dogs hunt the badger: to pester or worry. — *adj.* **badg′erly** like a badger: greyish-haired, elderly. — **badg′er-bait′ing, -drawing** the sport of set-

ting dogs to draw out a badger from a barrel; **badg′er= dog** the dachshund, a long-bodied and short-legged dog used in drawing the badger. — *adj.* **badg′er-legged** having legs of unequal length, as the badger was commonly supposed to have. [Prob. from **badge** and the noun-forming suffix *-ard*, in reference to the white mark borne like a badge on its forehead.]

badging-hook. See **bagging-hook.**

badinage *bad′in-äzh, n.* light playful talk: banter. [Fr. *badinage — badin,* playful or bantering.]

badious *bā′di-ɘs, (bot.) adj.* chestnut-coloured. [L. *badius.*]

badmash, budmash *bud′mash, (India) n.* an evil-doer. [Pers.]

badminton *bad′min-tɘn, n.* a cooling summer drink compounded of claret, sugar, and soda-water: a game played with shuttlecocks. [*Badminton* in Gloucester, a seat of the Dukes of Beaufort.]

Baedeker *bā′di-kɘr, n.* any of the series of travellers' guide-books published by Karl *Baedeker* (1801–59) or his successors: any similar guide-book: any handbook or vade-mecum (*fig.*).

bael, bel, bhel *bel, n.* a thorny Indian rutaceous tree (*Aegle marmelos*): its edible fruit, the Bengal quince. [Hind.]

baetyl *bē′til, n.* a magical or holy meteoric stone. [Gr. *baitÿlos.*]

baff *baf, v.t.* to strike the ground with the sole of a golf-club in playing, and so to send the ball up in the air. — *n.* **baffy** (*baf′i*) a club like a brassy, but with a somewhat shorter shaft and a more sloping face.

baffle *baf′l, v.t.* to frustrate, confound, bewilder, bring to nought, impede perplexingly: to cheat, hoodwink (*obs.*): to disgrace publicly, as by hanging by the heels (*obs.*): to regulate or divert (liquid, gas, sound-waves, etc.). — *n.* confusion, check (*obs.*): a plate or like device for regulating or diverting the flow of liquid, gas, sound-waves, etc. (also **baff′le-board, baff′le-plate, baff′ler**). — *ns.* **baff′lement; baff′ler** a bewilderer, confounder. — *adj.* **baff′ling.** — *adv.* **baff′lingly.** — **baff′legab** (*slang*) the professional logorrhoea of many politicians and salespeople, characterised by prolix abstract circumlocution and/or a profusion of abstruse technical terminology, used as a means of persuasion, pacification or obfuscation. [Perh. Scottish and connected with *bauchle,* to treat contemptuously; but cf. Fr. *bafouer,* or earlier *beffler,* from O.Fr. *befe,* mockery.]

baft¹ *bäft, n.* a coarse fabric, orig. Oriental, later made in and shipped from England. [Pers. *baft,* woven.]

baft² *bäft, (arch.) adv.* and *prep.* behind: abaft, astern (*naut.*). [O.E. *beæftan — be,* by, and *æftan,* behind.]

bag *bag, n.* a sack, pouch: specially the silken pouch to contain the back-hair of the wig: a bagful: measure of quantity for produce: a game-bag, hence the quantity of fish or game secured, however great: an udder: an unattractive, slovenly or immoral woman (*slang*): a person's line or vocation (*slang*): (in *pl.*) trousers (*coll.*). — *v.i.* to bulge, swell out: to drop away from the right course (*naut.*). — *v.t.* to cram full: to put into a bag, specially of game: hence to kill (game): to seize, secure or steal: to denigrate (*Austr.*): — *pr.p.* **bagg′ing;** *pa.p.* **bagged.** — *n.* **bag′ful** as much as a bag will hold: — *pl.* **bag′fuls.** — *adj.* **bagged** (*bagd*) in a bag: bulged slackly. — *adv.* **bagg′ily.** — *n.* **bagg′ing** cloth or material for bags. — *adj.* **bagg′it** (*Scot.*) bagged: full of spawn, etc. — *n.* a ripe female salmon that has failed to shed her eggs. — *adj.* **bagg′y** loose like a bag: bulged. — **bag′man** an old-fashioned name for a commercial traveller: one who carries a bag: one who collects or distributes money on behalf of another by dishonest means or for a dishonest purpose (*U.S.*): a swagman (*Austr.*): **bag′-net** a bag-shaped net for catching fish; **bag′wash** (a laundry offering) a laundry service by which rough unfinished washing is done; **bag′wig** an 18th-cent. wig with back-hair enclosed in an ornamental bag. — **bag and baggage** originally a military expression, as in the phrase, 'to march out with bag

and baggage', i.e. with all belongings saved: now used to mean 'completely' in sentences such as *to clear out bag and baggage*; **bag of bones** an emaciated living being; **bag of tricks** the whole outfit; **bags (I)** (*slang*) I lay claim to; **bags of** (*slang*) plenty of; **in the bag** secured or as good as secured; **let the cat out of the bag** to disclose a secret. [M.E. *bagge,* perh. Scand.; not Celtic, as Diez suggests.]

bagarre *ba-gär,* (Fr.) *n.* a scuffle, brawl, rumpus.

bagasse *bɘ-gas′, n.* dry refuse in sugar-making. — *n.* **bagassō′sis** industrial disease caused by inhaling bagasse. [Fr.; Sp. *bagazo,* husks of grapes or olives after pressing.]

bagatelle *bag-ɘ-tel′, n.* a trifle: a piece of music in a light style: a game played on a board with balls, usu. nine, and a cue or spring, the object being to put the balls into numbered holes or sections. [Fr., — It. *bagatella,* a conjuror's trick, a trifle.]

bagel *bā′gɘl, (U.S.) n.* a hard leavened roll in the shape of a doughnut. [Yiddish *beygel* — Ger. *Beugel.*]

baggage *bag′ij, n.* the tents, provisions, and other necessaries of an army: traveller's luggage: a worthless woman: a saucy woman. — *ns.* **bagg′age-animal; bagg′age-car** (*U.S.*) a railway luggage-van; **bagg′age-train** a train of baggage-animals, wagons, etc. [O.Fr. *bagage* — *baguer,* to bind up, from which we may infer all the meanings, without reference to Fr. *bagasse,* It. *bagascia,* a strumpet.]

bagging-hook *bag′ing-hōōk, (dial.) n.* a type of sickle. — Also **badging-hook** (*baj′-*). [Ety. uncertain.]

bagnio *ban′yō, n.* a bathing-house, esp. one with hot baths (*obs.*): an Oriental prison: a brothel: — *pl.* **bagn′ios.** [It. *bagno* — L. *balneum,* a bath.]

bagpipe *bag′pīp, n.* a wind-instrument consisting of a *bag* fitted with *pipes* (often in *pl.*). — *ns.* **bag′piper; bag′- piping.**

baguette *bag-et′, n.* a small moulding like an astragal (*archit.*): a precious stone cut in the shape of a long rectangle: a long narrow French loaf of white bread with a thick crust. [Fr., rod, dim. — L. *baculum.*]

baguio *bä-gē′ō, n.* a hurricane: — *pl.* **bagui′os.** [Philippine Islands Sp.]

bah *bä, interj.* expressing disgust or contempt. [Fr.]

bahada. See **bajada.**

Bahadur *bɘ-hä′dɘr,* or *-ö′, (India) n.* a title of respect often added to the names of officers and officials. [Hind. *bahädur,* hero.]

Bahai, Baha'i *bä-hä′ē,* or *bɘ-, n.* an adherent of an orig. Persian religion, a development of Babism (see **Babi**) following the teaching of *Baha-*Ullah, 'the Glory of God', (Mirza Husain Ali, 1817–92) who claimed to be the bringer of a new revelation from God: the religion itself. — Also *adj.* — *ns.* **Baha′ist; Baha′ism; Baha′ite.**

Bahasa Indonesia *bɘ-hä′sɘ in-dɘ-nē′zi-ɘ, -zhi-ɘ, -zhyɘ,* the Indonesian language. — **Bahasa Malaysia** Malay. [Malay, Indonesian *bahasa,* language.]

baht *bät, n.* the monetary unit of Thailand. [Thai *bāt.*]

bahuvrihi *bä-hōō-vrē′hē, n.* a class of compound words in which the first element governs or describes the second, but the qualified element cannot be substituted for the whole (exemplified by nouns like *turncoat, hunchback, blue-stocking*). — Also *adj.* [Sans. — *bahu,* much, *vrihi,* rice, together forming such a compound.]

baignoire *ben-wär, n.* a theatre box on a level with the stalls. [Fr., bath.]

bail¹ *bāl, n.* one who procures the release of an accused person by becoming security for his appearing in court: the security given: jurisdiction, custody (*Spens.*). — *v.t.* to set a person free by giving security for him: to release on the security of another: to deliver (goods) in trust upon a contract. — *adj.* **bail′able** — *ns.* **bailee′** one to whom goods are bailed; **bail′er** in U.S., a variant spelling of **bailor;** **bail′ment** a delivery of goods in trust: the action of bailing a prisoner; **bail′or** one who bails goods to a bailee. — **bail′bond** a bond given by a prisoner and his surety upon being bailed; **bail′-dock,**

bale′-dock a room at the Old Bailey, London, in which prisoners were formerly kept during the trials; **bail-out** see **bail out** below; **bails′man** one who gives bail for another. — **accept, admit to, allow bail** are all said of the magistrate; the prisoner **offers, surrenders to his bail;** the one who provides it **goes, gives** or **stands bail; bail out** (*coll.*) to stand bail for (a prisoner): to assist out of (financial) difficulties (*n.* **bail′-out**); **give leg bail** to be beholden to one's legs for escape. [O.Fr. *bail*, custody, handing over, *baillier*, to control, guard, hand over. — L. *bājulāre*, to bear a burden, carry, carry on.]

bail², **bayle** *bāl*, *n.* a barrier: a pole separating horses in an open stable: a frame for holding a cow's head during milking (*Austr.*). — *v.t.* **bail** (*Shak.* **bale**) to confine. — **bail up** (*Austr.*) to secure in a bail: to stop and disarm in order to rob: to put one's hands up in surrender: to bring, or be brought, to bay, to corner or be cornered. [O.Fr. *baile*, perh. from *baillier*, to enclose; or L. *baculum*, a stick.]

bail³ *bāl*, *n.* one of the cross pieces on the top of the wicket in cricket. — *ns.* **bail′-ball, bail′er** a bowled ball that hits or removes a bail without disturbing the stumps. [Prob. conn. with **bail².**]

bail⁴ *bāl*, *n.* on a typewriter, teleprinter, etc., a hinged bar that holds the paper against the platen. [Prob. conn. with **bail².**]

bail⁵ (also **bale**) *bāl*, *n.* a bucket or other vessel for ladling out water from a boat. — *v.t.* to clear of water with bails: to ladle (often with *out*). — *n.* **bail′er.** — **bale (bail) out** to escape from an aeroplane by parachute: to escape from a potentially difficult situation. [Fr. *baille*, bucket, perh. from L.L. *bacula*, dim. of *baca*, a basin.]

bail⁶ *bāl*, *n.* a hoop: a hoop-handle, as in a kettle. [Prob. O.N. *beygla*, hoop, from the Gmc. root *bug-*, to bend.]

bailey *bāl′i*, *n.* the outer wall of a feudal castle: hence the outer court, or any court within the walls. — **the Old Bailey** in London was in the ancient bailey between Ludgate and Newgate. [Fr. *baille*, palisade, enclosure, from L.L. *ballium*.]

Bailey bridge *bā′li brij*, a prefabricated bridge constructed speedily for emergency use. [Designed during World War II by Sir Donald *Bailey*.]

bailie *bāl′i*, *n.* in Scotland, title of magistrate who presides in borough court — elected by town council from among the councillors (now mainly *hist.*): sheriff's officer (*obs.*; cf. **water-bailie**): chief magistrate of Scottish barony or part of county (*obs.*). — *n.* **bail′ieship.** — Also **baill′ie, baill′ieship.** [O.Fr. *bailli, baillif*; see **bailiff.**]

bailiff *bāl′if*, *n.* formerly any king's officer, e.g. sheriff, mayor, etc., esp. the chief officer of a hundred, surviving in certain cases as a formal title: the first civil officer in Jersey and in Guernsey: a foreign magistrate: a sheriff's officer: an agent or land-steward. — *n.* **bail′iwick** the jurisdiction of a bailiff: jurisdiction in general. [O.Fr. *baillif* — L.L. *bājulivus* — *bājulus*, carrier, administrator. See **bail¹.**]

bailli *bī-yē*, (Fr.) *n.* a magistrate. — *n.* **bailliage** (*-äzh*) his jurisdiction.

baillie. See **bailie.**

Baily's beads *bā′liz bēds*, bright spots, resembling a string of beads, visible during the last seconds before a total eclipse of the sun. [Detected in 1836 by the astronomer F. *Baily.*]

bainin *bā-nēn′*, *n.* a type of wool produced in Ireland that is only partially scoured and therefore retains some natural oil. — Also *adj.* [Ir. *báinín*, homespun.]

bain-marie *ban-ma-rē′, be̜-ma-rē*, *n.* a water-bath (*chem.*): in cooking, a vessel of hot or boiling water into which another vessel is placed to cook slowly or keep hot. [Fr. *bain-marie*, bath of Mary — L. *balneum Mariae* — origin uncertain, perh. from *Mary* or Miriam, sister of Moses, who reputedly wrote a book on alchemy.]

Bairam *bī′räm, bī-räm′*, *n.* the name of two Muslim festivals — the *Lesser Bairam* lasting three days, after the feast of Ramadan, and the *Greater*, seventy days

later, lasting four days. [Pers.]

bairn *bārn*, (*Scot.*) *n.* a child. — *adjs.* **bairn′like, bairn′ly.** — **bairn′s′-part** see **legitim; bairn′-team, bairn′-time** brood of children. [O.E. *bearn* — *beran*, to bear.]

baisemain *bāz′mē̜*, (*obs.*) *n.* mostly in *pl.*, compliment paid by kissing the hand. [Fr. *baiser*, to kiss, *main*, hand.]

bait *bāt*, *n.* food put on a hook to allure fish or make them bite: any allurement or temptation: a refreshment, esp. taken on a journey (*arch.*): a stop for that purpose (*arch.*): a range (*slang*). — *v.t.* to set with food as a lure: to tempt: to give refreshment to, esp. on a journey (*arch.*): to set dogs on (a bear, bull, etc.): to persecute, harass: to exasperate, esp. with malice, tease. — *v.i.* to take, or stop for, refreshment on a journey (*arch.*). — *ns.* **bait′er; bait′ing.** — **bait′fish** fish used as bait: fish that may be caught with bait. [M.E. *beyten* — O.N. *beita*, to cause to bite — *bita*, to bite.]

baize *bāz*, *n.* a coarse woollen cloth with a long nap, used mainly for coverings, linings, etc.: a table cover. — *v.t.* to cover or line with baize. [Fr. *baies*, pl. (fem.) of *bai* — L. *badius*, bay-coloured.]

bajada, bahada *ba-hä′də*, (*geol.*) *n.* a slope formed by aggradation, consisting of rock debris. [Sp. *bajada*, a slope.]

bajan *bā′jən* (*Aberdeen*), **bejant** *bē′jənt* (*St Andrews*), *ns.* a freshman (so formerly at several continental universities). [Fr. *béjaune*, novice — *bec jaune*, yellow bill, unfledged bird.]

Bajocian *ba-jō′si-ən*, (*geol.*) *adj.* of a division of the Middle Jurassic. [L. *Bajocassēs*, a people living about Bayeux.]

bajra, bajri, bajree *bäj′rə*, or *-rä*, *bäj′rē*, *ns.* a kind of Indian millet. [Hind.]

bake *bāk*, *v.t.* to dry, harden, or cook by the heat of the sun or fire: to make or cook in an oven: to harden by cold (*Shak.*): to cake (*Shak.*). — *v.i.* to work as a baker: to become firm through heat: to be very hot (*coll.*): — *pa.p.* **baked** (*bākt*), **bak′en** (*arch.*); *pr.p.* **bāk′ing.** — *n.* (*Scot.*) a kind of biscuit. — *ns.* **bāk′er** one who bakes bread, etc: an artificial fly used in salmon-fishing; **bāk′ery** a bakehouse: a baker's shop; **bāk′ing** the process by which bread is baked: the quantity baked at one time. — **bake′apple** (*Can.*) the fruit of the cloudberry; **bake′board** (*Scot.*) a board for kneading dough on; **baked Alaska** a pudding consisting of ice-cream and cake covered with meringue baked rapidly; **baked beans** beans boiled and baked, now generally used of a variety tinned in tomato sauce; **bake′house** a house or place used for baking in; **bake′meat** (*B.*) pastry, pies; **baker's dozen** see **dozen; bake′stone** a flat stone or plate of iron on which cakes are baked in the oven; **bake′ware** heat-resistant dishes suitable for use in baking; **bak′ing-pow′der** a mixture (e.g. tartaric acid and sodium bicarbonate) giving off carbon dioxide, used as a substitute for yeast in baking; **bak′ing-so′da** sodium bicarbonate. [O.E. *bacan*; cog. with Ger. *backen*, to bake, Gr. *phōgein*, to roast.]

Bakelite® *bā′kəl-īt*, *n.* a synthetic resin made by condensation of cresol or phenol with formaldehyde. [From its inventor, L. H. *Baekeland* (1863–1944).]

Bakewell pudding, Bakewell tart *bāk′wel pŏŏd′ing, tärt* a dish consisting of a pastry base spread with jam and a filling made of eggs, sugar, butter and ground almonds. [*Bakewell*, Derbyshire.]

baklava, baclava *bak′lə-və*, *n.* a Turkish dessert made of pieces of flaky pastry, honey, nuts, etc. [Turk.]

baksheesh, bakhshish, backsheesh, bakshish *bak′* or *buk′-shēsh*, *n.* a gift or present of money in the East (India, Turkey, etc.), a gratuity or tip. [Pers. *bakhshīsh*.]

Balaam *bā′lam*, *n.* a prophet who strives to mislead, like Balaam in Num. xxii–xxiv: unimportant paragraphs kept in readiness to fill up a newspaper. — *n.* **Bā′laamite.** — *adj.* **Bālaamīt′ical.** — **Ba′laam-box** or **-bas′ket** a place in which such paragraphs are kept in readiness.

Balaclava cap, helmet *bal-ə-klä′və kap, hel′mit*, a warm knitted hat covering the head and neck, with an opening for the face. [*Balaklava* in Crimea.]

baladin *ba-la-dɛ̃*, (Fr.) *n.* a public dancer: a mountebank: — *fem.* **baladine** (*-dēn*).

balalaika *ba-lə-lī′kə*, *n.* a Russian musical instrument, like a guitar, with triangular body and ordinarily three strings. [Russ.]

balance *bal′əns*, *n.* an instrument for weighing, usu. formed of two dishes or scales hanging from a beam supported in the middle: act of weighing two things: equilibrium: harmony among the parts of anything: equality or just proportion of weight or power, as the *balance of power*: the sum required to make the two sides of an account equal, hence the surplus, or the sum due on the account: what is needed to produce equilibrium, a counterpoise: a contrivance that regulates the speed of a clock or watch: remainder. — *v.t.* to weigh in a balance: to poise: to set or keep in equilibrium: to counterpoise: to compare: to settle, as an account: to examine and test so as to make the debtor or creditor sides of an account agree (*bookkeeping*). — *v.i.* to have equal weight or power, etc.: to be or come to be in equilibrium: to hesitate or fluctuate: in dancing, to move in rhythm towards and away from one's partner. — *adj.* **bal′anced** poised so as to preserve equilibrium: well-arranged, stable. — *n.* **bal′ancer** one who, or that which, balances: a fly's rudimentary hindwing: an acrobat. — **bal′ance-sheet** a summary and balance of accounts; **bal′ance-wheel** a wheel in a watch or chronometer which regulates the beat or rate. — **balance of mind** sanity; **balance of payments** the difference over a stated period between a nation's total receipts (in all forms) from foreign countries and its total payments to foreign countries; **balance of power** a state of equilibrium of forces in which no nation or group of nations has the resources to go to war with another or others with likelihood of success; **balance of trade** the difference in value between a country's imports and exports; **in the balance** unsettled: undecided; **off balance** unstable, esp. mentally or emotionally: in a state of unreadiness to respond to an attack, challenge, etc.; **on balance** having taken everything into consideration. [Fr., — L. *bilanx*, having two scales — *bis*, double, *lanx*, *lancis*, a dish or scale.]

balancé *bul-ā-sā*, (Fr.) *n.* in ballet, a rocking step taking the weight from one foot to the other.

Balanus *bal′ə-nəs*, *n.* the acorn-shell genus. — *ns.* **balanitis** (*bal-ə-nī′tis*) inflammation of the glans penis in mammals; **Balanogloss′us** (Gr. *glōssa*, tongue) a genus of worm-like animals of the Hemichordata. [Gr. *balanos*, acorn, glans penis.]

balas *bal′as*, *n.* a rose-red spinel (usu. **balas ruby**). [O. Fr. *balais* (It. *balascio*) — L.L. *balascus* — Pers. *Badakhshān*, a place near Samarkand where they are found.]

balata *bal′ə-tə*, *n.* the gum of the bullet- or bully-tree of South America, used as a substitute for rubber and gutta-percha. [Prob. Tupí.]

balboa *bal-bō′ə*, *n.* the monetary unit of Panama. [Vasco Nuñez de *Balboa*, *c.* 1475–1517.]

Balbriggan *bal-brig′ən*, *n.* a knitted cotton fabric like that made at *Balbriggan*, Ireland: underclothing made of it.

balbutient *bal-bū′sh(y)ənt*, *adj.* stammering. [L. *balbūtiēns*, *-entis* — *balbūtīre*, to stutter.]

balcony *balk′ə-ni* (18th cent., *bal-kō′ni*), *n.* a stage or platform projecting from the wall of a building within or without, supported by pillars or consoles, and surrounded with a balustrade or railing: in theatres, usu. the gallery immediately above the dress circle (*U.S.* the dress circle itself). — *n.* **balconet(te)′** a miniature balcony. — *adj.* **bal′conied**. [It. *balcone* — *balco*, of Gmc. origin; O.H.G. *balcho* (Ger. *Balken*), Eng. **balk**.]

bald *böld*, *adj.* without hair, feathers, etc., on the head (or on other parts of the body): bare, unadorned: lacking in literary grace: paltry, trivial (*arch.*): undis-

guised. — *adjs.* **bald′ing** going bald; **bald′ish** somewhat bald. — *adv.* **bald′ly** plainly, without tactful circumlocution. — *n.* **bald′ness**. — **bald′-coot**, **bald′i-coot** the coot, from its pure white wide frontal plate; **bald′-eagle** a common but inaccurate name for the American white-headed eagle, used as the national emblem. — *adj.* **bald′-faced** having white on the face, as a horse. — **bald′-head** a person bald on the head. — *adj.* **bald′-headed** having a bald head. — *adj.* and *adv.* (*slang*) **bald′-head′ed** without restraint: out and out. — **bald′pate** one destitute of hair: a kind of wild duck. — *adjs.* **bald′pate**, **-d.** — **bald as a coot** see **coot**. [Perh. **balled**, rounded.]

baldachin, **baldaquin** *böl′də-kin*, *n.* silk brocade: a canopy over a throne, pulpit, altar, etc.: in R.C. processions, a canopy borne over the priest who carries the host. [It. *baldacchino*, Fr. *baldaquin*, a canopy, from It. *Baldacco*, Baghdad, whence was brought the stuff of which they were made.]

balderdash *böl′dər-dash*, *n.* mixture of liquids (*obs.*): idle senseless talk: anything jumbled together without judgment: obscene language or writing (*dial.*). [Origin unknown.]

balderlocks. See **badderlocks.**

baldi-coot. See under **bald.**

baldmoney *böld′mun-i*, *n.* spignel (*Meum athamanticum*), a subalpine umbelliferous plant: gentian of various kinds. [Ety. unknown.]

baldric, also **baldrick**, *böld′rik*, *n.* a warrior's belt or shoulder sash: (*Spens.* **baudricke**) the zodiac. [Cf. M.H.G. *balderich*, girdle.]

Baldwin *böld′win*, *n.* an American variety of apple. [Personal name.]

bale[1] *bāl*, *n.* a bundle, or package of goods: the set of dice for any special game (*obs.*). — *v.t.* to make into bales. — *n.* **bal′er**. [M.E. *bale*, perh. from O.Fr. *bale* — O.H.G. *balla*, *palla*, ball. See **ball.**]

bale[2]. See **bail**[5].

bale[3] *bāl*, *n.* evil, injury, mischief (*arch.*): misery, woe (*arch.*) — *adj.* **bale′ful** malignant, hurtful: of evil influence: painful (*arch.*): sorrowful (*arch.*): lugubrious. — *adv.* **bale′fully.** — *n.* **bale′fulness.** [O.E. *bealu*; O.H.G. *balo*; O.N. *böl*.]

balection. Same as **bolection.**

baleen *bə-*, *ba-lēn′*, *n.* horny plates growing from the palate of certain whales, the whalebone of commerce. — Also *adj.* [O.Fr. *baleine* — L. *balaena*, whale.]

bale-fire *bāl′-fīr*, *n.* a funeral pyre (*arch.*): a beacon-fire (*Scot.*): a bonfire. [O.E. *bǣl*; cf. O.N. *bāl*, bale, Gr. *phalos*, bright, white.]

Balfour declaration *bal′fə dek-lə-rā′shən*, the statement made in November 1917 by Arthur *Balfour*, the then British Foreign Secretary, that the British Government was in favour of the establishment of a national home for the Jewish people in Palestine.

balibuntal *bal-i-bun′tl*, *n.* (a hat made of) fine, closely-woven straw. [From *Baliuag*, in the Philippines, and *buntal*, Tagálog for the straw of the talipot palm.]

Balinese *bä-la-nēz′*, *adj.* pertaining to the island of Bali (east of Java), its people, or their language. — Also *n.*

balista. See **ballista.**

balk, baulk *bö(l)k*, *n.* an unploughed ridge: a place overlooked, an omission (*obs.*): a ridge (*obs.*): part of a billiard table marked off by the balk-line: a forbidden action of the pitcher in baseball: a squared timber: a tie-beam of a house, stretching from wall to wall, esp. when laid so as to form a loft (the balks): the beam of a balance (*obs.*): a rope to connect fishing-nets: a check, frustration: a disappointment: failure to take a jump or the like. — *v.t.* to ignore, pass over: to shirk: to decline: to avoid: to let slip: to put a stumbling-block in the way of: to thwart: to frustrate: to foil: to check: to chop (logic) (*Shak.*). — *v.i.* to pull up or stop short at a difficulty: to jib: to refuse a jump, etc.: to refrain: to desist: to lie out of the way (*Spens.*): to bandy words (*obs.*). — *adj.* **balk′d** (*Shak.*) prob., heaped in balks. — *n.* **balk′er.** — *n.* **balk′iness.** — *n.* and *adj.* **balk′ing.**

— *adv.* **balk'ingly.** — *adj.* **balk'y** apt to balk: perverse, refractory. — **balk'line** a line drawn across a billiard table: a boundary line for the preliminary run in a jumping competition or the like.   [O.E. *balca*, ridge; O.H.G. *balcho*, beam.]

Balkanise, -ize (also without *cap.*) *böl'kən-īz, v.t.* to reduce to the condition of the *Balkan* peninsula which was divided in the late 19th and early 20th centuries into a number of mutually hostile territories. — *n.* **Balk-, balkanisā'tion, -z-.**

ball[1] *böl, n.* anything spherical or nearly so: the orb of sovereignty: a globular body to play with: any rounded protuberant part of the body: a bullet, or solid missile thrown from an engine of war: a throw or delivery of the ball at cricket, etc.: a game played with a ball, esp. (*U.S.*) baseball or football: a spherical clew of yarn, string, etc.: the eyeball: a spherical cake of soap (*obs.*): a bolus for a horse: (in *pl.*) testicles (*vulg.*): (in *pl.*) nonsense (also *interj.*; *vulg.*): (in *pl.*) guts, courage (*slang*, esp. *U.S.*). — *v.t.* to form into a ball: to clog: to entangle. — *v.i.* to gather into a ball: to clog: to cluster, as swarming bees round the queen. — *adj.* **balled** formed into a ball. — *n.* **ball'ing** forming into a ball: snowballing: (*Scot.* **ba'ing** *bö'ing*, **ba'spiel** *bö'spēl*) a periodical game of football played by the population of a town in the streets and sometimes in the river. — *adj.* **ball'-and-claw'** see **claw-and-ball** under claw. — **ball'-barrow** a wheelbarrow with a ball-shaped wheel; **ball'-bear'ing(s)** a device for lessening friction by making a revolving part turn on loose steel balls: (in *sing.* only) one of the balls so used; **ball'cock** the stopcock of a cistern turned by a floating ball that rises and falls with the water; **ball'-flower** an ornament of Decorated Gothic architecture, resembling a ball within a globular flower; **ball'-game** any game played with a ball, esp. (*U.S.*) baseball or football: a situation, as in *a new ball-game* (*coll.*); **ball lightning** a slowly-moving luminous ball occasionally seen during a thunderstorm; **ball mill** a horizontal cylindrical vessel in which a substance is ground by rotation with steel or ceramic balls; **ball park** (*U.S.*) a baseball field: a sphere of activity (*coll.*). — *adj.* (*U.S.*) **ball'park** approximate (esp. in the phrase *ballpark figures*). — **ball'-player** (*U.S.*) a baseball-player; **ball'-point (pen)** a fountain-pen having a tiny ball rotating against an inking cartridge as its writing tip. — *adj.* **ball'-proof** proof against balls discharged from firearms. — **ballsed-up, balls-up** see **balls up** below. — **ball and socket** a joint formed of a ball partly enclosed in a cup; **ball of fire** a lively, dynamic person: a glass of brandy (*coll.*); **balls up** (*vulg.*) to make a muddle or mess of: to throw into confusion (*n.* **balls'-up**; *adj.* **ballsed'-up**); **ball up** to clog: to make a mess of (*slang*; *adj.* **balled'-up**); **keep the ball rolling** to keep things going; **make a balls of** (*vulg.*) to do badly, make a mess of; **no ball** (*cricket*) a delivery adjudged contrary to rule; **on the ball** properly in touch with the situation: on the alert; **play ball** see **play**; **set, start the ball rolling** to make the first move: to start things going; **the ball at one's feet** success in one's grasp; **the ball's in your court** the responsibility for the next move is yours; **three balls** the sign of a pawnbroker.   [M.E. *bal* — O.N. *böllr*; O.H.G. *ballo, pallo*.]

ball[2] *böl, n.* an assembly for dancing. — **ball'-dress; ball'-room.** — Also *adj.* — **have a ball** to enjoy oneself very much (*coll.*); **open the ball** to begin operations. [O.Fr. *bal* — *baller*, to dance — L.L. *ballāre*, perh. — Gr. *ballizein*, to dance.]

ballabile *bal-ä'bi-lā, n.* a part of a ballet danced by the whole corps de ballet, with or without the principal dancers: — *pl.* **-biles, -bili** (*-lē*).   [It. *ballabile*, fit to be danced — *ballare*, to dance — L.L.*ballāre*.]

ballad *bal'əd* (*Scot.* **ballant**, *bal'ənt*, **ballat, ballet** *-ət*), *n.* orig. a song accompanying a dance: a simple narrative poem in short stanzas (usu. of four lines, of eight and six syllables alternately): a popular song, often scurrilous, referring to contemporary persons or events

(chiefly *hist.*): formerly, a drawing-room song, usu. sentimental, in several verses sung to the same melody: any slow, sentimental song. — (*obs.*) *v.t.* to make ballads about. — *ns.* **balladeer'** one who sings ballads (also *v.i.*); **ball'adist** a writer or singer of ballads; **ball'adry** ballads collectively: ballad-making. — **ballad concert** a concert of drawing-room ballads; **ball'ad-monger** a dealer in, or composer of, ballads; **ballad opera** (*hist.*) an opera with spoken dialogue, and songs set to existing popular tunes.   [O.Fr. *ballade* — L.L. *ballāre*, to dance; see **ball**[2].]

ballade *ba-läd', n.* a poem of one or more terns or triplets of stanzas, each of seven, eight, or ten lines, including refrain, followed by an envoy, the whole on three (or four) rhymes: sometimes loosely, any poem in stanzas of equal length: an ill-defined form of instrumental music, often in six-eight or six-four time. — **ballade royal** rhyme royal (James VI and I's *ballat royal* has an additional line and rhymes *ababbcbc*).   [An earlier spelling of **ballad**, with old pronunciation restored.]

balladin(e). Same as **baladin(e).**

ballan *bal'ən, n.* a species of wrasse. — Also **ball'-anwrasse'.**   [Perh. Irish *ball*, spot.]

ballant *bal'ənt.* A Scots form of **ballad.**

ballast *bal'əst, n.* heavy material used to weigh down and steady a ship or balloon: broken stone or other material used as the bed of a road or railway: that which renders anything steady: quality giving stability to person's character. — *v.t.* to load with ballast: to make or keep steady: to load (*Shak.*): — *pa.p.* **ball'asted** (*Shak.* **ball'ast**). — **ball'ast-heav'er.** — **in ballast** carrying ballast only.   [Prob. Old Sw. *barlast* — *bar*, bare, and *last*, load.]

ballat. See **ballad, ballade.**

ballerina *bal-ə-rē'nə, n.* a female ballet-dancer: — *pl.* **balleri'ne** (*-nā*), **balleri'nas.**   [It.]

ballet *bal'ā, n.* a theatrical performance of dancing with set steps and pantomimic action: (a suite of) music for it: a troupe giving such performances: the art or activity of dancing in this way: a dance (*obs.*): (*bal'ət*) a form of madrigal: (*bal'ət*; *Scot.*) a ballad. — *adj.* **balletic** (*bal-et'ik*) of the art of ballet. — *adv.* **ballet'-ically.** — *ns.* **balletomane** (*-et'ō-mān*) an enthusiast for ballet; **balletomā'nia.** — **ball'et-dancer; ball'et-dancing; ball'et-girl; ball'et-master.**   [Fr.; dim. of *bal*, a dance.]

ballista, balista *ba-lis'tə, n.* a Roman military engine in the form of a crossbow for heavy missiles. — *adj.* **ballis'tic** projectile: relating to projectiles. — *n. sing.* **ballis'tics** the science of projectiles. — *ns.* **ballis'tite** a smokeless powder composed of guncotton and nitroglycerine; **ballistöcar'diogram** a record produced by a **ballistöcar'diograph**, an instrument for detecting the movements in the body caused by each heart-beat; **ballistöcardiog'raphy.** — **ballistic missile** a guided missile that ends in a ballistic descent, guidance being over only part of its course; **ballistic pendulum** a suspended block for finding the velocity of projectiles.   [L., — Gr. *ballein*, to throw.]

ballium *bal'i-əm, n.* the L.L. form of **bailey.**

ballocks. See **bollocks.**

ballon d'essai *ba-lɔ̃ de-sā,* (Fr.) an experimental balloon: a feeler or preliminary sounding of opinion.

balloon *bə-lōōn', n.* an apparatus for travel in the air, or for carrying recording instruments, consisting of a gas-bag and a car: a toy consisting of an inflatable rubber bag: anything inflated, empty (*fig.*): an ornamental ball on a pillar, etc. (*archit.*): a balloon-shaped drawing enclosing words spoken in a strip cartoon: a game played with a large inflated ball, or the ball itself (*obs.*; also **ballon** *ba-lɔ̃, ba-lōn'*). — *v.t.* to inflate: to send high in the air. — *v.i.* to ascend or travel in, or as if in, a balloon: to puff out like a balloon. — *ns.* **ballonet** (*bal-o-net'*) in a balloon or dirigible, a small bag from which air is allowed to escape, and into which air is forced, to compensate for changes of pressure in the gas-bag; **balloon'ing; balloon'ist.** — *adj.* **balloon'-back** (of a dining-room chair) having a circular or oval-shaped back-support, a style made in the 19th century. — **balloon barrage** a system of captive balloons as a protection against hostile aircraft; **balloon tyre** a large pneumatic tyre of low pressure; **balloon's-vine'** heartseed, a tropical American climber with bladdery pods. — **when the balloon goes up** when the trouble starts: when proceedings begin. [It. *ballone*, augmentative of *balla*, ball.]

ballot *bal'ət*, *n.* a little ball or ticket or paper used in voting: a secret vote or method of voting by putting a ball or ticket or paper into an urn or box: in U.S. extended to open voting. — *v.i.* to vote by ballot: to draw lots: — *pr.p.* **ball'oting**; *pa.t.* and *pa.p.* **ball'oted.** — *n.* **ballotee'.** — **ball'ot-box** a box to receive ballots; **ball'ot-paper** a paper on which a ballot vote is recorded. [It. *ballotta*, dim. of *balla*, ball. See **ball¹**.]

ballow *bal'ō*, (*Shak.*) *n.* a cudgel. — Other readings are **bat, battero.** [Perh. a misprint for **baton**.]

bally *bal'i*, (*slang*) *adj.* a euphemism for **bloody,** but almost meaningless.

ballyhoo *bal-i-hōō'*, (*slang*) *n.* noisy propaganda.

ballyrag *bal'i-rag*, *v.t.* to bullyrag (q.v.).

balm *bäm*, *n.* an aromatic substance: a fragrant and healing ointment: aromatic fragrance: anything that heals or soothes pain: a tree yielding balm: a labiate plant, *Melissa officinalis*, with an aroma similar to that of lemon: extended to *Melittis* (*bastard balm*) and other garden herbs. — *v.t.* to embalm (*arch.*): to anoint with fragrant oil (*Shak.*): to soothe (*arch.*). — *adv.* **balm'ily.** — *n.* **balm'iness.** — *adj.* **balm'y** fragrant: mild and soothing: bearing balm: a variant of **barmy.** — **balm,** or **balsam, of Gilead** the resinous exudation of trees of the genus *Commiphora* or *Balsamodendron*, from the belief that it is the substance mentioned in the Bible as found in Gilead: the balsam fir. [O.Fr. *basme* — L. *balsamum*. See **balsam**.]

bal masqué *bal mas-kā*, (Fr.) a masked ball.

balm-cricket *bäm-krik'it*, (*Tennyson*) *n.* a cicada. [Ger. *Baum*, tree, and **cricket¹**.]

balmoral *bal-mor'əl*, *n.* a flat Scottish bonnet: a figured woollen petticoat: a kind of boot lacing in front. — *n.* **balmorality** (*bal-mər-al'i-ti*; *jocular*) the Victorian type of morality. [**Balmoral,** royal residence in Aberdeenshire (Grampian Region) built in Queen Victoria's reign.]

balneal *bal'ni-əl*, *adj.* of baths or bathing. — *n.* **bal'neary** a bath: a bathing-place: a medicinal spring. — *adj.* of or for bathing. — *ns.* **balneā'tion** bathing; **balneol'ogist; balneol'ogy** the scientific study of bathing and mineral springs; **balneother'apy** treatment of disease by baths. [L. *balneum* — Gr. *balaneion*, bath.]

balneum Mariae *bal'ni-əm ma-rī'ē*, *bal'ne-ōōm ma-rē'ī*, (L.) a bain-marie.

baloney, boloney *ba-, bə-lō'ni*, (*slang*) *n.* deceptive talk: nonsense. [Thought to be from **Bologna** (**sausage**).]

baloo, balu *bä'lōō*, *n.* in India, a bear. [Hind. *bhālū*.]

bal paré *bal pa-rā*, (Fr.) a dress ball.

balsa *böl'sə, bäl'sə*, *n.* a raft or float: corkwood, a tropical American tree (*Ochroma lagopus*) of the silk-cotton family, with very light wood. [Sp., raft.]

balsam *böl'səm*, *n.* a plant of the genus *Impatiens* (family Balsaminaceae): a liquid resin or resinous oily substance, esp. balm of Gilead: any healing agent (*fig.*). — *v.t.* to heal: (*rare*) to embalm. — *adjs.* **balsamic** (*-sam'ik*); **balsamif'erous** producing balsam. — *n.* **Balsami'na** a discarded synonym of *Impatiens*, giving name to the balsam family **Balsaminaceae** (*-in-ā'si-ē*), close akin to the geraniums. — *adj.* **bal'samy** fragrant. — **balsam fir** an American fir (*Abies balsamea*); **balsam of Peru, of Tolu** see **Peru, Tolu; balsam poplar** an American species of poplar; **Canada balsam** a turpentine from the balsam fir. [L. *balsamum* — Gr. *balsamon*; prob. of Semitic origin.]

Balt *bölt*, *n.* a member of the former land-owning class (of German origin) in the Baltic provinces or states. — *adj.* **Balt'ic** of the sea separating Scandinavia from Germany and Russia: of the western division of the Baltoslavs. — *n.* **Balt'oslav'.** — *adjs.* **Balt'oslav, -ic, -on'ic** of a family of Indo-European languages including the Slavonic languages with Lettish, Lithuanian, and (extinct) Old Prussian. [From the *Baltic Sea* — L. *Baltia*, Scandinavia.]

balthazar, balthasar *bal'thə-zär*, *n.* a very large wine-bottle, in capacity usu. taken to equal 16 ordinary bottles (12·80 litres or 2·75 gallons). — Also **belshazzar** (*bel-shaz'ər*). — All forms also with *cap.* [Coined in reference to Dan. v. 1.]

Baltimore *böl'tim-ōr, -ör*, *n.* a common orange and black North American bird of the hang-nest family, called also *Baltimore oriole, fire-bird,* etc. [From Lord *Baltimore*, whose livery was orange and black.]

balu. See **baloo.**

Baluch, Baluchi *ba-lōōch', ba-lōō'chi*, *ns.* a native or inhabitant of Baluchistan: the language of the people of this region. — *adj.* of this region or its people. — *n.* **Baluchitherium** (*-thē'ri-əm*) a gigantic Tertiary fossil rhinoceros found in this region. [Gr. *therion*, wild beast.]

baluster *bal'əs-tər*, *n.* a small pillar supporting a stair rail or a parapet coping, often circular in section and curvaceous in outline. — *adj.* (of a vessel, its stem or handle) like a baluster in shape. — *adj.* **bal'ustered.** — *n.* **bal'ustrade** a row of balusters joined by a rail or coping. [Fr. *balustre* — L.L. *balaustium* — Gr. *balaustion*, pomegranate flower; from its form.]

balzarine *bal'zə-rēn*, *n.* a light dress material of mixed cotton and worsted. [Fr. *balzorine*.]

bam *bam*, (*coll.*) *n.* a hoax: a false tale. — *v.t.* to cheat or hoax. [See **bamboozle**.]

bambino *bam-bē'nō*, *n.* a child: a picture or image of the child Jesus: — *pl.* **bambi'nos, -i'ni** (*-nē*). [It.]

bamboo *bam-bōō'*, *n.* a gigantic tropical and subtropical grass with hollow-jointed woody stem. — **bamboo curtain** the impenetrable political barrier of Asiatic, esp. Chinese, communism (after **iron curtain**). [Perh. Malay *bambu.*]

bamboozle *bam-bōō'zl*, *v.t.* to deceive: to confound or mystify. — *n.* **bamboo'zlement.** [Origin unknown: first appears about 1700.]

bampot *bam'pot*, (*Scot.*) *n.* an idiot, fool. — Also **bamm'er**. [Ety. uncertain.]

ban¹ *ban*, *n.* a proclamation: sentence of banishment: outlawry: anathematisation: a denunciation: a curse: a prohibition: a vague condemnation. — *v.t.* to curse (*arch.*): to chide or rail upon (*dial.*): to anathematise: to proscribe: to forbid or prohibit. [O.E. *gebann*, proclamation, *bannan*, to summon: cf. **banns**.]

ban² *ban*, *n.* one hundredth part of a leu: — *pl.* **bani** (*bany*). [Rum.]

Ban *ban*, (*hist.*) *n.* the governor of a **Ban'at (Ban'ate, Bann'at),** a military district on the boundaries of the Hungarian kingdom. [Pers. *bān,* lord.]

banal *bən-al', bān'əl, ban'əl*, *adj.* commonplace, trivial, flat. — *n.* **banal'ity** triviality. — *adv.* **banal'ly.** [Fr.]

banana *bə-, ba-nä'nə*, *n.* a gigantic tree-like herbaceous plant (*Musa sapientum*) or its nutritious fruit. — **banana liquid, oil, solution** a solution having the odour of bananas, used for various purposes, e.g. in photography, as a solvent for paint, etc.; **banana republic** (*derog.*) any of the small republics in the tropics depending on exports of fruit and on foreign investment: hence any small country dependent on foreign capital; **banana skin** (*fig.*) something which causes a slip-up or a downfall; **banana split** a dish composed of a banana halved lengthways, ice-cream, and other ingredients. — **be, go bananas** (*slang*) to be, go crazy. [Sp. or Port., from the native name in Guinea.]

banausic *ban-ö'sik*, *adj.* mechanic: befitting or savouring of an artisan: vulgar: materialistic. — Also **banau'sian**. [Gr. *banausikos* — *banausos*, a handicraftsman.]

Banbury cake *ban'bər-i kāk*, a kind of mince-pie made in *Banbury*, Oxfordshire.

banc *bangk*, *n.* the judges' bench. — **in banc, in banco** in full court. [Fr.]

banco *bang'kō, n.* standard money in which a bank keeps its accounts, as distinguished from the current money of the place. [It. See **bank**[1,3].]

band[1] *band, n.* that by which loose things are held together: a moral bond of restraint or of obligation (*fig.*): a tie or connecting piece: (*pl.*) shackles, bonds, fetters: an agreement or promise given (*arch.*): security given (*arch.*): a pledge (*Spens.*). — *n.* **band'ster** one who binds the sheaves after the reapers. — **band'-stone** a stone set transversely in a wall to bind the structure. [M.E. *band, bond* — O.N. *band.* O.E. has *bend.* See **band**[2], **bind, bond**[1].]

band[2] *band, n.* a flat strip (of cloth, rubber, metal, etc.) to bind round anything, as a hat-band, waist-band, rubber-band, etc.: a stripe crossing a surface distinguished by its colour or appearance: a flat strip between mouldings, or dividing a wall surface: the neck-band or collar of a shirt, also the collar or ruff worn in the 17th century (termed a *falling-band* when turned down): a belt for driving machinery: (*pl.*) the pair of linen strips hanging down in front from the collar, worn by some Protestant clergymen and by barristers and advocates, formerly by others: a group or range of frequencies or wavelengths between two specified limits (*radio, electronics*): in sound reproduction, a separately recorded section of a record or tape: a group of close-set lines esp. in a molecular spectrum (*phys.*): a particular range, between an upper and lower limit, of e.g. intelligence, wealth, etc. — *n.* **band'age** a strip of cloth for winding round an injured part of the body: an adhesive plaster for protecting a wound or cut: a piece of cloth used to blindfold the eyes. — *v.t.* to bind with a bandage. — *adj.* **band'ed** fastened as with a band: striped with bands. — *n.* **band'ing** the division of children in the final year of primary school into three groups according to ability, in order to obtain an even spread in the mixed-ability classes usual in comprehensive schools. — **band'-box** (or *ban'boks*) a light kind of box for holding (originally bands) caps, millinery, etc.; **band'brake, band'-clutch** a brake, clutch in the form of a flexible band that can be tightened about a wheel or drum; **band'-fish** a bright red Mediterranean fish (*Cepola*), or other ribbon-shaped fish; **band'-saw** an endless saw, a toothed steel belt; **band'=string** an ornamental string for fastening bands or collar; **band'-wheel** a wheel on which a strap or band runs; **band'width** the width of a band of radio frequencies. [M.E. *bande* — O.Fr. *bande,* of Gmc. origin; cf. O.E. *bindan*; Ger. *Binde,* a band; Eng. **band**[1], **bind**.]

band[3] *band, n.* a number of persons bound together for any common purpose: a troop of conspirators, confederates, etc.: a body of musicians, esp. performers on wind and percussion instruments, often attached to a regiment: a herd or flock (*U.S.*). — *v.t.* to bind together. — *v.i.* to associate, assemble, confederate. — **band'master** the conductor of a band; **bands'man** a member of a band of musicians; **band'stand** a structure for accommodating a band of musicians; **band'wagon** the car that carries the band in a circus procession: a party drawing new members by the prestige or possible advantage it seems to offer: a fashionable movement. — **Band of Hope** an association of young persons pledged to lifelong abstinence from alcoholic drinks — first instituted about 1847; **beat the band** to be specially good or remarkable; **jump, leap on the bandwagon** to join in any popular and currently successful movement in the hope of gaining advantage from it; **then the band played** that was the end of it. [Fr. *bande,* of Gmc. origin, with changed sense; cf. **band**[1,2], **bend**[1], **bind**.]

band[4] *band, v.t.* (*Spens.*) to ban or banish.

band[5]. An obsolete *pa.t.* of **bind**.

band[6]. See **bund**.

Band *bant,* (*Ger.*) *n.* a volume of a book or journal: — *pl.* **Bände** (*ben'də*).

bandage. See under **band**[2].

Band-aid ® *band'-ād, n.* a type of sticking-plaster for covering minor wounds. — *adj.* (usu. without *cap.*) of policies, etc. makeshift, temporary.

bandalore *ban'də-lōr, -lör,* (*obs.*) *n.* an 18th cent. toy resembling a yo-yo (q.v.) which, through the action of a coiled spring, returned to the hand when thrown down. [Origin unknown.]

bandana, bandanna *ban-dan'ə, n.* a silk or cotton coloured handkerchief, with spots or diamond prints, originally from India. [Hind. *bādhnū,* a mode of dyeing.]

bandar *bun'där, n.* a rhesus monkey. [Hind.]

bandeau *ban'dō, ban-dō', n.* a band to bind the hair: a band within a hat: a bandage for the eyes: — *pl.* **bandeaux** (*ban'dōz, -dōz'*). [Fr.]

bandeirante *bã-dā-ē-rãt', (Port.) n.* a pioneer, explorer, or adventurer, esp. one who took part in expeditions (*bandeiras*) in search of gold and slaves in 17th-century Brazil.

bandelet *band'ə-let, (archit.) n.* a small flat moulding or fillet surrounding a column. [Fr. *bandelette.*]

bandelier *ban-də-lēr', n.* A form of **bandoleer**.

banderilla *ban-, bän-dā-rēl'yä, n.* a dart with a streamer, stuck by bullfighters in the bull's neck. — *n.* **banderillero** (*ban-, bän-dā-rēl-yā'rō*) a bullfighter who uses banderillas: — *pl.* **banderille'ros**.

banderol, banderole *ban'də-rōl,* **bandrol** *ban'drōl,* **bannerol** *ban'ə-rōl* (*Spens.* **bannerall** *-röl*) *ns.* a small banner or streamer, as that borne on the shaft of a lance: a flat band with an inscription, common in Renaissance buildings (*archit.*). [Fr.]

bandersnatch *ban'dər-snach, n.* a monster invented by Lewis Carroll.

bandh. Same as **bund**.

bandicoot *ban'di-kōōt, n.* the largest species of rat, found in India and Sri Lanka, called also *Malabar-rat* and *pig-rat*: a member of the genus *Perameles* of small marsupials. — *v.t.* (*Austr.*) to remove (potatoes) from the ground leaving the tops undisturbed. [Telugu *pandikokku,* pig-rat.]

bandit *ban'dit, n.* an outlaw: a brigand: in airmen's *slang,* an enemy plane: — *pl.* **ban'dits, banditti** (*ban-dit'ē*; also loosely used as *sing.*, a body of bandits). — *n.* **ban'ditry**. — **one-armed bandit** a fruit-machine, so called from the similarity to an arm of the lever pulled to operate it, and the heavy odds against the user. [It. *bandito,* pl. *banditi* — L.L. *bannīre, bandīre,* to proclaim. See **ban**.]

bandobast, bundobust *bun'dō-bust, (Ind.) n.* an arrangement, settlement. [Hind and Pers. *band-o-bast,* tying and binding.]

bandog *ban'dog, n.* a dog tied up as a watch-dog or because of its ferocity. [**band**[1] and **dog**.]

bandoleer, bandolier *ban-dō-lēr', n.* a shoulder belt, esp. for ammunition. [O.Fr. *bandouillere* — It. *bandoliera* — *banda,* a band.]

bandolero *ban-dō-lā'rō, n.* a highwayman: — *pl.* **bandole'ros**. [Sp.]

bandoline *ban'dō-lēn, n.* a gummy substance used for stiffening the hair. [Prob. from **band**[1].]

bandook. See **bundook**.

bandore *ban-dōr', -dör, n.* an Elizabethan wire-stringed instrument like a cittern, invented by John Rose. — Also **bando'ra**. [Sp. *bandurria,* Fr. *mandore*; L. *pandura,* Gr. *pandourā,* a three-stringed lute.]

bandrol *band'rōl, n.* Same as **banderol**.

bandura *ban-dōō'rə, n.* a Ukrainian twelve-stringed instrument of the lute family. [Ukrainian — Pol. — It. — L. *pandura* (cf. **bandore**).]

bandwagon. See **band**[3].

bandy[1] *ban'di, n.* a club bent at the end for striking a ball: a game at ball with such a club: a game played on ice, similar to ice-hockey but played with a ball and curved sticks. — **ban'dy-ball** hockey. [Origin obscure.]

bandy[2] *ban'di, v.t.* to beat to and fro: to toss from one to another (as words *with* any one): to pass from mouth to mouth (with *about*): to give and take (blows or reproaches): to fight, strive (*Shak.*): — *pr.p.* **ban'dying;**

pa.t. and *pa.p.* **ban'died.** — *n.* **ban'dying.** [Origin obscure.]

bandy[3] *ban'di, adj.* bent wide apart at the knee: having bandy or crooked legs. — *adj.* **ban'dy-legged'.** [Poss. **bandy**[1].]

bandy[4] *ban'di,* (*Ind.*) *n.* a carriage or (bullock) cart. — **ban'dyman.** [Telugu *bandi.*]

bane *bān, n.* destruction: death: mischief: poison: source or cause of evil. — *v.t.* to harm (*arch.*): to poison (*Shak.*). — *adj.* **bane'ful** destructive: pernicious: poisonous. — *adv.* **bane'fully.** — *n.* **bane'fulness.** — **bane'-berry** a black poisonous berry, the fruit of the ranunculaceous plant *Actaea spicata:* the plant itself. [O.E. *bana,* a murderer; O.N. *bani,* death.]

bang[1] *bang, n.* a heavy blow: a sudden loud noise: an explosion: *fig.* meanings as thrill, burst of activity, sudden success: an act of sexual intercourse (*slang*). — *v.t.* to beat: to strike violently: to slam, as a door: to beat or surpass: to have sexual intercourse with (*slang*). — *v.i.* to make a loud noise: to slam: to bounce (*dial.*). — *adv.* with a bang: abruptly: absolutely (as in *bang up-to-date, bang in the middle*). — *adj.* complete, total (used for emphasis, as in *the whole bang lot*). — *n.* **bang'er** something that bangs: an explosive firework: a decrepit old car (*coll.*): a sausage (*slang*). — *adj.* **bang'ing** dealing blows: overwhelming, very great (*coll.*). — *n.* **bang'ster** a violent person: a braggart: a victor. — *adj.* **bang'-up** (*arch. slang*) in the height of excellence or fashion. — **bang goes** (*coll.*) that's the end of; **bang off** (*coll.*) immediately; **bang on** (*coll.*) right on the mark: to speak at length, esp. assertively and repitiously; **bang out** to produce by banging: of printers, to mark someone's retirement or the end of someone's apprenticeship by banging tables, etc. with mallets, etc.; **bang to rights** orig., caught red-handed (*criminals' slang*): certainly, absolutely, no doubt (*coll.*); **bang up** (*slang.*) to imprison, shut up in a cell; **Big Bang** see **big; go with a bang** to go well, be a success. [O.N. *banga,* to hammer; cf. Ger. *Bengel,* a cudgel.]

bang[2] *bang, n.* hair cut square across the brow (often in *pl.*) — *v t* to cut square across. — *adj.* **banged** wearing the hair in such a way. — **bang'-tail** a tail with the end tuft squared: a beast whose tail hair is banged. [An Americanism, poss. from the phrase *bang off.*]

bang[3]. Same as **bhang.**

Bangalore torpedo *bang'gə-lör tör-pē'dō,* an explosive device for blowing gaps in barbed-wire obstacles, etc., invented by sappers and miners of the Indian army at *Bangalore.*

bangle *bang'gl, n.* a ring for arm or leg. — *adj.* **ban'gled** wearing bangles. [Hind. *bangrī, banglī.*]

bangsring. Same as **banxring.**

bania *ban'yə,* **banian, banyan,** *ban'yən, -yan, ns.* an Indian fig-tree with vast rooting branches: a Hindu trader, esp. from Gujarat: loosely, out of India, any Hindu: an Indian broker or financier: a loose jacket, gown, or under-garment worn in India. — **banian days** (*obs.*) days on which no meat was served out, hence days of short commons generally, from the abstinence from flesh of the Banian merchants. [Port. *banian,* perh. through Ar. *banyān,* from Hind. *baniyā* — Sans. *vānija* — *vanij,* a merchant.]

banish *ban'ish, v.t.* to condemn to exile: to drive away: to expel. — *n.* **ban'ishment** exile. [Fr. *bannir, baniss-* — L.L. *bannīre,* to proclaim.]

banister *ban'is-tər, n.* a stair-rail with its supports (often in *pl.*). [**baluster.**]

banjax *ban-jaks', ban',* (*slang*) *v.t.* to ruin, destroy. [Anglo-Irish; poss. combination of *bang* and *smash.*]

banjo *ban'jō, ban-jō', n.* a musical instrument played with the fingers or with a plectrum — having a long neck, a circular body of stretched parchment like a drum, and usu. five strings of catgut and wire: applied to various tools or devices shaped like a banjo: — *pl.* **ban'jos, ban'joes.** — *n.* **ban'joist** (*-ist*). [Negro pronunciation of **bandore.**]

banjulele *ban-jōō-lā'li, n.* a small banjo with gut strings. [**banjo** and **ukulele.**]

bank[1] *bangk, n.* a mound or ridge: an acclivity: the margin of a river, lake, etc.: the raised border of a road, railway cutting, etc.: the surface at a pit-mouth: the coal-face in a mine: a shoal or shallow: a bed of shellfish: a mass of cloud or mist: the tilt of an aeroplane. — *v.t.* to enclose with a bank: to deposit or pile up: to cover (a fire) so as to lessen the rate of combustion. — *v.t.* and *v.i.* (of aircraft) to tilt in turning. — *n.* **bank'er** a locomotive used to help pull a heavy load up a steep track (also **bank(ing) engine**): a fishing vessel on the Bank of Newfoundland, or a fisherman in such a vessel: a river full to the top of its banks (*Austr.*). — *adv.* **bank'-high** up to the top of the bank. — *n.* **banks'man** an overseer at a pit-mouth. — **from bank to bank** from the time the collier begins to descend for his spell of work till he reaches the top again. [M.E. *banke,* prob. Scand.; cog. with **bank**[2,3], **bench.**]

bank[2] *bangk, n.* a bench in a gallery: the bench on which judges sat: a tier or rank, e.g. of oars, keys on a typewriter, etc.: a range of apparatus or equipment: a working table in various crafts: a pottery: (of birds, esp. swans) a company. — *n.* **bank'er** a mason's bench: a builder's board on which cement, etc. is mixed. — **bank'er-mark** a mason's mark on a stone. [O.Fr. *banc,* of Gmc. origin; cog. with **bank**[1,3].]

bank[3] *bangk, n.* a bench, office, or institution for the keeping, lending, and exchanging, etc., of money: a money-box for savings: a stock of money, fund, or capital: in games of hazard, the money that the proprietor or other, who plays against all, has before him: a pool to draw cards from: any store of material or information, as **blood bank** (q.v.), **data bank** (q.v.), **eye bank.** — *v.t.* to deposit in a bank. — *v.i.* to have a bank account: to count, rely (on) (*coll.*). — *adj.* **bank'able.** — *ns.* **bank'er** one who keeps a bank: one employed in banking business: a betting card game: a certainty, something that can be banked on or betted on. — Also *adj.* — **bank'ing** the business of the banker. — *adj.* pertaining to a bank. — **bank'-ā'gent** formerly in Scotland, the head of a branch-bank (now **bank's man'ager**); **bank'-bill** (formerly) a bank-note: a bill drawn by one bank upon another; **bank'-book** a book in which record is kept of money deposited in or withdrawn from a bank; **bank'-cheque'** an order to pay issued upon a bank; **banker's card** a card issued by a bank guaranteeing the honouring of any cheque up to a specified value; **banker's order** a standing order (q.v.); **bank'-hol'iday** a day on which banks are legally closed, bills falling due on these being payable the following day — in England observed as a general holiday; **bank'-note** a note issued by a bank, which passes as money, being payable to bearer on demand; **bank'-pap'er** bank-notes in circulation; **bank'-rate** until 1972 the rate at which the Bank of England was prepared to discount bills (see **minimum lending rate** under **minim**); **bank'roll** money resources. — *v.t.* to finance. — **bank'-stock** a share or shares in the capital stock of a bank. — **bank of issue** one that issues its own notes or promises to pay; **break the bank** in gambling, to win from the management the sum fixed as the limit it is willing to lose on any one day; **clearing bank** a bank which is a member of the London Clearing-house; **joint-stock bank** one whose capital is subscribed by a large number of shareholders; **merchant bank** one whose functions include financing transit of goods and providing financial and commercial advice; **private bank** one carried on by fewer than ten persons. [Fr. *banque* — It. *banca;* of Gmc. origin, cog. with **bank**[1,2].]

banket *bang-ket',* (*S. Afr.*) *n.* an auriferous pebbly conglomerate. [Du. *banketje,* almond rock.]

bankrupt *bangk'rupt, n.* one who breaks or fails in business: an insolvent person. — *adj.* insolvent: destitute (with *of*). — *v.t.* to make bankrupt: to have (a person) declared bankrupt: to ruin, impoverish (*fig*). — *n.* **bank'ruptcy** (*-si*) the state of being or act of becoming bankrupt. [Fr. *banque-route*, It. *banca rotta* — *banca*, bank, and *rotto*, *-a* — L. *ruptus*, broken.]

Banksia *bangk'si-ə, n.* a genus of Australian Proteaceae: (without *cap.*) a shrub or tree of the genus. [After Sir Joseph *Banks* (1744–1820).]

banlieue *bä-lyø*, (Fr.) *n.* a precinct, extramural area, suburb.

Bannat. See **Ban.**

banner *ban'ər, n.* strictly, a square flag charged with a coat of arms: a military standard: a flag bearing some device, often carried on two poles, or hanging from a cross-piece, used in processions, etc.: those who serve under a banner, esp. in the Manchu army (*hist.*). — *adj.* **bann'ered** furnished with banners. — **banner cloud** a stationary lenticular cloud that forms on the lee side of a mountain; **banner headline** a large-type headline running right across a newspaper page. [O.Fr. *banere* — L.L. *bandum*, *bannum*; cog. with **band**[1] and **bind**.]

banneret *ban'ər-et*, (*hist.*) *n.* a knight of higher grade, orig. one bringing his vassals under his own banner, later, one dubbed on the field of battle (often confused with **baronet**). [O.Fr. *baneret*, lit. bannered.]

bannerol, bannerall. See **banderol.**

bannock *ban'ək*, (chiefly *Scot.*) *n.* a flat home-made cake of oatmeal, barley, or pease-meal, usually baked on a griddle. [O.E. *bannuc*.]

banns *banz, n.pl.* a proclamation of intended marriage. — **forbid the banns** to make formal objection to a projected marriage. [**ban**[1].]

banquet *bangk'wit, n.* a feast: a course of sweetmeats, fruit, and wine, separate, or after a meal — still used in the Scottish phrase, 'a cake and wine banquet'. — *v.t.* to give a feast to. — *v.i.* to fare sumptuously: — *pr.p.* **banq'ueting**; *pa.t.* and *pa.p.* **banq'ueted.** — *ns.* **banq'ueter; banqueteer'; banq'ueting**. — **banq'ueting-hall, -house.** [Fr., — *banc*, bench.]

banquette *bang-ket', n.* a raised way inside a parapet: the long seat behind the driver in a French diligence: a built-in wall-sofa used instead of individual seats, e.g. in a restaurant. [Fr.; It. *banchetta*, dim. of *banca*, seat.]

banshee *ban'shē, n.* a female fairy in Ireland and elsewhere who wails and shrieks before a death in the family to which she is attached. [Ir. *bean sidhe*, Old Ir. *ben side*, woman of the fairies.]

bant[1]. See **banting**[1].

bant[2] *bant*, (*dial.*) *n.* vigour, strength, springiness. [Cf. **bent**[1] and M.Du. *bant*, power, force.]

bantam *ban'təm, n.* a small variety of the common domestic fowl: a small man, esp. a soldier. — *adj.* of bantam breed: little and combative. — **ban'tam-weight**, a boxer over 8 st. and not over 8 st. 6 lb. (amateur 7 lb.). [Prob. *Bantam* in Java.]

banteng, banting *ban'teng, -ting, ns.* an East Indian wild ox. [Malay.]

banter *ban'tər, v.t.* to assail with good-humoured raillery: to joke or jest at: to impose upon, trick (*arch.*). — *n.* humorous raillery: jesting. — *n.* **bant'erer.** — *n.* and *adj.* **bant'ering.** — *adv.* **bant'eringly.** [Ety. quite unknown.]

Banthine® *ban'thēn, n.* a synthetic drug used against peptic ulcers.

banting[1] *bant'ing, n.* a system of diet for reducing superfluous fat. — *v.i.* **bant** (back-formation). — *n.* **bant'ingism.** [From W. *Banting* (1797–1878), a London cabinetmaker, who recommended it to the public in 1863.]

banting[2]. See **banteng.**

bantling *bant'ling, n.* a child. [Prob. Ger. *Bänkling*, bastard — *Bank*, bench.]

Bantu *ban'tōō, n.* a name given to a large group of African languages and the peoples speaking them in South and Central Africa: official name for African peoples of South Africa. — Also *adj.* — *n.* **Ban'tustan** the coined name for a semi-independent region of South Africa

populated and administered by Bantus: a region of similar status elsewhere.

banxring, bangsring *bangks'ring, n.* a tree-shrew. [Jav. *bangsring*.]

banyan. See **banian.**

banzai *bän'zä-ē, interj.* a Japanese battle-cry and salute to the emperor: a Japanese exclamation of joy uttered on happy occasions. [Jap. *banzai*, 10 000 years, forever.]

baobab *bā'ō-bab, n.* a gigantic tropical Western African tree, the monkey-bread tree (*Adansonia digitata*; family Bombacaceae). [Prob. African.]

bap *bap*, (*Scot.* and *Northern*) *n.* a large, flat and elliptical breakfast roll. [Ety. uncertain.]

Baphomet *baf'ō-met, n.* a mysterious idol the Templars were accused of worshipping. — *adj.* **baphomet'ic.** [For *Mahomet*.]

baptise, -ize *bapt-īz', v.t.* to administer baptism to: to christen, give a name to: to name at launching and break a bottle of wine on the bow of. — *n.* **bapt'ism** (*-izm*) immersion in or sprinkling with water as a religious ceremony: an experience regarded as initiating one into a society, group, etc. — *adj.* **baptis'mal.** — *adv.* **baptis'mally.** — *ns.* **bapt'ist** one who baptises: (with *cap.*) one of a body who approve only of baptising by immersion, and that only of persons who profess their faith in Christ; **bap'tistery, bap'tistry** a place for administration of baptism, whether a separate building or part of a church. — **baptismal name** one given at baptism, a Christian name; **baptismal regeneration** the doctrine of the remission of sin original and actual, and of the new birth into the life of sanctifying grace, in and through the sacrament of baptism. — **baptism by desire** the grace held to be given to a believer who ardently desires baptism, but dies before he can receive it; **baptism for the dead** the vicarious baptism of a living for an unbaptised dead Christian; **baptism of blood** martyrdom of the unbaptised Christian; **baptism of fire** the gift of the Holy Spirit: martyrdom by fire regarded as an equivalent to baptism: any trying ordeal, as a first experience of being under fire (*fig.*); **clinical baptism** baptism administered to the sick; **conditional** (or **hypothetical**) **baptism** baptism administered conditionally when it is doubtful whether the person was previously baptised validly or at all; **private baptism** baptism elsewhere than in church. [Gr. *baptizein* — *baptein*, to dip.]

bapu *bä'pōō, n.* spiritual father. [Hindi.]

bar[1] *bär, n.* a rod, strip or oblong block of any solid substance, as metal, soap, chocolate, wood: formerly used to indicate a variety of standards of weight or value: a pound, sovereign (*slang*): a strong rod or long piece used as a lever, door fastening, barrier, part of a gate or grate, etc.: a crossbar: a bolt: a barrier: an obstruction or impediment: that which completely puts an end to an action or claim: in salary statements, a level beyond which one cannot rise unless certain conditions, concerning e.g. the amount of advanced work one does, are met: a bank or shoal as at the mouth of a river or harbour: a counter across which liquor or food is served: (one room in) a public-house: a rail or the like marking off a space, as in a house of parliament, or that at which prisoners are arraigned: (usu. with *cap.*) barristers or advocates collectively: any body pronouncing judgment, often self-appointed: a ballet-dancer's exercise rail (usu. **barre**): an addition to a medal, a strip of metal below the clasp: a ridge: a stripe, esp. transverse: a horizontal band across a shield (*her.*): a vertical line across the staff marking off a measure (see also **double-bar**; *mus.*): the measure itself: (in *pl.*) the game of (prisoners'-) base (but see **base**[1]): a counter at which one particular article of food, clothing, etc., is sold, or one particular service is given. — *v.t.* to fasten, secure, shut (out, in), furnish or mark with a bar or bars: to hinder: to obstruct: to exclude the possibility or validity of: to preclude: to divide into bars: — *pr.p.* **barr'ing**; *pa.t.* and *pa.p.*

barred. — *prep.* except, but for. — *n.* barr'ing. — *prep.* except for: leaving out of consideration — *adj.* bar'ful (*Shak.* barrefull) full of obstructions. — bar'-bell a bar weighted at the ends for gymnastic exercises; bar'= chart, bar'-graph a graph showing comparative quantities by means of oblong sections produced to the appropriate length; bar code an arrangement, readable by computer, of thick and thin parallel lines, e.g. printed on, and giving coded details of, goods in a supermarket, etc.. — *adj.* bar'-cod'ed. — bar'fly (*coll.*) a drinker who spends his time in bars; bar'-iron iron in malleable bars; bar'keeper keeper of a refreshment bar or toll-bar; bar lunch a light meal or snack available in a bar; bar'-magnet a permanent magnet in the form of a straight bar; bar'maid, bar'man, bar'person a woman, man, who serves at a public-house bar; bar'= par'lour a small room adjoining a bar in a public-house; barr'ing-out' the shutting out of a schoolmaster from school by the pupils, to enforce demands; bar'= room a room in which there is a bar, taproom; bar'-sin'ister see baton; bar'tender a barman; bar'wood a red dye-wood imported in bars from Africa. — at the bar in court: in practice as a barrister or advocate; bar none (*coll.*) with no exceptions; behind bars in prison; called to the bar admitted as barrister or advocate; called within the bar made king's (or queen's) counsel.   [O.Fr. *barre* — L.L. *barra.*]
bar² *bär*, baur, bawr *bör*, (*Scot.*) *ns.* a jest: an amusing incident or story.   [Poss. Scot. *bar*, (the game of tossing the) caber.]
bar³ *bär, n.* a fish, the maigre.   [Fr.]
bar⁴ *bär, n.* a unit used in expressing atmospheric pressure (millibar equals a thousand dynes per square centimetre) (*meteor.*).   [Gr. *baros*, weight.]
baracan. Same as barracan.
baragouin *bä-rä-gwẽ, -gwin', n.* any jargon or unintelligible language.   [Fr.; from Bret. *bara*, bread, and *gwenn*, white, said to have originated in the Breton soldiers' astonishment at white bread.]
barathea *bar-ə-thē'ə, n.* a soft fabric of worsted, or of worsted and silk, etc.   [Origin unknown.]
barathrum *ba-rath'rŏŏm, n.* an abyss: hence, an insatiable extortioner or other person.   [L. — Gr. *barathron.*]
barb¹ *bärb, n.* the beard-like jag near the point of an arrow, fish-hook, etc.: one of the thread-like structures forming a feather's web: a sting (*fig.*): a wounding or wittily-pointed remark: a woven linen covering for the throat and breast (and sometimes the lower part of the face) worn by women in the Middle Ages, still part of the habit of certain orders of nuns. — *v.t.* to arm with barbs: to shave, trim, mow: to pierce, as with a barb. — *adjs.* barb'ate bearing a hairy tuft; barb'ated barbed: bearded. — *n.* barbe a Waldensian teacher. — *adj.* barbed furnished with a barb or barbs (e.g. barbed= wire, used for fences): (by confusion) barded. — *n.* barb'el a freshwater fish of the carp family with beard-like appendages at its mouth: such an appendage. — *adj.* barb'ellate (*bot.*) having barbed or bearded bristles. — *ns.* barb'et a tropical bird with bristly beak: a kind of poodle; barbicel (*bär'bi-sel*) a tiny hooked process on the barbule of a feather; barb'ule a small barb: a fish's barbel: a process on the barb of a feather.   [L. *barba*, a beard.]
barb² *bärb, n.* a swift kind of horse: a dark-coloured fancy pigeon.   [From *Barbary*, whence the breeds came.]
Barbados, also Barbadoes, *bär-bā'dōs, -dōz, adj.* of the West Indian island of Barbados. — *n.* and *adj.* Barbā'-dian. — Barbados cherry the cherry-like fruit of West Indian trees of the genus Malpighia; Barbados earth a diatomaceous marl found in Barbados; Barbados gooseberry the edible fruit of a West Indian climbing cactus, *Pereskia aculeata*; Barbados leg elephantiasis; Barbados pride a West Indian shrub, peacock-flower (*Caesalpinia*, or *Poinciana, pulcherrima*): an Asiatic mimosaceous tree (*Adenanthera pavonina*) naturalised in the West Indies, called red sandalwood.
barbarous *bär'bər-əs, adj.* falling short of the standard of

correctness, classical purity, and good taste: unscholarly: corrupt or ungrammatical or unidiomatic: uncultured: uncivilised: brutal: harsh. — *n.* barbār'ian orig. one who was not a Greek, later neither a Greek nor a Roman: a foreigner: one without taste or refinement: a somewhat uncivilised man (but usu. not a savage). — Also *adj.* — *adj.* barbar'ic (*-bar'ik*) foreign: uncivilised: characteristic of barbarians: rude: tastelessly ornate and ostentatious: wild and harsh. — *n.* barbarisation, -z- (*-bər-ī-zā'shən*). — *v.t.* bar'barise, -ize to make barbarous: to corrupt, as a language. — *ns.* bar'barism savage life: rudeness of manners: a form of speech offensive to scholarly taste; barbar'ity (*-bar'i-ti*) savageness: cruelty. — *adv.* bar'barously. — *n.* bar'-barousness.   [Gr. *barbaros*, foreign, lit. stammering, from the unfamiliar sound of foreign tongues.]
Barbary *bär'bər-i, n.* the country of the *Berbers*, in North Africa. — *adj.* barbaresque (*-esk'*). — Barbary ape the magot; Barbary sheep a North African wild sheep.   [Berber.]
barbasco *bär-bas'co, n.* any of a variety of S. American plants, the juice of whose roots is used in the preparation of fish-poisons, synthetic hormones, etc.: — *pl.* barbas'cos.   [Sp.]
barbastel(le) *bär-bəs-tel'*, or *bär', n.* a hairy-lipped bat.   [Fr. *barbastelle.*]
barbe. See barb¹.
barbecue *bär'bi-kū, v.t.* to roast whole: to cure on a barbecue. — *n.* a framework for drying and roasting meat: an animal roasted whole: an open floor on which coffee-beans and the like are spread out to dry: a large social entertainment, esp. in the open air, at which food is cooked over a charcoal fire: food so cooked, esp. with a highly seasoned sauce.   [Sp. *barbacoa* — Haitian *barbacòa*, a framework of sticks set upon posts.]
barbel. See barb¹.
barber *bär'bər, n.* one who shaves beards and dresses hair. — *v.t.* to shave or cut the hair of. — barb'er-mon'ger (*Shak.*) a man decked out by his barber, a fop; barber's block a round block on which wigs are made; bar'ber= shop a type of music originating in the U.S., played, or esp. sung, in close chromatic harmony, usu. in quartets; orig. sung by men waiting to have their hair cut. — Also *adj.* — barber's pole the barber's sign, a pole striped spirally, generally red and white, having often a brass basin hung at the end; barb'er-sur'geon (*hist.*) one who let blood and drew teeth as well as shaved.   [O.Fr. *barbour* — L. *barba*, a beard.]
barberry *bär'bər-i, n.* a thorny shrub (*Berberis*) of various species, most with yellow flowers and red berries, common in ornamental hedges.   [L.L. *berberis*; the Ar. *barbārīs* is borrowed; not connected with berry.]
Barbeton daisy *bär'bər-tən dā'zi*, (a plant of) the Gerbera genus of composites native to South Africa, flourishing esp. in the *Barberton* district of Transvaal.
barbet. See barb¹.
barbette *bär-bet', n.* an earthen terrace inside the parapet of a rampart, serving as a platform for heavy guns: a fixed cylinder which encloses and protects the rotating part of an armoured turret in a warship.   [Fr.]
barbican *bär'bi-kən, n.* a projecting watch-tower over the gate of a castle or fortified town: esp. the outwork intended to defend the drawbridge.   [O.Fr. *barba-cane*; origin unknown.]
barbicel. See barb¹.
barbie *bär'bi, (Austr. coll.*) a barbecue.
barbiturate *bärb-it-ū'rik, (chem.) adj.* applied to an acid got from malonic acid and urea, source of important sedatives. — *ns.* barb'itone (also barb'ital) a derivative of barbituric acid used as a sedative and hypnotic; barbit'urate (or *-tūr'*) a salt or ester of barbituric acid.   [From the lichen Usnea *barbata* and *uric* acid.]
barbola (work) *bär-bō'lə (wûrk), n.* ornamentation with small flowers, fruits, etc. made of plastic paste coloured.   [Orig. proprietary term from Fr. barbo-tine, a fine clay.]

barbotine *bär'bə-tin, n.* a fine clay used for ornamenting pottery: pottery ornamented with this. — Also *adj.* [Fr. — *barboter*, to dabble about noisily.]

barbs *barbz, (slang) n.pl.* short for **barbiturates**.

barbule. See **barb**[1].

barca *bär'ka,* (It.) *n.* a boat, barge.

barcarol(l)e *bär'kə-rōl, -rōl', -rol', n.* a gondolier's song: a musical composition of a similar character. [It. *barcarola,* a boat-song — *barca,* a boat.]

barchan(e). See **barkhan**.

Barclaycard *bär'kli-kärd, n.* credit card issued by Barclays Bank.

bard[1] *bärd, n.* a Celtic poet and singer: a strolling minstrel: a poet: a poet whose work has won a competition at the Eisteddfod. — *adj.* **bard'ic.** — *ns.* **bard'ling** a poetaster; **bardol'atry** Shakespeare-worship (Gr. *latreiā,* worship); **bard'ship.** — *adj.* **bard'y** (*Scot.*) insolent: impudent. — **bard'-craft.** — **the Bard** the poet regarded by a country as its national poet, e.g. Shakespeare, Burns. [Gael. and Ir. *bard.*]

bard[2] *bärd, n.* piece of bacon or pork fat used to cover meat or game during cooking to prevent drying-out: (*pl.*) the protective covering of a war-horse or a man-at-arms (*obs.*). — *v.t.* to cover a piece of meat or game with bards: to provide a horse or man with bards (*obs.*). — *adj.* **bard'ed** caparisoned. [Fr. *barde* — Sp. *albarda,* pack-saddle, perh. from Ar. *al-barda'ah,* — *al,* the, and *barda'ah,* the mule's pack-saddle.]

bard[3]. An old spelling of **barred**; also for **barded**.

bardash *bar-dash', (obs.) n.* a homosexual male, a catamite. [Fr. *bardache.*]

bare[1] *bār, adj.* uncovered: naked: open to view: uncovered, bare-headed: unsheathed: unarmed: disfurnished: napless, threadbare, worn: unprovided or scantily provided: poor: scanty: mere: unadorned: paltry (*Shak.*): laid waste (*Shak.; Milt.*): empty: plain, without luxury (*Spens.*). — *v.t.* to strip or uncover. — *adv.* **bare'ly** nakedly: plainly: explicitly: openly: hardly, scarcely: just and no more: not quite. — *n.* **bare'ness.** — *adj.* **bär'ish** somewhat bare. — *adj. and adv.* **bare'-back** without saddle. — *adjs.* **bare'backed** with bare back: unsaddled; **bare'boat** in shipping, used of a charter or hire in which the chartering company is totally responsible for manning, supplies, maintenance and insurance. — **bare'bone** (*Shak.*) a very lean person. — *adjs.* **bare'-breached** (*Scott*) trouserless; **bare'faced** with the face uncovered: beardless: avowed (*Shak.*): impudent. — *adv.* **barefacedly** (*-fāst'li, -fās'id-li*). — **bare'facedness.** — *adjs., advs.* **bare'foot, -ed** having the feet bare: discalced; **barehead'ed; bare-knuck'le** without gloves on: fiercely aggressive; **bare'legged.** — **barefoot doctor** orig. in China, an agricultural worker trained in the basic principles of health, hygiene and first-aid in order to treat his fellow-workers. [O.E. *bær;* Ger. *baar, bar;* O.N. *berr.*]

bare[2] *bār.* Old *pa.t.* of **bear**.

barege, barège *bä-rezh', n.* a light, mixed dress-stuff. — *n.* **baregine** (*bar'i-jēn*) a gelatinous mass of bacteria and sulphur deposited in thermal waters. [*Barèges* in Hautes-Pyrénées.]

baresark. Erroneous form of **berserk**.

barf *bärf, (U.S. slang) v.i.* to vomit. [Ety. unknown.]

bargain *bär'gən, n.* strife (*obs.*): a contract or agreement: a favourable transaction: an advantageous purchase: chaffering (*Shak.*). — *v.i.* to strive (*obs. Scot.*): to make a contract or agreement: to chaffer: to count (*on*), make allowance (*for* a possibility). — *v.t.* to lose by bad bargaining (with *away*). — *n.* **bar'gainer** — **bar'gain-basement, -counter** places in a shop where bargains are promised; **bar'gain-hunter** one who goes shopping in quest of bargains. — **bargain and sale** in law, a mode of conveyance whereby property may be assigned or transferred for valuable consideration; **into the bargain** as well, in addition; **make the best of a bad bargain** to do one's best in an adverse situation; **sell someone a bargain** (*Shak.*) to befool someone, esp. to trap him into saying something ridiculous or unseemly;

strike a bargain to come to terms. [O.Fr. *bargaine.*]

bargaist. See **barghest**.

bargander. See **bergander**.

barge *bärj, n.* a small sailing vessel (*obs.*): a flat-bottomed freight boat, with or without sails, used on rivers and canals: a lighter: the second boat of a man-of-war: a large pleasure or state boat. — *v.i.* to move clumsily: to bump (*into*): to push one's way rudely. — *n.* **barg'ee** a bargeman. — **barge'man** manager of a barge; **barge'-master** proprietor of a barge; **barge'pole** a pole for propelling a barge. — **barge in** to intrude: to interfere; **not touch with a bargepole** to refuse to have anything to do with. [O.Fr. *barge* — L.L. *barga;* cf. **bark**[2].]

barge-board *bärj'bōrd, -börd, n.* a board along the edge of a gable to cover the rafters and keep out rain. — **barge'-coup'le** gable rafters. — *n.pl.* **barge'-stones** those making up the sloping edge of a gable. [Perh. L.L. *bargus,* a gallows.]

bargello *bär'ji-lō, n.* a type of needlepoint or tapestry stitch that produces a zigzag pattern. [The *Bargello,* a Florentine museum having examples of this stitch.]

barghest, bargest, bargaist *bär'gest, -gäst, n.* a dog-like goblin portending death. [Perh. conn. with Ger. *Berggeist,* mountain-spirit.]

bargoose *bär'gōōs, n.* a large duck found on the seacoast, the shelduck. [Poss. from the band of brown on its shoulders, and its goose-like movement.]

baric. See **barium**.

barilla *bar-il'ə, n.* an impure sodium carbonate got by burning certain seaside plants. [Sp.]

barite. See under **barium, baryta**.

baritone *bar'i-tō n.* See **barytone**.

barium *bā'ri-əm, n.* a metallic element (at. numb. 56; symbol Ba) present in baryta. — *adj.* **bā'ric.** — *n.* **bā'rite** (*rare*) barytes. — **barium meal** a mixture of barium sulphate administered to render the alimentary canal opaque to X-rays. [See **baryta**.]

bark[1] *bärk, n.* the abrupt cry of a dog, wolf, etc.: report of a gun: cough (*coll.*). — *v.i.* to utter a bark: to clamour: to keep watch: to advertise wares noisily: to cough (*coll.*). — *v.t.* to utter with a bark (*Spens.*): to utter abruptly and peremptorily: to make by barking. — *n.* **bark'er** a dog: a barking dog: a tout advertising wares, a show, etc. in a loud voice to attract custom: a pistol or cannon (*slang*). — **barking deer** the muntjac. — **bark up the wrong tree** to follow a false scent; **chief barker** the title of the president of the Variety Club of Great Britain; **his bark is worse than his bite** his angry words are worse than his actual deeds. [O.E. *beorcan.*]

bark[2], **barque** *bärk, n.* formerly, any small sailing ship: a ship of small size, square-sterned, without head-rails: technically, a three-masted vessel whose mizzen-mast is fore-and-aft-rigged (instead of being square-rigged like the fore and main masts): any boat or sailing ship (*poet.*). — *n.* **bark'entine, barqu'entine** (*-ən-tēn*) a three-masted vessel, with the fore-mast square-rigged, and the main-mast and mizzen-mast fore-and-aft-rigged. [Fr. *barque* — L.L. *barca;* poss. from Gr. *bāris,* a Nile barge.]

bark[3] *bärk, n.* the rind or covering of the trunk and branches of a tree: that used in tanning or dyeing: that used in medicine (cinchona): an outer covering or skin. — *v.t.* to strip or peel bark or skin from: to encrust. — *v.i.* to form a bark. — *v.t. and v.i.* **bark'en** to dry up into a barky crust. — *adj.* (*poet.*) made of, composed of, bark. — *adjs.* **bark'less; bark'y.** — **bark'-bed** a hotbed of spent bark; **bark'-beet'le** any beetle of the family Scolytidae, tunnellers in and under bark. — *adj.* **bark'-bound** compressed by failure to shed the bark. [O.N. *börkr;* Dan. *bark.*]

Barker's mill *bärk'ərz mil,* a device rotated by water, invented by a 17th-cent. Dr *Barker.*

barkhan, barkan, barchan(e) *bär-kän', n.* a crescent-shaped sand-dune, of the type found in the Turkestan deserts. [Native word in Turkestan.]

barley[1] *bär'li, n.* a hardy grass (*Hordeum vulgare* and other species): its grain used for food, and for making malt liquors and spirits. — **bar′ley-bree, -broo, -broth** (*Scot.*) strong ale: whisky; **bar′leycorn** (personified as *John Barleycorn*) the grain from which malt is made: a single grain of barley: a measure of length = ⅓ of an inch: a V-shaped sight on a gun; **barley sugar** sugar candied by melting and cooling (formerly by boiling with a decoction of barley); **barley water** a decoction of pearl barley. — **pearl barley** the grain stripped of husk and pellicle, and completely rounded by grinding; **pot barley** the grain deprived by milling of its outer husk, used in making broth, etc. [O.E. *bærlic*, of barley, from root of **bear³**, and suffix *-līc*.]

barley² *bär′li*, (*Scot.*) *interj.* a word used in games in demand of a truce. — *n.* a truce: a breathing-space. [Perh. **parley**.]

barley-brake *bär′li-brāk*, *n.* an old country game, orig. played by three couples, of which one, left in a middle den called hell, had to catch the others, who could break or separate when about to be overtaken. [Perh. because often played in a *barley*-field; or perh. from the word preceding.]

barm *bärm*, *n.* froth of fermenting liquor: yeast. — *adj.* **barm′y** frothy: fermenting: mentally unsound (*slang*; also **balmy**). — *n.* **barm′iness.** — *adj.* **barm′y-brained.** [O.E. *beorma*, Dan. *bärme*, Ger. *Bärme*.]

barmbrack *bärm′brak*, *n.* a slightly sweet bread with dried peel, currants, etc. in it. [Ir. *bairigen* or *bairin, breac*, speckled cake.]

barm-cloth *bärm′-kloth*, (*arch.*) *n.* an apron. [O.E. *barm* (W.S. *bearm*) bosom, and **cloth.**]

Barmecide *bär′mi-sīd*, *n.* one who offers an imaginary or pretended banquet or other benefit. — *adjs.* **Bar′-mecide, Barmecī′dal.** [From an imaginary feast given to a beggar in the *Arabian Nights*, by one of the *Barmecide* family.]

bar mitzvah, bar mizvah, bar mitsvah *bär mits′və* (sometimes *caps.*; also hyphenated or as one word) in the Jewish religion, a boy attaining the age (usu. 13 years) of religious responsibility: the festivities held in recognition of this event. [Heb., son of the law.]

barmkin *bärm′kin*, (*arch*) *n.* a battlement, or a turret, on the outer wall of a castle: the wall itself. [Orig. obscure.]

barn¹ *bärn*, *n.* a building in which grain, hay, etc., are stored. — *v.t.* to store in a barn. — **barn dance** a social gathering at which square-dances and other traditional country-dances are danced: an American dance like a schottische; **barn′-door** the door of a barn: in cricket, a player who blocks every ball (*old facet.*): humorously, any broad target; **barn owl** a species of owl, generally buff-coloured above and white below; **barns′breaking** (*Scott*) a boisterous frolic: an injurious or mischievous activity; **barn′-stormer** a strolling player (as type of ranting actor): a peripatetic public speaker. — *v.i.* **barn′storm** to tour usu. country areas giving theatrical performances: to travel about speaking at meetings, usu. for election purposes. — Also *v.t.* — *n.* **barn′yard** — also *adj.* as in **barnyard fowl.** [O.E. *bere*-ern, contracted *bern*, from *bere*, barley, *ern*, a house.]

barn² *bärn*, *n.* unit of effective cross-sectional area of nucleus equal to 10^{-24}cm².

Barnaby *bärn′ə-bi*, *n.* a form of *Barnabas*. — *n.* **Bar′nabite** a member of the Congregation of Regular Clerics of St Paul, founded at Milan in 1530, so called from their church of St Barnabas there. — **Barnaby Day, Barnaby Bright** or **Long Barnaby** St Barnabas' Day, 11th June, in Old Style reckoned the longest day.

barnacle¹ *bär′nə-kl*, *n.* a barnacle-goose: a cirripede crustacean that adheres to rocks and ship bottoms: a companion not easily shaken off. — **bar′nacle-goose, ber′nicle-goose** a wild goose (*Branta leucopsis*) once believed to develop from a barnacle (the **goose′-bar′-nacle**) that attaches itself, esp. to floating wood, by a thick stalk. [O.Fr. *bernaque* — L.L. *bernaca*.]

barnacle² *bär′nə-kl*, *n.* an instrument put on a restless

horse's nose to keep him quiet: (in *pl.*) spectacles (*coll.*). — *adj.* **bar′nacled.** [O.Fr. *bernac*.]

barney *bär′ni*, (*coll.*) *n.* humbug: a prize-fight: a quarrel.

barocco, barock. See **baroque.**

barodynamics *bar-o-dī-nam′iks*, *n.sing.* mechanics applied to heavy structures, such as dams and bridges, which may collapse under their own weight. [Gr. *baros*, weight, and **dynamics.**]

barogram *bar′ō-gram*, *n.* a tracing produced by a barograph. [Gr. *baros*, weight, and **-gram.**]

barograph *bar′ō-gräf*, *n.* a recording barometer. [Gr. *baros*, weight, and **-graph.**]

barometer *bə-rom′i-tər*, *n.* an instrument for measuring atmospheric pressure: a weather-glass: an indicator of change (e.g. in public opinion; *fig.*; also *adj.*). — *adjs.* **barometric** (*bar-ō-met′rik*), **barometrical** (*-met′ri-kl*). — *adv.* **baromet′rically.** — *n.* **barometry** (*-rom′*). [Gr. *baros*, weight, *metron*, measure.]

barometz *bar′ō-mets*, *n.* the Scythian lamb, a plant at one time supposed to be also animal, growing on a stalk but eating grass like a lamb, near the Caspian Sea: a fern, *Cibotium* or *Dicksonia barometz*, of the East Indies and Pacific islands, whose woolly rootstock and leaf bases could easily be shaped into a lamb. [Erroneous form of Russ. *baranets*, club-moss, dim. of *baran*, ram.]

baron *bar′ən*, *n.* a title of rank, the lowest in the peerage: a foreign noble of similar grade: the owner of a freehold estate, whether titled or not (*Scot. hist.*): a husband (opposed to *feme*, wife; *her.* and *Eng. law*): the head of any organisation or institution who is regarded as wielding despotic power (as a *press baron*): formerly a title of the judges of the Court of Exchequer: in feudal times a tenant-in-chief of the crown: later a peer or great lord of the realm generally: till 1832, the name for the parliamentary representatives of the Cinque Ports. — *ns.* **bar′onage** the whole body of barons: a list or book of barons; **bar′oness** a baron's wife, or a lady holding a baronial title in her own right. — *adj.* **baronial** (*bə-rō′ni-əl*) pertaining to a baron or barony: applied to a turreted style of architecture favoured by the Scottish land-holding class. — *ns.* **baronne** (Fr.; *ba-ron*) a baroness; **bar′ony** the territory of a baron: in Ireland, a division of a county: in Scotland, a large freehold estate, or manor, even though not carrying with it a baron's title and rank: the rank of baron. — **bar′on-bail′ie** (*hist.*) a magistrate appointed by the lord superior in a burgh of barony; **bar′on-off′icer** (*Scott*) an estate official. — **baron of beef** a joint consisting of two sirloins left uncut at the backbone. [O.Fr. *barun, -on* — L.L. *barō, -ōnis*, man.]

baronet *bar′ən-et*, *n.* a lesser baron (*obs.*; confused with *banneret*): a baron's substitute (*obs.*): now the lowest British hereditary title (of England, now of Great Britain, since 1611; of Scotland, or of Nova Scotia, since 1625; of Ireland, since 1619). — *ns.* **bar′onetage** the whole body of baronets: a list or book of baronets; **bar′onetcy** the rank or title of baronet; **bar′onetess** a woman who succeeds to a Scottish baronetcy. — *adj.* **baronet′ical.** [Dim. of **baron.**]

baroque, barock *bə-rok′, -rōk′*, **barocco** *-rok′ō* (*pl.* **barocc′os**), *ns.* originally a jeweller's term applied to a rough pearl: a bold, vigorous, exuberant style in architecture, decoration, and art generally, that arose with the Counter-Reformation and prevailed in Louis XIV's time, degenerating into tasteless extravagance in ornament: comparable style in music, or literature. — *adj.* in baroque style: whimsical: flamboyant: sometimes rococo. [Fr. *baroque*, from Port. and Sp.; in architecture, from It.]

baroscope *bar′ō-skōp*, *n.* an instrument for indicating changes in the density of the air. [Gr. *baros*, weight, *skopeein*, to look at.]

barostat *bar′ō-stat*, *n.* an automatic device for regulating pressure, e.g. in an aircraft. [Gr. *baros*, weight, and **-stat.**]

barouche *ba-* or *bə-rōōsh'*, *n.* a double-seated four-wheeled carriage with a falling top. [Ger. *Barutsche* — It. *baroccio* — L. *bis*, twice, *rota*, a wheel.]

barp *bärp*, (*Scot. dial.*) *n.* a mound or cairn. [Gael. *barpa*, a burial cairn.]

barque, barquentine. See **bark²**.

barracan, baracan *bar'ə-kan*, (*obs.*) *n.* a thick, strong stuff resembling camlet. [Fr. *barracan* — Ar. *barrakān*, camlet, Pers. *barak*, a stuff made of camel's hair.]

barrace *bar'as*, (*obs.*) *n.* the lists in a tournament. [O.Fr. *barras* — *barre*, bar.]

barrack¹ *bar'ək*, *n.* a building for soldiers, esp. in garrison (generally in *pl*): a huge plain, often bleak, building, esp. for housing many persons. — *v.t.* and *v.i.* to lodge in barracks. — *adj.* **barr'ack-room** (of humour, etc.) somewhat coarse. — **barrack-room lawyer** an argumentative soldier given to disputing military procedure esp. with those in authority: hence any insistent but unqualified giver of advice. [Fr. *baraque* — It. *baracca*, or Sp. *barraca*, tent.]

barrack² *bar'ək*, *v.t.* and *v.i.* to make a hostile demonstration (against), esp. by cheering ironically, at a cricket-match, etc. — *v.i.* (with *for*; *Austr.* and *N.Z.*) to support, shout encouragement to. — *n.* **barr'acker**. — *n.* and *adj.* **barr'acking**. [Perh. two separate words — Aboriginal Austr. *borak*, for the first sense and poss. Northern Irish dialect *barrack*, meaning 'to brag', for the second sense.]

barracoon *bar-ə-kōōn'*, *n.* a depot for slaves. [Sp. *barracón*, augm. of *barraca*, tent.]

barracouta *bar-ə-kōō'tə*, *n.* a southern food-fish (*Thyrsites*) of the hairtail family, called snoek in South Africa and elsewhere: (also **barracoo'ta, -cuda** *-də*) a voracious West Indian fish (*Sphyraena*) akin to the grey mullets. [Sp. *baracuta*.]

barrage *bar'ij*, or (*mil.*) *bar-äzh'*, *bar'äzh*, *n.* an artificial bar across a river: the forming of such a bar: a barrier formed by continuous shower of projectiles along a fixed or a moving line (curtain-fire), or by captive balloons, or mines, or otherwise: a heavy or continuous fire, as of questions, criticisms, etc.: in sport, a heat or round to select contestants, or decide a dead-heat. — **barr'age-balloon; barr'age-fire** curtain-fire. [Fr. *barrage* — *barre*, bar.]

barramundi *bar-ə-mun'di*, *n.* an Australian river-fish, *Lates calcarifer*, esteemed as a food-fish: any of several other Australian river-fish such as a fish of the genus *Scleropages* (fam. Osteoglossidae), and the Australian lung-fish of the *Neoceratodus* genus. — Formerly also **barramun'da**. [Aboriginal.]

barranca *bar-ang'kə*, (*U.S.*) *n.* a deep gorge. — Also **barran'co** (*pl.* **barran'cos**). [Sp. *barranco*.]

barrat *bar'ət*, *n.* (*obs.*) deceit, strife or trouble. — *n.* **barr'ator** one who vexatiously stirs up lawsuits, quarrels, etc. — *adj.* **barr'atrous**. — *adv.* **barr'atrously**. — *n.* **barr'atry** fraudulent practices on the part of the master or mariners of a ship to the prejudice of the owners: vexatious litigation: stirring up of suits and quarrels, forbidden under penalties to lawyers: traffic in offices of church or state. [O.Fr. *barat*, deceit; traced by some to Gr. *prattein*, to do, by others to a Celt. or a Scand. origin.]

barre *bär*, *n.* a horizontal rail fixed to the wall at waist-level, which ballet-dancers use to balance themselves while exercising (sometimes **bar**): a capo on a guitar, lute, etc. — *adj.* **barré** (*ba-rā*) of a chord on a guitar, etc., played with the left forefinger laid across the strings. [Fr.]

barrefull (*Shak.*). See **barful** under **bar¹**.

barrel *bar'əl*, *n.* a wooden vessel made of curved staves bound with hoops; its contents or its capacity (36 imperial gallons, 31 U.S. gallons, of ale and beer; 35 imperial gallons, 42 U.S. gallons, of oil; various weights or quantities of other goods): a revolving drum: a cylinder: a tube as of a gun: a button on a braided coat: the trunk of a horse, etc. — *v.t.* to put in barrels. — *v.i.* to drive very fast (*U.S.*). — *ns.*

barr'elage; barr'elful (*pl.* **barr'elfuls**) as much as a barrel will hold. — *adj.* **barr'elled** having a barrel or barrels: put in barrels. — **barr'el-bulk** a measurement of five cubic feet. — *adj.* **barrel-chested** having a large, rounded, projecting ribcage. — **barr'el-house** a cheap saloon (*adj.* of jazz, crude and rough in style); **barr'el-or'gan** a mechanical instrument for playing tunes by means of a revolving drum set with pins turned by a handle; **barrel roll** in aerobatics, a complete revolution on the longitudinal axis; **barrel vault** a vault with a simple hemicylindrical roof (*adj.* **barr'el-vault'ed**). — **have someone over a barrel** to be in a position to get whatever one wants from someone. [Fr. *baril*; perh. conn. with **bar¹**.]

barren *bar'ən*, *adj.* incapable of bearing offspring: not producing fruit, seed, crops, vegetation, etc.: infertile: unproductive: unfruitful: arid: jejune: dull, stupid (*Shak.*). — *n.* (in *pl.* with *cap.*) in North America, plateaux with small trees but no timber. — *n.* **barr'enness**. — **barren strawberry** a plant (*Potentilla fragariastrum*) very like the wild strawberry, but with inedible fruit; **barr'enwort** a herb (*Epimedium*) of the barberry family. [O.Fr. *barain*, *brahain*, *brehaing*.]

barret *bar'it*, *n.* a flat cap: a biretta. — **barr'et-cap**. [Fr. *barette*; cf. **beret, biretta**.]

barrette *ba-ret'*, *n.* a bar-shaped hair-clip or hair ornament. [Dim. of Fr. *barre*, bar.]

barricade *bar'ik-ād*, *n.* a temporary fortification raised to block a street: a barrier. — *v.t.* to block: to close or enclose with a barricade. — *n.* (earlier form) **barricā'do:** — *pl.* **barricā'dos, -does**. — Also *v.t.* [Fr. *barricade* or Sp. *barricada*, perh. — Fr. *barrique* or Sp. *barrica*, cask, the first street barricades being casks filled with stones, etc.; or from L.L. *barra*, bar.]

barrico *bar-ē'kō*, *n.* a small cask: — *pl.* **barri'cos, -coes**. [Sp. *barrica*.]

barrier *bar'i-ər*, *n.* a defensive stockade or palisade: a fence or other structure to bar passage or prevent access: (in *pl.*) lists: (in *pl.*) a martial exercise of the 15th and 16th centuries in which the combatants were on opposite sides of a fence: a separating or restraining obstacle. — *v.t.* to shut by means of a barrier. — **barrier cream** a dressing for the skin used to prevent dirt from entering the pores and as a protection against oils and solvents; **barrier reef** a coral-reef fringing a coast with a navigable channel inside. — **Barrier Act** an act of the General Assembly of the Church of Scotland (1697) decreeing that changes in the law of the Church, even when approved by the Assembly, should not become law till approved by a majority of presbyteries. [O.Fr. *barrière* — L.L. *barrāria* — *barra*.]

barrio *bar'i-ō*, *n. esp.* in *U.S.* a Spanish-speaking, usu. poor, community or district: — *pl.* **barr'ios**. [Sp., district, quarter.]

barrister *bar'is-tər*, *n.* one who is qualified to plead at the bar in a law-court (in Scotland called *advocate*). — *adj.* **barristerial** (*-tē'ri-əl*). — *n.* **barr'istership**. — **revising barrister** a barrister formerly appointed to revise the voters' lists. [From L.L. *barra*, bar (i.e. orig. of the Inns of Court).]

barrow¹ *bar'ō*, *n.* a small usu. hand-propelled wheeled carriage used to convey a load. — **barr'ow-boy** a street-trader with wares displayed on a barrow; **barr'ow-tram** the shaft of a barrow. [O.E. *bearwe* — *beran*, to bear.]

barrow² *bar'ō*, *n.* a hill or hillock (*obs.* except in place-names): an ancient earth-built grave-mound, tumulus. [O.E. *beorg*; cf. Ger. *Berg*.]

barrow³ *bar'ō*, (*old*) *n.* a long, sleeveless flannel garment for infants. [Perh. O.E. *beorgan*, to protect.]

barrulet *bar'ū-lit*, (*her.*) *n.* a horizontal band one-quarter the width of a bar. [Dim. of *barrule*, assumed dim. of O.Fr. *barre*; cf. **bar¹**.]

barter *bär'tər*, *v.t.* to give in exchange (with *for*, *away*). — *v.i.* to traffic by exchange of commodities. — *n.* trade or traffic by direct exchange of goods. — *n.* **bar'terer**. [Prob. O.Fr. *barat*; see **barrat**.]

Bartholin's glands *bär'tə-linz glandz*, a pair of mucus-secreting glands in the vagina. [Discovered by Caspar *Bartholin* (1655–1738), a Danish anatomist.]
Bartholomew *bär-thol'ə-mū*, or (*obs.*) **Bartholmew, Bartlemew** *-t(h)l-mū*, **Bartlemy** *-tl-mi*, *adjs.* relating to the Apostle *Bartholomew*, his day (24th August), or the fair held about that time at West Smithfield, London (1133–1855): sold at Bartholomew Fair. — **Barthol'omew-tide** the time about St Bartholomew's Day. — **Black Bartholomew** 24th August 1662, when the Act of Uniformity came into force in England.
bartisan, bartizan *bär'ti-zan, -zan'*, *n.* a parapet or battlement: a projecting gallery on a wall-face: (erroneously) a corbelled corner turret. — *adj.* **bar'tisaned** (or *-zand'*). [Apparently first used by Scott, who found a reading *bertisene*, for **bratticing**; see **brattice**.]
barton *bär'tən*, *n.* a farmyard. [O.E. *bere-tūn*, yard — *bere*, barley, and *tūn*, enclosure.]
barycentric *bar-i-sen'trik*, *adj.* pertaining to the centre of gravity. [Gr. *barys*, heavy, *kentron*, centre.]
barye *bär'ē*. Same as **microbar**.
baryon *bar'i-on*, *n.* any one of the heavier class of subatomic particles, which includes protons and neutrons — opp. to *lepton*. — **baryon number** the number of baryons minus the number of antibaryons (antiparticles of baryons) in a system. [Gr. *barys*, heavy.]
barysphere *bar'is-fēr*, *n.* the heavy core of the earth within the lithosphere. [Gr. *barys*, heavy, *sphairā*, sphere.]
baryta *bə-rī'tə*, *n.* barium monoxide. — *n.* **bary'tes** (*-tēz*) heavy-spar, barium sulphate (also **barite** *bā'rīt*): (*loosely*) baryta. — *adj.* **barytic** (*ba-rit'ik*) of or containing baryta or barium. — **baryta paper** paper coated on one side with an emulsion of barium sulphate and gelatine. It is used in moving-pointer recording apparatus and for photographic printing papers. [Gr. *barys*, heavy.]
barytone *bar'i-tōn*, *n.* a deep-toned male voice between bass and tenor: a singer with such a voice (in these senses now usually **bar'itone**): (also **bar'yton**) a musical instrument like the viola da gamba with sympathetic strings added: a kind of saxhorn. — *adj.* of the pitch and compass of a baritone or barytone: in Greek, not having an acute accent on the last syllable. [Gr. *barytonos*, deep-sounding, not accented — *barys*, heavy, deep, and *tonos*, a tone.]
basal. See under **base¹**.
basalt *bas'ölt, bas-ölt'*, *n.* an igneous rock composed essentially of plagioclase and pyroxene, and commonly olivine and magnetite or titaniferous iron: esp. a compact rock of this kind. — *adj.* **basalt'ic**. [L. *basaltēs* — Gr. *basanītēs* (*lithos*), touchstone.]
basan *ba'zən*, *n.* a sheepskin roughly tanned and undressed. [Ar. *bitanah*, lining.]
basanite *bas'ən-īt*, *n.* a black jasper that serves as a touchstone: a variety of basalt containing nepheline, kuc . . . or analcime. [Gr. *basanos*, touchstone.]
bsbleu *ä-blø*, (Fr.) *n.* a bluestocking.
bascule *bas'kūl*, *n.* an apparatus of which one end rises as the other sinks. — **bascule bridge** a bridge that rises when a counterpoise sinks in a pit. [Fr. *bascule*, see-saw.]
base¹ *bās*, *n.* that on which a thing rests: foot: bottom: foundation: support: the part, e.g. of an organ of a plant or animal, nearest the place of attachment: the foot or lower member of a pillar, on which the shaft rests (*archit.*): the side or face on which a geometrical figure is regarded as standing: the lower part of a shield (*her.*): (in *pl.*) a skirt worn by knights on horseback (*Spens.*): a horse's housing (*Milt.*): a number on which a system of numeration or of logarithms is founded: the chief ingredient: an ingredient of a mixture that plays a subsidiary but important part, such e.g. as giving bulk: in dyeing, a mordant (q.v.): a starting-point: a standard against which comparisons can be made: a base-line: a fixed station in games such as baseball: an old game of which prisoners'-base and rounders are forms, and baseball a development (pos-

sibly a different word: see **bar¹**): a place from which operations are conducted or on which they depend: home or headquarters, of a fleet, with equipment for its safe-keeping, repairs and other needs: a substance that reacts with an acid to form a salt, or dissolves in water forming hydroxyl ions (*chem.*): that element in words to which suffixes and prefixes are added, the stem (*philol.*). — *v.t.* to found or place on a base: — *pr.p.* **bās'ing**; *pa.p.* **based** (*bāst*). — *adj.* **bās'al** pertaining to or situated at the base: at the lowest level: (*loosely*) fundamental. — *adj.* **base'less** without a base or foundation. — *ns.* **base'lessness; base'ment** an underlying support: the lowest storey of a building beneath the principal one, esp. one below ground level. — *adj.* **bās'ic** belonging to or of the nature of a base: containing excess of a base: in geol., poor in silica — opp. to *acid*: fundamental. — *n.* (in *pl.*) fundamental principles. — *adv.* **bās'ically** with reference to what is basic: fundamentally, essentially. — *n.* **bāsicity** (*-is'*). — *adj.* **basilar** (*bas'*) basal. — **basal anaesthesia** anaesthesia acting as a basis for further and deeper anaesthesia; **basal metabolism** the level of metabolism occurring in an individual in a resting state; **basal plane** (*crystallography*) a crystal face or form parallel to the horizontal axes; **base'ball** the American national game, a development of rounders, played nine-a-side with bat and ball, the players on the batting side making a circuit of four bases: a ball for the game; **base'baller; base'board** (*U.S.*) a skirting-board; **base'-line** an accurately measured line used as a base for triangulation: a line at the end of the court (*lawn tennis*): a line joining bases (*baseball*); **base'man** (*baseball*) any of the three fielders stationed near first, second, and third base (hence *first baseman*, etc.); **base'plate** the foundation plate of a piece of heavy machinery; **base rate** the rate, determined by a bank, on which it bases its lending rates of interest; **base ring** a strengthening band of metal round the breech of a muzzle-loading cannon; **base'runner** a baseball player in course of performing his circuit of bases; **Basic English** a reduced English vocabulary of 850 words for teaching foreigners or for use as an auxiliary language: (*without cap.*) English using few and simple words; **basic process** a steel-making process with a furnace lined with material rich in metallic oxides; **basic salt** a salt having one or more hydroxyl groups in place of an acid radical or radicals; **basic slag** a by-product of the basic process rich in lime, used as manure. — **base out** see **bottom out; get to, make, first base** (*U.S. coll.*) to complete the first stage in a process; **off base** (*U.S. coll.*) wrong, mistaken. [Fr. *base* — L. *basis* — Gr. *basis* — root of *bainein*, to go.]
base² *bās*, *adj.* low in place, value, estimation, or principle: mean: vile: worthless: debased: counterfeit: servile as opposed to *free* (*law*): humble: lowly (*B.* and *Shak.*): bass (*obs.*). — *adv.* **base'ly**. — *n.* **base'ness**. — *adj.* **base'-born** low-born: illegitimate. — **base coin** spurious coin; **base metal** any metal other than the precious metals: a metal that alters on exposure to air — opp. to *noble metal*. — *adjs.* **base'-mind'ed** of a low mind or spirit: mean; **base'-spirited** mean-spirited. [Fr. *bas* — L.L. *bassus*, thick, squat.]
base³ *bās*, *v.t.* A form of **abase**.
baseball. See **base¹**.
basecourt *bās'kōrt, -kört*, *n.* the outer court of a castle or mansion: an inferior court of justice. [Fr. *basse-court* (now *basse-cour*).]
baselard *bas'ə-lärd*, (*obs.*) *n.* a dagger or hanger. [A.Fr.]
basement. See under **base¹**.
basen. See **basin**.
basenji *bə-sen'jē*, *n.* a smallish erect-eared, curly-tailed African hunting dog that rarely barks. [Bantu, *pl.* of *mosenji, musengi*, native.]
bash *bash*, *v.t.* to beat, belabour: to smash: to attack harshly or maliciously, physically or verbally. — *v.i.* (*slang*) to solicit as a prostitute. — *n.* a heavy blow: a dint: a party (*coll.*). — *ns.* **bash'er** a person who, or

thing that, bashes (*sometimes used as suffix*): a straw hat (*slang*); **bash'ing** (*often used as suffix*, as in *queer-bashing, union-bashing*) the activity of making harsh or malicious physical or verbal attacks on individuals or (members of) groups one dislikes. — **have a bash** (*coll.*) to have a try: to make an attempt (at); **on the bash** (*slang*), on the spree: on the streets as a prostitute. [Prob. Scand.]

bashaw *ba-shö'*, *n.* a pasha (*arch.*): a haughty man. — *ns.* **bashaw'ism; bashaw'ship.** [Turk. *başa;* cf. **pasha.**]

bashful *bash'fŏol, adj.* easily confused: modest: shy, wanting confidence. — *v.i.* **bash** (*Spens.*) to be abashed. — *adv.* **bash'fully.** — *n.* **bash'fulness.** — *adj.* **bash'less** unashamed. [See **abash.**]

bashi-bazouk *bash-ē-bə-zōōk', n.* a Turkish irregular soldier. — *n.* **ba'shi-bazouk'ery.** [Turk. *başi-bozuk,* wild head.]

bashlyk *bash'lik, n.* a hood with long ends worn in Russia, esp. by soldiers. [Russ. *bashlyk,* a Caucasian hood — Turk. — Turk. *baş,* a head.]

basic. See **base¹.**

Basic, BASIC *bā'sik, n.* a computer language using a combination of simple English and algebra. [*B*eginners' *A*ll-purpose *S*ymbolic *I*nstruction *C*ode.]

basidium *bas-id'i-əm, n.* a fungal fructification from which spores (usually four) are abstricted: — *pl.* **basid'ia.** — *adj.* **basid'ial.** — *n.pl.* **Basidiomycetes** (*-ō-mī-sē'tēz*) one of the main groups of fungi, characterised by the possession of basidia, including the familiar toadstools as well as rusts and smuts. — *adj.* **basidiomycē'tous.** — *n.* **basid'iospore** a spore produced by a basidium. [Gr. *basis,* basis, and dim. ending, *-idion.*]

basifixed *bā'si-fikst, adj.* attached by the base. [**base** and **fixed.**]

basifugal *bās-,* or *bas-if'ū-gl, adj.* developing in a direction away from the base. [**base,** and L. *fugĕre,* to flee.]

basil¹ *baz'il, n.* an aromatic labiate plant (*Ocimum*): extended to calamint and other labiates. [O.Fr. *basile* — L. *basilisca,* representing Gr. *basilikon,* lit. royal, perh. with reference to *basiliskos,* basilisk, cobra, as a reputed cure for snakebite.]

basil² *baz'il.* Same as **basan.**

basil³. See **bezel.**

basilar. See **base¹.**

Basilian *ba-, bə-zil'i-ən,* or *sil', adj.* of St *Basil* (*c.* 329–379). — *n.* a monk or nun following his rule.

basilica *bə-sil'i-kə, n.* orig. a royal palace: a large oblong hall, with double colonnades and commonly a semicircular apse, used for judicial and commercial purposes: a magnificent church formed out of such a hall, or built after its plan: a Roman Catholic church with honorific privileges. — *adjs.* **basil'ical** royal; **basil'ican** of a basilica. — *n.* **basil'icon** an ointment of various kinds, as of sovereign virtue. [Gr. *basilikos, -ē, -on,* royal — *basileus,* king.]

basilisk *bas', baz'il-isk, n.* a fabulous creature, about a foot long, with fiery death-dealing eyes and breath, so named according to Pliny, from its crown-like crest: a harmless crested lizard of tropical America: an ancient brass cannon throwing a shot of about 200lb. [Gr. *basiliskos,* dim. of *basileus,* a king.]

basin *bā'sn,* (*arch.* **bason**) *n.* wide open vessel or dish: a basinful: any hollow place containing water, as a dock: the area drained by a river and its tributaries: a region of synclinal structure (*geol.*). — *n.* **ba'sinful** as much as will fill a basin: — *pl.* **ba'sinfuls.** — *adj.* **ba'sin-wide** (*Spens.* **basen wide**) wide as a basin. — **have a basinful** (*coll.*) to have an excess of. [O.Fr. *bacin* — L.L. *bachinus,* perh. from *bacca,* a vessel.]

basinet *bas'i-net,* **basnet** *bas'net, ns.* a light globular headpiece worn alone with a visor, or with the great helm over it. [Dim. of **basin.**]

basipetal *bās-* or *bas-ip'i-tl, adj.* proceeding or developing in the direction of the base. [**base¹,** and L. *petĕre,* to seek.]

basis *bās'is, n.* the foundation, or that on which a thing

rests: a pedestal: the groundwork or first principle: the fundamental ingredient: — *pl.* **bas'es** (*bās'ēz*). [See **base¹.**]

bask *bäsk, v.i.* to lie in the warmth or sunshine (often *fig.*). — **basking shark** a large but harmless shark that shows its great dorsal fin as it basks. [O.N. *bathask,* to bathe.]

Baskerville *bas'kər-vil, n.* a kind of printing type. [From the originator, J. *Baskerville,* 18th-cent. printer.]

basket *bäs'kit, n.* a receptacle of plaited or interwoven twigs, rushes, canes or other flexible materials: a basketful: a net used as goal at basketball: the back part of a stagecoach outside: a basket-hilt. — *ns.* **bas'ketful** as much as fills a basket: — *pl.* **bas'ketfuls; bas'ketry** basketwork. — **bas'ketball** a team game in which goals are scored by throwing a ball into a raised net (originally a basket); **bas'ket-chair'** a wicker chair; **bas'ket-hilt'** a sword hilt with a protective covering wrought like basketwork; **bas'ket-maker; bas'ket-making; bas'ket-stitch** in knitting, groups of plain and purl stitches alternating vertically and horizontally, resembling basketwork in effect; **bas'ket-weave** a form of weaving using two or more strands in the warp and weft; **bas'ketwork** articles made of interlaced twigs, canes, etc.: the art of making these. — **basket of currencies** (*econ.*) a name for the special monetary unit composed of various European currencies in fixed proportions, used as a standard against which to assess the value of any particular currency, or as a currency in its own right. [Origin obscure.]

bas mitzvah. See **bath mitzvah.**

basnet. See **basinet.**

basoche *ba-sosh,* (Fr.) *n.* a mediaeval gild of clerks of the parliament of Paris, performers of mystery plays.

bason. See **basin.**

ba'spiel. See **balling** under **ball¹.**

Basque *bäsk, n.* a member of a people (in their own tongue *Euscara, Eskuara*) inhabiting the western Pyrenees, in Spain and France: their agglutinative language: (without *cap.*) a short-skirted jacket, or a continuation of a bodice a little below the waist. — *adjs.* **Basque** of the Basques or their language or country; **basqued** (*bäskt*) furnished with a basque. — *n.* **basquine** (*-kēn'*) an outer petticoat worn by Basque and Spanish women. [Fr. *Basque* — L. *Vasconēs,* a people of Gascony.]

bas-relief *bas'-ri-lēf',* or (It.) **basso-rilievo** *bäs'sō-rēl-yā'vō,* popularly **-relievo** *bäs'ō-ri-lē'vō, n.* sculpture in which the figures do not stand far out from the ground on which they are formed. [Fr. and It. See **base²** and **relief.**]

bass¹ *bās, n.* the low or grave part in music: a bass singer — often in Italian form **basso** (*bäs'sō*), *pl.* **bas'sos, bas'si** (*-si*): a bass instrument, esp. (*coll.*) a double-bass: low frequency sound as output from an amplifier, etc. — *adj.* low, deep, grave: (of a musical instrument or voice) low in pitch and compass. — *v.t.* (*rare*) to sound in a deep tone. — *n.* **bass'ist** one who plays a double-bass or a bass guitar. — *adj.* **bass'y** somewhat bass: predominantly bass. — **bass'-bar** a strip of wood on the belly of a violin, etc., under the bass foot of the bridge, to distribute the vibrations; **bass clef** the F clef on the fourth line of the stave; **bass drum** the large drum of an orchestra or band; **bass fiddle** (*coll.*) a double-bass; **bass guitar** an electric guitar similar in sound and range to the double-bass; **bass horn** an old wind instrument, a modification of the serpent; **bass tuba** the lowest instrument of the saxhorn class — the bombardon; **bass viol** a four-stringed instrument, used for playing the bass in concerted music, the viola da gamba — double-bass (*coll.*). [See **base².**]

bass² *bas, n.* bast: a container made of bast or the like, used for carrying fish, etc. — **bass'wood** a lime-tree or its wood. [See **bast.**]

bass³, basse *bas, n.* a European sea-fish of the sea-perch family (*Labrax lupus* or *Morone labrax*): extended to other sea and freshwater fishes. [O.E. *bærs;* cf. Ger. *Bars,* the perch.]

basset *bas'it, n.* a hound (**bass'et-hound**) like a badger-dog, but bigger: an old Venetian game at cards, resembling faro, widely popular in the 18th century: an outcrop (*geol.*). — *v.i.* to crop out. — **basset horn** (It. *corno di bassetto*) the richest and softest of all wind instruments, similar to a clarinet in tone and fingering, but with a twice-bent wooden tube. — *n.* **bass'et= hornist.** [Fr., — *bas,* low.]

bassinet *bas'i-net, n.* a kind of basket with a hood used as a cradle: a similarly shaped perambulator: a bed in hospital, with necessary equipment, for care of a baby. [Fr. dim. of *bassin,* a basin.]

basso. See **bass**[1].

bassoon *bə-sōōn', -zōōn', n.* (It. *fagotto*) a woodwind instrument filling an important place in the modern orchestra, its compass from B flat below the bass stave to C or F in the treble. — The **double bassoon** (It. *contrafagotto*) sounds an octave lower. — *n.* **bassoon'-ist.** [It. *bassone,* augmentative of *basso,* low, from root of **base**[2], **bass.**]

basso profondo *bä'sō prō-fon'dō,* (It.) a deep bass voice or singer.

basso-rilievo. See **bas-relief.**

basswood. See **bass**[2].

bast *bast, n.* phloem: inner bark, esp. of lime: fibre: matting. — Also **bass** (*bas*). See **bass**[2] . [O.E. *bæst*; Ger. *Bast.*]

basta *bas'tə,* (*Shak.*) *interj.* enough. [It. and Sp.]

bastard[1] *bas'tərd, bäs', n.* a child born of parents not married to each other: a sweet Spanish wine (*Shak.*): vulgarly, a recalcitrant person or thing, an unpleasant person, an unfortunate person, or almost meaningless, a chap. — *adj.* born out of wedlock: not genuine: resembling, but not identical with, the species bearing the name: of abnormal shape or size: false. — *n.* **bastardisā'tion, -z-.** — *v.t.* **bas'tardise, -ize** to pronounce to be or prove to be a bastard: to reduce to a lower state or condition. — *v.i.* to beget bastards (*Shak.*): to degenerate. — *n.* **bast'ardism** bastardy. — *adj.* **bas'tardly.** — *n.* **bas'tardy** the state of being a bastard. — **bas'tard-bar** an inaccurate name for the baton-sinister in heraldry; **bastard file** file with teeth of a medium degree of coarseness; **bastard title** an abbreviated title of a book on an otherwise blank page preceding the full title-page; **bastard types** types cast with an extra deep bevel to obviate the use of leads, as longprimer face on pica body; **bas'tard-wing** three, four, or five feathers on the first digit (homologue of the thumb) of a bird's wing. [O.F. *bastard* (Fr. *bâtard*), child of the pack-saddle (O.Fr. *bast*).]

bastard[2] *bas'tərd,* (*S. Afr.*) *n.* a person of mixed white and coloured parentage, whether legitimately born or not. — Also *Afrik.* **baster** (*bas'tər*). [Du. *bastaard,* bastard.]

baste[1] *bāst, v.i.* to beat with a stick. — *n.* **bāst'ing.** [Prob. conn. with O.N. *beysta,* Dan. *böste,* to beat.]

baste[2] *bāst, v.t.* to drop fat or butter over, as in roasting. [Ety. unknown.]

baste[3] *bāst, v.t.* to tack in sewing. [O.Fr. *bastir* — O.H.G. *bestan,* to sew.]

bastel-house. See **bastille.**

baster. See **bastard**[2].

bastide *bas-tēd,* (Fr.) *n.* a French country-house.

bastille *bas-tēl', n.* a tower for the defence of a fortress (*hist.*): a movable tower used by besiegers: (with *cap.*) an old fortress and state prison in Paris, demolished in the Revolution (July 1789): hence any prison, esp. as a symbol of tyranny. — **bastel-house** (*bas'tl; Scot.* and *Northern.*) a fortified house, usu. with vaulted ground-floor. [Fr., — O.Fr., *bastir* (Fr. *bâtir*), to build.]

bastinado, bastinade *bast-in-ād'(ō), vs.t.* to beat with a baton or stick, *esp.* on the soles of the feet (an Eastern punishment): — *pr.p.* **bastinād'oing** or **bastinād'ing;** *pa.p.* **bastinād'oed** or **bastinād'ed.** — *ns.* **bastinade';** **bastinād'o:** — *pl.* **bastinā'does.** [Sp. *bastonada,* Fr. *bastonnade* — *baston, baton*; cf. **baton, batten.**]

bastion *bast'yən, n.* a kind of tower at the angle of a fortification: a defence (*fig.*). — *adj.* **bast'ioned.** [Fr., — It. *bastione* — *bastire,* to build.]

bastle, bastle-house. Same as **bastel-house** (see **bastille**).

basto *bäs'tō, n.* in quadrille, the ace of clubs: — *pl.* **bas'tos.** [Sp., club.]

Basuto *ba-sōō'tō n.* the Bantu people of Lesotho (form. Basutoland): a member thereof (*pl.* **Basu'tos**): their language (also **Sotho**). — Also **Basu'tu** (- *-tōo*).

bat[1] *bat, n.* a heavy stick: a flattish club for striking the ball in cricket: a club for baseball: in tennis, etc., a racket (*coll.*): a batsman: the clown or harlequin's lath: a piece of brick: speed (*slang*): a drunken spree (*slang*): a blow: a sheet of batting (also **batt**): a layer of felt used in hat-making (also **batt**). — *v.t.* and *v.i.* to hit with a bat in cricket, etc.: to hit as with a bat: — *pr.p.* **batt'ing;** *pa.t.* and *pa.p.* **batt'ed.** — *ns.* **batt'er; batt'ing** the management of a bat in playing games: cotton fibre prepared in sheets, for quilts, etc. — **bat'fowling** catching birds at night by showing a light and beating the bushes; **bat'man** a man on an aerodrome or aircraft carrier who assists planes to taxi to position using a pair of lightweight bats; see also under **bathorse; bat printing** a method of printing in which designs are transferred by means of a sheet of gelatine; **bats'man** one who wields the bat at cricket, etc.; **bats'manship.** — **bat around** (*slang*) to wander: to go on a bat; **carry (out) one's bat** (*cricket*) to be not-out at the end of an innings, esp. when one has gone in first and when all ten wickets have fallen; **off one's own bat** by one's own efforts (as a cricketer from his own hits): on one's own initiative; **take out one's bat** to be not-out at the end of an innings, esp. when one has gone in later than first and when all ten wickets have fallen. [Perh. from O.E. *bat* (a doubtful form), prob. Celt. *bat,* staff.]

bat[2] *bat, n.* a flying mammal with wings attached mainly to its arms and hands, but extending along its sides to the hind-feet and tail. — *adjs.* **bats** (*coll.*) batty; **batt'y** batlike: bat-infested: crazy (*coll.*). — **bats'wing** a gas-burner that gives a flame shaped like a bat's wing; **batwing sleeve** a sleeve that is very wide at the armhole and tight at the wrist. — **have, be bats in the belfry** (*coll.*) to be crazy, slightly mad; **like a bat out of hell** (*coll.*) very quickly [M.E. *bakke,* apparently from Scand.; cf. Dan. *aftenbakke,* evening-bat.]

bat[3] *bat, v.t.* to flutter, esp. an eyelid. — **not bat an eye(lid)** not to sleep a wink: to show no surprise, no emotion. [Cf. **bate**[3].]

bat[4] *bat, n.* a spoken language of India or farther east. — **sling the bat** to speak such a language. [Hindi, speech, word.]

batable *bāt'ə-bl, adj.* short for **debatable.**

batata *bə-tä'tə, n.* the sweet-potato. [Sp. from Haitian.]

Batavian *bə-tā'vi-ən, adj.* pertaining to the ancient *Batāvi* in the Low Countries, or to the modern Dutch, or to Batavia (Jakarta). — Also *n.*

batch *bach, n.* the quantity of bread baked, or of anything made or got ready, at one time: a set: quantity of material for one operation in glass-making, etc., or of concrete prepared at one time. — *v.t.* to collect into, or treat in, batches. — *adj.* **batch'ing.** — **batch process-ing** (*comput.*) a method of processing data in which similar items of data are collected together for processing at one time. [From the root of **bake.**]

bate[1] *bāt, v.t.* and *v.i.* to abate: to lessen, diminish: to blunt. — *adj.* **bate'less** not to be blunted (*Shak.*): not bated (*obs.*). — *n.* **bate'ment** reduction (*obs.*). — **batement light** a window whose sill is not horizontal. — **with bated breath** see **breath.** [Aphetic form of **abate**[1].]

bate[2] *bāt, n.* (*Spens.*) strife, contention. — *adj.* **bate'= breed'ing** (*Shak.*). [Aphetic form of **debate.**]

bate[3] *bāt, v.i.* to beat the wings impatiently, to try to fly from the fist or perch when still attatched by leash or jesses (*falconry*): to be impatient (*obs.*). [O.Fr. *batre* — L.L. *batěre.*]

bate[4]. Same as **bait,** a rage (*slang*).

bateau *bä-tō'*, *n.* a light river-boat, *esp.* on Canadian rivers: — *pl.* **bateaux** (*-tōz'*). [Fr.]
bateleur *bat'lər*, *n.* a short-tailed African eagle. [Fr., mountebank, app. from its characteristic movements.]
bath[1] *bäth*, *n.* water for immersing the body: an act of bathing: a receptacle or a house for bathing: a place for undergoing medical treatment by means of bathing: the act of exposing the body to vapour, mud, sunlight, etc.: a liquid or other material (as sand), or a receptacle, in which anything is immersed for heating, washing, or steeping (*chem.*): — *pl.* **baths** (*bädhz*, also *bäths*). — *v.t.* to give a bath to: to wash (oneself) in a bath. — *v.i.* to take a bath. — **bath'cube** bath-salts in the form of a solid cube; **bath'house; bath'robe** (*U.S.*) dressing-gown; **bath'room; bath'-salts** a usu. sweet-smelling substance used in baths to soften and perfume the water; **bath'tub.** — **Order of the Bath** an English order of knighthood, so named from the bath before installation. [O.E. *bæth;* Ger. *Bad.*]
bath[2] *bäth*, *n.* the largest Jewish liquid measure, containing about six gallons. [Heb.]
Bath *bäth*, a famous city in Somerset, with Roman *baths.* — *n.* **Bathō'nian** (*geol.*) a division of the Middle Jurassic (also *adj.*). — **Bath bun** a rich sweet bun; **Bath chair** (also without *cap.*) a large wheeled chair for invalids, long in general use in Bath; **Bath Oliver** a biscuit invented by Dr W. Oliver of Bath; **Bath stone** a building-stone quarried at Bath.
bath-brick *bäth'brik*, *n.* a preparation of siliceous silt, manufactured at Bridgwater in the form of bricks and used in cleaning knives. [Traditionally named after the first maker, one *Bath*, or from its resemblance to *Bath stone.*]
bathe *bädh*, *v.t.* to wash as in a bath: to wash or moisten, with any liquid: to moisten, suffuse, encompass. — *v.i.* to take a dip or swim: to bask. — *n.* the act of bathing: a swim or dip. — *n.* **bäth'er** one who bathes: (in *pl.*; *Austr.* and *N.Z.*) a swimming costume. — **bäth'ing= box', -hut'** a small structure for bathers to undress and dress in; **bäth'ing-cost'ume, -dress, -suit** a garb for bathing in; **bäth'ing-machine'** (*hist.*) a small carriage in which a bather may be carried out into water conveniently deep. [O.E. *bathian.*]
bathetic. See **bathos.**
bathmism *bath'mizm*, *n.* a supposed directive force in evolution, or inherent tendency to develop along divergent lines. — *adj.* **bath'mic.** [Gr. *bathmos*, step.]
bath mitzvah, bath mizvah, bath mitsvah *bäth mits'və* (also **bas** *bäs*, **bat** *bät*; sometimes with *caps.*; also hyphenated or as one word) *esp.* in the U.S., a girl of the Jewish religion attaining the age (usu. 13 years) of religious responsibility: the festivities held in recognition of this event. [Heb., daughter of the law.]
batholite *bath'ō-līt*, *n.* a mass of igneous rock that has risen from a great depth. — Also **bath'olith, bath'ylith, bath'ylith.** — *adjs.* **batholit(h)ic, bathylit(h)ic** (*-lit'*, *-lith'*). [Gr. *bathos*, depth, *bathys*, deep, *lithos*, a stone.]
bathometer *bath-om'it-ər*, *n.* a bathymeter. [Gr. *bathos*, depth, *metron*, measure.]
Bathonian. See **Bath.**
bathophobia *bath'ō-fō-bi-ə*, *n.* morbid fear of falling from a high place. [Gr. *bathos*, depth, *phobos*, fear.]
bathorse *bat'hörs, bät'* (formerly *bä'*), *n.* a pack-horse carrying an officer's baggage. — **batman** (*bat'mən;* formerly *bä'mən*) one who has charge of a bathorse: an officer's attendant; see also under **bat**[1]; **batwoman** (*bat'*). [Fr. *bât*, pack-saddle.]
bathos *bā'thos*, *n.* a ludicrous descent from the elevated to the mean in writing or speech. — *adj.* **bathetic** (*bə-thet'ik;* irregularly formed on the analogy of *pathos, pathetic*). [Gr. *bathos*, depth.]
bathy- *bath'i-, -i'*, in composition, deep. — *adj.* **bath'yal** (*-i-əl*) of ocean depths of between 200 and 2000 metres. — *n.* **bathyb'ius** (Gr. *bios*, life) a once supposed low form of life on the sea bottom. — *adj.* **bathygraph'ical** (Gr. *graphein*, to write) of maps, indicating depth of

water. — *ns.* **bathylite** etc. see **batholite; bathymeter** (*-im'*; Gr. *metron*, measure) a sounding instrument. — *adjs.* **bathymet'ric, -al.** — *n.* **bathym'etry** the science of sounding seas and lakes. — *adjs.* **bathyorograph'ical** (Gr. *oros*, mountain) representing height and depth — applied to maps that show height of land and depth of water; **bathypelagic** (*-aj'ik;* Gr. *pelagos*, sea) found in the depths of the sea. — *n.* **bath'ysphere** (Gr. *sphaira*, sphere) a submersible observation chamber (**bath'-yscaph(e), -scope,** later types). [Gr. *bathys*, deep.]
batik *bat'ik, ba-tē'k*, *n.* an orig. Indonesian method of producing designs on cloth by covering with wax, for each successive dipping, those parts that are to be protected from the dye. [Malay.]
bating *bāt'ing*, *prep.* abating, excepting. [**bate**[1].]
batiste *ba-tēst'*, *n.* a fine fabric of linen, cotton, or wool. [Fr., cambric — *Baptiste*, the original maker, or from its use in wiping the heads of children after baptism.]
batler *bat'lər*, (*Shak.*) *n.* a beetle for beating clothes. — Altered by some editors to **bat'let.** [**bat**[1].]
batman. See **bat**[1] and **bathorse.**
bat mitzvah. See **bath mitzvah.**
batology *ba-tol'ə-ji*, *n.* the study of brambles. — *adj.* **batological** (*-loj'*). — *n.* **batol'ogist.** [Gr. *batos*, bramble.]
baton *bat'(ə)n*, (*arch.*) **batoon** *bə-tōōn'* *ns.* a staff of office, e.g. that of a marshall: a policeman's truncheon: a short stick passed on from one runner to the next in a relay-race: a light wand used by the conductor of an orchestra: a knobbed staff carried, tossed and twirled by a drum major, etc., at the head of a marching band, etc: a baton round. — *v.t.* to strike with a baton. — **baton charge** a swift forward movement of police against a hostile crowd with truncheons drawn for use. — *v.t.* **bat'on-charge.** — **baton gun** a gun which fires **baton rounds**, plastic bullets, used in riot-control; **bat'on-sin'ister** a heraldic indication of illegitimacy, improperly called *bar-sinister*, a diminutive of a bend-sinister, not extending to the sides of the shield, so as to resemble a marshal's baton laid diagonally over the family arms from sinister to dexter. — **under the baton of** (of choirs and orchestras) conducted by. [Fr. *bâton.*]
batrachia *bə-trā'ki-ə*, (sometimes with *cap.*) *n.pl.* the Amphibia: the Salientia, tailless amphibia, or frogs and toads. — *adj.* and *n.* **batrā'chian.** [Gr. *batrachos*, a frog.]
batsman. See **bat**[1].
batswing. See **bat**[2].
batt. See **bat**[1].
batta *bat'ə*, *n.* an allowance in addition to ordinary pay: subsistence money. [Prob. Kanarese *bhatta*, rice.]
battailous *bat'ā-ləs*, (*Spens.*) *adj.* warlike. [O.Fr. *batail-los;* see **battle**[1].]
battalia *bət-äl'yə* or *-āl'*, *n.* order of battle (*arch.*): the main body of an army in array (*obs.*). [It. *battaglia;* see **battle**[1].]
battalia pie *bət-al'yə pī*, articles such as pin-cushions, embroidered by nuns in convents with scenes from the Bible: a pie containing sweetbreads, etc. [Fr. *béat-illes*, dim. from L. *beātus*, blessed, and perh. L. *pius*, pious.]
battalion *bə-tal'yən*, *n.* a body of soldiers consisting of several companies: a body of men drawn up in battle array. [Fr. *batallion* — It. *battaglione;* see **battle**[1].]
batteilant *bat'ā-lənt*, (*Spens.*) *adj.* combatant. [Fr. *bataillant.*]
battels *bat'lz*, *n.pl.* accounts for provisions received from college kitchens and butteries (*Oxford*): sums charged in college accounts generally. — *v.i.* **batt'el** to have such an account. — *n.* **batt'eler** one who battels: a student of rank below a commoner (*obs.*). [Poss. conn. with **battle**[2].]
battement *bat-mä*, *n.* in ballet, a movement in which one leg is extended to the front, side or back. [Fr., beating — *battre*, to beat.]
batten[1] *bat'n*, *v.i.* to thrive at the expense of (with *on*): to

grow fat: to feed abundantly (on; *lit.* and *fig.*). — *v.t.* (*obs.*) to fatten. [O.N. *batna*, to grow better — *bati*, advantage; cf. Du. *baten*, to avail.]

batten² *bat'n, n.* a piece of sawn timber used for flooring, support of laths, etc.: a strip of wood fastened across parallel boards, or used to fasten down hatches aboard ship, etc.: a row of electric lamps or a strip of wood carrying them. — *v.t.* to fasten or furnish with battens. — *n.* **batt'ening** battens forming a structure. [*baton*.]

Battenberg (cake) *bat'ən-bûrg* (*kāk*), *n.* a kind of cake usu. made in pink and yellow squares and covered with marzipan. [Perh. from *Battenberg*, a village in W. Germany.]

batter¹ *bat'ər, v.t.* to beat with successive blows: to wear with beating or by use: to attack with artillery. — *n.* ingredients beaten along with some liquid into a paste (*cook.*): paste for sticking. — *adj.* **batt'ered** suffering frequent violent assaults: in particular, suffering such attacks at the hands of one's parents or spouse: covered, treated, with batter. — **batt'ering-ram** a large beam with a metal head like a ram's used for battering down walls. — **battered baby** (or **child**) **syndrome** a collection of symptoms found in a baby or young child, caused by violence on the part of the parent or other adult suffering from social and psychological disturbance; **on the batter** (*slang*) on the bat, on a spree. [O.Fr. *batre* (Fr. *battre*) — L.L. *battĕre* (L. *ba*(*t*)*tuĕre*), to beat.]

batter² *bat'ər, n.* inward inclination from the perpendicular. — *v.i.* to slope inward. [Origin doubtful.]

batter³. See **bat¹**.

batterie *bat-(ə-)rē, n.* in ballet, a jump in which the dancer beats the calves together. — **batterie de cuisine** (*də kwē-zēn*, Fr.) a set of utensils for cooking. [Fr., — *battre*, to beat; see **batter¹**.]

battero see **ballow**.

battery *bat'ər-i, n.* the act of battering: a wound (*Shak.*): a number of cannon with their equipment: the place on which cannon are mounted: a unit of artillery or its personnel: a combination of Leyden jars, lenses, or other apparatus: a series of two or more electric cells arranged to produce, or store, electricity: a single voltaic or solar cell: an attack against a person, beating, wounding, or threatening by touching clothes or body (*law*): an arrangement of tiers of cages in which hens are kept, the eggs they lay running down into wire containers outside the cages: an arrangement of similarly restrictive compartments for rearing pigs or cattle intensively: an apparatus for preparing or serving meals: the pitcher and catcher (*baseball*). — **battery of tests** (*psych.*) a set of tests covering various factors relevant to some end purpose, e.g. job selection; **cross batteries** two batteries commanding the same spot from different directions; **masked battery** a battery out of the enemy's view.

battill. Spenser's spelling of **battle²**.

batting. See **bat¹**.

battle¹ *bat'l, n.* a contest between opposing armies: a fight or encounter: a battalion (*arch.*). — *v.i.* to fight: to struggle: to contend (with *against, with*). — *v.t.* to dispose in battalions (*arch.*): to contest. — *n.* **batt'ler** one who struggles, esp. (*Austr. and N.Z.*) unsuccessfully or to make a living. — **batt'le-axe, -ax** a kind of axe once used in battle: a formidable woman (*coll.*); **battle-axe block, section** (*Austr. and N.Z.*) a plot of land without a street frontage, with access to and from the street via a drive or lane; **batt'le-cruiser** a large cruiser with battleship qualities; **batt'le-cry** a war-cry, slogan; **batt'ledress** a simplified military uniform, close-fitting at the waist, allowing freedom of movement; **battle fatigue** same as **combat fatigue**; **batt'lefield, batt'leground** the place on which a battle is or was fought; **batt'le-piece** a picture or description of a battle; **batt'leplane** (*obs.*) a large fighting aeroplane; **battle royal** a general mêlée. — *adj.* **batt'le-scarred** scarred in battle. — **batt'leship** a warship of the first class. — **do battle** (often *fig.*) to fight; **half the battle** anything that

brings one well on the way to success; **join battle** to engage in fighting. [Fr. *bataille* — L. *battuālia*, fighting.]

battle² *bat'l, adj.* nourishing (*dial.*): fertile (*dial.*). — *v.t.* and *v.i.* (*arch.*) to feed: to fatten: to make or become fertile. [Perh. conn. with O.N. *bati*, improvement; see **batten¹**.]

battle³ *bat'l, v.t.* (*obs.*) to furnish with battlements (esp. in *pa.p*). — *n.* **batt'lement** a wall or parapet with embrasures. — *adj.* **batt'lemented.** [O.Fr. *batailler*, movable defences.]

battledore, battledoor *bat'l-dōr, -dör, n.* a wooden bat used for washing, etc.: a light bat for striking a ball or shuttlecock: a hornbook (*obs.*). — **not to know a B from a battledore** (*arch.*) to be thoroughly ignorant. [Perhaps Sp. *batidor*, a beater, a washing beetle.]

battology *bat-ol'ə-ji, n.* futile repetition in speech or writing. — *adj.* **battolog'ical.** [Gr. *battologiā*, stuttering, said to be from *Battos*, who consulted the Delphic oracle about his defect of speech (Herodotus iv. 155), and *legein*, to speak.]

battre la campagne *batr' la kã-pan-y'*, (Fr.) to scour the country, to beat the bush.

batts. See **bot²**.

battue *ba-tōō', ba-tū', bä-tü, n.* a hunt in which animals are driven into some place for the convenience of the shooters: indiscriminate slaughter. [Fr., — *battre*, to beat.]

battuta *bät'tōō'tä*, (It.) *n.* beat. — **a battuta** in strict time.

batty. See **bat²**.

batwing. See under **bat²**.

batwoman. See **bathorse**.

bauble *bö'bl, n.* a trifling piece of finery: a child's plaything: a jester's sceptre, a stick surmounted by a head with ass's ears: a piece of childish foolery: a foolish person (*Shak.*). — *adj.* **bau'bling** (*Shak.*) trifling. [O.Fr. *babel, baubel*, toy, trinket.]

bauchle *böhh'l*, (*Scot.*) *n.* a loose, down-at-heel, or badly worn, shoe: a worn-out, useless, or clumsy person or thing. — *v.i.* to shamble. — *v.t.* to make shapeless: to bungle or spoil. [Origin obscure.]

baud¹ *böd', (teleg.*) *n.* a unit of signalling speed.

baud². See **bawd²**.

baudckin *böd'i-kin.* Same as **baldachin.**

baudric, baudrick(e) *böd'rik.* Same as **baldric(k).**

Baudrons *böd'rəns, n.* Scottish quasi-proper name for the cat: also for the hare. [Origin obscure.]

Bauera *bow'ə-rə, n.* a genus of evergreen shrubs (fam. Saxifragaceae) found in Australia, with pink flowers: (without *cap.*) a plant of this genus. [F. and F.A. *Bauer*, 19th-century Austrian botanical painters.]

Bauhaus *bow'hows, n.* a German school of art and architecture (1919–33) having as its aim the integration of art and technology in design. [Lit. Building-house.]

Bauhinia *bö-hin'-i-ə n.* a genus of tropical trees of the family Caesalpinaceae: (without *cap.*) a plant of the genus. [J. and G. *Bauhin*, 17th-century Swiss botanists.]

bauk, baulk. Same as **balk.**

baur. See **bar²**.

bausond *bös'ənd, adj.* of animals, having white spots, esp. on the forehead, or a white stripe down the face. — *adj.* **baus'on-faced.** [O.Fr. *bausant*, black and white spotted.]

bauxite, beauxite *bök'sīt, -zīt, bō'zīt, ns.* a clay compound containing aluminium. — *adj.* **bauxitic** (*-it'ik*). [From Les *Baux*, near Arles, and *-ite*.]

bavardage *bäv-är-däzh', n.* chattering, prattle. [Fr. *bavard*, garrulous — *bave*, drivel.]

bavin *bav'in, n.* a fagot of brushwood. — **bavin wits** (*Shak.*) wits that blaze and die like bavins. [Origin unknown.]

bawbee *bö-bē', (Scot.*) *n.* a halfpenny: originally a silver coin worth three Scots pennies. [Prob. from a Scottish mint-master (1538), Alexander Orrok of Sillebawbe.]

bawble. Same as **bauble.**

bawcock *bö′kok*, (*Shak.*) *n.* a fine fellow. [From Fr. *beau*, fine, and *coq*, a cock.]

bawd[1] *böd, n.* a procuress (or till about 1700 procurer) of women for lewd purposes. — *adv.* **bawd′ily.** — *ns.* **bawd′iness; bawd′ry** procuring: unchastity: bawdy talk. — *adj.* **bawd′y** lewd. — *n.* bawdy talk. — *adj.* **bawd′=born** (*Shak.*) born of a bawd. — **bawd′y-house** a brothel. [Prob. M.E. *bawdstrot*, pander — O.Fr. *baldestrot*, prob. — *bald*, bold, gay, and the root of **strut.**]

bawd[2] (*Shak.* **baud**) *böd, n.* a hare. [Perh. **Baudrons.**]

bawdkin. Same as **baldachin.**

bawl *böl, v.t.* and *v.i.* to shout or cry out very loudly. — *n.* a loud cry or shout. — *ns.* **bawl′er; bawl′ing.** — **bawl out** (*coll.*) to reprimand bullyingly. [Perh. L.L. *baulāre*, to bark, but cf. Icel. *baula*, to low like a cow — O.N. *haula*, a cow.]

bawley *bö′li*, (*Essex* and *Kent*) *n.* a small fishing-smack. [Origin obscure.]

bawn *bön, n.* a fortification round a house: an enclosure for cattle. [Ir. *bábhun*, enclosure.]

bawr. See **bar**[2].

baxter *bak′stər*, (*obs.*) *n.* a baker. [**bake.**]

bay[1] *bā, adj.* reddish brown inclining to chestnut (of horses, usu. with a black mane and tail). — *n.* a bay horse. [Fr. *bai* — L. *badius*, chestnut-coloured.]

bay[2] *bā, n.* an inlet of the sea with a wider opening than a gulf: an inward bend of the shore: a similar recess in a land form, e.g. in a mountain range. — **bay salt** coarse-grained salt, orig. from sea-water. — **the Bay State** Massachusetts. [Fr. *baie* — L.L. *baia*, a harbour.]

bay[3] *bā, n.* the space between two columns, timbers, walls, etc.: the space under one house gable (*Shak.*): any recess or stall: a passing-place in a military trench: a side-line in a railway station (also **bay′-line**): a compartment (e.g. bomb bay) or section of an aircraft. — **bay window** any window forming a recess. — *adj.* **bay′-win′dowed.** [O.Fr. *baée* — *baer*, to gape, to open; prob. conn. **bay**[2].]

bay[4] *bā, n.* the laurel tree; extended to other trees and shrubs, species of *Magnolia, Myrica*, etc.: (in *pl.*) an honorary garland or crown of victory, originally of laurel: hence, literary renown. — **bay′berry** the berry of the bay tree, or of candle-berry: a tree (*Pimenta acris*) akin to allspice; **bay leaf** dried leaf of laurel tree (*Laurus nobilis*) used as flavouring agent in cooking; **bay rum** an aromatic liquid prepared from the leaves of *Pimenta acris* used medicinally and cosmetically: this liquid mixed with certain other substances. [O.Fr. *baie*, a berry — L. *bāca.*]

bay[5] *bā, n.* barking, baying (esp. of a dog in pursuit): the combined cry of hounds in conflict with a hunted animal: the last stand of a hunted animal when it faces the hounds at close quarters. — *v.i.* to bark (esp. of large dogs). — *v.t.* to bark at: to utter by baying: to follow with barking: to bring to bay. — **bay (at) the moon** to make a futile gesture; **keep at bay** to prevent from coming closer; **stand, be, at bay** to face the dogs at close quarters: to face one's pursuers. [Partly O.Fr. *abai*, barking, *bayer*, to bark, partly O.Fr. *bay*, open-mouthed suspense — L.L. *badāre*, to open the mouth.]

bay[6] *bā,* **bez** *bā, bāz, ns.* (in full **bay′-antler, -tine**) the second tine of a deer's horn. [O.Fr. *besantlier* — *bes-*, secondary (— L. *bis*, twice), *antlier*, antler.]

bay[7], **baye** *bā,* (*Spens.*) *v.t.* to bathe.

bayadère *bä-yä-der′, n.* a Hindu dancing-girl: a horizontally-striped woven fabric. [Fr., — Port. *bailadeira.*]

Bayard[1] *bā′är(d)*, Fr. *bä-yär, n.* a type of the knight 'without fear and without reproach'. [From the French knight *Bayard* (1476–1524).]

Bayard[2] *bā′ärd, -ərd, n.* in romance, Rinaldo's horse: (without *cap.*) a bay horse or horse generally: a type of blind recklessness or bold ignorance.

baye. See **bay**[7].

bayle. See **bail**[2].

bayonet *bā′ə-nit, n.* a stabbing instrument of steel fixed to the muzzle of a fire-arm: military force: a soldier armed with a bayonet: (also **bayonet fitting**) a type of fitting for a light bulb, camera lens, etc., in which prongs on its side fit into slots to hold it in place. — *v.t.* to stab with a bayonet: to force at the point of the bayonet. — *adj.* **bay′oneted** armed with a bayonet. — **bayonet joint, socket,** etc. one with, or for, a bayonet fitting. [Fr. *baïonnette*, perh. from *Bayonne*, in France; or from O.Fr. *bayon*, arrow.]

bayou *bī′oo*, (*U.S.*) *n.* the marshy offshoot of a lake or river. [Perh. Fr. *boyau*, gut, or Choctaw *bāyuk*, little river.]

bayt. A Spenserian spelling of **bate**[1]; also of **bait.**

bazaar, bazar *bə-zär′, n.* an Eastern market-place or exchange: a fancy fair in imitation of an Eastern bazaar: sometimes, a big shop. [Pers. *bāzār*, a market.]

bazooka *bə-zoo′kə, n.* a crude wind instrument with a slide used for humorous purposes: an anti-tank gun for rocket-driven projectiles: a rocket launcher situated on the wing of an aeroplane. [Invented name.]

baz(z)azz. See **bez(z)azz.**

bdellium *del′i-əm, n.* a gum got from *Commiphora* trees: used to translate, but prob. unconnected with, Heb. *b′dōlakh* (Gen. ii. 12; meaning unknown). [L., — Gr. *bdellion.*]

be *bē, v.i. infin.* to live: to exist: to have the state or quality mentioned: — *pr.p.* **bē′ing;** *pa.p.* **been** (*bēn, bin*); *pr.subj.* **be;** *arch.* and *dial.* pr.indic. **be** (see **am, art, is, are**); for *pa.t.* see **was, wast, were, wert.** — *n.* **be′-all** (*Shak.*) all that is to be (**be-all and end-all** now often = 'the supreme aim, issue'). [O.E. *bēon;* Ger. *bin* (1st pers.); Gael. *bi*, exist; W. *byw*, live; Gr. *phyein*, produce, grow; L. *fuī*, I was, *fīō*, I become; Sans. *bhavati*, he is; orig. to grow.]

be- *bi-, pfx.* used (1) to form words with the sense of around, on all sides, in all directions, thoroughly; (2) to form verbs from adjectives and nouns; (3) formerly, to make intransitive verbs transitive, as *bespeak.* [O.E. *bi-*, weak form of *bī.*]

beach *bēch, n.* the shore of a sea or of a lake, esp. when sandy or pebbly: a marginal terrace formed by waves: the strand. — *v.t.* to drive or haul up on a beach. — *adjs.* **beached** having a beach: driven on a beach; **beach′y** pebbly. — **beach′-ball** a large usu. inflatable, colourful ball for playing games on a beach; **beach′-comber** (-kōm-) a long rolling wave: a loafer about the wharfs in Pacific seaports: a settler on a Pacific island who maintains himself by pearl-fishery, or by gathering jetsam, etc. on beaches; **beach′combing; beach′head** an area held on an enemy's shore for purpose of landing; **beach′-master** an officer in charge of disembarking troops; **beach′-rescue** a person employed to save beach bathers in difficulties. [Orig. a dial. word for shingle.]

beach-la-mar *bēch-lä-mär′, n.* a South Sea jargon used in the bêche-de-mer trade. [Port. *bicho do mar*, seaslug, bêche-de-mer.]

beacon *bē′kən, n.* a fire on an eminence lit as a signal, e.g. to warn of danger: a hill on which it could be lighted: an erection with or without a light marking a rock or shoal in navigable waters: a light to guide airmen: a sign marking a street crossing — e.g. a **Belisha** (*bə-lē′shə, -ish′*) **beacon** named after the Minister of Transport 1934: a wireless transmitter in which the radiation is concentrated in one or more narrow beams, so as to act as a guide to shipping or aircraft: anything that warns of danger. — *v.t.* to act as a beacon to: to light up: to mark by beacons. — **floating beacon** a lightship. [O.E. *bēacn*, a beacon, a sign.]

bead *bēd, n.* a prayer (*obs.*): a little ball strung with others in a rosary, for counting prayers: a similar ball or the like pierced for stringing to form a necklace, etc.: a bead-like drop: the front-sight of a gun: a narrow moulding orig. of semi-circular section, sometimes

broken into bead-like parts, now in various shapes, used esp. for covering small gaps: the flange of a tyre. — *v.t.* to furnish with beads or beading. — *v.i.* to form a bead or beads. — *adj.* **bead′ed** having beads or a bead: in bead-like form. — *n.* **bead′ing** bead (moulding): work in beads. — *adj.* **bead′y** bead-like, small and bright (as eyes): covered with beads or bubbles. — **bead′-house** orig. a chapel: an almshouse whose inmates were required to pray for the founder's soul. — *adj.* **bead′-proof** of such proof or strength as to carry beads or bubbles after shaking, as alcoholic liquors. — **bead′-roll** orig. a list of the dead to be prayed for, hence a list of names, a long series: a rosary; **beads′man, bedes′man** one bound or endowed to pray for others: a licensed beggar (*Scot.*): —*fem.* **beads′woman.** — **draw a bead on** (*U.S.*) to take aim at; **tell one's beads** to say one's prayers. [O.E. *gebed*, prayer; see **bid**².]
beadle *bē′dl, n.* a mace-bearer, esp. (Oxford and Cambridge **bedel(l)** -*del′*, or *bēd′*) a vice-chancellor's: a petty officer of a church, college, etc.: a parish officer with the power of punishing petty offenders: in Scotland, the church-officer attending on the minister: a messenger or crier of a court (*obs.*). — *ns.* **bead′ledom, bead′lehood** stupid officiousness; **bead′leship, bedel(l)ship** the office of beadle or bedel. [O.E. *bydel* — *bēodan*, to proclaim, to bid; affected by O.Fr. form *bedel.*]
beadman, bedeman. Old forms of **beadsman** (see under **bead**).
beady. See **bead.**
beagle *bē′gl, n.* a small hound tracking by scent, formerly much used in hunting hares: sometimes, a harrier: a spy: a bailiff: a small kind of shark. — *v.i.* to hunt with beagles. — *ns.* **bea′gler; bea′gling** hunting with beagles. [Ety. unknown; prob. O.Fr. *beegueule*, clamourer — *beer,* to gape, *guele,* throat.]
beak *bēk, n.* a bird's bill: a hard or sharp snout: a nose (*jocular*): a pointed process or projection: in the ancient galley a pointed iron projecting from the bow for piercing the enemy's vessel: a magistrate, schoolmaster, or schoolmistress (*slang*). — *adj.* **beaked** (*bēkt*). — **beak′-iron** same as **bick-iron.** [O.Fr. *bec* — L. *beccus* (recorded by Suetonius), a cock's bill.]
beaker *bēk′ər, n.* a large drinking-bowl or cup, or its contents: a deep glass or other vessel used by chemists, generally with a lip for pouring: a usu. plastic tumbler: one of a set of similar cylindrical-shaped objects, a child's toy. — **Beaker Folk** a round-headed, heavy-browed, square-jawed people that appeared in Britain at the dawn of the Bronze Age, makers of round barrows in which bell-shaped pottery beakers are often found. [O.N. *bikarr,* prob. — L.L. *bicārium,* or *bīcārium,* app. — Gr. *bīkos,* a drinking bowl.]
beam *bēm, n.* a tree (*obs.* except in *hornbeam, whitebeam,* etc.): a large and straight piece of timber or iron forming one of the main structural members of a building, etc.: a great fault (*fig.*; from the figure of the mote and the beam — Matt. vii. 3): any of the transverse pieces of framing extending across a ship's hull: the greatest width of a ship or boat: breadth: the part of a balance from which the scales hang: the pole of a carriage: the stem, or main part of a deerhorn, an anchor, a plough: a cylinder of wood in a loom: a shaft or ray of light or other radiations: a gleam. — *v.t.* to send forth: to place on a beam: to transmit or direct, e.g. by beam system. — *v.i.* to shine: to smile radiantly. — *n.* **beam′er** a workman or machine that puts yarn on the beam of a loom: a fast, head-high ball that does not touch the ground (*cricket*): a beam trawler. — *adv.* **beam′ily** radiantly. — *n.* **beam′iness** radiance: breadth. — *n. and adj.* **beam′ing.** — *adv.* **beam′ingly.** — *adjs.* **beam′ish** radiant; **beam′less** without beams: emitting no rays; **beam′y** shining: radiant: massive like a weaver's beam: broad. — **beam′-ends** the ends of the transverse beams of a ship; **beam′-en′gine** a steam-engine with a beam connecting the piston-rod and the crank of the wheel-shaft; **beam sea** one rolling against

the ship's side; **beam system** a system whereby, with the aid of reflectors, short wireless waves are projected (like a lighthouse beam) in a particular direction, not radiated in all directions; **beam trawl** a trawling net kept open by a beam along its upper lip, resting on runners; **beam trawler; beam trawling; beam tree** a pleonastic name for the whitebeam; **beam weapon** any weapon whose destructive force consists of a beam of energy such as sub-atomic particles. — **abaft, before, the beam** behind, before, a line projected from the greatest width of a ship (its beam) at right angles to its course; **fly** or **ride the beam** to fly an aircraft in the direction shown by a radio beam; **lee, weather, beam** the side away from, or towards, the wind; **off** or **on the beam** off or on the course shown by a radio beam: off or on the right track (*fig.*); **on her beam-ends** of a ship, so much inclined to one side that the beams become nearly vertical; **on one's beam-ends** in acute distress, destitute; **on the beam** in the direction of a ship's beams, at right angles to her course: see **off the beam; on the port, starboard, beam** applied to any distant point out at sea, at right angles to the keel, and on the left, or right, side. [O.E. *bēam,* tree, stock of a tree, ray of light; Ger. *Baum,* tree; perh. akin to Gr. *phȳma,* a growth — *phyein,* to grow.]
bean *bēn, n.* the name of several kinds of leguminous plants and their seeds, esp. the common, or broad bean (*Vicia faba*) and the French kidney, or haricot bean (*Phaseolus vulgaris*): applied also to the seeds of other plants, from their bean-like form, as coffee: a coin (*coll.*): the head (*coll.*). — *v.t.* (*coll.*) to hit on the head. — *ns.* **bean′ie** (*coll.*) a small, close-fitting hat; **bean′o** (*coll.*) a beanfeast, a disturbance, a jollification: bingo: — *pl.* **bean′os.** — **bean′-bag** a small cloth bag containing dried beans or the like, used in games: a large cushion filled e.g. with chips or balls of plastic foam, used as seating; **bean caper** a genus (*Zygophyllum*) of steppe and desert shrubs whose flower-buds are used as capers; **bean′feast** an annual dinner given by employers to their workers at which beans used to be prominent: a jollification; **bean′-king** the king of the festivities on Twelfth Night, finder of a bean hidden in the Twelfth Cake; **bean′pole** a supporting pole up which a bean plant climbs: a tall, very thin person (*coll.*); **bean sprout** the young shoot of the mung bean or certain other beans, used as a vegetable esp. in Chinese cookery; **bean′stalk** the stem of a bean plant; **bean tree** a name given to several trees, as Moreton Bay chestnut, coral tree, and Catalpa. — **full of beans** in high spirits; **give someone beans** to treat someone severely; **know how many beans make five** (*coll.*) to be fully alert, know what's what; **old bean** see **old; spill the beans** see **spill**¹. [O.E. *bēan,* Ger. *Bohne.*]
bear¹ *bār, v.t.* to carry: to have: to convey: to remove from the board in the final stage of the game (*backgammon*): to sustain or support: to thrust or drive: to endure: to admit of: to purport: to be entitled to (*her.*): to afford: to behave or conduct (oneself): to bring forth, give birth to (*pa.p.* **born** (*börn*) in passive uses). — *v.i.* to suffer: to be patient: to have reference (with *on* or *upon*): to press (with *on* or *upon*): to lie in, take, a direction: to be capable of sustaining weight: to be productive: — *pr.p.* **bear′ing;** *pa.t.* **bore** (*arch.* **bare**); *pa.p.* **borne** (*börn, börn*). — *n.* (*Spens.* **beare** *bēr*) a burden: also (*Spens.*) a bier (see **bier**). — *adj.* **bear′able** that may be borne or endured. — *n.* **bear′ableness.** — *adv.* **bear′ably.** — *ns.* **bear′er** one who or that which bears: the actual holder of a cheque or the like: one who helps to carry a body to the grave: a carrier or messenger: in India a personal, household or hotel servant; **bear′ing** demeanour: direction: a supporting surface: relation: that which is borne upon an escutcheon: the part of a machine that bears friction, esp. a journal and its support (sometimes in *pl.*: see **ball-bearing**). — Also *adj.* — **bearer bond, share** security, etc. a bond, etc. the title to which is held by the person in possession of it; **bearing cloth** a mantle or

cloth in which a child was carried to the font; **bearing rein** a fixed rein between the bit and the saddle, by which a horse's head is held up and its neck made to arch. — **bear a hand** see **hand; bear away** to sail away: to carry away; **bear down** to overthrow: to press downwards: (with *upon* or *towards*) to sail with the wind (towards): (with *upon*) to approach (someone or something) rapidly and purposefully; **bear hard** (*Shak.*) to have ill-will to; **bear hard, heavily upon** (*lit.* and *fig.*) to press heavily on: to oppress, afflict; **bear in hand** to make out, maintain (*arch.*): to keep in expectation, to flatter one's hopes (*Shak.*); **bear in mind** to remember (that): to think of, take into consideration; **bear in upon** (usu. in *pass.*) to impress upon, or to make realise, esp. by degrees; **bear out** to corroborate; **bear up** to keep up one's spirits; **bear up for** to sail towards (a place); **bear with** to make allowance for; **bear witness** see **witness; bring to bear** to bring into operation (with *against, upon*); **find, lose one's bearings** to ascertain, or to become uncertain of, one's position or orientation. [O.E. *beran;* Goth. *bairan,* L. *ferre,* Gr. *pherein,* Sans. *bharati,* he carries.]

bear² *bār, n.* a heavy carnivorous animal with long shaggy hair and hooked claws: any rude, rough or ill-bred fellow: one who sells stocks for delivery at a future date, anticipating a fall in price — opp. to *bull* (the old phrase *a bearskin jobber* suggests an origin in the proverbial phrase, to sell the bearskin before one has caught the bear): the name of two constellations, the Great and Little Bear (Ursa major and minor). — *v.i.* to speculate for a fall. — *adj.* **bear'ish** like a bear in manners: inclining towards, anticipating, a fall in prices (*Stock Exchange*). — *n.* **bear'ishness.** — **bear'-animal'cule** a tardigrade — one of a group of degenerate arthropods; **bear'-baiting** the former sport of setting dogs to worry a bear; **bear'-berry** a trailing plant (*Arctostaphylos*) of the heath family: extended to various plants; **bear'bine** a bindweed; **bear'-cat** a panda; **bear garden** an enclosure for bear-baiting: a turbulent assembly; **bear'-leader** one who leads about a performing bear: the tutor of a youth on travel; **bear's'-breech** acanthus; **bear's'-ear** auricula; **bear's'-foot** black hellebore; **bear'skin** the skin of a bear: a shaggy woollen cloth for overcoats: the high fur cap worn by the Guards in England; **bear'ward** a warden or keeper of bears.   [O.E. *bera;* Ger. *Bär;* Du. *beer;* apparently from an Indo-European root *bhero-,* brown.]

bear³, bere *bēr, n.* barley: in Scotland now the little grown four-rowed (really six-rowed) variety.   [O.E. *bere.*]

bear⁴, beer *bēr.* See **bere².**

bearbine See **bear².**

beard *bērd, n.* the hair that grows on the chin and adjacent parts of a grown man's face: the tuft on the lower jaw of a goat, seal, etc.: a fish's barbel: an awn or threadlike spike as on the ears of barley (*bot.*): a tuft of hairs: a barb of a hook, an arrow, etc.: the gills of an oyster, etc. — *v.t.* to take by the beard: to oppose to the face. — *adj.* **beard'ed** having a beard: prickly: awned: barbed. — *n.* **beard'ie** (*coll.*) a bearded person. — *adj.* **beard'less.** — **beard'-grass** a kind of bearded grass (*Polypogon*).   [O.E. *beard;* Ger. *Bart,* Russ. *boroda.*]

beare. See **bear¹.**

béarnaise, Béarnaise (sauce) *bā-ar-nez (sōs),* a sauce made from egg yolks, butter, shallots, tarragon, chervil and wine vinegar.   [Fr. *béarnaise* (fem. of *béarnais*) of Béarn, region of south-western France.]

bearward. See **bear².**

beast *bēst, n.* an irrational animal, as opposed to man: a four-footed animal: a brutal person: anything beastly (*coll.*). — *ns.* **beast'hood** state or nature of a beast; **beast'ie** (orig. *Scot.*) a dim. form of **beast,** the four-footed animal: an insect, spider, etc. (*coll.*). — *adv.* **beast'ily** (*Shelley*) bestially. — *n.* **beast'liness.** — *adjs.* **beast'like** (also *adv.*); **beast'ly** like a beast in actions or behaviour: bestial: foul: sensual: vile, disagreeable (*coll.*). — *adv.* brutishly: abominably, frightfully (*coll.*).

— **beast fable** a story in which animals play human parts; **beast'ly-head** (*Spens.*) personality or self of a beast. — **mark of the Beast** a stamp on the forehead or right hand of a worshipper of the Beast (Antichrist) of the Book of Revelation, chap. xiii: hence a sign of whatever was considered to be of Antichrist, or (*loosely*) evil or even ill manners; **number of the beast** the apocalyptic number.   [O.Fr. *beste* (Fr. *bête*) — L. *bestia.*]

beastings. Same as **beestings.**

beat *bēt, v.t.* to strike repeatedly: to break or bruise (*B*): to pound: to batter: to whip up or switch: to flap: to strike (as bushes) in order to rouse game: to thrash: to defeat, to frustrate: to be too difficult for: to outdo, excel: to spread flat and thin by beating with a tool (as gold): to mark (time) with a baton, etc. — *v.i.* to give strokes repeatedly: to pulsate: to impinge: to mark time in music: to swindle (with *out of*): — *pr.p.* **beat'ing;** *pa.t.* **beat;** *pa.p.* **beat'en,** now rarely **beat.** — *n.* a recurrent stroke, its sound, or its moment, as of a watch or the pulse, or a conductor's baton: accent: pulsation, esp. that heard when two notes nearly in tune are sounded together: a round or course, as a policeman's: an area of land or stretch of river-bank on which sportsmen hunt or fish: a place of resort. — *adj.* weary: fatigued: relating to beatniks (*coll.*): affected with bursitis (as *beat elbow, knee*). — *adjs.* **beat'able; beat'en** made smooth or hard by beating or treading: trite: worn by use: exhausted (*Austr.* and *N.Z.; coll.*). — *ns.* **beat'er** one that beats or strikes: one who rouses or beats up game: a crushing or mixing instrument; **beat'ing** the act of striking: thrashing: pulsation or throbbing: rousing of game: exercising the brain. — **beat music** popular music with a very pronounced rhythm; **beatnik** (*bēt'nik*) one of the **beat generation** (orig. in *U.S.*), bohemian poets, etc., who, in the 1950s, dissociated themselves from the aims of contemporary society: later used loosely for a young person whose behaviour, dress, etc., were unconventional. — *adj.* **beat'-up** dilapidated through excessive use. — **beat about the bush** see **bush; beat a retreat** to retreat, originally to beat the drum as a signal for retreat (**beat the retreat** to perform the military ceremony (**beating the retreat**) consisting of marching and military music usu. performed at dusk (originally marking the recall of troops to their quarters)); **beat down** of a buyer, to try to reduce (the price of goods), to persuade (the seller) to settle for less; **beat it** (*slang*) to make off hastily or furtively; **beat off** to drive back; **beat one's brains** to puzzle one's brains about something; **beat one's breast** (*fig.*) to show extravagant signs of grief; **beat out** to flatten or reduce in thickness by beating; **beat someone to it** to manage to do something before someone else can; **beat the air** to fight to no purpose, or against an imaginary enemy; **beat the bounds** to trace out boundaries in a perambulation, certain objects in the line of journey being formally struck, and sometimes also boys whipped to make them remember; **beat the clock** to do or finish something within the time allowed; **beat up** to pound or whip into froth, paste, a mixture, etc.: to put up as by beating the bushes: to alarm by a sudden attack: to thrash, to subject to a violent and brutal attack (*coll.*; also in U.S. **beat upon**): to disturb: to arouse: to go about in quest of anything: to make way against wind or tide; **take a beating** to suffer physical or verbal chastisement; **take some, a lot of, beating** (*coll.*) to be of very high quality, i.e. to be difficult to excel.   [O.E. *bēatan,* pa.t. *bēot.*]

beatae memoriae *bi-ā'tē me-mō'ri-ē, -mō', be-ā'tī me-mo'ri-ī,* (L.) of blessed memory.

beath *bēdh,* (*Spens.*) *v.t.* to bathe, heat.   [O.E. *bethian,* to foment.]

beatify *bi-at'i-fī, v.t.* to make blessed or happy: to declare to be in the enjoyment of eternal happiness in heaven. — *adjs.* **beatific** (*bē-ə-tif'ik*), **-al** making supremely happy. — *adv.* **beatif'ically.** — *n.* **beatifica'tion** the act of beatifying: in the R.C. church, a declaration by the Pope that a person is blessed in heaven, authorising a certain definite form of public reverence payable to him — the first step to canonisation. — **beatific vision** a glimpse of the glory of heaven. [L. *beātus*, blessed, and *facĕre*, to make.]

beati pacifici *bi-ā'tī pa-sif'i-sī, be-ä'tē pa-kif'i-ke*, (L.) blessed are the peacemakers.

beatitude *bi-at'i-tūd, n.* heavenly happiness: happiness of the highest kind: a title given to patriarchs in the Orthodox Churches: (in *pl.*) sayings of Christ in Matt. v, declaring certain classes of person to be blessed. [L. *beātitūdō* — *beātus*, blessed.]

beatnik. See under **beat.**

beau¹ *bō, n.* a man attentive to dress or fashion: a fop or dandy: a lover: — *pl.* **beaux** (*bōz*): — *fem.* **belle** (*bel*). — *adj.* **beau'ish.** — **beau-ideal** (*bō'ī-dē'əl, bō-ē-dā-äl*) ideal beauty: (blunderingly) a type or embodiment of the highest excellence; **beau-pere** (*bū-pēr'; obs.;* Fr. *père,* father) a term of courtesy for father, used esp. of ecclesiastical persons: (*Spens.;* O.Fr. *per,* equal, peer) a companion. [Fr. *beau, bel* — L. *bellus,* fine, gay.]

beau² *bō,* (Fr.) *adj.* beautiful, handsome, fine; **beau garçon** (*gär-sɔ̄*) a handsome man: a dandy; **beau geste** (*zhest*) gracious gesture; **beau jour** (*zhōōr*) fine day, good times; **beau monde** (*mɔ̄d*) the gay or fashionable world.

beaufet, beauffet *buf-et', ns.* obs. forms of **buffet²**, sideboard, cupboard.

beaufin. A sophisticated spelling of **biffin.**

Beaufort *bō'fərt, adj.* devised by Sir Francis *Beaufort* (1774–1857), English admiral and hydrographer. — **Beaufort scale** a scale of wind velocity, with 0 for calm, 12 for hurricane.

Beaujolais *bō-zho-lā, n.* a red or white wine of east central France. [From *Beaujolais,* a subdivision of Lyonnais.]

beaumontag(u)e *bō-mon-tāg', -mon'tij, n.* a composition for hiding cracks and holes in wood or iron, varying in make-up. [Perh. from Elie de *Beaumont* (1798–1874), French geologist.]

Beaune *bōn, n.* a red or white wine from *Beaune* in eastern France.

beauté du diable *bō-tā dü dyäbl', (Fr.)* an irresistible or overpowering beauty: an attractiveness which the charm and sparkle of youth give to an otherwise unattractive person.

beauty *bū'ti, n.* the quality that gives pleasure to the sight, or aesthetic pleasure generally: a particular grace or excellence: a beautiful person (often *ironical*), esp. a woman: also applied collectively: a very fine specimen of its kind: (in *pl.*) beautiful passages or extracts. — *v.t.* (*Shak.*) to make beautiful. — *n.* **beaut** (*slang*) someone or something exceptionally beautiful or remarkable. — *adj., interj.* (esp. *Austr.*) excellent, fine. — *adj.* **beau'teous** (*-ti-əs*) a bookish word for beautiful. — *adv.* **beau'teously.** — *ns.* **beau'teousness; beautician** (*bū-tish'ən*) one engaged in women's hairdressing, facial make-up, manicuring, etc.; **beautificā'tion; beau'-tifier** one who or that which beautifies or makes beautiful. — *adj.* **beau'tiful** fair: with qualities that give delight to the senses, esp. the eye and ear, or which awaken admiration in the mind. — *adv.* **beau'tifully.** — *v.t.* **beau'tify** to make beautiful: to grace: to adorn. — *v.i.* (*rare*) to become beautiful, or more beautiful. — **beauty contest** a competition held for the selection of a beauty queen; **beauty parlour** an establishment for the hairdressing, manicuring, face-massaging, etc., of women; **beauty queen** a girl who is voted the most attractive or best-proportioned in a competition; **beauty sleep** the sleep before midnight, considered the most refreshing; **beauty spot** a patch placed on the face to heighten beauty: a birthmark resembling such a patch: a foil: a scene of outstanding beauty. [O.Fr. *biaute* (Fr. *beauté*) — L.L. *bellitās, -ātis* — L. *bellus.*]

beaux arts *bō-zär,* (Fr.) fine arts; **beaux esprits** (*-zes-prē*)

see **bel esprit; beaux yeux** (*-zyø*) fine eyes: a pretty woman.

beauxite. See **bauxite.**

beaver¹ *bēv'ər, n.* an amphibious rodent (*Castor*): its valuable fur: a hat of beaver fur or a substitute: a glove of beaver fur: a heavy woollen cloth: a boy belonging to the most junior branch of the scout movement (also **Beaver Scout**). — *n.* **beav'ery** a place where beavers are kept. — **beaverboard¹** (* ® with *cap.* in U.S.) a building board of wood-fibre; **beaver rat** the coypu: the musquash: Hydromys; **bea'ver-tree, -wood** a species of magnolia whose bark beavers eat. — **beaver away** (*coll.*) to work very hard (at); **mountain beaver** the sewellel. [O.E. *befer, beofor*; Du. *bever,* Ger. *Biber,* Gael. *beaghar,* L. *fiber.*]

beaver² *bēv'ər, n.* in mediaeval armour, the covering for the lower part of the face, the visor being that for the upper part — later the movable beaver was confounded with the visor: a beard or bearded man (*slang*). — *adj.* **beav'ered.** [O.Fr. *bavière,* child's bib — *bave,* slaver.]

bebeeru *bi-bē'rōō, n.* the greenheart tree of Guyana. — *n.* **bebee'rine** (*-rin, -rēn*) an alkaloid yielded by its bark, a substitute for quinine. [Native name.]

beblubbered *bi-blub'ərd, adj.* disfigured by weeping. [**be-** (1).]

bebop *bē'bop, n.* a variety of jazz music, from about 1940, which added new harmonies, melodic patterns, and rhythms to accepted jazz characteristics. — Also **bop.** — Also *v.i.* [Imitative of two quavers in the rhythm.]

bebung *bā'bŏong,* (*mus.*) *n.* a tremolo effect produced on the clavichord by fluctuating the pressure of the finger on the key. [Ger.]

becall *bi-köl', v.t.* to call names. [**be-** (1).]

becalm *bi-käm', v.t.* to make calm, still, or quiet. — *adj.* **becalmed'** motionless from want of wind. [**be-** (1).]

became *bi-kām', pa.t.* of **become.**

bécasse *bā-käs,* (Fr.) *n.* a woodcock: a fool, dupe.

because *bi-koz', bi-köz', adv.* and *conj.* for the reason that: on account (of). [**by, cause.**]

beccaccia *bāk-kä'chä,* (It.) *n.* a woodcock.

beccafico *bek-a-fē'kō, n.* a garden warbler or kindred bird, considered a delicacy *esp.* by the Italians: — *pl.* **beccafi'cos.** [It., from *beccare,* to peck, and *fico,* a fig.]

béchamel (sauce), bechamel *bā-sha-mel (sös), besh'ə-mel, n.* a white sauce flavoured with onion and herbs and sometimes enriched with cream. [Fr.; from name of steward of Louis XIV.]

bechance *bi-chäns', v.i.* (with *dat.*) to happen by chance: to befall. — *adv.* by chance: accidentally. [**be-** (1), and **chance,** *v.i.*]

becharm *bi-chärm', v.t.* to charm: to enchant. [**be-** (1).]

bêche-de-mer *besh'də-mer, n.* the trepang or sea-slug, a species of Holothuria, much esteemed in China as a food delicacy: South Sea English, or beach-la-mar. [Fr., — Port. *bicho do mar,* 'sea-worm', the sea-slug.]

Becher's Brook *bē'cherz brŏok,* a notoriously difficult jump in the Grand National steeplechase: a particularly difficult or critical obstacle, problem or possible stumbling-block.

beck¹ *bek, n.* a brook. [O.N. *bekkr;* Ger. *Bach.*]

beck² *bek, n.* a sign with the finger or head: a nod: a gesture of salutation (*Scot.*). — *v.i.* to make such a sign. — *v.t.* to call by a nod. — **at someone's beck (and call)** subject to someone's will. [A contr. of **beckon.**]

becke *bek,* (*Spens.*) *n.* Same as **beak.**

becket *bek'it,* (*naut.*) *n.* a loop of rope having a knot at one end and an eye at the other: a large hook, or a wooden bracket used to keep loose tackle or spars in a convenient place. [Perh. Du. *bogt, bocht,* a bend of rope.]

beck-iron. Same as **bick-iron.**

beckon *bek'n, v.t.* and *v.i.* to nod to or (now usu.) make a summoning sign (to). [O.E. *bīecnan* — *bēacn,* a sign. See **beacon.**]

becloud *bi-klowd'*, *v.t.* to obscure by clouds: to dim. [be-(2).]

become *bi-kum'*, *v.i.* to come to be: to arrive, have got (to a place) (*obs.*): to be the fate (followed by *of*). — *v.t.* to suit or befit: to grace: to adorn fittingly: to look well in. — *pa.t.* **became'**; *pa.p.* **become'**. — *adj.* **becom'-ing.** — *adv.* **becom'ingly.** — *n.* **becom'ingness.** [O.E. *becuman*; see **come**.]

becquerel *bek'ə-rel, -rəl, -rel'*, *n.* the derived SI unit of radioactivity, symbol Bq, equal to one disintegration per second. [A. H. *Becquerel* (1852–1908), French physicist.]

becurl *bi-kûrl'*, *v.t.* to curl. [be- (1).]

bed[1] *bed*, *n.* a couch or place to sleep on: a mattress: a bedstead: a garden plot: a layer of oysters, etc.: a place in which anything rests: conjugal union, sexual relationship, the marriage-bed, matrimonial rights and duties, or a marriage as a source of offspring: the channel of a river: sea or lake bottom: a layer or stratum. — *v.t.* to put to bed: to provide, or make, a bed for: to have sexual intercourse with: to plant in a bed: to lay in layers or on a surface: to embed. — *v.i.* to go to bed: to cohabit: — *pr.p.* **bedd'ing**; *pa.p.* **bedd'ed.** — *adj.* **bedd'able** sexually attractive. — *ns.* **bedd'er** a plant suitable for a flower bed: a bedmaker in a college (*coll.*); **bedd'ing** mattress, bedclothes, etc.: litter for cattle: stratification (*geol.*; **false bedding** see **false**). — *adv.* **bed'ward(s)** in the direction of bed: towards bedtime. — **bed'bug** the common bug (*Cimex lectularius*); **bed'chamber** a bedroom; **bed'-closet** a closet serving as a bedroom; **bed'clothes** sheets, blankets, etc, for a bed; **bed'cover** an upper covering for a bed; **bedd'y-bye(s)** bed, as a place to sleep (used in speaking to children or *facet.*). — *adj.* **bed'fast** confined to bed. — **bed'fellow** a sharer of a bed: a colleague: something or someone that associates with another; **bed'-jacket** light jacket worn when sitting up in bed; **bed'-key** a tool for tightening a bedstead; **bed'-linen** sheets and pillow-cases; **bed'maker** one who makes the beds and sweeps college rooms at Oxford, etc.; **bed'-of-hon'our** the grave of a soldier who has fallen in battle; **bed'-of-jus'tice** (Fr. *lit de justice*) the king's throne in the Parlement of Paris: a sitting at which the king was present, chiefly for the registration of his own decrees; **bed'pan** a chamber utensil for use in sick-bed: a warming-pan; **bed'-plate** (*mech.*) the metal base to which the frame of a machine, engine, etc. is attached; **bed'post** a corner support of a bedstead; **bed'presser** (*Shak.*) a heavy, lazy fellow. — *adjs.* **bed'rid(den)** confined to bed by age or sickness: worn out. — **bed'right, -rite** (*Shak.*) the privilege or due of the marriage-bed; **bed'rock** the solid rock underneath superficial formations: fundamental principles (*fig.*): the lowest state. — *adj.* bottom, lowest. — **bed'-roll** a sleeping-bag or bedclothes rolled up so as to be easily carried by a camper, etc.; **bed'room** a room with a bed: a sleeping apartment: room in bed, sleeping space. — *adj.* (esp. of a comedy or farce) involving or hinting at sexual activity between people in a bedroom, in night-clothes, etc. — **bed'side** position by a bed. — Also *adj.* [be- (2).] — **bedside book** one especially suitable for reading in bed; **bedside manner** that assumed by a doctor at a sickbed; **bed'-sitt'ing-room** a combined bedroom and sitting-room, e.g. in lodgings (shortened to **bed'-sit'**, **bed'-sitt'er**); **bed'socks** warm socks for wearing in bed; **bed'sore** an ulcer arising from long confinement to bed, esp. over the bony prominences; **bed'spread** a coverlet put over a bed by day; **bed'staff** a staff or stick formerly used for making or fixing a bed, a handy weapon; **bed'stead** a frame for supporting a bed; **bed'straw** any plant of the genus *Galium*, esp. (Our) Lady's bedstraw (*Galium verum*); **bed'-swerver** (*Shak.*) one who is false to his marriage vow; **bed'-table** a table for use by a person in bed; **bed'tick** (*old*) the case in which stuffing is put for a bed; **bed'time** the hour for going to bed; **bed'-wetting** the accidental passing of urine in bed; **bed'-work** (*Shak.*) work easily performed, as if done in bed.

— **bed and board** food and lodging: full connubial relations; **bed and breakfast** at a hotel, etc., overnight accommodation with breakfast (*adj.* **bed'-and-break'fast** of stock-exchange deals, in which shares standing at a loss are sold one day and rebought the next to establish a loss for tax purposes); **bed down** to (cause to) settle down, esp. in a makeshift bed, for sleep; **bed of down** or **roses** any easy or comfortable place; **bed out** to plant out in a flower-bed, etc.; **brought to bed** confined in childbirth (with *of*); **get out of bed on the wrong side** to start the day in a bad mood; **go to bed**, **put to bed** (of newspapers, magazines, etc.) to go to, send to, press; **keep one's bed** to remain in bed; **lie in the bed one has made** to have to accept the consequences of one's own acts; **Lords, Ladies, of the Bedchamber** officers in the royal household who wait in turn upon a king or queen; **make a bed** to put a bed in order; **take to one's bed** to go to bed because of illness, grief, age, etc. [O.E. *bed*(*d*); Ger. *Bett*, O.N. *bethr*; prob. akin to L. *fodĕre*, to dig (as orig. a hole).]

bed[2] *bed*, (*Spens.*). Same as **bid** (order, pray).

bedabble *bi-dab'l*, *v.t.* to dabble or wet. [be- (1).]

bedad *bi-dad'*, *interj.* an Irish minced oath, from **begad** = by God.

bedaggle *bi-dag'l*, *v.t.* to soil by dragging along the wet ground. [be- (1).]

bedarken *bi-därk'ən*, *v.t.* to cover with darkness. [be-(1).]

bedash *bi-dash'*, *v.t.* to bespatter, splash. [be- (1).]

bedaub *bi-döb'*, *v.t.* to daub over or smear. [be- (1).]

bedawin. Same as **bedouin**.

bedazzle *bi-daz'l*, **bedaze** *bi-dāz'*, *vs.t.* to dazzle or overpower by any strong light. — *pa.ps.* **bedazz'led**, **bedazed'** stupefied, besotted. — *n.* **bedazz'lement.** [be-(1).]

beddable. See **bed**[1].

bede (*obs.*). Same as **bead**, a prayer.

bedeafen *bi-def'n*, *v.t.* to make deaf: to stun. [be- (1).]

bedeck *bi-dek'*, *v.t.* to deck or ornament. [be- (1).]

bedeguar *bed'i-gär*, *n.* a soft spongy gall found on the branches of sweet-brier and other roses, called also the sweet-brier sponge. [Fr. *bédeguar* — Pers. and Ar. *bādā-war*, lit. wind-brought.]

bedel[1], **bedell**. Old spellings of **beadle**, still used at Oxford and Cambridge.

bedel[2] *bē'dl*, (*Bridges*) *n.* app. for **bevel**, i.e. bevel-wheel.

bedeman, bedesman, bedsman. Same as **beadsman**.

bederal. See **bedral**.

bedevil *bi-dev'l*, *v.t.* to throw into confusion: to play the devil with: to torment: to treat with devilish malignity: to possess as a devil: — *pr.p.* **bedev'illing**; *pa.t.* and *pa.p.* **bedev'illed.** — *n.* **bedev'ilment.** — [be- (2).]

bedew *bi-dū'*, *v.t.* to moisten gently, as with dew. [be-(2).]

bedide *bi-dīd'*, (*Spens.*). Same as **bedyed**.

bedight *bi-dīt'*, (*arch.* or *poet.*) *v.t.* to equip, array, furnish: to adorn: — *pa.t.* and *pa.p.* **bedight'.** [be- (1).]

bedim *bi-dim'*, *v.t.* to make dim or dark: — *pr.p.* **bedimm'ing**; *pa.t.* and *pa.p.* **bedimmed'.** — *n.* and *adj.* **bedimm'ing.** [be- (2).]

bedizen *bi-dīz'ən, bi-diz'ən*, *v.t.* to dress gaudily. — *adj.* **bediz'ened.** — *n.* **bediz'enment.** [be- (1).]

bedlam *bed'ləm*, *n.* an asylum for lunatics: a madhouse: a place of uproar: a madman (*obs.*). — *adj.* fit for a madhouse. — *ns.* **bed'lamism** anything characteristic of madness; **bed'lamite** a madman. [From the priory St Mary of *Bethlehem*, in London, afterwards a madhouse (Bethlehem Royal Hospital).]

Bedlington (terrier) *bed'ling-tən* (*ter'i-ər*), *n.* a long-bodied lightly-built terrier, swiftest of its kind. [*Bedlington*, near Morpeth, where it was first bred.]

Bedouin, Beduin, Bedawin *bed'oo-in, -ēn, bed'ä-win, -wēn, bed'win*, *n.* (also without *cap.*) a tent-dwelling nomad Arab (orig. *pl.*): — *pl.* **Bed'ouin, -ins.** — Also *adj.* — *n.* and *adj.* **Bedu** (*bed'oo*) (a) Bedouin. [Fr. *bédouin* — Ar. *badāwin*, dwellers in the desert.]

bedraggle *bi-drag'l*, *v.t.* to soil by dragging in the wet or dirt. — *adj.* **bedragg'led.** [**be-** (1).]

bedral, bederal *bed'(ə)rəl, (Scot.) n.* a beadle, church-officer, or minister's man: also a grave-digger. [**beadle.**]

bedrench *bi-drench', -drensh', v.t.* to drench or wet thoroughly. [**be-** (1).]

bedrop *bi-drop', v.t.* to drop upon. — *adj.* **bedropped', bedropt'** sprinkled as with drops: strewn. [**be-** (3).]

Bedu. See **Bedouin.**

beduck *bi-duk', v.t.* to duck or plunge under water. [**be-** (1).]

Beduin. Same as **Bedouin.**

bedung *bi-dung', v.t.* to manure: to befoul with dung. [**be-** (2).]

bedust *bi-dust', v.t.* to cover with dust. [**be-** (2).]

bedwarf *bi-dwörf', v.t.* to make dwarfish. [**be-** (2).]

bedye *bi-dī', v.t.* to dye or stain: — *pa.t.* and *pa.p.* **bedyed'** (*Spens.* **bedide'**, **bedyde'**). [**be-** (1).]

bee[1] *bē, n.* a four-winged insect that makes honey: a gathering of persons to unite their labour for the benefit of one individual or family, or for some joint amusement, exercise or competition (as *quilting-bee, husking-bee, spelling-bee*; from the bee's habit of combined labour): a busy person: (usu. in *pl.*) a lump of a type of yeast. — **bee balm** a species of Monarda; **bee'-bread** the pollen collected by bees as food for their young; **bee'-eat'er** any bird of a brightly-plumaged family (Meropidae) nearly allied to the kingfishers, which feed on bees; **bee'-flower** a flower pollinated by bees; **bee'-glue** propolis; **bee'hive** a case or box in which bees are kept, of straw-work, wood, etc. (*adj.* dome-shaped, like an old-fashioned beehive, as **beehive hairstyle, beehive tomb**); **bee'-house; bee'keeper; bee'-keeping; bee'-kite** the honey-buzzard; **bee'line** see **make a beeline for** below; **bee'-master** a beekeeper; **bee'-moth** a moth whose larvae are very destructive to young bees; **bee'-or'chis** an orchid whose flower resembles a bee; **bee'-skep** a beehive, properly of straw; **bees'wax** the wax secreted by bees and used by them in constructing their cells. — *v.t.* to polish with beeswax. — **bees'wing** a filmy crust of tartar formed in port and some other wines after long keeping. — *adj.* **bees'-winged** so old as to show beeswing. — **a bee in one's bonnet** a whimsical or crazy fancy on some point: an obsession; **make a beeline for** to take the most direct way towards (like the honey-laden bee's way home); **the bee's knees** (*coll.*) someone, something, particularly good, admirable, etc. [O.E. *bēo*; Ger. *Biene*.]

bee[2] *bē, n.* the second letter of the alphabet (B, b).

Beeb *bēb, n.* coll. for **BBC** — British Broadcasting Corporation.

beech *bēch, n.* a common forest tree of the genus *Fagus* with smooth grey bark: extended to the kindred genus *Nothofagus* and to many trees not related. — *adj.* **beech'en.** — **beech'-drops** cancer-root, an American orobanchaceous plant parasitic on beech roots; **beech'-fern** a fern of the polypody family (a mistranslation of Phegopteris; from Gr. *phēgos*, a kind of oak); **beech'-mar'ten** the stone-marten; **beech'-mast** the mast or nuts of the beech-tree, which yield a valuable oil, **beech'-oil; beech'-wood** a wood of beech-trees: beech timber. [O.E. *boece, bēce*; Ger. *Buche*, L. *fāgus*, Gr. *phēgos* (oak).]

beef *bēf, n.* the flesh of the ox as food: extended to that of some other animals, as the horse: muscle: vigorous muscular force: an ox, esp. one fattened for the butcher (*arch.*; *pl.* in this sense **beefs, beeves** *bēvz*): a complaint: an argument, quarrel. — *adj.* of beef. — *v.i.* to grumble. — *adj.* **beef'y** like beef: fleshy, muscular: stolid. — *adj.* **beef'-brained** stupid. — **beef'-brew'is** (*obs.*), **-broth** broth made from beef; **beef'burger** a round flat cake of finely chopped meat, usu. fried or grilled; **beef'cake** a picture of a muscle-man: brawn as distinct from brain; **beef'eater** the ox-bird or ox-pecker: a consumer of beef: a yeoman of the guard: a warder of the Tower of London (the form *buffetier* supposed to connect with *buffet* is not known); **beef'-ham'; beef olive** a thin

slice of beef rolled round a savoury stuffing and usu. stewed; **beef'steak** a thick slice of beef for broiling or frying; **beef'-tea'** stimulating rather than nutritious food for invalids, juice of beef strained off, after simmering in water. — *adj.* **beef'-witted** dull or heavy in wits: stupid. — **beef'-wood** the wood of Casuarina and other trees. — **beef up** (*coll.*) to add strength to, to reinforce. [O.Fr. *boef* (Fr. *bœuf*) — L. *bōs, bovis*; cf. Gr. *bous*, Gael. *bò*, Sans. *go*, O.E. *cū.*]

beefalo *bēf'ə-lō, n.* a cross between a cow and a N. American buffalo: — *pl.* **beef'aloes, -os.** [*beef*, buf-falo.]

beegah. Same as **bigha.**

Beelzebub *bi-el'zi-bub, n.* a form of Baal worshipped by the Philistines at Ekron: the prince of the evil spirits. [Heb. *ba'al z'būb*, fly-lord.]

been *bēn,* sometimes *bin, pa.p.* of **be**: *pres. infin.* and *pl. pres. indic.* of **be** (*arch.*).

beenah *bē'nä, n.* a form of marriage (in Sri Lanka etc.) in which the man goes to live with his wife's relatives and the children belong to her group. [Ar. *bīnah*, separate.]

beep *bēp, n.* the sound made by the horn of a car, etc., or an electronic device. — *v.i.* and *v.t.* to (cause to) make such a sound. — *n.* **beep'er.** [Imit.]

beer[1] *bēr, n.* an alcoholic beverage made by fermentation, in which the yeast settles to the bottom (cf. **ale**), from malted barley flavoured with hops: the generic name of malt liquor, including ale and porter: a glassful, etc., of this to drink. — *adj.* **beer'y** of, or affected by, beer. — *n.* **beer'iness; beer'-barrel; beer'-bottle; beer'-engine, beer'-pump** a machine for drawing beer up from the casks to the bar; **beer'-gar'den** a garden with tables where beer and other refreshments may be had; **beer'hall** (*S.Afr.*) a large public drinking place for non-whites; **beer'-house** a house where beer or malt liquors are sold; **beer'-mat** a small, usu. cardboard table-mat for a beer-glass, etc.; **beer'-money** money given in lieu of beer and spirits: a gratuity; **beer'=parlo(u)r** (*Can.*) a public room in a hotel, etc., where beer is served; **beer'-up** (*Austr. slang*) a drinking-bout. — **beer and skittles** idle enjoyment; **bitter beer** pale ale, a highly hopped beer made from the very finest selected malt and hops (**mild or sweet** ale being of greater gravity or strength, and comparatively lightly hopped); **black beer** a kind of beer made at Danzig, black and syrupy; **small beer** weak beer: something trifling or unimportant, esp. when compared with something else. [O.E. *bēor*; Ger. *Bier*, Du. *bier*, O.N. *bjorr*.]

beer[2], bear *bēr.* See **bere[2].**

beesome *bē'səm* (*Shak.*) *adj.* supposed to be for **bisson.**

beestings *bēst'ingz, n.* the first milk drawn from a cow after calving. [O.E. *bȳsting, bēost*; Ger. *Biest*, Du. *biest*.]

beet[1] *bēt, n.* a plant (genus *Beta*; esp. *Beta vulgaris*) of the goosefoot family, with a succulent root, used as food and as a source of sugar. — **beet'-fly** a fly whose larvae are injurious to beet and mangel-wurzel; **beet'-root** the root of the beet plant; **beet sugar.** [O.E. *bēte* — L. *bēta.*]

beet[2], bete *bēt, n.* (*obs. except dial.*) *v.t.* to improve: to mend (esp. a fire): to relieve, assuage. — *n.* **beet'mister** (*Scott,* **-master**) a help in need. [O.E. *bētan*; cf. *bōt,* **boot[2].**]

beetle[1] *bē'tl, n.* any insect of the Coleoptera, an order in which the fore-wings are reduced to hard and horny covers for the hind-wings: a game in which a drawing of a beetle is made up gradually of its component parts, body, head, etc., according to the throw of dice, the object being to produce a completed drawing: (esp. with *cap.*) a particular model of small Volkswagen car with rounded roof and bonnet, resembling a beetle (*coll.*). — *v.i.* to jut, to overhang (first found in *Shak.*): to scurry (*coll.*). — *adj.* (always applied to brows) overhanging, scowling. — *adj.* **beet'ling** jutting: prominent: overhanging. — *adj.* **beet'le-browed** with overhanging or prominent brows. — **beet'le-crusher** (*slang*) a big heavy foot or boot: a policeman: an infantryman:

beetle drive a progressive game of beetle. — *adj.*
beet'le-eyed blind. — **beetle off** to hurry away like a
beetle (*coll.*): to fly (*air-force jargon*); **black beetle** the
cockroach (properly not a beetle).   [M.E. *bityl* —
O.E. *bitula, bitela* — *bītan*, to bite; the connection of
beetle brows with the insect is not accepted by all.]
beetle² *bē'tl, n.* a heavy wooden mallet used for driving
wedges, crushing or beating down paving-stones, or
the like: a wooden pestle-shaped utensil for mashing
potatoes, beating linen, clothes, etc. — **beet'lehead,**
beet'lebrain a heavy stupid fellow. — *adj.* **bee'tle-**
headed, beet'lebrained.   [O.E. *bīetl* — *bēatan*, to beat.]
beetroot. See **beet¹.**
beeves *bēvz, n.pl.* cattle, oxen.   [See **beef.**]
befall *bi-föl', v.t.* (or *v.i.* with *dat.*) to fall or happen to:
to occur to. — *v.i.* to happen or come to pass: to befit
(*Spens.*): to fall in one's way: — *pr.p.* **befall'ing;** *pa.t.*
befell'; *pa.p.* **befall'en** (*Spens.* **befeld'**).   [O.E. *bef(e)al-*
lan; see **fall.**]
befana, beffana *be-fä'nə, n.* an Epiphany gift.   [It. *La*
Befana, a toy-bringing old woman, a personification
of Epiphany, Gr. *epiphaneia.*]
befit *bi-fit', v.t.* to be fitting, or suitable to: to beseem.
— *v.i.* to be right: — *pr.p.* **befitt'ing;** *pa.p.* **befitt'ed.** —
adj. **befitt'ing.** — *adv.* **befitt'ingly.**   [**be-** (1).]
beflower *bi-flow'ər, v.t.* to cover or besprinkle with flowers.   [**be-** (2).]
beflum *bi-flum',* (*Scott*) *v.t.* to befool, cajole.   [Cf.
flummery.]
befoam *bi-fōm, v.t.* to bespatter or cover with foam.   [**be-**
(2).]
befog *bi-fog', v.t.* to envelop in fog: to obscure.   [**be-**
(2).]
befool *bi-fōōl', v.t.* to make a fool of, or deceive: to treat
as a fool.   [**be-** (2).]
before *bi-för', -fōr', prep.* in front of: ahead of: in presence
or sight of: under the consideration or cognisance of:
previous to: previous to the expiration of: in preference
to: superior to. — *adv.* in front: sooner: earlier: in the
past: formerly. — *conj.* previous to the time when
(sometimes with *that*). — *adj.* (*Shak.*) previous. — *adv.*
before'hand before the time: in advance or anticipation: by way of preparation: in advance of one's needs.
— *adj.* **before'-men'tioned.** — *adv.* **before'time** in former time. — **be beforehand with** to forestall (a person);
before Christ (abbrev. **B.C.**) before the date formerly
assigned to the birth of Christ (corresponding to the
year 753 in Roman reckoning); **beforehand with the**
world comfortably provided for; **before the wind** in the
direction in which the wind is blowing, and hence
helped along by it.   [O.E. *beforan. See* **fore.**]
befortune *bi-för'tūn,* (*Shak.*) *v.t.* to happen to, to befall.
[**be-** (3).]
befoul *bi-fowl', v.t.* to make foul: to soil.   [**be-** (2).]
befriend *bi-frend', v.t.* to act as a friend to: to favour.
[**be-** (2).]
befringe *bi-frinj', v.t.* to adorn with fringes.   [**be-** (2).]
befuddle *bi-fud'l, v.t.* to reduce to a fuddled condition.
[**be-** (1).]
beg¹. Same as **bey.**
beg² *beg, v.i.* to ask alms or charity, esp. habitually: to
sit up on the hind quarters, as a dog for a reward. —
v.t. to ask earnestly: to beseech: to pray: to take
unwarrantedly for granted (esp. **beg the question,** to
fall into the fallacy of *petitio principii,* assuming what
is to be proved as part of the would-be proof): — *pr.p.*
begg'ing; *pa.t.* and *pa.p.* **begged** (*begd*). — *n.* **beggar**
(*beg'ər*) one who begs: one who lives by begging:
(hyperbolically) one who is indigent: a mean fellow: a
poor fellow: often used playfully and even affectionately. — *v.t.* to reduce to beggary: to exhaust or
impoverish: to go beyond the resources of, as of
description (*fig.*). — *ns.* **begg'ardom** the fraternity of
beggars; **begg'arliness.** — *adj.* **begg'arly** poor: mean:
worthless. — *adv.* meanly. — *n.* **begg'ary** extreme
poverty. — *n.* and *adj.* **begg'ing.** — *adv.* **begg'ingly.** —
begg'ar-man; begg'ar-my-neigh'bour a game that goes

on till one has gained all the others' cards: profitmaking at the expense of others (also *adj.*); **begg'ing-**
bowl a bowl carried by beggars, esp. certain orders of
monks, to receive food, money, etc.; **begg'ing-lett'er** a
letter soliciting alms or subscriptions. — **beg for a fool**
(*obs.*) to sue for the guardianship of, and administration of the estate of, on grounds of mental deficiency;
beg off to obtain another's release through entreaty:
to seek remission of some penalty or liability; **go**
(a-)begging to be in want of a purchaser, occupant,
etc.   [Perh. from **beghard** (q.v.), the verb being a
back-formation.]
begad *bi-gad',* **begar** *bi-gär'* (*Shak.*), *interjs.* minced oaths
for **by God.**
began *bi-gan', pa.t.* of **begin.**
begar¹ *bā'gär,* (*Ind.*) *n.* forced labour.   [Hind. *begār.*]
begar². See **begad.**
begat. See **beget.**
begem *bi-jem', v.t.* to adorn, as with gems.   [**be-** (2).]
beget *bi-get', v.t.* to produce or cause: to generate (commonly of the father): to produce as an effect, to cause:
— *pr.p.* **begett'ing;** *pa.t.* **begot'** (*arch.* **begat'**); *pa.p.*
begott'en (or **begot'**). — *n.* **begett'er** one who begets:
a father: the agent that occasions or originates anything.   [O.E. *begitan,* to acquire; see **get.**]
beggar. See **beg².**
beghard *beg'ärd, n.* in Flanders or elsewhere from the
13th century, a man living a monastic life without vows
and with power to return to the world.   [Flem.
beggaert; origin doubtful; cf. **béguine.**]
begift *bi-gift', v.t.* to present with gifts.   [**be-** (2).]
begild *bi-gild', v.t.* to gild: to cover or overlay with
gold-leaf.   [**be-** (1).]
begin *bi-gin', v.i.* to come into being: to take rise: to
perform the first act: to open: to have an opening. —
v.t. to perform the first act of: to enter on: to start: —
pr.p. **beginn'ing;** *pa.t.* **began'** (now rarely **begun'**); *pa.p.*
begun. — *ns.* **beginne'** (*Spens.*) beginning; **beginn'er** one
who begins: one who is in the early stages of learning
or doing anything; **beginn'ing** origin: a start: an entering upon action: an opening or first part: a rudiment.
— *adj.* **beginn'ingless.** — **to begin with** firstly: at first.
[O.E. *beginnan* (less usual than *onginnan*), from pfx.
be-, and *ginnan,* to begin.]
begird *bi-gûrd', v.t.* to gird or bind with a girdle: to
surround or encompass: — *pa.t.* and *pa.p.* **begirt'** (or
begird'ed).   [O.E. *begyrdan;* see **be-** (1), and **gird.**]
beglamour *bi-glam'ər, v.t.* to invest with glamour: to
bedazzle, infatuate or impress with glamour.   [**be-**
(2).]
beglerbeg *beg'lər-beg, n.* formerly, the governor of a
Turkish province, in rank next to the grand vizier.
[Turk., lit. bey of beys.]
begloom *bi-glōōm', v.t.* to render gloomy.   [**be-** (2).]
begnaw *bi-nö', v.t.* to gnaw or bite, to eat away.   [**be-**
(1).]
bego *bi-gō', v.t.* to beset (*obs.* except in compound
woebegone).   [O.E. *begān,* to beset, surround.]
begone *bi-gon', interj.* be gone: be off: get away.   [**be**
gone.]
Begonia *bi-gō'ni-ə, n.* a genus (giving name to a family
Boniā'ceae) of tropical, esp. American, plants cultivated in greenhouses for their pink flowers and their
remarkable unequal-sided and often coloured leaves:
(without *cap.*) a plant of the genus.   [Named from
Michel Bégon (1638–1710), patron of botany.]
begored *bi-gōrd', -görd',* (*Spens.*) *adj.* besmeared with
gore.   [**be-** (2).]
begorra, begorrah *bi-gor'ə, interj.* an Anglo-Irish modification of **by God.**
begot *bi-got',* **begotten** *bi-got'n.*   See **beget.**
begrime *bi-grīm', v.t.* to soil with grime.   [**be-** (2).]
begrudge *bi-gruj', v.t.* to grudge: to envy the possession
of.   [**be-** (1).]
beguile *bi-gīl', v.t.* to cheat or deceive: to pass with
diversion of attention from anything tedious or
painful: to wile into some course. — *ns.* **beguile'ment;**

beguil′er. — *adv.* **beguil′ingly.** [be- (1), and *obs. v.t.* **guile.**]

béguine, beguine *bāg′ēn, beg′in, ns.* a member of a sisterhood living as nuns but without vows, and with power to return to the world: — *masc.* **béguin, beguin** (*bāg-ē̆, beg′in*) a beghard. — *n.* **béguinage** (*bāg′ēn-äzh, beg′-in-ij*) an establishment for béguines. [Fr. *béguine*; see **beghard.**]

beguine *bə-gēn′, n.* a dance of French West Indian origin or its music, in bolero rhythm. [Fr.]

begum *bā′gəm, bē′gəm, n.* a Muslim princess or lady of rank: a deferential title given to any Muslim lady. [Urdu *begam*; cf. **beg¹, bey.**]

begun *bi-gun′, pa.p.* (sometimes *pa.t.*) of **begin.**

begunk *bi-gungk′,* (*Scot.*) *v.t.* to trick: to befool: to jape: to jilt. — *n.* a trick: a befooling. [Orig. uncertain; Scot. *gunk,* jilt, trick, recorded later.]

behalf *bi-häf′, n.* favour or benefit: cause: sake, account: part. — **on** (*U.S.* **in**) **behalf of, on** (*U.S.* **in**) **someone′s behalf** speaking, acting, etc. for (someone else). [M.E. *behalve* — O.E. *be healfe,* by the side. See **half.**]

behappen *bi-hap′n,* (*Spens.*) *v.t.* to happen to. [**be-** (1).]

behatted *bi-hat′id, adj.* wearing a hat. [**be-**(2).]

behave, *bi-hāv′, v.t.* to bear or carry: to wield, manage, conduct (commonly with *self*). — *v.i.* to conduct oneself (towards): to conduct oneself well: to act: to function: — *pa.t., pa.p.* **behaved′.** — *n.* **behaviour,** in U.S. **behavior,** (*bi-hāv′yər*) conduct: manners or deportment, esp. good manners: general course of life: treatment of others: mode of action: response to stimulus (*physiol.*). — *adj.* **behav′ioural** of or relating to behaviour. — *ns.* **behav′iourism** a psychological method which substitutes for the subjective element of consciousness, the objective one of observation of conduct in other beings under certain stimuli; **behav′iourist** an upholder of behaviourism. — **behavioural science** a science which studies the behaviour of human beings or other organisms (e.g. psychology, sociology); **behaviour therapy** treating a neurotic symptom (e.g. a phobia) by desensitising the patient, *i.e.* gradually conditioning him to react normally. — **(up)on one′s best behaviour** consciously trying to be as well-behaved as possible. [**be-** (1), and **have;** O.E. had *behabban,* to detain, restrain.]

behead *bi-hed′, v.t.* to cut off the head of. — *ns.* **behead′al** (*rare*); **behead′ing.** [**be-** (1), meaning off, away.]

beheld *bi-held′, pa.t.* and *pa.p.* of **behold.**

behemoth *bē′i-moth, bi-hē′moth, n.* an animal described in the book of Job, usually taken to be the hippopotamus: a great beast: something huge, gigantic. [Heb. *b′hēmōth,* pl. of *b′hēmāh,* beast, or a Hebraistic form of the Egyptian *p-ehe-mout,* water-ox.]

behest *bi-hest′, n.* promise (*obs.*): command: charge. [O.E. *behæs,* a promise; see **hest.**]

behight *bi-hīt′,* **behote** *bi-hōt′,* (*obs.*) *v.t.* to vow: to promise: to speak to, to ordain, to adjudge, to name (*Spens.*): — *pa.t.* and *pa.p.* **behight** or **behote.** [O.E. *behātan,* to vow — *be-* and *hātan,* to be called, to call, to command. For the confusion of tenses and voices and for reduplication, see **hight.**]

behind *bi-hīnd′, prep.* at the back of (in place, or as support): in the place or state left by: at the far side of: after (in time, rank, order): in inferiority to, or less far advanced than. — *adv.* at the back, in the rear: backward: past: in arrears. — *n.* the hinder part: rump. — *adj.* **behind′-door** surreptitious, clandestine. — *adj., adv.* **behind′-hand** being behind: tardy: ill-provided. — **behind someone′s back** without someone knowing (when he might feel entitled to know); **put something behind one** to think of something (usu. an unpleasant experience) as in the past, finished. [O.E. *behindan;* Ger. *hinten;* see **hind³.**]

behold *bi-hōld′, v.t.* to look upon: to contemplate: to view, see: perhaps, to restrain (*Spens.*). — *v.i.* to look: — *pa.t.* and *pa.p.* **beheld′.** — *imper.* or *interj.* see: lo: observe. — *adj.* **behold′en** bound in gratitude (to): under an obligation (to). — *n.* **behold′er** one who

beholds: an onlooker. — *adj.* **behold′ing** (*Shak.*) beholden. — *n.* (*Shak.*) sight, contemplation. [O.E. *behaldan* (W.S. *behealdan*), to hold, observe — *be-* and *h(e)aldan,* to hold.]

behoof *bi-hōōf′, n.* benefit: convenience. [O.E. *behōf.*]

behote. See **behight.**

behove, behoove *bi-hōōv′* (unhistorically *bi-hōv′*), *v.t.* and *v.i.* to be fit, right, or necessary — now only used impersonally with *it.* — *adjs.* **behove′ful** (*arch.*), **behove′ly** (*obs.*) useful: profitable. [O.E. *behōfian,* to be fit, to stand in need of.]

behowl *bi-howl′, v.t.* to howl at (Warburton′s emendation for ′beholds′ in *Midsummer Night′s Dream,* V. ii. 2).

beige *bāzh, n.* a woollen fabric of undyed wool. — *adj.* greyish: recently, buff with a slight suffusion of pink. [Fr.]

beigel *bā′gəl, n.* an alternative spelling of **bagel.**

beignet *ben′yā, n.* a fritter: a deep-fried ball of choux pastry. [Fr.]

bein *bēn,* (*Scot.*) *adj.* and *adv.* comfortable: well off: well found: good (*arch. slang*). — Also **bien.** — *n.* **bein′ness.** [M.E. *bene,* of dubious origin; O.N. *beinn,* L. *bene,* and Fr. *bien,* all offer difficulties.]

being *bē′ing, n.* existence: substance: essence: any person or thing existing. — *adj.* existing, present. — *adj.* **bē′ingless.** — *n.* **bē′ingness.** — **the Supreme Being** God. [Verbal noun and *pr.p.* of **be.**]

beinked *bē-ingkt′, adj.* smeared with ink. [**be-** (2).]

bejabers *bi-jā′bərs, interj.* an Anglo-Irish modification of by Jesus.

bejade *bi-jād′,* (*obs.*) *v.t.* to tire out. [**be-** (1).]

bejant. See **bajan.**

bejesuit *bi-jez′ū-it, v.t.* to initiate or seduce into Jesuitism. [**be-** (2).]

bejewel *bi-jōō′əl, v.t.* to deck with jewels. [**be-** (2).]

bekah *bē′kä,* (*B.*) *n.* a half-shekel. [Heb.]

bekiss *bi-kis′, v.t.* to cover with kisses. [**be-** (1).]

beknave *bi-nāv′, v.t.* to call or treat as a knave. [**be-**(2).]

beknown *bi-nōn′,* (*arch.* or *dial.*) *adj.* known. [**be-** (1).]

bel¹ *bel, n.* a measure for comparing intensity of noises, electric currents, etc., the number of bels being the logarithm to the base 10 of the ratio of one to the other. [From Graham *Bell* (1847–1922), telephone inventor.]

bel². See **bael.**

belabour *bi-lā′bər, v.t.* to beat soundly: to assail verbally. [**be-** (1).]

bel-accoyle *bel-a-koil′,* (*Spens.*) *n.* favourable or kind reception. [O.Fr. *bel acoil,* fair welcome. See **accoil.**]

belace *bi-lās′, v.t.* to adorn with lace. [**be-** (2).]

belah *bē′lä, n.* an Australian tree of the Casuarina genus. [Aboriginal.]

bel air *be-ler,* (Fr.) fine deportment.

belamoure, bellamoure *bel-a-mowr′,* (*Spens.*) *n.* a beloved one: some kind of flower. [Fr. *bel amour,* fair love.]

belamy *bel′a-mē,* (*Spens.*) *n.* a good or intimate friend. [Fr. *bel ami,* fair friend.]

belate *bi-lāt′, v.t.* to make late: to retard. — *adj.* **belāt′ed** coming too late: out of date: benighted. — *n.* **belāt′-edness.** [**be-** (2).]

belaud *bi-löd′, v.t.* to praise up. [**be-** (1).]

belay *bi-lā′, v.t.* to set, overlay, with ornament: to beset: to besiege: to waylay: to make fast: to secure by a turn about a cleat, belaying pin, point of rock, etc. — *interj.* enough: hold. — *n.* a turn of a rope in belaying: that about which a belay is made. — **belaying pin** a pin for belaying ropes about. [O.E. *belecgan;* Ger. *belegen,* Du. *beleggen.* See **lay³.**]

bel canto *bel kän′tō,* (It.) a manner of operatic singing that cultivates beauty of tone.

belch *belch, belsh, v.t.* and *v.i.* to void (wind) from the stomach by the mouth: to eject violently: to pour forth, as the smoke from a volcano, chimney, etc. — *n.* an eructation. [O.E. *bealcian;* Du. *balken.*]

belcher *bel′chər, n.* a dark-blue neckerchief with blue-centred white spots. [From Jim *Belcher*, a famous English boxer.]

beldam, beldame *bel'dəm, n.* a grandmother or remoter ancestress (*obs.*): an old woman (formerly a term of address): a hag: a furious woman. [Formed from **dam,** mother, and *bel-,* used like *grand-* — Fr. *bel, belle,* but not a French use.]

beleaguer *bi-lēg'ər, v.t.* to lay siege to. — *n.* **beleag'-uerment.** [Du. *belegeren,* to besiege — *be-,* and *leger,* camp. See **leaguer¹.**]

belee *bi-lē', (Shak.) v.t.* to place on the lee-side of something. [**be-** (2).]

belemnite *bel'əm-nīt, n.* a fossil pointed like a dart, being the internal shell of a cephalopod, formerly known as *thunderbolt, thunder-stone, elf-bolt.* [Gr. *belemnitēs* — *belemnon,* a dart.]

bel esprit *be-les-prē,* (Fr.) a wit or genius: — *pl.* **beaux esprits** (*bō-zes-prē*).

bel étage *be-lā-täzh,* (German Fr.) the best storey, the first floor.

belfry *bel'fri, n.* the part of a steeple or tower in which bells are hung: a bell-tower, sometimes standing apart: a movable wooden tower, used in the Middle Ages in attacking a fortification. — *adj.* **bel'fried** having a belfry. [Orig. and properly a watch-tower, from O.Fr. *berfroi* — M.H.G. *berchfrit* — *bergan,* to protect, *frid, frit,* a tower.]

belga *bel'gə, n.* a former currency unit of Belgium used in foreign exchange (from 1926 till the end of World War II), value five paper francs. [L. *Belga,* a Belgian.]

belgard *bel-gärd', (Spens.) n.* a fair or kind look. [It. *bel guardo,* lovely look.]

Belgian *bel'jən, adj.* of *Belgium,* a country of Europe. — *n.* a native or citizen of Belgium. — *adj.* **Bel'gic** of the *Belgae,* who anciently possessed Belgium, or of Belgium. — **Belgian hare** a hare-like breed of domestic rabbit. [L. *Belga, Belgicus.*]

Belgravian *bel-grā'vi-ən, adj.* belonging to *Belgravia* (a fashionable part of London), or to fashionable life.

Belial *bēl'yəl, n.* the devil: in Milton, one of the fallen angels. Not a proper name in O.T. [Heb. *b'li-ya'al,* — *b'li,* not, *ya'al,* use.]

belie *bi-lī', v.t.* to give the lie to: to speak falsely of: to present in a false character: to counterfeit: to be false to: to falsify: to fill with lies (*Shak.*): to fail to fulfil or justify: — *pr.p.* **bely'ing;** *pa.t.* and *pa.p.* **belied'.** — *n.* **belī'er.** [**be-** (3).]

believe *bi-lēv', v.t.* to regard as true: to accept as true what is said by: to suppose (followed by a noun clause). — *v.i.* to be firmly persuaded: to have faith (with *in, on*): to judge. — *n.* **belief'** persuasion of the truth of anything: faith: the opinion or doctrine believed: intuition, natural judgment (as used by some philosophers). — *adjs.* **belief'less; believ'able.** — *n.* **believ'er** one who believes: one who professes Christianity, Islam, or whatever religion is relevant. — *adj.* **believ'ing** trustful: having belief. — *adv.* **believ'ingly.** — **be unable, hardly able, to believe one's eyes, ears** to receive with incredulity what one has just seen, heard; **I (don't) believe so** I (don't) think so; **make believe** see **make; the belief** (*arch.*) the Apostles' Creed; **to the best of my belief** as far as I know. [M.E. *bileven* — *bi-, be,* and *leven,* superseding O.E. *gelēfan.*]

belike *bi-līk', (arch.) adv.* probably: perhaps. [O.E. pfx. *be-,* and **like¹.**]

Belisha beacon. See **beacon.**

belittle *bi-lit'l, v.t.* to make small: to cause to appear small, to disparage. — *n.* **belitt'lement.** — *adj.* **belitt'-ling.** [**be-** (2).]

belive *bi-līv', (arch.* and *Scot.) adv.* with speed: promptly. [M.E. *bi life;* bī, by, *līfe,* dat. of *līf,* life.]

bell¹ *bel, n.* an instrument for giving a ringing sound, typically a hollow vessel of metal with flared mouth struck by a tongue or clapper, but taking many other forms, as a hollow sphere containing a loose ball, a shallow cup, a tube, or a coiled spring struck by a

hammer: a corolla shaped like an ordinary bell: the body of a Corinthian or Composite capital, without the surrounding foliage: anything bell-shaped, as in diving-bell, bell-glass, the outward-turned orifice of a wind-instrument, etc.: the sound of a bell: a signal or intimation by bell: a stroke or double stroke of a bell to indicate the number of half-hours of the watch that have elapsed — 'two bells', 'three bells', etc., meaning that there are two, three, etc. half-hours past — the watch of four hours is eight bells (*naut.*). — *v.i.* to ring. — *v.t.* to furnish with a bell, esp. in **bell the cat** (q.v. below). — *v.t.* and *v.i.* to (cause to) flare out in the shape of a bell. — **bell beaker** the distinctive wide-necked pottery vessel found (sometimes inverted) in the graves of Beaker Folk; **bell'bind** (*dial.*) hedge or field bindweed; **bell'-bird** the campanero: any of several Australian and N.Z. birds with a bell-like note, such as either of the two species of honey-eater (*Manorina melanophrys* and *Anthornis melanura*) and a thick-head (*Oreoica gutturalis*) with a clear bell-like call: elsewhere, other birds with bell-like notes. — *adj.* **bell'-bottomed** (of trousers) widening towards the ankle. — **bell'-boy** (chiefly *U.S.*) a hotel porter or page; **bell'-buoy** a buoy carrying a bell, rung by the waves; **bell'cote** (*archit.*) an ornamental structure made to contain one or two bells, and often crowned by a small spire; **bell crank** a lever having two arms, usu. at right angles, with a common fulcrum at their junction; **bell'-flower** a campanula; **bell'-founder** one who casts bells; **bell'-foundry; bell'-glass** a bell-shaped glass for sheltering flowers, etc.; **bell'hanger** one who hangs and repairs bells; **bell'-heather** heath; **bell'hop** a bell-boy; **bell-housing** a tapered outer casing of part of a vehicle's transmission; **bell'-jar** a bell-shaped glass cover, in laboratories placed over apparatus to confine gases, etc.; **bell'man** one who rings a bell, esp. on the streets, before making public announcements: a town-crier; **bell'-metal** the metal of which bells are made — an alloy of copper and tin; **bell'-pull** a cord or handle used in ringing a bell; **bell'-punch** a ticket punch containing a signal-bell; **bell'push** a button used in ringing an electric or spring bell; **bell'-ringer** one who rings a bell on stated occasions: a performer with musical hand-bells; **bell'-ringing; bell'-rope** the rope by which a bell is rung. — *adj.* **bell'-shaped.** — **bell'-siller** (*-sil'ər; Scott*) a fee for bell-ringing at a funeral; **bell'-tent** a bell-shaped tent; **bell'-tower** a tower built to contain one or more bells, a campanile; **bell'-turret** a turret containing a chamber for a bell, usually crowned by a spire; **bell'-wether** the leading sheep of a flock, on whose neck a bell is hung: any loud, turbulent fellow, a ringleader (*fig.*): a setter of a standard, pattern or trend, a leader (*econ.* etc.); **bell'wort** any plant of the Campanulaceae: the liliaceous genus *Uvularia* (*U.S.*). — **bear** or **carry off,** or **away, the bell** to have or gain the first place; **bell, book, and candle** a phrase popularly used in reference to a form of excommunication ending, 'Do to (i.e. shut) the book, quench the candle, ring the bell'; **bells of Ireland** an annual plant, *Molucella laevis,* that has white flowers with green calyces, sometimes preserved for use in dried-flower arrangements; **bell the cat** to undertake the leading part in any hazardous enterprise, from the ancient fable of the mice who proposed to hang a warning bell round the cat's neck; **clear as a bell** (of a sound) distinct and pure in tone; **sound as a bell** in perfect condition, health, etc. [O.E. *belle;* cog. with Du. *bel.*]

bell² *bel, n.* a bubble formed in a liquid. [Ety. dub.; cf. Du. *bel,* a bubble in water, perh. from L. *bulla,* bubble in water.]

bell³ *bel, v.i.* to bellow, roar: to utter loudly. — *n.* the cry of a stag at rutting-time. [O.E. *bellan,* to roar; cf. Ger. *bellen.*]

belladonna *bel'ə-don'ə, n.* the deadly nightshade or dwale (*Atropa belladonna*), all parts of which are narcotic and poisonous from the presence of atropine: the drug prepared from it. — **belladonna lily** a pink-flowered

South African Amaryllis. [It. *bella donna*, fair lady; one property of belladonna is to enlarge the pupil of the eye.]

bella figura *bel-a-fi-goōr′ə*, good impression or appearance. [It.]

bellamoure. See **belamoure.**

bellarmine *bel′är-mēn, n.* a greybeard, or large jug with a big belly, decorated with a bearded face, said to represent Cardinal *Bellarmine* (1542–1621), made in mockery by Dutch Protestants.

Bellatrix *bel-ā′triks* (L. *-ā′trĕks*), *n.* a second-magnitude star in Orion, one of the corners of the quadrilateral. [L. *bellātrix*, female warrior.]

belle[1] *bel, n.* a handsome woman: the chief beauty of a place: a fair lady generally. — *n.* **belle-de-nuit** (*-də-nwē*; Fr., night beauty) the marvel of Peru (q.v.). [Fr. *belle* (*fem.*) — L. *bellus, -a, -um.*]

belle[2] *bel,* (Fr.) *adj. fem.* of **beau.** — **belle amie** (*be-la-mē*) a female friend, a mistress; **belle assemblée** (*be-la-sā-blä*) a fashionable gathering; **belle laide** (*bel led*) jolie laide; **belle-mère** (*bel-mer*) mother-in-law; **belle passion** (*pa-syõ*) tender passion; **belle peinture** (*pē-tür*) naturalistic painting; **belle vue** (*vü*) fine prospect. — **la belle époque** (*la-bel-ā-pok*; also with *caps.*) 'the fine period', the time of security and gracious living for the well-to-do, ended by World War I.

belles-lettres *bel-let′r′, n.pl.* polite or elegant literature, including poetry, fiction, criticism, aesthetics, etc. — *n.* **bellet(t)′rist.** — *adjs.* **belletris′tic, -al.** [Fr., lit. fine letters.]

belleter *bel′ə-tər, n.* a bell-founder. [For *bellyetter* — **bell**, and O.E. *gēotan*, to pour.]

bellibone *bel′i-bōn,* (*Spens.*) *n.* a beautiful and good woman. [Apparently Fr. *belle* (*et*) *bonne*.]

bellicose *bel′ik-ōs, adj.* contentious, war-like. — *adv.* **bell′icosely.** — *n.* **bellicosity** (*-kos′i-ti*). [L. *bellicōsus.*]

bellied. See **belly.**

belligerent *bel-ij′ər-ənt, adj.* waging war: recognised legally as waging war: aggressive. — *n.* a party or person waging war: one recognised as so doing. — *ns.* **bellig′erence; bellig′erency.** — *adv.* **bellig′erently.** [L. *belligerāre*, to wage war — *bellum*, war, *gerĕre*, to wage.]

Bellona *bel-ō′na, n.* the Roman goddess of war — hence (*fig.*) a woman of great spirit and vigour.

bellow *bel′ō, v.i.* to roar like a bull: to make any violent outcry. — *v.t.* to roar out. — *n.* the roar of a bull: any deep sound or cry. — *n.* **bell′ower.** [M.E. *belwen*; O.E. *bylgian*, to roar; cf. **bell**[3].]

bellows *bel′ōz,* or (old-fashioned) *bel′us, n.pl.* or *n.sing.* an instrument for producing a current of air to blow up a fire, or sound an organ, accordion, etc.: a contrivance for expanding a photographic camera or the like: that which fans the fire of hatred, jealousy, etc. (*fig.*): the lungs. — **bell′ows-fish** the trumpet-fish. — **bellows to mend** (esp. in sporting parlance) shortness of breath, e.g. in a horse. [Same as **belly**; the sing. did not survive the 15th century.]

bellum internecinum *bel′əm, -ōōm, in-tər-nes-īn′əm, -ter-nek-ēn′ōōm,* (L.) a war of extermination.

belly *bel′i, n.* the part of the body between the breast and the thighs, containing the bowels: the stomach, as the receptacle of the food: the bowels proper: the womb or uterus: the interior of anything: the bulging part of anything, as a bottle, or any concave or hollow surface, as of a sail: the front or under surface, as opposed to the *back*: in a violin or a leaf the upper surface: a sound-board. — *adj.* ventral, abdominal: belonging to the flesh, carnal (*theol.*). — *v.i.* to swell or bulge out (often with *out*): — *pa.t.* and *pa.p.* **bellied** (*bel′id*). — *adj.* **bell′ied** with a belly, esp. a big belly, pot-bellied: bulging: puffed out. — *n.* **bell′yful,** a sufficiency: more than enough — *n.* and *adj.* **bell′ying.** — **bell′y-ache** a pain in the belly: a persistent complaint, whine (*slang*). — *v.i.* (*slang*) to complain whiningly. — **bell′y-band** a saddle-girth: a band fastened to the shafts of a vehicle, and passing under the belly of the horse drawing it;

bell′y-button the navel (*coll.*); **bell′y-dance** a solo dance with very pronounced movement of abdominal muscles; **bell′y-dancer; bell′y-flop** an inexpert dive in which one lands face down, flat on the water: a belly-landing. — Also *v.i.* — **bell′y-god** one who makes a god of his belly, a glutton; **bell′y-landing** of an aircraft, a landing without using the landing-wheels; **bell′y-laugh** a deep unrestrained laugh; **bell′y-timber** (*arch.*) provisions. — **belly up to** (*U.S. slang*) to go directly or purposefully towards; **go belly up** (*U.S. slang*) to die, fail (as a dead fish, floating belly upwards). [M.E. *bali, bely* — O.E. *bælig, belig, bælg, belg,* bag.]

belomancy *bel′ō-man-si, n.* divination by means of arrows. [Gr. *belos,* a dart, *manteiā*, divination.]

Belone *bel′ə-ni, n.* a genus of needle-fish of the family **Belon′idae**, including the garfish. [Gr. *belone,* a needle — *belos,* a dart.]

belong *bi-long′, v.i.* (in all senses usu. with *to*) to go along (with): to pertain (to): to be the property (of): to be part or appendage (of), or in any way connected (with): to be specially the business (of): to be a native or inhabitant, or member (of). — *n.* **belong′er** one who qualifies as a member of a particular group. — *n.pl.* **belong′ings** matters connected with any person: possessions: persons connected, relatives (*obs.*): accessories. [M.E. *bi-, be-longen,* intens. of *longen.* See **long**[2].]

Belorussian, Byelorussian, *byel′ə-rush′ən, adj.* White Russian, of a region in European U.S.S.R. to the west of Moscow: of its language or people. — *n.* a native or citizen of White Russia: the language of White Russia, closely related to Russian proper. [Russ. *Belorossiya* — *beliy,* white.]

belove *bi-luv′, v.t.* (*obs.* except in *pa.p.* **beloved** *bi-luvd′*) to love. — *adj.* **beloved** (*bi-luv′id*) much loved, very dear — often compounded with *well-, best-,* etc. — *n.* (*bi-luv′id*) one who is much loved. — *adj.* **belov′ing** (*Shak.*) loving. [**be-** (1).]

below *bi-lō′, prep.* beneath in place, rank or quality: underneath: not worthy of. — *adv.* in a lower place: downstairs: on earth, or in hell (*fig.*). — *adj.* and *adv.* **below′stairs** downstairs: in, belonging to, the servants' quarters. — *adj.* **below′-the-line** of, pertaining to, that part of the government's spending and revenue not allowed for in its original estimates: of, pertaining to, business spending or income which, because of its unusual nature, is listed separately from the normal financial details on a company's accounts. [M.E. *bilooghe* — *bi,* by, *looghe,* low.]

bel paese® *bel pä-ā′zē,* a mild Italian cheese.

bel sangue *bel sän′gwä,* (It.) gentle blood.

belshazzar. See **balthasar.**

belt *belt, n.* a girdle, zone, or band: a band of leather or other material worn around the waist: a band of flexible material used to transmit motion in machinery: a broad stripe of anything, different in colour or material: that which confines or restrains: a zone of country, a district (*geog.*): a strait: a band for the waist awarded in recognition of a specific (grade of) achievement (see **black, Lonsdale**). — *v.t.* to surround with a belt, or to invest formally with one, as in conferring knighthood: to encircle: to thrash with a belt: to hit hard (*coll.*). — *v.i.* (*slang*) to hurry. — *adj.* **belt′ed** wearing a belt, of a knight: marked with a belt: having a belt. — *ns.* **belt′er** something outstanding or striking (*coll.*): a song for belting out (*coll.*); **belt′ing** belts collectively: material for making belts: a beating. — *adj.* **belt′-and-bra′ces** giving double security. — *n.* **belt′way** (*U.S.*) a ring-road. — **belt out** (*coll.*) to sing, play or send out vigorously or with great enthusiasm; **belt up** (*slang*) to be quiet; **hit,** etc., **below the belt** to hit, etc., an opponent's body lower than the waist (forbidden in some sports): hence (*fig.*) to deliver a mean blow, attack unfairly; **hold the belt** to hold the championship in wrestling, boxing, or the like; **tighten one's belt** to reduce one's demands or expenditure (*n.* **belt′-tightening**); **under one's belt** (*fig.*) firmly and irrevocably secured or in one's possession. [O.E. *belt* — L. *balteus*.]

Beltane *bel'tān, n.* an ancient Celtic festival, held in the beginning of May, when bonfires were lighted on the hills: the first day of May (O.S.) —one of the four old quarter-days of Scotland, the others being Lammas, Hallowmas, and Candlemas. — Also *adj.* [Gael. *bealltainn, beilteine,* apparently bright fire. It has nothing to do with **Baal.**]

beluga *bi-loō'gǝ, n.* the white whale, one of the dolphin family, closely allied to the narwhal, found in Arctic seas: a great Russian sturgeon — *Acipenser huso.* [Russ. *beliy,* white.]

belvedere *bel'vi-dēr, n.* a pavilion or raised turret or lantern on the top of a house, open for the view, or to admit the breeze: a summer-house on an eminence. [It. *belvedere* — *bel,* beautiful, *vedere,* to see.]

belying. See **belie.**

bema *bē'mǝ, n.* the tribune or rostrum from which Athenian orators made their speeches: hence the apse or chancel of a basilica. [Gr. *bēma,* a step.]

bemad *bi-mad', (arch.) v.t.* to madden. [**be-** (1).]

bemaul *bi-möl', (arch.) v.t.* to maul thoroughly. [**be-** (1).]

bemazed *bi-māzd', (arch.) adj.* stupefied, bewildered. [**be** (1).]

Bembex *bem'beks, n.* a genus of sand-wasps, noted for their loud buzz. [Gr. *bembix,* a buzzing insect.]

bemean¹ *bi-mēn', (arch.) v.t.* to make mean, to lower or debase. [**be-** (2).]

bemean² *bi-mēn', (obs.) v.i.* to signify. [**be-** (1).]

bemedal *bi-med'ǝl, (arch.) v.t.* to cover with medals. [**be-** (2).]

bemete *bi-mēt', (arch.) v.t.* to measure. [Pfx. **be-** (1).]

bemire *bi-mīr', (arch.) v.t.* to soil with mire. — *adj.* **bemired'.** [**be-** (2).]

bemoan *bi-mōn', v.t.* to lament, bewail: to pity. — *v.i.* to grieve. — *ns.* **bemoan'er; bemoan'ing.** [**be-** (1).]

bemock *bi-mok', (arch.) v.t.* to mock at, to deride. [**be-** (1).]

bemoil *bi-moil' (Shak.) v.t.* to bemire, to bedraggle. [**be-** (1).]

bemonster *bi-mon'stǝr, (arch.) v.t.* to make monstrous: to regard or treat as a monster. [**be-** (2).]

bemouth *bi-mowdh', (arch.) v.t.* to mouth about. [**be-** (1).]

bemud *bi-mud', (arch.) v.t.* to bespatter with mud: to confuse. [**be-** (2).]

bemuddle *bi-mud'l, (arch.) v.t.* to confuse or muddle completely. [**be-** (1).]

bemuffle *bi-muf'l, (arch.) v.t.* to wrap or muffle up completely. [**be-** (1).]

bemuse *bi-mūz', v.t.* to put in confusion: to stupefy. [**be-** (1).]

ben¹ *ben, n.* a mountain peak. [Gael. *beinn,* oblique case of *beann.*]

ben² *ben, (Scot.) prep.* and *adv.* in or toward the inner or better, or (vaguely) another, apartment (of). — *n.* the inner or better apartment of a house, as opposed to the *but* or kitchen through which formerly one had generally to pass first. — **a but and ben** a two-roomed house; **but and ben** backwards and forwards in the house (also *fig.*): out and in: at opposite ends of a house or passage; **far ben** on terms of great intimacy or favour. [M.E. *binne* — O.E. *binnan,* within.]

ben³ *ben, n.* any of several tropical trees of the Moringa genus, esp. the horseradish tree, *Moringa oleifera:* its seed (**ben'-nut**) yielding **ben'-oil** or **oil of ben,** used as a lubricant and in the preparation of perfumes and cosmetics. [Ar. *bān,* ben.]

bename *bi-nām', v.t.* to name, mention: to vow: — *pa.t.* and *pa.p.* **benamed'** (*arch.* **benempt'**). [O.E. *benemnan* — *nemnan,* to name.]

bench *bench, bensh, n.* a long seat or form with or without a back: a seat in a boat: a work-table or working-place: a judge's seat: the body or assembly of judges: a tribunal: an official seat: a level ledge or set-back in

the slope of masonry or earthwork: a level tract between a river and neighbouring hills (*Amer.*): a terrace: in a greenhouse or conservatory, a raised bed or a platform with sides for holding potted plants. — *v.t.* to place on or furnish with benches: to put plants in greenhouse benches: to show (dogs). — *ns.* **bench'er** a senior member of an inn of court; **bench'ership.** — **bench'-hole** (*Shak.*) a latrine; **bench'-mark** a surveyor's mark cut on a rock, etc. indicating a point of reference in levelling (from its horizontal line forming a bench for a levelling instrument): anything taken or used as a point of reference or comparison, a standard, criterion, etc. (also *adj.*); **bench'-warr'ant** one issued by a judge rather than a justice or magistrate. — **on the bench** holding the office of a judge or bishop: officiating as judge; **raise to the bench** to make a judge or bishop. [O.E. *benc;* cog. with Ger. *Bank* and Du. *bank.*]

bend¹ *bend, v.t.* to constrain: to subject to tension: to brace: to string: to nerve: to force into (or out of) a curved or angled form: to curve: to bow, turn downwards: to dispose, incline: to aim: to direct: to deflect: to subdue: to fasten (*naut.*): to drink hard at (*Scot.*). — *v.i.* to curve: to stoop: to bow: to give way, yield: to turn: to incline: to drink hard (perh. from the phrase *bend the bicker,* to turn up the cup in draining it) (*Scot.*): — *pa.t.* and *pa.p.* **bent;** also **bend'ed.** — *n.* a strengthening band (*Spens.*): a knot by which a line is tied to another, or to itself after passing through a ring, etc.: a band, strip: an ordinary bounded by two parallel lines crossing the shield from dexter chief to sinister base (**bend'-sin'ister** from sinister chief to dexter base), occupying a fifth of the shield, or a third if charged (*her.*): half a butt of leather cut lengthwise: an act of bending: state of being bent: a bent thing: a place of bending: a bow or stoop: a directing of the eye (*Shak.*): a pull of liquor, or a drinking bout (*Scot.*): (in *pl.*) caisson disease: (in *pl.*) aeroembolism. — *adj.* **bend'ed.** — *n.* **bend'er** one who, or that which bends: a sixpence (*obs. slang*): a thing very large or fine of its kind (*slang*): a (drunken) spree (*slang*): a temporary shelter consisting of a shell of woven branches covered with tarpaulins or plastic sheeting (*coll.*). — *n.* and *adj.* **bend'ing.** — *adv.* **bend'ingly.** — *n.* **bend'let** (*her.*) a half-width bend. — *adv.* **bend'wise** (*her.*) diagonally. — *adj.* **bend'y** divided into bends (*her.*): full of, characterised by, curves or bends: flexible. — *n.* and *adj.* **bent** see **bent¹.** — **bent'wood** wood artificially curved for chair-making, etc. — Also *adj.* — **bend over backwards** see **back¹; round the bend** (*coll.*) crazy, mad. [O.E. *bendan,* to constrain, bind, fetter, string (as a bow), *bend,* bond, fetter.]

bend² *bend, (Spens.) n.* Same as **band².**

bene¹ *bēn, (arch.; Wordsworth) n.* a prayer: a boon. [O.E. *bēn.*]

bene². An old spelling of **been.**

beneath *bi-nēth', adv.* and *prep.* below: in a lower position so as to have overhead, or nearly so, or to be covered: inside, behind, at the back (of): at a lower level relatively to. — *prep.* in a manner unworthy the dignity of, unbecoming to. — *adj.* (*Shak.*) lower. [O.E. *beneothan.*]

bene decessit *be'ne di-se'sit, dā-kā'sit,* (L.L.) he has left well — a leaving certificate given to a schoolboy, curate, etc.

benedicite *ben-i-dīs'i-ti, -dis'* (L. *-dēk'i-te*), *interj.* bless you (an old form of greeting). — *n.* a blessing: a grace at table: the canticle beginning *Benedicite omnia opera* (All ye works of the Lord, bless ye) from *The Song of the Three Holy Children.* [L. *benedīcite,* pl. imperative of *benedīcĕre,* to bless — *bene,* well, *dīcĕre,* to say, speak.]

Benedick *ben'i-dik,* or (blunderingly) **Ben'edict** *-dikt, n.* a name for a newly married man, esp. one who has long held out against marriage — from *Benedick* in Shakespeare's *Much Ado about Nothing.*

benedict *ben'i-dikt, (obs.) adj.* blessed: benign. — *n.*

benedic'tion (-shən) a blessing: a solemn invocation of the divine blessing on men or things: a blessing pronounced at the end of a religious service: a brief and popular service in the Roman Catholic Church: grace before or after a meal: blessedness. — *adjs.* **benedic'tional; benedict'ive; benedict'ory.** — *n.* **Benedict'us** the canticle of Zacharias (Luke, i. 68–79), used in the Roman and Anglican services. — *adj.* **benedight** (-dīt'; *Longfellow*) blessed. — **apostolic benediction** that at the end of 2 Cor. [L. *benedīcĕre, -dictum* — *bene,* well, *dicĕre,* to say, speak.]

Benedictine ben-i-dik'tin, -tīn, *adj.* pertaining to St *Benedict* of Nursia (480–543), or his monastic rule. — *n.* a monk or nun of the order founded by him at Monte Cassino: (-tēn) a cordial or liqueur resembling Chartreuse, distilled at Fécamp in Normandy — once distilled by Benedictine monks.

benefaction ben-i-fak'shən, *n.* the act of doing good: a good deed done or benefit conferred: a grant or endowment. — *v.t.* **ben'efact** to confer a benefit on. — *n.* **ben'efactor** (or -fak') one who confers a benefit: one who aids financially e.g. an institution, a patron: — *fem.* **ben'efactress** (or -fak'). — *adj.* **benefac'tory.** [L. *benefactiō, -ōnis;* cf. following words.]

benefic bi-nef'ik, *adj.* kindly: benign: beneficent: favourable (*astrol.*). — *n.* **benefice** (ben'i-fis) a church living, esp. with cure of souls: a fief (*hist.*). — *adj.* **ben'eficed** possessed of a benefice. — *n.* **beneficence** (bi-nef'i-səns) active goodness: kindness: charity: a beneficent gift. — *adjs.* **benef'icent; beneficential** (-sen'shl). — *adv.* **benef'icently.** — *adj.* **beneficial** (ben-i-fish'l) useful: advantageous: enjoying the usufruct of property (*law*). — *n.* (*Spens.*) app., a letter of presentation to a benefice. — *adv.* **benefic'ially.** — *ns.* **benefi'cialness; benefi'ciary** a holder of a benefice or a fief: one who receives a gift or advantage: one who enjoys, or has the prospect of enjoying, any interest or estate held in trust by others. [L. *beneficus,* kindly, beneficent, *beneficium,* a service, benefit — *bene,* well, *facĕre,* to do.]

beneficiate be-ni-fish'i-āt, *v.t.* to treat ores, etc. to get rid of impurities. — *v.i.* to receive profit from working a mine. — *n.* **beneficiā'tion** treatment of ores, etc. to get rid of impurities. [Sp. *beneficiar,* to benefit — L. *beneficium,* a service, benefit.]

benefit ben'i-fit, *n.* a kindness: a favour: any advantage, natural or other: a performance, match, etc., whose proceeds go to one of the company, a player, or other particular person or object (also *adj.*): a right in the form of money or services enjoyed under social security or insurance schemes. — *v.t.* to do good to. — *v.i.* to gain advantage (with *from* or *by*): — *pr.p.* **ben'efiting;** *pa.t.* and *pa.p.* **ben'efited.** — **benefit of clergy** see **clergy; benefit of inventory** (*Scots law*) an heir's privilege of securing himself against unlimited liability for his ancestor, by giving up within a year an inventory of his heritage or real estate, to the extent of which alone he was liable; **benefit of the doubt** favourable judgment when culpability is uncertain; **benefit society** a friendly society. [M.E. *benfet* — A.Fr. *benfet* — L. *benefactum.*]

Benelux ben'ə-luks, *n.* a name for (the economic union between) *Be*lgium, the *Ne*therlands and *Lux*embourg.

bene merentibus be'ne mer-ent'ib-us, -ōōs, (L.) to the well-deserving.

benempt. See **bename.**

beneplacito be-ne-plä'chē-tō, (It.) *interj.* good pleasure: by your leave.

Benesh ben'esh, *n.* a system of notation for detailing movements in dancing, introduced in 1955 by Joan and Rudolf *Benesh.*

benet¹ bi-net', *v.t.* to catch in a net, to ensnare. [be- (1) or (2).]

benet² ben'it, *n.* an exorcist, the third of the four lesser orders in the Roman Catholic church. [O.Fr. *beneit* — L. *benedictus,* blessed.]

bene vobis be'ne vō'bis, wō'bēs, (L.) health to you.

benevolence bi-nev'ə-ləns, *n.* disposition to do good: an act of kindness: generosity: a gift of money, esp. for support of the poor: a kind of forced loan or contribution, levied by kings without legal authority, first so called under Edward IV in 1473 (*Eng. hist.*). — *adj.* **benev'olent** charitable, generous, well disposed. — *adv.* **benev'olently.** [O.Fr. *benivolence* and L. *benevolentia.*]

Bengal ben-göl', beng-göl', *n.* a striped cotton woven in *Bengal,* or an imitation of it. — *adj.* of Bengal. — *n.* and *adj.* **Bengalese** (ben-gə-lēz', beng-) a native of Bengal: — *pl.* **Bengalese'.** — *adj.* **Bengali** (ben-gö'li, beng-) of or belonging to Bengal. — *n.* a native of Bengal: the language of Bengal. — *n.* **bengaline** (beng'gə-lēn) a light fabric usually of silk and cotton or silk and wool, with a crosswise rib. — **Bengal fire, Bengal light** a brilliant light, black sulphide of antimony, used as a shipwreck signal, to illuminate country at night, and in fireworks.

beni, beniseed. See **benne.**

benight bi-nīt, *v.t.* to involve in darkness: to cloud with disappointment. — *adj.* **benight'ed** overtaken by night: involved in darkness, intellectual or moral: ignorant. — *v.t.* **benight'en** (*rare*) to benight. — *ns.* **benight'ening; benight'er; benight'ing** (also *adj.*); **benight'ment.** [Pfx. be- (2) and **night.**]

benign bi-nīn', *adj.* favourable, esp. in astrology, as opposed to *malign:* gracious: kindly: of a mild type, as opposed to *malignant* (*med.*): salubrious. — *n.* **benignancy** (bi-nig'nən-si) benignant quality. — *adj.* **benig'nant** kind: gracious: beneficial. — *adv.* **benig'nantly.** — *n.* **benig'nity** goodness of disposition: kindness: graciousness: favourable circumstances — of climate, weather, disease, planets. — *adv.* **benign'ly** (-nīn'). [O.Fr. *benigne* — L. *benignus,* prob. — *bene,* well, and root of *genus,* birth, kind.]

benison ben'i-zən, -sən, *n.* a benediction, blessing, esp. blessing of God. [O.Fr. *beneiçun* — L. *benedictiō, -ōnis.*]

bénitier bā-nē'tyā, *n.* a holy-water font, or stoup. [Fr., — L.L. *benedictārium* — L. *benedictus.*]

benj benj, *n.* bhang. [Ar.]

Benjamin ben'jə-min, *n.* a youngest son: a favourite child. [As in Genesis xlii.]

benjamin¹ ben'jə-min, *n.* an old kind of overcoat. [Perh. alluding to **Joseph** (q.v.); or a tailor's name.]

benjamin² ben'jə-min, *n.* gum benzoin (also **gum benjamin**). — **ben'jamin-tree** Styrax: the American spice-bush: a kind of fig-tree. [**benzoin.**]

benne ben'ē, **benni, beni** ben'i, *ns.* sesame. — **benn'e-seed, benn'i-seed, ben'iseed** sesame seed. [From Malay *bene.*]

bennet¹ ben'it. See **herb-bennet** at **herb.**

bennet² ben'it, (*S. England*) *n.* a dry grass stalk. [**bent².**]

benny¹ ben'i, (*slang*) *n.* an overcoat. [Prob. abbrev. of **benjamin¹.**]

benny² ben'i, (*slang*) *n.* an amphetamine tablet. [Abbrev. of **benzedrine.**]

bent¹ bent, *pa.t.* and *pa.p.* of **bend.** — *adj.* curved: having a bend: intent, set (*on* or *upon* doing something): obedient, governed (*Spens.*): morally crooked, or criminal (*coll.*): homosexual, or otherwise sexually deviant (*slang*): stolen (*slang*). — *n.* curvature: curved part: tendency: trend: inclination: direction: leaning or bias: natural inclination of the mind: the extent to which a bow may be bent: degree of tension: capacity of endurance. — **to the top of one's bent** to the full measure of one's inclination. [**bend¹.**]

bent² bent, *n.* any stiff or wiry grass: the old dried stalks of grasses: a genus (*Agrostis*) of grasses, slender and delicate in appearance, some useful as pasture-grasses and for hay: a place covered with bents, a heath: a hillside. — Also **bent'-grass.** — *adj.* **bent'y.** — **take (to) the bent** (*Scot.*) to take flight. [O.E. *beonet,* found in place-names, as *Beonetlēah,* Bentley.]

Benthamism ben'thəm-izm, *n.* the social and political teaching of Jeremy *Bentham* (1748–1832), whose leading principle is the doctrine of utility, that happiness is identical with pleasure, summed up in Hutcheson's phrase, 'the greatest happiness of the greatest number'. — *n*. **Ben'thamite.**

benthos *ben'thos, n.* the flora and fauna of the sea-bottom — opp. to *plankton* and *nekton.* — *adjs.* **ben'thic; benthon'ic, benthoal** (*ben-thō'əl*) living on the sea-bottom. — *ns.* **benthopelagic** (*-thō-pi-laj'ik*) (of marine fauna) living just above the sea-bed; **ben'thoscope** a submersible sphere from which to study deep-sea life. [Gr. *benthos*, depth.]

bentonite *ben'tən-īt, n.* a valuable clay, consisting mainly of montmorillonite, widely used in industry as a bond, filler, etc. [Fort *Benton*, Montana, where it was found.]

ben trovato *ben trō-vä'tō*, (It.) aptly invented; **ben venuto** (*ven-ōōt'ō*) welcome.

bentwood. See **bend¹.**

benumb *bi-num', v.t.* to make insensible or powerless: to stupefy (now chiefly of *cold*): to deaden the feelings of: to paralyse generally. — *adj.* **benumbed'.** — *ns.* **benumbed'ness; benumb'ment.** [Pfx. **be-** (2).]

Benzedrine® *ben'zi-drēn, n.* a tradename for amphetamine.

benzene *ben'zēn, n.* simplest of the aromatic series of hydrocarbons, discovered by Faraday in 1825, now mostly prepared by destructive distillation of coal-tar, its molecule consisting of a ring or closed chain of six carbon atoms each with a hydrogen atom attached — formerly called benzine, benzol, names now used differently (see below). — *ns.* **ben'zal** or **benzyl'idine** a radical whose oxide is **benzal'dehyde** or oil of bitter almonds; **benz'idine** a base used in preparing azo-dyes; **ben'zil** a double benzoyl radical; **benzine** (*ben'zēn*) a mixture of hydrocarbons got by destructive distillation of petroleum, used as a solvent, motor fuel, etc.: improperly, benzene; **benz'oate** (*-zō-āt*) a salt of benzoic acid; **benzocaine** (*ben-zō-kā'in, ben'zō-kān*) a drug used as a local anaesthetic and in the treatment of gastritis (**benzine** and **cocaine**); **benzodiazepine** (*ben-zō-dī-az'ə-pēn, -pin, -pīn*) one of a group of non-addictive tranquillising and soporific drugs. — *adj.* **benzo'ic** pertaining to benzoin (see next article), as **benzoic acid,** an acid, $C_6H_5 \cdot COOH$, found in benzoin and other gums. — *ns.* **ben'zol(e)** crude benzene, used as a motor-spirit: improperly, benzene; **ben'zoline** benzine: impure benzene; **benzoyl** (*ben'zō-il*) the radical $C_6H_5 \cdot CO$; **benzpyrene** (*benz-pī'rēn*) a cancer-inducing hydrocarbon ($C_{20}H_{12}$) found in coal-tar and present in small quantities in smoke, including tobacco smoke (**benzene** and **pyrene**); **ben'zyl** (*zil*) the radical $C_6H_5CH_2$; **benzylidine** see **benzal** above. — **benzene hexachloride** (known as **BHC**) a chlorinated hydrocarbon, a very toxic insecticide. [From benzoin.]

benzoin *ben'zō-in,* or *-zoin, n.* gum benjamin, the aromatic and resinous juice of *Styrax benzoin,* a tree of Java and Sumatra, used in perfumery, in pastilles, for incense and court-plaster, and friar's balsam. — *adj.* **benzo'ic.** [In the 16th century, *benjoin*, most prob. through It. from Ar. *lubān jāwī,* frankincense of Jawa (i.e. Sumatra).]

bepaint *bi-pānt', (arch.) v.t.* to paint over: to colour. [Pfx. **be-** (1).]

bepat *bi-pat', (arch.) v.t.* to pat frequently, to beat. [Pfx. **be-** (1).]

bepatched *bi-pacht', (arch.) adj.* mended with patches: wearing patches on the face by way of adnornment. [Pfx. **be-** (1).]

bepearl *bi-pûrl', (arch.) v.t.* to cover over with pearls. [Pfx. **be-** (1).]

bepelt *bi-pelt', (arch.) v.t.* to pelt vigorously. [Pfx. **be-** (1).]

bepepper *bi-pep'ər, (arch.) v.t.* to pelt with a rain of shot or blows. [Pfx. **be-** (1).]

bepester *bi-pest'ər, (arch.) v.t.* to vex or pester greatly. [Pfx. **be-** (1).]

bepity *bi-pit'i, (arch.) v.t.* to pity greatly. [Pfx. **be-** (1).]

beplaster *bi-pläs'tər, (arch.) v.t.* to plaster thickly: to daub. [Pfx. **be-** (1).]

beplumed *bi-plōōmd', (arch.) adj.* adorned with feathers. [Pfx. **be-** (2).]

bepommel *bi-pum'l, (arch.) v.t.* to pommel soundly. [Pfx. **be-** (1).]

bepowder *bi-pow'dər, (arch.) v.t.* to powder over. [Pfx. **be-** (1).]

bepraise *bi-prāz', (arch.) v.t.* to lavish praise on. [Pfx. **be-** (1).]

beprose *bi-prōz', (arch.) v.t.* to reduce to prose: to discuss in prose and tediously. [Pfx. **be-** (2).]

bepuff *bi-puf', (arch.) v.t.* to puff out: to praise beyond measure. [Pfx. **be-** (1).]

bequeath *bi-kwēdh, v.t.* to leave by will to another (strictly of personal property): to transmit to posterity, to leave behind: to commit or entrust to anyone. — *adj.* **bequeath'able.** — *ns.* **bequeath'al; bequeath'ment.** [O.E. *becwethan* — pfx. *bi-, be-,* and *cwethan,* to say; see **quoth.**]

bequest *bi-kwest', n.* act of bequeathing: that which is bequeathed, a legacy. [M.E. *biqueste* — O.E. pfx. *bi-, be-, cwethan,* to say; see **quoth.**]

berate *bi-rāt', v.t.* to scold or chide vigorously. [Pfx. **be-** (1).]

beray *bi-rā', (obs.) v.t.* to befoul. — Also (erroneously) **bewray'.** [Pfx. **be-** (1), and **ray¹.**]

Berber *bûr'bər, n.* a member of one of the Hamitic peoples of Barbary: the language of the Berbers. — Also *adj.* [Ar. *barbar;* connection with Gr. *barbaros* doubtful.]

Berberis *bûr'bər-is, n.* the barberry genus, giving name to the family **Berberidā'ceae,** akin to the buttercup family: (without *cap.*) any shrub of this genus. — *adj.* **berberidā'ceous.** — *n.* **ber'berine** an alkaloid got from barberry roots. [Latinised from Ar.; see **barberry.**]

berceau *ber-sō', (Fr.) n.* a cradle: a covered walk: — *pl.* **berceaux** (*-sōz, -sō*).

berceuse *ber-sœz', n.* a cradle song: a musical composition in similar rhythm. [Fr.]

berdache, berdash *bər-dash', n.* amongst American Indians, a usu. male transvestite, adopting not only the dress but also the status and role of the opposite sex. [Fr. *bardache,* male homosexual.]

bere¹. Another spelling of **bear,** barley.

bere², beer, bear *bēr, n.* a pillow-case (usu. **pill'ow-bere**). [Origin obscure; cf. Ger. *Bühre.*]

Berean *be-rē'ən, n.* one of an extinct Scottish religious sect of the 18th century. — Also *adj.* [*Beroea,* Gr. *Beroia,* in Macedonia, where the people searched the scriptures daily (Acts, xvii. 11).]

bereave *bi-rēv', v.t.* to rob of anything valued: to deprive: to widow, orphan, or deprive by death of some dear relative or friend: to snatch away: — *pa.t.* and *pa.p.* **bereaved'** (usu. by death), **bereft'** (usu. in general sense); *arch. pa.p.* **bereav'en.** — *adj.* **bereaved'.** — *n.* **bereave'ment** loss by death of a relative or friend. [O.E. *berēafian,* to plunder; see **reave.**]

beret *ber'i,* **berret** *ber'et, ns.* a flat, round, woollen cap worn by Basques and others. [Fr. *béret.*]

berg¹ *bûrg, berhh, (S.Afr.), n.* a hill or mountain. — **berg'-add'er** a venomous S. African viper, living on hillsides; **berg'-ce'dar** a rare conifer (*Widdringtonia juniperoides*) of the Cedarbergen in South Africa; **bergfall** (*bûrg'föl, berk'fäl*) fall of mountain-rock (Ger., mountain fall); **berghaan** (*berhh'hän, bûrg'hän; S.Afr.*) the bateleur eagle (Du., mountain cock); **bergmehl** (*berk'mäl,* or *bûrg'*) a powdery deposit of diatom frustules (Ger., mountain flour); **bergschrund** (*berk'shrōont*) a crevasse formed where a glacier or snowfield starts away from a mountain wall (Ger., mountain cleft); **berg wind** in S. Africa, a hot, dry wind from the north, blowing in the coastal regions. [Ger. *Berg,* Du., *berg,* hill; cog. with **barrow** (O.E. *beorg*).]

berg² *bûrg, n.* short for **iceberg.**

bergamask *bûr'gə-mäsk, n.* a native of *Bergamo,* in Italy: a rustic dance associated with that district. — Also **ber'gomask.**

bergamot[1] *bûr'gə-mot, n.* a kind of citron or orange, whose aromatic rind yields oil of bergamot, used in perfumery: the essence so extracted: a mint of similar smell: a kind of woven tapestry made in Bergamo: a kind of rug made in Bergama (also **ber'gama**). [Said to be from *Bergamo* in Italy; or *Bergama* (Pergamum) in Asia Minor; or as next word.]

bergamot[2] *bûr'gə-mot, n.* a fine pear. [Fr., — It., — Turk. *begarmudi,* prince of pears.]

bergander, bargander *bər-gan'dər, n.* the shelduck. [Perh. formed from **burrow** and **gander.**]

Bergenia *bər-gē'ni-ə, n.*a genus of perennial plants of the family Saxifragaceae: (without *cap.*) a plant of the genus, having red, purple or pink flowers. [K.A. von *Bergen,* an 18th-cent. botanist and physician.]

bergère *ber-zher, adj.* denoting a type of easy chair or sofa with cane back and arms. [Fr., shepherdess.]

bergomask. See **bergamask.**

Bergsonian *bûrg-sō'ni-ən, adj.* pertaining to Henri *Bergson* (1859–1941) and his philosophy of creative evolution. — *n.* a follower of Bergson. — *n.* **Berg'sonism** (-*sən-izm*).

bergylt *bûr'gilt, n.* a red northern sea-fish of the Scorpaenidae. [Norw. *berggylta,* rock-pig.]

beribboned *bi-rib'ənd, participial adj.* decorated with ribbons. [Pfx. **be-** (2).]

beriberi *ber'i-ber-i, n.* an Eastern disease due to lack of vitamin B. [Sinh. *beri,* weakness.]

berk, burk *bûrk, (slang) n.* a fool. [Short for Cockney rhyming slang *Berkeley Hunt,* for *cunt.*]

Berkeleian *bärk'-lē'ən, bärk'li-ən,* in U.S. *bûrk'-, adj.* pertaining to Bishop *Berkeley* (1685–1753), who maintained that the world we see and touch is not an abstract independent substance, of which conscious mind may be an effect, but is the very world which is presented to our senses, and which depends for its actuality on being perceived. — *n.* a follower of Berkeley. — *n.* **Berkelei'anism** (or *bärk'*).

berkelium *bər-kē'li-əm* (earlier *bûrk'i-əm), n.* an element (at. numb. 97; symbol Bk), prepared in a cyclotron at *Berkeley,* California.

berley, burley *bûr'li, (Austr.) n.* bait, groundbait: legpulling, humbug (*coll.*). [Orig. unknown.]

berlin *bûr'lin, bər-lēn', -lin', n.* an old four-wheeled covered carriage, with a seat behind covered with a hood (also **ber'line**): a closed motor-car with the driver's seat partitioned off. — **Berlin blue** Prussian blue; **Berlin wool** a fine dyed wool for worsted work, knitting, etc. [From the city of *Berlin.*]

berm *bûrm, n.* a ledge: the area of level ground between the raised mound of a barrow or other earthwork and the ditch surrounding it (*archaeol.*). [Fr. *berme*; Ger. *Berme.*]

Bermudan *bər-mū'dən,* **Bermudian** *-di-ən, adjs., ns.* (a native or inhabitant) of Bermuda. — **Bermuda grass** (*bər-mū'də*) a type of grass native to Southern Europe, now growing widely in warm countries, with wiry rootstock, used in lawns and for binding sand dunes; **Bermuda rig** a sailing rig in which there is a large fore-and-aft sail fixed directly to a tall mainmast; **Bermuda shorts** shorts, for men or women, reaching almost to the knee. — Also **Bermu'das; Bermuda Triangle** the area between Florida, the Bahamas, and Cuba where ships and aeroplanes mysteriously disappear.

Bernardine *bûr'nər-din, -dēn, adj.* Cistercian. [From *Bernard* of Clairvaux, founder of the order.]

bernicle-goose. Same as **barnacle-goose.**

berob *bi-rob', (Spens.) v.t.* to rob or plunder.

berret. See **beret.**

berry[1] *ber'i, n.* any small succulent fruit: a simple fruit with pericarp succulent throughout (thus excluding strawberry, raspberry, blackberry, which are aggregate fruits) (*bot.*): a coffee-bean: a cereal grain: a lobster's or crayfish's egg: a knob on a swan's bill. — *v.i.* to come into berry, to swell: to gather berries. — *adj.* **berr'ied** bearing berries: of lobsters, etc., having

eggs. — *n.* **berr'ying.** — **berry bug** the harvest-mite or chigger, of the genus *Trombicula.* [O.E. *berie.*]

berry[2] *ber'i, n.* a pottage or sop (as in **ale-berry, bread=berry**). [O.E. *brīw,* pottage, porridge.]

bersaglieri *ber-säl-yä'rē, n.pl.* the riflemen or sharpshooters of the Italian army, first organised in the Sardinian army in 1836. [It.; pl. of *bersagliere* — *bersaglio,* a mark.]

berserk, berserker *ber-sûrk'(ər), -zûrk'(ər), ns.* a Norse warrior whom the sight of the field of battle would fill with a frenzied and resistless fury. — *adj.* **berserk'** violently frenzied or angry (*rare* **berserk'er**). — *advs.* **berserk'** in a violent frenzy; **berserk'ly.** [O.N. *berserkr,* probably bear-sark.]

berth *bûrth, n.* sea-room: a ship's station at anchor or at a wharf: a room or sleeping-place in a ship, sleeping-carriage, etc.: any allotted or assigned place: a situation or place of employment, usually a comfortable one. — *v.t.* and *v.i.* to moor. — *v.t.* to furnish with a berth. — *n.* **berth'age** accommodation, or dues paid, for mooring or anchoring. — **give a wide berth to** to keep well away from generally. [Ety. obscure.]

bertha *bûr'thə, n.* a woman's falling collar (also **berthe**): (with *cap.*; often **Big Bertha**) a big German gun (from Frau *Berta* Krupp of the Krupp steelworks); first used of guns shelling Paris 1918. — **bertha army worm** a type of cutworm of north central U.S. and Canada, destructive to crops. [Woman's name.]

Bertholletia *bûrth-ō-lē'sh(y)ə, n.* the brazil-nut genus of Lecythidaceae. [Named in honour of the chemist C. L. *Berthollet* (1748–1822).]

Berthon-boat *bûr'thon-bōt, n.* a type of collapsible boat. [Edward L. *Berthon* (1813–99), its inventor.]

bertillonage *ber-tē-yon-äzh, (Fr.) n.* a system of criminal identification by measurement, worked out by Alphonse *Bertillon* (1853–1914), a Paris police officer.

Berufsverbot *bə-rōofs'fər-bōt, (Ger.) n.* in Germany, the policy of excluding political extremists from public service.

beryl *ber'il, n.* a precious stone of which emerald and aquamarine are varieties, a silicate of beryllium and aluminium crystallising in the hexagonal system, green, colourless, yellow or blue, once esteemed as a magic crystal. — *adj.* pale greenish. — *ns.* **beryll'ia** the oxide of **beryll'ium**, a metallic element (at numb. 4; symbol Be), used as a moderator in nuclear reactors, and industrially to harden alloys, etc.; **berylliō'sis** a disease caused by exposure to the fumes or dust from beryllium salts, in which granulomata are formed esp. in the lungs. [O.Fr. *beryl* — L. *bēryllus* — Gr. *bēryllos.*]

besaint *bi-sānt', (arch.) v.t.* to make a saint of: — *pa.p.* **besaint'ed** canonised: haunted with saints. [Pfx. **be-** (2).]

bescatter *bi-skat'ər, (arch.) v.t.* to scatter over. [Pfx. **be-** (1).]

bescrawl *bi-scröl', (arch.) v.t.* to scrawl or scribble over. [Pfx. **be-** (1).]

bescreen *bi-skrēn', (arch.) v.t.* to screen: to overshadow. [Pfx. **be-** (1).]

bescribble *bi-skrib'l, (arch.) v.t.* to write in a scribbling hand: to scribble about, over, or upon. [Pfx. **be-** (1).]

besee *bi-sē' (obs.) v.t.* to look to: to provide for: to treat: to provide, furnish, apparel, adorn: — *pa.p.* **beseen'.** — *adj.* **beseen'** of good appearance, comely: furnished. [O.E. *besēon* — *be-,* pfx., *sēon,* to see.]

beseech *bi-sēch' (Spens.* **beseeke** *bi-sēk'), v.t.* to entreat, to implore: to ask or pray earnestly: to solicit: — *pa.t.* and *pa.p.* **besought** (*bi-söt'*) also **beseeched'.** — *n.* (*Shak.*) entreaty. — *n.* **beseech'er.** — *n.* and *adj.* **beseech'ing.** — *adv.* **beseech'ingly.** — *n.* **beseech'ingness.** [Pfx. **be-** (1), and M.E. *sechen*; see **seek.**]

beseem *bi-sēm', v.i.* to seem (*obs.*): to be fitting or becoming. — *v.t.* to be seemly for: to become: to be fit for or worthy of. — *n.* and *adj.* **beseem'ing.** — *adv.* **beseem'ingly.** — *n.* **beseem'ingness.** — *adj.* **beseem'ly** (*rare*). [Pfx. **be-** (1).]

beseen. See **besee.**

beset *bi-set'*, *v.t.* to surround or set round with anything (now only in *pa.p.*): to surround with hostile intentions, to besiege: to occupy so as to allow none to go out or in: to assail, perplex, endanger, as by temptations, obstacles, etc.: — *pr.p.* **besett'ing;** *pa.t.* and *pa.p.* **beset'.** — *ns.* **beset'ment; besett'er.** — *adj.* **besett'ing** constantly assailing: dominant: obsessive. [O.E. *besettan* — *settan*, to set.]

beshadow *bi-shad'ō*, (*arch.*) *v.t.* to cast a shadow over. [Pfx. **be-** (1).]

beshame *bi-shām'*, (*arch.*) *v.t.* to put to shame. [Pfx. **be-** (1).]

beshine *bi-shīn'*, (*arch.*) *v.t.* to light up. — *adj.* **beshone** (-*shon'*). [Pfx. **be-** (1).]

beshrew *bi-shrōō'*, (*arch.*) *v.t.* to invoke evil upon, to curse (latterly only in imprecations). [Pfx. **be-** (1) and obs. *v.t.* **shrew** to curse.]

beside *bi-sīd'*, *prep.* by the side of, near: over and above, besides (*rare*): outside of: away from: distinct from: apart from, not falling within, as of a question, resolution, etc. — *adv.* near by: besides: apart: to the side. — *adv.* **besides'** in addition: moreover: otherwise, else. — *prep.* over and above: else than: beside (*obs.*): away from, apart from (*obs.*). — **beside oneself** having lost self-possession; **beside the mark, point, question** irrelevant. [O.E. *besīdan*, by the side (dat.); the *s* is of the adverbial gen.]

besiege *bi-sēj'*, *v.t.* to lay siege to: to beset with armed forces: to throng round: to importune: to pester. — *ns.* **besiege'ment; besieg'er.** — *n.* and *adj.* **besieg'ing.** — *adv.* **besieg'ingly** (*rare*) urgently. [Pfx. **be-** (3).]

besigh *bi-sī'*, (*arch.*) *v.t.* to sigh over. [Pfx. **be-** (3).]

besing *bi-sing'*, (*arch.*) *v.t.* to celebrate in song. — *adj.* **besung'.** [Pfx. **be-** (3).]

besit *bi-sit'*, (*arch.*) *v.t.* to besiege: to sit well on, as clothes, to become. — *adj.* **besitt'ing** (*Spens.*) becoming. [O.E. *besittan* — *sittan*, to sit.]

beslave *bi-slāv'*, *v.t.* to make a slave of: to call slave. [Pfx. **be-** (2).]

beslaver *bi-slav'ər*, (*arch.*) *v.t.* to slaver or slobber upon: to cover with fulsome flattery. [Pfx. **be-** (1).]

beslobber *bi-slob'ər*, *v.t.* to besmear with the spittle running from one's mouth: to cover with drivelling kisses: to flatter fulsomely. [Pfx. **be-** (1).]

beslubber *bi-slub'ər*, *v.t.* to bedaub or besmear. [Pfx. **be-** (1).]

besmear *bi-smēr'*, *v.t.* to smear over: to bedaub: to pollute. [Pfx. **be-** (1).]

besmirch *bi-smûrch'*, *v.t.* to soil, as with smoke or soot: to sully. [Pfx. **be-** (1).]

besmut *bi-smut'*, *v.t.* to blacken with soot. — *adj.* **besmutt'ed.** [Pfx. **be-** (1).]

besmutch *bi-smuch'*, (*arch.*) *v.t.* to besmirch. [Pfx. **be-** (1).]

besognio *bi-zōn'yō*, *n.* a beggar: — *pl.* **besogn'ios.** [It.; see **bezonian.**]

besoin *bə-zwē̃*, (Fr.) *n.* need, want, desire.

beso las manos *bā'sō läs mä'nōs*, (Sp.) I kiss your hands.

besom[1] *bē'zəm, bez'əm*, *n.* a bunch of twigs for sweeping: (*Scot. biz'əm, buz'əm*) a broom: any cleansing or purifying agent (*fig.*). — **be'som-head** a blockhead; **be'som-rid'er** a witch. — **jump the besom** see **broom.** [O.E. *besema*; Ger. *Bezen*, Du. *bezem*.]

besom[2] *biz'əm, bē'zəm*, (Scot. and *dial.*) *n.* a term of reproach for a woman, implying generally slatternliness, laziness, impudence, or unscrupulous energy. [Perh. the same word as the preceding, perh. connected with O.E. *bysn, bisn*, example, or O.N. *bȳsn*, wonder.]

besort *bi-sört'*, (*Shak.*) *v.t.* to match, befit, become. — *n.* suitable company. [Pfx. **be-** (1).]

besot *bi-sot'*, *v.t.* to make sottish, dull, or stupid: to make a sot of: to cause to dote: to infatuate: — *pr.p.* **besott'ing;** *pa.p.* **besott'ed.** — *adj.* **besott'ed** infatuated. — *adv.* **besott'edly.** — *n.* **besott'edness.** [Pfx. **be-** (2).]

besought *bi-söt'*, *pa.t.* and *pa.p.* of **beseech.**

besouled *bi-sōld'*, (*arch.*) *adj.* endowed with a soul. [Pfx. **be-** (2).]

bespangle *bi-spang'gl*, *v.t.* to adorn with spangles, or with anything sparkling or shining. [Pfx. **be-** (1).]

bespatter *bi-spat'ər*, *v.t.* to spatter or sprinkle with dirt or anything moist: to defame. [Pfx. **be-** (1).]

bespeak *bi-spēk'*, *v.t.* to speak for or engage beforehand, to order or apply for: to stipulate or ask for: to betoken: to bewitch (*obs. dial.*). — *v.i.* (*obs.*) to speak: — *pa.t.* **bespoke'**, *arch.* **bespake';** *pa.p.* **bespōk'en,** also **bespoke'** (see also **bespoke, bespoken** below). — *n.* an actor's benefit, so called because his friends and patrons choose the piece to be performed: an application in advance. [Pfx. **be-** (3).]

bespeckle *bi-spek'l*, *v.t.* to mark with speckles or spots. [Pfx. **be-** (1).]

bespectacled *hi-spek'tə-kəld*, *adj.* having spectacles on. [Pfx. **be-** (2).]

bespeed *bi-spēd'*, (*arch.*) *v.t.* to help on: — *pa.t.* and *pa.p.* **besped'.** [Pfx. **be-** (1).]

bespice *bi-spīs'*, (*Shak.*) *v.t.* to season with spice. [Pfx. **be-** (2).]

bespit *bi-spit'*, (*arch.*) *v.t.* to spit upon, defile with spittle: — *pa.t.* and *pa.p.* **bespit', bespat';** *pa.p.* (*Browning*) **bespate'.** [Pfx. **be-** (1).]

bespoke *bi-spōk'*, **bespoken** *be-spōk'n*, *pa.p.* of **bespeak,** ordered to be made, as clothes, etc., made to order: (of a tailor, etc.) making clothes, etc. to order. [Pfx. **be-** (3).]

besport *bi-spōrt', -spört'*, *v.t.* to disport. [Pfx. **be-** (1).]

bespot *bi-spot'*, *v.t.* to cover with spots. — *adj.* **bespott'ed.** — *n.* **bespott'edness.** [Pfx. **be-** (1).]

bespout *bi-spowt'*, *v.t.* to spout over: to declaim pompously. [Pfx. **be-** (1).]

bespread *bi-spred'*, *v.t.* to spread over: to cover: — *pr.p.* **bespread'ing;** *pa.t.* and *pa.p.* **bespread'.** [Pfx. **be-** (3).]

besprent *bi-sprent'*, (*obs.*) *pa.p.* sprinkled over: scattered. [O.E. *besprengan*; see **sprinkle.**]

besprinkle *bi-spring'kl*, *v.t.* to sprinkle over. [Pfx. **be-** (1).]

Bessemer *bēs'əm-ər*, *adj.* pertaining to the steel-making process invented by Sir Henry *Bessemer* (1813–98). — **Bessemer iron, pig** pig-iron suitable for making Bessemer steel.

Besserwisser *bes'ər-vis-ər*, (Ger.; often *facet.*) *n.* someone who (thinks he) always knows better or more than anyone else.

best *best*, *adj.* (serving as *superl.* of **good**) good in the highest degree: first: highest: most excellent. — *n.* one's utmost endeavour: the highest perfection: the best share, part, success, or lot (as the *best of the bargain*, *the best of three* — tosses, games, etc.). — *adv.* (as *superl.* of **well**) in the highest degree: in the best manner. — *v.t.* (*coll.*) to get the better of. — **best-before date** the date (stamped, etc. on a package esp. with the wording 'best before (e.g.) 15 August') up to which a manufacturer can guarantee the good quality of a consumer product; **best boy, girl** (*coll.*) a favourite associate of the opposite sex; **best end** a cut of lamb, etc. from the part of the neck nearest the ribs; **best man, best maid** (*Scot.*) groomsman and bridesmaid at a wedding; **best part** greater part; **best'seller** a book that has had one of the biggest sales of the season: the writer of such a book. — *v.i.* **bestsell'** of a book, to be or become a bestseller. — **at best** on the most favourable supposition; **for the best** with the best of intentions or outcome; **give someone best** to concede the victory; **have the best of it** to gain the advantage in a contest; **I had best, I were best** (for earlier *me were best*) it were best for me; **make the best of one's way** to go as well as one can; **put one's best foot foremost** see **foot; with the best** as successfully as anyone. [O.E. *betst, betest*; see **better.**]

bestad(de). See **bestead**[2].

bestain *bi-stān'*, (*arch.*) *v.t.* to stain all over. [Pfx. **be-** (1).]

bestar *bi-stär'*, (*arch.*) *v.t.* to cover with stars. [Pfx. **be-** (2).]

bestead[1] *bi-sted'*, *v.t.* to help, relieve: to be of use to, avail. — *v.i.* to profit, be advantageous: — *pa.t.* **bestead'ed;** *pa.p.* **bestead', bested'.** [Pfx. **be-** (1) and obs. *v.t.* **stead.**]

bestead[2], **bested** *bi-sted'* (*Spens.* **bestad, bestadde** *bi-stad'*), *adj.* set about (*with*): beset (with *by*, of foes; with *with*, of dangers, etc.): situated — usually with *ill, hard*, etc. [Pfx. **be-** (2) and **stead**, placed.]

bestial *best'i-əl*, *adj.* like a beast: rude: brutally sensual. — *n.* (*Scot.*) a collective name for cattle. — *v.t.* **best'ialise, -ize** to make like a beast. — *ns.* **best'ialism** irrationality; **bestiality** (*-al'i-ti*) beastliness: disgusting vice: copulation between an animal and a person. [L. *bestiālis* — *bestia*, beast.]

bestiary *best'i-ər-i*, *n.* a book of a class popular in the Middle Ages, describing animals, a mixture of natural and unnatural history allegorised for edification. [L.L. *bestiārium*, a menagerie — *bestia*, a beast.]

bestick *bi-stik'*, *v.t.* to stick over, as with sharp points: to transfix: to stick about, adorn: — *pa.t.* and *pa.p.* **bestuck'.** [Pfx. **be-** (1).]

bestill *bi-stil'*, (*arch.*) *v.t.* to make quiet, to hush. [Pfx. **be-** (1).]

bestir *bi-stûr'*, *v.t.* to put into lively action: to arouse into activity. [Pfx. **be-** (1).]

bestorm *bi-störm'*, (*arch.*) *v.t.* to assail with storms or tumult. [Pfx. **be-** (1).]

bestow *bi-stō'*, *v.t.* to stow, place, or put by: to give or confer: to accommodate with quarters: to apply (with *on* and *upon*): (*refl., Shak.*) to acquit (oneself). — *ns.* **bestow'al** act of bestowing: disposal; **bestow'er; bestow'ment.** [Pfx. **be-** (1).]

bestraddle *bi-strad'l*, *v.t.* to bestride. [Pfx. **be-** (3).]

bestraught *bi-ströt'*, (*obs.*) *adj.* distraught: distracted: mad. [Pfx. **be-** (1); **distraught**, with change of pfx.]

bestreak *bi-strēk'*, *v.t.* to overspread with streaks. [Pfx. **be-** (1).]

bestrew *bi-strōō'*, *v.t.* to cover loosely with something strewn or scattered over: — *pa.p.* **bestrewed', bestrown** (*-strōn'*), **bestrewn'** (*with*). [Pfx. **be-** (1).]

bestride *bi-strīd'*, *v.t.* to stride over: to sit or stand across: to defend, protect, from the sense of standing over a fallen man to defend him: — *pa.t.* **bestrid, bestrode';** *pa.p.* **bestrid', bestridd'en.** — *adj.* **bestrīd'able.** [Pfx. **be-** (3).]

bestuck *pa.t.* and *pa.p.* of **bestick.**

bestud *bi-stud'*, *v.t.* to adorn as with studs, as the sky with stars. [Pfx. **be-** (1).]

bet *bet*, *n.* a wager: something staked to be lost or won on the result of a doubtful issue. — *v.t.* and *v.i.* to lay or stake, as a bet: — *pr.p.* **bett'ing;** *pa.t.* and *pa.p.* **bet** or **bett'ed.** — *ns.* **bett'er** one who bets — also **bett'or; bett'ing.** — **a better** a more hopeful proposition or possibility; **an even bet** an equal chance; **you bet** (*slang*) certainly. [Possibly shortened from the noun **abet.**]

beta *bē'tə*, *n.* the second letter (B, β) of the Greek alphabet: as a numeral β' = 2, ̦β = 2000: in classification, the second or one of the second grade, the grade below alpha: in a constellation, star second in brightness. — *adj.* in chemical classification, designating one of two or several isomeric forms of a compound. — *ns.* **be'tacism** (*-sizm*) pronunciation of the sound of b as that of v; **be'tatron** (Gr. *-tron*, agent suffix) see **accelerator** under **accelerate.** — **be'ta=block'er** a drug that reduces heart-rate and interferes with the action of stress hormones such as adrenaline, used to treat e.g. high blood-pressure and angina; **beta rays** streams of **beta particles** or electrons, given off by radium and other radioactive substances. [Gr. *bēta*; see **B, beth.**]

betaine *bē'tə-in, -ēn*, *n.* a crystalline, sweet-tasting alkaloid occurring in sugar beet and other plants, also found in animals. [L. *bēta*, beet, and *-ine.*]

betake *bi-tāk'*, *v.t.* to take (oneself) to, to go (with *self*):

to apply or have recourse to: — *pa.t.* **betook';** *pa.p.* **betāk'en.** [Pfx. **be-** (1).]

bete. See **beet**[2].

bête *bet*, (Fr.) *n.* a brute, a stupid person. — *n.* **bêtise** (*bet-ēz*) stupidity: a blunder. — **bête noire** (*nwär*) a black beast: a bugbear: a person or thing that one especially dislikes.

beteem, beteeme *bi-tēm'*, (*Spens., Shak.*) *v.t.* to grant, vouchsafe, allow. [Perh. from a lost O.E. word answering to Du. *betamen*, to beseem.]

betel *bē'tl*, *n.* the leaf of the **be'tel-pepp'er** (*Piper betle*) which is chewed in the East along with the areca-nut and lime. — **be'tel-nut** the areca-nut. [Through Port. from Malayalam *vettila*.]

Betelgeuse, Betelgeuz *bet'əl-jōōz*, *n.* a reddish first-magnitude star in Orion's shoulder. [Fr., — Ar. *bayt-al-jawzā'*, Orion.]

beth *beth, bāth*, *n.* the second letter of the Hebrew and Phoenician alphabets, resembling a house. [Heb. *bēth*, house; see **B, beta.**]

bethankit *bi-thangk'it*, (*Scot.*) *interj.* elliptical for *God be thanked.* — *n.* a grace.

Beth Din *bāt dēn*, a Jewish court, in London presided over by the Chief Rabbi. [Heb. *bēth*, house, *dīn*, judgment.]

bethel *beth'əl*, *n.* a Methodist or Baptist church: an old ship fitted as a place of worship for sailors. [Heb. *Bēth-ēl*, house of God.]

Bethesda *be-thez'də*, (Heb.) *n.* a healing pool at Jerusalem — (usu. without *cap.*) often applied to a Nonconformist church.

bethink *bi-thingk'*, *v.t.* to think on or call to mind: to recollect (generally followed by a reflexive pronoun and *of*): to propose to oneself. — *v.i.* to consider: — *pa.t.* and *pa.p.* **bethought** (*bi-thöt'*). [O.E. *bithencan*; cf. Ger. *bedenken*. See **think.**]

bethrall *bi-thröl'*, (*Spens.*) *v.t.* to enslave [Pfx. **be-** (2).]

bethumb *bi-thum'*, *v.t.* to mark with the thumbs: — *pa.p.* **bethumbed'.** [Pfx. **be-** (1).]

bethump *bi-thump'*, *v.t.* to thump or beat soundly. [Pfx. **be-** (1).]

bethwack *bi-thwak'*, *v.t.* to thrash soundly. [Pfx. **be-** (1).]

betide *bi-tīd'*, *v.t.* to befall, happen to (orig. *dat.* and formerly sometimes followed by *to, unto*): (*erroneous* and *rare*) to betoken: — *pa.t.* **beti'ded, betid** (*-tid'*); *pa.p.* **betid'** (*Spens.* **betight** *bi-tīt'*). [Pfx. **be-** (1); see **tide**[2].]

betime *bi-tīm'*, (*Shak.*) *v.i.* to betide. [Pfx. **be-** (2).]

betimes *bi-tīmz'*, *adv.* in good time: early: seasonably: speedily. [Pfx. **be-** (1), and **time**, with adverbial gen. *-s.*]

bêtise. See **bête.**

betitle *bi-tī'tl*, *v.t.* to give a name to. [Pfx. **be-** (2).]

betoil *bi-toil'*, *v.t.* to weary with toil. [Pfx. **be-** (1).]

betoken *bi-tō'kən*, *v.t.* to show by a sign: to foreshow: to mean: to symbolise (*arch.*). [Pfx. **be-** (1).]

béton *bā'tɔ̃*, *n.* lime concrete: concrete. [Fr.]

betony *bet'ən-i*, *n.* a common labiate plant (*Stachys* or *Betonica officinalis*) growing in woods, of great repute in ancient and mediaeval medicine: extended to various labiate and scrophulariaceous plants. [Fr. *bétoine* — L. *betonica, vettonica.*]

betook *bi-tōōk'*, *pa.t.* of **betake.**

betoss *bi-tos'*, (*Shak.*) *v.t.* to agitate. [Pfx. **be-** (1).]

betray *bi-trā'*, *v.t.* to give up treacherously: to disclose in breach of trust: to let go basely or weakly: to deceive (the innocent and trustful), to seduce: to discover or show: to show signs of. — *ns.* **betray'al** act of betraying; **betray'er** a traitor: the seducer of a trustful girl. [Pfx. **be-** (1) and O.Fr. *trair* (Fr. *trahir*) — L. *tradĕre*, to deliver up.]

betread *bi-tred'*, *v.t.* to tread over or walk upon: — *pa.t.* **betrod';** *pa.p.* **betrodd'en.** [Pfx. **be-** (1).]

betrim *bi-trim'*, *v.t.* to trim or set in order, to deck, to dress. [Pfx. **be-** (1).]

betroth *bi-trōdh'*, or *-trōth'*, *v.t.* to contract, or promise, to marry (a woman): to affiance: to pledge oneself to (*obs.*). — *ns.* **betroth'al, betroth'ment** an engagement to marry: ceremonious declaration of such an engagement. — *adj.* and *n.* **betrothed'.** [Pfx. **be-** (2), and **troth** or **truth.**]

better *bet'ər, adj.* (serves as *compar.* of **good**) good in a greater degree: preferable: improved: more suitable: larger: kinder: stronger in health: completely recovered, quite well again. — *adv.* (*compar.* of **well**) well in a greater degree: more fully or completely: over or more: with greater advantage. — *n.* superior (esp. in *pl.*). — *v.t.* to make better: to surpass. — *v.i.* to grow better. — *adjs.* **bett'ered; bett'ering.** — *ns.* **bett'ering** amelioration: improvement; **bett'erment** improvement, esp. in standard of life or value of property. — *adj.* **bett'ermost** best. — *n.* **bett'erness.** — **better half** a jocose term for a wife, once applied seriously to wife or husband, intimate friend, and even the soul as opposed to the body; **be better than one's word** to do more than one had promised; **better off** in superior circumstances: more fortunate: richer; **for better (or) for worse** whatever the result may be; **get the better of** to gain the advantage over, overcome; **had better see have; have seen, known better days** to be worse off or in worse condition now than formerly; **the better part of** more than half of; **think better of** to revise one's decision about, esp. to decide not to do: to have a higher opinion of. [O.E. *bet* (adv.), *betera* (adj.) better; Goth. *batiza*, Ger. *besser*; prob. cog. with **boot**².]

betty *bet'i, n.* a man who troubles himself with the women's work in a household: a burglar's jemmy (*old slang*). — **Betty Martin** an expression inviting incredulity (usu. *all my eye and Betty Martin*). [Dim. of *Elizabeth.*]

Betula *bet'ū-lə, n.* the birch genus, giving name to the family **Betulā'ceae,** which includes hazel and hornbeam. [L. *betŭla.*]

betumbled *bi-tum'bəld,* (*Shak.*) *participial adj.* tumbled or disordered. [Pfx. **be-** (1).]

between *bi-twēn', prep.* in, to, through, or across the space that separates: intermediate to: on the part of in reciprocal relation: by combined action or influence of: from one to another of: in joint possession of (generally of two). — *adv.* in or to an intermediate place: at intervals. — *n.* an interval (*Shak.*): an intermediate variety of needle. — *ns.* **between'ity** (*playful*), **between'ness** state of being between. — **between'-decks** the space between any two decks of a ship (also *adv.*); **between'-maid** a servant subsidiary to two others (esp. cook and tablemaid) — a tweeny. — *advs.* **between'-time(s), between'whiles** at intervals. — **between ourselves, between you and me** (*slang* **and the cat** or **post** or **bedpost,** etc.) in confidence; **between the devil and the deep sea** in a desperate dilemma; **go between** to act as a mediator (*n.* **go'-between).** [O.E. *betwēonum,* and *betwēon* — *be,* by, and *twēgen, twā,* twain, two.]

betwixt *bi-twikst', prep.* and *adv.* between. — **betwixt and between** in a middling position. [O.E. *betweox* — *twā,* two, and the suffix *-ix, -ish,* with added *-t,* as in *against,* and *amidst.*]

Beulah *bū'lə,* (Heb.) *n.* a land of rest — a name for Israel in its future condition, in Isa. lxii, 4: a Nonconformist chapel.

beurre *bær,* (Fr.) *n.* butter. — **beurre manié** (*ma-nyā*) a butter and flour mixture for thickening sauces; **beurre noir** (*nwär*)butter heated until it browns.

beurré *bæ-rā, n.* a soft pear of various kinds. [Fr., buttery.]

bevatron *bev'ə-tron, n.* See **accelerator** under **accelerate.** [from **Bev** (see List of abbreviations and Gr. agent suffix *-tron.*]

bevel *bev'l, n.* a slant or inclination of a surface: an instrument opening like a pair of compasses, and adjustable for measuring angles. — *adj.* having the form of a bevel: slanting. — *v.t.* to form with a bevel or slant: — *pr.p.* **bev'elling;** *pa.t.* and *pa.p.* **bev'elled.** — *adj.* **bev'elled** cut to an oblique angle, sloped off. —

ns. **bev'eller; bev'elling; bev'elment.** — **bev'el-gear, bev'el-wheels** (*mech.*) wheels working on each other in different planes, the cogs of the wheels being bevelled or at oblique angles to the shafts. [From the older form of Fr. *beveau,* bevel (instrument).]

bever¹. See **beverage.**

bever². An obsolete form of **beaver.**

beverage *bev'ər-ij, n.* any liquid for drinking, esp. tea, coffee, milk, etc.: a mixture of cider and water (*obs.*): a drink or drink-money to celebrate an occasion (*dial.*). — *n.* **bever** (*bēv'ər*) a small repast between meals (*dial.*): a time for drinking (*obs.*). — *adj.* **bevv'ied** (*slang*) drunk. — *n.* **bev(v)'y** (*coll.*) (an) alcoholic drink. — **beverage room** (*Can.*) a beer parlour. [O.Fr. *bevrage* (Fr. *breuvage*), *beivre* — L. *bibĕre,* to drink.]

bevue *bā-vü, n.* a blunder. [Fr. *bévue.*]

bevy *bev'i, n.* a company or flock of larks, quails, swans, roes, or ladies. [Origin obscure.]

bewail *bi-wāl', v.t.* to lament: to mourn loudly over (esp. the dead). — *v.i.* to utter lamentations. — *adj.* **bewailed'.** — *n.* and *adj.* **bewail'ing.** [Pfx. **be-** (1).]

beware *bi-wār', v.i.* (usu. with *of,* or with *that, lest*) to be on one's guard: to take heed (*obs.*): to take care (of) (*obs.*): to take warning (by) (*obs.*). — *v.t.* to be on one's guard against: to take care of (*obs.*): to take care (with *infin.* or clause) (*arch.*). Used normally only in infinitive and imperative; old writers have *was ware,* etc. [**be, ware.**]

beweep *bi-wēp', v.t.* to weep over, lament: to wet or disfigure by weeping: — *pa.t.* and *pa.p.* **bewept'.** [Pfx. **be-** (1).]

beweltered *bi-wel'tərd,* (*arch.*) *participial adj.* besmeared by weltering in blood. [Pfx. **be-** (1).]

bewet *bi-wet', v.t.* to wet or moisten (*Shak.*): — *pa.t* and *pa.p.* **bewett'ed, bewet'.** [Pfx. **be-** (1).]

bewhore *bi-hōr', -hör,* (*Shak.*) *v.t.* to call a whore: to make a whore of. [Pfx. **be-** (2).]

Bewick's swan *bū'iks swon,* a small white swan, *Cygnus bewickii,* native to N. Asia an N.E. Europe, that winters occasionally in W. Europe. [T. *Bewick* (d. 1828), Eng. wood-engraver, illustrator of *History of British Birds.*]

bewig *bi-wig', v.t.* to cover with a wig. — *adj.* **bewigged'.** [Pfx. **be-** (2).]

bewilder *bi-wil'dər, v.t.* to lead astray (*arch.*): to perplex, confuse. — *adjs.* **bewil'dered** lost (*arch.*): confused in mind: trackless (*arch.*): confused, mixed up (*arch.*); **bewil'dering.** — *adv.* **bewil'deringly.** — *n.* **bewil'derment.** [Pfx. **be-** (1) and obs. Eng. *wildern* — O.E. *wilddēoren,* wilderness — *wild,* wild, *dēor,* beast.]

bewitch *bi-wich', v.t.* to affect by witchcraft (mostly malignantly): to fascinate or charm. — *n.* **bewitch'ery.** — *adj.* **bewitch'ing** charming: enchanting. — *adv.* **bewitch'ingly.** — *n.* **bewitch'ment.** [Pfx. **be-** (1).]

bewray¹ *bi-rā',* (*arch.*) *v.t.* to reveal, esp. inadvertently: to betray: to divulge: to show up: to reveal the existence, presence, or whereabouts, of. [M.E. *bewreien* — *be-* , and O.E. *wrēgan,* to accuse.]

bewray². See **beray.**

bey *bā, n.* a Turkish governor. [Turk.]

beyond *bi-yond', prep.* on the farther side of: farther onward in comparison with: out of reach of: above, superior to: apart from. — *adv.* farther away. — *n.* the unknown: the hereafter. — **beyond measure** excessively; **beyond one** more than one is able to do: past one's comprehension; **beyond seas** abroad; **go beyond** to surpass: to circumvent: to overreach (*B., Shak.*); **the back of beyond** a place of extreme remoteness; **the (Great) Beyond** the afterlife. [O.E. *begeondan* — pfx. *be-,* and *geond,* across, beyond; see **yon.**]

bez, bez-antler, -tine. See **bay**⁶.

bezant *bez'ənt,* or *biz-ant', n.* a gold coin first struck at Byzantium or Constantinople: a small circle or (i.e. yellow), like a gold coin (*her.*).

bezazz. See **bez(z)azz.**

bezel *bez'l, n.* the part of the setting of a precious stone which encloses it: the oblique side or face of a cut gem:

the grooved rim in which a watch-glass is set, etc.: a sloped cutting edge (usually **basil** *baz'l*): an indicator light on a car dashboard. [From an O.Fr. word represented by mod. Fr. *biseau;* ult. origin uncertain.]

bezique *bi-zēk'*, *n.* a game at cards for two, three, or four, played with two to four packs, from which cards below the seven have been removed: the combination of the knave of diamonds and queen of spades. [Fr. *besigue*, of obscure origin.]

bezoar *bē'zōr*, *-zör*, *n.* a stony concretion found in the stomachs of goats, antelopes, llamas, etc., formerly esteemed an antidote to all poisons. — *adj.* **bezoardic** *(bez-ō-ärd'ik).* [Through Sp. *bezoar* and Ar. *bāzahr* — Pers. *pādzahr*, antidote — *zahr*, poison.]

bezonian *bi-zō'nyən*, *(Shak.) n.* a beggar. [It. *bisogno*, need.]

bez(z)azz, baz(z)azz, biz(z)azz *bə-zaz'*, *(coll.) n.* Variants of **piz(z)azz.**

bezzle *bez'l*, *(obs.) v.i.* to drink hard. — *v.t.* to squander: to despoil: to consume. [O.Fr. *besiler.* See **embezzle.**]

bhajan *buj'ən*, *n.* a Hindu religious song. [Sans.]

bhakti *buk'ti*, *n.* in Hinduism, devotion to a god, as a path to salvation. [Sans., portion.]

bhang *bang*, *n.* a narcotic and intoxicant, leaves and shoots of hemp. [Hind. *bhãg*; Pers. *bang*; Sans. *bhaṅga.*]

bharal *bur'əl*, *n.* the blue sheep of the Himalaya, connecting the true wild sheep with the goats. — Also **burrel, burrell, burrhel, burhel.** [Hind.]

Bharat *bu'rut*, *n.* Hindi name of the Republic of India. — *adj.* **Bha'rati.** [*Bharata*, legendary monarch.]

Bharata Natyam *bur'ə-tə nat'yəm*, a form of Hindu temple dance originating in the Madras region, first described by the sage *Bharata.*

bhel. See **bael.**

bhindi *bin'di*, *n.* the okra, frequently used in Indian cookery. [Hindi.]

bhisti, bheesty, bheestie, bhistee *bēs'tē*, *n.* an Indian water carrier. [Urdu *bhistī* — Pers. *behistī* — *bihisht*, paradise.]

bi-, *bī*, sometimes **bin-** *bin-* before a vowel, *pfx.* two, twice, double. [L. *bis*, twice, *bīnī*, two by two, for *duis*, *duīnī.*]

biannual *bī-an'ū-əl*, *adj.* happening, etc. twice a year, half-yearly: happening, etc. every two years, two-yearly. — *adv.* **biann'ually.** [L. *bi-*, twice, *annus*, year.]

bias *bī'əs*, *n.* an obliquity: an oblique line: a bulge or greater weight on one side of a bowl (in the game of bowling), making it turn to one side: a turning to one side: a one-sided inclination of the mind: a prejudice: any special influence that sways the mind. — *adj.* biased: cut slantwise. — *adv.* slantwise. — *v.t.* to cause to turn to one side: to prejudice, or prepossess: to cut obliquely: — *pr.p.* **bī'asing** (by some **bī'assing**); *pa.t.* and *pa.p.* **bī'ased** (**bī'assed**). — *n.* **bī'asing** a bias or inclination to one side. — **bias binding** a long narrow folded piece of material cut slantwise and used for finishing hems, seams etc., in sewing; **bī'as-drawing** *(Shak.)* a turn awry. [Fr. *biais*, slant; of unknown origin.]

biathlon *bī-ath'lon*, *n.* an international competition in skiing and shooting. [L. *bi-*, twice, Gr. *athlon*, a contest.]

biaxial *bī-aks'i-əl*, *adj.* having two (optic, etc.) axes. — Also **biax'al.** [L. *bi-*, and **axial.**]

bib *bib*, *n.* a cloth or plastic shield put under a child's chin: of an apron, overalls, etc., the front part above the waist: a vest bearing their number worn by competition skiers, etc.: the pout, a fish of the cod and haddock genus with a large chin barbel. — *v.t.* and *v.i.* to drink, to tipple. — *adj.* **bibā'cious.** — *ns.* **bibā'tion** tippling; **bibb'er** a tippler: chiefly used in composition as *(B.) wine-bibber;* **bib'ful** see **spill a bibful** below. — **bib'cock** a tap with down-turned nozzle. — **best bib and tucker** best clothes; **spill a bibful** *(slang)* to give away a secret, make an embarrassing revelation.

[Prob. from L. *bibēre*, to drink; perh. partly imit.]

bibble-babble *bib'l-bab'l*, *(Shak.) n.* idle talk. [Reduplication of **babble.**]

Bibby *bib'i*, *n.* in a ship, a stateroom on a passageway. [Name of shipping line.]

bibelot *bēb'lō*, *n.* a knick-knack. [Fr.]

Bible *bī'bl*, *n.* (also **bible**) the Scriptures of the Old and New Testaments: (also **bible**) a big or authoritative book: (without *cap.*) the third stomach of a ruminant, with many folds like the leaves of a book. — *adj.* **biblical** *(bib'li-kəl)* of, like or relating to the Bible. — *adv.* **bib'lically.** — *ns.* **bib'licism** *(-sizm)* biblical doctrine, learning, or literature: literal acceptance of the Bible; **bib'licist, bib'list** one versed in biblical learning: one who makes the Bible the sole rule of faith: one who adheres to its letter. — **Bible belt** those areas of the Southern U.S.A. of predominantly fundamentalist and puritanical religion; **Bible paper** very thin strong paper for printing; **Bi'ble-pound'er**, **-thump'er** a vigorous, aggressive or dogmatic preacher; **Bī'ble-pounding**, **-thumping.** — Also *adjs.* [Fr., — L.L. *biblia*, fem. sing., earlier neut. pl., from Gr. *biblia*, books, esp. the canonical books (sing. *biblion*, a book, dim. of *biblos*, papyrus, paper).]

bibli- *bib'li-*, in composition, book. — *n.* **bibliographer** *(-og'rə-fər)* versed in bibliography: the compiler of a bibliography. — *adjs.* **bibliographic** *(-ə-graf'ik)*, **-al.** — *ns.* **bibliog'raphy** study, description or knowledge of books, in regard to their outward form, authors, subjects, editions, and history: a descriptive list of books: a book containing such a list; **bibliolater** *(-ol'ə-tər)*, **bibliol'atrist** one given to bibliolatry. — *adj.* **bibliol'atrous.** — *n.* **bibliol'atry** (Gr. *latreiā*, worship) a superstitious reverence for a book, esp. the Bible. — *adj.* **bibliological** *(-ō-loj'i-kəl).* — *ns.* **bibliologist** *(-ol'ə-jist);* **bibliol'ogy** bibliography: book-lore; **bib'liomancy** *(-man-si;* Gr. *manteiā*, divination) divination by opening the Bible or other book at random; **bib'liomane;** **bibliomā'nia** (Gr. *maniā*, madness) a mania for collecting or possessing books: love of books; **bibliomā'niac.** — *adjs.* **bibliomaniacal** *(-mə-nī'ə-kəl);* **bibliopegic** *(-pej'-ik;* Gr. *pēgnynai*, to fix). — *ns.* **bibliopegist** *(-op'l-jist)* a bookbinder: a fancier of bindings; **bibliop'egy** the fine art of bookbinding; **bibliophagist** *(-of'ə-jist;* Gr. *phagein* to eat) a voracious reader; **bib'liophil(e)** *(-fil, -fīl;* Gr. *philos*, friend) a lover or collector of books. — Also *adj.* — *ns.* **bibliophilism; bibliophilist; bibliophi'ly; bibliophō'bia** (Gr. *phobein*, to fear) hatred of books; **bib'liopole** (Gr. *pōlēs*, seller) a bookseller. — *adjs.* **bibliopolic** *(-pol'ik)*, **-al.** — *ns.* **bibliop'olist; bibliop'oly** bookselling; **bibliothē'ca** (Gr. *bibliothēkē — thēkē, repository) a library; a bibliography: a series of books; **biblioth'ecary** *(rare)* a librarian. [Gr. *biblion*, book; cf. **Bible.**]

bibulous *bib'ū'ləs*, *adj.* drinking or sucking in: spongy: addicted to strong drink. — *adv.* **bib'ulously.** — *n.* **bib'ulousness.** [L. *bibulus — bibēre*, to drink.]

bicameral *bī-kam'ər-əl*, *adj.* having two chambers. — *n.* **bicam'eralist** an advocate of the bicameral parliamentary system. [L. *bi*, twice, and *camera*, chamber.]

bicarbonate *bī-kär'bən-āt*, *n.* an acid salt of carbonic acid: sodium bicarbonate, used in baking-powder or as an antacid *(coll.* contraction **bicarb'**). [L. *bi-*, twice, and **carbonate.**]

bice *bīs*, *n.* a pale blue or green paint. [Fr. *bis.*]

bicentenary *bi-sen-tēn'ər-i*, or *-ten'*, or *-sen'*, *adj.* pertaining to two hundred (years). — *n.* a bicentennial. [L. *bi-*, twice, *centēnārius*, pertaining to a hundred — *centum*, a hundred.]

bicentennial *bi-sen-ten'yəl*, *adj.* pertaining to two hundred years. — *n.* a two hundredth anniversary. [L. *bi*, twice, *centum*, a hundred, *annus*, a year.]

biceps *bī'seps*, *n.* a two-headed muscle: esp. one in front of the upper arm or one on the back of the thigh. — *adj.* **bicipital** *(-sip')* two-headed. [L. *biceps*, two-headed — *bis*, twice, and *caput*, head.]

bichord *bī'körd*, *adj.* of a musical instrument, having paired strings in unison for each note. [L. *bi-*, twice, and **chord**.]

bichromate *bī-krō'māt, n.* a dichromate, or salt of dichromic acid. [L. *bi-*, twice, and **chromate**.]

bicipital. See **biceps**.

bicker[1] *bik'ər, v.i.* to contend in a petty way: to quiver: to glitter: to brawl, as running water: to patter. — *n.* a fight, a quarrel, esp. (*Scot.*) a street or school encounter: a clattering noise: a strife (*Scot.*). [Poss. a freq. conn. with **beak**.]

bicker[2] *bik'ər, n.* a bowl, esp. of wood, for holding liquor: a vessel of wooden staves for porridge. [Scot. form of **beaker**.]

bick-iron *bik'ī-ərn, n.* a small anvil with one horn: the tapered end of an anvil. [From earlier *bickern*, a two-horned anvil — Fr. *bigorne* — L. *bicornis*, two-horned.]

biconcave *bī-kon'kāv, adj.* concave on both sides. [L. *bi-*, twice, and **concave**.]

biconvex *bī-kon'veks, adj.* convex on both sides. [L. *bi-*, twice, and **convex**.]

bicorporate *bī-kör'pər-āt,* (*her.*) *adj.* double-bodied, as the head of a lion to which two bodies are attached. [L. *bi-*, twice, and **corporate**.]

bicultural *bī-cul'chə-rəl, adj.* of, having, containing or consisting of, two distinct cultures. — *n.* **bicul'turalism**. [**bi-** and **cultural**.]

bicuspid *bī-kus'pid, adj.* having two cusps. — *n.* a premolar tooth. — *adj.* **bicusp'idate**. [L. *bi-*, twice, and **cusp**.]

bicycle *bī'si-kl, n.* a vehicle with two wheels, one before the other, driven by pedals or a motor. — *v.i.* to ride a bicycle. — *n.* **bī'cyclist**. — **bicycle chain** the chain transmitting motion from the pedals to the wheels of a bicycle; **bicycle clip** a metal clip for holding a cyclist's trousers closely to his leg; **bicycle polo** see **polo**[1]; **bicycle pump** a hand pump for inflating bicycle tyres. [L. *bi-*, twice, Gr. *kyklos*, a circle, wheel.]

bid[1] *bid, v.t.* to offer: to propose: to proclaim, as the banns of marriage: to command: to invite (*arch.*): to offer to pay at an auction: to call (in card games). — *v.i.* to make an offer or venture: — *pr.p.* **bidd'ing**; *pa.t.* **bade** (*bad*; also, as in the poets, *bād*), **bid**; *pa.p.* **bidd'en**, **bid**. — *n.* an offer of a price: a venturesome attempt or proposal: a call (at cards). — *adj.* **bidd'able** tractable. — *ns.* **bidd'er**; **bidd'ing** offer: command: calling. — **bid fair** to seem likely; **bid in** (of owner or his agent) in an auction, to overbid the highest offer; **bid up** to raise the market price of artificially, by means of specious bids, etc.. [O.E. *bēodan*; Goth. *biudan*, Ger. *bieten*, to offer.]

bid[2] *bid, v.t.* to ask for (*arch.*): to invite: to command: to pray (*obs.*): hence to salute with, say as a greeting: — Tenses are as in the preceding verb, with which it has been confused. — **bidd'ing-pray'er** originally the praying, or saying, of a prayer, then by confusion with the foregoing word taken to mean enjoining or inviting of prayer. [O.E. *biddan*; Goth. *bidjan*; Ger. *bitten*. See **bead**.]

biddy *bid'i, n.* a fowl (*dial.*), in *Shak.* applied to Malvolio: an old woman (*slang, derog.*). — **red biddy** see **red**. [Poss. the woman's name *Biddy* for *Bridget*.]

bide *bīd, v.i.* (*arch.* and *Scot.*) to wait: to dwell: to remain. — *v.t.* to await (*obs.* except in sense of *bide one's time*, to await a favourable moment): to face unshrinkingly (*poet.*): to endure: — *pa.t.* **bīd'ed, bode**, (*Shak.*) **bid**, (*Scot.*) **bade** (*bād*); *pa.p.* **bīd'ed**, (*obs.* and *Scot.*) **bidd'en**. — *n.* **bīd'ing** (*Shak.*) residence, habitation. — **bī'die-in** (*Scot., coll.*) a resident lover. [O.E. *bīdan*; but sometimes for **abide**.]

bident *bī'dənt, n.* a two-pronged tool: a two-year-old sheep. — *adj.* **bidental** (*bī-dent'l*) two-pronged: two-toothed. — *n.* a place struck by lightning (possibly consecrated by the Romans by sacrifice of a sheep). — *adjs.* **bīdent'ate, -d** two-toothed. [L. *bi-*, twice, *dēns, dentis*, a tooth.]

bidet *bē-dā, bi-det', n.* a nag: a bestridable basin on a low pedestal, for washing the genital and anal areas, etc. [Fr., pony.]

bi-directional *bī-dī-rek'shə-nəl, adj.* operating in two directions: printing the lines of a text snake-fashion, i.e. alternately left to right and right to left (*comput.* etc.).

bidon *bē'dō, n.* a vessel for holding liquids, as a wooden cup, water bottle, tin can or oil drum. — *n.* **bidonville** (*bē'don-vēl, bē-dō-*) in a French-speaking country, a shanty town with dwellings made from oil drums. [Fr.]

Biedermeier *bē'dər-mī-ər, adj.* of a style of furniture derived from the French empire style, common in Germany in the first half of the 19th cent.: (of German painting) of the Romantic Revival: bourgeois, hidebound (*derog.*). [Name of a fictitious German poet.]

bield *bēld,* (chiefly *Scot.*) *n.* shelter: protection. — *adj.* **bield'y**. [Northern; O.E. *beldo* (W.S. *bieldo*), courage, cf. **bold**.]

bien[1]. Another spelling of **bein**.

bien[2] *byẽ,* (Fr.) *adv.* well. — **bien-aimé** (*byẽ-ne-mā*) well-beloved; **bien chaussé** (*shō-sā*) well-shod; **bien élevé** (*-nā-ləv-ā*) well brought up, well mannered; **bien entendu** (*-nä-tä-dü*) of course: well designed: well versed: on condition; **bien-être** (*-netr*) a sense of well-being; **bien pensant** (*pä-sä*) right-thinking: orthodox; **bienséance** (*-sā-äs*) propriety: (in *pl.*) the proprieties.

biennial *bī-en'i-əl, -en'yəl, adj.* lasting two years: happening or appearing once in two years. — *n.* a plant that flowers and fructifies only in its second year, then dies. — *adv.* **bienn'ially**. [L. *biennium*, two years — *bi-*, twice, and *annus*, a year.]

bier *bēr, n.* a carriage or frame of wood for bearing the dead to the grave. — **bier right** (*hist.*) ordeal of appearing before a corpse believed murdered (expected to bleed in presence of murderer). [O.E. *bǣr*; Ger. *Bahre*, L. *feretrum*. From root of verb **bear**.]

bierkeller *bēr'kel-ər, n.* a German bar, selling beer. [Ger., beer cellar.]

biestings. Same as **beestings**.

bifacial *bī-fā'shl, adj.* two-faced: having two unlike sides. [L. *bi-*, twice, and **facial**.]

bifarious *bī-fā'ri-əs, adj.* double: in two rows. [L. *bifārius*, double.]

biff *bif,* (*coll.*) *n.* a blow. — *v.t.* to strike hard.

biffin *bif'in, n.* a variety of apple: such an apple slowly dried and flattened into a cake. [For *beefing*, from its colour of raw beef.]

bifid *bif'id, bī'fid, adj.* cleft in two. [L. *bifidus* — *bi-*, twice, and *findēre*, to cleave or split.]

bifilar *bī-fī'lər, adj.* having two threads. [L. *bi-*, twice, *fīlum*, thread.]

bifocal *bī-fō'kəl, adj.* composed of parts of different focal lengths. — *n.pl.* **bifo'cals** spectacles with bifocal lenses, for far and for near vision. [L. *bi-*, twice, and **focal**.]

bifold *bī'fōld, adj.* twofold: of two kinds (*Shak.*). [L. *bi-*, twice, and **fold**.]

bifoliate *bī-fō'li-āt, adj.* having two leaves or leaflets. — *adj.* **bifo'liolate** having two leaflets. [L. *bi-*, twice, *folium*, leaf.]

biform *bī'förm, adj.* having two forms. [L. *biformis* — *bi-*, twice, and *fōrma*, form.]

bifurcate *bī'fûr-kāt,* or *-fûr', adj.* two-forked; having two prongs or branches. — *v.i.* to divide into two branches. — *n.* **bifurca'tion** a forking or division into two branches. — *adj.* **bī'furcated**. [L. *bifurcus* — *bi-, bis*, twice, *furca*, a fork.]

big[1] *big, adj.* (*compar.* **bigg'er**; *superl.* **bigg'est** large or great: pregnant: grown up: older (as in *big sister, big brother*): magnanimous: great in air, mien, or spirit: loud: pompous: very important, as the *Big Three, Big Four*, etc., leaders, countries, organisations, etc. — *adv.* (*coll.*) boastfully or ambitiously, as in *talk big*: greatly or impressively. — *adj.* **bigg'ish**. — *ns.* **bigg'y, bigg'ie** (*coll.*) a large or important person or thing; **big'ness** bulk, size. — **Big Bang** the explosion of a small dense mass which some scientists believe to have been the origin of the universe: (also without *cap.*) the changes in the system and rules of the British Stock Exchange instituted on 27 October 1986, in effect de-regulating many of its practices and abolishing the distinction between jobbers and brokers. — **big′-bell′ied** having a big belly: pregnant (with). — **Big Brother** a dictator, as in George Orwell's *Nineteen Eighty-four* (1949): a powerful leader or organisation, perceived as ubiquitous and sinister; **Big Brotherism**; **big′-bud′** a swelling of currant buds owing to a gall-mite; **big business** large business enterprises and organisations, esp. collectively; **Big C** (*coll.*) cancer; **big cat** see **cat**; **big deal** (*coll.*) used as a scornful response to an offer, boast, etc.; **big Daddy** (*coll.*) a paternalistic or domineering head of an organisation, etc.; **big dipper** a switchback at a fair (orig. *U.S.*): (with *caps.*) the constellation Great Bear (*U.S.*); **big end** in an internal-combustion engine, the larger end of the connecting rod; **Big-endian** see **Little-endian** under **little**; **big fish** a powerful person, esp. one in a criminal organisation thought worthy of capture; **big guns** (*coll.*) the important persons in an organisation, etc.; **big′-head** (*coll.*) a swelled-headed person: conceit. — *adj.* **big′headed.** — **big′horn** the Rocky Mountain goat or sheep; **big house** prison (*slang*): the house of the local landowner, a wealthy citizen, or the like (*Scot.*); **big money** money in very large sums; **big mouth** (*slang*) a talkative and boastful person. — *adj.* **big′-mouthed′.** — **big name** (*coll.*) a celebrity; **big noise** (*coll.*) an important person. — *v.t.* **big′-note** (*Austr. coll.*) to promote or vaunt oneself. — **big science** scientific and technical research that requires large financial resources; **big shot** see **bigwig** below; **big stick** (*coll.*) a display of power; **big′-time** the top level in any pursuit. — *adj.* at the top level: important. — **big toe** see **toe**; **big top** a large circular tent used for circus performances; **big wheel** a Ferris wheel; **big′wig, big shot** (*coll.*) a leading man, a person of some importance. — **go over big (with)** (*coll.*) to have a great effect (on): to impress greatly; **in a big way** vigorously, enthusiastically; **that's big of him** etc. (usu. *iron.*) that action, etc. is generous on his, etc. part; **the Big Apple** (*coll.*) New York City; **too big for one's boots** conceited, self-important. [M.E. *big*; origin obscure.]

big² *big*, (*Scot.*) *v.t.* to build, to pile up. — *n.* **bigg′in** anything built, a house. [O.N. *byggja*, O.E. *būian.*]

biga *bī′gə, bē′ga*, (L.) *n.* a two-horse chariot (in L. earlier in *pl.* form **bigae** *bī′jē, bē′gī* — *bi-, jugum*, yoke).

bigamy *big′ə-mi, n.* the custom, crime, or fact of having two legal, or supposed, wives or husbands at once: a second marriage (*eccl. law*). — *n.* **big′amist** one who has committed bigamy. — *adj.* **big′amous.** — *adv.* **big′amously.** [L. *bi-*, twice; Gr. *gamos*, marriage.]

bigener *bī′jin-ər, n.* a hybrid between different genera. — *adj.* **bigeneric** (*-er′ik*). [L. *bīgĕner*, a hybrid.]

bigg *big, n.* four-rowed barley. [O.N. *bygg.*]

biggin¹ *big′in*, (*arch.*) *n.* a child's cap or hood: a nightcap: a serjeant-at-law's coif. [Fr. *béguin*, from béguine's cap.]

biggin². See **big².**

bigha *bē′ga, n.* a land measure in India, ⅓ to ⅔ of an acre. [Hindi.]

bight *bīt, n.* wide bay: a bend or coil. [O.E. *byht*; cf. Dan. and Sw. *bugt*, Du. *bocht.*]

Bignonia *big-nō′ni-ə, n.* a genus of tropical plants with trumpet-shaped flowers, giving name to the family **Bignoniā′ceae.** — *adj.* **bignoniā′ceous.** [Named after the Abbé *Bignon*, Louis XIV's librarian.]

bigot *big′ət, n.* one blindly and obstinately devoted to a particular creed or party. — *adj.* **big′oted** having the qualities of a bigot. — *n.* **big′otry** blind or excessive zeal, esp. in religious matters. [O.Fr.; origin disputed.]

bijection *bī-jek′shən*, (*math.*) *n.* a mapping function that is both an injection and a surjection. [*bi-*, and *-jection* from L. *-jicere*, to throw.]

bijou *bē′zhoo, n.* a trinket: a jewel: a little box: — *pl.* **bijoux** (*bē′zhooz*). — *adj.* small and elegant. — *n.*

bijouterie (*bē-zhoot′ər-ē*) jewellery, esp. trinkets. [Fr.]

bijwoner. Same as **bywoner.**

bike¹, byke *bīk*, (*Scot.*) *n.* a nest of wasps, wild bees, etc.: a swarm of people. — *v.i.* to swarm. [Origin unknown.]

bike² *bīk, n.* and *v.i.* coll. for **bicycle.** — *ns.* **bī′ker; bī′kie** (*Austr.* and *N.Z. coll.*) a member of a gang of motorcycle riders; **bī′king.** — **get off one's bike** (*Austr. slang*) to lose control of oneself; **on your bike** (*slang*) a contemptuous expression of dismissal.

bikini *bi-kē′ni, n.* a much reduced bathing-dress, in two parts, introduced early in the 1950s. [Said to be from *Bikini*, an atoll of the Marshall Islands, scene of atom-bomb experiments.]

bilabial *bī-lā′bi-əl, adj.* two-lipped: produced by contact or approximation of the two lips, as the sound of b, w, (*phon.*). — *n.* a bilabial consonant. — *adj.* **bīlā′biate** two-lipped, as some corollas. [L. *bi-*, twice, and *labium*, a lip.]

bilander *bī′land-ər, n.* a two-masted hoy, having her mainsail bent to the whole length of her yard, hanging fore and aft, and inclined to the horizontal at an angle of about 45°. — Also **by′lander.** [Du. *bijlander.*]

bilateral *bī-lat′ər-əl, adj.* having or involving two sides: affecting two parties or participants reciprocally. — *n.* **bilat′eralism** two-sidedness: equality in value of trade between two countries. — *adv.* **bilat′erally.** [L. *bi-*, twice, *latus, -eris*, side.]

bilberry *bil′bər-i, n.* a whortleberry or blaeberry shrub: its dark blue berry. [Cf. Dan. *böllebær.*]

bilbo *bil′bō, n.* a rapier or sword: — *pl.* **bil′boes, -os.** [From *Bilbao*, in Spain.]

bilboes *bil′bōz, n.pl.* a bar with sliding shackles. [Perh. connected with the foregoing.]

Bildungsroman *bil′dŏŏngs-rō-män′, -dŏŏngz-*, (Ger.) *n.* a novel concerning the early emotional or spiritual development or education of its hero.

bile *bīl, n.* a thick bitter fluid secreted by the liver — yellow in man and carnivorous animals, green in vegetable feeders: derangement of its secretion: ill-humour (*fig.*). — *adj.* **biliary** (*bil′yər-i*) of the bile, the bile ducts or the gall-bladder. — *n.* short for **biliary fever**, infectious canine jaundice. — *adj.* **bilious** (*bil′yəs*) pertaining to or affected by bile. — *adv.* **bil′iously.** — *n.* **bil′iousness.** — **bile′-ducts** the ducts that convey the bile to the small intestine. [Fr., — L. *bīlis.*]

bilge *bilj, n.* the bulging part of a cask: the broadest part of a ship's bottom: filth such as collects there: piffle (*slang*). — *v.i.* to spring a leak by a fracture in the bilge, as a ship. — *adj.* **bilg′y** having the appearance and disagreeable smell of bilge-water. — **bilge′-keel** a ridge along the turn of the bilge of a ship to check rolling; **bilge′-pump; bilge′-wat′er.** [Perh. **bulge**.]

Bilharzia *bil-här′zi-ə, -tsi-ə, n.* a genus of trematode worms parasitic in human and other blood with two larval stages, first in water-snails and then in man. — *ns.* **bilharz′ia, bilharzī′asis, bilharziō′sis** a disease caused by it, common in tropical countries, esp. Egypt and other parts of Africa (also known as schistosomiasis). [From the helminthologist, Theodor *Bilharz* (1825–62).]

bilian *bil′i-an, n.* a heavy ant-proof lauraceous timber tree of Borneo. [Malay.]

biliary. See **bile.**

bilimbi *bil-im′bi, n.* an East Indian tree of the wood-sorrel family: its acid fruit. — Also **bilim′bing, blim′bing.** [Dravidian and Malay.]

bilingual *bī-ling′gwəl, adj.* expressed in two languages: speaking two languages, esp. native or habitual languages. — *ns.* **bīling′ualism; bīling′uist.** [L. *bilinguis* — *bi-*, twice, *lingua*, tongue.]

bilious. See **bile.**

bilirubin *bil-i-rōō′bin, n.* a reddish pigment in bile. — *n.* **biliver′din** a green pigment in bile. [L. *bīlis*, bile, *ruber*, red, Fr. *verd*, green.]

biliteral *bī-lit′ər-əl, adj.* of or involving two letters: written

in two scripts. [L. *bi-*, twice, *lītera, littera*, a letter.]
biliverdin. See **bilirubin.**

bilk *bilk, v.t.* to elude: to cheat: to avoid paying what is due. — *n.* **bilk′er.** [Perh. a form of **balk**; at first a term in cribbage.]

bill[1] *bil, n.* a concave battle-axe with a long wooden handle: a kind of hatchet with a long blade and wooden handle in the same line with it, often with a hooked point, used in cutting thorn hedges or in pruning. — **bill′hook** a bill or hatchet with curved point; **bill′man** a soldier armed with a bill. [O.E. *bil*; Ger. *Bille*.]

bill[2] *bil, n.* the beak of a bird, or anything like it: a sharp promontory: the point of an anchor fluke. — *v.i.* to join bills as doves: to caress fondly. — *adj.* **billed** having a bill. — *n.* and *adj.* **bill′ing.** — **bill′board** a board used to protect the planking from injury by the bill when the anchor is weighed. [O.E. *bile*, prob. same as **bill**[1].]

bill[3] *bil, n.* an account of money: a draft of a proposed law: a written engagement to pay a sum of money at a fixed date: a bank-note (*U.S.*): a placard: a slip of paper serving as an advertisement: a list of performers, etc. in order of importance: a programme of entertainment: any written statement of particulars: a written accusation of serious crime (*Eng. criminal law*). — *v.t.* to announce or advertise by bill: to send an invoice (to). — *adj.* **billed** (*bild*) named in a list or advertisement. — *n.* **bill′ing** the making out or sending of bills or invoices: total amount of money received from customers or clients: advertising: naming in an announcement or poster. — **bill′board** a board on which placards are posted; **bill′book** a book used in commerce in which an entry is made of all bills accepted and received; **bill′-broker** one who deals in bills of exchange and promissory notes; **bill′-chamber** a department of the Scottish Court of Session dealing with summary business — so called because formerly both summonses and diligence or execution were usually commenced by a writ called a bill; **bill′-discounter** one who discounts or advances the amount of bills of exchange and notes which have some time to run; **bill′fold** (*U.S.*) a note-case; **bill′head** a form used for business accounts, with name and address printed at the top; **bill′poster, bill′sticker** one who sticks or posts up bills or placards. — **bill of adventure** a writing by a merchant stating that goods shipped by him, and in his name, are the property of another, whose adventure or chance the transaction is; **bill of costs** an account of a solicitor's charges and disbursements in the conduct of his client's business; **bill of exceptions** a statement of objections, by way of appeal against the ruling of a judge who is trying a case with a jury in the Court of Session; **bill of exchange** a document purporting to be an instrument of pecuniary obligation for value received, employed for the purpose of settling a debt in a manner convenient to the parties concerned; **bill of fare** a list of dishes or articles of food; **bill of health** an official certificate of the state of health on board ship before sailing (**clean bill of health** a certificate stating that there is no illness on board: proof that a person is healthy: proof that an organisation, etc. is in a good condition (*fig.*); **bill of indictment** a statement of a charge made against a person; **bill of lading** a paper signed by the master of a ship, by which he makes himself responsible for the safe delivery of the goods specified therein: a certificate stating that specified goods are aboard a vessel; **bill of mortality** (*hist.*) an official return of births and deaths — hence **within the bills of mortality**, within the London district for which such returns were made; **bill of rights** see **right**[1]; **bill of sale** in English law, a formal deed assigning personal property; **bill of sight** an entry of imported goods of which the merchant does not know the quantity or the quality; **bill of store** a licence from the customs authorities to reimport British goods formerly exported; **bill of victualling** a list of necessary stores shipped from the bonded warehouse, or for drawback on board vessels proceeding on oversea voyages; **double, triple**

bill a programme of entertainment consisting of two, three main items; **fill the bill** see **fill**[1]; **top the bill** to head the list of performers, to be the star attraction. [L.L. *billa* — L. *bulla*, a knob, a seal, hence a document bearing a seal, etc.; cf. **bull**[2].]

billabong *bil′ə-bong*, (*Austr.*) *n.* a cut-off loop of a river, replenished only by floods: an effluent from a river (strictly one that does not rejoin). [Aboriginal *billa*, river, *bung*, dead.]

billboard. See **bill**[2,3].

billet[1] *bil′it, n.* a little note or paper: a ticket assigning quarters to soldiers or others: quarters requisitioned: a destined resting-place: a post or occupation. — *v.t.* to quarter or lodge, as soldiers: — *pr.p.* **bill′eting;** *pa.t.* and *pa.p.* **bill′eted.** [O.Fr. *billette*, dim. of *bille*; see **bill**[3].]

billet[2] *bil′it, n.* a small log of wood used as fuel: a piece of timber sawn on three sides and rounded on the fourth: a bar of metal: an ornament in Norman architecture in the form of short cylinders with spaces between: a bearing in the form of an upright rectangle (*her.*). — **bill′et-head** a piece of wood round which the harpoon-line is turned. [Fr. *billette* — *bille*, the young stock of a tree; orig. unknown.]

billet-doux *bil-i-dōō′, n.* a love-letter: — *pl.* **billets-doux′** (same pron. as *sing.*). [Fr. *billet*, letter, *doux*, sweet.]

billiards *bil′yərdz, n. sing.* any of various games played with a cue and balls on a rectangular table, the table in one version having pockets at the sides and corners, into which the balls can be struck. — *adj.* **bill′iard.** — **bill′iard-ball; bill′iard-cloth** a green cloth for covering a billiard-table; **bill′iard-marker** a person who marks the points made by the players; **bill′iard-table.** [Fr. *billard* — *bille*, a stick, hence a cue.]

billie. See **billy.**

billingsgate *bil′ingz-gāt, n.* foul and abusive language like that once familiar to the ear at *Billingsgate* (the former London fish-market).

Billings method *bil′ingz meth′əd,* a rhythm method of contraception involving the examination of the discharge from the cervix. [Dr Evelyn *Billings*, an Australian physician.]

billion *bil′yən, n.* in Britain, France (since 1948), etc., a million millions (unit and twelve ciphers): in U.S., often now in Britain, one thousand millions (unit and nine ciphers), a milliard. — *n.* **billionaire′.** — *adj., n.* **bill′ionth.** [bi-, million.]

billon *bil′ən, n.* base metal: esp. an alloy of silver with copper, tin, or the like. [Fr., from same root as **billet**[2].]

billow *bil′ō, n.* a great wave: a wave, the sea (*poet.*). — *v.i.* to roll or swell in great waves: to bulge flowingly. — *adj.* **bill′owed; bill′owing; bill′owy.** [App. O.N. *bylgja*; Sw. *bölja*, Dan. *bölge*, wave.]

billy, billie *bil′i, n.* a brother (*Scot.*): a comrade, a companion-in-arms (*Scot.*): a cylindrical container for boiling water, cooking, etc. (*Austr.* and *N.Z.*; also **bill′y-can**): a truncheon (*U.S.*): — *pl.* **bill′ies.** — **bill′y-goat** a he-goat. [Prob. from *Bill*, a familiar abbrev. of *William*.]

billyboy *bil′i-boi, n.* a bluff-bowed one-masted trading-vessel. [Prob. conn. with **bilander**.]

Billy Bunter *bil′i bun′tər,* the type of a fat and ridiculous schoolboy. [Name of a character in stories by Frank Richards (pseudonym of Charles Hamilton, 1875–1961).]

billy-can. See **billy.**

billycock *bil′i-kok, n.* a hard felt hat. [Poss. from *William Coke*, nephew of Earl (1837) of Leicester, or from 19th-cent. Cornish hatter *William Cock*.]

billy-o(h) *bil′i-ō, n.* in phrase **like billy-o(h)** vigorously, fiercely. [Origin obscure.]

bilobar *bī-lō′bər,* **bilobate** *bī-lō′bāt,* **bilobed** *bī′lōbd,* adjs. having two lobes. — *adj.* **bilobular** (*bī-lob′ū-lər*) having two lobules. [L. *bi-*, twice, and **lobe, lobule**.]

bilocation *bī-lō-kā′shən, n.* the power of being in two places at the same time. [Coined from *bi-*, twice, and **location**.]

bilocular *bī-lok'ū-lər, adj.* divided into two cells. [L. *bi-*, twice, *loculus*, dim. of *locus*, place.]

biltong *bil'tong* (*S. Afr.*) *n.* sun-dried lean meat. [Du. *bil*, buttock, *tong*, tongue.]

Bim *bim*, (*slang*) *n.* an inhabitant of Barbados.

Bimana *bim'ə-nə, bī-mā'nə, n.pl.* two-handed animals, an obsolete name for mankind. — *adjs.* **bim'anal**, **bim'-anous**. [L. *bi-*, twice, *manus*, hand.]

bimbashi *bim-bä'shē, n.* a military officer (in Turkey or Egypt). [Turk. *bin*, thousand, *baş*, head.]

bimbo *bim'bō*, (*slang*) *n.* a woman, esp. one attractive but dim, naive or superficial: a youngster: — *pl.* **bim'bos**. [It., child.]

bimestrial *bī-mes'tri-əl, adj.* of two months' duration. [L. *bimestris* — *bi-*, and *mēnsis*, a month.]

bimetallic *bī-mi-tal'ik, adj.* composed of, or using, two metals: of a monetary system, in which gold and silver are on precisely the same footing as regards mintage and legal tender. — *n.* **bimetallism** (*bī-met'əl-izm*) such a system. — *n.* and *adj.* **bimet'allist**. — **bimetallic strip** a strip, formed by bonding two metals one of which expands more than the other, which bends with change of temperature, used in thermostatic switches, etc.

bimillenary *bī-mil'in-ər-i, n.* a period of two thousand years: two thousandth anniversary. — Also *adj.* [L. *bi-*, twice, **millenary**.]

bimillennium *bī-mil-en'i-əm, n.* Same as **bimillenary**. [L. *bi-*, twice, **millennium**.]

bimonthly *bī-munth'li, adj., adv.* (happening, etc.) once in two months: also twice a month. [L. *bi-*, two, and **month**.]

bin¹ *bin, n.* a receptacle for storing e.g. corn: a receptacle for rubbish: a stand or case with compartments in which to store bottled wine in a wine-cellar: the wine contained therein: a lunatic asylum (*slang*): gaol (*slang*): a pocket (*slang*). — *v.t.* to put (e.g. bottled wine) into a bin: — *pr.p.* **binn'ing**; *pa.t.* and *pa.p.* **binned**. — **bin'-liner** a usu. plastic bag for lining a rubbish bin. [O.E. *binn*, a manger.]

bin² *bin*, (*Shak.*) used for **be** and **been**.

bin-. See **bi-**.

binary *bī'nər-i, adj.* composed of two: twofold. — *n.* binary system, star. — *adj.* **bī'nate** growing in pairs: double: consisting of two leaflets. — **binary fission** (*biol.*) division of an organism or cell into two parts; **binary form** (*mus.*) a form of movement founded on two themes; **binary operation** in math., combining two elements in a collection of elements in such a way as to give another element from the same collection (as addition or multiplication in the ordinary number system); **binary pulsar** (*astron.*) a system consisting of a pulsar and a small companion star rotating round each other; **binary scale** the scale of notation whose radix or base is 2 (instead of 10); **binary star** binary system; **binary system** two stars revolving about their centre of gravity (also **binary star**): system using the binary scale of notation: system in which numbers are expressed by using two digits only, viz. 1 and 0; **binary weapon**, **munition** a bomb or shell loaded with two separate canisters of non-toxic chemicals, the chemicals combining at the time of firing to produce a lethal gas. [L. *bīnārius* — *bīnī*, two by two, *bis*, twice.]

binaural *bin-ö'rəl, adj.* having, employing, or relating to two ears: of reproduction of sound, using two sound channels. — *adv.* **binaur'ally**. — **binaural effect** the ability to tell the direction from which a sound is coming, arising from the difference in arrival times of the sound at a person's two ears. [L. *bīnī*, two by two, *auris*, ear.]

Binca® *bing'kə, n.* an open-weave canvas fabric used for embroidery, etc.

bind *bīnd, v.t.* to tie or fasten together with a band: to encircle round: to restrain: to fix: to make fast: to sew a border on: to tie up or bandage: to fasten together and put a cover on (a book): to impose an obligation

upon: to oblige by oath or promise: to indenture: to hold or cement firmly: to cause (dry ingredients) to cohere by adding a small amount of liquid (*cook.*): to render hard: to constipate. — *v.i.* to become bound: to complain (*slang*): — *pa.t.* and *pa.p.* **bound** (*bownd*). — *n.* a stalk of hop or other twiner: the indurated clay of coal-mines: in music, the tie for indicating that a note is to be held on, not repeated (of the same form as the slur or legato mark): capacity, measure (*Scot.*): a difficult or annoying situation, a bore (*slang*). — *ns.* **bind'er** one who binds (books, sheaves, etc.): anything that binds, as a rope, a bandage, a cementing agent, a tie-beam, a header in masonry, a case for binding loose papers: an attachment to a reaping-machine for tying the bundles of grain cut and thrown off: a reaping-machine provided with one; **bind'ery** a bookbinder's establishment. — *adj.* **bind'ing** restraining: obligatory. — *n.* the act of one who binds: anything that binds: the covering of a book. — **bind'weed** convolvulus: also (**black bindweed**) a species of *Polygonum*. — **be bound up in** to be wholly devoted to; **bind over** to subject to legal obligation; **I dare or will be bound** I will be responsible for the statement. See also **bound¹** and **bounden**. [O.E. *bindan*; Ger. *binden*, Sans. *badhnōti*, he binds.]

bindi-eye *bin'dī-ī, n.* an Australian herbaceous plant, esp. of the genus *Calotis*, having burr-like fruits. [Aboriginal.]

bine *bīn, n.* the slender stem of a climbing plant: a flexible shoot. [Orig. dial. form of **bind**.]

binervate *bī-nûrv'āt, adj.* with two ribs or nerves. [L. *bi-*, twice, and **nerve**.]

bing¹ *bing*, (*dial.*) *n.* a heap or pile (esp. of waste from a coal-mine): a bin. [O.N. *bingr*.]

bing² *bing*, (*obs. slang; Scott*) *v.i.* to go.

binge *binj, binzh, v.t.* and *v.i.* to soak (*dial.*). — *v.i.* to drink deep: to overeat (*coll.*). — *n.* a spree (*coll.*): a banquet, feast (*facet.*): a bout of indulgence esp. in overeating (*coll.*). — *n.* **bin'ger**.

bingle *bing'gl, n.* a hairstyle midway between bob and shingle. — Also *v.t.*

bingo¹ *bing'gō, n.* a familiar name for brandy. [Prob. B, for **brandy**, and **stingo**.]

bingo² *bing'gō, n.* a form of lotto in which, usu., the numbers in all the lines must be covered. — *interj.* the exclamation made by the first player to finish in this game: an exclamation expressing suddenness, unexpectedness, etc.: — *pl.* **bing'os**. [Orig. uncertain.]

bink *bingk*, (*Scot.*) *n.* a bench, a bank, a shelf: a plate-rack: a wasp's or bee's nest: a small heap of mortar. [Northern form of **bench**.]

binnacle *bin'ə-kl*, (*naut.*) *n.* the box in which a ship's compass is kept. [Formerly *bittacle* — Port. *bitácola* — L. *habitāculum*, a dwelling-place — *habitāre*, to dwell.]

binocle *bin'o-kl, -ə-kl, n.* a telescope for use with both eyes at once. — *adj.* **binocular** (*bī-*, *bi-nok'ū-lər*) with two eyes: suitable for use with two eyes: stereoscopic. — *n.* a binocular telescope (usu. in *pl.*) or microscope. — *adv.* **binoc'ularly**. [L. *bīnī*, two by two, *oculus*, an eye.]

binomial *bī-nōm'i-əl, adj.* (*alg.*) consisting of two terms, as *a* + *b*. — *n.* a binomial expression. — *adj.* **binominal** (*bī-nom'in-əl*) making use of two names, as the Linnaean nomenclature which names every species by giving first the generic and then the trivial name. — **binomial theorem** Newton's theorem giving any power of a binomial. [L. *bi-*, twice, and *nōmen*, a name, a term.]

bint *bint, n.* a girl, woman (with various shades of meaning). [Ar., daughter.]

binturong *bin'tū-rong, n.* an East Indian prehensile-tailed carnivore, akin to the civet. [Malay.]

bio- *bī-ō-*, in composition, life: living organisms: living tissue — as in, e.g. the following. — *n.* **bioassay** (*bī-ō-ə-sā', -as'*) the assessment of the strength and effect of a drug or other substance by testing it on a living organism and comparing the results with the known ones of another drug, etc. — *n.sing.* **bio-astronaut'ics** science dealing with the effects of travel in space on living organisms. — *n.* **bioavailabil'ity** the extent to which a drug, etc., after administration (e.g. by mouth), is available to the tissue it is intended to act on. — *adjs.* **bioavail'able; biobibliograph'ical** dealing with the life and writings of any one. — *ns.* **bi'oblast** (Gr. *blastos*, germ) a hypothetical unit of living matter: a minute granule in protoplasm; **biocat'alyst** a substance, e.g. an enzyme, that produces or speeds up a biochemical reaction. — *adj. and n.* **biochem'ical.** — *ns.* **biochem'ist; biochem'istry** the chemistry of living things, physiological chemistry. — *adj.* **biocidal** (-*sīd'*) killing living material, pesticidal. — *ns.* **bi'ocide; bioclimatol'ogy** an older name for **biometeorology; biocoenosis** (*bī-ō-sē-nō'sis*; Gr. *koinos*, common) an association of organisms ecologically interdependent. *adj.* **biocoenotic** (-*not'ik*) ecological. — *n.pl.* **biodā'ta** biographical information, curriculum vitae. — *adj.* **biodegrād'able** (of substances) able to be broken down by bacteria. — *n.* **biodegradā'tion** (also **biodeteriorā'tion**). — *adjs.* **biodestruct'ible** biodegradable; **biodynam'ic** dealing with activities of living organisms: (of system of land cultivation) fertilising with organic materials only. — *n.sing.* **biodynam'ics.** — *ns.* **bioecol'ogy** the branch of ecology dealing with the interrelationship of plant and animal life; **bioelectric'ity** electrical phenomena in plants and animals. — *n.sing.* **bioenerget'ics** the biology of energy relationships in living organisms or energy changes produced by them. — *ns.* **bioengineer'; bioengineer'ing** see **biological engineering** at end of article. — *n.sing.* **bioeth'ics** study of the ethical problems produced by medical and scientific research, etc. — *ns.* **biofeed'back** the clinical control of body functions in response to monitoring by electronic instruments such as an electrocardiograph; **bioflā'vonoid** (also called **citrin**) a vitamin that regulates the permeability of the capillary walls, found in citrus fruit, blackcurrents and rose-hips; **bi'ogas** domestic or commercial gas obtained by treating naturally-occurring materials; **bi'ogen** (-*jen*; Gr. *genos*, race, offspring) a hypothetical unit of protoplasm; **biogen'esis** (Gr. *genesis*, production) the derivation of living things from living things only: biogeny. — *adjs.* **biogenet'ic, biogen'ic** relating to biogens or to biogeny, or to biogenesis; **biogenous** (-*oj'*) parasitic. — *n.* **biog'eny** the course of organic evolution or development of the individual or the race. — *adj.* **biogeochem'ical.** — *n.* **biogeochem'istry** the science of plants and animals in relation to chemicals in the soil; **biogeog'rapher.** — *adj.* **biogeograph'ical.** — *ns.* **biogeog'raphy** the geography of living things: geographical distribution of plants and animals; **bi'ograph** (Gr. *graphein*, to write) a biography: a bioscope; **biog'rapher** one who writes biography. — *adjs.* **biograph'ic, -al.** — *adv.* **biograph'ically.** — *ns.* **biog'raphy** a written account or history of the life of an individual: the art of writing such accounts; **biohaz'ard** a danger of disease or pollution from living organisms, encountered e.g. during biological research. — *adj.* **biological** (-*loj'*) of, pertaining to, biology: physiological: produced by physiological means: effected by living organisms or by enzymes. — *adv.* **biolog'ically.** — *ns.* **biol'ogist; biol'ogy** the science of living things: sometimes restricted to ecology; **bioluminesc'ence** the emission of light by living organisms, as certain insects, marine animals, bacteria, fungi; **bi'omass** the quantity or weight of living material (animals, plants, etc.) in a unit of area: living material as a source of energy; **biomatē'rial** suitable material from which to produce artificial body parts that are to be in direct contact with living tissue. — *n.sing.* **biomathemat'ics** mathematics as applied to biological sciences. — *ns.* **biomathemati'cian; bi'ome** an extensive ecological community, usu. with a dominant vegetation. — *n.sing.* **biomechan'ics** the mechanics of movements in living creatures. — *adj.* **biomed'ical** of or

pertaining to both biology and medicine: applied to the study of the effects of stress, esp. space travel, on living organisms. — *n.* **biomed'icine.** — *adj.* **biomet'ric** (Gr. *metron*, measure). — *adj.* **biometeorolog'ical.** — *ns.* **biometeorol'ogy** the effect of weather and climate on plants, animals and man; **biometrician** (-*trish'an*); **biom'etry** the statistical or quantitative study of biology (also *n.sing.* **biomet'rics**); **bi'omorph** (Gr. *morphē*, form) a representation of a living thing in decoration. — *adjs.* **biomorph'ic; bion'ic** relating to, using, etc., bionics: superhuman (*coll.*). — *n.sing.* **bion'ics** the study of methods of working of living creatures and the application of the principles observed to design of computers, etc.: (*loosely*) the replacement of parts of the body with electronic or mechanical devices, such as power-controlled limbs, heart-valves, etc. — *adj.* **bionom'ic.** — *n.sing.* **bionom'ics** (Gr. *nomos*, law) the study of the relations between the organism and its environment: ecology. — *ns.* **bi'oparent** a biological parent, not a step-parent or guardian; **biophor(e)** (*bī'ō-fōr, -fōr*; Gr. *phoros*, carrying) Weismann's hypothetical unit of living matter. — *n.sing.* **biophys'ics** a form of biology dealing with biological structures and processes in terms of physics. — *ns.* **bi'oplasm** (Gr. *plasma*, form) protoplasm; **bi'oplast** (Gr. *plastos*, moulded) a minute portion of protoplasm; **biopoiesis** (-*poi-ēs'is*) creation of living from non-living material as an evolutionary process; **bi'opsy** a removal of tissue or fluid from a living body for diagnostic examination: such examination. — *n.sing.* **biorhyth'mics** the study of biorhythms. — *n.pl.* **bi'orhythms** physiological, emotional and intellectual rhythms or cycles, supposed to cause variations in mood or performance. — *ns.* **biosat'ellite** a satellite containing living organisms to be studied during flight; **biosci'ence** any one of the biological sciences. — *adj.* **bioscientif'ic.** — *ns.* **biosci'entist; bi'oscope** (Gr. *skopeein*, to look at) a cinematographic apparatus or theatre or, (*S.Afr.*), cinema; **bi'osphere** the part of the earth and its atmosphere in which living things are found. — *adjs.* **biostā'ble** not affected by the biological environment; **biostratigraph'ic(al).** — *ns.* **biostratig'raphy** the stratigraphy of sedimentary rocks; **biosyn'thesis** the production of chemical substances by a living organism. — *adjs.* **biosynthet'ic; biosystemat'ic.** — *n.sing.* **biosystemat'ics** the study of relationships of organisms and of laws of classification. — *n.* **biō'ta** flora and fauna of a region. — *adj.* **biotechnolog'ical.** — *ns.* **biotechnol'ogist; biotechnol'ogy** the utilisation of living organisms (e.g. bacteria) in industry, etc., e.g. in the creation of energy, destruction of waste, and the manufacture of various products: ergonomics (*U.S.*); **bi'otype** within a species, a distinct sub-group. — **biochemical oxygen demand** a measure of the amount of oxygen required by microorganisms in a volume of water; used as a guide to the state of pollution of the water; **biogenetic law** the law of recapitulation of the history of the race in that of the individual; **biological clock** an inherent mechanism which regulates the physiological rhythms and cycles of living organisms; **biological control** a method of reducing the numbers of a pest — plant, animal or parasite — by introducing or fostering one of its enemies; **biological engineering** provision of aids (electronic, electrical, etc.) to functioning of the body, as hearing aids, aids to movement, etc. (also **bioengineering**): engineering required for methods of biosynthesis of animal and plant products, e.g. for fermentation processes (also **bioengineering**): manipulating living cells so as to promote their growth in a desired way; **biological warfare** methods of fighting involving the use of disease bacteria.   [Gr. *bios*, life.]

bio *bī'ō* (*pl.* **bī'os**), **biog** *bī'og, -og'*, *ns.* short for **biography**.
biont *bī'ont*, *n.* a living organism. — *adj.* **bion'tic.** — **-biont** in composition, an organism belonging to a particular habitat or environment. — **-bion'tic** adjective combining form.   [Gr. *bios*, life, *ōn* (stem *ont-*) from *einai*, to be.]

biopic *bī'ō-pik, n.* a film, usu. an uncritically admiring one, telling the life-story of a celebrity. [*Bio*graphical *pic*ture.]

-biosis *-bi-ō'sis,* in composition, a specific way of living. — **-biotic** (*-ot'*) adjective combining form. [Gr. *biōsis,* way of life; adj. *biōtikos.*]

biotic *bī-ot'tik, adj.* pertaining to life. [Gr. *biōtikos.*]

biotin *bī'ō-tin, n.* one of the members of the vitamin B complex (also known as vitamin H). [Gr. *biotos,* means of living.]

biotite *bī'ō-tīt, n.* a black or dark ferro-magnesian mica. [Named after J. B. *Biot* (1774–1862), French physicist and astronomer.]

biparous *bip'ər-əs, adj.* bearing two at a birth: dichasial. [L. *bis,* twice, *parēre,* to bring forth.]

bipartite *bī-pärt'īt, adj.* divided into two parts: having two corresponding parts, as a document: affecting two parties, as an agreement. — *adj.* **bipart'isan** (*-i-zan*) pertaining to, supported by, or consisting of members of, two parties. — *n.* **bipartition** (*-tish'ən*) division into two parts. [L. *bi-, bis,* twice, *partītus,* divided — *partīre, -īrī,* to divide.]

biped *bī'ped, n.* an animal with two feet. — *adjs.* **bī'ped, bī'pedal** having two feet: using two feet for walking. — *n.* **biped'alism.** [L. *bipēs, -pedis* — *bi-,* twice, *pēs, pedis,* foot.]

bipetalous *bī-pet'əl-əs, adj.* having two petals. [L. *bi-,* twice, and **petal.**]

biphenyl *bī-fē'nīl, n., adj.* Same as **diphenyl.**

bipinnaria *bī-pin-ā'ri-ə, n.* a starfish larva with two ciliated bands. [L. *bi-,* twice, *pinna,* a feather.]

bipinnate *bī-pin'āt, adj.* pinnate with each pinna itself pinnate. [L. *bi-,* twice, and **pinnate.**]

biplane *bī'plān, n.* an aeroplane or glider with two sets of wings, one above the other. [L. *bi-,* twice, and **plane².**]

bipod *bī'pod, n.* a two-legged stand. [L. *bi-,* twice, Gr. *pous, podos,* a foot.]

bipolar *bī-pō'lər, adj.* having two poles or extremities (*lit.* and *fig.*). — *n.* **bipolar'ity.** [L. *bi-,* twice, and **polar.**]

bipyramid *bī-pir'ə-mid, n.* a form of two pyramids base to base, or with a pyramid at each end.

biquadratic *bī-kwəd-rat'ik, n.* a quantity twice squared, or raised to the fourth power. — **biquadratic equation** an equation involving the fourth, and no higher, power of the unknown quantity; **biquadratic root** the square root of the square root. [L. *bi-,* twice, and *quadrātus,* squared.]

biquintile *bī-kwin'tīl, n.* the aspect of planets when they are twice the fifth part of a great circle (i.e. 144 degrees) from each other. [L. *bi-,* twice, *quintus,* the fifth.]

birch *bûrch, n.* a hardy forest-tree (*Betula*), with smooth white bark and very durable wood: a rod for punishment, consisting of a birch twig or twigs. — *v.t.* to flog. — *adjs.* **birch, birch'en** made of birch. — **birch fly** see **black fly; birch rod** a birch for punishment. [O.E. *berc, bierce;* O.N. *björk,* Sans. *bhūrja.*]

bird *bûrd, n.* a general name for a feathered animal (orig. applied to the young): a warm-blooded, oviparous, feathered vertebrate of the class *Aves,* having forelimbs modified into wings: a person (*slang*): an object of admiration (*slang*): a prison sentence (*slang*; from **bird-lime,** rhyming slang for 'time'): a girl or woman (*arch., dial.;* later *slang*; orig. confused with **bride** or **burd¹** or **²**). — *v.i.* to shoot at, seek to catch or snare birds. — *ns.* **bird'er** (*coll.*) a bird-watcher; **bird'ie** (*dim.*) a little bird: the achievement of a hole in golf in one stroke less than par (also *v.i.* and *v.t.*); **bird'ing** hunting, shooting, snaring, or catching of birds. — *n., adj., adv.* **bird-alane** see **burd².** — **bird'bath** a basin set up for birds to bathe in; **bird'-batting** (*dial.*) batfowling; **bird'-bolt** (*Shak.*) a short thick blunted bolt or arrow for killing birds without piercing. — *adj.* **bird'-brained** (*coll.*) flighty, silly. — **bird'cage** a cage of wire or wicker for holding birds; **bird'call** a birdcatcher's instrument for imitating birds' notes; **bird's catcher** a professional catcher of birds. — *n.* and *adj.*

bird'-catching (**bird-catching spider** see **bird-spider**). — **bird'-cherry** a small wild cherry tree (*Prunus padus*): its astringent fruit; **bird'-dog** one trained to find or retrieve birds for hunters. — *adj.* **bird'-eyed** quicksighted. — **bird'-fancier** one who breeds birds, or keeps them for sale. — *adj.* **bird'-hipped** (of dinosaurs) having a pelvis slightly similar to a bird's, the pubis extending backwards to lie parallel with the upper pelvis, ornithischian. — **bird impact** bird strike; **bird'ing-piece** a fowling-piece; **bird'-louse** a louse-like insect of the Mallophaga, parasitical on birds and mammals (*pl.* **bird'-lice**); **bird'-lime** a sticky substance for catching birds: see also **bird** *n.,* above; **bird'man** an ornithologist or one otherwise concerned with birds; **bird'-of-par'-adise** see **paradise; bird-of-paradise flower** Strelitzia; **bird'-pepper** a species of capsicum; **bird'seed** seed (hemp, etc.) for cage-birds: a thing trifling in amount, chicken feed (*slang*); **bird's'eye** a kind of primrose, of speedwell, or of tobacco. — *adj.* such as might be seen by a flying bird: having markings like birds' eyes. — **bird's'-foot** a papilionaceous genus (*Ornithopus*) with clawlike pods; **bird'shot** pellets suitable for shooting birds; **bird'-skiing** water-skiing with a winglike device that enables the skier to rise off the water; **bird's'-nest** the nest in which a bird lays and hatches her eggs: a name given to several plants from their appearance, esp. Monotropa and *Neottia* (bird's-nest orchis); **bird's'-nesting, bird'-nesting** seeking and robbing birds' nests; **bird'-spider** a large spider (*Mygale*) that preys on small birds, found in Brazil: extended to others of the *Aviculariidae;* **bird strike** collision of a bird with an aircraft resulting in aircraft damage; **bird'-table** a table, inaccessible to cats, for wild birds to feed on; **bird'watcher; bird'-watching** observation of birds in their natural habitat; **bird'wing (butterfly)** any of various very large brightly coloured butterflies of south-east Asia. — *adj.* **bird'-witt'ed** flighty: incapable of sustained attention. — **a bird in the hand is worth two in the bush** a certainty is not to be thrown away for a poor chance of something better; **a little bird told me** I heard in a way I will not reveal; **bird's-eye view** a general view from above: a general view of a subject; **bird's-foot trefoil** a papilionaceous genus (*Lotus*) with clustered pods like birds' feet; **birds of a feather** see **feather; do bird** (*slang*; see **bird** *n.,* above) to serve a prison sentence; (**strictly) for the birds** (*slang*) not to be taken seriously, of little value; **get the bird** (i.e. the goose) in stage slang, to be hissed, hence dismissed; **in bird** (*slang*; see **bird** *n.,* above) in prison; **like a bird** with alacrity. [O.E. *brid,* the young of a bird, a bird.]

birefringent *bī-rə-frin'jənt, adj.* doubly refracting, as Iceland spar. — *n.* **birefrin'gence.** [L. *bi-,* twice, and **refringent.**]

bireme *bī'rēm, n.* an ancient vessel with two banks of oars. [L. *birēmis* — *bi-,* twice, and *rēmus,* an oar.]

biretta *bir-et'ə, n.* a square cap worn by clergy — by priests, black; bishops, purple; cardinals, red. [It. *berretta* — L.L. *birretum,* cap.]

bir(i)yani *bir-yä'ni, bi-ri-yä'ni, ns.* a spicy rice dish. [From Urdu.]

birk *birk, bûrk, n.* Scots and dial. for **birch.** — *adj.* **birk'en** (*Scot.*) birchen.

birkie *birk'i,* (*Scot.*) *n.* a strutting or swaggering fellow: a fellow generally. — *adj.* active. [Perh. conn. with O.N. *berkia,* O.E. *beorcan,* to bark.]

birl¹ *birl,* (*Scot.*) *v.t.* and *v.i.* to spin round: to toss (a coin): to spend (esp. on liquor). [Apparently onomatopoeic.]

birl², birle *birl,* (*Scot.*) *v.t.* and *v.i.* to pour out: to ply with drink: to carouse. — *ns.* **birl'er** (*Cumberland*); **birl'ing** the act of drawing liquor. [O.E. *byrelian* — *byrele,* a cup-bearer, *beran,* to bear.]

birlieman *bir'li-mən,* (*Scott*) *n.* Same as **byrlaw-man.**

birlinn *bir'lin, n.* a chief's barge in the Western Isles. [Gael. *birlinn* — O.N. *byrthingr* — *byrthr,* burden.]

Birminghamise, -ize *bûr'ming-əm-iz, v.t.* to make up artificially. [See **Brummagem.**]

Biro® *bī'rō, n.* a kind of ball-point pen: — *pl.* **Bi'ros.** [L. *Biró*, Hungarian inventor.]

birostrate *bī-ros'trāt, adj.* double-beaked. [L. *bi-*, twice, *rōstrātus*, beaked — *rōstrum*, a beak.]

birr¹ *bir, (Scot.) n.* impetuosity: a violent push: stress in pronunciation: any sharp whirring sound. [O.N. *byrr*, a favouring wind.]

birr² *bûr, bēr, n.* the monetary unit of Ethiopia. [Amharic.]

birse *birs, (Scot.) n.* bristle. —*adj.* **bir'sy.** — **lick the birse** to draw a hog's bristle through the mouth — as in admission as a burgess in Selkirk; **set up someone's birse** to rouse the wrath of someone, from the bristling up of enraged animals. [O.E. *byrst.*]

birsle *birs'l, (Scot.) v.t.* to scorch, to toast. [Origin unknown.]

birth¹ *bûrth, n.* a ship's station at anchor. [Same as **berth.**]

birth² *bûrth, n.* the act of bearing or bringing forth: coming into the world: the offspring born: dignity of family: origin. — *n.* **birth'dom** (*Shak.*) birthright. — **birth control** the control of reproduction by contraceptives; **birth'day** the day on which one is born, or (usually) its anniversary, or a day officially held instead. — *adj.* relating to the day of one's birth. — **birth'day-book** a book for (autograph) records of friends' birthdays; **birthday honours** titles, etc., conferred on the king's (or queen regnant's) official birthday; **birth'day-suit** the naked skin; **birth'mark** a mark, e.g. a pigmented area or spot, on one's body at birth: a distinguishing quality (*fig.*); **birth'night** the night on which one is born, or the anniversary of that night: the evening of the king's (or queen's) birthday (*obs.*); **birth pill** a contraceptive pill; **birth'place** the place of one's birth; **birth'-rate** proportion of births to population; **birth'right** the right or privilege to which one is entitled by birth: native rights. — *adj.* **birth's-strangled** (*Shak.*) strangled at birth. — **birth'wort** a plant (*Aristolochia clematitis*) formerly reputed to help parturition. [Prob. O.N. *byrthr.*]

biryani. See **bir(i)yani.**

bis *bis, adv.* twice: a direction for repetition (*mus.*). [L.]

biscacha. Same as **viscacha.**

Biscayan *bis'kā-ən,* or *-kā', adj.* of or pertaining to *Biscay* in Spain, or its people: Basque generally. — *n.* a native of Biscay: a long heavy musket, or its bullet.

biscuit *bis'kit, n.* a small, thin, crisp cake made of unleavened dough: a scone (*U.S.*): pottery that has been fired but not yet glazed: a square mattress (*mil. slang*). — *adj.* pale brown in colour. — *adj.* **bis'cuity** like a biscuit in flavour or texture. — **bis'cuit-root** camass. — **take the biscuit** to surpass everything else (*iron.*). [O.Fr. *bescoit* (mod. *biscuit*) — L. *bis,* twice, *coquěre, coctum,* to cook or bake.]

bise *bēz, n.* a cold north or north-east wind prevalent at certain seasons in and near Switzerland. [Fr.]

bisect *bī-sekt', v.t.* and *v.i.* to divide into two (usu. equal) parts. — *ns.* **bisec'tion; bisec'tor** a line that divides an angle, etc., into two equal parts. [L. *bi-,* twice, and *secāre, sectum,* to cut.]

biserial *bī-sē'ri-əl, adj.* arranged in two series or rows. [L. *bi-,* twice, and **series.**]

biserrate *bī-ser'āt, adj.* doubly serrate. [L. *bi-,* twice, and **serrate.**]

bisexual *bī-seks'ū-əl, adj.* hermaphrodite: attracted sexually to both sexes. [L. *bi-,* twice, **sexual.**]

bish *bish, (coll.) n.* a blunder, mistake. [Origin obscure.]

bishop¹ *bish'əp, n.* in the Western and Eastern Churches and in the Anglican communion, a clergyman consecrated for the spiritual direction of a diocese, usu. under an archbishop, and over the priests or presbyters and deacons: a spiritual overseer in the early Christian Church, whether of a local church or of a number of churches: a chessman whose move is in a diagonal line, its upper part carved into the shape of a bishop's mitre (formerly the *archer*): a wholesome hot drink compounded of red wine (claret, Burgundy, etc.) poured

warm or cold upon ripe bitter oranges, sugared and spiced to taste: any of several kinds of weaver-bird (**bish'op-bird**). — *v.t.* to play the bishop, to confirm (*jocularly*): to appoint to the office of bishop: to supply with bishops: to let (milk or the like) burn while cooking. — *ns.* **bish'opess** a bishop's wife: a she-bishop (*jocularly*): **bish'opric** the office and jurisdiction of a bishop: sometimes a diocese — also **bish'opdom.** — **bishop's cap** a genus (*Mitella*) of the saxifrage family, with one-sided inflorescences; **bishop's court** the court of a diocesan bishop: the Commissary Court (*Scots law*); **bishop sleeve** a full sleeve drawn in tightly at the wrist; **bishop('s) weed** goutweed or goatweed. — **the bishop has put his foot in it** it has burnt while cooking. [O.E. *biscop* — L. *episcopus* — Gr. *episkopos,* overseer — *epi,* upon, *skopeein,* to view.]

bishop² *bish'əp, v.t.* to fill, or otherwise tamper with, the teeth of (a horse, to make it seem younger). [From a person of the name.]

bisk. See **bisque¹.**

bismar *bis', biz'mər, (Orkney and Shetland) n.* a kind of steelyard. [O.N. *bismari.*]

bismillah *bis-mil'a, interj.* in the name of Allah. [Ar.]

bismuth *biz'məth, n.* a brittle reddish-white element (at. numb. 83; symbol Bi). [Ger. *Bismuth, Wissmuth* (now *Wismut*), origin unknown.]

bisociation *bī-sō-si-ā'shən, -shi-, n.* association at the same time of an idea or object with two quite different sets of facts or ideas. — *adj.* **bisō'ciative.** [L. *bi-,* twice, and **association.**]

bison *bī'sn, -zn, n.* a large wild ox with shaggy hair and a fatty hump — the European bison, almost extinct except in parks, and the American, commonly called buffalo in America. [From L. *bisōn, -ontis,* prob. of Gmc. origin; cf. O.H.G. *wisunt,* O.E. *wesend.*]

bisque¹, bisk *bisk, n.* a rich shellfish soup, made with wine and cream. [Fr.]

bisque² *bisk, n.* a kind of unglazed white porcelain: pottery that has undergone the first firing before being glazed. [See **biscuit.**]

bisque³ *bisk, n.* a term at tennis, golf, etc., for the handicap whereby a player allows a weaker opponent (at latter's choice of time) to score a point in a set, or deduct a stroke at a hole, to take an extra turn in croquet, etc. [Fr.]

bissextile *bis-ekst'īl, adj.* having an intercalary day. — *n.* leap year. [L. *bisextīlis* — *bis,* twice, *sextus,* sixth, the sixth day before the kalends of March (24th February) being doubled.]

bisson *bis'ən, adj. (Shak.* **beesome**) blind, purblind: (*Shak.* **bisson**) perh. blinding. [O.E. *bisene,* blind.]

bistable *bī'stā-bl, adj.* (of a valve or transistor circuit) having two stable states.

bistort *bis'tört, n.* adderwort or snakeweed, a plant (*Polygonum bistorta*) of the dock family with twisted rootstock. [L. *bistorta* — *bis,* twice, *tortus, -a, -um,* twisted.]

bistoury *bis'tər-i, n.* a narrow surgical knife for making incisions. [Fr. *bistouri.*]

bistre, bister *bis'tər, n.* a pigment of a warm brown colour made from the soot of wood, esp. beechwood. — *adj.* **bis'tred.** [Fr. *bistre;* origin unknown.]

bistro *bē'strō, n.* a small bar or restaurant: — *pl.* **bis'tros.** [Fr. slang.]

bisulcate *bī-sul'kāt, adj.* cleft in two (*zool.*): cloven-footed (*zool.*): with two furrows (*bot.*). [L. *bi-,* twice, *sulcus,* a furrow.]

bisulphate *bī-sul'fāt, n.* an acid sulphate. — *n.* **bīsulph'ide** a disulphide.

bit¹ *bit, n.* a bite, a morsel: a small piece: a coin: 12½ cents (*U.S.*) (used only in **two, four, six bits**): the smallest degree: a brief space of time: a small boring tool (see **brace**): the boring part of a drilling machine: the part of the bridle that the horse holds in his mouth: the part of a key that engages the lever of the lock: used with the effect of a diminutive as in *a bit of a laddie* (*pl.* *bits o' laddies*), *a bit laddie* (*dial., esp. Scot.*):

a girl, young woman (*slang*): an (area of) activity, an act, a role (*slang*). — *v.t.* to put the bit in the mouth of: to curb or restrain: — *pr.p.* **bitt′ing**; *pa.p.* **bitt′ed.** — *adj.* **bit′sy** (*coll.*) prettily small. — *ns.* **bitt′ie** (*Scot.*) a small piece, short distance, or short time; **bitt′ock** (*Scot.*) a little bit. — *adj.* **bitt′y** scrappy. disjointed, made up of odds and ends: not forming an artistic whole. — **bit′(-part)** a small part in acting; **bit player** an actor who plays bit-parts. — **a bit (of)** somewhat, rather, as in *a bit of a fool, a bit stupid*; **a bit of all right** (*slang*) a person or thing highly approved of; **a bit off** (*coll.*) in bad taste; **a bit on the side** (*slang*) (one's partner in) extra-marital sexual relations; **bit and sup** something to eat and drink; **bit by bit** piecemeal: gradually; **do one's bit** to do one's due share; **take, get, the bit in, between, one's teeth** to throw off control: to take up, have, a tenacious or keen interest (in) or occupation (with something). [From **bite.**]

bit² *bit*, the smallest unit of information in computers and communications theory. [Contracted *bi*nary dig*it*.]

bitch *bich*, *n.* the female of the dog, wolf, and fox: (abusively) a woman, very rarely a man: a malicious or arrogant woman: an act of grumbling (*slang*). — *v.i.* (*slang*) to complain, talk bitchily. — *v.t.* (*slang*) to mess up, spoil (often *bitch up*). — *n.* **bitch′ery** ill-tempered, malicious behaviour or talk. — *adv.* **bitch′-ily.** — *n.* **bitch′iness.** — *adj.* **bitch′y.** — **the bitch goddess** material success as an object of worship. [O.E. *bicce*; O.N. *bikkja*.]

bite *bīt*, *v.t.* and *v.i.* to seize or tear with the teeth: to puncture with the mouth-parts, as an insect: to cut or penetrate: to eat into chemically: to take effect: to grip: to wound by reproach (*arch.*): to deceive, to take in (now only in passive): to accept something offered as bait (also *fig.*): — *pa.t.* **bit**; *pa.p.* **bit** or **bitt′en.** — *n.* a grasp by the teeth: manner in which the teeth come together: a puncture by an insect: the wound or sore caused thereby: a nibble at the bait: something bitten off: a mouthful: biting quality: grip: pungency: incisiveness: corroding action: a playful imposition or befooling (*old slang*). — *ns.* **bīt′er** one who bites: an animal with a habit of biting: a fish apt to take the bait. a cheat (*obs.*, except in **the biter bit**, the cheater cheated: the wrongdoer paid back); **bit′ing.** — *adj.* which bites: sharp, cold: sarcastic. — **bīt′ing-louse** a bird-louse. — **bite in** (*etching*) to eat out the lines of with acid; **bite off more than one can chew** to over-estimate one's capacities: to undertake that which one cannot achieve; **bite (on) the bullet** to submit bravely to something unpleasant: to face up to an unpalatable fact or situation; **bite someone's head off** to speak to someone unnecessarily angrily; **bite the dust** to fall, to die; **bite the thumb** to express defiance by knocking the thumb-nail against the teeth; **what's biting you?** what is the matter with you? [O.E. *bītan*; Goth. *beitan*, O.N. *bīta*, Ger. *beissen*.]

bito *bē′tō*, *n.* a tree (*Balanites aegyptiaca*; family Zygophyllaceae) of dry tropical Africa and Asia; its oil-yielding fruit: — *pl.* **bi′tos.**

bitonal *bī-tōn′əl*, *adj.* using two musical keys simultaneously. — *n.* **bitonal′ity.**

bitt *bit*, (*naut.*) *n.* a post for fastening cables (usu. in *pl.*). — *v.t.* to fasten round the bitts. — *n.* **bitt′er** the turn of cable round the bitts, hence perhaps **the bitter end**, the end of the rope that remains aboard, and so the last extremity (but perhaps from **bitter** *adj.*). [Perh. O.N. *biti*, a cross-beam.]

bittacle. Same as **binnacle.**

bitte *bit′ə*, (Ger.) *interj.* please: don't mention it: I beg your pardon.

bitter *bit′ər*, *adj.* having a taste like that of quinine or hops: sharp: painful: acrimonious. — *n.* any substance having a bitter taste, esp. a type of ale. — *adj.* **bitt′erish.** — *adv.* **bitt′erly.** — *n.* **bitt′erness.** — *n.pl.* **bitt′ers** a liquid prepared from bitter herbs or roots, and used as a stomachic. — **bitt′er-app′le** colocynth; **bitt′er-**

cress′ Cardamine; **bitt′er-earth′** magnesia; **bitt′er-king** an intensely bitter shrub of the quassia family, growing in the Eastern Archipelago; **bitt′er-pit′** a disease of apples, etc., characterised by brown spots and depressions; **bitt′er-root** an American xerophytic plant of the purslane family; **bitt′er-spar′** dolomite; **bitt′ersweet′** the woody nightshade (*Solanum dulcamara*), whose stems when chewed taste first bitter, then sweet: an apple that tastes both sweet and bitter (*Shak.*): a mixture of sweet and bitter (also *fig.*; also *adj.*); **bitter vetch** see **vetch**; **bitt′erwood** various trees, esp. of the Simarubaceae. — **a bitter pill to swallow** something which is difficult or unpleasant to accept, as an unwelcome fact, etc.; **the bitter end** see **bitt.** [O.E. *biter* — *bītan*, to bite.]

bitterling *bit′ər-ling*, *n.* a small fish (*Rhodeus amarus*).

bittern¹ *bit′ərn*, *n.* a marsh bird of the heron family. [M.E. *bittour*, *botor* — O.Fr. *butor*.]

bittern² *bit′ərn*, *n.* an oily liquid remaining in salt-works after crystallisation of the salt. [**bitter**.]

bittock, bitty. See **bit¹.**

bittor, bittour, bittur *bit′ər*, (Spens., Dryden) *n.* the bittern.

bitumen *bit′ū-mən*, or *bi-tū′*, *n.* name applied to various inflammable mineral substances, as naphtha, petroleum, asphalt. — *v.t.* **bitū′minate** to mix with or make into bitumen — also **bitū′minise, -ize.** — *n.* **bituminisā′tion, -z-.** — *adjs.* **bitū′minous, bitūmed′** (or *bit′*; *Shak.*) impregnated with bitumen. — **bituminous coal** coal that flames in burning, from richness in volatile hydrocarbons. [L. *bitūmen, -inis*.]

bivalent *bī-vā′lənt* or *bi ′ə-lənt*, *adj.* having a valency of two (*chem.*): pertaining to one of a pair of homologous chromosomes (also *n.*). — *ns.* **bivalence, bivalency.** [L. *bi-*, twice, and **-valent**.]

bivalve *bī′valv*, *n.* an animal having a shell in two valves or parts, like the oyster — esp. a lamellibranch; a seed vessel of like kind. — *adj.* having two valves. — *adj.* **bivalv′ular.** [L. *bi-*, twice, *valva*, a door-leaf.]

bivariate *bī-vā′ri-āt*, *adj.* of, or involving, two variant qualities. — Also **bivā′riant.** — Also *ns.*

bivious *biv′i-əs*, *adj.* leading two, or different, ways. — *n.* **biv′ium** in echinoderms the two rays enclosing the madreporite. [L. *bivius* — *bi-*, twice, *via*, a way.]

bivouac *biv′ŏŏ -ak*, *n.* the resting at night of soldiers (or others) in the open air, instead of under cover in camp. — *v.i.* to pass the night in the open air: — *pr.p.* **biv′ouacking**; *pa.p.* **biv′ouacked.** — Also (*slang*) *n.* and *v.* **bivv′y.** [Fr., — Ger. *Beiwacht*, additional watch.]

bi-weekly *bī-wēk′li*, *adj.* occurring or appearing once in two weeks or twice a week or once every two weeks. — Also *adv.* — *n.* a periodical issued twice a week or once every two weeks.

Bixa *bik′sə*, *n.* a tropical American genus of plants yielding anatta, giving name to the **Bixā′ceae**, a family of parietal Archichlamydeae. [Sp. *bixa* (*bija*) — Taino *bixa*.]

bi-yearly *bī-yēr′li*, *adj., adv.* (happening, issued, etc.) twice a year or every two years.

biz *biz*. Slang for **business.**

bizarre *bi-zär′*, *adj.* odd: fantastic: extravagant. — *n.* **bizarr′erie.** [Fr., — Sp. *bizarro*, gallant, brave, poss. — Basque *bizarra*, beard.]

bizcacha. See **viscacha.**

bizone *bī′zōn*, *n.* a unit or country formed of two zones, e.g. that comprising the British and U.S. occupation zones in Germany after 1945. — *adj.* **bīzō′nal.**

biz(z)azz. See **bez(z)azz.**

blab¹ *blab*, *v.i.* to talk much: to tell tales. — *v.t.* to let out (a secret): — *pr.p.* **blabb′ing**; *pa.p.* **blabbed.** — *n.* one who lets out secrets (*Milt.*): a tattler: tattling. — *ns.* **blabb′er, blabber′mouth.** — *n.* and *adj.* **blabb′ing.** [M.E. *blabbe*, cf. O.N. *blabbra*, Ger. *plappern*.]

blab² *blab*, *n.* a blister (*obs.*). — *v.t.* to swell. — *adj.* **blabb′er** swollen. [**bleb.**]

black *blak*, *adj.* of the darkest colour: reflecting no light: used as a classification of pencil-leads to indicate softness in quality and darkness in use: obscure:

dismal: sullen: horrible: dusky: foul, dirty: malignant: dark-haired: wearing dark armour or clothes: illicit: (of income) not reported in tax returns: unofficial: under trade-union ban: Negro, of African, West Indian descent (often *offensive*; acceptable in the U.S., S. Africa): coloured, of mixed descent (esp. *S.Afr.*): (of an area or state) inhabited or controlled by a Negro population: of, belonging to, or relating to, Negroes and coloured people. — *n.* black colour or absence of colour: a Negro, a person of African, West Indian, etc., descent (often *offensive*; acceptable in U.S. and S. Africa): a black pigment: a smut: smut fungus: black clothes (formerly, still in Scotland, in *pl.*). — *v.t.* to make black: to soil or stain: to draw in black: to blackmail (*slang*): to put under trade-union ban. — *v.t.* **black'en** to make black: to defame. — *v.i.* to become black. — *n.* **black'ing** a substance used for blacking leather, etc. — *adj.* **black'ish.** — *n* **black'ness.** — *n.* **black'amoor** a black Moor: a Negro. — *adj.* **black'=and-blue'** livid in colour because of bruising. — *adj.* and *n.* **black'-and-tan'** (a dog) having black hair on the back, and tan or yellowish-brown elsewhere: (usu. **Black'-and-Tan'**) (of) an auxiliary policeman in Ireland, about 1920 (from his khaki uniform with black cap and armlet). — *n.* a drink that is a mixture of ale and stout or porter. — *adj.* **black'-and-white'** partly black, partly white: drawing or drawn in black on a white ground: not in colour (*TV*): consisting of extremes, not admitting any middle ground. — **black art** magic (perh. a translation of L. *nigromantia*, erroneously used for Gr. *nekromanteiā*, see **necromancy**). — *adj.* **black-a-vised** (*blak'ə-vīst, -vīzd*; perh. Fr. *à vis*, in the face) swarthy. — *v.t.* **black'ball** to vote against by putting a black ball into a ballot-box: to ostracise: to vote against, veto. — **black'balling; black'band** iron ore containing enough coal to calcine it; **black bass** a North American freshwater fish (*Micropterus*); **black'= bee'tle** a cockroach; **black belt** a belt showing the highest grade of proficiency in judo: an area with rich dark soil (*U.S.*): a region in which Negroes outnumber whites (*U.S.*); **black'berry** the fruit of the bramble: in some districts, the blackcurrant or the crowberry. — *v.i.* to gather blackberries. — **black'bird** a black species of thrush: a grackle or other bird of the *Icteridae* (*U.S.*): a Negro or Polynesian recruited or kidnapped for labour; **black'birder** a person or ship engaged in slave-trading; **black'birding; black'board** a board painted black, for writing on. — *adj.* **black'-bod'ing** of evil omen. — **black body** one that absorbs all incident radiation, reflecting none (**black body radiation** that emitted by a black body); **black book** an important book bound in black: a book recording the names of persons deserving punishment; **black bottom** an American dance of late 1920s with sinuous movement of hips; **black box** a type of seismograph for registering underground explosions: a unit of electronic equipment in package form which records all the flight details in an aircraft: a device or unit, esp. electronic, whose internal workings need not be understood by the user (*comput.*,etc.); **black'boy** the Australian grasstree; **black bread** rye-bread. — *adj.* **black'-browed'** having black eyebrows: sullen. — **black'buck** the common Indian antelope; **black'-bull'y** sapodilla; **black butt** any of several Australian trees of the genus Eucalyptus, used for timber; **black'cap** a warbler with a black crown: an apple roasted until it is black: a black American raspberry; **black cap** the cap put on by English judges to pronounce sentence of death (*hist.*); **black'-cat'** the pekan or fisher; **black cattle** at one time cattle of any colour, orig. Welsh and Scottish cattle; **black chalk** bluish-black clay-slate, used for drawing, and for making black paint. — *adj.* **black'= coated** wearing a black coat: of the professional class. — **black'cock** the male of the **black'grouse** or **black'- game,** a species of grouse, common in the north of England and in Scotland: — *fem.* **grey'-hen; black coffee** coffee without milk or cream; **black comedy** a

'pièce noire' (Jean Anouilh), a play in which, under fantasy and grotesque humour, the hopeless world of reality is clearly seen: also a comedy about dreadful events: a film of either type; **Black Country** the industrial Midland counties of England; **black'curr'ant** the small black berry of a garden shrub (*Ribes nigrum*) of the gooseberry genus; **black damp** air in which the oxygen has been displaced by carbon dioxide; **black death** (also with *caps.*) a deadly epidemic of bubonic plague that swept over Asia and Europe, reaching England in 1348 (from the black spots that appeared on the skin); **black diamond** same as **carbonado²**: (in *pl.*) coal; **black draught** a purgative medicine, chiefly senna and Epsom salts; **black drop** a liquid preparation of opium, vinegar, and sugar; **black earth** a fertile deposit covering wide regions in S. Russia and in Central India; **black economy** unofficial economic activity involving black money (q.v.) or payment in kind; **black eye** an eye of which the iris is dark: a discoloration around the eye due to a blow or fall; **black-eye(d) pea, bean** the cow-pea (q.v.); **black-eyed Susan** a N. American composite plant of the Rudbeckia genus, with dark centres and yellow or orange rays: a tropical African climbing plant (*Thunburgia alata*) that has yellow flowers with purple centres. — *adj.* **black'-faced.** — **black'-fellow** an Australian Aboriginal; **black'fish** a name given to several kinds of fish, e.g. the black ruff, a kind of perch: the ca'ing whale: a salmon after spawning; **black'-fisher** poacher of fish by night: **black'-fishing; black flag** the flag of a pirate: the banner of anarchism: that hoisted at the execution of a criminal: that waved to call a driver in from a racing circuit (also *v.t.*); **black fly** an aphid that infests beans, etc.: any of several black- or grey-bodied insects of the *Simuliidae*, hump-backed blood-suckers (also known as **birch fly** and **buffalo gnat**) some of which carry the nematode that causes onchocerciasis; **Black'- foot** a member of a tribe of Algonquin American Indians: — *pl.* **-foot** or **-feet.** — Also *adj.* **black'-fox'** the pekan; **Black Friar** (also without *caps.*) a Dominican, from his black mantle (over a white woollen habit); **black Friday** Good Friday: an unlucky Friday (*orig. hist.*); **black frost** frost without rime or snow; **black'game, blackgrouse** see **blackcock; black gold** (*coll.*) oil; **blackguard** (*blag'ärd*) originally applied to the lowest menials about a court, who took charge of the pots, kettles, etc.: a contemptible scoundrel: a low and scurrilous person. — Also *adj.* — *v.t.* to vituperate. — *v.i.* to play the blackguard. — **black'guardism.** — *adj.* and *adv.* **black'guardly.** — **black hand** a secret society or underground influence, often imaginary; **black'head** a bird of various kinds, as the blackheaded gull: a comedo: an infectious disease of turkeys, pheasants and other fowl. — *adj.* **black'headed** having a black head. — **black'heart** a dark kind of cherry. — *adj.* **black-heart'ed** of an evil disposition. — **black hole** a punishment cell, esp. (*caps.*) that at Calcutta (1756) in which 123 of 146 British prisoners were alleged to have died of suffocation: a field of such strong gravitational pull that matter and energy cannot escape from it, presumed to exist where a massive star has collapsed (*astron.*); **black house** an obsolescent type of house in the Scottish highlands and islands, built of turf; **black humour** humour which laughs at the tragedy of the human lot and mocks the idea that man can order his world successfully; **black ice** a thin layer of transparent ice on a road; **black'jack** a large jug for holding drink, originally made of leather: a pirate flag: zinc-blende: a short leather-covered club with weighted head: vingt-et-un, or a game like it: a combination of an ace and a face-card in the game of blackjack; **black'lead** a black mineral (plumbago, not lead) used in making pencils, blacking grates, etc.; **black'leg** black-quarter: a swindler, esp. at a racecourse: a worker continuing to work during a strike or one taking a striker's place (also **black'-neb**). — *v.i.* to work as a blackleg. — **black letter** the Old English (also called Gothic) type (𝕭lack-letter); **black light** invisible infrared or ultraviolet light; **black'list** a list of defaulters or persons against whom a warning is necessary, or who are liable to loss of employment or lack of full recognition because of their (usu. political) views. — *v.t.* **black'list'** to put on a blacklist. — **black'list'ing; black lung** a lung disease of miners, pneumoconiosis: **black'mail** tribute formerly paid to robbers for protection: hush-money extorted under threat of exposure, often baseless. — *v.t.* to extort money from (a person): to force by threats (into doing something). — **black'mailer; black Maria** (mə-rī'ə) a prison van: a shell that emits dense black smoke or a gun discharging it (*mil. slang*); **black mark** something known or noted to one's discredit; **black market** surreptitious trade in rationed goods: buying and selling that is against the law or official regulations (e.g. illegal traffic in drugs); **black'-marketeer'** one who operates on the black market; **black mass** a travesty of the mass in diabolism or devil-worship; **black Monday** Easter Monday: the day of return to school; **black money** income not reported for tax purposes; **Black Monk** a Benedictine (also without *caps.*); **black nationalism** a movement aimed at increasing Negro self-determination and reducing White influence in all areas with a Negro population; **black nationalist; black'out** total extinction or concealment of lights: a failure or cut in electrical power: sudden loss of consciousness, or failure of the mind to work: a complete stoppage or suppression (of news, communications, etc.): a stoppage in the transmission of television programmes. — *adj.* for blacking out with. — **black paper** an unofficial document similar in form to a government white paper, criticising official policy; **Black Pope** (*disparagingly*) the head of the Jesuits; **Black Power** (also without *caps.*) a militant movement to increase Negro influence, esp. in predominantly white countries; **black'-pudd'ing** a blood-pudding (q.v.); **black'-quart'er** an apoplectic disease of cattle; **black rat** the smaller of the two British rats (usually brown) now comparatively rare; **Black Rod** the usher of the chapter of the Garter and of the House of Lords; **black sheep** a disreputable member of a family or group; **Black'shirt** a member of a Fascist organisation, esp. in the Nazi SS and in Italy during World War II; **black'smith** a smith who works in iron; **black snake** a large agile non-poisonous snake (*Bascanium constrictor*) (*U.S.*): a very venomous snake (*Pseudechis porphyriacus*), nearly allied to the cobra (*Austr.*): a long whip; **black spot** name given to disease of various plants, e.g. roses: a small area which has bad conditions or a bad record; **Black Stone** an Islamic sacred stone in a shrine in Mecca; **black stump** (*Austr.* and *N.Z.*) a mythical distance-marker (esp. as **beyond the black stump** in the far outback); **black swan** a swan with black plumage and red beak native to Australia: something rare or non-existent (*fig.*); **black'thorn** a dark-coloured thorn bearing sloes, with white flowers that appear before its leaves in March and April: a stick made from its stem; **black tie** a black bow tie worn with a dinner jacket for formal occasions; **black'-top** (esp. *U.S.*) layers of bituminous material in specified arrangement used for surfacing roads, etc.: a road so surfaced: the apron or runways at an airport; **black velvet** champagne and stout. — *adj.* **black'-vis'aged** having a black visage or appearance. — **black vomit** vomit containing blood, usu. being a sign of some disease, e.g. yellow fever; **black'wash** a lotion of calomel and lime-water: anything that blackens; **Black Watch** see **watch; blackwater** a cattle disease (see **redwater**): (also **blackwater fever**) a fever in which the urine is dark-coloured; **black widow** a very venomous American and Far Eastern spider, the female with a black body and the habit of eating her mate; **black'-wood** the dark-coloured timber of several trees, including the American logwood, an Australian acacia, and the East Indian *Dalbergia labifolia*: any one of the trees themselves: (with *cap.*) a bidding convention in bridge

named after its American inventor. — **black in the face** purple through strangulation, passion, or effort; **black out** to obliterate with black: to extinguish or cover all lights: suddenly to lose consciousness: to suppress (news or radio communication); **in black and white** in writing or in print: in art, etc. in no colours but black and white; **in someone's black books**, having incurred someone's displeasure; **in the black** solvent, out of debt: making a profit; **put the black on** (*slang*) to blackmail. [O.E. *blæc*, black.]

blad. See **blaud.**

bladder *blad'ər, n.* a thin distended or distensible bag: any such bag in the animal body, esp. the receptacle for urine. — *adjs.* **bladd'ered, bladd'ery.** — **bladd'er-camp'ion** a species of Silene with inflated calyx; **bladd'er-cherry** the winter-cherry or strawberry tomato; **bladd'er-nut** a genus (*Staphylea*) of shrubs with inflated capsule; **bladd'er-worm** the asexual state of a tapeworm or cestode; **bladd'erwort** a genus (*Utricularia*) of floating plants with bladders that catch small animals; **bladd'er-wrack** a common brown seaweed with bladders. [O.E. *blǣdre* — *blāwan*, to blow; O.H.G. *blā(h)en, blāien*, to blow; Ger. *Blatter* — *blähen*; cf. L. *flātus*, breath.]

blade *blād, n.* the flat or expanded part of a leaf or petal, esp. a leaf of grass or corn: the cutting part of a knife, sword, etc.: the flat part of an oar: the paddle-like part of a propeller: the free outer part of the tongue: a dashing fellow. — *adj.* **blad'ed.** — **blade'-bone** the flat bone at the back of the shoulder, the scapula. [O.E. *blæd*; O.N. *blath*; Ger. *Blatt*.]

blae *blā, (Scot.) adj.* blackish or dark bluish: livid: bleak. — *n.sing.* or *pl.* **blaes, blaize** or **blaise** (*blāz*) hardened clay or somewhat carbonaceous shale, often blae (also red) in colour. — **blae'berry** the whortleberry or bilberry. [O.N. *blār*, livid.]

blag *blag, (slang) v.t., v.i.* to rob. — *n.* a theft, robbery. [Ety uncertain.]

blague *blāg, n.* humbug: bounce. — *n.* **blagueur** (*blä-gœr*) one given to blague. [Fr.]

blah *blä, (slang) n.* bunkum: pretentious nonsense. — Also **blah'-blah'.** — *v.i.* to talk stupidly or insipidly. — *adj.* **blah** (*slang*) dull, insipid. [Poss. imit.]

blain¹ *blān, n.* a boil or blister. [O.E. *blegen*.]

blain² *blān, n.* a fish (*Gadus luscus*), the bib or pout.

blaise, blaize. See **blae.**

blame *blām, v.t.* to find fault with: to censure: to impute fault to: to charge with being cause: to bring discredit upon (*Spens.; B.*). — *n.* imputation of a fault: culpability: responsibility for what is amiss: injury (*Spens.*). — *adj.* (*U.S.*) confounded (also *adv.*). — *adj.* **blā'mable, blame'able.** — *n.* **blā'mableness, blame'ableness.** — *adv.* **blā'mably, blame'ably.** — *adjs.* **blamed** (*U.S. slang*) damned, confounded (also *adv.*); **blame'ful** meriting blame. — *adv.* **blame'fully.** — *n.* **blame'fulness.** — *adj.* **blame'less** without blame: guiltless: innocent. — *adv.* **blame'lessly.** — *adj.* **blame'worthy** worthy of blame: culpable. — **be to blame** to be blameworthy as being the cause. [Fr. *blâmer*, O.Fr. *blasmer* — Gr. *blasphēmeein*, to speak ill; see **blasphemee.**]

blanc-de-Chine *blä-də-shēn, n.* a white porcelain made at Te-hua under the Ming dynasty. [Fr., white of China.]

blanch *blänch, blänsh, v.t.* to whiten: to immerse (fruit, vegetables, etc.) briefly in boiling water (*cook.*). — *v.i.* to grow white. — *adj.* and *adv.* see **blench².** [Fr. *blanchir* — *blanc*, white; see **blank.**]

blanchisseuse *blä-shē-sœz, (Fr.) n.* a laundress.

blancmange *blə-mäzh', -mönzh', n.* orig. fowl or other flesh with cream, etc.: a milk dessert thickened with cornflour or gelatine and set in a mould. [Fr. *blancmanger* — *blanc*, white, *manger*, food.]

blanco *blangk'ō, (mil.) n.* an opaque white, khaki, etc. substance for treating uniform belts, etc. — *v.t.* to treat with blanco. [*Blanco*, a trademark — Fr. *blanc*, white.]

bland¹ *bland, adj.* smooth: gentle: mild: polite: suave:

ironical. — *adv.* **bland′ly.** — *n.* **bland′ness.** [L. *blandus.*]

bland² *bland, n.* in Orkney and Shetland, buttermilk and water. [O.N. *blanda*.]

blandish *bland′ish, v.t.* to flatter and coax, to cajole. — *n.* **bland′ishment** an act of expressing fondness: flattery: (in *pl.*) winning expressions or actions. [Fr. *blandir, blandiss-,* from L. *blandīrī*.]

blank *blangk, adj.* without writing or marks, as white paper: empty: featureless: expressionless: nonplussed: sheer: unrhymed. — *n.* a paper without writing: a lottery-ticket that brings no prize: an empty space, a void or vacancy: a lapse of memory or concentration: the white mark in the centre of a target (*archery*): a form of document having blank spaces to be filled up (*arch.* except in *U.S.*): a roughly shaped piece to be fashioned into a manufactured article: a dash in place of an omitted word: a blank cartridge. — *v.t.* to make blank: to make pale: to disconcert (*Milton*): mincingly used for 'damn', from the once usual form of printing 'd — ': (esp. with *off*) to seal (an opening) with a plug, etc.: to prevent (one's opponent in a game) from making any score. — *v.t.* and *v.i.* to produce blanks during a manufacturing process. — *n.* **blank′ing** — *adv.* **blank′ly.** — *n.* **blank′ness.** — **blank cartridge** one without a bullet; **blank cheque** a signed cheque in which the sum is not filled in: complete freedom to act as one thinks best (*fig.*); **blank door, window** a recess imitating a doorway or window. — *n.* or *adj.* or *adv.* **blank′ety-blank′, blank′ety, blank′y, blankety blank** *blank* coll. for 'damned' as in **blank** *v.t.* above. — **blank verse** unrhymed verse esp. of five feet. — **draw a blank** (*coll.*) to get no result, to fail. [Fr. *blanc,* from root of Ger. *blinken,* to glitter — O.H.G. *blichen;* cf. Gr. *phlegein,* to shine.]

blanket *blangk′it, n.* originally a white woollen fabric: a covering, generally woollen, for a bed, or used as a garment by American Indians, etc.: a covering generally: fertile material put round a nuclear reactor core to breed new fuel: coverage: something that conceals or obscures. — *v.t.* to cover, obstruct, or extinguish with, or as with, a blanket (as a ship by taking the wind out of her sails, gun-fire by getting in the way): to toss in a blanket: to bring under a single coverage. — *adj.* applying generally or covering all cases. — *n.* **blank′eting** cloth for blankets: tossing in a blanket. — **blanket bath** the washing of a sick person in bed; **blanket finish** a very close finish to a race; **blanket Indian, Kaffir** one wearing a blanket, not European clothes; **blanket stitch** a stitch used for the edge of a blanket. — **on the wrong side of the blanket** illegitimately; **wet blanket** a damper of spirits: a killjoy. [O.Fr. *blankete,* dim. of *blanc,* white.]

blanquet *blä-ke,* (Fr.) *n.* a variety of pear.

blanquette *blä-ket,* (Fr.) *n.* a ragout of e.g. chicken or veal made with a white sauce.

blare *blār, v.i.* to roar: to sound loudly, usu. harshly, as a trumpet. — *n.* roar: noise. [M.E. *blaren*.]

blarney *blär′ni, n.* flattery or cajoling talk. — *v.t.* to cajole. — **blar′ney-land** Ireland. [*Blarney* Castle, near Cork, where a stone difficult to reach confers the gift of persuasive talk on those who kiss it.]

blasé *blä′zā, adj.* dulled to pleasures: surfeited with enjoyments. [Fr. *pa.p.* of *blaser,* to cloy.]

blash *blash,* (*Scot.*) *n.* a dash or splash of liquid or semi-liquid: battering rain: watery stuff. — *adj.* **blash′y.**

blaspheme *blas-fēm′, v.t.* to speak impiously of. — *v.i.* to speak profanely or impiously: to curse and swear. — *n.* **blasphem′er.** — *adj.* **blasphemous** (*blas′fi-məs; Spens., Milt. -fē′*). — *adv.* **blas′phemously** (*Spens. -fē′*). — *n.* **blas′phemy** (*Spens.* also *-fē′*) impious or profane speaking: contempt or indignity offered to God. [Gr. *blasphēmiā;* see **blame.**]

blast *bläst, n.* a blowing or gust of wind: a forcible stream of air: a sound of a wind instrument: an explosion or detonation: a golf stroke of explosive effect: any scorching, withering or pernicious influence: a blight. —

v.i. to emit blasts, blow: to use explosives: to swell (*dial.*): to wither (*obs.*): to curse: to smoke marijuana (*slang*). — *v.t.* to blow up: to rend asunder with an explosive: to blow into: to inflate (*dial.*): to strike with a blast: to blight, wither, scorch: to strike with a curse. — *adj.* **blast′ed** blighted: cursed, damned. — *n.* **blast′er** one who blasts: a kind of niblick. — *n.* and *adj.* **blast′ing.** — *n.* **blast′ment** (*Shak.*) blight. — **blast′-furnace** a smelting furnace into which hot air is blown; **blast′-furnaceman; blast′-hole** a hole in the bottom of a pump through which water enters; **blast′-off** the (moment of) launching of a rocket-propelled missile or space capsule (*v.t.* and *v.i.* **blast off**); **blast′-pipe** a pipe in a steam-engine, to convey the waste steam up the chimney. — **in, at, full blast** in a state of maximum activity. [O.E. *blǣst;* cf. O.N. *blāsa,* Ger. *blasen.*]

blastema *bla-stē′mə, n.* primordial material: the primordium of an organ: the protoplasmic part of an ovum, distinguished from the yolk: the axial part of a plant embryo. [Gr. *blastēma,* sprout].

blasto- *blas′tō-,* in composition, sprout, bud, germ. — *ns.* **blas′tocyst** the blastula in mammals; **blas′tocoel(e)** (*-sēl*) the cavity inside a blastula; **blas′toderm** (Gr. *derma,* skin; *embryology*) the layer or layers of cells arising from the germinal disc, or the portion of a partially segmenting egg which undergoes division; **blastogenesis** (*-jen′*) transmission of hereditary characters by the germ-plasm: reproduction by budding. — *adj.* **blastogen′ic** pertaining to the germ-plasm. — *adj.* and *n.* **blast′oid.** — *n.pl.* **Blastoid′ea** (Gr. *eidos,* form) a group of bud-like calcareous fossil echinoderms. — *ns.* **blas′tomere** (Gr. *meros,* part) a cell formed in an early stage of the cleavage of a fertilised ovum; **blas′topore** (Gr. *poros,* a passage) the orifice of a gastrula; **blas′tosphere** (Gr. *sphaira,* a sphere) a blastula; **blas′tula** a hollow sphere of cells, one cell thick, formed in the cleavage of a fertilised ovum. — *adj.* **blast′ular.** — *n.* **blastulā′tion.** [Gr. *blastos,* a sprout.]

blat¹ *blat, v.i.* to cry like a sheep or calf: to make an ineffectual noise: to talk with little sense. — Also *v.t.* [Imit.]

blat². See **blatt.**

blatant *blā′tənt,* (*Spens.* also **blattant,** prob. *blat′ənt*), *adj.* clamorous: calumniously clamorous: egregiously vulgar: (*loosely*) flagrant. — *adv.* **blat′antly.** [Prob. a coinage of Spenser: for the *blatant beast,* see *Faerie Queene,* V. xii. 37 onward.]

blate *blāt,* (*Scot.*) *adj.* bashful, timidly awkward. [Perh. O.E. *blā,* pale.]

blather, blatherskite. See **blether.**

blatt, blat *blat,* (*slang*) *n.* a newspaper. [Ger.]

blatter *blat′ər* (chiefly *Scot.*) *n.* a clattering rainy blast: a clatter or torrent of words. — *v.i.* to beat with clattering, like rain on a window. — *v.t.* to utter volubly. [L. *blaterāre,* to prate, with sense probably modified by sound.]

blaubok *blow′bok, Afrik.* **bloubok** *blō′bok, n.* a small South African antelope: also a large extinct species. [Du. *blauw,* blue, *bok,* goat.]

blaud, blad *blöd,* (*Scot.*) *n.* a fragment: a broken-off slab: a screed or selection of verse. — *v.t.* to strike: to disfigure. [Perh. conn. with O.E. *blāwan,* to blow.]

Blaue Reiter, Der *blow-ə rī′tər, der,* the name given to an important art book published by two artists in Munich and transferred (1911) to the group of expressionist painters formed round them. [Ger., the Blue Rider.]

blawort *blä′, blä′wərt, n.* the harebell: the corn bluebottle. — Also **blewart** (*blōō′ərt*). [Scot. **blae,** and O.E. *wyrt,* herb.]

blay, bley *blā, n.* the bleak (fish). [O.E. *blæge.*]

blaze¹ *blāz, n.* a rush of light or of flame: an area of brilliant light or colour: a bursting out or active display. — *v.i.* to burn with a strong flame: to throw out a brilliant light: to be furious (*coll.*). — *n.* **blaz′er** a light sporting jacket, originally bright-coloured. — *n.pl.* **blaz′es** the fires of hell, in imprecations like **to**

blazes; also **like blazes** with fury. — **blaze away** to fire a rapid and repeated stream of bullets: to work very hard (*coll.*); **blaze up** to burst into flames: to become furious (*coll.*). [O.E. *blǽse*, torch.]

blaze² *blāz, n.* a white mark on a beast's face: a mark on a tree made by chipping the bark or otherwise. — *v.t.* to mark (a tree or a track) with a blaze. — **blaze the trail** to show the way as a pioneer. [Perh. Du. *bles* or O.N. *blesi*; or **blaze¹**.]

blaze³ *blāz, v.t.* to proclaim, to spread abroad. — *n.* **blaz′er** (*Spens.*) one who spreads abroad or proclaims. [Connected with O.N. *blāsa*, to blow; confused with **blazon**.]

blazer. See **blaze¹′³**.

blazon *blā′zn,* (*her.*) *blaz′, v.t.* to make public: to display ostentatiously: to depict or to explain in heraldic terms (*her.*). — *n.* a coat-of-arms, heraldic bearings (also *fig.*): the science or rules of coats-of-arms. — *ns.* **blaz′oner** one who blazons: a herald: a slanderer; **blaz′onry** the art of drawing or of deciphering coats-of-arms: heraldry. [Fr. *blason*, a shield, confused with **blaze³**.]

bleach *blēch, v.t.* to make pale or white: to whiten, as textile fabrics. — *v.i.* to grow white. — *n.* a process or act of bleaching: a bleaching agent. — *n.* **bleach′er** one who or that which bleaches. — *n.pl.* **bleach′ers** (esp. *U.S.*) cheap, open-air seats for spectators at a sports ground, etc.: the people occupying such seats. — *n.sing.* a tier of such seats. — *n.* **bleach′ery**, a place for bleaching. — *n.* and *adj.* **bleach′ing.** — **bleach′-field** a place for bleaching cloth: a bleacher's office or works; **bleaching green** a green for bleaching clothes on; **bleaching powder** a compound of calcium, chlorine, and oxygen ($CaOCl_2$). [O.E. *blǽcan*.]

bleak¹ *blēk, adj.* colourless: dull and cheerless: cold, unsheltered. — *adv.* **bleak′ly.** — *n.* **bleak′ness.** — *adj.* **bleak′y** bleak. [Apparently O.N. *bleikr,* answering to O.E. *blǽc, blāc,* pale, shining, black; cf. **bleach**.]

bleak² *blēk, n.* a small silvery river-fish whose scales yield a pigment used in making artificial pearls. [O.N. *bleikja,* or a lost equivalent O.E. word.]

blear *blēr, adj.* dim, watery: blurred as with inflammation. — *v.t.* to blur: to dim the sight of: to hoodwink. — *adj.* **bleared.** — *n.* **blear′iness.** — *adj.* **blear′y.** — *adj.* **blear′eyed, blear′y-eyed.** [Cf. Ger. *Blerr*, soreness of the eyes.]

bleat *blēt, v.i.* to cry like a sheep: to complain, grumble: to talk nonsense. — *n.* a sheep's cry or similar quavering sound: a complaint, grumble. — *n.* **bleat′er** (*coll.*) a complainer. — *n.* and *adj.* **bleat′ing.** [O.E. *blǽtan*; imit.; cf. L. *bālāre*, to bleat; Gr. *blēchē*, a bleating.]

bleb *bleb, n.* a transparent blister of the cuticle: a bubble, as in water. [Prob. imit.]

bled *bled, pa.t.* and *pa.p.* of **bleed**.

blee *blē,* (*arch.*) *n.* complexion, colour. [O.E. *blēo*.]

bleed *blēd, v.i.* to lose blood or sap: to die by slaughter: to issue forth or drop as blood: to have money, etc., extorted from one: to feel great pity (*fig.*). — *v.t.* to draw blood from, esp. surgically: to draw sap from: to extort or extract from: (in bookbinding) to trim so as to encroach on letterpress or illustrations: to draw off (air) from a hydraulic braking system, or (liquid or gas) from other closed system or holder: — *pa.t.* and *pa.p.* **bled.** — *ns.* **bleed′er** one who bleeds: an extortioner: one who suffers from haemophilia: a (nasty) person (*slang*); **bleed′ing** a discharge of blood or sap: letting blood: diffusion or running of colouring matter: traces of copper showing through worn silver-plate. — *adj.* full of compassion: emitting sap: terribly weakened by war: bloody (*Shak., coll.*). — **bleeding heart** a name given to various plants of the genera *Dicentra, Colocasia,* etc.: a contemptuous name for a do-gooder. — **bleed like a pig** to bleed copiously. [O.E. *blēdan.* See **blood**.]

bleep *blēp, v.i.* to give out a high sound or radio signal. — *n.* such a sound or signal: a bleeper — *n.* **bleep′er**

a detecting device that bleeps on receiving a certain radio or other signal: such a device, carried on the person by e.g. a doctor, policeman, etc., by which he can be contacted. [Imit.]

blemish *blem′ish, n.* a stain or defect: reproach. — *v.t.* to mark with any deformity: to tarnish: to defame: to disrupt (the peace) (*law*). — *n.* **blem′ishment** (*Spens.*). [O.Fr. *blesmir, blemir,* pr.p. *blemissant,* to stain, of dubious origin.]

blench¹ *blench, blensh, v.i.* to shrink or start back: to flinch: to start aside, fly off (*Shak.*): to be inconstant (*Shak.*). — *n.* a starting aside (*Shak.*). [O.E. *blencan*.]

blench² *blench, blensh, adj.* or *adv.* on the basis of payment of a nominal yearly duty. — Also **blanch**. [See **blank**.]

blend¹ *blend, v.t.* to mix together, esp. intimately or harmoniously: to pollute, vitiate (*Spens.*). — *v.i.* to be mingled: to harmonise: to shade off: — *pa.t.* and *pa.p.* usu. **blend′ed,** also, esp. *poet.,* **blent.** — *n.* a mixture. — *ns.* **blend′er; blend′ing.** [M.E. *blenden;* cf. O.E. *blandan,* O.N. *blanda*.]

blend² *blend,* (*obs.*) *v.t.* to blind: to dazzle: to obscure: — *pa.p.* (*y*)**blent′.** [O.E. *blendan*.]

blende *blend, n.* a mineral, zinc sulphide. [Ger. *Blende* — *blenden,* to deceive, from its resemblance to galena.]

Blenheim *blen′əm, n.* a kind of spaniel named from the Duke of Marlborough's seat.

blennorrhoea *blen-ō-rē′ə, n.* a discharge of mucus. [Gr. *blennos,* mucus, *rhoiā,* flow.]

blenny *blen′i, n.* member of the genus **Blennius** of acanthopterygian fishes, usually slimy. [Gr. *blennos,* mucus.]

blent *blent, pa.t.* and *pa.p.* of **blend**¹′².

blepharism *blef′ər-izm, n.* spasm of the eyelid. — *ns.* **blepharī′tis** inflammation of the eyelid; **blepharoplas′ty** plastic surgery of the eyelids. [Gr. *blepharon,* eyelid.]

blesbok *bles′bok, n.* a South African antelope with a blazed forehead. [Du. *bles,* blaze, *bok,* goat.]

bless¹ *bles, v.t.* to consecrate: to make the sign of the cross over: to extol as holy: to pronounce holy or happy: to invoke divine favour upon: to wish happiness to: to make joyous, happy, or prosperous: to glorify: to approve officially: — *pa.p.* **blessed** (*blest*), or **blest.** — *adj.* **bless′ed,** **blest** happy: prosperous: in heaven: beatified: (euphemistically) accursed, confounded. — *adv.* **bless′edly.** — *ns.* **bless′edness; bless′ing** a wish or prayer for happiness or success: any means or cause of happiness: a gift or present (*B.*): a form of invoking the favour of God at a meal: official approval. — **blessed sacrament** the consecrated Host. — **be blessed with** to have the good fortune to possess; **a blessing in disguise** something proving unexpectedly advantageous; **bless you** for **God bless you,** used superstitiously to someone who has just sneezed; **single blessedness** the unmarried state. [O.E. *blēdsian, blētsian, bletsian,* to bless, prob. from *blōd,* blood.]

bless² *bles,* (*Spens.*) *v.t.* to brandish: to brandish around: — *pa.t.* **blest, blist.** [Perh. from **bless¹** as if to make the sign of the cross: or from **bless³**; or poss. conn. with **blaze¹**.]

bless³ *bles, v.t.* to wound: to beat. [Fr. *blesser,* to wound.]

blest *blest, pa.p.* of **bless.** — Also *adj.*

blet *blet, n.* incipient internal decay in fruit without external sign: a part so affected. — *v.i.* to become soft or sleepy: — *pr.p.* **blett′ing;** *pa.t.* and *pa.p.* **blett′ed.** [Fr.]

blether (*Scot.*) *bledh′ər,* **blather** (*U.S.* and *dial.*) *bladh′ər, vs.i.* to talk garrulous nonsense. — *n.* one who blethers: (often in *pl.*) fluent, garrulous nonsense. — *n.* **bletherā′tion.** — *n.* and *adj.* **bleth′ering.** — **bleth′erskate, bleth′eranskate** (*Scot.*), **blath′erskite** (*dial.*) a loquacious talker of nonsense. [M.E. *blather* — O.N. *blathra,* talk foolishly, *blathr,* nonsense; prob. **skate** (the fish).]

bleuâtre *blo-ätr′,* (Fr.) *adj.* bluish.

blew¹ *blōō, pa.t.* of **blow**.

blew² an old spelling (*Spens., Milt.*) of **blue**.

blewart. See **blawort**.

blewits *blū′its, n.* a kind of edible mushroom of the *Tricholoma* family, lilac-coloured when young. [Perh. from **blue**.]

bley *blā, n.* same as **blay**.

blight *blīt, n.* a disease in plants which blasts or withers them: a fungus, insect, or other cause of blight: anything that injures, destroys, depresses, or frustrates: a damp, depression, decay, set-back, check. — *v.t.* to affect with blight: to blast: to frustrate. — *adj.* **blight′ed** affected with blight: of a (usu. urban) area, becoming a slum. — *n.* **blight′er** a cause of blighting: a term of (usu. playful) abuse, scamp, beggar, wretch (*slang*). — *n.* and *adj.* **blight′ing.** — *adv.* **blight′ingly.** — **planning blight** a fall in value, and consequent neglect, of property in an area, caused by uncertainty about its planned future. [17th cent.: origin obscure; poss. conn. with **bleach, bleak**.]

blighty *blī′ti, (mil. slang) n.* the home country: a wound necessitating return home. [Hind. *bilāyatī,* foreign, European — Ar. *wilāyat* province, country. Cf. **vilayet**.]

blimbing. Same as **bilimbi.**

blimey, blimy *blī′mi, interj.* a Cockney vulgarism for *God blind me.*

blimp *blimp, n.* a small type of airship-like, heavier-than-air, craft for scouting, advertising, etc.: an incurably conservative elderly military officer, as Colonel *Blimp* of the cartoonist David Low (1891–1963), or any other person of similar views: soundproof housing for sound-film camera. — *adj.* **blimp′ish** like Colonel Blimp.

blimy. See **blimey.**

blin *blin, (Spens.) v.t.* and *v.i.* to cease from, to cease. — *n.* cessation: stoppage. [O.E. *blinnan,* to cease, pfx. **be-** (1), and *linnan,* to cease.]

blind *blīnd, adj.* without sight: dark: obscure: invisible: concealed: not directed, or affording no possibility of direction, by sight or by foresight: ignorant or undiscerning: unobserving: voluntarily overlooking: without an opening: failing to flower or fruit: in flying, using instruments only, without seeing course or receiving radio directions: drunk (*coll.*). — *n.* something intended to blind one to the facts: a window-screen: a shade: a stake put up without seeing one's cards (*poker*): a drinking spree (*slang*). — *v.t.* to make blind: to darken, obscure, or deceive: to dazzle: to render matt: to fill in the interstices of. — *v.i.* to curse, swear (*slang*). — *n.* **blind′age** (*mil.*) a temporary wooden screen faced with earth as a protection against splinters of shell and the like. — *adj.* **blind′ed** deprived of sight: without intellectual discernment. — *n.* **blind′er** one who or that which blinds: a horse's blinker: a spectacular piece of play, esp. in cricket or football (*coll.*): a drinking spree (*coll.*). — *n.* and *adj.* **blind′ing.** — *adj.* **blind′less.** — *adv.* **blind′ly.** — *n.* **blind′ness** want of sight: ignorance: folly. — **blind′-all′ey** a cul-de-sac: a situation, job, etc., which does not offer any prospect of improvement or advancement (also *adj.*); **blind′-coal** anthracite (as burning without flame): coal partly carbonised by an igneous intrusion; **blind date** an appointment with someone one has not seen, as with a dance partner chosen for one: the partner, etc., so chosen. — *adj.* **blind′-drunk′** so drunk as to be like a blind man. — **blind′fish** an eyeless fish (Amblyopsis) of the Kentucky Mammoth Cave. — *adj.* **blind′fold** (earlier **blind′-felled,** struck blind) having the eyes bandaged so as not to see: thoughtless: performed without seeing: reckless. — Also *adv.* — *v.t.* to cover the eyes of: to mislead. — *n.* a piece of fabric, handkerchief, etc. used for covering up the eyes. — **blind′-gut** the caecum; **blind′man's-buff′** (i.e. buffet) a game in which a blindfold player tries to catch the others; **blind road** a grassy track invisible to those that are on it; **blind′-side** the side on which a person is blind to danger: weak point: (*usu.* **blind side**) the part of the field between the scrum, etc. and the touch-line nearer it (*rugby*); **blind spot** the spot on the retina where the optic nerve joins and where there are no visual cells: a point within the normal range of a transmitter at which the field strength is abnormally small (*radio*): a point just outside the range of one's vision: a region of understanding in which one's intuition and judgment always fail; **blind′-storey** a triforium; **blind tooling, stamping** impression without gilding; **blind′worm** a slow-worm, a legless lizard with eyes so small as to be supposed blind. — **bake blind** to bake (a pastry case) separately, without its filling; **not a blind bit of** (*coll.*) not any; **the blind leading the blind** the ignorant trying to instruct the ignorant. [O.E. *blind;* O.N. *blindr.*]

blin(i). See **blintz(e).**

blink *blingk, v.i.* to glance, twinkle, or wink: to see obscurely: to look with the eyes half-closed: to shine unsteadily. — *v.t.* to shut out of sight: to ignore or evade. — *n.* a glimpse, glance, or wink: a gleam, esp. momentary. — *n.* **blink′ard** one who blinks or has bad eyes. — *adj.* **blinked** affected with blinking. — *n.* **blink′er** a leather flap to prevent a horse from seeing sidewise. — *v.t.* to obscure or limit the vision of (*lit.* and *fig.*). — *adj.* or intensive *adv.* **blink′ing** (*slang*) used to add force or emphasis, prob. as a substitute for bloody. — *n.* **blinks** a mud or water weed (*Montia*) of the purslane family, with minute flowers. — **on the blink** (of an electrical or electronic device) (going) out of order. [Cf. **blench**[1].]

blintz(e) *blints,* **blin(i)** *blin, blin′i, ns.* a thin filled pancake. [Yiddish *blintse* Russ. *blin,* pancake.]

blip *blip, n.* a sharp tap or blow: the image of an object on a radar screen, usu. a bright spot or sudden sharp peak on a line: the small, high sound made by a radar instrument. — *v.i.* to produce a blip. — *v.t.* to tap, hit, sharply.

bliss *blis, n.* the highest happiness: the special happiness of heaven. — *adj.* **bliss′ful.** — *adv.* **bliss′fully.** — *n.* **bliss′fulness.** — *adj.* **bliss′less.** [O.E. *blīths* — *blīthe,* blithe.]

blist *blist, (Spens.) pa.t.* and *pa.p.* of **bless**[1,2].

blister *blis′tər, n.* a thin bubble or bladder on the skin, often containing watery matter: a similar spot elsewhere, as on a leaf, metal, paint: the protective bulging outer hull of a double-hulled ship, to lessen risk of sinking (*naut.*): a plaster applied to raise a blister: a transparent bulge on the upper surface of an aeroplane forming part of its structure. — *v.t.* to raise a blister or blisters on: to burn with scathing words (*fig.*): to ornament with puffs (*Shak.*). — *v.i.* to develop blisters. — *adjs.* **blis′tery; blis′tering** of criticism, virulent, cruel (*fig.*): painfully intense or strenuous: of the weather, very hot: (of an action, pace, etc.) hard, fast. — **blis′ter-bee′tle, blis′ter-fly** an insect used for blistering, esp. Spanish fly (Cantharis); **blister card, pack** a bubble pack; **blister copper** copper at an intermediate stage of production, about 98% pure; **blis′ter-plas′ter** a plaster made of Spanish flies, used to raise a blister; **blis′ter-steel, blis′tered-steel** steel made from wrought-iron with blistered surface. [M.E.; most prob. O.Fr. *blestre,* conn. with O.N. *blāstr, blāsa,* to blow; Ger. *Blase.*]

blite *blīt, n.* a name for several plants of the goosefoot family. [Gr. *bliton.*]

blithe *blīdh, adj.* jocund: cheerful: gay: sprightly. — *adv.* **blithe′ly.** — *n.* **blithe′ness.** — *adj.* **blithe′some** joyous. — *adv.* **blithe′somely.** — *n.* **blithe′someness.** [O.E. *blīthe,* joyful. See **bliss**.]

blither *blidh′ər, v.i.* another form of **blather, blether.** — *adj.* **blith′ering** (used as an expression of contempt).

blitz *blits, n.* an attack or bombing from the air (also **blitzkrieg** *blits′krēg*): any sudden, overwhelming attack (also **blitzkrieg**): an intensive campaign (*coll.*): a burst of intense activity, in order to achieve something (*coll.*). — *v.t.* to attack or damage (as if) by air-raid: to deal with or complete by a burst of intense activity (*fig.*). [Ger. *Blitzkrieg,* lightning war, the German method in 1939 — *Blitz,* lightning, *Krieg,* war.]

blive *blīv*, (*Spens.*) *adv.* Same as **belive.**

blizzard *bliz'ərd, n.* a blinding storm of wind and snow, a snow-squall. — *adjs.* **blizz'ardly; blizz'ardous.** [A modern coinage, most prob. onomatopoeic, on the analogy of *blow, blast,* etc.]

bloat *blōt, v.t.* to swell or puff out: to dry partially by smoke (applied to fish). — *v.i.* to swell or dilate: to grow turgid. — *n.* hoove (also **bloat'ing**): bloatedness: a drunkard. — *adj.* puffed up, swollen, esp. with self-indulgence. — *adj.* **bloat'ed** having been bloated: swollen (often as a result of gluttony): swollen with riches (*fig.*). — *n.* **bloat'er** a herring partially dried in smoke, esp. at Yarmouth. [Cf. O.N. *blautr,* soft.]

blob *blob, n.* a drop or globule: anything soft and round, as a gooseberry: a round spot: zero. — *v.i.* to make a blob, to form into a blob. [Imit.]

bloc *blok, n.* a combination of parties, nations, or other units to achieve a common purpose. [Fr.]

block *blok, n.* a mass of wood or stone, etc., usu. flat-sided: a piece of wood or other material used as a support (as for chopping, beheading), or as a mould (as for hats), or for printing from (as wood-engravings, process-blocks), or as a toy (for building): (in *pl.*) starting-blocks (q.v.): a pulley with its framework or the framework alone: a compact mass, group or set, e.g. of seats, sheets of paper, shares, etc.: a group of buildings forming a square-shaped mass, bounded by intersecting streets: such a group regarded as a measure of distance (*U.S.*): a large building containing individual units of accommodation, etc.: a building lot (esp. *Austr.*): an obstruction: a head: a blockhead: an impassive person: a psychological barrier preventing intellectual development, progress, etc.: an instance of, or a cause of, blockage or blocking: an administrative unit in India: a bloc: (also **license block**) a section of sea within which a company is licensed to explore for and extract oil or gas: a cylinder block. — *adj.* in a block or lump: comprising a number grouped and dealt with together. — *v.t.* to enclose or shut up: to restrict: to obstruct: to make inactive: to shape as on a block, or to sketch out roughly (often with *in* or *out*): to stop (a ball) with bat resting upright on the ground: to print (usu. a fabric) from a block. — *n.* **blockade'** cutting a place off by surrounding it with troops or by ships: obstruction. — *v.t.* to block up by troops or ships. — *n.* **block'age** act or instance of obstructing, or state of being obstructed: resistance to understanding, learning, etc., set up by existing habits of thought and action. — *adj.* **blocked** meanings as *pa.p.* of verb: subject to restriction in use. — *ns.* **block'er** (*med.*) a substance, used as a drug, that prevents the production, or the operation, of some other substance in the body; **block'ing** interruption of a train of thought, esp. by unpleasant thoughts rising in the mind. — *adjs.* **block'ish** like a block: stupid: dull; **block'y** block-shaped: in blocks: stocky, chunky. — **blockade'-runner** a person or ship that passes through a blockading force; **block'board** board made up of plywood veneer enclosing thin strips of wood; **block'-book** a book printed from engraved blocks, not movable types; **block'buster** a bomb or explosive charge able to destroy a number of buildings simultaneously: a thing or person notably forceful, effective and overwhelming (also *adj.*); **block'busting.** — Also *adj.* — **block capital** a capital letter written in imitation of type: **block'-chain'** an endless chain of blocks and links; **block'-coal** coal that breaks into cuboidal blocks; **block grant** a fixed general grant made by the central government to a local authority for all its services, as distinct from a series of specific grants each a percentage of the amount spent locally on the various services; **block'-head** a wooden head: a dolt; **block'hole** (*cricket*) the place where a batsman rests his bat; **block'house** a small temporary fort: a house constructed of squared logs: a shelter of reinforced concrete, etc. used as an observation post and control centre for rocket launches, etc.; **blocking motion** notice of intention to bring up a

certain matter at a future date, thus preventing (or blocking) raising of the subject on a motion for adjournment; **block letter** a block capital: block type; **block release** release from employment for a period in order to complete a course of study; **block'-ship** a warship too old for action, but useful in port defence: **block'-system** a system in which no train is allowed on to a section of railway so long as any other is on it; **block'-tin** tin in the form of blocks or ingots; **block type** a heavy-letter type, without serifs; **block vote** a vote by a delegate at a conference, counted as the number of people he represents; **block'work** hollow blocks of precast concrete used for building. — **do one's block** (*Austr.* and *N.Z. coll.*) to be very angry; **on the block** up for auction. [Fr. *bloc,* probably Gmc.]

bloke *blōk, n.* a man (*slang*): the commander (*naut.*). [Origin obscure.]

bloncket *blongk'et,* (*Spens.*) *adj.* grey. [Fr. *blanquet, blanchet,* whitish, dim. of *blanc,* white.]

blond (*fem.* **blonde**) *blond, n.* a person of fair complexion and light-coloured hair — opp. to *brunet(te).* — *adj.* (of hair) between golden and light chestnut in colour: of a fair complexion: fair: light-coloured. — **blond beast** (or with *caps.*) blond type of primitive northern European man, admired, e.g. by Nietzsche, for his physical splendour: any predatory type of man; **blon-d(e)'-lace** lace made of silk, originally raw silk. [Fr.]

blood *blud, n.* the oxygenating fluid (red in the higher animals) circulating in the body: descent, good birth: relationship, kindred: (elliptically) a blood-horse, one of good pedigree: a swaggering dandy about town: the blood-royal (as in *princes of the blood*): temperament: bloodshed or murder: the juice of anything, esp. if red: the supposed seat of passion — hence temper, anger (as *his blood is up*), etc.: the sensual nature of man: sensational or melodramatic tale, a penny-dreadful (*slang*). — *v.t.* to bleed: to smear with blood: to initiate into blood sports or to war (also *fig.*). — *adj.* **blood'ed** having blood: of pure blood, pedigreed: initiated. — *adj.* **blood'ily.** — *adj.* **blood'less** without blood: dead: anaemic: without bloodshed: without spirit or activity (*Shak.*). — *n.* **blood'lessness.** — *adj.* **blood'y** of the nature of blood: stained with blood: murderous, cruel. — as an *adj.* emphasising anger or the like, or almost meaningless, as an *adv.* employed as an intensive — most prob. from the habits of the late 17th-century bloods (Etheredge, '*bloody*-drunk') (*coll.*). — *v.t.* to make bloody. — **blood agar** agar-agar for growing bacteria, to which blood has been added before the jelly set. — *adj.* **blood'-and-thund'er** sensational, melodramatic. — **blood bank** a supply of blood plasma, or the place where it is kept; **blood'-bath** a bath in warm blood: a massacre (also *fig.*). — *adj.* **blood'-bespott'ed** spotted, sprinkled with blood. — **blood'-bird** an Australian honey-eater, the male of which has scarlet plumage; **blood blister** a blister with blood in it, caused e.g. by a bruise. — *adjs.* **blood'-bol'tered** clotted or matted with blood; **blood'-bought** (*Shak.*) bought at the expense of blood or life. — **blood'-brother** a brother by blood: among primitive peoples, one who has entered a close and binding friendship with another by ceremonies involving the mixing of blood. — *adj.* **blood'-consuming** (*Shak.*). — **blood count** the number of red or white corpuscles in the blood. — *adj.* **blood'curdling** exciting horror with a physical feeling as if the blood had curdled. — **blood donor** one who gives blood for use in transfusion; **blood'-dust** haemoconia; **blood'-feud** a family feud arising out of an act of bloodshed: a vendetta; **blood'-flower** Haemanthus: a species of *Asclepias.* — *adj.* **blood'-froz'en** (*Spens.*) having the blood frozen or chilled. — **blood'-group** any one of the four types of human blood (designated O, A, B, AB) which may or may not prove incompatible on transfusion; **blood'-guilt, blood'-guiltiness** the guilt of shedding blood, as in murder. — *adj.* **blood'-guilty.** — **blood'heat** the temperature of human blood (37°C, about 98°F); **blood'-horse** a horse of the purest and most highly prized blood, origin, or stock. — *adj.* **blood'-hot** as hot or warm as blood. — **blood'hound** a large, keen-scented (sleuth) hound, noted for its powers of tracing: a detective (*fig.*); **blood'letter; blood'-letting** bleeding by opening a vein: bloodshed; **blood'-line** (of animals, etc.) all the individuals in a family line over a number of generations, esp. as considered with regard to some characteristic or other; **blood'lust** desire for bloodshed; **blood'-money** money earned by laying or supporting a capital charge against anyone, esp. if the charge be false or made by an accomplice: money paid to a hired assassin: compensation formerly paid to the next of kin of a victim slain; **blood orange** a variety of orange with red or red-streaked pulp; **blood'-plate** a platelet; **blood'-poisoning** a name popularly, but loosely, used of pyaemia and allied diseases; **blood pressure** the pressure of the blood on the walls of the blood-vessels, varying with age and physical condition; **blood'-pudding** a pudding made with blood and other materials; **blood purge** massacre or execution of large numbers believed by a government or ruler to be disloyal; **blood'-rain** rain coloured by red dust from the desert. — *adj.* **blood'-red'** of the colour of blood. — **blood'-rela'tion** one related by common ancestry; **blood'root** a plant (*Sanguinaria canadensis*) of the poppy family with red rootstock and sap; **blood-roy'al** royal descent; **blood'-sac'rifice** (*Shak.*) a sacrifice made with bloodshed; **blood'shed** the shedding of blood: slaughter. — *adjs.* **blood'shot** (of the eye) red or inflamed with blood; **blood'-sized** sized or smeared with blood. — **blood'-spav'in** a disease of horses consisting of the swelling of a vein on the inside of the hock, from a checking of the blood; **blood sports** those involving the killing of animals — fox-hunting and the like. — *adj.* **blood'sprent** sprinkled with blood. — **blood'stain.** — *adj.* **blood'stained** stained with blood: guilty of murder. — **blood'stock** pedigree horses collectively: young men available as dance partners; **blood'stone** a green chalcedony with blood-like spots of red jasper: haematite; **blood'stream** the blood flowing through the body: something playing a similarly vital part (*fig.*); **blood'sucker** an animal that sucks blood, esp. a leech: an extortioner: one who sponges upon another. — *adj.* **blood'sucking** that sucks or draws blood. — **blood'-tax** conscription or universal military service, as drawing from the nation, a number of lives or recruits annually; **blood test** an examination (chemical, microscopical, bacteriological) of a small specimen of blood usually drawn from a blood-vessel; **blood'thirstiness** eager desire to shed blood. — *adj.* **blood'thirsty.** — **blood transfusion** the taking of blood from the veins of one person and subsequent injection of it into those of another; **blood'-vessel** a vein or artery; **blood'-wagon** (*slang*) an ambulance; **blood'-wite, -wit** (*hist.*) a fine for shedding blood: the right to levy it; **blood'wood** a name for various trees with red wood or juice, of their timber, as a lythraceous tree of the East Indies (Lagerstroemia), eucalyptus of different kinds, logwood; **blood'-worm** a red aquatic midge larva (*Chironomus*); **blood'y-bones'** see rawhead. — *adjs.* **blood'y-eyed; blood'y-faced.** — **bloody flux** dysentery, in which the discharges from the bowels are mixed with blood; **bloody hand** see hand; **bloody Mary** a cocktail consisting of vodka, tomato juice and seasoning. — *adj.* **blood'y-mind'ed** liking bloodshed, cruel: in a mood of, or inclined to show, aggressive obstinacy. — **blood'y-mind'edness; blood'y-sweat** a sweat accompanied by the discharge of blood. — **after, out for (someone's) blood** having murderous intentions (towards someone) (*lit.* and *fig.*); **avenger of blood** the next of kin to a murdered man whose duty it was thought to avenge his death; **blood and iron** see Blut; **first blood** the first drawing of blood in a fight (also *fig.*); **fresh** or **new blood** new members in any association of people, to add liveliness; **in blood** in full vigour; **in hot** or **cold blood** under or free from excitement or sudden passion;

in one's blood in one's character, inborn; **make someone's blood boil** to arouse someone's fury. [O.E. *blōd*; O.Fris. *blōd*; Ger. *Blut.*]

bloom[1] *blōōm, n.* a blossom or flower (also collectively): the state of being in flower: the prime or highest perfection of anything: the first freshness of beauty of anything: rosy colour: the glow on the cheek: a powdery, waxy, or cloudy surface or appearance: an efflorescence. — *v.i.* to put forth blossoms: to flower: to be in a state of beauty or vigour: to flourish. — *v.t.* to give a bloom to. — *n.* **bloom'er** a plant that blooms: a floriated initial letter: an absurd and embarrassing blunder (*slang*): a longish crusty loaf of white bread with rounded ends and a number of slashes across the top. — *adj.* **bloom'ing** flowering: flourishing: fresh and youthful: bright: euphemistically for bloody (*slang*). — *adjs.* **bloom'less** without bloom; **bloom'y** flowery: flourishing, covered with bloom. [O.N. *blōm*; cf. Goth. *blōma*, Ger. *Blume.*]

bloom[2] *blōōm, n.* a mass or bar of iron or steel in an intermediate stage of manufacture, esp. one thicker than a *billet.* — *n.* **bloom'ery** a furnace for making iron ore or iron into blooms. [O.E. *blōma.*]

bloomer[1] *blōōm'ər, n. and adj.* a dress for women, advocated by Mrs *Bloomer* of New York about 1849 (although not devised by her), consisting of a jacket with close sleeves, a skirt falling a little below the knee, and Turkish trousers: (in *pl.*) bloomer trousers: (in *pl.*) a loose undergarment similar to knickers, but fuller.

bloomer[2]. See bloom[1].

Bloomsbury Group *blōōmz'bər-i grōōp,* a group of literary and artistic friends, some living in Bloomsbury, who wrote during and after the First World War; they included Virginia Woolf, Lytton Strachey, and E. M. Forster. — *n.* **Blooms'buryite** a member of the Bloomsbury Group.

bloop *blōōp, n.* a howling sound on a sound-track or made by a radio. — *v.i.* to make such a sound. — *n.* **bloo'per** a radio that makes such a sound: a stupid mistake (*slang.*) [Imit.]

bloosme *blōōm, n. and v.i.* Spenser's form of **blossom**, modified by **bloom**[1].

blore *blōr, blör, n.* a violent gust of wind. [Prob. related to **blare** and **blow.**]

blossom *blos'əm, n.* a flower or bloom, esp. one that precedes edible fruit: the state of being in flower, literally or figuratively. — *v.i.* (often with *out*) to put forth blossoms or flowers: to flourish and prosper. — *n.* **bloss'oming.** — *adj.* **bloss'omy** covered with flowers, flowery. [O.E. *blōstm, blōstma,* from the same root as **bloom**[1], and L. *flōs.*]

blot[1] *blot, n.* a spot, as of a drop of ink: an obliteration: a stain in reputation: a blemish. — *v.t.* to obliterate, destroy (with *out*): to spot or smudge: to disgrace: to blemish: to dry with blotting-paper: — *pr.p.* **blott'ing;** *pa.t.* and *pa.p.* **blott'ed.** — *ns.* **blott'er** one who blots: a bad author: a sheet, pad, or book of blotting-paper; **blottesque** (*-esk'*) a painting executed with heavy blot-like touches: a daub: a vigorous descriptive sketch (*fig.*). — Also *adj.* — *n.* **blott'ing** spotting as with ink: obliterating: smudging: drying with blotting-paper: blotting-paper. — *adjs.* **blott'o** (*slang*) helplessly drunk; **blott'y** blotted: smudged. — **blott'ing-pad** a pad of blotting-paper; **blott'ing-paper** unsized paper, used for absorbing ink. — **blot one's copybook** to blemish one's record, esp. by an indiscretion. [Origin obscure.]

blot[2] *blot, n.* a piece liable to be taken at backgammon: exposure of a piece: a weak place in anything. [Cf. Dan. *blot,* Du. *bloot,* naked, exposed.]

blot[3] *blot,* (*Spens.*) *n.* spawn. [Perh. conn. with **blow**[3].]

blotch *bloch, n.* an irregular discoloration: a pustule: any plant disease characterised by blotching. — *v.t.* to mark or cover with blotches. — *adj.* **blotched.** — *n.* **blotch'iness.** — *n. and adj.* **blotch'ing.** — *adj.* **blotch'y.** [Prob. formed on **blot**[1].]

bloubok. See blaubok.

blouse *blowz, n.* a loose sack-like, belted outer garment, like the smock-frock: a woman's usu. loose-fitting garment for the upper part of the body. — *v.t.* to arrange in loose folds. — *v.i.* to puff out loosely with air, as a sail. [Fr.]

blouson *blōō′zon, n.* a loose outer garment fastened at the waist by a belt, drawstring, etc. — **blouson noir** (*blōō-zõ nwär*) a rebellious young man, usu. one of a group, so called from the black windcheaters worn by many of them. [Fr.]

blow¹ *blō, n.* a stroke or knock: a sudden misfortune or calamity. — *adj.* **blow′-by-blow′** of a story or description, very detailed. — **at a blow** by a single action, suddenly; **come to blows** (of people quarrelling) to start fighting. [Found from the 15th century; perh. from **blow³** or conn. with Ger. *bläuen,* to beat.]

blow² *blō, v.i.* to bloom or blossom. — *v.t.* (*Milt.*) to put forth, as flowers: — *pr.p.* **blow′ing**; *pa.t.* **blew** (*blōō*); *pa.p.* **blown** (*blōn*). — *n.* blossom, bloom: display of blossom. [O.E. *blōwan*; Ger. *blühen*; cf. **bloom¹, blossom.**]

blow³ *blō, v.i.* to produce a current of air: to move, as air or wind (often *impers.*): to breathe hard: to spout, as whales: to boast: to act as an informer (*slang*): (of insects) to deposit eggs: of an electric fuse, to melt (also *v.t.*). — *v.t.* to drive air upon or into: to drive by a current of air: to sound, as a wind-instrument: to destroy or force by explosive: to spread by report: to inform upon: to fan or kindle: (of insects) to deposit eggs on: to curse: to squander (*slang*): to fail to succeed with or in when one has the chance (*slang*; usu. with *it*): — *pa.t.* **blew** (*blōō*); *pa.p.* **blown** (*blōn*), in imprecations **blowed** (*blōd*). — *n.* a blast: an insect egg. — *ns.* **blow′er** one who blows: a metal plate on the upper part of a fireplace to increase the draught: a machine for driving a blast of air: a speaking-tube, telephone, or similar means of sending messages (*coll.*): a communication system, esp. one used by bookmakers and their representatives, or one keeping police headquarters in touch with police cars (*coll.*); **blow′ie** (*Austr.* and *N.Z. coll.*) a blowfly. — *adjs.* **blown** out of breath, tired: swelled: stale, worthless; **blow′y** windy: gusty. — **blow′ball** the downy head of a dandelion in seed; **blow′down** an accident in a nuclear reactor. — *v.t.* **blow′-dry** to arrange (hair) by simultaneously brushing and drying it with a hand-held hair-drier. — Also *n.* — **blow′fly** a flesh-fly (*Sarcophaga*): a bluebottle (*Calliphora*); **blow′gun** a blowpipe (weapon); **blow′hard** a boastful person. — Also *adj.* — **blow′hole** a whale's nostril: a hole in ice to which seals, etc., come to breathe: a vent for escape of gas, etc.: a bubble in metal: a natural vent from the roof of a cave up to the ground surface, through which air and water are forced by rising tides; **blow job** (*vulg. slang*) an act of fellatio; **blow′lamp** a portable lamp producing heat by a blast; **blow′-mould′ing** a process used in fabricating plastic objects, the molten thermoplastic being blown against the sides of the mould; **blow′-out** a feast (*slang*): a tyre burst (*coll.*): a violent escape of oil and gas from an oilwell; **blow-out preventer** a valve in the well-head of an oilwell to prevent blow-outs; **blow′pipe** a pipe through which air is blown on a flame, to increase its heat, used in *blowpipe analysis,* etc.: a long straight tube from which an arrow, pellet, etc., is blown by the breath: a glass-blower's tube; **blow′torch** a blowlamp; **blow′-up** an explosion: an enlargement of (part of) a photograph, illustration, etc.; **blow′-valve** a snifting-valve. — **blow away** to kill, murder (*slang*); **blow hot and cold** to be favourable and unfavourable by turns, to be irresolute; **blow in** to turn up casually; **blow off** (steam, etc.) to allow to escape, to escape forcibly; **blow one's, someone's, mind** (*slang*) to go, cause to go, into a state of ecstasy under the influence of a drug or of an exhilarating experience; **blow one's top** (*coll.*) to explode in anger; **blow out** to extinguish by blowing: to force outwards by an explosion: of a tyre, to burst (*coll.*): of an oilwell, to emit an uncontrolled jet of oil and gas; **blow over** to pass away, as a storm, a danger

or a scandal; **blow someone's cover** (*slang*) to reveal someone's identity; **blow the whistle on** (*slang*) to inform on (a person); **blow up** to come into being: to destroy by explosion: to explode: to finish in disaster: to inflate: to scold: to lose one's temper: to enlarge, as an illustration: to go to pieces (*U.S.*); **blow upon** to take the bloom, freshness, or the interest off: to bring into discredit: to inform upon. [O.E. *blāwan*; Ger. *blähen, blasen*; L. *flāre.*]

blowze, blowse *blowz, n.* a ruddy, fat-faced wench. — *adjs.* **blowzed, blowz′y, blowsed, blowsy** fat and ruddy, or flushed with exercise: dishevelled: coarse, rowdy. [Perh. related to **blush** or **blow,** or of cant origin.]

blub *blub,* (*coll.*) *v.i.* to weep: — *pr.p.* **blubb′ing**; *pa.t.* and *pa.p.* **blubbed.** [Short for **blubber.**]

blubber *blub′ər, n.* a jellyfish: the fat of whales and other sea animals: excessive fat: a bout of weeping. — *v.i.* to weep effusively. — *adj.* **blubb′ered** of a face, swollen with weeping. [M.E. *blober, bluber*; prob. imit.]

blucher properly *blühh′ər,* often *blōōk′ər,* or *blōōch′ər, n.* a strong leather half-boot or high shoe. [Marshal *Blücher,* the Prussian general at Waterloo.]

blude *blüd, n.* a Scots form of **blood.** — *adj.* **blud′y, blud′ie.**

bludge *bluj,* (*slang*) *n.* a soft job. — *v.i.* to loaf about: to evade work or other responsibility. — *v.i.* and *v.t.* to scrounge. — *n.* **bludg′er.**

bludgeon *bluj′n, n.* a short stick with a heavy striking end. — *v.t.* to beat with a bludgeon: to assail heavily: to coerce (*coll.*). [First in 18th century; origin very obscure.]

blue¹ *blōō, adj.* of the colour of the unclouded sky or the like, applied also to that of wood-smoke, skim-milk, lead: livid: greyish: dismal: depressed: learned, pedantic: indecent or obscene: dressed in blue: symbolised by blue. — *n.* the colour of blue things: a blue object: the sky: the sea: a blue pigment: (also **wash′ing-blue**) a blue powder or liquid (indigo, Prussian blue, etc.) used in laundries: a member of a party whose colour is blue (as the opponents of the Greens in ancient Constantinople, *hist.* the Presbyterians, and later often the Conservatives): a present or past representative of Oxford or Harrow (dark), Cambridge or Eton (light blue) in sports: a similar representative of any university: the badge awarded to him or her, or the honour of wearing it: blue clothes: a bluestocking: a butterfly of the family *Lycaenidae*: a former squadron of the British fleet: (in *pl.*) depression, the blue devils: (in *pl.* usu. construed as *sing.*) a slow, sad song orig. an American Negro folksong, characteristically with three four-bar lines and blue notes, or any similar composition (sometimes neither slow nor sad). — *v.t.* to make blue: to treat with blue. — *v.i.* to turn blue. — *ns.* **blue′ing, blu′ing** the process of imparting a blue colour, esp. to metal, or of neutralising yellow: blue-rot in wood: laundress's blue (*U.S.*); **blue′ness.** — *adjs.* **blues′y** blues-like; **bluey** (*blōō′i*) inclined towards blue (esp. in compounds, as **blu′ey-green′**). — *n.* a bundle or swag, often in a blue cloth (*Austr.*): someone with ginger hair (*Austr. slang*). — *adj.* **blu′ish.** — **blue baby** a baby with congenital cyanosis; **blue′back** the sockeye, chief salmon of the North Pacific; **Blue′beard** a villainous character in European folkore, who murdered his wives in succession: (also without *cap.*) such a wife-murderer; **blue′bell** in S. England the wood-hyacinth: (*blōō′bel′*) in Scotland and N. England the harebell; **blue′berry** the fruit of *Vaccinium vacillans* and other American species; **blue′bird** a small American bird (*Sialia sialis*) akin to the warblers. — *n.* and *adj.* **blue′-black** black with a tinge of blue: blue changing in time to black. — **Blue Blanket** the banner of the Edinburgh craftsmen; **blue blood** aristocratic blood (Sp. *sangre azul,* from the blue veins of descendants of the Visigoths); **blue-bonn′et** a round flat blue woollen cap: hence a Scottish peasant, a Scotsman; **blue book** a report or other paper printed by parliament (from its blue paper wrapper); **blue′bottle** the blue cornflower: a large fly (*Calliphora*) with metallic blue abdomen, a blowfly: a policeman or beadle (*slang*): in Australia and New Zealand, the Portuguese man-of-war; **bluebreast** see **bluethroat; blue′buck** the blaubok; **blue′cap** a salmon of one year, with blue-spotted head: the blue titmouse: a Scotsman (*Shak.*); **blue′-cheese** blue-veined cheese, e.g. Gorgonzola; **blue′-chip′** a term applied to the most reliable industrial shares, or to anything of high value or prestige; **blue′coat** a servingman, almsman, or other wearing a blue coat (*arch.*): a pupil of Christ's Hospital or other *Bluecoat school,* whose garb is a blue coat. — Also *adj.* — *adj.* **blue′-coll′ar** relating to manual work or workers. — **blue devil** an evil demon: (in *pl.*) the apparitions seen in delirium tremens, hence deep despondency; **blue duck** a species of duck, *Hymenolaimus malacorhynchus,* of the mountains of New Zealand; **Blue Ensign** a blue flag with the Union Jack in canton, till 1864 flag of the Blue squadron, now flown by the Naval Reserve and certain yachts and merchant vessels; **blue′-eye** the Australian blue-faced honey-eater, a bird with blue eye-patches; **blue film, blue movie** a pornographic film; **blue′fish** a large voracious fish (*Pomatomus saltatrix*) of the Serranidae, on the U.S. Atlantic coast; **blue fox** an arctic fox; **blue funk** (*slang*) great terror; **blue′gown** one of a former class of licensed beggars in Scotland, a King's Bedesman; **blue′grass** a slightly glaucous permanent grass (*Poa pratensis,* etc.) of Europe and North America, esp. Kentucky: a simple style of country music, originating in Kentucky and popular in the Southern U.S. — *adjs.* **blue′-green′, blue′-grey′** between blue and green or grey (**blue-green algae** the *Cyanophyceae*). — **blue ground** a greyish-blue decomposed agglomerate in which diamonds are got: **blue gum** species of Eucalyptus, esp. *E. globulus;* **blue hare** the mountain hare; **blue′jacket** a seaman in the navy; **blue jay** an American jay (*Cyanocitta cristata*); **blue John** ornamental fluorspar; **blue laws** sumptuary laws; **Blue Mantle** one of the pursuivants of the English Heralds' College; **blue moon** a very long but quite indeterminate time (from the rare occurrence of the moon appearing to be blue becuse of dust particles in the atmosphere; **blue mould** a fungus that turns bread, cheese, etc., blue; **blue movie** see **blue film; blue murder** (*coll.*) extreme activity or commotion; **blue′nose** a straitlaced or puritanical person (*coll.*): (*cap.*) a nickname for a Nova Scotian; **blue note** a flattened note, usu. third or seventh, characteristic of the blues; **blue pencil** a pencil of the colour traditionally used for correcting, emending, etc. — *v.t.* **blue-pen′cil** to correct, edit, or censor (as if) with a blue pencil. — **Blue Peter** a blue flag with a white rectangle hoisted when a ship is about to sail: a call for trumps in whist; **blue pill** a mercurial pill; **blue pointer** a large voracious shark, *Prionace glauca*: the mako shark; **blue′print** a photographic print, white upon blue, on paper sensitised with a ferric salt and potassium ferricyanide from a photographic negative or a drawing on transparent paper — also called cyanotype, ferroprussiate print: a preliminary sketch or plan of work to be done, or a guide or model provided by agreed principles or rules or by conclusions from earlier experiment. — Also *v.t.* — **blue ribbon, riband** the ribbon of the Order of the Garter: any very high distinction or prize: the badge of the teetotal Blue Ribbon Army, founded in America in 1878; **blue′-rot′** a blue discoloration in coniferous wood, caused by a fungus, *Ceratostomella;* **blue ruin** (*slang*) gin; **blue sheep** the bharal. — *adj.* **blue sky, blue skies** (of research, etc.) having no immediate practical application. — **blue′stocking** a learned lady, esp. one inclining to pedantry (said to be from Benjamin Stillingfleet, a member of Mrs Montague's coterie, who preferred worsted to black silk); **blue′stone** or **blue vitriol** hydrated copper sulphate; **blue′throat** or **blue′-breast** a bird akin to the nightingale; **blue tit** a small bird, *Parus caeruleus,* with blue wings and tail and a blue-topped head; **blue tongue** a viral disease of sheep and cattle transmitted by mosquitoes; **blue′-tongue**

(*Austr.*) a rouseabout: a lizard of the genus Tiliqua; **blue water** open sea; **blue′weed** viper's bugloss (also **blue thistle**); **blue whale** Sibbald's rorqual, the biggest living animal; **blue whiting** a fish of the cod family, found in northern seas; **blue′wing** an American teal. — **blue-eyed boy** a favourite who can do no wrong, white-headed boy; **blue-sky laws** (*U.S.*) laws to prevent fraud in the sale of stocks (against capitalising of the blue skies); **blue water-gas** see **water; burn blue** to burn with a blue flame, as in the presence of sulphur, terrestrial or infernal; **full blues** full formal naval uniform (*Navy slang*); **out of the blue** from the cloudless sky: hence, entirely unexpectedly; **shout, scream, cry** etc. **blue murder** to shout loudly in pain, alarm, or rage; **the Blues** the Royal Horse Guards; **true blue** a person unswervingly faithful, esp. to political party of blue persuasion, orig. used of Covenanters (see above at **blue** *n.; adj.* **true′-blue**). [M.E. *blew* — O.Fr. *bleu,* of Gmc. origin; O.N. *blā* gave M.E. *bla, blo* and **blae.**]

blue² *blōō, v.t.* to squander. [Prob. for **blow.**]

bluette *blü-et,* (Fr.) *n.* a spark, flash: a short playful piece of music.

bluff¹ *bluf, adj.* steep or upright in front: blustering, surly (*dial.*): rough and hearty in a good-natured way: outspoken: (of the shape of a body) such that, when it moves through air or other fluid, it leaves behind it a large disorderly wake and experiences a large drag — opp. of *streamlined.* — *n.* a high steep bank. — *adv.* **bluff′ly.** — *n.* **bluff′ness.** [Perh. Du. *blaf* (*obs.*), broad, flat; or M.L.G. *blaff,* even, smooth.]

bluff² *bluf, v.t.* or *v.i.* to deceive or seek to deceive by concealment of weakness or show of self-confidence or threats (orig. in poker to conceal poor cards). — *n.* a bluffing act or behaviour; a horse's blinker. — *n.* **bluff′er.** — **call someone's bluff** to expose or challenge someone's bluff. [Perh. Du. *bluffen,* to brag, boast.]

bluggy *blug′i, adj.* jocularly for **bloody.**

bluid *blüd, n.* a Scots form of **blood.** — *adj.* **bluid′y.**

blunder *blun′dər, v.i.* to make a gross mistake: to flounder about. — *v.t.* to utter thoughtlessly: to mismanage, bungle: to achieve, put, render, by blundering. — *n.* a gross mistake. — *n.* **blun′derer.** — *n.* and *adj.* **blun′dering.** — *adv.* **blun′deringly.** [M.E. *blondren;* prob. conn. with **blend¹.**]

blunderbuss *blun′dər-bus, n.* a short hand-gun with a wide bore. [Du. *donderbus* — *donder,* thunder, *bus,* a box, gun-barrel, gun; Ger. *Donnerbüchse.*]

blunge *blunj,* (*pottery*) *v.t.* to mix (clay or the like) with water. — *n.* **blung′er** a machine for doing so: one who blunges. [From *bl*end and pl*unge.*]

blunk *blungk,* (*Scot.*) *v.t.* to spoil: to bungle. — *n.* **blunk′er** (*Scott*) a bungler, or according to Jamieson, one who prints cloth.

blunt *blunt, adj.* having a dull edge or point: rough: outspoken: dull: barren (*Spens.*) — *v.t.* to dull. — *v.i.* to become dull. — *n.* (*arch. slang*) money. — *adj.* **blunt′ish.** — *adv.* **blunt′ly.** — *n.* **blunt′ness.** — *adj.* **blunt′-witt′ed** (*Shak.*) dull, stupid. [Origin unknown.]

blur *blûr, n.* an ill-defined spot or smear: a confused impression. — *v.t.* to blot: to render indistinct in outline: to blemish. — *v.i.* to make blurs: — *pr.p.* **blurr′ing;** *pa.t.* and *pa.p.* **blurred.** [Perh. a variety of **blear.**]

blurb *blûrb, n.* a publisher's commendatory description of a book, commonly printed on the jacket: any brief commendatory advertisement. [Attributed to Gelett Burgess, American author.]

blurt *blûrt, v.t.* to utter suddenly or unadvisedly (with *out*). — *v.i.* (*Shak.*) to snort or puff in scorn. — *n.* an abrupt outburst. — *adv.* with a blurt. — *n.* and *adj.* **blurt′ing.** [Prob. imit.]

blush *blush, n.* a red glow on the skin caused by shame, modesty, etc.: any reddish colour or suffusion. — *adj.* pinkish. — *v.i.* to show shame or confusion by growing red: to grow red. — *ns.* **blush′er** one who blushes: a cosmetic, usu. pinkish, applied to the cheeks to add colour to them; **blush'et** (*Ben Jonson*) a blushing girl. — *adj.* **blush'ful.** — *n.* and *adj.* **blush'ing.** — *adv.* **blush'ingly.** — *adj.* **blush'less.** — *adv.* **blush'lessly.** — **blush'-rose'** a pink variety of rose. — **at (the) first blush** at the first glance or sight: offhand; **put to the blush** to cause to blush. [Cf. O.E. *blyscan*, to shine.]

bluster *blus'tər, v.i.* to blow boisterously: to storm, rage: to bully or swagger. — *v.t.* to utter stormily: to drive by storming. — *n.* a blast or roaring as of the wind: bullying or boasting language: a storm of anger. — *n.* **blust'erer.** — *n.* and *adj.* **blus'tering.** — *adv.* **blus'- teringly.** — *adjs.* **blus'terous** (*Shak.* **blus'trous**) noisy: boastful; **blus'tery** stormy: swaggering. [Cf. E. Frisian *blüstern*, to bluster.]

Blut *blōōt,* (Ger.) *n.* blood. — **Blut und Boden** (*ōont bō'dən*) blood and earth, and **Blut und Ehre** (*ā'rə*) blood and honour (Nazi party slogans); **Blut und Eisen** or **Eisen und Blut** (*ī'zən*) blood and iron (Bismarck), relentless force.

blutwurst *blōōt'vŏŏrst, n.* blood-pudding. [Ger.]

bo[1] (*pl.* **bos**), **boh,** *bō,* **boo** *bōō, interjs.* an exclamation used to drive geese, or, in fun, to startle someone. — **not be able to say bo(o) to a goose** to be inarticulate from extreme meekness.

bo[2]. See **bo tree.**

bo[3] *bō,* (*U.S. slang*) *n.* man (as term of address): — *pl.* **bos.**

Boa *bō'ə, n.* a genus, mainly South American, of large snakes that kill their prey by pressure: (without *cap.*) popularly any large constricting snake: long, serpent-like coil of fur, feathers, or the like worn round the neck by ladies. — **boa constrictor** properly the name of one species: popularly any boa, python, or similar snake. [L. *bŏa,* a kind of snake.]

boak. See **boke.**

Boanerges *bō-ən-ûr'jēz, n.* a noisy preacher or shouting orator (*sing.* and *pl.*). [Sons of thunder — Mark iii. 17.]

boar *bōr, bŏr, n.* the male swine, or its flesh. — *adj.* **boar'ish** swinish: brutal. — **boar'fish** a fish (*Capros*) of the horse-mackerel family with hoglike snout; **boar'= hound** a powerful dog used for hunting the wild boar, esp. the great Dane or German mastiff; **boar'-spear** a spear used in boar-hunting. [O.E. *bār;* Du. *beer.*]

board (*Spens.,* etc., **bord, boord, boorde**) *bōrd, bŏrd, n.* a broad and thin strip of timber: a table: supply of food: provision of meals (with or without lodging): a coun-cil-table: a council or authorised body: a slab, etc. prepared for playing a game (as a chessboard) or other special purpose (as a notice-board, blackboard, knife-board): (*obs.* except seaboard, and the side of a ship): (in *pl.*) the stage: a kind of thick stiff paper or sheets of paper pasted together, as in pasteboard, Bristol-board, esp. that used in the binding of books: a rectangular piece forming the side of a book-binding: conversation (*Spens.*): coast (*Spens.*). — *v.t.* to cover with boards: to supply with food (and bed) at fixed terms: to enter (a ship or orig. U.S., a train, bus, etc.): to accost, to attack (*Shak.*). — *v.i.* to receive food (and lodging): to border (*Spens.*). — *ns.* **board'er** one who receives board: one who boards a ship; **board'ing** the act of covering with boards: a structure or collection of boards: act of boarding a ship. — **board'-foot** a unit of **board'-measure** for timber, a piece one inch thick by 12 inches square; **board'-game** a game, e.g. chess, snakes-and-ladders, which is played with pieces, coun-ters, etc. on a specially designed board; **board'ing-house** a house where boarders are kept; **boarding pass** a card allowing one to board an aircraft, ship, etc.; **board'ing= pike** a pike used in boarding a ship, or in defending it when attacked; **board'ing-school** a school in which board and lodging are provided for pupils; **board'room** a room for meetings of a board of directors. — *adj.* taking place in a boardroom. — **board'sailor; board'- sailing** sailboarding; **board'-school** a school under con-trol of a schoolboard; **board'-wa'ges** payment to a servant in lieu of food; **board'walk** a footpath made

of boards. — **above board** openly; **Board of Trade unit** (*elect.*) a kilowatt-hour (contracted B.T.U.); **board out** to have board elsewhere than where one lives: to place in a house for board; **board with** to be a boarder in the house of; **go by the board** to go over the side of a ship: to be discarded or ignored: to meet disaster; **on board** aboard; **sweep the board** to take all the cards: to win everything; **take on board** to receive, accept (new notions, additional responsibilities, etc.). [O.E. *bord,* board, the side of a ship; O.N. *borth,* connected either with **bear**[1] or with **broad.**]

boart. See **bort.**

boast[1] *bōst, v.i.* to talk vaingloriously: to brag (with *of*). — *v.t.* to brag of: to speak proudly or confidently of, esp. justifiably: to possess with pride. — *n.* an expres-sion of pride: a brag: the cause of boasting. — *n.* **boast'er.** — *adj.* **boast'ful** given to bragging. — *adv.* **boast'fully.** — *ns.* **boast'fulness; boast'ing.** — *adj.* **boast'less** without boasting: simple, unostentatious. [M.E. *bōst;* origin unknown; apparently W. *bostio,* Gael. *bòsd,* a bragging, are borrowed from English.]

boast[2] *bōst, v.t.* in stonecutting, to shape roughly. — *n.* **boast'er** broad steel chisel used for boasting. [Origin unknown.]

boat *bōt, n.* a small open craft usually moved by oars: a ship: a boat-shaped utensil (as *sauce-boat*). — *v.i.* to sail about in a boat. — *v.t.* to put or convey in a boat: to ship (as oars): (with *it*) to go in a boat. — *ns.* **boat'er** one who boats: a straw hat; **boat'ing** the art, sport, or practice of sailing in boats. — **boat'bill** a bird of the heron family (from the shape of its bill); **boat'-builder** one who constructs boats; **boat'-deck** a ship's top deck, on which the small boats are carried; **boat'-fly** a water-bug (Notonecta), with boat-shaped body, that swims on its back; **boat'-hook** a hook fixed to a pole used for pulling or pushing off a boat; **boat'house** a house or shed for a boat; **boat'-load; boat'man** a man who has charge of a boat: a rower; **boat neck** a high slit-shaped neckline extending on to the shoulders. — *adj.* **boat'-necked.** — **boat people** refugees, esp. from Vietnam, who set off in boats to find a country that will admit them; **boat'race** a race of rowing boats: (*cap.*) annual boatrace between Oxford and Cam-bridge universities; **boat'-racing; boat'-song** a song sung by a boatman; **boat'tail** a grackle; **boat'-train** a train run in connection with a ship. — **have an oar in another's boat** to meddle with his affairs; **in the same boat** (of persons) in the same unfavourable circum-stances; **push the boat out** (*coll.*) to entertain, celebrate, etc., lavishly; **take to the boats** to escape in lifeboats from a sinking ship (also *fig.*). [O.E. *bāt;* cf. Du. *boot;* Fr. *bateau.*]

boatel. See **botel.**

boatswain (often **bosun, bo'sun, bo's'n, bos'n**) *bō'sn, n.* the foreman of a crew (warrant-officer in the navy) who looks after a ship's boats, rigging, flags, etc.: the skua (prob. from its aggressiveness): transferred (app.) to the tropic-bird (**boat'swain-bird**). — **boatswain's call, pipe, whistle** see **whistle; boatswain's chair** a wooden seat slung from ropes, for a man working on a ship's side, rigging, etc.; **boatswain's mate** boatswain's assis-tant. [**boat, swain.**]

bob[1] *bob, v.i.* to move quickly up and down: to curtsey: to ride a bobsled: to fish with a bob. — *v.t.* to move in a short jerking manner: to execute with a bob: to cut (hair) square across: to dock, to bobtail: — *pr.p.* **bobb'ing;** *pa.t.* and *pa.p.* **bobbed.** — *n.* a short jerking motion: a curtsey: a dance (*Scot.*): a slight blow (*obs.*): a jibe (*obs.*): anything that moves with a bob or swing: the weight of a pendulum, plumb-line, or the like: a pendant (*arch.*): a knot of hair: bobbed or docked hair: a bunch or cluster (as of cherries) (*dial.*): a bunch of lobworms, used in catching eels: any small roundish body: the refrain or burden of a song (*arch.*): a short line at or near the end of the stanza: a bobsled: a term (also **plain bob**) used in bell-ringing for a method of change-ringing —**bob minor** is rung upon six bells, **bob**

major on eight, **bob royal** on ten, **bob maximus** on twelve. — *adj.* **bobb'ish** in good spirits. — *n.* **bobb'le** the movement of water in commotion: a woolly ball for trimming dresses, hats, etc. — *v.t.* and *v.i.* to bob rapidly or continuously: (orig. *U.S.*) to fumble, to bungle. — **bobble hat** a usu. knitted tapering hat with a bobble at the top; **bob'cat** a kind of lynx; **bob'-cherry** the pastime of catching a swinging cherry with the teeth; **bob'(-fly')** the top drop-fly; **bob'sled, -sleigh** a short sledge: a sleigh made up of two of these, sometimes with common seat; a racing sledge for two or more people, with a continuous seat, steering mechanism, and brakes; **bob'tail** a short or cut tail: an animal with a bobbed tail (also *adj.*): a word applied in contempt to the rabble, as in *rag-tag and bobtail.* — Also *v.t.* — *adj.* **bob'tailed** with tail cut short. — **bob'wheel** in verse, the bob with the lines following it; **bob'wig** one with the ends turned up into short curls. — **bob up** to appear suddenly. [Poss. Gael. *baban, babag.*]

bob² *bob, (obs.) v.t.* to befool: to take by cheating (*Shak.*): to cheat (out of) (*Shak.*). [O.Fr. *bober.*]

bob³ *bob, (slang) n.* a shilling or 5 pence: — *pl.* **bob.** [Prob. not O.Fr. *bobe* = 1½d.]

boba *bō'bə. n.* another name for **yaws.**

bobak, bobac *bō'bak, n.* a species of marmot. [Pol. *bobak.*]

Bobadil *bob'ə-dil, n.* a swaggering boaster, from the soldier in Ben Jonson's *Every Man in his Humour.*

bobbery *bob'ər-i, n.* a noisy row. [Perh. Hind. *bāp re,* O father.]

bobbin *bob'in, n.* a reel or spool for winding yarn, wire, etc. — **bobb'in-lace'** lace made on a pillow with bobbins; **bobb'in-net'** or **bobb'inet** a fine machine-made netted lace. [Fr. *bobine.*]

bobbish, bobble. See **bob¹.**

bobby *bob'i, (slang) n.* a policeman. [Familiar form of *Robert,* from Sir Robert Peel, Home Secretary at the passing of the Metropolitan Police Act, 1828; cf. **peeler.**]

bobby calf *bob'i käf,* a calf slaughtered before it has been weaned.

bobby-dazzler *bob'i-daz-lər, (dial.) n.* anything overwhelmingly excellent, striking, or showy, esp. a woman; a young girl who sets out to make an impression.

bobby-pin *bob'i-pin, n.* a hairgrip.

bobbysock *bob'i-sok, (coll.* esp. formerly) *n.* an anklesock, esp. as worn by teenage girls. — *n.* **bobb'ysoxer** an adolescent girl, teenager.

bobolink *bob'ō-lingk, n.* a North American singing bird. [At first *Bob Lincoln,* from its note.]

bobsled, bobsleigh. See **bob¹.**

bobstays *bob'stāz, (naut.) n.pl.* ropes or stays used to hold the bowsprit down to the stem or cut-water, and counteract the strain of the foremast-stays.

bob-white *bob'-(h)wīt', n.* an American quail. [Imit.]

bocage. Same as **boscage.**

bocca *bok'ka, (It.) n.* mouth.

boche, bosche *bosh, n.* abusive French slang for a German.

bock¹ *bok, (Fr.,* from Ger.) *n.* a strong German beer — from *Einbocker bier, Eimbockbier* — beer from Einbeck (Eimbeck): now often a glass or mug of beer (quarter of a litre).

bock². See **boke.**

bod *bod, (orig. service slang) n.* a person. [Contraction of **body** (*coll.*).]

bodach *bōd'əhh, bod', Gael. bot', (Scot.) n.* an old man, a churl: a goblin or spectre. [Gael.]

boddle. See **bodle.**

bode¹ *bōd, v.t.* to portend: to foreshow: to augur: to have a presentiment of. — *v.i.* to augur. — *n.* (*Scot.*) a bid, offer. — *adj.* **bode'ful** boding, ominous. — *n.* **bode'ment** an omen, presentiment. — *adj.* **bod'ing** presaging. — *n.* an omen or portent. [O.E. *bodian,* to announce

— (*ge*)*bod,* a message; allied to **bid.**]

bode² *bōd.* See **bide.**

bodega *bo-dē'gə, Sp. bō-dā'ga, n.* a wine-shop. — *n.* **bodeguero** (-*gā'rō;* Sp.) one who owns or runs a bodega: — *pl.* **-os.** [Sp. — L. — Gr. *apothēkē,* a storehouse.]

bodge *boj, (dial.)* same as **botch** (*v.t.* and *v.i.*): (*Shak.*) prob. same as **budge.** — *n.* (*dial.*) a clumsy patch: a clumsy worker (also **bodg'er**).

bodger *boj'ər, (dial.) n.* a travelling pedlar who turns beechwood to make chairs, etc. [Origin uncertain.]

bodgie *boj'i, (Austr.) n.* a delinquent youth, usu. a member of a teenage gang. [From **bodge,** a clumsy worker.]

Bodhisattva *bō-di-sat'wə, (Buddhism) n.* one who postpones entry into nirvana in order to help others: a future Buddha. [Sans. — *bodhi,* enlightenment, *sattva,* existence.]

bodhi tree. See **bo tree.**

bodice *bod'is, n.* a stiffened inner garment (orig. *pl.* of **body**) (*arch.*): a woman's outer garment covering the waist and bust: the close-fitting waist or body of a woman's gown. — **bod'ice-ripp'er** a romantic (historical) novel involving violence.

bodikin *bod'i-kin, n.* dim. of **body,** in 'Od's bodikins, God's little body.

bodkin *bod'kin, n.* a small dagger: a small instrument for pricking holes, for dressing the hair, for correcting type, etc.: a large blunt needle. — **sit** or **ride bodkin** to be wedged in tight between two others. [Poss conn. with W. *bidog,* dagger.]

bodle, also **boddle,** *bod'l, bōd'l, n.* a 17th-century Scots copper coin, worth about one-sixth of an English penny, the smallest coin. [Origin unknown.]

bodrag *bod'rag, (Spens.) n.* a hostile attack, a raid. — Also **bord'raging.** [Perh. Ir. *buaidhreadh,* a disturbance.]

body *bod'i, n.* the whole frame of a man or lower animal: the main part of an animal, as distinguished from the limbs: the main part of anything: the part of a vehicle which carries the load or passengers: a garment or part of a garment covering the trunk: a bodice: a corpse: matter, as opposed to spirit: substance or substantial quality: fullness, as of flavour in a wine: solidity: opacity of a paint or pigment: a mass: a person (*coll.*): a number of persons united by some common tie: size of type: — *pl.* **bod'ies.** — *v.t.* to give form to: to embody: — *pr.p.* **bod'ying;** *pa.t.* and *pa.p.* **bod'ied.** — *adj.* **bod'iless** without a body: incorporeal. — *adj.* **bod'ily** of the body, esp. as opposed to the mind: actual, real (*Shak.*). — *adv.* in the flesh: as a whole. — **bodily function** any of the processes or activities performed by or connected with the body, such as breathing, hearing, eating, sleeping, walking, and dressing; **body blow** in boxing, a blow to the body: a serious setback; **bod'y-builder** a maker of vehicle bodies: an apparatus for exercising muscles: a nutritious food. — *n.* and *adj.* **bod'y-building.** — **bod'y-cavity** the coelom, or cavity in which the viscera of the higher animals lie; **body colour** degree of consistence, substance, and tingeing power of a paint: water-colour mixed with zinc or other white to give it body; **bod'y-check** a deliberate obstruction of an opposing player's movements, permitted in e.g. lacrosse and ice-hockey, not in soccer. — Also *v.t.* — **bod'y-checking; bod'y-cur'er** (*Shak.*) a doctor; **bod'yguard** a guard to protect the person, esp. of a sovereign; **body language** communication of information by means of conscious or unconscious gestures, attitudes, facial expressions, etc.; **bod'yline** see below; **body politic** the collective body of the people in its political capacity; **body-popping** a form of dancing with robot-like movements; **body servant** a personal attendant; **bod'yshell** bodywork; **body shop** a vehicle body repair or construction shop; **bod'y-snatcher** one who secretly disinters the bodies of the dead for the purposes of dissection; **body stocking** a one-piece, skintight undergarment for women; **bod'y-warmer** a padded sleeveless jacket; **bod'ywork** the metal outer frame of a motor vehicle. — **body and soul** one's entire self; **body forth** to give form to; **body-line bowling** in cricket, fast bowling delivered at the batsman's body (also **bod′yline**); **in a body** (acting) all together. [O.E. *bodig*.]

Boeotian *bi-ō′sh(y)ən, adj.* of *Boeotia* in Greece, proverbial for the dullness of its inhabitants: hence, stupid, dull. — Also *n.*

Boer *bōōr, (chiefly hist.) n.* a S. African of Dutch descent, esp. one engaged in farming. — Also *adj.* — **boerewors** (*bōōr′ə-vörs*; S. Afr.; Afrik. *boere-*, farmers', country style, *wors*, sausage) a traditional S. African sausage, usu. containing a mixture of beef and pork. [Du.; see **boor, bower**.]

boff *bof, (slang; esp. U.S.) n.* a punch: a hearty laugh: an entertainment. — *v.i.* and *v.t.* to hit, slug. — *v.i.* to copulate. [Ety. uncertain; perh. in part imit.]

boffin *bof′in, (orig. service slang) n.* a research scientist, esp. one employed by armed forces or government.

Bofors gun *bō′förz,* or *-förs, gun,* a single- or double-barrelled, quick-firing anti-aircraft gun. [From *Bofors*, Sweden, where orig. made.]

bog *bog, n.* spongy, usu. peaty, ground: a marsh: a type of vegetation growing on peat deficient in lime: a latrine, lavatory (*slang*). — *v.t.* to sink. — Also *v.i.* — *n.* **bogg′iness.** — *adj.* **bogg′y.** — **bog′-as′phodel** a yellow-flowered liliaceous bog-plant (*Narthecium ossifragum*); **bog′bean** buckbean; **bog′-butt′er** butter-like substance of animal origin found in Irish peat-bogs; **bog-iron** see **bog-ore; bog′land; bog′-Lat′in** Shelta; **bog′=moss′** the sphagnum genus; **bog′-myr′tle** sweet-gale (*Myrica gale*), a bog plant; **bog′oak′** trunks of oak embedded in bogs and preserved from decay — of a deep black colour, often used for making ornaments; **bog′-ore, bog′-iron** an iron ore found in boggy land, limonite; **bog′-spav′in** distension of the capsule of the hock-joint of the horse; **bog′trotter** one who lives in a boggy country, hence (*derog.*) an Irishman. — *n.* and *adj.* **bog′trotting.** — **bog down** to encumber with an overwhelming amount of work, a difficult task, etc. [Ir. and Gael. *bogach*; *bog*, soft.]

bogan *bō′gən, (Can.* and *U.S.) n.* a quiet tributary or backwater. [Algonquian *pokelogan*.]

bogey¹ *bō′gi, n.* in golf, the score, for a given hole or for the whole course, of an imaginary good player, Colonel *Bogey*, fixed as a standard — the bogey can be higher than par or sometimes equivalent to it, now usu. a score of one stroke above the par for any hole. [Perh. **bogy**.]

bogey². See **bogie, bogy**.

boggard *bog′ərd,* **boggart** *-ərt,* **boggle** *bog′l*. See **bogle**.

boggle *bog′l, v.i.* to stop or hesitate as if at a bogle: to start with fright: to make difficulties about a thing: to equivocate: (of one's mind, esp. in *the mind boggles*) to be unable to imagine or grasp something, to be astounded by something (*coll.*). — *n.* a scruple, objection: a bungle. — *n.* **bogg′ler** one who boggles: a doubter: one who hesitates or swerves (*Shak.*). [**bogle**.]

bogie, bogey *bō′gi, n.* a low heavy truck, a trolley: a railway coach: a pivoted undercarriage, as in a locomotive engine. [Ety. unknown: perh. conn. with **bogy**.]

bogle *bō′gl, n.* a spectre or goblin: a scarecrow (**tatt′ie=bo′gle**): a bugbear, or source of terror. — **bogg′le, bogg′ard, bogg′art** are North of England forms. — **bogle about the bush,** stacks a kind of hide-and-seek. [Scot.; possibly connected with **bug¹**.]

bogong *bō′gong, n.* a noctuid moth eaten by Australian Aborigines. — Also **bugong** (*bōō′-*). [Aboriginal.]

bogus *bō′gəs, adj.* counterfeit, spurious. [An American cant word, of very doubtful origin — it may possibly be ult. related to **bogy**.]

bogy, bogey *bō′gi, n.* a goblin: a bugbear or special object of dread: the devil: a policeman (*slang*): — *pl.* **bō′gies, bō′geys.** — *n.* **bō′g(e)yism.** — **bo′g(e)y-man** the Devil or other dreadful being with whom to threaten chil-

dren. [Perhaps a form of **bogle** and **boggard**.]

boh. See **bo¹**.

bohea *bō-hē′, n.* the lowest quality of black tea: black tea generally. [From the *Wu-i* hills in China.]

Bohemian *bō-hē′mi-ən, n.* a native or inhabitant of Bohemia: a Czech: a gypsy: a person of loose or irregular habits: an artist or man of letters, or indeed anyone, who sets social conventions aside: the Czech language. — Also *adj.* — *n.* **Bohē′mianism.** — **Bohemian ruby** rose quartz; **Bohemian topaz** citrine. [Fr. *bohémien*, a gypsy, from the belief that these wanderers came from *Bohemia*.]

bohunk *bō′hungk, (slang,* esp. *U.S.) n.* a Slav or Hungarian, esp. an unskilled labourer: his language. [Perh. *Bohemian Hungarian*.]

boil¹ *boil, v.i.* to pass rapidly from liquid into vapour with violent evolution of bubbles: to bubble up as if from the action of heat: to be heated in boiling liquid: to be hot: to be excited or angry. — *v.t.* to heat to a boiling state: to cook, dress, clean or otherwise treat by boiling. — *n.* act or condition of boiling: a swirling disturbance made at the surface of the water by a fish coming to the fly. — *ns.* **boil′er** one who boils: that in which anything is boiled: a vessel in which steam is generated: a vessel for heating water for baths, etc.: an electric apparatus for boiling a kettle or the like; **boil′ery** a place for boiling, esp. for obtaining salt; **boil′ing** the act of causing to boil: the condition of being boiled or at boiling-point: a quantity boiled at once: a boiled sweet (*Scot.*): collection, set (*coll.*). — *adj.* at boiling-point: very hot: bubbling: swelling with heat or passion. — **boil′ing-point** the temperature at which a liquid, esp. water, boils, esp. at atmospheric pressure; **boiled shirt** a dress shirt; **boiled sweet** a sweet of boiled sugar, flavouring, and often colouring; **boil′-er-maker; boiler suit** a workman's overall garment. — **boil down** to reduce in bulk by boiling: to extract the substance of: to epitomise; **boil down to** (*fig.*) to mean, to signify when reduced to essentials; **boil over** to bubble over the sides of the containing vessel: to break out into unrestrained indignation; **come to the boil** to arrive at boiling-point: to arrive at a critical state; **on the boil** boiling: active. [O.Fr. *boillir* — L. *bullīre* — *bulla,* a bubble.]

boil² *boil, n.* an inflamed swelling. [O.E. *bȳl*; Ger. *Beule*.]

boing *boing,* **boink** *boink, ns.* the sound of a bouncing impact. — *adj.* with this sound. — *vs.i.* to bounce or hit with such a sound. [Imit.]

boisterous *bois′tər-əs, adj.* wild: noisy and exuberant: turbulent: stormy. — *adv.* **bois′terously.** — *n.* **bois′-terousness.** [M.E. *boistous*.]

boîte de nuit *bwät də nwē, (Fr.)* a night-club.

bok *bok, (S. Afr.) n.* a goat: an antelope — used alike of male and female. [Du. *bok,* goat.]

boke, boak *bōk, (dial.) v.i.* to belch: to retch, vomit: to gush, spurt. — *v.t.* to vomit: to emit. — *n.* the act of boking: vomit. — Also (*Scot.*) **bock** (*bōk, bok*). [Prob. imit., but compare O. Scot *bolk,* M.E. *bolken,* and **belch**.]

boko *bō′kō, (slang) n.* the nose: — *pl.* **bō′kos.** [Origin unknown.]

bolas *bō′läs, n.* (properly *pl.*) a South American missile, consisting of two or more balls or stones strung together, swung round the head and hurled so as to entangle an animal. [Sp., balls.]

bold *bōld, adj.* daring: actively courageous: forward or impudent: presumptuous: executed with spirit: striking to the sense, standing out clearly, well marked: steep or abrupt: (of e.g. currants) full-flavoured, mature, plump: (of type) bold-faced. — *v.t.* **bold′en** (*obs.*) to make bold. — *adv.* **bold′ly.** — *n.* **bold′ness.** — *adj.* **bold′-faced** impudent: of type, having a heavy face. — **bold as brass** utterly unabashed; **make bold, be so bold as to** to venture, take the liberty. [O.E. *bald*; O.H.G. *bald,* O.N. *ballr*.]

bold-beating *bōld′-bēt′ing, (Shak.) adj.* poss. for 'bowl-

beating', tub-thumping, or a confusion of **bold** and **browbeating**.
bole[1] *bōl, n.* the trunk of a tree. [O.N. *bolr*; Ger. *Bohle*, a plank.]
bole[2] *bōl, n.* a friable earthy clay, usually red. [Gr. *bolos*, a clod.]
bole[3] *bōl, (Scot.) n.* a recess in a wall: an opening to admit light and air (also **win'dow-bole**). [Origin unknown.]
bolection, balection *bō-, bə-lek'shən, n.* a moulding around a panel, projecting beyond the surface of the framing. [Origin unknown.]
bolero *bə-lā'rō, n.* Spanish national dance: a tune to which it may be danced: (usu. *bol'ə-rō*) a jacket-like bodice, coming barely to the waist: — *pl.* **boleros.** [Sp.]
Boletus *bol-ē'təs, n.* a genus of fungi, edible and poisonous, with a pore-like surface instead of gills: (without *cap.*) a fungus of this genus: — *pl.* **bole'tuses, -tī.** [L. *bōlētus* — Gr. *bōlītēs*, mushroom.]
bolide *bō'līd, n.* a large meteor, esp. one that bursts: a fireball. [Fr., — L. *bolis, -idis* — Gr. *bolis*, missile.]
bolivar *bol-ē'vär, n.* the standard monetary unit of Venezuela. [From Simón *Bolívar* (1783–1830).]
boliviano *bol-ē-vi-ä'nō, n.* a Bolivian dollar (100 centavos): — *pl.* **bolivia'nos.**
bolix. See **bollocks.**
boll[1] *bōl, n.* a swelling: a knob: a round capsule, as in cotton, flax, poppy, etc. — *v.i.* to swell, to form bolls. — *adjs.* **bolled** (*bōld*) swollen, podded; **bollen** (*bō'lən*, *Shak. bōln; obs.*) swollen. — **boll'-weevil** a weevil (*Anthonomus grandis*) whose larvae infest cotton-bolls; **boll'-worm** a moth caterpillar that destroys cottonbolls, maize, tomatoes, etc. — in U.S. *Chloridea obsoleta*, in Egypt and India *Earias insulana* and *E. fabia*. [A form of **bowl** — O.E. *bolla*.]
boll[2] *bōl, n.* a measure of capacity for grain, etc., used in Scotland and the north of England — in Scotland usually = 6 imperial bushels; in England varying from 2 to 6 bushels: also a measure of weight, containing, for flour, 140 lb. [Prob. O.N. *bolli*.]
Bollandist *bol'ən-dist, n.* any of the Jesuit writers who continued the *Acta Sanctorum* by John *Bolland* (1596–1665).
bollard *bol'ərd, n.* a short post on a wharf or ship, etc., round which ropes are secured: one of a line of short posts barring passage of motor vehicles. [Prob. **bole**.]
bollen. See **boll**[1].
bolletrie *bol'ə-trē.* Same as **bully-tree.**
bollix. See **bollocks.**
bollock *bol'ək, (slang) v.t.* to reprimand severely. — *n.* **boll'ocking.** [Conn. with **bollocks** uncertain.]
bollocks *bol'əks,* **ballocks** *bol',* also *bal', n.pl.* (now generally considered *vulg.*) testicles. — *n.sing.* (*slang*) nonsense: a muddle, mess. — Also (*U.S. slang*) *n.sing.* **bollix, bolix** (*bol'iks*). — *v.t.* to make a botch of. [O.E. *beallucas*, testicles.]
bolo *bō'lō,* (esp. *U.S.*) *n.* in boxing, a long sweeping uppercut: — *pl.* **bo'los** — Also **bolo punch.** [Ety. uncertain.]
Bologna *bol-ōn'yä, adj.* of the town of *Bologna* in Italy. — *adj.* and *n.* **Bologn'ese** (or *-ēz'*). — **Bologna phial** an unannealed bottle that shatters on scratching; **Bologna phosphorus** barium sulphide; **Bologna sausage; Bologna stone** fibrous barytes. [L. *Bonōnia*.]
bolometer *bō-lom'i-tər, n.* an instrument for measuring radiant energy. — *adj.* **bolomet'ric.** — *n.* **bolom'etry.** [Gr. *bolē*, stroke, ray (*ballein*, to throw), *metron*, a measure.]
boloney. See **baloney.**
Bolshevik (or **bol-**) *bol'shə-vik, n.* a member of the Russian Majority (or Extreme) Socialist party, opp. to *Menshevik* (*hist.*): a violent revolutionary Marxian communist: anarchist, agitator, causer of trouble (used loosely as a term of disapprobation). — Also *adj.* — *n.* and *adj.* coll. contracted **bol'shie, bol'shy.** — *v.t.* **bol'shevise, -ize.** — *ns.* **bol'shevism; bol'shevist** a Bolshevik: an extreme revolutionary communist (of any country) — loosely used by opponents. — Also *adj.*

[Russ. — *bolshe*, greater, from its more thoroughgoing programme, or from its being in a majority (i.e. at the Russian Social Democratic Congress in 1903), -*vik*, agent suffix.]
bolster *bōl'stər, n.* a long, sometimes cylindrical, pillow or cushion: a pad: anything resembling it in form or use, esp. any piece of mechanism affording a support against pressure; a form of cold chisel with a broad, splayed-out blade, used in cutting stone slabs, etc.: the jutting-out part of a knife which abuts on the handle. — *v.t.* (also with *up*) to support as with a bolster: to hold up. — *adj.* **bol'stered** supported: swelled out. — *n.* and *adj.* **bol'stering** propping up or supporting. [O.E. *bolster*.]
bolt[1] *bōlt, n.* a bar used to fasten a door, etc.: a stout pin with a head: an arrow, esp. for a crossbow: a thunderbolt: a roll of a definite measure (of cloth, etc.): the uncut edge of a sheet folded for a book: a rush. *v.t.* to fasten with a bolt: to fetter: to throw or utter precipitately: to expel suddenly: to discharge, as a bolt: to swallow hastily: to break away from, withhold support from (*U.S.*). — *v.i.* to spring, dart: to rush away: to take flight: to run away: to start up: to withhold support from one's party, or its policy or nominee (*U.S.*): of a plant, to flower and run to seed. — *adv.* like a bolt. — *n.* **bolt'er** one who bolts: a horse given to running away. — **bolt'head** the head of a bolt; **bolt'hole** a hole to receive a bolt: a secret passage or way of escape: a refuge from danger: a secluded, private place for holidays, etc.: a distilling receiver (*arch.*); **bolt'-rope** a rope sewed all round the edge of a sail to prevent it from tearing. — **a fool's bolt is soon shot** a fool soon gives away the initiative, leaving himself unprotected; **bolt from the blue** an unexpected event; **bolt upright** upright and straight as an arrow: supine (*obs.*); **have shot one's bolt** to be unable to do more than one has done. [O.E. *bolt*; O.H.G. *bolz*.]
bolt[2], **bolting.** See **boult.**
bolus *bō'ləs, n.* a rounded mass: a large pill. [L. *bōlus* — Gr. *bōlos*, a lump.]
boma[1] *bō'mə, n.* a fenced enclosure. [Swahili.]
boma[2] *bō'mə, n.* a boa or anaconda. [Congo; thence carried by Portuguese to Brazil.]
bomb *bom* (old-fashioned *bum*), *n.* a hollow case containing explosive, incendiary, smoke-producing, poisonous, or other offensive material, deposited, thrown, dropped, or shot from a mortar: (also **volcanic bomb**) a rounded mass of lava thrown out by a volcano: an old worn-out car (*Austr.* and *N.Z. coll.*) — *v.i.* to throw, discharge, or drop bombs: (sometimes with *out*) to be a flop, fail (*slang*). — *v.t.* to attack, injure, or destroy with bombs. — *n.* **bombard** (*bom'bärd*) an early cannon, throwing stones, etc.: a large liquor-jug, a black-jack (*Shak.*): an old form of bassoon. — *v.t.* **bombard'** to attack with artillery: to batter or pelt: to subject to a succession of blows or impingements: to assail, as with questions (*fig.*): to subject, as the atom, to a stream of particles at high speed (*phys.*). — *ns.* **bombardier** (*bom-, bum-bər-dēr'*) the lowest non-commissioned officer in the British artillery, formerly a man employed about a bombard; **bombardment** (*bom-bärd'mənt*); **bombar'don** (or *bom'*) the bass tuba; **bomber** (*bom'ər*) one who bombs or plants bombs: a bombing aeroplane. — Also *adj.* — **bombardier beetle** a name given to beetles (*Brachinus*, etc.) that discharge an acrid volatile fluid with explosive force from the abdomen; **bomb'-calorim'eter** an apparatus for determining the calorific value of fuels by ignition in a thick-walled steel vessel; **bomb'-dispos'al** the act of removing and detonating previously unexploded bombs; **bomber jacket** a short jacket with zipped front and elasticated waist. — *adjs.* **bomb'-happ'y** in a state of mind for discharging bombs without compunction: with nerves shattered by exposure to bombing; **bomb'-proof** proof or secure against the force of bombs. — *n.* a bomb-proof structure. — **bomb'shell** a bomb: now only *fig.*, a sudden and surprising piece of news;

bomb′site an area which has been laid waste by air-raid(s); **bomb′-vessel, -ketch** (*hist.*) a vessel for carrying mortars used in bombarding from the sea. — **go like a bomb** to go very well or very quickly; **make a bomb** (*coll.*) to make or earn a great deal of money. [Fr. *bombe*, prob. — L. *bombus* — Gr. *bombos*, humming sound.]

bombasine, bombazine *bom′bə-zēn*, or *-zēn′*, formerly *bum′*, *n.* a twilled or corded fabric of silk and worsted, or of cotton and worsted. [Fr. *bombasin* — L.L. *bombȳcinus* — Gr. *bombȳkinos, bombȳx*, silkworm.]

bombast *bom′bast*, *n.* cottonwool: padding: stuffing: inflated or high-sounding language, fustian. — *adj.* (*Shak.*) inflated. — *v.t.* (*-bast′*, also *bom′*) to pad, stuff: to inflate, render grandiose. — *adj.* **bombas′tic** high-sounding: inflated. — *adv.* **bombas′tically.** — *n.* **Bom′-bax** a genus of tropical, chiefly S. Amer. trees, giving name to the silk-cotton family, **Bombacā′ceae:** (without *cap.*) any tree of the genus. — *adj.* **bombacā′ceous.** [L.L. *bombax*, cotton — Gr. *bombȳx*, silk.]

Bombay duck *bom′bā duk, a* fish, the bummalo.

bombe *bom, bõb, n.* a dessert, usually ice-cream frozen in a round or melon-shaped mould. [Fr.]

bombé *bom′bā, bõ-bā, adj.* of furniture, having a rounded, convex front. [Fr., bulging, convex.]

bomber. See **bomb.**

bombilate, bombinate *bom′bil-āt, -bin-āt, v.i.* to hum, buzz, drone, boom. — *ns.* **bombilā′tion, bombinā′tion.** [L. *bombilāre, bombināre.*]

bombo *bom′bō, (Austr. coll.) n.* cheap wine, plonk. [Ety. uncertain.]

bombora *bom-bō′rə, -bö, (Austr.) n.* a submerged reef: a dangerous current or rough sea over such a reef. [Aboriginal.]

Bombyx *bom′biks, n.* the silkworm genus, giving name to the family **Bombycidae** (*-bis′i-dē*). — *n.* **bom′bycid** an insect of the family. — Also *adj.* [Gr. *bombȳx.*]

bon *bõ, (Fr.) adj.* good. — **bon accueil** (*bo-na-kœy*) good reception, due honour; **bon ami** (*fem.* **bonne amie**) (*bo-na-mē*) good friend: lover; **bon appetit** (*bo-na-pə-tē*) good appetite, said politely to those who are (about to start) eating; **bon camarade** (*bõ ka-ma-rad*) good comrade; **bon chrétien** (*krā-tyē*) 'good Christian' — a kind of pear, the William; **bon diable** (*dē-äbl′*) a good-natured fellow; **bon goût** (*gōō*) good taste; **bon gré, mal gré** (*grä, mal grä*) willing or unwilling, willy-nilly; **bonjour** (*-zhōōr*) good day: good morning; **bon marché** (*mar-shä*) a bargain: cheapness: cheap: cheaply; **bon mot** (*pl.* **bons mots**) (*mō*) a witty saying; **bonsoir** (*-swär*) good evening; **bon ton** (*tõ*) the height of fashion; **bon vivant** (*vē-vä*) a jovial companion: one who lives well, esp. who enjoys fine food (**bonne vivante** is *not* according to French usage); **bon viveur** (*vē-vœr*; not used in Fr.) a bon vivant, esp. a man-about-town; **bon voyage** (*vwä-yäzh*) a good journey to you.

bona *bō′nə, bo′na* (L.) *n.pl.* goods. — **bona mobilia** (*mō-bi′li-ə, -a*) movable goods; **bona peritura** (*per-i-tū′rə, -tōō′ra*) perishable goods; **bona vacantia** (*va-kan′-shi-ə, wa-kan′ti-a*) unclaimed goods.

bona fide *bō′nə fīd, fī′də, -di, bo′nä fi′dä,* (L.) (*abl.*) in good faith — (used as *adj.*) genuine; **bona fides** (*fī′dēz, fid′ās*) good faith: genuineness.

bonamano. See **buonamano.**

bonanza *bon-an′zə, n.* a rich mass of gold: any mine of wealth or stroke of luck. — *adj.* very prosperous. [Sp., good weather.]

Bonapartean *bō-nə-pärt′i-ən, adj.* of Napoleon *Bonaparte* or his family. — *n.* **Bō′napartism** attachment to his dynasty or policy. — *n.* and *adj.* **Bō′napartist.**

bona-roba *bō′nə-rō′bə,* (*Shak.*) *n.* a showy wanton, courtesan. [It. *buona roba,* lit. good stuff (or dress).]

bonas(s)us *bon-as′əs, n.* a bison. [L., — Gr. *bonasos, bonassos.*]

bonbon *bon′bon, bõ-bõ, n.* a sweetmeat: a cracker (for pulling). — *n.* **bonbonnière** (*bõ-bon-yer′*) a fancy box for holding sweets. [Fr., redup. of *bon,* good.]

bonce *bons, n.* a large marble: the head (*coll.*). [Origin obscure.]

bond[1] *bond, n.* that which binds, a band: link or connection or union: a writing of obligation to pay a sum or to perform a contract: a debenture: a mortgage (*Scots law*): any constraining or cementing force: in building, the overlapping connection of one stone or brick with another, as in **English bond, Flemish bond,** etc.: (in *pl.*) imprisonment, captivity: the condition of goods retained in a warehouse, called a **bonded warehouse** or **bonded store,** until duties are paid. — *v.t.* to connect, secure, or bind with a bond: to put in a bonded warehouse: to put in a condition of bond: to cause to adhere (to) (e.g. metal to glass or plastic). — *adj.* **bond′ed** secured by bond. — *ns.* **bond′er** a bondstone or header; **bond′ing** act of bonding: the forming of the attachment between a mother and her newborn child (*psych.*). — **bonded debt** the debt of a corporation represented by the bonds it has issued, as contrasted with its floating debt; **bond′-hold′er** one who holds bonds of a private person or public company; **bond paper** a superior kind of paper, originally intended for bonds; **bonds′man** a surety; **bond′stone** a stone that reaches a considerable distance into or entirely through a wall for the purpose of binding it together; **bond′=timber** timber built into a wall as it is carried up for the purpose of binding it together in a longitudinal direction; **bond′-washing** an illegal series of deals in bonds designed to avoid payment of tax. [A variant of **band** — O.E. *bindan,* to bind.]

bond[2] *bond, adj.* in a state of servitude. — *ns.* **bond′age** captivity: slavery: sexual activity in which one partner is tied up by the other; **bond′ager** a female outworker in the Borders and North of England, whom the *hind* or married cottar was bound to provide for the farmwork. — **bond′maid, bond′-woman, bonds′woman** a woman-slave; **bond′man, bonds′man** a man-slave; **bond′manship; bond′servant** a slave; **bond′-service** the condition of a bondservant: slavery; **bond′-slave** a slave. [O.E. *bonda,* a boor, a householder, from O.N. *bōndi, būandi,* a tiller, a husbandman, *būa,* to till, cog. with O.E. *buan,* meaning affected by association with **bond[1].**]

bondsman. See **bond[1,2].**

bonduc *bon′duk, n.* the nicker seed. [Ar. *bonduq,* a kind of nut.]

bone *bōn, n.* a hard substance forming the skeleton of the higher animals: a separate piece of the skeleton: a piece of whalebone: a bobbin for lace-making: (in *pl.*) the skeleton or anything analogous: (in *pl.*) mortal remains: (in *pl.*) pieces of bone or the like held between the fingers of the hand and rattled together to keep time to music: (in *pl.*) dice. — *v.t.* to take the bones out of, as meat: to furnish with bones: to seize, to steal (*slang*). — *adjs.* **boned** having bones: having the bones removed; **bone′less** wanting bones: spineless (*fig.*). — **bō′niness; bō′ner** (*slang*) a howler, a blunder. — *adj.* **bō′ny** full of, or consisting of, or like bones: thin. — **bone′-ache** pain in the bones; **bone′-ash, bone′-earth** the remains of bones burned in an open furnace; **bone′-bed** a deposit of fossil bones; **bone′-brecc′ia** rock formed of broken fossil bones; **bone′-black** the carbonaceous remains of bones heated in a close vessel; **bone′-cave′** a cave containing deposits of fossil bones of animals that lived in it or their prey; **bone china** china in the making of which calcium phosphate, as in bone ash, is used. — *adj.* **bone′-dry** as dry as a bone: under total prohibition. — **bone′-dust** ground or pulverised bones, used in agriculture; **bone′head** a blockhead. — *adj.* **bone′-i′dle** utterly idle, idle to the bone. — **bone′-lace′** lace woven with bobbins, which were often made of bones; **bone′-meal** ground bones used as fertiliser and as animal feed; **bone′-mill** a mill where bones are ground; **bone′-oil′** a liquid got in dry distillation of bones; **bone′set** an American species of hemp agrimony; **bone′setter** one who treats broken or dislocated bones without being a duly qualified surgeon; **bone′-**

shaker a familiar name for earlier forms of bicycle: any crazy vehicle; **bone'-spav'in** a bony excrescence or hard swelling on the inside of the hock of a horse; **bone'-tur'quoise** blue fossil bone or tooth used as turquoise. — *adj.* **bone'-weary** utterly exhausted. — **bone'yard** (*slang*) a cemetery; **bony fishes** the Teleostei, an order of fishes including most of the living forms; **bony pike** the American (and fossil) garfish. — **bare bones** the essentials (of a subject); **bone of contention** something that causes strife; **bone to pick** something to occupy one (*arch*.): a difference to be cleared up (with somebody); **bone up on** (*slang*) to study or collect information about (a subject) for an immediate purpose; **feel in one's bones** to know instinctively, without proof; **make no bones of, about** to have no scruples about: to make no fuss, difficulty, about; **near the bone** mean: on the verge of the indecent or offensively pointed; **(never) make old bones** (not) to live to old age; **to the bone** to the inmost part: to the minimum; **work one's fingers to the bone** to work until one is exhausted. [O.E. *bān*; Ger. *Bein*, leg.]

bonfire *bon'fīr, n.* a large fire in the open air on occasions of public rejoicing, for consuming garden refuse, etc. — originally a fire in which bones were burnt. — **Bonfire night** 5 November, Guy Fawkes night (see **guy**). [**bone**, and **fire**.]

bong *bong, n.* a deep hollow or ringing sound. — *v.i.* to make such a sound. — Also *v.t.* [Imit.]

bongo *bong'gō, n.* an African bushbuck: — *pl.* **bong'os.** [Native name.]

bongo (drum) *bong'gō (drum), n.* a small Cuban drum played with the fingers — generally used in pairs: — *pl.* **bon'gos, bongo drums.** [Amer. Sp. *bongó*.]

bongrace *bon'grās, n.* a shade from the sun once worn by women on the front of the bonnet: a broad-brimmed hat or bonnet. [Fr. *bonne* (*fem.*) good, *grâce*, grace.]

bonheur-du-jour *bo-nœr-dü-zhōōr, n.* a small desk or writing-table popular esp. in 18th-cent. France. [Fr., happiness of the day.]

bonhom(m)ie *bon'o-mē, n.* easy good nature. — *adj.* **bon'homous.** [Fr.]

bonibell. See **bonnibell.**

bonie. See **bonny.**

boniface *bon'i-fās, n.* an innkeeper — from the hearty *Boniface* of Farquhar's *Beaux' Stratagem*, or the *Bonifazio* of Ariosto's *La Scolastica.*

bonilasse. See **bonnilasse.**

boning *bōn'ing, n.* estimation of straightness by looking along a row of poles, as in **bo'ning-rod** or **-telescope.**

bonism *bon'izm, n.* the doctrine that the world is good, but could be perfected. — *n.* **bon'ist.** [L. *bonus,* good.]

bonito *bo-nē'tō, n.* any of several large fish of the mackerel family, somewhat smaller than the tunas: — *pl.* **boni'-tos.** [Sp.]

bonk *bongk, n.* a blow or thump, or its sound: an act of sexual intercourse (*vulg*.). — *v.t.* to hit or thump: to have sexual intercourse with (*vulg*.). [Imit.]

bonkers *bong'kərz,* (*slang*) *adj.* slightly drunk: crazy.

bonne *bon,* fem. of **bon,** (Fr.) *adj.* good. — *n.* a French maid or nursemaid. — **bonne chance** (*shãs*) good luck; **bonne compagnie** (*kɔ̃-pa-nyē*) good society; **bonne foi** (*fwa*) good faith; **bonne grace** (*grãs*) good grace, gracefulness: (in *pl.*) favour; **bonne mine** (*mēn*) good appearance, pleasant looks.

bonne-bouche *bon-bōōsh', n.* a delicious morsel. [Fr., pleasant taste; *bonne* (fem.), good, *bouche,* mouth.]

bonnet *bon'it, n.* a woman's head-covering, tied on by strings: a soft cap: the velvet cap within a coronet: a small work before the salient or flanked angle of the ravelin (*fort*.): an additional part laced to the foot of jibs, or other fore-and-aft sails, to gather more wind (*naut*.): a wire-cowl over a chimney-top: the cover of a motor-car engine, or of various parts of machinery, etc.: the second stomach of a ruminant: a decoy or pretended player or bidder at a gaming-table or an auction, the accomplice of a thimble-rigger or other petty swindler. — *v.t.* to put a bonnet on: to crush his hat over the eyes of. — *adj.* **bonn'eted.** — **bonnet laird** (*Scot*.) a small landowner who wore a bonnet, not the hat of the gentry; **bonn'et-monkey** an Indian macaque (from the appearance of the head); **bonn'et-piece** a gold coin of James V of Scotland, on which the king wears a bonnet instead of a crown; **bonnet-rouge** (Fr.: *bon-ā-rōōzh*) the red cap of liberty of the French Revolution, in the form of a Phrygian cap. [O.Fr., — L.L. *bonnetum,* orig. the name of a stuff.]

bon(n)ibell *bon-i-bel', (Spens*.) *n.* a good and fair maid. [Fr. *bonne et belle,* good and fair: or for **bonny belle.**]

bon(n)ilasse *bon'i-läs, n.* (*Spens*.) for **bonny lass.**

bonny, bonnie *bon'i* (*Scot.* also *bō'ni; Burns* **bonie**) *adj.* comely, pretty: plump: healthy-looking: as a general term expressing appreciation, considerable, etc., often ironically: smiling, gay (*obs*.): stout, strong (*Shak*.). — *n.* a bonny person, a sweetheart. — Also *adv.* — *adv.* **bonn'ily** beautifully: gaily. — *n.* **bonn'iness** handsomeness: gaiety. [Origin obscure.]

bonny-clabber *bon'i-klab'ər, n.* milk naturally clotted on souring. [Ir. *bainne,* milk, *claba,* thick.]

bonsai *bon'sī, bōn', n.* a dwarf tree growing in a pot, produced by special methods of cultivation (*pl.* **bon'-sai**): the art of growing such trees. [Jap. *bon,* tray, bowl, *sai,* cultivation.]

bonspiel *bon'spēl, n.* a great match, now only a curling match. [App. from some Du. compound of *spel,* play; cf. **ba'spiel.**]

bontebok *bon'tə-bok, n.* a South African antelope. [Du. *bont,* particoloured, *bok,* goat.]

bonus *bō'nəs, n.* a premium beyond the usual interest for a loan: an extra dividend to shareholders: a policyholder's share of profits: an extra payment to workmen or others: a douceur or bribe: something good or desirable gained or given with something else. — **bonus issue** an issue of additional shares to a company's shareholders, representing a capitalisation of reserves. [L. *bonus,* good.]

bonxie *bongks'i, (Shetland*) *n.* the great skua. [O.N. *bunki,* heap.]

bonze *bonz, n.* a Buddhist priest. [Jap. *bonzô* or *bonzi,* a priest.]

bonzer *bon'zər, (coll.; Austr*.) *adj.* very good.

boo¹, booh *bōō, interj.* expressive of disapprobation or contempt. — *v.t.* and *v.i.* to hoot. — **boo'-hoo'** (*-hōō*) the sound of noisy weeping. — *v.i.* to weep noisily. — **boo'-word** a word denoting something disliked, disapproved of, or feared.

boo². See **bo¹.**

boob¹ *bōōb, (coll.) v.t.* to bungle. — *v.i.* to blunder. — *n.* a blunder (also **booboo** *bōō'bōō*): a stupid fellow (*U.S.*). [**booby.**]

boob² *bōōb, (slang) n.* a female breast (usu. in *pl.*). — **boob'-tube** (*slang*) a woman's clinging garment covering the torso from waist to armpit: television.

booboo. See **boob¹.**

boobook *bōō'bŏŏk, n.* an Australian owl (*Ninox boobook*). [Aboriginal; from its cuckoo-like cry.]

booby *bōō'bi, n.* a lubberly lout: a stupid fellow: a pupil at the bottom of the class: a sea-bird of the gannet tribe, absurdly easy to catch. — *adj.* **boo'byish** like a booby: stupid. — *n.* **boo'byism.** — **boo'by-prize** a prize for the worst score or the lowest marks; **boo'by-trap** a form of practical joke, by which something is made to fall upon someone entering a door, or the like: a harmless-looking object which on being touched sets off an explosion. — *v.t.* to set up a booby-trap in or on. [Perh. Sp. *bobo,* a dolt.]

boodie(-rat) *bōō'di-(rat), n.* a species of rat-kangaroo, found in the islands off W. Australia. [Aboriginal.]

boodle¹ *bōōd'l, n.* a crowd, pack: stock-in-trade, capital: counterfeit money: money got by political or official corruption: spoil. [Perh. Du. *boedel,* property.]

boodle² *bōōd'l, (slang) n.* a stupid noodle.

boody *bōōd'i, v.i.* to sulk or mope: — *pr.p.* **bood'ying;**

pa.t. and *pa.p.* **bood′ied.** [Fr. *bouder*, to pout.]
boogie-woogie *bōōg′i-wōōg′i, n.* a jazz rhythm in which the piano has an ostinato figure in the bass. — *n.* **boog′ie** boogie-woogie: dancing to jazz rhythms. — *v.i.* to dance to jazz: — *pr.p.* **boog′ieing,** *pa.t.* and *pa.p.* **boog′ied.** [From U.S. slang *boogie,* a Negro performer, and *woogie,* invented to rhyme.]
booh. See **boo**[1].
book *bŏŏk, n.* a collection of sheets of paper, etc., bound together or made into a roll, either printed, written on, or blank: a large-scale literary composition: a division of a volume or composition: (with **the**) the Bible: a betting-book, or record of bets made with different people: any source of instruction *(fig.)*: a libretto: a script: the first six tricks gained by a side in whist: a structure resembling a book: *(pl.)* formal accounts of transactions, as minutes of meetings, records kept of a business. — *v.t.* to write or enter in a book: to engage in advance: of police, to take the name of, for an alleged offence: hence, to arrest: of a referee, to enter a player's name in a notebook for an offence *(football).* — *v.i.* to make a reservation in advance. — *adjs.* **book′able; book′ful** full of information gathered from books. — *n.* **book′ie** *(coll.)* a bookmaker. — *n.* **book′ing** a reservation of e.g. a room in a hotel, a theatre seat, a seat on a plane, train, etc. — *adj.* **book′ish** fond of books: acquainted only with books: savouring of books. — *n.* **book′ishness.** — *adj.* **book′less** without books: unlearned. — *n.* **book′let** a small book. — *adjs.* **book′sie, book′sy** by way of being literary; **book′y** bookish. — **book′-account′** an account of debt or credit in a book; **book′binder** one who binds books; **book′binding** the cover of a book: the art or practice of binding or putting the boards on books; **book′-canvasser** one who goes around soliciting orders for a book; **book′case** a case with shelves for books; **book club** a society that buys, circulates on loan, or prints books for its members; **book′-debt** a sum owing to a seller as shown in his business-books. — *adjs.* **booked′-out, booked′-up** full up: unable to accept further reservations, bookings or appointments. — **book′= end** a prop for the end of a row of books; **book′ holder** one who holds the book of the play and prompts the actor in the theatre; **book′-hunter** one who hunts for rare books; **book′ing-clerk′** one who sells tickets; **book′-ing-hall; book′ing-off′ice** an office where names are booked or tickets sold; **book′keeper; book′keeping** the art of keeping accounts in a regular and systematic manner; **book′land** (O.E. *bōcland*) land taken from the *folcland* or common land, and granted by *bōc* or written charter to a private owner. — *adj.* **book′= learned** (-*lûrn′id*). — **book′-learning** learning got from books, as opposed to practical knowledge; **book′lore** (*Scot.* **book′-, buik′-lear** -*lār*) book-learning: bibliographical lore; **book′louse** a wingless insect of the Corrodentia, found among books and papers: — *pl.* **book′lice; book′maker** one who makes up books from the writings of others, a compiler: one who accepts bets at race-courses, etc. and pays out the winnings; **book′making; book′man** a scholar, student; **book′= mark(er)** a (decorative) strip of leather, fabric, paper, etc., or other object, for placing between the pages of a book to mark a particular opening; **book′-mate** (*Shak.*) a companion in study: a schoolfellow; **book′= mind′edness** habitual direction of the mind towards books; **book′-mus′lin** muslin used in book-binding: **book′-oath** (*Shak.*) an oath made on the Book or Bible; **book′plate** a label usually pasted inside the cover of a book, bearing the owner's name, crest, coat-of-arms, or peculiar device; **book′-post** arrangement in the Post Office for the transmission of books; **book price, book value** the officially-recorded value, not necessarily the market value, of a commodity; **book′rest** a support for a book, a bookstand; **book′-scor′pion** a scorpion-like arachnid found in libraries, probably feeding on booklice; **book′seller** one who sells books: formerly a publisher; **book′selling; book′shelf** a shelf for books; **book′-**

shop a shop where books are sold; **book′stall** a stall or stand, generally in the open air, where books are sold; **book′stand** a bookstall: a stand or support for holding up a book in reading; **book′store** *(U.S.)* a bookshop; **book′-token, -tally** a paper to be exchanged for books of a stated price, sent as a gift; **book trade** the trade of dealing in books; **book value** see **book price; book′-work** study from books, theoretical as opposed to practical work: work on account books, etc.; **book′-worm** a grub that eats holes in books, esp. a beetle larva (*Anobium*): a hard reader. — **be upon the books** to have one's name in an official list; **book in** to reserve a place or room (at): to register at a hotel; **book of words** directions for use; **book through** to book as a whole a journey to be made in parts; **bring to book** to bring to account; **closed book** a subject completely unknown or uncomprehended; **get one's books** to be dismissed; **in someone's good (bad) books** favourably (unfavourably) regarded by someone; **read like a book** to understand thoroughly (usu. a person's character or motives); **suit one's book** to be agreeable to or favourable to one; **take a leaf out of another's book** to profit by his example; **talk like a book** to talk pedantically, or with precision and readiness; **throw the book at** *(coll.)* to administer a lengthy and detailed reproof to; **without book** from memory: unauthorisedly. [O.E. *bōc,* book, beech; Ger. *Buche,* beech, *Buch,* book, supposed to be from early Germanic use of beechen boards.]
Boolean algebra *bōō′lē-ən al′ji-brə,* an algebra closely related to logic in which the symbols used do not represent arithmetical quantities. [Named after George *Boole* (1815–1864).]
boom[1] *bōōm, n.* a pole by which a sail is stretched: a chain or bar stretched across a harbour: a barrier of floating logs: an inflatable barrier used to control pollution at sea, esp. to contain oil from spillages, etc.: a long beam: a tree (in combination, as kaffir-boom, etc.; *S.Afr.*). — **boom′-iron** a ring in which a spar slides; **boom′slang** a venomous S. African tree-snake. [Du. *boom,* beam, tree.]
boom[2] *bōōm, v.t.* to make a hollow sound or roar. — *n.* a hollow roar, as of the sea, the cry of the bittern, etc. — **boom carpet** area affected by a particular sonic boom. [From a L.G. root found in O.E. *byme,* a trumpet, Du. *bommen,* to drum; like **bomb,** of imit. origin.]
boom[3] *bōōm, v.i.* to go on with a rush: to become suddenly prosperous: to increase sharply in value. — *v.t.* to push into sudden prominence: to boost by advertising. — *n.* a sudden increase of activity in business, or the like — often specially worked up: sudden rise in price or value. — *n.* and *adj.* **boom′ing.** — **boom town** one which has expanded suddenly and prospered because of e.g. the arrival of a valuable new industry. [Prob. from **boom**[2].]
boomer *bōōm′ər, n.* the sewellel: the chickaree: a large male kangaroo, esp. of the great grey species: anything large or very successful (*Austr. and N.Z. coll.*). [Partly from **boom**[2], partly from Eng. dial. *boomer,* anything very large of its type.]
boomerang *bōōm′ə-rang, n.* a curved missile used by the natives of Australia, sometimes so balanced that it returns towards the thrower: an act that recoils upon the agent *(fig.).* — *v.i.* to recoil thus *(fig.).* [Aboriginal.]
boon[1] *bōōn, n.* a petition: a gift, favour. [O.N. *bōn,* prayer: O.E. *bēn.*]
boon[2] *bōōn, adj.* gay, merry, or kind (as a *boon companion*). [Fr. *bon* — L. *bonus,* good.]
boondocks *bōōn′doks,* (*U.S. coll.*) *n.pl.* wild or remote country: a dull provincial place. — Also **boo′nies.** [Tagálog *bundok,* mountain.]
boondoggle *bōōn′dog-l,* (*U.S.*) *n.* a Scout's plaited cord of varicoloured leather strips: an article of simple handcraft: work, or operation, of little or no practical value, esp. work officially provided as a palliative for

unemployment. — *v.i.* to do such work. [Scout coinage.]

boong *boong*, (*offensive*) *n.* an Aborigine: a New Guinea native. [Aborigine word.]

boonies *boo'niz*. See **boondocks**.

boor *boor*, *n.* a countryman, a peasant: a Dutch colonist in South Africa: a coarse or awkward person. — *adj.* **boor'ish** like a boor: awkward or rude. — *adv.* **boor'-ishly.** — *n.* **boor'ishness.** [Du. *boer*; perh. partly O.E. *būr*, *gebūr*, farmer.]

boord, boorde *bōrd*, *börd*, old spellings of **board** (*Spens.*, etc.).

boortree. See **bourtree**.

boose. See **booze**.

boost *boost*, *v.t.* to push up: to raise, as price, morale: to advertise or promote: to supplement voltage of: to increase supply of air to, or pressure of: to push (a spacecraft) into orbit by means of a booster. — *v.i.* (*U.S.*) to shoplift: to steal. — Also *n.* — *n.* **boost'er** a person or thing which boosts: a keen supporter (*U.S.*): an auxiliary motor in a rocket, usually breaking away after delivery of its impulse: any device to increase effect of another mechanism: an additional dose of a vaccine to increase or renew the effect of the original dose: a shoplifter (*U.S.*). [Orig. U.S.; ety. dub.]

boot[1] *boot*, *n.* a covering for the foot and lower part of the leg, made of leather, rubber, etc.: an instrument of torture for the leg: a box or receptacle in a coach: a compartment in a motor-car for luggage, etc. — *v.t.* to put boots on: to kick: to turn out, dismiss (with *out*): to load the initial programs on (a computer) (often with *up*). — *adj.* **boot'ed** having boots on, equipped for riding: of a motor-car, having a boot. — *ns.* **bootee** (*boo'tē, -tē'*) a short boot: an infant's knitted boot; **boots** a hotel servant who cleans boots, runs messages, etc. — **boot'black** a shoeblack; **boot boy** same as **bovver boy**; **boot'-catcher** an inn servant who helped to pull off guests' boots; **boot'-closer** one who closes the upper leathers of boots. — *adj.* **boot'-faced** with an unsmiling, expressionless face. — **boot'-hook** an instrument for pulling on long boots; **boot'hose** (*Shak.*) a stocking used instead of a jack-boot: — *pl.* **boot'hose**; **boot'ikin** the boot for torture: a boot or mitten for the gouty; **boot'-jack** an instrument for taking off boots; **boot'lace** a lace for fastening boots (**bootlace tie** a very thin stringlike necktie); **boot'last, boot'tree** the last or foot-like mould on which boots or shoes are made or stretched to keep their shape; **boot'leg** the leg of a high boot. — *v.t.* to smuggle (liquor): to make, or deal in (illicit goods). — Also *v.i.* — *adj.* made or sold illicitly. — **boot'legger** one who smuggles alcoholic liquor in a bootleg or elsewhere: an illicit dealer, one who trades without licence; **boot'legging.** — *adj.* **boot'less** without boots. — **boot'licker** a toady (*U.S.* **boot'lick**; also *v.t.*); **boot'licking; boot'maker; boot'making; boot sale** same as **car boot sale; boot'-topping** the part of a ship's hull between the load-line and the water-line when the ship is without cargo: act of coating this: paint, etc., for the purpose. — **bet one's boots** to be quite certain; **boot and saddle** (a corr. of Fr. *boute-selle*, place saddle) the signal for mounting; **boots and all** (*Austr.* and *N.Z.*) without reservation; **die in one's boots** to die a sudden death, not in bed; **get the boot** (*slang*) to be dismissed; **have one's heart in one's boots** to have lost courage; **lick someone's boots** to try to ingratiate oneself with someone by obsequious behaviour; **like old boots** (*slang*) vigorously; **pull oneself up by one's bootstraps** to get on by one's own efforts; **put the boot in, put in the boot** (*slang*) to resort to physical or verbal bullying: to attack unfairly; **the boot is on the other leg, foot** responsibility (now) lies the other way; **tough as old boots** robust: indestructible. [O.Fr. *bote* (mod. *botte*). — L.L. *botta, bota*, of doubtful origin.]

boot[2] *boot*, *v.t.* to profit or advantage. — *n.* advantage: profit: in old law, any reparation or compensation paid: booty (*Shak.*). — *adj.* **boot'less** without boot or profit: useless. — *adv.* **boot'lessly.** — *n.* **boot'lessness.**

— **to boot** in addition. [O.E. *bōt*, compensation, amends, whence *bētan*, to amend.]

Boötes *bō-ō'tēz*, *n.* a northern constellation beside the Great Bear, containing the bright star Arcturus. [Gr. *Boōtēs*, lit. an ox-driver.]

booth *boodh, booth*, *n.* a hut or temporary erection formed of slight materials: a small shop of simple construction: a covered stall at a fair or market: a partly-enclosed compartment, as one in which to record one's vote, one containing a public telephone, or one formed by high-backed benches either side of a table in a restaurant. [O.N. *būth*, or a cognate word; cf. Ger. *Bude*.]

booty *boot'i*, *n.* spoil taken in war or by force: plunder, a prize. — **play booty** to join with others in order to cheat one player: to play a game with intention to lose. [O.N. *bȳti*, share — *bȳta*, to divide.]

booze, boose *booz*, (*arch.*) **bouse** *bowz*, (*coll.*) *v.i.* to drink deeply or excessively. — *n.* intoxicating liquor: a drinking bout. — *adj.* **boozed.** — *n.* **booz'er** one who boozes: a public house (*slang*). — *adv.* **booz'ily.** — *adjs.* **booz'ing** drinking: for drinking; **booz'y, booz'ey** inclined to booze: drunken. — **booze'-up** a drinking bout. See also **bouse**[1].

bop[1] *bop*, *n.* short for **bebop**, of which it was a development in the 1950s. — *v.i.* (*coll.*) to dance to pop music. — *n.* **bopp'er** a devotee of bebop.

bop[2] *bop*, (*slang*) *n.* a blow. — *v.t.* to strike. [Imit.]

bo-peep *bō-pēp'*, *n.* a simple play among children in which one peeps from behind something and cries 'Bo'.

bor *bö(r)*, *n.* neighbour, an East Anglian form of address to man or woman. [O.E. *būr*, usu. *gebūr*, farmer; cf. **neighbour**.]

bora[1] *bō'rä, bö'*, *n.* a strong north-east wind in the upper Adriatic. [Venetian variant of It. *borea* — L. *boreas*; or Slav.; cf. Serbian *bura*.]

bora[2] *bō'rə, bö'*, *n.* an Australian Aboriginal initiation rite. [Aboriginal.]

borachio *bor-ach'(i-)ō*, *n.* a Spanish wine-skin: a drunken fellow: — *pl.* **borach'ios.** [Sp. *borracha, borracho*.]

boracic, boracite. See **borax**.

borage *bur'ij, bor'ij*, *n.* a blue-flowered, bristly, aromatic herb, *Borago officinalis*, (fam. **Boraginā'ceae**, tubiflorous dicotyledons with cincinnate inflorescence and four nutlets), the leaves of which have a cucumber-like flavour and are used in salads and to flavour drinks. — *adj.* **boraginā'ceous.** [L.L. *borrāgō*.]

borane. See **boron**.

borax *bō'raks, bö'*, *n.* a mineral, hydrated sodium tetraborate, found on alkaline lake shores. — *adjs.* **bo'ric, boracic** (*bo-ras'ik*) of or relating to borax or boron. — *ns.* **bo'racite** (*-rə-sīt*) a mineral composed of magnesium borate and chloride; **bo'rate** a salt of boric acid. — **boric** or **boracic** or **orthoborac'ic acid** an acid (H_3BO_3) obtained by dissolving borax, and also found native in mineral springs in Italy, changing successively by loss of water on heating to metaboric acid, tetraboric or pyroboric acid, and boric anhydride. [Fr. and L.L. *borax* — Ar. *būraq*.]

borazon. See **boron**.

borborygmus *bör-bə-rig'məs*, *n.* sound of flatulence in the intestines. — *adj.* **borboryg'mic.** [Gr. *borborygmos*.]

bord, borde. Obs. spellings of **board**.

bordar *börd'ər*, *n.* a villein who held his hut at his lord's pleasure. [L.L. *bordārius*; of Gmc. origin. See **board**.]

Bordeaux *bör-dō'*, *n.* claret, wine of *Bordeaux*. — **Bordeaux mixture** a mixture of lime and copper sulphate, used to kill fungus and insect parasites on plants.

bordel *bör'dəl*, (*arch.*) *n.* a house for prostitution. — Also **bordello** (*-del'ō*; *It.*): — *pl.* **bordell'os.** [O.Fr. *bordel*, a cabin — L.L. *borda*.]

border *börd'ər*, *n.* the edge or margin of anything: the boundary of a country, etc., esp. (*cap.* — also in *pl.*) that between England and Scotland: a flower-bed in a garden: a piece of ornamental edging or trimming. — *adj.* of or on the border. — *v.i.* to come near or to be adjacent (with *on, upon, with*). — *v.t.* to furnish with a border: to bound. — *adj.* **bord'ered.** — *n.* **bord'erer**

one who dwells or was born on the border of a country. — *adj.* **bord'erless.** — **bordered pit** (*bot.*) a thin area in the wall between two vessels or tracheides, surrounded by a thickened border; **bord'erland** a border region. — *adj.* belonging to the undefined margin between two things, e.g. sanity and insanity. — *adj.* **bord'erline** marginal, hardly or doubtfully coming within the definition in question: verging on e.g. insanity or indecency. — Also *n.* — **Border Leicester** a sheep of a breed developed by cross-breeding Leicesters and Cheviots; **Border terrier** a small rough-haired terrier, originally from the Borders. [O.Fr. *bordure*; from root of **board.**]

bordereau *bor-d(ə-)rō,* (Fr.) *n.* a memorandum.

bordraging *börd'rag-ing, n.* See **bodrag.**

bordure *bör'dūr, -jōōr, n.* (*her.*) a border surrounding a shield. [See **border.**]

bore[1] *bōr, bör, v.t.* to pierce so as to form a hole: to weary or annoy with tediousness (perh. a different word — not known before mid-18th century). — *v.i.* to form a hole or borehole by drilling or piercing: of a race-horse, athlete, to push against another (to gain advantage in a race) (also *v.t.*). — *n.* a hole made by boring: the size of the cavity of a tube: in Australia, an artesian well: a person, thing, or activity that wearies: something that causes annoyance, a nuisance (*coll.*). — *ns.* **bore'dom** tedium; **bor'er** the person or thing that bores: a name common to many animals that pierce wood, rocks, etc. — *adj.* **bor'ing** causing boredom, tedious. — *n.* the act of making a hole in anything: a hole made by boring: (in *pl.*) the chips produced by boring. — **bore'hole** a bore in the earth's crust for investigation or for water, oil, etc. [O.E. *borian,* to bore; cf. Ger. *bohren*; allied to L. *forāre,* to bore, Gr. *pharynx,* the gullet.]

bore[2] *bōr, bör, pa.t.* of **bear**[1].

bore[3] *bōr, bör, n.* a tidal flood that rushes with great violence up the estuaries of certain rivers, also called eagre. [O.N. *bāra,* a wave or swell.]

Boreas *bor', bör', bör'i-as, n.* the North Wind. — *adj.* **bō'real** (or *bo', bö'*) of North Wind or North: (with *cap.*) of a biogeographical region consisting of the northern and mountainous parts of the Northern hemisphere: (with *cap.*) of a post-glacial period when the climate of Europe and North America resembled that of the present Boreal region. [L., Gr. *Boréas.*]

borecole *bōr'kōl, bör', n.* kale. [Du. *boerenkool,* lit. peasant's cabbage.]

boree *bō'rē, (Austr.) n.* any of several species of Acacia. [Aboriginal.]

boreen *bō-rēn', n.* a lane: byroad. [Ir. *bóithrín.*]

borel. See **borrel.**

borgo *bör'gō,* (It.) *n.* a borough, a market-town: — *pl.* **bor'gos.** — *n.* **borghetto** (*bor-get'tō*) a big village: — *pl.* **borghet'tos.**

boric. Same as **boracic.** [See **borax.**]

boride. See **boron.**

born *börn.* See **bear**[1]. — **born again** having received new spiritual life (*adj.* **born'-again'**); **born fool, mimic** etc., one whose folly, mimic ability, etc., is innate; **born to be** destined to be; **in (all) one's born days** in one's whole lifetime; **not born yesterday** not young in experience.

borne *börn, börn, pa.p.* of **bear** to carry.

borné *bor'nā, adj.* limited, narrow-minded. [Fr. *pa.p.* of *borner,* to limit.]

Bornholm disease *börn'hōm diz-ēz', epidemic pleurodynia, a rare infectious disease caused by a virus, named from the Baltic island *Bornholm,* where it was first described.

bornite *börn'īt, n.* a copper ore, sulphide of copper and iron. [I. von *Born* (1742–91), mineralogist.]

boron *bō'ron, bö', n.* a non-metallic element (at. numb. 5; symbol B), present in borax and boric acid, obtained as an amorphous powder or impure in diamond-like crystals. — *ns.* **borane** (*bōr'ān, bör'*) any boron hydride, efficient as high-energy fuel; **borazon** (*bör'a-zon, bör'*) a man-made substance, compound of boron and ni-trogen, hard as diamond; **boride** (*bōr'īd, bör'*) any of a class of substances made by combining boron chemically with a metal, some of which are extremely hard and heat-resistant; **borosil'icate** a salt of boric and silicic acids, used in making heat- and chemical-resistant glass. [See **borax.**]

Boronia *bo-rō'ni-ə, n.* a genus of Australian scented shrubs: (without *cap.*) any shrub of the genus. [F. *Borone* (1769–94), Italian botanist.]

borough *bur'ə, n.* a town with a corporation and special privileges granted by royal charter: a town that sends representatives to parliament: one of the local government divisions of London or New York. — **borough court** formerly an inferior court dealing with minor offences, etc., presided over by local magistrates; **bor'ough-English** a custom in some ancient English boroughs (till 1925), by which estates descended to the youngest son; **bor'ough-monger** a buyer or seller of the patronage of boroughs; **bor'ough-reeve** the chief municipal official in some unincorporated English towns prior to 1835; **close** or **pocket borough** a borough whose representation was in the nomination of some person — common before 1832; **county borough** a borough (by Acts of 1888, 1926, 1958, respectively above 50 000, 75 000, 100 000, inhabitants) with some of the characters of a county — abolished 1974; **rotten borough** one which still returned members to parliament although the constituency had disappeared — all abolished in 1832. — The Scottish terms are grouped under **burgh.** [O.E. *burg, burh,* a city, from *beorgan*; Ger. *bergen,* to protect.]

borrel, borrell, borel *bor'əl, (arch.) adj.* rustic, clownish. [O.Fr. *burel,* coarse cloth worn by peasantry.]

borrow *bor'ō, n.* a pledge or surety (*arch.*): a borrowing (*Shak.*): a slope on a green (*golf*). — *v.t.* and *v.i.* to obtain on loan or trust: to adopt from a foreign source: to derive from another (with *from, of*). — *v.i.* to allow for slope or wind, esp. by putting the ball uphill of the hole (*golf*). — *adj.* **borr'owed** taken on loan: counterfeit: assumed. — *n.* **borr'ower.** — *n.* and *adj.* **borr'owing.** — **borrowed time** an unexpected extension of life, or of the time allowed for some activity; **borrowing days** the last three days of March (O.S.), supposed in Scottish folklore to have been borrowed by March from April, and to be especially stormy. — **to borrow** for a pledge or surety. [O.E. *borgian* — *burg, burh,* a pledge, security.]

borsch(t) *börsh(t), ns.* a Russian soup with beetroot, etc. — Also **bortsch** (*börch*), etc. [Russ. *borshch.*]

borstal, borstall *bör'stəl, n.* a way up a hill, still used in the district of the Downs: an establishment for the detention of young adult delinquents. — **Borstal system** a system of detaining 'juvenile adult' delinquents, named from the first reformatory of the kind at Borstal, a suburb of Rochester, Kent; now replaced by a range of more or less similar detention systems. [O.E. *beorh,* a hill, and *stigel,* a stile, or *borg,* security, *steall,* place.]

bort, boart *bört, n.* diamond fragments or dust: a coarse diamond or semicrystallic form of carbon. [Fr.]

bortsch(t). See **borsch(t).**

borzoi *bör'zoi, n.* a dog like a huge greyhound, but with a soft coat about the length of a deer-hound's. [Russ. *borzii,* swift.]

bosbok. See **bush**[1].

boscage *bosk'ij, n.* thick foliage: woodland. [Fr. *boscage, bocage* — L.L. *boscus,* conn. with Ger. *Busch,* Eng. **bush.**]

boschbok, boschveld. See **bush**[1].

bosche. See **boche.**

Bose-Einstein statistics. See **boson.**

bosh *bosh, n.* nonsense: foolish talk. — Also *interj.* [Turk. *bosh,* worthless, frequent in Morier's novel *Ayesha* (1834).]

boshta, boshter *bosh'ta, -tər, (obs. Austr. coll.) adjs.* very good.

bosk *bosk, n.* a thicket: a little wood. — *ns.* **bosk'et** a thicket: a plantation; **bosk'iness.** — *adj.* **bosk'y** woody or bushy: shady: somewhat tipsy (*coll.*). [Cf. **bush, boscage.**]

bosker *bos'kər*, (*obs. Austr. coll.*) *adj.* very good.

bo's'n, bos'n. See **boatswain.**

bosom *bŏŏz'əm, n.* the breast of a human being: the part of the dress that covers it: (sometimes in *pl.*) a woman's breasts: the imagined seat of the passions and feelings: the heart: desire (*Shak.*): embrace, enclosure: any close or secret receptacle. — *attributively,* confidential: intimate. — *v.t.* to enclose in the bosom. — *adjs.* **bos'omed** having a bosom: enclosed; **bos'omy** of a woman, having large breasts. — **Abraham's bosom** the abode of the blessed dead. [O.E. *bōsm;* Ger. *Busen.*]

boson *bō'son, n.* any of a class of subatomic particles whose behaviour is governed by **Bose-Einstein statistics,** according to which, under certain conditions, particles of the same kind will accumulate in each low-energy quantum mechanical state. [S. N. *Bose* (1894–1974), Indian physicist.]

boss[1] *bos, n.* a knob or stud: a thickened part of a shaft, for strengthening or to allow attattchment of other parts (*mech.*): a wheel or propeller hub: a raised ornament in wood or leatherwork or (*archit.*) at the intersection of ribs in a vault: a dome-shaped protuberance of igneous rock exposed by erosion. — *v.t.* to ornament with bosses. — *adjs.* **bossed** embossed; **boss'y** having bosses. [O.Fr. *boce* (Fr. *bosse*) from O.H.G. *bôzan,* to beat.]

boss[2] *bos,* (*coll.*) *n.* a chief or leader: a master, manager, or foreman: the person who pulls the wires in political intrigues. — *adj.* chief: excellent. — *v.t.* to manage or control: to domineer over (sometimes with *about* or *around*). — *adv.* **boss'ily.** — *n.* **boss'iness.** — *adj.* **boss'y.** — *n.sing.* **boss'yboots** (*coll.*) a person who enjoys telling others what to do. [New York Dutch *baas,* master.]

boss[3] *bos,* (*Scot.*) *adj.* hollow: empty. [Obscure.]

boss[4] *bos, v.i.* (*dial.* and *slang*) to make a mess of. — *n.* a mistake. — *adj.* **boss'-eyed** with one good eye: squint-eyed: out of true. — **boss shot** a bungled shot or attempt. [Origin unknown.]

bossa nova *bos'ə nō'və,* a style of dancing originating in Brazil, or the music for it. [Port. *bossa,* trend, tendency, *nova,* new.]

bostangi *bos-tan'ji, n.* a Turkish palace guard. [Turk. *bostanji.*]

boston *bost'ən, n.* a game of cards, somewhat similar to whist: a kind of waltz. — **Boston terrier** a breed of dog arising from a cross between a bulldog and a bullterrier. [From *Boston,* U.S.A.]

bostryx *bos'triks,* (*bot.*) *n.* a cymose inflorescence in which each lateral axis arises on the same side (cyclically) of its parent axis. [Gr., curl.]

bosun, bo'sun. See **boatswain.**

Boswellian *boz-wel'i-ən, adj.* after the hero-worshipping, detailed and intimate manner of James Boswell in his biography of Samuel Johnson. — *v.i.* **Bos'wellise, -ize** (*-wəl-īz*) to write like Boswell. — *n.* **Bos'wellism.**

bot, bott *bot, n.* the maggot of a botfly, parasitic in the intestines of the horse and other animals: (in *pl.*) the diseased condition thereby caused: (*Scot.* **batts**) colic: (**bot**) a cadger (*Austr. coll.*) — *v.i.* and *v.t.* to cadge (*Austr. coll.*). — **bot'fly** a name for various flies of the family Oestridae that lay their eggs on horses, etc.; **bot'hole** a hole in a hide due to boring by a bot. [Origin unknown.]

botany *bot'ən-i, n.* the science of plants: the plants of an area: fine wool, orig. from Botany Bay (sometimes *cap.*; also *adj.*). — *adjs.* **botan'ic; botan'ical** (also *n.,* a vegetable drug). — *adv.* **botan'ically.** — *v.i.* **bot'anise, -ize** to seek for and collect plants for study. — *ns.* **bot'anist** one skilled in botany; **bot'anomancy** divination by means of plants, esp. the leaves of sage and fig. — **Botany Bay** an early convict settlement near what is now Sydney: convict settlements generally. [Gr. *botanē,* grass, fodder.]

botargo *bot-är'gō, n.* a relish made of mullet or tunny

roe: — *pl.* **botar'gos, -goes.** [It., — Ar. *butarkhah.*]

botch *boch, n.* a swelling on the skin: a boil, pimple, or sore (*Milt.*): a blemish: a clumsy patch: ill-finished work. — *v.t.* to patch or mend clumsily: to put together unsuitably or unskilfully: to bungle (often with *up*). — *v.i.* to do repairs: to bungle. — *ns.* **botch'er** a repairer: a bungler; **botch'ery.** — *n.* and *adj.* **botch'ing.** — *adj.* **botch'y** marked with or full of botches. [Partly perh. — O.N.Fr. *boche* (O.Fr. *boce*), ulcer; vb. prob. from M.E. *bocchen,* to bungle.]

botel, boatel *bō-tel',* (orig. *U.S.*) *n.* a waterside hotel catering especially for boat-owners: a boat or ship which functions as a hotel. [From *boat* and hot*el.*]

botfly. See **bot.**

both *bōth, adj.* and *pron.* the two: the one and the other. — *adv.* or *conj.* as well (sometimes of more than two). [O.N. *bāthar* (superseding O.E. *bēgen, bā*); Ger. *beide;* cf. L. *ambō,* Gr. *amphō,* Sans. *ubhau,* orig. *ambha.*]

bothan *bo'han, n.* a booth, hut: an illegal drinking den. [Gael.]

bother *bodh'ər, v.t.* to perplex or tease: to worry or concern: to fluster: to pester. — *v.i.* to stir oneself: to worry or be concerned (about). — *n.* petty trouble, difficulty, or perplexity. — *interj.* expressing irritation. — *n.* **botherā'tion** (*coll.*). — *adj.* **both'ersome.** — **I, they,** etc. **cannot be bothered** I, they, etc. consider it too much trouble (to do something): I, they, etc. find (someone or something) annoying (with *with*). [First found in 18th-cent. Irish-born writers; poss. Anglo-Irish for **pother;** some suggest conn. with Irish *bodhraim,* I deafen.]

bothy, bothie *both'i, n.* a humble cottage or hut: a one-roomed hut or temporary dwelling: in Scotland, a barely furnished dwelling for farm-servants. — **bothy ballad** a folk-song dealing with country matters, usu. bawdy; **both'yman.** [Cf. **booth.**]

botoné, bottony *bot'ən-i,* (*her.*) *adj.* having buds or knobs at the extremity, applied to a cross having each arm terminated in three buds, like trefoil. [O.Fr.; see **button.**]

bo tree, bodhi tree *bō trē, bōd'i,* in India and Sri Lanka the pipal (*Ficus religiosa*), holy tree of the Buddhists, under which Buddha found enlightenment, planted close by every temple. [Sinh. *bo,* from Pali *bodhi,* perfect knowledge.]

botryoid, -al *bot'ri-oid, -oid'əl, adjs.* like a bunch of grapes. — *adj.* **bot'ryose** botryoidal: racemose (*bot.*). — *n.* **Botrytis** (*bə-trī'tis*) a genus of fungi (fam. *Moniliaceae*), several of which cause plant diseases, and one of which (*Botrytis cinerea*) causes noble rot. [Gr. *botrys,* a bunch of grapes.]

bott. See **bot.**

botte *bot,* (Fr.) *n.* a pass or thrust in fencing.

bottega *bot-tā'gä,* (It.) *n.* a wine shop: the studio of an artist and his assistants or apprentices.

bottine *bot-ēn', n.* a high boot: a half-boot: a lady's boot: a small boot. [Fr., dim. of *botte,* boot.]

bottle[1] *bot'l, n.* a bundle (of hay). [O.Fr. *botel.*]

bottle[2] *bot'l, n.* a narrow-necked hollow vessel for holding liquids: the contents of such a vessel: liquor or drinking: a glass or plastic container with a teat for feeding milk to a baby: courage, firmness of resolve (*slang*). — *v.t.* to enclose in bottles: to preserve in bottles or jars: to block the entrance of (*fig.*). — *adj.* **bott'led** enclosed in bottles: preserved in bottles or jars: shaped or protuberant like a bottle: kept in restraint: drunk (*slang*). — *ns.* **bott'leful** as much as fills a bottle: — *pl.* **bott'lefuls; bott'ler** a person or machine that bottles; an excellent person or thing (*Austr. coll.*). — **bottle bank** a purpose-built skip in which empty glass bottles, jars, etc. may be deposited for collection for recycling; **bott'le-brush** a brush for cleaning bottles, with bristles standing out from a central axis: a name given to various plants of like appearance, as horse-tail, mare's-tail, *Banksia,* and *Callistemon;* **bott'le-chart** a chart showing currents from evidence of bottles thrown into the sea; **bott'le-coaster** a bottle-slider. — *v.t.* **bott'le=**

feed to feed milk to from a bottle rather than the breast. — **bott′le-fish** a fish, *Saccopharynx ampullaceus*, that can blow its body out like a bottle; **bott′le-gas, bottled gas** liquefied butane or propane gas in containers for use in lighting, cooking, heating, etc.; **bott′le-glass** a coarse green glass used in the making of bottles; **bott′le-gourd** or *false calabash*, a climbing, musky-scented Indian cucurbitaceous annual, whose fruit is shaped like a bottle, an urn, or a club. — *adj.* and *n.* **bott′le-green** dark green, like bottle-glass. — **bott′le-head** a bottle-nosed whale; **bott′le-holder** a boxer's attendant: a backer or supporter generally; **bott′le-imp** an imp confined in a bottle; **bott′le-neck** a narrow place in a road where traffic is apt to be congested (often *fig.*); **bott′le-nose** a large swollen nose: a bottle-nosed toothed whale (Hyperoodon). — *adj.* **bott′le-nosed.** — **bott′le-o(h)** (*Austr.*) a dealer in used bottles (from his cry); **bott′le-opener;** a device for opening bottles; **bott′-le-party** a more or less improvised drinking party where each brings a bottle. — *adj.* **bott′le-shouldered** with sloping shoulders like a champagne bottle. — **bott′le-slider** a tray for passing a decanter round the table; **bott′le-tree** an Australian sterculiaceous tree with swollen trunk; **bott′le-washer** one whose business it is to wash out bottles: a factotum generally. — **bottle off** to draw from the cask and put into bottles; **bottle out** (*slang*) to lose one's nerve and withdraw (from e.g. a contest); **bottle up** to enclose as in a bottle: to hold back; **bring up on the bottle** to rear artificially rather than by the breast; **pass the bottle of smoke** to acquiesce in some falsehood: to make pretence; **three-bottle man** one who could drink three bottles of wine without losing his decorum. [O.Fr. *bouteille*, dim. of *botte*, a vessel for liquids — L.L. *butis*, a vessel.]

bottom *bot′əm, n.* the lowest part or surface of anything: that on which anything rests or is founded: the sitting part of the body: the bed of the sea, a river, etc.: the part that supports the contents of a vessel: the seat of a chair: the less dignified end: the foot of a page, hill, etc.: low land, as by a river: the lower part of a ship, hence the ship itself: groundwork: fundamental character or ingredient: staying power: financial resources: the portion of a wig hanging down over the shoulder: a ball of thread (*Shak.*). — *adj.* undermost. — *v.t.* to ground or base: to wind (*Shak.*). — *v.i.* to find bottom: to found, rest. — *adjs.* **bott′omed; bott′omless** having no bottom: very deep: limitless; **bott′ommost** (*-mōst, -məst*) nearest the bottom. — **bottom drawer** a supposed receptacle for possessions hoarded by a young woman against marriage; **bottom end** the big end in a vertical internal combustion engine; **bott′om-fish** a fish that feeds on the bed of the sea, a lake, etc. (also collectively); **bott′om-glade** (*Milt.*) a glade or open space in a bottom or valley; **bott′om-grass** (*Shak.*) grass growing on low grounds. — *adj.* **bott′om-heav′y** having the lower part too heavy or large in proportion to the upper. — **bott′om-land** (*U.S.*) alluvial deposits; **bottomless pit** hell; **bottom line** the final line of a financial statement, showing net profit or loss: the essential factor in a situation; **bott′om-sawyer** the sawyer who works at the bottom of the saw-pit. — **at bottom** fundamentally; **at the bottom of** the real origin of; **bet one's bottom dollar** to bet all one has; **bottom out** (*U.S. base out*) of prices, etc., to reach and settle at the lowest level, esp. just before a rise; **from the bottom of the heart** with heartfelt sincerity; **get to the bottom of** to investigate exhaustively; **stand on one's own bottom** to be independent; **the bottom has fallen out of the market** there has been a sudden reduction in the market demand (for something); **touch, hit,** etc. **bottom** to reach the lowest point. [O.E. *botm*; Ger. *Boden*; conn. with L. *fundus*, bottom, Gael. *bonn*, the sole.]

bottony. See botoné.

botty *bot′i, n.* childish or slang for (a person's) **bottom.**

botulism *bot′ū-lizm, n.* sausage-poisoning, or poisoning by tinned or other food infected with *Bacillus botulinus* (or *Clostridium botulinum*). [L. *botulus*, sausage.]

bouche *bōōsh,* (Fr.) *n.* the staff of cooks in a large house.

bouché *bōō-shā,* (Fr.) *adj.* stoppered: corked while still fermenting.

bouchée *bōō-shā,* (Fr.) *n.* a small patty.

bouclé *bōō′klā, n.* a yarn having the threads looped to give a bulky effect: a fabric made of such a yarn. — Also *adj.* [Fr., curled, looped.]

bouderie *bōō-d(ə-)rē,* (Fr.) *n.* pouting, sulking.

boudoir *bōōd′wär, n.* a lady's private room. [Fr., *bouder*, to pout, to be sulky.]

bouffant *bōō-fā,* (Fr.) *adj.* puffed out, full, bulging.

bouffe. See opera bouffe.

Bougainvillaea *bōōg-ən-vil′i-ə,* or *-vil-ē′ə, n.* a Neotropical genus of Nyctaginaceae, frequently trained over trellises, its triplets of flowers almost concealed by rosy or purple bracts (also **Bougainvil′ia**): (without *cap.*) any member of the genus. [From the first French circumnavigator of the globe, Louis Antoine de *Bougainville* (1729–1811).]

bouge. A Shakespearian form of **budge**[1].

bouget. A Spenserian form of **budget.**

bough *bow, n.* a branch of a tree: the gallows. — **bough′pot, bow′pot** (*arch.*) a pot for boughs as an ornament: a flower-pot: a bunch of flowers. [O.E. *bōg, bōh,* an arm, the shoulder; Ger. *Bug,* shoulder, the bow of a ship — O.E. *būgan,* to bend.]

bought[1]**, boughten.** See buy.

bought[2] *bowt, n.* a bight or bend: a twist or coil (*Spens.*): the bend of a sling. [See bight.]

bougie *bōō′zhē, n.* a wax candle: an instrument (orig. of waxed linen) for distending contracted mucous canals. [Fr., — *Bougie* in Algeria.]

bouillabaisse *bōō-yä-bes′, n.* a Provençal thick, spiced soup made of fish and vegetables. [Fr.]

bouilli *bōō-yē, n.* boiled or stewed meat. — *n.* **bouillon** (*bōō′yõ*) a strong broth. [Fr.; see boil.]

bouillotte *bōō-yot′, n.* a gambling card game resembling poker. [Fr.]

bouk *bōōk,* (*Scot.*) *n.* body: bulk. [O.E. *būc,* belly, O.N. *būkr,* coalescing with bulk.]

boulder *bōld′ər, n.* a large stone rounded by the action of water: a mass of rock transported by natural agencies from its native bed (*geol.*). — *adj.* containing boulders. — **bould′er-clay** a stiff stony mass of finely ground rock, usually containing boulders and pebbles, formed as a ground moraine under land-ice. [Origin obscure; Sw. dial. *bullersten,* large stone in a stream, has been compared.]

boule[1]**.** Same as buhl.

boule[2] *bōō′lē, n.* in ancient Greece, a council or senate. [Gr. *boulē*.]

boules *bōōl, n.pl.* a French form of bowls, pétanque. [Fr.]

boulevard *bōōl′(ə-)vär(d), n.* a broad road, walk, or promenade bordered with trees, originally applied to those formed upon the demolished fortifications of a town: a broad main road. — *n.* **boulevardier** (*bōōl-vär-dyā*) a frequenter of boulevards or promenades, chiefly of Paris: a man-about-town. [Fr., — Ger. *Bollwerk*; see bulwark.]

bouleversement *bōōl-vers-mā, n.* an overturning: overthrow, ruin. [Fr.]

boulle. See buhl.

boult, bolt *bōlt, v.t.* to sift through coarse cloth: to examine by sifting. — *ns.* **bo(u)lt′er** a sieve: a machine for separating bran from flour; **bo(u)lt′ing.** — **bo(u)lt′ing cloth** a firm silk or nylon fabric with various mesh sizes used for boulting meal or flour, for embroidery, or for photographic enlargements; **bo(u)lt′ing-hutch** a hutch or large box into which flour falls when it is boulted. [O.Fr. *bulter — buleter,* app. from *bure* — L.L. *burra,* a coarse reddish-brown cloth — Gr. *pyrrhos,* reddish.]

boun, bowne *bōōn, bown, v.t.* (used *refl.*) and *v.i.* to prepare: to get ready: to dress: to set out. — *adj.* ready. [See bound[4]; revived by Scott.]

bounce[1] *bowns, v.i.* to jump or spring suddenly: to bound like a ball, to throw oneself about: to burst (into or out of a room, etc.): to boast, to exaggerate: to come back to one, as a cheque that cannot be cashed. — *v.t.* to beat (*obs.*): to cause to rebound: to turn out, eject, dismiss: to reprimand (*slang*): to bring to book: to hustle, force. — *n.* a thud: a leap or spring: a boast: dismissal (*U.S.*): a bold lie. — *adv.* and *interj.* expressing sudden or bouncing movement or (*formerly*) the noise of a gun. — *n.* **bounc'er** one who, or that which, bounces: something big: a bully: a liar: a cheque that bounces: in cricket, a ball bowled so as to bounce and rise sharply off the ground: one employed to eject undesirable people from a club, dance-hall, etc. — *adv.* **boun'cily.** — *n.* **boun'ciness.** — *adjs.* **bounc'ing** large and heavy: lusty: swaggering: **bounc'y** given to bouncing, cocky. — **bounce back** to recover quickly and easily. [Du. *bonzen*, to strike, from *bons*, a blow.]

bounce² *bowns*, *n.* the lesser spotted dogfish.

bound¹ *bownd*, *pa.t.* and *pa.p.* of **bind.** — in composition, restricted to, or by, as *housebound*, *stormbound.* — **bound'-bail'iff** a sheriff's officer, so called from his bond given to the sheriff for the discharge of his duty. — **bound to** obliged to (a person, etc.): certain to (do something) (perh. partly from **bound⁴**).

bound² *bownd*, *n.* a limit: (in *pl.*) the limit of that which is reasonable or permitted: (in *pl.*) a borderland, land generally within certain understood limits, the district. — *v.t.* to set bounds to: to limit, restrain, or surround. — *n.* **bound'ary** a limit: a border: termination: a hit to the limit of the ground (*cricket*): a score for such a hit. — *adjs.* **bound'ed** restricted, cramped; **bound'less** having no limit: vast. — *n.* **bound'lessness.** — **boundary layer** the very thin layer of air on the surface of an aircraft in which the viscosity of the air affects its velocity, causing turbulence to build up and thereby increasing drag (**boundary-layer control** the removal of the boundary layer by a suction system or other means); **bound'ary-rider** (*Austr.*) one who is responsible for the maintenance of (boundary) fences on a station. — **out of bounds** not to be visited, entered, etc.: in such a prohibited place. [O.Fr. *bonne* — L.L. *bodina*; cf. Bret. *bonn*, a boundary.]

bound³ *bownd*, *v.i.* to spring or leap. — *n.* a spring or leap. — *n.* **bound'er** one who bounds: an obtrusively ill-bred man: one whose moral conduct is objectionable. — *adj.* **bound'ing** moving forward with a bound: leaping. — **by leaps and bounds** by startlingly rapid stages. [Fr. *bondir*, to spring, in O.Fr. to resound — L. *bombitāre.*]

bound⁴ *bownd*, *adj.* ready, prepared (*obs.*): ready to start (for): on the way to (with *for*, or following an *adv.*, e.g. *homeward bound*; also in composition, as *southbound*). — See also **bound¹** . [O.N. *būinn*, pa.p. of *būa*, to prepare; cf. **boun.**]

bounden *bownd'n*, *adj.* obligatory. [Archaic pa.p. of **bind.**]

bountree *boon'tri.* See **bourtree.**

bounty *bown'ti*, *n.* liberality in bestowing gifts: the gift bestowed: money offered as an inducement to enter the army, or as a premium to encourage any branch of industry, or (**king's** or **queen's bounty**) to a mother who has three or more children at a birth. — *adjs.* **boun'teous**, **boun'tiful** liberal in giving: generous. — *advs.* **boun'teously**, **boun'tifully.** — *ns.* **boun'teousness**, **boun'tifulness**; **boun'tihood**; **boun'tyhed** (*Spens.*). — **Lady Bountiful** a character in Farquhar's *Beaux' Stratagem*: now used for the charitable great lady of a district. [O.Fr. *bontet* (*bonté*), goodness — L. *bonitās*, *-ātis* — *bonus*, good.]

bouquet *book'ā*, or *-ā'*, *n.* a bunch of flowers: a nosegay: the perfume exhaled by wine: a compliment, praise. — *n.* **bouquetière** (*boo-k(ə)-tyer*) a flower-girl. — **bouquet garni** (*boo'kā gär-nē*) a bunch or sachet of herbs used as flavouring, removed before serving (Fr., garnished bouquet). [Fr. *bouquet*, dim. of *bois*, a wood; cf. It. *bosco*; see **boscage**, **bush.**]

bourasque *boo-rask'*, *n.* a tempest. [Fr. *bourrasque*; It. *borasco*, a storm.]

Bourbon *boor'bon*, *n.* a reactionary (*U.S.*): a race of roses: (without *cap.*; usu. *bûr'bən*) maize whisky (orig. made in *Bourbon* County, Kentucky). — *ns.* **Bour'bonism; Bour'bonist** an adherent of the Bourbons. — **Bourbon biscuit** two chocolate-flavoured pieces of biscuit with chocolate cream between. [From the *Bourbon* family, which long reigned in France and Spain.]

bourd *boord*, (*obs.*) *n.* a jest, sport. — *n.* **bourd'er** (*obs.*) a jester. [O.Fr. *bourde*, origin unknown.]

bourdon¹ *boor'don*, *n.* the refrain of a song: a drone bass: a bass stop in an organ or harmonium. [See **burden.**]

bourdon² *boor'don*, (*obs.*) *n.* a pilgrim's staff: a club. [Fr., — L.L. *burdō*, *-ōnis*, a mule.]

bourg *boorg*, *n.* a town, esp. beside a castle: a market-town. [Fr.]

bourgeois¹ *hûr-jois'*, *n.* an old type size, larger than brevier and smaller than longprimer, approximately 9-point. [Fr.; perh. from the name of the type-founder.]

bourgeois² *boorzh'wä*, *n.* a citizen: a member of the middle class: a merchant or shopkeeper. — *adj.* middle class: conventional: humdrum: conservative: materialistic. — *n.* **bourgeoisie** (*boor'zhwä-zē*, *-zē'*) the middle class of citizens. [Fr. *bourgeois*, a citizen.]

bourgeon. See **burgeon.**

bourguignon *boor-gē-nyō̄*, (*cook.*) *adj.* of meat dishes, stewed with onion, mushrooms and Burgundy wine. [Fr., Burgundian.]

Bourignian *boor-in'yən*, *adj.* of or pertaining to Antoinette *Bourignon* (1616–80), a religious visionary for whom religion consisted in inward emotion, not in knowledge or practice.

bourkha. Same as **burk(h)a.**

bourlaw. See **byrlaw.**

bourn¹, **bourne** *boorn*, *bōrn*, *börn*, *n.* a boundary, limit, or goal: domain (*Keats*). [Fr. *borne*, a limit.]

bourn², **bourne.** Same as **burn¹.**

bourree *boor'ā*, *-ā'*, *n.* a brisk dance in duple time, originating in Auvergne or in the Basque provinces: a musical composition in the same rhythm, often introduced in old suites. [Fr.]

bourse *boors*, *n.* an exchange where merchants meet for business: a stock exchange, esp. (*cap.*) that in Paris. [Fr. *bourse*; see **purse.**]

boursier *boor-syā*, (Fr.) *n.* a foundation-scholar: a speculator on the exchange.

bourtree, **boortree** *boor'tri*, (*Scot.*) *n.* the elder-tree. — Also **bountree** (*boon'tri*). — **bour'tree-gun** a pop-gun made of an elder twig. [Ety. unknown.]

bouse¹ *booz*, *bowz*, *v.i.* and *n.* arch. form of **booze.** — *adjs.* **bous'ing; bous'y**, etc. — *n.* **bous'ingken** (*obs.* thieves' *slang*) a low drinking-shop.

bouse², **bowse** *bows*, *v.t.* and *v.i.* to haul with tackle. [Orig. unknown.]

boustrophedon *boo-* or *bow-strof-ē'don*, *adj.* and *adv.* (of ancient writing) ploughwise, alternately from right to left and from left to right. [Gr. *boustrophēdon* — *bous*, ox, *strophē*, a turning.]

bout *bowt*, *n.* a turn, round: a spell: a trial: in boxing or wrestling, a contest: a fit. [**bought²**.]

boutade *boo-täd'*, *n.* a sudden outburst: a caprice. [Fr., — *bouter*, to thrust.]

boutique *boo-tēk'*, *n.* a shop: a department in a shop: a tradesman's stock: about 1960, used esp. for a small, expensive, exclusive dress shop for women: now, a small shop, or a department in a shop, selling fashionable clothes, etc. [Fr.]

bouton *boo-tō̄*, *n.* an enlargement of the end of a nerve fibre in contact with part of another nerve fibre. — *adj.* **boutonné(e)** (*-ton-ā*) reticent, buttoned-up. — *n.* **boutonnière** (*-to-nyer*) a flower for the buttonhole, etc. [Fr., button.]

bouts rimés *boo rē-mā'*, rhyming words given out by someone as the line-endings of a stanza, for others to fill up the lines. [Fr., rhymed ends.]

bouzouki *boo-zoo'ki*, *n.* a plucked metal-stringed instrument, used esp. in Greece. [Mod. Gr.]

bovate *bō'vāt, (hist.) n.* an oxgang. [L.L. *bovāta — bōs, bovis,* an ox.]

bovine *bō'vīn, adj.* pertaining to cattle: stupid, dull. [L. *bōs, bovis,* an ox or cow.]

Bovril® *bov'ril, n.* a concentrated beef extract used to make drinks, to flavour meat dishes, etc. [L. *bōs, bovis,* ox, cow.]

bovver *bov'ər, (slang) n.* rowdy or violent behaviour by street gangs. — Also *adj.* — **bovver boy** *bov'ər boi,* a member of a gang of hooligans in the habit of engaging in street fights using heavy, hobnailed boots (**bovver boots**) to kick their opponents: a troublemaker, esp. one who uses rough methods. [Prob. Cockney pron. of **bother.**]

bow[1] *bow, v.i.* to bend: to bend the neck or body in saluting, acknowledging a compliment, etc.: to submit (to). — *v.t.* to bend or incline downwards: to crush down: to usher with a bow: to express by a bow. — *n.* a bending of the neck or body in salutation. — *adj.* **bowed** (*bowd*) bent forward, esp. in the back. — **a bowing acquaintance** a slight acquaintance; **bow in** to make a first appearance in public; **bow out** to withdraw or retire from a place, situation, etc.; **make one's bow** to retire ceremoniously: to leave the stage; **take a bow** to acknowledge applause or recognition. [O.E. *būgan,* to bend; akin to L. *fugere,* to flee, to yield.]

bow[2] *bō, n.* a piece of elastic wood or other material for shooting arrows, bent by means of a string stretched between its ends: anything of a bent or curved shape, as the rainbow: a yoke (*Shak.*): a rod strung with horsehair, by which the strings of a violin, etc., are sounded: a ring of metal forming a handle: a knot with one or two loops: a looped knot of ribbons: a necktie or the like, so tied (also **bow tie**): a single movement (up or down) or stroke of the bow in playing an instrument. — *v.i.* to handle the bow in playing. — *v.t.* to play with a bow: to distribute between up-bows and down-bows: to mark such distribution. — *n.* **bow'yer** a bowman: a maker of bows for archery. — *adjs.* **bow'-backed** with bent back; **bow'bent** (*Milton*) bent like a bow. — **bow'-boy** a boy archer: Cupid (*Shak.*). — *n.pl.* **bow'-compasses** a small pair of compasses, often with a bow-shaped spring instead of a hinge. — **bow'fin** a North American freshwater fish (*Amia*) of the Holostei. — *adj.* **bow'-fron'ted** having a convex front. — **bow'-hand** the hand in which the bow is held — normally in archery, the left, in violin-playing the right; **bowhead (whale)** the Greenland whale; **bow'-leg** a bandy leg like a bow. — *adj.* **bow'-legged** (*-legd* or *-leg-id*). — **bow'man** an archer; **bow'-saw** a saw with a narrow blade stretched like a bowstring in a strong bow-shaped frame (also **log'-saw**): a saw with a narrow blade stretched in an H-shaped frame and held taut by tightening a cord at the opposite end of the frame; **bow'shot** the distance to which an arrow can be shot from a bow; **bow'string** the string by which a bow is drawn: a string with which the Turks strangled offenders: a horizontal tie on a bridge or girder. — *v.t.* to strangle with a bowstring (*pa.t.* and *pa.p.* **bow'stringed**, sometimes **bow'strung**). — *adj.* of, for, having, a bowstring. — **bow'string-hemp** the genus Sansevieria or its fibre; **bow tie** see **bow**; **bow'-win'dow** a window projecting in a curve: a pot-belly (*slang*). — *adj.* **bow'-win'dowed.** — **draw the long bow** to make extravagant statements; **on the bow hand** wide of the mark; **two strings to one's bow** an alternative in reserve. [O.E. *boga;* cog. with Ger. *Bogen.*]

bow[3] *bow, n.* the forepart of a ship — often used in *pl.,* the ship being considered to have starboard and port bows, meeting at the stem. — *ns.* **bow'er, bow'er-anch'or** an anchor at the bow or forepart of a ship (*best-bower* and *small-bower*); **bow'-oar** the oar nearest the bow. — **bold** or **bluff bow** a broad bow; **lean bow** a narrow one; **on the bow** within 45° of the point right ahead. [From a L.G., Du. or Scand. word for shoulder; see **bough.**]

bowat, bowet, buat *bōō'ət, (Scot.) n.* a lantern. — **MacFarlane's buat** (*Scott*) the moon. [L.L. *boeta,* box.]

bowdlerise, -ize *bowd'lər-īz, v.t.* to expurgate a book or writing, by removing whatever might raise a blush, esp. to do so unnecessarily. — *ns.* **bowdlerisā'tion, -z-; bowd'leriser, -z-; bowd'lerism.** [From Dr T. *Bowdler* (1754–1825), who published an expurgated Shakespeare in ten volumes in 1818.]

bowel *bow'əl, n.* an interior part of the body: (in *pl.*) the entrails, intestines: (in *pl.*) the interior part of anything: (in *pl.*) the heart, pity, tenderness (the emotions being supposed to be seated in the bowels) (*obs., B.* and *Shak.*). — *v.t.* to take out the bowels of: — *pr.p.* **bow'elling;** *pa.p.* and *pa.t.* **bow'elled.** [O.Fr. *boel* — L. *botellus,* a sausage, an intestine.]

bower[1] *bow'ər, n.* a shady enclosure or recess in a garden, an arbour: an inner apartment: a lady's private room, boudoir: a dwelling (*poet.*). — *v.t.* to enclose: to embower (*Shak.*). — *v.i.* (*Spens.*) to lodge. — *adj.* **bow'ery** having bowers: shady. — **bow'er-bird** an Australian bird that makes a bower adorned with colourful feathers, shells, etc.; **bow'erwoman** (*arch.*) a chambermaid. [O.E. *būr,* a chamber; root of *būan,* to dwell.]

bower[2] *bow'ər, n.* the name in euchre for the two highest cards, the knave of trumps, and the other knave of the same colour, the *right* and *left* bower respectively. [Ger. *Bauer,* peasant.]

bower[3], **bower-anchor.** See **bow**[3].

bowery *bow'ə-ri (U.S. arch.) n.* a farm. — **the Bowery** a street in New York. [Du. *bouwerij.*]

bowes. A Miltonic spelling of **boughs.**

bowet. Same as **bowat.**

bowget. A variant of **budget.**

bowie knife *bō'i,* in U.S. *bōō'i, nīf,* a strong, one-edged dagger-knife with a blade about twelve inches long. [From Colonel *Bowie,* its inventor, died 1836.]

bowl[1] *bōl, n.* a ball (*obs.*): a heavy wooden ball with a bias: (in *pl.*) a game played by rolling such balls on a green towards a jack: (in *pl.*) sometimes the game of skittles (ninepins) or American bowls (tenpins): (*Scot. bōōl*) a marble: (in *pl.*) the game of marbles. — *v.i.* to play at bowls or ninepins or tenpins: to roll or trundle: to travel swiftly and smoothly in a wheeled vehicle: to pitch the ball to the batsman at the wicket (*cricket*): to be bowler. — *v.t.* to roll or trundle: to deliver by bowling (*cricket*): to put out by hitting the wicket with a bowled ball (also with *out; fig.* to overcome). — *ns.* **bowl'er** one who plays at bowls or bowls in cricket; **bowl'ing.** — **bowl'ing-alley** a long narrow covered place for ninepin- or tenpin-bowling; **bowl'ing-crease** see **crease; bowl'ing-green** a smooth grassy plot for bowls. — **bowl over** to knock down: to overwhelm. [Fr. *boule* — L. *bulla.*]

bowl[2] *bōl, n.* a vessel, characteristically of approximately hemispherical shape, for domestic use: a large vessel for brewing punch: a round drinking-cup, rather wide than deep — hence a synonym for conviviality: the round hollow part of anything: the pocket of a poundnet. [O.E. *bolla.*]

bowlder *bōld'ər, n.* Same as **boulder.**

bowler *bō'lər, n.* a stiff felt hat with a roundish brim. — Also **bow'ler-hat'.** — *v.t.* (*slang*) to discharge, dismiss in civil dress. [Said to be name of a hatter who made it in 1850.]

bowline *bō'lin, n.* a rope from the weather side of the square sails (to which it is fastened by *bridles*) to the larboard or starboard bow, to keep the sail close to the wind. — **bowline (knot)** a simple knot making a loop at the end of a rope which will not slip, used in fastening the bowline bridles to the cringles and also used widely in rock-climbing, etc. [M.L.G. *bōline,* M.Du. *boechlijne.*]

bowne. See **boun.**

bowpot. Same as **boughpot.**

bowr *bowr, (Spens.) n.* a muscle. [*bow,* to bend.]

bowse. Same as **bouse**[2].

bowser *bow'zər, n.* an early form of petrol pump: a light tanker used for refuelling aircraft on an airfield (also with *cap.*): a petrol pump (*Austr.* and *N.Z.*). [Orig. trade name.]

bowsprit *bō'sprit, n.* a strong spar projecting over the bows of a ship. [M.L.G. *bōgsprēt,* M.Du. *boech-spriet.*]

bowwow *bow'wow', n.* a dog's bark: a full-mouthed literary style (*Scott*): a dog (*childish* or *facet.*). [Imit.]

box[1] *boks, n.* an evergreen shrub or small tree (*Buxus sempervirens*) with hard smooth yellowish wood, often used to border garden-walks and flower-beds (also **box'-tree, box'wood**): its wood (also **box'wood**): extended to various other plants, esp. the Eucalyptus. — *adj.* **box'en** made of or like boxwood. [O.E. *box* — L. *buxus* — Gr. *pyxos,* the box-tree.]

box[2] *boks, n.* a case or receptacle for holding anything, usu. four-sided: the contents of a box: a fund: a (Christmas) present: a compartment: a ruled-off space: a pitcher's standing-place (*baseball*): a small house or lodge, as a *shooting-box,* etc.: in a theatre, a small enclosure with several seats: an old square pew or similar enclosure, as a *sentry-box, signal-box, bathing-box, witness-box,* etc.: the driver's seat on a carriage: the case of a ship's compass: a predicament: a light, padded shield covering the genitals (*cricket*): part of a page enclosed within lines, etc. — *v.t.* to put into or furnish with boxes: to enclose, confine (often with *in* or *up*): to panel, wainscot (*Scot.*): to overturn (a watchman) in his box (*slang*): to mix, as flocks of sheep (*Austr.*). — *ns.* **box'ful** as much as a box will hold: — *pl.* **box'fuls; box'iness.** — *adj.* **box'y** shaped like a box: of clothes, having a square appearance: of reproduced music, lacking the high and low tones. — **box'-bed** a kind of bed long common in Scottish cottages, having its ends, sides and roof of wood, and capable of being closed in front by two sliding panels; **box-cam'era** a simple box-shaped camera; **box canyon** (*U.S.*) a narrow canyon with almost vertical sides; **box'car** (*U.S.*) a box-wagon; **box'-cloth** a heavy cloth for riding garments; **box'-coat** a heavy overcoat for coaching; **box'-day** one of the Court of Session vacation days when papers ordered to be deposited in court must be lodged; **box'-frame** a box-shaped framework of a building; **box'-gird'er** a hollow, square or rectangular, girder. — *v.t.* **box'-haul** to veer (a square-rigged ship) hard round by bracing the foremast yards aback and turning the ship's head. — **Boxing Day** the day (now often the first weekday) after Christmas, when boxes or presents were traditionally given to employees, etc.; **box'-iron** a hollow smoothing-iron in which a heater is placed; **box junction** an area at a cross-roads or other road-junction, marked with yellow criss-crossed lines, into which a vehicle may not move unless its exit is clear; **box'keeper** an attendant who opens the doors of boxes at theatres, etc.; **box'-kite** a kite composed of open-ended boxes; **box'-lobb'y** the lobby leading to the boxes in a theatre; **box number** a number to which replies to advertisements may be sent; **box'-office** in a theatre, etc., the office at which seats may be booked: receipts from a play, etc.: ability to draw an audience: an attraction as judged by the box-office. — Also *adj.* — **box'-pleat** a type of double pleat formed by folding the cloth into two pleats facing opposite directions; **box'room** a room in which boxes, etc., are stored; **box'-seat** a driver's seat on a coach: a seat in a box in a theatre, etc.: a commanding or favourable position (*Austr. coll.*); **box van** a motor van with a box-shaped goods compartment; **box'-wag'on** a closed railway wagon; **box'wallah** (see **wallah**) a pedlar: a young man working in a business house in India (*derog.*). — **box the compass** to name the 32 points in their order in either or both directions: hence to make a complete roundabout in any opinion; **in the box-seat** (*Austr. slang*) in the best, most favourable, etc. position; **in the wrong box** in a false position, in a scrape; **the box** the television set: television (*facet.*); **the whole box and dice** (*Austr.* and *N.Z.*) the whole lot. [O.E. *box* —

L. *buxem,* acc. of *buxis* — Gr. *pyxis,* a box.]

box[3] *boks, n.* a blow on the head or ear with the hand. — *v.t.* to strike with the hand or fist. — *v.i.* to fight with the fists. — *v.t.* and *v.i.* (*Scot.*) to butt. — *ns.* **box'er** one who boxes or is skilled in boxing: a medium-sized, smooth-haired dog of a breed, with bulldog blood, developed in Germany, and used there in war and as a police dog: (with *cap.*) a member of a Chinese society hostile to foreigners — name arising from a Chinese phrase applied to them which meant 'righteous harmonious fist'; **box'ing** the act or art of fighting with the fists: a combat with the fists. — **box'ing-glove** a padded glove worn in boxing. — **box clever** to act in a clever or cunning way. [Possibly connected with Gr. *pyx,* with the fist.]

Box and Cox *boks and koks,* two people who never meet, or who alternate in a place, job, etc. — *adj.* and *adv.* **alternating** [From play, *Cox and Box* in which two men rent a room by night and day respectively; adapted (1847) by J. M. Morton from French farce, and made into comic opera by F. C. Burnand and A. S. Sullivan (1867).]

box-calf *boks'-käf, n.* a chrome-tanned calfskin with rectangular markings made by rolling. [Said to be named after one Joseph *Box,* shoemaker.]

boy *boi, n.* a male child: a lad: a son: a young man generally: (Ireland and elsewhere) a man: a camp-follower (*Shak.*): knave (*obs.*): in some countries a native or coloured servant or labourer (as a form of address, offensive in S. Africa): a slave: (in *pl.*) a group of men with whom a man is friendly or familiar (*coll.*): a man with a particular function, skill, etc., as in *backroom boy.* — *v.t.* (*Shak.*) to play (a female part) as a boy. — *n.* **boy'hood.** — *adj.* **boy'ish.** — *adv.* **boy'ishly.** — *n.* **boy'ishness.** — **boy bishop** a mock bishop formerly elected by choirboys or schoolboys, in office from St Nicholas' to Holy Innocents' Day (6–28 December); **boy'friend** a girl's favourite boy for the time being. — *adj.* **boy'-girl'** of a romantic relationship between a very young boy and girl: romantically sentimental. — **Boys' Brigade** an organisation of boys for the promotion of habits of obedience, reverence, discipline, and self-respect; (**Boy) Scout** a member of the (orig. Boy) Scouts Association, whose aim is to develop alertness and strong character; **boy's love** southernwood; **boy's play** trifling. — **boys in blue** (*facet.*) the police; **boys will be boys** one must expect and put up with foolish or childish behaviour; **(oh) boy** an expression of pleasure, enthusiasm, etc. [M.E. *boi,* boy; Fris. *boi;* Du. *boef,* Ger. *Bube.*]

boyar *bo-yär', boi'är, n.* a member of the old Russian aristocracy next in rank to the ruling princes, before the reforms of Peter the Great. [Russ. *boyarin.*]

boyau *bwo'yō, bwä'yō, boi'ō, (fort.) n.* a communication trench: — *pl.* **bo'yaux.** [Fr., bowel.]

boycott *boi'kot, v.t.* to shut out from all social and commercial intercourse: to refuse to take part in, deal with, handle by way of trade, etc. — *n.* an act of boycotting. [From Captain *Boycott* of County Mayo, who was so treated by his neighbours in Dec. 1880.]

boyg *boig, n.* an ogre: an obstacle, problem, difficult to get to grips with. [Norw. *bøig.*]

Boyle's law. See **law.**

boyo *boi'ō, (slang;* orig. Irish and Welsh) *n.* a boy, young man. [**boy**.]

boysenberry *boi'sən-ber-i, n.* a fruit growing on a bramble, a hybrid of certain raspberries and blackberries. [Rudolph *Boysen.*]

bozzetto *bot-set'tō, (It.) n.* a small model or sketch of a projected sculpture: — *pl.* **bozzet'ti** (*-tē*).

bra *brä, n.* short for **brassière.** — *adj.* **bra'less** not wearing a brassière.

brabble *brab'l, (arch.) v.i.* to babble or clamour: to brawl or wrangle. — *n.* a clamorous contest, a brawl (*Shak.*): a quibble. — *n.* **brabb'lement.** [Du. *brabbelen,* stammer, to jabber.]

braccate *brak'āt, adj.* having feathered legs or feet. [L. *brācātus*, wearing breeches.]

braccio *brät'chō, n.* an obsolete Italian measure of length, more than half a metre: — *pl.* **braccia** (*brät'chä*). [It., lit. arm.]

brace *brās, n.* armour for the arm (*Shak.*): anything that draws together and holds tightly: an instrument of wood or iron used by carpenters and metal-workers for turning boring tools: a mark ({ or }) connecting words, lines, staves of music, indicating that two are taken together, and also used as a bracket in algebra: a pair or couple (esp. of game shot): (in *pl.*) a combination of straps for supporting the trousers: (in *pl.*) ropes for squaring or traversing horizontally the yards of a ship: a piece of wire fitted over the teeth to straighten them. — *v.t.* to tighten or strengthen, to give firmness to: to tone up: to embrace, encompass (*Spens*). — *n.* **brāc'er.** — *adj.* **brāc'ing** giving strength or tone. — **brace'-and-bit** a brace with the drilling bit in place. [O.Fr. *brace* (Fr. *bras*), the arm, power — L. *brāchīum, brācchium*, Gr. *brāchīōn*.]

bracelet *brās'lit, n.* an ornament for the wrist: a handcuff (*coll*.). [Fr. dim., — L. *brāchiāle — brāchium*; see **brace.**]

brach *brach, n.* a dog for the chase, a bitch hound. — *n.* **brach'et, bratch'et** a brach: a whelp: a brat. [O.Fr. *brachet*, pl. *brachès*, dim. of *brac* — L.L. *braccō*, of Gmc. origin.]

brachial *brāk'* or *brak'i-əl, adj.* of the arm. — *n.* **brachiā'-tion** the use of arms as a supplementary means of locomotion. — **brachial artery** the great arterial trunk supplying the upper extremity between the armpit and the elbow, direct continuation of the axillary artery. [L. *brāchium*; see **brace.**]

brachiopod *brak'i-ō-pod, n.* a member of a class **Brachiopoda** (*-op'o-də*) of shelled animals allied to worms and Polyzoa, having usually two long arm-like processes serving to waft food particles to the mouth. [Gr. *brāchīōn*, an arm, and *pous, podos*, a foot.]

Brachiosaurus *brak-i-ō-sö'rəs, n.* a genus of huge lizard-hipped plant-eating dinosaurs, unusual in that their front legs were longer than their back legs: (without *cap.*) a member of the genus. [Gr. *brāchīōn*, an arm, *sauros*, a lizard.]

brachistochrone *bra-kis'tō-krōn, n.* the curve along which a particle acted on by a force (e.g. gravity) will pass in the shortest time from one given point to another. [Gr. *brachistos*, superl. of *brachys*, short, *chronos*, time.]

brachium civile *brā'kē-əm si-vī'lē, brä'ki-ōōm kē-wē'le,* (L.) the civil arm; **brachium seculare** (*sek-ū-lā'rē, sä-kōō-lä're*) the secular arm.

brachy-, *brak'i-, -i'-,* in composition, short. — *ns.* **brachyax'is** (*crystal.*) brachydiagonal; **brachycephal** (*-sef'əl*; Gr. *kephalē* a head) a short-headed person. — *adjs.* **brachycephalic** (*-si-fal'ik*), **brachycephalous** (*-sef'-ə-ləs*) short-headed, having a skull whose breadth is 80 (or 78) per cent or more of its length. — *n.* **brachyceph'-aly** short-headedness — opp. to *dolichocephaly*. — *adjs.* **brachydac'tyl, brachydactyl'ic, brachydac'tylous** (Gr. *daktylos*, finger, toe). — *ns.* **brachydac'tyly** abnormal shortness of fingers and toes; **brachydiag'onal** (*crystal.*) the shorter lateral axis; **brach'ydome** a dome parallel to the brachydiagonal; **brachyg'raphy** certain old systems of shorthand; **brachyl'ogy** condensed expression; **brachypin'akoid, brach'yprism** a pinakoid, prism, parallel to the brachydiagonal. — *adjs.* **brachyp'terous** (Gr. *pteron*, wing) short-winged: short-finned. — *n.pl.* **Brachyura** (*-ū'rə*; Gr. *ourā*, a tail) a group of decapod crustaceans having the abdomen reduced and bent forward under the thorax, the crabs. — *adjs.* **brachyū'ral, brachyū'rous.** [Gr. *brachys*, short.]

brack *brak, n.* a flaw in cloth. [See **break**[1].]

bracken *brak'ən, n.* a fern, esp. *Pteris aquilina*, the commonest British fern, abundant on hillsides, etc. [Ety. obscure.]

bracket *brak'it, n.* a projecting support: a small shelf fastened to a wall: a gas-pipe projecting from a wall: in printing, one of the marks used to enclose words or mathematical symbols: one of the side pieces of a gun-carriage, supporting the trunnions: the space intervening between overestimated and underestimated shots at a target in straddling (*artillery*): a bracketed group. — *v.i.* to support by brackets: to enclose by brackets: to group, as in an honour list, implying equality: to straddle (*artillery*). — **bracket clock** a rectangular clock with an internal pendulum, usu. with one or two handles and often an arched top, designed to stand on a table or wall-bracket. [Fr. *braguette* — Sp. *bragueta* — L. *brāca*, sing. of *brācae*, breeches.]

brackish *brak'ish, adj.* saltish, rather salt. — *n.* **brack'-ishness.** [Du. *brak*, brackish; prob. the same as *brak*, refuse.]

bract *brakt, n.* a leaf (often modified) that bears a flower in its axil. — *adj.* **bract'eal.** — *n.* **bract'eate** (*archaeology*) a thin-beaten plate of gold or silver. — *adj.* of metal beaten thin: having bracts. — *adj.* **bract'eolate** having bracteoles. — *n.* **bract'eole** a small leaf on the axis of a flower. — *adj.* **bract'less.** — *n.* **bract'let** a bracteole. [L. *bractea*, a thin plate of metal, gold-leaf.]

brad *brad, n.* a small tapering nail with a side projection instead of a head. — **brad'awl** a small boring tool. [O.N. *broddr*, spike.]

Bradshaw *brad'shō, n.* a noted railway-guide, 1839–1961, first issed by George *Bradshaw*.

brady- *brad'i,* in composition, slow. — *n.* **bradycard'ia** (Gr. *kardiā*, heart) slowness of heart-beat. — *adj.* **bradypept'ic** (Gr. *peptikos*, digesting) slow of digestion. — Also *n.* — *n.* **brad'yseism** (*-sīzm*; Gr. *seismos*, a shake) a slow up and down movement of the earth's crust. [Gr. *bradys*, slow.]

brae *brā*, (*Scot.*) *n.* the slope bounding a riverside plain: a hill-slope. [O.N. *brā*, eyelid; cf. **brow.**]

brag *brag, v.i.* and *v.t.* to boast or bluster: — *pr.p.* **bragg'ing;** *pa.t.* and *pa.p.* **bragged.** — *n.* a boast or boasting: a thing one boasts of or is proud of: a card game like poker. — *adj.* or *adv.* (*Spens.*) proud, proudly. — *advs.* **bragg'ingly; brag'ly** (*Spens.*). [Origin doubtful.]

bragadisme. See under **braggart.**

braggadocio *brag-ə-dō'shi-ō, -chiō, n.* a braggart or boaster (also with *cap.*): empty boasting: — *pl.* **braggado'cios.** [From *Braggadochio* (prob. *-dok'yō*) in Spenser's *Faerie Queene.*]

braggart *brag'ərt, adj.* boastful. — *n.* a vain boaster. — *n.* **bragg'artism** (*Shak.* **brag'adisme**) boastfulness. [Fr. *bragard*, vain, bragging.]

Brahma[1] *brä'mə, n.* a fowl of Chinese breed, modified in Europe and America. — Also *adj.* [*Brahmaputra*, whence it is said to have been brought.]

Brahma[2] *brä'mə* (*brä-mä'*), *n.* the first god of the Hindu triad, the creator of the Universe. — *n.* **Brah'man** (*-mən*), **Brah'min** one of the highest or priestly caste among the Hindus: (*-min; derog.*) a highly cultured person. — *adjs.* **Brahmanic** (*-man'*), **-al, Brahmin'ic, -al, Brah'minee** appropriated to the Brahmans. — *ns.* **Brah'manism,** or **-min-,** one of the religions of India, worship of Brahma; **Brahmi** (*brä'mē*) an ancient Indian alphabet. — **Brahma Samaj** (*su-mäj'*) or **Brah'mo Somaj'** a reformed Hindu theistic society or church, founded in 1830; **brahmin** (in U.S. **Brahman**) **bull** or **cow** zebu, or zebu cross.

braid[1] *brād, v.t.* to jerk, whip out (*obs.*): to plait, intertwine: to arrange in plaits: to thread, wind about, through: to trim, bind, or outline with braid. — *v.i.* (*obs.*) to start: to change colour or appearance. — *n.* a sudden movement, start (*obs.*): a plait, especially of hair: a band for the hair: a fabric woven in a narrow band: an interweaving, plaiting: embroidery. — *adj.* **braid'ed** plaited: entwined: trimmed with braid: tarnished, faded (*obs.*). — *n.* **braid'ing** plaiting: manufacture of braid: work in braid: embroidery: braids collectively. [O.E. *bregdan*, to move quickly, flash, change colour, plait, weave; O.N. *bregtha*.]

braid[2] *brād*, (*Shak.*) *v.t.* to upbraid, to reproach. [Prob. from **upbraid** or **braid**[1].]

braid[3] *brād*, *adj.* Scots form of **broad.**

braide *brād*, (*Shak.*) *adj.* dissembling, deceitful. [O.E. *brǣgd*, falsehood — *bregdan*, to weave.]

Braidism *brād'izm*, (*arch.*) *n.* hypnotism. [From Dr James *Braid*, who practised it *c.* 1842.]

brail *brāl*, *n.* a piece of leather to bind up a hawk's wing: (in *pl.*) the feathers about a hawk's rump: one of the ropes used to truss up a sail (*naut.*). — *v.t.* to haul in, as a sail, by pulling upon the brails. [O.Fr. *brail* — L. *brācāle*, a waist-belt — *brācae*, breeches.]

Braille *brāl*, *n.* a kind of type in relief for the blind, having arbitrary signs consisting of varying combinations of six points arranged thus (::), there being sixty-three distinguishable combinations. — Also *adj.* [From Louis *Braille* (1809–52), the inventor.]

brain *brān*, *n.* (sometimes in *pl.*) in vertebrates, that part of the central nervous system that is contained within the skull: in invertebrates, the nervous ganglia near the head end of the body: the seat of the intellect and of sensation: the intellect: (in *pl.*) intelligence, common sense: a person of exceptional intelligence (*coll.*): (in *pl.*) person(s) who plan and control an enterprise. — *v.t.* to dash out the brains of: to conceive of (*Shak.*). — *adjs.* **brained** having brains; **brain′ish** (*Shak.*) brain-sick: hot-headed: furious; **brain′less** without brains or understanding: silly; **brain′y** (*coll.*) well endowed with brains: intellectual. — *n.* **brain′iness.** — **brain′case** the cranium; **brain′child** an original thought or work; **brain coral** a coral with brain-like convolutions; **brain damage** general term covering all injury or disease of the brain, temporary or permanent. — *adj.* **brain′-dead′.** — **brain death** the cessation of function of the brain, thought by some doctors to be the true indication of death, rather than the cessation of the heartbeat (also **cerebral death**); **brain drain** the continuing loss of citizens of high intelligence and creativity through emigration; **brain fag** a tired condition of the nerves or brain; **brain fever** a loose popular term which includes congestion of the brain and its membranes, delirium tremens, and inflammation of the brain substance itself; **brain′pan** braincase. — *adj.* **brain′sick** diseased in the understanding, deranged. — *adv.* **brain′-sickly** (*Shak.*). — **brain′sickness; brain stem** the stem-like part of the brain connecting the spinal cord with the cerebral hemispheres, and controlling certain major functions, e.g. the operation of the heart and lungs and the ability to be conscious; **brain′storm** a sudden disturbance of the mind: a sudden inspiration; **brains trust** a committee of experts: a number of reputedly well-informed persons chosen to answer questions of general interest in public and without preparation; **brain′-teaser** a difficult puzzle or problem; **brain′wash, -ing** the subjection of a person to systematic indoctrination or mental pressure with a view to getting him to change his views or to confess to a crime. — *v.t.* **brain′wash.** — **brain′-wave** an electrical impulse produced by the brain: a sudden bright idea: an access of cleverness. — **brain-fever bird** an Indian cuckoo (*Cuculus varius*) that sings scales in the night; **on the brain** as an obsession; **pick someone's brains** see **pick**[1]. [O.E. *brægen*; Du. *brein*, dial. Ger. *Bregen.*]

braird *brārd*, **breer** *brēr*, *ns.* (orig. *Scot.*) the first shoots of corn or other crop. — *vs.i.* to appear above ground. [O.E. *brerd*, edge.]

braise[1] *brāz*, *v.t.* to stew in a closed vessel. [Fr. *braiser.*]

braise[2], **braize** *brāz*, *n.* a sea-bream or porgy. [Perh. conn. with **bream**[1], or with **bass(e).**]

brake[1] *brāk*, obsolete *pa.t.* of **break**[1].

brake[2] *brāk*, *n.* a fern: a bracken. [Perh. **bracken.**]

brake[3] *brāk*, *n.* a thicket. — *adj.* **brāk′y.** [Ety. obscure.]

brake[4] *brāk*, *n.* an instrument for breaking flax or hemp: a harrow: a contrivance for retarding by friction: a

kind of vehicle (see **break**[2]). — *v.t.* to slow down or stop with, or as if with, a brake. — *v.i.* to apply or operate a brake, esp. on a vehicle: to be slowed down or stopped by a brake. — *adj.* **brake′less** without a brake. — **brake′-block** a block pressed against a wheel as brake; **brake horsepower** the effective or useful power of a motor, measured by brake applied to the driving shaft; **brake′-shoe** the rubbing part of a brake; **brakes′-man** (in U.S. **brake′man**) the man whose business it is to manage the brake of a railway train; **brake′-van** the carriage wherein the brake is worked; **brake′-wheel** the wheel to which a brake is applied. [From root of **break**, cf. Du. *braak*, a flax-brake.]

brake[5] *brāk*, *n.* a handle, as of a pump: a lever for working a machine. [Prob. through O.Fr. *brac*, from L. *brāchium*, an arm.]

brake[6] *brāk*, (*Shak.*) *n.* an obscure word in *Measure for Measure* II, i. 39 (not made clearer by emendation of *ice* to *vice*).

Bramah-press *brām′a-pres*, *n.* a hydraulic press invented by Joseph *Bramah* (*c.* 1748–1814), inventor also of the **Bram′ah-lock**, etc.

bramble *bram′bl*, *n.* the blackberry bush, a wild prickly shrub of the raspberry genus (*Rubus*): any rough prickly shrub: a blackberry (*Scot.*). — *n.* **bram′bling** a bird nearly allied to the chaffinch. — *adj.* **bram′bly.** — **bram′ble-berry; bram′ble-bush** blackberry bush or thicket; **bram′ble-finch** the brambling. [O.E. *brēmel*; Du. *braam*, Ger. *Brombeere.*]

brame *brām*, (*Spens.*) *n.* sharp passion, longing. [Prob. It. *brama.*]

bran *bran*, *n.* the refuse of grain: the inner husks of corn sifted from the flour: the coarser part of anything. — *adj.* **brann′y.** — *n.* **bran′fulness.** — **bran′-mash; bran′= pie′, bran′-tub** a tub of bran from which Christmas presents, etc., are drawn. [O.Fr. *bran*, bran, perh. Celt.]

brancard *brangk′ard*, *n.* a horse litter. [Fr.]

branch *bränch, bränsh*, *n.* a shoot or arm-like limb of a tree: anything like a limb of a tree: any offshoot from a main trunk, as a minor road, railway line, etc. (also *adj.*): a subdivision, a section or department of a subject: any subordinate division of a business, subsidiary shop, office, etc. (also *adj.*): a tributary or (*rare*) brook (*U.S.*): a stage in a program where a choice is made to follow one of two or more sequences of instructions (*comput.*). — *v.t.* to divide into branches: to adorn with figures of branches, by embroidery or otherwise (*Spens.*, etc.). — *v.i.* to spread out as a branch (with *out*, *off*, *from*), or in branches. — *adj.* **branched.** — *ns.* **branch′er** a young hawk or other bird when it leaves the nest and begins to take to the branches; **branch′ery** branches collectively (*lit.* and *fig.*). — *n.* and *adj.* **branch′ing.** — *adj.* **branch′less** without branches. — *n.* **branch′let** a little branch. — *adj.* **branch′y.** — **branch′-off′icer** (*navy*; since 1949) any officer holding warrant; **branch′-pilot** one who holds the Trinity House certificate; **branch′-work** ornamental figured patterns. [Fr. *branche* — L.L. *branca*, a beast's paw.]

branchia *brangk′i-a*, *n.* a gill: — *pl.* **branch′iae** (*-ē*). — *adjs.* **branch′ial; branch′iate** having branchiae. [L. *branchia* — Gr. *branchion* (pl. *-a*).]

Branchiopoda *brangk-i-op′o-da*, *n.pl.* a class or subclass of Crustacea with numerous flattened, leaf-shaped, lobed swimming-feet that serve also as breathing organs. — *n.* and *adj.* **branch′iopod.** [Gr. *branchia*, gills, *pous, podos,* foot.]

brand *brand*, *n.* a piece of wood burning or partly burned: an instrument for branding: a mark burned into anything with a hot iron: a trademark, made by burning or otherwise, as on casks: a particular class of goods (as if distinguished by a trademark): a sword, from its glitter: a mark of infamy: a general name for the fungoid diseases or blights of grain crops (*bunt, mildew, rust,* and *smut*). — *v.t.* to burn or mark with a hot iron, or otherwise: to fix a mark of infamy upon (sometimes with *as*). — *adj.* **brand'ed.** — *n.* **brand'er** (*Scot.*) a gridiron. — *v.t.* to cook on the gridiron. — *adjs.* **brand'ered; brand'ering.** — *ns.* **brandise** (*brand'is*; O.E. *isen*, iron) a trivet; **brand'ling** a salmon-parr: an earthworm banded in red and yellow, found in dunghills, used by anglers; **brand'reth** (O.N. *brandreith* — *reith*, carriage) a stand of wood for a cask or hayrick: a rail round a well. — **brand'-image** the impression that the public has of a product or (*fig.*) a person; **brand'ing-iron; brand'-iron** a gridiron: an iron to brand with: a trivet or tripod to set a pot or kettle upon: (*Spens.* **brondyron**, etc.) a sword; **brand'-name** a tradename identifying a particular manufacturer's products. — *adj.* **brand'-new** quite new (as if newly from the fire) (also (*old*) **bran'-new**). — **a brand from the burning** one snatched out of a pressing danger — from Amos iv. 11. [O.E. *brand, brond*, O.N. *brandr*, from root of **burn²**.]

brandade *brã-däd, n.* a Provençal dish made of salt fish cooked with olive oil, garlic and cream. [Fr.]

brandish *brand'ish, v.t.* to wave or flourish as a brand or weapon. — *n.* a waving or flourish. [Fr. *brandir*, *brandiss-* from root of **brand.**]

brandy *brand'i, n.* an ardent spirit distilled from wine: a glass of this. — *adj.* **bran'died** heartened or strengthened with brandy. — **brand'y-ball** a kind of sweet; **brand'y-bott'le** (*dial.*) candock; **brandy butter** butter with brandy and sugar beaten in; **bran'dy-glass** a stemmed drinking-glass with a globular bowl; **brand'y-paw'nee** (Hind. *pānī* water) brandy and water; **brand'y-snap** a thin crisp biscuit flavoured with ginger and orig. brandy. [Formerly *brand-wine* — Du. *brandewijn* — *branden*, to burn, to distil, and *wijn*, wine; cf. Ger. *Branntwein*.]

brangle *brang'gl,* (*arch.*) *v.i.* to wrangle. — *n.* a brawl. — *n.* **brang'ling** disputing. [Fr. *branler*.]

brank¹ *brangk, n.* buckwheat. [Pliny says *brance* (doubtful reading, perh. *brace*) is the Gallic name of a kind of corn.]

brank² *brangk, v.i.* to prance, toss the head: to strut or swagger. — *adj.* **brank'y** (*Scot.*) showy. [Prob. a variant of **prank**.]

branks *brangks,* (*Scot.*) *n.pl.,* rarely in *sing.*, a bridle: a scold's bridle, having a hinged iron framework to enclose the head and a bit or gag. [Ety. very obscure; O.Fr. *bernac* (see **barnacle²**); Ger. *Pranger*, pillory, Du. *prang*, fetter, have been compared.]

brankursine *brangk'ər-sin*, or *-ūr', n.* acanthus, or bear's-breech. [L.L. *branca ursīna*, a bear's paw.]

branle. See **brawl²**.

bran-new. See **brand-new** under **brand.**

bransle. See **brawl²**.

brant-goose. See **brent-goose.**

brantle. See **brawl²**.

bras. A Spenserian spelling of **brass.**

brasero *brä-sā'rō, n.* a brazier: a place for burning criminals or heretics: — *pl.* **braser'os.** [Sp., — *brasa*, a live coal.]

brash¹ *brash, n.* angular fragments of rock, which occasionally form the basement bed of alluvial deposits: fragments of crushed ice: clippings of hedges or trees. — *adj.* **brash'y.** [Prob. Fr. *brèche*.]

brash² *brash, n.* an eructation or belching of acid water from the stomach — water-brash: a sudden burst of rain: a slight attack of illness (*Scot.*): an attack or bout (*obs.*). — *v.t.* (*obs.*) to disturb. [Prob. onomatopoeic.]

brash³ *brash, adj.* reckless, impetuous (*U.S.*): forward, bumptious: bold: of wood, brittle (*U.S.*).

brasier. Same as **brazier.**

brass *bräs, n.* an alloy of copper and zinc: bronze (*obs.*): effrontery (*slang*): money (*slang*): an article or fixture of brass: a monumental plate of brass, commonly with effigy: (*collectively*) the brass wind-instruments or their players in an orchestra or band. — *adj.* of brass. — *adv.* **brass'ily.** — *ns.* **brass'iness; brass'y** (a stroke with) a brass-soled wooden golf-club (also **brass'ie;** also *adj.*): a bronze-coloured fish, the bib or pout. —

adj. like brass in appearance, hardness, sound, or otherwise: brazen-faced. — **brass band** a band of players of (mainly) brass wind instruments: a small military band; **brass'-bounder** a midshipman: a privileged apprentice on a ship for whom a premium is paid (from his gold braid). — *adj.* **brass'-faced'** (*coll.*) impudent, shameless. — **brass farthing** a whit; **brass'-founder** one who casts objects in brass; **brass'founding; brass hat** (*mil. slang*) a staff officer (with gold braid on his hat); **brass neck** (*coll.*) effrontery; **brass plate** name plate on a professional person's office door, usu. made of brass: hence a symbol of membership of the professional class; **brass'-rubber; brass'-rubbing** the process of copying the design on a brass plate, etc., on to paper by laying the paper over the brass and rubbing it with coloured wax, chalk, etc.: the copy so obtained; **brass tacks** details of practical business. — **brassed off** (*slang*) dissatisfied or bored; **top brass** brass hats: those in authority at the top (also **the brass**). [O.E. *bræs.*]

brassard *bras'ärd, n.* a piece of armour for the arm (also **brassart** *bras'ert,* **brass'et**): an armband or armlet: a symbolic band for the arm. [Fr. — *bras,* arm.]

brasserie *bras'(ə-)rē, n.* a beer garden or restaurant. [Fr., brewery.]

Brassica *bras'i-kə, n.* the turnip and cabbage genus of Cruciferae: (without *cap.*) a plant of this genus. [L., cabbage.]

brassière *bras'i-er,* or *braz'* in U.S. sometimes *brə-zēr', n.* a woman's undergarment supporting the breasts. [Fr.]

brast *obs.* and *Northern* for **burst** (*pr.t., pa.t.,* and *pa.p.*).

brat *brat, n.* a contemptuous name for a child: an annoying child: any overgarment of coarse cloth (*obs.*): a child's pinafore (*obs.*): an apron (*obs.*). — *n.* **brat'ling** a little brat. — *adjs.* **bratt'ish; bratt'y.** [O.E. *bratt,* prob. Old Ir. *brat,* plaid, Gael. *brat,* apron.]

bratchet *brach'it.* See **brach.**

brattice *brat'is,* **brattish** *brat'ish,* **brettice** *bret'is, ns.* in mediaeval siege operations, a fixed tower of wood: a covered gallery on a castle wall, commanding the wall-face below (in these senses also **bretesse** *bri-tes',* **bretasche** *bri-tash'*): a wooden partition: a wooden lining: a partition to control ventilation in a mine. — *v.t.* to furnish with a brattice. — *ns.* **bratt'icing, bratt'-ishing** work in the form of brattices: cresting, or ornamental work along a ridge, cornice or coping (*archit.*). — **bratt'ice-cloth** strong tarred cloth used for mine brattices. [O.Fr. *breteshe* — L.L. *bretachia;* cf. **bartisan.**]

brattle *brat'l, n.* a clattering noise: a quarrel: tumult. — *v.i.* to make a clattering noise. — *n.* and *adj.* **bratt'ling.** [Imit.]

bratwurst *brat'vōorst, n.* a type of German sausage. [Ger.]

braunch. An old spelling of **branch.**

bravado *brav-ä'dō, n.* a display of bravery: a boastful threat: a swaggerer (*obs.*): — *pl.* **brava'do(e)s.** — *v.i.* to display bravado. [Sp. *bravada;* see **brave.**]

brave *brāv, adj.* daring, courageous: noble: making a fine appearance: finely dressed, showy, handsome (*Scot.* **braw**): a general word for excellent. — *v.t.* to meet boldly: to defy: to face (out). — *n.* a bully (*arch.*): a bravo (*arch.*): a hired assassin (*arch.*): a brave soldier, esp. among the North American Indians: bravado (*arch.*). — *adv.* bravely (*poet.*). — *adv.* **brave'ly.** — *n.* **brav'ery** bravado (*obs.*): courage: heroism: finery, showy dress. — **brave new world** a desirable or perfect future society (from Shak., *Tempest* V, i, 183), usu. used sardonically, specif. by Aldous Huxley as the title of his novel (1932) portraying a society where scientific, etc., progress has produced a repressive, totalitarian régime rather than a utopia. [Fr. *brave;* It. and Sp. *bravo;* origin unknown.]

bravo *brä'vō, n.* a daring villain: a hired assassin: — *pl.* **bra'vos, bra'voes.** — *interj.* (or *brä'vō'*) well done! excellent (also **bra'va** when addressed to a woman,

bra'vi -*vē*, to a number of persons). [Sp. and It.]
bravura *brä-vōō'rə*, *n*. spirit and dash in execution (*mus*.): a florid air with difficult and rapid passages (*mus*.): brilliant or daring display. — Also *adj*. [It.]
braw *brö*, *adj*. fine: attired in finery. — *adv*. **braw'ly**. — *predicative adj*. very well. — *n.pl*. **braws** fine clothes. [Scots form of **brave**.]
brawl[1] *bröl*, *n*. a noisy quarrel. — *v.i*. to quarrel noisily: to make a disturbance: to murmur or gurgle. — *n*. **brawl'er**. — *n*. and *adj*. **brawl'ing**. [M.E. *bralle*, of doubtful origin; perh. conn. with Du. *brallen*, Ger. *prahlen*, to boast.]
brawl[2] *bröl*, *n*. an old French dance or dance-tune. — Also **branle, bransle** (*bran'l*), **brantle** (*brant'l*). [Fr. *branle*.]
brawn *brön*, *n*. muscle, esp. of the arm or calf of the leg: thick flesh: muscular strength: a boar: a preparation of meat made from pig's head and ox-feet, cut up, boiled, and pickled. — *adj*. **brawned**. — *n*. **brawn'iness** quality of being brawny: muscularity. — *adj*. **brawn'y** fleshy: muscular: strong. [O.Fr. *braon*, flesh (for roasting); of Gmc. origin, cf. Ger. *braten*, to roast.]
braxy *brak'si*, (*Scot*.) *n*. a bacterial disease of sheep: applied loosely to various diseases of sheep: a sheep so infected: its flesh. — Also *adj*. — **braxy mutton** the flesh of a braxy sheep or generally of a sheep that has died of disease or accident. [Prob. orig. pl. of *brack*, variant of **break**.]
bray[1] *brā*, *v.t*. to break, pound, or grind small, as in a mortar. — *n*. **bray'er** an instrument for grinding or spreading ink in printing. [O.Fr. *breier* (Fr. *broyer*).]
bray[2] *brā*, *n*. the cry of the ass: any harsh grating sound. — *v.i*. to cry like an ass: to give forth harsh sounds, esp. of the trumpet. — *n*. **bray'er**. [O.Fr. *brai*, *brait*; *braire* — L.L. *bragīre*, perh. of Celt. origin.]
braze[1] *brāz*, *v.t*. to cover with, or make like, brass. — *adj*. **brā'zen** of or belonging to brass: impudent. — *v.t*. to face (out) with impudence. — *adv*. **brā'zenly**. — *ns*. **brā'zenness, brā'zenry** effrontery; **brazier** (*brāz'yər*, *brāzh'(y)ər*) a worker in brass. — **bra'zen-face** one remarkable for effrontery. — *adj*. **bra'zen-faced**. [**brass**.]
braze[2] *brāz*, *v.t*. to join with hard solder. — *adj*. **braze'less** without soldering. — *n*. **brazier** (*brāz'yər*, *brāzh'(y)-ər*) a vessel or tray for hot coals. [O.Fr. *braser*, to burn; perh. influenced by **brass**. Cf. **braise, brasero**.]
brazier. See **braze**[1,2].
brazil *brə-zil'*, *n*. usually **brazil'-wood**, the hard reddish wood of the East Indian sappan tree or other species of *Caesalpinia*, used in dyeing: also that of *Guaiacum*. — *n*. **Brazil'ian** a native or citizen of Brazil, in South America. — *adj*. of Brazil. — **Brazilian wax** carnauba; **Brazil nut** the edible seed of a large lecythidaceous Brazilian tree (*Bertholletia*). [O.Fr. *bresil* (Sp. *brasil*, It. *brasile*) — L.L. *brasilium*, a red dye-wood brought from the East, itself prob. a corr. of some Oriental word. When a similar wood was discovered in South America the country became known as *terra de brasil*, land of red dye-wood.]
breach *brēch*, *n*. a break: an act of breaking: an opening, or discontinuity: a breaking of law, contract, covenant, promise, etc.: a quarrel: a broken condition or part of anything: a gap made in a fortification: surf. — *v.t*. to make a breach or opening in. — **breach of promise** often used simply for breach of promise of marriage; **breach of the peace** a violation of the public peace by riot or the like. [O.E. *bryce*, *brice*, related to **break**.]
bread *bred*, *n*. food made of a baked paste of flour or meal: food: livelihood: money (*slang*). — *v.t*. to cover (a cutlet, etc.) with breadcrumbs before cooking. — *adj*. **bread'ed**. — **bread'-and-butt'er** bread sliced and buttered: livelihood. — *adj*. connected with making a living or with the consumption of bread-and-butter: materialistic, practical: youthfully insipid: ordinary, routine: descriptive of a letter of thanks for hospitality. — **bread'-basket** a basket for holding bread: the stomach (*slang*; also *fig*.); **bread'berry** a sop of bread in hot

milk; **bread'-board** a board on which bread is cut: a board on which temporary or experimental electronic circuits may be laid out; **bread'-chipper** (*Shak*.) one who chips bread, an under-butler; **bread'-corn** corn of which bread is made; **bread'crumb** the inner parts of a loaf: (usu. in *pl*.) bread crumbled down e.g. as a dressing (when commercially produced usu. coloured orange) for fish, etc. — *v.t*. to cover with breadcrumbs. — **bread'fruit** the fruit of a moraceous tree (*Artocarpus incisa*) of the South Sea Islands, which when roasted forms a good substitute for bread; **bread'head** (*slang*) a drug dealer who is not himself an addict; **bread'line** see **on the breadline** below; **bread'nut** the fruit of a tropical American tree (*Brosimum alicastrum*) akin to the breadfruit tree, used as bread when boiled or roasted; **bread'room** an apartment in a ship's hold where the bread is kept; **bread'root** the prairie-turnip, a North American papilionaceous plant (*Psoralea esculenta*) with an edible root: also the yam; **bread sauce** a thick milk-based sauce made with bread(-crumbs); **bread-'stick** a long, thin stick of bread dough baked until crisp; **bread study** any branch of study taken up as a means of gaining a living; **bread'stuff** bread in any form: any material of which bread is made; **bread tree** a name for various trees whose seeds or pith yield a substitute for bread, e.g. *Kaffir-bread*; **bread'winner** one who earns a living for a family. — **bread and circuses** translation of *panem et circenses* (q.v); **bread buttered on both sides** very fortunate circumstances; **know which side one's bread is buttered on** to know how to act from self-interest; **on the breadline**, at subsistence level, with just enough to make ends meet (from **breadline**, a queue of poor or derelict people waiting for free food, esp. from government sources); **take the bread out of someone's mouth** to deprive someone of the means of living. [O.E. *brēad*, prob. from a Gmc. root meaning a fragment; cf. Scots use of **piece**.]
breaded[1]. See **bread**.
breaded[2]. See **brede**.
breadth *bredth*, *n*. extent from side to side: width: liberality of mind: in art, subordination of details to the harmony of the whole. — *advs*. **breadth'ways, -wise** in the direction of breadth: broadside on. [O.E. *brǣdu*; Ger. *Breite*; see **broad**.]
break[1] *brāk*, *v.t*. to divide, part, or sever, wholly or partially, by applying a strain: to rupture: to shatter: to crush: to make by breaking: to destroy the continuity or integrity of: to interrupt (a fall, journey, etc.): to bruise or penetrate the surface of: to break a bone in, or separate the bones of: to subject, overcome, or wear out: to tame or habituate to obedience (also with *in*): to crush the spirit of: to cure (of a habit): to violate (as a law, promise, bounds, prison): to set aside (as a will): to cut up (an animal's body): to unfurl: to impart (esp. with delicacy): to make bankrupt: to degrade or cashier: to improve on (a particular time, number of strokes, etc., for a course or distance): to arpeggiate: to cause to change from a simple vowel to a diphthong. — *v.i*. to separate: to come apart, or go to pieces, esp. with suddenness: to give way: to start away: to burst forth: to force a passage: to pass suddenly into a condition or action (as into laughter, revolt, sweat, spots): to become variegated or striped: to open or come into view (as day, hope, a scene): (of news) suddenly to become generally known: to become bankrupt: to crack (as the voice): to collapse: to burst into foam: to sever a connection: to fall out (with a friend): to change direction (as a cricket-ball on pitching): to break the balls (see below): to change from a simple vowel to a diphthong under influence of a neighbouring sound: of the weather, to change suddenly, esp. after a settled period: — *pa.t*. **broke**, *arch*. **brake**; *pa.p*. **brō'ken**, less usu. **broke**. — *n*. an act of breaking: the state of being broken: an opening: a discontinuity: a pause, interval, or interruption: a pause for rest or refreshment: a consecutive series of

successful strokes (*billiards, croquet*): the number of points so scored at billiards: a continuous run of anything: the deviation of a ball on striking the pitch (*cricket*): an instance of breaking service (*tennis*): the dawn (*break of day*): onset (of the monsoon): a social blunder (*U.S.*): a chance (as in *an even break*, a fair or equal chance): a good chance. — *adj.* **break′able.** — Also *n.*, in *pl.* — *ns.* **break′ableness; break′age** act of breaking or its consequences: a broken place; **break′er** a person or machine that breaks: a wave broken on rocks or shore. — *n.* and *adj.* **break′ing.** — **break′away** revolt: secession: stampede, a stampeding animal (*Austr.*). — *adj.* having seceded. — *adj.* **break′back** crushing. — **breakbone fever** dengue; **break′dance, break′dancing** a form of dance to rock or disco music using some routines drawn from gymnastics; **break′-down** a stoppage through accident: collapse: disintegration: a vigorous and noisy Negro dance or the like: an analysis. — *adj.* assisting after a breakdown, etc., as in **breakdown truck, breakdown gang** vehicle, gang that clears and tows away wreckage after an accident. — *n.* and *adj.* **break′-even** see **break even.** — *n.* and *adj.* **break′-front** (a bookcase, wardrobe, etc.) having a centre section projecting beyond the two end sections. — **break′-in** an illegal (and sometimes violent) entering of a building; **break′ing-point** the point at which a person, relationship, situation, etc. breaks down under stress. — *adjs.* **break′-jaw** very difficult to pronounce accurately; **break′neck** headlong: very fast, usu. dangerously so: threatening to break the neck. — **break-out** see **break out; break point** a point giving one the opportunity to break service ((*tennis*): (also **break′point**) a point at which a computer program will stop running to allow checking, etc.; **break′-prom′ise, break′-vow** (both *Shak.*) one who habitually breaks promises or vows; **break′through** a forcible passage through a barrier: solving of a problem, esp. scientific, after much effort, opening the way to further developments: any comparable success; **break′-up** dissolution; **break-vow** see **break-promise; break′water** a barrier against force of waves; **break′-wind** a wind-break. — **break a jest** to utter a jest; **break a lance with** to enter into a contest with; **break a record** see **record; break a strike** see **strike; break away** to go away, escape, abruptly: to sever connection forcibly or abruptly: to be scattered, as clouds after a storm; **break bulk** to open the hold and take out a portion of the cargo: to begin to use goods supplied in bulk; **break camp** to dismantle and pack one's tents, etc.; **break cover** to burst forth from concealment, as a fox; **break down** to demolish: to crush: to collapse: to fail completely: to analyse; **break even** to avoid loss but fail to gain (*n.* and *adj.* **break′-e′ven**); **break forth** to burst out, issue; **break ground** see **ground²; break in** to make (shoes, etc.) less stiff by use (and see **break** *v.t.* above); **break in, in upon** or **into** to enter violently: to interpose abruptly; **breaking and entering** house-breaking; **break loose** to extricate oneself forcibly: to break through all restraint; **break no squares** to make no difference, do no harm, matter little; **break off** to detach by breaking: to put an abrupt end to: to leave off abruptly; **break one's mind** to communicate one's thoughts to somebody; **break out** to appear suddenly: to break through all restraint: to escape (*n.* **break′-out**): to come into sudden activity: to become covered with (a rash, etc.; with *in*); **break service, break someone's serve** to win a game in which one's opponent is serving (*tennis*, etc.); **break sheer** (said of a ship riding at anchor) to be forced by wind or tide out of a position clear of the anchor; **break someone's heart** to crush someone with grief; **break the balls** (or simply **break**) to open the game by striking the red ball or giving a miss, or to continue the game thus when a similar position occurs (*billiards*): to open the game by striking one of the red balls (*snooker*); **break the ice** (*fig.*) to get through first difficulties, esp. restraint on first meeting; **break through** to force a passage through (a barrier); **break**

up to break open: to break in pieces: to go to pieces: to put an end to: to disperse: to dig or plough up: to decay in health or faculties; **break upon the wheel** to punish by stretching on a wheel and breaking the bones; **break wind** to void wind; **break with** to cease relations with, esp. to quarrel with: to cease adherence to (tradition, a habit). [O.E. *brecan*; Ger. *brechen*.]

break², brake *brāk, n.* a long wagonette: a carriage frame all wheels and no body, used in breaking in horses: an estate car. [**break**, *v.t.*]

breaker¹. See **break¹.**

breaker² *brāk′ər, n.* a small water-cask, used on shipboard. [Prob. Sp. *bareca*, barrel.]

breakfast *brek′fəst, n.* a break or breaking of fast: the first meal of the day (also *adj.*). — *v.i.* to take breakfast. — *v.t.* to furnish with breakfast. — **break′fast-room; break′fast-set** the china or other ware used at breakfast; **break′fast-table.**

bream¹ *brēm, n.* a freshwater fish of the carp family, with high-arched back: a fish of the family Sparidae (sea-bream): a fish (Ray's bream, *Brama raii*) akin to the mackerel: extended to other fishes. [O.Fr. *bresme* (Fr. *brême*)—O.H.G. *brahsema* (mod. Ger. *Brassen*).]

bream² *brēm, v.t.* to clean, as a ship's bottom, by burning off seaweed, shells, etc. [Prob. conn. with **broom,** Du. *brem.*]

breare *brēr, (Spens.) n.* Same as **brier.**

breaskit. See **brisket.**

breast *brest, n.* the forepart of the human body between the neck and the belly: one of the two mammary glands in women (or rudimentary in men), forming soft protuberances on the chest: the corresponding part of any animal: a swelling slope: the part of a jacket, etc. which covers the breast: conscience, disposition, affections (*fig.*): voice (*obs.*). — *v.t.* to oppose the breast to: to oppose manfully: to mount. — *adj.* (usu. in composition) **breast′ed** having (a certain type of) breast(s). — **breast′bone** the sternum, the bone running down the middle of the breast, to which the first seven ribs are attached; **breast cancer** a malignant tumour of the breast. — *adv.* **breast′-deep′** deep, as up to the breast. — *v.t.* **breast′-feed** to give milk to from the breasts rather than from a bottle. — **breast′-feeding; breast′-girdle** the pectoral girdle. — *adv.* **breast′-high′** high as the breast: breast-deep. — **breast′-knot** a knot of ribbons worn on the breast; **breast′pin** an ornamental pin for the breast; **breast′plate** a plate or piece of armour for the breast: an embroidered square of linen with precious stones worn on the breast of the Jewish high-priest (*B.*); **breast′plough** a kind of spade for cutting turf, with a cross-bar against which the breast is pressed; **breast′rail** the upper rail of a breastwork; **breast′stroke** a swimming-stroke performed on the breast, with circling movements of the arms and legs; **breastsummer, bressummer** (*bres′ə-mər*) a summer or beam supporting the whole, or a great part, of the front of a building in the manner of a lintel; **breast wall** a retaining wall; **breast wheel** a water-wheel turned by water delivered upon it at about half its height; **breast′work** a hastily constructed earthwork. — **double-, single-breasted** see **double, single; make a clean breast** to make a full confession. [O.E. *brēost*; Ger. *Brust,* Du. *borst.*]

breath *breth, n.* the air drawn into and then expelled from the lungs: power of breathing: life: a single act of breathing: breathing without vibrating the vocal cords (*phon.*): a sound so produced: the time occupied by one breathing: a very slight breeze. — *adj.* produced by breath without voice. — *v.t.* **breath′alyze** (in *Britain,* usu. **breath′alyse**) to test with a breathalyzer. — *n.* **breathalyzer** (in *Britain,* usu. **breathalyser**) (*breth′ə-lī-zər*) a device which indicates amount of alcohol in a person's breath, by means of a plastic bag containing alcohol-sensitive crystals which change colour when a certain concentration of alcohol vapour is blown through them. — *adjs.* **breathed** (*bretht*) having a breath (esp. in compounds, as **long-breathed,** see also under **breathe**); **breath´ful** (*Spens.*) full of breath or air, also full of scent or odour; **breath´less** out of breath: with the breath held or taken away, from excitement, interest, etc.: breezeless: dead. — *adv.* **breath´lessly.** — *n.* **breath´lessness.** — *adj.* **breath´y** of a speaking voice, accompanied by much unvocalised breath: of a singer or instrument-player, without proper breath control, causing impure sound. — *adv.* **breath´ily.** — *n.* **breath´iness.** — *adj.* **breath´taking** astounding. **breath´-test** one carried out on a person's breath, by breathalyser or other device, to determine how much alcohol he has consumed. — **above one's breath** aloud; **below, under, one's breath** in a low voice; **catch one's breath** to stop breathing for an instant; **out of breath** having difficulty in breathing: panting from exertion, etc.; **spend** or **waste one's breath** to talk to no avail, profitlessly; **take breath** to recover freedom of breathing: to stop for breath, rest, or refreshment; **take someone's breath away** to render someone breathless through astonishment, delight, etc; **with bated breath** with breath restrained from reverence or fear. [O.E. *brǣth*; Ger. *Brodem*, steam, breath.]

breathe *brēdh*, *v.i.* to draw in or expel breath or air to or from the lungs or other respiratory organs: to respire: to take breath, to rest or pause: to live. — *v.t.* to draw into or expel from the lungs: to give out as breath: to utter by breath: to utter softly, whisper: to express: to keep in breath, to exercise: to tire by some brisk exercise. — *adj.* **breathed** (*brēdhd*) pronounced without voice (see also under **breath**). — *ns.* **breath´er** one who breathes or lives: a spell of exercise: a rest to recover breath; **breath´ing** the act of breathing: aspiration, secret prayer: respite: one or other of two signs used in Greek to signify presence ('rough breathing') or absence ('smooth breathing') of the aspirate. — *adj.* lifelike. — **breath´ing-space, breath´ing-time** time to breathe or rest: a brief respite; **breath´ing-while** time sufficient for drawing breath: any very short period. — **breathe again** to be relieved from an anxiety; **breathe down someone's neck** to keep too insistently close to someone, esp. by way of supervision; **breathe freely** to be at ease; **breathe one's last** to die; **breathe (up)on** (*old*) to tarnish the name of. [From **breath**.]

breccia *brech´yə*, *n.* a rock composed of angular fragments. — *adj.* **brecciated** (*brech´i-ā-tid*) reduced to or composed of breccia. [It.]

brecham *brehh´əm*, (*Scot.*) *n.* a horse-collar. [O.E. *beorgan*, to protect, *hama*, covering.]

Brechtian *brehht´iən*, *adj.* pertaining to, or suggestive of, the writings or dramatic theories and techniques of the German playwright, Bertolt *Brecht* (1898–1956).

bred *bred*, *pa.t.* and *pa.p.* of **breed**.

brede *brēd*, *n.* and *v.t.* an archaic form of **braid**. — *pa.t.* and *adj.* (Spens.) **bread´ed.**

bree¹ *brē*, *n.* (*Scot.*) the eyebrow. [O.E. *brǣw, brēaw*; cf. Ger. (*Augen*)*braue*; and **brae**.]

bree² *brē*, *n.* the liquor in which anything has been boiled. [O.E. *brīw*; cf. **berry²**, Ger. *Brei*.]

breech *brēch*, *n.* (almost always in *pl.*, **breeches** *brich´iz*; in Amer. also **britches**) a garment worn by men on the lower parts of the body — strictly, as distinguished from trousers, coming just below the knee, but often used generally for trousers: the lower part of the body behind (*arch.*): the hinder part of anything, esp. of a gun (*pl.* in these senses pron. *brēch´iz*). — *v.t.* (*brich, brēch*) to put into breeches: to flog. — *adj.* **breeched.** — *n.* **breeching** (*brich´ing*) a part of a horse's harness attached to the saddle, coming round the breech and hooked to the shafts: a strong rope attached to the breech of a gun to secure it to a ship's side. — *adj.* (*Shak.*) subject to whipping. — *adj.* **breech´less** trouserless. — **breech birth, breech delivery** one in which the buttocks come first; **Breeches Bible** the Geneva Bible (q.v.), with 'breeches' for 'aprons' in Gen. iii. 7; **breech´es-buoy** a life-saving apparatus enclosing the person like a pair of breeches; **breeches part** (*theat.*) a part in which an actress wears men's clothes; **breech´=**

loader a firearm loaded by introducing the charge at the breech instead of the muzzle. — *adj.* **breech´= loading.** — **wear the breeches** (said of a wife) to be master. [O.E. *brēc, pl.* of *brōc*; cf. Ger. *Bruch*, Du. *broek*.]

breed *brēd*, *v.t.* to generate or bring forth: to cause or promote the generation of, or the production of breeds of: to train or bring up: to cause or occasion. — *v.i.* to be with young: to produce offspring: to be produced or brought forth: to be in training, to be educated (*Scot.*): — *pa.t.* and *pa.p.* **bred.** — *n.* that which is bred, progeny or offspring: a strain, variety or race: a kind. — *ns.* **breed´er; breed´ing** act of producing: education: manners. — Also *adj.* — **breed´-bate** (*Shak.*) one who foments debate or strife; **breeder reactor** a nuclear reactor capable of creating more fissile material than it consumes in maintaining the chain reaction; **breed´- ing-ground** a place where animals, etc. go to breed: an attitude, environment, etc. which fosters or creates (esp. something considered undesirable) (*fig.*). — **breeding in-and-in** in-breeding, breeding from near kin. [O.E. *brēdan*, to cherish, keep warm; Ger. *brüten*, to hatch.]

breeks *brēks*, *n.pl.* Scots form of **breeches**, trousers.

breem. See **breme**.

breer. See **braird**.

breese. See **breeze²**.

breeze¹ *brēz*, *n.* a light wind: a disturbance or quarrel: a whispered rumour. — *v.i.* to blow as a breeze: to go briskly (*slang*): to do, achieve, etc. something with ease (with *through*). — *adj.* **breeze´less.** — *adv.* **breez´ily.** — *n.* **breez´iness.** — *adj.* **breez´y** fanned with or subject to breezes: bright, lively, exhilarating. — **breeze up** to freshen into a breeze; **get the breeze up** to get the wind up (see **wind¹**). [Old Sp. *briz*, north-east wind.]

breeze², **breese**, **brize** *brēz*, *n.* a gadfly, botfly, or other dipterous pest of horses and cattle. [O.E. *briosa*.]

breeze³ *brēz*, *n.* furnace refuse used in making **breeze brick, breeze blocks, breeze concrete** for building. [Perh. O.Fr. *brese*.]

bregma *breg´mə*, *n.* the part of the skull where the frontal and the two parietal bones join — sometimes divided into the right and left bregmata: — *pl.* **breg´mata.** — *adj.* **bregmat´ic.** [Gr.]

brehon *brē´hən*, *n.* an ancient Irish judge. — **Brehon Law(s)** the system of jurisprudence in use among the Irish until near the middle of the 17th century. [Ir. *breitheamh*, pl. *breitheamhuin*.]

breloque *brə-lok´*, *n.* an ornament attached to a watch-chain. [Fr.]

breme, breem *brēm*, (*Spens.*) *adj.* fierce, keen. [Perh. related to O.E. *brēman*, to rage.]

bremsstrahlung *bremz´shträ-lŏŏng*, *n.* electromagnetic radiation produced when an electron collides with, or is deflected by, a positively charged nucleus. [Ger. *bremsen*, to brake, *Strahlung*, radiation.]

bren, brenne *bren*, (*obs.*) *v.t.* and *v.i.* to burn: — *pa.t.* and *pa.p.* **brent.** — *adj.* **brent.** [See **burn²**.]

Bren (gun), bren bren (*gun*), *n.* a light machine-gun. [*Br*no, in Czechoslovakia, and *En*field, in England.]

brent *brent*, (*Scot.*) *adj.* lofty: steep: smooth, unwrinkled. [O.E. *brant*, steep; O.N. *brattr*.]

brent-goose *brent´gŏŏs*, *n.* a small wild goose, having the head, neck, long wing feathers, and tail black, the belly white, the rest slaty-grey, often confounded with the barnacle goose. — Also **brant´-goose** or **brent barnacle.** [Prob. *branded*, brindled.]

brer *brûr, brär*, *n.* (southern *U.S. dial.*) brother.

brere *brēr*, (*Spens.*) *n.* a form of **brier**.

bressummer. Same as **breastsummer**.

bretasche, bretesse. See **brattice**.

brethren *bredh´rən, pl.* of **brother**.

Breton *bret´ən, n.* a native of Brittany (*Bretagne*), France: the Celtic tongue of Brittany, Brezonek: (also without *cap.*; also **Breton hat**) a hat with a rounded crown and turned-up brim. — *adj.* of Brittany: Armoric.

brettice. See **brattice**.

Bretwalda *bret-wöl'də, n.* a title of certain kings of old English kingdoms, whose superiority over the others was more or less acknowledged. [Prob. Lord of the *Britons,* or of *Britain.* — O.E. *walda,* ruler.]

breve *brēv, n.* a pope's letter: the mark of a short vowel (as in *ĕ*), opp. to *macron:* an obsolescent note, ‖ ○ ‖, as long as the longest now used (the semibreve), but half (or in 'perfect' time one-third) as long as the obsolete long (*mus.*). [L. *brevis,* short.]

brevet *brev'it, n.* a military commission entitling an officer to take rank above that for which he receives pay. — *v.t.* to confer such rank on: — *pr.p.* **brev'eting;** *pa.t.* and *pa.p.* **brev'eted** (those who pronounce *bri-vet'* write **brevett'ing, brevett'ed**). [Fr., — L. *brevis,* short.]

brevet d'invention *brə-ve dē-vä-syɔ̃,* (Fr.) a patent.

breveté *brəv-tā,* (Fr.) *adj.* patented.

breviary *brēv'i-ər-i, n.* a book containing the daily service of the R.C. Church. [L. *brēviārium — brevis,* short.]

breviate *brē'vi-āt, n.* a short compendium: a lawyer's brief. [L. *brĕviātus — brĕviāre,* to shorten.]

brevier *brə-vēr', n.* an old type size (approx. 8-point) between bourgeois and minion, said (doubtfully) to have been used for breviaries.

brevi manu *brē'vī mān'ū, bre'wē man'oō,* (L.) with a short hand, off-hand.

brevipennate *brev-i-pen'ət, adj.* of birds, having short wings. [L. *brevis,* short, *penna,* wing.]

brevity *brev'it-i, n.* shortness: conciseness. — **brevity code** a code in which a single symbol is substituted for a group of words. [Poss. A.Fr. *breveté,* shortness, influenced by L. *brevitās, brevitātis,* — L. *brevis,* short.]

brew *broō, v.t.* to prepare by infusion, boiling and fermentation, as beer from malt and other materials, or by infusion, mixing, or boiling, without fermentation, as tea, punch: to contrive or plot. — *v.i.* to perform the operation of brewing ale or beer: to be gathering or forming. — *n.* a brewing: a brewage: a variety of making of a brewed beverage: a variety. — *ns.* **brew'age** something brewed: mixed liquor; **brew'er** one who brews; **brew'ery** a place for brewing; **brew'ing** the act of making liquor from malt: the quantity brewed at once; **brew'ster** (now mainly *Scot.*; orig. *fem.*) a brewer. — **brewers' yeast, brewer's yeast** a yeast used in brewing, esp. *Saccharomyces cerevisiae,* also used medically as a source of the vitamin B complex vitamins; **brew'-house** a brewery. [O.E. *brēowan;* cf. Ger. *brauen.*]

brewis *broō'is,* (*arch.* and *dial.*) *n.* broth, esp. beef broth: bread soaked in broth, fat, gravy, or the like. [O.Fr. *broez,* influenced by O.E. *brīw,* bree.]

Brezhnev Doctrine *brezh'nev dok'trin,* the Soviet doctrine which arose during the leadership of Leonid *Brezhnev* (d.1982), that the Soviet Union has the right to intervene in the internal affairs of another communist country to counter a perceived threat to socialism.

Brezonek *brez'ə-nek, n.* See **Breton.**

briar. See **brier**[1,2].

Briard *brē-är(d), n.* a large, heavy, hairy dog of a French breed. [*Brie,* district in N.E. France.]

Briarean *brī-ā'ri-ən, adj.* relating to *Briareus* (Gr. *Briărĕōs*), a hundred-handed giant: hence many-handed. [Gr. *briăros* — strong.]

bribe *brīb, n.* spoil (*obs.*): something offered to influence the judgment unduly or corrupt the conduct. — *v.t.* to steal (*obs.*): to influence by a bribe: to gain over. — *v.i.* to practise bribery. — *ns.* **brīb'er** one who bribes; **brīb'ery** the act of giving or taking bribes. — **brib'ery-oath** an oath taken by an elector that he had not been bribed. [O.Fr. *bribe,* a lump of bread; origin dub.]

bric-à-brac, bricabrac *brik'ə-brak, n.* old curiosities, knick-knacks, or other treasured odds and ends. [Fr.]

brick *brik, n.* baked or 'burned' clay: a shaped block of burned clay, generally rectangular (the standard dimensions being about 9 × 4½ × 3 inches): a brick-shaped block of other material, often compressed: a child's building block of wood, etc.: a loaf or a bun

more or less in the shape of a brick: a good, kind person (*coll.*). — *adj.* made of brick(s). — *v.t.* (with *in, up,* etc.) to fill with brick: to cover with brick or an appearance of brick: to wall in with brick. — *adj.* **brick'en** (*old*) made of brick. — *ns.* **brick'ie** a bricklayer; **brick'ing** brickwork: imitation brickwork. — *adj.* **brick'y** like or of brick. — *n.* a bricklayer. — **brick'bat** a piece of brick, esp. as a missile: a critical remark (*fig.*); **brick'clay** a clay containing sand and a good deal of iron: any clay, loam, or earth used for brick-making; **brick'-dust** powdered brick: the colour of powdered red brick; **brick'-earth** a clayey silt or loam used for brick-making; **brick'field** a place where bricks are made; **brick'fielder** (*Austr.*) a hot dry wind (orig. one bringing dust from the brickfields of Sydney suburbs); **brick'-kiln** a kiln in which bricks are made; **brick'layer** one who builds with bricks; **brick'laying; brick'maker; brick'making; brick'-nog, -nogging** see **nog**[2]. — *adjs.* **brick'-red'** of the colour of an ordinary red brick; **brick'shaped** of the shape of a standard brick. — **brick'-tea'** tea pressed into cakes; **brick'work** work constructed in brick: bricklaying: (in *pl.*) a factory for bricks; **brick'yard** a brickfield. — **drop a brick** to say or do something horrifyingly tactless or indiscreet; **like a ton of bricks** heavily and promptly; **like banging, knocking one's head against a brick wall** said of a laborious but unrewarding attempt, e.g. to persuade, inform, etc.; **make bricks without straw** to try to do a piece of work without the materials necessary for it: to make something that will not last; **see through a brick wall** to be unusually perspicacious. [Fr. *brique,* from the root of **break.**]

brickle *brik'l,* (*Spens.* and *Scot.*) *adj.* apt to break: weak: troublesome. [Cf. **bruckle.**]

brickwall *brik'wöl,* a corruption of **bricole.**

bricole *brik'əl,* or *-ōl,* or *brik-ōl', n.* an ancient engine for throwing stones: the rebound of a ball from the wall of a tennis-court: an indirect stroke: a similar stroke in billiards. [Fr., — L.L. *briccola.*]

bridal *brīd'əl, n.* a marriage feast: a wedding. — *adj.* belonging to a bride or a wedding: nuptial. [O.E. *brȳdealo,* lit. bride-ale; see **bride** and **ale** (feast).]

bride *brīd, n.* a woman about to be married or newly married. — *v.i.* and *v.t.* (with *it; Shak.*) to act the bride. — **bride'-ale** (*arch.*) the ale-drinking at a marriage feast (see **bridal**), **bride'-bed** the marriage bed; **bride'cake, bride's'-cake** a cake distributed at a wedding; **bride's-chamber** a nuptial apartment: the room in which a wedding is performed; **bride'groom** a man about to be married or newly married; **bride'maid(en), bride's'-maid, brides'maid, bride'man, bride's'-man, brides'man** young unmarried people who attend the bride and bridegroom at a wedding; **bride'wealth, bride-price** in tribal societies, etc., a price paid usu. in kind to a bride's family by the bridegroom. [O.E. *brȳd;* O.N. *brūthr,* Ger. *Braut.*]

bridewell *brīd'wəl, n.* a house of correction: a gaol. [From a palace near *St Bride's Well* in London.]

bridge[1] *brij, n.* a structure spanning a river, road, etc. giving communication across it: the narrow raised platform whence the captain of a ship gives directions: a thin upright piece of wood supporting the strings in a violin or similar instrument: the bony part of the nose: a support for a billiard cue: a bridge-like structure by which false teeth are borne by natural teeth or roots: in the theatre, a platform that rises above the stage: anything that connects across a gap. — *v.t.* to be or to build a bridge over: to connect the extremities of (a gap) (*fig.*): to make an electrical connection between. — *n.* **bridg'ing** the process of making, or the construction forming, a bridge: a brace or braces fixed between joists to strengthen them: provision of credit necessary for a business transaction: a method of keeping balance on overhanging rock. — Also *adj.* — *adj.* **bridge'less.** — **bridge'board,** a notch-board; **bridge'-builder** one who builds bridges: one who tries to reconcile hostile parties, etc., esp. in diplomacy;

bridge'-building; bridge'head a fortification covering the end of a bridge nearest to the enemy's position: a place suitable for such fortification: any advanced position seized in enemy territory; **bridge'-house** a house at the end of a bridge; **bridge'-of-boats'** a bridge resting on boats moored abreast across a piece of water; **bridging loan** a short-term loan, usu. for a fairly large sum and at a relatively high rate of interest, providing bridging for a business transaction, esp. house purchase. — **cross a bridge when one comes to it** not to bother about a future problem until it affects one. [O.E. *bryg*; Ger. *Brücke*, O.N. *bryggja*.]

bridge² *brij, n.* a modification of whist, in the earliest form of which (now called **bridge whist**, superceded by **auction bridge** and **contract bridge** (qq.v.), to which the word now refers) the dealer or his partner chose the trump suit, or no-trumps, and the dealer played his partner's hand as a dummy. — **Bridgera'ma** an apparatus which shows on large electronically-lit boards the steps of a bridge game in progress in another room; as a card is played, light behind it is switched off. — **bridge'-drive** a tournament of bridge-playing. [Earlier known as *bridge whist, biritch*; etymology unknown.]

bridie *brī'di*, (*Scot.*) *n.* a meat turnover.

bridle *brīd'l, n.* the apparatus on a horse's head by which it is controlled: any curb or restraint: a movement expressing resentment, scorn, or vanity — a throwing back of the head with a forward tilt, like a horse pulled up by the bridle. — *v.t.* to put a bridle on: to manage by a bridle: to check or restrain. — *v.i.* to make the movement described (often with *up*; *at* the thing taken amiss). — *adj.* **brī'dled** wearing a bridle. — *n.* **brī'dler** one who governs or restrains as by a bridle. — **bri'dle-hand** the hand that holds the bridle in riding — the left hand; **bri'dle-path, -road** a path or way for those riding or leading horses; **bri'dle-rein** the strap of a bridle. — **bite on the bridle** to be impatient, like a restive horse. [O.E. *brīdel*; O.H.G. *brittel*.]

bridoon *brid-ōōn', n.* the light snaffle usual in a military bridle in addition to the ordinary bit, controlled by a separate rein. [Fr. *bridon* — *bride*, a bridle.]

Brie *brē, n.* a white, soft cheese made in *Brie*, N.E. France.

brief *brēf, n.* a summary of a client's case for the instruction of counsel: a writ: a short statement of any kind: instructions: a lawyer, esp. a barrister (*slang*): (in *pl.*) close-fitting legless pants. — *adj.* short: concise: insubstantial, barely adequate. — *v.t.* to issue instructions to. — *n.* **brief'ing** action, or an instance, of making or giving a brief: instructions. — *adj.* **brief'less.** — *adv.* **brief'ly.** — *n.* **brief'ness.** — **brief'-bag, -case** a small case for carrying briefs, or for other papers, etc. — **hold a brief** to be retained as counsel: to assume the attitude of advocate rather than judge; **hold no brief for** not to support or advocate; **in brief** in few words; **king's briefs** royal mandates ordering collections to be made in chapels for building churches, etc.; **papal brief** a papal document issued without some of the solemnities proper to bulls; **take a brief** to undertake a case; **the brief and the long** (*Shak.*) the short and the long; **to be brief** in order to speak in few words. [Fr. *bref* — L. *brevis*, short.]

brier¹, briar *brīr, brī'ər, n.* a prickly shrub: a wild rose bush. — Also (*Spens.*, etc.) **brere** (*brēr*). — *adjs.* **briered, briared** caught in, covered with, briers; **briery** thorny: abounding in, beset with, briers. — **sweet brier** eglantine, a wild rose (*Rosa rubiginosa*) with scented leaves. [O.E. (Anglian) *brēr* (W.S. *brǣr*).]

brier², briar *brī'ər, n.* the white heath, a shrub grown in Algeria: a tobacco-pipe made of its root. — *ns.* and *adjs.* **bri'er-root, -wood.** [Fr. *bruyère*, heath.]

brig¹ *brig, n.* a two-masted, square-rigged vessel: a place of detention on board ship (*U.S.* navy): a prison (*U.S. slang*). [Shortened from **brigantine.**]

brig² *brig, n.* Northern form of **bridge¹.** [O.N. *bryggja*.]

brigade *brig-ād', n.* a body of troops consisting of a group of regiments, battalions, or batteries commanded by a general officer: a band of people more or less organised. — *v.t.* to form into brigades: to organise, esp. oppressively. — *n.* **brigadier** (*brig-ə-dēr'*) formerly **brig'adier-gen'eral** a general officer of the lowest grade, who has command of a brigade: (*brē-gä-dyā*) in the French army, a corporal. — **brigade'-ma'jor** a staff-officer attached to a brigade. [Fr. *brigade* — It. *brigata* — L.L. *briga*, strife.]

brigand *brig'ənd, n.* a bandit or freebooter. — *ns.* **brig'-andage, brig'andry** freebooting: plundering; **brigandine, brigantine** (*brig'ən-dēn, -tēn*) a coat-of-mail of steel rings or plates sewed upon linen or leather. [Fr., — It. *brigante* — L.L. *briga*, strife.]

brigantine *brig'ən-tēn, n.* a two-masted vessel, with the main mast of a schooner and the foremast of a brig. — See also under **brigand.** [Fr. *brigantin* — It. *brigantino*, pirate ship.]

bright *brīt, adj.* shining: full of light: vivid: clear: beautiful (*arch.*): cheerful: vivacious: clever: illustrious. — *adv.* brightly: clearly. — *v.t.* and *v.i.* **bright'en** to make or grow bright or brighter: to clear up. — *adv.* **bright'ly.** — *n.* **bright'ness.** — *adj.* **bright'some** bright: brilliant. — **bright and early** very early: in good time; **the bright lights** the places of entertainment in a city centre. [O.E. *byrht, beorht;* cog. with Goth. *bairhts,* clear.]

Bright's disease *brīts diz-ēz', a* generic name for diseases of the kidneys with albumen in the urine. [From Dr Richard *Bright* (1789–1858).]

brigue *brēg, v.i.* to intrigue. — *n.* strife: intrigue. — *n.* **briguing** (*brēg'ing*) canvassing. [Fr. *brigue.*]

brill *bril, n.* a fish akin to the turbot, spotted with white. [Ety. unknown.]

brilliant *bril'yənt, adj.* sparkling: glittering: splendid: superlatively bright, having a dazzling hard lustre: of outstanding or conspicuous ability: showily, strikingly, or superficially clever: performing or performed in a hard or showy manner or with great display of technical skill: very good, excellent (*coll.*): brilliant-cut. — *n.* a diamond or other gem cut in a many-faceted form resembling two truncated cones base to base: a very small type (about 4-point). — *v.t.* and *v.i.* to cut and polish the smaller triangular facets on a diamond. — *ns.* **brill'iance, brill'iancy; brill'iantine** (*-tēn*) a dressing for making the hair glossy. — *adv.* **brill'iantly.** — *n.* **brill'iantness.** — *adj.* **brill'iant-cut'** of gems, cut in a 58-faceted form. [Fr. *brillant*, pr.p. of *briller,* to shine, which like Ger. *Brille,* eyeglass, is from L.L. *beryllus,* a beryl.]

brim *brim, n.* the margin or brink of a river or lake: the upper edge of a vessel or of a similarly-shaped cavity: the rim of a hat. — *v.t.* to fill to the brim. — *v.i.* to be or become full to the brim: — *pr.p.* **brimm'ing;** *pa.t.* and *pa.p.* **brimmed.** — *adj.* **brim'ful, brim'-full'** full to the brim: brimming with tears. — *n.* **brim'ful(l')ness.** — *adjs.* **brim'less** without a brim; **brimmed** brim-full: having a brim (also in comp.). — *n.* **brimm'er** a bowl full to the brim. — *adv.* and *adj.* **brimm'ing.** [M.E. *brymme.*]

briming *brē'ming, bri', (dial.) n.* phosphorescence of the sea. [Origin unknown.]

brimstone *brim'stən, n.* sulphur: a virago (*fig.*): (in full, **brimstone butterfly**) a common yellow pierid butterfly (*Gonepteryx rhamni*). — *adj.* **brim'stony.** [Lit. burning stone; from O.E. *bryne,* a burning — *byrnan,* to burn, and **stone**; cf. Ger. *Bernstein.*]

brinded *brin'did,* **brindled** *brin'dld,* **brindle** *brin'dl, adjs.* marked with spots or streaks. — *n.* **brin'dle** the state of being brindled. [See **brand.**]

brindisi *brin'di-zi, brēn-dē'zē,* (It.) *n.* a toast: a drinking-song.

brine *brīn, n.* very salt water: the sea. — *v.t.* to treat with brine. — *adjs.* **brīn'ish** like brine: somewhat salt; **brīn'y** pertaining to brine or to the sea: salt. — **brine'-pan, -pit** a pan or pit in which brine is evaporated to obtain salt: a salt spring; **brine'-shrimp** a small phyllopod crustacean of salt-lakes and brine pools. — **the briny** (*coll.*) the sea. [O.E. *brȳne,* a burning.]

Brinell (hardness) test *bri-nel'* (*härd'nis*) *test*, (*metallurgy*, etc.) a test to determine the hardness (**Brinell hardness**) of a substance, expressed in terms of its **Brinell (hardness) number**, by pressing a steel ball into the substance being tested under a given pressure. [From the Swedish engineer, J. A. *Brinell* (1849–1925), who devised the test.]

bring *bring, v.t.* to fetch: to cause to come: to persuade: to adduce or institute (as an argument, charge, action): — *pa.t.* and *pa.p.* **brought** (*bröt*). — *ns.* **bring′er; bring′ing.** — **bringings forth** (*Shak.*) the fruits of his own actions; **bringing up** upbringing, rearing, training. — **bring about** to bring to pass, effect: to turn round; **bring down** to humble: to shoot: to overthrow: to lower; **bring down the house** to call forth a general burst of applause; **bring forth** to give birth to, produce; **bring forward** to advance: in bookkeeping (used in *pa.p.*), to transfer (a partial sum) to the head of the next column; **bring home** to prove: to impress; **bring in** to introduce: to yield: to pronounce (a verdict); **bring off** to bring away, as by a boat from a ship: to rescue: to achieve: to succeed; **bring on** to induce: to cause to advance: to advance the growth of (plants); **bring oneself to** to persuade or steel oneself to (do something unacceptable); **bring out** to make clear, or prominent: to put before the public, as a book, a play, a singer: to introduce (a young woman) formally into society; **bring over** to convert; **bring round** to restore from illness or unconsciousness: to win over; **bring to** to restore to consciousness: to bring to a standstill (*naut.*); **bring under** to subdue; **bring up** to rear or educate: to introduce to notice: to make prominent: to vomit; **bring up the rear** to come last. [O.E. *bringan*, to carry, bring; allied perh. to **bear**[1] .]

brinjal *brin′jäl, -jöl, n.* in India, the egg-plant, or its fruit. — Corrupted **brown jolly.** [Sans. *vātinganq,* through Pers., Ar. and Port.]

brinjarry *brin-jär′i, n.* a travelling dealer in grain and salt, in Southern India. [Hindi, *banjārā.*]

brink *bringk, n.* the edge or border of a steep place or of a river (often *fig.*). — **brink′man** one who practises **brink(s)′manship,** the action or art of going to the very edge of, but not into, war or other disaster in pursuit of a policy (first used 1956 following statement by J. Foster Dulles that U.S. Diplomacy had three times walked to the brink of war). — **on the brink of** (*fig.*) on the point of, very near. [Prob. Dan. *brink,* declivity.]

brio *brē′ō, n.* liveliness, vivacity, spirit. [It.]

brioche *brē-osh′, n.* a type of light, soft loaf or roll rich with butter and eggs. [Fr.]

briony. Same as **bryony.**

briquette, briquet *bri-ket′, n.* a brick-shaped block made of coal-dust: a small brick-shaped slab. [Fr. *briquette,* dim. of *brique,* **brick.**]

brisé *brē-zā, n.* in ballet, a movement in which the dancer jumps off one foot, strikes the feet or legs together and lands on two feet. — **brisé volé** (*vol-ā,* Fr. pa. p. of *voler,* to fly) a brisé performed with each leg alternately, completed by landing on one foot: — *pl.* **brisés volés** (*brē-zā volā(z)*). [Fr., of *briser,* to break.]

brise-soleil *brēz-sol-āy,* (Fr.) *n.* a louvred screen to keep sunlight from walls and windows of buildings.

brisk *brisk, adj.* spruce (*obs.*): pert (*obs.*): full of life and spirit: lively: promptly active: sharp: effervescing. — *v.t.* and *v.i.* to make or become brisk: to move briskly. — *v.t.* and *v.i.* **brisk′en** to make or become brisk. — *adjs.* **brisk′ish; brisk′y** (*Shak.*). — *adv.* **brisk′ly.** — *n.* **brisk′ness.** [First found in Shakespeare's time; poss. Welsh *brysg,* brisk of foot; perh. Fr. *brusque.*]

brisket *bris′kit* (Scott, **breaskit** *bres′kit*), *n.* the breast (*Scot.*): the breast of an animal, esp. the part next to the ribs: meat from this part of an animal. [Perh. conn. with Fr. *brechet, brichet.*]

brisling *bris′ling, n.* a Norwegian sprat. [Norw., sprat.]

brissel-cock *bris′l-kok,* (*obs. Scot.*) *n.* a fowl conjectured to be the turkey. [Ety. uncertain.]

bristle *bris′l, n.* a short stiff hair. — *v.i.* to stand erect, as bristles: to be set as with bristles: to be copiously furnished, be full (with *with; fig.*): to have or set bristles erect: to show rage or resistance (*fig.*). — *v.t.* to cover, as with bristles: to make bristly: to erect (as bristles): — *pr.p.* **brist′ling;** *pa.t* and *pa.p.* **brist′led.** — *adj.* **brist′led** furnished with bristles. — *n.* **brist′liness.** — *adj.* **brist′ly** set with bristles: rough. — **brist′le-fern′** a filmy fern (*Trichomanes radicans*) with a bristle on the receptacle; **brist′le-tail** any insect of the Thysanura; **brist′le-worm** a chaetopod. — **bristlecone (pine)** a western American pine (*Pinus aristata*) with bristle-like prickles on its cones; **set up one's bristles** to show resistance. [Conn. with O.E. *byrst;* Scot. *birse;* cog. with Ger. *Borste,* O.N. *burst.*]

Bristol *bris′tl, n.* a city in the county of Avon. — *n.pl.* **bris′tols** breasts (see **titty**[1]; *Cockney rhyming slang* from *Bristol city*). — **Bris′tol-board′** a smooth pasteboard; **Bris′tol-brick′** an earthy material for scouring cutlery, like bath-brick; **Bris′tol-di′amond** a kind of quartz crystal found near Bristol; **Bris′tol-milk′** sherry (17th-cent. joke). — **Bristol fashion** in good order.

brisure *brizh′yər, brē-zür′, n.* any part of a rampart or parapet which breaks off at an angle from the general direction (*fort.*): a variation of a coat-of-arms showing the relation of a younger to the main line (*her.*). [Fr. — *briser,* to break.]

brit, *brit, n.* a young herring, sprat, or other fish.

Brit *brit, n.* (*coll.*) shortening of **British**) a Briton.

Britannic *brit-an′ik, adj.* pertaining to Britannia or Britain (*arch.*, surviving officially in *Britannic majesty*). — **Britann′ia** a seated female figure with a trident and helmet, representing Britain or the British Commonwealth. — **Britannia metal** an alloy, mainly tin with copper, antimony, lead or zinc or a mixture of these, similar to pewter. [L. *Britannia, Brittan(n)ia,* Great Britain or the British Islands.]

britches. See **breech.**

British *brit′ish, adj.* pertaining to Britain, to its former or present inhabitants or citizens, or to the empire or commonwealth of nations of which it is the nucleus. — *n.* the language of the ancient Britons: Welsh (*obs.*): the British people. — *n.* **Brit** (*coll.*) a British person. — *v.t.* and *v.i.* **Brit′icise, -ize** to make or become British or like the British: to assimilate to the British. — *ns.* **Brit′ishism, Brit′icism** (*-sizm*) an expression characteristic of the English spoken in Britain. — **Brit′isher** (*orig. U.S.*) a native or citizen of Britain. — **British disease** extreme militancy in industrial relations, esp. excessive use of strikes; **British gum** dextrin; **British plate** a kind of German silver; **British Standard Time** (1968–71) time one hour ahead of Greenwich Mean Time; **British thermal unit** see **heat unit** under **heat; British warm** see **warm.** [O.E. *Brettisc* — *Bret,* a Briton, Welshman.]

Briton *brit′ən, n.* one of the Brythonic inhabitants of Britain before the coming of the English, or one of their present representatives the Welsh: a native or citizen of Great Britain or of any of the associated states: a Breton (*rare*): — *fem.* (*Spens.*) **Brit′oness.** — *adj.* **Britton′ic** Brythonic. [L. *Brittō, -ōnis,* or *-ōnis;* see **Brythonic.**]

brittle *brit′l, adj.* apt to break: easily broken: frail: sharp, edgy: sensitive. — *n.* a type of hard toffee made with caramelised sugar and nuts. — *n.* **britt′leness.** — **brittle bones** an inherited disease, *osteogenesis imperfecta,* characterised by abnormal fragility of the bones; **britt′le-star** an ophiuroid or sand-star. [O.E. *brēotan,* to break.]

britzka, britzska, britska *brits′kə,* **britschka** *brich′kə, ns.* an open four-wheeled carriage with one seat. [Polish *bryczka.*]

Brix Scale *briks skāl,* a scale used in measuring the density of sugar in a solution at a given temperature. [A. F. W. *Brix* (1798–1890), German scientist.]

brize. See **breeze**[2].

bro *brō, n.* a place for which one feels great affinity because of birth, upbringing, long residence, etc., there. [W., locality.]

broach *brōch*, *n.* a tapering, pointed instrument, used chiefly for boring or rounding holes: a spit: (also **broach'-spire**) a church spire, now restricted to one without parapets, consisting of a tall octagonal and a low square pyramid interpenetrating each other: a visible corner of the square pyramid in such a spire. — *v.t.* to pierce as a cask, to tap: to open up or begin: to utter. — *v.i.* and *v.t.* to (cause a sailing-ship to) veer dangerously when running downwind, so as to lie beam on to the waves (also *n.*). — *n.* **broach'er** a broach or spit: one who broaches or utters. — **broach the admiral** to steal some liquor from a cask in transit or in store; **broach to** (*naut.*) to turn to windward. [Fr. *broche*; cf. **brooch.**]

broad *brōd*, *adj.* wide: large, free or open: outspoken: coarse, indelicate: liberal minded: widely diffused: covering a wide range, spectrum, etc.: giving prominence to main elements, or harmony of the whole, without insisting on detail: slow and full-toned: strongly marked in pronunciation or dialect. — *n.* the broad part: (in East Anglia) a lake-like expansion of a river: a broadpiece: a woman (*slang*): sometimes, a prostitute (*slang*). — *advs.* **broad; broad'ly.** — *v.t.* and *v.i.* **broad'en** to make or grow broad or broader. — *adj.* **broad'ish.** — *n.* **broad'ness.** — **broad'-arr'ow** a mark (**↑**) on government property. — *adjs.* **broad'-band** across, involving, or designed to operate across, a wide range of frequencies: capable of accommodating data from a variety of input-sources, as voice, telephone, television *etc.* (*comput.*); **broad'-based'** including a wide range of opinions, subjects, political groups, etc. — **broad'-bean** the common bean, (*Vicia faba*); **broad'-brim** a hat with a broad brim, such as those once worn by Quakers: a Quaker (*coll.*). — *adjs.* **broad'brush** rough: not worked out in detail (*coll.*); **broad'cast** scattered or sown over the general surface: dispersed widely: communicated generally, by word of mouth, pamphlets, radio, TV, or any other means: by means of broadcast. — *adv.* in all directions. — *n.* sowing by broadcasting: general dissemination: the sending forth of material by radio or TV for reception by the public. — *v.t.* and *v.i.* to scatter, broadcast or disseminate freely by any means, esp. by radio or TV transmission: — *pa.t.* and *pa.p.* **broad'cast**, by some **broad'casted.** — *ns.* **broad'caster; broad'casting.** — **Broad Church** a party within the Church of England favouring a broad and liberal interpretation of dogmatic definitions and creed subscription — name used in 1853 by W. J. Conybeare: (esp. without *cap.*) a political or other group, party, etc. that is similarly liberal-minded or all-inclusive. — *adj.* **broad'-church.** — **broad'cloth** a fine, fulled woollen or worsted cloth; **broad day(light)** fully diffused daylight. — *adj.* **broad'-gauge** see **gauge.** — **broad jump** (*U.S.*) long jump. — *adjs.* **broad'-leaf, broad'-leaved** having broad leaves, not needles; **broad'loom** (of carpet) woven on a wide loom; **broad'-mind'ed** liberal: tolerant. — **broad'piece** (or **broad**) a 17th-century 20-shilling coin; **Broad Scots** (also **Scotch**) older or dialect forms of the Scottish tongue, a development of old English; **broad'sheet** a sheet of paper printed usu. on one side only, a broadside: a newspaper of large format, measuring approx. 40 × 60 centimetres (about 16 × 24 inches); **broad'side** the side of a ship: all the guns on one side of a ship of war: their simultaneous discharge: a critical attack (*fig.*): a sheet of paper printed usu. on one side only, containing a proclamation, a ballad, or other popular matter. — *adj.* **broad'-spectrum** wide-spectrum. — **broad'sword** a cutting sword with a broad blade: a man armed with such a sword; **broad'tail** fur prepared from the skin of very young Karakul lambs; **broad'way** a broad road, often the name of the chief thoroughfare of a town or district. — *advs.* **broad'ways, -wise** breadthwise. — **as broad as it is long** six of one and half-a-dozen of the other. [O.E. *brād*, Goth. *braiths*.]

Brobdingnagian *brob-ding-nag'i-ən*, *n.* an inhabitant of the fabulous region of *Brobdingnag* in *Gulliver's Travels*, where everything was gigantic. — *adj.* of Brobdingnag: (usu. without *cap.*) immense. — *adj.* **Brob'-dingnag** immense. — Also, erroneously, **Brobdigna-g(ian).**

brocade *brōk-ād'*, *n.* a silk stuff on which figures are wrought. — *adj.* **brocād'ed** woven or worked in the manner of brocade: dressed in brocade. [It. *broccato*, Fr. *brocart*, from It. *broccare*, Fr. *brocher*, to prick, stitch; from root of **broach.**]

brocage. See **brokage** under **broker.**

brocard *brōk'ärd*, or *-ərd*, *n.* an elementary law or principle: a canon: (*bro-kar*) a gibe (Fr.). [Fr. *brocard*, L.L. *brocarda*, from *Brocard* or Burchard, Bishop of Worms, who published a book of ecclesiastical rules.]

brocatel(le) *brok-ə-tel'*, *n.* a stiff, silk-and-linen, heavy-figured fabric like brocade. [Fr. — It. *brocatello*, gold tinscl — *broccato*, brocade.]

broccoli *brok'ə-li*, *n.* a hardy variety of cauliflower: (also **sprouting broccoli**) a variety of which the purple or green floret buds, and their stalks, are eaten as a vegetable. [It.; pl. of *broccolo*, a sprout, dim. of *brocco*, a skewer, a shoot.]

broch[1] *brohh*, *n.* a dry-built circular tower of the late Iron Age with galleries in the thickness of the wall, common in the north of Scotland, very rare in the south: a luminous ring around the moon. — Also **brogh** and **brough.** [Scots — O.N. *borg*; O.E. *burh*.]

broch[2] *brōch.* Obsolete spelling of **broach, brooch.**

brochan *brohh'ən*, (*Scot.*) *n.* gruel: sometimes porridge. [Gael.]

broché *brō'shā, adj.* of fabrics, woven with a pattern like brocade. — *n.* such a fabric. [Fr. pa.p. of *brocher*, to stitch.]

brochure *brō'shōōr, -shōōr'*, *bro'*, *n.* a pamphlet. [Fr., — *brocher*, to stitch — *broche*, a needle. See **broach.**]

brock[1] *brok*, *n.* a badger: a dirty, stinking fellow. — *adjs.* **brocked, brock'it** (*Scot.*) variegated, esp. black and white. [O.E. *brocc* — Celt. (as Gael. *broc*).]

brock[2] *brok*, (*Scot.*) *n.* food scraps: pigswill: rubbish. — *n.* **brock'age** fragments of crockery, furniture, etc. (*Scot.*): a mis-struck coin. [O.E. (*ge*)*broc*, fragment — *brecan*, to break.]

Brocken spectre *brok'ən spek'tər*, the shadow of an observer, enlarged and often surrounded by coloured lights, thrown onto a bank of cloud — a phenomenon sometimes encountered on mountain-tops. [*Brocken*, a peak in the Harz mountains.]

brocket *brok'it*, *n.* a stag in its second year, with its first, dagger-shaped, horns. [Fr. *brocard* — *broque*, a spike.]

brockram *brok'rəm*, (*N. England*) *n.* breccia.

brod[1] *brod*, *n.* a Scots form of **board**: esp. a church collection plate or box.

brod[2] *brod*, (*dial.*) *n.* a goad: a spike: a kind of nail: a prick. — *v.t.* to prod. [O.E. *brord*; O.N. *broddr*; cf. O.Ir. *brot* and Gael. *brod*, a goad, sting.]

brodekin, brodkin *brōd'kin*, (*obs.*) *n.* a buskin. [Fr. *brodequin*.]

broderie anglaise *brod-rē ã-glez', brō'də-ri ã'glāz*, open-work embroidery. [Fr., English embroidery.]

brog *brog*, (*Scot.*) *n.* an awl. — *v.t.* to prick. [Origin obscure.]

brogh. See **broch**[1].

brogue[1] *brōg*, *n.* a stout shoe (also **brō'gan**). [Ir. *brōg*, dim. *brògan* and Gael. *bròg*, a shoe.]

brogue[2] *brōg*, *n.* a dialectal accent, esp. Irish. [Perh. **brogue**[1], but Ir. *barróg*, hold, grip, speech impediment, is also suggested.]

broider *broid'ər*, *v.t.* and *v.i.* to embroider. — *ns.* **broid'erer; broid'ering; broid'ery.** [O.Fr. *brouder, broder*; see **embroider.**]

broil[1] *broil*, *n.* a noisy quarrel: a confused disturbance — (*Scot.*) **brulyie, bru(i)lzie** (*brōōl'i*). — *n.* **broil'er** one who stirs up broils. [Fr. *broullier*, to trouble.]

broil[2] *broil*, *v.t.* to cook over hot coals: to grill. — *v.i.* to be greatly heated. — *n*. **broil'er** a very hot day: a quickly-reared young chicken sold ready for broiling (also *adj*.). [Ety. dub.]

brokage. See **broker.**

broke *brōk, pa.t.* and old *pa.p.* of **break** surviving as *pa.p.* chiefly in the sense of hard up. — *pa.p.* **brōk'en.** — *adj.* **brōk'en** rent: infirm: humbled or crushed: thrown into disorder: dispersed, routed: altered in direction: shattered in health, spirit, estate or position: bankrupt: outlawed (*obs.*): trained to saddle or bridle: infringed: variegated: with surface interrupted: incomplete, fragmentary: interrupted: arpeggiated (*mus.*): uncertain: of a language, ill spoken, as by a foreigner. — *adv.* **brōk'enly.** — *n.* **brōk'enness.** — *adjs.* **brok'en-backed'** having the back dislocated: of a ship, so loosened in her frame as to droop at both ends; **brok'en-down** disintegrated: decayed: ruined in character or strength; **brok'en-heart'ed** crushed with grief: greatly depressed in spirit. — **broken home** the home of children whose parents are divorced or have separated; **broken man** one under outlawry, esp. in the Highlands and Border country (*hist.*): one whose life is completely shattered; **broken meats** the leavings of a banquet; **broken music** (*Shak.*) concerted music. — *adj.* **brok'en-wind'ed** having short breath or disordered respiration, as a horse. — **broke to the wide** completely penniless.

broker *brōk'ər, n.* one employed to buy and sell for others: a secondhand dealer: a go-between, negotiator or intermediary: a pander (*obs.*): a petty or disreputable trafficker (*obs.*): a stockbroker. — *v.i.* **broke** to bargain, negotiate: to act as broker (*Shak.*). — *ns.* **brōk'erage, brōk'age,** (*obs.*) **brōc'age** the business of a broker: commission for transacting business for others: procuring (*obs.*); **brō'ker-dealer** (*Stock exchange*) since 27 Oct. 1986, a firm or person officially combining the jobs of stockbroker and stockjobber; **brōk'ery** (*obs.*) the business of a broker: broker's wares; **brōk'ing.** [M.E. *brocour* — A.Fr. *brocour.* The original meaning seems to be tapster; cf. **broach.**]

brolga *brol'gə, n.* a tall grey Australian crane. — Also **Australian crane, native companion.** [Aboriginal.]

brolly *brol'i,* (*coll.*; a clipped form) *n.* an umbrella.

brome-grass *brōm'-gräs, n.* a grass (*Bromus*) strongly resembling oats. [Gr. *bromos,* a kind of oats.]

Bromelia *brə-mēl'yə, n.* a genus of plants giving name to the pineapple family, **Bromēliā'ceae,** a tropical American family of monocotyledons, mainly epiphytic and xerophytic, with stiff leaves in rosettes: (without *cap.*) any plant of this genus. — *adj.* **bromēliā'ceous.** — *n.* **bromēl'iad** any plant of the family. [Named in honour of the Swedish botanist Olaus *Bromel* (1639–1705).]

bromine *brō'mēn, -min, -mīn, n.* a non-metallic chemical element (at. numb. 35; symbol Br), a red liquid giving off an irritating, poisonous brown vapour. — *n.* **brō'mate** a salt of bromic acid. — *adj.* **brō'mic.** — *n.* **brō'mide** a salt of hydrobromic acid: a platitudinous person (from the use of bromides as sedatives): a platitude: a type of monochrome photographic print, loosely applied to other types. — *adj.* **brōmid'ic** conventionally commonplace. — *ns.* **brōm(h)idrō'sis** osmidrosis; **brō'moform** a bromine compound analogous to chloroform. — **bromic acid** a compound of hydrogen, bromine and oxygen, HBrO₃; **bromide paper** in photography, a paper with a sensitive surface containing silver bromide, used in printing from a negative. [Gr. *bromos,* stink.]

brommer *brom'ər,* (*Afrik.*) *n.* the bluebottle fly. [Onomatopoeic.]

broncho. See **bronco.**

broncho-. See **bronchus.**

bronchus *brong'kəs, n.* either of the main forks of the windpipe: — *pl.* **bronch'i** (*-ī*). — *n.pl.* **bronch'ia** (erroneously *bronchiae*) the ramifications of the bronchi. — *adj.* **bronch'ial** pertaining to the windpipe or the bronchia. — *ns.* **bronchiectasis** (*-ek'tə-sis*) a chronic viral disease caused by dilated bronchi; **bronch'iole**

(*-ōl*) any of the minute branches of the bronchi. — *adj.* **bronchitic** (*-it'ik*) pertaining to bronchitis. — *n.* one suffering from bronchitis. — *n.* **bronchitis** (*-ī'tis*) inflammation of the lining of the bronchial tubes. — **bron'cho-** (*-kō-*) in composition, relating to the bronchi. — *ns.* **bron'cho-constric'tor, bron'cho-dila'tor** any drug that causes the bronchi to narrow, expand; **bronch'oscope** an instrument which, when passed down into the bronchi, allows their examination, the removal of foreign bodies, etc. — *adjs.* **bronchoscop'ic, -al.** — *adv.* **bronchoscop'ically.** — *n.* **bronchos'copy.** [Gr. *bronchos,* windpipe; *bronchia,* bronchia.]

bronco, bronco *brong'kō,* (*U.S.*) *n.* a half-tamed horse: — *pl.* **bron'cos, bron'chos.** — **brenc'o-buster** one who breaks in broncos: a cowboy. [Sp. *bronco,* rough, sturdy.]

brond. An obsolete form of **brand.**

brondyron, etc. See under **brand.**

Brontosaurus *bron-tə-sör'əs, n.* a popular (and former) name for Apatosaurus, a genus of lizard-hipped, quadripedal, herbivorous dinosaurs, found fossil in Wyoming and Colorado: (without *cap.*) a member of this genus (also **bront'osaur**). [Gr. *brontē,* thunder, *sauros,* lizard.]

Bronx cheer *brongks chēr,* (*U.S.*) a vulgar sound of disapproval, a raspberry. [From the *Bronx* borough of New York City.]

bronze *bronz, n.* an alloy of copper and tin used in various ways since prehistoric times: a copper alloy without tin: anything cast in bronze: the colour of bronze: a bronze medal: impudence (*obs.*). — *adj.* made of bronze: coloured like bronze. — *v.t.* and *v.i.* to make or become bronze-like: to harden (*fig., obs.*). — *adjs.* **bronzed** coated with bronze: bronze-coloured, sunburned: hardened (*fig.,* obs); **bronz'en** (*rare*). — *v.t.* **bronz'ify** (*rare*) to make into bronze. — *ns.* **bronz'ing** the process of giving or assuming the appearance of bronze; **bronz'ite** an enstatite with bronzy lustre. — *adj.* **bronz'y** having the appearance of bronze. — **Bronze Age** a prehistoric condition or stage of culture marked by the use of bronze as the material for tools and weapons — coming between the Stone Age and the Iron Age; **bronzed skin** Addison's disease; **bronze medal** in athletics competitions, etc. the medal awarded as third prize; **bronze'-wing, bronze'-wing(ed) pigeon** an Australian pigeon of various species with lustrous bronze markings on the wings. [Fr., — It. *bronzo, bronzino* — perh. from L. (*aes*) *Brundusīnum,* (brass) from Brindisi; or perh. from Pers. *birinj, pirinj,* copper.]

broo¹ *brōō, brü,* (*Scot.*) *n.* liquor that comes off from anything or in which anything has been boiled. [Prob. O.Fr. *bro, breu,* broth.]

broo², brow *brōō,* (*Scot.*) *n.* brow in any sense: (perh. a different word) liking (with *of*). [**brow.**]

broo³ See **buroo.**

brooch *brōch, n.* an ornamental clasp with a joined pin fitting into a hook. — *v.t.* (*Shak.*) to adorn as with a brooch. [Fr. *broche,* a spit; see **broach.**]

brood *brōōd, n.* something bred: offspring, children, or family: a race, kind: parentage, extraction (*arch.*): the number hatched, produced, or cherished at once: condition of breeding or brooding. — *adj.* for breeding (as in *brood-mare,* etc.). — *v.t.* to sit upon or cover in order to breed or hatch: to hatch: to cover, as with wings: to mature or foster with care: to meditate moodily upon. — *v.i.* to sit as a hen on eggs: to hang envelopingly: to think anxiously for some time: to meditate silently (with *on, over*). — *ns.* **brood'er; brood'iness.** — *adv.* **brood'ingly.** — *adj.* **brood'y** inclined to sit or incubate: apt to brood or to breed. — **brood'mare** a mare kept for breeding; **brood'-pouch, brood'-sac** a body-cavity e.g. in viviparous cockroaches in which eggs or embryos are received and developed. [O.E. *brōd;* Du. *broed;* cf. **breed.**]

brook¹ *brōōk, n.* a small stream. — *n.* **brook'let** a little brook. — **brook'weed** water pimpernel (*Samolus*), a water-plant of the primrose family superficially like a crucifer. [O.E. *brōc*, water breaking forth; Du. *broek*, Ger. *Bruch*.]

brook[2] *brŏŏk*, *v.t.* to enjoy: to bear or endure. [O.E. *brūcan*, to use, enjoy; Ger. *brauchen*, L. *fruī, fructus*.]

brookite *brŏŏk'īt*, *n.* a mineral, titanium oxide. [After Henry James *Brooke* (1771–1857), English mineralogist.]

brooklime *brŏŏk'līm*, *n.* a speedwell that grows in brooks and ditches. [**brook**, and O.E. *hleomoc*, brooklime.]

brool *brŏŏl*, *n.* a deep murmur. [Ger. *Brüll*, a roar.]

broom *brŏŏm*, *n.* a papilionaceous shrub, *Cytisus scoparius*, or kindred kind: a besom made of its twigs or of anything else: a long-handled domestic sweeping brush. — *v.t.* to sweep with a broom. — *adj.* **broom'y** abounding in or consisting of broom. — **broom'ball** a team game played on ice orig. by British diplomatic staff in Moscow, using brooms and a plastic ball; **broom'-corn** a kind of millet of which brooms are made; **broom'rape** (L. *rapum*, a knob) a genus (*Orobanche*) of plants, parasitic on broom and other roots; **broom'staff, broom'stick** the handle of a broom. — **marry over the broomstick** or **jump the besom** or **broomstick** to go through an irregular form of marriage in which both jump over a broomstick; **new brooms sweep clean** people newly appointed to a position work very conscientiously, or try to sweep away abuses, old attitudes, old methods, etc.; **not know a B from a broomstick** to be very ignorant. [O.E. *brōm*.]

broose (*Scott*, **brouze**), *brŏŏz, brüz*, (*Scot.*) *n.* a race at a wedding. [Derivation unknown.]

brose *brōz*, *n.* a food made by pouring boiling water or milk on oatmeal or peasemeal, seasoned with salt and butter. — **Athole brose** a mixture of whisky and honey and sometimes oatmeal; **brose and bannock day** Shrove Tuesday. [Scot.; perh. conn. with **brewis, broo**[1].]

broth *broth*, *n.* an infusion or decoction of vegetable and animal substances in water, used as soup or (often with other substances added) as a medium for culture of bacteria. — **a broth of a boy** (*Irish*) the quintessence of a good fellow. [O.E. *broth* — *brēowan*, to brew; see **brew.**]

brothel *broth'l*, *n.* a house of prostitution. — **brothel creeper** (*coll.*) a man's soft shoe with thick crêpe sole. [M.E. *brothel*, worthless person — O.E. *brothen*, ruined, *brēothan*, to go to ruin; influenced in meaning by **bordel.**]

brother *brudh'ər*, *n.* a male in relation to another of either sex born of the same parents or parent (*half-brother*): any one closely united with or resembling another associated in common interests, occupation, etc.: a fellow-member of a religious order, a guild, etc.: a fellow-creature: a fellow-citizen: a co-religionist: a kinsman (*B.*): — *pl.* **broth'ers** and **breth'ren**, the latter esp. used in the sense of fellow-members and in the names of certain bodies, as *Christian Brethren, Moravian Brethren, Plymouth Brethren*, etc. — *adj.* associated in any relation (also in composition as **brother= man'**). — *n.* **broth'erhood** the state of being a brother: an association of men for any purpose. — *adj.* **broth'- erlike.** — *n.* **broth'erliness.** — *adj.* **broth'erly** like a brother: kind: affectionate. — **broth'er-ger'man** a full brother, one having both parents in common, in contradistinction to a *half-brother*; **broth'er-in-law** brother of a husband or wife: a sister's husband: a husband's or wife's sister's husband: — *pl.* **broth'ers= in-law.** [O.E. *brōthor*, pl. *brēther*; cog. with Ger. *Bruder*, Gael. *brathair*, L. *frāter*, Sans. *bhrātr*; Gr. *phrātēr*, fellow-clansman.]

Brotstudien *brŏt'shtŏŏ-dē-ən*, (Ger.) *n.pl.* bread studies, those by which one earns one's living.

brough. See **broch**[1].

brougham *brŏŏ'əm, brō'əm*, or *brŏŏm*, *n.* a one-horse close carriage, named after Lord *Brougham* (1778–1868): an early motor-car with uncovered driver's seat.

brought *brŏt*, *pa.t.* and *pa.p.* of **bring.**

brouhaha, *brŏŏ-hä'hä, brŏŏ'hä-hä*, *n.* fuss, excitement,

clamour, or an instance of this. [Fr.; perh. from Heb.]

brouze. See **broose.**

brow *brow*, *n.* the eyebrow: the ridge over the eyes: the forehead: the edge of a hill: a gallery in a coal-mine running across the face of the coal: a ship's gangway (*navy*): a pit-head: aspect, appearance (*fig.*). — *adj.* **brow'less** without eyebrows: without shame. — **brow'= antler, -tine** the first tine of a deer's horn. — *v.t.* **brow'beat** to bear down with stern looks or speech: to bully. — *adj.* **brow'-bound** crowned. [O.E. *brū*.]

brown *brown*, *adj.* of a dark or dusky colour, inclining to red or yellow: dark-complexioned: sunburnt: formerly conventionally applied to a sword, perh. burnished, perh. rusty, perh. bloodstained. — *n.* a dark-reddish colour: a copper coin (*slang*): a close-flying number of game-birds, usu. in **fire into the brown** to shoot into a mass without aiming at a particular bird. — *v.t.* to give a brown colour to: to roast brown. — *v.i.* to become brown. — *ns.* **brown'ie** a drudging domestic goblin (*folklore*): (with *cap.*; in full **Brownie Guide**) a member of the junior section of the Girl Guides, in brown garb: (a square piece of) a kind of rich, chewy chocolate cake containing nuts (*U.S.*): a kind of currant bread (*Austr.* and *N.Z.*); **brown'ing** the process of making or becoming brown: a preparation for the purpose. — *adj.* **brown'ish.** — *n.* **brown'ness.** — *adj.* **brown'y** of a brownish colour. — **brown algae, brown seaweeds** the Phaeophyceae, one of the main divisions of the algae; **brown bear** the common bear of Europe and Asia; **brown Bess** the old British flint-lock musket — from the brown walnut stock; **brown bill** a foot-soldier's or watchman's halberd, painted brown; **brown bread** any dark-coloured bread, esp. that made of unbolted flour; **brown coal** lignite; **brown dwarf** see **dwarf**; **brown fat** heat-producing fat cells of a brownish colour, found in various parts of the body, e.g. between the shoulder-blades, thought to be activated by over-eating and thus to have a bearing on weight-gain; **brown George** a hard biscuit: a brown earthen vessel; **brownie point** (*iron.*) a good mark for doing well, a commendation of little significance; **brown lung (disease)** byssinosis; **brown'out** (esp. *U.S.*) a reduction in electrical power, etc., a partial blackout; **brown owl** the tawny owl: (with *caps.*; correctly **Brownie Guider**) a woman who has charge of a group of Brownies; **brown paper** coarse and strong paper used chiefly for wrapping; **brown rat** the larger and commoner of the two British rats (often black); **brown rice** rice hulled but not polished; **Brown'shirt** a member of Hitler's organisation of storm-troopers: a Nazi; **brown spar** a brownish variety of dolomite; **brown'stone** (*U.S.*) a dark brown sandstone, regarded as the favourite building material of the prosperous classes: a house built of this; **brown stout** a kind of porter; **brown study** reverie: absent-mindedness; **brown sugar** unrefined or partially refined sugar; **brown trout** a kind of trout common in Europe, dark-coloured on the back and lighter underneath. — **browned off** (*slang*) fed up: bored: dejected; **do brown** (*slang*) to do thoroughly, to deceive or take in completely. [O.E. *brūn*; Du. *bruin*, Ger. *braun*.]

Brownian *brown'i-ən*, *adj.* pertaining to Robert *Brown* (1773–1858), who drew attention to **Brownian movement** or **motion**, an agitation of particles in a colloid solution caused by impact of molecules in the surrounding medium.

Brownist *brown'ist*, *n.* one holding the church principles of Robert *Browne* (*c.* 1550– *c.* 1633), which may be said to have given birth to the Independents or Congregationalists of England. — *n.* **Brown'ism.**

brown jolly *brown jol'i*, a corruption of **brinjal.**

browse *browz*, *v.i.* to feed on rough shoots of plants: to read desultorily. — *v.t.* to browse on. — *n.* a twig: a browsing. — *n.* **brows'ing** the shoots and leaves of plants: fodder: the action of the verb browse. [O.Fr. *brouster* (Fr. *brouter*) — *broust*, a sprout.]

browst *browst*, (*Scot.*) *n.* a brewing. [**brew.**]
brucellosis *broo-səl-ō'sis*, *n.* a disease of animals, also called **contagious abortion** (see **abortion**), communicable to man as Malta, or undulant, fever. [Sir David *Bruce*, bacteriologist, and *-ella*, *-osis*.]
bruchid *broo'kid*, *adj.*, *n.* (a beetle) of the family **Bruchidae** whose larvae live on peas, beans, etc. [GR. *brouchos*, locust.]
brucine *broos'ēn*, *n.* an alkaloid got from nux vomica, wrongly thought to come from the simarubaceous genus *Brucea*, named after James *Bruce* (1730–94), Scottish African traveller.
brucite *broos'īt*, *n.* a mineral, magnesium hydroxide. [Named after A. *Bruce*, American mineralogist.]
Brücke, Die *brü'kə*, *dē*, a group of expressionist painters formed in Dresden in 1905. [Ger., the Bridge.]
bruckle *bruk'l*, (*Scot.*) *adj.* liable to break, brittle and unstable. [O.E. *brucol* — *brecan*, to break.]
bruhaha. A spelling of **brouhaha.**
Bruin *broo'in*, *n.* the name of the bear in the beast-epic *Reynard the Fox*; hence in general use. [Du., brown.]
bruise *brooz*, *v.t.* to crush by beating or pounding without breaking the surface: to pound: to pulverise by pounding: to mark and discolour part of the surface of, e.g. skin of person, fruit, etc.: to hurt by unkind words. — *v.i.* to box (*obs.*): to ride recklessly (*hunting slang*): to be injured physically or in feelings. — *n.* an injury with discoloration of the human skin made by anything blunt and heavy: a similar injury to fruit or plants. — *n.* **bruis'er** one who bruises: a prize-fighter. — *n.* and *adj.* **bruis'ing.** [O.E. *brȳsan*, to crush, combined with O.Fr. *brisier*, *bruiser*, *bruser*, to break.]
bruit *broot*, *n.* noise (*arch.*): something noised abroad: a rumour or report: a murmur heard in auscultation. — *v.t.* to noise abroad: to report: to make famous. [Fr. *bruit*. — Fr. *bruire*; cf. L.L. *brugītus*; prob. imit.]
brûlé *brü-lā*, (Fr.) *adj.* cooked with brown sugar: compromised.
brulzie, bruilzie, brulyie *brool'(y)i*, *brül'yi*, *n.* Scottish form of **broil**[1].
Brum *brum*, *n.* contraction of **Brummagem** (q.v.) for Birmingham. — *n.* **Brumm'ie** (*coll.*) a person from Birmingham.
Brumaire *brü-mer'*, *n.* the second month in the French revolutionary calendar, about Oct. 22 to Nov. 20. [Fr. *brume*, fog — L. *brūma*, winter.]
brumby *brum'bi*, (*Austr.*) *n.* a wild horse. [Origin unknown.]
brume *broom*, *n.* fog. — *adjs.* **brum'al** relating to winter; **brum'ous** foggy, wintry. [L. *brūma*, winter, contr. from *brevima*, the shortest day.]
Brummagem *brum'ə-jəm*, *n.* a colloquial name for *Birmingham* derived from an older form of the word: a thing made in Birmingham. — *adj.* showy and worthless, sham, counterfeit.
brummer *broom'ər*, (*S. Afr.*) *n.* older form of **brommer**.
brumous. See **brume**.
brunch *brunch*, *brunsh*, *n.* a compromise between breakfast and lunch. [Portmanteau word.]
Brunella. See **prunella**.
brunette *broon-et'*, *n.* a woman with brown or dark hair and complexion. — Also (esp. *anthrop.*) in *masc.* **brunet'.** [Fr. dim. of *brun*, brown.]
Brunonian *broo-nō'ni-ən*, *adj.* relating to the system of medicine founded by Dr John *Brown* of Edinburgh (*c.* 1736–88) — all diseases are *sthenic* or *asthenic*, depending on excess or deficiency of excitement. [*Brūnō*, *-ōnis*, Latinisation of Brown.]
brunt *brunt*, *n.* the shock of an onset or contest: the force of a blow: the chief stress or crisis of anything. — *v.t.* to bear the brunt of. — **at the instant brunt** at the outset, at once. [Origin obscure.]
brush *brush*, *n.* an instrument set with bristles or the like for cleansing or for applying friction or a coating of some material: a painter's hair pencil: a manner of painting: a painter (*arch.*): a tuft: a bushy tail: a bundle of wires, strips, or the like, making electrical contact

between surfaces in relative motion: a brushlike discharge of electricity or any brushlike appearance: an application of a brush: a grazing contact: a skirmish: lopped or broken twigs: an assemblage of shrubs and small trees: an area covered with thickets: a forest (*Austr.*): the backwoods: a brisk run or race (*U.S.*). — *v.t.* to pass a brush over: to touch or rub as if with a brush: to remove by a sweeping motion (with *off*, or *away*). — *v.i.* to use a brush: to pass with light contact: to make off. — *adj.* **brushed** smoothed, rubbed, straightened, etc. with a brush: of cloth, with the surface roughened or raised. — *ns.* **brush'er** one who brushes; **brush'ing** the act or process of brushing. — *adj.* in a lively manner: brisk. — *adj.* **brush'y** like a brush: covered with brush. — **brush'-fire** a fire of dry bushes, etc., which usually spreads quickly and dangerously; **brush kangaroo** a wallaby; **brush'-off** (*coll.*) a curt or discourteous setting aside or ignoring: a rebuff; **brush turkey** an eastern Australian moundbird; **brush'wheel** a revolving brush: a friction wheel with bristles on the rubbing surface; **brush'wood** loppings and broken branches: underwood or stunted wood; **brush'work** work done with a brush: a painter's manner of using the brush. — **brush aside, brush off** to ignore, dismiss; **brush up** to freshen one's appearance: to clean and tidy: to renew one's knowledge of (a subject; sometimes with *on*). (*n.* **brush'-up**). [O.Fr. *brosse*, brushwood; prob. connected with **bristle**.]
brusque *broosk*, *brusk*, *adj.* blunt and abrupt in manner. — *adv.* **brusque'ly**. — *ns.* **brusque'ness; brusquerie** (*broos'kə-rē*). [Fr.]
Brussels *brus'əlz*, *n.* the capital of Belgium: (in full **Brussels carpet**) a kind of carpet in which the worsted threads are arranged in the warp, and are interwoven into a network of linen, the bulk of the carpet consisting of wool. — **Brussels lace** a fine lace with sprigs applied on a net ground; **Brussels sprouts** a variety of the common cabbage with sprouts like miniature cabbages.
brust *brust*, (*Spens.*). Same as **burst**.
brut *broot*, (Fr.) *adj.* of wines, raw, unsweetened.
brute *broot*, *adj.* belonging to the lower animals. irrational: stupid: rude: crude. — *n.* one of the lower animals, esp. the larger mammals: a brutal man: a large articulated goods trolley used on railway stations. — *v.t.* to girdle or shape (a diamond). — *adj.* **brut'al** like a brute: unfeeling: inhuman: stupidly cruel or sensual. — *n.* **brutalisā'tion, -z-.** — *v.t.* **brut'alise, -ize** to make like a brute, to degrade: to treat with brutality. — *v.i.* to live like a brute. — *n.* **brut'alism** deliberate crudeness of style in art, architecture, literature, etc. — *n.* and *adj.* **brut'alist.** — *n.* **brutal'ity.** — *adv.* **brut'ally.** — *n.* **brute'ness** brutelike state: brutality: stupidity (*Spens.*). — *v.t.* **brut'ify** to make brutal, stupid or uncivilised: — *pr.p.* **brut'ifying**; *pa.t.* and *pa.p.* **brut'ified.** — *adj.* **brut'ish** brutal: unwise (*B.*). — *adv.* **brut'ishly.** — *n.* **brut'ishness.** — **brute fact** a fact merely, presented without explanation; **brute force** sheer physical strength. [Fr. *brut*, rough, crude — L. *brūtus*, dull, irrational.]
brutum fulmen *broo'tum* (or *-toom*) *ful'* (or *fool'*)*men*, (L.) an ineffectual thunderbolt.
Brutus *broo'təs*, *n.* a kind of wig: a way of wearing the hair brushed back from the forehead, popular at the time of the French Revolution, when it was an affectation to admire the old Romans, as *Brutus*.
bruxism *bruks'izm*, *n.* habitual grinding of the teeth. [Gr. *brychein*, to gnash.]
bryology *brī-ol'ə-ji*, *n.* the study of mosses. — *adj.* **bryological** (*-ə-loj'i-kl*). — *n.* **bryol'ogist.** [Gr. *bryon*, moss, liverwort, and *logos*, discourse.]
bryony *brī'ə-ni*, *n.* a wild climbing plant (*Bryonia dioica*, **white bryony**) of the gourd family, common in English hedgerows. — **black bryony** a climbing plant (*Tamus communis*) of the yam family, similar to bryony in habit and disposition. [L. *bryōnia* — Late Gr. *bryōniā*.]

bryophyte *brī'ō-fīt, n.* a member of the **Bryophyta** (*-of'i-tə*), one of the main groups of the vegetable kingdom, mosses and liverworts. [Gr. *bryon*, a moss, a liverwort, *phyton*, plant.]

Bryozoa *brī-ō-zō'ə, n.pl.* an old name for the Polyzoa, from their resemblance to mosses. [Gr. *bryon*, moss, *zōia*, living things.]

Brython *brith'on, n.* a Celt of the group to which Welsh, Cornish, and Bretons belong — distinguished from Goidel. — *adj.* **Brython'ic.** [Welsh *Brython*, Briton — introduced in philological use by Sir John Rhys (1840–1915).]

buat. Same as **bowat.**

buaze, bwazi *bū'āz, bwä'zi, ns.* an African fibre-yielding polygalaceous shrub (*Securidaca*). [Native name.]

bub¹ *bub,* **bubby** *bub'i,* (*U.S.*) *ns.* boy (in addressing). [Cf. Ger. *Bube,* boy.]

bub² *bub,* (*arch. slang*) *n.* strong drink. [Origin unknown.]

buba *bōō'bə, n.* another name for **yaws.**

Bubalis *bū'bə-lis, n.* the genus (also called *Alcelaphus*) of antelopes, including the hartebeest: (without *cap.*; also **bubal** *bū'bəl*) a member of this genus. — *adj.* **bū'baline.** — *n.* **Bū'balus** the buffalo genus. [Gr. *boubalis, boubalos,* African antelope, Late Gr. *boubalos,* buffalo — *bous,* ox.]

bubble *bub'l, n.* a bladder of liquid or solidified liquid blown out with gas: anything empty: an unsound or fraudulent scheme: in television entertainment, etc. a spin-off from a soap opera (*coll.*). — *adj.* unsubstantial: deceptive: fleeting, transient: like a bubble in shape and lightness. — *v.i.* to rise in bubbles: to give off bubbles: to make sounds as of rising and bursting bubbles: (with *with*) to show (great joy, rage, etc.): to blubber (*Scot.*). — *v.t.* to cheat with bubble schemes (*arch.*). — *adj.* **bubb'ly.** — *n.* (*coll.*) champagne. — **bubb'le-and-squeak'** left-over potato, meat and cabbage, etc. fried together; **bubble bath** a cosmetic preparation that makes foam in bath-water; **bubb'le-car** a midget motor-car resembling a bubble in its rounded line and windowed top; **bubb'le-chamber** a device for showing the path of a charged particle by the string of bubbles left in its track — a variant of the cloudchamber; **bubb'le-gum** a kind of chewing-gum that can be blown into large bubbles. — *adj.* **bubb'le-headed** frivolous, flighty. — **bubble memory** (*comput.*) a memory composed of minute moving pockets of magnetism that represent, by their presence or absence in relation to fixed points, bits (q.v.) of digital information; **bubble pack** a type of packaging in which goods are enclosed in a transparent bubble of plastic, etc. backed by card; **bubb'le-shell** a gasteropod (*Bulla*) with thin globose shell; **bubb'ly-jock** (*Scot.*) a turkey-cock. — **bubble over** to show uncontrolled anger, mirth, etc. [Cf. Sw. *bubbla,* Du. *bobbel.*]

bubinga *bōō'bing-ə, n.* species of W. African tree, esp. *Didelotia africana,* its hard wood used in furniture-making. [Bantu.]

bubo *bū'bō, n.* an inflammatory swelling of the lymph nodes, *esp.* in the groin or armpit: — *pl.* **bū'boes.** — *adj.* **bubonic** (*-bon'*) relating to, characterised by, buboes. — *ns.* **bubonocele** (*bū-bon'ō-sēl;* Gr. *kēlē,* tumour) an inguinal hernia; **bū'bukle** (*Shak.*) a ridiculous word of Fluellen's (*Hen. V,* III, vi, 108) for a red pimple, compounded from *bubo* and *carbuncle.* — **bubonic plague** a form of plague characterised by buboes. [L. *būbō* — Gr. *boubōn,* the groin, a bubo.]

Bubo *bū'bō, n.* a genus of large horned owls, including the eagle owl. [L. *bubo, -onis,* a horned owl.]

buccal *buk'əl, adj.* of, towards, pertaining to, the cheek: pertaining to the mouth, oral. [L. *bucca,* cheek.]

buccaneer, buccanier *buk-ən-ēr', n.* one of the piratical adventurers in the West Indies during the 17th century, who plundered the Spaniards chiefly. — *v.i.* to act as a buccaneer. — *n.* and *adj.* **buccaneer'ing.** — *adj.* **buccaneer'ish.** [Fr. *boucanier* — *boucan,* a Carib

wooden gridiron (used by French settlers in the West Indies).]

buccina *buk'sin-ə,* a Roman curved trumpet. — *n.* **buc'cinator** a flat cheek muscle used in chewing and blowing. — *adj.* **buc'cinatory.** — *n.* **Buc'cinum** the whelk genus of molluscs, with trumpetlike shell. [L. *būcina,* trumpet, *būcinātor,* trumpeter.]

bucellas *bōō-sel'əs, bū-, n.* a white wine from *Bucellas* near Lisbon.

Bucentaur *bū-sen'tör, n.* the Venetian state barge used formerly in an Ascension-Day ceremony in which the doge dropped a ring into the sea, symbolising the marriage of Venice with the Adriatic. [It. *bucentoro, bucintoro,* explained as from *due cento,* as the vessel was orig. designed to carry two hundred — described by Francesco Sansovino.]

Bucephalus *bū-sef'ə-ləs, n.* Alexander the Great's famous war-horse: a familiar name for a riding-horse. [Gr. *Boukephalos* — *bous,* ox, *kephulē,* head.]

Buchmanism *bōōh'mən-izm, n.* the Oxford Group movement. — *adj.* and *n.* **Buch'manite** (*- īt*). [See **Oxford.**]

buchu, bucku *bōō'hhōō, -chōō, -kōō,* (*S. Afr.*) *n.* a rutaceous genus (*Barosma*) with leaves of medicinal value for wounds, etc. [Zulu.]

buck¹ *buk, n.* the body of a cart. — **buck'board** a board or rail projecting over cart-wheels: a plank on four wheels, with a light seat to hold two persons (*U.S.*); **buck'cart** a buckboard: a cart with boards projecting over the wheels; **buck'-wag'on** (*S. Afr., arch.*) a large canvas-covered trek wagon. [O.E. *būc,* body.]

buck² *buk, n.* the male of the deer, goat, hare, and rabbit (cf. *doe*): a male fallow-deer: a bok (q.v.): a dashing fellow: a male Negro or American Indian (*offensive*): a counter (*cards*): a dollar (*U.S.*): an act of bucking. — *v.i.* (of a horse or mule) to attempt to throw by rapid jumps into the air, coming down with the back arched, head down, and forelegs stiff. — *v.t.* to throw by bucking: to resist: to cheer, invigorate, tone up (*slang*). — *ns.* **buckeen'** a poor Irish gentleman, without means to support his gentility; **buck'er** an animal that bucks. — *adj.* **buck'ish** lively, frisky: dandified: goatish. — **buck'-eye** the American horse-chestnut (genus *Aesculus*): a native of the state of Ohio (*U.S.*). — *adj.* (*U.S.*) flashy, showy: corny. — **buck'horn, buck's'-horn** the material of a buck's horn (**buck's-horn plantain** a British plantain with pinnatifid leaves); **buck'hound** a small kind of staghound used for hunting bucks; **buck'-jumper** an animal that bucks; **buck-passing** see **pass the buck** below; **buck'-rabb'it** a male rabbit: a Welsh rabbit with poached egg; **buck'saw** a large saw consisting of a blade set in an H-shaped frame tightened by a cord, used with a saw-buck; **buck'shot** a large kind of shot, used in shooting deer; **buck'skin** a soft leather made of deerskin or sheepskin: a strong twilled woollen cloth, cropped of nap: a horse of buckskin (greyish-yellow) colour: a backwoods American: (in *pl.*) breeches or suit of buckskin. — *adj.* made of or like the skin of a buck. — **buck's party** (*Austr.*) a stag-party for a man about to be married; **buck'thorn** a genus (*Rhamnus*) of shrubs whose berry supplies the sap-green used by painters: see also **sea-buckthorn;** **buck'tooth** a projecting tooth. — **buck up** (*slang*) to bestir oneself: to cheer up: to improve: to stimulate: to dress up (*dial.*); **make a fast buck** (*coll.*) to earn some money quickly or easily but not necessarily honestly; **pass the buck** (*slang*) to shift the responsibility to someone else (as one passes a marker to the next dealer in forms of poker) (*n.* **buck'-passing**); **the buck stops here** the final responsibility rests here. [O.E. *buc, bucca;* Du. *bok,* Ger. *Bock,* a he-goat.]

buck³ *buk, v.t.* to soak or steep in lye, a process in bleaching. — *n.* lye in which clothes are bleached. — *n.* **buck'ing.** — **buck'-basket** a basket in which clothes are carried to be bucked; **buck'-wash, -ing.** [Ety. obscure: M.E. *bouken;* cog. words are Ger. *bäuchen, beuchen.*]

buckaroo, buckeroo *buk'ə-rōō,* or *-rōō',* (*U.S.*) *n.* a cowboy. — Also **buckay'ro:** — *pl.* **buckay'ros.** [Sp. *vaquero*.]

buckbean *buk'bēn, n.* a marsh plant (*Menyanthes trifoliata*) of the gentian family. — Also **bog'bean.** [Flem. *bocks boonen*, goat's beans.]

bucket *buk'it, n.* a vessel for drawing or holding water, etc.: one of the compartments on the circumference of a water-wheel: one of the scoops of a dredging-machine: a leather socket for holding a whip, carbine or lance: a waste-paper bin (*coll.*): the pitcher in some orchids: a bucketful. — *v.t.* to lift in a bucket. — *v.t.* and *v.i.* to drive or ride very hard or bumpily: to push forward mercilessly: to swindle (*arch.*). — *v.i.* (of rain) to pour heavily (*coll.*). — *ns.* **buck'etful** as much as a bucket will hold: — *pl.* **buck'etfuls; buck'eting.** — **bucket seat** a round-backed, often forward-tipping, seat for one in a motor-car, aeroplane, etc.; **bucket shop** (*coll.*) the office of an outside broker — a mere agent for bets on the rise or fall of prices of stock, etc.: thus, any agency operating along similar lines, e.g. one dealing in unsold airline tickets; **buck'et-wheel** a contrivance for raising water by means of buckets attached to the circumference of a wheel. — **give the bucket** to dismiss; **kick the bucket** (*slang*) to die (perh. from dial. *bucket*, a beam from which slaughtered animals are hung). [Prob. conn. with O.E. *būc*, a pitcher, or O.Fr. *buket*, a pail. Not Gael. *bucaid*, a bucket.]

buckie *buk'i*, (*Scot.*) *n.* a shellfish such as the whelk: a refractory person. [Prob. related somehow to L. *buccinum*, a shellfish.]

buckle *buk'l, n.* fastening for a strap or band, consisting of a rim and a tongue: a crisped, curled, or warped condition. — *v.t.* and *v.i.* to connect with a buckle: to prepare for action: to join closely as in fight or marriage: to bend or warp. — *n.* **buck'ler** a small shield used in parrying. — **buck'le-beggar** a hedge parson. — **buckle down** to apply oneself zealously (to); **buckle to** to buckle down; **buckle under** to give in, collapse, under strain. [Fr. *boucle*, the boss of a shield, a ring — L.L. *buccula*, dim. of *bucca*, a cheek.]

Buckley's (chance) *buk'liz (chäns)*, (*Austr. coll.*) no chance at all. [Origin unknown.]

buckling *buk'ling, n.* smoked Baltic herring. [Ger.]

bucko *buk'ō, n.* a swaggerer, domineering bully (orig. *naut. slang*). young lad, chap (*chiefly Irish*): — *pl.* **buck'oes.** [buck².]

buckra *buk'rə, n.* a word used by West Indian and American Negroes for a white man — said to mean 'demon' in a dialect of the Calabar coast.

buckram *buk'rəm, n.* a coarse open-woven fabric of jute, cotton, or linen made very stiff with size: stiffness in manners and appearance. — *adj.* made of buckram: stiff: precise. — *v.t.* to give the quality of buckram to. [O.Fr. *boquerant*.]

buckshish *buk'shēsh.* Same as **baksheesh.** — *n.* **buck'shee'** (*mil. slang*) spoil, a windfall. — *adj.* free, gratuitous: spare, extra. [See **baksheesh, bukshi.**]

bucksom. A Miltonic spelling of **buxom.**

buckthorn. See **buck².**

bucku. See **buchu.**

buckwheat *buk'(h)wēt, n.* a *Polygonum* or *Fagopyrum* used in Europe for feeding horses, cattle and poultry, in America made into cakes for the breakfast table. [Prob. Du. *boekweit*, or Ger. *Buchweizen*, beech-wheat, from the shape of the seeds.]

bucolic, -al *bū-kol'ik, -əl, adjs.* pertaining to the tending of cattle: pastoral: rustic, countrified. — *n.* **bucol'ic** a pastoral poem or poet: a rustic. [L. *būcolicus* — Gr. *boukolikos* — *boukolos*, a herdsman.]

bud¹ *bud, n.* a rudimentary shoot of a plant: a protuberance that develops asexually into a new individual (*biol.*): the first visible rudiment of a limb, horn *etc*: something undeveloped or immature: a young person (as a term of endearment): a débutante (*U.S.*). — *v.t.* to put forth as buds: to graft by inserting a bud under the bark of another tree. — *v.i.* to put forth buds: to come as a bud: to be in or issue from the bud: — *pr.p.*

budd'ing; *pa.t.* and *pa.p.* **budd'ed.** — *n.* **budd'ing.** — *adj.* in bud: beginning to develop, show talent in a particular way (as *a budding poet*). — *adjs.* **budd'y; bud'less.** — **bud'-scale** a leaf specialised as a scale protecting a bud. — **in bud** putting forth buds; **nip in the bud** to destroy at its very beginning. [M.E. *budde*; perh. related to Du. *bot*, a bud.]

bud². See **buddy¹.**

Buddha *bōōd'ə, bŏŏd', n.* a title applied to Sakyamuni or Gautama, the founder of a religion of spiritual purity: a general name for any one of a series of teachers of whom he is one. — *ns.* **Budd'hism** the religion founded by the Buddha; **Budd'hist** a believer in Buddhism. — *adj.* **Budd'hist, Buddhist'ic.** — **Buddhist cross** the swastika. [Sans. *buddha*, wise, from *bodhati*, he understands.]

buddle *bud'l, n.* an inclined hutch for washing ore. — *v.t.* to wash with a buddle. [Origin obscure.]

Buddleia *bud'li-ə, bud-lē'ə, n.* a genus of plants of the Loganiaceae, shrubs and trees with opposite leaves and showy clusters of purple or orange flowers: (without *cap.*) a plant of the genus. [Named in honour of Adam *Buddle* (d. 1715), botanist.]

buddy¹ *bud'i, n.* brother (*U.S.*): a pal, one's most constant companion. — Also (esp. in U.S. as form of address) **bud.** [Prob. from same root as *butty*.]

buddy². See **bud¹.**

budge¹ *buj, v.i.* and *v.t.* to move or stir. — *n.* **budg'er.** [Fr. *bouger* — L. *bullīre*, to bubble.]

budge² *buj, n.* lambskin fur. — *adj.* pompous: stiff. [Origin obscure.]

budge³. See **budgerigar.**

budgeree *buj'ər-ē*, (*Austr. obs. coll.*) *adj.* good. [Native word, *budgeri*.]

budgerigar *buj'ər-i-gär, -gär', n.* a cage and aviary bird, an Australian parrakeet. — *fam.* **budge** *buj,* **budgie** *buj'i.* [Aboriginal.]

budgerow, budgero (*pl.* **budgeros**) *buj'ər-ō*, (Hind.) *n.* a heavy keel-less barge.

budget¹ *buj'it, n.* a sack or its contents (*obs.*): a compact collection of things: news: a socket in which the end of a cavalry carbine rests: a financial statement and programme put before parliament by the Chancellor of the Exchequer: a plan of domestic expenditure or the like. — *adj.* cheap, economical, inexpensive. — *v.i.* to prepare a budget. — *v.t.* to provide for in a budget: — *pr.p.* **budg'eting;** *pa.t.* and *pa.p.* **budg'eted.** — *adj.* **bud'getary.** — **budget account** a special bank account, into which money is paid regularly by the bank from a customer's main account and from which payment of previously agreed recurring expenses, e.g. fuel bills, T.V. licence, is made: an account with a shop, into which the customer makes regular payments to cover purchases at the shop. — **budget for** to allow for, when planning one's expenditure. [Fr. *bougette*, dim. of *bouge*, a pouch — L. *bulga*.]

budget² *buj'it, n.* a fixed rudder on a barge. [Ety. uncertain.]

budgie. See **budgerigar.**

budmash. See **badmash.**

budo *bōō'dō, n.* the system or philosophy of the martial art. [Jap., the way the warrior.]

buenas noches *bwen'as noch'es*, (Sp.) good-night; **buenas tardes** *tar'dhes*, good-afternoon; **buenos dias** *bwen'os dē'as*, good-day, good-morning.

buff¹ *buf, n.* originally buffalo-hide: now white leather from which the grain surface has been removed, used for army accoutrements: a military coat: the colour of buff, a light yellow: the bare skin: a buff-stick or buff-wheel: (in *pl.*) certain regiments in the British army, from their former buff-coloured facings — e.g. East Kent Regiment, Ross-shire Buffs: a member of a party whose colour is buff: an enthusiast, fan (orig. a keen attender at fires, so called from the buff uniform of the former New York volunteer firemen) (*coll.*). — Also *adj.* — *v.t.* to polish with a buff. — *n.* **buff'er** one who buffs or polishes. — *ns.* **buff'-coat, buff'-jer'kin** a

strong, military coat: a soldier; **buff'-leather; buff⸗
stick, buff'-wheel** a stick or wheel covered with buff-
leather or the like, and charged with an abrasive for
polishing. — **in the buff** naked.   [Fr. *buffle*, a buffalo.]
buff² *buf, n.* a buffet, blow, or stroke (*obs.*): a dull blow
or its sound. — *v.t.* to strike, esp. with a dull sound:
to burst out. — *n.* **buff'er** a mechanical apparatus for
deadening the force of a concussion, as in railway
carriages: a ship's fender: a boatswain's mate: a fellow,
esp. a dull or ineffectual fellow (as in *old buffer*): in
chemistry, a substance or mixture which opposes
change of hydrogen-ion concentration in a solution:
a temporary store into which data can go while
awaiting transfer e.g. from computer to printer, acting
as an adjusting mechanism between processes of different speeds. — *v.t.* to treat with a buffer. — *v.i.* to
use, or be used as, a buffer. — *adj.* **buff'ered. — buffer
state, zone** a neutral country or zone lying between
two countries whose relations are or may become strained;
buffer stock stock held in reserve to minimise the effect
of price fluctuations.   [O.Fr. *buffe*, a blow.]
buffa. See **buffo.**
buffalo *buf'ə-lō, n.* a name for certain large animals of
the ox kind, esp. the tame, often domesticated Asiatic
buffalo, and the entirely wild and fierce Cape buffalo:
the American bison (*U.S.*): a bison: — *pl.* **buff'aloes.**
— *v.t.* to bewilder: to overawe. — **buff'alo-berry** a
North American shrub of the Elaeagnaceae, or its
edible fruit; **buff'alo-bird** an ox-pecker; **buffalo chips**
dried buffalo dung used as fuel; **buffalo gnat** see **black
fly** under **black**; **buff'alo-grass** a low creeping grass
(*Buchloe dactyloides*) growing on the western prairies
of the U.S.: any of several other prairie grasses;
buff'alo-nut a North American shrub of the sandalwood family: its oil-yielding nut; **buff'alo-robe** a bison-
hide rug or cloak.   [It. *buffalo*, through L. from Gr.
boubalos.]
buffe See **buffo.**
buffet¹ *buf'it, n.* a blow with the fist: a slap: a stroke, esp.
heavy and repeated, as of the wind, fortune, etc. —
v.t. to strike with the hand or fist: to knock or push
about roughly, to batter: to struggle against, beat back.
— *v.i.* to deal heavy blows. — *n.* **buff'eting** a striking
with the hand, boxing: contention: repeated blows:
irregular oscillation of any part of an aircraft, caused
and maintained by an eddying wake from some other
part.   [O.Fr. *buffet* — *buffe*, a blow, esp. on the
cheek.]
buffet² *buf'it, n.* a sideboard: a low (esp. rectangular)
stool (*Northern*): (usu. *boŏf'ā*) a refreshment counter
or bar: a meal set out on table, etc., from which the
diner serves himself. — Also *adj.* — **buffet car** (*boŏf'ā
kär*) a railway coach with light meal or snack service.
[Fr. *buffet*; origin unknown.]
buffi. See **buffo.**
bufflehead *buf'l-hed, n.* a N. American diving duck
resembling the golden-eye: a stupid fellow.   [From
buffalo and **head.**]
buffo *boŏf'fō, adj.* comic, — *n.* the comic actor in an
opera: — *pl.* **buff'fi** (*-fē*); *fem.* **buff'fa;** *pl.* **buff'fe** (*-fā*).
[It.]
buffoon *buf-oōn', n.* one who sets himself to amuse by
jests, grimaces, etc.: a low, vulgar, or indecent jester,
one without self-respect. — *n.* **buffoon'ery** the practices
of a buffoon: low or vulgar jesting.   [Fr. *bouffon* —
It. *buffone; buffare*, to jest.]
bufo *bū'fō,* (*Ben Jonson*) *n.* a black tincture in alchemy.
[L. *būfō*, toad.]
bug¹ *bug, n.* (*obs.*) an object of terror. — *n.* **bug'aboo** a
bogy, or object of terror: a cause of anxiety. —
bug'bear an object of terror, dislike, or annoyance;
bug'-word (*obs.*) a terrifying or theatening word.
[M.E. *bugge,* perh. W. *bwg,* a hobgoblin.]
bug² *bug, n.* a name applied loosely to certain insects,
esp. of the Hemiptera (Heteroptera), and specifically
to one (*Cimex lectularius*) that infests houses and beds:
any insect or small animal (*U.S.*): a disease-germ: a

viral disease (*coll.*): a craze, obsession: an enthusiast:
a crazy person: an important person (**big bug**): a snag,
a defect, a fault (*coll.*): a hidden microphone: a light
vehicle stripped of everything inessential: lunar excursion module (see **module**). — *v.t.* to plant a concealed
listening device in: to annoy, irritate (*slang*). — *adj.*
bugged. — *n. and adj.* **bugg'ing.** — **bug'bane, bug'wort**
a ranunculaceous plant (*Cimifuga foetida*) akin to
baneberry, reputed to drive away insects; **bug'house**
(*U.S.*) an insane asylum. — *adj.* insane. — **bug'-hunter**
a collecting entomologist.   [Perh. O.E. *budda,* beetle;
perh. same as **bug¹**.]
bug³ *bug,* (*U.S.*) *v.i.* to start or bulge: — *pr.p.* **bugg'ing;**
pa.t. and pa.p. **bugged.** — *adj.* **bug'-eyed'** with eyes
protruding in astonishment, etc.
bug⁴ *bug,* (*U.S.*) *v.i.* to leave, as in *n.* **bug'-out'** desertion:
a deserter. — **bug out** to desert, esp. in panic.   [Perh.
from **bugger (off).**]
buggan *bug'ən,* **buggane** *-ān,* **buggin** *-in,* (*dial.*) *ns.* an evil
spirit, a hobgoblin.   [Prob. W. *bwg,* hobgoblin; cf.
bogle and **bug¹**.]
bugger *bug'ər, n.* orig. a Bulgarian heretic, believed
capable of any crime: one guilty of bestiality and
unnatural, i.e. anal, sexual intercourse: a term of
abuse, often quite colourless or even kindly (*vulg.
coll.*): a rogue, scamp — applied inoffensively to child
or animal (*U.S.*): a difficult or unpleasant task, etc.
(*vulg. coll.*). — *v.t.* to have unnatural sexual, i.e. anal,
intercourse with: (the following all *vulg. coll.*) to
exhaust: to frustrate, ruin the plans of: to spoil, prevent
success in (also with *up*). — *v.i.* (with *off; vulg. coll.*)
to go away quickly. — *interj.* (*vulg. coll.*) used to
express annoyance. — *n.* **bugg'ery** (*law*) bestiality,
unnatural sexual, esp. anal, intercourse. — **bugger
about** (*vulg. coll.*) to potter about; **bugger all** (*vulg. coll.*)
none, nothing.   [Fr. *bougre* — L. *Bulgarus,* Bulgarian.]
Buggins's turn *bug'inz-əz tûrn,* turn for promotion, etc.,
in accordance with seniority, by rotation, etc.   [Ori-
gin unknown.]
buggy *bug'i, n.* a light carriage or gig of several kinds —
in America, a one-horse, four-wheeled vehicle with one
seat; in England, two-wheeled; in India, hooded: a
child's push-chair.   [By some conn. with **bogie;** ety.
really quite unknown.]
bugle¹ *bū'gl, n.* orig. a buffalo or wild ox: hence (also
bū'gle-horn) a horn used as a drinking vessel or hunting-horn: a treble instrument with or without keys,
usu. made of copper, like the trumpet, but having the
bell less expanded and the tube shorter and more
conical, used more for signalling than music. — *v.i.* to
sound a bugle. — *ns.* **bū'gler** one who sounds the bugle;
bū'glet a small bugle. — **bū'gle-band; bū'gle-call.**
[O.Fr. *bugle* — L. *būculus,* dim. of *bōs,* an ox.]
bugle² *bū'gl, n.* a slender elongated bead, usu. black, used
as a decoration on clothing. — *adj.* (*Shak.*) like bugles.
[Poss. conn. with L.L. *bugulus,* hair-pad, or with Du.
beugel, ring.]
bugle³ *bū'gl, n.* a genus (*Ajuga*) of labiate plants without
upper-lip.   [Fr., It. *bugola* — L.L. *bugula, būgillō.*]
bugloss *bū'glos, n.* a name for several plants of the borage
family, esp. *Lycopsis arvensis,* a common cornfield
weed, and **viper's bugloss** (q.v.).   [Fr. *buglosse* — L.
būglōssa — Gr. *bouglōssos — bous,* ox, *glōssa,* tongue.]
bugong. See **bogong.**
buhl *boōl, n.* a complicated form of inlay, gold, silver, or
brass and pewter, ivory and mother-of-pearl in tor-
toiseshell, etc., forming panels for furniture decoration: furniture thus decorated. — Also **boulle, boule.**
[From Charles André *Boulle* (1642–1732), a cabinet-
maker in the service of Louis XIV.]
buhrstone *bûr'stōn, n.* a variety of quartz, containing
many small empty cells, which give it a peculiar
roughness of surface particularly adapted for mill-
stones. — Also **burr'stone.**   [Perh. conn. with **burr,**
from its roughness.]

buik, buke *buk, bük, būk, n.* (*Scot.*) variants of **book** and of **bouk.**

build *bild, v.t.* to erect, as a house or bridge: to construct, as a railway, etc.: to establish (*fig.*): to base, as hopes (on): to form (combinations) (*cards*). — *v.i.* to depend (with *on, upon*). — *pa.t.* and *pa.p.* **built,** *arch.* **build′ed.** — *n.* form: make. — *ns.* **build′er** one who builds, or controls the work of building; **build′ing** the art or process of erecting houses, etc.: a substantial structure for giving shelter, e.g. a house, office-block: used as a collective noun for a gathering of rooks. — *adj.* **built** formed or shaped. — **builders′ merchant** a person whose job is to arrange deliveries and supplies of building materials to building-sites; **build′ing-block** a hollow or solid block made of concrete or other material, larger than a brick; **build′ing-board** an artificial material made in slabs for lining walls; **building society** a society that advances money to its members towards providing them with dwelling-houses; **build′-up** a building up, increasing, strengthening: the amount of this: a working up of favourable publicity: preliminaries leading up to a climax in a story, speech, etc. — *adjs.* **built′-in′** formed as part of a main structure, esp. if recessed: present as part of one′s genetic inheritance: inherent: included (as part of a deal, etc.): very firmly fixed; **built′-up** of an area, covered with buildings. — **build in** to enclose or fix by building; **build up** to close up by building, as a door: to cover with buildings: to create, or be created, or to increase, gradually (as a concentration of troops, a reputation, voltage, tension): to put together from parts already made: to edify spiritually. [O.E. *gebyld,* pa.p. of an assumed *byldan,* to build — *bold,* a dwelling.]

buirdly *bûrd′li,* (*Scot.*) *adj.* stalwart, large and well made. [Poss. a variant of **burly.**]

buist *büst,* (*Scot.*) *n.* a box: a tar-box: an owner′s mark on sheep or cattle. — *v.t.* to mark thus. [O.Fr. *boiste* (Fr. *boîte*), box.]

buke. See **buik.**

bukshi, bukshee *buk′shē, n.* a paymaster. See **buckshish.** [Pers. *bakhshī.*]

bulb *bulb, n.* a subterranean bud with swollen leaf-bases in which reserve materials are stored: a protuberance or swelling: the medulla oblongata: a dilatation or expansion of a glass tube: the glass of an electric light. — *v.i.* to form bulbs: to bulge out or swell. — *adjs.* **bulb′ar; bulbed; bulbif′erous** of a plant, producing bulbs. — *n.* **bulb′il** a small bud that may grow into an independent plant. — *adj.* **bulb′ous** bulging: swollen. — **bulb of percussion** a raised cone on a worked flint, marking where a blow was struck. [L. *bulbus* — Gr. *bolbos,* an onion.]

bulbul *bool′bool, n.* properly, a Persian nightingale: in India, extended to a genus (*Pycnonotus*) of birds akin to the babblers: a sweet singer. [Ar.]

Bulgarian *bul-gā′ri-ən, adj.* of *Bulgaria* or its language. — *n.* a native or citizen of Bulgaria: the Bulgarian language (Slavonic). — *n.* **Bul′gar** (*-gär*) a member of an ancient Finnic or Ugrian tribe that moved from the Volga towards Bulgaria. — *adj.* **Bulgaric** (*-gar′ik*). — *n.* the ancient language of the Bulgars.

bulge *bulj, n.* a protuberance, swelling: a salient (*mil.*): temporary increase. — *v.i.* and *v.t.* to swell out. — *ns.* **bul′ger** wooden golf-club with a convex face; **bul′giness.** — *adjs.* **bul′ging** swelling out: over-full; **bul′gy.** — **have, get the bulge on someone** (*slang*) to have or get a decided advantage over someone. [O.Fr. *boulge,* prob. L. *bulga,* a leather knapsack: a Gallic word; cf. **bilge.**]

bulgine. See **bul(l)gine.**

bulimia *bū-lim′i-ə, n.* morbid hunger (also *fig.*). — Earlier forms **būl′imy, bulī′mus.** — *adj.* and *n.* **bulim′ic.** — **bulimia nervosa** (*nər-vō′sə, -zə*) a pathological condition, characterised by the alternation of over-eating and self-induced vomiting, caused by an obsession with weight. [Gr. *boulīmiā* — *bous,* ox, *līmos,* hunger.]

bulk¹ *bulk, n.* a stall or framework built in front of a shop. — *n.* **bulk′er** (*arch.*) a street thief or strumpet. [Ety. dub.; cf. O.N. *bālkr,* beam, O.E. *bolca,* gangway of a ship.]

bulk² *bulk, n.* a heap (now only of tobacco): a cargo: the belly, trunk, or body: a hull or hold: volume or size: great size: the greater part: any huge body or structure: mass. — *v.i.* to be in bulk: to fill out (with *out* or *up*): to be of weight or importance. — *v.t.* to put or hold in bulk: (often with *out*; also with *up*) to cause to swell, make greater in size. — *adv.* **bulk′ily.** — *n.* **bulk′iness.** — *adj.* **bulk′y** having bulk: filling much space: unwieldy. — **bulk buying** large-scale purchase of a commodity, esp. on preferential terms and by a single buyer on behalf of a body of consumers: guaranteed purchase by one country of all or most of another′s output of a commodity; **bulk carrier** a vessel carrying cargo, such as grain, that is not in the form of separate packages. — **break bulk** see **break¹; bulk large** to be prominent or intrusive; **load in bulk** to put cargo in loose; **sell in bulk** to sell cargo as it is in the hold: to sell in large quantities. [Prob. (hypothetical) O.N. *bulki,* heap or cargo, confused with O.E. *buc,* belly; see **bouk.**]

bulkhead *bulk′hed, n.* any of the partitions separating one part of the interior of a ship, aircraft *etc* from another: a protecting barrier or structure: the roof of a bulk (**bulk¹**): the bulk itself. — **collision bulkhead** that nearest the bow. [**bulk¹** and **bulk².**]

bull¹ *bool, n.* an uncastrated male of the ox kind: a male whale, walrus, elephant, moose, etc.: (with *cap.*) Taurus (*astron.*): one who seeks to raise the price of stocks, and speculates on a rise (opp. to *bear*): a bull′s-eye (*musketry*): nonsense (*slang*): spit and polish (*mil. slang*): a policeman (*U.S. slang*). — *adj.* male: massive: favourable to the bulls, rising (*Stock Exchange*). — *v.t.* to try to raise the price of: to copulate with (a cow): to polish (*mil. slang*). — *v.i.* to be in heat, of a cow: to brag (*slang*): to talk rubbish (*slang*). — *adj.* **bull′ish** like a bull: obstinate: inclining towards rising prices (*Stock Exchange*). — *adv.* **bull′ishly.** — *ns.* **bull′ishness; bull′ock** an ox or castrated bull. — **bull ant** short for **bulldog ant; bull′-bait′ing** the sport of baiting or exciting bulls with dogs; **bull′bat** (*U.S.*) the night-hawk or goat-sucker; **bull′-beef** the beef or flesh of bulls, coarse beef: (*Shak.* in *pl.*) **bull′-beeves; bull′-begg′ar** (*dial.*) a hobgoblin, etc.; **bull′-calf** a male calf: a stupid fellow, a lout; **bull′-dance** a dance of men only; **bull′dog** a breed of dogs of great courage, formerly used for baiting bulls: hence a person of obstinate courage: a short-barrelled revolver of large calibre: a proctor′s attendant at Oxford or Cambridge: (with *cap.;* ®) a bulldog clip. — *v.t.* to assail like a bulldog: to wrestle with and throw (a steer, etc.) (*U.S.*). — **bulldog ant** a black or red Australian ant with a vicious sting; **bulldog clip** a clip with a spring, used for holding papers, etc. together or to a board; **bull′dust** (*Austr.* and *N.Z.*) euph. for **bullshit; bull fiddle** (*U.S. coll.*) a double-bass; **bull′fight** a popular spectacle in Spain, Portugal, Southern France, and Latin America, in which a bull is goaded to fury by mounted *picadores* armed with lances, and despatched by a specially skilful *espada* or swordsman; **bull′fighter; bull′fighting; bull′finch** a plump red-breasted finch: (perh. for *bull-fence*) a kind of high, thick hedge hard to jump; **bull′frog** a large frog. — *adj.* **bull′-fronted** having a forehead like a bull. — **bull′head** the miller′s thumb, a small river fish with large, flat head: extended to various similar fishes, as the pogge (*armed bullhead*). — *adj.* **bull′-head′ed** impetuous and obstinate. — **bull′-head′edness; bull′-hoof** a West Indian passion-flower (from the shape of its leaf); **bull′-horn** a megaphone; **bull′-mastiff** a cross between the bulldog and the mastiff, the mastiff strain predominating. — *adjs.* **bull′-necked′** thick-necked; **bull′-nosed** with a blunt nose, like a bull′s. — **bull′ock′s-heart** the custard-apple; **bull′-of-the-bog′** (*Scot.*) the bittern; **bull′-pen** a pen for a bull: a similar enclosure for prisoners (*U.S.*): a part of the ground where pitchers warm up (*baseball*); **bull point** (*coll.*) a key point, a salient point; **bull'-pup** a young bulldog; **bull'-ring** the enclosure for bull-fighting or bull-baiting: a ring for a bull's nose; **bull'-roarer** a child's plaything, made of an oblong slip of wood, whirled at the end of a string to give a loud whirring noise: a similar artefact used in an Australian Aboriginal ceremonial — the *turndun*: the similar *rhombos* of the Greek mysteries; **bull session** (esp. *U.S.*) an informal discussion esp. between men; **bull's'-eye** the central boss formed in making a sheet of spun glass: a thick lens, or round piece of glass, as in a lantern: a policeman's lantern: a round opening or window: the centre of a target: a shot that hits it: a big round hard peppermint sweet; **bull'shit** (*slang*) nonsense: deceptive humbug. — *v.i.* and *v.t.* to talk nonsense (to), often with the intention of deceiving. — **bull'shitter; bull's wool** (*Austr. coll.*) any fibrous bark: euph. for **bullshit; bull'-terr'ier** a breed of dog with a smooth, short-haired coat, orig. a cross between bulldog and terrier; **bull'-trout** a variety of sea-trout (*Salmo trutto eriox*): a large trout with a big head: a salmon that has re-entered fresh water after spawning; **bull'whack** a heavy whip. — *v.t.* to lash with a bull-whack. — **a bull in a china shop** one who lacks the delicacy that the situation calls for; **bull into** to plunge hastily into; **not know a B from a bull's foot** to be very ignorant; **take the bull by the horns** to grapple boldly with a danger or difficulty. [M.E. *bole*, prob. O.N. *bole, boli;* most prob. related to **bellow**.]

bull² *bool, n.* an edict of the pope with his seal affixed. — *n.* **bull'ary** a collection of papal bulls. [L. *bulla*, a knob, a leaden seal.]

bull³ *bool, n.* a ludicrous inconsistency in speech often said to be an especial prerogative of Irishmen — 'I was a fine child, but they changed me'. [Prob. O.Fr. *boul*, cheat.]

bull⁴ *bool, n.* drink made by pouring water into a cask that had held liquor. [Origin unknown.]

bull⁵ *bool, n.* a deck game in which pads are thrown at an inclined board, the **bull'-board**. [Origin unknown.]

bulla *bool'ə, n.* a round metal ornament worn by children of Ancient Rome: a seal attached to a document: a blister: anything rounded or globular: (with *cap.*) the bubble-shell genus. — *adj.* **bull'ate** blistered or puckered: bubble-like: knobbed: inflated. [L. *bulla*.]

bullace *bool'is, n.* a shrub closely allied to the sloe. [Cf. O.Fr. *beloce*.]

bullary See **bull²**.

bullate See **bulla**.

bulldoze *bool'dōz, v.t.* to intimidate: to bully: to level and clear by bulldozer: to demolish as if by bulldozer: to force or push through against opposition (*fig.*). — *n.* **bull'dozer** one who bulldozes: a pistol or other means of compulsion: a tractor machine for levelling and clearing land. [Origin obscure.]

buller *bool'ər, (Scot.) n.* turbulence in water: a bubbling: a bellow. — *v.i.* to seethe: to gurgle: to bellow. [Cf. Dan. *bulder*, Swed. *buller*, rumble, noise, roar; prob. partly from or influenced by O.Fr. *bullir*, Icel. *bulla*, to boil.]

bullet *bool'it, n.* a little ball (*obs.*): a projectile, now esp. one (round or conical) discharged from any kind of small-arm: a plumb or sinker in fishing. — **bull'et-head** a round head: an obstinate fellow (*U.S.*). — *adjs.* **bull'et-head'ed; bull'et-proof** proof against bullets. [Fr. *boulette*, dim. of *boule*, a ball — L. *bulla*.]

bulletin *bool'i-tin, n.* an official report of public news, or of a patient's progress. [Fr., — It. *bullettino*.]

bullet-tree, bulletrie. Same as **bully-tree**.

bul(l)gine *bool'jīn, (U.S. coll.) n.* a steam locomotive. [Said to be **bull¹** and en*gine*.]

bullion *bool'yən, n.* gold and silver in the mass and uncoined: occasionally, precious metal, coined and uncoined: a heavy twisted cord fringe, often covered with gold or silver wire. — *n.* **bull'ionist** one in favour of metallic currency. [Perh. conn. with L.L. *bullio, -ōnis*, a boiling.]

bullock. See **bull¹**.

bully¹ *bool'i, n.* a cruel oppressor of the weak: a blustering, noisy, overbearing fellow: a ruffian hired to beat or intimidate anyone (*arch.*): one who lives upon the gains of a prostitute (*obs.*): a term of genial familiarity, esp. to a man (*obs.*). — *adj.* blustering (*arch.*): excellent. — *v.i.* to bluster. — *v.t.* to oppress cruelly: to threaten in a noisy way: — *pr.p.* **bull'ying;** *pa.t.* and *pa.p.* **bull'ied.** — *interj.* good. — *n.* **bull'yism.** — **bull'y-boy** a ruffian hired to beat or intimidate someone; **bull'y-rook** a bully: a comrade. — **bully for you, him,** etc. (often *iron.*) good for you, him, etc. [Perh. Du. *boel*, a lover; cf. Ger. *Buhle*.]

bully² *bool'i, n.* a miner's hammer.

bully³ *bool'i, n.* a scrimmage (*football*): formerly in hockey, the opening (or reopening) of the game — two opposing players each striking the ground on his own side of the ball and his opponent's stick alternately, three times, and then trying to strike the ball (also **bull'y-off'**). — *v.t.* and *v.i.* **bull'y (-off')**. [Origin uncertain.]

bully⁴ *bool'i,* **bully-beef** *bool'i-bēf, ns.* canned or pickled beef. [Prob. Fr. *bouilli*, boiled beef, influenced by **bull¹**.]

bullyrag *bool'i-rag,* **ballyrag** *bal'i-rag, vs.t.* to assail with abusive language or horseplay: to badger. [Origin unknown; perhaps from **rag²**.]

bully-tree *bool'i-trē, n.* a name for several West Indian sapotaceous trees yielding good timber, edible fruits, and balata, esp. *Mimusops balata.* — Also **bull'et-tree, bull'etrie, boll'etrie.** [Perh. from **bullace;** perh. from **balata**.]

bulrush *bool'rush, n.* a name given to two distinct tall marsh or water plants — the reed-mace or cat's-tail, and clubrush, a plant of the sedge family (*Scirpus lacustris*). — *adj.* **bul'rushy.** — **bulrush millet** pearl millet. [Perh. **bole¹** or **bull¹** in sense of massive or coarse, and **rush²**.]

bulse *buls, n.* a bag for or of diamonds, etc. [Port. *bolsa* — L.L. *bursa*, a purse. See **purse**.]

bulwark *bool'wərk, n.* a fortification or rampart: a breakwater or sea-wall: the side of a ship projecting above the deck: any means of defence or security. — *v.t.* to defend: to fortify. [Cf. Ger. *Bollwerk*.]

bum¹ *bum, n.* (*coll.*) the buttocks: the anus (*vulg.*). — *v.t.* (*vulg.*) to have anal intercourse with. — **bum'bai'liff** (*Shak.* **bum'-bay'lie**) a bailiff who comes behind to make arrests: a sheriff's officer; **bum'freezer** (*slang*) an Eton jacket: a waist-length jacket; **bum roll** a bustle or dress-improver; **bum'sucker** (*vulg.*) a toady; **bum'sucking.** [Cf. **bump** in sense of swelling.]

bum² *bum, v.i.* to hum or make a murmuring sound, as a bee. — *v.t.* (*Scot.*) to toss, hurl: — *pr.p.* **bum'ming;** *pa.t.* and *pa.p.* **bummed.** — *n.* a humming sound. — *n.* **bumm'er** a person or thing that bums. — **bum'-bee** (*dial.*) a bumble-bee; **bum'-clock** (*Scot.*) a flying beetle that drones. — **head'-bumm'er** (*Scot.*) a manager or person in authority. [Imit.]

bum³ *bum, (U.S. slang) n.* a (drunken) spree: a dissolute fellow: a sponger. — *adj.* worthless: despicable: dud: wrong, false. — *v.i.* to loaf: to sponge: to live dissolutely. — *v.t.* to cadge. — *n.* **bumm'er** a plundering straggler or camp-follower (during the American Civil War): a dissolute fellow: a loafer: a sponger: a dismal failure (*coll.*): something worthless (*coll.*): a disappointment (*coll.*): a bad trip (q.v.; *coll.*): a nasty experience (*coll.*). — **bum steer** (*slang*) something misleading, false or worthless, a dud. — **give someone the bum's rush** (*slang*) to eject someone by force: to dismiss someone summarily, esp. from one's employment. [Cf. **bummel**.]

bumalo. See **bummalo**.

bumbaze *bum-bāz', (Scot.) v.t.* to confound, bamboozle. [Origin obscure.]

bumbershoot *bum'bər-shoōt*, (*U.S. facet.*) *n.* an umbrella. [Alteration of *umbr*ella, with para*chute*.]

bumble, bummle *bum'(b)l*, *v.i.* to bungle: to utter indistinctly: to bustle about blunderingly. — *n.* confusion: indistinct utterance: a bungler: an idler. — **bum'ble=bee'** a large wild loud-humming bee, a humble bee; **bum'ble-foot** cellulitis in a bird's foot, due to pusforming organisms: club-foot; **bum'ble-puppy** the old game of nine-holes: unscientific whist: a racket game in which a string is wound round a post by hitting a slung ball or bag. [Freq. of **bum²**.]

Bumble *bum'bl*, *n.* a beadle: a self-important minor official. — *n.* **Bum'bledom**. [From Mr *Bumble* in Dickens's *Oliver Twist*.]

bumbo *bum'bō*, *n.* a mixture of rum or gin, water, sugar, and nutmeg, or similar drink: — *pl.* **bum'bos**. [Perh. It. *bombo*, a child's word for drink.]

bum-boat *bum'bōt*, *n.* orig. a Thames scavenger's boat: a boat bringing vegetables, etc., for sale to ships. [Origin doubtful.]

bumf, bumph *bumf*, (*coll.*) *n.* lavatory paper: papers, official papers, documents (*disparagingly*). [Short for *bum-fodder*, **bum¹** and **fodder**.]

bumkin, bumpkin *bum'kin*, *n.* a short beam of timber projecting from each bow of a ship, for the purpose of extending the lower corner of the foresail to windward: a small outrigger over the stern of a boat, usually serving to extend the mizzen. [From **boom¹** and dim. termination *-kin*.]

bummalo, bumalo *bum'ə-lō*, *n.* the Bombay duck, a small Indian fish of a family (*Scopelidae*) akin to the salmon, dried and eaten as a relish: — *pl.* **bum(m)'alo**. — Also **bummalō'ti**. [Marathi *bombĭl*.]

bummaree *bum-ər-ē'*, *n.* orig. a middleman in Billingsgate fish-market: a porter at Smithfield meat-market. [Ety. unknown.]

bummel *bŏŏm'əl*, *n.* a stroll: a leisurely journey. [Ger. *Bummel*.]

bummer. See **bum²,³**.

bummle. See **bumble**.

bummock *bum'ək*, (*Orkney*) *n.* a brewing of ale for a feast. [Ety. unknown.]

bump¹ *bump*, *v.i.* to make a heavy or loud noise: to knock dully: to jolt: to move joltingly: (of a cricket-ball) to bound high on striking the pitch. — *v.t.* to strike with a dull sound: to strike against: to dislodge, knock, shove: in boat-racing, to overtake and impinge upon — the bumper consequently taking the place of the bumped in rank: to spread out in printing so as to fill any desired number of pages. — *n.* a dull heavy blow: a thump: (in *pl.*) a series of thumps against the ground administered esp.to a child celebrating his birthday, by others holding him by his arms and legs: a high rebound of a cricket-ball: a jolt: a lump or swelling: a protuberance on the head confidently associated by phrenologists with qualities or propensities of mind: hence (*coll.*) faculty. — *n.* **bump'er** any thing or person that bumps: a bar on a motor-car to lessen the shock of collision: a railway buffer (*U.S.*): a pad fitted round the inside of a cot to stop a baby bumping himself: a bumping race: a cup or glass filled to the brim for drinking a toast: anything large or generous in measure: a crowded house at a theatre or concert. — *adj.* full to overflowing: unusually large or plentiful. — *v.i.* to drink bumpers. — *ns.* **bump'iness; bumpol'ogy** (*jocose*) phrenology. — *adj.* **bump'y**. — **bumping race** a boat-race in which the boats seek to bump, not to pass. — **bump into** to happen to meet (someone); **bump off** (*slang*) to kill, murder; **bump start** (*n.* **bump'-start**) same as **jump start**; **bump up** (*coll.*) to raise (prices): to increase size of; **with a bump** with an unpleasant suddenness. [Imit.]

bump² *bump*, *n.* the booming cry of the bittern. — *v.i.* to utter that cry. [Imit.]

bumph. See **bumf**.

bumpkin¹ *bump'kin*, *n.* an awkward, clumsy rustic: a

clown. — *adj.* **bump'kinish**. [Prob. Du. *boomken*, a log.]

bumpkin². See **bumkin**.

bumptious *bump'shəs*, *adj.* offensively self-important. — *adv.* **bump'tiously**. — *n.* **bump'tiousness**. [Prob. formed from **bump¹**.]

bun¹ *bun*, *n.* a kind of sweet cake: a rounded mass of hair. — **bun'-fight** (*coll.*) a tea-party: a noisy occasion or assembly. [Perh. from O.Fr. *bugne*, a swelling.]

bun² *bun*, *n.* a dry stalk: a hare's scut. [Possibly Gael. *bun*, a root, a stump.]

bun³ *bun*, *n.* a playful name for a rabbit or a squirrel. [Origin unknown.]

buna *bōŏ'nə*, *n.* an artificial rubber made by the polymerisation of butadiene. [Orig. trademark.]

bunce *buns*, (*slang*) *n.* profit or gain. — *v.i.* (*slang*) to ring up wrongfully on every customer's bill the price of an item kept beside the till of a supermarket, etc., in order to defray losses by theft, etc. [Ety. uncertain, some say corr. of *bonus*.]

bunch *bunch, bunsh*, *n.* a lump: a lumpish gathering: a number of things aggregated or fastened together: a definite quantity fastened together, as of linen yarn (180000 yards), etc.: a cluster: a handful as of flowers: something in the form of a tuft or knot. — *v.i.* to swell out in a bunch: to cluster, form a tight group. — *v.t.* to make a bunch of: to concentrate. — *adj.* **bunched** humped, protuberant: lumpy. — *ns.* **bunch'iness; bunch'ing** the act of drawing together into a bunch: over-close grouping of cars on a motorway, etc. (esp. after a long gap), of ships arriving in port, etc. — *adj.* **bunch'y** growing in bunches or like a bunch: bulging. — *adj.* **bunch'-backed** (*Shak.*) hump-backed. — **bunch'-grass** a clumped Western American grass of several kinds. — **bunch of fives** see **five**. [Origin unknown.]

bunco. See **bunko**.

buncombe. See **bunkum**.

Bund *bŏŏnt*, (*Ger.*) *n.* a league or confederacy. — **Bundesbank** (*bŏŏn'des-bangk*) the state bank of the Federal Republic of Germany; **Bundesrat(h)** (*-rät*) federal council in Germany, etc.: upper house of the parliament of the Federal Republic of Germany; **Bun'destag** (*-tähh*) lower house of the Federal German parliament; **Bun'deswehr** (*-vār*) the Federal German armed forces.

bund, band(h) *bund*, *n.* (orig. in India, etc.) a man-made embankment or dam: a stoppage of work by employees. — *v.t.* to embank. [Hind. *band*, from Pers.]

bundle *bun'dl*, *n.* a number of things loosely bound together: a bunch: a loose parcel, esp. one contained in a cloth: a strand of conducting vessels, fibres, etc. (*biol.*): a definite measure or quantity, as two reams of paper, twenty hanks of linen yarn, etc. — *v.t.* to make into bundles: to put hastily or unceremoniously: to hustle. — *v.i.* to pack up one's things for a journey: to go hurriedly or in confusion (with *away, off, out*): to lie in bed together fully clad (an old custom in Wales, New England and parts of Scotland for sweethearts and others) (*n.* **bund'ling**). — **bundle of fun** an exuberant and entertaining person (sometimes *iron.* of one who is not); **go a bundle on** (*slang*) to like or be enthusiastic about. [Conn. with **bind** and **bond**.]

bundobust. Same as **bandobast**.

bundook, bandook *bun'dŏŏk*, (*mil. slang*) *n.* a rifle. [Hind. *bandūq*.]

bundu *bŏŏn'dŏŏ*, (*S.Afr*) *n.* a remote uncultivated region. [Bantu.]

Bundy® *bun'di*, (*Austr.*) *n.* a time-clock in a factory, etc.

bung¹ *bung*, *n.* the stopper of the hole in a barrel: a large cork. — *v.t.* to stop up or enclose with a bung (also *fig.*). — **bung'-hole** a hole for a bung; **bung'-vent** a small hole in a bung to let gases escape, etc. [Ety. dub.]

bung² *bung*, *n.* a purse (*obs.*; *thieves' cant*): a cutpurse (*Shak.*) — **nip a bung** to cut a purse. [Cf. O.E. *pung*, purse.]

bung³ *bung*, (*slang*) *v.t.* to throw or shove carelessly and hurriedly.

bung⁴ *bung*, (*Austral. coll.*) *adj.* dead: bust: ruined. — **go bung** to die: to fail, go bust: to go phut. [Aboriginal.]

bungalow *bung'gə-lō*, *n.* a lightly-built house, properly with a veranda and one storey: now loosely, a one-storey house. — *adj.* and *n.* **bung'aloid** (facetious formation, usu. *derog.*). — **dak bungalow** see **dak**. [Hindi *banglā*, (house) in the style of Bengal, house.]

bungee, bungey *bunj'i*, *n.* a tension device using springs, elastic cable or rubber in such a way as to facilitate the movement of the controls in aircraft, etc. [Prob. conn. with **bungie**.]

bungie, -gy, bunje, -jee, -jie, -jy *bunj'i*, (*slang*) *n.* india-rubber: a rubber or eraser. [Ety. dub.]

bungle *bung'gl*, *n.* anything clumsily done: a gross mismanagement. — *v.i.* to act in a clumsy manner. — *v.t.* to make or mend clumsily: to mismanage grossly: to make a failure of by want of skill. — *n.* **bung'ler.** — *adj.* **bung'ling** clumsy, awkward: unskilfully or ill done. — Also *n.* — *adv.* **bung'lingly.** [Ety. dub.; prob. onomatopoeic; cf. Sw. dial. *bangla*, to work ineffectually; Hindes Groome suggests Gypsy *bongo*, left, awkward.]

bunia. See **bunnia**.

bunion *bun'yən*, *n.* a lump or inflamed swelling on the first joint of the great toe. [Ety. unknown; poss. It. *bugnone*, a botch.]

bunje, -jee, -jie, -jy. See **bungie**.

bunk¹ *bungk*, *n.* a box or recess in a ship's cabin, a sleeping-berth anywhere: one of a pair of narrow beds one above the other (also **bunk bed**). — *v.i.* to occupy a bunk. — *n.* **bunk'er** a window-seat and chest (*Scot.*): a turf seat (*Scot.*): a large bin or chest, esp. for coals (*Scot.*): a slab beside a sink (*Scot.*): a compartment for fuel on shipboard: the fuel-oil carried by a ship for its own use: a sand-pit or sandy gap in turf, esp. as a hazard in a golf course. — *v.t.* to fuel: to play into a bunker. — *v.i.* to fuel. — *adj.* **bunk'ered** in a bunker: in difficulties. — **bunk'house** a building containing sleeping accommodation for labourers on a ranch *etc.* [Cf. O.N. *bunki*, Scand. *bunke*, heap.]

bunk² *bungk*, (*slang*) *n.* flight (esp. in phrase **to do a bunk**). — *v.i.* to flee: (with *off*) to do a bunk, to play truant.

bunk³. See **bunkum**.

bunker¹ *bung'kər*, *n.* an underground bombproof shelter. [Ger.]

bunker². See **bunk¹**.

bunko, bunco *bung'kō*, (*U.S.*) *n.* a form of confidence-trick by which a simple fellow is swindled or taken somewhere and robbed: — *pl.* **bunk'os, bunc'os.** — *v.t.* to rob or swindle in such a way. — **bunk'o-steer'er** that one of the swindling confederates who lures the victim.

bunkum *bung'kəm*, *n.* bombastic speechmaking intended for the newspapers rather than to persuade the audience: humbug: claptrap. — Also **bun'combe, bunk.** [From *Buncombe*, a county in North Carolina, whose member is said to have gone on talking in Congress, explaining apologetically that he was 'only talking for Buncombe'.]

bunnia, bunia *bun'i-ə*, *n.* a Hindu merchant. [Hind.]

bunny *bun'i*, *n.* a pet name for a rabbit. — **bunn'y-girl** (sometimes with *caps.*) a night-club hostess provocatively dressed in a brief, close-fitting costume with a white fluffy tail, and wearing rabbit-like ears. — **bunn'y-hug** a 20th-century American dance. — Also *v.i.* [Ety. unknown; cf. **bun³**.]

bunodont *bū'nō-dont*, *adj.* having tuberculate molars — opp. to *lophodont*. [Gr. *bounos*, a rounded hill, *odous*, *odontos*, a tooth.]

bunraku *boon-rä'koo*, *n.* a Japanese form of puppet theatre in which the puppets, usu. about 3 ft (1 metre) high, are each manipulated by 3 men who remain visible throughout the performance. [Jap.]

Bunsen (burner) *bun'sən* or *boon'sən* (*bûrn'ər*), *n.* a gas-burner in which a plentiful supply of air is caused to mingle with the gas before ignition, so that a smokeless flame of low luminosity but great heating power is the

result. [From the inventor R. W. *Bunsen* (1811–99), a German chemist.]

bunt¹ *bunt*, *n.* stink-brand, a disease of wheat: the fungus (*Tilletia*) that causes it. — *adjs.* **bunt'ed; bunt'y.** [Ety. unknown.]

bunt² *bunt*, *n.* the bagging part of a fishing-net, a sail, etc. — *v.i.* to belly, as a sail. — **bunt'line** a rope passing from the foot-rope of a square sail to prevent bellying in furling. [Ety. unknown.]

bunt³ *bunt*, *v.i.* to push with the horns, butt: to spring, rear: to block a ball with the bat (*baseball*; also *v.t.* and *n.*). — *n.* a push. — *n.* **bunt'ing** pushing: a boy's game, played with sticks and a small piece of wood: a strong timber, a stout prop.

bunter *bunt'ər*, *n.* a rag-picker: a low woman.

Bunter *boon'tər*, (*geol.*) *n.* the lowest division of the Trias. [From Ger. *bunt*, mottled.]

bunting¹ *bunt'ing*, *n.* a thin worsted stuff for ships' colours: flags, cloth decorations. [Ety. dub.]

bunting² *bunt'ing*, *n.* any of the small finch-like birds of the subfamily *Emberizinae* (fam. *Emberizidae* or perh. *Fringillidae*). [Orig. uncertain.]

bunting³. See **bunt³**.

bunya *bun'yə*, **bun'ya-bun'ya**, *ns.* an Australian tree, *Araucaria bidwillii*, the cones of which contain large edible seeds. [Aboriginal.]

bunyip *bun'yip*, *n.* a fabulous monster of Australian Aboriginal legend: an impostor. [Aboriginal.]

buonamano *bwō'na-mä'nō*, or **bonamano** *bo'na-*, (It.) *n.* a tip: — *pl.* **b(u)o'nama'ni** (*-nē*).

buona sera *bwō'na sā'ra*, (It.) good-evening.

buon giorno *bwōn jor'nō*, (It.) good-day.

buoy *boi* (in U.S. often *boo'ē* and in derivatives below, *boo'y-*), *n.* a floating secured mark, serving (by its shape, colour, light, sound, etc.) as a guide or as a warning. — *v.t.* to furnish or mark with buoys or marks: to keep afloat, bear up, or sustain (usu. with *up*): to raise, lift (usu. with *up*). — *v.i.* to rise. — *ns.* **buoy'age** a series of buoys or floating beacons to mark the course for vessels: the provision, or system, of buoys; **buoy'ance** (*rare*), **buoy'ancy** capacity for floating lightly on water or in the air: loss of weight owing to immersion in a fluid: lightness of spirit, cheerfulness (*fig.*). — *adj.* **buoy'ant** tending to float or to buoy up: light, cheerful, and elastic: of share prices, sales, profits, etc., tending to rise: of a firm, with rising profits, etc. — *n.* **buoy'antness.** [Du. *boei*, buoy, fetter, through Romance forms (Norman *boie*), from L. L. *boia*, a collar of leather.]

Buphaga *bū'fä-gə*, *n.* a small genus of African birds, nearly related to the starlings, feeding on the larvae of gadflies and the like which they find on the backs of cattle, camels, etc. — Also **beefeater** and **ox-pecker**. [Gr. *bous*, an ox, *phagein*, to eat.]

buplever *bū-plev'ər*, *n.* hare's-ear (*Bupleurum*). [Fr. *buplèvre* — L. *būpleurum* — Gr. *bous*, ox, *pleuron*, rib.]

Buprestis *bū-pres'tis*, *n.* a genus of beetles, typical of a large family, **Bupres'tidae**, those occurring in warmer countries having lively colour and metallic sheen — some known as golden beetles. [Gr. *bouprēstis*, a kind of poisonous beetle — *bous*, ox, *prēthein*, to swell.]

bur. See **burr¹,²**.

buran *boo-rän'*, *n.* a violent blizzard blowing from the north-east in Siberia and Central Asia. [Russ.]

Burberry *bûr'bər-i*, *n.* a kind of waterproof cloth: a raincoat made of this cloth. [From *Burberrys*, trademark of Burberrys Ltd., the manufacturers.]

burble¹ *bûrb'l*, *n.* a tangle. — *v.t.* to confuse. [Scot.; prob. conn. with O.Fr. *barbouiller*, to confound.]

burble² *bûrb'l*, *n.* a murmur. — *v.t.* and *v.i.* to murmur: to gurgle: to talk excitedly and rather incoherently (*coll.*). — *n.* **burb'ling** separation of the flow of air from the upper surface of a moving aerofoil. — **burble point, burbling point** the angle of attack at which the sharp drop in the ratio of lift to drag (an effect of burbling too near the leading edge) first appears. [Prob. onomatopoeic.]

burbot *bûr'bət, n.* a fresh-water fish, like the ling, with a longish barbel on its lower jaw. [Fr. *bourbotte, barbotte* — L.L. *borba,* mud, or L. *barba,* a beard.]

burd[1] *bûrd, (obs.) n.* a maiden: a lady. [O.E. *byrde,* well-born (or perh. *brȳd,* bride), prob. combined or confused with O.N. *byrthr,* O.E. *byrd,* birth, offspring.]

burd[2] *bûrd, (Scot.) n.* a bird: a young bird: a young animal of any kind: offspring, progeny: a term of endearment. — *n.* **burd'ie** (*dim.*). — **burd'-alane', bird'-alane'** the last remaining of a family. — *adj.* and *adv.* (*Morris* **bird**= **alone**) quite alone.

burdash *bûr-dash', n.* a fringed sash worn by gentlemen in the time of Anne and George I. [Origin unknown.]

burden[1] *bûr'dən (arch.* **burthen** *-dhən), n.* a load: weight: cargo: a ship's carrying capacity (still often **burthen**): that which is grievous, oppressive, or difficult to bear: an obligation: any restriction, limitation, or encumbrance affecting person or property (*Scots law*): a child in the womb (*obs.*): a birth: (in *pl.*) a boat's floorboards. — *v.t.* to load: to oppress: to encumber. — *adjs.* **bur'denous, bur'densome** heavy: oppressive. — **burden of proof** the obligation to prove one's contention. [O.E. *byrthen* — *beran,* to bear.]

burden[2] *bûr'dən, (arch.* **burthen** *-dhən), n.* bourdon or bass: part of a song repeated at the end of every stanza, refrain: the leading idea of anything. [Fr. *bourdon,* a humming tone in music — L.L. *burdō,* a drone bee; confused with **burden**[1].]

burden[3] *bûr'dən, n.* a pilgrim's staff. [See **bourdon**[2].]

burdock. See **burr**[1].

bureau *bū'rō, bū-rō', bü-rō', n.* a writing-table combined with chest of drawers: a room or office where such a table is used: a department or office for the transacting of business, such as collecting and supplying information: a government department: — *pl.* **bureaux, bureaus** (*-ōz*). [Fr. *bureau* — O.Fr. *burel,* russet cloth — L. *burrus,* red.]

bureaucracy *bū-rok'rə-si,* or *rōk', n.* a system of government by officials, responsible only to their departmental chiefs. — *ns.* **bur'eaucrat, bureau'cratist** one who practises or favours bureaucracy. — *adj.* **bureaucrat'ic.** — *adv.* **bureaucrat'ically.** — *n.* **bureaucratisā'tion, -z-.** — *v.t.* **bureau'cratise, -ize** to form into a bureaucracy: to make bureaucratic. [**bureau,** and Gr. *kratos,* power.]

bureau de change *bü-rō də shãzh,* (Fr.) an office where currency can be exchanged.

burette *bū-ret', n.* a graduated glass tube with a tap, for measuring liquids run off: an altar-cruet. [Fr.]

burg *bōorg, bûrg, n.* a fortress or a walled town (*hist.*): a town (*U.S. coll.; bûrg*). [West Gmc. *burg;* O.E. *burh.*]

burgage *bûr'gij, n.* a tenure in socage for a yearly rent: a tenure in Scotland in royal burghs under nominal service of watching. [L.L. *burgāgium,* from the root of **borough, burgh.**]

burganet, burgonet *bûr'gə-net, n.* a light 16th-century helmet with cheek-pieces. [Fr. *bourguignotte,* lit. Burgundian.]

burgee *bûr'jē, n.* a swallow-tailed flag or pennant: a kind of small coal for furnaces. [Origin unknown.]

burgeon, bourgeon *bûr'jən, v.i.* to put forth sprouts or buds: to grow. [Fr. *bourgeon,* a bud, shoot.]

burger *bûr'gər, (coll.) n.* short for **hamburger, cheeseburger,** etc. — **-burger** used as a compounding element as in *beefburger, cheeseburger,* to denote (a bread roll containing) a fried cake of meat, etc., made of, or accompanied by, the particular food mentioned.

burgess *bûr'jis, n.* a freeman or citizen of a borough: a member of a privileged class in a town: a member of parliament for a borough (*hist.*): a borough magistrate or town councillor (*hist.*). [O.Fr. *burgeis*].

burgh *bûr'ə,* spelling of **borough,** used for Scottish burghs, otherwise archaic. — *adj.* **burghal** (*bûrg'l*). — *n.* **burgher** (*bûrg'ər*) a freeman or citizen of a borough (burgh): a townsman: a Seceder who felt himself free to take the burgess oath (see **antiburgher**) (*Scot. eccles.*): a citizen of one of the South African Boer republics (*hist.*): in

Sri Lanka, a Eurasian of Dutch or Portuguese extraction, or a person of European race assimilated to the native population. — **burgh court** formerly in Scotland, an inferior court of summary jurisdiction presided over by a bailie. — **parliamentary burgh** one whose boundaries, as first fixed in 1832 for parliamentary representation, were adopted later for municipal purposes: a burgh which by itself or in combination elects a member of parliament: often applied to one that has ceased to do so; **police burgh** a burgh constituted by the sheriff for purposes of improvement and police; **royal burgh** a corporate body deriving its existence, constitution, and rights from a royal charter, actual or presumed to have existed. — **burgh of barony** a corporation under a feudal superior or baron, who sometimes nominated the magistrates; **burgh of regality** a burgh of barony enfranchised by crown charter, with regal or exclusive criminal jurisdiction within its territory. [See **borough.**]

burglar *bûrg'lər, n.* one who enters a building as a trespasser (before 1969, by night) to commit a felony, e.g. to steal. — Also (*obs.*) *v.i.* and *v.t.* — *adj.* **burglarious** (*-lā'ri-əs*). — *adv.* **burglār'iously.** — *v.t.* **burg'larise, -ize** (*U.S. coll.*). — *n.* **burg'lary.** — *v.i.* **burgle** (*bûr'gl;* a back-formation from **burglar**) to commit burglary. — *v.t.* to enter as a burglar. — **aggravated burglary** burglary involving the use of weapons or explosives. [Ety. dub.]

burgomaster *bûr'gō-mäs-tər, n.* the chief magistrate of an Austrian, Dutch, Flemish or German town. [Du. *burgemeester;* Ger. *Bürgermeister,* lit. borough-master.]

burgonet. See **burganet.**

burgoo *bûr-gōō', bûr'gōō, n.* a sailor's dish of boiled oatmeal with salt, butter, and sugar: a stew or thick soup for American picnics. [Derivation unknown.]

burgrave *bûr'grāv, n.* the governor or hereditary ruler of a town or castle. [Ger. *Burggraf.*]

burgundy *bûr'gən-di, n.* a French wine (generally red), made in *Burgundy:* a similar wine made elsewhere. — **Burgundy mixture** a fungicide composed of copper sulphate, sodium carbonate, and water; **Burgundy pitch** a resin prepared by melting and straining the exudation from Norway spruce (now got mainly elsewhere).

burhel. Same as **bharal.**

burial *ber'i-əl, n.* the act of burying: a tomb (*arch.*). — **bur'ial-ground** a ground set apart for burials: **bur'ial= place** a burial-ground: the place where anyone is buried; **burial society** an insurance society for providing the expenses of burial. [O.E. *byrgels,* a tomb; see **bury.**]

Buridan's ass *bū'ri-danz as, äs,* in the sophism doubtfully attributed to the French 14th-century schoolman Jean *Buridan,* an ass dying of starvation through inability to choose between two equidistant and equally desirable sources of food.

burin *būr'in, n.* a kind of chisel of tempered steel, used in copper engraving: the distinctive style of an engraver: a palaeolithic flint tool. — *n.* **bur'inist** an engraver. [Fr.; from root of **bore.**]

buriti *bōō-ri-tē', n.* the miriti palm. [Tupí.]

burk. See **berk.**

burke *bûrk, v.t.* to murder, esp. by stifling: hence (*fig.*) to put an end to quietly: to evade. [From *Burke,* an Edinburgh Irishman (hanged 1829), who committed murder in order to sell the bodies of his victims for dissection.]

burk(h)a *bōor'kə, n.* a loose garment, with veiled eyeholes, covering the whole body. [Urdu *burga'* — Ar.]

burl[1] *bûrl, n.* a small knot in thread: a knot in wood. — *v.t.* to pick knots, etc., from, in finishing cloth. — *n.* **bur'ler.** — *adj.* **bur'ly.** — **bur'ling-i'ron; bur'ling-machine'.** [O.Fr. *bourle,* tuft of wool.]

burl[2] *bûrl, (Austr.* and *N.Z. coll.) n.* an attempt, shot. [Prob. Scots. *birl, burl,* a twist, turn.]

burlap *bûr'lap, n.* a coarse canvas of jute or hemp for wrappings, or a lighter material, e.g. of flax, for wall-coverings, etc. — sometimes in *pl*. [Origin unknown.]

burlesque *bûr-lesk'*, *n*. ludicrous imitation: a piece of literature, of acting, or other performance that mocks its original by grotesque exaggeration or by combining the dignified with the low or the familiar: an entertainment combining often coarse jokes, strip-tease, songs, and dancing (*U.S.*): a playful or jocular composition (*mus*.). — *adj*. of the nature of burlesque: practising burlesque. — *v.t.* to mock by burlesque: to make a burlesque of. [It. *burlesco*; prob. from L.L. *burra*, a flock of wool, a trifle.]

burletta *bûr-let'ə*, *n*. a musical farce: comic opera. [It.; dim. of *burla*, a jest.]

burley. See **berley.**

burly[1] *bûr'li*, *adj*. big and sturdy. — *n*. **bur'liness.** [M.E. *borlich*; perh. the same as O.H.G. *burlīh*, high — *bōr*, a height.]

burly[2]. See **burl.**

Burmese *bûr'mēz*, *-mēz'*, *adj*. relating to *Burma* or its people or language. — *n*. a native of Burma: the language of Burma. — Also **Bur'man.** — **Burmese cat** a breed of short-haired domestic cat, similar to the Siamese, typically dark brown in colour, with golden eyes; **Burmese glass** a kind of unpolished semi-opaque coloured glass, popular in Victorian times.

burn[1] *bûrn*, (now chiefly *Scot*.) *n*. a small stream or brook. — **burn'side** the ground beside a burn. [O.E. *burna*, brook, spring; cf. Du. *born*, Ger. *Born*.]

burn[2] *bûrn*, *v.t.* to consume or injure by fire or great heat: to produce an effect of heat upon (as to bake pottery, calcine lime, scorch food, wither grass): to oxidise: to use (up), e.g. uranium, in a nuclear reactor (usu. with *up*): to corrode: to make by fire or analogous means. — *v.i.* to be burnt: to be on fire: to give out heat or light: to glow: to feel excess of heat: to be inflamed with passion: — *pa.t.* and *pa.p.* **burnt** or **burned.** — *n*. a hurt or mark due to burning: the firing of a rocket engine in order to produce thrust: a very fast ride, etc. on a motor-cycle, in a speed-boat, etc. — *ns*. **burn'er** one who burns: a fixture or part of a lamp, gas-jet or gas cooker from which a flame comes; **burn'ing** act of consuming by fire: conflagration: inflammation: a quantity burned at one time: controlled expenditure of rocket propellant for course adjustment purposes. — *adj*. very hot: scorching: ardent: excessive. — Also *adv*. — **burning bush** the emblem of the Church of Scotland and other Presbyterian churches with the motto, 'Nec tamen consumebatur', adopted from Exodus iii. 2, in memory of the unconquerable courage of the Covenanters under the cruel persecutions of the 17th century: applied to various plants, as dittany, whose volatile oil may catch fire in the air, some American species of spindle-tree with bright red fruits, artillery plant, etc.; **burn'ing-glass** a convex lens concentrating the sun's rays at its focus; **burn'ing-house** a kiln; **burn'ing-mirr'or** a concave mirror for producing heat by concentrating the sun's rays; **burning mountain** a volcano; **burn'ing-point** the temperature at which a volatile oil in an open vessel will take fire from a match held close to its surface; **burning question, issue** one keenly discussed; **burn-out** see **burn out** below; **burnt almonds** almonds in burnt sugar; **burnt'-cork'** charred cork used for blacking the face. — Also *v.t.* — **burnt cream** crème brûlée; **burnt'-ear** a smut in oats, wheat, etc.; **burn'-the-wind** (*Scot*.) a blacksmith; **burnt'-off'ering** something offered and burned upon an altar as a sacrifice; **burnt'-sienn'a** see **sienna**; **burn'-up** the using up of fuel in a nuclear reactor. — **burn a hole in one's pocket** said of money when one is eager to spend it; **burn blue** see **blue**; **burn daylight** (*Shak*.) to waste time; **burn down** to burn to the ground; **burned out** ineffective, exhausted; **burned up** (*U.S. slang*) angry; **burn in** to fix and render durable by intense heat: to imprint indelibly; **burn one's boats** to cut oneself off from all chance of retreat: to stake everything on success; **burn one's**

fingers, get one's fingers burnt to suffer as a result of interfering, embarking in speculations, etc.; **burn out** to destroy or drive out by burning: to burn till the fire dies down from want of fuel: to (cause to) become ineffective through overwork, exhaustion, etc. (*n*. **burn'-out**); **burn the candle at both ends** see **candle**; **burn the midnight oil** to study late into the night; **burn the water** to spear salmon by torchlight; **burn up** to consume completely by fire: to be burned completely: to increase in activity of burning: to make short or easy work of: to become or make angry (*U.S. slang*); **(money) to burn** (money) in great abundance. [O.E. the transitive weak verb *bærnan*, *bærnde*, *bærned*, has been confused with the intransitive strong verb *beornan*, *byrnan*, *barn*, *bornen*; cf. Ger. *brennen*, to burn.]

burnet *bûr'nit*, *adj*. dark brown (*obs*.). — *n*. a fine dark woollen cloth of the Middle Ages: the name of two closely related rosaceous plants, the great burnet (*Sanguisorba officinalis* or *Poterium officinale*), a meadow-plant, and common or salad burnet (*Sanguisorba minor*) found on the chalk and sometimes used in salads, cool-tankard, etc., both with close aggregates of brownish-purple flowers: the burnet moth. — **burnet moth** a moth of the Zygaenidae, esp. of the genus *Arthrocera*, with red-spotted or red-streaked fore-wings; **burnet(-leaved) rose** a wild rose (*Rosa spinosissima*) with leaves like burnet, the Scotch rose; **burnet saxifrage** a plant (*Pimpinella saxifraga*) neither burnet-coloured nor a saxifrage but a green umbellifer akin to anise, with burnet-like leaves. [O.Fr. *burnete*, *brunette*; see **brunette**.]

burnettise, -ize *bûr'nit-īz*, *v.t.* to treat with Burnett's fluid, a solution of zinc chloride, a preservative for timber, etc., against dry-rot and insects, introduced by Sir William *Burnett* (1779–1861).

burnish *bûrn'ish*, *v.t.* to polish: to make bright by rubbing. — *n*. polish: lustre. — *ns*. **burn'isher** an instrument employed in burnishing: one who burnishes; **burn'ishing; burn'ishment.** [Fr. *brunir*, *bruniss-*, to burnish — *brun*, brown.]

burnous *bûr-nōōs'*, **burnouse** *-nōōz'*, *ns*. a mantle with a hood much worn by the Arabs. [Fr., — Ar. *burnus*.]

Burnsian *bûrnz'i-ən*, *adj*. pertaining to Robert *Burns* (1759–96), the Scottish poet. — *n*. a student or admirer of Burns. — *n*. **Burns'ite** a devotee of Burns.

burnt *pa.t.* and *pa.p.* of **burn**[2]. — Also *adj*.

buroo *bə-rōō'* (*Scot.*and *Ir.*) *n*. the office at which people receive unemployment benefit: unemployment benefit. — Also **broo** (*brōō*). — **on the buroo** unemployed and receiving unemployment benefit. [*bureau*.]

burp *bûrp*, *v.i.* to belch (*coll.*). — Also *n*. — *v.t.* to rub or pat a baby's back after feeding to cause it to belch. [Imit.]

burqa *bûr'kə*. Same as **burk(h)a.**

burr[1], **bur** *bûr*, *n*. the prickly seed-case or head of certain plants, which sticks to clothes or animals: any impediment or inconvenient adherent: any lump, ridge, etc., more or less sharp, an excrescence on a tree, or markings representing it in wood (as in **burr'-wal'nut**): a knot in thread: a knob at the base of a deer's horn: the rough edge to a line made by an engraving tool, which, when the plate is inked, gives a further quality to the line: waste raw silk: the sweetbread or pancreas: club-moss (*Scot.*): the name for various tools and appliances, as the triangular chisel for clearing the corners of mortises, etc.: the blank driven out of a piece of sheet-metal by a punch: burrstone: a partly vitrified brick. — *adj*. **burr'y.** — **bur'dock** a composite plant (*Arctium lappa*) with hooked involucral bracts and docklike leaves: any species of *Xanthium*; **bur'marigold** any plant of the composite genus *Bidens*, with barbed pappus: a species of *Xanthium*; **bur'-reed** a reedlike genus (*Sparganium*) of water-plants with globular flower-heads; **burrstone** see **buhrstone**; **bur'this'tle** spear-thistle; **bur'weed** various burry plants as burdock, bur-reed, clot-bur (*Xanthium*), etc. — **burr in the throat** something seeming to stick in the throat, producing a choking sensation. [Cog. with Dan. *borre*, a bur.]

burr[2], **bur** *bûr, n.* the rough sound of *r* pronounced in the throat, as by many Northumberland people. — *v.i.* to whisper hoarsely, to murmur. [Usually associated with **burr**[1] but perh. imit.]

burramundi *bur-ə-mun'di,* an obs. variant of **barramunda.**

burra sahib *bur'ə sä'ib,* in India, a title of respect for the head of a family, a superior officer, etc. [Hind. *bara,* great, and **sahib.**]

burrel[1] *bur'əl, n.* a coarse russet cloth of mediaeval times. [See **bureau.**]

burrel[2], **burrell, burrhel.** Same as **bharal.**

burro *boor'ō, n.* a donkey: — *pl.* **burr'os.** [Sp.]

burrow *bur'ō, n.* a hole in the ground dug esp. by certain animals for shelter or defence: a passage, hole, or gallery dug or eaten through wood, stone, etc.: refuge. — *v.i.* to make holes underground as rabbits: to work one's way through earth, etc.: to dwell in a concealed place. — *v.t.* to make a burrow in: to make by burrowing. — **burr'ow-duck** the shelduck or bergander; **burr'owing-owl** a small long-legged diurnal American owl nesting in burrows. [Prob. a variant of **borough** — O.E. *beorgan,* to protect.]

burrowstown *bur'əs-toon,* (*Scot.*) *n.* a town that is a burgh. [**burgh.**]

bursa *bûr'sə, n.* a pouch or sac, esp. one containing viscid lubricating fluid at points of friction (*zool.*): — *pl.* **bur'sae** (-sē). — *adj.* **bur'sal** relating to a bursa: fiscal. — *n.* **bur'sar** one who keeps the purse, a treasurer: in Scotland, a student or pupil maintained at a university or school by funds derived from endowment. — *adj.* **bursarial** (-sā'ri-əl). — *ns.* **bur'sarship** the office of a bursar; **bur'sary** the treasury of a college or monastery: in Scotland, a scholarship; **burse** a purse: an obsolete form of **bourse.** — *adjs.* **bursic'ulate** resembling a small pouch; **burs'iform** pouch-shaped. — *n.* **bursī'tis** inflammation of a bursa. [L.L. *bursa,* a purse — Gr. *byrsa,* skin or leather.]

Bursch *boorsh, n.* a German student: — *pl.* **Bursch'en.** — *ns.* **Bursch'enism; Bursch'enschaft** (-shäft) a students' association. [Ger. *Bursch,* a companion, student.]

burse. See **bursa.**

Bursera *bûr'sər-ə, n.* a tropical American genus of trees yielding elemi and timber, giving name to the family **Bursera'ceae,** akin to the rue family. — *adj.* **bursera'ceous.** [Joachim *Burser* (1593–1689), German botanist.]

bursiculate, bursiform, bursitis. See **bursa.**

burst *bûrst, v.t.* to break into pieces: to break open or cause to give way suddenly or by violence: to make by bursting: to tear apart the perforated sheets of continuous stationery. — *v.i.* to fly open or in pieces, esp. owing to a force from within: to give way suddenly: to break forth or away: to force a way: to break suddenly into being, or into some condition, activity, or expression of feeling: — *pa.t.* and *pa.p.* **burst,** *arch., dial.,* and *U.S.* **burst'ed, bust'ed;** *obs. pa.p.* **burst'en.** — *n.* an act, occasion, or result of bursting: a sudden outbreak: a hard gallop: a spurt: a drunken bout: a measure of the strength of an envelope. — *n.* **burst'er** a person or thing that bursts: specif., a machine which bursts continuous stationery. — **burst binding** a unsewn book binding in which the gathered sections are perforated at the fold and glue is made to penetrate through the perforations; **burst'-up** a complete break: disruption: commotion: collapse: failure. [O.E. *berstan;* Ger. *bersten;* see also **bust**[2].]

burthen *bûr'dhən, n.* and *v.t.* See **burden**[1,2].

burton *bûr'tn, n.* a tackle of two or three blocks.

Burton *bûr'tn, n.* a town of Staffordshire famous for its beer: a drink. — **gone for a Burton** (*airmen's slang*) drowned, dead: absent: missing: no longer in existence.

bury *ber'i, bûr'i, v.t.* to hide in the ground: to cover: to consign to the grave, the sea, etc., as a dead body: to hide or blot out of remembrance: — *pr.p.* **bur'ying;** *pa.t., pa.p.* **bur'ied.** — *n.* (*dial.*) a burrow. — **bur'ying-**

beetle a beetle (*Necrophorus* or kindred genus) that buries small animals as food for its larvae; **bur'ying-ground** ground set apart for burying the dead: a graveyard; **bur'ying-place.** — **bury the hatchet** to renounce enmity. [O.E. *byrgan,* to bury; Ger. *bergen,* to hide.]

bus (*rare* **'bus;** *obs.* **buss**) *bus, n.* an omnibus: car, aeroplane, etc. (*slang*): a number of conductors forming a circuit or route along which data or power may be transmitted (also **highway** or **trunk;** *comput.*): — *pl.* **bus'es, buss'es.** — *v.t.* to transport by bus. — *v.i.* to go by bus: in a restaurant, etc., to clear dirty dishes from tables, replenish supplies of needed items, and otherwise assist the waiting staff. — *ns.* **bus'ing, buss'ing** the transporting by bus of people from one district to another, esp. children to school, to achieve a more even racial, etc. balance. — **bus'-bar** an electric conductor connecting with a number of circuits: **bus'boy, bus'girl** (*U.S.*) an assistant waiter or waitress, one who busses; **bus'-fare; bus'man** the driver or conductor of a bus; **bus'-stop** a halting-place for a bus, for passengers to board it or alight: the post or sign usu. marking such a place. — **busman's holiday** a holiday spent in activities similar to one's work; **miss the bus** to lose an opportunity. [Short for **omnibus.**]

busby *buz'bi, n.* a fur hat with a bag hanging on its right side, worn esp. by hussars. [Prob. Hung.]

bush[1] *boosh, n.* a woody plant in size between a tree and an undershrub: a shrub thick with branches: anything of bushy tuft-like shape: forest: wild uncultivated country (even though treeless): such country covered with bushes: the wild: a bunch of ivy hung up as a tavern sign: a tavern. — *v.i.* to grow thick or bushy. — *v.t.* to set bushes about: to support with bushes: to cover (seeds) by means of the bush-harrow. — *adj.* **bushed** lost in the bush: bewildered (*slang*): tired (*slang*). — *n.* **bush'iness.** — *adj.* **bush'y** full of or like bushes: thick and spreading. — *n.* (*Austr.* and *N.Z. coll.*) one who lives in the country as distinct from the town. — **bush'-baby** a small South African lemur (*Galago maholi*) also called **night-ape; bush'-buck** a small S. African antelope, or any other of the same genus (Tragelaphus). — Also (Du.) **boschbok** (*bos'-bok*), (Afrik.) **bosbok** (*bos'bok*); **bush'-cat** the serval; **bush'craft** practical knowledge of the bush and skill in its ways; **bush'fire** (esp. *Austr.* and *N.Z.*) a fire in forest or scrub; **bush'-fly** a small black Australian fly (*musca vetustissima* or other species) swarms of which are a great nuisance to people and animals in the bush; **bush'-fruit** a fruit growing on a bush, as gooseberry, raspberry; **bush'-harr'ow** a light harrow for covering grass-seeds, formed of a barred frame interwoven with bushes or branches; **bush'-lawyer** a prickly trailing plant (*Rubus cissoides*): one who feigns a knowledge of law (*Austr.*); **bush'man** a settler, or traveller, in uncleared land: a woodsman: (with *cap.*) one of a now almost extinct nomadic, short-statured, yellowish-brown, aboriginal race of huntsmen in S. Africa (Cape. Du. *Bos(jes)man*). — Also *adj.* — **bush'manship** bushcraft; **bush'master** a venomous South American snake (*Lachesis muta*); **bush pilot** an airline pilot operating over uninhabited country; **bush'ranger** in Australia, a lawless person, often an escaped criminal, who takes to the bush and lives by robbery: a woodsman: a rapacious person (*fig.*); **bush'-rope** a liana; **bush shirt, jacket** a cotton, etc., garment with four patch pockets and a belt; **bush'-shrike** the name of a number of birds belonging to certain genera of an African subfamily of the shrikes, applied collectively to the subfamily as a whole: applied by some, esp. formerly to birds of a sub-family of Formicariidae (ant-thrushes); **bush sickness** in Australia and New Zealand, a disease of cattle, sheep and goats, caused by a mineral deficiency in pastures; **bush telegraph** (*facet.*) the rapid transmission of news among primitive communities by drum-beating, etc.: gossip, rumour; **bush'-tit** a small long-tailed titmouse of West America, building a large hanging nest; **bush'veld, bosch'veld** (*bos'*) veld made up largely of woodland. — *v.i.* **bush'walk** to walk or hike through the bush as a leisure activity (*Austr.*) — Also *n.* — **bush'walker; bush'walking.** — *v.i.* **bush'whack** to range through the bush: to fight in guerrilla warfare: to travel through woods, esp. by clearing a way to do so. — *v.t.* to ambush. — **bush'whacker** a guerrilla fighter: a country lout: a short heavy scythe for cutting bushes: one who clears a way in the bush: a sniper; **bush'whacking** the habits or practice of bushwhackers: the process of forcing a way for a boat by pulling at the bushes overhanging a stream. — **beat about the bush** to go round about anything, to evade coming to the point; **go bush** (*Austr.*) to go off into the bush: to leave town or one's usual haunts: to abandon civilised life. [M.E. *busk, busch* — O.N. *buskr*, from a Gmc. root found in Ger. *Busch*, L.L. *boscus*, Fr. *bois*. Some uses are from the corresponding Du. *bosch*.]

bush² *bŏŏsh, n.* the metal box or lining of any cylinder in which an axle works. — *v.t.* to furnish with a bush. — **bush'-met'al** hard brass, gunmetal, a composition of copper and tin, used for journals, bearings, etc. [Du. *bus* — L. *buxus*, box-tree.]

bushel¹ *bŏŏsh'əl, n.* a dry measure of 8 gallons, no longer official, for grain, fruit, etc. (*imperial bushel*, 2219·36 cub. in.): a container for this quantity. — **hide one's light under a bushel** to keep quiet about or conceal one's talents or abilities. [O.Fr. *boissiel* — root of **box²**.]

bushel² *bŏŏsh'əl*, (*U.S.*) *v.t.* and *v.i.* to mend or alter, as men's clothes. — *ns.* **bush'eller; bush'elling.** — **bush'el= man, -woman.** [Cf. Ger. *bosseln*.]

bushido *bŏŏ'shi-dō, n.* a Japanese code of chivalry. [Jap. *bushi*, warrior, *dō*, doctrine.]

business *biz'nis, n.* employment: trade, profession, or occupation: a task or errand incumbent or undertaken: matter requiring attention: dealings, commercial activity: a commercial or industrial concern: one's concerns or affairs: a matter or affair: action as distinguished from dialogue (*theat.*): a thing, used quite indefinitely (*coll.*): (*biz'i-nis*, also written **busyness**) state of being busy. — Also *adj.* (*biz'nis*). — *adj.* **bus'iness-like** methodical, systematic, practical. — **business card** a card carried by business people, with their name and designation, and the name, address, telephone number and description, etc. of their firm; **business cycle** (*U.S.*) trade cycle; **business end** (*coll.*) the end or part of something that actually functions or does the work (as *business end of a fork*); **bus'inessman, bus'inesswoman** one engaged in commercial transactions. — **do the business for** to settle, make an end of: to ruin; **genteel business** (*theat.*) such parts as require good dressing; **like nobody's business** (*coll.*) keenly, energetically; **make it one's business** to undertake to accomplish something or see it done; **man of business** a law agent who conducts one's affairs; **mean business** to be in earnest; **mind one's own business** to confine oneself to one's own affairs; **place of business** the ordinary place for the practice of one's vocation; **send someone about his business** to dismiss someone unceremoniously. [**busy.**]

busk¹ *busk, v.t.* or *v.i.* to prepare: to dress. [O.N. *būa*, to prepare, and *-sk*, contr. of *sik*, the refl. pron. self.]

busk² *busk, n.* the piece of bone, wood, or steel in the front of a woman's stays: a corset. — *adj.* **busked.** [Fr. *busc.*]

busk³ *busk, v.i.* to cruise along a shore, to beat about (*naut.*): to seek: to play as a wandering musician or actor. — *ns.* **busk'er** a wandering musician or actor; **busk'ing.** [Prob. Sp. *buscar*, to seek.]

busket *busk'ət,* (*Spens.*) *n.* a little bush. [See **bush.**]

buskin *busk'in, n.* a high thick-soled boot worn in ancient times by actors in tragedy. — *adj.* **busk'ined** wearing buskins: tragic. [Ety. uncertain; cf. O.Fr. *brousequin*; Du. *brooseken*; Sp. *borcegui*.]

busky *busk'i,* (*Shak.*) *adj.* Same as **bosky.**

buss¹ *bus, n.* a rude or playful kiss, a smack. — *v.t.* to kiss, esp. in a rude or playful manner. [Cf. Ger. dial. *buss*, W. and Gael. *bus*, L. *bāsium*.]

buss² *bus, n.* a small two-masted Dutch vessel, used in the herring and mackerel fisheries. [O.Fr. *busse*, L.L. *bussa*; cf. Ger. *Büse*.]

buss³. See **bus.**

bussu *bŏŏs'ŏŏ, n.* a tropical American palm (*Manicaria*) with gigantic leaves and netted spathe that serves as cloth. [Port. from Tupí *bussú.*]

bust¹ *bust, n.* a sculpture representing the head and breast of a person: the upper front part of the human body, esp. a woman's. — *adjs.* **bust'ed** breasted: adorned with busts; **bust'y** (*coll.*) of a woman, having a large bust. [Fr. *buste*; It. and Sp. *busto.*]

bust² *bust,* (*coll.*) *v.t.* and *v.i.* to break, shatter: to make or become bankrupt. — *v.t.* to arrest: — *pa.t.* and *pa.p.* **bust'ed, bust.** — *n.* a drinking bout: a police raid (*slang*). — *adj.* ruined, penniless. — *n.* **bust'er** (*coll.*) something large: a frolic: a roisterer: a horsebreaker: a form of address to a man or boy: a strong south wind (*Austr.*): someone or something that destroys or shatters, esp. in combination, as *blockbuster.* — *n.* **bust'ing** (esp. in combination). — **busted flush** see **flush⁴; bust'-up** a quarrel or disruption: a disturbance or brawl. — **go bust** to become bankrupt. [Orig. a coll. form of **burst.**]

bustard *bust'ərd, n.* any bird of the genus *Otis*, sometimes made the type of a large family, usually ranked with cranes. [Fr. *bistard* — L. *avis tarda*, slow bird (a misnomer).]

bustee *bus'tē, n.* in India, a settlement or a collection of huts. [Hind. *bastī.*]

bustier *bü-styā,* (Fr.) *n.* a strapless brassière or bodice.

bustle¹ *bus'l, v.i.* to busy oneself noisily or fussily: to be full of or busy with (with *with*). — *n.* hurried activity: stir: tumult. — *n.* **bust'ler.** [M.E. *bustelen*, of doubtful etymology.]

bustle² *bus'l, n.* a frame or pad for causing a skirt to hang back from the hips: a car boot (*coll.*). [Origin doubtful.]

busy *biz'i, adj.* fully employed: active: diligent: meddling: fussily active: (of a telephone line) engaged: (of picture or design) unrestful because having too much detail. — *n.* (*slang*) a detective. — *v.t.* to make busy: to occupy: — *pr.p.* **bus'ying**; *pa.t.* and *pa.p.* **bus'ied.** — *adv.* **bus'ily.** — *n.* **bus'yness** the state of being busy (see **business**). — **bus'ybody** one who meddles in others' affairs: mirror(s) at a window arranged to show passers-by; **busy Lizzie** a plant of the *Impatiens* genus. [O.E. *bysig.*]

but¹ *but, prep.* without (*obs.*): except: in or toward the outer room of (*Scot.*). — *conj.* on the other hand: in contrast: nevertheless: unless, if not: otherwise than (that): introducing emphasis, as in *nobody, but nobody, must go*: except that (merging in *prep.*): that not (developing into a negative *rel. pron.*): than, sooner than (*arch.*). — *adv.* only: in or to the outer room, outwards (*Scot.*). — *n.* an objection (as in Mrs Centlivre's 'But me no buts'): an outer room (*Scot.*). — Also *adj.* — *v.t.* to put forward as an objection. — **anything but** certainly not; **but and** (*obs.*) and also; **but and ben** see **ben²; but for, but that** were it not for, or that; **but if** (*obs.*) unless: sometimes equivalent to **but** alone in various senses. [O.E. *be-ūtan, būtan*, without — *be*, by, and *ūtan*, out — near, and yet outside.]

but² *but, n.* Another spelling of **butt²,³,⁴.**

butadiene *bū-tə-dī'ēn, n.* (L. *dis*, twice) a hydrocarbon, C_4H_6, used in making synthetic rubber. — *ns.* **bu'tane** a hydrocarbon of the methane series, C_4H_{10}, widely used as a fuel (see **bottle-gas**); **bu'tanol** (*-tə-nol*) the name of two of the isomers of butyl alcohol. [**butyl.**]

Butazolidin ® *bū-ta-zol'i-din, n.* phenylbutazone. — sometimes shortened to **bute** (*būt; slang*; also with *cap.*).

butch *bŏŏch, n.* a very short haircut for men or women: an aggressively tough man (*slang*): the 'male' partner in a homosexual or lesbian relationship (*slang*). — *adj.*

tough: aggressively masculine. [Amer. boy's nick-name.]

butcher *bŏŏch′ər, n.* one whose business is to slaughter animals for food, or who deals in their flesh: one who delights in bloody deeds: a sweet-seller on a railway train (*U.S.*). — *v.t.* to slaughter and prepare (animals) for sale as food: to put to a bloody death, to kill cruelly: to spoil, as a bad actor or the like (*fig.*). — *ns.* **butch′ering, butch′ing** (back-formation) the act of killing for food, or cruelly. — *adj.* **butch′erly** butcher-like, cruel, murderous (formerly also *adv.*). — *ns.* **butch′er's** (orig. **butcher's hook;** *Cockney rhyming slang*) a look; **butch′ery** great or cruel slaughter: a slaughterhouse or shambles. — **butch′er-bird** a shrike: in Australia, a bird of the genus *Cracticus;* **butch′er('s) meat** the flesh of animals slaughtered by butchers, as distinguished from fish, fowls and game; **butch′er's-broom** an evergreen shrub (*Ruscus aculeatus*) of the lily family, with phyllodes, formerly used by butchers for sweeping their blocks. [O.Fr. *bochier, bouchier,* one who kills he-goats — *boc,* a he-goat; **buck.**]

bute, Bute. See **Butazolidin.**

Butea *būt′i-ə, n.* a genus of papiliaceous trees, including the dhak, yielding Bengal kino. [Named after Lord *Bute,* prime minister and botanist.]

but-end. Same as **butt-end** under **butt**[4].

butene *bū′tēn, n.* butylene.

butler *but′lər, n.* a servant who has charge of liquors, plate, etc.: an officer in a royal household. — *v.i.* to act as butler. — Also **butt′le** (back-formation). — *ns.* **but′lerage** duty on imported wine once paid to the king's butler (*obs.*): the office of butler (*obs.*): a butler's department; **but′lership; but′lery** the butler's pantry. [Norm. Fr. *butuiller* — L.L. *buticulārius.* See **bottle.**]

butment. Same as **abutment.**

butt[1] *but, v.t.* to strike with the head, as a goat, etc. — *v.i.* to strike with the head (also with *at, against*): to go or drive head first. — *n.* a push or blow with the head. — *n.* **butt′er** an animal that butts. — **butt in** to interfere, thrust oneself in. [O.Fr. *boter,* to push, strike.]

butt[2] *but, n.* a large cask: a wine butt = 126 gallons, a beer and sherry butt = 108 gallons. [Cf. Fr. *botte,* Sp. *bota,* L.L. *butta.*]

butt[3] *but, n.* a mark or mound for archery practice: a mound behind targets: one who is made an object of ridicule: a hiding place for grouse-shooters. — **butt′-shaft** (*Shak.*) a shaft for shooting at butts with. [Fr. *but,* goal.]

butt[4] *but, n.* the thick and heavy end: the stump: a tree-trunk: the hinder part of a hide: thick leather: the fag-end of a cigar or cigarette: the buttocks (*U.S. coll.*): the wooden, etc. handle or steadying shoulder-part of a pistol or rifle: a remnant: the square end of a plank meeting another. — *v.i.* to abut: to meet end to end. — **butted joint** a joint formed between the squared ends of the two jointing pieces, which come together but do not overlap; **butt′-end; butt welding** welding the seam formed by joining two butt-ends. [Ety. dub.; poss. connected with **butt**[3] and **abut.**]

butt[5] *but, n.* a flatfish of various kinds. [Poss. connected with root of **butt**[4]; cf. Sw. *butta,* turbot, Du. *bot,* Ger. *Butt,* flounder; **halibut, turbot.**]

butte *būt, n.* a conspicuous and isolated hill, cliff-sided, often flat-topped, in the western United States. [Fr.]

butter[1] *but′ər, n.* an oily substance obtained from cream by churning: extended to various substances resembling or containing it: an old chemical name for certain oily chlorides (butter of *antimony,* of *tin,* etc.): flattery. — *v.t.* to spread over with butter, mortar, or other soft substance: to flatter (usu. with *up*): to fail to catch, let slip (*arch.*). — *n.* **butt′erine** (*-ēn*) a margarine made partly from milk. — *adj.* **butt′ery** like butter: smeared with butter or the like. — **butt′er-bake** (*Scot.*), **-bis′cuit** a cake like a biscuit but softer; **butt′er-bean′** an American bean akin to the French bean; **butt′er-bird** in Jamaica, the bobolink; **butt′er-boat** a table vessel for

melted butter; **butt′er-box** a box for butter: an old nickname for a Dutchman; **butt′erbur′, butt′erdock′** a plant akin to coltsfoot with knobbed masses of flower heads and great rhubarb-like leaves; **butt′er-cloth′, -mus′lin** a loose-woven cloth suitable for wrapping butter; **butt′er-cool′er** a dish for keeping butter in water at table; **butt′ercup** a crowfoot (*Ranunculus*), esp. of one of those species that have golden-yellow cup-shaped flowers; **butt′er-dish, -plate** a dish or plate for holding butter at table; **buttered eggs** (*arch.*) scrambled eggs; **butt′er-fat′** the fat contained in butter, chiefly glycerides of palmitic and oleic acids. — *adj.* **butt′er-fingered** prone to let things slip. — **butt′er-fingers** (*sing.*) one who lets a ball, etc., he ought to catch slip through his fingers; **butt′er-fish** a name for various slimy fishes, notably the gunnel; **butt′erfly** a general name for any of the daylight Lepidoptera, roughly distinguished from moths by their clubbed antennae: a gay, flighty person (*fig.*): butterfly breast-stroke: — *pl.* **butt′erflies.** — *adj.* light, flighty, like a butterfly. — **butt′erfly-bow′** a bow whose loops and ends are spread like butterfly's wings; **butterfly (breast-)stroke** a swimming-stroke performed on the breast, the arms working simultaneously with an overarm action; **butt′erfly-fish′** a blenny with an eye-spot on the dorsal fin: any fish of the family Chaetodontidae; **butt′erfly-flower** one adapted for pollination by butterflies; **butt′erfly-or′chis, -or′chid** an orchid (of various kinds) with flowers resembling a butterfly; **butt′erfly-screw′, -nut′** a screw or nut, turned by winged finger-grips; **butterfly valve** a disc-shaped valve in a carburettor, etc.: a valve consisting of two hinged plates; **butt′erfly-weed′** pleurisy-root; **butterhead lettuce** a kind of soft-leaved lettuce; **butt′er-knife** a blunt knife for taking butter from a butter dish; **butt′er-milk** the milk that remains after the butter has been separated from the cream by churning; **butter-muslin** see **butter-cloth** above; **butt′ernut** the oily nut of the North American white walnut: the tree itself: its light-coloured close-grained wood: the souari-nut of Guiana; **butter oil** a dairy product consisting almost entirely of milk fat; **butt′er-paper** a translucent paper suitable for wrapping butter; **butt′er-pat** a pat of butter: a wooden instrument for working butter into shape; **butt′er-print′** a stamp for shaping butter: a child (*old slang*); **butt′erscotch** a kind of toffee containing much butter; **butt′er-tree** a name for many trees that yield a buttery substance, notably of the genera *Bassia, Butyrospermum, Caryocar, Pentadesma;* **butt′er-wife, butt′er-wom′an** a woman who makes and sells butter; **butt′erwort** any species of Pinguicula, a genus of insectivorous bog-plants, family *Lentibulariaceae*) with glistening leaves. — **butterflies in the stomach** nervous tremors in the stomach; **butter up** to flatter. [O.E. *butere;* Ger. *Butter;* both from L. *būtȳrum* — Gr. *boutȳron,* app. — *bous,* ox, *tȳros,* cheese.]

butter[2]. See **butt**[1].

butter-bump *but′ər-bump, n.* the bittern. [See **bittern**[1] and **bump**[2].]

butterine. See **butter**[1].

buttery[1] *but′ər-i, n.* a storeroom, often in a college, for provisions, esp. liquors. — **butt′ery-bar′** the ledge for holding tankards in the buttery; **butt′ery-hatch′** a half-door over which provisions are handed from the buttery. [Fr. *bouteillerie,* lit. place for bottles; **butler, bottle.**]

buttery[2]. See **butter**[1].

buttle. See **butler.**

buttock *but′ək, n.* the rump or protuberant part of the body behind: a cut of meat from the buttock, e.g. silverside: in wrestling, a throw by use of the buttock. — *v.t.* to throw in this way. — **butt′ock-mail** (*Scot.*) the fine formerly exacted by the church in commutation of sitting on the stool of repentance. [Dim. of **butt**[4].]

button *but′n, n.* a knob or disc, used as a fastening, ornament, or badge: a knob, e.g. that at the end of a foil, that for winding a watch, that to which a violin tailpiece is looped: a bud: the head of an unexpanded mushroom (also **button mushroom**): a pimple: the knob of an electric bell, etc.: anything of small value: a person who acts as a decoy: (in *pl.*) sheep's dung. — *adj.* like a button, used e.g. of small varieties of vegetables, blooms, etc. of a compact, globular shape. — *v.t.* to fasten by means of buttons: to close up tightly. — *v.i.* to admit of fastening with buttons. — *n.sing.* **butt'ons** a page in a hotel, etc. (also **boy in buttons**). — *adj.* **butt'ony** set with buttons: like a button. — **butt'on=bush** a North American shrub (*Cephalanthus*) of the madder family, having globular flower-heads; **button chrysanthemum** a kind of chrysanthemum with small round flowers. — *adj.* **butt'oned-up** (*slang*) uncommunicative. — **butt'onhole** the slit through which a button is passed: a flower or flowers for wearing in the buttonhole of a lapel. — *v.t.* to make buttonholes in: to work with a stitch suitable for defence of edges (*buttonhole-stitch*): to detain in talk (orig. **butt'onhold**). — **butt'on-hook** a hook for pulling buttons through buttonholes in boots, gloves, etc.; **button mushroom** see above; **butt'on-wood** a small tropical Atlantic coast evergreen tree (*Conocarpus erecta*) of the myrobalan family: a plane-tree (*U.S.*) — also **butt'on-ball**; **button scurvy** yaws; **butt'on-through** a woman's dress or skirt buttoning in front from top to bottom. — **button up!**, **button your lip!** (*coll.*) be quiet!; **buttoned up** (*slang*) successfully fixed up: safe in hand: ready for action: see also **buttoned-up** above; **in his buttons** a conjectural reading in *Merry Wives* where the quarto has *betmes*, prob. a misprint for *talons*; **press the button** to launch, or give the command for launching, nuclear weapons against an enemy target. [Fr. *bouton*, any small projection, from *bouter*, to push.]

buttress *but'rəs*, *n.* a projecting support built on to the outside of a wall: any support or prop. — *v.t.* to prop or support, as by a buttress. — **butt'ress-root** a root, often adventitious, that helps to keep a plant upright. [App. O.Fr. *bouterez* — *bouter*, to push, bear against.]

butty[1] *but'i*, (*dial.*) *n.* a chum, comrade, work-fellow, partner, esp. in a coal-mine (also **butt'yman**): one who takes a contract for work in a coal-mine: a barge towed by another. — **butt'y-collier**; **butt'y-gang.** [App. dim. of dial. *butt*, a companion.]

butty[2] *but'i*, (*dial.*) *n.* a sandwich, snack.

butyric *bū-tir'ik*, *adj.* pertaining to or derived from butter. — *ns.* **bū'tyl** (*-til*, *U.S. -təl*; Gr. *hȳlē*, matter) an alcohol radical C_4H_9; **bū'tylene** (also **bū'tene**) an olefine hydrocarbon (C_4H_8) in three isomers. — *adj.* **būtyrā'ceous** buttery, containing butter. — *n.* **bū'tyrate** a salt of butyric acid. — **butyl alcohol** any of four isomeric alcohols of formula $C_4H_9 \cdot OH$ used as solvents, etc.; **butyric acid** a volatile fatty acid ($C_3H_7 \cdot COOH$), smelling like rancid butter. [See **butter**[1].]

buvette *bü-vet*, (Fr.) *n.* a small road-side café selling drinks and snacks.

buxom *buks'əm*, *adj.* yielding, elastic: gay, lively, jolly: plump and comely. — *n.* **bux'omness.** [M.E. *buhsum*, pliable, obedient — O.E. *būgan*, to bow, yield, suff. *-some*.]

buy *bī*, *v.t.* to purchase for money: to bribe: to obtain in exchange for something: to accept, believe (*slang*): — *pr.p.* **buy'ing**; *pa.t.* and *pa.p.* **bought** (*böt*), *arch. pa.p.* **bought'en.** — *n.* something purchased. — *adj.* and *n.* **buy'able.** — *n.* **buy'er** one who buys: one employed to buy goods. — **buyers'** (or **buyer's**) **market** one in which buyers rule the price, supply exceeding demand. — **a good buy** (*coll.*) a wise purchase, a bargain; **buy and sell** (*Shak.*) to traffic in; **buy in** to collect a stock of by buying: to buy back for the owner at an auction (*n.* **buy'-in**); **buy into** to pay for a share or interest in; **buy off** to buy exemption or release for: to get rid of by paying; **buy out** to dispossess or take over possession from by payment (*n.* **buy'-out**); **buy off**; **buy over** to win over by payment: to bribe; **buy up** to purchase the whole stock of; **have bought it** (*slang*) to have been

killed; **I'll buy that** I'll accept that explanation though it seems surprising. [O.E. *bycgan*, *bohte*, *boht*; Goth. *bugjan*.]

buzz[1] *buz*, *v.i.* to make a noise like that of insects' wings: to murmur: to move quickly (*slang*). — *v.t.* to utter with a buzzing sound: to whisper or spread secretly: to transmit by Morse over a telephone wire by means of a key: to make a telephone call to: to throw (*slang*): to fly very low over or very close to: to interfere with in flight by flying very near to (*aero.*). — *n.* the noise of bees and flies: a humming sound: a voiced hiss: a whispered report: a telephone call (*coll.*): a pleasant feeling, stimulation (*coll.*): enthusiasm (*coll.*): a craze, fad (*coll.*). — *n.* **buzz'er** one who buzzes: a whisperer or tell-tale (*Shak.*): an apparatus that makes a buzzing sound, as a hooter, a circular saw, or an electrical device for signalling, etc. — *n.* and *adj.* **buzz'ing.** — *adv.* **buzz'ingly.** — *adj.* **buzz'y.** — **buzz bomb** a flying bomb; **buzz'-saw** (*U.S.*) a circular saw; **buzz'-wig** a great bushy wig; **buzz word** (*coll.*) a well-established term in the jargon of a particular subject, science, etc., its use conveying the impression of specialised knowledge. — **buzz off** (*slang*) to go away. [From the sound.]

buzz[2] *buz*, *v.t.* to drain (a bottle) to the last drop of wine. [Orig. uncertain.]

buzzard[1] *buz'ərd*, *n.* a large bird of prey of the genus *Buteo*, despised by falconers: extended to some others, as the *honey-buzzard*, *turkey-buzzard*: a blockhead, coward or sluggard. [Fr. *busard*.]

buzzard[2] *buz'ərd*, *n.* a blundering insect, as a cockchafer or night-flying moth: an ignorant blunderer (often *blind buzzard*). — **buzz'ard-clock** (*dial.*), a cockchafer. [**buzz**[1].]

bwana *bwä'nä*, *n.* master: sir. [Swahili.]

bwazi. See **buaze.**

by[1] *bī*, *prep.* at the side of: near to: along a route passing through, via: past: in oaths, in the presence of, or with the witness of: through (denoting the agent, cause, means, etc.): to the extent of: in quantity measurable in terms of: in accordance with: in respect of: of time, not after: during (day, night, etc.): multiplied into, or combined with another dimension of: in succession to: (of horses, etc.) sired by: besides (*Scot.*): in comparison with (*Scot.*). — *conj.* by the time that (*arch.* and *Scot.*): than (*Scot.*). — *adv.* near: aside: away: past: in reserve. — *n.* and *adj.* see **bye**[1]. — *adv.* **by'-and-by'** see **by and by** below. — **by'-blow** a side blow: an illegitimate child; **by'catch** immature fish, etc. caught along with the desired catch; **by'-corner** an out-of-the-way place; **by'-drinking** (*Shak.*) drinking between meals; **by'-election** a parliamentary election for a seat during the sitting of parliament; **by'-end** a subsidiary aim; **by'-form** a subsidiary form: a form varying from the usual one; **by'going** the action of passing by (esp. in **in the by-going**, in passing). — *adj.* **by'gone** (*-gon*). — *n.pl.* **by'gones** past happenings or grievances: ornaments, household articles, etc., of former times which are not fine enough, or not old enough, to be valued as antiques (also in *sing.*). — **by'-lane** a side lane or passage out of the common road; **bylaw**, **bye-law** see separate entry; **by'line** a line at the head of a newspaper or magazine article telling by whom it is written; **by'-mō'tive** an unavowed motive; **by'-name** a nickname. — *adj.* **by'-ordinar** (*Scot.*) extraordinary. — **by'pass** a road, route or passage for carrying traffic, fluids, electricity, etc., round an obstruction, congested place, etc. — *v.t.* to supply with a bypass: to direct (e.g. fluid) along a bypass: to go round and beyond by a bypass (also *fig.* to ignore, leave out): to evade. — **by'-passage** a side passage. — *adj.* **by'-past** (*Shak.*) past: gone by. — **by'path** a secluded or indirect path; **by'place** a retired place; **by'-play** action subordinate to and apart from the main action of a play; **by'-plot** a subsidiary plot; **by'-product** a product formed in the process of making something else; **by'road** a retired side road; **by'room** (*Shak.*) a side or private room;

by'-speech a casual speech; **by'stander** one who stands by or near one: a looker-on; **by'-street** an obscure street; **by'-thing** a thing of minor importance; **by'-time** leisure time; **by'way** a private, secluded, or obscure way; **by'word** a common saying, proverb: an object of scorn: a person noted for a specified characteristic; **by'work** work for leisure hours. — **by and by** in succession, in order of succession (*obs.*; *Spens.* **by'-and-by'**): at some future time: before long, presently: in the course of time; **by and large** whether close-hauled or before the wind (*naut.*): speaking generally: on the whole; **by oneself** alone; **by the by(e), by the way** in passing, incidentally; **let bygones be bygones** let past quarrels be ignored. — See also **bye!**. [O.E. *bī, bi, big*; Ger. *bei,* L. *ambi-.*]

by². See **bye¹**.

bycoket *bī'kok-it, n.* a turned-up peaked cap worn by noble persons in the 15th century. [O.Fr. *bicoquet,* prob. *bi-* (L. *bis*), double, *coque,* a shell.]

bye¹, by *bī, n.* anything of minor importance, a side issue, a thing not directly aimed at: in games, the state of one who has not drawn an opponent, and passes without contest to the next round: in cockfighting, a battle not forming part of a main: in golf, the holes remaining after the match is decided, played as a subsidiary game: in cricket, a run made from a ball bowled but not struck or touched by the batsman. — *adj.* subsidiary: part: indirect. — See also **by¹**. [See **by¹**.]

bye² *bī,* **bye-bye** *bī'bī, bə-bī',* coll. forms of **goodbye**.

bye-law. See **bylaw.**

Byelorussian. See **Belorussian.**

bygoing, bygones. See **by¹**.

byke. Same as **bike¹**.

bylander. Same as **bilander.**

bylaw, bye-law *bī'lö, n.* the law of a local authority or private corporation: a supplementary law or an inferred regulation. [The same as **byrlaw,** from O.N. *bȳjar-lög*; Dan. *by-lov,* town-law; from O.N. *būa,* to dwell. See **bower¹**.]

byline. See **by¹**.

bylive (*Spens.*). Same as **belive.**

bynempt. Obs. pa.t. of **bename.**

bypass, bypath, byplace. See **by¹**.

byre *bīr,* (mainly *Scot.*) *n.* a cowhouse. — **byre'man, byre'woman** a farm-servant with care of cows. [O.E. *bȳre.*]

byrlady *bər-lā'di,* **byrlakin** *bər-lā'kin,* (*arch.*) contractions for *By Our Lady, Ladykin.*

byrlaw *bir'lö, n.* a sort of popular jurisprudence long surviving in Scotland in villages and among husbandmen, concerning local matters in dispute. — Also **bourlaw** (*bōōr'*). — *n.* **byr'law-man** (*Scott* **bir'lieman**) an arbiter, oddsman, or umpire in such matters. [See **bylaw.**]

byrnie *bir'ni,* (*hist.*) *n.* a mail-coat: a breastplate. [A Scots form — O.N. *brynja*; O.E. *byrne.*]

byroad, bystander, byway, etc. See **by¹**.

Byronic *bī-ron'ik, adj.* possessing the characteristics of Lord *Byron* (1788–1824), or of his poetry, overstrained in sentiment or passion, cynical and libertine. — *adv.* **Byron'ically.** — *n.* **By'ronism.**

byssus *bis'əs, n.* a fine yellowish flax: linen made from it (the 'fine linen' of the Bible): the bundle of filaments by which some shellfish attach themselves. — *adjs.* **byssā'ceous** composed of a mass of fine threads: delicately filamentous; **byss'al** pertaining to a mollusc's byssus; **byss'ine** made of fine linen. — *n.* **byssinōs'is** an allergic lung disease of cotton workers. — *adj.* **byss'oid** byssaceous. [L., — Gr. *byssos,* a fine flaxen substance.]

byte *bīt,* (*comput.*) *n.* a set of usu. eight binary digits (bits) considered as a unit. [Poss. from *binary* digi*t* e*ight,* or from **bit²** and **bite.**]

bytownite *bī'town-īt, n.* a plagioclase intermediate between anorthite and labradorite. [*Bytown,* now Ottawa, where it occurs.]

bywoner *bī'wōn-ər, bī'vōn-ər, n.* an authorised squatter on another's farm: a poor white parasite. [Du. *bijwonen,* to be present.]

byzant *biz'ənt,* or *biz-ant'.* Same as **bezant.**

Byzantine *biz-an'tīn,* or *bīz-an'tīn,* or *-tin,* or *biz'ən-, adj.* relating to *Byzantium* (Constantinople, now Istanbul): rigidly hierarchic: intricate, tortuous. — *n.* an inhabitant of Byzantium. — *ns.* **Byzan'tinism** manifestation of Byzantine characteristics; **Byzan'tinist** a person who studies, or is expert in, Byzantine history, affairs, etc. — **Byzantine architecture** the style prevalent in the Eastern Empire down to 1453, marked by the round arch springing from columns or piers, the dome supported upon pendentives, capitals elaborately sculptured, mosaic or other incrustations, etc.; **Byzantine Church** the Eastern or Greek Church; **Byzantine Empire** the Eastern or Greek Empire from A.D. 395 to 1453; **Byzantine historians** the series of Greek chroniclers of the affairs of the Byzantine Empire down to its fall in 1453. [Gr. *Byzantion.*]

C

C, c sē, *n.* the third letter of our alphabet, a rounded form of the Greek *gamma* (see **G**), which the Romans used instead of *k*, and in some languages came to have the sound of *s* or one like it: one of the notes of the musical gamut, the sound on which the system is founded — the keynote of the natural scale, C major, having neither flats nor sharps: as a time signature, common time: as a Roman numeral, C = 100: C̄ = 100 000. — **C3** of poor physique; **C′-section** a Caesarean section (see under **Caesar**); **c-spring** see **cee=spring.**

ca′ kö, (*Scot.*) *v.t.* and *v.i.* to call: to drive: to propel: to knock (with *down, off, over,* etc.). — *n.* **ca″ing-** or **caa′ing-whale** a species of dolphin (*Globiocephalus melas*) often taken by ca'ing or driving ashore. — **ca′ canny** to go easy: deliberately to restrict output or effort. **[call.]**

caatinga kä-ting′gə, *n.* in Brazil, open, comparatively low forest, on white sandy soil derived from granite. [Tupí, white forest.]

cab¹ kab, *n.* a public carriage of various sizes and shapes, with two or four wheels, orig. horse-drawn, now usu. motor-driven: a taxi-cab: the driver's shelter on a locomotive, motor-lorry, etc. — *n.* **cabb′y, cabb′ie** a familiar dim. of **cab′man,** one who drives a horse cab, or of **cab′-driver,** a taxi-driver. — **cab′-rank, cab′-stand** a place where cabs stand for hire; **cab′-runner, cab′-tout** one whose business it is to call cabs. [Shortened from **cabriolet.**]

cab² kab, *n.* a Hebrew dry measure equal to nearly three pints. [Heb. *qab.*]

caba. U.S. form of **cabas,** having **cabas** as pl.

cabal kə-bal′, *n.* a small party united for some secret design: the plot itself: a name in English history esp. given to five unpopular ministers of Charles II (1672), whose initials happened to make up the word. — *v.i.* to form a party for a secret purpose: to intrigue: — *pr.p.* **caball′ing;** *pa.t.* and *pa.p.* **caballed′.** — *n.* **caball′er.** [Fr. *cabale;* from Heb. *qabbalah;* see **cabbala.**]

cabala, etc. See **cabbala.**

cabaletta ka-bə-let′ə, *n.* a simple operatic song or instrumental melody in rondo form, characterised by a uniform repetitive rhythm: the lively final section of an aria or duet: — *pl.* **-ett′as, -ett′e** (*-e*). [It., prob. — *coboletta,* dim. of *cobola,* a couplet, stanza — O.Prov. *cobla* — L. *copula;* perh. influenced by It. *cavallo,* horse, from being thought to be rhythmically similar to a horse's canter.]

caballero kab-al-yär′ō, *n.* a Spanish gentleman: — *pl.* **caballer′os.** [Sp., — L. *caballārius,* horseman — *caballus,* horse.]

caballine kab′ə-lin, *adj.* pertaining to, or suited to, a horse. [L. *caballīnus* — *caballus,* a horse.]

cabana kə-ban′(y)ə, (esp. *U.S.*) *n.* a small tentlike cabin, esp. used as a changing hut on the beach or by a swimming-pool: a cabin or chalet. [Sp. *cabaña.*]

cabaret kab′ə-rā, *n.* a restaurant with variety turns: the kind of entertainment there given: a tea or coffee service, often including a small tray. [Fr., tavern; prob. for *cabaneret* — *cabane,* a hut.]

cabas kab′ä, *n.* a woman's work-basket, reticule, or handbag. — See also **caba.** [Fr., flat basket.]

cabbage¹ kab′ij, *n.* a vegetable (*Brassica oleracea*) of the Cruciferae: the edible terminal bud of various palms: a dull, inactive person. — *adj.* **cabb′agy.** — **cabb′age-butt′erfly, cabb′age-white′** a large white butterfly (*Pieris*) whose larvae injure the leaves of cabbage and kindred plants; **cabb′age-fly** a fly (*Anthomyia brassicae*) whose maggots injure cabbage roots; **cabb′age-lett′uce** a lettuce with cabbage-like head; **cabb′age-moth** a moth (*Mamestra brassicae*) whose larva feeds on the cabbage; **cabb′age-palm** (also **cabb′age-tree**) *Oreodoxa oleracea* or other palm with an edible cabbage; **cabb′age-rose** a rose of bunchy cabbage-like form; **cabb′age-tree** the cabbage-palm (*Livistona australis*) of coastal areas of Eastern Australia: a New Zealand tree (*Cordyline australis*) with bushy heads of grass-shaped leaves; **cabb′age-worm** the larva of the cabbage-butterfly or of the cabbage-moth. — **cabbage=tree hat** (*Austr.*) a broad-brimmed hat made from the leaves of the cabbage-tree; **Kerguelen cabbage** (kûr′gə-lən) a wind-pollinated plant of the cabbage family growing on Kerguelen Island. [Fr. *caboche,* head; cf. It. *capocchia,* augmentative — *capo,* head — L. *caput.*]

cabbage² kab′ij, *v.t.* and *v.i.* to purloin, orig. of tailors who took portions of a customer's cloth as a perquisite. — *n.* cloth so appropriated.

cabbala, cabala kab′ə-lə or kə-bä′lə, *n.* a secret traditional lore, theological, metaphysical, and magical, of Jewish rabbis, who read hidden meanings into the Bible. — Also **kabala, kabbala(h).** — *ns.* **cab(b)′alism** the science of the cabbala; **cab(b)′alist** one versed in the cabbala. — *adjs.* **cab(b)alist′ic, -al** relating to the cabbala: having a hidden meaning. [Heb. *qabbālāh,* tradition, *qibbēl,* to receive.]

cabbie, cabby. See **cab¹.**

caber kāb′ər, *n.* a pole, generally the stem of a young tree, which is poised and tossed or hurled by Highland athletes. [Gael. *cabar.*]

cabin kab′in, *n.* a hut or cottage: a small room, esp. in a ship, for officers or passengers: a compartment for passengers in an aircraft: a railway signal-box. — *v.t.* to shut up in a cabin or in a cramped space: to hamper in action (*fig.*). — *v.i.* to dwell in a cabin. — **cab′in-boy** a boy who waits on the officers or cabin passengers of a ship; **cabin class** the class between tourist and first class; **cabin crew** members of aircraft crew who look after passengers; **cabin cruiser** a power-driven boat with full provision for living on board; **cabin passenger** formerly, one entitled to superior accommodation: a passenger having cabin accommodation; **cabin ship** a ship carrying only one class of passengers. [Fr. *cabane* — L.L. *capanna.*]

cabinet kab′(i-)nit, *n.* a little cabin or hut (*obs.*): the bed or nest of a beast or bird (*Shak.*): a small room, closet, or private apartment: a case for storing or displaying articles of value: a cupboard or drawer for storage: a private room for consultation, esp. a king's: hence (usu. *cap.*) a select inner group of the ministers who govern a country: in U.S., the president's advisory council, consisting of heads of government departments. — **Cabinet Council** an earlier name for the Cabinet; **cab′inet-edi′tion** one less in size and price than a library edition, but still elegant in format; **cab′-inetmaker** a maker of cabinets and other fine furniture; **cab′inetmaking** the occupation or art of the cabinet-maker: the getting together of a new set of cabinet ministers; **cabinet minister** a member of a cabinet; **cab′inet-pho′tograph** one of the size larger than a carte-de-visite; **cab′inet-pudd′ing** a cake-like pudding. [Dim. of **cabin;** cf. Fr. *cabinet.*]

Cabiri ka-bī′rī (L. kä-bē′rē), *n.pl.* ancient mystic divinities whose cult spread from Lemnos, Samothrace, and Imbros — also **Cabei′ri.** — *adjs.* **Cabir′ian; Cabir′ic.** [Latinised from Gr. *Kabeiroi.*]

cable kā′bl, *n.* a strong rope or chain for hauling or tying anything, esp. a ship's anchor: a cable-laid rope: a

cable-length: a line of submarine telegraph wires embedded in gutta-percha and encased in coiled strands of iron wire: a bundle of insulated wires laid underground: a cabled message: cable television. — Also *adj.* — *v.t.* and *v.i.* to provide with a cable, to tie up: to telegraph or send by cable. — *n.* **cā′bling** a bead or moulding like a thick rope: the filling of flutes on a column with a moulding like a cable. — **cā′ble-car** a car suspended from a moving cable, used as a method of transport up mountains, across valleys, etc.: a car on a cable-railway; **cā′ble-drilling** rope-drilling with the drill attached to a steel cable; **cā′blegram** a telegram sent by cable. — *adj.* **cā′ble-laid** composed of hawsers with a right-handed twist, twisted together to the left hand. — **cā′ble-length, cā′ble′s-length** a tenth of a nautical mile, approximately 200 yards or 100 fathoms; **cā′ble-mould′ing** a bead or moulding carved in imitation of a thick rope; **cā′ble-stitch** (a series of stitches producing) a pattern suggestive of cables; **cable television** the transmission of television programmes by cable to individual subscribers; **cā′ble-tram′way, -rail′way** one along which cars or carriages are drawn by an endless cable; **ca′blevision** cable television; **cā′bleway** a structure for transport of material in cars suspended from a cable. [Fr., — L.L. *caplum*, a halter — L. *capĕre*, to hold.]

cabob. Same as **kebab.**

caboc *ka′bok, n.* a double cream cheese rolled in oatmeal. [Same as **kebbock.**]

caboceer *kab-ō-sēr′, n.* a West African headman. [Port. *cabeceira* — *cabo* — L. *caput*, head.]

caboched, caboshed *kǝ-bosht′, (her.) adj.* in full face with no neck showing. [Fr. *caboché* — L. *caput*, head.]

cabochon *ka-bō-shõ, n.* a precious stone polished but uncut, or cut **en** (*ã*) **cabochon,** i.e. rounded on top and flat on back, without facets. — Also *adj.* [Fr., *caboche* — L. *caput*, head.]

caboodle *kǝ-bōō′dl, (slang) n.* crowd, collection. [Origin unknown.]

caboose *kǝ-bōōs′, n.* a ship's kitchen: an open-air cooking stove: a car, usu. at the rear of a goods or construction train for the train crew or workmen (*U.S.*): someone bringing up the rear (*U.S.*): a hut. [Du. *kombuis*; cf. Ger. *Kabuse.*]

caboshed. See **caboched.**

cabotage *kab′o-tij, n.* coastal trading: restriction of this within a country's territory: the use of lorries registered in one country to carry goods in another, for the purpose of evading certain taxes and licences. [Fr.]

cabré *kä′brä, adj.* rearing (*her.*): of an aeroplane, flying tail-down. [Fr. *cabrer,* to caper.]

cabrie *kab′rē, n.* a pronghorn. — Also **cab′rit.** [Sp. *cabrito,* kid.]

cabriole *kab′ri-ōl, n.* a capriole. — *adj.* of furniture legs, curved, often like an animal's paw. — *n.* **cabriolet** (*-lā′*) a light carriage with two wheels: (after 1830) a cab: a type of motor-car like a coupé, with folding top: a small armchair of curved design (18th century). [Fr., — L. *capra,* a goat.]

cacafogo *kak-ǝ-fō′gō,* **cacafuego** *-fū′gō* (Sp. *kä-kä-fwä′gō*), (*obs.*) *ns.* a spitfire, blusterer: — *pls.* **cacafo′gos, -fueg′os.** [Sp. and Port. *cagar,* to void excrement, Port. *fogo,* Sp. *fuego,* fire.]

cacao *kǝ-kä′ō, kǝ-kā′ō, n.* the tropical American tree *Theobroma cacao* (family *Sterculiaceae*) or its seeds from which cocoa and chocolate are made. [Mex. *cacauatl,* cacao tree.]

cachaemia *ka-kē′mi-ǝ, n.* a morbid state of the blood. — *adj.* **cachae′mic.** [Gr. *kakos,* bad, *haima,* blood.]

cachalot *kash′ǝ-lot, -lō, n.* the sperm-whale. [Fr.]

cache *kash, n.* a hiding-place for treasure, provisions, ammunition, etc.: stores so hidden. — *v.t.* to hide. — **cache-pot** (*kash′pō, -pot*) an ornamental flowerpot enclosing a common one; **cache-sexe** (*kash-seks′*) a piece of material, etc., covering the genitals. [Fr. *cacher,* to hide.]

cachet *kash′ā, n.* a seal: any distinctive stamp (*fig.*), esp.

something showing or conferring prestige: a capsule enclosing a medicine. — **lettre de cachet** (*hist.*) a letter under the private seal of the king of France, by which his pleasure was made known to individuals, and the administration of justice often interfered with. [Fr.]

cachexy, cachexia *ka-kek′si, -ǝ, ns.* a bad state of body: a depraved habit of mind. — *adjs.* **cachec′tic, -al.** [L., — Gr. *kachexiā* — *kakos,* bad, *hexis,* condition, from the root of *echein,* to have.]

cachinnate *kak′in-āt, v.i.* to laugh loudly. — *n.* **cachinnā′tion.** — *adj.* **cachinn′atory** (or *kak′*). [L. *cachinnāre,* to laugh loudly.]

cacholong *kach′o-long, n.* a variety of quartz or of opal, generally of a milky colour. [Fr. from Kalmuck.]

cacholot. Same as **cachalot.**

cachou *ka-shōō′, n.* a pill or lozenge of extract of liquorice, cashew-nut, or the like, used by some smokers in the hope of sweetening the breath. [Fr.]

cachucha *kǝ-chōō′chǝ, n.* a lively Spanish dance in 3–4 time, like the bolero. [Sp.]

cacique *ka-sēk′, n.* a West Indian chief: in Spain or Latin America, a political boss. — Also **cazique.** — *n.* **caciqu′ism** government by a cacique. [Haitian.]

cack-handed *kak′-hand′id, (slang) adj.* left-handed: clumsy. — Also **kack′-hand′ed.** — *n.* **cack′-hand′edness.** [Dial. *cack,* excrement, from L. *cacāre,* to defecate.]

cackle *kak′l, n.* the sound made by a hen or goose: talk or laughter of similar sound or value. — *v.i.* to make such a sound. — Also *v.t.* — *n.* **cack′ler** a fowl or person that cackles. — **cut the cackle** (*slang*) to stop the useless talk. [M.E. *cakelen*; cog. with Du. *kakelen.*]

cacodaemon, cacodemon *kak-ō-dē′mǝn, n.* an evil spirit: a nightmare (*Shak.*). [Gr. *kakos,* bad, *daimōn,* spirit.]

cacodoxy *kak′ō-dok-si, n.* a bad doctrine, wrong opinion, heterodoxy. [Gr. *kakos,* bad, *doxa,* an opinion.]

cacodyl *kak′ō-dil, n.* a colourless stinking liquid, composed of arsenic, carbon, and hydrogen. — *adj.* **cacodyl′ic.** [Gr. *kakōdēs,* stinking, *hȳlē,* matter.]

cacoepy *kak-ō′ǝ-pi, n.* bad or wrong pronunciation. [Gr. *kakos,* bad, *epos,* word.]

cacoethes *kak-ō-ē′thēz, n.* a bad habit or itch. [Gr. *kakoēthēs, -ēs,* ill-disposed — *kakos,* bad, *ēthos,* habit.] **cacoethes loquendi** *kak-ō-ē′thēz* (or *ka-ko-āth′ās*) *lō-kwen′dī* (or *lo-kwen′dē*), (L.) an itch for speaking; **cacoethes scribendi** *skrī-ben′dī* (or *skrē-ben′dē*) an itch for scribbling.

cacogastric *kak-ō-gas′trik, adj.* pertaining to a disordered stomach, dyspeptic. [Gr. *kakos,* bad, *gastēr,* the belly.]

cacogenics *kak-ō-jen′iks, n. sing.* dysgenics. [Gr. *kakos,* bad, *genos,* race.]

cacography *kak-og′rǝ-fi, n.* bad handwriting or spelling. — *n.* **cacog′rapher.** — *adjs.* **cacographic, -al** (*-ō-graf′ik, -ǝl*). [Gr. *kakos,* bad, and *graphē,* writing.]

cacolet *kak′ō-lā, n.* a military mule-litter. [Fr., prob. from Basque.]

cacology *ka-kol′ǝ-ji, n.* faulty vocabulary or pronunciation. [Gr. *kakos,* bad, *logos,* speech.]

cacomistle, cacomixl *ka′kǝ-mi(k)s-ǝl, ns.* a small carnivore (*Bassariscus*) found in south-west U.S. and Mexico. — Also **ringtail, ringtailed cat.** [Mex. Sp., — Nahuatl *tlaco,* half, *miztli,* cougar.]

cacoon *ka-kōōn′, n.* the large seed of a tropical climber (*Entada scandens*) of the mimosa family, used for making scent-bottles, snuff-boxes, etc.: the purgative and emetic seed of a tropical American climber (*Fevillea cordifolia*) of the gourd family. [Origin doubtful.]

cacophony *ka-kof′ǝ-ni, n.* a disagreeable sound: discord of sounds. — *adjs.* **cacoph′onous, cacophonic** (*-ō-fon′ik*), **-al, cacophonious** (*-fō′ni-ǝs*) harsh-sounding. [Gr. *kakos,* bad, *phōnē,* sound.]

cacotopia *kak-ō-tō′pi-ǝ, n.* a state, imaginary or otherwise, in which everything is as bad as possible — opp. of *Utopia.* — *adj.* **cacotō′pian.** [Gr. *kakos,* bad, *topos,* a place.]

For other sounds see detailed chart of pronunciation.

cacotrophy *ka-kot'rə-fi, n.* bad nourishment. [Gr. *kakos,* bad, *trophē,* nourishment.]

cactus *kak'tus, -təs, n.* a name given to any plant of the American family **Cactā′ceae** (now divided into several genera), fleshy xerophytes whose stems store water and do the work of leaves, which are generally reduced to spines: (also **cactus dahlia**) a type of double-flowered dahlia: — *pl.* **cac′tī** or **cac′tuses.** — *adjs.* **cactā′ceous; cac′tiform.** [L., — Gr. *kaktos,* a prickly plant found in Sicily.]

cacumen *ka-kū′men, n.* a top or point. — *adjs.* **cacū′minal** pertaining to the top: produced by turning the tip of the tongue up and back (*phon.*); **cacū′minous** with pointed or pyramidal top. [L. *cacūmen, -inis.*]

cad *kad, n.* an inferior assistant (*obs.*): a hanger-on, tavern-yard loafer, or errand-runner (*obs.*): a bus-conductor (*obs.*): a passenger taken by a conductor for his own profit (*obs.*): a townsman (at Oxford): a low vulgarian: one who lacks the instincts of a gentle-man. — *adj.* **cadd′ish.** — *n.* **cadd′ishness.** [Short for **cadet.**]

cadastral *ka-das′trəl, adj.* pertaining to a **cadastre** (*ka-das′tər*) or public register of the lands of a country for fiscal purposes: applied also to a survey on a large scale. [Fr., — L.L. *capitastrum,* register for a poll-tax. — L. *caput,* the head.]

cadaverous *kə-dav′ə-rəs, adj.* corpselike: sickly-looking: gaunt, haggard. — *n.* **cadāv′er** (or *-dav′; surg.* and *anat.*) a corpse. — *adj.* **cadāv′eric.** — *n.* **cadav′erousness.** [L. *cadāver,* a dead body — *cadēre,* to fall (dead).]

caddice. See **caddis²**.

caddie, caddy *kad′i, n.* one who attends a golfer at play, carrying the clubs. (18th cent.): a messenger or errand porter in Edinburgh and certain other towns (also **cad′ie**). — *v.i.* to carry clubs. — **caddie car** or **caddy car** a device running on two wheels for taking a bag of golf clubs round the course — also **caddie** (or **caddy**) **cart.** [See **cadet.**]

caddis¹ *kad′is,* (*Shak.* **caddyss**) *n.* worsted ribbon. [O.Fr. *cadaz, cadas,* tow.]

caddis², **caddice** *kad′is, n.* the larva of the **cadd′is-fly** (*Phryganea*) or other insect of the Trichoptera, which lives in water in a **cadd′is-case**, a silken sheath covered with fragments of wood, stone, shell, leaves, etc., open at both ends. — Also **cadd′is-worm.** [Origin obscure.]

caddy¹ *kad′i, n.* a small box for holding tea: any storage container (*U.S.*). [Malay *kati,* the weight of a small packet of tea.]

caddy². See **caddie.**
caddyss. See **caddis¹.**

cade¹ *kād, n.* a barrel or cask. [Fr. — L. *cadus,* a cask.]

cade² *kād, n.* a lamb or colt brought up by hand, a pet lamb. — Also *adj.* [Ety. unknown.]

cadeau *ka-dō,* (Fr.) *n.* a gift, present: — *pl.* **cadeaux** (*-ō*).

cadence *kā′dəns, n.* falling, sinking (*Milton*): the fall of the voice: rise and fall of sound, modulation: rhythm: a succession of chords closing a musical period (see **imperfect, perfect, plagal, cadence**). — *adj.* **cā′denced** rhythmical. — *n.* **cā′dency** rhythm: the relative status of younger sons (*her.*). — *adjs.* **cā′dent** (*Shak.*) falling; **cadential** (*kə-den′shəl*). [Fr. — L. *cadēre,* to fall.]

cadential. See **cadence, cadenza.**

cadenza *kä-dent′sa, kə-den′zə, n.* an outstanding virtuoso passage or flourish interpolated, sometimes improvised, given by a solo voice or instrument towards the end or at some important stage of a movement, usually the first of a concerto. — *adj.* **cadential** (*kə-den′shəl*). [It. *cadenza* — L. *cadēre,* to fall.]

cadet *kə-, ka-det′, n.* a younger son: a member of the younger branch of a family: one studying or qualifying for a commission in the army, navy, or other service, or (formerly) in the East India Company's service: a boy undergoing training for one of the armed forces: in New Zealand, a newcomer gaining experience in farming. — *n.* **cadet′ship.** — **cadet corps** an organised

body of boys undergoing military training. [Fr. *cadet,* formerly *capdet* — dim. of L. *caput,* the head.]

cadge¹ *kaj, v.t.* and *v.i.* to beg or go about begging: to sponge (money, etc.). — *n.* **cadg′er** a carrier who collects country produce for disposal: a hawker: a fellow who picks up his living about the streets: a sponger. [Prob. conn. with **catch.**]

cadge² *kaj, n.* a padded wooden frame on which a number of hawks may be carried. [Prob. **cage**; perh. **cadge¹.**]

cadgy *kaj′i,* (*dial.*) *adj.* cheerful and friendly: frolicsome: wanton. [Cf. Dan. *kaad,* wanton, O.N. *kātr,* merry.]

cadi *kä′di, kā′di, n.* a magistrate in Muslim countries. [Ar. *qādī,* a judge.]

cadie. See **caddie.**

Cadmean *kad-mē′ən, adj.* relating to *Cadmus* (Gr. *Kadmos*), who, according to legend, introduced the original Greek alphabet. — **Cadmean victory** one very costly to both sides (Cadmus sowed a dragon's teeth from which sprang soldiers who fought each other until only five were left).

cadmium *kad′mi-əm, n.* an element (at. numb. 51; symbol Cd), a white metal, occurring in zinc ores, used in magnets, metal-plating and as a control in nuclear reactors. — **cadmium yellow** cadmium sulphide used as pigment. [Gr. *kadmiā, kadmeiā* (*gē*), Cadmean (earth), calamine.]

cadrans *kad′rənz, n.* an instrument by which a gem is adjusted while being cut. [Fr. *cadran,* a quadrant, dial.]

cadre *kad′r′, käd′ri, kad′ər, kād′, n.* a framework, esp. the permanent skeleton of a military unit, the commissioned and non-commissioned officers, etc., around whom the rank and file may be quickly grouped: any nucleus of key persons: (prob. from Fr. through Russ.) a cell of trained Communist leaders: a member of such a cell. [Fr.]

caduac *kad′ū-ak,* (*obs.*) *n.* a casualty or windfall. [Scot. — L. *cadūcum.*]

caduceus *ka-dū′si-us,* (*myth.*) *n.* the rod of Hermes, messenger of the gods — a wand surmounted with two wings and entwined by two serpents: — *pl.* **cadū′ceī.** — *adj.* **cadū′cean.** [L. *cādūceus,* akin to Gr. *kērȳkeion,* a herald's wand — *kēryx, -ykos,* a herald.]

caducibranchiate *ka-dū-si-brang′ki-āt, adj.* losing the gills on attaining maturity. [L. *cadūcus,* caducous, *branchiae,* gills.]

caducous *ka-dū′kəs, adj.* falling early, as leaves or flowers: lapsing (*Rom. law*). — *n.* **caducity** (*ka-dū′si-ti*) transitoriness, senility: a lapse. [L. *cadūcus* — *cadēre,* to fall.]

Caecilia *sē-sil′i-ə, n.* a genus of legless burrowing Amphibia with hidden eyes. — *adj.* **caecil′ian.** — *n.* any member of the class to which Caecilia belongs. [L. *caecus,* blind.]

caecum *sē′kəm,* in U.S. **cecum,** *n.* a blind sac: a sac or bag having only one opening, connected with the intestine of an animal: — *pl.* **cae′ca.** — *adj.* **cae′cal.** [L., neut. of *caecus,* blind.]

caen-stone *kā′ən-stōn, n.* a cream-coloured limestone brought from Caen (*kä*) in France.

Caenozoic *sē-nō-zō′ik.* Same as **Cainozoic.**

caerulean. Same as **cerulean.**

Caesalpinia *ses-, sēz-al-pin′i-ə, n.* a genus, including brazil-wood and divi-divi, giving name to a family **Caesalpiniā′ceae** of leguminous plants. — *adj.* **caesalpiniā′ceous.** [Named after Andrea *Cesalpino* (1519–1603), Italian botanist.]

Caesar *sē′zər, n.* an absolute monarch, an autocrat, from the Roman dictator Gaius Julius *Caesar* (100–44 B.C.): (also without *cap.*) a Caesarean operation (*coll.*). — *adj.* **Caesarean, -ian** (*-ā′ri-ən*) relating to Julius Caesar. — *n.* an adherent of Caesar, an imperialist. — *ns.* **Cae′sarism; Cae′sarist; Cae′sarship.** — **caesaropapism** (also *cap.; sē-zə-rō-pā′pizm*) control of the church by a secular ruler or by the state (L.L. *pāpa,* pope). — **Caesarean operation, section** delivery of a child by cutting through walls of abdomen; in Roman times, enjoined by law if mother died (perh. *Lex Caesarea*, perh. *caedĕre*, to cut — Pliny connects with first bearer of cognomen *Caesar*).

caese. See **sessa.**

caesium *sēz'i-əm*, in U.S. **cesium**, *n.* an element (at. numb. 55; symbol Cs), a silver-white, soft, and extensile alkaline metal; used in form of compounds or alloys in photoelectric cells, etc. — *adj.* **caes'ious** bluish or greyish green. [L. *caesius*, bluish grey.]

caespitose *sēs'pi-tōs, adj.* tufted: turf-like. [L. *caespes, -itis*, turf.]

caestus. Variant of **cestus²**, or, less often, **cestus¹**.

caesura, cesura *si-zū'rə*, (*pros.*) *n.* division of a foot between two words: a pause in a line of verse (generally near the middle). — *adj.* **caesū'ral.** [L. *caesūra — caedĕre, caesum*, to cut off.]

cafard, *ka-fär', n.* depression, the blues.   [Fr.]

café, cafe *kaf'ā, ka'fi, n.* a coffee-house, a restaurant: (Fr. **café** *kaf-ā*) coffee(-house). — **café au lait** (*ō le*) coffee made with hot milk: coffee with milk added; **café-chantant** (*shã-tã*), **café-concert** (*kɔ̄-ser*) café providing musical entertainment; **café filtre** (*fēl-tr'*) strong black filtered coffee; **café noir** (*nwär*) black coffee (i.e. without milk); **café society** fashionable society.

cafeteria *ka-fi-tē'ri-ə, n.* a restaurant with a counter for self-service.   [Cuban Sp., a tent in which coffee is sold.]

caff. Slang term for **café**, coffee-house.

caffeine *kaf'ēn*, or *kaf-ē'in, n.* theine, an alkaloid present in coffee and tea. — *n.* **caff'e(in)ism** a morbid state caused by caffeine. [Fr. *caféine*; see **coffee.**]

Caffre. See **Kaffir, Kafir.**

cafila, caffila, kafila *ka'fēl-a, kä', -fil-, -ä, n.* a caravan, caravan train.   [Ar. *qāfilah*.]

caftan *kaf'tən, kaf-tan', n.* a long-sleeved Persian or Turkish garment, reaching to the ankles and often tied with a sash.   [Turk. *qaftān*.]

cage *kāj, n.* a box or compartment wholly or partly of open-work for captive animals: a prison: a frame with a platform or platforms used in hoisting in a vertical shaft: the framework supporting a peal of bells: a wire guard: any structure resembling a bird's cage: a structure of steel supports and netting to protect garden fruit and vegetables from birds: a squirrel's nest (*dial.*). — *v.t.* to imprison in a cage: — *pr.p.* **cag'ing;** *pa.t.* and *pa.p.* **caged.** — *adj.* **caged** confined. — *n.* **cage'ling** a bird that is or has been kept in a cage. — **cage'bird** a bird of a kind habitually kept in a cage; **cage'-cup** a kind of glass bowl of late Roman times, with a filigree-type glass decoration attached to the bowl by tiny struts (also **diatrē'tum**); **cage'work** open-work like the bars of a cage. — **cage in** to imprison (usu. *fig.*). [Fr., — L. *cavea*, a hollow place.]

cagey, cagy *kāj'i, (coll.) adj.* artfully shy, wary, chary: not frank, secretive. — *adv.* **cag'ily.** — *n.* **cag'iness, cag'(e)yness.** [Perh. conn. with **cadgy.**]

cagot *käg'ō, n.* one of an outcast class found scattered in the western Pyrenees, supposed to be the descendants of lepers.   [Fr.; origin unknown.]

cagoul(e), kagool, kagoul(e) *kə-gōōl', n.* a lightweight, weather-proof anorak, often knee-length.   [Fr. *cagoule*, a monk's hood.]

cagy. See **cagey.**

cahier *ka-yā, (Fr.) n.* a writing-book: a memorandum: a report memorial.

cahoot *kə-hōōt, n. (U.S.)* company or partnership. — **go cahoots** to go shares; **in cahoots** in collusion (with).

cailleach *kal'yahh, (Scot.) n.* an old woman. — Also **caillach, cailliach.**   [Gael. *cailleach*.]

caimac, caimacam. Same as **kaimakam.**

caiman. Same as **cayman.**

Cain *kān, n.* Adam's son, murderer of Abel (Gen. iv.), hence allusively a murderer. — *n.* **Cain'ite** a descendant of Cain: a member of a 2nd-century sect of Gnostics who revered Cain and Judas. — *adj.* **Cain'-col'oured** (*Shak.*) of the traditional colour of Cain's beard and hair, red. — **raise Cain** to make a determined or angry fuss.

cain, kain *kān, n.* in old Scots law, rent paid in kind, esp. in poultry, etc.: tribute. — **cain'-hen** a hen given up as cain. — **pay the cain** to pay the penalty.   [Ir. and Gael. *càin*, rent, tax.]

ca'ing-whale. See **ca'.**

Cainozoic *kī-nō-zō'ik, (geol.) adj.* and *n.* Tertiary.   [Gr. *kainos*, new, *zōē*, life.]

caique, caïque *kä-ēk', n.* a light skiff used on the Bosporus: the skiff of a galley.   [Fr., — Turk. *kaik*, a boat.]

caird *kārd, (Scot.) n.* a tramping tinker, a gypsy, a vagrant.   [Gael. and Ir. *ceard*.]

Cairene *kī'rēn, kī-rēn', adj.* relating to Cairo. — *n.* a native or citizen of Cairo.

cairn *kārn, n.* a heap of stones, esp. one raised over a grave, or as a landmark on a mountain-top or path: a small variety of Scottish terrier (in full **cairn terrier**) suitable for driving foxes from their earths among cairns. — *adj.* **cairned** marked with cairns. — *n.* **cairngorm' (-stone)** brown or yellow quartz found among the Cairngorm Mountains.   [Gael. *càrn*.]

caisson *kā'sən, kə-sōōn', n.* a tumbril or ammunition wagon: a chest of explosive materials: a strong case for keeping out the water while the foundations of a bridge are being built: an apparatus for lifting a vessel out of the water for repairs or inspection: the pontoon or floating gate used to close a dry-dock. — **caisson disease** bends, a painful, and sometimes fatal, disorder affecting divers, caisson-workers, etc. who are too suddenly subjected to decreased air pressure, caused by the formation of nitrogen bubbles in the body as nitrogen comes rapidly out of solution from the blood and other body fluids.   [Fr., from *caisse*, a case or chest. (See **case¹**.)]

caitiff *kā'tif, n.* a mean despicable fellow. — *adj.* mean, base. — *n.* **cai'tive** (*Spens.*) captive, subject.   [O.Fr. *caitif* (Fr. *chétif*) — L. *captīvus*, a captive — *capĕre*, to take.]

cajeput. See **cajuput.**

cajole *kə-jōl', v.t.* to coax (into): to cheat by flattery (into, out of). — *ns.* **cajole'ment** coaxing for the purpose of deluding: wheedling language: flattery; **cajol'er; cajol'ery.**   [Fr. *cajoler*, to chatter; ety. dub.]

Cajun *kā'jən, n.* a descendant of the French-speaking Acadians deported to Louisiana in 1755: the language of the Cajuns. — Also *adj.* (sometimes without *cap.*).   [Acadian.]

cajuput *kaj'ə-put, n.* a pungent, volatile, aromatic oil, distilled from leaves of an Indo-Malayan and Australian myrtaceous tree *Melaleuca leucodendron.* — Also **caj'eput.**   [Malay.]

cake *kāk, n.* a piece of dough that is baked: a small loaf of fine bread: any flattened mass baked, as *oatcake* (whence Scotland has been called the 'Land of Cakes'), or formed by pressure or drying, as of soap, clay, snow, blood: a breadlike composition enriched with additions such as sugar, spices, currants, peel, etc.: a separately made mass of such composition: a madcap or fool (*arch. slang*). — *v.t.* and *v.i.* to form into a cake or hard mass. — *n.* and *adj.* **cāk'ing.** — *adj.* **cāk'y.** — **cake hole** (*slang*) mouth; **cake'walk** a prancing movement once performed by American Negroes in competition for a *cake*: a dance developed therefrom: music for the dance: something accomplished with supreme ease. — *v.i.* to perform a cakewalk or execute similar movements. — **caking coal** a bituminous coal that fuses into a mass in burning. — **a piece of cake** (*coll.*) a thing easy to do; **cakes and ale** vaguely, all the good things of life; **go, sell, like hot cakes** see **hot¹; have one's cake and eat it, eat one's cake and have it** to have the advantage of both alternatives; **his cake is dough** his hope has failed; **take the cake** (*slang*) to carry off the honours, rank first (ironically).   [O.N. *kaka*, cog. with Ger. *Kuche(n)*, Du. *koek*.]

Calabar-bean *kal-ə-bär'-bēn*, or *kal', n.* the seed of the tropical African *Physostigma venenosum (Papil-*

ionaceae), used in emulsion in witchcraft ordeal, the accused being acquitted if he can vomit the poison.
calabash *kal'ə-bash, n.* a gourd, or its shell used as a vessel, tobacco-pipe, etc.: the fruit of the calabash tree or its shell similarly used. — **calabash nutmeg** the fruit of a tropical anonaceous tree *Monodora myristica*, whose seeds are used as nutmegs; **calabash tree** a bignoniaceous tree of tropical America (*Crescentia cujete*) with large melon-like fruit. [Fr. *calebasse* — Sp. *calabaza* — Pers. *kharbuz*, melon.]
calaboose *kal'ə-bōōs, -bōōs', (U.S.) n.* a prison. [Sp. *calabozo.*]
calabrese *kal-ə-brā'zā, n.* a kind of green sprouting broccoli. [It., Calabrian.]
Caladium *kal-ā'di-əm, n.* an American genus of plants of the arum family, with edible starchy root-stocks. [Latinised from Malay *kélády*, a kindred plant.]
calamanco *kal-ə-mangk'ō, n.* a satin-twilled woollen stuff, chequered or brocaded in the warp: a garment made of this: — *pl.* **calamanc'os.** [Du. *kalamink*, Ger. *Kalmank*, Fr. *calamande*; origin unknown.]
calamander *kal-ə-man'dər, n.* a hard and valuable cabinet-wood of the ebony genus, brownish with black stripes, brought from India and Sri Lanka. [Prob. Sinh.]
calamary *kal'ə-mər-i, n.* any of various species of squid. [L. *calamārius* — *calamus* — Gr. *kalamos*, pen, from their internal shell.]
calamine *kal'ə-mīn, -min, n.* a mineral, zinc carbonate (smithsonite): in U.S., hydrous zinc silicate (hemimorphite, or electric calamine). — **calamine lotion, ointment** a soothing lotion or ointment for the skin, containing zinc carbonate or oxide. [Fr. — L.L. *calamīna*, prob. — L. *cadmia*; see **cadmium.**]
calamint *kal'ə-mint, n.* a genus (*Calamintha*) of labiate plants allied to mint and thyme. [Fr. — Gr. *kalaminthē*, some related plant.]
calamite *kal'ə-mīt, n.* a general name for a family of fossil plants abundant in the Coal Measures, gigantic trees related to horse-tails. [L. *calamus*, a reed.]
calamity *kə-lam'i-ti, n.* a great misfortune: affliction. — *adj.* **calam'itous** making wretched, disastrous. — *adv.* **calam'itously.** — *n.* **calam'itousness.** [Fr. *calamité* — L. *calamitās, -ātis.*]
calamus *kal'ə-məs, n.* the traditional name of the sweet-flag: the reed pen used by the ancients in writing: a quill (*zool.*): (with *cap.*) a genus of palms whose stems make canes or rattans: a fistula: — *pl.* **cal'amī.** [L. — Gr. *kalamos*, reed, cane, pen.]
calando *kä-län'dō, (mus.) adj.* and *adv.* gradually slower with diminishing volume of tone. [It., falling off.]
calandria *kal-an'dri-ə, n.* a sealed vessel used in the core of certain types of nuclear reactor.
Calanthe *kal-an'thi, n.* a genus of orchids with tall spikes of long-lasting flowers: (without *cap.*) an orchid of this genus. [Gr. *kalos*, beautiful, *anthē*, blossom.]
Calanus *ka-lā'nəs, kal'ə-nəs, n.* a genus of copepods, swimming in plankton, important as whale and fish food.
calash *kə-lash', n.* a light low-wheeled carriage with a folding top: a hood with hoops formerly worn by ladies over the cap. [Fr. *calèche*; of Slav. origin.]
calavance *kal'ə-vans, n.* a name for certain varieties of pulse. — Also **car'avance.** [Sp. *garbanzo*, chick-pea, said to be Basque *garbantzu*.]
calcaneum *kal-kā'ni-əm, n.* the heel-bone. — *adj.* **calca'neal, calca'nean.** [L. *calcāneum*, the heel — *calx*, the heel.]
calcar[1] *kal'kär, n.* a spur or spur-like projection, esp. from the base of a petal (*bot.*): a bird's spur (*zool.*): the prehallux (*zool.*): the hippocampus minor or **cal'car ā'vis** (bird's spur) in the brain (*zool.*). — *adjs.* **cal'carate; calcar'iform; cal'carine.** [L., a spur — *calx*, the heel.]
calcar[2] *kal'kär, n.* a fritting furnace, an oven or furnace for calcining the materials of frit before melting: an arch or oven for annealing. [L. *calcāria*, a lime-kiln.]

calcareous *kal-kā'ri-əs, adj.* chalky: limy. [L. *calcārius*, from *calx*, lime.]
calceamentum *kal-si-ə-men'təm, n.* a red silk embroidered sandal forming part of the insignia of the Holy Roman Empire. [L. *calceāmentum*, a shoe.]
calced *kalst, adj.* shod, wearing shoes — opp. to *discalced* — of Carmelites. — *v.t.* **cal'ceate** to shoe. — *adjs.* **cal'ceate, -d** shod; **cal'cēiform, cal'ceolate** slipper-shaped. [L.L. *calceus*, a shoe — *calx*, the heel.]
calcedonio *kal-che-don'i-ō, n.* a type of Venetian coloured glass resembling natural stones like chalcedony. [It., chalcedony.]
calcedony. A form of **chalcedony.**
Calceolaria *kal-si-ō-lā'ri-ə, n.* a South American genus of Scrophulariaceae, largely cultivated for the beauty of the slipper-like flowers: (without *cap.*) any plant of the genus, slipperwort. [L. *calceolus*, dim. of *calceus*, a shoe.]
calces. See **calx.**
calciferol, etc. See **calcium.**
calcium *kal'si-əm, n.* the metal (at. numb. 20; symbol Ca) present in lime, chalk, gypsum, etc. — *adjs.* **cal'cic** containing calcium; **cal'cicole, calcic'olous** growing on limestone or limy soils. — *n.* **calcif'erol** vitamin D_2 (*calcif*erous and ergo*sterol*). — *adjs.* **calcif'erous** containing lime; **cal'cific** calcifying or calcified. — *n.* **calcifica'tion** the process of calcifying, a changing into lime. — *adjs.* **cal'cifuge** (*-fūj*), **calcif'ugous** (*-ū-gəs*) avoiding limestone. — *v.t.* and *v.i.* **cal'cify** to make or become limy, by secretion, deposition, or substitution. — *adjs.* **calcigerous** (*-sij'ə-rəs*) containing lime; **cal'cinable.** — *n.* **calcinā'tion.** — *v.t.* **cal'cine** (or *-sīn'*) to reduce to a calx by the action of heat: to subject to prolonged heating, esp. so as to oxidise, or so as to drive off water and carbon dioxide. — *v.i.* to become calx or powder by heat. — *ns.* **cal'cite** calcspar; **calcitō'nin** (*calcium* and *tone*, plus suffix *-in*) a hormone which regulates the amount of calcium in the blood and so inhibits loss of this element from bones; **calc'-sin'ter, calc'-tuff** travertine, a porous deposit from springs charged with calcium carbonate; **calcspar** (*kalk'spär*) a mineral, calcium carbonate crystallised in the hexagonal system. — **Calciferous Sandstone** the lowermost group of Carboniferous rocks in Scotland, answering to part of the English Carboniferous Limestone. [L. *calx, calcis*, lime, limestone.]
calculate *kal'kū-lāt, v.t.* to count or reckon: to think out, esp. mathematically: to think, purpose, suppose (*U.S.*). — *v.i.* to make a calculation: to estimate. — *adj.* **cal'culable.** — *adv.* **cal'culably.** — *adjs.* **cal'culāted** thought out: reckoned: computed: fitted, likely, of such a nature as probably; **cal'culāting** given to forethought: deliberately selfish and scheming. — *n.* **calculā'tion** the art or process of calculating: estimate: forecast. — *adjs.* **calculā'tional, cal'culātive** relating to calculation. — *n.* **cal'culātor** one who calculates: a book, table, or machine for obtaining arithmetical results. — **calculated risk** a possibility of failure, the degree of which has been estimated and taken into account before a venture is undertaken; **calculating machine** a machine for obtaining arithmetical results without calculation. [L. *calculāre, -ātum*, to reckon by help of little stones — *calculus*, dim. of *calx*, a stone.]
calculus *kal'kū-ləs, n.* a stone-like concretion which forms in certain parts of the body (*pl.* **cal'culī**): a system of computation used in the higher branches of mathematics (*pl.* **cal'culuses**). — *adjs.* **cal'cular** pertaining to the mathematical calculus; **cal'culary, cal'culose, cal'culous** pertaining to or affected with stone or with gravel. — **calculus of finite differences** is concerned with changes in functions due to finite changes in variables — it does not assume continuity; **differential calculus** a method of treating the values of ratios of differentials or the increments of quantities continually varying; **integral calculus** the summation of an infinite series of differentials; **predicate calculus** a

notation system by means of which the logical structure of simple propositions may be represented; **propositional calculus** a notation system in which symbols representing propositions and logical constants such as negation, conjunction and implication are used to indicate the logical relations between propositions. [L.; see foregoing.]

caldarium *kal-dār′i-əm, kal-där′i-ōōm,* (L.) *n.* a hot bath.
caldera *käl-dā′rə,* (*geol.*) *n.* a volcanic crater of great size. [Sp., cauldron.]
caldron. Same as **cauldron.**
Caledonian *kal-i-dō′ni-ən, adj.* pertaining to ancient *Caledonia,* to the Highlands of Scotland, or to Scotland generally, or (*geol.*) to a mountain-forming movement with folds and overthrusts trending generally N.E. and S.W. in Silurian and Old Red Sandstone times, well developed in Scotland. — *n.* a Scot. [L. *Călēdōnia.*]
calefaction *kal-i-fak′shən, n.* the act of heating: the state of being heated. — *adj.* **calefacient** (*-fā′shənt*) warming. — *n.* anything that warms: a blister or superficial stimulant. — *adj.* **calefac′tive** communicating heat. — *n.* **calefac′tor** a small stove. — *adj.* **calefac′tory** warming. — *n.* a room in which monks warmed themselves: a warming-pan, or pome. — *v.t.* and *v.i.* **cal′efy** to make or grow warm. [L. *calefacĕre — calēre,* to grow hot, *facĕre, factum,* to make.]
calembour *kal-ã-bōōr,* (Fr.) *n.* a pun.
calendar *kal′ən-dər, n.* the mode of adjusting the natural divisions of time with respect to each other for the purposes of civil life: an almanac or table of months, days, and seasons, or of special facts, etc.: a list of documents arranged chronologically with summaries of contents: a list of canonised saints, or of prisoners awaiting trial: a list of events, appointments, etc.: any list or record. — *v.t.* to place in a list: to analyse and index. — *ns.* **cal′endarer; calendarisa′tion, -z-.** — *v.t.* **cal′endarise, -ize** in accounting, to divide (something, e.g. a budget) into equal units of time within a year (usu. months). — *n.* **cal′endarist.** — **cal′endar-line** the date-line; **calendar month, year** see under **month, year; perpetual calendar** see **perpetual.** [O.Fr. *calandier* — L. *calendārium,* an account-book, *kalendae,* calends.]
calender[1] *kal′ən-dər, n.* a machine with bowls or rollers for finishing the surface of cloth, paper, etc., by combined moisture, heat, and pressure: a person who calenders (properly a calendrer). — *v.t.* to dress in a calender. — *ns.* **cal′endering; cal′endrer; cal′endry** a place where calendering is done. [Fr. *calandre* — L. *cylindrus* — Gr. *kylindros,* roller.]
calender[2] *kal′ən-dər, n.* a dervish. [Pers. *qalandar.*]
calends *kal′əndz, n.pl.* among the Romans, the first day of each month. [L. *kalendae — calāre,* Gr. *kaleein,* to call (because the beginning of the month was proclaimed).]
Calendula *ka-len′dū-lə, n.* the marigold genus: (without *cap.*) any plant of the genus: (without *cap.*) a preparation of marigold flowers formerly used in plasters, etc., for the healing of wounds. [L. *kalendae,* calends (but the connection is not obvious).]
calenture *kal′ən-chər, n.* a fever or delirium occurring on board ship in hot climates. [Fr. — Sp. *calentura* — L. *calēns, -entis — calēre,* to be hot.]
calescence *kal-es′əns, n.* increase in heat. [L. *calēscĕre,* inchoative of *calēre,* to be hot.]
calf[1] *käf, n.* the young of the cow, elephant, whale, and certain other mammals: calfskin leather: a stupid or loutish person: an iceberg in relation to its parent glacier: — *pl.* **calves** (*kävz*), (of calfskin) **calfs.** — *v.t.* and *v.i.* **calve** (*käv*) to bring forth a calf: to detach (an iceberg). — *adj.* **calf′-bound** bound in calfskin. — **calf′-country, -ground** the home of one's youth; **calf′-dozer** a small bulldozer; **calf′-lick** a cowlick; **calf′-love** a boy's or girl's transient amorous attachment; **calf's′=foot, calves′-foot** the foot of the calf, used in making a jelly; **calf′skin** the skin of the calf, making a good leather for bookbinding and shoes; **calf′-time** youth. — **divinity calf** a dark-brown calf bookbinding with

blind stamping, and without gilding — used on theological books; **golden calf** the image set up by Aaron during the absence of Moses on Sinai, or one of those erected by Jeroboam at Bethel and Dan: wealth as an object of worship; **half′-calf′** a bookbinding in which the back and corners are in calfskin; **in, with, calf** (of cows) pregnant; **mottled calf** a light-coloured bookbinding, decorated by the sprinkling of acid in drops; **smooth calf** a binding in plain or undecorated calf leather; **tree calf** a bright brown calf bookbinding, stained by acids with a pattern resembling the trunk and branches of a tree. [O.E. (Anglian) *cælf* (W.S. *cealf*); Ger. *Kalb.*]
calf[2] *käf, n.* the thick fleshy part at the back of the leg below the knee: — *pl.* **calves** (*kävz*). — *adj.* **calf′less** with a thin poor calf. [O.N. *kálfi.*]
caliature-wood *kal′i-ə-chər-wōōd, n.* red-sanders. — Also **caliatour, calliature,** etc.
Caliban *kal′i-ban, n.* a man of beastly nature, from the monster of that name in Shakespeare's *Tempest.*
calibre, caliber *kal′i-bər, n.* the size of the bore of a tube: diameter: character, capacity (*fig.*). — *v.t.* **cal′ibrate** to determine the calibre of, or the true values answering to the graduations of: to mark calibrations on. — *ns.* **calibra′tion; cal′ibrator.** — *adj.* **cal′ibred, cal′ibered.** [Fr. *calibre,* the bore of a gun; perh. L. *quā libra,* of what weight, or from Ar. *qālib,* a mould.]
caliche *kä-lē′chä, n.* Chile saltpetre. [Sp.]
calico *kal′i-kō, n.* a cotton cloth first brought from *Calicut* in India: plain white unprinted cotton cloth, bleached or unbleached: coarse printed cotton cloth: — *pl.* **cal′icos, cal′icoes.** — *adj.* made of calico: spotted. — **cal′ico-bush, -flower, -tree** kalmia; **cal′ico-print′er** one employed in printing calico(e)s; **cal′ico-wood** the snowdrop-tree.
calid *kal′id, adj.* warm. — *n.* **calid′ity.** [L. *calidus,* hot.]
calif. See **caliph.**
Califont® *kal′i-font,* (N.Z.) *n.* a gas-fuelled water-heater.
californium *kal-i-för′ni-əm, n.* an element (at. numb. 98; symbol Cf). [Produced at the University of *California.*]
caligo *kal-ī′gō, n.* dimness of sight. — *adj.* **caliginous** (*kal-ij′i-nəs*) dim, obscure, dark. — *n.* **caliginos′ity.** [L. *cālīgō, -ĭnis,* fog.]
caligraphy. A faulty spelling of **calligraphy.**
caliology *kal-i-ol′ə-ji, n.* the science of birds' nests. [Gr. *kaliā, kaliā,* a nest, *logos,* discourse.]
calipash *kal′i-pash, n.* the part of a turtle close to the upper shell, a dull greenish fatty gelatinous substance. — *n.* **cal′ipee** the light-yellowish portion of flesh from the turtle's belly. [Prob. from West Ind. words.]
calipers. See **callipers.**
caliph *kal′if,* or *kā′lif, n.* a successor of Mohammed: the spiritual leader of Islam. — Also **calif, kalif, khalif.** — *adj.* **cal′iphal.** — *n.* **cal′iphate** the office, rank, government or empire of a caliph. [Fr. *calife* — Ar. *khalīfah,* a successor.]
Calippic, Callippic *ka-lip′ik, adj.* pertaining to the Athenian astronomer *Kal(l)ippos* (c. 350 B.C.) whose cycle equalled four Metonic cycles less one day, or seventy-six years.
calisaya *kal-i-sā′yə, n.* a variety of Peruvian bark.
calisthenics. See **callisthenics.**
caliver *kal′i-vər,* (*Shak.*) *n.* a kind of light musket. [Same as **calibre.**]
calix *kā′liks, kal′iks, n.* a cup, chalice: a cup-like cavity or organ (*biol.*; often **calyx,** q.v.). [L. *calix,* a cup.]
Calixtin[1], **Calixtine** *kal-iks′tin, n.* a member of the more moderate party among the Hussites — a Utraquist. — Also *adj.* [From their demanding the cup (L. *calix*) as well as the bread for the laity.]
Calixtin[2], **Calixtine** *kal-iks′tin, n.* a follower of the syncretist Lutheran divine, Georg *Calixtus* (1586–1656).
calk[1]. Same as **caulk.**
calk[2] *kök, n.* a pointed piece on a horseshoe to prevent slipping — also **calk′in, calk′er, caulk′er.** — *v.t.* to

provide with a calk.   [O.E. *calc*, shoe — L. *calx*, a heel.]

calk³, calque *kök, kalk, v.t.* to copy by rubbing the back with colouring matter and then tracing with a blunt point. — *n.* (usu. **calque;** *kalk*) a loan-translation (q.v.). [L. *calcāre,* to tread, *calx,* the heel.]

calker, calkin. See **calk².**

call¹ *köl, v.i.* to cry aloud (often with *out*): to make a short visit (with *upon, for, at*): to make a telephone call: in poker, to demand a show of hands after repeated raising of stakes. — *v.t.* and *v.i.* in card games, to undertake to score: to declare (trump suit, etc.) in card games. — *v.t.* to name: to summon: to rouse: to appoint or proclaim: to designate or reckon: to select for a special office, as to the bar: to telephone: to read out the names in (a roll): to demand the repayment of (a debt, loan, redeemable bonds, etc.): to demand the playing of (an exposed card): to apply (offensive name) to (*coll.*): to broadcast a commentary on (a race, etc.) (*Austr.* and *N.Z.*). — *n.* a summons or invitation (to the witness-box, the telephone, before the curtain, etc.): a sense of vocation: a demand: a short visit: a signal by trumpet, bell, etc.: a telephone connection or conversation, or a request for one: in card games, a declaration or undertaking, or the right to make it in turn: a cry, esp. of a bird: an instrument mimicking a bird's cry: admission to the rank of barrister: an invitation to the pastorate of a congregation: on the stock exchange, an option of buying within a certain time certain securities or commodities at a stipulated price (also **call option**): the money paid to secure such an option: one instalment of the payment for newly issued securities: occasion, cause (*coll.*). — *ns.* **call'er** one who calls; **call'ing** vocation. — **call'-at-large** a form of pastoral call sometimes adopted by a presbytery where a congregation is not unanimous, in which the name of the person to be called is not inscribed beforehand, and the names cannot be adhibited by mandate; **call'-bird** a bird trained to allure others into snares; **call'-box** a public telephone-box; **call'-boy** a boy who waits upon the prompter in a theatre, and calls the actors when wanted on the stage; **call'-girl** a prostitute on call by telephone; **calling card** a visiting card; **call'ing-crab** the fiddler-crab, which waves its larger claw when disturbed; **call'-loan, call'-mon'ey** a loan or money payable when asked for; **call'-note** the note by which a bird or beast calls to its kind; **call option** see **call** above; **call sign, signal** in communications, a combination of letters and numbers, identifying a particular ship, aircraft, transmitter, etc.; **call'-up** an act of calling up, esp. conscription into the armed forces. — **at call** readily available; **boatswain's call** see under **whistle; call attention to** to point out; **call away** to divert the mind; **call back** to recall: to visit again: to telephone again; **call by** (*coll.*) to visit in passing; **call cousins** to claim kindred; **call down** to invoke: to rebuke (*arch.*); **call for** to come for and take away with one: to ask loudly for: to demand: to require (**called'-for** required, necessary; **not called for** uncalled-for); **call forth** to evoke; **call for trumps** to play a card as a signal to a partner to lead a trump; **call in** to bring in from circulation or public use, because no longer useful, applicable, etc., old currency notes, etc.: to demand repayment of (a debt, etc.): to call to one's help (as a doctor, the police); **call in(to) question** to challenge, throw doubt on; **call off** to summon away: to withdraw or back out: to cancel or abandon; **call of nature** (*euph.*) the need to urinate, etc.; **call on** or **upon** to invoke, appeal to: to make a short visit to; **call out** to challenge to fight a duel: to summon to service, bring into operation: to instruct (members of a trade union) to come out on strike; **call over** to read aloud (a list); **call the shots** (*U.S.*) to call the tune; **call the tune** to say what is to happen, to order; **call to account** see **account; call to mind** to recollect, or cause to recollect; **call to order** to call upon to observe the rules of debate: (of a chairman) to announce that a formal

meeting is starting; **call up** to summon, from beneath, or from another world, to a tribunal, to the colours, to memory; **on call** at call: ready to answer summons; **pay a call** (*coll. euph.*) to go to the lavatory, respond to a call of nature; **within call** within calling distance. [Found in O.E. (W.S.) as *ceallian;* O.N. *kalla.*]

call² *köl,* (*Spens.*) *n.* a caul or cap.

Calla *kal'ə, n.* a marsh plant of the arum family: (without *cap.*) erroneously (often **calla lily**) the lily of the Nile (*Zantedeschia*).   [Origin doubtful.]

callant *käl'ənt,* (*Scot.*) *n.* a lad.   [Du. *kalant.*]

caller *käl'ər, köl'ər,* (*Scot.*) *adj.* fresh: cool.   [Prob. the same as **calver.**]

callet *kal'it,* (*Shak.*) *n.* a scold, a woman of bad character, a trull.   [Origin obscure.]

calliature. See **caliature-wood.**

callid *kal'id, adj.* shrewd. — *n.* **callid'ity** shrewdness.   [L. *callidus,* expert.]

calligraphy *kə-lig'rə-fi, n.* fine penmanship: a characteristic style of writing: artistic script produced with a brush: a line or lines in art suggesting this. — *n.* **callig'rapher.** — *adjs.* **calligraphic** (*kal-i-graf'ik*), **-al.** — *ns.* **callig'raphist; call'igram(me)** a design using the letters of a word.   [Gr. *kallos,* beauty, *graphein,* to write.]

Calliope *kə-lī'ə-pi, kal-ī'o-pē, n.* the muse of epic poetry: (without *cap.*) a set of steam-whistles played by a keyboard.   [Gr. *Kalliopē.*]

callipers, (esp. *U.S.*) **calipers** *kal'i-pərz, n.pl.* compasses with legs suitable for measuring the inside or outside diameter of bodies. — Sometimes used in *sing.* — Also **call'iper-com'passes.** — *adj.* **call'iper.** — *v.t.* to measure with callipers. — **calliper (splint)** a splint fitted to the leg, so that the patient may walk without any pressure on the foot.   [**calibre.**]

Callippic. Same as **Calippic.**

callipygous *kal-i-pī'gəs, adj.* fair-buttocked. — Also **callipygean** (*-pij'i-ən*).   [Gr. *kallipȳgos,* an epithet of Aphrodite — *kallos,* beauty, *pȳgē,* buttock.]

Callistemon *kal-i-stē'mon, n.* an Australian genus of the myrtle family, bottle-brush shrubs.   [Gr. *kallos,* beauty, *stēmōn,* a thread (stamen).]

callisthenics *kal-is-then'iks, n.pl.* exercises for cultivating gracefulness and strength. — *adj.* **callisthen'ic.** — Also **calisthen'ics, -ic.**   [Gr. *kallos,* beauty, *sthenos,* strength.]

Callitriche *kal-it'ri-kē, n.* the water-starwort genus, constituting the **Callitrichā'ceae,** a family of uncertain affinities, placed by some beside the spurges and boxes, by others with the mare's-tails.   [Gr. *kallos,* beauty, *thrix, trichos,* hair.]

callous *kal'əs, adj.* hardened: unfeeling, cruel. — *n.* **callos'ity** a thickening of the skin: callousness. — *adv.* **call'ously.** — *n.* **call'ousness** lack of feeling, brutality.   [L. *callōsus* — *callus,* hard skin.]

callow¹ *kal'ō, adj.* not covered with feathers: unfledged, unbearded: inexperienced.   [O.E. *calu;* Ger. *kahl,* bald.]

callow² *kal'ō, adj.* low-lying and liable to be submerged. — *n.* an alluvial flat.   [Perh. Irish *calad,* a riverside meadow.]

Calluna *kə-lū'nə, n.* the heather genus.   [Gr. *kallȳnein,* to beautify, to sweep — *kalos,* beautiful.]

callus *kal'əs, n.* a thickening of the skin: new material by which fractured bones are consolidated (*path.*): soft tissue that forms over a cut surface (*bot.*).   [L.]

calm¹ *käm, adj.* still or quiet: (of person, action) serene, tranquil, assured: cool, impudent (*coll.*). — *n.* absence of wind — also in *pl.*: repose: serenity of feelings or actions. — *v.t.* and *v.i.* (also **calm down**) to make or become calm: to quiet. — *v.t.* to becalm. — *ns.* and *adjs.* (*med.*) **calmant, calmative** (both *kal'* or *kä'*). — *adj.* **calmed** (*kämd*). — *adv.* **calm'ly.** — *n.* **calm'ness.** — *adj.* **calm'y** (*Spens.*) characterised by calm.   [Fr. *calme* (It. *calma*), from L.L. *cauma* — Gr. *kauma,* noonday heat — *kaiein,* to burn.]

calm², **calmstane, -stone.** See **cam³.**

Calmuck. See **Kalmuck.**

calmy¹. See **calm¹.**

calmy². See **cam³.**

calomel *kal'ō-mel, n.* mercurous chloride, used in medicine. [Fr. *calomel,* apparently from Gr. *kalos,* beautiful, *melās,* black, possibly because, itself a colourless crystalline substance, it gives a black product with ammonia, or is got from a black mixture.]

caloric *ka-lor'ik, n.* heat (*arch.*): the once supposed material principle or cause of heat. — *ns.* **calorescence** (*kal-ər-es'əns;* an ill-formed word, meaning the contrary of what it should mean) the transmutation of heat rays into luminous rays; **cal'orie** the amount of heat needed to raise a gram of water (usu. at 15°C) 1° centigrade in temperature (*small* or *gram-calorie*) (in 1950 it was recommended that this should be superseded as unit by the *joule*; at 15°C, an *international table calorie* (cal$_{IT}$) = 4·1868 joules, a *thermochemical calorie* = 4·1840 joules): (sometimes with *cap.*) the amount of heat needed to raise a kilogram of water 1° centigrade in temperature (*great, large, kilogram-calorie, kilocalorie;* = 1000 small calories) (used in expressing the heat- or energy-producing value of foods): the hundredth part of the heat required to raise a gram from 0° to 100° (*mean calorie;* equal to 4·1897 joules). — *adj.* **calorif'ic** causing heat: heating. — *ns.* **calorifica'tion; calor'ifier** an apparatus for heating water in a tank, the source of heat being a coil of heated pipes immersed in the water; **calorim'eter** an instrument for measuring heat (not temperature) or thermal constants; **calorim'etry; cal'orist** one who held heat to be a subtle fluid called caloric. — **calor gas®** (sometimes with *caps.*) a type of gas for cooking, heating, etc. usually sold in large metal containers for use where there is no permanent supply of gas; **calorific value** of a food or fuel, the number of heat units got by complete combustion of unit mass. [L. *calor,* heat.]

calotte *kal-ot', n.* a plain skull-cap or coif worn by R.C. clergy. [Fr.]

calotype *kal'ō-tīp, n.* an early kind of photography (invented *c.* 1840 by W. H. Fox Talbot) by means of silver iodide and silver nitrate. — *n.* **cal'otypist.** [Gr. *kalos,* beautiful, *typos,* an image.]

caloyer *kal'o-yər, n.* a Greek monk, esp. of the order of St Basil. [Fr. — It. — Late Gr. *kalogēros.* — Gr. *kalos,* beautiful, *gēras,* old age.]

calp *kalp, n.* in Ireland, a dark shaly limestone occurring in the middle of the Carboniferous Limestone.

calpa. Same as **kalpa.**

calpac, calpack. See **kalpak.**

calque. See **calk³.**

Caltha *kal'thə, n.* a genus of flowers (fam. Ranunculaceae) to which the marsh marigold belongs: (without *cap.*) a plant of this genus. [L.]

caltrop *kal', köl'trop, n.* an instrument armed with four spikes, so arranged that one always stands upright, used to obstruct an enemy: a sponge spicule of like shape: a name for several plants with fruits so shaped, e.g. (esp. in *pl.*) water chestnut. — Also **cal'trap, cal'throp.** [O.E. *coltetræppe, calcatrippe* — L. *calx,* heel, and the root of **trap¹.**]

columba *ka-lum'bə, n.* the root of an East African plant (*Jateorhiza columba,* fam. Menispermaceae) used as a stomachic and tonic. [Perh. from *Colombo* in Sri Lanka.]

calumet *kal'ū-met, n.* the peace-pipe of the North American Indians, a tobacco-pipe smoked in token of peace. [Norman Fr. *calumet,* shepherd's pipe (Fr. *chalumet*) — L. *calamus,* reed.]

calumny *kal'əm-ni, n.* false accusation: slander. — *v.t.* **calumniate** (*kə-lum'ni-āt*) to accuse falsely: to slander. — *v.i.* to spread evil reports. —*ns.* **calumnia'tion; calum'niātor.** — *adjs.* **calum'niātory, calum'nious** of the nature of calumny: slanderous. — *adv.* **calum'niously.** [L. *calumnia,* prob. conn. with *calvī,* to deceive.]

Calvados *kal'və-dos,* or *-dos', n.* a liqueur made from cider or apple-pulp, esp. in the Calvados department of Normandy.

Calvary *kal'və-ri, n.* the name of the place where Jesus was crucified: a representation of Christ's crucifixion, or a series of scenes connected with it. — **Calvary cross** a Latin cross on three steps. [L. *calvāria,* Vulgate rendering of Gr. *krānion,* as that again of Aramaic *gogulthō* or *gogolthā* (Heb. *gulgōleth* — Grecised as *golgotha*), all three words meaning skull.]

calve, calves. See **calf.**

calver *kal'vər, v.t.* to prepare (salmon or other fish) when alive or freshly caught. — *adj.* **cal'vered.** [Cf. **caller.**]

Calvinism *kal'vin-izm, n.* the doctrines of the great Genevan religious reformer, John *Calvin* (1509–1564), as these are given in his *Institutio,* esp. on particular election, predestination, the incapacity for true faith and repentance of the natural man, efficacious grace, and final perseverance (continuance of the saints in a state of grace until the final state of glory). — *n.* **Cal'vinist.** — *adjs.* **Calvinist'ic, -al.**

calvities *kal-vish'i-ēz, n.* baldness. [L. *calvitiēs* — *calvus,* bald.]

calx *kalks, n.* the substance of a metal or mineral that remains after strong heating: — *pl.* **calxes** (*kalk'siz*) or **calces** (*kal'sēz*). [L. *calx, calcis,* lime.]

Calycanthus, etc. See under **calyx.**

calypso *ka-lip'sō, n.* a West-Indian folk-song, usually dealing with current events, usually made up as the singer goes along: — *pl.* **calyp'sos.** — *n.* **calypso'nian** a writer or singer of calypsos. [Poss. from 17th–18th cent. W. African *kaiso,* ceremonial song.]

calyptra *ka-lip'trə, n.* a Greek veil: a hood, covering, esp. that of a moss capsule, or of a root. — *adj.* **calyp'trate** capped. — *n.* **calyp'trogen** the group of cells giving rise to the root-cap. [Gr. *kalyptrā,* a veil.]

calyx *kā'liks, kal'iks, n.* the outer covering of a flower, its separate leaves termed sepals (*bot.*): applied to various cup-like structures, as the cup of a coral (*biol.*; by confusion with **calix,** q.v.): — *pl.* **ca'lyces** (*-sēz*) or **ca'lyxes.** — *n.pl.* **Calycanthaceae** (*kal-ik-an-thā'si-ē;* Gr. *anthos,* flower) the Carolina allspice family of plants, in which there is a transition from sepals to petals. — *ns.* **calycanthemy** (*kal-ik-an'thi-mi;* Gr. *anthemon,* flower) the condition of having the calyx like a corolla; **Calycan'thus** a small North American genus of shrubs, Carolina allspice or strawberry shrub: (without *cap.*) a shrub of the genus. — *n.pl.* **Calyciflorae** (*-is-i-flō'rē, -flō';* L. *flōs, flōris,* flower) a subclass of dicotyledons with a corolla of distinct petals. — *adjs.* **calyciform** (*kal-is'*) having the form of a calyx; **calyc'-inal, calycine** (*kal'i-sīn*) pertaining to a calyx. — *ns.* **cal'ycle, cal'ycule** a whorl of bracts, epicalyx or involucre (*bot.*): a calyx (*zool.*). — *adjs.* **cal'ycled** having a calycle; **cal'ycoid, calycoi'deous** like a calyx. [Gr. *kalyx,* a covering — *kalyptein,* to cover.]

calzone *kal-tsō'ne, n.* a pastry roll filled with cheese, tomato, etc.: — *pl.* **calzo'ni, calzo'nes.** [It.]

cam¹ *kam,* (*mech.*) *n.* an eccentric projection on a revolving shaft, shaped so as to give some desired linear motion to another part. — **cam'shaft, cam'-wheel** a shaft, wheel, bearing a cam or cams. [Du. *kam,* cam, comb; cf. **comb, kame.**]

cam² *adj.* and *adv.* See **kam.**

cam³, *caum, calm käm, köm,* (*Scot.*) *n.* pale blaes: a slate-pencil: pipeclay: limestone (*obs.*). — *v.t.* to whiten with camstone. — *adj.* **calm'y** clayey. — **cam'stone, caum'-, calm'-, cam'stane,** etc. a white argillaceous stone used for whitening hearthstones and doorsteps. [Origin unknown.]

Cama. See **Kama.**

camaieu *kam-a-yø', n.* a cameo: a painting in monochrome, or in simple colours not imitating nature: a style of printing pictures producing the effect of pencil-drawing: — *pl.* **camaieux** (*-yø'*). [Fr.; see **cameo.**]

Camaldolite *kam-al'dō-līt, n.* a member of a religious

order founded by St Romuald at *Camaldoli* early in the 11th century. — Also *adj.* — *n.* and *adj.* **Camal'- dolese.**

caman *kam'an, n.* a shinty stick. — *n.* **camanachd** (*kam-an-ahh(k)'*) shinty. [Gael.]

camaraderie *kam-ə-räd'ə-rē, n.* good fellowship: the intimacy of comradeship. [Fr.]

camarilla *kam-ə-ril'ə, n.* a body of secret intriguers, esp. of a court party against legitimate ministers: a small room. [Sp. dim. of *cámara,* a chamber.]

camaron *kam-ar-ōn', kam'ə-ron, n.* a kind of freshwater crustacean resembling a crayfish. [Sp. *camarón,* a shrimp — L. *cam(m)arus,* a sea-crab, — Gr. *kammaros.*]

camass, camas, camash, quamash *kam'as, -ash, kwom'ash, kwam-ash', ns.* a small plant (*Camassia*) of the lily family growing in the north-western United States: its nutritious bulb. — **cam'ass-rat** a small gopher rodent that devours the bulbs. [Chinook *kámass.*]

camber *kam'bər, n.* a slight convexity upon an upper surface (as on a road, a beam, the deck of a ship, the wing section of an aeroplane, etc.): a small dock for timber. — *v.t.* and *v.i.* to arch slightly. [Fr. *cambre* — L. *camerāre,* to vault.]

Camberwell beauty *kam'bər-wəl bū'ti,* (*Vanessa,* or *Nymphalis, antiopa*) a large and beautiful butterfly, first recorded in England in 1748 at *Camberwell,* then a rural place.

cambist *kam'bist, n.* one skilled in the science of financial exchange. — *ns.* **cam'bism, cam'bistry.** [It. *cambista* — L. *cambīre,* to exchange.]

cambium *kam'bi-əm,* (*bot.*) *n.* a layer or cylinder of meristem by whose differentiation into xylem and phloem new wood and bast are formed. — *adjs.* **cam'bial; cam'biform.** [L.L. — L. *cambīre,* to change.]

camboge. Obsolete form of **gamboge.**

cambrel *kam'brəl, n.* a bent stick or rod for hanging a carcase: an animal's hock. [Perh. conn. with **camber,** or with **gambrel.**]

Cambrian *kam'bri-ən, adj.* pertaining to *Cambria* or Wales: Welsh: the geol. system (well represented in Wales) next above the Archaean. — *n.* an inhabitant of Cambria, or Wales: the Cambrian system. [Latinised from W. *Cymry,* Welshmen, *Cymru,* Wales.]

cambric *kām'brik, n.* a fine white linen, originally manufactured at *Kamerijk* (Cambrai) in French Flanders: a cotton imitation. — **cambric tea** a beverage made of hot water, milk, sugar and sometimes a small amount of tea.

Cambridge *kām'brij, adj.* of or pertaining to *Cambridge,* an English university town. — **Cambridge blue** a light blue (see also **blue**); **Cambridge roller** a ring roller.

camcorder *kam'kör'dər, n.* a video *cam*era and sound re*corder* combined in one unit.

came[1] *kām, pa.t.* of **come.**

came[2]. See **kame[2].**

camel *kam'əl, n.* an animal of Asia and Africa with one or two humps on its back, used as a beast of burden and for riding: a watertight structure for raising a vessel in shallow water: a humped type of aeroplane: a light yellowish-brown colour. — *adj.* of the colour camel. — *ns.* **cam'eleer** one who drives or rides a camel; **cam'elid** an animal of the **Camel'idae,** the camel family of artiodactyls. — Also *adj.* — *n.* **cam'eline** a material made from camel's hair. — *adj.* of the nature of a camel. — *adjs.* **cam'elish** like a camel, obstinate; **cam'eloid** of the camel family. — Also *n.* — *n.* **cam'elry.** — **cam'elback** an inferior grade of rubber, made from reclaimed or synthetic rubber, used for retreading tyres. — *adj.* **cam'el-backed** hump-backed. — **cam'el-corps** troops mounted on camels; **camel('s) hair** the hair of the camel: the hair of the squirrel's tail used for paint-brushes; **camel spin** a type of spin in skating in which one leg is extended horizontally behind the skater; **camel's thorn** a papilionaceous manna-yielding desert plant (*Alhagi maurorum*) which camels eat

greedily. [L. *camēlus* — Gr. *kamēlos* — Phoenician or Heb. *gāmāl.*]

cameleon. Same as **chameleon.**

Camellia *ka-mēl'yə, -mel', n.* a genus of evergreen shrubs close akin to tea, natives of eastern Asia, grown for the singular beauty of their flowers: (without *cap.*) any shrub of the genus. [Named from Kamel, Latinised *Camellus,* a Moravian Jesuit, who collected plants in the Philippine Islands.]

camelopard *kam-el'ō-pärd,* or *kam'əl-ō-pärd, n.* the giraffe. — Also **cameleopard** (*kam-ə-lep'ərd*; as by Shelley, by confusion with **leopard**). — *n.* **Camelopardalis** (*kə-mel-ə-pär'də-lis*) a northern constellation. [L. *camēlopardus* — Gr. *kamēlopardălis*; from Gr. *kamēlos,* the camel, and *pardălis,* the panther.]

camelot *kam'lot, n.* Same as **camlet.**

Camembert *kam'əm-ber,* Fr. *kam-ā-ber, n.* a soft rich cheese made near *Camembert,* in Normandy.

cameo *kam'i-ō, n.* a gem with figure carved in relief, esp. one in which a differently coloured lower layer serves as ground: a short literary piece: a small rôle in a play or film, giving scope for character acting: — *pl.* **cam'eos.** — *adj.* miniature, small and perfect of its kind. — **cam'eo-part, -rôle; cam'eo-shell'** a helmet-shell; **cameo ware** pottery with relief figures against a different colour. [It. *cammeo* — L.L. *cammaeus,* of unknown origin.]

camera *kam'ər-ə, n.* a vaulted room: a judge's private chamber: a legislative chamber: the papal treasury: the photographer's apparatus, in which the outside image is recorded on a light-sensitive plate or film: the apparatus that receives the image of the scene and converts it into electrical impulses for transmission (*TV*): — *pl.* **cam'eras.** — *adjs.* **cam'eral; cam'erated** chambered: vaulted. — *n.* **camerā'tion.** — **camera lucida** (*lū'sid-ə*; L., light chamber) a drawing device by which the image of the object is made by reflection to appear as if projected on the paper; **cam'eraman** a photographer, esp. for press, television, or cinema; **camera obscura** (*ob-skūr'ə*; L., dark chamber) dark chamber in which an image of outside objects is thrown upon a screen. — *adj.* **cam'era-shy** (*coll.*) not liking to be photographed. — **cam'erawork.** — **in camera** in a (judge's private) room: in secret; **on camera** in front of a camera, being filmed. [L. *camera,* Gr. *kamarā,* vault.]

camerlengo *kam-ər-leng'gō,* **camerlingo** *-ling'gō, ns.* a papal treasurer: — *pls.* **camerleng'os, -ling'os.** [It.; conn. **chamberlain.**]

Cameronian *kam-ə-rōn'i-ən, n.* a follower of the Covenanter Richard *Cameron,* a member of the Reformed Presbyterian Church, a body that refused to accept the Revolution settlement (most united with the Free Church in 1876): a soldier of the Cameronian regiment (26th Foot, later First Battalion of Scottish Rifles, disbandment announced 1968), formed from a body of Cameronians (1689). — Also *adj.*

camese. See **camise.**

camiknickers. See under **camis.**

camino real *kä-mē'nō rā-äl',* (Sp.) lit. 'royal road': a highway.

camion *kam'i-ən, n.* a heavy lorry, wagon. [Fr.]

camis *kam'is,* **camus** *kam'əs, ns.* (*Spens.*) a loose light robe. — *ns.* **camisade', camisā'do** (*pl.* **camisā'dos**) (for Sp. *camisada*) a night attack, probably because shirts were often put on over armour; **cam'isard** (*-sär, -zär*) an insurgent Huguenot of the Cevennes, so called from the *camise* or blouse worn by the peasants; **cam'isole** a sleeved jacket, a woman's loose morning gown or jacket: a loose underbodice with or without sleeves. — *n.pl.* **cam'iknick'ers** combined camisole and knickers. [Sp. and Prov. *camisa,* shirt — L. *camisia.*]

camise, camese *kam-ēs', n.* the usual Arab shirt. [Ar. *qamīç,* perh. L. *camisia.*]

camlet *kam'lit, n.* a cloth perhaps originally of camel's hair, but now chiefly of wool and goat's hair. [Fr.

— L.L. *camelotum* — L. *camēlus*; or perh. Ar. *khamlat*, nap.]

camomile, chamomile *kam'ō-mīl, n.* a name for several plants akin to chrysanthemum, or their dried flowers, used in medicine, affording a bitter stomachic and tonic — esp. *Anthemis nobilis* (common camomile) and *Matricaria chamomilla* (wild camomile). — **c(h)amomile tea** medicinal tea made with dried camomile flowers. [Fr. *camomille* — L. *chamomilla* — Gr. *chamaimēlon*, lit. earth-apple, from the apple-like smell of its blossoms — *chamai*, on the ground, *mēlon*, an apple.]

Camorra *kam-or'ə, n.* a Neapolitan secret society similar to the Mafia. — *ns.* **Camorr'ism; Camorr'ist, Camorris'ta.** [It.]

camouflet *kä-mōō-flä', n.* a mine to destroy an underground hostile gallery: an underground cavern filled with gas and smoke formed by a bomb exploding beneath the surface. — *n.* **cam'ouflage** (*-fläzh*) any device or means (esp. visual) for disguising, or for deceiving an adversary: the use of such a device or means. — *v.t.* and *v.i.* to deceive, to counterfeit, to disguise. [Fr. *camouflet*, a whiff of smoke intentionally blown in the face, an affront, a camouflet.]

camp¹ *kamp, n.* a place on which a tent or tents or the like are pitched: a collection of temporary dwellings, or their inhabitants collectively: temporary quarters of an army, tribe, travellers, holiday-makers, or others: an old fortified site: a permanent military station: a mushroom town, as a mining camp: military service or life (*fig.*): a party or side. — *v.i.* to encamp, or pitch tents: to lodge in a camp (often with *out*, i.e. in the open). — *n.* **camp'er** one who camps: a motor vehicle purpose-built, or which can be converted, for use as temporary living accommodation. — **camp'-bed, -chair, -stool** a portable folding bed, etc.; **camp'-fe'ver** typhus, typhoid, or other fever apt to occur in camps; **camp'-fire** the fire of an encampment; a reunion, lodge, or section, of certain organisations; **camp'-foll'ower** a non-combatant who follows in the train of an army, as sutler, servant, etc.; a person associated with a (political, etc.) group without actually being a member; **camp'ground** (*U.S.*) a campsite; **camp'-meet'ing** a religious gathering in the open air or in a temporary encampment; **camp'-preach'er** one who preaches at such meetings; **camp'site** ground suitable, or specially laid out, for camping. — **camp on** (*telecomm.*) to put (a telephone call) through to an engaged extension, to be connected automatically when the extension is free; **camp out** to live temporarily in a tent or in the open air: to stay temporarily in improvised accommodation. [Fr. *camp*, camp — L. *campus*, a plain.]

camp² *kamp*, (*obs.*) *n.* conflict: an old form of the game of football. — *v.i.* to fight, struggle. — *v.i.* **cam'ple** to wrangle. [O.E. *camp*, battle; cf. Ger. *Kampf.*]

camp³ *kamp, adj.* theatrical, affected, exaggerated: homosexual: characteristic of homosexuals. — *n.* absurd extravagance in manner, deliberate (**high camp**) or without full awareness of the effect. — Also *v.i.* — *adj.* **camp'y.** — **camp up** to make exaggerated, etc.; **camp it up** to show camp qualities ostentatiously. [Ety. unknown.]

campaign *kam-pān', n.* champaign or open country (*arch.*): the time during which an army keeps the field: the operations of that time: an excursion into the country: an organised series of operations in the advocacy of some cause or object. — *v.i.* to serve in or conduct a campaign. — *ns.* **campagna** (*käm-pän'yä*; It.) once equivalent to *champaign*, now only a geographical proper name; **campaign'er** a person actively involved in a political or other campaign: one who has served in several campaigns, a veteran (also **old campaigner**). [Fr. *campagne* — L. *campania* — *campus*, a field.]

campana *kam-pā'nə, n.* a bell-shaped object, as the core of a Corinthian capital: a flower, perhaps the pasque-flower (*Drayton*). — *n.* **campanist** (*kam'pən-ist*) one

versed in bells. — *adjs.* **campaniform** (*-pan'*) bell-shaped; **campanolog'ical.** — *ns.* **campanol'ogist; campanol'ogy** the subject or science of bells or bell-ringing; **Campan'ula** a genus (giving name to a family **Campanulā'ceae**) commonly known as bell-flowers or bells, the best-known the harebell or Scottish bluebell. — *adjs.* **campanūlā'ceous; campan'ūlar.** — *n.* **Campanūlā'ria** a common genus of Hydrozoa, with stems simple or branched, the nutritive polyps surrounded by transparent bell-shaped sheaths. — *adj.* **campan'ūlate** bell-shaped. [It. *campana*, a bell.]

campanero *kam-pa-nē'rō, n.* the South American bell-bird or arapunga, a snow-white chatterer with a note like a church bell: — *pl.* **campane'ros.** [Sp., bellman.]

campanile *kam-pan-ē'lā, n.* a bell-tower, esp. a tall one detached from the church: — *pl.* **campani'les**, sometimes (It.) **campani'li** (*-lē*). [It., from *campana*, a bell.]

campanology, etc. See under **campana**.

Campari *kam-pä'ri, n.* a bitter-tasting, bright-red-coloured apéritif. [Name of manufacturers; trade name in U.S.]

Campbellite *kam'bəl-īt, n.* a member of the sect known as Disciples of Christ, founded by Alexander *Campbell* (1788–1866).

campeachy-wood *kam-pēch'i-wŏŏd, n.* logwood, first exported from Campeachy (*Campeche*, in Mexico).

campeador *kam-pi-ə-dör', n.* a champion, esp. the Cid. [Sp.]

campesino *kam-pə-sē'nō, n.* a Latin-American peasant farmer: — *pl.* **campesin'os.** [Sp., — *campo*, country, field — L. *campus*, field.]

campestral *kam-pes'trəl, adj.* growing in or pertaining to fields. — Also **campes'trian.** [L. *campester* — *campus*, field.]

camphire *kam'fīr, n.* an old name for camphor: henna (*Bible*). [**camphor.**]

camphor *kam'fər, n.* a solid essential oil, got from the camphor laurel (a species of cinnamon-tree) of Taiwan, etc., or synthetically manufactured, having a peculiar aromatic taste and smell: any similar compound of the terpene series. — *ns.* **camphane** (*kam'fān*) a terpene hydrocarbon ($C_{10}H_{18}$), parent substance of the camphor group; **camphene** (*kam'fēn, -fēn'*) a camphor-like terpene hydrocarbon ($C_{10}H_{16}$); **camphine** (*kam'fēn, -fīn*) an old name for rectified oil of turpentine. — *adj.* **camphorā'ceous** like camphor. — *v.t.* **cam'phorate** to impregnate with camphor. — *adj.* **camphoric** (*-for'ik*) pertaining to camphor. [Fr. *camphre* — L.L. *camphora* — Ar. *kāfūr.*]

campion *kam'pi-ən, n.* any plant of the genera *Lychnis* (or *Melandryum*) and *Silene.* [Origin obscure; poss. — obs. *campion*, champion.]

cample. See **camp².**

Campodea *kam-pō'di-ə, n.* a genus of bristle-tails. — *adj.* **campodē'iform** resembling a bristle-tail, as certain six-legged active insect grubs. [Gr. *kampē*, caterpillar, *eidos*, form.]

campo santo *kam'pō san'tō*, (It.) a burying-ground.

camp-sheathing, -shedding, -sheeting, -shot *kamp'shē'-dhing, -shed'ing, -shēt'ing, -shot, ns.* piles and boarding protecting a river bank or the like. [Origin unknown.]

Camptonite *kamp'tən-īt, n.* an igneous rock composed essentially of plagioclase and hornblende. [*Campton* in New Hampshire.]

campus *kam'pəs, n.* college grounds (and buildings), or college, or self-contained division of a university: a university: the academic world. [L., field.]

Campus Martius *kam'pəs mär'shəs, kam'pŏŏs mär'ti-ŏŏs*, (L.) field of Mars, used by the ancient Romans for athletic games, military drill, etc.

campylotropous *kam-pil-ot'rə-pəs, adj.* of an ovule, curved so as to bring the micropyle near the chalaza. [Gr. *kampylos*, curved, *tropē*, turning.]

camsho *kam'shō*, **camshoch, camsheugh** *kam'shuhh*, (*Scot.*) *adjs.* crooked. [Cf. **cam¹**, and O.E. *sceolh*, awry.]

For other sounds see detailed chart of pronunciation.

camstairy, camsteerie, camsteary *kam-stär'i, -stēr'i,* (chiefly *Scot.*) *adjs.* perverse, unruly. [Ety. dub.]
camstone. See **cam³**.
camus¹ *kam'əs, adj.* flat-nosed. [Prob. Fr. *camus.*]
camus². See **camis.**
cam-wood *kam'-wŏod, n.* the wood of *Baphia nitida,* a West African papilionaceous tree, at first white, turning red on exposure to air, used as a red dye. [Perh. from African name *kambi.*]
can¹ *kan, v.t.* (*obs.* in *infin.* except in Scots) to be able: to have sufficient power: to know (*obs.*): to have skill in: —*3rd pers.* **can**, *2nd sing.* **canst**; *parts. obs.* except **could** in Scots; *pa.t.* **could**. — **can** is used for *gan* in M.E. and in Spenser. [O.E. *cunnan,* to know (how to do a thing), to be able; *pres. indic. can*; Goth. *kunnan,* Ger. *können,* to be able. See **con², ken¹, know;** also **cannot, can't, couth.**]
can² *kan, n.* a vessel for holding or carrying liquids, generally of tinned iron, with a handle over the top: a chimney-pot: a tin, vessel of tin-plate in which meat, fruit, etc., are sealed up: a drinking-mug: a container for various things, as ashes, rubbish (*U.S.*), or film in quantity: a jacket in which a fuel rod is sealed in an atomic reactor: (with *the*) jail (*slang*): a lavatory (*slang*): (in *pl.*) headphones (*slang*). — *v.t.* to put up for preservation in tins: to store in containers: — *pr.p.* **cann'ing;** *pa.p.* and *pa.t.* **canned**. — *adj.* **canned** packed in tins (or in U.S. jars): drunk (*slang*): (of music) recorded for reproduction by e.g. gramophone. — *ns.* **can'ful** as much as a can will hold: — *pl.* **can'fuls; cann'er; cann'ery** a place where provisions are tinned. — **can'-opener** a tin-opener. — **can it!** (*slang*) stop talking about, doing, etc., that!; **can of worms** an unpredictable and potentially difficult situation or problem; **carry the can** (*slang*) to take the blame; **in the can** (of motion picture) ready for release: (of radio, TV, material), recorded and stored for future use. [O.E. *canne.*]
cañada *kän-yä'dä, n.* a narrow cañon. [Sp.]
Canadian *kə-nā'di-ən, adj.* pertaining to *Canada.* — *n.* a native or citizen of Canada. — **Canada balsam** see **balsam; Canada Day** a Canadian public holiday, the anniversary of the union of the provinces, 1 July 1867 (formerly called **Dominion Day**); **Canada goose** a common wild goose (*Branta canadensis*) of N. America; **Canada rice** see **Zizania; Canadian waterweed** see **Anacharis.**
canaigre *kə-nā'gər, kə-nī'grē, n.* a Texan dock whose root is used in tanning. [Mexican Sp.]
canaille *kan-äy', kan-ī', kən-āl', n.* the mob, the vulgar rabble. [Fr., — L. *canis,* a dog.]
canakin. See **cannikin.**
canal *kə-nal', n.* an artificial watercourse, esp. for navigation: a duct that conveys fluids (*biol.*): a groove. — *adjs.* **canalicular** (*kan-ə-lik'ū-lər*) like or pertaining to a canaliculus; **canalic'ulate, -d** channelled, grooved. — *ns.* **canalic'ulus** (*anat.*) a small furrow or channel: — *pl.* **canalic'ulī; canalisation, -z-** (*kan-əl-ī-zā'shən*) the construction of canals: formation of an artificial channel: conversion into a canal: direction into a fixed channel (*lit.* and *fig.*). — *v.t.* **can'alise, -ize** to make a canal through: to convert into a canal: to direct into a fixed channel (*lit.* and *fig.*). — **canal'-boat** a boat for canal traffic; **canal'-cell** a cell in the neck of an archegonium; **canal'-rays'** (*phys.*) positive rays, a stream of positively electrified particles through a perforation in the cathode of a vacuum-tube. [L. *canālis,* a water-pipe.]
canapé *ka'nə-pi, ka-na-pā, ns.* a small biscuit or piece of pastry or bread, etc., with a savoury filling or spread, usu. served with drinks: a sofa: a method of bidding in contract bridge in which a player bids a weak suit first, then rebids in his strongest suit. [Fr.]
canard *ka-när(d)', n.* a false rumour: a second wing fitted near the nose of an aircraft, esp. one smaller than the main wing and acting as the horizontal stabilizer: an aircraft with such a wing. — *adj.* denoting such a wing,

aircraft configuration, etc. [Fr., lit. duck.]
Canarese. See **Kanarese.**
canary *kə-nā'ri, n.* a light sweet wine from the *Canary* Islands: a song-bird (finch) found in the Canary Islands, bright yellow in domestic breeds: a lively dance said to have taken origin in the Canary Islands (often in *pl.*): an informer (*slang*). — *adj.* canary-coloured, bright yellow. — *v.i.* to dance the canary: to prance about. — **canā'ry-bird** a canary: a jail-bird (*slang*): a mistress; **canā'ry-cree'per** a yellow-flowered Tropaeolum (popularly but ungrammatically **canarien'sis**); **canā'ry-grass** a grass (*Phalaris canariensis*) whose seed (**canā'ry-seed**) is used to feed canaries, etc.; **canā'ry-wood** the timber of two species of *Persea* or *Laurus* of the Canary Islands, Azores and Madeira.
canasta *kə-nas'tə, n.* a card game of the rummy type, originating in South America. [Sp., basket.]
canaster *kə-nas'tər, n.* a kind of tobacco, so called from the rush basket in which it was originally brought from Spanish America. [Sp. *canastra, canasta* — Gr. *kanastron.*]
cancan *kan'kan, n.* a stage dance of French origin, orig. considered particularly indecorous. [Fr. *cancan,* chatter, scandal, the cancan; usually referred to L. *quamquam,* the pronunciation of which was long hotly disputed in the French schools; Littré quotes O.Fr. *caquehan,* a noisy assembly.]
cancel *kan'sl, v.t.* to cross out: to annul or suppress: to abolish or wipe out: to counterbalance or compensate for: (often with *out*) to remove as balancing each other, e.g. like quantities from opposite sides of an equation, like factors from numerator and denominator of a fraction. — *v.i.* (with *out*) to neutralise each other: — *pr.p.* **can'celling;** *pa.t.* and *pa.p.* **can'celled**. — *n.* the suppression of a printed leaf or sheet: the part so cancelled, or (usually) the new one substituted. — *adjs.* **can'cellate, -d** marked latticewise, reticulated. — *n.* **cancellā'tion** cancelling: crosswise marking. — *n.pl.* **cancelli** (*kan-sel'ī;* L. *kang-kel'ē*) cross-pieces forming a lattice-work or grating, as in the division between the choir and the body of a church: reticulations (*anat.*). — *adj.* **can'cellous.** [L. *cancellāre,* to cross out, *cancellī,* lattice-work, dim. of *cancer,* a lattice.]
cancelier, canceleer *kan-si-lēr', (Scott) v.i.* of a hawk, to turn on the wing before stopping. — Also *n.*
cancellarial, -ian *kan-səl-ār'i-əl, -i-ən, adjs.* relating to a chancellor. — *n.* **cancellā'riate** chancellorship. [L. *cancellārius;* see **chancellor.**]
Cancer *kan'sər, n.* the genus to which the edible crab belongs: a constellation (the Crab) between Gemini and Leo, and a sign of the zodiac (once coincident with it) whose first point marks the limits of the sun's course northward in summer: one born under this sign: (**cancer**) loosely any malignant new growth or tumour: properly a carcinoma or disorderly growth of epithelial cells which invade adjacent tissue and spread by the lymphatics and blood-vessels to other parts of the body: any corroding evil (*fig.*). — *v.i.* **can'cerate** to become cancerous. — *n.* **cancerā'tion**. — *adj.* **can'cerous** of, like, affected with, cancer. — *adjs.* **cancriform** (*kang'kri-förm*) crab-shaped: like cancer; **cancrine** (*kang'krīn*) crab-like: palindromic (from the false notion that a crab walked backwards); **cancrizans** (*kang'kri-zanz; mus.*) of a canon, having the answer repeating the subject backwards; **cancroid** (*kang'kroid*) crab-like: cancer-like. — Also *n.* — **can'cer-root** beech-drops; **can'cer-stick** (*slang*) a cigarette. [L., crab.]
cancionero *kän-thyō-nā'rō, n.* a collection of songs: — *pl.* **cancione'ros.** [Sp.]
cancriform, cancrizans, etc. See **Cancer.**
candela *kan-del'ə, -dē'lə, n.* a unit of luminous intensity such that the luminous intensity of a black body radiator at the temperature of solidification of platinum is 60 candelas per sq. cm. [**candle.**]
candelabrum *kan-di-lä'brəm,* or *-lä', n.* a branched and ornamented candlestick or lampstand: — *pl.* **candela'-bra** — also used as a false *sing.* with *pl.* **candela'bras.**

— **candelabrum tree** any of several African trees with branches arranged like a candelabrum. [L. *candēlābrum* — *candēla*, candle.]

candelilla *kän-dā-lēl'yə, n.* a Mexican wax-yielding spurge. [Sp., dim. of *candela*, candle.]

candent *kan'dənt, adj.* glowing: white-hot. — *n.* **candescence** (*kan-des'əns*) a white heat. — *adj.* **candesc'ent.** [L. *candēre*, to glow (inceptive *candēscĕre*).]

candid *kan'did, adj.* white (*obs.*): shining, clear: frank, ingenuous: free from prejudice: fair, impartial. — *adv.* **can'didly.** — *n.* **can'didness.** — **candid camera** a type of camera used for taking unposed photographs or films of people engaged in the normal occupations of their daily life: this style of photography. [L. *candidus*, white.]

candida *kan'did-ə, n.* one of the genus **Candida** of parasitic, yeastlike imperfect fungi. — *n.* **candidiasis** (*kan-di-dī'ə-sis*) an infection of the skin or mucous membranes caused by a candida (usu. *C. albicans* which causes thrush). [L. *candida*, fem. of *candidus*, white.]

candidate *kan'di-dāt, n.* one who offers himself for any office or honour, so called because, at Rome, the applicant used to dress in white: an examinee. — *ns.* **can'didature, can'didateship, can'didacy** (*-də-si*). [L. *candidātus* — *candidus*, white.]

candie. See **candy².**

candied. See **candy¹.**

candle *kan'dl, n.* a cylinder of wax, tallow, or the like surrounding a wick: a luminary: a candle-shaped object: a jet in a gas-stove: a photometric unit: (or **new candle**) candela: (**international candle** or **standard candle**) a former unit of luminous intensity. — *v.t.* to test (as an egg) by holding up before a candle or other light. — **can'dle-berry** wax-myrtle or bayberry (*Myrica cerifera*) of the spurge family, or its fruit; **can'dle-bomb** a small glass bomb filled with water, exploding in a candle-flame; **can'dle-coal** same as **cannel-coal**; **can'dle-dipp'ing** the method of making candles by dipping instead of moulding; **can'dle-doup** see **doup**; **can'dle-end** the end-piece of a burnt-out candle; **can'dle-fish** the eulachon: another West American fish, a cheek-armoured acanthopterygian (*Anoplopoma fimbria*) — the *black candle-fish*; **can'dle-holder** one who holds a candle to another while working — hence one who abets or connives; **can'dle-light** the light of a candle: illumination by candles: the time when candles are lighted; **can'dle-lighter** one whose business is to light the candles: a spill; **can'dle-nut** the oil-yielding fruit of a species of *Aleurites* (spurge family) of the Pacific Islands; **can'dle-power** illuminating power in terms of a standard candle — a name applied to various units of photometry; **can'dle-snuffer** a snuffer, instrument or person (see **snuff²**; also *fig.*); **can'dlestick** a portable stand for a candle, originally a stick or piece of wood; **can'dle-tree** a tropical American tree (*Parmentiera cerifera*) of Bignonia family, with candle-like pods; **can'dle-waster** one who studies late; **can'dlewick** the wick of a candle: a cotton tufted material used for bedspreads, etc.; **can'dle-wood** the wood of various West Indian and Mexican resinous trees. — **burn the candle at both ends** to waste or use up in two ways at once: to exhaust oneself by attempting to do too much, usu. by going to bed late and getting up early for work; **do a candle** of a parachute, to fail to inflate; **not fit to hold a candle to** not to be compared with; **sell by the candle** to offer for sale as long as a small piece of candle burns, the bid made just before it goes out being successful; **the game is not worth the candle** the thing is not worth the labour or expense of it. [O.E. *candel* — L. *candēla*, from *candēre*, to glow.]

Candlemas *kan'dl-məs, n.* the R.C. festival of the purification of the Virgin Mary, on 2nd February, when candles are blessed: a quarter-day in Scotland. [**candle, mass.**]

candock *kan'dok, n.* the yellow water-lily. [**can²** and **dock¹.**]

candour, in U.S. **candor,** *kan'dər, n.* whiteness (now *rare*):

purity (*obs.*): kindness (*obs.*): freedom from prejudice: sincerity: frankness. [Fr. *candeur* — L. *candor*, whiteness, from *candēre*, to shine.]

candy¹ *kan'di, n.* a sweetmeat of sugar boiled and crystallised (also **su'gar-can'dy**): any form of confectionery (*U.S.*): cocaine (*slang*): — *U.S. pl.* **can'dies.** — *v.t.* to preserve or dress with sugar: to crystallise as sugar or the like: to encrust. — *v.i.* to crystallise: to become encrusted. — *adj.* **can'died** encrusted with candy or sugar: sugared, flattering (*fig.*). — **candy floss** a fluffy sweetmeat consisting of a ball of spun coloured and flavoured sugar sold on the end of a stick: something insubstantial or ephemeral. — Also *adj.* — **candy stripe** a textile fabric pattern, consisting of narrow coloured stripes on a white background at intervals equal or nearly equal to the width of the stripe. [Fr. *candi*, from Ar. *qandah*, candy.]

candy² *kan'di, n.* a South Indian weight, generally containing 20 maunds, about 500 pounds English. — Also **can'die** and **kan'dy.** [Tamil.]

candytuft *kan'di-tuft, n.* a cruciferous plant (*Iberis*), with flowers in tufts or corymbs, the outer petals larger than the inner. [From *Candia* (Crete), whence a species was brought, and **tuft.**]

cane *kān, n.* the stem of one of the small palms (as calamus or rattan) or the larger grasses (as bamboo, sugarcane), or raspberry or the like: a slender rod for beating: a walking-stick. — *v.t.* to beat with a cane: to make or weave with canes, e.g. chairs. — *n.* **can'ing** a thrashing with a cane: a severe beating or defeat (*coll.*). — *adj.* **can'y** like, made of, or abounding in cane. — *adj.* **cane'-bottomed** having a seat of interwoven cane strips. — **cane'-brake** a thicket of canes, esp. (in Southern U.S.) of a giant reed; **cane'-chair** chair made of rattan; **cane'fruit** fruit borne upon canes, as raspberries, blackberries; **cane'-mill** a mill for crushing sugar-cane; **cane'-sugar** sucrose, esp. that obtained from the sugar-cane; **cane'-toad** (*Austr.*) the large toad (*Bufo marinus*) introduced to, and now abundant in, Queensland; **cane'-trash** refuse of sugar-cane used for fuel in boiling the juice. [Fr. *canne* — L. *canna* — Gr. *kannē*, a reed.]

caneh. See **kaneh.**

canella *kan-el'ə, n.* cinnamon (*obs.*): (with *cap.*) a genus of low aromatic trees of a small family **Canellā'ceae** (*-si-ē*), one of which yields white cinnamon or *canella* bark. [L.L., dim. of *canna*, reed.]

canephor *kan'i-fōr, -för*, (*archit.*). *n.* a female (or male) sculptured figure bearing a basket on the head. — Also **cane'phora, can'ephore, canephorus** (*ka-nē'for-əs*). [Gr. *kanēphoros*, a basket bearer, as at the Panathenaic festival — *kaneon*, basket, *phoros*, bearing.]

canescent *ka-nes'ənt, adj.* tending to white: hoary. — *n.* **canesc'ence.** [L. *cānēscēns* — *cānēre* — *cānus*, hoary.]

cang. See **cangue.**

cangle *kang'l, (Scot.) n.* noise, disturbance. — *v.i.* to argue, wrangle. [Cf. Norw. *kjangle*, to quarrel.]

cangue, cang *kang, n.* a Chinese portable pillory borne on the shoulders by petty offenders. [Fr. *cangue* — Port. *cango*, a yoke.]

canicular *ka-nik'ū-lər, adj.* pertaining to the Dogstar (**Canic'ula**) or to the Dog-days: pertaining to a dog (*facetious*). — **canicular year, cycle** Sothic year, cycle. [L. *canīculāris, canīcula*, dim. of *canis*, a dog.]

canid *kan'id*, (*zool.*) *n.* a member of the family **Can'idae** (*-i-dē*), including dogs, wolves, etc. [Mod. L. *Canidae* — L. *canis*, dog.]

canikin. See **cannikin.**

canine *kan'īn, kān'īn, adj.* like or pertaining to the dog. — *n.* any animal of the dog tribe: a canine tooth. — *ns.* **caninity** (*kə-* or *kā-nin'i-ti*); **Ca'nis** the dog genus, typical of the family **Can'idae.** — **canine appetite** a huge appetite: **canine letter** R (from its growling sound); **canine tooth** a sharp-pointed tooth between the incisors and the pre-molars. [L. *canīnus* — *canis*, a dog.]

canister *kan'is-tər, n.* a box or case, for holding tea, shot, etc.: (for **can′ister-shot**) case-shot. — *vs.t.* **can′ister, can′isterise, -ize** to put into, pack in, canister(s). — *n.* **canisterisā′tion, -z-.** [L. *canistrum*, a wicker-basket; Gr. *kanastron* — *kannē*, a reed.]

canities *ka-nish′i-ēz, n.* whiteness of the hair. [L.]

canker *kang′kər, n.* an eating sore: a gangrene: a fungus disease in trees, esp. one due to Nectria: inflammation in horses' feet: eczema of dogs' ears: an abscess or ulcer in birds: anything that corrupts, consumes, irritates or decays: a canker-worm: a dog-rose (*Shak.*). — *v.t.* to eat into, corrupt, or destroy: to infect or pollute: to make sour and ill-conditioned. — *v.i.* to grow corrupt: to decay. — *adj.* **cank′ered** corroded (*obs.*): polluted (*obs.*): malignant, soured, crabbed. — *adv.* **cank′eredly.** — *n.* **cank′eredness.** — *adjs.* **cank′-erous** corroding like a canker; **cank′ery** affected with canker: crabbed (*Scot.*). — **cank′er-worm** a larva that cankers or eats into plants. [L. *cancer*, a crab, gangrene.]

cann. Same as **con³.**

Canna *kan′ə, n.* the Indian shot (q.v.) genus of plants. [L., a reed.]

canna¹. See **cannot.**

canna² *kan′ə,* **cannach** *kan′əhh,* (*Scot.*) *ns.* cotton-grass. [Gael. *canach.*]

cannabic *kan′əb-ik,* or *-ab′, adj.* pertaining to hemp. — *ns.* **cann′abin** a resin obtained from the dried leaves and flowers of the hemp plant, containing the active principle of the drug cannabis; **cann′abinol** a crystalline phenol obtained from cannabin; **Cann′abis** the hemp (q.v.) genus: (without *cap.*) a narcotic drug variously known as hashish, bhang, marihuana, etc., obtained esp. from *Cannabis sativa* (common hemp) or *C. indica* (Indian hemp). — **cannabis resin** cannabin. [Gr. *kannabis;* cf. O.E. *hænep.*]

cannel *kan′l, n.* a bituminous coal that burns with a bright flame, used for making oils and gas. — Also **cann′el= coal, can′dle-coal.** [Prob. form of **candle.**]

cannelloni *kan-ə-lō′nē, n.* hollow tubelike pieces of pasta like macaroni, stuffed with cheese or meat. [It. *cannelloni,* augm. of *cannello,* small tube.]

cannelure *kan′i-lūr, n.* a groove or a fluting: a groove round the cylindrical part of a bullet. [Fr.]

cannibal *kan′i-bl, n.* an eater of the flesh of his own species. — *adj.* relating to or practising cannibalism. — *v.t.* **cann′ibalise, -ize** to repair (a vehicle, aircraft, etc.) with parts taken from other vehicles, etc.: to take (parts), or take parts from (aircraft), for repairs. — *n.* **cann′ibalism** the practice of eating one's own kind. — *adj.* **cannibalist′ic.** — *adv.* **cann′ibally** (*Shak.*). [Sp. *Caníbal, Caríbal,* Carib.]

cannikin *kan′i-kin, n.* a small can. — Also **can′akin, can′ikin.** [Dim. of **can.**]

cannon *kan′ən, n.* a great gun (*pl.* **cann′ons** or **cann′on**): a rapid-firing, large-calibre gun fitted to an aeroplane, ship or helicopter gunship (*pl.* **cann′ons** or **cann′on**): a cannon bone: a cannon bit: a stroke in billiards in which the cue-ball hits both the red and the opponent's ball (perh. for **carom**): a similar stroke in certain other games. — *v.i.* to cannonade: to make a cannon at billiards: to strike on the rebound: to collide. — *v.t.* to collide with. — *n.* **cannonade′** an attack with cannon. — *v.t.* to attack or batter with cannon. — *ns.* **cannoneer′, cannonier′** one who manages cannon; **cann′-onry** cannonading: artillery. — **cann′onball** a ball to be shot from a cannon; **can′nonball-tree** a South American tree (*Couroupita guianensis*) with a large woody fruit; **cannon bit** a smooth round bit; **cannon bone** in mammals in which the digits are reduced in number, a bone formed by the fusion of the persisting metacarpals or metatarsals, which supports the limb from 'knee' (wrist) or hock to fetlock: in birds, the tarsometatarsus; **cann′on-fodder** men regarded merely as material to be consumed in war; **cann′on-game** a form of billiards in which, the table having no pockets, the game consists in making a series of cannons; **cann′on-met′al** gun-metal. — *adj.* **cann′on-proof** proof

against cannon-shot. — **cann′on-shot** a cannonball: the distance to which a cannon will throw a ball. [Fr. *canon,* augmentative — L. *canna,* a reed.]

cannot *kan′ət, vb.* can not (contracted **can′t** *känt,* Scots **canna** *kan′ä, kan′ə,* **cannae** *kan′ä*). [**can, not.**]

cannula *kan′ū-lə, n.* a surgical tube, esp. one enclosing a trocar or perforator, or the breathing-tube inserted in the windpipe after tracheotomy: — *pl.* **cann′ulae** (*-ū-lē*) or **cann′ulas.** — *adj.* **cann′ulate.** [Dim. of *canna,* a reed.]

canny *kan′i, adj.* (*Scot.* and *Northern*) knowing: skilful: shrewd: lucky: of good omen: free from taint of the supernatural or dangerous: comfortable: sparing in money matters: gentle: innocent, harmless (sometimes euphemistically): sly or pawky. — Also *adv.* — *adv.* **cann′ily.** — *n.* **cann′iness.** — **ca′ canny** see **ca′; no′ canny** preternatural: dangerous. [App. conn. with **can¹.**]

canoe *kə-nōō′, n.* a boat made of the hollowed trunk of a tree, or of bark or skins: a skiff driven by paddling. — *v.i.* to paddle a canoe. — *ns.* **canoe′ing; canoe′ist.** [Sp. *canoa* — Haitian *canoa.*]

cañon, canyon *kan′yən, n.* a deep gorge or ravine. [Sp. *cañón,* a hollow, from root of **cannon.**]

canon¹ *kan′ən, n.* a law or rule, esp. in ecclesiastical matters: a general rule or principle: standard or criterion: the books of the Bible accepted as the standard or rule of faith by the Jewish or Christian faiths: works forming any similar standard: the recognised genuine works of any author: a species of musical composition constructed according to a rule, one part following another in imitation: a list of saints canonised: a large kind of type (*print.*). — *adjs.* **canonic** (*kə-non′ik*), **-al** of the nature of, according to, or included in a canon: regular: ecclesiastical. — *adv.* **canon′ically.** — *n.pl.* **canon′icals** the official dress of the clergy, regulated by the church canons. — *ns.* **canonicity** (*kan-ən-is′i-ti*) the state of belonging to the canon; **canonisā′tion, -z-.** — *v.t.* **can′onise, -ize** (*Shak. -non′*) to enrol in the canon or list of saints: to recognise as canonical. — *n.* **can′onist** one versed in canon law. — *adj.* **canonist′ic.** — **canonical hours** set hours for prayer: those wherein marriage may take place in an English parish church (formerly 8 a.m. to 12 noon, extended in 1886 to 3, in 1934 to 6 p.m.; **canon law** a digest of the formal decrees of councils, ecumenical, general, and local, of diocesan and national synods, and of patriarchal decision as to doctrine and discipline. — **canon of the mass** that part of the mass which begins after the 'Sanctus' with the prayer 'Te igitur', and ends just before the 'Paternoster'. [O.E. *canon* — L. *canon* — Gr. *kanōn,* a straight rod — *kannē,* a reed.]

canon² *kan′ən, n.* a member of a body of clergymen serving a cathedral or other church and living under a rule: a clerical dignitary belonging especially to a cathedral, enjoying special emoluments, and obliged to reside there part of the year. — *ns.* **can′oness** a member of a community of women living under a rule: a woman holding a prebend or canonry, often living in the world; **can′onry** the benefice of a canon. — **Canon Regular** a member of an order (Augustinian, Austin, or Black Canons) living under a rule based on St Augustine's teaching, or of an offshoot (Premonstratensians, White Canons), intermediate between monks and secular clergy; **canon residentiary** a canon obliged to reside at a cathedral and take a share in the duty; **canon secular** one other than a canon regular; **honorary canon** one having the titular rank of canon in a cathedral, but without duties or emoluments; **minor canon** one who conducts cathedral services but is not a member of the chapter. [O.E. *canonic* — L. *canonicus* — *canōn;* see previous article.]

canoodle *kə-nōōd′l,* (*slang*) *v.i.* to embrace amorously. [Origin obscure.]

canophilist *kə-nof′i-list,* **cynophilist** *si-, sī-,* (often *facet.*) *ns.* a lover of dogs. — *ns.* **canophilia** (*kan-ō-fil′i-ə*), **cynophilia** (*sin-, sīn-*) love of dogs. [L. *canis,* a dog, Gr. *phileein,* to love.]

canophobia *kan-ō-fō'bi-ə*, **cynophobia** *sin-*, *sīn-ō-*, *ns.* morbid fear of dogs. [L. *canis*, Gr. *kyon, kynos*, dog, Gr. *phobos*, fear.]

Canopus *kə-nō'pəs, n.* a bright star in the southern constellation *Argo navis*: an Egyptian human-headed vase for holding the entrails taken from an embalmed body (also **Canopic jar, vase**). — *adj.* **Cano'pic**. [L., — Gr. *Kanōpos*, Menelaus's steersman who died at Canopus in Egypt, was stellified as Canopus, and identified with an Egyptian god worshipped in the form of a jar with human head.]

canopy *kan'ə-pi, n.* a covering hung over a throne or bed: a covering of state held over the head: any overhanging covering, as the sky: the topmost layer of branches in a forest: a rooflike projection over a niche, tomb, statue, stall, altar, etc.: the transparent cover over the cockpit of an aircraft: the overhead fabric part of a parachute. — *v.t.* to cover with a canopy: — *pr.p.* **can'opying**; *pa.t.* and *pa.p.* **can'opied**. [Fr. *canapé* — L. *cōnōpium*, *cōnōpēum* — Gr. *kōnōpion*, a couch with a mosquito curtain — *kōnōps*, a mosquito.]

canorous *kan-ō'rəs, -ō', kan', adj.* musical: singing: resonant. — *adv.* **cano'rously** (or *kan'*). — *n.* **cano'rousness** (or *kan'*). [L. *canōrus* — *canor*, melody — *canēre*, to sing.]

canst. See **can¹**.

canstick *kan'stik*, (*Shak.*) *n.* a candlestick. [Contr.]

cant¹ *kant, v.i.* to speak whiningly: to use language whose meaning has evaporated from continued repetition: to use the language of thieves, etc.: to talk in an affectedly solemn or hypocritical way. — *n.* a hypocritical or affected or perfunctory style of speech or thought: the language peculiar to a sect: odd or peculiar talk of any kind: slang: a common saying: affected use of religious phrases or sentiments. — Also *adj.* — *n.* **cant'er** one who cants, a beggar: one who makes hypocritical professions. — *adj.* **cant'ing** whining, pretending to piety: in the form of a rebus, or implying a pun on the bearer's name, allusive (*her.*). [L. *cantāre*, freq. of *canēre*, to sing.]

cant² *kant, n.* an inclination from the level: a toss or jerk: a sloping or tilted position or face: one of the segments forming a side-piece in the head of a cask: a ship's timber lying obliquely to the line of the keel. — *v.t.* and *v.i.* to turn on the edge or corner: to tilt or toss suddenly: to tilt, slope. — Also **kant**. — *adj.* **cant'ed** tilted, sloping. — *n.* **cant'ing** tilting. — **cant'-board** a sloping board; **cant'dog, -hook** a metal hook on a long handle, for rolling logs; **cant'ing-coin** a piece of wood to prevent rolling of casks; **cant'ing-wheel** a wheel with bevelled cogs; **cant'-rail** a timber supporting the roof of a railway carriage. [Prob. conn. with Du. *kant*; Ger. *Kante*, corner.]

cant³ *kant, n.* sale by auction. — *v.t.* to sell by auction. [O.Fr. *encant*, auction; der. uncertain, cf. L.L. *in-cantāre*, to put up to auction.]

cant⁴ *kant*, (*Scot.*) *adj.* brisk: lively. [Cf. L.G. *kant*, and **canty**.]

can't *känt*, a colloquial contraction for **cannot**.

Cantab *kan'tab*, for **Cantabrigian** *kan-tə-brij'i-ən, adj.* of or pertaining to Cambridge (Latinised *Cantabrigia*). — Also *n.*

cantabank *kan'tə-bangk, n.* a strolling singer. [It. *cantambanco*.]

cantabile *kan-tä'bē-lā*, (*mus.*) *adj.* easy and flowing. — Also *n.* [It., suitable for singing.]

cantaloup(e) *kan'tə-lōōp, n.* a small, ribbed musk-melon: in U.S. extended to other varieties. [Fr., — It. *Cantalupo*, near Rome, where it was first grown in Europe.]

cantankerous *kən-tang'kər-əs, adj.* cross-grained: perverse in temper. — *adv.* **cantan'kerously.** — *n.* **cantan'kerousness.** [M.E. *contek*, strife.]

cantar. Same as **kantar**.

cantata *kan-tä'tə, n.* originally the name applied to a sort of musical narrative by one person, accompanied by a single instrument; subsequently an air was intro-

duced — the modern concert-aria: now also a choral work, a short oratorio or opera intended for concert performance only. — *n.* **cantatrice** (*kan-ta-trē'chä* or *kan'tə-trēs*) a female singer. [It., — L. *cantāre*, freq. of *canēre*, to sing.]

cantate *kan-tä'tä, kan-tä'tē, n.* the 98th Psalm, from its opening words in Latin, 'Cantate Domino'.

canteen *kan-tēn', n.* a vessel used by soldiers, etc., for holding liquids: a box of cooking utensils or of knives, forks and spoons: a barrack-tavern, or refreshment house for soldiers: a restaurant attached to an office, works, or the like: a public house (*S. Afr.*). — **wet, dry, canteen** one in which alcoholic liquors are, are not, sold. [Fr. *cantine* — It. *cantina*, a cellar; further der. uncertain.]

cante jondo *kän'tä hhon'dō*, (Sp.) an emotional and melancholy type of song sung esp. by Andalusian gypsies. — Also **cante hondo** [Sp., intense song.]

canter *kan'tər, n.* an easy gallop. — *v.i.* to move at an easy gallop. — *v.t.* to make to canter. [Orig. *Canter-bury-gallop*, from the easy pace at which the pilgrims rode to Canterbury.]

canterbury *kan'tər-bər-i, n.* a stand with divisions in it for holding books, music, etc.: — *pl.* **Canterburys, -ies.** — **Canterbury bells, bell** orig. the nettle-leaved bell-flower, or throatwort: transferred to a cultivated species *Campanula medium* with large blue, white, or pink bells, in some varieties double: loosely applied to other large-flowered bell-flowers.

cantharis *kan'thər-is, n.* a blister-beetle or Spanish fly (*Lytta* or *Cantharis*): in *pl.* **cantharides** (*kan-thar'i-dēz*) their dried bodies, used for blistering, etc. — *n.* **can'tharid** a member of the genus Cantharis, otherwise Lytta. — *adjs.* **canthar'idal, cantharid'ian, cantharid'ic.** — *n.* **canthar'idine** the active principle of blister-flies. [L. *cantharis* — Gr. *kantharis* (a blister-beetle), pl. *kantharidēs*.]

cantharus *kan'thə-rəs, n.* a large two-handled drinking-cup: a laver in the atrium before ancient churches: — *pl.* **can'tharī.** [L., — Gr. *kantharos*.]

canthus *kan'thəs, n.* the angle at the junction of the eyelids: — *pl.* **can'thī.** [Gr. *kanthos*.]

canticle *kan'ti-kl, n.* a song: a non-metrical hymn, esp. one used in church service as the *Benedicite*: a canto (*Spens.*): a short canto: (in *pl.*) the Song of Solomon. — *n.* **can'ticum** a canticle: a part-song in an ancient play. [L. *canticum*, dim. *canticulum*.]

cantico(y). See **kantikoy.**

cantilena *kan-ti-lē'nə, n.* a ballad or light song: a vocal or instrumental melody: a cantus firmus or melody for church use: a singing exercise or solfeggio. [L. *cantilēna*.]

cantilever *kan'ti-lēv-ər*, or *-lēv', n.* a large bracket for supporting cornices, balconies, and even stairs. — *adj.* **cantilevered.** — **cantilever bridge** one composed of arms projecting from the piers and connected together in the middle of the span. [Perh. **cant**, angle, and **lever.**]

cantillate *kan'ti-lāt, v.t.* and *v.i.* to chant, intone. — *n.* **cantillā'tion.** — *adj.* **can'tillatory.**

cantina *kan-tē'nə, n.* a bar, saloon: a wine-shop. [Sp. and It.]

cantion *kan'shən*, (*Spens.*) *n.* a song. [L. *cantiō, -ōnis.*]

cantle *kan'tl, n.* a corner, edge or slice of anything: the raised hind part of a saddle: the crown of the head or of the causeway (*Scot.*). — *v.t.* to cut a piece from: to divide. — *n.* **cant'let** a fragment. [cant, edge.]

canto *kan'tō, n.* a division of a long poem: the part that carries the melody (*mus.*): — *pl.* **can'tos.** — Also (*Shak.*) **can'ton.** — **canto fermo** plainsong, the unornamented melody used in the Western Church from the earliest times, to which later other parts in counterpoint were added. [It., — L. *cantus* — *canēre*, to sing.]

canton¹ *kan'tən, kan-ton', n.* a corner (*obs.*): a division or space (*obs.*): a division of territory, constituting in Switzerland a separate government, in France a subdivision of an arrondissement: a pilastered or quoined corner of a building: an ordinary of a shield, being a square occupying generally the dexter, sometimes the sinister, chief of the field (*her.*). — *v.t.* to divide into cantons: (mil. pron. *kən-tōōn'*) to allot quarters to. — *adjs.* **can'tonal** pertaining to or divided into cantons; **can'toned** ornamented at the corners with projecting pilasters (*archit.*): placed in the midst of charges occupying the corners (*her.*). — *n.* **canton'ment** (mil. pron. *kən-tōōn'mənt*) the temporary quarters of troops taking part in manoeuvres or active operations: in India, formerly, a permanent military town. [O.Fr. *canton*; It. *cantone*, corner, district — *canto*, a corner: cf. **cant²**.]

canton². See **canto**.

Cantonese *kan-ton-ēz'*, *adj.* belonging to or typical of Canton, a city in S. China: esp. of a style of cooking originating there. — *n.* a native of Canton: the dialect of Canton: — *pl.* **Cantonese'**.

cantor *kan'tör*, *n.* the leader of the singing in a church, a precentor: in a synagogue, the person who chants the liturgy and leads the congregation in prayer. — *adjs.* **cantorial** (*-tö'ri-əl*, *-tö'*); **cantö'ris** (*gen.* of L. *cantor*) of the cantor, i.e. on the north side of a choir (opposed to *decani*). [L., singer, *canere*, to sing.]

cantred *kan'tred*, **cantref** *kan'trev*, (*hist.*) *ns.* a division of the country — a hundred. [W. *cantref* — *cant*, hundred, and *tref*, town.]

cantrip *kan'trip* (*Scot.*) *n.* a freak or wilful piece of trickery: a witch's spell. [Ety. unknown.]

Cantuarian *kan-tū-ā'ri-ən*, *adj.* pertaining to Canterbury as the archiepiscopal see of the primate of the Church of England. [L.L. *Cantuārius*, *Cantuarensis* — O.E. *Cantware* (*pl.*) the people of Kent.]

cantus *kan'təs*, *n.* a melody, esp. an ecclesiastical style of music: — *pl.* **can'tus**. — **cantus firmus** canto fermo. [L., song — *canere*, to sing.]

canty *kan'ti* (*Scot.*) *adj.* cheerful, lively. — *n.* **can'tiness**. [**cant⁴**; cf. L.G. *kantig*.]

Canuck *kə-nuk'*, (*coll.*; *often derog.*) *n.* a Canadian (*U.S.*): a French-Canadian (*Can.*): a small horse. — *adj.* relating to Canada or to Canadians.

canvas *kan'vəs*, *n.* a coarse cloth made of hemp or other material, now esp. cotton, used for sails, tents, etc., and for painting on: the sails of a ship: a piece of stretched canvas, painted or to be painted: material for covering the ends of a racing-boat (whence a **canvas-length, win by a canvas**). — *v.t.* to cover with canvas. — **can'vas-back** a North American duck, very good eating, its back ashy white, crossed by broken, zigzag, dark lines; **can'vas-climb'er** (*Shak.*) a sailor; **can'vas-stretch'er** a wooden frame on which canvas is stretched for oil-painting; **can'vas-work** embroidery upon canvas, or upon cloth over which canvas has been laid to guide the stitches. — **under canvas** having the sails unfurled, under sail: living in tents. [O.Fr. *canevas* — L. *cannabis* — Gr. *kannabis*, hemp.]

canvass *kan'vəs*, *v.t.* to toss in canvas, or in a blanket (*Shak.*): to toss or turn about: to examine: to discuss: to solicit votes, orders, contributions, etc., from: (in American elections) to scrutinise. — *v.i.* to solicit votes, etc. (with *for*): to go from person to person seeking information. — *n.* close examination: a seeking or solicitation of votes, information, etc.: an election scrutiny (*U.S.*). — *n.* **can'vasser**. [**canvas**.]

cany. See **cane**.

canyon. Same as **cañon**.

canzone *kant-sö'nā*, **canzona** *kan-zō'nə*, *ns.* a song or air resembling a madrigal but less strict: an instrument piece of like character: a series of stanzas in Italian poetry, of various metrical arrangements: — *pls.* **canzo'ni** (*-nē*), **-nas**. — *ns.* (*dim.*) **canzonet** (*kan-zō-net'*), **canzonetta** (*kan-tsō-net'ə*; *pl.* **canzonet'te** *-tā*). [It., a song, L. *cantiō*, *-ōnis* — *canere*, to sing.]

caoutchouc *kow'chōōk*, *n.* india-rubber, gum-elastic: the latex of rubber trees. [Fr., — Carib *cahuchu*.]

cap¹ *kap*, *n.* a woman's light head-dress; brimless cover-

ing for the head: an official or symbolic head-dress or one appropriated to a special class or use, academic, athletic, etc.: membership of a team symbolised by a cap: a caplike covering of any kind: the top of a toadstool: the uppermost or terminal part of anything: a percussion-cap (see **percussion**): a paper disc enclosing a fulminating substance for use with toy pistols, etc.: a lifting of the cap in salutation: a collection of money at a hunt (orig. in a cap) from visitors, for hunt servants, etc.: (or **Dutch cap**) a contraceptive diaphragm. — *v.t.* to cover the end or top of: to touch with a cap in conferring a degree: to admit to membership of a team: to outdo or surpass by finishing with a better: to perplex, mystify (*U.S. dial.*): to set a limit to (esp. local authority rate increases). — *v.t.* and *v.i.* to salute by raising the cap: — *pr.p.* **capp'ing**; *pa.p.* and *pa.t.* **capped** (*kapt*). — *ns.* **capp'er; capp'ing** the action of the verb *cap*: a covering: a graduation ceremony. — **cap'-case** (*obs.*) a small travelling-case, a chest; **cap'-paper** a kind of wrapping paper: a size of writing paper; **cap pistol** a toy gun using paper caps; **cap rock** a stratum of (usu. impervious) rock overlying oil- or gas-bearing strata; **cap sleeve** a short sleeve, just covering the shoulder; **cap'stone** a coping stone: the top or finishing stone of a structure: a stone slab laid flat over the top of a cist (*archaeol.*): the horizontal stone of a dolmen (*archaeol.*): a flat stone acting as a cap e.g. to a shaft. — **black cap** see **black; cap and bells** the marks of a professional jester; **cap in hand** submissively: supplicatingly; **cap of liberty**, or *Phrygian cap*, the conical cap given to a Roman slave on enfranchisement, and for this reason popular during the French revolution, now the symbol of republicanism; **cap of maintenance** see **maintenance; cap verses** to quote verses in turn, according to rule; **college cap** a mortarboard or trencher-cap; **set one's cap at** of a woman, to set oneself to captivate (a man); **the cap fits** the allusion is felt to apply; **throw up one's cap** to make this gesture (*lit.* or *fig.*) in token of immoderate joy; **to cap it all** as a (usu. unpleasant) climax. [O.E. *cæppe* — L.L. *cappa*, a cape or cope.]

cap², **caup** *kap*, *köp*, (*Scot.*) *ns.* a wooden drinking-bowl, with two handles. [O.E. *copp*, a cup; or Scand. *koppr*.]

capa *kä'pə*, *n.* a Spanish cloak: fine Cuban tobacco for the outsides of cigars. [Sp.]

capable *kā'pə-bl*, *adj.* comprehensive (*Shak.*): having (esp. legal) right, or (with *of*) right to (*obs.*): having practical ability: able (often with *of*): qualified. — *ns.* **capabil'ity** quality or state of being capable: (usu. in *pl.*) a feature capable of being used or developed: ability for the action indicated, because provision and preparation have been made: manufacturing facilities, as factories, plant; **cā'pableness**. — **capable of** able to take in, contain, understand, etc. (*arch.*): able, good, wellmade, etc., enough to, or bad, foolish, etc., enough to (fol. by verbal noun or other action noun): susceptible of. [Fr., — L.L. *capābilis* — L. *capēre*, to hold, take.]

capacity *kə-pas'i-ti*, *n.* power of holding, containing, absorbing, or grasping: room: volume: ability: power of mind: character in which one does something: legal competence: maximum possible output or performance: capacitance: possession of industrial plant, technology, etc., with resulting ability to produce goods. — *adj.* attaining the full capacity. — *adj.* **capacious** (*kə-pā'shəs*) including much: roomy: wide: extensive. — *adv.* **capā'ciously**. — *ns.* **capā'ciousness; capac'itance** the property that allows a system or body to store an electric charge: the value of this expressed in farads (q.v.). — *v.t.* **capac'itate** to make capable: to qualify: to cause (sperm) to undergo capacitation. — *ns.* **capacitā'tion** a rendering capable: a change undergone by a sperm in the female reproductive tract to make it capable of fertilising an egg; **capac'itor** an electrical device having large capacitance. — **capacity for heat** power of absorbing heat; **legal capacity** the power to alter one's rights or duties by the exercise of free will, or responsibility for one's acts; **to capacity** to the utmost capacity, the fullest extent possible. [Fr. *capacité* — L. *capāx*, *-ācis*, able to receive — *capēre*, to hold.]

cap-à-pie *kap-ə-pē*, *adv.* from head to foot, referring to arming, as a knight. [O.Fr. *cap a pie* (mod. *de pied en cap*) — L. *caput*, head, *ad*, to, *pēs*, foot.]

caparison *kə-par'i-sən*, *n.* the covering of a horse: a rich cloth laid over a warhorse: dress and ornaments generally. — *v.t.* to cover with a cloth, as a horse: to dress very richly. — *adj.* **capar'isoned.** [Fr. *caparaçon* — Sp. *caparazón*, augm. of *capa*, cap, cover — L.L. *cappa*.]

cape[1] *kāp*, *n.* a covering for the shoulders attached as a tippet to a coat or cloak: a sleeveless cloak. — *n.* **cape'let** a small cape. [O.Fr. *cape* — L.L. *cappa*.]

cape[2] *kāp*, *n.* a head or point of land running into the sea or a lake. — *v.i.* (*naut.*) to keep a course. — **Cape cart** a two-wheeled vehicle with hood and pole; **Cape Coloured** (*S. Afr.*) a person of mixed race, mainly in the W. Cape area; **Cape doctor** a south-east wind in the Cape, so named (as being able to blow away germs) by Anglo-Indians formerly invalided there; **Cape Dutch** former name for the language now (officially and generally) known as *Afrikaans* (*q.v.*): an architectural style of the Cape, characterised by whitewashed, gabled, thatched-roof, single-storey houses; **Cape gooseberry** the strawberry-tomato (*Physalis peruviana*), a S. American solanaceous plant with bladdery calyx, naturalised in S. Africa: its edible fruit; **Cape hyacinth** see **hyacinth**; **Cape nightingale** a frog; **Cape pigeon** the pintado petrel; **Cape smoke** (*slang*) S. African brandy, dop; **Cape Sparrow** see **mossie**[2]. — **the Cape of Good Hope**: Cape Province, Capetown, and Cape Peninsula. [Fr. *cap* — L. *caput*, the head.]

capelet. See **cape**[1].

capelin *kap'ə-lin*, *n.* a small fish of the smelt family, abundant off Newfoundland, much used as bait. — Also **cap'lin.** [Fr. *capelan*.]

capeline *kap'ə-lin*, *n.* a small iron skullcap worn by archers: a light woollen hood for evening wear: a surgical bandage for the head. — Also **cap'elline.** [Fr., — L.L. *capella* — *capa*, a cap.]

Capella *ka-pel'ə*, *n.* a first-magnitude star in the constellation Auriga. [L., lit. she-goat.]

capellet *kap'ə-lit*, *n.* a wen-like swelling on a horse's elbow, or on the back part of his hock. [Fr., — L.L. *capella* — *capa*, a cap.]

capellmeister. Same as **kapellmeister.**

caper[1] *kā'pər*, *n.* the pickled flower-bud of a bush (*Capparis spinosa*) grown in Sicily. — *adj.* **cā'per-bush; cā'per-sauce** a sauce for boiled mutton, etc., made with capers; **cā'per-spurge** a kind of spurge whose capsules are sometimes pickled; **cā'per-tea** a black tea with a knotty curled leaf. [L. *capparis* — Gr. *kapparis*.]

caper[2] *kā'pər*, *v.i.* to leap or skip like a goat: to dance in a frolicsome manner. — *n.* a leap: a frisk: an escapade: any activity or pursuit (*coll.*): an illegal or questionable act (*slang*). — *n.* **cā'perer.** — **cut a caper** to execute a frisk. [See **capriole**.]

caper[3]. See **capercailzie.**

capercailzie, -llie *cap-ər-kā'l(y)i*, *n.* a species of grouse weighing up to 12 pounds. — Also **cap'er.** [Gael. *capull coille*, horse of the wood.]

Capernaite *ka-*, *kə-pûr'ni-īt*, *n.* an inhabitant of *Capernaum* in Galilee: (*polemically*) a believer in transubstantiation (John vi. 35, 51). — *adj.* **Capernaitic** (*-it'ik*). — *adv.* **Capernait'ically.**

capernoity, -ie, cappernoity *kap-ər-noi'ti*, (*Scot.*) *n.* the head, noddle. — *adj.* peevish: crabbed: capricious. — *adj.* **capernoit'ed** capernoity. [Origin unknown.]

capias *kā'pi-as*, *ka'*, (*law*) *n.* a writ which authorises the arrest of the person named in it. [L., you should seize, 2nd sing. pres. subj. of *capēre*, to take.]

capillaceous *kap-i-lā'shəs*, *adj.* hairlike. — *ns.* **capillaire** (*-lār'*) orig. an infusion of maidenhair fern (Fr. *capillaire*): a syrup flavoured with orange-flower water;

capillarity (*-lar'i-ti*) capillary quality: capillary attraction. — *adj.* **capillary** (*kə-pil'ə-ri*, sometimes *kap'*) having to do with hair: hairlike: of very small bore: relating to capillary attraction. — *n.* a fine-bored tube: a minute vessel such as those that connect arteries with veins. — *n.* **capillitium** (*kap-i-lish'i-əm*) a mass of threads. — **capillary attraction** the force that causes liquids to rise in capillary tubes and wicks, to spread through blotting-paper, etc.; **capillary watering** a system of plant watering using capillary attraction of water through a wick, sand, etc. [L. *capillus*, hair.]

capita. See **caput.**

capital[1] *kap'it-l*, *adj.* relating to the head: involving a death penalty: placed at the head: main, chief, principal: excellent: relating to capital. — *n.* the chief or most important thing: the chief town or seat of government: a large letter, in the form used at the beginning of a sentence, etc.: the stock (including property and equipment) and/or money used for carrying on a business: possessors of capital collectively, or their political and economic influence and interests: any advantage used as a means of gaining further advantages. — *interj.* excellent. — *n.* **capitalisā'tion, -z-.** — *v.t.* **cap'italise, -ize** to furnish with capital: to convert into capital or money: to turn to account: to print or write with capital letters. — *v.i.* to turn to one's advantage (with *on*). — *ns.* **cap'italism** the condition of possessing capital: the economic system which generates and gives power to capitalists; **cap'italist** one who derives income and power from capital. — Also *adj.* — *adj.* **capitalist'ic.** — *adv.* **cap'itally** chiefly: principally: excellently (*coll.*): by capital punishment. — **capital assets** fixed capital (see below); **capital cross** a Greek cross with terminations like Tuscan capitals; **capital expenditure** spending on capital assets: expenditure from which benefits may be expected in the long term; **capital gains** profits from the sale of bonds or other assets; **capital goods** goods to be used in production, not for consumption. — *adj.* **cap'ital-intens'ive** requiring a comparatively large amount of capital relative to the amount of labour involved. — **capital levy** an exaction by a state, for a specific purpose, of a proportion of the capital (money value — cash, securities, mortgages, houses, machinery, goodwill, etc.) of its members; **capital murder** a murder involving the death penalty; **capital punishment** the death penalty; **capital ship** a warship of the largest and strongest class; **capital sin** deadly sin; **capital sum** a lump sum payable on an insurance policy; **capital territory** the part of a country in which the capital city is situated. — **capital transfer tax** a tax payable on gifts of money or property over a certain value, made either during the lifetime of the giver or after his death; **circulating** or **floating capital** that which constantly changes hands, as wages paid to workmen, raw material used; **fixed capital** buildings, machines, tools, etc.; **make capital (out) of** to turn to advantage; **working capital** capital needed to carry on a business: liquid capital (see **liquid**): assets after debts have been paid. [O.Fr. *capitel* — L. *capitālis* — *caput*, the head.]

capital[2] *kap'it-l*, *n.* the head or top part of a column, etc.: a chapter of a book. [L. *capitellum*, dim. of *caput*, head.]

capitan *käp-i-tän'*, or *kap'i-tan*, (*hist.*) *n.* the chief admiral of the Turkish fleet. — *n.* **capitan'o** a head-man: — *pl.* **capitan'os** or **capitan'ī** (*-ē*). [Sp. *capitán*, and It. *capitano*; see **captain**.]

capitate *kap'it-āt*, *adj.* having a head, knob, or capitulum. — *n.* **capitā'tion** numbering of heads or individuals: a poll-tax. — **capitation allowance, grant** an allowance, grant of so much a head. [L. *capitātus*, headed, *capitātiō, -ōnis*, poll-tax — *caput*, head.]

capitayn *kap-i-tān'*, (*Spens.*) *n.* a captain.

capitellum. See **capitulum.**

Capitol *kap'it-ol*, *-əl*, *n.* the temple of Jupiter at Rome, built on the *Capitoline* hill: the house where Congress or a state legislature meets (*U.S.*). — *adjs.* **capitō'lian,**

capit'oline. [L. *Capitōlium* — *caput*, the head.]

capitular *kə-pit'ŭl-ər, n.* a statute passed in a chapter or ecclesiastical court: a member of a chapter. — *adj.* relating or belonging to a chapter in a cathedral. — *adj.* capit'ularly. — *n.* capit'ulary a collection of ordinances: a heading. — *adj.* of a chapter. [See chapter.]

capitulate *kə-pit'ŭl-āt, v.i.* to treat: to draw up terms of agreement: to yield or surrender on certain conditions or heads. — *ns.* capit'ulant one who capitulates; capitulā'tion. — *adj.* capit'ulatory. [L.L. *capitulātus,* pa.p. of *capitulāre,* to arrange under heads — *capitulum,* a chapter.]

capitulum *kə-pit'ū-ləm, n.* a close head of sessile flowers, as in Compositae (*bot.*): the head of a bone, esp. of a rib (also capitell'um) (*anat.*): — *pls.* capit'ula, capitell'a. — *adjs.* capit'ular; capit'ulate. [L., dim. of *caput,* head.]

caple, capul *kā'pl, n.* a horse. [M.E. *capel,* cf. O.N. *kapall;* Ir. *capall;* L.L. *caballus,* a horse.]

caplin. See capelin.

capnomancy *kap'nō-man-si, n.* divination by smoke. [Gr. *kapnos,* smoke, *manteiā,* divination.]

capo[1] *kap'ō,* (*U.S.*) *n.* the head of a branch of the Mafia: by extension, the leader of any band or organisation, criminal or otherwise: — *pl.* cap'os. [It. *capo* — L. *caput,* head.]

capo[2]. See capotasto.

capocchia *kä-pok'kyə,* (*Shak.*; also chipo'chia) *n.* a fool. [It.]

capodastro. See capotasto.

capon *kā'pn, n.* a castrated cock: (*jocularly*) a fish, esp. a herring: a letter (*Shak.*). — *v.t.* cā'ponise, -ize. [O.E. *capun;* L. *capō,* -*ōnis,* Gr. *kapōn* — *koptein,* to cut. See chop.]

caponiere *kap-ō-nēr', n.* a covered passage across the ditch of a fortified place. — Also caponier'. [Fr. *caponnière,* Sp. *caponera,* capon-coop.]

caporal *kap-or-äl', n.* a kind of shag tobacco. [Fr.]

capot *kə-pot', n.* the winning of all the tricks at the game of piquet, and scoring forty. — *v.t.* to score capot against. [Fr.]

capotasto *kap'ō-tas-tō,* capodastro *kap'ō-das-trō, ns.* a movable bridge secured over the fingerboard and strings of a lute or guitar, to alter the pitch of all the strings together: — *pls.* cap'otastos, -dastros. — Also cap'ō: — *pl.* cap'os. [It. *capo tasto, dastro,* head stop.]

capote *kə-pōt', n.* a long kind of cloak or mantle. [Fr. dim. of *cape,* a cloak; see cape.]

Cappagh-brown *kap'ä-brown, n.* a brown bituminous earth pigment, stained with oxide of manganese and iron from *Cappagh* near Cork. — Also Capp'ah-brown.

Capparis *kap'ər-is, n.* the caper genus, giving name to the family Capparidā'ceae, akin to the crucifers. — *adj.* capparidā'ceous. [See caper.]

cappuccino *ka-pōō-chē'nō, n.* black coffee with a little milk: white coffee, esp. from a machine, topped with froth: — *pl.* cappuccin'os. [It., Capuchin, perh. from the colour of a Capuchin's gown.]

capreolate *kap'ri-ō-lāt, adj.* tendrilled. [L. *căprěŏlus,* a tendril.]

capric *kap'rik,* caproic *kəp-rō'ik,* caprylic *kəp-ril'ik, adjs.* applied to three fatty acids obtained from butter, etc., with goat-like smell. — *ns.* cap'rate, cap'roate, cap'rylate salts respectively of these; caprolactam (*kap-rō-lak'tam*) a crystalline amide used in the production of nylon. [L. *caper,* a goat.]

caprice *kə-prēs', n.* a change of humour or opinion without reason: a freak: changeableness: a capriccio (*mus.*). — *n.* capriccio (*kä-prē'chō*) a sportive motion: a species of free composition, not subject to rule as to form or figure (*mus.*): — *pl.* capri'ccios, capricci (*-prē'chē*). — *adv.* capriccioso (*-chō'sō*) in a free style (*mus.*). — *adj.* capricious (*kə-prish'əs*) humorous (*Shak.*): full of caprice: changeable. — *adv.* capri'ciously. — *n.* capri'ciousness. [Fr. *caprice* and It. *capriccio;* perh. from L. *caper* (m.), *capra* (f.), a goat.]

Capricorn *kap'ri-körn, n.* a constellation and a sign of the zodiac represented as a horned ʟoat or monster: one born under this sign. — See also tropic. [L. *capricornus* — *caper,* a goat, *cornū,* a horn.]

caprid *kap'rid, n.* a member of the goat family, Capridae. — Also *adj.* — *n.pl.* Capridae (*kap'ri-dē*) in former classifications, the family of Artiodactyla comprising sheep, goats, etc. [L. *caper,* a goat.]

caprifig *kap'ri-fig, n.* a goat-fig, wild fig. — *n.* caprificā'tion a method of promoting the fertilisation and ripening of cultivated figs (which are practically dioecious) by hanging on the trees branches of caprifig (which have male flowers as well as sterile female or gall flowers) so that the gall-wasps emerging from the galls and flying to the cultivated fig to lay their eggs, carry with them some pollen. — *v.t.* cap'rify. [L. *caprīcus,* the wild fig — *caper,* a goat, and *ficus,* a fig.]

caprifole *kap'ri-fōl* (*Spens.* caprifoil *-foil'*) *n.* an old name for honeysuckle. — *n.pl.* Caprifoliā'ceae (*-si-ē*) the honeysuckle family. — *adj.* caprifoliā'ceous. [L. *caper,* goat, *folium,* leaf.]

capriform *kap'ri-förm, adj.* goatlike. [L. *caper,* goat, *förma,* form.]

caprify. See caprifig.

caprine *kap'rīn, adj.* goat-like. [L. *caprīnus* — *caper,* a goat.]

capriole *kap'ri-ōl, n.* a caper: a leap without advancing. — *v.i.* to leap: caper. [O.Fr. *capriole* — It. *capriola* — L. *caper* (m.), *capra* (f.), a goat.]

caproic, caprolactam, caprylic, etc. See capric.

caps *kaps,* (*coll.*) *n.pl.* for capitals, capital letters.

capsaicin. See Capsicum.

Capsian *kap'si-ən, adj.* of a Mediterranean culture answering to the Aurignacian. [L. *Capsa,* Gafsa, in Tunisia.]

Capsicum *kap'si-kəm, n.* a tropical shrubby genus of the potato family, yielding a fleshy, many-seeded fruit: (without *cap.*) the fruit of one species, eaten as a vegetable (also called *green* or *red pepper*): (without *cap.*) the dried seeds of other species, yielding paprika and cayenne pepper. — *n.* capsaicin (*kap-sā'i-sin*) the hot-tasting principle of capsicum. [Perh. L. *capsa,* a case.]

capsid *kap'sid, n.* the outer protein shell of some viruses. [L. *capsa,* case.]

capsid (bug) *kap'sid* (*bug*), *n.* any of several small active plant pests. [Gr. *kapsis,* gulping — *kaptein,* to gulp down.]

capsize *kap-sīz', v.t.* to upset. — *v.i.* to be upset. — *n.* an overturning. — *adj.* capsiz'able. — *n.* capsiz'al. [Origin unknown.]

capstan *kap'stən, n.* an upright machine turned by bars or otherwise so as to wind a cable upon it: the revolving shaft which controls the spin of a tape in a tape-recorder, etc. — capstan lathe a lathe with a revolving turret holding several tools which can be used in succession: capstan table a round-topped, often revolving table. [Fr. *cabestan, capestan,* through L.L. forms from L. *capere,* to take, hold.]

capsule *kap'sūl, n.* a dry dehiscent fruit of more than one carpel (*bot.*): the spore-bearing part of a moss (*bot.*): a fibrous or membranous covering (*zool.*): a gelatine case for holding a dose of medicine: a small dish: a metallic or other container: a self-contained spacecraft or a part of one, manned or unmanned, recoverable or non-recoverable: a similar craft, to be used on or under water. — *adjs.* cap'sular in the form of, resembling, a capsule: brief, condensed; cap'sulary; cap'sulate. — *v.t.* cap'sulise, -ize to condense. [Fr., — L. *capsula,* dim. of *capsa,* a case — *capěre,* to hold.]

captain *kap'tin, n.* a head or chief officer: the commander of a troop of horse, a company of infantry, a ship, or a portion of a ship's company: in the navy, an officer ranking with a colonel: in the army, an officer ranking with a naval lieutenant: the senior pilot of a civil aircraft: the overseer of a mine: the leader of a team or club: the head-boy of a school. — *v.t.* to lead or act as captain. — *ns.* **cap′taincy** the rank or commission of a captain; **cap′tainship,** (*obs.*) **cap′tainry** the rank or condition of a captain: skill in commanding. — **cap′-tain-gen′eral** the commander of an army; **captain's chair** a wooden armchair with back and arms in one semicircular piece supported on vertical spindles. — **captain of industry** a great industrial employer. [O.Fr. *capitaine* — L.L. *capitāneus,* chief — L. *caput,* head.]

captan *kap′tən, n.* a type of agricultural fungicide produced from mercaptan. [From **mercaptan.**]

caption *kap′shən, n.* the act of taking: an arrest: the formal title of an indictment or deposition which shows the authority under which it is executed or taken (*Eng. law*): in Scotland, before 1837, a formal warrant to apprehend a debtor or other defaulting obligant, given in the Bill Chamber after letters of horning had been executed: a heading, legend, or accompanying wording of an article, chapter, illustration, or cinematograph picture, etc. — *v.t.* to give a caption (heading, etc.) to. — *adj.* **cap′tious** ready to catch at faults or take offence: peevish. — *adv.* **cap′tiously.** — *n.* **cap′tiousness.** [L. *captiō, -ōnis* — *capĕre,* to take.]

captive *kap′tiv, n.* a prisoner: a person or animal kept in confinement. — *adj.* confined: kept in bondage: of an animal, living its whole life in a zoo or other controlled habitat: restrained by a line (as a balloon): charmed or subdued by anything (*fig.*): pertaining to captivity: that cannot refuse what is offered (as a *captive audience, market,* etc.). — *v.t.* (*kap′tiv*; also in *Spens., Milt. kap-tiv′*) to make captive or to captivate. — *v.t.* **cap′tivate** to charm: to engage the affections of. — *adj.* **cap′tivating.** — *ns.* **cap′tiva(u)nce** (*Spens.*) captivity; **captiv′ity; cap′tor** one who takes a captive or a prize; **cap′ture** the act of taking: the thing taken: an arrest: transference of a tributary to another river by more active denudation (*geol.*). — *v.t.* to take as a prize: to take by force: to succeed in representing (something intangible or elusive) in a fixed or permanent form: of an atomic or nuclear system, to acquire an additional particle (*phys.*): of a star or planet, to bring another body into orbit round it (*astron.*). — **captive bolt (pistol)** a gunlike device which fires a rod, used in slaughtering animals; **captive time** time during which a person is not working but must be available at the place of work. [L. *captīvus, captor, captūra* — *capĕre, captum,* to take.]

capuccio *kə-pōōt′chō,* (*Spens.*) *n.* a hood. [It.]

capuche *kə-pōōsh′, -pōōch′, n.* a hood, esp. that worn by the *Capuchins.* — *n.* **Capuchin** (*kap′ū-chin* or *kap-ōō-shēn′*) a friar of a branch of the Franciscan order so called from the hood he wears: (without *cap.*) a cloak like a Capuchin's: (usu. without *cap.*) a hooded pigeon: (without *cap.*) a capuchin monkey. — **capuchin cross** a cross with each arm terminated by a ball; **capuchin monkey** a South American monkey (*Cebus*) with hair like a cowl. [Fr., cowl — L.L. *cappa;* see **cap, cape.**]

capul. See **caple.**

caput *kap′ut, -ət, n.* a head: a knob: — *pl.* **cap′ita.** — **caput mortuum** the residuum after distillation: worthless residue. [L.]

capybara *kap-i-bä′rə, n.* the largest living rodent, a native of South America, allied to the guinea-pig. [Port. from Tupí.]

car *kär, n.* a vehicle moved on wheels, applied to very various forms — a large and splendid vehicle, as a triumphal car, a funeral car, the two-wheeled Irish jaunting-car, a motor-car: a street tramway carriage: in America, applied to all vehicles for railway travelling, as a passenger-car, freight-car, etc.: in Britain, to certain forms of railway carriage, as dining-car, sleeping-car, Pullman-car: a chariot (*poet.*): the part of a balloon, cable-car, or airship that carries passengers and load. — **car′-coat** a short coat designed for wearing in a car; **car ferry** a ferry boat designed so that cars can be driven on and off; **car′load** as much as a car will carry; **car′man** a man who drives a car or cart: a

carter; **car′park** an open space or a building for parking cars; **car pool** an arrangement by which several car owners take turns in giving lifts to each other; **car′port** a covered parking space, esp. a space under a roof projecting from a building. — *adj.* **car′-sick** affected with nausea by the movement of a car. — **car′-wash** a place specially equipped for the automatic washing of cars. — **car boot sale** a sale at which goods are sold direct from the boots of the owners' cars. [O.Fr. *carre* — L.L. *carra,* a Celt. word, seen in Ir. *carr,* Bret. *karr.*]

carabine. See **carbine.**

carabiniere *kä-rä-bē-nyā′rā,* (It.) *n.* a policeman armed with a rifle: — *pl.* **carabinie′ri** (*-rē*).

Carabus *kar′ə-bəs, n.* a genus of beetles giving name to the ground-beetle family, **Carabidae** (*kə-rab′i-dē*). [Gr. *kārabos,* a kind of beetle.]

caracal *kar′ə-kal, n.* the Persian lynx. [Fr., prob. — Turk. *qara-qulaq,* black ear.]

caracara *kä-rä-kä-rä′,* or *kä-rä-kä′rä, n.* a name for several South American vulture-like hawks. [Imit.]

carack. See **carrack.**

caracol, caracole *kar′ə-kōl, n.* a half-turn or wheel made by a horseman: a winding stair. — *v.i.* to turn half-round: to prance about. [Fr. *caracole* — It. *caracollo* — Sp. *caracol,* a spiral snail shell.]

caract *kar′əkt,* (*Shak.*) *n.* mark: sign. [App. Gr. *charaktos,* marked.]

caracul. See **karakul.**

carafe *kə-raf′, n.* a water-bottle or wine-flask for the table: the amount contained in a carafe. [Fr. *carafe,* prob. from. Ar. *gharafa,* to draw water.]

caramba *kär-äm′bə,* (Sp.) *interj.* expressing annoyance or surprise.

carambola *ka-rəm-bō′lə, n.* a small East Indian tree (*Averrhoa carambola*) of the wood-sorrel family: its acrid pulpy fruit used for tarts, etc. [Port.]

carambole *ka′rəm-bōl.* See **carom.**

caramel *kar′ə-mel, n.* a dark-brown substance produced from sugar by loss of water on heating, used in colouring puddings, whisky, wines, etc.: a tenacious sweetmeat made with sugar, butter, etc. — *adj.* made of or containing caramel: of the colour of caramel. — *n.* **caramelisā′tion, -z-.** — *vs.t.* and *vs.i.* **car′amel, car′amelise, -ize.** — Also (*rare*) **car′omel.** [Fr., — Sp. *caramelo.*]

carangid, carangoid. See **Caranx.**

caranna *kar-an′ə,* **carauna** *-ön′ə, ns.* a resinous substance yielded by various South American burseraceous trees. [Sp. *caraña,* from Tupí.]

Caranx *kar′angks, n.* the scad genus of fishes, giving name to a family **Carangidae** (*kar-an′ji-dē*): (without *cap.*) any fish of the genus: — *pl.* **car′anx.** — *adjs.* **carangid** (*-an′jid*), **carangoid** (*-ang′goid*) pertaining to or like the Carangidae. — Also *ns.* [Origin obscure.]

Carapa *kar′ə-pə, kə-rap′ə, n.* a genus of tropical trees of the mahogany family yielding **car′ap** (or **carap′,** also **crab′**)-**nuts, -oil, -wood.** — *n.* **car′ap** any tree of the Carapa genus. [*caraipi,* the native Guiana name.]

carapace *kar′ə-pās, n.* the shell of the crab, tortoise, etc.: official dress or reserved manner used as a protection aginst outside influences. — *adj.* **carapa′cial** (*-shl*). [Fr., — Sp. *carapacho.*]

carat *kar′ət, n.* a unit of weight (metric carat = 200 milligrams) used for gems: (also **karat**) a unit used in expressing fineness of gold, 24-carat gold being pure gold: worth, estimate (*obs.*). [Fr., — Ar. *qīrāt,* perh. from Gr. *keration,* a carob-seed used as a weight.]

carauna. See **caranna.**

caravan *kar′ə-van, -van′,* a company travelling together for security, esp. in crossing the deserts: a company of people: a fleet with convoy: a covered van: a house on wheels. — *v.i.* to travel in a caravan: — *pr.p.* **car′-avaning** or **caravann′ing;** *pa.p.* and *pa.t.* **car′avaned, caravanned′.** — *ns.* **caravaneer′** the leader of a caravan; **caravan(n)′er** a caravaneer: one who stays in a caravan, esp. for holidays; **caravanette′** a motorised mobile

home; **caravanserai** (*-van'sə-rī*) a kind of unfurnished inn or extensive enclosed court where caravans stop. — Also **caravansarai, -sary. — caravan site, park** an open space laid out for caravans. [Pers. *kārwān*, caravan; *kārwānsarāī* (*sarāī*, inn).]
caravance. See **calavance.**
caravel *kar'ə-vel, n.* a light Mediterranean sailing-ship. [Fr. *caravelle* — It. *caravella*; cf. L.L. *cārabus*, Gr. *kārabos*, a light ship.]
caraway *kar'ə-wā, n.* an umbelliferous plant (*Carum carvi*) with aromatic fruits (**caraway seeds**) used as a tonic and condiment. [Prob. Sp. *alcaravea* (*carvi*), Ar. *karwiyā* — Gr. *karon.*]
carb *kärb, n.* a coll. shortening of **carburettor.**
carbamate *kär'bə-māt, kär-bam'āt, n.* a salt or ester of carbamic acid, used esp. as a pesticide. — *ns.* **carbamide** (*kär'bə-mīd, kär-bam'īd*) urea; **car'baryl** (*-bə-ril*) a carbamate insecticide. — **carbamic acid** an acid, CH_3NO_2, a half amide of carbonic acid. [**carbon, amide, aryl.**]
carbide *kär'bīd, n.* a compound of carbon with another element, esp. calcium carbide. [**carbon.**]
carbine *kär'bīn,* **carabin(e)** *kar'ə-bin, -bīn, ns.* a short light rifle. — *ns.* **car(a)bineer', -ier** a soldier armed with a carbine: a light cavalryman: a soldier of the 6th Dragoon Guards (from 1939, 3rd Carabineers). [Fr. *carabine.*]
carbocyclic *kär-bō-sīk'lik, adj.* homocyclic. [**carbon, cyclic.**]
carbohydrate *kär-bō-hī'drāt, n.* a compound of carbon, hydrogen, and oxygen, the last two being in the same proportion as in water: extended to kindred compounds. [See **carbon, hydrate.**]
carbolic *kär-bol'ik, n.* (in full **carbolic acid**) phenol. [L. *carbō*, coal, *oleum*, oil.]
carbon *kär'bən, n.* a non-metallic element (at. numb. 6; symbol C), widely diffused, occurring uncombined as diamond and graphite: a piece of carbon (esp. an electrode or a lamp-filament), or of carbon paper: a carbon copy: a carbonado diamond. — Also *adj.* — *adj.* **carbonā'ceous** coaly: containing much carbon: like carbon. — *ns.* **carbon'alite** an intrusive carbonate rock; **car'bonate** a salt of carbonic acid. — *v.t.* to combine or impregnate with carbon dioxide: to carbonise. — *n.* **carbonā'tion.** — *adjs.* **carbonic** (*-bon'ik*) pertaining to carbon; **carbonif'erous** producing carbon or coal: (with *cap.*; *geol.*) belonging to the Carboniferous system. — *n.* **carbonisā'tion, -z-.** — *v.t.* **car'bonise, -ize** to reduce to carbon: to char or coke: to cover with carbon. — *v.i.* to become carbonised. — **carbon-14** a radioactive isotope of carbon used, e.g. as a tracer element in biological studies or in dating archaeological material; **carbon arc** an electric arc between two carbon electrodes, used for high-intensity lighting; **carbon black** a form of finely divided carbon produced by partial combustion of hydrocarbons; **carbon copy** a duplicate of writing or typed matter made by interleaving **carbon paper,** a paper coated with a pigment made of carbon or other material: any exact duplicate. — *v.t.* **car'bon-cop'y** to copy exactly. — **carbon dating** estimating the date of death of prehistoric organic material from the amount of carbon-14 still present in it; **carbon dioxide, carbonic anyhdride** an oxide of carbon (CO_2), a colourless, odourless, incombustible gas, present in the atmosphere, formerly called *carbonic acid gas,* which in solution in water forms **carbonic acid** (H_2CO_3), a weak acid; **carbon disulphide** (CS_2), a solvent for rubber; **carbon fibres** (see also **whiskers**) very fine filaments of carbon used in bundles, bound together by resins, to increase the strength of e.g. plastics; **carbon monoxide** (CO) a colourless, odourless, very poisonous gas which burns with a blue flame to form carbon dioxide; **carbon process** (*phot.*) a printing process using paper coated with gelatine and a pigment and sensitised with potassium bichromate; **carbon steel** steel containing carbon, with different properties according to the quantity of carbon used; **carbon tetrachloride** (CCl_4) a solvent, etc.; **the**

Carboniferous (System) one of the main divisions of the Palaeozoic rocks, overlying the Devonian or Old Red Sandstone, underlying the Permian, and including the Mountain or Carboniferous Limestone, the Millstone Grit, and the Coal Measures. [Fr. *carbone* — L. *carbō, -ōnis,* coal, charcoal.]
carbonado[1] *kär-bən-ā'dō, n.* a piece of meat cut crossways for broiling on coals (*obs.*): (also **carbon(n)ade'**) a beef stew made with beer: — *pl.* **carbona'do(e)s.** — *v.t.* to cut crossways for broiling (*obs.*): to slash (*obs.*). [Sp. *carbonada.*]
carbonado[2] *kär-bən-ā'dō, n.* a variety of crystalline carbon, black, opaque, harder than diamond, used in drilling, etc. — Also called **black diamond, carbon.** [Port., carbonated.]
Carbonari *kär-bon-är'ē, n.pl.* members of a secret society in Italy at the beginning of the 19th century, founded to help forward a republican government. — *n.* **Carbonar'ism.** [It., lit. charcoal burners.]
carbonyl *kär'bə-nil,* (*chem.*) *n.* the radical CO. — *v.t.* **carbonylate** (*kär-bon'i-lāt*) to introduce the carbonyl group into. — *n.* **carbonylā'tion.** [**carbon,** and Gr. *hȳlē,* matter.]
Carborundum® *kär-bər-un'dum, n.* a silicon carbide, used as a substitute for corundum. [**carbon** and **corundum;** a trademark in some countries.]
carboxyl *kär-boks'il, n.* the radical COOH. — *adj.* **carboxylic** (*-bok-sil'ik*). [**carbon, oxygen,** Gr. *hȳlē,* matter.]
carboy *kär'boi, n.* a large glass or plastic bottle, with basketwork or other casing, for dangerous chemicals. [Pers. *qarābah.*]
carbuncle *kär'bung-kl, n.* a mythical self-luminous gem: a fiery-red precious stone (almandine or precious garnet): a pimple on the nose: a local inflammation of the skin and subcutaneous tissues, caused by bacterial infection. — *adjs.* **car'buncled** set with the gem carbuncle: afflicted with carbuncles: having red inflamed spots; **carbun'cular** belonging to or like a carbuncle: red: inflamed. [L. *carbunculus,* dim. of *carbō,* a coal.]
carburet *kär'bū-ret,* or *-ret', n.* a carbide (*obs.*). — *vs.t.* **carburet, car'burate, car'burise, -ize** to combine with carbon: to charge with carbon compounds. — *ns.* **carburā'tion, carburetion** (*-rāsh'ən, -resh'ən*), **carburīsā'tion, -z-.** — *adj.* **car'buretted** (or *-ret'*). — *n.* **car'burettor, -er,** *U.S.* **carburetor, -er** (or *-ret'*) an apparatus for charging a gas with carbon compounds, esp. part of an internal-combustion engine in which air is mixed with volatile fuel in the desired proportion. — **carburetted gas** a mixed illuminant got by passing water-gas over hot hydrocarbons; **carburetted hydrogen** marsh-gas, olefiant gas, or other compound of carbon and hydrogen. [Fr. *carbure* — L. *carbō,* coal.]
carcajou *kär'kə-jōō, n.* the glutton or wolverene. [Canadian Fr., prob. from an Indian name.]
carcake *kär'kāk,* (*Scot.*) *n.* a kind of cake for Shrove Tuesday. [O.E. *caru,* grief, and **cake.**]
carcanet *kär'kə-net, n.* a collar of jewels: a jewelled head-ornament (*obs.*). [Fr. (and obs. Eng.) *carcan,* an iron collar used for punishment — L.L. *carcannum,* from Gmc.]
carcase, carcass *kär'kəs, n.* a dead body, no longer used of a human corpse: (*disrespectfully*) a live human body: the framework of anything: a ruin: an incendiary shell: the body of a tyre as distinct from the tread. — *v.t.* to put up the framework of: to make a carcase of. — **carcase meat, carcass meat** raw meat as prepared for the butcher's shop, not tinned. [O.Fr. *carquois* (mod. *carcasse*), a skeleton.]
carcinogen, -ic. See **carcinoma.**
carcinology *kär-si-nol'ə-ji, n.* the study of crustaceans. — *adj.* **carcinological** (*-ə-loj'i-kl*). — *n.* **carcinol'ogist.** [Gr. *karkinos,* a crab, *logos,* discourse.]
carcinoma *kär-si-nō'mə, n.* a cancer: — *pl.* **carcinō'mata, -nō'mas.** — *adj.* **carcinō'matous.** — *ns.* **carcin'ogen** (*-jen*) a substance that encourages the growth of cancer; **carcinogen'esis.** — *adj.* **carcinogen'ic.** — *ns.*

carcinogenic′ity; carcinō′sis, carcinōmatō′sis spread of cancer in the body. [Gr. *karkinōma — karkinos,* crab.]

card[1] *kärd,* a small piece of pasteboard: one with figures for playing a game, with a person's name and address, with a greeting, invitation, message, programme, etc. (*playing-card, visiting-card, Christmas card, wedding card, race-card,* etc.): a domino: the dial of a mariner's compass: a map: a perforated plate used as a guide in weaving: a personal announcement in a newspaper or elsewhere (*U.S.*): the programme of races at a race-meeting: an invitation: a person (*slang*): a wag or eccentric: (in *pl.*) a game played with cards. — *v.t.* to return on a scoring-card (*golf*): to enter in a card index. — **card′board** a stiff, finely finished pasteboard. — *adj.* made of cardboard: flimsy, insubstantial. — *adj.* **card′-carrying** openly expressing membership of or support for a party or group: orig. holding a membership card of a party, etc., esp. the Communist party. — **card′-case** a case for carrying visiting-cards; **card′castle** an erection of playing cards in storeys: any flimsy or precarious structure; **card catalogue** a card index; **card column** (*comput.*) one of the eighty vertical columns of a punched card; **card file** a card index; **card′-game** a game played with playing-cards; **card′-holder** one who has a membership card: hence a member of a club, organisation, etc.; **card index** one with entries on separate cards. — *v.t.* **card′-in′dex**. — **card′punch** (*comput.*) a machine which perforates cards to record data; **card reader** (*comput.*) a device which reads the data on a punched card and converts it to a form suitable for storage or processing; **card′-sharp(er)** one who cheats at cards; **card′-table** a table for playing cards on; **card′-vote** a voting system that gives each delegate's vote a value in proportion to the number he represents. — **cards in one's hands** everything under one's control; **cards on the table** one's resources and moves freely laid open; **card up one's sleeve** an advantageous factor or argument kept in reserve; **cooling card** see **cool**; **get one's cards** to be dismissed; **house of cards** a card-castle; **knowing card** one who is sharp, wide awake; **leading card** a strong point in one's case; **make a card** to win a trick in a card-game; **on the cards** not improbable; **play one's cards well, badly** to make, not to make, the best of one's chances; **show one's cards** to expose one's secrets or designs; **speak by the card** to speak with precision and to the point; **sure card** one who is wide awake; **the cards are stacked against (someone, something)** the circumstances, facts, are ranged against (a person, an argument, etc.); **throw up (or in) the cards** to give in: to confess defeat. [Fr. *carte* — L. *c(h)arta* — Gr. *chartēs,* paper; cf. **carte**[2].]

card[2] *kärd, n.* an instrument for combing wool or flax. — *v.t.* to comb (wool, etc.): to mix, adulterate (*Shak.*). — *n.* **card′er**. — **carding wool** short-stapled wool. [Fr. *carde* — L. *carduus,* a thistle.]

Cardamine *kär-dam′i-nē, n.* a genus of cress, including the cuckoo-flower or lady's smock: (without *cap.*) a member of the genus. [Gr. *kardaminē — kardamon,* cress.]

cardamom, cardamum *kär′də-məm, n.* the capsules of several tropical plants of the ginger family, which form an aromatic, pungent spice. — Also **card′amon**. [L. *cardamōmum* — Gr. *kardamōmon*.]

cardan joint *kär′dan joint* a type of universal joint invented by Geronimo *Cardano* (1501–76), Italian mathematician.]

cardecu, cardecue *kär′di-kū, (obs.) n.* an old French silver coin. [Fr. *quart d'écu,* quarter of a crown.]

cardi, cardy *kär′di, n.* coll. for **cardigan**.

cardiac *kär′di-ak, adj.* belonging to the heart or to the upper end of the stomach. — *n.* a cordial or heart stimulant: a person with cardiac disease. — *adj.* **cardiacal** (-*dī′ə-kl*) cardiac. — *ns.* **cardialgia** (-*di-al′ji-ə*; Gr. *algos,* pain), **car′dialgy** an uneasy sensation or burning pain at the upper orifice of the stomach, apparently at the heart — hence called heartburn;

car′diogram a tracing obtained from a cardiograph; **car′diograph** an instrument for recording movements of the heart; **cardiog′rapher** one who uses a cardiograph; **cardiog′raphy**. — *adj.* **car′dioid** heart-shaped. — *n.* a heart-shaped curve traced by a point on the circumference of a circle rolling on an equal circle. — *adj.* **cardiological** (-*log′i-kl*). — *ns.* **cardiol′ogist; cardiology** (-*ol′ə-ji*) the science that deals with the structure, function, and diseases of the heart. — *adj.* **cardiomō′tor** pertaining to the action of the heart. — *n.* **cardiomyop′-athy** myocardiopathy. — *adjs.* **cardiopul′monary** pertaining to the heart and lungs; **cardiorespir′atory** relating to the action of the heart and lungs; **cardiovascular** (-*vas′kū*) pertaining to, involving, heart and blood-vessels. — *n.* **cardī′tis** inflammation of the heart. — **cardiac arrest** stopping of the heart-beat; **cardiac failure** heart-failure; **cardiac massage** rhythmic massage of the heart, either directly or by pressure on the sternum, to restart or maintain blood-circulation after heart-failure. [Gr. *kardiā,* heart, the upper end of the stomach.]

cardigan *kär′di-gən, n.* a knitted woollen jacket, named after Lord *Cardigan* (1797–1868). — *adj.* **car′diganed** wearing a cardigan.

cardinal *kär′di-nl, adj.* pertaining to a hinge: on which a thing hinges: of fundamental importance: of a deep scarlet colour, like a cardinal's cassock or hat. — *n.* one of the princes of the church constituting the sacred college at Rome, to whom pertains the right of electing a new pope: a short cloak, formerly worn by ladies: a cardinal-bird. — *ns.* **car′dinalate, car′dinalship** the office or dignity of cardinal. — *adjs.* **cardinalā′tial, -li′tial** pertaining to a cardinal or to the office of cardinal. — *adv.* **car′dinally** fundamentally. — **car′-dinal-bird** a large American finch, the cock bright red with a crest, a song-bird; **car′dinal-bishop, car′dinal-priest, car′dinal-deacon** the three orders of cardinal in the sacred college; **car′dinal-flower** a scarlet-flowered American lobelia: extended to a blue species (*blue cardinal*); **cardinal numbers** numbers expressing how many (1, 2, 3, distinguished from *ordinals*); **cardinal points** the four chief points of the compass — north, south, east, and west; **cardinal virtues** justice, prudence, temperance, fortitude, upon which the whole of human nature was supposed to hinge. [L. *cardinālis — cardō, cardinis,* a hinge.]

cardiograph, cardioid, cardiovascular, carditis, etc. See **cardiac**.

cardoon *kär-dōōn′, n.* a Mediterranean plant close akin to the true artichoke, its leafstalks and ribs eaten like celery. [Obs. Fr. *cardon* — L. *carduus,* a thistle.]

cardophagus *kär-dof′ə-gəs, n.* a thistle-eater, a donkey. [Latinised from Gr. *kardos,* thistle; *phagos,* eater, glutton.]

carduus *kär′dū-əs,* (*Shak.*) *n.* a thistle. [L.]

cardy. See **cardi**.

care *kār, n.* affliction: anxiety: heedfulness: heed: charge, oversight: residential or non-residential medical or social welfare services: an object of anxiety or watchfulness. — *v.i.* to be anxious: to be inclined: to be concerned: to mind: to have liking or fondness: to provide, look after, watch over (with *for*). — *adj.* **care′ful** full of care: heedful: anxious (*B.*): grievous (*Spens.*): sorrowful (*Spens.*): painstaking, thorough. — *adv.* **care′fully**. — *n.* **care′fulness**. — *adj.* **care′less** without care: heedless, unconcerned. — *adv.* **care′-lessly**. — *ns.* **care′lessness; car′er** one who cares: one who takes responsibility for another, dependent person. — *adj.* **car′ing** compassionate: concerned professionally with social, medical, etc., welfare (as the *caring professions,* i.e. social workers, nurses, etc.). — *adjs.* **care′-crazed** (*Shak.*) crazed or broken with care and solicitude; **care′free** void of anxiety. — **care label** a label on a garment, giving washing, etc., instructions. — *v.t.* and *v.i.* **care′take** to act as caretaker (for a property, etc.). — **care′taker** one put in charge of anything, esp. a building. — *adj.* exercising temporary supervision or control, as *caretaker government.* — *adj.* **care'worn** worn or vexed with care. — **care and maintenance** the keeping of a discontinued plant in sound condition on possibility of its being restarted; **care (and protection) order** an order by a magistrate placing a child in care; **care of** to be delivered to the custody of, or at the address of; **for all I,** etc., **care it** is a matter of indifference to me, etc.; **have a care** to take care; **I,** etc., **couldn't care less** I, etc., do not care in the least; **in care** (of a child) in the guardianship of a local authority or other official organisation: (of an elderly person) in an old people's home or geriatric ward; **in care of** (*U.S.*) care of (see above); **take care** to be careful or cautious; **take care of** to look after with care: to make the necessary arrangements regarding (*coll.*). [O.E. *caru;* Goth. *kara,* sorrow; O.N. *kæra,* to lament.]

careen *kə-rēn',* *v.t.* to turn over on the side, esp. for repairing or cleaning — Also *v.i.* — *n.* a heeling position. — *n.* **careen'age** a place where ships are careened: the cost of careening. [L. *carīna,* keel.]

career *kə-rēr'* (*obs.* **cariere;** *Spens. kar'),* *n.* a racecourse or lists, a course passed over (*obs.*): a rush: progress through life: (advancement in) profession or occupation. — *adj.* having a career: dedicated to a career. — *v.i.* to gallop: to move or run rapidly. — *ns.* **career'ism; career'ist** one intent on his own advancement. — Also *adj.* — **careers master, mistress** a schoolteacher who advises pupils on their choice of career; **career woman** a woman who attaches great importance to her job, to promotion, etc. [Fr. *carrière,* a racecourse — L.L. *carrāria,* carriage-road — *carrus,* wagon.]

carème *ka-rem,* (Fr.) *n.* Lent.

caress *kə-res',* *v.t.* to touch endearingly: to fondle. — *n.* an endearing touch. — *n.* and *adj.* **caress'ing.** — *adv.* **caress'ingly.** [Fr. *caresser* — It. *carezza,* an endearment — L. *cārus,* dear.]

caret *kar'ət,* *n.* a mark, ∧, to show where to insert something omitted. [L., 'there is wanting'.]

Carex *kā'reks,* *n.* a genus of sedges: (without *cap.*) a member of the genus: — *pl.* **cā'rices** (*-ris-ēz*). [L. *cārex.*]

Carey Street *kā'ri strēt,* bankruptcy (name of a street in London where the Bankruptcy Court was formerly situated).

carfax, -fox *kär'faks, -foks, ns.* a place where four roads meet — now used mainly of particular examples, as at Oxford. [L. *quadrifurcus,* four-forked.]

carfuffle, curfuffle *kər-fuf'l,* (*orig. Scot.*) *n.* commotion, agitation. — *v.t.* to disorder. — Other present-day spellings include **ke(r)fuffle.** [Gael. pfx. *car-,* Scot. *fuffle,* to disorder.]

cargo *kär'gō, n.* the goods carried by a ship or aeroplane: any load to be carried: — *pl.* **-oes.** — *v.t.* to load, weigh down (with *with*). — **cargo cult** a type of religion in certain South Pacific islands based on the belief that ancestors or supernatural beings will return bringing products of modern civilisation and thus make the islanders rich and independent: any setting of too high a value on material possessions. [Sp., — root of **car.**]

cargoose *kär'gōōs, n.* the crested grebe: — *pl.* **car'geese.** [O.N. *kjarr,* copsewood, and **goose.**]

cariacou *kar'i-ə-kōō,* **carjacou** *kär'jə-kōō, ns.* any deer of the American genus or subgenus *Cariacus,* including the Virginian deer. [Tupi, *cariacu.*]

cariama *kä-ri-ä'mə, n.* Same as **seriema.**

Carib *kar'ib, n.* one of a race inhabiting parts of Central America and northern South America: their language. — Also *adj.* — *ns.* and *adjs.* **Caribbē'an** of, pertaining to, the West Indies, their inhabitants (not all of Carib origin), or their culture; **Caribbee'.** — **Caribbee bark** the bark of a West Indian rubiaceous genus (*Exostema*) once esteemed a substitute for cinchona. [Cf. **cannibal.**]

caribe *kä-rē'bā, n.* the piranha. [Sp., Carib, savage, piranha.]

caribou *kar-i-bōō', kar', n.* the American reindeer. [Can. Fr.]

Carica *kar'i-kə, n.* the papaw genus, giving name to a family **Caricā'ceae,** akin to the passion-flowers. [L. *Carica* (*fīcus*), a dried fig from Caria, an ancient region in Asia Minor.]

caricature *kar'i-kə-tūr,* or *-tūr',* or *-chōōr,* or *-chōōr', n.* a likeness of anything so exaggerated or distorted as to appear ridiculous (formerly **caricatū'ra**). — *v.t.* to turn into ridicule by distorting a likeness: to burlesque. — *adj.* **caricatūr'al.** — *n.* **caricatūr'ist.** [It. *caricatura* — *caricare,* to load, from root of **car.**]

carices. See **Carex.**

cariere. An obs. form of **career.**

caries *kā'ri-ēz, n.* decay, esp. of teeth. — *adjs.* **cariogenic** (*-ri-ō-jen'ik*) tending to give rise to caries; **cā'rious** decayed. [L. *cariēs.*]

carillon *kə-ril'yən, kar'il-yən, n.* a set of bells for playing tunes: a mechanism for playing them: a melody played on them. — *v.i.* to play a carillon. — *ns.* **carill'on(n)eur** (or *-nûr'),* **carill'onist** (or *kar').* [Fr., — L.L. *quadriliō, -ōnis,* a quaternary, as formerly rung on four bells.]

carina *kə-rī'nə, (biol.) n.* a keel or keel-like ridge: the boat-shaped structure formed by the two lower petals in the pea family. — *adj.* **carinate** (*kar'i-nāt*) keeled. [L. *carīna,* a keel.]

carioca *kar-ē-ō'kə, n.* a Brazilian dance or its tune, a maxixe or variety thereof: (with *cap.*) a native of Rio de Janeiro. — Also *adj.* [Port.]

cariogenic. See **caries.**

cariole, carriole *kar'i-ōl, n.* a small open carriage: a light cart. [Fr. *cariole* — root of **car.**]

caritas *ka'ri-tas* (or *kä'ri-täs*), (L.) *n.* (Christian) charity.

carious. See **caries.**

carjacou. See **cariacou.**

cark *kärk,* (*arch.*) *n.* care, anxiety, or solicitude. — *v.t.* to burden, harass. — *v.i.* to be anxious. — *adj.* **cark'ing.** [Norm. Fr. *kark(e)* — L.L. *carcāre* — *carricāre,* to load; see **charge.**]

carl *kärl, n.* a husbandman (*obs.*): a churl (*arch.*): a niggard (*Scot.*). — *n.* **car'line** (*-lin; Scot.*) an old woman: a witch. — *adj.* **carl'ish** (*arch.*) churlish: clownish. — *n.* **car'lot** (*Shak.; As You Like It*) a churl, peasant. — **carl'-hemp** the female plant of hemp (lit. male-hemp, as stronger than fimble, the true male). [O.N. *karl,* a man, a male; see **churl.**]

Carley float *kär'li flōt,* an emergency rubber raft. [From the inventor's name.]

carline[1] *kär'lin, n.* any plant of a genus (*Carlina:* **Carline thistle**) closely allied to the true thistles. [From a legend that an angel showed the root to *Carolus, Karl,* or Charlemagne, as a remedy for a plague.]

carline[2], carlish. See **carl.**

Carlist *kär'list, n.* a supporter of the claims of the Spanish pretender Don *Carlos* de Borbón (1788–1855), second son of Charles IV, and his representatives. — Also *adj.* — *n.* **Car'lism.**

carlock *kär'lok, n.* a Russian isinglass. [Russ. *karluk.*]

carlot. See **carl.**

Carlovingian. Same as **Carolingian.**

Carlylese *kär-līl-ēz', n.* the vigorous, irregular phraseology and vocabulary of Thomas *Carlyle* (1795–1881). — *adjs.* **Carlylesque'; Carlyl'ean.** — *n.* **Car'lylism** (or *-līl').*

carmagnole *kär-man-yōl', n.* a popular song and dance of the French Revolution: a kind of jacket worn by revolutionists at that time with short skirts, a broad collar and lapels, and several rows of buttons. [Prob. from *Carmagnola* in Piedmont.]

Carmelite *kär'mi-līt, n.* a White Friar, or friar of the order of Our Lady of Mount *Carmel,* in Palestine (now Israel), founded there *c.* 1156, made a mendicant order in 1247 — brown habit, white cloak and scapular: a nun of a similar order (from 1452): a variety of pear (*obs.*): (without *cap.*) a fine woollen stuff of beige or similar colour.

carminative *kär'min-ə-tiv*, or *-min'*, *adj.* expelling flatulence. — *n.* a medicine with that effect. [L. *cārmināre*, to card, comb out — *cārmen*, a card for wool.]

carmine *kär'mīn*, *-min*, *n.* the red colouring matter of the cochineal insect: its colour. — *adj.* of that colour. [Fr. *carmin* or Sp. *carmín* — Sp. *carmesí*, crimson — Ar. *qirmazī*, crimson — same root as **crimson**.]

carnage *kär'nij*, *n.* a heap of slain (*obs.*): slaughter. [Fr., — It. *carnaggio*, carnage — L. *carō*, *carnis*, flesh.]

carnahuba. See **carnauba**.

carnal *kär'nl*, *adj.* fleshly: sensual: unspiritual: bodily: sexual: murderous, flesh-eating (*Shak.*). — *v.i.* (*obs.*) to act carnally. — *v.t.* car'nalise, -ize to sensualise. — *ns.* car'nalism; car'nalist a sensualist; carnality (*-nal'i-ti*) the state of being carnal. — *adv.* car'nally. — *adj.* carnass'ial (Fr. *carnassier*) adapted for flesh-eating. — *n.* a carnivore's scissor-tooth, usually long and large, used for tearing flesh. — *adjs.* car'neous, car'nose fleshy: of or like flesh. — *n.* car'nifex (L.) an executioner. — *adj.* carnificial (*-fish'l*). — *n.* carnos'ity a fleshy excrescence growing in and obstructing any part of the body. — carnal knowledge (*law*) sexual intercourse. — *adj.* car'nal-mind'ed worldly-minded. [L. *carō, carnis*, flesh.]

carnallite *kär'nəl-īt*, *n.* a milk-white or pinkish hydrous chloride of potassium and magnesium. [Mineralogist Von *Carnall* (1804–74).]

carnaptious *kär-nap'shəs*, curnaptious *kər-*, (*Scot.* and *Ir.*) *adjs.* bad-tempered, cantankerous. [Origin obscure.]

carnassial. See **carnal**.

carnation *kär-nā'shən*, *n.* flesh-colour (*obs.*): a colour ranging from light pink to deep crimson: a florists' double-flowering variety of the clove pink. — *adj.* of the colour carnation. — *adj.* carnā'tioned ruddy. [L. *carnātiō, -ōnis*, fleshiness.]

carnauba, carnahuba *kär-nä-ōō'bə*, or *-now'*, *n.* a Brazilian palm (*Copernicia*): its yellowish wax — also *Brazilian wax*. [Braz.]

carnelian. See **cornelian**.

carneous. See **carnal**.

carnet *kär'nā*, *n.* a customs or other permit: a book of tickets, vouchers, or the like. [Fr.]

carney. See **carny**.

carnifex, -icial. See **carnal**.

carnival *kär'ni-vl*, *n.* a feast observed by Roman Catholics just before the fast of Lent: any season of revelry or indulgence: riotous feasting, merriment, or amusement: a fair-like entertainment. [It. *carnevale* — L.L. *carnelevārium*, apparently from L. *carnem levāre*, to put away flesh.]

Carnivora *kär-niv'ə-rə*, *n.pl.* an order of flesh-eating mammals. — *n.* car'nivore (*-vōr*, *-vör*) a carnivorous animal. — *adj.* carniv'orous flesh-eating. — *adv.* carniv'orously. — *n.* carniv'orousness. [L. *carō, carnis*, flesh, *vorāre*, to devour.]

carnose, carnosity. See **carnal**.

Carnot cycle *kär'nō sī'kl*, an ideal heat engine cycle of maximum thermal efficiency. [Nicolas *Carnot*, French physicist, d. 1832.]

carnotite *kär'nō-tīt*, *n.* a mineral (hydrated vanadate of uranium and potassium) important as a source of radium, later of vanadium, later of uranium. [Adolphe *Carnot*, French mine inspector, d. 1920.]

carny, carney *kär'ni*, (*dial.*) *v.t.* and *v.i.* to coax, wheedle. — *n.* flattery: a flatterer. — *adj.* cunning, sly.

carob *kar'ob*, *-əb*, *n.* the algarroba or locust-tree (*Ceratonia siliqua*), a caesalpiniaceous Mediterranean tree: its fruit: a substitute for chocolate prepared from the fruit. [Fr. *carobe* — Ar. *kharrūbah*; cf. **algarroba**.]

caroche *kä-rosh'*, *n.* a carriage, esp. a grand one (*hist.*). [Fr., — It. *caroccio*, *carro* — L. *carrus*, car.]

carol *kar'əl*, *n.* a ring-dance or the song accompanying it (*arch.*): a song of joy or praise: Christmas song or hymn: an enclosure for a study in a cloister, etc. (see also **carrel(l)**). — *v.i.* to dance or sing a carol: to sing or warble. — *v.t.* to praise or celebrate in song: — *pr.p.* car'olling; *pa.p.* and *pa.t.* car'olled. — *n.* car'oller.

[O.Fr. *carole*; It. *carola*, orig. a ring-dance, perh. — L. *chorus*, Gr. *choros*, or L. or Gr. *choraulēs*, a flute-player who accompanies a chorus.]

Carolina *kar-ə-lī'nə*, *n.* two states (North and South) of the United States. — Also *adj.* — *adj.* **Carolinian** (*-lin'i-ən*). — **Carolina allspice** see **Calycanthus** under **calyx**; **Carolina pink** an American species of Silene (bladder-campion): pinkroot (see **pink**[3]).

Carolingian *kar-ə-lin'ji-ən*, Carlovingian *kär-lō-vin'ji-ən*, *adjs.* relating to a dynasty of Frankish kings, so called from *Karl* (L. *Carolus*) the Great or Charlemagne (742–814). — **Carolingian** (or **Caroline**) **minuscule** a script developed in France at the time of Charlemagne.

Carolus *kar'ə-ləs*, *n.* a gold coin of the time of Charles I. — *adjs.* **Carolean** (*kar-ō-lē'ən*) belonging to the time of Charles I or II; **Car'oline** belonging to the time of Charles I or II, or Charlemagne, or any other Charles. — **Caroline minuscule** see **Carolingian**. [L. *Carolus*, Charles.]

carom *kar'əm*, *n.* and *v.i.* a shortened form of **carambole** (*kar'əm-bōl*), the same as **cannon** in billiards.

caromel. See **caramel**.

carotene *kar'ō-tēn*, carotin *-tin*, *ns.* any of a number of reddish-yellow pigments widely distributed in plants, precursors of vitamin A. — *n.* **carotenoid, carotinoid** (*kar-ot'in-oid*) any of a group of pigments similar to carotenes, some of which are precursors of vitamin A. [L. *carōta*, carrot, and suff. *-ene*.]

carotid *kə-rot'id*, *adj.* relating to the two great arteries of the neck. [Gr. *karōtídes* (pl.) — *karos*, sleep, the ancients supposing that deep sleep was caused by compression of them.]

carouse *kə-rowz'*, *adv.* (*obs.*) in drinking, all out. — *n.* a drinking-bout: a noisy revel. — *v.i.* to hold a drinking-bout: to drink freely and noisily. — *ns.* carous'al a carouse: a feast; carous'er. — *adv.* carous'ingly. [O.Fr. *carous*, Fr. *carrousse* — Ger. *gar aus*, quite out, that is, empty the glass.]

carousel, in U.S. carrousel, *kar-ōō-zel'*, *-ə-sel'*, *n.* a tilting match or tournament, to which were added games, shows, and allegorical representations: a merry-go-round (*U.S.*): a rotating conveyor, e.g. for luggage at an airport or air terminal. [Fr. *carrousel*.]

carp[1] *kärp*, *v.i.* to catch at small faults or errors (with *at*). — *n.* carp'er. — *n.* and *adj.* carp'ing cavilling: fault-finding. — *adv.* carp'ingly. [Most prob. Scand., — O.N. *karpa*, to boast, modified in meaning through likeness to L. *carpĕre*, to pluck, deride.]

carp[2] *kärp*, *n.* a fresh-water fish common in ponds. [O.Fr. *carpe* — L.L. *carpa*; poss. Gmc.]

carpal. See **carpus**.

carpe diem *kär'pē dī'em*, *kär'pe dē'em*, (L.) enjoy the present.

carpel *kär'pl*, *n.* a modified leaf forming the whole or part of the gynaeceum of a flower. — *adj.* car'pellary. — *n.* carpogō'nium the female organ in red seaweeds, indirectly producing carp'ospores. — *adj.* carpoph'agous fruit-eating. — *n.* carp'ophore a prolongation of a flower axis below or between the carpels. [Gr. *karpos*, fruit.]

carpenter *kär'pint-ər*, *n.* a worker in timber as used in building houses, etc. — *v.i.* to do the work of a carpenter. — *v.t.* to make by carpentry: to put together or construct, esp. clumsily. — *n.* car'pentry the trade or work of a carpenter. — car'penter-bee', -ant' a bee or ant that excavates its nest in wood. [O.Fr. *carpentier* — L.L. *carpentārius* — *carpentum*, a car, from root of **car**.]

carpet *kär'pit*, *n.* the woven, felted or tufted covering of floors, stairs, etc.: a tablecloth (*Shak.*): a smooth, or thin, surface or covering: the surface of the ground (*cricket*): a carpet-moth: a prison sentence of three months (*slang*). — *v.t.* to cover with or as if with a carpet: to have up for reprimand: — *pr.p.* car'peting; *pa.p.* and *pa.t.* car'peted. — *n.* car'peting material of which carpets are made: carpet, or carpets. — car'petbag' a travelling-bag made of carpeting; car'petbagger one who comes to a place for political or other ends (as if he carried his whole property qualification for citizenship with him in his carpet-bag); **car′pet-beat′ing** the removing of dust from carpets by beating; **car′pet-bed; car′pet-bedd′ing** a system of horticulture in which plants are arranged in mosaic or geometrical designs; **carpet beetle** any of several beetles or their larvae which are harmful to carpets and fabrics; **car′pet-bomb′ing** systematic bombing of a whole area; **car′pet-knight′** one dubbed a knight by mere court favour, not on account of his military exploits — hence an effeminate person; **car′petmonger** (*Shak.*) an effeminate person; **car′pet-moth′** any of the larger moths, with carpet-like markings, of the geometrid family Larentidae; **car′pet-rod** one of the rods used to keep a stair carpet in its place; **carpet shark** a shark of the genus *Orectolobus*, with a spotted back like a patterned carpet; **car′pet-slipper** a slipper whose upper was orig. made of carpeting; **car′pet-snake** a variegated python of Australia; **car′pet-sweeper** an apparatus with a revolving brush and a dust-pan, for sweeping carpets; **carpet tiles** small squares of carpeting which are laid together in such a way as to form an area of carpet. — **carpet-bag steak** a beefsteak stuffed with oysters; **on the carpet** under discussion (jocular trans. of Fr. *sur le tapis*): up before someone in authority for reprimand: at or near ground level (*airmen's slang*); **sweep under the carpet** to hide from notice, put out of mind (unpleasant problems or facts). [O.Fr. *carpite* — L.L. *carpeta, -pita,* coarse fabric made from rags pulled to pieces — L. *carpĕre,* to pluck.]

carphology *kär-fol′ə-ji, n.* floccillation, fitful plucking movements as in delirium. [Gr. *karphos,* straw, *logeiā,* gathering.]

carpogonium, carpophagous, etc. See **carpel.**

carpus *kär′pəs, n.* the wrist, or corresponding part of the fore-limb. — *adj.* **car′pal** pertaining to the carpus. — *n.* a bone of the carpus. — *n.* **carpometacar′pus** in birds, a bone of the wing formed by fusion of some of the carpals with the metacarpals. — **carpal tunnel syndrome** numbness and pain in the fingers caused by compression of the nerve as it passes through the **carpal tunnel** (between the bones of the wrist and the tendons). [Latinised from Gr. *karpos,* wrist.]

carr *kär, n.* (a copse in) boggy ground. [O.N. *kjarr.*]

carrack *kar′ək, (hist.) n.* a large ship of burden, which was also fitted for fighting. — Also **car′ack, carr′act, carr′ect.** [O.Fr. *carraque* — L.L. *carraca;* ety. dub.]

carrag(h)een *kar-ə-gēn′, n.* a purplish-red North Atlantic seaweed (*Chondrus crispus*) and a related species (*Gigartina mamillosa*), used for making soup and a kind of blancmange, as well as for size — also called *Irish moss.* — *n.* **carragee′nan, carrag(h)ee′nin** a colloid prepared from red algae, used in food processing, pharmaceuticals, etc. [Prob. Ir. *carraigín,* little rock — *carraig,* rock.]

carrat, carraway. Same as **carat, caraway.**

carrect. See **carrack.**

carrel(l) *kar′əl, n.* a carol (*hist.*): a desk or alcove in a library for private study. [See **carol.**]

carriage *kar′ij, n.* the act or cost of carrying: a vehicle for carrying, esp. a luxurious road vehicle, or a railway passenger-car: a wheeled support of a gun: the structures on which an aeroplane lands: a carrying part of a machine: the loop of a sword-belt (*Shak.*): behaviour (*arch.*): bearing: a burden (*Shak.*): baggage (*B.*). — *adj.* **carr′iageable** that may be conveyed in carriages. — **carriage clock** a small portable clock, usu. with a case with a handle on top; **carriage dog** a coachdog; **carr′iage-drive** a road for carriages through parks, etc.; **carriage driving** the competitive sport of driving a carriage and horse(s). — *advs.* **carr′iage-free′** without charge for transport; **carr′iage-for′ward** without prepayment of carriage. — **carriage horse** a horse that draws a carriage. — *adv.* **carr′iage-paid′** with prepayment of carriage. — **carriage trade** trade from the wealthy; **carr′iageway** a road, or part of a road, used

by vehicles. — **carriage and pair** a turn-out of a carriage and two horses. [See **carry.**]

carrick bend *kar′ik bend′ (naut.*) a knot for joining two ropes, formed by looping and interlacing the ends together. [Perh. conn. with **carrack,** and the root of **bind.**]

carrier. See **carry.**

carriole. See **cariole.**

carrion *kar′i-ən, n.* the dead and putrid body or flesh of any animal: anything vile. — *adj.* relating to, or feeding on, putrid flesh. — **carrion beetle** a beetle of the family *Silphidae,* which feeds on carrion; **carr′ion-crow′** the common crow: the black vulture (*U.S.*); **carr′ion-flower** a S. African asclepiad (*Stapelia*) with fleshy stem and stinking flowers. [Fr. *charogne* — L.L. *carōnia* — L. *carō, carnis,* flesh.]

carritch *kar′ich, (Scot.) n.* a catechism. [Fr. *catéchèse,* taken to be a plural.]

carriwitchet *kar-i-wich′it, n.* a quip: a quibble. [Origin unknown.]

carronade *kar-ən-ād′, (hist.) n.* a short cannon of large bore. [From *Carron,* a town in the Central Region of Scotland with ironworks.]

carron oil *kar′ən oil,* a liniment orig. of linseed-oil and lime-water. [Form. used for burns at *Carron* (see **carronade**) ironworks.]

carrot *kar′ət, n.* a plant of the *Umbelliferae,* having a tapering root of a reddish or yellowish colour: the root itself, which is edible and sweet: an incentive, enticement. — *adj.* **carr′oty** carrot-coloured, applied to the hair. — **carrot and stick** incentive and punishment, as alternative methods of persuasion. [Fr. *carotte* — L. *carōta.*]

carrousel. A U.S. spelling of **carousel.**

carry *kar′i, v.t.* to convey: to bear: to lead or transport: to take by force: to hold in saluting position (*mil.*): to effect: to gain: to behave or demean: (of money) to be sufficient for: to pass, by a majority: to add to another column (*arith.*): (of a newspaper) to publish (e.g. an item of news), or to publish as a regular feature: to do the work of, or perform in sport or entertainment well enough to cover up the deficiencies of (another): to keep (merchandise, etc.) in stock: to maintain: to be sufficient to maintain: to be pregnant with. — *v.i.* (of a voice, a gun, etc.) to reach, indicating its range: to be pregnant: — *pr.p.* **carr′ying;** *pa.p.* and *pa.t.* **carr′ied.** — *n.* the distance a golf ball goes when struck till it touches the ground: range: an act of carrying: the portage of a boat: land across which a boat has to be carried between one navigable stream or stretch and another: the position of 'carry arms': the sky, movement of clouds (*Scot.*). — *n.* **carr′ier** one who carries, esp. for hire: anything that carries: an instrument for carrying: a passenger aircraft: a basket, framework, or the like, for carrying luggage, as on a bicycle: one who transmits disease (without suffering from it) by harbouring germs, virus, etc.: a vehicle for communicating a signal in cases where the medium cannot convey the actual signal (as speech, etc., in radio transmission): (also **carrier wave**) a constant frequency in an amplitude-modulation transmission (*telecomm.*): non-active material mixed with, and chemically identical to, a radioactive compound (*nuc.*): a carrier-pigeon: a carrier bag: an aircraft carrier. — **carrier bag** a strong paper or plastic bag for carrying shopping, etc.; **carrier gas** a gas, e.g. helium, mixed with oxygen for breathing by divers when at great depths; **carr′ier-pig′eon** a pigeon with homing instincts, used for carrying messages: a pigeon of a fancy breed no longer so used; **carrier rocket** a rocket used to carry, e.g. a satellite into orbit; **carr′ycot** a small portable cot for a baby; **carr′y-out** (*Scot.*) a meal or drink bought and taken away to be consumed elsewhere; **carr′ytale** (*Shak.*) a tale-bearer. — **carry all before one** to bear down all obstacles; **carry away** to carry off: to deprive of self-control by exciting the feelings: to transport; **carry back** to set (a loss) against the previous year's profit, in order to lessen the total tax liability (*n.* **carr'y-back**); **carry forward** to transfer written or printed matter to the next page, or figures to the next column; **carry it** to behave, demean oneself: to gain the advantage, carry the day (also **carry it away**); **carry off** to cause the death of: to kidnap, abduct: to gain, to win, as a prize: to cause to pass muster, to make to pass by assurance or dissimulation; **carry on** to manage: to continue: to proceed: to complain or behave unrestrainedly (*ns.* **carr'y-on'**, **carry'ing-on'**): to flirt (*with*); **carry one's bat** see **bat**; **carry one's point** to overrule objections to one's plan or view; **carry out** to accomplish: to carry out for burial; **carry over** to bring into the other (political, etc.) party: to take to a new page, as an account, etc.: to postpone to next occasion: to postpone payment of (an account) to the next accounting period; **carry the can** to accept responsibility for a misdemeanour; **carry the day** to be successful: to win the day; **carry through** to support through difficulties: to succeed in putting into effect, to accomplish; **carry too far** to continue beyond reasonable limits; **carry up** to continue a building upward: to trace back; **carry weight** to possess authority: to have force. [O.Fr. *carier* — L.L. *carricāre*, to cart — L. *carrus*, a car.]

carry-all[1] *kar'i-öl*, (*U.S.*) *n.* a light four-wheeled one-horse carriage. [**cariole**, changed by folk-etymology.]

carry-all[2] *kar'i-öl*, *n.* (*U.S. and Can.*) an overnight bag, hold-all.

carse *kärs*, (*Scot.*), *n.* an alluvial river-side plain. [Perh. **carr**.]

cart *kärt*, *n.* a two-wheeled vehicle without springs, used for farm purposes, or for conveying heavy loads: a light two-wheeled vehicle with springs. — *v.t.* to convey in a cart: to carry publicly in a cart as a punishment — formerly done to bawds: to carry, esp. with difficulty (often with *around*). — *ns.* **cart'age** the act or cost of carting; **cart'er** one who drives a cart. — **cart'-horse** a horse suitable for drawing a cart; **cart'-house** a shed for keeping carts; **cart'load** as much as a cart can carry; **cart'road**, **cart'-track**, **cart'way** a road or way by which carts may pass; **cart's'-tail** the hind part of a cart, formerly a place of punishment; **cart'wheel** the wheel of a cart: a sideways somersault, or Catherine-wheel. — *v.i.* to make a sideways somersault. — **cart'wright** a carpenter who makes carts. — **cart off** (*coll.*) to remove; **in the cart** (*slang*) in the lurch: in a fix; **put the cart before the horse** to reverse the natural or sensible order of things; **village cart** an uncovered two-wheeled carriage for one horse, with a low body and one seat; **Whitechapel cart** or **chapel cart** a light two-wheeled spring-cart used in delivering shop goods. — See also **dogcart**, **mail-cart**, **tax-cart**, etc. [Ety. dub.; O.E. *cræt*, or O.N. *kartr*.]

carta. See **charta.**

carte[1]. See **quart**[1].

carte[2] *kärt*, *n.* a bill of fare: a playing-card (*Scot.*): a *carte-de-visite*. — **carte'-blanche'** (*-blāsh*) a blank paper, duly signed, to be filled up at the recipient's pleasure: freedom of action; **carte-de-visite** (*-də-vē-zēt'*) a small photographic portrait pasted on a card; **carte du jour** (*dü zhōōr*) menu (of the day). [Fr., — L. *c(h)arta*; see **card**.]

cartel *kär'təl*, *n.* a challenge: an agreement for exchange of prisoners: a card with writing on it: a political condition or bloc: (also *kär-tel'*) a combination of firms for certain purposes, esp. to keep up prices and kill competition. — *n.* **cartelisā'tion**, **-z-**. — *v.t.* and *v.i.* **car'telise**, **-ize**. — **cartel clock** a hanging wall-clock with the case usu. of metal. [Fr., — L. *c(h)arta*; see **card**.]

Cartesian *kär-tē'zi-ən*, or *-zhyən*, *adj.* relating to the French philosopher René *Descartes* (1596–1650), or his philosophy, or mathematical methods. — *n.* a follower of Descartes. — *n.* **Cartes'ianism.** — **Cartesian co-ordinates** co-ordinates of a point which have refer-

ence to two fixed lines that cross each other in a plane, or to three meeting surfaces; **Cartesian devil, diver,** or **bottle-imp** a scientific toy named after Descartes, a glass container with a floating figure that sinks when the top of the container is pressed.

carthamine *kär'thə-min*, *n.* a dye got from safflower. [L.L. *carthamus* — Ar. *qartum*, saffron.]

Carthusian *kär-thū'zi-ən*, or *-thōō'*, *n.* a monk or (since 1229) a nun of an order founded by St Bruno in 1086, noted for its strictness: a scholar of the Charterhouse School, founded on the site of a Carthusian monastery in London, now in Godalming. — *adj.* of or pertaining to the order or the school. [L. *Cartusiānus* — *Catorissium*, Chatrousse, a village in Dauphiné, near which their first monastery, La Grande Chartreuse, was founded.]

cartilage *kär'ti-lij*, *n.* gristle, a firm pearly white substance, often (*temporary cartilage*) converted later into bone. — *adj.* **cartilaginous** (*-laj'*). — **cartilaginous fishes** fishes with a cartilaginous skeleton — sharks, rays, chimaeras. [Fr., — L. *cartilāgō, -inis*; cog. with *crātis*, wickerwork, Gr. *kartallos*, a basket.]

cartography *kär-tog'rə-fi*, *n.* map-making. — *n.* **cartog'-rapher.** — *adjs.* **cartographic** (*-tō-graf'ik*), **-al.** — *ns.* **car'togram** a map presenting statistical information in diagrammatic form; **cartol'ogy** the science of maps and charts. — *adj.* **cartolog'ical.** [L. *c(h)arta* — Gr. *chartēs*, a sheet of paper, and Gr. *graphein*, to write.]

cartomancy *kär'tō-mən-si*, *n.* divination by playing-cards. [L.L. *carta*, a card, Gr. *manteiā*, divination.]

carton *kär'tən*, *n.* a thin pasteboard: a box made from it: a container of waxed cardboard for holding liquids: a small disc within the bull's-eye of the target: a shot that strikes it. — *v.t.* to put into a carton. — *n.* **car'ton(n)age** pasteboard: the outer covering of a mummy. — **carton-pierre** (*kär'tō-pyer*) a kind of papier-mâché, imitating stone. [Fr.; see **cartoon**.]

cartoon *kär-tōōn'*, *n.* a preparatory drawing on strong paper to be reproduced in fresco, tapestry, etc.: any large sketch or design on paper: a comic or satirical drawing commenting on current events or politics: a strip cartoon: a cinematograph film made by photographing a succession of drawings. — *v.t.* to make a cartoon or working design of: to caricature by a cartoon. — *n.* **cartoon'ist** one who makes cartoons. [Fr. *carton* or It. *cartone*, augm. of *carta*.]

cartophily *kär-tof'i-li*, *n.* cigarette-card collecting. — *ns.* **cartophile** (*kär'tō-fīl*), **cartoph'ilist.** — *adj.* **cartophil'ic.** [L. *c(h)arta* — Gr. *chartēs*, a sheet of paper, and Gr. *philiā*, a liking.]

cartouche *kär-tōōsh'*, *n.* a case for cartridges or formerly for mortar bullets: a scroll-like ornament with rolled ends (*archit.*): an ancient Egyptian oval figure enclosing royal or divine names. — Also **cartouch'.** [Fr., — It. *cartoccio* — L. *c(h)arta* — Gr. *chartēs*, paper.]

cartridge *kär'trij*, *n.* a case containing the charge for a gun (**blank'-car'tridge** with powder only; **ball'-car'-tridge** with a bullet as well): a small container which can easily be inserted into and removed from a machine, holding e.g. film for a camera, ink for a pen, a typewriter ribbon, part of the pick-up head of a record player: a cassette. — **car'tridge-belt** a belt having pockets for cartridges; **car'tridge-pā'per** a light-coloured, strong paper, originally manufactured for making cartridges. [A corr. of **cartouche**.]

cartulary *kär'tū-lər-i*, *n.* a register-book of a monastery, etc.: one who kept the records: the place where the register is kept. [L.L. *chartulārium* — L. *chartula*, a document — *charta*, paper.]

carucate *kär'ū-kāt*, *n.* as much land as a team of oxen could plough in a season. — *n.* **car'ucage** a tax on the carucate, first imposed by Richard I in 1198. [L.L. *carrūcāta*, ploughland — *carrūca*, plough, from root of **car**.]

caruncle *ka-*, *kə-rung'kl*, *n.* a small fleshy excrescence: an outgrowth on a seed near the micropyle. — *adjs.*

carun'cular, carun'culate, carun'culous. [Fr. — L. *caruncula*.]

carvacrol *kär'və-krol, n.* an isomer of and substitute for thymol, obtained from origanum, etc. [Fr. *carvi, caraway, L. acer, sharp, oleum, oil.*]

carve *kärv, v.t.* to cut into forms, devices, etc.: to make or shape by cutting: to cut up (meat) into slices or pieces: to apportion or distribute. — *v.i.* to exercise the art or perform the act of carving: app., to make affected gestures or amorous advances (*Shak.*): — *infin.* (*Spens.*) **carv'en**; *pa.p.* **carved**, *arch.* **carv'en**. — *adj.* **carv'en** carved. — *ns.* **carv'er** one who carves: a wood-carver: a sculptor: a carving-knife: a tree used for carving (*Spens.*): a dining chair with arms; **carv'ing** the act or art of sculpture esp. in wood or ivory: a carved device or figure: the act or art of cutting up meat at table. — **carv'ing-knife** a large knife for carving meat. — **carve out** to hew out: to gain by one's exertions; **carve up** (*slang*) to divide, esp. booty: to injure a person, esp. by slashing with a razor (*n.* **carve'-up**); **cut and carve** to refine. [O.E. *ceorfan,* to cut; Du. *kerven*; Ger. *kerben,* to notch.]

carvel *kär'vəl, n.* an older form of **caravel**. — *adj.* **car'vel-built** built without overlap of planks (distinguished from *clinker-built*).

carvy *kär'vi,* (*Scot.*) *n.* caraway: a caraway seed, esp. one coated with sugar. [Fr. *carvi*; see **caraway**.]

caryatid *kar-i-ät'id, n.* a female figure used instead of a column to support an entablature: — *pl.* **caryat'ids, caryat'ides** (-*i-dēz*) — *adjs.* **caryat'ic; caryat'idal; caryatidē'an; caryatid'ic.** [Gr. *Karyātis,* a priestess of Artemis at *Karyai* (*Caryae*), pl. *Karyātidĕs.*]

Caryocar *kär'i-ō-kär, n.* the butternut genus, giving name to the family **Caryocarā'ceae** (-*si-ē*). [Gr. *karyon,* nut, *karā,* head.]

caryophyllaceous *kar-i-ō-fi-lā'shəs, adj.* belonging to the pink family (**Caryophyllā'ceae**; - *si-ē*). [*Caryophyllus,* early botanical name for clove-pink — Gr. *karyophyllon,* clove-tree (from similar smell).]

caryopsis *kar-i-op'sis, n.* a dry indehiscent fruit in which the pericarp is united with the testa, characteristic of the grasses: — *pl.* **caryop'ses** (-*sēz*) or **caryop'sides** (-*si-dēz*). [Gr. *karyon,* a nut, *opsis,* appearance.]

casa *kä'zä,* (It.) *n.* a house.

Casanova *kas-ə-nō'və, n.* a person conspicuous for his amorous adventures, as was Giovanni Jacopo *Casanova* de Seingalt (1725–1798).

casbah. Same as **kasba(h).**

cascabel *kas'kə-bel, n.* the part behind the base-ring of a cannon. [Sp.]

cascade *kas-kād', n.* a waterfall: a trimming of lace or other material in a loose wavy fall: apparatus connected in series, each piece operating the next one in turn or acting on the output of the preceding one. — *v.i.* to fall in cascades: to form a cascade. [Fr., — It. *cascata* — L. *cadĕre,* to fall.]

cascara *kas-kä'rə* or *-kä'* or *kas'kə-rə, n.* a Californian buckthorn, *Rhamnus purshiana,* also known as the **cascara buckthorn:** the bark of the cascara, also known as **cascara sagrada** (*sə-grä'də* or *-grä'*; Sp., sacred) used as a tonic aperient. — *n.* **cascarill'a** the aromatic bitter bark of a West Indian croton, also known as **cascarilla bark:** the shrub itself. — **cascara amarga** (*ə-mär'gə*; Sp., bitter) the bitter bark of a tropical American tree of the quassia family, once used to treat syphilis and skin diseases. [Sp. *cáscara,* bark.]

caschrom *kas'krōm, n.* a sort of spade with a bent handle, formerly used in the Scottish Highlands for tilling the ground — Also **cas crom.** [Gael. *cas,* foot, handle, *chrom,* fem. of *crom,* bent, crooked.]

casco *kas'kō, n.* a Philippine lighter: — *pl.* **cas'cos.** [Sp.]

case¹ *kās, n.* a covering, box, or sheath: a set: a facing for walls: the boards and back of a book: the tray in which a compositor has his types before him. — *v.t.* to enclose in a case: to skin. — *n.* **cās'ing** the act of putting on a case, or of skinning: an outside covering of any kind, as of boards, plaster, etc.: a strong rigid pipe or tube lining a well, shaft, etc. — **case'-bottle** a bottle made to fit into a case with others, a bottle with a covering. — *adj.* **case'-bound** (of a book) with a hard cover. — *v.t.* **case'-hard'en** to harden on the surface, as by carbonising iron: to make callous or insensitive (*fig.*). — **case'-hard'ening; case'-knife** a large knife kept in a sheath; **case'maker** one who makes covers for books; **case'man** a compositor; **case'-shot** canistershot, an artillery projectile for use at close quarters; **case'-worm** caddis-worm. [O.N.Fr. *casse* (mod. Fr. *châsse* and *caisse*) — L. *capsa* — *capĕre,* to take.]

case² *kās, n.* that which falls or happens: event: state or condition: subject of question or inquiry: an instance of disease: (records relating to) a person under medical treatment or being dealt with by a social worker, etc.: an odd character (*slang*): a legal statement of facts: a lawsuit: a plausible contention, something to be said for a position or action: the grammatical relation of a noun, pronoun, or (in some languages) adjective to another word in the sentence, or its variation in form to express that relation — the nominative being imagined as a vertical line, and the oblique cases in various stages of falling or *declension.* — *v.t.* (*slang*) to reconnoitre or examine, usu. with a view to burglary. — **case'book** a book in which a doctor records the history of his cases: a book recording medical, legal, etc., cases which are valuable as examples for reference; **case history** a record of ancestry, environment, personal history, etc., for use in diagnosis and treatment, or for some other purpose; **case'-law** law as decided in previous cases; **case'-load** the number of cases a doctor, social worker, etc. has to deal with at a particular time; **case'-study** a study based on the analysis of one or more cases or case histories: (the gathering and organising of information for) a case history; **case'-work** the study of maladjusted individuals or families, their environment and history, often together with supervision and guidance; **case'-worker. — case in point** an example of what is under discussion; **in any case** at all events: at any rate; **in case** in the event that: lest; **in case to** in fit condition for; **make out one's case** to give good reasons for one's statements or position; **put (the) case** to suppose an instance: to take for example; **the case** the fact, the reality. [O.Fr. *cas* — L. *cāsus* — *cadĕre,* to fall.]

caseation, casein. See **caseous.**

casemate *kās'māt, n.* any bomb-proof vaulted chamber, even when merely used as quarters for a garrison: orig. a loopholed gallery, from which the garrison of a fort could fire upon an enemy who had obtained possession of the ditch. — *adj.* **case'mated.** [Fr.; der. uncertain.]

casement *kās'mənt, n.* the case or frame of a window: a window that opens on vertical hinges: a hollow moulding. — *adj.* **case'mented** having casements. — **case'-ment-cloth** a plain cotton fabric, suitable for casement-curtains; **case'ment-cur'tain** a curtain hung from a window-sash; **case'ment-win'dow.** [For **encasement** (Fr. *enchassement*), or L.L. *casamentum,* house-frame, or directly from **case¹.**]

caseous *kā'si-əs, adj.* cheeselike. — *ns.* **cāseā'tion** becoming cheeselike; **casein** (*kā'sē-, -si-in*) the principal albuminous constituent of milk, in which it is found as a calcium salt, obtainable by curdling. [L. *cāseus,* cheese.]

casern(e) *kä-zûrn', n.* a barrack. [Fr., — Sp. *caserna.*]

cash¹ *kash, n.* coin or money: ready money. — *adj.* using cash: paid for in cash. — *v.t.* to turn into or exchange for money. — *n.* **cashier'** one who has charge of the receiving and paying of money. — *adj.* **cash'less** operated, paid for, performed using credit cards or computer transfers, without the use of cash. — **cash'-account'** an account to which nothing is carried but cash (*book-k.*): a form of account with a bank, by which a person is entitled to draw out sums by way of loan — also called **cash'-cred'it.** — *adj.* **cash'-and-carr'y** denoting a business, method of trading, etc. which involves *cash and carry* (see below). — **cash'-**

book a book in which an account is kept of the receipts and disbursements of money; **cash card** a card issued by a bank that allows the holder to use a cash dispenser; **cash-credit** see **cash-account; cash crop** a crop intended for sale, not for consumption by the producer; **cash desk** a table, etc., with a till where money is taken for goods purchased; **cash dispenser** a machine, usually in or outside a bank, which dispenses money on the insertion of a special voucher; **cash flow** the movement of money in and out of a business; **cash'-keeper** cashier; **cash limit** a limit set on the total amount of money a company, institution, etc., may spend; **cash machine** a cash dispenser; **cash'-pay'ment** payment in ready money; **cash point** the place in a shop, supermarket, etc. where money is taken for goods purchased; **cash'-rail'way** a mechanical device for interchange of cash between counter and cash-desk in a shop; **cash'-reg'ister** a till that automatically and visibly records the amount put in. — **cash and carry** sale for cash, with delivery up to the buyer: a usu. large shop which trades in this way; **cash down** with payment at the time of purchase; **cash in** to exchange for money: to seize an advantage; **cash in on** to turn to one's advantage; **cash in (one's checks)** to exchange counters for money on leaving the gaming-table: to die (*slang*); **cash up** to count the money taken in a shop, department, etc., usu. at the end of the day; **hard cash** see **hard; out of cash, in cash** without, or with, money: out of, or in, pocket.   [A doublet of *case*, a box — O.Fr. *casse*, a box.]

cash² *kash, n.* a small Eastern coin.   [Port. *caixa* — Sinh. *kāsi*, coin — Tamil *kāsu*.]

cashaw *kə-shö', n.* a kind of pumpkin (*U.S.*; also **cushaw'**): a W. Indian mesquite.   [Algonkian.]

cashew *kə-shōō', kash'ōō, n.* a spreading tropical American tree (*Anacardium occidentale*) with kidney-shaped nuts (**cash'ew-nuts**) whose kernels and fleshy stalks (**cash'ew-app'les**) are used as food.   [Tupí *caju*; cf. **acajou.**]

cashier¹ *kash-ēr', v.t.* to dismiss from a post in disgrace: to discard or put away: to annul. — *ns.* **cashier'er; cashier'ing** a punishment for army and naval officers, severer than dismissal, in that it disqualifies from entering the public service in any capacity (abolished 1970); **cashier'ment** dismissal.   [Du. *casseren* (*kasseren*), to cashier — Fr. *casser* — L. *cassāre cassus*, void, empty.]

cashier². See **cash¹.**

cashmere *kash'mēr, n.* (a shawl or fabric made from) fine soft *Kashmir* goats' hair: any similar product. — Also *adj.*

casino *kə-sē'nō, n.* a room for public dancing: a building with public dance halls, gaming tables, etc.: an establishment with gambling as its main activity: a card-game (also **cassi'no**) — *pl.* **casi'nos.** [It., from L. *casa*, a cottage.]

cask *käsk, n.* a hollow round vessel for holding liquor, made of staves bound with hoops: a measure of capacity: a casque (*obs.*). — *v.t.* to put in a cask. — **cask'-stand.** [Fr. *casque* — Sp. *casco*, skull, helmet, cask.]

casket *käsk'it, n.* a little cask or case: a small case for holding jewels, etc.: a coffin (*U.S.*).   [Ety. uncertain; hardly a dim. of **cask.**]

Caslon *kaz'lən, n.* a style of printing type designed by William *Caslon* (1692–1766): a type-face imitating this style.

casque *käsk, n.* a cover for the head (*obs.* **cask**): a helmet (*obs.* **cask**): in certain species of birds, a process on the upper mandible or on the top of the head (*zool.*).   [A doublet of **cask.**]

Cassandra *kəs-an'drə, n.* a daughter of Priam, king of Troy, beloved by Apollo, who gave her the gift of prophecy, but not of being believed — hence any one who expresses gloomy views of the political or social future and is not listened to.

cassareep, cassaripe *kas'ə-rēp, n.* the juice of the bitter

cassava, a potent antiseptic, used in sauces, and in the West Indian pepper-pot (q.v.).   [From Tupí.]

cassata *ka-sä'tə, n.* an Italian ice-cream containing candied fruit and nuts.   [It.]

cassation *ka-sā'shən, n.* annulment: in French law, the quashing of a decision of a court — hence **court of cassation** the supreme tribunal: an 18th-cent. type of musical composition in several short movements.   [L.L. *cassātiō, -ōnis* — *cassāre*, to bring to nought.]

cassava *kə-sä'və, n.* a plant of the Manihot genus whose roots yield a nourishing starch. — Also **manioc, tapioca.** [From a Taino (language of extinct West Indian tribe) name.]

Cassegrain(ian) telescope *kas-ə-grän'(i-ən) tel'i-skōp,* a type of reflecting telescope devised by, and named after, a 17th-cent. Frenchman, N. *Cassegrain.*

casserole *kas'ə-rōl, n.* a stew-pan: a covered vessel in which food is both cooked and served: the food cooked in a casserole. — *v.t.* to cook in a casserole. — **casserole cookery** cooking in the dish in which the food is to be served.   [Fr.]

cassette *kas-et', n.* a small casket: a light-tight container for an X-ray film, or one for film that facilitates loading in a camera, projector, microfilm-reader, etc.: a holder with reel of magnetic tape, often with prerecorded material on it. — **cassette'-recorder, -play'er,** a machine using magnetic tape cassettes to record or play music, etc.   [Fr. dim. of *casse*, case.]

cassia *kas(h)'yə, n.* a coarser kind of cinnamon (**cass'ia= bark'**): the tree that yields it: (with *cap.*) a genus of shrubs of the Caesalpinia family, yielding senna, and the drug cassia fistula or purging cassia.   [L. *casia* — Gr. *kasiā* (also *kassiā*) — Heb. *qetsī'āh.*]

cassimere *kas'i-mēr, n.* a twilled cloth of the finest wools. — Also **ker'seymere.**   [Corr. of **cashmere.**]

cassino *kə-sē'nō, n.* a game at cards: — *pl.* **cassi'nos.** [See **casino.**]

Cassiopeia *kas-i-ō-pē'(y)ə, n.* a northern constellation named after the mother of Andromeda. — *n.* **cassiōpē'- ium** a discarded name for **lutetium.**

cassis *kä-sēs', n.* a syrupy blackcurrant drink or flavouring.   [Fr.]

cassiterite *ka-sit'ə-rīt, n.* a brown native tin dioxide.   [Gr. *kassiteros*, tin.]

cassock *kas'ək, n.* a long robe or outer coat, formerly in common wear, but now worn only by clergy and choristers: a shorter garment, usually of black silk, worn under the Geneva gown by Scottish ministers. — *adj.* **cass'ocked.**   [Fr. *casaque* — It. *casacca.*]

cassolette *kas'ō-let, n.* a censer: a perfume-box with perforated lid.   [Fr., — Sp. *cazoleta* — *cazo*, a saucepan.]

cassonade *kas-o-nād', n.* unrefined sugar.   [Fr.]

cassone *kä-sō'nā,* (It.) *n.* a large chest, elaborately carved and painted.

cassoulet *ka-sōō-le,* (Fr.) *n.* a stew consisting of beans and various kinds of meat.

cassowary *kas'ə-wər-i, n.* any member of a genus (*Casuarius*) of flightless birds, found esp. in New Guinea, closely related to the emu.   [Malay *kasuārī* or *kasavārī.*]

cassumunar *kas-ōō-mū'nər, n.* an East Indian ginger.   [Origin unknown.]

cast *käst, v.t.* to throw or fling: to throw off, shed, drop: to drop prematurely: to throw down: to throw up: to reckon: to add: to project: to reject, condemn, decide against (*arch.*): to mould or shape: to purpose, devise, consider (*arch.*): to appoint as actor (*for* a part): to assign as his part (*to* an actor): to cut and throw up to dry (peat) (*Scot.*). — *v.i.* to warp: — *pa.t.* and *pa.p.* **cast.** — *n.* the act of casting: a throw of anything, as the sounding-lead, a fishing-line: the thing thrown, esp. in angling: the distance thrown: a motion, turn, or squint, as of the eye: a turn or sample performance: a good turn, as a lift or conveyance in a vehicle (*Scot.*): matter ejected by a bird, earthworm, etc.: a throw or turn of fortune, a chance: a mould: a rigid casing, usu.

of plaster of Paris and, often, gauze, for holding a broken bone in place while it sets: form, manner, stamp, or quality: a shade of colour, a degree of guilt, etc.: the assignment of the various parts of a play, etc. to the several actors, etc.: the company of actors, etc. playing rôles: a couple of hawks. — *adj.* moulded: rejected, cast off: defeated at law: of an animal, on its back and unable to get up. — *adj.* cast'ed (*Shak.*) cast off. — *n.* cast'ing the act of casting or moulding: that which is cast: a mould. — cast'away one shipwrecked in a desolate place: an outcast. — *adj.* worthless, rejected. — casting couch (*facet.*) a couch on which girls are said to be seduced with the promise of a part in a film, play, etc.; cast'ing-net a species of net for fishing; cast'ing-vote' a chairman's deciding vote in case of equality; cast'ing-weight the weight that makes the balance cast or turn when exactly poised; cast'-i'ron an iron-carbon alloy distinguished from steel by its containing substantial amounts of cementite or graphite, which make it unsuitable for working. — *adj.* hard, rigid: unassailable. — *adj.* cast'-off rejected, laid aside, given away, no longer wanted, etc. — *n.* anything, esp. clothing, given or thrown away, no longer wanted, etc.: the act or result of casting off copy. — cast'-steel' steel that has been cast, not shaped by mechanical working. — cast about to contrive, to look about, to search for, as game or in one's mind: to turn, to go round (*B.*); cast a horoscope, nativity to make an astrological calculation; cast anchor to anchor a ship; cast an eye, a glance to look; cast a spell upon to put under an enchantment; cast a vote to record or make a vote; cast away to wreck: to waste; cast back to revert; cast down to deject or depress in mind: to turn downward; cast loose to set loose or adrift; cast lots see lot; cast off to reject: to loose (hawks, hounds): to unmoor: in knitting, etc., to eliminate stitches: to estimate amount of printed matter that copy will make; cast on in knitting, etc., to make stitches; cast out (*Scot.*) to quarrel; cast up to throw up: to bring up as a reproach: to turn up, appear, emerge (*Scot.*); cast water (*arch.*) to inspect urine in diagnosis; the last cast extremities.   [O.N. *kasta*, to throw.]

Castalian *kas-tā'li-ən, adj.* pertaining to *Castalia*, a fountain on Parnassus, sacred to Apollo and the Muses.

Castanea *kas-tān'i-ə, n.* the chestnut genus, of the beech family (*Fagaceae*). — *n.* Castanospermum (*kas-tan-ō-spûr'məm*; Gr. *sperma*, a seed) an Australian papilionaceous tree, the Moreton Bay chestnut, so called from the taste of its nuts.   [Gr. *kastanon*, chestnut.]

castanets *kas'tə-nets, -nets', n.pl.* two hollow shells of ivory or hard wood, bound by a band on the thumb, and struck by the finger to produce a clicking sound — much used in Spain as an accompaniment to dances and guitars.   [Sp. *castañeta* — L. *castanea*, a chestnut.]

caste *käst, n.* a social class in India: an exclusive social class: a type of individual in some polymorphic social insects. — *adj.* caste'less having no caste. — caste'=mark an indication of caste worn on the forehead (also *fig.*). — lose caste to descend in social rank.   [Port. *casta*, breed, race — L. *castus*, pure, unmixed.]

castellan, castellated, castellum. See castle.

caster. Same as castor[1].

castigate *kas'tig-āt, v.t.* to chastise: to criticise severely: to emend. — *ns.* castigā'tion; cas'tigātor. — *adj.* cas'-tigatory (*-ə-tər-i*).   [L. *castigāre, -ātum*, from *castus*, pure.]

Castilian *kas-til'yən, adj.* of Castile. — *n.* a native of Castile: the language thereof, standard Spanish. — Castile soap a hard soap made with olive-oil and soda.   [Sp. *Castellano*.]

castle *käs'l, n.* a fortified house or fortress: the residence of a prince or nobleman, or a large country mansion generally: a rook in chess: a defensive tower borne on an elephant's back: a large ship, esp. of war. — *v.t.* to enclose or fortify with a castle. — *v.i.* (*chess*) to move the king two squares towards the castle and place the

castle on the square the king has passed over. — *n.* castellan (*kas'təl-an*) the governor or captain of a castle. — *adj.* castellated (*kas'tel-āt-id*) having turrets and battlements like a castle. — *n.* castell'um a small Roman fort: a mile-castle. — *adj.* cas'tled furnished with castles. — cas'tle-building the act of building castles in the air or forming visionary projects; cas'tle=guard the guard for the defence of a castle. — castles in the air or in Spain groundless or visionary projects.   [O.E. *castel* — L. *castellum*, dim. of *castrum*, a fortified place.]

castock *kas'tək*, custock *kus', (Scot.) ns.* a cabbage stock.   [kale, stock[1].]

Castor *kas'tor, -tər, n.* one of the Dioscuri, twin brother of Pollux, son of Leda, famous for his skill in horse-taming: a bright star in the constellation Gemini (the Twins).   [L., — Gr. *Kastōr*.]

castor[1], caster *käst'ər, n.* a small solid swivelled wheel on a leg of furniture: a vessel with perforated top for sprinkling. — castor sugar, caster sugar white granulated sugar finely crushed.   [cast.]

castor[2] *käs'tər, n.* the beaver (genus *Castor*): castoreum: a hat of beaver-fur or substitute. — *ns.* castoreum (*-tō'ri-əm, -tö'*) the dried perineal sacs of the beaver, or a brown unctuous strong-smelling substance got from them, once used in medicine and perfumery; cas'tory (*Spens.*) a red or pink colour got from castoreum.   [L. *castōr, -ŏris* — Gr. *kastōr, -oros*, beaver.]

castor-oil *käs'tər-oil', n.* a medicinal and lubricating oil obtained from the seeds of a tropical African euphorbiaceous plant, *Ricinus communis*.   [Perh. from use as substitute for castor(eum).]

castral *kas'trəl, adj.* belonging to the camp.   [L. *castra.*]

castrametation *kas-trə-me-tā'shən, n.* the art of designing a camp.   [L. *castra*, a camp, *mētārī, -ātus*, to measure off — *mēta*, a boundary.]

castrate *kas-trāt', v.t.* to deprive of the power of generation: to remove the testicles from, to geld or emasculate: to take from or render imperfect. — *adj.* castrat'ed gelded: expurgated. — *ns.* castrā'tion; castrato (*käs-trä'tō*; from It.) a male singer castrated in boyhood so as to preserve a soprano or alto voice: — *pl.* castra'ti (*-tē*).   [L. *castrāre, -ātum.*]

casual *kaz(h)'ū-əl, adj.* accidental: unforeseen: occasional: off-hand: negligent: unceremonious: (of a worker) employed only for a short time, without fixed employment. — *n.* a chance or occasional visitor, labourer, pauper, etc.: a weed not naturalised. — *v.t.* cas'ualise, -ize to turn (regular workers) into casual labourers. — *ns.* casualīsa'tion, -z-; cas'ualism belief that chance governs all things — *adv.* cas'ually. — *n.* cas'ualness. — *n.pl.* cas'uals slip-on flat-heeled shoes: loose-fitting comfortable and informal clothing. — *n.* cas'ualty that which falls out: an accident: a misfortune: loss by wounds, death, desertion, etc. (*mil.*): an incidental charge or payment: a person injured or killed: a thing damaged or done for. — casual clothes informal clothing; casual labour workers without fixed employment; casual labourer; casualties of superiority in the feudal law of Scotland, payments to the superior in certain contingencies (e.g. death) — ultimately redeemed or extinguished by Act of 1914; casualty department, ward a hospital department, ward, in which accidents are treated; casual ward formerly, a workhouse department for labourers, paupers, etc.   [L. *cāsuālis* — *cāsus*; see case.]

Casuarina *kas-ū-ə-rī'nə, n.* the she-oak or beef-wood genus of trees, mainly Australian, constituting a family Casuārinā'ceae: (without *cap.*) a tree of the genus.   [Named from its resemblance to *Cassowary* plumage.]

casuist *kaz'ū-ist, n.* one who studies and resolves cases of conscience: often, one who argues sophistically in such cases. — *adjs.* casūist'ic, -al. — *adv.* casūist'ically. — *n.* cas'ūistry the science or doctrine of cases of conscience: the reasoning which enables a man to decide in a particular case between apparently conflicting duties — often with a suggestion of sophistry. [Fr. *casuiste* — L. *cāsus*; see **case**.]

casus belli *kā'səs be'lī, kä'zōōs be'lē*, whatever involves or justifies war; **casus conscientiae** (*kon-shi-en'shi-ē, kōn-skē-en'tē-ī*) a case of conscience; **casus foederis** (*fē'də-ris, foi'de-ris*) a case clearly coming within the provisions of a treaty.   [L.]

cat[1] *kat, n.* a carnivore of genus Felis, esp. the domesticated kind or any of the smaller wild species: a spiteful woman: a movable penthouse to protect besiegers: a double tripod with six legs: a piece of wood tapering at each end, struck with the **cat'-stick** in the game of tip-cat: the game itself: short for the **cat-o'-nine'-tails**, a whip with nine knotted tails or lashes, once used in the army and navy: a showily dressed man (*slang*): a man, fellow (*slang*): a jazz fan (*slang*): a caterpillar tractor. — *v.t.* to raise the anchor to the cathead: to vomit: to beat with a cat-o'-nine-tails. — *ns.* **cat'hood** the state of being a cat or having the nature of a cat; **cat'kin** a crowded spike or tuft of small unisexual flowers with reduced scale-like bracts, as in the willow, hazel, etc. — *adj.* **cat'-like** like a cat: noiseless, stealthy. — *ns.* **cat'ling** a little cat, a kitten: a catgut string (*Shak.*); **catt'ery** a place where cats are bred, or cared for in their owners' absence. — *adjs.* **catt'ish, catt'y** like a cat: spiteful: back-biting. — *advs.* **catt'ishly, catt'ily.** — *ns.* **catt'ishness, catt'iness.** — **cat'amount** the European wild cat: the puma, the lynx, or other beast of the cat family (*U.S.*); **catamoun'tain** or **cat o' mountain** a leopard, panther, or ocelot: a wild mountaineer. — *adj.* ferocious, savage. — *adjs.* **cat'-and-dog'** constantly quarrelling; **cat'-and-mouse'** consisting of harassing or toying with an opponent, victim, etc. before finally killing, defeating or otherwise disposing of him: consisting of waiting and watching for the right moment to attack and dispose of one's opponent. — **cat'bird** an American bird of the thrush family with a mewing note: an Australian bower-bird; **cat'-burglar** a burglar who performs nimble climbing feats; **cat'call** a squeaking instrument used in theatres to express disapprobation: a shrill whistle or cry expressing disapprobation. — *v.i.* to sound a catcall. — *v.t.* to assail with one. — **cat-cracker** see separate entry; **cat door** a cat flap. — *adj.* **cat'-eyed** having eyes like a cat: able to see in the dark. — **cat'fish** a fish with cat-like features, in Britain usually the wolf-fish, in America a salt- or fresh-water fish of the family Siluridae; **cat flap** a small door set in a larger door to allow a cat entry and exit; **cat'gut** a kind of cord made from the intestines of sheep and other animals used for violin strings, surgical ligatures, etc.: the violin or other stringed instrument (*old* or *facet.*): a coarse corded cloth. — *adj.* **cat'-hammed** with thin hams like a cat's. — **cat'head** one of two strong beams projecting from the bow of a ship through which passes the tackle by which the anchor is raised; **cat'-hole** one of two holes in the after part of a ship through which hawsers may pass for steadying the ship or for heaving astern; **cat'house** a brothel (*slang*): a place where cats are cared for; **cat'-lap** any thin or despised drink; **cat litter** a granular absorbent material used to line a tray, on which a cat may urinate and defecate; **cat'mint, cat'nep, cat'nip** a mint-like labiate plant (*Nepeta cataria*) of which cats are fond; **cat'nap** a brief sleep, in a chair, etc.; **cat o' mountain** see **catamountain** above; **cat-o'-nine-tails** see **cat**; **cat's'-cra'dle** a pastime in which a string looped about the fingers and passed from player to player is transformed from one symmetrical figure to another: an almost impenetrably intricate set of regulations, etc.; **cat's'-ear** a name given to two genera of British compositous plants — Hypochoeris, of the ligulate-flowered group, and Antennaria, or mountain-everlasting; **cat's'-eye'** a name for various chatoyant minerals, esp. a variety of chrysoberyl, also a fibrous quartz, and a quartz pseudomorph after crocidolite: ® a reflector set in a frame fixed in a road surface; **cat's'-foot** the mountain-everlasting: ground-

ivy; **cat'-sil'ver** a variety of silvery mica; **cat'skin; cat's'-meat** horse's flesh, or the like, sold for cats: any rather unappetising food; **cat's'-paw** a light breeze (*naut.*): a hitch in a rope providing two loops for a hook: one who is made the tool of another — from the fable of the monkey who used the paws of the cat to draw chestnuts out of the fire; **cat's'-tail** a catkin: timothy-grass: the reed-mace or bulrush; **cat'suit** a type of one-piece trouser suit; **cat's'-whisk'er** (*radio*) a delicate wire brought in contact with a crystal to rectify the current in some forms of crystal detector and produce audibility; **cat'-walk** a narrow footway, as on a bridge, above the stage in a theatre. — *adj.* **cat'-witted** small-minded, conceited, and spiteful. — **bell the cat** see **bell**; **big cats** see **the big cats** below; **catted and fished** (of an anchor) raised to the cathead and secured to the ship's side; **care killed the** (or **a**) **cat** worry killed the cat, even with his proverbial nine lives; **Cheshire cat** (*chesh'ər kat, chesh'ēr*) one proverbially notable for grinning, like the Cheshire cat in Lewis Carroll's *Alice's Adventures in Wonderland*; **enough to make a cat laugh** i.e. even the least inclined; **in the catbird seat** (*U.S.*) in an advantageous position; **Kilkenny cats** proverbial cats who fight till each destroys the other; **let the cat out of the bag** see **bag; like a cat on hot bricks, on a hot tin roof** (*coll.*) uneasy: nervous; **like something the cat brought in** bedraggled, slovenly in dress, etc.; **not have a cat in hell's chance** (*slang*) to have no chance at all; **play cat-and-mouse with** to deal with in a cat-and-mouse way; **put the cat among the pigeons** to stir up trouble; **rain cats and dogs** to pour down heavily; **room to swing a cat** a minimum of space; **see which way the cat jumps** to watch how things are going to turn before committing oneself; **the big cats** lions, tigers, leopards, etc.; **the cat's pyjamas, the cat's whiskers** (*slang*) the very thing that is wanted: anything very good; **turn (the) cat in (the) pan** to change sides with dexterity; **wait for the cat to jump** see **see which way the cat jumps; whip the cat** see **whip**.   [O.E. *cat*; found also in Celt., Slav., Ar., Finn., etc.]

cat[2] *kat, n.* an old name for a coal and timber vessel on the north-east coast of England. — *n.* **cat'boat** a cat-rigged boat. — *adj.* **cat'-rigged** having one great fore-and-aft main-sail spread by a gaff at the head and a boom at the foot, for smooth water only.   [Obscurely connected with **cat**[1].]

cat[3]. Short for **catamaran**.

catabolism. See **katabolism**.

catacaustic *kat-ə-kös'tik*, (*math., phys.*) *adj.* pertaining to or denoting a caustic curve or caustic surface formed by reflection. — *n.* a catacaustic curve or surface. [Gr. *kata*, against and **caustic**.]

catachresis *kat-ə-krē'sis*, (*rhet.*) *n.* misapplication of a word. — *adjs.* **catachrestic** (*-kres'tik*, or *-krēs'tik*), **-al.** — *adv.* **catachres'tically.**   [Gr. *katachrēsis*, misuse — *chrēsis*, use.]

cataclasm *kat'ə-klazm, n.* a disruption, breaking down. — *adjs.* **cataclas'mic** pertaining to or of the nature of a cataclasm; **cataclas'tic** (*geol.*) mylonitic, or granular in consequence of crushing.   [Gr. *kataklasma* — *kata*, down, *klaein*, to break.]

cataclysm *kat'ə-klizm, n.* a flood of water: a debacle: a great revolution. — *adj.* **cataclys'mic.** — *adv.* **cataclys'mically.**   [Gr. *kataklysmos* — *kata*, downward, *klyzein*, to wash.]

catacomb *kat'ə-kōm*, or *-kōōm, n.* a subterranean excavation used as a burial-place, esp. near Rome, where many of the early Christian victims of persecution were buried: any place built with crypt-like recesses for storing books, wine, etc. — *adj.* **catacumbal** (*-kum'bl*). [It. *catacomba* — L.L. *Catacumbas*, perh. in some way — Gr. *kata*, down, and *kymbē*, a cup.]

catacoustics *kat-ə-kōōs'tiks* or (*esp. formerly*) *-kows', n. sing.* the part of acoustics that treats of echoes or sounds reflected.   [Gr. *kata*, back, and **acoustics**.]

catacumbal. See **catacomb**.

catadioptric, -al *kat-ə-dī-op'trik, -l, adjs.* pertaining to both reflection and refraction. [See **catoptric, dioptric.**]

catadromous *kət-ad'rəm-əs, adj.* of fishes, descending periodically for spawning to the lower parts of a river or to the sea (opp. to *anadromous*). [Gr. *kata*, down, *dromos*, a run.]

catafalque *kat'ə-falk, n.* a temporary tomb-like structure used in funeral ceremonies: a funeral car. — Also **catafal'co:** — *pl.* **catafal'coes.** [Fr., — It. *catafalco.*]

Cataian, Catayan *kə-tā'ən, (Shak.) n.* a Cathayan, Chinese — a vague term of reproach. [*Cathay*, poetical name for China.]

Catalan *kat'ə-lan, adj.* of or belonging to *Catalonia*: of or concerning Catalan. — *n.* a native of Catalonia: the Romance language spoken esp. in Catalonia, Andorra and the Balearic Islands.

catalase. See **catalysis.**

catalectic *kat-ə-lek'tik, adj.* incomplete: wanting one syllable in the last foot (*pros.*). — *n.* **catalex'is.** [Gr. *katalēktikos*, incomplete — *katalēgein*, to stop.]

catalepsy *kat'ə-lep-si, n.* a state of more or less complete insensibility, with bodily rigidity: cataplexy in animals. — *adj.* and *n.* **catalep'tic.** [Gr. *katalēpsis*, seizure, catalepsy — *kata*, down, *lēpsis*, taking, seizure.]

catalexis. See **catalectic.**

catallactic *kat-ə-lak'tik, adj.* pertaining to exchange. — *adv.* **catallac'tically.** — *n. sing.* **catallac'tics** political economy. [Gr. *katallaktēs*, a money-changer.]

catalo. Same as **cattalo.**

catalogue *kat'ə-log*, in U.S. often **catalog**, *n.* a systematic list of names, books, pictures, etc.: a list of university courses and descriptions, usu. incl. a calendar (*U.S.*). — *v.t.* to put in a catalogue: to make a catalogue of. — *n.* **cat'aloguer**, in U.S. often **cat'aloger.** — *v.t.* **cat'aloguise, -ize**, in U.S. often **cat'alogize.** [Gr. *katalogos*, from *kata*, in order, *legein*, to reckon.]

catalogue raisonné *ka-ta-log re-zon-ā, (Fr.)* a classified descriptive catalogue.

Catalpa *kət-al'pə, n.* an American and Japanese genus of low bignoniaceous trees with profuse blossoms and long cigar-like pendent pods: (without *cap.*) a tree of the genus. [American Indian (Creek) *kutuhlpa.*]

catalysis *kə-tal'i-sis, n.* the chemical influence of a substance not itself permanently changed. — *n.* **cat'alase** an enzyme that reduces hydrogen peroxide. — *v.t.* **cat'alyse, -yze** (-*līz*) to subject to catalysis: to act as a catalyst for. — *ns.* **cat'alyser** (or -z-), **cat'alyst** (-*list*) a catalysing agent: a catalytic converter. — *adjs.* **catalytic** (-*lit'ik*), **-al.** — *adv.* **catalyt'ically.** — **catalytic converter** a device fitted to the exhaust of a motor vehicle to remove impurities from the exhaust gases. [Gr. *katalysis* — *kata*, down, *lyein*, to loosen.]

catamaran *kat'ə-mə-ran'*, or *kat-am'ə-ran, n.* a raft of logs lashed together: a boat with two hulls: an old kind of fire-ship, long superseded: an ill-natured woman. [Tamil, *kaṭṭu-maram*, tied wood.]

catamenia *kat-ə-mē'ni-ə, n. pl.* the menstrual discharge. — *adj.* **catame'nial.** [Neut. pl. of Gr. *katamēnios*, monthly — *kata*, against, *mēn*, a month.]

catamite *kat'ə-mīt, n.* a boy kept for homosexual purposes. [L. *catamītus* — Gr. *Ganymēdēs*, Ganymede.]

catamount, catamountain. See **cat¹.**

catapan *kat'ə-pan, n.* the governor of Calabria and Apulia for the Byzantine emperor. [Acc. to Littré, from Gr. *katepanō tōn axiōmatōn*, one placed over the dignities.]

cataphonics *kat-ə-fon'iks, n. sing.* catacoustics. — *adj.* **cataphon'ic.** [Gr. *kata*, back, *phōnē*, sound.]

cataphoresis *kat-ə-fə-rē'sis, n.* electrophoresis: the introduction into the body of medicinal substances by means of an electric current. [Gr. *kata*, down, *phorēsis*, a carrying.]

cataphract *kat'ə-frakt, n.* a suit of mail: a soldier in full armour (*Milt.*). — *adj.* **cataphrac'tic.** [Gr. *kataphraktēs*, a coat-of-mail — *kata*, intens., and *phrassein*, to enclose, protect.]

cataphyll *kat'ə-fil, n.* a rudimentary or simplified leaf. — *adj.* **cataphyll'ary.** [Gr. *kata*, down, *phyllon*, leaf.]

cataphysical *kat-ə-fiz'i-kl, (rare) adj.* unnatural. [Gr. *kata*, down, against, *physis*, nature.]

cataplasm *kat'ə-plazm, n.* a plaster or poultice. [Gr. *kataplasma.*]

cataplexy *kat'ə-plek-si, n.* a condition of immobility induced by emotion: in animals the state called shamming death. — *adj.* **cataplec'tic.** [Gr. *kataplēxis*, amazement — *kata*, down, *plēssein*, to strike.]

catapult *kat'ə-pult, n.* anciently, an engine of war (properly one resembling the ballista) for throwing stones, arrows, etc.: a small forked stick having an elastic string fixed to the two prongs, used by boys for throwing small stones: any similar device, as for launching aeroplanes. — *v.t.* and *v.i.* to shoot out from, or as if from, a catapult. — *adj.* **catapul'tic.** — *n.* **catapultier** (-*tēr'*). — **catapult fruit** one that shoots out its seeds. [L. *catapulta* — Gr. *katapeltēs.*]

cataract *kat'ə-rakt, n.* a portcullis (*obs.*): a water-spout, etc.: a waterfall: a floodgate (*Milt.*): an opaque condition of the lens of the eye, painless, unaccompanied by inflammation. [L. *cataracta* — Gr. *kataraktēs*, portcullis, waterfall.]

catarrh *kat-är', n.* a discharge of fluid from the inflammation of a mucous membrane, esp. of the nose, esp. when chronic: a cold in the head. — *adjs.* **catarrh'al, catarrh'ous.** [L. *catarrhus* — Gr. *katarrhous* — *kata*, down, *rheein*, to flow.]

catarrhine, catarhine *kat'ə-rīn, adj.* pertaining to that one of the two divisions of Primates, including all the Old World monkeys, having a narrow partition between the nostrils. [Gr. *katarrīs*, with hanging nose — *kata*, down, *rhīs, rhīnos*, nose.]

catasta *kət-as'tə, n.* a block on which slaves were exposed for sale: a stage or place for torture. [L.]

catastasis *kə-tas'tə-sis, n.* the part of a drama in which the action has reached its height. [Gr. *katastasis*, settlement.]

catastrophe *kət-as'trə-fi, n.* an overturning: a final event: the climax of the action of the plot in play or novel: an unfortunate conclusion: a sudden calamity: rear (*Shak.*): a sudden and violent upheaval in some part of the surface of the Earth (*geol.*): in catastrophe theory (q.v.), a discontinuous change (*math.*). — *adj.* **catastrophic** (*kat-ə-strof'ik*). — *adv.* **catastroph'ically.** — *ns.* **catas'trophism** the old theory of geological change by vast catastrophes and new creations (opp. to *uniformitarianism*); **catas'trophist.** — **catastrophe theory** that branch of mathematics dealing with continuous changes in the input of a system which cause a discontinuous change (i.e. a catastrophe) in the output of the system. [Gr. *kata*, down, *strophē*, a turning.]

catatonia *kat-ə-tō'ni-ə*, **catatony** *kət-at'ə-ni, ns.* a type of schizophrenia characterised by periodic states of stupor. — *adj.* and *n.* **catatonic** (-*ton'*). [Gr. *kata*, down, *tonos*, stretching, straining — *teinein*, to stretch.]

catawba *kə-tö'bə, n.* an American grape (*Vitis labrusca*): a red wine made from it. [*Catawba* River in Carolina.]

catbird, catcall. See **cat¹.**

catch *kach, v.t.* to take hold of, esp. of a thing in motion: to gather (the ball) after the batsman has hit it and before it touches the ground (*cricket*): to dismiss (a batsman) thus: to apprehend or understand: to seize after pursuit: to trap or ensnare: to come upon: to be in time for: to strike: to take (a disease) by infection: to take (fire): to take up by sympathy or imitation. — *v.i.* to be contagious: to be entangled or fastened (*infin.* in *Spens.* sometimes **catch'en, ketch;** *pa.t.* and *pa.p.* **caught** *köt*, also *obs.* and *dial.* **catched, catcht;** *pa.t.* in *Spens.* also **keight** *kīt*). — *n.* seizure: an act of catching, esp. the ball at cricket, etc.: a clasp, or anything that seizes or holds: that which is caught or is worth catching: a sudden advantage taken: a concealed difficulty or disadvantage: a round for three or more voices, later seeking comic effect by the interweaving of the words. — *adj.* **catch'able** that may be caught.

— *ns.* **catch′er; catch′ing** the action of the verb: a nervous or spasmodic twitching. — *adj.* infectious: captivating, attractive. — *n.* **catch′ment** river drainage. — *adj.* **catch′y** attractive: deceptive: readily caught up, or taking hold of the mind, as a tune, etc.: fitful. — *adj.* **catch′-all** covering or dealing with a number of instances, eventualities or problems, esp. ones not covered or dealt with by other provisions. — **catch′-as-catch′-can′** a style of wrestling in which any hold is allowed. — Also *adj.* and *adv.* — **catch′-basin, -pit** a trap for dirt in a drain; **catch′-crop** a secondary crop grown before, after, or at the same time as, and on the same piece of ground as, one's main crop; **catch′-drain** a drain on a hillside to catch the surface-water; **catch′-fly** a name for a species of campion (*Lychnis viscaria*) and several of bladder-campion (*Silene*) with sticky stems; **catchment area** the area from which a river or reservoir is fed (also **catchment basin**): the area from which are drawn, or are expected to be drawn, those served by some public facility such as a school, a library or a hospital; **catch′penny** a worthless thing made only to sell. — Also *adj.* — **catch′-phrase** a phrase that becomes popular and is much repeated: a slogan; **catch-pit** see **catch-basin; catch points** railway points which can derail a train to prevent it accidentally running on to a main line; **catch-the-ten′** a card game in which the aim is to capture the ten of trumps. — *adj.* **Catch 22** (title of novel by J. Heller, 1961) denoting an absurd situation in which one can never win, being constantly balked by a clause, rule, etc. which itself can change to block any change in one's course of action, or being faced with a choice of courses of action, both or all of which would have undesirable consequences. — *n.* such a situation; **catch′weed** goosegrass or cleavers; **catch′word** an actor's cue: the word at the head of the page in a dictionary or encyclopaedia: the first word of a page given at the bottom of the preceding page: any word or phrase taken up and repeated esp. as the watchword or symbol of a party. — **catch at** to snatch at; **catch cold (at)** to suffer a financial or other reverse (as a result of making an unwise venture); **catch fire** to become ignited: to become inspired by passion or zeal; **catch hold of** to seize; **catch it** to get a scolding or the like; **catch me, him,** etc., an emphatic colloquial phrase implying that there is not the remotest possibility of my or his doing something suggested; **catch on** to comprehend: to catch the popular fancy; **catch out** to put out at cricket by catching the ball after it has been hit and before it touches the ground: to detect in error or deceit; **catch sight of** to get a glimpse of; **catch up** to draw level and sometimes overtake; **catch up** or **away** to snatch or seize hastily. [From O.Fr. *cachier* — L.L. *captiāre* from *captāre*, intens. of *capĕre*, to take; see **chase**.]

catchpole, -poll *kach′pōl, n.* a constable, petty officer of justice. [Through O.Fr. from L.L. *cachepolus, chassipullus* one who chases fowls; see **chase** and **pullet**.]

catchup, catsup. See **ketchup**.

cat-cracker *kat′krak-ər, n.* (in full, **catalytic cracker**), a plant in which the cracking of petroleum is speeded up by the use of a catalyst. — *n.* **cat′-cracking**.

cate *kāt, (arch.) n.* (nearly always in *pl.*) a viand: a dainty, a delicacy. [Aphetic; see **acates**; cf. **cater**[1].]

catechise, -ize *kat′i-kīz, v.t.* to instruct by question and answer: to question as to belief: to examine systematically by questioning. — *adjs.* **catechetic** (-*ket′ik*), **-al** relating to catechism or oral instruction in the first principles, esp. of Christianity. — *adv.* **catechet′ically**. — *n. sing.* **catechet′ics** the art or practice of teaching by question and answer: that part of theology which treats of **catechesis** (-*kē′sis*), or primary oral instruction, as that given to catechumens. — *ns.* **cat′echiser, -z-; cat′echīsing, -z-; cat′echism** any compendious system of teaching drawn up in form of question and answer: a set of questions: an examination by questions; **cat′echist** one who catechises: a teacher of catechumens: a native teacher in a mission church. —

adjs. **catechis′tic, -al, catechis′mal** pertaining to a catechist or catechism. [L. *catēchismus*, formed from Gr. *katēchizein, katēcheein*, to din into the ears — *kata*, back, *echē*, a sound.]

catechu *kat′i-chōō, -shōō, n.* a dark extract of Indian plants (acacia, betel-nut, etc.) rich in tannin. — *ns.* **cat′echol** (-*kōl, -chōl*) a white crystalline phenol-alcohol derived from catechu; **catechō′lamine** (-*kō′lə-mēn, -chō′*) any of several sympathomimetic compounds (e.g. adrenaline and noradrenaline) that are derivatives of catechol. [Cf. Malay *cachu*.]

catechumen *kat-i-kū′mən, n.* one who is being taught the rudiments of Christianity: in the early Christian Church a converted Jew or heathen undergoing instruction preparatory to baptism. — *n.* **catechū′menate**. — *adj.* **catechūmen′ical**. — *adv.* **catechūmen′ically**. — *ns.* **catechū′menism, catechū′menship**. [Gr. *katēchoumenos*, being taught, pr.p. pass. of *katēcheein*, to teach; cf. **catechise**.]

category *kat′i-gər-i, n.* what may be affirmed of a class: a class or order: (in *pl.*) the highest classes under which objects of philosophy can be systematically arranged, understood as an attempt at a comprehensive classification of all that exists (*phil.*): (in *pl.*) in Kant's system, the root-notions of the understanding, the specific forms of the *a priori* or formal element in rational cognition (*quantity, quality, relation, modality*, etc.) (*phil.*). — *adjs.* **categorematic** (-*gor-i-mat′ik*) capable of being used by itself as a term; **categorial** (*ka-tə-gōr′i-əl, -gör′*) of or pertaining to a category. — *adv.* **categor′ially**. — *adj.* **categorical** (-*gor′*) positive: absolute: without exception. — *adv.* **categor′ically** absolutely: without qualification: expressly. — *n.* **categor′icalness** the quality of being absolute and unqualified. — *v.t.* **cat′egorise, -ize** to place in a category or list: to class. — *n.* **cat′egorist** one who categorises. — **categorical imperative** in the ethics of Kant, the absolute unconditional command of the moral law, irrespective of every ulterior end or aim — universally authoritative, belonging to the fixed law of nature. [Gr. *katēgoriā*, assertion, predication, accusation — *katēgoros*, an accuser, *kata*, down, against, *agorā*, assembly.]

catelog. An obs. spelling of **catalogue**.

catena *kə-tē′nə, n.* a chain or connected series, as in **catena patrum,** a chronological series of extracts from the Fathers on any doctrine of theology: — *pl.* **cate′nae** (-*nē*), **cate′nas**. — *adj.* **catenarian** (*kat-i-nā′ri-ən*) of, or of the nature of, a chain or a catenary. — *n.* **catē′nary** (*U.S. kat′*) the curve formed by a flexible homogeneous cord, hanging freely between two points of support, and acted on by no other force than gravity. — *adj.* relating to, like, a chain. — *v.t.* **catenate** (*kat′i-nāt*) to connect as in or by a chain. — *adj.* linked as in a chain. — *n.* **catenā′tion.** — **catenary system** on some electrified railways, an arrangement of wires, supported above the tracks, from which current is collected. [L. *catēna*, chain.]

cater[1] *kā′tər, n.* (*obs.*) an acater: one who provides (sometimes *fig.*). — *v.i.* to provide food, entertainment, etc. (*for*): to indulge, pander, give special consideration (with *to; U.S.*). — *v.t. (U.S.)* to provide food, entertainments, etc. for. — *ns.* **cā′terer; cā′teress; cā′tering.** [See **acater**.]

cater[2] *kā′tər, n.* (*obs.*) the four in dice. — *v.t. and v.i.* (*dial.*) to move diagonally. — Also *adj., adv.* — *advs., adjs.* **catercor′ner(ed)** diagonal(ly). [(M.) Fr. *quatre*, four — L. *quattuor*.]

cateran *kat′ər-ən, n.* a Highland reiver or freebooter: a robber or brigand generally. [Old Gael. *ceatharn, ceithern*, a band of soldiers (Ir. *ceithern*, foot-soldiers; see **kern**(e).).]

cater-cousin *kā′tər-kuz′n,* (*Shak.*) *n.* a person allied by familiarity, affection, sympathy, rather than kindred. [More prob. conn. with **cater,** to provide food, than *quatre* or *quarter*.]

caterpillar *kat′ər-pil-ər, n.* a butterfly or moth grub:

extended to other insect larvae: an unproductive consumer (*arch.*): (from **Caterpillar®**) a tractor or other
vehicle running on endless articulated tracks consisting of flat metal plates.   [Prob. O.Fr. *chatepelose*,
hairy cat; see **cat¹, pile¹**.]

caterwaul *kat'ər-wöl, n.* the shriek or cry emitted by the
cat when in heat. — *v.i.* to make such a noise: to make
any discordant sound: to behave lasciviously: to quarrel like cats. — *n.* **cat'erwauling.**   [**cat¹**; the second
part prob. imit.]

cates. See **cate.**

catfish, catgut. See **cat¹.**

Cathaian. See **Cathayan.**

Cathar *kath'ər, n.* a member of a mediaeval Manichaean
sect, chiefly in S. France and N. Italy, the Albigensians:
— *pl.* **Cath'arī, Cath'ars.** — *ns.* **Cath'arism; Cath'arist.**
[Gr. *katharos*, pure.]

cathartic, -al *kath-ärt'ik, -l, adjs.* cleansing, purifying:
having the power of cleansing the bowels: purgative:
causing emotional or psychological catharsis. — *n.*
cathart'ic a purgative medicine. — *v.t.* **cath'arise, -ize**
to render absolutely clean. — *n.* **cathar'sis** purification:
evacuation of the bowels: purification of the emotions,
as by the drama according to Aristotle: the purging
of the effects of a pent-up emotion and repressed
thoughts, by bringing them to the surface of consciousness (*psych.*): — *pl.* **cathar'ses** (*-sēz*).   [Gr. *kathar-
tikos*, fit for cleansing, *katharos*, clean.]

Cathayan, Cathaian *ka-thā'ən, n.* and *adj.* Chinese.   [See
Cataian.]

cathead. See **cat¹.**

cathectic. See **cathexis.**

cathedral *kə-thē'drəl, n.* the principal church of a diocese,
containing the bishop's throne. — *adj.* belonging to a
seat of authority or a cathedral: having a cathedral.
— *n.* **cathedra** (*-thē'drə, -thed'rə*) a bishop's seat: the
episcopal dignity: see also *ex cathedra.* — *adj.* **cathe-
drat'ic** promulgated *ex cathedra*, authoritative.   [L.
cathēdra, cathĕdra — Gr. *kathĕdrā*, a seat.]

Catherine-wheel *kath'(ə-)rin-(h)wēl, n.* a rose-window
(*archit.*): a wheel set round with teeth (*her.*): a rotating
firework: a sidewise somersault. — **Catherine pear** a
small and early variety of pear.   [From St *Catherine*
of Alexandria (4th cent.), who miraculously escaped
torture on a wheel.]

catheter *kath'i-tər, n.* a tube for admitting or removing
gases or liquids through channels of the body, especially for removing urine from the bladder. — *ns.*
cath'eterism the use of the catheter; **cathetom'eter** an
instrument for measuring small differences of level of
different liquids in tubes; **cath'etus** a straight line
perpendicular to another straight line or surface.
[Gr. *kathetos*, perpendicular, *kathetēr*, a catheter —
kathienai, to send down — *kata*, down, *hienai*, to send.]

cathexis *kə-thek'sis, (psych.) n.* a charge of mental energy
attached to any particular idea or object: — *pl.*
cathex'es (*-sēs*). — *adj.* **cathec'tic.**   [Gr. *kathexis*,
holding.]

cathisma *kə-thiz'mə, n.* in Greek use, a section of the
psalter: a troparion or short hymn used as a response.
[Gr. — *kathizein*, to sit down.]

cathode *kath'ōd, n.* the negative terminal of an electrolytic
cell at which positively charged ions are discharged
into the exterior electric circuit: in valves and tubes,
the source of electrons (opposed to *anode*). — *adjs.*
cath'ōdal; cathŏd'ic. — *ns.* **cathod'ograph** a photograph
by X-rays; **cathodog'rapher; cathodog'raphy.** —
cathode-ray oscillograph the complete equipment for
registering transient wave-forms on a photographic
plate within the vacuum of a cathode-ray tube; **cathode-ray oscilloscope** the complete equipment for observing repeated and transient wave-forms of current
or voltage, which present a display on a phosphor;
cathode rays streams of negatively charged particles,
electrons, proceeding from the cathode of a vacuum
tube; **cathode-ray tube** a device in which a narrow beam
of electrons, which can be deflected by magnetic

and/or electrostatic fields, impinges on a fluorescent
screen or photographic surface — used in television,
etc.; **cathodic protection** protection of a metal structure
underground or under water against electrolytic corrosion by making it the cathode in an electrolytic cell.
[Gr. *kathodos*, a going down — *kata*, down, *hodos*, a
way.]

catholic *kath'ə-lik, adj.* universal: general, embracing the
whole body of Christians: orthodox, as opposed to
heterodox and *sectarian*: liberal, the opposite of exclusive: (with *cap.*) belonging to the Christian Church
before the great schism between East and West, or to
any church claiming to be in historic continuity with
it, esp. after the schism the Western church, after the
Reformation the Church of Rome (Roman Catholic),
but applied also, e.g. to Anglicans: (with *cap.*) relating
to the Roman Catholics. — *n.* (with *cap.*) an adherent
of the R.C. Church. — *v.t.* and *v.i.* **cathol'icise, -ize**
(also with *cap.*) to make or become Catholic. — *ns.*
catholicisa'tion, -z- (also with *cap.*); **Cathol'icism** the
tenets of the R.C. Church: (without *cap.*) catholicity
(*rare*); **catholicity** (*-is'i-ti*) universality: liberality or
breadth of view: Catholicism (*rare*); **cathol'icon** (*-kon*)
a panacea; **cathol'icos** the Patriarch of Armenia. —
Catholic (and) Apostolic Church a body formed in
England about 1835, having an elaborate, symbolic
ritual and a complex ecclesiastical hierarchy, and
emphasising the existence in the present day of miracles and prophecy, and the imminent second coming
of Christ; **catholic creditor** (*Scots law*) one whose debt
is secured over two or more subjects belonging to the
debtor — e.g. over two or more heritable estates;
Catholic emancipation the relief of the Roman
Catholics from certain vexatious penal regulations and
restrictions, granted in 1829; **catholic** or **general epistles**
certain epistles in the canon addressed to the Church
universal or to a large and indefinite circle of readers;
Catholic King (*hist.*) the king of Spain; **German
Catholics** a body that broke away from the Roman
Catholic Church in Germany in 1844 on the occasion
of the exhibition of the Holy Coat at Trier; **Old
Catholics** a body that broke away from the Roman
Catholic church in Germany in opposition to the
dogma of papal infallibility proclaimed by the Vatican
Council in 1870.   [Gr. *katholikos*, universal — *kata*,
throughout, *holos*, the whole.]

Catiline *kat'i-līn, n.* the type of a daring and reckless
conspirator, L. Sergius *Catilina*, whose plot to destroy
Rome was foiled by Cicero, 63 B.C. — *adj.* **catilinarian**
(*-li-nā'ri-ən*).

cation, kation *kat'ī-ən, n.* an ion that travels towards the
cathode: a positively-charged ion.   [Gr. *kata*, down,
iŏn, neut. — pr.p. of *ienai*, to go.]

catkin, catling, catmint, catnep, -nip, etc. See **cat¹.**

Catonian *kə-tō'ni-ən, adj.* resembling or relating to *Cato*,
the Roman censor (234–149 B.C.), or *Cato Uticensis*
(95–46 B.C.), both remarkable for gravity of manners
— hence grave, severe, unbending.

catoptric *kat-op'trik, adj.* relating to reflection. — *n. sing.*
catop'trics the part of optics which treats of reflected
light.   [Gr. *katoptron*, a mirror — *kata*, back, and
the root of *opsomai*, I shall see.]

CAT scanner. Short for **computer-assisted** or **computed
axial tomography scanner** (qq.v. under **compute**).

catsup. See **ketchup.**

cattabu *kat'ə-bū, n.* a cross between common cattle and
zebu.   [From *cattle* and *zebu*.]

cattalo *kat'ə-lō, n.* a cross between the bison ('buffalo')
and the domestic cow: — *pl.* **catt'alo(e)s.**   [From
cattle and *buffalo*.]

cattle *kat'l, n.pl.* beasts of pasture, esp. oxen, bulls, and
cows: oxen, etc. and also horses, sheep, etc. (*arch.*). —
cattle cake a concentrated, processed food for cattle,
in the form of blocks or cakes; **cattle grid**, in U.S. **cattle
guard**, a frame of spaced bars covering a trench or
depression in a road where it passes through a fence,
crossable by motor vehicles or pedestrians but deter-

ring hoofed animals; **catt′le-lift′er** a stealer of cattle; **catt′le-lift′ing; catt′leman** one who tends cattle, or who rears them on a ranch; **catt′le-plague** plague among cattle, esp. rinderpest or steppe murrain; **cattle show** an exhibition of cattle or other domestic animals in competition for prizes. [O.Fr. *catel, chatel* — L.L. *captāle,* L. *capitāle* — *caput,* the head.]

catty *kat′i, n.* a unit of measurement used in S.E. Asia and China, equal to about 1·3 lb. avoirdupois in S.E. Asia and Hong Kong, and about 1·1 lb. avoirdupois (500 grammes) in China. — Also **kat′i, katt′i.** [Malay *kati.*]

Caucasian *kö-kā′z(h)i-ən, n.* as used by Blumenbach, a person belonging to that one of the main ethnological divisions of mankind which is native to Europe, North Africa and western and central Asia: as used by some later anthropologists, a member of the white race: now usu., in some places by law, a white person: a native of the *Caucasus* or the country around it. — *adj.* of or pertaining to a Caucasian or Caucasians in any of the above senses: pertaining to the Caucasus or the country around it: of or pertaining to the languages spoken in the Caucasus which do not belong to the Indo-European, Semitic, or Ural-Altaic groups (*linguistics*).

cauchemar *kōsh-mär,* (Fr.) *n.* a nightmare.

caucus *kö′kəs, n.* a meeting of members of a party to nominate candidates or delegates or to decide how to vote on any question, its decision binding on those who attend (*U.S.*): any small group which acts as a body within a larger group or organisation, esp. (*opprobriously*) one which is excessively influential. — *v.i.* to hold a caucus: to control by means of a caucus. [Ety. dub.; perh. John Smith's Algonkian word *Cawcawaassough,* an adviser; perh. a corr. of 'caulkers' meetings'.]

caudal *kö′dl, adj.* pertaining to the tail. — *adjs.* **cau′dad** (*zool.,* etc.) towards the tail; **cau′dāte, -d** tailed. — **caudal anaesthesia** a form of epidural anaesthesia. [L. *cauda,* tail.]

caudex *kö′deks,* (*bot.*) *n.* the stem of a tree, esp. of a palm or tree-fern: — *pl.* **caud′icēs** (*-i-sēz*), **caud′exes.** — *n.* **caud′icle** the stalk of the pollen-masses of certain orchids. [L.]

caudillo *kow-dēl′yō, n.* in Spanish-speaking countries, a leader: the head of the state: — *pl.* **caudil′los.** [Sp.]

caudle *kö′dl, n.* a warm drink, sweetened and spiced, given to the sick, esp. women in childbed. — *v.t.* to give a caudle to: to mix. — **caudle cup** a usu. silver two-handled cup with a bulbous or cylindrical body and usu. a lid. — **hempen caudle** (*Shak.*) the hangman's noose. [O.N.Fr. *caudel* — L. *calidus,* hot.]

caudron *kö′drən.* A Spenserian form of **cauldron.**

cauf. See **corf.**

caught *köt, pa.t.* and *pa.p.* of **catch.**

cauk, cawk *kök, n.* chalk (*dial.*): barytes in platy crystals. [A form of **chalk.**]

cauker. See **caulk.**

caul *köl, n.* a net or covering for the head: the membrane covering the head of some infants at their birth. [O.Fr. *cale,* a little cap, prob. Celt.; cf. Ir. *calla,* a veil, hood.]

cauld¹ *köld,* (*Scot.*) *n.* a dam in a stream, a weir. [Origin obscure.]

cauld² *köld,* (*Scot.*) *adj.* and *n.* cold. — *adj.* **cauldrife** (*köld′rif*) apt to feel chilly: chilling, lifeless, without vigour.

cauldron, caldron *köl′drən, n.* a large kettle for boiling or heating liquids. [O.Fr. *caudron* — L. *caldārium* — *calidus,* hot — *calēre,* to be hot.]

cauliflower *ko′, kö′li-flowr, n.* a variety of cabbage whose young inflorescence is eaten. — **cauliflower ear** an ear permanently thickened by injury, esp. from boxing. [Earlier *cole-florye, colie-florie* — L.L. *cauliflōra* — L. *caulis,* cabbage; see **cole** and **flower.**]

caulis *kö′lis* (L. *kow′lis*), *n.* the stem of a plant: one of the main stems at the angles of the Corinthian capital

(*archit.*). — *pl.* **cau′les** (*-lēz, -lās*). — *adj.* **caulesc′ent** having a stem rising above the ground. — *n.* **cau′licle** a rudimentary stem. — *adjs.* **caulic′olous** growing on a stem; **caulic′ūlāte.** — *ns.* **caulic′ūlus** one of the slender stems springing from the *caules* or main stalks supporting the volutes in the Corinthian capital; **cauliflo′ry** production of flowers on old stems from dormant buds.   *adjs.* **caul′iform** having the form of a stem; **caulig′enous** borne upon the stem; **caul′inary, cau′line** belonging to a stem. — *n.* **cau′lōme** a plant's stem-structure as a whole. [L. *caulis,* a stalk.]

caulk, calk *kök, v.t.* to render watertight by pressing oakum, etc. into the seams. — *v.i.* (*sailors' slang*), to snooze. — *ns.* **caulk′er** one who caulks: a dram: a big lie (also **cauk′er**); **caulk′ing.** — **caulk′ing-i′ron** an instrument like a chisel used for pressing oakum into the seams of ships.   [O.Fr. *cauquer,* to press — L. *calcāre,* to tread — *calx,* heel.]

caulker. See **calk²**.

caum, caumstane. See **cam³**.

caup. See **cap²**.

causa causans *kow′zə kow′zanz,* (*legal*) the immediate cause. — **causa sine qua non** (*sī′nē kwā non, si′ne kwä nōn; legal*) a necessary cause or condition allowing something, e.g. the causa causans, to be operative, but not itself a causa causans.

cause *köz, n.* that which produces an effect: that by or through which anything happens: a motive: an inducement: a legal action between contending parties: sake, advantage: that side of a question which is taken up by an individual or party: an accusation (*Shak.*): a matter, affair in general (*Shak.*). — *v.t.* to produce: to make to exist: to bring about: (*Spens.; infin.* **caus′en** to give excuses for. — *conj.* (*dial.* or *coll.*) because (usu. **'cause**). — *adj.* **caus′al** being the cause, that causes: relating to a cause or causes. — *n.* **causal′ity** the relation of cause and effect: the working of a cause. — *adv.* **caus′ally.** — *ns.* **causā′tion** the act of causing: the bringing about of an effect: the relation of cause and effect: **causā′tionism** the principle of universal causation; **causā′tionist.** — *adj.* **caus′ative** causal: of the nature of, or expressing, causation. — *n.* a form of verb expressing causation. — *adv.* **caus′atively.** — *adj.* **cause′less** without cause: without just cause. — *adv.* **cause′lessly.** — *ns.* **cause′lessness; caus′er.** — **efficient cause** the means by which a thing took its present form; **final cause** the end or object for which a thing is done, esp. the design of the universe; **first cause** the original cause or creator of all; **formal cause** the essence or idea of a thing; **have** or **show cause** to have to give reasons for a certain line of action; **hour of cause** (*Scot.*) hour or time of trial; **make common cause** (often with *with*) to unite for a common object; **material cause** that out of which a thing is framed; **occasional causes** see under **occasion; secondary causes** such as are derived from a primary or first cause; **show cause** (*Eng. law*) to argue against the confirmation of a provisional order or judgment.   [Fr., — L. *causa.*]

cause célèbre *köz sā-lebr′,* (Fr.) a very notable or famous trial: a notorious controversy.

causerie *köz′ər-ē, n.* a talk or gossip: a paragraph of chat about literature or art: a short and informal essay on any subject in a newspaper or magazine.   [Fr.]

causeway *köz′wā,* **causey** *köz′i, ns.* a raised way through a marsh or water: a pathway raised and paved with stone: a paved or cobblestoned road. — *vs.t.* to pave. — *p.adjs.* **cause′wayed, caus′eyed.**   [M.E. *causee* — O.Fr. *caucie* — L.L. (*via*) *calciāta,* a trodden way — L. *calx,* heel; **causeway** is for 'causey-way'.]

caustic *kös′tik, adj.* burning: corroding: pertaining to, or of the shape of, a caustic (*math., phys.*): bitter, severe, cutting (*fig.*). — *n.* a substance that exerts a corroding or disintegrating action on the skin and flesh: an envelope of rays proceeding from a fixed point and reflected (*catacaustic*) or refracted (*diacaustic*) by a curve (*math.*): a caustic curve or caustic surface (*phys.*). — *adv.* **caus′tically.** — *ns.* **causticity** (*-tis′i-ti*) quality of being caustic; **caus'ticness**. — **caustic ammonia** ammonia as a gas, or in solution; **caustic curve** a curve in the shape of a caustic, the form of a plane section through a caustic surface (*phys*.); **caustic lime** quicklime; **caustic potash** potassium hydroxide; **caustic soda** sodium hydroxide: **caustic surface** a caustic-shaped surface, the envelope of rays of light reflected or refracted by a curved surface (*phys*.). — **common caustic** potash: also silver nitrate; **lunar caustic** silver nitrate in sticks for surgical use.   [L. *causticus* — Gr. *kaustikos* — *kaiein*, fut. *kausein*, to burn.]

cautel *kö'tl, n*. craft (*Shak*.): insidious purpose (*Shak*.): caution (*obs*.): wariness (*obs*.): a traditionary caution or written direction about the proper manner of administering the sacraments (*obs*.). — *adj*. **cau'telous** cautious (*obs*.): insidious (*Shak*.): artful (*Shak*.).   [Fr. *cautèle* — L. *cautēla* — *cavēre, cautum*, to guard against.]

cauterise, -ize *kö'tər-īz, v.t.* to burn or destroy with a caustic, a hot iron, etc.: to sear (*fig*.). — *ns*. **cau'ter, cau'tery** burning or destroying with caustics, a hot iron, etc.: a burning iron, caustic, etc. for burning or destroying tissue. — *ns*. **cau'terant** a cauterising substance; **cauterīsā'tion, -z-**. — *adj*. **cauterīsing, -z-**. — *n*. **cau'terism**.   [Fr. *cautériser* — L.L. *cautērizāre* — Gr. *kautēr*, a hot iron — *kaiein*, to burn.]

caution *kö'shən, n*. heedfulness: a warning: a warning that what a person says may be used as evidence (*law*): an alarming, amusing, or astonishing person or thing (*coll*.): (also *kā'*) security, surety, bail (*Scots law*). — *v.t.* to warn to take care: to give (someone) a caution (*law*). — *adj*. **cau'tionary** containing caution or cautions: given as a pledge. — *ns*. **cau'tioner** one who cautions or advises: (also *kā'*) a surety (*Scots law*); **cautionry** (*Scots law; kā'*) the act of giving security for another. — *adj*. **cautious** (*kö'shəs*) possessing or using caution: watchful: prudent. — *adv*. **cau'tiously**. — *n*. **cau'tiousness**. — **caution money** money paid in advance as security for good behaviour.   [Fr., — L. *cautiō, -ōnis* — *cavēre*, to beware.]

cavalcade *kav-əl-kād', kav', n*. a train of persons on horseback: a parade. — *v.i.* to go in a cavalcade.   [Fr., through It. and L.L. — L. *caballus*, a horse.]

cavalier *kav-əl-ēr', n*. a knight: (with *cap*.) a Royalist in the great Civil War: a swaggering fellow: a gallant or gentleman in attendance upon a lady, as her escort or partner in a dance or the like: in military fortification, a raised work so situated as to command the neighbouring country. — *adj*. like a cavalier: gay: war-like: haughty, supercilious, free-and-easy, off-hand. — *v.i.* to act as cavalier. — *adj*. **cavalier'ish** like, characteristic of, a cavalier. — *n*. **cavalier'ism**. — *adv*. **cavalier'ly** off-hand: with supercilious disregard or curtness. — *adj*. **cavalierish**. — *n*. **cavaliero** (*kav-äl-yā'rō*; *pl*. **-s**; Sp. *caballero*). — **Cavalier King Charles spaniel** see **spaniel**.   [Fr., — It. *cavallo*; see **cavalcade**.]

cavaliere servente *kä-vä-lē-er'e ser-ven'te*, (It.) a gallant who waits with fantastic devotion upon a married woman.

cavalla *kə-val'ə*, **cavally** *kə-val'i, ns*. an American fish of the scad family, or any of several related carangoid fish.   [Sp. *caballa* and Port. *cavalla*, mackerel.]

cavalry *kav'əl-ri, n*. horse-soldiers: a troop of horse or horsemen. — *n*. **cav'alryman**. — **cavalry twill** see **twill**[1].   [Fr. *cavallerie* — It. *cavalleria* — L. *caballārius*, horseman — *caballus*, horse.]

cavass. See **kavass**.

cavatina *kav-ät-ē'nə, n*. a melody with no second part or da capo: loosely, a short operatic air, of a smooth and melodious character, often part of a grand scena.   [It.]

cave[1] *kāv, n*. a hollow place in a rock: a small faction of seceders from a political party (from the Cave of Adullam, 1 Sam. xxii, 1–2): the ash-pit under the furnace in glassworks. — *v.t.* to hollow out. — *v.i.* to lodge in a cave. — *ns*. **ca'ver** one who explores caves; **ca'ving** cave-exploration: collapse into a hollow, yield-

ing. — **cave'-bear** (*Ursus spelaeus*) a Pleistocene bear found fossil in caves; **cave'-dweller** one who lives in a cave, esp. one of the Stone Age of prehistoric times; **cave'-earth'** a fine deposit on cave floors; **cave-in** see **cave in** below; **cave'man** a cave-dweller: a modern male of primitive ways (*coll*.). — **cave in** to slip, to subside, to fall into a hollow (*n*. **cave'-in**): to yield to outside pressure, to give way, collapse.   [Fr. *cave* — L. *cavus*, hollow.]

cave[2] *kav'i, kāv'i, interj*. (*schoolboy slang*) beware. — *n*. **caveat** (*kā'vi-at*) a notice or warning: a formal warning, entered in the books of a court or public office, that no step be taken in a particular matter without notice to the person lodging the caveat. — **keep cave** (*schoolboy slang*) to keep watch.   [L. *cāvē*, imper. sing., *cāvĕat*, 3rd sing. pres. subj., of *cāvēre*, to take care.]

caveat actor *kā'vi-at* (*ka've-at, -we-*) *ak'tör*, (L.) let the doer beware; **caveat emptor** (*emp'tör*) it is the buyer's look-out.

cave canem *kā'vi* (*ka'vä, -wä*) *kā'nəm* (*ka'nem*), (L.) beware of the dog, a frequent inscription on Roman thresholds.

cavel *kāv'l,* (*Scot*.) *n*. a piece of wood, etc., used in casting lots: a lot.   [Du. *kavel*.]

cavendish *kav'ən-dish, n*. tobacco moistened and pressed into quadrangular cakes.   [Possibly from the name of the original manufacturer.]

cavendo tutus *kā-, ka-ven'dō* (*-wen'*) *tū'təs* (*tōō'tōōs*), (L.) safe through taking care.

cavern *kav'ərn, n*. a deep hollow place in rocks. — *v.t.* to put in a cavern: to hollow out. — *adjs*. **cav'erned** full of caverns: dwelling in a cavern; **cav'ernous** hollow: full of caverns. — *adv*. **cav'ernously**. — *adj*. **caver'nulous** full of little cavities.   [Fr. *caverne* — L. *caverna* — *cavus*, hollow.]

cavesson *kav'əs-ən, n*. a nose-band for a horse.   [Fr. *caveçon* — It. *cavezzone* — L. *capitia, capitium*, a head-covering.]

cavetto *ka-vet'ō, n*. a hollowed moulding whose curvature is the quarter of a circle, used chiefly in cornices: — *pl*. **cavett'i** (*-i*).   [It.; dim. of *cavo* — L. *cavus*, hollow.]

caviare, caviar *kav'i-är, kav-i-är'*, also *kav-yär'*, (*Shak*.) **caviar'ie**, (*obs*.) **cavier** (*kə-vēr'*), *ns*. salted roe of the sturgeon, etc.: something whose flavour is too fine for the vulgar taste (*fig*.).   [Prob. the 16th-cent. It. *caviale*; the Turk. *khāvyār* is prob. borrowed.]

cavicorn *kav'i-körn, adj*. hollow-horned, as a ruminant. — *n*. one of the **Cavicor'nia**, or Bovidae.   [L. *cavus*, hollow, *cornū*, a horn.]

cavie *kāv'i,* (*Scot*.) *n*. a hen-coop or cage.   [Cf. Du. *kevie*, Ger. *Käfig* — L. *cavus*.]

cavier. See **caviare**.

cavil *kav'il, v.i.* to make empty, trifling objections (with *at* or *about*): to use false arguments: — *pr.p.* **cav'illing;** *pa.t.* and *pa.p.* **cav'illed**. — *n*. a frivolous objection. — *ns*. **cavillā'tion, cav'illing; cav'iller**.   [O.Fr. *caviller* — L. *cavillārī*, to practise jesting.]

cavity *kav'it-i, n*. a hollow: a hollow place: hollowness: a decayed hollow in a tooth. — *v.i.* **cav'itate**. — *n*. **cavitā'tion** the formation of cavities in a structure, or of gas bubbles in a liquid, or of a vacuum, or of a partial vacuum as between a body moving in a fluid and the fluid: a cavity. — *adj*. **cav'itied**. — **cavity wall** a wall consisting of two layers with a space between.   [L. *cavitās* — *cavus*, hollow.]

cavo-rilievo *kä'vō-rē-lyä'vō, n*. a kind of relief in which the highest surface is level with the plane of the original stone, which is left round the outlines of the design. [It. *cavo*, hollow, *rilievo*, relief; see **cave** and **relief**.]

cavort *kə-vört', v.i.* to frolic, bound.   [Explained as a corr. of **curvet**.]

cavy *kāv'i, n*. a member of the guinea-pig genus (*Cavia*) of rodents.   [*Cabiai*, native name in French Guiana.]

caw *kö, v.i.* to cry as a crow. — *n*. the cry of a crow. — Also **kaw**. — *n*. **caw'ing**.   [From the sound.]

cawk. See **cauk**.

cawker. Same as **calker**.

caxon *kak'sən, n.* a kind of wig formerly worn. [Origin obscure.]

Caxton *kaks'tən, n.* a book printed by William *Caxton* (1422–91), the first English printer: a kind of printing-type in imitation of Caxton's.

cay *kā, n.* a low islet, the same as **key³.** [Sp. *cayo.*]

cayenne *kā-en', n.* a very pungent red pepper (**cayenne pepp'er**) made from several species of Capsicum. — *adj.* **cayenned'** seasoned with cayenne. [Usually referred to *Cayenne* in French Guiana; but prob. from Tupí.]

cayman *kā'mən, n.* any of the Central and South American crocodilian animals of the genus *Caiman* and related genera, similar to alligators: — *pl.* **cay'mans.** — Also **cai'man.** [Sp. *caimán*, most prob. Carib.]

cayuse *kī-ūs', (U.S.) n.* an Indian pony: a small or poor horse. [Amer. Indian.]

cazique. A form of **cacique.**

CB radio. See **Citizens' Band radio.**

Ceanothus *sē-ə-nō'thəs, n.* an American genus of shrubs of the buckthorn family. [Gr. *keanōthos*, corn-thistle.]

ceas(e). See **sessa.**

cease *sēs, v.t.* and *v.i.* to give over: to stop: to end. — *n.* an end: a cessation. — *adj.* **cease'less** without ceasing: incessant. — *adv.* **cease'lessly.** — *n.* **ceas'ing.** — **cease'= fire'** an order to cease firing: an agreed cessation of active hostilities. [Fr. *cesser* — L. *cessāre,* to give over — *cēdĕre,* to yield.]

ceaze. An obs. spelling of **seize.**

cebadilla. See **sabadilla.**

Cebus *sē'bəs, n.* the generic name of the capuchin monkeys. — *n.pl.* **Cebidae** *(seb'i-dē)* a family including all the New World monkeys except the marmosets. [Gr. *kēbos,* a kind of monkey.]

Cecidomyia *ses-id-o-mī'i-ə, n.* a gall-midge, a genus of flies destructive to vegetation. [Gr. *kēkis, -idos,* a gall, *myia,* a fly.]

cecils *ses', sēs'ilz, n.pl.* minced meat, bread-crumbs, onions, etc., made into balls and fried. [Ety. dub.]

cecity *sē'si-ti, n.* blindness. — *n.* **cecutiency** *(si-kū'shyən-si)* a tendency to blindness. [L. *caecus,* blind.]

Cecropia *si-krō'pi-ə, n.* a tropical American genus of trees of the mulberry family, some with hollow stems that give food and housing to a protective garrison of ants. [Named after the mythical Attic King *Cecrops* (Gr. *Kekrōps*).]

cecum. U.S. spelling of **caecum.**

cecutiency. See **cecity.**

cedar *sē'dər, n.* a large evergreen coniferous tree (*Cedrus,* including *Cedar of Lebanon, Atlantic cedar,* and *deodar*) remarkable for the durability and fragrance of its wood; applied also to many more or less similar trees, as the Barbados cedar, properly a juniper, and the Bastard Barbados cedar, a tree of the genus *Cedrela.* — *adj.* made of cedar. — *adjs.* **cē'dared** covered with cedars; **cē'darn** *(poet.)* of cedar; **cē'drine** belonging to the cedar-tree. — **ce'dar-bird** an American waxwing; **ce'dar-nut** the seed of the cembra pine; **ce'darwood** (also *adj.*). [L. *cedrus* — Gr. *kedros.*]

cede *sēd, v.t.* to yield or give up to another. — *v.i.* to give way. [L. *cēdĕre, cessum,* to yield, to give up.]

cedi *sed'i, n.* (**new cedi**) the unit of Ghana's decimal currency, equal to 100 (new) pesewas: — *pl.* **ced'is.**

cedilla *se-dil'ə, n.* a mark, originally a subscript Z, placed under the letter c (thus ç), formerly used in Spanish to indicate that the letter had the sound of (Spanish) z where that of k would be expected, still used esp. in French and Portuguese to indicate an *s*-sound as before *a, o, u,* and in other languages to denote other sounds, e.g. Turkish ş (*sh*) and ç (*ch*). [Sp. (Fr. *cédille,* It. *zediglia*), all dims. from *zēta,* the Greek name of *z*; see **z.**]

cedrate *sē'drāt, n.* citron. [Fr. *cédrat* — L. *citrus.*]

Cedrela *sed-rē'lə, n.* a tropical genus of Meliaceae, allied to mahogany. — *adj.* **cedrelā'ceous.** [Sp. dim. of

cedro, cedra, cedar; see **cedar.**]

cedrine. See **cedar.**

cedula *sed'ū-lə, n.* a S. American promissory-note or mortgage-bond on lands. [Sp.; cf. **schedule.**]

cee *cē, n.* the third letter of the alphabet (C, c): anything shaped like it. — **cee-spring, c-spring** *(sē'spring)* a spring in the shape of a C to support the frame of a carriage.

Ceefax® *sē'faks, n.* the teletext (q.v.) service of the British Broadcasting Corporation. [**see, facts.**]

ceil *sēl, v.t.* to overlay the inner roof of (*obs.*): to overlay or line: to provide with a ceiling. — *adj.* **ceiled.** — *n.* **ceil'ing** the inner roof of a room: the highest altitude at which an aircraft can fly: the height above the ground of the base of the cloud-layer: an upper limit. — *adj.* **ceil'inged** having a ceiling. — *n.* **ceilom'eter** an instrument for measuring the cloud ceiling. [Prob. conn. with Fr. *ciel,* It. *cielo,* L.L. *caelum,* a canopy.]

ceilidh *kā'li, n.* in Scotland and Ireland, an informal evening of song, story and dancing. — Also (*Ir.*) **ceili.** [Gael., a visit.]

ceinture *sē-tür,* (Fr.) *n.* a girdle, belt.

cel. See **celluloid** under **cell.**

celadon *sel'ə-don, n.* a pale-green colour: a Chinese pottery glaze of the colour: the pottery so glazed. [Fr., perh. after a character in D'Urfé's *Astrée.*]

celandine *sel'ən-dīn, n.* swallow-wort (*Chelidonium majus;* **greater celandine**), a plant of the poppy family, supposed to flower when the swallows came, and to perish when they went: also pilewort (*Ranunculus ficaria;* **lesser celandine**). [O.Fr. *celidoine* — Gr. *chelidonion* — *chelīdōn,* a swallow.]

celebrate *sel'i-brāt, v.t.* to make famous: to distinguish by solemn ceremonies, as a festival or an event: to perform with proper rites and ceremonies, as mass, the eucharist, marriage, etc.: to publish the praises of. — *v.i.* to do something enjoyable because of a feeling of pleasure at some event, achievement, etc. — *n.* **cel'ebrant** one who celebrates: the principal officiant at a rite. — *adj.* **cel'ebrated** distinguished: famous. — *ns.* **celebrā'tion** the act of celebrating: any solemn ceremony: an extolling; **cel'ebrator.** — *adj.* **cel'ebratory** — *n.* **celebrity** *(si-leb'ri-ti)* the condition of being celebrated: fame: notoriety: a person of distinction or fame (*slang abbrev.* **celeb'**). [L. *celebrāre, -ātum* — *celeber,* frequented.]

celerity *si-ler'i-ti, n.* quickness: rapidity of motion. [Fr. *célérité* — L. *celeritās* — *celer,* quick.]

celery *sel'ər-i, n.* an umbelliferous plant (*Apium grave-olens*) whose blanched leaf-stalks are eaten cooked or uncooked. — *n.* **celeriac** *(si-ler'i-ak)* a turnip-rooted variety of celery. [Fr. *céleri* — Gr. *selīnon,* parsley.]

celesta *si-les'tə, celeste si-lest', ns.* a keyboard instrument in which the hammers strike steel plates over wooden resonators. [Fr. *céleste,* heavenly.]

celeste *si-lest', adj.* sky-blue. — *n.* voix céleste: a kind of soft pedal on a piano. [Fr. *céleste.*]

celestial *si-lest'yəl, adj.* heavenly: dwelling in heaven: in the visible heavens: Chinese (*old coll.,* humorously). — *n.* an inhabitant of heaven: a Chinese (*old coll.*). — *adv.* **celest'ially.** — *n.* **celestine** *(sel'is-tēn, -tīn, -tin)* a mineral, strontium sulphate, sometimes sky-blue. — **the Celestial Empire** (*hist.*) China. [Through French from L. *caelestis* — *caelum,* heaven.]

Celestine *sel'is-tīn,* or *sil-es'tin, n.* a monk of an order founded 1264 by Pietro da Morrone, afterwards Pope *Celestine* V.

celiac. Same as **coeliac.**

celibacy *sel'i-bəs-i, n.* the unmarried state, esp. under a vow: abstention from sexual intercourse. — *adjs.* **celibatā'rian** favouring celibacy; **cel'ibate** *(-it)* living single: abstaining from sexual intercourse. — *n.* one who is unmarried, or bound not to marry. [L. *caelebs,* single.]

cell *sel, n.* a small room in a prison, monastery, etc.: a monastery or nunnery dependent on another: a hermit's one-roomed dwelling: a small cavity: one compartment of a comb in a hive: a vessel with electrodes and an electrolyte, for electrolysis or for generating an electric current by chemical action: a unit-mass of living matter, whether walled or unwalled, by itself or associated with others in a higher unity: a unit group, esp. of communist propagandists or other political activists: (a radio transmitter serving) one of the geographical areas into which Britain is divided for the coverage of cellular radio (q.v.): a part of the atmosphere that behaves as a unit (*meteor.*): the cavity containing pollen in an anther lobe (*bot.*): one chamber in an ovary (*bot.*): one of the spaces into which the wing of an insect is divided (*zool.*): a unit of homogenous reactivity in a nuclear reactor core: the unit of storage in computing. — *n.* **cell'a** the naos or inner chamber of a temple: — *pl.* **cell'ae** (-*ē*). — *adjs.* **celled** having cells, cellular; **cellif'erous** having or producing cells; **cell'ular** consisting of, characterised by or containing cells or compartments: relating to, involving, cells in the body: consisting of a number of separate rooms, as in *cellular office*: composed of ordinary cells without vessels (as the lower cryptogams): porous: of open texture; **cell'ūlāted**. — *n.* **cell'ule** a little cell. — *adj.* **cellūlif'erous** having or producing little cells. — *ns.* **cell'ūlite** deposits of fat, not responsive to dieting or exercise, which give the skin a dimpled, pitted appearance; **cellūlī'tis** spreading infection of subcutaneous tissue with pyogenic bacteria; **cell'ūloid** (® with *cap.* in U.S.) a thermoplastic, made from nitro-cellulose, camphor, and alcohol, which is elastic and very strong: (often shortened to **cel** (*sel*)) a sheet of this material on which the drawings, etc. for a cartoon film are made. — *adj.* **cell'ūlose** containing cells. — *n.* a carbohydrate forming the chief component of cell-walls of plants and of wood (cotton down, linen fibre, wood pulp being almost pure cellulose): extended to cellulose acetate, cellulose nitrate, etc., compounds used in making artificial silk, etc. — *adj.* **cellūlōs'ic** containing, or derived from cellulose. — *n.* a compound or substance containing cellulose. — **cell'**=**division** (*biol.*) the process in which cells each split into two new cells, so increasing in number during growth or reproduction; **cell'phone** a pocket telephone for use in a cellular radio system; **cellular** or **cell-mediated immunity** an acquired immunity in which lymphocytes play a major part; **cellular radio** a system of radio communication based on a network of roughly hexagonal geographical cells, each served by a transmitter. [O.Fr. *celle* — L. *cella*, conn. with *celāre*, to cover.]

cella. See **cell.**

cellar[1] *sel'ər, n.* any underground room or vault: a room for storing wine, beer, coal, etc.: a stock of wine. — *v.t.* to store in a cellar. — *ns.* **cell'arage** cellars: a charge for storing in cellars; **cell'arer, cell'arist** one who has charge of the cellar: an officer in a monastery who looks after the provisions; **cell'aret** a case for holding bottles. — *adj.* **cell'arous** (*Dickens*) belonging to a cellar: excavated: sunken. — **cell'ar-book** a record of wines kept in a cellar; **cell'ar-flap** a plate covering an entrance to a cellar; **cell'arman** one who has the care of a cellar. [O.Fr. *celier* — L. *cellārium* — *cella*.]

cellar[2]. See **salt-cellar.**

cello *chel'ō, n.* a shortened form of **violoncello** (sometimes written **'cello**): — *pl.* **cell'os.** — *n.* **cell'ist, 'cell'ist** for **violoncellist.**

cellophane® *sel'ō-fān, n.* a tough, transparent, paperlike wrapping material made from viscose. [*cellulose* and Gr. *phainein*, to show.]

cellulite, celluloid, cellulose. See **cell.**

celom. See **coelom(e).**

celsitude *sels'i-tūd, n.* loftiness. [L. *celsitūdō* — *celsus*, lofty.]

Celsius *sel'si-əs, adj.* pertaining to the centigrade scale used in the thermometer constructed by Anders *Celsius* (1701-44) in which the freezing-point of water is 0° and the boiling-point is 100° (to convert degrees Celsius to Fahrenheit multiply by ⁹/₅ and add 32).

celt *selt, n.* a prehistoric axe-like instrument. [Founded on *celte*, perh. a misreading for *certe* (surely), in the Vulgate, Job, xix. 24, taken to be from a supposed L. word *celtes*, a chisel.]

Celt *kelt, selt, n.* a Gaul (*hist.*): extended to include members of other Celtic-speaking or recently Celtic-speaking peoples — also **Kelt.** — *adjs.* **Celt'ic, Kelt'ic** pertaining to the Celts: of a branch of the Indo-European family of languages including Breton, Welsh, Cornish, Irish, Gaelic, Manx. — *ns.* **Celt'icism, Kelt'icism** a Celtic idiom or custom; **Celtomā'nia, Keltomā'nia.** — *adjs.* and *ns.* **P'-Celt'ic** (or **-Kelt'ic**), **Q'-Celt'ic** (or **-Kelt'ic**) (pertaining to) respectively, one of the Celtic languages in which Indo-European *qu* became *p* and one in which *qu* became *k* (written *c*). — **P'-Celt', -Kelt'; Q'-Celt', -Kelt'.** — **Celtic cross** a type varying from a cross incised on a flat slate to an elaborate monument essentially in the shape of a Latin cross, carved in the style common to the Celts, Scandinavians, and Northumbrian Angles, with a broad circle around the point of intersection of the crossbar and the upright, sometimes miscalled Runic cross; **Celtic Sea** the area of sea to the south of Ireland and west of Cornwall. [L. *Celtae*; Gr. *Keltoi* or *Keltai*.]

cembalo *chem'bä-lō, n.* a musical instrument with strings struck by hammers, a dulcimer: a similar instrument with a keyboard, as a harpsichord or pianoforte: — *pl.* **cem'balos.** — *n.* **cem'balist** one who plays a cembalo: (also *sem'*) one who plays the pianoforte in an orchestra (*rare*). [It.; see **cymbal.**]

cembra *sem'brə, n.* (also **cembra pine**) the Swiss stone-pine. [Modern L., from Ger. dial. *zember*, timber; cf. Ger. *Zimmer*, room.]

cement *si-ment', formerly sem'ənt, n.* anything that makes two bodies stick together: mortar: a bond of union: the bony substance forming the outer layer of the root of a tooth. — *v.t.* to unite with cement: to join firmly. — *ns.* **cementation** (*sem-ən-tā'shən*) the act of cementing: the process of impregnating the surface of one substance with another by surrounding it with powder and heating, as in steel-making, case-hardening, turning glass into porcelain: precipitation: the process of injecting fluid cement mixture for strengthening purposes; **cemen'tite** an iron carbide, Fe₃C; **cemen'tum** the boney outer covering of the root of a tooth. — *adjs.* **cemen'tatory, cementi'tious** having the quality of cementing or uniting firmly. — **cement'-copper** copper obtained by precipitation; **cement gun** an apparatus for spraying fine concrete or cement mortar; **cement'**=**stone** a clayey limestone, suitable for making hydraulic cement; **cement'-water** water containing copper salts, as in copper mines. [O.Fr. *ciment* — L. *caementum*, chip of stone used to fill up in building a wall, *caedimentum* — *caedĕre*, to cut.]

cemetery *sem'i-tri, n.* a burying-ground. [L.L. *coemētērium* — Gr. *koimētērion*, sleeping-place.]

cemitare. Spenser's spelling of **scimitar.**

cenacle *sen'ə-kl, n.* a supper-room, esp. that in which the Last Supper was eaten by Christ and the apostles: a coterie, or its meeting-place. [Fr. *cénacle* — L. *cēnāculum* — *cēna*, supper.]

cendré *sä-drā,* (Fr.) *adj.* ash-blond.

cenesthesis. Same as **coenaesthesis.**

cenobite. Same as **coenobite.**

cenotaph *sen'ō-täf, n.* an empty tomb: a sepulchral monument in honour of one or more people buried elsewhere. [Gr. *kenotaphion* — *kenos*, empty, and *taphos*, a tomb.]

cenote *si-nō'ti, n.* a deep, natural hole in the ground with a pool at the bottom of it, esp. in the Yucatan peninsula, often used by the Mayas as a place of sacrifice. [Sp. — Maya *conot, tyonot*.]

Cenozoic *sē-nō-zō'ik.* Same as **Cainozoic.**

cense[1] *sens, v.t.* to burn incense before. [**incense**[2].]

cense[2] *sens,* (*obs.*) *v.t.* to think: to assess. — *n.* a public rate of tax: rank, condition. [L. *cēnsēre,* to estimate.]

censer *sens'ər, n.* a pan in which incense is burned.

[O.Fr. *censier, encensier* (mod. *encensoir*) — L.L. *incēnsorium* — L. *incendĕre, incēnsum*, to burn.]

censor *sen'sör*, or *-sər, n.* a magistrate who kept account of the property of Roman citizens, imposed taxes, and watched over their morals (*hist.*): an official with analogous functions elsewhere: any of several university officials: an official who examines books, papers, telegrams, letters, films, etc., with powers to delete material, or to forbid publication, delivery, or showing: an unconscious inhibitive mechanism in the mind, that prevents what is painful to conscious aims from emerging into consciousness (*psych.*): one who censures or blames. — *v.t.* to subject to censorial examination or condemnation. — *adjs.* **censorial** (*-ō'ri-əl, -ō'*) belonging to a censor, or to the correction of public morals; **censo'rian** censorial; **censo'rious** expressing censure: fault-finding. — *adv.* **censo'riously.** — *ns.* **censo'riousness; cen'sorship** the office of censor: the time during which he holds office: the work of a censor, censoring. [L. *cēnsor, -ōris.*]

censor morum *sen'sər mör'əm, kān'sor mō'rŏŏm,* (L.) censor of morals.

censure *sen'shər, n.* an opinion or judgment (formerly general, now unfavourable only): blame: reproof. — *v.t.* to form or give an opinion or judgment (now unfavourable) of: to blame: to condemn as wrong: to sentence (*Shak.*). — *adj.* **cen'surable** deserving of censure: blamable. — *n.* **cen'surableness.** — *adv.* **cen'surably.** [L. *cēnsūra — cēnsēre*, to estimate.]

census *sen'səs, n.* an official enumeration of inhabitants with statistics relating to them. — *adj.* **cen'sual** (*-sū-əl*) relating to or containing a census. — *v.t.* to carry out a census of. [L. *cēnsus, -ūs*, a register.]

cent *sent, n.* a hundredth part, esp. of a dollar: a coin of that value. — *ns.* **cent'age** rate by the hundred; **cent'al** a weight of 100 lb. — **per cent** by the hundred. [L. *centum*, a hundred.]

centaur *sen'tör, n.* a mythical monster, half man, half horse. — *adj.* **centau'rian.** — *n.* **Centaur'us** a southern constellation containing Alpha Centauri and Beta Centauri. [Gr. *kentauros.*]

centaury *sen'tö-ri, n.* a name applied to plants of the gentianaceous genera Erythraea and Chlora, and to the composite genus **Centaurea** (knapweed, etc.). [The *centaur* Chiron is said to have healed a wound with *kentaurion*, one of these plants.]

centavo[1] *sen-tä'vō, n.* a Portuguese and Brazilian money of account, 100 centavos making 1 escudo or cruzeiro. [Port.]

centavo[2] *sen-tä'vō, n.* a Spanish American coin and money of account: — *pl.* **centa'vos.** [Sp.]

centenary *sen-tēn'ər-i* (also *-ten'* or *sen'*), *n.* a hundred: a century or hundred years: a centennial. — *adj.* pertaining to a hundred or to a centennial. — *ns.* **centenā'rian** one who is a hundred years old or more; **centenā'rianism; centenier** (*sen'tən-ēr*) a centurion: in Jersey, an honorary part-time police officer with judicial powers. [L. *centēnārius — centēnī,* a hundred each — *centum.*]

centennial *sen-ten'yəl, adj.* happening once in a hundred years: having lasted a hundred years. — *n.* a hundredth anniversary. [L. *centum*, a hundred, *annus*, a year.]

center[1]. The American spelling of **centre**.

center[2] *sen'tər,* (*Shak.*) *n.* a cincture, waist-belt.

centering, centreing, centring *sen'tər-ing,* (*archit.*) *n.* the framework upon which an arch or vault of stone, brick, or iron is supported during its construction.

centesimal *sen-tes'i-məl, adj.* hundredth: designating a centigrade thermometer. — *adv.* **centes'imally.** [L. *centēsimus — centum.*]

centesis *sen-tē'sis, n.* in surgery, a puncture (usu. used in compound terms): — *pl.* **centeses** (*sen-tē'sēz*). [Gr. *kentēsis — kentein*, to prick.]

centi- *sen-ti-,* in composition, 1/100 of the unit named. [L. *centum*, a hundred.]

centiare *sen'ti-är, n.* the hundredth part of an are, 1·196 sq. yards. [L. *centum*, a hundred, *area*, area.]

centigrade *sen'ti-grād, adj.* having a hundred degrees, as e.g. the **Celsius** scale (to convert degrees centigrade to Fahrenheit multiply by 9/5 and add 32). [L. *centum*, a hundred, and *gradus*, a step, a degree.]

centigram(me) *sen'ti-gram, n.* the hundredth part of a gram(me). [Fr., — L. *centum*, a hundred, and **gram(me).**]

centilitre *sen'ti-lē-tər, n.* the hundredth part of a litre, 10 cubic centimetres. [Fr., — L. *centum*, a hundred, and **litre.**]

centillion *sen-til'yən, n.* the hundredth power of a million — i.e. 1 followed by 600 ciphers: in U.S. the hundred-and-first power of a thousand — i.e. 1 followed by 303 ciphers. — *n.* **centill'ionth.** [L. *centum*, a hundred, and the ending of **million.**]

centime *sä'tēm, sä-tēm', n.* a French coin, 1/100 of a franc: other coins 1/100 of their standard. [Fr., — L. *centesimum*, a hundredth.]

centimetre, (*U.S.*) **centimeter,** *sen'ti-mē-tər, n.* a lineal measure, the hundredth part of a metre. — **centimetre=gram(me)-second** (contr. **C.G.S., CGS**) **system** a system of scientific measurement with the centimetre, etc., as units of length, mass, time. [Fr., — L. *centum*, a hundred, and **metre**[2].]

centinel(l) obs. spellings of **sentinel.** — **centinel (private)** a private soldier.

centipede *sen'ti-pēd, n.* any myriapod of the class Chilopoda, carnivorous flattened animals with many joints, most of which bear one pair of legs. [L. *centum*, a hundred, and *pēs, pedis*, a foot.]

centner *sent'nər, n.* a hundredweight, usually of 50 kg. [Ger., — L. *centēnārius*; cf. **centenary.**]

cento *sen'tō, n.* a poem manufactured by putting together verses or passages of one author, or of several authors, so as to make a new meaning: a composition formed by joining scraps from other authors: a mere string of commonplace phrases and quotations: — *pl.* usually **cen'tos.** — *adj.* **cen'tonate** (*bot.*) blotched. — *ns.* **cen'toist, cen'tonist.** [L. *centō, -ōnis,* Gr. *kentrōn*, patchwork.]

centonel(l). Spenserian spellings of **sentinel.**

central, etc. See **centre.**

centre (*U.S.* **center**), *sen'tər, n.* the middle point of anything, esp. a circle or sphere: the middle: a fixed point of reference: the point toward which all things move or are drawn: a nucleus: a resort: a stronghold: a meeting place: a place, institution, etc. devoted to a specified activity: the leader of an organisation, specif. of a group of Fenians, the overall chief being the **head-centre:** a player in a central position: a centre-forward: politicians of moderate political opinions, orig. those in the French Chamber, sitting right in front of the president: the Ultramontane party in Germany (*hist.*): a rod with a conical tip for supporting a workpiece in a lathe or other machine tool (*mach.*). — *v.t.* to place on or collect to a centre. — *v.i.* to be placed in the middle: to have a centre: to lie or move in relation to a centre (often with (*up*)*on*, (*a*)*round*): — *pr.p.* **cen'tring, cen'tering;** *pa.t.* and *pa.p.* **cen'tred, cen'tered.** — *adj.* **cen'tral** belonging to, in, or near, the centre: principal, dominant. — *ns.* **centralisā'tion, -z-, cen'tralism** the tendency to administer by the sovereign or central government matters which would be otherwise under local management; **cen'tralist** (also *adj.*). — *v.t.* **cen'tralise, -ize** to draw to or concentrate at a centre. — *n.* **centrality** (*-tral'i-ti*) central position. — *adv.* **cen'trally.** — *n.* **cen'treing** see separate article **centering.** — *adj.* **cen'tric** terete (*bot.*): relating to, placed in, or containing the centre. — *adj.* **cen'trical.** — *adv.* **cen'trically.** — *ns.* **cen'tricalness; centricity** (*-tris'i-ti*); **cen'tring** see separate article **centering.** — *n.* **cen'trism** the practice of sticking to the middle ground in politics: the holding of moderate, non-extreme political opinions. — *adj.* and *n.* **cen'trist.** — *n.* **cen'trum** the body of a vertebra. — **central conic** a conic section that has a centre — ellipse or hyperbola; **central**

fire a cartridge having the fulminate in the centre of the base; **central forces** forces causing an acceleration towards or from a fixed point, the centre of force; **central heating** a system of heating a building by water, steam or warm air conducted throughout the building from one point; **central locking** in a motor vehicle, the automatic locking of all the doors as the driver's door is locked; **central processor** see phrases below; **cen′tre= bit** a joiner's tool, turning on a centre, for boring circular holes — one of the chief tools of the burglar; **cen′tre-board** a movable plate, fitted to drop below the keel of a racing yacht; **cen′trefold, centre spread** the two facing centre pages of a newspaper, magazine, etc.: an article or set of photographs printed on these; **cen′tre-for′ward** in association football and hockey, the central player among the forwards; **cen′tre-half′** (= **back**) the central player among the half-backs; **cen′tre= piece** something placed at the centre, esp. an ornament for the middle of a table, ceiling, etc.; **cen′tre-rail** a rail between the ordinary rails. — **central nervous system** (*zool.*) the main ganglia of the nervous system with their associated nerve cords; **Central Powers** in and before the war of 1914–18, the German Empire and Austria-Hungary; **central processor, central processing unit** the part of a computer which performs the logical and arithmetical operations on the data and which controls other units of the computer system; **central to** important for the understanding or working of; **centre of attraction** the point to which bodies tend by the force of gravity or the like; **centre of buoyancy** or **displacement** the centre of gravity of the fluid displaced; **centre of excellence** a focal point, e.g. a university (or one of its departments) for work at the highest level (in a particular subject); **centre of gravity** the point at which the weight of a body may be supposed to act; **centre of inertia** or **mass** the point through which any plane divides a body into two parts of equal mass; **centre of oscillation** the point in a pendulum such that, if all the matter were concentrated there, the pendulum would have the same period; **centre of percussion** the point where the direction of a blow meets the plane in which lie the centre of inertia and a possible axis of rotation such that the blow imparts a rotation without pressure on the axis; **centre of pressure** the point on an immersed surface at which the pressure resultant may be taken to act; **centre of symmetry** a point in a figure such that any straight line through it meets the figure in two points at equal distances on either side. [Fr., — L. *centrum* — Gr. *kentron*, a sharp point.]

centri- *sen-tri′-*, *sen′tri-*, **centro-** *sen′tro-*, in composition, centre. — *adj.* **centrifugal** (*sen-trif′ū-gəl*, *sen′*, *-fū′*; L. *fugĕre*, to flee from) tending away from a centre: efferent: proceeding in development from the apex towards the base (*bot.*): using, or produced by centrifugal force. — *v.t.* **centrif′ugalise, -ize** (or *sen′*, *-fū′*) to subject to centrifugal force. — *adv.* **centrifugally.** — *n.* **cen′trifuge** (*-fūj*; also **centrifugal machine**) a machine which, by rapid rotation, separates substances of different densities — used in industry, biochemistry, etc. — *v.t.* to subject to such rotation. — *ns.* **centrifugation** (*-fū-gā′shən*), **centrifugence** (*-trif′ū-jəns*, *sen′*, *-fū′*) centrifugal tendency or force. — *adj.* **centrip′etal** (L. *petĕre*, to seek) tending towards a centre: afferent: proceeding from base towards apex. — *n.* **centrip′- etalism.** — *adjs.* **centrobaric** (*-bar′ik*; Gr. *baros*, weight) relating to the centre of gravity; **centroclī′nal** (Gr. *klīnein*, to lean; *geol.*) dipping towards a centre from all directions. — *ns.* **cen′trode** (Gr. *hodos*, a path) a locus traced out by the successive positions of an instantaneous centre of pure rotation; **cen′troid** (Gr. *eidos*, form) the point where the medians of a triangle intersect; **cen′tromere** the portion of DNA that attaches a chromosome to the spindle during cell-division; **cen′trosome** (Gr. *sōma*, a body) a small body found in the protoplasm of a cell, forming by division the two poles of the mitotic spindle; **cen′trosphere** the

barysphere. — **centrifugal force** the resistance of a revolving body, by virtue of its inertia, to an acceleration towards the centre, equal and opposite to the constraining force; **centrifugal machine** a centrifuge. [Gr. *kentron* and L. *centrum* (from Gr.) a sharp point.]

centric, etc. See **centre**.

centrifugal, centripetal, etc., **centrode**, etc. See **centri-**.

centry[1] *sen′tri*, *n.* centre (*Shak.*): centering (*obs.*).

centry[2]. An obs. spelling of **sentry**.

centum *sen′təm*, *ken′tŏŏm*, *n.* a hundred. — **centum languages** the group of Indo-European languages in which an original palatal consonant appears as a guttural (as in L. *centum*, hundred; cf. **satem languages**); **centumvir** (*sen-tum′vir*; L. *vir*, a man) one of the Roman judges chosen annually for civil suits, orig. 105 in number (three from each of the thirty-five tribes): — *pl.* **centum′virī**. — *n.* **centum′virate**. [L. *centum*, a hundred.]

centuple *sen′tū-pl*, *adj.* hundredfold. — *v.t.* to multiply or increase a hundred times. — *n.* **centuplicā′tion.** — *adj.* **centū′plicate.** — *n.* one of a hundred like things or copies. — *v.t.* to centuple. [L. *centuplus* and *centuplex* — *centum*, *plicāre*, to fold.]

century *sen′tū-ri*, *n.* a set or series of a hundred, as Roman soldiers, runs at cricket, or miles ridden, or consecutive years (esp. reckoned from the conventionally accepted date of Christ's birth). — *adj.* **centū′rial.** — *ns.* **centuriā′- tion** division into hundreds; **centū′riātor** one of a company of 16th-century Reformed divines of Magdeburg who compiled a church history in 13 vols., each volume covering a century; **centū′rion** in the Roman army, the commander of a century: one who has scored or achieved a hundred in any way. — **century plant** see **agave**. [L. *centuria*, a century — *centum*, a hundred.]

ceòl mór *kyol mōr*, *mōr*. Same as **pibroch**. [Gael., great music.]

ceorl *chā′örl*, *kā′örl*, *n.* before the Norman Conquest an ordinary freeman not of noble birth. [O.E. *ceorl*; see **churl**.]

cep *sep*, *n.* a type of edible mushroom of the Boletus genus. [Fr. *cèpe*, — L. *cippus*, a stake.]

cephal- *sef′əl-*, *si-fal′*, *kef′al-*, *ki-fal′* in composition, head. — *adjs.* **ceph′alad** (*zool.*) towards the head; **ceph′alate** having a head; **cephal′ic** of, belonging to, the head: for curing pains in the head. — *n.* a remedy for head-pains. — **-cephal′ic, -ceph′alous** adjective combining forms. — *adj.* **ceph′alous** having a head. — *ns.* **cephalag′ra** (Gr. *agrā*, a catching) gout in the head; **cephalal′gia** (Gr. *algos*, pain) headache. — *adj.* **cephalal′gic.** — *ns.* **Cephalas′pis** (Gr. *aspis*, shield) an Upper Silurian and Old Red Sandstone genus of fishes or fishlike animals (ostracoderms) with a head-shield; **cephalī′tis** inflammation of the brain. — *n.pl.* **Cephalochorda** (*-ō-kör′də*; Gr. *chordē*, cord) a lowly class of chordate animals in which the persisting notochord projects beyond the nerve-cord to the end of the snout — the lancelets or amphioxus. — *ns.* **ceph′alopod** (*-pod*; Gr. *pous*, *podos*, foot) a member of the **Cephalopoda** (*-op′od-ə*), the highest class of molluscs, usu. large animals, exclusively marine, with the foot modified into arms surrounding the mouth — *cuttle-fish*, etc.; **cephalospō′rin** any of a group of wide spectrum antibiotics derived from the *Cephalosporium* genus of fungi; **cephalōthō′- rax** the fused head and thorax in some arthropods; **cephalotomy** (*kef-al-ot′ə-mi*; Gr. *tomē*, a cut) the dissection of the head. — **cephalic index** the ratio of the breadth to the length of the skull expressed as a percentage; **cephalic presentation** the usual position of a child in the womb just before birth, head downwards. [Gr. *kephalē*, head.]

Cepheus *sē′fūs*, *-fē-əs*, *n.* a northern constellation named after Andromeda's father. — *n.* **cepheid** (*sē′fē-id*) any star of the type of the star δ Cephei ('classical' cepheid) or of a similar short-period 'cluster-type', from whose rhythmically varying brightness its distance can be inferred — useful in estimating the dimensions of the

Milky Way and the distances of extragalactic bodies. [Gr. *Kēpheus*.]

ceramic *se-* or *ke-ram'ik, adjs.* pertaining to a ceramic or to ceramics: made of a ceramic. — *n.* **ceram'ic** any product that is first shaped and then hardened by means of heat, or the material from which it is formed — including not only traditional potter's clays but also a large range of new dielectric materials: (in *pl.*) articles made of ceramic material. — *n. sing.* **ceram'ics** the potter's art. — *ns.* **cer'amet** a cermet; **ceram'ist, ceram'- icist** one who makes a scientific study of clays and other ceramic materials, or who puts them to practical use; **ceramog'raphy** the description or study of pottery; **cer'met** a combination of *ceramic* particles and a *metal* matrix. — Also (now *rare*) **keramic**, etc. [Gr. *keramos*, potter's earth.]

cerargyrite *ser-är'jər-īt, n.* horn-silver — a horn-like mineral, silver chloride. [Gr. *keras*, horn, *argyros*, silver.]

cerasin *ser'ə-sin, n.* the insoluble portion of cherry-tree gum. [L. *cerasus*, Gr. *kerasos*, the cherry-tree.]

cerastes *se-ras'tēz, n.* the North African horned viper, with a horny process over each eye: — *pl.* **ceras'tes.** — *n.* **Ceras'tium** the genus of mouse-ear chickweed, with horn-shaped capsules. [Gr. *kerastēs* — *keras*, a horn.]

cerate, cerated. See cere.

ceratitis. Same as **keratitis.**

Ceratodus *ser-at'ō-dəs, n.* a genus formerly including the barramunda, an Australian lung-fish, now called Neoceratodus, the name Ceratodus being reserved for a fossil genus: (without *cap.*) a fish or fossil of the genus. [Gr. *keras, -atos*, horn, *odous*, tooth.]

ceratoid *ser'ə-toid, adj.* horny. [Gr. *keratoeidēs — keras*, horn, *eidos*, form.]

Ceratopsian *ser-ə-top'si-ən, n.* a member of a large group of bird-hipped dinosaurs of the late Cretaceous, being quadrupedal, herbivorous, horned and beaked. — Also *adj.* [Gr. *keras*, horn, and *ops*, face.]

Cerberus *sûr'bər-əs, (myth.) n.* the monster that guarded the entrance to Hades, a dog with (at least) three heads. — *adj.* **cer'bē'rian.** [L. — Gr. *Kerberos*.]

cercal. See cercus.

cercaria *sər-kā'ri-ə, n.* a larval stage of many trematodes. — *adj.* **cercā'rian.** [Gr. *kerkos*, a tail.]

Cercopithecus *sûr-kō-pi-thē'kəs, n.* an African genus of long-tailed monkeys, including the Diana monkey, vervet, and mona. [Gr. *kerkos*, tail, *pithēkos*, monkey.]

cercus *sûr'kəs*, a tail-like appendage. — *adj.* **cer'cal** pertaining to a tail. [Gr. *kerkos*, tail.]

cere *sēr, v.t.* to cover with wax. — *n.* the bare waxlike patch at the base of the upper part of a bird's beak. — *adj.* **cerā'ceous** waxy. — *n.* **cēr'ate** a paste or stiff ointment containing wax. — *adjs.* **cēr'ated** (of a bird) having a cere; **cēr'eous** waxy. — *n.* **cere'-cloth, cerement** (*sēr'mənt*) a cloth dipped in melted wax to wrap a dead body in: a winding-sheet or grave-clothes generally. [L. *cēra*, wax.]

cereal. See Ceres.

cerebellum *ser-i-bel'əm, n.* the hinder and lower part of the brain, whose function is to co-ordinate voluntary movements and maintain balance: — *pls.* **cerebell'a** or **cerebell'ums.** — *adjs.* **cerebell'ar, cerebell'ic, cerebell'- ous.** [L., little brain, dim. of *cerebrum*.]

cerebrum *ser'i-brəm, n.* the front and larger part of the brain. — *adj.* **cer'ebral** (also *sə-rē'brəl*) pertaining to the brain or the cerebrum: intellectual, as opposed to practical: of consonant sounds, produced by inverting the tip of the tongue on the palate (*phon.*). — *ns.* **cer'ebralism** the theory that all mental operations originate in the brain; **cer'ebralist.** — *v.i.* **cer'ebrate** to show brain action. — *n.* **cerebrā'tion** action of the brain, esp. unconscious. — *adjs.* **cer'ebric** (or *sər-eb'rik*) cerebral; **cereb'riform** brain-shaped. — **cerebrī'- tis** inflammation of the cerebrum. — *adj.* **cer'- ebrōspīn'al** relating to the brain and spinal cord to-

gether. — *n.* **cerebrotonia** (*-tō'ni-ə*) the temperament associated with ectomorphic body type — introversive, hypersensitive (L. *tonus*, tone). — *adjs.* **cerebrŏtŏn'ic; cer'ebrōvas'cūlar** relating to the cerebrum and its blood vessels. — **cerebral death** see **brain death** under **brain; cerebral haemorrhage** haemorrhage of the blood-vessels in the brain; **cerebral hemispheres** the two great divisions of the cerebrum; **cerebral palsy** a form of congenital paralysis marked by lack of muscular co-ordination, etc.; **cerebrospinal fever** meningitis; **cerebrovascular accident** a paralytic stroke. [L. *cerebrum*, the brain; prob. cog. with Gr. *kara*, the head, *krānion*, the cranium.]

cerement, cereous. See cere.

ceremony *ser'i-mə-ni, n.* a rite: a formal act: the outward form, religious or other: any empty form without inwardness: pomp or state. — *adj.* **ceremonial** (*-mō'ni-əl*) relating to ceremony. — *n.* outward form: a system of ceremonies. — *n.* **ceremō'nialism** adherence to outward form. — *adv.* **ceremō'nially.** — *adj.* **ceremō'nious** full of ceremony: particular in observing forms: precise. — *adv.* **ceremō'niously.** — *n.* **ceremō'niousness.** — **master of ceremonies** the person who directs the form and order of the ceremonies to be observed on some public occasion: a compère; **stand on ceremony** to be punctilious about forms; **without ceremony** informally: without formalities. [L. *caerimōnia*, sanctity.]

Ceres *sē'rēz, n.* the Roman name for the Greek Demeter, goddess of tillage and corn: one of the minor planets. — *adj.* **cereal** (*sē'ri-əl*) relating to edible grain. — *n.* a grain used as food, such as wheat, barley, etc.: a food prepared from such grain, esp. a breakfast food easily got ready. — *n.* **cē'realist** a specialist in cereals: a feeder on cereals. [L. *Cěrēs, -eris*, prob. from root of *creāre*, to create.]

ceresin, ceresine *ser'ə-sin, -sēn, ns.* a kind of hard, whitish wax prepared from ozokerite. [L. *cera*, wax.]

Cereus *sē'ri-əs, n.* a large genus of cactuses, including some of the most imposing forms. [L. *cēreus*, waxen, wax-taper (from their stiff form).]

cerge *sûrj, n.* a large wax-candle burned before the altar. — Also **cierge, serge.** [O.Fr., — L. *cēreus — cēra*, wax.]

ceria. See cerium.

Cerinthian *sər-in'thi-ən, adj.* pertaining to *Cerinthus*, one of the earliest heretics in the Christian Church, against whose crude Gnosticism the Gospel of John was written, according to Irenaeus.

ceriph. Same as **serif.**

cerise *sər-ēz'*, also *-ēs', n.* and *adj.* light and clear red. [Fr., cherry.]

cerium *sē'ri-əm, n.* a metallic element (at. numb. 58; symbol Ce). — *ns.* **cē'ria** its oxide; **cē'rite** a mineral, its hydrous silicate. [Named from the planet *Ceres* discovered about the same time.]

cermet. See under **ceramic.**

cerne *sûrn* (*Shak.*), a short form of **concern.**

cernuous *sûr'nū-əs, (bot.) adj.* nodding, bowing down, drooping. [L. *cernuus*, inclined forwards.]

cerograph *sē'rō-gräf, n.* a writing on wax: an encaustic painting: engraving by means of a plate spread with wax. — *adjs.* **cērographic** (*-graf'ik*), **-al.** — *ns.* **cērographist** (*-rog'rə-fist*); **cērog'raphy.** [Gr. *kēros*, wax, *graphein*, to write.]

ceromancy *sē'rō-man-si, n.* divination by dropping melted wax in water. [Gr. *kēros*, wax, *manteiā*, divination.]

ceroon. A U.S. spelling of **seron.**

ceroplastic *sē-rō-plas'tik, adj.* pertaining to wax-modelling. — *n. sing.* **ceroplas'tics** the art of wax-modelling. [Gr. *kēros*, wax, *plastikos*, plastic — *plassein*, to mould.]

cerris *ser'is, n.* the Turkey oak (*Quercus cerris*). — *adj.* **cerr'ial.** [L. *cerreus*.]

cert. See **certain.**

certain *sûr'tn, adj.* sure: not to be doubted: resolved: fixed: determinate: regular: inevitable: some: one. — *adv.* **cer'tainly** without doubt, undoubtedly: in a resolved, fixed, etc. manner. — *interj.* yes, of course. — *ns.* **cer′tainty** (*slang* **cert**, sometimes in the phrase **dead cert**); **cer′titude.** — **a certain person** implying some degree of contempt; **a lady of a certain age** one no longer young; **for certain** assuredly; **in a certain condition** a euphemism for pregnant; **make certain** see **make;** **moral certainty** see **moral.** [O.Fr., — L. *certus* — *cernĕre*, to decide.]

certes *sûr′tiz, adv.* certainly: in sooth. — **my cer′tie, cer′ty** (*Scot.*) assuredly. [Fr.]

certificate *sər-tif′i-kāt, -kət, n.* a written declaration, official or formal, of some fact: a statement of qualification(s) or recognised professional status. — *v.t.* to give a certificate to. — *adj.* **cer′tifiable** (*-fī-ə-bl*) capable of being certified (esp. as insane). — *adv.* **cer′tifiably.** — *adj.* **certif′icated** (of e.g. a teacher) holding a certificate of training and fitness. — *ns.* **certificā′tion; certif′icatory** a certificate. — Also *adj.* — *n.* **cer′tifier** one who certifies. — *v.t.* **cer′tify** to make known as certain: to inform: to declare in writing: to certify as insane: to refer by certiorari (*law*): — *pr.p.* **cer′tifying;** *pa.p.* **cer′tified.** — **certified milk** milk certified as yielded by tuberculin-tested herds, fulfilling required conditions as to bacterial content, etc. [Fr. *certificat* — L. *certificāre*, *certus*, certain, and *facĕre*, to make.]

certiorari *sûr-shi-ō-rā′rī, n.* a writ by which causes are removed from inferior courts into the High Court of Justice. [L.L. *certiōrārī*, to be informed of — *certior*, compar. of *certus*, certain.]

certitude. See **certain.**

certy. See **certes.**

cerulean, caerulean *si-rōō′li-ən, adj.* sky-blue: dark-blue: sea-green. — *adjs.* **caerule** (*sēr′ūl*; *Spens.*) sky-blue; **cerū′leous.** — *n.* **cerū′lein** (*-lē-in*) a coal-tar colour, producing fast olive greens. [L. *caerŭleus*, dark blue or green.]

cerumen *si-rōō′men, n.* ear wax. — *adj.* **ceru′minous.** [L. *cēra*, wax.]

ceruse *sē′rōōs*, or *si-rōōs′, n.* white lead. — *n.* **cē′rus(s)ite** native lead carbonate. [Fr., — L. *cērussa*, conn. with *cēra*, Gr. *kēros*, wax.]

cervelat *ser′ve-lä, n.* a kind of smoked sausage, made of pork. [Fr. — It. *cervellata*.]

cervix *sûr′viks, n.* the neck of an organ, esp. the uterus. — *adj.* **cervical** (*sûr′vi-kl, sər-vī′kl*). — **cervical smear** the collection of a sample of cells from the neck of the womb and the examination of these cells under a microscope, as a test for early cancer. [L. *cervīx, cervīcis*, neck.]

cervine *sûr′vīn, adj.* relating to deer: like deer: fawn-coloured. [L. *cervīnus* — *cervus*, a stag.]

Cesarean. Esp. U.S. spelling of **Caesarean.**

cesarevitch, -witch, cesarevna. See **tsar.**

cesium. U.S. spelling of **caesium.**

cespitose. Same as **caespitose.**

cess *ses,* (*obs.*) *n.* a tax, a local rate. — *v.t.* to impose a tax. — **bad cess to** (in Ireland) ill luck to; **out of all cesse** (*Shak.*) excessively, immoderately. [Shortened from **assess.**]

cessation *ses-ā′shən, n.* a ceasing or stopping: a rest: a pause. [L. *cessātiō, -ōnis*; see **cease.**]

cesse¹ *ses,* (*Spens.*) *v.i.* Same as **cease.**

cesse². See **cess.**

cesser *ses′ər,* (*law*) *n.* the cessation of a term or liability upon fulfilment of an obligation. [Fr. *cesser*, to cease.]

cession *sesh′ən, n.* a yielding up. — *n.* **cess′ionary** one to whom an assignment has been legally made. — **cessio** (*ses′i-ō, sesh′i-ō*) **bonō′rum** (*Scots law*) a debtor's surrender of his estate to his creditors in return for a judicial protection from imprisonment in respect of his debt — after 1880 a summary process in small bankruptcies, finally abolished 1913. [L. *cēssiō, -ōnis*; see **cede.**]

cesspit *ses′pit,* **cesspool** *-pōōl, ns.* a pit or pool for collecting filthy water. [Origin obscure.]

cestode *ses′tōd, n.* a tapeworm or bladder-worm. — *n.*

ces′toid a cestode: a ribbon-like ctenophoran (Venus's girdle). — Also *adj.* — *n.* and *adj.* **cestoid′ean.** [Gr. *kestos*, a girdle, a strap, and *eidos*, form.]

Cestracion *ses-trā′si-on, n.* an antiquated type of shark represented by the Port Jackson shark. [Perh. Gr. *kestrā*, a kind of fish, or *kestros*, sharp, *akē*, point.]

cestui *set-ē′, sest′wē, n.* that one — in such phrases as **cestui que trust** (*ki-trust*) a person entitled to the benefit of a trust. [O.Fr., dat. of *cest*, that.]

cestus¹ *ses′təs, n.* a girdle, esp. Aphrodite's. [L., — Gr. *kestos*, girdle.]

cestus² *ses′təs, n.* an ancient boxing-glove loaded with metal. [L. *caestus*.]

cesura. See **caesura.**

cesure *sē′zūr,* (*Spens.*) *n.* a break: interruption. [**caesura.**]

Cetacea *si-tā′shi-ə, -shyə, n.pl.* an order of mammals of aquatic habit and fish-like form including the toothed whales, or *Odontoceti* (sperm whales, bottle-noses, dolphins, etc.) and the baleen whales, or *Mystacoceti* (right whale, hump-backs, rorquals). — *n.* and *adj.* **cetā′cean.** — *adj.* **cetā′ceous.** — *ns.* **cete** (*sēt*) a whale or sea-monster; **cetol′ogy** the study of whales; **Ceteosau′rus** (Gr. *sauros*, lizard) a large Jurassic dinosaur. [Gr. *kētos*, a sea-monster.]

cetane *sē′tān, n.* a paraffin hydrocarbon found in petroleum. — **cetane number** a measure of the ignition quality of diesel engine fuel; **cetyl** (*sē′til,* U.S. *sē′təl;* Gr. *hȳlē*, matter) the univalent radical $C_{16}H_{33}$. — **cetyl alcohol** a waxy crystalline solid used in detergents and pharmaceuticals, so called because compounds of it occur in spermaceti. [Gr. *kētos*, a sea-monster.]

cete¹ *sēt, n.* a collective noun for a company of badgers. [Poss. L. *coetus*, assembly.]

cete². See **Cetacea.**

Ceteosaurus. See **Cetacea.**

Ceterach *set′ər-ak, n.* the scale-fern genus: (without *cap.*) a scale-fern. [Mediaeval L. *ceterach* — Ar. *shītarakh*.]

cetera desunt *set′ə-rə dē′sunt, kā′te-ra dā′sŏŏnt,* (L.) the rest is missing.

ceteris paribus *set′ər-is par′i-bus, kā′te-rēs pa′ri-bŏŏs,* (L.) other things being equal.

cetology. See **Cetacea.**

cetyl. See **cetane.**

cetywall. See **setwall.**

cevadilla. See **sabadilla.**

cevitamic acid *sē-vi-tam′ik a′sid,* ascorbic acid. [The letter *c* and *vitamin*.]

Ceylon *si-lon′, n.* the name (until 1972) of the island of Sri Lanka. — *adj.* and *n.* **Ceylonese** (*se-* or *sē-lə-nēz′*). — *ns.* **cey′lonite, cey′lanite** a magnesia-iron spinel.

ch *ch,* (*obs.*) *pron.* S.W. dialect for **ich,** I, fused with the verb, as **cham** I am, **chave** I have, **chill** I will. [M.E. *ich* — O.E. *ic.*]

cha *chä, n.* tea: rolled tea. [Chin. *ch′a.*]

chabazite *kab′ə-zīt, n.* a zeolite, a hydrated calcium-aluminium silicate, in pink and glassy white crystals. [From a misreading of Gr. *chalazios*, a kind of stone — *chalaza*, hailstone.]

Chablis *shab′lē, n.* a very dry white Burgundy wine made at *Chablis*, department of Yonne, in France.

chabouk *chä′bŏŏk, n.* a horsewhip. [Pers. *chābuk.*]

chace. See **chase¹.**

cha-cha (-cha) *chä′-chä′ (-chä′), n.* a West Indian dance, a later form of the mambo.

chack *chak, chäk, n.* (*Scot.*) a snack or slight hasty meal: a snapping or pinching, as by a door or window. — *v.t.* to pinch or nip in such a way. [Imit.]

chacma *chak′mə, n.* a large South African baboon. [From Hottentot.]

chaco. Same as **shako.**

chaconne *sha-, shə-kon′, n.* an old dance, with slow movement: its music, a series of variations on a ground bass, in triple time, appearing in vocal and instrumental music as well as in ballets. [Fr., — Sp. *chacona* — Basque *chucun*, pretty.]

chad[1] *shad, n.* a kind of fish. [See **shad.**]

chad[2] *chad, (comput.) n.* the little bits of paper or cardboard punched out of paper tape or cards. [Origin uncertain.]

Chad *chad, n. (usu.* **Mr Chad**) a character in facetious sketches esp. of the 1940s, portrayed as a bald head peering over a wall, with a caption beginning 'Wot no...?', in protest at post-war shortages, etc. [Origin uncertain.]

chadar, chaddar, chador, chuddah, chuddar *chud'ə(r), ns.* the large veil worn by Muslim and Hindu women, covering head and body: a cloth spread over a Muslim tomb. [Pers. *chaddar,* Hindi *caddar,* a square cloth.]

chaeta *kē'tə, n.* a chitinous bristle on the body of the earthworm and other invertebrates: — *pl.* **chaetae** (*kē'tē*). — *ns.* **Chaetodon** (*kē'tō-don;* Gr. *odous, odontos,* tooth) a tropical genus of fishes with slender teeth, giving name to the family **Chaetodon'tidae:** (without *cap.*) any fish of this genus; **chaetognath** (*kē'təg-nath;* Gr. *gnathos,* jaw) a coelomate, worm-like marine invertebrate, having bristles round the mouth; **chaetopod** (*kē'tō-pod;* Gr. *pous, podos,* foot) a worm (as earthworm, lobworm, sea-mouse) of the class **Chaetop'oda,** that crawls with the help of bristles. [Gr. *chaitē,* hair, spine.]

chafe *chāf, v.t.* to heat, fret, or wear by rubbing: to cause to fret or rage. — *v.i.* to fret or rage (with *against, at*). — *n.* heat caused by rubbing: rage: passion. — *n.* **chaf'er** (*obs.*) a chafing-dish, a saucepan. — **chaf'ing-dish** a vessel for heating by hot coals, etc.: a dish for cooking on the table; **chaf'ing-gear** mats, spun-yarn, battens, etc., put upon the rigging and spars of a ship to prevent their being chafed. [Fr. *chauffer* — L. *calefacēre* — *calēre,* to be hot, and *facēre,* to make.]

chafer *chāf'ər, n.* a beetle, esp. of the Scarabaeidae. [O.E. *cefer;* Du. *kever;* Ger. *Käfer.*]

chaff *chäf, chaf, n.* husks of corn as threshed or winnowed: cut hay and straw: strips of metallic foil, bits of wire, etc. fired into the air to deflect radar signals and so interfere with detection: refuse, or worthless matter: light banter, badinage (perh. a different word). — *v.t.* to banter. — *n.* and *adj.* **chaff'ing.** — *adv.* **chaff'ingly.** — *adjs.* **chaff'less; chaff'y.** — **chaff'-cutt'er, chaff'-en'gine** a machine for cutting up straw or hay. [O.E. *ceaf;* cf. Du. *kaf.*]

chaffer *chaf'ər, v.i.* to bargain: to haggle about price: to sell, exchange, or bandy (*Spens.*). — *ns.* **chaff'erer** a haggler; **chaff'ery** buying and selling: haggling (*Spens.*). [M.E. *chapfare,* a bargain, from O.E. *cēap,* price, *faru,* way.]

chaffinch *chaf'inch, -insh, n.* a little song-bird of the finch family. [Said to delight in *chaff;* see **finch.**]

chaffron. See **chamfrain.**

chaft *chaft, chäft, (Scot.) n.* the jaw. [O.N. *kjaptr;* cf. Sw. *kaft,* Dan. *kieft.*]

chagan *kä-gän', n.* an early form of **khan.**

chagrin *shag'rin, shə-grēn', n.* that which wears or gnaws the mind: vexation: annoyance. — *v.t.* to vex or annoy. — *p.adj.* **chagrined'.** [Fr. *chagrin,* shagreen, rough skin, ill-humour.]

chai, chi *chī, fem.* of **chal.**

chain *chān, n.* a series of links or rings passing through one another: a number of things connected in series: a linked series: a mountain range: a string of islands: something that binds: a connected course or train of events: a measure of 100 links, or 66 feet (see **Gunter's chain** under **gunter**): a measure of 100 feet (see **engineer's chain** at **engineer**): a succession of cigars or cigarettes smoked without intermission: a series of shops, hotels, restaurants, etc. under the same management: a number of atoms linked in succession (*chem.*): (in *pl.*) fetters, bonds, confinement generally: (in *pl.*) a circular apparatus of metal links fitted to the wheels of a car in icy conditions to prevent skidding. — *v.t.* to fasten (also **chain up, down**): to fetter: to restrain: to embrace (*Shak.*): to measure, with chain or tape (*surveying*). — *p.adj.* **chained** bound or fastened, as

with a chain: fitted with a chain. — *adj.* **chain'less** without chains: unfettered. — *n.* **chain'let** a small chain. — **chain'-arm'our** chain-mail; **chain'-bolt** a large bolt used to secure the chain-plates to the ship's side; **chain'-bridge** a bridge suspended on chains: a suspension-bridge; **chain'-cable** a cable composed of iron links; **chain'-drive** transmission of power by chaingear. — *adj.* **chain'-driven.** — **chain'-gang** a gang of convicts wearing leg-irons, esp. chained together; **chain'-gear, -gearing** gearing consisting of an endless chain and (generally) sprocket-wheels; **chain'-harrow** a harrow composed of chainwork; **chain'-letter** a letter soliciting (among other things) the sending, by the recipient, of similar letters with or without a limit to other people; **chain'-light'ning** forked or zigzag lightning: a harsh whisky; **chain locker** (*naut.*) a compartment at the forward end of a ship for storing the anchor chain when the anchor is not being used; **chain'-mail** armour of connected links, much used in Europe in the 12th and 13th centuries; **chain'-mould'ing** moulding in the form of a chain; **chain'-pier** a pier supported by chains like a chain-bridge. — *n.pl.* **chain'-plates** on shipboard, iron plates bolted below the channels to serve as attachments for the dead-eyes, through which the standing rigging or shrouds and backstays are rove and secured. — **chain'-pump** a pump consisting of an endless chain, usually with discs; **chain reaction** a process in which each reaction is in turn the stimulus of a similar reaction; **chain reactor** a nuclear reactor; **chain'-rule** an arithmetical rule, so called from the terms of the problem being stated as equations, and connected, as if by a chain, so as to obtain by one operation the same result as would be obtained by a number of different operations in simple proportion: the rule for solving problems by compound proportion; **chain'saw** a power saw with teeth linked in an endless chain; **chain'-shot** two bullets or half-bullets fastened together by a chain, used formerly to destroy ships' rigging. — *v.t.* and *v.i.* **chain'-smoke'** to smoke (cigarettes, etc.) non-stop. — **chain'-smok'er; chain'-stitch** a stitch resembling the links of a chain; **chain'-store** one of a series of shops, esp. department stores, under the same management; **chain'wheel** a toothed wheel, as on a bicycle, which meshes with a chain to transmit motion; **chain'work** work looped or linked like a chain: network. — **chain of command** a series of military or civic functionaries, each taking orders from the one immediately senior to himself. [O.Fr. *chaeine* — L. *catēna.*]

chair *chār, n.* a movable seat for one, with a back to it: a chariot (*hist.*): a vehicle, wheeled or carried, for one person (*hist.*): the seat or office of one in authority, as a judge, a bishop, or the person presiding over any meeting: the chairman: the seat from which a professor delivers his lectures: a professorship: a pulpit (*obs.*): the instrument or the punishment of electrocution: a support for a railway rail securing it to a sleeper. — *v.t.* to place in a seat of authority: to carry publicly in triumph: to conduct as chairman, etc. (a meeting). — **chair'-bed** a chair capable of being turned into a bed. — *adjs.* **chair'borne** (*coll.*) working at a desk; **chair'-bound** unable to walk: confined to a wheel-chair. — *n.pl.* **chair'days** (*Shak.; fig.*) the evening of life. — **chair'lift** a set of seats suspended from cables used to take skiers uphill; **chair'man** one who takes the chair, or presides at an assembly or meeting (also **chair'-person;** *fem.* **chair'woman**): one who carries a sedan or draws a Bath chair; **chair'manship; chair'-or'gan** a choir-organ (perhaps because it sometimes formed the back of the organist's seat); **chairperson, chairwoman** see **chairman.** [Fr. *chaire* — L. — Gr. *kathedrā.*]

chaise *shāz, n.* a light open carriage for one or more persons: a travelling carriage (see **post-chaise**). — *adj.* **chaise'less.** — **chaise'-cart** a light vehicle for going about in; **chaise'-longue'** (- *lõg'*) a couch with back at one end and short armrest. [Fr., a form of *chaire;*

see **chair**; **chay** and **shay** are vulgar singulars of imaginary *pl.* **chaise.**]

chakra *chak'ra, n.* amongst the Sikhs, a disc-shaped knife used as a missile: a discus representing the sun, as in portrayals of Hindu Gods: in Yoga, a centre of spiritual power in the body. [Sans. *cakra*, wheel.]

chal *chal, n.* fellow: person: — *fem.* **chai** or **chi** (*chī*). [Romany.]

chal(l)an *chul'ən, (Ind.) n.* a way-bill: a pass: the sending up of an accused person before a magistrate: a form used when money due to a government department is paid, not to the department itself, but to the government Treasury. — Also *v.t.* [Hindi *calan.*]

chalaza *ka-lā'za, n.* in a bird's egg, the string that holds the yolk-sac in position (*zool.*): the base of the ovule (*bot.*). — *adj.* **chalazogamic** (*kal-az-ō-gam'ik*). — *n.* **chalazogamy** (*-og'ə-mi*; *bot.*) entrance of the pollen-tube through the chalaza (opp. to *porogamy*). [Gr. *chalaza*, hail, lump.]

chalcedony *kal-sed'ə-ni,* or *kal', n.* a beautiful mineral composed of silica, usually banded, translucent, of waxy lustre, generally white or bluish-white, apparently amorphous but consisting of crystalline fibres. — *adj.* **chalcedonic** (*-si-don'ik*). — *n.* **chalced'onyx** (or *-on'*; from **onyx**) an agate of alternating white opaque and greyish translucent chalcedony. [Gr. *chalkēdōn*, possibly from *Chalcedon*, in Asia Minor.]

Chalcidian *kal-sid'i-ən, adj.* pertaining to *Chalcis* in Euboea, or its people. — **Chalcidian alphabet** the alphabet used by Chalcidian settlers in southern Italy and Sicily, from which the Latin alphabet developed.

chalcography *kal-kog'rə-fi, n.* the art of engraving on copper or brass. — *ns.* **chalcog'rapher, chalcog'raphist.** [Gr. *chalkos*, copper, *graphein*, to write.]

Chalcolithic *kal-kō-lith'ik.* Same as **Aeneolithic.** [Gr. *chalkos*, copper, *lithos*, stone.]

chalcopyrite *kal-kō-pī'rīt, n.* copper pyrites. [Gr. *chalkos*, copper, and **pyrite.**]

Chaldaic *kal-dā'ik,* **Chaldee** *kal'dē, adjs.* relating to *Chaldaea.* — *n.* the language of the Chaldaeans: an ancient inhabitant of Chaldaea: a soothsayer: a member of the Chaldaean church. — *n.* **chal'dāism** a Chaldaic idiom. — *adj.* **Chaldae'an, Chalde'an** (*-dē'ən*) Chaldaic. — *n.* a native of Chaldaea.

chalder *chöl'dər, n.* an old Scottish dry measure, containing 16 bolls. [Prob. a form of **chaldron.**]

chaldron *chöl'drən, n.* an old coal-measure, holding 36 heaped bushels (= 25½ cwt.). [Fr. *chaudron*; see **cauldron.**]

chalet *shal'ā, n.* a summer hut used by Swiss herdsmen in the Alps: a wooden villa: a small house, usu. of wood, built for use by holidaymakers, etc. [Fr.; *châlet* is wrong.]

chalice *chal'is, n.* a cup or bowl: a communion-cup. — *adj.* **chal'iced** cup-like. [O.Fr. *chalice* — L. *calix, calicis*; cf. Gr. *kylix*, a cup; **calyx** is a different word.]

chalk *chök, n.* white soft rock, composed of calcium carbonate, chiefly shells of Foraminifera: a substitute for this used for writing, etc. — *v.t.* to write, rub, mark, or manure, with chalk. — *n.* **chalk'iness.** — *adj.* **chalk'y.** — **chalk'board** a blackboard; **chalk'face** (*coll.,* usu. **at the chalkface**) the classroom, as the centre of the teacher's activities; **chalk'pit** a pit in which chalk is dug; **chalk'stone** a stone or piece of chalk: (in *pl.*) the white concretions formed round the joints in chronic gout. — **as like, as different, as chalk and cheese** completely unalike; **by a long chalk** by a considerable distance or degree, orig. referring to the habit of scoring with chalk; **chalk (and) talk** the formal teaching method of writing on the blackboard and expounding; **chalking the door** in Scotland, a form of warning tenants to remove from burghal tenements; **chalk out** to trace out, as with chalk, to plan; **chalk up** to make a special note of: to record (a score, etc.): to charge or ascribe (to e.g. a person); **not know chalk from cheese** to know nothing about the matter; **the Chalk** (*geol.*) the uppermost part of the Cretaceous system in England. [O.E. *cealc* — L. *calx*, limestone.]

challan. See **chal(l)an.**

challenge *chal'inj, v.t.* to call on to settle a matter by fighting or by any kind of contest: to claim as one's own: to accuse: to object to: to track (*Spens.*). — *n.* a summons to a contest of any kind, but esp. a duel: a calling of anyone or anything in question: exception to a juror: the demand of a sentry: an accusation: a claim: a difficulty which stimulates interest or effort: a task, undertaking, etc. to test one's powers and capabilities to the full. — *adj.* **chall'engeable** that may be challenged. — *n.* **chall'enger** one who challenges to a combat of any kind: a claimant: one who objects, calls in question. — *adj.* **chall'enging.** — *adv.* **chall'-engingly.** [O.Fr. *chalenge*, a dispute, claim — L. *calumnia*, a false accusation — *calvī* or *calvēre*, to deceive.]

challis, shalli *chal'is, shal'is, shal'i, ns.* a soft glossless silk and worsted fabric, later applied to other materials. [Origin uncertain.]

chalone *kāl', kal'ōn, n.* an internal secretion which inhibits action as a hormone excites it. — *adj.* **chalon'ic.** [Gr. *chalaein*, to relax.]

chalumeau *shal-ū-mō', shal-ü-mō', n.* an early reed instrument that developed into the clarinet: the lowest register of the clarinet: — *pl.* **chalumeaux** (*-mōz'*). [Fr., — O.Fr. *chalemel* — L.L. *calamellus*, dim. of *calamus*, a pipe, a reed.]

Chalybean *kal-ib-ē'ən,* or *ka-lib'i-ən, adj.* forged by the Chalybes (*Milt.*): well tempered. — *adj.* **chalyb'eate** containing iron. — *n.* a water or other liquid containing iron. — *n.* **cha'lybite** siderite, a common iron ore, ferrous carbonate. [Gr. *chalyps, chalybos*, steel, or *Chalyps*, one of the *Chalybĕs*, a nation in Pontus famous for steel.]

cham¹ *kam, n.* an obs. form of **khan:** an autocrat (*fig.*).

cham². See **ch.**

chamade *shə-mäd', n.* a drum or trumpet call for a parley or surrender. [Fr.]

chamaeleon. See **chameleon.**

Chamaerops *kə-mē'rops.* See **palmetto** (**palm²**).

chamber *chām'bər, n.* a room: the place where an assembly meets: a house of a legislature, esp. the French Chamber of Deputies: an assembly or body of men met for some purpose, as a chamber of commerce: a hall of justice: a compartment: a cavity: the back end of the bore of a gun: a small cannon (*Shak.*): (in *pl.*) a suite of rooms in a house occupied separately, esp. by lawyers: (in *pl.*) a judge's room for hearing cases not taken into court. — *v.t.* to put in a chamber: to confine. — *v.i.* to be wanton (*arch.*). — *adj.* **cham'bered** confined: having rooms or room, or (of a shell) parts separated by a succession of walls. — *ns.* **cham'berer** a man of intrigue (*arch.*): a gallant (*Shak.*); **cham'bering** (*B.*) lewd behaviour. — **chamber concert** a concert of chamber music; **chamber council** (*Shak.*) a private or secret council; **cham'ber-counsel, -counsellor** a counsel who gives his advice privately, but does not plead in court; **cham'ber-fellow** (*arch.*) one sharing a chamber. — *n.pl.* **cham'ber-hangings** (*Shak.*) the hangings or tapestry of a chamber. — **cham'ber-lye** (*Shak.*) urine; **cham'bermaid** a female servant who has the care of bedrooms in hotels, etc.: formerly, and still in U.S., a housemaid; **chamber music** music, performed by a small group such as a quartet, suitable for a room rather than a theatre or a large hall; **chamber of commerce** (sometimes with *caps.*) a group of businessmen working together to promote local trade; **chamber organ** a small organ suitable for a room; **cham'berpot** a bedroom vessel for urine — often merely **cham'ber** or **pot**; **chamber practice** the business of a chamber-counsel; **cham'ber-stick** a candlestick designed to be carried. [Fr. *chambre* — L. *camera* — Gr. *kamarā*, a vault, a room.]

chamberlain *chām'bər-lin, n.* an officer appointed by a king or nobleman, or by a corporation, to perform domestic and ceremonial duties or to act as factor or steward. — *n.* **cham'berlainship.** — **Lord Chamberlain** an officer of high standing in the royal household, having control over all the officers and servants 'above stairs', except those of the bedchamber, over the establishment attached to the Chapel Royal, the physicians, surgeons, and apothecaries of the household; **Lord Great Chamberlain** a hereditary officer who has the government of the palace of Westminster and to whom on solemn occasion the keys of Westminster Hall and of the Court of Requests are delivered. [O.Fr. *chambrelenc*; O.H.G. *chamerling* — L. *camera*, a chamber, and affix *-ling* or *-lenc* = Eng. *-ling* in *hireling*.]

Chambertin *shã-ber-tẽ, n.* a famous red Burgundy from the vineyard of that name near Dijon.

chambré *shã-brã,* (Fr.) *p.adj.* of wine, at room temperature.

chameleon, chamaeleon *kə-mēl'yən, n.* a small lizard famous for changing its colour: an inconstant, changeable, or readily adaptable person (*fig.*). — Also *adj.* — *adjs.* **chameleonic** (*-i-on'ik*); **chamel'eon-like.** [L. *chamaeleōn* — Gr. *chamaileōn* — *chamai* (cf. L. *humī*), on the ground (i.e. dwarf) and *leōn*, a lion.]

chamelot *cham',* or *kam'e-lot,* (*Spens.*) *n.* same as **camlet.**

chamfer *cham'fər, n.* a bevel or slope made by paring off the edge of anything originally right-angled: a groove, channel, or furrow. — *v.t.* to cut or grind off bevelwise, as a corner: to channel or make furrows upon: to flute, as a column. — *adj.* **cham'fered** bevelled: furrowed, grooved, wrinkled. [Fr. *chanfrein*—O.Fr. *chanfraindre*, apparently from *chant fraindre* — L. *cantum frangĕre*, to break the edge or side.]

chamfrain *cham'frən, n.* a piece of leather or plate of steel to protect the face of a horse in battle. — Also **cham'fron, chaf'fron.** [Fr. *chanfrein*; origin unknown.]

chamiso *shə-mē'sō,* **chamise** *shə-mēz', ns.* a rosaceous shrub (*Adenostoma fasciculatum*) of California: — *pls.* **chami'sos, -mis'es.** — *n.* **chamisal'** a chamiso thicket. [Sp. *chamiza*, cane.]

chamlet *cham'* or *kam'let, n.* Same as **camlet.**

chamois *sham'wä, n.* a goat-like antelope inhabiting high mountains in southern and central Europe (*pl.* **chamois** *sham'wä*): (*sham'i*) a soft kind of leather originally made from its skin (see also **shammy**). [Fr., perh. from Swiss Romanic; cf. Ger. *Gemse*, a chamois.]

chamomile. See **camomile.**

champ[1] *champ, v.i.* to make a snapping noise with the jaws in chewing. — *v.t.* to bite or chew: to munch: to crush: to mash. — *n.* a champing: esp. in Northern Ireland, a dish made of potatoes, leeks and spring onions. — **champ at the bit** (of a horse) to gnaw at the bit in impatience to move off: to show signs of impatience while waiting for something (*fig.*). [Poss. onomatopoeic; conn. with **jam**[2].]

champ[2] *champ,* (*her.*) *n.* field. [Fr.]

champ[3] *champ, n.* slang shortening of **champion.**

champac. See **champak.**

champagne *sham-pān', n.* a white sparkling wine, strictly from *Champagne* in France (sometimes still or coloured red): the amber-like colour of white champagne.

champaign *cham'pān',* also *sham-pān', adj.* level, open. — *n.* an open level country. [Doublet of **campaign**, from O.Fr. *champaigne* — L. *campānia*, a plain.]

champak, champac *chum'puk, cham'pak, n.* an Indian tree (*Michelia champaca*) of the magnolia family, of great beauty, with oppressively scented flowers. [Hind.]

champers *sham'pərz,* (*coll.*) *n.* champagne.

champerty *cham'pər-ti, n.* an illegal bargain whereby the one party is to assist the other in a suit, and is to share in the proceeds. — *n.* **cham'part** the division of the produce of land, the right of the feudal lord. [Norm. Fr. — L. *campī pars*, part of the field.]

champignon *sham'pin-yõ, n.* a mushroom or other edible fungus, esp. the fairy-ring champignon (*Marasmius oreades*).

champion *cham'pi-ən, n.* one who fights in single combat for himself or for another: one who defends a cause: a successful combatant: in sports, one who has excelled all others: a hero. — *adj.* acting or ranking as champion, first: excellent (*coll.*). — *v.t.* to challenge (*obs.*): to defend: to support. — *ns.* **cham'pioness; cham'pionship** the position of honour gained by being champion: a contest held to decide who is the champion: the act of championing. [Fr., — L.L. *campiō, -ōnis* — L. *campus*, a plain, a place for games.]

champlevé *shã-lə-vã, n.* enamel work done with vitreous powders in channels cut in a metal base. — Also *adj.* [Fr.]

Champs Elysées *shã-zā-lē-zā,* (Fr.) Elysian Fields (Elysium): also a famous open space and avenue in Paris.

chance *chäns, n.* that which falls out or happens fortuitously, or without assignable cause: fortune: an unexpected event: risk: opportunity: possibility of something happening: (sometimes in *pl.*) probability: (in *pl.*) misfortunes (*arch.*). — *v.t.* to risk. — *v.i.* to happen: (with (*up*)*on*) to happen to find or meet. — *adj.* happening by chance. — *adv.* perchance. — *adjs.* **chance'ful** full of risk or danger (*arch.*): full of chance(s); **chance'less** without an opportunity. — *n.* **chanc'er** (*coll.*) a person prepared to take risks for his own advancement. — *adj.* **chanc'y** lucky, safe (*Scot.*): risky, uncertain. — **chance'-com'er** one who comes by chance or unexpectedly. — **by chance** accidentally; **chance one's arm** to take a chance, often recklessly; **chance upon** to find by chance; **chance would be a fine thing** (*coll.*) some hope!; **even chance** equal probability for or against; **how chance?** (*Shak.*) how does it happen that?; **stand a good chance** to have a reasonable expectation; **take one's chance** to accept what happens: to risk an undertaking; **the main chance** the chief object (esp. **an eye to the main chance** thought for selfenrichment). [O.Fr. *cheance* — L.L. *cadentia* — L. *cadĕre*, to fall.]

chancel *chän'sl, n.* the eastern part of a church, originally separated from the nave by a screen of latticework, so as to prevent general access thereto, though not to interrupt either sight or sound. [O.Fr., — L. *cancellī*, lattices.]

chancellor *chän'səl-ər, n.* secretary (*Shak.*): a chief minister: the president, or a judge, of a court of chancery or other court: the official who keeps the registers of an order of knighthood: the titular (or in U.S. active) head of a university: the foreman of a jury (*Scot.*). — *ns.* **chan'cellorship; chan'cellery, -ory** the position, department, etc., of a chancellor: the office attached to an embassy or consulate. — **chancellor of a cathedral** an officer who had charge of the chapter library, custody of the common seal, superintendence of the choir practices, and headship of the cathedral schools; **chancellor of a diocese** an ecclesiastical judge uniting the functions of vicar-general and official principal, appointed to assist the bishop in questions of ecclesiastical law, and hold his courts for him; **Chancellor of the Exchequer** the chief minister of finance in the British government; **Lord Chancellor, Lord High Chancellor** the Speaker of the House of Lords, presiding judge of the Chancery Division, keeper of the Great Seal. [Fr. *chancelier* — L.L. *cancellārius*, orig. an officer that had charge of records, and stood near the *cancelli* (L.), cross-bars surrounding the judgment seat.]

chance-medley *chäns-med'li, n.* a casualty that is not pure chance but has a mixture of chance in it: esp. unintentional homicide in which the killer is not entirely without blame: action with an element of chance: (wrongly) pure chance. [O.Fr. *chance medlée*, mingled chance.]

Chancery *chän'sər-i, n.* formerly the highest court of justice next to the House of Lords, presided over by the Lord High Chancellor — now a division of the High Court of Justice: a court of record generally: the office of a chancellor: the political office in an embassy or legation (*Brit. diplomatic*). — **Chancery Office** in Scotland, an office in the General Register House at Edinburgh, managed by a director, in which all royal charters of novodamus, patents of dignities, gifts of offices, remissions, legitimations, presentations, commissions, and other writs appointed to pass the Great and Quarter Seals are recorded; **in chancery** (of an estate, etc.) in litigation: (of a wrestler's or boxer's head) held firmly under his adversary's arm (*slang*): in an awkward predicament (*slang*). [Fr. *chancellerie*.]

chancre *shang'kər, n.* the hard swelling that constitutes the primary lesion in syphilis. — *n.* **chanc'roid** a non-syphilitic ulceration of the genital organs due to venereally contracted infection. — *adjs.* **chanc'roid; chanc'rous.** [Fr.; a form of **canker**.]

chancy. See **chance**.

chandelier *shan-di-lēr', n.* a frame with branches for holding lights. — *ns.* **chandler** (*chand'lər*) a candle-maker: a dealer in candles, oil, soap, etc.: a dealer generally (as in *corn-chandler, ship-chandler*); **chand'lering.** — *adj.* **chand'lerly.** — *n.* **chand'lery** goods sold by a chandler. [Fr., — L.L. *candēlārius,* a candle-maker, *candēlāria,* a candlestick — L. *candēla,* a candle.]

Chandler('s) wobble *chand'lər(z) wob'l,* the very small displacement of the earth's axis of rotation which causes variation in latitude (and also longitude). [S.C. *Chandler* (1846–1913), American astronomer.]

change *chānj, v.t.* to alter or make different: to put or give for another: to make to pass from one state to another: to exchange. — *v.i.* to suffer change: to change one's clothes or vehicle. — *n.* the act of changing: alteration or variation of any kind: exchange (*Shak.*): fickleness (*Shak.*): a shift: variety: money given for money of a different kind, or in adjustment of a payment: small coin: satisfaction (*coll.*): an exchange (now usu. **'change**). — *ns.* **changeabil'ity, change'ableness** fickleness: the power of being changed. — *adj.* **change'able** subject or prone to change: fickle: inconstant: admitting possibility of change: showing change of colours, shot (*Shak.*). — *adv.* **change'ably.** — *adj.* **change'ful** full of change: changeable. — *adv.* **change'fully.** — *n.* **change'fulness.** — *adj.* **change'less** without change: constant. — *ns.* **change'ling** a surreptitious substitute: a child substituted for another, esp. one supposed to be left by the fairies: hence, an undersized crabbed child: a half-wit: one apt to change (*arch.*); **chāng'er** one who changes the form of anything: one employed in changing or discounting money (*obs.*). — **change'-house** (*Scot.*) a small inn or alehouse; **change'-over** transition to a new system or condition; **change-ringing** see **ring the changes** below; **chang'ing-piece** (*Shak.*) a fickle person. — **change colour** to blush or turn pale; **change down** to change to a lower gear; **change gear** to select a higher or lower gear; **change of life** the time of life at which menstruation is about to cease — the menopause; **change oneself** (now *Scot.*) to change one's clothes; **change one's mind** to form a different opinion; **change one's tune** to change from joy to sorrow: to change one's manner of speaking; **change up** to change to a higher gear; **put the change on** to delude, trick; **ring the changes** to go through all the possible permutations in ringing a peal of bells (*n.* **change'-ringing**): to go over in every possible order: to do, use, etc. a limited number of things repeatedly in varying ways, order, etc.: to pass counterfeit money: to bemuddle a shopman into giving too much change; **small change** small coin: a petty thing. [Fr. *changer* — L. *cambīre,* to barter.]

chank *changk,* **chank-shell** *changk'-shel, ns.* the shell of several species of Turbinella, gasteropod molluscs of the East Indian seas, sliced into bangles for Hindu women. [Hind. *chankh;* cf. **conch**.]

channel[1] *chan'l, n.* the bed of a stream of water: a strait or narrow sea: a navigable passage: a passage for conveying a liquid: a groove or furrow: a gutter: means

of passing or conveying: gravel (*Scot.*): (in *pl.*) means of communication: a one-way path for a signal: a path for information in a computer: a narrow range of frequencies, part of a frequency band, for the transmission of radio and television signals without interference from other channels. — *v.t.* to make a channel: to furrow: to convey (through): to direct (into a particular course; *lit.* and *fig.*): — *pr.p.* **chann'elling;** *pa.t.* and *pa.p.* **chann'elled.** — *adj.* **chann'elled.** — **channel seam** a seam on clothing outlined by stitching running along both sides; **channel seaming; chann'el-stone, -stane** (*Scot.*) a curling-stone. — **the Channel** the English Channel. [O.Fr. *chanel, canel* — L. *canālis,* a canal.]

channel[2] *chan'l, n.* a flat piece of wood or iron projecting horizontally from a ship's side to spread the shrouds and keep them clear of the bulwarks — **fore, main,** and *mizzen* channels. [For *chain-wale*.]

chanoyu *chä'no-ū, n.* a Japanese tea ceremony. [Jap., tea of hot water.]

chanson *shã'sɔ̃, n.* a song. — *ns.* **chansonette** (-*son-et'*) a little song, a ditty; **chansonnier** (-*son'ē-ā*) a collection of songs, esp. old French: a cabaret performer of satirical songs. — **chanson de geste** (*də zhest;* see **gest**[2]) an old French epic poem. [Fr.]

chant, chaunt *chänt, v.t.* to sing: to celebrate in song: to recite in a singing manner: to intone: to sell (a horse) fraudulently. — *n.* song: melody: a kind of church music, in which prose is sung. — *ns.* **chant'er, chaunt'er, chant'or** a singer: a precentor: in a bagpipe, the pipe with fingerholes, on which the melody is played: one who cries up horses; **chant'ress, chaunt'ress; chant'ry, chaunt'ry** an endowment, or chapel, for the chanting of masses; **chanty** see **shanty**[2]. [Fr. *chanter* — L. *cantāre* — *canēre,* to sing.]

chantage *shä-täzh', n.* blackmail. [Fr.]

chanterelle[1] *shan-, shä-tər-el', n.* the highest string of a musical instrument. [Fr., — L. *cantāre,* to sing.]

chanterelle[2], **chantarelle** *chan-tər-el', n.* a yellowish edible fungus (*Cantharellus cibarius*). [Fr., dim. from Gr. *kantharos,* cup.]

chanteuse *shan'tōōs* or -*tōōz, shä-tøz, n.* a female nightclub singer. [Fr.]

chantey. See **shanty**[2].

chanticleer *chant'i-klēr, -klēr', n.* a cock. [From the name of the cock in the old beast-epic of *Reynard the Fox* — O.Fr. *chanter,* to sing, *cler,* clear.]

chantie. See **shanty**[2].

Chantilly *shan-ti'li, shä-tē-yē, n.* a silk or linen bobbin lace, black or white, of delicate floral or scrolled pattern. — Also **Chantilly lace** (*lās*). — *adj.* of cream, sweetened and whipped, and usu. flavoured with vanilla: prepared or served with such cream. [From *Chantilly,* France, where the lace was first made.]

chantor, chantress, chantry. See **chant**.

chanty[1]. See **shanty**[2].

chanty[2] *chan'ti,* (*Scot. slang*) *n.* a chamber-pot. [Orig. unknown.]

Chanuk(k)ah. See **Hanukkah**.

chaos *kā'os, n.* the shape of matter before it was reduced to order: disorder: shapeless mass. — *adj.* **chaot'ic** confused. — *adv.* **chaot'ically.** [Gr.]

chap[1] *chap, v.i.* to crack: to strike (of a clock, etc., or to knock at a door (*Scot.*). — *v.t.* to fissure. — *n.* a crack: an open fissure in the skin, caused by exposure to cold: a knock. — *adjs.* **chap'less; chapped** cracked, of a heavy soil in dry weather, or of the skin in cold weather: cut short; **chapp'y.** [M.E. *chappen;* cog. with Du. and Ger. *kappen.*]

chap[2] *chap, n.* a customer (for **chap'man**) (*obs.* or *dial.*): a fellow (*coll.; facet. fem.* **chap'(p)ess**). — *n.* **chapp'ie** a familiar dim. of **chap**. — **chap'book** a book or pamphlet of a popular type such as was hawked by chapmen; **chap'man** one who buys or sells (*arch.*): an itinerant dealer: a pedlar: a purchaser (*obs.*). [O.E. *cēap,* trade, *cēapman,* trader; cf. **cheap**; Ger. *kaufen, Kaufmann.*]

chap³ *chap, n.* a chop or jaw: a cheek. — *adjs.* **chap'fall'en** same as **chopfallen; chap'less,** without a lower jaw. [Cf. **chop**³; Northern Eng. and Scot. *chaft,* O.N. *kjaptr,* jaw.]

chaparajos *shap-ə-rä'ōs, chä-pä-rä'hhos,* **chaparejos** *-rä', -rē', ns.pl.* cowboy's leather riding leggings (short forms **chaps, shaps**). [Mex. Sp.]

chaparral *shap-ə-ral', chäp-ä-räl', n.* dense tangled brush-wood. — **chaparral cock** a ground-cuckoo of the Californian and Mexican chaparral. [Sp., — *chaparro,* evergreen oak, one of its constituents.]

chapati, chapatti *chəp-ät'i, n.* a thin flat loaf of unleavened bread. [Hind.]

chapbook. See **chap**².

chape *chāp, n.* the plate of metal at the point of a scabbard: the catch or hook by which the sheath of a weapon was attached to the belt. — *adj.* **chape'less.** [Fr., — L.L. *capa,* a cap.]

chapeau *shä-pō, n.* a hat. — **chapeau-bras** (*brä*) a three-cornered hat formerly carried under the arm. [Fr.]

chapel *chap'l, n.* a place of worship inferior or subordinate to a regular church, or attached to a house or institution: an oratory in a mausoleum, etc.: a cell of a church containing its own altar: a dissenters' place of worship, as of Nonconformists in England, Roman Catholics or Episcopalians in Scotland, etc.: a chapel service (*to keep one's chapels,* to make the requisite number of attendances in chapel): a body of musicians, as a choir, an orchestra, or both, whether connected with a chapel or not: a printing office, or an association or trade union of workmen therein. — *adj.* Nonconformist. — *n.* **chap'elry** the jurisdiction of a chapel. — **chapel cart** see **cart; chap'el-master** (Ger. *Kapellmeister*) a music-director; **chapel royal** the oratory of a royal palace. — **chapel of ease** a chapel for worshippers at some distance from the parish church; **father, mother, of the chapel** the president of a printing office or chairman or chairwoman of a printers' association or trade union branch; **lady chapel** see **lady; proprietary chapel** one that is private property. [O.Fr. *capele* — L.L. *cappella,* dim. of *cappa,* a cloak or cope; orig. from the cloak of St Martin.]

chapelle ardente *sha-pel är-dät,* (Fr.) a chapel or chamber in which a corpse lies in state before burial, surrounded by lighted candles.

chaperon (*now often* **chaperone**) *shap'ə-rōn, n.* a kind of hood or cap: one (esp. an older woman) who accompanies a girl for protection, restraint, or appearance's sake. — *v.t.* to attend in such a capacity. — *n.* **chap'eronage.** [Fr., a large hood — *chape,* a hooded cloak — L.L. *cappa;* see **cape**¹.]

chapess. See **chap**².

chapiter *chap'i-tər, n.* the head or capital of a column. [Fr. *chapitre* — L. *capitulum,* dim. of *caput,* the head.]

chapka, czapka *chap'kə, n.* a military cap of a shape adapted from the traditional Polish peasant cap, worn by lancer regiments. — Also **schapska** (*shaps'kə*). [Pol. *czapka,* a cap.]

chaplain *chap'lin, n.* a clergyman attached to an institution, establishment, organisation, or family. — *ns.* **chap'laincy, chap'lainry, chap'lainship.** [O.Fr. *chapelain* — L.L. *cappellānus* — *cappella;* see **chapel.**]

chaplet *chap'lit, n.* a garland or wreath for the head: a circlet of gold, etc.: a string of beads used in counting prayers, one-third of a rosary in length: anything in a string: a metal support of a cylindrical pipe. — *adj.* **chap'leted.** [O.Fr. *chapelet* — *chape,* a head-dress.]

chapman, chappie. See **chap**².

chaprassi *chu-präs'i, n.* an office messenger: a household attendant: an orderly. [Hind. *chaprāsi,* badge-wearer, messenger — *chaprās,* a badge.]

chaps. See **chaparajos.**

chaptalise, -ize *chap'tə-līz, v.t.* to add extra sugar to wine during its fermentation — usually a prohibited or closely controlled practice. — *n.* **chaptalisa'tion, -z-.** [From the originator, *Chaptal,* a late 19th-cent. French chemist.]

chapter *chap'tər, n.* a main division of a book, or of anything: a subject or category generally: a division of the Acts of Parliament of a session: an assembly of the canons of a cathedral or collegiate church, or the members of a religious or military order (from the custom of reading a chapter of the rule or of the Bible): its members collectively: an organised branch of a society or fraternity: a Roman numeral on a clock or watch face: a chapter (*Spens.*). — *v.t.* to put into chapters: to take to task. — **chap'ter-house** a building used for meetings of a cathedral, church, etc. chapter. — **chapter and verse** the exact reference to the passage of the authority of one's statements; **chapter of accidents** see **accident; to the end of the chapter** throughout. [O.Fr. *chapitre* — L. *capitulum,* dim. of *caput,* the head.]

chaptrel *chap'trəl, n.* the capital of a pillar which supports an arch. [Dim. of **chapiter.**]

char¹, **charr** *chär, ns.* a small fish (*Salvelinus*) of the salmon kind, found in mountain lakes and rivers. [Prob. Celt.; cf. Gael. *ceara,* red, blood-coloured.]

char² *chär, vs.t.* to reduce to carbon. — *v.t.* and *v.i.* to scorch: — *pr.p.* **charr'ing;** *pa.t.* and *pa.p.* **charred.** — *adj.* **charr'y** pertaining to charcoal. [Origin obscure.]

char³ *chär,* **chare** *chār, ns.* a turn (*obs.*): an occasional piece of work, an odd job: (in *pl.*) household work (see **chore**): a charwoman. — *vs.i.* to do odd jobs of work: to do house-cleaning. — *vs.t.* (*Scott*) to do, accomplish: — *pr.p.* **charr'ing, chär'ing;** *pa.t.* and *pa.p.* **charred, chäred.** — **char'woman, char'lady** a woman hired to do rough cleaning. [O.E. *cerran, cierran,* to turn; also **jar**³, **ajar.**]

char⁴ *chär, n.* (*slang*) tea. [Cockney spelling of **cha.**]

Chara *kā'rə, n.* a genus of freshwater plants of a family and class (stoneworts, **Charā'ceae, Charoph'yta**) more or less akin to the green seaweeds, having stems encrusted with calcareous matter and whorled branches: (without *cap.*) any plant of the genus. [L., some plant]

charabanc, char-à-banc *shar'ə-bang, -bä, n.* formerly a long open vehicle with rows of transverse seats: more recently, a tourist coach. — *vulg.* contr. **cha'ra:** — *pl.* **char'abancs, char'-à-bancs** or **chars'-à-bancs.** [Fr. *char à bancs,* carriage with benches.]

Characidae *ka-ras'i-dē, n.pl.* a family of freshwater fishes to which belong the dorado and the piranha. — Also **Characin'idae.** — *n.* **char'acin** a fish of this family. — Also *adj.* — *adj.* **chara'cinoid.** [Gr. *charax,* a fish of some kind.]

character *kar'ək-tər* (*Spens., Shak.,* etc. *-ak'*), *n.* a letter, sign, figure, stamp, or distinctive mark: a mark of any kind, a symbol in writing, etc.: writing generally, handwriting: a secret cipher: one of a set of symbols, e.g. letters of the alphabet, numbers, punctuation marks, that can be arranged in groups to represent data for processing (*comput.*): any essential feature or peculiarity: a quality: nature: personal appearance (*obs.*): the aggregate of peculiar qualities which constitutes personal or national individuality: esp. moral qualities: the reputation of possessing these: a formal statement of the qualities of a person who has been in one's service or employment: official position, rank, or status, or a person who has filled it: a person noted for eccentricity or well-marked personality: a personality as created in a play or novel (*Shak.* **char'act**) or appearing in history: a literary genre, consisting in a description in prose or verse of a human type, or of a place or object on that model, a dominant form of literature in the 17th century under the influence of Theophrastus and the theory of humours: a person (*slang*). — *v.t.* (*arch.*) to engrave, imprint, write: to represent, delineate, or describe. — *n.* **characterisa'tion, -z-.** — *v.t.* **char'acterise, -ize** to describe by peculiar qualities: to be a distinguishing mark or quality of. — *ns.* **char'acterism** a characteristic: a characterisation; **characteris'tic** that which marks or constitutes the character: the integral part of a logarithm. — *adjs.* **characteris'tic, -al.** — *adv.* **characteris'tically.** — *adj.* **char'acterless** without character or distinctive qualities. — *ns.* **char'acterlessness; characterol'ogy** the science or study of the variety and development of character; **characterol'ogist; char'actery** (in *Shak. -ak'*) (*arch.*) writing: impression: that which is charactered. — **character actor** one who plays character parts; **character assassination** the destruction of a person's reputation by slander, rumour, etc.; **character essay; characteristic radiation** the wavelength of radiation that characterises a particular substance; **characteristic X-rays** see under **X; character literature; character part** a stage or film rôle portraying an unusual or eccentric personality type; **character sketch** a short description of the main traits in a person's character. — **in character** in harmony with the part assumed, appropriate: in keeping with the person's usual conduct or attitudes: dressed for the part; **out of character** not in character, unlike what one would expect from the person concerned. [Fr. *caractère* — L. *charactēr* — Gr. *charaktēr*, from *charassein*, to cut, engrave.]

charade *shə-räd'*, in U.S. usu. *-rād'*, *n.* a species of riddle, the subject of which is a word proposed for solution from an enigmatical description of its component syllables and of the whole: an acted riddle in which the syllables and the whole are uttered or represented in successive scenes: a piece of ridiculous pretence. [Fr., perh. — Prov. *charrada*, chatter, or Sp. *charrada*, clownishness.]

Charadrius *kar-ad'ri-əs*, *n.* the plover genus, giving name to the family **Charad'riidae.** [Gr. *charadrios*, a bird, prob. the thick-knee.]

charas, churrus *chär'əs, chur'əs, ns.* the resinous exudation of hemp, a narcotic and intoxicant. [Hind.]

charcoal *chär'kōl*, *n.* charred wood, or coal made by charring wood: the carbonaceous residue of substances that have undergone smothered combustion. — *n.* and *adj.* (also **charcoal grey**) (of) a dark grey colour. — **charcoal burner** a person whose job is to burn wood to produce charcoal. [**char²**, **coal**.]

charcuterie *shär-küt-rē*, *n.* a pork-butcher's shop: a delicatessen, or the meats sold in it. [Fr.]

chard *chärd*, *n.* the edible leafstalk of cardoon, artichoke, or a variety (*Swiss chard*) of white beet. [L. *carduus*, thistle.]

chardonnay *shär-do-nā'*, *n.* a type of grape used in making dry white wine: the wine itself. [Fr.]

chare. See **char³**.

charet *char'et*, (*Spens.*) *n.* same as **chariot**.

charge *chärj*, *v.t.* to load, to put something into, to fill: to load heavily, burden: to fill completely: to cause to accumulate electricity: to lay a task upon, to enjoin, command: to deliver an official injunction, exhortation, or exposition to: to accuse: to place a bearing upon (with *with*; *her.*): to exact or demand from, to ask as the price: to set down as a liability against: to attack at a rush: to advance in accusation (that). — *v.i.* to make an attack. — *n.* that which is laid on: cost or price: the load of powder, fuel, etc., for a gun, furnace, etc.: an attack or onset: care, custody: the object of care: an accumulation of electricity: a command: an exhortation: an accusation (*law*): a device borne on a shield (*her.*): (in *pl.*) expenses. — *adj.* **charge'able** liable to be charged, imputable: blamable: burdensome (*B.*). — *n.* **charge'ableness.** — *adv.* **charge'ably.** — *adj.* **charge'ful** (*Spens., Shak.*) burdensome, or expensive. — *adj.* **charge'less.** — *n.* **char'ger** a flat dish capable of holding a large joint, a platter: a war-horse. — **charge account** an account in which goods obtained are entered to be paid for later; **charge'-hand, -man** the leader of a group of workmen; **charge'-house** (*Shak.*) a school; **charge'-nurse** a nurse in charge of a ward; **charge'-sheet** a police list of accused and the charges against them. — **bring a charge** to accuse (with *against; law*); **charge down** in rugby football, to run towards (a kicked ball) and block it; **give in charge** to hand over

to the police; **in charge** in control or authority, responsible (often with *of*); **take charge of** to assume the care of. [Fr. *charger* — L.L. *carricāre*, to load — L. *carrus*, a wagon; see **car**, **cargo**.]

chargé-d'affaires *shär'zhä-dä-fer'*, *n.* a diplomatic agent of lesser rank, accredited not to the sovereign but to the department for foreign affairs and holding his credentials from the minister: the person in charge for the time: — *pl.* **chargés-d'affaires** (*shär'zhä-*). [Fr.]

charily, chariness. See **chary**.

chariot *char'i-ət*, *n.* a pleasure or state car: a god's car: a car used in ancient warfare or racing: a light four-wheeled carriage with back seats and box. — *v.t.* (*arch.*) to carry in a chariot. — *v.i.* (*arch.*) to ride in a chariot. — *n.* **charioteer'** one who drives a chariot. — *v.t.* and *v.i.* (*arch.*) to drive or to ride in such. [Fr., dim. of *char*, a car.]

Charis *kar'is* (Gr. *hhär'is*), *n.* any one of the three **Char'ites** (*-tēz*, Gr. *-tes*), the Graces (Aglaia, Euphrosyne, Thalia), Greek goddesses of whatever imparts graciousness to life. — *ns.* **char'ism, charis'ma** a spiritual power given by God: personal quality or gift that enables an individual to impress and influence many of his fellows: a similar quality felt to reside in an office or position. — *adj.* **charismat'ic** of, pertaining to, or having a charism or charisma. — **charismatic movement** a non-denominational religious movement based on a belief in the divinely-inspired gifts of speaking in tongues (see **glossolalia**), healing, prophecy, etc. [Gr. *charis, -itos*, grace.]

charity *char'i-ti*, *n.* universal love (*N.T.*): the disposition to think favourably of others, and do them good: almsgiving: a use. non-profit-making foundation, institution, or cause, devoted to caring for those in need of help, etc.: (in *pl.*) affections. — *adj.* **char'itable** of or relating to, showing, inspired by charity: (of an institution, etc.) having the status of, being in the nature of, a charity. — *n.* **char'itableness.** — *adv.* **char'itably.** — **char'ity-boy', -girl'** a pupil in a **char'ity-school,** a school for the poor supported by endowments or gifts. — **charity begins at home** usually an excuse for not allowing it to get abroad; **cold as charity** see **cold.** [Fr. *charité* — L. *cāritās, -ātis* — *cārus*, dear.]

charivari *shär-i-vär'i*, *n.* a cacophonous mock serenade, rough music, e.g. with kettles, pans, lids, etc.: cacophony of sound. [Fr., — L.L. *caribaria*, a headache.]

chark *chärk*, *v.t.* to burn to charcoal. — *n.* charcoal, coke. [**charcoal**.]

charlady. See **char³**.

charlatan *shär'lə-tən*, *n.* a mere talking pretender, esp. one who claims to have medical knowedge: a quack. — *adjs.* **charlatanic** (*-tan'ik*), **-al.** — *ns.* **char'latanism; char'latanry.** [Fr., — It. *ciarlatano* — *ciarlare*, to chatter; imit.]

Charles's wain *chärlz'iz wān*, the seven bright stars in the Plough. [O.E. *Carles wægn*, Carl being Charlemagne.]

Charleston *chärls'tən*, *n.* a 20th-century dance characterised by spasmodic knee action. [*Charleston* in South Carolina.]

Charley, Charlie (also without *cap.*), *chär'li*, *n.* a nightwatchman (*obs.*): the small triangular beard familiar in the portraits of *Charles* I: a small moustache, resembling that worn by *Charlie* Chaplin: a credulous person: an inefficient, forceless person, a fool (often in the phrase *a proper Charlie*): the fox. — **Char'ley-pitch'er** (*slang*) a thimble-rigger. [From the name *Charles*.]

charlock *chär'lək*, *n.* wild mustard, a common yellow-flowered cornfield weed. [O.E. *cerlic*.]

charlotte *shär'lət*, *n.* a dish of cooked apple or the like, covered with crumbs of toast: a kind of tart containing fruit. — **charlotte russe** (*rüs*) a custard or cream enclosed in a kind of sponge-cake. [From the name *Charlotte*.]

charm¹ *chärm*, *n.* a spell: something thought to possess occult power, as an amulet, a metrical form of words, etc.: an amulet, etc.: a trinket: power of fascination: attractiveness: (in *pl.*) personal attractions: that which can please irresistibly: a song (*Spens.*): in particle physics, (the quantum number used to account for) the unusual properties and behaviour of certain elementary particles. — *v.t.* to influence by a charm: to subdue by secret influence: to enchant: to delight: to allure: to tune or play. — *adj.* **charmed** bewitched: delighted: protected as by a special charm: in particle physics, having charm. — *n.* **charm′er**. — *adjs.* **charm′ful** abounding in charms; **charm′ing** highly pleasing: delightful: fascinating. — *adv.* **charm′ingly**. — *adj.* **charm′less** wanting or destitute of charms. — *adv.* **charm′lessly**. [Fr. *charme* — L. *carmen*, a song.]

charm². Same as **chirm**.

charmeuse *shär′mõõz*, Fr. *shar-mœz*, *n.* a soft satin material made originally of silk, but now also of synthetic fibres. [Originally a tradename.]

charneco *chär′ni-kō*, (*Shak.*) *n.* a kind of sweet wine. [Prob. from a village near Lisbon.]

charnel *chär′nəl, n.* (*obs.*) a burial place. — *adj.* sepulchral: death-like. — **char′nel-house** a place where the bones thrown up by grave-diggers are put (also *fig.*). [O.Fr. *charnel* — L.L. *carnāle* — L. *carnālis* — *carō, carnis*, flesh.]

Charolais *shar′ō-lā, n.* a breed of cattle named after an old district of France (Charolais) of which Charolles was the capital.

Charon *kā′rən, n.* in Greek mythology, the ferryman who rowed the shades of the dead across the river Styx in the lower world: a ferryman. [Gr. *Charōn*.]

charoset(h). See **haroset(h).**

charpie *shär′pē*, or *-pē′, n.* lint shredded down to form a soft material for dressing wounds. [O.Fr. *charpir* — L. *carpĕre*, to pluck.]

charpoy *chär′poi, n.* the common Indian bedstead, sometimes handsomely wrought and painted. [Hind. *chārpāī* — Pers. *chahār-pāī*, four feet.]

charqui *chär′kē, n.* beef cut into long strips and dried in the sun — jerked beef. [Quechua.]

charr. Same as **char¹**.

chart *chart, n.* a marine or hydrographical map, exhibiting part of a sea or other water, with the islands, contiguous coasts, soundings, currents, etc.: an outline-map, curve, or a tabular statement giving information of any kind: (usu. in *pl.*) the lists of the ten, twenty, etc. most popular records, i.e. those which have sold the most copies, each week. — *v.t.* to map. — *ns.* **chart′ist** one who makes and/or studies charts of past performances, esp. of stocks and shares, with a view to forecasting future trends; **chart′ism**. — *adj.* **chart′less**. — *adj.* **chart′-busting** (*slang*; esp. of records) very successful. — **chart′-buster**; **chart′house**, **chart′=room** the room in a ship where charts are kept. [O.Fr. *charte* — L. *c(h)arta*, a paper — Gr. *chartēs*.]

charta, carta *kär′tə, n.* a charter. — *adj.* **chartā′ceous** papery. [L. *c(h)arta* — Gr. *chartēs*, a sheet of paper.]

charter *chärt′ər, n.* any formal writing in evidence of a grant, contract, or other transactions, conferring or confirming titles, rights, or privileges, or the like: the formal deed by which a sovereign guarantees the rights and privileges of his subjects: a document creating a borough or other corporation: any instrument by which powers and privileges are conferred by the state on a body of persons for a special object: a patent: grant: allowance: immunity. — *v.t.* to establish by charter: to let or hire, as a ship, on contract. — *adj.* hired, as *charter plane*: made in a hired aeroplane, as *charter flight*. — *n.* **chart′erer**. — *adj.* **chart′ered** granted or protected by a charter: privileged: licensed: hired by contract. — **chart′er-chest** a box in which charters are preserved; **chartered accountant, engineer, surveyor,** etc. one qualified under the regulations of the relevant institute or professional body which has a royal charter; **chartered company** a trading company acting under a charter from the crown; **chart′er-hand′**

court-hand; **chart′er-may′or** the mayor of a borough at the time of its granting its charter; **char′ter-mem′ber** an original member of an incorporation; **chart′erparty** see separate entry below. [O.Fr. *chartre* — L. *cartula*, *c(h)arta* — Gr. *chartēs*, a sheet of paper.]

Charterhouse *chärt′ər-hows, n.* a Carthusian monastery: the famous hospital and school instituted in London in 1611, on the site of a Carthusian monastery. — *n.* **Chartreuse** (*shär-trœz′*) a Carthusian monastery, esp. the original one, La Grande Chartreuse near Grenoble in France: (sometimes without *cap.*) a famous liqueur, usu. green, or yellow, long manufactured there by the monks from aromatic herbs and brandy: (sometimes without *cap.*) a kind of enamelled pottery: (without *cap.*) a mould of rice or blancmange enclosing some other food: (without *cap.*) a pale greenish colour. — *adj.* of this colour. — *n.* **Chartreux** (*shär-trœ*) a Carthusian: the Charterhouse School. [See **Carthusian.**]

charterparty *chärt′ər-pär-ti, n.* the common written form in which the contract of affreightment is expressed — viz. the hiring of the whole or part of a ship for the conveyance of goods. — Also **charter party**. [Fr. *charte partie*, lit. a divided charter, as the practice was to divide it in two and give a half to each person — L. *c(h)arta partīta*; see **charta.**]

Chartism *chärt′izm, n.* a movement in Great Britain for the extension of political power to the working-classes — its programme, the People's Charter (1838), since achieved, except annual parliaments. — *n.* **Chart′ist**. — Also *adj.* [See **charta.**]

chartist, chartism. See **chart.**

chartography *kär-tog′rə-fi.* Same as **cartography.**

Chartreuse, Chartreux. See **Charterhouse.**

chartulary *kär′tū-lər-i.* Same as **cartulary.**

charwoman. See **char³.**

chary *chā′ri, adj.* fastidious, shy (*Shak.*): precious (*obs.*): careful (of) (*arch.*): cautious: wary (of doing, saying, giving, etc.). — *adv.* **chār′ily**. — *n.* **chār′iness**. [O.E. *cearig* — *cearu*, care.]

Charybdis *kə-rib′dis, n.* in the Odyssey a dangerous monster that dwelt under a rock opposite to Scylla, and three times a day swallowed and threw up the waters of the sea, later a current or a whirlpool on the Sicilian side of the Straits of Messina — with Scylla providing a proverbial alternative of evil or disaster.

chase¹ (*obs.* **chace**) *chās, v.t.* to pursue: to hunt: to seek: to drive away: to put to flight: to follow with a chaser or chasse. — *v.i.* (*coll.*) to hurry (about, around, after). — *n.* pursuit: a hunting: that which is hunted: an unenclosed game preserve: the second impact of an unreturned ball, for which the player scored unless his opponent bettered it (and scored) by a like impact nearer the end wall (*real tennis*). — *n.* **chas′er** a pursuer: a hunter: a horse for steeplechasing: an aeroplane for pursuing hostile aircraft: a woman over-assiduous in pursuit of men: a cooling drink, or sometimes food, after spirits: a chasse. — **chase′-port** the porthole at bow or stern (through which a gun is fired during pursuit). — **beasts of chase** properly the buck, doe, fox, marten, and roe: wild beasts that are hunted generally; **chase rainbows** see **rainbow-chaser** under **rain¹**; **give chase** to set off in pursuit; **go and chase yourself** (*slang*) go away, clear out; **wild-goose chase** a chase hither and thither: any foolish or profitless pursuit of the unattainable. [O.Fr. *chacier, chasser* — L. *captāre*, freq. of *capĕre*, to take.]

chase² *chās, v.t.* to enchase, to decorate by engraving. — *ns.* **chās′er** one who practises chasing: a tool for chasing; **chās′ing** the art of engraving on the outside of raised metal work: the art of cutting the threads of screws. [Short for **enchase.**]

chase³ *chās, n.* a case or frame for holding types: a groove. [Fr. *châsse*, a setting — L. *capsa*, a chest. See **case¹**.]

Chasid, Chasidic, etc. See **Hasid.**

chasm *kaz′əm, n.* a yawning or gaping hollow: a gap or opening: a void space. — *adjs.* **chas′med; chasmic**

(*kaz'mik*); **chas'my**. [Gr. *chasma*, from *chainein*, to gape; cf. **chaos**.]

chasmogamy *kaz-mog'ə-mi*, (*bot*.) *n*. the condition of having open, not cleistogamic, flowers, allowing cross-fertilisation. — *adj*. **chasmogamic** (*-mō-gam'ik*). [Gr. *chasma*, a gape, *gameein*, to marry.]

chasse *shas*, *n*. a dram or liqueur taken after coffee. — Also **chasse-café'**. [Fr. *chasser*, to chase.]

chassé *shas'ā*, *n*. a gliding step in dancing. — *v.i.* to make such a step. — *v.t.* (*slang*) to dismiss. — **cha'ssé-croi'sé** (*-krwä'zā*) a dance movement in which partners change places by means of a chassé. [Fr.]

Chassepot *shas'pō*, *n*. a rifle adopted by the French army in 1866. [From the inventor's name.]

chasseur *shas-œr'*, *n*. a hunter or huntsman: one of a select body of French light infantry or cavalry: a liveried attendant. [Fr., — *chasser*, to hunt; see **chase**[1].]

Chassid, Chassidic, etc. See **Hasid**.

chassis *shas'ē*, *-i*, *n*. the frame, wheels, and machinery of a motor-car: the framework of a radio, television, etc.: an aeroplane's landing-carriage: a casemate gun carriage: a frame, sash (*obs*.): — *pl*. **chassis** (*shas'ēz*, *-iz*). [Fr. *chassis*, frame.]

chaste *chāst*, *adj*. sexually virtuous: modest: refined and pure in taste and style. — *adv*. **chaste'ly**. — *v.t.* **chasten** (*chās'n*) to free from faults by punishing: hence, to punish: to purify or refine: to restrain or moderate. — *p.adj*. **chās'tened** purified: modest: tempered. — *ns*. **chās'tener**; **chaste'ness**; **chās'tenment**. — *v.t.* **chastise** (*chas-tīz'*) to refine, purify, correct (*obs*.): to moderate, restrain (*arch*.): to inflict punishment upon for the purpose of correction: to reduce to order or to obedience. — *adj*. **chastis'able**. — *ns*. **chastisement** (*chas'tiz-mənt*); **chastity** (*chas'ti-ti*) sexual purity: virginity: refinement of style: moderation. — **chaste tree** agnus castus; **chastity belt** a device said to have been worn by e.g. wives of absent crusaders, to prevent their having sexual intercourse: a device made in modern times according to its supposed design. — Also *fig*. [O.Fr. *chaste* — L. *castus*, pure.]

chasuble *chaz'* or *chas'ū-bl*, *n*. a sleeveless vestment worn over the alb by the priest while celebrating mass. [Fr. — L.L. *casubula* — L. *casula*, dim. of L. *casa*, a hut.]

chat[1] *chat*, *v.i.* to talk easily or familiarly. — *v.t.* (often with *up*) to talk to lightly and informally but with a purpose, e.g. in order to cajole: — *pr.p.* **chatt'ing**; *pa.t.* and *pa.p.* **chatt'ed**. — *n*. familiar, easy talk. — *n*. **chatt'iness**. — *adj*. **chatt'y** given or inclined to chat: of the nature of chat. — **chat'-show** (*coll*.) a radio or television programme in which invited personalities talk informally with their host. — Also **talk'-show**. [From **chatter**.]

chat[2] *chat*, *n*. a genus (*Saxicola*) of small birds in the thrush family, including the stonechat and the whinchat. [From the sound of their voice.]

chat[3] *chat*, (*dial*.) *n*. a small potato of poor quality.

chat[4] *chat*, (*obs. slang* and *Austr. and N.Z. coll*.) *n*. a louse. — *adj*. **chatt'y** lousy, flea-infested: dirty (*Austr. and N.Z. coll*.). [Orig. cant *chat(t)s*, lice.]

château *shä'tō*, *n*. a castle: a great country-seat, esp. in France: a vineyard estate around a castle, house, etc., esp. in Bordeaux (common in names of wines associated with such, e.g. Château Lafite, Château Margaux): — *pl*. **chât'eaux** (*-tōz*). — *ns*. **châtelain** (*shat'ə-lē*) a castellan; **chât'elaine** (*-len*) a female castellan: an ornamental bunch of short chains bearing keys, scissors, etc., attached to the waist-belt: a similar thing in miniature attached to the watch-chain. — **château bottled** bottled on the estate in which it has been produced; **châteaux en Espagne** (*shä-tō-zä-nes-päny'*) (Fr.) castles in Spain, castles in the air. [Fr. *château* (O.Fr. *chastel*) — L. *castellum*, dim. of *castrum*, a fort.]

Chateaubriand (also without *cap*.) *shä-tō-brē-ä'*, *n*. a grilled thick fillet steak. [François René, Vicomte de *Chateaubriand*, 1768–1848, French author and statesman.]

chaton *shä-tō'*, *n*. the head of a finger-ring. [Fr.]

chatoyant *shat-wä-yä*, *shat-oi'ənt*, *adj*. with a changing lustre, like a cat's eye in the dark: iridescent. — *n*. **chatoyance** (*shat-wä-yäs*, *shat-oi'ons*). [Fr.]

chatta *chät'ä*, *n*. an umbrella. [Hind.]

chattel *chat'l*, *n*. any kind of property which is not freehold, distinguished further into *chattels-real* and *chattels-personal*, the latter being mere personal movables — plate, cattle, and the like — the former including leasehold interests. — **goods and chattels** all corporeal movables. [O.Fr. *chatel* — L.L. *captāle* — L. *capitāle*, etc., property, goods.]

chatter *chat'ər*, *v.i.* to talk idly or rapidly: (of birds) to utter a succession of rapid short notes: to sound as the teeth when one shivers. — *n*. noise like that made by a magpie, or by the striking together of the teeth: idle talk. — *ns*. **chatt'erer** one that chatters: an idle talker: a name applied to two families of birds, the waxwings and the cotingas; **chatt'ering**. — **chatt'erbox** one who talks or chatters incessantly. [From the sound.]

chatty[1]. See **chat**[1].

chatty[2] *chat'i*, (*India*) *n*. a usu. earthen water-pot. [Hindi *chātī* — Dravidian.]

chatty[3]. See **chat**[4].

Chaucerian *chö-sē'ri-ən*, *adj*. like or pertaining to Chaucer. — *n*. a student or follower of Chaucer. — *n*. **Chau'cerism** anything characteristic of Chaucer.

chaudfroid *shō-frwä*, *n*. a jellied sauce, or a dish, e.g. of chicken, including it. [Fr., (*lit*.) hot-cold.]

chaud-mellé *shōd-mel'ā*, (*Scots law*) *n*. a fight arising in the heat of passion: the killing of a man in such a fight. [O.Fr. *chaude-mellee*, hot fight; see **mêlée**.]

chaufe, chauff (*Spens*.) *chöf*. Forms of **chafe**.

chauffer *chö'fər*, *n*. a metal box for holding fire, a portable furnace or stove. [See **chafer** under **chafe**.]

chauffeur *shō'fər*, *-fœr'*, *n*. one employed to drive a motor-car: — *fem*. **chauffeuse** (*-føz'*). — *v.i.* and *v.t.* to drive, act as a chauffeur (for): — (*facet*., of women) **chauffeuse'**. [Fr., stoker.]

chaulmoogra, chaulmugra *chöl-mōō'grə*, *n*. a name for various Indian trees of the family Flacourtiaceae, yielding **chaulmoogra oil**, used, esp. formerly, in the treatment of leprosy. [Beng.]

chaumer *chö'mər*, (*Scot*.) *n*. formerly, a room or building in which male farm-workers sleep. [**chamber**.]

chaunce, chaunge. Old forms of **chance, change**.

chaunt(er), chauntress, chauntry. See **chant**.

chausses *shōs*, or *shō'zis*, *n.pl*. any closely fitting covering for the legs, hose generally: the defence-pieces for the legs in ancient armour. — *n*. **chaussure** (*-ür'*) a general name for boots and shoes. [O.Fr. *chauces* — L. *calcia*, hose.]

Chautauqua *shə-tök'wə*, *n*. a village and lake in U.S. where summer educational meetings were instituted in the late 19th cent.: (also without *cap*.) a meeting of this type, with lectures, etc. — *adj*. **Chautauquan** (*shə-tö'kwən*) pertaining to a system of instruction for adults by home reading and study under guidance, evolved from the *Chautauqua* (New York State) Literary and Scientific Circle, organised in 1878.

chauvinism *shō'vin-izm*, *n*. an absurdly extravagant pride in one's country, with a corresponding contempt for foreign nations: extravagant attachment to any group, place, cause, etc. — *ns*. **chau'vin; chau'vinist**. — *adjs*. **chau'vinist; chauvinist'ic**. [From Nicolas *Chauvin*, an ardent veteran of Napoleon's, who figures in Cogniard's *La Cocarde tricolore*.]

chave. See **ch**.

chavender *chav'ən-dər*, *n*. the chub. [Cf. **cheven**.]

chaw[1] *chö*, (*Spens*.) *n*. a jaw. [See **jaw**[1].]

chaw[2] *chö*, *v.t.* to chew (still used of tobacco and in *dial*.). — *n*. a quantity for chewing. — **chaw'-bā'con** a country clown, a rustic fellow. — **chawed up** (*dial*. or *old U.S. slang*) destroyed: defeated: crushed: reprimanded. [By-form of **chew**.]

chawdron *chö'drən*, (*Shak*.) *n*. the entrails of an animal. [O.Fr. *chaudun*.]

chay[1]. A vulgar form of **chaise**.

chay² *chī, chā,* **chaya** *chī'ə,* **shaya** *shī'ə, ns.* an Indian plant (Oldenlandia) of the madder family whose root (**chay**= **root,** etc.) yields a red dye.   [Cf. Tamil *saya*.]

chayote *chä-yō'tē, chī-ō'tē, n.* a tropical American cucurbitaceous plant (*Sechium edule*): its edible fruit. — Also **chō'chō.**   [Sp. — Nahuatl *chayotli*.]

che *chə,* (*Shak.*) *pron.* a S.W. dialect form of I.   [O.E. *ic*; cf. **ch.**]

cheap *chēp, n.* (*obs.*) bargain, buyer's advantage. — *adj.* (from the phrase *good cheap*) low in price or cost: charging low prices: of a low price in relation to the value: easily obtained: of small value, or so reckoned: paltry: inferior: vulgar. — Also *adv.* — *v.t.* **cheap'en** to ask the price of (*arch.*): to make cheap, to lower the price of: to lower the reputation of: to beat down the price of. — *ns.* **cheap'ener; cheap'ie, -y** (*coll.*) somethng which is low in price or cost. — Also *adj.* — *adv.* **cheap'ly.** — *n.* **cheap'ness.** — *adj.* **cheap'o** (*coll.*; *usu. derog.*) cheap, esp. with connotations of inferiority or tawdriness. — **cheap'-jack** (*orig.* **cheap Jack** or **John**) a travelling hawker who professes to give great bargains. — *adj.* inferior, of bad quality. — **cheap labour** labour paid at a poor rate; **cheap'skate** (*slang*) a miserly or despicable person. — **cheap and nasty** offensively inferior and of low value; **cheap of** (*Scot.*) having got off lightly with: served right; **dirt cheap** ridiculously cheap; **feel cheap** to have a sense of inferiority and humiliation; **on the cheap** cheap or cheaply.   [O.E. *cēap,* price, a bargain, *ceapian*; O.N. *kaupa,* Ger. *kaufen,* to buy.]

cheat¹ *chēt, n.* an escheat, a forfeit (*obs.*): a piece of plunder, a stolen thing (*obs.*): a thing in general, esp. the gallows (*thieves' cant*; see also **nubbing-cheat**): a fraud: a deception: a card-game in which deception is allowed: one who cheats. — *v.t.* to deceive, defraud, impose upon. — *v.i.* to practise deceit. — *ns.* **cheat'er** one who cheats: an officer who collected the fines to be paid into the Exchequer (*Shak.*): (in *pl.*) spectacles (*U.S. slang*): (in *pl.*) falsies (*slang*); **cheat'ery** (*coll.*) cheating. — **cheat on** (*coll.*) to deceive, esp. to be unfaithful to one's wife, husband, lover, etc.; **put a cheat upon** to deceive; **tame cheater** (*Shak.*) a decoy.   [**escheat.**]

cheat² *chēt,* **cheat bread** *chēt'-bred,* (*obs.*) *ns.* bread of a lower quality than manchet, made of a somewhat coarser wheat flour.   [Orig. uncertain.]

chechako, chechaqua, chechaquo. Same as **cheechako.**

chéchia *shā'shya, n.* a cylindrical skull-cap, worn by Arabs and adopted by French troops in Africa.   [Fr., — Berber *tashashit,* pl. *tishushai,* skull-cap.]

check *chek, v.t.* to bring to a stop: to restrain or hinder: to rebuke: to control by comparison: to verify: to punch (as a ticket): to nip, pinch, crush, as by biting or shutting (*Scot.* also **chack**): to deposit or receive in exchange for a number (*U.S.*): to send (baggage) on a passenger's ticket (*U.S.*): to place in check at chess: to mark with a pattern of crossing lines. — *v.i.* to forsake the quarry for some other bird (with *at*; *falconry*): to come to a stop: to make investigations. — *n.* a position in chess when one party obliges the other either to move or guard his king: anything that checks: a sudden stop, repulse, or rebuff: restraint: control: a rebuke (*B., Shak.*): a mark put against items in a list: an order for money (usually written **cheque** except in U.S.): a means of verification or testing: any counter-register used as security, a counterfoil: a token, given for example to a person leaving his seat in a theatre with the intention of returning (see also **raincheck** under **rain¹**): a restaurant bill: a counter used in games at cards (hence *pass in one's checks =* to die): a mechanism that holds a piano hammer after striking: a pattern of cross lines forming small squares, as in a chessboard: any fabric woven with such a pattern. — *adj.* divided into small squares by crossing lines. — *n.* **check'er** one who hinders, rebukes, or scrutinises: (in *pl.*; *U.S.*) the game of draughts. — **check'-ac'tion** piano action with checks; **check'-book** (*U.S.*) a cheque-book; **check'-clerk** a clerk

who checks accounts, etc.; **check digit** (*comput.*) a digit carried in computer processes to discover errors, check accuracy, etc.; **checked square** a square in a crossword that belongs to the solution of two clues; **check'er= board** a checked board on which checkers or draughts is played; **check'-in** see **check in** below; **check'-key** a latch-key; **check'list** a list for verification purposes: a comprehensive list: an inventory; **check'mate** in chess, a check given to the adversary's king when in a position in which it can neither be protected nor moved out of check, so that the game is finished: a complete check: defeat: overthrow. — *v.t.* in chess, to put in checkmate: to defeat. — **check'-off** see **check off** below; **check'-out** the cash-desk where one pays for goods bought in a supermarket, etc.: the act of checking out (see below); **check'point** a place where an official check of documents, etc. is made; **check'-rein** a coupling rein, a strap hindering a horse from lowering its head; **check'room, check'ing-room** (*U.S.*) a cloakroom, luggage-room or room where goods are checked; **check'-string** a string by which the occupant of a carriage may attract the driver's notice; **check'-tak'er** one who takes tickets; **check'-till** a till that records sums received; **check'-up** a testing scrutiny: one of a series of regular medical examinations; **check'-weigh'er, -weigh'man** one who on the part of the men checks the weight of coal sent up to the pit-mouth. — **check in, out** to record one's arrival or departure from work: to perform the necessary business at a hotel office, airport, etc., on arriving, or leaving (*ns.* **check'-in, check'-out**); **check off** to mark off on a list as having arrived, been completed, etc.: to deduct (trade union dues) from a worker's pay before he or she receives it (*U.S.*; *n.* **check'-off**); **check out** (*coll.*) to test, examine, investigate (*n.* **check'-out**): see also at **check in; check up** to investigate: to examine and test (often with *on*). — **hold, keep, in check** to restrain, keep back.   [O.Fr. *eschec, eschac,* through Ar. from Pers. *shāh,* king, **checkmate** being O.Fr. *eschec mat* — Ar. *shāh māt(a),* the king is dead.]

checker. See **check;** also under **cheque.**

checker-berry *chek'ər-ber-i, n.* the American winter-green (*Gaultheria*).

checklaton, s(c)hecklaton *chek-, shek-lat'ən, ns.* understood and explained by Spenser as gilded leather used for making embroidered jacks.   [**ciclaton,** perh. with association with **latten.**]

checky. See **cheque.**

Cheddar *ched'ər, n.* a kind of cheese first made at *Cheddar* in Somerset. — **Cheddar pink** a species of pink (*Dianthus gratianopolitanus*) found on the limestone cliffs at Cheddar.

cheechako *chē-chä'kō,* (*Canada* and *Alaska*) *n.* a tenderfoot: — *pl.* **cheecha'kos, -koes.** — Also **checha'ko, cheechal'ko, chechaqua, checha'quo.**   [Chinook jargon, new-come.]

chee-chee *chē'chē, n.* in India, a Eurasian: affected Eurasian English. — Also *adj.* — Also **chi'-chi.**   [Perh. Hind. *chī-chī,* dirt, fie!]

cheek *chēk, n.* the side of the face below the eye, the fleshy lateral wall of the mouth: effrontery, impudence (*coll.*): a side-post of a door, window, etc.: the cheek strap of a horse's bridle: the ring at the end of a bit: anything arranged in lateral pairs: a buttock (*coll.*). — *v.t.* (*coll.*) to address insolently. — *adv.* **cheek'ily.** — *adj.* **cheek'y** (*coll.*) rude: saucy. — **cheek'-bone** the bone above the cheek; **cheek'-piece** the part of a helmet, bridle, etc. that covers the cheek; **cheek'-pouch** a dilatation of the cheek, forming a bag, as in monkeys, etc.; **cheek'-tooth** a molar tooth. — **cheek by jowl** side by side.   [O.E. *cēce, cēace,* cheek, jaw; cf. Du. *kaak*.]

cheep *chēp, v.i.* to chirp, as a young bird. — *n.* a sound of cheeping. — *n.* **cheep'er** a young bird, esp. of game.   [Imit.]

cheer *chēr, n.* face (*arch.*): disposition, frame of mind (with *good,* etc.): joy: a shout of approval or welcome: kind treatment (*obs.*): entertainment: fare, food. — *v.t.* to comfort: to encourage: to applaud: to inspirit. —

v.i. to take comfort (*obs.*): to be of good cheer (*obs.*): to shout encouragement or applause. — *n.* **cheer'er.** — *adj.* **cheer'ful** in, of, promoting, or accompanied by good spirits. — *adv.* **cheer'fully.** — *n.* **cheer'fulness.** — *adv.* **cheer'ily.** — *n.* **cheer'iness.** — *interjs.* **cheerio',** **cheer'o** a bright informal goodbye: — *pl.* **cheerios',** **-ros.** — *n.* **cheer'ishness** (*Milton*) cheerfulness. — *adjs.* **cheer'less** comfortless. — *n.* **cheer'lessness.** — *adj.* **cheer'ly** (*arch.*) cheerful. — *adv.* (*arch.*) in a cheery manner: heartily. — *interj.* **cheers!** (*coll.*) good health! (used when drinking a toast): thank you!: cheerio, goodbye! — *adj.* **cheer'y** cheerful: promoting cheerfulness. — **cheer'-leader** (esp. *U.S.*) one who directs organised cheering, as at team games. — **cheer up** (*coll.*) to make, or become, more cheerful; **what cheer?** (*arch.*) how are you? [O.Fr. *chiere*, face — L.L. *cara*, the face.]

cheerio¹. See **cheer.**

cheerio² *chē'ri ō', n.* (*Austr.* and *N.Z.*) a small frankfurter.

cheese¹ *chēz, n.* a wholesome article of food, made from the curd of milk coagulated by rennet, separated from the whey, and pressed into a solid mass: a compressed cake of various nature: the receptacle of a thistle-head: the flattened cheese-shaped bowl used in skittles. — *n.* **chees'iness.** — *adj.* **chees'y** having the nature of cheese. — **cheese'-board** a flat wooden board on which cheese is served; **cheese'burger** a hamburger cooked with cheese on top of it; **cheese'cake** a cup of pastry containing orig. cheese, later a curd of various types: a kind of cake having a base of pastry or biscuit crumbs, with a filling of cream cheese, sugar, eggs, flavouring, etc.: a pin-up, esp. of a lightly clad woman (*slang*): female shapely charms (*slang*): a show of leg (*slang*); **cheese'cloth** a loose-woven cloth suitable for pressing cheeses: a stronger type of loosely-woven cotton cloth used for making shirts, etc.; **cheese'-cutter** a square-peaked cap; **cheese'-hopper** the larva of a small fly, remarkable for its leaping power, found in cheese; **cheese'-mite** a very small arachnid that breeds in cheese; **cheese'-monger** a dealer in cheese; **cheese'- paring** paring, or rind, of cheese (*Shak.*): a very thin man: parsimony. — *adj.* mean and parsimonious. — **cheese'-press** a machine in which curds for cheese are pressed; **cheese'-renn'et** the plant lady's bedstraw, said to have been used as rennet in curdling milk; **cheese straw** a long thin biscuit flavoured with cheese; **cheese'- taster** a scoop for taking a sample from the inside of a cheese; **cheese'-vat** a vat or wooden case in which curds are pressed; **cheese'wire** a thin wire used for cutting cheese; **cheese'-wring** a cheese-press. — **green cheese** cheese not yet dried; **hard cheese** (*slang*) hard luck; **make cheeses** (*arch.*) to whirl round and then sink down suddenly so as to make the skirt stand out like a cheese. [O.E. *cēse, cȳse,* curdled milk (cf. Ger. *Käse,* cheese) — L. *cāseus.*]

cheese² *chēz, n.* the correct thing (*obs. slang*): anything of excellent quality. — **big cheese** (*slang*) a person of importance. [Prob. Pers. and Hindi *chīz,* thing.]

cheese³ *chēz, v.t.* (*slang*) in the phrases **cheese it** to stop, have done, run off; **cheesed off** (also **cheesed**) fed up.

cheetah *chē'tə, n.* an Eastern animal like the leopard, used in hunting. [Hindi *cītā* — Sans. *citraka, citrakāya,* having a speckled body.]

cheewink. Same as **chewink.**

chef *shef, n.* a usu. male cook, esp. a head-cook (in full **chef de cuisine** (*də kwē-zēn*) the head of a kitchen): a reliquary in the shape of a head. — **chef d'œuvre** (*shā-dœ-vr'*) a masterpiece: — *pl.* **chefs d'œuvre** (*shā-*). [Fr. head, chief; see **chief.**]

cheiro- *kī'rō-, kī-ro'-,* (see also **chiro-**) in composition, hand. — *ns.* **cheirog'nomy, chirog'nomy** (Gr. *gnōmē,* understanding) palmistry; **chi'rograph** a written or signed document; **ch(e)irog'rapher** (*obs.*) an official of the Court of Common Pleas; **ch(e)irog'raphist** an expert in handwriting: a palmist (*Pope*); **ch(e)irog'- raphy** handwriting, penmanship; **ch(e)irol'ogist**; **ch(e)irol'ogy** gesture-language: the study of the hand;

ch(e)i'rōmancy (*-man-si*) fortune-telling by the hand (Gr. *manteiā,* divination). — *adjs.* **ch(e)irōmant'ic, -al.** — *n.* **ch(e)iron'omer** (Gr. *nomos,* law) a gesticulator. — *adj.* **ch(e)irōnom'ic.** — *ns.* **ch(e)iron'omy** the art of gesticulation or of pantomime; **ch(e)irop'teran** (Gr. *pteron,* wing) a member of the **Ch(e)irop'tera,** the order of bats. — *adjs.* **ch(e)iropteroph'ilous** (Gr. *phileein,* to love) pollinated by bats; **ch(e)irop'terous.** — *n.* **Cheirōthē'rium** (Gr. *thērion,* beast) a Triassic laby- rinthodont with hand-like footprints. [Gr. *cheir,* hand.]

cheka *chā'kə, n.* the Russian secret police of 1917–1922. — *n.* **chek'ist** a member of the cheka. [Russ. *che ka,* names of the initial letters of the words for extra- ordinary commission.]

Chekhovian *che-kō'vi-ən, adj.* pertaining to the Russian writer Anton *Chekhov* (1860–1904), or to (the style of) his stories and plays.

chela¹ *kē'lə, n.* the prehensile claw of an arthropod: — *pl.* **chē'lae** (*-ē*). — *adj.* **chē'late.** — *n.* a co-ordination compound (e.g. haemoglobin) in which a central metallic ion is attached to an organic molecule at two or more positions. — *v.i.* to form a chelate. — *ns.* **chēlā'tion; chēlā'tor; Chē'lifer** the book-scorpion. — *adj.* **chēlif'erous** having a chela or chelae. — *n.* **chē'liped** one of the pair of legs carrying the chelae. — **chelation therapy** the treatment of heavy metal (e.g. lead) poison- ing or certain other diseases by substances (**chelating agents**) which combine chemically with the toxic sub- stances and render them harmless. [Latinised from Gr. *chēlē.*]

chela² *chā'lə, n.* a novice in Buddhism: a disciple of a religious teacher or leader. — *n.* **che'laship.** [Hindi *celā,* servant, disciple.]

chelicera *kē-lis'ə-rə, n.* a biting appendage in Arachnida: — *pl.* **chēlic'erae** (*-rē*). [Gr. *chēlē,* a crab's claw, *keras,* horn.]

Chelifer, cheliferous, cheliped. See **chela¹.**

Chellean *shel'i-ən, adj.* belonging to an early Palaeolithic culture, older than Acheulean. [*Chelles,* near Paris, where flints of this stage are found.]

cheloid. See **keloid.**

Chelonia *ki-lō'ni-ə, n.* an order of reptiles with horny shell and horny beak, tortoises and turtles. — *adj.* and *n.* **chelō'nian.** [Gr. *chelōnē,* a tortoise.]

Chelsea *chel'sē, n.* a district of London formerly noted as an artists' quarter. — **Chelsea bun** a rolled bun filled with currants and raisins; **Chelsea pensioner** an elderly, often disabled, ex-soldier, connected with the Chelsea Royal Hospital; **Chelsea ware** a variety of china made in the 18th century.

chemic, etc. See under **chemistry.**

chemin de fer *shə-mē də fer', n.* a variety of baccarat (familiarly **chemmy** *shem'i*). [Fr. railway.]

chemise *shə-mēz', n.* a woman's shirt, a smock or straight dress. — *n.* **chemisette'** a kind of bodice worn by women: lace or muslin filling up the open front of a woman's dress. [Fr. *chemise* — L.L. *camisia,* a nightgown, surplice.]

chemistry *kem'is-tri,* formerly **chymistry** *kim'is-tri, n.* the science of the properties of substances elementary and compound, and the laws of their combination and action one upon another. — *adjs.* **chemiat'ric** iatro- chemical; **chem'ic** alchemical (*obs.*): iatrochemical (*obs.*): chemical. — *n.* an alchemist or a chemist (*obs.*): bleaching powder (*arch.*). — *v.t.* to treat with bleaching powder: — *pr.p.* **chem'icking;** *pa.t.* and *pa.p.* **chem'- icked.** — *adj.* **chem'ical** alchemical (*obs.*): iatrochemical (*obs.*): relating to chemistry: versed in or studying chemistry. — *n.* a substance obtained by chemical means or used in chemical operations. — *adv.* **chem'- ically.** — *ns.* **chemiluminesc'ence** luminescence arising from chemical processes, e.g. that of the glow-worm; **chem'ism** chemical action; **chem'ist** an alchemist (*obs.*): one skilled in chemistry: a manufacturer or dealer in chemicals and drugs: a pharmacist; **chem'itype** any chemical process for obtaining impressions from an engraving; **chem'itȳpy;** (the following words in **chemo-** also *kē-*, esp. in U.S.) **chemoattrac'tant** a chemical which provokes a chemotactic movement of e.g. cells or bacteria towards its area of highest concentration; **chem'ōnasty** nastic movement under diffuse chemical stimulus; **chemōpsychī'atry** treatment of mental illness by drugs. — *adjs.* **chemōpsychīat'ric; chemōrecep'tive.** — *ns.* **chemōreceptiv'ity; chemōrecep'tion; chemōrecep'tor** a sensory nerve-ending, receiving a chemical stimulus; **chem'ōstat** an apparatus for growth of bacteria, fungi, tissue, etc.; **chemōsyn'thesis** (*bot.*) the formation of organic material by some bacteria by means of energy derived from chemical changes. — *adj.* **chemōtac'tic** pertaining to chemotaxis. — *ns.* **chemōtax'is** movement of a whole organism in a definite direction in response to chemical stimulus; **chemōtherapeu'tics** (*n. sing.*), more commonly **chemōther'apy** treatment of infectious diseases or cancer by means of chemical compounds which act against micro-organisms or cancerous tissue; **chemōt'ropism** (*bot.*) orientation by differential growth in response to chemical stimulus. — *adj.* **chemōtrop'ic.** — *n.* **chemurgy** (*kem'ər-ji*) a branch of applied chemistry concerned with the use of agricultural products, or other organic raw materials, for industry. — *adjs.* **chemur'gic, -al.** — **chemical affinity** the tendency to combine with one another exhibited by many substances, or the force by which the substances constituting a compound are held together; **chemical closet, toilet** a kind of toilet containing deodorising and liquefying chemicals, used when running water is not available; **chemical dependency** addiction to alcohol and/or drugs; **chemical engineering** design, construction, and operation of chemical plant and works, esp. in industrial chemistry; **chemical warfare** warfare involving the use of irritating or asphyxiating gases, oil flames, etc. — **chemist and druggist** one who has passed the lower, **pharmaceutical chemist** one who has passed the higher examinations, qualifying him to practise as a pharmacist. [See **alchemy.**]

chemmy. See **chemin de fer.**

chenar *chē-när', n.* the oriental plane (*Platanus orientalis*). [Pers. *chinār.*]

chenet *shə-ne,* (Fr.) *n.* an andiron.

chenille *shə-nēl', n.* a thick, velvety cord of silk or wool resembling a woolly caterpillar: a velvet-like material used for table-covers, etc. [Fr. *chenille,* caterpillar — L. *canicula,* a hairy little dog, *canis,* a dog.]

Chenopodium *ken-ō-pō'di-əm, n.* the goosefoot genus, giving name to the family **Chenopodiā'ceae,** akin to the pink family. — *adj.* **chenopodiā'ceous.** [Gr. *chēn,* goose, *pous, podos,* foot.]

cheong-sam *chong'sam', n.* a tight-fitting high-necked dress with slits at the sides. [Chin. (Cantonese), long dress.]

cheque, in U.S. **check,** *chek, n.* a counterfoil (*obs.*): a money order on a bank. — *n.* **cheq'uer** a chess-board, also a chess-man (*arch.*): alternation of colours, as on a chess-board (see also **checker**). — *v.t.* to mark in squares of different colours: to variegate: to interrupt. — *adjs.* **cheq'uered, check'ered** variegated, like a chessboard: varying in character: eventful, with alternations of good and bad fortune. — *adv.* **cheq'uerwise.** — *adj.* **cheq'uy, check'y** (*her.*) chequered. — **cheque'-book** a book of cheque forms; **cheque card** a card issued by a bank to a client, undertaking payment of cheques up to a certain limit; **chequered flag** the black and white flag shown to the winner and subsequent finishers in a motor race; **cheq'uer-work** any pattern having alternating squares of different colours. — **blank cheque** a cheque signed by the drawer without having the amount indicated: concession of power without limit (*fig.*); **cheque-book journalism** news, articles, etc., based on information bought, usu. at a high price; **crossed cheque** an ordinary cheque with two transverse lines drawn across it, which have the effect of making it payable only through a bank account. [See **check.**]

cher, *fem.* **chère,** *sher,* (Fr.) *adj.* dear.

cheralite *cher'ə-līt, n.* a radioactive mineral rich in thorium and uranium. [*Chera,* anc. name of Travancore, where discovered, Gr. *lithos,* a stone.]

cherchef't. A Miltonic spelling of **kerchiefed.**

cherimoya, cherimoyer *cher-i-moi'ə, -ər, ns.* a Peruvian fruit (*Anona cherimolia*) resembling the custard-apple. [Quechua.]

cherish *cher'ish, v.t.* to protect and treat with affection: to nurture, nurse: to entertain in the mind. — *adj.* **cher'ished** (of number plates) with a combination of letters and numbers specially chosen by the owner of the vehicle. — *n.* **cher'ishment.** [Fr. *chérir, chérissant* — *cher,* dear — L. *cārus.*]

Cherkess *chər-kes', n.* a Circassian: the Caucasian language of the Cherkesses: — *pl.* **-kesses.** [Russ.]

chernozem *chûr'nō-zem, n.* a very fertile soil of sub-humid steppe, consisting of a dark topsoil over a lighter calcareous layer. [Russ., black earth.]

Cherokee *cher'ə-kē, n.* (a member of) a tribe of Iroquoian Indians: the language of the Cherokee.

cheroot *shə-rōōt', n.* a cigar not pointed at either end. [Fr. *cheroute,* representing the Tamil name *shuruttu,* a roll.]

cherry[1] *cher'i, n.* a small stone-fruit: the tree (*Cerasus,* a subgenus of *Prunus*) that bears it: extended to many fruits resembling it in some way, as **Barbados cherry:** in cricket slang, the new ball, taken after so many runs have been scored or overs bowled: virginity (*slang*). — *adj.* like a cherry in colour: ruddy. — **cherr'y-bean** cow-pea; **cherr'y-bob'** in children's games, two cherries joined by the stalks; **cherr'y-bounce'** cherry brandy: brandy and sugar; **cherry brandy** a liqueur made by steeping Morello cherries in brandy; **cherr'y-coal** a soft shining coal; **cherr'y-lau'rel** a species of cherry with evergreen laurel-like leaves; **cherr'y-pepp'er** a West Indian capsicum; **cherr'y-picker** a crane-like device consisting of a platform at the end of a long arm with an elbow-like joint in it, the platform being raised as the arm is raised; **cherr'y-pie'** a pie made of cherries: the common heliotrope; **cherr'y-pit** a game in which cherry-stones are thrown into a small hole; **cherr'y-plum** a plum of flavour approaching a cherry; **cherr'y-stone** the hard endocarp of the cherry; **cherry tomato** a more or less cherry-sized red tomato. **have** or **take two bites** at or **a second bite at the cherry** (*coll.*) to have a second chance, opportunity. [O.E. *ciris* — L. *cerasus* — Gr. *kerasos,* a cherry-tree; it is said to have been introduced from *Kerasous* (*Cerasus*) in Pontus, by Lucullus, but was known in Europe long before his time.]

cherry[2] *cher'i,* (Spens.) *v.t.* to cheer. [See **cherish.**]

chersonese *kûr'sə-nēz, -nēs, n.* a peninsula. [Gr. *chersonēsos* — *chersos,* land, dry land, *nēsos,* an island.]

chert *chûrt, n.* a compact flinty chalcedony. — *adj.* **chert'y.** [Etymology doubtful.]

cherub *cher'əb, n.* a winged creature with human face, represented as associated with Jehovah: a celestial spirit: a chubby-faced person, esp. a child: — *pl.* **cher'ubs, cher'ubim** (*-ə, -ū, -bim*), **cher'ubims.** — *adjs.* **cherubic** (*-ōō'bik*), **-al, cherubim'ic** angelic. — *adv.* **cheru'bically.** — *n.* **cher'ubin** (*Shak.*) a cherub. [Heb. *k'rub,* pl. *k'rubim.*]

cherup *cher'up.* Same as **chirrup.**

chervil *chûr'vil, n.* an umbelliferous plant (*Anthriscus cerefolium*) cultivated as a pot-herb: also other species of Anthriscus (*common, wild,* and *rough chervil*): extended to sweet cicely (*sweet chervil*). [O.E. *cerfille* — L. *caerefolium* — Gr. *chairephyllon.*]

Cheshire cat. See **cat**[1].

Cheshvan. See **Hesvan.**

chesil *chez'il, n.* gravel: shingle: bran. — Also **chis'el.** [O.E. *cisil.*]

chesnut. See **chestnut.**

chess[1] *ches, n.* a game of skill for two, played with figures or men of different kinds which are moved on a chequered board. — **chess'board** the board on which chess is played: a chequered design; **chess'man.** [O.Fr. *eschès* (Fr. *échecs*; It. *scacchi*; Ger. *Schach*) — Pers. *shāh*, a king.]

chess² *ches, n.* one of the parallel planks of a pontoon-bridge — generally in *pl.*

chessel *ches'l, n.* a cheese mould. [**cheese¹.**]

chessylite *ches'i-līt, n.* basic carbonate of copper, vivid blue in colour, azurite. [*Chessy*, near Lyons, where it occurs.]

chest *chest, n.* a large strong box: the part of the body between the neck and the abdomen, the thorax: a treasury: a chestful. — *adj.* **chest'ed** having a chest: placed in a chest. — *n.* **chest'ful** enough to fill a chest. — *adj.* **chest'y** of the quality of the chest-voice: suggestive of disease of the chest (*coll.*): self-important (*slang*). — **chest freezer** a long, low freezer which opens at the top; **chest'-note** in singing or speaking, a deep note; **chest'-protec'tor** a covering to keep the chest warm; **chest'-register, -tone, -voice** the lowest register of the voice. — **chest of drawers** a case in which drawers slide; **chest of viols** (*arch.*) a set of viols (two trebles, two tenors, two basses); **off one's chest** (*coll.*) off one's mind: admitted, stated, declared openly. [O.E. *cyst* — L. *cista* — Gr. *kistē*; Scot. *kist*.]

chesterfield *chest'ər-fēld, n.* a long overcoat: a heavily padded sofa. [Lord *Chesterfield*.]

chestnut (*now rarely* **chesnut**) *ches'nut, n.* a tree of genus Castanea, esp. the *Spanish* or *Sweet Chestnut*: its edible nut, encased (three together) in a prickly husk: its hard timber: the **horse-chestnut** (*Aesculus hippocastanum*), its fruit or nut: a chestnut horse: a horny knob of a horse's foreleg: a stale joke or cliché (*slang*). — *adj.* of chestnut colour, reddish-brown. — **pull the chestnuts out of the fire** to take control and rescue someone from a difficult situation. [O.Fr. *chastaigne* — L. *castanea* — perh. from *Castana*, in Thessaly.]

Chesvan. See **Hesvan.**

cheval de bataille *shə-val də bä-tä-y', (*Fr.; *lit.* warhorse) a favourite topic.

cheval-de-frise *shə-val'-də-frēz', n.* a spiky defensive structure used esp. to stop cavalry: — *pl.* **chevaux-de-frise** (*shə-vō'-*). [Fr., *cheval*, horse, *de*, of, *Frise*, Friesland.]

chevalet *shə-va'lā, she', n.* the bridge of a stringed instrument (*mus.*). [Fr. dim. of *cheval*, a horse.]

cheval-glass *shə-val'-gläs, n.* a large glass or mirror supported on a frame and able to swivel in it. — Also **cheval mirror.** [Fr. *cheval*, horse, stand.]

chevalier *shev-ə-lēr', n.* a cavalier: a knight: a gallant. [Fr., — L.L. *caballārius* — L. *caballus*, a horse.]

chevalier d'industrie *shə-va-lyā dē-düs-trē, (*Fr.) *lit.* a knight of industry: an adventurer, one who lives by his wits.

chevelure *shev'(ə-)lür, n.* a head of hair: a periwig: the nebulous part of a comet. [Fr., — L. *capillātūra* — *capillus*, hair.]

cheven *chev'ən, n.* the chub. — Also **chev'in.** [Fr. *chevin*, *chevanne*.]

cheverel, -il *chev'ər-əl, n.* a kid: soft, flexible kidskin leather. — *adj.* like kid leather, pliable. — *ns.* **chev(e)ron** (*shev'*; *obs.*) a kid glove; **chevrette** (*shəv-ret'*) a thin kind of goat-skin. [Fr. *chevreau*, *chevrette*, a kid — *chèvre*; L. *capra*, a she-goat.]

cheverye (*Spens.*). See **chiefery** under **chief.**

chevesaile *chev'ə-sāl, n.* an ornamental collar of a coat. [O.Fr. *chevesaile* — *chevece*, the neck.]

cheville *shə-vē', n.* the peg of a stringed instrument (*mus.*): a redundant word or expression used in a verse or sentence for purposes of metre or balance only. [Fr., peg — L. *clāvicula*, dim. of *clāvis*, a key.]

chevin. See **cheven.**

Cheviot *chē'vi-ət* (or *chev'i-ət*), *n.* a hardy breed of short-woolled sheep reared on the *Cheviot* Hills: a cloth made from their wool.

chevisance *chev'i-zəns, n.* (*obs.*) achievement: resource: gain: money dealings: performance (*Spens.*): an unidentified flower. [Fr., — *chevir*, to accomplish; *chef*, the head, the end.]

chevron *shev'rən, n.* a rafter: the representation of two rafters of a house meeting at the top (*her.*): a V-shaped band on the sleeve, a mark of non-commissioned rank or (in army and R.A.F., inverted) of long service and good conduct: see under **cheverel.** — *adjs.* **chev'roned; chev'rony** (*her.*). — **chevron board** a road sign consisting of a line of horizontal V-shapes, used to indicate a sharp change in direction. [Fr. *chevron*, rafter — L. *capreolus*, dim. of *caper*, a goat.]

chevrotain *shev'rō-tān*, or *-tən, n.* a mouse-deer, any member of the Tragulidae, an Old World tropical family of small deerlike animals not very near the deer but forming a separate section of artiodactyls. [Fr., dim. of *chèvre* — L. *capra*, she-goat.]

chevy *chev'i*, **chiv(v)y** *chiv'i, ns.* a hunting cry: a pursuit: prisoner's base. — *vs.t.* to chase: (usu. **chivv'y**) to harass. — *vs.i.* to scamper. [Perh. from the Border ballad of battle, *Chevy Chase.*]

chew *chōō, v.t.* to bruise and grind with the teeth: to masticate: to meditate, reflect (*fig.*). — *n.* the action of chewing: a quid of tobacco. — *adj.* **chew'y** soft, able to be chewed, like toffee. — **chew'ing-gum** a preparation made from chicle gum, produced by the sapodilla plum tree, sweetened and flavoured. — **chew out** (*coll.*) to tell off, reprimand; **chew the cud** of cows, etc., to masticate a second time food that has already been swallowed and passed into the first stomach: to ruminate in thought (*fig.*; also **chew over**); **chew the rag, the fat** (*slang*) to keep on arguing the point. [O.E. *cēowan*; Ger. *kauen*; cf. **jaw¹.**]

chewet¹ *chōō'it, n.* a chough (*obs.*): a chatterer (*Shak.*). [Fr. *chouette*, chough (now owl).]

chewet² *chōō'it, (obs.) n.* a pie or pudding of miscellaneous chopped meats.

chewink *chə-wingk', n.* a large finch of eastern N. America, the red-eyed towhee. [Imit.]

Cheyenne *shī-an', -en', n.* (a member of) a tribe of N. American Indians now living in Montana and Oklahoma: the Algonkian language of the tribe. [Canadian Fr. — Siouan (Dakota) *Shahiyena*, people who speak unintelligibly.]

chez *shā, prep.* at the home or establishment of. [Fr.]

chi¹ *kī, hhē, n.* the twenty-second letter (X, χ) of the Greek alphabet, representing an aspirated *k* sound: as numeral χ' = 600, χ = 600 000: in inscriptions χ = 1000 (*chīlioi*). [Gr. *chei, chī.*]

chi² *chī.* Same as **chai.**

chiack *chī'ak, (Austr. coll.) v.t.* to tease, deride, jeer at. — Also *n.* — Also **chy'ack.** — *n.* **chī'acking.** [Brit. obs. slang, to greet, salute.]

Chian *kī'an, adj.* pertaining to Chios in the Aegean Sea.

Chianti *kē-an'ti, -än', It.* kyän'tē, *n.* a red (or white) wine of Tuscany. [*Chianti* Mountains.]

chiao *jow, n.* a coin of the People's Republic of China, one-tenth of 1 yuan: — *pl.* **chiao.** [Chin.]

chiaroscuro *kyär-ō-skōō'rō, n.* management of light and shade in a picture: a monochrome painting: the effect of light and shade (also *fig.*): —pl. **chiaroscu'ros.**

chiasm *kī'azm, (anat.) n.* a decussation or intersection, esp. that of the optic nerves. — Also **chīas'ma.** — *n.* **chīas'mus** (*rhet.*) contrast by parallelism in reverse order, as *Do not live to eat, but eat to live.* — *adj.* **chīas'tic.** — *n.* **chīas'tolite** (*min.*) a variety of andalusite with black cruciform inclusions. [Gr. *chiasma*, a cross-shaped mark, *chiastos*, laid crosswise, like the Greek letter X (*chi, chei*), *lithos*, a stone.]

chiaus *chows.* Same as **chouse.**

chibol. See **cibol.**

chibouk, chibouque *chi-bōōk', n.* a long straight-stemmed Turkish pipe. [Turk. *chibūk.*]

chic *shēk, n.* style, elegance: artistic skill. — *adj.* having chic: smart and fashionable. — *adv.* **chic'ly.** [Fr.]

chica *chē'kə, n.* an orange-red dye-stuff, got by boiling the leaves of a South American Bignonia. [From a native name.]

Chicago *shi-kä'gō, n.* a form of contract bridge played in sets of four deals, not in rubbers.

chicane *shi-kān'*, *v.i.* (*arch.*) to use shifts and tricks. — *v.t.* (*arch.*) to deceive. — *n.* a trick or artifice: a bridge hand without trumps, for which a score above the line used to be allowed: a barrier or obstacle in motor-racing, etc. — *ns.* **chicā'ner** one who chicanes: a quibbler; **chicā'nery** trickery or artifice, esp. in legal proceedings: quibbling; **chicā'ning** quibbling. [Fr. *chicane*, sharp practice at law, from Late Gr. *tzykanion*, a game at mall, *tzykanizein*, to play at mall — Pers. *tchugagan*, a crooked mallet.]

chicano *chi-kä'nō*, *shi-*, *n.* (*U.S.*, sometimes considered *derog.*; also with *cap.*) an American of Mexican descent: — *pl.* **chica'nos.** — Also *adj.* [Sp. *mejicano*, Mexican.]

chiccory. See **chicory.**

chich *chich.* Same as **chick-pea**; see under **chickling[1].**

chicha *chēch'ə*, *n.* a South American liquor fermented from maize. [Said to be Haitian.]

chichi, chi-chi *shē'shē, chē'chē, adj.* pretentious: fussy, precious, affected: stylish, chic, self-consciously fashionable. — *n.* something that is, or quality of being, chichi: red tape: fuss. [Fr.]

chi-chi. See **chee-chee.**

chick[1] *chik*, *n.* the young of fowls, esp. of the hen: a child, as a term of endearment: a girl or young woman (*slang*). — *n.* **chick'en** the young of birds, esp. of the domestic fowl: the flesh of a fowl, not always very young: a prairie chicken: a youthful person, esp. a girl: a faint-hearted person (*coll.*): a type of sometimes competitive game in which one dares to perform some physically dangerous activity (*coll.*). — *adj.* (*coll.*) cowardly, frightened. — *v.i.* (*coll.*) to show fear. — *n.* **chick'ling** a little chicken. — **chick'-a-biddy, chick'-a=didd'le** terms of endearment addressed to children; **chick'en-feed** poultry food: small change (*coll.*): something of little value (*coll.*); **chick'en-haz'ard** a game at hazard for low stakes. — *adj.* **chick'en-heart'ed, -liv'-ered** timid, cowardly. — **chick'en-pox** a contagious febrile disease, chiefly of children, not unlike a mild form of smallpox; **chick'en-run** a run for hens; **chick'en-wire** wire-netting; **chick'-pea** see **chickling[1]**; **chick'weed** a species of stitchwort, one of the commonest of weeds, much relished by fowls and cagebirds (**mouse-ear chickweed** the kindred genus *Cerastium*); **chickweed=wintergreen** see **wintergreen** under **winter.** — **chicken-and-egg situation** one in which it is impossible to tell which is the cause and which the effect; **chicken out** (*coll.*; often with *of*) to desert, quit, through cowardice; **the chickens have come home to roost** see **roost[1]**. [O.E. *cicen*; cf. Du. *kieken*, Ger. *Küken*.]

chick[2] *chik*, (*Ind.*) *n.* a hanging door-screen or sun-blind of laced bamboo slips, etc. [Hindi *ciq*.]

chickadee *chik-ə-dē'*, *n.* an American titmouse. [From its note.]

chickaree *chik-ə-rē'*, *n.* an American red squirrel. [From its cry.]

chickling[1] *chik'ling*, *n.* a species of pea (also **chickling vetch** *Lathyrus sativus*). — **chick'-pea** gram, a plant of the pea family (*Cicer arietinum*): its edible seed. [Earlier *chich, chichling, chich-pease* — Fr. *chiche* — L. *cicer*, chick-pea.]

chickling[2]. See **chick[1].**

chicle *chik'l, chik'li, n.* the gum of the sapodilla tree, chewing-gum. [Sp., — Mex.]

chicly. See **chic.**

chicory (also **chiccory**) *chik'ə-ri, n.* succory, a blue-flowered composite (*Cichorium intybus*): its carrot-like root (ground to mix with coffee). — *n.* **chic'on** (*-ən*) the shoot of the chicory plant, eaten like lettuce. [Fr. *chicorée* — L. *cichorēum* — Gr. *kichorion*.]

chide *chīd*, *v.t.* to scold, rebuke, reprove by words: to be noisy about, as the sea. — *v.i.* to make a snarling, murmuring sound, as a dog or trumpet: — *pr.p.* **chīd'ing**; *pa.t.* **chīd**, sometimes **chīd'ed, chode** (*arch.*); *pa.p.* **chīd, chīdd'en**, sometimes **chīd'ed.** — *ns.* **chīd'er** (*Shak.*) a quarrelsome person; **chīd'ing** scolding.

[O.E. *cīdan* (a weak verb).]

chidlings. See **chitterling.**

chief *chēf, adj.* head: principal, highest, first: outstanding, important (with *compar.* **chief'er**, *superl.* **chief'est**): intimate (*Scot.*). — *adv.* chiefly. — *n.* a head or principal person: a leader: the principal part or top of anything: the greater part: an ordinary, consisting of the upper part of the field cut off by a horizontal line, generally made to occupy one-third of the area of the shield (*her.*). — *ns.* **chief'dom, chief'ship** state of being chief: sovereignty; **chief'ery, chief'ry** (in *Spens.* **chev-erye**) an Irish chieftaincy: the dues paid to a chief or the supreme lord: a chief's lands; **chief'ess** a female chief. — *adj.* **chief'less** without a chief or leader. — *n.* **chief'ling.** — *adv.* **chief'ly** in the first place: principally: for the most part. — *ns.* **chief'tain** the head of a clan: a leader or commander: — *fem.* **chief'tainess; chief'-taincy, chief'tainry; chief'tainship.** — **chief'-bar'on** the President of the Court of Exchequer; **Chief Constable** (in Britain) an officer commanding the police force in an administrative area; **chief-justice** see **justice.** — **-in-chief** in composition, at the head, as *commander-in-chief*. — **chief of staff** (*mil.*) a senior staff officer: (with *cap.*) the senior officer of each of the armed forces (in the U.S. of the army and air force); **in chief** borne in the upper part of the shield (*her.*): of a tenure, held directly from the sovereign: most importantly. [Fr. *chef* — L. *caput*, the head.]

chield *chēld*, (*Scot.*) *n.* a lad, a man. — Also **chiel.** [Apparently a form of **child.**]

chiff-chaff *chif'chaf, n.* a small warbler. [Imit.]

chiffon *shif'on, shē'fõ, n.* (in *pl.*) trimmings, or other adornments: a thin fine clothing fabric of silk, nylon, etc. — *n.* **chiffonier** (*shif-ən-ēr'*) an ornamental cabinet. [Fr., rag, adornment — *chiffe*, rag.]

chigger. See **chigoe.**

chignon *shē'nyõ, n.* a fold or roll of hair worn on the back of the head and neck. [Fr., meaning first the nape of the neck (jointed like a chain) — *chaînon*, link of a chain — *chaîne*, a chain.]

chigoe *chig'ō*, **chigre, chigger** *chig'ər, ns.* a tropical American, African and Indian flea (*Tunga penetrans*), the gravid female of which buries itself, esp. beneath the toe-nails: the larva of a harvest-mite (*Trombicula*) of America, Europe, and Asia that burrows in the skin. — Also **jigg'er.** [W. Indian name; cf. Carib *chigo*, and Wolof (W. African language) *jiga*, an insect.]

chihuahua *chi-wä'wä, n.* a very small dog (2 lb. or so) with big eyes and pointed ears. [*Chihuahua* in Mexico.]

chik. Same as **chick[2].**

chikara[1] *chi-kä'rə, n.* a four-horned Indian antelope: an Indian gazelle (also **chinka'ra**). [Hindi.]

chikara[2] *chik'ə-rə, n.* an Indian instrument of the violin class. [Hindi *cikārā*.]

chik(h)or. See **chukor.**

chilblain *chil'blān, n.* a painful red swelling, esp. on hands and feet in cold weather. [**chill[1]** and **blain[1]**.]

child *chīld, n.* a very young person (up to the age of sixteen for the purpose of some acts of parliament, under fourteen in criminal law): a female infant (*Shak.*): a son or daughter: one standing in a relationship of adoption or origin (to a person, place, etc.): disciple: a youth of gentle birth, esp. in ballads, etc. (*arch.*; also **childe, chylde**): (in *pl.*) offspring: (in *pl.*) descendants: (in *pl.*) inhabitants: — *pl.* **children** (*chil'drən*; double pl. from older and dial. **chil'der**). — *v.t., v.i.* (*arch.*) to bring forth. — *adj.* **chīld'ed** (*Shak.*) possessed of a child. — *n.* **child'hood** the state of being a child: the time of being a child. — *adjs.* **child'ing** (*Shak.*) fruiting, teeming; **child'ish** of or like a child: silly: trifling. — *adv.* **child'ishly.** — *n.* **child'ishness** what is natural to a child: puerility. — *adjs.* **child'less** without children; **child'like** like a child: becoming a child: docile: innocent; **child'ly** (*arch.*) natural or becoming to a child. — *n.* **child'ness** (*Shak.*) the nature or character of a child. — **child abuse** physical or mental cruelty to or neglect of a child by a parent or guardian; **child'bearing** the act of bringing forth children; **child'bed** (*arch.*) the state of a woman brought to bed with child; **child benefit** an allowance granted by the government to parents for children; **child'birth** the giving birth to a child: parturition; **child'crowing** a nervous affection with spasm of the muscles closing the glottis; **child endowment** (*Austr.*) family allowance from a government source; **child'-minder** a person, usu. with little training, officially recognised as being fit to look after children. — *adjs.* **child'-proof, -resis'tant** not able to be damaged, opened, worked, etc., by a child. — **Children's Panels** a system of legal hearing for child crime, etc. which in 1970 replaced the Juvenile Courts in Scotland; **child's play** something very easy to do; **child'-study** the psychology and physiology of children; **child welfare** health and well-being of young children as an object of systematic social work; **child'-wife'** a very young wife. — **second childhood** the childishness of old age; **with child** pregnant. [O.E. *cild,* pl. *cild,* later, *cildru, -ra.*]

Childermas *chil'dər-məs, n.* Innocents' Day, a festival (Dec. 28) to commemorate the slaying of the children by Herod. [O.E. *cildra,* gen. pl. of *cild,* child, *mæsse,* mass.]

Chile *chil'i, adj.* of Chile. — *n.* and *adj.* **Chil'ean** (*obs.* **Chil'ian).** — **Chile(an) pine** the monkey-puzzle; **Chile saltpetre** sodium nitrate.

chile *chīl.* Variant form of **child.**

chili¹, chile *chil'i.* Variant forms of **chilli.**

chili² *shil'ē, n.* a hot dry wind of North Africa. [Berber.]

chiliad *kil'i-ad, n.* the number 1000: 1000 of anything (e.g. years). — *ns.* **chil'iagon** a plane figure with 1000 angles: **chiliahē'dron** a solid figure with 1000 plane faces; **chiliarch** (*kil'i-ärk*) a leader or commander of a thousand men; **chil'iarchy** the position of chiliarch; **chil'-iasm** the doctrine that Christ will reign bodily upon the earth for 1000 years; **chil'iast** one who holds this opinion: one who believes in a coming happier time on earth. — *adj.* **chilias'tic.** [Gr. *chīlias, -ados — chīlioi,* 1000.]

chill¹ *chil, n.* coldness: a cold that causes shivering: anything that damps or disheartens: a foundry mould. — *adj.* shivering with cold: slightly cold: opposite of *cordial.* — *v.i.* to grow cold. — *v.t.* to make chill or cold: to cool: to preserve by cold: to injure with cold: to discourage: to cloud or bloom the surface of (by cold air): to take the chill off (*dial.*). — *adj.* **chilled** made cold: hardened by chilling, as iron: preserved by cold, as beef. — *n.* **chill'er** — *adv.* **chill'ily.** — *n.* **chill'iness.** — *n.* and *adj.* **chill'ing.** — *n.* **chill'ness.** — *adj.* **chill'y** cold: chilling: sensitive to cold. — **chill factor** the degree by which weather conditions, e.g. wind, increase the effect of low temperatures. — **take the chill off** to warm slightly: to make lukewarm. [O.E. *cele, ciele,* cold; see **cold, cool.**]

chill². See **ch.**

chilli *chil'i, n.* the pod of the capsicum, extremely pungent and stimulant, used in sauces, pickles, etc., and dried and ground to form cayenne pepper: — *pl.* **-is, -ies.** — Also **chili, chile.** — **chilli con carne** (*kon kär'nē*) a dish of minced meat, beans and chillis, originating in Mexico. [Nahuatl.]

Chillingham cattle *chil'ing-əm kat'l,* an ancient breed of wild, white-coated cattle, now confined to a single herd which roams the Chillingham estate in Northumberland.

chillum *chil'um, n.* the part of a hookah containing the tobacco and charcoal balls: a hookah itself: the act of smoking it. [Hind. *chilam.*]

Chilognatha *kī-log'nä-thə, n.pl.* millipedes. [Gr. *cheilos,* lip, *gnathos,* jaw.]

Chilopoda *kī-lop'o-də, n.pl.* centipedes. [Gr. *cheilos,* lip, *pous, podos,* foot.]

Chiltern hundreds. See **hundred.**

chimaera. Older spelling of **chimera.**

chimb. See **chime².**

chime¹ *chīm, n.* a set of bells tuned in a scale: (often in *pl.*) the ringing of such bells in succession: a definite sequence of bell-like notes sounded as by a clock: the harmonious sound of bells or other musical instruments: agreement of sound or of relation: harmony: rhyme: jingle. — *v.i.* to sound a chime or in chime: to accord or agree: to jingle: to rhyme: to say words over mechanically. — *v.t.* to strike, or cause to sound in chime: to indicate by chiming. — **chime in** to join in, in agreement. [M.E. *chimbe,* prob. O.Fr. *cymbale* — L. *cymbalum,* a cymbal.]

chime², chimb *chīm, n.* the rim formed by the ends of the staves of a cask: a hollowed or bevelled channel in the waterway of a ship's deck (*naut.*). — Also **chine.** [Cog. with Du. *kim,* Ger. *Kimme,* edge.]

chimer *chim'ər,* **chimere** *chi-mēr', ns.* a long sleeveless tabard: the upper robe worn by a bishop. [O.Fr. *chamarre;* cf. **cymar;** Sp. *zamarra, chamarra,* sheepskin.]

chimera, chimaera *kī-, ki-mē'rə, n.* (often with *cap.*) a fabulous, fire-spouting monster, with a lion's head, a serpent's tail, and a goat's body: any idle or wild fancy: a picture of an animal having its parts made up of various animals: (only **-ae-**) a genus of cartilaginous fishes, often ranked with the sharks and rays: (only **-ae-**) a fish of the genus: an organism made up of two genetically distinct tissues. — *n.* **chimaer'id** a fish of the genus Chimaera or related genera of the family **Chimaer'idae** (*-i-dē*). — *adjs.* **chimeric** (*-mer'ik*), **-al** of the nature of a chimaera: wild: fanciful. — *adv.* **chimĕr'ically.** [L., — Gr. *chimaira,* a she-goat.]

chimere. See **chimer.**

chimney *chim'ni,* (*dial.* **chimley, chumley** *chim', chum'li*), *n.* a passage for the escape of fumes, smoke, or heated air from a fireplace or furnace: a glass tube surrounding a lamp flame: a volcanic vent: a cleft in a rock-face just large enough for a mountaineer to enter and climb. — *v.t.* to climb (a narrow crevice) with back against one wall and feet against the other. — **chim'ney-board** a board blocking up a fireplace; **chim'ney-breast** the part of a wall that projects into a room and contains the fireplace and chimney; **chim'ney-can** a chimney-pot; **chim'ney-cor'ner, -nook** (*Scot.* **-nuik**) in old chimneys, the space between the fire and the side-wall of the fireplace: fireside, commonly spoken of as the place for the aged and infirm; **chim'ney-piece** a shelf over the fireplace; **chim'ney-pot** a cylindrical pipe of earthenware or other material at the top of a chimney: a top-hat (in full **chimney-pot hat**); **chim'ney-shaft** the stalk of a chimney which rises above the building; **chim'ney-stack** a group of chimneys carried up together: a chimney-stalk; **chim'ney-stalk** a very tall chimney; **chim'ney-swallow** the common swallow: a species of swift (*U.S.*); **chim'ney-sweep, chim'ney=sweeper** one who sweeps or cleans chimneys; **chim'ney=top** the top of a chimney. [Fr. *cheminée* — L. *camīnus,* a furnace.]

chimpanzee *chim-pən-zē', n.* one of the African anthropoid apes: —often shortened to **chimp.** [West African.]

chin *chin, n.* the jutting part of the face below the mouth. — *adj.* **chin'less** having a receding chin: upper-class and not very clever, esp. in *chinless wonder* (*facet.*). — **chin'strap** the strap on a helmet, etc. that goes under the chin. — *n.* and *v.i.* **chin'wag** (*slang*) talk. — **keep one's chin up** to keep cheerful in a difficult situation (usu. reduced to **chin up!** in exhortation): **take it on the chin** to be courageous in misfortune. [O.E. *cin;* Ger. *Kinn,* Gr. *genys* (jaw).]

china¹ *chī'nə, n.* (orig. **Chi'na-ware**) articles of porcelain brought from China in 16th cent.: Chinese porcelain or, esp., Western imitation or version of it: (*Cockney rhyming slang*) mate (from *china plate*). — *adj.* of china: (*cap.*) of, from, etc., China. — *n.* **Chinese** (*chī-nēz'*) a native or citizen of China (*pl.* **Chinese'** — *arch. coll. sing.* **Chinee'**): the language of China. — *adj.* (in names of commodities, sometimes without capital) of, concerning or relating, etc. to China, its language or its people. — **China aster** see **aster; china clay** kaolin (q.v.), fine white clay used in making porcelain, etc.; **China goose** the Chinese goose; **China grass** rami; **China ink** see **ink; China jute** a species of Abutilon; **Chi′naman** a Chinese (derog.): off-break bowled by a left-handed bowler to a right-handed batsman; **chi′naroot** root-stock of Smilax china; **China rose** any of several garden roses; **china stone** partly decomposed granite; **China tea** a kind of tea grown in China and smoke-cured; **Chi′natown** a Chinese quarter in a town; **Chinese block** see **Chinese (temple) block; Chinese boxes** a set of boxes nesting one inside another, so that when one opens one box, one finds yet another to open inside it; **Chinese cabbage** either of two kinds of plant, Brassica chinensis or Brassica pekinensis, with edible leaves; **Chinese checkers** a board game similar to draughts which can be played by 2, 4, or 6 people; **Chinese goose** the largest living goose (Anser, or Cygnopsis, cyg-noides), domesticated in East Asia; **Chinese gooseberry** subtropical vine (Actinidia chinensis) with edible fruit; **Chinese lantern** a paper lantern; **Chinese lantern plant** same as **winter-cherry; Chinese leaves** Chinese cabbage; **Chinese paper** a fine soft brownish paper-like material made from bamboo bark, giving fine impressions of engravings: also the so-called rice paper; **Chinese pavilion** see **pavilion; Chinese puzzle** a very difficult puzzle or problem; **Chinese sugar-cane** see under **sorghum; Chinese wall(s)** the strict demarcation barriers which must exist between e.g. the corporate finance and investment advisory departments of a bank, etc. in order to ensure that privileged information available to one department is not available to the other and so prevent conflicts of interest from arising; **Chinese white** a zinc oxide pigment. — **Chinese restaurant syndrome** a set of symptoms including chest pain, dizziness and flushing, attributed to the consumption of too much monosodium glutamate, usu. in Chinese food; **Chinese (temple) block** a percussion instrument consisting of a hollow wooden block that is struck with a hammer. [Prob. from the Ch'in dynasty, third cent. B.C.]

china² kī′nə, kēn′ə. See **quina**.

chinampa chin-am′pə, n. a 'floating garden', of earth piled on floating mats of twigs. [Sp., — Nahuatl china-mitl.]

Chinagraph® chī′nə-gräf, n. a kind of pencil that writes on glass, porcelain, etc. [**china**, Gr. graphein, to write.]

chinar. Same as **chenar**.

chincapin. See **chinkapin**.

chinch chinch, n. the bed-bug in America. [Sp. chinche — L. cimex.]

chincherinchee, chinkerinchee ching′kə-rin-chē′, chin-kə-rin′chē, n. a white-flowered S. African plant of the star-of-Bethlehem genus. — Also (coll.) **chinks.** [Said to be imitative of the flower-stalks rubbing together in the wind.]

chinchilla chin-chil′ə, n. a small rodent of South America valued for its soft grey fur: the fur itself: (with cap.) a breed of rabbits, or of cats, with soft grey fur. [Sp.]

chin-chin chin′chin′, (coll.) interj. hello or good-bye: good health! (as a toast). [Anglo-Chin. — Chin. ts'ing ts'ing.]

chincough chin′kof, (dial.) n. whooping-cough. [For chink-cough; cf. Scot. king-hoast, Du. kinkhoest; see **chink³** and **cough**.]

chindit chin′dit, n. a member of General Wingate's commando force in Burma during World War II. [Burmese chinthey, a griffin, the force's badge.]

chine¹ chīn, n. the spine or backbone (arch.): a piece of the backbone and adjoining parts (esp. of a pig) for cooking: the back (Spens.): a ridge crest. — v.t. to break the back of. [O.Fr. eschine, prob. from O.H.G. scina, pin, thorn.]

chine² chīn, n. a ravine. [O.E. cinu, a cleft.]

chine³. Variant form of **chime²**.

chiné shē-nā′, adj. mottled, with the pattern printed on

the warp. [Fr., dyed in a (supposedly) Chinese way.]

Chinee, Chinese. See **China**.

chink¹ chingk, n. a cleft, a narrow opening. — v.i. to crack. — v.t. to fill up cracks. — adj. **chink′y** full of chinks. [Apparently formed upon M.E. chine, a crack — O.E. cinu, a cleft.]

chink² chingk, n. the clink, as of coins: money (in Shak. chinks) (slang). — v.i. to give forth a sharp sound. — v.t. to clink together. [Imit.]

chink³ chingk (Northern **kink** kingk), (dial.) n. a gasp for breath. — v.i. to gasp. [Cf. Du. kinken, to cough; Ger. keichen, to gasp.]

Chink chingk, **Chinkie, Chinky** chingk′i, (coll. offensive) n. and adj. Chinese. — **chink′ie, chink′y** (coll.) a meal of Chinese food. [China.]

chinkapin, chincapin, chinquapin ching′kə-pin, n. the dwarf chestnut of the U.S. [Algonquian.]

chinkara. See **chikara¹**.

chinkerinchee, chinks. See **chincherinchee**.

chino chē′nō, (U.S.) n. strong khaki-like twilled cotton: (in pl.) trousers made of it: — pl. **chi′nos.** [Amer. — Sp.]

chinoiserie shē-nwä-z(ə)rē, (Fr.) n. Chinese objects, decoration, behaviour, etc.

Chinook chin-ook′, n. a traders' jargon, consisting of words from French, English, Chinook, and other American-Indian tongues (also **Chinook Jargon**): (without cap.) a warm dry wind blowing down the eastern side of the Rocky Mts, making winter grazing possible: also a warm moist wind from the Pacific.

chinovnik chin-ov′nik, n. a high official in the Russian civil service: a bureaucrat. [Russ., — chin, rank.]

chinquapin. See **chinkapin**.

chintz chints, n. a cotton printed generally in several colours on a white or light ground. — adj. **chintz′y** covered with, or like, chintz: cheap, gaudy. [Orig. pl. — Hindi chīt, spotted cotton-cloth.]

Chionodoxa kī-ō-nō-dok′sə, n. glory of the snow, an early-blooming blue-flowered genus of liliaceous plants: (without cap.) any plant of the genus. [Gr. chiōn, snow, doxa, glory.]

chip chip, v.t. to strike with small sharp cutting blows: to strike small pieces off the surface of (also with at): to remove by chipping (often with away or off): to slice or pare: (of hatching chickens) to crack by pecking: to cut as with an adze: to chaff, tease (coll.). — v.i. to become chipped: to play a chip-shot: — pr.p. **chipp′ing;** pa.t. and pa.p. **chipped.** — n. an act of chipping: a piece chipped off, esp. a flattish fragment: a small fragment of stone (also **chipp′ing**): a surface flaw: a thin slice of fruit, etc.: a potato-chip: a thin strip of wood, used for making boxes, baskets, etc.: a chip-basket: a small, flat piece of wood, plastic, etc. used to represent money in certain games: a minute piece of silicon or other semiconducting material on which one or more microcircuits can be printed (also **microchip, silicon chip**): a piece of money (slang): a piece of dried dung of cow or bison: in sport, a hit or kick which sends a ball high into the air over a short distance: a key on a musical instrument (Shak.). — n. **chipp′ing** see **chip** above. — adj. **chipp′y** abounding in chips: dry as a chip: seedy from an overdose of liquor: touchy, quarrelsome, aggressive (Can. coll.): having a chip on one's shoulder (see below; coll.). — n. (a meal from) a chip-shop (coll.; also **chipp′ie**): see also **chips** and separate entry **chippy.** — n. **chips** (slang) a carpenter (also **chipp′y**): a regimental pioneer sergeant — usually a carpenter: money. — n.pl. fried potato-chips (coll.). — **chip′-basket** a fruit basket of interwoven chips: a metal basket in which potato-chips are placed for frying; **chip′board** reconstructed wood made by consolidation of chips from woodland trimmings, workshop waste, etc., with added resin: a wastepaper cardboard used in box-making; **chip′-carving** wood carving by removal of splinters; **chip′-hat** a hat of palm-leaf strips; **chip′-shop** a restaurant selling take-away meals of fish and chips, etc.; **chip′-shot** (golf) a short lofted approach. — **chip in** to enter the game by putting chips on the table: to interpose: to pay part of the cost of something (*coll.*); **chip off** (orig. **of**) **the old block** one with the characteristics of his father; **chip on one's shoulder** a defiant manner, as if daring anyone to knock it off: readiness to take offence: bitterness, grievance; **have had one's chips** to have died: to have had one's chance; **when the chips are down** at a critical moment when it is too late to alter the situation. [M.E. *chippen*; M.L.G., M.Du. *kippen*, to hatch by chipping shell.]

chipmunk, chipmuck *chip'mungk, -muk, ns.* a terrestrial squirrel of N. America and parts of Asia, with dark stripes on the back and cheek pouches for storing and carrying food. [From Indian name.]

chipochia. See **capocchia.**

chipolata *chip-ə-lä'tə, n.* a small sausage, used as a garnish, etc. [Fr., — It. *cipolla*, onion.]

Chippendale *chip'ən-dāl, adj.* applied to a style of furniture, after the name of a well-known cabinetmaker of the 18th century: also applied to a style of book-plates.

chipper *chip'ər, adj.* briskly cheerful: well, fit. [Perh. same word as Northern dial. *kipper*, lively.]

chippy *chip'i, (U.S.) n.* a flirtatious or promiscuous woman. — See also under **chip.** [chip, variant of **cheep.**]

chiquichiqui *chē-kē-chē'kē, n.* a piassava palm (Leopoldinia). [Tupí.]

chiragra *kī-rag'rə, n.* gout in the hand. — *adjs.* **chirag'ric, -al.** [Gr. *cheiragrā* — *cheir*, hand, *agrā*, a catching.]

chirality *kī-ral'i-ti, n.* the property of a chemical of existing in left-handed and right-handed structural forms: the handedness of such a chemical. — *adj.* **chī'ral.** [Gr. *cheir*, hand.]

chi-rho *kī'rō', n.* a monogram of XP (*chī, rhō*, ch, r), the first letters of the Greek *Chr*istos (Christ).

chirimoya. Same as **cherimoya.**

chirk *chûrk, v.i.* to chirp or squeak: to grate (*Scot.*). [O.E. *cearcian*, to creak.]

chirl *chirl, (Scot.) v.i.* to emit a low sound: to warble. — *n.* a kind of musical warble. [Imit.]

chirm *chûrm, v.i.* to cry out: to chirp. — *n.* noise, din, hum of voices: a flock of goldfinches (also **charm**). [O.E. *cirman*, to cry out; cf. Du. *kermen*.]

chiro-. See **cheiro-.**

Chironomus *kī-ron'ō-məs, n.* a large genus of common midges, giving name to the family **Chironomidae** (*kī-rō-nom'i-dē*). — *n.* **chīron'omid** any member of the family. [Gr. *cheironomōn*, gesticulator.]

chiropodist *ki-rop'ə-dist,* older *kī-,* also *shi-, n.* one who treats minor ailments of the feet, e.g. corns, verrucas. — *adj.* **chiropō'dial.** — *n.* **chirop'ody.** [App. Gr. *cheir*, hand, and *pous, podos*, foot; but *cheiropodēs* means having chapped feet.]

chiropractic *kī-rə-prak'tik, n.* a method of healing concerned with disorders of the locomotor system, which relies upon the removal of nerve interference by manual adjustment of the spinal column: a chiropractor. — *n.* **chīroprac'tor** one who practises chiropractic. [Gr. *cheir*, hand, *praktikos*, concerned with action — *prattein*, to do.]

chirp *chûrp, n.* the sharp thin sound of certain birds and insects. — *v.i.* to make such a sound: to talk in a cheerful and lively strain. — *v.t.* to urge by chirping. — *n.* **chirp'er** a little bird. — *adv.* **chirp'ily.** — *n.* **chirp'iness.** — *adjs.* **chirp'ing; chirp'y** lively: merry. [Imit.]

chirr *chûr, v.i.* to chirp like a cricket or grasshopper. [Imit.]

chirrup *chir'əp, v.i.* to chirp: to make a sound with the mouth to urge on a horse: to cheer up. — *adj.* **chirr'upy** cheerful. [Lengthened form of **chirp,** associated with **cheer up.**]

chirt *chûrt, n.* a squeeze: a squirt. — *v.t.* to squeeze: to squirt. [Conn. with **chirr.**]

chirurgeon, chirurgery, chirurgical *kīr-ûr'jən, -jər-i, -ji-kl,* old forms of **surgeon, surgery, surgical,** with pronun-

ciation readjusted to the ultimate Greek etymology. — *adv.* **chirur'geonly** (*Shak.*) in a manner becoming a surgeon. [Fr. *chirurgien* — Gr. *cheirourgos* — *cheir*, hand, *ergon*, a work.]

chisel¹ *chiz'l, n.* a tool with the end bevelled to a cutting edge, in literature esp. the tool of the sculptor. — *v.t.* to cut, carve, etc. with a chisel: to cheat (*slang*): — *pr.p.* **chis'elling;** *pa.t.* and *pa.p.* **chis'elled.** — *adj.* **chis'-elled** cut with a chisel: having sharp outlines, as cut by a chisel (*fig.*). — *n.* **chis'elling.** — **chis'el-tooth** a rodent's chisel-shaped incisor. [O.Fr. *cisel* — L. *caedēre*, to cut.]

chisel² *chiz'l, n.* See **chesil.**

Chislev. Same as **Kislev.**

chit¹ *chit, n.* a short informal letter: a bill which one signs and pays at a later date, esp. in a club, service mess, etc.: an order or pass: testimonial. — Also **chitt'y.** [Hindi *citthī*.]

chit² *chit, n.* a child; a girl (*slightingly*). — *adjs.* **chitt'y; chitt'y-faced.** [Same as **kit³.**]

chit³ *chit, (dial.) n.* a shoot. — *v.i.* to sprout. — *v.t.* to cause or encourage to sprout. [Perh. O.E. *cīth*, a shoot.]

chital *chē'təl, n.* the axis deer. [Hind.]

chitarrone *kēt-ə-rō'nä, n.* a large lute-like instrument with a long neck. [It.]

chitchat *chit'chat, n.* chatting or idle talk: prattle: gossip. — *v.i.* to chat, gossip. [A reduplication of **chat¹.**]

chitin *kī'tin, n.* the substance which forms most of the hard parts of arthropods. — *adj.* **chī'tinous.** [Fr. *chitine* — Gr. *chitōn*, a tunic.]

chitlings. See **chitterling.**

chiton *kī'ton, n.* the ancient Greek tunic: (with *cap.*) a genus of marine molluscs with shell of movable plates. [Gr. *chitōn*, a tunic.]

chittagong *chit'ə-gong, n.* an Indian variety of domestic fowl. — **chitt'agong-wood'** a cabinetmaker's wood, usu. that of *Chickrassia tabularis* (mahogany family). [*Chittagong* in Bangladesh.]

chitter *chit'ər, (Scot.) v.i.* to shiver: to chatter. — *n.* **chitt'ering.** [Cf. **chatter.**]

chitterling *chit'ər-ling, n.* (also in *pl.*) the smaller intestines of a pig or other edible animal, prepared as a dish: a frill (*obs.*). — Also (*dial.*) **chid'lings, chit'lings.** [Ety. dub.]

chiv *chiv, shiv, (slang) n.* and *v.t.* knife. — Also **shiv.** [From older *chive*, knife (*thieves' slang*) or perh. Romany *chiv*, blade.]

chivalry *shiv'əl-ri* (orig. *chiv'), n.* the usages and qualifications of chevaliers or knights: bravery and courtesy: the system of knighthood in feudal times and its social code. — *adjs.* **chivalric** (*-al'*), **chiv'alrous** pertaining to chivalry: bold: gallant. — *adv.* **chiv'alrously.** — *n.* **chiv'alrousness.** [Fr. *chevalerie* — *cheval* — L.L. *caballus*, a horse.]

chive¹ *chīv, n.* a herb like the leek and onion, with tufts of leaves (used in cooking) and clustered bulbs: a small bulb (*arch.*). — Also **cive** (*sīv*). [Fr. *cive* — L. *cēpa*, an onion.]

chive², *chiv.* Same as **chiv.**

chivy, chivvy *chiv'i, v.t.* to harass, pester, urge. [Same word as **chevy.**]

Chladni figures. Same as **sonorous figures.**

chlamys *klam'is, n.* a short cloak for men: a purple cope: — *pl.* **chlam'ydes** (*-i-dēz*). — *adjs.* **chlam'ydate** (*zool.*) having a mantle; **chlamyd'eous** (*bot.*) having a perianth. — *ns.* **Chlamydia** (*klə-mid'i-ə*) a genus of microorganisms, resembling viruses and bacteria, which cause disease in man and birds: (without *cap.*) an organism of this genus: (without *cap.*) a sexually transmitted disease caused by *Chlamydia trachomatis*; **Chlamydō'mōnas** a genus of fresh-water algae; **chlam'ydospore** a thick-walled spore. [Gr. *chlamys,* pl. *chlamydes.*]

chloasma *klō-az'mə, n.* a skin disease marked by yellowish-brown patches. [Gr. *chloasma*, greenness, yellowness — *chloē*, verdure.]

chloracne *klör-ak′ni, n.* a type of disfiguring skin disease resembling acne in appearance, caused by contact with chlorinated hydrocarbons.

chlorine *klō′, klō′rēn, -rin, -rīn, n.* a yellowish-green gas (Cl) with a peculiar and suffocating odour, used in bleaching, disinfecting, and poison gas warfare. — *ns.* **chlor′al** (or *-al′*) a limpid, colourless, oily liquid (CCl₃·CHO), of penetrating odour, formed when anhydrous alcohol is acted on by dry chlorine gas: loosely *chloral hydrate,* a white crystalline substance used as a hypnotic; **chlo′ralism** the habit, or the morbid effects, of using chloral hydrate; **chloram′bucil** (*-byōō-sil*) an oral drug used to treat some cancers, e.g. leukaemia; **chloramphenicol** same as **Chloromycetin; chlorargyrite** (*klō-rär′ji-rīt, klö-*; Gr. *argyros,* silver) horn silver; **chlo′rate** a salt of chloric acid; **chlor′dan(e)** (*-dan, -dān*) a highly poisonous liquid insecticide; **Chlorella** (*klo-rel′ə*) a genus of green freshwater algae (Gr. *chlōros,* pale green). — *adjs.* **chlo′ric, chlo′rous** of or from chlorine. — *n.* **chlo′rīde** a compound of chlorine with another element or radical: bleaching powder (*chloride of lime*), not a true chloride. — *v.t.* **chlo′ridise, -ize** to convert into a chloride: to cover with chloride of silver (*phot.*). — Also **chlo′ridate.** — *n.* **chlorim′eter** same as **chlorometer.** — *adj.* **chlorimet′ric.** — *n.* **chlorim′etry.** — *v.t.* **chlor′inate** to treat with chlorine (as in sterilisation of water, extraction of gold from ore). — *n.* **chlorinā′tion.** — *v.t.* **chlo′rinise, -ize** to chlorinate. — *n.* **chlo′rite** a salt of chlorous acid (*chem.*): a general name for a group of minerals, hydrated silicates of magnesia, iron, and alumina — dark green and rather soft, like mica but not elastic. — *adj.* **chlorīt′ic** pertaining to, of the nature of, or containing, the mineral chlorite. — *ns.* **chloritīsā′tion, -z-** the alteration of ferro-magnesian minerals into chlorite or similar material; **chlorobrō′mide** a compound of chlorine and bromine with a metal or organic radical: a photograph taken on paper coated with this; **chlorocru′orin** a green respiratory pigment found in some Polychaeta; **chlo′rodyne** a patent medicine — anodyne and hypnotic, containing chloroform; **chloroform** (*klor′ō-förm* or *klō′rō-förm*) a limpid, mobile, colourless, volatile liquid (CHCl₃) with a characteristic odour and a strong sweetish taste, used to induce insensibility. — *v.t.* to administer chloroform to. — *ns.* **chlor′oformer, -ist; chlorom′eter** apparatus for measuring available chlorine in bleaching powder, etc. — *adj.* **chloromet′ric.** — *ns.* **chlorom′etry; Chloromy′cetin** ® (or *-mī-sēt′in*) a drug used against typhoid, cerebrospinal meningitis, etc. — Also **chloramphen′icol.** — *n.pl.* **Chlorophyceae** (*-fis′i-ē*; Gr. *phȳkos,* seaweed) the green seaweeds and their kindred, one of the main divisions of the Algae. — *ns.* **chlorophyll, -phyl** (*klor′ō-fil,* or *klō′rō-fil*; Gr. *phyllon,* leaf) the ordinary green colouring matter of vegetation; **chlo′roplast** (Gr. *plastos,* moulded), a chlorophyll-bearing plastid; **chlor′oprene** a colourless fluid derived from acetylene and hydrochloric acid and used in the production of neoprene; **chlo′roquin(e)** a drug taken to suppress malaria; **chlorō′sis** properly *green sickness,* a form of anaemia affecting young women: blanching of the green parts of a plant, esp. for want of iron (*bot.*). — *adj.* **chlorŏt′ic** pertaining to or affected by chlorosis. — *n.* **chlorprō′mazine** see **Largactil.** — **chloric acid** (HClO₃), a monobasic acid, a vigorous oxidising agent; **chlorine water** an aqueous solution of chlorine; **chlo′rite-schist′** a schistose rock composed of chlorite, usu. with quartz, epidote, etc.; **chloritic marl** a marl at the base of the English Chalk stained green with glauconite (not chlorite); **chlorous acid** a hypothetical acid (HClO₂), known in solution and by its salts; **chlorprom′azine hydrochloride** a drug which induces a feeling of well-being. [Gr. *chlōros,* pale green.]

chobdar *chōb′där, n.* in India, an usher. [Pers.]

choc *chok,* (*coll.*) *n.* and *adj.* a short form of **chocolate.** — **choc′-ice, choc′-bar** an ice-cream with a chocolate covering.

chocho. See **chayote.**

chock *chok, v.t.* to fasten as with a block or wedge. — *n.* a wedge to prevent movement: a log. — *adjs.* **chock′-a-block′, chock′-full′, choke′-full′** quite full; **chock′er** full up (*Austr. slang*): annoyed, fed up (*Brit. slang*). — **chock′stone** stone(s) jammed in a mountain crack, chimney or crevice. — *adj.* **chock′-tight** very tight. [See **choke.**]

chocolate *chok′(ə-)lit, n.* a paste made of the ground seeds of *Theobroma cacao* (cocoa), with sugar and flour or similar material: a sweetmeat made of, or covered with, the paste: beverage made by dissolving the paste, or a powder prepared from it, in hot water or milk. — *adj.* chocolate-coloured, dark reddish-brown: made of or flavoured with chocolate. — *adj.* **choc′olate-box** pretty-pretty or over-sentimental, esp. of a painting. [Sp. *chocolate*; from Nahuatl, *chocólatl,* a mixture containing chocolate.]

Choctaw *chok′tö, n.* an American Indian of a tribe formerly chiefly in Mississippi: the tribe, or its language: (sometimes without *cap.*) a skating movement, forward on the edge of one foot, then backward on the opposite edge of the other (cf. **Mohawk).** [Choctaw *Chahta.*]

chode *chōd,* an archaic *pa.t.* of **chide.**

choenix, chenix *kē′niks, n.* in ancient Greece, a dry measure equivalent to rather more than a quart. [Gr., in Rev. vi. 6.]

Chogyal *chog′yäl, n.* a title of the ruler of Sikkim.

choice *chois, n.* the act or power of choosing: the thing chosen: an alternative: a preference: the preferable or best part: variety from which to choose. — *adj.* worthy of being chosen: select: appropriate. — *adj.* **choice′ful** (*Spens.*) making many choices, fickle. — *adv.* **choice′ly** with discrimination or care. — *n.* **choice′ness** particular value: excellence: nicety. — *adj.* **choice′-drawn** (*Shak.*) selected with care. — **by, for, from choice** by preference; **Hobson's choice** the choice of a thing offered or nothing, from *Hobson,* a Cambridge horsekeeper, who lent out the horse nearest the stable door, or none at all; **make choice of** to select; **take one's choice** to take what one wishes. [Fr. *choix — choisir*; cf. **choose.**]

choir *kwīr, n.* a chorus or band of singers, esp. those belonging to a church: the part of a church appropriated to the singers: the part, the eastern end, often separated from the nave by a rail or screen: a group of instruments of the same class playing together. — *v.i.* (*Shak.*) to sing in chorus. — **choir′boy, choir′-girl, choir′man** a boy, girl or man who sings in a choir; **choir′-master** the director of a choir; **choir′-organ** a department of a large organ, probably originally called chair-organ (renamed as if an organ suitable for accompanying a choir); **choir school** a school usu. maintained by a cathedral to educate boys who also sing in the choir; **choir′-screen** a screen of latticework, separating the choir from the nave. — *n.pl.* **choir′-stalls** fixed seats in the choir of a church, generally of carved wood. [Fr. *chœur —* L. *chorus —* Gr. *choros*; see **chorus.**]

choke *chōk, v.t.* to stop or interfere with the breathing of (whether by compression, blocking, fumes, emotion, or otherwise): to injure or suppress by obstruction, overshadowing, or deprivation of air, etc.: to constrict: to block: to clog: to obstruct. — *v.i.* to be choked: to die (*slang*): to lose one's nerve when facing an important challenge. — *n.* a complete or partial stoppage of breath: the sound of choking: a constriction: a device to prevent the passage of too much petrol, oil, gas, electric current, etc., e.g. a choking-coil. — *adj.* **choked** (*coll.*) angry: upset. — *ns.* **chŏk′er** that which or one who chokes: a large neck-cloth: a very high collar: a close-fitting necklace or jewelled collar; **chokey** see separate entry **choky.** — *adj.* **chŏk′y** tending to, or inclined to, choke. — **choke′berry** a small astringent American fruit akin to the apple; **choke′bore** a gun-bore narrowed at the muzzle: a shot-gun so bored; **choke′cherry** an astringent American cherry;

choke'-coil a choking-coil; **choke'damp** carbon dioxide or other suffocating gas in mines. — *adj.* **choke-full** see **chock-full.** — **choke'-pear** an astringent pear: anything that reduces one to silence; **chok'ing-coil** a coil of thick wire, used to limit the supply of electric light. — **choke back, down** to repress as if by a choking action; **choke off** to get rid of: to deter by force, to discourage; **choke up** to fill completely: to block up. [Ety. dub.]

choky, chokey *chō'ki, n.* a prison: a toll-station: a chokidar. — *n.* **chokidar, chowkidar** (*chō', chow'ki-där*) a watchman. [Hindi *caukī, caukīdār.*]

cholaemia *ko-lē'mi-ə, n.* a morbid accumulation of the constituents of bile in the blood. — *adj.* **cholae'mic.** [Gr. *cholē*, bile, *haima*, blood.]

cholagogue *kol'ə-gog, n.* a purgative causing evacuations of bile. — *adj.* **cholagog'ic** (*-gog'ik, -goj'ik*). [Gr. *cholē*, bile, *agōgos*, leading.]

cholangiography *kol-an-ji-og'rə-fi, n.* the examination by X-ray of the gall-bladder and bile-ducts. [Gr. *cholē*, bile, *angeion*, case, vessel.]

cholecyst *kō'li-sist, n.* the gall-bladder. — *ns.* **cholecystec'-tomy** excision of the gall-bladder; **cholecystī'tis** inflammation of the gall-bladder; **cholecystos'tomy** (Gr. *stoma*, mouth), **cholecystot'omy** (Gr. *tomē*, a cut) surgical opening of the gall-bladder. [Gr. *cholē*, bile, *kystis*, a bladder.]

cholelith *ko'lə-lith, n.* a gall-stone. — *n.* **cholelithiasis** (*ko-lə-li-thī'ə-sis*) the presence of gall-stones. [Gr. *cholē*, bile, *lithos*, stone.]

choler *kol'ər, n.* the bile: biliousness (*Shak.*): anger, irascibility. — *adj.* **chol'eric** full of choler: passionate. — *adv.* **chol'erically** (also *-er'*). [Gr. *cholerā* — *cholē*, bile, partly through Fr.]

cholera *kol'ər-ə, n.* a highly infectious and deadly disease characterised by bilious vomiting and purging. — *adj.* **choleraic** (*kol-ər-ā'ik*). — **cholera belt** a waist-band of flannel or other material worn as a precaution against disease. — **British cholera** an acute catarrhal affection of the mucous membrane of the stomach and small intestines; **chicken, fowl cholera** a contagious septicaemia of birds; **hog cholera** swine fever. [Gr. *cholerā* — *cholē*, bile.]

choleric. See **choler.**

cholesterol *ko-les'tər-ol, n.* an alcohol ($C_{27}H_{45}OH$), occurring abundantly in gall-stones, nerves, bloodstream, etc., a white crystalline solid, thought to be a cause of arteriosclerosis — formerly **choles'terin.** — *adj.* **cholester'ic.** [Gr. *cholē*, bile, *stereos*, solid.]

choli *chō'lē, n.* a short, short-sleeved blouse often worn under a sari. [Hindi *colī*; from Sans. but prob. of Dravidian origin.]

choliamb *kō'li-amb, n.* a variety of iambic trimeter having a spondee for an iambus as the sixth foot. — *n.* and *adj.* **choliam'bic.** [Gr. *chōliambos* — *chōlos*, lame, *iambos*, iambus.]

cholic *kol'ik, kōl'ik, adj.* pertaining to bile, as **cholic acid** ($C_{24}H_{40}O_5$) got from bile. — *n.* **chol'ine** (*kō'lin, -lēn*) an alcohol ($C_5H_{15}NO_2$) found in bile, used in the synthesis of lecithin, etc., and in preventing accumulation of fat in the liver. — *adj.* **choliner'gic** (Gr. *ergon*, work) (of nerve fibres) releasing acetylcholine; activated or transmitted by acetylcholine; (of an agent) having the same effect as acetylcholine. — *n.* **cholinesterase** (*-est'ər-āz*) an enzyme which breaks down a choline ester into choline and an acid, esp. acetylcholine into choline and acetic acid. [Gr. *cholē*, bile.]

choltry *chōl'tri, n.* a caravanserai: a shed used as a place of assembly. — Also **choul'try.** [From Malayalam.]

chomp *chomp,* (*coll.*) *v.t.* and *v.i.* to munch with noisy enjoyment. — *n.* the act or sound of munching thus. [Variant of **champ**[1].]

chondrus *kon'drəs, n.* a cartilage: a chondrule: (*cap.*) a genus of cartilaginous red seaweeds to which carrageen belongs: — *pl.* **chon'drī.** — *adj.* **chon'dral.** — *ns.* **chondre** (*kon'dər*) a chondrule; **chondrificā'tion** formation of

chondrin or development of or change into cartilage. — *v.t.* and *v.i.* **chon'drify** to change into cartilage. — *ns.* **chon'drin** a firm elastic, translucent, bluish-white gelatinous substance, the ground-substance of cartilage; **chon'driosome** a minute body in the cytoplasm of a cell; **chon'drite** a meteorite containing chondrules: a fossil resembling *Chondrus.* — *adj.* **chondrit'ic.** — *ns.* **chondrocrān'ium** a cartilaginous skull, as in embryos, fishes, etc.; **chondrogen'esis** chondrification. — *adj.* **chon'droid** like cartilage. — *ns.pl.* **chondropterygii** (*kon-drop-tər-ij'i-ī*; Gr. *pteryx, -ygos,* fin) the selachians or elasmobranchs; **Chondrostei** (*kon-dros'ti-ī*; Gr. *osteon,* bone) an order of fishes including the sturgeon. — *n.* **chon'drule** a rounded granule found in meteorites and in deep-sea deposits. [Gr. *chondros,* a grain, grit, cartilage.]

choo-choo *chōō'chōō, n.* a child's word for a railway train. [Imit.]

chook *chōōk,* (*coll.,* esp. *Austr.*) *n.* a hen, chicken. — Also **chook'ie** (also *Scot.*). [Imit.]

choom *chōōm,* (*Austr. coll.*) *n.* an Englishman.

choose *chōōz, v.t.* to take or pick out in preference to another thing: to select: to will or determine: to think fit. — *v.i.* to make a choice (between, from, etc.): — *pa.t.* **chose** *chōz; pa.p.* **chos'en.** — *n.* **choos'er.** — *adj.* **choos'(e)y** (*coll.*) difficult to please, fastidious. — **cannot choose** (*arch.*) can have no alternative (but); **choosers of the slain** the Valkyries; **not much to choose between** each about equally good or bad; **pick and choose** to select with care or at leisure; **the chosen people** the Israelites (1 Chron. xvi. 13). [O.E. *cēosan,* Du. *kiesen.*]

chop[1] *chop, v.t.* to cut with a sudden blow (away, down, off, etc.): to cut into small pieces: to thrust or clap (*arch.*): to reduce greatly or abolish (*coll.*). — *v.i.* to hack: to come suddenly or accidentally (*arch.*): to thrust (*arch.*): to crack or fissure: to take a direction (running into **chop**[2]): — *pr.p.* **chopp'ing;** *pa.t.* and *pa.p.* **chopped.** — *n.* an act of chopping: chopped food: a piece cut off: a slice of mutton or pork, containing a rib: (*W. African coll.*) food: a crack: a sharp downward blow. — *n.* **chopp'er** one who or that which chops: a cleaver: a helicopter (*slang*): (in *pl.*) teeth (*slang*). — *n.* and *adj.* **chopp'ing.** — *adj.* **chopp'y** full of chops or cracks: (of the sea, etc.) running in irregular waves (also **chopp'ing**). — **chop'-house** a house where muttonchops and beefsteaks are served: an eating-house; **chopp'ing-block, -board** one on which material is to be chopped is placed; **chopp'ing-knife** a knife for chopping or mincing meat. — **chop at** to aim a blow at; **chop in** to break in, interrupt; **chop up** to cut into small pieces; **for the chop** (*slang*) about to get the chop; **get the chop** (*slang*) to be dismissed from one's job, etc.: to be killed. [A form of **chap**[1].]

chop[2] *chop, v.t.* and *v.i.* to buy and sell, barter, or exchange (*Milton*): to change direction (running into **chop**[1]): — *pr.p.* **chopp'ing;** *pa.t.* and *pa.p.* **chopped.** — *n.* an exchange: a change. — **chop'-log'ic** chopping of logic: one who chops logic. — **chop and change** to buy and sell: to change about; **chop logic** to argue contentiously; **chops and changes** vicissitudes. [Connection with **chop**[1] and with **chap**[2] is not clear.]

chop[3] *chop, n.* the chap or jaw: (in *pl.*) a person with fat cheeks: the mouth or jaws of anything, as a cannon or a vice. — *v.t.* to eat. — *v.i.* to snap: — *pr.p.* **chopp'ing;** *pa.t.* and *pa.p.* **chopped.** — *adj.* **chop'fallen** lit. having the chop or lower jaw fallen down: cast-down: dejected. — **lick one's chops** (*coll.*) to await eagerly or greedily. [See **chap**[3].]

chop[4] *chop, n.* in China and India, a seal: a brand: a sealed document. — **first chop** best quality; **no chop** no good. [Hindi *chāp,* seal, impression.]

chop-chop *chop'chop', adv.* promptly. [Pidgin English.]

chopin[1] *chop'in, n.* an old French liquid measure containing nearly an English imperial pint: a Scottish measure containing about an English quart. [O.Fr. *chopine,* Old Du. *schoppe;* Scot. *chappin,* Ger. *Schoppen,* a pint.]

chopin², chopine *chop-ēn', chop'in, n.* a high clog or patten introduced into England from Venice during the reign of Elizabeth I. [Sp. *chapin.*]

chopping *chop'ing, adj.* stout, strapping, plump. [Perh. **chop¹**; cf. **thumping.**]

chop-stick *chop'stik, n.* (usu. in *pl.*) either of two small sticks used by the Chinese instead of a fork. [**chop=chop**, and **stick².**]

chop-suey *chop-soō'i, n.* a miscellaneous Chinese dish, fried in sesame-oil. [Chin., mixed bits.]

choragus, choregus *ko-rā'gəs, -rē'gəs, n.* in Athens the organiser of a chorus: the leader of a choir. — *adj.* **choragic, choregic** (*-raj', -rāj', -rēj'ik*). [Gr. *chorāgos, chorēgos — choros,* chorus, and *agein,* to lead.]

choral, chorale. See **chorus.**

chord¹ *körd, (mus.) n.* the simultaneous union of sounds of a different pitch. — *adj.* **chord'al.** — **common chord** a note with its third and perfect fifth reckoned upwards. [From **accord.**]

chord² *körd, n.* a string of a musical instrument (*poet.*): a sensitive area of the emotions (*fig.*): a straight line joining any two points on a curve (*geom.*): a cord (see **spinal, vocal**): the straight line joining the leading and the trailing edges of an aerofoil section (*aero.*). — *adj.* **chord'al.** — *n.pl.* **Chordāt'a** the highest phylum of the animal kingdom, including the vertebrates, ascidians, and Hemichordata — animals possessing a notochord. — *n.* **chor'date** a member of the Chordata. — Also *adj.* — *n.* **chordophone** (*kör'dō-fōn, mus.*) a stringed instrument. — *adj.* **chordophonic** (*-fon'ik*). — *n.* **chordotomy** see **cord.** — **strike a chord** to prompt a feeling of recognition, familiarity, etc. [Gr. *chordē,* a string, intestine.]

chore *chōr, chör, n.* a household task: an unenjoyable task. [Form (orig. *U.S.*) of **char³.**]

chorea *ko-rē'ə, n.* St Vitus's dance, a nervous disease, causing irregular involuntary movements of the limbs or face. [L., — Gr. *choreiā,* a dance.]

choree *kō'rē, kö', n.* a trochee. — Also **chorē'us.** [Gr. *choreios.*]

choreography, choreographer, etc. See **chorus.**

chorepiscopal *kō-ri-pis'kə-pl, kö-, adj.* pertaining to a local or suffragan bishop. [Gr. *chōrā,* place, country.]

choriamb *kor'i-amb, n.* a foot of four syllables, the first and last long, the others short. — *adj.* and *n.* **choriam'bic.** [Gr. *choriambos — choreios,* a trochee, *iambos,* iambus.]

choric, chorine. See **chorus.**

chorion *kō'ri-on, kö', n.* the outer foetal envelope: — *pl.* **cho'ria.** — *adjs.* **cho'rioid; cho'roid.** — Also *ns.* — **choroid (coat)** the vascular tunic of the eye, between the retina and the sclerotic. — *adj.* **chorion'ic** of or pertaining to the chorion. — **chorionic gonadotrophin** a hormone produced when an embryo begins to form in the uterus. [Gr. *chorion.*]

chorisis *kō'ris-is, kö', (bot.) n.* multiplication of parts by branching. — *n.pl.* **choripet'alae** a series of dicotyledons having the petals separate if present at all. — *ns.* **cho'rizont, -zont'ist** one who disputes identity of authorship, as of the *Iliad* and *Odyssey.* [Gr. *chōrisis,* separation, *chōrizōn, -ontos,* separating.]

chorist, etc. See **chorus.**

chorizo *cho-rē'zō, n.* a dry, highly-seasoned sausage, made from pork. [Sp.]

chorizont, etc. See **chorisis.**

chorography *kō-rog'rə-fi, kö-, n.* geography: topography. — *adjs.* **chorographic** (*-ro-graf'ik*), **-al; chorolog'ical.** — *ns.* **chorol'ogist; chorol'ogy** the science of geographical distribution. [Gr. *chōrā,* region, country.]

choroid. See **chorion.**

chortle *chört'l, v.i.* to chuckle: to utter a low, deep laugh. — Also *n.* [Coined by Lewis Carroll in 1872.]

chorus *kō'rəs, kö', n.* a band of singers and dancers: in Greek plays, a number of persons who between the episodes danced, and chanted comment and counsel: a person who performs similar functions by himself:

a company of singers: that which is sung by a chorus: the combination of voices in one simultaneous utterance: a refrain, in which the company may join: an obsolete kind of bagpipe. — *v.t.* to sing or say together: — *pr.p.* **cho'rusing;** *pa.t.* and *pa.p.* **cho'rused.** — *adj.* **chor'al** pertaining to a chorus or a choir. — *n.* (*ko-rāl'*; often altered to **chorale'**) a simple harmonised composition with slow rhythm: a psalm or hymn tune: in R.C. usage, any part of the service sung by the whole choir. — *adv.* **chor'ally** in the manner of a chorus: suitable for a choir. — *adj.* **choric** (*kor'ik, kō'rik*). — *ns.* **chorist** (*kor'ist, kō'rist*), **chŏr'ister,** (*obs.*) **quīr'ister** a member of a choir; **chorine** (*kōr'ēn, kör'*) (*slang*) a chorus-girl. — *v.t.* **chor'eograph** to arrange (a dance, dances, etc.). — *v.i.* to practise choreography. — *ns.* **chor'eograph, choreographer** (*kor-i-og'rə-fər*). — *adj.* **choreograph'ic** (*-graf'ik*). — *ns.* **choreog'raphy, choreog'raphy** the art, or the notation, of dancing, esp. ballet-dancing: the art of arranging dances, esp. ballets: arrangement of a ballet; **choreol'ogist; choreol'ogy** the study of ballets and their history. — **chor'us-girl** a woman employed to sing or dance in a chorus on the stage; **chorus master** the director of a choir. [L., — Gr. *choros,* dance; see also **choir.**]

chose¹, chosen. See **choose.**

chose² *shōz, (law) n.* a thing: a piece of personal property. [Fr. — L. *causa,* thing.]

chose jugée *shōz zhü-zhā,* (Fr.) a settled matter.

chota-hazri *chō'tə-haz'ri, häz', (Anglo-Indian) n.* early light breakfast. — **chota peg** a small drink, usu. whisky with soda or water. [Hind. *chotā,* little, *haziri,* breakfast.]

chou *shoō, n.* a cabbage: a soft rosette: a cream bun: dear, pet: — *pl.* **choux** (*shoō*). — **choux pastry** very light, rich pastry. [Fr.]

chough¹ *chuf, n.* the red-legged crow, or any bird of the genus *Fregilus* or *Pyrrhocorax:* a jackdaw (*obs.*). [Perh. from its cry.]

chough². See **chuff.**

choultry. See **choltry.**

chouse *chows, n.* a cheat: one easily cheated (*obs.*): a trick. — *v.t.* to cheat, swindle. [Prob. from Turk, *chaush,* a messenger or envoy.]

chout *chowt, n.* one-fourth part of the revenue, extorted by the Mahrattas as blackmail: blackmail, extortion. [Hind. *chauth,* the fourth part.]

choux. See **chou.**

chow-chow *chow'chow,* shortened as **chow,** *n.* food: a Chinese mixed condiment: a mixed fruit preserve: a dog of a Chinese breed. — *adj.* mixed, miscellaneous. — *n.* **Chow** a Chinese (*arch. slang*). [Pidgin Eng., food.]

chowder *chow'dər, n.* a stew or thick soup made of fish with vegetables: a similar soup made with other main ingredients. [Fr. *chaudière,* a pot.]

chowkidar. See **choky.**

chow-mein *chow'mēn', -mān', n.* fried noodles: a dish of seasoned shredded meat and vegetables, served with fried noodles. [Chin., fried noodles.]

chowry, chowri *chow'ri, n.* an instrument used for driving away flies. [Hindi *caurī.*]

choy-root. Same as **chay².**

chrematist *krē'mə-tist, n.* a political economist. — *adj.* **chrematis'tic** pertaining to finance, money-making, or political economy. — *n. sing.* **chrematis'tics** the science of wealth. [Gr. *chrēmatistēs,* a money-getter — *chrēma, -atos,* a thing, possession, money.]

chrestomathy *kres-tom'ə-thi, n.* a book of selections esp. in a foreign language, usu. for beginners. — *adjs.* **chrestomathic** (*-tō-math'ik*), **-al.** [Gr. *chrēstos,* useful, *mathein,* (aorist) to know.]

chrism *krizm, n.* consecrated or holy oil: unction: confirmation: chrisom. — *adj.* **chris'mal** pertaining to chrism. — *n.* a case for containing chrism: a pyx: a veil used in christening. — *ns.* **chris'matory** a vessel for holding chrism; **chris'om, christ'om** a white cloth or robe (also **chris'om-cloth**) put on a child newly anointed with chrism after its baptism: the child itself. — **chrisom child** (*Shak.*) a child still wearing the chrisom-cloth: a child that died in its first month, buried in its chrisom-cloth: an innocent child. [O.Fr. *chresme* (Fr. *chrême*) — Gr. *chrīsma* — *chrīein*, to anoint.]

Christ *krīst, n.* the Anointed, a name given to Jesus: a Messiah. — *v.t.* **christen** (*kris'n*) to baptise in the name of Christ: to give a name to: to use for the first time (*coll.*). — *ns.* **Christendom** (*kris'n-dəm*) that part of the world in which Christianity is the received religion: the whole body of Christians; **christening** (*kris'ning*) the ceremony of baptism; **Christ'hood** the condition of being the Christ or Messiah; **Christian** (*kris'chən*) a believer in the religion of Christ or one so classified: a follower of Christ: one whose behaviour is considered becoming to a follower of Christ: often a vague term of approbation, a decent, respectable, kindly, charitably minded person: a human being (*coll.*). — *adj.* relating to Christ or his religion: in the spirit of Christ. — *n.* **christianīsā'tion, -z-**. — *v.t.* **christ'ianise, -ize** to make Christian: to convert to Christianity. — *ns.* **christ'ianiser, -z-; Christ'ianism; Christianity** (*kris-ti-an'i-ti*) the religion of Christ: the spirit of this religion. — *adjs.* **Christ'ianlike; Christ'ianly**. — Also *adv.* — *ns.* **Christ'ianness; christ'ingle** a Christmas symbol for children, usu. consisting of an orange containing a candle, with fruit and nuts and red paper or ribbon, representing Christ as the light of the world, its creation and his passion; **Christ'liness**. — *adjs.* **Christ'less; Christ'like; Christ'ly** like Christ. — **criss-, Christ-cross-row** (*kris'kros-rō*) the alphabet, from the use in hornbooks of having a cross at the beginning; **Christian era** the era counted from the date formerly assigned to the birth of Christ; **Christian name** the name given at christening: the personal name as distinguished from the surname; **Christian Science** a religion which includes spiritual or divine healing, founded in 1866 by Mrs Eddy; **Christian Scientist; Christian Socialism** a mid-nineteenth century movement for applying Christian ethics to social reform: the principles of a pre-World War II Austrian Roman Catholic political party; **Christ's'-thorn** a prickly shrub (*Paliurus spina-christi*) of the buckthorn family common in the Mediterranean region, from which the crown of thorns is fancied to have been made: a kind of jujube tree (*Zizyphus spina-christi*) with the like legend. [O.E. *Crīst* — Gr. *Chrīstos* — *chrīein*, to anoint.]

Christadelphian *kris-tə-del'fi-ən, n.* a member of a small religious body believing in conditional immortality — sometimes called *Thomasites* from Dr John *Thomas* (1805–71). [Gr. *Chrīstos*, Christ, and *adelphos*, brother.]

christiana. Variant of **Christiania**.

Christiania *kris-ti-än'i-ə*, **Chris'tie, -ty** (also without *caps.*) *ns.* a turn with skis parallel executed when descending at speed. [Former name of Oslo.]

christingle. See under **Christ**.

Christmas *kris'məs, n.* an annual festival, orig. a mass, in memory of the birth of Christ, held on the 25th of December: the season at which it occurs: evergreens, esp. holly, for Christmas decoration (*arch.*). — Also *adj.* — *adj.* **Christ'mas(s)y** savouring of Christmas. — **Christmas box** a box containing Christmas presents: a Christmas gift, often of money to tradesmen, etc.; **Christmas cactus** a S. American cactus with red flowers; **Christmas cake** a rich fruit-cake, usu. iced, made for Christmas; **Christmas card** a card, more or less ornamented, sent to one's friends at Christmas; **Christmas daisy** the aster; **Christmas eve** Dec. 24; **Christmas pudding** a rich, spicy fruit-pudding, eaten at Christmas; **Christmas rose** or **flower** *Helleborus niger* flowering in winter: **Christmas stocking** a stocking that children hang up on Christmas eve to be filled with presents; **Christ'mas-tide, -time** the season of Christmas; **Christmas tree** a tree, usu. fir, set up in a room or a public place, and loaded with Christmas gifts and/or gauds:

an apparatus fitted to the outlet of an oilwell to control the flow of oil or gas. [**Christ** and **mass²**.]

Christolatry *kris-tol'ə-tri, n.* worship of Christ. [Gr. *Chrīstos*, Christ, *latreiā*, worship.]

Christology *kris-tol'ə-ji, n.* that branch of theology which treats of the nature and person of Christ. — *adj.* **Christological** (*-to-loj'i-kl*). — *n.* **Christol'ogist**. [Gr. *Chrīstos*, and *logos*, discourse.]

christom *kriz'əm*. See **chrisom** under **chrism**.

christophany *kris-tof'ə-ni, n.* an appearance of Christ to men. [Gr. *Chrīstos*, and *phainesthai*, to appear.]

Christy. See **Christiania**.

Christy-minstrel *krist'i-min'strəl, n.* one of a troupe of minstrels imitating Negroes. [Instituted by George *Christy*, in New York.]

chroma *krō'mə, n.* quality of colour: a hue. — *n.* **chrō'mate** a salt of chromic acid. — *adj.* **chrōmat'ic** pertaining to, or consisting of, colours: coloured: relating to notes in a melodic progression, which are raised or lowered by accidentals, without changing the key of the passage, and also to chords in which such notes occur (*mus.*). — *adv.* **chrōmat'ically**. — *ns.* **chrōmat'icism** (*mus.*) the state of being chromatic: the use of chromatic tones; **chrōmaticity** (*-tis'*) the colour quality of light depending on hue and saturation (i.e. excluding brightness), one method of defining it being by its purity and dominant wavelength. — *n.sing.* **chrōmat'ics** the science of colours. — *n.* **chrō'matin** a readily stained substance in the nucleus of a cell. — *adj.* **chrōmatograph'ic**. — *ns.* **chrōmatog'raphy** methods of separating substances in a mixture which depend on selective adsorption, partition between non-mixing solvents, etc., using a **chrōmat'ograph**, and which present the substances as a **chrōmat'ogram**, such as a series of visible bands in a vertical tube; **chrōmat'ophore** a pigment-cell, or a pigment-bearing body in protoplasm or photosynthetic bacteria; **chrōmatop'sia** (Gr. *opsis*, sight) coloured vision; **chromatosphere** see **chromosphere** below; **chrō'matype, chrō'motype** a photographic process that uses chromium salts; a photograph in colours: a sheet printed in colour; **chrome** chromium or a chromium compound. — Also *adj.* — *v.t.* in dyeing, to treat with a chromium solution: to plate with chromium. — *adj.* **chrō'mic** pertaining to trivalent chromium. — *ns.* **chrōmid'ium** an algal cell in a lichen: a free fragment of chromatin: — *pl.* **chrōmid'ia; chrō'minance** (*TV*) the difference between any colour and a reference colour (usu. a white of specified chromaticity) of equal luminance; **chrō'mite** a mineral, a double oxide of chromium and iron; **chrō'mium** a metallic element (at. numb. 24; symbol Cr) remarkable for the beautiful colour of its compounds; **chrō'mō** a chromolithograph: — *pl.* **chrō'mos; chrō'mōgram** a combination of photographs in different colours to give an image in natural colours; **chrō'mōlith'ograph**, or merely **chrōmō**, a lithograph printed in colours; **chrō'mōlithog'raphy; chrō'mōplast** (*bot.*) a chromatophore: **chrō'mōscope** an apparatus for combining coloured images; **chrō'mōsome** a rod-like portion of the chromatin of a cell-nucleus, performing an important part in mitotic cell-division, and in the transmission of hereditary characters. — *adj.* **chrōmosō'mal**. — *ns.* **chrō'mōsphere** a layer of incandescent gas surrounding the sun through which the light of the photosphere passes — also **chrō'matosphere; chrō'mōtypog'raphy** printing in colours; **chrō'mōxy'lograph** (Gr. *xylon*, wood) a picture printed in colours from wooden blocks; **chrō'mōxylog'raphy**. — **chromakey** (*TV*) a special effect in which a coloured background can be removed from a picture and a different background substituted; **chromatic aberration** blurring of an optical image, with colouring of the edges, caused by light of different wavelengths being focused at different distances; **chromatic scale** (*mus.*) a scale proceeding by semitones; **chrome'-al'um** potassium chromium sulphate; **chrome'-leath'er** leather prepared by chrome-tanning; **chrome'-plat'ing**

electroplating with chromium; **chrome'-spinel** picolite; **chrome'-steel'** an alloy steel containing chromium; **chrome'-tann'ing** tanning with salts of chromium; **chrome'-yell'ow** a pigment of lead chromate; **chromic acid** an acid of chromium (H_2CrO_4), of an orange-red colour, much used in dyeing and bleaching; **chromosome number** the number of chromosomes in a cell nucleus, constant for any given species. [Gr. *chrōma, -atos,* colour.]

chron-, chrono- *kron', -ō-, -ə-, krən-, kron-o',* in composition, time. — *adj.* **chron'ic** relating to time (*obs.*): lasting a long time: of a disease, deep seated or long continued, as opp. to *acute:* deplorable (*slang*). — *n.* a chronic invalid: a student who repeatedly fails in examinations (*slang*). — *adj.* **chron'ical** chronic. — *adv.* **chron'ically.** — *ns.* **chronic'ity; chron'icle** a bare record of events in order of time: a history: a story, account: (in *pl.,* with *cap.*) the name of two of the O.T. books. — *v.t.* to record as in a chronicle. — *ns.* **chron'icler** a writer of a chronicle; **chronobiol'ogy** the science of biological rhythms, esp. where the properties of the rhythms are measured; **chron'ogram** (Gr. *gramma,* letter) an inscription from which a date is got by adding the values of such letters as are Roman numerals; **chron'ograph** (Gr. *graphein,* to write) a chronogram: an instrument for taking exact measurements of time, or for recording graphically the moment or duration of an event; **chronog'rapher** a chronicler; **chronog'raphy** chronology; **chronol'oger.** — *adjs.* **chronolog'ic, -al.** — *adv.* **chronolog'ically.** — *ns.* **chronol'ogist; chronol'ogy** (Gr. *logos,* discourse) the science of computing time: a scheme of time: order of time; **chronom'eter** (Gr. *metron,* measure) an instrument for accurate measurement of time. — *adjs.* **chronomet'ric, -al.** — *ns.* **chronom'etry** the art of measuring time by means of instruments: measurement of time; **chrō'non** (*phys.*) a unit of time — that required for a photon to travel the diameter of an electron, 10^{-24} seconds; **chron'oscope** (Gr. *skopeein,* to look) an instrument used for measuring extremely short intervals of time, especially in determining the velocity of projectiles; **chron'otron** a device which measures very small time intervals by comparing the distance between electric pulses from different sources. — **chronicle play** a drama which follows closely historical events and characters; **chronological age** age in years, etc., opp. e.g. to *mental age.* [Gr. *chronos,* time; adj. *chronikos;* partly through A.Fr. *cronicle* (O.Fr. *cronique*).]

chronique scandaleuse *kro-nēk skā-da-lœz,* (Fr.) a story full of scandalous events or details.

chrys- *kris-,* **chryso-** *kris'ō-, -ə-, kris-ō',* in composition, gold. — *ns.* **chrys'alid, chrys'alis** (Gr. *chrȳsallis*) orig. a golden-coloured butterfly pupa: a pupa generally: a pupa case: — *pls.* **chrysalides** (*kris-al'i-dēz*), **chrys'alises, chrys'alids; Chrysan'themum** (*kris-* or *kriz-;* Gr. *anthemon,* flower) a genus of composite plants to which belong the corn marigold and ox-eye daisy: (without *cap.*) any plant of the genus: (without *cap.*) any of several cultivated plants of the genus, with colourful double flower-heads (often shortened to **chrysanth'**); **chrysarō'bin** (see **araroba**) a yellow crystalline mixture got from Goa powder and from rhubarb root: also one of its components, an active purgative. — *adj.* **chryselephant'ine** (Gr. *elephantīnos,* made of ivory — *elephas, -antos,* ivory) made of gold and ivory. — *ns.* **chrysober'yl** a mineral, beryllium aluminate, of various shades of greenish-yellow or gold colour; **chrysocoll'a** (Gr. *chrȳsokolla,* gold-solder, perh. applied to this mineral — *kolla,* glue) a silicate of copper, bluish-green; **chrysoc'racy** (Gr. *krateein,* to rule) the rule of wealth; **chrys'olite** (Gr. *lithos,* stone) olivine, esp. yellow or green precious olivine; **chrys'ophan** (Gr. *phainesthai,* to appear) an old name for chrysarobin. — *adj.* **chrysophan'ic** (**chrysophanic acid** an oxidation product of chrysarobin used against skin diseases). — *ns.* **chrysoph'ilite** (Gr. *phileein,* to love) a lover of gold; **chrys'oprase** (*-prāz;* Gr. *prason,* a leek)

a green chalcedony; **chrys'otile** (Gr. *tilos,* a shred) a fibrous serpentine, a form of asbestos. [Gr. *chrȳsos,* gold.]

chthonian *thō'ni-ən, adj.* pertaining to the earth or the underworld and the deities inhabiting it: ghostly. — Also **chthonic** (*thon'ik*). [Gr. *chthōn, chthŏnos,* the ground.]

chub *chub, n.* a small fat river-fish of the carp family. — *adjs.* **chubbed, chubb'y** short and thick, plump. — *n.* **chubb'iness.** — *adj.* **chub'-faced** plump-faced. [Origin unknown.]

Chubb® *chub, n.* a lock invented by Charles *Chubb* (1772–1846), a locksmith in London. — Also **chubb'-lock.**

chuck¹ *chuk, n.* the call of a hen: a chicken (dim. **chuck'ie**): a word of endearment. — *v.i.* to call, as a hen. [A variant of **cluck.**]

chuck² *chuk n.* a gentle blow under the chin: a toss or throw, hence dismissal (*coll.*): a pebble or small stone — usu. **chuck'ie, chuck'ie-stone, -stane** (*Scot.*): (in *pl.*) a game with such stones, often called **chuck'ies:** any game of pitch and toss. — *v.t.* to tap under the chin: to toss: to pitch: to abandon or dismiss. — **chuck'er-out'** (*coll.*) one who expels undesirable people; **chuck'-far'thing** a game in which a farthing is chucked into a hole. — **chuck it** (*coll.;* sometimes with *in*) to stop, give over; **chuck out** (*coll.*) to expel (a person): to throw away, get rid of; **chuck up** (*coll.*) to give up: to give in: to throw up (the sponge): to vomit. [Fr. *choquer,* to jolt; allied to **shock.**]

chuck³ *chuk, n.* a lump or chunk: an instrument for holding an object so that it can be rotated, as upon the mandrel of a lathe: food (*slang*): a cut of beef, the neck and shoulder-blade. — **chuck'-wagon** a wagon carrying food, cooking apparatus, etc. [Der. uncertain; cf. It. *cioco,* a block, stump.]

chuck-full. Same as **chock-full.** [See **chock.**]

chuckle¹ *chuk'l, n.* a quiet laugh: the cry of a hen. — *v.t.* to call, as a hen does her chickens. — *v.i.* to laugh in a quiet, suppressed manner, in derision or enjoyment. — *n.* **chuck'ling.** [Cf. **chuck¹.**]

chuckle² *chuk'l, adj.* clumsy. — **chuck'le-head** a loutish fellow. — *adj.* **chuck'le-head'ed** stupid: awkward, clumsy. [Prob. **chock,** a log.]

chuddah, chuddar. Variants of **chadar.**

chufa *chōō'fə, n.* a sedge with edible tubers. [Sp.]

chuff, though *chuf, n.* a clown: a surly fellow. — *n.* **chuff'iness** boorishness. — *adjs.* **chuffed** disgruntled; **chuff'y** coarse and surly. [M.E. *chuffe, choffe,* a boor (ety. dub.).]

chuffed *chuft, (coll.) adj.* very pleased. [Dial. *chuff,* chubby.]

chug *chug, n.* a rapid explosive noise, as of an internal-combustion engine. — *adj.* **chugg'ing.** — *v.i.* **chug** to make a chugging noise: of a vehicle, to move while making such a noise. [Imit.]

chukker, chukka *chuk'ər, -ə, ns.* a period of play in polo. [Hindi *cakkar,* a round.]

chukor *chu-kōr',* **chukar** *-kär',* **chik(h)or** *chi-kör', ns.* an Indian partridge. [Hindi *cakor.*]

chum¹ *chum, n.* a chamber-fellow: a friend or associate. — *v.i.* to share a room: to be or become a chum. — *v.t.* to assign as chum (with *on*): to be or become a chum to: to accompany. — *n.* **chumm'age** the quartering of two or more persons in one room: a fee demanded from a new chum. — *adj.* **chumm'y** sociable. — *n.* a chum: a compact motor-car body for a small company. — **chum up with** to become intimate with. [Perh. a mutilation of **chamber-fellow.**]

chum² *chum, n.* a dog-salmon or keta.

chumley. See **chimney.**

chummy *chum'i, (old slang) n.* a chimney sweeper's boy. — See also **chum¹.** [**chimney.**]

chump *chump, n.* an end lump of wood, mutton, etc.: a thick lump: a blockhead: the head. — **off one's chump** out of one's mind. [Perh. related to **chunk.**]

chunder *chun'dər, (Austr. slang) v.i.* to vomit. — Also *n.*

chunk *chungk, n.* a thick piece of anything, as wood, bread, etc. — *adj.* **chunk'y** in chunks: short and broad: of sweaters, etc., thick and heavy. [Perh. related to **chuck**.]

Chunnel *chun'l, n.* (also without *cap.*) the proposed tunnel underneath the English Channel, connecting England and France. [*Channel* t*unnel*.]

chunter *chun'tər, (coll.) v.i.* (often with *on*) to mutter: to grumble: to chatter unceasingly. — Also (*obs.* or *dial.*) **choun'ter, chun'der, chunn'er.** [Imit.]

chupati, chupatti. Same as **chapati, chapatti.**

chuprassy *chup-räs'i.* Same as **chaprassi.**

church *chûrch, n.* a house set apart for public worship, esp. that of a parish, and esp. that of an established or once established form of religion: a church service: the whole body of Christians: the clergy: any particular sect or denomination of Christians: any body professing a common creed, not necessarily Christian. — *adj.* of the church: ecclesiastical: belonging to the established church (*coll.*). — *v.t.* to perform a service in church with (e.g. a woman after childbirth, a newly-married couple, a new town council). — *n.* **churchian'ity** religion centring in the church rather than in Christ; **church'ing; church'ism** adherence to the form of principles of some church, esp. established. — *adjs.* **church'less** not belonging to a church: without church approval (*Tennyson*); **church'ly** concerned with the church: ecclesiastical. — *advs.* **church'ward(s)**. — *adj.* **church'y** obtrusively devoted to the church: savouring of church. — **church'-ale** a church festival; **Church Army** an organisation of the Church of England, resembling the Salvation Army; **church'-bench** (*Shak.*) a seat in the porch of a church; **church'-court** a court for deciding ecclesiastical causes: a kirk session: a presbytery, synod, or general assembly; **church'-goer** one on the way to, or who habitually goes to, church; **church'-going** the act or habit of going to church; **church'man** a clergyman or ecclesiastic: a member or upholder of the established church; **church militant** the church on earth in its struggle against evil; **church'-mouse** a mouse inhabiting a church, a proverbial example of poverty; **church'-off'icer** a church attendant or beadle; **church'-parade'** a uniformed parade of a military or other body for the purpose of church-going: the promenade of fashionable church-goers after service; **church'people; church'-rate** an assessment for the sustentation of the fabric, etc., of the parish church; **church'-ser'vice** a religious service in a church: the form followed: a book containing it; **church'-text** a thin and tall form of black-letter print; **church triumphant** the portion of the church which has overcome and left this world; **church'-war'den** an officer who represents the interests of a parish or church: a long clay-pipe; **church'way** the public way or road that leads to the church. — Also *adj.* (*Shak.*). — **church'-woman** a female member or upholder of a church, esp. the Anglican Church; **church'yard** a burial-ground round a church. [O.E. *cirice, circe* — Gr. *kȳriakon*, belonging to the Lord — *kȳrios*, lord.]

Churchillian *chûr-chil'iən, adj.* of, in the manner of, resembling Sir Winston *Churchill* (1874–1965), British prime minister.

churinga *choo-ring'gə, n.* a sacred amulet. [Australian Aboriginal.]

churl *chûrl, n.* a rustic, labourer: an ill-bred, surly fellow. — *adj.* **churl'ish** rude: surly: ungracious. — *adv.* **churl'ishly**. — *n.* **churl'ishness.** [O.E. *ceorl*, a countryman; O.N. *karl*, Ger. *Kerl*, a man; Scot. *carl*.]

churn *chûrn, n.* an apparatus used for the production of butter from cream or from whole milk: a large milk-can suggestive of an upright churn. — *v.t.* to agitate so as to obtain butter: to stir, agitate, violently (often with *up*): to turn over persistently (ideas in the mind). — *v.i.* to perform the act of churning: to move restlessly and with violence. — *n.* **churn'ing** the act of making butter: the quantity of butter made at once. — **churn'-drill** a drill worked by hand, not struck with the

hammer, a jumper; **churn'-milk** buttermilk; **churn'-staff** the plunger of an upright churn: the sun-spurge. — **churn out** to produce continuously with effort. [O.E. *cyrin*; O.N. *kirna*, a churn, Du. *karnen*, and Ger. *kernen*, to churn.]

churn-owl *chûrn'-owl, n.* the nightjar. [App. **churr** and **owl**.]

churr *chûr, n.* a low sound made by certain birds and insects. — *v.i.* to make this sound. — **churr'-worm** the fen-cricket. [Prob. imit.]

churrus. See **charas.**

chuse *chooz*, an *obs.* spelling of **choose.**

chut *chut, interj.* an expression of impatience.

chute[1], **shoot** *shoot, n.* a waterfall, rapid: a passage or sloping trough for sending down goods, water, logs, rubbish, etc.: a slide in a park, etc.: a narrow passage for controlling cattle. [Fr. *chute*, fall, combined with **shoot.**]

chute[2] *shoot*, abbrev. for **parachute**. — *n.* **chut'ist** a parachutist.

chutney *chut'ni, n.* an East Indian condiment, of mangoes, chillies, etc.: an imitation made with home materials, as apples. [Hindi *catnī*.]

chutzpah *hhoot'spə, n.* effrontery, nerve. [Yiddish.]

chyack. See **chiack.**

chylde. See **child.**

chyle *kīl, n.* a white fluid, mainly lymph mixed with fats derived from food in the body. — *n.* **chylu'ria** (Gr. *ouron*, urine) the presence of chyle in the urine. [Gr. *chȳlos*, juice — *cheein*, to pour.]

chyme *kīm, n.* the pulp to which food is reduced in the stomach. — *n.* **chymifica'tion** the act of being formed into chyme. — *v.t.* **chym'ify** to form into chyme. — *adj.* **chym'ous.** [Gr. *chȳmos*, chyme, juice — *cheein*, to pour.]

chymistry. See **chemistry.**

chymous. See **chyme.**

chynd *chīnd, (Spens.) p.adj.* cut into chines.

chypre *shē'pr', n.* a scent made from sandalwood, orig. from Cyprus. [Fr., Cyprus.]

ciao *chä'ö, Eng. chow, interj.* an informal greeting used on meeting or parting: — *pl.* **ciaos.** [It.]

cibation *si-bā'shən, (obs.) n.* the seventh of the twelve processes employed in the search for the philosopher's stone, 'feeding the matter': taking food, feeding. [L. *cibātiō*, -ōnis, feeding.]

cibol *sib'əl,* **chibol** *chib'əl, ns.* a variety of onion. [Fr. *ciboule* (Sp. *cebolla* — L.L. *cēpola*, dim. of L. *cēpa*, an onion; see **sybo(w)**).]

ciborium *si-bō'ri-əm, -bō', n.* a vessel closely resembling a chalice, usu. with an arched cover, in which the host is deposited: a canopy supported on four pillars over the high altar: — *pl.* **cibo'ria.** [L., a drinking-cup — Gr. *kibōrion*, the seed-vessel of the Egyptian water-lily.]

cicada *si-kä'də, -kä'də,* **cicala** *-kä'lə, ns.* a homopterous insect remarkable for its loud chirping sound. [L. *cicāda*; It. *cicala*.]

cicatrice *sik'ə-tris, n.* a scar over a healed wound: scar in the bark of a tree: the mark left where a leaf, etc., has been attached: mark, impression (*Shak.*): — *pl.* **cica-trī'cēs.** — Also **cicatrix** (*sik-ā'-triks, sik'ə-triks*): — *pl.* **cic'atrixes.** — *ns.* **cicatric'ula** the germinating point in the yolk of an egg; **cicatrīsā'tion, -z-,** the process of healing over. — *v.t.* **cic'atrīse, -ize** to help the formation of a cicatrix on: to scar. — *v.i.* to heal. [L. *cicātrīx, -īcis*, a scar.]

cicely *sis'ə-li, n.* a name for several umbelliferous plants allied to chervil, esp. *Myrrhis odorata* (**sweet cicely**). [L. and Gr. *seseli*.]

Cicero *sis'ə-rō* (L. *kik-e-rō), n.* a famous Roman orator: (without *cap.*) a type-body between pica and English. — *n.* **cicerone** (*chich-ə-rō'ni,* also *sis-ə-rō-ni*) one who shows strangers the curiosities of a place: a guide: — *pl.* **cicerō'ni** (*-nē*). — *v.i.* to act as cicerone. — *adjs.* **Cicerō'nian** (*sis-*), **Ciceronic** (*-ron'ik*). — *n.* **Cicerō'nianism** the character of Cicero's Latin style. [L.

Cicerō, -ōnis; It. *Cicerone.*]

cichlid *sik'lid, n.* any fish of the family **Cich'lidae,** to which the angel-fish of the Amazon belongs. — *adj.* **cich'loid.** [Gr. *kichlē*, a kind of wrasse.]

Cichorium *si-kō'ri-əm, -kō', n.* the chicory and endive genus of Compositae. — *adj.* **chichorā'ceous.** [L. *cichōrium* — Gr. *kichorion.*]

Cicindela *si-sin-dē'lə, n.* a genus of carnivorous beetles, type of the family **Cicinde'lidae,** the tiger-beetles, active in running down their insect prey. [L. *cicindēla*, glow-worm — *candēla*, a candle.]

cicinnus *si-sin'əs, n.* a cincinnus. [Latinised from Gr. *kinkinnos*, a ringlet.]

cicisbeo *chē-chēz-bā'ō, chi-chiz-, n.* a married woman's gallant or *cavaliere servente* in Italy: — *pl.* **cicisbe'i (-ē)**. — *n.* **cicisbē'ism.** [It.]

ciclaton, ciclatoun *sik'lə-tən, -tōōn, (obs.) n.* cloth of gold or other rich stuff: misunderstood by Spenser (see **checklaton**). [O.Fr. *ciclaton*, from Ar., perh. from the root of **scarlet.**]

Cicuta *si-kū'tə, n.* a genus of poisonous umbelliferous plants: (without *cap.*) a plant of the genus, water-hemlock or cowbane. [L. *cicūta*, hemlock.]

Cid *sid, sēd, n.* a chief, captain, hero — title of the 11th-cent. Castilian champion Rodrigo, or Ruy, Diaz. [Ar. *sayyid*, lord.]

cidaris *sid'ə-ris, n.* a Persian tiara: (with *cap.*) a genus of sea-urchins, mostly fossil. [Gr. *kidaris.*]

cide *sīd, v.t.* a proposed emendation for Shakespeare's **side,** as if aphetic for **decide,** to adjudge.

-cide *-sīd*, in composition, (1) killing, murder; (2) killer, murderer. — **-cī'dal** adjective combining form. [L. *caedere*, to kill.]

cider (sometimes **cyder**) *sī'dər, n.* an alcoholic drink made from apples. — *n.* **cī'derkin** an inferior cider. — *adj.* **cī'dery.** — **ci'der-and** a mixture of cider and spirits; **ci'der-cup** a drink of sweetened cider, with other ingredients; **ci'der-press** an apparatus for pressing the juice from apples. [Fr. *cidre* — L. *sīcera* — Gr. *sikera*, strong drink — Heb. *shēkār.*]

ci-devant *sē-də-vä, (Fr.) adj.* and *adv.* before this, former, formerly.

ciel, cieling. Variants of **ceil, ceiling.**

cierge. See **cerge.**

cig, etc. See **cigar.**

cigar *si-gär', n.* a roll of tobacco-leaves with a pointed end for smoking. — *ns.* **cigarette** *(sig-ə-ret')* finely-cut tobacco rolled in thin paper *(coll.* shortened forms **cig, cigg'ie, cigg'y**); **cigarillo** *(sig-ə-ril'ō)* a small cigar: — *pl.* **cigarill'os.** — **cigarette'-card** a picture card formerly given away with a packet of cigarettes, valued by cartophilists; **cigarette'-end, cigarette'-butt** the unsmoked remnant of a cigarette; **cigarette'-holder, cigar'-holder** a mouthpiece for a cigarette or cigar; **cigarette'-lighter** a mechanical contrivance for lighting cigarettes; **cigarette'-paper** paper for making cigarettes. — *adj.* **cigar'-shaped** cylindrical with tapered ends. — **cigar'-tree** a species of Catalpa with long cigar-like pods. [Sp. *cigarro.*]

ci-gît *sē-zhē, (Fr.)* here lies.

cilice *sil'is, n.* haircloth: a penitential garment made of haircloth. — *adj.* **cilicious** *(-ish'əs).* [L., — Gr. *kilikion*, a cloth made of Cilician goat's hair.]

cilium *sil'i-əm, n.* a hair-like lash borne by a cell: a flagellum: — *pl.* **cil'ia.** — *adj.* **cil'iary.** — *n.pl.* **Cilia'ta** a subclass of Infusoria retaining cilia throughout life. — *adjs.* **cil'iate, -d** bearing a cilium or cilia: fringed with hairs; **cil'iolate** fringed with very short fine hairs. — *n.pl.* **Cilioph'ora** (Gr. *phoros*, bearing) the Infusoria. [L. *cilium*, eyelash.]

cill *sil, (building) n.* an old variant of **sill,** now usual in the trade.

cimar. See **cymar.**

cimelia *sī-mē'li-ə, n.pl.* treasures. [Gr. *keimēlia.*]

Cimex *sī-meks, n.* the bed-bug genus of Hemiptera, giving name to the family **Cimicidae** *(sī-* or *si-mis'i-dē)*:

(without *cap.*) a member of the genus: — *pl.* **cimices** *(sim'i-sēz).*

cimier *sē-myā', n.* the crest of a helmet. [Fr.]

ciminite *sim'in-īt, n.* a rock intermediate between trachyte and andesite, containing olivine. [Monte *Cimini*, in Italy.]

Cimmerian *sim-ē'ri-ən, adj.* relating to the Cimmerii, a tribe fabled to have lived in perpetual darkness.

cimolite *sim'ō-līt, n.* a species of clay, or hydrous silicate of aluminium, used as fuller's earth. [Gr. *kimōliā*, prob. from *Kimōlos*, an island of the Cyclades.]

cinch *sinch, n.* a saddle-girth *(U.S.)*: a secure hold *(coll.)*: a certainty *(coll.)*: something easy *(coll.)*. — *v.i.* to tighten the cinch. — *v.t.* to bind firmly, esp. with a belt around the waist: to make sure of *(coll.)*: to pull (clothing) in tightly at the waist. [Sp. *cincha* — L. *cingula.*]

Cinchona *sing-kō'nə*, a rubiaceous genus of trees, yielding the bark from which quinine and its congeners are obtained —also called *Peruvian bark:* (without *cap.*) a tree of the genus: (without *cap.*) the dried bark of these trees. — *adjs.* **cinchonaceous** *(-kən-ā'shəs)*, **cinchonic** *(-kon'ik)*. — *n.* **cinch'onine** an alkaloid obtained from cinchona bark. — *adj.* **cinchoninic** *(-nin'ik)*. — *n.* **cinchonīsā'tion, -z-.** — *v.t.* **cinch'onise, -ize** to bring under the influence of cinchona or quinine. — *n.* **cinch'onism** a morbid state due to overdoses of cinchona or quinine. [Said to be so named from the Countess of *Chinchón*, who was cured of a fever by it in 1638.]

cincinnus *sin-sin'əs, (bot.) n.* a uniparous cymose inflorescence in which the plane of each daughter axis is at right angles, alternately to right and left, with that of its parent axis. — *adj.* **cincinn'ate.** [L., a curl.]

cincture *singk'chər, n.* a girdle or belt: a moulding round a column. — *v.t.* to gird, encompass. — *adjs.* **cinct** surrounded; **cinc'tured** having a cincture. [L. *cinctūra* — *cingĕre, cinctum*, to gird.]

cinder *sin'dər, n.* the refuse of burned coals: an ember: anything charred by fire: a scoriaceous fragment of lava: a strong stimulant put in tea, soda-water, etc. *(slang).* — *n.* **Cinderell'a** a scullery-maid: the despised and neglected one of a set. — Also *adj.* — *adj.* **cin'dery.** — **cin'der-cone** a hill of loose volcanic materials; **Cinderell'a-dance** a dancing-party ending at midnight — from the nursery tale; **cin'der-path, -track** a path, racing-track, laid with cinders. [O.E. *sinder*, slag; cf. Ger. *Sinter*; not connected with Fr. *cendre.*]

cine-, ciné- *sin'i-*, in composition, cinema, cinematograph. — **cin'e-biol'ogy, cin'é-** the study of biological phenomena by means of cinematographic records; **cin'e-cam'era, ciné-** a camera for taking moving photographs; **cin'e-film** film suitable for use in a cine-camera; **cinemicrog'raphy** cinematographic recording of changes under the microscope; **cin'e-project'or, ciné-; Cinerama®** *(-ə-rä'mə)* a method of film projection on a wide curved screen to give a three-dimensional effect — the picture is photographed with three **cineramic** cameras. — **ciné vérité** cinéma vérité.

cinéaste, cineast(e) *sin'ē-ast, n.* one who takes an artistic interest in, or who makes, motion pictures. [Fr.]

cinema *sin'ə-mə, -mä, n.* a cinematograph: a building in which motion pictures are shown: (with *the)* motion pictures collectively, or as an art: material or method judged by its suitability for the cinema. — Also **kin'ema** *(old).* — *n.* **cin'emathèque, -theque** *(-tek)* a small, intimate cinema. — *adj.* **cinemat'ic** pertaining to, suitable for, or savouring of, the cinema. — **cin'ema-go'er** one who goes (regularly) to the cinema; **cin'ema-or'gan** an organ with showier effects than a church organ; **Cin'emaScope®** name of one of the methods of film projection on a wide curved screen to give a three-dimensional effect — the picture is photographed with a special type of lens; **cinéma vérité** realism in films sought by photographing scenes of real life. [**cinematograph.**]

cinematograph *sin-ə-mat'ə-gräf, n.* apparatus for projecting a series of instantaneous photographs so as to give a moving representation of a scene, with or without reproduction of sound: an exhibition of such photographs. — Also **kinemat′ograph** (*old*). — *n.* **cinematog′rapher**. — *adjs.* **cinematograph′ic, cinematograph′ical**. — *ns.* **cinematog′raphist; cinematog′raphy** the art of making motion pictures. [Fr. *cinématographe* — Gr. *kīnēma, -atos,* motion, *graphein,* to write, represent.]

cineol, -ole *sin′i-ol, -ōl, n.* eucalyptol, a camphor-smelling disinfectant liquid (C₁₀H₁₈O) got from several essential oils, as eucalyptus, wormwood, cajeput. [From *Artemisia cīna,* a species of wormwood, and L. *oleum,* oil.]

cineraria¹ *sin-ə-rā′ri-ə, n.* a brightly-flowered variety of plants close akin to Senecio, with ashy down on the leaves. [L. *cinerārius,* ashy — *cinis, cineris,* ash.]

cineraria². See **cinerarium** under **cinerary**.

cinerary *sin′ə-rə-ri, adj.* pertaining to ashes: for containing ashes of the dead. — *ns.* **cinerā′rium** a place for depositing the ashes of the dead: — *pl.* **cinerā′ria; cinerā′tion; cinerā′tor; cinē′rea** grey nerve matter. — *adjs.* **cinē′real** ashy: cinerary; **cinē′reous** ashy-grey: ashy; **cineri′tious** ashy-grey: pertaining to grey nerve matter. [L. *cinereus,* ashy — *cinis, cineris,* ash.]

Cingalese. See **Sinhalese.**

cingulum *sing′gū-ləm, n.* a girdle: a girdle-like structure. [L. *cingĕre,* to gird.]

cingulum Veneris *sing′gū-ləm ve′nə-ris, king′gōō-lōōm ve′ne-ris (we′)* (L.) the girdle of Venus.

cinnabar *sin′ə-bär, n.* a mineral, sulphide of mercury, called vermilion when used as a pigment. — *adj.* vermilion-coloured. — *adjs.* **cinnabaric** (- *bär′ik*); **cinn′abarine** (*-bə-rēn*). — **cinnabar moth** a large red moth whose black and yellow caterpillars feed on ragwort. [Gr. *kinnabari,* from Persian.]

cinnamon *sin′ə-mən, n.* the spicy bark of a lauraceous tree of Sri Lanka: the tree: a light yellowish brown. — Also *adj.* — *adjs.* **cinnamic** (*-am′ik*), **cinnamonic** (*-ə-mon′ik*) obtained from, or consisting of, cinnamon. — **cinn′amon-bear** a cinnamon-coloured variety of grizzly or American black bear; **cinn′amon-stone** a yellowish grossular garnet. [Gr. *kinnamōmon,* later *kinnamon* — Heb. *qinnāmōn.*]

cinquain *sing′kān, n.* a poetic form consisting of five lines of two, four, six, eight and two syllables respectively. [Fr.]

cinque *singk, n.* the number five as on dice. — **cinque′-foil** a common bearing representing a flower with five petals borne full-faced and without a stalk (*her.*): a similar figure formed by cusps in circular window or the head of a pointed arch (*archit.*): species of the genus Potentilla (*bot*): the five-bladed clover (*bot.*); **cinque=pace** (*Shak.* also **sinke′-a-pace**) a kind of dance, the pace or movement of which is characterised by five beats. — *adj.* **cinque′-spott′ed** (*Shak.*) having five spots. — **Cinque Ports** the five ancient ports on the south of England lying opposite to France — Sandwich, Dover, Hythe, Romney, and Hastings (later associated with Winchelsea, Rye, and a number of subordinate ports). [Fr.]

cinquecento *ching′kwe-chen-tō, n.* the 16th century — the art and architecture of the Renaissance period. [It., five hundred, *mil,* one thousand, being understood.]

cion. A spelling of **scion** still used in U.S.

cipher (sometimes **cypher**) *sī′fər, n.* the character 0 (*arith.*): any of the Arabic numerals: any person or thing of little value: a nonentity: an interweaving of the initials of a name: a secret code: in an organ, continuous sounding of a note not played, due to a mechanical defect. — *v.i.* to work at arithmetic: of an organ, to sound a note continuously when it is not played. — *v.t.* to write in cipher: to calculate: to decipher (*Shak.*). — *n.* **cī′phering.** — **cī′pher-key** a key to a cipher or piece of secret writing. [O.Fr. *cyfre,* Fr. *chiffre* — Ar. *çifr,* zero, empty.]

cipollino *chē-pol-lē′nō, n.* a marble with green bands in

which calcite is interfoliated with mica or talc: — *pl.* **cipolli′nos.** — Also **cipolin** (*sip′ō-lin*). [It. *cipolla,* an onion.]

cippus *sip′əs, n.* the stocks: a monumental pillar: — *pl.* **cipp′ī.** [L. *cippus,* a post.]

circa *sûr′kə, prep.* and *adv.* about, around. [L.]

circadian *sûr-kā′di-ən, adj.,* esp. in **circadian rhythm,** pertaining to any biological cycle (e.g. of varying intensity of metabolic or physiological process, or of some feature of behaviour) which is repeated, usu. approx. every 24 hours. [From L. *circa,* about, *di(em),* day, and suff. *-an.*]

Circaean *sûr-sē′ən, adj.* relating to the beautiful sorceress Circe, who transformed the companions of Ulysses into swine by a magic beverage: infatuating and degrading. — Also **Circe′an.** — *n.* **Circae′a** the enchanter's nightshade genus. [L. *Circē* — Gr. *Kirkē.*]

circar. Same as **sircar.**

Circassian *sûr-kas(h)′yən, adj.* belonging to Circassia, the country of the Cherkesses in the western Caucasus. — *n.* a Cherkess: the language of the Cherkesses: (without *cap.*) a kind of light cashmere (also **circassienne′**). — **Circassian circle** a progressive dance in reel time.

circensian *sûr-sen′shi-ən, adj.* relating to the Circus Maximus, Rome, where the games were held. — Also **circen′sial** (*obs.*). [L. *circēnsis* — *circus.*]

circinate *sûr′sin-āt, adj.* ring-shaped: rolled inwards (*bot.*). [L. *circināre, -ātum,* make round.]

circiter *sûr′si-tər, prep.* (with dates) about, around. [L.]

circle *sûr′kl, n.* a plane figure bounded by one line every point of which is equally distant from a fixed point called the centre: the circumference of the figure so defined: a circular object: a ring: a planet's orbit: a parallel of latitude: a series ending where it began: a figure in magic: a group of things in a circle: a company surrounding or associating with the principal person: those of a certain class or group: an administrative unit. — *v.t.* to move round: to encompass: to draw a circle around. — *v.i.* (often with (*a*)*round*) to move in a circle: to stand in a circle. — *adj.* **cir′cled** circular: encircled. — *ns.* **cir′cler; cir′clet** a little circle: a little circular band or hoop, esp. a metal headband. — *n.* and *adj.* **cir′cling** moving in a circle. — **cir′cle-rider** one who rides in circles to round up cattle; **cir′cle-riding.** — **come full circle** to return to the beginning: to regain or turn out to be in a former state; **dress circle** see **dress; go round in circles** to get no results in spite of effort: not to get anywhere; **great, small, circle** a circle on the surface of a sphere whose centre is, is not, the centre of the sphere; **reasoning in a circle** assuming what is to be proved as the basis of the argument; **run round in circles** to act in too frenzied a way to achieve anything useful. [O.E. *circul* — L. *circulus,* dim. of *circus;* allied to O.E. *hring,* a ring.]

circs *sûrks,* (*slang*) *n.pl.* a shortened form of **circumstances.**

circuit *sûr′kit, n.* a journey round: a way round: perimeter: a roundabout way: an area enclosed: the path, complete or partial, of an electric current: a round made in the exercise of a calling, esp. in England (till 1972) by judges: the judges making the round: a district in which such a round is made, as by Methodist preachers, commercial travellers: a group of theatres, cinemas, etc., under common control, through which an entertainment circulates: the venues visited in turn and regularly by sports competitors, performers, etc.: a motor-racing track: diadem (*Shak.*). — *v.t.* to go round. — *n.* **circuiteer′** a judge who goes on a circuit. — *adj.* **circuitous** (*-kū′i-təs*) roundabout. — *adv.* **circū′itously.** — *ns.* **circū′itousness; circuitry** (*sûr′kit-ri*) the detailed plan of a circuit, as in radio or television, or its components; **circū′ity** motion in a circle: an indirect course. — **circuit board** a printed circuit board; **cir′cuit-breaker** a switch or other device for interrupting an electric circuit; **circuit judge** a judge in a county or crown court; **cir′cuit-rider** a preacher who goes on a circuit; **circuit training** a form of athletic training

consisting of repeated series of exercises. [Fr., — L. *circuitus* — *circuīre* — *circum*, round, *īre*, to go.]
circuitus verborum *sûr-kū'it-əs vûr-bō'rəm, -bō', kir-koō'-it-ōōs ver-, wer-bō'rōom,* (L.) a circumlocution.
circular *sûr'kū-lər, adj.* of or pertaining to a circle: in the form of a circle: round: ending in itself: recurring in a cycle: addressed to a circle of persons. — *n.* an intimation sent to a number of persons. — *v.t.* **cir'-cularise, -ize** to make circular: to send circulars to. — *n.* **circularity** (*-lar'i-ti*). — *adv.* **cir'cularly.** — **circular file** (*comput.*) one in which each item has a pointer to the next, the last leading back to the first; **circular function** any of the trigonometrical functions with argument in radians; **circular letter** a letter of which copies are sent to several persons; **circular measure** the reckoning of angles in radians; **circular note** a letter of bank-credit for the use of a traveller, being a kind of bill personal to the bearer, who also bears a letter of indication addressed to foreign bankers; **circular saw** a power-driven saw in the shape of a flat disc with a serrated edge. [L. *circulāris.*]
circulate *sûr'kū-lāt, v.t.* to make to go round as in a circle: to spread. — *v.i.* to move round: to be spread about: to repeat in definite order (of decimals). — *adj.* **cir'culable** capable of being circulated. — *n.* and *adj.* **cir'culating.** — *n.* **circulā'tion** the act of moving in a circle or in a closed path (as the blood): spreading or moving about: dissemination: the sale of a periodical: the money in use at any time in a country. — *adjs.* **cir'culātive, cir'culatory** circulating. — *n.* **cir'culātor.** — **circulating library** one from which books are circulated among subscribers; **circulatory system** the system of blood and lymph vessels, including the heart. — **in, out of, circulation** in, out of, general use, activity, etc. [L. *circulāre, -ātum.*]
circum- *sûr'kəm-, sər-kum'-, sûr'kəm-,* in composition, around. [L. *circum.*]
circumambages *sûr-kəm-am-bā'jēz, -am'bi-jiz, n. sing.* and *pl.* roundabout speech. — *adj.* **circumambā'gious** (*-jəs*) roundabout in speech. [L. *circum*, around, *ambāgēs*, a winding.]
circumambient *sûr-kəm-am'bi-ənt, adj.* going round about, encompassing. — *ns.* **circumam'bience, circumam'biency.** [L. *ambīre*, to go round.]
circumambulate *sûr-kəm-am'bū-lāt, v.i.* to walk round about. — *n.* **circumambulā'tion.** [L. *circum*, around, *ambulāre, -ātum*, to walk.]
circumbendibus *sûr-kəm-ben'di-bəs, n.* a roundabout way or expression. [Jocular formation from L. *circum*, round, **bend**, and L. abl. pl. ending *-ibus.*]
circumcentre *sûr'kem-sen-tər, n.* the centre of the circumscribed circle or sphere. [**circum-.**]
circumcise *sûr'kəm-sīz, v.t.* to cut or cut off all or part of the foreskin (male) or (*rare*) all or part of the clitoris (female), often as a religious rite: to purify (*fig.*). — *ns.* **cir'cumciser; circumcision** (*-sizh'n*) the act of circumcising: the state of being circumcised: those who are circumcised, esp. the Jews. [L. *circumcīdēre, -cīsum* — *caedēre*, to cut.]
circumdenudation *sûr-kəm-den-ū-dā'shən,* (*geol.*) *n.* denudation or erosion of surroundings, leaving an isolated elevation. [**circum-.**]
circumduct *sûr'kəm-dukt, v.t.* to lead around or about, to cause to revolve round an imaginary axis so as to describe a cone. — *v.t.* **circumduce** (*-dūs'*) in Scots law, to declare at an end (of the term for bringing proof). — *n.* **circumduc'tion.** — *adj.* **circumduct'ory.** [L. *circum*, round, *dūcěre, ductum*, to lead.]
circumference *ser-kum'fər-əns, n.* the boundary-line, esp. of a circle: compass: distance round. — *adj.* **circumferential** (*-en'shl*). — *n.* **circum'ferentor** (*-en-tər*) an instrument for measuring horizontal angles, consisting of a graduated circle, sights, and a magnetic needle: a graduated wheel for measuring the circumference of wheels. [L. *circum*, around, *ferre*, to carry.]
circumflect *sûr-kəm-flekt', v.t.* to bend round: to mark with a circumflex. — *ns.* **cir'cumflex** an accent (ˆ)

originally denoting a rising and falling of the voice on a vowel or syllable — also *adj.*; **circumflexion** (*-flek-shən*) a bending round. [L. *circum*, around, *flectěre, flexum*, to bend.]
circumfluence *sər-kum'flōō-əns, n.* a flowing round: the engulfing of food by surrounding it (as by protozoa, etc.). — *adjs.* **circum'fluent, circumflu'ous.** [L. *circum*, around, *fluěre*, to flow.]
circumforaneous *sûr-kəm-fō-rā'ni-əs, -fō-, adj.* wandering about as from market to market, vagrant. — Also **circumforā'nean.** [L. *circum*, around, *forum*, the forum, market-place.]
circumfuse *sûr-kəm-fūz', v.t.* to pour around. — *p.adj.* **circumfused'.** — *adj.* **circumfus'ile** molten. — *n.* **circumfusion** (*-fū'zhən*). [L. *circum*, around, *funděre, fūsum*, to pour.]
circumgyrate *sûr-kəm-ji'rāt, v.i.* to whirl round. — *n.* **circumgyrā'tion.** — *adj.* **circumgy'rātory.** [L. *circum*, around, *gyrāre, -ātum*, to turn.]
circumincession, -insession *sûr-kəm-in-sesh'ən, n.* the reciprocity of existence in one another of the three persons of the Trinity. [L. *circum*, around, and *incessus*, pa.p. of *incēdere*, to go, proceed.]
circumjacent *sûr-kəm-jā'sənt, adj.* lying round: bordering on every side. — *n.* **circumjā'cency.** [L. *circum*, around, *jacēns, -entis*, lying — *jacēre*, to lie.]
circumlittoral *sûr-kəm-lit'ə-rəl, adj.* adjacent to the shoreline. [L. *circum*, around, *littus*, for *lītus, -oris*, shore.]
circumlocution *sûr'kəm-lō-kū'shən, n.* expressing an idea in more words than are necessary: an instance of this: evasive talk. — *v.i.* **circumlocūte'** to use circumlocution. — *n.* **circumlocū'tionist** one who does this. — *adj.* **circumlocutory** (*-lok'ū-tər-i*). — **Circumlocution Office** in Dickens's *Little Dorrit*, a very dilatory government department. [L. *circum*, around, *loquī, locūtus*, to speak.]
circumlunar *sûr-kəm-loō'nər, -lū', adj.* situated or moving round the moon. [L. *circum*, around, *lūna*, the moon.]
circummure *sûr-kəm-mūr',* (*Shak.*) *v.t.* to wall around. [L. *circum*, around, *mūrus*, a wall.]
circumnavigate *sûr-kəm-nav'i-gāt, v.t.* to sail round. — *adj.* **circumnav'igable.** — *ns.* **circumnavigā'tion; circumnav'igātor.** [**circum-.**]
circumnutation *sûr-kəm-nū-tā'shən, n.* rotation in a nodding position, as in the growing point of a plant. — *v.i.* **circumnū'tate.** — *adj.* **circumnū'tatory.** [L. *circum*, around, *nūtāre, -ātum*, to nod.]
circumpolar *sûr-kəm-pō'lər, adj.* situated or ranging round the pole. — **circumpolar stars** stars so near the pole of the heavens that (for places at the latitude in question) they never set but merely revolve round the pole. [**circum-.**]
circumpose *sûr-kəm-pōz', v.t.* to place round. — *n.* **circumposi'tion** the act of placing round. [L. *circumpōnēre*, by analogy with *impose*, etc.]
circumscissile *sûr-kəm-sis'il, adj.* opening by a circular rent. [L. *circum*, around, *scissilis*, cleavable.]
circumscribe *sûr-kəm-skrīb', v.t.* to draw a line round: to describe a curve or figure touching externally: to enclose within certain limits, to curtail, abridge. — *adj.* **circumscrīb'able** able to be circumscribed. — *ns.* **circumscrīb'er** one who circumscribes; **circumscription** (*-skrip'shən*) limitation: the line that limits: the act of circumscribing: an inscription running round: a defined district. — *adj.* **circumscrip'tive** marking the external form or outline. [L. *circum*, around, *scrībēre, scrīptum*, to write.]
circumsolar *sûr'kəm-sō'lar, adj.* situated or moving round the sun. [L. *circum*, around, *sōl*, the sun.]
circumspect *sûr'kəm-spekt, adj.* looking round on all sides watchfully: cautious: prudent. — *n.* **circumspec'tion** watchfulness: caution: examining. — *adj.* **circumspec'tive** looking around: wary. — *adv.* **cir'cumspectly.** — *n.* **cir'cumspectness.** [L. *circum*, around, *specěre, spectum*, to look.]
circumstance *sûr'kəm-stəns, n.* the logical surroundings

of an action: an attendant fact: an accident or event: ceremony: detail: (in *pl.*) the state of one's affairs. — *v.t.* to place in particular circumstances. — *adj.* **circumstantial** (*-stan'shl*) consisting of details: minute. — *n.* **circumstantiality** (*-stan-shi-al'i-ti*) the quality of being circumstantial: minuteness in details: a detail. — *adv.* **circumstan'tially**. — *n.pl.* **circumstan'tials** incidentals: details. — *v.t.* **circumstan'tiate** to prove by circumstances: to describe exactly. — **circumstantial evidence** evidence which is not positive nor direct, but which is gathered inferentially from the circumstances in the case; **in good** or **bad circumstances** prosperous or unprosperous; **in, under, no circumstances** never; **in, under, the circumstances** conditions being what they are; **not a circumstance to** (*old U.S. coll.*) nothing in comparison to.   [L. *circum*, around, *stāns*, *stantis*, standing — *stāre*, to stand.]

circumterrestrial *sûr-kəm-ti-res'tri-əl*, *adj.* situated or moving round the earth.   [L. *circum*, around, *terrestris*, — *terra*, the earth.]

circumvallate *sûr-kəm-val'āt*, *v.t.* to surround with a rampart. — *n.* **circumvallā'tion** a surrounding with a wall: a wall or fortification surrounding a town or fort: engulfing of food by surrounding it (as by protozoa) (*zool.*).   [L. *circum*, around, *vallum*, rampart.]

circumvent *sûr-kəm-vent'*, *v.t.* to go round: to encompass: to surround so as to intercept or capture: to get round, or to outwit. — *n.* **circumven'tion**. — *adj.* **circumvent'ive** deceiving by artifices.   [L. *circum*, around, *venīre*, *ventum* to come.]

circumvolve *sûr-kəm-volv'*, *v.t.* to roll round. — *v.i.* to revolve. — *n.* **circumvolution** (*-lōō'*, *-lū'*) a turning or rolling round: anything winding or sinuous.   [L. *circum*, around, *volvēre*, *volūtum*, to roll.]

circus *sûr'kəs*, *n.* a circular building for the exhibition of games: a place, building, or tent for the exhibition of feats of horsemanship and other performances: a show of this kind or the company of performers (also *fig.*): a group of houses arranged in the form of a circle: an open place at a street junction: a natural amphitheatre: a group of people who travel around putting on a display (as *flying circus*), often in the form of a competition (as *tennis circus*): a noisy entertainment or scene. — *adj.* **cir'cus(s)y**. — *n.* **cirque** (*sûrk*; from Fr.) a circus: a ring (*poet.*): a deep round hollow, a natural amphitheatre (*geog.*).   [L. *circus* — Gr. *kirkos*.]

ciré *sē'rā*, *n.* (a fabric with) a highly glazed finish.   [Fr. pa.p. of *cirer*, to wax.]

cire perdue *sēr per-dü*, (Fr.) lit. 'lost wax', a method of casting in metal, the mould being formed round a wax model which is then melted away.

cirl *sûrl*, *n.* a species of bunting (usu. **cirl bunting**).   [It. *cirlo*.]

cirque. See under **circus**.

cirrate, cirriform, etc. See **cirrus**.

cirrhopod *sir'ə-pod*, **Cirrhopoda** *sir-ə-pō'də*, older forms of **cirripede, Cirripedia** (as if from Gr. *kirrhos*, tawny, *pous, podos*, foot); also by confusion, **cirrh'ipede, Cirrhipe'dia**.

cirrhosis *si-rō'sis*, *n.* a wasting of the proper tissue of the liver, accompanied by abnormal growth of connective tissue. — *adj.* **cirrhŏt'ic**.   [Gr. *kirrhos*, tawny — from the colour of the liver so diseased.]

cirripede *sir'i-pēd*, *n.* one of the **Cirripe'dia**, a degenerate class of Crustacea, the barnacles and acorn-shells. — Also **cirr'iped** (*-ped*).   [L. *cirrus*, a curl, *pēs, pedis*, foot.]

cirrus *sir'əs*, *n.* the highest form of clouds, consisting of curling fibres: a tendril (*bot.*): any curled filament (*zool.*): — *pl.* **cirr'ī**. — *adjs.* **cirr'ate, cirr'iform** like a cirrus; **cirr'igrade** moving by cirri; **cirr'ose** with tendrils; **cirr'ous** having a cirrus. — **cirr'o-cū'mulus** a cloud of small white flakes or ripples (also *mackerel sky*); **cirr'o-strā'tus** a high thin sheet of haze-like cloud.   [L., a curl, tuft; the common spellings cirrhus, etc., are due to confusion with Gr. *kirrhos*, tawny.]

Cisalpine *sis-alp'in, -īn, adj.* on this (i.e. the Roman) side of the Alps. — *adjs.* **Cisatlan'tic; Cisleithan** (*-lī't(h)ən*) on this side of the Leitha (which once in part separated Austria and Hungary): Austrian; **cislu'nar** on this side of the moon, i.e. between the moon and the earth; **cismon'tane** on this side of the mountains — opp. to *ultramontane*; **Cispadane** (*-pā'dān, sis'pa-dān*; L. *Padus*) on this (Roman) side of the Po; **cispon'tine** on this side of the bridges, viz. in London, north of the Thames.   [L. *cis*, on this side.]

cisco *sis'kō*, *n.* a variety of Coregonus (*Leucichthys*) found in Great Lakes of North America — also *lake herring*: — *pl.* **cis'coes, cis'cos**.   [Fr.-Canadian, *cisco(ette)* — Ojibwa, *pemitewiskawet*, that which has oily flesh.]

ciselure *sēz'lōōr*, *n.* the art or operation of chasing: the chasing upon a piece of metalwork. — *n.* **cis'eleur** (*-lər*), a chaser.   [Fr.]

cissoid *sis'oid*, *n.* a plane curve consisting of two infinite branches symmetrically placed with reference to the diameter of a circle, so that at one of its extremities they form a cusp, while the tangent to the circle at the other extremity is an asymptote.   [Gr. *kissoeidēs*, ivy-like — *kissos*, ivy, *eidos*, form.]

cissy *sis'i*, (*slang*) *n.* an effeminate person. — Also *adj.* [Partly from the name *Cecily*, partly from **sister;** cf. **sis**.]

cist *sist*, *n.* a tomb consisting of a stone chest covered with stone slabs. — *adjs.* **cist'ed** containing cists; **cist'ic** like a cist.   [See **chest**.]

Cistercian *sis-tûr'shən*, *n.* a member of the order of monks established in 1098 in the forest of Cîteaux, (*Cistercium*), in France — an offshoot of the Benedictines. — Also *adj.*

cistern *sis'tərn*, *n.* an artificial reservoir or tank for holding water or other liquid: a natural reservoir.   [L. *cisterna* — *cista*, a chest.]

cistic. See **cist**.

cistron *sis'trən*, *n.* the section of a chromosome which controls protein structure.   [*cis-trans* (test, to define the unit of genetic function).]

Cistus *sis'təs*, *n.* the rock-rose genus of shrubby plants, giving name to the family **Cistā'ceae**, cultivated for the beauty of their flowers: (without *cap.*) any plant of the genus: — *pl.* **cis'tuses**.   [Gr. *kistos*, rock-rose.]

cistvaen. See **kistvaen**.

cit *sit*, (*arch. slang*) *n.* a term of contempt for a townsman, not a gentleman: — *fem.* **cit'ess** (*Dryden*). — *n.pl.* **cits** (*U.S. slang*) civilian clothes.   [**citizen**.]

citadel *sit'ə-dəl*, *n.* a fortress in or near a city: the place where the guns are kept in a warship: in the Salvation Army, the hall in which meetings are held.   [It. *cittadella*, dim. of *città*, a city; see **city**.]

cite *sīt*, *v.t.* to call or summon: to summon to appear in court: to quote: to name: to adduce as proof. — *adj.* **cīt'able** that can be cited. — *ns.* **cīt'al** summons to appear; **citā'tion** (*sīt-, sit-*) an official summons to appear: a document containing the summons: the act of quoting: the passage or name quoted: mention in dispatches: official recognition of achievement. — *adj.* **cit'atory** having to do with citation: addicted to citation. — *n.* **cīt'er**.   [L. *citāre, -ātum*, to call, intens. of *ciēre, cīre*, to make to go.]

cithara *sith'ə-rə*, *n.* an ancient Greek musical instrument differing from the lyre in its flat shallow sound-chest. — *n.* **cith'arist** a player on it. — *adj.* **citharist'ic**. — *ns.* **cith'er, cith'ern, citt'ern** an early modern metal-stringed musical instrument, played with a plectrum: the Tirolese zither.   [L., — Gr. *kitharā*; cf. **guitar, zither**.]

citify. See **city**.

citigrade *sit'i-grād, adj.* moving quickly: applied to a tribe of spiders that run down their prey — Lycosidae or wolf-spiders.   [L. *citus*, quick, *gradus*, a step.]

citizen *sit'i-z(ə)n*, *n.* an inhabitant of a city: a member of a state: a townsman: a freeman: a civilian (*U.S.*): — *fem.* **cit'izeness**. — *adj.* (*Shak.*) like a citizen. — *v.t.* **cit'izenise, -ize** to make a citizen of — *ns.* **cit'izenry** the general body of citizens; **cit'izenship** the state of being or of having rights and duties of a citizen: conduct in relation to these duties. — **citizen's arrest** an arrest, legally allowable, made by a member of the public; **Citizens' Band** (orig. *U.S.*) a band of radio frequencies on which the public are permitted to broadcast personal messages, etc.; **Citizens' Band radio** (also **CB radio**). [M.E. *citesein* — O.Fr. *citeain*; see **city**.]

cito *sī'*, *ki'tō*, (L.) *adv.* quickly.

citole *sit'ōl*, *sit-ōl'*, *n.* a mediaeval stringed instrument, prob. an earlier form of **cither** (see under **cithara**).

citron *sit'rən*, *n.* the fruit of the citron tree, resembling a lemon: the tree that bears it (*Citrus medica*), considered to be the parent of the lemon and lime-fruit. — *ns.* **cit'range** (*-rənj*) a hybrid between citron and orange; **cit'rate** a salt of citric acid. — *adjs.* **cit'reous** citrine; **cit'ric** derived from the citron (**citric acid** the acid to which lemon and lime juice owe their sourness, $C_6H_8O_7$). — *n.* **cit'rin** the water-soluble vitamin P, found in citrus fruits, etc. — *adj.* **cit'rine** (*-rin*) dark and greenish yellow, like a citron or lemon. — *n.* citrine colour: a rock-crystal of this colour. — *n.* **citronell'a** a Ceylon grass (**citronell'a-grass,** *Cymbopogon nardus*) yielding **citronell'a-oil,** used in perfumery. — *adj.* **cit'rous.** — *n.* **cit'rus** a citron tree: (with *cap.*) a genus of Rutaceae including the citron, lemon, orange, etc. — **citron tree; citron wood, citrus wood** the most costly furniture wood of the ancient Romans (perhaps sandarach); **citrus fruits** citrons, lemons, limes, oranges, grapefruit. — **citric acid cycle** a cycle of chemical changes in living material (e.g. muscle), in course of which citric acid is oxidised, and by which acetic acid or acetyl is converted to carbon dioxide and water, the chemicals released in the process being important to the tissue. [L. *citrus*, from which comes also Gr. *kitron*, a citron.]

cittern. Same as **cither.** [See under **cithara**.]

city *sit'i*, *n.* a large town: an incorporated town that has or had a cathedral: a town on which the dignity has been conferred by tradition or grant: in various countries a municipality of higher rank, variously defined: the business centre or original area of a large town: (often with *cap.*) the centre of British financial affairs, most banks, etc., being in the City of London. — *n.* **citificā'tion.** — *v.t.* **cit'ify** to give the characteristics or attitudes of the city, or city culture, to (a person, etc.). — **city article** in a newspaper, a financial or commercial article; **City Company** a London corporation representing any of the mediaeval trade guilds; **city desk** the desk or (*fig.*) the department or field of work of a city editor: **city editor** the financial editor of a newspaper: the editor in charge of local news, etc. of a newspaper (*U.S.*); **city fathers** the magistrates: the town or city council; **city farm** a farm established within an urban area in order to let city children learn about agriculture; **city hall** a town hall; **city man** a man engaged in commercial or financial work in a city; **city manager** a man appointed by an elected body to manage the administrative affairs of a city; **city mission** a mission for evangelising the poor classes in the large cities; **cit'yscape** a view or picture of a city (following *landscape*); **cit'y-slick'er** a city-dweller perceived as over-sophisticated and untrustworthy; **city state** a sovereign state consisting of a city with a small surrounding territory. — **city of God, heavenly city**, etc., the ideal of the Church of Christ in glory; **city of refuge** by the Jewish law a city where the perpetrator of an accidental homicide might flee for refuge; **Eternal City** Rome; **Holy City** Jerusalem. [Fr. *cité*, a city — L. *civitās*, *-ātis*, the state — *cīvis*, a citizen.]

cive *sīv*. See **chive**.

civet *siv'it*, *n.* a perfume obtained from the **civet** or **civet cat**, a small cat-like carnivore (*Viverra*) of Africa, India, etc. [Fr. *civette* — Ar. *zabād*.]

civic *siv'ik*, *adj.* pertaining to a city or citizen. — *adv.* **civ'ically.** — *n. sing.* **civ'ics** the science of citizenship. — **civic centre** a place in which the chief public

buildings of a town are grouped; **civic crown** an oak wreath awarded to a Roman solider for saving a citizen's life in battle. [L. *cīvicus* — *cīvis*, citizen.]

civil *siv'il*, *adj.* pertaining to the community: polite (in any degree short of discourtesy): pertaining to ordinary life, not military: lay, secular, temporal, not ecclesiastical: pertaining to the individual citizen: relating to private relations amongst citizens, and such suits as arise out of these, as opposed to *criminal* (*law*): naturally good, as opposed to good through regeneration (*theol.*). — *n.* **civil'ian** a professor or student of civil law (not canon law): one engaged in civil as distinguished from military and naval pursuits. — Also *adj.* — *v.t.* **cīvil'ianise, -ize** to convert from military to civilian use: to replace military personnel in (a factory, etc.) by civilians. — *ns.* **civ'ilist** (*arch.*) one versed in civil law; **civil'ity** civilisation (*arch.*): good-breeding (*obs.*): politeness: polite attentions. — *adv.* **civ'illy.** — *ns.* **civ'ism** good citizenship: state of being well-affected to French Revolution principles; **civv'y** (*slang*) civilian: (in *pl.* **civv'ies**) civilian clothes. — Also *adj.* — **civil aviation** non-military flying, esp. commercial airlines and their operation; **civil day, year, time** the day, year, time, as reckoned for ordinary purposes; **civil death** the loss of all civil and legal privileges; **civil defence** a civilian service for the wartime protection of the civilian population against the effects of enemy attack by air, etc.; **civil disobedience** refusal to obey laws and regulations, pay taxes, etc., used as non-violent means of forcing concessions from government; **civil engineer** one who plans and builds railways, docks, etc., as opposed to a military engineer, or to a mechanical engineer, who makes machines, etc.; **civil law** as opposed to criminal law, the law laid down by a state regarding the rights of the inhabitants, esp. that founded on Roman law; **civil liberty** (often in *pl.*) personal freedom of thought, word, action, etc.; **civil list** formerly a list of charges for civil government purposes: now the expenses of the sovereign's household only (**civil list pensions** those granted by royal favour); **civil rights** (often with *caps.*) the rights of a citizen to personal freedom, i.e. political, racial, legal, social, etc. — Also *adj.* — **civil servant; civil service** the paid service of the state, in so far as it is not military or naval. — *adj.* **civ'il-suited** (*Milton*) sombrely clad. — **civil war** a war between citizens of the same state; **civvy street** (*coll.*) civilian life after the Services. [L. *cīvīlis* — *cīvis*, citizen.]

civilise, -ize *siv'il-īz*, *v.t.* to reclaim from barbarism: to instruct in arts and refinements. — *adj.* **civilīs'able, -z-.** — *n.* **civilīsātion, -z-** the state of being civilised: culture: cultural condition or complex. — *adj.* **civ'ilised, -z-** (having) advanced beyond the primitive savage state: refined in interests and tastes: sophisticated, self-controlled and fair-spoken. — *n.* **civ'ilīser, -z-.** [See **civil**.]

civvies. See **civil**.

cizers. An old spelling (*Shak.*) of **scissors**.

clabber *klab'ər*, (esp. *Ir.*) *n.* mud. [Ir. *clabar*, mud.]

clachan *klä'* or *kla'hhən* (*Scot.*) *n.* a small village. [Gael. *clachan* — *clach*, stone.]

clack *klak*, *v.i.* to make a noise as of a flat thing flapping: to chatter: to cackle. — *n.* a noise of this kind: an instrument making it: sound of voices: the tongue (*coll.*). — *n.* **clack'er.** — **clack'box** the box containing the clack-valve of an engine; **clack'dish** (*Shak.*) a wooden dish carried by beggars, having a movable cover which they clacked to attract attention; **clack'-valve** a valve consisting of a hinged flap or other device that falls back with a clacking noise. [Prob. from the sound.]

clad *klad*, *pa.t.* and *pa.p.*, also (*Spens.*) *pres. infin.*, of **clothe.** — *adj.* clothed, or covered. — *v.t.* to cover one material with another, e.g. one metal with another (as in nuclear reactor), or brick or stonework with a different material (in building). — *ns.* **cladd'er; cladd'ing.**

clade *klād*, (*biol.*) *n.* a group of organisms that have evolved from a common ancestor. — *ns.* **clād'ism** adherence to cladistic theories; **clād'ist.** — *adj.* **clădis-t'ic.** — *ns.* **clădist'ics** a taxonomic theory which classifies organisms according to the shared characteristics which distinguish a group from other groups; **clădo-gen'esis** evolution of clades as if by branching from a common ancestor; **clād'ogram** a tree-like diagram showing the development of a clade. [Gr. *klados*, branch.]

cladode *klad'ōd*, (*bot.*) *n.* a branch with the appearance and functions of a leaf. [Gr. *klados*, a shoot.]

claes *klāz*, *n.pl.* Scots for **clothes.**

clag *klag*, (*dial.*) *v.i.* to stick. — *v.t.* to bedaub: — *pr.p.* **clagg'ing;** *pa.t.* and *pa.p.* **clagged.** — *n.* a sticky mass or clot of dirt, etc. — *adj.* **clagg'y** tenacious. [Prob. Scand.; Dan. *klag*, mud; cf. **clay.**]

claim *klām*, *v.t.* to call for: to demand as a right: to maintain or assert. — *v.i.* to make a claim (*on* one's insurance policy, etc.). — *n.* a demand for something supposed due: a right or ground for demanding: the thing claimed, esp. a piece of land appropriated by a miner or other: (*Spens.* **clame**) a call, shout. — *adj.* **claim'able** that can be claimed. — *ns.* **claim'ant,** **claim'er** one who makes a claim. — **claiming race** a race in which any horse having taken part in the race may be bought at a previously fixed price by anyone starting a race at the meeting (cf. *selling race*); **claim'-jumper** one who takes possession of another's mining claim; **claims assessor** an assessor employed by an insurance company, usu. in motor accident claims. — **lay claim to** to assert a right to; **stake a claim** see **stake**[1]. [O.Fr. *claimer* — L. *clāmāre*, to call out.]

clairaudience *klār-öd'i-əns*, *n.* the alleged power of hearing things not present to the senses. — *n.* and *adj.* **clairaud'ient.** [Fr. *clair* — L. *clārus*, clear, and **audience.**]

claircolle. See **clearcole.**

clair-obscure, clare-obscure *klār-ob-skūr'*. Same as **chiaroscuro** (q.v.). [Fr. *clair* — L. *clārus*, clear, and Fr. *obscur* — L. *obscūrus*, obscure.]

clairschach *klār'shähh.* A variant of **clarsach.**

clairvoyance *klār-voi'əns*, *n.* the alleged power of seeing things not present to the senses. — Also **clairvoy'ancy.** — *n.* and *adj.* **clairvoy'ant.** [Fr. *clair* — L. *clārus*, clear, and Fr. *voir* — L. *vidēre*, to see.]

clam[1] *klam*, *n.* a gripping instrument: a very reticent person (*coll.*): a scallop or scallop-shell (Pecten): in America an edible shellfish of various kinds, esp. the round clam or quahog (*Venus mercenaria*) and the long clam (*Mya arenaria*). — *v.i.* to gather clams: — *pr.p.* **clamm'ing;** *pa.t.* and *pa.p.* **clammed.** — **clam'bake** a baking of clams on hot stones, with layers of potatoes, fish, Indian corn, etc., popular at picnic parties in U.S.: such a party: any informal party. — **clam-chow'der** chowder made with clams; **clam'-shell.** — **clam up** (*coll.*) to be silent. [O.E. *clam*, fetter; cf. Ger. *Klamm;* Dan. *klamme.*]

clam[2] *klam*, *v.t.* to clog (*dial.*): to smear (*dial.*): — *pr.p.* **clamm'ing;** *pa.t.* and *pa.p.* **clammed.** — *n.* dampness (*dial.*). — *adv.* **clamm'ily.** — *n.* **clamm'iness.** — *adj.* **clamm'y** sticky: moist and adhesive. [O.E. *clǣman*, to anoint: cf. Du., Dan. *klam*, damp.]

clam[3] *klam*, *n.* noise produced by ringing two or more bells together. — Also *v.t.* and *v.i.* [Prob. onomatopoeic.]

clamant *klam'ənt, klām'ənt*, *adj.* calling aloud or earnestly. — *n.* **clam'ancy** urgency. — *adv.* **clam'antly.** [L. *clāmāre*, to cry out.]

clambe *klām*, (*Spens.*) *pa.t.* of **climb.**

clamber *klam'bər*, *v.i.* to climb with difficulty, grasping with hands and feet. — *n.* the act of clambering. [From the root of **climb;** cf. Ger. *klammern* — *klemmen*, to squeeze or hold tightly.]

clame (*Spens.*). Same as **claim.**

clamjamphrie, clamjamfry *klam-jam'fri*, (*Scot.*) *n.* rub-bish: nonsense: rabble. — Also **clanjam'fray.** [Der. uncertain.]

clammed, clamming, clammy. See **clam**[1], **clam**[2].

clamour[1], in U.S. **clamor**, *klam'ər*, *n.* a loud continuous outcry: uproar: any loud noise: persistent expression of dissatisfaction. — *v.i.* to cry aloud in demand (often with *for*): to make a loud continuous outcry. — *adj.* **clam'orous** noisy, boisterous. — *adv.* **clam'orously.** — *ns.* **clam'orousness; clam'ourer.** — **clamour down, into, out of** to force an objective by clamouring. [L. *clāmor, -ōris.*]

clamour[2] *klam'ər*, (*Shak*) *v.t.* to silence, check the ringing of. [Perh. conn. with **clam**[3].]

clamp[1] *klamp*, *n.* a piece of timber, iron, etc., used to fasten things together or to strengthen any framework: any instrument for holding: a wheel clamp. — *v.t.* to bind with a clamp: to grasp or press firmly: to put (on) authoritatively, impose. — **clamp down on** to suppress, or suppress the activities of, firmly (*n.* **clamp'down**). [From a root seen in O.E. *clam*, fetter; Du. *klamp*, a clamp; akin to **clip, climb.**]

clamp[2] *klamp*, *n.* a heavy tread. — *v.i.* to tread heavily. [Prob. from the sound.]

clamp[3] *klamp*, *n.* a stack, as of bricks for burning, peats, etc.: a heap: a covered heap of root vegetables. — *v.t.* to put in clamps. [Prob. Du. *klamp*, heap.]

clamper *klam'pər*, (*Scot.*) *v.t.* to botch up. [Der. unknown; prob. conn. with **clamp**[1].]

clan *klan*, *n.* a tribe or collection of families subject to a single chieftain, commonly bearing the same surname, and supposed to have a common ancestor: a clique, sect: a collective name for a number of persons or things. — *adj.* **clann'ish** closely united and holding aloof from others, like the members of a clan. — *adv.* **clann'ishly.** — *ns.* **clann'ishness; clan'ship** association of families under a chieftain: feeling of loyalty to a clan. — **clans'man, clans'woman** a member of a clan. [Gael. *clann*, offspring, tribe — L. *planta*, a shoot.]

clandestine *klan-des'tin*, *adj.* concealed or hidden: private: sly. — *adv.* **clandes'tinely.** — *ns.* **clandes'tineness, clan-destin'ity.** [L. *clandestīnus* — *clam*, secretly.]

clang[1] *klang*, *v.i.* to produce a loud deep ringing sound. — *v.t.* to cause to clang. — *n.* a ringing sound, like that made by striking large pieces of metal, or that of a trumpet: the sonorous cry of some birds, as cranes or geese. — *n.* **clang'er** a singularly ill-timed remark or comment: a stupid mistake. — *n.* and *adj.* **clang'ing.** — *adj.* **clangorous** (*klang'gər-əs*). — *adv.* **clang'orously.** — *n.* **clang'our,** in U.S. **clang'or,** a clang: a loud ringing noise. — *v.i.* to make a clangour. — **drop a clanger** (*coll.*) to say something tactless: to make a stupid blunder. [L. *clangĕre*, to sound; *clangor*, noise of birds or wind instruments.]

clang[2]. See **klang.**

clanjamfray. See **clamjamphrie.**

clank *klangk*, *n.* a metallic sound, less prolonged than a clang, such as is made by chains hitting together. — *v.i.* or *v.t.* to make or cause to make a clank. — *n.* **clank'ing.** — *adj.* **clank'less** without clank. [Prob. formed under the influence of **clink**[1] and **clang**[1].]

clap[1] *klap*, *n.* a sudden blow or stroke (*lit.* or *fig.*): a slap: a pat (*Scot.*): the noise made by the sudden striking together of two things, as the hands: a burst of sound, esp. thunder. — *v.t.* to strike together so as to make a noise: to thrust or drive together suddenly: to fasten promptly: to pat (*Scot.*): to applaud with the hands: to bang: to put suddenly (e.g. in prison). — *v.i.* to strike the hands together: to strike or slam with noise: to applaud: to come or go suddenly (*arch.*): — *pr.p.* **clapp'ing;** *pa.t.* and *pa.p.* **clapped.** — *n.* **clapp'er** one who claps: that which claps, as the tongue of a bell: a contrivance for shaking a mill hopper: an instrument for making a noise, as a rattle, or (in *pl.*) bones for keeping musical time: the tongue (*slang*). — *v.i.* to make a noise like a clapper. — *v.t.* to ring by pulling on a clapper. — *n.* and *adj.* **clapp'ering.** — *n.* **clapp'ing** noise of striking: applause. — **clap'board** (or *klab'ərd*) wood for barrel staves, wainscot (*arch.*): a thin board used in covering wooden houses (*U.S.*); **clap'bread** a kind of hard-baked oatmeal cake; **clap'dish** same as **clackdish; clap'net** a net made to clap together suddenly by pulling a string. — *adj.* **clapped'-out'** (*coll.*) tired, exhausted: finished, of no more use. — **clapp'er-board(s)** (a set of) hinged boards clapped together in front of camera before or after shooting a piece of film to help to synchronise sound and vision; **clapp'erboy** the person who works the clapperboards. — *v.t.* **clapp'erclaw** (*arch.*) to claw or scratch: to scold. — **clapp'erclawer; clap'-sill** a lock-sill, the bottom part of the frame on which lock-gates shut; **clap'trap** a trick to gain applause (*arch.*): flashy display: empty words. — Also *adj.* — **claptrapp'ery.** — **clap eyes on** to catch sight of; **clap hands** to applaud with the hands: to make an agreement (*Shak.*); **clap hold of** to seize roughly; **clap on** (*coll.*) to put on quickly (of clothes); **clap up** (*Shak.*) to conclude suddenly; **like the clappers** (*coll.*) at top speed. [O.N. *klappa*, to pat; Du. and Ger. *klappen*.]

clap² *klap*, (*slang*) *n.* gonorrhoea. — *v.t.* to infect with gonorrhoea. [Cf. Du. *klapoor*.]

clapper *klap'ər, n.* (esp. in Devon) a rude bridge of slabs or planks laid across supports (*dial.*): a raised footpath (*dial.*). — See also **clapper** under **clap¹.** [L.L. *claperium*, heap of stones, rabbit-hole.]

claque *klak, n.* an opera hat: an institution for securing the success of a performance, by pre-concerted applause: a body of hired applauders: supporters who are after their own ends. — *n.* **claqueur** (*kla-kûr'*) a member of a claque. [Fr., — *claquer*, to clap.]

clarabella *klar-ə-bel'ə, n.* an organ-stop of a sweet, fluty tone. [L. *clārus*, clear, *bellus*, beautiful.]

Clare *klār, n.* a nun of a Franciscan order founded by St *Clare* (1212). — Also **Poor Clare.**

clarence *klar'əns, n.* a four-wheeled carriage, seated inside for two or more persons. [Named after the Duke of *Clarence* (William IV.).]

Clarenceux, Clarencieux *klar'ən-sū, (her.) n.* the second king-of-arms in England, so named from the Duke of *Clarence*, son of Edward III.

clarendon *klar'ən-dən, (print.) n.* a form of type having a heavy face.

clare-obscure. See **clair-obscure.**

claret *klar'ət, n.* originally applied to wines of a light-red colour, but now used in Britain for the dark-red wines of Bordeaux: a dark red colour (also *adj.*): blood (*slang*). — *v.i.* to drink claret. — **clar'et-cup** a drink made up of iced claret, brandy, sugar, etc.; **clar'et-jug** a fancy jug for holding claret. [Fr. *clairet* — *clair* — L. *clārus*, clear.]

clarichord *klar'i-körd, n.* a clavichord. [As if from L. *clārus*, clear; see **clavichord.**]

clarify *klar'i-fī, v.t.* to make clear or pure, esp. butter, etc.: to make clear, easily understood. — *v.i.* to become clear: — *pr.p.* **clar'ifying;** *pa.t.* and *pa.p.* **clar'ified.** — *ns.* **clarificā'tion; clar'ifier.** [L. *clārus*, clear, and *facĕre*, to make.]

clarinet, (*arch.*) **clarionet** *klar-in-et', klar', n.* a wind instrument, usually of wood, in which the sound is produced by a single thin reed, the compass being approximately that of the violin. — *n.* **clarinett'ist.** — **bass clarinet** one pitched an octave lower than the ordinary clarinet. [Fr., — L. *clārus*, clear.]

clarino *kla-rē'nō, n.* in baroque music, the highest register of the trumpet: an organ stop imitating this: a trumpet, a clarion: — *pl.* **clari'ni** or **clarin'os.** — *adj.* relating to the trumpet's highest register.

clarion *klar'i-ən, n.* a kind of trumpet whose note is clear and shrill: the sound of a trumpet, or a sound resembling that of a trumpet. — **clarion call** (*fig.*) a stirring summons (to duty, etc.). [Fr. *clairon* — *clair* — L. *clārus*, clear.]

clarionet. See **clarinet.**

clarity *klar'i-ti, n.* clearness. [M.E. *clarte* — L. *clāritās, -ātis.*]

Clarkia *klärk'i-ə, n.* a North American genus of the evening-primrose family, a favourite border plant: (without *cap.*) any plant of the genus. [Named in honour of Captain *Clark*, of Lewis and Clark's expedition.]

clarsach *klär'səhh, n.* the old Celtic harp strung with wire. [Gael. *clàrsach* and Ir. *cláirsach*, a harp.]

clart *klärt,* (*Scot.* and *N. Eng.*) *n.* mud: dirt. — *v.t.* to dirty. — *adj.* **clart'y** sticky and dirty. [Der. unknown.]

clary *klā'ri, n.* a plant of the sage genus (*Salvia sclarea*) with pale-blue flowers and large coloured bracts: extended to others of the genus. [L.L. *sclarea*; origin unknown.]

clash *klash, n.* a loud noise, such as is caused by the striking together of sheets of metal: opposition: contradiction: an outbreak of fighting: chatter, country talk (*Scot.*). — *v.i.* to dash noisily together: to meet in opposition: to act in a contrary direction: to disagree: of events, to coincide disturbingly: to gossip (*Scot.*). — *v.t.* to strike noisily against: to bang, slam (*dial.*). — *n.* **clash'ing** a striking against: opposition, conflict, disagreement. — **clash'-ma-clā'vers** (*Scot.*, by analogy with **clishmaclaver**) idle chat, gossip. [Imit; cf., Ger. *Klatsch*, Sw. *klatsch.*]

clasp *kläsp, n.* a fastening: a supplementary decoration in the form of a bar on the ribbon of a medal: an embrace: a grasp. — *v.t.* to fasten with a clasp: to enclose and hold in the hand or arms: to embrace. — *ns.* **clas'per** that which clasps: the tendril of a plant: a clasping organ (*zool.*); **clasp'ing.** — **clasp'-knife** a knife whose blade folds into the handle. [M.E. *clapse.*]

class *kläs, n.* a rank or order of persons or things: high rank or social standing: the system or situation in any community in which there is division of people into different social ranks: a number of students or scholars who are taught together, or are in the same year of their course: a scientific division or arrangement in biological classification, a division above an order: a grade, as of merit in examination, accommodation in a ship or railway train: a section of a Methodist congregation: style, quality (*coll.*). — *v.t.* to form into a class or classes: to arrange methodically. — *v.i.* to take rank. — *adj.* (*slang*) of high class. — *adjs.* **class'able, class'ible** capable of being classed; **classed.** — *n.* **classic** (*klas'ik*) any great writer, composer, or work: a student of the ancient classics: a standard work: something of established excellence: something quintessentially typical or definitive: any of five flat races (e.g. the Derby) for three-year-olds, or other established sporting event: something delightful, as a good story (*coll.*): (in *pl.*) Greek and Latin studies. — *adjs.* **class'ic, -al** of the highest class or rank, esp. in literature or art (usu. **classic**): (**classical** of music, orchestral and chamber, etc., as opposed to jazz, folk music, etc.: (usu. **classical**) used of the best Greek and Roman writers: (usu.**classical**) pertaining to Greek and Latin Studies: (usu. **classical**; i.e. opposed to *romantic*) like in style to the authors of Greece and Rome or the old masters in music: chaste, refined, restrained, in keeping with classical art: (usu. **classic**) having literary or historical associations: traditionally accepted, long or well established: (usu. **classic**) excellent, standard (*slang*): (**classical**; **classic** in *Milt.*) Presbyterian, of a classis: (usu. **classic**) of clothes, made in simple tailored style that does not soon go out of fashion. — *n.* **classical'ity.** — *adv.* **class'ically.** — *ns.* **class'icalness.** — *v.t.* **class'icise, -ize** to make classic or classical. — *v.i.* to imitate a classical style in literature, music, etc. — *ns.* **class'icism** (*-sizm*) a classical idiom: in literature, music, etc., a principle, character, or tendency such as is seen in Greek classical literature, marked by beauty of form, good taste, restraint, and clarity — opposed to *romanticism*; **class'icist** one versed in the classics, or devoted to their being used in education: one who is for classicism rather than romanticism; **class'iness** (*coll.*) the quality of being classy. — *adjs.* **class'less**

having no class distinctions: not belonging obviously to any social class: in sports, etc., not confined to any particular category: pertaining to sports with events of this sort; **class'y** (*coll.*) of or characteristic of high or upper class. — **class action** (*law*) in the U.S., an action taken by one or more persons on their own behalf and on that of all others adduced as having the same grievance; **class'-book** a book used in class teaching. — *adj.* **class'-con'scious** clearly or acutely conscious of membership of a social class. — **class= con'sciousness; class-distinc'tion; class'-fellow, class'- mate** a pupil in the same class at school or college; **classic car** a motor car of classic design, esp. manu- factured between 1925 and 1942; **classic races** the five chief annual horse-races — the Two Thousand Guineas, One Thousand, Derby, Oaks, and St Leger; **class'-lead'er** the leader of a class in a Methodist church; **class legislation** legislation in the interests of a class; **class'man** one who has gained honours of a certain class at the Oxford examinations — opp. to *passman*; **class'room** a room in which a class is held; **class'-war'** hostility or hostilities between different social ranks or classes, esp. between the proletariat and the combined middle and upper classes. — **in a class of, on, its own** so good as to be without an equal; **take a class** to take honours in an examination, as opposed to the mere pass. [L. *classis*, a division of the Roman people.]

classes aisées *klas e-zā*, (Fr.) the well-off classes.
classify *klas'i-fī*, *v.t.* to arrange in classes: to make secret for security reasons: — *pr.p.* **class'ifying;** *pa.p.* **class'i- fied.** — *adjs.* **class'ifiable** (or *-fī'*) capable of being classified; **classif'ic** denoting classes. — *n.* **classificā'- tion** the act or a system of arranging in classes. — *adjs.* **classificā'tory; class'ified** arranged in classes: of a road, in a class entitled to receive a government grant. — *n.* **class'ifier.** — **classified advertisements** advertisements in a newspaper or periodical grouped according to the goods or services offered. [L. *classis*, and *facĕre*, to make.]
classis *klas'is*, *n.* a group: a presbytery (*obs.*): a bay of a library (*obs.*). [L.]
clastic *klas'tik*, (*geol.*) *adj.* (of sedimentary rock) com- posed of fragments of older rock, fragmental. [Gr. *klastos* — *klaein*, to break.]
clat. See **claut.**
clatch *klach, kläch*, (*Scot*), *n.* a splashy slapping sound: a slap: anything sloppy and pasty: anything lumbering or clumsy, as an old gig: an ungainly person: a slut: a botched piece of work. — *v.i.* to dabble or work in miry matter. — *v.t.* to daub, plaster: to work up into a pasty mess: to botch. [Cf. Ger. *Klatsch*, slap.]
clathrate *klath'rit, -rāt, adj.* lattice-shaped (*biol.*): of a molecular compound, having one component enclosed in the cavities of the crystals of another component (*chem.*). [L. *clāthrāre*, to furnish with a lattice.]
clatter *klat'ǝr*, *n.* a repeated rattling noise: a repetition of abrupt, sharp sounds: noisy talk: gossip (*Scot.*, often in *pl.*). — *v.i.* to make rattling sounds: to chatter. — *v.t.* to cause to rattle. — *n.* **clatt'erer.** — *adv.* **clatt'er- ingly.** [O.E. *clatrung*, clattering (verbal noun).]
claucht. See **claught.**
Claude Lorraine glass *klöd lor-ān' gläs*, a convex mirror, usu. coloured, employed for viewing landscape. [Named after the painter *Claude Gelée*, known as *le Lorrain* (1600–82).]
Claudian *klö'di-ǝn, adj.* pertaining to the Romans of the name of *Claudius*, esp. the emperors of that gens (Tiberius, Caligula, Claudius, Nero), or to their period (A.D. 14–68).
claudication *klö-di-kā'shǝn, n.* a limp. [L. *claudicātio, -ōnis — claudus*, lame.]
claught, claucht *klöhht*, (*Scot.*) *v.t.* and *v.i.* to snatch: to clutch. — See also **cleek.** — *n.* a hold: a snatch: a clutch. [From the pa.t. of **cleek.**]
clause *klöz, n.* a sentence: part of a sentence with subject and predicate: an article or part of a contract, will, act

of parliament, etc. — *adjs.* **claus'al; claus'ular** pertain- ing to, or consisting of, a clause or clauses. — **depen- dent clause** a part of a sentence which cannot stand in isolation as a sentence in itself (opp. to **independent clause).** [Fr. *clause* — L. *claudĕre*, to shut.]
claustral *klös'trǝl, adj.* cloistral, secluded: pertaining to a claustrum: narrow-minded (*fig.*). — *ns.* **claustrā'tion** the act of shutting in a cloister; **claus'trum** a thin layer of grey matter in the brain hemispheres: — *pl.* **claus'tra; claustrophō'bia** (Gr. *phobos*, fear) a morbid dread of confined places. — *adj.* **claustrophō'bic** (or *-fob'*). [L. *claustrum*, an enclosed place.]
clausula *klö'zhǝ-lǝ, klow'sōō-la, n.* a short clause ending a period in Latin prose: — *pl.* **clau'sulae** (*-ē, -ī*). [L.]
clausular. See **clause.**
claut *klöt*, **clat** *klat, klät*, (*Scot.*) *ns.* a claw: a scratch: a blow: a grasp: a scraping hoe: something scraped together, a lump. — *v.t.* to scratch, claw: to scrape: to hoe. [Perh. conn. with **claw.**]
clavate, -d *klā'vāt, klav'āt, -ĭd, adjs.* (*biol.*) club-shaped. — *n.* **clavā'tion** articulation in a socket. — *adj.* **clav'i- form** in the form of a club. — *n.* **clav'iger** (*-i-jǝr*) a club-bearer. — *adjs.* **clavigerous** (*-ij'ǝr-ǝs*) club-bearing (see also under **clavis**); **clav'ūlate** somewhat club- shaped. [L. *clāva*, a club.]
clave¹ *klāv, pa.t.* of **cleave¹,²**.
clave² *klā'vä, n.* one of a pair of small wooden cylinders held in the hands and struck together to mark S. American dance rhythm. [Sp., key to code, etc., clef — L. *clāvis*, key.]
clavecin *klav'ǝ-sin, n.* a harpsichord. — *n.* **clav'ecinist.** [Fr. *clavecin* — L. *clāvis*, a key.]
claver *klā'vǝr*, (*Scot.*) *n.* idle talk, gossip. — *v.i.* to talk idly. [Der. uncertain; cf. Gael. *clabair*, a prater.]
clavicembalo *klav-i-chem'bǝ-lō, n.* a cembalo with keys — a harpsichord: — *pl.* **clavicem'balos.** [It., — L. *clāvis*, key, and **cembalo.**]
clavichord *klav'i-körd, n.* an old keyboard stringed in- strument in which the tangent striking the string and producing the sound also determines the vibrating length. [L. *clāvis*, a key, *chorda*, a string.]
clavicle *klav'i-kl, n.* the collar-bone: a merry-thought of birds. — Also **clavic'ūla.** — *adj.* **clavic'ūlar.** [Fr. *clavicule* — L. *clāvicula*, dim. of *clāvis*, a key.]
clavicorn *klav'i-körn, adj.* having clavate antennae. — *n.* a member of the **Clavicorn'ia**, a group of beetles. [L. *clāva*, a club, *cornū*, a horn.]
clavicytherium *klav-i-sī-thēr'i-ǝm, n.* an upright form of spinet. [L. *clāvis*, key, *cytherium — cithara*.]
clavie *klā'vi*, (*Scot*) *n.* tar barrel burnt for luck at Burghead on Hogmanay (O.S.). [Unknown.]
clavier *klä-vēr', n.* the keyboard of a musical instrument: a stringed keyboard instrument, esp. the clavichord or the pianoforte. [Fr., (or Ger. *Klavier*, — Fr.), — L. *clāvis*, a key.]
claviform. See under **clavate.**
claviger, clavigerous. See under **clavate, clavis.**
clavis *klā'vis* (L. *klä'wis*), *n.* a key, hence a clue or aid for solving problems, interpreting a cipher, etc.: — *pl.* **clā'ves** (*-vēz*; L. *klä'wās*). — *n.* **claviger** (*klav'i-jǝr*) one who keeps a key, a custodian. — *adj.* **clavig'erous** (see also under **clavate**). [L. *clāvis*, a key.]
clavulate. See under **clavate.**
claw *klö, n.* the hooked nail of a beast or bird, or the creature's foot with a number of such nails: the leg of a crab, insect, etc., or its pointed end or pincer: an instrument shaped like a claw: the narrow basal part of a petal (*bot.*): anything like a claw. — *v.t.* to scratch: to tear: to scrape: to seize: to flatter, fawn on (*fig.*). — *adjs.* **clawed** having claws; **claw'less.** — *adj.* **claw'= and-ball'** of furniture, having feet carved to represent an animal's claw holding a ball (also **ball'-and-claw'**). — **claw'back** a toady, flatterer: an arrangement by which the financial benefit from family allowances, etc., is partially recouped by the government in extra taxation from the higher-paid: extended to other situ-

ations where a seeming financial benefit proves to be almost non-existent; **claw'-hammer** a hammer with one part of the head divided into two claws, for drawing nails; **claw'-hamm'er-coat** a facetious name for a dress-coat. — **claw back** to recoup money by means of taxation, etc.; **claw me and I'll claw thee** favour me and I shall do you good in return. [O.E. *clawu*; cog. with Ger. *Klaue*; akin to **cleave²**.]

clay *klā, n.* earth in very fine particles, tenacious and impervious (*agri.*): a tenacious ductile earthy material, hydrated aluminium silicates more or less impure (*chem.* and *min.*): earth in general: the human body: (in full **clay'-pipe'**) a tobacco-pipe of baked clay. — *v.t.* to purify with clay, as sugar. — *adjs.* **clayed** clay-like; **clay'ey** made of clay: covered with clay: like clay; **clay'ish** of the nature of clay. — *adjs.* **clay'-bank** (*U.S.*) brownish yellow. — *n.* (*U.S.*) a horse of this colour. — *adjs.* **clay'-brained** (*Shak.*) stupid; **clay'-cold** cold as clay, lifeless. — **clay'-court** a type of hard-surfaced tennis-court; **clay'-eater** one addicted to chewing a fatty clay — in Brazil and elsewhere; **clay'-ground** ground consisting mainly of clay; **clay'=ir'onstone** a clayey chalybite; **clay'-marl** a whitish chalky clay; **clay'-mill** a mill for preparing clay; **clay'-pan** (*Austr.*) a shallow depression in clay soil, holding water after rain; **clay pigeon** a clay (or usu. other material) disc (or other shape) thrown from a trap and shot at as a substitute for a pigeon; **clay'-pit** a pit from which clay is dug; **clay'-slate** hard, fissile argillaceous rock. — **feet of clay** (*fig.*) faults and weaknesses of character not at first suspected; **wet one's clay** to drink. [O.E. *clæg*; cf. Dan. *klæg*, Ger. *Klei*.]

claymore *klā-mōr', -mör', n.* a large sword formerly used by the Scottish Highlanders: the old Celtic one-handed, two-edged longsword: now applied inaccurately to the basket-hilted sword of the officers of Highland regiments: (also **claymore mine**) a type of explosive mine. [Gael. *claidheamhmór* — Gael. and Ir. *claidheamh*, sword, *mór*, great.]

clean *klēn, adj.* clear (*Spens.*): clear-cut: sharply defined: even: neat: free from dirt, stain, or whatever defiles: pure: guiltless: honest, without corruption: having nothing of an incriminating nature on one's person (*slang*): (of a driving licence) without any endorsements for motoring offences: (of e.g. an athlete) clear of drugs when tested; complete: without a catch (*angling*): free of radioactive fall-out: of a design that causes little turbulent wake (*aerodynamics*). — *adv.* quite: entirely: smoothly: without mishap. — *v.t.* to make clean, or free from dirt. — *n.* an act of cleaning: in weight-lifting, a lift of the weight to the shoulders, where it is held with arms bent. — *n.* **clean'er** one who or that which cleans. — *n.* and *adj.* **clean'ing** (the act of) making clean. — *n.* **cleanliness** (*klen'li-nis, -nes*) habitual cleanness or purity. — *adj.* **cleanly** (*klen'li*) clean in habits and person: pure: neat. — *adv.* (*klēn'li*) in a clean manner. — *n.* **cleanness** (*klēn'nis, -nes*). — *adj.* **clean'-cut'** neat, well-shaped: with a neat, respectable appearance. — **clean hands** freedom from guilt or corruption; **cleaning lady, cleaning woman** a woman employed to clean a house, premises, etc. — *adjs.* **clean'-limb'ed** with shapely limbs: trim; **clean'=liv'ing** morally upright: respectable; **clean'-shav'en** with all facial hair shaved off; **clean'skin** (*Austr.*) an unbranded animal (also **clear'skin**): a person with a clean police record (*coll.*); **clean'-tim'bered** (*Shak.*) well-proportioned. — **clean'-up** an act of thorough cleaning: the stamping out of an evil (see also **clean up** below). — **a clean sheet, slate** a fresh start; **a clean sweep** a complete change: the winning or gaining of all the prizes, votes, etc. (usu. with *of*); **clean as a whistle** completely emptied; **clean bowled** (*cricket*) bowled out by a ball which hits the stumps without hitting the bat; **clean out** to clean the inside of: to take away all someone's money from (someone) (*coll.*); **clean up** to make clean: to free from vice, corruption, etc.: to make (large profits) (*n.* **clean'-up**); **come clean** (*slang*) to

confess, to divulge, everything; **make a clean break** to sever a relationship, etc. completely; **show a clean pair of heels** to escape by running; **take (someone) to the cleaners** (*slang*) to take all, or a great deal of, a person's money, etc.: to beat or criticise (someone) severely. [O.E. *clæne*; Ger. *klein*, small.]

cleanse *klenz, v.t.* to make clean or pure. — *adj.* **cleans'-able.** — *ns.* **cleans'er** one who, or that which, cleanses: cleansing-cream or the like; **cleans'ing** purification. — **cleans'ing-cream** a type of cream used to remove make-up from the face; **cleansing department** the section of local administration that deals with the collecting and disposing of refuse and the cleaning of streets. [O.E. *clænsian*.]

clear *klēr, adj.* pure, bright, undimmed, unclouded, undulled: free from obstruction, difficulty, complication, contents, blame, or accusation: disengaged: plain: distinct: obvious: without blemish, defect, drawback, or diminution: perspicuous: transparent: not coded. — *adv.* in a clear manner: plainly: wholly: quite: out of the way (of). — *v.t.* to make clear: to empty: to free from obscurity, obstruction, or guilt: to free, acquit, or vindicate: to leap, or pass by or over: to make as profit: to settle, as a bill: to move on, as wounded from a temporary field hospital (**casualty clear'ing-station**): to set free for sailing: to decode: to unscramble: to declare free from security, etc., restrictions: of a cheque, etc., to pass through a clearing-bank: to pass through (customs, etc.). — *v.i.* to become clear: to grow free, bright, transparent: to sail after satisfying all demands and obtaining permission. — *ns.* **clear'age** a piece of land cleared; **clear'ance** the act of clearing: general removal or emptying: eviction from lands: removal of hindrances: intervening space: play between parts, as of a machine: a certificate that a ship has been cleared at the custom-house: a declaration of freedom from restrictions; **clear'er** someone or something that clears; a clearing bank; **clear'ing** the act of making clear: the tract of land cleared of wood, etc., for cultivation: the method by which bankers change cheques and drafts, and arrange the differences. — *adv.* **clear'ly** in a clear manner: distinctly. — *n.* **clear'ness.** — **clearance cairn** (*archeol.*) a heap of stones merely cleared from agricultural land, as distinct from a burial cairn; **clearance sale** a sale of goods at reduced prices in order to make room for new stock. — *adjs.* **clear'-cut'** sharp in outline: free from obscurity; **clear'-eyed** clear-sighted, discerning: **clear felling** the wholesale felling of all the trees in a particular area; **clear'-head'ed** having a clear understanding. — **clearing bank** a bank that is a member of the London Bankers' Clearing House, through which it makes credit and cheque transfers to and from other banks; **clear'ing-house** an office where financial clearing business is done (**railway clearing-house** an office for adjusting claims of different railways for shares of freights and through tickets); a central source or pool of information, etc. (*fig.*); **clear'ing-nut** the seed of *Strychnos potatorum* used in the East Indies for clearing muddy water; **clear'-obscure'** same as **chiaroscuro**. — *adj.* **clear'-sight'ed** having clearness of sight: discerning. — **clear'-sight'edness; clear'skin** see **cleanskin** under **clean; clear'-starch'er** a laundress; **clear'-starch'-ing** the act of stiffening linen with clear starch; **clear'=story** see **clerestory; clear'way** a stretch of road on which motorists are not allowed to stop; **clear'wing** a transparent-winged moth. — **clear as a bell** see **bell; clear off** to get rid of, dispose of: to go away, esp. in order to avoid something (*coll.*); **clear one's throat** to give a slight cough; **clear out** to get rid of: to empty: of a ship, to clear and leave port: to take oneself off; **clear the air** to simplify the situation and relieve tension; **clear the decks** (*fig.*) to clear away everything surplus, so as to prepare for action; — **clear the way** to make the way open; **clear up** to make or to become clear: to explain (a mystery, misunderstanding, etc.); **in the clear** free of suspicion: out of a difficulty: solvent.

[Fr. *clair* — L. *clārus*, clear.]

clearcole *klēr′kōl, n.* a priming coat consisting of size or glue with whiting. — Also **clere′cole, claircolle** (*klār′*). [Fr. *claire colle*, clear glue.]

cleat *klēt, n.* a wedge: one of several pieces attached to the sole of a shoe for protection or grip: a piece of wood, etc., nailed across anything to keep it in its place or give it an additional strength: a piece attached to parts of a ship for fastening ropes. — *v.t.* to strengthen with a cleat: to fasten to or by a cleat. [From a supposed O.E. *clēat*; cf. Du. *kloot*; Dan. *klode*; Ger. *Kloss*.]

cleave[1] *klēv, v.t.* to divide, to split: to separate with violence: to go through: to pierce. — *v.i.* to part asunder: to crack: — *pr.p.* **cleav′ing**; *pa.t.* **clōve** or **cleft**, (*arch.*) **clāve**; *pa.p.* **clōv′en** or **cleft**. — *adj.* **cleav′able** capable of being cleft. — *ns.* **cleav′ableness; cleav′age** a split: a tendency to split, esp. (in rocks and minerals) in certain directions: mitotic cell-division: the hollow between a woman's breasts, esp. as shown by a low-cut dress; **cleav′er** one who or that which cleaves: a butcher's chopper. — *adj.* **cleav′ing** splitting. — *n.* a cleft. — **cleft palate** see **palate**. — **in a cleft stick** (*fig.*) in a difficult situation: in a dilemma. [O.E. *clēofan*, cog. with Ger. *klieben*.]

cleave[2] *klēv, v.i.* to stick or adhere: to unite: — *pa.t.* **cleaved** or **clāve**; *pa.p.* **cleaved**. — *ns.* **cleav′ers, clivers** (*kliv′ərz*) goose-grass (*Galium aparine*) which cleaves to fur or clothes by its hooks; **cleav′ing** the act of adhering. — Also *adj.* [O.E. *clifian*; cog. with Ger. *kleben*.]

cleché *klech′ā, klesh′ā*, (*her.*) *adj.* voided or hollowed throughout, showing only a narrow border. [Fr.]

cleck *klek*, (*Scot.*) *v.t.* to hatch. — *n.* **cleck′ing** a brood. [O.N. *klekia*; cf. Dan. *klække*, to hatch.]

cleek *klēk, n.* a large hook (*Scot.*): a narrow-faced iron-headed golf-club. — *v.t.* to seize, to hook. — *v.i.* (*Scot.*) to go arm in arm: to link: to marry: — *pa.t.* and *pa.p.* **cleeked, cleek′it, claught** (*klöhht*). [Northern, perh. related to **clutch**.]

cleep. See **clepe**.

cleeve. See **cleve**.

clef *klef, n.* a character placed on the stave by which the absolute pitch of the notes is fixed. [Fr. *clef*, key — L. *clāvis*; Gr. *kleis*, a key.]

cleft[1] *kleft, pa.t.* and *pa.p.* of **cleave**[1]. — **cleft palate** see **palate**.

cleft[2] *kleft, n.* an opening made by cleaving or splitting: a crack, fissure, or chink. — Also **clift** (*B.*). [Cf. Ger. *Kluft*, Dan. *klyft*, a hole.]

cleg *kleg, n.* a gadfly, horse-fly. [O.N. *kleggi*.]

cleistogamy, clistogamy *klīs-tog′ə-mi*, (*bot.*) *n.* production of small flowers, often simplified and inconspicuous, which do not open, and in which self-pollination occurs. — *adjs.* **cleistogamic** (*-tə-gam′ik*), **cleistog′- amous.** [Gr. *kleistos*, closed, *gamos*, marriage.]

cleithral, clithral *klī′thrəl, adj.* completely roofed over. [Gr. *kleithron*, a bar.]

clem *klem, v.i.* and *v.t.* to starve. [Dial. Eng. *clam*; Ger. *klemmen*, to pinch.]

Clematis *klem′ə-tis, klə-mā′tis, n.* a genus of Ranunculaceae, including virgin's-bower or traveller's-joy: (without *cap.*) a plant of the genus. [L., — Gr. *klēmatis*, a plant, prob. periwinkle — *klēma*, a twig.]

clement *klem′ənt, adj.* mild: gentle: kind: merciful. — *ns.* **clem′ence** (*Spens.*), **clem′ency** the quality of being clement: mildness: readiness to forgive. — *adv.* **clem′- ently.** [Fr., — L. *clēmēns, -entis.*]

clementine *klem′ən-tēn, -tīn, n.* a type of orange.

Clementine *klem′ən-tēn, -tīn, adj.* relating to any of the popes named *Clement*, esp. Clement I or Clement V. — *n.* a follower of a leader called Clement.

clench *klench, klensh, v.t.* to close tightly: to grasp: to clinch. [Same as **clinch**.]

clepe, cleep *klēp*, (*arch.*) *v.t.* to call: to name: — *pa.p.* **yclept** (*i-klept′*), also **ycleped′** (*Milt.*), **ycleap'd** (*i-klēp′- id, i-klēpt′*). [O.E. *clipian*, to call.]

clepsydra *klep′si-drə, n.* an instrument for measuring time by the trickling of water, a water-clock. [L., — Gr. *klepsydrā — kleptein*, to steal, *hydōr*, water.]

clerecole. See **clearcole**.

clerestory, clear-story *clēr′stō-ri, -stö-, n.* an upper storey or part with its own row of windows — esp. the storey above the triforium in a church. [**clear**, prob. in sense of lighted, and **storey**.]

clergy *klûr′ji, n.* the ministers of the Christian or other religion, as holders of an allotted office, in contradistinction to the laity: learning, education (*arch.*). — *adjs.* **cler′gyable, cler′giable** entitled to or admitting of the benefit of clergy; **cleric, -al** (*kler′ik, -əl*) belonging to the clergy: pertaining to a clerk or scribe. — *ns.* **cler′ic** a clergyman; **cler′icalism** undue influence of the clergy: sacerdotalism; **cler′icalist.** — *n.pl.* **cler′icals** clerical garb. — *ns.* **cler′icate** clerical position; **clericity** (*klər-is′-ti*) the state of being a clergyman; **clerisy** (*kler′i-si*, introduced by Coleridge, imitating Ger. *Klerisei*, clergy) the class of learned men, scholars. — **cler′gyman** one of the clergy, a regularly ordained minister; **cler′gy-woman** a woman who is a minister of religion: a woman belonging to a clergyman's family (*facet.*); **clerical collar** the white collar worn by many Christian clergy, fastening behind the neck. — **benefit of clergy** originally an exemption of clergymen, in certain cases, from criminal process before a secular judge, but later covering the first offence of all who could read; **black clergy** in Russia, all the regular or monastic, as distinct from the secular or parochial, clergy; **clergyman's sore throat** chronic pharyngitis. [Fr. *clergé* — L. *clēricus* — Gr. *klērikos*, from *klēros*, a lot, a heritage, then the clergy.]

cleric, etc. See **clergy, clerk**.

clerihew *kler′i-hū, n.* a jingle in two short couplets purporting to quintessentialise the life and character of some notable person. [Started by E. *Clerihew* (Bentley) in his *Biography for Beginners* (1905).]

clerisy. See **clergy**.

clerk *klärk* (*U.S. klûrk*), *n.* a clergyman or priest: a scholar: one who leads the responses in the English Church service: in common use, one employed as a writer, assistant, copyist, account-keeper, or correspondent in an office: a hotel receptionist (*U.S.*): a shop-assistant (*U.S.*). — *v.i.* to act as clerk. — *adj.* **cler′ical** of, done by, etc., clerks (see also under **clergy**). — *ns.* **clerk′dom; clerk′ess** a female clerk. — *adj.* **clerk′ish** like a clerk; **clerk′less** ignorant; **clerk′-like** scholarly. — *n.* **clerk′ling** a young clerk. — *adj.* **clerk′ly** scholarly. — *adv.* in a scholar-like or learned manner. — *n.* **clerk′ship.** — **Bible clerk** a scholar who reads the lessons in some college chapels; **clerk of the course** in horse- or motor-racing, an official in charge of administration; **clerk of the weather** an imaginary functionary facetiously supposed to direct the weather; **clerk of works** one who superintends the erection and maintenance of a building, etc.; **Lord Clerk-Register** see **register; St Nicholas's clerks** (*arch.*) thieves; **town clerk** see **town**. [O.E. *clerc*, a priest — L.L. *clēricus*; see **clergy**.]

cleromancy *kler′ə-man-si, n.* divination by lot. [Gr. *klēros*, lot, *manteiā*, divination.]

cleruch *kler′ook, -uk*, (*Greek hist.*) *n.* an allotment-holder in foreign territory retaining his Athenian citizenship. — *n.* **cler′uchy, cleruch′ia.** [Gr. *klērouchos — klēros*, allotment, *echein*, to have.]

cleuch, cleugh *klōōhh*, Scottish form of **clough**.

cleve, cleeve *klēv*, (*dial.*) *n.* a cliff: a hillside. [M.E. *cleof*, a variant of **cliff**[1].]

cleveite *klē′vīt, klā′və-īt, n.* a pitchblende in octahedral crystals containing helium. [P.T. *Cleve*, Swedish chemist.]

clever *klev′ər, adj.* dexterous, deft: able: ingenious: skilful: good-natured (*U.S. dial.*). — *ns.* **cleveral′ity** (*Scot.*); **clev′erness.** — *adj.* **clev′erish** somewhat clever. — *adv.* **clev′erly.** — *adj.* **clev′er-clev′er** flaunting a superficial knowledgeableness: too clever. — **clever dick** (*slang*) a person who thinks himself clever. [Orig. dial.; poss. conn. with M.E. *clivers*, claws.]

clevis *klev'is*, *n*. a U-shaped piece of metal through which tackle may pass, fixed at the end of a beam. [Ety. dub.]

clew, clue *kloō̄*, *n*. a ball of thread, or the thread in it (*arch*.): a thread that guides through a labyrinth: the corner of a sail. — *v.t.* to coil up into a clew or ball: to tie up to the yards (usu. with *up*): to fix up (*fig*.). — **clew'-garnet** (*naut*.) a tackle for clewing up the smaller square sails for furling. — *n.pl.* **clew'-lines** ropes on the smaller square sails by which they are clewed up for furling. [O.E. *cliwen*; cf. Du. *kluwen*; Ger. *Knäuel*.]

Clianthus *kli-an'thɔs*, *n*. an Australian genus of shrub or vine with hanging red flowers: (without *cap*.) any plant of the genus. [L., — G. *kleos*, glory, *anthos*, flower.]

cliché *klē'shā*, *n*. the impression made by a die in any soft metal: an electrotype or stereotype plate: a stereotyped phrase, or literary tag: something hackneyed as idea, plot, situation. — *adjs*. **cli'ché-ridden, cli'ché(')d** filled with clichés. [Fr.]

click *klik*, *n*. a short, sharp ticking sound: anything that makes such a sound, as a small piece of iron falling into a notched wheel: a clucking sound produced by sudden retraction of the tongue from the upper teeth, palate, or elsewhere, characteristic of certain South African native languages, represented, e.g. in Zulu, by C (dental), Q (retroflex), and X (lateral): a latch for a gate. — *v.i.* to make a light, sharp sound: to fit into place opportunely or successfully, esp. to succeed in coming into relations of sociability with a person of the other sex (*slang*). — *v.t.* (*dial*.) (of a gate) to fasten the latch. — *ns*. **click'er** the compositor who distributes the copy among a companionship of printers, makes up pages, etc.: one who cuts up leather for the uppers and soles of boots; **click'ing** the action of the verb. — **click'-bee'tle** any beetle of the family Elateridae, which are characterised by leaping in the air with a click when laid on their backs; **click'-clack** a persistent clicking noise. — **click'ety-click', -clack'** a continuous, usu. regular, clicking sound. [Dim. of **clack**.]

clicket *klik'ət*, *n*. a latch. — *v.i.* to make a clicking sound. [O.Fr. (and Fr.) *cliquet*.]

client *klī'ənt*, *n*. a vassal, dependant, or hanger-on: one who employs a lawyer or other professional adviser: a customer. — *n*. **cli'entage** the whole number of one's clients: the client's relation to the patron. — *adj*. **cliental** (-*ent'l*). — *ns*. **clientèle** (*klē-ā-tel'*), **clientele** (*klī'ən-tēl*) a following: the whole connection of a lawyer, shopkeeper, etc.; **cli'entship**. — **client state** a state which depends on another for protection, economic aid, etc. [L. *cliēns, -entis*, a dependant upon a *patrōnus*.]

cliff[1] *klif*, *n*. a high steep rock: the steep side of a mountain. — *adjs*. **cliffed, cliff'y** having cliffs: craggy. — **cliff'-face'** the sheer or steep front of a cliff; **cliff'hanger** a tense, exciting adventure or contest: an ending line of an episode of a serial, etc. that leaves one in suspense: a serial, film, etc. that keeps one in suspense. — *v.i.* **cliff'hang**. — *n*., *adj*. **cliff'hanging**. [O.E. *clif*; Du. *clif*; O.N. *klif*.]

cliff[2] *klif*, (*mus*.) *n*. Same as **clef**.

clift[1]. See **cleft**[2].

clift[2] *klift*, *n*. same as **cliff**[1] (through the influence of **cleft**). — *adjs*. **clift'ed, clift'y** broken into cliffs.

climacteric *klī-mak'tər-ik* or *klī-mak-ter'ik*, *n*. a critical period in human life, in which some great bodily change takes place: a critical time. — *adj*. pertaining to such a period: critical. — *adj*. **climacter'ical**. — **the grand climacteric** (generally) the sixty-third year, supposed to be a critical period for men. [Gr. *klīmaktēr* — *klīmax*, a ladder.]

climatic, -al. See **climax**.

climate *klī'mit, -māt, n.* the condition of a country or place with regard to temperature, moisture, etc. (also *fig*.): the character of something (*fig*.): a region (*Shak*.).

— *v.i.* (*Shak*.) to remain in a certain place. — *adjs*. **cli'matal; climatic** (-*mat'ik*), **-al**. — *v.t.* **cli'matise, -ize** see **acclimatise**. — *n*. **cli'mature** (*Shak*.) a region. — *adj*. **climatograph'ical**. — *n*. **climatog'raphy** a description of climates. — *adj*. **climatolog'ical**. — *ns*. **climatol'ogist; climatol'ogy** the science of climates, or an investigation of the causes on which the climate of a place depends. — **climate of opinion** the critical atmosphere or complex of opinions prevalent at a particular time or in a particular place. [Fr. *climat* — L. *clima* — Gr. *klima, -atos*, slope — *klīnein*, to slope.]

climax *klī'maks*, *n*. the arranging of discourse in order of increasing strength (*rhet*.): (*loosely*) the last term of the rhetorical arrangement: hence, a culmination: of a story, play, piece of music, etc., the most interesting and important or exciting part: the relatively stable culmination of a series of plant and animal communities developing in an area (also **climax community**): sexual orgasm. — *v.i.* to ascend in a climax: to culminate (in). — *adjs*. (wrongly formed) **climact'ic, -al** pertaining to a climax. — *adv*. **climact'ically**. [Gr. *klīmax, -akos*, a ladder — *klīnein*, to slope.]

climb *klīm*, *v.i.* or *v.t.* to ascend or mount by clutching with the hands and feet: to ascend with difficulty: to mount: of plants, to ascend by clinging to other objects, by means of hooks, tendrils, twining stems, or otherwise: extended to similar downward movement (to *climb down*): — *pa.t.* and *pa.p.* **climbed**, (*arch*.) **clomb** (*klōm*). — *n*. an act of climbing: an ascent. — *adjs*. **climb'able**. — *n*. **climb'er** one who or that which climbs: one who is intent upon his own social advancement: an old-fashioned name for a bird whose feet are mainly adapted for climbing: a climbing plant (*bot*.). — *n*. and *adj*. **climb'ing**. — **climb down** to become more humble: to abandon a firmly stated opinion or resolve, or an excessive or overweening demand, position or attitude (*n*. **climb'-down**). — **climbing boy** formerly, a small boy employed by a chimney-sweep to climb chimneys; **climb'ing-frame** a wooden or metal structure on or through which children can climb; **climbing iron** a metal frame with a horizontal spike, worn strapped to the feet as an aid in climbing trees, telegraph poles, etc. [O.E. *climban*; cf. Ger. *klimmen*; **clamber, cleave**[2].]

clime *klīm*, *n*. a country, region, tract. [**climate**.]

clinamen *klin-ā'mən*, *n*. inclination. [L. *clīnāmen*.]

clinch *klinch, klinsh, v.t.* to fasten or rivet a nail by bending and beating down the point: to clench (*obs*.): to drive home (an argument; *fig*.): to settle or confirm (*fig*.). — *v.i.* to grapple. — *n*. something set firmly: the fastening of a nail by beating it back: a holding grapple (*boxing*): an embrace (*coll*.): a pun: a punning retort. — *n*. **clinch'er** one that clinches: a decisive argument. — *adj*. **clinch'er-built** same as **clinker-built**. — **clinch'er-work** the disposition of the side planks of a vessel, when the lower edge of one row overlaps the row next under it. [Same as **clench**; causal form of **clink**[4].]

cline *klīn*, (*biol*.) *n*. a gradation of differences of form, etc., seen, e.g. within one species over a specified area of the world. [See **clino-**.]

cling *kling, v.i.* to stick close by adhesive surface or by clasp: to adhere in interest or affection: to remain by an opinion: of wood, to shrink. — *v.t.* (*arch*.) to attach: to shrivel: — *pa.t.* and *pa.p.* **clung**. — *n*. adherence. — *adjs*. **cling, cling'stone** (of peaches, etc.) having the pulp adhering firmly to the stone (opp. to *freestone*). — *ns*. **cling'er; cling'iness**. — *adj*. **cling'y** sticky. — **cling film** a type of transparent plastic film used to seal food containers, etc. — *adj*. **clingstone** see **cling** above. — *n*. a clingstone fruit. [O.E. *clingan*.]

clinic *klin'ik*, *n*. one confined to bed by sickness (*arch*.): the instruction of medicine or surgery at the bedside of hospital patients: a session of such instruction: a private hospital or nursing-home: an institution, or a department of one, or a group of doctors, for treating patients or for diagnosis or giving advice: any group meeting for instruction, often remedial, in a particular field. — Also *adj.* — Also **clinique** (*klin-ēk'*). — *adj.* **clin'ical** hospital-like: concerned with, based on, observation: strictly objective: plain, functional in appearance. — *adv.* **clin'ically.** — *n.* **clinician** (*-ish'ən*) a doctor, etc. who works directly with patients: a doctor, etc. who runs, or works in, a clinic. — **clinical baptism** baptism administered to persons on their sick-bed; **clinical convert** one converted on his death-bed; **clinical death** a state of the body in which the brain has entirely ceased to function, though artificial means can be used to maintain the action of the heart, lungs, etc.; **clinical medicine** or **surgery** medicine or surgery as taught by clinics; **clinical lecture** one to students at the bedside of the sick; **clinical thermometer** one for taking the temperature of patients.   [Gr. *klīnikos* — *klīnē*, a bed.]

clink[1] *klingk, n.* a ringing sound made by striking metal, glass, etc. — *v.t.* to cause to make a ringing sound. — *v.i.* to ring: to go with a clink. — *n.* **clink'er** a hard brick (also **klink'er** as Dutch): a scale or globule of black iron oxide obtained from red-hot iron under the hammer: the incombustible residue of fused ash raked out of furnaces: furnace slag: the cindery crust of some lava-flows. — **clink'er-block** a block for building made from ash from furnaces; **clink'stone** phonolite (from its metallic clink when struck).   [A form of **click** and **clank**.]

clink[2] *klingk, n.* (*slang*) prison.   [Appar. orig. one in Southwark.]

clink[3] *klingk,* (*Spens.*) *n.* said to mean a keyhole, or a latch.   [Cf. Du. *klink*, latch.]

clink[4] *klingk, v.t.* to clinch: to rivet. — *n.* **clink'er** a nail used as a protective stud in footwear, esp. in climbing boots: anything worthy of warm admiration in its kind (*slang*): a mistake or blunder (*slang*). — *adj.* (*slang*) **clink'ing.** — *adj.* **clink'er-built** made of planks which overlap those below (as distinguished from carvel-built) and fastened with clinched nails.   [Northern form, of **clinch**.]

clinker. See **clink**[1,4].

clino- *klī'nō-*, in composition, oblique. — *ns.* **clī'nōaxis** (*crystal.*) the clinodiagonal; **clīnōdiag'onal** in a monoclinic crystal, that lateral axis which is not perpendicular to the vertical axis; **clinometer** (*klīn-, klin-om'i-tər*) any of various instruments for measuring slope, elevation, or inclination. — *adj.* **clinomet'ric.** — *ns.* **clinom'etry; clīnōpin'acoid, -pin'akoid** a form consisting of two faces parallel to the clinoaxis and the vertical axis.   [Gr. *klīnein*, to lean.]

clinochlore *klī'nō-klōr, -klör, n.* a green mineral, a distinctly mono*clinic* variety of *chlor*ite.

clinquant *klingk'ənt, adj.* tinselly (*Shak.*): glittering. — *n.* tinsel: glitter.   [Fr., — Du. *klinken*, to clink.]

clint *klint,* (*geol.* and *dial.*) *n.* a vertical fissure or grike in an exposed limestone surface: (usu. *pl.*) one of a series of limestone outcrops or ridges divided by grikes: any exposed outcrop of flinty rock on a hillside or stream bed.   [M.E., cliff, conn. with Sw., Dan. and M.L.G. *klint*, crag, cliff; cf. O.N. *klettr*, rock.]

Clio[1] *klī'ō, n.* the muse of history.   [Gr. *Kleiō*, proclaimer.]

Clio[2] *klī'ō, n.* a genus of shell-less pteropods, 'whales' food'.   [Gr. *Kleiō*, a sea-nymph.]

cliometrics *klī-ō-met'riks, n. sing.* the application of econometrics in economic history.   [**Clio**[1], econo*metrics*.]

clip[1] *klip, v.t.* to cut with shears: to cut off: to trim or cut off the hair, twigs, ends, edges, etc. of: to cut out (a magazine article, etc.): to excerpt a section from (a film, etc.): to pare down: to reduce or curtail: to shorten (a sound) in indistinct utterance: to abbreviate (a word) esp. in speech, as 'sec' for 'second': to punch a piece from (a ticket, etc.): to cheat, overcharge (*coll.*): to hit sharply. — *v.i.* to go at a good speed: — *pr.p.* **clipp'ing;** *pa.p.* **clipped, clipt.** — *n.* an act of clipping: the thing removed by clipping: yield of wool: a smart

blow: a high speed: a piece taken from a film for separate showing. — *adj.* **clipped, clipt.** — *ns.* **clipp'er** one who clips: a clipping instrument: a swift mover: a sharp-built fast sailing-vessel: a showy spirited person or anything admired (*slang*); **clipp'ie** (*slang*) a woman bus or tram conductor; **clipp'ing** the act of clipping, esp. the edges of coins: a small piece clipped off, shred, paring: a newspaper cutting. — *adj.* superb: fast-going. — **clip'-joint** a place of entertainment, e.g. a night-club, where customers are overcharged or cheated. — **clip coin** to pare the edges of coins; **clip the wings** to cut the feathers of a bird's wings to prevent it from flying: to restrain ambition (*fig.*): to deprive of the means of rising.   [Prob. from O.N. *klippa*, to cut; Dan. *klippe*.]

clip[2] *klip, v.t.* to embrace (*arch.*): to encircle: to hold firmly. — *n.* a device for gripping, clasping, fastening, or holding things together: a container for ammunition which is clipped on to, and from which the bullets pass directly into, a pistol, rifle, etc. — **clip'board** a firm board to which papers can be clipped in order to take notes easily; **clip'-fas'tener** a name for a press-stud; **clip'-hook** a sister-hook. — *adj.* **clip'-on** fastening on to something by means of a clip.   [O.E. *clyppan*, to embrace; Ger. *Kluppe*, pincers.]

clip-clop. See **clop**.

clipe. See **clype**.

clipt. See **clip**[1].

clique *klēk, n.* an exclusive group of persons: a faction: a coterie — used generally in a bad sense. — *adjs.* **cliqu'(e)y, cliqu'ish** relating to a clique: exclusive. — *ns.* **cliqu'iness; cliqu'ishness; cliqu'ism** the tendency to form cliques.   [Fr., orig. in sense of claque; prob. conn. with **click**.]

clish-clash *klish'klash,* **clishmaclaver** *klish'mə-klāv'ər,* (*Scot.*) *ns.* gossip.   [See **clash, claver**.]

clistogamy. See **cleistogamy**.

clitellum *kli-, klī-tel'əm, n.* a glandular belt on a worm, secreting a cocoon: — *pl.* **clitell'a.** — *adj.* **clitell'ar.**   [L. *clītellae*, pack-saddle.]

clithral. Same as **cleithral**.

clitic *klit'ik,* (*linguistics*) *adj.* (of a word, e.g. French 'me', 'te', 'le') not capable of being stressed, usually pronounced as though part of the preceding or following word. — Also *n.*   [Back-formation from **proclitic, enclitic**.]

clitoris *kli', klī'tə-ris, n.* a small elongated erectile organ at the front of the vulva in females, the counterpart, in miniature, of the male penis. — *adj.* **clit'oral.** — *n.* **clitoridec'tomy** surgical removal of part or all of the clitoris, female circumcision.   [Gr. *kleitoris*.]

clitter *klit'ər, v.t.* and *v.i.* to make, or cause to make, a shrill rattling noise. — **clitt'er-clatt'er** idle talk, chatter.   [Related to **clatter**.]

clivers. Same as **cleavers**.

cloaca *klō-ā'kə* (L. *-ā'ka*), *n.* a sewer: a privy: a cavity in birds and reptiles, in which the intestinal and urinary ducts terminate: a sink of moral filth: — *pl.* **cloacae** (*klō-ā'sē;* L. *ä'kī*). — *adjs.* **clōā'cal, clōā'calin(e), cloacinal** (*klō-ə-sī'nl*).   [L. *cloāca* — *cluēre*, to purge.]

cloak *klōk, n.* a loose outer garment: a covering: that which conceals: a disguise, pretext. — *v.t.* to clothe with a cloak: to cover: to conceal (usu. with *with* or *in*). — Also (*arch.*) **cloke.** — *adjs.* **cloak'-and-dagg'er** concerned with plot and intrigue esp. espionage; **cloak'-and-sword** concerned with fighting and romance. — **cloak'-bag** (*obs.*) a portmanteau; **cloak'room** a room for keeping coats and hats: a room in a place of public assembly, e.g. a theatre, in which outer garments and luggage may be temporarily deposited: a lavatory.   [O.Fr. *cloke, cloque* — L.L. *cloca*, a bell, horseman's bell-shaped cape; see **clock**[1].]

cloam *klōm, n.* and *adj.* earthenware, clay, or made of such.   [O.E. *clām*, mud.]

clobber *klob'ər, n.* a paste used by shoemakers to hide the cracks in leather. — *v.t.* to overpaint a piece of porcelain and enamelled decoration.   [Origin uncertain.]

clobber[2] *klob'ər*, (*slang*) *n.* clothing, gear. [Origin uncertain.]

clobber[3] *klob'ər*, (*slang*) *v.t.* to strike very hard: to attack, cause to suffer (*fig.*): to defeat overwhelmingly. [Origin unknown.]

clochard *klo-shär*, (Fr.) *n.* a tramp.

cloche *klosh, n.* a glass under which plants are forced: a lady's close-fitting hat. [Fr.; see **clock**[1].]

clock[1] *klok, n.* a machine for measuring time, strictly one with a bell: a time-measurer in general: the striking of the hour (*Shak.*): a speedometer (*coll.*). — *v.t.* to time by a clock or stop-watch: to achieve (a certain officially attested time for a race): to hit (*slang*): to observe, notice (*slang*). — *v.i.* to register a time by a recording clock. — *adv.* **clock′wise** in the manner or direction of the hands of a clock. — **clock card** a card on which the hours worked by an employee are recorded by a time-clock; **clock′-golf** a putting game on a green marked like a clock dial, in which the player putts from each hour-figure to a hole near the centre; **clock′maker; clock′-ra′dio** an electronic apparatus combining the functions of alarm-clock and radio, esp. for bedside use. — Also **alarm′-ra′dio; clock tower** a usu. a square tower having a clock at the top with a face on each exterior wall; **clock-watcher, clock-watching** see **watch the clock** below; **clock′work** the works or machinery of a clock: machinery steady and regular like that of a clock (see also **like clockwork** below). — *adj.* automatic. — **against the clock** with effort to overcome shortage of time or achieve the shortest time; **beat the clock** to finish a job, etc., before the time limit runs out; **clock in, out, on, off** to register time of coming or going, in, out, on, off; **clock up** (*coll.*) to reach (a certain speed, score, etc.); **know what o'clock it is** to be wide awake, to know how things are; **like clockwork** as smoothly as if driven by clockwork (*fig.*); **o'clock**, for earlier **of the clock**, as reckoned or shown by the clock: in a direction corresponding to that which would be taken by the hour-hand of a horizontal clock relative to a person at the centre and facing twelve; **put back the clock, put the clock back** to return to earlier time and its conditions; **put the clock(s) back, forward** to alter the clocks to allow for the change from or to summer time; — **round the clock** for the whole of the twenty-four hours; **watch the clock** to wait eagerly for one's work-time to finish, i.e. to skimp one's work, do no more than is necessary (*ns.* **clock′= watcher; clock′-watching**. [M.E. *clokke*, prob. through O.Fr. from L.L. *cloca, clocca*, a bell; mod. Fr. *cloche*, bell, Du. *klok*, bell, clock, Ger. *Glocke*, bell.]

clock[2] *klok, n.* an ornament on the side of a stocking. — *adj.* **clocked** ornamented with such clocks. [Ety. dub.]

clock[3] *klok, klōk,* (*Scot.* and *dial.*) *n.* a beetle. — *n.* **clock′er** a large beetle. [Origin unknown; cf. Swed. dial. *klocka*, beetle, earwig.]

clock[4] *klok,* (*Scot.*) *v.i.* to cluck: to brood or sit. — *n.* a brooding hen's cry: a cluck. — *n.* **clock′er** a clocking hen. [O.E. *cloccian*; Du. *klokken*.]

clod *klod, n.* a thick round mass or lump, that sticks together, esp. of earth or turf: a concreted mass: the ground: a bed of fireclay in a coal-mine: the body of a man, as formed of clay: a stupid fellow. — *v.t.* to pelt (*arch.*): to throw (*Scot.*). — *v.i.* (*arch.*) to throw clods: — *pr.p.* **clodd′ing;** *pa.t.* and *pa.p.* **clodd′ed.** — *adj.* **clodd′ish.** — *n.* **clodd′ishness.** — *adj.* **clodd′y** abounding in clods: earthy. — *adv.* **clod′ly.** — **clod′-hopper** a countryman: a peasant: a dolt: a heavy, clumsy shoe (*slang*). — *adj.* **clod′hopping** boorish. — **clod′pate, clod′pole, clod′poll** a stupid fellow. — *adj.* **clod′pated.** [A later form of **clot**.]

cloff[1] *klof,* (*Scot.*) *n.* a cleft. [Cf. O.N. *klof.*]

cloff[2] *klof, n.* an allowance on buying goods wholesale, of 2 lb. in every 3 cwt., after tare and tret have been deducted. [Origin obscure.]

clog *klog, n.* a block or log of wood: a heavy block of wood fastened to a man or animal to restrict move-

ment: anything hindering motion: an obstruction: an impediment: a wooden shoe: a shoe with a wooden sole. — *v.t.* to fasten a piece of wood to: to choke up with an accumulation (often with *up*): to obstruct: to encumber: to sole with wood. — *adj.* **clogged** encumbered. — *ns.* **clogg′er** one who makes clogs; **clogg′iness.** — *adj.* **clogg′y** lumpy, sticky. — **clog′-al′manac** an early form of almanac having the indicating characters notched on wood, horn, etc.; **clog box** a Chinese temple block; **clog′dance** a dance performed with clogs, the clatter keeping time to the music. [Ety. dub.]

cloison *klwä-zō, kloi′zn, n.* a partition, dividing fillet or band. — *n.* **cloisonnage** (*klwäz-on-äzh′*) cloisonné work or process. — *adj.* **cloisonné** (*klwäz-on-ā, kloi-zon′ā,* or *-ā′*) decorated in enamel, in compartments formed by small fillets of metal. — *n.* work of this kind. [Fr.]

cloister *klois′tər, n.* a covered arcade forming part of a monastic or collegiate establishment: a place of religious retirement, a monastery or nunnery: an enclosed place: monastic life. — *v.t.* to confine in a cloister: to confine within walls. — *adj.* **clois′tered** dwelling in or enclosed by cloisters: sheltered from reality and the full experience of life. — *n.* **clois′terer** one belonging to a cloister. — *adj.* **clois′tral** claustral, pertaining or confined to a cloister: secluded. — *n.* **clois′tress** (*Shak.*) a nun. — **clois′ter-garth** the court or yard enclosed by a cloister. [O.Fr. *cloistre* (O.E. *clauster*) — L. *claustrum* — *claudĕre, clausum,* to shut.]

cloke. Same as **cloak.**

clomb *klōm,* old *pa.t.* and *pa.p.* of **climb.**

clomiphene *klom′i-fēn, n.* a synthetic drug used to stimulate ovulation in apparently infertile women. [Coined from *chloramine* and **phene**.]

clone *klōn,* (*biol.*) *n.* the whole stock of individuals derived asexually from one sexually produced: any of such individuals: a person or thing closely similar to another, a copy, replica (*coll.*). — *v.t.* to reproduce as a clone: to produce a clone or clones of. — *adj.* **clō′nal.** [Gr. *klōn,* shoot.]

clonic. See **clonus.**

clonk *klongk, n.* the sound of something heavy falling on to a surface. — *v.i.* to make or go with such a sound. — *v.t.* to hit. [Imit.]

clonus *klō′nəs, n.* a spasm of alternate contractions and relaxations of the muscles. — *adj.* **clonic** (*klon′ik*). [Latinised from Gr. *klōnos,* tumult.]

cloop *kloŏp, n.* the sound of drawing a cork. [Imit.]

cloot[1] *kloŏt,* Scot. *klüt, klit, n.* a division of a cloven hoof: (*loosely*) a hoof. — *ns.* **Cloot′ie, Cloots** the devil. [Scot.; ety. dub.]

cloot[2] *kloŏt, klüt, klit,* (*Scot.*) *n.* a cloth. — **clootie dumpling** a suet pudding, containing currants, raisins, etc., steamed or boiled in a cloth. [**clout**.]

clop *klop, n.* the sound of a horse's hoof-tread. — *adv.* with a clop. — *v.i.* to make, or go with, such a sound. — Also **clip′-clop′, clop′-clop′.** [Imit.]

cloqué *klo-kā′, n.* an embossed material. — Also *adj.* [Fr.]

close[1] *klōs, adj.* shut up: with no opening: confined, unventilated: stifling: narrow: stingy: near, in time or place (often with *to* or *by*): intimate: compact: crowded: hidden: reserved: private: secret: thorough, in detail: (of a vowel) pronounced with slight opening, or with the tongue tense. — *adv.* in a close manner: tightly: nearly: densely: secretly. — *n.* an enclosed place: a small enclosed field: a narrow passage off a street, esp. leading to a tenement stairway or courtyard: the precinct of a cathedral. — *adv.* **close′ly.** — *n.* **close′ness.** — *adjs.* **close′-band′ed** closely united; **close′-barred** firmly closed; **close′-bod′ied** fitting close to the body. — **Close Brethren** the Exclusive Brethren, a branch of the Plymouth Brethren whose members will not associate with (e.g. eat in company with) people outside their group; **close call** a narrow escape; **close company** a firm controlled by five, or fewer, people; **close corporation** a corporation which fills up its own vacancies, without outside interference; **close encounter**

a direct personal confrontation with an extra-terrestrial being (also *fig.*). — *adjs.* **close′-fist′ed, close′-hand′ed** penurious, covetous; **close′-fitt′ing** of clothes, designed to fit tightly; **close′-grained** with the particles, fibres, etc., close together, compact. — **close harmony** harmony in which the notes of chords lie close together. — *adj.* **close′-hauled′** in trim for sailing as near as possible to the wind. — *n.* **close-head** (*Scot.*) the entrance to a close, or the gossips that congregate there. — *adjs.* **close′-knit′** of communities, etc., closely connected, bound together; **close′-lipped′, -mouthed′** reticent, saying little; **close′-reefed′** having all reefs taken in. — **close season, time** a time of the year when it is illegal to kill certain game or fish — the breeding season: a prohibited or inactive period; **close shave, thing** a close call; **close′-stool** a chamberpot enclosed in a box or stool; **close tennis** tennis properly so called, distinguished from lawn-tennis. — *adj.* **close′-tongued** (*Shak.*) cautious in speaking. — **close′-up′** a photograph or film taken near at hand and thus detailed and big in scale: a close scrutiny. — **close on** almost, nearly; **close to the chest** without revealing one's intentions. [Fr. *clos*, shut — L. *claudĕre*, *clausum*, to close, shut up.]

close² *klōz*, *v.t.* to make close: to draw or to bring together: to unite: to narrow: (of ships) to come or pass near to: to place (a door, etc.) so as to cover an opening, to shut: to block, make impassable or impenetrable: to forbid access to: to end: to complete, conclude: to terminate: to put an end to discussion of: to cease operating or trading. — *v.i.* to come together: to unite: to narrow: to grapple: to come to an end: of currency, a financial index, etc., to measure, be worth, at the end of the day's business (with *at*): to agree (with). — *n.* the manner or time of closing: a pause or stop: a cadence: the end: junction: encounter (*Shak.*). — *adj.* **closed** shut: blocked: not open to traffic: with permanent sides and top: with lid, etc.: exclusive, having few contacts outside itself (e.g. *a closed community*): not open to all, restricted: continuous and finishing where it began. — *ns.* **clos′er** one who or that which concludes: any portion of a brick used to close up the bond next to the end brick of a course; **clos′ing** enclosing: ending: agreement; **clos′ure** the act of closing: something that closes or fastens: the end: the stopping of a parliamentary debate by vote of the House. — *v.t.* to apply the closure to. — **closed book** (*fig.*) a mystery: something about which one knows nothing. — *adj.* **closed′-chain′** (*chem.*) having a molecule in which the atoms are linked ringwise, like a chain with the ends united. — **closed circuit** (*television*) a system in which the showing is for restricted not general viewing. — *adj.* **closed-door** see **with closed doors** below. — **close-down** see **close down** below; **closed shop** an establishment in which only members of a trade union, or of a particular trade union, will be employed: the principle or policy implied in such a regulation: an establishment boycotted by the trade unions: a situation where only specialist personnel have access to a computer (opp. to *open shop*); **closed syllable** one ending in a consonant; **closing price** the value of shares on the stock-market when business stops for the day; **clos′ing-time** the time at which business stops, esp. in public houses. — **close a bargain** to make an agreement; **close down** to come to a standstill or stoppage of work: to give up business (*n.* **close′-down**); **close in upon** to surround and draw near to; **close on** to catch up with; **close one's eyes** (*euph.*) to die; **close one's eyes to** to ignore purposely; **close ranks** (of soldiers drawn up in line) to stand closer together in order to present a more solid front to the enemy: to unite, make a show of solidarity in the face of a common danger; **close with** to accede to: to grapple with; **with closed doors** in private, the public being excluded, as in special cases in court, etc. (*adj.* **closed′-door′**). [Fr. *clore*, *clos* — L. *claudĕre*, *clausum*.]

closet *kloz′it*, *n.* a small private room: a recess off a room:

a privy: the private chamber of a sovereign, an apartment for private audience or council, or for private or domestic devotions: a horizontal band one-half the width of a bar (*her.*). — *adj.* secret, private. — *v.t.* to shut up in or take into a closet: to conceal: — *pr.p.* **clos′eting;** *pa.t.* and *pa.p.* **clos′eted.** — **clos′et-play, -drama** a play to be read rather than acted; **closet queen** (*slang*) a homosexual who does not openly admit his homosexuality; **clos′et-strat′egist** a mere theorist in strategy. [O.Fr. *closet*, dim. of *clos*, an enclosure; see **close.**]

clostridium *klos-trid′i-əm*, *n.* an ovoid or spindle-shaped bacterium: (with *cap.*) a genus of spindle-shaped anaerobic bacteria (fam. Bacillaceae) incl. several species pathogenic to man and animals: — *pl.* **clostrid′ia.** — *adj.* **clostrid′ial.** [Gr. *klōstēr*, a spindle.]

closure. See **close².**

clot *klot*, *n.* a mass of soft or fluid matter concretcd, as blood: a fool. — *v.t.* and *v.i.* to form into clots: — *pr.p.* **clott′ing;** *pa.t.* and *pa.p.* **clott′ed.** — *v.t.* **clott′er** to coagulate. — *ns.* **clott′iness; clott′ing** coagulation. — *adj.* **clott′y.** — **clot′poll** (*Shak.*) a clodpoll, a blockhead; **clotted** (also **clouted**) **cream** a famous Devonshire delicacy, prepared by scalding milk. [O.E. *clott*, a clod of earth; cf. Du. *klos*, block; Dan. *klods*; Ger. *Klotz*.]

clote *klōt*, *n.* the burdock: extended to other plants of burry character. — *n.* **clotbur** (*klot′bər*) the burdock: a species of Xanthium. — Also **clote′bur, cockle-bur.** [O.E. *clāte*.]

cloth *kloth*, *klöth*, *n.* woven material from which garments or coverings are made: a piece of this material: clothing: the usual dress of a trade or profession, esp. the clerical: a table-cloth: sails: a theatre curtain: — *pl.* **cloths** (*kloths*, *klödhz*). — *v.t.* **clothe** (*klōdh*) to cover with a garment: to provide with clothes: to invest as with a garment (*fig.*): to cover: — *pr.p.* **clothing** (*klōdh′ing*); *pa.t.* and *pa.p.* **clothed** (*klōdhd*) or **clad.** — *n.pl.* **clothes** (*klōdhz*; *coll.* *klōz*) garments or articles of dress: blankets, sheets and cover for a bed. — *ns.* **clothier** (*klō′dhi-ər*) one who makes or sells cloth or clothes; **clothing** (*klō′dhing*) clothes, garments: covering. — **cloth cap** a flat cap. — *adjs.* **cloth′-cap′** symbolic of the working-class; **cloth′-eared** (*slang*) deaf, usu. because inattentive. — **clothes′-basket** a large basket for holding and carrying clothes for the wash; **clothes′-brush** a brush for clothes. — *adj.* **clothes′-conscious** concerned about one's clothes and appearance. — **clothes′-horse, clothes′-screen** a frame for hanging clothes on to dry; **clothes′-line** a rope or wire for hanging clothes on to dry; **clothes′-moth** one of various tineas whose larvae feed on woollens; **clothes′-peg, -pin** a forked piece of wood or a wooden or plastic clamp to secure clothes on a line; **clothes′-pole** a pole from which clothes-lines are hung; **clothes′-press** a place for holding clothes: an apparatus for pressing clothes; **clothes′-prop** a movable notched pole for raising or supporting a clothes-line; **clothes′-sense** dress-sense; **cloth′-hall** an exchange building or market for the cloth trade; **cloth-yard** the yard by which cloth was measured, formerly 37 inches. — **clothe in words** to express in words; **clothe on** or **upon** to invest: to cover; **cloth of gold** a tissue of threads of gold and silk or wool; **cloth of state** a canopy; **cloth-yard shaft** an arrow a cloth-yard long; **the cloth** the clerical profession: the clergy. [O.E. *clāth*, cloth; Ger. *Kleid*, a garment.]

Clotho *klō′thō*, *n.* in Gr. myth., the Fate that holds the distaff from which Lachesis spins the thread of life: the puff-adder genus. [Gr. *klōthō*.]

cloture *klō′chər*, Fr. *klō-tür*, *n.* closure: the limitation of a debate in a legislative assembly, usu. by calling for an immediate vote (*U.S.*). — Also *v.t.* [Fr. *clôture*; see **closure.**]

clou *klōō*, *n.* the chief point of interest: a dominant idea. [Fr., nail.]

cloud *klowd*, *n.* a mass of fog, consisting of minute particles of water, often in a frozen state, floating in the atmosphere: anything unsubstantial (*fig.*): a great number or multitude of anything (as cloud of witnesses) (*fig.*): anything that obscures, as a cloud: a dullness: a dark or dull spot: a dark spot on a horse's face (*Shak.*): a great volume of dust or smoke: a loosely-knitted headscarf for ladies, a fascinator: anything gloomy, overhanging or bodeful. — *v.t.* to overspread with clouds: to darken: to defame: to stain with dark spots or streaks: to dull. — *v.i.* to become clouded or darkened. — *n.* **cloud'age**. — *adj.* **cloud'ed** hidden by clouds: darkened, indistinct, dull (*fig.*): variegated with spots. — *adv.* **cloud'ily**. — *ns.* **cloud'iness**; **cloud'ing** a cloudy appearance. — *adj.* growing dim. — *adj.* **cloud'less** unclouded, clear. — *adv.* **cloud'lessly**. — *n.* **cloud'let** a little cloud. — *adj.* **cloud'y** darkened with, or consisting of, clouds: obscure: gloomy: stained with dark spots: 'shady' (*coll.*). — **cloud base** the under-surface of cloud(s): the height of this above sea-level; **cloud'berry** a low plant related to the bramble, found on elevated moors in Britain, with an orange-red berry of delightful flavour. — *adj.* **cloud'-built** made of clouds, unsubstantial. — **cloud'-burst** a sudden flood of rain over a small area. — *adj.* **cloud'-capt** (*Shak.*) capped with or touching the clouds. — **cloud'-castle, cloud'land, cloud'-cuck'oo-land** or **-town** an imaginary situation or land esp. as the product of impractical or wishful thinking (the last translating Aristophanes's *Nephelokokkȳgiā*); **cloud ceiling** the height of the cloud base above the ground; **cloud'-chamber** an apparatus in which the path of charged particles is made visible by means of waterdrops condensed on gas ions. — *adj.* **cloud'-compell'ing** driving or collecting the clouds, an epithet of Zeus. — **clouded leopard** an arboreal cat (*Felis nebulosa*) smaller than a leopard. — *adj.* **cloud'-kiss'ing** (*Shak.*) touching the clouds. — **cloud'-seeding** the induction of rainfall by scattering particles, e.g. dry ice, silver iodide, on clouds from aircraft. — *adj.* **cloud'-topped** covered with or touching the clouds. — **on cloud nine** (*coll.*) intensely happy; **under a cloud** in trouble, disgrace, or disfavour; **with one's head in the clouds** in a dreamy impractical way or state. [O.E. *clūd*, a hill (as still in Derbyshire), then a cloud, the root idea being a mass or ball; cf. **clod, clot**.]

clough *kluf*, or *klow, n.* a ravine: a valley. [O.E. would be *clōh*; Scot. *cleuch*.]

clour *klōōr*, (*Scot.*) *n.* a knock: a swelling caused by a knock, a bruise. — *v.t.* to knock: to raise a bump. [Origin doubtful.]

clout *klowt, n.* a piece of cloth, esp. used for mending: a patch: a protective plate or nail: a rag: in archery, the mark or target, usually in long-distance shooting: a shot that hits: a blow or cuff: influence, power (*coll.*). — *v.t.* to mend with a patch: to protect with a plate or with nails: to cover with a cloth: to cuff: to hit with great force. — *adj.* **clout'ed** (*Shak.*) heavy and patched or having nails in the soles, as shoes; covered with a clout. — *n.* **clout'er**. — *adj.* **clout'erly** clownish. — **clout'-nail** a large-headed nail: **clout'-shoe** a shoe with clout-nails: a clown. [O.E. *clūt*; cf. O.N. *klūtr*, a kerchief; Dan. *klud*, rag.]

clouted *klowt'id, adj.* clotted. [See **clot**.]

clove¹ *klōv, pa.t.* of **cleave¹**. — **clove'-hitch'** a kind of hitch knot, used to connect ropes of different thicknesses, or a rope to an object; **clove'-hook** a sister-hook.

clove² *klōv, n.* a division of a bulb, as in garlic. [O.E. *clufu*; cf. **cleave¹**.]

clove³ *klōv, n.* an old weight (7, 8, or 10 pounds) for wool and cheese. [Fr. *clou* — L. *clāvus*, nail.]

clove⁴ *klōv, n.* the flower-bud of the **clove'-tree** (*Eugenia caryophyllata*) a native of the Moluccas, dried as a spice, and yielding an essential oil, **oil of cloves**, used in medicine (in *pl.*) a cordial got therefrom. — **clove'=gill'yflower, clove'-pink** a variety of pink, smelling of cloves. [Fr. *clou*, nail, from its shape — L. *clāvus*, a nail.]

cloven *klōv'n, p.adj.* split: divided. — *adjs.* **clov'en-foot'ed,**

clov'en-hoofed' having the hoof divided, as the ox or sheep. — **the cloven hoof** applied to any indication of devilish agency or temptation, from the early representation of the devil with cloven hoofs — prob. from Pan, some of whose characteristics he shares. [*Pa.p.* of **cleave**, to divide.]

clover *klō'vər, n.* a genus (Trifolium) of papilionaceous plants, with heads of small flowers and trifoliate leaves, affording rich pasturage. — *adj.* **clov'ered** covered with clover. — *adj.* **clov'ery** abounding in clover. — **clov'er= grass** clover; **clov'erleaf** a traffic arrangement in which one road passes over the top of another and the roads connecting the two are in the pattern of a four-leafed clover: any interlinked arrangement of this shape. — Also *adj.* — **live in clover** to live luxuriously or in abundance. [O.E. *clāfre* (usu. *clǣfre*); Du. *klaver*; Dan. *klöver*; Ger. *Klee*.]

clow *klow, n.* a Scots form of **clove⁴**. — **clow'-gill'ieflower**.

clowder *klow'dər, (rare) n.* a collective name for a number of cats. [Variant of **clutter**.]

clown *klown, n.* a rustic or country-fellow: one with the awkward manners of a countryman: an ill-bred fellow: a fool or buffoon, esp. of the harlequinade or the circus: a stupid person (*coll.*). — *v.i.* to play the clown. — *ns.* **clown'ery** a clown's performance; **clown'ing**. — *adj.* **clown'ish** of or like a clown: coarse and awkward: rustic. — *adv.* **clown'ishly**. — *ns.* **clown'ishness; clown'-ship**. [Perh. — L. Ger., cf. Fris. *klönne, klünne*.]

cloy *kloi, v.t.* to prick (a horse in shoeing) (*obs.*): to gore (*arch.*): to spike (a cannon) (*arch.*): to block up (*arch.*): to overcharge with food, to satiate, esp. with sweetness: to disgust, weary. — *v.i.* to cause distaste, become distasteful from excess. — *adjs.* **cloyed; cloy'ing; cloy'-less** (*Shak.*) that cannot cloy. — *n.* **cloy'ment** (*Shak.*) satiety, surfeit. — *adj.* **cloy'some** satiating. [Aphetised from *accloy* — O.Fr. *encloyer* (Fr. *enclouer*) — L.L. *inclāvāre*, to drive in a nail — in, in, *clāvus*, a nail.]

cloye *kloi, (Shak.) v.t.* app., to claw, stroke with the claw. [Perh. **claw**.]

cloze *klōz, (education) adj.* denoting a type of exercise in which the reader is required to supply words that have been deleted from a text, as a test of comprehension in reading. [Formed from **closure**.]

club *klub, n.* a heavy tapering stick, knobby or massy at one end, used to strike with: a cudgel: a bat used in certain games: an instrument for playing golf, with a wooden, iron, or aluminium head, or a wooden head with brass sole: a bunch: a card of one of the four suits: a combination: a clique, set: an association of persons for social, political, athletic, or other ends: an association of persons who possess a building as a common resort for the members: a club-house, or the house occupied by a club. — *v.t.* to beat with a club: to gather into a bunch: to combine: to use as as a club: to throw into confusion (*mil.*). — *v.i.* (esp. with *together*) to join together for some common end: to combine together: to share in a common expense. — *adjs.* **club'(b)able** sociable; **clubbed** enlarged at the end like a club. — *n.* **clubb'ing** beating: combination: a thickening, as of finger-ends, or of cabbage-stems attacked by insect larvae. — *adj.* **clubb'ish** given to clubs. — *ns.* **clubb'ism** the club system; **clubb'ist** a clubman. — *n. sing.* **clubs** see **clumps**. — **club'-face** the face of a golf-club; **club'-foot** a deformed foot. — *adj.* **club'-foot'ed**. — *v.t.* **club'-haul** (*naut.*) to tack by dropping the lee anchor and slipping the cable. — **club'-head** the head of a golf-club. — *adj.* **club'-head'ed** having a thick head. — **club'house** a house for the accommodation of a club; **club'land** the area around St James's in London, where many of the old-established clubs are: an area or region containing a large number of e.g. working-men's clubs; **club'-law** government by violence; **club'-line** a short line at the end of a paragraph; **club'man** one who carries a club: a member of a club: a frequenter of clubs, man-about-town; **club'-master** the manager of, or purveyor for, a club;

club'-moss a lycopod; club'room the room in which a club meets; club'root a fungal disease which attacks the roots of plants of the Cruciferae; club'-rush any sedge of the genus Scirpus; club sandwich a sandwich of toast, usu. three slices, containing chicken or turkey, bacon or ham, lettuce, tomato, and mayonnaise; club soda soda water; club'woman. — in the (pudding) club (*slang*) pregnant; join the club (*coll.*) we are all in the same position: me too; on the club certified unfit to work. [O.N. and Sw. *klubba*; same root as clump.]

cluck *kluk, n.* the call of a hen to her chickens: any similar sound: a fool (*U.S.*; now also dumb'-cluck). — *v.i.* to make such a sound. — *adj.* cluck'y (*Austr. slang*) obsessed with babies, broody. [Imit; cf. Du. *klokken*, Ger. *glucken*, Dan. *klukke*, and clock[4].]

cludgie *klud'ji*, (*Scot. slang*) *n.* a (public) lavatory. [Origin uncertain.]

clue[1] *klōō, n.* anything that points to the solution of a mystery. — *adj.* clue'less without a trace: trackless: ignorant: stupid. — *adj.* clued'-up' (*coll.*) (well-)informed. — clue in (*coll.*) to inform; not have a clue to have no information; to have no idea, no notion at all. [See clew.]

clue[2]. See clew.

clumber *klumb'ər, n.* a kind of spaniel, formerly bred at *Clumber*, in Nottinghamshire.

clump *klump, n.* a thick, short, shapeless piece of anything: a cluster: a clot: a thick additional sole: a blow. — *v.i.* to walk heavily: to clot: to cluster. — *v.t.* to put in a clump: to beat. — *n.* clump'iness. — *adj.* clump'ing (*coll.*) clumsy. — *n. sing.* clumps a parlour game of question and answer — also clubs. — *adj.* clump'y abounding in clumps: heavy. [Prob. Scand.; Dan. *klump*, a lump. Cf. Ger. *Klump*, and club.]

clumsy *klum'zi, adj.* shapeless: ill-made: unwieldy: awkward: ungainly. — *adv.* clum'sily. — *n.* clum'siness. [ME. *clumsen*, to be stiff or benumbed.]

clunch *klunch, -sh, n.* a tough clay. [Prob. related to clump.]

clung *klung, pa.t.* and *pa.p.* of cling.

Cluniac *klōōn'i-ak, n.* a monk or nun of a branch of the Benedictine order originating at *Cluny* in France in A.D. 910. — Also *adj.*

clunk *klungk, n.* the gurgling sound of a liquid or the sound of a cork being drawn from a bottle (*Scot.*): a metallic noise: a thump: a dolt (*U.S.*). — *v.i.* to fall with a thumping sound. — *v.t.* (*dial.*) to gurgle while swallowing. [Imit.]

Clupea *klōō'pi-ə, n.* the herring genus. — *ns.* clu'peoid, clu'peid any fish of the herring family, Clupē'idae. — Also *adjs.* [L. *clupea*, a kind of river fish.]

Clusia *klōō'zi-ə, n.* a typical American genus of (mostly) climbing plants, giving an alternative name Clusiā'ceae to the Guttiferae: (without *cap.*) any plant of the genus. [After the French botanist Charles de Lécluse (L. *Clusius*).]

cluster *klus'tər, n.* a number of things of the same kind growing or joined together: a bunch: a mass: a crowd. — *v.i.* to grow in or gather into clusters. — *v.t.* to collect into clusters: to cover with clusters. — *adjs.* clus'tered grouped; clus'tering; clus'tery. — clus'ter= bean the guar (q.v.); clus'ter-bomb a bomb that opens on impact to throw out a number of small bombs; clus'ter-cup an aecidium; clustered column a pier which consists of several columns or shafts clustered together; cluster fly a large dark-brown fly akin to the blue-bottle, that gathers in large numbers in attics, etc. during autumn; clust'er-pine the pinaster (*Pinus pinaster*), a pine with clustered cones. [O.E. *clyster*; L.G. *kluster*; cf. clot.]

clutch[1] *kluch, v.t.* to close the hand upon: to hold firmly: to seize or grasp. — *v.i.* to make a snatching movement (with *at*). — *n.* a claw (often in *pl.*): a hand (often in *pl.*): a device by which two shafts or rotating members may be connected or disconnected either while at rest or in relative motion: grasp: a snatching movement: (in *pl.*) power, control. — clutch bag a kind of handbag

without strap or handle, carried in the hand or under the arm. [O.E. *clyccan*, to clench.]

clutch[2] *kluch, n.* a brood of chickens: a sitting of eggs: (*loosely*) a number, group. — *v.t.* to hatch. [Cf. cleck.]

clutter *klut'ər, n.* a clotted or confused mass: a disorderly accumulation: confusion: stir (*dial.*): noise (*dial.*): irregular interference on radar screen from echoes, rain, buildings, etc. — *v.i.* to crowd together: to go about in noisy confusion (*dial.*). — *v.t.* to litter, clog with superfluous objects, material, etc. (often with *up*). [From clot; influenced in meaning by cluster and clatter.]

cly *klī,* (*slang*) *v.t.* to seize, steal. — cly'-fāk'er a pickpocket; cly'-fāk'ing pocket-picking. [Prob. related to claw; referred by some to Du. *kleed, a garment, to fake a cly,* to take a garment.]

Clydesdale *klīdz'dāl, adj.* (of a breed of cart-horses) originating in *Clydesdale,* the area of Scotland through which the Clyde flows. — *n.* a Clydesdale horse. — *adj.* Clyde'side relating to *Clydeside,* the area along the Clyde; or to ship-building, its main industry. — *n.* Clyde'sider an inhabitant of Clydeside.

clype, clipe *klīp,* (*Scot.*) *v.i.* to tell tales. — Also *n.* [M.E. *clepien,* to call.]

clypeus *klip'i-əs, n.* the shield-like part of an insect's head. — *adjs.* clyp'eal of the clypeus; clyp'eate, clyp'ēiform buckler-shaped. [L. *clipeus* (*clypeus*), a round shield.]

clyster *klis'tər, n.* a liquid injected into the intestines. — clys'ter-pipe (*Shak.*) a pipe or syringe for injecting a clyster. [Gr. *klystēr,* a clyster-pipe — *klyzein,* to wash out.]

Cnicus (*k*)*nī'kəs, n.* a genus of thistles. [Gr. *knēkos.*]

cnida (*k*)*nī'də, n.* a nematocyst: — *pl.* cnī'dae (-*dē*). — *n.pl.* cnīdā'ria a division of the Coelenterata characterised by cnidae. — *n.* cnī'doblast the mother-cell of a cnida. [Gr. *knīdē,* a nettle, a sea-anemone.]

co-. See com-.

co' *kə.* Scots form of quoth.

co. *kō.* An abbreviation for company.

coacervate *kō-as'ər-vāt* (or -*ûr'*), *v.t.* to heap: to cause to mass together. — Also *adj.* — *n.* (also coacervā'tion) a reversible aggregation of particles of an emulsoid into liquid droplets before flocculation. [L. *coacervāre, -ātum — acervus,* heap.]

coach *kōch, n.* formerly, a private carriage: a large, close, four-wheeled carriage, esp. one for state occasions or one plying for conveyance of passengers: a railway carriage: a bus for tourists and sightseers: a ship's cabin near the stern: a private tutor: a professional trainer in athletics, football, etc.: a decoy animal. — *v.t.* to carry in a coach (*arch.*): to tutor, instruct, prepare for an examination, boat-race, etc. — *v.i.* to go by coach: to act as tutor: to study with a tutor. — *ns.* coach'ee, coach'y a coachman; coach'er one who coaches: a coach-horse; coach'ing travelling by coach: tutoring: instruction. — *adj.* coach'y pertaining to a coach — *n.* see coachee. — coach bolt a large mushroom-headed bolt with a shank that is square-sectioned at the top; coach'-box the driver's seat on a coach; coach'builder a person who builds the bodies of cars, lorries, railway carriages, etc.; coach'-building. — *adj.* coach'-built of prams, of solid construction and upholstered. — coach'dog a spotted dog, kept chiefly as an attendant on carriages, a Dalmatian dog; coach'-hire money paid for the use of a hired coach; coach'-horn a post-horn; coach'-horse a horse used for drawing a coach; coach'= house a house to keep a coach in; coach'-line an ornamental line along the body of a motor vehicle; coach'man the driver of a coach: a servant employed to drive a carriage; coach'-office a coach booking-office; coach'-road; coach'-stand a place where coaches stand for hire; coach'-way; coach'-wheel; coach'whip a coachman's whip: a kind of whip-snake; coach'whip= bird either of two Australian birds of the genus Psophodes that utter a sound like the crack of a whip; coach'work the fine work of a motor-car body. [Fr.

coche — Hung. *kocsi*, from *Kocs*, in Hungary.]
coact[1] *kō-akt'*, *v.i.* to act together. — *n.* **coaction** (*kō-ak'-shən*) mutual relations. — *adj.* **cōac'tive** acting together. — *n.* **cōactiv'ity**.   [Pfx. **co-** and **act**.]
coact[2] *kō-akt'*, *v.t.* to compel. — *n.* **coaction** (*kō-ak'shən*) compulsion. — *adj.* **coac'tive** compulsory.   [L. *cōgěre*, *cōāctum*, to compel.]
coadjacent *kō-ə-jās'ənt*, *adj.* contiguous. — *n.* **coadja'-cency**.
coadjutant *kō-aj'ə-tənt*, *adj.* mutually helping. — *n.* one who helps another. — *ns.* **coadj'utor** a helper, assistant, esp. of a bishop: an associate: — *fem.* **coadj'utress, coadj'utrix; coadj'utorship**.   [L. *adjūtor*, a helper — *ad*, to , *juvāre*, to help.]
coadunate *kō-ad'ū-nāt*, *v.t.* to unite: to combine. — *n.* **coadūnā'tion**. — *adj.* **coad'ūnative**.   [L. *adūnāre*, *-ātum*, to unite — *ad*, to, *unus*, one.]
co-agent *kō-ā'jənt*, *n.* a joint agent. — *n.* **co-ā'gency**.
coagulate *kō-ag'ū-lāt*, *v.t.* to make to curdle, clot, or set by a chemical reaction. — *v.i.* to curdle, clot, or set irreversibly. — *adj.* clotted (*rare*): curdled. — *n.* **cōagūlabil'ity**. — *adj.* **cōag'ūlable**. — *ns.* **cōag'ūlant** a substance that causes coagulation; **cōagūlā'tion**. — *adj.* **cōag'ūlative**. — *n.* **cōag'ūlator**. — *adj.* **cōag'ūlatory**. — *n.* **cōag'ūlum** what is coagulated.   [L. *coāgulāre*, *-ātum* — *agěre*, to drive.]
coaita *kō-ī-tä'*, *n.* the red-faced spider monkey.   [Tupí.]
coal *kōl*, *n.* charcoal (*obs.*): a piece of charcoal, esp. glowing: a firm, brittle, generally black combustible carbonaceous rock derived from vegetable matter (the usual sense now): a piece of this rock: a cinder: an ember. — *v.i.* to take in coal. — *v.t.* to supply with coal: to char. — *ns.* **coal'er** a ship or train carrying or transporting coal; **Coal'ite®** a smokeless fuel got by low-temperature carbonisation of coal. — *adj.* **coal'y** of or like coal: covered with coal. — **coal'ball** a calcareous nodule found in coal; **coal'-bed** a stratum of coal. — *adj.* **coal'-black** black as coal, very black. — **coal'-box** a box for holding coal: a shell that emits black smoke (*mil. slang*); **coal'-brass** iron pyrites found with coal; **coal'-bunker** a box, recess, or compartment for holding coal; **coal'-cellar** a cellar or similar place for storing coal; **coal'-cutter** a machine for under-cutting a coal-bed; **coal'-dust** coal in fine powder; **coal'-face'** the exposed surface of coal in a mine: **coal'field** a district containing coal strata. — *adj.* **coal'-fired** burning or fuelled by coal. — **coal'fish** a dusky fish of the cod family, with a green back — the saith or sillock; **coal'-flap, coal'-plate** a flap or plate covering the entrance from the pavement to a coal-cellar; **coal'-gas** the mixture of gases produced by the distillation of coal, used for lighting and heating; **coal'-heaver** one employed in carrying coal; **coal'-hole** a small coal-cellar: a hole in the pavement for filling a coal-cellar; **coal'-house** a covered-in place for keeping coal; **coaling station** a port at which steamships take in coal; **coal'man** one who has to do with coals; **coal'master** the owner or lessee of a coalfield; **Coal Measures** (*geol.*) the uppermost division of the Car-boniferous; **coal'-merchant** a dealer in coal; **coal'-mine, -pit** a pit or mine from which coal is dug; **coal'-miner**; **coal-mouse** see **coal-tit**; **coal'-oil** (*U.S.*) rock-oil, shale-oil, petroleum; **coal'-own'er** one who owns a colliery; **coal'-plant** a fossil plant of the Carboniferous strata; **coal'-porter** one who carries coal; **Coal Sack** (*astron.*) a dark patch in the Milky Way; **coal'-scuttle** a fireside vessel for holding coal; **coal'-tar** gas-tar, a thick, black, opaque liquid formed when coal is distilled; **coal'-tit, coal'-tit'mouse, coal'-mouse** (also **cole-**) a dark species of tit; **coal'-trimmer** one who stores or shifts coal on board vessels; **coal'-whipper** one who unloads coal from vessels to barges. — **blow the coals** to excite passion, foment strife; **carry coals to Newcastle** to take a thing where it is already most abundant; **coal-scuttle bonnet** a bonnet shaped like a coal-scuttle upside down; **haul** or **call over the coals** to reprimand — from the discipline applied to heretics; **heap coals of fire on**

someone's head to excite someone's remorse and re-pentance by returning good for evil (Rom. xii. 20).   [O.E. *col*; cog. with O.N. *kol*, Ger. *Kohle*.]
coalesce *kō-ə-les'*, *v.i.* to grow together or unite into one body. — *n.* **coalesc'ence** growing into each other: fusion. — *adj.* **coalesc'ent**. — *v.t.* and *v.i.* **coalise, -ize** (*kō'ə-līz*) to bring or come into coalition. — *n.* **cōalition** (*-lish'ən*) combination or alliance short of union, esp. of states or political parties. — *adj.* **cōali'tional**. — *ns.* **cōali'tioner; cōali'tionism; cōali'tionist**. — **coalition gov-ernment** government by a coalition of parties, some-times called a national government.   [L. *coalēscěre* — *alēscěre*, to grow up.]
Coalport *kōl'pōrt, -pört*, *n.* porcelain ware made at *Coalport*, near Shrewsbury, during the 19th century.
coaming *kōm'ing* (*naut.*) *n.* (usu. in *pl.*) raised work about the edges of the hatches of a ship to keep water out.   [Der. unknown.]
Coanda effect *kō-an'də i-fekt'*, the tendency of liquid, when it encounters a curved surface, to run along it.   [Henri Marie *Coanda*, 1885–1972, French engineer.]
coapt *kō-apt'*, *v.t.* to adjust. — *n.* **coaptā'tion**.   [L. *coaptāre* — *aptāre*, to fit.]
coarb *kō'ärb*, (*hist.*) *n.* the head of a family in an Irish sept: an ecclesiastical successor. — Also **comarb** (*kō'ärb*).   [Ir. *comharba*, successor.]
coarctate *kō-ärk'tāt*, *adj.* compressed: constricted. — *n.* **cōarctā'tion**.   [L. *coar(c)tāre*, *-ātum* — *ar(c)tāre*, to draw together.]
coarse *kōrs, körs*, *adj.* common, base, inferior: rough: rude: uncivil: harsh: gross: large in grain, fibre, or mesh, etc.: without refinement: roughly approximate. — *adv.* **coarse'ly**. — *v.t.* and *v.i.* **coars'en** to make or become coarse. — *n.* **coarse'ness**. — *adj.* **coars'ish** somewhat coarse. — **coarse fish** freshwater fish other than those of the salmon family , but including the grayling, which, though of a salmon family, is classed as a coarse fish, because of its time of spawning; opp. to *game fish*; **coarse fishing**. — *adj.* **coarse'-grained** large in grain: coarse in nature (*fig.*): gross. — **coarse metal** impure cuprous sulphide got in course of smelt-ing.   [From phrase 'in course', hence *ordinary*.]
coast *kōst*, (*obs.*) **cost** *kōste kōst*, (also, e.g. *Spens.*) *kost*, *n.* a side (*obs.*): the border of land next to the sea: the seashore: a limit or border (*obs.*): a region (*obs.*): direction (*obs.*): footing, terms (*Spens.*): a hill suitable for coasting: an act or spell of coasting. — *v.i.* (also *obs.* **cost**) to approach (*obs.*): to sail along or near a coast: to travel downhill on a sledge, on a cycle without pedalling or in a motor-car out of gear: to glide: to succeed or proceed without effort. — *v.t.* to sail by or near to. — *adj.* **coast'al**. — *n.* **coast'er** a vessel that sails along the coast: a foot-rest on a bicycle: a container or mat for a decanter or glasses on a table. — *adj.* **coast'ing** keeping near the coast: trading be-tween ports in the same country. — *ns.* the act of sailing, or of trading, along the coast: advances to-wards acquaintance (*obs.*): sliding downhill. — *advs.* **coast'ward, -s** toward the coast; **coast'wise** along the coast. — *adj.* carried on along the coast. — **coast'guard** a body of men, and now also women, organised to watch along the coast for prevention of smuggling, for life-saving, defence, etc.: a member thereof; **coast'-guard(s)man** (*obs.* or *U.S.*); **coast'line** the line or bound-ary of a coast: shoreline. — *adj.* **coast'-to-coast'** cov-ering the whole country, nationwide. — **coast'-wait'er** a custom-house officer for coasting shipping. — **the coast is clear** there is no obstacle or danger in the way.   [O.Fr. *coste* (Fr. *côte*) — L. *costa*, rib, side.]
coat[1] *kōt*, *n.* an outer garment with sleeves: an overcoat: the hair or wool of a beast: vesture or habit: any covering: a membrane or layer, as of paint, etc.: a coat of arms (see below): a skirt or petticoat (*dial.*). — *v.t.* to clothe: to cover with a coat or layer. — *ns.* **coat'ee** a short close-fitting coat; **coat'er** a worker, machine, etc., that applies a layer or covering; **coat'ing** a cover-ing, layer: cloth for coats. — *adj.* **coat'less** without a

coat or a coat of arms. — **coat'-arm'our** a coat of arms, or heraldically embroidered garment worn over armour: armorial devices; **coat'-card** a card bearing the representation of a coated figure, the king, queen, or knave — now, less correctly, called *court-card*; **coat'= frock** a dress for use without coat or jacket: a tailored dress with fastening from neckline to hem (also **coat'= dress**); **coat'-hanger** a curved piece of wood, etc., with a hook, by which clothes may be hung and kept in shape; **coat'rack, coat'stand** a rack or stand with pegs for hanging coats on. — *adj.* **coat'-style** of a shirt, buttoning all the way down in front. — **coat tails** the long back-pieces of a tail-coat; **coat-trailing** see **trail one's coat (tails)** below. — **coat of arms** the family insignia embroidered on the surcoat worn over the hauberk, or coat of mail: the heraldic bearings of a gentleman; **coat of mail** a piece of armour for the upper part of the body, made of metal scales or rings linked one with another; **trail one's coat (tails)** (orig. *Ir.*) to be aggressive, pick a quarrel (*n.* **coat'-trailing**); **turn one's coat** to change one's principles, or to turn from one party to another. [O.Fr. *cote* (Fr. *cotte*) — L.L. *cottus, cotta*, a tunic; the further etymology is uncertain.]

coat², **coate**. Shakespearian forms of **quote**.
coati *kō-ä'tē* or *-ti*, or *kə-wä'tē, n.* an American plantigrade carnivorous mammal allied to the raccoons. — Also **coati-mun'di, -mon'di**. [Tupí.]
co-author *kō-ö'thər, n.* a joint author.
coax *kōks, v.t.* to persuade by fondling or flattery: to humour or soothe: to pet. — *ns.* **coax, coax'er** one who coaxes. — *adv.* **coax'ingly**. [cokes, a simpleton.]
coaxial *kō-ak'si-əl, adj.* having the same axis. — *adv.* **coax'ially**. — **coaxial cable** a cable consisting of one or more **coaxial pairs**, each a central conductor within an outer tubular conductor.
cob¹ *kob, n.* a big or notable man (*dial.*): a short-legged strong horse: a male swan (also **cob'-swan**): a lump (esp. of coal, ore, clay): a rounded object: a herring's head (*obs.*): a cobloaf: the axis of a head of maize, a corncob: a cobnut: an irregularly-shaped Spanish-American dollar (*hist.*). — *adj.* **cobb'y** like a cob: stout, brisk, lively, arrogant (*dial.*). — **cob'loaf** a rounded, round-headed or misshappen loaf: an expression of contempt (*Shak.*); **cob'nut** a large hazelnut: a game played by children with nuts; **cob'-pipe** a tobacco pipe made from a corncob. [Perh. conn. with **cop¹**.]
cob² *kob, n.* a kind of composition of clay and straw for building. — **cob'-wall; cob cottage**. [Origin unknown.]
cob³ *kob, (dial.) n.* a wicker basket used by sowers. [Origin unknown.]
cob⁴ *kob, v.t.* to strike: to thump on the buttocks.
cob⁵, cobb *kob, (arch.) n.* a gull, esp. the greater black-backed gull. [Cf. Du. *kob*, gull.]
cobalt *kō'bölt, n.* a metallic element (at. numb. 27; symbol Co), having similarities to nickel: a blue pigment prepared from it — also **cō'balt-blue'**. — *adj.* of this deep-blue colour. — **cobalt-60** a radioactive isotope of cobalt used in the gamma-ray treatment of cancer. — *adjs.* **cobalt'ic; cobaltif'erous**. — *n.* **cō'baltite** a mineral containing cobalt, arsenic, and sulphur (also **cobalt glance**). — **cobalt bloom** erythrite; **cobalt bomb** a suggested bomb consisting of a hydrogen bomb encased in cobalt — made more dangerous than ever by the cobalt-60 dust released. [Ger. *Kobalt*, from *Kobold*, a demon, a nickname given by the German miners, because they supposed it to be a mischievous and hurtful metal.]
cobb. See **cob⁵**.
cobber *kob'ər, (Austr.; coll.) n.* mate, chum, buddy. [Origin unknown.]
cobble¹ *kob'l*, **cobblestone** *-stōn, ns.* a rounded stone, esp. used in paving. — *v.t.* to pave with cobblestones. [Ety. dub.]
cobble² *kob'l, v.t.* to mend shoes: to patch up, assemble, put together, or mend coarsely (often with *together* or

up). — *n.* see **coble**. — *ns.* **cobb'ler** one who cobbles or mends shoes: an iced drink made up of wine or spirits, sugar, lemon, etc.: (a (usu. fruit) pie with) a thick pastry crust: (in *pl.; slang*) nonsense; **cobb'lery; cobb'ling**. — **cobbler's punch** a hot drink made of beer, with the addition of spirit, sugar, and spice. [Der. unknown.]
cobble³. See **coble**.
Cobdenism *kob'dən-izm, n.* the policy of Richard *Cobden* (1804–1865), the English 'Apostle of Free Trade'. — *n.* **Cob'denite** a supporter of Cobdenism, esp. a free-trader.
co-belligerent *kō-bi-lij'ə-rent, adj.* co-operating in warfare. — Also *n.*
cobia *kō'bi-ə, n.* the sergeant-fish. [Perh. of West Indian origin.]
coble, cobble *kōb'l, kob'l, ns.* a small flat-bottomed boat for use on rivers (*Scot.*): a single-masted sea-fishing boat with a flat bottom and square stern (*N.E. England*). [Cf. W. *ceubal*, a hollow trunk, a boat.]
Cobol *kō'bōl, -bol, n.* a computer programming language, for commercial use, which uses English words. [*Common business oriented language*.]
cobra, cobra de capello *kō'brə, kob'rə, di ka-pel'ō, n.* a poisonous snake, found in India and Africa, which dilates its neck so as to resemble a hood. — *adjs.* **cob'ric; cob'riform** like or akin to the cobra. [Port., snake of the hood.]
coburg *kō'bûrg, n.* a thin fabric of worsted with cotton or silk, twilled on one side: the name of various pieces of bakery and confectionery, including a type of round loaf and a type of sponge cake (also *adj.*). [*Coburg*, in Germany.]
cobweb *kob'web, n.* a spider's web or net: any snare or device intended to entrap: anything flimsy or easily broken: anything that obscures. — Also *v.t.* — *n.* **cobwebb'ery**. — *adj.* **cob'webby**. [Prob. *attercop-web*; see **attercop, web**.]
coca *kō'kə, n.* a Peruvian shrub (*Erythroxylon coca*) of a family akin to flax, whose leaves furnish an important narcotic and stimulant. — *ns.* **cocaine** *(ko-kān', kō'kā-in, kō'kä-in)* an alkaloid obtained from coca-leaves or produced synthetically, used as a local anaesthetic and as an intoxicant; **cocainisā'tion, -z-**. — *v.t.* **cocain'ise, -ize**. — *ns.* **cocain'ism** a morbid condition induced by addiction to cocaine; **cocain'ist**. [Sp. — Quechua *coca*.]
Coca-Cola® *kō'kə-kō'lə, n.* a carbonated soft drink first made in the U.S. (often shortened to **Coke**). — **coca= colonisā'tion** (*facet.*) the invasion of other parts of the world by American culture.
Cocagne, Cocaigne. Same as **Cockaigne**.
cocaine, etc. See **coca**.
coccid, etc. See **coccus**.
coccineous *kok-sin'i-əs, (obs.) adj.* bright red. [L. *coccineus* — *coccum*, cochineal.]
cocco *kok'ō*, **coco** *kō'kō, ns.* the taro or other edible araceous tuber: — *pls.* **cocc'os, co'cos**.
coccolite *kok'ō-līt, n.* a variety of pyroxene: a small rounded body found in deep-sea ooze (also **cocc'olith**). [Gr. *kokkos*, a berry, *lithos*, a stone.]
coccus *kok'əs, n.* a one-seeded portion of a dry fruit that breaks up (*bot.*): a spherical bacterium: (with *cap*) a genus of insects in the Hemiptera, type of a family **Coccidae** *(kok'si-dē)*: — *pl.* **cocci** *(kok'sī)*. — *adj.* **coccal** *(kok'əl)*. — *n.* **coccid** *(kok'sid)* any of the Coccidae. — Also *adj.* — *ns.* **coccidioidomycosis** *(-oi-də-mī-kō-sis)* infection resulting from the inhalation of the spores of the fungus *Coccidioides immitis*, occurring either as an influenza-like respiratory illness, or as a severe, progressive disease affecting the skin, viscera, nervous system and lungs; **coccidium** *(kok-sid'i-əm)* a protozoan parasite of the order **Coccid'ia**: — *pl.* **-ia; coccidiosis** *(kok-sid-i-ōs'is)* a contagious infection of birds and animals by coccidia; **coccidiostat** *(kok-sid'i-ō-stat)* an agent which builds up a resistance by the host to coccidia by retarding the latter's life-cycle, etc. — *adj.* **coccoid** *(kok'oid)*. — *n.* **Cocc'ulus** a tropical genus of

climbing plants (*Menispermaceae*). — **cocculus indicus** the dried fruit of *Anamirta cocculus* (same family), narcotic and poisonous. [L., — Gr. *kokkos*, a berry.]

coccyx *kok′siks* (*anat.*) *n.* the terminal triangular bone of the vertebral column: — *pl.* **coccyges** (*kok-sī′jēz*). — *adjs.* **coccygeal** (*kok-sij′i-əl*), **coccyg′ian**. [Gr. *kokkyx, -ȳgos*, cuckoo, coccyx (as resembling its bill).]

coch *kōch*, (*Spens.*) *n.* Same as **coach**.

Cochin *koch′in*, *n.* a large feathery-legged domestic hen, originally from Cochin-China, now part of Vietnam. — Also **Cochin-China** (*-chī′nə*).

cochineal *koch′i-nēl, -nēl′*, *n.* a scarlet dyestuff consisting of the dried bodies of a Coccus insect gathered from a cactus in Mexico, the West Indies, etc.: the insect itself. [Sp. *cochinilla*, dim. of L. *coccinus*, scarlet — *coccum* (Gr. *kokkos*), a berry, as the similar kermes insect was formerly supposed to be the berry or seed of an oak.]

cochlea *kok′li-ə*, *n.* anything spiral-shaped, esp. a snail-shell, a medick-pod, a winding stair: the spiral cavity of the ear (*anat.*). — *adj.* **coch′lear** (*-li-ər*) pertaining to the cochlea of the ear: spoon-shaped. — *ns.* **coch′-lear, cochleăr′e** (L.) a spoon. — *n.pl.* **Cochleăr′ia** the scurvy-grass genus. — *adjs.* **cochleăr′iform** spoon-shaped; **coch′leāte, coch′leated** twisted spirally: spoon-like. [L. *coc(h)lea*, a shell, screw, and *coc(h)leare*, a spoon — Gr. *kochlias*, a snail.]

cock[1] *kok*, *n.* a male bird, esp. of the domestic fowl (often compounded, as **cock′bird, cock-rob′in, cock-spar′r′ow**): a male crab, lobster or salmon: the time of cock-crowing (*obs.*): a weathercock (*obs.*): a plucky chap, a term of familiarity (sometimes *old cock*; *slang*): a strutting chief or leader: anything set erect: a tap: part of the lock of a gun, held back by a spring, which, when released by the trigger, produces the discharge: upward turn or upturned part, as of a hat-brim: a penis (*vulg.*): nonsense (*coll.*). — *v.t.* to set erect or upright (often with *up*): to set up the brim of: to draw back, as the cock of a gun: to turn up or to one side: to tilt up knowingly, inquiringly, or scornfully. — *v.i.* to strut: to swagger. — *adj.* **cocked** set erect: turned up or to one side. — *ns.* **cock′er** one who follows cockfighting: a small spaniel employed in pheasant and woodcock shooting: a term of familiarity (*slang*); **cock′erel** a young cock: a young man — also **cock′le**, whence **cock′le-brained** foolish. — *adv.* **cock′ily**. — *ns.* **cock′iness; cocks′iness, cox′iness** — *adj.* **cocks′y, cox′y** self-important, bumptious; **cock′y** pert. — *ns.* **cock′-a-dood′le(-doo′)** the crow of a cock. — *v.t.* to crow. — *adj.* **cock-a-hoop′** in exultant spirits. — **cockaleekie** see **cockieleekie; cockalō′rum** a bumptious little person: a boys' jumping game. — *adj.* **cock′-and-bull′** (of a story) fabricated and incredible. — **cock′-broth** the broth made from a boiled cock; **cock′chafer** a large greyish brown beetle (*Melolontha vulgaris*), most destructive to vegetation; **cock′-crow, -ing** early morning, when cocks crow; **cocked hat** an old-fashioned three-cornered hat; **cocker spaniel** a cocker; **cock′eye** a squinting eye: the loop by which a trace is attached to the whippletree. — *adj.* **cock′eyed** having a cockeye: off the straight, awry (*coll.*): tipsy (*coll.*). — **cock′fight, -ing** a fight or contest between game-cocks: a fight; **cockhorse′** a child's imaginary or toy horse: a trace-horse for a coach: a spirited animal. — *adj.* prancing, proud. — *adv.* properly **a-cockhorse′** (i.e. on cock-horse) on horseback: exultingly. — **cockieleek′ie, cockyleek′y, cock(-)a(-)leek′ie** (*Scot.*) soup made from a fowl and leeks; **cock′laird** (*Scot.*) a yeoman; **cock′loft** a room just under the roof; **cock′match** a cockfight; **cock′-of-the-rock′** a South American bird of the cotinga family; **cock-pad(d)le, -paidle** see **paddle**[2]; **cock′pit** a pit or enclosed space where game-cocks fought: a frequent battleground: part of a ship-of-war's lower regions used for the wounded in action: a sheltered depression in the deck of a yacht or small ship: in aircraft, a compartment in the fuselage for pilot or passenger: the driver's seat in a racing car; **cock′s′=**

comb, cocks′comb the comb or crest on a cock's head: a jester's cap: a head (*Shak.*): a crest-like crystalline mineral aggregate (as in *cockscomb pyrites*): a name for various plants, esp. a monstrous *Celosia* (fam. Amarantaceae) with fasciated inflorescence like a cock's comb, also yellow-rattle (*Rhinanthus*), and sain-foin: a coxcomb; **cocks′foot** a genus (Dactylis) of grasses with inflorescences like a cock's foot; **cock′-shoot** (*obs.*) a glade where woodcock were netted as they shot through; **cock′shot** a shy at a mark; **cock′shut** (*Shak.*) twilight, probably referring to the time when poultry are shut up, or when woodcock shoot; **cock′shy** a throw at a thing, originally a cock, as for amusement: the object set up, or a showman's outfit for the purpose (also *fig.*); **cock′-sparr′ow** a male sparrow: a small, lively person; **cock′spur** a spur on the leg of a cock: a type of catch used on casement windows; **cockspur grass** (*Echinochloa crus-galli*) an invasive grass of warmer, orig. only tropical, climates. — *adj.* **cock′sure′** quite sure, self-confident, esp. offensively. — **cock′tail** a racing horse that is not thoroughbred: one who apes the gentleman: a concoction of spirituous or other liquors, used as an appetiser: a non-alcoholic appetiser consisting e.g. of sea-food with a sauce: generally, a mixture of substances. — Also *adj.* — **cocktail bar, lounge** a superior kind of bar, e.g. in a hotel; **cocktail dress** one for semi-formal wear. — *adj.* **cock′tailed** having the tail cocked or tilted up. — **cocktail shaker, mixer** a container for mixing cocktails; **cocktail stick** a small wooden or plastic stick for a cherry, olive, small sausage, etc., when eaten with drinks; **cock′teaser** (*vulg.*) a woman who deliberately arouses a man's sexual appetite, then refuses to comply with his desires. — *adjs.* **cock-thropp′led, -thrapp′led** of a horse, bending the windpipe on bridling. — **cock′-throw′ing** the old sport of throwing sticks at a cock. — *adj.* **cock′-up** turned up: rising above the tops of the other letters, superior (*print.*). — *n.* (*coll.*) a muddle, mess, confusion. — **cockyleeky** see **cockieleekie; cockyolly** (*kok-i-ol′i*) a nursery or pet name for a bird. — **beat cockfighting** (*slang*) to be excellent; **cock a snook** see **snook**[2]; **cock of the walk** the chief of a set: a person who (thinks he) is the most important in a group; **go off at half cock** (*coll.*) to begin too soon, when not properly prepared; **knock into a cocked hat** to give a profound beating; **live like fighting cocks** to have every luxury. [O.E. *coc*; O.N. *kokkr*.]

cock[2] *kok*, *n.* a small pile of hay, dung, etc. — *adj.* **cocked** heaped up in cocks. [Cf. O.N. *kökkr*, a lump.]

cock[3] *kok*, (*Shak.*) *n.* a cockboat. — **cock′boat** a ship's small boat: a small frail boat; **cockswain** see **coxswain**. [Cf. **cog**[3].]

cock[4] *kok*, corr. of **god**. — **cock and pie** see **pie**[2].

cock-a-bondy *kok′ə-bon′di* (coll. *kok-i-bun′di*), *n.* a fly for angling. [Welsh *coch a bon ddu*, red, with black stem.]

cockade *kok-ād′*, *n.* a rosette worn on the hat as a badge. [Fr. *cocarde* — *coq*, cock.]

Cockaigne, Cockayne *kok-ān′*, *n.* an imaginary country of luxury and delight. [Ety. dub.; Fr. *cocagne*, acc. to some from L. *coquĕre*, to cook.]

cock-a-leekie. See **cockieleekie** under **cock**[1].

cockalorum. See **cock**[1].

cockatoo *kok-ə-tōō′*, *n.* any of a number of large crested parrots of the Australian region: a small farmer (also **cock′y**) (*Austr.*): a lookout (*Austr. coll.*). — *n.* **cock-atiel, cockateel** (*-tēl′*) a small crested parrot of Australia. — **cow cocky** (*Austr.*) a dairy farmer. [Malay *kakatua*.]

cockatrice *kok′ə-trīs, -tris, n.* a fabulous monster like a serpent, often confounded with the basilisk: a cock-like monster with a dragon's tail (*her.*): a prostitute (*obs.*). [O.Fr. *cocatris*.]

cockboat. See **cock**[3].

cockchafer. See **cock**[1].

cocker[1] *kok′ər*, *v.t.* to pamper: to fondle: to indulge. [Ety. dub.; cf. Du. *kokelen*, O.Fr. *conqueliner*, to dandle.]

cocker², **cockerel**. See **cock¹**.

Cocker *kok'ər*, *n.* a standard of accuracy and orthodoxy. [From Edward *Cocker* (1631–75), author of a popular arithmetic book.]

cockernony *kok-ər-non'i*, (*obs. Scot.*) *n.* the gathering of hair in a fillet: a coiffure: a pad of false hair: a starched cap. [Origin obscure.]

cocket *kok'it*, *n.* the custom-house seal (*hist.*): a custom-house certificate. [Origin doubtful.]

cock-eye(d), **cockhorse**. See **cock¹**.

cockieleekie. See under **cock¹**.

cockle¹ *kok'l*, *n.* a cornfield weed, esp. now the corn-cockle. — **cock'le-bur** clotbur (Xanthium). [O.E. *coccel*.]

cockle² *kok'l*, *n.* a large bivalve mollusc (*Cardium edule* or other species) with thick, ribbed, heart-shaped, equal-valved shell: its shell: a bivalve shell generally. — *adj.* **cock'led** shelled like a cockle. — **cock'le-hat** a hat bearing a scallop-shell, the badge of a pilgrim; **cock'leshell** the shell of a cockle: a frail boat. — **cockles of the heart** the heart itself. [Fr. *coquille* — Gr. *konchylion* — *konchē*, a cockle.]

cockle³ *kok'l*, *n.* a pucker. — *v.i.* to pucker. — *v.t.* to cause to pucker. [Perh. Fr. *coquiller*, to blister — *coquille*; see **cockle²**.]

cockle⁴ *kok'l*, *n.* a furnace or stove. [Perh. Du. *kachel*.]

cockle-brained. See **cock¹**.

cockney *kok'ni*, *n.* an egg, esp. a small misshapen egg (*obs.* or *dial.*): a coddled child (*obs*): a milksop (*Shak.*): one whose experience and knowledge are exclusively townish: (still in *U.S.*, usu. *disparaging*) a townsman: (often with *cap.*) one born in London, strictly, within hearing of Bow Bells: London dialect. — *adj.* (often with *cap.*) characteristic of a Cockney. — *ns.* **cock'-neydom** the domain of Cockneys; **cockneyficā'tion**. — *v.t.* **cock'neyfy** to make Cockney. — *adj.* **cock'neyish**. — *n.* **cock'neyism** a Cockney idiom or characteristic. — **the Cockney School** an old nickname for a supposed school of writers belonging to London — Leigh Hunt, Keats and others. [M.E. *coken-ey*, cock's egg; others would connect with Fr. *coquin*, a rogue — L. *coquus*, a cook.]

cockroach *kok'rōch*, *n.* an orthopterous insect, the so-called black beetle. [Sp. *cucaracha*, woodlouse, cockroach.]

cockscomb, **cocksfoot**, **cockshoot**, **cockshy**, **cocktail**, etc. See **cock¹**.

cocky. See **cock¹**, **cockatoo**.

cockyleeky. See **cockieleekie** under **cock¹**.

coco¹ *kō'kō*, *n.* a tropical seaside palm-tree (*Cocos nucifera*) with curving stem (also **co'co-palm**, **co'conut=palm**, **co'co-tree**), producing the coco-nut: — *pl.* **cō'cos**. — **co'co-de-mer** (-*də-mer'*; Fr.) the double coconut (see below); **co'conut**, (less correctly) **co'coanut** or **co'kernut**, a large edible nut, yielding **co'conut-butt'er** or **co'conut-oil'**, and **co'conut-milk'**; **co'conut-matt'ing** matting made from the husk of the coconut; **co'conut-shy** a cockshy with coconuts as targets or as prizes. — **double coconut** the large two-lobed nut of the Seychelles palm, *Lodoicea seychellarum*. [Port. and Sp. *coco*, a bugbear; applied to the nut from the three marks at the end of it, which form a grotesque face.]

coco². See **cocco**.

cocoa *kō'kō*, *n.* the seed of the cacao or chocolate tree: a powder made from the seeds: a drink made from the powder. — **co'coa-beans** the seeds, esp. when dried and fermented; **co'coa-butt'er**, **co'coa-fat'** a fat got from the seeds (different from *coconut*-butter); **co'coa-nibs** cocoa-beans shelled and bruised; **cocoa-wood** see **coco=wood** below. [cacao.]

coconscious *kō-kon'shəs*, *adj.* conscious in a subsidiary stream, apart from the main stream. — *n.* **cocon'-sciousness**.

cocoon *ko-kōōn'*, *n.* the silken sheath spun by many insect larvae in passing into the pupa stage and by spiders for their eggs: the capsule in which earthworms and leeches lay their eggs: a preservative covering for military and other equipment. — *v.t.* to wrap carefully as in a cocoon. — *n.* **cocoon'ery** a place for keeping silkworms when feeding and spinning cocoons. [Fr. *cocon*, from *coque*, a shell — L. *concha*, a shell.]

cocoplum *kō'kō-plum*, *n.* a West Indian rosaceous tree (*Chrysobalanus icaco*): its edible fruit. [Sp. *icaco*, and **plum**.]

cocotte *ko-kot'*, *n.* a light-o'-love: a loose woman: a small fireproof dish, usu. for an individual portion.

coco-wood, **cocoa-wood** *kō'kō-wŏŏd*, *n.* the wood of a West Indian mimosaceous tree, *Inga vera*: kokra-wood.

coction *kok'shən*, *n.* boiling: cooking. — *adj.* **coc'tile** baked: hardened by fire, as a brick. [L. *coquĕre*, *coctum*, to boil, cook.]

cocus-wood *kō'kəs-wŏŏd*, *n.* the so-called Jamaica ebony (*Brya ebenus*; Papilionaceae): a tradename for kokra-wood.

cod¹ *kod*, **codfish** *kod'fish*, *ns.* a food fish (*Gadus morrhua*) of northern seas: any fish of the genus Gadus or the family Gadidae. — *n.* **cod'ling** a small cod. — **cod'=fisher**; **cod'-fish'ery**; **cod'-fishing**. — **cod'-liver oil'** a medicinal oil extracted from the fresh liver of the common cod or related fish. [Ety. dub.]

cod² *kod*, (*obs.*) *n.* a bag: a pod: the scrotum. — *adjs.* **codd'ed** enclosed in a cod; **codd'ing** (*Shak.*) lecherous. — **cod'-piece** a baggy appendage once worn in front of tight hose. [O.E. *codd*, a small bag; cf. next word.]

cod³ *kod*, (*Scot.*) *n.* a pillow or cushion. [O.N. *koddi*, a pillow; cf. foregoing word.]

cod⁴ *kod*, (*slang*) *n.* a fellow: a codger: a Charterhouse pensioner: a jest: a hoax. — *adj.* mock: done, intended, etc. as a joke or take-off. — *v.t.* to hoax: to poke fun at: — *pr.p.* **codd'ing**; *pa.t.* and *pa.p.* **codd'ed**. [Ety. dub.]

coda *kō'də*, *n.* a passage forming the completion of a piece, rounding it off to a satisfactory conclusion (*mus.*): any similar passage or piece in a story, dance sequence, etc. [It., — L. *cauda*, a tail.]

coddle *kod'l*, *v.t.* to pamper, mollycoddle: to fondle: to parboil. — *n.* an effeminate person. [Ety. dub.]

code *kōd*, *n.* a collection or digest of laws: a system of rules and regulations (*specif.* regarding education): established principles or standards (of art, moral conduct, etc.): a volume: a system of signals: a system of words, letters, or symbols which represent sentences or other words, to ensure economy or secrecy in transmission: a cipher: a set of rules and characters for converting one form of data to another (*comput.*): the characters of the resulting representation of data (*comput.*). — *v.t.* to codify: to express in code. — *ns.* **codificā'tion** (*kod-*, *kōd-*); **codifier** (*kod'*, *kōd'*), **cod'ist** one who codifies. — *v.t.* **codify** (*kod'*, *kōd'*) to put into the form of a code: to digest: to systematise: — *pr.p.* **cod'ifying**; *pa.t.* and *pa.p.* **cod'ified**. — *n.* and *adj.* **cod'ing**. — **code'-book** a book containing the words, symbols, etc., of a code or codes; **code'-breaker** a person who tries to interpret secret codes; **code'=breaking**; **code'-name**, **-number** a name or number used for convenience, economy, secrecy, etc. — *adj.* **code'=named**. — **code of conduct**, **practice** an established method or set of rules for dealing with, behaving in, etc., a particular situation. [Fr. *code*; see **codex**.]

codeine *kō'dēn*, *-di-in*, *n.* an alkaloid, obtained from opium, used as an analgesic and sedative. [Gr. *kōdeia*, poppy-head.]

codex *kō'deks*, *n.* a code: a manuscript volume: — *pl.* **codices** (*kōd'i-sēz*). — *n.* **cōdicol'ogy** the study of manuscript volumes. — *adj.* **cōdicolog'ical**. [L. *cōdex* or *caudex*, *-icis*, the trunk of a tree, a set of tablets, a book.]

codger *koj'ər*, *n.* a mean fellow: an old person: a chap. [Prob. a variant of **cadger**.]

codicil *kod'i-sil*, *n.* a supplement to a will. — *adj.* **codicill'-ary**. [L. *cōdicillus*, dim. of *cōdex*.]

codicology. See **codex**.

codification, etc. See **code**.

codilla *kō-dil'ə*, *n.* the coarsest part of hemp or flax. [Dim. of It. *coda* — L. *cauda*, a tail.]

codille *kō-dil'*, *n.* a situation in ombre when the challenger loses. [Fr.]

codling[1] *kod'ling*, **codlin** *kod'lin*, *ns.* an elongated apple. — **cod'lin-moth** the moth whose larvae cause 'wormeaten' apples to fall prematurely. [Ety. dub.]

codling[2]. See **cod**[1].

codon *kō'don*, *n.* a triplet of bases in the messenger-RNA molecule, which determines a particular amino-acid in protein synthesis. [**code**, *-on.*]

co-driver *kō'-drī'vər*, *n.* one of two alternating drivers, esp. in a race or rally.

cod's(-)wallop, codswallop *kodz'wol-əp*, (*coll.*) *n.* nonsense, rubbish. [Origin unknown.]

coeducation *kō-ed-ū-kā'shən*, *n.* education of the sexes together. — *n.* **co'ed** a girl or woman educated at a coeducational institution (usu. *U.S.*): a coeducational school. — *adjs.* **co'ed; coeducā'tional.**

coefficient *kō-if-ish'ənt*, *n.* that which acts together with another thing: a numerical or literal expression for a factor of a quantity in an algebraic term (*math.*): a numerical constant used as a multiplier to a variable quantity, in calculating the magnitude of a physical property (*phys.*).

coehorn, cohorn *kō'hörn*, *n.* a small mortar for throwing grenades. [Baron van *Coehoorn* (1641–1704).]

coelacanth *sē'lə-kanth*, *n.* any of a group of crossopterygian fishes of very great antiquity. [From Gr. *koilos*, hollow, *akantha*, spine.]

coelanaglyphic *sēl-an-ə-glif'ik*, *adj.* in cavo-rilievo. [Gr. *koilos*, hollow, *ana*, up, *glyphein*, to carve.]

Coelenterata *sə-len-tər-ā'tə*, *sē-*, *n.pl.* a phylum of manycelled animals, radially symmetrical, with a single body-cavity, the enteron — Hydrozoa, Scyphozoa, Anthozoa, Ctenophora. — *adj.* and *n.* **coelen'terate.** [Gr. *koilos*, hollow, *enteron*, intestine.]

coeliac, celiac *sē'li-ak*, *adj.* relating to the belly: pertaining to coeliacs, coeliac disease, etc. — *n.* a person suffering from coeliac disease. — **coeliac disease** a disease of the intestines in which a sensitivity to gluten prevents the proper absorption of nutrients through the stomach, etc. lining. [Gr. *koiliakos* — *koiliā*, the belly.]

coelom(e), celom *sē'lōm*, *-lom*, *n.* the body-cavity, or space between the intestines and the body-wall in animals above the Coelenterates. — *n.pl.* **Coelō'mata** animals possessing a coelom. — *adj.* **coe'lomate** having a coelom. — *n.* a coelomate animal. — *adjs.* **coelomat'ic, coelom'ic.** [Gr. *koilōma, -atos*, a cavity.]

coelostat *sē'lō-stat*, *n.* a clock-driven mirror on an axis parallel to the earth's, so as to reflect continuously the same region of the sky. [L. *caelum* (misspelt *coelum*), sky, Gr. *statos*, fixed.]

coemption *kō-emp'shən*, *n.* the buying up of the whole of a commodity: a mode of marriage under the fiction of a mutual sale (*Roman law*). [L. *coemptiō, -ōnis* — *emēre*, to buy.]

coenaesthesis, cenesthesis *sē-nēs-thē'sis*, or *-nis-*, **coenesthesia, cenesthesia** *-thē'zi-ə*, *-zyə*, *ns.* the general bodily consciousness. [Gr. *koinos*, common, *aisthēsis*, perception.]

coenenchyma *sē-neng'ki-mə*, (*bot.*) *n.* gelatinous material uniting the polyps of an anthozoan colony. [Gr. *koinos*, common, *enchyma*, infusion.]

coenobite, cenobite *sēn'o-bīt*, *n.* a monk who lives in a community. — *adjs.* **coenobitic** (*-bit'ik*), **-al.** — *ns.* **coen'obitism; coenō'bium** a religious community: a colony of unicellular organisms (*biol.*): — *pl.* **coenō'bia.** [Gr. *koinóbion* — *koinos*, common, *bios*, life.]

coenosarc *sēn'ō-särk*, *n.* the common tissue uniting the polyps of a coral or the like. [Gr. *koinos*, common, *sarx*, flesh.]

coenzyme *kō-en'zīm*, *n.* the non-protein part of an enzyme system, which is unaffected by heat.

coequal *kō-ē'kwəl*, *adj.* equal with another of the same rank or dignity. — *n.* one of the same rank. — *n.* **cōequality** (*-i-kwol'*). — *adv.* **coē'qually.**

coerce *kō-ûrs'*, *v.t.* to restrain by force: to compel. — *adj.* **cōer'cible.** — *adv.* **cōer'cibly.** — *ns.* **cōer'cion** restraint: government by force; **cōer'cionist.** — *adj.* **cōer'cive** having power to coerce: compelling: tending to or intended to coerce. — *adv.* **cōer'cively.** — *ns.* **cōer'civeness; coerciv'ity** the coercive force needed to demagnetise a material that is fully magnetised. — **coercive force** the reverse magnetising force required to bring the magnetisation of a ferromagnetic material to zero. [L. *coercēre* — *arcēre*, to shut in.]

co-essential *kō-is-en'shəl*, *-es-*, *adj.* partaking of the same essence. — *n.* **co-essentiality** (*-shi-al'i-ti*).

coetaneous *kō-i-tā'ni-əs*, *adj.* of the same age: contemporary. [L. *aetās, aetātis*, age.]

co-eternal *kō-i-tûr'nəl*, *-ē-*, *adj.* alike eternal with another. — *adv.* **co-eter'nally.** — *n.* **co-eter'nity.**

coeval *kō-ē'vəl*, *adj.* of the same age. — *n.* one of the same age: a contemporary. [L. *coaevus* — *aevum*, age.]

co-exist *kō-igz-ist'*, *-egz-*, *v.i.* to exist at the same time or together. — *n.* **co-exist'ence.** — *adj.* **co-exist'ent.** — **peaceful co-existence** a living side by side in mutual toleration.

co-extend *kō-iks-tend'*, *-eks-*, *v.i.* to extend equally. — *n.* **co-exten'sion.** — *adj.* **co-exten'sive.**

coff *kof*, (*Scot.*) *v.t.* to buy. [A new present formed from **coft**, *pa.t.* and *pa.p.* originally of **cope**[2] — M.Du. *copen, cofte*, (*ghe*)*coft* (Mod. Du. *koopen, kocht, gekocht*) to buy.]

coffee *kof'i*, *n.* a powder made by roasting and grinding the seeds of a tree (*Coffea arabica, robusta*, etc.) of the madder family: a drink made from the powder. — **coffee bar, shop** a small restaurant where coffee, tea, cakes, etc. are served; **coff'ee-bean** the seed of the coffee-tree; **coff'ee-berr'y** the fruit or the seed of the coffee-tree; **coffee break** a break for coffee during the working day; **coff'ee-bug** a coccus destructive to the coffee-tree; **coff'ee-cup** a cup for coffee; **coff'ee-disease'** a leaf-disease of coffee caused by a rust fungus, *Hemileia vastatrix*; **coffee grounds** the sediment left after coffee has been infused; **coff'ee-house** a house where coffee and other refreshments are sold; **coff'ee-mill** a machine for grinding coffee-beans; **coffee morning** a morning social gathering at which coffee is drunk; **coff'ee-pot** a pot in which coffee is prepared and served; **coff'ee-room** a room in a hotel where coffee and other refreshments are served: a public room; **coffee service, set** a set of utensils for serving and drinking coffee; **coffee shop** see **coffee bar; coff'ee-stall** a movable street stall for coffee and other refreshments; **coff'ee-table** a small low table; **coff'ee-tree; coff'ee-whitener** whitener (*q.v.*) for coffee. — **coffee-table book** (orig. *facet.*, sometimes *derog.*) a large, expensive and profusely illustrated book of the kind one would set out on a coffee-table for visitors to admire; **white, black coffee** coffee respectively with and without milk. [Turk. *kahveh* — Ar. *qahwah*, orig. meaning wine.]

coffer *kof'ər*, *n.* a chest for holding money or treasure: a deep panel in a ceiling. — *v.t.* to hoard up. — *adj.* **coff'ered.** — **coff'er-dam** a watertight structure allowing underwater foundations to be built dry; **coff'er-fish** a fish (*Ostracion*) enclosed in a box of bony scales. [O.Fr. *cofre*, a chest — L. *cophinus*, a basket — Gr. *kophinos*, a basket.]

coffin *kof'in*, *n.* a pie-crust (*obs.*): a chest for a dead body: a thick-walled container, usu. of lead, for transporting radioactive materials. — *v.t.* to place in a coffin. — **coff'in-bone** a bone enclosed in a horse's hoof; **coff'in-nail** (*slang*) a cigarette; **coff'in-ship** a dangerously unsound ship. — **drive a nail in one's coffin** to do something tending to hasten death or ruin. [O.Fr. *cofin* — L. *cophinus* — Gr. *kophinos*, a basket.]

coffinite *kof'in-īt*, *n.* a uranium-yielding ore. [From Reuben Clare *Coffin*, a worker of the ore in Colorado.]

coffle *kof'l*, *n.* a gang, esp. of slaves. [Ar. *qāfilah*, a caravan.]

coffret *kof'rət*, *n.* a small coffer: a small presentation box. [Fr., dim. of *coffre*, coffer.]

coft, *koft, (Scot.) pa.t* and *pa.p.* of **coff.**

cog¹ *kog, v.t.* to cheat or deceive: to wheedle: to manipulate (dice) so that they may fall in a given way. — *n.* the act of cheating: deception. — *n.* **cogg'er.** [Thieves' slang.]

cog² *kog, n.* a catch or tooth as on a wheel: an unimportant person in a large organisation (*fig.*). — *v.t.* to furnish with cogs: to stop (a wheel) by putting a block before it: — *pr.p.* **cogg'ing;** *pa.t.* and *pa.p.* **cogged.** — **cog'-wheel** a toothed wheel. [M.E. *cogge*; ety. dub.; cf. Sw. *kugge.*]

cog³ *kog, n.* formerly a large ship of burden or for war: a small boat: a cockboat. [M.E. *cogge*, perh. from O.Fr. *cogue*, a ship, or O.N. *kuggr*, a merchant ship.]

cog⁴. See **coggie.**

cog⁵. See **cogue.**

cogener *kō'ji-nər, n.* a variant of **congener.**

cogent *kō'jənt, adj.* powerful: convincing. — *ns.* **cō'gence,** **cō'gency** convincing power. — *adv.* **cō'gently.** [L. *cōgēns, -entis,* pr.p. of *cōgĕre co-* — *agĕre,* to drive.]

coggie, cogie *kog'i, kōg'i, (Scot.) n.* a small wooden bowl. — Also **cog.** [Dim. of **cogue.**]

coggle *kog'l, v.i.* to be unsteady. — *n.* a cobblestone. — *adv.* **cogg'ly** (*Scot.*) shaky. [Origin doubtful.]

cogitate *koj'i-tāt, v.i.* to turn a thing over in one's mind: to meditate: to ponder. — *adj.* **cog'itable** capable of being thought. — *n.* **cogitā'tion** deep thought: meditation. — *adj.* **cog'itātive** having the power of thinking: given to cogitating. [L. *cōgitāre, -ātum,* to think deeply — *co-, agitāre,* to put in motion.]

Cognac *kon'yak, n.* a French brandy made near *Cognac,* in Charente.

cognate *kog'nāt, adj.* of the same family, kind, or nature: derived from the same ancestor, root, or other original: related or allied. — *n.* one related by blood, a kinsman (whether agnate or not) (*Roman law* and *gener.*): often, any kinsman on either side other than an agnate: a relative on one's mother's side (*Scots law*). — *ns.* **cog'nateness; cogna'tion.** — **cognate object** a word akin in origin or meaning to a normally intransitive verb, and used as its object. — **cognatic succession** the succession to the throne of the eldest child, irrespective of sex. [L. *cognātus — co-, (g)nāscī,* to be born.]

cognition *kog-nish'ən, n.* a knowledge: apprehension: knowing, in the widest sense, including sensation, perception, etc., distinguished from emotion and conation (*psychol.*). — *adj.* **cognisable, -z-** (*kog'niz-ə-bl*; also *kon'iz-*) that may be known or understood: that may be judicially investigated. — *adv.* **cog'nisably, -z-.** — *ns.* **cog'nisance, -z-** (or *kon'iz-*) knowledge or notice, judicial or private: observation: jurisdiction: that by which one is known, a badge. — *adj.* **cog'nisant, -z-** (or *kon'iz-*) having cognisance or knowledge of. — *v.t.* **cognise', -ize'** to become conscious of. — *adjs.* **cognit'ional; cog'nitive** capable of, or pertaining to, cognition. — *adv.* **cog'nitively.** — *n.* **cognitiv'ity.** — **take cognisance of** to recognise, take into consideration. [L. *cognitiō, -ōnis — cognōscĕre, cognitum — co-, (g)nōscĕre,* to know.]

cognomen *kog-nō'mən, n.* a surname: a nickname: a name: the last of the three names of a Roman, indicating the house or family to which he belonged: — *pl.* **cognō'mens** or **-mina.** — *adj.* **cognominal** (*-nom'*) like-named: relating to a cognomen. — *v.t.* **cognom'inate** to name. — *n.* **cognominā'tion.** [L. *cognōmen, -inis — co-, (g)nōmen,* a name.]

cognosce *kog-nos', (Scots law) v.t.* to examine: to give judgment upon: to declare to be an idiot. — *adj.* **cognosc'ible.** [L. *cognōscĕre — co-,* intens., *(g)nōscĕre,* to know.]

cognoscente *ko-nyō-shent'ā, n.* one professing a critical knowledge of works of art, music, literature, etc.: a connoisseur: — *pl.* **cognoscent'i** (*-ē*). [It. (mod. *conoscente*) — L. *cognōscĕre,* to know.]

cognovit *kog-nō'vit, (law) n.* an acknowledgment by a defendant that the plaintiff's cause is just. [L. *cognōvit actiōnem,* (he) has confessed the action.]

cogue, cog *kōg, kog, (esp. Scot.) ns.* a round wooden vessel, usu. of staves and hoops. [Ety. dub.]

cohabit *kō-hab'it, v.i.* to dwell together as husband and wife, or as if husband and wife. — *ns.* **cohab'itant** one dwelling with others; **cohabitā'tion; cohabitee'.** [L. *cohabitāre — co-,* habitāre, to dwell.]

co-heir *kō-ār', n.* a joint heir: — *fem.* **co-heir'ess.** — *n.* **coheritor** (*kō-her'it-ər*) a co-heir.

cohere *kō-hēr', v.i.* to stick together: to be consistent. — *v.t.* to fit together in a consistent, orderly whole. — *ns.* **cohēr'ence** a sticking together: consistency; **cohēr'ency.** — *adj.* **cohēr'ent** sticking together: connected: consistent in thought or speech: (of a system of units) such that one unit multiplied or divided by another gives a third unit in the system exactly: (of beam of radiation) showing definite, not random, relationships between points in a cross-section. — *adv.* **cohēr'ently.** — *n.* **cohēr'er** an apparatus for detection of electric waves by reduced resistance of imperfect contact, as if by cohesion. — *adj.* **cohēsible** (*-hēz'*) capable of cohesion. — *n.* **cohē'sion** (*-zhən*) the act of sticking together: a form of attraction by which particles of bodies stick together: concrescence of like parts (*bot.*): logical connection. — *adj.* **cohē'sive** (*-siv, -ziv*) having the power of cohering: tending to unite into a mass. — *adv.* **cohe'sively.** — *ns.* **cohe'siveness; cohesibil'ity** (*-hēz-*). [L. *cohaerēre, -haesum — co-, haerēre,* stick.]

coheritor. See **co-heir.**

cohibit *kō-hib'it, v.t.* to restrain. — *n.* **cohibition** (*-ish'ən*). — *adj.* **cohib'itive.** [L. *cohibēre — co-,* habēre, to have, hold.]

coho, cohoe *kō'hō, n.* a Pacific salmon, a species of *Oncorhynchus:* — *pl.* **co'ho(e)s.** [Ety. unknown.]

cohog. Same as **quahog.**

cohorn. See **coehorn.**

cohort *kō'hört, n.* a tenth part of a Roman legion: any band of warriors: (*formerly*) a division of plants between a class and an order or, according to some, between a suborder and a family: in the classification of higher animals, one of the divisions between subclass and order: a group of individuals: (*popularly*) a companion or follower. [L. *cohors, -tis,* an enclosed place, a multitude enclosed, a company of soldiers.]

cohortative *kō-hör'tə-tiv, adj.* encouraging. — *n.* (*Heb. gram.*) lengthened form of the imperfect. [L. *cohortārī, -ātus — co-,* intens., *hortārī,* to exhort.]

cohune *kō-hōōn', n.* a Central and South American palm (*Attalea cohune*) yielding **cohune nuts** and **cohune oil.** [From Amer. Sp.]

co-hyponym *kō-hī'pō-nim, n.* a word which is one of two or more hyponyms of another word.

coif *koif, n.* a covering for the head, esp. the close-fitting cap of white lawn or silk originally worn by serjeants-at-law: a covering for the head worn by women. — *v.t.* to provide with a coif: to dress (the hair). — *ns.* **coiffeur** (*kwä-fær'*) a hairdresser: — *fem.* **coiffeuse** (*-øz'*); **coiffure** (*kwä-für'*) a style of hairdressing: a head-dress. — Also *v.t.* [Fr. *coiffe* — L.L. *cofia,* a cap.]

coign, coigne *koin.* Same as **coin** (esp. first sense — after *Shak.*), **quoin.** — **coign(e) of vantage** an advantageous salient corner: hence, a good position generally.

coil¹ *koil, v.t.* to wind in rings: to enclose in twists. — *v.i.* to wind. — *n.* a coiled object: one of the rings into which anything is coiled: a wire wound spirally to conduct electricity: a contraceptive device consisting of a metal or plastic coil fitted in the uterus. [O.Fr. *coillir* (Fr. *cueillir*) — L. *colligĕre — col-,* together, *legĕre,* to gather; cf. **cull, collect.**]

coil² *koil, n.* tumult: hubbub: noise: fuss. — **mortal coil** (*Hamlet* III. i. 68) the toil and trouble of human life. [Der. unknown.]

coin *koin, n.* a corner-stone, quoin, or coign (*Shak.*): a piece of metal legally stamped and current as money: money. — *v.t.* to convert into money: to stamp: to invent, fabricate, esp. a new word: to gain money by means of (*Shak.*). — *ns.* **coin'age** the act of coining money: the currency: the pieces of metal coined: the invention, or fabrication, of something new, esp. a word or phrase: what is invented; **coin′er** one who coins money: a maker of counterfeit coins: an inventor; **coin′ing** minting: invention. — **coin′-box** a telephone which one operates by putting coins in a slot. — *adjs.* **coin′-op′erated, coin′-op′, coin′-in-the-slot′** of a machine, operated by inserting a coin in a slot. — **coin a phrase** to use a new phrase or expression (usu. *iron.*, i.e. to repeat a cliché); **coin money** to make money rapidly; **pay a man in his own coin** to give tit for tat: to give as good as one got. [Fr. *coin*, a wedge (see **quoin**), also the die to stamp money — L. *cuneus*, a wedge.]

coincide *kō-in-sīd′, v.i.* to occupy the same place or time: to agree: to correspond: to be identical. — *ns.* **coincidence** (*kō-in′si-dəns*) fact, event, or condition of coinciding: the occurrence of events simultaneously and consecutively in a striking manner but without any causal connection between them; **coin′cidency.** — *adjs.* **coin′cident, coincidental** (*-dent′l*). — *advs.* **coincident′ally; coin′cidently.** [L. *co-, incidĕre* — *in*, in, *cadĕre*, to fall.]

co-inhere *kō-in-hēr′, v.i.* to inhere together. — *n.* **co-inher′ence.**

co-inheritor *kō-in-her′it-ər, n.* a joint heir. — *n.* **co-inher′itance.**

co-instantaneous *kō-in-stən-tā′ni-əs, adj.* exactly simultaneous. — *ns.* **co-instantaneity** (*-stan-tə-nē′i-ti*), **co-instantā′neousness.** — *adv.* **co-instantā′neously.**

co-insurance *kō′in-shōō′rəns, n.* insurance jointly with another, esp. when the insurer bears part of the risk.

Cointreau® *kwē-trō′, kwän′, n.* an orange-flavoured liqueur.

coir *koir, n.* the strong fibre of coconut husk. [From Tamil or Malayalam.]

coistrel, coistril *kois′tril, n.* a groom (*obs.*): a knave (*Shak.*). [See **custrel.**]

coition *kō-ish′ən*, **coitus** *kō′it-əs, ns.* sexual intercourse. — *adj.* **cō′ital.** — **coitus interrup′tus** coitus intentionally interrupted by withdrawal before semen is ejaculated; **coitus reserv′atus** coitus in which ejaculation is avoided. [L. *coitiō, -ōnis* — *co-*, together, *īre, ītum*, to go.]

cojoin *kō-join′*, (*Shak.*) *v.t.* Same as **conjoin.**

coke[1] *kōk, n.* a form of fuel obtained by the heating of coal in confined space whereby its more volatile constituents are driven off: the residue when any substance (e.g. petrol) is carbonised. — *v.t.* and *v.i.* to make into, or become, coke. — *adj.* **cō′ky** like coke. — **coking coal** bituminous coal good for coking. [Ety. dub.; not before 17th century.]

coke[2] *kōk, n.* cocaine (*slang*): (®; with *cap.*) Coca-Cola.

cokernut *kō′kər-nut, n.* a faulty form of **coconut.**

cokes *kōks, (obs.) n.* a simpleton. [Ety. dub.]

col *kol, n.* a depression or pass in a mountain-range (*geog.*): a region between two anticyclones giving a similar figure when represented in contour (*meteor.*). [Fr., — L. *collum*, a neck.]

col-. See **com-.**

cola, kola *kō′lə, n.* (with *cap.*) a genus of West African trees (*Cola acuminata, C. nitida*) producing nuts used in drugs and for flavouring soft drinks: a soft drink so flavoured. [African name.]

colander, cullender *kul′ən-dər, n.* a perforated vessel used as a strainer in cookery. — *ns.* **colation** (*kə-lā′shən*), **colature** (*kol′ə-chər*) straining. — *adj.* **cō′liform** like a sieve. [L. *cōlāre*, to strain.]

colatitude *kō-lat′i-tūd, n.* the complement of the latitude. [**complement, latitude.**]

Colbertine *kol′bər-tin, n.* a kind of lace, so called from Jean Baptiste *Colbert* (1619–83), Minister of Finance to Louis XIV, a great patron of the arts.

colcannon *kol-kan′ən, n.* an Irish dish, consisting of pounded cabbage and potatoes with butter. [**cole,** cabbage, Ir. *ceannan*, white-headed.]

Colchicum *kol′ki-kəm, n.* a genus of *Liliaceae* including

meadow saffron: (without *cap.*) its corm and seeds, used for gout and rheumatism and yielding **col′chicine** (*-chi-* or *-ki-sēn*), an alkaloid used to produce polyploidy, etc.: (without *cap.*) a plant of the genus: — *pl.* **col′chica, col′chicums.** [L., — Gr. *kolchikon*, meadow saffron, neut. of *Kolchikos*, relating to *Kolchis*, the sorceress Medea's country.]

colcothar *kol′kō-thär, n.* a dark-red iron peroxide formed by calcining iron sulphate: a reddish-brown colour. [Ar. *qolqotār*.]

cold *kōld, adj.* giving or feeling a sensation that is felt to be the opposite of hot: chilly: low in temperature: without passion or zeal: spiritless: unfriendly: indifferent: reserved: suggesting cold rather than heat, as blue or grey (*paint.*): without application of heat: used of operations formerly requiring heat, e.g. **cold′-cast′ing, -forg′ing, -mould′ing, -weld′ing;** in marketing, politics, etc., involving contacting people thought to be potential customers or supporters, without the contact having been prearranged or primed, and with no knowledge of the people's likely reactions or opinions, as in **cold calling, cold canvassing.** — *n.* a relative want of heat: the feeling or sensation caused by the absence of heat: coldness: a spell of cold weather: a catarrhal inflammation of the mucous membrane of the respiratory organs, caused by a virus, usually accompanied by hoarseness and coughing (**cold in the head** coryza): catarrh: chillness. — *adj.* **cold′ish** somewhat cold. — *adv.* **cold′ly.** — *n.* **cold′ness.** — *n.* and *adj.* **cold′blood** (of) a horse belonging to the heavy draught breeds (cf. *hot-* and *warmblood*). — *adj.* **cold-blood′ed** having body-temperature depending upon environment, as fishes: without feeling: (of persons or actions) hardhearted. — *adv.* **cold′-blood′edly.** — **cold′-blood′edness; cold cathode** (*elect.*) an electrode from which electron emission results from high-potential gradient at the surface at normal temperatures; **cold′-chis′el** a strong and finely-tempered chisel for cutting cold metal: a tool used with a heavy hammer to cut or break stone, concrete, etc.; **cold comfort** see **comfort; cold′-cream′** a creamy ointment orig. usu. of almond-oil, spermaceti, white wax, and rosewater, used to remove make-up or as a cooling dressing for the skin. — *v.t.* (*coll.*) to apply cold-cream to. — **cold cuts** slices of cold cooked meat. — *adj.* **cold′-drawn** drawn through a die without heating: (of vegetable oil) subjected to pressure without heat. — **cold feet** loss of nerve: cooling off of courage or ardour; **cold fish** a person with no emotion; **cold′-frame′, cold′house** a plant frame, greenhouse, without artificial heat; **cold front** the surface of an advancing mass of cold air where it meets a retreating mass of warmer air; **cold harbour** a wayside travellers' shelter. — *adj.* **cold′-heart′ed** wanting feeling: indifferent. — *adv.* **cold-heart′edly.** — **cold-heart′edness; cold pack** a wet pack prepared with cold water, to counteract inflammation, etc.; **cold pig** (*coll.*) an application of cold water to rouse a sleeper; **cold rubber** a hardwearing synthetic rubber made at a temperature of 41°F (5°C). — *adj.* **cold′-short** brittle when cold: (of feelings) brittle, sensitive. — *v.t.* **cold′-should′er** to give the cold shoulder to (see below). — **cold slaw** cole-slaw; **cold snap** a sudden spell of cold weather; **cold sore** a blister or group of blisters on or near the mouth, caused by a viral infection (*herpes simplex*); **cold steel** cutting or stabbing weapons, opp. to bullets; **cold storage** storage and preservation of goods in refrigerating chambers: abeyance (*fig.*); **cold turkey** the plain unvarnished truth: sudden withdrawal of narcotics (also *fig.*): narcotics hangover; **cold war** see **war; cold water** water at its natural temperature in ordinary conditions; **cold wave** (*hairdressing*) an artificial wave produced by a chemical solution; **cold′-without′** brandy with cold water and no sugar. — *v.t.* **cold′-work** to shape (metals) at or near atmospheric temperature by rolling, pressing, etc. — **catch cold** to contract a cold; **cold as charity** a proverbial phrase expressing ironically great coldness or indifference; **give, show, the cold**

shoulder to show studied indifference: to give a rebuff; **in a cold sweat** (as if) sweating with fear; **in cold blood** with deliberate intent, not under the influence of passion; **leave one cold** to fail to impress; **leave out in the cold** to neglect, ignore; **pour, throw cold water on** to discourage. [O.E. (Anglian) *cald* (W.S. *ceald*); Scot. *cauld*, Ger. *kalt*; cf. **cool**, O.N. *kala*, to freeze, L. *gelidus* — *gelū*, frost.]

cole *kōl*, *n.* a general name for all sorts of cabbage. — **cole'-garth** a cabbage garden; **cole'-seed** the seed of rape: rape; **cole'-slaw** (-*slö*; Du. *koolsla*, for *kool salade*, cole salad) cabbage salad; **cole'-wort** cole — esp. heartless kinds. [O.E. *cawel*; Ger. *Kohl*, Scot. **kail**; all from L. *cōlis, caulis*, a stem, esp. of cabbage.]

cole-mouse. See under **coal.**

Coleoptera *kol-i-op'tər-ə, n.pl.* an order of insects having the fore-wings hard or horny, serving as wing-cases for the functional wings — the beetles. — *adjs.* **coleop'-teral, coleop'terous.** — *n.* **coleop'terist** a student of beetles. [Gr. *koleos*, a sheath, and *pteron*, a wing.]

coleor(r)hiza *kol-i-ō-rī'zə, n.* a protective layer on the radicle of some plants. [Gr. *koleos*, sheath, *rhiza*, root.]

cole-slaw. See **cole.**

cole-tit, cole-titmouse. See under **coal.**

Coleus *kō'li-əs, n.* a genus of plants with variegated coloured leaves often used for indoor decoration: (without *cap.*) a plant of the genus. [Gr. *koleos*, a sheath.]

coley *kō'li, n.* the coalfish.

colibri *kol'ib-rē, -lē', n.* a humming-bird. [Sp. *colibrí*, Fr. *colibri*, said to be the Carib name.]

colic, colicky. See **colon².**

coliform. See **colon², colander.**

colin *kol'in, n.* the Virginian quail. [Ety. uncertain; perh. Sp.]

coliseum. See **colosseum** under **colossus.**

colitis. See **colon².**

coll *kol, (obs.) v.t.* to embrace. — *n.* **coll'ing** embracing. [Fr. *col* — L. *collum*, the neck.]

collaborate *kəl-ab'ər-āt, v.i.* to work in association (sometimes invidiously, with an enemy). — *n.* **collabora'tion.** — *adj.* **collab'orative.** — *ns.* **collab'orator; collabora'tionist** (in invidious sense). [L. *collabōrāre, -ātum* — *labōrāre*, to work.]

collage *kol-äzh', n.* a picture made from scraps of paper and other odds and ends pasted out: any work put together from assembled fragments. — *n.* **collag'ist.** [Fr., pasting.]

collagen *kol'ə-jen, n.* a protein in fibrous connective tissue, readily turned into gelatine. — *adj.* **collag'enous.** [Gr. *kolla*, glue, and *gen-*, the root of *gignesthai*, to become.]

collapse *kəl-aps', n.* a falling away or breaking down: any sudden or complete breakdown or prostration. — *v.i.* to cave in: to close or fold up: to break down: to go to ruin: to lose heart. — *n.* **collapsibil'ity, -abil'ity.** — *adj.* **collaps'ible, -able** capable of collapsing. [L. *collāpsus* — *col-*, together, and *lābī, lāpsus*, to slide or fall.]

collar *kol'ər, n.* something worn round the neck by man, horse, dog, etc.: the part of a garment at the neck: the part of an animal's skin or coat, or a bird's feathers, round the neck: a ring: a surrounding band: the junction of root and stem in a plant: a piece of meat rolled up and tied. — *v.t.* to seize by the collar: to put a collar on: to seize (*slang*). — *adj.* **coll'ared** having, or ornamented with, a collar: rolled up and bound with a string, as a piece of meat having the bones removed: captured. — *n.* **collarette'** a small collar. — **coll'ar-beam** a horizontal piece of timber connecting or bracing two opposite rafters, to prevent sagging; **coll'ar-bone** the clavicle, a bone connecting the shoulder-blade and breast-bone; **coll'ar-stud** a stud for fastening a collar; **coll'ar-work** hard work against the horse-collar: drudgery. — **hot under the collar** see **hot¹.** [O.Fr. *colier* — L. *collāre* — *collum*, the neck.]

coll' arco *kol är'kō*, (It.) with the bow.

collard *kol'ərd, n.* cole-wort. [**cole-wort.**]

collate *kol-āt', v.t.* to bring together for comparison: to examine and compare, as books, and esp. old manuscripts: to place in or confer a benefice upon: (to place in order, as sheets of a book for binding, and) to examine with respect to completeness and sequence of sheets, etc.: to merge two or more files, sets of records, etc. (*comput.*). — *adj.* **collā'table.** — *n.* **collā'tion** the act of collating: a bringing together for examination and comparison: the presentation of a clergyman to a benefice: a description of a book as collated: a repast between meals, from the habit of reading the *Collationes* of Johannes Cassianus during a slight meal in monasteries. — *adj.* **collā'tive** having the power of conferring: of livings where the bishop and patron are one and the same person. — *n.* **collā'tor** one who collates or compares: one who bestows or presents: a machine which merges sets of punched cards or separates cards from a set. [L. *collātum*, used as supine of *conferre* — pfx. *col-* and *lātum* (*ferre*, to bring).]

collateral *kol-at'ər-l, adj.* side by side: running parallel or together: corresponding: descended from the same ancestor, but not in direct line. — *n.* a collateral relation: a contemporary: a rival: collateral security. — *adv.* **collat'erally.** — **collateral security** an additional and separate security for repayment of money borrowed. [L. *col-, latus, lateris*, a side.]

colleague¹ *kol'ēg, n.* one associated with another in some employment — not a partner in business. — *n.* **coll'- eagueship.** [Fr. *collègue* — L. *collēga* — *col-, legĕre*, to choose.]

colleague² *kol-ēg', (obs.) v.i.* to ally: to conspire: — *pr.p.* **colleaguing** (*kol-ēg'ing*); *pa.t.* and *pa.p.* **colleagued** (*kol-ēgd'*). [O.Fr. *colliguer*, to join in alliance — L. *colligāre*, to bind together.]

collect *kəl-, kol-ekt', v.t.* to assemble or bring together: to infer: to put (one's thoughts) in order: to receive payment of: to call for and remove. — *v.i.* to run together: to accumulate. — *n.* **collect** (*kol'*) a short prayer, peculiar to the liturgies of the Western Church, consisting of one sentence, conveying one main petition. — *adj.* and *adv.* (-*ekt'; U.S.*) of a telephone call, telegram, etc., paid for by the recipient. — *adj.* **collect'- able, -ible.** — *n.* one of a set of toys or ornaments each purchasable separately but priced and marketed in such a way as to encourage the purchase of all or much of the range. — *n.pl.* **collectā'nea** a collection of passages: a miscellany. — *adj.* **collect'ed** gathered together: (of a poet's or other writer's works) assembled in one volume, one set of volumes, etc.: having unscattered wits: cool: firm. — *adv.* **collect'edly.** — *n.* and *adj.* **collect'edness** self-possession: coolness. — *n.* and *adj.* **collect'ing.** — *n.* **collec'tion** the act of collecting: the gathering of contributions, esp. of money: the money collected: money intended for collection in church: an assemblage: a book of selections: inference (*Shak.*): composure: (in *pl.*) an examination at the end of the terms in certain colleges: the range of new fashion clothes shown by a couturier: the regular uplifting of mail by a postal official. — *adj.* **collect'ive** considered as forming one mass or sum: congregated: common: inferential (*Milt.*): expressing a number or multitude (*gram.*). — *n.* a gathering, assemblage: a unit of organisation in a collectivist system: (*loosely*) a group of people who run a business, etc., for their mutual benefit, often with no specifically designated jobs. — *adv.* **collect'ively.** — *v.t.* **collect'ivise, -ize** to give a collectivist organisation to. — *ns.* **collect'ivism** the economic theory that industry should be carried on with a collective capital — a form of socialism: a system embodying this; **collect'ivist.** — Also *adj.* — *ns.* **collectiv'ity; collect'or** that which, or one who (esp. in composition, as *ticket-collector, tax-collector*) collects: one who sets himself to acquire and set together examples or specimens, as of books, minerals, curiosities: in India, the chief official of a district, collecting revenue and acting as a magistrate; **collect'orate**, **collect'orship**. — **collect'ing-box** a field-naturalist's box for specimens: a box for receiving money contributions; **collective agreement** one reached by collective bargaining; **collective bargaining** negotiation on conditions of service between an organised body of workers on one side and an employer or association of employers on the other; **collective farm** a state-controlled farm consisting of a number of small-holdings operated on a co-operative basis; **collective fruit** (*bot.*) a multiple fruit — one derived from several flowers, as fig, mulberry; **collective security** general security among nations to be achieved through guarantee of each nation's security by all; **collective unconscious** (*psych.*) the part of the unconscious mind that originates in ancestral experience; **collector's item, piece** an object beautiful, valuable, interesting, etc. enough to be included in a collection. [L. *colligĕre, collēctum* — *legĕre*, to gather.]

colleen *kol'ēn, kol-ēn', n.* a girl. [Irish *cailín.*]

college *kol'ij, n.* an incorporation, company, or society of persons joined together generally for literary or scientific purposes, and often possessing peculiar or exclusive privileges: a body or society that is a member of a university or is co-extensive with a university: a seminary of learning: a literary, political, or religious institution: the edifice appropriated to a college. — *n.* **coll'eger** a member of a college: one of the foundationers at Eton College. — *adj.* **collegial** (*ka-lē'ji-al*) pertaining to a college or university, or to a collegium. — *ns.* **collē'gialism** the theory that the church is a self-governing body independent of the state; **collegial'ity** sharing by bishops in papal decision-making: colleagueship: adherence to the theory of collegialism; **collē'gian** a member or inhabitant of a college: an inmate of a prison (*slang*), **collē'gianer** a member of a college, a student. — *adj.* **collē'giate** pertaining to or resembling a college: containing a college, as a town: instituted like a college: corporate. — *n.* (*obs. slang*) an inmate of a prison, etc. — **college pudding** a kind of steamed dried fruit pudding; **collegiate church, collegial church** a church having a college or chapter, consisting of a dean or provost and canons, attached to it: in Scotland, a church occupied by two or more pastors of equal rank (also **collegiate charge**). — **College of Arms, Heralds' College** a collegiate body incorporated in 1483, presided over by the Earl Marshal, and including Garter, principal King-of-arms, Clarenceux, and Norroy, besides six heralds and four pursuivants; **college of cardinals** the whole body of cardinals, electors of the pope; **College of education** a college for training teachers; **College of Justice** in Scotland, a great forensic society, composed of judges, advocates, writers to the signet, and solicitors. [Fr. *collège* — L. *collēgium*, from *col-*, and *legĕre*, gather.]

collegium *ko-lēj'i-am, n.* college of cardinals: an administrative board: — *pl.* **collegia, collegiums**. — **collegium musicum** (*ko-lēj'i-am mū'si-kam, ko-lāg'i-ōōm mōō'si-kōōm*) a group of amateur musicians, often connected with a university. [L. *collēgium*; see **college**.]

col legno *kol len'yō, kō lān'yō*, (It.) with the wood (of the violin bow).

Collembola *kol-em'bō-la, n.pl.* an order of wingless Apterygota, formerly classified as insects, whose abdomen has six segments or fewer, a forward-pointing springing fork and an adhesive apparatus — the springtails. — *n.* **collem'bolan** an insect of this order. [Gr. *kolla*, glue, *embolos*, a peg.]

collenchyma *kol-eng'ki-ma*, (*bot.*) *n.* the strengthening tissue of thick-cornered cells. — *adj.* **collenchym'atous.** [Gr. *kolla*, glue, *en*, in, *chyma*, that which is poured.]

Colles' fracture *kol'is frak'char*, a fracture of the radius near the wrist, with backward displacement of the hand. [Abraham *Colles*, 1773–1843, Irish surgeon.]

collet *kol'it, n.* a ring or collar: the collar of a plant: the part of a ring which contains the stone. [Fr., — L. *collum.*]

collide *ka-līd', v.i.* to dash together: to clash. — *v.t.* to cause to collide. — *n.* **collision** (*-lizh'n*) the state of being struck together: a violent impact, a crash: conflict: opposition: clashing. — **collision course** a course which, if persisted in, will result in a collision (*lit.* and *fig.*); **colli'sion-mat** a mat for covering a hole in a ship's side caused by a collision. — **elastic collision** a collision in which both kinetic energy and momentum are conserved (*phys.*): a collision in which the bombarding particle does not excite or break up the struck nucleus, and is simply scattered (**elastic scattering**) (*nuc.*); **inelastic collision** a collision in which momentum, but not kinetic energy, is conserved (*phys.*): a collision in which there is a change in the total energies of the particles involved, the resultant scattering being termed **inelastic scattering** (*nuc.*). [L. *collīdĕre, collīsum* — *col-, laedĕre*, to strike.]

collie, colly *kol'i, n.* a long-haired, intelligent breed of sheep-dog, originating in Scotland. [Ety. dub.]

collier *kol'yar, n.* a charcoal-burner or dealer in charcoal or coal (*obs.*): a coal-miner: a ship that carries coal: a sailor in such a ship. — *n.* **coll'iery** a coal-mine. [**coal.**]

collieshangie *kol-i-shang'i*, (*Scot.*) *n.* a noisy wrangling: an uproar: a disturbance. [Origin unknown.]

colligate *kol'i-gāt, v.t.* to bind together. — *n.* **colligā'tion** conjunction: bringing together under a general principle or conception. — *adj.* **coll'igative** (*physical chem.*) depending on the concentration, not the nature, of the substance. [L. *colligāre, -ātum* — *col-, ligāre*, to bind.]

collimate *kol'i-māt, v.t.* to make parallel: to adjust accurately parts of (an optical instrument, as a surveying telescope). — *ns.* **collimā'tion; coll'imātor** a device for obtaining a beam of parallel rays of light or other radiation, or one for obtaining a beam of particles moving in parallel paths: a subsidiary telescope for collimating other instruments. [*collīmāre*, a wrong reading for L. *collīneāre*, to bring into line with — *col-*, together, *līnea*, a line.]

collinear *ko-lin'i-ar, adj.* in the same straight line.

Collins *kol'inz, n.* a letter of thanks for hospitality. [From the notable example sent by Mr *Collins* in *Pride and Prejudice*.]

colliquate *kol'i-kwāt*, (*obs.*) *v.t.* to melt: to fuse. — *adjs.* **colliq'uable, colliq'uant** (*obs.*) melting, wasting. — *n.* **colliquā'tion**, melting: wasting away. — *adj.* **colliq'uative** profuse in flow: wasting. — *n.* **colliquesc'ence** readiness to liquefy. [L. *col-*, together, *liquāre, -ātum*, to make melt.]

collision. See **collide.**

collocate *kol'ō-kāt, v.t.* to place together: to set: to arrange. — *n.* **collocā'tion.** [L. *collocāre, -ātum*, — *col-, locāre*, to place.]

collocutor, collocutory. See **colloquy.**

collodion *kol-ō'di-an, n.* a gluey solution of nitrated cotton (or cellulose nitrates) in alcohol and ether, used in surgery and photography. [Gr. *kollōdēs* — *kolla*, glue, *eidos*, form, appearance.]

collogue *ka-lōg', v.i.* to simulate belief (*obs.*): to conspire (*dial.*): to converse confidentially. — *v.t.* to coax (*obs.*): to flatter. [Prob. from L. *colloquī*, to speak together.]

colloid *kol'oid, n.* a substance in a state in which, though apparently dissolved, it cannot pass through a membrane: a substance that readily assumes this state: a colloidal system. — *adj.* **colloid'al. — colloidal system** a dispersed substance plus the material in which it is dispersed. [Gr. *kolla*, glue, *eidos*, form.]

collop *kol'ap, n.* an egg fried with bacon (*obs.*): a slice of meat, fried or not (*dial.*): a child (*Shak.*). — **Collop Monday** the day before Shrove Tuesday, when collops-and-eggs were eaten. — **minced collops** (*Scot.*) minced meat. [Origin obscure.]

colloquy *kol'a-kwi, n.* a speaking together: mutual discourse: conversation. — *v.i.* (*rare*) to converse. — *n.*

For other sounds see detailed chart of pronunciation.

collocutor (*kol-ok'ū-tər*). — *adj.* colloc'ūtory. — *v.i.* colloque (*kol-ōk'*) to hold colloquy. — *adj.* colloquial (*kə-lō'kwi-əl*) pertaining to or used in common conversation. — *ns.* collō'quialism a form of expression used in familiar talk; collō'quialist. — *adv.* collō'quially. — *v.i.* coll'oquise, -ize to converse. — *ns.* coll'oquist a speaker in a colloquy; collō'quium a conference: a meeting for discussion: a seminar: — *pl.* collō'quia, -iums. [L. *colloquium* — *col-*, *loquī*, to speak.]

collotype *kol'ō-tīp, n.* a form of gelatine process in book illustration and advertising. [Gr. *kolla*, glue, and type.]

colluctation *kol-uk-tā'shən, n.* strife: opposition. [L. *colluctārī* — *col-*, *luctārī*, to wrestle.]

collude *kol-ūd', -ōōd', v.i.* to play into each other's hands: to act in concert, esp. in a fraud. — *ns.* collud'er; collu'sion the act of colluding: a secret agreement to deceive, esp. one made between the opposing parties in a lawsuit: deceit: in *Love's Lab. Lost*, Goodman Dull's blunder for *allusion*. — *adj.* collu'sive fraudulently concerted: deceitful. — *adv.* collu'sively. [L. *collūdĕre*, *collūsum*, from *col-*, and *lūdĕre*, to play.]

colluvies *ko-lū', ko-lōō'vi-ēz, n.* accumulated filth: a rabble. [L. *colluviēs*, washings — *colluĕre*, to wash thoroughly.]

colly[1] *kol'i, v.t.* to begrime with coal-dust (*arch.*): to darken (*Shak.*). — *n.* soot, smut (*obs.* or *dial.*): (also colly bird) a blackbird (*dial.*). — *p.adj.* coll'ied. [See coal.]

colly[2]. See collie.

collyrium *ko-lir'i-əm, n.* eye-wash: — *pl.* collyria, collyriums. [Latinised from Gr. *kollyrion*, eye-salve, dim. of *kollyrā*, a roll of bread.]

collywobbles *kol'i-wob-lz, n.* (*facet.*) abdominal pain or disorder. [Prob. colic and wabble, wobble.]

Colmar *kol'mär, n.* a kind of fan fashionable in Queen Anne's time. [Perh. *Colmar* in Alsace.]

Colobus *kol'ō-bəs, n.* an African genus of monkeys, almost thumbless: (without *cap.*) any of several monkeys of the genus, including the guereza: — *pl.* col'obi (-*bī*, -*bē*), col'obuses. [Gr. *kolobos*, maimed.]

Colocasia *kol-ō-kā'zi-ə, -si-ə,* (*bot.*) *n.* a genus of plants of the arum family — taro, etc. [Gr. *kolokāsiā*, water-lily root.]

colocynth *kol'o-sinth, n.* a kind of cucumber (*Citrullus colocynthis*): a cathartic drug got from it. [Gr. *kolokynthis*.]

Cologne-earth *kə-lōn'-ûrth, n.* a brown earth prepared from lignite, found originally near *Cologne.* — Cologne water or eau de Cologne (*ō də kə-lōn'*) a perfumed spirit first made at Cologne in 1709 by Johann Farina.

colon[1] *kō'lən, n.* the punctuation mark (:), used to indicate a distinct member or clause of a sentence, or to introduce a list, spoken or reported words, etc. [Gr. *kōlon*, a limb, member.]

colon[2] *kō'lən, n.* the large intestine from the caecum to the rectum. — *n.* colic (*kol'ik*) a disease attended with severe pain and flatulent distention of the abdomen, without diarrhoea. — *adjs.* col'ic; col'icky like, suffering or causing colic. — *ns.* coliform (bacillus) (*kol'i-förm*) any of several bacilli living in the intestines (also colon bacillus); colitis (*kō-, ko-lī'tis*) inflammation of the colon. — *adj.* colon'ic of the colon. — *n.* a colonic irrigation. — *adj.* colorec'tal pertaining to the colon and rectum. — *ns.* colos'tomy (*kə-*) the making of an artificial anus by surgical means; colot'omy (*kə-*) cutting of or incision into the colon. — colonic irrigation the injection of large amounts of water or other liquid into the colon in order to clean it out (*med.*). [Gr. *kōlon*, the large intestine.]

colon[3] *kō-lōn', n.* the monetary unit of El Salvador and Costa Rica. [From Columbus (Sp. *Colón*).]

colonel *kûr'nəl, n.* an officer who has command of a regiment, or one of equivalent rank — between a lieutenant-colonel and a brigadier (in U.S. brigadier-general): in U.S., also an officer in the marines and one in the air force: in some regiments, an honorary rank given usu. to a distinguished former member of the regiment: in U.S. sometimes, an honorary title given to one not connected with the armed forces. — *ns.* col'onelcy (*-si*) the office or rank of colonel; col'onelling (or *kor-ō-nel'ing*) playing the colonel; col'onelship colonelcy: the quality of being a colonel. — Colonel Blimp see blimp; col'onel-comm'andant the commander of a brigade (sometimes given as an honorary rank); col'onel-in-chief' an honorary colonel, in Britain generally a member of the Royal Family. [Older Fr. and Sp. *coronel* — It. *colonello*, the leader of a *colonna*, or column — L. *columna*; spelling assimilated to mod. Fr.]

colonial, etc. See colony.

colonic. See colon[2].

colonnade *kol-ən-ād', n.* a range of columns placed at regular intervals: a similar row, as of trees. — *adj.* colonnād'ed. [Fr., — L. *columna*.]

colony *kol'ən-i, n.* a name vaguely applied to a state's dependencies overseas or abroad (distinguished from a *dominion*): a military settlement planted in subject territory (*Rom. hist.*): a band of emigrants or their new home, connected with the mother city by no political tie (*Gr. hist.*): a body of persons settled in a foreign country, or forming a separate group in any way (as by common occupation), or organised for purposes of support, labour, treatment, etc.: the settlement so formed: the place they inhabit: a number of organisms, esp. of one kind, living together as a community (*biol.*): a coenobium: a group or company of Beaver Scouts. — *adj.* colonial (*kə-lō'ni-əl*) pertaining to, of the nature of, or dating from the time when a territory was, a colony. — *n.* an inhabitant, citizen, or member of a colony, a colonist. — *ns.* colō'nialism a trait of colonial life or speech: the colonial system (see below): policy of obtaining, or maintaining hold over, colonies, esp. with the purpose of exploiting them. — *adj.* and *n.* colōn'ialist. — *adv.* colōn'ially. — *n.* colonisā'tion, -z- the act or practice of colonising: state of being colonised. — *v.t.* col'onise, -ize to plant or establish a colony in: to form into a colony: to plant fraudulent voters in (*U.S.*). — *v.i.* to settle. — *n.* col'onist an inhabitant of a colony: a voter set up for election purposes: a weed of cultivated ground (*bot.*). — colonial animals organisms consisting of numerous individuals in bodily union; colonial experience man (*Austr.*) a jackaroo; colonial goose (*Austr.* and *N.Z.*) a joint of mutton, boned, stuffed and roasted; Colonial Office (*hist.*) the government office dealing with the colonies; colonial system the theory that the settlements abroad should be treated as proprietary domains exploited for the benefit of the mother country. [L. *colōnia* — *colōnus*, a husbandman — *colĕre*, to till.]

colophon *kol'ə-fon, -fən, n.* an inscription at the end of a book or literary composition, often naming the author and scribe or printer, with place and date of execution, etc., as on a modern title-page: a publisher's imprint or device, with name, date, etc. [L. *colophōn* — Gr. *kolophōn*, summit, finishing touch.]

colophony *kol-of'ə-ni,* or *kol', n.* rosin. [Gr. *kolophōniā* (*rhētinē*, gum) from *Kolophōn*, Colophon, in Asia Minor.]

coloquintida *kol-o-kwin'ti-də.* Same as colocynth.

color. U.S. spelling of colour.

Colorado beetle *kol-ər-ä'dō bē'tl,* an American beetle, yellow with black stripes, a potato pest. [State of *Colorado*.]

coloration. See under colour.

coloratura *kol-or-ət-ōō'rə,* (*mus.*) *n.* florid vocal passages. — *adj.* florid. — coloratura soprano a high and flexible soprano voice, capable of singing coloratura passages: a singer with such a voice. [It., colouring.]

colorectal. See under colon.

colorific, etc. See under colour.

colossus *kəl-os'əs, n.* a gigantic statue, esp. that of Apollo at (but not astride of) the entrance of the harbour of Rhodes: a person or organisation of gigantic power and influence (*fig.*): — *pl.* **coloss'i** (*sī*), **coloss'uses**. — *adj.* **coloss'al** like a colossus: gigantic. — *ns.* **colossē'um, colisē'um** a large place of entertainment, from Vespasian's amphitheatre at Rome, which was the largest in the world. — **coloss'us-wise** (*Shak.*) astride. [L., — Gr. *kolossos*.]

colostomy. See **colon²**.

colostrum *ko-los'trəm, n.* a mammal's first milk after parturition. — *n.* **colostrā'tion** a disease of infants due to colostrum. — *adjs.* **colos'tric, -trous.** [L.]

colotomy. See **colon²**.

colour, also, esp. in U.S., **color,** *kul'ər, n.* a sensation of light induced in the eye by electromagnetic waves of a certain frequency - the colour being determined by the frequency: a property whereby bodies have different appearances to the eye through surface reflection or absorption of rays: hue, one of the constituents into which white light can be decomposed: appearance of blood in the face: race or race-mixture other than Caucasian: appearance: plausibility: reason, pretext: tint: shade: paint: particle of gold: rhetorical figure: false show: vividness: timbre (*mus.*): variety: (in *sing.* or *pl.*) a flag, ensign, or standard: (in *pl.*) a symbol of membership of a party, club, college, team, etc.: in particle physics, any of six varieties of a particular characteristic of quarks and antiquarks, used to define possible combinations of these particles in baryons and mesons. — *v.t.* to put colour on: to stain: to paint: to set in a fair light: to exaggerate: to disguise: to misrepresent. — *v.i.* to take on colour: to blush. — *ns.* **col'orant** (also **col'ourant**) a substance used for colouring; **colorā'tion** (also **colourā'tion**) colouring: mode of colouring: disposition of colours. — *adj.* **colorif'ic** (*kol-, kul-*) producing colours. — *ns.* **colorim'eter** (*kol-, kul-*) an instrument for comparison of colours; **colorim'etry.** — *adj.* **colourable** (*kul'*) plausible: feigned. — *adv.* **col'ourably.** — *adj.* **col'oured** having colour: having a specious appearance, deceitful (*Spens.*): of the complexion, other than white: (*loosely*; often *derog.*) belonging to a dark-skinned race: (usu. with *cap.*) in South Africa, of mixed racial descent — partly Caucasian, partly of darker race and with English or Afrikaans as mother tongue: (also with *cap.*) in South Africa, of one of the official racial groups, neither white nor African: not of Caucasian race. — *n.* (usu. with *cap.*) in South Africa, a person of mixed racial descent speaking either English or Afrikaans as his mother tongue: (also with *cap.*) in South Africa, a member of one of the official racial groups, one who is neither white nor African. — *n.* **col'ourer.** — *adj.* **col'ourful** full of colour: vivid. — *ns.* **col'ouring** any substance used to give colour: the actual colours of anything, and their arrangement: manner of applying colours: appearance, esp. a person's hair and skin colour: tone; **col'ourist** one who colours or paints: one who excels in colouring. — *adjs.* **col'ourless** without colour: transparent: pale: neutral: lacking distinctive character; **col'oury** having much colour. — **colour bar** social discrimination between whites and other races. — *adj.* **col'our-blind** unable to distinguish some colours from others, or to see them at all. — **colour blindness; colour code** a system of identification, e.g. of electrical wires, by different colours. — *v.t.* **col'our-code** to mark with different colours for identification. — **coloured pencil** one containing a coloured lead as distinct from graphite or blacklead. — *adj.* **col'our-fast** of material, etc., with colours that will not run when washed. — **colour film** a film for making colour photographs; **colour filter** a film or plate transparent for the required colours only or chiefly; **colour hearing** the association of colours with sounds heard; **colour line** a social and political distinction between white and other races; **col'ourman** one who prepares or sells paints; **colour music** the art of displaying colours on a screen with effect analogous to music; **colour organ** an instrument for doing this; **colour party** a guard carrying colours; **colour scheme** general conception of combination of

colours in a design; **colour screen** a colour filter; **col'our-sergeant** the sergeant who guards the colours of a regiment; **colour supplement** an illustrated magazine printed in colour and published as a usu. weekly part of a newspaper. — *adj.* of a style often pictured in such a magazine, i.e. expensive and rather exclusive. — **col'our-wash** a cheap form of distemper coating. — *v.t.* to paint with this. — *n.pl.* **col'our-ways** combinations of colours. — **colour a pipe** to cause a pipe, esp. a meerschaum, to darken by smoking; **colour in** to fill in an area on a piece of paper, etc. with colour; **colour up** to blush, flush; **come off with flying colours** to do something with éclat; **come out in one's true colours** to appear in one's real character; **false colours** a false pretence; **fear no colours** to fear no enemy; **give colour to** give plausibility; **high colour** ruddiness of complexion; **in one's true colours** as one really is; **join the colours** to enlist; **lose colour** to lose one's good looks: to become pale: to appear less probable (*fig.*); **nail one's colours to the mast** to commit oneself to some party or plan of action; **off colour** faded: indisposed: past one's best: slightly indecent; **pair of colours** see **pair¹**; **primary colours** see **primary; see the colour of a person's money** to be sure that a person has money to pay for an article about to be bought. [O.Fr. *color* — L. *color, -ōris*; akin to *cēlāre*, to cover, to conceal.]

colporteur *kol-pōr-tûr', -pör,* or *kol'pört-ər, n.* a pedlar, esp. one selling religious tracts and books. — *n.* **col'portāge** (or *-täzh'*) the distribution of books by colporteurs. [Fr. *colporteur*, from *col* — L. *collum*, the neck, and *porter* — L. *portāre*, to carry.]

colposcope *kol'pō-skōp, n.* an instrument for examining the neck of the uterus, used esp. for early detection of cancer. — *adj.* **colposcop'ical.** — *adv.* **colposcop'ically.** — *n.* **colpōs'copy** examination using a colposcope. [Gr. *kolpos*, the womb, *skopeein*, to see.]

colt *kōlt, n.* a young horse: an awkward fellow: an inexperienced youth: in sports and games, a young, inexperienced player: a young camel or ass (*B.*): a rope's end (*naut.*). — *v.i.* (*Spens.*) to frisk like a colt. — *v.t.* to cheat (*Shak.*): to give the rope's end, to beat. — *adj.* **colt'ish** like a colt: frisky: wanton. — **colts'foot** a composite plant (*Tussilago farfara*) with shaggy stalk and large soft leaves; **colt's tooth** one of a horse's first set of teeth: love of youthful pleasures (*Shak.*): wantonness; **colt'wood** (*Spens.*) a plant used by Glauce in her incantations (F.Q. III. ii. 49. 8) — said to be coltsfoot, which is not woody. [O.E. *colt*; Sw. *kult*, a young boar, a stout boy.]

Colt *kōlt, n.* a pistol invented by Samuel *Colt* (1814–62).

colter. Same as **coulter.**

Coluber *kol'ū-bər, n.* an extensive genus of non-venomous snakes: (without *cap.*) any snake of the genus. — *ns.* **colūb'riad** (*Cowper*) the epic of a snake; **Colū'bridae** the largest family of snakes — in which some include cobras and other venomous snakes. — *adj.* **colubriform** (*-ōō', -ū'*) resembling Coluber; **col'ūbrine** snakelike: colubriform. [L. *coluber*, a snake.]

colugo *ko-lōō'gō, n.* the flying lemur (q.v.): — *pl.* **colu'gos.** [Prob. from Malaysian word.]

Columba *kəl-um'bə, n.* a large genus consisting of the pigeons: one of the southern constellations. — *adj.* **Colum'ban** pertaining to St. *Columba* (521–597), the Irish apostle who founded a monastery at Iona and converted the Northern Picts to Christianity. [L. *columba*, dove.]

columbarium, columbary. See **columbine.**

Columbian *kəl-um'bi-ən, adj.* American: (of type) in size between English and Great Primer — 16-point. — *n.* **colum'bate** niobate. — *adj.* **colum'bic** niobic. — *ns.* **columb'ite** a mineral, niobate and tantalate of iron and manganese; **colum'bium** the former name for niobium. [*Columbus*, discoverer of America.]

columbine *kol'əm-bīn, adj.* of or like a dove: dove-coloured. — *n.* any plant of the ranunculaceous genus Aquilegia, with coloured sepals and spurred petals, giving the appearance of a bunch of pigeons: (with *cap.*) in pantomime, the sweetheart of Harlequin. — *ns.* **columbä′rium** a dovecot: a niche for a sepulchral urn: a recess in a wall to receive the end of a rafter: — *pl.* **columbaria; col′umbary** a dovecot. [L. *columba,* a dove.]

column *kol′əm, n.* a long round body, used as support or adornment: any upright body or mass like a column: a body of troops with narrow front: a perpendicular row of figures, etc.: a perpendicular section of a page or of a table: a special section in a newspaper: a bundle of nerve-fibres: the central part of an orchid. — *ns.* **col′umel** a small column; **columell′a** the central axis of a spiral univalve: the auditory ossicle in lower vertebrates: the central axis of the spore-case of mosses: in the opening of fruits, what remains in the centre after the carpels have split away: — *pl.* **columell′ae** (*lē*). — *adjs.* **columnal** (*kə-lum′nl*), **colum′nar** pertaining to columns: like a column: formed in columns. — *n.* **columnar′ity.** — *adjs.* **columnated** (*kol′əm-nāt-id*, or *kə-lum′*), **columned** (*kol′əmd*), **colum′niated** having columns. — *ns.* **columniation** (*kə-lum-ni-ā′shən*) the use or arrangement of columns; **columnist** (*kol′əm-ist, -nist; illit.* or *facet.* kol′ūm-ist*) one who conducts a column in a newspaper. [L. *columna,* akin to *celsus,* high; Gr. *kolōnē,* a hill; see **hill.**]

colure *kō-lūr′, kōl′, kol′yər, n.* a great circle of the celestial sphere passing through the poles of the equator and either the solstitial or the equinoctial points. [Gr. *kolouros — kolos,* docked, *ourā,* tail.]

colza *kol′zə, n.* cole-seed, yielding **col′za-oil.** [Du. *koolzaad,* cabbage-seed.]

com- kom-, con- kon-, co- ko-, kō-, also, by assimilation, **col- kol-, cor- kor-,** *pfxs.* together, with: similar: used as intensive. [L. *com,* old form of *cum,* with.]

coma¹ *kō′mə, n.* deep sleep: stupor. — *adj.* **com′atose** affected with coma: drowsy. [Gr. *kōma, -atos.*]

coma² *kō′mə, n.* a tuft (*bot.*): the head of a tree: the nebulous envelope of the head of a comet (*astron.*): (the manifestation of) a defect in an optical system (e.g. in a telescope) in which the image of a point appears as a blurred pear-shaped patch (*optics*): — *pl.* **com′ae** (*mē*). — *adjs.* **cō′mal, cō′mate, cō′mose, cō′mous.** — **Coma Berenices** (*ber-ə-nī′sēz*) Berenice's Hair, a small northern constellation. [Gr. *kŏmē,* hair of head.]

comanchero *kō-man-che′rō, n.* in the 19th cent., one who traded with plains Indians of south-west N. America: — *pl.* **comanche′ros.** [Mex.-Sp. — *Comanche* tribe.]

comarb. See **coarb.**

comart *kō-märt′,* (*Shak.*) *n.* an agreement. [Perh. pfx. **co-** and **mart;** or a misprint for *cou′nant,* i.e. **covenant.**]

comate¹ *kō′māt′,* (*Shak.*) *n.* a mate or companion.

comate². See **coma².**

comatose. See **coma¹.**

comb¹ *kōm, n.* a toothed instrument for separating and cleaning hair, wool, flax, for graining paint, etc.: anything of similar form: the fleshy crest of some birds: the top or crest of a wave, of a roof, or of a hill: an aggregation of cells for honey. — *v.t.* to separate, to arrange, or clean by means of a comb or as if with a comb: to dress with a comb: to search thoroughly: to beat (*Shak.*). — *v.i.* to break with a white foam, as the top of a wave. — *adj.* **combed.** — *n.* **comb′er** one who or that which combs wool, etc.: a long foaming wave. — *n.pl.* **comb′ings** hairs combed off. — *adjs.* **comb′less; comb′y.** — *adv.* **comb′wise.** — **comb out** to arrange hair by combing after rollers, etc. have been removed: to remove (tangles, etc.) from hair by combing: to search for and remove, e.g. lice, men for military service (*n.* **comb′-out**). [O.E. *camb.*]

comb², combe. See **coomb¹,².**

combat *kom′bət, kum′* (U.S. usu. *kəm-bat′;* not standard in U.K.), *v.i.* to contend or struggle. — *v.t.* to beat against: to contest: to oppose: to debate: — *pr.p.* **com′bating;** *pa.t.* and *pa.p.* **com′bated.** — *n.* (*kom′, kum′*) a struggle: a fight. — *adjs.* **com′batable; com′batant** disposed to combat: taking part or liable to

take part in action. — *n.* one who takes part in a combat. — *adj.* **com′bative** inclined to quarrel. — *n.* **com′bativeness.** — **combat fatigue** mental disturbance in a fighting soldier, formerly called shell-shock; **combat jacket** a jacket (in the style of those) worn by soldiers when fighting, usu. khaki with camouflage markings. [Fr. *combattre,* to fight — L. pfx. *com-,* mutual, and *bātuĕre,* to strike.]

comber¹ *kom′bər, n.* the gaper (a sea-perch): a species of wrasse.

comber². See under **comb¹.**

combine *kəm-bīn′, v.t.* to join together: to unite intimately (with): to bind, restrict (*Shak.*). — *v.i.* to come into close union (with): to co-operate: to unite and form a new compound (*chem.*). — *n.* (*kom′bīn*) a syndicate, a trust, an association of trading companies: a combine harvester: a painting into which articles of everyday use have been fixed. — *adj.* **combinate** (*kom′bin-āt*) combined: betrothed (*Shak.*). — *n.* **combinā′tion** the act of combining: union of individual things: a motor-cycle with sidecar: persons united for a purpose: in mathematics, a possible set of a given number of things selected from a given number, irrespective of arrangement within the set (distinguished from a *permutation*): the series of letters or numbers that must be dialled to move the mechanism of a combination lock and so open it. — *n.pl.* **combinā′tions** (*coll.* shortened form **com(b)s** (*komz*)) an undergarment comprising vest and drawers. — *adjs.* **com′binātive; combinato′rial** concerned with arrangement (*math.*); **combin′atory; combīned′; combīn′ing.** — *n.* **combo** (*kom′bō*) a small jazz or dance band: any combination (*coll.*): a white man who cohabits with an Aboriginal woman (*Austr.*): — *pl.* **com′bos.** — **combination lock** a lock used on safes, etc., with numbered dials which must be turned in a special order a certain number of times to open it; **combination room** at Cambridge, a fellows' common room; **combined operations** (*mil.*) operations in which army, navy and air force work together; **combine harvester** a combined harvesting and threshing machine. [L. *combīnāre,* to join — *com-, bīnī,* two and two.]

comble *kõ-bl′,* (Fr.) *n.* the acme.

combo. See under **combine.**

Combretum *kom-brē′təm, n.* a tropical and subtropical genus of trees and shrubs noted for the beauty of their flowers, giving name to the **Combretā′ceae,** a family akin to the myrtles: (without *cap.*) a plant of the genus. [L. *combrētum,* an unknown plant.]

combs *komz.* Short for **combinations.**

comburgess *kom-bûr′jis, n.* a fellow-burgess.

combust *kom-bust′, adj.* burnt by the sun (*obs.*): in conjunction with the sun, or apparently very near it, so as to be obscured by its light, said of a planet when it is not more than $8\frac{1}{2}°$ from the sun. — *n.* that which is burnt. — *v.t.* to burn up. — *n.* **combustibil′ity.** — *adj.* **combust′ible** liable to take fire and burn: excitable. — *n.* anything that will take fire and burn. — *ns.* **combust′ibleness** quality of being combustible; **combust′ion** (*-yən*) a burning: the action of fire on combustible substances: confusion, turmoil: oxidation or analogous process with evolution of heat. — *adjs.* **combust′ious** (*Shak.*) combustible, inflammable: turbulent; **combust′ive** disposed to take fire. — **spontaneous combustion** burning caused by heat generated in the substance itself. [L. *combūrĕre, combūstum,* to consume — *com-,* intens., *ūrĕre,* to burn.]

come *kum, v.i.* to move toward the place that is the point of view (the opposite of *go*): to draw near: to arrive at a certain state or condition: to issue: to happen: to yield (*Shak.*): to become: to turn out: to amount (to): to reach: to begin to be in some condition: to achieve a sexual orgasm, to ejaculate (*slang*): to be had, got, gained: (only *3rd pers. sing.;* esp. in *subj.*) when (a certain time) comes (as in *Come five o'clock, I shall be exhausted*). — *v.t.* (*coll.*) to act the part of, assume the behaviour of, as in *Don't come the innocent with me:*

(with *it*) to try to impress, assert one's authority over, etc.: — *pr.p.* **com′ing;** *pa.t.* **came** *kām;* *pa.p.* **come.** — *interj.* (or *imper.*) expressive of encouragement, protest, or reproof (often in phrases **come come, come now).** — *n.* **com′er** (*Spens.* **comm′er**) one who comes or has come: one who shows promise; **com′ing** arrival or approach: (esp. with *cap.*) the Advent, or the hoped-for return (also **Second Coming**) of Christ. — *interj.* or *pr.p.*, used as a promise of attention. — *adj.* future: of future importance: ready to make or meet advances (*arch.*). — **come′-and-go′** passage to and fro. — *adj.* **come-at′-able** accessible. — **come′-back** a return, esp. to a former good, popular, successful, etc., state: a revival: a retort: cause or ability to complain; **come′down** a descent: a disappointment: a degradation; **come-hith′er** an invitation to approach: allure. — *adj.* of a look, manner, etc., inviting. — **come′-off** a conclusion: an evasion of duty; **come′-on** encouragement, esp. sexual: persuasion; **come′-o′-will** something that comes of its own accord: an illegitimate child (also **come′-by-chance**); **come(-)up(p)′ance** (*coll.*) deserved rebuke or punishment. — *n.pl.* **com′ings-in′** income. — **all comers** anyone that likes; **as they come** as they are made, as they are to be had, as they turn up; **come about** to happen; **come across** see **across; come again?** (*slang*) what did you say?: pardon?; **come and go to** fluctuate: to have freedom of action; **come at** to reach: to attack; **come away** to become detached; **come back** to return to popularity, office, etc.: to retort; **come by** to come near: to pass: to obtain: to come in; **come down** to descend: to be reduced: to lose esp. financial status; **come down upon** to be severe with; **come down with** to pay down: to become ill with (a disease); **come for** to arrive in order to collect: to attack; **come forward** to identify oneself (to the police, etc.); **come high, low** to cost much, little; **come home** to return to one's house: to touch one's interest or feelings closely (with *to*): to drag or slip through the ground — of an anchor (*naut.*); **come in** to enter: to reply to a radio signal or call: to give in, to yield: to get within the opponent's guard (*fencing; Shak.*); **come in for** to receive as, or as if as, one's share: to receive incidentally; **come into** to fall heir to; **come it strong** (*coll.*) to do or say much, go to great lengths, exaggerate; **come of** to descend from: to be the consequence of, arise from: to become of; **come of age** to reach full legal age; **come off** to come away: to become detached: to turn out: to escape: to pay up (*Shak.*): to desist from: to prove successful; **come off it!** (*coll.*) don't be ridiculous!; **come on** to advance: to thrive: to proceed: to begin: often in *imper.* as a challenge or invitation to attack; **come on stream** of oil-wells, to start regular pumping (also *fig.*); **come on strong** (*coll.*) to speak or act forcefully or aggressively; **come out** to result: to be published: to become known or evident: to enter society: to declare openly one's homosexuality (*slang*): to stop work, strike: to declare oneself (against or in favor of); **come out with** to utter: to exclaim; **come over** to surpass (*Shak.*): to befall: to come into the mind of: to overreach (*slang*): to experience a certain feeling (*coll.*); **come round** to come by a circuitous path: to happen in due course: to veer: to become favourable: to recover from a faint, etc.; **come short** to fail; **come short of** to fail to attain; **come to** to obtain: to amount to: to recover consciousness; **come to grief** to meet with disaster; **come to oneself** to return to normal state of mind; **come to pass** to happen; **come to stay** to become permanent; **come true** to be fulfilled; **come under** to be included under; **come undone, unfastened,** etc. to become detached, loose, etc.; **come up to** present itself in discussion, etc.; **come up against** to encounter (an obstacle, difficulty); **come upon** to attack: to affect: to hold answerable: to meet; **come up with** to overtake: to suggest; **give someone the come-on** to invite or entice, esp. sexually; **have it coming (to one)** (*coll.*) to have no chance of avoiding one's just deserts; **how come?** how does it happen that …?; **to come** future. [O.E. *cuman;* Ger. *kommen.*]

Comecon *kom′i-kon, n.* a Communist organisation, the Council for Mutual *Econ*omic Aid, or Assistance.

co-meddle *kō-med′l, v.t.* to mix (*obs.*): to temper (*Shak.*).

Comédie Française, La *ko-mā-dē frā-sez, la,* (Fr.) the official name of the Théâtre Français, the French national theatre; **Comédie Humaine, La** (*ü-men*) (Fr.) the human comedy — Balzac's collection of novels, planned to form a complete picture of contemporary society.

comedo *kom′i-dō, n.* a blackhead, a small, black-tipped white mass sometimes found in the sebaceous glands: — *pl.* **com′edos.** [L. *comedō, -ōnis,* glutton — *comedēre,* to eat up, from its wormlike appearance.]

comedy *kom′i-di, n.* a dramatic piece of a pleasant or humorous character: a story with a happy ending: an incident suggesting comic treatment. — *n.* **comedian** (*kə-mē′di-ən*) one who acts or writes comedies: an entertainer who tells jokes, etc. — *fem.* **comedienne** (*ko-me-, -mē-, -di-en′;* orig. French, and still often spelt **comédienne**). — *adj.* **comē′dic** (or *-mēd′-*) of or pertaining to comedy. — *n.* **comēdiett′a** a short comic piece. — **comedy of manners** satirical comedy dealing with the manners or fashions of a social class. [Fr. *comédie* — L. *cōmoedia* — Gr. *kōmōidiā* — *kōmos,* revel, or *kōmē,* village, *ōidē,* song.]

comely *kum′li, adj.* pleasing: graceful: handsome. — *adv.* in a comely manner. — *n.* **come′liness.** [Conn. O.E. *cȳmlic* — *cȳme,* suitable, *lic,* like.]

comestible *kom-est′ibl, adj.* eatable. — *n.* (usu. in *pl.*) food. [Fr., — L. *comedēre,* to eat up.]

comet *kom′it, n.* a heavenly body with a very eccentric orbit, having a definite nucleus, a nebulous light surrounding the nucleus, and commonly a luminous tail turned away from the sun. — *adjs.* **com′etary; cometic** (*-et′ik*). — *ns.* **cometog′raphy; cometol′ogy.** — **com′et-finder** a telescope of low power used to search for comets. [Gr. *komētēs,* long-haired — *komē,* hair.]

comether *kəm-edh′ər,* (*dial.*) *n.* wheedling: charm. [come **hither,** a call to cows, etc.]

comfit *kum′fit, n.* a sweetmeat: a sugar-coated seed or almond. — *n.* **com′fiture** (*obs.*) conserve. [A doublet of **confect;** Fr. *confit, confiture.*]

comfort *kum′fərt* (Spens. *kom-fort′*), *v.t.* to strengthen (*obs.*): to relieve from pain or distress: to soothe, cheer. — *n.* relief: encouragement: ease: quiet enjoyment: freedom from annoyance: whatever gives ease, enjoyment, etc.: a subject of satisfaction: a bed quilt (*U.S. coll.*). — *adj.* **com′fortable** imparting or enjoying comfort: easy (*fig.*): having enough money to live well. — *adv.* **com′fortably.** — *n.* **com′forter** one who administers comfort: the Holy Ghost (*B.; A.V.*): a long narrow woollen scarf: a dummy teat: a bed quilt (*U.S.*). — *adj.* **com′fortless.** — *n.* **com′fortlessness.** — *adj.* **com′fy** (*coll.*) comfortable. — **cold comfort** little, if any, comfort; **comfort station** (*U.S.*) a (public) lavatory. [O.Fr. *conforter* — L. *con-,* intens., and *fortis,* strong.]

comfrey *kum′fri, n.* a rough boraginaceous plant (*Symphytum*). [O.Fr. *confirie.*]

comic *kom′ik, adj.* relating to comedy: raising mirth: droll. — *n.* the quality or element that arouses mirth: an actor of droll parts: a humorous entertainer on stage, in clubs, on TV, etc.: an amusing person (*coll.*): a paper or magazine, esp. for children, with illustrated stories, strip cartoons, etc. (orig. comic, later also serious, even horrific; also **comic book**). — *adj.* **com′ical** funny. — *ns.* **comical′ity, com′icalness.** — *adv.* **com′ically.** — *n.* **comique** (*kō-mēk′*) a comic actor or singer. — **comic strip** a strip cartoon. [See **comedy.**]

Cominform *kom′in-förm, n.* the Communist *Inform*ation Bureau (1947–56), which succeeded the Comintern. — *n.* **Com′informist.**

Comintern *kom′in-tûrn, n.* the Communist *Intern*ational (1919–43), or Third International (see under **international**).

comitadji. Same as **komitaji.**

comitatus *kom-i-tā′təs, n.* a prince's escort: a county or shire. — *adjs.* **com′ital** relating to a count, earl, or county; **com′itative** of a grammatical case, expressing accompaniment. — *n.* a comitative case. [L. *comitātus, -ūs* — *comes, -itis,* companion, count.]

comitia *ko-mish′i-ə, ko-mi′ti-a, n.pl.* the assemblies of the Romans for electing magistrates, passing laws, etc. — **comitia centuriata** (*sen-tū-ri-ā′ta, ken-tōō-ri-ä′ta*) the assembly of Roman people, voting by centuries; **comitia curiata** (*kū-ri-ā′ta, kōō-ri-ä′ta*) that of the patricians, voting by curiae; **comitia tributa** (*tri-bū′ta, tri-bōō′ta*) that of the people, voting by tribes. [L., — *com,* together, *īre, itum,* to go.]

comity *kom′i-ti, n.* courteousness: civility. — **comity of nations** (*comitas gentium*) the international courtesy by which effect is given (within limits) to the laws of one state within the territory of another state: a group of nations adhering to this code of behaviour. [L. *cōmitās, -ātis* — *cōmis,* courteous.]

comma *kom′a, n.* a phrase (*rhet.; Shak.*); in punctuation, the point (,) that marks the smallest division of a sentence: the smallest interval, break, discontinuity: hence perh. (*Shak.*) a connecting link: a name for various minute intervals, esp. the difference between twelve perfect fifths and seven octaves (*mus.*). — **comma bacillus** the micro-organism that causes cholera; **comma (butterfly)** a nymphaline butterfly (Polygonia) with a white comma-shaped mark on the under side of the hind-wing; **inverted commas** a set of double or single superscript commas used to introduce and close a quotation, the introductory one(s) being inverted (". .", ′. .′). [L., — Gr. *komma,* a section of a sentence, from *koptein,* to cut off.]

command *kəm-änd′, v.t.* to order: to bid: to exercise supreme authority over: to demand: to cause to act (*Shak.*): to exact (*Shak.*): to have within sight, range, influence, or control. — *v.i.* to have chief authority: to govern. — *n.* an order: authority: control: power to overlook, influence or use: the thing commanded: a military division under separate control: ability or understanding: in a remote-control guidance system, a signal activating a mechanism or setting in motion a sequence of operations by instruments: a command paper. — *ns.* **commandant** (*kom-ən-dant′*) an officer who has the command of a place or of a body of troops; **commandant′ship.** — *v.t.* **commandeer′** to compel to military service, or seize for military use (orig. *Cape Dutch*): to take arbitrarily. — *ns.* **command′er** one who commands: an officer in the navy next in rank under a captain: a high-ranking police officer in charge of a district: a member of a higher class in an order of knighthood: a district administrator in religious military orders: the highest ranking officer in the Royal Society for the Prevention of Cruelty to Animals; **command′ership; command′ery** the district under a commander, esp. in the religious military orders. — *adj.* **command′ing** fitted to impress or control: strategic. — *adv.* **command′ingly.** — *ns.* **command′ment** a command: a precept; **command′o** a military party (*S. Afr.* from *Port.*): a unit of a special service raiding brigade equivalent to a battalion (*mil.*): one serving in such a unit: — *pl.* **command′os.** — **command′er-in-chief′** the officer in supreme command of an army, or of the entire forces of the state; **command module** the part of a spacecraft from which operations are directed; **command paper** one laid before Parliament, theoretically by command of the crown; **command performance** a performance by royal command; **command post** a military unit's (temporary) headquarters. — **at command** available for use; **commander of the faithful** a title of the caliphs; **on commando** on military service in the field; **ten commandments** the ten Mosaic laws: the fingernails, esp. a woman's (*Shak.*). [Fr. *commander* — L.L. *commandāre* (L. *commendāre*) — L. *mandāre,* to entrust.]

commeasure *kəm-ezh′ər, v.t.* to equal in measure: to coincide with. — *adj.* **commeas′urable** same as **commensurable.**

commedia dell′arte *ko-mā′dē-a de-lär′te,* (It.) guild com-

edy, Italian Renaissance comedy, mainly improvised and with stock characters, performed by a guild of professional actors.

comme il faut *ko-mēl-fō,* (Fr.) as it should be: correct: approved by the fashionable world: genteel.

Commelina *kom-ə-lī′nə, n.* a tropical genus of monocotyledons, giving name to the fam. **Commelinaceae** (*-li-nā′si-ē*). [After the Dutch botanists Johannes (1629–72) and Caspar (1667–1731) *Commelin.*]

commemorate *kəm-em′ə-rāt, v.t.* to call to remembrance by a solemn or public act: to celebrate: to preserve the memory of. — *adj.* **commem′orable.** — *n.* **commemorā′tion** preserving the memory of some person or thing, esp. by a solemn ceremony: the specification of individual saints in the prayers for the dead: the great festival of the Oxford academic year, usually taking place on the third Wednesday after Trinity Sunday. — *adjs.* **commem′orative, commem′oratory** tending or serving to commemorate. — *n.* **commem′orātor.** [L. *commemorāre, -ātum,* to remember — *com-,* intens., and *memor,* mindful.]

commence *kəm-ens′, v.i.* to begin: to originate: to take rise. — *v.t.* to begin: to originate: to enter upon: to take a university degree (as *commence M. A.; rare*). — *n.* **commence′ment** the beginning: at certain universities the act of taking the degrees: the ceremony when these are conferred (esp. *U.S.*). [O.Fr. *com(m)encier* — L. *com-,* intens., and *initiāre,* to begin — *in,* into, and *īre,* to go.]

commend *kəm-end′, v.t.* to commit as a charge: to recommend as worthy: to praise: to adorn, set off (*obs.*). — (*Shak.*) *n.* a greeting: praise. — *adj.* **commend′able.** — *n.* **commend′ableness.** — *adv.* **commend′ably.** — *ns.* **commend′am** (L.L. accus.) an ecclesiastical benefice held, or the tenure or grant of a benefice held, *in commendam,* i.e. theoretically till a pastor was provided for it, but often for life and without duties; **commendation** (*kom-ən-dā′shən*) the act of commending, esp. of commending the dying or dead to the favour and mercy of God: praise: declaration of esteem; **comm′endator** one who holds a benefice *in commendam:* a titular abbot, etc.: the head of a commandery. — *adj.* **commend′atory** commending: containing praise or commendation: presenting to favourable notice or reception: held, or holding, *in commendam.* — **commend me to** (*arch.*) remember me kindly to: give me by preference. [L. *commendāre* — *com-,* intens., and *mandāre,* to trust.]

commensal *ka-men′səl, adj.* eating at the same table: living together for mutual benefit (*biol.*): esp. an association of less intimate kind than that called symbiosis. — *n.* a messmate: an organism living in partnership (not parasitism) with another. — *ns.* **commen′salism; commensal′ity.** — *adv.* **commen′sally.** [L. *com-,* together, *mēnsa,* a table.]

commensurable *kəm-en′shə-rə-bl, -sū-, adj.* having a common measure: capable of being measured exactly by the same unit: in due proportion. — *ns.* **commensurabil′ity; commen′surableness.** — *adv.* **commen′surably.** — *adj.* **commen′surate** equal in measure or extent: in due proportion. — *adv.* **commen′surately.** — *ns.* **commen′surateness; commensurā′tion.** [L. *com-, mēnsūra,* a measure — *mētīrī, mēnsus,* to measure.]

comment *kom′ənt, -ent, n.* a note conveying illustration or explanation: a remark, observation, criticism. — *v.i.* (or *kəm-ent′*) to make critical or explanatory notes (on): to annotate: to meditate (*Shak.*). — *v.t.* to say in comment: to expound (*Spens.*). — *n.* **comm′entary** a comment: a remark: a series or book of comments or notes: a continuous description of a sport, event, etc., as it is filmed or broadcast on television or radio (also **running commentary**). — *v.i.* **comm′entate** to give a running commentary. — *ns.* **commentā′tion** annotation; **comm′entātor** one who comments: the writer of a commentary: a broadcaster of a running commentary. — *adj.* **commentatō′rial** (*-tō′*) pertaining to the making of commentaries. — *n.* **comm′enter, -or** (or

-ment'). — **no comment** (coll.) I have nothing to say (usu. to a newspaper or television reporter). [L. commentārī, to devise, contrive — com- and L. mēns, mentis, the mind.]

commer (Spens.). See **come**.

commerce kom'ûrs, n. interchange of merchandise on a large scale between nations or individuals: extended trade or traffic: intercourse. — v.i. **commerce** (kəm-ûrs') to trade: to have communication (with). — adj. **commer'cial** (-shl) pertaining to commerce: mercantile: having profit as the main aim (sometimes implying disregard of quality): commercially viable. — n. a commercial traveller: (formerly) a commercially-sponsored programme on radio or TV: an advertisement in such a programme: a commercial vehicle. — n. **commercialese'** business jargon. — v.t. **commer'cialise, -ize** to reduce to a branch of commerce: to subject to the commercial spirit: to turn (something) into a source of profit (often derog.). — ns. **commer'cialism** the commercial spirit: an expression characteristic of commercial language; **commer'cialist; commerciality** (-shi-al'i-ti). — adv. **commer'cially.** — **commercial room** a room in a hotel set apart for commercial travellers; **commercial traveller** an accredited travelling representative of a trading house; **commercial vehicle** generally, a goods-carrying vehicle: by some, understood to include passenger-carrying vehicles such as buses. [Fr., — L. commercium — com-, mutual, merx, mercis, merchandise.]

commère kom-er', n. fem. of **compère**. [Fr., godmother; cf. **cummer**.]

commerge kə-mûrj', v.i. to merge together.

commie kom'i, (coll.) n. and adj. a contraction for **communist**.

comminate kom'in-āt, v.t. to threaten. — n. **commina'tion** threatening, denunciation: a recital of God's threatenings made on Ash Wednesday and at other times in the English Church. — adjs. **comm'inative, comm'inatory** threatening punishment. [L. comminārī, -ātum - com-, intens., and minārī, to threaten.]

commingle kəm-ing'gl, v.t. and v.i. to mingle or mix together. — adj. **comming'led.**

comminute kom'in-ūt, v.t. to reduce to minute particles: to pulverise. — n. **comminū'tion. — comminuted fracture** see **fracture**. [L. comminuĕre, -ūtum, to break into pieces — com-, intens., minuĕre, to make small — root of minus, less.]

Commiphora kom-if'ər-ə, n. a genus of plants of the family Burseraceae, natives of tropical Asia and Africa, yielding myrrh, bdellium, and other resins. [Gr. kommi, gum, phoreein, to bear.]

commis ko'mē, n. an agent, deputy: an apprentice waiter, steward or chef (also in composition, as commis-waiter, etc.). [Fr.]

commiserate kəm-iz'ər-āt, v.t. to feel or express compassion for: to pity: to condole with. — Also v.i. (often with with). — adj. **commis'erable** requiring commiseration: pitiable. — n. **commiserā'tion** pity. — adj. **commis'erative** feeling or expressing sympathetic sorrow. — n. **commis'erator.** [L. com-, with, miserāri, to deplore — miser, wretched.]

commissary kom'is-ər-i, n. one to whom any charge is committed: a deputy: the judge in a commissary court (Scots law): a higher officer of police: an officer representing a bishop, and performing his duties in distant parts of the diocese (eccles.): an officer who furnishes provisions, etc., to an army: a store supplying equipment and provisions (U.S.): (the supply of) provisions, commissariat (U.S.): a restaurant or canteen, esp. in a film studio (orig. U.S.): a commissar. — n. **commissar'** a commissary: (also **People's Commissar**) formerly, in the Soviet Union, a head of a government department (since 1946 called **minister**): (also **political commissar**) in the Soviet Union, a Communist Party official responsible for political education, encouragement of party loyalty, etc., esp. in military units. — adj. **commissā'rial** pertaining to a commissary. — ns.

commissā'riat the department charged with the furnishing of provisions, as for an army: the supply of provisions: the office of a commissary or of a commissar: a body of commissars; **comm'issaryship.** — **commissary court** a Scottish court, abolished in 1836, with jurisdiction in matters that had belonged to the bishops' courts; **commissary general** the head of the department for supplying provisions, etc., to an army. [L.L. commissārius — committĕre, commissum.]

commission kəm-ish'ən, n. the act of committing: the state of being commissioned or committed: that which is committed: an instrument conferring authority, or the authority itself, esp. that of a military, naval, or air officer, or a justice of the peace: a percentage paid to an agent: a body of persons appointed to perform certain duties: an order for a piece of work, esp. of art: (of a warship, etc.) the state of being manned, equipped, and ready for service: (of an office) temporary or permanent delegation to a number of persons who act jointly. — v.t. to give a commission to or for: to empower: to appoint: to put in commission. — v.i. to be put in commission. — n. **commissionaire** (-ār') a messenger or door-keeper in uniform: a member of a corps of former soldiers and sailors employed as door-keepers, etc. — adj. **commiss'ioned.** — ns. **commiss'ioner** one who holds a commission to perform some business: a member of a commission: the representative of high authority in a district, etc.; **commiss'ionership.** — **commiss'ion-ag'ent, -mer'chant** one who transacts business for another for a commission; **commissioned officer** one appointed by commission. — **High Commission** the embassy representing one country that is a member of the British Commonwealth in another such country; **High Commission Court** a court established in 1529 to investigate ecclesiastical cases, abolished as illegal in 1641; **High Commissioner** the chief representative in a High Commission; **in, out of, commission** (of warships) prepared, unprepared for service: in, not in, usable or working condition; **Lord High Commissioner** the representative of the crown at the General Assembly of the Church of Scotland. [See **commit**.]

commissure kom'is-ūr, n. a joint: a surface of junction· a suture: a bundle of nerve-fibres connecting two nerve-centres. — adj. **commissū'ral.** [L. commissūra, a joining; see **commit**.]

commit kə-mit', v.t. to give in charge or trust: to consign: to become guilty of, perpetrate: to compromise or involve: to pledge: — pr.p. **committ'ing**; pa.t. and pa.p. **committ'ed.** — ns. **commit'ment** the act of committing: an order for sending to prison: imprisonment: an obligation undertaken: declared attachment to a doctrine or cause; **committ'al** commitment: (the ceremony of) the placing of a coffin in a grave, crematorium furnace or the sea: a pledge, actual or implied. - adj. **committ'ed** having entered into a commitment: (of literature) written from, (of author) writing from, a fixed standpoint or with a fixed purpose, religious, political, or other. — ns. **committ'ee** a portion selected from a more numerous body (or the whole body) to which some special business is committed: (kom-i-tē') a person to whom something is committed: one charged with the care of a lunatic or imbecile (law); **committ'eeship.** — **committee stage** the stage in the passage of a bill through parliament, between the second and third readings, when it is discussed in detail in committee. — **commit oneself** to make a definite decision or judgment (on): to make a definite agreement; **Committee of the whole House** the House of Commons or other legislative body, when it resolves itself into a committee with chairman, etc.; **commit to memory** to learn by heart; **go into committee** to resolve itself into a committee; **in committee** during the deliberations of a committee. [L. committĕre — com-, with, mittĕre, to send.]

commix kə-miks', v.t. to mix together. — v.i. to mix. — ns. **commix'tion** (-chən), **commix'ture** the act of mixing together: the state of being mixed: the compound formed by mixing: the rite of putting a piece of the host into the chalice, emblematic of the reunion of body and soul at the resurrection: sexual intercourse (*obs.*).

commo *kom'ō*, (*Austr. coll.*) *n.* a communist: — *pl.* **comm'os.**

commodious *kə-mō'dyəs, adj.* suitable or convenient (*arch.*): roomy, spacious: serviceable (*Shak.*): comfortable. — *n.* **commode'** a small sideboard: an ornamental chest of drawers: a chair containing a chamberpot: a large, high head-dress formerly worn by ladies. — *adv.* **commo'diously.** — *ns.* **commo'diousness; commodity** (-*mod'*) convenience (*arch.*): profit, expediency, advantage, privilege (*Shak.*): parcel, portion (*Shak.*): an article of traffic: (in *pl.*) goods, produce. [L. *commodus* — *com-*, together, *modus*, measure.]

commodore *kom'ə-dōr, -dör, n.* an officer intermediate between an admiral and a captain: the senior captain in a fleet of merchantmen: the president of a yachtclub: a commodore's ship. [Perh. from Du. *kommandeur*.]

common *kom'ən, adj.* belonging equally to more than one: public: general: usual: frequent: ordinary: easy to be had: of little value: vulgar: of low degree. — *n.* the commonalty (*Shak.*): a tract of open land, used in common by the inhabitants of a town, parish, etc.: a right to take something from the land of another (*law*). — *v.i.* to share (*Shak.*): to converse (*Spens.*): to board (*arch.*). — *adj.* **comm'onable** held in common. — *ns.* **comm'onage** right of pasturing on a common: the right of using anything in common: a common; **commonal'ity** frequency, widespreadness: (esp. *Scot.*) the common people; **comm'onalty** the general body of the people: the common people; **comm'oner** one who is not a noble: a member of the House of Commons: at Oxford, a student who pays for his commons; **comm'oney** an ordinary playing marble. — *adv.* **comm'only** in a common manner: meanly, vulgarly: ordinarily: usually: generally: familiarly, intimately (*Spens.*): publicly (*B.*). — *n.* **comm'onness.** — *n.pl.* **comm'ons** the common people: (with *cap.*) their representatives — i.e. the lower House of Parliament or **House of Commons:** common land: food at a common table: at Oxford, rations served at a fixed rate from the college buttery: food in general, rations. — **common carrier** a person or company that deals with the transporting of goods, messages, etc. for which he or it is legally responsible; **common chord** a tone with its third (major or minor) and perfect fifth; **common debtor** (*Scots law*) a debtor who is also a creditor — the sum owed to him may be arrested (q.v.) and transferred directly to his creditor; **Common era** the Christian era; **common forms** the ordinary clauses which are of frequent occurrence in identical terms in writs and deeds; **common gender** the gender of a noun or pronoun having one form for male and female, as L. *bōs*, bull, cow, Eng. *student*; **common ground** a common subject of interest, argument, etc.; **comm'onhold** a freehold held in common by a number of owners, who have joint responsibility for managing the property (e.g. a block of flats); **common law** in England, the ancient customary law of the land; **common-law husband, wife** non-legal terms used to describe a man and woman who, because of long standing cohabitation, have come to be regarded as husband and wife; **common-law marriage** in England, any of various informal types of marriage ceremony given legal recognition till 1753, some of which if performed abroad, are still legally valid: loosely, the bond between a common-law husband and wife; **common market** an association of countries as a single economic unit with internal free trade and common external tariffs: **(European) Common Market** the common market formed in 1957 by Treaty of Rome by France, West Germany, Italy, Belgium, the Netherlands and Luxembourg; joined in 1973 by the United Kingdom, Denmark and the

Republic of Ireland, and in 1981 by Greece; **common measure** a quantity that is a measure of several quantities (*math.*): common time (*mus.*); **common metre** a four-line hymn stanza with eight syllables in first and third lines, six in second and fourth; **common noun** a name that can be applied to all the members of a class — opp. to *proper* noun. — *adj.* **comm'on-or-gar'den** ordinary. — **comm'onplace** a common topic or subject (*obs.*): a note (*obs.*): a platitude. — *adj.* lacking distinction: hackneyed. — *v.t.* to make notes of: to put in a commonplace book. — *v.i.* to platitudinise. — **commonplace book** a note or memorandum book; **comm'on-rid'ing** the Scottish equivalent of beating the bounds; **common room** in schools, colleges, etc., a room to which the members have common access; **common school** (*U.S.*) a public elementary school; **common sense** an inner consciousness unifying the five outer senses (*obs.*): average understanding: good sense or practical sagacity: the opinion of a community: the universally admitted impressions of mankind. — *adjs.* **comm'onsense'; commonsens'ical.** — **comm'on-shore'** see **shore⁴; common stair** an interior stair giving access to several independent flats or dwellings; **common time** (*mus.*) four-beat or two-beat rhythm. — **common in the soil** (*law*) the ancient right to take stone, sand, gravel and minerals from common land; **common of pasture** (*law*) the ancient right to graze animals on common land; **Common Prayer (Book of)** the liturgy of the Church of England; **Court of Common Bench, Common Pleas** one of the divisions of the High Court of Justice; **in common** together (*arch.*): together (with): shared or possessed equally; **make common cause with** to cast in one's lot with: to have the same interest and aims as; **philosophy of common sense** that school of philosophy which takes the universally admitted impressions of mankind as corresponding to the facts of things without any further scrutiny; **short commons** scant fare; **the common** that which is common or usual; **the common good** the interest of the community at large: the corporate property of a burgh in Scotland; **the common people** the people in general. [Fr. *commun* — L. *commūnis*, prob. from *com-*, together, and *mūnis*, serving, obliging.]

commonweal *kom'ən-wēl, n.* the common good, welfare of the community: commonwealth (*arch.*). — *n.* **comm'onwealth** (-*welth*) the public or whole body of the people: a form of government in which the power rests with the people, esp. that in England after the overthrow of Charles I: a state or dominion, esp. applied to the Australian federation and certain states of America: a group of states united by a strong but elastic link as *the British Commonwealth*. — **Commonwealth Day** the second Monday in March, kept as a day of celebration in the British Commonwealth; **comm'onwealth'sman, comm'onwealthsman** (*obs.*) a (good) citizen: an adherent of Cromwell's Commonwealth. [See **wealth.**]

commorant *kom'ər-ənt, n.* and *adj.* resident (esp. at a university). [L. *commorāns, -antis,* pr.p. of *commorārī,* to abide.]

commorientes *kom-mor-i-en'tēz,* (*law*) *n.pl.* persons who die together on the same occasion, where it cannot be ascertained which died first. [L.]

commot, commote *kum'ət,* (*hist.*) *n.* a subdivision of a cantred. [Mediaeval L. *commotum* — W. *cymwd.*]

commotion. See commove.

commove *kə-mōōv',* (*arch.*) *v.t.* to put in motion: to agitate: to disturb, excite. — *n.* **commotion** (-*mō'shən*) a violent motion or moving: excited or tumultuous action, physical or mental: agitation: tumult. — *adj.* **commō'tional.** [L. *com-,* intens., and *movēre, mōtum,* to move.]

commune¹ *kom'ūn, n.* a corporation: in France, etc., a small territorial division with some self-government and a mayor: in some communist countries, an agricultural community: a group of people living communally. — *adj.* **communal** (*kom'ū-nl, kə-mū'*) pertaining to a commune or a community: owned in common, shared. — *ns.* **commūnalīsā'tion, -z-.** — *v.t.* **commū'-nalise, -ize** (or *kom'*) to make communal. — *ns.* **commū'nalism; commū'nalist.** — *adv.* **comm'ūnally.** — *n.* **Comm'ūnard** (or *-ärd'*) an adherent of the Paris *Commune* in 1871: (without *cap.*) a communist: (without *cap.*) a member of a commune. — **the Commune** at Paris in 1871 was a revolt against the national government, the principle of the revolt being that each city or district should be ruled independently by its own commune or local government.   [Fr. *commune*; see **common.**]

commune² *kə-mūn'*, *kom'ūn*, *v.i.* to converse or talk together: to have intercourse, esp. spiritual: to receive Holy Communion. — *n.* **comm'une** converse. — *n.* and *adj.* **commūn'ing.**   [O.Fr. *communer*, to share.]

commune bonum *ko-mū'nē bō'nəm*, *ko-mōō'ne bo'nōōm*, (L.) common good.

communibus annis *ko-mū'ni-bəs an'ēs*, *ko-mōō'ni-bōōs an'ēs*, (L.) on the annual average.

communicate *kə-mū'ni-kāt*, *v.t.* to give a share of, impart: to reveal: to bestow. — *v.i.* to have something in common with another: to have communication: to have means of passage: to have intercourse: to partake of Holy Communion: to succeed in conveying one's meaning to others. — *ns.* **commū'nicability** (*-kə-bil'i-ti*), **commū'nicableness.** — *adj.* **commū'nicable** that may be communicated (esp. of a disease): affable. — *adv.* **commū'nicably.** — *ns.* **commū'nicant** one who partakes of Holy Communion; **commūnicā'tion** an act of communicating: that which is communicated: intercourse: correspondence: a means of communicating, a connecting passage or channel: (in *pl.*) means of giving information, as the press, cinema, radio, and television: a means of transporting, esp. troops and supplies. — *adj.* **commū'nicātive** inclined to communicate or give information: unreserved. — *adv.* **commū'nicātively.** — *ns.* **commū'nicātiveness; commū'nicātor.** — *adj.* **commū'nicātory** imparting knowledge. — **communique, communiqué** (*kom-ū'ni-kā*) an official announcement. — **communicating door** a door which gives access from one room, etc. to another; **communication cord** a cord in the wall or ceiling of a railway train which can be pulled in an emergency to stop the train; **communications satellite** an artificial satellite in orbit around the earth, used to relay radio, television and telephone signals; **communication(s) theory** the theory of the transmitting of information, esp. to, from, or between machines.   [L. *communicāre*, *-ātum* — *communis*, common.]

communi consensu *ko-mū'nī kon-sen'sū*, *ko-mōō'nē kon-sen'sōō*, (L.) by common consent.

communion *kəm-ūn'yən*, *n.* act of communing: spiritual intercourse: fellowship: common possession: interchange of transactions: union in religious service: the body of people who so unite: (**Holy Communion**) sacrament commemorating the Last Supper. — **communion card** a card used esp. in the Presbyterian church to invite to, or register attendance at, Holy Communion; **commun'ion-cloth, -cup, -table** those used at a service of Holy Communion; **communion rail** the rail in front of the altar in some churches, at which the communicant kneels. — **Communion of Saints** the spiritual fellowship of all true believers, the blessed dead and the faithful living — in R.C. doctrine held to involve a mutual exchange of examples, prayers, merits and satisfactions; **take communion** to receive the bread and wine at a service of Holy Communion.   [L. *communiō*, *-ōnis*, from *communis*, common.]

communique, communiqué. See **communicate.**

communism *kom'ūn-izm*, *n.* a theory or condition of things according to which society should be classless, private property should be abolished, and land, factories, etc., collectively owned and controlled: (often with *cap.*) Marxian socialism as understood in Russia. — *v.t.* **comm'ūnise, -ize** to make common property: to make communist. — *n.* **comm'ūnist** a believer in com-

munism. — *adjs.* **comm'ūnist, commūnist'ic,** of, or pertaining to, communism: believing in or favouring communism: (**commūnistic**) of or favouring communal living and ownership.

community *kəm-ūn'i-ti*, *n.* common possession or enjoyment: agreement: communion: commonness (*Shak.*): people having common rights, etc.: the public in general: a body of persons in the same locality: a body of persons leading a common life, or under socialistic or similar organisation: a monastic body. — *adj.* of, for, or by a local community. — *n.* **communitā'rian** a member of a community. — **community centre** a place where members of a community may meet for social and other activities; **community chest** (*U.S.*) a fund of voluntary contributions for local welfare; **community college** same as **village college**; **community council** a lay body elected to look after local interests; **community home, school** successor to approved school (see **approve**); **community nurse** a nurse employed by a local health authority, e.g. a health visitor or district nurse, to visit patients in their own homes, staff various clinics, etc.; **community physician** a physician, appointed by the local health authority, with administrative responsibility for the medical and social welfare of an area; **community property** (*law*; *U.S.*, etc.) property held jointly by husband and wife; **community radio** broadcasts made from stations independent of local radio, aimed at involving people in their own community, and serving specialist groups, e.g. ethnic minorities, jazz enthusiasts, etc.; **community relations commission** a national body formed to ensure good relations between people of different races in Britain; **community school** a school that is open outside school hours for the use and recreation of the community; **community-service order** a court order by which an offender is required to do unpaid work of benefit to the community as an alternative to a prison sentence; **community singing** organised singing by a gathering; **community work** a form of social work based on the needs of local communities; **community worker.** [O.Fr. *communité* — L. *communitās*, *-ātis* — *communis*, common.]

commute *kə-mūt'*, *v.t.* to exchange: to exchange for a punishment less severe: to compound for (by a single payment, a simple or more convenient method, etc.): to change (electric current) from alternating to direct or vice versa. — *v.i.* (orig. in U.S., using a **commutation ticket,** valid for a set number of journeys at reduced fare) to travel regularly, esp. between suburban home and town office. — *n.* **commūtabil'ity.** — *adj.* **commūt'-able** that may be commuted or exchanged. — *v.t.* **commūtate** (*kom'*; *elect.*) to commute. — *n.* **commūtā'-tion** the act of commuting: change or exchange of one thing for another: the change to a lighter penalty, simpler or easier mode of payment, etc. — *adj.* **commū'-tative** (or *kom'ū-tā-tiv*) relating to exchange: interchangeable: such that $x*y = y*x$ — where * denotes a binary operation (*math.*). — *adv.* **commūtatively.** — *ns.* **comm'ūtātor** an apparatus for reversing electric currents; **commūt'er** (orig. *U.S.*) one who commutes. — **commutation ticket** (*U.S.*) a season ticket.   [L. *commūtāre* — *com-*, with, *mūtāre*, to change.]

commutual *kə-mū'chōō-əl*, *adj.* mutual, reciprocal.

comose, comous. See **coma².**

comp *komp*, *n.* contracted form of **compositor.**

compact¹ *kəm-pakt'*, *adj.* closely placed or fitted together: composed or framed: close: firm: close: brief: of a car, medium-sized and economical (*U.S.*). — *n.* **compact** (*kom'*) a compacted body or structure, a combination: a small case containing face-powder for carrying in the handbag (**powder compact**). — *v.t.* (*-pakt'*) to press closely together: to consolidate: to confirm (*Shak.*). — *adj.* **compact'ed.** — *adv.* **compact'edly.** — *n.* **compact'-edness.** — *adv.* **compact'ly.** — *ns.* **compac'tion** act of compacting, or state of being compacted: sediments compacted by pressure from above (*geol.*): an area formed by dumping rock waste, etc., pressing it together by means of heavy machines, and causing or allowing grass to grow over the whole; **compact'ness; compact'or** a machine which crushes solid waste into the ground; **compac'ture** (*Spens.*) close union or knitting together; **compact disc** (abbrev. **CD**) a small audio disc on which digitally recorded sound is registered as a series of pits that are readable by laser beam; **compact-disc player** a machine that plays compact discs by means of a laser beam. [L. *compāctus, pa.p.* of *compingĕre* — *com-, pangĕre*, to fix.]

compact² *kom'pakt, n.* a mutual bargain or agreement: a league, treaty, or union: league, in bad sense (*Shak.*). — *adj.* (*kom-pakt'*) united: leagued: agreed upon, arranged (*Spens.*). [L. *compactum* — *compacīscī*, from *com-*, with *pacīscī*, to bargain.]

compages *kəm-pā'jēz, n.* structure (also *obs.* **compage'**): — *pl.* **compa'ges.** — *v.t.* **compag'inate** to join, connect. — *n.* **compagination** (*-paj-i-nā'shən*). [L. *compāgēs, compāgināre, -ātum* — *com-* and root of *pangĕre*, to fasten.]

compagnie anonyme *kɔ̃-pa-nyē a-no-nēm,* (Fr.). Same as **société anonyme.**

compagnon de voyage *kɔ̃-pa-nyɔ̃ də vwa-yäzh,* (Fr.) travelling companion.

compander, compandor *kəm-pand'ər, n.* a system of transmitting or reproducing sound by compressing and then re-expanding the volume-range so as to produce a clearer signal by reducing the contrast. [*com*press, ex*pand*, and *-er, -or*.]

companing (*Spens.*). See **company.**

companion¹ *kəm-pan'yən, n.* one who keeps company or frequently associates with another: a partner (*obs.*): spouse (*obs.*): higher rank of servant, who, though receiving pay, stands rather in the relation of a friend: fellow, rascal (*Shak.*): a member of an order, esp. in a lower grade: one of a pair or set of things: an often pocket-sized book on a particular subject (as in *angler's companion*). — *v.t.* to accompany. — *adj.* of the nature of a companion: accompanying. — *adjs.* **pan'iable** (*obs.*) sociable; **compan'ionable** fit to be a companion: agreeable. — *n.* **compan'ionableness.** — *adv.* **compan'ionably.** — *adjs.* **compan'ionate** shared in companionship; **compan'ioned** having a companion. — *n.* **compan'ionhood.** — *adj.* **compan'ionless.** — *n.* **compan'ionship** state of being a companion: company: fellowship: a body of companions. — **companionate marriage** a form of marriage proposed in the 1920s with legalised birth-control and divorce by mutual consent; **companion set** a set of fireside implements on a stand; **companion star** a star appearing to be close to another though not necessarily near it in space, e.g. the fainter component of a double star. — **Companion of Literature, C.Litt.** an honour (instituted 1961) conferred by the Royal Society of Literature. [Fr. *compagnon*, from L.L. *compānium*, a mess — L. *com-*, with, and *pānis*, bread.]

companion² *kəm-pan'yən,* (*naut.*) *n.* the skylight or window-frame through which light passes to a lower deck or cabin: companion-ladder. — **compan'ion-hatch** the covering of an opening in a deck; **compan'ion-ladd'er** the ladder or stair leading from the deck to a cabin or to the quarter-deck; **compan'ion-way** a staircase from the deck to a cabin. [Cf. Du. *kompanje*; O.Fr. *compagne*; It. *compagna*, store-room.]

company *kum'pə-ni, n.* a person or persons associating with one: any assembly of persons, or of beasts and birds: persons associated for trade, etc.: a society: a sub-division of a regiment: the crew of a ship: a collective noun for a flock of widgeon: state of being a companion: presence in association: fellowship: social intercourse. — *adj.* belonging to, relating to, or associated with, a commercial company. — *v.t.* (*arch.*) to accompany. — *v.i.* to associate: to cohabit: — *pr.p.* **com'panying,** *Spens.* **companing;** *pa.t.* and *pa.p.* **com'-panied.** — **company promoter** one who promotes or superintends the formation of joint-stock companies. — **bad company** unsuitable, esp. criminal, companions

or associates; **good, bad, company** having, lacking companionable qualities; **in company** in the presence of other people; **keep company** to associate (with): to court; **know a man by his company** to determine his character by the quality of his friends; **part company** to separate, go different ways. [Fr. *compagnie*; same root as **companion¹**.]

compare¹ *kəm-pār', v.t.* to set together so as to ascertain how far things agree or disagree (often with *with*): to liken or represent as similar (with *to*): to give the degrees of comparison of (*gram.*). — *v.i.* to make comparison: to stand in comparison: to vie. — *n.* (*obs.*) compeer: comparison. — *n.* **comparabil'ity.** — *adj.* **comparable** (*kom'pər-ə-bl*). — *n.* **com'parableness.** — *adv.* **com'parably.** — *adj.* **comparative** (*kəm-par'ə-tiv*) pertaining to or making comparison: estimated by comparing with something else: not positive or absolute: expressing more (*gram.*; also *n.*). — *adv.* **compar'-atively.** — *ns.* **compar'ator** any device for comparing accurately, so as e.g. to detect deviations from a standard or to confirm identity; **comparison** (*-par'i-sən*) the act of comparing: capacity of being compared: a comparative estimate: a simile or figure by which two things are compared: the inflection of an adjective or adverb to express different relative degrees of its quality (*gram.*). — **comparability study** a comparison of wages, conditions, etc., in different jobs, or the same job in different areas, usu. in order to determine level of wages; **comparison microscope** a microscope in which there are two objective lenses, so that images from each can be examined side by side. — **beyond compare** without any rival or like; **compare notes** to share or exchange one's ideas. [L. *comparāre*, to match, from *com-, parāre*, to make or esteem equal. — *par*, equal.]

compare² *kəm-pār',* (*Spens.*) *v.t.* to get or provide. [L. *comparāre* — *com-*, intens., *parāre*, to prepare.]

compartment *kəm-pärt'mənt, n.* a partitioned-off or marked-off division of an enclosed space or area: a division of a railway carriage: a division of anything. — *v.t.* **compart'** to divide into parts. — *n.* **compartmentalisā'tion, -z-.** — *v.t.* **compartment'alise, -ize** to divide into categories or into units, esp. units with little intercommunication. — *adv.* **compartment'ally.** [Fr. *compartiment* — L. *com-*, intens., *partīrī*, to divide — *pars, partis*, a part.]

compass *kum'pəs, n.* a circuit or circle: space: limit: range of pitch of a voice or instrument: circumference: girth: an instrument consisting of a magnetised needle, used to find directions: (*pl.*) a pair of jointed legs, for describing circles, etc. — *v.t.* to pass or go round: to surround or enclose: to besiege: to grasp, comprehend: to bring about, accomplish, achieve, or obtain: to devise: to contrive or plot: to curve, bend (*Shak.*). — *adj.* **com'passable** capable of being compassed. — *n.* **com'passing** contrivance, design. — *adj.* **com'past** (*Spens.*) rounded. — **com'pass-card** the circular card of a compass; **com'pass-plane** a plane, convex on the underside, for smoothing curved timber; **com'pass-plant** any plant (as species of lettuce and *Silphium*) that places its leaves north and south to avoid the midday sun; **compass rose** the circular arrangement showing the principal directions on a map or chart; **com'pass-saw** one for cutting in curves; **com'pass-sig'nal** a signal denoting a point in the compass; **com'pass-tim'ber** curved timber, used for shipbuilding, etc.; **com'pass-win'dow** a semicircular bay-window. — **box the compass** see **box²; fetch a compass** to go round in a circuit. [Fr. *compas*, a circle, prob. from L.L. *compassus* — L. *com-*, intens., *passus*, a step.]

compassion *kəm-pash'ən, n.* fellow-feeling, or sorrow for the sufferings of another: pity. — *v.t.* (*arch.*) to pity. — *adjs.* **compass'ionable** pitiable; **compass'ionate** inclined to pity or mercy: merciful. — *v.t.* to have compassion for: to have pity or mercy upon. — *adv.* **compass'ionately.** — *n.* **compass'ionateness.** — **compassionate leave, discharge,** etc. leave, discharge, etc. in exceptional circumstances for personal reasons. [Fr., — L.L. *compassiō, -ōnis* — *com-*, with, *patī, passus,* to suffer.]

compatible *kəm-pat'i-bl, adj.* consistent (with), congruous: capable of co-existence: admissible in combination: able to be transplanted into another's body without rejection (*med., biol.*): able to form grafts, or capable of self-fertilisation (*bot.*): of drugs, able to be combined without untoward interaction (*chem.*): of a television system, enabling colour transmissions to be received in black and white by monochrome sets: enabling stereophonic signals to be treated as monophonic by mono equipment. — *ns.* **compatibil'ity; compat'ibleness.** — *adv.* **compat'ibly.** [Fr., — L. *com-*, with, *patī,* to suffer.]

compatriot *kəm-pāt'ri-ət,* or *-pat', n.* a fellow-countryman. — Also *adj.* — *adj.* **compatriotic** (*-ot'ik*). — *n.* **compa'triotism.** [Fr. *compatriote* — L. *compatriōta;* see **patriot.**]

compear *kəm-pēr', (Scots law) v.i.* to appear in court. — *ns.* **compear'ance; compear'ant.** [Fr. *comparoir* — L. *compārēre* — *com-*, intens., *pārēre,* to appear.]

compeer *kəm-pēr', kom'pēr, n.* an equal: a companion: an associate. — *v.t.* (*-pēr'; Shak.*) to equal. [L. *compār* — *com-*, intens., *pār,* equal.]

compel *kəm-pel', v.t.* to drive or urge on forcibly (to): to bring with urgency (*Spens.*): to oblige: to force: to obtain by hard labour: — *pr.p.* **compell'ing;** *pa.t.* and *pa.p.* **compelled'.** — *adjs.* **compell'able; compell'ing** forcing attention. [L. *com-*, intens., *pellēre, pulsum,* to drive.]

compellation *kom-pə-lā'shən, n.* style of address: an appellation. — *adj.* **compellative** (*kəm-pel'ə-tiv*). — *n.* compellation. [L. *compellāre, -ātum,* to address, freq. of *compellēre.*]

compendium *kəm-pen'di-əm, n.* a shortening or abridgement: a book or treatise containing the substance of a larger one: an epitome: an abstract: a comprehensive, generally compressed, treatise: a collection of board-games in one box: — *pl.* **-diums, -dia.** — Also **com'pend** (*old*). — *adj.* **compen'dious** short: concise, comprehensive. — *adv.* **compen'diously.** — *n.* **compen'diousness.** [L. *compendium,* what is weighed together, or saved (opp. to *dispendium,* what is weighed out or spent) — *com-*, together, *pendēre,* to weigh.]

compensate *kom'pən-sāt,* or *kəm-pen'sāt, v.t.* to make amends (for), or to recompense: to counterbalance. — *v.i.* to make up (for). — *n.* **compensā'tion** (*kom-*) act of compensating: amends, esp. financial, for loss, injury, etc., sustained: the neutralisation of opposing forces (*phys.*): payment, remuneration (*U.S.*): process of compensating for sense of failure or inadequacy by concentrating on achievement or superiority, real or fancied, in some other sphere: the defence mechanism involved in this (*psych.*). — *adjs.* **compensā'tional, com'pensātive** (or *kəm-pen'sə-tiv*), **compen'satory** (also *sā'*) giving compensation. — *n.* **com'pensātor** one who or that which compensates. — **compensation balance, pendulum** a balance-wheel or pendulum so constructed as to counteract the effect of the expansion and contraction of the metal under variation of temperature. [L. *com-*, intens., and *pēnsāre,* freq. of *pendēre,* to weigh.]

compère *kõ-per, kom'per, n.* one who introduces and interlinks items of an entertainment: — *fem.* **commère'.** — *v.t.* to act as compère to. [Fr., god-father, god-mother.]

compesce *kəm-pes', (arch. Scot.) v.t.* to restrain. [L. *compēscere.*]

compete *kəm-pēt', v.i.* to seek or strive for something in opposition to others: to contend for a prize. — *n.* **competition** (*kom-pi-tish'ən*) the act of competing: rivalry in striving for the same object: a match or trial of ability. — *adj.* **competitive** (*kəm-pet'i-tiv*) pertaining to or characterised by competition: (of e.g. price) such as to give a chance of successful result in conditions of rivalry. — *ns.* **compet'itiveness; compet'itor** one who

competes: a rival or opponent: an associate, confederate, fellow (*Shak.*). — **in competition** competing (with). [L. *competēre,* to strive together — *com-, petēre,* to seek, strive after.]

competent *kom'pi-tənt, adj.* suitable: sufficient: fit: efficient: belonging: legally qualified: legitimate. — *ns.* **com'petence, com'petency** fitness: efficiency: capacity: sufficiency: enough to live on with comfort: legal power or capacity. — *adv.* **com'petently.** [L. *competēre,* to come together, be convenient — *com-, petēre,* to seek.]

compile *kəm-pīl', v.t.* to write or compose by collecting the materials from other books: to draw up or collect: to compose: to heap up, to put or bring together (*Spens.*): to compose (in peace and rest) (*Spens.*): to pile up a score of (*cricket slang*). — *ns.* **compilā'tion** (*-pil-* or *-pīl-*) the act of compiling: the thing compiled, a usu. literary work made by gathering the material from various authors, sources, etc.; **com'pilātor** one who compiles. — *adj.* **compī'latory.** — *ns.* **compile'ment** a compilation; **compīl'er** one who compiles: a complex program which translates a whole program of computer instructions written in a program-language into machine code before the computer acts on any of the instructions in that program (*comput.*) (cf. **interpreter**). [Fr. *compiler,* prob. from L. *compīlāre* — *com-*, together, *pīlāre,* to plunder, or *pīlāre,* to pound down; influenced by **pile.**]

compital *kom'pit-əl, adj.* pertaining to crossroads, or to the intersection of leaf-veins: acutely intersecting. [L. *compita,* cross-roads.]

complacent *kəm-plā'sənt, adj.* showing satisfaction: self-satisfied, usu. with insufficient regard to problems, dangers, etc.: pleased: inclined to please (*arch.*). — *ns.* **complā'cence, complā'cency** pleasure: (self-)satisfaction: complaisance. — *adv.* **complā'cently.** [L. *complacēre* — *com-*, intens., *placēre,* to please.]

complain *kəm-plān', v.i.* (formerly also *refl.*) to express grief, pain, censure (at, about): to murmur or express a sense of injury: to accuse: to make a mournful sound: to indicate that one has an illness (with *of*). — *v.t.* to deplore: to utter as a complaint. — *n.* (*obs.* or *poet.*) complaint. — *ns.* **complain'ant** one who complains: one who raises a suit, a plaintiff (*law*); **complain'er** a murmurer: complainant. — *n.* and *adj.* **complain'ing.** — *adv.* **complain'ingly.** — *n.* **complaint'** a complaining: an expression of grief and dissatisfaction: a poem setting forth matter of grief or dissatisfaction: a representation of pains or injuries: a finding fault: the thing complained of: a grievance: a disease: an ailment. [Fr. *complaindre* — L.L. *complangēre* — L. *com-*, intens., *plangēre,* bewail.]

complaisant *kəm-plā'zənt, kom'ple-zant,* esp. form. *-zant', adj.* desirous of pleasing: obliging: facile, ready to condone. — *n.* **complais'ance** (or *kom'ple-zans,* or *-zans'*) care or desire to please, esp. in excess: an obliging civility. — *adv.* **complaisantly.** [Fr., *complaire* — L. *complacēre.*]

complanate *kom'plən-āt, adj.* flattened. — *n.* **complanā'tion.** [L. *complānāre, -ātum,* make flat.]

compleat. See **complete.**

complect *kəm-plekt', v.t.* to embrace: to interweave. — *adj.* **complect'ed** interwoven. [L. *complectī,* to embrace — *com-*, *plectēre,* to twine.]

complected. See **complexion.**

complement *kom'pli-mənt, n.* that which completes or fills up: that by which an angle or arc falls short of a right angle or quadrant: one of the parallelograms not intersected by the diagonal of a given parallelogram when it is divided into four parallelograms by straight lines through a point in the diagonal: that by which a logarithm falls short of 10: that which is added to certain verbs to make a complete predicate: that by which an interval falls short of an octave: one of two colours which together give white: full number or quantity: consummateness, completeness (*Spens.*): fullness (of the moon) (*her.*): politeness (*Spens.; Shak.*):

all members of a set not included in a given subset (*math*.): a series of proteins in blood serum that combine with antibodies to destroy antigens (*immunology*). — *v.t.* **complement** (*-ment'* or *kom'pli-mənt*) to be the complement of: to compliment (*arch*.). — *adj.* **complement'al** completing: complimental (*Shak.*). — *adv.* **complement'arily.** — *n.* **complementar'ity** a concept, first adopted in microphysics, which accepts the existence of superficially inconsistent views of an object or phenomenon e.g. which accepts a dual aspect of light (consisting of particles, as shown by certain experiments, and of waves, as shown by others). — *adj.* **complement'ary** completing: together making up a whole, right angle, ten, an octave, white: of medical treatment, therapies, etc., alternative (q.v. under **alternate**). [L. *complēmentum* — *com-*, intens., and *plēre*, to fill.]

complete *kəm-plēt'*, *adj.* free from deficiency: perfect: finished: entire: fully equipped: consummate. — Also **compleat** (*-plēt'*; *arch*.). — *v.t.* to finish: to make perfect or entire: to accomplish. — *adjs.* **complēt'able; com-plēt'ed.** — *adv.* **complete'ly.** — *ns.* **complete'ness; com-plē'tion** the fact of completing: the state of being complete: fulfilment. — *adjs.* **complēt'ive; complēt'ory** fulfilling: completing. [L. *complēre*, *-ētum*, to fill up — *com-*, intens., and *plēre*, to fill.]

complex *kom'pleks*, *adj.* composed of more than one, or of many parts: not simple: intricate: difficult. — *n.* a complex whole: a group of (repressed and forgotten) ideas or impressions to which are ascribed abnormal mental conditions and abnormal bodily conditions due to mental causes (*psychology*): loosely applied to the mental condition itself: a complex chemical substance such as a co-ordination compound (q.v.): a collection of interrelated buildings, units, etc., forming a whole, as a *sports complex.* — *v.t.* **complex'** to complicate: to combine into a complex. — *ns.* **complex'edness, com'plexness, complex'ity** state of being complex: complication. — *v.t.* and *v.i.* to make or become complex or complicated. — *n.* **complexificā'-tion.** — *adv.* **com'plexly.** — *n.* **complex'us** a complicated system: a large muscle of the back, passing from the spine to the head. — **complex number** the sum of a real and an imaginary number; **complex sentence** one consisting of a principal clause and one or more subordinate clauses. [L. *complex — com-*, together, and root of *plicāre*, to fold; see **complicate**.]

complexion *kəm-plek'shən*, *n.* disposition: colour: quality: colour or look of the skin, esp. of the face: general appearance, temperament, or texture: bodily constitution (*Shak*.): general character or nature (*fig*.). — *v.t.* to give a colour to. — *adjs.* **complex'ional** pertaining to the complexion; **complex'ioned** (*U.S.* com-plect'ed) having a certain complexion, or temperament; **complex'ionless** colourless: pale. [Fr., — L. *complexiō, -ōnis*, a combination, physical structure of body — *com-*, and *plectĕre*, to plait.]

compliance *kəm-plī'əns*, *n.* a yielding: agreement, complaisance: assent: submission (in bad sense): under the deregulated stock-market, self-policing by securities firms to ensure that the rules to prevent information passing between departments with potentially conflicting interests are being obeyed. — *adj.* **complī'able** disposed to comply. — *n.* **complī'ancy** compliance. — *adj.* **complī'ant** yielding: pliant: civil. — *adv.* **complī'antly.** [See **comply**.]

complicate *kom'pli-kāt*, *v.t.* to twist or plait together: to render complex: to entangle. — *adj.* complex: involved: folded together. — *n.* **com'plicacy** (*-kə-si*) the quality or state of being complicated. — *adjs.* **com'plicant** overlapping; **com'plicated** intricate, confused. — *n.* **complicā'tion** an intricate blending or entanglement: a complexity: (usu. in *pl.*) disease or illness starting during treatment of or recovery from an existing medical condition: something which causes or adds to difficulty or confusion. — *adj.* **com'plicātive** tending to complicate. — **complicated fracture** a fracture where

there is some other injury (e.g. a flesh wound not communicating with the fracture, a dislocation, a rupture of a large blood-vessel). — **complication of diseases** a number of diseases present at the same time. [L. *com-*, together, and *plicāre*, *-ātum*, to fold.]

complice *kom'plis*, *n.* an associate (*Shak.*): an accomplice (*obs*.). — *n.* **complic'ity** the state or condition of being an accomplice: complexity.

complied, complier. See **comply**.

compliment *kom'pli-mənt*, *n.* an expression of regard or praise: delicate flattery: an expression of formal respect or civility: a present. — *v.t.* **compliment** (*-ment'* or *kom'pli-mənt*) to pay a compliment to: to express respect for: to praise: to flatter: to congratulate: to present in compliment. — *v.i.* to make compliments. — *adjs.* **compliment'al** expressing or implying compliment; **compliment'ary** conveying, or expressive of, civility or praise: using compliments: bestowed in compliment, given free. — *n.* **compliment'er** one who pays compliments. — **compliments of the season** compliments appropriate to special times, as Christmas, etc.; **left-handed compliment** a saying intended to seem a compliment, but in reality the reverse; **pay or present one's compliments** to give one's respects or greeting. [Fr. *compliment* — L. *complīmentum*; see **comply**.]

complin, compline *kom'plin*, *n.* in the Christian liturgy, the seventh and last service of the day, at 9 p.m., completing the canonical hours. [O.Fr. *complie* (mod. *complies*) — L. *complēta* (*hōra*); *n* unexplained.]

complish *kom'plish*, (*Spens*.) *v.t.* to accomplish.

complot *kom'plot*, *n.* a conspiracy. — *v.i.* **complot'** (*kəm-*) to plot together: to conspire. — *v.t.* to plan: — *pr.p.* **complott'ing**; *pa.t.* and *pa.p.* **complott'ed.** [Fr.]

compluvium *kom-plōō'vi-əm*, *n.* a quadrangular open space in the middle of a Roman house. [L.]

comply *kəm-plī'*, *v.i.* to yield to the wishes of another: to agree or consent to (with *with*): to use ceremony (*Shak.*): — *pr.p.* **comply'ing**; *pa.t.* and *pa.p.* **complied.** — *n.* **complī'er** one who complies. — *p.adj.* **comply'ing** compliant. [It. *complire*, to fulfil, to suit, to offer courtesies — L. *complēre*, to fulfil; see **complete**.]

compo[1] *kom'pō*, *n.* a mortar of cement: a mixture of whiting, resin, and glue for ornamenting walls and cornices: a bankrupt's composition: — *pl.* **com'pos.** — **compo ration** (*mil*.) a composite 'hard' ration for use in the field when no fresh food is available. [Abbrev. of **composition**.]

compo[2] *kom'pō*, (*coll*.) *n.* compensation for industrial injuries, paid out of a central fund: — *pl.* **com'pos.** [Abbrev. of **compensation**.]

component *kəm-pō'nənt*, *adj.* making up: forming one of the elements or parts. — *n.* one of the parts or elements of which anything is made up, or into which it may be resolved. — *n.* **compō'nency.** — *adjs.* **componental** (*kom-pō-nent'l*); **componential** (*-nen'shəl*). [L. *com-pōnĕre*.]

compony, componé *kom-pō'ni*, (*her*.) *adj.* consisting of a row of squares of alternate tinctures. [Origin doubtful.]

comport[1] *kəm-pōrt', -pört', v.i.* to agree, suit (with *with*). — *v.t.* (*refl*.) to bear: to behave. — *n.* manner of acting. — *ns.* **comport'ance** (*Spens*.), **comport'ment** behaviour. [L. *comportāre — com-*, with, *portāre*, to carry.]

comport[2] *kom'pört*, **compote** *kom'pōt*, **compotier** *k3-po-tyā*, *kom-pō'*, *ns.* a dish, usu. stemmed, for serving desserts, fruit, etc. [See **compot**.]

compose *kəm-pōz', v.t.* to form by putting together or being together: to set in order or at rest: to settle or soothe: to dispose artistically: to set up for printing: to create (esp. in literature and music). — *v.i.* to write (esp.) music: to set type. — *p.adj.* **composed'** settled: quiet: calm. — *adv.* **compōs'edly.** — *ns.* **compōs'edness; compōs'er** a writer or author, esp. of music; **composition** see **composite**; **composure** (*kəm-pōzh'(y)ər*) calmness: self-possession: tranquillity: composition: temperament, character (*Shak.*). — **compōs'ing-stick** a boxlike instrument for holding type before it is placed

on the galley. [Fr. *composer* — L. *com-*, with, *pausāre*, to cease, rest; confused and blended in meaning with words from *pōnĕre, positum*, to place.]
composite *kom'pɔ-zit*, formerly *-poz'*, *adj.* made up of distinct parts or elements: (esp. with *cap.*) blending Ionic and Corinthian (*archit.*): belonging to the **Compositae** (*kɔm-poz'i-tē*), a great family akin to the bell-flowers but having small flowers crowded together in heads on a common receptacle surrounded by bracts so as to resemble single flowers: of an insurance company, etc., combining several different lines: of a proposal, etc., combining points from several sources. — *n.* a composite thing: something made up of distinct parts or diverse elements: a plant of the Compositae. — *v.t.* (*-zīt*) to pool and combine (proposals from various sources, e.g. local branches of a political party) so as to produce a satisfactory list for discussion at a higher, esp. national level. — *ns.* **com'positeness; composi'tion** the act or art of composing: the nature or proportion of the ingredients of anything: a thing composed: a work of art, esp. in music: an exercise in writing prose or verse: disposition of parts: congruity: combination: an artificial mixture, esp. one used as a substitute: mental or moral make-up: a compromise: a percentage accepted by a bankrupt's creditors in lieu of full payment: the compounding of vector quantities, as velocities, forces, into a single resultant: a picture, photograph formed from several images: the transition from a concept or assertion about individuals to one about the class to which they belong (*philos.*). — *adjs.* **composi'tional; compositive** (*-poz'*). — *n.* **compos'itor** one who sets up type. — *adj.* **compos'itous** (*bot.*) composite. — *n.* **compost** (*kom'post*), **compŏst'ure** (*Shak.*) a mixture: a manure consisting of a mixture of decomposed organic substances. — *v.t.* **com'post** to treat with compost: to convert into compost. — *n.* **com'poster** an apparatus for converting garden waste into compost. — **composite carriage** a railway carriage with compartments of different class; **composite portrait** a blend of several portraits: a photograph printed from several negatives representing different persons or the same person at different times; **composite resolution** a resolution or proposal made up from several similar resolutions and incorporating all their main points; **com'post-heap** a pile of plant refuse, soil, and often chemical fertiliser, which decomposes to form compost. — **composition of felony** compounding of felony; **metal composite** a metal with steel wires or glass fibres incorporated in it. [L. *compositus, compostus* — *com-*, together, *pōnĕre*, to place.]
compos mentis *kom'pos men'tis*, (L.) of sound mind, sane.
compossible *kɔm-pos'i-bl, adj.* possible in co-existence with something else. — *n.* **compossibil'ity.**
compost, composture. See composite.
composure. See compose.
compot, compote *kom'pot,* or *kom'pōt, n.* fruit preserved in syrup: stewed fruit. [Fr. *compote*; cf. **composite.**]
compotation *kom-pō-tā'shɔn, n.* a carouse together. — *ns.* **compotā'tionship; com'potātor** a bottle-companion. — *adj.* **compot'ātory.** [L. *compōtātiō, -ōnis* — *com-*, together, *pōtāre*, to drink.]
compote, compotier. See compot, comport[2].
compound[1] *kɔm-pownd', v.t.* to make up: to combine: to settle or adjust by agreement: to agree for a consideration not to prosecute (a felony): to intensify, make worse or greater. — *v.i.* to agree, or come to terms: to bargain in the lump. — *adj.* (*kom'*) mixed or composed of a number of parts: in chem., resolvable into two or more elements, so united that the whole has properties of its own which are not necessarily those of its constituents, as in the case of a mixture: in arith., not simple, dealing with numbers of various denominations of quantity, etc., as in *compound addition*, etc., or with processes more complex than the simple process, as in *compound proportion.* — *n.* a mass made up of a number of parts: a word made up of two or more words: a compound substance (*chem.*): a com-

pounded drug. — *n.* **compound'er.** — **compound animals** same as **colonial animals; compound engine** a condensing engine in which the mechanical action of the steam is begun in one cylinder, and ended in a larger cylinder; **compound eye** in insects, etc., an eye made up of many separate units; **compound fracture** see **fracture; compound householder** one who pays his rates in his rent, the landlord being immediately chargeable with them; **compound interest** interest added to the principal at the end of each period (usu. a year) to form a new principal for the next period; **compound interval** (*mus.*) any interval plus an octave; **compound leaf** one divided into leaflets by divisions reaching the mid-rib; **compound quantity** (*alg.*) a quantity consisting of more than one term, as *a + b*; **compound ratio** the product of ratios; **compound sentence** (*gram.*) one containing more than one principal clause; **compound time** (*mus.*) time in which each bar is made up of two or more simple measures. [O.Fr. *compundre* from L. *compōnĕre* — *com-*, together, *pōnĕre*, to place.]
compound[2] *kom'pownd, n.* an enclosure round a house or factory (in India), or for housing labourers (S. Africa). [Malay *kampong, kampung,* enclosure.]
comprador(e) *kom-prä-dōr', -dör', n.* an intermediary through whom a foreign firm trades with Chinese dealers: an agent of a foreign power. [Port., buyer — L. *com-*, intens., *parāre*, to furnish.]
comprehend *kom-prɔ-hend', v.t.* to seize or take up with the mind, to understand: to comprise or include. — *ns.* **comprehensibil'ity; comprehen'sibleness.** — *adj.* **comprehen'sible** capable of being understood. — *adv.* **comprehen'sibly.** — *n.* **comprehen'sion** power of the mind to understand: the intension of a term or the sum of the qualities implied in the term (*logic*): the inclusion of Nonconformists within the Church of England. — *adj.* **comprehen'sive** having the quality or power of comprehending or containing much: inclusive: compendious. — *n.* a comprehensive school: a detailed layout or proof. — *adv.* **comprehen'sively.** — *n.* **comprehen'siveness.** — *n.* **comprehensivīsā'tion, -z-** the act of converting schools to comprehensives. — *v.t.* **comprehen'sivise, -ize.** — **comprehensive school** a secondary school, serving a particular area, that provides education for pupils of all levels and types. [L. *comprehendĕre, -hēnsum* — *com-, prehendĕre,* to seize.]
compress *kɔm-pres', v.t.* to press together: to force into a narrower space: to condense or concentrate: to embrace (*arch.*). — *n.* (*kom'; surg.*) a pad used to apply pressure to any part: a folded cloth applied to the skin. — *adj.* **compressed'** pressed together: compacted: laterally flattened or narrowed (*biol.*). — *n.* **compressibil'ity** the property of being reduced in volume by pressure: the ratio of the amount of compression per unit volume to the compressing force applied: a shock-wave phenomenon causing increased drag, which asserts itself when an aircraft in flight approaches the speed of sound, the hypothesis of the air as an incompressible fluid being no longer valid (*aero.*). — *adj.* **compress'ible** that may be compressed. — *ns.* **compress'ibleness; compression** (*kɔm-presh'ɔn*) the act of compressing: state of being compressed: condensation: flattening: deformation by pressure: the stroke that compresses the gases in an internal-combustion engine. — *adjs.* **compress'ional; compress'ive** able to compress. — *ns.* **compress'or** anything that compresses or raises pressure, as a device that compresses air or gas: a muscle that compresses certain parts; **compressure** (*-presh'ɔr*). — **compressed air** air at more than atmospheric pressure; **compression-ignition engine** an internal-combustion engine in which ignition of the liquid fuel injected into the cylinder is performed by the heat of compression of the air charge. [L. *compressāre, com-,* together, and *pressāre,* to press — *premĕre, pressum,* to press.]
comprimario *kom-prē-mä'ri-ō, n.* in opera or ballet, a rôle of secondary importance: a singer or dancer playing

such a rôle: — *pl.* **comprimar'ios.** [It.]

comprint *kəm-print'*, *v.t.* to share in printing — of the former privilege shared with the Stationers' Company and the King's Printer by Oxford and Cambridge universities.

comprise *kəm-prīz'*, *v.t.* to contain, include: to comprehend: to consist of: to hold together (*Spens.*). — *adj.* **compris'able.** — *n.* **compris'al** the act, condition, or fact of comprising. [Fr. *compris*, pa.p. of *comprendre* — L. *comprehendĕre*; see **comprehend.**]

compromise *kom'prə-mīz*, *n.* arbitration (*Shak.*): a settlement of differences by mutual concession: partial waiving of theories or principles for the sake of settlement: anything of intermediate or mixed kind, neither one thing nor another. — *v.t.* to settle by mutual concession: to involve or bring into question: to expose to risk of injury, suspicion, censure, or scandal. — *v.i.* to make a compromise. [Fr. *compromis* — L. *comprōmittĕre*, *-missum* — *com-*, together, *prōmittĕre*, to promise.]

comprovincial *kom-prə-vin'shəl*, *adj.* belonging to the same province.

Compsognathus *komp-sog'nə-thəs*, *n.* one of the smallest known dinosaurs, lizard-hipped, bipedal and carnivorous. [Gr. *kompsos*, elegant, *gnathos*, jaw.]

compt, compter, comptible *kownt*, *-ər*, *-ə-bl*, obs. forms of **count**, etc. — *n.* **Comptometer**® (*komp-tom'*) a machine that adds, subtracts, multiplies and divides.

compte rendu *kɔ̃t rã-dü*, (Fr.) an account rendered: a report.

comptroll, comptroller. See under **control.**

compulse *kəm-puls'*, *v.t.* (*obs.*) to compel. — *adjs.* **compul'satory, compul'sative** (*Shak.*) compulsory. — *ns.* **compul'sion** the act of compelling: force: a strong irrational impulse; **compul'sionist** a believer in compulsion; **compul'sitor** (*Scots law*) a means of compelling. — *adj.* **compul'sive** with power to compel: pertaining to compulsion: (of person) driven by, (of action) caused by, a specific constant and irresistible impulse: irresistible. — *advs.* **compul'sively, compul'sorily.** — *adj.* **compul'sory** compelled: obligatory: compelling. — *n.* an exercise comprising specified compulsory figures, movements, or dances, e.g. in ice-skating. — **compulsion neurosis** a disorder in which the patient suffers from compulsions and/or obsessions, depression, etc.; **compulsory purchase** enforced purchase by a public authority of property needed for public purposes. [L. *compulsāre*, freq. of *compellere*; see **compel.**]

compunction *kəm-pungk'shən*, *n.* pricking or uneasiness of conscience (*obs.*): remorse tinged with pity. — *adj.* **compunc'tious** of the nature of compunction: feeling compunction. — *adv.* **compunc'tiously.** [O.Fr., — L. *compunctiō*, *-ōnis* — *com-*, intens., and *pungĕre*, *punctum*, to prick.]

compurgation *kom-pûr-gā'shən*, *n.* in Old English and other Germanic law, the clearing of the accused by witnesses joining their oaths to his: evidence in favour of the accused: vindication. — *n.* **com'purgator** one who testifies to the innocence or veracity of another. — *adjs.* **compurgatō'rial** (*kom-*); **compur'gatory.** [L. *compūrgāre*, to purify wholly — *com-*, intens., *pūrgāre*, to purify: taken as if meaning to clear together; see **purge.**]

compursion *kəm-pûr'shən*, (*Sterne*) *n.* a pursing together.

compute *kəm-pūt'*, *v.t.* to calculate: to number: to estimate. — *adj.* **computable** (*kom'* or *-pūt'*) calculable. — *ns.* **com'putant, com'putātor, com'putist** a calculator; **comput'er** a calculator: a machine or apparatus, mechanical, electric or electronic, for carrying out, esp. complex, calculations, dealing with numerical data or with stored items of other information: also used for controlling manufacturing processes, or co-ordinating parts of a large organisation; **computā'tion** the act of computing: reckoning: estimate: arithmetic. — *adjs.* **computā'tional** involving calculation; **com'putative** (or *-pūt'*) given to computation. — *n.* **computerese'** (*facet.*) computer language: the jargon used by people who

deal with computers. — *v.t.* **comput'erise, -ize** to bring computer(s) into use to control (operation, system of operations): to process (data) by computer. — *n.* **computerisā'tion, -z-.** — **computer-assisted** or **computed axial tomography scanner** a machine which produces X-ray pictures of sections of the body with the assistance of a computer (shortened to **CAT scanner**); **computer crime, fraud** crime such as embezzlement, perpetrated through the manipulation of company finances, etc., by computer; **computer game** a game on cassette for playing on a home computer, the player attempting to manipulate moving images on the screen by operating certain keys; **computer graphics** diagrammatic or pictorial matter produced by computer, on a screen or in printed form; **computer language** a system of alphabetical or numerical signs used for feeding information into a computer; **computer literacy.** — *adj.* **comput'er-lit'erate** competent in the use of computers. — **computer science** the sciences connected with computers, e.g. computer design, programming, data processing, etc.; **computer scientist; computer typesetting** the use of electronic equipment to process an unjustified input of keyed material into an output of justified and hypenated, etc., lines, the output being either a new tape to be used on a typesetting or filmsetting machine or, in some systems, the final product. [L. *computāre* — *com-*, intens., *putāre*, to reckon.]

comrade *kom'rid, kum'rid* (*Shak.*, *Milt.*; *-rād'*), *n.* a close companion: an intimate associate: a fellow-soldier: in some socialist and communist circles used as a term of address, or prefixed to a name: a communist (*slang*; *derog.*). — *n.* **com'radeship.** — *adj.* and *adv.* **com'radely.** [Sp. *camarada*, a roomful, a room-mate — L. *camera*, a room — Gr. *kamarā.*]

coms. See **combinations** under **combine.**

comsat. Abbrev. for *com*munications *sat*ellite.

Comsomol. Variant of **Komsomol.**

comstockery *kum'stok-ə-ri*, or *kom'*, *n.* prudery. — *ns.* **com'stocker; com'stockism.** [From Anthony *Comstock* (1844–1915), an American denunciator of the nude in art.]

Comtism *komt'izm, kɔ̃t-ēzm*, *n.* the philosophical system of Auguste *Comte* (1798–1857), the founder of Positivism. — *ns.* and *adjs.* **Comt'ian; Comt'ist.**

Comus *kō'məs*, *n.* a god of mirth (*Milt.*): (without *cap.*) a revel. [L., — Gr. *kōmos*, a revel.]

con[1] *kon*, *adv.* and *n.* a contraction of L. *contrā*, against, as in **pro and con**, for and against.

con[2] (*Spens.* **conne, kon**) *kon*, *v.t.* to know (*Spens.*): to learn (*Spens.*): to study carefully, scan, pore over: to commit to memory: to acknowledge (as *to con thanks*; *obs.*): to teach, show (*obs.*): — *pr.p.* **conn'ing**; *pa.t.* and *pa.p.* **conned**, *Spens.* **cond** (*kond*). — *ns.* **conn'er; conn'ing.** [Another form of **can**, O.E. *cunnan*, to know; perh. partly *cunnian*, to seek to know, examine. (See **conner**[2].)]

con[3], **conn** *kun, kon*, (*naut.*) *v.t.* to direct the steering of. — Also *v.i.* — *n.* the act or station of conning. — *ns.* **con'der, conner** (*kun'ər, kon'ər*) one who directs steering: a lookout on land, who signals the movements of fish to fishermen; **conn'ing.** — **conn'ing-tower** the pilothouse of a warship or submarine. [Older forms *cond*, *condue*, etc., apparently — Fr. *conduire* — L. *condūcĕre*; see **conduct.**]

con[4] *kon*, (*dial.*) *n.* a knock. [Fr. *cogner*, to knock.]

con[5] *kon*, (*slang*) *adj.* short for **confidence**, as in **con game, con trick** a swindle, **con man** a swindler, esp. one with a persuasive way of talking. — *v.t.* **con** to swindle: to trick: to persuade by dishonest means. — *n.* a trick, swindle.

con[6] *kon*, (*slang*) *n.* a prisoner. [Abbrev. of **convict.**]

con-. See **com-.**

conacre *kon'ā-kər*, *n.* the custom of letting land in Ireland in small portions for a single crop, for rent in money or labour; a form of this is still found in Eire. — Also corn'acre. — *v.t.* to sublet in conacre. — *n.* con'acreism. [corn[1], acre.]

con amore *kon am-ōr'e, -ö're*, (It.) with love: very earnestly.

conarium *kō-nā'ri-əm, n.* the pineal gland: — *pl.* conā'ria. — *adj.* conā'rial. [Gr. *kōnarion*, pineal gland, dim. of *kōnos*, cone.]

conation, conative. See conatus.

conatus *kō-nā'təs, n.* an effort: an impulse: a tendency, nisus: — *pl.* conā'tus. — *n.* conā'tion the active aspect of mind, including desire and volition. — *adj.* conative (*kon', kōn'ə-tiv*). [L. *cōnātus, -ūs*, effort.]

con brio *kon brē'ō*, (It.) with spirit.

concatenate *kən-kat'ə-nāt, v.t.* to chain or link together: to connect in a series. — *n.* concatenā'tion a series of links united: a series of things depending on each other. [L. *con-, catēna*, a chain.]

concause *kon'köz, n.* a co-operating cause.

concave *kon'kāv, kon-kāv', adj.* curved inwards (opp. to *convex*). — *n.* a hollow: an arch or vault. — *v.t.* and *v.i.* to make or become hollow. — *adv.* con'cavely (or *-kāv'*). — *n.* concavity (*kən-kav'i-ti*) the quality of being concave: a hollow. — *adjs.* concā'vō-con'cave or doub'-le-con'cave (both also *-kon-kāv'*) concave on both sides; concā'vō-con'vex (or *-kon-veks'*) concave on one side, and convex on the other. [L. *concavus*, from *con-*, intens., and *cavus*, hollow; see cave[1].]

conceal *kən-sēl', v.t.* to hide completely or carefully: to keep secret: to disguise: to keep from telling. — *adj.* conceal'able. — *n.* conceal'ment hiding: keeping secret: secrecy: disguise: hiding-place: a mystery (*Shak.*). [O.Fr. *conceler* — L. *concēlāre*, from *con-*, intens., and *cēlāre*, to hide.]

concede *kən-sēd', v.t.* to yield or give up: to admit, allow. — *v.i.* to make concession. — *n.* conced'er. [L. *concēdĕre, -cēssum* — *con-*, wholly, and *cēdĕre*, to yield.]

conceit *kən-sēt', n.* overweening self-esteem: fancy: thought (*obs.*): wit: a witty thought, far-fetched, affected or over-ingenious: idea (*Spens.*): understanding (*Shak.*): estimate. — *v.t.* (*obs.*) to conceive: to think. — *adj.* conceit'ed clever, witty (*obs.*): fantastical (*dial.*): having a high opinion of oneself: egotistical. — *adv.* conceit'edly. — *n.* conceit'edness. — *adjs.* conceit'ful (*Spens.*) thoughtful; conceit'less (*Shak.*) without conceit, stupid; conceit'y (*dial.*) characterised by conceit. — out of conceit with displeased with. [From conceive on the analogy of deceive, deceit.]

conceive *kən-sēv', v.t.* to receive into or form in the womb: to form in the mind: to imagine or think: to understand: to grasp as a concept: to express. — *v.i.* to become pregnant: to think. — *ns.* conceivabil'ity, conceiv'ableness. — *adj.* conceiv'able. — *adj.* conceiv'ably. [O.Fr. *concever* — L. *concipĕre, conceptum*, from *con-*, together, and *capĕre*, to take.]

concelebrate *kon-sel'ə-brāt, v.t.* of two or more priests, to celebrate (mass) jointly. — *ns.* concel'ebrant a priest taking part in a concelebrated mass; concelebrā'tion. [L. *con-*, together, and celebrate.]

concent *kən-sent', (arch.) n.* a harmony or concord of sounds: concert of voices. — *v.t.* (*Spens.*) to fit, adjust duly. [L. *concentus*, pa.p. of *concinĕre* — *con-*, *canĕre*, to sing.]

concentrate *kon'sən-trāt*, sometimes *kən-sen'-, v.t.* to bring towards a common centre: to focus: to direct with exclusive attention upon the matter in hand: to condense, to increase the quantity in unit space. — *v.i.* to draw towards a common centre: to direct one's thoughts or efforts towards one object. — *n.* a product of concentration. — *adj.* con'centrate concentrated. — *n.* something concentrated, as animal feed. — *n.* concentrā'tion the act of concentrating: condensation: the proportion of molecules or ions to unit volume: the keeping of the mind fixed on something. — *adj.* concen'trative tending to concentrate. — *ns.* concen'trativeness; con'centrator apparatus for concentrating solutions or for obtaining minerals from ores by

physical means. — concentration camp a settlement for segregating persons who might be in the way of, or obnoxious to, the authorities. [A lengthened form of concentre.]

concentre, (*U.S.*) concenter *kən-sent'ər, v.i.* to tend to or meet in a common centre: to be concentric. — *v.t.* to bring or direct to a common centre or point: — *pr.p.* concent'ring, -cent'ering; *pa.t.* and *pa.p.* concent'red, concent'ered. — *adjs.* concen'tric, -al having a common centre. — *adv.* concen'trically. — *n.* concentricity (*kon-sən-tris'i-ti*). [Fr. *concentrer* — L. *con-, centrum* — Gr. *kentron*, point.]

concept *kon'sept, n.* a thing conceived, a general notion: an idea, invention. — *ns.* conceptacle (*kən-sep'tə-kl*; *obs.*) a receptacle: a reproductive cavity; concep'tion the act of conceiving: the fertilisation of an ovum: the formation, or power of forming in the mind, of a concept, plan, thought, etc.: a concept: a notion: a mere fancy (*Shak.*): a plan: a thing conceived, esp. in some seaweeds; Concep'tionist a nun of an order founded in Portugal in 1489 in honour of the Immaculate Conception. — *adjs.* concep'tious (*Shak.*) fruitful; concept'ive capable of conceiving; concep'tual pertaining to conception or concepts. — *n.* conceptualisā'tion, -z-. — *v.t.* concep'tualise, -ize to form a concept of. — *v.i.* to form concepts: to think abstractly. — *ns.* concep'tualism the doctrine in philosophy that universals exist only in the mind; concep'tualist. — *adj.* conceptualis'tic. — *n.* concep'tus (*-təs*) the foetus and surrounding tissue forming in the uterus immediately on fertilization: — *pl.* concep'tuses or (erron.-formed) concep'tī (classically concep'tūs). — Conceptual Art a revolutionary type of art of the 1960s and 1970s, concentrating not so much on a completed image as on the means of producing an image or concept. [L. *concipĕre, -ceptum*, to conceive.]

concern *kən-sûrn', v.t.* to relate or belong to: to affect or interest: to involve by interest, occupation or duty: to implicate: to make uneasy: to trouble. — *n.* that which concerns or belongs to one: affair: business: interest: regard: anxiety: a business establishment: in Quaker terminology, a spiritual directive to act in a given matter. — *n.* concern'ancy (*Shak.*, in burlesque) bearing, relevancy. — *adj.* concerned' interested: involved: taking an active interest in current social, etc., problems: troubled: under the influence of liquor, drunk (*obs.*). — *adv.* concern'edly. — *n.* concern'edness. — *prep.* concern'ing regarding: about. — *n.* concern'ment concern: importance. — as concerns as regards. [L. *concernĕre*, to distinguish, later to have respect to — *con-*, intens., *cernĕre*, to distinguish.]

concert *kon'sərt, n.* union or agreement in any undertaking: harmony: musical harmony: a musical entertainment. — *v.t.* (*kən-sûrt'*) to frame or devise together: to arrange, adjust. — *n.* concertante (*kon-sər-tan'tē*; It. *kon-cher-tän'te*) a symphonic composition with parts for solo instruments. — *adj.* providing an opportunity for brilliant virtuosity by an instrumentalist. — *adj.* concerted (*-sûrt'*) mutually planned: arranged in parts (*mus.*). — *n.* concertina (*kon-sər-tē'nə*) a musical instrument consisting of a pair of bellows, usually hexagonal, the sounds produced by free vibrating reeds of metal, as in the accordion. — *v.i.* to collapse or fold up like a concertina. — *ns.* concertino (*kon-chər-tē'nō*) a short concerto: — *pl.* concerti'nos; concerto (*kon-chûr'tō*) a composition for solo instrument(s) and orchestra in sonata form: applied by the older composers to various combinations and forms: — *pl.* concer'tos. — con'cert-goer a habitual attender of concerts; con'cert-grand a grand piano suitable for concerts; con'cert-hall; con'cert-master (*U.S.* or as a translation of Ger. *Konzertmeister*) the leader of an orchestra; concerto grosso a musical work in which solo parts are played by a small group of instruments, usu. alternating with strings or an orchestra; concert overture a piece of music like an overture, but composed specially to be played at a concert; concert party a group of often amateur performers of musical entertainment, recitations, sketches, etc.: an arrangement by which a number of people buy shares separately to use them later as one holding; **concert pitch** a standard of pitch that has varied (see **international concert pitch, French pitch**): also *fig.* — **in concert** working or conspiring together: performing at a concert. [It. *concertare*, to sing in concert, perh. — L. *con-, certāre*, to strive.]

concession *kən-sesh'ən, n.* the act of conceding: the thing conceded: a grant: in Canada, a piece of land granted by the government: the grant of such land: the right, granted under government licence, to drill for oil or gas in a particular area. — *adj.* **concessible** (*-ses'*). — *n.* **concession(n)aire'** one who has obtained a concession. — *adj.* **concess'ionary.** — *n.* **concess'ionist.** — *adj.* **concess'ive** implying concession. — **concession road** in Canada, a road running between concessions. [See **concede.**]

concetto *kon-chet'tō, n.* an ingenious turn of expression: a conceit: — *pl.* **concet'ti** (*-tē*). — *ns.* **concet'tism** the use of concetti; **concet'tist.** [It., — L. *conceptum*, conceit.]

conch *kongk, konch, n.* the name for various marine gasteropods, esp. chank and Strombus, and for their shells: a shell used as a trumpet, as by the Tritons: a poor white or other native of the Bahamas or Florida Keys (from their feeding on conchs): a concha: a shell-like device for kneading and mixing chocolate during manufacture: — *pl.* **conchs** (*kongks*), **conches** (*kon'chiz*). — *n.* **conch'a** in archit., the semi-dome of an apse: the apse itself: the outer ear, or its cavity: — *pl.* **conchae** (*kong'kē, -chē*). — *adjs.* **conch'ate, conch'iform** shaped like a shell, esp. one valve of a bivalve shell; **conchif'erous** having a shell: shelly. — *v.t.* **conche** (*kongk, konch*) to knead and mix (chocolate) during manufacture. — *ns.* **conchī'tis** inflammation of the concha; **conch'oid** a plane curve, $(x^2 + y^2)(x - a)^2 = l^2x^2$, the locus of a point making with a fixed straight line a constant intercept on the ray of a pencil through a fixed point. — *adjs.* **conchoid'al** pertaining to a conchoid: shell-like, applied to a fracture like that seen in glass (*min.*); **concholog'ical.** — *ns.* **conchol'ogist; conchol'ogy** the study of molluscs and their shells. [L. *concha* — Gr. *konchē*, a cockle or mussel; Sans. *śankha*, a shell; conn. with **chank, cockle².**]

conchy, conchie *kon'shi*, (*slang*) *n.* a conscientious objector: an overconscientious person (*Austr.*).

concierge *kɔ̃-si-erzh', n.* a warden: a janitor: a porter or a portress. [Fr.; ety. unknown.]

conciliar *kən-sil'i-ər, adj.* pertaining to an ecclesiastical council. — Also **concil'iary.** [L. *concilium*, council.]

conciliate *kən-sil'i-āt, v.t.* to gain, or win over: to reconcile, bring together (esp. opposing sides in an industrial dispute). — *v.i.* to make friends. — *adj.* **concil'iable** (*obs.*). — *n.* **concilia'tion** the act of conciliating. — *adj.* **concil'iātive** (or *-ā-tiv*). — *n.* **concil'iātor.** — *adj.* **concil'iātory.** [L. *conciliāre, -ātum — concilium*, council.]

concinnity *kən-sin'i-ti, n.* harmony: congruity: elegance. — *adj.* **concinn'ous** elegant: harmonious. [L. *concinnus*, well adjusted.]

concipient *kən-sip'i-ənt, adj.* conceiving. — *n.* **concip'iency.** [L. *concipiēns, -entis*, pr.p. of *concipĕre*, to conceive.]

concise *kən-sīs', adj.* cut short: brief. — *v.t.* (*Milt.*) to mutilate. — *adv.* **concise'ly.** — *ns.* **concise'ness** the quality of being concise: terseness; **concision** (*-sizh'ən*) mutilation: circumcision (*B.*): conciseness. [L. *concīsus*, pa.p. of *concīdĕre — con-*, intens., *caedĕre*, to cut.]

conclamation *kon-klə-mā'shən, n.* a shout of many together. [L. *conclāmātiō, -ōnis*.]

conclave *kon'klāv, n.* a private room (*obs.*): the room in which cardinals meet to elect a pope: the body of cardinals: any close assembly. — *n.* **con'clāvist** an attendant on a cardinal in conclave. [L. *conclāve — con-*, with, *clāvis*, a key.]

conclude *kən-klōōd', v.t.* to enclose (*arch.*): to include (*obs.*): to restrain or debar (*obs.*): to close: to end: to decide: to settle or arrange finally: to infer. — *v.i.* to end: to form a final judgment: to state the object sought (*Scots law*). — *p.adj.* **conclud'ed** finished: settled. — *adj.* **conclud'ing** final, closing. — *n.* **conclu'sion** (*-zhən*) the act of concluding: the end, close, or last part: inference: judgment: an experiment (*obs.*): a problem, a riddle (*Shak.*). — *adjs.* **conclusive** (*-klōō'siv*), **conclu'sory** final: convincing. — *adv.* **conclus'ively.** — *n.* **conclus'iveness.** — **in conclusion** finally; **jump to conclusions** see **jump; try conclusions** to experiment: to engage in a contest (with). [L. *conclūdĕre, conclūsum — con-*, intens., *claudĕre*, to shut.]

concoct *kən-kokt', v.t.* to digest: to prepare or mature: to make up or put together: to plan, devise: to fabricate. — *ns.* **concoct'er, concoct'or; concoc'tion** the action of concocting: ripening: preparation of a medical prescription, etc.: a made-up story. — *adj.* **concoct'ive.** [L. *concoquĕre, concoctum — con-*, together, and *coquĕre*, to cook, to boil.]

concolor *kon'kul-ər, adj.* of uniform colour. — Also **concol'orate, concol'orous.** [L., — *con-*, together, *color*, colour.]

concomitant *kən-kom'i-tənt, adj.* accompanying: conjoined: occurring along with, because of, or in proportion to, (something else). — *n.* one who or that which accompanies. — *ns.* **concom'itance, concom'itancy** the state of being concomitant. — *adv.* **concom'itantly.** [L. *con-*, intens., *comitāns, -antis*, pr.p. of *comitārī*, to accompany — *comes*, a companion.]

concord *kon'körd*, or *kong'-, n.* the state of being of the same heart or mind: harmony: agreement: a combination of sounds satisfying to the ear. — *v.i.* **concord'** (*kən-*) to agree: to harmonise. — *n.* **concord'ance** agreement: an index of the words or passages of a book or author. — *adj.* **concord'ant** harmonious, united. — *adv.* **concord'antly.** — *n.* **concord'at** a pact or agreement, esp. between the pope and a secular government. — *adj.* **concor'dial** harmonious. [Fr. *concorde* — L. *concordia — concors*, of the same heart, from *con-, cor, cordis*, the heart.]

concorporate *kən-kör'pər-āt*, (*arch.*) *v.t.* to unite in one body. — *adj.* united in the body.

concours *kɔ̃-kōōr*, (Fr.) *n.* a contest, competition. — **concours d'élégance** (*dā-lā-gãs*) a competition among cars in which marks are allotted for appearance, not speed.

concourse *kon'kōrs, kong', -körs, n.* the assembly of persons or things running or drawn together: concurrence of an officer who has the legal right to grant it (*Scots law*): a large hall: an open space, esp. in a railway station, airport, etc. [Fr. *concours* — L. *concursus — con-, currĕre*, to run.]

concreate *kon'krē-āt*, (*arch.*) *v.t.* to create with: to create at the same time.

concremation *kon-kri-mā'shən, n.* complete burning: cremation: burning together: suttee. [L. *concremāre, -ātum — con-*, intens., *cremāre*, to burn.]

concrescence *kən-kres'əns, n.* a coalescence or growing together. — *adj.* **concresc'ent.** [L. *concrēscentia — con-, crēscĕre*, to grow.]

concrete *kon'krēt* (or *kən-krēt'*), *adj.* formed into one mass: the opposite of *abstract*, and denoting a particular thing: (*kon'*) made of concrete. — *n.* (*kon'*) a mass formed by parts growing or sticking together: a mixture of sand, gravel, etc., and cement, used in building. — *v.t.* (*-krēt'*) to form into a solid mass: (*kon'*) to cover or fix with concrete. — *v.i.* (*-krēt'*) to harden. — *adv.* **concrēte'ly** (or *kon'*). — *ns.* **concrēte'ness** (or *kon'*); **concrētion** (*-krē'shən*) a mass concreted: a nodule or lump formed within a rock by materials rearranging themselves about a centre (*geol.*): a solid mass formed within an animal or plant body, whether by deposition or by accumulation of foreign matter. — *adj.* **concrē'tionary.** — *n.* **concretrisā'tion, -z-.** — *v.t.* **con'cretise, -ize** to render concrete, realise. — *n.* **con'cretism** re-

garding, representing, abstract things as concrete. —
n., *adj.* **con'cretist.** — *adj.* **concrēt'ive** having power to
concrete. — **concrete jungle** (*facet.*) an area of bleakly
ugly esp. high-rise buildings; **concrete mixer** a machine
with a large revolving drum for mixing concrete;
concrete music see **musique concrète**; **concrete poetry**
an art form which seeks to introduce a new element
into poetry by means of visual effects such as the
arrangement of letters on the printed page; **concrete
steel** reinforced concrete. [L. *concrētus* — *con-*,
together, and *crēscĕre, crētum* to grow.]
concrew *kon-krōō'*, (*Spens.*) *v.i.* to grow together. [Fr.
concrû, pa.p. of *concroître* — L. *concrēscĕre.*]
concubine *kong'kū-bīn, n.* one (esp. a woman) who cohabits without being married. — *n.* **concubinage** (*kon-
kū'bin-āj*) the state of living together as man and wife
without being married. — *adj.* **concū'binary.** — *ns.*
concū'bitancy a custom by which marriage between
certain persons is obligatory; **concū'bitant** one subject
to such an obligation. — Also *adj.* [Fr., — L.
concubīna — *con-*, together, *cubāre*, to lie down.]
concupiscence *kən-kū'pis-əns, n.* a violent desire: sexual
appetite: lust. — *adjs.* **concū'piscent; concū'piscible.**
[L. *concupīscentia* — *concupīscĕre* — *con-*, intens.,
cupĕre, to desire.]
concupy *kon*(g)*'kū-pi*, (*Shak.*) *n.* a shortened form of
concupiscence (or perh. of **concubine**).
concur *kən-kûr'*, *v.i.* to run together: to meet in one point:
to coincide: to act together: to agree: to assent: — *pr.p.*
concurr'ing; *pa.p.* **concurred'.** — *ns.* **concurrence** (*-kur'*)
the meeting of lines in one point: coincidence: joint
action: assent: competition (*arch.*); **concurr'ency.** —
adj. **concurr'ent** meeting in the same point: running,
coming, acting, or existing together: coinciding: accompanying. — *n.* one that concurs: a competitor
(*arch.*): one who accompanies a sheriff's officer as
witness. — *adv.* **concurr'ently.** — *adj.* **concurr'ing** agreeing. [L. *concurrĕre* — *con-*, *currĕre*, to run.]
concuss *kən-kus'*, *v.t.* to disturb: to shake: to overawe
(*arch.*): to coerce (*arch.*). — *n.* **concussion** (*-kush'*) the
state of being shaken: a violent shock caused by the
sudden contact of two bodies: a violent blow, esp. on
the head: the resulting injury to the brain, causing
temporary loss of consciousness: any undue pressure
or force exerted upon anyone. — *adj.* **concuss'ive**
having the power or quality of concussion. [L.
concussus, pa.p. of *concutĕre* — *con-*, together, *quatĕre*,
to shake.]
concyclic *kon-sī'klik*, (*geom.*) *adj.* lying on the circumference of the same circle. — *adv.* **concy'clically.** [L.
con-, together, Gr. *kyklos*, wheel.]
cond. See **con².**
condemn *kən-dem'*, *v.t.* to pronounce guilty: to censure
or blame: to sentence: to give up to some fate: to
pronounce unfit for use: to reject. — *adj.* **condemnable**
(*-dem'nə-bl*) blamable. — *n.* **condemnation** (*kon-dəm-
nā'shən*) the state of being condemned: the act of
condemning. — *adj.* **condem'natory** expressing or implying condemnation. — *p.adj.* **condemned'** pronounced to be wrong, guilty, or useless: belonging or
relating to one who is sentenced to punishment (e.g.
condemned cell): declared dangerous or unfit. [L.
condemnāre, from *con-*, intens., and *damnāre*, to hurt.]
condense *kən-dens'*, *v.t.* to reduce to smaller compass: to
render more dense or more intense: to reduce to a
denser form, as vapour to liquid: to subject to condensation (*chem.*). — *v.i.* to become condensed. — *n.*
condensabil'ity. — *adj.* **condens'able.** — *v.t.* and *v.i.*
condens'ate to condense. — *n.* a product of condensation. — *ns.* **condensā'tion** (*kon-*) the act of condensing:
the union of two or more molecules of the same or
different compounds with the elimination of water,
alcohol, or other simple substances (*chem.*): loosely
applied to almost any reaction in which a product of
higher molecular weight than the reactant is obtained;
condens'er an apparatus for reducing vapours to a
liquid form: a mirror or lens for focusing light: a

capacitor; **condens'ery** a condensed-milk factory. —
condensation trail see **contrail; condensed milk** milk
reduced by evaporation, and sugared; **condensed type**
printing type of narrow face. [L. *condēnsāre* — *con-*,
intens., and *dēnsus*, dense.]
conder. See **con³.**
condescend *kon-di-send'*, *v.i.* to descend willingly from a
superior position: to act graciously to inferiors: to
deign: to stoop to what is unworthy: to comply (*obs.*):
to agree, consent (*obs.*). — *v.t.* to concede or grant
(*obs.*): to specify (*Scot.*). — *n.* **condescend'ence** condescension: an articulate statement annexed to a summons, setting forth the allegations in fact upon which
an action is founded (*Scots law*). — *adj.* **condescend'ing**
gracious to inferiors: offensively patronising. — *adv.*
condescend'ingly. — *n.* **condescen'sion.** — **condescend
upon** to specify: to mention. [L. *con-*, intens., and
dēscendĕre, to descend — *dē*, down from, *scandĕre*, to
climb.]
condiddle *kən-did'l*, (*Scott*) *v.t.* to steal. [L. *con-*, intens.,
and **diddle.**]
condign *kən-dīn'*, *adj.* well merited (usu. of punishment):
worthy, deserving (*Spens.*). — *adv.* **condign'ly.** — *n.*
condign'ness. [L. *condīgnus* — *con-*, intens., *dīgnus*,
worthy.]
condiment *kon'di-mənt, n.* a seasoning. — *v.t.* to season.
[L. *condīmentum* — *condīre*, to preserve, to pickle.]
condisciple *kon-di-sī'pl, n.* a fellow-disciple: a schoolfellow: a fellow-student. [L. *con-*, together, and
disciple.]
condition *kən-dish'ən, n.* the state in which things exist: a
good or fit state: a particular manner of being: quality:
rank (as *a person of condition*): prerequisite: temper
(*obs.*): a term of a contract: (in *pl.*) circumstances: that
which must precede the operation of a cause (*logic*):
a provision upon which an obligation depends (*law*):
obligation of passing a future examination to make
up a deficiency (*U.S.*). — *v.i.* to make terms. — *v.t.* to
agree upon: to restrict, limit: to determine: to put into
the required state: to allow to proceed in an education
course on condition of passing a future examination
(*U.S.*): to prepare, train (person, animal) for a certain
activity or for certain conditions of living: to secure
by training (a certain behavioural response to a stimulus). — *adj.* **condi'tional** depending on conditions:
expressing condition. — *n.* **conditional'ity.** — *adv.*
condi'tionally. — *v.t.* **condi'tionate** (*obs.*) to condition:
to qualify. — *adj.* **condi'tioned** having a certain condition, state, or quality: circumstanced: depending: relative — the opposite of *absolute*: subject to condition.
— *ns.* **condi'tioner** a person, substance, or apparatus
that brings something into good or required condition;
condi'tioning. — conditioned reflex, response a reflex
response to a stimulus which depends upon the former
experience of the individual; **conditioning house** an
establishment in which the true weight, length, and
condition of articles of trade and commerce are determined scientifically. — **in, out of, condition** in good,
bad, condition: physically fit, unfit. [L. *condicio*
(wrongly *conditiō*), *-ōnis*, a compact — *condīcĕre*, —
con-, together, *dīcĕre*, to say.]
condole *kən-dōl'*, *v.i.* to grieve with another: to express
sympathy in sorrow: to grieve (*Shak.*). — *adj.* **condol'-
atory** expressing condolence. — *ns.* **condole'ment, condol'ence** an expression of sympathy with another's
sorrow. — *adj.* **condol'ent.** [L. *con-*, with, *dolēre*, to
grieve.]
con dolore *kon do-lō're, -lö're*, (It.) with grief.
condom *kon'dom* or *-dəm', n.* a contraceptive rubber
sheath. [Perh. from the name of the inventor in the
18th cent.]
condominium *kon-do-min'i-əm, n.* joint sovereignty: a
country whose government is controlled by two or
more other countries: a block of flats in which each
flat is separately owned (*U.S.*): such a flat (*U.S.*). [L.
con-, together, *dominium*, lordship.]
condone *kən-dōn'*, *v.t.* to forgive: to pass over without

blame, overlook: to excuse, atone for. — *n.* **condonā'-tion** (*kon*-) forgiveness: such forgiveness granted by the injured party as may be urged against divorce for adultery (*law*). [L. *con*-, intens., *dōnāre*, to give; see **donation**.]

condor *kon'dör, -dər, n.* a large South American vulture. [Sp. *cóndor* — Quechua *cuntur*.]

condottiere, *kon-dot-tyā'rā, n.* a leader of a mercenary band of military adventurers: — *pl.* **condottie'ri** (*-rē*). [It., — *condotto*, way — L. *condūcĕre*, to assemble — *con*-, together, and *dūcĕre*, to lead.]

conduce *kən-dūs', v.i.* to help to bring about, contribute (towards a result): app., to go on, conduct itself, or poss. to assemble (*Shak.*). — *n.* **conduce'ment** (*Milt.*). — *adjs.* **conduc'ible, conduc'ive** leading or tending: having power to promote: advantageous: favourable to or helping towards something. — **conducive to** helping towards or encouraging. [L. *con*-, together, *dūcĕre*, to lead.]

conduct *kən-dukt', v.t.* to lead or guide: to convey (water, blood, sap, etc.): to direct: to manage: to behave: to carry or transmit (*elect.*): to beat time for and co-ordinate (*mus.*): — *n.* (*kon'dukt*), the act or method of leading or managing: guidance: escort: guide: management: behaviour. — *ns.* **conduct'ance** a conductor's power of conducting electricity, the reciprocal of the resistance; **conductibil'ity**. — *adj.* **conduct'ible** capable of conducting heat, etc.: capable of being conducted or transmitted. — *n.* **conduc'tion** act or property of conducting or transmitting: transmission by a conductor, as heat. — *adj.* **conduct'ive** having the quality or power of conducting or transmitting. — *ns.* **conductiv'ity** the power of transmitting heat, electricity, stimuli: a substance's specific power of conducting electricity, conductance across a unit cube, reciprocal of the resistivity; **conduct'or** the person or thing that conducts: a leader: a manager: a director of an orchestra or choir: one in charge of a bus, etc.: a railway guard (*U.S.*): that which has the property of transmitting electricity, heat, etc.: — *fem.* **conduct'ress; conduct'orship** the office of conductor; **conduct'us** a style of choral composition of the 12th and 13th cents., monophonic or polyphonic, orig. processional: — *pl.* **conduc'tī.** — **conducted tour** a sightseeing tour led by a guide; **conductor rail** a rail which transmits electricity to an electric train. [L. *conductus* — *condūcĕre*. See **conduce.**]

conduit *kon'dit,* or *kun'*, also *kon'dū-it, -dwit n.* a channel or pipe conveying water or other fluid, or covering electric wires, etc.: a fountain for supplying the public with water. [Fr. *conduit* — L. *conductus* — *condūcĕre, to lead.*]

conduplicate *kən-dūp'li-kāt* or *-dōōp', adj.* folded together lengthwise. [L. *conduplicāre, -ātus,* to double — *con*-, and *duplex,* double.]

condyle *kon'dil, -dīl, n.* a protuberance at the end of a bone serving for articulation with another bone. — *adjs.* **con'dylar, con'dyloid.** — *n.* **condylō'ma** an overgrowth of skin about the mucous passages: — *pl.* **condylō'mata.** — *adj.* **condylō'matous.** [Gr. *kondylos,* knuckle.]

cone *kōn, n.* an infinite solid figure generated by a straight line passing through a fixed point and intersecting some curve in space: esp. (*right circular cone*) one generated by revolution of a triangle about one of its sides: a portion of such a figure terminated at the vertex: a surface generated by a line one point of which is fixed and one point of which describes a fixed plane curve: anything shaped like a cone: a form of weather signal: a tapering part of a machine, as a race for ball-bearings: a volcanic hill: a fan of alluvium where a torrent is checked at the foot of a declivity or in a lake: the typical flower (or fruit) or inflorescence of the Coniferae, a more or less conical mass of scale-like sporophylls set closely about an axis: a similar structure in other plants, e.g. horsetails: a sensory body in the retina: an ice-cream cornet: one of a series of plastic cone-shaped bollards placed round obstacles, etc. in the road in order to divert traffic. — *v.t.* to shape like a cone. — *v.i.* to bear cones. — *adjs.* **conic** (*kon'ik*), **-al** having the form of or pertaining to a cone. — *n.* a conic section. — *adv.* **con'ically.** — *n. sing.* **con'ics** the geometry of the cone and its sections. — *adj.* **cō'niform** in the form of a cone. — *adj.* **cone'-in-cone'** (*petrology*) showing a series of cones, one within another. — **cone shell** a Gasteropod mollusc of a family (*Conidae*) with substantial conical shells; **cone wheat** a bearded variety of wheat; **conic section** a figure made by the section of a cone by a plane. — **cone off** to close off (e.g. one carriage-way of a motorway) with cones. [Gr. *kōnos.*]

coney. See **cony.**

confabulate *kən-fab'ū-lāt, v.i.* to chat (*coll.* **confab'**): to imagine experiences to compensate for loss of memory (*psych.*). — *adjs.* **confab'ūlar; confab'ūlatory.** — *ns.* **confabūlā'tion** (*coll.* **confab'** (or *kon'*)); **confab'ūlātor.** [L. *cōnfābulārī* — *con*-, *fābulārī,* to talk.]

confarreation *kən-far-i-ā'shən, n.* a Roman patrician mode of marriage, in which a spelt cake was offered up. — *adj.* **confarr'eāte.** [L. *cōnfarreātiō* — *con*-, with, *fār,* spelt.]

confect *kon'fekt, n.* fruit, etc., prepared with sugar: a sweetmeat: a comfit. — *v.t.* (*kən-fekt'*) to prepare: to preserve. — *n.* **confec'tion** composition, compound: a composition of drugs (*obs.*): a sweetmeat: a ready-made article of dress for women's wear. — *v.t.* to make (into a confection). — *n.* **confec'tionary** a confectioner (*B.*): a sweetmeat: a place where confections are made or kept. — *adj.* pertaining to or of the nature of confectionery. — *ns.* **confec'tioner** one who makes or sells sweets; **confec'tionery** confectioners' work or art: sweetmeats in general. [L. *cōnficĕre, cōnfectum,* to make up together — *con*-, *facĕre,* to make.]

confederate *kən-fed'ər-āt, adj.* leagued together: allied (esp. the seceding American states of the Civil War). — *n.* one united in a league: an ally: an accomplice. — *v.i.* and *v.t.* to league together or join in a league. — *n.* **confed'eracy** a league or mutual engagement: persons or states united by a league: a conspiracy: (*cap.*; *U.S. hist.*) the league of eleven seceding states in the Civil War. — *adj.* **confed'eral** belonging, or pertaining, to a confederation. — *n.* **confederā'tion** a league: alliance, esp. of princes, states, etc.: an association of more or less autonomous states united permanently by a treaty. — *adj.* **confed'erātive** of or belonging to a federation. [L. *cōnfoederāre, -ātum* — *con*-, *foedus, foedĕris,* a league.]

confer *kən-fûr', v.t.* to give or bestow: to compare (*obs.*) — in use as abbrev. **cf.** — *v.i.* to talk or consult together: — *pr.p.* **conferr'ing;** *pa.t.* and *pa.p.* **conferred'.** — *ns.* **conferee'** (*kon*-) one conferred with: one on whom something is conferred: one taking part in a conference; **conference** (*kon'*) the act of conferring: an appointed meeting for instruction or discussion: (with *cap.*) a kind of pear. — *n.* **con'ferencing** participation in discussion by computer terminal, teleconferencing. — *adj.* **conferential** (*kon-fər-en'shl*). — *n.* **confer'ment** bestowal: a thing bestowed. — *adj.* **conferr'able.** — *n.* **conferr'er.** — **in conference** attending a meeting: engaged. [L. *cōnferre* — *con*-, together, *ferre,* to bring.]

conférence *kõ-fā-räs,* (Fr.) *n.* a lecture. — *n.* **conférencier** (*-rā-syā*) a lecturer.

Conferva *kon-fûr'və, n.* a genus of freshwater algae (*Heterocontae*) forming slimy masses or tufts of unbranched filaments: (without *cap.*) an alga of the genus — often loosely applied to any filamentous alga: — *pl.* **confer'vae** (*-vē*). — *adj.* **confer'void** like conferva. [L. *cōnferva,* a kind of water-plant.]

confess *kən-fes', v.t.* to acknowledge fully (esp. something wrong): to own or admit: to make known, as sins to a priest: to hear a confession from, as a priest: to reveal, betray, or make manifest (*poet.*). — *v.i.* to make confession. — *ns.* **confession** (*kən-fesh'ən*) acknowledgment of a crime or fault: avowal: the thing confessed:

a statement of religious belief: acknowledgment of sin to a priest (*auricular confession*): a religious body of common belief; **confess'ional** the seat or enclosed recess where a priest hears confessions: the institution of confession. — *adj.* pertaining to confession. — *ns.* **confess'ionalism; confess'ionalist.** — *adj.* **confess'ionary** of or belonging to confession. — *n.* a confessional. — *ns.* **confess'or** (or *kon'*) a priest who hears confessions and grants absolution: one who makes avowal, esp. of religious faith: one who endures persecution but not death: — *fem.* **confess'oress; confess'orship.** — *adjs.* **confessed', confest'** admitted: avowed: evident. — *advs.* **confess'edly, confest'ly.** — **confession of faith** a formulary embodying the religious beliefs of a church or sect: a creed; **confess to** to admit, acknowledge; **stand confessed** to be revealed. [Fr. *confesser* — L. *cōnfitērī, cōnfessus* — *con-*, sig. completeness, and *fatērī,* to confess — *fārī,* to speak.]

confetti *kən-fet'i, kon-fet'tē, n.pl.* sweetmeats or comfits: plaster or paper imitations of them flung in carnival: bits of coloured paper flung at brides and bridegrooms. — **confetti money** paper money which is virtually worthless, esp. as a result of acute inflation. [It. (sing. *confetto*); see **comfit, confect.**]

confide *kən-fīd', v.i.* to trust wholly or have faith (with *in*): to impart secrets to someone with trust (with *in*). — *v.t.* to entrust: to impart with reliance upon secrecy. — *ns.* **confidant** (*kon-fi-dant'*) one confided in or entrusted with secrets, esp. in love affairs: a bosom friend: — *fem.* **confidante'; confidence** (*kon'fi-dəns*) firm trust or belief: faith: trust in secrecy: self-reliance: firmness: boldness: presumption: admission to knowledge of secrets or private affairs: a confidential communication; **con'fidency.** — *adj.* **con'fident** trusting firmly: having full belief: assured: bold. — *n.* a confidential friend. — *adj.* **confidential** (*-den'shl*) given in confidence: admitted to confidence: private. — *n.* **confidential'ity.** — *advs.* **confiden'tially; con'fidently.** — *n.* **confid'er** one who confides. — *adj.* **confid'ing** trustful. — *adv.* **confid'ingly.** — *n.* **confid'ingness.** — **confidence trick** a swindler's trick, whereby a person is induced to hand over money as a mark of confidence in the swindler; **confident person** (*Scots law*) a confidential person, partner, agent, etc. [L. *cōnfīdĕre* — *con-*, sig. completeness, and *fīdĕre,* to trust.]

configuration *kən-fig-ū-rā'shən, n.* external figure or shape: outline: relative position or aspect, as of planets: spatial arrangements of atoms in a molecule (*chem.*): Gestalt, the organised whole (*psych.*): a computer system, esp. as a complex of physical components. — *adj.* **configura'tional.** — *vs.t.* **config'urate, config'ure** to shape. [L. *cōnfigūrāre,* to form.]

confine *kon'fīn, n.* a border, boundary, or limit — generally in *pl.*: (*kən-fīn'*) confinement (*arch.*): a prison (*Shak.*). — *v.t.* **confine'** to border (*obs.*): to be adjacent to (*obs.*): to limit, enclose: to imprison. — *adjs.* **confin'able; confined'** limited: imprisoned: narrow; **confine'less** (*Shak.*) without bound: unlimited. — *ns.* **confine'ment** the state of being shut up: restraint: imprisonment: accouchement; **confin'er** one within the confines (*obs.*): an inhabitant (*Shak.*). — *adj.* **confin'ing** bordering: limiting. — **be confined** to be limited: to be restrained to bed or indoors in childbirth. [L. *cōnfīnis,* bordering — *con-*, together, *fīnis,* the end.]

confirm *kən-fûrm', v.t.* to strengthen: to fix or establish: to ratify: to verify: to assure: to admit to full communion. — *adj.* **confirm'able.** — *ns.* **con'firmand** a candidate for confirmation; **confirmā'tion** a making firm or sure: convincing proof: the rite by which persons are admitted to full communion in many churches: ratification by a competent court of the appointment of an executor, constituting his right to act (*Scots law*). — *adj.* **confirm'ative** tending to confirm. — *n.* **con'firmator.** — *adjs.* **confirm'atory** giving additional strength to: confirming; **confirmed'** settled: inveterate. — *ns.* **confirmee'** one to whom a confirmation is made; **confirm'er; confirm'ing; confirm'or.** [O.Fr. *confermer*

— L. *cōnfirmāre* — *con-*, intens., and *firmāre* — *firmus,* firm.]

confiscate *kon'fis-kāt,* (*obs.*) *kən-fis', v.t.* to appropriate to the state, as a penalty: to take possession of by authority. — *adj.* forfeited. — *adjs.* **con'fiscable** (or *-fis'*); **confiscatory** (*kon'fis-kā-tər-i* or *kən-fis'kə-tər-i*) of the nature of confiscation. — *ns.* **confiscā'tion** the act of confiscating, **con'fiscātor** one who confiscates. [L. *cōnfiscāre, -ātum* — *con-*, together, *fiscus,* a basket, purse, treasury.]

confiserie *kō-fēs-ə-rē,* (Fr.) *n.* a confectionery. — *n.* **confiseur** (*kō-fēs-œr*) a confectioner.

confit *kon'fit, n.* (*obs.*). Same as **comfit.**

confiteor *kon-fit'i-ör, n.* a form of prayer or confession used in the Latin Church. [L. *cōnfiteor,* I confess.]

confiture *kon'fit-ūr, n.* (*obs.*). Same as **comfiture.**

confix *kən-fiks', (Shak.) v.t.* to fix firmly. [L. *cōnfīgĕre, -fīxum* — *con-,* intens., *fīgĕre,* to fix.]

conflagrate *kon'flə-grāt, v.t.* and *v.i.* to burn up. — *adj.* **conflāg'rant** (*Milt.*) burning. — *n.* **conflagrā'tion** a great burning or fire. [L. *cōnflagrāre* — *con-*, intens., and *flagrāre,* to burn; see **flagrant.**]

conflate *kən-flāt', v.t.* to fuse: to combine (two variant readings of a text) into one. — *n.* **conflā'tion.** [L. *cōnflāre, -ātum,* to blow together — *con-*, and *flāre,* to blow.]

conflict *kon'flikt, n.* violent collision: a struggle or contest: a battle: a mental struggle. — *v.i.* (*kən-flikt'*) to fight: contend: to be in opposition: to clash. — *adj.* **conflict'ing** clashing: contradictory. — *n.* **conflic'tion.** — *adj.* **conflict'ive** tending to conflict. — **in conflict** incompatible, or irreconcilable (with). [L. *cōnflīgĕre, -flīctum* — *con-*, together, and *flīgĕre,* to strike.]

confluence *kon'floō-əns, n.* a flowing together: a meeting-place, as of rivers: a concourse: the act of meeting together. — *adj.* **con'fluent** flowing together: running into one: uniting. — *n.* a stream uniting and flowing with another. — *adv.* **con'fluently.** — *n.* **con'flux** (*-fluks*) a flowing together. [L. *cōnfluĕre* — *con-*, together, *fluĕre, fluxum,* to flow.]

conform *kən-förm', v.t.* to make like or of the same form: to adapt. — *v.i.* to be or become of the same form: to comply: to obey. — *adj.* and *adv.* (*Scot.*) in conformity. — *n.* **conformabil'ity** state of being conformable. — *adj.* **conform'able** corresponding in form: suitable: compliant: in unbroken continuity of bedding (*geol.*). — *adv.* **conform'ably.** — *adj.* **conform'al** of a map, representing small areas in their true shape. — *ns.* **conformā'tion** particular form, shape, or structure: adaptation; **conform'er, conform'ist** one who conforms, esp. to the worship of the Established Church; **conform'ity** likeness: compliance: consistency: conformability (*geol.*). — **conformal transformation** see **transformation; conformation theory** the theory of the structure of molecules, particularly of the arrangement of atoms in very complex molecules. — **in conformity with** in accordance with. [L. *cōnfōrmāre* — *con-*, *fōrmāre* — *fōrma,* form.]

confound *kən-fownd', v.t.* to overthrow, defeat: to mingle so as to make the parts indistinguishable: to confuse, fail to distinguish: to throw into disorder: to defeat in argument: to perplex: to astonish: used in the imperative as a mild curse: — *pa.p.* (*Spens.*) **confound'.** — *adj.* **confound'ed** confused: astonished: consummate, egregious (a term of disapprobation; *coll.*). — *advs.* **confound'edly** (*coll.*) hatefully, shamefully: cursedly; **confound'ingly** astonishingly. — **confound you** a gentle execration or curse. [O.Fr. *confondre* — L. *cōnfundĕre, -fūsum* — *con-*, together, *fundĕre,* to pour.]

confraternity *kon-frə-tûr'ni-ti, n.* a brotherhood: clan: brotherly friendship. [L. *con-*, *frāter,* brother.]

confrère *kō-frer, n.* a colleague: a fellow-member or associate. — *n.* **confrérie** (*kō-frā-rē*) a brotherhood. [Fr., — L. *con-*, together, *frāter,* a brother.]

confront *kən-frunt', v.t.* to come or be face to face with: to face in opposition: to bring face to face: to compare. — *ns.* **confrontā'tion** (*kon-*), **confront'ment** the bringing of people face to face: continued hostile attitude, with hostile acts but without declaration of war. — *adj.* **confrontā'tional** involving, causing, etc. confrontation. — *n.* **confrontā'tionism** the favouring of confrontation as a political means. — *n.* and *adj.* **confrontā'tionist.** — *adj.* **confronté** (*kon-frunt'ā*) (*her.*) face to face. [Fr. *confronter* — L. *con-*, together, and *frōns, frontis*, forehead; see **front**.]

Confucian *kən-fū'shyən, adj.* of or belonging to *Confucius*, the Chinese philosopher (551–479 B.C.). — *ns.* **Confū'cianism; Confū'cianist.**

con fuoco *kon foo-ök'ō, kon fwō'kō,* (It.; *mus.*) with fire.

confuse *kən-fūz', v.t.* to pour or mix together so that things cannot be distinguished: to throw into disorder: to perplex: to fail to distinguish. — *v.i.* to be confused. — *adj.* **confu'sable, confu'sible** liable to be confused. — Also *n.* — *adj.* **confused'** perplexed: disordered. — *adv.* **confu'sedly** in a confused manner: disorderly. — *ns.* **confu'sedness** state of being confused: disorder; **confu'sion** (*-zhən*) the state of being confused: disorder: shame: overthrow: perdition: perplexity: embarrassment: turmoil. [See **confound**.]

confute *kən-fūt', v.t.* to prove to be false: to refute: to bring to naught. — *adj.* **confūt'able.** — *n.* **confūtā'tion** (*kon-*). — *adj.* **confūt'ative** tending to confute. — *n.* **confute'ment.** [L. *cōnfūtāre*.]

conga *kong'gə, n.* a Cuban dance in which dancers follow a leader, usu. in single file: music for it. — Also *v.i.* — **conga drum** a narrow drum beaten with the hands. [Amer. Sp., Congo.]

congé *kɔ̄-zhā,* **congee** *kon'ji, ns.* a bow: dismissal: leave to depart. — *v.i.* to take leave: to bow. — **congé d'élire** (*dā-lēr';* Fr.) permission to elect: the crown's formal permission to a dean and chapter to elect a certain person as bishop. [Fr. *congé* — L. *commeātus*, leave of absence — *com-*, together, *meāre*, to go.]

congeal *kən-jēl', v.t.* to freeze: to change from fluid to solid by cold: to solidify, as by cold. — *v.i.* to pass from fluid to solid, as by cold: to stiffen: to coagulate. — *adj.* **congeal'able.** — *ns.* **congeal'ableness; congeal'ment, congelation** (*kon-ji-lā'shən*) the act or process of congealing: anything congealed. [L. *congelāre*, from *con-*, intens., and *gelū*, frost.]

congee. See **congé, conjee.**

congener *kon'ji-nər, n.* a person or thing of the same kind or nature: a member of the same genus: a secondary product in an alcoholic beverage that helps to determine its flavour, colour and power to intoxicate. — *adj.* akin. — *adjs.* **congeneric** (*-ner'ik*), **-al** of the same genus, origin, or nature: of the congeners of an alcoholic beverage. — *n.* **congener'ic** member of the same genus: in the manufacturing of alcoholic beverages, a congener. — *adjs.* **congenerous** (*kən-jen'ər-əs*) of the same nature or kind; **congenetic** (*kon-ji-net'ik*) alike in origin. [L. *con-*, with, and *genus, generis*, kind.]

congenial *kən-jē'ni-əl, adj.* of the same genius, spirit, or tastes: kindred, sympathetic: to one's taste: suitable. — *n.* **congēniality** (*-al'i-ti*). — *adv.* **congē'nially.** [L. *con*, with, and *geniālis*, see **genial**[1].]

congenital *kən-jen'i-təl, adj.* begotten or born with one — said of diseases or deformities dating from birth: innate. — *adv.* **congen'itally.** [L. *congenitus*, from *con-*, together, *gignĕre, genitum*, to beget.]

conger[1] *kong'gər, n.* a large sea-fish of the eel family — also **con'ger-eel'.** [L., — Gr. *gongros*.]

conger[2] *kong'gər,* (*hist.*) *n.* a company of co-operating booksellers. [Origin unknown.]

congeries *kon-jer'i-ēz, -jēr', n.* an aggregation: — *pl.* **conger'ies;** — false *sing.* **congery** (*kon'jər-i*). [L. *congeriēs* — *con-*, together, *gerĕre, gestum*, to bring.]

congest *kən-jest', v.t.* to bring together, or heap up: to accumulate: to cause congestion in. — *adjs.* **congest'ed** affected with an unnatural accumulation of blood: overcrowded: packed closely: overcharged: clogged: incapable of supporting its population; **congest'ible.** — *n.* **congestion** (*-jes'chən*) an accumulation of blood in part of the body: fullness: an overcrowded

condition. — *adj.* **congest'ive** indicating or tending to congestion. [L. *congerĕre, congestum* — *con-*, together, and *gerĕre, gestum*, to bring.]

congiary *kon'ji-ər-i, n.* a gift to the Roman people or soldiery, originally in corn, oil, etc., later in money. [L. *congiārium* — *congius*, the Roman gallon.]

conglobe *kən-glōb', v.t.* or *v.i.* to collect together into a globe or round mass. — *adj.* **conglobate** (*kon'glō-bāt, kən-glō'bāt*) formed into a globe or ball. — *v.t.* or *v.i.* to form into a globe or ball. — *n.* **conglobā'tion.** — *v.i.* **conglobūlate** (*-glob'*) to gather into a globule or small globe. — *n.* **conglobūlā'tion.** [L. *con-*, together, and *globāre, -ātum* — *globus*, a ball, globe.]

conglomerate *kən-glom'ər-it, adj.* gathered into a clew or mass: bunched: composed of pebbles cemented together (*geol.*). — *v.t.* and *v.i.* (*-āt*) to gather into a ball. — *n.* (*-it*) a conglomerate rock (*geol.*): a miscellaneous mass or collection: an industrial group made up of companies which often have diverse and unrelated interests. — *adj.* **conglomeratic** (*-at'ik; geol.*) of the nature of conglomerate. — *n.* **conglomerā'tion** the state of being conglomerated: a collection or jumble of things. [L. *conglomerāre, -ātum* — *con-*, together, and *glomus, glomeris*, a clew, akin to *globus*.]

conglutinate *kən-gloo'tin-āt, v.t.* to glue together: to heal by uniting. — *v.i.* to unite or grow together. — *adj.* **conglu'tinant.** — *n.* **conglutinā'tion** a joining by means of some sticky substance: healing. — *adj.* **conglu'tinātive** having power to conglutinate. — *n.* **conglu'tinator.** [L. *conglūtināre, -ātum* — *con-*, together, and *glūten*, glue.]

congo. See **congou.**

Congolese *kong-gōl-ēz', kong',* or, now *rare,* **Congoese** *kong-gō-ēz', ns.* a native of the Congo. — Also *adjs.*

congou *kong'goo, n.* a kind of black tea. — Also **con'go.** [Chinese *kung hu*, labour, referring to that expended in producing it.]

congratulate *kən-grat'ū-lāt, v.t.* to express pleasure in sympathy with: to felicitate: to pronounce or deem happy (esp. *refl.*). — *adjs.* **congrat'ūlable; congrat'ūlant** expressing congratulation. — *n.* a congratulator. — *ns.* **congratūlā'tion; congrat'ūlator.** — *adjs.* **congrat'ūlative, congrat'ūlatory** (or *lā'*) expressing congratulation. [L. *congrātulārī, -ātus* — *con-*, intens., *grātulārī* — *grātus*, pleasing.]

congree *kən-grē',* (*Shak.*) *v.i.* to agree together: to accord. [L. *con-*, together, and Fr. *gré*, goodwill — L. *grātus*, pleasing.]

congreet *kən-grēt',* (*Shak.*) *v.t.* to salute mutually. [L. *con-*, together, and **greet**.]

congregate *kong'grə-gāt, v.t.* to gather together: to assemble. — *v.i.* to flock together. — *p.adj.* (*Spens.*) congregated. — *p.adj.* **con'gregated** assembled: aggregated. — *ns.* **con'gregant** a member of a congregation, esp. of a Jewish congregation; **congregā'tion** the act of congregating: an assemblage of persons or things: a name given to the children of Israel (*O.T.*): a body of people actually or habitually attending a particular church: the body of Protestant Reformers in Scotland in the time of Mary: a board charged with some department of administration in the Roman Catholic Church: a name given to certain religious orders without solemn vows: an academic assembly — at Cambridge, the senate, at Oxford, the resident masters, doctors, etc., or a smaller degree-conferring body. — *adj.* **congregā'tional** pertaining to a congregation: (with *cap.*) pertaining to the Independent Church. — *ns.* **Congregā'tionalism** a form of church government in which each congregation is independent in the management of its own affairs — also called *Independency;* **Congregā'tionalist** an Independent. — **Congregation for the Doctrine of the Faith** see **Inquisition**. [L. *congregāre, -ātum* — *con-*, together, and *grex, gregis*, a flock.]

congress *kong'gres, n.* the act of meeting together: intercourse: an assembly of delegates, specialists, ambassadors, etc., for the discussion or settlement of prob-

lems: (with *cap.*) the federal legislature of the United States and of some other American republics. — *v.i.* to meet in congress. — *adj.* **congressional** (*-gresh'*). — *n.* **Con'gressman** a member of Congress, esp. of the House of Representatives: — *fem.* **Con'gresswoman.** [L. *con-*, together, and *gradi, gressus*, to step, to go.]
Congreve *kong'grēv, n.* a rocket for use in war. — **Con'greve-match** a kind of friction match. [Both poss. invented by Sir William *Congreve* (1772–1828).]
congrue *kong-grōō', v.i.* (*Shak.*) to agree. — *ns.* **con'gruence, con'gruency** the quality of being congruent: agreement: suitableness. — *adj.* **con'gruent** agreeing: suitable: congruous: of two numbers, having the same remainder when divided by a third number (*math.*): capable of coincident superposition (*geom.*). — *n.* **congru'ity** agreement, between things: consistency: fitness. — *adj.* **con'gruous** suitable: fit: consistent. — *adv.* **con'gruously.** — *n.* **con'gruousness.** [L. *congruĕre*, to run together.]
conia. See **coniine.**
conic, -al. See **cone.**
conidium *kon-id'i-əm, n.* a spore produced by abstriction, not in a sporangium: — *pl.* **conid'ia.** — *adj.* **conid'ial.** — *ns.* **conid'iophore** (Gr. *phoros,* bearing) a hypha that produces conidia; **conid'iospore** a conidium. [Gr. *konis,* dust.]
conifer *kon'* or *kōn'i-fər, n.* a member of the **Conif'erae,** an order of gymnosperms, including yews, pines, firs, etc., which typically bear cones. — *adj.* **conif'erous** cone-bearing: of the Coniferae. [L. *cōnus* (Gr. *kōnos*), a cone, *ferre,* to bear.]
coniform. See **cone.**
coniine *kō'ni-ēn, n.* a liquid, highly poisonous alkaloid ($C_8H_{17}N$) found in hemlock (*Conium*). — Also **cō'nia, cō'nine.** [Gr. *kōneion,* hemlock.]
conima *kon'i-mə, n.* the fragrant resin of a tropical American burseraceous tree (*Protium*). [Carib name.]
conine. See **coniine.**
conirostral *kōn-i-ros'trəl, adj.* having a strong conical beak. [L. *cōnus* (Gr. *kōnos*), cone, *rōstrālis* — *rōstrum,* a beak.]
conject *kən-jekt', v.i.* (*Shak.*; also as a mod. back-formation) to conjecture. — *n.* **conject'ure** a forecast: an opinion formed on slight or defective evidence or none: an opinion without proof: a guess: an idea. — *v.t.* to make conjectures regarding: to infer on slight evidence: to guess. — *v.i.* to guess. — *adjs.* **conject'urable** that may be conjectured; **conject'ural** involving conjecture: given to conjecture. — *adv.* **conject'urally.** [L. *conjicĕre, conjectum,* to throw together — *con-, jacĕre,* to throw.]
conjee, congee *kon'jē, n.* water in which rice has been boiled. — *v.t.* to starch with conjee. [Tamil *kañji.*]
conjoin *kən-join', v.t.* to join together: to combine. — *v.i.* to unite. — *adjs.* **conjoined'** united: in conjunction; **conjoint'** joined together: united. — *adv.* **conjoint'ly.** [Fr. *conjoindre* — L. *con-, jungĕre, junctum,* to join; see **join.**]
conjugal *kon'jōō-gəl, adj.* pertaining to marriage. — *n.* **conjugality** (*-gal'i-ti*). — *adv.* **con'jugally.** — **conjugal rights** the right of sexual relations with a spouse. [L. *conjugālis* — *conjux,* a husband or wife — *con-*, together, and *jugum,* a yoke.]
conjugate *kon'jōō-gāt, v.t.* to give the various inflections or parts of (a verb) (*gram.*): to unite (*biochemistry*). — *v.i.* to undergo inflection (*gram.*): to unite. — *adj.* joined: connected: coupled: occurring in pairs (*bot.*): reciprocally related: of two complex numbers, having their real parts equal and their imaginary parts equal but of opposite sign (*math.*). — *n.* a word agreeing in derivation with another word: anything conjugate with another — joined, or from same root, or reciprocally related. — *n.* **con'jugant** (*biol.*) one of a pair of cells or individuals undergoing conjugation. — *n.pl.* **Conjuga'tae** (*-tē*) class of freshwater algae reproducing by conjugation of like gametes, including desmids,

Spirogyra, etc. — *adjs.* **con'jugated** conjugate: (of atoms, groups, bonds, or the compounds in which they occur) showing a special type of mutual influence, esp. characterised by an arrangement of alternate single and double bonds between carbon atoms (*chem.*); **conjuga'tional, con'jugative** conjugate. — *n.* and *adj.* **con'jugating.** — *n.* **conjuga'tion** the act of joining: union: a connected view or statement of the inflectional forms of a verb (*gram.*): a class of verbs similarly inflected (*gram.*): temporary or permanent union of two cells or individuals preparatory to the development of new individuals esp. the union of isogametes (*biol.*): in Infusoria, an exchange of nuclear material. — **conjugate diameters** two diameters in a conic section, such that each is parallel to the tangent at the extremity of the other; **conjugate foci** see **focus; conjugate mirrors** mirrors set so that rays from the focus of one are reflected to that of the other. [L. *conjugāre, -ātum — con-*, together, and *jugāre — jugum,* a yoke.]
conjunct *kən-junkt',* or *kon', adj.* conjoined: joint. — *n.* **conjunc'tion** connection, union: combination: a word that connects sentences, clauses, and words (*gram.*): one of the aspects of the planets, when two bodies have the same celestial longitude or the same right ascension (formerly when they were in the same sign). — *adj.* **conjunc'tional** relating to a conjunction. — *adv.* **conjunc'tionally.** — *n.* **conjunctiva** (*kon-jungkt-ī'və*) the modified epidermis of the front of the eye, covering the cornea externally and the inner side of the eyelid. — *adjs.* **conjuncti'val** of the conjunctiva; **conjunc'tive** closely united: serving to unite: connective: copulative (*gram.*): of the nature of, or introduced by, a conjunction. — *adv.* **conjunc'tively.** — *ns.* **conjunc'tiveness; conjunctivitis** (*-iv-ī'tis*) inflammation of the conjunctiva. — *adv.* **conjunct'ly** conjointly: in union. — *n.* **conjunc'ture** combination of circumstances: important occasion, crisis. — **conjunctive mood** the subjunctive mood generally, or when used in a principal clause, or in the principal clause of a conditional sentence; **conjunct tetrachords** (*Greek music*) tetrachords in which the highest note of the lower is the lowest note of the higher. [L. *conjunctiō, -ōnis — conjungĕre*; see **conjoin.**]
conjure *kun'jər, v.i.* to practise magical arts: to make an invocation: to conspire (*obs.*). — *v.t.* (usu. *kən-jōōr'*) to call on or summon by a sacred name or in a solemn manner: to implore: to implore earnestly: (*kun'jər*) to compel (a spirit) by incantations: to put a spell upon: to call before the imagination (often with *up*): to render, effect, cause to be or become, by magic or jugglery. — *ns.* **conjura'tion** conspiracy: act of summoning by a sacred name or solemn: enchantment; **con'jurator** a conspirator; **conjure'ment** adjuration; **conjurer, -or** (*kun', kon'*) one who practises magic: one who produces magical effects by sleight-of-hand, etc.; **conju'ror** one bound by oath with others; **con'juring** magic-working: the production of effects apparently miraculous by natural means; **con'jury** magic. — **to conjure with** meriting being regarded as influential, powerful or important. [Fr. *conjurer* — L. *conjūrāre,* to swear together — *con-,* and *jūrāre,* to swear.]
conk¹ *kongk, n.* the fructification of a fungal parasite on a tree (*U.S.*): timber disease due to the parasite (*U.S.*): the nose (*slang*). — *ns.* **conk'er** a strung snail-shell or horse chestnut used in the game of **conkers,** in which each seeks to break his opponent's: a horse chestnut; **conk'y** (*slang*) a large-nosed person. — *adj.* affected by the disease of conk. [**conch.**]
conk² *kongk,* (*slang*) *v.i.* to get out of order, fail, break down (often with *out*): to fall asleep, collapse from exhaustion (with *out*). [Origin unknown.]
conk³ *kongk,* (*slang*) *n.* the head: a blow on the head. — *v.t.* to strike (a person) on the head.
con moto *kon mō'tō,* (*mus.*) with movement: briskly. [It.]
conn. See **con³.**
connascent *kən-ās'ənt, adj.* born or produced at the same

time. — *ns.* **connasc'ence; connasc'ency.** — *adj.* **connate** (*kon'āt*) inborn: innate: allied: congenital: united in growth. — *n.* **connā'tion** (*biol.*) union, esp. of like parts. — *adj.* **connatural** (*kon-ach'ər-əl*) of the same nature as another. — *v.t.* **connat'uralise, -ize.** — *n.* **connatural'ity.** — *adv.* **connat'urally.** — *ns.* **connat'uralness; connā'ture.** — **connate water** water which has been trapped in sediments since their deposition. [L. *con-, nāscī, nātus*, to be born.]

conne. See **con².**

connect *kən-ekt'*, *v.t.* to tie or fasten together: to establish a relation between: to associate. — *v.i.* to be, or become, joined: to be significant (*coll.*): to hit (a target) with a blow, a kick, etc. (*coll.*): to find a source of illicit drugs (*slang*). — *adj.* **connect'able, -ible** capable of being connected. — *p.adj.* **connect'ed** joined: linked: coherent: related. — *adv.* **connect'edly** in a connected manner. — *ns.* **connect'er, -or** one who or that which connects; **connection, connexion** (-*ek'shən*) the act of connecting: that which connects: a religious body or society held together by a set of shared beliefs: coherence: intercourse: context: relation: intimacy: opportunity of change of trains, buses, etc.: a relative, esp. a distant one, or one by marriage: (in *pl.*) the owner and trainer of a racehorse and their associates: the supplying of narcotic drugs (*slang*): a supplier of such drugs (*slang*). — *adj.* **connect'ive** binding together (also **connex'ive** (*obs.*)). — *n.* a word that connects sentences and words. — *adv.* **connect'ively.** — *n.* **connectiv'ity.** — **connect'ing-rod** in a reciprocating-engine or pump, the rod connecting the piston or cross-head to the crank; **connective tissue** an animal tissue including a great variety — e.g. bone, cartilage, ligaments, and enswathing membranes. — *adj.* **well-connect'ed** related to people of good social standing. — **in connection with** concerning. [L. *con-*, and *nectĕre, nexum*, to tie.]

conner¹. See **con².³.**

conner² *kun'ər*, *n.* an inspector or tester. [O.E. *cunnere* — *cunnian*, to learn, seek to know.]

conner³, cunner *kun'ər*, *n.* a kind of wrasse, the goldsinny or corkwing: an allied American fish. [Origin obscure.]

connexion, connexive. See **connect.**

conning-tower. See **con³.**

conniption (fit) *kə-nip'shən* (*fit*) *n.* a fit of hysterical excitement or rage. [Origin unknown.]

connive *kən-īv'*, *v.i.* to wink (usu. *fig.*, as at a fault): to take no notice: to have a private understanding: to converge (*biol.*). — *ns.* **conniv'ance, -ancy, conniv'ence, -ency.** — *adj.* **conniv'ent** (*biol.*) converging and meeting, but not joining. — *n.* **conniv'er.** [L. *con nīvēre, cōnīvēre*, to wink.]

connoisseur *kon-əs-ûr'*, *kon'*, *n.* a well-informed judge in the arts, etc. — *n.* **connoisseur'ship** the skill of a connoisseur. [Fr. (now *connaisseur*), — *connoître* (*connaître*) — L. *cognōscĕre*, to know.]

connote *kon-ōt'*, *v.t.* to signify secondarily: to imply as inherent attributes: to include. — *v.t.* **connotate** (*kon'ō-tāt*) to connote. — *n.* **connotā'tion** the implication of something more than the denotation of an object: an attribute, or the aggregation of attributes, connoted by a term. — *adjs.* **conn'otātive** (or *-nō'tə-tiv*), **connō'tive.** [L. *con-*, with, *notāre*, to mark.]

connubial *kən-ū'bi-əl*, *adj.* pertaining to marriage. — *n.* **connubiality** (*-al'i-ti*). — *adv.* **connū'bially.** [L. *con-, nūbĕre*, to marry.]

connumerate *kən-ū'mə-rāt*, *v.t.* to count together. — *n.* **connumerā'tion.**

conodont *kon'ə-dont, kōn-*, *n.* a tiny conical or tooth-like Palaeozoic fossil derived from an extinct phylum now known as the **Conodon'ta**, app. related to the hagfish. — Also *adj.* [Gr. *konos*, cone, *odont*.]

conoid *kōn'oid*, *n.* anything like a cone in form: a solid generated by the revolution of a conic section about its axis. — *adjs.* **cōn'oid, cōnoid'al, cōnoid'ic, -al.** [Gr. *kōnos*, a cone, *eidos*, form.]

conquer *kong'kər*, *v.t.* to gain by force or with an effort:

to overcome or vanquish. — *v.i.* to be victor. — *adj.* **con'querable.** — *n.* **con'querableness.** — *adj.* **con'quering.** — *adv.* **con'queringly.** — *ns.* **con'queror** one who conquers: a victor: — *fem.* **con'queress; conquest** (*kong'kwest*) the act of conquering: that which is conquered or acquired by physical or moral force: the act of gaining the affections of another: the person whose affections have been gained: acquisition otherwise than by inheritance (*Scots law*). — **the Conqueror** William I of England (L. *conquestor*); **the Conquest** the acquisition of the throne of England by William, Duke of Normandy, in 1066. [O.Fr. *conquerre* — L. *conquīrĕre, conquaerĕre* — *con-*, intens., *quaerĕre*, to seek.]

conquistador *kong'kēs-ta-dōr', -dör* or *-kwis'*, *n.* a conqueror, applied to the conquerors of Mexico and Peru: — *pl.* **-dors, -dores** (*-dōr'es, -dör'es*). [Sp., — L. *conquīrĕre.*]

con-rod *kon'rod*, *n.* short for **connecting-rod.**

consanguine *kon-sang'gwin*, *adj.* related by blood: of the same family or descent — also **consanguin'eous.** — *n.* **consanguin'ity** relationship by blood as opposed to affinity or relationship by marriage. [L. *cōnsanguineus* — *con-*, with, *sanguis*, or *sanguīs*, blood.]

conscience *kon'shəns*, *n.* inmost thought, consciousness (*Shak.*): moral sense: scrupulousness, conscientiousness: —in genitive case commonly written **conscience'.** — *interj.* (*Scot.*) an expression of surprise (also **my conscience!**). — *adjs.* **con'scienceless; con'scient** aware: conscious; **conscientious** (*-shi-en'shəs*) regulated by a regard to conscience: scrupulous. — *adv.* **conscien'tiously.** — *ns.* **conscien'tiousness; conscientisā'tion, -z-.** — *v.t.* **con'scientise, -ize** to make (someone) aware of (political or social rights, etc.). — *adj.* **con'scionable** (*-shən-ə-bl; obs.*) governed or regulated by conscience. — *n.* **con'scionableness.** — *adv.* **con'scionably.** — **conscience clause** a clause in a law to relieve persons of conscientious scruples, esp. against religious instruction; **conscience money** money given to relieve the conscience, by discharging a claim previously evaded. — *adjs.* **con'science-proof** unvisited by any compunctions of conscience; **con'science-smitten, -stricken** stung by conscience. — **conscientious objector** one who objects on grounds of conscience, esp. to military service. — **case of conscience** a question in casuistry; **crisis of conscience** a state of acute unease over a difficult moral decision; **freedom of conscience** the right to hold religious or other beliefs without persecution; **good** or **bad conscience** an approving or reproving conscience; **in all conscience** certainly: by all that is right and fair (*coll.*); **make a matter of conscience** to have scruples about; **on one's conscience** causing feelings of guilt; **prisoner of conscience** a person imprisoned on account of his or her political beliefs; **speak one's conscience** (*Shak.*) to speak frankly: to give one's opinion; **upon conscience, o' my conscience** truly. [Fr., — L. *cōnscientia*, knowledge — *cōnscīre*, to know well, in one's own mind — *con-*, intens., *scīre*, to know.]

conscious *kon'shəs*, *adj.* having the feeling or knowledge of something: aware: having consciousness. — *n.* the conscious mind. — **-conscious** in composition, being very aware of and concerned about, as *clothes-conscious, cost-conscious.* — *adv.* **con'sciously.** — *n.* **con'sciousness** the waking state of the mind: the knowledge which the mind has of anything: awareness: thought. — **con'sciousness-rais'ing** development of awareness of one's identity and potential. — Also *adj.* [L. *cōnscius* — *cōnscīre*, to know; see **conscience.**]

conscribe *kən-skrīb'*, *v.t.* to enlist by conscription. — *adj.* **conscript** (*kon'skript*) enrolled, registered, esp. compulsorily. — *n.* one enrolled and liable to serve compulsorily. — *v.t.* (*kən-skript'*) to enlist compulsorily. — *n.* **conscrip'tion** a compulsory enrolment for service, in a narrower sense, of a number drawn, but now usu. employed of universal service: the obtaining of recruits by compulsion. — *adj.* **conscrip'tional.** — *n.* and *adj.* **conscrip'tionist.** — **conscript fathers** (L. *patrēs cōn-*

scrīptī) the senators of ancient Rome. [L. *cōnscrībere*, to enrol — *con-*, together, *scrībere*, *scrīptum*, to write.]

consecrate *kon'si-krāt*, *v.t.* to set apart for a holy use: to render holy or venerable: to hallow: to devote. — *adj.* **consecrated:** devoted: sanctified. — *ns.* **con'secratedness; consecrā'tion** the act of devoting to a sacred use. — *adj.* **con'secrative.** — *n.* **con'secrator.** — *adj.* **consecratory** (*-krā'tər-i*) making sacred. [L. *cōnsecrāre*, *-ātum*, to make wholly sacred — *con-*, intens., *sacrāre*, to set apart as sacred — *sacer*, sacred.]

consectaneous *kon-sek-tā'ni-əs*, *adj.* following as a natural consequence. — *n.* **consect'ary** a deduction, corollary. [L. *cōnsectārī*, freq. of *cōnsequī*; see next.]

consecution *kon-si-kū'shən*, *n.* a train of consequences or deductions: a series of things that follow one another: succession of similar intervals in harmony (*mus.*). — *adj.* **consecutive** (*kən-sek'ū-tiv*) following in regular order or one after another; expressing consequence (*gram.*). — *adv.* **consec'utively.** — *n.* **consec'utiveness.** [L. *cōnsequī* — *con-*, intens., *sequī*, *secūtus*, to follow.]

conseil *kō-sāy*, (Fr.) *n.* advice: council. — **conseil de famille** (*də fa-mē-y'*) a family consultation; **conseil d'état** (*dā-ta*) a council of state.

consenescence *kon-sən-es'əns*, *n.* general decay. — Also **consenesc'ency.** [L. *con-*, intens., *senēscēre*, to grow old.]

consensus *kən-sen'səs*, *n.* agreement of various parts: agreement in opinion: unanimity: (*loosely*) trend of opinion. — *n.* **consen'sion** mutual consent. — *adj.* **consen'sual** relating to consent: involving voluntary and involuntary action in correlation. — *adv.* **consen'sually.** — **consensual contract** a contract requiring merely the consent of the parties. [L. *cōnsēnsus* — *cōnsentīre*; see next word.]

consent *kən-sent'*, *v.i.* to be of the same mind: to agree: to give assent: to yield: to comply. — *v.t.* to agree: to allow (*Milt.*). — *n.* agreement: accordance with the actions or opinions of another: concurrence. — *adj.* **consentaneous** (*kon-sən-tā'ni-əs*) agreeable or accordant: consistent. — *adv.* **consentā'neously.** — *ns.* **consentā'neousness, consentaneity** (*kon-sen-tə-nē'i-ti*); **consentience** (*kən-sen'shəns*) agreement: power of unifying impressions below the level of consciousness: imperfect consciousness. — *adj.* **consen'tient** agreeing: having consentience. — *adv.* **consent'ingly.** — **consenting adult** a person over the age of 21, legally able to enter into a homosexual relationship (also *fig.*). — **age of consent** the age at which a person is legally competent to give consent to certain acts, esp. marriage, sexual intercourse; **be of consent** (*Shak.*) to be accessory; **with one consent** unanimously. [L. *cōnsentīre* — *con-*, *sentīre*, to feel, to think.]

consequence *kon'si-kwəns*, *n.* that which follows or comes after as a result or inference: effect: the relation of an effect to its cause: importance: social standing: consequentiality: (in *pl.*) a game describing the meeting of a lady and gentleman and its consequences, each player writing a part of the story, not knowing what the others have written. — *v.i.* (*Milt.*) to draw inferences. — *adj.* **con'sequent** following, esp. as a natural effect or deduction: flowing in the direction of the original slope of the land (distinguished from *subsequent* and *obsequent*, *geol.*). — *n.* that which follows: the natural effect of a cause. — *adj.* **consequential** (*-kwen'shl*) following as a result, esp. an indirect result: significant, important: self-important. — *advs.* **consequen'tially** or **con'sequently.** — **in consequence (of)** as a result (of); **of no consequence** trivial, unimportant; **take the consequences** to accept the results of one's actions. [Fr., — L. *cōnsequī* — *con-*, intens., *sequī*, to follow.]

conserve *kən-sûrv'*, *v.t.* to keep entire: to retain: to preserve: to preserve in sugar (*obs.*). — *n.* (also *kon'*) something preserved, as fruits in sugar. — *adj.* **conser'vable.** — *n.* **conser'vancy** a court or board having authority to preserve the fisheries, navigation, banks, etc., of a river: the act of preserving: esp. official care

of a river, forest, etc. — *p.adj.* **conser'vant.** — *n.* **conservā'tion** (*kon-*) the act of conserving (as old buildings, flora and fauna, environment): the keeping entire. — *adj.* **conservā'tional.** — *ns.* **conservā'tionist** one who is actively interested in conservation, esp. of the environment or natural resources; **conser'vātism** (with *cap.*) the opinions and principles of a Conservative: dislike of innovations. — *adj.* **conser'vātive** tending or having power to conserve: averse to change: (*loosely*) moderately estimated or understated: (with *cap.*) belonging, or pertaining, to the Conservative party. — *n.* one averse to change: (with *cap.*) one belonging to or supporting the political party which favours the preservation of existing institutions and seeks to promote free enterprise. — *ns.* **conser'vativeness; conservatoire** (*kɔ̃-ser-va-twär, kən-sûrvə-twär'*), **conservato'rium** a school of music; **con'servātor** (or *kən-sûr'və-tər*) one who preserves from injury or violation: a guardian, custodian: — *fem.* **conservā'trix; conser'vātorship; conser'vātory** a storehouse: a greenhouse or place in which exotic plants are kept: a school of music. — *adj.* preservative. — *n.* **conser'ver.** — **conservation area** an area designated as being of special architectural or historic interest, and therefore protected from any alterations which would destroy its character; **conservation of mass and energy** the principle that the sum of the total amount of mass and energy in a given isolated system is constant. [L. *cōnservāre* — *con-*, *servāre*, to keep.]

consider *kən-sid'ər*, *v.t.* to look at attentively or carefully: to think or deliberate on: to take into account: to attend to: to regard as: to think, hold the opinion (that): to reward. — *v.i.* to think seriously or carefully: to deliberate. — *adj.* **consid'erable** worthy of being considered: of some importance: more than a little. — *n.* **consid'erableness.** — *adv.* **consid'erably.** — *n.* **consid'erance** (*Shak.*) consideration. — *adj.* **consid'erate** (*-it*) considered, deliberate (*arch.*): thoughtful for the feelings and interests of others. — *adv.* **consid'erately.** — *adj.* **consid'erative** (*obs.*) thoughtful: prudent: considerate. — *adv.* **consid'eratively** (*obs.*). — *ns.* **consid'erateness** thoughtfulness for others; **considerā'tion** considerateness: careful thought: importance: motive or reason: recompense, payment: the reason or basis of a compact: the thing given or done or abstained from by agreement with another, and in view of that other giving, doing, or abstaining from something (*law*). — *adj.* **consid'ered** carefully thought out, deliberate. — *n.* and *adj.* **consid'ering** (*pl.* in *Shak.*). — *prep.* in view of. — *conj.* seeing that. — *adv.* everything considered. — *adv.* **consid'eringly** with consideration. — **in consideration of** as payment for; **take into consideration** to allow for; **under consideration** being considered or dealt with. [L. *cōnsīderāre*, perh. orig. a term of augury and from *con-*, and *sīdus, sīderis*, star; conn. **desiderate**.]

consign *kən-sīn'*, *v.t.* to sign or seal: to devote: to transfer: to entrust: to commit: to transmit. — *adj.* **consign'able.** — *ns.* **consignation** (*kon-sig-nā'shən*); **consignatory** (*kən-sig'nə-tər-i*) a co-signatory. — *adj.* **consigned'** given in trust. — *ns.* **consignee** (*kon-sīn-ē'*) one to whom anything is consigned or entrusted; **consign'er, consign'or; consign'ment** the act of consigning: the thing consigned: a set of things consigned together. [L. *cōnsignāre*, to attest.]

consignify *kon-sig'ni-fī*, *v.t.* to mean when taken along with something else. — *n.* **consignificā'tion.** — *adv.* **consignif'icative.**

consilience *kən-sil'i-əns*, *n.* concurrence: coincidence. — *adj.* **consil'ient** agreeing. [L. *con-*, together, and *salīre*, to leap.]

consimilar *kən-sim'i-lər*, *adj.* like each other. — *ns.* **consimilar'ity; consimil'itude; consimil'ity.** [L. *cōnsimilis*.]

consist *kən-sist'*, *v.i.* to exist, subsist (*obs.*): to be composed (of): to insist (*Shak.*): to co-exist (*obs.*): to agree: to hold together (*obs.*). — *ns.* **consist'ence** substance; **consist'ency** consistence: degree of density or thickness: agreement: self-consistency. — *adj.* **consist′ent** fixed: not fluid: agreeing together, compatible: free from self-contradiction: true to principles. — *adv.* **consist′ently.** — *adjs.* **consistō′rial; consistō′rian.** — *n.* **con′sistory** (or *-sist′*) properly, a place of assembly: the place where the privy council of the Roman emperor met: the council itself: an assembly or council: a spiritual or ecclesiastical court. — Also *adj.* — **consist in** to inhere in (*obs.*): to have as essence: to be composed of; **consist of** to be made up of. [L. *cōnsistĕre* — *con-*, together, *sistĕre*, to set, stand.]

consociate *kon-sō′shi-āt, v.t.* and *v.i.* to associate together. — *p.adj.* **consō′ciated.** — *n.* **consociation** (*-si-* or *-shi-ā′shən*) companionship: association: alliance, esp. of churches: a federal council of Congregational churches: a subdivision of an association dominated by one particular species (*bot.*). — *adj.* **consocia′tional.** [L. *cōnsociāre, -ātum* — *con-*, *sociāre*, to associate — *socius*, a companion.]

console[1] *kən-sōl′, v.t.* to give solace or comfort to: to cheer in distress. — *adj.* **consōl′able.** — *v.t.* **consolate** (*kon′sol-āt; Shak.*) to console. — *n.* **consolā′tion** solace: alleviation of misery: a comforting circumstance. — *adj.* **consolatory** (*kən-sol′ə-tər-i,* or *-sōl′*) comforting. — *n.* (*Milt.*) a message of comfort. — *ns.* **console′ment; consol′er:** — *fem.* **consolā′trix.** — **consolā′tion-match, -prize, -race,** etc., a match, prize, race, etc., for the otherwise unsuccessful. [L. *cōnsōlāri* — *con-*, intens., *sōlārī*, to comfort.]

console[2] *kon′sōl, n.* a projection resembling a bracket, frequently in the form of the letter S, used to support cornices, or for placing busts, vases, or figures on: the key-desk of an organ: a large cabinet radio or television set or radiogram: a cabinet for this or similar apparatus: a panel or cabinet with dials, switches, etc., control unit of an electrical, electronic, or mechanical system. — **con′sole-ta′ble** a table supported against a wall by consoles or brackets. [Fr. *console;* prob. conn. with **consolidate.**]

consolidate *kən-sol′i-dāt, v.t.* to make solid: to form into a compact mass: to unite into one: to merge: to rearrange and strengthen (*mil.*). — *v.i.* to grow solid or firm: to unite. — *adj.* made firm or solid: united. — *p.adj.* **consol′idated.** — *n.* **consolidā′tion.** — *adj.* **consol′idative** tending to consolidate: having the quality of healing. — *n.* **consol′idator.** — **consolidated annuities** that part of the British national debt which consists of several stocks consolidated into one fund; **consolidated fund** a fund made up by uniting the yield of various taxes, etc., from which are paid interest on national debt, grants to royal family, etc.; **consolidation acts** acts of parliament which combine into one general statute several special enactments. [L. *cōnsolidāre, -ātum* — *con-*, intens., and *solidus*, solid.]

consols *kon′solz,* or *kon-solz′, n.pl.* short for **consolidated annuities.**

consommé *kɔ̄-som-ā, kən-som′ā, n.* a soup made from meat by slow boiling: a clear soup. [Fr., pa.p. — L. *cōnsummāre, -ātum,* to consummate.]

consonant *kon′sən-ənt, adj.* consistent (with): suitable: harmonious. — *n.* any speech sound other than a vowel: a letter of the alphabet representing such a sound. — *ns.* **con′sonance** a state of agreement: agreement or unison of sounds: a combination of musical notes which can sound together without the harshness produced by beats: concord; **con′sonancy** harmony. — *adj.* **consonantal** (*-ant′l*). — *adv.* **con′sonantly.** — *adj.* **con′sonous** harmonious. [L. *cōnsonāns, -antis,* pr.p. of *cōnsonāre,* to harmonise. — *con-, sonāre,* to sound.]

con sordino *kon sör-dē′nō,* (It.; *mus.*) of an instrument, played with a mute.

consort *kon′sört, -sərt* (*Spens., -sört′), n.* a partner: a companion: a wife or husband: an accompanying ship: a number of people (*obs.*): partnership: company: agreement: accord: formerly (by confusion) for **concert:** a group of instruments played or musicians playing together. — *v.t.* **consort′** to accompany: to

associate. — *v.i.* to associate or keep company: to agree. — *adj.* **consort′ed** associated. — *ns.* **consort′er** one who consorts; **con′sortism** symbiosis; **consortium** (*kon-sör′ti-əm, -shəm, -shi-əm*) fellowship: association: a combination of several banks, business concerns, or other bodies: the association of fungus and alga in a lichen: a lichen thallus: — *pl.* **consor′tia.** — **in consort** in company: in harmony. [L. *cōnsors, -sortis* — *con-, sors,* a lot.]

conspecific *kon-spə-sif′ik, adj.* of the same species. — *n.* a plant or animal of the same species. [L. *con-,* with, and **specific;** see **species.**]

conspectus *kən-spek′təs, n.* a comprehensive view or survey: a synopsis. — *n.* **conspectuity** (*kon-spek-tū′i-ti; Shak.*) sight. [L. *cōnspectus* — *cōnspicĕre,* to look at; see next.]

conspicuous *kən-spik′ū-əs, adj.* catching the eye: prominent. — *ns.* **conspicū′ity** (*kon-*), **conspic′uousness.** — *adv.* **conspic′uously.** — **conspicuous consumption** extravagant, ostentatious spending on luxury goods in order to impress other people. [L. *cōnspicuus* — *cōnspicĕre* — *con-,* intens., *specĕre,* to look.]

conspire *kən-spīr′, v.i.* to plot or scheme together: to devise: to act together to one end. — *v.t.* to plan, devise. — *n.* **conspiracy** (*-spir′ə-si*) the act of conspiring: a banding together for a purpose, often secret, usu. unlawful: a plot: joint action, concurrence. — *adj.* **conspir′ant** conspiring. — *ns.* **conspirā′tion** conspiracy; **conspir′ator** one who conspires: — *fem.* **conspir′atress.** — *adj.* **conspiratō′rial.** — *n.* **conspir′er** (*Shak.*) conspirator. — *adv.* **conspir′ingly.** — **conspiracy of silence** an agreement not to talk about a particular matter. [L. *cōnspīrāre* — *con-,* together, *spīrāre,* to breathe.]

con spirito *kon spir′i-tō, spēr′ē-tō,* (It.) with spirit.

conspurcation *kon-spür-kā′shən,* (*obs.*) *n.* defilement. [L. *cōnspurcāre, -ātum,* to defile.]

constable *kun′stə-bl,* or *kon′, n.* formerly a state-officer of the highest rank: the warden of a castle: a peace-officer: a policeman of the lowest rank. — *ns.* **con′stableship; con′stablewick** (*arch.*) the district of a constable; **constabulary** (*kən-stab′ū-lər-i*) an organised body of constables: a police force. — *adj.* of or pertaining to constables, or peace-officers. — **Constable of France** chief of the household under the old French kings, then commander-in-chief of the army, judge in questions of chivalry, tournaments, and martial displays; **High Constable** one of two constables formerly ordained in every hundred or franchise, to make the view of armour, and to see to the conservation of the peace; **Lord High Constable of England** an officer of the crown, formerly a judge in the court of chivalry; **Lord High Constable of Scotland** a similar officer (now a mere hereditary title); **outrun the constable** to go too fast: to get into debt; **petty constable** a parish constable who was under the High Constable; **special constable** a person sworn in by the justices to preserve the peace, or to execute warrants on special occasions. [O.Fr. *conestable* (Fr. *connétable*) — L. *comes stabulī,* count or companion of the stable.]

constant *kon′stənt, adj.* fixed: unchangeable: firm: continual: faithful. — *n.* (*math.*) a fixed quantity. — *n.* **con′stancy** fixedness: unchangeableness: faithfulness: perseverance (*Shak.*): certainty (*Shak.*). — *adv.* **con′stantly.** [L. *cōnstāns, -stantis,* from *cōnstāre,* to stand firm — *con-,* intens., *stāre,* to stand.]

constantan *kon′stən-tan, n.* an alloy of about 40% nickel and 60% copper, having a high and constant resistance to flow of electricity or heat. [**constant.**]

Constantia *kən-stan′shi-ə, n.* a sweet wine produced around *Constantia,* near Cape Town.

constantia et virtute *kon-stan′shi-ə (-ti-ä) et vûr-tū′tē (vir-tōō′te, wir-),* (L.) by constancy and virtue.

Constantinian *kon-stən-tin′yən, adj.* pertaining to Constantine I (A.D. *c.* 274–337; emperor 306–337).

Constantinopolitan *kon-stan-ti-nō-pol′it-ən, adj.* of or pertaining to *Constantinople.*

constate *kən-stāt′, v.t.* to assert (*Gallicism*). — *n.* **con-**

statation (*kon-stə-tā'shən*) a statement, assertion: ascertaining, verification. — *adj.* **constative** (*kon'stə-tiv, -stā'tiv*) of a statement, that can be true or false: that implies assertion rather than performance. — *n.* such a statement (opp. to *performative*). [Fr. *constater*.]

constellate *kon'stəl-āt*, or *kən-stel'āt*, *v.t.* to cluster: to compel or affect by stellar influence. — *v.i.* to cluster together. — *n.* **constellā'tion** a group of stars: an assemblage of persons distinguished in some way: any grouping of persons, ideas, factors in a situation, etc.: in astrol., a particular disposition of the planets, supposed to influence the course of human life or character. — *adj.* **constell'atory**. [L. *cōnstellātus*, studded with stars — *con-, stellāre — stella*, a star.]

conster. See **construe**.

consternate *kon'stər-nāt, v.t.* to fill with dismay. — *n.* **consternā'tion** terror that throws into confusion: dismay. [L. *cōnsternāre, -ātum*, from *con-*, wholly, *sternĕre*, to strew.]

constipate *kon'stip-āt, v.t.* to stop up, close (*obs.*): to press together (*obs.*): to make costive, cause an irregular and insufficient action of the bowels of: to deprive of vigour (*fig.*). — *adj.* **con'stipated**. — *n.* **constipā'tion**. [L. *cōnstīpāre, -ātum*, to press together — *con-, stīpāre*, to pack.]

constitute *kon'stit-ūt, v.t.* to set up: to establish: to form or make up: to appoint: to give being to. — *n.* **constituency** (*kən-stit'ū-ən-si*) the whole body of voters, or a district, or population, represented by a member of parliament or the like: a set of people supporting, patronising, or forming a power-base for, a business organisation, pressure group, etc. — *adj.* **constit'uent** constituting or forming: essential: elemental: component: electing: constitution-making. — *n.* an essential or elemental part: one of those who elect a representative, esp. in parliament: an inhabitant of one's constituency. — *n.* **constitū'tion** (*kon-*) the act of constituting: the natural condition of body or mind: disposition: a system of laws and customs established by the sovereign power of a state for its own guidance: an established form of government: a particular law or usage: in chem., molecular structure, taking into account not only the kinds and numbers of atoms but the way in which they are linked. — *adj.* **constitū'tional** inherent in the natural frame: natural: agreeable to the constitution or frame of government: essential: legal: reigning subject to fixed laws: supporting the existing constitution. — *n.* a walk for the sake of one's health. — *v.t.* **constitū'tionalise, -ize** to make constitutional. — *ns.* **constitū'tionalism** adherence to the principles of the constitution; **constitū'tion(al)ist** one who favours or studies a constitution or the constitution; **constitutional'ity**. — *adv.* **constitū'tionally**. — *adj.* **con'stitutive** that constitutes or establishes: having power to constitute: essential: component. [L. *cōnstituĕre, cōnstitūtum — con-*, intens., *statuĕre*, to make to stand, to place.]

constrain *kən-strān', v.t.* to urge with irresistible power: to bring about by force: to force, compel: to distress: to violate: to confine: to limit: to cause constraint to: to restrict by a condition. — *adj.* **constrain'able**. — *p.adj.* **constrained'** forced, compelled: lacking ease and spontaneity of manner: embarrassed. — *adv.* **constrain'edly**. — *n.* **constraint'** irresistible force: compulsion: confinement: repression of one's feelings: embarrassment: a restricting condition. [O.Fr. *constraindre* — L. *cōnstringĕre — con-, stringĕre*, to press; see following words and **strain**[1].]

constrict *kən-strikt', v.t.* to press together: to contract: to cramp: to narrow locally. — *p.adj.* **constrict'ed** narrowed: cramped: narrowed in places (*bot.*). — *n.* **constric'tion** a pressing together: contraction: tightness: a narrow place. — *adj.* **constrict'ive**. — *n.* **constrict'or** that which constricts or draws together: a muscle that compresses an organ or structure: a snake that crushes its prey in its folds. [L. *cōnstringĕre, -strictum*; see preceding and following.]

constringe *kən-strinj', v.t.* to draw together: to cause to contract. — *v.i.* to contract. — *n.* **constrin'gency**. — *adj.* **constrin'gent** having the quality of contracting. [L. *cōnstringĕre*; see preceding.]

construct *kən-strukt', v.t.* to build up: to compile: to put together the parts of: to make: to compose: to put in grammatical relation. — *adj.* **constructed**. — *n.* (*kon'-strukt*) a thing constructed, esp. in the mind: an image or object of thought constructed from a number of sense-impressions or images (*psych.*). — *adjs.* **construct'able, construct'ible** able to be constructed. — *ns.* **construct'er, construct'or; construc'tion** the act of constructing: anything piled together: building: a stage structure: manner of forming: the syntactic relations of words in a sentence (*gram.*): interpretation: meaning. — *adj.* **construc'tional** pertaining to construction: used for structures: making use of structures. — *n.* **construc'tionism** use of structures: principle of using structures or of following structure. — *adj.* **construct'ive** capable of, tending towards, or concerned in, constructing: embodying positive advice — opp. to *destructive*: not direct or expressed, but inferred. — *adv.* **construct'ively**. — *ns.* **construct'iveness; construct'ivism** constructionism: a non-representational style of art, originating in Russia about 1920 and affecting esp. sculpture and architecture, using man-made industrial materials and processes such as twisting, welding: a simplified, non-realistic style in stage sets, using steps, platforms, etc.; **construct'ure**. — **constructive dismissal** action by an employer which forces an employee to resign; **construct state** in Semitic languages, the state of a noun depending on another noun, where in Indo-European languages the other would be in the genitive case — e.g. House of God — house being in the construct state. — **bear a construction** to allow of a particular interpretation. [L. *cōnstruĕre, -structum — con-, struĕre*, to build.]

construe *kən-strōō', kon'strōō*, (old form **conster** *kon'stər*), *v.t.* to exhibit in another language the grammatical structure and literal meaning of: to translate: to explain: to interpret: to construct grammatically: to infer. — *v.i.* to admit of grammatical analysis. — *n.* (*kon'-strōō*) an act of construing: something construed, a piece of translation. — *n.* **construabil'ity**. — *adj.* **constru'able**. — *n.* **construer** (*kon'*, or *-strōō'*). [L. *cōnstruĕre, constructum*, to pile together.]

constuprate *kon'stū-prāt* (*obs.*) *v.t.* to ravish. — *n.* **constuprā'tion**. [L. *cōnstuprāre — con-*, intens., *stuprum*, defilement, disgrace.]

consubsist *kon-sub-sist', v.i.* to subsist together.

consubstantial *kon-sub-stan'shl, adj.* of the same substance, nature, or essence, esp. of the Trinity. — *ns.* **consubstan'tialism** the doctrine of consubstantiation; **consubstan'tialist** one who believes in consubstantiation; **consubstantiality** (*-shi-al'i-ti*). — *adv.* **consubstan'tially** with sameness of substance. — *v.t.* and *v.i.* **consubstan'tiate** (*-shi-āt*) to unite in one common substance or nature. — *adj.* so united. — *ns.* **consubstantiā'tion** the Lutheran doctrine of the actual, substantial presence of the body and blood of Christ co-existing in and with the bread and wine used at the Lord's Supper (cf. **transubstantiation); consubstantiā'tionist**. [L. *con-*, with, and **substantial**, etc.]

consuetude *kon'swi-tūd, n.* custom: familiarity. — *adj.* **consuetu'dinary** customary. — *n.* an unwritten law established by usage, derived by immemorial custom from antiquity: a ritual of customary devotions. [L. *cōnsuētūdō, -inis*, custom.]

consul *kon'səl, n.* one of the two chief magistrates in the Roman republic: one of the three heads of the French republic, 1799–1804: an agent for a foreign government appointed to attend to the interests of its citizens and commerce. — *n.* **con'sulage** duty paid to a consul for protection of goods. — *adj.* **con'sular** (*-sū-lər*) pertaining to a consul. — *n.* a man of consular rank. — *ns.* **con'sulate** (*-sūl-*, or *-səl-*) the office, residence, jurisdiction, government, or time of a consul or con-

suls; con'sulship the office, or term of office, of a consul. — **consul general** a consul of the first rank: — *pl.* **consuls general; consulate general.** [L. *cōnsul.*]
consult *kən-sult', v.t.* to ask advice of: to decide or act in favour of: to look up for information or advice: to discuss: to consider: to take measures for the advantage of. — *v.i.* to consider jointly: to take counsel. — *n.* (*kən-sult'*, or *kon'sult*) consultation: council: a meeting for conspiracy or intrigue. — *ns.* **consult'ancy** the post of consultant: an agency which provides professional advice; **consultant** (*kən-sult'ənt*) one who seeks advice or information: one who gives professional advice or takes part in consultation: the most senior grade of doctor in a given speciality in a hospital. — Also *adj.* — *n.* **consultā'tion** (*konsəl-*, *-sul-*) deliberation, or a meeting for deliberation, esp. of physicians or lawyers. — *adj.* **consult'ative** of or pertaining to consultation, esp. of bodies without vote on the decision; **consult'atory** of the nature of consultation. — *ns.* **consultee'** the person consulted; **consult'er** one who consults. — *adjs.* **consult'ing** of a physician, lawyer, etc., prepared to give professional advice to others in the same field; **consult'ive** consultative. — *n.* **consult'or.** — *adj.* **consult'ory** consultatory. — **consult'ing-room** the room in which a doctor sees a patient. [L. *cōnsultāre,* intens. of *cōnsulěre,* to consult.]
consulta *kon-sool'tä,* (It. and Sp.) *n.* a meeting of council.
consume *kən-sūm', -soom', v.t.* to destroy by wasting, fire, evaporation, etc.: to use up: to devour: to waste or spend: to exhaust. — *v.i.* to waste away. — *adj.* **consum'able.** — *n.* something that can be consumed. — *adv.* **consum'edly** exceedingly — originally a fantastic variant of *confoundedly,* and prob. influenced in meaning by *consummately.* — *ns.* **consum'er** one who consumes: one who uses an article produced (opp. to *producer*); **consum'erism** (the promotion of) the protection of the interests of buyers of goods and services against defective or dangerous goods, etc.: an economic system based on the continued increase in consumer goods; **consum'erist.** — *n.* and *adj.* **consum'ing** wasting or destroying: engrossing. — **consumer durables** consumer goods for domestic use and needing infrequent replacement; **consumer(s') goods** goods to be used without further manufacturing process to satisfy human needs; **consumer research** the study of the needs and preferences of consumers. [L. *cōnsūmere, -sūmptum,* to destroy — *con-,* sig. completeness, *sūmere,* to take.]
consummate *kon'sum-āt, -səm-,* or *-sū- v.t.* to raise to the highest point: to perfect or finish: to make (marriage) legally complete by sexual intercourse. — *adj.* (*kənsum'āt, -it, kon'sū-*), complete, supreme, perfect of its kind. — *adv.* **consumm'ately** perfectly. — *n.* **consummā'tion** the act of completing: perfection: conclusion of life or of the universe: the subsequent intercourse which makes a marriage legally valid. — *adj.* **consumm'ative.** — *n.* **con'summātor.** — *adj.* **consumm'atory.** [L. *cōnsummāre, -ātum,* to perfect — *con-,* intens., *summus,* highest, perfect, *summa,* a sum.]
consumption *kən-sum(p)'shən, n.* the act or process of consuming or using up: the quantity consumed: wasting of the body: an earlier name for pulmonary tuberculosis. — *n.* **consumpt** (*kon'sum(p)t, kənsum(p)t'*) a quantity consumed. — *adj.* **consump'tive** wasting away: inclined to the disease consumption. — *n.* one affected by consumption. — *adv.* **consump'tively.** — *ns.* **consump'tiveness, consumptiv'ity** (*kon-*) a tendency to consumption. [See **consume.**]
contabescent *kon-tab-es'ənt, adj.* wasting away, atrophied: failing to produce pollen. — *n.* **contabesc'ence.** [L. *contābēscēns, -entis — contābēscěre,* to waste away.]
contact *kon'takt, n.* touch: meeting in a point without intersection (*math.*): close approximation allowing passage of electric current or communication of disease: a place or part where electric current may be allowed to pass: association: means or occasion of communication: a person who has been exposed to

contagion: a person one can call upon for assistance, information, introductions, etc., in a business or other organisation. — *adj.* involving contact: caused or made active by contact. — *v.t.* and *v.i.* (also *kon-takt'*) to bring or to come into contact: to get in touch with, or establish a connection with. — *adj.* **contact'able** able to be contacted. — *n.* **con'tactor** a device for repeatedly making and breaking an electric circuit. — *adj.* **contact'ual** pertaining to contact. — **contact flight** navigation of an aircraft by ground observation alone; **contact lens** a lens, usu. of plastic material, worn in contact with the eyeball, instead of spectacles, to correct defects of vision; **contact man** (*coll.*) an intermediary in transactions, esp. shady ones; **con'tact= metamor'phism** alteration of rocks in the neighbourhood of igneous materials; **contact poison** one which can penetrate the skin, and which can act without being swallowed or inhaled; **contact print** (*phot.*) a print made by putting a negative or positive transparency in direct contact with a sensitised paper or film and exposing to light. [L. *contingěre, contactum,* to touch — *con-,* wholly, *tangěre,* to touch.]
contadino *kon-tä-dē'nō, n.* an Italian peasant: — *pl.* **contadi'ni** (*-nē*): — *fem.* **contadi'na** (*-nä*): — *pl.* **contadi'ne** (*-nä*), **contadi'nas.** [It.]
contagion *kən-tā'jən, n.* transmission of a disease by direct contact with an infected person or object: a disease or poison so transmitted: the means of transmission: a hurtful influence. — *n.* **contā'gionist** one who believes in the contagiousness of a disease. — *adj.* **contā'gious** communicable by contact: carrying disease or other contagion: noxious (*obs.*): spreading easily (*fig.; coll.*). — *adv.* **contā'giously.** — *ns.* **contā'giousness; contā'gium** contagion: contagious matter. — **contagious abortion** see **brucellosis.** [L. *contāgiō, -ōnis — con-, tangěre,* to touch.]
contain *kən-tān', v.t.* to have within, enclose: to comprise, include: to restrain: to keep fixed: to hold back: to keep in check: to retain (*Shak.*). — *adj.* **contain'able.** — *ns.* **contain'er** that which contains: that in which goods are enclosed for transport, esp. a large box-like receptacle of standard shape and size to fit on a lorry, train or ship: a vessel for holding gas; **containerisā'tion, -z-.** — *v.t.* **contain'erise, -ize** to put (freight) into standard sealed containers: to use such containers for (e.g. a transport operation). — *n.* **contain'ment** the act of containing: the act or policy of preventing the spread beyond certain limits of a power or influence regarded as hostile, by means other than war: the successful result of this. — **container crane** a very large bridge-type quayside crane for handling large containers; **container ship** a ship designed for the most efficient stowing and transport of such containers; **container terminal** a port, railway station, etc., or part of one, set aside and equipped for handling containers. [O.Fr. (Fr.) *contenir* — L. *continēre — con-, tenēre,* to hold.]
contaminate *kən-tam'i-nāt, v.t.* to defile by touching or mixing with: to pollute, esp. by radioactivity: to corrupt: to infect. — *adj.* contaminated. — *adj.* **contam'inable.** — *ns.* **contam'inant; contaminā'tion** pollution: the blending into one of several stories, legends or plots: the blending of two or more linguistic forms to produce one new form: the blending into one manuscript of several readings. — *adj.* **contam'inative.** [L. *contāmināre, -ātum — contāmen* (for *contagmen*), pollution; see **contact.**]
contango *kən-tang'gō, n.* a percentage paid by the buyer to the seller of stock for keeping back its delivery to the next settling-day, continuation (opp. to *backwardation*): — *pl.* **contang'os.** — Also *v.t.* — **contang'o-day** see **continuation-day.** [Arbitrarily from **continue.**]
conte *kõt, n.* a short story (as a literary genre). [Fr.].
conté *kõ-tā', kon'tā, n.* (sometimes with *cap.*) a hard crayon, usu. black, brown, or red, made of graphite and clay. [N. J. *Conté,* Fr. chemist.]
conteck *kon'tek,* (*Spens.*) *n.* strife. [O.Fr. *contek,* prob.

conn. with *contekier*, to touch.]

contemn *kən-tem′*, *v.t.* to despise: — *pr.p.* **contemning** (*-tem′ing*); *pa.t.* and *pa.p.* **contemned′**, *Spens.* *pa.p.* **contempt′**. — *ns.* **contem′ner, contem′nor** (*-ər, -nər*) one who contemns: one who has been found guilty of contempt of court. [L. *contemnĕre, -temptum*, to value little — *con-*, intens., *temnĕre*, to slight.]

contemper *kən-temp′ər*, *v.t.* to blend together, to qualify by mixture: to adapt. — *ns.* **contemperā′tion** (*obs.*); **contem′perature**. [L. *contemperāre*.]

contemplate *kon′tem-plāt*, older *kən-tem′plāt*, *v.t.* to consider or look at attentively: to meditate on or study: to intend. — *v.i.* to think seriously: to meditate (on, upon). — *adj.* **contemp′lable**. — *ns.* **contem′plant; contemplā′tion** meditation: a meditative condition of mind: attentive viewing or consideration: matter for thought: purpose; **contemp′latist**. — *adj.* and *n.* **con′templātive** (or *kən-tem′plə-*) given to contemplation. — *adv.* **con′templatively** (or *-tem′*). — *ns.* **con′templativeness** (or *-tem′*); **con′templātor** one who contemplates: a student. — **contemplative life** (*theol.* and *philos.*) life devoted to meditation (opposed to the *active life*). — **in contemplation of** in the expectation of: bearing in mind as a possiblity. [L. *contemplārī, -ātus*, to mark out carefully a *templum* or place for auguries — *con-*, sig. completeness, and *templum*.]

contemporaneous *kən-tem-pə-rā′nyəs*, *adj.* living, happening, or being at the same time: in geol., belonging approximately to the same relative place in the succession, not necessarily strictly synchronous. — *n.* and *adj.* **contemporā′nean** contemporary. — *n.* **contemporaneity** (*-ə-nē′i-ti*). — *adv.* **contemporā′neously**. — *ns.* **contemporā′neousness; contem′porariness**. — *adj.* **contem′porary** belonging to the same time (with): of the same age: present-day (an inaccurate use), esp. up-to-date, fashionable: of a style of house decoration and furnishing popular in the 1950s. — *n.* one who lives at the same time: a newspaper or magazine of the same time. — *v.t.* **contem′porise, -ize** to make contemporary in mind. [L. *con-, tempus, -oris*, time.]

contempt *kən-tempt′*, *n.* scorn (with *for*): disgrace: disregard of the rule, or an offence against the dignity, of a court, etc., as in *contempt of court, contempt of Parliament*. — *ns.* **contemptibil′ity, contempt′ibleness**. — *adj.* **contempt′ible** (*Spens kən′*) despicable. — *adv.* **contempt′ibly**. — *adj.* **contempt′ūous** haughty, scornful. — *adv.* **contempt′ūously**. — *n.* **contempt′uousness**. [See **contemn**.]

contend *kən-tend′*, *v.i.* to strive: to struggle in emulation or in opposition: to dispute or debate (with *against, for, with, about*): to urge one's course. — *v.t.* to maintain in dispute (that). — *ns.* **contend′ent** (*rare*), **contend′er** one who contends. — *n.* and *adj.* **contend′ing** striving. — *n.* **conten′tion** a violent straining after any object: strife: debate: a position argued for. — *adj.* **conten′tious** quarrelsome: given to dispute: in, or relating to, dispute. — *adv.* **conten′tiously**. — *n.* **conten′tiousness**. [L. *contendĕre, -tentum* — *con-*, *tendĕre*, to stretch.]

contenement *kən-ten′i-mənt*, (*obs.*) *n.* property necessary to maintain one's station. [L. *con-*, intens., see **tenement**.]

content¹ *kon′tent*, *n.* that which is contained: capacity: the substance: (in *pl.*) the things contained: (in *pl.*) the list of chapters, sections, etc., in a book. — **content word** a word which has a meaning independent of its context (opp. to *function word*). [See **contain**.]

content² *kən-tent′*, *adj.* having the desire limited by present enjoyment: satisfied: quietly happy. — *n.* satisfaction. — *interj.* I am content, agreed! — the formula of assent in the House of Lords. — *v.t.* to make content: to satisfy the mind: to quiet: to please. — *n.* **contentā′tion** (*obs.*). — *adj.* **content′ed** content. — *adv.* **content′edly**. — *ns.* **content′edness; content′ment**. — *adj.* **content′less** without content: discontented. [Fr., — L. *contentus*, contained, hence, satisfied — *con-*, and *tenēre*, to hold.]

conterminous *kən-tûr′min-əs*, *adj.* adjacent, meeting along a common boundary: meeting end to end: coincident: co-extensive in range. — *adjs.* **conter′minal** adjacent: end to end; **conter′minant, conter′minate** adjacent. [L. *conterminus*, neighbouring — *con-, terminus*, a boundary.]

contesseration *kon-tes-ər-ā′shən*, *n.* (the act of) forming friendship or union — in Roman times by dividing a square tablet as token. [From L. *contesserāre* — *con-, tessera*, square stone, token (*hospitalis*, given by guest to host).]

contest *kən-test′*, *v.t.* to call in question or make the subject of dispute: to strive to gain. — *v.i.* to contend. — *n.* (*kon′*) a struggle for victory: a competition: strife: a debate, dispute, argument. — *adj.* **contest′able**. — *ns.* **contest′ant** one who contests; **contestā′tion** the act of contesting: contest, strife: emulation. — *p.adj.* **contest′ed**. — *n.* **contest′er**. — *p.adj.* **contest′ing**. — *adv.* **contest′ingly**. — **contested election** one in which there are more candidates than are to be elected: one whose validity is disputed (*U.S.*). [Fr. *contester* — L. *contestārī*, to call to witness — *con-*, intens., *testārī*, to be a witness — *testis*, a witness.]

context *kon′tekst*, *n.* the parts of a discourse or treatise which precede and follow a special passage and may fix its true meaning: associated surroundings, setting. — *adj.* **context′ūal**. — *n.* **contextūalisā′tion, -z-**. — *v.t.* **context′ūalise, -ize** to place in context: to study (words, etc.) in their context. — *adv.* **context′ūally**. — *n.* **context′ure** the process or manner of weaving together: structure: fabric. [L. *contextus, contexĕre* — *con-*, *texĕre, textum*, to weave.]

conticent *kon′tis-ənt*, (*Thackeray*) *adj.* silent. [L. *conticēns, -entis* — *con-*, intens., *tacēre*, to be silent.]

contignation *kon-tig-nā′shən*, (*arch.*) *n.* joining together of timber: framework boarding. [L. *contignātiō, -ōnis* — *contignāre* — *con-, tignum*, beam.]

contiguous *kən-tig′ū-əs*, *adj.* touching, adjoining: near. — *ns.* **contigū′ity; contig′uousness**. — *adv.* **contig′uously**. [L. *contiguus* — *contingĕre*, to touch on all sides — *con-*, wholly, *tangĕre*, to touch.]

continent *kon′ti-nənt*, *n.* that which contains (*arch.*): a bank or shore (*arch.*): sum and substance (*arch.*): a great extent of land not broken up by seas: one of the great divisions of the land surface of the globe: the mainland portion of one of these: (usu. with *cap.*) the mainland of Europe: solid earth (*obs.*): the main or whole body of anything (*obs.*). — *adj.* restraining within due bounds, or absolutely abstaining from, the indulgence of pleasure, esp. sexual: able to control one's evacuations: temperate: virtuous. — *ns.* **con′tinence, con′tinency** self-restraint or abstinence, esp. sexual: chastity: ability to control one's evacuations. — *adj.* **continental** (*ent′l*) of, characteristic of, or of the nature of, a continent, esp. the European continent, the colonies of North America at the period of independence, or the main body of the United States. — *n.* a native or inhabitant of a continent: an American soldier of the War of Independence: a currency note of the Continental Congress. — *ns.* **continent′alism** anything peculiar to the usage of a continent, esp. Europe; **continent′alist**. — *adv.* **con′tinently** in a continent manner. — **continental breakfast** a light breakfast of rolls and coffee (cf. **English breakfast**); **continental climate** the climate characteristic of the interior of a continent, with hot summers, cold winters, and little rainfall; **Continental Congress** an assembly of delegates of the revolting American colonies, before the United States constitution was in force; **continental divide** a range of mountains forming the watershed of a continent; **continental drift** hypothetical slow drifting apart of land masses, as e.g. in A. L. Wegener's theory of the formation of world continents from one original land mass; **continental plate** a plate (q.v.) of the lithosphere; **continental quilt** a duvet; **continental shelf** a gently sloping zone, under relatively shallow seas, offshore from a continent or island; **Continental Sys-**

tem Napoleon's plan for shutting out England from all commercial connection with Europe. [L. *continēns*, *-entis* — *continēre*, to contain — *con-*, *tenēre*, to hold.]

contingent *kən-tin'jənt*, *adj.* dependent on something else: liable but not certain to happen: accidental. — *n.* an event liable but not certain to occur: a share, quota, or group, esp. of soldiers. — *ns.* **contin'gence** contact: contingency (*obs.*); **contin'gency** the quality or state of being contingent: contact (*obs.*): close connection: uncertainty: chance: a chance happening or concurrence of events: a possible future event: something dependent on such (also *adj.*): an incidental. — *adv.* **contin'gently**. — **contingency plans** plans or arrangements made in case a particular situation should arise. [L. *contingēns*, *-entis* — *con-*, mutually, *tangĕre*, to touch.]

continue *kən-tin'ū*, *v.t.* to draw out or prolong: to extend: to maintain: to go on with: to resume: to adjourn: to be a prolongation of. — *v.i.* to remain in the same place or state: to last or endure: to persevere. — *adjs.* **contin'uable; contin'ual** without interruption: unceasing: persistent. — *adv.* **contin'ually**. — *n.* **contin'uance** duration: uninterrupted succession: stay. — *adj.* **contin'uant** continuing: capable of continuing. — *n.* an open consonant. — *adj.* **contin'uāte** closely united (*obs.*): unbroken (*Shak.*). — *n.* **continuā'tion** going on: persistence: constant succession: extension: resumption: a further instalment. — *adj.* **contin'uative** continuing. — *n.* **contin'uator** one who continues: one who keeps up a series or succession. — *adj.* **contin'ued** uninterrupted: unceasing: extended: resumed: in instalments. — *adv.* **contin'uedly**. — *ns.* **contin'uedness; contin'uer** one who continues: one who has the power of persevering; **continū'ity** the state of being continuous: uninterrupted connection: a complete scenario of a motion-picture: the person who writes it (in full **continuity writer**): the ordering or arrangement of film or television shots and scenes, or of parts of a radio broadcast, in a correct or consistent way; **continuo** (*kon-tin'ū-ō*; It. *-tēn'wō*) thorough-bass: the part as written for a keyboard instrument, with or without an accompaniment: the instruments playing this part: — *pl.* **contin'uos**. — *adj.* **contin'uous** joined together without interruption. — *adv.* **contin'uously**. — *ns.* **contin'- uousness; contin'ūum** that which is continuous: that which must be regarded as continuous and the same and which can be described only relatively: — *pl.* **contin'ua**. — **continuation class** (*old*) a class for continuing the education of those who have left school; **continuā'tion-day** the same as **contango-day**, that on which contangos are fixed; **continuity announcer** (*radio, TV*) one who supervises the continuity of a sequence of programmes, by linking programmes, filling gaps with interlude material, etc.; **continuity girl, man** a person responsible for film, television or radio continuity; **continuous assessment** the assessment of the progress of a pupil or student by intermittent checks, e.g. class tests, essays, etc, thoughout the year; **continuous creation** the notion of creation as going on always, not as a single act at one particular time (*philos.*): the theory that the universe is in a steady state showing no overall change, although new systems are continually being formed to replace those carried away by recession (*astron.*); **continuous stationery** (*comput.*) stationery consisting of a long sheet of paper with regular perforations, usu. folded fan-wise and fed through a printer. — **space-time continuum** see **space**. [L. *continuāre* — *continuus*, joined, connected, from *continēre*, to hold together.]

contline *kont'līn*, *n.* the space between stowed casks: a spiral interval between the strands of a rope. [Prob. **cant²**, **line².**]

conto *kon'tō*, *n.* a Portuguese and Brazilian money of account, 1000 escudos or cruzeiros: — *pl.* **con'tos**. [Port., million (reis) — L. *computus*, a sum.]

contorno *kon-tör'nō*, *n.* contour or outline: — *pl.* **contor'-**

nos. — *n.* **contor'niate** a coin or medal with a deep groove round the disc. — *adj.* having this. [It. *contorno*, circuit, contour.]

contort *kən-tört'*, *v.t.* to twist or turn violently: to writhe. — *adj.* **contort'ed** twisted: twisted, as some flower-buds when each floral leaf overlaps its neighbour always on the same side round the circle: much and irregularly plicated (*geol.*). — *n.* **contor'tion** a violent twisting: deformation. — *adjs.* **contor'tional, contor'tionate**. — *ns.* **contor'tionism; contor'tionist** a gymnast who practises contorted postures: one who twists words and phrases. — *adj.* **contort'ive**. [L. *con-*, intens., and *torquēre*, *tortum*, to twist.]

contour *kon'tŏŏr*, *n.* outline: the line that bounds the figure of any object: general character or aspect: artistic quality of outline: a contour line: a point, line, or surface, at, along, or on which some property or characteristic is constant, or its representation in a map or diagram. — *adj.* having, showing, or based on contours: contoured. — *v.t.* to mark with contour lines: to follow the contour lines of. — *adj.* **con'toured** of chairs, etc., shaped to fit the lines of the human body. — **contour cultivation, farming, ploughing** the ploughing (and planting) of sloping land along the contour lines to counter erosion; **contour feathers** those that determine the contours of a bird's body; **contour line** a line on the ground whose points are all at the same height above sea-level, or the intersection of the ground surface by a level surface of constant elevation: representation of such a line on a map; **contour map** a map in which the configuration of land is shown by contour lines. [Fr. *contour* (It. *contorno*) — It. *contornare*, to surround, outline — L. *con-*, *tornāre*, to turn in a lathe — *tornus* (Gr. *tornos*), a lathe.]

contra- *kon'tra*, *-trə*, *pfx.* against: contrary. [L. *contrā*.]

contra *kon'tra*, *-trə*, *adv.* and *prep.* against. — *n.* an argument against: the other side.

contraband *kon'trə-band*, *adj.* excluded by law: prohibited. — *n.* illegal traffic: smuggled or prohibited goods: in the American Civil War, a refugee slave. — *ns.* **con'trabandism** trafficking in contraband goods; **con'trabandist** a smuggler. — **contraband of war** commodities not to be supplied by neutral to belligerent powers. [Sp. *contrabanda* — It. *contrabbando* — L.L. *contrā*, L.L. *bandum*, ban.]

contrabass *kon'trə-bās*, *n.* the double-bass. — *adj.* applied to other instruments taking a similar part. — Also **contrabasso** (*-bäs'ō*; *pl.* **-bass'os**) and (*rare*) **coun'terbase**. [It. *contra(b)basso* — pfx. *contra-* indicating an octave lower, and *basso*, bass.]

contrabassoon *kon'trə-bas-ōōn'*, *n.* the double bassoon. [*contra-* (see **contrabass** above), and **bassoon**.]

contra bonos mores *kon'tra bō'nōs* (*bo'*) *mō'rēz* (*-rās*), (L.) against good manners or morals.

contraception *kon-trə-sep'shən*, *n.* prevention of conception. — *n.* **contracep'tive** a drug, device or other means of contraception. — Also *adj.* [L. *contrā*, against, and **(con)ception**.]

contract *kən-trakt'*, *v.t.* to draw together: to lessen: to shorten: to effect by agreement: to come into, become the subject of: to incur, catch (a disease): to bargain for: to betroth. — *v.i.* to shrink: to become less: to become shorter: to make a contract (with *or* for). — *n.* (*kon'trakt*), an agreement on fixed terms: a bond: a betrothal: the writing containing an agreement: a season-ticket: contract bridge: a final bid in contract bridge: an undertaking: in criminal circles, an undertaking to kill a particular person, esp. for an agreed sum of money (*slang*). — *n.* **contractabil'ity**. — *adjs.* **contract'able** (*kən-*) able to be contracted, esp. of a disease or habit; **contract'ed** drawn together: shortened: narrow: mean: affianced. — *adv.* **contract'edly**. — *ns.* **contract'edness; contractibil'ity**. — *adjs.* **contract'ible** capable of being contracted, shortened; **contract'ile** tending or having power to contract or to draw in. — *ns.* **contractil'ity** (*kon-*); **contrac'tion** (*kən-*) the act of contracting: a word shortened in speech or spelling: a symbol for shortening in palaeography, etc.: a tightening of the muscles or muscle fibres, esp. of the uterine muscles or fibres involved in the process of giving birth. — *adjs.* **contrac'tional, contrac'tionary** having the effect of contracting; **contract'ive** tending to contract. — *n.* **contract'or** one of the parties to a bargain or agreement: one who engages to execute work or furnish supplies at a stated rate. — *adj.* **contract'ual.** — *n.* **contract'ure** persistent muscular contraction: shortening due to spasm or paralysis of muscles, etc.: tapering of a column (*archit.*). — **contract bridge** a development of auction bridge, in which tricks beyond the number bid for count only like honours; **contract in** to agree to participate on certain conditions; **contract out** to arrange that certain conditions shall not apply: to withdraw from an obligation, agreement, etc.: to decide not to participate in a pension scheme, etc. [L. *contractus* — *con-*, together, *trahĕre, tractum,* to draw.]

contracyclical *kon'trə-sī'kli-kl, adj.* of an economic policy, offsetting fluctuation cycles in the economy by reducing taxes during a recession and raising them during a boom. [L. *contrā,* against, and **cyclical** (see **cycle**).]

contra-dance. Same as **country-dance.**

contradict *kon-trə-dikt', v.t.* to oppose by words (*obs.*): to deny what is affirmed by: to assert the contrary of: to deny: to be contrary to in character. — *adj.* **contradict'able.** — *n.* **contradic'tion** act of contradicting: a speaking against: denial: inconsistency. — *adj.* **contradic'tious** prone to contradiction. — *adv.* **contradic'tiously.** — *adj.* **contradict'ive** contradicting. — *adv.* **contradict'ively.** — *n.* **contradict'or.** — *adv.* **contradict'orily.** — *n.* **contradict'oriness** the quality of being contradictory. — *adj.* **contradict'ory** affirming the contrary: inconsistent. — *n.* a word, principle, that contradicts another: either of two propositions such that both cannot be true, or both cannot be false (*log.*). — **contradiction in terms** a group of words containing a contradiction. [L. *contrādīcĕre, -dictum* — *contrā-,* against, *dīcere,* to say.]

contradistinguish *kon'trə-dis-ting'gwish, v.t.* to distinguish by contrasting different qualities or conditions. — *n.* **contradistinc'tion.** [L. *contrā,* against, and **distinguish.**]

contrafagotto *kon-trə-fə-got'tō, n.* the contrabassoon: — *pl.* **-fagot'tos.** [It. *contra-,* indicating an octave lower, and *fagotto,* bassoon.]

contraflow *kon'trə-flō, n.* a system of traffic regulation on motorways, when one carriageway is closed and the other is arranged for two-way traffic. [L. *contrā,* against, and **flow.**]

contrahent *kon'trə-hənt, adj.* entering into a contract. — *n.* a contracting party. [L. *contrahēns, -entis* — *contrahĕre,* to contract.]

contrail *kon'trāl, n.* a trail of condensed vapours left by a high-flying aircraft. [**con(densation)** and **trail.**]

contraindicate *kon'trə-in'di-kāt, v.t.* to point to (a particular treatment or procedure) as unsuitable (*med.*): to show or give as reason for not being, doing or having, etc.: to forbid. — *ns.* **contrain'dicant; con'traindicā'tion.** — *adj.* **contraindic'ative.** [L. *contrā,* against, and **indicate.**]

contrair *kon-trār',* an obsolete dial. form of **contrary.**

contralto *kon-tral'tō* or *-träl', n.* the lowest musical voice in women: a singer with such a voice: a part for such a voice: — *pl.* **contral'ti** (*-tē*), **-tos.** — Also *adj.* [It., *contra-,* and **alto.**]

contra mundum *kon'trə mun'dum* or *kon'tra mōōn'dōōm,* (L.) against the world.

contranatant *kon-trə-nā'tənt, adj.* swimming upstream. [L. *contrā, natāns, -antis,* pr.p. of *natāre,* to swim.]

contraplex *kon'trə-pleks,* (*teleg.*) *adj.* having messages passing opposite ways at the same time. [L. *contrā,* against, and *-plex,* as in **complex.**]

contraposition *kon-trə-pō-zish'ən, n.* opposition, contrast: an immediate inference, which consists in denying the original subject of the contradictory of the original predicate (*log.*). — *adj.* and *n.* **contrapos'itive.** — *n.*

contrapposto (*kon-trə-po'stō; art*) a pose of the human body with hips, shoulders, and head in different planes: — *pl.* **contrappo'stos.**

contraprop *kon'trə-prop.* Contraction of **contrarotating propeller.**

contraption *kən-trap'shən, n.* a contrivance. [Perh. *con-*trivance ad*aption.*]

contrapuntal, contrapuntist. See **counterpoint.**

contrarotating propeller *kon-trə-rō-tā'ting prə-pel'ər,* one of a pair of propellers rotating in opposite directions. — Also **contrapropell'er.**

contrary *kon'trə-ri, adj.* opposite: contradictory: (usu. *kən-trā'ri*) perverse. — *n.* an extreme opposite: a proposition so related to another that both cannot be true though both may be false (*log.*). — *v.t.* and *v.i.* to oppose: to contradict: to annoy. — *n.* **contrariety** (*-rī'i-ti*) opposition: inconsistency. — *adv.* **contrarily** (*kon'* or *-trā'*). — *n.* **contrariness** (*kon'* or *-trā'*). — *adj.* **contrarious** (*kən-trā'ri-əs; arch.*) showing contrariety. — *advs.* **contra'riously** (*arch.*) contrarily; **con'trariwise** (or *-trā'* or *-tra'*) in the contrary way: on the other side: on the other hand. — **contrary motion** (*mus.*) movement of parts in opposite directions—one up, another down. — **on the contrary** far otherwise; **to the contrary** to the opposite effect. [L. *contrārius* — *con*trā, against.]

contrast *kən-träst', v.i.* to stand in opposition. — *v.t.* to set in opposition to, in order to show difference. — *n.* (*kon'träst*) opposition or unlikeness in things compared: exhibition of differences: the (degree of) difference in tone between the light and dark parts of a photograph or a television picture. — *adjs.* **contrast'ive; contrast'y** (*phot.*) of prints or negatives, showing a high degree of contrast. — **contrast medium** a suitable substance used in diagnostic radiology in order to give contrast. [Fr. *contraster* — L. *contrā,* opposite to, *stāre,* to stand.]

contrasuggestible *kon-trə-suj-est'i-bl,* (*psych.*) *adj.* responding to suggestion by believing or doing the opposite. [L. *contrā,* against, and **suggestible.**]

contrate *kon'trāt, adj.* of wheels (esp. in watchmaking), having cogs parallel to the axis. [L. *contrā,* opposite.]

contra-tenor. Same as **counter-tenor.**

contraterrene *kon-trə-ter'ēn, adj.* opposite in character to earthy or terrestrial. [L. *contrā,* against, and **terrene.**]

contrat social *kɔ̃-tra sos-yal,* (Fr.) social contract.

contravallation *kon-trə-val-ā'shən, n.* a fortification built by besiegers about the place invested. [L. *contrā,* against, *vallāre, -atum,* to fortify.]

contravene *kon-trə-vēn', v.t.* to oppose: to infringe. — *n.* **contraven'tion.** [L. *contrā,* against, *venīre, ventum,* to come.]

contrayerva *kon-trə-yûr'və, n.* a tropical American plant of the mulberry family, once esteemed as an antidote: a Jamaican birthwort of like reputation. [Sp. (now *contrahierba*) — L. *contrā,* against, *herba,* a herb.]

contrecoup *kɔ̃-tr'-kōō,* (*med.*) *n.* an injury, esp. to the skull, resulting from a blow on the side exactly opposite to it. [Fr., counterblow.]

contretemps *kɔ̃-tr'-tã, n.* something happening inopportunely or at the wrong time, anything embarrassing, a hitch. [Fr. *contre* (L. *contrā*), against, *temps* (L. *tempus*), time.]

contribute *kən-trib'ūt* (*dial. kon'*), *v.t.* to give along with others: to give for a common purpose: to add towards a common result, to a fund, etc.: to write and send for publication with others. — *v.i.* to give or bear a part: to be a contributor. — *adj.* **contrib'utable** payable: subject to contribution. — *n.* **contribū'tion** (*kon-*) the act of contributing: something contributed: a levy or charge imposed upon a number of persons: anything furnished to a common stock or done towards a common end: a written composition supplied to a periodical, etc. — *adjs.* **contrib'utive, contrib'utory** (**contrib'utary** *obs.*) giving a share: helping. — *n.*

contrib'utor a person who contributes: a person who sends written articles for publication. — contributory negligence failure to take adequate precautions against an accident, etc., resulting in partial legal responsibility for injury, damage, etc. [L. con-, tribĕre, -ūtum, to give.]

contrist kən-trist', (obs.) v.t. to sadden. — n. contristā'tion. [Fr. contrister — L. contristāre — con-, intens., and tristis, sad.]

contrite kon'trīt, or kən-trīt', adj. brokenhearted for sin: penitent. — adv. contritely. — ns. contriteness; contrition (kon-trish'ən) deep sorrow for sin: remorse. [L. contrītus — conterĕre — con-, wholly, terĕre, to bruise.]

contriturate kən-trit'ū-rāt, (rare) v.t. to pulverise. [con-, intens., and triturate.]

contrive¹ kən-trīv', v.t. to plan: to invent: to bring about or effect: to manage, arrange: to plot: to conceive, understand (Spens.). — adj. contriv'able that may be contrived. — n. contriv'ance. — adj. contrived' laboured, artificially intricate. — ns. contrive'ment an act of contriving: the thing contrived: invention: design: artifice; contriv'er a schemer, a manager. [O.Fr. controver — con-, intens., trover, to find.]

contrive² kən-trīv', (Shak.) v.t. to spend, as time. [L. conterĕre, contrītum, perf. contrīvī, to wear out.]

control kən-trōl', n. restraint: authority: command: regulation: a check: a means of controlling or testing: a station for doing so: an experiment performed to afford, to provide a standard of comparison for other experiments (also control experiment): a subject or group of subjects (control group) providing such a standard of comparison: a disembodied spirit or other agency supposed to direct a spiritualistic medium: a lever ('joy-stick') or wheel to move ailerons and elevator, and so control the movements of aircraft (also control column, lever, stick): an aerofoil that controls the movements of an aircraft, as rudder, elevator, stabiliser (also control surface): a secret service agent who supervises other agents. — adj. pertaining to control. — v.t. to check: to restrain: to govern: — pr.p. contrōll'ing; pa.t. and pa.p. contrōlled'. — Formerly comptroll', countrol', controul'. — n. contrōllabil'ity. — adj. controll'able capable of, or subject to, control. — ns. controll'er one who checks the accounts of others by a counter-roll (also comptroll'er) an official authorised to control some activity or department: one who controls or regulates: an apparatus for regulating — e.g. the speed of an electric car; controll'ership; control'-ment the act or power of controlling: the state of being controlled: control. — control character (comput.) one which, in a suitable context, produces a particular effect, e.g. start, delete, etc.; controlling interest number of shares sufficient to ensure control over the running of a company; control panel, board a panel or board containing dials, switches and gauges for operating and monitoring electrical or other apparatus; control register (comput.) one which stores the instructions controlling the operation of a computer for one cycle; control room a room in which control instruments are placed, e.g. in a broadcasting station; control tower a building at an aerodrome from which take-off and landing instructions are given; control unit (comput.) the part of a computer which interprets instructions and controls the execution of a program. [Fr. contrôle, from contre-rôle, a duplicate register — L. contrā, against, rotulus, a roll.]

controvert kon'trə-vûrt, v.t. to oppose: to argue against: to dispute. — n. con'troverse (Spens.) dispute. — adj. controver'sial (-shəl) relating to controversy: arousing controversy. — n. controver'sialist one given to controversy. — adv. controver'sially. — n. con'troversy (also kən-trov') a debate: contention: dispute: a war of opinions, in books, pamphlets, etc. — adj. contro-vert'ible. — adv. controvert'ibly. — n. con'trovertist (or -vûrt'). [L. contrā, against, and vertĕre, to turn.]

contubernal (Chaucer, contubernyal) kən-tūb'ər-nəl, adj. living together (in the same tent): pertaining to com-

panionship. [L. contubernālis (n.) — cum, with, together, taberna, hut, tavern.]

contumacious kon-tū-mā'shəs, adj. opposing lawful authority with contempt: obstinate: stubborn. — adv. contumā'ciously. — ns. contumā'ciousness; contumacity (-mas'i-ti); con'tumacy (-məs-i) obstinate disobedience or resistance. [L. contumāx, -ācis, insolent, from con-, intens., and tumēre, to swell, or temnĕre, to despise.]

contumely kon'tūm-li (or kon'tū-mi-li), n. scornful insolence. — adj. contumē'lious haughtily insolent. — adv. contumē'liously. — n. contumē'liousness. [L. contumēlia, prob. from the same source as contumāx.]

contund kən-tund', (arch.) v.t. to bruise or pound. — v.t. contuse (-tūz') to beat or bruise: to crush. — n. contusion (-tū'zhən) the act of bruising: the state of being bruised: a bruise. — adj. contū'sive apt to bruise. [L. contundĕre, contūsum — con-, intens., tundĕre, to bruise.]

conundrum kən-un'drəm, n. a riddle turning on some odd or fanciful resemblance between things quite unlike: any puzzling question. [Ety. dub.]

conurbation kon-ûr-bā'shən, n. an aggregation of towns. — adj. conur'ban. — n. conurbia (kən-ûr'bi-ə) the world of conurbations. [L. con-, together, urbs, city.]

convalesce kon-vəl-es', v.i. to regain health. — ns. convalesc'ence, (rare) convalesc'ency gradual recovery of health and strength. — adj. convalesc'ent gradually recovering health: promoting or encouraging convalescence. — n. one recovering health. [L. con-, intens., valēscĕre — valēre, to be strong.]

Convallaria kon-və-lā'ri-ə, n. the lily-of-the-valley, a genus of Liliaceae. [L. convallis, a sheltered valley.]

convection kən-vek'shən, n. a transmission, esp. that of heat or electricity through liquids or gases by means of currents: vertical movement, esp. upwards, of air or atmospheric conditions (meteor.). — adjs. convec'-tion; convec'tional; convec'tive. — n. convec'tor apparatus for heating by convection. [L. convectiō, -ōnis, bringing together — con-, and vehĕre, to carry.]

convenable. See convenance, convene, convenient.

convenance kɔ̄-və-näs, kon'vən-äns, n. what is suitable or proper: (in pl.) the conventional usages or social proprieties. — adj. convenab'le (-äbl', or kon') conforming to the convenances. [Fr.]

convene kən-vēn', v.i. to come together: to assemble. — v.t. to call together. — adj. convēn'able. — n. convēn'er, convēn'or one who convenes a meeting: the chairman of a committee. [Fr. convenir — L. convenīre — con-, together, and venīre, to come.]

convenient kən-vēn'yənt, adj. suitable: handy: commodious. — adj. convenable (kon'vən-ə-bəl) (obs.) fitting. — ns. convēn'ience suitability: an advantage: any means or device for promoting (esp. domestic) ease or comfort: a lavatory or water-closet, esp. (public convenience) a building containing several for use by the public; convēn'iency (rare) convenience. — adv. convēn'iently. — convenience food food (partly) prepared before sale so as to be ready, or almost ready, for the table. — at one's (earliest) convenience (on the first occasion or at the earliest time) when it is suitable or opportune. [L. convenīre.]

convent¹ kon'vənt, n. an association of persons secluded from the world and devoted to a religious life: the house in which they live, a monastery or (now usu.) nunnery. — adj. convent'ual belonging to a convent. — n. a monk or nun: (with cap.) a member of one of the two divisions of the Franciscans, following a mitigated rule — the other being the Observants. [Though Fr. from L. conventum, convenīre, to come together.]

convent² kən-vent', (Spens., Shak.) v.t. to convene, summon, cite. — v.i. (Shak.) to be suitable. [L. convenīre, conventum — con-, venīre, to come.]

conventicle kən-vent'i-kl (earlier kon'vənt-), n. a secret, illegal, or forbidden religious meeting, applied esp. to those of English dissenters and to the Scottish Presbyterian field-preachings in the persecutions under Charles II and James VII: any private, clandestine, or irregular meeting. — *v.i.* to hold such a meeting. — *n.* **conven'ticler.** [L. *conventiculum*, a secret meeting of monks.]

convention *kən-ven'shən, n.* the act of convening: an assembly, esp. of representatives or delegates for some common object: any extraordinary assembly called upon any special occasion: a parliament not summoned by the sovereign: an assembly for framing or revising a constitution: a meeting of political party delegates for nominating a candidate for the presidency or other purpose (*U.S.*): any temporary treaty: an agreement: established usage: fashion: in card games, a mode of play in accordance with a recognised code of signals, not determined by the principles of the game. — *adj.* **conven'tional** formed or adopted by convention: bound or influenced by convention: growing out of tacit agreement or custom: customary: not spontaneous: stylised: arbitrary: of weapons, warfare, energy sources, not nuclear. — *v.t.* **conven'tionalise, -ize** to make conventional: to delineate according to a convention rather than nature. — *ns.* **conven'tionalism** that which is established by tacit agreement, as a mode of speech, etc.; **conven'tionalist** one who adheres to a convention, or is swayed by conventionalism; **conventional'ity** state of being conventional: that which is established by use or custom. — *adv.* **conven'tionally.** — *adj.* **conven'tionary** acting under contract. — *ns.* **conven'tioner, conven'tionist.** [L. *conventiō, -ōnis*; see **convene.**]

converge *kən-vûrj', v.i.* to tend towards or meet in one point or value: to acquire like character independently. — *n.* **conver'gence** the act or point of converging (also **conver'gency**): the moving inwards of the eyes in focusing on a near object (*physiol.*): the property of having a limit, for infinite series, sequences, products, etc. (*math.*): the accumulation of air over a particular region, giving rise to upward air currents (*meteor.*). — *adjs.* **conver'gent** converging: due to or characterised by convergence; **conver'ging** meeting in a point: coming nearer together: with gradually approaching tips (*bot.*). [L. *con-, vergĕre*, to bend, to incline.]

conversazione *kon-vər-sat-si-ō'ni, n.* a meeting for conversation, particularly on learned subjects: — *pl.* **conversazio'nes** or **conversazió'ni** (*-nē*). [It.]

converse *kən-vûrs', v.i.* to have social intercourse: to talk familiarly: to commune. — *n.* **converse** (*kon'*) familiar intercourse: conversation: communing. — *adj.* **convers'able** disposed to converse: sociable. — *adv.* **convers'ably.** — *ns.* **convers'ance, convers'ancy** (also *kon'*) the state of being conversant: familiarity. — *adj.* **convers'ant** (also *kon'*) acquainted by study: familiar: concerned or occupied: associating: dwelling (*obs.*). — *n.* **conversā'tion** intercourse: talk: familiar discourse: behaviour or deportment (*B.*). — *adj.* **conversā'tional.** — *ns.* **conversā'tionalist, conversā'tionist** one who excels in conversation; **conversā'tionism** (*rare*) a colloquialism. — *adj.* **conver'sative** (*obs.*) ready to talk. — **conversation piece** a painting of a number of persons, grouped indoors or outside: a play, etc., in which the dialogue is as important as, or more important than, the action: an object that arouses comment by its novelty. [Fr. *converser* — L. *conversārī*, to turn about, go about, associate, dwell — *con-*, intens., and *versāre*, to keep turning — *vertĕre*, to turn.]

convert *kən-vûrt', v.t.* to turn about (*obs.*): to change or turn from one thing, condition, opinion, party or religion to another: to change from an irreligious to a holy life: to change by a spiritual experience: to change into the converse: to alter into something else (esp. iron into steel, a try into a goal, a large house into several flats, a merchant ship into a cruiser): to apply to a particular purpose: to exchange for an equivalent, as paper money for specie. — *v.i.* to undergo conversion: to be convertible (from one form into another): to switch (religious or political) allegiance. — *n.* (*kon'*)

one who is converted. — *adj.* **con'verse** reversed in order or relation. — *n.* that which is the opposite of another: a proposition in which the subject and predicate have changed places (*log.*): a proposition in which that which is given and that which is to be proved in another proposition are interchanged (*math.*). — *adv.* **converse'ly.** — *ns.* **conver'sion** a change from one condition, use, opinion, party, religion or spiritual state to another: appropriation to a special purpose: the act of constructing a proposition in accordance with the rules of direct inference, in which the terms of another proposition are interchanged (*log.*); **con'-vertend** the proposition to be converted (*log.*); **convert'er** one who or that which converts: a vessel in which materials are changed from one condition to another (esp. iron into steel): apparatus for making a change in electric current (also **conver'tor**): a device which converts data from one form into another (*comput.*): a reactor which converts fertile material into fissile material; **convertibil'ity.** — *adj.* **convert'ible** that may be converted: of currency, that may be converted into gold (or dollars) at a fixed price: equivalent. — *n.* anything convertible: a car with a folding top. — *adv.* **convert'ibly.** — *n.* **con'vertite** (*arch.*) a convert: a reformed woman. — **convertiplane** (*kən-vûr'tə-plān*) an earlier name for a vertical take-off and landing aircraft. — **conversion course** a course of study designed to facilitate the change from one subject to another. [L. *convertĕre, conversum — con-, vertĕre*, to turn.]

convex *kon'veks*, also *kon-veks', adj.* rising into a round form on the outside, the reverse of concave. — *n.* a convex figure, surface, body, or part: the vault of heaven, etc. — *adj.* **convexed'** made convex. — *adv.* **convex'edly.** — *ns.* **convex'ity** roundness of form on the outside: a convex part or figure; **con'vexness** (or *-veks'*). — *adv.* **con'vexly** (or *-veks'*). — *adjs.* **convex'o= con'cave** (or *-kāv'*) convex on one side, and concave on the other; **convex'o-con'vex** (or *-veks'*) convex on both sides. [L. *convexus — convehĕre — con-, vehĕre*, to carry.]

convey *kən-vā', v.t.* to carry: to transmit: to impart: to steal: to communicate, as ideas: to make over in law. — *adj.* **convey'able.** — *ns.* **convey'al; convey'ance** act or means of conveying: trickery: a vehicle of any kind: the act of transferring property (*law*): the writing that transfers it; **convey'ancer** one who prepares deeds for the transference of property; **convey'ancing; convey'er, convey'or** a person or thing that conveys in any sense: a mechanism for continuous transport of materials, packages, goods in process of manufacture, etc. (also **convey'or-belt**). [O.Fr. *conveier* — L. *con-, via*, a way.]

convicinity *kon-vi-sin'i-ti,* (*rare*) *n.* a neighbourhood.

convict *kən-vikt', v.t.* to prove guilty: to pronounce guilty. — *n.* (*kon'*) one convicted or found guilty of crime: one who has been condemned to penal servitude. — *ns.* **convic'tion** act of convincing: strong belief: a proving guilty: the condition of being consciously convicted of sin (*theol.*); **con'victism** the convict system. — *adj.* **convict'ive** able to convince or convict. — **carry conviction** to bear irresistibly the stamp or proof of truth. [Root as **convince.**]

convince *kən-vins', v.t.* to overcome, get the better of (*Shak., Spens.*): to subdue the mind of by evidence: to satisfy as to truth or error: to convict (*B.*): to refute (*obs.*) — *n.* **convince'ment** (*obs.*). — *adjs.* **convinc'ible; convinc'ing** producing conviction: certain, positive, beyond doubt by a large or significant margin. — *adv.* **convinc'ingly.** [L. *convincĕre, con-,* sig. completeness, and *vincĕre, victum,* to conquer.]

convivial *kən-viv'i-əl, adj.* feasting or drinking in company: relating to a feast: social: jovial. — *v.i.* **convive** (*-vīv'; Shak.*) to feast together. — *n.* (*kə̄-vēv, kon'vīv*) a companion at table. — *ns.* **conviv'ialist** a convivial fellow; **convivial'ity.** — *adv.* **conviv'ially.** [L. *convīvium,* a living together, a feast — *con-,* together, *vīvĕre,* to live.]

convoke *kən-vōk', v.t.* to call together: to assemble (also **convocate** (*kon'vō-kāt*)). — *n.* **convocā'tion** the act of convoking: a provincial synod of clergy, esp. those of the provinces of Canterbury and York in the Church of England: the great legislative assembly of the university at Oxford and elsewhere. — *adj.* **convocā'tional.** — *n.* **convocā'tionist.** [L. *convocāre* — *con-*, together, and *vocāre*, *-ātum*, to call.]

convolve *kən-volv', v.t.* to roll together, or one part on another. — *adjs.* **convolute** (*kon'və-lōōt*, *-lūt*), rolled together, or one part on another (also **convoluted**): coiled laterally with one margin within, one without (*bot.*): of a flower-bud, contorted (*bot.*): of a gasteropod shell, having the inner whorls concealed or overlapped by the outer (*zool.*); **con'voluted** of argument, style of speech or writing, intricate, tortuous. — *n.* **convolution** (*-lōō'*, *-lū'*) twisting: a fold or sinuosity, esp. of the brain surface. [L. *con-*, together, *volvĕre*, *-ūtum*, to roll.]

Convolvulus *kən-vol'vū-ləs*, *n.* the bindweed genus of twining or trailing plants, giving name to the family **Convolvūlā'ceae**, akin to the nightshade family: (without *cap.*) a plant of the genus or of the kindred *Calystegia*. [L. *convolvĕre*; see above.]

convoy *kon-voi', now usu. kon'voi, v.t.* to accompany for protection. — *n.* (*kon'*) the act of convoying: protection: that which convoys or is convoyed, esp. a ship or ships of war guarding a fleet of merchant-vessels: also the ships so protected: an honourable escort: a supply of stores, etc., under escort: a train of military wagons or the like. [Fr. *convoyer*; see **convey**.]

convulse *kən-vuls', v.t.* to agitate violently: to affect by spasms. — *n.* **convuls'ant** an agent that causes convulsions. — Also *adj.* — *adj.* **convul'sible** subject to convulsion. — *n.* **convul'sion** any involuntary contraction of the voluntary muscles of the body, esp. such seizures in which the body is thrown into violent spasmodic contractions: any violent disturbance: (in *pl.*) fits of immoderate laughter (*coll.*). — *adjs.* **convul'sional, convul'sionary** pertaining to convulsions. — *ns.* **convul'sionary** one who has convulsions, esp. one of a fanatical sect of Jansenists who sprang up in France, about 1730; **convul'sionist** a religious convulsionary: a believer in the importance of convulsions in geological history (opposed to *uniformitarian*). — *adj.* **convuls'ive** attended with convulsions: spasmodic. — *adv.* **convuls'ively.** — *n.* **convuls'iveness.** [L. *con-*, intens., and *vellĕre*, *vulsum*, to pluck, to pull.]

cony, coney *kō'ni*, or (historically right) *kun'i*, *n.* a rabbit: rabbit-skin: a hyrax (*B.*): a term of endearment for a woman (*obs.*): a dupe (*obs.*). — **co'ny-burr'ow** a rabbit-burrow. — *v.t.* **co'ny-catch** (*Shak.*) to cheat. — **co'ny-catcher** (*obs.*) a cheat; **co'ny-wool** rabbits' fur. [Prob. through O.Fr. *conil*, from L. *cunīculus*, a rabbit.]

coo¹ *kōō, v.i.* to make a sound as a dove: to converse fondly. — *v.t.* to murmur softly or ingratiatingly: to effect as by cooing: — *pr.p.* **coo'ing**; *pa.t.* and *pa.p.* **cooed** (*kōōd*) — *n.* the sound emitted by doves. — *n.* and *adj.* **coo'ing.** — *adv.* **coo'ingly.** [Imit.]

coo² *kōō*, (*slang*) *interj.* expressive of surprise.

cooee, cooey *kōō'ē*, *n.* an Australian signal-call: a call to attract attention. — *v.i.* to utter the call. — *interj.* attracting attention. — **within cooee** nearby. [Aboriginal.]

coof *kōōf*, *køf*, *kif*, (*Scot.*) *n.* a lout. [Origin obscure.]

cook¹ *kōōk, v.t.* to prepare as food by heat: to subject to great heat: to manipulate for any purpose, or falsify, as accounts, etc.: to concoct (often with *up*): to ruin, tire out (*slang*): to spoil (as a chess-problem, by finding another way out): to prepare (a drug) by heating (*slang*). — *v.i.* to practise cookery: to undergo cooking. — *n.* one who undertakes or is skilled in cooking: a process of heating: an unforeseen alternative that ruins a chess-problem. — *adj.* **cook'able.** — *ns.* **cook'er** a stove, special vessel, or other apparatus for cooking: a variety (e.g. of apple) suitable for cooking; **cook'ery** the art or practice of cooking food. — **cooked breakfast** a breakfast which comprises or includes cooked food such as grilled or fried bacon, eggs, sausages, etc.; **cooker hood** a canopy over a cooker, containing filters, for the extraction of steam and smells; **cook'ery-book** a book of recipes for cooking dishes (*U.S.* **cook'-book**); **cook'-gen'eral, cook'-house'maid** a servant combining the functions of cook and general servant or housemaid; **cook'house** a building or room for cooking in; **cook'ing-apple**, etc., an apple, etc., specially suitable for cooking; **cook'ing-range** a stove adapted for cooking several things at once; **cook'maid** a maid who cooks or assists a cook; **cook'out** (*U.S.*) a barbecue party; **cook'room** a room in which food is cooked; **cook'shop** an eating-house; **cook'ware** (orig. *U.S.*) pans, dishes, etc., used for cooking. — **cook someone's goose** (*slang*) to finish off, to kill, to ruin, to spoil someone's plans; **cook the books** (*coll.*) to falsify accounts, etc.; **what's cooking?** (*coll.*) what is afoot? [O.E. *cōc*, a cook (cf. Ger. *Koch*) — L. *coquus*.]

cook² *kōōk, v.i.* to make the sound of the cuckoo.

cook³, kook *kōōk*, (*Scot.*) *v.i.* to appear and disappear by turns: to peep. [Origin obscure.]

cookie *kōōk'i*, *n.* in Scotland, a plain bun: in U.S. (usu. **cook'y**), a small sweet biscuit or cake: a person (*U.S. slang*). — **cook'ie-shine** (*facet.*) a tea-party. — **that's how, the way, the cookie crumbles** (*coll.*; esp. *U.S.*) that's what the situation is: that's just what one would expect to happen. [Du. *koekje*, a cake.]

cool *kōōl, adj.* slightly cold: free from excitement: calm: not zealous, ardent or cordial: indifferent: impudent: colloquially of a large sum of money, as *a cool thousand*: a slang term of approval meaning intellectual, not sensual: of jazz, unemotional and relaxed: excellent and up to date: pleasing, satisfying, pleasant (often *coll.*). — *v.t.* to make cool: to allay or moderate, as heat, excitement, passion, etc. — *v.i.* (often with *down*) to grow cool: to lose radioactivity. — *n.* that which is cool: coolness: coolness, self-possession. — *ns.* **cool'ant** a cooling agent: a fluid used to cool the edge of a cutting tool (*eng.*): a fluid used as the cooling medium in an engine (*eng.*); **cool'er** anything that cools: a vessel in which something is cooled: jail (*slang*). — *adj.* **cool'ish** somewhat cool. — *adv.* **cool'ly** in a cool manner: indifferently: impudently. — *ns.* **cool'ness** moderate cold: indifference: diminution of friendship: want of zeal: lack of agitation: self-possession; **coolth** (*dial.*) coolness. — *adj.* **cool'y** (*Spens.*) cool. — **cool box, bag** an insulated box, bag, used to keep food, etc., cool. — *adj.* **cool'head'ed** not easily excited: capable of acting with composure. — **cool'-house** a greenhouse kept at a cool temperature; **cooling card** (*Shak.*) anything that discourages, or dashes hopes; **cooling-off** see **cool off**; **cooling tower** a large structure in which water heated industrially is cooled for re-use; **cool'-tank'ard** a cooling drink of wine and water, with lemon-juice, spices, and borage: a local name of borage. — **cool it** (*slang*) to calm down, act in a relaxed fashion; **cool off** to become less angry and more amenable to reason (*n.* and *adj.* **cooling-off'**): to grow less passionate (*n.* and *adj.* **cool'ing-off'**); **cool one's heels** to be kept waiting; **keep one's cool** (*coll.*) to remain calm, keep one's head; **lose one's cool** to become flustered. [O.E. *cōl*; cf. Ger. *kühl*.]

coolabah, coolibah, -bar *kōōl'ə-bä(r)*, *n.* any of several species of Australian eucalypt. [Aboriginal.]

coolamon *kōōl'ə-mon*, (*Austr.*) a wooden or bark vessel used by Australian aborigines to hold liquids, etc. [Aboriginal.]

coolie, cooly *kōōl'i*, *n.* an Indian or Chinese labourer who has emigrated under contract to a foreign land: a European's name for a hired native labourer in India and China (*offensive*): in South Africa, an Indian (*offensive*). [Prob. *Kolī*, a tribe of W. India; or Tamil, *kūlī*, hire.]

coolly, coolth, etc. See **cool**.

coom¹ *kōōm*, *n.* soot: coal-dust: dust of various kinds. —

v.t. to begrime. — *adj.* **coom'y.** [App. Northern form of **culm².**]

coom² *kōōm*, (*Scot.*) *n.* the wooden centering on which a bridge is built: anything arched or vaulted. — *adj.* **coom'ceiled** said of a garret with the inside ceiling sloping from the wall. [Origin obscure.]

coomb¹, comb(e) *kōōm*, *n.* a deep little wooded valley: a hollow in a hillside. [O.E. *cumb*, a hollow.]

coomb², comb *kōōm*, *n.* an old measure of capacity = 4 bushels. [O.E. *cumb*, a measure.]

coon *kōōn*, *n.* the raccoon: a sly fellow: a Negro (*offensive*). — **coon'-song** a Negro-song. — **a gone coon** one whose case is hopeless. [U.S.; for **raccoon**.]

coon-can *kōōn'kan*, *n.* a card game in which one tries to form sequences. [Sp. *con quién*, with whom.]

coontie, coonty *kōōn'ti*, *n.* an American cycad yielding a sort of arrowroot. [Seminole *kunti*.]

coop *kōōp*, *n.* a wicker basket: a box or cage for fowls or small animals: a prison: a confined, narrow place. — *v.t.* (often with **up**) to confine in a coop or elsewhere. [Perh. from an unknown O.E. *cūpe*, collateral with *cȳpe*, cask; cf. L. *cūpa*, cask.]

co-op *kō-op', kō'op*, (*coll.*) *n.* short for **co-operative society** or **store.**

cooper¹ *kōōp'ər*, *n.* one who makes tubs, casks, etc.: a mixture of stout and porter. — *v.t.* to repair (tubs, etc.): to prepare, patch up. — *ns.* **coop'erage** the work or workshop of a cooper: the sum paid for a cooper's work; **coop'ering; coop'ery** the business of a cooper. [Also L.G., — L.L. *cūpārius* — *cūpa*, cask; cf. **coop.**]

cooper² *kōp'ər.* See **coper¹.**

co-operate (*also* **coop-** in all words) *kō-op'ər-āt*, *v.i.* to work together. — *n.* **co-opera'tion** joint operation: combination in co-operative societies. — *adjs.* **co-op'erative** (*also n.*); **co-op'erant** working together. — *n.* **co-op'erator** one who co-operates: a member of a co-operative society. — **co-operating grace** (*theol.*) the R.C., Arminian, and Socinian doctrine that the human will co-operates with the divine in the matter of saving grace; **co-operative society** an association for supplying goods or for carrying on some branch of industry, the profits going to the members; **co-operative store** the shop of a co-operative society. [Pfx. **co-**, together, and **operate.**]

co-opt *kō-opt'*, *v.t.* to elect into any body by the votes of its members. — *ns.* **co-opta'tion, co-op'tion.** — *adjs.* **co-op'tative, co-op'tive.** [L. *cooptāre, -ātum* — *co-*, together, *optāre*, to choose.]

co-ordinate (*also* **coor-** in all words) *kō-ör'di-nāt*, *adj.* of the same order or rank: pertaining to or involving co-ordination or co-ordinates. — *v.t.* to place or classify in the same order or rank: to adjust the relations or movements of: to combine or integrate harmoniously: to harmonise: to match. — *n.* an element of the same order as another: each of a system of two or more magnitudes used to define the position of a point, line, or surface by reference to a fixed system of lines, points, etc.: (in *pl.*) outer garments in harmonising colour, material and pattern (cf. **separates**). — *n.* **co-or'dinance** a joint ordinance. — *adv.* **co-or'dinately.** — *ns.* **co-or'dinateness; co-ordina'tion.** — *adj.* **co-or'dinative** co-ordinating: co-ordinated, indicating co-ordination. — **co-ordinate geometry** geometry by the use of co-ordinates, analytical geometry; **co-ordination compounds** (*chem.*) compounds in which the atoms or groups are united by **co-ordinate bonds**, secondary valences supplementary to the principal valences (e.g. addition compounds), esp. (**co-ordination complex compounds**) ones in which there is a central atom or ion.

coosen, coosin. Obs. spellings of **cousin, cozen.**

cooser. See **cusser.**

coost *køst*, a Scottish form of **cast** (*pa.t.*).

coot¹ *kōōt*, *n.* a short-tailed water-fowl, with a characteristic white spot — an extension of the bill — on the forehead (hence called *bald*, as in the phrase, *bald as*

a coot): a foolish person (*coll.*). [M.E. *cote*; cf. Du. *koet.*]

coot², cootikin. See **cuit.**

cop¹ *kop*, *n.* a top or head of anything: a conical ball of thread on a spindle. — Also **copp'in.** — *adj.* **copped** rising to a cop or head. [O.E. *cop, copp.*]

cop² *kop*, (*slang*) *v.t.* to capture: to catch: to acquire, get. — *n.* a policeman: a capture. — *n.* **copp'er** (*slang*) a policeman. — **cop'-shop** (*slang*) police station. — **cop out** (*slang*) not to take responsibility for, to refuse to participate in (*n.* **cop'-out**). [Perh. Fr. *caper*, to seize — L. *capěre, captum*, to take; cf. Du. *kapen*, to steal.]

copacetic, copesettic *kō-pə-set'ik*, (*U.S. slang*) *adj.* sound: excellent. — *interj.* all clear. [Origin obscure.]

copaiba, copaiva *kō-pī'bä, -vä*, or *-pā'*, *ns.* a balsam obtained from S. American caesalpiniaceous trees (*Copaifera*) much used in medicine: a tree of the genus *Copaifera.* [Sp. and Port. from Tupí.]

copal *kō'pəl*, *n.* a hard resin got from many tropical trees, and also fossil. [Sp., — Nahuatl *copalli*, resin.]

coparcener *kō-pär'sən-ər*, *n.* a joint heir to an undivided property. — *n.* and *adj.* **copar'cenery, -ary.**

copartner *kō-pärt'nər*, *n.* a joint partner. — *ns.* **copart'nership; copart'nery.**

copataine *kop'ə-tān*, (*Shak.*) *adj.* high-crowned like a sugar-loaf. [Ety. obscure.]

copatriot. A form of **compatriot.**

cope¹ *kōp*, *n.* a covering: a cap or hood: anything spread overhead: a coping: a semicircular, sleeveless hooded vestment worn over the alb or surplice in processions, at solemn lauds and vespers. — *v.t.* to cover as with a cope. — *n.* **cop'ing** the covering course of masonry of a wall. — **cope'-stone, cop'ing-stone** a stone that copes or tops a wall. [M.E. *cape* — hypothetical O.E. *cāpe* — L.L. *cāpa*; cf. **cap¹.**]

cope² *kōp*, (*dial.*) *v.t.* and *v.i.* to barter or exchange. — *n.* **cōp'er** a dealer, esp. in horses. [Cf. Du. *koopen.*]

cope³ *kōp*, *v.i.* (esp. with **with**) to contend: to deal (with) successfully. — *v.t.* to encounter, meet (*Shak.*): to match (*obs.*). — **copes'-mate** a companion (*Shak.*): an accomplice (*obs.*): a partner (*obs.*): an adversary (*obs.*): a paramour (*obs.*). [Fr. *couper* — L. *colaphus* (Gr. *kolaphos*), a buffet.]

cope⁴ *kōp*, (*obs.*) *v.t.* to tie or sew up the mouth of (a ferret). [Origin obscure; cf. **uncape, uncope.**]

cope⁵ *kōp*, *v.t.* to cut (a piece of moulding) so that it fits over another piece. — **cop'ing-saw** a narrow saw blade held under tension in a wide, U-shaped metal frame, used for cutting curves. [Prop. Fr. *couper*, to cut.]

copeck. Same as **kopeck.**

copepod *kō'pi-pod*, *n.* a member of the **Copep'oda**, a class of Crustacea, minute animals with oarlike swimming feet. [Gr. *kōpē*, handle, oar, *pous, podos*, foot.]

coper¹, often **cooper**, *kōp'ər*, *n.* a ship employed in surreptitiously supplying strong drink to deep-sea fishermen. — *v.i.* to supply liquor in such a way. [Du. *kooper* — *koopen*, to trade; cf. Ger. *kaufen*, to buy; O.E. *cēapan.*]

coper² *kōp.* See **cope².**

Copernican *ko-pûr'ni-kən*, *adj.* relating to *Copernicus*, famous Polish astronomer (1473–1543), or to his system, in which the earth revolves about the sun.

copesettic. See **copacetic.**

copia verborum *kō'pi-ə vûr-bō'rəm, kō'pi-a ver-bō'rŏŏm, wer-*, (L.) plenty of words, fluency.

copier. See **copy.**

coping. See **cope¹.**

co-pilot, copilot *kō'pī-lət*, *n.* a fellow pilot.

copious *kō'pi-əs*, *adj.* plentiful: overflowing: abounding: rich in words: not concise. — *adv.* **cō'piously.** — *n.* **cō'piousness.** [L. *cōpiōsus* — *cōpia*, plenty — *co-*, intens., and *ops, opis*, wealth.]

copita *ko-pēt'ə*, *n.* a tulip-shaped sherry glass. [Sp.]

co-polymer *kō-pol'i-mər*, *n.* a substance polymerised along with another, the result being a chemical compound, not a mixture. — *v.t.* **co-pol'ymerise, -ize.** — *n.* **co-polymerisa'tion, -z-.**

co-portion kō-pōr'shən, -pŏr', (Spens.) n. share.
copper¹ kop'ər, n. a reddish moderately hard metallic element (at. numb. 29; symbol Cu for L. cuprum), perhaps the first metal used by man: money, or a coin, made orig. of copper: a copper vessel: a boiler (orig. of copper) for clothes, or soap, etc. — adj. made of copper: copper-coloured. — v.t. to cover with copper. — n. copp'ering the act of sheathing with copper: a covering of copper. — adjs. copp'erish somewhat like copper; copp'ery like copper. — Copper Age a stage in culture in some regions leading up to the Bronze Age, characterised by the use of copper unmixed with tin; copp'er-beech' a variety of the common beech with purplish, copper-coloured leaves. — v.t. copp'er-bott'om to cover the bottom of with copper. — adj. copp'er-bott'omed having the bottom covered with copper: sound, reliable, esp. financially. — copp'er=cap'tain one who styles himself captain without grounds. — adjs. copp'er-faced faced with copper, as type; copp'er-fastened fastened with copper bolts. — copp'er-glance' redruthite, cuprous sulphide; copp'-erhead a venomous United States snake akin to the rattlesnake: in U.S. a northern sympathiser with the South in the Civil War; copp'er-nick'el niccolite, a copper-red mineral, arsenide of nickel; copp'er-nose a red nose; copp'erplate a plate of polished copper on which something has been engraved: an impression taken from the plate: faultless handwriting; copp'er=pyrī'tēs a yellow double sulphide of copper and iron; copp'erskin an American Indian; copp'ersmith a smith who works in copper; copp'er-work work in copper: (also n. sing. -works) a place where copper is wrought or manufactured; copp'er-worm the ship-worm. — hot coppers a parched tongue and throat after a bout of drinking. [O.E. copor — L.L. cuper — L. cuprum, a form of cyprium (aes), Cyprian (brass), because found in Cyprus.]
copper². See cop².
copperas kop'ər-əs, n. a name formerly applied to copper and other sulphates, now only to ferrous sulphate. [Fr. couperose (It. coparosa), perh. — L. cuprī rosa, rose of copper, or aqua cuprōsa, copper water.]
coppice kop'is, copse kops, ns. a wood of small growth for periodical cutting: a wood of sprouts from cut stumps. — v.t. to make into coppice: to cover with coppice. — n. copp'icing. — adj. cop'sy. — copse'wood. [O.Fr. copeiz, wood, newly cut — L.L. colpare, to cut — L. colaphus — Gr. kolaphos, a buffet.]
coppin. See cop¹.
copple kop'l, (obs.) n. a bird's crest. — copp'le-crown. — adj. copp'le-crowned. [App. from cop¹.]
copple-stone. An obsolete form of cobblestone.
coppy kop'i, (dial.) n. a small stool. — Also copp'y-stool. [Orig. uncertain.]
copra kop'rə, n. the dried kernel of the coconut, yielding coconut oil. [Port., from Malayalam.]
co-presence, copresence kō-prez'əns, n. presence together. — adj. co'pres'ent.
copro-, in composition, dung. — n. coprōlāl'ia (Gr. lalia, talk; psychiatry) obsessive use of obscene language. — adj. coprōlāl'iac. — n. coprolite (kop'rə-līt; Gr. lithos, stone) a piece of fossil dung: loosely applied to the phosphatic concretions. — adj. coprolitic (-lit'ik). — ns. coprol'ogy (Gr. logos, discourse) the unclean in literature and art; coproph'agan (Gr. phagein, to eat) a dung-beetle. — adj. coprophag'ic (-aj'ik) — n. coproph'agist (-jist) a dung-eater. — adj. coproph'agous (-gəs). — ns. coproph'agy (-ji); coprophil'ia (Gr. philiā, love) morbid pleasure in dung or filth. — adj. coproph'-ilous delighting in dung or filth: growing on or in dung. — n. copros'terol a compound formed from cholesterol in the intestine. [Gr. kopros, dung.]
copse, copsewood, copsy. See coppice.
Copt kopt, n. a Christian descendant of the ancient Egyptians. — adj. Copt'ic. — n. the language of the Copts. [Gr. Aigyptios, Egyptian.]
copula kop'ū-lə, n. that which joins together: a bond or

tie: copulation: the word joining the subject and predicate (log. or linguistics). — adj. cop'ular. — v.t. to unite. — v.i. cop'ulāte to unite in sexual intercourse. — n. copulā'tion. — adj. cop'ulātive uniting: indicating combination, not alternative or adversative relation. — n. in gram., a conjunction that indicates combination. — adj. cop'ulatory. [L. cōpula — co-, apĕre, to join.]
copy kop'i, n. abundance, copiousness (obs.): an imitation: a transcript: a reproduction: an exemplar: that which is imitated or reproduced: a specimen to be imitated: matter (e.g. a newspaper article) for printing: something newsworthy. — v.t. to write, paint, etc. in the manner of: to imitate closely: to transcribe: to reproduce or duplicate by copying-press or otherwise. — v.i. to make a copy: to follow: to look on a schoolfellow's work and filch the result: — pr.p. cop'ying; pa.t. and pa.p. cop'ied. — ns. cop'ier one who or that which copies: an imitator; cop'yism servile or plagiaristic copying; cop'yist one whose business is to copy documents: a mere copier. — cop'ybook a writing or drawing book of models printed for imitation: a letter-book, or collection of copies of documents. — adj. conventional, commonplace: (of example, operation, etc.) perfect, or carried out flawlessly. — cop'y-cat (slang) a term applied in resentful derision to an imitator. — v.t. and v.i. to imitate. — cop'yhold (Eng. law) a species of estate or right of holding land, according to the custom of a manor, by copy of the roll originally made by the steward of the lord's court; cop'yholder a holder of land by copyhold: an assistant who reads copy to a proof-reader; cop'ying-ink ink suitable for copying by impression; cop'ying(-ink)=pencil an ink-pencil; cop'ying-press a machine for copying manuscript letters by pressure; cop'yright the sole right to reproduce a literary, dramatic, musical, or artistic work — also to perform, translate, film, or record such a work (in the United Kingdom, since 1 July 1912, for books the term is the author's lifetime and fifty years after his death). — adj. protected by copyright. — v.t. to secure the copyright of. — adj. cop'yrightable. — cop'y-taster a person who selects items for publication or broadcast from the range of material submitted by reporters, etc.; cop'y-typing; cop'y-typist a typist who copies written, printed, etc. matter, not working from shorthand or recorded sound; cop'ywriter a writer of copy (esp. advertisements) for the press. — a copy of verses a set of verses, esp. a college exercise. [Fr. copie, from L. cōpia, plenty; in L.L. a transcript.]
coquelicot kok'li-kō, (Jane Austen) n. a brilliant red, the colour of the red poppy. [Fr., poppy.]
coquet, coquette ko-, kō-ket', v.i. to flirt: to dally. — v.t. (obs.) to flirt with: — pr.p. coquett'ing; pa.p. and pa.t. coquett'ed. — ns. cō'quetry (-kit-ri) the act of coquetting: the attempt to attract admiration, without serious affection: deceit in love: any artful prettiness; coquette' a woman (rarely a man) who seeks admiration from mere vanity: a flirt. — Also adj. — adj. coquett'ish practising coquetry: befitting a coquette. — adv. co-quett'ishly. — n. coquett'ishness. [Fr. coqueter, coquet, dim. of coq, a cock.]
coquilla kō-kil'yə, n. the nut of the piassava palm (Attalea), whose mottled, dark-brown endosperm is used by button-makers and turners. [Sp.; dim. of coca, shell.]
coquille ko-kē', n. (often in pl.) a scallop: a dish or pastry case in the shape of a scallop or shell. [Fr., — L. conchȳlium, — Gr. konchylion, a cockle or mussel.]
coquimbite kō-kim'bīt, n. a yellowish hydrous sulphate of iron found in Coquimbo.
coquito kō-kē'tō, n. a beautiful Chilean palm, Jubaea spectabilis: — pl. coqui'tos. [Sp.; dim. of coco, coco-palm.]
cor¹ kör, (coll.) interj. an expression of surprise. — cor blimey a form of gorblim(e)y. [Vulg. form of God.]
cor² kör, n. a Hebrew measure, the homer, 10 ephahs or

baths (roughly 11 bushels). [Heb. *kōr*, round vessel.]

cor-. See **com-**.

coracle *kor'ə-kl, n.* a small oval rowing-boat used in Wales, made of skins or tarred or oiled canvas stretched on wickerwork, etc. [Conn. W. *corwg,* anything round; Gael. *curach,* see **currach**.]

coracoid *kor'ə-koid, adj.* shaped like a crow's beak. — *n.* (*anat.*) a paired ventral bone in the breast-girdle, forming along with the scapula the articulation for the fore-limb: in mammals, except monotremes, reduced to a **coracoid process** fused to the scapula. [Gr. *korax, korakos,* a crow, and *eidos,* form.]

co-radicate, coradicate *kō-rad'i-kāt, (philol.) adj.* of the same root. [Pfx. **co-,** together, and **radicate** — see **radical**.]

coraggio *kor-ad'jō, interj.* courage: — *pl.* **corag'gios.** [It.]

coral *kor'əl, n.* a hard substance of various colours deposited on the bottom of the sea, skeleton, mostly calcareous, of Anthozoa and of some Hydrozoa: the animal or colony that produces it: a young child's toy of coral or other material for biting: lobster roe, coral red when cooked: (in *pl.*) a necklace of coral: a deep orange-pink colour. — *adj.* made of or like coral, esp. red coral. — *adj.* **coralla'ceous** like, or having the qualities of, coral. — *n.* **Corallian** (-*al'; geol.*) a Jurassic formation overlying the Oxfordian, including the Coral Rag and Coralline Oolite. — *adjs.* **corallif'erous** containing coral; **coralliform** (-*al'*) having the form of coral: **corallig'enous** producing coral; **cor'alline** of, like, or containing coral. — *n.* a common limy seaweed (*Corallina*) of a delicate pinkish or purplish colour: a coral-like substance or animal. — *n.* **cor'allite** the cup of a simple coral or of one polyp: a fossil coral. — *adjs.* **cor'alloid, coralloid'al** in the form of coral: resembling coral. — *n.* **corallum** (-*al'*) the skeleton of a coral colony: — *pl.* **corall'a.** — **cor'al-berr'y** an American shrub of the snowberry genus, or its red berry; **cor'al-fish** a tropical, spiny-finned fish of many kinds abundant about coral reefs; **cor'al-is'land; Coralline Crag** (*geol.*) a division of the English Pliocene, shelly sands and clays with fossil polyzoa; **Coralline Oolite** a massive limestone underlying the Coral Rag; **Coral Rag** a coarse limestone rock formed chiefly of coral in the Corallian formation; **cor'al-reef'** a reef or bank formed by the growth and deposit of coral; **cor'al-rock'** a limestone composed of coral; **cor'al-root'** a species of Cardamine with knobbed root stock: a plant of a genus of orchids (*Corallorhiza*) with coral-like root-stock; **cor'al-snake** an American genus, Elaps (or Micrurus), of small venomous snakes; **cor'al-tree** a tropical genus (Erythrina) of trees and shrubs with red coral-like flowers; **cor'al-wort** coral-root, in either sense. [L. *corallum* — Gr. *korallion*.]

coram domino rege *kō', kō'ram dom'i-nō rē'jē, rā'ge,* (L.) before our lord the king; **coram nobis** *nō'bis, -bēs,* before us (*i.e.* the monarch), in our presence; **coram populo** *pop'ū-lō, -ōō-,* in the presence of the public.

coramine *kor'a-mīn.* See **nikethamide**.

coranach. Same as **coronach**.

cor anglais *kör ã'glā, ong'-,* an oboe set a fifth lower than the ordinary oboe — also called (It.) **corno inglese** (*kör'nō ing-glā'sā*): — *pl.* **cors anglais** (*körz*), **cor'ni inglesi** (*kör'nē in-glā'sē*). [Fr., English horn, but probably not English.]

coranto *ko-ran'tō, n.* a rapid and lively dance: the music for it, in triple time: — *pl.* **coran'to(e)s.** — Also **courante** (*kōō-rät*). [Fr. *courante,* lit. running — L. *currēre,* to run — (It. *coranta,* from Fr.).]

corban *kör'bən, n.* anything devoted to God in fulfilment of a vow. [Heb. *qorbān,* an offering, sacrifice.]

corbe *körb* (*Spens.*). See **corbel, courb**.

corbeau *kor-bō', n.* a blackish green colour. [Fr., raven.]

corbeil *kör'bel, -bāy', n.* a basket filled with earth, set up as a protection (*fort.*): a carved representation of a basket (*archit.*). — *n.* **corbeille'** a basket of flowers. [Fr. *corbeille* — L. *corbicula,* dim. of *corbis,* a basket.]

corbel *kör'bəl, (archit.) n.* a projection from the face of a wall, supporting a weight (*Spens.* **corbe**). — *adj.* **cor'belled.** — *n.* **cor'belling.** — **cor'bel-ta'ble** a row of corbels and the parapet or cornice they support. [O.Fr. *corbel* — L.L. *corvellus,* dim. of *corvus,* a raven.]

Corbett *kör'bət, n.* a Scottish mountain of between 2 500 and 2 999 feet that has a re-ascent of 500 feet on all sides. [Orig. list of these made by J. R. *Corbett*.]

corbicula *kör-bik'ū-lə, n.* the pollen basket of bees, consisting of the dilated posterior tibia with its fringe of long hairs: — *pl.* **corbic'ulae** (-*lē*). — *adj.* **corbic'ulate.** [L. dim. of *corbis,* a basket.]

corbie *kör'bi, (Scot.) n.* a raven: a crow. — **corbie messenger** one who returns too late, or not at all; **cor'bie-steps** crow-steps. [O.Fr. *corbin* — L. *corvus,* a crow.]

corcass *kör'kəs, n.* in Ireland, a salt-marsh, or readily flooded land by a river. [Ir. *corcach*.]

Corchorus *kör'kə-rəs, n.* the jute genus. [Gr. *korchoros,* the name of a plant.]

cord *körd, n.* a small rope or thick string: something resembling a cord (as spinal cord, umbilical cord), anything that binds or restrains: a measure of cut wood (128 cubic feet), orig. determined by use of a cord or string: a raised rib on cloth: ribbed cloth, esp. corduroy (also *adj.*): (in *pl.*) corduroy trousers: a string crossing the back of a book in binding: a flex for an electrical apparatus (esp. *U.S.*). — *v.t.* to supply with a cord: to bind with a cord. — *n.* **cord'age** a quantity of cords or ropes, as the rigging of a ship, etc. — *adj.* **cord'ed** fastened with cords: wound about with cords (*her.*): ribbed: piled in cords. — *ns.* **cord'ing** the act of binding: cordage; **cord'ite** a cord-like smokeless explosive. — *adj.* **cord'less** (of an electrical device) operating without a flex, battery-powered. — *n.* **cordot'omy** cutting in certain parts of the spinal cord to relieve great pain (also **chordot'omy**). — **cord'-grass** a grass of the genus *Spartina* which is found in muddy salt-marshes and is used for making ropes; **cord'-wood** wood put up in cords. [Fr. *corde* — L. *chorda*; see **chord**.]

Cordaites *kör-dā-ī'tēz, n.* a Palaeozoic genus of fossil plants, typical of the family **Cordaita'ceae,** gymnosperms nearer the conifers than the cycads. [Named after A. K. J. *Corda* (1809–49), Bohemian botanist.]

cordate *kör'dāt, adj.* heart-shaped: having the base indented next to the petiole (*bot.*). — *adj.* **cord'iform** heart-shaped. [L. *cordātus* (in modern sense) — L. *cor, cordis,* the heart.]

Cordelier *kör-də-lēr', n.* a Franciscan friar, from the knotted cord worn as a girdle: (in *pl.*) a club in the French Revolution, meeting in an old Cordelier convent. [O.Fr. *cordele,* dim. of *corde,* a rope.]

cordial *kör'di-əl, adj.* hearty: with warmth of heart: sincere: affectionate: reviving the heart or spirits. — *n.* anything which revives or comforts the heart: a medicine or drink for refreshing the spirits: a beverage containing alcohol or sugar or stimulating drugs. — *v.i.* **cor'dialise, -ize** to become cordial, to fraternise — *ns.* **cordiality** (-*al'i-ti*); **cor'dialness.** — *adv.* **cor'dially.** [Fr., — L. *cor, cordis,* the heart.]

cordierite *kör'di-ər-īt, n.* the mineral iolite or dichroite. [After P. L. A. *Cordier* (1777–1861), Fr. mineralogist.]

cordiform. See **cordate**.

cordillera *kör-dil-yā'rə, n.* a chain of mountains, as the Andes and Rocky Mountains. [Sp., — Old Sp. *cordilla* — L. *chorda,* cord — Gr. *chordē*.]

cordiner *kör'di-nər.* See **cordovan**.

cordite. See **cord**.

córdoba *kor'dō-bə, -bä, n.* the monetary unit of Nicaragua. [Named after Francisco Fernandez de *Córdoba* (d. about 1518).]

cordon *kör'don, -dən, n.* a cord or ribbon bestowed as a badge of honour: a row of stones along the line of a rampart (*fort.*): a line of police, soldiers, etc., or a system of road-blocks, encircling an area so as to prevent or control passage into or out of it: a single-stemmed fruit-tree. — *v.t.* to close (off) an area with a cordon of men, ring of barriers, etc. — **sanitary cordon** (now more *usu.*) cordon sanitaire. [Fr.]

cordon bleu *kor-dɔ̃ blø,* (Fr.) blue ribbon: a cook of the highest excellence. — *adj.* (of a cook or cookery) of a very high standard.

cordon sanitaire *kor-dɔ̃ sa-nē-ter,* (Fr.) a sanitary cordon, a line of sentries posted to restrict passage into and out of an area and so keep contagious disease within that area: neutral states keeping hostile states apart: a barrier (*lit.* or *fig.*) isolating a state, etc., considered dangerous — sometimes called **sanitary cordon.**

cordotomy. See **cord.**

cordovan *kör'də-vən,* (*arch.*) **cordwain** *körd'wān, ns.* goatskin leather, originally from *Cordova* (*Córdoba*) in Spain. — *ns.* **cord'wainer, cord'iner** (*arch.*) a worker in cordovan or cordwain: a shoemaker; **cord'wainery** (*arch.*).

corduroy *kör-də-roi',* or *kör', n.* a ribbed fustian, a cotton stuff made after the fashion of velvet: (in *pl.*) corduroy trousers. — *adj.* of corduroy. — **corduroy road** a track laid transversely with tree-trunks. [Perh. Fr. *corde du roi,* king's cord, although the term is not used in French; perh. **cord** and **duroy.**]

cordwain, cordwainer. See **cordovan.**

Cordyline *kör-di-lī'nē, n.* a tropical and subtropical liliaceous genus of trees similar to the dragon-tree: (without *cap.*) a tree of the genus. [Gr. *kordylē,* club.]

core[1] *kōr, kör, n.* in an apple, pear, etc. the central casing containing the seeds: the innermost or most essential part of something: the central part of the earth (*geol.*): a cylindrical sample of rock, soil, etc. extracted by an annular drill: the lump of stone or flint remaining after flakes have been struck off it (*archaeol.*): the part of a nuclear reactor containing the fissile material (*phys.*): (also **magnetic core**) a small ferromagnetic ring which, charged or uncharged by electric current, can thus assume two states corresponding to the binary digits 0 and 1; used for computer memory. — *v.t.* to take out the core of (an apple, etc.). — *adjs.* **cored** having the core removed: cast by means of a core: having a core; **core'less** without core: pithless: hollow. — *n.* **cor'er** an instrument for removing the core. — **core time** see **flexitime.** [Poss. L. *cor,* the heart, or Fr. *cor,* horn, corn (on the foot), or *corps,* body.]

core[2] *kōr, kör, n.* a company, gang, shift. [**corps.**]

co-regent *kō-rē'jənt, n.* a joint-regent.

Coregonus *kor-i-gō'nəs, kör-, n.* whitefish, a genus of herring-like fishes of the salmon family, pollan, vendace, etc. — *adj.* **corego'nine** (or -*nin*). [Gr. *korē,* pupil of the eye, *gōniā,* angle.]

co-relation, co-relative. See **correlate.**

co-religionist *kō-rə-lij'ən-ist, n.* one of the same religion as another.

corella *kə-rel'ə, n.* an Australian long-billed cockatoo. [Aboriginal.]

Coreopsis *kor-i-op'sis, n.* a genus of annual or perennial composite plants mostly native to America, some species of which are cultivated for their showy flowers: (without *cap.*) a plant of the genus. [Gr. *koris,* a bug, *opsis,* appearance, from the shape of the seed.]

co-respondent *kō-rə-spond'ənt,* (*law*) *n.* a man or woman charged with adultery, and proceeded against along with the wife or husband who is the *respondent.* — **co-respondent shoes** two-coloured shoes for men, generally black or brown and white.

corf *körf, n.* a coal-miner's basket, now usu. a tub or trolley: a cage for fish or lobsters: — *pl.* **corves** (*körvz*). — Also *dial.* **cauf** (*köf*): — *pl.* **cauves** — **corf'-house** (*Scot.*) a salmon-curing house. [Du., — L. *corbis,* basket.]

corgi *kör'gi, n.* a Welsh breed of dog, having a fox-like head and short legs. [Welsh *corr,* dwarf, *ci,* dog.]

coriaceous. See **corium.**

coriander *kor-i-an'dər, n.* an umbelliferous plant (*Coriandrum sativum*), whose seeds are used as spice, etc. — **corian'der-seed.** [Fr. *coriandre* — L. *coriandrum* — Gr. *koriannon.*]

Corinthian *kor-inth'i-ən, adj.* of Corinth (Gr. *Korinthos*) in Greece: of an ornate style of Greek architecture, with acanthus capitals: over-brilliant in literary style: profligate. — *n.* a native or inhabitant of Corinth: a profligate: a man of fashion: an amateur sportsman. — *n.* **Cor'inth** (*obs.*) a brothel. — *v.i.* **corinth'ianise, -ize** to be licentious. — **Corinthian brass, bronze** an alloy made in Corinth, much valued in ancient times: assurance or effrontery.

Coriolis effect *kor-i-ō'lis i-fekt',* (*phys., meteor.*) the deflection (to the right in the Northern, left in the Southern, hemisphere) and acceleration of bodies, etc. moving relative to the earth's surface, caused by the earth's rotation. [First studied by G. B. *Coriolis,* (1792–1843).]

corium *kō'ri-əm, kö', n.* leather armour (*ant.*): the true skin, under the epidermis (*anat.*). — *adjs.* **coriā'ceous, co'rious** leathery. [L. *corium* — Gr. *chorion,* skin, leather.]

co-rival, co-rivalry, co-rivalship. Variant forms of **corival,** etc.

cork *körk, n.* the outer bark of the cork-tree, an oak found in S. Europe, N. Africa, etc.: a stopper made of cork: any stopper: a tissue of close-fitting, thickwalled cells, almost airtight and watertight, forming bark or covering the surfaces of wounds (*bot.*): a piece of cork: a float of cork. — *adj.* made of cork. — *v.t.* to stop with a cork: to stop up: to bottle up, repress (with *up; fig.*). — *n.* **cork'age** corking or uncorking of bottles: a charge made by hotel-keepers for uncorking of bottles when the liquor has not been supplied from the house. — *adj.* **corked** stopped as by a cork: of wine, tainted as if by the cork, generally in fact by a fungus which develops on the cork: blackened by burnt cork: drunk (*slang*). — *ns.* **cork'er** something conclusive, a finisher (*slang*): a person or thing that surpasses (*slang*): a person or device that inserts corks; **cork'iness.** — *adjs.* **cork'ing** (*slang*) surpassing; **cork'y** of, or resembling, cork: withered (*Shak.*). — **cork'-borer** an instrument for boring holes in corks to receive glass tubes in chemical apparatus; **cork'-cam'bium** phellogen; **cork'-car'pet, -lino'leum, -mat** a floor-covering, mat, made of pieces of cork with rubber and linseed oil; **cork'-cutter** one employed in cutting corks for bottles, etc.: an instrument used for this; **cork'-heel** a shoe-heel of cork. — *adj.* **cork'-heeled** having cork heels: wanton. — **cork'-jacket** a jacket made of or lined with cork, to aid in swimming; **cork'-leg** an artificial leg; **cork'-oak** a species of oak (*Quercus suber*) which supplies the cork of commerce in Spain and Portugal; **cork'-screw** a screw for drawing corks from bottles. — *adj.* like a cork-screw in shape. — *v.i.* to move in a spiral manner. — *v.t.* to pull out with difficulty, as a cork: to obtain information from by force or cunning. — **cork'-sole'** an inner shoe-sole made of cork; **cork'-tree** the cork-oak: applied to various trees with corky bark or very light wood; **cork'wing** the goldsinny; **cork'wood** very light wood: applied to many trees with light wood, e.g. balsa, alligator apple. [Perh. from Sp. *alcorque,* cork slipper, which may be from L. *quercus,* oak, with the Arabic article *al*; Sp. has also *corche, corcha, corcho,* perh. L. *cortex,* bark, rind.]

corking-pin *körk'ing-pin, n.* a pin of the largest size. [Perh. for **calking-pin.**]

corkir, korkir *kör'kər,* (*Scot.*) *n.* a lichen used for dyeing (red or purple). [Gael. *corcur* — L. *purpura,* purple.]

corm *körm, n.* a short, bulbous, subterranean stem as in the crocus. — *n.* **corm'ophyte** (-*fīt*) a plant differentiated into leaf, stem, and root. — *adjs.* **cormophytic** (-*fīt'*); **corm'ous** producing corms. — *n.* **corm'us** the differentiated body of a cormophyte: the whole body of a compound animal. [Gr. *kormos,* the lopped trunk of a tree.]

cormorant *kör'mə-rənt, n.* a member of a genus (*Phalacrocorax*) of web-footed sea-birds, of great voracity: a glutton. [Fr. *cormoran,* from L. *corvus marīnus,* sea crow.]

corn¹ *körn, n.* a grain, hard particle: a kernel, small hard seed: collectively seeds of cereal plants, or the plants themselves — esp. (in England) wheat, (in Scotland and Ireland) oats, (in North America) maize: something old-fashioned or hackneyed. — *adj.* of, for, pertaining to, made from, growing among, feeding upon, corn: granular. — *v.t.* to make granular: to sprinkle with grains of salt: to salt: to give corn to, as a horse (*Scot.*): to intoxicate (*slang*). — *v.i.* to form seed. — *p.adj.* **corned** granulated: salted (e.g. **corned beef** — also **corn'-beef**). — *adj.* **corn'y** like corn: produced from corn: tipsy (*slang*): old-fashioned, uninteresting from frequent use, dull (*slang*). — **cornacre** see **conacre**; **corn'-baby** see **kirn**; **corn'-ball** (*U.S.*) a sweetened ball of popcorn: a yokel: an unsophisticated person: something trite, banal or sentimental. — Also *adj.* — **corn-beef** see **corned**; **corn'-bin** a bin for corn; **corn'-bor'er** a European moth (*Pyrausta nubilalis*) whose larvae have become a maize pest in America; **corn'-brake'** a maize plantation; **corn'-bran'dy** spirits made from grain: whisky; **corn'brash** (*geol.*) a clayey limestone of the Oolite, giving good corn soils; **corn'-bread, -cake** (*U.S.*) bread, a cake, made of maize meal; **corn'-chandler** a retailer of grain; **corn'-chandlery**; **corn'-cob** the woody axis of a maize ear: a corn-cob pipe; **corn'cockle** a tall, beautiful cornfield weed (*Agrostemma* (or *Lychnis*) *githago*) akin to the campions; **corn'-cracker** (*U.S.*) a poor white: a Kentuckian; **corn'-crake** a rail with characteristic cry, inhabiting cornfields; **corn'-dealer, -factor, -merchant** one who buys and sells corn; **corn'-dodger** (*U.S.*) a cake, small loaf, or dumpling of maize; **corn-dollie** see **kirn**¹; **corn'-exchange'** a mart for trade in corn. — *adj.* **corn'-fed** fed on corn: well fed. — **corn'field** a field in which corn is growing; **corn'-flag** a gladiolus: **corn'flakes** toasted flakes of maize, eaten esp. as a breakfast cereal; **corn'flour** finely ground maize, rice, or other grain: a pudding made of it; **corn'flower** the bluebottle, a beautiful blue-flowered cornfield weed of the Compositae (*Centaurea cyanus*); **corn'fly** the gout-fly; **corn'-husk** (*U.S.*) a corn-shuck; **corn'husker** a person or machine that removes cornhusks; **corn'husking; corn'-ing-house** a place where gunpowder is granulated; **corn'-kist** (*Scot.*) a stable grain-chest; **corn'-kister** a farm-worker's song of his life and work; **corn'land** ground suitable for growing grain; **corn'-law** a law regulating trade in grain, esp. (in *pl.*) laws that restricted importation to Britain by a duty, repealed 1846; **corn'loft** a granary; **corn'-maiden** see **kirn**; **corn'-mar'igold** a yellow cornfield chrysanthemum; **corn'-mill** a flour-mill; **corn'-miller; corn'-moth** a moth of the clothes-moth genus (*Tinea granella*) whose larvae feed on grain; **corn'pipe** a musical instrument made of a stalk of an oat or other cereal; **corn'-pit** (*U.S.*) part of an exchange where business is done in maize; **corn'-pone** (*U.S.*) maize-bread: a maize loaf; **corn'-popper** a pan or grating for popping corn; **corn'-rent** rent paid in corn, not money; **corn'-rig** (*Scot.*) a ridge or strip on which oats are grown; **corn'-sal'ad** lamb's lettuce, a genus (*Valerianella*) of humble weeds of the valerian family, sometimes used as salads; **corn'-shuck** (*U.S.*) the leaves enclosing a maize ear; **corn'-shucking** the removal of corn-shucks: an assembly for the purpose; **corn'-snow** granulated snow; **corn'-spirit** a vegetation god or spirit concerned in the growth of corn; **corn'-stalk** a stalk of corn: a tall thin person, esp. one born in New South Wales; **corn'starch** maize starch or flour, for puddings; **corn'stone** a silicious limestone, favourable for corn-growing; **corn'-thrips** a minute insect of the Thysanura, that sucks the sap of grain; **corn'-van** an instrument for winnowing corn; **corn'-weevil** a small weevil (*Calandra granaria*), destructive in granaries; **corn'-whisky** an American whisky made from maize; **corn'worm** a corn-weevil: a corn-moth larva. — **corn-cob pipe** a tobacco-pipe with the bowl made of a maize cob; **corn in Egypt** abundance (Gen. xlii. 2); **corn on the cob** a cob of maize with grains still attached, boiled whole and eaten as a vegetable. [O.E. *corn*; Goth. *kaurn*; akin to L. *grānum*.]

corn² *körn, n.* a small hard growth chiefly on the toe or foot, resulting from an increase of thickness of cuticle, caused by pressure or friction. — *adj.* **corn'eous** horny. — *ns.* **corn'icle, cornic'ulum** a little horn: a hornlike process; esp. one of the wax-secreting tubes of a greenfly. — *adjs.* **cornic'ulate** horned: horn-shaped; **cornif'erous** containing hornstone; **cornif'ic** producing or forming horn or horns. — *n.* **cornifica'tion**. — *adjs.* **corn'iform** shaped like a horn; **cornigerous** (*kör-nij'ər-əs*) horned. — *n.* **cor'nū** (L. *kör'nōō*) a horn, hornlike part, or process: — *pl.* **cor'nūa**. — *adj.* **cor'nūal**. — *adj.* **corn'y** of or pertaining to horns or corns: having corns: horny. — **corn'-cure** a remedy for corns; **corn'-cutter** one who cuts corns; **corniferous limestone** a coral limestone with chert nodules in the Devonian of North America; **corn plaster** a remedial plaster for corns. — **tread on someone's corns** to hurt someone's feelings. [L. *cornū*, a horn.]

Cornaceae. See **cornel**.

cornage *körn'ij*, (*hist.*) *n.* a feudal service or rent fixed according to number of horned cattle — horngeld. [O.Fr., — L. *cornū*, horn.]

cornea *kör'ni-ə, n.* the transparent horny membrane that forms the front covering of the eye. — *adj.* **cor'neal.** — **corneal lens** a contact lens covering the transparent part of the eye only. [L. *cornea* (*tēla*), horny (tissue).]

cornel *kör'nəl, n.* the so-called cornelian-cherry or cornelian-tree, a small tree (*Cornus mas*) of middle and southern Europe: any species of the genus **Cor'nus**, type of the family **Corna'ceae** (akin to Umbelliferae), such as **dwarf cornel**, an alpine herb with four white bracts surrounding its umbel, and dogwood. — **cor'nel-tree; cornē'lian-tree.** [L.L. *cornolium* — L. *cornus*, cornel.]

cornelian *kör'nē'li-ən, n.* a fine chalcedony, generally translucent red. — Also **carnē'lian** (*kär-*). [Fr. *cornaline* — L. *cornū*, a horn, or *cornum*, cornelian-cherry, from its appearance; confused with *carō, carnis*, flesh.]

cornemuse *kör'ni-mūz, n.* a French bagpipe. [Fr.]

corneous. See **corn**².

corner *kör'nər, n.* the point where two lines or several planes meet: an angular projection or recess: a secret or confined place: an embarrassing position, difficulty: a point in a rubber at whist (*obs.*): a free shot, taken from the corner of the field, given to the opposite side when a player in football or hockey e.g. plays the ball over his own goal-line: an operation by which the whole of a stock or commodity is bought up so that the buyers may resell at their own price. — *v.t.* to supply with corners: to put in a corner: to put in a fix or difficulty: to form a corner against: to get control of by forming a corner. — *v.i.* to turn a corner. — *adj.* **corn'ered** having corners: put in a difficult position. — *adv.* **corn'erwise** with the corner in front: diagonally. — **corn'er-boy** a loafer: a street-corner rough: the man at the end of the row in a negro-minstrel performance (also **corn'er-man**); **corn'er-stone** a stone that unites the two walls of a building at a corner: the principal stone, esp. the corner of the foundation of a building: something of prime importance (*fig.*). — *n.pl.* **corn'er-teeth** the lateral incisors of a horse. — **cut corners** see **cut**; **fight, stand, one's (own) corner** to defend strongly, maintain, one's (own) position, stand, argument, etc.; **turn the corner** to go round the corner: to get past a difficulty or danger, begin to pick up; **within the four corners of** contained in. [O.Fr. *corniere* — L. *cornū*, horn.]

cornet¹ *kör'nit* (*U.S.* also *-net'*), *n.* an old woodwind instrument (usu. **cornett**): an organ stop of various kinds: a treble brass valve instrument, more tapering than the trumpet (also **cornetto** (*-net'ō*: — *pl.* **cornett'i** (*-ē*) It.), **cornō'pean, cornet-à-piston(s)** (*kor-nā-ā-pēs-tɔ̄*)): a cornet-player: any funnel-shaped object, as a piece of gold for assaying, a shopkeeper's screwed paper bag, an ice-cream-filled wafer cone, a cream-filled pastry. — *ns.* **cor'netist, cornett'ist** a cornet-player; **cornettino** (-*tē'nō*) an instrument of the cornet family with a compass a fourth above that of a cornet (also **small cornet**). [Fr. *cornet*, dim. of *corne* — L. *cornū*, horn.]

cornet² *kör'nit, n.* an old form of lady's head-dress, with side lappets: a lappet of this: a cavalry standard (*obs.*): till 1871 a cavalry officer — later sub-lieutenant: a standard-bearer at riding the marches. — *n.* **cor'netcy** the commission or rank of cornet. [Fr. *cornette*, ult. from L. *cornū*, horn.]

cornet³. See **coronet**.

cornett, cornettino, cornettist, cornetto. See **cornet¹**.

cornice *kor'nis, n.* the uppermost member of the entablature, surmounting the frieze (*classical archit.*): a projecting moulding along the top of a building, window, etc.: a plaster moulding round a ceiling: a moulded ridge for supporting picture-hooks: an overhanging crest of snow. — *v.t.* to furnish with a cornice. — *adj.* **cor'niced.** — **cor'nice-hook, -pole, -rail** a hook, pole, rail for hanging pictures, curtains, etc.; **cor'nice-ring** a ring or moulding on a cannon next below the muzzle-ring. [Fr., — It., poss. Gr. *korōnis*, a curved line, cf. L. *corōna*.]

corniche *kor-nēsh*, (Fr.) *n.* a coast road built along a cliff-face: in Egypt, a boulevard along a bank of the Nile.

cornicle, corniculate, corniferous, cornigerous, etc. See **corn²**.

Cornish *kör'nish, adj.* pertaining to Cornwall. — *n.* the Celtic language of Cornwall, dead since the later 18th cent. — **Cornish clay** china-clay; **Cornish pasty** a pasty (**pasty²**) with meat and vegetables.

corno *kör'nō, n.* the French horn: — *pl.* **cor'ni** (-*nē*). — *n.* **corn'ist** a horn-player. — **corno di basset'to** the basset horn: an organ-stop; **corno inglese** see **cor anglais**. [It., — L. *cornū*, a horn.]

cornopean. See **cornet¹**.

cornu, cornual. See **corn²**.

cornucopia *kör-nū-kō'pi-ə, n.* the horn of plenty — according to one fable, the horn of the goat that suckled Jupiter, placed among the stars as an emblem of plenty: an ornament consisting of a horn overflowing with fruits: an abundant source of supply. — *adj.* **cornucō'pian.** [L. *cornū cōpiae* — *cornū*, horn, *cōpia*, plenty.]

Cornus. See **cornel**.

cornute *kör-nūt', v.t.* (*obs.*) to cuckold. — *adjs.* **cornute', -d** horned: hornlike: cuckolded (*obs.*). — *n.* **cornūt'o** (or -*nōō'*; It.; *obs.*) a cuckold: — *pl.* **cornut'os.** [L. *cornūtus*, horned — *cornū*, horn.]

corny. See **corn¹,²**.

corocore *kor'ō-kōr, -kör, -ō, n.* a Malay form of boat. — Also **cor'ocorō** (*pl.* **cor'ocoros**). [Malay *kurakura*.]

corody. See **corrody**.

corolla *kor-ol'ə, -ōl'ə, n.* the inner circle or whorl of the floral envelopes. — *adj.* **corollā'ceous.** — *n.pl.* **Corolliflorae** (-*i-flō'rē*; L. *flōs, flōris*, flower) in some classifications the Gamopetalae or Sympetalae. — *adjs.* **corolliflo'ral; corolliflo'rous; corolli'form; coroll'ine** (or *kor'*). [L. *corolla*, dim. of *corōna*, a crown.]

corollary *kər-ol'ə-ri* (rare *kor'ol-ə-ri*), *n.* an easy inference: a consequence or result: a supplement, surplus, or supernumerary. [L. *corollārium*, a garland, money for a garland, a tip — *corolla*.]

Coromandel *ko-rə-man'dəl, -rō-*, (sometimes without *cap.*) *n.* or *adj.* (also **Coromandel wood**) calamander: (also **Coromandel ebony**) a wood of the same genus (*Diospyros*) as calamander: the colour colcothar. — **Coromandel screen** a Chinese folding lacquered screen; **Coromandel work** lacquer work in which an incised design is filled with colour or with gold. [*Coromandel* Coast in south-east India.]

corona *ko-rō'nə, kə-, n.* the large, flat, projecting member of a cornice crowning the entablature (*archit.*): the trumpet of a daffodil, etc., composed of ligules of the perianth leaves (*bot.*): a coloured ring round the sun or moon, distinguished from halo by having red

outermost: convergence point of auroral rays: one of the sun's envelopes, outside the chromosphere, observable during total eclipse (*astron.*): a similar atmospheric envelope of a star (*astron.*): a round pendent chandelier: — *pl.* **corō'nas, corō'nae** (-*ē*). — *n.* **cor'onal** (-*ə-nl*) a circlet, small crown or garland. — *adjs.* **corō'nal** pertaining to a crown, a corona, or to the top of the head: like a crown; **cor'onary** (-*ən-ə-ri*) coronal: surrounding a part (**coronary arteries** those that supply the muscle of the heart-wall with blood; so **coronary circulation**). — *n.* a coronary thrombosis. — *adjs.* **cor'onāte, -d** crowned: applied to shells with a row of projections round the apex. — *ns.* **coronā'tion** the ceremony of crowning; **corō'nium** the name given to a hypothetical element in the solar corona assumed to explain spectral lines now known to be due to iron and nickel atoms that have lost a large number of electrons; **coronagraph, coronograph** (-*ōn'ə-gräf*) a special telescope used to observe prominences and the corona around the edge of the sun. — **coronary thrombosis** stoppage of a branch of a coronary artery by a clot of blood. [L. *corōna*, a crown.]

coronach *kor'ə-näkh, -nəhh, n.* a dirge. [Said to be a Gaelic word *corranach* (cf. Ir. *coránach* — *comh-*, with, together, and *rànach*, a cry), but evidence insufficient.]

coronal, coronary, etc. See **corona**.

coronation¹ (*Spens.*), for **carnation**.

coronation². See **corona**.

coroner *kor'ə-nər, n.* orig. the guardian of the pleas of the crown: now an officer whose chief duty is to enquire into the causes of accidental or suspicious deaths: in the Isle of Man, the principal officer of a sheading. [O.Fr. *corouner* — L. *corōna*, crown.]

coronet *kor'ə-nit, n.* a small crown worn by the nobility: an ornamental head-dress: the part of a horse's pastern just above the coffin (also **cor'net**). — *adj.* **cor'oneted.** [O.Fr. *coronete*, dim. of *corone*, crown — L. *corōna*.]

coronis *ko-rō'nis, n.* in Greek, a sign (') marking a crasis, as κἄν = καὶ ἄν. [Gr. *korōnis*, a curved line.]

coronium, coronograph. See **corona**.

coronoid *kor'ə-noid*, or *kor-ō'noid*, (*anat.*) *adj.* like a crow's bill, as the *coronoid process* of the lower jaw. [Gr. *korōnē*, a crow, and *eidos*, form, shape.]

corozo *kor-ō'sō, n.* a South American short-stemmed palm (*Phytelephas*) whose seed (**corozo nut**) gives vegetable ivory: also the cohune palm, or other: — *pl.* **corō'zos.** [Sp. from an Indian language.]

corpora. See **corpus**.

corporal¹ *kör'pə-rəl, n.* a non-commissioned officer next under a sergeant: in the navy, a petty officer under a master-at-arms: the leader of a gang of miners, etc. — *n.* **cor'poralship.** [Fr. *caporal* — It. *caporale* — *capo*, the head — L. *caput*, the head.]

corporal² *kör'pə-rəl, adj.* belonging or relating to the body: having a body: material: not spiritual. — *n.* in Catholic and episcopal churches, the cloth on which the bread and wine of the Eucharist are laid out and with which the remains are covered. — Also **cor'poras** (*obs.*). — *n.* **corporality** (-*al'i-ti*). — *adv.* **cor'porally.** — *adj.* **cor'porate** legally united into a body so as to act as an individual: belonging or pertaining to a corporation: united. — *adv.* **cor'porately.** — *ns.* **cor'porateness; corporā'tion** a body or society authorised by law to act as one individual: a town council: a company (*U.S.*): a belly, esp. a pot-belly (*coll.*); **cor'poratism** (the policy of) control of a country's economy through the combined power of the trade unions, large businesses, etc. — *n.* and *adj.* **cor'poratist.** — *adj.* **cor'porative.** — *n.* **cor'porā'tor** a member of a corporation. — *adj.* **corporeal** (*kor-pō'ri-əl, -pö'*) having a body or substance: material. — *v.i.* and *v.t.* **corpō'realise, -ize.** — *ns.* **corpō'realism** materialism; **corpō'realist; corpōreality** (-*al'i-ti*). — *adv.* **corpō'really.** — *ns.* **corporeity** (-*pə-rē'i-ti*); **corporificā'tion** the act of corporifying. — *v.t.* **corpor'ify** to embody: to solidify. — **corporal punishment** punishment inflicted on the body, as flogging, etc.; **corporate state** a system of government by corporations representing employers and employed, its purpose being to increase national production and obviate party politics; **corporation aggregate** a corporation consisting of several persons; **corporation sole** a corporation which consists of one person and his successors; **corporation tax** a tax levied on the income of companies. [L. *corpus, corpŏris,* the body.]

corposant *kör'pə-zant, n.* St Elmo's fire, an electrical discharge forming a glow about a mast-head, etc. [Port. *corpo santo* — L. *corpus sanctum,* holy body.]

corps *kōr, kör, n.* a division of an army forming a tactical unit: a branch or department of an army: an organised body: a German students' society: a set of people working more or less together: — *pl.* **corps** (*kōrz, körz*). [Fr., — L. *corpus,* body.]

corps de ballet *kor də ba-le,* (Fr.) the company of ballet dancers at a theatre; **corps d'élite** (*kor dā-lēt*) (Fr.) a small number of people picked out as being the best in any group; **corps diplomatique** (*dē-plō-ma-tēk*) (Fr.) the whole diplomatic staff at a particular capital.

corpse *körps,* or *körs, n.* a dead human body. — *v.i.* (*coll.*) of an actor on stage, to begin to laugh, forget one's lines, etc. — *v.t.* (*coll.*) to cause (an actor) to corpse. — **corpse'-can'dle** a light seen hovering over a grave — an omen of death; **corpse'-gate** a lich-gate. [M.E. *corps,* earlier *cors* — O.Fr. *cors* — L. *corpus,* the body.]

corpus *kör'pəs, n.* a body, esp. a dead body: any special structure in the body: a body of literature, law, etc.: — *pl.* **cor'pora** (*-pə-rə*). — *ns.* **cor'pulence, cor'pulency** fleshiness of body: excessive fatness. — *adj.* **cor'pulent.** — *adv.* **cor'pulently.** — *n.* **cor'puscle** (*-pus-l;* sometimes *-pus'l*) a cell or other minute body suspended in fluid, esp. a red or white cell in the blood: a minute particle (also **corpus'cule**). — *adjs.* **corpus'cular; corpuscūlā'rian.** — *ns.* **corpuscūlā'rian** one who holds the corpuscular theory; **corpuscular'ity.** — **corpus callosum** (*kə-los'əm;* L. *callosus,* callous, hard-skinned) in humans and higher mammals. a connecting column of nerve fibre between the two cerebral hemispheres: — *pl.* **corpora callosa; corpus cavernosum** (*ka-vər-nō'səm;* L. *cavernosus,* cavernous, hollow) a section of erectile tissue in the penis or clitoris: — *pl.* **corpora cavernosa; Corpus Christi** (*kris'tē, -tī*) the festival in honour of the Eucharist, held on the Thursday after the festival of the Trinity; **corpus delicti** (*di-lik'tī, de-lik'tē; law*) the essential facts of the crime charged, e.g. in a murder trial, that somebody is actually dead and has been murdered; **corpus luteum** (*lōō'ti-əm;* L. *luteus,* yellow) a mass of yellow tissue that develops in a Graafian follicle after the discharge of an ovum and secretes progesterone: — *pl.* **cor'pora lu'tea; corpus vile** (*vī'lē, vē'le, wē-*) a person or thing considered so expendable as to be a fit object for experimentation, regardless of consequences: — *pl.* **cor'pora vi'lia.** — **corpuscular theory of light** Newton's theory that light consists in the emission of material particles; **Corpus Juris Canonici** (*jōō'ris* (*ū'ris*) *ka-non'i-sī* (*-i-kē*)) the body of the canon law; **Corpus Juris Civilis** (*si-vi'lis* (*kē-vē', -wē'*)) the body of the civil law. [L. *corpus,* the body.]

corrade *kə-rād', kor-,* (*geol.*) *v.t.* to wear away through the action of loose solid material, e.g. pebbles in a stream or wind-borne sand. — *n.* **corrasion** (*-rā'zhən*). [L. *corrādĕre,* to scrape together — *con-,* together, *rādĕre, rāsum,* to scratch.]

corral *kə, ko-ral' n.* a pen for cattle: an enclosure to drive hunted animals into: a defensive ring of wagons. — *v.t.* to pen: to form into a corral: — *pr.p.* **corall'ing:** *pa.t.* and *pa.p.* **corralled'.** [Sp.]

correct *kə-* or *ko-rekt', v.t.* to make right or supposedly right: to remove or mark faults or supposed faults from or in: to do this and evaluate: to set (a person) right: to punish: to counterbalance: to bring into a normal state: to reduce to a standard. — *adj.* right: according to standard: free from faults. — *adjs.* **correct'able, correct'ible.** — *adv.* **correct'ly.** — *n.* **correc'tion** emendation or would-be emendation: amendment: punishment: reduction: compensation: quantity

to be added to bring to a standard or balance an error: bodily chastisement: a period of reversal or counter-action during a strong market trend (*U.S. finance*). — *adj.* **correc'tional.** — *ns.* **correc'tioner** (*Shak.*) one who administers correction; **correct'itude** correctness of conduct or behaviour. — *adj.* **correct'ive** of the nature of, by way of, correction: tending to correct: correcting. — *n.* that which corrects. — *ns.* **correct'ness; correct'or** he who, or that which, corrects: a director or governor: a proof-reader. — *adj.* **correct'ory** corrective. — **corrective training** reformative imprisonment for persistent offenders of 21 and over for periods from 2 to 4 years. — **under correction** subject to correction — often used as a formal expression of deference to a superior authority. [L. *corrigĕre, corrēctum* — *cor-,* intens., *regĕre,* to rule.]

corregidor *ko-rehh'i-dōr, n.* the chief magistrate of a Spanish town. [Sp., corrector.]

correlate *kor'i-lāt, v.i.* to be related to one another. — *v.t.* to bring into relation with each other: to establish relation or correspondence between. — *n.* either of two things so related that one implies the other or is complementary to it: an analogue (*rare*). — *adj.* (*rare*) correlated. — *adj.* **correlā'table.** — *n.* **correlā'tion** the state or act of correlating: mutual relation, esp. of phenomena regularly occurring together: interdependence, or the degree of it. — *adj.* **correlative** (*-el'ə-tiv*). — *n.* a person or thing correspondingly related to another person or thing. — *adv.* **correl'atively.** — *ns.* **correl'ativeness, correlativ'ity.** [L. *cor-,* with, and **relate.**]

correligionist. Same as **co-religionist.**

correption *kər-ep'shən,* (*obs.*) *n.* shortening in pronunciation: a reproof. [L. *correptiō, -ōnis* — *cor-,* intens., and *rapĕre,* to seize.]

correspond *kor-i-spond', v.i.* to answer, suit, agree (with *to, with*): to hold intercourse, esp. by letter. — *ns.* **correspond'ence, correspond'ency** suitability: harmony: relation of agreement, part to part, or one to one: friendly intercourse (*arch.*): communication by letter: a body of letters. — *adj.* **correspond'ent** answering: agreeing: suitable. — *n.* one with whom intercourse is kept up by letters: one who contributes letters, or is employed to send special reports (e.g. *foreign correspondent, war correspondent*) to a periodical: a person or firm that regularly does business for another elsewhere. — *adv.* **correspond'ently.** — *adj.* **correspond'ing** correspondent: answering: similar, comparable, matching: suiting: carrying on correspondence by letters. — *adv.* **correspond'ingly.** — *adj.* **correspon'sive** corresponding: answering. — **correspondence course, school,** etc., one conducted by postal correspondence; **corresponding member** a member living at a distance who communicates with a society without taking part in its administration. — **doctrine of correspondences** the theory of Swedenborg that there is a spiritual antitype corresponding to every natural object and that Scripture contains the key to these correspondences. [L. *cor-,* with, and *respondēre.*]

corrida (de toros) *kō-rē'dhä* (*dä tō'rōs*) (Sp.) a bullfight.

corridor *kor'i-dör, n.* a passageway or gallery communicating with separate rooms or dwellings in a building or compartments in a railway train: a strip of territory by which a country has access to a port, etc.: (in *pl.*) places outside the administrative centre where unofficial news circulates and gossip is carried on (*politics*). — **corr'idor-carr'iage, -train** a carriage, train, in which one can pass along from one compartment to another; **corridor work** informal discussion behind the scenes at a meeting. — **corridors of power** (*fig.*) the higher reaches of government administration. [Fr., — It. *corridore* — It. *correre,* to run — L. *currĕre.*]

corrie *kor'i, n.* a semicircular mountain recess or cirque. [Gael. *coire,* a cauldron.]

corrigendum *kor-i-jen'dəm* or *-gen'dōōm, n.* that which requires correction: — *pl.* **corrigen'da,** esp. corrections to be made in a book. [L., gerundive of *corrigĕre*, to correct.]

corrigent *kor'i-jənt, adj.* and *n.* corrective. — *adj.* **corr'-igible** that may be corrected: open to correction. — *n.* **corrigibil'ity.** [L. *corrigĕre*, to correct; see **correct.**]

corrival *kor-ī'vəl, n.* a rival: a competitor: an equal. — *adj.* contending: emulous. — *v.t.* to rival. — *v.i.* to vie. — *ns.* **corrī'valry; corrī'valship.** [L. *con-*, with, and **rival.**]

corroborate *kər-ob'ə-rāt, v.t.* to confirm: to make more certain. — *adj.* confirmed: used blunderingly by Ancient Pistol, perh. for *corroded* or *corrupt* (*Shak.*). — *adjs.* **corrob'orable; corrob'orant; corrob'orative** tending to confirm. — *n.* that which corroborates. — *ns.* **corroborā'tion** confirmation; **corrob'orātor.** — *adj.* **corrob'oratory** corroborative. [L. *cor-*, intens., and *rōborāre, -ātum*, to make strong; see **robust.**]

corroboree *kə-rob'ə-rē, n.* a ceremonial dance of Australian aborigines: a song for such a dance: a festive gathering. — *v.i.* to hold a corroboree. [Aboriginal.]

corrode *kər-ōd', v.t.* to eat away by degrees, esp. chemically: to rust. — *v.i.* to be eaten away. — *adj.* **corrōd'ent** having the power of corroding. — *n.* that which corrodes. — *n.pl.* **Corrodentia** (*ko-rə-den'shyə*) the Psocoptera, or book-lice, etc. — *n.* **corrōsibil'ity.** — *adj.* **corrōs'ible** (also **corrōd'ible**). — *n.* **corrosion** (*-rō'zhən*) the act or process of eating or wasting away. — *adj.* **corrōs'ive** having the quality of eating away. — *n.* that which has the power of corroding. — *adv.* **corrōs'ively.** — *n.* **corrōs'iveness.** — **corrosive sublimate** mercuric chloride. [L. *cor-*, intens., *rōdĕre, rōsum*, to gnaw.]

corrody, corody *kor'ō-di, n.* an allowance: a pension: originally the right of the lord to claim free lodging from the vassal. [O.Fr. *conrei, conroi.*]

corrugate *kor'ə-* or *kor'ōō-gāt, v.t.* to wrinkle or draw into folds. — *ns.* **corrugā'tion** the act of wrinkling or state of being wrinkled: a wrinkle; **corr'ugator** (*anat.*) a wrinkling muscle. — **corrugated iron** sheet iron bent by ridged rollers into a wavy form for the sake of strength; **corrugated paper** a wrinkled paper used as wrapping material. [L. *cor-*, intens., *rūgāre, -ātum*, to wrinkle — *rūga*, a wrinkle.]

corrupt *kər-upt', v.t.* to make putrid: to taint: to debase: to spoil: to destroy the purity of: to pervert: to bribe. — *v.i.* to rot: to lose purity. — *adj.* putrid: depraved: defiled: not genuine: much vitiated or debased in transcription: bribed: dishonest, venal: of the nature of, or involving, bribery: (of a computer program or data in store) containing errors arising e.g. from a fault in the hardware or software. — *ns.* **corrupt'er; corruptibil'ity.** — *adj.* **corrupt'ible** liable to be corrupted. — *n.* **corrupt'ibleness.** — *adv.* **corrupt'ibly.** — *ns.* **corrup'-tion** rottenness: putrid matter: impurity: bribery; **corrup'tionist** one who defends or who practises corruption. — *adj.* **corrupt'ive** having the quality of corrupting. — *adv.* **corrupt'ly.** — *n.* **corrupt'ness.** — **corruption of blood** the former inability of an attainted person to inherit or transmit lands, titles or dignities. [L. *cor-*, intens., and *rumpĕre, ruptum*, to break.]

corsage *kor-säzh', n.* the bodice or waist of a woman's dress: a bouquet to be worn there or elsewhere. [O.Fr., — *cors* — L. *corpus*, the body.]

corsair *kor'sār, n.* a privateer (esp. of Barbary): a privateering ship: a pirate. [Fr. *corsaire*, one who courses or ranges — L. *cursus*, a running — *currĕre*.]

corse *kors, n.* a poetic form of **corpse.**

corselet, corselette. See **corslet.**

corset *kor'sit, n.* a close-fitting stiff inner bodice: stays: a stiff belt coming down over the hips: a term for the controls imposed by the Bank of England to restrict banks' capacity to lend money, e.g. by limiting the amount of new interest-bearing deposits a bank can accept. — Also *adj.* — *v.t.* to furnish with a corset: — *pr.p.* **cor'seting;** *pa.t.* and *pa.p.* **cor'seted.** — *ns.* **corsetier** (*kor-sə-tyā*, also *-tēr'*), *fem.* **corsetière** (*kor-sə-tyer*, also *-tēr'*) a maker or seller of corsets; **cor'setry** corsets: the

making or selling of corsets. [Dim. of O.Fr. *cors* — L. *corpus*, the body.]

corsive *kor'siv,* (*obs.*) *n.* and *adj.* Same as **corrosive.**

corslet, corselet *körs'lit, n.* a cuirass, a protective body-covering of leather, or steel, etc.: a modified corset, or combined belt and brassière. — Also **corselette'.** — *adj.* **cors'leted.** [Fr. *corselet*, dim. of O.Fr. *cors* — L. *corpus*, the body.]

corsned *körs'ned,* (*hist.*) *n.* the ordeal of swallowing a piece of bread or cheese, taken to prove guilt if it stuck in the throat. [O.E. *corsnæd* — *gecor* (cf. *coren*, pa.p. of *cēosan*, to choose) and *snæd*, a piece, from *snīdan*, to cut.]

corso *kor'sō, n.* a race, run, course: a race of riderless horses: a procession of carriages: a street where these are held: an avenue, wide street: — *pl.* **cor'sos.** [It.]

Cortaderia *kör-tə-dēr'i-ə, n.* a genus of tall-stemmed S. American grasses with large thick panicles. [Amer. Sp. *cortadera*, a plant with sharp-edged leaves.]

cortège *kör-tezh', n.* a train of attendants: a procession, a funeral procession. [Fr., — It. *corte*, court.]

Cortes *kor'tes, n.* the parliament of Spain and of Portugal. [Sp. and Port. pl. of *corte*, a court.]

cortex *kor'teks, n.* the bark or skin of a plant between the epidermis and the vascular bundles (*bot.*): the outer layer of an organ, esp. of the brain (*zool.*): — *pl.* **cortices** (*kör'ti-sēz*), sometimes **cor'texes.** — *adjs.* **cor'-tical** pertaining to the cortex: external; **cor'ticāte, -d** furnished with bark. — *ns.* **cor'ticoster'oid, cor'ticoid** any of the steroids, e.g. cortisone, extracted from the adrenal cortex; **cortico'trophin** adrenocorticotrophin. [L. *cortex, cortĭcis*, bark.]

cortile *kör-tē'lā, n.* an enclosed courtyard within a building, generally roofless. [It.]

cortisol *kör'ti-sol, n.* hydrocortisone. [*cortis*one.]

cortisone *kör'ti-zōn, -sōn, n.* 'compound E', a steroid isolated from the adrenal cortex, or prepared from ox bile, etc., an anti-inflammatory agent.

Corti's organ. Same as **organ of Corti.**

corundum *kə-run'dəm, n.* a mineral consisting of alumina, second in hardness only to the diamond — including sapphire, ruby, emery. [Tamil *kurundam.*]

coruscate *kor'əs-kāt, v.i.* to sparkle: to throw off flashes of light. — *adj.* **coruscant** (*-rus'*) flashing; **cor'uscating** (esp. *fig.* of wit). — *n.* **coruscā'tion** a glittering: sudden flash of light. [L. *coruscāre, -ātum*, to vibrate, glitter.]

corvée *kör-vā', n.* the obligation to perform gratuitous labour (such as the maintenance of roads) for the sovereign or feudal lord. [Fr., — L.L. *corrogāta* — L. *corrogāre* — *cor-*, together, *rogāre*, to ask.]

corves. See **corf.**

corvet. Same as **curvet.**

corvette *kör-vet', n.* formerly a flush-decked vessel, with one tier of guns: now an escort vessel specially designed for protecting convoys against submarine attack. [Fr., — Sp. *corbeta* — L. *corbīta*, a slow-sailing ship — *corbis*, a basket.]

Corvus *kor'vəs, n.* the crow genus, typical of the family **Cor'vidae** and subfamily **Corvī'nae;** a southern constellation: (without *cap.*) a grappling-hook in ancient Roman naval warfare: (without *cap.*) a hooked ram for destroying walls. — *n.* **cor'vid** (*zool.*) a member of the Corvidae. — *adj.* **cor'vine** (*-vīn*). [L. *corvus*, a raven.]

corybant *kor'ə-bant, n.* a priest of Cybele, whose rites were accompanied with noisy music and wild dances (Eng. *pl.* **cor'ybants;** L. *pl.* **corybant'es**). — *adj.* **coryban'tic** wildly excited. — *n.* **cor'ybantism.** [Gr. *korybās, korybantos.*]

Corydalis *kor-id'ə-lis, n.* a genus akin to fumitory. — *n.* **cor'ydaline** (or *-rid'*) an alkaloid ($C_{22}H_{27}O_4N$) obtained from Corydalis root. [Gr. *korydallis*, crested lark, from a fancied resemblance of the flower.]

Corydon *kor'i-don, n.* a generic proper name for a rustic. [L., — Gr. *Korydōn*, a shepherd's name in Theocritus and Virgil.]

Corylus *kor'i-ləs, n.* the hazel genus. [L.]

corymb *kor'imb, (bot.) n.* a flattish-topped raceme. — *adj.* **cor'ymbose** (or *-imb'*). [L. *corymbus* — Gr. *korymbos,* a cluster.]

Corypha *kor'i-fə, n.* the talipot genus of gigantic tropical Asian palms. [Gr. *koryphē,* top.]

coryphaeus *kor-i-fē'əs, n.* the chief or leader, esp. the leader of a chorus: — *pl.* **coryphaei** *(-fē'ī).* — Also *(arch.)* **coryphe** *(kor'if).* — *n.* **coryphee** *(kor-ē-fā';* Fr. *coryphée)* orig. a male dancer *(n.* is *masc.* in Fr.): now, one of a group between soloists and corps de ballet (also **cor'yphe**). [L., — Gr. *koryphaios* — *koryphē,* the head.]

coryphene *kor'i-fēn, n.* a fish of the genus *Coryphaena,* called the dolphin. [Gr. *koryphaina.*]

coryza *ko-rī'zə, n.* a cold in the head: nasal catarrh. [L., — Gr. *koryzu.*]

cos¹ *kos, n.* a long-leaved lettuce. — Also **cos lettuce.** [Introduced from the Aegean island of Cos (Gr. *Kōs*).]

cos². See **cosine.**

'cos *koz, kəz, (coll.) adv.* and *conj.* because.

Cosa Nostra *kō'zə nos'trə,* the Mafia organisation, esp. in U.S. [It., 'our thing'.]

coscinomancy *kos'i-nō-man-si, n.* an ancient mode of divination by a sieve and pair of shears. [Gr. *koskinon,* a sieve, *manteiā,* divination.]

cose *kōz, v.i.* to make oneself cosy. [See **cosy.**]

cosecant *kō-sek'ənt, -sēk', n.* the secant of the complement of an angle — *abbrev.* **cosec** *(kō'sek).* — *n.* **cosech** *(kōs-ek')* a conventional shortening of *hyperbolic cosecant.*

coseismal *kō-sīz'məl, adj.* experiencing an earthquake shock simultaneously. — Also **coseis'mic.** [L. *co-,* together, Gr. *seismos,* earthquake.]

co-sentient *kō-sen'sh(y)ənt, (arch.) adj.* perceiving together.

cosh¹ *kosh, (Scot.) adj.* cosy, snug. [Orig. unknown.]

cosh² *kosh, (slang) n.* a bludgeon, truncheon, leadpipe, piece of flexible tubing filled with metal, or the like, used as a weapon. — Also *v.t.* [Prob. Romany, from *koshter,* a stick.]

cosh³. See **cosine.**

cosher¹ *kosh'ər, (dial.) v.t.* to pamper, to coddle. — *v.i.* to chat in a friendly way.

cosher². Same as **kosher.**

coshery *kosh'ər-i, n.* the ancient right of an Irish chief to quarter himself and his retainers on his tenantry — also **cosh'ering.** — *v.i.* **cosh'er** to live on dependants. — *n.* **cosh'erer.** [Ir. *coisir,* a feast.]

cosier. See **cozier.**

co-signatory *kō-sig'nə-tə-ri, adj.* uniting with others in signing. — *n.* one who does so. — *adj.* **co-signif'icative** *(rare)* having the same signification.

cosine *kō'sīn, n.* the sine of the complement of an angle — *abbrev.* **cos** *(kos).* — *n.* **cosh** *(kosh* or *kos-āch')* a conventional abbrev. for *hyperbolic cosine.*

cosmea *koz'mi-ə, n.* a plant of the genus *Cosmos.*

cosmetic *koz-met'ik, adj.* purporting to improve beauty, esp. that of the complexion: correcting defects of the face, etc., or supplying deficiencies (as *cosmetic surgery, hands*): involving or producing an apparent or superficial concession, improvement, etc. without any real substance to it. — *n.* (usu. in *pl.*) a preparation for the improvement of beauty, etc., sometimes including shampoo, deodorant, toothpaste, etc. — *n.* **cosmē'sis** cosmetic surgery or treatment. — *adj.* **cosmet'ical.** — *adv.* **cosmet'ically.** — *n.* **cosmetic'ian** one who produces, sells, or is skilled in the use of, cosmetics (sometimes *fig.*). — *v.t.* **cosmet'icise, -ize.** — *ns.* **cosmet'icism; cosmetol'ogy** the art or profession of applying cosmetics or hairdressing, or of carrying out plastic surgery. [Gr. *kosmētikos* — *kosmeein,* to adorn — *kosmos,* order.]

Cosmos *koz'mos, n.* an American plant genus of composites akin to the dahlia: (without *cap.*) any plant of the genus. [Gr. *kosmos,* ornament.]

cosmos *koz'mos, n.* the world or universe as an orderly or systematic whole — opp. to chaos: order. — *adjs.* **cos'mic** relating to the cosmos: universal: orderly; **cos'mical** cosmic: happening at sunrise *(astron.)*: rising with the sun *(astron.).* — *adv.* **cos'mically.** — *ns.* **cos'mism** the notion of the cosmos as a self-existing whole; **cos'mist** a secularist. — *adj.* **cosmochem'ical.** — *ns.* **cosmochem'istry** the chemistry of stars, planets etc. — **cos'mocrat** *(rare)* a ruler of the world. — *adj.* **cosmocrat'ic.** — *n.* **cos'modrome** *(-drōm;* Russian *kosmodrom)* a launching-site for spacecraft, esp. in the Soviet Union. — *adjs.* **cosmogon'ic, -al** relating to cosmogony. — *ns.* **cosmog'onist** one who speculates on the origin of the universe; **cosmog'ony** (Gr. *kosmogoniā*) a theory or a myth of the origin of the universe, esp. of the stars, nebulae, etc. — Also **cosmogeny** *(-moj');* **cosmog'rapher.** — *adjs.* **cosmograph'ic, -al.** — *ns.* **cosmog'raphy** a description of the world: the science of the constitution of the universe; **cosmol'atry** (Gr. *latreiā,* worship) *(rare)* the worship of the world. — *adj.* **cosmolog'ical.** — *ns.* **cosmol'ogist; cosmol'ogy** the science of the universe as a whole: a treatise on the structure and parts of the system of creation; **cos'monaut** an astronaut (Russian *kosmonaut;* Gr. *nautēs,* sailor). — *n.* **cosmonau'tics.** — *adj.* **cosmoplas'tic** (Gr. *plassein,* to form) moulding the universe: world-forming. — *ns.* **cosmopol'icy** *(Shelley)* cosmopolitanism; **cosmop'olis** (Gr. *polis,* city, state) an international city: a world-city; **cosmopol'itan** a citizen of the world: one free from local or national prejudices: a communist sympathetic towards or tolerant of non-communism in other countries. — *adj.* belonging to all parts of the world: unprejudiced. — *n.* **cosmopol'itanism.** — *n.* and *adj.* **cosmopolite** *(koz-mop'ə-līt).* — *adjs.* **cosmopol'itic, -polit'ical.** — *n. sing.* **cosmopol'itics** world politics. — *n.* **cosmop'olitism** (or *-pol'*); **cosmorama** *(-rä'mə;* Gr. *horāma,* a spectacle) a view, or a series of views, of different parts of the world, tricked out with mirrors, lenses, etc. — *adj.* **cosmoramic** *(-ram').* — *ns.* **cos'mosphere** an apparatus for showing the position of the earth at any given time with reference to the fixed stars; **cosmothē'ism** (Gr. *theos,* god) the belief that identifies God with the cosmos: pantheism. — *adjs.* **cosmothet'ic, -al** assuming an external world. — **cos'motron** see **accelerator** under **accelerate.** — **cosmical constant** a number, at present of the order of 10⁷⁸, believed to be fundamental to the structure of the universe; **cosmic rays** radiation first discovered by Hess in 1911–1912, thought by Millikan to be electromagnetic but now known to consist of protons, electrons, positrons, neutrinos, and other particles originating for the most part within the Galaxy; **cosmological principle** according to the cosmology of general relativity, the principle that, at a given time, the universe would look the same to observers in other nebulae as it looks to us. [Gr. *kosmos,* order, world, universe.]

co-sphered *kō-sfērd', (arch.) adj.* being in the same sphere.

cosponsor *kō'spon'sər, v.t.* to sponsor jointly. — Also *n.*

coss *kos, n.* a measure of distance in India, averaging about 1¾ mile. [Hindi *kōs* — Sans. *krośa,* a call.]

Cossack *kos'ak, n.* one of a people in south-eastern Russia, formerly holding by military tenure and serving as cavalry. — **Cossack boots** Russian boots; **Cossack hat** a brimless hat of fur or similar material; **Cossack post** a small group of mounted troops on outpost duty. [Turk. *quzzāq,* freebooter.]

cosset *kos'it, n.* a hand-reared lamb: a pet. — *v.t.* to fondle: to pamper: — *pr.p.* **coss'eting;** *pa.t.* and *pa.p.* **coss'eted.** [Perh. O.E. *cot-sæta, cot-setla,* cot-dweller.]

cossie *koz'i, (Austr. coll.) n.* a swimming costume.

cost¹ *kost, v.t.* or *v.i.* to be obtainable at a price of: to involve an expenditure of: to require to be laid out or suffered or lost: — *pa.t.* and *pa.p.* **cost.** — *v.t.* to estimate the cost of production of: — *pa.t.* and *pa.p.* **costed.** — *n.* what is or would have to be laid out or suffered or lost to obtain anything: (in *pl.*) expenses of a law-suit. — *n.* **cost′liness.** — *adj.* **cost′ly** high-priced: valuable. — **cost′-account′ant** one who analyses and classifies elements of cost, as material, labour, etc., or who devises systems of doing this; **cost′-account′ing** (*v.t.* **cost′-account′**). — *adj.* **cost′-effec′tive** giving adequate return for outlay. — **cost′-effec′tiveness, cost efficiency.** — *adj.* **cost′-free′** free of charge. — Also *adv.* — **cost plus** a work contract where payment is based on the actual production cost plus an agreed percentage of that cost as profit. — *adj.* **cost′-plus′.** — **cost price** the price the merchant pays for goods bought; **cost push** (*econ.*) inflation due to rising production costs. — Also **cost-push inflation.** — **at all costs,** (*old*) **cost what may** no matter what the cost or consequences may be; **cost-benefit analysis** (or **assessment**) the comparison of the cost of a particular course of action with the benefits (to be) derived from it; **cost of living** the total cost of goods ordinarily required in order to live up to one's usual standard; **cost of living index** an official number showing the cost of living at a certain date compared with that at another date taken as a standard; **prime cost** the price of production, without regard to profit or overhead expenses. [O.Fr. *couster* (Fr. *coûter*) — L. *cōnstāre,* to stand at.]

cost², coste *kost,* (*Spens.*) *n.* See **coast.** — *v.t.* and *v.i.* (*Shak., Spens.*) to approach. [**coast.**]

costa *kos′tə, n.* a rib: a rib-like structure, vein, ridge: the fore-edge of an insect's wing: the nervure next to it: — *pl.* **cos′tae** (*-ē*). — *adj.* **cos′tal** of or near the ribs, the costa, or the side of the body. — *n.* the costal nervure. — *adjs.* **cos′tāte, -d** having or resembling ribs. [L. *costa,* a rib.]

co-star *kō′stär, n.* a cinema, etc. star appearing with other stars. — *v.i.* to appear with other stars: — *pr.p.* **co′-starr′ing;** *pa.t.* and *pa.p.* **co′-starred′.**

costard *kos′tərd, n.* a large kind of apple: the human head (contemptuously) (*arch.*). — *ns.* **cos′tardmonger, cos′-termonger, cos′ter** a seller of apples and other fruit: a seller of fruit and other wares from a barrow: a term of abuse (*Shak.*). [Perh. L. *costa,* a rib.]

costate, -d; coste. See **costa; cost².**

costean *kos-tēn′, v.i.* to dig down to bedrock in prospecting. — *n.* **costean′ing.** — **costean′-pit.** [Said to be from Cornish *cothas,* dropped, *stean,* tin.]

coster, costermonger. See under **costard.**

costive *kos′tiv, adj.* constipated. — *adv.* **cos′tively.** — *n.* **cos′tiveness.** [Fr. *constipé;* see **constipate.**]

costmary *kost′mār-i, n.* alecost (*Chrysanthemum balsamita*), a composite of southern Europe, grown in gardens for its fragrant leaves. [L. *costum* — Gr. *kostos,* costus, and *Maria,* the Virgin Mary.]

costrel *kos′trəl,* (*obs.* or *dial.*) *n.* an eared bottle or small keg, to be hung at the waist. [O.Fr. *costerel.*]

costume *kos′tūm,* in U.S. *-tōōm, n.* a manner of dressing: dress, garb: a woman's outer dress as a unit: fancy dress: (a piece of) clothing for a particular purpose, as in *swimming-costume.* — *v.t.* (*kos-tūm′,* in U.S. *-tōōm′*), to dress. — *adj.* **costumed′.** — *ns.* **costum′er, costum′ier** one who makes or deals in costumes. — **costume drama, piece, play** one in which the actors wear the costumes of an earlier era; **costume jewellery** jewellery worn as an adornment only, without pretence of being genuine gems. [Fr., — It. *costume* — L. *cōnsuētūdō, -inis,* custom.]

Costus *kos′təs, n.* a genus of plants of the ginger family: (without *cap.*) an aromatic root wrongly assigned to it, really that of a composite of Kashmir, *Saussurea hypoleuca* (also **cos′tus arab′icus, cos′tus-root**). [Latinised from Gr. *kostos.*]

cosy, in U.S. **cozy,** *kō′zi,* (orig. *Scot.*) *adj.* snug: comfortable. — *n.* a covering used for a teapot, to keep the tea warm (also **tea′-cosy**): a similar covering for a boiled egg. — *adv.* **cō′sily.** — *n.* **cō′siness.** — **cosy along** (*coll.*) to reassure, often with falsehoods; **cosy up** (*coll.* esp. *U.S.;* with *to* or *with*) to try to gain someone's favour or friendship. [Ety. dub.]

cot¹ *kot,* (*poet.*) *n.* a small dwelling, a cottage. — *adj.*

cott′ed lined with cots. — **cot′-folk** (*Scot.*) cottars; **cot′-house** (*Scot.*) a house occupied by a cottar; **cot′land** land belonging to a cottage; **cot′quean** (*obs.*) a scolding woman: a man who busies himself with women's affairs (*Shak.*); **cot′town** (*Scot.*) a group of cot-houses. [O.E. *cot;* cf. O.N. and Du. *kot.*]

cot² *kot, n.* a small bed, esp. one with high sides for a young child: a swinging bed of canvas (for officers, sick, etc.) (*naut.*): a camp-bed (*U.S.*): a hospital bed. — Also **cott.** — **cot death** the sudden, unexplained death in sleep of an apparently healthy baby. — Also **sudden infant death syndrome.** [Anglo-Ind., — Hindi *khāt.*]

cot³ (*Spens.* **cott**) *kot, n.* a small boat. [Ir.]

cot⁴. See **cotangent.**

cotangent *kō-tan′jənt, n.* the tangent of the complement of an angle — *abbrev.* **cot** (*kot*). — *n.* **coth** (*koth*) a conventional shortening of *hyperbolic cotangent.*

cote¹ *kōt, n.* a cot: a place for animals, as *dovecote* or *dovecot, sheep-cote.* [O.E. *cote;* cf. **cot¹.**]

cote² *kōt, v.t.* to pass by (*Shak.*): to outstrip (as one dog another) (*obs.*). [Poss. conn. with **coast.**]

cote³. Shakespearian form of **quote.**

coteau *ko′tō,* (*U.S.; old*) *n.* a hilly upland area: a valley side. — *pl.* **cot′eaux** (*-tō* or *-tōz*). [Canadian Fr. — Fr., a sloping hillside — O.Fr. *costel,* dim. of *coste,* slope.]

cote-hardie *kōt′-här′di, n.* a mediaeval close-fitting tight-sleeved body garment. [O.Fr.]

côtelette *kōt-let,* (Fr.) *n.* a cutlet, a chop.

coteline *kōt-lēn′, n.* a kind of muslin, corded or ribbed. [Fr. *côte,* a rib — L. *costa.*]

cotemporaneous, etc. Forms of **contemporaneous,** etc.

co-tenant *kō-ten′ənt, n.* a joint tenant. — *n.* **co-ten′ancy.**

coterie *kō′tə-ri, n.* a social, literary, or other exclusive circle. [Fr.; orig. a number of peasants holding land jointly from a lord — L.L. *cota,* a cot.]

coterminous. A form of **conterminous.**

coth. See **cotangent.**

cothurnus *kō-thûr′nəs,* **cothurn** *kō′thûrn,* or *-thûrn′, ns.* the tragedian's buskin: — *pl.* **cothur′nī.** [Latinised from Gr. *kothornos.*]

coticular *kō-tik′ū-lər,* (*obs.*) *adj.* pertaining to whetstones. [L. *cōticula,* dim. of *cos, cotis,* whetstone.]

co-tidal *kō-tīd′l, adj.* having high tide at the same time.

cotillion *ko-til′yən,* **cotillon** *ko-tē′yō, ns.* a sort of country dance. [Fr., petticoat — *cotte,* a coat — L.L. *cotta,* a tunic; see **coat.**]

Cotinga *kō-ting′gə, n.* a tropical American genus of bright plumaged passerine birds: (without *cap.*) any bird of its fam., **Cotingidae** (*-tin′ji-dē*). [Of Tupi origin.]

cotise, cottise *kot′is,* (*her.*) *n.* one of the diminutives of the bend. — *v.t.* to border with cotises, barrulets, etc. [Fr. *cotice;* origin obscure.]

Cotoneaster *ko-tō-ni-as′tər, n.* a genus of shrubs or small trees akin to hawthorn: (without *cap.*) a plant of this genus. [L. *cotōnea,* quince.]

Cotswold *kots′wōld, n.* a breed of sheep. — **Cotswold lion** (*jocular*) a sheep. [*Cotswold* Hills.]

cott. See **cot²,³.**

cotta *kot′ə, n.* a surplice. [L.L. *cotta.*]

cottabus *kot′ə-bəs, n.* an amusement in ancient Greece among young men, consisting in throwing wine into a vessel, success at which betokened fortune in love. [L., — Gr. *kottabos.*]

cottage *kot′ij, n.* a small dwelling-house: a country residence: a summer residence (*U.S.*): a one-storey house, a bungalow (*Austr.*). — *adj.* **cott′aged** covered with cottages. — *n.* **cott′ager** one who dwells in a cottage, esp. of labourers. — *adj.* **cott′agey** cottage-like. — **cottage cheese** soft white loose cheese made from skim-milk curds; **cottage hospital** a small, rural hospital without resident doctors: one housed in a cottage or cottages; **cottage industry** one in which the work is done wholly or largely by people in their own homes; **cottage loaf** a loaf consisting of a smaller lump on the top of a bigger one; **cottage orné** (Fr. *ko-täzh or-nā*) an ornately-designed small country house built in rustic style; **cottage piano** a small upright piano; **cottage pie** shepherd's pie. [L.L. *cottagium* — O.E. *cot*; see **cot**[1].]

cottar, cotter *kot'ər, n.* one of a class of mediaeval villeins: a peasant occupying a cot or cottage for which he has to give labour (*Scot.*). [**cot**[1].]

cotter *kot'ər, n.* a pin or wedge for fastening and tightening. — *n.* **cott'er-pin** a pin for keeping a cotter in place. [Origin obscure.]

cottier *kot'i-ər, n.* a cottar: an Irish tenant holding land as the highest bidder. — *n.* **cott'ierism** the cottier system of land tenure. [Fr. *cotier*; see **cot**[1].]

cottise; cottoid. See cotise; Cottus.

cotton *kot'n, n.* a soft substance like fine wool, the long hairs covering the seeds of the cotton-plant: the plant itself, individually or collectively: yarn or cloth made of cotton. — *adj.* made of cotton. — *v.t.* (*arch.*) to provide with cotton. — *v.i.* to agree (the connection of the intransitive meaning is unknown). — *ns.* **cottonade'** an inferior cotton cloth; **cottonoc'racy** the cotton planting or the cotton manufacturing interests. — *adj.* **cott'ony** like cotton: soft: downy. — **cotton belt** (sometimes with *caps.*) the region in the south-eastern United States in which much cotton is produced; **cott'on-boll** the pod of the cotton-plant; **cotton cake** cakes or pellets of compressed cotton-seed, used as an animal feed; **cotton candy** (*U.S.*) candy floss; **cott'on-gin** a machine for separating the seeds from the fibre of cotton; **cott'on-grass** a genus (Eriophorum) of sedges with long, silky, or cottony hairs about the ripened ovary; **cott'on-mill** a factory where cotton is spun or woven; **cott'onmouth** the venomous water mocassin snake (from the white inside of its mouth). — *adj.* **cott'on-pick'ing** (*U.S. slang*; sometimes *facet.*) used as a relatively mild pejorative. — **cott'on-plant** one of various species of Gossypium (family Malvaceae), yielding cotton; **cott'on-press** a press for compressing cotton into bales; **cott'onseed** the seed of the cotton-plant, yielding a valuable oil; **cott'on-spinner** one who spins cotton, or employs those who do; **cott'ontail** any of several species of rabbits of the genus Sylvilagus, the ordinary United States rabbit; **cott'on-thistle** a strong thistle (Onopordon acanthium) covered with a cottony down; **cott'on-tree** the American cotton-wood: the Indian Bombax malabaricum: an Australian hibiscus; **cott'on-waste** refuse from cotton mills, used for cleaning machinery, etc.; **cott'on-weed** cudweed, a cottony seaside composite (Diotis maritima); **cott'on-wood** any one of several American species of poplar; **cott'on-wool'** cotton in its raw or woolly state: loose cotton pressed in a sheet as an absorbent or protective agent, for stuffing, etc.; **cott'on-worm** the caterpillar of an owlet moth (Aletia xylina) destructive to American cotton crops. — **cotton on to** (*slang*) to take to: to understand. [Fr. *coton* — Ar. *qutun*.]

Cottus *kot'əs, n.* a genus of fishes including the bullhead and father-lasher. — *n. and adj.* **cott'oid.** [Gr. *kottos*, a fish, perhaps the bullhead.]

cotwal. See kotwal.

cotyle *kot'i-lē, n.* an ancient Greek drinking-cup: a cup-like cavity (*zool.*): — *pl.* **cot'ylae** (-*lē*) or **cot'ylēs.** — *adjs.* **cotyl'iform** (*bot.*) disc-shaped with raised rim; **cot'yloid** cup-shaped. [Gr. *kotylē.*]

cotyledon *kot-i-lē'dən, n.* a seed-leaf (*bot.*): a tuft or patch of villi on the placenta, as in most ruminants (*zool.*): (with *cap.*) a genus of S. Afr. plants (fam. Crassulaceae): a plant of this genus. — *adjs.* **cotylē'donary; cotylē'donous** pertaining to or having cotyledons. — *n.pl.* **Cotyloph'ora** the Pecora, or ruminants other than camels and chevrotains. [Gr. *kotylēdōn* — *kotylē*, a cup.]

coucal *kōō'käl, n.* any member of a genus (Centropus) of common bush-birds in Africa, India and Australia, the lark-heeled cuckoos. [Imit.]

couch[1] *kowch, v.t.* to lay down: to lower: to cause to lie close: to spread: to level: to arrange in language, to

express: to depress or remove (a cataract in the eye). — *v.i.* to lie down for the purpose of sleep, concealment, etc.: to bend or stoop. — *n.* any place for rest or sleep: a bed: a kind of sofa with half back and one raised end: the lair of a wild beast: a layer: that on which something is spread. — *adj.* **couch'ant** couching or lying down: lying down with head up (*her.*). — *n.* **couch'ing** embroidery in which the surface is covered with threads and these are secured by stitches forming a pattern. — **couch a spear** to fix it in its rest at the side of the armour. [Fr. *coucher*, to lay down — L. *collocāre*, to place — *col-*, together, *locus*, a place.]

couch[2], **couch grass** *kowch', kōōch'* (*gräs*), *ns.* a grass akin to wheat, a troublesome weed owing to its creeping rootstocks. [A variant of **quitch**[1].]

couchee *kōō'shā, n.* an evening reception. — Also formerly **couchée, couché.** [Fr. *couché*, a reception before going to bed; see **couch**[1].]

couchette *kōō-shet', n.* a sleeping-berth on a continental train or a cross-channel boat, convertible from and into ordinary seating. [Fr.]

coudé *kōō-dā', adj.* bent like an elbow: (of a reflecting telescope) in which one or more plane mirrors reflect the light down the polar axis. [Fr.]

Couéism *kōō'ā-izm, n.* psychotherapy by auto-suggestion. — *n.* **Cou'éist.** [Emile *Coué* (1857–1926), its expounder.]

cougar *kōō'gär, -gər,* **couguar** -*gwär, ns.* a puma. [Fr. *couguar* — Port. *cucuarana*, adapted from a Tupí-Guaraní name.]

cough *kof, v.i.* to expel air with a sudden opening of the glottis and a characteristic sound. — *v.t.* to expel by coughing. — *n.* the act or the sound of coughing: an ailment of which coughing is a symptom. — *ns.* **cough'er; cough'ing.** — **cough'-drop** a cough-lozenge: a person of spicy character; **cough'-lozenge** a medicated lozenge to allay coughing; **cough'-mixture.** — **cough down** to put to silence by coughing; **cough up** (*slang*) to pay out, hand over, under compulsion. [M.E. *coughen*; cf. Du. *kuchen*, Ger. *keuchen, keichen,* to gasp.]

could *kŏŏd, pa.t.* of **can**[1]. [M.E. *coude, couth* — O.E. *cūthe* for *cunthe*, was able; *l* is inserted from the influence of *would* and *should.*]

coulée *kōō-lā', n.* a lava-flow: a ravine (*U.S. and Can.*). [Fr. *couler*, to flow.]

couleur de rose *kōō-lær də rōz,* (Fr.) rose-coloured: seen or presented in a way that exaggerates attractiveness.

coulis *kōō-lē, (Fr.)* a thin purée of fish, fowl, or vegetables.

coulisse *kōō-lēs', n.* a piece of grooved wood, as the slides in which the side-scenes of a theatre run — hence (in *pl.*) the wings. [Fr. *couler,* to glide, to flow — L. *cōlāre,* to strain.]

couloir *kōōl-wär', n.* a gully. [Fr., passage.]

coulomb *kōō-lom', n.* the MKSA and SI unit of electric charge (static or as a current), furnished by one ampere flowing for one second. — *n.* **coulom'eter** a voltameter. — Also **coulomb'meter.** — *adj.* **coulomet'ric.** — *n.* **coulom'etry** (chemical analysis by) the measuring of the number of coulombs used in electrolysis. [From the French physicist, C. A. de *Coulomb* (1736–1806).]

Coulommiers *kōō-lom-yā, n.* a white, soft cheese, fresh or cured, made near *Coulommiers* in central France.

coulter, colter *kōl'tər (Scot. kōō'tər), n.* the iron cutter in front of a ploughshare. [O.E. *culter* — L. *culter,* knife.]

coumarin, cumarin *kōō'mə-rin, n.* a crystalline compound ($C_9H_6O_2$) obtained from Tonka beans, woodruff, melilot, etc. — *adjs.* **coumaric** (-*mar'*); **coumaril'ic.** [Tupí *cumarú,* Tonka bean.]

council *kown'sl, -sil, n.* an assembly called together for deliberation advice, administration or legislation: the persons constituting such an assembly: the body directing the affairs of a town, county, parish, etc.: an assembly of ecclesiastics met to regulate doctrine or discipline: a governing body in a university: a committee that arranges the business of a society. — Also adj. — ns. **coun′cillor,** (*U.S.*) **coun′cilor,** a member of a council; **coun′cilman** (*London* and *U.S.*) a member of a municipal council. — adj. **councilman′ic** (*U.S.*). — **coun′cil-board** the board or table round which a council meets for deliberation: the council itself; **coun′-cil-cham′ber** the room where a council is held; **council estate** an area set apart for council-houses; **coun′cil-house′** a house in which a council meets: a house erected by a municipal council; **council school** a school governed by a town or county council. — **Council of Europe** a consultative body of European states, at first (1949) thought of as the parliament of a future European federation; **Council of Ministers** in the EEC, the decision-making body comprising ministers of the member countries; **Council, House, of States** the upper house of the Indian parliament; **council of war** a conference of officers called to consult with the commander (also *fig.*); **European Council** the body comprising the French head of state and the prime ministers of the other EEC countries; **general council** one called by an invitation to the church at large, also **oecumenical** if received by the Catholic Church in general — as the first seven, 325–787; **in council** in the council-chamber: in consultation; **legislative council** a council to assist a governor, with power to make laws. [Fr. *concile* — L. *concilium.*]

counsel *kown′sl, n.* consultation: deliberation: advice: plan: purpose: a confidential matter: one who gives counsel, a barrister or advocate. — v.t. to advise: to warn: — pr.p. **coun′selling;** pa.t. and pa.p. **coun′selled.** — adj. **couns′ellable** that may be counselled. — n. **coun′selling** (orig. *U.S.*) (a service consisting of) helping people to adjust to or deal with personal problems, etc. by enabling them to discover for themselves the solution to the problems while receiving sympathetic attention from a counsellor: (sometimes) the giving of advice on miscellaneous problems. — Also adj. — ns. **coun′sellor** one who counsels: one involved in counselling: a barrister; **coun′sellorship.** — **coun′sel-keep′er** (*Shak.*) one who can keep counsel or a secret. — adj. **coun′sel-keep′ing** (*Shak.*). — **counsel of perfection** commendation of something beyond the binding minimum, something not absolutely imperative, but commended as the means of reaching greater 'perfection': an impractical ideal; **keep counsel** to keep a secret; **King′s, Queen′s Counsel** (K.C., Q.C.) a barrister or advocate appointed by letters-patent — the office is honorary, but gives the right of precedence in all the courts. [Fr. *conseil* — L. *consilium,* advice — *consulĕre,* to consult.]

count[1] *kownt, n.* an imperial official (*Rom. hist.*): on the Continent, a noble equal in rank to an earl. — n. **count′ess** a lady of the same rank as a count or earl: the wife of a count or earl: a size of roofing slate, 20 × 10 inches (508 × 254 mm). — ns. **count′ship** a count's dignity or domain (also used as a title); **coun′ty** a count (*obs.*): a countship (*obs.*): a portion of a country separated for administrative, parliamentary or other purposes, a shire. — adj. of a, or the, county: of county family. — **county borough** see **borough; county council** a council for managing the public affairs of a county; **county councillor; county court** the highest court of law within a county; **county cricket** cricket played in matches between clubs representing counties; **county family** a family of nobility or gentry (**coun′ty-people**) with estates and a seat in the county; **County school** a school provided and maintained by a local education authority; **county seat** (*U.S.*) the seat of county government; **county town** the town in which the public business of the county is transacted; **Count of the Saxon Shore** in Roman Britain, an official in charge of the S.E. coast (liable to attacks by Saxons). [O.Fr. *conte* — L. *comes, comitis,* a companion, *con-,* with, *īre,* to go.]

count[2], *obs.* **compt,** *kownt, v.t.* to number, sum up: to name the numerals up to: to take into account, reckon as significant or to be recognised: to ascribe: to reckon,

esteem, consider. — v.i. to number: to be numbered: to be of account: to be recognised in reckoning: to have a certain value: to reckon: to name the numerals in order. — n. the act of numbering: reckoning: the number counted: a number indicating size of yarn: the counting of the seconds in which a fallen man may rise and resume (also **count′-out**) (*boxing*): esteem, consideration, account: a particular charge in an indictment. — adj. specifying a noun which, since it denotes an entity of which there can be one or more than one, is able to form a plural. — adjs. **count′able** (*obs.* **compt′able, -ible**) capable of being counted: to be counted: accountable: sensitive (*Shak.*): of a noun, count; **count′ed** accounted, reckoned. — n. **count′er** he who or that which counts: that which indicates a number: a disc or the like, used in reckoning or, in games, as a substitute for a coin or a marker of one's position on a board: a table on which money is counted or goods laid: the name of certain prisons (officially **compt′er;** *obs.*). — adj. **count′less** that cannot be counted: innumerable. — **count′-down** a descending count or counted check to a moment of happening regarded as zero, as in the firing of a rocket; **count′er-caster** (*Shak.*) an arithmetician, reckoner; **count′er-jumper, -skipp′er** contemptuous names for a shopman; **coun′terman** (*arch.*) one who serves at a counter; **count′ing-house, count′ing-room** a room in which a merchant keeps his accounts and transacts business; **count-out** see **count** above; **count′-wheel** a wheel with notched edge controlling the stroke of a clock in sounding the hours. — **count out** of a meeting (esp. of the House of Commons), to bring to an end by pointing out that a quorum is not present: in children's games, to eliminate players by counting while repeating a rhyme (**counting-out rhyme**): in boxing, etc., to adjudge defeated by counting seconds; **keep count** to keep an accurate numerical record (of); **lose count** to fail to keep count (of); **out for the count** (*fig.*) unconscious, or completely exhausted; **over the counter, o′ver-the-count′er** involving trading in shares not on the official Stock Exchange list; **under the counter** hidden from customers' sight (adj. **un′der-the-count′er** reserved for the favoured: secret, furtive).   [O.Fr. *cunter* (Fr. *compter*) — L. *computāre.*]

countenance *kown′tən-əns, n.* the face: the expression of the face: appearance: demeanour shown towards a person: favour: approbation: acquiescence. — v.t. to favour or approve: to make a show of (*Spens.*). — n. **coun′tenancer.** — **change countenance** to change the expression of the face; **in countenance** unabashed; **out of countenance** abashed.   [O.Fr. *contenance* — L. *continentia,* restraint, demeanour — *continēre,* to contain.]

counter[1] *kown′tər, adv.* the opposite way: in opposition. — adj. contrary: opposing: opposite. — n. that which is counter or opposite: the voice-part set in immediate contrast with the air (*mus.*): an encounter (*Spens.*): a parry in which one foil follows the other in a small circle (*fencing*): the part of a horse's breast between the shoulders and under the neck: the part of a ship's stern from the lower moulding to the water-line (*naut.*). — v.t. to encounter: to contradict: to meet or answer by a stroke or move: to strike while receiving or parrying a blow (*boxing*). — **run counter to** to move in the opposite direction (to): to act, happen, in a way contrary (to instructions, expectations, etc.).   [Partly aphetic for **encounter,** partly directly from A.Fr. *countre,* O.Fr. (Fr.) *contre* — L. *contrā,* against.]

counter[2]. See **count**[2].

counter- *kown′tər-,* in composition, against. — v.t. **counteract′** to act counter or in opposition to: to hinder or defeat: to neutralise. — **counterac′tion.** — adj. **counterac′tive** tending to counteract. — n. one who or that which counteracts. — adv. **counteract′ively.** — **coun′ter-ag′ent** anything which counteracts; **coun′ter-approach′** a work thrown up outside a besieged place to command or check the approaches of the besieger;

coun'ter-attack an attack in reply to an attack. — Also
v.t. and v.i. — coun'ter-attrac'tion attraction in an
opposite direction: a rival show. — adj. coun'ter=
attract'ive. — v.t. counterbal'ance to balance by weight
on the opposite side: to act against with equal weight,
power, or influence. — coun'terbalance an equal
weight, power, or agency working in opposition; coun-
terbase see contrabass; coun'ter-batt'ery (mil.) a battery
erected to oppose another; coun'ter-bid a bid made in
opposition to another bid; coun'ter-bidder; coun'-
terblast a defiant pronouncement or denunciation;
coun'terblow a return blow; coun'terbluff actions or
words intended as a bluff, made in opposition to
someone else's bluff; coun'terbond a bond to protect
from contingent loss one who has given bond for
another. — coun'ter-bore a straight-sided widening of
the end of a bored hole: a drill for making this. — v.t.
to form a counter-bore in. — v.t. coun'ter-brace (naut.)
to brace or fasten (the head-yards and after-yards) in
opposite ways. — n. the lee-brace of the foretopsail-
yard. — coun'terbuff a stroke that stops motion or
causes a recoil: a reaction: a return blow: a rebuff. —
v.t. to rebuff. — coun'ter-cast (Spens.) a contrary cast,
counter-plot, trick; coun'terchange exchange (Shak.):
reciprocation (Shak.): a balanced contrast in a picture,
etc. between e.g. light on a dark background and dark
on a light background. — adj. coun'terchanged' exchanged: having the tinctures reversed or interchanged
(her.). — coun'tercharge a charge brought forward in
opposition to another charge. — v.t. coun'tercharm to
destroy or dissolve the effects of (another charm). —
n. that which destroys the effects of another charm.
— v.t. countercheck' to check by some obstacle: to
rebuke. — coun'tercheck a check in opposition to
another: a rebuke; coun'ter-claim (esp. law) a claim
brought forward as a partial or complete set-off
against another claim. — adv. coun'ter-clock'wise in a
direction contrary to that of the hands of a clock. —
coun'ter-culture a way of life deliberately different
from that which is normal or expected; coun'ter=
current a current flowing in an opposite direction;
coun'ter-drain a drain alongside a canal, etc., to carry
off water oozing out. — v.t. coun'terdraw to trace on
oiled paper or other transparent material. — coun'ter=
esp'ionage espionage directed against the enemy's spy
system or action taken to counter it in one's own
country; coun'ter-ev'idence evidence brought forward
in opposition to other evidence. — adj. coun'ter-fleury
(-floo'ri, -flu'ri), -flo'ry, -flow'ered with flowers placed
the contrary way. — coun'terfoil the corresponding
part of a bank cheque, postal order, ticket, etc.,
retained by the giver (see foil²); coun'ter-force an
opposing force; coun'terfort a buttress or arch supporting a retaining wall; coun'ter-gauge an adjustable
scribing gauge for marking the measurements of a
mortise on a piece to be tenoned; coun'ter-glow gegenschein; coun'ter-guard (fort.) an outwork consisting of
two lines of rampart running parallel to the faces of
the bastion, to guard the bastion from being breached;
coun'ter-in'fluence an opposing influence; coun'ter=
insur'gency action taken against insurgents. — Also
adj. — coun'ter-intell'igence activities, as censorship,
camouflage, use of codes, etc., aimed at preventing an
enemy from obtaining information, or the organisation that carries these out; coun'ter-irr'itant an irritant used to relieve another irritation; coun'ter-irrita'-
tion; coun'terlight (paint.) a light opposite to any
object, disturbing the effect of its light. — v.i. coun'-
termarch to march back or in a direction contrary to
a former one. — n. a marching back or in a direction
different from a former one: an evolution by which a
body of men change front, and still retain the same
men in the front rank (mil.): change of measures. —
coun'termark an additional mark put on a bale of
goods belonging to several merchants, so that it may
not be opened except in the presence of all the owners:
a mark put on standard metal by the London Goldsmiths' Company in addition to the artificer's: an
artificial cavity made in the teeth of horses to disguise
their age; coun'termeasure an action intended to
counteract the effect of another action or happening.
— v.t. countermine' to make a mine in opposition to:
to oppose by means of a countermine: to frustrate by
secret working (fig.). — n. (kownt') a mine or chamber
excavated by the besieged to counteract or destroy the
mines made by the besiegers: any means of counter-
action (fig.). — coun'ter-mo'tion an opposite motion;
coun'ter-move, -move'ment a contrary move, movement; coun'termure a wall-facing: a supplementary
wall: a wall raised by besiegers against a wall. — v.t.
(-mūr') to defend with a countermure. — coun'ter=
offen'sive counter-attack: an attack by the defenders;
coun'ter-o'pening an aperture or vent on the opposite
side, or in a different place; coun'ter-pace a step in
opposition to another, a contrary measure. — adj.
coun'ter-paled (her.) divided equally, as an escutcheon,
first palewise, then by a line fesswise, with tinctures
counterchanged. — coun'ter-parole' a word in addition
to the password; coun'terpart the part that answers to
another part: that which fits into or completes another,
having the qualities which another lacks, and so an
opposite: a duplicate: a double. — adj. coun'ter=
pass'ant (her.) passing each other contrary ways. —
coun'terplea a replication to a plea or request. — vs.t.
counterplead' to plead the contrary of; coun'ter-plot'
to plot against in order to frustrate another plot. —
n. a plot or stratagem opposed to another plot. — v.t.
coun'terpoise (obs. coun'terpeise -pēz) to poise or weigh
against or on the opposite side: to act in opposition
to with equal effect. — n. an equally heavy weight in
the other scale. — coun'ter-poison a poison used as the
antidote of another; coun'ter-pressure opposing pressure. — adj. coun'ter-produc'tive acting against productivity, efficiency, or usefulness. — coun'terproof an
inverted impression obtained from a newly printed
proof of an engraving, by laying it, while the ink is
still wet, upon plain paper, and passing it through the
press; coun'ter-proposal one which proposes an alternative to a proposal already made; Coun'ter-Reforma'-
tion (hist.) a reform movement within the Roman
Catholic Church, following and counteracting the
Reformation; coun'ter-revolu'tion a subsequent revolution counteracting the effect of a previous. — n. and
adj. coun'ter-revolu'tionary (a person) opposing a particular revolution or opposed to revolutions. — coun'-
ter-roll a copy of the rolls relating to appeals, inquests,
etc., serving as a check on another's roll; coun'ter-
round a body of officers to inspect the rounds. — adj.
coun'ter-sa'lient (her.) salient in opposite directions. —
coun'terscarp (fort.) the side of the ditch nearest to the
besiegers and opposite to the scarp. — v.t. counterseal'
(Shak.) to seal along with others. — coun'ter-secur'ity
security given to one who has become surety for
another; coun'ter-sense an interpretation contrary to
the real sense; coun'tershaft an intermediate shaft
driven by the main shaft. — v.t. countersign' to sign
on the opposite side of a writing: to sign in addition
to the signature of a superior, to attest the authenticity
of a writing. — n. (kownt') a military private sign or
word, which must be given in order to pass a sentry:
a counter-signature. — coun'ter-sig'nal a signal used
as an answer to another; coun'ter-sig'nature a name
countersigned to a writing. — v.t. coun'tersink to bevel
the edge of (a hole), as for the head of a screw-nail:
to set the head or top of on a level with, or below, the
surface of the surrounding material. — coun'ter-spy;
coun'ter-spying counter-espionage; coun'ter-stand opposition, resistance; coun'ter-state'ment a statement in
opposition to another statement; coun'terstroke
(Spens.) a stroke in return. — v.t., v.i. coun'tersue to
sue a person by whom one is being sued. — coun'ter=
sub'ject (mus.) part of a figure in which the first voice
accompanies the answer of the second; coun'ter-tall'y
a tally serving as a check to another; coun'ter-ten'or

the highest alto male voice (so called because a contrast to tenor); **coun'ter-time** the resistance of a horse that interrupts his cadence and the measure of his manège: resistance, opposition; **coun'ter-trading** trading by barter; **coun'ter-turn** a turn in a play different from what was expected. — *v.t.* **countervail'** to be of avail against: to act against with equal effect: to be of equal value to: to compensate. — *adj.* **countervail'able.** — **coun'ter-view** an opposing view: a posture in which two persons face each other: opposition: contrast. — *vs.t.* **counter-vote'** to vote in opposition to; **counter=weigh'** to weigh against, counterbalance. — **coun'ter-weight** weight in an opposite scale: a counterbalancing influence or force. — *v.i.* **coun'ter-wheel** to wheel in an opposite direction. — **coun'ter-work** a work raised in opposition to another. — *v.t.* **counter'work'** to work in opposition to. — *p.adj.* **coun'ter-wrought.** [A.Fr. *countre*, O.Fr. *contre* — L. *contrā*, against.]

counterfeit *kown'tər-fit, -fēt, v.t.* to imitate: to copy without authority: to forge. — *n.* something false or copied, or that pretends to be true and original. — *adj.* (*Spens.* **coun'terfect**) pretended: made in imitation: forged: false. — *n.* **coun'terfeiter** one who counterfeits. — *adv.* **coun'terfeitly** in a counterfeit manner: falsely. — *n.* **coun'terfeis'ance** (*-fēz'əns*; *Spens.* **coun'terfē'-saunce**) an act of counterfeiting: forgery. [O.Fr. *contrefet*, from *contrefaire*, to imitate — L. *contrā*, against, *facĕre*, to do.]

countermand *kown-tər-mänd', v.t.* to give a command in opposition to one already given: to revoke. — *n.* (*kownt'*) a revocation to a former order. — *adj.* **countermand'able.** [O.Fr. *contremander* — L. *contrā*, against, and *mandāre*, to order.]

counterpane *kown'tər-pān, n.* a coverlet for a bed. — Older form (*Shak.*) **coun'terpoint.** [O.Fr. *contrepoint* — *coultepointe* — L. *culcita puncta*, a stitched pillow; see **quilt.**]

counterpoint[1] *kown'tər-point, n.* the art of combining melodies (*mus.*): a melody added to another (*mus.*): app. a trick (*Spens.*): an opposite point. — *adj.* **contra-punt'al.** — *n.* **contrapunt'ist** a composer skilled in counterpoint. [Fr. *contrepoint* and It. *contrappunto* — L. *contrā*, against, *punctum*, a point, from the pricks, points or notes placed against those of the melody; in some senses **counter-** and **point.**]

counterpoint[2]. See **counterpane.**

countrol. See **control.**

country *kun'tri, n.* a region: a state: a nation: rural districts as distinct from town: the land of one's birth or citizenship: the district hunted by a pack of fox-hounds: the rock surrounding a mineral lode (also **coun'try-rock'**): country music. — *adj.* belonging to the country: rural: rustic: rude. — *adj.* **coun'trified, coun'tryfied** like or suitable for the country in style: like a person from the country in style or manner. — **coun'try-and-west'ern** a popularised form of music deriving from the rural folk-music of the United States. — Also *adj.* — **coun'try-box** a small country-house; **country club** a club in the country which has facilities for sport, leisure and social activities; **country cousin** a relative from the country, unaccustomed to town sights or manners; **coun'try-dance'** a dance as practised by country people: a type of dance in which either an indefinite number of couples in a circle or two lines, or groups of fixed numbers of couples in two lines, can take part, tracing a precise and sometimes complex pattern of movements; **coun'try-dan'cing; coun'try-folk** fellow-countrymen: rural people; **country gentleman** a landed proprietor who resides on his estate in the country; **coun'try-house', -seat'** the residence of a country gentleman; **coun'tryman** one who lives in the country: a farmer: one belonging to the same country, fellow-countryman; **country music** the folk-music of the rural areas of the United States: country-and-western music: both of these taken together; **country party** (*hist.*) the party opposed to the court; **country rock** electrically amplified music which combines the styles of rock-and-roll and country-and-western music; **country-rock** see **country** above; **coun'tryside** a district or part of the country: rural districts in general; **country town** a small town in a rural district. — *adj.* **countrywide'** all over the country. — **coun'trywoman** a woman who dwells in the country: a woman of the same country. — **go to the country** to appeal to the community by calling a general election; **the country** (*cricket slang*) the outfield. [O.Fr. *contrée* — L.L. *contrāta, contrāda*, an extension of L. *contrā*, over against.]

county. See **count[1].**

coup[1] *kōō, n.* a blow, stroke: a clever and successful stroke in a board or card game: a masterstroke, clever and successful stratagem (*fig.*): the act of putting a ball in a pocket without having hit another ball (*billiards*): a coup d'état. — **coup d'essai** (*de-sā*) an experimental work: a first attempt; **coup de foudre** (*də fōō-dr'*) a sudden and astonishing happening: love at first sight; **coup de grâce** (*də gräs*) a finishing blow to put out of pain: a finishing stroke generally; **coup de main** (*də mē*) a sudden overpowering attack; **coup de maître** (*də metr'*) a masterstroke; **coup de poing** (*də pwē*) a typical Old Stone Age axe, a roughly pointed piece of stone held in the hand; **coup d'état** (*dā-tä*) a violent or subversive stroke of state policy; **coup de théâtre** (*də tā-atr'*) a sudden and sensational turn as in a play; **coup d'oeil** (*dœy*) a general view at a glance. [Fr., — L.L. *colpus* — L. *colaphus* — Gr. *kolaphos*, a blow.]

coup[2] *kowp, (Scot.) v.t.* to exchange or barter. — *n.* **coup'er** a dealer. [O.N. *kaupa*, to buy.]

coup[3], cowp *kowp (Scot.) v.t. and v.i.* to overturn: to tip up. — *n.* an upset: a tip for rubbish. [O.Fr. *colp, blow.*]

coupe[1] *kōōp, (Fr.). n.* a dessert, usu. made with ice-cream and often fruit, served in a glass bowl: a glass container for serving such a dessert, usu. with a shallow bowl and a short stem.

coupe[2] *kōōp, (U.S.) n.* a coupé (motor-car).

coupé *kōō-pā', n.* the front part of a French stagecoach: a four-wheeled carriage seated for two inside, with a separate seat for the driver: an end compartment of a railway carriage with a seat on one side only: a two-door motor-car with a roof sloping towards the back. — *adj.* (*her.*) cut off evenly, as the head or limb of an animal. — Also **couped** (*kōōpt*). — *n.* **coupee** (*kōō-pē'*) in dancing, a salute to a partner, while swinging one foot. [Fr., pa.p. of *couper*, to cut.]

couple *kup'l, n.* that which joins two things together: two of a kind joined together, or connected: two: a pair, esp. of married or betrothed persons, dancers, golfers, hunting-dogs: a rafter: a pair of equal forces acting on the same body in opposite and parallel directions (*statics*). — *v.t.* to join together. — *v.i.* to pair sexually. — *ns.* **coup'lement** union: a couple; **coup'ler** one who or that which couples or unites: an organ mechanism by which stops of one manual can be played from another or from the pedals; **coup'let** a pair, couple: a twin: two successive lines of verse that rhyme with each other; **coup'ling** that which connects: an appliance for transmitting motion in machinery, or for connecting vehicles as in a railway train. — **coup'ling-box** the box or ring of metal connecting the contiguous ends of two lengths of shafts. — *adj.* **well'-coup'led** of a horse, well formed at the part where the back joins the rump. — **a couple of** (loosely) two or three: a few. [O.Fr. *cople* — L. *cōpula.*]

coupon *kōō'pon, -pən, -pō, -pong, n.* a billet, check, or other slip of paper cut off from its counterpart: a separate ticket or part of a ticket: a voucher that payments will be made, services performed, goods sold, or the like: a piece cut from an advertisement entitling one to some privilege: a party leader's recommendation of an electoral candidate: a printed betting form on which to enter forecasts of sports results: rate of interest. [Fr. *couper*, to cut off.]

coupure *kōō-pūr', n.* an entrenchment made by the besieged behind a breach: a passage cut to facilitate sallies. [Fr. *couper*, to cut.]

cour, coure. Obsolete forms of **cover, cower.**

courage *kur'ij, n.* the quality that enables people to meet danger without giving way to fear: bravery: spirit: desire (*obs.*). — *interj.* take courage. — *adjs.* **cour'ageful; courageous** (*ka-rā'jas*) full of courage: brave. — *adv.* **courāgeously.** — *n.* **courā'geousness.** — **Dutch courage** a factitious courage induced by drinking; **pluck up courage, take one's courage in both hands** to nerve oneself: to gather boldness; **the courage of one's convictions** courage to act up to, or consistently with, one's opinions. [O.Fr. *corage* (Fr. *courage*), from L. *cor*, the heart.]

courant *kōō-rant', (her.) adj.* in a running attitude. — *n.* **courante, courant** (*kōō-ränt'*) an old dance with a kind of gliding step, a coranto: music for it: (*kōō-rant'*) a newspaper (now in titles only). [Fr., pr.p. of *courir*, to run; see **current.**]

courb, curb *kōōrb, kûrb, (Shak.) v.i.* to bend, stoop to supplicate. — *adj.* bent (*Spens.* **corbe**). [Fr. *courber* — L. *curvāre*, to bend.]

courbaril *kōōr'ba-ril, n.* the West Indian locust-tree: its resin, gum anime. [Fr. from Carib.]

courbette *kōōr-bet', n.* the French form of **curvet.**

courd (*Spens.*), for **covered.**

courgette *kōōr-zhet', n.* a small marrow. [Fr. *courge*, gourd.]

courier *kōō'ri-ar, n.* a runner: a messenger: a state messenger: an official guide who travels with tourists: a frequent title of newspapers. [Fr., — L. *currĕre*, to run.]

courlan *kōōr'lan, n.* any bird of the American genus *Aramus*, akin to the rails. [Fr., from a South American name.]

course *kōrs, körs, n.* a run (*arch.*): the path in which anything moves: the ground over which a race is run, golf is played, or the like: a channel for water: the direction pursued: a voyage: a race: regular progress from point to point: a habitual method of procedure: a prescribed series, sequence, process, or treatment, as of lectures, training, pills, etc.: each of the successive divisions of a meal — soup, fish, etc.: conduct: a range of bricks or stones on the same level in building: in the lute, etc., one of two or more strings tuned in unison or in octaves: in bell-ringing, the series of positions of a bell in the changing order in which a set of bells is struck: (*naut.*) one of the sails bent to a ship's lower yards (mainsail = *main course*: foresail = *fore course*: cross-jack = *mizzen course*): (in *pl.*) the menses. — *v.t.* to run, chase, or hunt after: to use in coursing. — *v.i.* to run: to move with speed, as in a race or hunt. — *ns.* **cours'er** a runner: a swift horse (*orig.* a charger): one who courses or hunts: a swift running bird (*Cursorius*); **cours'ing** hunting of esp. hares with greyhounds, by sight rather than by scent. — **cours'ing-joint** a joint between two courses of masonry. — **in course** in regular order: of course (*arch*); **in due course** eventually: at a suitable later time; **in the course of** during: in the process of: undergoing (something); **in the course of time** eventually: with the passing of time; **of course** by natural consequence: indisputably (often a mere apology for making a statement): it must be remembered (often used to introduce a comment on a preceding statement); **run** or **take its** or **their course** to proceed or develop freely and naturally, usu. to a point of completion or cessation; **stay the course** see **stay; the course of nature, the normal,** etc. **course of events** the usual way in which things happen or proceed. [Fr. *cours* — L. *cursus*, from *currĕre, cursum*, to run.]

court *kōrt, kört, n.* space enclosed: space surrounded by houses: a piece of ground or floor on which certain games are played: a division marked off by lines on such a place: a ferret's hutch: the palace of a sovereign: the body of persons who form his suite or council: an assembly of courtiers: attention, civility, as *to pay court*: a hall of justice (*law*): the judges and officials

who preside there: any body of persons assembled to decide causes: a sitting of such a body: a court shoe. — *v.t.* to pay attentions to: to woo: to solicit: to seek. — *ns.* **court'ier** one who frequents courts or palaces: one who courts or flatters; **court'ierism** the behaviour or practices of a courtier. — *adj.* and *adv.* **court'ierlike.** — *adv.* **court'ierly.** — *ns.* **court'ing** paying addresses, wooing: attendance at court (*Spens.*); **court'let** a petty court. — *adj.* **court'like** courtly: polite. — *ns.* **court'liness; court'ling** a hanger-on at court. — *adj.* **court'ly** having manners like those of, or befitting, a court: politely stately: fair and flattering. — *n.* **court'ship** courtly behaviour: wooing. — **court'-bar'on** the assembly of freehold tenants of a manor under a lord; **court'-card** see **coat-card; court'craft** the courtier's art, intrigue; **court'-cup'board** (*Shak.*) a movable cupboard or sideboard on which plate was displayed; **court'-day** a day on which a judicial court sits; **court'-dress** the special regulation costume worn on state or ceremonious occasions; **court'-dress'er** (*obs.*) a flatterer; **court'-fool** a fool or jester, formerly kept at court for amusement; **court'-guide** a guide to, or directory of, the names and residences of the nobility in a town; **court'-hand** a modification of the Norman handwriting, as distinguished from the modern or Italian handwriting, in use in the English law-courts from the 16th century to the reign of George II; **court'-house** a building where the law-courts are held; **court'-leet** a court of record held in a manor before the lord or his steward; **courtly love** a conception and tradition of love, originating in late mediaeval European literature, in which the knight sublimates his love for his lady in submission, service, and devotion; **court'-mar'tial** a court held by officers of the army, navy or air force for the trial of offences against service laws (one improvised in time of war round an upturned drum for summary judgment was a **drumhead court-martial**): — *pl.* **courts'-mar'tial,** (*coll.*) **court'-mar'tials.** — *v.t.* to try before a court-martial: — *pr.p.* **court'-mar'tialling;** *pa.t.* and *pa.p.* **court'-mar'tialled.** — **court order** a direction or command of a justiciary court. — **court'-plas'ter** sticking-plaster made of silk, originally applied as patches on the face by ladies at court; **court'-roll** the record of a court of justice; **court'room** a room in a court-house in which lawsuits and criminal cases are heard; **court shoe** a light high-heeled dress shoe; **court'-sword** a light sword worn as part of court-dress; **court tennis** the game of tennis, distinguished from lawn tennis (also **real** or **royal tennis**); **court'yard** a court or enclosed ground attached to a house. — **court holy water** (*obs.*) empty compliments: flattery; **go to court** to institute legal proceedings against someone; **hold court** to preside over admiring followers, etc.; **laugh out of court** see **laugh; out of court** without a trial in a law-court: without claim to be considered. [O.Fr. *cort* (Fr. *cour*) — L.L. *cortis*, a courtyard — L. *cors, cohors, -tis,* an enclosure; akin to Gr. *chortos,* an enclosed place; L. *hortus,* a garden. See **yard²**.]

court bouillon *kōōr bōō-yõ', n.* a seasoned stock made with water, vegetables and wine or vinegar, in which fish is boiled. [Fr. *court,* short — L. *curtus;* and **bouillon.**]

Courtelle® *kōōr-tel', n.* a synthetic acrylic wool-like fibre.

courteous *kûrt'yas, kört'yas, adj.* polite, considerate or respectful in manner and action: obliging. — *adv.* **court'eously.** — *ns.* **court'eousness; courtesy** (*kûrt'a-si,* or *kört'*) courteous behaviour: an act of civility or respect: a curtsy: the life interest of the surviving husband in his wife's estate (*law.*). — *v.i.* to make a curtsy: — *pr.p.* **court'esying;** *pa.t.* and *pa.p.* **court'esied.** — **courtesy light** a small light in a motor vehicle usu. operated by the opening and closing of the doors; **courtesy title** a title really invalid, but allowed by the usage of society — as to children of peers. — **remember your courtesy** (*obs.*) please put on your hat; **strain courtesy** see **strain.** [O.Fr. *corteis, cortois;* see **court.**]

courtesan, -zan *kûrt'i-zan, kört', or -zan', n.* a court mistress: a whore. [Fr. *courtisane* — It. *cortigiana,*

couscous

orig. a woman of the court.]

couscous, kouskous *ko͞os'ko͞os,* **couscousou** *-o͞o', ns.* granulated wheat flour: a N. African dish of steamed couscous with meat, vegetables, etc. [Fr., — Ar. *kuskus — kaskasa,* to pound; see **cuscus**[1].]

cousin *kuz'n, n.* formerly a kinsman generally: now, the son or daughter of an uncle or aunt: a term used by a sovereign in addressing another, or to one of his own nobles: a person belonging to a group related by common ancestry, interests, etc.: something kindred or related to another. — *ns.* **cous'inage; cous'inhood; cous'inship.** — *adj.* **cous'inly** like, or having the relation of, a cousin. — *n.* **cous'inry** cousins collectively. — **cous'in-ger'man** a first cousin: something closely related; **Cousin Jack** a native of Cornwall. — **cross'-cous'in** the son or daughter of one's father's sister or mother's brother; **first cousin** the child of one's aunt or uncle, a full cousin; **first cousin once removed** the son or daughter of a cousin-german — sometimes loosely called *second cousin*; **forty-second cousin** vaguely, a distant relative; **second cousin** the child of one's parent's first cousin: (*loosely*) a first cousin once removed. [Fr., — L. *consōbrīnus — con-,* sig. connection, and *sobrīnus,* applied to the children of sisters from the root of *soror,* a sister.]

couter *ko͞o'tər,* (*slang*) *n.* a sovereign. [Said to be from Gypsy *cuta,* a gold piece.]

couth *ko͞oth,* obsolete *pa.t.* and *pa.p.* of **can:** could: knew: known: did. — *adj.* known (*obs.*): famed, well-known (*obs.*): familiar (*obs.*): now in occasional use meaning good-mannered, sophisticated, etc., as a back-formation from **uncouth.** [O.E. *pa.t. cūthe,* pa.p. *cūth*; see **could.**]

couthie, couthy *ko͞oth'i,* (*Scot.*) *adj.* friendly, kindly: comfortable: snug. [Prob. O.E. *cūth,* known.]

coutil, coutille *ko͞o-til', n.* a strong cotton fabric used in mattresses, etc. [Fr. *coutil.*]

couture *ko͞o-tür,* in U.S. *-to͝or', n.* dressmaking or dress designing. — *n.* **couturier** (*ko͞o-tür'yā,* in U.S. *-to͝or-*), *fem.* **couturière** (*-yer'*) a dressmaker or dress designer. [Fr.]

couvade *ko͞o-väd', n.* a custom among primitive peoples in many parts of the world for the father to take to his bed at the birth of a child, and submit to certain restrictions of food, etc. [Erroneously attributed to the Basques; the O.Fr. *couvade,* from *couver,* to hatch, never had this special meaning.]

couvert *ko͞o-ver,* (Fr.) *n.* a cover (at table).

covalency *kō-vā'lən-si, n.* the union of two atoms by the sharing of a pair of electrons, one from each atom — cf. **electrovalency.** — *adj.* **covā'lent.** [L. *co-,* together, and **valency.**]

covariance *kō-vār'i-əns, n.* the property of varying concomitantly (*math.*): the mean value of the products of the deviations of two or more variates from the respective mean values of these variates (*statistics*). — *n.* and *adj.* **cōvār'iant.** — *v.i.* **cōvār'y.** [**co-.**]

cove[1] *kōv, n.* a small inlet of the sea: a bay: a cavern or rocky recess: a curved junction of wall and ceiling (*archit.*): the moulding covering the junction of wall and ceiling (also **cō'ving**). — *v.t.* to overarch. — *adj.* **coved** formed with an arch. — *n.* **cove'let** a small cove. [O.E. *cofa,* a room; O.N. *kofi,* Ger. *Koben.*]

cove[2] *kōv,* (*slang*) *n.* a fellow, a customer: — *dim.* **cōv'ey.** [Origin obscure.]

covellite *kō-vel'īt, kō'vəl-, n.* a blue mineral, cupric sulphide. [*Covelli,* its discoverer.]

coven *kuv'in,* or *-ən, n.* a gathering of witches: a gang of thirteen witches. [See **covin.**]

covenant *kuv'ə-nənt, n.* a mutual agreement: the writing containing the agreement: an engagement entered into between God and a person or a people — a dispensation, testament. — *v.i.* to enter into an agreement. — *v.t.* to agree to: to stipulate. — *adj.* **cov'enanted** agreed to by covenant: bound by covenant: holding a position under a covenant or contract. — *ns.* **covenantee'** the person to whom a covenant is made; **cov'enanter** (usually in Scotland *kuv-ə-nant'ər*) one who signed or adhered to the *Scottish National Covenant* of 1638 (the *Solemn League and Covenant* of 1643 was in effect an international treaty between Scotland and England for securing civil and religious liberty); **cov'enantor** that party to a covenant who subjects himself to the penalty of its breach. — **covenant of grace, redemption** in Christian theology, that by which life is freely offered to sinners on condition of faith in Christ; **covenant of works** that made with Adam as federal representative of the human race on condition of obedience. [O.Fr., — L. *con-,* together, and *venīre,* to come.]

covent *kov'ənt, kuv'ənt,* (*Shak.*) *n.* a variant of **convent.**

Coventry *kov', kuv'ənt-ri, n.* a city in the West Midlands of England. — **Coventry blue** a blue thread once made there. — **send to Coventry** to exclude from social intercourse.

cover *kuv'ər, v.t.* to put or spread something on, over or about: to come or be on, over or about: to hide: to clothe: to protect: to screen: to brood or sit on: to suffice for: to provide for or against: to comprise: to traverse: to take as field of operations: to play a higher card upon: to table upon a coin of equal value in wagering: to set as for a meal: to copulate with — esp. of a stallion: to command with a weapon: to report. — *v.i.* to lay a table for a meal (*obs.*): to put one's hat on. — *n.* that which covers or is intended to cover: a bedcover: a lid: the binding of a book: an envelope: an envelope with a stamp and postmark, as *first-day cover*: undergrowth, thicket, concealing game, etc.: the table requisites for one person — plate, knife, fork, napkin, etc.: a pretext: a disguise: an apparently genuine identity, job, etc. used as a front, esp. by spies: a confederate: a cover version: a cover point. — *adj.* intended to conceal the true nature or identity of a person, organisation, etc. — Also in composition. — *n.* **cov'erage** the area or (*fig.*) amount covered or included: the group or section of the community reached by an advertising medium: the protection provided by an insurance: the amount available to cover liabilities: the (extent of) reporting of a topic, event, etc. on television, in the press, etc. — *adj.* **cov'ered** having a cover: sheltered, concealed: roofed over: with a hat on. — *n.* **cov'ering** anything that covers. — *adj.* **cov'ert** covered: concealed: secret: concealing (*Spens.*). — *n.* a feather covering the quill-bases of wings and tail: (usu. pron. *kuv' ər*) a cover for game: a shelter. — *adv.* **cov'ertly** in a covered or concealed manner. — *n.* **cov'erture** covering, shelter: disguise: secret proceedings (*Spens.*): the condition of a married woman as legally deemed under the protection of her husband (*law.*). — **cov'erall** a boiler suit (*U.S.*; *often in pl.*): a one-piece garment for babies, covering arms, legs and body. — *adj.* covering or including everything. — **cover charge** a charge per person made by a restaurant, in addition to charge for food; **cover crop** a subsidiary crop grown partly to protect the soil; **cover drive** (*cricket*) a drive past cover point; **covered wagon** a large wagon with bonnet-shaped canvas hood, esp. that used by pioneers to the American West: symbol of pioneering spirit; **covered way, covert way** (*fort.*) a path outside the ditch of a fort, sunk below the crest of the glacis to afford cover; **cover girl** a girl pictured on a magazine cover; **cover glass** a thin glass placed over the object on a microscope slide; **covering letter** a letter to explain documents enclosed with it; **cover note** (*insurance*) a note certifying that the holder has a current insurance policy: a note issued to an insured person certifying that he has insurance coverage while his policy is being prepared; **cover point** in cricket, etc., (the position of) the player who supports point and stands to his right: in lacrosse, (the position of) one of the defending players; **cov'erslip** a loose cover for a duvet; **cov'er-slut** an outer garment worn to hide rags or dirty clothes; **covert coat** a short light overcoat; **covert coating** cloth for such; **covert way** see **covered way** above; **cover-up** see **cover up; cover version** a

recording of a song, etc. which has been recorded by someone else, usu. very similar to the original. — **cover for** to act in the place of (one who is absent, etc.); **cover in** to fill in: to complete the covering of, esp. of roof of building; **cover into** to transfer into; **cover shorts** to buy in such stocks as have been sold short, in order to meet one's engagements, etc.; **cover the buckle** to execute a certain difficult step in dancing; **cover up** to cover completely: to conceal, withhold information (*coll.*; *n.* **cov'er-up**); **under cover of** see **undercover.** [Fr. *couvrir* (It. *coprire*)—L. *cooperīre*—*co-*, and *operīre*, to cover.]

coverlet *kuv'ər-lit, n.* a bedcover. — Also **cov'erlid.** [Fr. *couvrir,* to cover, *lit* (L. *lectum*), a bed.]

covert, covertly, coverture. See **cover.**

covet *kuv'it, v.t.* to desire or wish for eagerly: to wish for wrongfully. — *v.i.* (*Shak.*) to desire (with *for*): — *pr.p.* **cov'eting;** *pa.t.* and *pa.p.* **cov'eted.** — *adjs.* **cov'etable; cov'eted.** — *adv.* **cov'etingly.** — *ns.* **cov'etise** (*obs.*) covetousness: ardent desire; **cov'etiveness** (*obs.*) acquisitiveness. — *adj.* **cov'etous** inordinately desirous: avaricious. — *adv.* **cov'etously.** — *n.* **cov'etousness.** [O.Fr. *coveit(i)er* (Fr. *convoiter*)—L. *cupiditās,* -*ātis*—*cupĕre,* to desire.]

covey[1] *kuv'i, n.* a brood or hatch of partridges: a small flock of game birds: a party, a set. [O.Fr. *covée*—L. *cubāre,* to lie down.]

covey[2]. See **cove**[2].

covin, covyne *kōv'in, kuv'in, n.* a compact (*arch.*): a conspiracy: a coven. — *adj.* **covinous** (*kuv'*) (*arch.*) fraudulent. — **cov'in-tree'** a tree before a Scottish mansion at which guests were met and parted from. [O.Fr. *covin* — L.L. *convenium* — *con-*, together, *venīre,* to come.]

coving *kō'ving, n.* the projection of upper storeys over lower: the vertical sides connecting the jambs with the breast of a fireplace: a quadrant moulding covering the joint between wall and ceiling. [See **cove**[1].]

covyne. See **covin.**

cow[1] *kow, n.* the female of the bovine animals: the female of certain other animals, as the elk, elephant, whale, etc.: an ugly, ungainly, slovenly, or objectionable woman (*vulg*): an objectionable or rather despicable person or thing (*Austr. slang*): a trying situation or occurrence (usu. *a fair cow*) (*Austr. slang*): — *pl.* **cows,** older **kine** (*kīn*) and (still in *Scots*) **kye** (*kī*). — *adj.* **cow'ish** like a cow: cowardly (*Shak.*). — **cow'bane** the water hemlock (*Cicuta virosa* or other species), often fatal to cattle; **cow'bell** a bell for a cow's neck; **cow'-berry** the red whortleberry (*Vaccinium vitis-idaea*); **cow'bird, cow blackbird** an American bird (*Molothrus*) of the troupial family, that accompanies cattle, and drops its eggs into other birds' nests; **cow'boy** a boy who has the care of cows: a man who has the charge of cattle on a ranch (*U.S.*): any rather rough male character in stories, etc. of the old American West, such as a gunfighter or a man involved in fighting Indians: a rodeo performer (*U.S.*): a young inexperienced lorry-driver, or anyone who drives an unsafe or overloaded lorry (*slang*): a person who behaves wildly or irresponsibly (*slang*): a derogatory term for an often inadequately qualified person providing inferior services (*coll.*). — Also *adj.* — **cowboy boots** high-heeled boots, usu. with ornamental stitching, etc. worn by, or reminiscent of styles worn by, cowboys and ranchers; **cow'-calf** a female calf; **cow'catcher** (*U.S.*) an apparatus on the front of a railway engine to throw off obstacles; **cow cocky** see **cockatoo; cow'-cher'vil, -pars'ley, -weed** wild chervil; **cow'-dung; cow'feeder** a dairyman; **cow'fish** a coffer-fish (with cowlike head): a manati: any small cetacean; **cow'girl** a young woman who dresses like and does the work of a cowboy; **cow'grass** perennial red clover: zigzag clover; **cow'hand** a cowboy (*U.S.*); **cow'heel** an oxfoot stewed to a jelly; **cow'herd** one who herds cows: cowheard (see separate entry); **cow'hide** the hide of a cow: the hide of a cow made into leather: a coarse whip made of twisted strips

of cowhide. — *v.t.* to whip with a cowhide. — **cow'-house** a building in which cows are stalled, a byre; **cow'-leech** a cow-doctor; **cow'lick** a tuft of turned-up hair on the forehead (also **cow's lick**); **cow'man** one who tends cows: one who owns a cattle ranch (*U.S.*); **cow-parsley** see **cow-chervil; cow'-pars'nip** an umbelliferous plant, hogweed (*Heracleum sphondylium*) used as fodder; **cow'pat** a roundish lump of cow-dung; **cow'-pea** a leguminous plant (*Vigna sinensis*) indigenous to Asia but cultivated in other parts of the world and used like French beans: a similar plant, *V. catjang*; **cow'-pil'ot** a West Indian demoiselle fish, said to accompany the cowfish; **cow'-plant** an asclepiadaceous plant of Ceylon (*Gymnema lactiferum*) with a milky juice; **cow'poke** (*U.S. coll.*) a cowboy; **cow'pox** a disease that appears in pimples on the teats of the cow, the matter thereof used for vaccination; **cow'puncher** (*U.S. coll.*) a cowboy: a driver of cows; **cow's arse** (*vulg.*) a mess, botched job, etc.; **cow'shed** a cowhouse; **cow's lick** see **cowlick; cow'-tree** a South American tree (*Brosimum galactodendron*) of the mulberry family, that produces a nourishing fluid resembling milk; **cow-weed** see **cow-chervil; cow'-wheat** a yellow-flowered scrophulariaceous plant (*Melampyrum*), with seeds somewhat like grains of wheat. — **till the cows come home** for a long time of unforeseeable duration. [O.E. *cū,* pl. *cȳ;* Ger. *Kuh;* Sans. *go,* a bull, cow.]

cow[2], **kow** *kow,* (*Scot.*) *n.* a branch, bunch of twigs, besom. [Poss. O.Fr. *coe*—L. *cauda,* tail.]

cow[3] *kow, v.t.* to subdue the spirit of: to keep under. — *adj.* **cowed** abjectly depressed or intimidated. [Perh. from O.N. *kūga;* Dan. *kue,* to subdue.]

cow[4] *kow,* (*Dickens*) *n.* a chimney cowl. [Variant of **cowl**[1].]

cowage. See **cowhage.**

cowan *kow'ən,* (*Scot.*) *n.* a dry-stone-diker: a mason who never served an apprenticeship: one who tries to enter a Freemason's lodge, or the like, surreptitiously. [Origin doubtful.]

coward *kow'ərd, n.* a reprehensibly faint-hearted person: one without courage: often applied to one who, whether courageous or not, brutally takes advantage of the weak. — *v.t.* to make cowardly. — *adj.* cowardly: with tail between legs (*her.*). — *ns.* **cow'ardice** (-*is*) want of courage: timidity; **cow'ardliness.** — *adj.* **cow'ardly** having the character of a coward: befitting a coward: characteristic of a coward. — *adv.* like a coward: with cowardice. — *ns.* **cow'ardry** (*Spens.* **cow'ardree); cow'ardship** (*Shak.*). [O.Fr. *couard* (It. *codardo*)—L. *cauda,* a tail.]

cowdie-gum, -pine. Same as **kauri-gum, -pine.**

cower *kow'ər, v.i.* to sink down through fear, etc.: to crouch shrinkingly. — *adv.* **cow'eringly.** [Cf. O.N. *kūra,* Dan. *kure,* to lie quiet.]

cowhage, cowage, cowitch *kow'ij, -ich, ns.* a tropical leguminous climber (*Mucuna*): the stinging hairs on its pod, used as a vermifuge: its pods. [Hindi *kavāc.*]

cowheard, cowherd. Spenserian spellings of **coward.**

cowitch. See **cowhage.**

cowl[1] *kowl, n.* a cap or hood: a monk's hood: the badge of monkhood: a monk: a cover for a chimney: an engine bonnet: a cowling. — *v.t.* to make a monk of: to cover like a cowl. — *adj.* **cowled** wearing a cowl. — *n.* **cowl'ing** the casing of an aeroplane engine. — *adj.* **cowl'-necked** (of a dress, sweater, etc.) having a collar which lies over the shoulders, etc. in a way reminiscent of a monk's cowl. [O.E. *cugele;* O.N. *kofl;* akin to L. *cucullus,* hood.]

cowl[2] *kōl, kōōl, kowl,* (*dial.* or *arch.*) *n.* a tub or large vessel for liquids. — **cowl'-staff** (*Shak.*) a pole on which a basket or vessel is slung. [O.E. *cūfel* or O.Fr. *cuvele,* both—L. *cūpella,* dim. of *cūpa,* a cask.]

co-worker *kō-wûr'kər, n.* an associate: one who works (on a project, etc.) with another. [**co-**.]

cowp *kowp.* See **coup**[3].

Cowper's glands *kow'pərz glandz, kōō'* a pair of glands near the prostate in mammals which under sexual stimulation secrete mucus into the urethra. [Discovered by William *Cowper* (1666–1709), an English anatomist.]

cowrie, cowry *kow'ri, n.* a mollusc of a large genus (Cypraea) of gasteropods the shells of which are used in certain primitive societies as money and magical objects: a shell of the mollusc. [Hindi *kaurī*.]

cowrie-pine. Same as **kauri-pine.**

cowslip *kow'slip, n.* a species of primrose, with flowers in umbels, common in pastures: in U.S., the marsh-marigold. — *adj.* **cow'slip'd** covered with cowslips. [O.E. *cūslyppe*—*cū,* cow, *slyppe,* slime, i.e. cow-dung.]

cox *koks.* A shortened form of **coxswain.**

coxa *koks'ə, n.* the hip: the proximal joint of an arthropod's leg: — *pl.* **cox'ae** (*-ē*). — *adj.* **cox'al.** — *n.* **coxal'gia** (*ji-ə*) pain in the hip. [L.]

coxcomb *koks'kōm, n.* a strip of red cloth notched like a cock's comb, which professional fools used to wear: the head (*Shak.*): a fool: a fop. — *adjs.* **coxcombic** (*-kōm', -kom'*), **-al, coxcom'ical** foppish: vain. — *n.* **coxcombical'ity.** — *adv.* **coxcomb'ically.** — *n.* **cox'-combry** the manner of a coxcomb. [**cock's comb.**]

coxiness. See **cock**[1].

Coxsackie virus *kōok-sä'kē vīrəs,* (sometimes without *cap.*) any of several disease-causing viruses that occur in the human intestinal tract. [From *Coxsackie,* in the state of New York, where the virus was first discovered.]

coxswain, cockswain *kok'sn,* or *kok'swān, n.* one who steers a boat: a petty officer in charge of a boat and crew. — *v.t.* and *v.i.* to act as coxswain (for). — Often contr. **cox.** — *adj.* **coxed** having a cox. [**cock,** a boat, and **swain.**]

coxy. See **cock**[1].

coy *koi, adj.* bashful: affectedly shy. — *v.t.* to caress (*Shak.*): to disdain (*Shak.*): to affect coyness (with *it*) (*arch.*). — *adj.* **coy'ish.** — *adv.* **coy'ishly.** — *n.* **coy'-ishness.** — *adv.* **coy'ly.** — *n.* **coy'ness.** [Fr. *coi*—L. *quiētus,* quiet.]

coyote *koi'ōt, koi-ōt'(i), kī-ōt'i, kī'ōt, n.* a prairie-wolf, a small wolf of N. America: — *pl.* **coyo'tes** or **coyo'te.** [Mex. *coyotl.*]

coypu *koi'pōo,* or *-pōō',* or *-pū, n.* a large South American aquatic rodent (*Myopotamus* or *Myocastor coypus*) yielding nutria fur — now found wild in Europe. [Native name.]

coystrel, coystril. Same as **coistrel.**

coz *kuz,* (*arch.*) *n.* a contraction of **cousin.**

coze *kōz, v.i.* to chat. — Also *n.* [Fr. *causer.*]

cozen *kuz'n, v.t.* to cheat. — *ns.* **coz'enage** deceit; **coz'ener.** [Perh. Fr. *cousiner,* to claim kindred; see **cousin.**]

cozier, cosier *kō'zi-ər,* (*Shak.*) *n.* a cobbler. [O.Fr. *cousere,* tailor — L. *cōnsuĕre,* to sew together.]

cozy. See **cosy.**

crab[1] *krab, n.* any of the Brachyura or short-tailed decapod crustaceans: Cancer (sign of the zodiac and constellation): a portable winch: (in *pl.*) the lowest throw at hazard — two aces: a crab-louse. — *v.i.* to drift or fly sideways: to fish for crabs: to catch a crab in rowing. — *adj.* **crabb'y** crab-like. — *adjs.* and *advs.* **crab'like; crab'wise.** — **crab'-eat'er** a sergeant-fish: an antarctic seal. — *adj.* **crab'-faced** having a peevish countenance. — **crab'-louse** a crab-shaped louse infesting the hair of the pubis, etc.; **Crab Nebula** the expanding cloud of gas in the constellation of Taurus, being the remains of a supernova observed in 1054 A.D.; **crab's'-eyes, crab'-stones** prayer-beads, the scarlet and black seeds of the Indian liquorice tree (*Abrus precatorius*): a limy concretion in the crayfish's stomach. — *v.i.* **crab'-sī'dle** to go sideways like a crab. — **crab'-yaws** framboesia tumours on the soles and palms. — **catch a crab** to sink the oar too deeply (or not enough) in the water and fall back in consequence. [O.E. *crabba;* Ger. *Krebs.*]

crab[2] *krab, n.* a wild bitter apple: a sour-tempered person. — *ns.* **crab'-apple; crab'stick; crab'-tree.** [Ety. doubtful.]

crab[3] *krab, v.t.* (of hawks) to claw: to decry, criticise: to obstruct, wreck, or frustrate. — *n.* dejection: fault-finding. [**crab**[1].]

crabbed *krab'id, adj.* ill-natured: harsh: rough (*arch.*): crooked (*arch.*): undecipherable: cramped. — *adj.* **crabb'edly.** — *n.* **crabb'edness.** — *adj.* **crabb'y** bad-tempered, ill-natured. — *adv.* **crabb'ily.** — *n.* **crabb'-iness.** [**crab**[1] intermixed in meaning with **crab**[2].]

crab-nut, -oil, -wood. See **Carapa.**

crack *krak, v.t.* and *v.i.* to make or cause to make a sharp sudden sound: to split: to break partially or suddenly: to fracture, the parts remaining in contact: to (cause to) give way under strain, torture, etc.: (of the voice) to change tone or register suddenly: (of petroleum, etc.) to break into simpler molecules: to boast (*obs.*). — *v.i.* (*Scot.*) to chat. — *v.t.* to break open (a safe, etc.): to solve the mystery of (a code, etc.). — *n.* a sudden sharp splitting sound: a partial fracture: a flaw: a blow, a smack: a moment: break (of day): a friendly chat (*Scot.*): house-breaking (*slang*): an expert: a pert boy (*Shak.*): a quip, gibe: a try (*slang*): a highly addictive form of cocaine. — *adj.* (*coll.*) excellent: expert. — *adj.* **cracked** rent: damaged: crazy. — *n.* **crack'er** one who or that which cracks: a liar, boaster (*arch.*): a lie (*arch.*): the pin-tail duck: a thin crisp biscuit (esp. *U.S.*): a colourful tubular package that comes apart with a bang, when the ends are pulled, to reveal a small gift, motto, etc.: a small, noisy firework: the apparatus used in cracking petroleum: something exceptionally good or fine of its type (*coll.*): a poor white (*U.S.*): a curl-paper or curling rag: a rapid pace (*slang*). — *adjs.* **crack'ers** crazy: unbalanced; **crack'ing** (*coll.*) of speed, etc., very fast: very good. — **crack'brain** a crazy person. — *adj.* **crack'brained.** — **crackdown** see **crack down on; crack'erjack, crack'ajack** a person or thing of highest excellence. — Also *adj.* —*adj.* **crack'er-barr'el** (*U.S.*) of homely philosophy. — **crack'-halt'er, crack'-hemp, crack'-rope** (*obs.*) one likely or deserving to be hanged. — *adj.* **crack'jaw** hard to pronounce. — **crack'pot** a crazy person. — Also *adj.* — **cracks'man** a burglar; **crack'-tryst** (*obs.*) one who breaks an engagement. — **crack a bottle, can,** etc. to open or drink a bottle, can, etc.; **crack a crib** (*thieves' slang*) to break into a building; **crack a joke** to utter a joke with some effect; **crack credit** to destroy one's credit; **crack down on** to take firm action against (*n.* **crack'down**); **crack the whip** to assert authority suddenly or forcibly; **crack up** to praise: to fail suddenly, to go to pieces; **fair crack of the whip** a fair opportunity; **get cracking** to get moving quickly. [O.E. *cracian,* to crack; cf. Du. *kraken,* Gael. *crac.*]

crackle *krak'l, v.i.* to give out slight but frequent cracks. — *n.* the giving out of slight cracks: a kind of china-ware, purposely cracked in the kiln as an ornament. — *n.* **crack'ling** the rind of roast pork: (in *pl.*) the skinny part of suet without tallow. — *adj.* **crack'ly** brittle. — *n.* **crack'nel** a light, brittle biscuit: (in *pl.*) pieces of fat pork fried crisp. [Freq. of **crack.**]

Cracovian *kra-kō'vi-ən, adj.* pertaining to *Cracow.* — *ns.* **cracovienne** (*-en'*) a lively Polish dance: music for it, in 2–4 time. — Also **krakowiak** (*kra-kō'vi-ak*); **cracowe** (*krak'ow*) a long-toed boot fashionable under Richard II.

-cracy *-krə-si, suffix* used to indicate rule, government (by a particular group, etc.) as in *democracy, mobocracy.* — *suffix* **-crat** (*-krat*) person supporting, or partaking in, government (by a particular group, etc.). — *adj.* suffixes **-cratic, -cratical.** [Gr. *-kratia,* from *kratos,* power.]

cradle *krā'dl, n.* a bed or crib in which a child is rocked: infancy (*fig.*): one's place of origin or nurture: a stand, rest or holder for supporting something: a suspended platform or trolley which can be raised and lowered and from which work can be carried out on the side of a ship, building, etc.: a framework, esp. one for keeping bedclothes from pressing on a patient, or one under a ship for launching: a rocking box for gold-washing: an engraver's knife used with a rocking motion. — *v.t.* to lay or rock in a cradle: to nurture. — *n.* **cra'dling** (*archit.*) a wooden or iron framework within a ceiling. — **cra'dle-scythe** a broad scythe used in a cradle framework for cutting grain; **cra'dle-snatcher** (usu. *derog.*) someone who choses as a lover or marriage partner someone much younger than himself or herself (also **baby-snatcher**); **cra'dle-snatching; cra'dle-song** a lullaby; **cra'dlewalk** (*obs.*) an avenue arched over with trees. — **from the cradle to the grave** throughout one's life. [O.E. *cradol*; ety. obscure.]

craft *kräft, n.* cunning: artifice (*obs.*): dexterity: art: creative artistic activity involving construction, carving, weaving, sewing, etc. as opposed to drawing (also **craft'work**): skilled trade: occupation: a ship or ships (of any kind, orig. small): aircraft, spacecraft. — *v.i.* to exercise one's craft (Shak., *Cor.* IV, vi. 118). — *v.t.* to make or construct, esp. with careful skill. — *adv.* **craft'ily.** — *n.* **craft'iness. — adjs. craft'less** free from craft: unskilled in any craft; **craf'ty** having skill (*arch.*): cunning: wily. — **craft'-broth'er** a person engaged in the same trade as another; **craft'-guild** an association of people engaged in the same trade; **craft shop** a shop in which materials and tools for creative activities such as embroidery, basketry, model-making, etc. are sold; **crafts'man** one engaged in a craft; **crafts'manship, craft'manship; crafts'master** (*obs.*) one skilled in a craft; **craft'work** see **craft.** — **arty-crafty** see **art**[2]. [O.E. *cræft*; Ger. *Kraft*, power.]

crag[1] *krag, n.* a rough steep rock or point, a cliff: a shelly deposit mixed with sand, found in the Pliocene of East Anglia (*geol.*). — *adj.* **cragg'ed** craggy. — *ns.* **cragg'edness, cragg'iness.** — *adj.* **cragg'y** full of crags or broken rocks: rough: rugged. — **crag'-and-tail'** (*geol.*) a hillform with steep declivity at one end and a gentle slope at the other. — *adj.* **crag'fast** unable to move from a position on a crag. — **crags'man** one skilled in rockclimbing. [App. conn. with Gael. *creag, carraig*.]

crag[2] *krag, n.* neck: throat. [Cf. Du. *kraag*, Ger. *Kragen*, the neck.]

craig *krāg, n.* Scots form of **crag** (cliff) and of **crag** (neck). — **craig'fluke** the witch (*Pleuronectes cynoglossus*), a flat fish.

crake[1] *krāk, (dial.) n.* a crow, raven: a corncrake: a croak: the cry of the corncrake. — *v.i.* to utter a crake. **crake'-berry** crowberry. [Cf. **corncrake, croak**.]

crake[2] *krāk, (Spens.) n., v.t.* and *v.i.* (to) boast. [**crack**.]

cram *kram, v.t.* to press close: to stuff: to fill to superfluity: to overfeed: to feed with a view to fattening: to make believe false or exaggerated tales (*slang*): to teach, or prepare, hastily for a certain occasion (as an examination, a lawsuit), to the extent required for the occasion. — *v.i.* to eat greedily: to prepare for an examination, etc. by cramming: — *pr.p.* **cramm'ing;** *pa.t.* and *pa.p.* **crammed.** — *n.* a crush: a lie (*slang*): information that has been crammed: the system of cramming. — *adjs.* **cramm'able; crammed.** — *n.* **cramm'er** a person or machine that crams poultry: one who, or an establishment that, crams pupils or a subject: a lie (*slang*). — *adj.* **cram'-full'.** [O.E. *crammian*; O.N. *kremja*, to squeeze; Dan. *kramme*, to crumple.]

crambo *kram'bō, n.* a game in which one gives a word to which another finds a rhyme: rhyme: — *pl.* **cram'boes.** — **cram'boclink, -jingle** rhyming. [Prob. from L. *crambē repetīta*, cabbage served up again.]

crame *krām, (Scot.) n.* a booth for selling goods. [From Du. or Low Ger.]

cramoisy, cramesy *kram'əz-i* (or *-oi-zi*), *adj.* and *n.* crimson. [See **crimson**.]

cramp *kramp, n.* an involuntary and painful contraction of a voluntary muscle or group of muscles (in U.S. often in *pl.*): restraint: a cramp-iron: a contrivance with a movable part that can be screwed tight so as to press things together. — *adj.* (*old*) hard to make out (used of handwriting): cramped: narrow. — *v.t.* to affect with spasms: to confine: to hamper: to fasten with a cramp-iron. — *adj.* **cramped** of handwriting, small and

closely written: compressed: restricted, without enough room, confined. — *n.* **cramp'et, cramp'it** a scabbard-chape: a cramp-iron: a crampon: an iron foot-board for curlers. — *adj.* **cramp'ing** restricting, confining. — *n.* **cramp'on** a grappling-iron: a spiked contrivance attached to the boots for climbing mountains or telegraph poles or walking on ice. — *adj.* **cramp'y** affected or diseased with cramp: producing cramp. — **cramp'-bark** (*U.S.*) the guelder-rose, or its medicinal bark; **cramp'-bone** the patella of the sheep, an old charm for cramp; **cramp'-fish** the electric ray or torpedo; **cramp'-iron** a piece of metal bent at both ends for binding things together; **cramp'-ring** a ring formerly blessed by the sovereign on Good Friday against cramp and falling sickness. — **bather's cramp** paralysis attacking a bather; **writer's cramp** or *scrivener's palsy* a common disease affecting those in the habit of constant writing, the muscles refusing to obey only when an attempt to write is made. — **cramp someone's style** to restrict someone's movements or actions. [O.Fr. *crampe*; cf. Du. *kramp*, Ger. *Krampf*.]

crampon. See **cramp.**

cran *kran, n.* a measure of capacity for herrings just landed in port — 37½ gallons. — **coup the cran** (*Scot.*) to upset, or be upset, as plans. [Prob. from Gael. *crann*, a measure.]

cranberry *kran'bər-i, n.* the red acid berry of a small evergreen shrub (*Vaccinium oxycoccos*; Ericaceae) growing in peaty bogs and marshy grounds or the larger berry of an American species (*V. macrocarpum*), both made into jellies, sauces, etc.: extended loosely to other species of the genus: the shrub itself. — **cran'berry-bush, -tree** (*U.S.*) the guelder-rose. [For *craneberry*; a late word; origin obscure; cf. Ger. *Kranbeere* or *Kranichbeere*.]

cranch *kranch, n.* and *v.t.* Same as **crunch.**

crane[1] *krān, n.* any bird of the *Gruidae*, large wading birds with long legs, neck, and bill: a bent pipe for drawing liquor out of a cask: a machine for raising heavy weights, usu. having a rotating boom from the end of which the lifting gear is hung: a travelling platform for a film camera. — *v.t.* to raise with a crane: to stretch as a crane does its neck. — *v.i.* to stretch out the neck: to pull up before a jump. — *n.* **cran'age** the use of a crane: the price paid for the use of it. — **crane'-fly** a fly (Tipula) with very long legs — the daddy-long-legs. — *adj.* **crane'-necked.** — **cranes'bill, crane's'-bill** any wild species of Geranium, from the beaked fruit. [O.E. *cran*; Ger. *Kranich*, W. *garan*.]

crane[2]. Same as **cranium.**

cranium *krā'ni-əm, n.* the skull: the bones enclosing the brain: — *pl.* **crā'niums, crā'nia.** — *adj.* **crā'nial.** — *n.pl.* **Crānia'ta** (*zool.*) the main division of Chordata, having a cranium. — *ns.* **crāniec'tomy** the surgical removal of a piece of the skull (Gr. *ektomē*, cutting out); **crāniog'nomy** (Gr. *gnōmē*, knowledge) cranial physiognomy. — *adj.* **crāniolog'ical.** — *ns.* **crāniol'ogist; crāniol'ogy** the study of skulls: phrenology; **crāniom'eter** an instrument for measuring the skull; **crāniom'etry; crānios'copist** a phrenologist; **crānios'copy** phrenology; **crāniot'omy** (Gr. *tomē*, a cut) the act of crushing the skull of a foetus in obstructed deliveries (*obstetrics*): incision of the skull esp. for the purpose of neurosurgery. — **cranial index** the breadth of a skull as a percentage of the length. [L.L. *crānium* — Gr. *krānion*, the skull.]

crank[1] *krangk, n.* a crook or bend: a conceit in speech: a whim: a faddist: an arm on a shaft for communicating motion to or from the shaft (*mach.*). — *v.i.* to move in a zigzag manner: to turn a crank (often with *up*). — *v.t.* to shape like a crank: to provide with a crank: to move or seek to move by turning a crank. — *adj.* crooked: crabbed: loose or slack. — *adv.* **crank'ily.** — *n.* **crank'iness.** — *adj.* **crank'y** crooked: infirm: full of whims: cross. — **crank'case** a box-like casing for the crankshaft and connecting-rods of some types of reciprocating-engine; **crank'shaft** the main shaft of an engine or other machine, which carries a crank or cranks for the attachment of connecting rods.   [O.E. *cranc*, cf. Ger. *krank*, ill.]

crank² *krangk*, *adj.* brisk: merry. — Also *adv.* [Origin unknown.]

crank³ *krangk*, **crank-sided** *krangk-sī′did*, (*naut.*) *adjs.* liable to be upset. — *n.* **crank′ness** liability to be upset. [Ety. uncertain.]

crankle *krangk′l*, *n.* a turn, winding, or wrinkle, an angular protuberance. — *v.t.* and *v.i.* to bend: to twist. [Freq. of **crank¹**.]

crannog *kran′og*, *n.* in Scotland and Ireland a fortified island (partly natural and partly artificial) in a lake: a lake-dwelling.   [Gael. *crann*, a tree.]

cranny *kran′i*, *n.* a rent: a chink: a secret place. — *v.i.* to enter crannies. — *adj.* **crann′ied** having crannies, rents, or fissures.   [Fr. *cran*, a notch.]

cranreuch *krän′ruhh*, (*Scot.*) *n.* hoar-frost.   [Origin obscure; poss. from Gaelic.]

crants *krants*, (*Shak.*) *n.* the garland carried before the bier of a maiden and hung over her grave.   [Ger. *Kranz*, a wreath, a garland.]

crap¹ *krap*, *kräp*, *n.* Scots form of **crop**. — *v.t.* to crop: to cram, stuff. — **crappit-head, -heid** (*krap′it-hēd, kräp′*) a haddock's head stuffed with a compound of oatmeal, suet, onions, and pepper.

crap² *krap*, *n.* money (*obs. slang*): excrement (*vulg.*): rubbish (*slang*): nonsense (*slang*). — *v.i.* to defecate (*vulg.*). — *v.t.* to fear (something) (*vulg.*; also **crap it**). — **crap out** (*vulg.*) to give up, opt out, chicken out. [M.E. *crappe*, chaff — M.Du. *krappe*, prob. from *krappen*, to tear off.]

crape *krāp*, *n.* a thin silk fabric, tightly twisted, without removing the natural gum — usually dyed black, used for mournings. — *adj.* made of crape. — *v.t.* to clothe with crape: to frizzle (hair). — *adj.* **crāp′y.** — **crape′-hanger, crepe′hanger** (*coll.*) a pessimist; **crape′hanging, crepe′hanging.**   [O.Fr. *crespe* (Fr. *crêpe*) — L. *crispus*, crisp.]

craple *krap′l*, (*Spens.*) *n.* Same as **grapple**.

craps *kraps*, *n. sing.*, a gambling game in which a player rolls two dice. — **shoot craps** to play this game. [**crab¹**, lowest throw at hazard.]

crapulence *krap′ū-ləns*, *n.* sickness caused by excessive drinking: intemperance. — *adjs.* **crap′ulent; crap′ulous.** — *n.* **crapulos′ity.**   [Fr. *crapule* — L. *crāpula*, intoxication.]

craquelure *krak′ə-lūr, -loor*, *n.* the fine cracking that occurs in the varnish or pigment of old paintings: this effect or pattern.   [Fr.]

crare, crayer *krār*, *n.* a trading vessel.   [O.Fr. *craier*.]

crases. See **crasis.**

crash¹ *krash*, *n.* a noise as of things breaking or being crushed by falling: the shock of two bodies meeting: a collision between vehicles, etc.: the failure of a commercial undertaking: economic collapse: a fall or rush to destruction: the complete breakdown of a computer system or program. — *adj.* intended to lessen effects of a crash: planned to meet an emergency quickly: involving suddenness, speed or great effort. — *v.t.* and *v.i.* to dash, or fall, to pieces with a loud noise: to move with a harsh noise: to (cause a vehicle to) collide with another vehicle, etc.: to (cause an aircraft to) fall violently to earth or into the sea, usu. with extensive damage: to gatecrash (*coll.*): to (cause a computer system or program to) have a complete breakdown. — *v.i.* to come to grief, fail disastrously. — *adj.* **crash′ing** (*coll.*) extreme, overwhelming, esp. in *a crashing bore.* — **crash barrier** a protective barrier usu. of steel placed e.g. along the edge of a road or the central reservation of a motorway; **crash course** a short-lasting but intensive programme of instruction; **crash′-dive** a sudden dive of a submarine (also *v.i.* and *v.t.*); **crash′-helmet** a padded safety head-dress for motor-cyclists, racing motorists, etc. — *v.i.* and *v.t.* **crash′-land′** in an emergency, to land (an aircraft) abruptly, with resultant damage. — **crash′-land′ing;**

crash′pad padding inside a motor vehicle to protect the occupants in case of accident: a place providing temporary accommodation (*slang*). — *adj.* **crash′proof.** — **crash out** (*slang*) to fall asleep: to become unconscious.   [Imit.]

crash² *krash*, *n.* a coarse strong linen.   [Perh. from Russ. *krashenina*, coloured linen.]

crasis *krā′sis*, *n.* the mixture of different elements in the constitution of the body: temperament: the mingling or contraction of two vowels into one long vowel, or into a diphthong (*gram.*): — *pl.* **crā′sēs** (*-sēz*).   [Gr. *krāsis*, mixture.]

crass *kras*, *adj.* gross: thick: dense: stupid: tactless, insensitive. — *ns.* **crassament′um** the thick part of coagulated blood: the clot; **crass′itude** coarseness: density: stupidity. — *adv.* **crass′ly.** — *n.* **crass′ness.** — *n.pl.* **Crassūlā′ceae** a family of succulent plants including stone-crop and house-leek.   [L. *crassus*.]

-crat, -cratic(al). See **-cracy.**

Crataegus *kra-tē′gəs*, *n.* the hawthorn genus.   [Latinised from Gr. *krataigos*.]

cratch *krach*, *n.* a crib to hold hay for cattle, a manger. — *n.pl.* **cratch′es** a swelling on a horse's pastern, under the fetlock.   [Fr. *crèche*, manger; from a Gmc. root, whence also **crib**.]

crate *krāt*, *n.* a wickerwork case for packing crockery in, or for carrying fruit: a packing-case: an open framework of spars: a decrepit aeroplane or car (*coll.*). — *v.t.* to pack in a crate.   [L. *crātis*, a hurdle.]

crater *krāt′ər*, *n.* a large bowl for mixing wine (*ant.*): the mouth of a volcano: a hole in the ground where a meteor has fallen, or a shell, mine, or bomb exploded: a cavity formed in the carbon of an electric arc. — *n.* **Crāterell′us** a genus of funnel-shaped fungi. — *adjs.* **crateriform** (*krat-er′i-förm*, or *krāt′er-i-förm*) cup-shaped; **crat′erous.** — **crater lake** one formed in the crater of an extinct volcano.   [L., — Gr. *krātēr*, a mixing bowl.]

craton *krāt′on*, (*geol.*) *n.* any of the comparatively rigid areas in the earth's crust.   [Gr. *kratos*, strength.]

cratur *krāt′ər*, (*Ir.* and *Scot.*) *n.* a creature. — **the cratur** whisky.

craunch *krönch.* A form of **crunch.**

cravat *krə-vat′*, *n.* a neckcloth worn chiefly by men. — *v.t.* to dress in a cravat.   [Fr. *cravate* — introduced in 1636 from the *Cravates* or Croatians.]

crave *krāv*, *v.t.* to beg earnestly: to beseech: to require: to long for. — *n.* a longing: a claim (*Scots law*). — *ns.* **crav′er** one who craves: a beggar; **crav′ing** a longing. [O.E. *crafian*, to crave; O.N. *krefja*.]

craven *krāv′n*, *n.* a coward: a spiritless fellow. — *adj.* cowardly: spiritless. — *v.t.* (*Shak.*) to render spiritless. — *adv.* **crav′enly.** — *n.* **crav′enness.** — **cry craven** to surrender.   [Origin obscure.]

craw *krö*, *n.* the crop, throat, or first stomach of fowls: the crop of insects: the stomach of animals generally. [M.E. *crawe*; not found in O.E.; cf. Du. *kraag*, neck.]

crawfish. See **crayfish.**

crawl¹ *kröl*, *v.i.* to move slowly with the body on or close to the ground: to move on hands and knees: to creep: to move slowly or stealthily: to behave abjectly: to warp: to be covered with crawling things: to swim using the crawl stroke. — *n.* the act of crawling: a slow pace: an alternate overhand swimming stroke. — *n.* **crawl′er** one who or that which crawls: an abject person: a sluggish person: a creeping thing: a cab moving slowly in hope of a fare: a caterpillar tractor: a baby's overall, a romper-suit. — *n.* **crawl′ing.** — *adj.* creeping: lousy, verminous. — *adj.* **craw′ly** (*coll.*) with, or like the feeling of, something crawling over one: creepy. — **crawling peg** (*econ.*) a system of stabilising prices or exchange rates by allowing a limited amount of rise or fall at predetermined intervals.   [Scand.; O.N. *krafla*, to paw; Dan. *kravle*.]

crawl² *kröl*, *n.* a pen for keeping fish: a kraal.

Crax *kraks*, *n.* a genus of birds of the curassow family.

[Gr. *kreks*, a long-legged bird.]

crayer. See **crare.**

crayfish *krā′fish*, **crawfish** *krö′fish*, *ns.* a large freshwater decapod crustacean: the Norway lobster: the spiny lobster. [M.E. *crevice* — O.Fr. *crevice* (Fr. *écrevisse*, a crayfish) — O.H.G. *krebiz*, a crab.]

crayon *krā′ən*, *n.* a pencil made of chalk, wax or pipe-clay, variously coloured, used for drawing: a drawing done with crayons. — *v.t.* and *v.i.* to draw with a crayon. [Fr. *crayon* — *craie*, chalk, from L. *crēta*, chalk.]

craze *krāz*, *v.t.* to shatter (*Milt.*): to crack: to cover with fine cracks (as pottery): to weaken: to impair: to derange (of the intellect). — *v.i.* to develop fine cracks: to become mad. — *n.* a crack, flaw: a finely cracked condition: insanity: fashion, fad: a small structural defect in plastic. — *adj.* **crazed.** — *adv.* **crāz′ily.** — *n.* **crāz′iness.** — *adj.* **crāz′y** frail: cracked: insane: demented: composed of irregular pieces (as a pavement): extravagantly enthusiastic or passionate (about) (*coll.*). — *n.* a crazy person (*coll.*): — *pl.* **cra′zies.** — **crazing mill** a mill for crushing tin-ore; **crazy golf** a form of putting in which balls have to be hit past, through, over, etc. obstacles (humps, tunnels, bends, etc.) to reach the hole; **crazy quilt** a patchwork quilt in which irregular pieces of material are sewn together with no regular pattern or design: a jumble, mess, hotch-potch (*fig.*) — *adj.* **craz′y-quilt** (*fig.*). [Scand.; cf. Sw. *krasa*, Dan. *krase*, to crackle; also Fr. *écraser*, to crush.]

creagh, creach *krehh,* (*Scot.*) *n.* a foray: booty. [Gael. *creach.*]

creak *krēk*, *v.i.* to make a sharp, grating sound, as of a hinge, etc. — *n.* a grating noise, as of an unoiled hinge. — *adv.* **creak′ily.** — *adj.* **creak′y.** [From the sound, like *crake*, and *croak*.]

cream *krēm*, *n.* the oily substance that rises on milk, yielding butter when churned: that which rises to the top: the best part of anything: the pick of a group of things or people: a food largely made of, or like, cream, as *ice-cream*: a cream-like substance, as *cold-cream* for skin. — *v.t.* to take off the cream from: to select (the best) from a group, etc. (with *off*) (*fig.*): to treat with cream: to make creamy (e.g. a mixture of sugar and butter in cake-making). — *v.i.* to gather or form as or like cream. — *adj.* of the colour of cream: prepared with cream: of sherry, sweet. — *ns.* **cream′er** a device for separating cream from milk: a small jug for cream; **cream′ery** an establishment where butter and cheese are made from the milk supplied by a number of producers: a shop for milk, butter, etc.; **cream′iness.** — *adj.* **cream′y** full of cream, or like cream in appearance, consistency, etc.: gathering like cream. — **cream′-bun, -cake** a kind of bun, cake, filled with cream or creamy material, etc.; **cream′-cheese** cheese made with cream. — *adj.* **cream′-coloured** of the colour of cream, light yellow. — **cream cracker** a crisp, unsweetened type of biscuit. — *adj.* **cream′-faced** pale-faced. — **cream horn** a horn-shaped pastry containing cream, etc. — *adj.* **cream′-laid** of paper, of a cream colour or white with a laid watermark. — **cream′-nut** the Brazil nut; **cream puff** a confection of puff pastry filled with cream; **cream′-slice** a wooden blade for skimming cream from milk; **cream soda** (chiefly *U.S.*) a vanilla-flavoured fizzy drink. — *adj.* **cream′-wove** of paper, of a cream colour or white, and wove. — **cream of chicken, mushroom,** etc. **soup** chicken, mushroom, etc. soup made with milk or cream; **cream of tartar** a white crystalline compound made by purifying argol, potassium hydrogen tartrate; **cream of tartar tree** the baobab: an Australian tree of the same genus, *Adansonia gregorii.* [O.Fr. *cresme, creme* — L. *chrisma* — Gr. *chrīsma,* to anoint.]

creance *krē′əns*, *n.* the cord which secures the hawk in training. [Fr. *créance.*]

creant *krē′ənt, adj.* creating: formative. [L. *creāns, -antis,* pr.p. of *creāre*; see **create.**]

crease[1] *krēs*, *n.* a mark made by folding or doubling anything: such a mark pressed centrally and longitudinally into a trouser-leg: a regulative line, of three kinds — *bowling crease,* from behind or astride of which the bowler must bowl, *popping-crease,* 4 feet in front of it, at which the batsman plays and behind which is his ground, *return crease,* marking the sideward limits of the bowler (*cricket*): in ice-hockey and lacrosse, a marked area round the goal. — *v.t.* to make creases in. — *v.i.* to become creased — *v.t.* and *v.i.* (*coll.*) to double up with laughter (often with *up*). — *adj.* **creas′y** full of creases. — *adj.* **crease-resist′ant, -resist′ing** of a fabric, not becoming creased in normal wear. [Origin uncertain.]

crease[2]. See **kris.**

creasote. See **creosote.**

create *krē-āt′, v.t.* to bring into being or form out of nothing: to bring into being by force of imagination: to make, produce, or form: to design: to invest with a new form, office, or character: to institute: to be the first to act (a part). — *v.i.* (*slang*) to make a fuss. — *adj.* (*Milt.*) created. — *adj.* **creāt′able.** — *n.* **creation** (*krē-ā′shən*) the act of creating, esp. the universe: that which is created: the world, the universe: a specially designed, or particularly striking, garment. — *adj.* **crea′tional.** — *ns.* **crea′tionism** the theory that everything that exists had its origin in special acts of creation by God (opp. to *evolutionism*): the theory that God immediately creates a soul for every human being born (opp. to *traducianism*; also **crea′tianism**); **crea′tionist.** — *adj.* **crea′tive** having power to create: that creates: showing, pertaining to, imagination, originality. — *adv.* **crea′tively.** — *ns.* **crea′tiveness; creativity** (*krē-ə-tiv′*) state or quality of being creative: ability to create; **crea′tor** one who creates: a maker: — *fem.* **crea′trix, crea′tress; crea′torship.** — *adjs.* **creatural** (*krē′chər-əl*), **crea′turely** pertaining to a creature or thing created. — *ns.* **creature** (*krē′chər*) anything that has been created, animate or inanimate, esp. an animated being, an animal, a man: a term of contempt or of endearment: a dependent, instrument, or puppet: (*coll.* — usu. with *the*) alcoholic liquor; **crea′tureship.** — **creation science** creationism treated as a scientific viewpoint or theory; **creature comforts** material comforts, food, etc.: liquor, esp. whisky; **the Creator** the Supreme being, God. [L. *creāre, -ātum,* to create, *creātūra,* a thing created.]

creatine *krē′ə-tin, -tēn, n.* a constant and characteristic constituent of the striped muscle of vertebrates ($C_4H_9N_3O_2$). — *adj.* **creatic** (*kri-at′ik*) relating to flesh. — *n.* **crē′atinine** (*-nin, -nēn*) dehydrated creatine ($C_4H_7N_3O$) found in urine and muscles. [Gr. *kreas, kreatos,* flesh.]

creative, creator, creature. See **create.**

crèche *kresh, n.* a public nursery for children: a model representing the scene of Christ's nativity. [Fr. *crèche,* manger.]

credal. See **creed.**

credence *krē′dəns, n.* belief: trust: precautionary tasting of food for a great man's table (*obs.*): a sideboard: the small table beside the altar on which the bread and wine are placed before being consecrated (also **credence table**): a shelf over a piscina (also **credence shelf**). — *n.* **credendum** (*kri-den′dəm*) a thing to be believed, an act of faith: — *pl.* **creden′da.** — *adjs.* **crē′dent** credible: credulous: believing; **credential** (*kri-den′shl*) giving a title to belief or credit. — *n.* that which entitles to credit or confidence: (in *pl.*) esp. the letters by which one claims confidence or authority among strangers. — *ns.* **credenza** (*kri-den′zə,* It. *krā-dent′sa*) a sideboard: a bookcase of similar design, esp. if without legs; **credibil′ity** (*kred-*) the quality of being worthy of belief or trust: the capacity for believing or trusting. — *adj.* **cred′ible** that may be believed: seemingly worthy of belief or of confidence: reliable: of a nuclear weapon, in whose use and effectiveness one can believe — *n.* **cred′ibleness.** — *adv.* **cred′ibly.** — *n.* **cred′it** belief: esteem: reputation: honour: distinction: good character: acknowledgment: sale on trust: time allowed for payment: a balance in a person's favour in an account: an entry in an account making acknowledgment of a payment (*book-k.*): the side of an account on which such entries are made: a sum placed at a person's disposal in a bank up to which he may draw: certified completion of a course of study counting towards a final pass: (in *pl.*) credit titles: (in *pl.*) a list of acknowledgments in a book, etc. — *v.t.* to believe: to trust: to sell or lend to on trust: to enter on the credit side of an account: to set to the credit of (with *to* or *with*): to mention in the credit titles. — *adj.* **cred'itable** trustworthy: bringing credit or honour: praiseworthy. — *n.* **cred'itableness.** — *adv.* **cred'itably.** — *ns.* **cred'itor** one to whom a debt is due; **crē'dō** (L. *crēdō*, pron. *krā'dō*, I believe) the Apostles' Creed or the Nicene Creed, or a musical setting of either of these for church services: a belief or set of beliefs:— *pl.* **crē'dōs; credulity** (*kri-dū'li-ti*) credulousness: disposition to believe on insufficient evidence. — *adj.* **credūlous** (*kred'*) easy of belief: apt to believe without sufficient evidence: unsuspecting. — *adv.* **cred'ūlously.** — *n.* **cred'ūlousness.** — **credence shelf, table** see credence above; **credibility gap** (*politics,* etc.) the discrepancy between what is claimed or stated and what actually is, or seems likely to be, the case; **credit card** a card obtainable from a credit card company which, in places where the card is recognised, enables the holder to have purchases, services, etc. debited to an account kept by the company: a similar card issued by other organisations, or by certain banks (to be used with a cheque-book); **credit rating** (an assessment of) the level of a person's or business's creditworthiness; **credit scoring** the calculation of a person's credit rating by adding up points awarded acccording to the person's age, marital status, occupation, address, etc.; **credit titles** acknowledgments of the work of participators shown at the beginning or end of a cinema film, television programme, etc.; **credit union** a non-profit-making co-operative savings association which makes loans to its members at low interest; **cred'itworthiness** entitlement to credit as judged from earning capacity, promptness in debt-paying, etc. — *adj.* **cred'itworthy. — be a credit to someone,** etc. to be proof of time, trouble, etc. well-invested in one by someone, etc. [L. *crēdĕre, crēditum,* to believe.]

credenza. See credence.

crédit *krā-dē,* (Fr.) *n.* credit. — **crédit foncier** (*fɔ̃-syā*) lending of money on security of landed property, repayable by terminable annuity; **crédit mobilier** (*mō-bē-lyā*) lending of money on movable property.

credit, etc., **credulity,** etc. See credence.

cree *krē, v.t.* and *v.i.* of grain, to soften by boiling or soaking. [Fr. *crever,* to burst.]

Cree *krē, n.* a member of a N. American Indian tribe living in Montana and parts of Cananda: the Algonquian language of this people, or its syllabic writing system. [Short for Can. Fr. *Christianaux* — Algonquian *kiristino, kinistino.*]

Creed *krēd, n.* a form of teleprinter. [From the inventor, Frederick George *Creed* (1871–1957).]

creed *krēd, n.* a summary of articles of religious belief, esp. (esp. with *cap.*) those called the Apostles', Nicene, and Athanasian: any system of belief. — *adjs.* **creed'al, cred'al. — the Creed** the Apostles' Creed or the Nicene Creed. [O.E. *crēda* — L. *crēdō,* I believe.]

creek *krēk, n.* a small inlet or bay, or the tidal estuary of a river: any turn or winding: in America, Australia and New Zealand, a small river or brook. — *adj.* **creek'y** full of creeks: winding. — **up the creek** (*slang*) in dire difficulties. [Prob. Scand., O.N. *kriki,* a nook; cf. Du. *kreek,* a bay; Fr. *crique.*]

Creek *krēk, n.* a member of any of the tribes of American Indians who formed the **Creek Confederacy.** [Prob. **creek,** a river.]

creel *krēl, n.* a basket, esp. a fish basket. [Origin obscure.]

creep *krēp, v.i.* to move with the belly on or near the ground: to move or advance slowly or stealthily: to slip or encroach very gradually: to grow along the ground or on supports, as a vine: to fawn or cringe: to have the physical sensation of something creeping over or under the skin: to shudder: to drag with a creeper (*naut.*): to undergo creep (*metallurgy*). — *v.t.* (*Milt.,* etc.) to creep on: — *pa.t.* and *pa.p.* **crept.** — *n.* a crawl: a slow slipping or yielding to stress: crystallisation or rise of a precipitate on the side of a vessel above the surface of a liquid: gradual alteration of shape under stress (*metallurgy*): a narrow passage: an enclosure in which young farm animals may feed, with an approach too narrow to admit the mother: a silent, boring, or unpleasant person (*slang*). — *ns.* **creep'er** anything that creeps: a creeping plant, esp. a Virginia creeper: a small bird that runs up trees (*Certhia*): a kind of grapnel used for dragging the seabed, etc.: an endless chain or conveyor: a crêpe-soled, or other soft-soled, shoe (*coll.*): a wheeled board on which one may lie and move about while working under a vehicle e.g. as a mechanic: a ball bowled so as to stay low (*cricket*). — *adj.* **creep'ered** covered with a creeper. — *n.* **creep'ie** a low stool: a stool of repentance. — *adj.* **creep'ing.** — *adv.* **creep'ingly.** — *adj.* **creep'y. — creep'hole** a hiding hole: a subterfuge. — *adj.* **creep'mouse** silent and shrinking. — *n.* **creep'y-crawl'y** a creeping insect (also *adj.*). — **creeping Jenny** moneywort, a creeping plant (*Lysimachia nummularia*); **creeping Jesus** (*slang*) a slinking person. — **the creeps** a feeling of horror or revulsion. [O.E. *crēopan;* Du. *kruipen.*]

creese. See **kris.**

creesh *krēsh,* (*Scot.*) *v.t.* to grease. — *n.* grease. — *adj.* **creesh'y.** [O.Fr. *craisse* — L. *crassus,* fat.]

crémaillère *krā-mī-yer',* *n.* a zigzag line of fortification: a rack railway. [Fr., pot-hook.]

cremaster *kri-mas'tər, n.* a muscle of the spermatic cord: the organ of attachment in lepidopterous pupae. [Gr. *kremastēr,* suspender — *kremannynai,* to hang.]

cremate *kri-māt', v.t.* to burn (esp. a dead body). — *ns.* **cremā'tion; cremā'tionist** one who advocates cremation; **cremāt'or** one who cremates: a furnace for cremation: an incinerator. — *adj.* **crematorial** (*krem-ə-tō'ri-əl, -tō'*). — *n.* **cremātō'rium** a place for cremating dead bodies. — *adj.* **crem'atory** (*-ə-tər-i*). — *n.* a crematorium. [L. *cremāre, -ātum,* to burn.]

crème, crême *krem,* (Fr.) *n.* cream — applied to various creamy substances. — **crème brûlée** (*brü-lā*) a dish of egg yolks, cream and vanilla topped with caramelised sugar; **crème caramel** (*kar-a-mel*) an egg custard baked in a dish lined with caramel; **crème de menthe** (*də māt*) a peppermint-flavoured liqueur.

crème de la crème *krem də la krem,* (Fr.) cream of the cream, the very best.

cremocarp *krem'ō-kärp,* (*bot.*) *n.* the characteristic fruit of the Umbelliferae, composed of two one-seeded halves which split apart and dangle from the top of the axis. [Gr. *kremannynai,* to hang, *karpos,* fruit.]

Cremona *krim-ō-nə, n.* the name applied to any of the superior violins or stringed instruments made at *Cremona* in Italy (16th-18th cent.) incl. those made by Stradivari.

cremona, cremorne *kri-mō'nə, kri-mör'nə.* Erroneous forms of **cromorna.**

cremor *krē'mör, n.* thick juice. [L.]

cremosin, cremsin *krem'zin,* (*Spens.*) *adj.* crimson.

crenate, -d *krēn'āt, kren'āt, kren-āt', -id,* (*bot.*) *adjs.* having rounded teeth between sharp notches. — *n.* **crē'na** a notch or tooth; **crēnā'tion; crenature** (*krē', kren'*). — *adjs.* **crěn'ulate, -d** finely notched or crenate. [From an inferred L. *crēna,* a notch.]

crenel *kren'l,* (*archit.*) *n.* a notch in a parapet. — *v.t.* to indent with crenels. — *v.t.* **cren'ellate,** U.S. **cren'elate,** to embattle. — *adjs.* **cren'ellate, -d** embattled: indented. — *n.* **crenellā'tion.** — *adj.* **cren'elled.** [O.Fr. *crenel* — inferred L. *crēna,* a notch.]

crenulate. See **crenate.**

---

creodont *krē'ō-dont, n.* any member of a group of primitive fossil carnivores, appearing in Eocene times. [Gr. *kreas*, flesh, *odous, odontos*, tooth.]

creole *krē'ōl, krē-ōl', n.* (usu. with *cap.*) strictly applied in the former Spanish, French, and Portuguese colonies of America, Africa and the East Indies to natives of pure European blood (in opposition to immigrants born in Europe or to coloured natives): (usu. with *cap.*) a native, but not aboriginal or indigenous: (*loosely;* usu. with *cap.*) a native of mixed blood: (usu. with *cap.*) applied to the native French or Spanish stock in Louisiana (*U.S.*): (usu. with *cap.*) a colonial patois (French, Spanish, etc.): (usu. with *cap.*) a Negro born in America (*obs.*; earlier **creō'lian**): (also **creolised,** or **creolized, language**) a language formerly a pidgin which has developed and become the accepted language of a region. — *adj.* (sometimes with *cap.*) pertaining to a Creole or creole. — *n.* and *adj.* **creō'lian** see **creole.** — **creōlisā'tion, -z-,** the development of a pidgen into a creole; **crē'ōlist** one who studies creole languages. [Fr. *créole* — Sp. *criollo*, dim. of *criado*, nursling — *criar*, lit. to create, hence to bring up, nurse — L. *creāre*.]

creophagous *krē-of'ə-gəs, adj.* flesh-eating. [Gr. *kreas*, flesh, *phagein*, to eat.]

creosote, creasote *krē'ə-sōt, n.* an oily liquid obtained by destructive distillation of wood-tar: a somewhat similar liquid got from coal-tar (**creosote oil** or **coal-tar creosote**). — *v.t.* to treat with creosote. — **cre'osote=plant** an American bush (*Larrea mexicana*; fam. Zygophyllaceae) that smells of creosote and forms dense scrub. [Gr. *kreas*, flesh, *sōtēr*, saviour — *sōzein*, to save.]

crepance *krē'pəns, n.* a wound on a horse's hind ankle-joint, caused by the shoe of the other hind-foot. [L. *crepāre*, to break.]

crêpe, crepe *krāp, krep, n.* a crape-like fabric: rubber rolled in thin crinkly sheets (**crêpe rubber**): generally written with the accent, as in French) a pancake. — *v.t.* to frizz, as hair. — *ns.* **crep'oline** a light crape-like dress material; **crep'on** a similar fabric made of silk or nylon. — *adj.* **crêp'y, crep'y** wrinkled, crêpe-like, crape-like. — **crêpe-de-chine** (*də shēn;* also **crepe-**) a crape-like fabric, originally of silk; **crepe'hanger** see **crape; crêpe paper** thin crinkled paper. — *adj.* **crêpe'-soled** soled with crêpe rubber. — **crêpe suzette** (*sü-zet*) a thin pancake in a hot orange- or lemon-flavoured sauce, usu. flambéed: — *pl.* **crêpes suzettes.** [See **crape.**]

crepitate *krep'i-tāt, v.i.* to crackle, snap: to rattle: (of beetles) to discharge an offensive fluid. — *adj.* **crep'itant** crackling. — *n.* **crepitā'tion** the act of crepitating: crackle: a sound detected in the lungs by auscultation in certain diseases. — *adj.* **crep'itative.** — *n.* **crep'itus.** [L. *crepitāre, -ātum*, freq. of *crepāre*, to crack, rattle.]

crept *krept, pa.t.* and *pa.p.* of **creep.**

crepuscular *kri-pus'kū-lər, adj.* of or pertaining to twilight — also **crepus'culous.** — *ns.* **crepuscule** (*krep'əs-kūl*, or *-ūs'*), **crepuscle** (*krep'əs-l*, or *-us'*) twilight. [L. *crepusculum* — *creper*, dusky, obscure.]

crescendo *kresh-en'dō*, (*mus.*) *adj.* and *adv.* gradually increasing in loudness. — *n.* increase of loudness: a passage of increasing loudness: a high point, a climax (*fig.*): — *pl.* **crescen'dos.** — Also *v.i.* [It., increasing.]

crescent *kres'ənt, krez', adj.* increasing: shaped like the waxing moon. — *n.* the waxing moon: a figure like the crescent moon: the Turkish (originally Byzantine) standard or emblem: the Turkish power: the Muslim faith: a curved range of buildings (sometimes applied at random): a crescent-shaped roll or bun. — *n.* **cresc'entade** a religious war for Islam. — *adjs.* **cresc'ented, crescentic** (*-ent'ik*) formed like a crescent; **cresc'ive** increasing. [L. *crēscĕre*, to grow, pr.p. *crēscēns, -entis.*]

cresol *krēs'ol, n.* a product of distillation of coal-tar resembling phenol — C₇H₈O. [From *creos*ote and alco*hol*.]

cress *kres, n.* a name for many pungent-leaved crucifer-ous plants of various genera, e.g. *Lepidium* (garden cress), *Rorippa* (watercress), *Arabis* (rock cress): extended to other plants of similar character, as Indian cress (*Tropaeolum*). — *adj.* **cress'y** abounding in cresses. [O.E. *cresse, cerse*; cf. Du. *kers*, Ger. *Kresse.*]

cresset *kres'it, n.* an iron basket, or the like, for combustibles, placed on a beacon, lighthouse, wharf, etc.: a torch generally. [O.Fr. *cresset, crasset* (Fr. *creuset*) — Old Du. *kruysel*, a hanging lamp.]

crest *krest, n.* the comb or tuft on the head of a cock or other bird: the summit of anything, as a roof-ridge, hill, wave: the mane of a horse, etc.: a ridge along the surface of a bone (*anat.*): a plume of feathers or other ornament on the top of a helmet: an accessory figure originally surmounting the helmet, placed on a wreath, etc., also used separately as a personal cognisance on plate, etc. (*her.*). — *v.t.* to furnish with a crest or serve as a crest for: to surmount. — *adjs.* **crest'ed** having a crest: having an elevated appendage like a crest (*bot.*); **crest'less** without a crest: not of high birth. — *adj.* **crest'fallen** dejected: cast-down. — **on, riding, the crest of a wave** enjoying a run of success. [O.Fr. *creste* (Fr. *crête*) — L. *crista.*]

cretaceous *kri-tā'shəs, adj.* composed of or like chalk: (*cap.*) belonging to the uppermost system of the Secondary or Mesozoic rocks, including in England the Wealden, the Gault and Greensand, and the Chalk. — Also *n.* [L. *crētāceus* — *crēta*, chalk.]

Cretan *krē'tən*, **Cretic** *krē'tik, adjs.* belonging to Crete. — *ns.* a native or inhabitant of Crete. — *ns.* **crē'tic** a metrical foot consisting of one short syllable between two long; **crē'tism** a lie. [Gr. *krētikos* — *Krētē*, Crete.]

cretin *kret'in, krēt'in, n.* a child suffering from a congenital deficiency of thyroid hormone, which, if untreated, can lead to mental deficiency and incomplete physical development: a person affected by these conditions as a result of such a deficiency: an idiot (*coll.*). — *n.* **cret'inism.** — *adjs.* **cret'inous; cret'inised, -ized; cret'inoid.** [Fr. *crétin* — L. *christiānus*, human creature.]

cretonne *kret-on', or kret'on, n.* a strong printed cotton fabric used for curtains or for covering furniture. [Fr., prob. from *Creton* in Normandy.]

creutzer. Same as **kreutzer.**

crevasse *kriv-as', n.* a crack or split, esp. applied to a cleft in a glacier: a breach in a canal or river bank (*U.S.*). — *v.t.* to fissure with crevasses. — *n.* **crevice** (*krev'is*) a crack or rent: a narrow opening. [O.Fr. *crevace* — L. *crepāre*, to creak, break.]

crève-cœur *krev-kœr*, (Fr.) *n.* heartbreak.

crevice. See **crevasse.**

crew¹ *krōō, n.* a set, gang: a ship's company: the oarsmen and steersman manning a racing boat: a group in charge of a bus, train or aeroplane. — *v.i.* to act as a crew member on a ship, etc. (esp. with *for*). — **crew cut** a very short style of haircut; **crew neck** a round, close-fitting style of neck on a jersey (*adj.* **crew'= necked**). [O.Fr. *creue*, increase — *croistre*, to grow.]

crew² *krōō, pa.t.* of **crow.**

crewe *krōō*, (Spens.) *n.* a pot. [O.Fr. *crue.*]

crewel *krōō'əl, n.* a fine worsted yarn used for embroidery and tapestry: work in crewels. — *v.t.* to work in crewel. — *ns.* **crew'elist; crew'ellery; crew'elwork.** [Orig. a monosyllable, *crule, crewle*; ety. dub.]

crewels, cruel(l)s *krōō'əlz*, (*Scot.*) *n.pl.* the king's evil, scrofula. [Fr. *écrouelles.*]

criant *krī'ənt, krē-ã, adj.* garish, discordantly coloured. [Fr.]

crib *krib, n.* a manger or fodder-receptable: a stall for oxen: a bin: a crate: a model representing the scene of Christ's nativity: a child's bed usu. with closed sides, a cot (*esp. U.S.*): a cabin or hut: a confined place: a house (*thieves' slang*): a job (*slang*): a timber framework for a dam, a pier foundation: a mine-shaft lining, etc.: a pilfering, or the thing pilfered: a plagiarism: a key or baldly literal translation, used by students, etc.: the discarded cards at cribbage, used by the dealer in scoring. — *v.t.* to put in a crib: to confine: to pilfer: to plagiarise: — *pr.p.* **cribb'ing**; *pa.t.* and *pa.p.* **cribbed.** — *n.* **cribb'age** a card game in which each player discards a certain number of cards for the *crib*, and scores by holding certain combinations and by bringing the sum of the values of cards played to certain numbers. — **cribb'age-board** a scoring-board for cribbage, with holes for pegs; **crib'-bit'ing** in horses, a vicious habit of biting the manger, etc., and swallowing air; **crib death** (*U.S.*) cot death; **crib'work** work formed of cribs. [O.E. *crib*; Ger. *Krippe*.]

cribbage. See **crib.**

cribble *krib'l, n.* a coarse screen or sieve used for sand, gravel or corn: coarse flour or meal (*obs.*). — *v.t.* to sift or riddle (*obs.*): in engraving, to produce a dotted effect. — *adj.* **cribb'led.** — *n.* **cribell'um** an accessory spinning-organ of certain spiders: — *pl.* **cribell'a.** — *adjs.* **cribell'ar, criblé** (Fr.; *krē-blä*; *engraving*) punctured like a sieve, dotted; **crib'rate** (or *krīb'*), **crib'rose** perforated like a sieve. — *n.* **cribrā'tion** sifting. — *adj.* **crib'riform** perforated. [L. *crībrum*, dim. *crībellum*, a sieve.]

cribellar, criblé, cribrate, etc. See **cribble.**

Cricetus *kri-sē'tэs, n.* the hamster genus. [Mod. L. — Slav. name of hamster.]

crick *krik, n.* a spasm or cramp of the muscles, esp. of the neck. — *v.t.* to produce a crick in. [Prob. imit.]

cricket[1] *krik'it, n.* a saltatory, orthopterous insect, allied to grasshoppers and locusts. [O.Fr. *criquet*; cf. Du. and L.G. *krekel.*]

cricket[2] *krik'it, n.* an outdoor game played with bats, a ball, and wickets, between two sides of eleven each: that which is fair and sporting (*coll.*). — *v.i.* to play at cricket. — *n.* **crick'eter.** — *n.* and *adj.* **crick'eting.** [Fr. *criquet*; not O.E. *crycc*, a stock.]

cricket[3] *krik'it* (*now dial.*) *n.* a low stool. — **cricket table** a small low table with a circular foldable top on a triangular base. [Ety. unknown.]

crickey, cricky. See **crikey.**

cricoid *krī'koid, (anat.) adj.* ring-shaped. — *n.* a cartilage of the larynx. [Gr. *krīkoeides — krikos*, a ring, and *eidos*, form.]

cri de cœur *krē dэ kœr,* (Fr.) a cry from the heart — heartfelt, passionate entreaty, complaint, reproach.

cried, crier, cries. See **cry.**

crikey, cricky, crickey *krīk'i, krik'i, (slang) interjs.,* a mild oath or expression of surprise. [Euphemism for *Christ.*]

crime *krīm, n.* a violation of law, esp. if serious: an act punishable by law: such acts collectively or in the abstract: an act gravely wrong morally: sin: an accusation (*Spens.*): a cause or motive of wrongdoing (*Spens.*). — *v.t.* (*mil.*) to charge or convict of an infraction of law. — *adjs.* **crime'ful** criminal; **crime'less** without crime, innocent; **criminal** (*krim'*) relating to crime: guilty of crime: violating laws. — *n.* one guilty of crime. — *ns.* **criminalēse'** criminals' slang; **criminalīsā'tion, -z-.** — *v.t.* **crim'inalise, -ize** to declare someone or something criminal. — *ns.* **crim'inalist** one versed in criminal law; **criminal'ity** guiltiness. — *adv.* **crim'inally.** — *v.t.* **crim'inate** to accuse. — *n.* **criminā'tion** the act of criminating: accusation. — *adjs.* **crim'inative, crim'inatory** involving crimination; **criminogen'ic** causing crime. — *ns.* **criminol'ogist; criminol'ogy** the science dealing with crime and criminals. — *adj.* **crim'inous** criminal — chiefly in the ecclesiastical phrase 'a criminous clerk'. — *n.* **crim'inousness.** — **crime sheet** (*mil.*) a record of offences; **crime wave** a sharp rise in the level of criminal activity (see **wave**); **criminal conversation,** often **crim. con.,** adultery. [Fr., — L. *crīmen, -inis.*]

crimen falsi *krī'men fal'sī, krē'men fal'sē,* (L.) crime of perjury; **crimen laesae majestatis** (*lē'sē maj-эs-tā'tis, lī'sī ma-yes-tä'tis*) high treason.

crime passionel *krēm pa-syo-nel,* (Fr.) a crime due to (sexual) passion.

criminal, etc., **criminologist,** etc. See **crime.**

crimine, crimini *krim'i-ni, (arch.) interj.* an ejaculation of surprise or impatience. [Perh. from *Christ*; see **crikey.**]

crimmer. See **krimmer.**

crimp *krimp, adj.* made crisp or brittle. — *v.t.* to press into folds: to curl (hair): to bend into shape: to gash: to seize or decoy. — *n.* a curl or wave: a hindering factor (*coll.*): one who presses or decoys (sailors, etc.). — *n.* **crimp'er** one who or what crimps or corrugates: a hairdresser (*slang*). — *v.t.* **crimp'le** to contract or draw together: to plait: to curl. — *adj.* **crimp'y** frizzy. — **crimp'ing-iron** an iron instrument used for crimping hair or material; **crimp'ing-machine** a machine for forming crimps or plaits on ruffles. [O.E. *gecrympan*, to curl; cf. **cramp,** and Du. *krimpen*, to shrink.]

Crimplene® *krim'plēn, n.* (a grease-resistant, synthetic fabric made from) a thick polyester yarn.

crimson *krim'zn, n.* a deep red colour, tinged with blue: red in general — *adj.* deep red. — *v.t.* to dye crimson. — *v.i.* to become crimson: to blush. [M.E. *crimosin* — O.Fr. *cramoisin*; from Ar. *qirmizī*, scarlet — *qirmiz*, kermes, from which it is made.]

crinal *krī'nэl, adj.* of or belonging to the hair. — *adjs.* **crīn'ate, -d** having hair; **crīnig'erous** hairy; **crī'nite** hairy: resembling a tuft of hair (*bot.*); **crī'nose** hairy. — *adj.* **crīnicul'tural** relating to the culture or growth of the hair. [L. *crīnis*, the hair.]

crine *krīn, (Scot.) v.i.* to shrink or shrivel. [Gael. *crion*, dry.]

cringe *krinj, v.i.* to bend or crouch with servility: to submit: to fawn: to flatter with mean servility: (*loosely*) to wince or flinch. — *n.* a servile obeisance. — *ns.* **cringe'ling, crin'ger** one who cringes. — *n.* and *adj.* **crin'ging.** — *adv.* **crin'gingly** in an obsequious manner. [Related to O.E. *crincan, cringan,* to shrink; cf. **crank**[1].]

cringle *kring'gl, n.* a small piece of rope worked into the bolt-rope of a sail, and containing a metal ring or thimble. [Gmc.; cf. Ger. *Kringel.*]

crinicultural, crinigerous. See **crinal.**

crinite. See **crinal, crinum.**

crinkle *kringk'l, v.t.* to twist, wrinkle, crimp. — *v.i.* to wrinkle up, curl. — *n.* a wrinkle: (also **crink'ly**) paper money, money in general (*slang*). — *adj.* **crink'ly** wrinkly. — *ns.* and *adjs.* **crink'le-crank'le** (mainly *dial.*) (something) zigzag or winding; **crink'um-crank'um** a word applied familiarly to things intricate or crooked. [Related to O.E. *crincan*; see **cringe.**]

crinoid. See **crinum.**

crinoline *krin'э-lin, -lēn, n.* originally a stiff fabric of horsehair and flax: this or other means to distend women's attire: a hooped petticoat or skirt made to project all round by means of steel wire: a netting round ships as a guard against torpedoes. — *n.* **crinolette'** a small crinoline causing the dress to project behind only. — *adj.* **crin'olined.** [Fr., *crin* — L. *crinis,* hair, and *lin* — L. *linum,* flax.]

crinose. See **crinal.**

crinum *krī'nэm, n.* any of various plants of the Amaryllis family, characterised by luxuriant clusters of lily-like flowers. — *ns.* **crinite** (*krin', krīn'*) an encrinite or fossil crinoid; **crinoid** (*krin', krīn'*) a feather-star or sea-lily, an echinoderm of the class **Crinoid'ea,** with cup-shaped body and branching arms and well developed skeleton, usually attached by a jointed stalk, mouth upwards, well known in fossil forms as encrinites or stone-lilies. — Also *adj.* — *adj.* **crinoid'al** (Gr. *krīnoeidēs*, like a lily — *eidos*, form). — *adj.* and *n.* **crinoid'ean.** [Gr. *krīnon*, a lily.]

criollo *krē-ōl'ō, n.* a Latin American native of European, esp. Spanish, blood: any of several South American breeds of animal: the name given to a fine variety of cocoa: — *pl.* **criollʹos.** [Sp., native, indigenous; see **creole.**]

crio-sphinx *krī'ō-sfingks, n.* a ram-headed sphinx. [Gr. *krīos*, a ram, *sphinx*, a sphinx.]

cripes *krīps, (slang) interj.* expression of surprise or worry.   [Euphemism for *Christ*.]

cripple *krip'l, n.* a lame person: one who is deficient in some way: a bracket attached to a ladder on the ridge of a roof to support scaffold boards. — *adj.* lame. — *v.t.* to make lame: to lame: to disable, impair the efficiency of. — *ns.* **cripp'ledom; cripp'ling** a prop set up as a support against the side of a building.   [O.E. *crypel*; conn. with **creep**.]

crise *krēz*, (Fr.) *n.* a crisis: an instance of mental or physical distress. — **crise de conscience** (*də-kɔ̃-syãs*) a crisis of conscience, a moral dilemma; **crise de foi** (*də-fwä*) an attack of doubt, distrust or disillusionment; **crise de nerfs** (*də-ner*) an emotional upset.

crisis *krī'sis, n.* a crucial or decisive moment: a turning-point: a time of difficulty or distress: an emergency: — *pl.* **crises** (*krī'sēz*).   [Gr. *krisis*, from *krinein*, to decide.]

crisp *krisp, adj.* curling closely: having a wavy surface: so dry as to be crumbled easily: brittle: short (of pastry): fresh and bracing: firm, the opposite of limp or flabby. — *v.t.* to curl or twist: to make crisp or wavy: to ripple. — *n.* a piece of food fried or roasted to crispness: (in *pl.*) potato-crisps. — *adjs.* **crisp'āte, -d** having a crisp or wavy appearance. — *ns.* **crispā'tion; crisp'ature** a curling; **crisp'er** one who or that which crisps. — *adv.* **crisp'ly.** — *n.* **crisp'ness.** — *adj.* **crisp'y.** — **crisp'bread** a brittle, unsweetened type of biscuit of rye or wheat, eaten instead of bread; **crisp'ing-iron,** **-pin** a curling-iron.   [O.E., — L. *crispus*.]

crispin *kris'pin, n.* a shoemaker, from *Crispin* of Soissons, the patron saint of shoemakers, martyred 25 October 287.

criss-cross *kris'-kros, n.* the cross at the beginning of the alphabet on a hornbook (see **criss-cross-row** at **Christ**): a mark formed by two lines in the form of a cross, as the signature of a person unable to write his name: a network of crossing lines: repeated crossings: cross-purposes: a game of noughts and crosses. — *adj.* and *adv.* crosswise. — *v.t.* and *v.i.* to cross repeatedly.   [From **christ-cross**.]

crissum *kris'əm, n.* the area round a bird's vent, with the under-tail coverts: — *pl.* **criss'a.**   [L. *crissāre*, to move the thighs sensuously.]

crista *kris'tə, n.* a crest: a ridge or fold (*biol.*): — *pl.* **cris'tae** (*-ē*). — *adjs.* **crist'ate** crested; **crist'iform.**   [L.]

cristobalite *kris-tō'bəl-īt, n.* one of the principal forms of silica, produced from quartz at high temperatures, occurring in volcanic rocks, slags, etc.   [Cerro San Cristóbal in Mexico, where it was discovered.]

crit *krit,* (*coll.*) *n.* short for **criticism**.

criterion *krī-tē'ri-ən, n.* a means or standard of judging: a test: a rule, standard, or canon: — *pl.* **critē'ria.** — *adj.* **crite'rion-referenced** of an examination or assessment) judging examinees on the basis of their demonstrated mastery of certain skills and abilities (rather than by comparison with the achievements of their peers; cf. *norm-referenced*). — **crite'rion referencing.**   [Gr. *kritērion* — *kritēs*, a judge.]

crith *krith, n.* a unit of mass, that of 1 litre of hydrogen at standard temperature and pressure.   [Gr. *krithē,* barleycorn, a small weight.]

crithomancy *krith'ō-man-si, n.* divination by the meal strewed over the victims of sacrifice.   [Gr. *krithē,* barley, and *manteiā,* divination.]

critic *krit'ik, n.* one skilled in estimating the quality of literary or artistic work: a professional reviewer: one skilled in textual studies, various readings, and the ascertainment of the original words: a fault-finder. — *adj.* **crit'ical** at or relating to a turning-point, transition or crisis: decisive: (*loosely*) seriously ill: relating to criticism: rigorously discriminating: captious: of a condition in which a chain reaction is self-sustaining. — *adv.* **crit'ically.** — *ns.* **crit'icalness, critical'ity; crit'- icaster** a petty critic (see **-aster**). — *adj.* **criticisable** (*-sīz'*). — *v.t.* **crit'icise, -ize** to pass judgment on: to censure. — *ns.* **crit'icism** the art of judging, esp. in literature or the fine arts: a critical judgment or

observation; **critique** (*kri-tēk'*) a critical examination of any production: a review. — **critical angle** the least angle of incidence at which a ray is totally reflected; **critical mass** (*nuc.*) the minimum amount of fissile material needed to sustain a chain reaction; **critical philosophy** that of Kant which is based on a critical examination of the faculty of knowledge; **critical tem- perature** that temperature above which a gas cannot be liquefied by pressure alone. — **critical path analysis** the working out with the aid of a computer the sequence of operations that must be followed in order to complete a complex piece of work in the minimum time; **higher** or **historical criticism,** as distinguished from **textual** or **verbal criticism,** the inquiry into the composition, date, and authenticity of the books of the Bible, from historical and literary considerations.   [Gr. *kritikos* — *krinein,* to judge.]

critter, crittur *krit'ər,* (*dial.* and *coll.*; now esp. *U.S.*) *n.* creature: animal.

crivens, crivvens *kriv'ənz,* (*dial.*) *interj.* an exclamation expressive of amazement or dismay.   [Perh. from *Christ* combined with *heavens*.]

croak *krōk, v.i.* to utter a low hoarse sound, as a frog or raven: to grumble: to forebode evil: to die (*slang*). — *v.t.* to utter croakingly: to kill (*slang*). — *n.* the sound of a frog or raven. — *n.* **croak'er** a person or animal that croaks: any of several types of tropical sea-fish of the Sciaenidae family that emit croaking noises. — *adv.* **croak'ily.** — *n.* **croak'ing.** — *adj.* **croak'y.**   [Imit.]

Croat *krō'at, n.* a native or inhabitant of Croatia in Yugoslavia: the language of Croatia. — Also *adj.* — *adj.* **Croatian** (*-ā'shən*) belonging to Croatia or its people. — *n.* a Croat: the Croat language.   [Serbo-Croatian *Hrvat.*]

croc *krok,* (*coll.*) *n.* short for **crocodile**.

croceate, croceous. See **crocus**[1].

croche *krōch, n.* a knob at the top of a deer's horn.   [Fr.]

crochet *krō'shā, n.* looping work done with a small hook. — *v.i.* and *v.t.* to work in crochet: — *pr.p.* **crocheting** (*krō'shā-ing*); *pa.t.* and *pa.p.* **crocheted** (*krō'shād*). — *n.* **cro'cheting** the action of crochet: crochetwork.   [Fr. *crochet* — *croche, croc,* a hook.]

crocidolite *krō sid'ə līt, n.* a fibrous mineral consisting mainly of silicate of iron and sodium, called *blue asbestos:* in S. Africa also a golden alteration product or pseudomorph of this mineral, largely quartz.   [From Gr. *krokis, -idos,* nap of cloth, and *lithos,* stone.]

crock[1] *krok, n.* a pot or jar: a potsherd. — *n.* **crock'ery** earthenware: all types of domestic pottery.   [O.E. *croc;* Ger. *Krug;* perh. of Celt. origin, as in W. *crochan,* a pot, Gael. *crogan,* a pitcher.]

crock[2] *krok,* (*dial.*) *n.* dirt, smut. — *v.t.* to besmut.   [Origin doubtful.]

crock[3] *krok, n.* an old ewe: an old horse: a broken down or decrepit person or thing. — *v.i.* to break down (often with *up*). — *v.t.* to disable.   [Cf. Norw. and Sw. *krake,* a poor beast.]

crockery. See **crock**[1].

crocket *krok'it,* (*archit.*) *n.* an ornament on the sloping sides of a pediment, pinnacle, etc., usu. like curled leaves or flowers.   [See **croquet**.]

crocodile *krok'ə-dīl, n.* a large reptile of the Nile with bony scutes and horny scales: extended to others of the genus **Crocodi'lus** or order **Crocodil'ia** or *Loricata* (alligators, gavials, etc.): leather from crocodile skin: a double file of school pupils taking a walk. — *adj.* and *n.* **crocodilian** (*-dil'*). — *n.* **crocodil'ite** (*obs.*) captious arguing — from a sophistical problem about a crocodile. — **crocodile bird** a bird, perh. a plover, said to pick the crocodile's teeth or take leeches from its throat; **crocodile tears** hypocritical grief — from the old story that crocodiles (which have large lachrymal glands) shed tears over the hard necessity of killing animals for food.   [L. *crocodīlus* — Gr. *krokodeilos,* a lizard.]

crocus[1] *krō'kəs, n.* a bulbous iridaceous plant with brilliant yellow, purple, or white flowers: in old chemistry, various yellow or red powders (*crocus of Mars*, colcothar). — *adjs.* **croceate** *krō'si-āt* (*obs.*), **croceous** (*krō'shi-əs*) saffron-coloured. — *ns.* **crocoite** (*krō'-kō-īt*), **crocoisite** (*krō'*, or *-kō'*) a bright red mineral, lead chromate. [L. *crocus* — Gr. *krokos*; prob. of Eastern origin; cf. Heb. *karkom*, and Ar. *kurkum*, saffron.]

crocus² *krō'kəs*, (*slang*) *n.* a quack doctor.

Croesus *krē'səs*, *n.* a very rich man. [*Croesus*, king of Lydia, of fabulous wealth.]

croft *kroft*, *n.* a small piece of arable land esp. adjoining a dwelling: a small farm. — *ns.* **croft'er; croft'ing.** [O.E. *croft*; perh. cog. with Du. *kroft*, hillock.]

Crohn's disease *krōnz diz-ēz'*, a medical condition involving severe inflammation of the ileum. [B. *Crohn* (b.1884), Amer. physician.]

croissant *krwä'sã*, *n.* a crescent roll. [Fr.]

croix de guerre *krwä də ger*, (Fr.) military decoration for heroism in action.

cromack. Same as **crummock, crummack.**

Cro-Magnon *krō-mag'nən, krō-man'yõ, adj.* pertaining to a type of man, long-skulled but short-faced, surviving from Aurignacian times to recent times. [From *Cro-Magnon*, in Dordogne, where the first skulls of this race were found.]

crombie *krom'bi*, *n.* a woollen cloth manufactured in Aberdeen, used for overcoats, etc.: a garment from such cloth.

crome, cromb *krōm, krōōm*, (*dial.*) *n.* a hook or crook. — *v.t.* to draw with a crome. [Cf. Du. *kram*.]

cromlech, *krom'lehh, -lek, n.* a stone circle: formerly applied to a dolmen. [W. *cromlech* — *crom*, curved, circular, and *llech*, a stone.]

cromorna, cromorne *krō-mörn'(ə), ns.* a krummhorn: a krummhorn stop. [Fr. *cromorne* — Ger. *Krummhorn.*]

Cromwellian *krom-wel'i-ən, adj.* of or relating to Oliver Cromwell, Puritan and Lord Protector of the Commonwealth (1653–8). — *n.* a supporter of Cromwell: a settler in Ireland in the settlement of 1652: a chair of plain design with leather seat and back, said to have been popularised by the Puritans.

crone *krōn, n.* an old woman, usually in contempt — rarely an old man: an old ewe. [Perh. O.Fr. *carogne*, carrion, hag, directly or through Du.]

cronet *krō'net*, (*obs.*) *n.* the hair growing over the top of a horse's hoof. [**coronet.**]

cronk *krongk*, (*Austr. coll.*) *adj.* ill: of poor quality: unfavourable. [From **crank¹.**]

crony *krōn'i, n.* an intimate companion. — *n.* **crō'nyism** (*U.S. coll.*) the appointment of friends to well-paid posts regardless of their fitness for these posts. [Said to be orig. university slang — Gr. *chronios*, longcontinued, perennial.]

croodle¹ *krōōd'l*, (*Scot.*) *v.i.* to cower down, snuggle. [Origin unknown.]

croodle² *krōōd'l, krōōd'l*, (*Scot.*) *v.i.* to murmur like a dove. [Imit.]

crook *krōōk*, *n.* a bend, anything bent: a curved tube used to lower the pitch of a wind instrument: the bending of the body in reverence (*obs.*): a staff bent at the end, as a shepherd's or bishop's: an artifice or trick (*obs.*): a gibbet (*Spens.*): a professional swindler or thief. — *adj.* (*Austr. coll.*) ill: angry: unfair: unscrupulous. — *v.t.* to bend or form into a hook: to turn from the straight line or from what is right (*obs.*). — *v.i.* to bend or be bent. — *adj.* **crook'ed** bent like a crook: not straight: deviating from rectitude, perverse: dishonest (*coll.*). — *adv.* **crook'edly.** — *n.* **crook'edness.** — *n.* **crook'back** (*Shak.*) a hunchback. — *adjs.* **crook'-backed; crook'-kneed; crook'-shoul'dered.** — **a crook in the lot** any trial in one's experience; **go crook** (*Austr. coll.*) to lose one's temper; **go crook on** (*Austr. coll.*) to upbraid, rebuke. [Prob. O.N. *krōkr*, hook; cf. Sw. *krok*, Dan. *krog*.]

Crookes glass *krōōks gläs*, a type of glass that inhibits the passage of ultraviolet light, used in sunglasses, etc.;

Crookes tube (*phys.*) a sealed, evacuated tube in which stratification in electric discharges can be observed. [Sir William *Crookes* (1832–1919), British scientist.]

croon *krōōn, v.i.* (*Scot. krün*) to utter a low, monotonous inarticulate sound like a bull: to murmur: to lament murmuringly: to sing or hum in an undertone. — *v.t.* and *v.i.* to sing softly in a sentimentally contemplative manner. — Also *n.* — *ns.* **croon'er; croon'ing.** [Cf. Du. *kreunen*, to groan.]

crop *krop, n.* the top or end of anything, as a tree or twig (*arch.*): a sprout: a finial (*archit.*): a whip-handle: a hunting whip with loop instead of lash: an end cut off: an act or mode of cutting: mode of cutting or wearing short hair: the total quantity produced, cut, or harvested: the total growth or produce: a cultivated plant, collectively: a number, quantity (of products, ideas, etc.) produced or appearing at a time, a supply: a season's yield: an entire hide: the craw, a dilatation of a bird's oesophagus: a similar structure in another animal: an outcrop. — *v.t.* to cut off the top, ends, margins, or loose parts of: to cut short: to mow, reap, or gather: to bite off in eating: to raise crops on: to cut the hair of. — *v.i.* to yield a crop: to come to the surface (with *up* or *out*): hence, to come (up) casually, as in conversation: — *pr.p.* **cropp'ing;** *pa.t.* and *pa.p.* **cropped.** — *n.* **crop'ful** as much as the crop can hold: — *pl.* **crop'fuls.** — *adj.* **crop'full** (*Milt.*) satiated. — *ns.* **cropp'er** one who or that which crops: a plant that yields a crop: one who raises a crop for a share of it: a kind of pigeon noted for its large crop: a small platen printing machine: a fall (*coll.*): a failure (*coll.*); **cropp'ing** the act of cutting off: the raising of crops: an outcrop (*geol.*); **cropp'y** one of the Irish rebels of 1798 who cut their hair short, like the French Revolutionists. — *adj.* **crop'bound'** suffering from impaction of the crop. — **crop'dusting** the spraying of crops with fungicides or insecticides from the air; **crop'-duster** one who does this; **crop'-ear** a person, horse, dog, etc., with cropped ears. — *adj.* **crop'-eared** having ears cropped, or hair cropped to show the ears (a Cavalier jibe at a Puritan). — **crop'land** land used for growing crops; **crop'-marks** (*archaeol.*) variations in the depth or colour of a crop growing in a field, which, viewed from the air, can show the presence of a structure beneath the soil. — *adj.* **crop'sick** sick of a surfeit. — **come a cropper** (*coll.*) to have a fall, perhaps from the phrase *neck and crop*. [O.E. *crop*, the top shoot of a plant, the crop of a bird; Du. *crop*, a bird's crop.]

croquet *krō'kā, n.* a game in which wooden balls are driven by means of long-handled mallets, through a series of hoops. — *v.t.* to drive away by striking another ball in contact. [North Fr. *croquet*, a dial. form of *crochet*, dim. of *croc, croche*, a crook.]

croquette *krō-ket', n.* a ball or round cake, usu. of minced and seasoned meat, fish, or potato, coated in breadcrumbs and fried. [Fr., — *croquer*, to crunch.]

croquis *kro-kē*, (Fr.) *n.* an outline or rough sketch.

crore *krōr, krör, n.* ten millions, or one hundred lakhs. [Hind. *karor.*]

crosier, crozier *krō'z(h)yər, n.* the pastoral staff or crook of a bishop or abbot: erroneously, an archbishop's cross. — *adj.* **cro'siered.** [M.E. *crose* or *croce* — Late L. *crocia*, a crook.]

cross *kros, n.* a gibbet on which the Romans exposed malefactors, typically consisting of two pieces of timber, one placed tranversely to the other: (with *cap.*) the particular one on which Christ suffered: (*cap.*) the symbol of the Christian religion, or of the crusades: the Christian doctrine of atonement: a representation of Christ's cross: any object, figure, or mark formed by two parts or lines transverse to each other, with or without elaboration: such a mark used instead of a signature by an illiterate person: such a mark used to symbolise a kiss in a letter: a staff surmounted by a cross: a monument not always in the form of a cross, where proclamations are made, etc.: a place in a town or village where such a monument stands or stood: a cross-shaped pendant or medal: the transverse part of an anchor, or the like: a surveyor's cross-staff: a crossing or crossway: anything that crosses or thwarts: adversity or affliction in general, or a burden or cause of suffering, as in *bear one's cross*: mixing of breeds: a hybrid: something intermediate in character between two other things: unfairness or dishonest practices, esp. in sport where a contestant corruptly allows himself to be beaten: a game or race lost by collusion: the obverse of a coin, formerly often stamped with a cross (*obs.*): hence, a coin (*arch.*): a transverse pass, esp. towards the opposing team's goal (*football*). — *adj.* lying across or crosswise: transverse: oblique: adverse: interchanged: peevish: angry, displeased (with): hybrid: dishonest: balancing, neutralising. — *adv.* and *prep.* across (as *prep.* often written 'cross in poetry). — *v.t.* to mark with a cross: to make the sign of the cross over: to set something, or draw a line, across: to set in position athwart the mast (*Spens.*): to place crosswise: to cancel by drawing cross lines: to pass from one side to the other of: to pass transversely, esp. in the direction of the opposing team's goal (*football*): to extend across: to interbreed: to draw two lines across (a cheque), thereby restricting it to payment through a bank: to obstruct: to thwart: to annoy: to confront (*arch.*): to bestride. — *v.i.* to lie or pass across: to meet and pass: to interbreed: — *pa.t.* and *pa.p.* **crossed,** sometimes **crost.** — *adj.* **crossed.** — *n.* **cross'ing** the act of making the sign of the cross: the act of going across: a place where a roadway, etc., may be crossed: intersection: esp. transepts and nave: act of thwarting: cross-breeding. — *adjs.* **cross'ing, cross'-ish.** — *n.* **cross'let** a small cross. — *adv.* **cross'ly.** — *n.* **cross'ness.** — *adv.* **cross'wise** in the form of a cross (*arch.*): across. — **cross action** (*law*) an action brought by the defender against the pursuer; **cross aisle** (*obs.*) a transept; **cross'-and-pile'** (or **-or-**) (*arch.*) heads or tails: a toss-up. — *adj.* **cross'-armed** having the arms crossed. — **cross'-assem'bler** (*comput.*) one which runs on one computer, producing a machine code for a different computer. — *adj.* **cross'band'ed** having the grain of the veneer run across that of the rail — of a handrail. — **cross'band, cross'banding; cross'bar** a transverse bar: a kind of lever. — *adj.* **cross'barred.** — **crossbar switch** a switch having two sets of paths, one vertical and one horizontal, with an electromagnetically operated means of connecting any path in the one set with any path in the other; **crossbar switching** using a crossbar switch system; **cross'beam** a large beam stretching across a building and serving to hold its sides together; **cross'bearer** one who carries a cross in a procession; **cross'-bedd'ing** (*geol.*) false bedding; **cross'bench** a bench laid crosswise: a bench on which independent members of parliament sometimes sit. — *adj.* **indcpcndcnt:** impartial. — **cross'bencher; cross'=bill** a bill brought by the defendant in a Chancery suit against the plaintiff; **cross'bill** a finch of the genus Loxia with mandibles crossing near the points; **cross'=birth** a birth in which the child lies transversely in the uterus. — *v.t.* **cross'bite** (*arch.*) to bite in return: to cheat in return: to outwit: to entrap. — **cross'bones** a figure of two thigh-bones laid across each other — forming with the skull a conventional emblem of death or piracy; **cross'bow** a weapon for shooting arrows, formed of a bow placed crosswise on a stock; **cross'-bower, -bowman** one who uses a crossbow. — *adj.* **cross'bred.** — **cross'breed** a breed produced by crossing: the offspring of a cross; **cross'breed'ing; cross'-bun** see **hot cross-bun; cross'-butt'ock** a particular throw over the hip in wrestling. — *v.t.* **cross'-check'** to test the accuracy of e.g. a statement by consulting various sources of information. — Also *v.i.* and *n.* — **cross'=claim** a claim made by the defendant against the plaintiff; **cross'-compil'er** (*comput.*) one which runs on one computer, producing a machine code for a different computer; **cross correspondence** (*psychical re-*

search) fitting together of communications separately unintelligible to give an intelligible whole. — *adj.* and *adv.* **cross'-coun'try** through fields, woods, over hills, etc., rather than by road, esp. (of running, skiing, etc.) over a long distance. — **cross'-cross'let** a cross with its ends crossed. — *adj.* **cross'-cul'tural** pertaining to the differences between cultures: bridging the gap between cultures. — **cross'-current** in the air, sea, or a river, a current flowing across the main current; **cross'cut** a crosswise cutting: a short way across from one point to another. — *v.t.* (*-kut'*) to cut across. — **crosscut saw** a large saw worked by two men, one at each end, for cutting beams crosswise; **cross'cutting** (*cinema, TV*) cutting and fitting together film sequences so that in the finished picture the action moves from one scene to another and back again, thus increasing dramatic tension; **cross'-dā'ting** (*archaeol.*) dating one site, level, etc., by comparison with others; **cross'-divi'sion** division into groups or classes that overlap; **cross'-dress'-ing** transvestism: wearing unisex clothes; **crossed line** a telephone line connected in error to a different line or circuit; **cross'-examinā'tion.** — *v.t.* **cross'-exam'ine** to question minutely, or with a view to checking evidence already given: to subject to examination by the other side. — **cross'-eye.** — *adj.* **cross'-eyed** squinting. — *v.t.* **cross'-fade** (*television, radio*) to cause (a sound source or picture) to fade away while gradually introducing another (also *v.i.*). — **cross'fall** the transverse inclination on a road; **cross'-fertilisā'tion** the fecundation of a plant by pollen from another: fruitful interaction of ideas from e.g. different cultures. — *adj.* **cross'field** (*football*) of a pass, etc., usu. long and transverse in direction. — **cross'fire** (*mil.*) the crossing of lines of fire from two or more points (also *fig.*); **cross'fish** the common sea-urchin Asterias rubens; **cross'-gar'net** a T-shaped hinge. — *adjs.* **cross'-gar'-tered** (*Shak.*) wearing the garters crossed on the leg; **cross'-grained** having the grain or fibres crossed or intertwined: perverse: contrary: intractable. — *adv.* across the grain: perversely. — **cross'-grained'ness; cross guard** the bar, at right angles to the blade, forming the hilt-guard of a sword. — *n.pl.* **cross'-hairs** two fine lines crossing at right angles at the centre of the lens of an optical instrument, used for focusing. — **cross'-hatch'ing** in drawing, etc. shading by intersecting sets of parallel lines; **cross'-head** a beam across the head of something, esp. the bar at the end of the piston-rod of a steam-engine; **cross-infec'tion** infection of an already ill or injured person with germs unrelated to his own complaint, liable to occur e.g. in hospitals where a variety of diseases are being treated: infection from one species to another. — *v.t.* **cross'-infect'.** — **cross'ing-o'ver** (*biol.*) interchange of parts of two chromosomes when they separate again after synapsis; **cross'ing-sweeper** one who sweeps a street crossing; **cross'ing-ward'en** a lollipop man or woman; **cross'jack** a mizzen course; **cross'-kick** a crossfield kick; **cross=lat'eral** a person affected with cross-laterality. — Also *adj.* — **cross-lateral'ity** a mixture of physical one-sidedness, as the combination of a dominant left eye with a dominant right hand. — *adjs.* **cross'-leaved** having leaves in four rows, set crosswise; **cross'-legged** having the legs crossed. — Also *adv.* — **cross'light** a light whose direction makes an angle with that of another light, and which illumines additional parts or regions. — *adjs.* **cross'-lighted; cross'-magnet'ic** diamagnetic. — *v.t.* **cross'-match'** to test (blood samples from a donor and a recipient) for compatibility by checking that agglutination does not occur when red cells from each are put into the other's serum. — **cross'over** a road passing over the top of another: a place or point at which a crossing or transfer is made: crossing-over (*biol.*). — *adj.* **cross'-part'y** covering, drawn from, all political parties. — **cross'patch** an ill-natured person (see **patch**[2]); **cross'piece** a piece of material of any kind crossing another: a timber over the windlass, with pins for belaying the running rigging (*naut.*); **cross-ply tyre** tyre in which the plies of fabric in the carcass are wrapped so as to cross each other diagonally; **cross'-pollina'tion** transfer of pollen from one flower to the stigma of another; **cross'-pur'pose** a contrary purpose: (in *pl.*) a game in which answers to questions are transferred to other questions: (in *pl.*) confusion in conversation or action by misunderstanding; **cross-quar'ters** an ornament of tracery like the four petals of a cruciform flower: a quatrefoil. — *v.t.* **cross'-ques'tion** to cross-examine. — **cross-ra'tio** of four points in a range, or rays in a pencil, the quotient of the position ratios of two with respect to the other two; **cross'-ref'erence** a reference in a book to another title or passage. — *v.i.* and *v.t.* **cross-refer'**. — **cross'-rib** an arch supporting a vault; **cross'road** a road crossing the principal road, a bypath: a road joining main roads: (often *pl.*) a place where roads cross — in U.S. often a hamlet: (in *pl.*) a stage at which an important decision has to be made. — *adj.* **cross'roads**. — **cross'-row** same as **christ-cross-row**; **cross'-ruff'** alternate ruffing by partners, each leading a suit that the other lacks; **cross sea** a sea that sets at an angle to the direction of the wind; **cross'-sec'tion** a transverse section: a comprehensive representation: the effective target area of a nucleus for a particular reaction under specified conditions, measured in barns (1 barn = 10^{-24} sq. cm.) — when no reaction can take place, the cross-section is zero. — *v.t.* to make a cross-section of. — *adj.* **cross-sec'tional**. — **cross'-sill** a railway sleeper; **cross'-spring'er** a cross-rib in a groined vault; **cross'-staff** a surveying instrument consisting of a staff surmounted with a frame carrying two pairs of sights at right angles; **cross'-stitch'** a stitch in the form of a cross; needlework of such stitches; **cross'-stone** chiastolite: staurolite: harmotome; **cross'-talk** interference of one telephone conversation with another: backchat: repartee; **cross'-tie** a supporting tie placed transversely: a railway sleeper; **cross'-tīn'ing** a mode of harrowing crosswise. — *adj.* **cross'-town** (*U.S.*) extending over, or crossing, a town. — **cross'tree** a piece of timber or metal placed across the upper end of a ship's mast; **cross'-vault'ing** vaulting formed by the intersection of simple vaults; **cross'walk** (*U.S.*) a pedestrian crossing; **cross'way** a way that crosses another or links others; **cross'wind** a wind blowing across the path of, e.g. an aeroplane; **cross'word (puzzle)** a type of puzzle invented in America in 1913, in which a square with blank spaces is to be filled with letters which, read across or down, will give words corresponding to clues given; **cross'wort** a bedstraw with leaves set crosswise. — **cross as two sticks** particularly perverse and disagreeable; **cross one's fingers, keep one's fingers crossed** to place one finger across another to ensure good luck; **cross one's heart (and hope to die)** to emphasise that one is being truthful by making the sign of a cross over one's heart; **cross someone's lips** to be uttered by someone; **cross someone's mind** to flash across someone's mind; **cross someone's palm** to put a coin in someone's hand; **cross someone's path** to come in someone's way: to thwart someone; **cross swords** to enter into a dispute (with); **on the cross** diagonally: dishonest (*slang*). [O.E. *cros* — O.N. *kross* — L. *crux, crucis*.]

crosse *kros, n.* the stick with which the game of lacrosse is played, having at its top end a network of leather thongs enclosed in a triangular frame. [Fr.]

crossette *kro-set', n.* a small projecting part of an impost-stone at the extremity of an arch: a shoulder in an arch-stone fitting into the stone next to it. [Fr.]

Crossopterygii *kros-op-tər-ij'i-ī, n.pl.* a subclass of fishes, nearly extinct, whose paired fins have an axis fringed with rays. — *adj.* and *n.* **crossopteryg'ian**. [Gr. *krossoi*, tassels, fringe, *pteryx, -gos,* fin.]

crost. See **cross**.

crotal[1] *krō'təl, n.* a crotalum: a small spherical bell. — *n.* **Crotalaria** (*krot-, krŏt-ə-lā'ri-ə*) the sunn-hemp genus of Papilionaceae, including the American rattle-boxes

(from their inflated pods): (without *cap.*) any plant of the genus. — *n.pl.* **Crotalidae** (*-tal'*) the rattlesnake family. — *adj.* **crotaline** (*krot'ə-līn*) like a rattlesnake. — *ns.* **crot'alism** poisoning by crotalaria; **crotalum** (*krot'ə-ləm*) a clapper or castanet used in ancient Mysteries: — *pl.* **crot'ala Crotalus** (*krot'*) the rattlesnake genus. [Gr. *krotalon,* a rattle, castanet.]

crotal[2], crottle *krot'l, n.* a lichen (of various kinds) used for dyeing. [Gael. *crotal*.]

crotch *kroch, n.* a fork, as of a tree: the bifurcation of the human body. — *adj.* **crotched**. [Ety. obscure.]

crotchet *kroch'it, n.* a hook: a note in music, equal to half a minim, ♩: a crooked or perverse fancy: a whim, or conceit. — *adjs.* **crotch'eted, crotch'ety** having crotchets or peculiarities: whimsical: short-tempered. — *n.* **crotch'eteer** a crotchety person. [Fr. *crochet,* dim. of *croche,* a hook; see **crochet**.]

Croton *krō'tən, n.* a genus of tropical plants of the spurge family: (without *cap.*) any plant of the genus: (without *cap.*) extended by gardeners, etc., to a tropical hedge-plant, *Codiaeum variegatum,* of a related genus. — **croton oil** a powerful purgative got from the seeds of *Croton tiglium.* [Gr. *krŏtōn,* a sheep-tick, which the seed resembles.]

crottle. See **crotal[2]**.

crouch *krowch, v.i.* to squat or lie close to the ground, as an animal preparing to spring: to bend low with legs doubled: to cringe: to fawn. — *v.t.* to bend. — *n.* act or position of crouching. [Possibly connected with **crook**.]

Crouched-friars, Crutched-friars. See **crutch**.

crouch-ware *krowch'-wār, n.* an old salt-glazed stoneware made at Burslem. [Origin unknown.]

croup[1] *krōōp, n.* inflammation of the larynx and trachea in children, associated with difficulty in breathing and a peculiar ringing cough: a burr. — *v.i.* to croak or speak hoarsely. — *n.* **croup'iness**. — *adjs.* **croup'ous; croup'y**. [From the sound made.]

croup[2], croupe *krōōp, n.* the rump of a horse: the place behind the saddle. — *n.* **croup'on** (*obs.*) the croup; the human buttocks. [Fr. *croupe,* a protuberance; allied to **crop**.]

croupade *krōō-pād', n.* a leap in which the horse draws up his hind-legs toward the belly. [Fr.]

croupe. See **croup[2]**.

crouper *krōōp'ər, n.* obsolete form of **crupper**.

croupier *krōō'pi-ər,* or *-pi-ā, n.* one who sits at the lower end of the table as assistant chairman at a public dinner: a vice-president: one who officiates at a gaming-table, collecting the stakes and paying the winners. [Fr., one who rides on the croup.]

croupon. See **croup[2]**.

croupous, croupy. See **croup[1]**.

crouse *krōōs,* (*Scot.*) *adj.* lively, cheerfully confident. — *adv.* boldly, pertly. — *adv.* **crouse'ly**. [M.E. *crūs;* cf. L.G. *krūs,* gay, Ger. *kraus,* Du. *kroes,* crisp, cross.]

croustade *krōōs-täd', n.* a case of fried bread or pastry for serving game, etc. [Fr.]

crout *krowt, n.* Same as **sauerkraut**.

croûte *krōōt, n.* a thick slice of fried bread for serving entrées. — *n.* **croûton** (*-tō, -ton'*) a small cube of fried bread. — **en croûte** (*cook.*) wrapped in pastry and baked. [Fr. *croûte,* crust.]

crow *krō, n.* any of several large black birds of the genus Corvus esp. *C. corone* (the so-called *carrion crow*): extended to other birds of this genus, esp. the rook: inferior coal: the defiant or triumphant cry of a cock: a child's inarticulate cry of joy: a crow-bar. — *v.i.* to croak: to utter a crow: to boast, swagger, triumph (often with *over*): — *pa.t.* **crew** (*krōō*), or **crowed;** *pa.p.* **crowed,** also **crown** (*krōn*). — **crow'-bar** a large iron bar mostly bent at the end, to be used as a lever; **crow'-berry** a small creeping moorland shrub (*Empetrum*) producing small black berries; **crow'-flower** (*Shak.*) perhaps crowfoot; **crow'foot** a buttercup, sometimes extended to other plants (*pl.* in this sense **crow'foots**): crow's-foot: a number of lines rove through a long wooden block, supporting the backbone of an awning horizontally; **crow'-keeper** (*Shak.*) a scarecrow; **crow'-quill** a pen made of the quill of a crow, etc., for fine writing or etching; **crow's'-bill, crow'-bill** (*surg.*) a kind of forceps for extracting bullets, etc., from wounds; **crow's'-foot** one of the wrinkles produced by age, spreading out from the corners of the eyes: a caltrop (*mil.*); **crow'-shrike** a piping crow (see **pipe**); **crow's'-nest** (*naut.*) an elevated shelter for a man on the lookout. — *n.pl.* **crow'-steps** steps on a gable. — **crow'-toe** (*Milt.*) probably the same as **crowfoot**. — **as the crow flies** in a straight line; **eat crow, eat (boiled) crow** to be forced to do something very disagreeable, humiliate oneself; **have a crow to pluck with** to have something to settle with someone; **Royston crow** the hooded crow (*Corvus corone cornix*) — said to be common near Royston in Herts; **stone the crows** (*slang*) an expression of amazement, horror, etc. [O.E. *cráwe*, a crow, *cráwan*, to crow.]

crowd¹ *krowd, n.* a number of persons or things closely pressed together, without order: the rabble: multitude: a set. — *v.t.* to gather into a lump or crowd: to fill by pressing or driving together: to compress: to thrust, put pressure on. — *v.i.* to press on: to press together in numbers: to swarm. — *adj.* **crowd'ed.** — **crowd'-pull'er** a person, event, etc., attracting a large audience. — **crowd sail** to carry a press of sail for speed. [O.E. *crúdan*, to press.]

crowd² *krowd, n.* (*obs.*) the crwth. — *n.* **crowd'er** (*obs.*) a fiddler. [See **crwth**.]

crowdie *krowd'i,* (*Scot.*) *n.* a mixture of meal and water: brose: a cheese-like preparation of soured milk. [Der. unknown; perh. in part for **crud**.]

crown¹ *krown, n.* a circular head ornament, esp. as a mark of honour: the diadem or state-cap of royalty: kingship: the sovereign: governing power in a monarchy: honour: the top of anything, as a head, hat, tree, arch: a species of spire or lantern, formed by converging flying buttresses (*archit.*): a stag's surroyals: the visible part of a tooth: a substitute for this, made of gold or synthetic material, etc., fitted over a broken or bad tooth: in gem-cutting, the upper of the two conical surfaces of a brilliant: the junction of root and stem: a short rootstock: a clasping metal cap for a bottle: chief ornament: completion or consummation: a coin originally stamped with a crown, esp. a 5s. piece: used to translate various coin names, as krone: the old French écu: a British size of paper before metrication (a U.S. size of paper 15 × 19 in.), originally watermarked with a crown. — *v.t.* to cover or invest with a crown: to cap: to invest with royal dignity: to fill with foaming liquor: in draughts, to convert into a king or crowned man by the placing of another draught on the top on reaching the crown-head: to adorn: to dignify: to complete happily: to hit on the head (*slang*). — *adj.* **crowned.** — *ns.* **crown'er** (*Shak.*) a coroner; **crown'et** a coronet: that which crowns or accomplishes (*Shak.*); **crown'ing.** — *adj.* **crown'less.** — *n.* **crown'let** a small crown. — **crown agent** a solicitor in Scotland who prepares criminal prosecutions: (with *caps.*) one of a British body of business agents operating internationally, appointed by the Ministry for Overseas Development; **crown'-ant'ler** the uppermost tine of an antler; **crown'-bark'** a kind of cinchona bark; **crown'-cap** a lined metal cap for a bottle; **crown colony** colony administered directly by the home government; **crown courts** the system of courts replacing assize courts and quarter sessions; **crown Derby** a late 18th-century porcelain made at Derby, marked with a crown; **crowned head** a monarch; **crown'-gall'** a bacterial disease of plants, forming tumours; **crown'-glass** alkali-lime glass: window-glass formed in circular plates or discs; **crown'-graft** insertion of scions between bark and wood; **crown'-green** a bowling-green with a crown or arched surface; **crown'-head'** in draughts, the back row of squares, where a man is crowned; **crown'-impe'rial** a plant, a species of fritillary; **crown'-jew'el** a

jewel pertaining to the crown or sovereign; **crown'-land** land belonging to the crown or sovereign; **crown'-law'yer** the lawyer who acts for the crown in criminal cases; **crown living** a church living in the gift of the crown; **crown octavo** an octavo 5 × 7¹⁄₂ in.; **Crown Office** the office for the business of the crown side of the King's Bench: the office in which the great seal is affixed; **crown-of-thorns starfish** a starfish that eats living coral; **crown'-piece** a five-shilling piece; **crown'-post** a king-post; **crown prince** the heir apparent to the crown; **crown princess** the female heir to a throne: the wife of a crown prince; **crown roast** roast ribs of lamb or pork arranged in a circle like a crown; **crown'-saw** a saw consisting of a rotating teeth-edged cylinder; **crown'-wheel** a wheel with teeth set at right angles to its plane; **crown witness** a witness for the crown in a criminal prosecution instituted by it; **crown'work** (*fort.*) an outwork composed of a bastion between two curtains, with demi-bastions at the extremes. — **crown and anchor** a dicing game; **crown of the causeway** the middle of the street. [O. Fr. *corone* — L. *corōna*; cf. Gr. *koronos*, curved.]

crown². See **crow.**

croze *krōz, n.* the groove in the staves of a cask in which the edge of the head is set. [Perh. O.Fr. *croz* (Fr. *creux*), groove.]

crozier. See **crosier.**

cru *krü,* (Fr.) *n.* a vineyard or group of vineyards.

crubeen *krōō-bēn', krōō', n.* a pig's trotter, as food. [Ir. *crúibín,* dim. of *crúb,* hoof.]

cruces, crucial, cruciate. See **crux.**

crucian, crusian *krōō'shən, n.* the German carp, without barbels. [L.G. *karusse* (Ger. *Karausche*) — L. *coracīnus* — Gr. *korakīnos,* a black perch-like fish — *korax,* raven.]

crucible *krōō'si-bl, n.* an earthen pot for melting ores, metals, etc. [L.L. *crucibulum.*]

crucifer *krōō'si-fər, n.* a cross-bearer in a procession: a member of the Cruciferae. — *n.pl.* **Crucif'erae** a family of archichlamydeous dicotyledons, with cross-shaped flowers, including cabbage, turnip, cress, wallflower. — *adj.* **crucif'erous** bearing or marked with a cross: with four petals placed crosswise: of the Cruciferae. [L. *crux, crucis,* a cross, *ferre,* to bear.]

cruciform, crucigerous. See **crux.**

crucify *krōō'si-fī, v.t.* to expose or put to death on a cross: to fasten to a wheel or the like, as a military field punishment: to subdue completely: to mortify: to torment: to treat harshly or cruelly: to hold up to scorn or ridicule: — *pr.p.* **cru'cifying;** *pa.t.* and *pa.p.* **cru'cified.** — *ns.* **cru'cifier** one who crucifies; **cru'cifix** a figure or picture of Christ fixed to the cross; **crucifixion** (*-fik'shən*). [O.Fr. *crucifier* — L. *crucifīgĕre, crucifixum — crux,* cross, and *fīgĕre,* to fix.]

cruck *kruk, n.* in crude building, one of a pair of curved timbers supporting a roof. [Cf. **crook.**]

crud *krud, krōōd, n.* obs. and dial. form of **curd**: dirt, filth, esp. if sticky (*slang*): radioactive waste (*slang*): a contemptible person (*slang*). — *v.t.* (*Spens.*) and *v.i.* **crudd'le** to curdle. — *adj.* **crudd'y** curdy (*Spens.*): dirty (*slang*): contemptible (*slang*).

crude *krōōd, adj.* raw, unprepared: not reduced to order or form: unfinished: undigested: immature: unrefined: coarse, vulgar, rude: inartistic. — *n.* crude oil. — *adv.* **crude'ly.** — *ns.* **crude'ness; crud'ity** rawness: unripeness: that which is crude. — *adj.* **crud'y** (*Shak.*) crude, raw. — **crude oil** petroleum in its unrefined state. [L. *crūdus,* raw.]

crudités *krü-dē-tā,* (Fr.) *n.pl.* raw fruit and vegetables served as an hors d'oeuvre.

crue. A Miltonic spelling of **crew** (*n.*).

cruel *krōō'əl, adj.* disposed to inflict pain, or pleased at suffering: void of pity, merciless, savage: severe. — *adj.* **cru'elly.** — *ns.* **cru'elness** (*obs.*); **cru'elty.** — *adj.* **cru'el-heart'ed** delighting in cruelty. [Fr. *cruel* — L. *crūdēlis.*]

cruels, cruells. Same as **crewels.**

cruet *krōō'it, n.* a small jar or phial for sauces and condiments for the table: a vessel for wine, oil, or water for religious ceremonies. — **cru'et-stand** a stand or frame for holding cruets. [A.Fr., dim. of O.Fr. *cruye,* jar, from root of **crock**[1].]

cruise *krōōz, v.i.* to sail to and fro: (of a vehicle, aircraft, etc.) to progress smoothly at a speed economical in fuel, etc.: to wander about seeking something (with *about,* etc.; *coll.*): to go round public places looking for a sexual partner (*slang*). — *n.* a sailing to and fro: a wandering voyage in search of an enemy or for the protection of vessels or for pleasure or health: a land journey of similar character. — *ns.* **cruis'er** one who or that which cruises: a speedy warship, specially for cruising: a privateer: a cruising yacht: a cruiser-weight boxer. — **cruise missile** a subsonic guided missile using the air for support; **cruis'er-weight** a boxer between middle and heavy, a light-heavyweight; **cruise'way** a canal for exclusively recreational use. [Du. *kruisen,* to cross.]

cruisie. See **crusie.**

cruive, cruve *krōōv* (*Scot. krøv, kriv*)*, n.* a pen, sty: a hovel: a wattled fish-trap.

cruller *krul'ər,* (*U.S.*) *n.* a friedcake. [Cf. Du. *krullen,* to curl.]

crumb *krum, n.* a small bit or morsel of bread: a small particle of anything: the soft part of bread: a worthless person (*slang*). — *v.t.* to break into crumbs: to put crumbs in or on: to remove crumbs from. — *v.i.* to crumble. — *adjs.* **crumb'y** in crumbs: soft; **crum'my** crumby: plump (*slang*): covered in lice (*slang*): not good, worthless, inferior, unpleasant, out of sorts, etc. (*coll.*). — **crumb'-brush** a brush for sweeping crumbs off the table: **crumb'-cloth** a cloth laid under a table to keep crumbs from the carpet: a drugget; **crumb'-tray** a tray on to which crumbs are brushed from the table or one on which crumbs collect at the base of a toaster. [O.E. *cruma*; Du. *kruim*; Ger. *Krume*; **crimp.**]

crumble *krum'bl, v.t.* to break into crumbs. — *v.i.* to fall into small pieces: to decay. — *n.* a crumb: that which crumbles easily: a sweet dish consisting of a layer of stewed fruit covered with a crumbled mixture of flour, butter and sugar. — *n.pl.* **crum'blies** (*slang*) very old people. — *adj.* **crum'bly.** [Orig. dim. of **crumb**; Du. *kruimelen*; Ger. *krümeln.*]

crumbs *krumz,* (*schoolchildren's slang*) *interj.* expressive of surprise, dismay, etc. [Euphemism for *Christ.*]

crumen *krōō'mən, n.* a deer's tear-pit. — *n.* **cru'menal** (*Spens.*) a purse. [L. *crumēna,* a purse.]

crumhorn. See **krummhorn.**

crummock, crummack *krum'ək, n.* a crook, stick with curved head. [Gael. *cromag,* hook, crook.]

crummy. See **crumb, crump**[2].

crump[1] *krump,* (*mil. slang*) *n.* (the sound of) an exploding bomb, etc. — *v.i.* to make such a sound. [Imit.]

crump[2] *krump, adj.* crooked: wrinkled: crisp, friable (*Scot.*). — *ns.* **crumm'y** a cow with a crumpled horn: **crump'et** a soft, unsweetened griddle cake: the head (*slang*): a girl (*slang*). — *adj.* **crump'y** (*dial.*) crisp. [O.E. *crump* — *crumb,* crooked; Ger. *krumm.* Cf. **crimp.**]

crumple *krump'l, v.t.* to crush into irregular wrinkles: to wrinkle: to cause to collapse. — *v.i.* to wrinkle: to collapse. — *adj.* **crump'led.** — *n.* **crump'ling.** — **crumple zones** the front and rear portions of a motor car designed to crumple and absorb the impact in a collision while the passenger area remains intact. [**crump**[2].]

crunch *krunch, v.t.* to crush with harsh noise, with the teeth, under foot, or otherwise: to chew anything hard, and so make a noise. — *v.i.* to make such a noise: to chew with, or as with, such a noise. — *n.* the act or sound or crunching: (with *the*) the real testing or critical moment, trial of strength, time or cause of difficulty, etc. (*coll.*): a crisis, emergency (*coll.*). — *n.* **crunch'iness.** — *adj.* **crunch'y.** — **number cruncher, crunching** see under **number.**

crunkle *krunk'l, v.i.* to crumple. [Cf. **crinkle.**]

cruor *krōō'ör, n.* coagulated blood. [L.]

crupper *krup'ər, n.* a strap of leather fastened to the saddle and passing under the horse's tail to keep the saddle in its place: the hind part of a horse. [O.Fr. *cropiere* — *crope,* the croup.]

crural *krōō'rəl, adj.* belonging to or like a leg. [L. *crūrālis,* from, *crūs, crūris,* the leg.]

crusade *krōō-sād', n.* a military expedition under the banner of the cross to recover the Holy Land from the Muslims: any daring or romantic undertaking: concerted action to further a cause. — *v.i.* to go on a crusade. — *n.* **crusād'er** one engaged in a crusade. [Fr. *croisade* — Prov. *crozada* — *croz* — L. *crux,* a cross.]

crusado *krōō-sā'dō, n.* a Portuguese coin, so called because marked with a cross: — *pl.* **crusā'dos.** [Port. *cruzado.*]

cruse *krōōz,* also *krōōs, n.* an earthen pot: a small cup or bottle. [Cf. O.N. *krūs*; Ger. *Krause.*]

cruset *krōō'sit, n.* a goldsmith's crucible. [Cf. Fr. *creuset,* M.Du. *kruysel,* M.L.G. *krusel.*]

crush *krush, v.t.* to break or bruise: to squeeze together: to beat down or overwhelm: to subdue: to ruin. — *v.i.* to become broken or crumpled under pressure. — *n.* a violent squeezing: a close crowd of persons or things: a drink made from fruit juice; a set of people (*slang*): a narrowing passage for cattle: an infatuation (with *on*), or its object (*slang*). — *adjs.* **crush'able; crushed.** — *n.* **crush'er** one who, or that which, crushes or subdues: a policeman (*slang*). — *adj.* **crush'ing.** — *adv.* **crush'ingly.** — **crush bar** a bar in a theatre for selling drinks in the intervals of a play, etc.; **crush'-barrier** a barrier erected to restrain a crowd; **crushed strawberry** the pinky colour of strawberries that have been crushed. — Also *adj.* — **crush'-hat** an opera-hat; **crush'-room** a room where an audience may promenade during the intervals of the entertainment. — **crush a cup** to empty a cup: to quaff. [O.Fr. *croissir*; perh. cog. with M.H.G. *krosen,* to crunch.]

crusian. See **crucian.**

crusie, crusy, cruisie *krōōz'i,* (*Scot.*) *n.* an open iron lamp used with a rush wick. [From **cruset.**]

crust *krust, n.* the hard rind or outside coating of anything: the outer part of bread: a dried-up scrap of bread: hence, a livelihood (*slang*): the covering of a pie, etc.: the solid exterior of the earth: the dry scaly covering on a skin lesion: a layer of sediment on the side of the bottle in some wines and ports: impertinence (*slang*). — *v.t.* to cover with a crust or hard case. — *v.i.* to gather into a hard crust. — *adjs.* **crust'al** pertaining to a crust esp. the earth's; **crust'ate, crustāt'ed** covered with a crust. — *n.* **crustā'tion** an adherent crust. — *adv.* **crust'ily.** — *n.* **crust'iness.** — *adjs.* **crust'less; crust'y** of the nature of or having a crust, as port or other wine: having a hard or harsh exterior: hard: snappy: surly. [L. *crusta,* rind.]

crusta *krus'tə, n.* a piece prepared for inlaying: a hard coating: a cocktail served in a glass, its rim encrusted in sugar: — *pl.* **crus'tae** (*-tē*). [L.]

Crustacea *krus-tā'sh(y)ə, -shi-ə, n.pl.* a large class of arthropod animals with hard shells, almost all aquatic — crabs, lobsters, shrimps, sand-hoppers, wood-lice, water-fleas, barnacles, etc. — *adj.* and *n.* **crustā'cean.** — *adj.* **crustā'ceous** crusty. [L. *crusta,* shell.]

crusy. See **crusie.**

crutch *kruch, n.* a staff with a cross-piece at the head to place under the arm of a lame person: any support of like form: a bifurcation, crotch: a small figure inserted to show the number to be carried (*arith.*). — *v.t.* to support: to prop: to clip wool from the hindquarters of (a sheep) (*Austr.*). — *v.i.* to go on crutches. — *adj.* **crutched** marked by the sign of, or wearing, a Cross. — *n.pl.* **Crutch'ed-fri'ars** an order of friars so called from the sign of the cross which they wore — *Crouched-* or *Crossed-friars.* [O.E. *crycc.*]

cruve. See **cruive.**

crux *kruks, n.* a cross: something that occasions difficulty or perplexity (*fig.*): that on which a decision turns: the essential point, as of a problem: — *pl.* **crux'es, cruces** (*krōō'sēz*). — *adjs.* **crucial** (*krōō'shəl*) crosslike: of the nature of a crux: testing or decisive, as if of the nature of a finger-post at a cross-road: essential or very important; **cruciate** (*krōō'shi-āt*) cross-shaped. — *v.t.* to torment. — *adjs.* **cruciform** (*krōō'si-förm*) cross-shaped; **crucigerous** (*krōō-sij'ər-əs*) bearing a cross. [L. *crux, crucis,* a cross.]
crux ansata *kruks* (*krōōks*) *an-sä'tə* (*an-sä'ta*), (L.) the ankh. — **crux criticorum** (*krit-i-kō'rəm, -kö', -rōom*) a puzzle for the critics.
cruzeiro *krōō-zā'rō, n.* the monetary unit of Brazil: — *pl.* **cruzei'ros.** [Port. *cruz,* cross.]
crwth *krōōth, n.* the crowd, an old Welsh stringed instrument, four of its six strings played with a bow, two plucked by the thumb. [W. *crwth,* a hollow protuberance, a fiddle; Gael., Ir. *cruit.*]
cry *krī, v.i.* to utter a shrill loud sound, esp. one of pain or grief: to lament: to weep: to bawl: to call (*Scot.*). — *v.t.* to utter loudly: to exclaim: to proclaim or make public: to offer for sale by crying: to call (*Scot.*): to proclaim the banns of marriage of (*Scot.*): — *3rd pers. sing.* **cries;** *pr.p.* **cry'ing;** *pa.t.* and *pa.p.* **cried** (*krīd*). — *n.* any loud sound, esp. of grief or pain: a call or shout: a fit of weeping: a pack of hounds, hence of people: a particular sound uttered by an animal: the creak of bent tin: bawling: lamentation: prayer: clamour: report or rumour: a general utterance: a watchword, battle-cry, or slogan: a street call of wares for sale or services offered: — *pl.* **cries.** — *ns.* **cri'er** one who cries, esp. an official maker of proclamations; **cry'ing** the act of calling loudly: weeping. — *adj.* calling loudly: claiming notice and usu. redress, as in *a crying shame:* notorious. — **cry'-baby** one who cries childishly. — **a far cry** a great distance; **cry against** to protest against; **cry down** to decry; **cry for the moon** to beg, or sigh, for something unattainable; **crying in the wilderness** voicing opinions or making suggestions that are not (likely to be) heeded; **cry off** to withdraw from an agreement; **cry on** (*Scot.*) to call upon; **cry one's eyes, heart, out** to weep copiously or bitterly; **cry out** to be in childbirth (*obs. Scot.*): to give a shout or shriek, e.g. of alarm, pain, etc.; **cry out for** to be in urgent or obvious need of; **cry out to be (done, used,** etc.) to be someone or something that very much ought to be (done, used, etc.); **cry over spilt milk** to waste time in bemoaning what is irreparable; **cry quits** to declare a thing even; **cry stinking fish** to decry one's own goods; **cry up** to praise; **cry you mercy** (*obs.*) I beg your pardon; **for crying out loud** (*slang*) an expression of frustration, impatience, etc.; **great cry and little wool** much ado about nothing; **hue and cry** see **hue; in full cry** in full pursuit, used of dogs in hunt; **out of cry** (*obs.*) beyond measure: beyond dispute; **within cry of** within hearing distance. [Fr. *crier* — L. *quirītāre,* to scream.]
cryo- *krī'ō-, krī-o'-,* in composition, frost, icc. — *n.* **cryobiol'ogy** the biology of organisms below their normal temperature. — *adj.* **cryobiolog'ical.** — *ns.* **cryobiol'ogist; cryoc'onite** (Gr. *konis,* dust) dust found on the surface of polar ice; **cry'ogen** (*-jen*) (Gr. root of *gignesthai,* to become) a substance used for obtaining low temperatures, a freezing mixture. — *adj.* **cryogen'ic** pertaining to the science of cryogenics, or to work done, apparatus used, or substances kept, at low temperatures. — *n. sing.* **cryogen'ics** the branch of physics concerned with phenomena at very low temperatures. — *ns.* **cryogeny** (*-oj'ə-ni*) refrigeration: cryogenics; **cry'olite** (Gr. *lithos,* a stone) an ice-stone or Greenland spar, sodium aluminium fluoride, earliest source of aluminium; **cryom'eter** (Gr. *metron,* measure) a thermometer for low temperatures. — *adjs.* **cryomet'ric; cryon'ic.** — *n. sing.* **cryon'ics** the practice of preserving human corpses by freezing them, with the idea that advances in science may enable them to be revived at some future time. — *adj.* **cryophīl'ic** (Gr.

phileein, to love; *biol.*) able to thrive at low temperatures. — *n.* **cryoph'orus** (Gr. *pherein,* to bear) an instrument for showing the decrease of temperature in water by evaporation. — *n. sing.* **cryophys'ics** low temperature physics. — *ns.* **cryopreservā'tion** cryonics; **cry'oprobe** a fine instrument with a cooled tip used in cryosurgery; **cry'oscope** an instrument for determining freezing-points. — *adj.* **cryoscop'ic.** — *ns.* **cryos'copy** the study of the effect of dissolved substances on the freezing-points of solvents; **cry'ostat** apparatus for achieving or demonstrating cooling by evaporation: any apparatus for maintaining a low temperature; **cryosur'gery** surgery using instruments at very low temperatures; **cryother'apy** medical treatment using extreme cold; **cry'otron** a tiny form of electronic switch operating in a bath of liquid helium a few degrees above absolute zero. — **cryonic suspension** cryonics. [Gr. *kryos,* frost.]
crypt *kript, n.* an underground cell or chapel: a small cavity, a tubular gland (*zool.*). — *adjs.* **cryp'tal** pertaining to, or of the nature of, a crypt; **cryp'tic, -al** hidden: secret: unseen: mysteriously obscure: protectively concealing (*zool.*). — *adv.* **cryp'tically.** [L. *crypta* — Gr. *kryptē* — *kryptein,* to hide; cf. **grot.**]
crypt-, crypto- *kript-, -ō-, -o-,* in composition, hidden. — *n.* **cryptaesthesia** (*kript-ēs-thē'zyə, -zhə;* Gr. *aisthēsis,* perception) supranormal perception, e.g. clairvoyance. — *adj.* **cryptaesthĕt'ic.** — *n.pl.* **cryptadia** (*kript-ā'di-ə;* Gr.) things to be kept secret. — *ns.* **cryptanal'ysis** the art of deciphering codes, etc.; **cryptan'alyst; cryp'to-Chris'tian; cryp'to-comm'unist.** — *adj.* **cryptocryst'alline** with crystalline structure visible only under the microscope. — *n.* **cryp'togam** any member of the **Cryptogamia** (*krip-tō-gā'mi-ə*), the class of flowerless plants, so named by Linnaeus in the expectation that sexual reproduction would one day be discovered in them. — *adjs.* **cryptogā'mian; cryptogamic** (*-gam'ik*); **cryptŏg'amous.** — *ns.* **cryptŏg'amist; cryptog'amy.** — *adj.* **cryptogen'ic** of diseases, of unknown origin. — *ns.* **cryp'togram, cryp'tograph** anything written in cipher. — *ns.* **cryptŏg'rapher, -ist.** — *adj.* **cryptograph'ic.** — *n.* **cryptŏg'raphy.** — *adj.* **cryptolog'ical.** — *ns.* **cryptol'ogist; cryptol'ogy** secret language: the scientific study of codes; **Cryptomēr'ia** (Gr. *meros,* part) the Japanese cedar; **cryptomnesia** (*-mnē'zi-ə, -zhə*) latent or subconscious memory. — *adj.* **cryptomnēs'ic.** — *ns.* **crypton** same as **krypton; cryp'tonym** (Gr. *onyma,* name) a secret name. — *adj.* **cryptŏn'ymous.** [Gr. *kryptos,* hidden.]
crypto *krip'tō, n.* a secret member of a party, sect, organisation, etc., esp. a crypto-communist: — *pl.* **cryp'tos.** [See **crypt-, crypto-.**]
crystal *kris'tl, n.* ice (*obs.*): rock-crystal, a clear quartz, like ice: a body, generally solid, whose atoms are arranged in a definite pattern, outwardly expressed by geometrical form with plane faces: a crystalline element, of piezoelectric or semiconductor material, functioning as e.g. a transducer, oscillator, etc. in an electronic device: a globe of rock-crystal or the like in which one may see visions (also **crystal ball**): anything bright and clear: a superior glass of various kinds: cut glass: a watch-glass. — *adj.* composed of or like crystal. — *adj.* **crys'talline** (*-īn, -in;* in the poets also *-tal'*) like crystal or a crystal: composed of crystal, crystals, or parts of crystals: having the structure of a crystal. — *n.* a crystalline substance: aniline (*obs.*): a shining fabric of silk and wool. — *n.* **crystallin'ity.** — *adj.* **crystallī'sable, -z-.** — *n.* **crystallīsā'tion, -z-.** — *v.t.* and *v.i.* **crys'tallise, -ize** to form into crystals: to make or become definite or concrete: of fruit, to coat with sugar crystals. — *ns.* **crys'tallite** a small, imperfectly formed or incipient crystal: a minute body in glassy igneous rocks; **crystallī'tis** inflammation of the crystalline lens; **crystallogen'esis** origination of crystals. — *adj.* **crystallogenet'ic.** — *n.* **crystallog'rapher.** — *adj.* **crystallograph'ic.** — *ns.* **crystallog'raphy** the science of the structure, forms, and properties of crystals; **crys'talloid**

a substance in a state in which it dissolves to form a true solution which will pass through a membrane: a minute crystalline particle of protein (*bot.*). — *adj.* like a crystal: of the nature of a crystalloid. — *n.* **crys'-tallomancy** (Gr. *manteiā*, divination) divination by transparent bodies. — *adj.* **crys'tal-clear'** very, completely clear. — **crys'tal-gazer; crys'tal-gazing** gazing in a crystal or the like to obtain visual images, whether in divination or to objectify hidden contents of the mind; **crystalline heaven, sphere** in ancient astronomy a sphere between the fixed stars and the *primum mobile*, assumed to explain precession of the equinoxes; **crystalline lens** the transparent refractive body of the eye; **crystal rectifier** rectifier that depends on differential conduction in semiconductor crystals suitably doped; **crystal set** a simple wireless receiving apparatus in which a crystal and a cat's-whisker rectify the current; **crystal violet** an antiseptic dye, hexamethylpararosaniline hydrochloride. [O.Fr. *cristal* — L. *crystallum* — Gr. *krystallos*, ice — *kryos*, frost.]

csárdás *chär'däsh, n.* a Hungarian dance, or its music, in two movements, one slow and the other fast. — Also (wrongly) **czar'das.** [Hung.]

CS gas. See **CS** in Abbreviations.

c-spring. See **cee-spring.**

ctene *tēn, n.* a comb-like swimming organ in the Ctenophora. — *adjs.* **cteniform** (*tēn'*, or *ten'*), **cten'oid** comb-shaped. — *n.pl.* **Ctenoph'ora** a class of Coelenterates — beautifully delicate, free-swimming marine organisms, moving by means of meridionally placed comb-like plates. — *n., adj.* **ctenoph'oran.** — *n.* **cten'-ophore** any member of the Ctenophora. [Gr. *kteis, ktenos,* comb.]

Ctesiphon arch *tes'i-fon ärch,* an arch of inverted catenary shape, such as the great ruined arch at Ctesiphon, on the Tigris south-east of Baghdad.

cub¹ *kub, n.* the young of certain animals, as foxes, etc.: a whelp: a young boy or girl (playful or contemptuous, esp. of the ill-conditioned, unmannerly, raw, or conceited): (in full **Cub Scout**) an embryo Scout: a beginner, novice, apprentice: a young or inexperienced reporter. — *v.t.* and *v.i.* to bring forth: to hunt (fox-cubs): — *pr.p.* **cubb'ing;** *pa.t.* and *pa.p.* **cubbed.** — *n.* **cubb'ing** cub-hunting. — *adj.* **cubb'ish** like a cub: awkward or ill-mannered. — *n.* **cub'hood.** — *adj.* **cub'less.** — *adj.* **cub'-drawn** (*Shak.*) drawn or sucked by cubs. — *cub'-hunting* hunting of young foxes. [Ety. dub.]

cub² *kub, n.* a cattle-pen: a chest. — *ns.* **cubb'y, cubb'y-hole** a snug enclosed place. [Prob. from L.G.]

Cuban *kū'bən, adj.* pertaining to *Cuba* or its people. — *n.* a native of Cuba. — **Cuban heel** on footwear, a medium high heel without curves.

cubby-hole. See **cub².**

cube *kūb, n.* a solid body having six equal square faces, a solid square: the third power of a quantity. — *v.t.* to raise to the third power: to cut into cubes: to calculate the amount or contents of in cubic units. — *ns.* **cūb'age, cū'bature** the act of finding the solid or cubic content of a body: the result thus found. — *adjs.* **cū'bic, -al** pertaining to a cube: solid: isometric (*crystal.*): (**cubic**) of or involving the third power or degree. — *adv.* **cū'bically.** — *n.* **cū'bicalness.** — *adj.* **cū'biform.** — *n.* **cū'bism** a modern movement in painting, which seeks to represent several aspects of an object seen from different standpoints arbitrarily grouped in one composition, making use of cubes and other solid geometrical figures. — *n.* and *adj.* **cū'bist.** — *n.* **cū'boid** a rectangular parallelepiped esp. one whose faces are not all equal. — *adjs.* **cū'boid, cū'boidal** resembling a cube in shape. — **cube root** the quantity of which the given quantity is the cube. [Fr., — L. *cubus* — Gr. *kybos,* a die.]

cubeb *kū'beb, n.* the dried berry of *Piper cubeba,* a Sumatran climbing pepper shrub — used in medicine. [Fr. *cubèbe* — Ar. *kabābah.*]

cubic. See **cube.**

cubica *kū'bi-kə, n.* a fine worsted for linings. [Sp. *cubica.*]

cubicle *kū'bi-kl, n.* a bedroom: part of a dormitory or other large room which is partitioned off: a cell or compartment. [L. *cubiculum — cubāre,* to lie down.]

cubic zirconia. See under **zircon.**

cubism, etc. See **cube.**

cubit *kū'bit, n.* an old measure, the length of the arm from the elbow to the tip of the middle finger, from 18 to 22 inches. — Also **cū'bitus.** — *adj.* **cū'bital** of the length of a cubit. [L. *cubitum,* the elbow; cf. L. *cubāre,* to lie down.]

cuboid, etc. See **cube.**

cucking-stool *kuk'ing-stōōl, n.* a stool in which scolds and other culprits were placed, usually before their own door, to be pelted by the mob. [Mentioned in the Domesday Book as in use in Chester, and called *cathedra stercoris;* from an obs. word *cuck,* to defecate; cf. O.N. *kūka.*]

cuckold *kuk'əld, n.* a man whose wife has proved unfaithful. — *v.t.* to make cuckold. — *v.t.* **cuck'oldise, -ize** to make a cuckold. — *adj.* **cuck'oldly** (*Shak.*). — *ns.* **cuck'oldom, cuck'oldry** the state of a cuckold: the act of making a cuckold. — *adj.* **cuck'oldy.** — **cuck'old=maker.** [O.Fr. *cucuault — cucu,* cuckoo.]

cuckoo *kŏŏ'kŏŏ, n.* a bird, *Cuculus canorus,* that cries *cuckoo,* remarkable for depositing its eggs in the nests of other birds: any bird of this or related genera: a silly person. — *adj.* (*coll.*) silly. — **cuck'oo-bud** (*Shak.*) the name of a plant; **cuck'oo-clock** a clock in which the hours are told by a cuckoo-call; **cuck'oo-flower** a species of Cardamine — lady's-smock: ragged robin; **cuck'oo-fly** a gold-wasp — from laying its eggs in wasps' and bees' nests; **cuck'oo-pint** (*-pint, -pīnt*) the wake-robin, *Arum maculatum;* **cuck'oo-spit, -spitt'le** a froth secreted by frog-hoppers on plants, surrounding the larvae and pupae. [Imit.; cf. Fr. *coucou,* Ger. *Kuckuck,* L. *calcūlus,* Gr. *kokkyx, -ȳgos.*]

cucullate, -d *kū'kul-āt,* or *-kul', -id, adjs.* hooded: shaped like a hood. [L. *cucullatus — cucullus.*]

cucumber *kū'kum-bər, -kəm-, n.* a creeping plant (*Cucumis sativus*) of the Cucurbitaceae, with bristly lobed leaves and tendrils: its long cylindrical fruit, used as a salad and pickle: a cucumber-tree (*U.S.*). — **cū'cumber-tree** the bilimbi tree: a magnolia (*U.S.*): also a tulip-tree (*U.S.*). — *adj.* **cūcūm'iform.** — **cool as a cucumber** calm, imperturbable. [L. *cucumis, -eris.*]

cucurbit *kū-kûr'bit, n.* a chemical vessel used in distillation, originally shaped like a gourd: a cucurbitaceous plant. — *adjs.* **cucur'bital, cucurbitā'ceous** pertaining to the **Cucurbitā'ceae,** a family of sympetalous dicotyledons, including gourd, melon, etc.: gourd-like. [L. *cucurbita,* a gourd.]

cud *kud, n.* food brought back from first stomach of a ruminating animal to be chewed again. — **cud'weed** a woolly composite plant of the genus Gnaphalium: extended to kindred plants. — **chew the cud** (*coll.*) to meditate, to reflect. [O.E. *cwidu.*]

cudbear *kud'bär, n.* a purple dyestuff, a powder prepared from various lichens. [From Dr *Cuthbert* Gordon, who made it an article of commerce.]

cuddeehih. See **cuddy².**

cudden. See **cuddy⁴, cuddie.**

cuddie. See **cuddy³·⁴.**

cuddin. See **cuddy⁴.**

cuddle *kud'l, v.t.* to hug: to embrace: to fondle. — *v.i.* to lie close and snug together. — *n.* a close embrace. — *adjs.* **cudd'lesome, cudd'ly** pleasant to cuddle, being e.g. attractively plump, soft, etc.: suggestive of, conducive to, cuddling. [Origin unknown.]

cuddy¹ *kud'i, n.* a small cabin or cookroom, in the fore-part of a boat or lighter: in large vessels, the officers' cabin under the poop-deck. [Origin uncertain; cf. Fr. *cahute;* Du. *kajuit;* Ger. *Kajüte.*]

cuddy² *kud'i,* (*hist.*) *n.* the right of a lord to entertainment from his tenant: rent — (*Spens.*) **cuddeehih.** [Ir. *cuid oidhche — cuid,* a share, *oidche,* night.]

fāte; fär; hûr; mīne; mōte; för; mūte; mōōn; fŏŏt; dhen (then); *el'ə-mənt* (element)

cuddy[3], **cuddie** *kud'i*, (*Scot.* and *dial.*) *n.* a donkey: a horse: a stupid person. [Perh. *Cuthbert*.]

cuddy[4] *kud'i*, (*Scot.*) *n.* a young coalfish. — Also **cudd'en, cudd'in.** [Gael. *cudainn, cudaig.*]

cudgel *kuj'l*, *n.* a heavy staff: a club. — *v.t.* to beat with a cudgel: — *pr.p.* **cudg'elling**; *pa.t.* and *pa.p.* **cudg'elled.** — *ns.* **cudg'eller; cudg'elling.** — **cud'gel-play.** — *adj.* **cudg'el-proof** not to be hurt by beating. — **cudgel one's brains** to think hard; **take up the cudgels** to join in defence. [O.E. *cycgel*.]

cue[1] *kū*, *n.* the seventeenth letter of the alphabet (Q, q).

cue[2] *kū*, *n.* the last words of an actor's speech serving as a hint to the next speaker: any hint: the part one has to play. — *v.t.* to give a cue to: to insert (e.g. a film sequence, sound effect, etc.) into a script: — *pr.p.* **cue'ing, cū'ing**; *pa.t.* and *pa.p.* **cued.** — **cue someone in** (orig. *U.S. slang*) to inform (someone); **on cue** just at the right moment. [Acc. to some from Fr. *queue*, tail (see next word); in 17th cent. written Q, and derived from L. *quando*, when, i.e. when the actor was to begin.]

cue[3] *kū*, *n.* a twist of hair at the back of the head: a rod used in playing billiards, etc. — *v.t.* to form a cue in (hair): to hit (a ball) with a cue (also *v.i.*): — *pr.p.* **cue'ing, cū'ing**; *pa.t.* and *pa.p.* **cued.** — *n.* **cue'ist** a billiard-player. — **cue-ball** the ball struck by the cue. [Fr. *queue* — L. *cauda*, a tail.]

cuerpo. See **en cuerpo.**

cuesta *kwes'tə*, *n.* a hill ridge having a steep scarp on one side and a gradual slope on the other, caused by denudation of gently dipping hard rock strata. [Sp.]

cuff[1] *kuf*, *n.* a stroke with the open hand. — *v.t.* to strike with the open hand: to beat. [Origin obscure; cf. Sw. *kuffa*, to knock.]

cuff[2] *kuf*, *n.* the end of the sleeve near the wrist: a covering for the wrist: a handcuff: a turned-up fold at the bottom of a trouser leg (*U.S.*). — **cuff'-link** either of a pair of usu. decorative fasteners, orig. consisting of two buttons linked together, now usu. one button-like object attached to a pivoting bar, used for fastening a shirt cuff. — **off the cuff** unofficially and offhand: improvised; **on the cuff** (*U.S.*) on tick: on the house. [Prob. cog. with **coif.**]

cuff[3] *kuf*, *n.* a Scottish form of **scuff**[1], **scruff**[1].

cuffin *kuf'in*, *n.* a man. — **queer cuffin** a justice of the peace: a churl. [Thieves' slang.]

cuffle *kuf'l*, (*Spens.*) *v.i.* to scuffle.

cuffo *kuf'ō*, (*old U.S. slang*) *adv.* without any admission charge. [Prob. der. from **on the cuff** see **cuff**[2].]

Cufic. Same as **Kufic.**

cui bono? *kī', kwē', bō'nō, kōō'ē bo'nō*, (L.) for whose benefit is it?: who is the gainer?

cuif. Same as **coof.**

cuirass *kwi-ras'* (or *kū'*), *n.* a defensive breastplate and backplate fastened together: a breastplate alone. — *v.t.* to furnish with a cuirass. — *n.* **cuirassier** (*-ēr'*) a horse-soldier wearing a cuirass. [Fr. *cuirasse* — *cuir*, leather — L. *corium*, skin, leather.]

cuir-bouilli *kwēr-bōō'yē*, *n.* leather boiled or soaked in hot water and moulded. — Also **cuir-bou'illy.** [Fr., boiled leather.]

Cuisenaire rods *kwē-zə-nār' rodz*, a set of small wooden rods, of significant related sizes and colours, used in teaching arithmetic. [Georges *Cuisenaire*, a Belgian educationalist.]

cuish. See **cuisse.**

cuisine *kwē-zēn'*, *n.* a kitchen or cooking department: cookery. — *n.* **cuisin'ier** (*-yā*) a cook. — **cuisine minceur** (*mē̃-sœr*; Fr., slenderness) a style of cooking characterised by imaginative use of light, simple ingredients. [Fr., — L. *coquina* — *coquĕre*, to cook.]

cuisse *kwis*, **cuish** *kwish*, (*Shak.* **cush** *kush*) *ns.* thigh armour. — **cuisse-madame** (*-däm'*) a jargonelle pear. [Fr. *cuisse* — L. *coxa*, hip.]

cuisser. See **cusser.**

cuit, cute, coot *køt, küt, kit,* (*Scot.*) *n.* the ankle. — *n.*

cuit'ikin, cut'ikin, coot'ikin a gaiter. [Cf. Du. *koot*, Flem. *keute*.]

cuiter *küt'ər*, (*Scot.*) *v.t.* to wheedle: to cocker, pamper.

cuittle *küt'l*, (*Scot.*) *v.t.* to coax: to cajole: to curry (favour): (perh. by confusion with **kittle**[1]) to tickle. [Origin obscure.]

culch, cultch *kulch*, (*S. England*) *n.* rubbish: the flooring of an oyster-bed: oyster-spawn. [Origin doubtful.]

Culdee *kul'dē*, *n.* one of a fraternity of monks living in Scotland from the 8th century in groups of cells. [Old Ir. *cēle de*, servant or companion of God — Latinised by Boece into *Culdei* (pl.) as if *cultōrēs Deī*.]

cul-de-four *kü(l)-də-fōōr* (Fr. *kü*), *n.* (*archit.*) a sort of low spherical vault, oven-like. — **cul-de-lampe** (*läp*) an ornamental design used in filling up blank spaces in a book; **cul-de-sac** (*kōōl'də-sak, kul'*) a street, etc., closed at one end: a blind-alley. [Fr. *cul*, bottom — L. *cūlus*; Fr. *de*, of, *four*, furnace, *lampe*, lamp, *sac*, sack.]

culet *kū'lit*, *n.* the back of a brilliant-cut diamond: armour protecting the hips. [O.Fr. *culet*, dim. of *cul*; see foregoing.]

Culex *kū'leks*, *n.* the typical genus of **Culic'idae** or gnats: (without *cap.*) an insect of this genus: — *pl.* **culices** (*kū'li-sēz*). — *adjs.* **culiciform** (*-lis'*); **cu'licine.** — *n.* **cu'licid.** [L. *culex, -icis*.]

culinary *ku'lin-ər-i, kū'*, *adj.* pertaining to the kitchen or to cookery: used in the kitchen. [L. *culīnārius* — *culīna*, a kitchen.]

cull[1] *kul*, *v.t.* to gather: to select: to pick out and destroy, as inferior or superfluous members of a group, e.g. of seals, deer. — *n.* an act of culling: an unsuitable animal eliminated from a flock or herd. — *ns.* **cull'er; cull'ing.** [Fr. *cueillir*, to gather — L. *colligĕre* — *col-*, together, *legĕre*, to gather.]

cull[2]. See **cully.**

cullender. See **colander.**

cullet *kul'it*, *n.* waste glass, melted up again with new material. [Fr. *collet* — L. *collum*, neck.]

cullion *kul'yən*, *n.* a wretch: a rascal. — *adj.* **cull'ionly** (*Shak.*) mean, base. [Fr. *couillon*, testicle, poltroon (It. *coglione*) — L. *cōleus*, a leather bag — Gr. *koleos*, sheath.]

cullis[1] *kul'is*, (*rare*) *n.* a strong broth. [O.Fr. *coleis* — L. *cōlāre*, to strain.]

cullis[2] *kul'is*, *n.* a roof gutter or groove. [Fr. *coulisse*.]

cully *kul'i*, (*rare*) *n.* a dupe: fellow, mate, a man generally. — *v.t.* to deceive meanly: — *pr.p.* **cull'ying**; *pa.t.* and *pa.p.* **cull'ied.** — *ns.* **cull** a dupe; **cull'yism** the state of being a cully. [Prob. a contr. of **cullion**.]

culm[1] *kulm*, *n.* a grass or sedge stem. — *v.i.* to form a culm. — *adj.* **culmif'erous** having a culm. [L. *culmus*, a stalk.]

culm[2] *kulm*, *n.* coal-dust: anthracite dust: in some parts of England, anthracite. — *adj.* **culmif'erous** producing culm. — **Culm, Culm Measures** a Lower Carboniferous formation of Europe and Southwest England, with grits, sandstones, shales, etc. [Origin unknown; cf. **coom.**]

culmen *kul'men*, *n.* the highest point: the top ridge of a bird's bill. [L.; see **culminate.**]

culmiferous. See **culm**[1,2].

culminate *kul'min-āt*, *v.i.* to be on, or come to, the meridian, and thus the highest (or lowest) point of altitude (*astron.*): to reach the highest point (with *in*). — *v.t.* to bring to the highest point. — *adj.* **cul'minant** at its highest point. — *n.* **culminā'tion** the act of culminating: the top: the highest point: transit of a body across the meridian (*astron.*). [L.L. *culmināre*, -*ātum* — *culmen*, or *columen*, -*inis*, a summit.]

culottes *kū-lot', kōō-*, *n.pl.* a divided skirt. — Also in *sing.* **culotte'.** — **sansculotte** see **sans.** [Fr. *culotte*, breeches.]

culpable *kul'pə-bl*, *adj.* faulty: criminal. — *ns.* **culpabil'ity, cul'pableness** liability to blame. — *adv.* **cul'pably.** — *adj.* **cul'patory** expressive of blame. [L. *culpa*, a fault.]

culpa levis *kul'pǝ lē'vis, kōōl'pa le'vis, -wis,* (L.) a slight fault.

culprit *kul'prit, n.* one in fault: a criminal: a prisoner accused but not yet tried (*Eng. law*). [From the fusion in legal phraseology of *cul.* (*culpable, culpābilis*), and *prit, prist* (O.Fr. *prest*), ready.]

cult *kult, n.* a system of religious belief: formal worship: a sect: an unorthodox or false religion: a great, often excessive, admiration for a person or idea: the person or idea giving rise to such admiration: (with *of*) a fad. — Also **cult′us.** — *adj.* applied to objects associated with pagan worship: pertaining to, giving rise to, a cult, extremely fashionable. — *adjs.* **cult′ic, cult′ish** pertaining to, characteristic of a cult. — *ns.* **cult′ism** adherence to a cult; **cult′ist.** [L. *cultus* — *colěre,* to worship.]

cultch. Same as **culch.**

culter *kul'tǝr, n.* An obs. form of **coulter.** — *adjs.* **cul′trate, -d, cul′triform** knife-shaped. [L., knife.]

cultigen. See under **cultivate.**

cultism *kult'izm, n.* Gongorism. — *ns.* **cult′ist, cult′orist.** [Sp. *culto,* elegant — L. *cultus.*]

cultivar. See under **cultivate.**

cultivate *kul'ti-vāt, v.t.* to fill or produce by tillage: to prepare for crops: to devote attention to: to civilise or refine. — *n.* **cultigen** (*kul'ti-jen*) a cultivated type of plant of uncertain origin (Gr., root of *gignesthai,* to become). — *adjs.* **cul′tivable, cultivāt′able** capable of being cultivated. — *ns.* **cultivar** (*kul'ti-vär*) a plant variety produced from a naturally occurring species, that has been developed and maintained by cultivation (*culti*vated *var*iety); **cultivā′tion** the art or practice of cultivating: civilisation: refinement; **cul′tivātor** one who cultivates: an agricultural implement — a grubber. — **cultivate someone's friendship** to seek to gain or foster it. [L.L. *cultivāre, -ātum* — L. *colěre,* to till, to worship.]

cultrate, cultriform. See **culter.**

culture *kul'chǝr, n.* cultivation: the state of being cultivated: refinement: the result of cultivation: a type of civilisation: a crop of experimentally-grown bacteria or the like. — *v.t.* to cultivate: to improve. — *adjs.* **cul′turable; cul′tural.** — *adv.* **cul′turally.** — *adj.* **cul′tured** cultivated: well educated: refined. — *adj.* **cul′tureless.** — *n.* **cul′turist** a devotee of culture: one who grows cultures in a laboratory. — **cultural anthropology** social anthropology; **cultural, culture shock** disorientation caused by an abrupt change from one environment, culture, ideology, etc., to another; **cultured pearl** a pearl grown round a small foreign body deliberately introduced into an oyster's shell; **culture medium** a nutritive substance on which cultures can be grown; **culture vulture** derogatory term for one who has an extravagant interest in the arts. [L. *cultūra* — *colěre.*]

cultus. See **cult.**

culver *kul'vǝr, n.* a dove, a pigeon: a wood-pigeon. — **cul′ver-key** (often in *pl.*), the wild hyacinth: the cowslip: (in *pl.*) ash-keys. — *adj.* **cul′vertailed** dove-tailed. [O.E. *culfre.*]

culverin *kul'vǝr-in, n.* an early form of cannon of great length, generally an 18-pounder, weighting 50 cwt. — *n.* **culverineer′.** [Fr. *coulevrine* — *couleuvre,* snake — L. *colubrīnus,* snake-like — *coluber,* snake.]

Culver's physic, root *kul'vǝrz fiz'ik, rōōt,* the rhizome of speedwell *Veronica virginica,* used medicinally. [From one Dr *Culver.*]

culvert *kul'vǝrt, n.* an arched channel for carrying water beneath a road, railway, etc. [Perh. from Fr. *couler,* to flow — L. *colāre.*]

culvertage *kul'vǝrt-tij, n.* degradation of a vassal to the position of a serf. [O.Fr. *culvert,* a serf.]

cum *kum, prep.* combined with: with the addition of (as *cum-dividend,* of shares, including the right to the next dividend): used in combination to indicate dual function, nature, etc., as in *kitchen-cum-dining-room.* [L.]

cumarin. See **coumarin.**

cumbent *kum'bǝnt, adj.* lying down: reclining. [L. *cumbēns, -entis,* pr.p. of *cumběre,* to lie down.]

cumber *kum'bǝr, v.t.* to trouble or hinder with something useless: to get in the way of: to occupy obstructively. — *n.* encumberance: cumbering. — *adj.* **cum′bered** hampered: obstructed. — *n.* **cum′berer.** — *adj.* **cum′-berless** unencumbered. — *n.* **cum′berment.** — *adj.* **cum′bersome** unwieldy. — *n.* **cum′brance** encumbrance. — *adj.* **cum′brous** hindering: obstructing: unwieldy. — *adv.* **cum′brously.** — *n.* **cum′brousness.** — **cum′ber=ground** a useless thing, from Luke xiii. 7. [Apparently O.Fr. *combrer,* to hinder — L.L. *cumbrus,* a heap — L. *cumulus,* a heap.]

cumec *kū'mek,* (*eng.*) *n.* short for *cubic metre per second,* a unit for measuring volumetric rate of flow.

cum grano salis *kum grā'nō sā'lis, kōōm grä'nō sa'lis,* (L.) with a grain of salt.

cumin, cummin *kum'in, n.* an umbelliferous plant (*Cuminum cyminum*) of the Mediterranean region, with seeds like caraway, valuable as carminatives. [O.E. *cymen* — L. *cumīnum* — Gr. *kymīnon,* cog. with Heb. *kammon.*]

cum laude. See **maxima cum laude.**

cummer *kum'ǝr,* **kimmer** *kim'ǝr,* (*Scot.*) *ns.* a godmother (*obs.*): a gossip: a woman: a girl. [Fr. *commère* — L. *con-,* with *māter,* mother.]

cummerbund *kum'ǝr-bund, n.* a waist-belt, a sash. [Pers. *kamarband,* a loin-band.]

cummin. See **cumin.**

cum multis aliis *kum mul'tis ā'lē-is, kōōm mōōl'tēs a'lē-ēs,* (L.) with many other things.

cum notis variorum *kum nō'tis vā-ri-ō'rǝm, -ō', kōōm no'tēs va-ri-ō'rōōm, wa-,* (L.) with notes of various (critics).

cum privilegio *kum priv-i-lē'ji-ō, kōōm prē-vi-lā'gi-ō, -wi-,* (L.) with privilege.

cumquat. Same as **kumquat.**

cum-savvy *kum-sav'i,* (slang) *n.* know-how.

cumshaw *kum'shö, n.* a gift, a tip. [Pidgin-English.]

cumulate *kūm'ū-lāt, v.t.* and *v.i.* to heap together: to accumulate. — *adjs.* **cum′ulate, -d** heaped up. — *n.* **cumulā′tion** accumulation. — *adj.* **cum′ulative** increasing by successive additions. — *adv.* **cum′ulatively.** — **cumulative vote** a system by which a voter may distribute a number of votes at will among the candidates, giving more than one to a candidate if he chooses. [L. *cumulāre, -ātum* — *cumulus,* a heap.]

cumulus *kū'mū-lǝs, n.* a heap: a kind of cloud consisting of rounded heaps with a darker horizontal base: — *pl.* **cū′mulī.** — *adjs.* **cū′muliform; cū′mulose.** — *ns.* **cū′mulo-cirr′us** a delicate cirrus-like cumulus; **cū′mulo-nim′bus** a cumulus discharging showers. [L. *cumulus,* a heap.]

cunabula *kū-nab'ū-lǝ, n.pl.* a cradle: incunabula. [L. *cūnābula.*]

cunctator *kungk-tā'tǝr, n.* one who delays or puts off. — *n.* **cunctā′tion** delay. — *adjs.* **cunctā′tious, cunc′tative, cunc′tatory** inclined to delay. [L. *cunctātor* — *cunc-tārī,* to delay.]

cuneal *kū'ni-ǝl,* **cuneate** *kū'ni-āt, adjs.* wedge-shaped. — *adjs.* **cuneat′ic** cuneiform; **cuneiform** (*kū-nē'i-förm, kū'ni(i-)förm*) wedge-shaped — specially applied to the old Hittite, Babylonian, Assyrian and Persian writing, of which the characters were impressed by the wedge-shaped facets of a stylus. — *n.* cuneiform writing. [L. *cuneus,* a wedge.]

cunette *kū-net', n.* a cuvette. [Fr.]

cunjevoi *kun'ji-voi,* (*Austr.*) *n.* a marine animal: a large-leaved araceous plant. [Aboriginal.]

cunner. See **conner**[3].

cunnilingus *kun-i-ling'gǝs, n.* oral stimulation of the female genitalia. [L. *cunnus,* vulva, *lingěre,* to lick.]

cunning *kun'ing, adj.* knowing: skilful: artful: crafty: dainty or quaintly pleasing (*U.S.*). — *n.* knowledge: skill: faculty of using stratagem to accomplish a purpose: craftiness: artifice. — *adv.* **cunn′ingly.** — *n.* **cunn′ingness** the quality of being cunning: artfulness, slyness. [O.E. *cunnan,* to know.]

cunt *kunt, n.* the female genitalia: a woman regarded as a sexual object (*vulg.*): an unpleasant, contemptible person (*vulg.*).   [M.E. *cunte*; ety. dub.]

cup *kup, n.* a drinking-vessel, usu. roughly hemispherical: a hollow: a cup-shaped structure (*biol.*): either of the two cup-shaped supports for the breasts in a brassière: a cupful: a dry or liquid measure used in cooking, half a pint (*U.S.*): the liquid contained in a cup: a mixed beverage made with wine (as *claret-cup*): an ornamental vessel offered as a prize: a competition with such a vessel as a prize: the hole, or its metal lining, on the green (*golf.*): the chalice, or the consecrated wine, at the Eucharist: that which we must receive or undergo: afflictions: blessings. — *v.t.* to form into a cup: to lodge in or as if in a cup: to extract blood from by means of cupping-glasses: to make drunk (*Shak.*). — *v.i.* to become cup-shaped: — *pr.p.* **cupp′ing**; *pa.t.* and *pa.p.* **cupped.** — *ns.* **cup′ful** as much as fills a cup: — *pl.* **cup′fuls; cup′pa** (*coll.*) a cup of tea; **cupp′er** a cupbearer: one professionally engaged in cupping; **cupp′ing** the application of cups from which the air has been exhausted in order to draw blood. — **cup′-and-ball′** a ball and socket joint: the game of catching a tethered ball in a cup on the end of a stick; **cup′-and-ring′(mark)** (*archeol.*) a cup-mark surrounded by one or more incised rings, carved on stones; **cup′bearer** one who attends at a feast to fill and hand out wine cups; **cupboard** (*kub′ərd*) a place for keeping victuals, dishes, etc. — *v.t.* to store. — **cup′board-love, faith** love or faith with a material end; **cup′-cake** a small round cake baked in a foil or paper case; **cup′-cor′al** a simple cup-shaped coral; **cup′gall** a cup-shaped gall in oak-leaves; **cup′head** a hemispherical (or nearly so) bolt-head or rivet-head; **cup′-li′chen** or **-moss** any lichen with cup-shaped structures; **cup′man** a boon companion; **cup′-mark** a cup-shaped hollow made by prehistoric man on rocks, standing-stones, etc.; **cupp′ing= glass** a glass used in cupping; **cup′-tie** one of a series of games to determine the winners of a cup. — **cry cupboard** to cry for food; **in one′s cups** under the influence of liquor; **one′s cup of tea** see **tea; there′s many a slip ′twixt the cup and the lip** failure is possible at the last moment.   [O.E. *cuppe* — L. *cūpa, cuppa*, a tub.]

cupel *kū′pəl, n.* a small vessel used by goldsmiths in assaying precious metals: the movable hearth of a reverberatory furnace for refining. — *v.t.* to assay in a cupel: — *pr.p.* **cū′pelling**; *pa.t.* and *pa.p.* **cū′pelled.** — *n.* **cūpellā′tion** recovery of precious metal in assaying.   [L. *cūpella*, dim. of *cūpa*; see **cup**.]

Cupid *kū′pid, n.* the Roman love-god, identified with Greek Eros: (without *cap.*) a winged figure of a young boy representing the love-god (*art*, etc.): (without *cap.*) a kind of jam-tart (*U.S.*). — *adj.* **cūpid′inous** full of desire, esp. amorous. — *n.* **cūpid′ity** covetousness.   [L. *Cūpīdo, -inis* — *cupĕre*, to desire.]

cupola *kū′pə-lə, n.* a spherical vault, or concave ceiling, on the top of a building: the internal part of a dome: a dome: a lantern on the top of a dome: an armoured dome or turret to protect a gun: a furnace used in iron-foundries. — *v.t.* to furnish with a cupola. — *adjs.* **cū′pola'd** (or **cū′polaed); cū′polar; cū′polated.**   [It., — L. *cūpula*, dim. of *cūpa*, a cask.]

cuppa. See **cup.**

cuprammonium *kū-prä-mō′ni-əm, n.* a solution of cupric hydroxide in ammonia. — **cuprammonium rayon** artificial silk made by dissolving cellulose in cuprammonium.   [L. *cuprum*, copper, and **ammonium.**]

cupreous *kū′pri-əs, adj.* of, containing, or like copper. — *adjs.* **cū′pric** of or containing bivalent copper; **cūprif′- erous** yielding copper. — *n.* **cū′prite** red copper ore, ruby copper, cuprous oxide (Cu_2O). — *adj.* **cū′prous** of or containing univalent copper. — *n.* **cū′pro-nick′el** an alloy of copper and nickel.   [L. *cupreus* — *cuprum*; see **copper.**]

Cupressus *kū-pres′əs, n.* the cypress genus.   [L.]

cupric, etc., **cuprous.** See **cupreous.**

cupule *kū′pūl, n.* a small cup in a liverwort containing

gemmae: a cup-shaped envelope on the fruit of some trees, e.g. oak, beech, chestnut. — *adjs.* **cū′pūlar, cū′pūlate** cup-like: pertaining to a cupule. — *n.pl.* **Cūpūlif′erae** (*-ə-rē*) in some classifications a family including beech, oak, chestnut, with or without birch, hazel, and hornbeam. — *adj.* **cūpūlif′erous** of the Cupuliferae: bearing cupules.   [L. *cūpula*, dim. of *cūpa*, tub.]

cur *kûr, n.* a worthless dog, of low breed: a contemptible scoundrel. — *adj.* **curr′ish.** — *adv.* **curr′ishly.** — *n.* **curr′ishness.**   [M.E. *curre*; cf. O.N. *kurra*, to grumble.]

curaçao, curaçoa, *kōō-rä-sä′ō, kū′rə-sō, kū-ra-sō′, ns.* a liqueur flavoured with bitter orange peel.   [*Curaçao*, island in West Indies, where first made.]

curacy. See **curate.**

curare, curari *kū-* or *kōō-rä′ri, n.* a paralysing poison extracted from wourali root (*Strychnos toxifera*), etc., by South American Indians for arrows — now a source of valuable drugs. — Also **cura′ra.** — *n.* **cura′rine** a highly poisonous alkaloid therefrom, used, e.g. in surgery, as a muscle relaxant. — *v.t.* **cu′rarise, -ize.**   [Port. from Carib *kurari*.]

curassow *kū′rə-sō, kū-räs′ō, n.* a large turkey-like S. American bird.   [From the island of *Curaçao*.]

curat *kū′rət, (Spens.) n.* a cuirass.   [See **cuirass.**]

curate *kūr′it, n.* one who has the cure of souls: a clergyman in the Church of England, assisting a rector or vicar: a small poker (*coll.*): a cake-stand. — *ns.* **cur′acy** (*-ə-si*), **cur′ateship** the office, employment, or benefice of a curate. — **curate′s egg** anything of which parts are excellent.   [L.L. *cūrātus*, L. *cūra*, care.]

curative. See **cure[1].**

curator *kūr-ā′tər* (in Scots law *kūr′ə-tər*), *n.* one who has the charge of anything: a superintendent, esp. of a museum: one appointed by law as guardian: a member of a board for electing university professors and the like: — *fem.* **curā′trix.** — *adj.* **curatorial** (*-ə-tō′ri-əl*). — *n.* **curā′torship.**   [L. *cūrātor*.]

curatory. See **cure[1].**

curb *kûrb, n.* a chain or strap attached to the bit for restraining a horse: another spelling for **kerb** (chiefly *U.S.*): a check or restraint: a disease of horses, marked by hard swellings on the leg: the swelling itself. — *v.t.* to furnish with or guide by a curb: to restrain or check. — *adjs.* **curb′able; curb′less.** — **curb′-roof** a mansard-roof. — See also **courb.**   [Fr. *courbe* — L. *curvus*, bent.]

curch *kûrch, n.* a covering for the head, a kerchief.   [See **kerchief.**]

Curculio *kûr-kū′li-ō, n.* a genus of weevils: (without *cap.*) any member of the genus: — *pl.* **curcu′lios.**   [L.]

Curcuma *kûr-kū′mə, n.* a genus of the ginger family yielding turmeric: (without *cap.*) any plant of the genus. — *n.* **cur′cumine** the colouring matter of turmeric.   [Ar. *kurkum*, saffron.]

curd *kûrd, n.* milk thickened or coagulated by acid: the cheese part of milk, as distinguished from the whey: any similar substance: in soap-making the granular soap that rises in the lye upon salting: the fatty matter between the flakes of salmon flesh: the flowering head of cauliflower, broccoli, etc. — *v.t.* and *v.i.* to curdle. — *n.* **curd′iness.** — *v.t.* and *v.i.* **curd′le** to turn into curd: to coagulate: to thicken. — *adj.* **curd′y** like or full of curd. — **curd cheese** a mild white cheese made from skimmed milk curds.   [Prob. Celt.; Gael. *gruth*, Ir. *cruth*.]

cure[1] *kūr, n.* care of souls or spiritual charge: care of the sick: an act of healing: that which heals: a remedy, or course of remedial treatment: a means of improving a situation: a course or method of preserving or arresting decomposition: the total quantity cured: treatment by which a product is finished or made ready for use. — *v.t.* to heal or make better: to preserve as by drying, salting, etc.: to finish by means of chemical change, e.g. to vulcanise (a rubber), or to use heat or chemicals in the last stage of preparing (a thermosetting plastic).

— *v.i.* to undergo a process or course of curing. — *adj.* **cūr′able**. — *ns.* **cūr′ableness; cūrabil′ity**. — *adjs.* **cūr′ative, cūr′atory** tending to cure. — *adj.* **cūre′less** that cannot be cured. — *n.* **cūr′er**. — **cūre′-all** a panacea. [O.Fr. *cure* — L. *cūra*, care.]

cure² *kūr*, (*slang*) *n.* an odd or queer person. [Ety. dub.]

curé *kū′rā, n.* a parish priest in France. [Fr.; see **curate**.]

curettage *kū-ret′ij, n.* scraping of a body cavity by means of a surgeon's instrument known as a **curette′**. — *v.t.* **curette′** to scrape with a curette. — *n.* **curette′ment** curettage. [Fr. *curer*, to clean, clear.]

curfew *kûr′fū, n.* in feudal times the ringing of a bell as a signal to put out all fires and lights: the ringing of a bell at a certain hour continued as a traditional custom: a signal for the imposition of restrictions of other kinds, e.g. from being abroad in the streets at night: the time of curfew: the bell itself: a regulation obliging persons to be indoors within certain hours. — **cur′few-bell**. [O.Fr. *covrefeu; couvrir,* to cover, *feu,* fire — L. *focus*.]

curfuffle. See **carfuffle**.

curia *kū′ri-ə, n.* one of the ten divisions of a Roman tribe: a building in which the senate met: a provincial senate: a court, legislative or judicial: the court of the papal see. — *ns.* **cū′rialism; cū′rialist.** — *adj.* **cūrialist′ic.** — **curia regis** see **aula**. [L. *cūria*.]

curie *kü-rē′, kū′rē, n.* orig., the quantity of radon in radioactive equilibrium with a gram of radium: now, a unit of radioactivity, defined as 3.7 × 10¹⁰ disintegrations per second (becquerels), or the quantity of a radioactive substance which undergoes this number of disintegrations. — *n.* **curium** (*kū′*) a chemical element (at. numb. 96; symbol Cm). — **curiether′apy** treatment of disease by radium. [After Marie and Pierre *Curie,* discoverers of radium.]

curiet *kū′ri-et, (Spens.) n.* a cuirass. [See **cuirass**.]

curio *kū′ri-ō, n.* any article of virtu or bric-à-brac, or anything considered rare and curious: — *pl.* **cū′rios**. [For **curiosity**.]

curiosa *kū-ri-ō′sə, n.pl.* strange or unusual objects: books, manuscripts, etc. which are pornographic or erotic. [Mod. L., from same root as **curious**.]

curious *kū′ri-əs, adj.* anxious to learn: inquisitive: showing great care or nicety (*obs.*): solicitous (*Shak.*): skilfully made: singular: rare: (in booksellers' catalogues) indecent: odd. — *n.* **curiosity** (-*os′i-ti*) state or quality of being curious: inquisitiveness: that which is curious: anything rare or unusual. — *adv.* **cū′riously.** — *n.* **cū′riousness.** — **curious arts** (*B.*) magical practices. [Fr. *curieux* — L. *cūriōsus* — *cūra*.]

curium. See **curie**.

curl *kûrl, v.t.* to twist into ringlets: to coil: to cause to move in a curve: to ripple. — *v.i.* to shrink into ringlets: to move in curves: to writhe: to ripple: to eddy: to play at the game of curling. — *n.* a ringlet of hair, or what is like it: a wave, bending, or twist: an eddy: a plant disease in which leaves curl: a curled condition. — *adj.* **curled.** — *ns.* **curl′er** one who, or that which, curls: a player at the game of curling; **curl′iness; curl′ing** a game common in Scotland, consisting in sliding heavy smooth stones along a sheet of ice. — *adj.* **curl′y** having curls: full of curls. — *adj.* **curled′-pate** (*Shak.*) having curled hair. — **curl′iewurlie** (*Scot.*) any fantastic round ornament; **curl′ing-īrons, curl′ing-tongs** an instrument used for curling the hair; **curl′ing-pond** a pond on which curling is played; **curl′ing-stone** a heavy stone with a handle, used in playing curling; **curl′-pap′er** a paper twisted into the hair to give it curl; **curl′y-greens′** kale. — *adj.* **curl′y-head′ed.** — **curl up** (*coll.*) to be embarrassed; **out of curl** lacking energy, limp. [M.E. *crull*; Du. *krullen,* Dan. *krolle,* to curl.]

curlew *kûr′lōō, -lū, n.* a moorland bird (*Numenius arquata*) of the woodcock family with long curved bill and long legs, and plaintive whistling cry — the whaup: any bird of the genus *Numenius:* the thick-knee (**stone′=cur′lew**). — **cur′lew-berry** crow-berry. [O.Fr. *corlieu,* prob. from its cry.]

curlicue *kûr′lə-kū, n.* a fantastic curl: a fancy twist. [**curly,** and **cue²**.]

curliewurlie. See **curl**.

curmudgeon *kər-muj′ən, n.* an avaricious, ill-natured churlish fellow: a miser. — *adj.* and *adv.* **curmud′-geonly**. [Origin unknown.]

curmurring *kər-mûr′ing, n.* a rumbling sound, esp. that made in the bowels by flatulence. [Imit.]

curn *kûrn,* (*Scot.*) *n.* a grain: a particle: a small quantity, a little. — *adj.* **curn′y, curn′ey** granular, coarse-grained. [**corn**.]

curnaptious. See **carnaptious**.

curpel *kûr′pl, n.* a Scots form of **crupper**.

curr *kûr,* (*Wordsworth*) *v.i.* to make a purring sound. [Imit.]

currach, -agh *kur′ə(hh), n.* a long-shaped boat of similar construction to a coracle. [Ir. *curach*.]

currajong. See **kurrajong**.

currant *kur′ənt, n.* a small black raisin or dried seedless grape (imported from eastern Mediterranean countries): extended to several species of Ribes (*black, red, white, flowering currant*), and to various other plants, and their fruits. — *adj.* **curr′anty** full of currants. — **curr′ant-bread′** a sweetened bread with some (grape) currants in it; **curr′ant-bun, curr′ant-loaf′** a dark spiced cake full of currants; **curr′ant-cake′** a cake with currants in it; **curr′ant-jell′y** a jelly made from red or black currants; **curr′ant-wine′**. [Corinth.]

currawong *kur′ə-wong, n.* any of several Australian birds of the genus *Strepera.* [Aboriginal.]

current *kur′ənt, adj.* running or flowing: passing from person to person: generally or widely received: now passing: present: belonging to the period of time now passing. — *n.* a running or flowing: a stream: a portion of water or air moving in a certain direction: a flow of electricity: course. — *n.* **curr′ency** circulation: that which circulates, esp. the money of a country: general estimation. — *adv.* **curr′ently**. — *n.* **curr′entness**. — **currency note** paper-money, esp. that issued by the Treasury in 1914–28 as legal tender; **current account** a bank account on which one is usu. not paid interest and from which money may be withdrawn by cheque; **current bedding** (*geol.*) false bedding. — **pass current** to be received as genuine. [L. *currēns, -entis* — pr.p. of *currĕre,* to run.]

currente calamo *ku-ren′tē (kōō-ren′te) ka′la-mō,* (L.) with a running pen, offhand.

curricle *kur′i-kl, n.* a two-wheeled open chaise, drawn by two horses abreast. [L. *curriculum,* course, race, racing chariot — *currĕre,* to run.]

curriculum *kə-rik′ū-ləm, n.* a course, esp. the course of study at a university, etc.: — *pl.* **curric′ula** or **-ums**. — *adj.* **curric′ular** of or relating to a curriculum or to courses of study. — **curriculum vitae** (*kə-rik′ūl-əm vī′tē, kōōr-ik′ōō-lōōm vē′tī, wē′tī*) (a biographical sketch of) the course of one's life. [L.; see **curricle**.]

currie. See **curry³**.

curried, currier. See **curry²**.

currish, currishly, etc. See **cur**.

curry¹ *kur′i, n.* a meat or other dish prepared with turmeric and mixed spices. — *v.t.* to make a curry of. — **curr′y-leaf** a rutaceous Indian tree (*Murraya koenijii*) whose leaves are an ingredient in curry-powder; **curr′y-pow′der** ground spices and turmeric. [Tamil *kari,* sauce.]

curry² *kur′i, v.t.* to dress (leather): to rub down and dress (a horse): to beat: to scratch: — *pr.p.* **curr′ying**; *pa.t.* and *pa.p.* **curr′ied**. — *ns.* **curr′ier** one who curries or dresses tanned leather; **curr′ying**. — **curr′y-comb** an iron instrument or comb used for currying or cleaning horses. — **curry favour** (orig. **curry favell** to curry the chestnut horse) to seek to ingratiate onself. [O.Fr. *correier* (Fr. *corroyer*), *conrei,* outfit, from L. *con-,* with, and the root seen in **array**.]

curry³, currie. Obsolete forms of **quarry²**.

cursal. See **cursus**.

curse *kûrs, v.t.* to invoke or wish evil upon: to blaspheme:

to afflict with: to utter doom or damnation against: to excommunicate. — *v.i.* to utter imprecations: to swear. — *n.* an invocation or wishing of evil or harm: evil invoked on another: excommunication sentence: an imprecation: any great evil: (with *the*) menstrual period (*coll.*). — *adj.* **curs'ed** under a curse: hateful. — *adv.* **curs'edly.** — *ns.* **curs'edness; curs'er; curs'ing.** — *adj.* **curst** cursed: ill-tempered (*arch.*) — *n.* **curst'ness** the state of being curst: peevishness: perverseness. — **curse of Scotland** the nine of diamonds (origin unknown). [O.E. *cursian* — *curs*, a curse; ety. doubtful; not conn. with **cross.**]

curselarie, cursenary. See **cursorary** under **cursor.**

cursitor *kûr'si-tər, n.* a clerk or officer in the Court of Chancery who made out original writs *de cursu*, i.e. of ordinary course: a vagrant (*obs.*). [L.L. *cursitor.*]

cursive *kûr'siv, adj.* (of handwriting) written with a running hand: flowing: of a typeface, designed to imitate handwriting. — *adv.* **cur'sively.** [L.L. *cursivus* — L. *currĕre*, to run.]

cursor *kûr'sər, n.* a sliding part of a measuring instrument: one of several (usu. flashing) devices appearing on a VDU screen used to indicate position, e.g. of the next input character, of a correction, etc. — *adj.* (*obs.*) **cur'sorary** (*Shak.*; other readings **cur'senary, cur'selarie;** prob. intended for **cursitory**) cursory. — *n.pl.* **cursores** (*-sō'rēz, -sö'*) in old classifications, running birds, variously limited. — *adj.* **curso'rial** adapted for running. — *adv.* **cur'sorily** (*-sər-*). — *n.* **cur'soriness.** — *adj.* **cur'sory** running quickly over: hasty: superficial. [L. *cursor*, pl. *cursōrēs*, a runner — *currĕre, cursum*, to run.]

curst. See **curse.**

cursus *kûr'səs,* (*rare*) *n.* a racecourse: a form of daily prayer or service: an academic curriculum: an elongated earthwork, consisting of parallel banks with ditches outside. — *adj.* **cur'sal.** [L.]

curt *kûrt, adj.* short: concise: discourteously brief or summary. — *adj.* **curt'āte** shortened or reduced — applied to the distance of a planet from the sun or earth projected on the plane of the ecliptic. — *n.* **curtā'tion.** — *adv.* **curt'ly.** — *n.* **curt'ness.** [L. *curtus*, shortened.]

curtail *kər-tāl', v.t.* to cut short: to cut off a part of: to abridge. — *n.* **curtail'ment.** — **cur'tail-step** a round-ended step at the bottom of a flight. [Old spelling *curtal*, O.Fr. *courtault* — L. *curtus*, shortened.]

curtain *kûr'tən, n.* hanging drapery at a window, around a bed, etc.: the part of a rampart between two bastions: a curtain wall: a screen of cloth or metal concealing the stage, or restricting the spread of fire (*theat.*): the fall of the curtain, close of a scene or act (*theat.*): a protective barrier in general, as the fire of many guns directed along a certain line to prevent the passage of an enemy (also called **cur'tain-fire**). — *v.t.* to enclose or furnish with curtains: (with *off*) to separate with, or as if with, a curtain. — **curtain call** a summons from the audience to appear at the end of a scene; **curtain lecture** a lecture or reproof given in bed by a wife to her husband; **cur'tain-raiser** a short play preceding the main performance: an event which precedes and foreshadows a more important event; **curtain speech** a speech made before a theatre curtain; **curtain wall** a wall that is not load-bearing, e.g. does not support a roof; **curtain walling** prefabricated large framed sections of lightweight, usu. predecorated, material used in building. — **bamboo curtain** see **bamboo; be curtains (for)** to be the end or death (of) (*coll.*); **behind the curtain** away from public view; **draw the curtain** to draw it aside, so as to show what is behind, or to draw it in front of anything so as to hide it; **iron curtain** see **iron.** [O.Fr. *cortine* — L.L. *cortīna;* prob. L. *cŏrs, cŏrtis*, a court.]

curtal *kûr'təl,* (*obs.*) *n.* a horse or other animal with a docked tail: anything docked or cut short. — *adj.* docked or shortened. — **curtal friar** (*Scott*) a friar with a short frock. [See **curtail.**]

curtal-ax *kûr'təl-aks,* **curtaxe** *kûrt'aks,* (*Spens*) *ns.* a short, broad sword. [A corr. of the earlier forms *coutelas, curtelas.* See **cutlass.**]

curtana *kûr-tä'nə, -tā'nə, n.* a sword without a point, symbolic of mercy, carried at coronations. [L. *curtus*, short.]

curtate, curtation. See **curt.**

curtaxe. See **curtal-ax.**

curtilage *kûr'til-ij, n.* a court or area of land attached to and including a dwelling-house, etc. [O.Fr. *courtillage;* see **court.**]

curtsy, curtsey *kûrt'si, n.* an obeisance, esp. by women, made by bending the knees. — *v.i.* to make or 'drop' a curtsy. [See **courtesy.**]

curule *kū'rool, adj.* like a camp-stool with curved legs, applied to the chair of a higher Roman magistrate. [L. *curūlis* — *currus*, a chariot.]

curvaceous, curvate, etc. See **curve.**

curve *kûrv, n.* anything bent: a line that is not straight: a line (including a straight line) answering to an equation: a graph: the curved line on a graph representing the rise and fall of measurable data, e.g. birth-rate: a curved surace: an arch: (in *pl.*) the rounded contours of a woman's body (*coll.*). — *v.t.* to bend: to form into a curve. — *v.i.* to bend: to move in a curve. — *adjs.* **curvaceous, curvacious** (*kûr-vā'shəs; coll.*) (of a woman) having shapely curves; **curv'āte, -d** curved or bent in a regular form. — *n.* **curvā'tion.** — *adj.* **cur'vative** (*-və-tiv*). — *n.* **cur'vature** (*-və-chər*) a curving or bending: the continual bending, or the amount of bending, from a straight line: the reciprocal of the radius at any point. — *adjs.* **curved; curve'some** curvaceous; **curvicau'date** having a crooked tail; **curvicos'tate** having curved ribs; **curvifo'liate** having curved leaves; **cur'viform; curvilin'eal, curvilin'ear** bounded by curved lines. — *n.* **curvilinear'ity.** — *adjs.* **cur'ving; curviros'tral** with the bill curved downward; **cur'vital** of or pertaining to curvature. — *n.* **cur'vity** the state of being curved. — *adj.* **curv'y.** [L. *curvus*, crooked.]

curvet *kûr'vet, kər-vet', n.* a light leap of a horse in which he raises his forelegs together, next the hind-legs with a spring before the forelegs touch the ground: a leap, frolic. — *v.i.* (*kər-vet', kûr'vet*), to leap in curvets: to frisk: — *pr.p.* **curvett'ing, cur'veting;** *pa.t.* and *pa.p.* **curvett'ed, cur'veted.** [It. *corvetta*, dim. of *corvo* — L. *curvus.*]

curvicaudate, curvifoliate, curvilineal, etc. See **curve.**

cus-cus *kus'-kus,* or *kŏos'-kŏos, n.* a phalanger of the Malay Archipelago. [Native name in the Moluccas.]

cuscus[1] *kus'kus, n.* the grain of the African millet. [Same as **couscous.**]

cuscus[2] *kus'kus, n.* the fragrant fibrous root of an Indian grass (*Andropogon squarrosus*), used for making fans, etc. [Pers. *khas khas.*]

cusec *kū'sek,* (*eng.*) *n.* short for *cu*bic feet per *sec*ond, a unit for measuring volumetric rate of flow.

cush. See **cuisse, cushion.**

cushat *kush'ət,* (*Scot.*) *n.* the ringdove or wood-pigeon. [O.E. *cūscute*, perh. from its note, and *scēotan*, to shoot.]

cushaw *kə-shö', ku', kŏo'shö.* See **cashaw.**

Cushing's disease, syndrome *kŏosh'ingz diz-ēz', sin'drōm,* a disease characterised by obesity, high blood pressure, metabolic disorders, etc., caused by excess hormonal secretion due to an adenoma of the pituitary or adrenal gland. [Described by H. W. *Cushing* (1869–1939), American surgeon.]

cushion *kŏosh'ən, n.* a case filled with some soft, elastic stuff, e.g. feathers, foam rubber, for resting on: a pillow: a pad: the pillow used in making bone-lace: an engraver's pad: the rubber of an electrical machine: a pad supporting a woman's hair: the cap of a pier (*archit.*): the elastic lining of the inner side of a billiard-table (*coll.* **cush**): a body of steam remaining in the cylinder of a steam-engine, acting as a buffer to the piston: anything that serves to a deaden a blow. — *v.t.* to seat on, or furnish with, a cushion: to serve as a cushion for or against: to suppress (complaints) by ignoring. — *adj.* **cush′ioned** furnished with a cushion, padded: having cushion-tyres. — *n.* **cush′ionet** a little cushion. — *adj.* **cush′iony** like a cushion, soft. — **cush′ion-plant** a plant of cushion-like form reducing transpiration; **cush′ion-tyre, -tire** a cycle tyre of rubber tubing, with rubber stuffing. [O.Fr. *coissin* — L. *coxīnum, coxa*, hip, or perh. L. *culcita*, mattress, cushion.]

Cushite, Kushite *kōōsh′īt, n.* a group of languages of eastern Africa: a (member of a) race speaking any of these languages. — *adj.* of or relating to the languages or the race. — Also **Cushitic, Kushitic** *(-it′).* [*Cush*, an ancient kingdom in the Nile valley, and **-ite.**]

cushy *kōōsh′i, (slang) adj.* easy and comfortable: not dangerous. [Perh. Hind. *khush*, pleasant, *khushī*, happiness.]

cusk *kusk, n.* the torsk: the burbot.

cusp *kusp, n.* a point: the point or horn of the moon, etc.: a tooth-like meeting of two branches of a curve, with sudden change of direction: a tooth-like ornament common in Gothic tracery *(archit.):* a prominence or a tooth: a division between signs of the zodiac *(astrol.).* — *adjs.* **cus′pate; cusped; cus′pid; cus′pidal; cus′pidate, -d** *(biol.)* having a rigid point. [L. *cuspis, -idis,* a point.]

Cusparia bark *kə-spar′i-ə bärk,* Angostura bark (q.v.).

cuspidor(e) *kus′pi-dōr* or *-dör, (U.S.) n.* a spittoon. [Port., — L. *conspuěre,* to spit upon.]

cuss *kus, (slang) n.* a curse: a fellow. — *v.t.* and *v.i.* to curse. — *adj.* **cuss′ed** cursed: obstinate. — *n.* **cuss′-edness** contrariness. — **cuss′-word.** [*curse*; prob. sometimes associated with **customer.**]

cusser, cuisser, cooser *kus′ər, kōōs′ər, küs′ər, (Scot.) n.* a stallion. [**courser.**]

custard *kus′tərd, n.* a baked mixture of milk, eggs, etc., sweetened or seasoned (now usu. **egg custard**): a cooked mixture of similar composition, thickened with cornflour. — **cus′tard-apple** the fruit of a W. Indian tree *(Anona reticulata)* with eatable pulp, like a custard; **cus′tard-coff′in** *(Shak.)* paste or crust covering a custard: **custard-pie (comedy)** slapstick, esp. of early U.S. films in which comedians threw custard pies at each other; **custard powder** a flavoured preparation containing cornflour, sugar, etc. for using with milk to make custard. [Earlier *custade,* a corr. of *crustade,* a pie with a crust; see **crust.**]

custock. See **castock.**

custody *kus′tə-di, n.* a watching or guarding: care: security: imprisonment. — *adj.* **custō′dial.** — *ns.* **custō′dian, cus′tode, custō′dier** one who has care, esp. of some public building; **custō′dianship.** [L. *custōdia,* guard, *custōs, -ōdis,* a keeper.]

custom *kus′təm, n.* what one is wont to do: what is usually done by others: usage: frequent repetition of the same act: regular trade or business: any of the distinctive practices and conventions of a people or locality, esp. those of a primitive tribe (applied, *hist.*, to a periodical massacre in parts of West Africa): usages of a manor or of a district: a tax on goods: (in *pl.*) duties on imports and exports: (in *pl.*) the collecting authorities. — *adj.* (esp. *U.S.*) made to order. — *adj.* **cus′tomable** *(arch.)* customary: common: dutiable. — *adv.* **cus′tomarily.** — *n.* **cus′tomariness.** — *adj.* **cus′tomary** according to use and wont: usual: holding or held by custom: copyhold. — *n.* (also **customary** *kus′tūm-ər-i*) a body or book of the customs of a manor, etc. or the ritual of a religious community. — *adj.* **cus′tomed** accustomed: usual. — *n.* **cus′tomer** one accustomed to a frequent a certain place of business: a buyer: a prostitute *(Shak.):* a person *(slang).* — *v.t.* **cus′tomise, -ize** to make in such a way as to suit specified individual requirements. — *adj.* **cus′tomized, -z-.** — *adjs.* **cus′tom‑built′, cus′tom-made′** built (as e.g. a motor-car) or made to a customer's order. — **cus′tom-house** the place, esp. at a port, where customs or duties on exports and imports are collected. — *adj.* **cus′tom‑**

shrunk *(Shak.)* having fewer customers than formerly. — **customs union** a group of states having free trade between themselves, and a common tariff policy toward non-member states. [O.Fr. *custume, costume* — L. *cōnsuētūdō, -inis* — *cōnsuēscěre,* to accustom.]

custos *kus′tos, n.* a guardian: a superior in the Franciscan order: — *pl.* **custō′des** *(-dēz).* — **custos rotulorum** *(ro-tū-lō′rəm, kōō′stōs ro-tōō-lō′rōōm),* (L.) keeper of the rolls.

custrel *kus′trəl, (hist.) n.* an attendant on a knight: a knave. [O.Fr. *coustillier* — *coustille,* dagger; cf. **coistrel.**]

custumary. See **custom.**

cut *kut, v.t.* to penetrate with a sharp edge: to make an incision in: to cleave or pass through: to divide: to carve, hew, or make or fashion by cutting: to sever: to reap: to excise: to intersect: to divide (a pack of cards) by lifting the upper portion at random: to expose (a card or suit) in this way: in tennis, golf, etc., to strike obliquely, imparting spin to: to reduce or lessen: to abridge: to trim (a book) by guillotine: to wound or hurt: to affect deeply: to shorten: to break off acquaintance with: to pass intentionally without greeting: to renounce, give up: to stay away from: to castrate: to perform or execute (as a caper): to make (a sound recording, e.g. a disc): to grow (teeth) through the gums (see also **cut one's teeth (on)** below). — *v.i.* to make an incision: to intersect: to strike obliquely: to be cut: to dash, go quickly: to run away, to be off *(slang):* to twiddle the feet rapidly in dancing: in film-making, to cease photographing: (of a film) to change rapidly to another scene: — *pr.p.* **cutt′ing;** *pa.t.* and *pa.p.* **cut.** — *n.* a cleaving or dividing: an excavation for a road, railway, etc.: a cross passage: a stroke or blow: in various games, a particular stroke, generally implying obliquity and spin: in cricket, a stroke to the off side with horizontal bat: the spin imparted to the ball: a reduction or diminution: an act of unkindness: the result of fashioning by cutting, carving, etc. (e.g. clothes, hair, gemstones): the act, or outcome, of cutting a pack of cards: an incision or wound: an excision: a piece cut off: total quantity cut: a varying unit of length for cloth and yarn: an engraved block or the picture from it: manner of cutting, or fashion: a working horse *(Shak.):* a general term of abuse (as in 'call me cut') *(Shak.):* a rake-off or share *(slang):* in films, the action of cutting or its result. — *adj. (slang)* of a drug, adulterated or diluted. — *ns.* **cutt′er** a person or thing that cuts: a cut-throat *(obs.):* a tailor who measures and cuts out the cloth: a small vessel with one mast, a mainsail, a forestay-sail, and a jib set to bowsprit-end: any sloop of narrow beam and deep draught: in quarrying, a joint parallel to the dip of the rocks: a small whisky bottle holding half a mutchkin, shaped for carrying in the hip pocket *(Scot.):* a medium-sized pig carcase, from which joints and fillets are taken; **cutt′ing** a dividing or lopping off: an incision: a piece cut from a newspaper: a piece of a plant cut off for propagation: an open excavation for road, railway, etc.: editing of film or recording. — *adj.* of a remark, etc., intended to be cruel or hurtful: of wind, penetrating. — *adj.* **cut-and-thrust** see **cut and thrust** below. — **cut′away** a coat with the skirt cut away in a curve in front: a model or picture showing the interior workings of something, with the overlying parts removed: in films or television, a shot of action that is related to, or happening simultaneously to, the central events. — *adj.* having parts cut away. — **cut′back** a going back in a plot to earlier happenings: a reduction or decrease, esp. in expenditure, workforce, production, etc.; **cut flowers** flowers cut from their plants for display in vases, etc.; **cut glass** flint glass shaped by cutting or grinding; **cut′-in** the act of cutting in. — *adj.* **cut′-leaved** having leaves deeply cut. — **cut′line** *(U.S.)* a caption; **cut′-off** that which cuts off or shortens, e.g. a straighter road, a shorter channel cut across a bend of a river: a bend thus cut off: a

device for shutting off steam, water, light, electricity, supply of cartridges in a magazine rifle, etc.: the point at which something ceases to operate or apply (also *adj.*); **cut'-out** the act of cutting out: something which has been cut out: a safety device, e.g. for breaking an electric circuit. — *adjs.* **cut'-over** (*U.S.*) (of land) having had its timber removed; **cut'-price** at a reduced rate. — **cut'purse** one who stole by slitting purses worn at the girdle: a pickpocket; **cut'-throat** an assassin: a ruffian: a modification of bridge, etc., played by three, each for himself; an open razor; **cutting edge** a part or area (of an organisation, branch of study, etc.) that breaks new ground, effects change and development, etc. — *adj.* murderous: ruinous. — **cut'-up** (orig. *U.S.*) a person who makes jokes or plays tricks: a literary collage, composed of cut-up and rearranged passages of prose or verse (also *adj.*); **cut'-water** the forepart of a ship's prow: the angular edge of a bridge-pier; **cut'worm** a caterpillar, esp. of the moth genus *Agrotis*, that cuts off young plants near the ground. — **a cut above** something distinctly better; **cut a dash** or **figure** to have a striking appearance; **cut and come again** abundant supply, from the notion of cutting a slice, and returning at will for another; **cut and cover** a method of forming a tunnel by making an open cutting, arching it over, and covering in; **cut and dry** or **cut and dried** ready made, fixed beforehand — from the state of herbs in the shop instead of the field; **cut and run** to be off quickly; **cut and thrust** in fencing, the use of the edges and the point of the weapon: swift, shrewd, and cleverly-calculated action or reaction, argument, etc. (*adj.* **cut'-and-thrust'**); **cut back** to prune close to the stem: to revert to a previous scene: to reduce; **cut both ways** of a decision, action, situation, etc., to have or result in both advantages and disadvantages; **cut corners** to turn corners by the quickest way, not keeping close to the edge of the road: to do something (e.g. a piece of work) with the minimum of effort and expenditure and therefore often imperfectly; **cut dead** to refuse to recognise; **cut down** to take down by cutting the rope on which one has been hanged: to bring down by cutting: to reduce, curtail; **cut down to size** to cause (a person) to feel less important or to be less conceited; **cut in** to interpose: to deprive someone of a dancing partner: to intercept on the telephone: to take one's place in a line of traffic in front of an overtaken vehicle, etc., esp. when meeting others: to come into a game by cutting a card: to give a share; **cut it fine** to take risks by calculating too narrowly; **cut it out** (*coll.*) to make an end of it, leave off; **cut it too fat** to overdo a thing; **cut loose** to break free from constraints; **cut no ice** see **ice**; **cut off** to sever: to isolate: put to an untimely death: to intercept: to stop: of an electrical device, to stop working, usu. automatically, esp. as a safety measure: to disinherit; **cut off with a shilling** to bequeath only a shilling: to disinherit; **cut one's coat according to one's cloth** to adapt oneself to circumstances; **cut one's losses** to have done with an unprofitable matter; **cut one's stick** to take one's departure; **cut one's teeth (on)** (*coll.*) to gain experience (by means of): to practise (on); **cut out** to shape: to contrive: to debar: to supplant: to separate from a herd: to pass out of a game on cutting a card: to pass out of a line of traffic in order to overtake: to capture and carry off (a ship) as from a harbour, etc., by getting between her and the shore: of an engine, suddenly to stop functioning; **cut out for** naturally fitted for; **cut short** to abridge: to make short by cutting: to silence by interruption; **cut teeth** to have teeth grow through the gums, as an infant; **cut up** to cut into pieces: to criticise severely: to turn out (well or ill) when divided into parts: (in *pass.*) to be deeply afflicted: to make jokes or play tricks (*U.S.*); **cut up rough** to take something amiss; **draw cuts** (*arch.*) to cast lots; **short cut** see **short**. [Origin unknown.]
cutaneous. See **cutis**.
cutch¹ *kuch, n.* catechu. [Malay *kachu*.]

cutch², kutch *kuch, n.* a set of vellum or tough paper sheets used by gold-beaters. [App. — Fr. *caucher*, cutch — L. *calcāre*, to tread.]
cutcha *kuch'ə, adj.* of dried mud: makeshift. [Hindi *kaccā*, raw.]
cutcherry, cutchery. Same as **kachahri**.
cute¹ *kūt, adj.* an aphetic form of **acute**: daintily or quaintly pleasing. — *adj.* **cute'sy** (esp. *U.S.*) sentimentally or affectedly cute, twee. — *n.* **cū'tie, cū'tey** a smart girl: something cute. — **cū'tie-pie** (*slang*) someone cute or sweet, a poppet.
cute². See **cuit**.
Cuthbert *kuth'bərt, n.* the apostle of Northumbria (c. 635–687): a derisive name given to one suspected of evading military service, and hence to any shirker. — **(St) Cuthbert's beads** perforated joints of encrinites found on Holy Island; **(St) Cuthbert's duck** the eiderduck.
cuticle, etc. See **cutis**.
cutikin. Same as **cuitikin**.
cutis *kū'tis, n.* the skin: the true skin, as distinguished from the cuticle. — *adj.* **cūtān'eous** belonging to the skin. — *n.* **cū'ticle** the outermost or thin skin: the dead skin at the edge of finger- and toenails: the waxy or corky layer on the epidermis in plants (*bot.*). — *adj.* **cūtic'ular** — *ns.* **cū'tin** material forming plant cuticle; **cūtinisā'tion, -z-.** — *v.t.* and *v.i.* **cū'tinise, -ize.** [L.]
cutlass *kut'ləs, n.* a short, broad sword, with one cutting edge, formerly used in the navy. [Fr. *coutelas*, augmentative from L. *cultellus*, dim. of *culter*, a ploughshare, a knife.]
cutler *kut'lər, n.* one who makes or sells knives. — *n.* **cut'lery** the business of a cutler: edged or cutting instruments in general: implements for eating food. [Fr. *coutelier* — O.Fr. *coutel* — L. *culter*, knife.]
cutlet *kut'lit, n.* rib and the meat belonging to it or similar piece of mutton, veal, etc.: other food made up in the shape of a cutlet. [Fr. *côtelette*, dim. of *côte*, from L. *costa*, a rib.]
cuttle¹ *kut'l, n.* a cephalopod mollusc (Sepia) remarkable for its power of ejecting a black, inky liquid (also **cutt'lefish**): extended to other cephalopods. — **cutt'le-bone** the internal shell of the cuttlefish, used for making tooth-powder, for polishing the softer metals and for cage-birds to sharpen their beaks on. [O.E. *cudele*.]
cuttle² *kut'l, n.* a knife (*obs.*): a bully (*Shak.*). [Perh. L. *cultellum*, knife; perh. also for **cut-throat, cutpurse**, or **cuttlefish**.]
cutto, cuttoe *kut'ō, n.* a large knife: — *pl.* **cutt'oes.** [Fr. *couteau.*]
cutty *kut'i, (Scot.) adj.* short, curtailed. — *n.* a short clay pipe: a short, dumpy girl: applied to a woman, a term of reprobation, serious or playful: a mischievous or teasing girl or woman. — **cutt'y-sark'** a short shift, or its wearer; **cutt'y-stool** the stool of repentance in old Scottish church discipline. [**cut.**]
cuvée *kü-vā, kōō-vā', n.* a vat of blended wine of uniform quality. [Fr.]
cuvette *küv-et, kü-vet', n.* a trench sunk along the middle of a dry ditch or moat, a cunette. [Fr.]
cuz (*kuz*). An obsolete spelling of **coz**.
cwm *kōōm, n.* the Welsh name for a valley or glen: a cirque (*geol.*). [W., cf. **coomb¹**, and Fr. **combe**.]
cyan *sī'an, n.* a greenish blue: printers' blue ink. — *adj.* of a greenish blue colour. — **cyan(o)-** in composition, blue or dark blue: relating to, indicating, cyanide or cyanogen. — *ns.* **cyan'amide** the amide of cyanogen, a white crystalline substance ($NCNH_2$): loosely applied to **calcium cyanamide** ($NCNCa$) a fertiliser; **cyanate** (*sī'ən-āt*) a salt of cyanic acid. — *adj.* **cyan'ic** of or belonging to cyanogen. — *n.* **cy'anide** a direct compound of cyanogen with a metal. — *v.t.* to treat with a cyanide. — *ns.* **cy'aniding** extraction of gold or silver from ore by means of potassium cyanide; **cy'anin** a plant pigment, blue in cornflower, but red in the rose because of its reaction with acids; **cy'anine** any of a group of dyes used as sensitisers in photography. —

v.t. **cy'anise, -ize** to turn into cyanide. — *ns.* **cyanite** see **kyanite; cyanoac'rylate** any of several strong, fast-setting adhesives derived from acrylic acid; **cyanocobal'amin** (*cobal*t and vit*amin*) vitamin B$_{12}$, which has a large and complicated molecule, in one form including a cyanide group, in all forms including a cobalt atom; **cyan'ogen** (*-jen*) a compound of carbon and nitrogen (CN)$_2$ forming a colourless, poisonous gas with an almond-like odour, an essential ingredient of Prussian blue; **cyanom'eter** an instrument for measuring the blueness of the sky or ocean. — *adj.* **cy'anosed** (*coll.*). — *n.* **cyanō'sis** morbid blueness of the skin. — *adj.* **cyanŏt'ic.** — *ns.* **cyan'otype** blue-print; **cyan'ūret** (*obs.*) a cyanide. — **cyanic acid** an acid composed of cyanogen, oxgen and hydrogen (HCNO). [Gr. *kyanos*, blue.]

Cyanophyceae *sī-ən-ō-fish'i-ē, n.pl.* the blue-green algae, simply organised unicellular or filamentous thallophytes growing in water and on damp earth, rocks or bark. [See **cyan.**]

cyathus *sī'ə-thəs, n.* the ancient Greek filling or measuring cup — about $^1/_{12}$ of a pint. — *n.* **Cyath'ea** a genus of tree-ferns, often with cup-shaped indusium, giving name to the family **Cyatheā'ceae.** — *adj.* **cy'athiform** (or *-ath'*) cup-shaped. — *ns.* **cyath'ium** the characteristic inflorescence of the spurges (*pl.* **cyath'ia**); **Cyathophyll'um** (Gr. *phyllon*, leaf) a fossil genus of cup-corals. [Gr. *kyathos*.]

Cybele *sib'i-lē, n.* a flora, treatise on the plants of a region. [L. *Cybelē* — Gr. *Kybelē*, the mother goddess.]

cybernetics *sī-bər-net'iks, n. sing.* the comparative study of automatic communication and control in functions of living bodies and in mechanical electronic systems (such as in computers). — *adj.* **cybernet'ic.** — *n.* **cybernet'icist** (*-sist*). [Gr. *kybernētēs*, a steersman.]

cycad *sī'kad, n.* one of an order of gymnospermous plants, more or less akin to conifers but superficially resembling ferns and palms. — *adj.* **cycadā'ceous.** [Formed from supposed Gr. *kykas*, a misreading of *koīkas*, accus. pl. of *koīx*, doum-palm.]

cycl-. See **cycl(o)-.**

cyclamate *sik'la-māt, sīk', n.* any of a number of very sweet substances derived from petrochemicals, formerly used as sweetening agents in food, soft drinks, etc.

Cyclamen *sik'lə-mən, n.* a S. European genus of Primulaceae, with nodding flowers and bent-back petals: (without *cap.*) a plant of the genus. [Gr. *kyklamīnos.*]

Cyclanthaceae *sī-klan-thā'si-ē, n.pl.* a tropical S. American family of plants aking to the screw-pines, with a spadix sometimes resembling a pile of discs. — *adj.* **cyclanthā'ceous.** [Gr. *kyklos*, wheel, *anthos*, flower.]

cycle *sī'kl, n.* a period of time in which events happen in a certain order, and which constantly repeats itself: a recurring series of changes: an age: an imaginary circle or orbit in the heavens: a series of poems, romances, etc., centring in a figure or event (also **cy'clus**): a group of songs with related subjects: a bicycle or tricycle: complete series of changes in a periodically varying quantity, e.g. an alternating current, during one period: sequence of computer operations which continues until a criterion for stoppage is reached, or the time of this. — *v.t.* to cause to pass through a cycle of operations or events: to transport or accompany on a cycle. — *v.i.* to move in cycles: to ride on a cycle. — *n.* **cy'cler** (*U.S.*) a cyclist. — *adjs.* **cy'clic, -al** pertaining to or containing a cycle: recurring in cycles: arranged in a ring or rings. — *n.* **cyclical'ity.** — *adv.* **cy'clically.** — *ns.* **cy'clicism; cyclic'ity; cy'cling; cy'clist** one who rides on a cycle; **cy'cloid** a figure like a circle: a curve traced by a point on the circumference of a circle which rolls along a straight line: a person of cyclothymic temperament, or one suffering from a cyclic type of manic-depressive psychosis. — *adj.* nearly circular: (of fish) having scales with evenly curved border: cyclothymic: characterised by swings of mood (*psych.*). —

adj. **cycloid'al.** — *ns.* **cycloid'ian** a fish with cycloid scales; **cyclō'sis** circulation: — *pl.* **cyclō'ses** (*-sēz*). — **cy'cle-car** a small light motor-car; **cy'cleway** a track or path, often running alongside a road, constructed and reserved for cyclists; **cyclic compound** a closed-chain or ring compound in which the ring consists of carbon atoms only (*carbocyclic compound*) or of carbon atoms linked with one or more other atoms (*heterocyclic compound*); **cy'clo-cross** a pedal-bicycle race over rough country in the course of which bicycles have to be carried over natural obstacles. — **cycle per second** see **hertz.** [Gr. *kyklos*, circle.]

cycl(o)- *sīk-l(ō)-*, in composition, cycle: ring: circle: cyclic compound. [Gr. *kyklos*, circle.]

cyclo *sī'klō, (coll.) n.* a trishaw: — *pl.* **cy'clos.** [**cycle**.]

cyclograph *sī'klō-gräf, n.* an instrument for describing arcs of circles without compasses: a camera that can reproduce the whole surface of a cylindrical object as a single photograph. — *adj.* **cyclograph'ic.** [**cyclo-**, and **graph.**]

cyclohexane *sī-klō-heks'ān, n.* a highly flammable chemical, C$_6$H$_{12}$, with a pungent odour, used in making synthetic fibres, as a paint solvent, etc. [**cyclo-** and **hexane.**]

cycloid. See **cycle.**

cyclolith *sī'klō-lith, n.* a peristalith or stone circle. [**cyclo-**, and Gr. *lithos*, a stone.]

cyclone *sī'klōn, n.* a system of winds blowing spirally inwards towards a centre of low barometric pressure: loosely, a wind-storm: a separating apparatus, a kind of centrifuge. — *adj.* **cyclŏn'ic.** [Gr. *kyklōn*, contr. pr.p. of *kykloein*, to whirl round.]

cyclopaedia, cyclopedia *sī-klō-pē'di-ə, n.* a shortened form of **encyclopaedia.** — *adj.* **cyclopae'dic, cyclope'dic.**

cyclopean, -pian, etc. See **Cyclops.**

cyclopropane *sī-klō-prō'pān, n.* a cyclic hydrocarbon C$_3$H$_6$, a general anaesthetic. [**cyclo-** and **propane.**]

Cyclops *sī'klops, n.* one of a fabled race of giants who lived chiefly in Sicily, with one eye in the middle of the forehead (*pl.* **Cy'clops, Cyclō'pes,** or **Cy'clopses**): (without *cap.*) a one-eyed monster (*pl.* **cyclō'pes**): a genus of minute freshwater copepods with an eye in front: (without *cap.*) a member of the genus (*pl.* **cy'clops**). — *adjs.* **cyclopē'an, cyclō'pian, cyclŏp'ic** relating to or like the Cyclopes: giant-like: vast: pertaining to a prehistoric style of masonry with immense stones of irregular form. [Gr. *kyklōps*, pl. *kyklōpĕs* — *kyklos*, a circle, and *ōps*, an eye.]

cyclorama *sī-klō-rä'mə, n.* a circular panorama: a curved background in stage and cinematograph sets, used to give impression of sky distance, and for lighting effects. — *adj.* **cycloram'ic.** [**cyclo-**, and Gr. *horāma*, view.]

cycloserine *sī-klō-sēr'in, n.* an antibiotic used against tuberculosis. [**cyclo-**, and *serine*, an amino acid.]

cyclospermous *sī-klō-spûr'məs, (bot.) adj.* with embryo bent round the endosperm. [**cyclo-**, and Gr. *sperma*, seed.]

cyclosporin A *sī-klō-spör'in ā, n.* an extract of a soil fungus, used as an anti-rejection drug in transplant surgery. [**cyclo-**, and Gr. *spora*, seed.]

Cyclostomata *sī-klō-stō'mə-tə, n.pl.* a class of animals with fixed open mouth, including the lampreys. — *n.* **cy'clostome** a member of the class. — *adj.* **cyclostomous** (*-klos'to-məs*). [**cyclo-**, and Gr. *stŏma*, mouth.]

cyclostyle *sī'klō-stīl, n.* an apparatus for multiplying copies of a writing by use of a pen with a small puncturing wheel. — Also *v.t.* [**cyclo-** and **style.**]

cyclothymia *sī-klō-thī'mi-ə, n.* a temperament inclined to alternation of high and low spirits. — *n.* **cy'clothyme** a person having such a temperament. — *adj.* **cyclothy'mic.** [**cyclo-**, and Gr. *thymos*, spirit.]

cyclotron *sī'klō-tron, n.* See **accelerator** under **accelerate.**

cyder. Same as **cider.**

cyesis *sī-ē'sis, n.* pregnancy: — *pl.* **cyē'ses** (*-sēz*). [Gk. *kyēsis.*]

cygnet *sig'nit, n.* a young swan. [Dim. from L. *cygnus*, directly or through Fr. *cygne*, which seems to be a reshaping of *cisne* — L.L. *cicinus*, L. *cycnus* — Gr. *kyknos*, a swan.]

cylinder *sil'in-dər, n.* a solid figure of uniform cross-section generated by a straight line remaining parallel to a fixed axis and moving round a closed curve — ordinarily in a circle perpendicular to the axis (giving a *right circular cylinder*): a roller-shaped object: a cylindrical part, solid or hollow, as a rotating part of a printing press, the tubular chamber in which a piston works (*mech.*). — *adjs.* **cylindrā'ceous** somewhat cylindrical; **cylin'dric, -al.** — *adv.* **cylin'drically.** — *n.* **cylindricity** (*-dris'i-ti*). — *adj.* **cylin'driform** in the form of a cylinder. — *ns.* **cylin'drite** a mineral of cylindrical habit, compound of tin, lead, antimony, and sulphur; **cyl'indroid** a body like a cylinder. — Also *adj.* — **cyl'inder-block** a casing in which the cylinders of an internal-combustion engine are contained; **cyl'inder= head** the closed end of the cylinder of an internal-combustion engine; **cylinder lock** a type of lock comprising a movable cylinder which can be rotated inside a fixed cylinder only when the correct key is inserted; **cyl'inder-seal'** (*ant.*) a stone engraved in intaglio, used in the ancient East for sealing clay tablets by rolling. — **firing, working,** etc. **on all cylinders** working at full strength or perfectly: in good condition. [Gr. *kylindros*, roller, *kylindein*, to roll.]

cylix *sil'* or *sīl'iks, n.* a shallow two-handled stemmed drinking cup: — *pl.* **cyl'ices** (*-sēz*). — Also **kyl'ix.** [Gr. *kylix, -ikos*.]

cyma *sī'mə, n.* an ogee moulding of the cornice (**cy'ma rec'ta** concave in front, convex behind; **cy'ma rever'sa** convex in front, concave behind). — *ns.* **cy'mograph** (improperly **cy'magraph**) an instrument for tracing the outline of mouldings (see also **kymograph**); **cymā'tium** a cyma. [Gr. *kyma*, a billow.]

cymar, cimar *si-mär', n.* a loose coat of various styles, formerly worn by women: an undergarment, a shift: a chimer: [Fr. *simarre*, of comparable meanings, — Sp. *zamarra*, sheepskin; cf. **chimer.**]

cymbal *sim'bəl, n.* a hollow brass plate-like musical instrument, beaten with a stick, etc. or against another of a pair. — *ns.* **cym'balist** a cymbal-player; **cym'balo** the dulcimer: — *pl.* **cym'baloes, -os.** — *adj.* **cym'biform** boat-shaped. [L. *cymbalum* — Gr. *kymbalon* — *kymbē*, the hollow of a vessel.]

cymbidium *sim-bid'i-əm, n.* any orchid of the genus **Cymbidium**, with colourful, long-lasting flowers: — *pl.* **cymbid'iums** or **-ia.** [Mod. L. *Cymbidium* — L. *cymba*, a boat.]

cyme[1] *sīm*, (*bot.*) *n.* a young shoot: any sympodial inflorescence, the main shoot ending in a flower, the subsequent flowers growing on successive lateral branches. — *adjs.* **cym'oid, cym'ose, cym'ous.** [L. *cyma, cīma* — Gr. *kyma*, a sprout.]

cyme[2] *sī'əm, n.* (*Shak.*) app. for **Sium.**

cymograph. See under **cyma.**

cymoid. See **cyme**[1].

cymophane *sī'mō-fān, n.* cat's eye, a variety of chrysoberyl with wavy opalescence. — *adj.* **cymophanous** (*-mof'ə-nəs*) opalescent. [Gr. *kyma*, wave, *phainein*, to show.]

cymose, cymous. See **cyme**[1].

cymotrichous *sī-mot'ri-kəs*, (*anthrop.*) *adj.* wavy-haired. — *n.* **cymot'richy.** [Gr. *kyma*, wave, *thrix*, gen. *trichos*, hair.]

Cymric *kim'rik, kum'*, or *sim'*, *adj.* Welsh. — *n.* **Cym'ry** the Welsh. [W. *Cymru*, Wales.]

cynanche *si-nang'kē, n.* disease of the throat, esp. quinsy. [Gr. *kyōn*, a dog, *anchein*, to throttle.]

cynegetic *sin-ē-jet'ik, adj.* relating to hunting. [Gr. *kynēgetēs*, huntsman — *kyōn, kynos*, dog, *hēgetēs*, leader.]

cynic, -al *sin'ik, -əl, adjs.* dog-like: surly: snarling: disinclined to recognise or believe in goodness or selflessness. — *ns.* **Cyn'ic** one of a sect of philosophers founded by Antisthenes of Athens (born c. 444 B.C.), characterised by an ostentatious contempt for riches, arts, science, and amusements — so called from their morose manners: (without *cap.*) a morose man: (without *cap.*) a snarler: (without *cap.*) one who takes a pessimistic view of human motives and actions; **cyn'icism** (*-i-sizm*) surliness: contempt for and suspicion of human nature: heartlessness, misanthropy: a cynical remark. — *adv.* **cyn'ically.** — *n.* **cyn'icalness.** [Gr. *kynikos*, dog-like — *kyōn, kynos*, dog, or perh. from *Kynosarges*, the gymnasium where Antisthenes taught.]

Cynips *sin'ips, sīn'ips, n.* a genus of gall-wasps, giving name to the family **Cynip'idae.** [Origin doubtful.]

Cynocephalus *sin-* or *sīn-ō-sef'ə-ləs, n.* the so-called flying lemur or Galeopithecus: the dog-faced baboon: a dog-headed man. [Gr. *kyōn, kynos*, dog, *kephalē*, head.]

cynomolgus *sin-ə-mol'gəs, n.* a type of macaque: — *pl.* **cynomol'gī.** [Gr. *Kynamolgoi*, a Libyan tribe, lit. 'dog-milkers', — *kyon, kynos*, dog, *amelgein*, to milk.]

cynophilist, -ia, cynophobia. See **canophilist, canophobia.**

cynosure *sin'* or *sīn'ō-shōōr, n.* the dog's tail, or Lesser Bear (*Ursa Minor*), the constellation containing the North Star: the North Star itself: hence anything that strongly attracts attention or admiration. — *n.* **Cynosur'us** dog's-tail grass. [Gr. *kyōn, kynos*, a dog, *ourā*, a tail.]

Cyperus *sip-, sīp-ē'rus, n.* a tropical genus of the sedge family, **Cyperā'ceae**, including papyrus. — *adj.* **cyperaceous** (*-ə-rā'shəs*) belonging to, or like, sedge plants. [From Gr. *kypeiros*, sedge.]

cypher. Same as **cipher.**

cy pres *sē prā*, in the law of charitable trusts in England, the principle of applying the money to some object *as near as possible* to the one specified, when that is impracticable. [O.Fr., so near.]

cypress[1] *sī'prəs, -pris, n.* a coniferous tree (Cupressus), whose branches used to be carried at funerals: hence a symbol of death: extended to various other trees, esp. in America to the swamp-growing deciduous conifer *Taxodium distichum.* — **cy'press-knee** a hollow upgrowth from the root of the swamp-cypress, a breathing organ; **cy'press-swamp'.** [O.Fr. *ciprès* (Fr. *cyprès*) — L. *cupressus* — Gr. *kyparissos*.]

cypress[2] *sī'prəs, -pris, n.* a thin transparent black stuff like crape. — *adj.* of cypress. — Also **cy'prus.** [Prob. from the island of *Cyprus*.]

Cyprian *sip'ri-ən, adj.* of the island of Cyprus: lewd, licentious — Cyprus being the place where Aphrodite was worshipped. — *n.* a Cypriot: (also without *cap.*) a lewd woman. — *n.* **Cyp'riot(e)** a native of Cyprus. — **Cyp'ro-Mino'an** an undeciphered Bronze Age script of Cyprus. — Also *adj.*

cyprid. See **Cypris.**

Cyprinus *si-prī'nəs, n.* the carp genus of fishes, giving name to the fam. **Cyprinidae** (*si-prin'i-dē*). — *adjs.* **cyprine** (*sip'rīn*). — *n.* **Cyprin'odont** (Gr. *odous, odontos*, tooth) any of several esp. marine types of soft-finned tropical or sub-tropical fishes related to the carp, but with toothed jaws, including guppies and sword-tails. — Also *adj.* — *adj.* **cyp'rinoid** (*-rin-oid*) resembling the carp. [L. — Gr. *kyprīnos*, a kind of carp.]

Cypriot(e). See **Cyprian.**

Cypripedium *sip-ri-pē'di-əm, n.* a genus of orchids: (without *cap.*) a plant of the genus, lady's slipper: — *pl.* **cypripē'dia.** [Gr. *Kypris*, Aphrodite, *podion*, a little foot, modified by L. *pēs*, foot.]

Cypris *sip'ris, n.* a genus of freshwater ostracod crustaceans: (without *cap.*) a bivalved barnacle (*pl.* **cyp'-ridēs**). — *n.* **cyp'rid** a member of the genus: a cypris. [Gr. *Kypris*, Aphrodite.]

Cypro-Minoan. See **Cyprian.**

cyprus. Same as **cypress**[2].

Cyrenaic *sī-rin-ā'ik, adj.* pertaining to *Cyrēnē*, or to the hedonism of its philosopher Aristippus.

Cyrillic *sir-il'ik, adj.* pertaining to the alphabet attributed to St Cyril (9th cent.), distinguished from the other

Slavonic alphabet, the Glagolitic.

cyst *sist, n.* (*biol.*) a bladder or bag-like structure, whether normal or containing morbid matter: a membrane enclosing an organism in a resting stage. — *adjs.* **cyst'ic, cyst'iform.** — *ns.* **cysticercō'sis** infestation by cysticerci; **cysticer'cus** (Gr. *kerkos,* tail) a bladder-worm: — *pl.* **-cercī; cyst'id, cystid'ean** a cystoid; **cystī'tis** inflammation of the bladder; **cyst'ocarp** (Gr. *karpos,* fruit) the fructification in red seaweeds; **cys'tocele** (Gr. *kēlē,* tumour) hernia of the bladder; **cyst'oid** any echinoderm of the extinct class **Cystoid'ea,** globular or bladder-like animals enclosed in calcareous plates, stalked or sessile; **cyst'olith** (Gr. *lithos,* stone) a stalked limy concretion in some plant cells; **cyst'oscope** (Gr. *skopeein,* to view) an instrument for examining the inside of the bladder; **cystos'copy; cystot'omy** (Gr. *tomē,* a cut) the operation of cutting into the bladder. — **cystic fibrosis** (*fī-brō'sis*) a hereditary disease, appearing in infancy or childhood, characterised by too great production of mucus and of fibrous tissue, and the presence of cysts, conditions which interfere with digestion, breathing, etc. [L.L. *cystis* — Gr. *kystis,* a bladder.]

cyte *sīt, ns.* (*biol.; rare*) a cell. — *ns.* **cyt'ase** an enzyme that breaks down cellulose. — **cyto-** in composition, cell. — *n.* **cyt'ochrome** any of a group of substances in living cells, of great importance in cell oxidation; **cyt'ode** a protoplasm body without nucleus; **cytodiagnos'is** medical diagnosis following the close examination of the cells of the body tissues or fluids, e.g. the smear test for cervical cancer; **cytodifferentiā'tion** the process of specialisation, in cell development; **cytogen'esis** cell formation. — *adj.* **cytogenet'ic.** — *adv.* **cytogenet'ically.** — *n.* **cytogenet'icist.** — *n. sing.* **cytogenet'ics** genetics in relation to cytology. — *adj.* **cyt'oid** cell-like. — *n.* **cytokīn'in** (Gr. *kineein,* to move) any of numerous substances which regulate plant growth by inducing cell division. — *adj.* **cytolog'ical.** — *ns.* **cytol'ogist; cytol'ogy** that part of biology that deals with cells; **cytol'ysis** (Gr. *lysis,* loosening) dissolution of cells; **cy'tomegalovī'rus** any of a group of DNA-containing viruses which cause **cytomegalic inclusion disease,** a disease characterised by cell enlargement in the brain, liver, lungs, etc. of newborn babies; **cyt'on** the body of a nerve-cell; **cytopathol'ogy** the study of cells in illness; **cyt'oplasm** (Gr. *plasma,* form, body) the protoplasm of a cell apart from that of the nucleus; **cy'tosine** one of the four bases in deoxyribonucleic acids, in close association with guanine; **cytoskel'eton** the internal fibrous structure within cytoplasm, determining the shape of a cell, and influencing its movement. — *adjs.* **cytoskel'etal; cytotox'ic.** — *ns.* **cytotoxic'ity; cytotox'in** a substance poisonous to cells. [Gr. *kȳtos,* vessel, hollow.]

Cytherean *sith-ə-rē'ən, adj.* pertaining to Aphrodite. [L. *Cytherēa* — Gr. *Kythereia,* Cytherean (goddess), Aphrodite, worshipped in the island of *Kythēra.*]

Cytisus *sit'i-səs, n.* the broom genus of Papilionaceae: (without *cap.*) a plant of the genus: — *pl.* **cyt'isī.** — *n.* **cyt'isine** a poisonous alkaloid found in laburnum. [Gr. *kytisos,* a kind of medick, laburnum.]

cyto-, cytochrome, etc., **cytology,** etc., **cytotoxin.** See **cyte.**

czapka. See **chapka.**

czar, czarina, etc. See **tsar,** etc.

czardas. A faulty spelling of **csárdás.**

Czech *chek, n.* a member of a westerly branch of the Slavs, the Bohemians, and sometimes also the Moravians: a Czechoslovak: the language of the Czechs, Bohemian, closely allied to Polish. — Also *adj.* — *adj.* (*rare*) **Czech'ic.** — *n.* **Czechoslō'vak** a native or citizen of *Czechoslovakia:* a member of the Slavic people including the Czechs and the Slovaks. — Also *adj.* — *adj.* **Czechoslovak'ian.** [Polish.]

D

D, d dē, n. the fourth letter in our alphabet, as well as in the Phoenician, Hebrew, Greek, and Latin, from which last it was immediately derived — its sound the voiced dental stop: the second note in the natural scale (*mus.*): as a Roman numeral, D = 500: the semicircular marking on a billiards table. — **D-day** (dē′dā; D for unnamed *d*ay) the opening day (6 June 1944) of the Allied invasion of Europe in World War II: any critical day of action: decimal day (15 February 1971), day of conversion from £.s.d. to decimal money; **D′-mark** Deutsche mark (see **mark**²); **D′-notice** (D for defence) a notice officially sent to newspapers, etc., asking them not to publish certain information; **D′-ring** a metal ring or clip in the shape of a capital D, used in mountaineering and parachuting harnesses, etc.

'd *d*, a shortened form of **had, would.** See also **'dst.**

da¹, dah dä, *n.* a heavy Burmese knife. [Burmese *da.*]

da² dä, *n.* dialect form of **dad¹.**

dab¹ *dab, v.t.* to strike gently with something soft or moist: to peck: to smear: to dress (the face of stone) using a steel point: — *pr.p.* **dabb′ing;** *pa.t.* and *pa.p.* **dabbed.** — *n.* a gentle blow: a small lump of anything soft or moist: (usu. in *pl.*) a fingerprint (*slang*): (with *cap.*, in *pl.*) Fingerprint Department of New Scotland Yard: a species (*Limanda limanda*) of fish of the Pleuronectidae: applied to other (esp. to small) flatfish. — *ns.* **dabb′er** a pad for dabbing ink on blocks or plates; **dabb′ity** (*Scot.*) a cheap pottery figure sold at fairgrounds, etc. — **dab′chick** the little grebe. [Cf. M. and early Mod. Du. *dabben*, to pinch; Ger. *Tappe*, a pat; confused with **daub** and **tap.**]

dab² *dab, n.* an expert person. — Also *adj.* — *n.* **dab′ster** (*coll.*). — **a dab hand at** an expert at. [Origin unknown.]

dabble *dab′l, v.t.* to shake about in liquid: to spatter with moisture. — *v.i.* to play in liquid with hands or feet: to do anything in a trifling or small way. — *n.* the act of dabbling. — *n.* **dabb′ler.** — *n.* and *adj.* **dabb′ling.** — *adv.* **dabb′lingly.** [Freq. of **dab.**]

dabchick. See **dab¹.**

Daboecia. See **St Dabeoc's heath** under **saint.**

da capo dä kä′pō, (*mus.*) an indication in music that the performer must return to the beginning of the piece and conclude at the double bar marked *Fine*: — abbrev. **D.C.** [It., from the head or beginning.]

d'accord da-kör, (*Fr.*) *interj.* and *adv.* agreed: in tune.

dace dās, **dare** dār, **dart** därt, *ns.* a small river fish (*Leuciscus vulgaris*) of the carp family and chub genus. [M.E. *darce* — O.Fr. *dars* — L.L. *dardus*, a dart or javelin — of Gmc. origin; from its quickness.]

dacha dä′chə, *n.* a country house in Russia. [Russ., orig. gift (esp. from a ruler).]

dachshund däks′hŏŏnt, daks′hŏŏnd, -hŏŏnt, *n.* a badger-dog or teckel, of German origin, with long body and very short legs. [Ger. *Dachs,* badger, *Hund,* dog.]

dacite dā′sīt, *n.* a fine-grained eruptive rock composed of quartz and plagioclase, with mica, etc. [From *Dacia*, a Roman province.]

dacker dak′ər, **daker, daiker** dā′kər, (*Scot.*) *vs.i.* to lounge, saunter: to potter. [Origin unknown.]

dacoit, dakoit dä-koit′, *n.* one of a gang of robbers in Indian and Burma. — *ns.* **dacoit′y, dakoit′i, dacoit′age** robbery by gang-robbers, brigandage. [Hind. *dākait, dakait,* a robber.]

Dacron® dak′ron, *n.* U.S. name for **Terylene®.**

dactyl dak′til, *n.* a digit (*zool.*): a foot of three syllables, one long followed by two short, like the joints of a finger (*classical pros.*): in English, etc., a foot of three syllables, the first accented. — *adjs.* **dac′tylar, dactyl′ic.**

— *adv.* **dactyl′ically.** — *ns.* **dactyliog′raphy, dactyliol′ogy** the study or lore of finger-rings or engraved gems; **dactyl′iomancy** divination by means of a finger-ring; **Dac′tylis** the cocksfoot grass genus; **dac′tylist** a writer of dactylic verse; **dactyl′ogram** (or *dak′*) a fingerprint; **dactylog′raphy** the study of fingerprints: dactylology; **dactylol′ogy** the art of talking with the fingers, like the deaf and dumb; **dactylos′copy** identification by, or classification of, fingerprints. [Gr. *daktylos,* a finger, *daktylios,* a finger-ring.]

dad¹ *dad,* **daddy** dad′i, (*childish* and *coll.*) *ns.* father: used familiarly in addressing any older man. — **dadd′y=long′-legs** the crane-fly. — **the daddy of them all** (*coll.*) the biggest, best, etc. [History uncertain.]

dad², daud *dad, död,* (*dial.*) *vs.t.* to throw against something: to dash, thump. — *ns.* a lump: a blow, thump. [Der. unknown.]

Dada, Dadaism dä′dä(-izm), *ns.* a short-lived (from 1916 — *c.* 1920) movement in art and literature which sought to abandon all form and throw off all tradition. — *n.* **Da′daist.** — *adj.* **Dadais′tic.** [Fr., *dada,* hobby-horse, a name said to have been arbitrarily chosen by the German writer Hugo Ball.]

daddle¹ dad′l, (*dial.*) *v.i.* to walk in an unsteady manner, as a child or very old person: to totter. [Perh. conn. with **dawdle.**]

daddle² dad′l, (*dial.*) *n.* the hand. [Uncertain.]

daddock dad′ək, (*dial.*) *n.* the heart of a rotten tree. [Perh. conn. with **dodder².**]

daddy. See **dad¹.**

dado dā′dō, *n.* the cubic block forming the body of a pedestal (*classical archit.*): a skirting of wood along the lower part of the walls of a room, often merely represented by wall-paper, painting, etc.: — *pl.* **dā′dos, dā′does.** — *v.t.* to furnish with a dado. [It.; see **die².**]

daedal, daedale dē′dəl, **Daedalian** dē-dā′li-ən, *adjs.* formed with art: displaying artistic or inventive skill: intricate, varied. — *adj.* **daedal′ic.** — Also **dē′dal, dēdā′lian.** [From L. *Daedalus,* Gr. *Daidalos,* the mythical artist who constructed the Cretan labyrinth and made wings for his son Icarus and himself.]

daemon dē′mən, **daimon** dī-′mōn, *ns.* a spirit holding a middle place between gods and men, as the daemon or good genius of Socrates. — *adjs.* **daemonic, daimonic** (-mon′ik) supernatural: of power or intelligence more than human: inspired. [L. *daemōn, -onis* — Gr. *daimōn, -onos,* a spirit, a genius, and later a devil; see **demon.**]

dae-nettle. See **day-nettle.**

daff¹ *daf,* (*arch.*) *v.i.* to make sport, to play the fool. — *n.* **daff′ing** foolery, gaiety. [Origin doubtful.]

daff² *daf,* (*Shak.*) *v.t.* to put off: to turn aside, dismiss, put by. [A variant of **doff.**]

daff³. Short for **daffodil.**

daffodil daf′ə-dil, often *coll.* **daff, daff′y,** *ns.* a yellow-flowered narcissus. — Also (*poet.*) **daffadowndilly** (*daf′ə-down-dil′i*), **daffodill′y.** — *adj.* pale yellow. [M.E. *affodille* — O.Fr. *asphodile* — Gr. *asphodelos,* asphodel; the *d* is unexplained.]

daffy¹ *daf′i, n.* an 'elixir of health' invented by one Thomas *Daffy* (d. 1680).

daffy² *daf′i,* (*coll.*) *adj.* daft, crazy. [**daff¹.**]

daffy³. Short for **daffodil.**

daft däft, (*coll.*) *adj.* silly: weak-minded: insane: unreasonably merry. — *n.* **daft′ie.** — *adv.* **daft′ly.** — *n.* **daft′ness.** — **daft days** (*Scot.*) the period of festivity and leisure at Christmas and New Year: the carefree days of one's youth. [M.E. *daffte,* mild, meek. See **deft.**]

daftar *daf'tär*, (*Ind.*) *n.* an office, esp. a military orderly room: a bundle of documents. [Hindi.]

dag[1] *dag, n.* a heavy pistol of the 15th and 16th centuries. [Origin uncertain.]

dag[2] *dag, n.* a tag, scallop, or laciniation (*obs.*): a dirt-clotted tuft of wool on a sheep (also **dag'lock**). — *v.t.* to cut into dags: to bedraggle (*obs.*): to cut off a sheep's dags. [Origin uncertain.]

dagaba. See **dagoba.**

dagga *dag'ə, duhh'ə, n.* Indian hemp (called true dagga): an African labiate plant *Leonotis leonurus* or other species (Cape or red dagga) smoked as a narcotic, called the love-drug. [Hottentot *dachab.*]

dagger *dag'ər, n.* a knife or short sword for stabbing at close quarters: an obelus, a mark of reference † (*print.*). — **dagg'erboard** (*naut.*) a light, narrow, completely removable centreboard. — **at daggers drawn** in a state of hostility; **double dagger** diesis ‡; **look daggers** to look in a hostile manner. [M E. *dagger*; cf. Fɪ. *dague.*]

daggle *dag'l, v.t.* and *v.i.* to wet or grow wet by dragging or sprinkling. — **dagg'le-tail** a draggle-tail. [Freq. of **dag**[2].]

daglock. See **dag**[2].

dago *dā'gō,* (*offensive*) *n.* a man of Spanish, Portuguese, or Italian origin: — *pl.* **dā'goes.** [Prob. Sp. *Diego* — L. *Jacōbus,* James.]

dagoba, dagaba *dä'gə-bä, n.* in Sri Lanka, a tope (for Buddhist relics). [Sinh. *dāgaba.*]

Dagon *dā'gən, -gon, n.* the national god of the Philistines, half-man, half-fish. [Heb. *dāgōn — dāg,* fish.]

daguerreotype *də-ger'ō-tīp, n.* a method of photography by mercury vapour development of silver iodide exposed on a copper plate: a photograph so taken: a faithful representation (*obs.*). — *v.t.* to photograph by that process. — *adj.* **daguerr'ean.** — *ns.* **daguerre'otyper, daguerre'otypist; daguerre'otypy** the art of daguerreotyping. [Fr., from Louis *Daguerre* (1789–1851).]

dagwood. Same as **dogwood** (see under **dog**).

dah[1] *dä, n.* a word representing the dash in the spoken form of Morse code. See also **dit.**

dah[2]. See **da**[1].

dahabiyah, -iyeh, -ieh, -eeah *dä-hä-bē'(y)ä, -ə, n.* a Nile sailing boat. [Ar. *dhahabīyah,* golden.]

dahl. See **dal.**

Dahlia *dāl'yə,* in U.S. *däl'yə, n.* a Mexican genus of perennial garden composites with large brightly-coloured flowers and tuberous roots: (without *cap.*) any plant of this genus. [From *Dahl,* an 18th-cent. Swedish botanist.]

daidle *dā'dl,* (*Scot.*) *v.i.* to waddle: to stagger: to idle about: to trifle: to potter. — *adj.* **daid'ling** feeble: dawdling. [**daddle**[1].]

daiker[1] *dā'kər,* (*Scot.*) *v.i.* to deck out. [Perh. Fr. *décorer.*]

daiker[2]. See **dacker.**

daikon *dī'kon, n.* a long white Japanese root vegetable of the radish family, similar to a mooli. [Jap.]

Dáil (Eireann) *doil (ār'ən), n.* the lower house of the legislature of the Republic of Ireland. [Ir., 'assembly (of Ireland)'.]

daily *dā'li, adj.* and *adv.* every day. — *n.* a daily paper: a non-resident servant: (in *pl.*) film rushes (*U.S.*). — **daily bread** one's living, livelihood; **daily double** in horse racing, a single bet on the winners of two races on the same day; **daily dozen** physical exercises done regularly, usu. every morning (*coll.*). [**day.**]

daimen *dem'ən, däm'ən,* (*Scot.*) *adj.* occasional. [Origin obscure.]

daimio *dī'myō, n.* a Japanese territorial noble under the old feudal system: — *pl.* **dai'mios.** [Jap.]

daimon. See **daemon.**

daine (*Shak.*). Same as **deign.**

dainty *dān'ti, adj.* pleasant to the palate: delicate: tasteful: fastidious: choicely or fastidiously neat: elegant (*Spens.*). — *n.* that which is dainty, a delicacy, esp. a small cake. — *adj.* (*Spens.*) **daint, daynt.** — *adv.*

dain'tily. — *n.* **dain'tiness.** [M.E. *deintee,* anything worthy or costly — O.Fr. *daintié,* worthiness — L. *dignitās, -ātis — dignus,* worthy.]

daiquiri *dī'kə-ri, dak'ə-ri, n.* a cocktail containing rum and lime-juice. [*Daiquirí,* Cuban place name.]

dairy *dā'ri, n.* a place where milk is kept, and butter and cheese made: a shop where milk and other dairy produce is sold. — *n.* **dai'rying.** — **dairy cattle** cattle reared mainly for the production of milk, as distinct from *beef cattle,* reared primarily for their meat products; **dairy cream** cream made from milk, not artificial substitutes; **dai'ry-farm; dai'rymaid; dai'ryman; dairy products** milk and its derivatives, butter, cheese, etc.; **dayr'house** (*Spens.*) a dairy. [M.E. *deye* — O.E. *dæge,* a dairymaid; orig. a kneader of dough; see **dough.**]

dais *dās* (*dā'is* is only a guess from the spelling), *n.* a raised floor at the upper end of the dining-hall where the high table stood: a raised floor, usually with a seat and perhaps a canopy: the canopy over an altar, etc. [O.Fr. *deis* — L.L. *discus,* a table — L. *discus,* a quoit — Gr. *diskos,* a disc.]

daisy *dā'zi, n.* a composite plant (*Bellis perennis*) growing in pastures and meadows: extended to other plants, as the *Ox-eye daisy,* which is a chrysanthemum: a general term of admiration, often ironical. — *adj.* **dai'sied** covered with daisies. — **dai'sy-chain** a succession of daisies strung one upon another; **dai'sy-cutter** a fast-going horse that does not lift its feet high (*arch.*): a cricket-ball skimmed along the ground; **dai'sy-wheel** a flat, horizontal, wheel-shaped device with printing characters at the end of the spokes. — **fresh as a daisy** bright and vigorous, with strength and spirits unimpaired; **New Zealand daisy bush** a half-hardy shrub of the genus Olearia, with daisy-like flowers. [O.E. *dæges ēage,* day's eye.]

dak *däk,* **dawk** *dök, ns.* in India, the mail-post: hence mail, a letter, a parcel, etc.: method of travelling like that of the mail (orig. by relays of bearers or horses). — **dak bungalow** a house for travellers in India; **dak runner** a runner or horseman who carries mail. [Hind. *dāk,* a relay of men.]

daker. See **dacker.**

Dakin's solution *dā'kinz səl-, sol-ōō'shən, -ū'shən* (*chem.*) *n.* a dilute solution of sodium hypochlorite and boric acid, used as an antiseptic. [From Henry *Dakin,* British chemist (1880–1952).]

dakoit. See **dacoit.**

dal *däl, n.* the pigeon-pea, a pea-like plant (*Cajanus indicus*) cultivated in India and the tropics: pulse: a purée of pulse. — Also **dahl, dhal, dholl.** [Hind. *dal,* to split.]

dalai lama *dä'lī läm'ə,* the head of the Tibetan Buddhist hierarchy. [Mongolian *dalai,* ocean, Tibetan *lama,* high-priest.]

dale *dāl, n.* the low ground between hills: the valley through which a river flows. — **dales'man** specifically, a man of the dales of Yorkshire. [O.E. *dæl,* reinforced by O.N. *dalr*; cf. Sw. *dal*; Ger. *Tal.*]

Dalek *dä'lek, n.* a mobile mechanical being. [From a children's television series.]

dali *dä'li, n.* a tropical American tree akin to nutmeg yielding staves, etc., and wax seeds. [Native name.]

Dalila, Dalilah. See **Delilah.**

dalle *däl, n.* a slab or tile, esp. decorative: (in *pl.*) a rapid where a river runs in a gorge between steep rocks (*U.S.*). [Fr.]

dallop. See **dollop.**

dally *dal'i, v.i.* to lose time by idleness or trifling: to play (with): to exchange caresses: — *pr.p.* **dall'ying;** *pa.t.* and *pa.p.* **dall'ied.** — *ns.* **dall'iance** dallying, toying, or trifling: interchange of embraces: delay; **dall'ier** a trifler. [O.Fr. *dalier,* to chat.]

dalmahoy *däl'mə-hoi, -hoi', n.* a bushy bob-wig worn in the 18th cent. [Said to be named from a wearer.]

Dalmatian *dal-mā'shən, adj.* belonging to *Dalmatia* (now a part of Yugoslavia): denoting a Dalmatian (dog).

Dalmatian (dog) the spotted coach-dog, like the pointer in shape.

dalmatic *dal-mat'ik, n.* a loose-fitting, wide-sleeved ecclesiastical vestment, worn specially by deacons in the R.C. Church, also sometimes by bishops. [L.L. *dalmatica,* a robe worn by persons of rank, on the pattern of a dress worn in *Dalmatia.*]

Dalradian *dal-rā'di-ən, adj.* applied to a series of Pre-Cambrian rocks well represented in the Scottish Highlands. — Also *n.* [From the ancient kingdom of *Dalriada.*]

dal segno *däl sān'yō,* an indication in music that the performer must return to the sign (𝄋) — abbrev. **D.S.** [It. *dal segno,* from the sign.]

dalt, dault *dölt,* (*Scot.*) *n.* a foster-child. [Gael. *dalta.*]

dalton *döl'tən, n.* another name for **atomic mass unit** (q.v. under **atom**). — *n.* **Dal'tonism** colour-blindness: inability to distinguish red from green. — *adj.* **Dalto'nian.** [From the chemist and physicist John *Dalton* (1766–1844), who described his own case of colour-blindness.]

Daltonism[1] *döl'tən-izm, n.* a school method (the Dalton plan) by which each pupil pursues separately in his own way a course suited to himself, mapped out into monthly instalments. [First tried in 1920 at *Dalton,* Massachusetts.]

Daltonism[2]. See **dalton.**

dam[1] *dam, n.* an embankment to restrain water: the water thus confined: a mill-stream (*Scot.*): a restraint (*fig.*). — *v.t.* to keep back by a bank: — *pr.p.* **damm'ing**; *pa.t.* and *pa.p.* **dammed.** [Gmc.; Du. *dam,* Ger. *Damm,* etc.]

dam[2] *dam, n.* a mother, usu. of cattle, horses, etc., or contemptuous. [A form of **dame**[1].]

dam[3] *däm, n.* an obsolete Indian copper coin, one fortieth of a rupee. [Hind. *dām.*]

dam[4] *dam,* (*obs. Scot.*) *n.* a draughtsman. — *n.sing.* **dams** the game of draughts. — **dam'board, dam'brod** a draughtboard. [Fr. *dame,* lady.]

dam[5] *dam,* a coll. form of **damn, damned.** — *adj.* **dam'fool'** stupid, ridiculous. — *interjs.* **damme** (*dam'(m)ē*) damn me; **damm'it** damn it. — **as near as dammit** see **near.**

damage *dam'ij, n.* hurt, injury, loss: the value of what is lost: cost (*coll.*): (*pl.*) the financial reparation due for loss or injury sustained by one person through the fault or negligence of another. — *v.t.* to harm. — *v.i.* to be injured. — *adj.* **dam'ageable.** — *n.* **damageabil'ity.** — *adv.* **dam'agingly.** — **damage feasant** (*fez'ənt*) doing damage (of beasts trespassing); **direct** or **general damages** damages awarded for the immediate consequences of a hurt as distinct from **indirect** or **special damages** turning on the remoter consequences; **what's the damage?** (*coll.*) how much do I owe? what is the cost? [O.Fr. *damage* (Fr. *dommage*) — L. *damnum,* loss.]

daman *dam'an, n.* the Syrian hyrax, the cony of the Bible. [Ar.]

damar. Same as **dammar.**

damascene *dam'ə-sēn, dam-ə-sēn', n.* a Damascus or damascened sword: inlay of metal (esp. gold) or other materials on steel, etc.: the structure or surface appearance of Damascus steel: a damson: (with *cap.*) a native or inhabitant of Damascus. — *v.t.* to decorate (esp. steel) by inlaying or encrusting: to ornament with the watered or wavy appearance of Damascus steel, or in imitation of it. — Also **damasceene, damaskeen, -kin, -quin** (*-kēn*). — *n.* **damascen'ing** inlaying upon steel: the production of watered appearance on steel. — **Damascus blade** a Damascus sword, the surface marked by wavy pattern. [From *Damascus,* famous for its steel and (see **damask**) silk work.]

damask *dam'əsk, n.* figured material, originally of silk, now usually of linen, also of cotton or wool, the figure woven not printed: Damascus steel or its surface appearance: the red colour of the damask rose. — *v.t.* to flower or variegate (cloth): to damascene. — *adj.* red, like a damask rose. — *n.* **dam'assin** damask with flowered patterns in gold or silver thread. — **damask plum** the damson; **damask rose** a fragrant pink or red variety of rose; **dam'ask-steel** Damascus steel. [From *Damascus* (see **damascene**).]

damboard, dambrod. See **dam**[4].

dame[1] *dām, n.* the mistress of a house, a matron (now usu. jocular or patronising): a mother: a woman (*slang*): the comic vulgar old woman of the pantomime, usu. played by a male actor: a noble lady: (title of) a lady of the same rank as a knight: a baronet's or knight's wife (as a formal title prefixed to the lady's name) (*obs.*): a name given to members of certain orders of nuns, esp. Benedictine; **dame'-school** (*hist.*) a school for young children usu. kept by a woman; **dame's'-vī'olet** a cruciferous plant (*Hesperis matronalis*) formerly cultivated in pots by ladies for its sweet scent at night. [Fr. *dame* — L. *domina,* a lady.]

dame[2] *dam,* (Fr.) *n.* woman, lady. — **dame d'honneur** (*don-œr*) maid of honour; **dames de la halle** (*də la al*) market women.

damfool. See **dam**[5].

dammar *dam'ər, n.* a copal used for making varnish, obtained from various conifers. — Also **damm'er.** [Malay *damar.*]

damme, dammit. See **dam**[5].

damn *dam, v.t.* to censure: to sentence to eternal punishment: to doom: to curse or swear at. — *v.i.* to utter curses. — *n.* an interjection expressing annoyance, disgust or impatience (*coll.*): something of little value (*coll.*): a curse. — *adj.* **damnable** (*dam'nə-bl*) deserving or tending to damnation: hateful: pernicious. — *ns.* **dam'nableness, damnabil'ity.** — *adv.* **dam'nably.** — *n.* **damnation** (*-nā'shən*) condemnation: the punishment of the impenitent in the future state (*theol.*): eternal punishment. — *adjs.* **dam'natory** (*-nə-tər-i*) consigning to damnation; **damned** (*damd;* poet. *dam'nid*) sentenced to everlasting punishment (**the damned** *damd,* those so sentenced): hateful: thorough, complete: very surprised (as in *I'll be damned!*). — *adv.* very, exceedingly. — *n.* **damnification** (*dam-ni-fi-kā'shən*) infliction of injury or loss. — *v.t.* **dam'nify** to cause loss to. — *adj.* **damning** (*dam'ing, -ning*) exposing to condemnation. — **damn all** (*coll.*) nothing at all; **damn with faint praise** to condemn in effect by expressing too cool approval; **do one's damnedest** (*damd'əst; coll.*) to do one's very best; **not give a damn** (*coll.*) to be completely unconcerned; **not worth a damn** (*coll.*) of no value; **the damned** see **damned** above. [Fr. *damner* — L. *damnāre,* to condemn — *damnum,* loss.]

Damoclean *dam-ō-klē'ən, adj.* like *Damoclēs,* flatterer of Dionysius of Syracuse, taught the insecurity of happiness by being made to sit through a feast with a sword suspended over his head by a single hair: hence, carrying the threat of imminent calamity.

damo(i)sel, damozel *dam'ō-zel, n.* Same as **damsel.**

damp *damp, n.* vapour, mist: moist air: in mines, etc., any gas other than air: lowness of spirits (*arch.*): a gloom: discouragement. — *v.t.* to wet slightly: to discourage: to check: to make dull: to slow down the rate of burning (of a fire) (often with *down;* see also **damp down**): to diminish the amplitude of. — *adj.* moist: foggy: unenthusiastic (*coll.*). — *v.t.* and *v.i.* **damp'en** to make or become damp or moist: to stifle (*fig.*). — *ns.* **damp'er** one who or that which damps: a depressive influence: a door or shutter for shutting off or regulating a draught: a device for diminishing the amplitude of vibrations or cycles: a mute (*mus.*): in a piano, harpsichord, etc., the pad which silences a note after it has been played: a kind of unleavened bread (orig. *Austr.*): a cake of this; **damp'ing** reduction in vibration through dissipation of energy (*phys.*): diminution in sharpness of resonance through the introduction of resistance (*electronics*). — *adj.* **damp'ish.** — *n.* **damp'ishness.** — *adv.* **damp'ly.** — *n.* **damp'ness.** — *adj.* **damp'y** (*poet.*) damp. — **damp'-course** a layer of moisture-proof material in a masonry wall. — **damp down** to close down a furnace, etc. (*n.* **damp'ing-down'**). —

damp'ing-off a disease of seedlings caused by Pythium or other fungus in an excess of moisture. — *adj.* **damp'-proof** impervious to moisture. — **damp-proof course** a damp course. — **damp squib** something that fails to go off with the expected bang. [M.E. *dampen*; akin to Du. *damp*, Ger. *Dampf*, vapour.]

damsel *dam'zəl, n.* a young unmarried woman: a girl. — **dam'selfish** a small brightly-coloured tropical fish of the family *Pomacentridae*; **dam'selfly** an insect of the order Odonata, resembling the dragonfly; [O.Fr. *dameisele* (Fr. *demoiselle*) — L.L. *domicella*, dim. of L. *domina*, lady.]

damson *dam'zən, n.* a rather small, oval, dark-purple plum. — **damson cheese** damsons pressed into a solid cake. [Shortened from *Damascene* — *Damascus*.]

Dan *dan, n.* a title of honour equivalent to Master or Sir formerly applied esp. to poets, and now by the poets to great poets, etc. [O.Fr. *dan* (Sp. *don*; Port. *dom*) — L. *dominus*, lord.]

dan[1] *dan,* (*dial.*) *n.* a box for carrying coal: a tub.

dan[2] *dan, n.* in Japanese combative sports, a level of proficiency (usu. 1st rising to 10th): a person who has gained such a level. [Jap.]

dan[3] *dan, n.* a small sea marker-buoy. — Also **dan buoy**. [Origin obscure.]

dance *däns, v.i.* to move with measured steps, esp. to music: to spring. — *v.t.* to make to dance or jump: to perform, execute, as a dance. — *n.* a movement of one or more persons with measured steps: the tune to which dancing is performed: the musical form of a dance-tune: a meeting for dancing: a series of dance-like movements performed by birds *etc*, e.g. as a mating display. — *adj.* **dance'able.** — *ns.* **danc'er; danc'ing.** — **dance'-band; dance'-hall** a public hall providing facilities for dancing to patrons on receipt of an admission fee; **dance'-music** music specially arranged for accompanying dancing; **dance'-tune; danc'ing-girl** a professional dancer; **danc'ing-master.** — **dance a bear** (*obs.*) to exhibit a performing bear; **dance attendance** to wait assiduously (on); **dance of death** a series of allegorical paintings symbolising the universal power of death, represented as a skeleton; **dance upon nothing** to be hanged; **lead someone a (merry) dance** to keep someone involved unnecessarily in a series of perplexities and vexations; **merry dancers** (*dial.*) the aurora borealis. [O.Fr. *danser*, from Gmc.; O.H.G. *dansôn*, to draw along.]

dancette *dän-set', n.* a zigzag or indented line or figure (*her.*): the chevron or zigzag moulding common in Romanesque architecture. — *adj.* **dancetté, -ee, -y** (*dän'set-i,* or *-set'*) deeply indented. [O.Fr. *dent, dant,* tooth, notch — L. *dēns, dentis.*]

dandelion *dan'di-lī-ən, n.* a common yellow-flowered composite (*Taraxacum officinale*) with jagged-toothed leaves. [Fr. *dent de lion,* lion-tooth.]

dander[1] *dan'dər, dauner, daunder, dawner dön'(d)ər,* (*Scot.*) *vs.i.* to stroll, saunter. — *ns.* a stroll, saunter. [Origin unknown.]

dander[2] *dan'dər, n.* a form of **dandruff**: anger: passion. — **get someone's, one's dander up** or **raise someone's, one's dander** to make or become angry.

dander[3] *dan'dər,* (*Scot.*) *n.* furnace cinders. [Origin unknown.]

Dandie Dinmont *dan'di din'mənt,* a short-legged rough-coated terrier of Scottish Border breed, of pepper or mustard colour. [From *Dandie Dinmont* in Scott's *Guy Mannering,* whose Peppers and Mustards are represented as the origin of the breed.]

dandify, etc. See **dandy**[1].

dandiprat, dandyprat *dan'di-prat,* (*obs.*) *n.* a silver three-halfpenny piece: an insignificant person: a little boy. [Origin unknown.]

dandle *dan'dl, v.t.* to play with: to fondle, toss in the arms or dance lightly on the knee (a baby). — *n.* **dand'ler.** [Origin unknown.]

dandruff, dandriff *dand'rəf, n.* a scaly scurf on the skin under the hair. [Origin unknown.]

dandy[1] *dan'di, n.* a foppish, silly fellow: one who pays much attention to dress: a dandy-cock: a dandy-roll. — *adj.* (*coll.*) smart, fine — a word of general commendation. — *adjs.* **dandï'acal, dand'ified** inclined to be a dandy. — *v.t.* **dan'dify** to dress up. — *adv.* **dan'dily.** — *adj.* **dan'dyish.** — *n.* **dan'dyism.** — **dan'dy-brush** a hard horse brush of whalebone bristles; **dan'dy-cart** a light spring-cart; **dan'dy-cock, -hen** a bantam; **dan'dy-horse** an early bicycle without pedals, driven by kicking the ground; **dan'dy-roll** a wire-gauze cylinder that impresses the ribs and water-mark on paper. [Origin unknown; orig. Scots; poss. one spoiled by overmuch dandling.]

dandy[2] *dan'di, n.* a sloop-like vessel with jigger-mast abaft. — *adj.* **dan'dy-rigged.**

dandy-fever. Same as **dengue.**

dandyfunk. See **dunderfunk.**

dandyprat. See **dandiprat.**

Dane *dān, n.* a native or citizen of Denmark: a Northman: a very large dog (great Dane): a Dalmatian dog (lesser Dane). — *adj.* **Danish** (*dān'ish*) belonging to Denmark. — *n.* the language of the Danes. — Also **Dan'isk** (*Spens.*). — **Danish blue** a blue-veined, strongly-flavoured cheese; **Danish pastry** a flaky confection of sweetened dough, containing jam or other fillings and often iced. [Dan. *Daner* (pl.); O.E. *Dene.*]

danegeld, danegelt *dān'geld, -gelt, ns.* a tax imposed in the 10th cent., to buy off the Danes or to defend the country against them. [O.E. *Dene,* Danes, *geld,* payment.]

dane-hole *dān'hōl, n.* Same as **dene-hole.**

Danelaw, Danelagh *dān'lō, n.* that part of England, N.E. of Watling Street, occupied (9th–11th cent.) by the Danes: (without *cap.*) the Danish law which prevailed there. [O.E. *Dena lagu,* Danes' law.]

dang[1] *dang, v.t.* a minced form of **damn.**

dang[2]. See **ding**[1].

danger *dān'jər, n.* peril, hazard, or risk: insecurity: power (*obs.*). — *v.t.* (*Shak.*) to endanger. — *adj.* **dan'gerous** full of danger: arrogant, stand-offish (*obs.*): unsafe: insecure. — Also *adv.* (*Shak.*). — *adv.* **dan'gerously.** — *n.* **dan'gerousness.** — **danger line** the boundary between safety and danger; **danger money** extra money paid for doing a more than usually perilous job; **danger point** the place where safety gives way to danger; **dangerous drugs** certain specific drugs, including morphine, cocaine, heroin, etc., to the dispensing of which stringent regulations apply (**Dangerous Drugs Act** the act under which these drugs are scheduled). — **in danger of** liable to, on the point of; **on the danger list** in a hospital, etc., categorised as being dangerously ill (also *fig.*). [O.Fr. *dangier,* absolute power (of a feudal lord), hence power to hurt, — L.L. *dominium,* feudal authority — L. *dominus,* a lord.]

dangle *dang'gl, v.i.* to hang loosely or with a swinging motion: to follow about. — *v.t.* to make to dangle (often with intent to entice or encourage). — *n.* **dang'ler** one who dangles about others, esp. about women. — *n. and adj.* **dang'ling.** — **dangling participle** (*U.S.*) a misrelated participle. [Cf. Dan. *dangle* — O.N. *dingla.*]

Daniel *dan'yəl, n.* a wise judge (in phrases as *a second Daniel, a Daniel come to judgment* — both *Merchant of Venice*). [From Daniel in the Apocryphal *Book of Susannah.*]

Daniell cell *dan'yəl sel* (*chem.; hist.*) *n.* a type of primary cell with zinc and copper electrodes. [From John Daniell, British scientist (1790-1845).]

danio *dā'ni-ō, n.* any of several brightly-coloured tropical freshwater fish: — *pl.* **da'nios.** [Origin obscure.]

Danish. See **Dane.**

Danite *dan'īt, n.* one of a secret society amongst the early Mormons. [*Dan*; cf. Gen. xlix. 16, 17.]

dank *dangk, adj.* unpleasantly moist, wet. — *n.* (*Milt.*) a wet place. — *adj.* **dank'ish.** — *n.* **dank'ness.** [Origin uncertain.]

danke schön *dang'kə shœn,* (Ger.) many thanks.

---

fāte; fär; hûr; mīne; mōte; för; mūte; moon; foot; dhen (then); *el'ə-mənt* (element)

dannebrog *dan'e-brog*, *n.* the Danish national flag: the second of the Danish orders instituted by King Valdemar in 1219. [Dan.]

danse macabre *däs ma-käbr'*, (Fr.) dance of death (q.v.).

danseur *dä-sœr*, *n.* a male ballet dancer. — *n.* **danseuse** *(dä-sœz)* a female dancer: a ballet dancer. — **danseur noble** *(nobl')* a principal male ballet-dancer: — *pl.* **danseurs nobles** *(dä-sœr nobl')*. [Fr.]

Dansker *dan'skər*, (*Shak.*) *n.* a Dane.

dant, danton. Earlier forms of **daunt, daunton.**

Dantean *dan'ti-ən*, **Dantesque** *dan-tesk'*, *adjs.* like the poet *Dante*: sublime: austere. — *ns.* **Dan'tist** a Dante scholar; **Dantŏph'ilist** a lover of Dante.

dap[1] *dap*, *v.i.* to bounce: to drop bait gently into the water. — *n.* a bait so used: a bounce. — *n.* **dapp'er**. [Origin obscure.]

dap[2] *dap*, (*dial.*) *n.* a gym shoe, plimsoll. [Prob. **dap**[1].]

Daphne *daf'ni*, *n.* a genus (fam. *Thymelaeaceae*) of shrubs, including mezereon and spurge-laurel: (without *cap.*) any plant of this genus. [Gr. *daphnē*, sweet bay.]

Daphnia *daf'ni-ə*, *n.* a genus of water flea. — *n.* **daph'nid** (*-nid*) any member of the genus. [Gr. *Daphne*.]

dapper[1] *dap'ər*, *adj.* quick: little and active: neat: spruce. — *n.* **dapp'erling** a dapper little fellow. — *adv.* **dapp'-erly**. — *n.* **dapp'erness**. [Du. *dapper*, brave; cf. Ger. *tapfer*, quick, brave.]

dapper[2]. See **dap**.

dapple *dap'l*, *adj.* marked with spots. — *v.t.* to variegate with spots. — *adj.* **dapp'led**. — *adjs.* and *ns.* **dapp'le= bay'** (an animal, esp. a horse) of bay colour, variegated with dapples; **dapp'le-grey'** (an animal, esp. a horse) of a pale grey colour with darker spots. [Origin unknown.]

dapsone *dap'sōn*, *n.* a drug widely used in the treatment of leprosy, dermatitis, etc. [*di*aminodiphenylsulph*one.*]

daraf *dar'af*, (*elect.*) *n.* a unit of elastance, the reciprocal of capacitance in farads. [*Farad* backwards.]

darbies *där'biz*, (*slang*) *n.pl.* handcuffs. [App. from the personal name *Darby.*]

Darby and Joan *där'bi-ənd-jōn'*, a devoted elderly married couple. [Poss. from characters in an 18th-cent. song.]

Darbyite *där'bi-īt*, *n.* one of the Plymouth Brethren, more particularly of the Exclusive branch of the sect. [From their principal founder, J. N. *Darby* (1800–82).]

Dard *därd*, *n.* a person belonging to any of the peoples who speak Dardic languages. — *adj.* and *n.* **Dard'ic** (of or relating to) a particular Indo-European language group spoken in parts of Northern India, Pakistan and Afghanistan.

Dardan *där'dən*, **Dardanian** *där-dā'ni-ən*. Same as **Trojan.**

dare[1] *där*, *v.i.* and *v.t.* to be bold enough (to): to venture: — *3rd pers. sing.* **dare(s)**; *pa.t.* **durst** (now rare, used esp. in subjunctive sense), **dared**; *pa.p.* **dared.** — *v.t.* to challenge: to defy: to face: — *3rd pers. sing.* **dares**; *pa.t.* and *pa.p.* **dared.** — *n.* boldness (*Shak.*): an act of daring or a challenge to perform it. — *adjs.* **dare'ful** (*Shak.*) full of daring, adventurous; **dar'ing** bold: courageous: fearless. — *n.* boldness. — *adv.* **dar'ingly**. — **dare'-devil** a rash, venturesome fellow. — *adj.* unreasonably rash and reckless. — **dare'-dev'ilry; dar'ing-do** same as **derring-do.** — *adj.* **dar'ing-hard'y** (*Shak.*) fool-hardy. — **I dare say, I daresay** I suppose. [O.E. *durran* (preterite-present vb.), pres.t. *dearr*, pret. *dorste*; Goth. *daursan*; akin to Gr. *tharseein.*]

dare[2] *där*, (*obs.*) *v.i.* to lurk, crouch, shrink, be dismayed, doze, be fascinated, stare. — *v.t.* (*Spens., Shak.*) to daze: to frighten. — *n.* a contrivance with mirrors used to fascinate larks. [O.E. *darian*, to lurk, be hidden.]

dare[3] *där*. Same as **dace.**

darg *därg*, (*Scot.*) *n.* a day's work: a task. [Contr. from *dawerk, day-wark*, day-work.]

darga *dûr'gä*, *n.* (a structure over) a place where a holy person was cremated or buried. [Hind. *dargāh.*]

dargle *där'gl*, (*Scott*) *n.* a dell. [Prob. from the *Dargle*

in Co. Wicklow, mistaken by Scott for a common noun.]

dari. See **durra.**

daric *dar'ik*, *n.* an old gold or silver coin larger than an English sovereign named after *Darius* I of Persia.

dariole *da'rē-ōl, dar'yöl*, *n.* a shell of pastry, etc., or small round mould: a dish comprising such a shell and its filling. [Fr.]

dark *därk*, *adj.* without light: black, or somewhat blackish: (of hair and skin colouring) not of a fair or light hue: gloomy: (of a theatre) closed: difficult to understand: unenlightened: secret: sinister. — *n.* absence of light: nightfall: a state of ignorance. — *adv.* (*Shak.*) in a state of dark. — *v.t.* **dark'en** to make dark or darker: to render ignorant: to sully. — *v.i.* to grow dark or darker. — *n.* **dar'kie** a darky. — *adj.* **dark'ish**. — *v.i.* **dark'le** to grow dark (a back-formation from *darkling*). — *adv.* and *adj.* **dark'ling** dark: in the dark. — *advs.* **dark'lings** (*poet.*) in the dark; **dark'ly**. — *adj.* **dark'-some** dark: gloomy (*poet.*). — *ns.* **dark'(e)y** a Negro (*offensive, old-fashioned*): a dark-lantern (*slang*); **dark'-ness.** — **Dark Ages** the period of intellectual darkness in Europe, from the 5th to the 9th or 12th (or 15th) century; **Dark Continent** Africa; **darkfield microscope** an ultramicroscope (q.v.); **dark horse** in racing, a horse whose capabilities are not known; also *fig.* of a person (usu. implying undisclosed ability): a candidate not brought forward till the last moment (esp. *U.S.*); **dark'-house** (*Shak.*) a mad-house; **dark'-lant'ern** a lantern whose light can be covered; **dark'mans** (*thieves' slang*) night; **dark'room** a room for developing and printing photographs free from such light as would affect photographic plates; **dark star** a star that emits no visible light, and can be detected only by its radiowaves, gravitational effect, etc. — **darken some-one's door** (often with negative, often implying unwelcomeness) to appear as a visitor; **in the dark** ignorant, unaware; **keep dark** to be silent or secret; **keep it dark** to conceal it; **prince of darkness** Satan. [O.E. *deorc.*]

darling *där'ling*, *n.* and *adj.* (one) dearly beloved (often *voc.*): (a) favourite. [O.E. *dēorling*; see **dear**[1].]

Darlingtonia *där-ling-tō'ni-ə*, *n.* a Californian pitcher-plant of the Sarracenia family. [Named after William *Darlington* (1782–1863), American botanist.]

darn[1] *därn*, *v.t.* to mend by interwoven stitches: to embroider or sew with the stitches used in mending holes. — *n.* a darned place. — *ns.* **darn'er; darn'ing. darn'ing-needle.** [Etymology uncertain.]

darn[2], **darned** *därn(d)*, minced forms of **damn, damned.**

darnel *där'nəl*, *n.* a species of rye-grass: perh. the tares of the Bible. [Poss. conn. with O.Fr. *darne*, stupid, from its supposed narcotic properties.]

darraign(e), darrain(e), darrayn, deraign *də-rān'*, (*obs.*) *v.t.* to vindicate: to justify: to prove: to claim: to challenge: to decide: to set in battle array, or to do (battle) (*Spens., Shak.*). [O.Fr. *derainier, desraisnier*, to plead, vindicate — L.L. *dē-, disratiōnāre* — L. *dē-* or *dis-, ratiō*, reason; cf. **arraign.**]

darre *där* (*Spens.*). Same as **dare**[1]. — **darred** (*därd*) *pa.p.* of **dare**[2].

darshan *där'shən*, *n.* a blessing conferred by seeing or touching a great or holy person. [Hindi.]

dart[1] *därt*, *n.* a pointed weapon or toy for throwing with the hand: anything that pierces: a tapering fold sewn on the reverse of material in order to shape it: (in *pl.*) a game in which darts are thrown at a board: in some snails, a calcareous needle supposed to be used as a sexual stimulus: a sudden forward movement: a plan, scheme (*Austr. coll.*): a cutworm moth (*Agrotis*) with a dart-like mark on the forewing (in full **dart'-moth**). — *v.t.* to hurl suddenly: to send or shoot forth. — *v.i.* to move, start or shoot forth rapidly — freq. **dart'le.** — *n.* **dar'ter** one who or that which darts: a freshwater diving bird (*Plotus*) allied to cormorants: an archer-fish: applied also to various small American fishes akin to perch. — *adj.* **dart'ing.** — *adv.* **dart'ingly.** — **dart'= board** the target used in the game of darts; **dart'-sac**

the gland that secretes the dart in snails. — **Old Dart** (*Austr. slang*) Great Britain. [O.Fr. *dart*; cf. O.E. *daroth*.]

dart². See **dace**.

dartle. See **dart¹**.

dartre *där'tər, n.* herpes. — *adj.* **dar'trous.** [Fr.]

Darwinism *där'win-izm, n.* the theory of the origin of species propounded by Charles *Darwin* (1809–82). — *adj.* and *n.* **Darwin'ian.**

darzi *där'zē, dûr'zē, n.* a tailor. [Hind. *darzī*.]

dash¹ *dash, v.t.* to throw, thrust, or drive violently: to break by throwing together: to bespatter: to blotch: to frustrate: to confound: to modify by dilution or admixture. — *v.i.* to rush with violence. — *n.* a violent striking: a rush: a violent onset: a blow: a splash: a splash of colour: a stroke of the pen or similar mark: a mark (—) at a break in a sentence or elsewhere: a euphemism for damn (sometimes represented by this sign): a staccato mark: an acute accent used in algebra and in lettering of diagrams as a discriminating mark: a long element in the Morse code: verve. ostentation: a slight admixture: a dashboard. — *n.* **dash'er** one who dashes: one who makes a great show (*coll.*). — *adj.* **dash'ing** spirited: showy: ostentatiously fashionable. — *adv.* **dash'ingly.** — **dash'board** a board, screen or partition in front of a driver, on a horse-vehicle to keep off splashes of mud, in a motor-car or aeroplane to carry instruments; **dash'-pot** a device for damping vibration by a piston moving in a cylinder containing liquid; **dash'-wheel** a washing-machine in the form of a partitioned drum. — **dash off** to throw off or produce hastily: to leave abruptly; **dash out** to knock out by striking against something. [M.E. *daschen, dassen,* to rush, or strike with violence — cf. Dan. *daske,* to slap.]

dash² *dash, n.* a gift accompanying a commercial transaction: a gratuity: a bribe. [Port. *das,* will you (*sing.*) give?]

dasheen *da-shēn', n.* the taro. [Poss. Fr. *de Chine,* of China.]

das heisst *das hīst,* (Ger.) that is: — *abbrev.* **d.h.** equivalent to English *i.e.*

dashiki, dasheki *da-shē'ki, n.* a type of loose shirt worn in Africa, and also in the U.S. [West African.]

dassie *das'i,* (*S. Afr.*) *n.* the hyrax. [Du. *dasje, dim.* of *das,* badger: Afrik. *dassie.*]

dastard *däs'tərd, n.* a cowardly fellow: loosely, one who does a brutal act without giving his victim a chance. — *adj.* shrinking from danger: cowardly. — *adj.* and *adv.* **das'tardly.** — *ns.* **das'tardness, das'tardliness, das'-tardy.** [Prob. conn. with **dazed.**]

dasyphyllous *das-i-fil'əs, adj.* having crowded, thick, or woolly leaves. [Gr. *dasys,* thick, bushy, hairy, *phyllon,* leaf.]

Dasypus *das'i-pŏos, -pəs, n.* a genus of armadillos. — *n.* **das'ypod** any member of the genus. — *n.pl.* **Dasipod'-idae** the armadillo family. [Gr. *dasypous,* a hare — *dasys,* hairy, *pous, podos,* foot.]

dasyure *das'i-ūr, n.* any marsupial of the flesh-eating genus *Dasyu'rus* (called native cat) or the fam. **Dasyu'-ridae** (Tasmanian devil, Tasmanian wolf, etc.). [Gr. *dasys,* shaggy, *ourā,* tail.]

DAT, Dat, dat *dat.* See **digital audio tape** under **digit.**

data *dā'tə,* (in U.S. and technical Eng. *dä'tə*), *n.pl.* (commonly treated as *sing.*) facts given, from which others may be inferred: — *sing.* **da'tum** (q.v.) — *n.* **datamā'tion** shortened term for **automatic data processing.** — **da'tabank, da'tabase** a large body of information stored in a computer, which can process it and from which particular pieces of information can be retrieved when required; **databus, data highway** (*comput.*) a path for transferring data; **data processing** see **process.** — (**direct**) **data capture** the putting of information, esp. concerning (cash) sales, into a form that can be fed directly into a computer. [L. *dāta,* things given, pa.p. neut. pl. of *dāre,* to give.]

datal¹. See **date¹**.

datal². See **daytale** under **day**.

datary *dā'tə-ri, n.* an officer of the papal court charged with registering and dating bulls, etc., and with duties relating to the granting of indults and graces: his office (also **datā'ria**). [L.L. *datārius* — L. *dāre,* to give.]

date¹ *dāt, n.* a statement of time, or time and place, of writing, sending, executing, as on a letter, book, document, etc.: a particular day of the month: the time of an event: duration, or end, of existence (*arch.*): term of life: death-day, doom (with pun on *debt; Spens.*): an appointment or engagement (*coll.*): the person dated (in the last sense of the *v.t.*). — *v.t.* to affix a date to: to ascertain the date of: to suggest the date of: to make an appointment with (*coll.*): to go out with (a member of the opposite sex), esp. regularly (*coll.*). — *v.i.* to reckon: to take beginning: to savour of a particular time: hence, to become old-fashioned. — *adjs.* **dāt'able, dāt'eable; dāt'al; dat'ed** old-fashioned, out of date; **date'less** without date or fixed limit: free from engagements. — *ns.* **dāt'er; dāt'ing.** — **date'=coding** marking in code on the container a date after which food should not be used; **date line** short for International Date Line; **date'-line** a line giving the date and location, as on a newspaper; **date'-stamp** (the impression made by) a device for stamping the date on documents, etc. — **out of date** see **out; to date** until now; **up to date** abreast of the times: adapted or corrected to the present time: modern. [O.Fr. *date* — L. *dătum,* given.]

date² *dāt, n.* the fruit of the date-palm. — **date'-palm, -tree** a palm (*Phoenix dactylifera*) of N. Africa and S.W. Asia; **date'-plum** a fruit of the ebony genus, persimmon; **date'-shell** the date-shaped shell of *Lithodomus,* or the animal itself, of the mussel family, a borer in limestone rocks; **date'-su'gar.** [Fr. *datte* — L. *dactylus* — Gr. *daktylos,* a finger, a date.]

Datel® *dā'tel, n.* a facility provided by British Telecom for the transfer of data between computers. [*data* and *tel*ex.]

Datin. See **Datuk.**

dative *dāt'iv, adj.* given or appointed: expressing an indirect object (*gram.*). — *n.* the dative case: a word in the dative. — *adj.* **dātī'val.** [L. *dătīvus* — *dăre,* to give.]

datolite *dat'ə-līt, n.* a hydrated silicate of boron and calcium. [Gr. *dateesthai,* to divide, *lithos,* stone.]

Datuk *da-tŏŏk, n.* a member of a senior chivalric order in Malaysia: — *fem.* **Datin** (*da-tēn'*). [Malay *datu,* chief.]

datum *dā'təm.* See **data.** — **dā'tum-line, -level, -plane** the horizontal base-line from which heights and depths are measured. [L. *dătum,* given — *dăre,* to give.]

Datura *də-tū'rə, n.* the thorn-apple genus of the potato family, with strongly narcotic properties: (without *cap.*) any plant of this genus: (without *cap.*) the poison got from these plants. — *n.* **datū'rine** atropine, or a mixture of atropine with other alkaloids. [Hind. *dhatūrā.*]

daub *döb, v.t.* to smear: to paint coarsely. — *n.* a coarse painting. — *ns.* **daub'er** one who daubs: a coarse painter; **daub'ery** (*Shak.* **dawb'ry**) a daubing, or crudely artful device, false pretence; **daub'ing.** — *adj.* **daub'y** sticky. — **wattle and daub** see **wattle¹.** [O.Fr. *dauber,* to plaster — L. *dealbāre,* to whitewash; see **dealbate.**]

daube *dōb,* (Fr.) *n.* a meat stew.

daud, dawd, dod *död,* (*Scot.*) *v.t.* to knock, thump. — *n.* a lump: large piece. [**dad²**.]

daughter *dö'tər, n.* a female in relation to her parent: a female descendant: woman (generally). — *adj.,* proceeding, formed, as from a parent: of a cell, formed by division (*biol.*); derived of a nuclide, formed by the radioactive decay of another (*phys.*). — *ns.* **daugh'terliness; daugh'terling** a little daughter. — *adj.* **daugh'terly** like or becoming a daughter. — **daugh'ter-in-law** a son's wife: formerly, a step-daughter: — *pl.* **daugh'ters-in-law.** [O.E. *dohtor;* Scot. *dochter,* Ger. *Tochter,* Gr. *thygatēr.*]

dault. See **dalt.**

daunder, dauner. Same as **dander¹.**

daunt *dönt*, or *dänt*, *v.t.* to frighten: to discourage: to subdue. — *n.* **daunt′er.** — *adj.* **daunt′less** not to be daunted. *adv.* **daunt′lessly.** — *n.* **daunt′lessness.** — *v.t.* **daun′ton** (*Scot.*) to subdue: to dare. [O.Fr. *danter* (Fr. *dompter*) — L. *domitāre* — *domāre*, tame.]

dauphin *dö′fin*, *n.* the eldest son of the king of France (1349–1830). — *ns.* **dau′phiness, dauphine** (*dö-fēn′*) his wife. [O.Fr. *daulphin* (Fr. *dauphin*) — *Delphinus*, family name of the lords of the Viennois — hence dolphins in their crest and name Dauphiné for their province (ceded to the king, 1349).]

daur *dör*. A Scots form of **dare.**

daut, dawt *döt*, (*Scot.*) *v.t.* to pet. — *n.* **daut′ie, dawt′ie** a pet. [Origin unknown.]

davenport *dav′n-pört, -pört*, *n.* a small ornamental writing-desk — also **dev′onport**: a large sofa. [Prob. from the maker.]

davenport-trick *dav′n-pört-trik, -pört-*, *n.* an artifice by which a man can free himself from ropes wound round him and tied. [From two impostors who practised it (fl. 1845–65).]

Davis apparatus *dā′vis ap-ər-ā′təs*, a device making possible escape from a crippled submarine. [From the inventor.]

davit *dav′it, dā′vit, n.* one of a pair of erections for hoisting and lowering, e.g. on a ship, for lowering a boat. [App. from the name *David.*]

Davy *dā′vi*, **Davy-lamp** *-lamp*, *ns.* the safety-lamp used in coalmines invented by Sir Humphry *Davy* (1778–1829).

Davy Jones *dā′vi jōnz*, a sailor's familiar name for the (malignant) spirit of the sea, the devil. — **Davy Jones's locker** the sea, as the grave of men drowned at sea. [Origin unknown.]

daw¹ *dö*, (*obs.*) *v.i.* to dawn. [O.E. *dagian* — *dæg*, day.]

daw² *dö*, *n.* a bird of the crow kind, a jackdaw: a simpleton (*arch.*). — *adj.* **daw′ish.** — **daw′cock** (*arch.*) a cock jackdaw: a noodle. [M.E. *dawe.*]

dawbry (*Shak.*). See **daub.**

dawd. See **daud.**

dawdle *dö′dl*, *v.i.* to waste time by trifling: to act or move slowly. — *n.* **daw′dler.** — *adv.* **daw′dlingly.** [Cf. **daddle.**]

dawk. See **dak.**

dawn *dön*, *v.i.* to become day: to begin to grow light: to begin to appear. — *n.* daybreak: beginning. — Also **dawn′ing.** — **dawn chorus** the singing of birds at dawn; **dawn cypress** or **redwood** a conifer, abundant as a fossil, found living in China in the 1940s and since planted widely; **dawn′-man** Eoanthropus (q.v.); **dawn raid** a stock market operation in which a large proportion of a company's shares are suddenly bought at a price much higher than their prevailing market rate. — **dawn on** to begin to become evident to or be understood by. [Appears first as **dawning**, prob. from O.N.; cf. Sw. and Dan. *dagning*.]

dawner. See **dander¹.**

dawt, dawtie. See **daut.**

day *dā*, *n.* the time of light, from sunrise to sunset, morning till night: twenty-four hours, from midnight to midnight (formerly by some reckoned from sunrise, or sunset, or — by astronomers — from noon): the time the earth takes to make a revolution on its axis this being the *sidereal* day (between two transits of the first point of Aries, or approximately of the same star), distinguished from the *apparent solar* day (between two transits of the sun), and the *mean solar* day (between two transits of the mean, or imaginary uniformly moving, sun): morning and afternoon, as opp. to evening and night: the hours devoted to work (*working-day*): a day set apart for a purpose, as for receiving visitors: lifetime: time of existence, vogue, or influence: a time: daylight: the space between mullions of a window: ground surface over a mine. — *adv.* (*coll.*) **days** during the day, each day. — **day′-bed** a kind of

couch or sofa: a hospital-bed for patients for one day only or for part of a day; **day′-blind′ness** a defect of vision in which objects are best seen by a dim light, hemeralopia; **day′-board′er** a pupil who eats but does not sleep at a boarding-school; **day′-book** a book for entering the transactions of each day; **day′-boy, -girl** see **day scholar** below; **day′break** dawn; **day care** daytime supervision and help given by trained nursing and other staff to a group of pre-school children, or elderly or handicapped people; **day (care) centre** a centre which provides social amenities and/or supervision for elderly or handicapped people, vagrants, alcoholics, petty offenders, etc.; **day′-coal** the upper stratum of coal; **day′dream** a dreaming or musing while awake. — Also *v.i.* — **day′dreamer; day′-fly** a mayfly; **day′-lā′bour** labour paid by the day; **day′-lā′bourer; day′-level** (*mining*) a level driven from the surface; **day′light** the light of day: a clear space, **day′light= sav′ing** reduction or loss of daylight, for work or play, by advancing the clock; **day′-lil′y** a liliaceous plant (*Hemerocallis*) whose blossoms last only for a day. — *adj.* **day′long** during the whole day. — **day′mark** an unlighted sea-mark. — *adj.* **day′-old** one day old. — **day′-peep** (*Milt.*) dawn; **day′-release′** a system by which workers are freed from employment during the day so as to attend an educational course. — Also *adj.* — **day′-return′** a usu. reduced rail or bus fare for a journey to a place and back on the same day: a ticket for this type of journey; **day room** a room used as a communal living-room in a school, hospital, hostel, etc.; **day= scholar** a pupil who attends a boarding-school during the school-hours, but boards at home (also **day′-boy, day′-girl**); **day′-school** a school held during the day, as opposed both to a night-school and to a boarding-school; **day′-shift** a group of workers that takes its turn during the day: the daytime period of work; **day′-sight** night-blindness; **days′man** one who appoints a day to hear a cause: an umpire; **day′spring** dawn; **day′star** the morning star; **day′tale** (*-tāl, -təl*), **dā′tal** (*-təl*) (*old*) reckoning by the day, esp. of work or wages; **day′taler, da′taller** (*-təl-ər*) a day-labourer; **day′time** the time of daylight: day, as opp. to evening and night. — Also *adj.* — *adj.* **day′-to-day′** daily, routine. — **day trip** a trip made to somewhere and back within one day; **day′-tripper.** — *adj.* **day′-wea′ried** (*Shak.*) wearied with the work of the day. — **day′-work.** **at the end of the day** (*fig.*) when all is said and done; **call it a day** to announce a decision to leave off; **day about** on alternate days; **day by day** daily; **day in, day out** for an indefinite succession of days; **day off** a day's holiday; **day out** a servant's free day: a day spent away from home for pleasure, as a holiday, etc.; **days of grace** three days allowed for payment of bills, etc., beyond the day named; **from day to day** concerned only with the present; **in this day and age** at the present time; **knock, beat the (living) daylights out of** (*coll.*) to beat severely; **make someone's day** to make the day memorable for someone; **one day, one of these days** some indefinite time in the near future; **scare the (living) daylights out of** (*coll.*) to terrify; **see daylight** to arrive at some comprehension, illumination, prospect of a solution; **that will be the day** (*coll.*) that is very unlikely; **the day** the time spoken of or expected: to-day (*Scot.*); **the day after the fair** too late; **the other day** not long ago; **the time of day** the hour of the clock: a greeting; **win the day** to gain the victory. [O.E. *dæg*; Ger. *Tag*; not L. *diēs.*]

Dayak. See **Dyak.**

dayes-man; daynt; dayr'house (all *Spens.*). See **day (daysman); dainty; dairy.**

dayglo *dā′glō*, *adj.* of a luminously brilliant green, yellow, pink or orange. [*Day-glo*®, a brand of paint.]

day-nettle *dā′net′l, n.* a dead-nettle: (in Scotland and N. England) the hemp-nettle: a gathering on the finger. — Also **dae′-nett′le.** [Perh. for **dead-nettle;** but cf. O.N. (*akr*)*dai*, hemp-nettle.]

day-woman (*Shak.*). Same as **dey-woman.**

daze *dāz, v.t.* to stun, to stupefy. — *n.* (a state of) bewilderment: mica (*arch.*). — *adj.* **dazed** (*dāzd*). — *adv.* **dazedly** (*dāz'id-li*). — **in a daze** stunned. [O.N. *dasa-sk* (refl.), to be breathless.]

dazzle *daz'l, v.t.* to daze or overpower with strong light: to confound by brilliancy, beauty, or cleverness. — *v.i.* to be dazzled. — *ns.* **dazz'le, dazz'lement** the act of dazzling: that which dazzles; **dazz'ler; dazz'ling** (also *adj.*). — *adv.* **dazz'lingly.** — **dazz'le-paint'ing** fantastic painting for camouflage. [Freq. of **daze.**]

DDT. See **dichlor(o)-**.

de- *dē-, di-, pfx.* (1) meaning down from, away: (2) indicating a reversal of process, or deprivation: (3) used intensively. [L., or Fr. — L.]

deacon *dē'kən, n.* in Episcopal churches, a member of the order of clergy under priests: in some Presbyterian churches, an officer, man or woman, distinct from the elders, who attends to the secular affairs of the church: in Congregational and some other churches, an officer who advises the pastor, distributes the elements at communion, and dispenses charity· in Scotland, the master of an incorporated company: an adept (*Scot.*): the skin of a very young calf. — *n.* **dea'coness** a female servant of the Christian society in the time of the apostles: in a convent, a nun who has the care of the altar: one of an order of women in some Protestant churches whose duties are pastoral, educational, social and evangelical. — *ns.* **dea'conhood; dea'conry; dea'conship.** — **permanent deacon** an officer in the Roman Catholic church, minimally below a priest. — See also **diaconate.** [L. *diāconus* — Gr. *diākonos*, a servant.]

deactivate *dē-ak'tiv-āt, v.t.* to diminish or remove the activity of. — *n.* **deactiva'tion.** [Pfx. **de-** (2).]

dead *ded, adj.* no longer alive: inanimate: deathlike: of a ball, at rest, out of play: of a golf-ball, within a certain putt, or into the hole: out of use: obsolete: inactive: cold and cheerless: dull: numb: insensitive: unproductive: as good as dead: inelastic: without vegetation: utter, complete, absolute: unerring. — *v.t.* (*obs.*) to deaden, dull: to benumb. — *v.i.* (*obs.*) to lose vitality: to become numb. — *adv.* in a dead manner: absolutely: utterly: directly: exactly (*coll.*). — *n.* the time of greatest stillness, as *the dead* of night. — *v.t.* **dead'en** to make dead: to deprive partly of vigour, sensibility, or sensation: to blunt: to lessen: to make soundproof. — *ns.* **dead'ener; dead'ening** (also *adj.*); **dead'er** (*coll.*) a corpse; **dead'liness.** — *adj.* **dead'ly** causing death: fatal: implacable: very great (*coll.*). *adv.* in a manner resembling death: extremely (*coll.*). — *n.* **dead'ness.** — *adjs.* **dead'-alive', dead'-and-alive'** dull, inactive. — **dead'-beat** (*coll.*) a down-and-out. — *adj.* **dead'-beat'** (*coll.*) quite overcome, exhausted. — **dead'-bolt', -lock** one moved by turning key, knob, without intervention of a spring. — *adj.* **dead'-born** still-born. — **dead'-cart** a cart for collecting the bodies of those dead of a pestilence. — **dead centre** in a reciprocating engine or pump, either of the positions, at top and bottom of a piston stroke, at which the crank and connecting-rod are in line and there is no actual turning effect (usu. **top,** or **bottom dead centre**): a non-rotating centre in the tail-stock of a lathe; **dead'-clothes** clothes to bury the dead in; **dead'-col'ouring** the first broad outlines of a picture; **dead'-deal** a board for measuring and lifting a corpse. — *adjs.* **dead'-do'ing** (*Spens.*) putting to death, destructive; **dead'-drunk'** completely drunk. — **dead duck** (*coll.*) a plan, idea, person, etc., that has no chance of success or survival; **dead'-end'** a pipe, passage, etc., closed at one end: a blind alley (*lit.* and *fig.*). — *adj.* leading nowhere (*lit.* and *fig.*). — **dead'-eye** (*naut.*) a round, flattish wooden block with a rope or iron band passing around it, and pierced with three holes for a lanyard; **dead'-fall** a trap with a weight that falls when its support is removed; **dead'-fin'ish** (*Austr.*) a thicket or a thicket-forming shrub of the mimosa family (*Albizzia, Acacia*): a complete standstill or vanquishment; **dead'-fire** an appearance of fire taken as a death-omen; **dead'-freight** money paid for the empty space in a ship by a person who engages to freight her, but fails to make out a full cargo; **dead'=ground** (*mil.*) ground that cannot be covered by fire; **dead'-hand** mortmain; **dead'-head** one who enjoys privileges without paying, as in a theatre, etc.: an ineffective, unproductive person: a sprue. — *v.t.* to remove the withered heads of flowers, in order to encourage further growth. — **dead'-heat'** (the result of) a heat or race in which two or more competitors are equal. — Also *v.i.* — **dead'house** a mortuary; **dead language** one no longer spoken; **dead'-lett'er** a letter undelivered and unclaimed at the post-office: a law or ordinance made but not enforced; **dead'-lev'el** a stretch of land without any rising ground: sameness; **dead'-lift, -pull** a lift, pull, made without help, leverage, etc.: hence an effort under discouraging conditions; **dead'-lights** storm-shutters for a cabin window; **dead'line** line in a military prison, on going beyond which a prisoner was liable to be shot: closing date, last possible minute; **dead'lock** the case when matters have become so complicated that all is at a complete standstill: see also **dead'-bolt'.** — *v.i.* and *v.t.* to reach or bring to a standstill because of difficulties, etc. — **dead loss** a complete loss: a useless ally (*fig.*); **dead'ly-night'shade** belladonna; **deadly sin** a mortal sin (see **seven**); **dead'-march** a piece of solemn music played at funeral processions, esp. of soldiers; **dead'-meat** the flesh of animals ready for the market; **dead'-men** (*coll.*) empty bottles after a carouse: the poisonous parts of a crab or other edible shellfish; **dead'-nett'le** any species of *Lamium,* labiate plants superficially like nettles but stingless; **dead'pan** an expressionless face: one having or assuming such. — *adj.* expressionless: emotionless: dead serious or mock serious. — **dead'-pay** continued pay dishonestly drawn for men actually dead; **dead point** another name for **dead centre; dead'-reck'oning** an estimation of a ship's place simply by the log-book; **dead ringer** (*slang*) a person who, or a thing which, looks exactly like someone or something else; **dead'-rope** a rope not running in any block; **dead'-set'** a complete standstill, as of a setting dog: a determined and prolonged onslaught, esp. with a view to captivation; **dead'-shot** an unerring marksman; **dead's part** (*Scots law*) the part of a man's moveable property which he may bequeath by will, and which is not due to wife and children. — *adj.* **dead'stroke** without recoil. — **dead'-wall** wall unbroken by windows or other openings; **dead'-wa'ter** still water: eddy water closing in behind a ship's stern; **dead'-weight'** unrelieved weight: heavy and oppressive burden: difference in a ship's displacement loaded and light; **dead'-wind** calm (in the vortex of a storm): head wind (*obs.*); **dead'-wood** pieces of timber laid on the upper side of the keel at either end: useless material; **dead'-work** work, itself unprofitable, but necessary as a preliminary. — **dead as a dodo, door-nail, herring, mutton** absolutely dead; **dead man's handle** a device, e.g. on an electric train, which allows current to pass only so long as there is pressure on it; **dead man's pedal** a foot-operated safety device on the same principle, used esp. on diesel trains; **dead-men's bells** the foxglove; **dead men's fingers** a very common actinozoan coelenterate (*Alcyonium digitatum*); **dead men's shoes** succession to one who dies; **dead on** (used of time, musical notes, etc.) exact(ly); **Dead Sea apple, fruit** apple of Sodom; **dead set** see **set; dead** (set) against utterly opposed to; **dead spit** exact image; **dead to the world** very soundly asleep: unconscious; **leave for dead** to abandon, presuming dead: to surpass spectacularly (*coll.*); **over my dead body** when I am beyond caring, and not until; **put the dead wood on** (*slang*) to gain a great advantage over. [O.E. *dēad*; Goth. *dauths,* Ger. *tot,* from root of **die.**]

deaf *def, adj.* dull of hearing: unable to hear at all: not willing to hear: inattentive: hollow, with no kernel. — *v.t.* **deaf'en** to make deaf: to stun: to render impervious to sound. — *n.* **deaf'ening** stuffing put into floors, partition-walls, etc., to prevent sounds from passing through. — *adj.* making deaf (with noise): very loud. — *adv.* **deaf'ly.** — *n.* **deaf'ness.** — **deaf'-aid** a hearing-aid; **deaf'-mute'** one who is both deaf and dumb; **deaf'-mut'ism.** — **deaf-and-dumb alphabet** (language) digital and manual signs used to express letters (and words and phrases) visually; **turn a deaf ear** to pretend not to have heard: to ignore.   [O.E. *dēaf;* Du. *doof,* Ger. *taub.*]

deal[1] *dēl, n.* a portion: an indefinite quantity: a large quantity: the act of dividing cards: a business transaction (esp. a favourable one): treatment. — *v.t.* to divide, to distribute: to throw about: to deliver. — *v.i.* to transact business (in): to act: to distribute cards: *pa.t.* and *pa.p.* **dealt** (*delt*). — *ns.* **deal'er** one who deals or whose turn it is to deal, or who has dealt the hand in play: a trader; **deal'ership** the state of being a dealer: dealers as a group; **deal'ing** (often in *pl.*) manner of acting towards others: intercourse of trade. — **deal with** to have to do with, to treat of: to take action in regard to.   [O.E. *dǣlan* — *dǣl,* a part; Ger. *teilen* — *Teil,* a part or division; cf. **dole**[1].]

deal[2] *dēl, n.* a fir or pine board of a standard size: soft wood. — *adj.* of deal. — **deal'fish** a ribbon-fish (*Trachypterus*).   [M.L.G. *dele;* cf. O.E. *thel, thille,* and mod. **thill**[1].]

dealbate *dē-al'bāt, adj.* whitened. — *n.* **dealba'tion.**   [L. *dealbāre, -ātum,* to whitewash — pfx. *de-,* in sense of over a surface, *albus,* white.]

dealt. See **deal**[1].

deambulatory *dē-am'bū-lə-tər-i, n.* a place for walking about in: a passage or aisle round the choir and apse of a church.   [L. *deambulāre, -ātum,* to walk about.]

dean[1], **dene** *dēn, n.* a small valley.   [O.E. *denu,* a valley; cf. **den.**]

dean[2] *dēn, n.* a dignitary in cathedral and collegiate churches who presides over the canons: a rural dean: the chief cardinal-bishop of the College of Cardinals: the president of a faculty in a college or of the Faculty of Advocates: a resident fellow of a college who has administrative and disciplinary functions: the senior member of a corps or body: the chief chaplain of the Chapel Royal: the chief judge of the Court of Arches: the president of a trade-guild. — *ns.* **dean'ery** the office of a dean: a group of parishes presided over by a dean: a dean's house; **dean'ship** the office or dignity of a dean. — **Dean of Arches** dean of the Court of Arches (see **arch**); **Dean of Faculty** president of the Faculty of Advocates in Scotland; **Dean of Guild** form. a municipal functionary in Scotland who had authority over building and altering of houses; **rural dean** one who, under the bishop, has the special care and inspection of the clergy in certain parishes.   [O.Fr. *deien* (Fr. *doyen*) — L.L. *decānus* or Gr. *dekānos,* a chief of ten — L. *decem* or Gr. *deka,* ten.]

deaner *dēn'ər, (old slang) n.* a shilling.   [Prob. L. *denārius.*]

dear[1] *dēr, adj.* high in price: costly: characterised by high prices: scarce: highly valued: beloved: a conventional form of address used in letter-writing: earnest (*Shak.*). — *n.* one who is dear or beloved. — *adv.* at a high price: dearly. — *interj.* indicating surprise, pity, or other emotion. — *n.* and *adj.* **dear'ling** (*Spens.*) darling. *adv.* **dear'ly.** — *ns.* **dear'ie, dear'y** (*coll.*) one who is dear; **dear'ness.** — *adj.* **dear'bought** (*poet.*) precious. — **dear(y) me** an expression of various emotions; **Dear John letter** (*coll.;* orig. *U.S.*) a letter from a girl to her husband, fiancé, etc. ending their relationship; **dear knows** an expression of ignorance.   [O.E. *dēore, dȳre;* cog. with Ger. *teuer.*]

dear[2], **deare, deere** *dēr,* (*Spens.; Shak.; Milt.*) *adj.* grievous. — Also *adv.*   [O.E. *dēor.*]

deare. See **dere.**

dearn, dearnful, dearnly. See **dern**[2], etc.

dearth, *dûrth, n.* dearness, high price: scarcity: want: famine: barrenness.   [**dear.**]

dearticulate *dē-är-tik'ū-lāt, v.t.* to disjoint.   [Pfx. **de-** (2).]

deasil *dēz'l, des'l, desh'l, dēsh'l,* (*Scot.*) *n.* sunwise motion

— opp. to *withershins.* — *adv.* sunwise. — Also **dea'soil, dei's(h)eal, dea'siul.**   [Gael. *deiseil.*]

deaspirate *dē-as'pir-āt, v.t.* to remove the aspirate from. — *n.* **deaspira'tion.**   [Pfx. **de-** (2).]

death *deth, n.* state of being dead: extinction or cessation of life: manner of dying: mortality: a deadly plague: cause of death: spiritual lifelessness: the killing of the animal in hunting. — *adjs.* **death'ful** deadly, destructive: mortal: deathlike; **death'less** never dying: everlasting. — *n.* **death'lessness.** — *adj.* **death'like** like death. — *n.* **death'liness.** — *adj.* **death'ly** deadly: deathlike. — *advs.* **death'ward, -s.** — *adj.* **death'y.** — **death'-add'er** a poisonous Australian snake (*Acanthophis antarcticus*); **death'-ag'ony** the struggle often preceding death; **death angel** death-cap; **death'-bed** the bed on which one dies: the last illness; **death'-bell** the passing bell; **death'-blow** a blow that causes death; **death'-cap, -cup** a very poisonous toadstool (*Amanita phalloides*) often mistaken for an edible mushroom; **death'-cell** a prison cell for condemned prisoners awaiting execution; **death certificate** a legal certificate on which a doctor states the fact and usu. cause of a person's death; **death'-damp** a cold sweat preceding death. — *adj.* **death'-dealing.** — **death'-duty** (often in *pl.*) duty paid on inheritance of property; **death'-fire** a light supposed to presage death; **death'-knell** the ringing of a bell to announce a death: something that announces the end of one's hopes, ambitions, etc. (*fig.*). — *adj.* **death'-marked** marked for or by death, destined to die. — **death'-mask** a plaster-cast taken from the face after death; **death penalty** the taking of a person's life as punishment for crime. — *adj.* **death'= prac'tised** (*Shak.*) threatened with death by malicious arts. — **death'-rate** the proportion of deaths to the population; **death'-ratt'le** a rattling in the throat that sometimes precedes death; **death'-ray** an imaginary ray that could destroy all life; **death'-roll** a list of the dead; **death row** (*U.S.*) the part of a prison containing death-cells; **death's'-head** the skull of a human skeleton, or a figure of it: a memorial ring bearing such a figure; **deaths'man** (*Shak.*) an executioner; **death'-song** a song sung before dying; **death squad** an unofficial terrorist group who murder those whose views or activities they disapprove of, often operating with the tacit or covert support of the government of the country; **death'-stroke** a death-blow; **death'-throe** the dying agony; **death'-token** (*Shak.*) a sign or token of impending death, a plague-spot; **death'-trap** an unsafe structure or place that exposes one to great danger of death; **death'-warrant** an order from the authorities for the execution of a criminal; **death'-watch** a watch by a dying person: an insect that produces a ticking noise, esp. a beetle of the genus *Anobium* (also **death'-watch beetle**); **death wish** (*psych.*) a wish, conscious or unconscious, for death for oneself or another; **death'= wound** a wound that causes death. — **at death's door** very near to death; **catch one's death (of cold)** (*coll.*) to catch a very bad cold; **death-bed repentance** repentance for one's faults, sins, etc., when it is too late to reform one's life; **death's-head moth** a hawk-moth with pale markings on the back of the thorax somewhat like a skull; **death on** fatal to, fond of, good at; **do or put to death** to kill: to cause to be killed; **gates or jaws of death** the point of death; **in at the death** up on the animal before the dogs have killed it: present at the finish, crux, climax, etc. of anything (*fig.*); **like death warmed up, over** (*coll.*) very unwell; **like grim death** tenaciously; **sign one's own death-warrant** to do something that makes one's downfall inevitable; **to death** (until) dead: to a state of exhaustion; **to the death** to the uttermost.   [O.E. *dēath;* Ger. *Tod;* see **dead** and **die**[1].]

deave, deeve *dēv,* (*Scot.* and *dial.*) *v.t.* to deafen: to worry (esp. with noise): to bother: to break.   [See **deaf.**]

deaw, deawy, -ie (*Spens.*). Same as **dew, dewy.**

deb. Coll. form of **débutante.**

debacle, débâcle *di-bak'l, dā-bäk'l', n.* a breaking up of ice on a river: a sudden flood of water leaving its path strewed with debris (*geol.*): a complete break-up or collapse: a stampede. [Fr. *débâcle*; *dé-*, *des-*, and *bâcler*, to bar — L. *baculus*, a stick.]

debag *di-bag'*, (*coll.*) *v.t.* to remove the trousers of, as a prank or punishment. — *n.* **debagg'ing.** [Pfx. **de-** (2), bags.]

debar *di-bär'*, *v.t.* to bar out: to exclude: to hinder: — *pr.p.* **debarr'ing;** *pa.t.* and *pa.p.* **debarred'.** — *n.* **debar'ment.** [Pfx. **de-**(3).]

debark *di-bärk'*, *v.t.* or *v.i.* to disembark. — *n.* **dēbarka'tion, dēbarcā'tion.** [Fr. *débarquer* — *des* (— L. *dis-*), away, and Fr. *barque*, a ship.]

debarrass *di-bar'əs*, *v.t.* to disembarrass, disentangle, free. [Fr. *débarrasser*; *dé-*, *des-*, and *barre*, a bar.]

debase *di-bās'*, *v.t.* to lower: to make mean or of less value: to adulterate. — *adj.* **debased'** degraded: reversed (*her.*). — *ns.* **debās'edness; debase'ment** degradation; **debās'er.** — *adj.* **debās'ing.** — *adv.* **debās'ingly.** [Pfx. **de-**(1).]

debate *di-bāt'*, *n.* a contention in words or argument: a (parliamentary) discussion: fight, strife (*obs.*). — *v.t.* to contend for in argument: to argue about: to fight for (*arch.*). — *v.i.* to fight, contend (*obs.*): to deliberate: to consider: to join in debate. — *adjs.* **debāt'able,** also **debate'able,** liable to be disputed: open to argument: contentious; **debate'ful** (*Spens.*) quarrelsome. — *ns.* **debate'ment** (*Spens.*; *Shak.*) controversy; **debāt'er.** — *adv.* **debāt'ingly.** — **Debat(e)able Land** a tract of border land between Esk and Sark, formerly claimed by both England and Scotland. [O.Fr. *debatre* — L. *dē*, and *batuère*, to beat.]

debauch *di-böch'*, *v.t.* to lead away from duty or allegiance: to corrupt with lewdness: to seduce: to vitiate. — *v.i.* to over-indulge. — *n.* a fit or period of intemperance or debauchery. — *adj.* **debauched'** corrupt: profligate. — *adv.* **debauch'edly.** — *ns.* **debauch'edness; debauchee** (*di-böch-ē'*, *-bösh-ē'*) a libertine; **debauch'er; debauch'ery** excessive intemperance: habitual lewdness; **debauch'ment.** [O.Fr. *desbaucher* (Fr. *débaucher*), to corrupt — *des-* (L. *dis-*), and *baucher*, to hew.]

debby. See **début.**

debel *di-bel'*, (*Milt.*) *v.t.* to conquer in war: — *pr.p.* **debell'ing;** *pa.t.* and *pa.p.* **debelled'.** [L. *dēbellāre* — *dē*, down, *bellāre*, to war — *bellum*, war.]

debenture *di-ben'chər*, *n.* a written acknowledgment of a debt: a security issued by a company for money borrowed on the company's property, having a fixed rate of interest and usually fixed redemption rates: a certificate entitling an exporter of imported goods to a repayment of the duty paid on their importation. — *adj.* **debent'ured** entitled to drawback or debenture, as goods. [L. *dēbentur*, there are due, 3rd pers. pl. pass. of *dēbēre*, to owe — the first word of the receipt.]

debilitate *di-bil'i-tāt*, *v.t.* to make weak: to impair the strength of. — *adj.* **debile** (*deb'il*, *dē'bīl*; *arch.*) weak, feeble. — *n.* **debilitā'tion.** — *adjs.* **debil'itating; debil'itative.** — *n.* **debil'ity** weakness and languor: a weak action of the animal functions. [L. *dēbilitāre*, *-ātum* — *dēbilis*, weak — *dē*, from, *habilis*, able. See **ability.**]

debit *deb'it*, *n.* a debt or something due: an entry on the debtor side of an account, recording a sum owing (*book-k.*). — *v.t.* to charge with debt: to enter on the debtor side of an account. — *n.* **deb'itor** (*Shak.*) a debtor. — **debit card** a card used by a purchaser by means of which money is directly transferred from his account to the retailers. [L. *dēbitum*, what is due, from *dēbēre*, to owe.]

de-blur *dē-blûr'*, *v.t.* to make (blurred photographs) sharp, esp. with the aid of computers: — *pr.p.* **de-blurr'ing;** *pa.t.* and *pa.p.* **de-blurred'.** [Pfx. **de-** (2).]

debonair, debonnaire *deb-ə-nār'*, *adj.* of good appearance and manners: elegant: courteous: gay. — *adv.* **debonair'ly.** — *n.* **debonair'ness.** [Fr. *de*, of, *bon*, good, and the old word *aire* (*masc.*), manner, origin; mod. Fr. *débonnaire*.]

debosh *di-bosh'*. An old form of **debauch.**

debouch *di-bowch'*, *di-bōōsh'*, *v.i.* to issue, emerge, to march or flow out from a narrow pass or confined place. — *ns.* **débouché** (*dā-bōō-shā'*) an outlet; **debouch'ment** an act or place of debouching; **debouchure** (*di-bōōshūr'*) the mouth of a river or strait. [Fr. *déboucher* — *de*, from, *bouche*, mouth — L. *bucca*, cheek.]

Debrett *di-bret'*, *n.* a peerage edited and published from 1784 until his death by John Field *Debrett*, still in publication and the type of all exclusive lists.

débridement *dā-brēd-mā*, *dā-brēd'mənt*, *n.* the removal of foreign matter or dead or infected tissue from a wound. — *v.t.* **débride** to clean or treat (a wound) by débridement: to remove (dead tissue, etc.) by débridement. [Fr., lit. unbridling.]

debrief *dē-brēf'*, *v.t.* to gather information from a soldier, astronaut, etc., on his return from a mission. — *n.* **debrief'ing.** [Pfx. **de-** (2).]

debris, débris *deb'rē*, *dəb-rē'*, or *dāb'rē*, *n.* wreckage: ruins: rubbish: a mass of rocky fragments. [Fr., from *briser*, akin to **bruise.**]

debruised *di-brōōzd'*, (*her.*) *adj.* surmounted or partly covered by one of the ordinaries. [O.Fr. *debruisier* — *de-*, apart, *bruiser*, to break.]

debt *det*, *n.* what one owes to another: what one becomes liable to do or suffer: a state of obligation or indebtedness: a duty: a sin (*B.*). — *adj.* **deb'ted** (*Shak.*) indebted, obliged. — *ns.* **debtee'** a creditor; **debt'or** one who owes a debt. — **bad debt** a debt of which there is no prospect of payment; **debt of honour** a debt not recognised by law, but binding in honour — esp. a gambling or betting debt; **debt of nature** death; **floating debt** miscellaneous public debt, like exchequer and treasury bills, as opposed to *funded debt*, that which has been converted into perpetual annuities like consols in Britain; **in someone's debt** under an obligation (not necessarily pecuniary) to someone; **national debt** see **nation**[1]. [O.Fr. *dette* — L. *dēbitum*, *dēbēre*, to owe.]

debug *dē-bug'*, *v.t.* to remove concealed listening devices from: to find faults or errors in and remove them from (something mechanical): to remove insects from (*coll.*). [L. *dē*, from, and **bug.**]

debunk *dē-bungk'*, *v.t.* (*slang*) to clear of bunk or humbug: to remove the whitewash from (a reputation): to show up (e.g. a theory) as false. [Pfx. **de-** (2).]

debus *dē-bus'*, *v.t.* and *v.i.* to unload from or get out of a bus or other vehicle: — *pr.p.* **debuss'ing;** *pa.t.* and *pa.p.* **debussed'.** [Pfx. **de-** (1).]

début *dā-bü'*, *n.* a beginning or first attempt: a first appearance before the public, or in society. — *n.* **débutant** (*dā-bü-tā*, *deb'ü-tənt*) one who makes his first appearance: — *fem.* **débutante** (*-tāt*, *deb'ü-tənt*) esp. of one making her first appearance in society (*coll.* shortenings **deb, debb'y**). — *adj.* **debb'y** (*coll.*) of or like a deb or debs. [Fr. *début*, a first stroke — *débuter* — *de*, from, *but*, aim, mark.]

Debye (unit) *də-bī'* (*ū'nit*), *n.* a unit of electric dipole moment. [P. J. W. *Debye*, Dutch physicist.]

deca- *dek-ə-*, prefix signifying ten. [Gr. *deka*.]

decachord *dek'ə-körd*, *n.* an old ten-stringed musical instrument. [Gr. *dekachordos* — *deka*, ten, and *chordē*, a string.]

decade, decad *dek'ād*, *dek-ād'*, *-ad*, *ns.* a series of ten years: any group or series of ten. — *adj.* **dec'adal.** [Gr. *dekas*, *-ados* — *deka*, ten.]

decadence *dek'ə-dəns*, or *di-kā'*, **dec'adency** (or *di-kā'*), *ns.* state of decay: a decline from a superior state, standard or time: applied to a school in late 19th-century French literature, the symbolists, and their like. — *adj.* **dec'adent** (or *di-kā'*) decaying: lacking in moral and physical vigour: symbolist. — *n.* one who is degenerate: a symbolist. — *adv.* **decadently.** [Fr. *décadence* — L.L. *dēcadentia*, from L. *dē*, down, *cadēre*, to fall.]

decaffeinate *dē-kaf'i-nāt*, *v.t.* to extract (most of) the caffeine from coffee. [Pfx. **de-** (2).]

decagon *dek'ə-gon, n.* a plane figure of ten angles and sides. — *adj.* **decagonal** (*-ag'ən-əl*). [Gr. *deka*, and *gōniā*, an angle.]

decagramme, decagram *dek'ə-gram, n.* a weight of ten grammes. [Fr. *décagramme* — Gr. *deka*, ten, and **gramme.**]

Decagynia *dek-ə-jin'i-ə, (bot.) n.pl.* in the Linnaean system a class of plants with ten pistils. — *adjs.* **decagyn'ian, decagynous** (*-aj'*). [Gr. *deka*, ten, *gynē*, a woman.]

decahedron *dek-ə-hē'drən, n.* a solid figure having ten faces. — *adj.* **decahē'dral.** [Gr. *deka*, and *hedrā*, a seat.]

decal *dē'kal, dek'al, n.* a transfer (picture or design). [From Fr. *décalquer*, to trace, copy.]

decalcify *dē-kal'si-fī, v.t.* to deprive of lime. — *n.* **decalcificā'tion.** [Pfx. **de-** (2).]

decalescence *dē-kəl-es'əns, n.* the behaviour of iron or steel which in heating from red to white reaches a point where it seems to go back for a little — the opposite of *recalescence.* [L. *dē*, down, *calēscĕre*, to grow hot.]

decalitre *dek'ə-lēt-ər, n.* ten litres, 2·20 imperial gallons, 2·64 U.S. gallons. [Fr. *décalitre* — Gr. *deka*, ten, and *lītrā*, a pound.]

decalogue *dek'ə-log, n.* the ten commandments. — *n.* **decalogist** (*di-kal'ə-jist*) an exponent as of the decalogue. [Gr. *deka*, ten, *logos*, a discourse.]

Decameron *di-kam'ə-ron, -rən, n.* Boccaccio's book of a hundred tales, supposed to be told in ten days. — *adj.* **decameron'ic.** [Gr. *deka*, ten, *hēmerā*, a day.]

decamerous *di-kam'ər-əs, adj.* having the parts in tens. [Gr. *deka*, ten, *meros*, part.]

decametre *dek'ə-mēt-ər, n.* ten metres. [Fr. *décamètre* — Gr. *deka*, ten, *metron*, a measure.]

decamp *di-kamp', v.i.* to make off, esp. secretly: to break camp. — *n.* **decamp'ment.** [Fr. *décamper.*]

decanal *dek-ān'əl, adj.* pertaining to a dean or deanery: decani. — *adj.* **decān'ī** dean's, i.e. south (of the side of a choir where the dean sits, opposed to **cantoris**): used (*mus.*) in antiphonal singing. [L.L. *decānus, -ī.*]

Decandria *de-kan'dri-ə, (bot.) n.pl.* in Linnaean system a class of plants with ten stamens. — *adjs.* **decan'drian; decan'drous** with ten stamens. [Gr. *deka*, ten, and *anēr, andros,* a man, male.]

decane *dek'ān, n.* a hydrocarbon ($C_{10}H_{22}$), tenth of the methane series. [Gr. *deka*, ten.]

decani. See **decanal.**

decant *di-kant', v.t.* to pour off, leaving sediment: to pour from one vessel into another: to move (people) to another area, etc. — *ns.* **decantā'tion** (*dē-*); **decant'er** an ornamental stoppered bottle for holding decanted liquor. [Fr. *décanter* (It. *decantare*) — L. *dē*, from, *canthus*, beak of a vessel — Gr. *kanthos*, corner of the eye.]

decantate *dē-kant'āt, (obs.) v.t.* and *v.i.* to chant or say repeatedly. [L. *dēcantāre* — pfx. *dē-, cantāre,* intens. of *canĕre*, to sing.]

decapitalisation, -z- *di-kap-it-əl-ī-zā'shən, n.* loss or draining away of capital in industry. — *v.t.* **decap'italise, -ize.** [Pfx. **de-** (2).]

decapitate *di-kap'i-tāt, v.t.* to behead. — *n.* **decapitā'tion.** [L.L. *dēcapitāre* — L. *dē*, from, and *caput, capitis*, the head.]

Decapoda *di-kap'ə-də, n.pl.* an order of higher crustaceans with ten feet (including pincers) — crabs, lobsters, shrimps, prawns, etc.: an order of cephalopods with ten arms. — *n.* **dec'apod** a member of either of these orders. — Also *adj.* — *adjs.* **decap'odal, decap'odan, decap'odous.** [Gr. *deka*, ten, and *pous, podos*, a foot.]

decarbonise, -ize *dē-kär'bən-īz, v.t.* to remove carbon or carbon dioxide from (also **decar'būrise**, -ize; **decar'bonate**). — *ns.* **decarbonā'tion; decarbonīsā'tion, -z-; decarburīsā'tion, -z-.** See also **decarb** under **decoke.** [Pfx. **de-** (2).]

decare *dek'är, dek-är', n.* 1000 square metres — 10 ares. [Gr. *deka*, ten, and **are**[1].]

decastere *dek'ə-stēr, n.* ten steres. [Gr. *deka*, ten, and **stere.**]

decastich *dek'ə-stik, n.* a poem of ten lines. [Gr. *deka*, ten, and *stichos*, a row, a verse.]

decastyle *dek'ə-stīl, n.* a portico with ten columns in front. — Also *adj.* [Gr. *deka*, ten, *stȳlos*, a column.]

decasyllable *dek-ə-sil'ə-bl, n.* a verse-line, or a word, of ten syllables. — *adj.* **decasyllabic** (*-ab'ik*). [Gr. *deka*, ten, *syllabē*, a syllable; see **syllable.**]

decathlon *dek-ath'lon, n.* a two-day contest of ten events held at the modern Olympic Games since 1912. — *n.* **decath'lete.** [Gr. *deka*, ten, *athlon*, a contest.]

decaudate *dē-kö'dāt, v.t.* to cut off the tail of. [L. *dē*, from, *cauda*, tail.]

decay *di-kā', v.i.* to fall away from a state of health or excellence: to waste away: to rot. — *v.t.* to cause to waste away: to impair. — *n.* a falling into a worse or less perfect state: a wearing away: rotting: bad or rotten matter (e.g. in a tooth): loss of fortune: ruin, downfall (*obs.*): disintegration of a radioactive substance. — *adj.* **decayed'** rotten: reduced in circumstances, impoverished. [O.Fr. *decair* — L. *dē*, from, *cadĕre*, to fall.]

Decca® *dek'ə, n.* the **Decca Navigator System**, consisting of a series of chains of long-wave radio transmitting stations, each chain formed of a master station and three slaves, providing a navigator or pilot with meter readings that have to be interpreted by special charts, or, alternatively, with a direct picture of his track on a **Decca Flight Log.**

deccie *dek'i, (slang) n.* short for interior decoration or (also with *cap.*) an interior decoration enthusiast, interior designer.

decease *di-sēs', n.* death. — *v.i.* to die. — *adj.* **deceased'** dead: lately dead. — *n.* the dead person in question. [O.Fr. *deces* (Fr. *décès*) — L. *dēcessus*, departure, death — *dē*, away, *cēdĕre, cēssum*, to go.]

decedent *di-sē'dənt, n.* (*U.S. law*) a deceased person. [L. *dēcēdēns, -entis*, pr.p. of *dēcēdĕre*, to depart — *dē*, away, *cēdĕre*, to go.]

deceit *di-sēt', n.* act of deceiving: anything intended to mislead another: fraud: falseness. — *adj.* **deceit'ful** full of deceit: disposed or tending to deceive: insincere. — *adj.* **deceit'fully.** — *n.* **deceit'fulness.** [O.Fr. *deceite* — L. *dēcipĕre, dēceptum*, to deceive.]

deceive *di-sēv', v.t.* to mislead or cause to err: to cheat: to disappoint (*arch.*). — *adj.* **deceiv'able** that may be deceived: exposed to imposture. — *ns.* **deceiv'ableness, deceivabil'ity.** — *adj.* **deceiv'ably.** — *n.* **deceiv'er.** [Fr. *décevoir* — L. *dēcipĕre, dēceptum*, to deceive.]

decelerate *dē-sel'ər-āt, v.t.* and *v.i.* to retard. — *ns.* **decelerā'tion; decel'erator; decelerom'eter** an instrument for measuring deceleration. [L. *dē*, down, *celer*, swift.]

December *di-sem'bər, n.* formerly the tenth, now the twelfth month of the year. — *adjs.* **Decem'berish, Decem'berly** wintry, cold. — *n.* **Decem'brist** one of those who took part in the Russian conspiracy of December, 1825. [L. *December* — *decem*, ten.]

decemvir *di-sem'vər, n.* a member of a body of ten men: esp. of those who drew up the Laws of the Twelve Tables at Rome (451–450 B.C.): — *pl.* **decem'virs** or **decem'virī** (L. *dek'em-wi-r ē*). — *adj.* **decem'viral.** — *n.* **decem'virāte** a body of ten men in office: the term of office of decemvirs. [L. *decem*, ten, and *vir*, a man.]

decency. See **decent.**

decennary *di-sen'ər-i, n.* a period of ten years — also **decenn'ium.** — *adj.* **decenn'ial** consisting of, or happening every, ten years. [L. *decem*, ten, and *annus*, a year.]

decennoval *di-sen'ō-vəl, (obs.) adj.* pertaining to the number 19. [L. *decennovalis* — *decem*, ten, *novem*, nine.]

decent *dē'sənt, adj.* becoming: seemly: proper: modest: moderate: fairly good: passable: showing tolerant or kindly moderation (*coll.*): nice, pleasant (*coll.*). — *n.* **dē'cency** becomingness: modesty: considerateness, sense of what may be fitly expected of one (*coll.*): (in

pl.) the conventions of respectable behaviour. — *adv.*
dē'cently. [L. *decēns, -entis,* pr.p. of *decēre,* to be
becoming.]
decentralise, -ize *dē-sen'trəl-īz, v.t.* to withdraw from the
centre: to transform by transferring functions from a
central government, organisation or head to local
centres. — *n.* **decentralisā'tion, -z-.** [Pfx. **de-** (2).]
deception *di-sep'shən, n.* act of deceiving: state of being
deceived: means of deceiving or misleading: trick:
illusion. — *n.* **deceptibil'ity.** — *adjs.* **decept'ible** capable
of being deceived; **decep'tious** (*Shak.*) deceitful; **decep'-
tive** tending to deceive: misleading. — *adv.* **decep'tively.**
— *n.* **decep'tiveness.** — *adj.* **decep'tory** tending to
deceive. — **deceptive cadence** (*music*) same as **interrupted cadence.** [O.Fr., — L.L. *dēceptiō, -ōnis —
dēcipĕre,* to deceive.]
decerebrate *dē-ser'ə-brāt, v.t.* to deprive of cerebrum. —
Also **decer'ebrise, -ize.** — *n.* **decerebrā'tion.** [Pfx. **de-**
(2).]
decern *di-sûrn', (Scots law) v.t.* and *v.i.* to judge: to decree.
to pass judgment. [O.Fr. *decerner —* L. *dēcernĕre
— de,* and *cernĕre,* to distinguish.]
decession *di-sesh'ən, (rare) n.* departure. [See **decease.**]
déchéance *dā-shā-ās,* (Fr.) *n.* forfeiture.
dechristianise, -ize *dē-krist'yən-īz, v.t.* to turn from Christianity. — *n.* **dechristianiza'tion.** [Pfx. **de-** (2).]
deci- *des'i-,* prefix signifying one-tenth. [L. *decimus,*
tenth.]
deciare *des'i-är, n.* the tenth part of an are. [Fr., — L.
deci- (in *decimus*), and **are.**]
decibel *des'i-bel, n.* the tenth part of a bel — unit more
commonly used than **bel** (q.v.). [L. *deci-,* and **bel.**]
decide *di-sīd', v.t.* to determine: to end: to settle: to
resolve. — *v.i.* to make up one's mind. — *adjs.*
decid'able capable of being decided; **decid'ed** determined: clear, unmistakable: resolute. — *adv.* **decid'-
edly.** — *n.* **decid'er** one who, or that which, decides:
an action, etc., that proves decisive, as the winning
goal in a match (*coll.*). [O.Fr. *decider —* L. *dēcīdĕre
— dē,* away, *caedĕre,* to cut.]
deciduous *di-sid'ū-əs, adj.* liable to be shed at a certain
period: transitory, not permanent: shedding all the
leaves together (opp. to *evergreen*) (*bot.*): shedding
wings (as some insects). — *n.* **decid'ua** a membrane of
the uterus discharged after parturition. — *adjs.* **decid'-
ual; decid'uate.** — *n. adj.* **decid'uousness.** [L. *dēciduus —
dēcīdĕre — dē,* from, *cadĕre,* to fall.]
decigram(me) *des'i-gram, n.* the tenth part of a gram(me).
decilitre *des'i-lē-tər, n.* a tenth part of a litre.
decillion *di-sil'yən, n.* a million raised to the tenth power:
in American notation, a thousand raised to the
eleventh power. — *adj.* and *n.* **decill'ionth.** [L. *decem,*
ten, and **million.**]
decimal *des'i-məl, adj.* numbered or proceeding by tens.
— *n.* a decimal fraction. — *v.t.* **dec'imalise, -ize** to
convert to a decimal system, esp. the metric system.
— *ns.* **decimalisā'tion, -z-; dec'imalism** use or advocacy
of a decimal system; **dec'imalist.** — *adv.* **dec'imally.** —
decimal currency one in which the basic unit is divided
into ten, or a multiple of ten, parts; **decimal fraction** a
fraction expressed by continuing ordinary decimal
notation into negative powers of ten, a point being
placed after the unit figure; **decimal notation** a system
of writing numbers based on ten and powers of ten,
our ordinary system; **decimal places** the number of
figures written after the point (**decimal point**) which
separates the unit and the decimal fraction; **decimal
system** a system in which each unit is ten times the
next below it, esp. the metric system of weights and
measures. [L. *decima* (*pars*), a tenth (part).]
decimate *des'i-māt, v.t.* to take the tenth part of: to punish
by killing every tenth man: (*loosely*) to reduce very
heavily. — *ns.* **decimā'tion; dec'imātor.** [L. *decimāre,
-ātum — decimus,* tenth — *decem,* ten.]
décime *dā-sēm,* (*hist.*) *n.* a French coin equal to ¹/₁₀ franc.
[Fr., — L. *decima* (*pars*), tenth (part).]
decimetre *des'i-mē-tər, n.* a tenth of a metre.

decinormal *des-i-nör'məl,* (*chem.*) *adj.* of one-tenth of
normal concentration. [L. *decimus,* tenth, and **normal.**]
decipher *di-sī'fər, v.t.* to uncipher: to read or transliterate
or interpret from secret, unknown, or difficult writing:
to make out: to detect (*Shak.*): to reveal (*Shak.*): to
show forth (*obs.*). — *n.* **decī'pherabil'ity.** — *adj.* **decī'-
pherable.** — *ns.* **decī'pherer; decī'pherment.** [Pfx. **de-**
(2).]
decision *di-sizh'ən, n.* the act or product of deciding:
settlement: judgment: the quality of being decided in
character. — *adj.* **decisive** (*-sīs'iv*) having the power of
deciding: showing decision: final: positive. — *adv.*
decī'sively. — *n.* **decī'siveness.** — *adj.* **decī'sory** decisive.
— **decision table** (*log.* and *comput.*) a table comprising
four sections showing a number of conditions and
actions to be taken if these are or are not met,
indicating the action to be taken under any condition
or set of conditions. [See **decide.**]
declstere *des'i-stēr, n.* one-tenth of a stere.
decitizenise, -ize *dē-sit'i-zən-īz, v.t.* to deprive of citizenship. [Pfx. **de-** (2).]
decivilise, -ize *dē-siv'i-līz, v.t.* to reduce from a civilised
to a more savage state. [Pfx. **de-** (2).]
deck *dek, v.t.* to cover: to clothe: to adorn: to furnish
with a deck: to pile up on a platform. — *n.* a covering:
a horizontal platform extending from one side of a
vessel to the other, thereby joining the sides together,
and forming both a floor and a covering (*naut.*): the
floor, platform, or tier as in a bus, bridge, etc.: the
ground (*slang*): a pile of things laid flat: a pack of
cards: the part of a pack used in a particular game, or
the undealt part: the turntable of a record-player: that
part of a tape-recorder or computer in which the
magnetic tapes are placed, and the mechanism for
running them: a set of punched cards. — *adj.* **decked**
(*dekt*) adorned, decorated. — *ns.* **deck'er** the person
or thing that decks: a vessel, vehicle, or other structure
that has a deck or decks (used only in composition,
as *three-decker*): one who adorns; **deck'ing** adornment:
a platform. — **deck'-bridge** a bridge whose upper
stringer carries the roadway; **deck'-cargo** cargo stowed
on the deck of a vessel; **deck'chair** a chair, usually
folding and made of canvas, such as passengers sit or
lie on deck in; **deck'-game** a game played on a ship's
deck; **deck'-hand** a person employed on deck: an
ordinary sailor; **deck'-house** a house, room, or box on
deck; **deck'-load** a deck-cargo; **deck officer** a ship's
officer dealing with navigation, cargo, etc., rather than
engineering; **deck'-passage** a passage securing only the
right of being on deck, without cabin accommodation;
deck'-pass'enger; deck'-quoits quoits as played on a
ship's deck, with rope rings; **deck'-tenn'is** lawn-tennis
modified for playing on board ship. — **clear the decks**
to tidy up, remove encumbrances, esp. in preparation
for action (orig. naval action, now often *fig.*); **deck out**
to adorn, decorate; **hit the deck** (*slang*) to lie, fall, or
be pushed down quickly; **pedestrian deck** a safe-way
for pedestrians. [Verbal meanings — Du. *dekken,*
to cover: cf. **thatch;** Ger. *decken;* L. *tegĕre;* substantive
meanings — M.Du. *dec,* roof, covering.]
deckle *dek'l, n.* in paper-making a contrivance for fixing
width of sheet: a deckle-edge. — *adj.* **deckled** (*dek'ld*)
deckle-edged. — **deck'le-edge** the raw or ragged edge
of handmade paper or an imitation of it. — *adj.*
deck'le-edged having a rough uncut edge. [Ger.
Deckel, lid.]
decko. See **dekko.**
declaim *di-klām', v.i.* to make a set or rhetorical speech:
to harangue: to recite. — *v.t.* to utter, repeat, or recite
declamatorily. — *ns.* **declaim'ant, declaim'er.** — *n.* and
adj. **declaim'ing.** — *n.* **declamation** (*dek-lə-mā'shən*) act
of declaiming: a set speech in public: display in speaking. — *adv.* **declamatorily** (*di-klam'ə-tə-ri-li*). — *adj.*
declam'atory of the nature of declamation: appealing
to the passions: noisy and rhetorical. [L. *dēclāmāre
— de-,* intens., *clāmāre,* to cry out.]

declare *di-klār′, v.t.* to make known: to announce: to assert: to make a full statement of, as of goods at a custom-house: to expose and claim a score for (*bezique*, etc.): to announce one's choice of trump-suit or no trumps (*bridge*). — *v.i.* to make a statement: to announce one's decision or sympathies: to show cards in order to score: to end an innings voluntarily before ten wickets have fallen (*cricket*). — *adj.* **declar′able** capable of being declared, exhibited, or proved. — *ns.* **declar′ant** one who makes a declaration; **declaration** (*dek-lə-rā′shən*) act of declaring: that which is declared: a written affirmation: a formal announcement (e.g. of war): an official announcement of entry for a race, etc.: in the criminal law of Scotland, the statement made by the prisoner before the magistrate: in common law, the pleading in which the plaintiff in an action at law sets forth his case against the defendant. — *adjs.* **declarative** (*di-klar′ə-tiv*) making a statement or declaration: declaratory; **declar′atory** explanatory: declarative. — *advs.* **declar′atively, declar′atorily.** — *n.* **declar′ator** a form of action in the Court of Session, with the view of having a fact judicially ascertained and declared. — *adj.* **declared′** avowed. — *adv.* **declar′edly** avowedly. — *n.* **declar′er** one who declares. — **declaratory act** an act intended to explain an obscure or disputed law. — **declare an interest** (of member of parliament, etc.) formally to make known that he has (financial) connections with an organisation with which parliamentary discussions are concerned; **declare off** to renounce: to withdraw: to cancel; **(well) I declare!** *interj.* expressing surprise. [L. *dēclārāre*, -*ātum* — pfx. *dē-*, wholly, *clārus*, clear (partly through Fr. *déclarer*).]

declass *dē-kläs′, v.t.* to remove or degrade from one's class. — *adj.* **déclassé,** *fem.* **déclassée** (*dā-klä-sā*; Fr.) having lost caste or social standing. [Fr. *déclasser.*]

declassify *dē-klas′i-fī, v.t.* to take off the security list. [Pfx. **de-** (2).]

declension *di-klen′shən, n.* a falling off: decay: descent: system of cases and case-endings (*gram.*): a class of words similarly declined: a statement in order of the cases of a word. — *adj.* **declen′sional.** [See **decline**.]

decline *di-klīn′, v.i.* to bend or turn away: to deviate: to refuse: to bend or slope down: to fail or decay e.g. in health, fortune: to stoop or condescend: to draw to an end. — *v.t.* to bend down: to turn away from: to refuse: to avoid: to give the various cases of (*gram.*). — *n.* a falling off: deviation: decay: a gradual sinking of the bodily faculties, consumption (*arch.*): a down-slope. *adjs.* **declin′able** having inflection for case; **declī′nal** bending downward; **declinant** (*dek′lin-ənt; her.*) having the tail hanging down; **dec′linate** (*bot.*) curving downwards. — *ns.* **declinā′tion** act of declining (*U.S.*): sloping or bending downwards: deviation: angular distance of a heavenly body from the celestial equator (*astron.*); **dec′linātor** an instrument determining declination. — *adj.* **declin′atory** containing a declination or refusal. — *ns.* **declin′ature** act of declining or refusing: a plea declining the jurisdiction of a judge (*law*); **declinom′eter** an instrument for measuring declination in various senses, esp. the **declination of the compass** or **magnetic declination** (i.e. the deviation of the magnetic needle from the true north), or the declination or dip of a compass needle (see **dip of the needle**). — **on the decline** in the process of becoming less, deteriorating. [L. *dēclīnāre* — *dē*, down, away from, *clīnāre*, to bend (partly through Fr. *décliner*).]

declivity *di-kliv′i-ti, n.* a place that declines, or slopes downward, opposite of *acclivity*: inclination downwards. — *adjs.* **decliv′itous; declī′vous.** [Fr. *déclivité* — L. *dēclīvitās, -ātis* — *dē*, downward, *clīvus*, sloping, akin to *clīnāre.*]

declutch *dē-kluch′, v.i.* to release the clutch. [Pfx. **de-** (2).]

deco, Deco *dek′ō, adj.* pertaining to art deco (q.v.).

decoct *di-kokt′, v.t.* to prepare by boiling: to extract the substance of by boiling: to boil: to devise. — *adjs.*

decoc′tible, decoc′tive. — *ns.* **decoc′tion** an extract of anything got by boiling; **decoc′ture** a substance prepared by decoction. [L. *dēcoquĕre, dēcoctum* — *dē*, down, *coquĕre*, to cook.]

decode *dē-kōd′, v.t.* to translate from a code. — *v.t.* and *v.i.* to convert from sound or writing to meaning, or from a foreign language to one's own language (*ling.*). — *n.* (*dē′kōd*) a decoded message. — *n.* **decō′der.** [Pfx. **de-** (2).]

decoherer *dē-kō-hē′rər, n.* a device for bringing a coherer back to its former condition after it has been affected by an electric wave. [Pfx. **de-** (2).]

decoke *dē-kōk′,* earlier **decarb** *dē-kärb′,* (*coll.*) *vs.t.* to decarbonise (an internal combustion engine). [Pfx. **de-** (2).]

decollate *dē-kol′āt, v.t.* to behead. — *adj.* **decoll′ated** rounded off, as the apex of a shell. — *n.* **decollā′tion** the act of beheading: a picture of a decapitation, esp. of the head of St John the Baptist on a charger: the festival of the Baptist, 29th Aug. [L. *dēcollāre* — *dē*, from, *collum*, the neck.]

décolleté *dā-kol-tā, adj.* with neck uncovered: of dress, low cut. — *n.* **décolletage** (*dā-kol-täzh′*) (a dress with) a low-cut neckline. [Fr., pa.p. of *décolleter*, to bare the neck and shoulders — *collet*, collar. Cf. **decollate.**]

decolonise, -ize *dē-kol′ə-nīz, v.t.* to release from being a colony, grant independence to. — *n.* **decolonisā′tion, -z-.** [Pfx. **de-** (2).]

decolour, decolor *dē-kul′ər, v.t.* to deprive of colour — also **decol′o(u)rise, -ize.** — *n.* and *adj.* **decol′orant** (a substance) that bleaches or removes colour. — *v.t.* **decol′orate** to deprive of colour. — *adj.* without colour. — *ns.* **decolorā′tion** removal or absence of colour; **decolo(u)rīsā′tion, -z-.** [L. *dēcolōrāre* — *dē*, from, *color*, colour.]

decommission *dē-kəm-ish′ən, v.t.* to take out of commission or operation, e.g. a warship, atomic reactor. — *ns.* **decommiss′ioner; decommiss′ioning.** [Pfx. **de-** (2).]

decomplex *dē′kom-pleks, adj.* repeatedly compound. [Pfx. **de-** (3).]

decompose *dē-kom-pōz′, v.t.* to separate the component parts of: to resolve into elements. — *v.i.* to decay, rot — *n.* **decompōsabil′ity.** — *adj.* **decompōs′able.** — *n.* **decompōs′er.** [Fr. *décomposer* — pfx. *dé-* (L. *dis-*, apart), and *composer*; see **compose**.]

decomposition[1] *di-kom-pə-zish′ən, n.* act or state of decomposing: decay. — *v.t.* **decompound** (*dē-kəmpownd′*) to decompose. — *adj.* **decompound′able.** [Fr. pfx. *dé-* (L. *dis-*), apart, and **composition**; accidentally associated in meaning with **decompose**.]

decomposition[2] *dē-kom-ə-zish′ən, n.* the compounding of things already compound. — *adj.* **decomp′osite** (or *-oz′-*) doubly or further compounded. — *v.t.* **decompound** (*-kəm-pownd′*) to compound again, or further. — *adj.* (*dē′*) compounded more than once: having leaflets themselves composed of separate parts (*bot.*). [Pfx. **de-** (3).]

decompound. See **decomposition**[1,2].

decompress *dē-kəm-pres′, v.t.* to release from pressure. — *n.* **decompression** (*-presh′ən*) the act or process of releasing from pressure: the gradual release of air pressure on persons (as divers, construction workers, etc.) on returning to normal atmospheric conditions: any operation to relieve excessive pressure (*surg.*). — *adj.* **decompress′ive.** — *n.* **decompress′or.** — **decompression chamber** a chamber in which excessive pressure can be reduced gradually to atmospheric pressure, or in which a person can be subjected gradually to decreased atmospheric pressure; **decompression sickness** same as **caisson disease.** [Pfx. **de-** (2).]

decongest *dē-kən-jest′, v.t.* to relieve or end the congestion of. — *ns.* **deconges′tant** (*med.*) an agent that relieves congestion; **decongest′ion** (*-yən*). — *adj.* **deconges′tive.** [Pfx. **de-** (2).]

deconsecrate *dē-kon′si-krāt, v.t.* to deprive of the character given by consecration: to secularise. — *n.* **deconsecrā′tion.** [Pfx. **de-** (2).]

decontaminate *dē-kən-tam'in-āt*, *v.t.* to free from contamination. — *ns.* **decontam'inant; decontaminā'tion.** — *adj.* **decontam'inative.** — *n.* **decontam'inātor.** [Pfx. **de-** (2).]

decontrol *dē-kən-trōl'*, *v.t.* to remove (esp. official) control from. — *n.* removal of control. [Pfx. **de-** (2).]

décor *dā'kör*, *n.* scenery and stage embellishments: ornament: general decorative effect (colour-scheme, furnishings, etc.) of a room. [Fr., decoration.]

decorate *dek'ə-rāt*, *v.t.* to ornament, to beautify: to paint, put wallpaper on (a house, etc.): to honour with a badge or medal. — *adj.* **dec'orated.** — *n.* **decorā'tion** ornament: the applied paint and wallpaper in e.g. a house: badge of an order: (in *pl.*) flags, bunting, paper chains, etc., put out or hung at a time of rejoicing. — *adj.* **dec'orative** (*-rə-tiv*) ornamental. — *adv.* **dec'oratively.** — *n.* **dec'orativeness; dec'orātor** one who decorates, esp. houses. — **Decorated style** (*archit.*) a style of Gothic architecture, elaborate and richly decorated, which prevailed till near the end of the 14th century; **Decoration Day** see **Memorial Day.** [L. *decorāre*, *-ātum* — *decus*, what is becoming — *decēre*, to be becoming.]

decorous *de'kə-rəs*, or (*old-fashioned*) *-kō'*, *-kö'*, *adj.* becoming: suitable: proper: decent. — *adv.* **decorously.** — *ns.* **decorousness; decō'rum** that which is in keeping, congruous: that which is becoming in outward appearance: propriety of conduct: decency. [L. *decōrus*, becoming; L. *decēre*, to be becoming.]

decorticate *dē-kör'ti-kāt*, *v.t.* to deprive of the bark, husk, or peel: to remove the cortex of (*med.*). — *n.* **decorticā'tion.** [L. *decorticāre*, *-ātum* — *dē*, from, and *cortex*, bark.]

decoupage, découpage *dā-koo-päzh'*, *n.* the craft, originating in the 18th century, of applying decorative paper cut-outs to e.g. wood surfaces: a picture produced in this way. [Fr. *découper*, to cut out.]

decouple *dē-kup'l*, *v.t.* to reduce or prevent unwanted coupling within (a circuit or circuits) (*elect.*): to separate from, end the connection with. — *n.* **decoup'ling.** [Pfx. **de-** (2).]

decoy *di-koi'*, *v.t.* to allure: to entrap: to lure into a trap. — *n.* (*dē'koi*) anything intended to lure into a snare (also *fig.*): apparatus of hoops and network for trapping wild-ducks — sometimes *duck-coy.* — **de'coy= duck** a wild duck tamed and trained to entice others into a trap: one employed to allure others into a snare (*fig.*; also **de'coy**). [Perh. Du. *de*, the, or L. pfx. *dē*, down, and Du. *kooi* — L. *cavea*, a cage; or poss. Du. *eendekooi*, a duck-trap.]

decrassify *dē-kras'i-fī*, *v.t.* to make less crass. [Pfx. **de-** (2), and **crass.**]

decrease *di-krēs'*, *v.i.* to become less. — *v.t.* to make less. — *n.* (*dē'krēs*) a growing less: loss. — *adv.* **decreas'ingly.** [O.Fr. *decrois*, a decrease — L. *dēcrēscĕre* — *dē*, from, and *crēscĕre*, to grow.]

decree *di-krē'*, *n.* an order by one in authority: an edict or law: a judicial decision: a predetermined purpose (*theol.*). — *v.t.* to decide or determine by sentence in law: to appoint. — *v.i.* to make a decree: — *pr.p.* **decree'ing;** *pa.t.* and *pa.p.* **decreed'.** — *adj.* **decree'able** capable of being decreed. — *n.* **decreet'** (*Scots law*) a court judgment. — *adj.* **decrē'tal** (*Spens. dec'*) pertaining to a decree. — *n.* decree, esp. of the pope: book containing decrees: (specif. in *pl.*; often with *cap.*) the second part of the canon law, the decrees of various popes determining points of ecclesiastical law. — *n.* **decrē'tist** in mediaeval universities, a student of the decretals, a student of law. — *adjs.* **decrē'tive; decrē'tory** pertaining to a decree, judicial: having the force of a decree. — **decree nisi** (*nī'sī*; L. *nisi*, unless) a decree that becomes a **decree absolute** unless cause be shown to the contrary granted esp. in divorce cases. [O.Fr. *decret* and L. *dēcrētālis* — L. *dēcrētum* — *dēcernĕre*, to decide.]

decrement *dek'ri-mənt*, *n.* the act or state of decreasing: the quantity lost by decrease: the decrease in value of

a variable (*math.*): the ratio of successive amplitudes in an oscillator (*phys.*). — *v.t.* to decrease the value of by a given amount. [L. *dēcrēmentum.*]

decrepit *di-krep'it*, *adj.* worn out by the infirmities of old age: in the last stage of decay. — *ns.* **decrep'itness; decrep'itude** state of being decrepit or worn out with age. [L. *dēcrepitus*, noiseless, very old — *dē*, from, *crepitus*, a noise.]

decrepitate *di-krep'i-tāt*, *v.i.* to crackle, as salts when heated. — *v.t.* to roast so as to cause a continual crackling, to calcine. — *n.* **decrepitā'tion.** [L. *dē-*, intens., *crēpitāre*, to rattle much, freq. of *crepāre*.]

decrescent *di-kres'ənt*, *adj.* becoming gradually less. — *n.*, *adj.* and *adv.* **decrescendo** (*dā-kre-shen'dō; mus.*; It.) diminuendo: — *pl.* **decrescend'os.** [L. *dē*, *crēscĕre.*]

decretal, etc. See decree.

decrew *di-krōō'*, (*Spens.*) *v.i.* to decrease. [O.Fr. *decru*, pa.p. of *decroistre.* See decrease.]

decriminalise, -ize *dē-krim'in-əl-īz*, *v.t.* to make a practice, etc., no longer a criminal offence in law. — *n.* **decriminalisā'tion, -z-.** [Pfx. **de-** (?) .]

decrown *dē-krown'*, *v.t.* to discrown. [Pfx. **de-** (2).]

decrustation *dē-krus-tā'shən*, *n.* removal of a crust. [Pfx. **de-** (2).]

decry *di-krī'*, *v.t.* to cry down: to condemn: to censure as worthless: to blame: — *pr.p.* **decry'ing;** *pa.t.* and *pa.p.* **decried'.** — *ns.* **decrī'al; decrī'er.** [Fr. *dé-*, *des-* (L. *dis-*), and *crier*, to cry; see **cry.**]

decrypt *dē-kript'*, *v.t.* to decode. — *n.* **decryp'tion.** [**de-** (2) and **crypt-.**]

dectet *dek-tet'*, *n.* a group of ten (musicians, lines of verse, etc.): a composition for ten musicians. [L. *decem*, ten, and **quartet, quintet,** etc.]

Dectra® *dek'trə*, *n.* a long-range modification of **Decca.**

decubitus. See under decumbent.

decuman *dek'ū-mən*, *adj.* principal, large — of waves, etc.: connected with the principal gate of a Roman camp (near which the 10th cohort of the legion was stationed). — *n.* a great wave, as every tenth wave was supposed to be. [L. *decumānus* — *decem*, ten.]

decumbent *di-kum'bənt*, *adj.* lying down: reclining on the ground: lying flat with rising top (*bot.*). — *ns.* **decubitus** (*-kūb'i-təs; med.*) posture in bed; **decum'bence, decum'-bency** the act or posture of lying down. — *adv.* **decum'bently.** — *n.* **decum'biture** the time when a sick person takes to bed. — **decubitus ulcer** a bed-sore. [L. *dēcumbēns*, *-entis* — *dē*, down, and *-cumbĕre* (in compounds only), to lie.]

decuple *dek'ū-pl*, *adj.* tenfold. — *n.* a number ten times repeated. — *v.t.* to make tenfold. [Fr. *décuple* — L. *decuplus.*]

decurion *di-kū'ri-ən*, *n.* in a Roman army, an officer over ten soldiers: any overseer of ten: a councillor. — *ns.* **decū'ria, decury** (*dek'ū-ri*) a company of ten (or more); **decū'rionate.** [L.]

decurrent *di-kur'ənt*, *adj.* running or extending downward: continued down the stem (*bot.*). — *n.* **decurr'-ency.** — *adv.* **decurr'ently.** — *n.* **decursion** (*-kûr'*) a running down: a military manoeuvre or parade. — *adj.* **decur'sive.** — *adv.* **decur'sively.** [L. *dēcurrēns*, *-entis* — *dē*, down, *currĕre*, *cursum*, to run.]

decurve *di-kûrv'*, (*biol.*) *v.i.* to curve downwards. — *n.* **decurvā'tion.** — *adj.* **decurved'.** [Pfx. **de-** (1).]

decury. See decurion.

decussate *di-kus'āt*, *v.t.* to divide in the form of an X. — *v.i.* to cross in such a form: to cross, intersect, as lines, etc. — *adjs.* **decuss'ate, -d** crossed: arranged in pairs which cross each other, like some leaves. — *adv.* **decuss'ately.** — *n.* **decussā'tion** (*dek-*). [L. *decussāre*, *-ātum* — *decussis*, a coin of ten asses (*decem asses*) marked with X, symbol of ten.]

dedal, dedalian. See daedal.

dedans *də-dā*, *n.* an open gallery at the end of the service side of a (real) tennis-court: spectators at a court tennis match. [Fr.]

dedicate *ded'i-kāt*, *v.t.* to set apart and consecrate to some sacred purpose: to devote wholly or chiefly: to inscribe to anyone: to inaugurate or open (*U.S.*). — *adj.* devoted: dedicated (*Shak.*). — *n.* **ded'icant** one who dedicates. — *adj.* **ded'icated** consecrated: giving one's whole interest and work to a particular cause or belief: single-minded: manufactured or set aside for a specific purpose, as a *dedicated calculator*. — *ns.* **dedicatee** (*ded-i-kə-tē'*) one to whom a thing is dedicated; **dedica̅'tion** the act of dedicating: an address to a patron, prefixed to a book; **ded'icator**. — *adjs.* **dedica̅'tional**, **dedicatorial** (-kə-tō'ri-əl, -tö'), **ded'icatory** (-kə- or -kā-), **ded'icative**. — **Feast of Dedication** a name for **Hanukkah**. [L. *dēdicāre, -ātum* — *dē*, down, *dicāre*, to declare.]

dedifferentiation *dē-dif-ər-en-shi-ā'shən*, (*biol.*, *med.*) *n.* a change by which specialised or heterogeneous tissue reverts to a generalised or homogeneous form. [Pfx. **de-** (2)]

dedimus *ded'i-məs, n.* a writ commissioning one not a judge to act as a judge. [From the opening, L. *dedimus* (*potestātem*), we have given (power) — *dāre*, to give.]

dedramatise, -ize *dē-drä'mə-tīz, v.t.* to play down the importance of, lessen or keep low the tension or friction caused by. [Pfx. **de-** (2).]

deduce *di-dūs', v.t.* to derive: to infer from what precedes or from premises. — *n.* **deduce'ment** what is deduced. — *adj.* **dedūc'ible** that may be deduced or inferred. — *ns.* **dedūcibil'ity**, **dedūc'ibleness** the quality of being deducible. — *v.t.* **deduct** (*-dukt'*) to take away: to separate: to subtract: to reduce, weaken (*Spens.*): to deduce (*obs.*). — *adj.* **deduct'ible**. — *ns.* **deductibil'ity**; **deduc'tion** the act of deducing: that which is deduced: the drawing of a particular truth from a general, antecedently known, as distinguished from *induction*, rising from particular truths to a general: the act of deducting: that which is deducted: abatement. — *adj.* **deduct'ive** concerned with deduction from premises or accepted principles. — *adv.* **deduct'ively**. — **deducted spaces** see **tonnage**. [L. *dēdūcĕre, dēductum* — *dē*, from, *dūcĕre*, to lead.]

dee¹ *dē, v.i.* Scottish form of **die**.

dee² *dē, n.* the fourth letter of the alphabet (D, d): anything shaped like it. *n., v.t., interj.* a substitute for **damn**.

deed¹ *dēd, n.* something done: an act: an exploit: a legal transaction, esp. involving the transference of property: the written evidence of it, signed, sealed and delivered. — *v.t.* (*arch.*) to transfer (property). — *adj.* **deed'ful** (*Tenn.*) marked by deeds or exploits. — *adv.* **deed'ily**. — *adjs.* **deed'less** (*Shak.*) not having performed deeds; **deed'y** industrious, active. — **deed poll** a deed executed by one party, esp. one by which a person changes his/her name, originally having the edge *polled* or cut even, not indented. — **deed of saying** (*Shak.*) performance of what has been said or promised; **in deed** in reality. [O.E. *dǣd* — *dōn*, to do; Ger. *Tat.*]

deed² *dēd*, a Scottish form of **indeed**; also for **died, dead**.

dee-jay, deejay *dē'jā, or -jā', (coll.) n.* a phonetic representation of the initials **D.J.**, abbrev. of **disc-jockey**. — *v.i.* to act as a dee-jay.

deem *dēm, v.t.* or *v.i.* to judge: to think: to believe: — *pa.t.* and *pa.p.* **deemed**, *Spens.* **dempt**. — *n.* (*Shak.*) opinion. — *ns.* **deem'ster** a judge — now only in the Isle of Man; **dempster** (*dem'stər*) a judge (*obs.*): formerly in Scotland an officer who repeated the sentence after the judge (also **doom'ster**). [O.E.*dēman*, to form a judgment *dōm*, judgment; see **doom**.]

de-emphasise, -ize *dē-em'fə-sīz, v.t.* to take the emphasis away from, treat or consider as of little or less importance. [Pfx. **de-** (2).]

deen *dēn*, (*Spens.*) for **din**.

deep *dēp, adj.* extending or placed far down or far from the outside: deep-penetrating: far recessed: far involved: engrossed (in): difficult to understand: secret: wise and penetrating: profoundly versed: cunning: very still: profound: intense: excessive: heartfelt: sunk

low: low in pitch: (of a road) encumbered with mud, sand, or ruts: in the out-field, not close to the wickets (*cricket*). — *adv.* in a deep manner: at or to a great depth: far (in time): deeply, intensely, profoundly. — *n.* that which is deep: the sea: a deep place: the middle, deepest, or most intense part: anything profound or incomprehensible. — *v.t.* **deep'en** to make deeper in any sense: to increase. — *v.i.* to become deeper. — *n.* **deep'ie** (*coll.*) a three-dimensional cinematograph film. — *adv.* **deep'ly**. — *adj.* **deep'most** deepest. — *n.* **deep'ness**. — *adjs.* **deep'-browed** of high intellectual powers; **deep'-draw'ing** (of ships) requiring considerable depth to float in; **deep'-drawn**; **deep'-dyed** thoroughgoing, extreme in a bad sense; **deep'felt**; **deep'-fet** (*Shak.*) fetched from a depth. — **deep field** fielding position deep behind the bowler; **deep'-freeze'** storage of foodstuffs, or other perishable substances, at very low temperature: the container in which the material is stored. — Also *v.t.* — *v.t.* **deep'-fry'** to fry food completely submerged in fat. — **deep kiss** a French kiss (q.v.); **deep kissing**. — *adj.* **deep'-laid**. — **deep litter** a method of keeping hens in a henhouse with a peat material on the floor. — *adjs.* **deep'-mouthed** with deep voice; **deep'-read** profoundly versed; **deep-root'ed**; **deep'-sea** pertaining to the deeper parts of the sea; **deep'-seat'ed** not superficial. — **deep'-sink'er** (*Austr.*) a drinking vessel of the largest size; **Deep South** the region of the S.E. United States that clings to old ways, roughly Georgia, Alabama, Mississippi and Louisiana; **deep space** the area of space beyond the moon's orbit; **deep structure** (*linguistics*) the underlying grammatical concepts and relations of a sentence from which its **surface structure** (q.v.) derives; **deep therapy** the treatment of disease by deep X-rays or gamma rays. — *adj.* **deep'-toned'** having a deep tone. — **deepwa'terman** a sea-going ship: — *pl.* **deepwa'termen**. — **go, dive** or **be thrown in at the deep end** to plunge, or be plunged, straight into an activity, job, etc., with little or no experience; **go (in) off the deep end** to express strong feelings with abandonment; **in deep water** in difficulties; **two deep, three deep**, etc., in two, three, etc., layers or rows. [O.E. *dēop*; Ger. *tief*; cf. **dip, dive**.]

deer *dēr, n.* any kind of animal (as in *small deer*; *obs.*): any animal of the Cervidae, a family of even-toed ungulates characterised by the possession of antlers by the males at least — including stag, reindeer, etc.: — *pl.* **deer**. — *n.* **deer'let** a chevrotain. — **deer'berry** the huckleberry (*Gaylussacia*): the fruit of Gaultheria: that of *Vaccinium stamineum*, an inedible American whortleberry; **deer'-fence** a very high fence that deer cannot jump over; **deer'-forest** wild tract (not necessarily woodland) reserved for deer; **deer'-hair** a small species of club-rush; **deer'(-)horn** a deer's antler or its material: a fresh-water mussel (*U.S.*); **deer'-hound** a large rough-coated greyhound; **deer'-lick** a spot of salt ground whither deer come to lick the earth; **deer'-mouse** the American deer-footed mouse — so called from its agility; **deer'-neck** a thin ill-shaped neck of horses; **deer'-park**; **deer'skin** skin of the deer, or leather therefrom; **deer'stalker** one who stalks deer: a sportsman's helmet-shaped cap; **deer'stalking**. [O.E. *dēor*; Ger. *Tier*, Du. *dier*; O.N. *dyr*.]

deere. See **dear²**.

deev *dēv*. Same as **div²**.

deeve. See **deave**.

deface *di-fās', v.t.* to destroy or mar the face or external appearance of, to disfigure: to obliterate: to put out of countenance (*Spens.*): to defame (*Spens.*). — *ns.* **deface'ment** act of defacing: injury to form or appearance: that which defaces; **defa'cer**. — *adv.* **defa'cingly**. [O.Fr. *desfacer* — L. *dis-*, away, *faciēs*, face.]

de facto *dē, dä fak'tō*, (L.) actual, if not rightful or legally recognised (e.g. *the de facto ruler*): in fact, actually. — *n.* (*Austr.*) a de facto husband or wife.

defaecate. Same as **defecate**.

defalcate *dē' or de'fal-kāt, or di-fal'kāt or (rare) -föl', v.t.*

(*obs.*) to deduct a part of. — *v.i.* to embezzle money held on trust. — *ns.* **defalca'tion** a diminution: a defection: a misappropriation of funds entrusted to one: the amount misappropriated; **de'falcator** a defaulter. [L.L. *dēfalcāre, -ātum*, to cut away — L. *dē*, from *falcāre*, to cut — *falx, falcis*, a sickle.]

defame *di-fām'*, *v.t.* to take away or destroy the good fame or reputation of: to speak evil of: to charge falsely (*arch.*). — *n.* (*Spens.*) infamy. — *n.* **defamation** (*def-ə-mā'shən*) the act of defaming: calumny: slander. — *adv.* **defamatorily** (*di-fam'ə-tər-i-li*). — *adj.* **defām'atory** containing defamation: injurious to reputation: calumnious. — *n.* and *adj.* **defā'ming**. [O.Fr. *diffamer* — L. *diffāmāre* — *dis-*, away, *fāma*, report.]

defast(e). Spenserian spellings of **defaced** (*pa.p.*).

defat *dē-fat'*, *v.t.* to remove fat or fats from: — *pr.p.* **defatt'ing**; *pa.t.* and *pa.p.* **defatt'ed.** [Pfx. **de-** (2).]

default *di-fölt'*, *n.* a fault, failing, or failure: defect: neglect to do what duty or law requires: failure to fulfil a financial obligation: fault or offence (*arch.*). — *v.i.* to fail through neglect of duty: to fail to appear in court when called upon: to fail to fulfil a financial obligation (with *on* or *in*). — *n.* **default'er** one who fails to appear in court, or to account for money entrusted to his care, or to settle an ordinary debt or debt of honour: a military offender. — **judgment by default** judgment given against a person because he fails to plead or make an appearance in court; **in default of** in the absence of: for lack of. [O.Fr. *defaute* (noun) and *default* (3rd sing. of *defaillir*) — L. pfx. *dē-* and *fallēre*; see **fault**.]

defeasance *di-fēz'əns*, *n.* undoing (*obs.*): defeat: a rendering null or void (*law*): a condition whose fulfilment renders a deed void. — *adjs.* **defeas'anced** liable to be forfeited; **defeas'ible** that may be annulled. — *ns.* **defeasibil'ity; defeas'ibleness.** — **deed of defeasance** (*Eng. law*) an instrument which defeats the operation of some other deed or estate. [O.Fr. *defesance* — *desfaire*; see **defeat**.]

defeat *di-fēt'*, *v.t.* to win a victory over: to get the better of: to ruin: to frustrate: to undo (*Shak.*): to annul (*legal*): to disfigure (*Shak.*). — *n.* a frustration of plans: ruin: overthrow, as of an army in battle: loss of a game, race, etc: annulment (*legal*). — *ns.* **defeat'ism** disposition to accept, welcome, help to bring on, defeat; **defeat'ist.** — Also *adj.* — *n.* **defeat'ure** undoing (*Spens.*): defeat: disfigurement (*Shak.*; from **feature**). — *v.t.* to disfigure. [O.Fr. *defait* — *desfaire*, to undo — L. *dis-*, neg., *facēre*, to do.]

defecate *def'*, *dēf'i-kāt*, *v.t.* to clear of dregs or impurities: to purify from extraneous matter. — *v.i.* to void excrement. — *ns.* **defeca'tion; def'ecātor.** [L. *dēfaecāre, -ātum*, to cleanse — *dē*, from, *faex, faecis*, dregs.]

defect *di-fekt'*, *dē'fekt*, *n.* a deficiency: a want: imperfection: blemish: fault. — *v.i.* (*di-fekt'*) to desert one's country, a cause, transferring one's allegiance (to another). — *n.* **defectibil'ity.** — *adj.* **defect'ible** liable to imperfection: deficient. — *ns.* **defec'tion** desertion: a failure, a falling away from duty: revolt; **defec'tionist.** — *adj.* **defect'ive** having defect: wanting in some necessary quality: imperfect: faulty: insufficient: incomplete in inflexions or forms (*gram.*). — *n.* a person deficient in physical or mental powers. — *adv.* **defect'ively.** — *ns.* **defect'iveness; defect'or** one who deserts his country, etc. — **defective equation** (*math.*) an equation derived from another, but with fewer roots than the original. — **the defects of one's qualities** virtues carried to excess, the faults apt to accompany or flow from good qualities. [L. *dēficĕre, dēfectum*, to fail — *dē*, down, and *facĕre*, to do.]

defence, in U.S. **defense**, *di-fens'*, *n.* a defending: capability or means of resisting an attack: protection: a protective piece of armour: vindication: a defendant's plea (*law*): the defending party in legal proceedings: the members of a (football, hockey, etc.) team who are in defending positions, e.g. halves, backs, goalkeeper. — *adjs.* **defenced'** fortified; **defence'less.** — *adv.*

defence'lessly. — *n.* **defence'lessness.** — *v.t.* **defend** (*di-fend'*) to keep off anything hurtful from: to guard or protect: to maintain against attack: to prohibit, forbid (*obs.*): to ward off: to resist, as a claim (*law*): to contest. — *v.i.* to have the responsibility for preventing scoring (*sport*). — *adj.* **defend'able** that may be defended. — *n.* **defend'ant** a defender: a person accused or sued (*law*). — *adj.* **defend'ed** guarded: protected: maintained against attack: forbidden (*Milt.*). — *ns.* **defend'er** one who defends: a player who defends the goal: the holder of a championship, etc., who seeks to maintain his title: one who accepts a challenge (*obs.*): a person sued or accused (*Scots law*): (in *pl.* with *cap.*; *hist.*) an Irish Roman Catholic society formed at the end of the 18th century in opposition to the Peep-o'-day Boys and the Orangemen; **Defend'erism** (esp. *hist.*) the policies of the Defenders; **defen'sative** a protection; **defensibil'ity.** — *adj.* **defens'ible** that may be defended. — *adv.* **defens'ibly**, — *adj.* **defens'ive** serving to defend: in a state or posture of defence. — *n.* that which defends: posture of defence. — *adv.* **defens'ively.** — **defence'man, defense'man** (esp. *U.S.*) in ice-hockey and lacrosse, a player (other than the goalkeeper) who defends the goal; **defence mechanism** an unconscious mental process by which an individual excludes ideas or emotions painful or unacceptable to him (*psych.*): a response by the body in reaction to harmful organisms (*med.*). — **defender of the faith** a title borne by the sovereigns of England since Henry VIII, on whom it was conferred in 1521 for his book against Luther; **stand, be, on the defensive** to be in the attitude of self-defence. [L. *dēfendĕre, dēfēnsum*, to ward off — *dē*, off, and *fendĕre*, to strike (found in compounds).]

defenestration *dē-fen-is-trā'shən*, *n.* a flinging out of a window. [L. *dē*, from, *fenestra*, window.]

defense. See **defence**.

defer¹ *di-fûr'*, *v.t.* to put off to another time: to delay: — *pr.p.* **deferr'ing**; *pa.t.* and *pa.p.* **deferred'.** — *adj.* **defer(r)'able.** — *ns.* **defer'ment; deferr'al; deferr'er** a procrastinator. — **deferred annuity** see **annuity; deferred pay** an allowance paid to soldiers on their discharge, or to their relations on their death: a government servant's pension; **deferred payment** payment by instalments; **deferred shares** shares not entitling the holder to a full share of profits, and sometimes to none at all, until the expiration of a specified time or the occurrence of some event. [L. *differre* — *dis-*, asunder, *ferre*, to bear, carry; cf. **differ**.]

defer² *di-fûr'*, *v.i.* to yield (to the wishes or opinions of another, or to authority). — *v.t.* to submit to or lay before somebody: — *pr.p.* **deferr'ing**; *pa.t.* and *pa.p.* **deferred'.** — *n.* **deference** (*def'ər-əns*) a deferring or yielding in judgment or opinion: respectful compliance: submission. — *adj.* **def'erent** bearing away, carrying off: deferential. — *n.* a deferent duct (as opposed to an *afferent* one) in the body: in the Ptolemaic system of astronomy, any of the large eccentric circles which with the smaller epicycles were used to account for the apparent movements of the moon and the planets round the earth. — *adj.* **deferential** (*-en'shl*) showing deference. — *adv.* **deferen'tially.** [L. *dēferre* — *dē*, down, and *ferre*, to bear.]

defervescence *dē-fər-ves'əns*, *n.* abatement of heat: coolness: decrease of feverish symptoms. — Also **defervesc'ency.** [L. *dēfervēscĕre*, to cease boiling — *dē*, down, and *fervēscĕre*, from *fervēre*, to boil.]

defeudalise, -ize *dē-fū'dəl-īz*, *v.t.* to deprive of feudal character. [Pfx. **de-** (2).]

deffly (*Spens.*) for **deftly**.

defiance *di-fī'əns*, *n.* the act of defying: a challenge to combat: aggressiveness: contempt of opposition. — *adj.* **defi'ant** full of defiance, insolently bold. — *adv.* **defi'antly.** — *n.* **defi'antness** (*rare*). — **bid defiance to** to defy. [**defy**.]

defibrillator *dē-fib'ri-lā-tər* or *-fīb'*, (*med.*) *n.* a machine which applies an electric current to the chest or heart

to stop fibrillation of the heart.   [Pfx. **de-** (2).]
defibrinate *dē-fī'bri-nāt, v.t.* to deprive of fibrin — also
defī'brinise, -ize. — *n.* **defibrinā'tion.**   [Pfx. **de-** (2),
and **fibrin.**]
deficient *di-fish'ənt, adj.* wanting (in): less than complete:
defective. — *n.* a defective. — *n.* **defic'iency** (sometimes
defic'ience) defect: shortage: the amount which is
lacking for completeness. — *adv.* **defic'iently.** — *ns.*
defic'ientness; deficit (*def'i-sit,* or *-fis'*) deficiency, esp.
of revenue, as compared with expenditure: amount of
the deficiency. — **deficiency disease** a disease due to
lack of necessary substances (as vitamins) in the diet,
such as rickets, scurvy, beri-beri, pellagra.   [L. *defi-
cĕre;* see **defect.**]
de fide *dē fī'dē, dā fē'de,* (L.) (of a teaching) in which
belief is obligatory.
defied, defier, etc. See **defy.**
defilade. See **defile¹.**
defile¹ *di-fīl', v.i.* to march off in file or line, or file by
file. — *n.* (*dē'fīl, di-fīl'*) a long narrow pass or way, in
which troops can march only in file, or with a narrow
front: a gorge. — *v.t.* **defilade** (*def-i-lād'*) to plan a
fortification so as to protect it from enfilading fire. —
Also *n.* — *n.* **defile'ment** act of defilading.   [Fr. *défiler*
— L. *dis-,* and *fīlum,* a thread.]
defile² *di-fīl', v.t.* to befoul: to pollute or corrupt: to
violate. — *ns.* **defile'ment** act of defiling: foulness;
defīl'er.   [L. *dē,* and O.E. *fȳlan* — *fūl,* foul; confused
with O.Fr. *defouler,* to trample, violate.]
defilement. See **defile¹,².**
defiliation *dē-fil-i-ā'shən, n.* depriving a parent of his
child.   [L. *dē,* from, and *filius,* a son.]
define *di-fīn', v.t.* to bring to an end (*obs.*): to decide: to
fix the bounds or limits of: to determine with precision:
to describe accurately: to fix the meaning of. — *n.*
definabil'ity. — *adj.* **defin'able.** — *adv.* **defin'ably.** —
ns. **define'ment** (*Shak.*) description; **defin'er.** — *adj.*
definite (*def'i-nit*) defined: having distinct limits: fixed:
exact: clear: sympodial or cymose (*bot.*): referring to
a particular person or thing (*gram.;* see also **article**).
— *adv.* **def'initely** in a definite manner: determinately:
yes indeed (*coll.*). — *ns.* **def'initeness; defini'tion** a
defining: a description of a thing by its properties: an
explanation of the exact meaning of a word, term, or
phrase: sharpness of outline. — *adjs.* **defini'tional;
definitive** (*di-fin'i-tiv*) defining or limiting: positive:
final: authoritative. — *n.* (*gram.*) an adjective used to
limit the extent of signification of a noun. — *adv.*
defin'itively. — *ns.* **defin'itiveness; defin'itude.**   [L.
definīre, -ītum, to set bounds to — *dē, fīnis,* a limit.]
deflagrate *def'lə-grāt, v.i., v.t.* to burn suddenly, generally
with flame and crackling noise. — *n.* **deflagrabil'ity.**
— *adj.* **deflag'rable** which deflagrates: deflagrating
readily. — *ns.* **deflagrā'tion; def'lagrātor** apparatus for
deflagration. — **def'lagrating-spoon** a cup with long
vertical shank for handling chemicals that deflagrate.
[L. *deflagrāre* — *dē,* down, *flagrāre,* to burn.]
deflate *dē-flāt', v.t.* to reduce from a state of inflation.
v.i. to become deflated. — *n.* **deflā'tion** the act or
process of deflating: the state of being deflated: a
financial condition in which there is an undue decrease
in the amount of money available relative to its buying
power — the converse of **inflation** (*econ.*): removal of
loose material by the wind. — *adj.* **deflā'tionary.** — *n.*
deflā'tionist one who favours deflation of currency. —
Also *adj.* — *ns.* **deflā'ter; deflā'tor.**   [L. *dē,* from, *flāre,*
to blow.]
deflect *di-flekt', v.i.* or *v.t.* to turn aside: to swerve or
deviate from a right line or proper course. — *adj.*
deflect'ed (*bot.*) bent abruptly downward. — *ns.* **deflec'tion, deflex'ion** (L. *deflexiō*) bending: turning:
deviation. — *adjs.* **deflec'tional, deflex'ional; deflec'tive**
causing deflection. — *n.* **deflec'tor** a device for deflecting a flame, electric arc, etc. — *v.t.* **deflex'** (*zool., bot.*)
to bend down. — *adj.* **deflexed'.** — *n.* **deflex'ure**
deviation.   [L. *dē,* from, down, and *flectĕre, flexum,*
to bend, turn.]

deflorate *dē-flō'rāt, -flō', adj.* past flowering: of an anther,
having shed its pollen. — *v.t.* to deflower. — *n.*
deflorā'tion the act of deflowering.   [L. *dēflōrāre;* see
next.]
deflower *di-flowr', v.t.* to deprive of flowers: to deprive
of grace and beauty, or of virginity: to ravish. — *n.*
deflower'er.   [O.Fr. *desflorer* — L.L. *dēflōrāre,* to
strip flowers off — L. *dē,* from, *flōs, flōris,* a flower.]
defluent *def'lōō-ənt, adj.* running down, decurrent. — *n.*
defluxion (*di-fluk'shən; obs.*) a downflow: a disease
supposedly due to a flow of humour: a discharge of
fluid in the body.   [L. *dēfluĕre* — *dē,* down, *fluĕre,*
fluxum, to flow.]
defoliate *di-fō'li-āt, v.t.* to deprive of leaves. — *adjs.*
defōl'iate, -d. — *ns.* **defō'liant** a chemical preparation
used to remove leaves; **defoliā'tion** the falling off of
leaves: the time of shedding leaves; **defō'liātor.**   [L.L.
dēfoliāre, -ātum — *dē,* off, *folium,* a leaf.]
deforce *di-fōrs', -förs', v.t.* to keep out of possession by
force (*law*): to resist (an officer of the law in the
execution of his duty) (*Scots law*). — *ns.* **deforce'ment;
deforc'iant** one who deforces; **deforciā'tion** (*obs.*) a
legal distress.   [A.Fr. *deforcer* — *de-* (L. *dis-*); see
force¹.]
deforest *dē-for'ist, v.t.* to disforest, to deprive of forests.
— *n.* **deforestā'tion.**   [Pfx. **de-** (2).]
deform *di-förm', v.t.* to alter or injure the form of: to
disfigure: to change the shape of without breach of
continuity. — *adj.* (*Milt.,* etc.) hideous, unshapely. —
adj. **deform'able.** — *ns.* **deformabil'ity; deforma'tion.** —
adj. **deformed'** misshapen. — *adv.* **deform'edly.** — *ns.*
deformed'ness; deform'er; deform'ity state of being
deformed: want of proper form: ugliness: disfigurement: anything that destroys beauty: an ugly feature
or characteristic.   [L. *dēförmis,* ugly — *dē,* from,
förma, beauty.]
defoul *di-fowl', v.t.* to befoul, defile.   [O.E. *fūl,* foul,
with *de-* from confusion with O.Fr. *defouler,* to trample; cf. **defile².**]
defraud *di-fröd', v.t.* to deprive by fraud (of): to cheat or
deceive. — *ns.* **defraudā'tion, defraud'ment; defraud'er.**
[L. *dēfraudāre* — *dē,* from, *fraus, fraudis,* fraud.]
defray *di-frā', v.t.* to pay: to satisfy, appease (*Spens.*): —
pr.p. **defray'ing;** *pa.t.* and *pa.p.* **defrayed'.** — *adj.*
defray'able. — *ns.* **defray'al, defray'ment; defray'er.**
[O.Fr. *desfrayer* — *des-* L. *dis-,* and *frais,* expenses.]
defreeze *de-frēz', v.t.* to thaw out, esp. frozen foods.
[Pfx. **de-** (2).]
defrock. Same as **unfrock.**
defrost *dē'frost', v.t.* to remove frost or ice from: to thaw
out. — Also *v.i.* — *n.* **de'frost'er** a device for defrosting
esp. a windscreen.   [Pfx. **de-** (2).]
deft *deft, adj.* handy, clever, esp. in movement. — *adv.*
deft'ly. — *n.* **deft'ness.**   [M.E. *defte, dafte,* simple,
meek; O.E. *gedæfte,* meek — *dæftan, gedæftan,* prepare, make fit; the stem appears in *gedafen,* fit.]
defunct *di-fungkt', adj.* having finished the course of life,
dead: finished, no longer working (*fig.*). — *n.* a dead
person. — *n.* **defunc'tion** (*Shak.*) death. — *adj.* **defunc'-
tive** pertaining to the dead.   [L. *dēfungī, dēfunctus,*
to finish — *dē,* intens., *fungī,* to perform.]
defuse¹ *de-fūz', (Shak.) v.t.* to disorder. — *adj.* **defūs'd'.**
[For **diffuse¹.**]
defuse², defuze *dē-fūz', v.t.* to remove the fuse of (a bomb,
etc.), so making it harmless. — Also *fig.*
defy *di-fī', v.t.* to challenge (*arch.*): to brave, dare: to
flout, or to resist (e.g. convention, order, person): to
discard, dislike (*obs.*). — *pr.p.* **defy'ing;** *pa.t.* and *pa.p.*
defied'; *3rd pers. sing. pres. ind.* **defies'.** — *n.* (*Dryden*)
a defiance. — *n.* **defī'er.**   [O.Fr. *defier* — L.L.
diffīdāre, to renounce faith or allegiance — L. *dis-,*
asunder, and *fīdĕre,* to trust — *fīdēs,* faith.]
dégagé *dā-gä-zhā, (Fr.) adj.* unembarrassed, unconstrained, easy: uninvolved.   [Pa.p. of Fr. *dégager,* to
disentangle.]
degarnish. Same as **disgarnish.**
degas *dē-gas', v.t.* to remove gas from: to eject or emit

in the form of a gas. [Pfx. **de-** (2).]

degauss *dē-gows'*, *v.t.* to protect against magnetic mines by equipment for neutralising a ship's magnetic field: to remove the magnetic field from. [Pfx. **de-** (2), **gauss.**]

degender *di-jen'dər*, (*Spens.*) *v.i.* to degenerate. [Fr. *dégénerer*, influenced by **gender²**.]

degenerate *di-jen'ər-it, adj.* having departed from the high qualities of race of kind, become base. — *n.* one who is degenerate. — *v.i.* (*-āt*) to fall from a nobler state: to be or to grow worse. — *v.t.* (*Milt.*) to cause to degenerate. — *ns.* **degen'eracy, degenerā'tion** the act or process of becoming degenerate: the state of being degenerate. — *adv.* **degen'erately.** — *n.* **degen'erateness.** — *adj.* **degen'erating.** — *n.* **degenerā'tionist** one who believes that the tendency of man is not to improve, but to degenerate. — *adj.* **degen'erative** tending or causing to degenerate. — *adj.* **degen'erous** (*obs.*). — **degenerative joint disease** same as **osteo-arthritis.** [L. *degenerāre, -ātum*, to depart from its kind — *dē*, from, down, *genus, genĕris*, kind.]

deglutinate *di-glōō'tin-āt, v.t.* to separate (things glued together): to remove gluten from. — *n.* **deglutinā'tion.** [L. *dēglūtināre, -ātum — dē*, from, *glūtināre — glūten* glue.]

deglutition *dē-glōō-tish'ən, n.* the act or power of swallowing. — *adjs.* **deglu'titive; deglu'titory.** [L. *dē*, down, and *glūtīre*, to swallow; see **glut.**]

dégoût *dā-gōō*, (Fr.) *n.* distaste.

degrade *di-grād', v.t.* to lower in grade or rank: to deprive of office or dignity: to lower in character, value, or position, or in complexity: to disgrace: to wear down (*geol.*): to decompose (*chem.*). — *v.i.* to decompose (*chem.*). — *adj.* **degrād'able** able to decompose chemically or biologically (also **biodegradable**). — *n.* **degradation** (*deg-rə-dā'shən*) degrading: disgrace: degeneration: abortive structural development: a lowering in dignity: decomposition (*chem.*). — *adjs.* **degrād'ed** reduced in rank: base: low: placed on steps (*her.*); **degrād'ing** debasing: disgraceful. [O.Fr. *degrader* — L. *dē*, down, and *gradus*, a step. See **grade.**]

degras *deg'räs, n.* a fat got from sheepskins. [Fr. *dégras* — *dégraisser*, to degrease.]

degrease *dē-grēs', v.t.* to deprive of, or cleanse from, grease. — *n.* **degreas'ant** a substance which removes grease. [Pfx. **de-** (2).]

degree *di-grē', n.* a grade or step (*arch.*): a gradation on a scale, or that which it measures: a unit of temperature: one of a series of advances or steps: relative position: rank: extent: a mark of distinction conferred by universities, whether earned by examination or granted as a mark of honour: the 360th part of a revolution: 60 geographical miles: nearness of relationship: comparative amount of criminality, severity, etc.: one of the three stages (*positive, comparative, superlative*) in the comparison of an adjective or adverb: the highest sum of exponents in any term (*alg.*): the number of points in which a curve may be met by a straight line. — **degree'-day'** a unit used in measuring the heating requirements in a building — a fall of one degree of heat in one day. — **by degrees** by little and little, gradually; **degree of freedom** any one of the independent variables defining the state of a system (e.g. temperature, pressure, concentration): a capability of variation (e.g. a system having two variables one of which is dependent on the other has one degree of freedom); **first, second, third degree burn** (*med.*) the three categories of seriousness of a burn, third degree being most serious; **first, second, third degree murder** (*U.S.*) the three categories of criminality of a murder, first degree being most serious; **forbidden degrees** the degrees of consanguinity within which marriage is not allowed; **Songs of degrees** or **Songs of ascents**, Psalms cxx-cxxxiv, either because sung by the Jews returning from captivity, or by the Jews coming up annually to attend the feasts at Jerusalem; **third degree** an American police method of extracting a confession by

bullying or torture: any ruthless interrogation; **to a degree** to a certain degree: to a great degree, to an extreme. [Fr. *degré* — L. *dē*, down, *gradus*, a step.]

degression *di-gresh'ən, n.* a gradual decrease, esp. on tax rates. — *adj.* **degressive** (*di-gres'iv*). [L. *dēgredī, dēgressus*, to descend.]

dégringoler *dā-grē-go-lā*, (Fr.) *v.i.* to descend rapidly or steeply: to decline, fail. — *n.* **dégringolade** (*-go-läd*) a sudden descent: a quick deterioration. — Also *v.i.*

degum *dē-gum', v.t.* to free from gum. [Pfx. **de-** (2).]

degust *dē-gust', v.t.* to taste, to relish. — *v.i.* to have a relishing taste. — *v.t.* **degust'āte** to degust. — *n.* **degustā'tion** the act of tasting. — *adj.* **degust'atory.** [L. *dē*, down, and *gustāre*, to taste.]

dehisce *di-his', v.i.* to gape, burst open (*bot.*, etc.). — *n.* **dehisc'ence.** — *adj.* **dehisc'ent.** [L. *dēhīscēns*, pr.p. of *dēhīscĕre — dē*, intens., and *hīscĕre*, inceptive of *hiāre*, to gape.]

dehorn *dē-hörn', v.t.* to dishorn: to prune (a tree). — *n.* **dehorn'er.** [Pfx. **de-** (2).]

dehort *di-hört', v.t.* to dissuade. — *n.* **dehortā'tion** (*dē-*) dissuasion. — *adjs.* **dehor'tative, dehor'tatory** dissuasive. — *n.* **dehort'er.** [L. *dēhortārī — dē*, off, *hortārī*, to exhort.]

dehumanise, -ize *dē-hū'mən-īz, v.t.* to deprive of specifically human qualities. [L. *dē*, from, down, and **humanise.**]

dehumidify *dē-hū-mid'i-fī, v.t.* to rid of moisture, dry. — *ns.* **dehumidificā'tion; dehumid'ifier.** [Pfx. **de-** (2).]

dehydrate *dē-hī'drāt, v.t.* to deprive of water chemically: to remove moisture from, dry: to deprive of strength, interest, etc. (*fig.*). — *v.i.* to lose water. — *ns.* **dēhydrā'tion** loss or withdrawal of moisture: excessive loss of water from the tissues of the body (*med.*): the removal of water from oil or gas; **dēhy'drātor, dēhy'drater.** [L. *dē*, from, Gr. *hydōr*, water.]

dehypnotise, -ize *dē-hip'nə-tīz, v.t.* to bring out of a hypnotic trance. — *n.* **dehypnotisā'tion, -z-.** [Pfx. **de-** (2).]

de-ice *dē'īs', v.t.* to dislodge ice from (aircraft surfaces, etc.), or to treat them so as to prevent its formation. — *n.* **dē'-īc'er** any means of doing this, whether a fluid, a paste, or a mechanical or pneumatic device. [Pfx. **de-** (2).]

deicide *dē'i-sīd, n.* the killing or killer of a god. — *adj.* **deicī'dal.** [L. *deus*, a god, and *caedĕre*, to kill.]

deictic. See **deixis.**

deid *dēd*, Scots form of **dead, death.** — **deid'-thraw** death-throe.

deify *dē'i-fī, v.t.* to exalt to the rank of a god: to worship as a deity: to make godlike: — *pr.p.* **dē'ifying;** *pa.t.* and *pa.p.* **dē'ified.** — *adjs.* **dēif'ic, -al** making godlike or divine. — *ns.* **dēificā'tion** the act of deifying: a deified embodiment; **dē'ifier.** — *adj.* **dē'iform** formed or appearing like a god. [Fr. *déifier* — L. *deificāre — deus*, a god, and *facĕre*, to make.]

deign *dān, v.i.* to condescend. — *v.t.* to condescend to give or (*Shak.*) take. [Fr. *daigner* — L. *dīgnārī*, to think worthy — *dīgnus*, worthy.]

dei gratia *dē'i grā'shi-ə, dā'ē grä'ti-a*, (L.) by the grace of God.

deil *dēl, n.* Scots form of **devil.**

deindustrialise, -ize *dē-in-dus'tri-əl-īz, v.t.* to disperse or reduce the industrial organisation and potential of a nation, area, etc. — *n.* **deindustrialisā'tion, -z-.** [Pfx. **de-** (2).]

deino-, Deinoceras, Deinornis, deinosaur, Deinotherium. See **dino-.**

de integro *dē in'ti-grō, dā in-teg'rō* (L.) anew.

deiparous *dē-ip'ə-rəs, adj.* bearing a god — used of the Virgin. [L. *deus*, a god, *parĕre*, to bring forth.]

deipnosophist *dīp-nos'ə-fist, n.* one who converses learnedly at dinner, a table-philosopher — from Athenaeus's work, *Deipnosophistai* (end of 2nd century). [Gr. *deipnon*, dinner, *sophos*, wise.]

deis(h)eal. Same as **deasil.**

deist *dē'ist, dā'ist, n.* one who believes in the existence of

God, but not in a revealed religion. — *n.* **de′ism.** — *adjs.* **deist′ic, -al.** — *adv.* **deist′ically.** [L. *deus*, a god.]

deity *dē′i-ti, dā′i-ty, n.* godhood: divinity: godhead: a god or goddess: (*cap.*; with **the)** the Supreme Being. [Fr. *déité* — L.L. *deitās* — L. *deus*, god; Sans. *deva.*]

deixis *dīk′sis, (gram.) n.* the use of words relating to the time and place of utterance, e.g. personal pronouns, demonstrative adverbs, adjectives and pronouns. — *adj.* **deictic** (*dīk′tik*) designating words relating to the time and place of utterance (also *n.*): proving directly. — *adv.* **deic′tically.** [Gr. *deiknynai*, to show.]

déjà vu *dā-zhä vü*, in any of the arts, unoriginal material, old stuff: an illusion of having experienced before something that is really being experienced for the first time, a form of paramnesia (*psych.*). [Fr., already seen.]

deject *di-jekt′, v.t.* to cast down the countenance or spirits of. — *adj.* (*Shak.*) cast down. — *adj.* **deject′ed** cast down: dispirited. — *adv.* **deject′edly.** — *ns.* **deject′edness; dejec′tion** lowness of spirits: (often in *pl.*) faecal discharge (also **dejec′ta**): defecation. — *adj.* **dejec′tory** promoting evacuations. [L. *dējicĕre, -jectum* — *dē*, down, *jacĕre*, to cast.]

dejeune *di-jōōn′,* (*arch.*) *n.* breakfast or luncheon. See **disjune, déjeuner.**

déjeuner *dā-zhø-nā,* (Fr.) *n.* breakfast or lunch. — **petit déjeuner** (*pɘ-tē*) (little breakfast) coffee and rolls on rising; **déjeuner à la fourchette** (*a la fōōr-shet*) meat (lit. fork) breakfast, early lunch.

de jure *dē jōō′rē, dā zhōō′re,* (L.) by right: rightful.

Dekabrist *dek′ɘ-brist, n.* a Decembrist. [Russ. *Dekabr′,* December.]

dekalogy *de-kal′ɘ-ji, n.* a group of ten novels. [Gr. *deka*, ten, and *logos*, discourse, by analogy with **trilogy.**]

dekko, decko *dek′ō,* (*slang*) *n.* a look: — *pl.* **dekk′os, deckos.** — *v.i.* to look. — **have, take, a dekko** to have a (quick) look. [Hind. *dekho,* imp. of *dekhnā,* to see.]

del *del, n.* another name for **nabla.**

delaine *di-lān′, n.* an untwilled light dress material, originally of wool. [Fr. *mousseline de laine,* wool muslin.]

delaminate *di-lam′i-nāt, v.i.* to split into layers. — *n.* **delaminā′tion.** [L. *dēlamināre* — *dē, lāmina,* a layer.]

delapse *di-laps′,* (*obs.*) *v.i.* to sink down. — *n.* **delap′sion.** [L. *dē,* down, *lābī, lapsus,* to slip.]

délassement *dā-las-mä,* (Fr.) *n.* relaxation.

delate[1] *di-lāt′, v.t.* to pass on: to publish (*obs.*): to charge with a crime. — *ns.* **delā′tion; delā′tor.** [L. *dēlātum,* used as supine of *dēferre,* to bring a report against, to inform — *dē-,* intens., *ferre, lātum,* to bear.]

delate[2] (*Shak.*), for **dilate.**

delay[1] *di-lā′, v.t.* to put off to another time: to defer: to hinder or retard. — *v.i.* to pause, linger, or put off time: — *pr.p.* **delay′ing;** *pa.t.* and *pa.p.* **delayed.** — *n.* a putting off or deferring: the time during which something is put off: a lingering: hindrance. — *n.* **delay′er.** — *adv.* **delay′ingly.** — **delayed action** a method of operating a switch, detonating explosive, etc., some time after the mechanism has been set; **delayed drop** (*aero.*) a live parachute descent in which the parachutist deliberately delays pulling the ripcord; **delayed neutrons** those neutrons resulting from fission which are emitted with a measurable time delay. [O.Fr. *delaier.*]

delay[2] *di-lā′,* (*Spens.*) *v.t.* to temper, dilute, weaken. [Fr. *délayer,* to dilute — L. *dēliquāre,* to clarify or *dis-, ligāre,* to bind.]

del credere *del krād′ɘr-i,* applied to an agent who becomes surety for the solvency of persons to whom he sells. [It. *del,* of the, *credere,* to believe, trust.]

dele *dē′lē, v.t.* delete, efface, a direction in proof-reading to remove a letter or word, indicated by δ or other sign. — *adj.* **deleble, delible** (*del′*) that can be deleted. — *n.pl.* **delen′da** things to be deleted. [L. *dēlē,* imper. of *dēlēre,* to delete; or for *dēlēātur,* subj. pass.; *dēlenda,* neut. pl. of gerundive.]

delectable *di-lekt′ɘ-bl* (*Spens., Shak., del′*), *adj.* delightful: pleasing. — *ns.* **delect′ableness; delectabil′ity.** — *adv.*

delect′ably. — *n.* **delectā′tion** (*dē-*) delight. [Fr., — L. *dēlectābilis* — *dēlectāre,* to delight.]

delegate *del′i-gāt, v.t.* to send as a legate or representative: to entrust or commit. — *n.* one who is delegated: a deputy or representative: a person elected to represent a Territory in Congress, as distinguished from the representatives of the States (*U.S.*). — *adj.* delegated, deputed. — *adj.* **del′egable.** — *ns.* **del′egacy** act or system of delegating: a delegate's appointment or authority: a body of delegates; **delegā′tion** a delegating: a deputation: a body of delegates (*U.S.*): a body of delegates that was appointed every ten years by each of the two portions of the Dual Monarchy to negotiate a treaty between the Austrian Empire and the Kingdom of Hungary (*hist.*). — **delegated legislation** rules and orders with the force of law made by the executive under statutory authority. [L. *dē,* away, and *lēgāre, -ātum,* to send as ambassador.]

delete *di-lēt′, v.t.* to blot out: to erase: to destroy. — *n.* **delē′tion.** — *adjs.* **delē′tive, delē′tory.** [L. *dēlēre, dēlētum,* to blot out.]

deleterious *del-i-tē′ri-ɘs, adj.* hurtful or destructive: poisonous. — *adv.* **delete′riously.** — *n.* **delete′riousness.** [Gr. *dēlētērios,* hurtful — *dēleesthai,* to hurt.]

delf[1], delph *delf,* **delft** *delft, ns.* (in full **Delft′ware**), a kind of earthenware originally made at *Delft,* Holland.

delf[2], delph *delf, n.* a drain, ditch, excavation: a charge representing a square sod (*her.*): — *pl.* **delfs, delphs, delves.** [O.E. *delf; delfan,* to dig.]

deli. Short for **delicatessen.**

Delian *dē′li-ɘn, adj.* pertaining to *Dēlos,* in the Aegean Sea, birthplace of Apollo and Artemis.

delibate *del′i-bāt,* (*obs.*) *v.t.* to sip. — *n.* **delibā′tion.** [L. *dēlībāre* — *dē,* from, *lībāre,* to take, taste.]

deliberate *di-lib′ɘr-āt, v.t.* to weigh well in one's mind. — *v.i.* to consider the reasons for and against anything: to reflect: to consider: to take counsel: to debate. — *adj.* (*-it*) well considered: not impulsive: intentional: considering carefully: slow in determining: cautious. — *adv.* **delib′erately** in a deliberate manner: (*loosely*) quietly, without fuss or haste. — *ns.* **delib′erateness; deliberā′tion** the act of deliberating: mature reflection: calmness: coolness. — *adj.* **delib′erative** proceeding or acting by deliberation. — *adv.* **delib′eratively.** — *ns.* **delib′erativeness; delib′erātor.** [L. *dēlīberāre, -ātum* — *dē-,* intens., and *lībrāre,* to weigh — *lībra,* a balance.]

delible. See **dele.**

delicate *del′i-kit, adj.* pleasing to the senses, esp. the taste: dainty: nicely discriminating or perceptive: fastidious: of a fine, slight texture or constitution: tender: not robust: pale: requiring nice handling: refined in manners: not immodest: gentle, polite: luxurious. — *n.* a luxurious or fastidious person: a luxury: a delicacy (*arch.*). — *n.* **del′icacy** (*-kɘ-si*) state or quality of being delicate: refinement: nicety: tenderness, weakness: luxuriousness: anything delicate or dainty, esp. to eat. — *adv.* **del′icately.** — *n.* **del′icateness.** [L. *dēlicātus,* prob. conn. with *dēliciae,* allurements, luxury — *dēlicĕre* — *dē-,* intens., *lacĕre,* to entice.]

delicatessen *del-i-kɘ-tes′n, n.pl.* or *sing.* prepared foods, esp. cooked meats, pâtés, and unusual or foreign foods: (*sing.*; coll. short form **del′i**) a shop selling these. [Ger. pl. of Fr. *délicatesse,* delicacy.]

delicious *di-lish′ɘs, adj.* pleasing to the senses, esp. taste: affording exquisite pleasure. — *n.* **delice** (*di-lēs′; Spens. del′is*) delight: a delight: a delicacy. — *adv.* **deli′ciously** in a delicious manner: luxuriously (*B.*). — *n.* **deli′ciousness.** — **flower delice** (*Spens.,* also *del′is*) see **fleur-de-lis.** [L. *dēliciōsus* — *dēliciae,* or *dēlicium,* delight.]

delict *di-likt′,* (*legal,* esp. *Scot.*) *n.* a transgression: a misdemeanour. [L. *dēlictum,* an offence; see **delinquent.**]

deligation *del-i-gā′shɘn, n.* a binding up, ligature. [L. *dēligāre,* to bind up — *dē,* intens., and *ligāre,* to bind.]

delight *di-līt′, v.t.* to please highly. — *v.i.* to have or take great pleasure: to be greatly pleased. — *n.* a high degree of pleasure: extreme satisfaction: that which gives great pleasure. — *adj.* **delight'ed** greatly pleased: delightful (*Shak.*): capable of delight ((*Shak.*). — *adv.* **delight'edly.** — *n.* **delight'edness.** — *adjs.* **delight'ful,** (*arch.*) **delight'some** causing, or full of delight. — *adv.* **delight'fully.** — *n.* **delight'fulness.** — *adj.* **delight'less** affording no delight. [O.Fr. *deliter* — L. *dēlectāre,* intens. of *dēlicēre*; cf. **delicate, delicious;** spelling influenced by confusion with **light.**]

Delilah *di-lī'lə, n.* the Philistine woman who befooled Samson: a courtesan: a temptress: an alluring object. — Also **Dali'lah, Dalila** (*Milt. dal'i-lə*).

delimit *di-lim'it,* **delimitate** *di-lim'i-tāt, vs.t.* to fix or mark the limit of. — *n.* **delimitā'tion.** — *adj.* **delim'itative.** [L. *dēlīmitāre* — *dē,* intens., *līmitāre*; see **limit.**]

delineate *di-lin'i-āt, v.t.* to mark out with lines: to represent by a sketch or picture: to draw: to describe. — *adj.* **delin'eable.** — *n.* **delineā'tion** the act of delineating: a sketch, representation, or description. — *adj.* **delin'eative.** — *n.* **delin'cātor.** [L. *dēlīneāre, ātum   dē,* down, and *līnea,* a line.]

delineavit *di-lin-i-ā'vit, -ā'wit,* (he) drew (this), sometimes added to the signature of the artist or draughtsman. [L.]

delinquent *di-ling'kwənt, adj.* failing in duty. — *n.* one who fails in or leaves his duty: an offender: a person lacking in moral and social sense, without showing impairment of intellect. — *n.* **delin'quency** failure in or omission of duty: a fault: a crime. — *adv.* **delin'quently.** [L. *dēlinquēns, -entis,* pr.p. of *dēlinquĕre — dē-,* intens., and *linquĕre, lictum,* to leave.]

deliquesce *del-i-kwes', v.i.* to melt and become liquid by absorbing moisture, as certain salts, etc. — *n.* **deliquesc'ence.** — *adj.* **deliquesc'ent** liquefying in the air: breaking up into branches, as the veins of a leaf (*bot.*). [L. *dēliquēscĕre — dē-,* intens., *liquēscĕre,* to become fluid — *liquēre,* to be fluid.]

deliquium *di-lik'wi-əm, n.* swoon (*obs.*): eclipse (*arch.*): melting away (*Carlyle*). [Really two different words, partly confused (1) L. *dēliquium — dēlinquĕre,* to leave, fail; (2) L. *dēliquium — dēliquāre,* to melt.]

delirious *di-lir'i-əs, adj.* wandering in mind: lightheaded: insane. — *n.* **delirā'tion** (*del-*) madness, aberration. — *adjs.* **delir'iant; delirifacient** (*di-lir-ifā'shənt*) producing delirium. — *ns.* that which produces delirium. — *adv.* **delir'iously.** — *ns.* **delir'iousness; delir'ium** state of being delirious: strong excitement: wild enthusiasm: — *pl.* **delir'iums, delir'ia.** — **delirium tremens** (*trē'menz; coll. abbrev.* **DT's**) a delirious disorder of the brain produced by over-absorption of alcohol, often marked by convulsive or trembling symptoms and hallucination. [L. *dēlīrus,* crazy — *dēlīrāre,* lit. to turn aside — *dē,* from, and *līra,* a furrow; *tremēns,* the pr.p. of *tremĕre,* to tremble.]

delitescent *del-i-tes'ənt, adj.* latent. — *n.* **delitesc'ence.** [L. *dēlitēscēns, -entis,* pr.p. of *dēlitēscĕre — dē,* from, and *latēscĕre — latēre,* to lie hid.]

deliver *di-liv'ər, v.t.* to liberate or set free from restraint or danger: to rescue from evil or fear: to give up: to hand over, distribute: to communicate: to pronounce: to give forth, as a blow, a ball, etc.: to discharge, as water: to assist (a mother) at the birth (of). — *adj.* nimble. — *adj.* **deliv'erable.** — *ns.* **deliverabil'ity; deliv'erance** liberation: release: parturition: the utterance of a judgment or authoritative opinion; **deliv'erer.** — *adv.* **deliv'erly.** — *n.* **deliv'ery** the act of delivering: a giving up: the act or manner of speaking in public, of discharging a shot, or water, of throwing a cricket-ball, etc.: withdrawal of a pattern from a mould: a distribution: a round of distribution: the act of giving birth. — **deliv'ery-man** a man who goes round delivering goods; **deliv'ery-pipe, -tube** one that delivers water, etc., at the place where it is required; **deliv'ery-van** a tradesman's van for delivering goods at customers' houses. — **be delivered of** (*arch.*) to give birth to; **deliver the goods** (*slang*) to carry out what is required or promised; **general delivery** the delivery of letters at a

post-office to the persons to whom they are addressed opp. to house-to-house delivery; **jail** or **gaol delivery** see **jail.** [Fr. *délivrer* — L. *dē,* from, *līberāre,* to set free — *līber,* free.]

dell[1] *del, n.* a deep hollow or small valley, usually covered with trees: a hole (*Spens.*). [O.E. *dell;* cf. **dale.**]

dell[2] *del,* (*arch. slang*) *n.* a young girl: a trull.

Della-Cruscan *del-ə-krus'kən, del-la-krōōs'kən, n.* a member of the old Florentine Accademia *della Crusca* (It., academy of the bran, as sifters of the language; 1582), or of a group of sentimental poetasters crushed by Gifford's *Baviad* and *Maeviad* (1794 and 1796). — Also *adj.*

Della-Robbia *del-la-rob'bya, n.* a term applied to enamelled terracotta, said to have been invented by Luca *della Robbia.*

delouse *dē-lows', v.t.* to free from lice, or (*fig.*) from land-mines, etc. [Pfx. **de-** (2).]

delph. See **delf**[1,2].

Delphic *del'fik, adj.* relating to *Delphi,* a town of ancient Greece, or to its famous oracle: (also without *cap.*) oracular, esp. if ambiguous or difficult to interpret. — Also **Del'phian.** — *adv.* **del'phically.** [Gr. *Delphikos — Delphoi.*]

delphin *del'fin, adj.* pertaining to the *dauphin* (q.v.) of France, or to an edition of the Latin classics prepared for his use, 64 vols., 1674–1730.

Delphinidae *del-fin'i-dē, n.pl.* a family of cetaceans, including dolphins, grampuses, etc. — *adj.* **del'phinoid.** [L. *delphīnus* — Gr. *delphīs, -īnos,* a dolphin.]

Delphinium *del-fin'i-əm, n.* a genus of Ranunculaceae, comprising the larkspurs and stavesacre: (without *cap.*) any plant of the genus: — *pl.* **delphin'iums, delphin'ia.** [Latinised from Gr. *delphīnion,* larkspur, dim. of *delphīs,* dolphin, from the appearance of the flowers.]

Delphinus *del'fin-us,* (*astron.*) *n.* the Dolphin, a northern constellation between Pegasus and Aquila. [L.]

delta *del'tə, n.* the fourth letter (Δ δ) of the Greek alphabet, answering to *d*: an alluvial deposit at the mouth of a stream, Δ-shaped in the case of the Nile: as an ancient Greek numeral Δ' = 4, ͵Δ = 4000: in classification, the fourth or one of the fourth grade, the grade below gamma. — *adjs.* **deltā'ic** belonging to a delta; **del'toid** of the form of the Greek Δ: triangular. — **del'ta-wing** (*aeroplane*) a jet aeroplane with triangular wings; **deltoid muscle** the large triangular muscle of the shoulder. [Gr., — Heb. *daleth,* a tent-door.]

deltiology *del-ti-ol'ə-ji, n.* the study and collection of picture postcards. — *n.* **deltiol'ogist.** [Gr. *deltion,* small writing-tablet.]

delubrum *di-lū'brəm, -lōō', n.* a temple, shrine, sanctuary: a church having a font: a font. [L. *dēlūbrum.*]

deluce. See **fleur-de-lis.**

delude *di-lōōd', di-lūd', v.t.* to play with (someone) so as to frustrate him or his hopes (*obs.*): to elude (*obs.*): to deceive, cause to accept what is false as true. — *adjs.* **delud'able; delud'ed** holding or acting under false beliefs. — *n.* **delud'er.** [L. *dēlūdĕre,* to play false — *dē,* down, *lūdĕre, lūsum,* to play.]

deluge *del'ūj, n.* a great overflow of water: a flood, esp. Noah's: an overwhelming flow (*fig.*). — *v.t.* to inundate: to overwhelm as with water. [Fr. *déluge* — L. *dīluvium — dīluĕre — dis-,* away, *luĕre,* to wash.]

delundung *del'ən-dung, n.* the weasel-cat of Java and Malacca, a small carnivore akin to the civet. [Javanese.]

delusion *di-lōō'zhən, di-lū'zhən, n.* the act of deluding: the state of being deluded: a hallucination: a false belief (esp. *psych.*): error. — *adj.* **delu'sional** pertaining to delusions, afflicted with such. — *n.* **delu'sionist.** — *adjs.* **delu'sive** (*-siv*), **delu'sory** apt or tending to delude: deceptive. — *adv.* **delu'sively.** — *n.* **delu'siveness.** [See **delude.**]

de luxe *də lüks', di lōōks', luks',* sumptuous, luxurious: having refinements or superior qualities. [Fr., of luxury.]

delve *delv, v.t.* and *v.i.* to dig, esp. with a spade: to make deep research (*fig.*): to dip, slope suddenly. — *n.* (*Spens.*) a hollow, hole, depression, a cave. — *n.* **delv'er.** [O.E. *delfan,* to dig; conn. with **dale, delf², dell¹.**]

delves. See **delf².**

demagnetise, -ize *dē-mag'nit-īz, v.t.* to deprive of magnetic properties. — *ns.* **demagnetīsā'tion, -z-; demag'netiser, -z-.** [Pfx. **de-** (2).]

demagogue *dem'ə-gog, n.* a leader of the people: a popular and factious orator. — *adjs.* **demagogic, -al** (*-gog'* or *-goj'*). — *ns.* **demagogism, demagoguism** (*dem'ə-gog-ism*); **dem'agoguery** (*-gog-*); **dem'agogy** (*-goj-*). [Gr. *dēmagōgos* — *dēmos,* people, *agōgos,* leading — *agein,* to lead.]

demain. See **demesne.**

demaine. See **demean¹.**

demanning *dē-man'ing, n.* the deliberate reduction of the number of employees in a particular industry, etc. — *v.t.* **deman'.** [Pfx. **de-** (2).]

demand *di-mänd', v.t.* to claim: to ask peremptorily or authoritatively for: to require: to ask (a question) (*obs.*). — *n.* the asking for what is due: peremptory asking for something: a claim: desire shown by consumers: the amount of any article, commodity, etc., that consumers will buy: inquiry. — *adj.* **demand'able** that may be demanded. — *ns.* **demand'ant** one who demands: a plaintiff; **demand'er.** — *adj.* **demand'ing** requiring much attention, effort, etc. — **demand feeding** the practice of feeding a baby when it wants food, rather than at set times. — **in (great) demand** much sought after; **on demand** whenever required. [Fr. *demander* — L.L. *dēmandāre,* to demand — L. *dē-,* intens., and *mandāre,* to put into one's charge.]

demarcation, demarkation *dē-märk-ā'shən, n.* the act of marking off or setting bounds: separation: a fixed limit: in trade unionism, the strict marking off of the field of one craft from that of another. — *v.t.* **dē'marcate** (or *di-märk'*) to mark off or limit. — Also **demark'.** — **demarcation dispute** a disagreement between trade unions in a particular factory or industry about which union's members are responsible for performing a particular task. [Sp. *demarcación — de,* from, *marcar,* to mark. See **mark¹.**]

démarche *dā-märsh,* (Fr.) *n.* a step or measure (esp. diplomatic).

dematerialise, -ize *dē-mə-tē'ri-əl-īz, v.t.* to deprive of material qualities or character. — *v.i.* to become immaterial. — *n.* **dematerialisā'tion, -z-.** [Pfx. **de-** (2).]

demayne. See **demean¹.**

deme *dēm, n.* a subdivision of ancient Attica and of modern Greece, a township: a group of plants or animals that are closely related and live in a single distinct locality (*biol.*). [Gr. *dēmos,* people.]

demean¹ *di-mēn', v.t.* to bear, behave, conduct (*refl.*): to treat (*Spens.*): to ill-treat (*Spens.*; *obs. Scot.*). — *n.* (*Spens.* **demaine', demayne', demeane'**) air, bearing: treatment. — *n.* **demeanour,** *U.S.* **demean'or,** (*di-mēn'-ər; Spens.* **demeasnure**) behaviour: bearing towards another. [O.Fr. *demener — de-,* intens., and *mener,* to lead — L. *mināre,* to drive — *minārī,* to threaten.]

demean² *di-mēn', v.t.* to lower in status, reputation, or (often *refl.*) dignity. [Prob. on the analogy of *debase,* pfx. **de-** (1) and **mean.**]

dement *di-ment', (rare) v.t.* to drive crazy, render insane. — *adj.* (*arch.*) insane, demented. — *n.* a demented person. — *v.t.* **dement'āte** to dement. — *adj.* **dement'ed** out of one's mind: insane: suffering from dementia. — *adv.* **dement'edly.** — *ns.* **dement'edness; dementia** (*di-men'shi-ə; psychol.*) any form of insanity characterised by the failure or loss of mental powers: the organic deterioration of intelligence, memory, and orientation. — **dementia praecox, precox** (*prē'koks*) schizophrenia. [L. *dēmēns, dēmentis,* out of one's mind — *dē,* from, and *mēns,* the mind.]

démenti *dā-mä-tē, n.* a contradiction, denial. [Fr. *démentir,* to give the lie to.]

demerara *dem-ə-rä'rə, -rä', n.* brown sugar in large crystals: a type of rum. [*Demerara* in Guyana.]

demerge¹ *dē-mûrj', v.t.* to immerse, plunge. [L. *dē,* down, *mergĕre,* to plunge.]

demerge² *dē-mûrj', v.i.* of companies, etc., to undergo a reversal of a merger, to become separate again. — *n.* **demer'ger.** [Pfx. **de-** (2).]

demerit *dē-, di-mer'it, n.* desert (*obs.*): ill-desert: fault: a mark given for a fault or offence, esp. in schools or the army, etc. (*U.S.*). [L. *dēmerērī, dēmeritum,* to deserve fully, later understood as to deserve ill — *dē-,* fully, *merēri,* to deserve.]

demerse *də-mûrs', v.t.* (*obs.*) to immerse. — *adjs.* **demer'sal** subaqueous: found on or near the bottom; **demersed'** (*bot.*) growing under water. — *n.* **demer'sion.** [L. *dē,* down, *mergĕre, mersum,* to plunge.]

demesne *di-mān', -mēn', demain* *di-mān', n.* a manor-house with lands adjacent to it not let out to tenants: any estate in land. [Forms of **domain.**]

demi- *dem'i,* in composition, half, half-sized. — *ns.* **dem'i-bast'ion** a kind of half-bastion, consisting of one face and one flank; **dem'i-cann'on** (*Shak.*) an old kind of gun which threw a ball of from 30 to 36lb.; **demi-caractère** (*də-mē-kar-ək-tār;* Fr., half-character) in ballet, a character dance that uses the the classical technique. — Also *adj.* — **dem'i-cul'verin** an old kind of cannon which threw a shot of 9 or 10lb. — *v.t.* **dem'i-de'ify** to treat as a demigod: to go halfway towards deifying. — *ns.* **dem'i-dev'il** a half-devil; **dem'i-dis'tance** (*fort.*) the distance between the outward polygons and the flank; **dem'i-dī'tone** (*mus.*) a minor third; **dem'igod** a half-god: one whose nature is partly divine, esp. a hero fabled to be the offspring of a god and a mortal: — *fem.* **dem'igoddess; dem'i-gorge** (*fort.*) the part of the polygon remaining after the flank is raised, going from the curtain to the angle of the polygon; **dem'i-lance** a short, light spear of the 16th century: a soldier armed with such a weapon; **dem'i-lune** (*-lōon; fort.*) a half-moon: an old name for *ravelin;* **demi-monde** (*dem'i-mond, də-mē-mɔ̃d*) a class of women in an equivocal social position, the kept mistresses of society men: the shady section of a profession or group; **demi-mondaine** (*-en'*) a woman member of the demi-monde. — Also *adj.* — **demi-pension** (*də-mē-pä-syɔ̃;* Fr., boarding-house) the provision of bed, breakfast and one other meal, in hotels, etc. — *adj.* **demipique** (*dem'i-pēk*) of an 18th-century war-saddle, having a lower peak than usual. — Also *n.* — *ns.* **dem'irep** (for *demi-reputable*) a person, esp. a woman, of dubious reputation; **demirep'dom; demi-semiquaver** (*dem-i-sem'i-kwā-vər; mus.*) a note equal in time to the half of a semiquaver; **dem'i-volt(e)** a half-turn of a horse, the forelegs being raised in the air; **dem'i-wolf** (*Shak.*) a half-wolf, the offspring of a dog and a wolf. [Fr. *demi* — L. *dīmidium* — *di-,* apart, *medius,* the middle.]

demic. See **demos.**

demigration *dem-i-grā'shən, n.* change of abode. [L. *dēmigrāre, -ātum,* depart — *dē, migrāre.*]

demijohn *dem'i-jon, n.* a glass bottle with a full body and narrow neck often enclosed in wickerwork. [Fr. *dame-jeanne,* Dame Jane, analogous to **bellarmine, greybeard;** not from the town *Damaghan.*]

demi-jour *də-mē-zhōōr,* (Fr.) *n.* half-light, twilight, subdued light.

demilitarise, -ize *dē-mil'i-tər-īz, v.t.* to release from military control. — *n.* **demilitarīsā'tion, -z-.** [Pfx. **de-** (2).]

demineralise, -ize *dē-min'ə-rə-līz, v.t.* to remove salts from (water, the body). — *n.* **demineralīsā'tion, -z-.** [Pfx. **de-** (2).]

demipique, demirep. See **demi-.**

demise *di-mīz', n.* a transferring by lease: death, esp. of a sovereign or a distinguished person: a transfer of the crown or of an estate to a successor. — *v.t.* to send down to a successor: to bequeath by will: to transfer by lease. — *adj.* **demī'sable.** [O.Fr. *demise,* pa.p. of *desmettre*, to lay down. — L. *dis-*, aside, *mittĕre*, *missum*, to send.]

demiss *di-mis'*, (*rare*) *adj.* humble. — *n.* **demission** (*di-mish'ən*) lowering: degradation: depression: relinquishment: resignation. — *adj.* **demiss'ive** (*obs.*) humble. — *adv.* **demiss'ly** (*arch.*). [L. *dēmittĕre, -missum* — *dē*, down, *mittĕre*, to send.]

demist *dē-mist'*, *v.t.* to clear (e.g. a car windscreen) of condensation. — Also *v.i.* — *n.* **demist'er** a mechanical device which does this, usu. by blowing hot air. [Pfx. **de-** (2).]

demit[1] *di-mit'*, *v.t.* to send down: to lower. [See **demiss**.]

demit[2] *di-mit'* (esp. *Scot.*) *v.t.* to dismiss: to relinquish: to resign. [Fr. *démettre* — L. *dimittĕre* — *dis-*, apart, *mittĕre*, to send.]

demitasse *dem'i-tas*, *n.* a small cup of, or for, (esp. black) coffee. [Fr., half-cup.]

demiurge *dem'i-ûrj*, *n.* the maker of the world: among the Gnostics, the creator of the world and man, subordinate to God the supreme — also **demiur'gus** (*-gəs*). — *adjs.* **demiur'geous** (*-jəs*), **demiur'gic** (*-jik*), **-al.** — *adv.* **demiur'gically.** [Gr. *dēmiourgos* — *dēmos*, the people, and *ergon*, a work.]

demo *dem'ō*, (*coll.*) *n.* short for **demonstration**, esp. in the sense of a public expression of feeling: — *pl.* **dem'os.**

demobilise, -ize *di-mōb'il-īz*, *v.t.* to take out of mobilisation: to disband: to discharge from the army (*coll.*). — *n.* **demobilisā'tion, -z-.** — *n.* and *v.t.* **demob'** (*pr.p.* **demobb'ing**; *pa.p.* **demobbed'**) coll. shortening of *demobilisation, demobilise.* — Also *adj.* [Pfx. **de-** (2).]

democracy *di-mok'rə-si*, *n.* a form of government in which the supreme power is vested in the people collectively, and is administered by them or by officers appointed by them: the common people: a state of society characterised by recognition of equality of rights and privileges: political, social or legal equality: (usu. with *cap.*) in the U.S., the Democratic party (*arch.*). — Also **democraty** (*-ok'*; *Milt.*). — *n.* **democrat** (*dem'ō-krat*) one who adheres to or promotes democracy as a principle: a member of the Democratic party in the United States, the party generally inclining to look to the rights of States against centralisation of government, and favouring a low tariff: a light four-wheeled cart with several seats (*U.S. hist.*; also **democrat wagon**). — *adjs.* **democrat'ic, -al** relating to democracy: insisting on equal rights and privileges for all. — *adv.* **democrat'ically.** — *adj.* **democratifi'able** capable of being made democratic. — *v.t.* **democratise, -ize** (*di-mok'*) to render democratic. — *ns.* **democratīsā'tion, -z-;** **democ'ratist** a democrat. [Fr. *démocratie* — Gr. *dēmokratiā* — *dēmos*, the people, *kratos*, strength.]

démodé *dā-mō-dā*, (Fr.) *adj.* out of fashion.

demoded *dē'mōd'id*, *adj.* (*disparagingly*) no longer in fashion. [Pfx. **de-** (2).]

demodulate *dē-mod'ū-lāt*, (*radio*) *v.t.* to perform demodulation on (a wave). — *n.* **demodulā'tion** the inverse of modulation, a process by which an output wave is obtained that has the characteristics of the original modulating wave. — *n.* **demod'ulator.** [Pfx. **de-** (2).]

Demogorgon *dē-mō-gör'gən*, *n.* a mysterious infernal deity first mentioned about A.D. 450. [Apparently Gr. *daimōn*, deity, *gorgō*, Gorgon, *gorgos*, terrible.]

demography *dē-mog'rə-fi*, *n.* the study of population. — *n.* **demog'rapher.** — *adj.* **demographic** (*-ō-graf'ik*). [Gr. *dēmos*, the people, *graphein*, to write.]

demoiselle *dəm-wä-zel'*, *n.* a young lady (*arch.* or *playful*): a graceful kind of crane (*Anthropoides virgo*): a dragonfly: a fish of the genus *Pomacentrus* or its family (akin to the wrasses): a tiger-shark. [Fr.; see **damsel.**]

demolish *di-mol'ish*, *v.t.* to lay in ruins: to destroy, put an end to. — *ns.* **demol'isher; demol'ishments; demoli'tion** (*dem-ō-*) act of pulling down: ruin; **demoli'tionist.** [Fr. *démolir* — L. *dēmōliri*, to throw down — *dē*, down, and *mōlīrī*, to build — *mōlēs*, a heap.]

demology *dē-mol'ə-ji* *n.* demography: the theory of the origin and nature of communities. [Gr. *dēmos*,

people, *logos*, a discourse.]

demon *dē'mən*, *n.* an evil spirit, a devil: sometimes like **daemon**, a friendly spirit or good genius: a person of great energy or enthusiasm (*fig.*): — *fem.* **dē'moness.** — *adj.* **demoniac** (*di-mōn'i-ak*). — *n.* one possessed by a demon or evil spirit. — *adj.* **demoniacal** (*dē-mə-nī'ə-kl*) pertaining to or like demons or evil spirits: influenced by demons. — *adv.* **demonī'acally.** — *n.* **demonī'acism** (*-ə-sizm*) state of being a demoniac. — *adj.* **demō'nian** (*Milt.*). — *n.* **demō'nianism** possession by a demon. — *adj.* **demonic** (*dē-mon'ik*) demoniac. — *v.t.* **dē'monise, -ize** to convert into a demon: to control or possess by a demon. — *ns.* **dē'monism** a belief in demons; **dē'monist; demonŏc'racy** the power of demons; **dēmonŏl'ater; dēmonŏl'atry** the worship of demons. — *adjs.* **dēmonolog'ic, -al.** — *ns.* **dēmonol'ogist; dēmonŏl'ogy** an account of, or the study of, demons and their agency; **dēmonomā'nia** a form of mania in which the subject believes himself possessed by devils; **dē'monry** demoniacal influence. [L. *daemōn* — Gr. *daimōn*, a spirit, genius; in N.T. and Late Greek, a devil; see **dacmon.**]

demonetise, -ize *dē-mon'i-tīz*, or *-mun'*, *v.t.* to divest of value as money. — *n.* **demonetīsā'tion, -z-.** [Pfx. **de-** (2).]

demonstrate *dem'ən-strāt* (or *di-mon'strāt*), *v.t.* to make manifest: to give proof of: to prove with certainty: to teach, expound, explain, or exhibit by practical means. — *v.i.* to exhibit one's feelings: to act as demonstrator. — *adj.* **demon'strable** (or *dem'ən-*) that may be demonstrated. — *ns.* **demon'strableness, -strabil'ity.** — *adv.* **demon'strably** (or *dem'*). — *n.* **demonstrā'tion** a pointing out: proof beyond doubt: expression of the feelings by outward signs: a public expression of feelings, as by a mass-meeting, a procession, etc. : show: a movement to exhibit military intention, or to deceive an enemy: a practical lesson or exhibition. — Also *adj.* — *adj.* **demon'strative** pointing out (as a *demonstrative adjective*): making evident: proving with certainty: of the nature of proof: given to the manifestation of one's feelings. — *adv.* **demon'stratively.** — *ns.* **demon'strativeness; dem'onstrātor** one who proves beyond doubt: a teacher or assistant who helps students with practical work: one who goes about exhibiting the uses and merits of a commodity: one who takes part in a public demonstration: a vehicle or other piece of merchandise used for demonstration to customers. — *adj.* **demon'stratory** demonstrative. [L. *dēmōnstrāre, -ātum* — *dē-*, intens., and *mōnstrāre*, to show.]

demoralise, -ize *dē-mor'əl-īz*, *v.t.* to corrupt in morals: to lower the morale of — that is, to deprive of spirit and confidence: to throw into confusion. — *n.* **demoralīsā'tion, -z-** act of demoralising: corruption or subversion of morals. — *adj.* **demoralīs'ing, -z-.** [Pfx. **de-** (2).]

demos *dē'mos*, *n.* the people (esp. *contemptuously*). — *adjs.* **dem'ic** (*rare*) of the people; **demot'ic** pertaining to the people: popular: of a simplified kind of writing distinguished from the hieratic, or priestly, and from hieroglyphics (*Egypt ant.*). — *ns.* **demot'icist, demot'ist** a student of demotic script. [Gr. *dēmos*.]

Demosthenic *de-mos-then'ik*, *adj.* of or like *Dēmosthenēs*, the Athenian orator: oratorical: eloquent.

demote *dē-mōt'*, *v.t.* to reduce in rank. — *n.* **demō'tion.** [On the analogy of **promote; de-** (2).]

demotivate *dē-mōt'i-vāt*, *v.t.* to cause a loss of motivation (in or for someone, etc.). [Pfx. **de-** (2).]

demount *dē-mownt'*, *v.t.* to take down from a support, etc.: to take (e.g. a building) to pieces in such a way that it can be reassembled. — *adj.* **demount'able.** [Pfx. **de-** (2), **mount**, to set in position.]

dempster. Same as **deemster.** [See under **deem.**]

dempt *demt* (*Spens.*), *pa.p.* and *pa.t.* of **deem.**

demulcent *di-mul'sənt*, *adj.* soothing. — *n.* a medicine that allays irritation. [L. *dēmulcēns, -entis* — *dē*, down, *mulcēre*, to stroke, to soothe.]

demulsify *dē-mul'si-fī*, *v.t.* to separate from an emulsion: to make resistant to emulsification. — *ns.* **demulsificā'-**

tion, **demul'sifier**. [Pfx. **de-** (2), **emulsify**.]

demur *di-mûr'*, *v.i.* to hesitate from uncertainty or before difficulty (*arch.*): to object. — *v.t.* (*Milt.*) to hesitate about: — *pr.p.* **demurr'ing**; *pa.t.* and *pa.p.* **demurred'**. — *n.* (also **demurr'al**) a stop: a pause, hesitation (*arch.*). — *adj.* **demurr'able**. — *ns.* **demurr'age** undue delay or detention of a vessel, railway wagon, etc.: compensation for such detention: a charge made by the Bank of England for exchanging notes or gold for bullion; **demurr'er** one who demurs: an objection: a plea in law that, even if the opponent's facts are as he says, they yet do not support his case (*law*). [Fr. *demeurer* — L. *dēmorārī*, to loiter, linger — *de-*, intens., and *morārī*, to delay — *mora*, delay.]

demure *di-mūr'*, *adj.* sober: staid: modest: affectedly modest: making a show of gravity. — *v.i.* (*Shak.*) app., to look demurely. — *adv.* **demure'ly**. — *n.* **demure'ness**. [O.Fr. *meur* (Fr. *mûr*) — L. *matūrus*, ripe; pfx. unexplained.]

demy *di-mī'*, *n.* before metrication a size of printing and writing paper approximating to **A2**: in U.S. a writing paper, 21 by 16 in: a holder of certain scholarships in Magdalen College, Oxford, orig. allowed half the commons assigned to a fellow: — *pl.* **demies'**. — *n.* **demy'ship**. [Fr. *demi* — L. *dīmidium*, half — *dis-*, apart, *medius*, the middle.]

demyelinate *dē-mȳ'ə-lin-āt*, (*med.*) *v.t.* to destroy the myelin of (nerve fibres). — *n.* **demyelina'tion**. [Pfx. **de-** (2).]

demystify *dē-mis'ti-fī*, *v.t.* to clear of mystification. — *n.* **demystifica'tion**. [Pfx. **de-** (2).]

demythologise, -ize *dē-mith-ol'ə-jīz*, *v.t.* to remove mythology from, esp. the Bible, in order to arrive at the basic meaning. — *n.* **demythologīsa'tion, -z-**. [Pfx. **de-** (2).]

den[1] *den*, *n.* the hollow lair of a wild beast: a pit, cave: a haunt of vice or misery: a private retreat for work or pleasure (*coll.*): a narrow valley, a dean (*Scot.*). — *v.i.* to retire to a den. [O.E. *denn*, a cave, lair; akin to *denu*, a valley.]

den[2] *den*, (*obs.*) *n.* for **good-e'en, good-even**.

denary *dēn'ər-i*, *adj.* containing or depending on the number ten: ten. — *n.* the number ten: a group of ten. — *n.* **denarius** (*di-nā'ri-əs*) the chief Roman silver coin under the Republic, divided into ten asses about 8d.; translated *penny* in the N.T. — hence the use of d. for penny (before the introduction of decimal coinage). [L. *dēnārius* — *dēnī*, ten by ten — *decem*, ten.]

denationalise, -ize *dē-nash'ən-əl-īz*, *v.t.* to deprive of national rights or character: to return from state to private ownership. — *n.* **denationalisa'tion, -z-**. [Pfx. **de-** (2).]

denaturalise, -ize *dē-nach'ər-əl-īz*, *v.t.* to make unnatural: to deprive of naturalisation. — *n.* **dēnaturalīsa'tion, -z-**. [Pfx. **de-** (2).]

denature *dē-nā'chər*, **denaturise, -ize** *dē-nā'chər-īz*, *vs.t.* to change the nature or properties of, as a protein by heat or other treatment: of alcohol, etc., to render unfit for consumption: to add (non-radioactive material) to radioactive material, in order to prevent its being used in an atomic bomb (*nuc.*). — *n.* **denā'turant** a substance used to denature another. [Pfx. **de-** (2).]

denay *di-nā'*, obs. form of **deny, denial**.

denazify *dē-nät-si-fī*, *v.t.* to free from Nazi influence and ideology. — *n.* **denazifica'tion**. [Pfx. **de-** (2).]

dendron *den'dron*, *n.* a branching process of a nerve-cell. — *n.* **dendrachate** (*den'drə-kāt;* Gr. *achātēs*, agate) arborescent agate. — *adj.* **den'driform** tree-like. — *n.* **den'drite** (Gr. *dendrītēs*, of a tree) a tree-like crystalline aggregate or skeleton crystal: a dendron. — *adjs.* **dendrit'ic, -al** tree-like, arborescent: marked with branching figures like plants. — *ns.* **Dendrō'bium** (Gr. *bios*, life) a genus of epiphytic orchids, chiefly of tropical Asia: (without *cap.*) any plant of the genus; **Dendrocal'amus** (Gr. *kalamos*, cane) a genus of bamboos. — *adj.* **dendrochronolog'ical**. — *ns.* **dendrochron-ol'ogist; dendrochronology** (*den-drō-kron-ol'ə-ji*) fixing

of dates in the past by comparative study of the annual growth rings in ancient trees; **dendroclimatol'ogy** the study of growth rings in trees as evidence of climatic change; **den'droglyph** (*-glif;* Gr. *glyphē*, carving) an ancient carving on a tree; **den'drogram** a diagram with branches indicating the relationships of items in a classification. — *adjs.* **den'droid, -al** tree-like. — *n.* **dendrōl'atry** (Gr. *latreiā*, worship) the worship of trees. — *adjs.* **dendrolŏg'ical, dendrŏl'ogous**. — *ns.* **dendrŏl'ogist; dendrŏl'ogy** a treatise on trees: the natural history of trees; **dendrŏm'eter** an instrument for measuring trees; **Den'drophis** (Gr. *ophis*, snake) a genus of tree-snakes, Indian and Australian. [Gr. *dendron*, tree.]

dene[1] *dēn*, *n.* a small valley. [See **dean**[1].]

dene[2] *dēn*, *n.* a sandy tract, a dune. [Ety. doubtful.]

Deneb *den'eb*, *n.* the brightest star in the constellation Cygnus. — *n.* **Deneb'ola** a star at the tail of the constellation Leo. [Ar. *dhanab*, tail, *al-asad*, of the lion.]

denegation *den-i-gā'shən*, *n.* a denial. [L. *dēnegāre*, *-ātum*, to deny — *dē-*, intens., and *negāre*, to deny.]

dene-hole *dēn'hōl*, *n.* a prehistoric artificial chamber in the chalk, in Kent, Essex, etc., perhaps a flint-mine or a storehouse. [Perh. from **dene**[1], or O.E. *Dene*, Danes, from popular association; and **hole**[1].]

dengue *deng'gā*, *n.* an acute tropical epidemic fever, seldom fatal — also **breakbone fever, dan'dy-fever**. [Apparently Swahili, *dinga*.]

deniable, denial, denier, etc. See **deny**.

denier *də-nēr'*, *n.* an old small French silver coin (*Shak.*): also later, a copper coin of the value of ¹/₁₂ sou — hence a very trifling sum: a unit of silk, rayon, and nylon yarn weight (usu. *den'i-ər*). [Fr. — L. *dēnārius*.]

denigrate *den'i-grāt*, *v.t.* to blacken (esp. a reputation). — *adj.* blackened. — *ns.* **denigrā'tion; den'igrātor**. [L. *dē-*, intens., *nigrāre*, to blacken, *niger*, black.]

denim *den'im*, *n.* coloured twilled cotton fabric for overalls, etc.: (in *pl.*) a garment made of denim. [Fr. *de*, of, and *Nîmes*.]

denitrate *dē-nī'trāt*, *v.t.* to free from nitric acid or other nitrogen compounds. — *ns.* **denītrā'tion; denītrifica'-tion**, removal of nitrogen or its compounds; **denī'-trificātor**. — *v.t.* **denī'trify**. [Pfx. **de-** (2).]

denizen *den'i-zn*, *n.* an inhabitant (human or animal): one admitted to the rights of a citizen: a wild plant, probably foreign, that keeps its footing: a naturalised foreign word, etc. — Also *adj.* — *v.t.* to make a denizen: to provide with occupants. — *v.i.* to inhabit. — *ns.* **denizā'tion** act of making one a citizen; **den'izenship**. [O.Fr. *deinzein* — *deinz, dens* (Fr. *dans*), within — L. *dē intus*, from within.]

dennet *den'it*, *n.* a light gig. [Prob. a surname.]

denominate *di-nom'in-āt*, *v.t.* to give a name to: to call. — *adj.* **denom'inable**. — *n.* **denomina'tion** the act of naming: a name or title: a class or group, esp. of units in weights, money, etc.: a collection of individuals called by the same name: a sect. — *adj.* **denomina'tional** belonging to a denomination or sect. — *adv.* **denomina'tionally**. — *ns.* **denomina'tionalism** a denominational or class spirit or policy: devotion to the interests of a sect; **denomina'tionalist**. — *adj.* **denom'inative** giving or having a title. — *adv.* **denom'inatively**. — *n.* **denom'inator** he who, or that which, gives a name (*arch.*): the lower number in a vulgar fraction, which names the parts into which the integer is divided (*arith.*). — **common denominator** a number that is a multiple of each of the denominators of a set of fractions, esp. the least: something that makes comparison, communication, agreement, etc., possible. [L. *dē-*, intens., *nōmināre*, to name — *nōmen*, name.]

denote *di-nōt'*, *v.t.* to note or mark off: to indicate by a sign: to signify or mean: to indicate the objects comprehended in a class (*log.*). — *adj.* **denō'table**. — *v.t.* **dē'nōtate** to denote. — *n.* **dēnotā'tion** (*log.*) that which a word denotes, in contradistinction to that which it connotes. — *adj.* **denō'tative** (or *dē'*). — *adv.* **denō'tatively** (or *dē'*). — *n.* **denōte'ment** (*Shak.*) a sign or indication. [Fr. *dénoter* — L. *dēnotāre, -ātum* — *dē,* intens., and *notāre*.]

dénouement *dā-nōō'-mā, n.* the unravelling of a plot or story: the issue, event, or outcome. [Fr. *dénouement* or *dénoûment*; *dénouer,* O.Fr. *desnoer,* to untie — L. *dis-, nodāre,* to tie — *nodus,* a knot.]

denounce *di-nowns', v.t.* to inform against or accuse publicly: to inveigh against: to proclaim as imminent: to notify formally termination of (treaties, etc.): to announce (*obs.*): to give formal notice of a claim for mining rights covering (*U.S.*; through Sp.). — *ns.* **denounce'ment** denunciation; **denounc'er.** [Fr. *dénon-cer* — L. *dēnuntiāre* — *dē-,* intens., and *nuntiāre,* to announce.]

de novo *dē nō'vō, dā nō'wō,* (L.) anew.

dense *dens, adj.* thick, close, compact: impenetrably stupid. — *adv.* **dense'ly.** — *ns.* **dense'ness; dens'ifier.** — *v.t.* **dens'ify** to increase the density of (wood, etc.) by compression. — *n.* **dens'ity** the quality of being dense: the proportion of a mass to bulk or volume: the quantity of matter per unit of bulk; **densim'eter** an instrument for measuring the relative density or the closeness of grain of a substance. — *adj.* **densimet'ric.** — *ns.* **densim'etry; densitŏm'eter** any instrument for measuring the optical transmission or reflecting properties of a material. — *adj.* **densitomet'ric.** — *n.* **densitŏm'etry.** [L. *dēnsus,* thick, dense.]

dent¹ *dent, n.* a hollow in a surface, caused by a blow. *v.t.* to make such a hollow in. — Also *fig.* — See also **dint, dunt¹.** [Confused with next.]

dent² *dent, n.* a notch. — *v.t.* to notch. — *adj.* **dent'al** pertaining to or concerned with the teeth or dentistry: produced by the aid of the teeth. — *n.* a sound pronounced by applying the tongue to the teeth or (*loosely*) the gums. — *ns.* **Dentā'lium** a genus of scaphopod molluscs with shell like an elephant's tusk —tooth-shell or tusk-shell: (without *cap.*) any mollusc or shell of the genus: — *pl.* **dentā'liums** or **-ia; Dentā'ria** a genus of plants including the cruciferous toothwort: (without *cap.*) any plant of the genus. — *adj.* **dent'ary** belonging to dentition: bearing teeth. — *n.* a bone of the lower jaw of some vertebrates usually bearing teeth. — *adjs.* **dent'ate, -d** toothed: notched: set as with teeth. — *ns.* **dentā'tion** condition of being dentate: a tooth-like projection; **dent'el** see **dentil** below; **dent'ex** a strongly toothed voracious fish akin to perch, found in the Mediterranean; **dent'icle** a small tooth-like structure: a dentil. — *adjs.* **dentic'ulāte, -d** notched: having dentils. — *n.* **denticulā'tion.** — *adj.* **dent'iform** having the form of a tooth or of teeth. — *n.* **dent'ifrice** (L. *fricāre,* to rub) a substance used in rubbing or cleaning the teeth — toothpaste or tooth-powder. — *adj.* **dentigerous** (-*ij'*) bearing teeth. — *n.* **dent'il** a denticle: one of a series of square blocks or projections as in the bed-moulding of a cornice of columns. — Also **dent'el.** — *adj.* **dentilin'gual** (L. *lingua,* tongue) formed between the teeth and the tongue, as *th* in *thin, this.* — *n.* a consonant so formed. — *ns.* **dent'ine** (-*ēn*), **den'tin** the substance of which teeth are mainly composed. — *adj.* **dentiros'tral** (L. *rōstrum,* a beak) with notched bill. — *ns.* **dent'ist** one qualified to treat diseases and malformations of, and injuries to, teeth; **dent'istry** the art or work of a dentist; **dent'ition** the cutting or growing of teeth: the conformation, number, and arrangement of the teeth. — *adj.* **dent'oid** (Gr. *eidos,* form) formed or shaped like a tooth. — *n.* **dent'ure** a set of (esp. artificial) teeth. — **dental floss** see **floss; dental formula** a formula showing the number and distribution of the different kinds of teeth in an animal's jaws. [L. *dēns, dentis,* a tooth; dim. *denticulus.*]

dental, dentate. See **dent².**

dentelle *den-tel', dā-tel, n.* lace, lacework: an ornamental pattern or border resembling lace and featuring toothed outlines, used in decorating book covers. [Fr., lit. little tooth — O.Fr. *dentele,* dim. of *dent,* tooth.]

dentifrice, dentine, dentist, denture, etc. See **dent².**

denuclearise, -ize- *dē-nū'klē-ə-rīz, v.t.* to remove nuclear weapons from (a country, state, etc.) — *n.* **denuclearīsā'tion, -z-.** [Pfx. **de-** (2).]

denude *di-nūd', v.t.* to make nude or naked: to lay bare (also rarely **denud'ate**). *v.i.* to divest oneself of a title, etc. — *n.* **denudation** (*den-ū-dā'shən*) a making nude or bare: the wearing away of rocks whereby the underlying rocks are laid bare (*geol.*). [L. *dēnūdāre* — *dē-,* intens., *nūdāre, -ātum,* to make naked.]

denumerable *di-nū'mər-əbl,* (*math.*) *adj.* able to be put in a one-to-one correspondence with the positive integers. — *adv.* **denū'merably.** [Pfx. **de-** (3).]

denunciate *di-nun's(h)i-āt, v.t.* to denounce. — *n.* **denunciā'tion** any formal declaration: act of denouncing: a threat; **denun'ciātor** one who denounces. — *adj.* **denun'ciatory** containing a denunciation: threatening. [L. *dēnunciāre* or *dēnuntiāre;* see **denounce.**]

deny *di-nī', v.t.* to gainsay or declare not to be true: to reject: to refuse: to refuse to admit: to refuse a visitor access to: to disown: — *pr.p.* **deny'ing;** *pa.t.* and *pa.p.* **denied'.** — *n.* **deniabil'ity.** — *adj.* **denī'able.** — *adv.* **denī'ably.** — *ns.* **denī'al** the act of denying: refusal: rejection; **denī'er.** — *adv.* **deny'ingly.** — **deny oneself** to refuse to allow oneself gratification: to exercise self-denial. [Fr. *dénier* — L. *dēnegāre* — *dē-,* intens., and *negāre,* to say no.]

Deo *dē'ō, dā'ō,* (L.) to, for, with God. — **Deo favente** *fə-ven'tē, -wen'tā,* with God's favour; **Deo gratias** *grā'shi-əs, grä'tē-äs,* thanks to God; **Deo Optimo Maximo** (abbrev. **D.O.M.**) *op'ti-mō mak'si-mō,* to God, the best, the greatest (the motto of the Benedictines); **Deo volente** (abbrev. **D.V.**) *vo-len'tē, wo-len'tā,* God willing.

deobstruent *dē-ob'strōō-ənt,* (*med.*) *adj.* removing obstructions. — Also *n.* [L. *dē,* away; see **obstruct.**]

deoch-an-doruis *dohh'ən dō'ris, dō', n.* a stirrup-cup, a parting cup. — Also **doch-an-doris, doch-an-dorach** (-*əhh*), **deuch-an-doris.** [Gael. *deoch,* drink, *an,* the, *doruis,* gen. of *dorus,* door.]

deodand *dē'ō-dand, n.* in old English law, a personal chattel which had been the immediate accidental cause of the death of a human being, forfeited to the crown for pious uses. [L. *deō,* to God, *dandum,* that must be given — *dāre,* to give.]

deodar *dē'ō-där, n.* a cedar (*Cedrus deodara*) of the Himalayas, much praised by Indian poets: its hard, sweet-smelling wood. [Sans. *deva-dāru,* divine tree.]

deodate *dē'ō-dāt, n.* a gift to God: extended to mean a gift from God. [L. *deō,* to God (*ā Deō,* by God), *dātum,* given, pa.p. of *dāre,* to give.]

deodorise, -ize *dē-ō'dər-īz, v.t.* to take the odour or smell from: to make inoffensive by euphemism, evasion, etc. — *ns.* **deō'dorant, deō'doriser, -z-** a substance that destroys or conceals unpleasant smells; **deō'dorīsā'tion, -z-.** [Pfx. **de-** (2).]

dcontology *dē-on-tol'ə-ji, n.* the science of duty, ethics. — Also *n. sing.* **deon'tics.** — *adjs.* **deon'tic; deontological** (-*tə-loj'*). — *n.* **deontol'ogist.** [Gr. *deon, -ontos,* neut. pr.p. of *deein,* to be necessary, to behave, *logos,* discourse.]

deoppilate *dē-op'i-lāt, v.t.* to free from obstruction. — *n.* **deoppilā'tion.** — *adj.* **deopp'ilative.** [Pfx. **de-** (2).]

deoxidate *dē-oks'i-dāt, v.t.* to take oxygen from, or reduce. — Also **deox'idise, -ize.** — *ns.* **deoxidā'tion; deoxidīsā'tion, -z-; deox'idīser, -z-** a substance that deoxidises. — *v.t.* **deoxygenate** (*dē-oks'ij-ən-āt*) to deprive of oxygen. — Also **deox'ygenise, -ize.** — *pfxs.* **deoxy-, desoxy-** containing less oxygen. — **deoxyribonucleic acids** (*dē-oks-i-rī'bō-nū-klē'ik*) nucleic acids containing **deoxyrī'bōse** (sugar), consisting of complex molecules, present in chromosomes of all plant and animal cells, and carrying in coded form instructions for passing on of hereditary characteristics — abbrev. **DNA.** [Pfx. **de-** (2).]

depaint *di-pānt',* (*Spens.*) *v.t.* to paint: to depict. [Fr. *dépeindre* — L. *dēpingĕre;* see **depict.**]

depart *di-pärt', v.i.* to go away: to quit or leave: to die:

to separate from one another (*obs.*). — *v.t.* (*obs.*) to separate, divide. — *n.* (*Shak.*; *Spens.*) departure, parting. — *ns.* **depart'er; depart'ing; depart'ure** act of departing: a going away from a place: deviation: the distance in nautical miles made good by a ship due east or west: death. — **a new departure** a change of purpose or method, a new course of procedure; **the departed** the deceased. [Fr. *départir* — L. *dis-*, apart, and *partīre* (*partīrī*), to part, to divide.]

department *di-pärt'mənt, n.* a part: a special or allotted function, sphere of activity, duty, or competence: a section of an administration, university, office or other organisation: a division of a country, esp. of France. — *adj.* **departmental** (*dē-pärt-ment'l*). — *v.t.* **department'alise, -ize** to form into separate departments: to deal with by allotting a specific share to different departments. — *ns.* **departmentalisā'tion, -z-; department'alism** too strict division of work among departments with little intercommunication. — *adv.* **department'ally.** — **department store** (orig. *U.S.*) a big shop selling a variety of goods in different departments. [Fr. *département* — *départir* (see **depart**).]

depasture *di-päs'chər, v.t.* to eat bare: to put to pasture: to afford pasture for. — *v.i.* to graze. [Pfx. **de-** (2).]

depauperise, -ize *di-pö'pər-īz, v.t.* to remove from the state of pauper. — *v.t.* **depau'perate** to impoverish. — *adj.* impoverished. [Pfx. **de-** (2), (3).]

dépêche *dā-pesh,* (Fr.) *n.* dispatch, message.

depeinct *di-pānt',* (*Spens.*) *v.t.* to paint. [**depaint.**]

depend *di-pend', v.i.* to hang down: to be sustained by or connected with anything: to be pending: to rely (on): to rest (on). — *adj.* **depend'able** that may be depended on: reliable. — *adv.* **depend'ably.** — *n.* **depend'ant** (also **-ent**) one who depends on another for support or otherwise: a hanger-on. — *adj.* **depend'ent** (also **-ant**) depending, relying, contingent, relative: awaiting settlement. — *ns.* **depend'ence** (rarely **-ance**) state of being dependent: reliance, trust: that on which one depends: a quarrel or duel pending (*arch.*); **depend'ency** that which depends: connected consistency (*Shak.*): a foreign territory dependent on a country, a kind of subordinate colony without self-government: dependence (*rarely*; *Shak.* **depend'acie** submissiveness). — *adj.* **depend'ing** still undetermined. — *adv.* **depend'ingly.** [Fr. *dépendre* — L. *dēpendēre* — *dē,* from, and *pendere,* to hang.]

depersonalise, -ize *dē-pûr'sən-əl-īz, v.t.* to take away the characteristics or personality of. — *n.* **dēpersonalisā'tion, -z-.** [Pfx. **de-** (2).]

dephlegmate *di-fleg'māt,* (*old chem.*) *v.t.* to free from water: to concentrate, rectify. — *ns.* **dephlegmā'tion** (*dē-*); **dephlegmā'tor.** [Pfx. **de-** (2).]

dephlogisticate *dē-flo-jis'ti-kāt, v.t.* to deprive of phlogiston. — **dephlogisticated air** Priestley's name for oxygen. [Pfx. **de-** (2).]

depict *di-pikt', v.t.* to paint carefully: to make a likeness of: to describe minutely. — *ns.* **depict'er, -or; depic'tion.** — *adj.* **depict'ive.** [L. *dēpingĕre, dēpictum* — *dē-,* intens., *pingĕre,* to paint.]

depicture *di-pik'chər, v.t.* to picture: to paint: to represent. — *n.* depicting, representation. [Pfx. **de-** (3), and **picture** vb.]

depilate *dep'i-lāt, v.t.* to remove the hair from. — *ns.* **depilā'tion** removal or loss of hair; **dep'ilātor; depilatory** (*di-pil'ə-tər-i*) an application for removing superfluous hairs. — *adj.* possessing this quality. [L. *dēpilāre, -ātum* — *dē,* out, *pilus,* hair.]

deplane *dē-plān', v.i.* to disembark from an aeroplane. [Pfx. **de-** (2), and **plane**[2].]

deplete *di-plēt', v.t.* to empty, reduce, exhaust. — *n.* **deplē'tion** the act of emptying or exhausting: the act of relieving congestion or plethora (*med.*). — *adjs.* **deplē'table; deplē'tive, deplē'tory.** [L. *dēplēre, dēplētum,* to empty, *dē-,* neg., *plēre,* to fill.]

deplore *di-plōr', -plör', v.t.* to feel or express deep grief for: to disapprove strongly of: to give up as hopeless (*obs.*). — *adj.* **deplor'able** lamentable: sad: hopelessly bad. — *ns.* **deplor'ableness, deplorabil'ity.** — *adv.* **deplor'ably.** — *n.* **deplorā'tion** (*dep-, dēp-*) lamentation. — *adv.* **deplor'ingly.** [L. *dēplōrāre* — *dē-,* intens., *plōrāre,* to weep.]

deploy *di-ploi', v.t.* to unfold: to open out or extend: to spread out and place strategically (any forces). — *v.i.* to open: to extend from column into line, as a body of troops. — *ns.* **deploy', deploy'ment.** [Fr. *déployer* — L. *dis-,* apart, and *plicāre,* to fold.]

deplume *di-ploom', v.t.* to take the plumes or feathers from. — *n.* **deplumā'tion** (*dē-*). [Pfx. **de-** (2).]

depolarise, -ize *dē-pō'lər-īz, v.t.* to deprive of polarity. — *n.* **depolarīsā'tion, -z-.** [Pfx. **de-** (2).]

depoliticise, -ize *dē-po-lit'i-sīz, v.t.* to remove the political nature or awareness from. [Pfx. **de-** (2).]

depolymerise, -ize *dē-pol'i-mər-iz, v.t.* to break a large molecule into simpler ones that have the same empirical formula. — *v.i.* to decompose in this way. — *n.* **depolymerisā'tion, -z-.** [Pfx. **de-** (2).]

depone *di-pōn',* (mainly *Scot.*) *v.t.* to lay down: to deposit: to testify upon oath. — *adj.* **depō'nent** (*gram.*) having a passive form but active signification (as if having laid aside the passive — really middle or reflexive — meaning). — *n.* a deponent verb: one who makes a deposition, esp. under oath, or whose written testimony is used as evidence in a court of justice. [L. *dēpōnĕre*; pr.p. *dēpōnēns, -entis* — *dē,* down, *pōnĕre,* to place, lay.]

depopulate *dē-, di-pop'ū-lāt, v.t.* to overrun and lay waste (*obs.*): to deprive of population, to dispeople. — *v.i.* to become dispeopled. — *adj.* depopulated. — *ns.* **depopulā'tion** act of depopulating: havoc: destruction; **depop'ulātor.** [L. *dēpopulārī, -ātus* — *dē-,* intens., and *populārī,* to swarm over, to spread over a country, said of hostile people (L. *populus*) — hence to ravage, to destroy; later understood as to deprive of people.]

deport[1] *di-, dē-pōrt', -pört', v.t.* to transport, to exile: to expel (e.g. as an undesirable alien). — *ns.* **deportā'tion; deportee'.** [Fr. *déporter* — L. *dēportāre* — *dē-,* away, and *portāre, -ātum,* to carry.]

deport[2] *di-pōrt' -pört', v.t.* to behave (*refl.*). — *n.* **deport'ment** behaviour: bearing: manners. [O.Fr. *deporter* — L. *dē-,* intens., *portāre,* to carry.]

depose *di-pōz', v.t.* to remove from a high station: to degrade: to set down: to remove: to attest: to examine or put upon oath (*Shak.*). — *v.i.* to bear witness: to swear (*Shak.*). — *adj.* **depōs'able.** — *ns.* **depōs'al; depōs'er.** [Fr. *déposer* — L. *dē,* from, *pausāre,* to pause, (late) to place.]

deposit *di-poz'it, v.t.* to put or set down: to place: to lay: to lay up or past: to entrust: to lodge as a pledge: to lay down as a coating, bed, vein or the like. — *n.* that which is deposited or put down: a sum of money paid to secure an article, service, etc., the remainder of the cost being paid later: an accumulation by sedimentation, precipitation, sublimation, or other natural means: something entrusted to another's care, esp. money put in a bank: a pledge: a bailment where one entrusts goods to another to be kept without recompense (in *Scots law,* **depositā'tion**): the state of being deposited. — *n.* **depos'itary** a person with whom anything is left for safe keeping: a guardian — sometimes **depos'itory.** — *adj.* **depos'itive.** — *ns.* **depos'itor; depos'itory** a place where anything is deposited sometimes **depos'itary.** — **deposit account** a bank account in which money is deposited to gain interest, and for which cheques are not used; **depos'it-receipt'** a receipt for money deposited in a bank, etc. [L. *dēpositum,* placed — *dēpōnĕre, dē,* down, and *pōnĕre,* to place.]

deposition *dēp-ə-zish'ən, n.* act of deposing: act of deponing: declaration, testimony taken authoritatively, to be used as a substitute for the production of the witness in open court: removal: act or process of depositing: what is deposited, sediment. — *adj.* **deposi'tional.** [**deposit;** blended with root of **depose.**]

depot, dépôt *dep'ō, di-pō', dā'pō* or *dē'pō, n.* a place of deposit: a storehouse: a military station where stores

are kept and recruits trained: the headquarters of a regiment: the portion of a regiment left at home: a railway station (*U.S.*): a place where buses or tramcars are kept. [Fr. *dépôt* — L. *dēpōnĕre, -pŏsitum*, to put down, to place.]

deprave *di-prāv'*, *v.t.* to represent as bad (*obs.*): to make morally bad or worse: to corrupt. — *n.* **depravation** (*dep-rə-vā'shən*) act of depraving: state of being depraved: depravity. — *adj.* **deprāved'** corrupt. — *adv.* **deprāv'edly**. — *ns.* **deprāv'edness; deprāve'ment** vitiation. — *adv.* **deprāv'ingly**. — *n.* **depravity** (*di-prav'i-ti*) a vitiated or corrupt state of moral character: extreme wickedness: corruption: the hereditary tendency of man toward sin (*theol.*): original sin (*theol.*). — *adv.* **dep'recātorily**. [L. *dēprāvāre — dē-*, intens., *prāvus*, bad.]

deprecate *dep'ri-kāt*, *v.t.* to try to ward off by prayer (*arch.*): to desire earnestly the prevention or removal of: to invoke or beseech with a view to the averting or withholding of evil (*arch.*): to regret deeply: to argue or protest against: to express disapproval of: to disparage, belittle. — *adjs.* **dep'recable** to be deprecated; **dep'recating** expressing deprecation, disapproval, disparagement. — *n.* **depreca'tion** act of deprecating, earnest prayer, esp. a special petition against some evil, in litanies. — *adv.* **dep'recatingly**. — *adjs.* **dep'recātive, dep'recātory**. — *n.* **dep'recātor**. — *adv.* **dep'recātorily**. [L. *dēprecāri, -ātus — dē*, away, and *precāri*, to pray.]

depreciate *di-prē'shi-āt*, *v.t.* to lower the worth of: to undervalue: to disparage. — *v.i.* to fall in value. — *adv.* **deprē'ciātingly**. — *n.* **depreciātion** (*-s(h)i-ā'shən*) the falling of value: disparagement. — *adjs.* **deprē'ciative, deprē'ciatory** tending to depreciate or lower. — *n.* **deprē'ciātor**. [L. *dēpretiāre, -ātum — dē*, down, and *pretium*, price.]

depredate *dep'ri-dāt*, *v.t.* to plunder or prey upon: to rob: to lay waste: to devour. — *ns.* **depredā'tion** act of plundering: state of being depredated; **dep'redātor**. — *adj.* **depredatory** (*di-pred'ət-ə-ri*). [L. *dēpraedārī, -ātus — dē-*, intens., and *praedārī — praeda*, plunder.]

deprehend *dep-ri-hend'*, (*obs.*) *v.t.* to catch, seize: to apprehend: to detect. [L. *dēpraehendĕre — dē-*, aside, and *praehendĕre*, to take.]

depress *di-pres'*, *v.t.* to press down: to let down: to lower: to cause to sink: to humble: to make subject: to dispirit or cast a gloom over. — *n.* **depress'ant** that which lowers activity: a sedative: a chemical that causes a mineral to sink in flotation (*mining*). — Also *adj.* — *adj.* **depressed'** pressed down: lowered: flattened or slightly hollowed: humbled: dejected: dispirited: of a market, trade, etc., reduced, not flourishing. — *adjs.* **depress'ible; depress'ing** able or tending to depress. — *adv.* **depress'ingly**. — *n.* **depression** (*di-presh'ən*) a falling in or sinking: a lowering: a region of low barometric pressure: a hollow: abasement: dejection: a reduced condition of trade and prosperity. — *adj.* **depress'ive** tending to depress: suffering from periods of depression. — *n.* one suffering from these. — *n.* **depress'or** an oppressor: that which lowers activity: a muscle that draws down: a surgical instrument for pressing down. — **depressed area** a region suffering from depression of trade: a region of specially heavy unemployment. [L. *dēprimĕre, -pressum — dē*, down, *premĕre*, to press.]

depressurise, -ize *dē-presh'ər-īz*, *v.t.* to release, e.g. an aircraft cabin, from controlled air-pressure. — *n.* **depressurisā'tion, -z-**. [Pfx. **de-** (2).]

deprive *di-prīv'*, *v.t.* to dispossess: to keep out of enjoyment: to degrade (esp. a clergyman) from office: to bereave. — *adj.* **depriv'able**. — *ns.* **depriv'al, depriva'tion** (*dep-ri-* or *dē-prī-*) the act of depriving: the state of being deprived: degradation from office: loss: bereavement. — *adj.* **deprived'** having been dispossessed (of): suffering from hardship, esp. the lack of good educational, social, medical, etc., facilities. — *adj.* **depriv'ative**. — *n.* **deprive'ment**. [L.L. *dēprīvāre*, to

degrade — L. *dē*, from, and *prīvāre*, to deprive — *prīvus*, one's own.]

de profundis *dē prə-fun'dis, dā pro-fŏŏn'dēs*, (L.) out of the depths — Psalm cxxx.

deprogram *dē-prō'gram*, *v.t.* to remove a program from (a computer): (usu. **deprō'gramme**) to prevail upon (a person) to reject obsessive beliefs, fears, etc. [Pfx. **de-** (2).]

depside *dep'sīd* (*chem.*) *n.* a product formed from hydroxy-aromatic acids by the condensation of the carboxyl group of one molecule with the phenol group of a second, functioning in plant cells. [Gr. *depsein*, to knead.]

depth *depth*, *n.* deepness: the measure of deepness down or inwards: a deep place: intensity: the innermost or intensest part, as *depth of winter*: abstruseness: extent of sagacity and penetration. — *adj.* **depth'less** having no depth: bottomless. — **depth'-bomb, -charge** a powerful bomb that explodes under water (dropped over or near submarines); **depth psychology** the psychology of the unconscious; **depth psychologist**. — **depth of field** the distance between the nearer and farther planes in an area photographed, seen through a microscope, etc., over which the image is in reasonably sharp focus; **depth of focus** the distance between a camera lens and the film at which the image will be clear; **in depth** extending far inwards: (of defence) consisting of several successive lines: extensive(ly) and thorough(ly) (*adj.* **in'-depth'** see **in**); **out of one's depth** in water where one cannot touch bottom, or too deep for one's safety: beyond one's understanding; **the depths** the lowest pitch of humiliation and misery. [Not in O.E.; possibly O.N. *dȳpth*; or formed from **deep**, on analogy of **length**, etc.]

depurate *dep'ū-rāt, di-pū'rāt*, *v.i.* to purify. — *adj.* and *n.* **dep'ūrant**. — *ns.* **depūrā'tion; dep'ūrātor**. — *n.* and *adj.* **depurative** (*dep'ū-rā-tiv, di-pūr'ə-tiv*). — *adj.* **depū'ratory**. [L.L. *dēpūrāre, -ātum*, to purify — L. *dē-*, intens., and *pūrāre*, to purify — *pūrus*, pure.]

depute *di-pūt'*, *v.t.* to appoint or send as a substitute or agent: to send with a special commission: to make over (one's authority). — *adj.* (*dep'ūt*) in Scotland, appointed deputy (as in *sheriff-depute* — often simply *the depute*). — *n.* **deputation** (*dep-ū-tā'shən*) act of deputing: the person or persons deputed or appointed to transact business for another: a body of persons sent to state a case: the privilege of shooting game, or a document granting it, formerly given by the lord of a manor, nominally as to a gamekeeper. — *v.t.* **dep'ūtise, -ize** to appoint as deputy. — *v.i.* to act as deputy. — *n.* **dep'ūty** one deputed or appointed to act for another, esp. (*London*) for an alderman or (*U.S.*) for a sheriff: a delegate or representative, or substitute: a legislator, member of a chamber of deputies: one who attends to protective arrangements in a coal-mine. [L. *dēputāre*, to prune, (later) to select.]

deracialise, -ize *dē'rāsh'əl-īz, -yə-līz*, *v.t.* to divest of racial character. [Pfx. **de-** (2) and **racial**.]

deracinate *dē-ras'i-nāt*, *v.t.* to root up. — *n.* **deracinā'tion**. — *adj.* **deraciné** (*dā-ras-ē-nā*; Fr.) uprooted (*lit.* and *fig.*). [Fr. *déraciner* — L. *dē*, from, L.L. *rādicīna*, dim. of L. *rādix*, a root.]

deraign. See **darraigne**.

derail *di-rāl'*, *v.t.* to cause to leave the rails. — *v.i.* to go off the rails. — *ns.* **derail'er; derail'ment**. [Pfx. **de-** (2).]

dérailleur (gear) *dā-ra-yœr* (*gēr*), *də-rāl'yər*, *n.* a variable bicycle-gear depending on a mechanism by means of which the chain can be transferred from one sprocket wheel to another of different size. [Fr. *dérailler*, to derail.]

derange *di-rānj'*, *v.t.* to put out of place or order: to disorder: to make insane. — *adj.* **deranged'** disordered: insane. — *n.* **derange'ment** disorder: insanity: obs. psychiatric term for psychosis. [Fr. *déranger* — *dé-* (L. *dis-*), asunder, *ranger*, to rank.]

derate *dē-rāt'*, *v.t.* to relieve (wholly or partially) from local rates: to reduce the maximum capacity ratings of electrical equipment to allow for deterioration, etc. — *n.* **derat'ing**. [Pfx. **de-** (2).]

deration *dē-ra'shən, v.t.* to free from rationing. [Pfx. **de-** (2).]

deray *di-rā', (obs.) v.t.* to derange. — *v.i.* to go wild. — *n.* tumult, disorder. [O.Fr. *desreer* — *des-*, neg., and *rei, roi,* order; see **array**.]

Derby *där'bi, n.* a kind of porcelain made at *Derby:* a horse-race held annually on Epsom Downs (from Derby stakes, instituted by Earl of *Derby,* 1780): (*dûr'bi*) one run at Churchill Downs, Kentucky: (often without *cap.*) any race attracting much interest, or a keen sporting contest, esp. one of local importance: (*dûr'bi; U.S.;* often without *cap.*) a bowler hat: (sometimes without *cap.*) a strong type of boot. — **Derby dog** a dog straying on a race-course: an intruder or an interruption (*fig.*); **Derbyshire neck** a form of goitre; **Derbyshire spar** fluorite.

der-doing *dûr'doo'ing,* (*Spens.*) *adj.* doing daring deeds. [See **derring-do.**]

dere, deare, *dēr, (obs.) v.t.* to injure. — *n.* (*Spens.*) injury. [O.E. *derian.*]

derecognise, -ize *dē-rek'əg-nīz, v.t.* to withdraw recognition from. — *n.* **derecogni'tion**. [Pfx. **de-** (2).]

deregister *dē-rej'is-tər, v.t.* to remove from a register. — *n.* **deregistrā'tion**. [Pfx. **de-** (2).]

de règle *də regl', (Fr.)* according to rule.

deregulate *dē-reg'ū-lāt, v.t.* to free from regulations or controls. — *n.* **deregulā'tion**. [Pfx. **de-** (2).]

derelict *der'i-likt, adj.* forsaken: abandoned, falling in ruins: neglectful of duty (chiefly *U.S.*). — *n.* anything (esp. a ship) forsaken or abandoned: a person abandoned by society, a down-and-out. — *n.* **derelic'tion** act of forsaking, unfaithfulness or remissness: state of being abandoned: land gained from the water by a change of water-line. [L. *dērelinquĕre, -lictum* — *dē,* intens., *re-,* behind, and *linquĕre,* to leave.]

dereligionise, -ize *dē-ri-lij'ən-īz, v.t.* to make irreligious. [Pfx. **de-** (2).]

derequisition *dē-rek-wi-zi'shən, v.t.* to return (something that has been used for a military purpose) to civilian use. [Pfx. **de-** (2).]

derestrict *dē-ri-strikt', v.t.* to free from restriction, esp. a road from a speed limit. — *n.* **derestric'tion**. [Pfx. **de-** (2).]

derham. See **dirhem.**

deride *di-rīd', v.t.* to laugh at: to mock. — *n.* **derid'er**. — *adv.* **derid'ingly**. — *adj.* **derisible** (*-riz'*). — *n.* **derision** (*di-rizh'-ən*) act of deriding: mockery: a laughing-stock. — *adjs.* **derisive** (*di-rīs'iv,* or *riz'*) scoffing; **deris'ory** scoffing: ridiculous. — *adv.* **deris'ively** (or *-riz'*). — *n.* **deris'iveness** (or *-riz'*). [L. *dērīdēre, -rīsum* — *dē,* intens., and *ridēre,* to laugh.]

de rigueur *də rē-gœr', (Fr.)* required by strict etiquette, or by fashion, etc.

derision, derisive, etc. See **deride.**

derive *di-rīv', v.t.* to conduct, draw, take, obtain, or receive (from a source or origin): to bring down (upon oneself; *Shak.*): to infer: to trace to an origin. — *v.i.* to descend or issue. — *adj.* **deriv'able**. — *adv.* **deriv'ably**. — *adj.* **derivate** (*der'i-vāt*) derived. — *n.* a derivative. — *n.* **derivā'tion** act of deriving: a drawing off: the tracing of a word to its root: source: that which is derived: descent or evolution of man or animals: a sequence of statements showing how a certain result must follow from other statements already accepted, as in a mathematical formula, logical progression, etc. — *adj.* **derivā'tional**. — *n.* **derivā'tionist**. — *adj.* **derivative** (*di-riv'ə-tiv*) derived or taken from something else: not radical or original. — *n.* that which is derived: a word formed from another word: a differential coefficient (*math.*). — *adv.* **deriv'atively**. — **derived unit** a unit of measurement derived from the fundamental units of a system. [Fr. *dériver* — L. *dērīvāre* — *dē,* down, from, and *rīvus,* a river.]

derm *dûrm, n.* the true skin — also **der'ma, der'mis.** —

n. **dermabrā'sion** a cosmetic operation in which the facial skin is scrubbed, peeled away and allowed to heal. — *adjs.* **der'mal, dermat'ic, der'mic** pertaining to the skin: consisting of skin. — *n.pl.* **Dermap'tera** an order of insects with forewings, when present, in the form of firm elytra — the earwigs. — *ns.* **dermatī'tis** inflammation of the skin; **dermat'ogen** (*bot.*) the layer from which epidermis is formed at the growing-point; **dermatoglyph'ics** (Gr. *glyphein,* to carve) skin patterns, esp. of the skin on the under-surfaces of the hands and feet: (*n. sing.*) the science of the study of skin patterns; **dermatograph'ia** a type of urticaria in which the physical allergy causes stroking or scratching, etc. to raise a red weal on the skin. — *adj.* **dermatograp'ic**. — *n.* **dermatog'raphy** anatomical description of the skin — also **dermog'raphy**. — *adjs.* **der'matoid** of the form of skin: skin-like; **dermatolog'ical**. — *ns.* **dermatol'ogist**; **dermatol'ogy** the branch of science that treats of the skin; **derm'atome** (Gr. *tomos,* a slice, section, — *temnein,* to cut) a surgical instrument for cutting layers of skin, esp. for grafting: the part of an embryonic somite that produces the dermis: the area of skin supplied with nerves from a single spinal root; **dermatomyosī'tis** a disease characterised by inflammation of the skin and muscles, and wasting of the muscles; **der'matophyte** a parasitic fungus of the skin. — *adj.* **dermatoplas'tic**. — *n.* **dermatoplas'ty** (Gr. *plassein,* to mould) a plastic operation on the skin, esp. grafting; **dermatō'sis** any skin disease: — *pl.* **dermatō'ses** (*-sēz*) **der'moid** a cyst of congenital origin, containing such structures as hair, skin and teeth, occurring usu. in the ovary. — *n.pl.* **Dermop'tera** an order of mammals, the flying lemurs, sometimes included in Insectivora. [Gr. *derma, -atos,* the skin.]

dern[1]. See **durn.**

dern[2], **dearn** *dûrn, (arch.* and *dial.) adj.* secret: hidden: dreadful (*Shak.*). — *n.* secrecy: hiding. — *adjs.* **dern'ful, dearn'ful** solitary: mournful. — *advs.* **dern'ly, dearn'ly** secretly: sorrowfully: grievously. [O.E. *dyrne, derne,* secret.]

dernier *der-nyā,* (Fr.) *adj.* last. — **dernier cri** (*krē*) the last word (lit. cry), the latest fashion; **dernier ressort** (*ressör*) a last resort.

derogate *der'ō-gāt, v.i.* to lessen by taking away: to detract. — *adj.* (*Shak.*) degenerate. — *adv.* **der'ogately** (*Shak.*) in a derogatory manner. — *n.* **derogā'tion** a taking from: detraction: depreciation: the allowed breaking of a rule. — *adj.* **derog'ative**. — *advs.* **derog'atively**; **derogatorily** (*di-rog'ə-tər-i-li*). — *n.* **derog'atoriness**. — *adj.* **derog'atory** detracting: injurious. [L. *dērogāre, -ātum,* to repeal part of a law — *dē,* down, from, and *rogāre,* to propose a law.]

derrick *der'ik, n.* an arrangement for hoisting materials, by a boom stayed from a central post: a framework or tower over a borehole or the like. — *v.t.* to luff (the jib of a crane). [From *Derrick,* a 17th-century hangman.]

derrière *der-yer, der'i-er,* (Fr.) *n.* the behind, buttocks.

derring-do, derring do, doe *der'ing-doo, (false archaic) n.* daring action. — *adj.* **der-do'ing**. — **derr'ing doo'er**. [Spenser mistook Lydgate's *dorryng do,* i.e. daring (to) do (misprinted *derrynge do*) for a noun.]

derringer *der'in-jər, n.* a short American pistol. [Inventor's name.]

Derris *der'is, n.* a tropical genus of papilionaceous plants whose roots yield an insecticide powder: (without *cap.*) any plant of the genus. [Gr. *derris,* a leather coat.]

derry *der'i, (slang,* esp. *Austr.) n.* a feeling of dislike or resentment, esp. in the phrase **have a derry on** (**someone**). [Prob. from old refrain **derry down**.]

der Tag *där tähh, täg,* (Ger.) the day when the struggle begins (orig., in Germany, the day when a career of conquest by Germany was to begin).

derth *dûrth, (Spens.) n.* Same as **dearth.**

derv *dûrv, n.* diesel engine fuel oil. [From *d*iesel *e*ngined *r*oad *v*ehicle.]

dervish *dûr'vish, n.* a member of one of numerous Muslim fraternities, professing poverty and leading an austere life. [Turkish *dervīsh* — Pers. *darvish*, a dervish — lit., a poor man.]

désagrément *dāz-ag-rā-mã*, (Fr.) *n.* something disagreeable.

desalinate *dē-sal'in-āt*, *v.t.* to remove salt from (esp. sea water). — Also **desal'inise, -ize.** — *ns.* **desalinā'tion; desal'inātor; desalinisā'tion, -z-.** [Pfx. **de-** (2).]

desalt *dē-sölt'*, *v.t.* to remove salt from. — *n.* **desalt'ing.** [Pfx. **de-** (2).]

descale *dē-skāl*, *v.t.* to scale: to scrape away an encrustation from. [Pfx. **de-** (2).]

descant *des'kant*, *n.* an accompaniment above and harmonising with the air: counterpoint (*obs.*): a discourse or disquisition under several heads. — *adj.* (of a musical instrument) with a higher register and pitch than most others of the same family. — *v.i.* **descant'** (*Shak. des'*) to sing a descant: to discourse at length: to comment. [O.N.Fr. *descant* — L. *dis-*, apart, and *cantus*, a song.]

descend *di-send'*, *v.i.* to climb down: to pass from a higher to a lower place or condition: to pass from general to particulars: to make an invasion: to be derived (from): (of the testes) to move from the abdominal cavity into the scrotum. — *v.t.* to go down upon, to traverse downwards. — *n.* **descend'ant** one who descends, as offspring from an ancestor: the point on the ecliptic opposite the ascendant (*astrol.*). — *adjs.* **descend'ed** derived by descent; **descend'ent** going down: proceeding from an ancestor. — *n.* **descend'er** the part of a letter such as *j, p,* etc. that comes below the line of type (*print.*). — *adjs.* **descend'ible** (also **-able**) that may descend or be descended: capable of transmission by inheritance, heritable. — *adj.* **descend'ing.** — *n.* (*Shak.*) lineage. — *n.* **descen'sion.** — *adj.* **descen'sional.** — *n.* **descent'** an act of descending: transmission by succession: motion or progress downward: slope: a raid or invasion: derivation from an ancestor: a generation, a degree in genealogy: descendants collectively. — **descent from the cross** a picture representing Christ being taken down from the cross. [Fr. *descendre* — L. *dēscendēre* — *dē*, down, *scandēre*, to climb.]

deschool *dē-skōōl'* *v.t.* and *v.i.* to free children from the restrictions of traditional classroom learning and a set curriculum, and educate them in a less formal way, esp. at home. — *ns.* **deschool'er; deschool'ing.** [Pfx. **de-** (2).]

descramble *dē-skram'bəl*, *v.t.* to unscramble. [Pfx. **de-** (2).]

describe *di-skrīb'*, *v.t.* to trace out or delineate: to give an account of. — *adj.* **describ'able.** — *ns.* **describ'er; description** (*di-skrip'shən*) act of describing: an account of anything in words: (*loosely*) sort, class, or kind. — *adj.* **descrip'tive** containing description. — *adv.* **descrip'tively.** — *ns.* **descrip'tiveness; descrip'tivism** the use of, or belief in, descriptive linguistics (see below): a theory of ethics by which only empirical statements are acceptable; **descrip'tor** (*comput.*) a symbol or form of words that identifies a particular subject in a storage system, or gives information on how particular material is stored: a key word or a heading. — **descriptive geometry** the study of three-dimensional figures when projected onto a two-dimensional surface; **descriptive linguistics** the study of the description of a language structure as it occurred individually at a particular time, i.e. with no reference to its history, any other language, etc. [L. *dēscrībēre* — *dē*, down, *scrībēre*, *scrīptum*, to write.]

descrive *di-skrīv'*, (*obs.*) *v.t.* to describe. [O.Fr. *descrivre* — L. *dēscrībēre.*]

descry *di-skrī'*, *v.t.* to reveal (*Spens.*): to discover by the eye: to espy: — *pr.p.* **descry'ing;** *pa.t.* and *pa.p.* **descried'.** — *n.* discovery: a thing discovered (*Shak.*). [App. two words: O.Fr. *descrire* for *descrivre* — L. *dēscrībēre*, and O.Fr. *descrier, decryer*, proclaim, announce — *des-, de-*, and *crier*, to cry; cf. **describe, decry.**]

desecrate *des'i-krāt*, *v.t.* to divert from a sacred purpose: to profane. — *ns.* **des'ecrater, -or; desecrā'tion** act of desecrating: profanation. [Coined on the analogy of **consecrate** — L. *dē*, from. L. *dēsecrāre* meant to consecrate.]

desegregate *dē-seg'ri-gāt*, *v.t.* to abolish racial segregation in (e.g. a university). — *n.* **desegregā'tion.** — *n.* and *adj.* **desegregā'tionist.** [Pfx. **de-** (2).]

deselect *dē-sə-lekt'*, *v.t.* (of a political party at constituency level) not to select (the candidate who is already an M.P.) for re-election. — *n.* **deselec'tion.** [Pfx. **de-** (2).]

desensitise, -ize *dē-sen'sit-īz*, *v.t.* and *v.i.* to make or become less sensitive. — *ns.* **desensitīsā'tion, -z-; desen'sitiser, -z-.** [Pfx. **de-** (2).]

deserpidine *di-zûrp'i-din, -dēn, n.* a synthetic sedative drug of which the natural base is *Rauwolfia serpentina.*

desert[1] *di-zûrt', n.* that which is deserved: claim to reward: merit. — *adj.* **desert'less** without merit. [O.Fr., pa.p. of *deservir*; see **deserve.**]

desert[2] *di-zûrt', v.t.* to leave: to forsake. — *v.i.* to run away: to quit a service, as the army, without permission. — *ns.* **desert'er** one who deserts or quits a service without permission; **deser'tion** act of deserting: state of being deserted: wilful abandonment of a legal or moral obligation. — **desert the diet** (*Scots law*)) to give up a charge. [L. *dēserēre, dēsertum* — *dē-*, neg., and *serēre*, to bind.]

desert[3] *dez'ərt, adj.* deserted: desolate: uninhabited: uncultivated. — *n.* a desolate or barren tract: a waste: a solitude. — *ns.* **desertificā'tion, desertīsā'tion, -z-** the deterioration or reversion of land to desert conditions, owing to over-grazing, erosion, etc. — **desert boots** laced suede ankle boots with rubber soles; **desert pea** (usu. **Sturt's desert pea**) an Australian glory-pea (Clianthus) with a predominantly scarlet flower; **desert rat** (from the divisional sign, a jerboa) a soldier of the British 7th Armoured Division with service in North Africa in 1941–42. [O.Fr. *desert* — L. *dēsertum* — *dēserēre*, to desert, unbind.]

deserve *di-zûrv'*, *v.t.* to be entitled to by merit: to merit. — *v.i.* to be worthy of reward. — *adj.* **deserved'.** — *adv.* **deserv'edly.** — *ns.* **deserv'edness; deserv'er.** — *adj.* **deserv'ing** worthy. — *adv.* **deserv'ingly** according to desert: justly. [O.Fr. *deservir* — L. *dēservīre* — *dē*, intens., *servīre*, to serve.]

desex *dē-sex'*, *v.t.* to desexualise. [Pfx. **de-** (2).]

desexualise, -ize *dē-seks'ū-əl-īz*, *v.t.* to deprive of sexual character or quality. — *n.* **desexualīsā'tion, -z-.** [Pfx. **de-** (2).]

déshabillé. Same as **dishabille.**

desiccate *des'i-kāt*, formerly *di-sik'āt, v.t.* to dry up: to preserve by drying. — *v.i.* to grow dry. — *adjs.* **des'iccant, desiccative** (*di-sik' ə-tiv*) drying: having the power of drying. — *ns.* a drying agent. — *ns.* **desiccā'tion** the act or process of drying up: state of being dried up; **des'iccātor** apparatus for drying. [L. *dēsiccāre, -ātum*, to dry up — *dē-*, intens., *siccus*, dry.]

desiderate *di-sid'ər-āt*, *v.t.* to long for or earnestly desire: to want or miss. — *n.* **desiderā'tion** the act of desiderating: the thing desiderated. — *adj.* **desid'erative** implying desire (as in *desiderative verb*). — *ns.* **desiderā'tum** (or *ä'*) something desired or much wanted: — *pl.* **desidera'ta; desiderium** (*des-i-dē'ri-əm*) longing: grief for what is lost. [L. *dēsīderāre, -ātum*, to long for; *dēsīdērium*, longing. A doublet of **desire.**]

design *di-zīn'*, *v.t.* to indicate (*Shak.; Spens.*): to draw: to plan and execute artistically: to form a plan of: to contrive: to intend: to set apart or destine. — *n.* a drawing or sketch: a plan in outline: a plan or scheme formed in the mind: plot: intention. — *adj.* **design'able.** — *v.t.* **designate** (*dez'ig-nāt*) to mark out so as to make known: to show: to name: to be a name for: to appoint or nominate. — *adj.* nominated to but not yet in possession of an office (used after the *n.*, as in *chairman designate*). — *n.* **designā'tion** a showing or pointing out: a name: a title: an appellation descriptive of occupation, standing, etc.: nomination to office. — *adjs.* **des′ignative, designā′tory.** — *n.* **des′ignātor.** — *adv.* **designedly** (*di-zīn′id-li*) by design: intentionally. — *n.* **design′er** one who furnishes designs or patterns: a draughtsman: a plotter: one who designs sets for plays, operas, films, etc. — *adj.* of or pertaining to a designer: designed by (and bearing the name of) a known fashion designer: (*loosely*) designed, created, to follow the fashionable trend or image: (*slightly derog.*) for effect. — *adjs.* **design′ful** full of design; **design′ing** artful: scheming: working secretly for self-interest. — *n.* the art of making designs or patterns. — *adv.* **design′ingly.** — *adj.* **design′less.** — *n.* **design′-ment** the design or sketch of a work: intention, purpose, enterprise (*Shak.*). — **design engineer** a designer in engineering. — **argument from design** the argument for the existence of God from evidence of design in creation; **by design** intentionally. [Fr. *désigner* — L. *dēsignāre, -ātum* — *dē-*, off, and *signum*, a mark.]

desilver *dē-sil′vər, v.t.* to remove silver from — also **desil′verise, -ize.** — *n.* **desilverisā′tion, -z-.** [Pfx. **de-** (2).]

desine (*Spens.*). Same as **design.**

desinent *des′in-ənt,* **desinential** *des-i-nen′shəl, adjs.* terminal. — *n.* **des′inence** ending. [L. *dēsinēns, -entis,* pr.p. of *dēsinĕre,* to leave off — *dē,* from, *sinĕre,* to allow.]

desipient *di-sip′i-ənt, adj.* playing the fool: trifling. — *n.* **desip′ience.** [L. *dēsipiēns, -entis,* pr.p. of *dēsipĕre* — *dē-,* neg., *sapĕre,* to be wise.]

desire *di-zīr′, v.t.* to long for: to wish for: to ask: to regret the loss of (*B.*). — *v.i.* to be in a state of desire. — *n.* an earnest longing or wish: a prayer or request: the object desired: lust. — *adj.* **desīr′able** worthy of desire: to be approved of: pleasing: agreeable. — *n.* a desirable person or thing. — *ns.* **desīr′ableness, desīrabil′ity.** — *adv.* **desīr′ably.** — *adj.* **desire′less.** — *n.* **desīr′er.** — *adj.* **desīr′ous** (usu. with *of*) full of desire: wishful: eager: desirable (*obs.*). — *adv.* **desīr′ously.** — *n.* **desīr′ousness.** [Fr. *désirer* — L. *dēsīderāre.*]

desist *di-zist′, -sist′, v.i.* to leave off. — *n.* **desist′ance, -ence.** [L. *dēsistĕre* — *dē-,* away from, and *sistĕre,* to cause to stand.]

desk *desk, n.* a sloping or flat table for writing or reading, often fitted with drawers, etc.: a shut-up writing-box: a pulpit or lectern: a counter in a public place for information, registration, etc.: a department of a newspaper office, e.g. *the news desk:* a music-stand: in an orchestra, esp. among strings, (players in) a seating position determined by rank (e.g. *the first desk*). — *adjs.* **desk′bound** confined to a desk, i.e. doing paper work and administration rather than active or practical work; **desk′top** of a computer, etc., designed for use on a desk. — **desk′-work** work done at a desk, as by a clerk or author. [M.E. *deske* — L. *discus* — Gr. *diskos;* see **dish¹, disc.**]

deskill *dē-skil′, v.t.* to remove the element of human skill from (a job, process, operation, etc.) through automation, computerisation, etc. [Pfx. **de-** (2).]

desman *des′mən, n.* a Russian aquatic insectivore with long snout and musk-glands: a kindred Pyrenean species. [Sw. *desman,* musk.]

desmid *des′mid, n.* one of a group of microscopic algae, unicellular or strung in chains. — *ns.* **desmine** (*des′mēn, -min*) the mineral stilbite occurring in bundles; **Desmōd′ium** the telegraph-plant genus: (without *cap.*) a plant of the genus: — *pl.* **desmo′diums.** — *adjs.* **desmodrom′ic** (*mech.*; Gr. *dromos,* running) denoting a system, used in some motor-cycle and racing car engines, that employs e.g. cams, rockers, etc. to ensure that the opening and closing of valves, when the vehicle is at high speed, is fully controlled; **des′moid** arranged in bundles; **desmosō′mal.** — *n.* **des′mosome** a small thickened patch on the membrane of a cell, such patches serving as points of adhesion between cell and cell, e.g. in the skin. [Gr. *desmos,* a chain, fetter, *desmē,* a bundle, *eidos,* form.]

désobligeante *dāz-ob-lēzh-ät, n.* a carriage for one. [Fr., unaccommodating.]

désœuvré *dāz-œv-rā,* (Fr.) *adj.* unoccupied: at a loose end.

desolate *des′ō-lāt, v.t.* to make lonely or forlorn: to make joyless: to deprive of inhabitants: to lay waste. — *adj.* (*-lit*) comfortless: dreary: forlorn: lonely: destitute of inhabitants: laid waste. — *adv.* **des′olately.** — *ns.* **des′olateness; des′olāter, -or; desolā′tion** waste: destruction: a place desolated: misery, wretchedness. — *adj.* **des′olatory.** [L. *dēsōlāre, -ātum* — *dē-,* intens., and *sōlāre,* to make alone — *sōlus,* alone.]

desorb. See **desorption.**

désorienté *dāz-or-ē-ä-tā,* (Fr.) *adj.* having lost one's bearings, confused.

desorption *dē-sörp′shən, n.* release from an adsorbed state. — *v.t.* **desorb′.** [Pfx. **de-** (2).]

desoxy-. See **deoxy-** under **deoxidate.**

despair *di-spār′, v.i.* to be without hope (of). — *n.* hopelessness: that which causes despair. — *adjs.* **despair′ful** (*Spens.*); **despair′ing** apt to despair: full of despair. — *adv.* **despair′ingly.** [O.Fr. *desperer* — L. *dēspērāre, -ātum* — *dē-,* neg., and *spērāre,* to hope.]

despatch. Same as **dispatch.**

desperado *des-pər-ä′dō, -ā′dō, n.* a desperate fellow: one reckless of danger: a wild ruffian: — *pl.* **despera′dos, -oes.** [Old Sp. (mod. *desesperado*), — L. *dēspērātus.*]

desperate *des′pər-it, adj.* in a state of despair: hopeless: beyond hope: despairingly reckless: (*loosely*) furious: extremely bad: extremely anxious or eager (for, to do, etc.) (*coll.*). — *adv.* **des′perately.** — *ns.* **des′perateness, desperā′tion** state of despair: despairing: disregard of danger: fury. [See **despair.**]

despicable *des′pik-ə-bl, dis-pik′, adj.* deserving to be despised: contemptible: worthless. — *ns.* **despicabil′ity, des′picableness** (or *-pik′*). — *adv.* **despic′ably** (or *des′*). [See **despise.**]

despight *di-spīt′.* An old spelling of **despite.**

despise *di-spīz′, v.t.* to look down upon with contempt. — *adj.* **despīs′able.** — *ns.* **despīs′al** contempt; **despīs′-edness** (*Milt.*); **despīs′er.** [O.Fr. *despire* (*despis-*) — L. *dēspicĕre* — *dē,* down, *specĕre,* to look.]

despite *di-spīt′, n.* a looking down with contempt: violent malice or hatred. — *prep.* in spite of: notwithstanding. — *adj.* **despite′ful.** — *adv.* **despite′fully.** — *n.* **despite′-fulness.** — *adj.* **despiteous** (*dis-pit′i-əs; Spens.*). [O.Fr. *despit* (mod. *dépit*) — L. *dēspectus* — *dēspicĕre;* see **despise.**]

despoil *di-spoil′, v.t.* to plunder completely: to strip: to bereave: to rob. — *ns.* **despoil′er; despoil′ment.** [O.Fr. *despoiller* (mod. *dépouiller;* see next).]

despoliation *di-spōl-i-ā′shən, n.* despoiling. [L. *dēspoliāre* — *dē-,* intens., and *spolium,* spoil.]

despond *di-spond′, v.i.* to be wanting in hope, to be dejected. — *n.* (*Bunyan*) despondency. — *ns.* **despond′-ence, despond′ency.** — *adj.* **despond′ent.** — *adv.* **despond′ently.** — *n.* and *adj.* **despond′ing.** — *adv.* **despond′-ingly.** [L. *dēspondēre,* to promise, to devote, to resign, to despond — *dē,* away, and *spondēre,* to promise.]

despot *des′pot, -pət, n.* one invested with absolute power: a tyrant. — *n.* **des′potat(e)** a territory governed by a despot. — *adjs.* **despotic** (*dis-pot′ik*), **-al** pertaining to or like a despot: having absolute power: tyrannical. — *adv.* **despot′ically.** — *ns.* **despot′icalness; des′potism** absolute power: a state governed by a despot; **despot-oc′racy** government by a despot. [O.Fr. *despot* — Gr. *despotēs,* a master.]

despumate *di-spū′māt,* or *des′pū-māt, v.i.* to throw off impurities in foam or scum. — *v.t.* to skim. — *n.* **despumā′tion.** [L. *dēspūmāre, -ātum* — *dē-,* off, and *spūma,* foam.]

desquamate *des′kwə-māt, v.i.* to scale off. — *n.* **desquamā′-tion** a scaling off: the separation of the cuticle or skin in scales. — *adjs.* **desquamative** (*di-skwam′ə-tiv*), **desquam′atory.** [L. *dēsquāmāre, -ātum* — *dē,* off, and *squāma,* a scale.]

desse *des,* (*Spens.*) *n.* a desk. [**dais.**]

dessert *diz-ûrt'*, *n.* a final course of a meal, pudding or other sweet item: fruit, sweetmeats, etc. served at the end of a meal. — **dessert'-serv'ice** the dishes used for dessert; **dessert'spoon** a spoon smaller than a tablespoon and larger than a teaspoon; **dessert'spoon'ful.** [O.Fr. *dessert, desservir*, to clear the table — *des-* (L. *dis-*), away, and *servir*, to serve — L. *servīre*.]

dessiatine, dessyatine, desyatin *des'yə-tēn*, *n.* a Russian measure of land, 2·7 English acres (about 1·1 hectares). [Russ. *desyatīna*, a measure of land, a tenth; *desyat'*, ten.]

destabilise, -ize *dē-stā'bil-īz*, *v.t.* to make unstable or less stable (*lit.* and *fig.*). — *n.* **destā'biliser, -z-.** [Pfx. **de-** (2).]

de-Stalinise, -ize *dē-stä'li-nīz*, *v.t.* to remove the influence of Joseph Stalin (from Russian politics, etc.). — *n.* **de-Stalinīsā'tion, -z-.**

destemper. See **distemper¹.**

De Stijl *də stīl*, an (orig. Dutch) artistic movement of the 1920s, embracing neoplasticism and Dada, and having an influence on contemporary architecture and design. [Du., the style, the title of the movement's magazine.]

destine *des'tin*, *v.t.* to ordain or appoint to a certain use or state: to intend: to fix: to doom — also **des'tinate** (*obs.*). — *ns.* **destinā'tion** the purpose or end to which anything is destined or appointed: end: purpose: design: fate: place to which one is going: (the nomination of) the series of heirs to whom property, etc. is to pass (*Scots law*); **des'tiny** the purpose or end to which any person or thing is appointed: unavoidable fate: necessity. [Fr. *destiner* — L. *dēstināre* — *dē-*, intens., and root of *stāre*, to stand.]

destitute *des'ti-tūt*, *adj.* left alone, forsaken (*obs.*): in utter want: entirely lacking in (with *of*). — *v.t.* (*obs.*) to forsake: to deprive. — *n.* **destitu'tion** the state of being destitute: deprivation of office: poverty. [L. *dēstituĕre, -ūtum* — *dē-*, away, and *statuĕre*, to place.]

destrier *des'tri-ər*, *des-trēr'*, (*arch.*) *n.* a warhorse. [Fr., — L. *dextrārius*, led by the (squire's) right hand.]

destroy *di-stroi'*, *v.t.* to unbuild or pull down: to overturn: to ruin: to put an end to: — *pr.p.* **destroy'ing;** *pa.t.* and *pa.p.* **destroyed'.** — *adj.* **destroy'able.** — *n.* **destroy'er** a person or thing that destroys: a small, fast-moving warship. — **destroying angel** *Amanita phalloides* or *amanita virosa*, two poisonous toadstools, whitish in colour, with a volva at the base of the stalk. [O.Fr. *destruire* (Fr. *détruire*) — L. *dēstruĕre, dēstructum* — *dē-*, down, and *struĕre*, to build.]

destruction *di-struk'shən*, *n.* act or process of destroying: overthrow: physical or moral ruin: death: a cause of destruction. — *v.t.* **destruct'** to destroy a rocket or missile in flight. — Also *v.i.* — *adj.* **destruc'tible** liable to be destroyed. — *ns.* **destructibil'ity, destruc'tibleness.** — *adj.* **destruc'tional.** — *n.* **destruc'tionist** one engaged in destruction: one who believes in the final annihilation of the damned. — *adj.* **destruc'tive** causing or concerned with destruction: mischievous. — *n.* a destroying agent. — *adv.* **destruc'tively.** — *ns.* **destruc'tiveness; destruc'tivist** a representative of destructive principles; **destructiv'ity** (*dē-*); **destruc'tor** (*di-*) a destroyer: a furnace for burning up refuse. — **destructive distillation** the distillation of solid substances accompanied by their decomposition. [L. *dēstruĕre, -structum;* see **destroy.**]

desuetude *di-sū'i-tūd, des'wi-tūd*, *n.* disuse: discontinuance. [L. *dēsuētūdō* — *dēsuētum, dēsuēscĕre* — *dē-*, neg., and *suēscĕre*, to become used.]

desulphur *dē-sul'fər*, *v.t.* to remove sulphur from — also **desul'phūrāte, desul'phūrise, -ize.** — *ns.* **desulphūrā'tion; desulphūrīsā'tion, -z-; desul'phūriser, -z-.** [Pfx. **de-** (2).]

desultory *des'əl-tər-i*, *adj.* jumping from one thing to another: without rational or logical connection: rambling: hasty: loose. — *adv.* **des'ultorily.** — *n.* **des'ultoriness.** [L. *dēsultōrius* — *dēsultor*, a vaulter, *dēsilīre, -sultum*, to leap — *dē*, from, and *salīre*, to jump.]

desyatin. See **dessiatine.**

desyne (*Spens.*). Same as **design.**

detach *di-tach'*, *v.t.* to unfasten: to take away or separate: to withdraw: to send off on special service. — *v.i.* to separate. — *adj.* **detach'able.** — *adj.* **detached'** unconnected: separate: aloof: free from care, passion, ambition, and worldly bonds. — *adv.* **detach'edly.** — *ns.* **detach'edness; detach'ment** the state of being detached: the act of detaching: that which is detached, as a body of troops. [Fr. *détacher* — O.Fr. pfx. *des-* (L. *dis-*), apart, and root of **attach.**]

detail *di-tāl'*, *v.t.* to relate minutely: to enumerate: to set apart for a particular service. — *v.i.* to give details about anything. — *n.* (*dē'tāl*, also *di-tāl'*) a small part: an item: a particular account: (chiefly *mil.*) a small body set apart for special duty. — *adj.* **detailed'** giving full particulars: exhaustive. — **go into detail** to study, discuss, etc., a matter deeply, considering the particulars; **in detail** circumstantially, point by point: piecemeal. [Fr. *détailler* — *de-*, intens., and *taillr*, to cut.]

detain *di-tān'*, *v.t.* to hold back: to withhold: to stop: to keep: to keep in custody. — *n.* (*Spens.*) detention. — *adj.* **detain'able.** — *ns.* **detain'ee** a person kept in custody; **detain'er** one who detains: the holding of what belongs to another (*law*): a warrant to a sheriff to keep in custody a person already in confinement; **detain'ment** detention. [O.Fr. *detenir* — L. *dētinēre;* see **detent.**]

detect *di-tekt'*, *v.t.* to uncover, expose (*obs.*): to accuse (*Shak.*): to discover: to discern: to find out (esp. something elusive or secret). — *adjs.* **detect'able, -ible.** — *n.* **detec'tion** discovery of something hidden or not easily observed: state of being found out. — *adj.* **detect'ive** employed in or concerned with detection. — *n.* a policeman, usually not in uniform, or other person (*private detective*) who investigates cases of crime or watches behaviour of suspected persons. — *ns.* **detect'ivist** a writer of detective fiction; **detect'ōphone** a secret telephone for eavesdropping; **detec'tor** one who detects: an apparatus for detecting something, as smoke, tampering with a lock, pressure of electric currents, of electric waves. — **detective story** one in which clues to the detection of a criminal are set forth and unravelled. [L. *dētegĕre, -tēctum* — *dē-*, neg., *tegĕre*, to cover.]

detent *di-tent'*, *n.* that which checks motion: a catch, esp. for regulating the striking of a clock. — *n.* **deten'tion** act of detaining: state of being detained: confinement, or restriction of liberty, esp. of a political prisoner, a military offender, a pupil out of school hours: delay. **detention centre** a place of confinement for young offenders from 14 to 20 years old for periods of up to 6 months. [L. *dētinēre, dētentum* — *dē*, from, *tenēre*, to hold.]

détente *dā-tãt*, (Fr.) *n.* relaxation of strained relations (esp. between countries).

détenu *dā-tə-nü*, (Fr.) *n.* a prisoner, esp. a political prisoner in India: — *fem.* **détenue.**

deter *di-tûr'*, *v.t.* to frighten from: to hinder or prevent: — *pr.p.* **deterr'ing;** *pa.t.* and *pa.p.* **deterred'.** — *ns.* **deter'ment; deterrence** (*di-ter'əns*). — *adj.* **deterrent** (*di-ter'ənt*) serving to deter. — *n.* anything that deters: (*specif.*), a nuclear weapon. [L. *dēterrēre — dē*, from, *terrēre*, to frighten.]

deterge *di-tûrj'*, *v.t.* to wipe off: to cleanse (as a wound). — *ns.* **deterg'ence, deterg'ency; deterg'ent** (also *rarely* **deters'ive**) that which cleanses: a cleansing agent, as an abrasive, a solvent or mixture of solvents, and certain water-soluble oils, esp (commonly) a soapless cleanser. — *adj.* (also **deters'ive**) cleansing: purging. [L. *dētergēre, dētersum* — *dē*, off, and *tergēre*, to wipe.]

deteriorate *di-tē'ri-ə-rāt*, *v.t.* to make worse. — *v.i.* to grow worse. — *ns.* **detēriorā'tion** the act of making worse: the process of growing worse; **detēriorā'tionist** a believer in deterioration. — *adj.* **detē'riorātive.** — *ns.* **detē'riorism** the doctrine that the world grows worse; **detē'riority** (*-or'i-ti;* *obs.*) worseness. [L. *dēteriōrāre, -ātum*, to make worse — *dēterior*, worse — *dē*, down.]

determine dē-tûr'min, v.t. to put terms or bounds to: to limit: to fix or settle: to define: to decide: to resolve: to cause to resolve: to put an end to. — v.i. to come to a decision: to come to an end: to cease to exist (*Shak.*): to take part in a dispute, esp. in completing the degree of bachelor of arts (*obs.*). — n. **determinabil'ity.** — adj. **deter'minable** capable of being determined, decided, or finished. — n. **deter'minableness.** — adv. **deter'minably.** — n. **deter'minacy** (-ə-si). — adj. **deter'minant** serving to determine. — n. that which serves to determine: the sum of all the products got by taking one from each row and column of a square block of quantities, each product being reckoned positive or negative according as an even or an odd number of transpositions reduces it to the order of the rows (or of the columns) — used for the solution of equations and other purposes (*math.*): a hypothetical unit in the germ-plasm determining the course of development of a cell (*bot.*): a determining candidate for the B.A. degree (*obs.*). — adj. **deter'mināte** determined or limited: fixed: decisive: cymose (*bot.*). — v.t. (*Shak.*) to determine. — adv. **deter'minately.** — n. **determinā'tion** the act of determining: condition of being determined: that which is determined or resolved on: end: direction to a certain end: resolution: fixedness of purpose: decision of character. — adj. **deter'minātive** that determines, limits, or defines. — n. in hieroglyphics an additional sign attached to a word as a guide to its meaning. — adj. **deter'mined** ascertained: fixed: firm in purpose: resolute. — adv. **deter'minedly.** — ns. **deter'miner** one who, or that which, determines: a determinant (*bot.*): a limiting adjective or modifying word such as *any, each, that, my*, etc. (*gram.*); **deter'minism** the doctrine that all things, including the will, are determined by causes — the converse of free-will: necessitarianism. — n. **deter'minist.** — adj. **determinis'tic.** [L. *dētermināre, -ātum* — *dē*, intens., and *terminus*, a boundary.]

deterrent. See deter.

detersion di-tûr'shən, n. act of cleansing. — adj. and n. **deter'sive** detergent. [See deterge.]

detest di-test', v.t. to hate intensely. — adj. **detest'able** (*Spens.* and *Shak.* dē') worthy of being detested: extremely hateful: abominable. — ns. **detestabil'ity, detest'ableness.** — adv. **detest'ably.** — n. **detestation** (dē-tes-tā'shən) (an object of) extreme hatred. [Fr., — L. *dētestāri* — *dē*, intens., and *testāri*, to call to witness, execrate — *testis*, a witness.]

dethrone di-thrōn', v.t. to remove from a throne. — ns. **dethrone'ment; dethrōn'er; dethrōn'ing.** [Pfx. de- (2).]

detinue det'in-ū, (*law*) n. wrongful detention of property. [O.Fr. *detenue*, fem. pa.p. of *detenir*; see detain.]

detonate det'ō-nāt or dēt'ō-nāt, v.t. and v.i. to explode or cause to explode rapidly and loudly: in an internal-combustion engine, to explode by spontaneous combustion with a hammering sound (pinking or knock). — ns. **detonā'tion** an explosion with report: knock; **det'onātor** a substance that detonates: a substance or contrivance whose explosion initiates that of another explosive. [L. *dētonāre, -ātum* — *dē*, down, and *tonāre*, to thunder.]

detort di-tört', v.t. to distort: to untwist: to twist the other way. — ns. **detor'sion, detor'tion.** [L. *dētorquēre, dētortum*; *dē*, away, also neg., and *torquēre*, to twist.]

detour dē', dā'tōōr, di-tōōr', n. a winding: a circuitous way. — Also v.t. and v.i. [Fr. *dé*- (L. *dis*-) asunder, and *tour*, turning.]

detoxicate dē-toks'i-kāt, **detox'ify** -i-fī, vs.t. to rid of poison or the effects of it. — n. **detox'icant** a substance that detoxicates. — Also adj. — ns. **detoxicā'tion, detoxificā'tion.** — **detoxification centre** a centre for the cure of alcoholism. [Pfx. de- (2).]

detract di-trakt' v.t. to take away, abate: to defame. — v.i. to take away (with *from*): to reduce in degree: to diminish. — n. **detract'or:** — fem. **detract'ress.** — n. and adj. **detract'ing.** — adv. **detract'ingly.** — n. **detrac'tion** depreciation: slander. — adjs. **detract'ive, detract'-**

ory tending to detract: derogatory. — adv. **detract'ively.** [L. *dētrahēre* — *dē*, from, *trahēre, tractum*, to draw.]

detrain dē-trān', v.t. to set down out of a railway train. — v.i. to alight from a train. — n. **detrain'ment.** [Pfx. de- (2).]

détraqué dā-trä-kā, n. a person who is deranged: — fem. **détraquée.** [Fr., upset, out of order.]

detribalise, -ize dē-trī'bə-līz, v.t. to cause to lose tribal characteristics, customs, etc., usu. in favour of an urban way of life. — n. **detribalīsā'tion, -z-.** [Pfx. de- (2).]

detriment det'ri-mənt, n. diminution: damage: loss. — adj. **detrimental** (-ment'l). — n. (*arch.*) a suitor undesirable owing to lack of means or other defect: one whose presence lessens the chances of a good match. — adv. **detriment'ally.** [L. *dētrīmentum* — *dē*, off, and *terēre, tritum*, to rub.]

detritus di-trī'tas, n. a mass of substance gradually worn off solid bodies: an aggregate of loosened fragments, esp. of rock: accumulated debris. — adj. **detrī'tal.** — ns. **detrition** (di-trish'ən) wearing away. [L. *dētrītus*, worn — *dē*, off, and *terēre, trītum*, to rub.]

de trop də trō, (Fr.) superfluous: in the way.

detrude di-trōōd', v.t. to thrust down. — n. **detru'sion.** [L. *dētrūdēre* — *dē*, down, *trūdēre*, to thrust.]

detruncate di-trung'kāt, v.t. to cut short: to lop: to mutilate. — n. **detruncā'tion** (dē-). [L. *dētruncāre, -ātum* — *dē*, off, *truncāre*, to lop.]

detumescence dē-tū-mes'əns, n. diminution of swelling — opp. to *intumescence*. [Pfx. de- (2).]

deuce¹ dūs, n. a card or die with two spots: a situation ('forty all') in which one side must gain two successive points to win the game, or ('five all', 'games all') two successive games to win the set (*lawn-tennis*): two dollars (*U.S. slang*). **deuce'-ace** a throw of two dice turning up deuce and ace: bad luck. [F. *deux*, two — L. *duōs*, accus. of *duo*, two.]

deuce² dūs, n. the devil — in exclamatory phrases. — adj. **deuced** (dū'sid, or dūst) devilish: excessive. — adv. confoundedly. — Also **deuc'edly.** [Prob. from the **deuce** (see foregoing), the lowest throw at dice.]

deuch-an-doris. See deoch-an-doruis.

deuddarn dī'dhärn, n. a Welsh dresser or sideboard in two stages. [W.]

deus dē'əs, dā'ŏŏs, (L.) n. god. — **Deus avertat** (a-vûr'tat, ä-wer'tat) God forbid; **Deus det** (det) God grant; **deus ex machina** (usu. *eks mak'in-a*, sometimes *mə-shē'nə*) a god brought on the stage by a mechanical device: a contrived and inartistic solution of a difficulty in a plot; **Deus vobiscum** (vō-bis'kəm, wō-bēs'kŏŏm) God be with you; **Deus vult** (vult, wŏŏlt) God wills it (the Crusaders' cry).

deuter(o)- dū-tər(-ō)-, in composition, second, secondary. — ns. **deuterag'onist** the second actor in a Greek drama; **deu'teranope** a person suffering from deuteranopia; **deuteranō'pia** (Gr. *ops*, eye) a type of colour-blindness in which red and green are confused, blue and yellow only being distinguished. — adj. **deuteranōp'ic.** — v.t. **deu'terate** to add deuterium to, or to replace hydrogen by deuterium in (molecules). — ns. **deuterā'tion; deu'teride** a hydrogen compound containing another element; **deuterium** (-tē'ri-əm) heavy hydrogen, an isotope of hydrogen of double mass. — adj. **deuterocanon'ical** (Gr. *kanōn*, rule) pertaining to a second canon of inferior authority — the O.T. Apocrypha and the N.T. Antilegomena. — ns. **deuterog'amy** (Gr. *gamos*, marriage) second marriage, esp. of the clergy, after the death of the first wife; **deuterog'amist** one who allows or practises it; **deu'teron** the nucleus of heavy hydrogen, carrying unit positive charge; **Deuteronomy** (-on'ə-mi, or dū'; Gr. *nomos*, law) the fifth book of the Pentateuch, containing a repetition of the decalogue and laws given in Exodus. — adjs. **Deuteronom'ic, -al.** — n. **Deuteron'omist** the author of the book of Deuteronomy or part of it. — ns. **deu'teroplasm** same as **deutoplasm;**

deuton — 386 — devil

deuteros'copy (Gr. *skopiā*, a look-out) a second view or meaning (*obs.*): second sight. — *adj.* **deuteroscop'ic.** — **deuterium oxide** heavy water. [Gr. *deuteros*, second.]

deuton *dū'ton*, older form of **deuteron.**

deutoplasm *dū'tō-plazm, n.* the food material, such as yolk or fat, within an egg or cell. — *adj.* **deutoplas'mic.** [Fr. *deutoplasme.*]

Deutschmark *doich'märk, n.* (also **Deutsche Mark** *doich'ə märk*) the standard monetary unit of West Germany. [Ger.]

Deutzia *dūt'si-ə* or *doit'si-ə, n.* a genus of saxifragaceous plants with panicles of white flowers, introduced from China and Japan. [After Jan *Deutz*, 18th-cent. Dutch naturalist.]

Deuxième Bureau *də-zyem bü-rō*, (Fr.) the French Department of Military Intelligence.

deva *dā'vä*, (*Hindu myth.*) *n.* a god: a good spirit. [Sans. *deva*, a shining one, a god.]

devall *di·völ', v.i.* to sink, decline (*obs.*): to cease (*Scot.*). — *n.* (*Scot.*) a stop. [Fr. *dévaler* — L. *dē-*, down, *vallis*, a valley.]

devalue *dē-val'ū, v.t.* to reduce the value of. — Also *v.i.* (esp. of currency). — *ns.* **devalorisā'tion, -z-, devaluā'tion.** — *vs.t.* **deval'orise, -ize, deval'uate.** [Pfx. **de-** (2).]

devanagari *dā-və-nä'gə-ri, n.* the character in which Sanskrit is usually written and printed: the official script for Hindi: used also for other Indian languages. — Also with *cap.* [Sans. *devanāgari*, town-script of the gods; see **nagari.**]

devastate *dev'əs-tāt, v.t.* to lay waste, plunder. — *adj.* **dev'astating** ravaging: (*coll.*) overpoweringly effective. — *adv.* **dev'astatingly.** — *n.* **devastā'tion** act of devastating: state of being devastated: havoc: waste of property by an executor. — *adj.* **dev'astātive.** — *ns.* **dev'astātor; dēvastā'vit** (L., has wasted) a writ lying against an executor for devastation: the offence of devastation. [L. *dēvastāre, -ātum* — *dē-*, intens., *vastāre*, to lay waste.]

devel. See **devvel.**

develop (*earlier also* **develope**), *di-vel'əp, v.t.* to unroll: to lay open by degrees: to free from integuments or that which envelops: to bring out what is latent or potential in: to bring to a more advanced or more highly organised state: to work out the potentialities of: to elaborate: to cause to grow or advance: to evolve: to contract (a disease): to make more available: to exploit the natural resources of (a region): to build on or prepare (land) for building on: to bring into a position useful in attack (*chess*): to disclose: to express in expanded form (*math.*): to unroll into a plane surface (*geom.*): to render visible the image on a negative by the use of chemicals (*phot.*). — *v.i.* to open out: to evolve: to advance through successive stages to a higher, more complex, or more fully grown state: — *pr.p.* **devel'oping;** *pa.t.* and *pa.p.* **devel'oped.** — *adjs.* **devel'opable; devel'oped.** — *ns.* **devel'oper** one who develops: a reagent for developing photographs: an apparatus for developing muscles; **develop'ment** the act or process of developing: state of being developed: a gradual unfolding or growth: evolution: the expression of a function in the form of a series (*math.*): elaboration of a theme, or that part of a movement in which this occurs (*mus.*): new situations that emerge. — *adj.* **development'al** pertaining to development. — *adv.* **development'ally.** — **development area** a region of heavy unemployment where new industry is given official encouragement. [Fr. *développer*, opposite to *envelopper*, of obscure origin.]

devest *di-vest', v.t.* to undress (*Shak.*): to alienate (*law*): to take off: to strip. [A form of **divest.**]

Devi *dā'vē, n.* in India, used as a title for a married woman (following her name). [Sans., goddess.]

deviate *dē'vi-āt, v.i.* to go from the way: to turn aside from a certain course: to diverge, differ, from a standard, mean value, etc.: to err. — *v.t.* to cause to

diverge. — *n.* (*dē'vi-ət; psych.*) one who deviates much from the normal. — *ns.* **dē'viance, dē'viancy.** — *adj.* **dē'viant** which deviates from the norm, esp. sexually. — Also *n.* — *ns.* **dēviā'tion; dēviā'tionism; dēviā'tionist** a communist whose doctrine deviates from the strictly orthodox; **dē'viātor.** — *adj.* **dēviā'tory.** — **deviation of the compass** departure of the mariner's compass from the magnetic meridian, owing to the ship's magnetism or other local causes; **standard deviation** the square root of the variance of a number of observations. [L. *dēviāre, -ātum* — *dē*, from, *via*, a way.]

device *di-vīs', n.* that which is devised or designed: contrivance: power of devising: an emblem (*her.*): a motto: a conceit (*obs.*): a masque (*obs.*). — *adj.* **device'ful** (*Spens.*) full of devices. — **leave someone to his own devices** to leave someone alone, not distracting or interfering with him. [O.Fr. *devise*; see **devise.**]

devil *dev'l, -il, n.* an evil spirit: (*cap.*) the supreme spirit of evil: wicked person: reckless, lively person: (usu. pitying) a fellow: an animal, thing, problem, difficult to deal with: one who excels or exceeds in anything: a printer's devil: a drudge (esp. legal or literary): a firework: a grilled or highly seasoned dish: a duststorm: fighting spirit: a plumber's portable furnace: a machine of various kinds, esp. for tearing: used as a mild oath, an expression of impatience, irritation, etc., or a strong negative. — *v.t.* to season highly and broil. — *v.i.* to perform another person's drudgery: to do very menial work: — *pr.p.* **dev'illing;** *pa.t.* and *pa.p.* **dev'illed.** — *ns.* **dev'ildom;** *adj.* **dev'iless;** *n.* **dev'ilet, dev'iling,** **dev'ling** a young devil: a swift (*dial.*). — *adj.* **dev'ilish** fiendish, malignant: very bad. — *adv.* (often *dev'lish; coll.*) very, exceedingly. — *adv.* **dev'ilishly.** — *ns.* **dev'ilism; dev'ilkin.** — *adj.* **dev'illed.** — *ns.* **dev'ilment** frolicsome mischief; **dev'ilry; dev'ilship; dev'iltry** (*U.S.*). **dev'il-crab** the velvet crab; **dev'il-dodger** (*slang*) a preacher, esp. of the ranting kind: one who attends churches of various kinds, to be on the safe side; **dev'il-fish** the fishing-frog or angler: the giant ray of the United States: the octopus; **dev'il-in-a-bush** a garden flower, love-in-a-mist. — *adj.* **dev'il-may-care'** reckless, audacious. — **dev'il-on-the-neck** an old instrument of torture; **dev'il-on-two-sticks** older name for diabolo; **devil's advocate** advocatus diaboli, the Promoter of the Faith, an advocate at the papal court whose duty it is to propose objections against a canonisation: a person who states the case against a proposal, course of action, etc., usu. for the sake of argument; **dev'il's-bit** a species of scabious (*Succisa pratensis*) with rootstock as if bitten off; **devil's bones** dice; **devil's books** playing-cards; **devil's coach-horse** a large dark-coloured beetle (*Ocypus olens*); **devil's dozen** thirteen; **devil's dung** asafoetida; **devil's dust** shoddy made by a machine called the **devil; devil's food cake** (chiefly *U.S.*) a kind of chocolate cake; **dev'ils-on-horse'back** same as **angels-on-horseback; devil's own** name given to the 88th Regiment in the Peninsular War, as also to the Inns of Court Volunteers; **devil's picture-books** (also in *sing.*) same as **devil's books; devil's snuff-box** a puff-ball; **devil's tattoo** see **tattoo[1]; dev'il-worship** the worship of the Devil, or of devils: Satanism: the Yezidi religion; **dev'il-worshipper.** — **between the devil and the deep (blue) sea** in a desperate dilemma; **devil a bit, a one, a thing** etc., not at all, not one, etc.; **devil of a mess** a very bad mess; **devil take the hindmost** each man for himself; **go to the devil** to become ruined: (*interj.*) go away!; **play the devil** to make havoc (with); **printer's devil** the youngest apprentice in a printing-office: a printer's errand-boy; **raise hell, the devil** see **raise; talk of the devil** here comes the person we were talking of; **the devil and all** much ado: turmoil; **the devil to pay** serious trouble (as a consequence of an action, etc.). [O.E. *dēofol, dēoful* — L. *diabolus* — Gr. *diabolos*, from *diaballein*, to throw across, to slander, from *dia*, across, and *ballein*, to throw; cf. Ger. *Teufel*, Fr. *diable*, It. *diavolo*, Sp. *diablo*.]

devious *dē'vi-əs, adj.* remote: out of the way: roundabout: winding: erring: tortuous of mind: deceitful. — *adv.* **dē'viously.** — *n.* **dē'viousness.** [L. *dēvius*; see **deviate**.]

devise *di-vīz', v.t.* to imagine: to compose: to suppose, guess (*Spens.*): to purpose (*Spens.*): to meditate (*obs.*): to describe (*obs.*): to depict (*obs.*): to scheme: to contrive: to bequeath. — *v.i.* to consider: to talk (*obs.*): to scheme. — *n.* act of bequeathing: a will: property bequeathed by will. — *adj.* **devīs'able.** — *ns.* **devīs'al; devīsee** (*dev-ī-zē'*) one to whom real estate is bequeathed; **devī'ser** one who contrives; **devīs'or** one who bequeaths. — **devisal of arms** formerly synonymous with **grant of arms**, now used by the English College of Arms where the petitioner is an American corporate body and therefore ineligible for a grant of arms. [O.Fr. *deviser, devise* — L.L. *dīvīsa*, a division of goods, a mark, a device — L. *dīvidere, dīvīsum*, to divide.]

devitalise, -ize *dē-vi'tə-līz, v.t.* to deprive of vitality or life-giving qualities. — *n.* **devitalīsā'tion, -z-.** [Pfx. **de-** (2).]

devitrify *dē-vit'ri-fī, v.t.* to change from glassy to minutely crystalline. — *n.* **devitrification** (*-fi-kā'*). [Pfx. **de-** (2).]

devling. See **devilet** under **devil**.

devocalise, -ize *dē-vō'kə-līz*, **devoice** *dē-vois', vs.t.* to make voiceless. [Pfx. **de-** (2).]

devoid *di-void', adj.* (*with of*) destitute, free: empty. [O.Fr. *desvoidier* — *des-* (L. *dis-*, away), *voider* — L. *viduāre* — *viduus*, deprived.]

devoir *dev'wär* (historically *dev'ər*), *n.* (often in *pl.*) what is due, duty: service: an act of civility. [Fr., — L. *dēbēre*, to owe.]

devolution *dēv-, dev-ə-lōō'shən, -lū', n.* a passing from one person to another: a handing over of powers: a modified home rule, the delegation of certain powers to regional governments by a central government. — *adj.* **devolu'tionary.** — *n.* **devolu'tionist.** [See **devolve**.]

devolve *di-volv', v.t.* to roll down: to hand down: to deliver over, esp. powers to regional governments by a central government. — *v.i.* to roll down: to fall or pass over in succession (with *on*). — *n.* **devolve'ment.** [L. *dēvolvēre, -volūtum* — *dē*, down, *volvēre*, to roll.]

Devonian *di-vō'ni-ən, adj.* belonging to *Devonshire*: belonging to a system above the Silurian and below the Carboniferous, and esp. to the marine type, well seen in Devon — the continental type being the Old Red Sandstone (*geol.*). — *n.* a native of Devonshire: the Devonian system. — **Devon (minnow)** an angler's lure that imitates a swimming minnow; **Devonshire cream** clotted cream.

devonport *dev'n-pōrt, -pört.* Same as **davenport**.

dévot *dā-vō*, (Fr.) *n.* a devotee: — *fem.* **dévote** (*dā-vōt*).

devote *di-vōt', v.t.* to set apart or dedicate by a vow or solemn act: to doom (*obs.*): to give up wholly. — *adj.* (*Shak.*) devoted. — *adj.* **devōt'ed** given up, as by a vow: doomed: strongly attached (to): zealous. — *adv.* **devōt'edly.** — *ns.* **devōt'edness; devotee** (*dev-ə-tē'*, or *dev'*) one wholly or superstitiously devoted, esp. to religion: a votary: one strongly and consistently interested in something (with *of*); **devōte'ment** (*Shak.*); **devō'tion** the act of devoting: state of being devoted: consecration: giving up of the mind to the worship of God: piety: prayer: strong affection or attachment: ardour: faithful service: (in *pl.*) prayers: religious offerings (*obs.*): alms (*obs.*). — *adj.* **devō'tional.** — *ns.* **devō'tionalist; devotional'ity, devō'tionalness; devō'tionist.** — *adv.* **devō'tionally.** [L. *dēvovēre, dēvōtum* — *dē*, away, and *vovēre*, to vow.]

devour *di-vowr', v.t.* to swallow greedily: to eat up: to consume or waste with violence or wantonness: to take in eagerly by the senses or mind. — *n.* **devour'er.** — *adj.* **devour'ing.** — *adv.* **devour'ingly.** — *n.* **devour'ment.** [O.Fr. *devorer* — L. *dēvorāre* — *dē*, intens., and *vorāre*, to swallow.]

devout *di-vowt', adj.* given up to religious thoughts and exercises: pious: solemn: earnest. — *adv.* **devout'ly.** — *n.* **devout'ness.** [O.Fr. *devot* — L. *dēvōtus*; see **devote**.]

devvel, devel *dev'l*, (*Scot.*) *n.* a hard blow. — *v.t.* to hit hard: to stun with a blow. [Ety. dub.]

dew¹ *dū, n.* moisture deposited from the air on cooling, esp. at night, in minute specks upon the surface of objects: a similar deposit or exudation of other kinds: early freshness. — *v.t.* to wet with dew: to moisten. — *adv.* **dew'ily.** — *n.* **dew'iness.** — *adj.* **dew'y.** — **dew=berry** a kind of bramble or blackberry (*Rubus caesius*; in America other species) having a bluish, dew-like bloom on the fruit; **dew'-bow** a rainbow-like appearance seen on a dewy surface; **dew'-claw** a rudimentary inner toe, esp. on a dog's leg; **dew'-drop; dew'-fall** the deposition, or time of deposition, of dew; **dew'point** the temperature at which a given sample of moist air becomes saturated and forms dew; **dew'-pond** a hollow supplied with water by mist; **dew'-retting** the process of rotting away the gummy part of hemp or flax by exposure on the grass to dew and rain; **dew'-worm** common earthworm. — *adj.* **dew'y-eyed** fresh, innocent (often *iron.*). — **mountain dew** (*coll.*) whisky. [O.E. *dēaw*; cf. O.N. *dögg*, Ger. *Tau*, dew.]

dew² *dū, n.* an obsolete spelling of **due**. — *adj.* **dew'full** (*Spens.*) due.

Dewali. Same as **Diwali**.

dewan, diwan *dē-wän', n.* in India, a financial minister: a state prime minister: the native steward of a business house. — *n.* **dewani, dewanny** (*dē-wä'nē*) the office of dewan. [Pers. *dīwān*; see **divan**.]

Dewar-flask *dū'ər-fläsk, n.* a type of vacuum flask. [From Sir James Dewar (1842–1923), its inventor.]

dewater *dē-wö'tər, v.t.* to drain or pump water from (e.g. coal). [Pfx. **de-** (2).]

Dewey decimal system, classification *dū'i des'i-məl sis'tim, klas'i-fi-kā'shən,* a system of library classification, based on the division of books into numbered classes, with further subdivision shown by numbers following a decimal point. — Also **decimal classification.** [Invented by Melvil Dewey (1851–1931), U.S. librarian.]

dewitt *di-wit', v.t.* to lynch — from the fate of Jan and Cornelius *De Witt* in Holland in 1672.

dewlap *dū'lap, n.* the pendulous skin under the throat of oxen, dogs, etc.: the fleshy wattle of the turkey. — *adj.* **dew'lapped, dew'lapt.** [Prob. **dew** and O.E. *læppa*, a loose hanging piece.]

Dexedrine® *dek'sə-drēn, n.* dextroamphetamine.

dexiotropic *deks-i-ō-trop'ik, adj.* turning to the right. [Gr. *dexios*, right, *tropos*, turning.]

dexter¹ *deks'tər, adj.* on the right-hand side: right: of that side of the shield on the right-hand side of the bearer, the spectator's left (*her.*): so sometimes in description of a picture, to avoid ambiguity. — *n.* **dexterity** (*-ter'i-ti*) skill of manipulation, or generally: adroitness: right-handedness. — *adj.* **dex'terous, dex'trous** right-handed: adroit: subtle. — *adv.* **dex't(e)rously.** *n.* **dex't(e)rousness.** — *adv.* **dex'terwise.** — *adj.* **dex'tral** right: turning to the right: of flatfish, lying right-side-up: of a spiral shell, turning in the normal manner, i.e. anticlockwise from the top. — *n.* **dextral'ity** right-handedness. — *adv.* **dex'trally.** — *ns.* **dex'tran** a carbohydrate formed in sugar solutions by a bacterium, *Leuconostoc mesenteroides*, a substitute for blood plasma in transfusion; **dex'trin, dex'trine** British gum, a gummy mixture got from starch by heating or otherwise. — **dextro-** in composition, pertaining to, or towards, the right. — *ns.* **dextroamphet'amine** the dextrorotatory isomer of amphetamine, used as a stimulant; **dextrocar'dia** (Gr. *kardiā*, heart) a condition in which the heart lies in the right side of the chest, not the left; **dextrocar'diac** one who has this condition. — *adjs.* **dextrogyrate** (*-jī'*), **dex'trogyre** (*-jīr*) causing to turn to the right hand; **dextrorō'tatory** rotating to the right (clockwise), esp. rotating thus the plane of polarisation of light. — *ns.* **dextrorōtā'tion; dex'trōse** glucose. [L. *dexter*; Gr. *dexios*, Sans. *dakṣiṇa* on the right, on the south.]

dexter² *deks'tər, n.* a small breed of Kerry cattle. — Also *adj.* [Prob. breeder's name.]

dextral, dextro-; etc. See **dexter**[1].

dextrorse *deks-trörs'*, or *deks'*, (*biol.*) *adj.* rising spirally and turning to the left, i.e. crossing an outside observer's field of view from left to right upwards (like a screw-nail): formerly used in the contrary sense (sinistrorse). [L. *dextrōrsus*, towards the right — *dexter*, and *vertĕre*, to turn.]

dextro tempore *deks'trō tem'pər-ē*, *-por-e*, (L.) at a lucky moment.

dey[1] *dā, n.* a dairy-maid. — Also **dey'-woman**. [See **dairy**.]

dey[2] *dā, n.* the pasha or governor of Algiers before the French conquest. [Turk. *dāi*, orig. a maternal uncle, a familiar title of the chief of the janizaries.]

dhak *däk, n.* an Indian Butea. [Hind. *dhāk*.]

dhal. Same as **dal**.

dharma *där'mə, dûr', n.* the righteousness that underlies the law: the law. [Sans.]

dharmsala *dûrm-sä'lä, n.* a building having a religious or charitable purpose, as a free or cheap lodging for travellers. — Also **dharmshala**. [Hindi *dharmsālā* — Sans. **dharma**, *śālā*, hall.]

dharna *dûr'nä, n.* calling attention, esp. to injustice, by sitting or standing in a place where one will be noticed, esp. sitting and fasting at the door of an offender. [Hindi.]

dhobi *dō'bi, n.* an Indian washerman. — **dhobi itch** a tropical allergic dermatitis. [Hindi *dhobī*.]

dhole *dōl, n.* the Indian wild dog. [Supposed to be from an Indian language.]

dholl. Same as **dal**.

dhooly. Same as **doolie**.

dhoti *dō'ti*, **dhooti** *doo'ti, ns.* the Hindu loin-cloth: a cotton fabric used for this. [Hindi *dhotī*.]

dhow, better **dow**, *dow, n.* an Arab lateen-sailed vessel of the Indian Ocean. [Origin unknown; cf. Ar. *dāw*, Marathi *dāw*.]

dhurra. Same as **durra**.

dhurrie. Same as **durrie**.

di- *dī, pfx.* two, twice, double. [Gr. *dis*, twice.]

dia- *dī'a-, -ə-, pfx.* through: across: during: composed of. [Gr.]

diabase *dī'əbās, n.* (*formerly*) diorite: an altered dolerite or basalt. — *adj.* **diabā'sic**. [Appar. orig. a faulty derivative of Gr. *di-*, double, *basis*, base; associated with *diabasis*, transition.]

diabetes *dī-ə-bē'tēz, n.* a disease marked by a morbid and excessive discharge of urine — **diabetes insip'idus** caused by a disorder of the pituitary gland leading to malfunction of the kidney, **diabetes melli'tus** (L., honied) caused by insulin deficiency or, rarely, an excess of insulin, with excess of sugar in the blood and urine. — *adjs.* **diabetic** (*-bēt'* or *-bet'*), **-al** relating to, or suffering from, diabetes: for the use of diabetics. — *ns.* **diabet'ic** one suffering from diabetes; **diabetol'ogist** a doctor specialising in the study and treatment of diabetes and the care of diabetics. [Gr. *diabētēs*, a siphon, *dia*, through, and *bainein*, to go.]

diablerie, diablery *dē-äb'lə-rē, n.* magic: the black art: sorcery: mischief. [Fr. *diable*; see **devil**.]

diabolic, -al *dī-ə-bol'ik, -əl, adjs.* devilish: (usu. **-al**) extremely unpleasant, very bad (*coll.*; used for emphasis). — *adv.* **diabol'ically**. — *v.t.* **diabolise, -ize** (*-ab'ə-līz*) to render devilish. — *ns.* **diab'olism** devil worship: devilry; **diab(ol)ol'ogy** the doctrine of devils: devil-lore. [Gr. *diabolikos* — *diabolos*; see **devil**.]

diabolo *di-a'bol-ō*, or *dī-, n.* a game in which a two-headed top is spun, tossed, and caught on a string attached to two sticks, held one in each hand. [Gr. *diaballō*, I throw over, toss, or *diabolos*, devil; see also **devil**.]

diacatholicon *dī-ə-kə-thol'i-kon*, (*obs.*) *n.* a purgative electuary: a panacea. [Gr. *dia katholikōn*, of universal (ingredients).]

diacaustic *dī-ə-kös'tik*, (*math., phys.*) *adj.* pertaining to or denoting a caustic curve or caustic surface formed by refraction. — *n.* a curve so formed. [Pfx. **dia-**, and **caustic** (*math.*).]

diacetylmorphine. See **diamorphine**.

diachronic *dī-ə-kron'ik, adj.* of the study of a subject (esp. a language) through its historical development — opp. of *synchronic*. — *adv.* **diachron'ically**. — *n.* **diachronism** (*dī-ak'*). — *adjs.* **diachronist'ic; diach'ronous**. [Pfx. **dia-**, and Gr. *chronos*, time.]

diachylon *dī-ak'i-lon*, **diachylum** *-i-ləm, ns.* form. a plaster of plant juices: now lead-plaster. [Gr. *dia chŷlōn*, through (i.e. composed of) juices or *diachŷlōn* (*neut.*), juicy.]

diacid *dī-as'id, adj.* having two replaceable hydrogen atoms: capable of replacing two hydrogen atoms of an acid. [Pfx. **di-**.]

diacodion *dī-ə-kō'di-on*, **diacodium** *-əm, ns.* a syrup of poppies. [L., — Gr. *dia kōdeiōn*, composed of poppy-heads — gen. pl. of *kōdeia*, a poppy-head.]

diaconate *dī-ak'ə-nāt, n.* the office of a deacon. — *adj.* **diac'onal** pertaining to a deacon. [See **deacon**.]

diaconicon *dī-ə-kon'i-kən, n.* a sacristy for sacred vessels, in a Greek church, on the south side of the bema or sanctuary. [Gr. *diākonikon*.]

diacoustic *dī-ə-koo'stik*, old-fashioned *-kow'*, *adj.* pertaining to the refraction of sound. — *n.* **diacoust'ics** the branch of physics that deals with refracted sounds. [Pfx. **dia-**, and **acoustic**.]

diacritic, -al *dī-ə-krit'ik, -əl, adjs.* distinguishing — used of marks (e.g. accents, cedillas, etc.) attached to letters to indicate modified sound, value, etc. — *n.* **diacrit'ic** such a mark. [Gr. *diakritikos* — *dia*, between, and *kritikos*; see **critic**.]

diact *dī'akt, adj.* two-rayed. — *adjs.* **diactinal** (*-ak'*, or *-tī'*), **diact'ine**. [Pfx. **di-**, and Gr. *aktīs, aktīnos*, ray.]

diactinic *dī-ak-tin'ik, adj.* capable of transmitting actinic rays. [Pfx. **dia-**, and Gr. *aktīs, aktīnos*, ray.]

diadelphous *dī-ə-del'fəs, adj.* of stamens, united by the filaments in two bundles: having stamens so joined. — *n.pl.* **Diadel'phia** in the Linnaean classification, a class with stamens so joined. [Pfx. **di-**, and Gr. *adelphos*, brother.]

diadem *dī'ə-dem, n.* a crown, head-band, or the like: an arch of a crown. — *adj.* **dī'ademed** wearing a diadem. **diadem spider** the common garden spider (from its markings). [O.Fr. *diademe* — L. *diadēma* — Gr. *diadēma* — *dia*, round, and *deein*, to bind.]

diadochi *dī-ad'o-kī, n.pl.* the generals who became monarchs of the various kingdoms (Syria, Egypt, etc.) into which the empire of Alexander the Great split after his death (323 B.C.). [Gr. *diadochos*, succeeding, a successor; *diadechesthai*, to succeed.]

diadrom *dī'ə-drom, n.* a course or passing: a vibration. — *adj.* (of leaf nerves) radiating fanwise. [Gr. *dia*, across, *dromos*, a run.]

diaeresis, dieresis *dī-ēr'i-sis, -er', n.* a mark (¨) placed over a vowel-letter, esp. the second of two adjacent ones to show that it is to be pronounced separately, as *naïf*: a pause or break where the end of the word coincides with the end of a foot (*pros.*): — *pl.* **diaer'eses, dier'eses** (*-ēz*). [Gr. *diairesis*, separation — *dia*, apart, *haireein*, to take.]

diagenesis *dī-ə-jen'i-sis, n.* the conversion of sediment into rock: reconstitution of crystals to form a new product. — *adj.* **diagenetic** (*-ji-net'ik*). [Pfx. **dia-**, and **genesis**.]

diageotropic *dī-ə-jē-ō-trop'ik*, (*bot.*) *adj.* taking a position perpendicular to the direction of gravity. — *adv.* **diageotrop'ically**. — *n.* **diageotropism** (*-ot'*). [Pfx. **dia-**, **geotropic**.]

diaglyph *dī'ə-glif, n.* an intaglio. [Gr. *dia*, through, *glyphein*, to carve.]

diagnosis *dī-əg-nō'sis, n.* the identification of a disease by means of its symptoms: a formal determining description: — *pl.* **diagnō'ses** (*-ēz*). — *n.* **diagnosabil'ity**. — *adj.* **dī'agnosable** (or *-nō'*). — *v.t.* **dī'agnose** (or *-nōz'*, esp. *U.S.*) *-nōs, -nōs'*) to ascertain from symptoms, as a disease. — *adj.* **diagnŏs'tic** distinguishing: differentiating. — *n.* that by which anything is known: a symptom. — *n. sing.* **diagnos'tics** diagnosis as a branch of medicine. — *n.* **diagnosti'cian** (*-nos-tish'ən*) one skilled in diagnosis. [Gr., *dia*, between, *gnōsis*, knowing.]

diagometer *dī-ə-gom'i-tər, n.* a form of electroscope for ascertaining electric conductivity. [Gr. *diagein*, to conduct, *metron*, a measure.]

diagonal *dī-ag'ə-nəl, adj.* through the corners, or joining two vertices that are not adjacent, of a polygon: (of a plane) passing through two edges, not adjacent, of a polyhedron: slantwise. — *n.* a straight line or plane so drawn. — *adv.* **diag'onally.** — **diagonal scale** a scale for laying down small fractions of the unit of measurement, by lengthwise parallel lines intersected by two sets of parallel lines, crosswise and oblique. [L. *diagōnālis*, from Gr. *diagōnios* — *dia*, through, and *gōniā*, a corner.]

diagram *dī'ə-gram, n.* a figure or plan intended to explain rather than represent actual appearance: an outline figure or scheme: a curve symbolising a set of facts: a record traced by an automatic indicator. — *adj.* **diagrammatic** (*-grə-mat'ik*). — *adv.* **diagrammat'ically.** — *n.* **dī'agraph** (*-gräf*) an instrument for copying, enlarging, or projecting drawings. — *adj.* **diagraphic** (*-graf'-ik*). [Gr. *diagramma* — *dia*, round, *graphein*, to write.]

diagrid *dī'ə-grid, n.* a structure of diagonally intersecting beams, used for support. [*diagonal grid*.]

diaheliotropic *dī-ə-hē-li-ō-trop'ik, (bot.) adj.* turning transversely to the light. — *n.* **diaheliotropism** (*-ot'rə-pizm*). [Pfx. **dia-**, **heliotropic**.]

dial *dī'əl, n.* an instrument for showing the time of day by the sun's shadow (as in *sundial*): a timepiece (*obs.*): the face of a watch or clock: graduated plate on which a movable index shows the value of some quantity measured, or can be set to make an adjustment (as in getting a telephone connection, tuning a radio): a miner's compass with sights for surveying: a face (*slang*). — *v.t.* to measure or indicate or get into communication with by dial. — *v.i.* to use a telephone dial: — *pr.p.* **di'alling;** *pa.t.* and *pa.p.* **di'alled.** — *ns.* **di'alist** a maker of dials: one skilled in dialling; **di'aller** one who surveys by dial; **di'alling** the art of constructing sundials: the science which explains the measuring of time by the sundial: surveying by dial. — **dialling code** a group of numbers dialled to obtain the desired exchange in an automatic dialling system; **dialling tone,** (*U.S.*) **dial tone,** the continuous sound heard on picking up a telephone receiver which indicates that one may begin dialling; **di'al-plate** the plate to which the pillars of a watch are fixed. [L.L. *diālis*, daily — L. *diēs*, a day.]

dialect *dī'ə-lekt, n.* a variety or form of a language peculiar to a district or class, esp. but not necessarily other than a literary or standard form: a peculiar manner of speaking: any of two or more variant forms of a particular computer language. — *adj.* **dialect'al.** — *adv.* **dialect'ally.** — *ns.* **dialect'icism; dialectol'ogist; dialectol'ogy.** [Through Fr. and L. from Gr. *dialektos*, speech, manner of speech, peculiarity of speech — *dia*, between, *legein*, to speak.]

dialectic, -al *dī-ə-lek'tik, -əl, adjs.* pertaining to dialect or to discourse or to dialectics: logical. — *n.* **dialec'tic,** or *n. sing* **dialec'tics,** the art of discussing: that branch of logic which teaches the rules and modes of reasoning. — *adv.* **dialec'tically.** — *n.* **dialecti'cian** one skilled in dialectics, a logician. — **dialectical materialism** see **materialism.** [Gr. *dialektikos*.]

diallage[1] *dī-al'ə-jē, (rhet.) n.* a figure of speech by which arguments, after having been considered from various points of view, are all brought to bear upon one point. [Gr. *diallagē*; see next word.]

diallage[2] *dī'əl-āj, n.* a mineral nearly allied to augite, brown, grey, or green, with play of colour. — *adjs.* **diallagic** (*-aj'ik*), **diallagoid** (*-al'ə-goid*). [Gr. *diallagē*, change — *dia*, between, *allassein*, to change — *allos*, other.]

dialogite *dī-al'ə-jīt, n.* a rose-red manganese carbonate. [Gr. *dialogē*, selection, doubt.]

dialogue, *U.S.* **dialog,** *dī'ə-log, n.* conversation between two or more persons, esp. of a formal or imaginary nature: an exchange of views in the hope of ultimately reaching agreement. — *v.i.* (*Shak.*) to converse. — *v.t.* (*Shak.*) to put into dialogue form. — *adjs.* **dialog'ic** (*-loj'*), **dialogist'ic, -al.** — *v.i.* **dialogise, -ize** (*dī-al'ə-jīz*) to discourse in dialogue. — *n.* **dial'ogist** a speaker in, or writer of, dialogue. [Fr., — L. *dialogus* — Gr. *dialogos*, a conversation — *dialegesthai*, to discourse.]

dialypetalous *dī-ə-li-pet'ə-ləs, adj.* having the petals separate, polypetalous. [Gr. *dialyein*, to separate — *dia*, asunder, *lyein*, to loose, and *petalon*, a leaf.]

dialysis *dī-al'i-sis, (chem.) n.* the separation of substances by diffusion through a membranous septum or partition: diaeresis: dissolution: separation: removal of impurities from the blood by a kidney machine (q.v.) (*med.*): — *pl.* **dial'yses** (*-sēz*). — *adj.* **dialysable, -z-** (*dī-ə-līz'ə-bl*). — *v.t.* **dialyse,** (*U.S.*) **-yze** (*dī'ə-līz*) to separate by dialysis. — *v.i.* to use a kidney machine. — *n.* **di'alyser, -z-.** — *adj.* **dialytic** (*-lit'ik*). [Gr. *dialysis* — *dia*, asunder, *lyein*, to loose.]

diamagnetic *dī-ə-mag-net'ik, adj.* applied to any substance of which a rod suspended between the poles of a magnet arranges itself across the lines of force (opp. to *paramagnetic*). — *n.* **diamag'net** a diamagnetic substance. — *adv.* **diamagnet'ically.** — *n.* **diamag'-netism** the form of magnetic action possessed by diamagnetic bodies: the branch of magnetism which deals with diamagnetic phenomena. [Pfx. **dia-**, **magnetic**.]

diamanté *dē-a-mä-tā, dī-ə-man'ti, n.* a decoration, e.g. on a dress, consisting of glittering particles: a fabric so decorated. — Also *adj.* — *adj.* **diamantine** (*dī-ə-man'-tīn*) of, or resembling, diamonds. [Fr., *diamant*, diamond.]

diamantiferous *dī-ə-man-tif'ər-əs, adj.* yielding diamonds. [Fr. *diamantifère*.]

diameter *dī-am'i-tər, n.* the measure through or across: a straight line passing through the centre of a circle or other figure, terminated at both ends by the circumference: in the parabola a straight line parallel to the axis extending from the curve to infinity. — *adjs.* **diam'etral, diametric** (*dī-ə-met'rik*), **-al** in the direction of a diameter: pertaining to the diameter: as of opposite ends of a diameter (as in *diametrical opposition*). — *advs.* **diam'etrally** in a diametral manner; **diamet'-rically** along a diameter: as at the ends of a diameter. — **tactical diameter** the perpendicular distance between a ship's courses before and after turning 180°. [Through Fr. and L. from Gr. *diametros* — *dia*, through, across, and *metron*, a measure.]

diamond *dī'ə-mənd, n.* a highly prized gem stone, and the hardest of all minerals, carbon crystallised in the cubic system: a rhombus: a card of a suit distinguished by pips of that form: a baseball field, or the part between bases (*U.S.*): one of the smallest kinds of English printing type (about 4½ -point). — *adj.* resembling diamonds: made of diamonds: marked with diamonds: lozenge-shaped, rhombic. — *adjs.* **dī'amonded** furnished with diamonds; **diamondif'erous** yielding diamonds. — **di'amond-back** a N. American terrapin with diamond-shaped markings on its shell: a N. American rattlesnake, *Crotalus adamanteus*, with diamond-shaped markings; **di'amond-bee'tle** a beautiful sparkling S. American weevil; **diamond dove** a small Australian dove (*Geopelia cuneata*) with white markings on the wings, often kept in cage or aviary; **di'amond-drill** a borer whose bit is set with bort; **di'amond-dust, -pow'der** the powder made by the friction of diamonds on one another in the course of polishing; **di'amond-field** a region that yields diamonds; **di'amond-hitch** a mode of fastening a rope for heavy burdens; **diamond jubilee** a sixtieth anniversary (of marriage, **di'amond-wedd'ing**); **diamond snake** a carpet snake with diamond-shaped markings; **di'amond-wheel** a wheel covered with diamond-dust and oil for polishing diamonds, etc. — **black diamonds**

(*fig.*) coal; **diamond cut diamond** an encounter between two very sharp persons; **rough diamond** an uncut diamond: a person possibly of great worth, but of rude exterior and unpolished manners. [M.E. *diamaunt* — O.Fr. *diamant* — L.L. *diamas, -antis* — Gr. *adamas, -antos*; see **adamant.**]

diamorphine *dī-ə-mör′fēn, n.* a contraction of **diacetyl-mor′phine** (*dī-as′ə-til-*) an acetyl derivative of morphine, commonly known as heroin.

diamyl *dī-am′il, adj.* having two amyl groups. [Pfx. **di-, amyl.**]

Diana *dī-an′ə, n.* Roman goddess of light, the moon-goddess, representative of chastity and hunting — identified with the Greek Artemis: a huntress. — Also **Dī′an.** — **Diana monkey** a large long-tailed W. African monkey (*Cercopithecus diana*) with a white crescent on the forehead; **Diana's tree** tree of silver (see **tree**). — **Diana of the Ephesians** a goddess of fertility worshipped at Ephesus. [L. *Diāna.*]

diandrous *dī-an′drəs, adj.* having, or allowing, two husbands or male mates (at a time): having two stamens or antheridia. — *n.pl.* **Dian′dria** in Linnaeus's classification, a class of plants with two stamens. — *n.* **dian′dry** the practice or condition of being diandrous. [Gr. *dis*, twice, *anēr, andros*, a man, male.]

dianetics® *dī-ə-net′iks, n. sing.* a method of diagnosing and treating psychosomatic ills (held to be caused by pre-natal experiences). [Gr. *dia*, through, *nous*, mind.]

dianodal *dī-ə-nō′dəl,* (*math.*) *adj.* passing through a node. [Pfx. **dia-, nodal.**]

dianoetic *dī-ə-nō-et′ik, adj.* capable of or relating to thought. [Gr. *dianoētikos* — *dia*, through, *noeein*, to think.]

Dianthus *dī-an′thəs, n.* the genus of herbaceous flowers to which carnations and pinks belong: (without *cap.*) any plant or flower of the genus. [Poss. Gr. *Dios anthos*, Zeus's flower; or *dianthēs* flowering in succession.]

diapason *dī-ə-pā′zən, -sən, n.* a whole octave: a bass part: a harmony: a full volume of various sounds in concord: the whole range or compass of tones: a standard of pitch: a foundation-stop of an organ (*open* or *stopped diapason*) extending through its whole compass. — (*Spens.*) **dī′apase.** [Gr. *dia pasōn chordōn symphōniā*, concord through all the notes.]

diapause *dī′ə-pöz, n.* in insects and the embryos of some animals, a period of suspended animation and growth. [Gr. *diapausis*, pause — *diapauein*, to pause — *dia*, between, *pauein*, to stop.]

diapedesis *dī-ə-pi-dē′sis,* (*physiol.*) *n.* the migration of white blood-corpuscles through the walls of the blood-vessels without apparent rupture. — *adj.* **diapedetic** (*-det′ik*). [Gr. *dia*, through, *pēdēsis*, leaping.]

diapente *dī-ə-pen′ti, n.* the interval of a fifth (*mus.*): a medicine of five ingredients. [Gr. *dia*, through, *pente*, five.]

diaper *dī′ə-pər, n.* linen or cotton cloth with a square or diamond pattern, used chiefly for table linen and towels: esp. in U.S., a baby's napkin: a pattern for ornamentation, woven, not coloured, in textiles: a floral or geometric pattern in low relief in architecture, often repeated over a considerable surface: paving in a chequered pattern. — *v.t.* to variegate with figures, as diaper. — *n.* **dī′apering.** [O.Fr. *diaspre, diapre* — L.L. *diasprus* — Byzantine Gr. *diaspros, dia*, through, *aspros*, white.]

diaphanous *dī-af′ə-nəs, adj.* transparent: translucent: pellucid: clear: light, delicate. — *ns.* **diaphaneity** (*dī-ə-fə-nē′i-ti*); **dīaphanom′eter** an instrument for measuring the transparency of the air. — *adv.* **dīaph′anously.** — *n.* **dīaph′anousness.** [Gr. *diaphanēs* — *dia*, through, and *phainein*, to show, shine.]

diaphone *dī′ə-fōn, n.* a siren-like fog-signal: an organ stop made louder by vibrating material: all the variants of a phoneme. [Gr. *dia*, across, *phōnē*, voice.]

diaphoresis *dī-ə-for-ē′sis, n.* sweat, esp. artificially in-duced. — *adj.* **diaphoretic** (*-et′ik*) promoting sweating. — *n.* a sudorific. [Gr. *diaphorēsis*, sweating — *dia*, through, *pherein*, to carry.]

diaphototropic *dī-ə-fō-tō-trop′ik, adj.* diaheliotropic. — *ns.* **diaphototrōp′ism; diaphototropy** (*-tot′rə-pi*). [Pfx. **dia-, phototropic.**]

diaphragm *dī′ə-fram, -frəm, n.* a thin partition or dividing membrane: the midriff, a structure separating the chest from the abdomen: a metal plate with a central hole, for cutting off side-rays in optical instruments: a strengthening or stiffening plate (*engineering*): in a telephone, a thin vibrating disc that converts electrical signals into sound waves and vice versa: a contraceptive device, a thin rubber or plastic cap placed over the mouth of the cervix. — *adjs.* **diaphragmatic** (*-frag-mat′*), **diaphrag′mal.** — *n.* **diaphragmatī′tis** inflammation of the diaphragm. — **diaphragm pump** a pump which has a flexible membrane instead of a piston. [Gr. *diaphragma*, partition, midriff — *dia*, across, *phragma*, a fence.]

diaphysis *dī-af′i-sis, n.* an abnormal elongation of the axis (*bot.*): the shaft of a long bone (*anat.*). [Gr. *diaphysis*, a separation — *dia*, through, *phyesthai*, to grow.]

diapir *dī′ə-pēr, n.* an anticlinal fold in which the overlying rock has been pierced by material from beneath. — *adj.* **diapi′ric.** — *n.* **diapi′rism** the upward movement of material through denser rocks to form diapirs. [Gr. *diapeirainein*, to pierce.]

diapophysis *dī-ə-pof′i-sis, n.* a dorsal transverse process of a vertebra: — *pl.* **dīapoph′ysēs** (*-sēz*). — *adj.* **diapophysial** (*dī-ap-ō-fiz′i-əl*). [Gr. *dia*, apart, *apophysis*, offshoot.]

diapositive *dī-ə-poz′i-tiv, n.* a transparent photographic positive. [Pfx. **dia-, positive.**]

diapyesis *dī-ə-pī-ē′sis, n.* suppuration. — *adj.* **diapyetic** (*-et′ik*) producing suppuration. — *n.* a medicine of this property. [Gr. *diapyēsis* — *dia*, through, *pyon*, pus.]

diarch *dī′ärk,* (*bot.*) *adj.* having two xylem strands. [Gr. *di-*, twice, *archē*, origin.]

diarchy *dī′är-ki, n.* a form of government in which two persons, states, or bodies are jointly vested with supreme power — less correctly **dī′narchy, dy′archy.** *adjs.* **diarch′al, diarch′ic.** [Gr. *di-*, twice, *archein*, to rule.]

diarrhoea, (*U.S.*) **diarrhea,** *dī-ə-rē′ə, n.* a persistent purging or looseness of the bowels: an excessive flow of anything (*fig.; coll.*). — *adjs.* **diarrhoe′al, diarrhoe′ic** (also *U.S.* **-rhē′al,** etc.). [Gr. *diarroia* — *dia*, through, *rhoiā*, a flow.]

diarthrosis *dī-är-thrō′sis, n.* articulation admitting free movement. [Gr. *diarthrōsis*, jointing — *dia*, through, *arthron*, joint.]

diary *dī′ə-ri, n.* a daily record: a book for making daily records, noting engagements, etc. — *adjs.* **diarial** (*dī-ā′ri-əl*), **diā′rian.** — *v.t.* or *v.i.* **dī′arise, -ize.** — *n.* **dī′arist** one who keeps a diary. [L. *diārium* — *diēs*, day.]

diascope *dī′ə-skōp, n.* an optical projector used for showing transparencies on a screen. [Pfx. **dia-,** and Gr. *skopeein*, to view.]

diascordium *dī-ə-skör′di-əm, n.* a medicine made from water-germander, etc. [Medical L., — Gr. *dia skordiōn*, composed of *skordiōn* (perhaps water-germander).]

diaskeuast *dī-ə-skū′ast, n.* a reviser: an interpolator. [Gr. *diaskeuazein*, to make ready — *dia*, through, *skeuos*, a tool.]

Diasone® *dī′ə-sōn, n.* a proprietary name for a sulphonamide (a derivative of diaminodiphenylsulphone) used against leprosy.

diaspora *dī-as′por-ə, n.* (with *cap.*) dispersion, used collectively for the dispersed Jews after the Babylonian captivity, and also in the apostolic age for the Jews living outside of Palestine, now, for Jews outside Israel: a similar dispersion or migration of other peoples or communities. — Also *adj.* [Gr. *diasporā* — *dia*, through, *speirein*, to scatter.]

diaspore *dī'ə-spōr, -spör, n.* a mineral, aluminium hydroxide, AlO(OH). [Gr. *diasporā*, scattering, from its decrepitation.]

diastaltic *dī-ə-stal'tik, (Greek mus.) adj.* of intervals, extended: of style, bold. [Gr. *diastaltikos*, expanding.]

diastase *dī'ə-stās, n.* an enzyme that converts starch into sugar, produced in germinating seeds and in pancreatic juice. — *adjs.* **diastā'sic; diastatic** *(-stat'ik).* [Gr. *diastasis*, division — *dia*, apart, *stasis*, setting.]

diastasis *dī-as'tə-sis, (surg.) n.* separation of bones without fracture. [See foregoing.]

diastema *dī-ə-stē'mə, n.* a natural space between two consecutive teeth, or series of teeth: — *pl.* **diastē'mata.** *adj.* **diastemat'ic.** [Gr. *diastēma, -atos*, interval.]

diaster *dī-as'tər, (biol.) n.* in cell-division, a stage in which the daughter chromosomes are situated in two groups near the poles of the spindle, ready to form the daughter nuclei. [Gr. *di-*, twice, and *astēr*, a star.]

diastereoisomer *dī-ə-stē-ri-ō-ī'sō-mər, (chem.) n.* a stereoisomer which is not an enantiomorph. — *adj.* **diastereoisomeric** *(-me'rik).* — *n.* **diastereoisom'erism.** [Pfx. **dia-**, and **stereoisomer.**]

diastole *dī-as'tə-lē, n.* dilatation of the heart, auricles, and arteries — opp. to *systole*, or contraction: the lengthening of a short syllable, as before a pause. — *adj.* **diastolic** *(dī-ə-stol'ik).* [Gr. *diastolē* — *dia*, asunder, and *stellein*, to place.]

diastrophism, *dī-as'trō-fizm, (geol.) n.* processes of deformation of the earth's crust. — *adj.* **diastrophic** *(dī-ə-strof'ik).* [Gr. *diastrophē*, distortion — *dia*, aside, *strophē*, a turning.]

diastyle *dī'ə-stīl, (archit.) adj.* with columns about three diameters apart. — *n.* a building or colonnade so proportioned. [Gr. *diastȳlos* — *dia*, apart, *stȳlos*, column.]

diatessaron, *dī-ə-tes'ə-ron, -rən, n.* a harmony of the four gospels, especially the earliest, that of Tatian (prob. A.D. 110–180): the interval of a fourth *(mus.)*: a medicine of four ingredients. [Gr. *dia tessarōn*, through, or composed of, four.]

diathermic *dī-ə-thûr'mik, adj.* permeable by radiant heat. — Also **diather'mal, diather'manous, diather'mous.** — *ns.* **diather'macy, diather'mancy, diathermanē'lty** permeability by radiant heat; **di'athermy** heating of internal parts of the body by electric currents. [Gr. *dia*, through, *thermē*, heat.]

diathesis *dī-ath'i-sis, n.* a particular condition or habit of body, esp. one predisposing to certain diseases: a habit of mind. — *adj.* **diathetic** *(dī-ə-thet'ik).* [Gr. *diathesis* — *dia*, asunder, *tithenai* to place.]

diatom *dī'ə-təm, n.* one of a class of microscopic unicellular algae with flinty shells in two halves, fitting like box and lid. — *adj.* **diatomā'ceous.** — *ns.* **dī'atomist** one who studies diatoms; **diatomite** *(dī-at'əm-īt,* or *dī'ət-)* diatomaceous earth or kieselguhr, a powdery siliceous deposit of diatom frustules. — **diatom ooze** a deep-sea deposit of diatom frustules. [Gr. *diatomos*, cut through — *dia*, through, *temnein*, to cut.]

diatomic *dī-ə-tom'ik, adj.* consisting of two atoms: having two replaceable atoms or groups: bivalent. [Pfx. **di-**, **atom.**]

diatonic *dī-ə-ton'ik, adj.* proceeding by the tones and intervals of the natural scale in music. — *adv.* **diaton'ically.** [Gr. *diatonikos* — *dia*, through, *tonos*, tone.]

diatretum. See **cage-cup.**

diatribe *dī'ə-trīb, n.* a continued discourse or disputation: an invective harangue. — *n.* **dī'atribist** a writer or utterer of such. [Gr. *diatrībē*, a spending of time — *dia*, through, *tribein*, to rub, wear away.]

diatropism *dī-at'rō-pizm, n.* orientation at right angles to the direction of a stimulus. — *adj.* **diatropic** *(dī-ə-trop'-ik).* [Gr. *dia*, across, *tropos*, turning.]

diaxon *dī-aks'on, adj.* having two axes or two axis-cylinder processes. — *n.* a bipolar nerve-cell. [Gr. *di-*, twice, *axōn*, an axis.]

diazepam *dī-az'i-pam, n.* a tranquilliser which relieves tension and acts as a muscle relaxant. [Pfx. **di-**, *azo-*, *epoxide.*]

diazeuxis *dī-ə-zūk'sis, (Greek mus.) n.* the separation of two tetrachords by a whole tone. — *adj.* **diazeuc'tic.** [Gr. *diazeuxis*, disjunction — *dia*, apart, *zeuxis*, yoking.]

diazo *dī-az'ō, adj.* of compounds containing two nitrogen atoms and a hydrocarbon radical: of a photocopying process using a diazo compound decomposed by exposure to light (also **dye'line**). — *n.* a copy made by the diazo method: — *pl.* **diaz'os** or **diaz'oes.** — Also **dye'line.** — **diazonium** *(dī-ə-zō'ni-əm)* **salts** a group of diazo compounds used in the manufacture of certain dyes. [Pfx. **di-**, and **azo-**.]

dib¹ *dib, v.i.* to dip, as in angling: — *pr.p.* **dibb'ing;** *pa.t.* and *pa.p.* **dibbed.** [Prob. a form of **dab.**]

dib² *dib, n.* one of the small bones of a sheep's leg: *(pl.)* a children's game, played by throwing up such small bones or stones **(dib'-stones)** from the palm and catching them on the back of the hand — also *jacks*, in Scots *chuckie-stanes*, or *chucks*: *(pl.)* money *(slang;* also **dibbs**). [Ety. uncertain.]

dibasic *dī-bā'sik, adj.* capable of reacting with two equivalents of an acid: (of acids) having two replaceable hydrogen atoms. [Pfx. **di-**, **basic.**]

dibber. See **dibble.**

dibble *dib'l, n.* a pointed tool used for making holes for seeds or plants. — Also **dibb'er.** — *v.t.* **dibb'le** to plant with a dibble. — *v.i.* to make holes: to dip, as in angling. — *n.* **dibb'ler** one who, or that which, dibbles: a dibber: a small carnivorous Australian marsupial *Antechinus apicalis*, with long snout and short hairy tail. [Prob. connected with **dab¹**.]

dibranchiate *dī-brang'ki-āt, adj.* having two gills. — *ns.pl.* **Dibran'chia, Dibranchiā'ta** the two-gilled subclass of cephalopods. [Gr. *di-*, twice, *branchia*, gills.]

dibromo- *dī-brō'mō-,* in composition, having two atoms of bromine, esp. replacing hydrogen.

dibutyl *dī-bū'til, adj.* having two butyl groups. — **dibutyl phthalate** *(thal'āt)* the dibutyl ester of phthalic acid, used to keep off insects.

dicacity *di-kas'i-ti, n.* raillery, pert speech. — *adj.* **dicacious** *(di-kā'shəs).* [L. *dicāx*, sarcastic.]

dicarpellary *dī-kar'pəl-ər-i,* or *-pel', adj.* of or with two carpels. [Px. **di-**.]

dicast, dikast *dik'ast, n.* one of the 6000 Athenians annually chosen to act as judges. — *n.* **dicas'tery** their court. — *adj.* **dicas'tic.** [Gr. *dikastēs* — *dikē*, justice.]

dice¹, dicey, dicing. See **die².**

dice² *dīs, v.t. (Austr. coll.)* to reject.

Dicentra *dī-sen'trə, n.* a genus of the fumitory family including bleeding-heart *(D. spectabilis)* with the two outer petals broadly pouched: (without *cap.*) any plant of the genus. — Also **Dielytra, dielytra** *(dī-el'i-trə;* orig. a misprint). [Gr. *di-*, double, *kentron*, a point, spur.]

dicephalous *dī-sef'ə-ləs, adj.* two-headed. [Gr. *dikephalos* — *di-*, double, *kephalē*, a head.]

dich *dich, (Shak.,* Timon) supposed to be for **do it**, may it do.

dichasium *dī-kā'zi-əm, n.* a cymose inflorescence in which each axis in turn produces a pair of nearly equal branches: — *pl.* **dichā'sia.** — *adj.* **dichā'sial.** [Gr. *dichāsis*, division, halving.]

dichlamydeous *dī-klə-mid'i-əs, adj.* having both a calyx and a corolla. [Gr. *di-*, double, *chlamys, -ydos*, mantle.]

dichlor(o)- *dī-klōr(-ō)-, -klör-,* in composition, having two atoms of chlorine, esp. replacing hydrogen. — *n.* **dichlo'rodiphēn'yltrichlo'roeth'ane** known as DDT, a white powder orig. used to kill lice and thus prevent the spread of typhus; effective also against other insects, but having long-term disadvantages.

dichloralphenazone *dī-klōr-əl-phen'ə-zōn, -klör-, n.* a drug, $C_{15}H_{18}CI_6N_2O_5$, used as a hypnotic and sedative. [Pfx. **di-, chloral hydrate, and** *phenazone*, an antipyretic drug.]

dichogamy *dik-* or *dīk-og'ə-mi, n.* an arrangement for preventing the self-fertilisation of hermaphrodite flowers, the stamens and stigmas ripening at different times. — *adj.* **dichog'amous.** [Gr. *dicha*, in two, *gamos*, marriage.]

dichord *dī'körd, n.* an ancient two-stringed lute. [Gr. *dichordos.*]

dichotomy *dik-* or *dīk-ot'ə-mi, n.* a division into two strongly contrasted groups or classes: repeated branching. — *v.t.* and *v.i.* **dichot'omise, -ize.** — *n.* **dichot'omist.** — *adj.* **dichot'omous.** — *adv.* **dichot'omously.** [Gr. *dichotomiā* — *dicha*, in two, *tomē*, a cut — *temnein*, to cut.]

dichroism *dī'krō-izm, n.* the property of showing different colours exhibited by doubly refracting crystals when viewed in different directions by transmitted light. — *adjs.* **dichrō'ic, dichrōït'ic.** — *ns.* **dī'chrōite** a strongly dichroic mineral, iolite or cordierite; **dī'chrō(o)scope** an instrument for testing the dichroism of crystals. — *adj.* **dichrō(o)scop'ic.** [Gr. *dichroos*, two-coloured — *di-*, twice, *chroā*, colour.]

dichromate *dī-krō'māt*, a salt of **dichro'mic acid** ($H_2Cr_2O_7$) containing two chromium atoms. — Also **bīchrō'mate.** [Pfx. **di-, chromate.**]

dichromatic *dī-krō-mat'ik, adj.* having two colours, esp. in different individuals of the same species: able to see two colours and two only, as in red-green colour-blind persons who see only blue and yellow. — *n.* a person of dichromatic vision, a dichromat. — *ns.* **dī'chrōmat(e)** a person who can distinguish two colours only; **dichrō'matism.** — *adj.* **dichrō'mic** dichroic: dichromatic. — *n.* **dichrō'mism.** [Gr. *di-*, twice, *chrōma, -atos*, colour.]

dichromic. See (1) **dichromate**; (2) **dichromatic.**

dicht, dight *dihht, (Scot.) v.t.* to wipe. — *n.* a wipe. [**dight.**]

dick *dik, (slang) n.* fine words (for **dictionary**): also for **declaration,** as *to take one's dick*, and prob. *up to dick*, excellent (up to declared value).

Dick (*also without cap.*) *dik, (slang) n.* a man: detective: (without *cap.*) a penis (*vulg.*). — **clever Dick** one who thinks himself to be cleverer than he is. [*Dick*, for Richard.]

dickcissel *dik-sis'l, n.* the black-throated bunting, an American migratory bird. [Imit. of call.]

dickens *dik'ənz, n.* the deuce, the devil, as in *what the dickens, play the dickens.* [App. *Dickon*, Richard, as a substitute for **devil.**]

Dickensian *dik-en'zi-ən, adj.* pertaining to Charles *Dickens* (1812–70), the novelist: pertaining to conditions, esp. squalid social or working conditions, like those described in his novels. — *n.* an admirer or student of Dickens.

dicker *dik'ər, (U.S.) n.* haggling, bargaining: petty trade by barter, etc. — *v.i.* to haggle: to hesitate, dither. [Prob. the obs. *dicker*, the number ten, esp. of hides or skins. — L. *decuria*.]

dickey¹, dicky, dickie *dik'i, n.* a leathern apron for a gig, etc.: the driver's seat in a carriage: a seat for servants at the back of a carriage: a folding seat at the back of a motor-car: a false shirt-front. [Perh. from *dick*, a dial. Eng. word for a leathern apron; perh. Du. *dek*, a cover.]

dickey²,³. See **dicky¹,².**

dickie. See **dickey¹.**

Dickin medal *dik'in med'əl*, a British award for animal heroism in wartime, instituted in 1943. [Maria Elisabeth *Dickin*, founder of the People's Dispensary for Sick Animals, which makes the awards.]

Dicksonia *dik-sōn'i-ə, n.* a tropical and southern genus of ferns, mainly tree-ferns. [After James *Dickson* (d. 1822), botanist.]

dickty. See **dicty.**

dicky¹, dickey *dik'i, (E. Anglian) n.* an ass. — **dick'y-bird** a small bird (*childish*): a word (*rhyming slang*). [*Dick*, for Richard.]

dicky², dickey *dik'i, (coll.) adj.* shaky: not in good condition. [Origin unknown.]

dicky³. See **dickey¹.**

diclinous *dī'kli-nəs,* or *-klī', adj.* having the stamens and pistils in separate flowers, whether on the same or on different plants. — *n.* **dī'clinism.** [Gr. *di-*, twice, double, *klīnē*, a bed.]

dicotyledon *dī-kot-i-lē'dən, n.* (often shortened to **dī'cot**) a plant of the **Dīcotylē'donēs** (*-ēz*) or **Dīcot'ylae** (*-i-lē*), one of the two great divisions of Angiosperms, having embryos with two cotyledons, leaves commonly net-veined, the parts of the flowers in twos, fives, or multiples of these, and the vascular bundles in the axes usually containing cambium. — *adj.* **dicotylē'donous.** [Gr. *di-*, twice, and **cotyledon.**]

dicrotic *dī-krot'ik, adj.* of the pulse, having two beats to one beat of the heart. — Also **dī'crotous.** — *n.* **dī'crotism.** [Gr. *di-*, twice, double, and *krotos*, beat.]

dict. See **dictate.**

dicta. See **dictum.**

Dictaphone® *dik'tə-fōn, n.* a recording apparatus for dictating letters, etc. [L. *dictāre*, to dictate, Gr. *phōnē*, sound.]

dicta probantia *dik'tə prō-ban'shi-ə, dik'ta prō-ban'ti-a,* (L.) proof texts.

dictate *dik-tāt'*, formerly *dik'tāt, v.t.* to say or read for another to write: to lay down with authority: to command. — *v.i.* to give orders: to behave dictatorially. — *n.* (*dik'tāt*) an order, rule, direction: impulse. — *n.* **dict** (*obs.*) a saying. — *v.t.* (*obs.*) to dictate. — *ns.* **dictā'tion** act, art, or practice of dictating: speaking or reading of words for a pupil, amanuensis, etc., to write: overbearing command; **dicta'tor** one invested with absolute authority — originally an extraordinary Roman magistrate: one who, or that which, dictates: — *fem.* **dictā'tress, dictā'trix.** — *adj.* **dictatorial** (*dik-tə-tō'ri-əl, -tō'*) like a dictator: absolute: overbearing. — *adv.* **dictātō'rially.** — *ns.* **dictā'torship, dictā'ture.** — *adj.* **dic'tatory.** [L. *dictāre, -ātum*, freq. of *dīcĕre*, to say.]

diction *dik'shən, n.* a saying or speaking: manner of speaking or expressing: choice of words: style: (*U.S.*) enunciation. [L. *dictio, -ōnis* — *dīcĕre, dictum*, to say.]

dictionary *dik'shən-ə-ri, n.* book containing the words of a language alphabetically arranged, with their meanings, etymology, etc.: a lexicon: a work containing information on any department of knowledge, alphabetically arranged. [L.L. *dictiōnārium*; see **diction.**]

Dictograph® *dik'tō-gräf, n.* a telephone for transmitting speech from room to room, with or without the speaker's knowledge. [L. *dictum*, thing said, Gr. *graphein*, to write.]

dictum *dik'təm, n.* something said: a saying: an authoritative saying: — *pl.* **dic'ta.** [L.]

dicty, dickty *dik'ti, (U.S. slang) adj.* proud, snobbish: high-class: excellent. [Origin unknown.]

dictyogen *dik'ti-ō-jen, (obs.) n.* a monocotyledon with net-veined leaves. [Gr. *diktyon*, a net; *gennaein*, to produce.]

dicyclic *dī-sīk'lik, adj.* having two whorls or rings. [Gr. *di-*, twice, double, *kyklos*, wheel.]

dicynodont *dī-sin'ō-dont, n.* an extinct tusked reptile, showing affinities with mammals. [Gr. *di-*, twice, *kyōn, kynos*, dog, and *odous, odontos*, tooth.]

did *did, didst didst, pa.ts.* of **do.**

didactic, -al *di-dak'tik, -əl, dī-, adjs.* fitted or intended to teach: instructive (sometimes pedantically or dictatorially so): preceptive. — *adv.* **didac'tically.** — *n.* **didac'ticism** (*-sizm*). — *n. sing.* **didactics** the art or science of teaching. [Gr. *didaktikos* — *didaskein*, to teach; akin to L. *docēre, discēre*.]

didactyl *dī-dak'til, adj.* two-fingered, two-toed, or two-clawed. — Also *n.* — *adj.* **didac'tylous.** [Gr. *di-*, twice, *daktylos*, finger, toe.]

didakai, didakei. See **did(d)icoy.**

didapper *dī'dap-ər, n.* the dabchick or little grebe: one who disappears and bobs up again. [**dive** and **dapper,** a variant of **dipper;** cf. O.E. *dūfedoppa*, pelican.]

didascalic *did-as-kal'ik, adj.* didactic. [Gr. *didaskalikos* — *didaskalos*, teacher.]

didder *did'ər, (dial.) v.i.* to shake. [See **dither**.]

did(d)icoy, -coi *did'i-koi,* **didakai, -kei** *did'ə-kī, ns.* an itinerant tinker or scrap-dealer, not a true gypsy. [Romany.]

diddle *did'l, v.t.* to cajole, swindle. — *n.* **didd'ler.** [Origin uncertain.]

didelphic *dī-del'fik, adj.* having or pertaining to a double womb. — *n.pl.* **Didel'phia** the marsupials. — *adjs.* **didel'phian, didel'phic, didel'phine, didel'phous.** — *ns.* **didel'phid** an animal of the **Didel'phidae** (*-ē*) or, less commonly, **Didelphyidae** (*-fī'i-dē*), the opossum family; **Didel'phis** (*-fis;* less commonly **Didelphys**) an American genus of opossums. [Gr. *di-,* double, *delphys,* womb.]

didgeridoo *did'jər-i-dōō', n.* an Australian Aboriginal musical instrument, consisting of a very long tube producing a low-pitched resonant sound. [Aboriginal word.]

dido *dī'dō, (slang) n.* an antic, caper: a frivolous or mischievous act: — *pl.* **dī'does, dī'dos.** — **act dido** to play the fool; **cut up didoes** to behave in an extravagant way. [Origin unknown.]

didrachma *dī-drak'mə,* **didrachm** *dī'dram, ns.* a double drachma. [Gr. *di-,* double, and **drachma**.]

Didunculus *di-dung'kū-lus, n.* a genus of birds — the tooth-billed pigeon of Samoa. [Dim. of *Didus,* zoological name of the dodo, from its similar bill.]

didymium *di-* or *dī-dim'i-əm, n.* a supposed element discovered in 1841, later resolved into neodymium and praseodymium. [Gr. *didymos,* twin, from its constant association with *lanthanum.*]

didymous *did'i-məs, adj.* twin: twinned: growing in pairs: composed of two parts slightly connected. [Gr. *didymos,* twin.]

Didynamia *did-i-nā'mi-ə, n.pl.* a class of plants in the Linnaean system with two long stamens and two short. — *adjs.* **didynā'mian, didyn'amous.** [Gr. *di-,* double, *dynamis,* strength.]

die¹ *dī, v.i.* (or *v.t.* with object *death*) to lose life: to perish: to wither: esp. **be dying** hyperbolically, to languish, suffer, or long, be very eager (for): to become insensible: to merge: — *pr.p* **dy'ing;** *pa.t.* and *pa.p.* **died** *dīd.* — *adj.* **die'-away'** languishing. — **die'-hard** an irreconcilable conservative. — Also *adj.* — **die away** to disappear by degrees, become gradually inaudible; **die back** (*bot.*) to die by degrees from the tip backwards (*n.* **die'back**); **die down** to subside: to die above ground, leaving only roots or rootstocks; **die game** to keep up one's spirit to the last; **die hard** to struggle hard against death, to be long in dying: to be difficult to suppress or eradicate; **die off** to die quickly or in large numbers; **die out** to become extinct, to disappear; **die the death** (*theat. slang*) to arouse no response from one's audience; **never say die** never give up. — See also **dying.** [Prob. from a lost O.E. (Anglian) *dēgan;* but commonly referred to a Scand. root seen in O.N. *deyja, döyja;* akin to M.H.G. *touwen,* whence Ger. *Tod.* The O.E. word in use was *steorfan* (see **starve**).]

die² *dī, n.* (also **dice** *dīs*) a small cube with faces numbered or otherwise distinguished, thrown in gaming, etc.: (also **dice**) a small cubical piece: (also **dice**) hazard: a stamp for impressing coin, etc.: applied to various tools for shaping things by stamping or cutting: — *pl.* (gaming, cookery, and the like) **dice;** (stamping and shaping) **dies** (*dīz*). — *v.i.* **dice** to play with dice. — *v.t.* to cut into dice: to chequer: — *pr.p.* **dic'ing;** *pa.t.* and *pa.p.* **diced.** — *adj.* **diced** ornamented with a chequered pattern: cut into dice. — *ns.* **dic'er; dic'ing** a chequered pattern: dice-playing. — *adj.* **dic'ey** (*coll.*) risky: tricky: uncertain in result. — **dice'-box** an hour-glass-shaped box from which dice are thrown; **dice'-coal** a coal that breaks into cubical blocks; **dice'-play; dice'-player.** — *v.t.* **die'-cast'** to shape (metal or plastic) by casting in a metal mould. — **die'-casting; die'-sink'er; die'-sink'ing** the engraving of dies for embossing, etc.; **die'-stock**

a contrivance for holding the dies used in screw-cutting; **die'-work** ornamentation of a metal surface by impressions with a die. — **dice with death** to take great risks; **no dice** no answer, or a negative answer: no success; **straight as a die** (i.e. a gaming die; *fig.*) completely honest; **the die is cast** an irrevocable step has been taken: there is no turning back now. [O.Fr. *de,* pl. *dez* (Prov. *dat,* It. *dado*), from L.L. *dadus* = L. *datus,* given or cast.]

dieb *dēb, n.* a jackal of northern Africa. [Ar. *dhīb.*]

diedral. Same as **dihedral.**

dièdre *dē-edr', n.* a rock angle, or re-entrant corner, usu. with a crack in it. [Fr.]

diegesis *dī-ē-jē'sis, (rhet.) n.* in an oration, the narration of the facts. [Gr. *diēgēsis.*]

dieldrin *dēl'drin, n.* a crystalline organochlorine compound used as a contact insecticide. [O. *Diels* (1876–1954), German chemist, and **aldrin**.]

dielectric *dī-i-lek'trik, adj.* non-conducting: transmitting electric effects without conducting. — *n.* a substance, solid, liquid or gas, capable of supporting an electric stress, and hence an insulator. — **dielectric constant** relative permittivity (see **permit**); **dielectric heating** the heating of a non-conducting substance as a result of loss of power in dielectric. [Gr. *dia,* through, and **electric**.]

Dielytra *dī-el'i-trə, n.* an erroneous name for *Dicentra* (q.v.). [As if Gr. *di-,* double, and *elytron,* cover.]

diencephalon *dī-en-sef'ə-lon, -kef', n.* the posterior part of the forebrain in vertebrates connecting the cerebral hemispheres with the midbrain. [Pfx. **dia-,** and **encephalon.**]

diene *dī'ēn, n.* an organic compound containing two double bonds between carbon atoms. [Pfx. **di-,** and *-ene* as in **alkene, benzene,** etc.]

dieresis. Same as **diaeresis.**

dies *dī'ēz, dē'ās,* (L.) *n.* day: — *pl.* **dies.** — **dies fasti** or **profesti** (*fas'tī, fäs'tē, pro-fes'tī, -tē*) days on which judgment could be pronounced, on which courts could be held in ancient Rome, lawful days; **dies faustus** (*fös'təs, fows'tōōs*) lucky day; **dies festi** or **feriae** (*fes'tī, -tē, fer'i-ē, -ī*) days of actual festival; **dies infaustus** (*in-fös'təs, in-fows'tōōs*) unlucky day; **dies irae** (*īr'ē, ēr'ī*) the day of wrath: the day of judgment (from a Latin hymn); **dies nefasti** (*ni-fas'tī, ne-fäs'tē*) days on which a judgment could not be pronounced or assemblies of the people be held, in ancient Rome; **dies non** (*non, nōn*) a day on which judges do not sit, or one on which normal business is not transacted.

diesel *dēz'l, n.* a diesel engine: a locomotive, train, etc., driven by a diesel engine: diesel oil. — *v.t.* and *v.i.* **dies'elise, -ize** to equip, or be equipped with, a diesel engine, locomotive or train. — *n.* **dieselisā'tion, -z-.** — *adj.* **dies'el-elec'tric** using power obtained from a diesel-operated electric generator. — **diesel engine** a compression-ignition engine in which the oil fuel is introduced into the heated compressed-air charge as a jet of liquid under high pressure. — *adj.* **dies'el-hydraul'ic** using power transmitted by means of one or more mechanisms (torque convertors) filled with oil. — **diesel oil** heavy fuel oil used in diesel engines. [Rudolph *Diesel* (1858–1913), German engineer.]

diesis *dī'i-sis, n.* the difference between a major and a minor semitone (*mus.*): the double-dagger (‡) (*print.*): — *pl.* **dī'eses** (*-sēz*). [Gr. *diesis,* a quarter-tone.]

diet¹ *dī'ət, n.* mode of living, now only with especial reference to food: planned or prescribed selection of food: allowance of provisions (*obs.*). — *v.t.* to furnish with food: to prescribe a diet for, put on a diet: to keep fasting. — *v.i.* to feed: to take food according to rule. — *n.* **dietā'rian** one who observes prescribed rules for diet. — *adj.* **dī'etary** pertaining to diet or the rules of diet. — *n.* course of diet: allowance of food, esp. in large institutions. — *n.* **dī'eter** one who regulates diet (*Shak.*): one who is on a diet. — *adjs.* **dietet'ic, -al** pertaining to diet. — *adv.* **dietet'ically.** — *n. sing.* **dietet'ics** the study of, or rules for regulating, diet. —

ns. **dī′etist, dīetitian, -cian** (*-ish′ən*) an authority on diet. — **dietary fibre** roughage; **di′et-bread** bread designed for persons on a diet; **di′et-drink** medicated liquor; **diet sheet** a list of permitted foods for a person on a diet. [Fr. *diète* — L.L. *diaeta* — Gr. *diaita*, mode of living, diet.]

diet² *dī′ət, n.* a national, federal, or provincial assembly, council, or parliament, esp. (usu. with *cap.*) the national legislature of Japan: a conference: the proceedings under a criminal libel (*Scots law*): a clerical or ecclesiastical function in Scotland, as a *diet of worship*. — *n.* **dī′etine** a minor or local diet. — **desert the diet** to abandon criminal proceedings under a particular libel — in Scottish usage. [O.Fr. *diete* — L.L. *dīēta* — Gr. *diaita*; or acc. to Littré from L. *diēs*, a (set) day, with which usage cf. Ger. *Tag*, day, *Reichstag*.]

diethyl *dī-eth′il, adj.* having two ethyl groups. — *n.* **diethylamine** (*-mēn′*) a liquid resembling ethylamine, answering to ammonia, with ethyl groups replacing two hydrogen atoms. [Pfx. **di-**.]

Dieu *dyø*, (Fr.) *n.* God. — **Dieu avec nous** (*a-vek noō*) God with us; **Dieu et mon droit** (*ā mõ drwä*) God and my right.

diffarreation *di-far-i-ā′shən, n.* a divorce from a Roman marriage by *confarreation*. [L. *dif-* (*dis-*), asunder.]

differ *dif′ər, v.i.* to be unlike, distinct, or various (used by itself, or followed by *from*): to disagree (with *with*, sometimes *from*): to fall out, dispute (*with*). — *n.* (*Scot.*) difference. — *ns.* **diff′erence,** (*arch.*) **diff′erency** dissimilarity: the quality distinguishing one thing from another: a contention or quarrel: the point in dispute: the excess of one quantity or number over another: differentia: a distinguishing mark: a modification to distinguish the arms of a branch from those of the main line (*her.*): discrimination. — *v.t.* to make or perceive a difference between or in. — *adj.* **diff′erent** distinct: separate: unlike: not the same (with *from*, also *to*, not now *than*): out of the ordinary (*slang*): novel. — *n.* **differentia** (*-en′shi-ə; L.*) in logic, that property which distinguishes a species from others: — *pl.* **differen′tiae** (*-ē*). — *adj.* **differen′tial** (*-shəl*) constituting or pertaining to a difference or differentia: discriminating: pertaining to infinitesimal differences (*math.*). — *n.* an infinitesimal difference: a differential gear: a price or wage difference. — *adv.* **differen′tially.** — *v.t.* **differentiate** (*-en′shi-āt*) to make different, cause to develop difference(s): to classify as different: to constitute a difference between: to obtain the differential coefficient of (*math.*). — *v.i.* to become different by specialisation: to distinguish (*from, between*). — *ns.* **differentiā′tion** the act of distinguishing: description of a thing by giving its differentia: exact definition: a change by which what was generalised or homogeneous became specialised or heterogeneous: the act or process of differentiating, or determining the ratio of the rates of change of two quantities one of which is a function of the other (*math.*); **differen′tiātor** one who or that which differentiates. — *adv.* **diff′erently.** — **difference tone, differential tone** a tone heard when two tones are sounded together, its frequency the difference of their frequencies; **differential calculus** see **calculus; differential coefficient** the ratio of the rate of change of a function to that of its independent variable; **differential equation** one involving total or partial differential coefficients; **differential gear** a gear permitting relative rotation of two shafts driven by a third; **differential motion** a mechanical movement in which the velocity of a driven part is equal to the difference of the velocities of two parts connected to it; **differential thermometer** a thermometer for measuring difference of temperature. — **agree to differ** to agree to accept amicably a difference of opinion without further argument; **difference of opinion** a matter about which two or more people or groups disagree; **with a difference** with something special: in a special way. [L. *differre* — *dif-* (for *dis-*), apart, *ferre*, to bear.]

difficile *di-fis′il, dif′i-sil,* (*arch.* or reintroduced) *adj.*

difficult. [O.Fr. and Fr. *difficile*; see **difficult.**]

difficult *dif′i-kəlt, adj.* not easy: hard to be done: requiring labour and pains: hard to please: not easily persuaded: unmanageable: hard to resolve or extricate oneself from, potentially embarrassing, etc. — *adv.* **diff′icultly** (mainly *chem.*; e.g. *difficultly soluble*). — *n.* **diff′iculty** the quality or fact of being difficult: a difficult situation: laboriousness: obstacle: objection: that which cannot be easily understood or believed: embarrassment of affairs: a quarrel. — **make difficulties** to be hard to please: to make objections. [The adj. was formed from *difficulty* — Fr. *difficulté* — L. *difficultās, -ātis* — *difficilis* — *dif-*(*dis-*), neg., and *facilis*, easy.]

diffident *dif′i-dənt, adj.* distrusting: wanting in selfconfidence. — *n.* **diff′idence.** — *adv.* **diff′idently.** [L. *diffīdēns, -entis*, pr.p. of *diffīdēre*, to distrust — *dif-*(*dis-*), neg., *fīdēre*, to trust — *fīdēs*, faith.]

diffluent *dif′loō-ənt, adj.* readily flowing away: fluid: deliquescent. [L. *dis-*, apart, *fluēns, -entis*, pr.p. of *fluĕre*, to flow.]

difform *di-förm′, adj.* unlike: irregular in form. — *n.* **difform′ity.** [L. *dis-*, apart, *förma*, form.]

diffract *di-frakt′, v.t.* to break up: to subject to diffraction. — *n.* **diffrac′tion** the spreading of light or other rays passing through a narrow opening or by the edge of an opaque body or reflected by a grating, etc., with interference phenomena, coloured and other. — *adj.* **diffrac′tive.** — *ns.* **diffractom′eter** an instrument used in examination of the atomic structure of matter by means of diffraction of X-rays, electrons, or neutrons; **diffrangibil′ity** (*-franj-*). — *adj.* **diffrang′ible** capable of being diffracted. [L. *diffringĕre, diffrāctum* — *dis-*, asunder, *frangĕre*, to break.]

diffuse¹ *di-fūz′, v.t.* to pour out all round: to send out in all directions: to scatter: to circulate: to publish. — *v.i.* to spread. — *adj.* **diffūsed′** spread widely: loose. — *adv.* **diffūs′edly.** — *ns.* **diffūs′edness; diffūs′er; diffūsibil′ity.** — *adj.* **diffūs′ible.** — *ns.* **diffū′sion** a spreading or scattering abroad: extension: distribution: mixture through each other of gases or liquids in contact: spread of cultural elements from one region or community to another (*anthrop.*); **diffū′sionism** (*anthrop.*) the theory that diffusion is mainly responsible for cultural similarities; **diffū′sionist.** — *adj.* **diffū′sive** (*-siv*) extending: spreading widely. — *adv.* **diffū′sively.** — *ns.* **diffū′siveness; diffūsiv′ity.** — **diffused lighting** lighting that is transmitted or reflected in all directions and, being evenly distributed, produces no glare; **diffu′sion= tube** an instrument for determining the rate of diffusion for different gases. [L. *diffundĕre, diffūsum* — *dif-*(*dis-*), asunder, *fundĕre*, to pour out.]

diffuse² *di-fūs′, adj.* diffused: widely spread: wordy: not concise. — *adv.* **diffuse′ly.** — *n.* **diffuse′ness.** [Root as above.]

dig *v.t.* to excavate: to turn up with a spade or otherwise: to get or put by digging: to poke or thrust: to taunt: to understand, approve (*slang*): to take note of (*slang*). — *v.i.* to use a spade: to seek (for) by digging (*lit.* and *fig.*): to burrow: to mine: to lodge (*slang*): to study hard (*U.S. slang*): — *pr.p.* **digg′ing;** *pa.t.* and *pa.p.* **dug,** (*B.*) **digged.** — *n.* an act or course of digging: an archaeological excavating expedition: an excavation made by archaeologists: a poke: a taunt: a hardworking student (*U.S. slang*). — *adj.* **digg′able.** — *ns.* **digg′er** a person or animal that digs: a miner, esp. a gold-miner: an Australian or New Zealand soldier: an Australian coll. form of address: a machine for digging. — *n.pl.* **digg′ings** places where mining is carried on, esp. for gold: lodgings, rooms (abbrev. **digs;** *coll.*; *orig. U.S.*). — **digg′er-wasp** a burrowing wasp of various kinds; **digging stick** a primitive tool, a pointed stick, sometimes weighted, for digging the ground. — **dig in** to cover over by digging: to work hard: to take up a defensive position (*lit.* or *fig.*): to begin eating (*coll.*); **dig oneself in** to entrench oneself: to establish oneself in a position; **dig one's heels in** to refuse to be moved or persuaded; **dig out** to decamp (*U.S. slang*):

to unearth (*lit.* or *fig.*); **dig up** to remove from the ground by digging: to excavate: to obtain by seeking (*coll.*): to produce, esp. reluctantly (*coll.*).   [Prob. O.Fr. *diguer*, to dig; of Gmc. origin.]

digamma *dī-gam'ə, n.* vau, the obsolete sixth letter (F, Ϛ later ϛ) of the Greek alphabet with the sound of our *w*: as a numeral ϛ' = 6, ͵ϛ = 6000. See **episemon.**   [Gr. *di-*, twice, and *gamma*, from its form like one capital Γ over another.]

digamy *dig'ə-mi, n.* a second marriage. — *n.* **dig'amist.** — *adj.* **dig'amous.**   [Gr. *di-*, twice, *gamos*, marriage.]

digastric *dī-gas'trik, adj.* double bellied, or fleshy at each end, as is one of the muscles of the lower jaw.   [Gr. *di-*, double, *gastēr*, the belly.]

digest¹ *di-jest'* (also *ī-*), *v.t.* to dissolve in the stomach: to soften by heat and moisture: to distribute and arrange: to prepare or classify in the mind: to think over, to take in gradually, the meaning and implications of: to endure without protest (e.g. insult). — *v.i.* to be dissolved in the stomach: to be softened by heat and moisture. — *adv.* **digest'edly.** — *n.* **digest'er** one who digests: a close vessel in which by heat and pressure strong extracts are made from animal and vegetable substances. — *n.* **digestibil'ity.** — *adj.* **digest'ible** that may be digested. — *n.* **digestion** (*di-jest'yən*) the dissolving of the food in the stomach: orderly arrangement: exposing to slow heat, etc. — *adj.* **digest'ive** pertaining to digestion: promoting digestion. — *n.* something which promotes digestion: (also **digestive biscuit**) a round, semi-sweet biscuit, the basic ingredient of which is meal. — *adv.* **digest'ively.** — **digestive tract** the alimentary canal.   [L. *dīgerĕre*, *dīgestum*, to carry asunder or dissolve — *dī-* (*dis-*), asunder, and *gerĕre*, to bear.]

digest² *dī'jest, n.* a body of laws collected and arranged, esp. the Justinian code of civil laws: a synopsis: an abstract: a periodical abstract of news or current literature.   [L. *dīgesta*, neut. pl. of *dīgestus*, pa.p. of *dīgerĕre*, to carry apart, to arrange.]

dight *dīt, v.t.* to adorn (*arch.*): to equip (*arch.*): (*dihht*) another spelling of **dicht.** — *adj.* disposed: adorned.   [O.E. *dihtan*, to arrange, prescribe, from L. *dictāre*, to dictate (whence Ger. *dichten*, to write poetry).]

digit *dij'it, n.* a finger or toe: a finger's breadth or ³/₄ inch: a figure used in arithmetic to represent a number: the twelfth part of the diameter of the sun or moon. — *adj.* **dig'ital** pertaining to the fingers, or to arithmetical digits: showing numerical information by a set of digits to be read off, instead of by a pointer on a dial, etc. (as *digital clock*, *digital thermometer*): of electronic circuits, responding to and producing signals which at any given time are at any one of a number of possible discrete levels, generally either one of two levels: of continuous data (e.g. sound signals), separated into discrete units to facilitate transmission, processing, etc., or of the transmission, etc., of sound, etc., in this form. — *n.* a finger: a key of a piano, etc. — *ns.* **digitalin** (*dij-i-tā'lin,* or *dij'it-ə-lin*) a glucoside or mixture of glucosides got from foxglove; **Digitā'lis** the foxglove genus: (without *cap.*) dried foxglove leaves used as a drug. — *adjs.* **dig'itate, -d** consisting of several finger-like sections. — *adv.* **dig'itately.** — *n.* **digitā'tion** finger-like arrangement: a finger-like division. — *adjs.* **digit'-iform** formed like fingers; **dig'itigrade** walking on the toes. — *n.* an animal that walks on its toes. — *n.* **digitīsā'tion, -z-.** — *v.t.* **dig'itise, -ize** to put (data) into digital form, e.g. for use in a digital computer. — *ns.* **dig'itiser, -z-** a machine which does this; **digitō'rium** a pianist's dumb keyboard for finger exercises. — **digital audio tape** (abbrev. **DAT, Dat, dat**) a magnetic audio tape on which sound has been recorded digitally: this form of recorded sound, affording greater clarity and compactness, and less distortion than conventional recording; **digital clock, watch** a clock, watch, without a conventional face, on which the time is indicated directly by numbers; **digital computer** an electronic calculating machine using arithmetical digits, gener-

ally binary or decimal notation; **digital recording** a digital means of storing and transmitting information electronically, e.g. in sound recording where frequency and amplitude features of the sound wave are measured, expressed and stored in digital form (as on compact disc, digital audio tape); **digital socks** socks with individual toe-coverings similar to the fingers of gloves; **digitising board, pad, table, tablet** a device consisting of a flat surface on which diagrams may be drawn with a special stylus, the co-ordinates of the position of the stylus at any given point on the diagram being digitised for storage, etc.   [L. *digitus*, finger, toe.]

digladiate *dī-glad'i-āt, v.i.* to fight with swords: to fence: to wrangle. — *ns.* **digladiā'tion; diglad'iātor.**   [L. *dīgladiārī*, to contend fiercely — *dis-*, this way and that, and *gladius*, sword.]

diglot *dī'glot, adj.* bilingual. — *n.* a bilingual person or book.   [Gr. *diglōttos* — *di-*, double, *glōtta*, tongue.]

diglyph *dī'glif, (archit.) n.* an ornament consisting of a double groove.   [Gr. *di-*, double, *glyphē*, carving.]

dignify *dig'ni-fī, v.t.* to invest with honour: to exalt: to lend an air of dignity to (as *dignify with the name of*): — *pr.p.* **dig'nifying;** *pa.t.* and *pa.p.* **dig'nified.** — *n.* **dignificā'tion.** — *adj.* **dig'nified** marked or consistent with dignity: exalted: noble: grave: ranking as a dignitary.   [L.L. *dīgnificāre* — *dīgnus*, worthy, *facĕre*, to make.]

dignity *dig'ni-ti, n.* the state of being dignified: elevation of mind or character: grandeur of mien: elevation in rank, place, etc.: degree of excellence: preferment: high office: a dignitary. — *n.* **dig'nitary** one in a high position or rank, esp. in the church. — **beneath one's dignity** degrading, at least in one's own estimation; **stand on one's dignity** to assume a manner that asserts a claim to deference.   [Fr. *dignité* — L. *dīgnitās, -ātis* — *dīgnus*, worthy.]

digonal *dig'ə-nl, adj.* of symmetry about an axis, such that a half-turn (180°) gives the same figure.   [Gr. *di-*, twice, *gōniā*, angle.]

digoneutic *dig-ə-nūt'ik, adj.* breeding twice a year.   [Gr. *di-*, twice, *goneus*, a parent.]

digraph *dī'gräf, n.* two letters expressing but one sound, as *ph* in *digraph.*   [Gr. *di-*, twice, *graphē*, a mark, a character — *graphein*, to write.]

digress *dī-gres', di-gres', v.i.* to depart from the main subject: to introduce irrelevant matter. — *n.* **digression** (*-gresh'ən*) a going from the main point: a part of a discourse not upon the main subject. — *adj.* **digress'-ional, digress'ive** of the nature of a digression: departing from the main subject. — *adv.* **digress'ively.**   [L. *dīgredī, digressus* — *dī-*(*dis-*), aside, *gradī*, to step.]

Digynia *dī-jin'i-ə, n.pl.* in various Linnaean classes of plants, an order with two styles or a deeply cleft style. — *adjs.* **digyn'ian; digynous** (*dij'* or *dīj'i-nəs*) digynian: with two styles or two carpels.   [Gr. *di-*, twice, and *gynē*, a woman.]

dihedral *dī-hē'drəl,* sometimes **diedral,** *dī-ē'drəl, adjs.* bounded by two planes, or two plane faces. — *n.* a dihedral angle. — *n.* **dihē'dron** the limiting case of a double pyramid when the vertices coincide. — **dihedral angle** the angle made by the wing of an aeroplane with the horizontal axis.   [Gr. *di-*, twice, *hedrā*, a seat.]

dihybrid *dī-hī'brid, n.* a cross between parents that differ in two independently heritable characters. — Also *adj.* [Gr. *di-*, double, twice, and **hybrid.**]

dihydric *dī-hī'drik, adj.* having two hydroxyl groups. [Pfx. *di-.*]

dijudicate *dī-joō'di-kāt, v.t.* and *v.i.* to judge: to decide. — *n.* **dijudicā'tion.**   [L. *dī-*(*dis-*), asunder, and *jūdicāre*, judge.]

dika *dī'kə, dē'kə, n.* a West Indian simarubaceous tree, *Irvingia gabonensis,* the so-called wild mango. — **di'ka-bread** a compressed mass of dika and other seeds, smelling like chocolate; **di'ka-butter, -oil** a fat expressed from its seeds.   [From a W. African name.]

dikast. See **dicast.**

dik-dik *dik'dik, n.* a name for several very small E. African antelopes, species of *Madoqua*, etc. [Said to be a name in Ethiopia.]

dike¹, dyke *dīk, n.* a trench, or the earth dug out and thrown up: a ditch: a mound raised to prevent inundation: in Scotland, a wall (**dry-stane dike** a wall without mortar; **fail'-dike** a wall of turf), sometimes even a thorn-hedge: an igneous mass injected into a fissure in rocks, sometimes weathered out into wall-like forms (*geol.*): a lavatory (*slang*). — *v.t.* to provide with a dike. — *v.i.* to make a dike. — *n.* **dīk'er** one who makes dikes. [O.E. *dīc,* whence also **ditch,** this and related words in the Germanic languages denoting both a trench dug out and the mound of earth so formed; cf. Ger. *Teich,* a pond, *Deich* (orig. L. Ger.) an embankment, Du. *dijk,* a bank, dam, Dan. *dige,* a bank, dam, Sw. *dike,* a ditch, trench.]

dike², dyke *dīk, (slang) n.* a lesbian. — *adj.* **dīk'ey, dyk'ey.** [Origin unknown.]

diktat *dik·tät', n.* a harsh settlement forced on the defeated or powerless: an order or statement admitting of no opposition. [Ger., something dictated.]

dilacerate *di-las'ər-āt, v.t.* to rend or tear asunder. — *n.* **dilacerā'tion.** [L. *dī-,* asunder, and **lacerate.**]

dilapidate *di-lap'i-dāt, v.t.* to pull down, stone from stone: to waste: to suffer to go to ruin. — *adj.* **dilap'idated** in ruins. — *ns.* **dilapidā'tion** the state of ruin: (*pl.*) damage done to a building during tenancy: impairing of church property during an incumbency: (*pl.*) money paid at the end of an incumbency by the incumbent or his heirs for the purpose of putting the parsonage, etc., in good repair; **dilap'idātor.** [L. *dīlapidāre* — *dī-,* asunder, *lapis, lapidis,* a stone.]

dilate *dī-lāt', di-lāt', v.t.* to spread out in all directions: to enlarge: to set forth at full length (*Shak.*). — *v.i.* to widen: to swell out: to speak at length. — *n.* **dilātabil'-ity.** — *adj.* **dilāt'able** that may be dilated or expanded. — *n.* **dilāt'ancy** the property shown by some colloidal systems of thickening or solidifying under pressure or impact. — *adj.* **dilāt'ant** tending to dilate: showing dilatancy. — *ns.* **dilatation** (-lə-tā'shən) or (irregularly formed) **dilā'tion** expansion: a transformation which produces a figure similar to, but not congruent with, the original (*math.*); **dil'atātor** an instrument or a muscle that expands. — *adj.* **dilāt'ed** expanded and flattened. — *n.* **dilātor** a dilatator: one who dilates (also **dilāt'er**). — *adj.* **dilāt'ive.** [L. *dīlātus* (used as pa.p. of *differre*), from *dī-* (*dis-*), apart, and *lātus,* wide.]

dilatory *dil'ə-tə-ri, adj.* slow: given to procrastination: loitering: tending to delay. — *adv.* **dil'atorily.** — *n.* **dil'atoriness.** [L. *dīlātōrius.* See **dilate.**]

dildo *dil'dō, n.* an object serving as an erect penis substitute (also **dil'doe;** *slang*): word used in refrains of songs (*obs.*): a weak or effeminate man (*obs.*): a cylindrical curl: a W. Indian spiny cactus (*Lemaireocereus hystrix*): — *pl.* **dil'dos, dildoes.** — **dil'do-glass** a cylindrical glass. [Origin uncertain.]

dilemma *di-, dī-lem'ə, n.* a form of argument in which the maintainer of a certain proposition is committed to accept one of two propositions each of which contradicts his original contention (the argument was called a 'horned syllogism', and the victim compared to a man certain to be impaled on one or other of the horns of an infuriated bull, hence the **horns of a dilemma** a position where each of two alternative courses (or of all the feasible courses) is eminently undesirable: (*loosely*) a predicament, problem. — *adj.* **dilemmat'ic.** — **on the horns of a dilemma** in a dilemma (see comments above). [L., — Gr. *dilēmma* — *di-,* twice, double, *lēmma,* an assumption — *lambanein,* to take.]

dilettante *dil-et-an'ti, n.* one who loves the fine arts but in a superficial way and without serious purpose (the *amateur* usually practises them): a dabbler in art, science, or literature: — *pl.* **dilettan'ti** (-tē). — *adj.* **dilettan'tish.** — *ns.* **dilettan'tism, dilettan'teism.** [It., pr.p. of *dilettare* — L. *dēlectāre,* to delight.]

diligent *dil'i-jənt, adj.* steady and earnest in application:

industrious. — *n.* **dil'igence** steady application: industry: a warrant to produce witnesses, books, etc., or a process by which persons or goods are attached (*Scots law*): a French or continental stage-coach (also pronounced *dē-lē-zhäs*) (also **dill'y**). — *adv.* **dil'igently.** [Fr., — *dīligēns, -entis,* pr.p. of L. *dīligĕre,* to choose.]

dill¹ *dil, n.* an umbelliferous annual akin to parsnip, the fruits or 'seeds' used as condiment and carminative. — **dill pickle** pickled cucumber flavoured with dill; **dill'-wat'er** a medicinal drink prepared from the seeds. [O.E. *dile;* Ger. *Dill,* Sw. *dill.*]

dill² *dil, (Austr. coll.) n.* a fool. [Prob. **dilly³.**]

dilli. See **dilly-bag.**

dilling *dil'ing, n.* a darling: the youngest child: the weakling of a litter. [Origin doubtful.]

dilly¹. See **diligence, dilly-bag.**

dilly² *dil'i, (coll.) n.* an excellent or very pleasing person or thing. — Also *adj.* [Perh. contr. of **delightful.**]

dilly³ *dil'i, (Austr. coll.) adj.* foolish, silly. [Prob. **daft** and **silly.**]

dilly-bag *dil'i-bag, n.* an Australian Aboriginal bag, made of woven grass or fibre: a small bag. — Also **dill'i.** **dill'y.** [Aboriginal *dilli,* and **bag.**]

dilly-dally *dil'i-dal'i, v.i.* to loiter, trifle. [Reduplication of **dally;** cf. **shilly-shally.**]

dilucidate *di-lū'si-dāt, di-lōō', (obs.) v.t.* to elucidate. — *n.* **dilucidā'tion.** [L. *dīlūcidāre, -ātum.*]

dilute *di-lūt', di-lōōt',* or *dī, v.t.* to make thinner or more liquid: to diminish the concentration of, by mixing, esp. with water: of labour, to increase the proportion of unskilled to skilled in. — *v.i.* to become mixed. — *adj.* (*di-* or *dī-lūt', -lōōt',* or *dī'*) diminished in concentration by mixing. — *adj.* **diluent** (*dil'ū-ənt*) diluting. — *n.* that which dilutes. — *adj.* **dilut'able.** — *n.* a drink such as a fruit squash which is diluted before being drunk. — *ns.* **dilut'ee** an unskilled worker introduced into a skilled occupation; **dilute'ness; dilut'er, dilut'or** one who or that which dilutes; **dilu'tion.** — *adj.* **dilu'tionary** tending to dilute. [L. *dīluĕre, dīlūtum* — *dī-,* away, *luĕre,* to wash.]

diluvium *dil-ū'vi-əm, dil-ōō', n.* an inundation or flood: a deposit of sand, gravel, etc., made by extraordinary currents of water (*geol.; obs.*). — Also **dilu'vion.** — *adjs.* **dilu'vial, dilu'vian** pertaining to a flood, esp. Noah's: caused by a deluge: composed of diluvium. — *n.* **dilu'vialist** one who explains geological phenomena by the flood. [L. *dīluvium,* a deluge — *dīluĕre,* to wash away.]

dim *dim, adj.* not bright or distinct: obscure: not seeing clearly: mentally dull, stupid (*coll.*). — *v.t.* to make dark: to obscure. — *v.i.* to become dim: — *pr.p.* **dimm'ing;** *pa.t.* and *pa.p.* **dimmed.** — *adv.* **dim'ly.** — *n.* **dimm'er** an arrangement for regulating the supply of light. — *adj.* **dimm'ish** somewhat dim. — *n.* **dim'ness.** — **dim'wit** (*coll.*) a stupid person. — **a dim view** (*coll.*) an unfavourable view; **dim out** to reduce the lighting (of) gradually (*n.* **dim'-out'**). [O.E. *dimm;* akin to O.N. *dimmr,* dark, and Ger. *Dämmerung,* twilight.]

di majorum gentium *dī mə-jō'rəm, -jō', jen'sh(y)əm, dē ma-yō'rŏŏm gen'ti-ŏŏm,* (L.) the divinities of superior rank, i.e. the twelve greater gods of classical mythology.

dimble *dim'bl, n.* a dell, dingle.

dime *dīm, n.* the tenth part of an American dollar, 10 cents. — **dime museum** a cheap show; **dime novel** a cheap novel, usually sensational; **dime store** (*U.S.*) a shop selling cheap goods — orig. costing not more than a dime. — **a dime a dozen** cheap, commonplace. [Fr., orig. *disme,* from L. *decima* (*pars*), a tenth (part).]

dimension *dī-* or *di-men'shən, n.* measure in length, breadth, or thickness (the three dimensions of space): scope, extent (also *fig.*): size: the sum of the indices in a term (*alg.*) a factor, aspect: a concept, development in range or quality, etc. — *v.t.* to give the dimensions of: to make to specified dimensions. — *adjs.* **dimen'sional** concerning dimension: in composition, of so many dimensions; **dimen'sioned; dimen'sionless.** — **di-**

mension work masonry in stones of specified size. — **fourth dimension** an additional dimension attributed to space: in relativity theory, etc., time; **new dimension** (*fig.*) a fresh aspect; **third dimension** depth, thickness: a rounding out, completeness, given by added information, detail, etc. (*fig.*). [Fr., — L. *dīmēnsiō, -ōnis* — *dīmētīrī, dīmēnsus* — *dī* (*dis-*), apart, *mētīrī*, to measure.]

dimer *dī'mər, n.* a compound whose molecule has twice as many atoms as another compound of the same empirical formula (the *monomer*). — *adj.* **dīmeric** (*-mer'ik*). — *n.* **dīmerisā'tion, -z-.** — *v.t.* **dī'merise, -ize.** [Pfx. **di-**, and mono*mer*.]

dimerous *dim'ə-rəs, adj.* consisting of two parts: with two members in each whorl (*bot.*): having two-jointed tarsi (*entom.*). — *adj.* **dimeric** (*dī-mer'ik*) bilaterally symmetrical: dimerous. — *n.* **dimerism** (*dim'ər-izm*). [Gr. *di-*, double, twice, and *meros*, a part.]

dimeter *dim'i-tər, adj.* containing two measures. — *n.* a verse of two measures. [L., — Gr. *dimetros* — *di-*, twice, *metron*, a measure.]

dimethyl *dī-meth'il, n.* ethane. — *adj.* containing two methyl radicals in combination. — *ns.* **dimeth'ylamine** (*-ə-mēn*) a compound answering to ammonia with methyl replacing two hydrogen atoms; **dimethylan'iline** an oily liquid, aniline heated with methyl alcohol and hydrochloric acid — from which dyes are obtained. [Pfx. **di-**, methyl.]

dimetric *dī-met'rik,* (*crystal.*) *adj.* tetragonal. [Pfx. **di-**, and **metric**, pertaining to distance.]

dimidiate *di-mid'i-āt, adj.* divided into halves: having a shape that appears as if halved: having only one side developed: split on one side. — *v.t.* (*her.*) to represent the half of. — *n.* **dimidiā'tion.** [L. *dīmidiāre, -ātum,* to halve — *dīmidius,* half — *dis-,* apart, *medius,* the middle.]

diminish *di-min'ish, v.t.* to make less: to take a part from: to degrade. — *v.i.* to grow or appear less: to subside. — *adjs.* **dimin'ishable; dimin'ished** made smaller: humbled: of a semitone less than perfect or minor (*mus.*). — *n.* and *adj.* **dimin'ishing.** — *adv.* **dimin'ishingly.** — *n.* **dimin'ishment.** — **diminished responsibility** limitation in law of criminal responsibility on ground of mental weakness or abnormality, not merely of actual insanity; **diminishing glass** a lens or combination of lenses that makes objects appear smaller. — **law of diminishing returns** the fact that there is a point beyond which any additional amount of work, expenditure, taxation, etc. results in progressively smaller output, profits, yields, etc. [Coined from **minish**, in imitation of L. *dīminuĕre,* to break in pieces (— *dī-,* — *dis-,* apart, *minuĕre,* to make less) which in L.L. replaced the earlier *dēminuĕre,* to lessen (— *dē,* from, and *minuĕre*).]

diminuendo *di-min-ū-en'dō,* (*mus.*) *adj.* and *adv.* letting the sound die away. — Also *n.:* —*pl.* **-o(e)s.** [It., — L.L. *dīminuendus,* for L. *dēminuendus,* ger. of *dēminuĕre,* to lessen (see **diminish**).]

diminution *dim-in-ū'shən, n.* a lessening: degradation. — *adj.* **dimin'utive** of a diminished size: very small: contracted. — *n.* (*gram.*) a word formed from another to express a little one of the kind. — *adv.* **dimin'utively.** — *n.* **dimin'utiveness.** [L.L. *dīminūtiō,* a lessening, *dīminūtīvus,* diminutive, for earlier *dēminūtiō, dēminūtīvus; see* **diminish**.]

dimissory *dim'is-ə-ri, di-, dī-mis'ə-ri, adj.* sending away or giving leave to depart to another jurisdiction. [L. *dīmissōrius* — *dīmittĕre, dīmissum* — *dis-,* apart, *mittĕre,* to send.]

dimity *dim'i-ti, n.* a stout white cotton, striped or figured in the loom by weaving with two threads. [Gr. *dimitos* — *di-,* twice, *mitos,* a thread.]

dimmer, dimming. See **dim**.

dimorphism *dī-mör'fizm, n.* the occurrence of two forms in the same species (*biol.*): the property of crystallising in two forms (*chem.*). — *n.* **dī'morph** either of the two forms of a dimorphous species or substance. — *adjs.*

dimor'phic, dimor'phous. [Gr. *di-,* twice, *morphē,* form.]

dimple *dim'pl, n.* a small hollow, esp. on the surface of the body. — *v.i.* to form dimples. — *adj.* **dim'pled.** — *n.* **dim'plement.** — *adj.* **dim'ply.** [Apparently cogn. with Ger. *Tümpel,* pool.]

dim sum *dim sum,* a Chinese dish, often eaten as an appetiser, consisting of steamed dumplings with various fillings. [Chin.]

dimyarian *dim-i-* or *dī-mī-ā'ri-ən, adj.* having two adductor muscles. [Gr. *di-,* twice, *mȳs, myos,* muscle.]

din *din, n.* a loud continued noise. — *v.t.* to assail (the ears) with noise: to annoy with clamour: to obtrude noisily and persistently: — *pr.p.* **dinn'ing;** *pa.t.* and *pa.p.* **dinned.** — *adj.* **din'ful.** — **din into** (*coll.*) to instil knowledge into (a person) by forceful repetition. [O.E. *dynn, dyne;* cf. O.N. *dynr,* Dan. *dön,* noise.]

dinanderie *dē-nä-də-rē, n.* domestic decorative brassware, originally that made at *Dinant* in Belgium: extended to Indian and Levantine brassware. [Fr.]

Dinantian *din-an'shi-ən,* (*geol.*) *adj.* Lower Carboniferous. [*Dinant* in Belgium.]

dinar *dē-när', n.* an ancient Arab gold coin of 65 grains' weight: the monetary unit of Yugoslavia, and of Algeria, Tunisia, Iraq, and other Arab countries. [L. *dēnārius.*]

dinarchy. See **diarchy**.

dindle. See **dinnle**.

dine *dīn, v.i.* to take dinner. — *v.t.* to furnish with a dinner. — *n.* (*obs.*) dinner, dinner-time. — *ns.* **din'er** one who dines: a dining-car: a small, cheap restaurant (esp. *U.S.*); **dinette'** an alcove or other part of a room or kitchen set apart for meals. — **din'er-out** one who goes much to dinner parties; **din'ing-car** a railway carriage in which meals are served; **din'ing-hall; din'ing-room; din'ing-table.** — **dine off, on** to have as one's dinner; **dine out** to dine elsewhere than at home; **dine out on** to be invited to dinner, or, loosely, to enjoy social success, on the strength of one's possession of e.g. interesting information; **dine with Duke Humphrey** (*hist.*) to go without a meal, loiter about Duke Humphrey's Walk in Old St Paul's. [O.Fr. *disner* (Fr. *dîner*) prob. — L. *dis-,* expressing undoing, and *jējūnus,* fasting (cf. **disjune**); according to others — L. *dē-,* intens. and *cēna,* a meal.]

ding[1] *ding, v.t.* to dash: to beat: to thump: to knock: to surpass (*Scot.*). — *v.i.* to beat: to dash: — *pa.t.* **dinged, dang, dung;** *pa.p.* **dinged, dung.** — *n.* **ding'er** (*slang*) anything superlative in its kind. — **ding doun** (*dōōn, Scot.*) to knock or throw down. [M.E. *dingen, dyngen;* cf. O.N. *dengja,* Sw. *dänga,* to bang.]

ding[2] *ding, v.i.* to ring, keep sounding. — *v.t.* to reiterate to a wearisome degree. — **ding'-dong'** the sound of bells ringing: monotony: sameness: an argument or fight. — *adj.* and *adv.* like a bell ringing: hammer-and-tongs: keenly contested with rapid alternations of success. — *v.t.* and *v.i.* to ring: to nag. [Imit., but partly confounded with preceding.]

Ding an sich *ding an zihh,* (Ger.; *philos.*) the thing-in-itself, noumenon.

dingbat *ding'bat,* (*U.S. slang*) *n.* something whose name one has forgotten, or does not want to use: a foolish or eccentric person: a tramp: money. — *adj.* **ding'bats** (*Austr.* and *N.Z. coll.*) daft, crazy. — **the dingbats** (*Austr.* and *N.Z. coll.*) delirium tremens. [Perh. **ding**[1] and **bat**[1].]

dinge. See **dingy**.

dinges *ding'əs, n.* an indefinite name for any person or thing whose name one cannot or will not remember. — Also **ding'us.** [Du., — Afrik. *ding,* thing; cf. Eng. **thingummy, thingumbob**.]

dinghy, dingy, dingey *ding'gi, n.* a small rowing-boat or ship's tender: an airman's collapsible rubber boat. [Hind. *dingī,* a small boat.]

dingle *ding'gl, n.* a dell. [Origin uncertain.]

dingle-dangle *ding'gl-dang'gl, adv.* swinging to and fro. [Reduplication of **dangle**.]

dingo *ding'gō, n.* the wild dog of Australia: — *pl.* **ding'oes.** [Name in obs. Aboriginal dialect.]

dingus. See **dinges.**

dingy *din'ji, adj.* of a dim or dark colour: dull: soiled. — *n.* **dinge** dinginess. — *v.t.* to make dingy. — *n.* **din'giness.** — See also **dinghy.** [Origin obscure.]

dinic *din'ik, adj.* relating to vertigo or dizziness. — *n.* a remedy for dizziness. [Gr. *dīnos,* whirling.]

dinitro- *dī-nī'trō-,* in composition, having two nitro-groups (NO₂), esp. replacing hydrogen. — *n.* **dinitro-ben'zene** $C_6H_4(NO_2)_2$, answering to *benzene,* C_6H_6.

dink[1] *dingk, (Scot.) adj.* neat, trim. — *v.t.* to dress neatly. — *adj.* **dink'y** *(coll.)* neat: dainty: trivial, insignificant *(U.S.).*

dink[2] *dingk, (tennis) n.* a drop-shot, esp. one that drops just past the net. — *v.t.* and *v.i.* to play such a shot. [Imit.]

dinkum *ding'kəm, (Austr. coll.) adj.* real, genuine: square, honest. — Also *adv.* — Emphatically **fair dinkum.** — Also **dink'y-di(e).** [E. dial. *dinkum,* a fair share of work.]

dinky[1] *ding'ki, n.* double- (or dual-) income *no kids* — coll. acronym applied to a member of a young, childless (usu. married) couple both earning a good salary, who thus enjoy an affluent life-style: — *pl.* **dink'ies.**

dinky[2]. See **dink**[1].

dinmont *din'mənt, n.* a Border name for a male sheep between the first and second shearing. [Origin obscure.]

dinner *din'ər, n.* the chief meal of the day: a feast. — *v.i.* to dine. — *v.t.* to provide with dinner. — *adj.* **dinn'erless.** — **dinn'er-dance** a dance following a dinner; **dinn'er-gown** a less formal evening dress; **dinn'er-hour;** **dinn'er-jacket** a tailless dress-coat; **dinner lady** one who cook and/or serves meals in a school canteen; **dinn'er-pail** a vessel in which a workman carries his dinner; **dinner party** a party at which dinner is served; **dinn'er-service, -set** a complete set of plates and dishes for a company at dinner; **dinn'er-table; dinn'er-time; dinn'er-wagon** orig. a shelved trolley for a dining-room: a sideboard in two tiers. [O.Fr. *disner,* prop. breakfast; see **dine.**]

dinnle *din'l, (Scot.) v.i.* to tingle: to shake, vibrate. — *v.t.* to cause to tingle, shake or vibrate. — *n.* a thrill, vibration, tremor, tingling. — Also **din'dle.** [Prob. imitative.]

dino-, *(arch.)* **deino-** *dī-nō-,* in composition, huge, terrible. — *ns.* **Dinoceras, Deinoceras** *(-nos'ə-rəs;* Gr. *keras,* horn)* a large Eocene fossil stump-footed ungulate of Wyoming, otherwise Uintatherium, named from three pairs of protuberances on the skull; **Dinornis, Deinornis** *(dī-nör'nis;* Gr. *ornis,* a bird)* a genus of moas, including the biggest; **dinosaur, deinosaur** *(dī'nə-sör;* Gr. *sauros,* a lizard) any extinct (Mesozoic) reptile of the order **Dinosaur'ia** in length from two to eighty feet: a chance survivor of a type characteristic of a bygone era *(fig.);* **Dinotherium, Deinotherium** *(-thē'ri-əm;* Gr. *thērion,* a beast) a huge extinct (Tertiary) proboscidean, with elephant-like tusks and trunk. [Gr. *deinos,* terrible.]

dinoflagellate *dī-nō-flaj'ə-lāt, n.* a unicellular organism, a plant-like flagellate with two flagella. [Gr. *dīnos,* whirl, and **flagellate.**]

Dinornis, dinosaur, etc. See **dino-.**

dint *dint, n.* a blow or stroke: the mark of a blow (often **dent**): force (as in *by dint of*). — *v.t.* to make a dint in. [O.E. *dynt,* a blow; cf. **dunt;** O.N. *dyntr.*]

diocese *dī'ə-sis, -sēs, n.* the circuit or extent of a bishop's jurisdiction. — *adj.* **diocesan** *(dī-os'i-sn, -zn)* pertaining to a diocese. — *n.* a bishop in relation to his diocese: one of the clergy in the diocese. [Through Fr. and L. from Gr. *dioikēsis* — *dioikeein,* to keep house — *di-,* for *dia-,* sig. completeness, *oikeein,* to keep house — *oikos,* a house.]

diode *dī'ōd, n.* the simplest electron tube with heated cathode and anode: a two-electrode semiconductor device evolved from primitive crystal rectifiers. [Gr. *di-,* twice, *hodos,* way.]

Diodon *dī'ə-don, n.* a genus of globe-fishes with all the teeth in each jaw consolidated. [Gr. *dis-,* twice, double, *odous, odontos,* a tooth.]

dioecious *dī-ē'shəs, adj.* having the sexes separate: having male or female flowers on different plants. — *n.pl.* **Dioe'cia** a class in the Linnaean system, dioecious plants. — *n.* **dioe'cism** *(-sizm).* [Gr. *di-,* twice, *oikos,* a house.]

dioestrus *(U.S. diestrus) dī-ēs'trəs, n.* a sexually quiescent period following ovulation, in the oestrous cycle in mammals.

Diogenic *dī-ə-jen'ik, adj.* pertaining to the Cynic philosopher *Diogenes (c.* 412–323 B.C.): cynical.

Dionaea *dī-ə-nē'ə, n.* Venus's fly-trap, Venus Fly Trap *(Dionaea muscipula)* an American droseraceous insectivorous plant. [L., — Gr. *Dīōnaiā,* Aphrodite, from her mother *Dīōnē.*]

Dionysia *dī-ə-niz'i-ə,* or *nis', n.pl.* dramatic and orgiastic festivals in honour of *Dīonȳsos* (Bacchus), god of wine. — *adjs.* **Dionys'iac** Bacchic; **Dionys'ian** relating to *Dīonȳsos* or to *Dīonȳsios* (Dionysius — of Syracuse, the Areopagite, Exiguus, or any other of the name).

Diophantine *dī-ə-fan'tīn, adj.* pertaining to the Alexandrian mathematician *Diophantos (c.* A.D. 275). — **Diophantine analysis** the part of algebra which treats of finding particular rational values for general expressions under a surd form; **Diophantine equations** *(math.)* indeterminate equations for which integral or rational solutions are required.

Diophysite. See **Diphysite.**

diopside *dī-op'sīd, n.* a strongly birefringent monoclinic calcium-magnesium pyroxene. [Gr. *di-,* double, *opsis,* a view.]

dioptase *dī-op'tās, n.* an emerald-green acid copper silicate. [L., — Gr. *dia,* through, *optazein,* to see; from its internal glitter.]

dioptric, -al *dī-op'trik, -əl, adjs.* pertaining to dioptrics or a diopter: transparent (as a *dioptric beehive*). — *n.* **diop'ter** an ancient form of theodolite: the index-arm of a graduated circle: (also **diop'tre**) a unit of measurement of the power of a lens, the reciprocal of the focal distances in metres, negative for a divergent lens. — *adj.* **diop'trate** *(entom.)* having the compound eye divided transversely. — *n. sing.* **diop'trics** the part of optics that treats of refraction. [Gr. *dioptrā,* a levelling instrument, *dioptron,* a spyglass — *dia,* through, and the root of *opsesthai,* used as fut. of *horaein,* to see.]

diorama *dī-ə-rä'mə, n.* an exhibition of translucent pictures seen through an opening with lighting effects: a miniature three-dimensional scene with figures: a display of e.g. a stuffed animal in a naturalistic setting: a miniature film or television set. — *adj.* **dioräm'ic.** [Gr. *dia,* through, *horāma,* a sight.]

diorism *dī'ə-rizm, n.* distinction, definition. — *adjs.* **dioris'tic, -al.** — *adv.* **dioris'tically.** [Gr. *diorizein,* to divide, *dia,* through, *horos,* a boundary.]

diorite *dī'ə-rīt, n.* a crystalline granular igneous rock composed of plagioclase and hornblende. — *adj.* **diorit'ic.** [Gr. *diorizein,* to distinguish — *dia,* through, *horos,* a boundary.]

diorthosis *dī-ör-thō'sis, n.* the reduction of a dislocation *(surg.):* the correction of a deformity: a critical revision of a text. — *adj.* **diorthot'ic.** [Gr. *dia,* through, *orthos,* straight.]

Dioscorea *dī-os-kör'i-ə, -kōr'i-ə, n.* the yam genus, of the monocotyledonous family **Dioscoreā'ceae.** — *adj.* **dioscoreā'ceous.** [From the 1st-century (A.D.) Greek physician *Dioskoridēs.*]

Dioscuri *dī-os-kū'rī, n.pl.* Castor and Pollux, as sons of Zeus. [Gr. *Dios,* gen. of *Zeus,* and *koros* (Ionian *kouros*), a son, a lad.]

diosgenin *dī-os'jən-in, n.* a crystalline substance obtained from the Mexican yam (genus Dioscorea), used in the preparation of steroid hormones.

diota *dī-ō'tə, n.* a two-handled ancient vase.   [Gr. *dīotos*, two-handled — *di-*, twice, *ous, ōtos*, ear.]

Diothelism, Diothelite. See **ditheletism.**

dioxan *dī-oks'ən*, **dioxane** *-ān*, (*chem.*) *ns.* a colourless, flammable, toxic liquid, $C_4H_8O_2$, used as a solvent for waxes, resins, etc.

dioxide *dī-ok'sīd, n.* an oxide with two atoms of oxygen in the molecule.   [Pfx. **di-**, **oxide.**]

dioxin *dī-ok'sin, n.* an extremely toxic poison found in certain weedkillers which causes cancer, skin, liver, and kidney disease, and birth defects.

dip *dip, v.t.* to immerse for a time: to lower: to lower and raise again (as a flag): to baptise by immersion: to lift by dipping (usu. with *up*): to dye or clean by dipping: to moisten, suffuse (*Milt.*): to involve in money difficulties (*coll.*): to mortage: to pawn. — *v.i.* to plunge and emerge: to sink: to reach down into something: to enter slightly: to fish by lowering the bait slightly into the water, then bobbing it gently on the surface: to look cursorily: to incline downwards: to dip snuff (see below): — *pr.p.* **dipp'ing**; *pa.t.* and *pa.p.* **dipped.** — *n.* the act of dipping: a hollow: a sag: that which is taken by dipping: inclination downwards: a sloping: the angle a stratum of rock makes with a horizontal plane (*geol.*): a bath: a short swim: a liquid in which anything is dipped (as sheep, garments, etc.): a creamy mixture into which bread, biscuits, etc., are dipped: a candle made by dipping a wick in tallow: a pickpocket (*slang*). — *ns.* **dipp'er** one that dips: a ladle: a bucket or scoop of a dredge or excavator: a contrivance for directing motor-car headlights upwards or downwards (also **dip'-switch**): a dipping bird (*Cinclus*), the water-ouzel: dabchick (*U.S.*): (with *cap.*) the Plough (*astron.*): a nickname for a Baptist, esp. a Dunker; **dipp'ing** the action of the verb: snuff-dipping. — **dip'-circle** or **dipp'ing-needle** an instrument for determining magnetic dip: **dip'-net** a long-handled net for dipping up fish: **dip'-pipe** a pipe with submerged outlet, esp. in gas-works; **dip'-sec'tor** an instrument for determining the dip of the visible horizon; **dip'-slope'** (*geol.*) a slope of ground coinciding with the dip of the rocks; **dip-stick** a rod for measuring depth of liquid in a sump, etc.; **dip'-switch** see **dipper**; **dip'-trap** a bend in a pipe containing liquid to cut off gases. — **dip in** to take a share; **dip into** to put one's hand into to remove something: to read cursorily in; **dip of the horizon** the angle of the visible horizon below the level of the eye; **dip of the needle** the angle a balanced magnetic needle makes with the horizontal plane; **dip snuff** orig., in the southern U.S., to rub the gums and teeth with a wet stick dipped in snuff: to suck a pinch or small bag of snuff held between one's cheek and gum (*ns.* **snuff'-dipper**; **snuff'-dipping**).   [O.E. *dyppan*, causal of *dȳpan*, to plunge in — *dēop*, deep; cf. Dan. *dyppe*; Ger. *taufen*, to immerse.]

dipchick *dip'chik*. Same as **dabchick.**

di penates *dī pə-nā'tēz, dē pe-nä'tās*, (L.) household gods.

dipeptide *dī-pep'tīd*, (*chem.*) *n.* a peptide formed by the combination of two amino-acids.   [Pfx. **di-**, and **peptide** (see **pepsin**).]

dipetalous *dī-pet'ə-ləs, adj.* having two petals.   [Gr. *di-*, twice, and *petalon*, a leaf.]

diphenyl *dī-fē'nil, n.* a hydrocarbon, $C_{12}H_{10}$, consisting of two phenyl groups, used as a fungicide, in dye-manufacture, etc. (also **bīphē'nyl**) — *adj.* having two phenyl groups, esp. replacing hydrogen.

diphone *dī'fōn, n.* a shorthand sign representing a diphthongal sound.   [Gr. *di-*, twice, *phōnē*, sound.]

diphtheria *dif-thē'ri-ə, n.* an infectious throat disease in which the air-passages become covered with a leathery membrane. — *adjs.* **diphtheric** (*-ther'ik*), **diphtheritic** (*-thər-it'ik*). — *n.* **diphtherī'tis** diphtheria. — *adj.* **diph'-theroid.**   [Fr. *diphthérie*, *diphthérite* (now *diphtérie*) — Gr. *diphtherā*, leather.]

diphthong *dif'thong, n.* two vowel-sounds pronounced as one syllable (as in *out, mind*): (*loosely*) a digraph: the ligature æ or œ. — *adjs.* **diphthongal** (*-thong'gəl*),

diphthongic (*-thong'gik*). — *adv.* **diphthong'ally.** — *v.t.* **diph'thongise, -ize** (*-gīz*).   [O. Fr. *di(p)tongue* (Fr. *diphtongue*), — L. *dip(h)thongus* — Gr. *diphthongos* — *di-*, twice, *phthongos*, sound, vowel, reconstructed to more closely resemble the Greek.]

diphycercal *dif-i-sûr'kəl, adj.* having the tail symmetrical about the vertebral column, which runs horizontally (of fishes, etc.).   [Gr. *diphyēs*, of double nature, twofold, *kerkos*, a tail.]

diphyletic *di-*, *dī-fil-et'ik*, (*biol.*) *adj.* of dual origin: descended from two distinct ancestral groups.   [Gr. *di-*, double, *phÿletikos*, pertaining to a tribesman — *phÿlē*, a tribe.]

diphyodont *dif'i-ō-dont, adj.* having two sets of teeth (milk and permanent). — *n.* a mammal with these.   [Gr. *diphyēs*, of double nature, *odous, odontos*, a tooth.]

Diphysite *dif'i-zīt, -sīt, n.* a believer in the existence of two natures in Christ, a divine and a human — opp. to *Monophysite.* — Also **Dyoph'ysite,** less correctly **Dioph'ysite.** — *n.* **Diph'ysitism** (*-it-izm*). — All words also without *cap.*   [Gr. *di-*, double, *physis*, nature.]

dipleidoscope *di-plī'də-skōp, n.* an instrument for ascertaining the moment of meridian passage by observing the coincidence of two images.   [Gr. *diploos*, double, *eidos*, appearance, *skopeein*, to view.]

diplex *dī'pleks, adj.* pertaining to the transmission of two simultaneous messages over one wire in the same direction.   [**duplex**, with substitution of Gr. *di-*, double.]

dipl(o)- *dip-l(-ō)-*, in composition, double. — *ns.* **Diplod'ocus** (Gr. *dokos*, beam, bar, from its appearance) a gigantic, quadrupedal, herbivorous dinosaur of the sauropod group, remains of which have been found in the Jurassic rocks of the Rocky Mountains; **dip'logen** (from **hydrogen**) an alternative name for deuterium or heavy hydrogen; **diplogen'esis** (Gr. *genesis*, generation) doubling of parts normally single. — *adj.* **dip'loid** (Gr. *eidos*, form; *biol.*) having the full or unreduced number of chromosomes characteristic of the species, as in body cells: opp. to *haploid.* — *ns.* **diploid'y; dip'lon** an alternative name for deuteron, the nucleus of heavy hydrogen; **diplont** (Gr. *on, ontos, pr.p.* of *einai*, to be; *biol.*) an animal or plant body containing diploid nuclei; **diplō'pia** (Gr. *ōps*, eye) double vision. — *adj.* **diplostē'monous** (Gr. *stēmōn*, a thread; *bot.*) having two whorls of stamens, the outer alternating with the petals, the inner with the outer. — *n.* **Diplozō'on** (Gr. *zōion*, an animal) a flat-worm that lives fused together in pairs parasitically upon the gills of minnows, etc.   [Gr. *diploos*, double.]

diploe *dip'lō-ē*, (*anat.*) *n.* the spongy tissue between the hard inner and outer tables of the skull.   [Gr. *diploē*, doubling, fold.]

diplogen, -genesis, diploid. See **dipl(o)-.**

diploma *di-plō'mə, n.* a document conferring some honour or privilege, as a university degree, etc. — *v.t.* to furnish with a diploma. — *ns.* **diplomacy** (*di-plō'mə-si*, or *-plo'*) the art of negotiation, esp. in relations between states: tact in management of persons concerned in any affair; **diplomat** (*dip'lə-mat*) one employed or skilled in diplomacy; **diplomate** (*dip'lə-māt*) one who holds a diploma. — *v.t.* to confer a diploma on. — *ns.* **diplomatese** (*-ēz'*; *coll.*) the jargon or obscure language used by diplomats; **diplomatic** (*-mat'ik*) a minister at a foreign court: diplomatics. — *n. sing.* **diplomat'ics** the science of deciphering ancient writings, as charters, etc. — palaeography. — *adjs.* **diplomat'ic, -al** pertaining to diplomacy: tactful and skilful in negotiation. — *adv.* **diplomat'ically.** — *v.i.* and *v.t.* **diplo'matise, -ize** to practice, or effect by, diplomacy. — *ns.* **diplo'matist** a diplomat; **diplomatol'ogy** the study or science of diplomatics, charters, decrees, etc. — **diplomatic bag** a bag used for sending documents, etc., to and from embassies, free of customs control: the contents of such a bag; **diplomatic corps** the whole body of foreign diplomatists resident in any capital; **diplomatic immunity** immunity from local laws and taxation enjoyed by diplomats abroad; **diplomatic relations** formal relations between states marked by the presence of diplomats in each other's country. [L., — Gr. *diplōma*, a letter folded double — *diploos*, double.]

diplon, diplopia, etc. See **dipl(o)-**.

Dipnoi *dip'nō-ī, n.pl.* the lung-fishes. — *adj.* and *n.* **dip'nōan.** — *adj.* **dip'nōous** having both lungs and gills. [Gr. *di-*, double, *pnoē*, breath.]

Dipodidae *dī-pod'i-dē, n.pl.* the jerboa family of rodents. [Gr. *dipous,* two-footed — *di-,* twice, and *pous, podos* a foot.]

dipody *dip'ə-di, (pros.) n.* a double foot. [Gr. *di-,* double, *pous, podos,* foot.]

dipolar *dī-pō'lər, adj.* having two poles. — *n.* **di'pole** two equal and opposite electric charges or magnetic poles of opposite sign a small distance apart: a body or system having such: a type of aerial. [Pfx. **di-**.]

dippy *dip'i, (coll.) adj.* crazy: insane. [Origin obscure.]

diprionidian *dī-prī-ə-nid'i-ən, adj.* serrated on both sides (of graptolites). [Gr. *di-,* twice, *prīōn,* a saw.]

diprotodont *dī-prō'tō-dont, n.* any marsupial of the **Diprotodont'ia,** the suborder (in some classifications) including kangaroos, wombats, etc., with one pair of incisors in the lower jaw. — *ns.* **Dīprō'tōdon** an extinct genus, the largest known marsupials: (without *cap.*) an animal of this genus; **diprotodon'tid** an animal of the **Diprotodon'tidae** (-*ē*), an extinct family of marsupials including the genus Diprotodon. [Gr. *di-,* twice, *prōtos,* first, *odous, odontos,* tooth.]

Dipsacus *dip'sə-kəs, n.* the teasel genus, giving name to the **Dipsacā'ceae,** akin to the valerian and madder families. [Gr. *dipsakos,* teasel — *dipsa,* thirst, because the leaf-axils hold water.]

dipsas *dip'sas, n.* a snake whose bite was believed to cause intense thirst: (*pl.* **dip'sades** (-*dēz*): (with *cap.*) a genus of non-venomous snakes. [Gr. *dipsas* — *dipsa,* thirst.]

dipsomania *dip-sō-mā'ni-ə, n.* an intermittent morbid craving for alcoholic stimulants. — *n.* **dipsomā'niac** one who suffers from dipsomania (coll. **dip'sō:** — *pl.* **dip'sōs**). [Gr. *dipsa,* thirst, *maniā,* madness.]

Diptera *dip'tər-ə, n.pl.* two-winged insects or flies. — *adj.* **dip'teral** two-winged: with double peristyle. — *ns.* **dip'teran** a dipterous insect; **dip'terist** a student of flies; **dip'teros** a building with double peristyle or colonnade. — *adj.* **dip'terous** with two wings or winglike expansions. [Gr. *dipteros,* two-winged, *di-,* twice, *pteron,* a wing.]

dipterocarp *dip'tər-ō-kärp, n.* any tree of the genus **Dipterocarp'us** or its family **Dipterocarpā'ceae** (chiefly Indian), in which some of the sepals enlarge as wings for the fruit. — *adjs.* **dipterocarpā'ceous, dipterocarp'ous.** [Gr. *di-,* double, *pteron,* wing, *karpos,* fruit.]

diptych *dip'tik, n.* a double-folding writing-tablet: a register of bishops, saints, etc., read aloud during the eucharist: a pair of pictures as folding-tablets. [Gr. *diptychos* — *di-,* and *ptychē,* a tablet, a fold.]

dirdum, dirdam *dir'dəm, (Scot.) n.* uproar: a scolding, punishment. [Origin obscure.]

dire *dīr, adj.* dreadful: calamitous in a high degree. — *adj. (poet.)* **dire'ful.** — *adv.* **dire'fully.** — *n.* **dire'fulness.** [L. *dīrus.*]

direct *di-rekt', dī'rekt, adj.* straight: straightforward: by the shortest way: forward, not backward or oblique: at right angles: immediate: without intervening agency or interposed stages: (of a dye) fixing itself without a mordant: in the line of descent: outspoken: sincere: unambiguous: unsophisticated in manner. — *n. (mus.)* an indication of the first note or chord of next page or line. — *adv.* straight: by the shortest way: without deviation, intervening agency or interposed stages. — *v.t.* to keep or lay straight: to point or aim: to point out the proper course to: to guide: to order: to address, mark with the name and residence of a person: to plan and superintend (the production of a film or play). — *v.i.* to act as director: to direct letters, etc. — *n.*

direc'tion aim at a certain point: the line or course in which anything moves or on which any point lies: guidance: command: the body of persons who guide or manage a matter: the address, or written name and residence of a person. — *adjs.* **direc'tional** relating to direction in space; **direc'tionless** not moving, looking, etc. in any particular direction: aimless; **direct'ive** having power or tendency to direct. — *n.* a general instruction. — *n.* **directiv'ity** the property of being directional. — *adv.* **direct'ly** in a direct manner: without intermediary: immediately (in time and otherwise). — *conj.* (often with *that; coll.*) as soon as. — *ns.* **direct'ness; direct'or** one who directs: one who directs the shooting of a motion picture: a manager or governor: a member of a board conducting the affairs of a company: a counsellor: a father confessor or spiritual guide: part of a machine or instrument which guides the motion: in automatic trunk dialling, the apparatus which obtains a channel through exchange junctions to the required exchange. a device that continuously calculates the position of a moving target and supplies firing data: — *fem.* **direct'ress, direct'rix.** — *ns.* **direct'orate** the office of director: a body of directors: (with *cap.*) the French Directory or Directoire. — *adjs.* **directorial** (-*tō', -tō'*); **direct'ory** containing directions: guiding. — *n.* a body of directions: a guide: a book with the names and residences of the inhabitants of a place: a body of directors: (with *cap.*) the *Directoire,* or French Republican government of 1795–99. — *ns.* **direc'torship; direct'rix** a directress: a line serving to describe a conic section, which is the locus of a point whose distances from focus and directrix have a constant ratio (*geom.*): — *pl.* **directrices** (-*trī'sēz*). — **direct access** same as **random access; direct action** coercive methods of attaining industrial or political ends as opposed to pacific, parliamentary, or political action; **direct current** an electric current flowing in one direction only; **direct debiting** an arrangement by which a creditor can claim payment direct from the payer's account; **direct drilling** the ploughing and sowing of a field in one operation; **directional aerial** one that can receive or transmit radio waves in one direction only; **direc'tion-finder** a wireless receiver that determines the direction of arrival of incoming waves; **direct labour** labour employed directly, not through a contractor; **direct method** a method of teaching a foreign language through speaking it, without translation, and without formal instruction in grammar; **direct motion** (*mus.*) progression of parts in the same direction; **direct object** word or group of words denoting that upon which the action of a transitive verb is directed; **director circle** the locus of the intersection of a pair of tangents to a conic at right angles to each other; **direct'or-gen'eral** a chief administrator of a usu. non-commercial organisation; **director's chair** a light folding chair with seat and back of canvas or similar material and arm-rests; **direct speech** speech reported as spoken, in the very words of the speaker (L. *ōrātiō recta*); **direct tax** one levied directly from those on whom its burden falls. — **directed-energy weapon** a weapon whose destructive force consists of beams of light, electromagnetic pulses, subatomic particles, or the like; **direct-grant school** until 1979, a fee-paying school which received a state grant on condition that it took a specified number of non-fee-paying pupils. [L. *dirigĕre, dirēctum* — *di-,* apart, *regĕre,* to rule.]

Directoire *dē-rek-twär, n.* the French Directorate of 1795–99. — *adj.* after the fashion in dress or furniture then prevailing: of knickers, knee-length, with elastic at waist and knee. [Fr.; see **direct.**]

directrix. See **direct.**

diremption *dī-remp'shən, n.* separation into two, disjunction. — *v.t.* **dirempt'.** [L. *diremptiō, -ōnis* — *dirimĕre, diremptus,* to separate, cf. **diriment.**]

dirge *dûrj, n.* a funeral song or hymn: a slow and mournful piece of music. [Contracted from *dīrige* (imper. of L. *dīrigĕre,* to direct), the first word of an antiphon sung in the office for the dead — the words from the Vulgate, Psalm v. 8.]

dirham *dûr-ham', də-ram', dē'ram*, **dirhem** *dûr-hem', ns.* an oriental unit of weight, orig. two-thirds of an Attic drachma (usu. **dirhem**): (the following usu. **dirham**) the monetary unit of Morocco: a coin equal to this in value: a coin used in several N. African and Middle Eastern countries, with varying value. — Also **derham'**. [Ar., Pers., and Turk. forms of the Greek *drachmē*, a drachma or dram.]

dirige *dir'i-ji, n.* a dirge.

dirigible *dir'i-ji-bl, -rij', adj.* that can be directed. — *n.* a navigable balloon or airship. — *adj.* **dir'igent** directing. [See **direct**.]

dirigism(e) *dē-rēzh-ēzm', n.* control by the State in economic and social spheres. — *adj.* **dirigiste** *(-ēst').* [Fr., — It. *dirigismo*.]

diriment *dir'i-mənt, adj.* nullifying. [L. *dirimĕre*.]

dirk¹ *dûrk, n.* a Highland dagger: a side-arm worn by midshipmen and naval cadets *(hist.)*. — *v.t.* to stab with a dirk. [Orig. Scots, in form *durk*; ety. uncertain, but cf. Du., Dan., Sw. *dolk*, dagger; Ir. *duirc* is probably from the English word.]

dirk², dirke *dûrk, adj., adv.* and *v.t. (Spens.)* for **dark, darkly, darken.**

dirl *dirl, (Scot.) v.i.* and *v.t.* to (cause to) thrill, vibrate. — *n.* vibration: a tingling as after a blow. [**drill, thrill.**]

dirndl *dûrn'dl, n.* an Alpine peasant woman's dress with close-fitting bodice and full skirt: an imitation of this, esp. a full skirt with a tight, often elasticated, waistband. [Ger. dial., dim. of *dirne*, girl.]

dirt *dûrt, n.* any filthy substance, such as dung, mud, etc.: foreign matter adhering to anything: loose earth: rubbish: obscenity: spiteful gossip. — *v.t.* to make dirty. — *adv.* **dirt'ily.** — *n.* **dirt'iness.** — *adj.* **dirt'y** foul, filthy: stormy: obscene: unclean in thought or conversation: despicable: mean: sordid: dishonest, treacherous. — *v.t.* to soil with dirt: to sully: — *pr.p.* **dirt'ying;** *pa.t.* and *pa.p.* **dirt'ied.** — **dirt'-bed** a quarryman's term for a layer representing an old soil, esp. in the Purbeck group. — *adj.* **dirt'-cheap'** cheap as dirt, very cheap. — **dirt'-eating** a practice of eating clay as among various primitive peoples: a morbid impulse to eat dirt; **dirt farmer** *(U.S.)* one who farms his own land, esp. without hired help; **dirt'-pie** mud moulded by children in play; **dirt'-road** *(U.S.)* a soft road, unpaved and unmacadamised. — *adj.* **dirt'-rott'en** *(Shak.)* wholly decayed. — **dirt'-track** a rough unsurfaced track: a motor-cycling racing-track, with earthy or cindery surface; **dirty bomb** one that produces a large amount of radioactive contamination; **dirty dog** *(slang)* a dishonest or contemptible person; **dirty look** *(coll.)* a threatening or malevolent look; **dirty money** money earned by base means: in dock labour, extra pay for unloading offensive cargo: extra pay for any unpleasant, dirty, etc. task; **dirty trick** a dishonest or despicable act; **dirty word** an obscene word: a word for something, as a feeling, principle, or belief, that is regarded with disfavour at the present time; **dirty work** work that dirties the hands or clothes: dishonourable practices, esp. undertaken on behalf of another: foul play. — **dirty old man** *(coll.)* a man whose sexual aspirations and actions are considered appropriate only to a younger man; **do the dirty on** to play a low trick on, cheat; **eat dirt** to acquiesce submissively in a humiliation; **throw dirt** to besmirch a reputation. [M.E. *drit*, prob. O.N. *drit*, excrement; cf. O.E. *gedrītan*, to defecate.]

Dis *dis, dēs, n.* a name for Pluto, hence, the infernal world. [L. *Dīs*, cog. with *deus, dīvus*.]

dis-, di-, *dis-, di-, pfx.* (1) meaning in two, asunder, apart: (2) meaning 'not' or a reversal: (3) indicating a removal or deprivation: (4) used intensively. [L. *dis-, dī-*.]

Disa *dī'sə, dīzə, n.* a genus of African orchids with dark green leaves: (without *cap.*) an orchid of this genus or certain other genera. [Orig. unknown.]

disable *dis-ā'bl, v.t.* to deprive of power: to weaken: to cripple, incapacitate: to disqualify: to depreciate, disparage, undervalue *(Shak.)*. — *adj.* **disā'bled.** — *ns.* **disā'blement; disābil'ity** want of power: want of legal qualification: a disqualification: a handicap, esp. physical. [Pfx. **dis-** (2).]

disabuse *dis-ə-būz', v.t.* to undeceive or set right. [Pfx. **dis-** (2).]

disaccharide *dī-suk'ə-rīd, n.* a sugar that hydrolyses into two molecules of simple sugars. [Pfx. **di-**]

disaccommodate *dis-ə-kom'ə-dāt, v.t.* to put to inconvenience. — *n.* **disaccommodā'tion.** [Pfx. **dis-** (2).]

disaccord *dis-ə-körd', v.i.* to refuse to accord: to be at discord: not to agree. — Also *n.* — *adj.* **disaccord'ant.** [Pfx. **dis-** (2).]

disaccustom *dis-ə-kus'təm, v.t.* to make to be lost through disuse. [Pfx. **dis-** (2).]

disacknowledge *dis-ək-nol'ij, v.t.* to refuse to acknowledge, disown. [Pfx. **dis-** (2).]

disadorn *dis-ə-dörn', v.t.* to deprive of ornaments. [Pfx. **dis-** (3).]

disadvance *dis-əd-väns', v.t.* to cause to retreat: to draw back, cease to put forward *(Spens.)*. [Pfx. **dis-** (2).]

disadvantage *dis-əd-vänt'ij, n.* unfavourable circumstance or condition: loss: damage. — *adjs.* **disadvan'tageable** *(obs.)*; **disadvan'taged** deprived of the resources and privileges, usu. social, enjoyed by the majority of people: in unfavourable conditions relative to other (specified) people; **disadvantageous** *(dis-ad-vont-ā'jəs)* attended with disadvantage: unfavourable. — *adv.* **disadvantā'geously.** — *n.* **disadvantā'geousness.** [Pfx. **dis-** (2).]

disadventurous *dis-əd-ven'chə-rəs, adj.* unfortunate. — *ns.* **disadven'ture, disaven'ture** *(Spens.)* a mishap. — *adj.* **disaven'trous** *(Spens.)* unfortunate. [Pfx. **dis-** (2).]

disaffect *dis-ə-fekt', v.t.* to take away the affection of: to make discontented or unfriendly: — *pa.p.* and *adj.* **disaffect'ed** ill-disposed: tending to break away. — *adv.* **disaffect'edly.** — *ns.* **disaffect'edness; disaffec'tion** the state of being disaffected: want of affection or friendliness: alienation: ill-will: political discontent or disloyalty. — *adj.* **disaffec'tionate.** [Pfx. **dis-** (3).]

disaffiliate *dis-ə-fil'i-āt, v.t.* and *v.i.* to end an affiliation (to): to separate oneself (from). — *n.* **disaffiliā'tion.** [Pfx. **dis-** (2).]

disaffirm *dis-ə-fûrm', v.t.* to contradict: to repudiate. — *ns.* **disaffirm'ance, disaffirmā'tion** *(dis-a-)*. [Pfx. **dis-** (2).]

disafforest *dis-ə-for'ist, v.t.* to bring out of the operation of forest laws: to clear of forest, disforest. — *ns.* **disafforestā'tion, disaffor'estment.** [L. *dis-*, reversal, and L.L. *afforestāre*, to make into a forest. See **forest**.]

disaggregate *dis-ag'ri-gāt, v.t.* to separate (something) into its component parts. — *n.* **disaggregā'tion.** [Pfx. **dis-** (1).]

disagree *dis-ə-grē', v.i.* to differ or be at variance: to disaccord: to dissent: to quarrel: to prove unsuitable or a source of annoyance, as of food disagreeing with the stomach. — *adj.* **disagree'able** not amicable: unpleasant: offensive. — *ns.* **disagree'ableness, disagreeabil'ity.** — *n.pl.* **disagree'ables** annoyances. — *adv.* **disagree'ably.** — *n.* **disagree'ment** want of agreement: difference: unsuitableness: dispute. [Pfx. **dis-** (2).]

disallow *dis-ə-low', v.t.* to dispraise *(obs.)*: not to allow: to refuse to sanction: to deny the authority, validity, or truth of: to reject, to forbid. — *v.i. (obs.)* to disapprove. — *adj.* **disallow'able.** — *n.* **disallow'ance.** [Pfx. **dis-** (2).]

disally *dis-ə-lī', v.t.* to break the alliance of: to separate, sunder *(Milt.)*. [Pfx. **dis-** (2), (1).]

di salto *dē säl'tō*, (It.) at a leap.

disamenity *dis-ə-mē'ni-ti, -men'-, n.* a lack of amenity: a disadvantage or drawback (of a property or district). [Pfx. **dis-** (3).]

disanalogy *dis-an-a'lə-ji, n.* a non-correspondence, an aspect or feature in which something is not analagous to something else. — *adj.* **disanal'agous**. [Pfx. **dis-** (2).]

disanchor *dis-angk'ǝr, v.t.* to free from the anchor. — *v.i.* to weigh anchor. [Pfx. **dis-** (3).]

disanimate *dis-an'i-māt, v.t.* to deprive of spirit or animation: to deject (*Shak.*). [Pfx. **dis-** (3).]

disannex *dis-ǝ-neks', v.t.* to disjoin. [Pfx. **dis-** (1).]

disannul *dis-ǝ-nul', v.t.* to annul completely. — *ns.* **disannull'er; disannul'ment, disannull'ing.** [Pfx. **dis-** (4).]

disanoint *dis-ǝ-noint', v.t.* to undo the anointing or consecration of. [Pfx. **dis-** (2).]

disapparel *dis-ǝ-par'ǝl, v.t.* to disrobe. [Pfx. **dis-** (2).]

disappear *dis-ǝ-pēr', v.i.* to vanish from sight. — *n.* **disappear'ance** a ceasing to be in sight: removal from sight, flight, secret withdrawal. [Pfx. **dis-** (3).]

disapply *dis-ǝ-plī', v.t.* to render (a law) inapplicable. — *n.* **disapplicā'tion.** [Pfx. **dis-** (2).]

disappoint *dis-ǝ-point', v.t.* to deprive of what is appointed (*obs.*): to frustrate the hopes or expectations of: to defeat the fulfilment of. — *v.i.* to cause disappointment. — *adjs.* **disappoint'ed** balked: frustrated: unequipped or ill-equipped (*Shak.*); **disappoint'ing** causing disappointment. — *n.* **disappoint'ment** the defeat of one's hopes or expectations: frustration: the vexation accompanying failure. [O.Fr. *desapointer, des-* (L. *dis-*), away, and *apointer*, to appoint. See **appoint.**]

disapprobation *dis-ap-rō-bā'shǝn, n.* disapproval. — *adjs.* **disapp'robātive, disapp'robātory.** [Pfx. **dis-** (2).]

disappropriate *dis-ǝ-prō'pri-āt, v.t.* to take away from the condition of being appropriated. — *adj.* (*-it*) deprived of appropriation. [Pfx. **dis-** (3).]

disapprove *dis-ǝ-prōōv', v.t.* and *v.i.* to give or have an unfavourable opinion (of): to reject. — *n.* **disapprov'al.** — *adv.* **disapprov'ingly.** [Pfx. **dis-** (2).]

disarm *dis-ärm', v.t.* to deprive of arms: to strip of armour: to render defenceless: to deprive of the power of hurt: to conciliate (*fig.*): to deprive of suspicion or hostility: to reduce to a peace footing. — *v.i.* to disband troops, reduce national armaments. — *ns.* **disarm'ament; disarm'er** one who disarms: one in favour of disarmament. — *adj.* **disarm'ing** charming. [Pfx. **dis-** (3).]

disarrange *dis-ǝ-rānj', v.t.* to undo the arrangement of: to disorder: to derange. — *n.* **disarrange'ment.** [Pfx. **dis-** (2).]

disarray *dis-ǝ-rā', v.t.* to break the array of: to throw into disorder: to strip of array or dress. — *n.* want of array or order: undress. [Pfx. **dis-** (2), (3).]

disarticulate *dis-är-tik'ūl-āt, v.t.* to separate the joints of. — *v.i.* to separate at a joint. — *n.* **disarticulā'tion.** [Pfx. **dis-** (1).]

disassemble *dis-ǝ-sem'bl, v.t.* to take apart. — *n.* **disassem'bly.** [Pfx. **dis-** (1).]

disassimilate *dis-ǝ-sim'i-lāt, v.t.* to subject to katabolism. — *n.* **disassimilā'tion.** — *adj.* **disassim'ilative.** [Pfx. **dis-** (2).]

disassociate *dis-ǝ-sō'shi-āt, v.t.* (with *from*) to disconnect: to dissociate. — *n.* **disassociā'tion.** [Pfx. **dis-** (2).]

disaster *diz-äs'tǝr, n.* an adverse or unfortunate event: a great and sudden misfortune: calamity. — *adj.* **disas'trous** calamitous, ruinous: gloomy, foreboding disaster. — *adv.* **disas'trously.** — **disaster area** an area in which there has been a disaster (e.g. flood, explosion), requiring special official aid: (*loosely*) any place where a misfortune has happened: anything which is untidy, ugly, disadvantageous, etc. (*coll.*); **disaster movie** a film which has as its main theme or focus of action a disaster or catastrophe. [O.Fr. *desastre, des-* (L. *dis-*), with evil sense, *astre,* a star, destiny — L. *astrum,* Gr. *astron,* star.]

disattire *dis-ǝ-tīr', (Spens.) v.t.* to undress. [Pfx. **dis-** (2).]

disattune *dis-ǝ-tūn', v.t.* to put out of harmony. [Pfx. **dis-** (2).]

disauthorise, -ize *dis-ö'thǝr-īz, v.t.* to deprive of authority. [Pfx. **dis-** (3).]

disavaunce (*Spens.*). Same as **disadvance.**

disaventure. See **disadventure.**

disavouch *dis-ǝ-vowch', v.t.* to disavow. [Pfx. **dis-** (2).]

disavow *dis-ǝ-vow', v.t.* to disclaim knowledge of, or connection with: to disown: to deny. — *n.* **disavow'al.** [O.Fr. *desavouer, des-* (L. *dis-*), away, *avouer,* to avow. See **avow.**]

disband *dis-band', v.t.* to disperse, break up, esp. of troops. — *v.i.* to break up. — *n.* **disband'ment.** [O.Fr. *desbander,* to unbind, *des-* (L. *dis-*), reversal, *bander,* to tie.]

disbar *dis-bär', v.t.* to expel from the bar. — *n.* **disbar'ment.** [Pfx. **dis-** (3).]

disbark¹ *dis-bärk', v.t.* to land from a ship: to disembark. [O.Fr. *desbarquer, des-* (L. *dis-*), reversal, *barque,* bark.]

disbark² *dis-bärk', v.t.* to strip of bark, to bark. [Pfx. **dis-** (3).]

disbelieve *dis-bǝ-lēv', v.t.* to believe to be false: to refuse belief or credit to. — *v.i.* to have no faith (*in*). — *ns.* **disbelief'; disbeliev'er.** [Pfx. **dis-** (2).]

disbench *dis-bench', -bensh', v.t.* to drive from a bench or seat (*Shak.*): to deprive of the privilege of a bencher (e.g. in the Inns of Court). [Pfx. **dis-** (3).]

disbenefit *dis-ben'i-fit, n.* drawback, disadvantage, loss, inconvenience, etc.: absence or loss of a benefit. [Pfx. **dis-** (2), (3).]

disbodied *dis-bod'id, adj.* disembodied. [Pfx. **dis-** (3).]

disbosom *dis-booz'ǝm, v.t.* to make known, reveal. [Pfx. **dis-** (1).]

disbowel *dis-bow'ǝl, (fig.) v.t.* to disembowel. — *pr.p.* **disbow'elling;** *pa.t.* and *pa.p.* **disbow'elled.** [Pfx. **dis-** (3).]

disbranch *dis-bränch', -bränsh', v.t.* to remove branches from: to sever. [Pfx. **dis-** (3).]

disbud *dis-bud', v.t.* to remove buds from. [Pfx. **dis-** (3).]

disburden *dis-bûr'dn,* **disburthen** *dis-bûr'dhn, vs.t.* to rid of a burden: to free: to unload, discharge. [Pfx. **dis-** (3).]

disburse *dis-bûrs', v.t.* to pay out. — *ns.* **disburs'al, disburse'ment** a paying out: that which is paid. [O.Fr. *desbourser, des-* (L. *dis-*), apart, and *bourse,* a purse.]

disc, disk *disk, n.* a quoit thrown by ancient Greek athletes: any flat thin circular body or structure: a circular figure, as that presented by the sun, moon, and planets: the enlarged torus of a flower: the inner part of a capitulum in composite plants: a layer of fibrocartilage between vertebrae, the slipping of which (*slipped disc*) causes pressure on spinal nerves and hence pains: a gramophone record: a disc file (*comput.*). — *v.t.* and *v.i.* to work with a disc harrow. — *adjs.* **disc'al** pertaining to, or of the nature of, a disc; **disc'oid, discoid'al** in the form of a disc: of a capitulum, without ray-flowers (*bot.*). — *ns.* **discog'raphy** collection, description, etc., of gramophone records: the history or description of musical recording: a list of recordings by one composer or performer; **discog'rapher; disc'ophile** (*-ō-fīl*) one who makes a study of and collects gramophone records; **diskette** (*dis-ket'; comput.*) a floppy disc. — **disc brake** one in which the friction is obtained by pads hydraulically forced against a disc on the wheel; **disc drive** a computer peripheral with a head that records data on, and retrieves data from, discs; **disc file, store** (*comput.*) a random access device consisting of discs coated with magnetisable material, on which data is stored in tracks; **disc'-flower', -flor'et** one of the tubular inner flowers of a capitulum — opp. to *ray-flower*; **disc'= harr'ow, -plough** a harrow, or plough, in which the soil is cut by inclined discs; **disc'-jockey** a person who introduces and plays records (esp. of popular music) on a radio or television programme, etc.; **disc parking** a system according to which the motorist himself is responsible for affixing to his car special disc(s) showing his time of arrival and the time when permitted parking ends, there being no charge during the permitted period; **disc player** a machine for playing videodiscs; **disc wheel** a wheel on a motor vehicle, etc. in which the hub and rim are connected by a solid of metal. [Gr. *diskos*.]

discage *dis-kāj'*, *v.t.* to free from a cage. [Pfx. **dis-** (2).]

discalced *dis-kalst'*, *adj.* without shoes, bare-footed, as a branch of the Carmelite order. — *n.* and *adj.* **discal'ceate.** [L. *discalceātus* — *dis-*, neg., and *calceāre*, *-ātum*, to shoe, *calceus*, a shoe — *calx*, the heel.]

discandie, discandie *dis-kan'di*, (*Shak.*) *v.i.* to dissolve or melt from a state of being candied. — *n.* **discan'dering** (*Shak.*) supposed to be for **discandying.** [Pfx. **dis-** (2).]

discant *dis'kant*. Same as **descant.**

discapacitate *dis-kə-pas'i-tāt*, *v.t.* to incapacitate. [Pfx. **dis-** (2).]

discard *dis-kärd'*, *v.t.* and *v.i.* to throw away, as not needed or not allowed by the game, said of cards: in whist, etc., to throw down a (useless) card of another suit when one cannot follow suit and cannot or will not trump: to cast off: to discharge: to reject. — *n.* (also *dis'*) the act of discarding: the card or cards thrown out of the hand: discharge, dismissal, abandonment: a cast-off, anything discarded. — *n.* **discard'ment.** — **throw into the discard** (*U.S.*) to throw on the scrap-heap. [Pfx. **dis-** (3).]

discarnate *dis-kär'nit*, *-nāt*, *adj.* disembodied: separated from its or the body. [Pfx. **dis-** (1), and L. *carō*, *carnis*, flesh.]

discase *dis-kās'*, (*Shak.*) *v.t.* to remove a case or covering from, to undress. [Pfx. **dis-** (3).]

discept *di-sept'*, (*Browning*) *v.i.* to dispute, debate. — *n.* **disceptā'tion.** — *adj.* **disceptā'tious.** — *n.* **disceptā'tor.** — *adj.* **disceptatō'rial.** [L. *disceptāre*, *-ātum*, to contend — *dis-*, *captāre*.]

discern *di-sûrn'*, *-zûrn'*, *v.t.* to make out: to distinguish by the eye or understanding: to judge (*obs.*, a blunder for **decern**). — *n.* **discern'er.** — *adj.* **discern'ible.** — *adv.* **discern'ibly.** — *adj.* **discern'ing** discriminating, acute. — *n.* **discern'ment** power or faculty of discriminating: judgment: acuteness. [L. *discernĕre* — *dis-*, thoroughly, and *cernĕre*, to sift, perceive.]

discerp *di-sûrp'*, *v.t.* to separate. — *n.* **discerpibil'ity** capability of being disunited. — *adjs.* **discerp'ible** (*obs.*), **discerp'tible.** — *n.* **discerp'tion.** — *adj.* **discerp'tive.** [L. *discerpĕre*, to tear in pieces — *dis-*, apart, *carpĕre*, to pluck.]

discharge *dis-chärj'*, *v.t.* to free from or relieve of a charge of any kind (burden, explosive, electricity, liability, accusation, etc.): to set free: to acquit: to dismiss: to fire (as a gun): to take the superincumbent weight from: to set down or send forth: to eject: to pour out: to emit or let out: to perform: to pay: to give account for: to distribute (as weight): to forbid (*obs.*). — *v.i.* to unload: to become released from a charged state: to allow escape of contents: to flow away or out. — *n.* (usu. *dis'*) the act of discharging: release from a charge of any kind: unloading: liberation: acquittal: dismissal: outflow: rate of flow: emission: release of tension: payment: performance: that which is discharged. — *ns.* **discharg'er** one who discharges: an apparatus for discharging, esp. electricity, e.g. a spark-gap, discharging tongs: apparatus for firing an explosive. — **discharge'-tube'** a tube in which an electric discharge takes place in a vacuum or in a gas at low pressure; **discharging arch** an arch built in a wall to protect a space beneath from the weight above; **discharging tongs** metal tongs used for discharging condensers. [O.Fr. *descharger* — *des-*, apart, *charger*; see **charge.**]

dischurch *dis-chûrch'*, *v.t.* to deprive of church rank or privileges. [Pfx. **dis-** (3).]

discide *di-sīd'*, (*Spens.*) *v.t.* to cut asunder, to divide. [L. *dis-*, asunder, and *caedĕre*, to cut.]

discinct *di-singkt'*, *adj.* ungirded. [L. *discingĕre*, *-cinctum*, to ungird.]

disciple *dis-ī'pl*, *n.* one who professes to receive instruction from another: one who follows or believes in the doctrine of another: a follower, esp. one of the twelve apostles of Christ. — *v.t.* (*Spens.*) to teach. — *n.* **discī'pleship.** — **Disciples of Christ** a sect that seeks a restoration of New Testament Christianity — by some called Campbellites. [Fr., — L. *discipulus*, from *discĕre*, to learn: akin to *docēre*, to teach.]

discipline *dis'i-plin*, *n.* instruction: a branch of learning, or field of study: a branch of sport: an event in a sports meeting: training, or mode of life in accordance with rules: subjection to control: order: severe training: mortification: punishment: an instrument of penance or punishment. — *v.t.* to subject to discipline: to train: to educate: to bring under control: to chastise. — *adjs.* **disc'iplinable; disc'iplinal** (or *-plī'*). — *ns.* **disc'iplinant** one who subjects himself to a discipline, esp. one of an order of Spanish flagellants; **disciplinā'rian** one who enforces strict discipline. — *adj.* disciplinary: advocating or practising strict discipline. — *n.* **disciplinā'rium** a scourge for penitential flogging. — *adj.* **disc'iplinary** pertaining to or of the nature of discipline. — *n.* **disc'ipliner** one who disciplines. — **First, Second, Book of Discipline** two documents (1560 and 1578) embodying the constitution and order of procedure of the Church of Scotland from the period of the Reformation. [L. *disciplīna*, from *discipulus*.]

discission *di-sish'ən*, *n.* an incision into a tumour or cataract. [L. *discissiō*, *-ōnis* — *discindĕre*, *-scissum* — *dī-*, apart, *scindĕre*, to cut.]

disclaim *dis-klām'*, *v.t.* to renounce all claim to: to refuse to acknowledge or be responsible for: to repudiate: to reject: to cry out against the claim of. — *v.i.* to make a disclaimer: to declaim, cry out (*obs.*). — *ns.* **disclaim'er** a denial, disavowal, or renunciation; **disclamā'tion** (*-kləm-*) a disavowal. [O.Fr. *disclaimer* — L. *dis-*, apart, *clāmāre*, to cry out.]

disclose *dis-klōz'*, *v.t.* to unclose: to open: to lay open: to bring to light: to reveal: to hatch (*Shak.*): to transform and give vent to (*Spens.*): — *pa.p.* (*Spens.*) **disclōst.** — *n.* a disclosure: emergence from the egg (*Shak.*). — *n.* **disclō'sure** (*-zhər*) act of disclosing: a bringing to light or revealing: that which is disclosed or revealed. — **disclosing tablet** a tablet which, when chewed, reveals by means of a coloured dye areas of plaque to be removed from the teeth. [O.Fr. *desclos* — L. *dis-*, apart, *claudĕre*, *clausum*, to shut.]

disco *dis'kō*, *n.* short for **discothèque:** — *pl.* **dis'cos.** — *adj.* suitable, or specially produced, for discothèques, as *disco dancing*, *disco dress*, *disco music*. — *n.* **dis'coer** one who frequents discos.

discobolus *dis-kob'ə-ləs*, *n.* a disc-thrower: the name of a famous lost statue ascribed to Myron, of which copies exist. [L., — Gr. *diskobolos* — *diskos*, a quoit, *ballein*, to throw.]

discographer, -graphy, discoid, -al, etc. See **disc.**

discolour *dis-kul'ər*, *v.t.* to take away colour from: to change or to spoil the natural colour of: to alter the appearance of: to mark with other colours, to stain: to dirty, disfigure. — *v.i.* to become discoloured. — *n.* **discolo(u)rā'tion** act of discolouring: state of being discoloured: stain. — *adj.* **discol'oured** stained, etc.: many-coloured (*Spens.*). [O.Fr. *descolorer* — L. *dis-*, apart, and *colōrāre* — *color*, colour.]

discombobulate, -boberate *dis-kəm-bob'ōō-lāt*, *-ū-lāt*, *-bob'ər-āt*, (*U.S. slang*) *vs.t.* to disconcert, upset. [Orig. obscure.]

Discomedusae *dis-kō-me-dū'sē*, *n.pl.* an order of jellyfishes with flattened umbrella. — *n.* and *adj.* **discomedū'san.** [Gr. *diskos*, disc, and **medusa.**]

discomfit *dis-kum'fit*, *v.t.* to disconcert, to balk: to defeat or rout: — *pr.p.* **discom'fiting**; *pa.t.* and *pa.p.* **discom'fited.** — *n.* (*Milt.*) defeat. — *n.* **discom'fiture.** [O.Fr. *desconfit*, pa.p. of *desconfire* — L. *dis-*, neg., *conficĕre*, to prepare — *con-*, intens., *facĕre*, to make.]

discomfort *dis-kum'fərt*, *n.* want of comfort: uneasiness. — *v.t.* to deprive of comfort: to make uneasy. — *adj.* **discom'fortable** causing discomfort: uncomfortable.

[O.Fr. *desconforter*—*des-*, priv., *conforter*, to comfort; see **comfort**.]

discommend *dis-kəm-end'*, *v.t.* to blame: to dispraise. — *adj.* **discommend'able.** — *ns.* **discommend'ableness, discommendation** (*dis-ko-mən-dā'shən*). [Pfx. **dis-** (2).]

discommission *dis-kə-mish'ən*, (*Milt.*) *v.t.* to deprive of a commission. [Pfx. **dis-** (3).]

discommode *dis-kə-mōd'*, (*arch.*) *v.t.* to incommode. — *adj.* **discommō'dious.** — *adv.* **discommō'diously.** — *n.* **discommŏd'ity** inconvenience. [Pfx. **dis-** (2), obs. vb. *commode*, to suit.]

discommon *dis-kom'ən*, *v.t.* to deprive of the right of common, or, at Oxford and Cambridge, of dealing with undergraduates. [Pfx, **dis-** (3), **common**, n.]

discommunity *dis-kə-mūn'i-ti*, *n.* want of community. [Pfx. **dis-** (2).]

discompose *dis-kəm-pōz'*, *v.t.* to deprive of composure, disturb, agitate: to disarrange, disorder. — *n.* **discompō'sure** (*-zhər, -zhyər*). [Pfx. **dis-** (2).]

Discomycetes *dis-kō-mī-sē'tēz*, *n.pl.* a group of fungi (Ascomycetes) with open apothecia.—*n.* **dis'comycete.** — *adj.* **discomycē'tous.** [Gr. *diskos*, disc, *mykētĕs*, pl. of *mykēs*, a fungus.]

disconcert *dis-kən-sûrt'*, *v.t.* to throw into confusion: to disturb: to frustrate: to defeat: to put out of countenance. — *ns.* **disconcert** (*dis-kon'sərt*) disunion; **disconcer'tion** confusion; **disconcert'ment.** [Obs. Fr. *disconcerter*, *des-* (L. *dis-*), apart, and *concerter*, to concert.]

disconformable *dis-kən-förm'ə-bl*, *adj.* not conformable. — *n.* **disconform'ity** want of conformity: unconformity (*geol.*). [Pfx. **dis-** (2).]

disconnect *dis-kən-ekt'*, *v.t.* and *v.i.* to separate or disjoin (from). — *adj.* **disconnect'ed** separated: loosely united, as of a discourse. — *adv.* **disconnect'edly.** — *ns.* **disconnec'tion, disconnex'ion.** [Pfx. **dis-** (1).]

disconsent *dis-kən-sent'*, *v.i.* to differ, dissent. [Pfx. **dis-** (2).]

disconsolate *dis-kon'sə-lit*, *adj.* without consolation or comfort. — *adv.* **discon'solately.** — *ns.* **discon'solateness, disconsolā'tion.** [L. *dis-*, neg., and *consōlārī*, *consōlātus*, to console.]

discontent *dis-kən-tent'*, *adj.* not content: dissatisfied. — *n.* want of contentment: dissatisfaction: a discontented person (*Shak.*). — *v.t.* to deprive of content: to stir up to ill-will. — *adj.* **discontent'ed** dissatisfied. — *adv.* **discontent'edly.** — *n.* **discontent'edness.** — *adjs.* **discontent'ful; discontent'ing** not contenting or satisfying: discontented (*Shak.*).—*n.* **discontent'ment.** [Pfx. **dis-** (2), (3).]

discontiguous *dis-kon-tig'ū-əs*, *adj.* not contiguous, not in contact. — *n.* **discontigū'ity.** [Pfx. **dis-** (2).]

discontinue *dis-kən-tin'ū*, *v.t.* to cease to continue: to put an end to: to leave off: to stop. — *v.i.* to cease: to be separated. — *ns.* **discontin'uance, discontinuā'tion** a breaking off or ceasing; **discontinu'ity** (*-kon-*). — *adj.* **discontin'uous** not continuous: broken off: separated: interrupted by intervening spaces. — *adv.* **discontin'uously.** [O.Fr. *discontinuer* — L. *dis-*, reversal, and *continuāre*, to continue.]

discophile. See **disc**.

Discophora *dis-kof'ə-rə*, *n.pl.* the Discomedusae.—*n.* and *adj.* **discoph'oran.** — *adj.* **discoph'orous.** [Gr. *diskos*, disc, *phoros*, carrying.]

discord *dis'körd*, *n.* opposite of *concord*: disagreement, strife: difference or contrariety of qualities: a combination of inharmonious sounds: uproarious noise: a dissonance, esp. unprepared. — *v.i.* **discord'** to disagree. — *ns.* **discord'ance, discord'ancy.** — *adj.* **discord'ant** without concord or agreement: inconsistent: contradictory: harsh: jarring. — *adv.* **discord'antly.** — *adj.* **discord'ful** (*Spens.*). — **apple of discord** see **apple**. [O.Fr. *descord* — L. *discordia* — *dis-*, apart, and *cor, cordis*, the heart.]

discorporate *dis-kör'pər-rit*, *adj.* disembodied. [Pfx. **dis-** (2).]

discothèque, -theque *dis'kə-tek, dēs-kō-tek*, *n.* a club or party where music for dancing is provided by records:

the equipment and records used to provide such music. — Coll. **dis'co** (q.v.) [Fr., a record-library — Gr. *diskos*, disc, *thēkē*, case, library.]

discounsel *dis-kown'səl*, (*Spens.*) *v.t.* to dissuade. [O.Fr. *desconseillier*—*des-*, apart, and *conseillier*, to counsel.]

discount *dis'kownt*, *n.* a sum taken from the reckoning: a sum returned to the payer of an account: the rate or percentage of the deduction granted: a deduction made for interest in advancing money on a bill: the amount by which the price of a share or stock unit is below the par value. — *v.t.* **discount'** to allow as discount: to allow discount on: to pay (rarely to receive) beforehand the present worth of: to put a reduced value on, as in an extravagant statement or fabulous story or an event foreseen: to ignore. — *v.i.* to practise discounting. — *adj.* **discount'able.** — *n.* **discount'er.** — **dis'count-brok'er** one who cashes notes or bills of exchange at a discount; **discount house** a company trading in bills of exchange, etc.: (also **discount store**) a shop where goods are sold at less than the usual retail price; **discount rate** the rate at which a discount is granted: the rate at which banks can borrow funds using bills as security: in U.S., bank rate. — **at a discount** below par: not sought after: superfluous: depreciated in value. [O.Fr. *descompter*, *des-* (L. *dis-*), away, *compter*, to count.]

discountenance *dis-kown'tən-əns*, *v.t.* to put out of countenance: to abash: to refuse countenance or support to: to discourage. — *n.* cold treatment: disapprobation. [O.Fr. *descontenancer*—*des-*, reversal, *contenance*, countenance.]

discourage *dis-kur'ij*, *v.t.* to take away the courage of: dishearten: to oppose by showing disfavour. — *n.* **discour'agement** act of discouraging: that which discourages: dejection. — *n.* and *adj.* **discour'aging** disheartening, depressing. — *adv.* **discour'agingly.** [O.Fr. *descourager*. See **courage**.]

discoure *dis-kowr'*, (*Spens.*) *v.t.* to discover.

discourse *dis-kōrs', -körs'*, or *dis'*, *n.* speech or language generally: conversation: the reasoning faculty: a treatise: a speech: a sermon: apparently, process of combat (*Spens.*). — *v.i.* to talk or converse: to reason: to treat formally. — *v.t.* to utter or give forth. — *n.* **discours'er** (*Shak.*). — *adj.* (*obs.*) **discours'ive.** [Fr. *discours* — L. *discursus* — *dis-*, away, *currĕre*, to run.]

discourteous *dis-kûrt'yəs* (or *-kört', -kört'*), *adj.* wanting in courtesy: uncivil. — Also (*Spens.*) **discour'teise.** — *adv.* **discourt'eously.** — *ns.* **discourt'eousness, discourt'esy.** [Pfx. **dis-** (2).]

discover *dis-kuv'ər*, *v.t.* to uncover: to lay open or expose: to exhibit: to reveal: to make known: to find out: to espy. — Also (*Spens.*) **discoure', discure'.** — *adj.* **discov'erable.** — *ns.* **discov'erer** one who makes a discovery, esp. of something never before known: an informer (*obs.*): a scout (*Shak.*); **discov'ery** the act of finding out: the thing discovered: gaining knowledge of the unknown: the unravelling of a plot: exploration or reconnaissance (*obs.* except in **voyage of discovery** voyage of exploration). — **discovery well** an exploratory oil-well which proves to yield a commercially viable amount of oil. [O.Fr. *descouvrir, des-* (L. *dis-*), away, *couvrir*, to cover; see **cover**.]

discovert *dis-kuv'ərt*, (*law*) *adj.* not under the bonds of matrimony, of a spinster or widow. — *n.* **discov'erture.** [Lit. uncovered, unprotected, O.Fr. *descovert*; see **discover, cover**.]

discredit *dis-kred'it*, *n.* want of credit: bad credit: ill-repute: disgrace. — *v.t.* to refuse credit to, or belief in: to deprive of credibility: to deprive of credit: to disgrace. — *adj.* **discred'itable** not creditable: disgraceful. — *adv.* **discred'itably.** [Pfx. **dis-** (2), (3).]

discreet *dis-krēt'*, *adj.* having discernment: wary: circumspect: prudent: discrete, separate, detached (*arch.*). — *adv.* **discreet'ly.** — *n.* **discreet'ness.** [O.Fr. *discret* — L. *discrētus* — *discernĕre*, to separate, to perceive; see **discern, discrete**.]

discrepancy *dis-krep'ən-si*, or *dis'*, *n.* disagreement, variance of facts or sentiments. — *n.* **discrep′ance** (or *dis′*). — *adj.* **discrep′ant** (or *dis′*) contrary, disagreeing. [L. *discrepāns, -antis,* different — *dis-,* asunder, and *crepāns,* pr.p. of *crepāre,* to sound.]

discrete *dis′krēt, dis-krēt′, adj.* separate: discontinuous: consisting of distinct parts: referring to distinct objects: abstract — opp. to *concrete.* — *adv.* **discrete′ly.** — *n.* **discrete′ness.** — *adj.* **discret′ive** separating: disjunctive. — *adv.* **discret′ively.** [L. *discrētus;* cf. *discreet.*]

discretion *dis-kresh′ən, n.* quality of being discreet: prudence: liberty to act at pleasure. — *adjs.* **discre′tional, discre′tionary** left to discretion: unrestricted. — *advs.* **discre′tionally, discre′tionarily.** — **age, years, of discretion,** mature years; **at discretion** according to one's own judgment; **be at someone's discretion** to be completely under someone's power or control; **surrender at discretion** to surrender unconditionally, that is, to another's discretion. [O.Fr. *discrecion* — L. *discrētiō, -ōnis* — *discernĕre, -crētum.*]

discriminate *dis-krim′i-nāt, v.t.* to note the difference of or between: to distinguish: to select from others: (with *in favour of* or *against*) to treat differently, esp. because of one's feelings or prejudices about a person's sex, race, religion, etc. — *v.i.* to make or note a difference or distinction: to distinguish. — *adj.* (*-nit*) discriminated: discriminating. — *adj.* **discrim′inant** discriminating. — *n.* a special function of the roots of an equation, expressible in terms of the coefficients — zero value of the function showing that at least two of the roots are equal. — *adv.* **discrim′inately.** — *adj.* **discrim′ināting** noting distinctions: gifted with judgment and penetration. — *adv.* **discrim′inātingly.** — *n.* **discriminā′tion** the act or process of discriminating: judgment: good taste: the selection of a signal having a particular characteristic (frequency, amplitude, etc.) by the elimination of all the other input signals (*telecomm.*). — *adj.* **discrim′inative** that marks a difference: characteristic: observing distinctions. — *adv.* **discrim′inatively.** — *n.* **discrim′inātor** a person who, or thing which, discriminates: a device which affects the routing and/or determines the fee units for a call originating at a satellite exchange (*telecomm.*). — *adj.* **discrim′inatory** discriminative: favouring some, not treating, or falling on, all alike. — **positive discrimination** discrimination in favour of those who were formerly discriminated against, esp. in the provision of social and educational facilities and employment opportunities. [L. *discrīmināre, -ātum* — *discrīmen,* that which separates; cf. *discernĕre,* discern.]

discrown *dis-krown′, v.t.* to deprive of a crown. [Pfx. **dis-** (3).]

disculpate *dis-kul′pāt, v.t.* to free from blame. [Pfx. **dis-** (3).]

discumber *dis-kum′bər, v.t.* to disencumber. [Pfx. **dis-** (2).]

discure *dis-kūr′,* (*Spens.*) *v.t.* to discover. [Pfx. **dis-** (2).]

discursive *dis-kûr′siv, adj.* running from one thing to another: roving, desultory: proceeding regularly from premises to conclusion: intellectual, rational. — *ns.* **discur′sion** desultory talk: act of reasoning; **discur′sist** a disputer. — *adv.* **discur′sively.** — *n.* **discur′siveness.** — *adj.* **discur′sory** discursive. — *n.* **discur′sus** (L.L.), discourse, reasoned treatment. [See **discourse.**]

discus *dis′kəs, n.* a disc, flat circular image or object: a heavy wooden disc, thickening towards the centre, thrown for distance in athletic contests. [L., — Gr. *diskos.*]

discuss *dis-kus′, v.t.* to examine in detail, or by disputation: to debate: to sift: to consume, as a bottle of wine (*facet.*): to throw off (*Spens.*): to dispel: to settle, decide (*obs.*): to declare, make known (*Shak.*). — *adj.* **discuss′able, -ible.** — *n.* **discussion** (*dis-kush′ən*) debate: the dispersion of a tumour (*surg.*). — *adjs.* **discuss′ive, discutient** (*-kū′shi-ənt*) able or tending to discuss or disperse tumours. — *n.* **discū′tient** a medicine with this property. [L. *discutĕre, discussum* — *dis-,* asunder, *quatĕre,* to shake.]

disdain *dis-dān′,* or *diz-, v.t.* to think unworthy: to scorn. — *n.* a feeling of contempt, generally tinged with superiority: haughtiness. — *adjs.* **disdained′** (*Shak.*) disdainful; **disdain′ful.** — *adv.* **disdain′fully.** — *n.* **disdain′fulness.** [O.Fr. *desdaigner* with substitution of *des-* (L. *dis-*) for L. *dē* in L. *dēdīgnārī — dīgnus,* worthy.]

disease *diz-ēz′, n.* uneasiness (in this sense often written **dis-ease** and pron. *dis′ēz′; arch.*): a disorder or want of health in mind or body: an ailment: cause of pain. — *v.t.* (*Spens.*) to make uneasy. — *adj.* **diseased′** affected with disease. — *n.* **diseas′edness.** — *adj.* **disease′ful.** [O.Fr. *desaise* — *des-* (L. *dis-,* not), *aise,* ease; see **ease.**]

diseconomy *dis-ə-kon′ə-mi, n.* (an instance of) something which is economically wasteful or unprofitable. [Pfx. **dis-** (2).]

disedge *dis-ej′,* (*Shak.*) *v.t.* to deprive of the edge: to blunt: to dull. [Pfx. **dis-** (3).]

disembark *dis-im-bärk′, v.t.* to set ashore: to take out of a ship. — *v.i.* to quit a ship: to land. — *ns.* **disembarkā′tion** (*dis-em-, dis-im-*), **disembark′ment.** [O.Fr. *desembarquer* — *des-* (L. *dis-,* removal), *embarquer.* See **embark.**]

disembarrass *dis-im-bar′əs, v.t.* to free from embarrassment or perplexity. — *n.* **disembarr′assment.** [Pfx. **dis-** (2).]

disembellish *dis-im-bel′ish, v.t.* to deprive of embellishment. [Pfx. **dis-** (2).]

disembitter *dis-im-bit′ər, v.t.* to free from bitterness. [Pfx. **dis-** (2).]

disembody *dis-im-bod′i, v.t.* to take away from or out of the body (esp. of spirits): to discharge from military embodiment. — *adj.* **disembod′ied.** — *n.* **disembod′iment.** [Pfx. **dis-** (3).]

disembogue *dis-im-bōg′, v.t.* and *v.i.* to discharge at the mouth, as a stream. — *n.* **disembogue′ment.** [Sp. *desembocar — des-* (L. *dis-*), asunder, *embocar,* to enter the mouth — *en* (L. *in*), into, *boca* (L. *bucca*), cheek, mouth.]

disembosom *dis-im-bŏŏz′əm, v.t.* to separate from the bosom: to disburden. [Pfx. **dis-** (1).]

disembowel *dis-im-bow′əl, v.t.* to take out the bowels of: to tear out the inside of. — *n.* **disembow′elment.** [Pfx. **dis-** (3).]

disembrangle *dis-im-brang′gl, v.t.* to free from dispute. [Pfx. **dis-** (2).]

disembroil *dis-im-broil′, v.t.* to free from broil or confusion. [Pfx. **dis-** (2).]

disemburden *dis-im-bûr′dn, v.t.* to disburden. [Pfx. **dis-** (3).]

disemploy *dis-im-ploi′, v.t.* to remove from employment. — *adj.* **disemployed′.** — *n.* **disemploy′ment.** [Pfx. **dis-** (2).]

disenable *dis-in-ā′bl, v.t.* to make unable: to disable: to deprive of power (*obs.*). [Pfx. **dis-** (2).]

disenchain *dis-in-chān′, v.t.* to free from restraint. [Pfx. **dis-** (2).]

disenchant *dis-in-chänt′, v.t.* to free from enchantment, to disillusion. — *ns.* **disenchant′er;** — *fem.* **disenchant′ress; disenchant′ment.** [Pfx. **dis-** (2).]

disenclose *dis-in-klōz′, v.t.* to free from the condition of being enclosed: to dispark. — Also **disinclose′.** [Pfx. **dis-** (2).]

disencumber *dis-in-kum′bər, v.t.* to free from encumbrance: to disburden. — *n.* **disencum′brance.** [Pfx. **dis-** (2).]

disendow *dis-in-dow′, v.t.* to take away the endowments of (esp. of an established church). — *adj.* **disendowed′.** — *n.* **disendow′ment.** [Pfx. **dis-** (3).]

disenfranchise *dis-in-fran′chīz, -shīz, (rare) v.t.* to disfranchise: to deprive of suffrage. — *n.* **disenfran′chisement** (*-chiz-, -shis-*). [Pfx. **dis-** (2).]

disengage *dis-in-gāj′, v.t.* to separate or free from being engaged: to separate: to set free: to release. — *v.i.* to come loose. — *adj.* **disengaged′** at leisure, without engagement. — *ns.* **disengag′edness; disengage′ment** a separating, releasing: a mutual withdrawal from a position. [O.Fr. *desengager* — *des-* (L. *dis-*, neg.), *engager*, to engage.]

disennoble *dis-i-nō′bl, v.t.* to deprive of title, or of what ennobles: to degrade. [Pfx. **dis-** (2).]

disenrol *dis-in-rōl′, v.t.* to remove from a roll. [Pfx. **dis-** (2).]

disenshroud *dis-in-shrowd′, v.t.* to divest of a shroud, to unveil. [Pfx. **dis-** (3).]

disenslave *dis-in-slāv′, v.t.* to free from bondage. [Pfx. **dis-** (2).]

disentail *dis-in-tāl′, v.t.* to break the entail of (an estate): to divest. — *n.* the act of disentailing. [Pfx. **dis-** (2).]

disentangle *dis-in-tang′gl, v.t.* to free from entanglement or disorder: to unravel: to disengage or set free. — *n.* **disentang′lement.** [Pfx. **dis-** (2).]

disenthral, disenthrall *dis-in-thröl′, v.t.* to free from enthralment. — *n.* **disenthral(l)′ment.** [Pfx. **dis-** (2).]

disenthrone *dis-in-thrōn′,* (*Milt.*) *v.t.* to dethrone. [Pfx. **dis-** (2).]

disentitle *dis-in-tī′tl, v.t.* to deprive of title or right. [Pfx. **dis-** (2).]

disentomb *dis-in-tōōm′, v.t.* to take out from a tomb. [Pfx. **dis-** (2).]

disentrail, disentrayle *dis-in-trāl,* (*Spens.*) *v.t.* to let forth as if from the entrails. [Pfx. **dis-** (3).]

disentrain *dis-in-trān′, v.t.* to set down from a train. — *v.i.* to alight from a train. — *n.* **disentrain′ment.** [Pfx. **dis-** (3).]

disentrance *dis-in-träns′, v.t.* to awaken from a trance or entrancement: to arouse from a reverie. — *n.* **disentrance′ment.** [Pfx. **dis-** (2).]

disentrayle. See **disentrail.**

disentwine *dis-in-twīn′, v.t.* to untwine. [Pfx. **dis-** (2).]

disenvelop *dis-in-vel′ap, v.t.* to free from that in which a thing is enveloped: to unfold. [Pfx. **dis-** (2).]

disenviron *dis-in-vī′ran, v.t.* to deprive of environment. [Pfx. **dis-** (3).]

disepalous *dī-sep′a-las,* (*bot.*) *adj.* having two sepals. [Pfx. **di-**, sepal.]

disequilibrium *dis-ek-wi-lib′ri-am, n.* lack of balance, esp. in economic affairs: — *pl.* **disequilib′ria.** — *v.t.* **disequil′ibrate** to cause a disequilibrium in. [Pfx. **dis-** (2).]

disespouse *dis-is-powz′,* (*Milt.*) *v.t.* to separate after espousal or betrothal. [Pfx. **dis-** (1).]

disestablish *dis-is-tab′lish, v.t.* to undo the establishment of: to deprive (a church) of established status. — *n.* **disestab′lishment.** [Pfx. **dis-** (2).]

disesteem *dis-is-tēm′, n.* lack of esteem: disregard. — *v.t.* to disapprove: to dislike. — *n.* **disestimā′tion** (*-es-tim-*). [Pfx. **dis-** (2).]

diseuse *dē-zœz′, masc.* **diseur** *dē-zœr′,* (*Fr.*) *ns.* a reciter or entertainer.

disfame *dis-fām′, n.* evil reputation. [Pfx. **dis-** (2).]

disfavour (*U.S.* **disfavor**) *dis-fā′var, n.* lack of favour: displeasure: dislike. — *v.t.* to withhold favour from: to disapprove: to oppose. — *n.* **disfā′vourer.** [Pfx. **dis-** (2).]

disfeature *dis-fē′char, v.t.* to deprive of a feature: to deface. [Pfx. **dis-** (3).]

disfellowship *dis-fel′ō-ship, n.* lack of, or exclusion from, fellowship. — *v.t.* to excommunicate. [Pfx. **dis-** (2).]

disfigure *dis-fig′ar, v.t.* to spoil the figure of: to change to a worse form: to spoil the beauty of: to deform. — *ns.* **disfigurā′tion, disfig′urement.** [O.Fr. *desfigurer* — L. *dis-*, neg., *figūrāre*, to figure.]

disflesh *dis-flesh′, v.t.* to deprive of flesh, to disembody. [Pfx. **dis-** (3).]

disfluency *dis-flōō′an-si, n.* a lack of fluency in speech, with hesitations, repetitions, stammering, etc. — *adj.* **disflu′ent.** [Pfx. **dis-** (2)]

disforest *dis-for′ist, v.t.* to strip of trees: to disafforest. [Pfx. **dis-** (2).]

disform *dis-förm′, v.t.* to alter the form of. [Pfx. **dis-** (2).]

disfranchise *dis-fran′chīz, -shīz, v.t.* to deprive of a franchise, or of rights and privileges, esp. that of voting for an M.P. — *n.* **disfran′chisement.** [Pfx. **dis-** (2).]

disfrock *dis-frok′, v.t.* to unfrock, deprive of clerical garb or character. [Pfx. **dis-** (3).]

disfurnish *dis-fûr′nish,* (*Shak.*) *v.t.* to strip, render destitute. — *n.* **disfur′nishment.** [Pfx. **dis-** (2).]

disgarnish *dis-gär′nish, v.t.* to despoil. [Pfx. **dis-** (3).]

disgarrison *dis-gar′i-sn, v.t.* to deprive of a garrison. [Pfx. **dis-** (3).]

disgavel *dis-gav′l, v.t.* to relieve from the tenure of gavelkind. [Pfx. **dis-** (3).]

disgest *dis-jest′, -jēst′,* **disgest′ion** (*-yan*), *obs.* or *dial.* forms of **digest, digestion.**

disglorify *dis-glō′ri-fī, -glō′,* (*Milt.*) *v.t.* to deprive of glory. [Pfx. **dis-** (3).]

disgodded *dis-god′id, adj.* deprived of divinity. [Pfx. **dis-** (2).]

disgorge *dis-görj′, v.t.* to discharge from the throat: to vomit: to throw out with violence: to give up: to remove sediment from (champagne) after fermentation in the bottle. — *n.* **disgorge′ment.** [O.Fr. *desgorger, des,* away, gorge, throat. See **gorge.**]

disgospelling *dis-gos′pal-ing,* (*Milt.*) *adj.* withholding the gospel, stopping the channel of the gospel. [Pfx. **dis-** (3).]

disgown *dis-gown′, v.t.* or *v.i.* to strip of a gown: to deprive of or to renounce orders or a degree. [Pfx. **dis-** (3).]

disgrace *dis-grās′, n.* the state of being out of grace or favour, or of being dishonoured: a cause of shame: dishonour: disfigurement: ugliness: defect of grace. — *v.t.* to put out of favour: to bring disgrace or shame upon. — *adj.* **disgrace′ful** bringing disgrace: causing shame: dishonourable. — *adv.* **disgrace′fully.** — *ns.* **disgrace′fulness; disgra′cer.** — *adj.* **disgracious** (*-grā′shas; Shak.*) ungracious, unpleasing. — **in disgrace** out of favour: shamed. [Fr. *disgrâce* — L. *dis-*, not, and *grātia*, favour, grace.]

disgrade *dis-grād′, v.t.* to deprive of rank or status. — *n.* **disgradation** (*-gra-dā′shan*). [O.Fr. *desgrader,* with substitution of *des-* (L. *dis-*), for L. *dē* in L.L. *dēgradāre* — *gradus,* a step.]

disgregation *dis-gri-gā′shan, n.* separation: scattering. [L. *disgregātiō, -ōnis* — *dis-*, apart, *grex, gregis,* flock.]

disgruntle *dis-grun′tl,* (*coll.*) *v.t.* to disappoint, disgust. — *adj.* **disgrun′tled** out of humour. — *n.* **disgrun′tlement.** [Pfx. **dis-** (4), and **gruntle,** freq. of **grunt.**]

disguise *dis-gīz′, v.t.* to change the guise or appearance of: to conceal the identity of, e.g. by a dress intended to deceive, or by a counterfeit manner and appearance: to intoxicate (*usu. disguised in liquor; arch.* and *slang*). — *n.* a dress intended to disguise the wearer: a false appearance: change of behaviour in intoxication (*arch.* and *slang*). — *adjs.* **disguis′able; disguised′.** — *adv.* **disguis′edly.** — *n.* **disguis′edness.** — *adj.* **disguise′less.** — *ns.* **disguise′ment; disguis′er; disguis′ing.** [O.Fr. *desguiser* — *des-* (L. *dis-*, reversal), *guise,* manner; see **guise.**]

disgust *dis-gust′, n.* (formerly, e.g. in Milton, Johnson, Jane Austen) distaste, disfavour, displeasure: (now) loathing, extreme distaste, extreme annoyance. — *v.t.* to cause disgust in. — *adj.* **disgust′ed.** — *adv.* **disgust′edly.** — *n.* **disgust′edness.** — *adj.* **disgust′ful.** — *adv.* **disgust′fully.** — *n.* **disgust′fulness.** — *adj.* **disgust′ing.** — *adv.* **disgust′ingly.** — *n.* **disgust′ingness.** — **in disgust** with or because of a feeling of disgust. [O.Fr. *desgouster* — *des-* (L. *dis-*), and *gouster* — L. *gustāre,* to taste.]

dish[1] *dish, n.* a vessel, esp. one that is flat, or shallow, or not circular, or one for food at table: a dishful: the food in a dish: a cup (of tea, coffee, etc.) (*arch.*): a particular kind of food: a hollow: concavity of form, as in a wheel, a chair-back: a concave reflector used for directive radiation and reception, esp. for radar or radio telescopes: a good-looking person, esp. of the opposite sex (*coll.*). — *v.t.* to put in a dish, for serving at table: to make concave: to outwit, circumvent (*coll.*): to ruin (*coll.*). — *adj.* **dished** having a concavity: of a pair of wheels on a car, etc., sloping in towards each other at the top: completely frustrated (*coll.*). — *ns.* **dish'ful; dish'ing** putting in a dish: a hollow, a concavity. — *adj.* hollow like a dish. — *adj.* **dish'y** (*coll.*) good-looking, attractive. — **dish aerial** a dish-shaped aerial used esp. in satellite communications; **dish'=cloth, dish'-clout** a cloth for washing, drying, or wiping dishes; **dish'-cover** a cover for a dish to keep it hot. — *adj.* **dish'-faced** having a round, flat face, or (in animals) a concavity in the face. — **dish'-rag** a dish-cloth; **dish'-towel** a tea-towel; **dish'-washer** a machine which washes dishes, cutlery, etc.; **dish'-water** water in which dishes have been washed: a liquid deficient in strength or cleanliness. — **dish out** to serve out: to share (food) among several people: to give, give out (*fig.*; *coll.*; usu. *disparagingly*, esp. with *it*, of rough treatment, punishment, etc.); **dish up** to serve up, esp. *figuratively* of old materials cooked up anew. [O.E. *disc*, a plate, a dish, a table — L. *discus* — Gr. *diskos*; cf. **disc, desk;** Ger. *Tisch*, table.]

dish² *dish* (*print.*) *v.t.* to distribute (type).

dishabilitate *dis-(h)ə-bil'i-tāt, v.t.* to disqualify: to attaint. — *n.* **dishabilitā'tion.** [Pfx. **dis-** (2).]

dishabille *dis-ə-bēl', n.* a negligent toilet: undress: an undress garment. — Also **déshabillé** (*dā-zä-bē-yā*). [Fr. *déshabillé*, pa.p. of *déshabiller*, to undress — *des-* (L. *dis-*), apart, *habiller*, to dress.]

dishabit *dis-hab'it*, (*Shak.*) *v.t.* to drive from a habitation. [O.Fr. *deshabiter* — L. *dis-*, priv., *habitāre*, to inhabit.]

dishable *dis-hā'bl*, an obs. form (*Spens.*) of **disable.**

dishallow *dis-hal'ō, v.t.* to desecrate. [Pfx. **dis-** (2).]

disharmony *dis-här'mə-ni, n.* lack of harmony: discord: incongruity. — *adjs.* **disharmonic** (*-mon'*) out of harmony: discordant: incongruous: dysharmonic; **disharmonious** (*-mō'*). — *adv.* **disharmō'niously.** — *v.t.* and *v.i.* **dishar'monise, -ize** to put out of, or be out of, harmony. [Pfx. **dis-** (2).]

dishearten *dis-härt'n, v.t.* to deprive of heart, courage, or spirits: to discourage: to depress. — *adjs.* **disheart'ened; disheart'ening.** — *adv.* **disheart'eningly.** [Pfx. **dis-** (2).]

dishelm *dis-helm', v.t.* to divest of a helmet. [Pfx. **dis-** (3).]

disherit *dis-her'it*, (*Spens.*) *v.t.* to disinherit. — *ns.* **disher'ison** (*-zən*); **disher'itor.** [O.Fr. *desheriter* — L. *dis-*, neg., L.L. *hērēditāre*, to inherit — L. *hērēs*, heir.]

dishevel *di-shev'l, v.t.* to disorder, as hair: to cause to hang loose: to ruffle. — *v.i.* to spread in disorder: — *pr.p.* **dishev'elling;** *pa.t.* and *pa.p.* **dishev'elled.** — *n.* **dishev'elment.** [O.Fr. *discheveler* — L.L. *discapillāre*, to tear out or disorder the hair — L. *dis-*, in different directions, *capillus*, the hair.]

dishome *dis-hōm', v.t.* to deprive of a home. [Pfx. **dis-** (3).]

dishonest *dis-on'ist, adj.* not honest: lacking integrity: disposed to cheat: insincere: unchaste (*Shak.*). — *adv.* **dishon'estly.** — *n.* **dishon'esty.** [O. Fr. *deshoneste — des-* (L. *dis-*), neg., *honeste* (L. *honestus*), honest.]

dishonour, (*U.S.* **dishonor**), *dis-on'ər, n.* want of honour: disgrace: shame: reproach. — *v.t.* to deprive of honour: to disgrace: to cause shame to: to seduce: to degrade: to refuse the payment of, as a cheque. — *adjs.* **dishon'orary** causing dishonour; **dishon'ourable** not in accordance with a sense of honour: disgraceful. — *n.* **dishon'ourableness.** — *adv.* **dishon'ourably.** — *n.* **dishon'ourer. — dishonourable discharge** dismissal from the U.S. armed forces for serious misconduct (such as theft or desertion). [O.Fr. *deshonneur — des-* (— L. *dis-*), neg., *honneur* (— L. *honor*), honour.]

dishorn *dis-hörn', v.t.* to deprive of horns. [Pfx. **dis-** (3).]

dishorse *dis-hörs', v.t.* to unhorse. [Pfx. **dis-** (3).]

dishouse *dis-howz', v.t.* to deprive of house or housing: to turn out of doors: to clear of houses. [Pfx. **dis-** (3).]

dishumour *dis-(h)ū'mər, n.* ill-humour. — *v.t.* to put out of humour. [Pfx. **dis-** (2).]

disillude *dis-i-lood', -lūd', v.t.* to free from illusion. — *n.* **disillusion** (*dis-i-loo'zhən, -lū'*) a freeing from illusion:

state of being disillusioned. — *v.t.* to free from illusion, disenchant. — *adjs.* **disillu'sionary; disillu'sioned** freed from illusion: often, bereft of comfortable beliefs whether they were false or true. — *v.t.* **disillu'sionise, -ize.** — *n.* **disillu'sionment.** — *adj.* **disillu'sive** (*-siv*). [Pfx. **dis-** (3).]

disilluminate *dis-i-loo'mi-nāt, -lū', v.t.* to destroy the light of, to darken. [Pfx. **dis-** (2).]

disimagine *dis-i-maj'in, v.t.* to banish from the imagination: to imagine not to be. [Pfx. **dis-** (3), (2).]

disimmure *dis-i-mūr', v.t.* to release from walls. [Pfx. **dis-** (2).]

disimpassioned *dis-im-pash'ənd, adj.* free from the influence of passion, tranquil. [Pfx. **dis-** (2).]

disimprison *dis-im-priz'n, v.t.* to free from prison or restraint. — *n.* **disimpris'onment.** [Pfx. **dis-** (2).]

disimprove *dis-im-prōōv', v.t.* to render worse. — *v.i.* to grow worse. [Pfx. **dis-** (2).]

disincarcerate *dis-in-kär'sər-āt, v.t.* to free from prison. — *n.* **disincarcerā'tion.** [Pfx. **dis-** (2).]

disincentive *dis-in-sen'tiv, n.* a discouragement to effort. — Also *adj.* [Pfx. **dis-** (2).]

disinclination *dis-in-kli-nā'shən, n.* lack of inclination: unwillingness. — *v.t.* **disincline** (*-klīn'*) to turn away inclination from: to excite the dislike or aversion of. — *adj.* **disinclined'** not inclined: averse. [Pfx. **dis-** (2).]

disinclose. Same as **disenclose.**

disincorporate *dis-in-kör'pə-rāt, v.t.* to deprive of corporate rights. — *n.* **disincorporā'tion.** [Pfx. **dis-** (2).]

disindividualise, -ize *dis-in-di-vid'ū-əl-īz, v.t.* to deprive of individuality. [Pfx. **dis-** (2).]

disindustrialise, -ize *dis-in-dus'tri-əl-īz, v.t.* to deprive of industry, reduce the amount of industry in. — *n.* **disindustrialisā'tion, -z-.** [Pfx. **dis-** (2).]

disinfect *dis-in-fekt', v.t.* to free from infection: to purify from infectious germs. — *n.* **disinfect'ant** anything that destroys the causes of infection. — Also *adj.* — *ns.* **disinfec'tion; disinfect'or.** [Pfx. **dis-** (2).]

disinfest *dis-in-fest', v.t.* to free from infesting animals. — *n.* **disinfestā'tion.** [Pfx. **dis-** (2).]

disinflation *dis-in-flā-shən, n.* return to the normal condition after inflation: deflation which reduces or stops inflation. — *adj.* **disinflā'tionary.** [Pfx. **dis-** (2).]

disinformation *dis-in-fər-mā'shən, n.* deliberate leakage of misleading information. [Pfx. **dis-** (2).]

disingenuous *dis-in-jen'ū-əs, adj.* not ingenuous: not frank or open: crafty. — *n.* **disingenu'ity** (*rare*). — *adv.* **disingen'uously.** — *n.* **disingen'uousness.** [Pfx. **dis-** (2).]

disinherit *dis-in-her'it, v.t.* to cut off from hereditary rights: to deprive of an inheritance. — *ns.* **disinher'ison** (*-zən*) act of disinheriting; **disinher'itance.** [Pfx. **dis-** (3).]

disinhibit *dis-in-hib'it, v.t.* to remove restraints on — used esp. of drugs affecting behaviour. — *n.* **disinhibition** (*-hi-bish'ən*). — *adj.* **disinhib'itory.** [Pfx. **dis-** (2).]

disinhume *dis-in-hūm', v.t.* to take out of the earth, to disinter. [Pfx. **dis-** (2).]

disintegrate *dis-in'ti-grāt, v.t.* and *v.i.* to separate into parts: to break up: to crumble. — *adjs.* **disin'tegrable; disin'tegrative.** — *ns.* **disintegrā'tion** the act or state of disintegrating: a process in which a nucleus ejects one or more particles, esp. in spontaneous radioactive decay (*nuc.*); **disin'tegrātor** a machine for crushing or pulverising. [Pfx. **dis-** (1).]

disinter *dis-in-tûr', v.t.* to take out of the earth, from a grave, or from obscurity. — *n.* **disinter'ment.** [Pfx. **dis-** (2).]

disinterest *dis-in'tər-ist, n.* disadvantage: disinterestedness: lack of interest. — *v.t.* to free from interest. — *adj.* **disin'terested** not influenced by private feelings or considerations: not deriving personal advantage: impartial: unselfish, generous: (revived from obsolescence) uninterested. — *adv.* **disin'terestedly.** — *n.* **disin'terestedness.** — *adj.* **disin'teresting** (*obs.*) uninteresting. [Pfx. **dis-** (2).]

disinthral. Same as **disenthral.**

disintricate *dis-in'tri-kāt, v.t.* to free from intricacy. [Pfx. **dis-** (2).]

disinure *dis-in-ūr', (Milt.) v.t.* to render unfamiliar. [Pfx. **dis-** (2).]

disinvest[1] *dis-in-vest', v.t.* to divest. — *n.* **disinvest'iture** the action of disinvesting. [Pfx. **dis-** (2).]

disinvest[2] *dis-in-vest', v.i.* and *v.t.* to remove investment (from; with *in*). — *n.* **disinvest'ment.** [Pfx. **dis-** (2).]

disinvigorate *dis-in-vig'ər-āt, v.t.* to weaken. [Pfx. **dis-** (2).]

disinvolve *dis-in-volv', v.t.* to unfold: to disentangle. [Pfx. **dis-** (2).]

disjaskit *dis-jas'kit, (Scot.) adj.* jaded: worn out. [Prob. **dejected.**]

disject *dis-jekt', v.t.* to dismember: to scatter. — *n.* **disjec'tion.** [L. *disjicĕre, -jectum* — *dis-*, apart, *jacĕre,* to throw.]

disjoin *dis-join', v.t.* to separate after having been joined: to form a disjunction of. — *adj.* **disjoin'ing** disjunctive. — *v t* **disjoint'** to put out of joint: to separate united parts of: to break the natural order or relations of: to make incoherent. — *adj.* **disjoint'ed** incoherent, esp. of discourse: badly assorted. — *adv.* **disjoint'edly.** — *n.* **disjoint'edness.** [O.Fr. *desjoindre* — L. *disjungĕre* — *dis-*, apart, *jungĕre,* to join.]

disjunct *dis-jungkt',* also *dis', adj.* disjoined: having deep constrictions between the different sections of the body (*zool.*): of tetrachords, having the highest note of the lower and the lowest of the upper a tone or semitone apart (*ancient Gr. mus.*). — *n.* (*log.*) one of the propositions in a disjunction: a disjunctive proposition. — *n.* **disjunc'tion** the act of disjoining: disunion: separation: the separation during meiosis of the two members of each pair of homologous chromosomes (*biol.*): a compound statement comprising propositions connected by an element denoting 'or', an *inclusive disjunction* being true when at least one proposition is true, an *exclusive disjunction* being true when at least one but no more than one of the propositions is true (*log.*). — *adj.* **disjunct'ive** disjoining: tending to separate: of conjunctions, indicating an alternative or opposition (*gram.*): relating to, containing, forming, or being part of, a disjunction (*log.*). — *n.* a disjunctive word or element. — *adv.* **disjunct'ively.** — *ns.* **disjunct'or** a device for breaking an electric circuit: a weak place where separation between conidia occurs (*bot.*); **disjunct'ure.** [O.Fr. *desjoinct, desjoindre.* See above.]

disjune *dis-jōōn', (Scot.; arch.) n.* breakfast. [O.Fr. *desjun* — L. *dis-*, expressing undoing, *jējūnus,* fasting.]

disk, diskette. See **disc.**

disleaf *dis-lēf', v.t.* to deprive of leaves. — Also **disleave'.** [Pfx. **dis-** (2).]

disleal *dis-lē'əl, (Spens.) adj.* disloyal, dishonourable. [See **disloyal.**]

disleave. See **disleaf.**

dislike *dis-līk', v.t.* to be displeased with: to disapprove of: to have an aversion to: to displease (*obs.*). — *n.* (*dis-līk'*, sometimes *dis'*) disinclination: aversion: distaste: disapproval. — *adjs.* **dislike'able, dislīk'able; dislike'ful.** — *v.t.* **dislik'en** (*Shak.*) to make unlike. — *n.* **dislike'ness** (*obs.*) unlikeness. [Pfx. **dis-** (2) and **like**[2]; the genuine Eng. word is *mislike*.]

dislimb *dis-lim', v.t.* to tear the limbs from: to dismember. [Pfx. **dis-** (1).]

dislimn *dis-lim', (Shak.) v.t.* to efface. [Pfx. **dis-** (3).]

dislink *dis-lingk', v.t.* to unlink, to separate. [Pfx. **dis-** (2).]

disload *dis-lōd', v.t.* to unload, to disburden. [Pfx. **dis-** (3).]

dislocate *dis'lō-kāt, v.t.* to displace: to put out of joint. — *adv.* **dis'locatedly.** — *n.* **disloca'tion** a dislocated joint: displacement: disorganisation: derangement (of traffic, plans, etc.): a fault (*geol.*). [L.L. *dislocāre, -ātum* — L. *dis-*, apart, *locāre,* to place.]

dislodge *dis-loj', v.t.* to drive from a lodgment or place of rest: to drive from a place of hiding or of defence. — *v.i.* to go away. — *n.* **dislodg(e)'ment.** [O.Fr.

desloger — *des-* (L. *dis-*), apart, *loger,* to lodge.]

disloign *dis-loin', (Spens.) v.t.* to put far apart or at a distance, to remove. [O.Fr. *desloignier* — *des-* (L. *dis-*), apart, *loignier,* to remove.]

disloyal *dis-loi'əl, adj.* not loyal: unfaithful. — *adv.* **disloy'ally.** — *n.* **disloy'alty.** [O.Fr. *desloyal* — *des-* (L. *dis-*), neg., *loyal, leial* — L. *lēgālis,* legal.]

dislustre *dis-lus'tər, v.t.* to deprive of lustre. — *v.i.* to lose lustre. [Pfx. **dis-** (3).]

dismal *diz'məl, adj.* gloomy: dreary: sorrowful: depressing. — *n.* unlucky days (*obs.*): (with *cap.*, usu. in *pl.*) a swamp (*old U.S. dial.*): a dismal person: (in *pl.*) the dumps: (in *pl.*) mournings (*obs.*). — *adv.* **dis'mally.** — *ns.* **dis'malness, dismality** (*-mal'i-ti*). — **dismal day** (*Spens.*) a day of ill omen; **dismal Jimmy** a confirmed pessimist. — **the dismal science** political economy. [O.Fr. *dismal* — L. *diēs malī,* evil, unlucky days.]

disman *dis-man', v.t.* to deprive of men (of a country, or ship): to unman: to deprive of human character (of the body by death). [Pfx. **dis-** (3).]

dismantle *dis-man'tl, v.t.* to strip: to deprive of furniture, fittings, etc., so as to render useless: to raze the fortifications of: to take to bits, pull down. — *ns.* **disman'tlement; disman'tler.** [O.Fr. *desmanteller* — *des-* (L. *dis-*), away, *manteler—mantel,* a mantle.]

dismask *dis-mäsk', v.t.* to strip a mask from: to remove a disguise from: to uncover. [O.Fr. *desmasquer* — *des-* (L. *dis-*), neg., *masquer,* to mask.]

dismast *dis-mäst', v.t.* to deprive of a mast or masts. — *n.* **dismast'ment.** [Pfx. **dis-** (3).]

dismay *dis-, diz-mā', v.t.* to appal: to discourage: to distress (*Spens.*). — *v.i.* (*Shak.*) to be daunted. — *n.* the loss of strength and courage through fear: a discouraging onslaught (*Spens.*). — *n.* **dismay'edness.** — *adj.* **dismay'ful.** — *adv.* **dismay'fully** (*Spens.*). [App. through O.Fr. — L. *dis-*, neg., and O.H.G. *magan* (Ger. *mögen*; O.E. *magan*), to have might or power; see **may**[1].]

dismayd *dis-mād', (Spens.) adj.* (*apparently*) misshapen, deformed, mismade. [Pfx. **dis-** (2).]

dismayl *dis-māl', (obs.) v.t.* to deprive of mail (armour): to break mail from (*Spens.*). [O.Fr. *desmailler* — *des-* (L. *dis-*), priv., *maille,* mail.]

disme *dīm, (Shak.) n.* a tenth or tithe. [O.Fr.; see **dime.**]

dismember *dis-mem'bər, v.t.* to divide member from member: to separate a limb from: to disjoint: to tear to pieces: to carve (certain birds — herons, cranes) for the table (*obs.*). — *adj.* **dismem'bered** (*her.*) without limbs or with limbs detached. — *n.* **dismem'berment.** [O.Fr. *desmembrer* — *des-* (L. *dis-*), apart, *membre,* a member (L. *membrum*).]

dismiss *dis-mis', v.t.* to send away: to dispatch: to discard: to remove from office or employment: to reject, to put out of court, to discharge (*law*): in cricket, to put out (batsman, -men): (*imper.*) as a military command, to fall out. — *ns.* **dismiss'al, dismission** (*-mish'ən*). — *adjs.* **dismiss'ible; dismiss'ive, dismiss'ory.** — **dismissal with disgrace** dismissal from the British armed forces for serious misconduct. — a court-martial ruling. [Pfx. **dis-** (3), and L. *mittĕre, missum,* to send; L. *dimissus.*]

dismoded *dis-mōd'id, adj.* out of fashion. [Pfx. **dis-** (2), and **mode.**]

dismount *dis-mownt', v.i.* to come down: to come off a horse, bicycle, etc. — *v.t.* to throw or bring down from any elevated place: to unhorse, to remove from a stand, framework, setting, carriage, or the like. [O.Fr. *desmonter* — *des-* (L. *dis-*), neg., *monter,* to mount.]

dismutation *dis-mū-tā'shən, n.* in biochemistry, simultaneous oxidation and reduction. [Pfx. **dis-** (2).]

disnatured *dis-nā'chərd, adj.* unnatural, devoid of natural affection. — *v.t.* **disnaturalise, -ize** (*-nat', -nach'*) to make alien or unnatural. [Pfx. **dis-** (2).]

disnest *dis-nest', v.t.* to dislodge from a nest: to clear as of nestlings. [Pfx. **dis-** (3).]

Disneyesque *diz-ni-esk', adj.* in the style of the characters, etc. appearing in the cartoon films of Walt *Disney* (1901–66), American cartoonist and film producer:

fantastical, whimsical, unreal.

disobedient *dis-ō-bēd'yənt, adj.* neglecting or refusing to obey. — *n.* **disobed'ience.** — *adv.* **disobed'iently.** [Pfx. **dis-** (2).]

disobey *dis-ō-bā', dis-ə-bā', dis', v.t.* and *v.i.* to neglect or refuse to obey. [O.Fr. *desobeir* — *des-* (L. *dis-*), neg., and *obeir*, to obey.]

disoblige *dis-ō-blīj', -ə-blīj', v.t.* to relieve from an obligation: to refuse or fail to oblige or grant a favour to: to offend or injure thereby. — *n.* **disobligation** (*dis-ob-li-gā'shən*) freedom from obligation: act of disobliging. — *adj.* **disob'ligatory** (*-gə-tə-ri*) releasing from obligation. — *n.* **disobligement** (*-blīj'*). — *adj.* **disoblīg'ing** not obliging: not careful to attend to the wishes of others: unaccommodating: unkind. — *adv.* **disoblīg'ingly.** — *n.* **disoblīg'ingness.** [Pfx. **dis-** (2).]

disoperation *dis-op-ər-ā'shən,* (*ecology*) *n.* a mutually harmful relationship between two organisms in a community. [Pfx. **dis-** (2).]

disorbed *dis-örbd',* (*Shak.*) *adj.* thrown from its sphere, as a star: deprived of the orb of sovereignty. [Pfx. **dis-** (3).]

disorder *dis-ör'dər, n.* want of order: confusion: disturbance: breach of the peace: disease. — *v.t.* to throw out of order: to disarrange: to disturb: to produce disease in. — *adj.* **disor'dered** confused, deranged. — *n.* **disor'derliness.** — *adj.* **disor'derly** out of order: in confusion: irregular: lawless: defying the restraints of decency. — *adv.* confusedly: in a lawless manner. — *n.* a disorderly person. — **disorderly conduct** (*legal*) any of several minor infringements of the law likely to cause a breach of the peace; **disorderly house** a brothel: a gaminghouse. [O.Fr. *desordre* — *des-* (L. *dis-*), neg., *ordre,* order.]

disordinate *dis-ör'di-nit, adj.* not in order (*rare*): disorderly (*rare*): inordinate (*Milt.*). — *adv.* **disor'dinately.** [Pfx. **dis-** (2).]

disorganise, -ize *dis-ör'gən-īz, v.t.* to destroy the organic structure of: to disorder. — *adjs.* **disor'ganised, -z-** disordered: unsystematic, muddled; **disorganic** (*-gan'*). — *n.* **disorganisā'tion, -z-.** [Pfx. **dis-** (2).]

disorient *dis-ō'ri-ənt, -ö', v.t.* to turn from the east: to confuse as to direction: to throw out of one's reckoning. — Also **diso'rientate.** — *n.* **disorientā'tion.** [Pfx. **dis-** (2).]

disown *dis-ōn' v.t.* to refuse to own or acknowledge as belonging to oneself: to deny: to repudiate, cast off. — *n.* **disown'ment.** [Pfx. **dis-** (2).]

dispace *dis-pās',* (*Spens.*) *v.i.* to range about. — Also *v.t.* (*refl.*) [Perh. L. *di-*, apart, *spatiāri*, to walk about; — or **dis-**(1), and **pace**[1].]

disparage *dis-par'ij, v.t.* to dishonour by comparison with what is inferior: to match in marriage with an inferior: to lower in rank or estimation: to talk slightingly of: to dishearten (*Spens.*). — *ns.* **dis'parage** (*Spens.*) an unequal match; **dispar'agement; dispar'ager.** — *adv.* **dispar'agingly.** [O.Fr. *desparager* — *des-* (L. *dis-*), neg., and *parage;* see **parage.**]

disparate *dis'pər-it, -āt, adj.* unequal: incapable of being compared. — *adv.* **dis'parately.** — *n.* **dis'parateness.** — *n.pl.* **dis'parates** things or characters of different species. [L. *disparātus* — *dis-*, not, and *parāre,* make ready; influenced by *dispar,* unequal.]

disparity *dis-par'i-ti, n.* inequality: unlikeness so great as to render comparison difficult and union unsuitable. [L. *dispar,* unequal — *dis-*, neg., *par,* equal.]

dispark *dis-pärk', v.t.* to throw open, deprive of the character of a park: to remove from a park. [Pfx. **dis-** (2, 3).]

dispart *dis-pärt', v.t.* to part asunder: to divide, to separate. — *v.i.* to separate. — *n.* the difference between the thickness of metal at the breech and the mouth of a gun. [Pfx. **dis-** (1).]

dispassion *dis-pash'ən, n.* freedom from passion: a calm state of mind. — *adj.* **dispass'ionate** (*-it*) free from passion: unmoved by feelings: cool: impartial. — *adv.* **dispass'ionately.** [Pfx. **dis-** (2).]

dispatch, despatch *dis-pach', v.t.* to send away hastily: to send out of the world: to put to death: to dispose of: to perform speedily. — *v.i.* (*Shak.*) to make haste. — *n.* a sending away in haste: dismissal: rapid performance: haste: the taking of life: the sending off of the mails: that which is dispatched, as a message, esp. telegraphic: (in *pl.*) state-papers or other official papers (diplomatic, military, etc.). — *n.* **dispatch'er.** — *adj.* **dispatch'ful** (*Milt.*) swift. — **dispatch'-boat** a vessel for carrying dispatches; **dispatch'-box, -case** a box or case for holding dispatches or valuable papers; **dispatch'-rider** a carrier of dispatches, on horseback or motorcycle. — **mentioned in dispatches** as a distinction, commended in official military dispatches for bravery, etc.; **with dispatch** (*arch.*) quickly: without delay. [It. *dispacciare* or Sp. *despachar* — L. *dis-*, apart, and some L.L. word from the root of *pangĕre, pactum,* to fasten; not connected with Fr. *dépêcher.*]

dispathy. A misspelling of **dyspathy.**

dispauperise, -ize *dis-pö'pər-īz, v.t.* to free from pauperism or from paupers. — *v.t.* **dispau'per** to declare no longer a pauper. [Pfx. **dis-** (2).]

dispeace *dis-pēs', n.* lack of peace: dissension. [Pfx. **dis-** (2).]

dispel *dis-pel', v.t.* to drive away and scatter: to make disappear. — *v.i.* to scatter or melt away: — *pr.p.* **dispell'ing;** *pa.t.* and *pa.p.* **dispelled'.** [L. *dispellĕre* — *dis-*, away, *pellĕre,* to drive.]

dispence *dis-pens'* (*Spens.*). Same as **dispense.**

dispend *dis-pend',* (*obs.*) *v.t.* to expend, pay out. [O.Fr. *despendre* — L. *dis-*, out, and *pendĕre,* to weigh.]

dispensary. See **dispensation.**

dispensation *dis-pən-sā'shən, n.* the act of dispensing or dealing out: administration: a dealing of Providence, or of God, or nature: a method or stage of God's dealing with man (*Patriarchal, Mosaic, Christian*): licence or permission to neglect a rule, esp. of church law in the R.C. church: ground of exemption. — *adj.* **dispens'able** that may be dispensed, or dispensed with: pardonable (*arch.*). — *ns.* **dispensabil'ity, dispens'-ableness.** — *adv.* **dispens'ably.** — *n.* **dispens'ary** a place where medicines are dispensed (esp. form. gratis): an out-patient department of a hospital. — *adjs.* **dispensā'tional; dispens'ative** granting dispensation. — *adv.* **dispens'atively.** — *n.* **dis'pensātor** a dispenser: a distributor: an administrator. — *adv.* **dispens'atorily.** — *adj.* **dispens'atory** granting dispensation. — *n.* a book containing medical prescriptions. — *v.t.* **dispense'** to deal out: to distribute: to administer: to make up for distributing or administering. — *v.i.* (*Spens.*) to make amends: to compound. — *n.* expense: expenditure: supplies: dispensation (*Milt.*). — *adj.* **dispensed'.** — *n.* **dispens'er** one who dispenses, esp. a pharmacist who dispenses medicines: a container, or machine that gives out in prearranged quantities. — **dispense with** to permit the want of: to do without. [Fr. *dispenser* — L. *dis-*, *pēnsāre,* to weigh.]

dispeople *dis-pē'pl, v.t.* to empty of inhabitants. [Pfx. **dis-** (2).]

dispermous *dī-spûr'məs,* (*bot.*) *adj.* having or yielding two seeds. [Pfx. **di-**, Gr. *sperma,* seed.]

disperse *dis-pûrs', v.t.* to scatter in all directions: to spread: to diffuse: to drive asunder: to cause to vanish: to put in a colloidal state. — *v.i.* to separate: to spread abroad: to vanish. — *ns.* **dispers'al** dispersion: distribution: the spread of a species to new areas; **dispers'ant** a substance causing dispersion. — *adv.* **dispers'edly.** — *ns.* **dispers'edness; dispers'er; dispersion** (*dis-pûr'shən*) a scattering, or state of being scattered: the removal of inflammation (*med.*): the spreading out of rays owing to different refrangibility (*phys.*): the scattering of values of a variable from the average (*statistics*): the state of a finely divided colloid: a substance in that state: the diaspora. — *adj.* **dispers'ive** tending or serving to disperse. — *n.* **dispers'oid** a substance in a state of dispersion — also **disperse phase.** — **dispersal prison** a prison designed to accommodate particularly

dangerous or high-risk prisoners. [L. *dīspergĕre,
dīspersum — dī-*, asunder, apart, *spargĕre*, to scatter.]
dispirit *dis-pir'it, v.t.* to dishearten: to discourage. — *adj.*
dispir'ited dejected: feeble, spiritless. — *adv.* **dispir'-
itedly.** — *n.* **dispir'itedness.** — *adj.* **dispir'iting** disheartening. — *adv.* **dispir'itingly.** — *n.* **dispir'itment.** [Pfx.
dis- (2).]
dispiteous *dis-pit'i-əs, (obs.) adj.* despiteous: pitiless. —
adv. **dispit'eously.** — *n.* **dispit'eousness.** [See **despite**;
influenced by **piteous.**]
displace *dis-plās', v.t.* to put out of place: to disarrange:
to remove from a state, office, or dignity: to supplant:
to substitute something for. — *adj.* **displace'able.** — *n.*
displace'ment a putting or being out of place: the
difference between the position of a body at a given
time and that occupied at first: the quantity of water
displaced by a ship afloat or an immersed body: the
disguising of emotional feelings by unconscious transference from one object to another (*psychol.*). —
displaced person one removed from his country as a
prisoner or as slave labour: a refugee or stateless
person. [O.Fr. *desplacer — des-* (L. *dis-*), neg., and
place, place.]
displant *dis-plänt', v.t.* to remove from a fixed position:
to drive from an abode. — *n.* **displantā'tion.** [O.Fr.
desplanter — L. *dis-*, neg., and *plantāre*, to plant.]
display *dis-plā', v.t.* to unfold or spread out: to exhibit:
to set out ostentatiously: to make prominent by large
type, wide spacing, etc. (*print.*). — *n.* a displaying or
unfolding: exhibition: ostentatious show: an animal's
or bird's behaviour when courting, threatening intrud-
ers, etc., in which the crest is raised, feathers spread,
etc.: the 'picture' on a cathode-ray tube screen making
the information visible (*electronics*). — *adj.* **displayed'**
unfolded: spread: printed in prominent letters: erect,
with wings expanded, as a bird (*her.*). — *n.* **display'er.**
[O.Fr. *despleier* — *des-* (L. *dis-*), neg., and *plier, ploier*
— L. *plicāre*, to fold; doublet **deploy**; see **ply**[1].]
disple *dis'pl, (Spens.) v.t.* to discipline, chastise. [Ap-
parently from **discipline.**]
displease *dis-plēz', v.t.* to offend: to make angry in a slight
degree: to be disagreeable to. — *v.i.* to raise aversion.
— *n.* **displeasance** (*dis-plez'əns; Spens.*) displeasure. —
adjs. **displeas'ant** (*obs.*); **displeased'** vexed, annoyed. —
adv. **displeas'edly.** — *n.* **displeas'edness.** — *adj.* **displeas'ing** causing displeasure: giving offence. — *adv.*
displeas'ingly. — *ns.* **displeas'ingness; displeasure** (*dis-
plezh'ər*) the feeling of one who is offended: anger: a
cause of irritation. — *v.t. (arch.)* to displease, offend.
[O.Fr. *desplaisir — des-* (L. *dis-*), reversal, *plaisir*, to
please.]
displenish *dis-plen'ish, v.t.* to deprive of plenishing or
furniture, implements, etc.: to sell the plenishing of.
— *n.* **displen'ishment.** [Pfx. **dis-** (3).]
displode *dis-plōd', (Milt.) v.t.* to discharge, to explode. —
v.i. to explode. — *n.* **displō'sion** (*-plō'zhən*). [L. *dis-
plōdĕre* — *dis-*, asunder, *plaudĕre*, to beat.]
displume *dis-plōōm', v.t.* to deprive of plumes or feathers.
[Pfx. **dis-** (3).]
dispondee *dī-spon'dē, n.* a double spondee. — *adj.*
dispondā'ic. [Gr. *dispondeios — di-*, twice, *spondeios,*
spondee.]
dispone *dis-pōn', v.t.* to set in order, dispose (*arch.*): to
make over to another (*Scots law*): to convey legally.
— *ns.* **disponee'** the person to whom anything is
disponed; **dispon'er.** [L. *dispōnĕre*, to arrange.]
disponge. See **dispunge.**
disport *dis-pōrt', -pört', v.t. (usu. refl.)* and *v.i.* to divert,
amuse: to move in gaiety. — *n.* **disport'ment.** [O.Fr.
(*se*) *desporter*, to carry (oneself) away from one's work,
to amuse (oneself) — *des-* (L. *dis-*), and *porter* — L.
portāre, to carry; see **sport.**]
dispose *dis-pōz', v.t.* to arrange: to distribute: to place:
to apply to a particular purpose: to make over by sale,
gift, etc.: to bestow: to incline. — *v.i.* to settle things:
to ordain what is to be: to make a disposition: (usu.
with *of*) to get rid of. — *n.* disposal, management:

behaviour, disposition. — *ns.* **dispōsabil'ity, dispōs'-
ableness.** — *adj.* **dispōs'able** able to be disposed of:
intended to be thrown away or destroyed after use. —
n. **dispōs'al** the act of disposing: order: arrangement:
management: right of bestowing: availability for use,
control, service, etc. — *adj.* **disposed'** inclined: of a
certain disposition (with *well, ill*, etc. *towards*). — *adv.*
dispōs'edly in good order: with measured steps. — *n.*
dispōs'er. — *n.* and *adj.* **dispōs'ing.** — *adv.* **dispōs'ingly.**
— *n.* **disposure** (*-pō'zhər*) disposal, arrangement: disposition. — **disposable income** one's net income after
tax has been paid, available for spending, saving,
investing, etc. — **dispose of** to settle what is to be done
with: to make an end of: to have done with: to part
with: to get rid of: to sell. [Fr. *disposer — dis-* (L.
dis-), asunder, *poser*, to place — L. *pausāre*, to pause,
(late) to place.]
disposition *dis-pə-zish'ən, n.* an arrangement: distribution: a plan for disposing one's property, etc.: natural
tendency: temper: ministration (*N.T.*): a giving over
to another, conveyance or assignment — often *disposition and settlement*, a deed for the disposal of a man's
property at his death (*Scots law*). — *adjs.* **disposi'tional;
disposi'tioned; dispositive** (*-poz'i-tiv*). — *adv.* **dispos'-
itively.** — *n.* **dispos'itor** a planet that disposes or
controls another. [Fr., — L., from *dis-*, apart,
pōnĕre, positum, to place.]
dispossess *dis-pə-zes', v.t.* to put out of possession. — *adj.*
dispossessed' deprived of possessions, property, etc.:
deprived of one's home or country: deprived of rights,
hopes, expectations, etc. — *ns.* **dispossession** (*dis-pə-
zesh'ən*); **dispossess'or.** [Pfx. **dis-** (2).]
dispost[1] *dis-pōst', v.t.* to displace from a post. [Pfx. **dis-**
(2).]
dispost[2] *dis-pōst', (Spens.)* for **disposed.**
disposure. See **dispose.**
disprad (*Spens.*). See **dispread.**
dispraise *dis-prāz', n.* the expression of an unfavourable
opinion: blame: reproach. — *v.t.* to blame: to censure.
— *n.* **dispraise'er.** — *adv.* **disprais'ingly.** [O.Fr. *des-
preisier* — *des-* (L. *dis-*), reversal, *preisier*, to praise.]
dispread *dis-pred', v.t.* to spread in different ways. — *v.i.*
to spread out: to expand. — Spenser has the forms
dispred, dispredden (*plur.*), **disprad** (*pa.p.*). [Pfx. **dis-**
(1).]
disprinced *dis-prinst', (Tenn.) adj.* deprived of the appearance of a prince. [Pfx. **dis-** (3).]
disprison *dis-priz'n, v.t.* to set free. [Pfx. **dis-** (2).]
disprivacied *dis-priv'ə-sid, adj.* deprived of privacy.
[Pfx. **dis-** (3).]
disprivilege *dis-priv'i-lij, v.t.* to deprive of a privilege.
[Pfx. **dis-** (3).]
disprize *dis-prīz', (arch.) v.t.* to set a low price upon: to
undervalue. [Pfx. **dis-** (2).]
disprofess *dis-prə-fes', v.t.* to cease to profess, renounce.
[Pfx. **dis-** (3).]
disprofit *dis-prof'it, n.* loss, damage. [Pfx. **dis-** (2).]
disproof *dis-prōōf', n.* a disproving: refutation. [Pfx.
dis- (2).]
disproove *dis-prōōv', (Spens.) v.t.* to disapprove of. [Pfx.
dis- (2).]
disproperty *dis-prop'ər-ti, (Shak.) v.t.* to deprive one of
possession of. [Pfx. **dis-** (3).]
disproportion *dis-prə-pōr'shən, -pör', n.* want of suitable
proportion. — *v.t.* to make unsuitable in form or size,
etc. — *adj.* **dispropor'tionable** (*arch.*). — *n.* **dispropor'-
tionableness.** — *adv.* **dispropor'tionably.** — *adj.* **dispro-
por'tional.** — *adv.* **dispropor'tionally.** — *adj.* **dispropor'-
tionate.** — *adv.* **dispropor'tionately.** — *n.* **dispropor'-
tionateness.** [Pfx. **dis-** (2).]
dispropriate *dis-prō'pri-āt, v.t.* to disappropriate. [Pfx.
dis- (3).]
disprove *dis-prōōv', v.t.* to prove to be false or wrong: to
disapprove (*arch.*): — *pa.p.* **disproved', disapproved**
(*-prōv'; -prōōv'*). — *adj.* **disprov'able.** — *n.* **disprov'al.**
[O.Fr. *desprover*; see **prove.**]

disprovide *dis-prō-vīd'*, *v.t.* to leave or render unprovided. [Pfx. **dis-** (2).]

dispunge *dis-punj'*, (*Shak.*) *v.t.* to sprinkle or discharge as if from a sponge. [Pfx. **dis-** (1).]

dispurse *dis-pûrs'*, (*Shak.*) *v.t.* to disburse. [Pfx. **dis-** (1).]

dispurvey *dis-pər-vā'*, (*arch.*) *v.t.* to deprive of provisions. — *n.* **dispurvey'ance** (*Spens.*). [Pfx. **dis-** (3).]

dispute *dis-pūt'*, *v.t.* to make a subject of argument: to contend for: to oppose by argument: to call in question. — *v.i.* to argue: to debate. — *n.* a contest with words: an argument: a debate: a quarrel. — *adj.* **dis'putable** (also *-pūt'*) that may be disputed: of doubtful certainty. — *ns.* **disputabil'ity, dis'putableness.** — *adv.* **dis'putably.** — *n.* and *adj.* **dis'putant.** — *ns.* **disput'er; disputā'tion** a contest in argument: an exercise in debate. — *adjs.* **disputā'tious, disput'ative** inclined to dispute, cavil, or controvert. — *advs.* **disputā'tiously, disput'atively.** — *ns.* **disputā'tiousness, disput'ativeness.** — **beyond** or **without dispute** indubitably, certainly. [O.Fr. *desputer* — L. *disputāre—dis-*, apart, and *putāre*, to think.]

disqualify *dis-kwol'i-fī*, *v.t.* to deprive of the qualities or qualifications necessary for any purpose: to make unfit: to disable: to debar: to declare to be disqualified. — *adj.* **disqualifi'able.** — *ns.* **disqualificā'tion** state of being disqualified: anything that disqualifies or incapacitates; **disqual'ifier.** [Pfx. **dis-** (3).]

disquiet *dis-kwī'ət*, *adj.* (*arch.*) unquiet, uneasy, restless. — *n.* want of quiet: uneasiness, restlessness: anxiety. — *v.t.* to render unquiet: to make uneasy: to disturb. — Also **disqui'eten.** — *adjs.* **disqui'etful; disqui'etive, disqui'eting.** — *advs.* **disqui'etingly; disqui'etly** (*Shak.*). — *n.* **disqui'etness.** — *adj.* **disqui'etous.** — *n.* **disqui'etude.** [Pfx. **dis-** (2).]

disquisition *dis-kwi-zish'ən*, *n.* a careful inquiry into any matter by arguments, etc.: an essay. — *adjs.* **disquisi'tional, disquisi'tionary, disquisi'tory, disquis'itive** pertaining to or of the nature of a disquisition. [L. *disquīsītiō, -ōnis — disquīrĕre*, *dis-*, intens., *quaerĕre, quaesītum*, to seek.]

disrank *dis-rangk'*, *v.t.* to reduce to a lower rank: to throw into confusion. [Pfx. **dis-** (3).]

disrate *dis-rāt'*, (*naut.*) *v.t.* to reduce to a lower rating or rank, as a petty officer. [Pfx. **dis-** (3).]

disregard *dis-ri-gärd'*, *v.t.* to pay no attention to. — *n.* want of attention: neglect: slight. — *adj.* **disregard'ful.** — *adv.* **disregard'fully.** [Pfx. **dis-** (2).]

disrelish *dis-rel'ish*, *v.t.* not to relish: to dislike the taste of: to dislike. — *n.* distaste: dislike: disgust. — *adj.* **disrel'ishing** offensive. [Pfx. **dis-** (2).]

disremember *dis-ri-mem'bər*, (*dial.* or *U.S. coll.*) *v.t.* not to remember, to forget. [Pfx. **dis-** (2).]

disrepair *dis-ri-pār'*, *n.* the state of being out of repair. [Pfx. **dis-** (2).]

disrepute *dis-ri-pūt'*, *n.* bad repute: discredit. — Also **disreputā'tion** (*dis-rep-*). — *adj.* **disrep'utable** in bad repute: disgraceful: not repectable: disordered and shabby. — *ns.* **disrep'utableness, disreputabil'ity** (*rare*). — *adv.* **disrep'utably.** [Pfx. **dis-** (2).]

disrespect *dis-ri-spekt'*, *n.* want of respect: discourtesy: incivility. — *v.t.* (*arch.*) not to respect. — *adjs.* **disrespect'able** (*rare*) not respectable; **disrespect'ful** showing disrespect: irreverent: uncivil. — *adv.* **disrespect'fully.** — *n.* **disrespect'fulness.** [Pfx. **dis-** (2).]

disrobe *dis-rōb'*, *v.t.* and *v.i.* to undress: to uncover: to divest of robes. [Pfx. **dis-** (2), (3).]

disroot *dis-rōōt'*, *v.t.* to uproot. [Pfx. **dis-** (3).]

disrupt *dis-rupt'*, *v.t.* and *v.i.* to burst asunder, to break up: to interrupt (growth, progress, etc.). — *ns.* **disrupt'er, disrupt'or; disrup'tion** the act of breaking asunder: the act of bursting and rending: breach: (with *cap.*) in Scottish ecclesiastical history, the separation of the Free Church from the Established Church for the sake of spiritual independence (1843). — *adj.* **disrup'tive** causing, or accompanied by, disruption. — *adv.* **rupt'ively.** [L. *disruptus, dīruptus — dīrumpĕre —*

dis-, asunder, *rumpĕre*, to break.]

diss *dis*, *n.* an Algerian reedy grass (*Ampelodesma tenax*) used for cordage, etc. [Ar. *dīs*.]

dissatisfactory *dis-sat-is-fak'tər-i*, *adj.* causing dissatisfaction. — *ns.* **dissatisfac'tion** state of being dissatisfied: discontent: uneasiness; **dissatisfac'toriness.** [Pfx. **dis-** (2).]

dissatisfy *dis-sat'is-fī*, *v.t.* to fail to satisfy: to make discontented: to displease. — *adj.* **dissat'isfied** discontented: not pleased. [Pfx. **dis-** (2).]

disseat *dis-sēt'*, *v.t.* to unseat. [Pfx. **dis-** (2), (3).]

dissect *di-sekt'*, *v.t.* to cut asunder: to cut into parts for the purpose of minute examination: to divide and examine: to analyse and criticise. — *adjs.* **dissect'ed** deeply cut into narrow segments (*bot.*): cut up by valleys (*geol.*); **dissect'ible.** — *ns.* **dissect'ing; dissec'tion** the act or the art of cutting in pieces a plant or animal in order to ascertain the structure of its parts: anatomy. — *adj.* **dissect'ive** tending to dissect. — *n.* **dissect'or.** — **dissected map, picture** a map or picture on a board cut up, so as to form a puzzle; **dissecting microscope** a form of microscope that allows dissection of the object under examination; **dissecting room, table** a room in, table on, which anatomical dissection is practised. [L. *dissecāre, dissectum — dis-*, asunder, *secāre*, to cut.]

disseise, disseize *dis-sēz'*, *v.t.* to deprive of seisen or possession of an estate of freehold: to dispossess wrongfully. — *ns.* **disseis'in, disseiz'in; disseis'or, disseiz'or.** [Pfx. **dis-** (3).]

dissemble *di-sem'bl*, *v.t.* to disguise: to mask: to feign (*obs.*). — *v.i.* to assume a false appearance: to play the hypocrite: to dissimulate. — *ns.* **dissem'blance** (*rare*) want of resemblance: the act of dissembling; **dissem'bler; dissem'bling.** — *adj.* deceiving, hypocritical. — *adv.* **dissem'blingly.** [L. *dissimulāre — dissimilis*, unlike — *dis-*, neg., and *similis*, like; perh. remodelled on *resemble*.]

dissembly *dis-em'bli*, *n.* the breaking up of an assembly: a Dogberryism for assembly (*Shak.*). [Pfx. **dis-** (1).]

disseminate *di-sem'i-nāt*, *v.t.* to sow or scatter abroad: to propagate: to diffuse. — *adj.* scattered. — *n.* **disseminā'tion.** — *adj.* **dissem'inative.** *ns.* **dissem'inātor; dissem'inule** any part or organ of a plant that serves for dissemination. — **disseminated sclerosis** a chronic progressive disease in which patches of thickening appear throughout the central nervous system, resulting in various forms of paralysis. [L. *dissēminare, -ātum — dis-*, asunder, *sēminare*, to sow — *sēmen, sēminis*, seed.]

dissent *di-sent'*, *v.i.* to think differently: to disagree in opinion: to differ (with *from*). — *n.* the act of dissenting: difference of opinion: a protest by a minority: a differing or separation from an established church. — *ns.* **dissen'sion** disagreement in opinion: discord: strife; **Dissent'er** one (esp. a Protestant) who is separate from an established church: a nonconformist: (without *cap.*) a dissentient. — *adj.* **dissent'erish.** — *n.* **dissent'erism.** — *adj.* **dissen'tient** (*-shənt*) declaring dissent: disagreeing. — *n.* one who disagrees: one who declares his dissent. — *adj.* **dissent'ing.** — *adv.* **dissent'ingly.** — *adj.* **dissen'tious** (*-shəs*; *Shak.*) disposed to discord, contentious. [L. *dissentīre, dissēnsum — dis-*, apart, *sentīre*, to think.]

dissepiment *di-sep'i-mənt*, *n.* a partition in an ovary (*bot.*): a partition partly cutting off the bottom of a coral cup (*zool.*). — *adj.* **dissepimental** (*-ment'l*). [L. *dissaepīmentum*, a partition — L. *dissaepīre — dis-*, apart, *saepīre*, to hedge in, to fence.]

dissertate *dis'ər-tāt*, *v.i.* to discourse —(*arch.*) **dissert'.** — *n.* **dissertā'tion** a formal discourse: a treatise. — *adjs.* **dissertā'tional, disser'tātive.** — *n.* **disser'tātor.** [L. *dissertāre*, intens. of *disserĕre*, to discuss — *dis-*, *serĕre*, to put together.]

disserve *dis-sûrv'*, (*arch.*) *v.t.* to do an ill turn to: to clear (a table). — *n.* **disserv'ice** injury: mischief: an ill turn.

— *adj.* **disserv'iceable.** [O.Fr. *desservir* — L. *dis-*, neg., *servīre*, to serve.]

dissever *di-sev'ər*, *v.t.* to sever: to part in two: to separate: to disunite. — *ns.* **dissev'erance, disseverā'tion, dissev'erment** a dissevering or parting. — *adj.* **dissev'ered** disunited. [O.Fr. *dessevrer* — L. *dis-*, apart, *sēparāre*, to separate.]

dissheathe *dis-shēdh'*, *v.t.* to unsheathe. [Pfx. **dis-** (2).]

disshiver *dis-shiv'ər*, *v.t.* (*Spens.*) and *v.i.* to shiver in pieces. [Pfx. **dis-** (1).]

dissident *dis'i-dənt*, *adj.* dissenting. — *n.* a dissenter, esp. one who disagrees with the aims and procedures of the government. — *n.* **diss'idence** disagreement. [L. *dissidēns, -entis*, pr.p. of *dissidēre* — *dis-*, apart, *sedēre*, to sit.]

dissight *di(s)-sīt'*, *n.* an unsightly object. [Pfx. **dis-** (2).]

dissilient *di(s)-sil'yənt*, *adj.* springing asunder: bursting open with force (*bot.*). — *n.* **dissil'ience.** [L. *dissiliēns, -entis* — *dis-*, asunder, *salīre*, to leap.]

dissimilar *di-sim'ilər*, *adj.* unlike. — *n.* **dissimilarity** (*-ar'*) unlikeness. — *adv.* **dissim'ilarly.** — *v.t.* **dissim'ilate** to make unlike. — *ns.* **dissimilā'tion** the act of rendering dissimilar: katabolism; **dissimile** (*di-sim'i-li*) the opposite of a simile, a comparison by contrast; **dissimil'itude.** [Pfx. **dis-** (2).]

dissimulate *di-sim'ū-lāt*, *v.t.* to pretend the contrary of: to conceal or disguise: to dissemble. — *v.i.* to practise dissimulation, play the hypocrite. — *n.* **dissimulā'tion** the act of dissembling: a hiding under a false appearance: false pretension: hypocrisy. — *adj.* **dissim'ulative.** — *n.* **dissim'ulātor.** [L. *dissimulāre, -ātum*, to dissimulate — *dis-*, neg., *similis*, like.]

dissipate *dis'i-pāt*, *v.t.* to scatter: to squander: to waste: to dispel. — *v.i.* to separate and disappear: to waste away: to be dissolute in conduct: to indulge in trivial amusements. — *adjs.* **diss'ipable** that may be dissipated; **diss'ipated** dissolute, esp. addicted to drinking. — *adv.* **diss'ipatedly.** — *n.* **dissipā'tion** dispersion: state of being dispersed: scattered attention: a course of frivolous amusement or of dissolute life. — *adj.* **diss'i-pātive** tending to dissipate or disperse: connected with the dissipation of energy. — **dissipation of energy** degradation of energy, or progressive loss of availability of a portion for doing work at each transformation. [L. *dissipāre, -ātum* — *dis-*, asunder, and (archaic) *supāre*, to throw.]

dissociate *di-sō'shi-āt*, *v.t.* and *v.i.* to separate from society or from association of any kind: to separate: to subject to or suffer dissociation. — *adj.* **separated.** — *ns.* **dissōciabil'ity** (*-shə-*); **dissō'ciableness.** — *adj.* **dissō'ciable** not sociable: ill associated: incongruous: capable of being dissociated. — *adv.* **dissō'ciably.** — *adj.* **dissō'cial** (*arch.*) not social. — *v.t.* **dissō'cialise, -ize** to make unsocial. — *ns.* **dissociality** (*-sō-shi-al'*); **dissociā'tion** (*-sō-shi-* or *-sō-si-*) act of dissociating: state of being dissociated: separation into simpler constituents, esp. a reversible separation caused by heat, or separation into ions (*chem.*): splitting of personality (*psych.*): splitting off from consciousness of certain ideas and their accompanying emotions: breaking of associations. — *adj.* **dissō'ciative** (*chem.*) tending to dissociate. [L. *dissociāre, -ātum* — *dis-*, asunder, *sociāre*, to associate.]

dissoluble *dis-ol'ū-bl* or *dis'əl-ū-bl, -ōō-bl, adj.* capable of being dissolved. — *ns.* **dissolūbil'ity, dissol'ūbleness.** — *adj.* **diss'olute** (*-lōōt* or *-lūt*) loose, esp. in morals, debauched. — *n.* a dissolute person. — *adv.* **diss'olutely.** — *ns.* **diss'oluteness; dissolution** (*-lōō'* or *-lū'*) the breaking up of an assembly: loosening: melting: break-up: death: dissoluteness or dissolute behaviour (*arch.*); **dissolu'tionism; dissolu'tionist.** — *adj.* **diss'olutive.** — *n.* **dissolvabil'ity** (*diz-*); **dissolv'ableness.** — *adj.* **dissolv'able** capable of being dissolved. — *v.t.* **dissolve** (*di-zolv'*) to loose asunder: to undo: to separate or break up: to put an end to (as a parliament): to melt in solution (formerly also in fusion): to disperse: to resolve (as doubts, riddles; *arch.*). — *v.i.* to go into

solution: to break up: to waste away: to fade away: in films and television, to fade out one scene gradually while replacing it with another (also *n.*): to melt. — *n.* **dissolv'ent** (*rare*) a solvent. — *adj.* having power to melt. — *n.* and *adj.* **dissolv'ing.** [L. *dissolvĕre, dissol-ūtum* — *dis-*, asunder, *solvĕre, -ūtum*, to loose.]

dissonant *dis'ə-nənt, adj.* not agreeing or harmonising in sound: without concord or harmony: disagreeing. — *n.* **diss'onance** disagreement of sound: want of harmony: discord: disagreement: *specif.*, a combination of musical sounds that calls for resolution or produces beats (also **diss'onancy**). — *adv.* **diss'onantly.** [L. *dissonāns, -antis* — *dis-*, apart, *sonāre*, to sound.]

dissuade *di-swād'*, *v.t.* to give advice against (*obs.*): to seek to divert by advice (*obs.*): to divert by advice (from). — *ns.* **dissuā'der; dissuā'sion** (*-zhən*). — *adj.* **dissuā'sive** (*-siv*) tending to dissuade. — *n.* that which tends to dissuade. — *adv.* **dissuā'sively.** — *n.* and *adj.* **dissuā'sory** (*rare*). [L. *dissuādēre* — *dis-*, apart, *suādēre, suāsum*, to advise.]

dissunder *dis-sun'dər*, (*arch.*) *v.t.* to sunder. [Pfx. **dis-** (4).]

dissyllable. A variant of **disyllable.**

dissymmetry *dis-sim'i-tri*, *n.* want of symmetry: enantiomorphy — the symmetry of right and left hand, object and mirror-image. — *adjs.* **dissymmetric, -al** (*-et'*). — *adv.* **dissymmet'rically.** [Pfx. **dis-** (2).]

distaff *dis'täf*, *n.* the stick that holds the bunch of flax, tow, or wool in spinning. — **distaff side** the female part, line, side, or branch of a family or descent. [O.E. *distæf*, from the root found in L.G. *diesse*, the bunch of flax on the staff; and *stæf*, staff; see **dizen.**]

distain *dis-tān'*, *v.t.* to stain: to sully. [O.Fr. *desteindre*, to take away the colour of — L. *dis-*, neg., and *tingĕre*, to colour.]

distal *dis'təl*, (*biol.*) *adj.* far apart, widely spaced: pertaining to or situated at the outer end: farthest from the point of attachment — opp. to *proximal.* — *adv.* **dis'tally.** [Formed from **distance** on the analogy of *central.*]

distance *dis'təns*, *n.* measure of interval between: remoteness: a remote place or region: the remote part of the field of view or the part of a picture representing it: degree of remoteness: opposition: stand-offishness or aloofness of manner: the scheduled duration of a boxing match, etc.: in horse-racing, the space measured back from the winning-post which a horse, in heat-races, must reach when the winner has covered the whole course, in order to run in the final heat. — *adj.* in athletics, of races, over a long distance. — *v.t.* to place at a distance: to leave at a distance behind. — *adj.* **dis'tanceless** not allowing a distant view (of hazy weather): having no indications of distance (of pictures). — **go the distance** to complete what one has started (*coll.*): to endure to the end of a (boxing, etc.) bout; **keep someone at a distance** to treat someone with aloofness; **keep one's distance** to abstain from familiarity (with): to keep aloof (from). — **distance education, teaching** the provision of educational courses, e.g. by television or correspondence course, for students unable to attend in person the educational institution concerned; **distance learning** the following of such educational courses. [See **distant.**]

distant *dis'tənt*, *adj.* at a certain distance: at a great distance: remote, in time, place, resemblance, or connection: indistinct: reserved or aloof in manner. — *adv.* **dis'tantly.** — *n.* **dis'tantness.** — **dis'tant-signal** on a railway, a signal farther from the destination than the home-signal. [Fr., — L. *dīstāns, -antis* — *dī-*, apart, *stāns, stantis*, pr.p. of *stāre*, to stand.]

distaste *dis-tāst'*, *n.* disrelish (for): dislike (for): an unpleasant experience (*obs.*): an offence (*obs.*). — *v.t.* to dislike (*arch.*): to offend (*obs.*): to spoil the taste of (*Shak.*). — *v.i.* (*Shak.*) to be distasteful. — *adj.* **distaste'ful** unpleasant to the taste: unpleasant: indicating distaste (*Shak.*): full of distaste. — *adv.* **distaste'fully.** — *n.* **distaste'fulness.** [Pfx. **dis-** (2).]

distemper[1] *dis-temp'ər, n.* a mode of painting in size, water-glass, or other watery vehicle giving body to the pigment: paint of this kind — for indoor walls, scenery, etc. — *v.t.* to paint in distemper. — Also **destemp'er**. [L. *dis-*, reversal, *temperāre*, to regulate, mix in proportion; cf. next word.]

distemper[2] *dis-temp'ər, n.* a morbid or disorderly state of body or mind (*arch.*): disease, esp. of animals: *specif.* a disease of the dog and ferret families caused by a virus: ill-humour (*arch.*). — *v.t.* (*arch.*) to derange the temper: to disorder or disease. — *adj.* **distemp'erate** not temperate, immoderate: diseased. — *n.* **distemp'erature** (*arch.*) want of proper temperature: intemperateness, disturbance: uneasiness of mind: indisposition. — *adj.* **distem'pered** disordered: intemperate, ill-humoured, put out of sorts. [O.Fr. *destemprer*, to derange — L. *dis-*, apart, *temperāre*, to govern, regulate.]

distend *dis-tend', v.t.* to stretch forth or apart: to stretch in three dimensions: to swell: to exaggerate. — *v.i.* to swell. — *n.* **distensibil'ity** capacity for distension. — *adjs.* **disten'sible** that may be stretched; **disten'sile** (*-sīl*) distensible: able to cause distension. — *n.* **disten'sion** act of distending or stretching: state of being stretched: breadth (*rare*; sometimes **disten'tion**). — *adjs.* **disten'sive** capable of stretching or of being stretched; **distent'** (*Spens.*) extended: distended, swollen. [L. *distendĕre* — *dis-*, asunder, *tendĕre*, *tēnsum* or *tentum*, to stretch.]

disthene *dis'thēn, n.* kyanite — so called from its difference in hardness when scratched in different directions. [Gr. *di-*, twice, *sthenos*, strength.]

disthrone *dis-thrōn', v.t.* to dethrone —(*Spens.*) **disthrōn'ize.** [Pfx. **dis-** (2), (3).]

distich *dis'tik, n.* a couple of lines or verses, making complete sense: a couplet: — *pl.* **distichs** (*-tiks*). — *adj.* having two rows. — *adjs.* **dis'tichal; dis'tichous** in or having two rows: (esp. *bot.*) arranged in, having, two opposite vertical rows. [Gr. *distichos* — *di-*, twice, *stichos*, a line.]

distil now rarely **distill** *dis-til', v.i.* to fall in drops: to flow gently: to use a still. — *v.t.* to let or cause to fall in drops: to convert from liquid into vapour by heat, and then to condense again: to extract by evaporation and condensation. — *pr.p.* **distill'ing**; *pa.t.* and *pa.p.* **distilled'.** — *adj.* **distill'able.** — *ns.* **dis'tilland** that which is to be, or is being, distilled; **dis'tillate** the product of distillation; **distillā'tion** the act of distilling. — *adj.* **distill'atory** of or for distilling; — *ns.* **distill'er; distill'ery** a place where distilling, esp. of alcoholic spirits, is carried on; **distill'ing; distil'ment** (*Shak.*) that which is distilled. — **destructive distillation** the collection of volatile matters released when a substance is destroyed by heat in a close vessel (as coal in making gas); **fractional distillation** the separation by distilling of liquids having different boiling-points, the heat being gradually increased and the receiver changed; **vacuum distillation** distillation under reduced pressure (effecting a lowering of the boiling point). [O.Fr. *distiller*, with substitution of prefix — L. *dēstillāre, -ātum* — *dē*, down, *stillāre*, to drop — *stilla*, a drop.]

distinct *dis-tingkt', adj.* distinguished, differentiated (*Milt.*): separate: different: well-defined: clear: marked, variegated (*Spens., Milt.*). — *n.* **distinction** (*dis-tingk'shən*) separation or division: discrimination: a distinguishing mark or character: distinctness (*obs.*): difference: a mark or honorific recognition of excellence: an honour: discriminating favour: noticeable eminence: outstanding merit: impressive and meritorious individuality. — *adj.* **distinc'tive** marking or expressing difference: characteristic. — *adv.* **distinct'ively.** — *n.* **distinct'iveness.** — *adv.* **distinct'ly.** — *ns.* **distinct'ness; distincture** (*-tingk'chər, -tyər*) distinctness. [See **distinguish**.]

distingué *dē-stē̃-gä,* (Fr.) *adj.* distinguished: striking: — *fem.* **distinguée.**

distinguish *dis-ting'gwish, v.t.* to mark off, set apart (often with *from*): to recognise by characteristic qualities: to make out: to make distinctions in or concerning (*obs.*): to bring by drawing distinctions: to separate by a mark of honour: to make eminent or known: to hold to be not directly comparable (*Scots law*). — *v.i.* to make or show distinctions or differences, to recognise a difference (often with *between*). — *adj.* **disting'uishable** capable of being distinguished. — *adv.* **disting'uishably.** — *adj.* **disting'uished** illustrious: dignified in appearance or manner. — *n.* **disting'uisher.** — *adj.* **disting'uishing** peculiar. — *n.* **disting'uishment** (*Shak.*) distinction. — **Distinguished Conduct Medal (D.C.M.), Distinguished Flying Cross (D.F.C.), Distinguished Service Medal (D.S.M.;** also *U.S.*), **Distinguished Service Order (D.S.O.)** military decorations awarded for distinguished conduct in action. [L. *dīstinguĕre, dīstinctum* — *dī-*, asunder, *stinguĕre*, orig. to prick, and *-ish*, in imitation of Fr. vbs. in *-ir*.]

distort *dis-tört', v.t.* to twist aside: to put out of shape without breach of continuity: to turn aside from the true meaning: to pervert: to misrepresent. — *adj.* **distort'ed.** — *n.* **distortion** (*-tör'shən*) a twisting awry: deformation without breaking: change of wave-form in course of transmission: crookedness: perversion. — *adj.* **distort'ive** causing distortion. [L. *dis-*, asunder, *torquēre, tortum*, to twist.]

distract *dis-trakt', v.t.* to draw aside, apart, or in different directions — esp. of the mind or attention: to confuse: to harass: to render crazy. — *adj.* separate (*Shak., dis'-*): distracted (*Milt., -trakt'*). — *adj.* **distract'ed.** — *adv.* **distract'edly.** — *ns.* **distract'edness; distractibil'ity.** — *adjs.* **distract'ible; distract'ing.** — *adv.* **distract'ingly.** — *n.* **distrac'tion** state of being distracted: that which distracts: perplexity: agitation: madness: recreation, relaxation. — *adj.* **distract'ive** causing perplexity. — *adv.* **distract'ively.** [L. *distrahĕre, -tractum* — *dis-*, apart, *trahĕre*, to draw.]

distrain *dis-trān', v.t.* to seize (esp. goods for debt, esp. for non-payment of rent or rates): to pull apart, burst (*Spens.*). — *v.i.* to seize the goods of a debtor. — *adj.* **distrain'able.** — *ns.* **distrainee'** a person whose property has been distrained; **distrain'er; distrain'ment; distrain'or** (*law*); **distraint'** seizure of goods. [O.Fr. *destraindre* — L. *dī-*, asunder, *stringĕre*, to draw tight.]

distrait *dēs-tre,* (Fr.) *adj.* absent-minded: — *fem.* **distraite** (*dēs-tret*).

distraught *dis-tröt', adj.* drawn aside (*Spens.*): distracted: mad: perplexed. [**distract**, modified by association with words like **caught, taught**.]

distress *dis-tres', n.* extreme pain or suffering: that which causes suffering: calamity: misfortune: acute poverty: exhaustion: peril: difficulty: compulsion (*arch.*): act of distraining goods: in a structure, a sign of weakness arising from stress. — *v.t.* to afflict with pain or suffering: to harass: to grieve: to distrain: to treat (antique furniture, etc.) by knocking, scraping, etc., so that it appears older than it is (*coll.*). — *adj.* **distressed'.** — *n.* **distress'er.** — *adj.* **distress'ful.** — *adv.* **distress'fully.** — *n.* **distress'fulness.** — *adj.* **distress'ing.** — *adv.* **distress'ingly.** — **distressed area** a region of unusually severe unemployment; **in distress** (of a ship or aircraft) in danger, needing help. [O.Fr. *destresse* — L. *dīstringĕre*; see **distrain**.]

distribute *dis-trib'ūt,* or *dis', v.t.* to divide amongst several: to deal out or allot: to classify: to disperse about a space: to spread out: to separate and put back in compartments (*print.*): to use with full extension, including every individual to which the term is applicable (*log.*). — *n.* **distrib'uend** that which is to be distributed. — *adjs.* **distrib'utable** that may be divided; **distrib'utary** distributing. — *n.* a branch of a distributing system: an off-flow from a river that does not return to it. — *ns.* **distrib'utor, distrib'uter** one who, or that which, distributes: an agent, or middleman, between manufacturer and retailer: a device in a petrol engine whereby high tension current is transmitted in correct sequence to the sparking plugs; **distribu'tion** the act or process of distributing: dispersal: division:

range: allotment: classification: the application of a general term to all the objects denoted by it: the manner in which the products of industry are shared among the people (*econ.*). — *adjs.* **distribu'tional; distrib'utive** that distributes, separates, or divides: giving to each his own: such that $a.(x+y+z+ ...) = a.x+a.y+a.z+ ...$(*math.*). — *n.* a word, like *each* or *every*, that indicates the several individuals of a number taken separately. — *adv.* **distrib'utively.** — *n.* **distrib'utiveness.** — **distributed processing** (*comput.*) the distribution of processing power away from the centre to other terminals. — **geographical distribution** the department of science that treats of the range and dispersal of animal and plants about the world. [L. *distribuĕre* — *dis-*, asunder, *tribuĕre*, *tribūtum*, to allot.]

district *dis'trikt*, *n.* a portion of territory defined for political, judicial, educational, or other purposes (as a registration district, a militia district, the District of Columbia): a region: the smaller of the two local-government administrative units in Scotland (cf. **region**): a subdivision of English and Welsh non-metropolitan counties: a constituency (*U.S.*): a subdivision of a division (*India*). — *v.t.* to divide into districts. — **district attorney** (*U.S.*) a public prosecutor for a district; **district council** the council of an urban or rural district: the council elected to govern a Scottish district; **district court** (*U.S.*) the federal court for a district; **district heating** the distribution of heat from a central source to buildings in the surrounding area; **district nurse** a nurse appointed to attend to cases in their own homes; **district visitor** a church worker who visits parishioners in a district. [Fr., — L.L. *dīstrictus*, jurisdiction — *dīstringĕre*; see **distrain**.]

distringas *dis-tring'gas*, *n.* an old writ directing a sheriff or other officer to distrain. [Second pers. sing. pres. subj. of L. *dīstringĕre*; see **distrain**.]

distrouble *dis-trub'l*, (*Spens.*) *v.t.* to trouble greatly, to perplex, to disturb. [L. *dis-*, intens., and **trouble**.]

distrust *dis-trust'*, *n.* want of trust: want of faith or confidence: doubt. — *v.t.* to have no trust in: to disbelieve: to doubt. — *adj.* **distrust'ful** full of distrust: apt to distrust: suspicious: to be distrusted (*rare*). — *adv.* **distrust'fully.** — *n.* **distrust'fulness.** — *adj.* **distrust'less.** [Pfx. **dis-** (2), (3).]

distune *dis-tūn'*, (*arch.*) *v.t.* to put out of tune. [Pfx. **dis-** (3).]

disturb *dis-tûrb'*, *v.t.* to throw into confusion: to agitate: to disquiet: to interrupt: to inconvenience. — *n.* disturbance. — *n.* **disturb'ance** agitation: tumult: interruption: perplexity. — *adj.* and *n.* **disturb'ant** disturbing. — *adjs.* **disturb'ative; disturbed'** worried: confused, esp. emotionally. — *n.* **disturb'er.** [O.Fr. *destourber* — L. *disturbāre*, *dis-*, asunder, *turbāre*, to agitate — *turba*, a crowd.]

distyle *dis'tīl*, *dī'stīl*, *n.* a portico with two columns. [Gr. *di-*, twice, and *stȳlos*, column.]

disulfiram *dī-sul-fē'ram*, *n.* a drug used to treat chronic alcoholism, acting by inducing nausea, etc., if alcohol is taken.

disulphate *dī-sul'fāt*, *n.* a pyrosulphate: formerly, an acid sulphate. — *n.* **disul'phide** a sulphide containing two atoms of sulphur to the molecule. — Also (*obs.*) **disul'phuret.** — *adj.* **disulphu'ric** pyrosulphuric. [Pfx. **di-**.]

disunion *dis-ūn'yən*, *n.* want of union: breaking up of union or concord: separation. — *n.* **disun'ionist** one who favours dissolution of a union. — *v.t.* **disunite'** to separate from union: to sever or sunder. — *v.i.* to fall asunder: to part. — *n.* **disu'nity** state of disunion. [Pfx. **dis-** (2), (1).]

disuse *dis-ūs'*, or *dis'ūs*, *n.* the state of being out of use. — *v.t.* (*dis-ūz'*) to cease to use or practise: to leave out of use. — *n.* **disusage** (*dis-ūz'ij*) gradual cessation of use or custom. [Pfx. **dis-** (2), (3).]

disutility *dis-ū-til'i-ti*, *n.* an inconvenience, drawback, disadvantage. [Pfx. **dis-** (2).]

disvalue *dis-val'ū*, *v.t.* to disparage. [Pfx. **dis-** (3).]

disvouch *dis-vowch'*, (*Shak.*) *v.t.* to disavow. [Pfx. **dis-** (3).]

disworship *dis-wûr'ship*, (*Milt.*) *n.* dishonour, disgrace. [Pfx. **dis-** (2).]

disyllable *dīs-il'ə-bl*, *n.* a word of two syllables. — *adj.* **disyllabic** (-*ab'ik*). — *n.* **disyllabifica'tion.** — *v.t.* **disyllab'ify** to make into two syllables. — *n.* **disyll'abism** the character of having two syllables. [Through Fr. *dissyllabe*, *dissilabe*, and L. from Gr. *di-*, twice, *syllabē*, a syllable; with *l* as in **syllable**.]

disyoke *dis-yōk'*, (*Tenn.*) *v.t.* to free from the yoke. [Pfx. **dis-** (3).]

dit[1], **ditt** *dit*, (*arch.*) *n.* a poem: the words of a song. [Apparently formed by Spenser from **dite**[1] influenced by **ditty**.]

dit[2] *dit*, (now *Scot.*) *v.t.* to stop, block: — *pa.t.* and *pa.p.* **ditt'ed**, **ditt'it**; *pa.p.* also **dit.** [O.E. *dyttan*, to shut.]

dit[3] *dē*, (Fr.) *adj.* named: reputed.

dit[4] *dit*, *n.* a word representing the dot in the spoken form of Morse code. See also **dah.**

dita *dē'tə*, *n.* an apocynaceous tree (*Alstonia scholaris*) of India and the Philippines, with tonic bark. [Tagálog or Visayan.]

dital *dī'təl*, *n.* a thumb key for sharpening a lute or guitar string by a semitone. [It. *dito*, finger, with -*al* after **pedal, manual.**]

ditch *dich*, *n.* a trench dug in the ground: any long narrow depression carrying water: the border of a bowling-green: the sea (*slang*). — *v.i.* to make, repair or clean a ditch or ditches: of an aircraft, to come down in the sea (*coll.*). — *v.t.* to dig a ditch in or around: to drain by ditches: to throw, or drive, into a ditch: to abandon, or get rid of (*slang*): to escape from or leave in the lurch (a person) (*slang*): to derail (*U.S.*): to bring (an aircraft) down in the sea (*coll.*). — *n.* **ditch'er** a man or machine that makes, cleans or repairs ditches. — **ditch'-dog** (*Shak.*) a dead dog rotting in a ditch; **ditch'-water** stagnant foul water such as is found in ditches, proverbially dull. [O.E. *dīc*, whence also **dike**; see notes at **dike**[1].]

dite[1] *dīt*, (*obs.*) *n.* writing: a composition. — *v.t.* (*obs.*) to compose, indite: to dictate: to indict. [O.Fr. *dit*, saying, *ditier*, *diter*, to write — L. *dictum*, an utterance, *dictāre*, freq. of *dīcĕre*, to say.]

dite[2] (*Spens.*) *v.t.* Same as **dight** (*arch.*).

dithecal *dī-thē'kl*, *adj.* having two thecae. — Also **dithē'cous.** [Pfx. **di-**.]

ditheism *dī'thē-izm*, *n.* the doctrine of the existence of two supreme gods. — *n.* **di'theist.** — *adjs.* **ditheist'ic, -al.** [Gr. *di-*, twice, and *theos*, a god.]

Ditheletism *dī-thel'ət-izm*, *n.* the doctrine that Christ on earth had two wills, human and divine — opp. to *Monotheletism.* — Also **Di'thelism, Dīo-, Dyoth'elism, Dyothel'etism, Dīthel'itism.** — *n.* **Di'thelete** a believer in the doctrine. — Also **Dīo-, Dyoth'elēte, -ite.** — *adjs.* **Dīthelet'ic, -al.** — Also **Dīo-, Dyothelet'ic, -it'ic, -al.** — All words also without *cap.* [Gr. *di-*, twice (or *dyo*, two), *thelētēs*, a willer — *thelein*, to will.]

dither *didh'ər*, *v.i.* to tremble, shiver, quake: to waver. — *v.t.* to perturb, confuse. — *n.* a trembling condition: a quaking fit: tremulous excitement: perturbation. — Also **didd'er.** — *n.* **dith'erer.** — *adj.* **dith'ery.** — **all of a dither** nervous, agitated. [Prob. imit.]

dithionate *dī-thī'ən-āt*, *n.* a salt of **dithionic** (-*on'ik*) **acid**, otherwise hyposulphuric acid ($H_2S_2O_6$). [Gr. *di-*, twice, *theion*, sulphur.]

dithyramb *dith'i-ram(b)*, *n.* an ancient Greek hymn sung in honour of Bacchus: a short poem of a like character. — *adj.* **dithyram'bic** of or like a dithyramb: rapturous: wild and boisterous. — *adv.* **dithyram'bically.** — *n.* **dithyram'bist.** [Gr. *dīthyrambos.*]

ditokous *dit'o-kəs*, *adj.* producing two at a birth or in a clutch. [Gr. *di-*, twice, *tokos*, birth.]

ditone *dī'tōn*, *n.* in ancient Greek music, an interval of two major tones. [Pfx. **di-**.]

ditriglyph *dī-trī'glif*, *n.* a space for two triglyphs in the entablature between columns. — *adjs.* **ditriglyph′ic.** [Pfx. **di-.**]

ditrochee *dī-trō′kē, n.* a trochaic dipody. — *adj.* **dī-troche̅′an.** [Pfx. **di-.**]

ditt. See **dit¹.**

dittander *di-tan′dər, n.* a pepperwort (*Lepidium latifolium*), a pungent cruciferous plant: dittany. [A form of **dittany.**]

dittany *dit′ə-ni, n.* an aromatic rutaceous plant (*Dictamnus albus*), secreting much volatile oil. [O.Fr. *dictame* — L. *dictamnus* — Gr. *diktamnos*; prob. from Mt. *Diktē* in Crete.]

dittay *dit′ā,* (*Scots law*) *n.* an indictment, charge. [O.Fr. *ditté* — L. *dictātum*; cf. **ditty, dictate.**]

dittit. See **dit².**

ditto *dit′ō,* contracted **do.,** *n.* that which has been said: the same thing. — *adv.* as before, or aforesaid: in like manner. — *v.t.* to duplicate. — *n.pl.* **ditt′os** a suit of clothes of the same colour throughout. [It. *ditto* — L. *dictum,* said, *pa.p.* of *dīcĕre,* to say.]

dittography *di-tog′rə-fi, n.* unintentional repetition of letters or words in copying a manuscript. [Gr. *dittos,* double, *graphein,* to write.]

dittology *di-tol′ə-ji, n.* a double reading or interpretation. [Gr. *dittologiā* — *dittos,* double, *legein,* to speak.]

ditty *dit′i, n.* a song: a little poem to be sung. — *v.t.* to set to music. [O.Fr. *ditie* — L. *dictātum,* neut. perf. part. (pass.) of *dictāre,* to dictate.]

ditty-bag *dit′i-bag, n.* a sailor's bag for personal belongings. — Also **ditt′y-box.** [Origin unknown.]

diuretic *dī-ū-ret′ik, adj.* promoting the discharge of urine. — *n.* a medicine causing this discharge. — *n.* **diure̅′sis** discharge of urine, esp. in excess. [Gr. *diourētikos* — *dia,* through, *ouron,* urine.]

diurnal *dī-ûr′nəl, adj.* daily: relating to or performed in or lasting a day: (of animals) having one period of rest and one of activity in twenty-four hours (*biol.*): belonging to the daytime. — *n.* a service-book containing the day hours, except matins (a night-office): a diary, journal. — *n.* **diur′nalist** a journalist. — *adv.* **diur′nally.** [L. *diurnālis* — *diēs,* a day; see **journal.**]

diuturnal *dī-ū-tûr′nəl, adj.* lasting long. — *n.* **diutur′nity.** [L. *diūturnus* — *diū,* long.]

div¹ *div,* (*Scot.;* in *pres. indic.* only) *v.t.* a form of **do** (auxiliary).

div² *dēv, n.* an evil spirit of Persian mythology. [Pers. *dīv.*]

div³ *div, n.* short for **dividend.**

diva *dē′vä, n.* a popular female singer: a prima donna. [It., — L. *dīva,* fem. of *dīvus,* divine.]

divagate *dī′və-gāt, v.i.* to wander about: to digress. — *n.* **divagā′tion.** [L. *dīvagārī,* to wander.]

divalent *dī-vā′lənt* or *div′əl-ənt, n.* a chemical element or atom capable of uniting with two atoms of hydrogen or their equivalent. — *adj.* having two combining equivalents. — Also **bivalent.** [Gr. *di-,* twice, L. *valēre,* to be worth.]

Divali. Same as **Diwali.**

divan *di-van′, n.* a collection of poems: a council of state: a court of justice: poetically, any council or assembly: a council-chamber with cushioned seats: an Eastern couch: a couch of similar type (without back or sides) often used as couch and bed (**divan′-bed′**): a smoking-room: a dewan. [Ar. and Pers. *dīwān,* a long seat.]

divaricate *dī-var′i-kāt, v.i.* to part into two branches, to fork: to diverge. — *v.t.* to divide into two branches. — *adj.* widely divergent, spreading apart. — *n.* **divaricā′tion.** [L. *dīvaricāre, -ātum* — *dis-,* asunder, *vāricāre,* to spread the legs — *varus,* bent apart.]

dive *dīv, v.i.* to dip or plunge into or down through water or down through the air: to go headlong into a recess, forest, etc.: to plunge or go deeply into any matter. — *v.t.* to plunge, dip. — *n.* a plunge: a swoop: a headlong descent: a refuge: a resort, generally disreputable, often underground (*slang*): a subway. — *n.* **div′er** one who dives or can dive: one who dives for pearls: one who works from a diving-bell or in a diving-suit

beneath water: a bird expert at diving, esp. the loon, loosely applied to auks, grebes, penguins, etc.: a pickpocket (*slang*). — *n.* and *adj.* **div′ing.** — *v.t.* and *v.i.* **dive′-bomb** to attack with, or as if with, a dive-bomber: to discharge bombs while diving; **dive′-bomber** an aeroplane that discharges a bomb while in a steep dive; **dive′-bombing; dive-dapp′er** (*Shak.*) a didapper, dabchick; **div′ing-bell** a hollow vessel or chamber, originally bell-shaped, open at the bottom and supplied with air by a tube from above, in which one may descend into and work under water; **div′ing-board** a board for diving from; **div′ing-suit, -dress** a watertight costume for a diver, with special provision for receiving air, etc. [O.E. *dȳfan, dūfan* — O.N. *dȳfa.*]

divellent *dī-vel′ənt, adj.* drawing asunder. — *v.t.* **divell′icate** to pull in pieces: to pluck apart. [L. *dī-,* apart, *vellĕre, vellicāre,* to pluck.]

diverge *di-* or *dī-vûrj′, v.i.* to incline or turn apart: to tend from a common point in different directions: to vary from the standard. — *ns.* **diverge′ment; diverg′ence** (also **diverg′ency**): the act, or amount, of diverging: the condition of being divergent: the flow of air away from a particular region, usu. associated with fine weather (*meteor.*): the property of having no limit, of an infinite series, etc. (*math.*): the turning outward of the eyes in focusing on a distant object (*physiol.*): initiation of a chain reaction in which more neutrons are released than are absorbed and lost (*nuc.*). — *adj.* **diverg′ent.** — *adv.* **diverg′ently.** — *adj.* **diverg′ing.** — *adv.* **diverg′ingly.** [L. *dī-,* asunder, *vergĕre,* to incline.]

divers *dī′vərz, adj.* sundry: several: more than one: same as **diverse** (*B.*). — *adv.* (*Milt.*) in different directions. — *adj.* **diverse** (*dī′vərs, dī′-, dī′vûrs′*) different: unlike: multiform: various: distracting (*Spens.*). — *v.i.* (*Spens.*) to turn aside. — *adv.* **di′versely** or **diverse′ly.** — *adj.* **diversifi′able.** — *n.* **diversificā′tion.** — *adj.* **diver′sified.** — *v.t.* **divers′ify** to differentiate (*obs.*): to give variety to: to make (investments) in securities of different types so as to lessen risk of loss: to engage in production of a variety of (manufactures, crops). — Also *v.i.:* — *pr.p.* **diver′sifying;** *pa.t., pa.p.* **diver′sified.** — *n.* **diver′sion** act of diverting or turning aside: that which diverts: amusement, recreation: something done to turn the attention of an opponent: a detour round part of a road which is temporarily closed. — *adj.* **diver′sionary** of the nature of a diversion, designed to distract the attention of an opponent. — *ns.* **diver′sionist** a deviationist; **diver′sity** state of being diverse: difference: unlikeness: variety. — *adv.* **dī′versly** in divers ways. — *v.t.* **divert** (*di-vûrt′, dī-*) to turn aside (also *arch., v.i.*): to change the direction of: to turn from business or study: to amuse. — *n.* (*Scot.*) amusing person or thing. — *adj.* **divert′ible.** — *ns.* **divertibil′ity; dīvertimen′to** diversion (*obs.*): (the following meanings all *mus.*) a piece in several movements: a pot-pourri: a light piece of music: a ballet-interlude: — *pl.* **-ti** (*-tē*). — *adj.* **divert′ing.** — *adv.* **divert′ingly.** — *ns.* **divertisement** (*di-vûrt′iz-mənt*) diversion: a divertimento; **divertissement** (Fr.; *dē-ver-tēs′mä*) a divertimento. — *adj.* **divert′ive** tending to divert. [Fr., — L. *dīvertĕre, dīversum* — *dī-,* aside, *vertĕre,* to turn.]

diverticulum *dī-vər-tik′ū-ləm,* (*anat.*) *n.* a blind tubular branch, esp. in the intestinal wall. — *adjs.* **dīvertic′ular, dīvertic′ulate, -d.** — *ns.* **dīverticulī′tis** inflammation of the diverticula; **dīverticulō′sis** the presence of several diverticula in the intestines. [L. *dīverticulum,* a byway, retreat.]

divertimento, divertissement. See **divert** under **divers.**

Dives *dī′vēz, n.* the rich man at whose gate Lazarus lay (Luke xvi. 19): a rich and luxurious person. [L. *dīves,* rich (man), understood as a proper name.]

divest *dī-* or *di-vest′, v.t.* to strip or deprive of anything. — *adj.* **divest′ible.** — *ns.* **divest′iture, divest′ment** (*rare*). [O.Fr. *desvestir,* with change of prefix (*dis-* for *dē-*) from L. *dēvestīre* — *dē,* away from, *vestīre,* to clothe — *vestis,* a garment.]

divi. See **divvy.**

divide *di-vīd'*, *v.t.* to break up, or mark off, into parts, actually or in imagination: to separate or distinguish the parts of: to classify: to share: to allot: to deal out: to ascertain how many times a quantity is contained in (*math.*): to perform with division or floridly (*mus.*): to be a boundary or a subject of difference between: to keep apart: to cause to vote for and against a motion: to sever. — *v.i.* to separate: to fall apart: to branch: to vote for and against a motion: to admit of or be susceptible of division. — *n.* the act of dividing (*coll.*): a watershed (esp. in U.S.): something that divides or separates, a gap. — *adjs.* **divīd'able** (or *div'id-*) divisible: divided (*Shak.*); **divīd'ant** (*Shak.*) distinguishable, separable. — *adv.* **divīd'edly.** — *n.* **divīd'er** one who or that which divides: a soup-ladle (*Scot.*): (in *pl.*) a kind of compasses for measuring. — *adj.* **divīd'ing** separating. — *n.* separation. — *adjs.* **divīd'ual** divisible: separable (*Milt.*): shared in common with others (*Milt.*); **divīd'uous** divided, special, accidental. — **divided highway** (*U.S.*) a dual carriageway; **divīd'ing-en'gine** an instrument for marking accurate subdivisions or graduating scales. [L. *dīvidĕre*, *dīvīsum* — *dis-*, asunder, root *vid*, to separate.]

dividend *div'i-dend*, *n.* that which is to be divided: the share of a sum divided that falls to each individual, by way of interest or otherwise. — **dividend stripping** a method of evading tax on dividends by a contrived arrangement between a company liable to tax and another in a position to claim repayment of tax; **div'idend-warr'ant** a certificate entitling to payment of dividend. — **declare a dividend** to announce the sum per cent. a trading concern is prepared to pay its shareholders. [L. *dīvidendum*, to be divided, *dīvidĕre*.]

dividivi *div'i-div-i*, *n.* the curved pods of *Caesalpinia coriaria*, imported for tanning and dyeing. [Carib name.]

divine *di-vīn'*, *adj.* belonging to or proceeding from a god: holy: excellent in the highest degree: prescient, having forebodings (*Milt.*). — *n.* one skilled in divine things: a minister of the gospel: a theologian. — *v.t.* to foresee or foretell as if divinely inspired: to guess or make out: to prognosticate: to make divine (*Spens.*): to search for (underground water, etc.), esp. with a divining-rod. — *v.i.* to profess or practise divination: to have forebodings. — *ns.* **divīnā'tion** the act or practice of divining: seeking to know the future or hidden things by magical means: instinctive prevision: prediction: conjecture; **div'īnātor**, **divīn'er** one who divines or professes divination: a conjecturer: — *fem.* **divīn'eress.** — *adjs.* **divīnatō'rial**, **divīn'atory** relating to divination, conjectural. — *adv.* **divīne'ly.** — *n.* **divīne'ness.** — *vs.t.* **div'īnise**, **-ize**, **divīn'ify** to treat as divine. — **divine right** the concept that kings rule by the authority of God rather than by consent of the people: any authority supposed to be unquestionable (*coll.*); **divīn'ing-rod** a rod, usually of hazel, used by those professing to discover water or metals under ground. [O.Fr. *devin*, soothsayer, and L. *dīvīnus* — *dīvus*, *deus*, a god.]

diving. See **dive**.

divinity *di-vin'i-ti*, *n.* godhead: the nature or essence of a god: a celestial being: a god: the science of divine things: theology. — **divinity hall** (*Scot.*) a theological college or department. [O.Fr. *devinite* — L. *dīvīnitās*, *-tātis*; see **divine**.]

divisim *di-vī'zim*, *dē-wē'sim*, (L.) *adv.* separately.

division *di-vizh'ən*, *n.* act of dividing: state of being divided: that which divides: a partition: a barrier: a portion or section: the taking of a vote: a florid passage or performance in which many short notes may be regarded as taking the place of a long note (*mus.*; *arch.*): one of the parts of a territorial, business, etc., unit, divided for administrative, etc., purposes: in India, a part of a province under a commissioner, divided into districts: an army unit (usually half an army corps) containing almost all branches of the service: separation: difference in opinion, etc.: dis-

union: the process of finding how many times one quantity is contained in another (*math.*). — *n.* **divisibil'ity** (*-viz-*). — *adj.* **divis'ible** capable of being divided or separated: capable of being divided without remainder. — *adv.* **divis'ibly.** — *adjs.* **divisional** (*-vizh'*) pertaining to or marking a division or separation (also **divis'ionary**): pertaining to a part of a larger unit. — *ns.* **divis'ionism** (often *cap.*; *paint.*) pointillism; **divis'ionist.** — *adj.* **divisive** (*-vīz'*) forming division or separation: creating discord. — *ns.* **divīs'iveness**; **divīs'or** (*math.*) the number which divides the dividend. — **division-lobby** see **lobby**. — **division of labour** the assigning of different functions to different agents; **fallacy of division** (*log.*) the fallacy of assuming that the part or individual partakes of the characteristic of the whole or group. [L. *dīvīsiō*, *-ōnis*, *dīvīsor*, *-ōris* — *dīvīdĕre*, to divide.]

divorce *di-vōrs'*, *-vörs'*, *n.* the legal dissolution of marriage: separation (*fig.*). — *v.t.* to dissolve the marriage of: to put away by divorce: to separate. — *v.i.* to obtain a divorce. — *adj.* **divorce'able.** — *ns.* **divorcee'** a divorced person; **divorce'ment** (*B.*) divorce; **divor'cer.** — *adj.* **divor'cive** having power to divorce. [Fr., — L. *dīvortium* — *dīvortĕre*, another form of *dīvertĕre*; see **divert**.]

divot *div'ət*, *n.* a thin sod, cut for roofing, etc., (*Scot.*), or accidentally by golfers when hitting the ball. — **feal and divot** (*Scots law*) a right of cutting sods. [Origin unknown.]

divulge *di-* or *dī-vulj'*, *v.t.* to spread abroad among the vulgar or the people: to make public: to reveal. — *v.t.* **divul'gate** (*-gāt*) to publish. — *n.* **dīvulgā'tion.** [L. *dīvulgāre* — *dī-*, abroad, *vulgāre*, to publish — *vulgus*, the common people.]

divulsion *di-* or *dī-vul'shən*, *n.* act of pulling or rending asunder or away. — *adj.* **divul'sive** tending to pull asunder. [L. *dīvulsiō*, *-ōnis* — *dī-*, *vellĕre*, *vulsum*, to pull.]

divvy *div'i*, (*slang*) *n.* a dividend: a share. — *v.t.* and *v.i.* (often with *up*) to divide: to go shares. — Also **divi**. [Abbrev. of **divide**, **dividend**.]

Diwali *di-wä'lē*, *n.* the Hindu or Sikh festival of lamps held in October or November. — Also **Dewali**, **Divali**. [Hindi *dīvālī*.]

diwan. Same as **dewan.**

dixi *dik'sē*, (L.) I have spoken.

dixie, **dixy** *diks'i*, *n.* a military cooking-pail or camp-kettle. [Perh. Hindi *degcī* — Pers. *degcha*, dim. of *dīg*, large metallic cooking utensil.]

Dixieland *dik'si-land*, *n.* an early style of jazz in New Orleans, played by small combinations of instruments. [*Dixie*, name given to southern states of U.S.]

DIY *dee'ī-wī'*, *n.* and *adj.* abbrev. of **do-it-yourself**.

dizain *di-zān'*, *n.* a ten-line stanza or poem. [Fr. *dix*, ten — L. *decem*, ten.]

dizen *dī'zn*, or *diz'n*, (*obs.*) *v.t.* to dress or charge (a distaff) with flax: to dress up, dress gaudily. [From root seen in **distaff**.]

dizygotic *dī-zī-got'ik*, *adj.* developed from two zygotes or fertilised eggs. — **dizygotic twins** fraternal twins so developed.

dizzard *diz'ərd*, *n.* a blockhead. [Perh. M.E. and O.Fr. *disour*, story-teller.]

dizzy *diz'i*, *adj.* giddy: confused: causing giddiness: silly (*coll.*): extreme (*coll.*). — *v.t.* to make dizzy: to confuse. — *adv.* **dizz'ily.** — *n.* **dizz'iness.** — *adj.* **dizz'ying** making dizzy. — *adv.* **dizz'yingly.** [O.E. *dysig*, foolish: cf. Dan. *dösig*, drowsy; also **doze**.]

djebel. See **jebel.**

djellaba, **djellabah** *jə-lä'bə*, *n.* a cloak with a hood and wide sleeves. — Also **jellab'a**, **jelab'**. — See also **gal(l)abi(y)a(h).** [Ar. *jallabah*, *jallāb*.]

djibbah *jib'ä*. Same as **jubbah.**

djinn, **djinni.** See **jinn.**

DNA *dē-en-ā*, *n.* deoxyribonucleic acid (q.v.).

do¹ *dōō*, *v.t.* to put, place (*obs.*): to cause (*obs.*): to put in some condition: to render: to confer: to bestow: to perform: to accomplish: to finish: to exhaust: to work at: to perform work upon: to beat up, thrash (*slang*): to prepare, set in order: to cook: to cheat, or overreach (*slang*): to raid, rob (*slang*): to treat: to make the round of, see the sights of: to spend in prison. — *v.i.* to act, be active: to behave: to fare: to thrive: to suffice: to be good enough to pass: — *2nd sing.* **do'est, dost** *dust*, *3rd* **does** *duz*, also **do'eth, doth** *duth*; *pa.t.* **did**; *pr.p.* **do'ing**; *pa.p.* **done** *dun*; in *Spens, infin.* **doen, done, donne,** *3rd pl. pa.t.* **doen.** — *Do* serves as a substitute for a verb that has just been used. It is used as an auxiliary verb (where there is no other auxiliary) with an infinitive in negative, interrogatory, emphatic, and rhetorically inverted sentences, in some dialects merely periphrastically, and in verse sometimes to gain a syllable or postpone the accent; but these uses are limited with the verbs *have* and *do*. — *n.* activity: what one has to do: fuss (*arch.*): a feast, celebration: a swindle, hoax (*slang*): — *pl.* **do's** or **dos.** — *adj.* **do'able** that can be done. — *n.* **do'er** one who does, or habitually does, anything: an agent. — *adj.* **do'ing** active (as in *up and doing*). — *n.* (*coll.*) a scolding: thrashing: severe treatment: (in *pl.*) activities, behaviour: (in *pl.*) fancy dishes or adjuncts (*U.S.*): (in *pl.*) what's-its-name (*slang*). — **done** *pa.p.* of **do:** *infin.* of **do** (*Spens.*). — *adj.* utterly exhausted: socially acceptable. — *interj.* agreed. — *n.* (*cook.*) **done'ness** the state of being, or degree to which something is, cooked. — **do'-all** a factotum; **do'-good'er** a slighting name for one who tries to benefit others by social reforms, etc., implying that his, her, efforts are unwelcome or ineffectual; **do'-good'ery** (*slang*); **do'-good'ism.** — *adj.* **do'-it-yourself** designed to be built, constructed, etc. by an amateur rather than by someone specially trained. — Also *n.* — **do'-it-yourself'er; do'-naught, do'-nought, do'-noth'ing** a lazy or idle person: a fainéant (see **donnot**); **do'-noth'ingism; do'-noth'ingness.** — **all done** completely finished, used up; **be done** to be at an end: to have done, finished (*Scot.*); **be, have done with** to finish with, end contact or dealings with; **do away with** to abolish, destroy; **do brown** to cook or roast to brownness: to hoax, swindle (*slang*); **do by** to act towards; **do down** to put down, subdue (*obs.*): to cheat, get the better of (*slang*); **do for** to suit: to provide for: to ruin: to kill (*coll.*): to do domestic work for (*coll.*); **do in** (*coll.*) to deceive, to get the better of: to exhaust: to ruin, to murder; **do or die** to make a final desperate attempt to do, achieve, etc. something, no matter what the cost or consequences (*adj.* **do'-or-die'**); **do out** (*coll.*) to clean thoroughly (a room, etc.); **do out of** to deprive of by cheating; **do over** to do again: to cover over, as with paint: to beat up (*slang*); **do's and don'ts** advice or rules for action, esp. in particular circumstances; **do someone proud** (*coll.*) to make someone feel flattered: to treat lavishly; **do to death** to murder: to repeat too often; **do up** to fasten up: to put up, make tidy, arrange, tie up: to redecorate: to apply cosmetics to: to dress: to fatigue utterly; **do well** to be justified: to prosper; **do with** to make use of: to meddle with: to get on with; **do without** not to be dependent on, to dispense with; **have done** to cease: to desist: to stop it: to have no more dealings; **have to do with** to have any sort of connection with; **have you done?** are you finished?; **how do you do?** a conventional phrase used on greeting; **nothing doing** no; **that's done it** it is completed: (*interj.* indicating dismay) it is spoiled, ruined; **what's to do?** what is the matter? [O.E. *dōn, dyde, gedōn*; Du. *doen*, Ger. *tun*; conn. with Gr. *tithenai*, to put, place.]

do² *dō*, (*mus.*) n. a syllable representing the first note of the scale — anglicised as **doh:** — *pl.* **dos** or **do's.** [Perh. from G.B. *Doni* (1593–1647), who is said to have substituted it for the Aretinian syllable *ut* (see **gamut**).]

doab *dō'āb*, n. a tongue of land between two rivers (esp. the Ganges and Jumna). [Pers. *dōāb*, two waters.]

doat, etc. See **dote.**

dob *dob* (*Austr. coll.*). — **dob in** (*pr.p.* **dobb'ing;** *pa.t.* and

pa.p. **dobbed**) to betray, inform on: to contribute. — *ns.* **dobb'er-in, dobb'er.**

dobbin *dob'in*, n. a workhorse. [An altered dim. of *Robert.*]

dobby, dobbie *dob'i*, n. a dotard: a brownie: an attachment to a loom for weaving small figures. [Perh. from *Robert.*]

dobchick *dob'chik.* Same as **dabchick.**

Doberman(n) pinscher *dōb'ər-mən pin'shər*, a breed of terrier — large, smooth-coated, with long forelegs. [*Dobermann*, the first breeder, and Ger. *Pinscher*, terrier.]

dobhash *dō'bash*, n. an interpreter. [Hind. *dōbāshī, dūbhāshiya* — *dō, dū*, two, *bhāshā*, language.]

doc *dok*, n. a familiar contraction of **doctor.**

docent *dō'sənt, dō-sent'*, (*U.S.*) n. a college teacher or lecturer. [From Ger., see **privat-dozent.**]

Docetism *dō-sē'tizm*, n. a 2nd-century heresy, that Christ's body was only a semblance, or else of ethereal substance. — *ns.* **Do'cēte, Docē'tist** a holder of this belief: — *pls.* **Docē'tae** (-*tē*), **Docētists.** — *adjs.* **Docetic** (-*sēt', -set'*), **Docetist'ic.** [Gr. *dokēsis*, phantom, semblance — *dokeein*, to seem.]

doch-an-doris, -dorach. See **deoch-an-doruis.**

dochmius *dok'mi-əs*, n. a foot of five syllables, typically with first and fourth short, the rest long. — *adjs.* **doch'miac, dochmī'acal.** [L. — Gr. *dochmios.*]

docht. See **dow².**

docile *dō'sīl*, or *dos'il, adj.* teachable: ready to learn: easily managed. —(*obs.*) **do'cible.** — *ns.* **docibil'ity, doc'ibleness, docil'ity.** [Fr., — L. *docilis* — *docēre*, to teach.]

docimasy *dos'i-mə-si*, n. scrutiny: application of tests: assaying: examination of drugs. — *adj.* **docimastic** (-*mas'tik*). — *n.* **docimol'ogy** the art of assaying. [Gr. *dokimasiā*, examination — *dokimazein*, to test — *dechesthai*, to take, approve.]

dock¹ *dok*, n. a polygonaceous weed (*Rumex*) with large leaves and a long root. — *n.* **dock'en** (*Scot.*, perh. orig. *pl.*) a dock. — **dock'-cress** the nipplewort. [O.E. *docce.*]

dock² *dok, v.t.* to cut short: to curtail: to cut off: to clip: to deprive of pay. — *n.* the part of a tail left after clipping: the rump (*Scot.*). [M.E. *dok*, prob. — O.N. *dokkr*, stumpy tail.]

dock³ *dok*, n. (often used in *pl.*) an artificial basin for the reception of vessels and cargo: the waterway between two wharves or two piers: a wharf or pier: the enclosure in court for the accused: in a railway station, the place of arrival and departure of a train: in the theatre, a space for storing scenery. — *v.t.* to embed in sand or ooze (*Shak.*): to place in a dock: to bring into dock: to equip with docks: to join (spacecraft) together in space. — *v.i.* to enter a dock: to join together in space. — *ns.* **dock'age** accommodation in docks for ships: dock-dues; **dock'er** one who works in the docks; **dock'ing; dockīsā'tion, -z-.** — *v.t.* **dock'īse, -ize** to convert into docks. — **dock'-dues** payments for use of a dock; **dock'-la'bourer** a docker; **dock'land** a district about docks; **dock'-master** the person superintending a dock; **dock'-warrant** a warehouse receipt; **dock'yard** a naval establishment with docks, building-slips, stores, etc. — **dry dock** a dock from which the water can be pumped, in order to effect repairs to the underside of a ship (*v.t.* **dry'-dock** to put in dry dock); **in the dock** (*lit.* and *fig.*) accused of, charged with some misdemeanour. [Origin obscure; cf. O.Du. *dokke.*]

docket *dok'it*, n. a summary of a larger writing: a bill or ticket affixed to anything indicating its contents: a label: a list or register of cases in court, or of legal judgments, or (*U.S.*) business to be transacted: an official permit to buy: a customhouse certificate of payment. — *v.t.* to make a summary of the heads of a writing: to enter in a book: to mark the contents of papers on the back: — *pr.p.* **dock'eting;** *pa.t.* and *pa.p.* **dock'eted.** — Also **docquet** (as if French). [Perh. a dim. of **dock,** to curtail.]

doctor *dok'tər, n.* a teacher (*arch.*): a learned father of the church: a cleric especially skilled in theology or ecclesiastical law: one who has received from a university (or the Archbishop of Canterbury) the highest degree in any faculty (originally implying competency to teach): a physician or medical practitioner, whatever be his degree in medicine: in U.S. extended to a dentist or druggist: a mender: in some warm countries, a cool sea-breeze conducive to health: a ship's cook: a name for various contrivances for removing defects or superfluities in manufacture: material used for sophistication: brown sherry: counterfeit coin: (in *pl.*) loaded dice: a fish, the sea-surgeon: an angler's fly. — *v.t.* to treat, as a doctor does: to patch up, repair: to sophisticate, tamper with, falsify: to address as doctor: to confer a doctor's degree upon: to spay, castrate (*coll.*). — *v.i.* to practise medicine. — *adj.* **doc'toral**. — *n.* **doc'torand** a candidate for the doctorate. — *v.t.* **doc'torate** to confer the degree of doctor upon. — *n.* an academic degree of doctor. — *ns.* **doc'toress, doc'tress** (*facet.*) a female doctor: a doctor's wife. — *adjs.* **doctorial** (-tō'ri-əl, -tō'ri-əl); **doc'torly**. — *n.* **doc'torship**. — **doc'tor-fish** a sea-surgeon; **Doctors' Commons** before the establishment of the Divorce Court and Probate Court in 1857, the college of the doctors of civil law in London, incorporated by royal charter in 1768; **doctor's stuff** medicine. — **what the doctor ordered** (*coll.*) the very thing that's needed.   [L., a teacher — *docēre*, to teach.]

doctrinaire *dok-tri-nār', n.* an unpractical theorist, disposed to carry principles to logical but unworkable extremes: in France, in 1815–30, one of a school who desired constitutional government. — *adj.* theoretical: dogmatic: showing doctrinairism. — *n.* and *adj.* **doctrinā'rian** doctrinaire. — *ns.* **doctrinair'ism, doctrinā'rianism** blind adhesion to one-sided principles.   [Fr., — L.L. *doctrīnārius.*]

doctrine *dok'trin, n.* teaching (*arch.*): a thing taught: a principle of belief. — *adj.* **doctrī'nal** (or *dok'tri-nl*). — *adv.* **doctrī'nally** (or *dok'*).   [L. *doctrīna* — *docēre*, to teach.]

docudrama *dok'ū-drä-mə, n.* a play or film reproducing real events and characters.   [*docu*mentary *drama.*]

document *dok'ū-mənt, n.* instruction (*Spens.*): warning (*obs.*): a paper or other material thing affording information, proof, or evidence of anything. — *v.t.* -*ment'* to furnish with documents: to support or prove by documents. — *adjs.* **documental** (-*ment'*), **document'ary** relating to or found in documents: aiming at presentation of reality. — *ns.* **document'alist** one who specialises in documentation: one who collects and classifies documents; **document'ary** a film or radio or TV programme about real people or events, without fictional colouring or professional actors; **documentā'tion** instruction (*arch.*): preparation, setting forth, or use of documentary evidence and authorities: in fiction, realistic reproduction of records, real or supposed: the written information on the structure and operation of hardware or software (*comput.*). — **document reader** (*comput.*) a form of optical character reader which convert the characters into code and feeds them automatically into the computer.   [Fr., — L. *documentum* — *docēre*, to teach.]

dod[1] *dod, (obs.* or *dial.*) *v.t.* to cut the hair of: to poll: to pollard: to clip. — *n.* (*Scot.*) a rounded hill-top, esp. a shoulder of a greater hill. — *adj.* **dodd'ed** polled: hornless: pollard. — *n.* **dodd'y** (*Scot.*) a hornless cow.   [M.E. *dodden.*]

dod[2] *dod, (Scot.) n.* a slight fit of ill-humour: (in *pl.*; often with *the*) the sulks. — *adj.* **dodd'y.**   [Gael. *dod*, peevishness.]

dod[3] *dod, n.* a minced form of **God**, in oaths.

dod[4]. See **daud.**

dodder[1] *dod'ər, n.* a leafless, twining, pale parasitic plant (*Cuscuta*) or akin to the convolvulus family.   [M.E. *doder*; cf. Ger. *Dotter.*]

dodder[2] *dod'ər, v.i.* to shake: to tremble: to totter: to

potter: to ramble in talk: to be decrepit in mind or body. — *n.* **dodd'erer**. — *adjs.* **dodd'ering; dodd'ery.**   [Perh. conn. with **doddered.**]

doddered, doddard *dod'ərd, adj.* orig. perh. pollard: decayed with loss of branches.   [Cf. **dod**[1].]

doddle *dod'l, (coll.) n.* something very easily accomplished.   [Poss. — **dodder**[2].]

doddy. See **dod**[1,2].

doddypoll, doddipoll *dod'i-pōl, (obs.) n.* a blockhead. — Also **dottipoll.**   [App. **dote** and **poll**.]

dodeca- *dō-dek-ə-,* in composition, twelve. — *n.* **dodec'agon** (Gr. *gōniā*, an angle) a plane figure with twelve angles and sides. — *n.pl.* **Dodecagyn'ia** (-*jin'i-ə*; Gr. *gynē,* a woman, female) in some classes of the Linnaean classification an order of plants with twelve styles. — *adjs.* **dodecagyn'ian, dodecag'ynous** (-*aj'i-nəs*). — *n.* **dodecahedron** (-*hē'dron*; Gr. *hedrā,* a seat) a solid figure, having twelve faces (equal pentagons in a *regular* dodecahedron, rhombs in a *rhombic dodecahedron*). — *adj.* **dodecahē'dral**. — *n.pl.* **Dodecan'dria** (Gr. *anēr, andros,* a man, male) a Linnaean class of plants, having twelve stamens. — *adjs.* **dodecan'drous; dodecaphon'ic** (*mus.*; Gr. *phōnē,* voice) twelve-tone. — *ns.* **dodecaph'onism** twelve-tone music; **dodecaph'onist** a composer or admirer of twelve-tone music; **dodecaph'ony**. — *adj.* **dodecastyle** (*dō'dek-ə-stīl, dō-dek'ə-stīl; archit.*; Gr. *stȳlos,* a pillar) having twelve columns in front. — *n.* a portico so built. — *n.* **dodecasyll'able** (*pros.*) a line of twelve syllables. — *adj.* **dodecasyllab'ic.**   [Gr. *dōdeka,* twelve.]

dodge *doj, v.i.* to start aside or shift about: to evade or use mean tricks: to shuffle or quibble. — *v.t.* to evade by a sudden shift of place: to evade: to trick. — *n.* an evasion: a trick: a quibble. — *ns.* **dodg'er** one who dodges: a screen on a ship's bridge for shelter in rough weather: an advertising leaflet (*U.S.*); **dodg'ery** trickery. — *adj.* **dodg'y** artful, tricky: difficult to do or carry out: risky. — **dodge the column** (*slang*) to evade one's duties.   [Origin obscure.]

Dodgem(s)® *doj'əm(z), n.* (also without *cap.*) an amusement in which drivers of small electric cars within an enclosure strive to bump others without being bumped.

dodkin *dod'kin, n.* a doit. — Also **doit'kin.**   [**doit.**]

dodman *dod'mən, (dial.) n.* a snail.   [Origin unknown.]

dodo *dō'dō, n.* a clumsy flightless bird, about the size of a turkey, a native of Mauritius, extinct about the end of the 17th century: an old-fashioned or stupid person (*coll.*): — *pl.* **do'do(e)s.**   [Port. *doudo,* silly.]

Dodonaean *dō-dō-nē'ən,* pertaining to *Dodona* in Epirus, or its oracle sacred to Zeus, situated in a grove of oaks. — Also **Dodō'nian.**

Doe *dō.*—**John Doe** and **Richard Roe,** imaginary plaintiff and opponent in the old legal action for ejectment, proverbial as a legal fiction.

doe *dō, n.* the female of the fallow-deer or buck: extended to the female of other deer, of antelope, rabbit, hare, and sometimes other animals. — *adj.* **doe'-eyed** having large, dark eyes like those of a deer; **doe'-skin** the skin of a doe: a smooth, close-woven, woollen cloth.   [O.E. *dā*; Dan. *daa,* deer.]

doen, doer, does, etc. See **do**[1].

doff *dof, v.t.* to take off: to put off: to remove. — *n.* **doff'er** part of a carding machine that strips the cotton from the cylinder when carded: one who removes full bobbins from a machine.   [**do**[1], **off.**]

dog[1] *dog, n.* a wild or domestic animal of the same genus (Canis) as the wolf: a male of the species: a mean scoundrel: a term of contempt: a fellow (as *a jolly dog*): either of the two constellations, the Greater and the Lesser Dog (Canis Major and Minor): an andiron: a hook for holding logs: a gripping appliance of various kinds: a cock, as of a gun: a dogfish: a prairie dog: heavy ostentation (*slang*): (in *pl.*) greyhound races (*coll.*): a boring or unattractive woman (*U.S. slang*). — *adj.* (*and in composition*) of dogs: male (opposed to *bitch*): spurious, base, inferior. — *adv.* (*esp.* in composition) utterly. — *v.t.* to follow as a dog: to track and watch constantly: to worry, plague, infest: to hunt with dogs: to fasten with a dog: — *pr.p.* **dogg'ing;** *pa.t.* and *pa.p.* **dogged.** — *adj.* **dogg'ed** doglike: sullen: pertinacious. — *adv.* (*slang*) very. — *adv.* **dogg'edly.** — *ns.* **dogg'edness; dogg'er** one who dogs; **dogg'ery** doggish ways or doings; dogs collectively: rabble: a drinking resort (*U.S.*); **dogg'ess** (*facet.*) a bitch; **dogg'-iness; dogg'ing** shooting with dogs: following like a dog. — *adj.* **dogg'ish** doglike: characteristic of dogs: churlish: brutal. — *adv.* **dogg'ishly.** — *n.* **dogg'ishness.** — *adj.* **dogg'y** fond of dogs: doglike: dashing, beauish. — *n.* (also **dogg'ie**) *dim.* of **dog.** — *n.* **dog'ship** the quality or personality of a dog. — **dog'-ape** a baboon (from the form of its head); **dog('s)'bane** a plant (*Apocynum*) said to be poisonous to dogs; **dog'-bee** a drone; **dog'-belt** a broad belt put round the waist for hauling; **dog'berry** the fruit of the wild cornel or dogwood: extended to many other plants and their fruits: (with *cap.*) a pompous, muddle-headed fellow (from the character in Shakespeare's *Much Ado About Nothing*); **Dog'berrydom; Dog'berryism** an utterance worthy of Dogberry, wordy consequential blundering and malapropism; **dog'-bis'cuit** a biscuit for feeding dogs; **dog'bolt** *orig.* a kind of arrow: a contemptible fellow (*obs.*); **dog'cart** a two-wheeled horse-vehicle with seats back to back, originally used to carry sporting dogs. — *adj.* **dog'-cheap** extremely cheap. — **dog'-collar** a collar for a dog: a clerical collar fastened behind: a woman's stiff collar or neck ornament; **dog'-crab** a very small crab; **dog'-dai'sy** the common daisy: the ox-eye daisy; **dog'days** the period when the Dogstar rises and sets with the sun (generally reckoned July 3rd to August 11th) — erroneously supposed to be the time when dogs are specially liable to hydrophobia; **dog'-ear** a dog's-ear. — *adj.* **dog'-eared** of pages of a book, turned down like the ears of a dog: hence, shabby, scruffy. — **dog'-eat-dog'** a ruthless pursuit of one's own interests, savage self-concern. — Also *adj.* — **dog'-end** (*slang*) a cigarette-end. — *adj.* **dog'-faced.** — **dog'-fancier** a breeder or seller of dogs; **dog'fight** a fight between dogs: a confused fight or mêlée: a fight between fighter aircraft, esp. at close quarters; **dog'fish** a small shark of various kinds; **dog'fox** a male fox; **dog'-grass, dog'-wheat** couch-grass or kindred species; **dog'gy-bag** a bag used by diners to carry home leftover food from a restaurant (for their pets); **dog'gy-paddle, dog'-paddle** a crude swimming stroke used by humans in imitation of a dog; **dog'=hand'ler** a policeman, etc., in charge of a specially trained dog; **dog'-head** hammer of a gunlock; **dog'-hip, -hep** (*dial.*) hip or fruit of the dog-rose; **dog'hole** a hole fit only for a dog: a wretched dwelling; **dog'-house** a dog-kennel: a place of disgrace (*fig.*); **dog'-kennel; dog'-Lat'in** barbarous Latin; **dog'-leech** one who treats diseases of dogs; **dog'-leg** a sharp bend, like that in a dog's hind leg: something so bent, e.g. (*golf*) a hole with a bent fairway. — *adj.* (also **dog'-legged**) bent like a dog's hind leg: (of stairs) having successive flights running opposite ways without a well-hole: (of a fence) made of poles laid on cross-shaped supports. — *v.i.* to become, or be, bent like a dog's leg. — *v.t.* to make such a bend in. — **dog'-lett'er** *r*, from its growling sound; **dog'-louse; dog-paddle** see **dog'gy-paddle; dog'=pars'ley** fool's parsley; **dog'-per'iwinkle** species of Purpura (also **dog'-whelk); dog'-rose** species of wild rose, *Rosa canina;* **dog's age** (*coll.*) a long time; **dog'-salmon** keta and humpback, Pacific species of salmon; **dog's'=body** (*orig. naut. slang*) pease-pudding: dish of biscuit, water, and sugar: junior naval (or other) officer: (usu. **dogs'body**) a general drudge; **dog's breakfast, dinner** anything very untidy; **dog's chance** a bare chance; **dog's disease** (*Austr. coll.*) any minor ailment; **dog('s)'-ear** a fold at the corner of a leaf in a book. — *v.t.* to fold at the corner. — **dog's'-fenn'el** mayweed, **dog'shores** pieces of timber used to shore up a vessel before launching. — *adj.* **dog'-sick'** thoroughly sick, sick as a dog. — **dog'skin** leather made of or in imitation of

dog's skin. — Also *adj.* — **dog'-sled** one pulled by a team of dogs; **dog'sleep** a light sleep, very easily broken; **dog's life** a wretched, miserable life; **dog's'-meat** scraps and refuse sold as food for dogs; **dog's'-mer'cury** a euphorbiaceous plant *Mercurialis perennis;* **dog's'-nose** gin and beer, or similar mixture; **dog's'-tail-grass'** a common British pasture grass (Cynosurus); **Dog'star** Sirius, in the constellation of the Greater Dog, brightest star in the heavens and giving name to the dogdays; **dog's'-tongue** hound's-tongue; **dog's'-tooth** a brokencheck pattern used extensively in the weaving of tweeds; **dog's-tooth-grass'** a seaside sand-binding grass (Cynodon); **dog tag** a metal identity disc for a dog or (*coll.*) a soldier; **dog'-tick.** — *adjs.* **dog'-tired', (**Shak.**)** **dog'-wea'ry** tired as a dog, completely worn out. — **dog'tooth** a moulding in later Norman architecture, consisting of a series of ornamental square pyramids: a canine tooth; **dog'tooth-spar'** calcite crystals like canine teeth; **dog'tooth-vi'olet** any plant of the liliaceous genus Erythronium; **dog'town** a prairie-dog community; **dog'-trick** a low trick; **dog'trot** a gentle trot like a dog's; a jogtrot; **dog'vane** (*naut.*) a small vane to show direction of wind; **dog'-vi'olet** a scentless wild violet, esp. *Viola canina;* **dog'-watch** (*naut.*) on shipboard, a watch 4–6 p.m. or 6–8 p.m., consisting of two hours only, instead of four; **dog-wheat** see **dog-grass; dog'-whelk'** a gasteropod of the genus Nassa, like a small whelk: a dog-periwinkle; **dog'wood** the wild cornel (*Cornus,* or *Swida, sanguinea*), a small tree with white flowers and purple berries, the shoots and leaves turning red in autumn: extended to many other shrubs and trees. — **dog in the manger** one who will not let others enjoy what he has himself no use for; **dogs of war** (*fig.*) troops, aggressors, mercenaries, warlike people (from Shak., *Jul. Caes.* III, i, 270); **go to the dogs** to be ruined; **hot dog** a roll containing a hot sausage; **like a dog's dinner** (*slang*) very smart, dressed up flamboyantly; **not to lead the life of a dog** to lead a life so wretched that even a dog would not be content with it; **throw, give** or **send to the dogs** to throw away or abandon. [Late O.E. *docga* — cf. Du. *dog,* a mastiff; Ger. *Dogge.*]

dog² *dog,* (*obs.*) *n.* used in oaths for **God.** — *interj.* **doggone** (*dog-gon'*) (*U.S.*) expressing vexation (*adj., adv.* **doggone(d)'**), from **dog on** (**it**), God damn (it).

doge *dōj,* or *dō'jā, n.* the chief magistrate in republican Venice and Genoa. — *ns.* **dogaressa** (*do-gä-res'a*) a doge's wife; **dogate** (*dō'gāt*); **dogeate** (*dō'jāt*); **doge'ship.** [It. (Venetian dial.) for *duce,* duke — L. *dux,* a leader.]

dogger¹ *dog'ər, n.* a two-masted Dutch fishing-vessel. — **dogg'erman.** [Du.]

dogger² *dog'ər, n.* a concretion, esp. of ironstone: a sandy ironstone or ferruginous sandstone: (with *cap.*) part of the Middle Jurassic. [Origin uncertain; a northern word.]

doggerel *dog'ər-əl, n.* irregular measures in burlesque poetry, so named in contempt: worthless verses. — *adj.* irregular in rhythm, mean. — Also **dogg'rel.** [Origin unknown.]

doggo *dog'ō,* (*coll.*) *adv.* hidden. [Poss. from **dog¹.**]

dogie, dogy *dō'gi,* (*U.S.*) *n.* a motherless calf. [Origin obscure.]

dogma *dog'mə, n.* a settled opinion: a principle or tenet: a doctrine laid down with authority. — *adjs.* **dogmatic** (*-mat'ik*), **-al** pertaining to a dogma: asserting a thing as if it were a dogma: asserting positively: overbearing. — *adv.* **dogmat'ically.** — *n. sing.* **dogmat'ics** (*theol.*) the statement of Christian doctrines, systematic theology. — *v.i.* **dog'matise, -ize** (*-mə-tīz*) to state one's opinion dogmatically or arrogantly. — *ns.* **dog'matiser, -z-;** **dog'matism** dogmatic or positive assertion of opinion; **dog'matist** one who makes positive assertions; **dogmatol'ogy** the science of dogma. — *adj.* **dog'matory.** [Gr. *dogma, -atos,* an opinion — *dokeein,* to think, seem.]

doh. See **do².**

doilt *doilt*, (*Scot.*) *adj.* crazy, foolish. — Also **doiled.** [Origin obscure.]

doily *doi'li*, *n.* an old kind of woollen stuff (*obs.*): a small lace or lacy paper, etc. ornamented napkin, often laid on or under dishes. — Also **doy'ley, doyly.** [From *Doily* or *Doyley*, a famous haberdasher.]

doit *doit*, *n.* a small Dutch coin worth about half a farthing: a thing of little or no value. — Also **doit'kin.** [Du. *duit*.]

doited, doitit *doit'id, -it*, (*Scot.*) *adjs.* in dotage. [Origin obscure.]

dojo *dō'jō n.* a place where judo, karate, etc. are taught or practised: — *pl.* **do'jos.** [Jap.]

dolabriform *dō-lab'ri-form, adj.* like a hatchet or cleaver. [L. *dolābra*, a cleaver, *fōrma*, form.]

Dolby® *dol'bi*, *n.* an electronic device which reduces the amount of extraneous noise on recorded or broadcast sound. [R. *Dolby* (b. 1933), its inventor.]

dolce *dol'chā, adj., adv.* sweet(ly), esp. of music. — *n.* a soft-toned organ-stop. — *adv.* **dolcemente** (*-men'tā; mus.*) softly and sweetly. — **dolce far niente** (*fär nē-en'tā*) sweet doing-nothing, pleasant idleness; **dolce vita** (*vē'ta*; It., sweet life) a life of wealth, pleasure and self-indulgence. [It., — L. *dulcis*.]

doldrums *dol'drəmz, n. pl.* those parts of the ocean about the equator where calms and baffling winds prevail (*naut.*): low spirits. [Prob. conn, with obs. *dold*, stupid, or *dol*, dull.]

dole[1] *dōl, n.* a share: a dealing out: something given in charity: state pay to unemployed (*coll.*): a small portion. — *v.t.* (usu. with *out*) to deal out in small portions. — **on the dole** (*coll.*) living on unemployment or other benefit. [O.E. *dāl*; cf. **deal**[1].]

dole[2] *dōl, n.* pain: grief: heaviness at heart (*arch.* and *poet.*). — Also **dool,** (*obs.*) **doole.** — *adj.* **dole'ful** full of dole or grief: melancholy. — *adv.* **dole'fully.** — *n.* **dole'fulness.** — *adjs.* **do'lent** (*obs.*); **dole'some** dismal. — *adv.* **dole'somely.** [O.Fr. *doel* (Fr. *deuil*), grief — L. *dolēre*, to feel pain.]

dole[3] *dōl, n.* guile (*obs.*): criminal intention (*Scots law*). [L. *dolus* — Gr. *dolos*, guile.]

dolerite *dol'ər-it, n.* a basic igneous rock like basalt in composition but coarser grained. — *adj.* **doleri̇t'ic.** [Fr. *dolérite* — Fr. *doleros*, deceptive.]

dolia. See **dolium.**

dolicho- *dol-i-kō-*, in composition, long. — *n.* **dolichocephal** (*-sef'əl*), a long-headed person. — *adj.* **dolichocephalic** (*-sif-al'ik*; Gr. *kephalē*, the head) long-headed — having a breadth of skull (from side to side) less than 75 (or 78) per cent. of the length (front to back) — opp. to *brachycephalic*. — Also **dolichoceph'alous.** — *ns.* **dolichoceph'aly, dolichoceph'alism; Dolichos** (*dol'i-kos*; Gr., long, also a podded plant) a genus of long-podded leguminous plants allied to the haricot: (without *cap.*) any plant of the genus; **Dolichosaurus** (*-sö'rəs*; Gr. *sauros*, lizard) the typical genus of **Dolichosau'ria,** a group of Cretaceous fossil reptiles; **Dolichotis** (*-kō'tis*; Gr. *ous, ōtos*, the ear) a genus of long-eared S. American rodents — the mara or Patagonian hare. [Gr. *dolichos*, long.]

dolichurus *dol-i-kū'rəs, n.* a dactylic hexameter with a redundant syllable at the end. [Gr. *dolichouros*, long-tailed.]

dolium *dō'li-əm, n.* a Roman earthenware jar for wine, oil, grain, etc.: — *pl.* **dō'lia.** [L. *dōlium*.]

doll *dol, n.* a puppet: a toy in human form: an insipid woman, esp. one who is over-dressed and silly: a young woman: the smallest or pet pig in a litter. — *v.i.* and *v.t.* to dress showily (often with *up*). — *ns.* **doll'dom; doll'hood; doll'iness.** — *adj.* **doll'ish.** — *ns.* **doll'ishness; doll'y** dim. of doll, an attractive young girl (also **dolly girl** or **bird**): formerly, a dolly-mop: a slow, easy catch (*cricket*) or shot. — Also *adj.* — **doll's'-house** (*U.S.* **doll'-house**); **doll'y-mixture** a mixture of small brightly-coloured sweets: one of these sweets; **doll'y-mop** a slut: a prostitute; **doll'y-shop** a marine store — a low pawn-shop — often having a black doll as sign.

[Prob. from *Dolly*, familiar dim. of *Dorothy*.]

dollar *dol'ər, n.* a silver coin (= 100 cents) of U.S.A., Canada, Australia, New Zealand, Mexico, Hong-Kong, etc.: a thaler: five shillings (*old slang*). — *adjs.* **doll'ared; doll'arless.** — *ns.* **dollaroc'racy; doll'arship.** — **dollar area** those countries as a whole whose currencies are linked to the U.S. dollar; **dollar diplomacy** diplomacy dictated by financial interests: diplomacy that employs financial weapons to increase political power; **dollar gap** the excess of imports from a dollar country over exports to it, necessitating settlement by dollar exchange or in gold. [Ger. *T(h)aler* (L. G. *daler*), short for *Joachimsthaler* because first coined at the silver-mines in Joachimsthal (Joachim's dale) in Bohemia.]

dollop *dol'əp, n.* a tuft of grass or weeds: a rank patch in a field: a lump. — Also **dall'op.** [Prob. conn, with Norw. dial. *dolp*, a lump.]

dolly[1] *dol'i, n.* a complimentary offering of flowers, sweetmeats, etc., on a tray. [Anglo-Ind., — Hindi *dālī*.]

dolly[2]. See **doll.**

dolly[3] *dol'i, n.* a wooden shaft attached to a disc with projecting arms, used for beating and stirring clothes in a washing-tub: somewhat similar apparatus in mining, pile-driving, etc.: a tool for holding the head of a rivet: a trolley, truck, or platform on wheels or roller. — *v.t.* to operate upon, yield, or obtain, with a dolly: to beat with a hammer. — *adj.* **doll'ied.** — *n.* **doll'ier.** — **dolly camera** a camera moving on a dolly; **doll'y-shop** see **doll; dolly shot** a shot taken with a dolly camera; **dolly switch** a switch, for an electric light, etc., consisting of a pivotal lever pushed up and down vertically; **doll'y-tub** a tub for washing clothes or ores with a dolly. [Prob. from *Dolly*, the familiar form of *Dorothy*.]

Dolly Varden *dol'i var'dən*, a flowered muslin dress for women, with pointed bodice and tucked-up skirt: a large hat, one side bent downwards, abundantly trimmed with flowers: a large American fish of the char genus. [Named from a character in Dickens's *Barnaby Rudge*.]

dolma *dol'mə, n.* a vine or cabbage leaf with a savoury stuffing: — *pl.* **dol'mas, dolmades** (Gr., *-mä'des*). [Turk.]

dolman *dol'mən, n.* a Turkish robe with slight sleeves and open in front: a hussar's jacket, worn like a cloak, with one or both sleeves hanging loose: a woman's mantle. — **dolman sleeve** a kind of sleeve which tapers from a very wide armhole to a tight wrist. [Turk. *dōlāmān*.]

dolmen *dol'mən, n.* a stone table: a prehistoric sepulchral chamber of erect unhewn stones, supporting a flattish stone. [Fr. *dolmen*; usually explained as — Bret. *dol, taol*, table, *men*, stone; but *tolmēn* in Cornish meant hole of stone.]

dolomite *dol'ə-mīt, n.* a mineral, double carbonate of calcium and magnesium: a rock composed of that mineral, magnesian limestone. — *adj.* **dolomitic** (*-mit'-ik*). — *n.* **dol'omitisātion, -z-.** — *v.t.* **dol'omitise, -ize** to convert into dolomite. [After the French geologist D. Guy de *Dolomieu* (1750–1801).]

dolour *dol'ər, dōl'ər*, historically *dul'ər, n.* pain: grief: anguish. — *adjs.* **dolorif'erous, dolori'fic** causing or conveying dolour, pain, or grief. — *adv.* **doloro'sō** (It.; *mus.*) in a soft and pathetic manner. — *adj.* **dol'orous** full of dolour, pain, or grief: doleful. — *adv.* **dol'orously.** — *n.* **dol'orousness.** [O.Fr., — L. *dolēre*, to grieve.]

dolphin *dol'fin, n.* any of a group of animals of the whale kind belonging to the family Delphinidae, about 8 to 10 feet long, with a beak-like snout: sometimes used loosely in the U.S. to include the porpoise: either of two fish of the genus *Coryphaena* about 5 feet in length, esp. *C. hippurus*, noted for the brilliancy of its colours when dying (also **dol'phin-fish**): (with *cap.*) a northern constellation (see **Delphinus**): a buoy or pile for mooring. — *ns.* **dolphinarium** (*-ā'ri-əm*) an aquarium for

dolphins: — *pl.* **-ā′riums, -ā′ria** (*-ə*); **doi′phinet** (*Spens.*) a female dolphin. — **dol′phin-fish** see **dolphin; dol′phin-fly** a black aphis or plant-louse, destructive to bean-plants. [O.Fr. *daulphin* — L. *delphinus* — Gr. *delphīs, -phīnos.*]
dolt *dōlt, n.* a dull or stupid fellow. — *adj.* **dolt′ish** dull: stupid. — *adv.* **dolt′ishly.** — *n.* **dolt′ishness.** [For **dulled** or blunted; see **dull.**]
Dom *dom, n.* the Portuguese form of *Don:* also a title given to certain Catholic dignitaries and members of some monastic orders, esp. the Benedictine. [L. *dominus,* lord.]
-dom *-dom, -dəm, suff.* forming nouns, denoting dominion, power, state or condition: a group of people (with a specified characteristic). [O.E. *dōm,* judgment; Ger. *-tum.*]
domain *dō-mān′, n.* what one is master of or has dominion over: an estate: territory: ownership of land: the scope or range of any subject or sphere of knowledge: an aggregate to which a variable belongs (*math.*). — *adjs.* **domain′al, domā′nial.** [Fr. *domaine* — L. *dominicum* — *dominus,* a master.]
domal *dōm′əl, adj.* relating to a house. [L. *domus,* a house.]
domatium *do-mā′sh*(*y*)*əm, n.* a plant structure that harbours mites or other symbiotic organisms: — *pl.* **domā′tia.** [Latinised form of Gr. *dōmation,* dim. of *dōma,* house.]
Domdaniel *dom-dan′yəl, n.* a hall under the sea inhabited by a sorcerer and his disciples (*Southey*): an infernal cave, den of iniquity generally (*Carlyle*). [Fr., — Gr. *dōma Daniēl,* house of Daniel; from Chavis and Cazotte's French continuation of the *Arabian Nights.*]
dome[1] *dōm, n.* a structure, usually hemispherical, raised above a large building: a large cupola: a cathedral: a building, esp. a great or stately building (*poet.*): anything approaching the form of a hemispherical vault, esp. a head, the cover of a reverberatory furnace, the steam-chamber on a locomotive boiler, a clip-fastener that fits into a hold: a pair of crystal-faces parallel to a lateral axis, meeting in a roof-like edge (*crystal.*). — *v.t.* to furnish with a dome: to form into a dome. — *v.i.* to swell or rise as a dome. — *adjs.* **domed, domical** (*dōm′, dom′*) having a dome; **dōm′y.** [L. *domus,* a house; Fr. *dôme,* It. *duoma,* Ger. *Dom.*]
dome[2] (*Spens.*). Same as **doom.** — **Domesday-, Doomsday-book** (*dōōmz′dā-bŏŏk*) a book compiled by order of William the Conqueror, containing a survey of all the lands in England, their value, owners, etc. — so called from its authority in judgment (O.E. *dōm*) on the matters contained in it.
domestic *dō-, də-mes′tik, adj.* belonging to the house: remaining much at home: private: tame: not foreign. — *n.* a servant in the house: (in *pl.*) articles of home manufacture, esp. homemade cotton cloths. — *adjs.* **domes′ticable; domes′tical** (*arch.*). — *adv.* **domes′tically.** — *vs.* **domes′ticate, domes′ticise, -ize** to make domestic or familiar: to tame. — *adj.* **domes′ticated** adapted to or content with home life and activities: tamed. — *ns.* **domesticā′tion; domes′ticātor.** — *v.t.* **domesticise, -ize** see **domesticate.** — *n.* **domesticity** (*dō-, do-mis-tis′*) domestic or domesticated state: home life: (in *pl.*) home conditions and arrangements. — **domestic architecture** the architecture of mansions, dwelling-houses, cottages, etc.; **domestic economy** the principles of efficient ordering of a household; **domestic science** the household arts, as catering, cookery, laundry-work, studied in the light of physiological, chemical, etc., knowledge. [L. *domesticus* — *domus,* a house.]
domett *dom′ət, -it, n.* a plain cloth with cotton warp and woollen weft. [Perh. a proper name.]
domical. See **dome**[1].
domicile *dom′i-sīl, -sil,* **dom′icil** *-sil ns.* a dwelling-place, abode: one's legally recognised place of residence. — *v.t.* **dom′icile** (*-sīl*) to establish in a fixed residence. — *adjs.* **dom′iciled; domiciliary** (*-sil′*) pertaining to the domicile: dealing with, or available to, people in their own homes. — *v.t.* **domiciliāte** (*-sil′*) to establish in a permanent residence. — *n.* **domiciliā′tion.** — **domiciliary visit** a visit, under authority, to a private house for the purpose of searching it: a visit made by a doctor, etc. to a patient's or client's home. [Fr., — L. *domicilium* — *domus,* a house.]
dominant *dom′in-ənt, adj.* prevailing: predominant: over-topping: of an ancestral character, appearing in the first generation of cross-bred offspring to the exclusion of the alternative character in the other parent, which may yet be transmitted to later generations (*genetics*). — *n.* the fifth above the tonic (*mus.*): a dominant gene or the character determined by it: one of the prevailing species in a plant community. — *ns.* **dom′inance, dom′inancy** ascendancy: the state of being dominant. — *adv.* **dom′inantly.** [L. *domināns, -antis,* pr.p. of *domināri,* to be master.]
dominate *dom′in-āt, v.t.* to be lord over: to govern: to prevail over: to tower over: to command a view of: to be the controlling position of: to be predominant in: to project one's personality, influence, etc. strongly over. — Also *v.i.* — *n.* the Roman Empire in its later more avowedly absolute form. — *n.* **dominā′tion** government; absolute authority: tyranny: (in *pl.*) the (angelic) dominions (q.v.). — *adj.* **dom′inātive** governing: arbitrary (*rare*). — *n.* **dom′inātor** a ruler or governor (*Shak.*): a ruling influence. [L. *domināri, -ātus,* to be master — *dominus,* master — *domāre,* to tame.]
domineer *dom-in-ēr′, v.i.* (often with *over*) to rule arbitrarily: to command haughtily: to be overbearing. — *adj.* **domineer′ing** overbearing. [Prob. through Du. from O.Fr. *dominer* — L. *dominārī.*]
dominical *do-min′i-kl, adj.* belonging to the Lord, as the Lord's Prayer, the Lord's Day. — **dominical letter** one of the first seven letters of the alphabet, used in calendars to mark the Sundays throughout the year. [L.L. *dominicālis* — L. *dominicus* — *dominus,* lord, master.]
Dominican *do-min′i-kən, adj.* belonging to St. *Dominic* or to the Dominicans. — *n.* a friar or monk of the order of St. Dominic — *Fratres Predicatores,* founded in 1215, or *Black Friars,* from their black mantle.
dominie *dom′i-ni, n.* a schoolmaster, a tutor (esp. *Scots.*): a clergyman (*U.S. dial.*). [L. *domīne,* voc. of *dominus,* master.]
dominion *dō-, də-min′yən, n.* lordship: sovereignty: a domain or territory with one ruler, owner or government: a completely self-governing colony, not subordinate to but freely associated with the mother-country: control: (in *pl.*) a class of angelic spirits (Col. i, 16). — **Dominion Day** until 1983, the name of Canada Day (q.v.). [L.L. *dominiō, -ōnis* — *dominus,* master.]
domino *dom′i-nō, n.* a cape with a hood worn by a master or by a priest: a long cloak of black silk with a hood, used at masked balls, or its wearer: a mask: one of the oblong pieces with which the game of **dom′inoes** (*-nōz*) is played, usually twenty-eight in number, divided into two compartments, each of which is a blank or marked with from one to six spots: a card game played in a similar way: the end: — *pl.* **dom′ino(e)s.** — **domino theory** the theory that one event (orig. the fall of one S.E. Asian country to Communism) sets off a series of similar events (i.e. the neighbouring countries following suit), thus exhibiting the **domino effect,** the fall of one domino standing on end causing the whole row to fall in turn. [Apparently Sp. *dominó, dómino,* in some way conn. with L. *dominus,* master.]
domy. See **dom**[1].
don[1] *don, n.* (with *cap.*) a Spanish title, corresponding to English Sir, Mr, formerly applied only to noblemen, now to all classes (*fem.* **Doña** (*dōn′ya*) Italian form **Don′na**): a Spanish nobleman, a Spaniard: a fellow of a college, a college authority: a swell, adept (*coll.*). — *n.* **dona(h)** (*dō′nə*) a sweetheart (corr. of **Doña** or **Donna**). — *adj.* **donn′ish** pertaining to a don: with the airs of a don. — *ns.* **donn′ism** self-importance; **don′ship** the rank or dignity of a don. — **Don Juan** (*hwän, jōō′ən*)

a libertine of Spanish legend, subject of plays, poems, and operas in several European languages: an attractive profligate. [Sp., — L. *dominus*.]

don[2] *don, v.t.* to do or put on: to assume: — *pr.p.* **donn'ing**; *pa.t.* and *pa.p.* **donned.** [**do, on.**]

dona(h). See **don**[1].

Donat, Donet *dō'nət, n.* a grammar, a primer. [O.Fr. *donat*, from Aelius *Dōnātus*, author about 358 A.D. of a long-famous Latin grammar.]

donation *dō-nā'shən, n.* an act of giving: that which is given, a gift of money or goods: the act by which a person freely transfers his title to anything to another (*law*). — *ns.* **dō'nary** a thing given to a sacred use; **dō'nătary** (*Scots law*) one to whom lands escheated to the crown are made over. — *v.t.* **dōnate'** (a backformation from **donation**) to give as gift: to contribute, esp. to charity. — *n.* **dōnătive** (or *don'*), a gift: a gratuity: a benefice presented by the founder or patron without reference to the bishop. — *adj.* vested or vesting by donation. — *ns.* **dōnā'tor** one who makes a gift, a donor; **dōn'ătory** (or *don'*) a recipient; **dōnee'** the person to whom a gift is made; **dō'ning** (*coll.*; back formation from **donor**) the act of donating (as blood); **dō'nor** a giver: a benefactor: a person who (or animal which) provides blood, semen, or tissue or organs for use in transplant surgery. — **donor card** a card carried by a person willing to have parts of his body used in transplant surgery in the event of his death. — **dona nobis** the last section of the mass, beginning *Dona nobis pacem*, Give us peace. [Fr. — L. *dōnāre, -ātum* — *dōnum*, a gift — *dāre*, to give.]

Donatist *dōn', don'ə-tist, n.* a member of an African Christian sect of the 4th and 5th centuries, who protested against any diminution of the extreme reverence paid to martyrs, treated the lapsed severely, and rebaptised converts from the Catholic Church. — *n.* **dōn'atism.** — *adjs.* **dōnatis'tic, -al.** [From *Dōnātus*, one of their leaders.]

done. See **do**[1].

doner kebab *don'ər kə-bab'*, a Middle Eastern dish, thin slices cut from a block of minced and seasoned lamb grilled on a spit, eaten in a split piece of unleavened bread.

Donet. See **Donat.**

dong[1] *dong, n.* a deep ringing sound, as that of a large bell. — Also *v.i.* [Imit.]

dong[2] *dong,* (*vulg.*) *n.* the penis.

donga *dong'gə,* (orig. *S. Afr.*) *n.* a gully made by soil erosion. [Zulu, bank, side of a gully.]

dongle *dong'gl, n.* a device plugged into a computer which prevents the use of software on a different machine.

doning. See **donation.**

donjon *dun'jən, n.* a strong central tower in ancient castles, to which the garrison retreated when hard pressed. [A doublet of **dungeon.**]

donkey *dong'ki, n.* an ass: a stupid person: — *pl.* **don'keys.** — **don'key-en'gine** a small auxiliary engine; **donkey jacket** a strong jacket, with shoulders of leather or (usu.) a substitute, and patch pockets; **don'key-man** (*-man*) a man in charge of a donkey: (*-mən*) in the merchant navy, (*formerly*) a man in charge of a donkey-engine, (*now*) a petty officer or senior rating in a ship's engine-room; **don'key-pump** an extra steampump; **donkey vote** (*Austr.*) in a preferential system of voting, a vote accepting the order of candidates on the ballot paper: such votes collectively; **don'key-work** drudgery. — **argue, talk, the hindleg(s) off a donkey** to do so with invincible pertinacity; **donkey's years** a long time (a pun on *ears*). [Still regarded as slang in 1823; perh. a double dim. of *dun*, from its colour; or from *Duncan*.]

Donna. See **don**[1].

donnard, donnart. See **donnered.**

donnat. See **donnot.**

donne. See **do**[1].

donné(e) *do'nā, n.* a datum: basic assumption(s), as e.g. a given situation, on which a work of literature is founded: the main fact or condition determining the character and timing of an action: — *pl.* **donn'é(e)s** (*-ā(z)*). [Fr.]

donnered, donnerd, donnert, donnard, donnart *don'ərd, -ərt,* (*Scot.*) *adjs.* stupid: dull-witted.

Donnerwetter *don'ər-vet-ər,* (Ger.) *n.* thunderstorm (used as an interjection of annoyance, etc.).

donnot, donnat *don'ət,* (*Yorkshire*) *n.* a good-for-nothing: an idler. [App. partly **do-naught,** partly *dow-nought* (**dow**[2]).]

Donnybrook *don'i-brook, n.* a riotous assembly. [From the fair at *Donnybrook*, Dublin.]

donor. See **donation.**

donsie *don'si,* (*Scot.*) *adj.* unlucky, perverse: neat: trim: sickly. [Origin unknown.]

don't *dōnt,* for **do not.** — *n.* something one must not do. — **don't'-know** (the answer given by) one whose mind is not made up with regard to some, esp. political, issue.

donut. Same as **doughnut.**

donzel *don'zəl,* (*obs.*) *n.* a squire, aspirant to knighthood. [It. *donzello* — L.L. *domnicellus*, dim. of L. *dominus*, lord.]

doo *dōō, n.* A Scots form of **dove.** — **doocot, dooket** (*dōōk'ət*) a dovecote.

doob *dōōb, n.* dog's-tooth grass. [Hind. *dūb*.]

doodad, doodah *dōō'dad, -dä, n.* a small ornament or trinket: a piece of decoration: a gadget: thingamy. — **all of a doodah** in a state of agitation. [Both coined from **do**[1].]

doodle[1] *dōōd'l,* (*Scot.*) *v.t.* to dandle.

doodle[2] *dōōd'l,* (*Scot.*) *v.t.* to drone or play, as a bagpipe. [Ger. *dudeln*.]

doodle[3] *dōōd'l, v.i.* to scrawl, scribble, meaninglessly. — *n.* something doodled. — *n.* **dood'ler.**

doodlebug *dōōd'l-bug, n.* the larva of an ant-lion or other insect (used in divination in America; *U.S.*): any instrument, scientific or unscientific, used by prospectors to indicate the presence of minerals: a flying bomb (*war slang*).

dook[1] *dōōk,* (*Scot.*) *n.* a plug of wood driven into a wall to hold a nail, etc.: a bung. [Unknown.]

dook[2] *dōōk,* (*Scot.*) *v.t.* and *v.i.* to duck: to bathe. — *n.* an act of plunging, dipping, or bobbing: a bathe: an inclined mine-adit. [**duck.**]

dook[3]. See **duke.**

dooket. See **doocot** under **doo.**

dool[1], **doole.** See **dole**[2], **dule.**

dool[2] *dōōl,* **dule** (*Scot.*) *dül, ns.* a boundary mark: a goal. — **hail the dules** to score a goal. [Cf. Du. *doel,* L. Ger. *dole,* Fris. *dôl, dôle*.]

doolie *dōō'li, n.* a litter or palanquin. [Hindi *dolī*.]

doom *dōōm, n.* judgment: condemnation: destiny: ruin: catastrophe: death: final judgment: a picture of the Last Judgment. — *v.t.* to pronounce judgment on: to sentence: to condemn: to destine: — *pr.p.* **doom'ing**; *pa.t.* and *pa.p.* **doomed.** — *adjs.* **doomed** under sentence: fated: destined to inevitable death, failure or ruin; **doom'ful** (*Spens.*) dispensing judgment. — *adv.* **dooms** (*Scot.*) very, exceedingly. — *n.* **doom'ster** a judge: a dempster: a pessimist (*coll.*): a doomwatcher (*coll.*). — *adj.* **doom'y** (*coll.*) pessimistic: depressed: depressing. — **doom'-merchant** (*coll.*) a pessimist: one continually expecting, and forecasting, disaster; **dooms'day** the day of doom, the last judgment: a day of reckoning; **dooms'man** one who pronounces doom or sentence, a judge: a pessimist (*coll.*); **doom'watch** pessimism about the contemporary situation and about the future, esp. of the environment: observation of the environment to prevent its destruction by pollution, over-population, etc.: a generally pessimistic view of the future. — Also *adj.* and *v.i.* — **doom'watcher; doom'watching.** — **Doomsday-book** see **dome**[2]. — **crack of doom** the last trump; **till doomsday** forever. [O.E. *dōm,* judgment.]

doom-palm. See **doum-palm.**

door *dōr, dör, n.* the usual entrance into a house, room, or passage: a frame for closing up the entrance: a house, etc., as in *three doors away*: a means of approach or access. — **door'bell; door'-case** the frame which encloses a door; **door'-cheek** (*Scot.*) a side-post of a door; **door'-keeper; door'knob; door'knock** (*Austr.*) a fundraising appeal in which agents go from door to door soliciting donations. — Also *adj.* and *v.i.* — **door'-knocker** a knocker on a door: one who doorknocks (*Austr.*); **door(s)'-man** a porter, doorkeeper; **door'mat** a mat for wiping shoes or other purpose at a door: a person whom others trample upon (*coll.*); **door'nail** a stud for a door, proverbially dead; **door'= plate** a plate on or at a door with the householder's name on it; **door'post** the jamb or side-piece of a door; **door'-sill** the threshold of a doorway; **door'-stead** a doorway; **door'step** a step at a door: a thick slice of bread (*coll.*) — *v.t.* to go from door to door round (an area), e.g. canvassing in an election: — *pr.p.* **door'-stepping;** *pa.t.* and *pa.p.* **door'stepped.** — **door'stepper; door'stepping; door'stone; door'stop** a wedge to prevent a door swinging shut: a knob fixed to floor or wall to prevent a door opening too far. — *adj.* **door'-to-door'** calling at each house in an area for purposes of selling, canvassing, etc. — **door'way** an opening where there is or might be a door; **door'-yard** (*U.S.*) a yard about the door of a house. — **close, open the door to** to make impossible, possible; **doorstep selling** going from house to house to (try to) sell goods or services; **lay at someone's door** to blame someone (for); **leave the door open** to preserve a situation in which something remains possible; **next door (to)** in the next house: near, bordering upon: very nearly (*fig.*); **on one's doorstep** close to one's house, etc.; **out of doors** see **out; show someone the door** to turn someone out of the house. [O.E. *duru* (fem.) and *dor* (neut.); cf. Ger. *Tür, Tor,* Gr. *thyrā,* L. *forīs,* Sans. *dvār,* a door.]

doorn *dōōrn,* (*S. Afr.*) *n.* thorn. — **doorn-boom** (*dōōrn'-bōōm*) a S. African acacia. [Du. *doorn,* thorn, *boom,* tree.]

dop[1] *dop, n.* a copper cup in which a gem is fastened for cutting or polishing: Cape brandy made from grapeskins: a drink container (about one third of a bottle): an empty shell (as of a nut): a cartridge-case (usu. **dopp'ic.**)([Du. *dop,* shell, husk.]

dop[2] *dop, v.t.* and *v.i.* to dip: to dap. — *n.* (*obs.*) a curtsy: a bob. — *ns.* **dopp'er** a didapper: a rod for dapping; **dopp'ing** a flock of sheldrake. [O.E. *dop-* (in compounds); connected with **dip.**]

dopa *dō'pə, n.* a naturally-occurring amino-acid, a form of which, L-**dopa** is used in the treatment of Parkinson's disease. [From *di*oxyphenylalanine, a former name for the compound.]

dopamine *dō'pə-mēn, n.* a chemical found e.g. in brain tissue that acts as a neurotransmitter, necessary for the normal functioning of the brain. [**dopa** and **amine.**]

dope *dōp, n.* a thick liquid, semi-liquid, or pasty material: an absorbent: lubricating grease: aeroplane varnish: a substance added to improve the efficiency or modify the properties of anything: opium: a drug, esp. one administered to a racehorse or taken by an addict: drug-taking: confidential or fraudulent information in advance (*coll.*): information in general (*coll.*): anything supplied to dull, blind, or blunt the conscience or insight: a fool (*coll.*). — *v.t.* to give or apply dope to: to drug: to add impurities to (a semiconductor) to modify or improve its properties (*electronics*). — *v.i.* to take dope. — *ns.* **dōp'ant** (*electronics*) a substance used in doping; **dōp'er** one who applies, administers, deals in, or takes dope. — *adj.* **dope'y, dōp'y** narcotic: stupefied: stupid. — *n.* **dōp'ing** drugging: the addition of known impurities to a semiconductor, to achieve the desired properties in diodes and transistors (*electronics*). — **dope'-fiend** a drug addict. [Du. *doop,* a dipping, sauce; *doopen,* to dip.]

doppelgänger *dop'l-geng'ər, n.* a double: a wraith. — Also **doppelgang'er** (*-gang'*). [Ger., lit. double-goer.]

Dopper *dop'ər, n.* a Baptist or Anabaptist: a member of a strict and conservative denomination, an offshoot of the Dutch Reformed Church in S. Africa. [Du. *dooper* — *doopen,* to dip.]

doppie. See **dop**[1].

doppio movimento *dop'pi-ō mo-vē-men'tō,* (It.; *mus.*) double speed.

dopplerite *dop'lər-it, n.* a black elastic substance (calcium salts of humus acids) found in peat beds. — **Doppler('s) principle** the law of change of wavelength when a source of vibrations is moving towards or from the observer, explaining the fall of pitch of a railway whistle when the engine passes, and enabling astronomers to measure the radial velocity of stars by the displacement of known lines of the spectrum; **Doppler effect, shift** this observed change, used in e.g. Doppler radar to determine velocities of observed objects. [From Christian *Doppler* (1803–53), an Austrian physicist, who announced the principle in 1842.]

dor[1] *dōr,* (*obs.*) *n.* a scoff, mockery, as *to give* (any one) *the dor.* — *v.t.* to mock, put out of countenance. [Prob. O.N. *dār,* scoff.]

dor[2], **dorr** *dōr, n.* a kind of dung-beetle, also called **dor'-beetle** and **dor'-fly:** a cockchafer (in U.S. called **dor'-bug**): a drone (*obs.*). — **dor'hawk** the nightjar. [O.E. *dora,* a humble-bee.]

Dora *dō'rä, dō', (coll.) n.* the Defence of the Realm Act (1914) which imposed wartime restrictions. [From the initials — Defence Of Realm Act.]

dorado *də-rä'dō, n.* the coryphene, so called from its beautiful colour when dying: the so-called golden salmon, a S. American river fish (*Salminus*) of the Characinidae: (with *cap.*) a small southern constellation, the Swordfish: — *pl.* **dora'dos.** [Sp. from *dorar,* to gild — L. *deaurāre, -ātum;* see **dory, el Dorado.**]

Doras *dō'rəs, dō', n.* a S. American genus of Siluridae, bony-plated river fish with spines, with the habit of walking overland when drought threatens. — *n.* **do'rad** any member of the genus, or of the group to which it belongs. [Gr. *dory,* spear.]

Dorcas *dör'kəs, n.* in Acts, ix, 36, the Greek translation (*Dorkas*) of *Tabitha* (Aramaic, gazelle), the name of a woman famous for good works — hence **Dorcas society** a ladies' society for making and providing clothes for the poor. [Gr. *dorkas,* gazelle.]

doree. See **dory**[1].

Dorian *dō'ri-ən, dō', adj.* belonging to *Doris* in Greece or to the Dorians: Doric. — *n.* a native of Doris: a member of one of the main divisions of the ancient Greeks who arrived about 1100 B.C. and made their home in Doris, S.E. Peloponnese, Crete, Rhodes, etc. — **Dorian mode** a mode of ancient Greek music consisting of two tetrachords with a semitone between the two lowest notes in each, the tetrachords separated by a whole tone (as efga; bcde — but reckoned downwards by the Greeks), traditionally of a stirring, solemn, simple and martial quality: an authentic mode of old church music, extending from d to d with d as its final. [L. *Dōrius* — Gr. *Dōrios* — *Dōris.*]

Doric *dor'ik, adj.* belonging to *Doris* in Greece, or the Dorians, or their dialect: denoting one of the Greek orders of architecture, distinguished by its simplicity and massive strength. — *n.* a Greek dialect: any dialect imagined to resemble it, esp. Scottish. — *n.* **Doricism** (*dor'i-sizm*), a peculiarity of the Doric dialect. — *v.t.* and *v.i.* **dōr'ise, -ize** to render or become like the Dorians, in language, manners, etc. — *n.* **Dō'rism** Doricism: a Dorian characteristic. [L. *Dōricus* — Gr. *Dōrikos* — *Dōris.*]

Doris *dō'ris, dō', n.* a genus of nudibranchiate gasteropods, shell-less molluscs with a plumy tuft of gills on the back, giving name to the family **Dorid'idae.** — *n.* and *adj.* **do'ridoid.** [Gr. *Dōris,* a sea-goddess.]

Dorking *dörk'ing, n.* a square-bodied breed of poultry, variously coloured, and with five claws on each foot —so named from *Dorking* in Surrey.

dorlach *dör'lahh, n.* a bundle, a truss: a sheaf: a valise. [Gael.]

dorm *dörm*, (*coll.*) *n.* short for **dormitory**.

dormant *dör'mənt*, *adj.* sleeping: hibernating: of seeds, etc., alive but not active or growing: of volcanoes, inactive but not extinct: torpid: at rest: not used, in abeyance (as a title): in a sleeping posture (*her.*). — *n.* a crossbeam: a joist. — *n.* **dor'mancy.** [O.Fr. *dormant*, pr.p. of *dormir* — L. *dormīre*, to sleep.]

dormer *dör'mər*, *n.* a dormitory or bedroom (*obs.*): a dormer-window. — **dor'mer-win'dow** a small window with a gable, projecting from a sloping roof (orig. a dormitory window). [O.Fr. *dormeor* — L. *dormītōrium* — *dormīre*, to sleep.]

dormie. See **dormy**.

dormient *dör'mi-ənt*, *adj.* sleeping: dormant. [L. *dormiēns*, *-entis*, pr.p. of *dormīre*, to sleep.]

dormition *dör-mish'ən*, *n.* falling asleep: death. — *n.* and *adj.* **dor'mitive** soporific. [Fr., — L. *dormīre*, to sleep.]

dormitory *dör'mi-tər-i*, *n.* a large sleeping-room with many beds, whether in separate cubicles or not: a resting-place: a college hostel (*U.S.*): a small town or a suburb (also **dormitory town, suburb**), the majority of whose residents work elsewhere. — **dor'mitory-car** (*U.S.*) a railway sleeping-carriage. [L. *dormītōrium* — *dormīre*, to sleep.]

dormouse *dör'mows*, *n.* any member of the Myoxidae, a family of rodents akin to mice but somewhat squirrel-like in form and habit: — *pl.* **dor'mice.** [Perh. connected with L. *dormīre*, to sleep (from their hibernation); prob. **mouse**.]

dormy, dormie *dör'mi*, *adj.* in golf, as many holes up or ahead as there are yet to play. [Conjecturally connected with L. *dormīre*, to sleep; the player who is *dormy* cannot lose though he go to sleep.]

dornick *dör'nik*, *n.* a kind of stout figured linen, originally made at *Doornik*, or Tournai, in Belgium.

Dorothy bag *dor'ə-thi bag*, a type of ladies' handbag closed by draw-strings at the top and hung from the wrist.

dorp *dörp*, *n.* a Dutch or S. African village or small town: a town considered as provincial and backward(*coll.*; *derog.*). [Du., Afrik., *dorp*; O.E. *thorp*.]

dorr. See **dor²**.

dorsal *dör'sl*, *adj.* pertaining or belonging to the back. — *n.* a dorsal fin: a dorsal vertebra: a dossal. — *adv.* **dor'sally.** — *ns.* **dorse** (*obs.*) the back of a book or writing: a dossal: the back; **dor'sel** a dossal; **dor'ser** a dosser. — *adjs.* **dorsibranchiate** (*-brangk'*) having gills on the back; **dorsif'erous** having sori on the back: carrying young on the back; **dor'sifixed** (*bot.*) of an anther, attached by the whole length of the back to the filament; **dor'siflex** bent towards the back. — *n.* **dorsiflex'ion** a bending backwards: a bending of the back, a bow. — *adjs.* **dor'sigrade** walking on the back of the toes; **dorsiven'tral** possessing two sides distinguishable as upper or ventral and lower or dorsal, as a leaf. — *n.* **dorsiventral'ity.** — *adj.* **dorsolum'bar** of or relating to the dorsal and lumbar vertebrae, or the area of the body which they occupy. — *n.* **dor'sum** the back: — *pl.* **dor'sa.** — **dorsal suture** the seam at the midrib of a carpel. — **send to dorse** to throw on the back. [L. *dorsum*, the back.]

dorse *dörs*, *n.* a small cod. [Low Ger. *dorsch*.]

dort *dört*, (*Scot.*) *v.i.* to sulk. — *n.pl.* **dorts** sulks. — *adj.* **dor'ty** pettish: delicate. [Origin unknown.]

dorter, dortour *dör'tər*, (*arch.*) *n.* a dormitory, esp. monastic. [O.Fr. *dortour* — L. *dormītōrium*; see **dormer**, **dormitory**.]

dory¹ *dō'ri*, *dö'*, *n.* a golden-yellow fish (*Zeus faber*) of the mackerel family. — Also **John Dory** and **doree.** [Fr. *dorée*, from *dorer*, to gild — L. *deaurāre*, to gild — *dē-*, in the sense of over, *aurum*, gold.]

dory² *dō'ri*, *dö'*, (esp. *Amer.*) *n.* a small boat, with flat bottom, sharp bow and stern, especially suited for surf-riding. [Perh. — a Central Amer. language.]

dos-à-dos *dō-za-dō'*, *adv.* (*arch.*) back to back. — *n.* a sofa constructed for sitting so: a square-dance figure

in which dancers pass each other back to back (*dō-sē-dō'*); also **dosi-do':** — *pl.* **dosi-dos'.** [Fr.]

dose *dōs*, in Scotland commonly *döz*, *n.* the quantity of medicine, electric current, X-rays, etc., administered at one time: a portion, esp. a measured portion, of something given or added: anything disagreeable or medicinal to be taken: a bout, esp. of a venereal disease (*slang*). — *v.t.* to order or give in doses: to give doses to. — *ns.* **dōs'age** the practice, act, or method of dosing: the regulation of dose: the addition of an ingredient: the proper size of dose; **dōsim'eter** an instrument for measuring radiation, a small ionisation chamber with a scale on which can be read the dose which has caused it partially to discharge (also **dose'-meter); dōsim'etry; dōs(i)ol'ogy** the science of doses. — **dose equivalent** a quantity of absorbed radiation dosage, measured in sieverts or (esp. formerly) in rems, being the value of the absorbed dose (q.v.) adjusted to take acount of the different effects different types of radiation have on the human body, etc. — **absorbed dose** the amount of radiation absorbed by a body, etc., measured in grays or (esp. formerly) rads. [Fr., — Gr. *dósis*, a giving — *didonai*, to give.]

doseh *dō'se*, *n.* a religious ceremony at Cairo (abolished 1884), during the festival of the Prophet's birth, when the sheikh of the Sa'di dervishes rode on horseback over the prostrate bodies of his followers. [Ar. *dawsah*, treading.]

dosi-do. See **dos-à-dos**.

doss *dos* (*slang*) *n.* a bed, sleeping-place: a sleep. — *v.i.* to sleep: to go to bed. — *n.* **doss'er** one who lodges in a doss-house, or wherever he can. — **doss'-house** a very cheap lodging-house. — **doss down** to go to bed in a doss-house, or in a makeshift bed elsewhere. [Perh. from *doss*, a dial. Eng. name for a hassock; or perh. **dorse** (see under **dorsal**).]

dossal, dossel *dos'əl*, *n.* a cloth hanging for the back of an altar, sides of a church chancel, etc. [L.L. *dossāle*, *dorsāle* — L. *dorsum*, back.]

dosser *dos'ər*, *n.* a rich hanging or tapestry for the walls of a hall or of a chancel: a pannier. [O.Fr. *dossier* — *dos* — L. *dorsum*, back.]

dossier *do'si-ā*, *do-syā'*, *dos'i-ər*, *n.* a bundle of documents relating to a person or case: a brief. [Fr., — *dos* — L. *dorsum*, back.]

dossil *dos'il*, *n.* a plug, spigot: a cloth roll for wiping ink from an engraved plate in printing: a pledget of lint for dressing a wound (*surg.*). [O.Fr. *dosil* — L.L. *ducillus*, a spigot.]

dost *dust*, 2nd pers. sing. pres. indic. of **do**.

dot¹ *dot*, *n.* a very small spot: a short element in the written representation of Morse code. — *v.t.* to mark with a dot or dots: to scatter with objects: to jot: to hit: to place, stand, etc. at irregular and relatively widely spaced intervals. — *v.i.* to form dots: to limp: — *pr.p.* **dott'ing;** *pa.t.* and *pa.p.* **dott'ed.** — *adj.* **dott'ed** composed of dots: marked with a dot or dots. — *n.* **dott'iness.** — *adj.* **dott'y** composed of, covered with, dots: unsteady (*coll.*): feeble (*coll.*): crazed (*coll.*). — **dotted line** a line composed of dots or dashes that (on printed forms, etc.) one is instructed to sign on, tear along, etc.; **dotted note, rest** (*mus.*) one whose length is increased by one half by a dot placed after it; **dotted rhythm** one characterised by dotted notes; **dot matrix** (*comput.*) a method of printing using a rectangular matrix consisting of lines of pins, a selection of which is used to make each letter shape. — **dot and carry** (*arith.*) to set down the units and carry over the tens to the next column; **dot one's i's and cross one's t's** to pay great attention to detail; **dotted around, over,** etc., here and there; **on the dot (of)** exactly (at) (a given time); **the year dot** (*coll.*) the very beginning of time. [O.E. has *dott*, head of a boil; Du. *dot*, tuft, knot.]

dot² *dot*, *n.* a marriage portion. — *adj.* **dōt'al** pertaining to dowry or to dower. — *n.* **dōtā'tion** the bestowing of a dowry: an endowment. [Fr., — L. *dōs*, *dōtis*.]

dote, doat *dōt*, *v.i.* to be stupid or foolish (*arch.*): to be weakly affectionate: to show excessive love (with *upon*, *on*): of timber, to decay. — *ns.* **dōt′age** a doting: the childishness of old age: excessive fondness; **dōt′ant** (*Shak.*) a dotard; **dōt′ard** one who dotes: one showing the weakness of old age, or excessive fondness. — *adj.* **dōt′ed** (*Spens.*) stupid. — *n.* **dōt′er, doat′er** one who dotes. — *adj.* and *n.* **dōt′ing, doat′ing.** — *adjs.* **dōt′ish** silly; **dōt′y** decaying (of timber). — **dot′ing-piece, doat′-ing-piece** one who is doted on. [Cf. Old Du. *doten*, to be silly; Fr. *radoter*, to rave, is from the same root.]

doth *duth*, 3rd pers. sing. pres. indic. of **do.**

dotterel, dottrel *dot′(ə)rəl, n.* a kind of plover, named from its apparent stupidity in allowing itself to be approached and caught: a stupid fellow, a dupe. [dote.]

dottipoll. See **doddypoll.**

dottle[1] *dot′l, n.* a plug, esp. of tobacco left at the bottom of a pipe. [**dot**[1].]

dottle[2] *dot′l*, (*Scot.*) *n.* a fool, a silly person, a dotard. — *adj.* foolish, crazy: in dotage. — Also *adj.* **dott′led.** [dote.]

douane *dōō-än′, dwän, n.* a custom-house. — *n.* **douanier** (*dwä-nyä′*), a custom-house officer. [Fr., — Ar. *dīwān* cf. **divan, diwan.**]

douar *dōō′är.* See **duar.**

Douay *dōō′ā*, among Catholics often *dow′i, n.* the town of *Douai* in France (Nord), historically famous for its English and other Catholic colleges. — **Douay Bible** an English Roman Catholic translation of the Bible, the New Testament in the Rhemish version, the Old done at Douai in 1609–10.

double *dub′l, adj.* twofold: twice as much: of about twice the weight, size, or quality: two of a sort together: in pairs: paired: for two people: acting two parts, insincere: folded once: sounding an octave lower: having stamens in the form of petals, or having ligulate in place of tubular florets. — *adv.* to twice the extent: twice over: two together: deceitfully. — *v.t.* to multiply by two: to make twofold: to make twice as much or as many: to be the double of: in acting, to play by doubling: to be a substitute for or counterpart of: in bridge, to double the scoring value of: to sound in another octave: to line (*her.*): to fold: to clench: to pass (esp. sail) round or by. — *v.i.* to increase to twice the quantity: to turn sharply back on one's course in running: to act as substitute: in acting, to play two different parts in the same piece: in bridge, to make a double (bid). — *n.* a quantity twice as much: a score of twice the amount shown, as in the outer ring of a dartboard: a combination of two things of the same kind (as a binary star): (in *pl.*) in tennis, etc., a game with two players on each side: in tennis, two faults in succession: in bridge, a bid which, if successful, would double one's score for the hand: a win, or a defeat, in two events on the same programme: a combined bet on two races, stake and winnings from the first being bet on the second: a Guernsey copper coin, 1/8th of a penny: a duplicate: an actor's substitute: a quick pace (short for **double-quick**): one's wraith or apparition: an exact counterpart: a turning upon one's course: a trick: a feast on which the antiphon is said both before and after the psalms (*eccles.*): a size of roofing slate, 13 × 6 inches (330 × 152 mm.). — *ns.* **doub′leness** the state of being double: duplicity; **doub′ler** one who or that which doubles; **doub′leton** (the possession of) two cards of a suit in a hand; **doub′ling** the act of making double: a turning back in running: a trick: a plait or fold: mantling (*her.*). — *adj.* shifting, manoeuvring. — *adv.* **doub′ly.** — **double act** (*theat.*) a variety act for two people: the two entertainers. — *adj.* **doub′le-act′ing** applying power in two directions: producing a double result. — **doub′le-a′gent** one secretly acting simultaneously for two opposing powers; **doub′le-axe′** a religious symbol of Minoan Crete and the Aegean, a double-headed axe, associated with the mother-goddess and her son (Zeus). — *adj.* **doub′le-banked′** having two men at each oar, or having two tiers of oars one

above the other, as in ancient galleys. — **doub′le-bar′** a double vertical line marking the end of a movement or piece of music or one of its important divisions. — *adj.* **doub′le-barr′elled** having two barrels: of a surname, hyphened: of a compliment, ambiguous. — **doub′le-bass′** the largest and lowest-pitched instrument of the violin family, playing an octave below the 'cello; **double bed** a wide bed for two people; **double bill** see under **bill**[3]; **double bind** (*psych.*) a situation in which conflicting cues are given so that any choice of behaviour will be considered wrong. — *adjs.* **doub′le-bit′ing** cutting on either side; **doub′le-blind′** denoting a comparative experiment, trial, etc. in which the identities of the control group are known neither to the subjects nor to the experimenters; **double bond** (*chem.*) a covalent bond involving the sharing of two pairs of electrons. — **doub′le-bott′om (lorry)** an articulated lorry pulling a second trailer. — Also **drawbar outfit.** — *adj.* **doub′le-breast′ed** of a coat, having two breasts, one to be folded over the other. — *v.t.* **doub′le-charge′** to load with double measure. — *v.t.* and *v.i.* **doub′le-check′** to check a second time. — Also *n.* — **double chin** a chin with a fold of flesh; **doub′le-co′conut** the coco-de-mer; **double concerto** a concerto for two solo instruments; **double cream** a cream with a higher fat content than single cream; **doub′le-cross** a betrayal or deceiving of someone for whom one was supposed to be betraying or deceiving someone else. — *v.t.* to betray by double-cross. — **doub′le-cross′er; doub′le-dagg′er** a diesis (‡); **doub′le-deal′er** a deceitful person; **doub′le-deal′ing** duplicity. — *adj.* **doubl′le-decked** having two decks. — **doub′le-deck′er** a double-decked ship: a bus, tram-car, etc., in two stories or tiers: a sandwich having three pieces of bread and two layers of filling: a novel, film, etc., in two separate parts. — *v.i.* **doub′le-declutch′** (*motoring*) to change into a different gear by first changing to neutral, increasing the engine speed, then engaging the chosen gear, disengaging the clutch at both stages. — **doub′le-decomposi′-tion** a chemical action in which two compounds exchange some of their constituents. — *adjs.* **doub′le-dens′ity** (*comput.*) of a disc which can record double the normal number of bytes; **doub′le-dig′it** double-figure. — **double door(s)** a door consisting of two parts hung on opposite posts; **double-dotted note, rest** (*mus.*) one whose length is increased by three-quarters by two dots placed after it; **double-dotted rhythm** one characterised by double-dotted notes; **doub′le-Dutch** incomprehensible talk. — *adj.* **doub′le-dyed** twice-dyed: deeply imbued. — **doub′le-eagle** (*U.S.*) a gold coin worth $20: a heraldic representation of an eagle with two heads, as in the old arms of Russia and Austria. — *adj.* **doub′le-edged′** having two edges: cutting or working both ways. — **doub′le-end′er** anything having two ends alike: a cross-cut sawing machine with two adjustable circular saws for sawing both ends of timber; **doub′le-en′try** (*book-k.*) a method by which two entries are made of each transaction; **double exposure** (*phot.*) accidental or deliberate superimposition of one image on another. — *adjs.* **doub′le-eyed** doubly keen of sight; **doub′le-faced** hypocritical, false. — **doub′le-fa′cedness** (-*sid-*); **double fault** (*tennis*, etc.) two faults served in succession, causing the loss of a point. — *v.i.* **doub′le-fault′.** — **double feature** a cinema programme involving two full-length films. — *adj.* **doub′le-fig′ure.** — **double figures** a score, total, etc. of any number equal to or greater than 10 but less than 100; **double first** a university degree with first-class honours in two different subjects: one who has such a degree; **doub′le-flat′** a note already flat flattened again by a semitone: a sign indicating this. — *adjs.* **doub′le-flow′er′ed** having double flowers, as a plant; **doub′le-form′d′** having, or combining, two forms; **doub′le-fount′ed** having two sources; **doub′le-front′ed** of a house, having main-room windows on both sides of the front door. — *v.t.* **doub′le-gild** to gild with double coatings of gold: to gloze over. — **doub′le-glaz′ing** a double layer of glass in a window with an air-space between the layers to act as insulation. — *adj.* **doub'le-glazed'.** — **double Gloucester** (*glos'tər*), (*rarely*) **Gloster** a Gloucestershire cheese of extra richness. — *adjs.* **doub'le-hand'ed** having two hands: two-handled; **doub'le-head'ed** having two heads; **doub'le-heart'ed** treacherous. — **double helix** the DNA molecule. — *adj.* **doub'le-hung'** (of a window) having top and bottom sashes each balanced by sash-cord and weights, so as to be capable of vertical movement in its own groove. — **double jeopardy** second trial for the same offence. — *adjs.* **doub'le-joint'ed** having loose joints admitting some degree of movement backward; **doub'le-līved'** having two lives; **doub'le-locked'** locked with two locks or bolts: locked by two turns of the key, as in some locks and many novels; **doub'le-manned'** furnished with twice the complement of men; **doub'le-mean'ing** ambiguous. — Also *n.* — *adj.* **doub'le-mind'ed** undetermined, wavering. — **doub'le-mind'edness.** — *adjs.* **doub'le-mouth'd'** speaking with contradictory voices; **doub'le-na'tured** having a twofold nature. — **double negative** a construction consisting of two negatives, esp. when only one is logically required. — *v.t.* and *v.i.* **doub'le-park'** to park (a car, etc.) alongside vehicles already parked at the kerb. — **double pneumonia** pneumonia of both lungs. — *adj.* and *adv.* **doub'le-quick'** at a pace approaching a run: very fast. — *n.* the double-quick pace. — **double salt** a salt whose crystals dissolve to give two different salts in solution. — *v.t.* **doub'le-shade'** (*Milt.*) to double the darkness of. — **doub'le-sharp'** a note already sharp sharpened again by a semitone: a sign indicating this. — *adj.* **doub'le-shott'ed** of cannon, with double charge. — **doub'le-shuff'le** a scraping movement made twice with each foot: a dance of such steps: a trick. — *v.t.* and *v.i.* **doub'le-space'** to type with a space of one line between each typed line. — **doub'le-speak** double-talk; **double standard** bimetallism: a principle, etc. applied in such a way as to allow different standards of behaviour to different people, groups, etc.: (in *pl.*) the practice of advocating (for others) certain moral, etc. standards not followed by oneself; **double star** (*astron.*) a binary star: two unrelated stars appearing close together when seen through a telescope; **doub'le-stopp'-ing** playing on two stopped strings of an instrument at once. — *adj.* **doub'le-sto'rey** of a building, having two floors, tiers. — **doub'le-stout'** extra strong stout or porter; **doub'le-take'** a second look impelled by surprise or admiration: delayed reaction; **doub'le-talk** talk that sounds to the purpose but amounts to nothing: ambiguous, deceptive talk; **doub'le-think** the faculty of simultaneously harbouring two conflicting beliefs — coined by George Orwell in his *Nineteen Eighty-Four* (1949); **double time** payment to a worker at twice the usul rate: a time twice as fast as the previous time (*mus.*): a fast marching pace (*U.S.*). — *adj.* **doub'le-tongued'** having two tongues or a cleft tongue: self-contradictory: deceitful. — **double vision** seeing two images of the same object, because of lack of co-ordination between the two eyes; **double-you, -u** (*dub'l-ū*) the twenty-third letter of the alphabet (W, w). — **double back** to go back in the direction one has just come, usu. not by the same path; **double or quits** in gambling, the alternative, left to chance, of doubling or cancelling payment (*adj.* **double'-or-quits'**); **double up** to fold double: to bend over (as with laughter): to come at the double: to share with another. [O.Fr. *doble* — L. *duplus*, double — *duo*, two, and the root seen in Eng. **fold**, Gr. *haploos*.]

double entendre *doo-blä-tä'dr'*, (the use of) a word or phrase with two meanings, one usually more or less indecent. [Fr. of 17th century, superseded now by (*mot*) *à double entente*.]

doublet *dub'lit, n.* a close-fitting garment for the upper part of the body — with *hose*, the typical masculine dress in the 14th–17th cent.: a thing that is repeated or duplicated: one of a pair, esp. one of two words orig. the same but varying in spelling and meaning,

e.g. *balm, balsam.* [O.Fr., dim. of *double.*]

doubletree *dub'l-trē, n.* the horizontal bar on a vehicle to which the whippletree (with harnessed animals) is attached.

doubloon *dub-loon', n.* an obsolete Spanish gold coin, orig. = 2 pistoles. [Sp. *doblón*, aug. of *doble*, double; see **double.**]

doubt *dowt, v.i.* to be undecided in opinion: to be apprehensive (*obs.*). — *v.t.* to hold in doubt: to hesitate or scruple: to incline to believe with fear or hesitation: to distrust: to incline to think (esp. *Scot.*): to suspect (*arch.*; also *refl.*): to cause to doubt or fear (*obs.*). — *n.* uncertainty of opinion: a suspicion: fear (*obs.*): a thing doubtful or questioned (*obs.*): danger (*Spens.*). — *adj.* **doubt'able.** — *adj.* **doubt'ed** (*Spens.*) redoubted: feared: questioned. — *n.* **doubt'er.** — *adj.* **doubt'ful** full of doubt: undetermined: subject to doubt: not clear: insecure: suspicious: not confident: not likely or not certain to participate, co-operate, etc. — *n.* a doubtful person or thing. — *adv.* **doubt'fully.** — *n.* **doubt'fulness.** — *n.* and *adj.* **doubt'ing.** — *adv.* **doubt'ingly.** — *adj.* **doubt'less** free from doubt or (*Shak.*) fear. — *adv.* without doubt: certainly: no doubt (often a mere concession of possibility). — *adv.* **doubt'lessly.** — **doubting Thomas** a doubter or sceptic: one who needs proof before believing something (from the doubting of *Thomas*, in John, xx, 25). — **beyond (a shadow of) doubt** certain(ly); **in doubt** not certain, undecided; **no doubt** see **no.** [O.Fr. *douter* — L. *dubitāre*, akin to *dubius*, doubtful, moving in two (*duo*) directions.]

douc *dook, n.* a variegated monkey of S.E. Asia. [Fr., from Cochin name.]

douce *doos, adj.* sweet (*obs.*): sober, peaceable, sedate (*Scot.*). — *adv.* **douce'ly.** — *ns.* **douce'ness; doucet, dowset** (*doo', dow'sit; obs.*) a sweet dish: (in *pl.*) a deer's testicles; **douceur** (*doo-sûr'*) sweetness of manner (*obs.*): a compliment (*arch.*): a conciliatory present, bribe, or tip. [Fr. *doux, douce*, mild — L. *dulcis*, sweet.]

doucepere. See **douzepers.**

douche *doosh, n.* a jet of water directed upon or into the body from a pipe: an apparatus for throwing it. — *v.t.* to turn a douche upon. [Fr., — It. *doccia*, a water-pipe — L. *dūcĕre*, to lead.]

doucine *doo-sēn', (archit.) n.* a cyma recta. [Fr.]

dough *dō, n.* a mass of flour or meal moistened and kneaded, but not baked: money (*slang*). — *n.* **dough'-iness.** — *adj.* **dough'y** like dough: soft: of complexion, pallid, pasty (*coll.*). — *adj.* **dough'-baked** half-baked, defective in intelligence. — **dough'-boy** boiled flour dumpling (also **dough'-ball**): an American infantryman (*mil. slang*). — *adjs.* **dough'faced** over-persuadable, specif. of N. American politicians too inclined to favour the South at the time of the Civil War; **dough'-kneaded** (*Milt.*) soft. — **dough'nut** sweetened dough fried in fat: an accelerating tube in the form of a toroid (*nuc.*): a toroidal assembly of enriched fissile material for increasing locally the neutron intensity in a reactor for experimental purposes (*nuc.*). [O.E. *dāh*; Ger. *Teig*, O.N. *deig*, dough; cf. **duff.**]

dought. See **dow².**

doughty *dow'ti, adj.* able, strong: brave. — *adv.* **dough'tily.** — *n.* **dough'tiness.** [O.E. *dyhtig*, later *dohtig*, valiant — *dugan*, to be strong; Ger. *tüchtig*, able.]

Douglas fir *dug'las fûr*, a tall western American coniferous timber tree (*Pseudotsuga douglasii*). [David *Douglas* (1798–1834), who introduced it to Britain.]

Doukhobor. See **Dukhobor.**

douleia, doulocracy. See **dulia.**

douma. See **duma.**

doum-palm *dowm', doom'-päm, n.* an African palm (*Hyphaene*), with a branched stem, and a fruit with the taste of gingerbread. — Also **doom'-, dum'-palm.** [Ar. *daum, dūm.*]

doup *dowp, (Scot.) n.* the bottom section of an egg-shell: the buttocks: the bottom or end of anything. — **can'dle-doup** a candle-end. [Cf. O.N. *daup*, a hollow.]

dour *door, (Scot.) adj.* obstinate: sullen: grim. — *n.*

dour'ness. [Apparently L. *dūrus*, hard.]

doura. See **durra.**

dourine *dōō-rēn', dōō'rēn, n.* a contagious disease of horses due to a trypanosome. [Fr. *dourin.*]

douroucouli, durukuli *dōō-rōō-kōō'lē, n.* a night-ape, any monkey of the S. American genus *Nyctipithecus.* [S. Amer. name.]

douse[1], **dowse** *dows, v.t.* to plunge into water. — *v.i.* to fall suddenly into water. [Cf. Sw. *dunsa,* fall heavily; prob. from sound; cf. *souse.*]

douse[2], **dowse** *dows, v.t.* to strike: to strike or lower (a sail). — *n.* a heavy blow. [Prob. related to Old Du. *dossen,* to beat.]

douse[3], **dowse** *dows, v.t.* to put out, extinguish (esp. in the *slang* **douse the glim,** to put out the light). — *n.* **dous'er** a shutter for cutting off light in a cinema projector. [Perh. connected with **dout** or with **douse**[2].]

dout[1] *dowt, v.t.* to put out, extinguish. — *n.* **dout'er.** [**do out.**]

dout[2] See **dowt.**

douzepers *dōō'zə-pär, n.pl.* the twelve peers of Charlemagne, or similar group: — *sing.* **dou'zeper, dou'cepere** (*Spens.*) a champion, great knight or noble. [O.Fr. *douze pers,* twelve peers.]

dove[1] *duv, n.* a pigeon (esp. in comp., as *ring-dove, turtle-dove,* etc., and used esp. of the smaller species): a word of endearment: an emblem of innocence, gentleness, also of the Holy Spirit (Matt. iii. 16): in politics, industrial relations, etc., a person who seeks peace and conciliation rather than confrontation or war (opp. to *hawk*). — *v.t.* to treat as a dove. — *n.* **dove'let** a small dove. — *adjs.* **dove'-like** like a dove: innocent; **dov'ish, dove'ish** dove-like: seeking peace and conciliation rather than confrontation or war. — **dove'-colour** a greyish, bluish, pinkish colour; **dove'cot, -cote** a small cot or box in which pigeons breed: a pigeon-house. — *adjs.* **dove'-drawn** (*Shak.*) drawn by doves; **dove'-eyed** meek-eyed. — **dove'-house** a dovecot; **dove's'-foot** a name for some species of cranesbill (*Geranium dissectum, Geranium molle,* etc.); **dove'tail** a tenon shaped like a dove's spread tail, for fastening boards: a joint of alternate tenons and mortises of that shape. — *v.t.* and *v.i.* to fit by, or as if by one or more dovetails. — **dove'tailing.** — **flutter the dovecots** to disturb commonplace, conventional people, as the eagle would a dovecot (see Shak., *Cor.* V, vi, 115). [O.E. *dūfe,* found only in the compound *dūfe-doppa,* a diving bird; Ger. *Taube.*]

dove[2] *dōv, (Scot.) v.i.* to be half asleep or stupefied. — *v.i.* **dōv'er** (*Scot.*) to snooze, doze. — *v.t.* to stun. — *n.* a snooze: a swoon: half-consciousness. — *adj.* **dō'vie** (*Scot.*) stupid. [O.E. *dofian,* to be stupid.]

dove[3] *dōv, U.S. pa.t.* of **dive.**

dovekie *duv'ki, n.* the little auk or rotch: the black guillemot. [Dim. of **dove.**]

Dover's powder *dō'vərz pow'dər,* a sudorific compounded of ipecacuanha root, opium and potassium sulphate (or, in the U.S.A., lactose). [First prescribed by Dr. Thomas *Dover* (1660–1742).]

dow[1]. See **dhow.**

dow[2] *dow, (obs.* and *Scots) v.i.* to be good for a purpose: to avail: to be able: —3rd pers. sing. **dow, dows;** *pa.t.* **docht, dought** (*dohht*), **dowed.** — **dow'na** (*neg.*) cannot: cannot be bothered. — **dow'na-do** powerlessness. [O.E. *dugan.*]

dowable. See **dower.**

dowager *dow'ə-jər, n.* a widow with a dower or jointure: a title given to a widow to distinguish her from the wife of her husband's heir (also *adj.*): an elderly woman of imposing appearance. [O.Fr. *douagere* — L.L. *dōtārium,* dower — L. *dōtāre,* to endow.]

dowar. See **duar.**

dowd *dowd,* **dowdy** *dowd'i, ns.* a woman who wears dull-looking, clumsy, ill-shaped clothes. — *adv.* **dowd'ily.** — *n.* **dowd'iness.** — *adjs.* **dowd'y; dowd'yish.** — *n.* **dowd'yism.** [Origin unknown.]

dowel *dow'əl, n.* a pin for fastening things together by

fitting into a hole in each. — *v.t.* to fasten by means of dowels. — *n.* **dow'elling** long, thin, usu. wooden rod of circular section. — **dow'el-joint; dow'el-pin; dow'el-rod.** [Prob. related to Ger. *Döbel, Dübel,* a plug.]

dower *dow'ər, n.* a jointure: a dowry: an endowment. — *v.t.* to bestow a dowry upon: to endow. — *adj.* **dow'able** that may be endowed. — *adj.* **dow'erless.** — **dow'er-house** the house set apart for the widow, usu. on her late husband's estate. [O.Fr. *douaire* — L.L. *dōtārium* — L. *dōtāre,* to endow.]

dowf *dowf, (Scot.) adj.* dull, heavy, spiritless. — *n.* **dowf'ness.** [Prob. O.N. *daufr,* deaf.]

dowie *dow'i, (Scot.) adj.* dull, low-spirited, sad: dismal. [Prob. O.E. *dol,* dull.]

Dow-Jones average, index *dow'jōnz' av'ər-ij, in'deks,* (*U.S.*) an indicator of the relative prices of stocks and shares on the New York Stock exchange, based on the average price of a certain agreed list of securities. [Charles H. *Dow* (1851–1902), and Edward D. *Jones* (1856–1920), American economists.]

dowl, dowle *dowl, (Shak.) n.* a portion of down in a feather: a piece of fluff. [Origin obscure.]

dowlas *dow'ləs, n.* a coarse linen cloth. [From *Daoulas* or *Doulas,* near Brest, in Brittany.]

down[1] *down, n.* soft feathers: a soft covering of fluffy hair. — *adj.* **downed** filled or covered with down. — *ns.* **Down'ie®** a duvet; **down'iness.** — *adj.* **down'y** covered with or made of down: like down: knowing (*slang*). — **down'-bed; down'-quilt.** — **the downy** (*old slang*) bed. — The spellings **dowlne, dowlney** (*Shak.*) show confusion with **dowl.** [O.N. *dūnn;* Ger. *Daune,* L.G. *dune.*]

down[2] *down, n.* a bank of sand thrown up by the sea (same as **dune**): a treeless upland: (in *pl.*) an undulating upland tract of pasture-land, esp. in S.E. England (**the Downs**), also the roadstead off E. Kent. — *n.* **down'-land.** [O.E. *dūn,* a hill — Celt. *dun.*]

down[3] *down, adv.* (passing into *adj.* in predicative use), to a lower position, level or state: away from a centre (capital, great town, university, etc.): southward: to leeward: in a low or lowered position or state: below: on or to the ground: downstairs: under the surface: from earlier to later times: to a further stage in a series: from greater to less (in size, grain, activity, intensity, etc.): to a standstill, exhaustion, or conclusion: to a final state of defeat, subjection, silence, etc.: in a fallen state: in adversity: at a disadvantage: ill: behindhand: in writing or record, in black and white: in flood: on the spot, in cash: in readiness to pounce: in a state of alert awareness and understanding: in watchful opposition or hostility (with *on, upon*): broken, not operational (*comput.*). — Also elliptically, passing into an interjection or verb by omission of *go, come, put,* etc., often followed by *with.* — *adj.* going, reaching, or directed towards a lower position or level: depressed: low: broken, not operational (*comput.*). — *prep.* in a descent along, through, or by: to or in a lower position on or in: along in the direction of the current: along. — *n.* a descent; a low place: a reverse of fortune: an act of throwing or putting down: a tendency to be down on one. — *v.t.* to knock, throw, shoot or set down: to put down, overthrow: to dispirit. — *n.* **down'er** (*slang*) a depressant drug: any depressing experience, etc. — *advs.* **down'ward, down'wards** (-*wərd(z)*), from higher to lower: from source to outlet: from more ancient to modern: in the lower part. — *adj.* **down'ward.** — *adv.* **down'wardly.** — *n.* **down'-wardness** a sinking tendency: a state of being low. — *adj.* **down'-and-out'** at the end of one's resources. — *ns.* **down'-and-out'(er).** — *adj.* **down'-at-heel'** having the back of the shoe trodden down: generally shabby. — **down'beat** a downward movement of the conductor's baton: an accented beat. — *adj.* (*coll.*) relaxed, unworried: unemphatic: depressed: gloomy: depressing. — **down'bow** (*mus.*) a movement of the bow over the strings beginning at the nut end; **down'burst** same as microburst. — *adj.* **down'cast** dejected. — *n.* a current of air into a mine: a shaft carrying it (**down'cast-shaft'**):

a downward throw: a down-throw. — **down'-come** a fall, ruin: a heavy pour of rain; **down'-draught** a current of air downwards; **down'-east'er** one living *down east* from the speaker, a New Englander, and esp. an inhabitant of Maine; **down'fall** fall, failure, humiliation, ruin: a falling down, as of rain. — *adj.* **down'fallen** ruined. — **down'flow** a running or flowing down: something which runs or flows down; **down'force** aerodynamically-caused downward force in a car, etc. which e.g. improves its road holding. — *adj.* **down'going**. — **down-go'ing** (or *down'*); **down'grade** a downward slope or course. — *adj.* and *adv.* downhill. — *v.t.* to reduce in status, etc.: to belittle, underrate. — *adj.* **down'-gyved** (*Shak.*) hanging down like fetters. — **down'-haul** a rope by which a jib, etc., is hauled down when set. — *adjs.* **down'-heart'ed** dejected; **down'hill** descending, sloping. — Also *n.* — *adv.* **downhill'**. — *adj.* **down'-home** (*U.S. coll.*) characteristic of the southern states of the U.S.A.: characteristic of the country or country-dwellers· homemade: friendly. — **down'-line** the line of a railway leading from the capital, or other important centre, to the provinces; **down'lighter** a downward directed light-fitting, attatched to or recessed in the ceiling. — *adj.* **down'looked** (*Dryden*) downcast, gloomy. — **down'-ly'ing** (*dial.*) time of retiring to rest: a woman's lying-in. — *adj.* **down'-mar'ket** of (buying, selling or using) commodities relatively low in price, quality or prestige. — Also *adv.* — *adv.* and *adj.* **down'most** superlative of *down*. — **down payment** a deposit on an article, service, etc.; **down'pipe** a drainpipe which takes rainwater from the gutter of a roof; **down'pour** a heavy fall of rain, etc. — *adv.* **down'right** perpendicular (*obs.*): in plain terms: utterly. — *adj.* plain-spoken: brusque: utter, out-and-out (as in *downright madness*). — **down'rightness; down'rush** a rushing down (as of gas, hot air, etc.); **down'-sett'ing** a setting down, a snub; **down'-sitt'ing** sitting down, time of rest (Ps. cxxxix, 2): a sitting, session (*Scot.*): a settlement, establishment (esp. by marriage; *Scot.*). — *advs.* **down'stage'** towards the footlights (also *adj.*); **downstairs'** in, or towards, a lower storey: belowstairs, in the servants' quarters. — *n.* a lower storey, usu. the ground floor. — *adj.* **down'stair(s)**. — *adv.* **downstream'** with the current. — *adj.* **down'stream** further down the stream: going with the current: in the hydrocarbons industry, denoting any stage subsequent to oil production, e.g. refining, the production of oil derivatives, etc. (sometimes with *of*). — **down'stroke** a downward line made by the pen in writing; **down'swing** a downward trend in volume of trade, etc.: the part of the swing where the club is moving down towards the ball (*golf*). — *adj.* **down'-the-line** of a ballet-dancer, inconspicuously placed, unimportant. — **down'-throw** act of throwing down, or state of being thrown down: the amount of vertical displacement of the relatively lowered strata at a fault (*geol.*); **down'time** a period when work is halted, due to equipment failure, bad weather, etc. — *adj.* **down'-to-earth'** sensible: practical: realistic. — *adj.* and *adv.* **down'-town'** in or towards the lower part or (esp. *U.S.*) the business and shopping centre of the town. — *n.* this part of a town. — **down'-train** a railway train proceeding from the chief terminus; **down'trend** a downward trend. — *adj.* **down'-trod, -trodden** trampled on: tyrannised over. — **down'turn** a downward trend, decline. — *adj.* and *adv.* **down'wind'** in the direction in which the wind is blowing: in or to a position (relative to someone or something) in this direction (often with *of*). — **down east** (*U.S.*) in or into Maine and adjoining parts of New England; **down in the mouth** in low spirits; **down on one's luck** in ill-luck; **down south** in the southern states; **down to** (*slang*) the fault or responsibility of; **down tools** to stop work, strike; **down to the ground** (*coll.*) completely; **down town** in or towards the centre of a town; **down under** in or to Australia and New Zealand; **down with** put down: swallow: (as *interj.*) depose, get rid of, abolish; **go down** (often with *with*) to be received (well or badly) (by):

(often with *with*) to be acceptable (to): (with *with*) to contract (illness); **go downhill** to deteriorate (in health, prosperity, morality); **go downstream** to begin operating the downstream stages of oil exploitation; **up and down** often merely to and fro. [M.E. *a-down, adun* — O.E. *of dūne*, from the hill (dat. case of *dūn*, hill; see foregoing and **adown**).]

downa. See **dow**[2].

Downie®. See **down**[1].

Downing Street *down'ing strēt,* the street in London where the Prime Minister's official residence is, as well as the Foreign and Commonwealth Office: the government.

Down's syndrome *downz' sin'drōm,* a congenital disease caused by chromosomal abnormality, in which there is mental deficiency and a broadening and flattening of the features. — Also known as **Mongolism.** [John L. H. *Down,* (1828–96), English physician.]

dowp. Same as **doup**.

dowry *dow'ri, n.* the property which a woman brings to her husband at marriage — sometimes used for dower: sometimes a gift given to or for a wife at marriage: a natural endowment. [See **dower**.]

dowse[1] *dows, v.t.* and *v.i.* See **douse**[1,2,3].

dowse[2] *dowz, v.i.* to use the divining-rod. — *n.* **dows'er** a water-diviner. [Origin unknown.]

dowset. See **douce**.

dowt, dout *dowt,* (*Scot.*) *n.* a cigarette-end. [From **dout**[1].]

doxographer *doks-og'rə-fər, n.* a compiler of opinions of philosophers. — *ns.* **doxog'raphy; doxol'ogy** a hymn or liturgical formula ascribing glory to God. [Gr. *doxa,* opinion, reputation, glory, *graphein,* to write, *logos,* discourse.]

doxy[1] *dok'si, n.* a mistress (*Shak.*): a woman of loose character. [Origin unknown.]

doxy[2] *dok'si, n.* an opinion — 'Orthodoxy', said Warburton, 'is my doxy — heterodoxy is another man's doxy'. [Gr. *doxa,* opinion.]

doyen *doi'ən, dwä-yã, n.* a dean, senior member (of an academy, diplomatic corps, class, profession, etc.): —*fem.* **doyenne** (*doi-en', dwä-yen*). [Fr. — L. *decānus.*]

doyley. See **doily**.

doze *dōz, v.i.* to sleep lightly, or to be half-asleep: to be in a dull or stupefied state. — *v.t.* to spend in drowsiness (with *away*). — *n.* a short light sleep. — *adj.* **dozed** drowsy. — *v.t.* **dō'zen** (*Scot.*) to stupefy. — *v.i.* to become stupefied. — *ns.* **dō'zer; dō'ziness; dō'zing.** — *adj.* **dō'zy** drowsy: beginning to decay. [Cf. O.N. *dūsa,* Dan. *döse.*]

dozen *duz'n, n.* a set of twelve: also used, esp. in *pl.,* for a less exact number: — *pl.* **doz'en** when preceded by a numeral, otherwise **doz'ens.** — *adj.* and *n.* **doz'enth.** — **baker's, devil's, long, dozen** thirteen; **daily dozen** see **daily; half'-a-doz'en** six: approximately six; **round dozen** full dozen. [O.Fr. *dozeine* — L. *duodecim* (*duo,* two, and *decem,* ten), and neut. pl. ending *-ēna* (Cf. Sp. *docena*).]

dozer. Coll. for **bulldozer, calfdozer.**

drab[1] *drab, n.* a low, sluttish woman: a whore. — *v.i.* to associate with drabs. — *ns.* **drabb'er** one who herds with drabs; **drabb'iness.** — *adjs.* **drabb'ish, drabb'y** sluttish. [Poss. Gael. *drabag;* Ir. *drabog,* slut; or L.G. *drabbe,* dirt.]

drab[2] *drab, n.* thick, strong, grey cloth: a grey or dull-brown colour, perh. from the muddy colour of undyed wool: uninteresting unvaried dullness. — *adj.* of the colour of drab: dull and monotonous. — *n.* **drabb'et** a coarse linen fabric used for smock-frocks. — Also **drabette'.** — *adv.* **drab'ly.** — *n.* **drab'ness.** [Perh. Fr. *drap,* cloth — L.L. *drappus,* prob. Gmc.; see **drape**.]

drabble *drab'l, v.t.* to besmear, bedraggle. — *n.* **drabb'ling** a manner of fishing for barbels with a rod and long line passed through a piece of lead. — *n.* **drabb'ler, drab'ler** an additional piece of canvas, laced to the bottom of the bonnet of a sail, to give it greater depth.

[L. Ger. *drabbeln*, to wade about.]

Dracaena *drä-sē′nə, n.* the dragon-tree genus.   [L.L. *dracaena*, a she-dragon — Gr. *drakaina*, fem. of *drakōn*, dragon.]

drachm *dram, n.* a drachma: a dram,

drachma *drak′mə, n.* an ancient Greek weight, and a silver coin of different values: the standard unit of modern Greek currency, 100 lepta. — *pl.* **drach′mas, drach′mae** (*-mē*), **drach′mai** (*-mī*).   [Gr. *drachmē* — *drassesthai*, to grasp with the hand.]

Draco *drā′kō, n.* the Dragon, a northern constellation: a dragon-lizard. — *n.* **dracone** (*dra′kōn*, sometimes *dra-kō′ni*; also with *cap.*; Ⓡ in U. S.) a large sausage-shaped, bag-like container for transporting liquids, towed on the surface of the sea, etc. — *adjs.* **draconian** (*drək-, drak-ō-ni-ən*), **draconic** (*-on′ik*) of, of the nature of, a dragon. — *ns.* **draconites** (*drak-ə-nī′tēz*) a precious stone fabled to come from a dragon's brain; **dracontiasis** (*drak-ən-tī′ə-sis*) guinea-worm disease; **Dracontium** (*drə-kon′shi-əm*) a S. American araceous genus once of medical repute; **dracunculus** (*drə-kungk′-ū-ləs*) (with *cap.*) the green dragon genus of Araceae: the dragonet: the guinea-worm.   [L. *dracō, -ōnis*, and Gr. *drakōn, -ontos*, a dragon or snake, dims. L. *dracunculus*, Gr. *drakontion*, prob. from the root of Gr. *derkesthai*, to look.]

Draconian *drə-* or *drā-kō′ni-ən*, **Draconic** (*-kon′ik*), **Dracontic** (*-kont′ik*) *adjs.* extremely severe, as the laws of *Draco* (Gr. *Drakōn*), archon at Athens 621 B.C. — *n.* **Draconism** (*drak′ən-izm*). — All words also without *cap.*

drad *drad,* (*Spens.*) *pa.t.* and *pa.p.* of **dread.** — *adj.* (*Spens.*) dread.

draff *dräf, n.* dregs: the refuse of malt after brewing. — *adjs.* **draff′ish, draff′y** worthless.   [Prob. related to Du. *draf*, Ger. *Treber, Träber*.]

draft *dräft, n.* anything drawn: the selecting of a smaller body (of men, animals, things) from a larger: the body so selected (esp. *mil.*): a member of it: conscription (*U.S.*): an order for the payment of money: a demand (upon resources, credulity, patience, etc.): a plan: a preliminary sketch: (occasional and *U.S.*) a draught (in various senses). — *v.t.* to draw an outline of: to draw up in preliminary form: to draw off: to detach. — *ns.* **draftee′** a conscript; **draft′er, draught′er** one who drafts: a draught-horse. — **draft′-bar** a draw-bar; **draft′-dodger** (*U.S. coll.*) one who avoids conscription; **draft′-dodging.** — **draft′-horse, draft′-ox, drafts, drafts′man, drafts′manship** see **draught.**   [draught.]

drag *drag, v.t.* to draw by force: to draw slowly: to pull roughly and violently: to trail: to explore with a drag-net or hook: to apply a drag to. — *v.i.* to hang so as to trail on the ground: to be forcibly drawn along: to move slowly and heavily: to lag: to give the feeling of being unduly slow or tedious: — *pr.p.* **dragg′ing;** *pa.t., pa.p.* **dragged.** — *n.* anything dragged: an act of dragging: a dragging effect: the component of the aerodynamic force on a body travelling through a fluid (esp. a vehicle travelling through air) that lies along the longitudinal axis (*aero.*): a net or hook for dragging along to catch things under water: a heavy harrow: a device for guiding wood to the saw: a car, lorry or wagon (*slang*): a mail-coach: a long open carriage, with transverse or side seats: a contrivance for retarding a wheel, esp. an iron shoe that drags on the ground: any obstacle to progress: a tedious, dreary occupation or experience (*slang*): influence, pull (*U.S. slang*): a trail of scent left by an animal, or a trail of broken undergrowth caused by an animal dragging off its prey: an artificial scent dragged on the ground for foxhounds to follow: a short 'draw' on a cigarette (*slang*): a retarded motion of the cue-ball imparted by striking somewhat under the centre (*billiards*, etc.): (the wearing of) transvestite clothing, now usu. women's dress worn by a man, or a form of entertainment involving this (*slang*; also *adj.*): a homosexuals' party (*slang*). — *adj.* (*slang*.) **dragg′y** boring, tedious. — *n.*

drag′ster a car for drag-racing. — **drag′-bar** a draw-bar; **drag′-chain** a chain used as drag to a wheel: a chain for coupling railway vehicles; **drag′hound** a foxhound trained to follow a drag; **drag′-hunt; drag′-line** an excavating machine, crane-like in appearance, moving on articulated tracks (or, **walking dragline** on 'legs' having steel plates as 'feet'), and drawing towards itself a bucket suspended from a long jib; **drag′-man** a fisherman who uses a drag-net; **drag′-net** a net to be dragged along the bottom of water or the ground: a systematic police search for a wanted person; **drag′-parachute** a small parachute attached to the rear of an aircraft, which opens on landing to assist deceleration; **drag′-queen** a homosexual who likes wearing women's clothes; **drag race** a contest in acceleration, with standing start and quarter-mile course; **drag′-racing; drag′-shot** a shot that imparts drag to a billiard-ball; **drags′man** the driver of a drag or coach. — **drag by** to pass slowly; **drag on** to continue slowly and tediously; **drag one's feet, heels** to hang back deliberately in doing something (*n.* **foot′-dragging**); **drag out** to prolong unnecessarily or tediously; **drag out of** to get (information, etc.) from (someone) with difficulty, sometimes by force; **drag up** (*coll.*) to mention, quote (a story, etc., esp. defamatory) inappropriately or unnecessarily.   [North. — O.E. *dragan* or O.N. *draga*.]

dragée *drä′zhä, n.* a sweetmeat enclosing a drug, or a nut or fruit, etc.: a chocolate drop: a small silvered ball for decorating a cake.   [Fr.]

draggle *drag′l, v.t.* or *v.i.* to make or become wet and dirty, as by dragging along the ground: to trail. — **dragg′le-tail** a slut. — *adj.* **dragg′le-tailed.**   [Freq. of **drag**, and a doublet of **drawl.**]

dragoman *drag′ō-mən, n.* an interpreter or guide in Eastern countries: — *pl.* **drag′ōmans.**   [Fr., from Ar. *tarjumān* — *tarjama*, to interpret.]

dragon *drag′ən, n.* a fabulous winged scaly-armoured fire-breathing monster, often a guardian of treasure, ravaging a country when its hoard is rifled: a fierce, intimidating, or watchful person: a paper kite: a dragon lizard: applied to various plants, esp. Dracunculus (green dragon), and Dracontium: (with *cap.*) a northern constellation (Draco). — *ns.* **drag′oness** a she-dragon; **drag′onet** a little dragon: a fish of the genus Callionymus. — *v.t.* **drag′onise -ize** to turn into a dragon: to watch like a dragon. — *adjs.* **drag′onish; drag′onlike.** — *n.* **drag′onism** unremitting watchfulness. — *adj.* **dragonné** (*drag-o-nā′; her.*) like a dragon in the hinder part. — **drag′on-fish** a dragonet: a fish of the genus *Pegasus*; **drag′onfly** a predaceous long-bodied often brilliantly-coloured insect of the Odonata; **drag′onhead, drag′on's-head** a labiate garden plant (*Dracocephalum*) — from the shape of the corolla; **dragon lizard** a small tree-dwelling E. Indian lizard (*Draco*) with parachute of ribs and skin: a S.American lizard (*Thorictis*): a monitor, esp. a species (*Varanus komodoensis*) found in Komodo (in Indonesia), reaching 10 feet in length; **drag′on-root** (*U.S.*) an araceous plant (Arisaema) or its tuberous root, used in medicine; **drag′on's-blood** a red resinous exudation from the dragon-tree and many other trees, used for colouring varnishes, etc.; **drag′on-stand′ard** a standard in, or bearing, the form of a dragon; **drag′on-tree′** a great tree of the Canary Islands (*Dracaena draco*), of the Liliaceae, remarkable for its resin (a variety of dragon's blood), its growth in thickness like a dicotyledon, and the great age it attains. — **chase the dragon** (*slang*) to smoke heroin by heating it and inhaling the fumes.   [Fr., — L. *dracō, -ōnis* — Gr. *drakōn, -ontos*, perh. — root *drak*, as in *edrakon*, aorist of *derkesthai*, to see clearly.]

dragonnade *drag-ən-ād′, n.* the persecution of French Protestants under Louis XIV by means of dragoons: any persecution by military means (usu. in *pl.*).   [Fr., from *dragon*, dragoon.]

dragoon *drə-gōōn′, n.* an old fire-spitting musket: a mounted infantryman armed with it (*obs.*): a heavy cavalryman, as opp. to hussars and lancers — surviving in the names of certain regiments. — *v.t.* to compel by military bullying: to coerce. — **dragoon'-bird** the umbrella-bird. [Fr. *dragon*, dragon, dragoon.]

dragsman. See **drag.**

drail *drāl*, *n.* the iron bow of a plough from which the traces draw: a piece of lead round the shank of the hook in fishing. — *v.i.* to draggle. [Prob. a combination of **draggle** and **trail.**]

drain *drān*, *v.t.* to draw off by degrees: to filter: to draw off water, sewage, or other liquid from: to furnish means of withdrawal of liquid from: to make dry: to drink dry: to exhaust. — *v.i.* to flow off gradually: to part with liquid by flowing, trickling or dripping: to discharge. — *n.* a water-course: a channel for escape of liquid: a ditch: a sewer: a drink (*slang*): exhausting expenditure. — *adj.* **drain'able.** — *ns.* **drain'age** act, process, method, or means of draining: mode of discharge of water: the system of drains in a town; **drain'er** a device on which articles are placed to drain. — **drain'age-basin** the area of land that drains into one river; **drain'age-tube** a tube for discharge of pus, etc.; **drain'ing-board** a sloping surface beside a sink, where dishes, etc. are placed to drain when washed; **drain'= pipe** a pipe to carry away waste water or rainwater: (in *pl.*; *coll.*; also **drainpipe trousers**) very narrow trousers; **drain'-tile; drain'-trap** a contrivance for preventing the escape of foul air from drains, while admitting water to them. — **down the drain** (*slang*) gone for good: wasted. [O.E. *drēahnian.*]

draisine, draisene *drā-zēn*, *n.* dandy-horse. [Invented in early 19th cent. by Baron *Drais*, of Mannheim.]

drake[1] *drāk*, *n.* the male of the duck: a flat stone thrown so as to skip along the surface of water in playing *ducks and drakes* (also **drake'stone**). [Ety. obscure; cf. provincial Ger. *draak*; O.H.G. *antrahho*, Ger. *Enterich*, the first element usually explained as *eend, end, anut*, duck.]

drake[2] *drāk*, *n.* a dragon: a fiery meteor: a beaked galley, or viking ship of war; an angler's name for species of Ephemera. [O.E. *draca*, dragon — L. *dracō*.]

Dralon® *drā'lon*, *n.* a type of acrylic fibre.

dram *dram*, *n.* a contraction of **drachm:** ¹/₁₆th of an ounce avoirdupois: formerly, with apothecaries, ¹/₈th of an ounce: a small drink of alcoholic liquor: a tipple. — *v.i.* to drink a dram. — *v.t.* to give a dram to. — **dram'-drink'er; dram'-shop** a bar. [Through Fr. and L., from Gr. *drachmē*; see **drachma.**]

drama *drä'mə*, *n.* a story of life and action for representation by actors: a composition intended to be represented on the stage: dramatic literature: theatrical entertainment: a dramatic situation, or series of absorbing events. — *adjs.* **dramat'ic** (*drə-mat'ik*), **-al**, belonging to the drama: appropriate to or in the form of drama: with the force and vividness of the drama: impressive or important because of speed, size, suddenness, etc. — *adv.* **dramat'ically.** — *n.* **dramat'icism.** — *n.* (usu. *sing.*) **dramat'ics** the acting, production, study of plays: a show of excessive, exaggerated emotion (*coll.*). — **dramatīs'able** (*dram-*), **-z-.** — *n.* **dramatīsā'tion, -z-** the act of dramatising: the dramatised version of a novel or story. — *v.t.* **dram'atise, -ize** to compose in, or turn into, the form of a drama or play: to exaggerate the importance of or emotional nature of. — *n.* **dram'atist** a writer of plays. — **drama documentary** see **faction; dramatic irony** a situation, etc. in a play, the irony of which is clear to the audience but not to the characters; **dram'atis persōnae** (*-e, -ī*) the characters of a drama or play. [L., — Gr. *drama, drāmatos* — *drāein*, to do.]

dramaturgy *dram'ə-tûr-ji*, *n.* the principles of dramatic composition: theatrical art. — *ns.* **dram'aturg** (from Ger.) a member of a theatrical company who selects the repertoire and may assist in the arranging and production of the plays, compiling notes for the programme, etc.; **dram'aturge, dram'aturgist** a playwright. — *adjs.* **dramatur'gic(al).** [Through Fr. from

Gr. *drāmatourgiā, drāmatourgos*, playwright — *drāma*, and *ergon*, a work.]

Drambuie® *dram-boo'i*, *-bū'*, a Scotch whisky liqueur. [**dram**, and Gael. *buidhe*, yellow, golden.]

dramma giocoso *dräm'mä jō-kō'sō* (It., comic drama) comic opera. — **dramma per musica** (*per moo'zē-kä*; It., drama through music) an esp. 17th- and 18th-century term for opera, or for the musical drama that was its forerunner.

drammock *dram'ək*, *n.* meal and water mixed raw. — Also **dramm'ach.** [Cf. Gael. *drama(i)g*, a foul mixture.]

Drang nach Osten *drang nahh ō'stən*, (Ger., *hist.*) eastward thrust — policy of German expansionists.

drank *drangk*, *pa.t.* of **drink.**

drant, draunt *dränt, drönt*, (*dial.*) *vs.i.* and *vs.t.* to drawl, to drone. — *ns.* a droning tone.

drap *drap*, *n.* and *v.* Scots for **drop.** — *n.* **drapp'ie, drapp'y** (*Scot.*) a little drop, csp. of spirits.

drap-de-Berry *drä-də-ber-ē'*, (*obs.*) *n.* a woollen cloth made in Berry, in France. — Also *adj.* [Fr., Berry cloth.]

drape *drāp*, *v.t.* to cover as with cloth: to hang cloth in folds about: (*refl.*) to assume a casual and graceful pose. — *n.* a hanging or curtain (*U.S.* and *theatre*): (in *pl.*) a drape suit. — *adj.* **draped.** — *n.* **drāp'er** a dealer in cloth and cloth goods. — *adj.* **drāp'eried** draped. — *n.* **drāp'ery** cloth goods: hangings: the draper's business: the representation of clothes and hanging folds of cloth (*art*): — *pl.* **drāp'eries.** — *v.t.* to drape. — *ns.* **drapet** (*drap'it; Spens.*) a cloth covering; **drapier** (*drāp'-i-ər; obs.*) a draper. — **drape suit** a man's suit with narrow trousers and a **drape coat** or **jacket**, a very long jacket (esp. with velvet collar and cuffs). [O.Fr. *draper*, to weave, drape, *drapier*, draper — *drap*, cloth, prob. Gmc.; see **drab.**]

drastic *dras'tik*, *adj.* forcible, powerful in action: violent: unsparing: great and quick or sudden: dramatic: bad, unpleasant: extreme. — *n.* a severe purgative. — *adv.* **dras'tically.** [Gr. *drastikos* — *drāein*, to act, to do.]

drat *drat*, *interj.* a minced oath used to express vexation, (sometimes with an object). — *adj.* **dratt'ed.** [Aphetic from **God rot.**]

dratchell *drach'l*, (*dial.*) *n.* a slut.

draught *dräft*, *n.* drawing or pulling: a pull: attraction: the thing or quantity drawn: readiness for drawing from the cask: the act of drinking: the quantity drunk in one breath: a dose of liquor or medicine: the outline of a picture, or a preliminary sketch or plan (usu. **draft**): that which is taken in a net by drawing: a chosen detachment of men (usu. **draft**): a current of air: the depth to which a ship sinks in the water: a move in a game (*obs.*): a thick disc used in the game of draughts: (in *pl.*) a game played by two persons moving draughtmen alternately on a chequered board: a cesspool or privy (*Shak.*). — *adj.* on draught. — *v.t.* to sketch out, make a preliminary plan of or attempt at (also **draft**): occasionally for **draft** in sense of draw off, set apart from a larger body. — *n.* **draught'iness.** — *adj.* **draught'y** full of draughts or currents of air. — **draught'-animal, -horse, -ox**, etc., one used for drawing heavy loads; **draught-bar** see **draw-bar; draught'board** a chessboard used for playing draughts; **draught'= en'gine** the engine over the shaft of a coal-pit. — *n.pl.* **draught'-hooks** large iron hooks fixed on the cheeks of a cannon-carriage. — **draught'-house** (*B.*) a sink, privy; **draught'man** a piece used for playing draughts; **draught'-net** a drag-net. — *adj.* **draught'-proof** sealed, filled, etc. to prevent draughts. — Also *v.t.* — **draught'= proofing; draught'-screen** a screen for warding off a current of air; **draughts'man** a piece used in playing draughts: one skilled or employed in drawing: one who draughts or draws up documents (in this sense usually **draftsman**). — **feel the draught** (*fig.*) to be unpleasantly conscious of difficult conditions, esp. economic; **on draught** of liquor, sold from the cask. [O.E. *draht*

— *dragan*, to draw; see **drag, draw**.]
draunt. See **drant**.
drave *drāv*, old *pa.t.* of **drive**.
Dravidian *drə-vid'i-ən, adj.* belonging to a dark, long-headed, wavy-haired race of the Deccan: belonging to a group of languages in Southern India, including Tamil, Malayalam, Kannada, Telugu, etc. — Also *n.* [Sans. *Drāviḍa,* an ancient province of Southern India.]
draw *drö, v.t.* to pull: to drag: to pull along: to bring forcibly towards or after one: to pull into position: to pull back: to pull back the string of: to pull together or away: to take at random from a number: to entice, attract: to coax into giving information: to stimulate to self-expression (usu. **draw out**): to inhale: to take out: to unsheathe: to withdraw: to cause to flow out: to evoke or bring out by some artifice: to extract by pulling: to extract the essence of: to eviscerate: to pull through a small hole, as in making wire: to deduce: to lengthen: to extend to the full length: to force to appear (as a badger from its hole): to receive or take from a source or store: to demand by a draft: to get by lot: to trace: to construct in linear form: to make a picture of, by lines drawn: to describe: to put into shape, frame: to write out (as a cheque): to require as depth of water for floating: to finish without winning or losing: to glance (*cricket*): to hit (the ball) too much to the left (if right-handed) or to the right (if left-handed) (*golf*): to deliver (a bowl) so that it draws (*bowls*): to deliver gently (*curling*): to force one's opponents to play (all their cards of a suit, esp. trumps) by continually leading cards of that suit (*bridge,* etc.): to hit (the cue ball) so that it recoils after striking another ball (*billiards,* etc.). — *v.i.* to pull: to practise drawing: to move: to make one's way, betake oneself: to resort: to approach: to make a draught: to allow a free current: to act as drawer: to draw a card, a sword, lots: to infuse: to end a game without winning or losing: to move in a curve to the point aimed for (*bowls*): — *pa.t.* **drew** (*drōō*); — *n.* the act of drawing: assignment by lot, as of prizes, opponents in a game: anything drawn: a drawn or undecided game: an attraction: a drawer (of a chest of drawers; *U.S.*). — *adj.* **draw'able.** — *ns.* **drawee'** the person on whom a bill of exchange is drawn; **draw'er** he or that which draws: one who draws beer or fetches liquor in a tavern: (*drör*) a thing drawn out, as the sliding box in a **chest of drawers**: (in *pl.*) a close undergarment for the lower part of the body and the legs; **draw'ing** the art of representing objects or forms by lines drawn, shading, etc.: a picture in lines: an assigning by lot: the act of pulling, etc. — *adj.* **drawn** pulled together: closed: neither won nor lost: unsheathed: eviscerated: strained, tense: etiolated. — **draw'back** a disadvantage: a receiving back some part of the duty on goods on their exportation; **draw'-bar** a sliding bar: a bar used in coupling railway vehicles (also **drag'-, draught'-bar**); **drawbar outfit** a double-bottom lorry; **draw'-boy** the boy who pulls the cords of the harness in figure-weaving: a mechanical device for this purpose; **draw'bridge** a bridge that can be drawn up or let down at pleasure: bridge played by two persons, with two dummy hands, not exposed; **draw'-gear** the apparatus by which railway-cars are coupled; **draw'ing-board** a slab on which paper can be pinned for drawing on: the planning stage of a project, etc. (*fig.*); **draw'ing-frame** a machine in which carded wool, cotton, or the like is drawn out fine; **draw'ing-knife** a knife with a handle at each end, used by a cooper for shaving hoops by drawing it towards him; **draw'ing-master; draw'ing-paper; draw'ing-pen; draw'-ing-pencil; draw'ing-pin** a short broad-headed pin for fastening paper to a drawing-board; **draw'ing-room** in engineering, a room where plans and patterns are drawn (see also separate article); **draw'ing-table** (also **draw-leaf table, draw-table, draw-top table**) a table which can be extended in length by drawing out sliding leaves; **draw'-net** same as **drag-net; drawn'-(thread') work** ornamental work done by pulling out some of

the threads of a fabric; **draw'-plate** a plate supporting dies for drawing wire or tubing; **draw'-sheet** a hospital sheet that can be drawn out from under a patient; **draw'-string** a string, cord, etc., in a casing in, or threaded through, material, by which the material may be drawn or gathered up. — *adj.* having, closed by, such a string. — **draw-table, draw-top table** see **drawing-table; draw'-tube** a tube sliding within another, as in a form of telescope; **draw'-well** a well from which water is drawn up by a bucket and apparatus. — **at daggers drawn** openly hostile; **draw a bead on** see **bead; draw a blank** to get a lottery ticket that wins no prize: to get no result; **draw a cover (covert)** to send the hounds into a cover to frighten out a fox; **draw back** to recoil: to withdraw; **draw blank** to draw a cover, but find no fox; **draw, hang, and quarter** see **hang; draw in** to reduce, contract: to become shorter; **draw it fine** to be too precise; **draw it mild** (*coll.*) to refrain from exaggeration; **draw near** to approach; **draw off** to cause to flow from a barrel, etc.: to withdraw; **draw on** to approach: to pull on; **draw on, upon** to make a draught upon: to make a demand upon (one's credulity, patience, resources): to draw one's sword, pistol, against; **draw on one's imagination** to make imaginative or lying statements; **draw on one's memory** to try to remember: to make use of what one remembers; **draw out** to leave the place (of an army, etc.): to lengthen: to entice into talk and self-expression; **draw rein** to slacken speed, to stop; **draw stumps** to end play in cricket by removing the wickets; **draw the cloth, board, table** (*arch.*) to clear up after a meal; **draw the line** to fix a limit: **draw the long bow** see **bow²; draw the teeth of** to render harmless; **draw to a head** to mature; **draw up** to form in regular order: to compose, put into shape: to stop; **in drawing** correctly drawn; **out of drawing** inaccurately drawn, or drawn in violation of the principles of drawing; **out of the top drawer** of top grade, esp. socially. [O.E. *dragan*; cf. **drag**.]
Drawcansir *drö-kan'sər, n.* a blustering bully. [*Drawcansir* (parodying Dryden's *Almanzor*), who 'kills 'em all on both sides' in Buckingham's *Rehearsal* (performed 1671).]
drawing-room *drö'ing-rōōm, n.* a room to which the company withdraws after dinner, a sitting-room: a reception of company at court: a private compartment of a 'parlor-car' (*U.S.*). — *adj.* suitable for the drawing-room. [Orig. **withdrawing-room.**]
drawl *dröl, v.i.* to dawdle (*obs.*): to speak in a slow lengthened tone. — *v.t.* to utter in a slow and sleepy manner. — *n.* a slow, lengthened utterance. — *n.* **drawl'er.** — *adv.* **drawl'ingly.** — *n.* **drawl'ingness.** [Connected with **draw**.]
drawn *drön, pa.p.* of **draw**, and *adj.*
dray¹ *drā, n.* a low strong cart for heavy goods: a timber sledge: that which is dragged or drawn. — *n.* **dray'age.** — **dray'-horse; dray'man; dray'-plough.** [Cf. O.E. *dræge,* drag-net — *dragan*, to draw; see **drag, draw**.]
dray². Same as **drey**.
drazel *dräz'l,* (*dial.*) *n.* a slut. [Origin unknown.]
dread *dred, n.* great fear: awe: an object of fear or awe: fury (*Spens.*). — *adj.* dreaded: inspiring great fear or awe. — *v.t.* to fear greatly: to reverence: to cause to fear, to affright (*obs.*). — *n.* **dread'er.** — *adj.* **dread'ful** orig., full of dread: producing great fear or awe: terrible: very bad, unpleasant (*coll.*). — *adv.* **dread'fully** in a dreadful way: very (much) (*coll.*). — *n.* **dread'fulness.** — *adj.* **dread'less.** — *adv.* (*Spens.*) doubtless. — *adv.* **dread'lessly.** — *n.* **dread'lessness.** — *adv.* **dread'ly.** — **dread locks, dread'locks** the long-plaited hairstyle adopted by Rastafarians; **dread'nought, dread'naught** one who dreads nothing: hence, a thick cloth or garment thereof: a powerful type of battleship or battle-cruiser (dating from 1905–6). — **penny dreadful** a cheap sensational serial or tale. [M.E. *dreden* — O.E. *ondrǣdan,* to fear; O.N. *ondrēda,* O.H.G. *intratan,* to be afraid.]
dream¹ *drēm,* (*obs.*) *n.* joy: mirth: minstrelsy: music:

sound. — **dream′hole** a hole in the wall of a steeple, tower, etc., for admitting light. [O.E. *drēam*, joy, mirth.]

dream² *drēm, n.* a train of thoughts and fancies during sleep, a vision: something only imaginary: a distant hope or ideal, probably unattainable. — *v.i.* to fancy things during sleep: to think idly (with *of*): to think (of) as possible, contemplate as imaginably possible. — *v.t.* to see or imagine in, or as in, a dream: — *pa.t.* and *pa.p.* **dreamed** or **dreamt** (*dremt*). — *ns.* **dream′er; dream′ery** a place favourable to dreams: dream-like fancies. — *adj.* **dream′ful** (*Tenn.*) dreamy. — *adv.* **dream′ily.** — *n.* **dream′iness.** — *n.* and *adj.* **dream′ing.** — *adv.* **dream′ingly.** — *adj.* **dream′less.** — *adv.* **dream′lessly.** — *n.* **dream′lessness.** — *adj.* **dream′y** full of dreams: given to dreaming: appropriate to dreams: dream-like: lovely (*coll.*). — **dream′boat** (*slang*) someone wonderful and desirable — usu. of the opposite sex; **dream′-land** the land of dreams, reverie, or imagination; **dream′time** in the mythology of Australian Aboriginals, the time when the earth and patterns of life on earth took shape; **dream′while** the duration of a dream; **dream′-world** a world of illusions. — **dream up** to plan in the mind, often unrealistically; **go like a dream** to work, progress, etc. very well. [M.E. *dream, drēm*; perh. the same word as the foregoing.]

dreary *drēr′i, adj.* gloomy: cheerless. — *adj.* **drear** dreary. — *n.* (*obs.; Spens.*) **dreare, drere**) dreariness: gloom: mishap. — *ns.* **drear′ihead, drear′iment, drear′iness, drear′ing** (all *Spens.*), **drear′ihood.** — *adv.* **drear′ily.** — *adj.* **drear′isome** desolate, forlorn. [O.E. *drēorig*, mournful, bloody — *drēor*, gore.]

dreck *drek,* (*slang*) *n.* rubbish, trash. [Yiddish *drek*, Ger. *Dreck*, dirt, filth, dung.]

dredge¹ *drej, n.* a bag-net for dragging along the bottom to take oysters, biological specimens, mud, etc.: a machine for deepening a harbour, canal, river, etc., for excavating under water or on land, or for raising alluvial deposits and washing them for minerals, by means of buckets on an endless chain, pumps, grabs, or other devices. — *v.t.* and *v.i.* to gather, explore, or deepen with a dredge. — *n.* **dredg′er** one who dredges: a machine for dredging: a boat, ship, or raft equipped for dredging. [Conn. with **drag, draw.**]

dredge² *drej, v.t.* to sprinkle. — *ns.* **dredg′er, dredge′-box, dredg′ing-box** a vessel with perforated lid for dredging. [O.Fr. *dragie*, sugar-plum — Gr. *tragēmata*, dessert.]

dree *drē,* (*Scot.*) *v.t.* to endure, bear. — **dree one′s weird** to undergo one's destiny. [O.E. *drēogan*, suffer, accomplish.]

dregs *dregz, n.pl.* impurities in liquor that fall to the bottom, the grounds: dross: the vilest part of anything. — *n.* **dregg′iness.** — *adj.* **dregg′y** containing dregs: muddy: foul. [O.N. *dregg.*]

dreich *drēhh,* (*Scot.*) *adj.* long drawn out: tedious: dreary. [See **dree.**]

dreikanter *drī′kän-tər, n.* a pebble faceted by wind-blown sand, properly having three faces: — *pl.* **drei′kanter(s).** [Ger. *Dreikant*, solid angle — *drei*, three, *Kante*, edge.]

drench *drench, drensh, v.t.* to fill with drink or liquid: to wet thoroughly: to soak: to physic by force: to drown (*obs.*). — *v.i.* (*obs.*) to drown. — *n.* a draught: a dose of physic forced down the throat. — *n.* **drench′er.** [O.E. *drencan*, to cause to drink (*drincan*, to drink), *drenc*, drink, drowning; Ger. *tränken*, to soak; see **drink.**]

drent *drent* (*Spens.*), obsolete *pa.p.* of **drench,** to drown.

drepanium *dri-pā′ni-əm, n.* a cymose inflorescence in which each daughter axis is on the same side of its parent axis, and all in one plane. [Latinised from Gr. *drepanion*, dim. of *drepanon*, a reaping-hook.]

drere, dreryhead, etc. Spenserian forms of **drear,** etc.

Dresden (**china, porcelain, ware**) *drez′dən* (*chī′nə, pōrs′lin, wār*), fine decorated china made in Saxony (Royal Saxon porcelain factory established at Meissen, 1710).

dress *dres, v.t.* to straighten: to flatten: to smooth: to erect: to set in order: to prepare: to draw (fowl): to

manure: to add seasoning to (food): to finish or trim: to treat: to tend: to apply suitable materials to: to clothe: to adorn: to treat with severity: to chide: to thrash: to tie (a fly) (*angling*). — *v.i.* to come into line: to put on clothes: to put on finer, more elaborate, or more formal clothes: — *pa.t.* and *pa.p.* **dressed,** sometimes **drest.** — *n.* the covering or ornament of the body: a lady's gown: manner of clothing: ceremonial or formal clothing. — *adj.* pertaining to evening dress. — *ns.* **dress′er** one who dresses: a medical student who dresses wounds: a tirewoman: a person who assists an actor to dress in a theatre: a tool or machine for dressing: a table on which meat is dressed or prepared for use: a kitchen sideboard, esp. with a high back and shelves: a chest of drawers or dressing-table (*U.S.*); **dress′ing** dress or clothes: material applied to land, a wound, manufactured goods, etc.: matter used to give stiffness and gloss to cloth: sauce, stuffing, etc., used in preparing a dish for the table, etc.: an ornamental moulding: a thrashing. — *adj.* **dress′y** fond of dress: showy: indicating care in dressing. — **dress′-cir′cle** part of a theatre (usually the first gallery), orig. intended for people in evening dress; **dress′-coat** a fine black coat with narrow or cut-away skirts, worn in full dress; **dressed day** formerly, the second day of a three days' visit; **dress′-form** a dressmaker's (usu. adjustable) model. — *n.pl.* **dress′-goods** cloths for making women's and children's gowns, frocks, etc. — **dress′guard** (*arch.*) an arrangement of strings to protect the rider's dress from contact with a bicycle wheel; **dress′-improver** (*obs.*) a bustle; **dress′ing-case** a case of toilet requisites; **dress′ing-down** a severe scolding: a thrashing; **dress′ing-gown** a loose garment used in dressing, or in dishabille; **dress′ing-jacket,** (*obs.*) **dress′ing-sack** a jacket worn by women in dressing; **dress′ing-room; dress′ing-station** a place where wounded are collected and tended by members of a field-ambulance; **dress′ing-table; dress′-length** enough to make a dress; **dress′maker** one who makes clothes: one who makes clothes for women and children as a living; **dress′making** the art or process of making clothes; **dress′-reform** a late 19th-cent. movement seeking to make dress more practical; **dress′-rehears′al** a full rehearsal in costume with everything as for the performance. — Also *fig.* — **dress sense** sense of style in dress, knowledge of what suits one; **dress′-shield** a device to protect the armpit of a dress against sweat; **dress′-shirt′, dress′-suit′, dress′-tie′** one for formal evening dress; **dress uniform** a formal, ceremonial uniform. — **dress down** to handle with severity: to reprimand: to thrash: to dress deliberately informally; **dress up** to dress elaborately: to dress for a part: to masquerade: to treat so as to make appear better, more interesting, etc., than it really is; **evening dress, full dress** the costume prescribed by fashion for evening receptions, dinners, balls, etc. — **get dressed** to put one's clothes on. [O.Fr. *dresser,* to prepare — an inferred L.L. *dīrectiāre*, to straighten; see **direct.**]

dressage *dres′äzh, n.* training of a horse in deportment and response to controls. [Fr.]

drest *drest, pa.t.* and *pa.p.* of **dress.**

drevill *drev′il,* (*Spens.*) *n.* a foul person. [Cf. M.Du. *drevel,* scullion.]

drew *droo, pa.t.* of **draw.**

drey, dray *drā, n.* a squirrel's nest. [Ety. dub.]

drib *drib, v.i.* (*obs.*) to trickle: to go little by little. — *v.t.* (*obs.*) to let trickle: to take a little, filch: to lead gradually: to shoot (an arrow) short or wide. — *n.* a drop: a trickle: a small quantity. — *ns.* **dribb′er** (*obs.*); **dribb′let, drib′let** a drop: a trickle: a small quantity. — **dribs and drabs** small quantities at a time. [Akin to **drip.**]

dribble *drib′l, v.i.* to fall in small drops: to drop quickly: to trickle: to slaver, as a child or an idiot. — *v.t.* to let fall in drops: to give out in small portions: to drib (*archery; Shak.*). — *v.t.* and *v.i.* to move the ball forward little by little, tricking opponents (*football,*

hockey, etc.): — Also *n.* — *n.* **dribb'ler.** — *adj.* **dribb'ly.** [Freq. of **drib.**]
dricksie. See **druxy.**
dried, drier, dries, driest. See **dry.**
drift *drift, n.* a driving: a drove (*arch.*): a heap of matter driven together, as snow: floating materials driven by water: a driving shower: a streaming movement: the direction in which a thing is driven: a slow current caused by the wind: leeway: passive travel with the current, wind, etc.: abandonment to external influences: tendency: a cattle-track, drove-road: a pin or bar driven into a hole, e.g. to enlarge it (also **drift'pin**): a drift-net: a set of nets: the object aimed at: the meaning or implication of words used: loose superficial deposits, esp. glacial or fluvio-glacial (*geol.*): a horizontal or oblique excavation or passage (*mining*): a ford (*S. Afr.*; from *Du.*). — *v.t.* to drive: to carry by drift: to cause or allow to drift: to pierce or tunnel. — *v.i.* to be floated along: to be driven into heaps: to leave things to circumstances: to wander around, or live, without any definite aim. — *ns.* **drift'age** that which is drifted: the amount of deviation from a ship's course due to leeway; **drift'er** one who or that which drifts: an aimless shiftless person: a fisherman or a fishing-boat that uses a drift-net. — *adjs.* **drift'less** without drift; **drift'y** full of or forming drifts. — **drift'-anchor** an anchor for keeping the ship's head to the wind; **drift'-bolt** a steel bolt used to drive out other bolts; **drift'-ice** floating masses of ice drifting before the wind; **drift'-land** an old tribute paid for the privilege of driving cattle through a manor; **drift'-mining** gold-mining by means of drifts in the gravel and detritus of old river-beds: coal-mining by means of drifts; **drift'-net** a net which is allowed to drift with the tide; **drift'pin** see **drift** *n.* above; **drift'-sail** a sail immersed in the water, used for lessening the drift of a vessel during a storm; **drift'-way** a road over which cattle are driven: drift (*min.*); **drift'-weed** gulf-weed: tangle: sea-weed thrown up on the beach; **drift'-wood** wood drifted by water. [M.E.; O.N. *drift*, snowdrift; root as **drive.**]
drill¹ *dril, v.t.* to bore, pierce: to make with a drill: to pierce with a bullet or bullets (*slang*): to exercise (soldiers, pupils, etc.) by repeated practice: to sow in rows. — *n.* an instrument for boring stone, metal, teeth, or other hard substances, actuated by a kind of bow, by a brace, or otherwise: a large boring instrument used in mining: a type of shellfish which bores into the shells of oysters: training exercise: a spell of it: a drill-master: a ridge with seed or growing plants on it (turnips, potatoes, etc.): the plants in such a row: the machine for sowing the seed in drill-husbandry: correct procedure or routine (*coll.*). — *n.* **drill'er.** — **drill'-barrow** a grain-drill driven by hand; **drill'-harrow** a harrow for working between drills; **drill'-hole** a hole bored in the ground e.g. for rock samples; **drill'-husbandry** the method of sowing seed in drills or rows; **drill'ing-machine, drill'ing-lathe, drill'-press** a machine for boring with a drill or drills; **drill'-master** one who teaches drill, or who trains in anything, esp. in a mechanical manner; **drill'-plough** a plough for sowing grain in drills; **drill'-sergeant** a sergeant who drills soldiers; **drill'ship** a free-floating ship-shaped drilling platform. [Prob. borrowed from Du. *drillen*, to bore; *dril, drille*, a borer; cf. **thrill.**]
drill² *dril, n.* a W. African baboon, smaller than the mandrill. [Perh. a W. African word.]
drill³ *dril, n.* a stout twilled linen or cotton cloth. — Also **drill'ing.** [Ger. *Drillich*, ticking — L. *trilīx*, three-threaded; *trēs, tria*, three, *līcium*, thread.]
drily. See under **dry.**
drink *dringk, v.t.* to swallow as a liquid: to smoke (tobacco; *obs.*): to empty, as a glass, bowl, etc.: to absorb: to take in through the senses. — *v.i.* to swallow a liquid: to take intoxicating liquors to excess: — *pr.p.* **drink'ing**; *pa.t.* **drank,** *arch.* **drunk**; *pa.p.* **drunk.** — *n.* an act of drinking: a quantity drunk: something to be drunk: a beverage: intoxicating liquor. — *adj.* **drink'-**

able. — *ns.* **drink'ableness; drink'er** one who drinks: a tippler; **drink'ing.** — *adj.* fit to drink: for drinking. — **drink-dri'ver** one who drives a vehicle after having drunk more than the legally permitted amount of alcohol. — *n.* and *adj.* **drink-dri'ving.** — *interj.* **drink'=hail** an Early Middle English reply to a pledge in drinking (*waes hail* (later **wassail**), be healthy, or lucky, was answered with *drinc hail*, drink healthy or lucky — *hail* being O.N. adj. *heill*, not O.E. *hāl*). — **drink'ing=bout; drinking-fountain; drink'ing-horn; drinking-up time** in a public house, the few minutes allowed after official closing time for customers to finish their last drinks before leaving; **drink'-mon'ey** a gratuity, ostensibly given to buy liquor for drinking to the health of the giver; **drink'-offering** an offering of wine, oil, blood, etc., to a god. — **drink oneself drunk** to drink until one is drunk; **drink in** to absorb (rain, etc.), as dry land does: to take in eagerly (something seen, said, etc.); **drink off** to quaff wholly and at a gulp; **drink the others under the table** to continue drinking and remain (comparatively) sober after the others have completely collapsed; **drink to, drink (to) the health of** to drink wine, etc., with good wishes for the health, prosperity, etc. of; **drink up** to exhaust by drinking; **in drink** (while) intoxicated; **strong drink** alcoholic liquor; **the drink** (*slang*) the sea. — See also **drunk.** [O.E. *drincan*; Ger. *trinken.*]
drip *drip, v.i.* to fall in drops: to let fall drops. — *v.t.* to let fall in drops: — *pr.p.* **dripp'ing**; *pa.t.* and *pa.p.* **dripped.** — *n.* a falling in drops: that which falls in drops: the edge of a roof: a device for passing a fluid slowly and continuously, esp. into a vein of the body (also **drip'-feed**): the material so passed: a forceless person (*coll.*): drivel, esp. sentimental (*slang*). — *n.* **dripp'ing** that which falls in drops, as fat from meat in roasting. — *adj.* **dripp'y** (*coll.*) silly, inane. — *adj.* **drip'-dry'** (of a material or garment) which, when allowed to dry by dripping, requires no, or little, ironing. — Also *v.i., v.t.* — **drip'-feed** a drip (see above). — *v.t.* to treat (a patient, etc.) with a drip. — **drip irrigation** a system of irrigation in which water is supplied through pipes to the roots of a crop; **drip'ing=pan** a pan for receiving the dripping from roasting meat; **dripping roast** a source of easy and continuous profits; **drip'-stone** a projecting moulding over doorways, etc., serving to throw off the rain; **drip'-tip** (*bot.*) a prolonged leaf-tip, serving to shed rain. — **right of drip** a right in law to let the drip from one's roof fall on another's land. [O.E. *dryppan* — *drēopan.*]
drisheen *dri-shēn', n.* a type of Irish sausage made with sheep's blood. [Ir. *drisín.*]
drive *drīv, v.t.* to urge along: to hurry on: to control or guide the movements or operations of: to convey or carry in a carriage: to force in: to push briskly: to furnish motive power to: to urge, as a point of argument: to carry through, as a bargain: to impel: to compel: to send away with force, as a ball, esp. in golf, to play from the tee or with a driver, in cricket to hit strongly down the pitch, in tennis, to return forcibly underarm: to chase: to excavate (e.g. tunnel): to sort out (feathers) in a current of air. — *v.i.* to control an engine, vehicle, draught-animal, etc.: to press forward with violence: to be forced along, as a ship before the wind: to be driven: to go in a carriage: to aim or tend towards a point (with *at*): to strike with a sword, the fist, etc. (with *at*): — *pr.p.* **drīv'ing**; *pa.t.* **drōve,** *arch.* **drāve,** *Spens.* **drive** (*driv*); *pa.p.* **driv'en.** — *n.* an excursion in a vehicle: a road for driving on, esp. the approach to a house within its own grounds: a driving stroke in games: impulse: impulsive force: power of getting things done: the chasing of game towards the shooters, or the sport so obtained, or the ground over which the game is driven: pushing sales by reducing prices: an organised campaign to attain any end: a meeting in order to play certain games, e.g. whist: apparatus for driving. — *n.* **driv(e)abil'ity.** — *adj.* **driv(e)'able.** — *n.* **driv'er** one who or that which drives,

in all senses: a club used in golf to propel the ball from the teeing-ground. — *adj.* **driv′erless** running or able to run, without a driver. — **drive′-in** a refreshment halt, store, cinema, etc., where patrons are catered for while still remaining in their motor-cars. — Also *adj.* — **drive′way** a carriage drive: a driving road; **driv′ing-band** the band or strap that communicates motion from one machine, or part of a machine, to another; **driv′ing-box** a box on which a driver sits; **driv′ing-gear** apparatus by which power is transmitted from shaft to shaft; **driving licence** an official licence to drive a motor vehicle; **driv′ing-mirror** a small mirror in which a driver can see what is behind his vehicle; **driv′ing-shaft** a shaft from a driving-wheel communicating motion to machinery; **driving test** a test of ability to drive safely, esp. an official and obligatory test; **driv′ing-wheel** a main wheel that communicates motion to other wheels: one of the main wheels in a locomotive. — **drive a coach and horses through** (*coll.*) to demolish (an argument, etc.) by demonstrating the obvious faults in it: to brush aside, ignore completely; **drive home** to force (e.g. a nail) completely in: to make completely understood or accepted; **let drive** to aim a blow. [O.E. *drīfan*, to drive; Ger. *treiben*, to push.]

drivel *driv′l*, *v.i.* to slaver like a child: to be foolish: to speak like an idiot: — *pr.p.* **driv′elling;** *pa.t.* and *pa.p.* **driv′elled.** — *n.* slaver: nonsense. — *n.* **driv′eller.** [M.E. *drevelen, draveln*; O.E. *dreflian.*]

driven. See **drive.**

drizzle *driz′l*, *v.i.* to rain in small drops. — *v.t.* to shed in small drops. — *n.* a small, light rain. — *adj.* **drizz′ly.** [Freq. of M.E. *dresen* — O.E. *drēosan*, to fall; Goth. *driusan.*]

droger, drogher *drō′gər*, *n.* a W. Indian coasting vessel, with long masts and lateen sails. [Du. *droogen*, to dry — orig. a vessel on which fish were dried.]

drogue *drōg*, *n.* the drag of boards, attached to the end of a harpoon-line, checking the progress of a running whale: a conical canvas sleeve open at both ends, used as one form of sea-anchor, or to check the way of an aircraft, etc.: a parachute used to reduce speed of a falling object, e.g. one fired from a descending space capsule: a funnel device on the end of the hose of a tanker aircraft: a wind-sock: an air target of similar shape. [Origin obscure.]

droguet *dro-gā′*, *n.* a ribbed woollen dress fabric, a variety of rep. [Fr.; cf. **drugget.**]

droich *drōhh*, (*Scot.*) *n.* a dwarf. — *adj.* **droich′y** dwarfish. [Gael. *troich* or *droich*; orig. from O.E. (see **dwarf**).]

droil *droil*, *v.i.* to drudge. [Perh. Du. *druilen*, to loiter.]

droit *drwä* (before a vowel *drwät*; Eng. *droit*), *n.* right, legal claim. — **droit administratif** (*ad-mēn-ē-stra-tēf*) in France, administrative law; **droit au travail** (*ō-tra-vä-y′*) right to work; **droit des gens** (*dā zhã*) international law; **droit du seigneur** (*dü se-nyœr*) same as *jus primae noctis* (q.v.). [Fr.]

drôle *drōl*, *n.* a rogue, a knave. — *adj.* amusing: odd. [Fr.]

droll *drōl*, *adj.* odd: amusing: laughable. — *n.* one who excites mirth: a jester. — *v.i.* to practise drollery: to jest. — *ns.* **droll′ery** drollness: waggery: a comic show, picture, story: a jest: a puppet-show; **droll′ing.** — *adjs.* **droll′ish** rather droll. — *n.* **droll′ness.** — *adv.* **drolly** (*drōl′li*). [Fr. *drôle*, prob. from Du. *drollig*, odd — *trold*, a hobgoblin; cf. Ger. *Droll*, a short thick person.]

drome *drōm*, (*coll.*) *n.* an aerodrome.

dromedary *drum′i-dər-i, drom′*, *n.* a thoroughbred camel: a one-humped Arabian camel. — *Spens.* **drom′edare.** [O.Fr. *dromedaire* — L.L. *dromedārius* — Gr. *dromas, dromados*, running — *dromos*, a course, run.]

dromond *drom′, drum′ənd*, *n.* a swift mediaeval ship of war. — Also **drom′on.** [O.Fr., — L.L. *dromō, -ōnis* — Byzantine Gr. *dromōn* — *dromos*, a running, *dramein* (aor.) to run.]

dromophobia *drom-ō-fō′bi-ə*, *n.* a morbid fear of crossing streets. [Gr. *dromos*, public walk, *phobos*, fear.]

dromos *drom′os*, *n.* a Greek race-course: an entrance-passage or avenue, as to a subterranean tomb, etc.: — *pl.* **drom′oi.** — *adjs.* **drom′ic, -al** pertaining to a race-course: basilican. [Gr.]

drone *drōn*, *n.* the male of the honey-bee: one who lives on the labour of others, like the drone-bee: a lazy, idle fellow: a deep humming sound: a bass-pipe of a bagpipe: its note: a pedal bass: the burden of a song: a monotonous speaker or speech: an aircraft piloted by remote control. — *v.i.* to emit a monotonous humming sound. — *v.t.* to utter with such a tone. — *adv.* **drōn′ingly.** — *adj.* **drōn′ish** like a drone: lazy, idle. — *adv.* **dron′ishly.** — *n.* **drōn′ishness.** — *adj.* **drōn′y.** — **drone′-pipe** a pipe producing a droning sound. [O.E. *drān*, bee, but the quantity of the *a* is doubtful, and relations obscure: perh. — Old Saxon.]

drongo *drong′gō*, *n.* any member of the family *Dicruridae*, glossy-black fork-tailed insect-catching birds of the Old World tropics: a nitwit, a no-hoper (*Austr. slang*): — *pl.* **drong′o(e)s.** — Also **drong′o-shrike.** — **drong′o= cuck′oo** a cuckoo that resembles a drongo. [From Malagasy.]

drook, drookit. See **drouk.**

drool *drōōl*, *v.i.* to slaver: to drivel: to show effusive or lascivious pleasure (with *over*). — *n.* drivel. [**drivel.**]

droome *drōōm*, (*Spens.*) *n.* another form of **drum**[1].

droop *drōōp*, *v.i.* to hang down: to grow weak or faint: to decline. — *v.t.* to let hang down. — *n.* a drooping position. — *advs.* **droop′ily, droop′ingly.** — *n.* **droop′- iness.** — *adj.* **droop′y.** [O.N. *drūpa*, to droop; see **drop.**]

drop *drop*, *n.* a small rounded blob of liquid that hangs or falls at one time: a very small quantity of liquid: anything hanging like a drop: a pendant: a round sweetmeat: a curtain dropped between acts (also **drop′= cur′tain**): (in *pl.*) a medicine taken in drops: a fall: a vertical descent, difference of level: a landing by parachute: an instance of dropping anything: an unpleasant surprise: a trap in the gallows scaffold, the fall of which allows the criminal to drop: a device for lowering goods into a ship's hold. — *v.i.* to fall in drops: to let drops fall: to fall suddenly, steeply or sheer: to let oneself fall gently: to sink: to lapse: to diminish: to subside into a condition, come gradually to be: to come casually or accidentally: to move slowly with the tide. — *v.t.* to let fall in drops: to let fall: to let go, relinquish, abandon: to omit: to lower: to lay: to give birth to: to spot, bespatter, sprinkle: to utter casually: to write and send (a note) in an offhand manner: to set down, part with: to cause to fall, e.g. by shooting: to hole, etc. (a ball): to score (a goal) with a drop-kick: to set down from a vehicle, a ship: to cease to associate with: to lose (a sum of money, a game as part of a contest): to take one more (shot, stroke) than par (*golf*): to cause to fall: to bring down by a shot: — *pr.p.* **dropp′ing;** *pa.t.* and *pa.p.* **dropped.** — *ns.* **drop′let** a little drop; **dropp′er** one who or that which drops: a tube or contrivance for making liquid issue in drops: a shoot that grows downward from a bulb and develops a new bulb (*hort.*): a setter or dog that drops to earth on sighting game: an artificial fly attached to the leader (also **drop′fly); dropp′ing** that which is dropped: (usu. in *pl.*) dung, excrement; **drop′p′le** a trickle. — *adv.* **drop′wise** by drops. — **drop′-drill** an apparatus for dropping seed and manure into the soil simultaneously; **drop′-forging** the process of shaping metal parts by forging between two dies, one fixed to the hammer and the other to the anvil of a steam or mechanical hammer; **drop′-goal** (*Rugby*) a goal secured by a drop-kick; **drop′-hamm′er, drop′-press** a swaging, stamping, or forging machine; **drophead coupé** one whose top can be opened; **drop′-kick** a kick made when the ball rebounds from the ground after dropping from the hand (*Rugby football*; also *v.t.*): a kick made by both feet while jumping in the air (*wrestling*); **drop′-lett′er** (*U.S. old*) a letter left at a post-office merely for local delivery; **drop′-net** a net suspended from a boom, to be suddenly dropped on a passing shoal of fish; **drop-out** see **drop out** below; **dropp'ing-well** (*fig.* in Tennyson) a well supplied by water falling in drops from above. — *adj.* **drop'-ripe** so ripe as to be ready to drop from the tree. — **drop'-scene** a drop-curtain; **drop(ped)'-scone** a scone made like a pancake; **drop serene** (*Milt.*) an old medical name for amaurosis, literally translated from L. *gutta serēna*; **drop'-shot** (*tennis*, etc.) a ball made to drop close to the net; **drop'stone** a stalactitic calcite; **drop tank** (*aero.*) a tank, esp. for fuel, that can be dropped during flight; **drop'-wort** a species of spiraea (*S. filipendula*) with bead-like root tubercles. — **a drop in the bucket, ocean** a quantity infinitesimal in proportion; **at the drop of a hat** immediately: on the smallest provocation; **drop a brick** see **brick; drop a curtsy** to curtsy; **drop astern** (*naut.*) to get left more and more behind; **drop away, off** to depart, disappear; **drop down** to sail, move, or row down a coast, or down a river to the sea; **drop in** to come, fall, set, etc. in casually, unintentionally, or one by one; **drop off** to fall asleep: to become less, to diminish; **drop on, drop down on** to single out for reproof or an unpleasant task; **drop out** to disappear from one's place: to make a drop-kick (*Rugby football*): to withdraw, esp. from an academic course or from conventional life in society (*n.* and *adj.* **drop'-out**); **dropping fire** unremitting irregular discharge of small-arms; **drop someone a line** (*coll.*) to write someone a letter; **get the drop on one** (*U.S.*) to be ready to shoot first; hence to have at a disadvantage; **let drop** to disclose inadvertently, or seemingly so; **(Prince) Rupert's drops** drops of glass that have fallen in a melted state into cold water, and have assumed a tadpole-like shape, the whole falling to dust with a loud report if the point of the tail be nipped off. [O.E. *dropa*, a drop, *dropian, droppian,* to drop; Du. *drop,* Ger. *Tropfe.*]

dropsy *drop'si, n.* a morbid accumulation of watery fluid in any part of the body. — *adjs.* **drop'sical, drop'sied** (*Shak.*) affected with dropsy. [Aphetic for **hydropsy**.]

Drosera *dros'ə-rə, n.* the sundew genus of **Droserā'ceae,** a family of insectivorous plants: (without *cap.*) any plant of the genus. — *adj.* **droserā'ceous.** [Fem. of Gr. *droseros,* dewy — *drosos,* dew.]

droshky *drosh'ki,* **drosky** *dros'ki, ns.* a low four-wheeled open carriage used in Russia: a German four-wheeled cab. [Russ. *drozhki.*]

drosometer *dros-om'i-tər, n.* an instrument for measuring dew. [Gr. *drosos,* dew, *metron,* measure.]

Drosophila *dros-of'i-lə, n.* a genus of small yellow flies —fruit-flies — which breed in fermenting fruit juices and are utilised in experiments in heredity: (without *cap.*) any fly of the genus. [Gr. *drosos,* dew, moisture, *phileein,* to love.]

dross *dros, n.* the scum of melting metals: waste matter: small or waste coal: refuse: rust: lucre. — *n.* **dross'iness.** — *adj.* **dross'y** like dross: impure: worthless. [O.E. *drōs.*]

drostdy *dros'dā,* (*S. Afr.*) *n.* formerly the house and office of a landdrost. [Afr. — Du. *drost,* bailiff, sheriff; cf. Ger. *Drost, Drostei.*]

drought *drowt,* **drouth** *drowth* (*Scot.* drōōth), *ns.* dryness: want of rain or of water: a condition of atmosphere favourable to drying: thirst. — *ns.* **drought'iness, drouth'iness.** — *adjs.* **drought'y, drouth'y** very dry: wanting rain: thirsty. [O.E. *drūgath,* dryness — *drūgian,* to dry.]

drouk, drook *drōōk,* (*Scot.*) *v.t.* to drench. — *n.* **drouk'ing, drook'ing.** — *adj.* **drouk'it, drook'it.** [Origin obscure; cf. O.N. *drukna,* to be drowned; Dan. *drukne.*]

drouth, etc. See **drought.**

drove *drōv, pa.t.* of **drive.** — *n.* a number of cattle, or other animals, driven: a crowd, horde, e.g. of people, moving along together: a broad-edged chisel for dressing stone. — *n.* **drov'er** one whose occupation is to drive cattle: a fishing boat, drifter (*Spens.*). — **drove'=road** an old generally grassy track used or once used by droves of cattle. [O.E. *drāf, drīfan,* to drive.]

drow[1] *drow,* (*Shetland and Orkney*) a form of **troll**[1].

drow[2] *drow,* (*Scot.*) *n.* a drizzling mist: a squall. [Origin obscure.]

drown *drown, v.i.* to die of suffocation in liquid. — *v.t.* to kill by suffocation in liquid: to submerge: to flood: to extinguish: to make indistinguishable or imperceptible. — *adj.* **drownd'ed** (*Spens.*; *now illiterate*) drowned. — *n.* **drown'er.** — *n.* and *adj.* **drown'ing.** — **drown someone out** to make someone inaudible by making a louder noise. [M.E. *drounen;* origin obscure; the word used in O.E. was *druncnian.*]

drowse *drowz, v.i.* to doze, sleep lightly. — *v.t.* to make heavy with sleep, cause to doze: to stupefy: to pass in a half-sleeping state. — *n.* a half-sleeping state. — *ns.* **drows'ihe(a)d** (*Spens.*) drowsiness, sleepiness. — *adv.* **drows'ily.** — *n.* **drows'iness.** — *adj.* **drows'y** sleepy: heavy: dull: inducing sleep. [Apparently O.E. *drūsian,* to be sluggish; but not known between O.E. times and the 16th century.]

drub *drub, v.t.* to beat or thrash: — *pr.p.* **drubb'ing;** *pa.t.* and *pa.p.* **drubbed.** — *n.* **drubb'ing** a cudgelling: in games, a thorough defeat. [Ar. *daraba,* to beat, bastinado — *darb,* a beating, has been suggested.]

drucken *druk'ən,* (*Scot.*) *adj.* drunken. — Used also as *pa.p.* of **drink.** — *n.* **druck'enness.** [O.N. *drukkinn,* pa.p. of *drekka,* to drink.]

drudge *druj, v.i.* to do dull, laborious or very mean work. — *n.* one who does heavy monotonous work: a slave: a menial servant: dull task-work. — *ns.* **drudg'er; drudg'ery, drudg'ism** the work of a drudge: uninteresting toil: hard or humble labour. — *adv.* **drudg'ingly.** [Ety. unknown; perh. from root of O.E. *drēogan,* to perform, undergo.]

drug[1] *drug, n.* any substance used in the composition of medicine: a substance used to stupefy or poison or for self-indulgence: an article that cannot be sold, generally owing to overproduction. — *v.t.* to mix or season with drugs: to administer a drug to: to dose to excess: to poison or stupefy with drugs. — *v.i.* to administer drugs or medicines: to take drugs, esp. narcotics, habitually: — *pr.p.* **drugg'ing;** *pa.t.* and *pa.p.* **drugged.** — *ns.* **drugg'er** a druggist (*obs.*): one who drugs; **drugg'ist** one who deals in drugs: a pharmacist (*U.S.*). — **drug'-add'ict, drug'-fiend** a habitual taker of drugs; **drug'-pusher** a pusher, one who peddles narcotics illegally; **drug'-store** (*U.S.*) a chemist's shop (usually in America selling a variety of goods, including refreshments). [O.Fr. *drogue,* of uncertain origin.]

drug[2] *drug,* (*Shak.*) *n.* a form of **drudge.**

drugget *drug'it, n.* a woven and felted coarse woollen fabric: a protective covering, made of such fabric, for a floor or carpet. [O.Fr. *droguet.*]

druid *drōō'id, n.* (also with *cap.*) a priest among the ancient Celts of Britain, Gaul and Germany: a member of a benefit society (founded 1781), its lodges called *groves:* an Eisteddfod official: — *fem.* **dru'idess** (also with *cap.*). — *adjs.* **druid'ic, -al.** — *n.* **dru'idism** the doctrines which the druids taught: the ceremonies they practised. — **druidical circle** a fanciful 18th-century name for a stone circle (not made by the druids). [L. pl. *druidae,* from a Celtic stem *druid-,* whence O.Ir. *drai,* Ir. and Gael. *draoi,* magician.]

drum[1] *drum, n.* an instrument of percussion, a skin stretched on a frame: anything shaped like a drum: the tympanum of the ear: the upright part of a cupola (*archit.*): a cylinder, esp. a revolving cylinder: a magnetic drum (*comput.*; see under **magnet**): a cylindrical barrel: a bundle or swag (*Austr.*): formerly, a large and tumultuous evening party (said to be so called because rival hostesses vied with each other in drumming up crowds of guests): a drumfish. — *v.i.* to beat a drum: to beat rhythmically: to solicit orders (*U.S.*). — *v.t.* to expel to the sound of a drum or drums (with *out;* esp. *milit.;* also *fig.*): to summon (with *up*): to impress by iteration: — *pr.p.* **drumm'ing;** *pa.t.* and *pa.p.* **drummed.** — *n.* **drumm'er** one who drums: a commercial traveller: a swagman (*Austr.*). — **drum'beat; drum brake** a type of brake in which two shoes grip the inside of the brake drum; **drum'fish** any fish of the Sciaenidae; **drum'fire** massed artillery-fire with a rolling sound; **drum'head** the head or skin of a drum: the top part of a capstan (also **drumhead cabbage**) a type of flat-headed cabbage. — *adj.* (*mil.*) improvised in the field (see **court-martial**). — **drum'-ma'jor** the marching leader of a military band; **drum majorette** a girl who heads a marching band, usu. twirling a baton, in a parade, etc.: a majorette; **drum'stick** the stick with which a drum is beaten: the tibia of a dressed fowl; **drum table** a round, deep-topped table on a central leg, usu. with drawers. — **beat, bang the drum** to indulge in publicity. [From a Gmc. root found in Du. *trom,* Ger. *Trommel,* a drum; prob. imit.]

drum² *drum, n.* a ridge, drumlin (in many place names). — *n.* **drum'lin** (*geol.*) a usu. oval ridge formed under the ice-sheet of the Glacial Period (also **drum**). [Ir. and Gael. *druim,* back.]

drumble *drum'bl,* (*Shak.*) *v.i.* to be sluggish. — *n.* **drum'-bledor** a dumbledore.

drumlin. See **drum²**.

drumly *drum'li,* (*Scot.*) *adj.* turbid, muddy: gloomy.

drummock *drum'ək.* Same as **drammock**.

Drummond light *drum'ənd līt,* the limelight or oxyhydrogen light invented by Captain T. *Drummond* (1797–1840).

drunk *drungk, pa.p.* and old-fashioned *pa.t.* of **drink**. — *adj.* intoxicated (also *fig.*): saturated. — *n.* drunken bout: a drunk person. — *n.* **drunk'ard** one who frequently drinks to excess: a habitual drinker. — *adj.* **drunk'en** given to excessive drinking: worthless, besotted: resulting from intoxication: (sometimes) drunk. — *adv.* **drunk'enly.** — *n.* **drunk'enness** intoxication: habitual intoxication.

drupe *drōōp, n.* a fleshy fruit with a stone. — *adj.* **drupā'ceous** producing or pertaining to drupes or stone-fruits. — *ns.* **drup'el, drupe'let** a little drupe, forming part of a fruit, as in the raspberry. [L. *drūpa* — Gr. *dryppā,* an olive.]

druse *drōōz, n.* a rock cavity lined with crystals (by geologists usu. called a **drusy cavity**), a geode. — *adj.* **dru'sy** rough with, composed of, minute crystals: miarolitic. [Ger. *Druse* — Czech. *druza,* a piece of crystallised ore.]

Druse, Druze, Druz *drōōz, n.* one of a people inhabiting chiefly a mountainous district in the south of Syria, whose religion contains elements found in the Koran, the Bible, Gnosticism, etc. — *adj.* **Drus'ian.** [Perh. from *Darazi,* an early exponent of the religion.]

druxy *druk'si, adj.* of timber, having decayed spots concealed by healthy wood. — Also **drick'sie.** [Origin unknown.]

Druz, Druze. See **Druse**.

dry *drī, adj.* without water or liquid, contained or adhering: free from, or deficient in, moisture, sap, rain: thirsty: out of water: failing to yield water, or milk, or other liquid: of a fruit, not fleshy: not green: unbuttered: not drawing blood: of wines, etc., free from sweetness and fruity flavour: legally forbidding the liquor trade: enforcing or subjected to prohibition: uninteresting: frigid, precise, formal: of humour, quiet, restrained, uttered in a matter-of-fact way, as if not intended to be humorous : of manner, distantly unsympathetic: of natural gas, containing only small amounts of liquid constituents: — *compar.* **drī'er; *superl.* **drī'est.** — *v.t.* to free from or exhaust of water or moisture (often with *off*). — *v.i.* to become dry (often with *off*): to evaporate entirely:—*pr.p.* **dry'ing;** *pa.t.* and *pa.p.* **dried;** *3rd pers. sing. pr.t.* **dries.** — *n.* a prohibitionist: one who favours strict adherence to hardline right-wing Conservative policies (*U.K.pol.*). — *n.* **drī'er, dry'er** one who or that which dries: a machine for extracting moisture from cloth, grain, etc.: a drying agent for oils, paint, etc. — *adv.* **drī'ly, dry'ly** in a dry manner. — *n.* and *adj.* **dry'ing.** — *adj.* **dry'ish.** — *n.* **dry'ness.** — **Dry'asdust** a character in the prefa-

tory matter of some of Scott's novels: a dull, pedantic, learned person. — Also *adj.* — **dry battery** (*elect.*) a battery composed of dry-cells. — *v.t.* **dry'beat** (*Shak.*) to drub, but without shedding blood. — **dry'-bi'ble** a disease of horned cattle in which the third stomach, or bible, is very dry; **dry bob** at Eton, a boy who plays cricket, football, etc. — opp. to the *wet bob,* who rows. — **dry'-cell** an electric cell in which the electrolyte is not a liquid but a paste. — *v.t.* **dry'-clean** to clean (clothes, etc.) using e.g. a petroleum-based solvent rather than water. — **dry'-cupping** application of cups without previous scarification. — *vs.t.* **dry'-cure** to cure by drying; **dry'-dock** see **dry dock** at **dock³**. — *adj.* **dry'-eyed** tearless. — **dry farming** a system of tillage in dry countries, surface soil being kept constantly loose, so as to retain scanty rains and reduce evaporation; **dry-'fist** a niggard. — *adj.* and *adv.* **dry-fist'ed** taking payment for gains and owing for losses. — *adj.* **dry'-fly** (of fishing) without sinking the fly in the water. — *adv.* **dry'-foot** (*Shak.*) by scent of the foot alone. — *n.pl.* **dry'-goods** drapery and the like distinguished from groceries, hardware, etc. — **dry hole** a well which does not yield commercially viable quantities of oil or gas: an unsuccessful project (*fig.*); **dry ice, dry-iced** see **ice**. — *n.pl.* **drying oils** vegetable or animal oils which harden by oxidation when exposed to air. — **dry land** land as opposed to sea; **dry light** an undeceptive light: an unprejudiced view; **dry Mass, service** *Missa sica,* a rite in which there is neither consecration nor communion; **dry measure** a system of measure by bulk, used for grain, etc. (see **bushel¹, peck¹, pint**); **dry'mouth** xerostomia; **dry'-nurse** a nurse who does not suckle. — Also *v.t.* — **dry'-plate** a sensitised photographic plate, with which a picture may be made without the preliminary use of a bath; **dry'-point** a sharp needle by which fine lines are drawn in copper-plate engraving: a plate or impression produced with it; **dry riser** a vertical pipe with an outside access through which water can be pumped from the street to the individual floors of a building in the event of a fire; **dry'-rot** a decay of timber caused by *Merulius lacrymans* and other fungi which reduce it ultimately to a dry brittle mass: a concealed decay or degeneration (*fig.*); **dry run** a practice exercise (*mil.*): a rehearsal. — *v.t.* **dry'-salt'** to cure (meat) by salting and drying. — *n.* **dry'salter** a dealer in gums, dyes, etc., or (*obs.*) in salted or dry meats, pickles, etc.; **dry'saltery**. — *adj.* and *adv.* **dry'=shod** without wetting the shoes or feet. — **dry ski** an adaptation of a ski with which one can practise skiing on a dry surface; **dry skiing; dry steam** steam unmixed with liquid drops. — *adj.* **dry'-stone** built of stone without mortar, as some walls. — **dry'-stove** a kind of hot-house with dry heat; **dry'-wall'er** one who builds walls without mortar; **dry'-wash'** the bed of an intermittent stream. — **cut and dried** see **cut; dry out** (*coll.*) to take or give a course of treatment to cure oneself or another person of alcoholism; **dry up** to dry thoroughly or completely: to cease to produce liquid (water, milk, etc.): to forget one's lines or part (as an actor, etc.; *coll.*): to stop talking (*slang*); **go dry** to adopt liquor prohibition; **high and dry** see **high; the dry** (sometimes with *cap.*) the dry season in central and northern Australia. [O.E. *drȳge;* cf. Du. *droog,* Ger. *trocken.*]

dryad *drī'ad, -əd, n.* a wood nymph: a forest-tree: — *pl.* **dry'ads, -adēs.** [Gr. *dryas, -ados,* — *drȳs,* oak tree.]

dso, dsobo, dsomo. See under **zho**.

'dst *dst,* a shortened form of **hadst, wouldst,** etc.

duad. See **dual**.

dual *dū'əl, adj.* two-fold: consisting of two: expressing or representing two things (*gram.*). — *n.* a grammatical form indicating duality: a word in the dual number. — *ns.* **dū'ad** a dyad: a pair (*rare*) **dū'alin** an explosive mixture of sawdust, saltpetre, and nitroglycerine; **dū'alism** (*philos.*) that view which seeks to explain the world by the assumption of two radically independent and absolute elements — e.g. (1) the doctrine of the entire separation of spirit and matter, thus being opposed both to *idealism* and to *materialism;* (2) the doctrine of two distinct principles of good and evil, or of two divine beings of these characters; **dū′alist** a believer in dualism. — *adj.* **dūalis′tic** consisting of two: relating to dualism. — *adv.* **dūalis′tically.** — *n.* **duality** (*dū-al′i-ti*) doubleness: state of being double. — *adv.* **dū′ally.** — *n.* **dū′archy** a faulty form of **diarchy.** — **dual carriageway** a road consisting of two separated parts, each for use of traffic in one direction only; **dual control** joint control or jurisdiction. — *adj.* **du′al-control′** able to be operated by either or both of two persons. — **dual monarchy** two (more or less) independent states with one and the same monarch: *specif.*, Austria-Hungary (before 1918); **dual personality** a condition in which the same individual shows at different times two very different characters. — *adj.* **du′al-pur′pose** serving or intended to serve two purposes: (of cattle) bred to produce meat and milk. — **dual school** on for both boys and and girls. [L. *duālis* — *duo*, two.]

duan *dōō′än, -an, n.* a division of a poem, canto. [Gael.]

duar *dōō′är, n.* a circular Arab encampment or tent village. — Also **douar, dowar.** [Ar. *dūār*.]

duarchy. See **dual.**

dub¹ *dub, v.t.* to confer knighthood upon, from the ceremony of striking the shoulders with the flat of a sword: to confer any name or dignity upon: to smooth with an adze: to trim: to cut the comb and wattles from: to rub a softening and waterproof mixture into (leather): to dress (a fly) for fishing: — *pr.p.* **dubb′ing;** *pa.p.* **dubbed.** — *n.* **dubb′ing** the accolade: (also **dubb′in**) a preparation of grease for softening leather. [O.E. *dubbian*, to dub knight.]

dub² *dub,* (*Scot.*) *n.* a pool of foul water: a puddle: (in *pl.*) mud. [Cf. L.G. *dobbe*.]

dub³ *dub, v.t.* to give (a film) a new sound-track, e.g. one in a different language: to add sound effects or music: to transfer (recorded music, etc.) to a new disc or tape: to combine so as to make one record (music, etc., from more than one source, e.g. a live performance and a recording). [Abbrev. of **double.**]

dubbin. See **dub¹.**

dubious *dū′bi-əs, adj.* doubtful, causing doubt: uncertain: of uncertain event or issue: arousing suspicion or disapproval: hesitating (about). — *n.* **dūblety** (*-bī′i-ti*) doubt. — *adv.* **dū′biously.** — *ns.* **dūbios′ity, dū′biousness.** [L. *dubius*.]

dubitate *dū′bi-tāt, v.i.* to doubt, hesitate. — *adj.* **dū′bitable.** — *adv.* **dūbitably.** — *ns.* **dū′bitancy, dūbitā′tion.** — *adj.* **dū′bitative.** — *adv.* **dū′bitatively.** [L. *dubitāre, -ātum*.]

ducal *dū′kəl, adj.* pertaining to a duke. — *adv.* **dū′cally.** [Fr., — L.L. *ducālis* — L. *dux*, leader.]

ducat *duk′ət, n.* a gold or silver coin of varying values, formerly much used on the Continent. — *n.* **ducatoon′** an old silver coin in Venice and elsewhere. [O.Fr. *ducat* — It. *ducato* — L.L. *ducātus*, a duchy.]

ducdame *dōōk′də-mi, dōōk-dä′mi,* (Shak. *As You Like It*), *interj.* perh. a meaningless refrain: explained as L. *duc ad mē,* bring to me, as Welsh *dewch 'da mi,* come with me, as Romany *dukrā′mē,* I tell fortunes, etc.

duce *dōō′chä, n.* the title assumed by the Italian dictator Mussolini. [It., leader — L. *dux*.]

duchess, duchesse. See **duchy.**

duchy *duch′i, n.* the territory of a duke, a dukedom. — *ns.* **duch′ess** the consort or widow of a duke: a woman of the same rank as a duke in her own right: a size of roofing slate, 24 × 12 inches (610 × 305 mm.); **duchesse** (*duch′es, dü-shes′;* Fr., duchess) a table-cover or centre-piece. — Also **duchesse cover.** — **duchesse lace** Flemish pillow lace with designs in cord outline; **duchesse potatoes** piped shapes of mashed potato, butter, milk and egg-yolk baked until light brown; **duchesse set** a set of covers for a dressing-table; **duchy court** the court of a duchy. [O.Fr. *duché* — L.L. *ducātus*; Fr. *duchesse* — L.L. *ducissa*.]

duck¹ *duk, n.* a kind of coarse cotton, linen, etc. cloth for small sails, sacking, etc.: (in *pl.*) garments made of duck. [Du. *doek*, linen cloth; Ger. *Tuch*.]

duck² *duk, v.t.* to dip for a moment in water: to avoid (*coll.*). — *v.i.* to dip or dive: to lower the head suddenly: to cringe, yield. — *n.* a quick plunge, dip: a quick lowering of the head or body, a jerky bow. — *ns.* **duck′er** one who ducks: a diving-bird; **duck′ing.** — **duck′ing-pond; duck′ing-stool** a stool or chair in which offenders were formerly tied and ducked in the water. — **duck out of** to shirk, avoid (responsibilities, etc.). [M.E. *douken* from an assumed O.E. *dūcan*, to duck, dive; Ger. *tauchen*, Du. *duiken*.]

duck³ *duk, n.* any bird of the family Anatidae, the prominent marks of which are short webbed feet, with a small hind-toe not reaching the ground, the netted scales in front of the lower leg, and the long bill: the female duck as distinguished from the male *drake*: in cricket (originally *duck's egg*), the zero (O), which records in a scoring-sheet that a player made no runs: a darling, sweetheart (*coll.*): a defaulter, bankrupt: an oscillating shape used in wave-power technology (also **nodding duck**). — *ns.* **duck′ing** duck-hunting; **duck′ling** young duck; **ducks, duck′y** (*coll.*) a term of endearment. — *adj.* **duck′y.** — **duck′-ant** a Jamaican termite nesting in trees; **duck′bill** a platypus. — *adj.* **duck′-billed** having a bill like a duck. — **duck′-board** planking for swampy ground, trenches, etc.; **duck′-hawk** moor-buzzard or marsh-harrier: (*U.S.*) peregrine falcon. — *adj.* **duck′-legged** short-legged. — **duck′mole** the duck-bill; **duck′-pond; duck′s arse** (*slang: abbrev.* **DA**) a man's hairstyle in which the hair is swept back to a point on the neck resembling a duck's tail — worn esp. by Teddy boys; **duck′s′-foot** lady's-mantle; **duck′=shot** shot for shooting wild-duck. — *v.i.* **duck′shove** (*Austr.* and *N.Z., coll.*) to jump a queue (orig. of taxi-drivers): to cheat: to steal: to avoid responsibilities. — **duck′shover** (*Austr.* and *N. Z., coll.*); **duck′s′=meat** duckweed; **duck soup** (*U. S. slang*) something very easy, a cinch: someone easy to handle, a pushover; **duck′-tail** white Teddy boy of S. Africa; **duck′weed** any plant of the family Lemnaceae, monocotyledons most of which consist of a small flat green floating plate, from which one or more roots dangle. — **Bombay duck** bummalo; **break one's duck** (*cricket*) to make one's first run (see above); **lame duck** a defaulter: a bankrupt: anything disabled: an inefficient or helpless person or organisation; **like a dying duck** languishing; **make, play, ducks and drakes** to make flat stones skip on the surface of water: to use recklessly: to squander, waste (with *of, with*); **sitting duck** an easy target, helpless victim; **wild′-duck** the mallard, esp. the hen-bird. [O.E. *dūce* (or *duce*?), a duck; cf. **duck².**]

duck⁴ *duk, n.* a kind of amphibious military transport vehicle or landing craft. [From manufacturers' code initials, DUKW.]

duct *dukt, n.* a tube conveying fluids in animal bodies or plants: a pipe for an electric cable: a hole, pipe, or channel for carrying a fluid: an air-passage. — *v.t.* to carry along, or as if along, a duct. — *adj.* **duct′less.** — **ductless glands** masses of glandular tissue that lack ducts and discharge their products directly into the blood. [L. *ductus* — *dūcĕre*, to lead.]

ductile *duk′tīl, -til, adj.* easily led: yielding: capable of being drawn out into threads. — *ns.* **ductility** (*-til′*), **duc′tileness** capacity of being drawn out without breaking. [Fr., — L. *ductilis* — *dūcere*, to lead.]

dud¹ *dud,* (*coll.*) *n.* (in *pl.*) poor or ragged clothes, tatters: (in *pl.*) clothes. — *n.* **dudd′ery** a shop where old clothes are sold: rags collectively. — *adj.* **dudd′ie** ragged. — **duddie weans** (*wānz; Burns*) ragged children: (with *cap.*) a Scottish literary society. [There is a M.E. *dudde, birrus,* a cloak; cf. O.N. *duthi,* swaddling-clothes.]

dud² *dud,* (*coll.*) *n.* a bomb or projectile that fails to go off: a dishonoured cheque: a counterfeit: any person or thing useless or ineffective: a failure. — Also *adj.* [Origin unknown.]

dudder *dud′ər,* (*dial.*) *n.* confusion. [Cf. **dither.**]

dude *dūd, dōōd,* (orig. *U.S. slang*) *n.* a fop or dandy: a townsman: a fellow. — *adj.* **du'dish.** — *n.* **du'dism.** — **dude ranch** ranch run as a holiday resort or for training in ranching. [Origin unknown.]

dudeen *dōō-dēn', -dhēn', n.* a short clay tobacco-pipe. — Also **dudheen'.** [Ir. *dúidín,* dim. of *dúd,* pipe.]

dudgeon¹ *duj'ən, n.* resentment: offended indignation, as in *in high dudgeon.* [Origin unknown.]

dudgeon² *duj'ən, n.* the haft of a dagger: a small dagger (*arch.*). [Anglo-Fr. *digeon,* knife-handle.]

due¹ *dū, adj.* owed: that ought to be paid or done to another: proper: appointed, under engagement, to be ready, arrive, etc. — *adv.* exactly, directly. — *n.* that which is owed: what one has a right to, has earned: fee, toll, charge, or tribute: (in *pl.*) subscription to a club or society. — *adj.* **due'ful, dewfull** (*Spens.*) proper, fit. — **due date** the date on which a bill of exchange, etc. must be paid. — **due to** caused by: (*wrongly*) owing to, because of; **give someone his/her due** to be fair to someone; **give the devil his due** to give a fair hearing or fair-play to one of notorious character; **in due course** in the ordinary way when the time comes. [O.Fr. *deü,* pa.p. of *devoir* — L. *debēre,* to owe.]

due² *dū,* (*Shak.*) *v.t.* to endue.

duel *dū'əl, n.* a combat between two persons, prearranged and fought under fixed conditions, generally on an affair of honour: single combat to decide a quarrel: any fight or struggle between two parties. — *v.i.* to fight in a duel: — *pr.p.* **dū'elling;** *pa.t.* and *pa.p.* **dū'elled.** — *ns.* **dū'eller; dū'elling; dū'ellist; duello** (*dōō-el'ō*) a duel: duelling: the laws which regulate duelling: — *pl.* **duell'os.** — *adj.* **dū'elsome** given to duelling. [It. *duello* — L. *duellum,* the original form of *bellum* — *duo,* two.]

duenna *dū-en'ə, n.* a lady who acts the part of governess in Spain: a lady who watches over or chaperons a younger. [Sp. *dueña,* a form of *doña,* mistress — L. *domina,* fem. of *dominus,* lord.]

duet, duett *dū-et', duetto dōō-et'ō, ns.* a composition in music for two performers: the performance of such: the performers of such: any action involving two parties: — *pls.* **duet(t)s', duett'os, duett'i** (*-ē*). — *v.i.* to perform a duet: — *pr.p.* **duett'ing;** *pa.t.* and *pa.p.* **duett'ed.** — *ns.* **duettino** (*-tē'nō*) a simple duet: — *pl.* **duettin'os; duett'ist** (*dū-*). [It. *duetto,* dim. of *duo — due,* two — L. *duo.*]

duff¹ *duf, n.* dough: a stiff flour pudding boiled in a bag: decaying vegetable matter, fallen leaves: coal-dust. [A form of **dough.**]

duff² *duf, v.t.* to make to look new: to alter brands on (stolen cattle): to steal cattle. — *ns.* (*slang*) **duff'ing, duff'ing-up, duff'ing-over.** — **duff up, over** (*slang*) to beat up. [Perh. a back-formation from **duffer²**.]

duff³ *duf, v.t.* to play amiss by hitting the ground behind the ball (*golf*): to bungle. [Back-formation from **duffer¹**.]

duff⁴ *duf,* (*coll.*) *adj.* no good: broken, not working. [Prob. **duff³**.]

duffel *duf'l, n.* a thick, coarse woollen cloth, with a thick nap — also **duff'le:** sporting or camping kit (*U.S.*). — **duffel bag** a canvas bag, cylindrical in shape, orig. used for a sailor's kit; **duffel coat** a jacket or coat, usu. hooded, made of duffel. [Du., from *Duffel,* a town near Antwerp.]

duffer¹ *duf'ər, n.* an unskilful person: a fogy, a useless old fellow: a counterfeit coin: an unproductive mine. — *ns.* **duff'erdom, duff'erism.** [Origin unknown.]

duffer² *duf'ər, n.* a peddler of sham jewellery, etc.: one who fakes up sham articles or duffs cattle. [Origin unknown: thieves' slang.]

duffle. See **duffel.**

dug¹ *dug, n.* a nipple or udder of a cow or other beast. [Cf. Sw. *dægga,* Dan. *dægge,* to suckle.]

dug² *dug, pa.t.* and *pa.p.* of **dig.** — **dug'out** a boat made by hollowing out the trunk of a tree: a rough dwelling or shelter dug out of a slope or bank or in a trench: a

superannuated person brought back to employment (*slang*).

dugong *dōō'gong, n.* a herbivorous marine mammal of the order Sirenia — the supposed original of the mermaid. [Malayan *dūyong.*]

duiker, duyker *dī'kər, dä'kər, n.* a small S. African antelope: (*dī'kər*) a cormorant (*S. Afr.*). [Du., diver, from plunging into the bush, or into the sea.]

duke *dūk, n.* a sovereign prince of a small state: a nobleman of the highest order: a chief (*B.*): (*dōōk; slang*) the fist (also **dook**). — *v.t.* (with *it*) to play the duke. — *ns.* **duke'dom** the title, rank, or lands of a duke; **duke'ling** a petty duke; **dūk'ery** a duke's territory or seat; **duke'ship.** — **the Dukeries** a group of ducal seats in Notts. [O.Fr. *duc* — L. *dux, ducis,* a leader — *dūcĕre,* to lead.]

Dukhobor, Doukhobor *dōō'hhō-bör, dōō'kō-bör, n.* a member of a Russian sect who trust to an inner light, reject the doctrine of the Trinity, and refuse military service, many of them settled in Canada since 1899: — *pl.* **D(o)ukhobors, Dukhobort'sy.** [Russ. *Dukhoborets* — *dukh,* spirit, *borets,* fighter — *boroty',* to fight.]

dukkeripen *dook-ə-rip'ən, n.* fortune-telling. [Romany *drukeriben.*]

DUKW. See **duck⁴**.

dulcamara *dul-kə-mä'rə, -mä'rə, n.* the bittersweet. [L. *dulcis,* sweet, *amāra* (fem.) bitter.]

dulcet *duls'it, adj.* sweet: melodious, harmonious. — *ns.* **dul'cian** (*dul'si-ən; obs.* or *hist.*) a small bassoon; **dulciana** (*dul-si-ä'nə*) an open diapason organ stop of pleasing tone and small scale; **dulcifica'tion.** — *adj.* **dulcif'luous** flowing sweetly. — *v.t.* **dul'cify** (*rare*) to make sweet. — *ns.* **dulcil'oquy** a soft manner of speaking; **dul'cite, dul'citol, dul'cose** (*-kōs*) a saccharine substance derived from various plants — in its crude form, *Madagascar manna;* **Dul'citone®** a keyboard instrument in which graduated tuning-forks are struck by hammers; **dul'citude** sweetness. — **dulcified spirit** a compound of alcohol with mineral acid. [L. *dulcis,* sweet.]

dulcimer *dul'si-mər, n.* a musical instrument like a flat box, with sounding-board and wires stretched across bridges: a Jewish musical instrument, probably a bagpipe. [Sp. *dulcemele* — L. *dulce melos,* a sweet song — *dulcis,* sweet, Gr. *melos,* a song.]

Dulcinea *dul-sin-ē'ə, dul-sin'i-ə, n.* a sweetheart. [From *Dulcinea* del Toboso, the name given by Don Quixote to the mistress of his imagination.]

dulcify, dulcite, dulcose, etc. See **dulcet.**

dule¹ *dül,* (*Scot.*) *n.* woe. — Also **dool,** (*obs.*) **doole.** — **dule'-tree** the gallows. [See **dole²**.]

dule². See **dool²**.

dulia, douleia *dū-, dōō-li'ə,* (*R.C. Church*) *n.* the inferior veneration accorded to saints and angels, as opposed to **hyperdulia,** that accorded to the Virgin Mary, and **latria,** that accorded to God alone. — *ns.* **d(o)uloc'racy** government by slaves; **dulō'sis** enslavement, practised by certain ants upon other kinds. — *adj.* **dulŏt'ic.** [Gr. *douleiā,* servitude, *doulōsis,* enslavement — *doulos,* a slave.]

dull *dul, adj.* slow of learning, or of understanding: wanting in keenness of hearing or other sense: insensible: without life or spirit: uninteresting: slow of motion: drowsy: sleepy: sad: downcast: cheerless: lacking brightness or clearness: cloudy: dim: muffled: obtuse: blunt. — *v.t.* to make dull or stupid: to blunt: to damp: to cloud. — *v.i.* to become dull. — *n.* **dull'ard** a dull and stupid person: a dunce. — *adj.* **dull'ish.** — *ns.* **dull'ness, dul'ness** the state or quality of being dull. — *adj.* **dull'y** somewhat dull. — *adv.* **dully** (*dul'li*). — *adjs.* **dull'-brained** (*Shak.*); **dull'-browed; dull'-eyed** (*Shak.*); **dull'-sighted; dull'-witted.** [Related to O.E. *dol,* foolish, and *dwellan,* to err; Du. *dol,* Ger. *toll,* mad.]

dulocracy, etc. See **dulia.**

dulse *duls, n.* an edible red seaweed, esp. *Rhodymenia* *palmata.* [Gael. *duileasg*, poss. — *duille*, a leaf, *uisge*, water.]

duly *dū'li, adv.* properly: fitly: at the proper time. [See **due¹**.]

duma, douma *dōō'mə, n.* an elected council, esp. the Russian parliament of 1906–17. — *n.* **dum'aist** a duma member. [Russ. *duma*, of Gmc. origin; cf. **doom**.]

dumb *dum, adj.* without the power of speech: silent: soundless: stupid (*U.S.* after Ger. or Du.). — *v.t.* (*Shak.*), to render dumb. — *adv.* **dumb'ly** in silence: mutely. — *ns.* **dumb'ness; dumm'erer** (*old slang*) a dumb person, esp. a rogue who feigns dumbness; **dumm'iness; dumm'y** one who is dumb: a mere tool, man of straw: a block or lay-figure: a sham or counterfeit article taking the place of a real one: an unprinted model of a book: a rubber teat: an exposed hand of cards: a game in which a hand is exposed: the imaginary player of such a game or hand: a feint of passing or playing the ball (*Rugby football,* etc.). — *v.t.* and *v.i.* to sell the dummy (to; see below). — *adj.* silent: sham. — **dumb'-bell** a double-headed weight swung in the hands to develop the muscles: any object or figure of the same shape: a stupid person (*U.S.*); **dumb blonde** in films, etc., the stock character of the blonde-haired beauty of limited intelligence; **dumb'-cane** a tropical American araceous plant (*Dieffenbachia seguine*) whose acrid juice swells the tongue; **dumb'-cluck** a fool (orig. *U.S.*: same as **cluck**). — *vs.t.* **dum(b)found', -er** to strike dumb: to confuse greatly: to astonish. — **dumb'-pia'no** a soundless keyboard for piano practice; **dumb'-show'** gesture without words: pantomine. — *adj.* **dumb'struck** silent with astonishment. — **dumb'= wait'er** a movable platform used for conveying food, dishes, etc., at meals: a stand with revolving top for holding dessert, etc.: a small lift for food and dishes; **dummy run** an experimental run: a try-out or testing. — **sell the dummy** (*Rugby football,* etc.) to deceive an opponent by a feint of passing or playing the ball (also *fig.*); **strike dumb** to silence with astonishment. [O.E. *dumb*; Ger. *dumm*, stupid, Du. *dom*.]

dumbledore *dum'bl-dōr, -dör, (dial.) n.* the bumble-bee: the brown cockchafer.

dumdum *dum'dum, n.* a soft-nosed expanding bullet, first made at *Dum Dum* near Calcutta. — **dumdum fever** kala-azar.

dumka *dōōm'kə, (mus.) n.* a lament: a slow movement or piece: — *pl.* **-ky** (*-kē*). [Czech.]

dummerer, dummy, etc. See **dumb.**

dumortierite *dū-mör'ti-ə-rīt, n.* a blue, greenish-blue, pink or violet semi-precious gemstone, aluminium borosilicate. [From the 19th-cent. French palaeontologist Eugène *Dumortier*, who discovered it.]

dumose *dū'mōs, adj.* bushy (also **dū'mous**). — *n.* **dumōs'-ity.** [L. *dūmus*, a thorn-bush.]

dump¹ *dump, v.t.* to set down heavily or with a thump: to unload: to land and sell at prices below cost of production in the exporting country — or (according to some) in the importing country (*econ.*): to tip (esp. rubbish): to get rid of. — *n.* a thud: a place for the discharge of loads, or for rubbish: a deposit: store (*mil.*): a dirty, dilapidated place. — *n.* **dump'er** one who, or that which dumps: a dumper truck: in surfing, a wave that crashes suddenly downwards with great force, causing surfers to fall. — **dump'bin** in a shop, a display stand or a container for usu. random display of e.g. bargain items; **dump(er) truck** a lorry which can be emptied by raising the front of the carrier to allow the contents to slide out the back (also **dump'er**); **dump on** (*U.S. slang*) to do down, belittle: to take advantage of. [Cf. Dan. *dumpe*, Norw. *dumpa*, to fall plump.]

dump² *dump, n.* dullness or gloominess of mind, ill-humour, low spirits — now only used in the pl.: an obsolete slow dance or dance-tune in 4-4 time: a melancholy strain (*Shak.*): any tune (*obs.*). — *adj.* **dump'ish** depressed in spirits. — *adv.* **dump'ishly.** — **dump'ishness.** — **(down) in the dumps** (*coll.*) in bad spirits: depressed. [Prob. related to O.Du. *domp,*

mist; or Ger. *dumpf*, gloomy.]

dump³ *dump, n.* a deep hole in a river-bed, a pool. [Prob. Norw. *dump*, pit.]

dump⁴ *dump, n.* a short thick person or thing: a marble: a counter: small coin: (in *pl.*) money (*slang*). [Perh. a back-formation from **dumpy.**]

dum-palm. Same as **doum-palm.**

dumper. See **dump¹.**

dumple. See **dumpy.**

dumpling *dump'ling, n.* a kind of thick pudding or mass of paste: a dumpling-shaped person or animal: a silly person. [Origin obscure.]

dumpy *dump'i, adj.* short and thick. — *n.* a dumpy person or animal, esp. one of a breed of very short-legged fowls: a short umbrella. — *n.* **dump'iness.** — *v.t.* **dump'le** to make or cook, as a dumpling: to round into a dumpy shape. — **dump'y-lev'el** a surveyor's level with rigid connection of the telescope to the vertical spindle. [18th cent.; perh. from **dumpling.**]

dun¹ *dun, adj.* greyish brown: mouse-coloured: dingy: dusky. — *n.* a dun colour: a horse of dun colour. — *v.t.* (*New England*) to cure and brown, as cod. — *v.i.* to become dun-coloured. — *n.* **dunn'ing.** — *adj.* **dunn'-ish** somewhat dun. — **dun'-bird** the pochard, esp. the hen-bird; **dun'-cow** a ray with a skin of shagreen; **dun'-div'er** the merganser; **dun'-fish** codfish cured by dunning. [O.E. *dun*, prob. not Celt.]

dun² *dun, v.t.* to importune for payment: to plague, pester: — *pr.p.* **dunn'ing;** *pa.t.* and *pa.p.* **dunned.** — *n.* one who duns: a demand for payment. [Perh. allied to **din.**]

dun³ *dun, n.* a hill: a fortified mound. [Celt.; in many place names; adopted in O.E. as *dūn*; see **down².**]

dunce *duns, n.* one slow at learning: a stupid person. — *ns.* **dunce'dom** the class of dunces; **dun'cery** stupidity; **Dun'ciad** Pope's epic of dunces. — **dunce's cap** a tall conical hat, formerly worn at school to indicate stupidity. [*Duns* Scotus (died 1308), the Subtle Doctor, leader of the schoolmen, from him called *Dunses*, who opposed classical studies on the revival of learning — hence any opposer of learning, a blockhead.]

dunch, dunsh, *dunsh, (Scot.) v.t.* to jog, nudge, bump: to butt. — Also *n.* [Ety. doubtful.]

dunder *dun'dər, n.* lees, dregs of sugar-cane juice. [Sp. *redundar*, to overflow.]

dunderfunk *dun'dər-fungk, n.* ship-biscuit, soaked in water, mixed with fat and molasses, and baked in a pan. — Also **dan'dyfunk.**

dunderhead *dun'dər-hed, n.* a stupid person — also **dun'-derpate.** — *adj.* **dun'derheaded.** — *ns.* **dun'derheadism; dun'derheadedness.** [Origin uncertain.]

Dundonian *dun-dō'ni-ən, n.* and *adj.* (a person) belonging to, coming from, born in, Dundee, Scotland.

Dundreary *dun-drēr'i, adj.* like Lord *Dundreary*, in Tom Taylor's *Our American Cousin* — in Sothern's creation of the part, a lisping and brainless dandy, wearing long side-whiskers.

dune *dūn, n.* a low hill of sand, esp. on the seashore. — **dune'-bugg'y** (orig. *U.S.*) a usu. small car with large tyres, used for driving on beaches. [Fr., — O.Du. *duna*: cf. **down².**]

dung¹ *dung, n.* excrement: manure: a tailor or other worker submitting to low rates of pay (opp. to *flint*; *obs. slang*). — *v.t.* to manure with dung. — *v.i.* to void excrement. — *adj.* **dung'y.** — **dung'-bee'tle** the dor-beetle: a scarabaeid beetle generally; **dung'-cart; dung'= fly** any of a number of small dipterous flies (*Scatophagidae*) that breed on dung or decaying vegetable matter; **dung'-fork** a fork used for moving stable manure; **dung'-heap, dung'-hill** a heap of dung: any mean situation; **dung'-hunt'er** a skua; **dung'mere** a manure-pit. [O.E. *dung*; cf. Dan. *dynge*, a heap; Ger. *Dung*.]

dung². See **ding¹.**

dungaree *dung-gə-rē', or dung', n.* a coarse Indian calico: (in *pl.*) overalls, esp. ones including trousers, made of it: (in *pl.*) a similar garment for casual wear. [Hindi *dūgrī*.]

dungeon *dun'jən, n.* orig. the principal tower of a castle: a close, dark prison: a cell under ground. — *v.t.* to confine in a dungeon. — *n.* **dun'geoner** a gaoler. [O.Fr. *donjon* — L.L. *domniō, -ōnis* — L. *dominus*, a lord.]

duniewassal, dunniewassal, duniwassal *dōōn-i-wos'l, n.* a Highland gentleman of inferior rank. [Gael. *duine*, man, *uasal*, of gentle birth.]

dunite *dun'īt, n.* crystalline rock composed almost entirely of olivine. [*Dun* Mountain, near Nelson, in New Zealand.]

duniwassal. See **duniewassal.**

dunk *dungk, v.t.* and *v.i.* to dip cake, etc., that one is eating in one's coffee or other beverage. [Ger. *tunken*, to dip; cf. **Dunker.**]

Dunker *dungk'ər, n.* a member of a sect of German-American Baptists who practise triple immersion. — Also **Tunk'er.** [Ger., dipper.]

Dunkirk *dun-kûrk',* or *dun', n.* a successful military evacuation by sea against odds, as by the British in 1940 at *Dunkirk*: a complete abandonment of one's position: a rapid or desperate withdrawal.

dunlin *dun'lin, n.* the red-backed sandpiper, *Calidris alpina*, a gregarious shore-bird, also known as the **ox-bird.** [Dim. of **dun**[1].]

Dunlop *dun-lop', n.* a cheese made of unskimmed milk — from *Dunlop* in Ayrshire.

dunnage *dun'ij, n.* loose wood of any kind laid in the bottom of the hold to keep the cargo out of the bilge-water, or wedged between parts of the cargo to keep them steady: sailor's baggage. [Ety. unknown.]

dunnakin *dun'ə-kin,* (*Brit.*) *n.* same as **dunny**[2].

dunniewassal. See **duniewassal.**

dunnite *dun'īt, n.* a kind of explosive based on ammonium picrate. [From its inventor, the U.S. army officer, Col. B. W. *Dunn* (1860–1936).]

dunno *də-nō'.* Coll. contr. of (I) don't know.

dunnock *dun'ək, n.* the hedge-sparrow. [Dim. of **dun**[1].]

dunny[1] *dun'i,* (*dial.*) *adj.* deaf: stupid. [Origin obscure.]

dunny[2] *dun'i,* (*coll.* or *dial.*) *n.* a lavatory (esp. *Austr.* and *N. Z.*): an outside lavatory (esp. *Scot.*).

dunsh. See **dunch.**

Dunstable *dun'stə-bl, n.* a kind of straw-plait, first made at *Dunstable* in Bedfordshire: a straw hat, etc. — **Dunstable road, highway** anything plain and direct.

dunt[1] *dunt,* (*Scot.*) *n.* a thump: the wound or mark made thereby. — *v.t.* to thump, beat. [See **dint.**]

dunt[2] *dunt,* (*dial.*) *n.* gid or sturdy in sheep, etc. [Origin obscure.]

dunt[3] *dunt, v.t.* (of ceramics) to crack in the oven because of too rapid cooling. [Origin obscure.]

duo *dōō'ō, dū'ō, n.* a duet: two persons, etc., associated in some way, e.g. a pair of musicians or variety artists: — *pl.* **dū'os.** [It. — L. *duo*, two.]

duodecennial *dū-ō-di-sen'yəl, adj.* occurring every twelve years. [L. *duodecim*, twelve, *annus*, year.]

duodecimal *dū-ō-des'i-ml, adj.* computed by twelves: twelfth: (in *pl.*) a method of calculating the area of a rectangle when the length and breadth are stated in feet and inches. — **duodecimal system** a system of numbers in which each denomination is twelve times the next, instead of ten times, as in ordinary (decimal) arithmetic: the name given to the division of unity into twelve equal parts. [L. *duodecim*, twelve — *duo*, two, and *decem*, ten.]

duodecimo *dū-ō-des'i-mō, adj.* formed of sheets folded so as to make twelve leaves. — *n.* a book of such sheets — usually written 12mo: an interval of a twelfth (*mus.*): — *pl.* **-s.** [L. *in duodecimō*, in twelfth (abl. of *duodecimus*, twelfth) — *duo*, two, *decem*, ten.]

duodenary *dū-ō-dē'nə-ri, adj.* relating to twelve, twelvefold. [L. *duodēnārius*.]

duodenum *dū-ō-dē'nəm, n.* the first portion of the small intestine, so called because about twelve fingers'-breadth in length: — *pl.* **duodē'na.** — *adj.* **duodē'nal.** — *ns.* **duodenec'tomy** excision of the duodenum; **duo-dēnī'tis** inflammation of the duodenum. [Formed

from L. *duodēnī*, twelve each.]

duologue *dū'ō-log, n.* a piece spoken between two. [Irregularly formed from L. *duo* (or Gr. *dyo*), two, Gr. *logos*, discourse.]

duomo *dwō'mō, n.* a cathedral: — *pl.* **duō'mos, duō'mi** (*-ē*). [It. See **dome**[1].]

duopoly *dū-op'ə-li, n.* a situation in which two companies, etc., monopolise trading in a commodity. [L. *duo* (or Gr. *dyo*), two, and mono*poly.*]

duotone *dū'ō-tōn, n.* and *adj.* (a drawing, print, etc.) done in two tones or colours. [L. *duo*, two, and **tone.**]

dup *dup,* (*Shak.*) *v.t.* to undo, open. [**do up;** cf. **don** and **doff.**]

dupe *dūp, n.* one who is cheated. — *v.t.* to deceive: to trick. — *n.* **dūpabil'ity.** — *adj.* **dū'pable.** — *ns.* **dū'per; dū'pery** the art of deceiving others. [Fr. *dupe;* of uncertain origin.]

dupion *dū'pi-ən, -on, n.* a double cocoon, made by two silk-worms spinning together: a kind of coarse silk made from these cocoons. [Fr. *doupion*, from It. *doppione*, double.]

duple *dū'pl, adj.* double, twofold: having two beats in the bar (*mus.*). — *n.* **dū'plet** a like throw of two dice: a pair of electrons forming a single bond between two atoms: a group of two notes occupying the time of three. [L. *duplus;* cf. **double.**]

duplex *dū'pleks, adj.* twofold, double: having some part doubled: allowing communication, transmission, in both directions simultaneously (*comput., teleg.*, etc.). — *adj.* **duplic'itous.** — *n.* **duplicity** (*dū-plis'i-ti*) doubleness, esp. in conduct and intention: insincerity: double-dealing. — **duplex (apartment)** a flat on two floors; **duplex (house)** (*U.S.*) a house, divided either horizontally or vertically, providing accommodation for two families. [L. *duplex, -icis.*]

duplicate *dū'pli-kit, adj.* double: twofold: like, equivalent or alternative. — *n.* another (esp. subsidiary or spare) thing of the same kind: a copy or transcript: condition of being in two copies. — *v.t.* (*-kāt*) to double: to copy: repeat: to fold. — *ns.* **dūplicand'** (*Scots law*) double feu-duty, due on certain occasions; **dūplica'tion.** — *adj.* **dū'plicative.** — *ns.* **dū'plicātor** a copying apparatus; **dū'plicāture** a doubling: anything doubled: the fold of a membrane; **dūply'** a second reply in Scots law. — *v.t.* to say in duply. — **duplicate bridge** a form of competition bridge in which each pair or four plays the same set of hands as all other pairs or fours; **duplicate ratio** ratio of the squares of the quantities. — **in duplicate** in two copies, or original accompanied by a copy; **duplication of the cube** the problem eagerly discussed by the early Greek geometers, of constructing a cube equal to twice a given cube, impossible by use of straight line and circle only, but soluble by means of other curves. [L. *duplicāre, -ātum*, duo, two, *plicāre*, to fold.]

duplicitous, duplicity. See **duplex.**

duply. See **duplicate.**

dupondius *dū-pon'di-əs,* (*hist.*) *n.* an ancient Roman coin: — *pl.* **dupon'diī.** [L.]

duppy *dup'i, n.* a ghost. [West Indian Negro word.]

Dupuytren's contracture *dū-pwē'trenz kən-trak'chər,* a condition in which one or more fingers (or, more rarely, toes) are caused to be bent towards the palm of the hand (or sole of the foot) by the contraction of a fibrous chord in the palmar or plantar) tissue. — Also **Dupuytren's contraction.** [Baron Guillaume *Dupuytren* (1777–1835), French surgeon.]

dura. Same as **durra.**

durable *dūr'ə-bl, adj.* able to last or endure: hardy: permanent. — *n.* something that will endure, esp. (*pl.*) goods that do not need replacing frequently. — *ns.* **durabil'ity, dur'ableness.** — *adv.* **dur'ably.** — *ns.* **dur'-ance** continuance (*obs.*): durability (*obs.*): a durable cloth (*obs.*): imprisonment (*arch.*): **dur'ant** a strong cloth in imitation of buff-leather; **durā'tion** continuance in time: time indefinitely: power of continuance: length of time. — *adj.* **durā'tional.** — **for the duration**

(*coll.*) as long as the war (or the situation under discussion) continues. [L. *dūrāre*, to harden, endure, last.]

Duralumin® *dūr-al'ū-min, n.* (also without *cap.*; also **dūr'al, dūralumin'ium**) a strong, light, aluminium alloy containing copper. [L. *dūrus*, hard, and *alumin*ium.]

dura mater *dū'rə mā'tər*, L. *dōō'ra mä'ter*, the exterior membrane of the brain and spinal column distinguished from the other two, the arachnoid and the pia mater. [L. *dūra māter*, hard mother, a translation of the Ar. name.]

duramen *dū-rā'mən, n.* heartwood. [L. *dūrāmen*, hardness — *dūrus*, hard.]

durance, duration, etc. See **durable.**

durante bene placito *dū-ran'tē ben'ē plas'i-tō, dōō-ran'te ben'e plak'i-tō*, (L.L.) during good pleasure; **durante vita** (*vī'tə, vē', wē'tä*) during life.

durbar *dûr'bär, n.* an audience-chamber: a reception or levee: a court: the body of officials at an Indian court. [Pers. *darbār*, a prince's court, lit. a door of admittance.]

durchkomponi(e)rt *dōōrhh-kom-pon-ērt', (Ger.; now **-komponiert**) adj.* having the music specially adapted to each stanza.

Durchlaucht *dōōrhh'lowhht*, (Ger.) *n.* Serene Highness.

Durchmusterung *dōōrhh-mōōs'tər-ōong*, (Ger., examination, scrutiny) *n.* a star-catalogue.

durdum. Same as **dirdum.**

dure *dūr, (obs.) v.i.* to endure, last or continue. — *adj.* **dure'ful** (*Spens.*) enduring, lasting. [Fr. *durer* — L. *dūrāre* — *dūrus*, hard.]

duress, duresse *dūr-es', dūr'es, n.* constraint: imprisonment: constraint illegally exercised to force a person to perform some act. [O.Fr. *duresse* — L. *dūritia* — *dūrus*, hard.]

durgan *dûr'gən, n.* a dwarf, any undersized creature. — *adj.* **dur'gy.** (*-gi, -ji*). [Related to **dwarf.**]

Durham *dur'əm, n.* one of a particular breed of short-horned cattle — from the English county. — Also *adj.*

durian *dōō'ri-ən,* or *dū', n.* a lofty Indian and Malayan bombacaceous fruit-tree (*Durio zibethinus*), with leaves like a cherry's: its large fruit, with hard rind and pulp of foul smell but fine flavour. — Also **du'rion.** [Malay *dūrī*, thorn.]

during *dū'ring, prep.* throughout the time of: in the course of. [Orig. *pr.p.* of **dure.**]

durmast *dûr'mäst, n.* a variety of sessile-fruited oak with leaves downy below (*Quercus petraea* or *sessiliflora*). [Origin unknown: perhaps a blunder for *dun mast.*]

durn *dûrn, (dial.) n.* a doorpost. — Also **dern.** [Prob. Norse.]

duro *dōō'rō, n.* a Spanish peso: — *pl.* **dur'os.** [Sp. (*peso*) *duro*, hard (peso).]

duroy *dōō-roi', (obs.) n.* a type of coarse woollen fabric. [Orig. uncertain.]

durra *dōō'rə, n.* Indian millet, a grass (*Sorghum vulgare*) akin to sugar-cane, much cultivated for grain in Asia and Africa, or other species of the genus. — Also **dou'ra, dhu'rra, du'ra** and **dari** (*dur'i*). [Ar. *dhurah*.]

durrie *dur'i, n.* an Indian cotton carpet fabric with fringes, used for curtains, covers, etc. [Hind. *darī*.]

durst *dûrst, pa.t.* of **dare¹**, to venture. [O.E. *dorste*, pa.t. of *durran*, to dare.]

durukuli. See **douroucouli.**

durum (wheat) *dū'rəm ((h)wēt), n.* a kind of spring wheat (*Triticum durum*), grown esp. in Russia, North Africa and North America, whose flour is used in making spaghetti, etc. [L. *trīticum dūrum*, hard wheat.]

dush *dush, (Scot.) v.t.* to strike heavily against: to throw down. — *n.* a heavy impact.

dusk *dusk, adj.* darkish: of a dark colour. — *n.* twilight: partial darkness: darkness of colour. — *v.t.* and *v.i.* to make or become dusky: to dim. — *v.t.* and *v.i.* **dusk'en** to make or grow dark. — *adv.* **dusk'ily.** — *n.* **dusk'iness.** — *adj.* **dusk'ish.** — *adv.* **dusk'ishly.** — *n.* **dusk'ishness.** — *adv.* **dusk'ly.** — *n.* **dusk'ness.** — *adj.* **dusk'y** partially dark or obscure: dark-coloured: sad: gloomy. [Ap-

parently connected with O.E. *dox*, dark.]

dust *dust, n.* fine particles of solid matter: a cloud of powdery matter: powder: earth: the grave: a mean condition: (with *the*) pneumoconiosis (*miners' slang*): gold-dust — hence money: turmoil (*slang*): a disturbance, a brawl. — *v.t.* to free from dust (also *v.i.*): to sprinkle. — *n.* **dust'er** one who dusts: a cloth or brush for removing dust: a sprinkler: a dust-coat (*U.S.*). — *adv.* **dust'ily.** — *n.* **dust'iness.** — *adjs.* **dust'less; dust'y**, covered or sprinkled with dust: like dust; contemptible, bad (in phrase *not so dusty; slang*). — **dust'-ball**, a ball of grain-dust, etc., in a horse's intestine; **dust'-bath** the action of birds in rubbing dust into their feathers, prob. to get rid of parasites; **dust'bin**, a receptacle for household rubbish: a repository for anything unwanted, unimportant, etc. (*fig.*); **dust'-bowl** a drought area subject to dust-storms (**Dust Bowl** the region of the U.S. along the western edge of the Great Plains); **dust'-brand** smut; **dust'-brush** a light brush for removing dust; **dust'-cart** a cart for taking away household rubbish; **dust'-coat** an overall: a light overcoat; **dust'=cover** the jacket of a book; **dust'-devil, -storm** a small storm in which a whirling column of dust or sand travels across a dry country; **dust'-hole** (*obs.*) dustbin; **dusting powder** fine powder, esp. talcum powder; **dust'=jacket** the jacket or dust-cover of a book; **dust'man** one who removes household rubbish; **dust'-pan** a pan or shovel for removing dust swept from the floor. — *adj.* **dust'proof** impervious or inaccessible to dust. — **dust'=sheet** a cloth for protecting furniture from dust; **dust'=shot** the smallest size of shot; **dust-storm** see dust-devil; **dust'-up** a quarrel, a brawl; **dusty answer** an unsatisfying, unfruitful, or sordid response (*fig.*); **dust'y-foot** see piepowder; **dust'y-mill'er** the auricula, from the white dust upon its leaves and flowers. — **bite the dust** see bite; **dust someone's jacket** to give someone a drubbing; **kick up, raise a dust** see kick; **throw dust in someone's eyes** to deceive someone. [O.E. *dūst*; cf. Ger. *Dunst*, vapour.]

Dutch *duch, adj.* pertaining to the Netherlands, its people, or language: German, Teutonic (*obs.*, except *rare* or *arch. U.S.*): heavy, clumsy, as in *Dutch-built*. — *n.* the language of the Netherlands: German (*High and Low Dutch, Hoch* and *Nieder* or *Platt Deutsch*, High and Low German; *obs.* and *U.S.*): (*pl.*) the people of the Netherlands: Germans (*obs.* and *U.S.*). — **Dutch'man** a native or citizen of the Netherlands: an Afrikaner (*S. Afr.; derog.*): a German or Teuton (*U.S.*): — *pl.* **Dutch'men;** *fem.* **Dutch'woman:** — *pl.* **Dutch'women.** — **Dutch auction** see auction; **Dutch bargain** a one-sided bargain; **Dutch barn** a storage barn consisting of a roof on a steel framework; **Dutch cap** see cap¹; **Dutch carpet** a mixed material of cotton and wool for floor coverings; **Dutch cheese** a small round cheese made on the Continent from skim-milk; **Dutch clinker** a hard yellow brick for paving, etc.; **Dutch clock** a clock of wood and wire with brass wheels, made in the Black Forest; **Dutch clover** white clover; **Dutch comfort** 'Thank God it's no worse'; **Dutch concert** a concert in which singers sing their various songs simultaneously, or each one sings a verse of any song he likes between bursts of some familiar chorus; **Dutch courage** see courage; **Dutch doll** a wooden doll with jointed legs; **Dutch drops** a once popular medicine, composed of oil of turpentine, tincture of guaiacum, etc.; **Dutch gold, leaf, metal** a copper-zinc alloy, a substitute for gold-leaf; **Dutch hoe** a hoe with blade attached as in a spade; **Dutch liquid** ethylene dichloride (C₂H₄Cl₂), an anaesthetic discovered by Dutch chemists; **Dutch lunch, supper, treat** one at which each brings or pays for his own share; **Dutchman's breeches** Dicentra; **Dutchman's pipe** a species of Aristolochia; **Dutch oven** a cooking-pot used by burying in coals: a tin for roasting before an open fire; **Dutch pink** see pink⁴; **Dutch rush** a horse-tail (*Equisetum hyemale*) with much silica in its stem, used for polishing; **Dutch tiles** see tile; **Dutch wife** an open frame of rattan or cane used in the East Indies, to rest the limbs upon in bed. — **double Dutch** any unknown or unintelligible language; **Dutch elm disease** a fungal, often fatal, disease of elm trees, spread by bark beetles, causing a gradual withering; **go Dutch** (*coll.*) to pay each for himself; **High Dutch** see above: formerly, Dutch as spoken in the Netherlands as opp. to S. African Dutch: double Dutch (*obs.*); **Pennsylvania Dutch** the mixed German dialect of the descendants of German settlers in Pennsylvania; **talk like a Dutch uncle** to utter a rebuke.   [Ger. *deutsch*, (lit.) belonging to the people — O.H.G. *diutisc;* cf. O.E. *thēod*, Goth. *thiuda*, nation; see **Teutonic.**]

dutch *duch*, (*costermongers' slang*) *n.* a wife.   [Probably **duchess.**]

duty *dū′ti*, *n.* that which is due: what one is bound by any (esp. moral) obligation to do: one's proper business: service: attendance: supervision of pupils out of school hours: performance of function or service: the work done by a machine under given conditions, or for a specified amount of energy supplied: the amount of water needed to irrigate in area for a particular crop: respect: tax on goods, etc. — *adj.* **dū′teous** devoted to duty: obedient. — *adv.* **dū′teously.** — *n.* **dū′teousness.** — *adjs.* **dū′tiable** subject to custom duty; **dū′tied** subjected to duties and customs; **dū′tiful** attentive to duty: respectful: expressive of a sense of duty. — *adv.* **dū′tifully.** — *n.* **dū′tifulness.** — *adjs.* **du′tybound′** obliged by one's feeling of duty: honour-bound; **du′ty-free′** free from tax or duty. — *n.* (*coll.*) a shop, usu. at an airport or on board a ship, where duty-free articles are on sale: an article on sale at such a shop; **duty officer** the officer on duty at any particular time. — *adj.* **du′ty-paid′** on which duty has been paid. — **do duty for** to serve as, to act as substitute for; **on duty** performing one's duties, or liable to be called upon to do so, during a specified period of time (*opp.* **off duty**).   [Anglo-Fr. *dueté;* see **due**[1].]

duumvir *dōō-*, *dū-um′vir*, *-vər*, *n.* one of two associated in the same office: — *pl.* **duum′virs, duum′viri** (*-ī;* L. *dōō-ōōm-wir′ē*). — *adj.* **duum′viral.** — *n.* **duum′virate** an association of two men in one office: a government by duumvirs.   [L. *duumvirī*, for *duovirī* — *duo*, two, and *vir*, a man.]

duvet *dōō′vā*, (Fr. *dü-vā*), *n.* a quilt stuffed with eiderdown, swan's-down or man-made fibres, used on a bed in place of blankets, etc.   [Fr.]

duvetyn *dū′və-tēn*, *duv′tin*, *n.* a soft fabric with a nap, made of cotton, wool, silk, or rayon, and often used for women's clothes. — Also **duvetyne, duvetine.**   [Fr *duvetine* — *duvet*, down.]

dux *duks*, *n.* a leader: the top academic prize-winner in a school or class.   [L., a leader.]

duxelles *duk-sel′*, *dōōk-*, *-z*, *n.* a seasoning made from chopped mushrooms, onions or shallots, and parsley.   [The Marquis *d'Uxelles*, 17th-cent. French nobleman.]

duyker. See **duiker.**

dvandva *dvän′dvä*, (*gram.*) *n.* a compound word, each element being equal in status (e.g. *tragicomedy, bittersweet*).   [Sans. *dvaṁdva*, a pair.]

dvornik *dvor′nek, dvŏr′*, *n.* a Russian concierge or porter.   [Russ., caretaker — *dvor*, yard, court.]

dwale *dwāl*, *n.* deadly nightshade (*bot.*): a stupefying drink: a black colour (*her.*).   [O.N. *dvöl, dvali*, delay, sleep.]

dwam, dwalm, dwaum *dwäm, dwöm*, (*Scot.*) *ns.* a swoon (*obs.*): a sudden sickness: a dream, state of inattention. — *vs.i.* to swoon (*obs.*): to fail in health.   [O.E. *dwolma*, confusion.]

dwarf *dwörf*, *n.* a diminutive person: a small manlike mythological being, esp. a metal-worker: an animal or plant much below the ordinary height: anything very small of its kind: a small star of high density and low luminosity (**white dwarf, red dwarf, brown dwarf**, etc. according to colour): — *pl.* **dwarfs**, (*rare*) **dwarves.** — *adj.* **dwarfed:** dwarfish: very small. — *v.t.* to hinder from growing: to make to appear small. — *v.i.* to become dwarfed. — *adjs.* **dwarfed; dwarf′ish** like a

dwarf: very small: despicable. — *adv.* **dwarf′ishly.** — *ns.* **dwarf′ishness; dwarf′ism** condition of being a dwarf. — **dwarfed tree** bonsai.   [O.E. *dweorg;* Du. *dwerg*, O.N. *dverg*, Ger. *Zwerg.*]

dwell *dwel*, *v.i.* to abide: to reside: to remain: to rest attention (on): to continue long (in; *obs.*). — *v.t.* (*Milt.*) to inhabit: to cause to dwell: — *pr.p.* **dwell′ing;** *pa.t.* and *pa.p.* **dwelt** or **dwelled.** — *n.* a pause, hesitation in the working of a machine (*eng.*): a part of a cam shaped so as to allow a pause in operation at the point of maximum lift (*eng.*); — *ns.* **dwell′er; dwell′ing** the place where one dwells: a house: habitation: continuance. — **dwell′ing-house** a house used as a dwelling, in distinction from a place of business or other building; **dwell′ing-place** a place of residence.   [O.E. *dwellan*, to go astray, delay, tarry.]

dwindle *dwind′l*, *v.i.* to grow less: to waste away: to grow feeble: to become degenerate. — *v.t.* to lessen — *n.* decline. — *n.* **dwin′dlement.**   [Dim. of **dwine.**]

dwine *dwīn*, *v.i.* to pine: to waste away (*Scot.*).   [O.E. *dwīnan*, to fade: cf. O.N. *dvīna*, Dan. *tvine*, to pine away.]

dyad *dī′ad*, *n.* a pair of units treated as one: a bivalent atom, radical, or element (*chem.*). — *adj.* **dyad′ic.**   [Gr. *dyas, -ados* — *dyo*, two.]

Dyak, Dayak *dī′ak*, *n.* a member of any of the indigenous, generally non-Muslim tribes of the interior of Borneo: their languages and dialects.   [Malay *dayak*, up-country.]

dyarchy *dī′ärk-i*, *n.* a common but undesirable spelling of **diarchy.**

dybbuk *dib′ək*, (*Jewish folklore*) *n.* evil spirit, or soul of dead person, that enters the body of a living person and controls his actions.   [Heb. *dibbūq.*]

dye[1] *dī*, (*Spens.*) *n.* Same as **die**[2].

dye[2] *dī*, *v.t.* to stain: to give a new colour to: — *pr.p.* **dye′ing;** *pa.t.* and *pa.p.* **dyed.** — *n.* colour: tinge: stain: a colouring liquid. — *adjs.* **dye(e)′able; dyed.** — *ns.* **dye′ing; dye′er** one whose trade is to dye cloth, etc.; **dyester** (*dī′stər; Scot.*) a dyer. — **dye′-house** a building in which dyeing is done; **dyeline** (*dī′līn*) see **diazo;** **dy′er's-green′weed** or **dy′er's-broom** a papilionaceous shrub (*Genista tinctoria*), a source of yellow colouring matter; **dy′er's-rock′et, -weld, -yell′owweed** a plant (*Reseda luteola*) akin to mignonette yielding a yellow dye; **dy′er's-weed** a name for various plants that yield dyes — woad, weld, dyer's-greenweed, etc.; **dye′stuff** a material used in dyeing; **dye′-wood** any wood from which material is obtained for dyeing; **dye′-work(s)** an establishment for dyeing. — **dye in the wool** to dye (the wool) before spinning, to give a more permanent result (*adj.* **dyed-in-the-wool** (*fig.*) (too) fixed in one's opinions or attitudes).   [O.E. *dēagian*, to dye, from *dēag, dēah*, colour.]

dying *dī′ing, pr.p.* of **die**[1]. — *adj.* destined for death: mortal: declining: occurring immediately before death, as *dying words*: pertaining to death: last, final. — *n.* death. — *adv.* **dy′ingly.** — *n.* **dy′ingness.** — **dying declaration** (*law*) declaration made by a dying person who does not survive through the trial of the accused.   [See **die**[1].]

dyke, dykey. See **dike**[1,2].

dynamic *dīn-am′ik*, or *din-*, *adj.* relating to force: relating to dynamics: relating to the effects of forces in nature: relating to activity or things in movement: relating to dynamism: causal: forceful, very energetic. — *n.* a moving force: any driving force instrumental in growth or change (esp. social): pattern of growth or change. — *adj.* **dynam′ical.** — *adv.* **dynam′ically.** — *n.* **dynam′icist** a person who studies dynamics. — *n.sing.* **dynam′ics** the science of matter and motion, mechanics, sometimes restricted to kinetics: (often *n.pl.*) (signs indicating) varying levels of loudness (*mus.*). — *v.t.* **dyn′amise, -ize** to make dynamic. — *n.* **dyn′amism** a theory which explains the phenomena of the universe by some immanent energy: operation of force: dynamic quality: quality of restless energy: quality of suggesting forceful movement (*art*, etc.); **dyn'amist.** — *adj.* **dynamis'tic.** [Gr. *dynamikos* — *dynamis*, power — *dynasthai*, to be able.]

dynamite *dīn'ə-mīt* (formerly also *din'*), *n.* explosive consisting of absorbent matter, as porous silica, saturated with nitroglycerine: something highly dangerous to deal with. — *v.t.* to blow up with dynamite. — *ns.* **dyn'amiter, dyn'amitard** (*-mit-ärd*) (*arch.*) a user of dynamite, esp. for political purposes. [Gr. *dynamis*, power.]

dynamo *dīn'ə-mō*, *n.* contraction for **dynamo-electric machine,** a machine for generating electric currents by means of the relative movement of conductors and magnets: — *pl.* **dyn'amos.** — *adjs.* **dyn'amo-elec'tric, -al.** — *ns.* **dynamogen'esis, dynamog'eny** production of increased nervous activity; **dynamograph** (*-am'*) a recording dynamometer; **dynamom'eter** an instrument for measuring force, or power. — *adjs.* **dynamomet'ric, -al.** — *ns.* **dynamom'etry; dyn'amotor** an electrical machine with two armature windings, one acting as a motor and the other as a generator, and a single magnetic field, for converting direct current into alternating current; **dyn'atron** (*electronics*) a four-electrode thermionic valve used to generate continuous oscillation. — **human dynamo** a person of exceptional energy. [Gr. *dynamis*, power.]

dynast *din'ast, -əst*, also *dīn'*, *n.* a ruler. — *adjs.* **dynas'tic, -al** relating to a dynasty. — *adv.* **dynast'ically.** — *n.* **dyn'asty** (*-əs-ti*) a succession of kings of the same family, or of members of any powerful family or connected group. [Fr. *dynastie*, or L.L. *dynastīa* — Gr. *dynasteia*, power, dominion — *dynasthai*, to be able.]

dyne *dīn*, *n.* the C.G.S. unit of force — the force which, acting on a mass of one gramme, produces an acceleration of one centimetre per second per second, equal to 10^{-5} of a newton. — *n.* **dyn'ode** (*electronics*) an intermediate electrode (between the cathode and final anode) which causes amplification by secondary emission of electrons. [Gr. *dynamis*, force.]

Dyophysite. Same as **Diphysite.**

Dyothelete, Dyotheletism, Dyothelism. See **Ditheletism.**

dys- *dis-*, *pfx.* ill, bad, abnormal. [Gr.]

dysaesthesia *dis-əs-thē'si-ə, -zhi-ə, -zhə*, or *-ēs-*, *n.* impaired sensation, partial insensibility. — *adj.* **dysaesthetic** (*-thet'ik*). [Pfx. **dys-**, and Gr. *aisthēsis*, sensation — *aisthanesthai*, to feel.]

dysarthria *dis-är'thri-ə*, *n.* impaired ability to articulate speech resulting from damage to the central or peripheral nervous system. [Pfx. **dys-**, and Gr. *arthron*, a joint.]

dyschroa *dis'krō-ə*, *n.* discoloration of the skin from disease. — Also **dyschroia** (*-kroi'ə*). [Pfx. **dys-**, and Gr. *chroā*, *chroia*, complexion.]

dyscrasia *dis-krā'si-ə, -zhi-ə, -zhə*, (*path.*) *n.* a disordered condition of the body attributed originally to unsuitable mixing of the body fluids or humours. [Pfx. **dys-**, and Gr. *krāsis*, a mixing.]

dyscrasite *dis'kras-īt*, *n.* a mineral composed of silver and antimony. [Pfx. **dys-**, and Gr. *krāsis*, mixture.]

dysentery *dis'ən-tər-i, -tri*, *n.* a term formerly applied to any condition in which inflammation of the colon was associated with the frequent passage of bloody stools: now confined to *amoebic dysentery*, the result of infection with the *Entamoeba histolytica*; and to *bacillary dysentery*, due to infection with *Bacterium dysenteriae*. — *adj.* **dysenteric** (*-ter'ik*). [Gr. *dysenterīa* — *dys-*, amiss, *enteron*, intestine.]

dysfunction *dis-fung(k)'shən*, *n.* impairment or abnormality of the functioning of an organ. — *adj.* **dysfunc'tional.** [Pfx. **dys-**.]

dysgenic *dis-jen'ik*, *adj.* unfavourable to race-improvement. — *n.sing.* **dysgen'ics** the study of race degeneration: cacogenics. [Pfx. **dys-**, and the root of *gennaein*, to beget.]

dysgraphia *dis-graf'i-ə*, *n.* inability to write, arising from brain damage or other cause. — *adj.* **dysgraph'ic.**

[Pfx. **dys-**, and Gr. *graphein*, to write.]

dysharmonic *dis-här-mon'ik*, *adj.* unbalanced, wanting in harmony of proportion. [Pfx. **dys-**.]

dyskinesia *dis-kin-ē'zi-ə*, *n.* lack of control over bodily movements: impaired performance of voluntary movements. [Pfx. **dys-**, and Gr. *kīnēsis*, movement.]

dyslexia *dis-leks'i-ə*, *n.* word-blindness, great difficulty in learning to read or spell, of which the cause (not lack of intelligence) has not been established. — *adjs.* and *ns.* **dyslec'tic, dyslex'ic.** [Pfx. **dys-**, and Gr. *lexis*, word.]

dyslogistic *dis-lə-jis'tik*, *adj.* conveying censure, opprobrious. — *adv.* **dyslogis'tically.** — *n.* **dys'logy** dispraise. [Pfx. **dys-**, and Gr. *logos*, discourse.]

dysmelia *dis-mēl'i-ə, -mel'*, *-yə*, *n.* the condition in which one or more limbs are misshapen or incomplete. — *adj.* **dysmel'ic.** [Pfx. **dys-**, and Gr. *melos*, limb.]

dysmenorrhoea, -rhea *dis-men-ō-rē'ə*, *n.* difficult or painful menstruation. — *adjs.* **dysmenorrh(o)e'al, dysmenorrh(o)e'ic.** [Pfx. **dys-**, and Gr. *mēn*, month, *rhoiā*, flow.]

dysodyle, -ile, -il *dis'ō-dīl, -dil*, *ns.* a yellow or greyish laminated bituminous mineral, often found with lignite, burning vividly, with an odour of asafoetida. [Gr. *dysōdēs*, stinking — *dys-*, ill, *ozein*, to smell, *hȳlē*, matter.]

dyspathy *dis'pə-thi*, *n.* antipathy, dislike. — *adj.* **dyspathet'ic.** [Pfx. **dys-**, and Gr. *pathos*, feeling.]

dyspepsia *dis-pep'si-ə*, *n.* indigestion. — Also **dyspep'sy.** — *n.* **dyspep'tic** a person afflicted with dyspepsia. — *adjs.* **dyspep'tic, -al** afflicted with, pertaining to, or arising from, indigestion: gloomy, bad-tempered. — *adv.* **dyspep'tically.** [Gr. *dyspepsiā* — *dys-*, ill, *pepsis*, digestion — *peptein*, to digest.]

dysphagia *dis-fā'ji-ə*, *n.* difficulty in swallowing — also **dys'phagy** (*-fə-ji*). — *adj.* **dysphagic** (*-faj'ik*). [Pfx. **dys-**, and Gr. *phagein* (aorist), to eat.]

dysphasia *dis-fāz'i-ə, -fā'zhə*, *n.* difficulty in expressing or understanding thought in spoken or written words, caused by brain damage. [Pfx. **dys-**, and Gr. *phasis*, speech.]

dysphemism *dis'fə-mizm*, *n.* the replacing of a mild or inoffensive word or phrase by an offensive one: the offensive word or phrase substituted. — *adj.* **dysphemis'tic.** [From pfx. **dys-**, and **euphemism**.]

dysphonia *dis-fō'ni-ə*, *n.* difficulty in producing sounds. — *adj.* **dysphon'ic.** [Pfx. **dys-**, and Gr. *phōnē*, sound.]

dysphoria *dis-fō'ri-ə, -fō'*, *n.* impatience under affliction: morbid restlessness: uneasiness: want of feeling of well-being. — *adj.* **dysphor'ic.** [Gr. *dysphōriā*, affliction, pain — *dys-*, ill, and the root of *pherein*, to bear.]

dysplasia *dis-plā'zi-ə*, *n.* abnormal development or growth of a cell, tissue, organ, etc. [Pfx. **dys-**, and Gr. *plāsis*, moulding.]

dyspnoea *disp-nē'ə*, *n.* difficulty of breathing. — *adjs.* **dyspnoe'al, dyspnoe'ic.** — Also **dyspnea**, etc. [Gr. *dyspnoia* — *dys-*, ill, *pnoē*, breathing.]

dyspraxia *dis-prak'si-ə*, *n.* an impaired ability to perform deliberate actions. [Pfx. **dys-**, and Gr. *prāxis*, doing.]

dysprosium *dis-prōz'i-əm*, *n.* a metal of the rare earths, the element of atomic number 66 (symbol Dy). [Gr. *dysprositos*, difficult to reach — *dys-*, ill, difficult, *pros*, to, *ienai*, to go.]

dystectic *dis-tek'tik*, *adj.* not easily fused. [Gr. *dystēktos* — *dys-*, ill, *tēkein*, to melt.]

dysteleology *dis-tel-i-ol'ə-ji*, *n.* the doctrine of purposelessness, or denial of final causes: the study of functionless rudimentary organs in animals and plants. — *adj.* **dysteleological** (*-i-ə-loj'i-kl*). — *n.* **dysteleol'ogist.** [Pfx. **dys-** (in a negative sense).]

dysthesia *dis-thē'si-ə*, *n.* a morbid habit of body, resulting in general discomfort and impatience. — *adj.* **dysthetic** (*-thet'ik*). [Gr. *dysthesiā* — *dys-*, ill, *thesis*, position.]

dysthymia *dis-thī'mi-ə*, *n.* morbid anxiety and despondency. — *n.* **dysthȳm'iac** one who suffers from dysthymia. — *adj.* **dysthȳm'ic.** [Pfx. **dys-**, and Gr. *thymiā*, despair.]

dystopia *dis-tō'pi-ə, n.* a place thought of as the opposite to Utopia, i.e. where everything is as bad as possible. — *adj.* **dysto'pian.** [From pfx. **dys-**, and **utopia.**]

dystrophy *dis'trə-fi, (biol.) n.* imperfect nutrition: any of several disorders in which there is wasting of muscle tissue, etc. — Also **dystrō'phia.** — *adj.* **dystrophic** (*-tro'fik*) of a lake, over-acidic and lacking sufficient nutrients. — **muscular dystrophy** see **muscle.** [Pfx. **dys-**, and Gr. *trophē*, nourishment.]

dysuria *dis-ū'ri-ə, n.* a difficulty or pain in passing urine — also **dys'ury.** — *adj.* **dysū'ric.** [Gr. *dysouriā* — *dys-*, ill, *ouron*, urine.]

Dytiscus *di-* or *dī-tis'kəs, n.* a genus of carnivorous water-beetles, including a common large British species, *D. marginalis.* — Also **Dyticus** (*dit'*). — *adj.* and *n.* **dytiscid** (*di-* or *dī-tis'id*). [Gr. *dўtikos*, diving — *dyein*, to dive.]

dyvour *dī'vər, (Scot.) n.* a bankrupt. — *n.* **dyv'oury** bankruptcy. [Perh. from Fr. *devoir*, to owe.]

dzeren *dzē'rən, n.* a Central Asian antelope. [Mongolian.]

dziggetai *dzig'ə-tī, n.* a Central Asian wild ass (*Equus hemionus*), rather like a mule. [Mongolian *tchikhitei*.]

dzo. See **zho.**

fāte; fär; hûr; mīne; mōte; för; mūte; mōon; fŏot; dhen (then); *el'ə-mənt* (element)

E

E, e $\bar{e}$, *n.* the fifth letter in our own and cognate alphabets, with various sounds (as in me, get, *E*ngland, h*e*r, pr*e*y) and often mute (commonly an indication of a preceding long vowel or diphthong — cf. not, not*e*; bit, bit*e*): in music the third note or sound of the natural diatonic scale, the major third above the tonic C: *e* represents the base of the natural system of logarithms (see **Napierian**): as a mediaeval Roman numeral E = 250; $\bar{E}$ = 250 000. — **E'-boat** (enemy *boat* or Ger. *Eilboot* — *File*, speed) a fast German motor torpedo-boat; **E. coli** see **Escherichia coli; E-layer, -region** see **Kennelly-Heaviside layer; E number** an identification code required by EEC law for food additives such as colourings and preservatives, consisting of the letter E followed by a number.

ea $\bar{e}'\partial$, $\bar{e}$, (*dial.*) *n.* a river: running water: a drainage canal in the Fens — sometimes **eau**, as if taken from French. [O.E. *ēa*; akin to L. *aqua*, water.]

each *ēch, adj.* and *pron.* every one separately considered. — *adv.* **each'where** (*obs.*) everywhere. — **each other** a compound reciprocal pronoun, one another, by some restricted in application to two; **each way** in betting, for a win and for a place (*adj.* **each'-way'**). [O.E. *ǣlc* — *ā*, ever, *gelīc*, alike.]

eadish. Obsolete form of **eddish.**

eager[1] $\bar{e}'g\partial r$, *adj.* excited by desire: ardent to do or obtain: earnest (*obs.*): keen, severe: (*Shak.* **aygre**) sour, acid, bitter (*obs.*). — *adv.* **ea'gerly.** — *n.* **ea'gerness.** — **eager beaver** an enthusiast: a zealous person: one over-eager for work. [O.Fr. *aigre* — L. *ācer, ācris,* sharp.]

eager[2]. Same as **eagre.**

eagle $\bar{e}'gl$, *n.* a name given to many large birds of prey of the family Falconidae: a military standard carrying the figure of an eagle: a lectern in the form of an eagle: the badge of certain orders, as the Prussian **black** (1701) and **red** (1705) **eagle,** the Polish, afterwards Russian, **white eagle** (1705): a gold coin of the United States, worth ten dollars: a colonel's shoulder insignia (*U.S.*): a hole at golf played in two strokes less than par. — *n.* **ea'glet** a young or small eagle. — *adjs.* **ea'gle-eyed, ea'gle-sight'ed** having a piercing eye: discerning; **ea'gle-flight'ed** mounting high. — **ea'gle-hawk** a name applied to several eagles of comparatively small size; **ea'gle-owl** any of a number of large horned owls of the genus Bubo; **ea'gle-ray** a large sting-ray; **ea'gle-stone** a hard-encrusted nodule of argillaceous oxide of iron. — *adj.* **ea'gle-winged** having an eagle's wings. [O.Fr. *aigle* — L. *aquila.*]

eaglewood $\bar{e}'gl$-$w\bar{oo}d$, *n.* a genus (Aquilaria) of the daphne family, large spreading trees of Eastern India, whose heartwood contains a resinous substance fragrant in burning. [From the accidental resemblance of its name in some Eastern language to **eagle,** L. *aquila*; cf. **agalloch, agila.**]

eagre $\bar{a}'g\partial r$, $\bar{e}'g\partial r$, *n.* a bore or sudden rise of the tide in a river. [Origin doubtful; hardly from O.E. *ēgor,* flood.]

ealdorman. See **alderman** (first meaning and derivation).

eale prob. *ēl,* (Shak., *Hamlet* I, iv, 36) *n.* various conjectures, generally supposed to be for **evil,** but perh. a misprint.

ean *ēn,* (*Shak.*) *v.t.* and *v.i.* to bring forth. — *n.* **ean'ling** a young lamb. [O.E. *ēanian.*]

ear[1] *ēr, n.* a spike, as of corn. — *v.i.* to put forth ears. — *adj.* **eared** of corn, having ears. — **ear'-cock'le** a disease of wheat caused by a thread-worm (*Tylenchus*). [O.E. *ēar;* Ger. *Ähre.*]

ear[2] *ēr,* (*obs.*) *v.t.* to plough or till. — *n.* **ear'ing** (*obs.*) ploughing. [O.E. *erian;* cf. L. *arāre,* Gr. *aroein.*]

ear[3] *ēr, n.* the organ of hearing, or the external part merely: the sense or power of hearing: the faculty of distinguishing sounds esp. of a different pitch: attention: anything projecting or shaped like an ear, as the auricle of a leaf, lug of a vessel, a projecting part for support, attachment, etc. — *adj.* **eared** having ears, or external ears. — *ns.* **ear'ful** (*coll.*) rough or scolding words, a reprimand; **ear'ing** (*naut.*) one of a number of small ropes to fasten the upper corner of a sail to the yard. — *adj.* **ear'less** without ears, or external ears. — **ear'ache** an ache or pain in the ear. — *v.i.* **ear'bash** to talk incessantly (*Austr. coll.*). — **ear'bob** an earring; **ear'-bone.** — *adj.* **ear'-bussing** (*Shak.*; another reading **ear'-kissing**) whispered. — **ear'-cap** (*arch.*) an earflap; **ear'drop** an ornamental pendant hanging from the ear: (in *pl.*) a medicine taken in the form of drops introduced into the outer ear; **ear'drum** the drum or middle cavity of the ear, tympanum; **ear'flap** one of two coverings for the ears, attached to a cap, to protect them from cold or injury; **ear'-hole** the aperture of the ear; **ear'lap** the tip of the ear: an earflap; **ear'lock** a curl near the ear worn by Elizabethan dandies; **ear'-mark** an owner's mark on an animal's ear: a distinctive mark. — *v.t.* to put an earmark on: to set aside, intend, for a particular purpose. — **ear'muffs** a pair of ear coverings joined by a band of material across the head; **ear'phone** a headphone; **ear'pick** an instrument for clearing the ear; **ear'piece** the part of a telephone, etc. that is placed next to the ear. — *adj.* **ear'-pierc'ing** shrill, screaming. — *n.* the piercing of the lobe of the ear (in order to insert earrings). — **ear'plug** a plug of soft material inserted into the outer ear to exclude unwanted sound, water, etc.; **earring** (*ēr'ing*) a piece of jewellery hung from, or fixed on or in, the ear; **ear'-shell** any shell of the family Haliotidae; **ear'-shot** the distance at which a sound can be heard. — *adj.* **ear'-splitt'ing** ear-piercing. — **ear'-trum'pet** a tube to aid in hearing; **ear'wax** a waxy substance secreted by the glands of the ear; **ear'wig** (O.E. *ēarwicga, ēare,* ear, *wicga,* insect, beetle) any dermapterous insect of the family Forficulidae, once supposed to creep into the ear: a flatterer. — *v.t.* to gain the ear of (*arch.*): to bias (*arch.*): to torment by private importunities (*arch.*): to eavesdrop (*slang*). — *adj.* **ear'wiggy.** — **ear'-witness** a witness that can testify from his own hearing. — **about one's ears** said of something falling about one (e.g. house), or assailing one all around (also *fig.*); **be all ears** to give every attention; **fall on deaf ears** of a remark, request, etc., to be ignored; **give ear** to attend (to); **go in (at) one ear and out (at) the other** to make no permanent impression; **have someone's ear** to be secure of someone's favourable attention; **have itching ears** to be desirous of hearing novelties (2 Tim. iv. 3); **have, keep, one's ear to the ground** to keep oneself well informed about what is going on around one; **lend an ear** to listen (to); **make a pig's ear of** see **pig**[1]; **make someone's ears burn** to discuss someone in his absence; **out on one's ear** (*coll.*) turned out, dismissed; **over head and ears** (*arch.*) overwhelmed: deeply engrossed or involved; **pin back one's ears** to listen attentively; **pin back someone's ears** to subdue someone by beating; **set by the ears** to set at strife; **tickle the ear of** to gratify, pander to the taste of, flatter; **turn a deaf ear** to refuse to listen (to); **up to one's ears in** deeply involved in; **walls have ears** there may be listeners. [O.E. *ēare;* cf. Ger. *Ohr,* L. *auris.*]

eard, eard-hunger. See **yird.**

earl *ûrl, n.* a British nobleman ranking between a marquis and a viscount: — *fem.* **count'ess.** — *n.* **earl'dom** the dominion or dignity of an earl. — **Earl Marshal** an English officer of state, president of the Heralds' College — the Scottish form **Earl Marischal.** [O.E. *eorl*, a warrior, hero, a Danish under-king, later a nobleman equivalent to count; cf. O.N. *jarl*.]

early *ûr'li, adv.* near the beginning (of a time, period, series): soon: in good time: before appointed time: — *compar.* **ear'lier;** *superl.* **ear'liest.** — *adj.* belonging to or happening in the first part of time, period, or series: belonging to or happening in the first stages of development: beforehand: ready, advanced, astir, or on the spot in good time: happening in the remote past or near future. — *v.t.* **ear'lierise, -ize** to do at a date earlier than that arranged. — *n.* **ear'liness.** — **early bird** the proverbial catcher of the (early) worm: an early riser: (with *caps.*) a name given to a type of communications satellite; **early closing** observance of a weekly half-holiday: closing of public houses early in the night; **early door** an entrance to a theatre or hall open before the ordinary door at a higher price; **Early English** see **English** (*philol.*): the form of Gothic architecture in which the pointed arch was first employed in Britain — succeeding the *Norman* towards the end of the 12th century, merging into the *Decorated* at the end of the 13th. — *adjs.* **ear'ly-Victor'ian** belonging to or characteristic of the early part of Queen Victoria's reign (reigned 1837–1901); **ear'ly-warn'ing** (also as two words) pertaining to or part of an early warning system (see below). — **early and late** at all times; **earlier on** previously; **early day motion** a parliamentary motion for consideration on a day when business finishes early, i.e. (as such days rarely exist) merely to draw attention to a matter; **early on** before much time has elapsed; **early warning system** a system of advance warning or notice, esp. of nuclear attack; **(it's) early days** (*coll.*) (it's) too soon to know, have a result, etc.; **keep early hours** to rise and go to bed early. [O.E. *ǣrlīce* (adv.) — *ǣr*, before.]

earn[1] *ûrn, v.t.* to gain by labour: to acquire: to deserve: to bring to one. — *n.* **earn'er** one who earns: something, esp. illegal or slightly shady, that brings a good income or profit (*slang*). — *n.pl.* **earn'ings** what one has earned: money saved. [O.E. *earnian*, to earn; cf. O.H.G. *aran*, harvest; Ger. *Ernte*.]

earn[2] *ûrn,* (*dial.*) *v.t.* and *v.i.* to curdle (of milk). — *n.* **earn'ing** rennet. — Also **yearn, yearning.** [O.E. *iernan* = *rinnan*, to run, and *ærnan* = *rennan*, to cause to run; *gerinnan*, causative *gerennan*, to curdle.]

earn[3] *ûrn, v.i.* (*Spens., Shak.*). See **yearn**[1].

earnest[1] *ûr'nist, adj.* intent: sincere: serious. — *n.* seriousness: reality. — *adv.* **ear'nestly.** — *n.* **ear'nestness.** [O.E. *eornost*, seriousness; Ger. *Ernst*.]

earnest[2] *ûr'nist, n.* payment given in token of a bargain made (also **ear'nest-money, ear'nest-penny**): a pledge: first-fruits. [Ety. obscure: possibly conn. with **arles**.]

earst. Obsolete form of **erst**.

earth *ûrth, n.* the third planet in order from the sun (often with *cap.*): the matter on the surface of the globe: soil, a mixture of disintegrated rock and organic material in which plants are rooted: dry land, as opposed to sea: the world: the inhabitants of the world: dirt: dead matter: the human body: a burrow: an electrical connection with the earth, usually by a wire soldered to a metal plate sunk in moist earth: an old name for certain oxides of metals (see **alkaline earth, rare earth**). — *v.t.* to bury, inter (*obs.*): to hide or cause to hide in the earth, or in a hole: to connect to earth electrically: to clog, cover, smear, or partially cover with earth (often with *up*). — *v.i.* to burrow: to hide. — *adj.* **earth'en** made of earth or clay: earthly. — *ns.* **earth'-iness; earth'liness; earth'ling** a dweller on the earth: a worldly-minded person. — *adj.* **earth'ly** belonging to the earth: vile: worldly: conceivably possible on earth. — *n.* (*coll.*) chance (for *earthly chance*). — *adv.* **earth'-ward** toward the earth. — *adj.* **earth'y** consisting of, relating to, or resembling earth: inhabiting the earth: gross: unrefined. — **earth'-bag** a sack of earth used in

fortifications; **earth'-bath** a bath of earth or mud; **earth'-board** the board of a plough, or other implement, that turns over the earth. — *adjs.* **earth'born** born from or on the earth; **earth'bound** bound to earth; **earth'-bred** bred from earth: mean, grovelling. — **earth'-closet** a closet in which earth is used for the deodorisation of faecal matters. — *adj.* **earth'-crea'ted** made of earth. — **earth'enware** crockery: coarse pottery; **earth'fall** a landslide. — *adjs.* **earth'fast** fixed in the earth; **earth'-fed** contented with earthly things. — **earth'flax** asbestos; **earth'-hog** the aardvark; **earth'=house** an underground stone-lined gallery associated with the Iron Age, which may have functioned as a storehouse or possibly dwelling, also called **Picts' house; earth'-hunger** passion for acquiring land; **earthing tyres** aircraft tyres that discharge static electricity on grounding; **earth-light** see **earth-shine.** — *adj.* **earth'ly-mind'ed** having the mind intent on earthly things. — **earth'ly-mind'edness; earth'man, -woman** esp. in science fiction, a person who lives on the planet earth; **earth mother** the earth personified as a goddess: a woman, typically fertile and of generous proportions, who seems to symbolise motherhood; **earth'=move'ment** elevation, subsidence, or folding of the earth's crust; **earth'mover** any piece of plant designed to move earth, e.g. a bulldozer. — *adj.* **earth'moving.** — **earth'-nut** the edible root-tuber of *Conopodium flexuosum*, a woodland umbelliferous plant: the plant itself (also *arnut, pig-nut, earth-chestnut*): the peanut (Arachis); **earth'-pea** the peanut; **earth'-pillar** a column of soft material protected from erosion by an overlying stone; **earth'-plate** a buried plate of metal forming the earth connection of a telegraph-wire, lightning-conductor, etc.; **earth'quake** a quaking or shaking of the earth: a heaving of the ground. — *adjs.* **earth'quaked** shaken, destroyed or visited by an earthquake; **earth'-quaking.** — **earth science** any of the sciences dealing with the earth, e.g. geography, geology. — *adjs.* **earth'-shaking, earth'shattering** of great importance or consequence. — **earth'-shine, earth'-light** the faint light visible on the part of the moon not illuminated by the sun; **earth'-smoke** fumitory; **earth'-star** a fungus (*Geaster*) akin to the puffballs that opens out into a starlike form; **earth'-table** a course of stone or brick just above the ground; **earth'-tremor** a slight earthquake; **earth'wax** ozokerite; **earth'wolf** the aardwolf; **earthwoman** see **earthman; earth'work** a fortification of earth: an embankment: work of excavation and embanking; **earth'worm** the common worm: a mean person, a poor creature. — **cost the earth** (*coll.*) to be very expensive; **down, back to earth** back to reality; **go to earth** to seek a hole or hiding-place (also *fig.*); **green earth** see **green**[1]; **on earth** used for emphasis in phrases such as *how on earth, why on earth*, etc.; **run to earth** to search out, find; **the Earthshaker** (*myth.*) Poseidon (q.v.), the god responsible for causing earthquakes. [O.E. *eorthe*; cf. Du. *aarde*, Ger. *Erde*.]

ease *ēz, n.* freedom from pain or disturbance: rest from work: quiet: freedom from difficulty: naturalness: unconstrained manner. — *v.t.* to free from pain, trouble, or anxiety: to relieve: to relax: to calm: to move gently. — *v.i.* to become less great or severe (often *ease off, up*): to move very gradually: to become less in demand. — *adj.* **ease'ful** ease-giving: quiet, fit for rest. — *n.* **ease'ment** relief, easing (*rare*): assistance (*obs.*): support (*obs.*): gratification (*obs.*): legally, the right to use something (esp. land) not one's own or to prevent its owner from making an inconvenient use of it. — *adv.* **eas'ily.** — *n.* **eas'iness.** — *adj.* **eas'y** at ease: free from pain: tranquil: unconstrained: giving ease: not difficult: convenient: yielding: not straitened (in circumstances): not tight: not strict: in plentiful supply: (*of market*) not showing unusually great activity. — Also *adv.* — *interj.* command to lower, to go gently, to stop rowing, etc. — *adj.* **eas'y-care'** esp. of materials, easy to look after, clean, etc. — **eas'y-chair** an armchair for ease or rest. — *adj.* **eas'y-go'ing** (*coll.*) indolent: placid. — **easy money** money made without much exertion or difficulty. — *adj.* **eas′y-ō′sy** (*coll.*) easy-going: without strong feelings, indifferent. — **easy street** (*coll.*) a situation of comfort or affluence; **easy terms** a phrase used in describing a hire-purchase agreement to imply or emphasise that the payments will not be a burden to the customer; **easy touch** see **touch.** — **be easy** to be quite willing to fall in with one arrangement or another; **chapel of ease** see **chapel; ease off** to slacken gradually: to make or become less intense; **ease oneself** (*arch. euph.*) to urinate or defecate; **easy does it!** take your time, do (it) slowly, carefully; **easy on the eye** (*coll.*) good to look at; **go easy on** to be lenient with: to use sparingly; **honours easy** honours evenly divided (at cards, etc.); **ill at ease** uncomfortable; **stand at ease** used of soldiers, when freed from attention; **stand easy** used of a still easier position; **take it easy** to avoid exertion: to be in no hurry; **take one's ease** to make oneself comfortable. [O.Fr. *aise*; cog. with It. *agio*, Prov. *ais*, Port. *azo*; ult. — L. *adjacēns*, see **adjacent.**]

easel *ēz′l, n.* the frame for supporting a picture during painting. [Du. *ezel*, or Ger. *Esel*, an ass.]

easle, aizle *āz′l,* (*Burns*) *n.* hot ashes. [O.E. *ysle.*]

eassel, eassil *ēs′l,* (*Scot.*) *adv.* eastward: easterly. — *advs.* **eass′elgate, eass′elward.** [east.]

east *ēst, n.* that part of the heavens where the sun rises at the equinox: one of the four cardinal points of the compass: the east part of a region: the east wind. — *adj. and adv.* toward the rising of the sun: (blowing) from the east. — *v.i.* (*arch.*) to move or turn east. — *adjs.* **east′er, east′ern** toward the east: connected with the east: dwelling in the east. — *n.* **east′erling** a native of the east: a trader from the shores of the Baltic. — *adj.* **east′erly** situated in the east: coming from the eastward: looking toward the east. — *adv.* on the east: toward the east. — *n.* an east wind. — *n.* **east′erner** a native or inhabitant of the east, esp. of the United States. — *adjs.* **east′ernmost, east′most** situated furthest east. — Also **east′ermost** (*obs.*). — *ns.* **east′ing** the course gained to the eastward: distance eastward from a given meridian; **east′land** the land in the East. — *adjs.* **east′ling, -lin** (*Scot.*) easterly. — *advs.* **east′-lings, -lins** (*Scot.*) eastward; **east′ward, east′wards** toward the east. — *adj.* **east′ward. — east′-by-north′ (south)** 11¼ degrees north (south) from due east; **East End** the eastern part of London or other town, often an area inhabited by people of the poorer classes; **East′-end′er; Eastern Church** the Greek Church; **East= Ind′iaman** a vessel used in the East Indian trade; **East Indian, Indies** see **Indian; east′-north-(south)-east′** 22½ degrees north (south) from the east; **East Side** the eastern part of New York. — **about east** (*old U.S. slang*) in proper manner; **East Coast fever,** also called **African coast fever,** a protozoan cattle disease resembling redwater, transmitted by ticks; **the East** countries between the Balkans and China (see also **Near East, Middle East, Far East**): the eastern part of the United States, used relatively and vaguely, but commonly that part between the Mississippi and the Ohio. [O.E. *ēast*; Ger. *Ost*; akin to Gr. *ēōs,* the dawn.]

Easter *ēst′ər, n.* a Christian festival commemorating the resurrection of Christ, held on the Sunday after Good Friday. — **Easter cactus** a S. American cactus having coral flowers; **Easter Day** Easter Sunday; **Easter dues, offerings** customary sums paid to the parson by his people at Easter; **Easter egg** a painted, decorated, stained or artificial (esp. made of chocolate) egg, given as a present at Easter; **Easter lily** any of several white-flowered lilies; **East′ertide, East′ertime** either Easter week or the fifty days from Easter to Whitsuntide. [O.E. *ēastre*; Ger. *Ostern*; Bede derives the word from *Eostre* (*Eastre*), a goddess whose festival was held at the spring equinox.]

easy. See **ease.**

eat *ēt, v.t.* to take into the body by the mouth as food:

to consume: to corrode. — *v.i.* to take food: to be eatable, to taste: — *pr.p.* **eat′ing;** *pa.t.* **ate** (*et* or *āt*); *pa.p.* **eaten** (*ē′tn*) or, *obs.,* **eat** (*et.*) — *n.* (*arch.* in *sing.,* *coll.* in *pl.*) food. — *adj.* **eat′able** edible, fit to be eaten. — *n.* anything used as food (chiefly in *pl.*; *coll.*). — *ns.* **eat′age** grass or fodder for horses, etc.: the right to eat; **eat′er** one who, or that which, eats or corrodes: variety suitable for eating uncooked; **eat′ery** (*slang*) a restaurant. — *n. and adj.* **eat′ing. — eat′ing-apple** etc., one suitable for eating uncooked; **eat′ing-house** a restaurant. — **eat away** to destroy gradually: to gnaw; **eat crow, dirt, humble pie** see **crow, dirt, humbles; eat in** of acid, to corrode, etch, etc., a metal: to eat at home; **eat into** of acid, to corrode, etc.: to consume, use up; **eat off** to clear (a crop) by setting cattle to eat it; **eat one's hat** an undertaking promised on conditions one thinks very improbable; **eat one's head off** to cost more for food than one is worth; **eat one's heart out** to pine away, brooding over misfortune; **eat one's terms** to study for the bar, with allusion to the number of times in a term that a student must dine in the hall of an Inn of Court; **eat one's words** to take back what one has said; **eat out** to finish eatables: to encroach upon: to eat in a restaurant; **eat the air** (*Shak.*) to be deluded with hopes; **eat up** to devour entirely: to consume, absorb: to derive pleasure from (*fig.*); **what's eating you?** (*coll.*) what is irking you? [O.E. *etan*; cf. Ger. *essen,* O.N. *eta,* L. *edĕre,* Gr. *edein.*]

Eatanswill *ēt′ən-swil, n.* in *Pickwick Papers,* a pocket borough at which an election takes place: any corrupt election or selection.

eatche *ēch,* (*Scott*) *n.* a Scots form of **adze.**

eath, eathe, ethe *ēth, eth,* (*Spens.,* etc.) *adj.* easy. — *adv.* easily. — *adv.* **eath′ly.** [O.E. *ēathe,* easy, easily.]

eau¹ *ō, n.* the French word for water, used in English in various combinations. — **eau des creoles** (*dā krā-ol′*) a fine Martinique liqueur, made by distilling the flowers of the mammee-apple with spirit of wine; **eau de Cologne** see **Cologne water; eau de Javelle** see **Javel water; eau de Nil** a pale-green colour, Nile green; **eau de vie** (*də vē*) brandy.

eau². See **ea.**

eaves *ēvz, n.pl.* (orig. *sing.*) the projecting edge of the roof: anything projecting. — **eaves′drip, eaves′drop** the water that falls from the eaves of a house: the place where the drops fall: (**eavesdrop**) an act of eavesdropping. — *v.i.* **eaves′drop** to stand under the eaves or near the windows of a house to listen: to listen for secrets. — Also *v.t.* — **eaves′dropper** one who thus listens: one who tries to overhear private conversation; **eaves′dropping.** [O.E. *efes,* the clipped edge of thatch; cf. Icel. *ups.*]

ébauche *ā-bōsh,* (Fr.) *n.* rough draft, sketch.

ebb *eb, n.* the going back or retiring of the tide: a decline. — *v.i.* to flow back: to sink: to decline. — *adj.* (*obs.* or *dial.; Scott*) shallow. — *adj.* **ebb′less. — ebb′tide** the ebbing tide. — **at a low ebb** (*fig.*) in a low or weak state. [O.E. *ebba.*]

ebenezer *eb-ən-ēz′ər, n.* a memorial stone set up by Samuel after the victory of Mizpeh (1 Sam. vii. 12): a name sometimes applied to a chapel or meeting-house. [Heb. *eben-hā-'ezer,* stone of help.]

ébéniste *ā-bā-nēst,* (Fr.) *n.* a cabinet-maker.

Ebionite *ē′bi-ən-īt, n.* an early Christian holding the Mosaic law binding and denying the apostolate of Paul and the miraculous birth of Jesus. — *v.t.* **e′bionise, -ize.** — *adj.* **ebionitic** (*-it′ik*). — *ns.* **e′bionītism, e′bionism.** [Heb. *ebyōn,* poor.]

Eblis *eb′lis,* **Iblis** *ib′lis, n.* the chief of the fallen angels in Muslim mythology. [Ar. *Iblīs.*]

Ebola disease *ē-bō′lə diz-ēz′,* a virus disease occurring in Africa, similar to, but with a much higher mortality rate than, green monkey disease (q.v. under **green**).

ebony *eb′ən-i,* (*rare* esp. *poet.* **ebon** *eb′ən*), *n.* a kind of wood furnished by various species of *Diospyros* (family **Ebenā′ceae**) almost as heavy and hard as stone, usually black, admitting of a fine polish: a tree yielding it: a black person (*U.S. arch. derog.*), now black people in general, their concerns and sensibilities. — *adj.* made of ebony: black as ebony. — *v.t.* and *v.i.* **eb'onise, -ize** to make or become like ebony. — *ns.* **eb'onist** a worker in ebony; **eb'onite** black vulcanised rubber, vulcanite. [L. (*h*)*ebenus* — Gr. *ebenos*; cf. Heb. *hobnīm*, pl. of *hobni, obni* — *eben*, a stone.]

éboulement *ā-boōl'mā, n.* the falling in of the wall of a fortification: a landslide or landslip. [Fr.]

ebracteate *ē-brak'ti-āt, (bot.) adj.* without bracts. — *adj.* **ebract'eolate** without bracteoles. [L. *ē-*, without, from, *bractea*, a thin plate.]

ebriate, ebriated *ē'bri-āt, -id, adjs.* intoxicated. — *n.* **ebriety** (*ē-brī'i-ti*) drunkenness. — *adj.* **e'briōse** drunk. — *n.* **ebriŏs'ity.** [L. *ēbriāre, -ātum*, to make drunk.]

ébrillade *ā-brē-(l)yäd', n.* the sudden jerking of a horse's rein when he refuses to turn. [Fr.]

ebullient *i-bul'yənt, adj.* boiling up or over: agitated: enthusiastic. — *ns.* **ebull'ience, ebull'iency** a boiling over: cheerful enthusiasm; **ebull'ioscope** an apparatus for determining the boiling-points of liquids. — *adjs.* **ebullioscop'ic, -al.** — *adv.* **ebullioscop'ically.** — *ns.* **ebullios'copy; ebullition** (*eb-ə-lish'ən*) the act of boiling: agitation: an outbreak. [L. *ēbulliēns, -entis* — *ēbullīre* — *ē*, out, and *bullīre*, to boil.]

eburnean *eb-ûr'ni-ən, adj.* of or like ivory — also **ebur'neous.** — *ns.* **eburnā'tion** (*ēb-* or *eb-*) a morbid change of bone by which it becomes very hard and dense; **eburnificā'tion** the art of making like ivory. [L. *eburneus* — *ebur*, ivory.]

ecad *ek'ad, (bot.) n.* a plant form which is assumed to have adapted to its environment. [*ecology*, and suff. *-ad.*]

ecardinate *ē-kärd'in-āt, adj.* hingeless. — *n.pl.* **Ecard'inēs** a class of brachiopods without hinge or arm skeleton. [L. *ē-*, without, *cardō, -inis*, hinge.]

écarté¹ *ā-kär'tā, n.* a game in which cards may be discarded for others. [Fr., discarded — *é-*(L. *ēx*, out of, from), *carte*, a card.]

écarté² *ā-kär'tā, n.* in ballet, a position in which the arm and leg are extended to the side. [Fr., spread, separated.]

ecaudate *ē-kö'dāt, adj.* tailless. [L. *ē-*, without, *cauda*, tail.]

ecblastesis *ek-blas-tē'sis, (bot.) n.* proliferation of a floral axis. [Gr. *ekblastēsis*, budding forth — *ek*, out of, *blastos*, a sprout.]

ecbole *ek'bo-lē, n.* a digression (*rhet.*): the raising or sharpening of a tone (*mus.*). — *adj.* **ecbol'ic** (*med.*) inducing contractions of the uterus leading to parturition or abortion. — *n.* a drug with this quality. [Gr. *ekbolē*, throwing out — *ek*, out of, *ballein*, to throw.]

eccaleobion *e-kal-i-ō-bī'on, n.* a kind of incubator. [Gr. *ekkaleō bion*, I call forth life.]

ecce *ek'si, ek'ā, ek'e, ech'ā, (L.) interj.* behold. — **ecce homo** (*hō'mō, hom'ō*; L., man) behold the man (John xix. 5): a portrayal of Christ crowned with thorns (*art*); **ecce signum** (*sig'nəm, -nōom*) behold the sign or proof.

eccentric *ek-sen'trik, adj.* departing from the centre: not having the same centre as another, said of circles: out of the usual course: not conforming to common rules: odd. — *n.* a circle not having the same centre as another: a contrivance for taking an alternating rectilinear motion from a revolving shaft (*mech.*): an eccentric person. — *adj.* **eccen'trical.** — *adv.* **eccen'trically.** — *n.* **eccentricity** (*-sən-tris'*) the condition of being eccentric: in a conic section, the constant ratio of the distance of a point on the curve from the focus to its distance from the directrix (usually represented by *e*): singularity of conduct: oddness. [Gr. *ek*, out of, *kentron*, centre.]

ecchymosis *ek-i-mō'sis, n.* discoloration due to extravasation of blood. — *adjs.* **ecch'ymosed; ecchymŏt'ic.** [Gr. *ekchȳmōsis* — *ek*, out of, and *chȳmos*, juice.]

Eccles cake *ek'lz kāk*, a cake like a Banbury cake. [*Eccles* in Lancashire.]

ecclesia *i-klē'zi-ə, n.* a popular assembly, esp. of Athens,

where the people exercised full sovereignty, and every male citizen above twenty years could vote: applied by the Septuagint commentators to the Jewish commonwealth, and from them to the Christian Church. — *adj.* **ecclē'sial.** — *ns.* **ecclē'siarch** (*-ärk*) a ruler of the church; **ecclē'siast** the preacher — as the author of Ecclesiastes: an ecclesiastic; **Ecclesias'tes** one of the books of the Old Testament, traditionally ascribed to Solomon; **ecclesias'tic** one consecrated to the church, a priest, a clergyman. — *adjs.* **ecclesias'tic, -al** relating to the church. — *adv.* **ecclesias'tically.** — *ns.* **ecclesias'ticism** (*-sizm*) attachment to ecclesiastical observances, etc.: the churchman's temper or spirit; **Ecclesias'ticus** one of the books of the Apocrypha; **ecclesiol'atry** (Gr. *latreiā*, worship) excessive reverence for church forms and traditions; **ecclesiŏl'ater.** — *adj.* **ecclesiolŏg'ical.** — *ns.* **ecclesiŏl'ogist; ecclesiŏl'ogy** the science of church forms and traditions, of building and decorating churches: the science relating to the church. — **ecclesiastical year** see **year.** [L.L., — Gr. *ekklēsia*, an assembly called out of the world, the church — *ek*, out of, and *kaleein*, to call.]

ecco *ek'kō, (It.) imper.* here is: there: look there.

eccoprotic *ek-ō-prot'ik, adj.* laxative, mildly cathartic. — *n.* a laxative. [Gr. *ekkoprōtikos* — *ek*, out of, *kopros*, dung.]

eccrinology *ek-ri-nol'ə-ji, n.* the branch of physiology that relates to the secretions. — *adj.* **eccrine** (*ek'rīn*) of a gland, esp. the sweat glands, secreting externally. [Gr. *ek*, out of, *krīnein*, to separate, secrete.]

eccrisis *ek'ri-sis, n.* expulsion of waste or morbid matter. — *n.* **eccrit'ic** a medicine having the property of effecting this. [Gr. *ekkrisis*, secretion — *ek*, out, and *krisis*, separation.]

ecdysis *ek'di-sis, n.* the act of casting off an integument, sloughing. — *n.* **ecdysiast** (*-diz'; facet.*) a stripteaser. [Gr. *ekdysis* — *ek*, out of, *dyein*, to put on.]

échappé *ā-sha-pā, (Fr.) n.* in ballet, a leap with change of foot position.

eche *ēch, (Shak.) v.t.* to eke out: to augment. — Also **ech, eech, ich.** [O.E. *ēcan*; akin to L. *augēre*, to increase; see **eke.**]

echelon *esh'ə-lon, āsh-lō, n.* a stepwise arrangement of troops, ships, planes, etc.: a group of persons of one grade in an organisation. [Fr. *échelon* — *échelle*, ladder, stair; see **scale².**]

Echeveria *ech-ə-vē'ri-ə, ek-, n.* a genus of succulent plants of the Crassulaceae family: (without *cap.*) a plant of the genus. [Named after 19th-cent. Mexican botanical artist.]

Echidna *ek-id'nə, n.* a genus (also **Tachyglossus** *tak-iglos'əs*) of Australian toothless, spiny, egg-laying, burrowing monotremes: (without *cap.*) any member of the genus. — *n.* **echid'nine** snake-poison. [Gr. *echidna*, viper.]

echinus *e-kī'nəs, n.* a sea-urchin: the convex projecting moulding (of eccentric curve in Greek examples) supporting the abacus of the Doric capital (*archit.*). — *adjs.* **echinate, -d** (*ek'in-āt, -id*) prickly like a hedgehog: bristly. — *ns.* **Echī'nocac'tus** a large genus of ribbed, generally very spiny, cactuses; **echī'nococc'us** the bladder-worm stage (parasitic in cow, sheep, pig, man) of the dog tapeworm; **echī'noderm** any one of the **Echinoder'ma** or **Echīnoder'mata**, a phylum of radially symmetrical marine animals, having the body-wall strengthened by calcareous plates, and moving usually by tube-feet, distensible finger-like protrusions of a part of the coelom known as the water-vascular system — starfishes, sea-urchins, brittle-stars, sea-cucumbers, and sea-lilies. — *adjs.* **echinoder'mal; echinoder'matous; echī'noid** like a sea-urchin. — *n.* a sea-urchin. — *n.pl.* **Echīnoid'ea** the sea-urchins, a class of Echinoderma. — *n.* **Echīn'ops** a genus of Compositae found in southern Europe, the globe thistle, with flowers in globular clusters. [Gr. *echīnos*, a hedgehog.]

echo *ek'ō, n.* the sending back or reflection of sound or other waves: the repetition of sound by reflection: a

echt

echt 449 **e converso**

reflected sound: a soft-toned organ forming a part of some large organs: a device in verse in which a line ends with a word which recalls the sound of the last word of the preceding line: response: repetition: imitation: an imitator: conventional play to indicate what cards one holds: — *pl.* **echoes** (*ek′ōz*). — *v.i.* to reflect sound: to be sounded back: to resound: to play a card as echo. — *v.t.* to send back (sound or other waves): to send back the sound of: to repeat: to imitate: to follow slavishly: — *pr.p.* **ech′ōing**; *pa.t.* and *pa.p.* **ech′oed** (*-ōd*). — *n.* **ech′ōer**. — *adj.* **echō′ic** of the nature of an echo: onomatopoeic (*philol.*). — *v.i.* **ech′ōise**, **-ize**. — *ns.* **ech′ōism** the formation of imitative words; **ech′ōist** one who repeats like an echo. — *adj.* **ech′ōless** giving no echo: unresponsive. — *ns.* **echocar′diogram** the record produced by **echocardiog′raphy**, the investigation by means of ultrasound of certain internal parts of the heart and the ways in which they move in order to detect disease esp. of the heart valves; **echoenceph′alogram** the record produced by **echoencephalog′raphy**, the investigation of brain tissues by means of ultrasound waves beamed through the head; **ech′ogram** the record produced in echo-sounding; **echolalia** (*ek-ō-lā′li-ə*; Gr. *laliā*, talk) senseless or compulsive repetition of words heard, occurring in disease of the brain or in insanity; **echoprax′ia, echoprax′is** (Gr. *praxis*, doing) imitation by an insane person of postures or movements of those near him. — **echo chamber** a room in which sound can be echoed, for recording or radio effects, or when measuring acoustics; **echo location** determining (as a bat does) the position of objects by means of supersonic vibrations echoed from them; **ech′o-sounder** the apparatus used in echo-sounding; **ech′o-sounding** a method of measuring depth of water, locating shoals of fish, etc., by noting time for return of echo from the bottom, or bottom and shoal, etc.; **echo virus** any of a group of viruses which can cause respiratory and intestinal diseases, and meningitis (enteric cytopathogenic *h*uman *o*rphan virus). — **cheer to the echo** to applaud most heartily. [L., — Gr. *ēchō*, a sound.]

echt *ehht*, (Ger.) *adj.* genuine, authentic.

éclair *ā-kler′*, or *-klār′, n.* a cake, long in shape but short in duration, with cream filling and chocolate or other icing. [Fr. *éclair*, lightning.]

éclaircissement *ā-kler-sēs′mā, n.* the act of clearing up anything: explanation. **come to an éclaircissement** to come to an understanding: to explain conduct that seemed equivocal. [Fr. *éclaircir* — L. *ex*, out, *clārus*, clear.]

eclampsia *i-klamp′si-ə, n.* a condition resembling epilepsy: now confined to acute toxaemia with convulsive fits about the time of childbirth. — Also **eclamp′sy**. — *adj.* **eclamp′tic**. [Gr. *eklampsis* — *eklampein*, to flash forth, to burst forth violently (as a fever) — *ek*, out of, *lampein*, to shine.]

éclat *ā-klä, n.* a striking effect: showy splendour: distinction: applause. [Fr. *éclat*, from O.Fr. *esclater*, to break, to shine.]

eclectic *ek-lek′tik, adj.* selecting or borrowing: choosing the best out of everything: broad, the opposite of exclusive. — *n.* one who selects opinions from different systems, esp. in philosophy. — *adv.* **eclec′tically**. — *n.* **eclec′ticism** (*-sizm*) the practice of an eclectic: the doctrine of the **eclec′tics**, a name applied to certain Greek thinkers in the 2nd and 1st centuries B.C., later to Leibniz and Cousin. [Gr. *eklektikos* — *ek*, from, *legein*, to choose.]

eclipse *i-klips′, n.* the total or partial disappearance of a heavenly body by the interposition of another between it and the spectator, or by passing into its shadow — can be *total, partial,* or *annular* (q.v.): a throwing into the shade: loss of brilliancy: darkness. — *v.t.* to hide wholly or in part: to darken: to throw into the shade, to cut out, surpass. — *n.* **eclip′tic** the great circle in which the plane containing the centres of the earth and sun cuts the celestial sphere: hence, the apparent path of the sun's annual motion among the fixed stars: a great circle in which that plane cuts the earth's surface at any moment. — *adj.* pertaining to an eclipse or the ecliptic. — **eclipse plumage** dull plumage apparent in certain usu. brilliant-coloured birds out of the mating season. [O.Fr. — L. *eclīpsis* — Gr. *ekleipsis*, failure — *ek*, out of, *leipein*, to leave.]

eclogite, eklogite *ek′lə-jīt, n.* a crystalline rock composed of red garnet and green omphacite or smaragdite. [Gr. *eklogē*, selection (from the unusual minerals that compose it) — *ek*, out of, *legein*, to choose.]

eclogue *ek′log, n.* a short pastoral poem like Virgil's *Bucolics*. [L. *ecloga* — Gr. *eklogē*, a selection, esp. of poems — *ek*, out of, *legein*, to choose.]

eclosion *i-klō′zhən, n.* emergence, esp. of insect from pupal case or larva from egg. — *v.i.* **eclose′**. [Fr. *éclosion* — L., *ex-, claudĕre*, to shut.]

eco-, *ēk′, ek′ō-,* in composition, concerned with habitat and environment in relation to living organisms, as in ecology. — *ns.* **ec′ocīde** the destruction of the aspects of the environment which enable it to support life; **ec′ofreak, ec′onut** (*derog. slang*) a person much concerned about the effects of man's behaviour on the environment; **ecophō′bia** fear of one's home surroundings; **ec′ospecies** a group of ecotypes; **ec′osphere** the parts of the universe, or esp. the earth, in which life is possible; **ec′osystem** a unit consisting of a community of organisms and their environment; **ec′otype** a group of organisms which have adapted to a particular environment, and so have become different from other groups within the species.

ecology *ē-kol′ə-ji, ek-ol′, ik-, n.* a study of plants, or of animals, or of peoples and institutions, in relation to environment. — *adjs.* **ecologic** (*-ko-loj′ik*), **-al**. — *adv.* **ecolog′ically**. — *n.* **ecol′ogist**. — Also **oecology**, etc. [Gr. *oikos*, house, *logos*, discourse.]

economy *ē-kon′ə-mi, i-kon′, e-, n.* the management of a household (*arch.*): the administration of the material resources of an individual, community, or country: the state of these resources: a frugal and judicious expenditure of money: thrift: a dispensation, as *the Christian economy*: the efficient use of something, e.g. speech, effort, etc.: making one's presentation of doctrine, etc. suit the needs or not offend the prejudices of one's hearers (*theol.*): an organised system: regular operations, as of nature. — *adj.* pertaining to a cheaper class of air or sea travel: (of goods) of a larger size, so costing less than several small sizes (of packets, etc.). — *adj.* **economet′ric**. — *n.* **econometrician** (*-mə-trish′ən*). — *n. sing.* **economet′rics** statistical analysis of economic data and their interrelations. — *n.* **economet′rist**. — *adjs.* **economic** (*ē-kə-nom′ik, ek-ə-*) pertaining or having reference to economy or to economics: relating to industry or business, e.g. *economic geography, history,* etc., from the utilitarian viewpoint: operated at, or capable of yielding, a profit: economical; **econom′ical** conducive to thrift: frugal: careful: economic. — *adv.* **econom′ically**. — *n. sing.* or *n.pl.* **econom′ics** the science of household management (*obs.*; but see **home economics** under **home**): pecuniary position and management: financial or economic aspects. — *n.sing.* political economy. — *n.* **economisā′tion, -z-** the act of economising. — *v.i.* **econ′omise, -ize** to manage with economy: to spend money carefully: to save. — *v.t.* to use prudently: to spend with frugality. — *ns.* **econ′omīser, -z-** one who is economical: a device for saving heat, fuel, etc.; **econ′omism** a (sometimes too great) belief that economic causes and theories are of primary importance; **econ′omist** one who studies or is an expert on political economy: an economiser. — **economic zone** the coastal sea-area which a country claims as its own territory (for fishing, mining, etc.). [L. *oeconomia* — Gr. *oikonomiā* — *oikos*, a house, *nomos*, a law.]

e contra *ē* (*ā*) *kon′tra*, (L.L.) contrariwise, conversely.

e contrario *ē kon-trär′i-ō, ā kon-trä′ri-ō*, (L.L.) on the contrary.

e converso *ē kon-vûr′sō, ā kon-ver′,* (*-wer′*), (L.L.)

conversely, by logical conversion.

écorché *ā-kör-shā'*, *n.* a figure in which the muscles are represented stripped of the skin, for the purposes of artistic study. [Pa.p. of Fr. *écorcher*, to flay.]

écossaise *ā-ko-sez'*, *n.* originally a dance or dance-tune of Scottish origin in 3-4 or 2-4 time: later a lively country-dance or its music in 2-4 time. — **douche écossaise** the alternation of hot and cold douches. [Fr., fem. of *écossais*, Scottish.]

ecostate *ē-kos'tāt*, *adj.* ribless. [L. *ē*, from, *costa*, rib.]

ecphonesis *ek-fō-nē'sis*, *n.* exclamation (*rhet.*): in the Greek Church, the part of the service spoken in an audible tone: — *pl.* **-nē'ses.** [Gr. *ekphōnesis* — *ek*, out, *phōnē*, voice.]

ecphractic *ek-frak'tik*, (*obs. med.*) *adj.* serving to remove obstructions. — *n.* a drug with such properties. [Gr. *ekphraktikos* — *ek*, from, *phrassein*, to enclose.]

écraseur *ā-kra-zœr'*, *n.* a surgical instrument in the form of a wire or chain loop which cuts as it tightens. [Fr. *écraser*, to crush.]

écritoire *ā-krē-twär*, (Fr.) *n.* the modern form of **escritoire.**

ecru *e-*, *ā-krōō'*, *-krü'*, *n.* unbleached linen: its colour. — *adj.* like unbleached linen. [Fr. *écru* — L. *ex*, intensive, *crūdus*, raw.]

ecstasy *ek'stə-si*, *n.* a state of temporary mental alienation and altered or diminished consciousness: excessive joy: enthusiasm, or any exalted feeling. — *v.t.* to fill with joy. — *adj.* **ec'stasied** enraptured. — *n.* **ec'stasis** ecstasy. — *v.t.* and *v.i.* **ec'stasise, -ize.** — *adj.* **ecstat'ic** causing ecstasy: amounting to ecstasy: rapturous. — *n.* one given to ecstasy: something spoken in a state of ecstasy. — *adv.* **ecstat'ically.** [Gr. *ekstasis* — *ek*, from, and root of *histanai*, to make to stand.]

ectasis *ek'tə-sis*, *n.* the lengthening of a short syllable: dilatation: — *pl.* **-ases.** [Gr. *ektasis*, stretching.]

ecthlipsis *ek-thlip'sis*, *n.* suppression of a sound, esp. of a syllable ending in *m* in verse before a vowel: — *pl.* **-ses** (*-sēz*). [Gr. *ekthlīpsis* — *ek*, from, *thlībein*, to rub or squeeze.]

ecthyma *ek-thī'mə*, *n.* a skin eruption in large pustules. [Gr. *ekthȳma*, a pustule.]

ecto- *ek-tō-*, in composition, outside, often opp. to **endo-, ento-.** See also **exo-.** — *n.* **ec'toblast** (Gr. *blastos*, a shoot, bud) the outer cell-layer of a gastrula, the epiblast. — *adj.* **ectoblas'tic.** — *ns.* **ec'tocrine** an organic substance, released in minute amounts by an organism into the environment, which exerts an effect on its own and other species' form, development or behaviour; **ec'toderm** (Gr. *derma*, skin) the external germinal layer of epiblast of the embryo, or any part of the mature animal derived from it. — *adjs.* **ectoderm'al; ectoderm'ic.** — *n.* **ec'tomorph** (Gr. *morphē*, form) a person of light and delicate build. — *adj.* **ectomorph'ic.** — *ns.* **ec'tomorphy; ectopar'asite** an external parasite; **ec'toplasm** (Gr. *plasma*, mould) the outer layer of cytoplasm of a cell (*biol.*): an emanation of bodily appearance believed by some spiritualists to come from a medium. — *adjs.* **ectoplas'mic; ectoplas'tic.** — *n.* **ec'tosarc** (Gr. *sarx, sarkos*, flesh) ectoplasm; **ec'totherm** a cold-blooded animal. — *adjs.* **ectotherm'ic; ectotroph'ic** (Gr. *trophē*, food; *bot.*) of a mycorrhiza, having its hyphae mainly on the outside of the root that it feeds. — *n.* and *adj.* **ectozō'an.** — *adj.* **ectozō'ic.** — *n.* **ectozō'on** (Gr. *zōion*, animal) an animal ectoparasite: — *pl.* **ectozō'a.** [Gr. *ektos*, outside.]

ectogenesis *ek-tō-jen'i-sis*, *n.* development outside the body: variation in response to outside conditions. — *adjs.* **ectogenetic** (*-jən-et'ik*) produced by or pertaining to ectogenesis; **ectogen'ic** of external origin: ectogenous; **ectogenous** (*ek-toj'ə-nəs*) capable of living independently, or outside the body of the host (as some parasites). — *n.* **ectog'eny** the effect of pollen on the tissues of a plant. [Gr. *ektos*, outside, *genesis*, generation.]

ectomorph, etc., **ectoparasite.** See **ecto-.**
ectophyte *ek'tō-fīt*, *n.* a vegetable ectoparasite. — *adj.*

ectophytic (*-fit'ik*). [Gr. *ektos*, outside, *phyton*, a plant.]

ectopia *ek-tō-pi-ə*, **ectopy** *ek'to-pi*, (*path.*) *ns.* morbid displacement of parts: a condition in which the foetus is outside the womb. — *adj.* **ectop'ic.** [Gr. *ek*, from, *topos*, place.]

ectoplasm... to ... ectozoon. See **ecto-.**

ectropion, -um *ek-trōp'i-on, -əm*, *ns.* eversion of the margin of the eyelid, so that the red inner surface is exposed. — *adj.* **ectrop'ic.** [Gr. *ek*, out of, *trepein*, to turn.]

ectype *ek'tīp*, *n.* a reproduction or copy. — *adj.* **ectypal** (*ek'ti-pəl*). — *n.* **ectypog'raphy.** [Gr. *ek*, from, and *typos*, a stamp.]

écu *ā-kü*, or *ā-kü'*, *n.* a French silver coin, usually considered as equivalent to the English crown, a French gold coin weighing about 60 grains, etc. (*hist.*): formerly, a common name for the five-franc piece. [Fr., — L. *scutum*, a shield.]

écuelle *ā-kwel'*, or *ā-kü-el'*, *n.* a two-handled soup bowl. [Fr., — L. *scutella*, drinking-bowl.]

ecumenic, -al *ē-kū* or *ek-ū-men'ik, -əl*, *adjs.* general, universal, belonging to the entire Christian Church: of or relating to the ecumenical movement. — *adv.* **ecumen'ically.** — *ns.* **ecumen'icalism, ecumen'icism** (*-is-izm*), **ecumen'ism** doctrines and practice of the Christian ecumenical movement (also *fig.*). — *n. sing.* **ecumen'ics** the study of ecumenical awareness and the ecumenical movement in the Christian church. — Also **oecumenic,** etc. — **ecumenical movement** a movement within the Christian church towards unity on all fundamental issues of belief, worship, etc. [L. *oecumenicus* — Gr. *oikoumenikos* — *oikoumenē* (*gē*), inhabited (world).]

écurie *ā-kü-rē*, (Fr.) *n.* lit. stable: a team of cars under individual or joint ownership which take part in motor racing.

eczema *ek'si-mə*, *n.* a skin disease, in which part of the skin is red, with numerous small papules that turn into vesicles. — *adj.* **eczematous** (*-sem'*, or *-zem'ət-əs*). [Gr. *ekzeein* — *ek*, out of, *zeein*, to boil.]

edacious *i-*, *ē-*, *e-dā'shəs*, *adj.* given to eating: gluttonous. — *adv.* **edā'ciously.** — *ns.* **edā'ciousness; edacity** (*i-das'i-ti*). [L. *edāx, edācis* — *edĕre*, to eat.]

Edam *ē'dam*, *n.* a type of mild Dutch cheese, shaped into globes with a red outer skin. [After *Edam* near Amsterdam.]

edaphic *i-daf'ik*, *adj.* pertaining to the soil. — *n.* **edaphology** (*ed-ə-fol'ə-ji*). [Gr. *edaphos*, ground.]

Edda *ed'ə*, *n.* the name of two Scandinavian books — the *Elder Edda*, a collection of ancient mythological and heroic songs (9th–11th century, or earlier); and the *Younger* or *Prose Edda*, by Snorri Sturluson (*c.* 1230), mythological stories, poetics, and prosody. — *adjs.* **Eddā'ic; Edd'ic.** [O.N. apparently akin to *ōdr*, mad, *ōthr*, spirit, mind, poetry; cf. **wood²**; Ger. *Wut*, fury; L. *vātēs*, poet, seer.]

eddish *ed'ish*, *n.* pasturage, or the eatable growth of grass after mowing. [Dubiously referred to O.E. *edisc*, a park.]

eddoes *ed'ōz*, *n.pl.* the tubers of various plants, especially of taro (*Colocasia*): — *sing.* **edd'o.** [From a W. African word.]

eddy *ed'i*, *n.* a current running back, contrary to the main stream, thus causing a circular motion: a whirlpool: a whirlwind. — *v.i.* to move round and round: — *pr.p.* **edd'ying;** *pa.t.* and *pa.p.* **edd'ied.** — **eddy current** an electric current caused by varying electromotive forces which are due to varying magnetic fields, and causing heating in motors, transformers, etc. — Also **Foucault current** (*fōō-kō'*). [Cf. O.N. *itha*; prob. conn. with O.E. pfx. *ed-*, back.]

edelweiss *ā'dəl-vīs*, *n.* a small white composite (*Leontopodium alpinum*), with woolly heads, found in damp places on the Alps. [Ger. *edel*, noble, *weiss*, white.]

edema, edematose, -ous. See **oedema.**

Eden *ē'dən*, *n.* the garden of Adam and Eve: a paradise.

— *adj.* **Edenic** (*-den'*).   [Heb. *ēden*, delight, pleasure.]

edentate *ē-den'tāt, adj.* without teeth: wanting front teeth. — *n.* a member of the **Edentā'ta**, a New World order of mammals having no front teeth or no teeth at all — sloths, ant-eaters, armadillos, and, formerly, certain Old World edentate animals, as the pangolins. — *adjs.* **eden'tal** of the edentates; **eden'tulous** toothless.   [L. *ēdentātus*, toothless — *ē*, out of, *dēns, dentis*, a tooth.]

edge *ej, n.* the border of anything: a rim: thc brink: the intersection of the faces of a solid figure: a ridge or crest: the cutting edge of an instrument: something that wounds or cuts: keenness: sharpness of mind or appetite: irritability: advantage (*coll.*). — *v.t.* to put an edge on: to place a border on: to border: to egg, urge on (*arch.*): to move gradually: to thrust edgewise: to strike with the edge. — *v.i.* to move sideways: to move gradually. — *adjs.* **edged; edge'less** without an edge: blunt. — *n.* **edg'er** someone or something that edges: a garden tool for trimming the edge of a lawn. — *advs.* **edge'ways, edge'wise** in the direction of the edge: sideways. — *ns.* **edg'iness** angularity, over-sharpness of outline: the state of being on edge; **edg'ing** any border or fringe round a garment: a border of box, etc., round a flower-bed. — *adj.* **edg'y** with edges: sharp, hard in outline: irritable, on edge. — **edge coal** a steeply dipping coal-seam; **edge rail** a rail of such form that the carriage-wheels roll on its edges, being held there by flanges; **edge tool, edged tool** a tool with a sharp edge. — **edge in a word, get a word in edgeways** to get a word in with difficulty; **edge out** to remove or get rid of gradually: to defeat by a small margin (*U.S.*); **go, be over the edge** (*coll.*) to go, have gone, beyond what can be endured: to have, have had, a nervous breakdown; **have the, an, edge on, against** to have the, an, advantage over; **inside, outside, edge** a skating movement on the inner or outer edge of the skate; **on edge** in a state of expectant irritability: nervous, tense: all agog; **play with edge tools** to deal carelessly with dangerous matters; **set on edge** to excite; **set one's teeth on edge** to cause a strange grating feeling in the teeth: to give a feeling of abhorrent discomfort: formerly, to make eager, stimulate desire.   [O.E. *ecg;* cf. Ger. *Ecke,* I., *aciēs.*]

edgebone. Same as **aitchbone.**

edh. See **eth.**

edible *ed'ĭ-bl, adj.* able to bc eaten. — *n.* something for food. — *ns.* **edibil'ity, ed'ibleness** fitncss for being eaten.   [L. *edibilis* — *edēre*, to eat.]

edict *ē'dikt, n.* something proclaimed by authority: an order issued by a king or lawgiver. — *adj.* **edict'al.** — *adv.* **edict'ally.**   [L. *ēdictum* — *ē*, out of, *dīcěre, dictum,* to say.]

edifice *ed'i-fis, n.* a building: a large building or house. — *adj.* **edificial** (*-fish'l*) structural.   [Fr. *édifice* — L. *aedificium* — *aedificāre;* see **edify.**]

edify *ed'i-fī, v.t.* to build (*arch.*): to establish (*obs.*): furnish with buildings (*Spens.*): to build up the faith of: to strengthen spiritually towards faith and holiness: to improve the mind of: — *pr.p.* **ed'ifying;** *pa.t.* and *pa.p.* **ed'ified.** — *n.* **edificā'tion** instruction: progress in knowledge or in goodness. — *adj.* **edif'icatory** (or *ed'*) tending to edification. — *n.* **ed'ifier** one who edifies. — *adj.* **ed'ifying** instructive: improving. — *adv.* **ed'ifyingly.**   [L. *aedificāre* — *aedēs,* a temple, house, *facěre,* to make.]

edile. Same as **aedile.**

Edinburgh rock *ed'in-bə-rə rok',* a sweetmeat in the form of brittle pastel-coloured sticks.   [First manufactured by an Edinburgh confectioner in 1822.]

edit *ed'it, v.t.* to prepare for publication, broadcasting, etc.: to superintend the publication of: to compile: to garble, cook up: to revise: to censor, bowdlerise: to make up the final version of a motion picture by selection, rearrangement, etc., of material photographed previously. — *ns.* **edi'tion** the publication of a book (*obs.*): one of the different forms in which a book is published: the form given to a text by its editor: the number of copies of a book printed at a time, or at different times without alteration: number of identical articles, as e.g. copies of a work of art, issued at one time: reproduction; **ed'itor** one who edits books, etc.: one who conducts a newspaper, periodical, etc., or a section of it: — *fem.* **ed'itress.** — *adj.* **editō'rial** (or *-tö'*) of or belonging to an editor. — *n.* an article in a newspaper written by an editor or leader writer. — *v.i.* **edito'rialise, -ize** to introduce personal opinions or bias into reporting: to expound one's views in an editorial or in the style of one. — *n.* **editorialisā'tion, -z-.** — *adv.* **edito'rially.** — *n.* **ed'itorship.** — **edit out** to remove (a piece of film, tape, etc.) during editing.   [L. *ēdere, ēdītum* — *ē,* from, *dāre,* to give.]

edite, bibite *e'di-tē, bi'bi-tē, e'di-te, bi'bi-te,* (L.) eat, drink.

edition. See **edit.**

édition de luxe *ā-dē-syɔ̃ də lüks,* (Fr.) a splendid and expensive edition of a book.

editio princeps *i-dish'i-ō prin'seps, ā-dit'i-ō prin'keps,* (L.) original edition (esp. of a work till then known only in MS).

editor, etc. See **edit.**

edriophthalmic *ed-ri-of-thal'mik, adj.* (of crustaceans) with stalkless eyes. — Also **edriophthal'mian, edriophthal'mous.**   [Gr. *hedrion,* dim. of *hedrā,* seat, *ophthalmos,* eye.]

educate *ed'ū-kāt, v.t.* to bring up and instruct: to teach: to train. — *adj.* **ed'ucable.** — *ns.* **educabil'ity; educātabil'ity; educā'tion** bringing up or training, as of a child: instruction: strengthening of the powers of body or mind: culture. — *adj.* **educā'tional.** — *adv.* **educā'tionally.** — *ns.* **educā'tion(al)ist** one skilled in methods of educating or teaching: one who promotes education. — *adj.* **ed'ucātive** of or pertaining to education: tending to teach. — *n.* **ed'ucātor.** — *adj.* **educatory** (*ed'* or *-kā'tə-ri*).   [L. *ēducāre, -ātum,* to rear — *ēducěre* — *ē,* from, *dūcěre,* to lead.]

educe *i-* or *ē-dūs', v.t.* to draw out: to extract: to cause to appear, elicit. — *n.* **educe'ment.** — *adj.* **educ'ible.** — *ns.* **educt** (*ē'dukt*) what is educed; **eduction** (*ē-duk'shən*) the act of educing: exhaust of an engine; **educ'tor** he who, or that which, educes.   [L. *ēdūcěre, ēductum* — *ē,* from, and *dūcěre,* to lead.]

edulcorate *ι-dul'kə-rāt, v.t.* to sweeten (*obs.*): to free from soluble particles by washing. — *adj.* **edul'corant.** — *n.* **edulcorā'tion.** — *adj.* **edul'corātive.** — *n.* **edul'corātor.**   [L. *ē-,* intens., *dulcōrāre,* to sweeten — *dulcis,* sweet.]

eduskunta *ā-dōos-kōon'tä, n.* the unicameral Finnish parliament, elected every four years.   [Finn.]

Edwardian *ed-wörd'i-ən* (*arch.* and *U.S.* also *-wärd'*), *adj.* belonging to or characteristic of the reign of (any) King *Edward,* esp. Edward VII: (of a motor-car) built in the period 1905 to 1918, coming between veteran and vintage cars. — Also *n.* — *n.* **Edward'ianism.**

ee *ē.* Scottish form of **eye**[2]. — *pl.* **een.**

eech. See **eche.**

eek *ēk, interj.* of fright, used conventionally in children's comics, etc.   [Representative of a shriek or squeal.]

eel *ēl, n.* any fish of the *Anguillidae, Muraenidae,* or other family of *Apodes,* fishes with long smooth cylindrical or ribbon-shaped bodies, scaleless or nearly, without pelvic fins: extended to various other fishes of similar form, as the **sand eel** (or launce), **electric eel:** extended also to some eel-like thread-worms (also **eel'worm**): a slippery person. — *adj.* **eel'y.** — **eel'-bas'ket** a basket for catching eels; **eel'fare** (O.E. *faran,* to travel) a migratory passage of young eels: a brood of young eels: a young eel; **eel'grass, eel'wrack** grasswrack (*Zostera*), a grasslike flowering plant of the pondweed family, growing in sea-water; **eel'pout** (*-powt;* O.E. *ælepūte*) the burbot: the viviparous blenny; **eel'-set** a net placed across a river to catch eels; **eel'-spear** an instrument with broad prongs for catching eels; **eel'-worm** a nematode. — **salt eel** (*obs.*) a rope's end.   [O.E. *ǣl;* Ger. *Aal,* Du. *aal.*]

een. See **ee.**

e'en *ēn.* A contraction of **even**[1,2].

e'er *ār*. A contraction of **ever**.

eerie, eery *ē'ri, adj.* exciting fear: weird: affected with fear, timorous (*dial.*). — *adv.* **ee'rily.** — *n.* **ee'riness.** [Scot.; M.E. *arh, eri* — O.E. *ærg* (*earg*), timid.]

eeven, eevn, eev'n, eevning. Old spellings (*Milt.*) of **even** (*n., adj., adv.*) and **evening.**

ef *ef, n.* the sixth letter of the alphabet (F, f).

eff *ef, euph.* for **fuck**, esp. in *adj.* **eff'ing** and *v.i.* **eff off.** — **eff'ing and blinding** swearing.

effable *ef'ə-bl,* (*arch.*) *adj.* capable of being expressed. [Fr., — L. *effārī* — *ex*, out, *fārī,* to speak.]

efface *i-, e-fās', v.t.* to destroy the surface of: to rub out: to obliterate, wear away. — *adj.* **efface'able.** — *n.* **efface'ment.** — **efface oneself** to avoid notice. [Fr. *effacer* — L. *ex,* out, *faciēs,* face.]

effect *i-fekt', n.* the result of an action: the impression produced: purport: reality: (in *pl.*) goods, property: (in *pl.*) sound, and also lighting, devices contributing to the illusion of the place and circumstance in which the action is carried on (*theatre, cinema,* etc.). — *v.i.* to produce: to accomplish, bring about. — *n.* **effec'ter.** — *adjs.* **effec'tible** that may be effected; **effec'tive** having power to effect: causing something: successful in producing a result or effect: powerful: serviceable: actual: in force. — *n.* a soldier, or a body of soldiers, ready for service. — *adv.* **effec'tively.** — *n.* **effec'tiveness.** — *adj.* **effect'less** without effect, useless. — *n.* and *adj.* **effec'tor** (*biol.*) (an organ or substance) that effects a response to stimulus. — *adj.* **effec'tual** successful in producing the desired effect: decisive (*Shak.*). — *ns.* **effectual'ity; effec'tualness.** — *adv.* **effec'tually.** — *v.t.* **effec'tuate** to accomplish. — *n.* **effectuā'tion.** — **effective rate** (also **sterling effective rate**) the percentage deviation of sterling from its Smithsonian parity (q.v.) against an average of selected foreign currencies, weighted according to their U.K. trade importance; **effectual calling** (*theol.*) the invitation to come to Christ received by the elect. — **for effect** so as to make a telling impression; **general effect** the effect produced, by a picture, etc., as a whole; **give effect to** to carry out, perform; **in effect** in truth, really: substantially; **leave no effects** to die without property to bequeath; **take effect** to begin to operate: to come into force. [O.Fr., — L. *effectus* — *ex,* out, *facĕre,* to make.]

effeir[1], **effere** *e-fēr',* (*Scot.*) *n.* affair: appearance, show, array. [**affair**.]

effeir[2], **effere** *e-fēr',* (*obs.*) *v.i.* to appertain: to suit. [O.Fr. *afferir* — L. *ad,* to, *ferīre,* to strike.]

effeminate *i-fem'in-ət, adj.* womanish: unmanly: weak: soft: voluptuous: feminine (*Shak.*). — *n.* an effeminate person. — *v.t.* (*-āt; arch.*) to make womanish: to weaken, unman. — Also *v.i.* (*arch.*). — Also **effem'inise, -ize.** — *n.* **effem'inacy** (*-ə-si*) womanish softness or weakness: indulgence in unmanly pleasures. — *adv.* **effem'inately.** — *n.* **effem'inateness.** [L. *effēmināre, -ātum,* to make womanish — *ex,* out, and *fēmina,* a woman.]

effendi *e-fen'di, n.* a title for civil officials and educated persons generally (abolished in Turkey in 1934). [Turk.; from Gr. *authentēs,* an absolute master.]

efferent *ef'ə-rənt, adj.* conveying outward or away, as (*zool.*) **efferent nerve,** a nerve carrying impulses away from the central nervous system. — *n.* **eff'erence.** [L. *ē,* from, *ferēns, -entis,* pr.p. of *ferre,* to carry.]

effervesce *ef-ər-ves', v.i.* to boil up: to bubble and hiss: to froth up. — *ns.* **effervesc'ence; effervesc'ency.** — *adjs.* **effervesc'ent** boiling or bubbling from the disengagement of gas; **effervesc'ible.** — *adv.* **effervesc'ingly.** [L. *effervēscĕre* — *ex,* intens., and *fervēre,* to boil.]

effete *e-fēt', adj.* exhausted: degenerate, decadent: become barren (*obs.*). — *adv.* **effete'ly.** — *n.* **effete'ness.** [L. *effētus,* weakened by having brought forth young — *ex,* out, *fētus,* a bringing forth young.]

efficacious *ef-i-kā'shəs, adj.* able to produce the result intended. — *adv.* **efficā'ciously.** — *ns.* **efficā'ciousness; efficacity** (*-kas'i-ti*), **eff'icacy** (*-kə-si*) the power of

producing an effect: effectiveness. [L. *efficāx, -ācis* — *efficĕre;* see **efficient.**]

efficient *i-fish'ənt, adj.* capable of doing what may be required: effective. — *n.* (*arch.*) the person or thing that effects. — *ns.* **effi'cience** (*arch.*) efficient action or power; **effi'ciency** power to produce the result intended, adequate fitness: ratio of a machine's output of energy to input. — *adv.* **effi'ciently.** [Fr., — L. *efficiēns, -entis,* pr.p. of *efficĕre* — *ex,* out, *facĕre,* to make.]

effierce *e-fērs',* (*Spens.*) *v.t.* to make fierce.

effigurate *e-fig'u-rāt, adj.* having a definite shape. — *n.* **effigurā'tion** an axial outgrowth in a flower. [L. *ef-, ex-,* intens., and **figurate.**]

effigy *ef'i-ji, n.* a likeness or figure of a person: the head or impression on a coin — (*arch.*) **effigies** (*ef-ij'i-ēz*): — *pl.* **effigies** (*ef'i-jiz; arch. ef-ij'i-ēz*). — **burn, hang, in effigy** to burn or hang a figure of a person, as an expression of dislike. [L. *effigiēs* — *effingĕre* — *ex,* intens., *fingĕre,* to form.]

effing. See **eff.**

effleurage *ef-lə-räzh', n.* a stroking movement in massage. — Also *v.i.* and *v.t.* [Fr., glancing, grazing.]

effloresce *ef-lo-res', v.i.* to blossom forth: to become covered with a powdery crust (*chem.*): to form such a crust. — *n.* **effloresc'ence** production of flowers: the time of flowering: a redness of the skin: a powdery surface crust: the formation of such a crust: giving up of water of crystallisation to the atmosphere. — *adj.* **effloresc'ent.** [L. *efflōrēscĕre* — *ex,* out, *flōrēscĕre,* to blossom — *flōs, flōris,* a flower.]

effluent *ef'loo-ənt, adj.* flowing out. — *n.* a stream that flows out of another stream or lake: liquid industrial waste: outflow from sewage during purification. — *n.* **eff'luence** a flowing out: emanation. [L. *effluēns, -entis,* pr.p. of *effluĕre* — *ex,* out, *fluĕre,* to flow.]

effluvium *e-floo'vi-əm, n.* minute particles that flow out from bodies: disagreeable vapours rising from decaying matter: — *pl.* **efflu'via.** — *adj.* **efflu'vial.** [L.L., — L. *effluĕre.*]

efflux *ef'luks, n.* the act of flowing out: that which flows out. — Also **effluxion** (*e-fluk'shən*). [L. *effluĕre* — *ex,* out, *fluĕre, fluxum,* to flow.]

efforce *e-förs', -förs',* (*obs.*) *v.t.* to compel: to force: to force open: to do violence to: to put forward with force. [Fr., *efforcer* — L.L. *exfortiāre* — *ex,* out, *fortis,* strong.]

effort *ef'ərt, n.* a putting forth of strength: attempt: struggle: a piece of work produced by way of attempt: anything done or produced (*coll.*). — *adjs.* **eff'ortful** done with effort, laboured; **eff'ortless** making no effort, passive: easy, showing no sign of effort. [Fr., — L. *ex,* out, *fortis,* strong.]

effray, effraide. Obsolete forms of **affray, afraid.**

effrontery *i-, e-frunt'ər-i, n.* shamelessness: impudence: insolence. [Fr. *effronterie* — L. *effrōns, effrontis* — *ex,* out, without, *frōns, frontis,* forehead.]

effulge *i-, e-fulj', v.i.* to shine forth: to beam: — *pr.p.* **efful'ging;** *pa.t.* and *pa.p.* **efful'ged'.** — *n.* **efful'gence** great lustre or brightness: a flood of light. — *adj.* **efful'gent** shining forth: extremely bright: splendid. — *adv.* **efful'gently.** [L. *effulgēre,* to shine out, pr.p. *effulgēns, -entis,* — *ex,* out, *fulgēre,* to shine.]

effuse *e-fūz', v.t.* to pour out: to pour forth (as words): to shed (as blood): to spread: to let loose (*Thomson*). — *v.i.* to flow out. — *n.* (*e-fūs'; Shak.*) effusion, shedding. — *adj.* (*e-fūs'*) poured out: loosely spreading (*bot.*): (of shells) with the lips separated by a groove. — *ns.* **effusiometer** (*e-fūz-i-om'i-tər*) an apparatus for comparing molecular weights of gases by observing the relative time taken to stream out through a small hole; **effusion** (*e-fū'zhən*) pouring or streaming out: emission: shedding (as of blood): an abnormal outpouring of fluid into the tissues or cavities of the body (*med.*): an outpouring, esp. in poetic form: effusiveness. — *adj.* **effusive** (*e-fū'ziv*) poured out abundantly: gushing: poured out at the surface in a state of fusion, volcanic (*geol.*): expressing emotion in a copious and demonstrative manner. — *adv.* **effus'ively.** — *n.* **effus'-iveness.** [L. *effundĕre, effūsum — ex,* out, *fundĕre,* to pour.]

Efik *ef'ik, n.* (a member of) a people of S.E. Nigeria: the language of this people.

eft[1] *eft, n.* a lizard (*obs.*): a newt. [O.E. *efeta*; see **newt.**]

eft[2] *eft,* (*obs.*) *adv.* afterwards: again: forthwith: moreover. — *adv.* **eftsoons** (*eft-sōōnz'*; *obs.*) soon afterwards, forthwith. [O.E. *æft, eft,* after, again; see **aft.**]

eftest *eft'ist,* (*Warwickshire, Worcestershire; Shak.* Much Ado, IV, ii. 38) *adj. superl.* readiest: most convenient.

eftsoons. See **eft**[2].

egad *i-gad', interj.* a minced oath. [Perh. orig. **ah! God!**]

egal *ē'gəl, adj.* (*Shak.*) equal. — *adj.* and *n.* **egalitā'rian** (*i-gal-*) equalitarian. — *ns.* **egalitā'rianism; egality** (*ē-, i-gal'*) equality. — *adv.* **ē'gally** (*Shak.*) [O.Fr. *egal* — L. *aequālis — aequus,* equal.]

égarement *ā-gar-mã,* (Fr.) *n.* confusion, bewilderment.

egence *ē'jəns,* **egency** *-si, ns.* need. [L. *ēgēre,* to be in need.]

eger *ē'gər, n.* Same as **eagre.**

Egeria *ē-jē'ri-ə, e-, n.* a female adviser. [L. *Ēgĕrĭa,* or *Aegĕrĭa,* the nymph who instructed Numa Pompilius.]

egest *ə-jest', ē-jest', v.t.* to discharge: to expel from the body in any way. — *n.pl.* **egest'a** things thrown out: excreta: waste materials removed from the body. — *n.* **egestion** (*e-jest'yən*). — *adj.* **egest'ive.** [L. *ēgerĕre, ēgestum — ē,* out, *gerĕre,* to carry.]

egg[1] *eg, n.* an oval body laid by birds and certain other animals from which the young is hatched: an ovum or female gamete (also **egg'-cell**): a zygote: anything shaped like a hen's egg: a bomb or mine (*slang*). — *ns.* **egg'er** one who gathers wildfowl's eggs: any moth of the family *Lasiocampidae,* whose cocoons are eggshaped (also **egg'ar**); **egg'ery** (*arch.*) a place where eggs are laid; **egg'ler** (*arch.*) a dealer in eggs. — *adj.* **egg'y** abounding in eggs: having just laid or about to lay an egg: savouring of, or marked with, eggs. — **egg'-and-anch'or, egg'-and-dart', egg'-and-tongue'** ornaments on mouldings in the form of eggs alternating with anchors, darts or tongues; **egg'-apparatus** (*bot.*) the egg and the synergidae in the embryo-sac of an angiosperm; **egg'-apple** the egg-fruit; **egg'-beater** an egg-whisk: a helicopter (*slang*); **egg'-binding** inability to expel an egg; **egg'-bird** the sooty tern. — *adj.* **egg'=bound** in the state of being unable to expel eggs. — **egg'-box** a cardboard, etc. container with specially shaped compartments for holding eggs. — *adj.* used of a type of building appearing as if made of numbers of unadorned rectangular sections. — **egg'-capsule, -case, -purse** a protective covering in which the eggs of some animals are enclosed; **egg'-cōsy** a cover for keeping a boiled egg hot; **egg'cup** a cup for holding a boiled egg at table; **egg custard** see **custard; egg'-dance** a dance performed blindfold among eggs; **egg'-flip** a drink made of ale, wine, spirits, or milk, with eggs, sugar, spice, etc.; **egg'-fruit** the fruit of the egg-plant; **egg'-glass** an egg-timer; **egg'head** (*coll.*) an intellectual; **egg'mass** (*coll.*) intellectuals as a group. — Also *adj.* — **egg'nog** a drink of eggs and hot beer, spirits, etc.; **egg'-plant** the aubergine or brinjal, an East Indian annual plant (*Solanum melongena*) with edible egg-shaped fruit; **egg'-plum** a yellowish egg-shaped plum; **egg'-powder** a powder of dried eggs, or a substitute; **egg'-purse** egg-capsule; **egg'shell** the calcareous covering of a bird's egg: a smooth gastropod shell: a very thin kind of porcelain. — *adj.* thin and delicate: (of paint, etc.) having a slight gloss. — **egg'-slice** a utensil for lifting fried eggs out of a pan; **egg'-spoon** a small spoon used in eating boiled eggs from the shell; **egg'-tim'er** a small sand-glass for timing the boiling of eggs; **egg'-tooth** a hard point on the beak by which an unhatched bird or reptile breaks the egg-shell; **egg'=whisk** an instrument for beating raw eggs. — **a bad egg** (*coll.*) a worthless person; **egg-and-spoon race** a race in which each competitor carries an egg in a

spoon; **good egg!** (*coll.*) an exclamation of approval; **have, put, all one's eggs into one basket** to risk all on one enterprise; **have, get, egg on one's face** (*slang*) to be left looking foolish; **lay an egg** (*slang,* chiefly *U.S.*) of a joke, comedian, theatrical performance, etc., to fail, flop; **take eggs for money** to be put off with mere promises of payment; **teach your grandmother to suck eggs** spoken contemptuously to one who would teach those older and wiser than himself; **tread upon eggs** to walk warily, to steer one's way carefully in a delicate situation. [O.N. *egg;* cf. O.E. *æg,* Ger. *Ei,* perh. L. *ōvum,* Gr. *ōon.*]

egg[2] *eg, v.t.* (now with *on*) to incite, urge on. [O.N. *eggja* — *egg,* an edge; cog. with O.E. *ecg;* see **edge.**]

eggar, egger, eggery, eggler, eggy. See **egg**[1].

egis. Same as **aegis.**

eglandular *ē-glan'dū-lər, adj.* having no glands. — *adj.* **eglan'dulose.** [L. *ē-,* without, *glandula,* gland.]

eglantine *eg'lən-tin, n.* the sweet-brier: perhaps the honeysuckle (*Milt.*). [Fr., — O.Fr. *aiglent,* as if from a L. *aculentus,* prickly — *acus,* a needle, and suff. *-lentus.*]

eglatere *eg-lə-tēr', (arch.) n.* eglantine.

egma *eg'mə, n.* Costard's attempt at *enigma* (*Shak.,* Love's Lab. Lost III, i. 73.).

ego *e'gō, ē'gō, n.* the 'I' or self — that which is conscious and thinks: an image of oneself: self-confidence: egotism. — *adj.* **egocen'tric** self-centred: regarding or regarded from the point of view of the ego. — *ns.* **egocentri'city; e'gōism** the doctrine that we have proof of nothing but our own existence (*philos.*): the theory of self-interest as the principle of morality (*ethics*): selfishness: egotism; **e'gōist** one who holds the doctrine of egoism: one who thinks and speaks too much of himself or of things as they affect himself: an egotist. — *adj.* **egōist'ic, -al** pertaining to or manifesting egoism. — *adv.* **egōis'tically.** — *ns.* **egō'ity** the essential element of the ego; **egomā'nia** morbid egotism; **egomā'niac.** — *adj.* **egomānī'acal.** — *n.* **e'gotheism** (or *-thē'*) the deification of self: identification of oneself with God. — *v.i.* **e'gotise, -ize** to talk much of oneself. — *ns.* **e'gotism** a frequent use of the pronoun I: thinking or speaking too much of oneself: self-exaltation; **e'gotist** one full of egotism. — *adjs.* **egotis'tic, -al** showing egotism: self-important: conceited. — *adv.* **egotist'-ically.** — **ego ideal** (*psych.*) one's personal standards, ideals, ambitions, etc. acquired as one recognises parental and other social standards, formed into a composite of characteristics to which one would like to conform: one's idealised picture of oneself; **e'go-trip** (*slang*) an action or experience which inflates one's good opinion of oneself; **e'go-tripper.** [L. *ego, egō,* and Gr. *egō,* I.]

egregious *i-grē'jəs, adj.* prominent, distinguished (*arch.*): outrageous: notorious. — *adv.* **egrē'giously.** — *n.* **egrē'giousness.** [L. *ēgregius,* chosen out of the flock — *ē,* out of, *grex, gregis,* a flock.]

egress *ē'gres, n.* the act of going out: departure: the way out: the power or right to depart. — *n.* **egression** (*i-, ē-gresh'ən*) the act of going out: departure. [L. *ēgredī, ēgressus — ē,* out of, *gradī, to go.*]

egret *ē'gret, n.* a white heron of several species: an aigrette. [See **aigrette.**]

egurgitate *ē-gûr'ji-tāt, (rare) v.t.* to vomit: to cast forth. [L. *ēgurgitāre, -ātum — ē,* out of, *gurges, -itis,* a whirlpool.]

Egypt *arch.* **Aegypt,** *ē'jipt, n.* a country of N.E. Africa. — *adj.* **Egyptian** (*ē-jip'shən*) belonging to Egypt: (of type) antique. — *n.* a native or citizen of Egypt: a gypsy (*arch.*). — *adj.* **Egyptolog'ical.** — *ns.* **Egyptol'ogist; Egyptol'ogy** the science of Egyptian antiquities. — **Egyptian darkness** darkness like that of Exod. x. 22.

eh *ā, interj.* expressing inquiry, failure to hear, or slight surprise. — *v.i.* to say 'Eh'.

eident *ī'dənt, (Scot.) adj.* busy, diligent. [M.E. *ithen* — O.N. *ithinn,* diligent.]

eider *ī'dər, n.* the **ei'der-duck',** a northern sea-duck, sought after for its fine down. — **ei'derdown'** the soft down of the eider-duck, used for stuffing quilts: a quilt. [Prob. through Sw. from O.N. *æthar*, gen. of *æthr*, an eider-duck.]

eidetic *ī-det'ik, adj.* vividly clear: reproducing, or able to reproduce, a vividly clear visual image of what has been previously seen. — *n.* a person with this ability. — *adv.* **eidet'ically.** [Gr. *eidētikos*, belonging to an image — *eidos*, form.]

eidograph *ī'dō-gräf, n.* an instrument used for copying drawings. [Gr. *eidos*, form, and *graphein*, to write.]

eidolon *ī-dō'lon, n.* an image: a phantom or apparition: a confusing reflection or reflected image: — *pl.* **eidō'la.** [Gr.; see idol.]

eigen- *ī-gən-,* in composition, proper, own. — *ns.* **ei'genfre'quency** one of the frequencies with which a particular system may vibrate; **ei'gentone'** a tone characteristic of a particular vibrating system; **ei'genval'ue** any of the possible values for a parameter of an equation for which the solutions will be compatible with the boundary conditions. [Ger.]

eight *āt, n.* the cardinal number one above seven: a symbol (8, viii, etc.) representing that number: a set of eight things or persons (syllables, leaves, oarsmen, etc.): an eight-oar boat: an eight-cylinder engine or car: a card with eight pips: a shoe or other article of a size denoted by 8: the eighth hour after midday or midnight: a score of eight points, tricks, etc.: the age of eight years. — *adj.* of the number eight: eight years old. — *adj.* and *adv.* **eight'fold** in eight divisions: eight times as much. — *adj.* **eighth** (*ātth*) last of eight: next after the seventh: equal to one of eight equal parts. — *n.* an eighth part: a person or thing in eighth position: an octave (*mus.*). — *adv.* **eighthly** (*ātth'li*) in the eighth place. — *n.* **eight'some** a group of eight together: a Scottish reel for eight dancers (also *adj.*). — *n.* and *adj.* **eight'vo** same as **octavo:** — *pl.* **eight'vos.** — *adj.* **eight'-day** lasting or running for eight days. — **eight'-foil** (*her.*) an eight-leaved flower. — *adj.* **eight'foot** eight feet in measure (also *adv.*): (*mus.*) see **foot.** — *adjs.* **eight'-hour** consisting of eight hours, or eight working hours; **eight'-oar** manned by eight oarsmen. — *n.* an eight-oar boat. — **eight'pence** the value of eight pennies. — *adj.* **eight'penny** costing eightpence. — *n.* and *adj.* **eight'score** eight times twenty. — **eights'man** one of a crew or team of eight. — *adj.* **eight'-square** regularly octagonal. — **an eight days** a week; **figure of eight** a figure shaped like an 8 made in skating, etc.; **one over the eight** (*coll.*) one drink too many; **piece of eight** an old Spanish coin worth eight reals; **the eights** annual bumping boat-races in the summer term between the various Oxford colleges. [O.E. (Anglian) *æhta* (W.S. *eahta*); Ger. *acht,* L. *octō,* Gr. *oktō.*]

eighteen *ā-tēn', ā'tēn, n.* and *adj.* eight and ten. — *adj.* and *n.* **eighteen'mo** octodecimo: — *pl.* **eighteen'mos.** — *adj.* **eigh'teenth** (or -*tēnth'*) last of eighteen: next after the seventeenth: equal to one of eighteen equal parts. — *n.* an eighteenth part: a person or thing in eighteenth position. — *adv.* **eighteenth'ly.** — *adj.* **eigh'teen-hole** having eighteen golf-holes. — **eigh'teen-pence.** — **eighteen-penny piece** an obsolete English coin. — *adj.* **eigh'teen-penn'y.** [O.E. (Mercian) *æhtatēne* (W.S. *eahtatīene*).]

eighty *ā'ti, n.* and *adj.* eight times ten. — *n.pl.* **eight'ies** the numbers eighty to eighty-nine: the years so numbered in life or any century: a range of temperatures from eighty to just less than ninety degrees. — *adj.* **eigh'tieth** last of eighty: next after the seventy-ninth: equal to one of eighty equal parts. — *n.* an eightieth part: a person or thing in eightieth position. [O.E. *æhtatig* (W.S. *eahtatig,* or *hundeahtatig*).]

eigne *ān, adj.* first born. [Fr. *aîné.*]

eik *ēk.* Scots form of **eke.**

eikon. Same as **icon.**

eild¹. Same as **eld.**

eild² *ēld,* (*Scot.*) *adj.* not yielding milk. [See **yeld.**]

eilding. See **eldin.**

eine *īn, ēn,* (*obs.*) *n.pl.* eyes. [See **een,** under **ee.**]

Einsteinian *īn-stī'ni-ən, adj.* of, pertaining to, Albert *Einstein,* physicist and mathematician (1879–1955) or his theories, esp. that of relativity. — *n.* **einstein'ium** the element (symbol Es) of atomic number 99, artificially produced and named after Einstein.

eirack *ē'rək,* (*Scot.*) *n.* a young hen. [Gael. *eireag.*]

eirenicon, irenicon *ī-rē'ni-kon,* a proposition or scheme for peace: a peace-making message: the deacon's litany at the beginning of the Greek liturgy — from its opening petitions for peace. — *adj.* **eire'nic** same as **irenic.** [A partly Latinised spelling of Gr. *eirēnikon,* neut. of *eirēnikos,* peaceful, peaceable — *eirēnē,* peace.]

eisel(l) *ā'səl, ī'səl,* (*obs.*) *n.* vinegar. [O.Fr. *aisil, aissil,* from L.L. dim. of L. *acētum,* vinegar.]

Eisen und Blut. See **Blut und Eisen.**

eisteddfod *īs-tedh'vod, U.S. ās-, n.* orig. a competitive congress of Welsh bards and musicians, now any of several gatherings in Wales for competitions in music, poetry, drama, etc., *esp.* (with *cap.*) the Royal National Eisteddfod: — *pl.* **-fodau** (-*vo-dī*), **-fods.** — *adj.* **eisteddfod'ic.** [W., lit. session — *eistedd,* to sit.]

either *ī'dhər, ē'dhər, adj.* or *pron.* the one or the other: one of two: each of two. — *conj.* correlative to *or:* or (*B.*). — *adv.* (used in conjunction with a neg.) also, likewise (not), as in *He isn't hungry and she isn't either:* (after a neg.) moreover, besides. [O.E. *ægther,* contraction of *æghwæthar — ā,* aye, pfx. *ge-,* and *hwæther,* whether; see also **each.**]

ejaculate *i-jak'ū-lāt, v.t.* to eject: to utter with suddenness. — *v.i.* to utter or make an ejaculation: to emit semen. — *n.* (-*lət*) semen. — *n.* **ejaculā'tion** ejection, emission: a sudden utterance in prayer or otherwise: an unpremeditated emotional prayer or remark: emission of semen. — *adjs.* **ejac'ūlative** (or -*lā*-); **ejac'ūlatory** (or -*lā*-). [L. *ē,* from, and *jaculārī, -ātus — jacēre,* to throw.]

eject *ē-jekt', i-, v.t.* to cast out: to dismiss: to turn out: to expel. — *v.i.* to cause oneself to be ejected as from an aircraft or spacecraft. — *n.* eject (*ē'jekt*) a mental state other than one's own, a thing thrown out of one's own consciousness, as distinguished from *object,* a thing presented in one's consciousness. — *ns.pl.* **eject'a, ejectament'a** matter thrown out, esp. by volcanoes. — *n.* **ejec'tion** discharge: expulsion: the state of being ejected: vomiting: that which is ejected. — *adj.* **ejec'tive.** — *ns.* **eject'ment** expulsion: dispossession: an action for the recovery of the possession of land (*law*); **eject'or** one who ejects or dispossesses another of his land: any mechanical apparatus for ejecting or discharging. — **eject'or-seat,** (*U.S.*) **ejection seat,** a seat that can be shot clear with its occupant in an emergency. [L. *ējectāre,* freq. of *ējicēre, ējectum — ē,* from, *jacēre,* to throw.]

ejusdem generis *ē-jus'dəm jen'ə-ris, ā-ūs'dem ge'ne-ris,* (L.) of the same kind.

eka- *ā'kə-, ē'kə-, pfx.* formerly prefixed to the name of an element to give a provisional name for the hypothetical undiscovered element that should follow in the periodic table. [Sans. *eka,* one.]

ek dum *ek dum,* at once. [Hind. *ek dam.*]

eke¹ (*Scot.* **eik**) *ēk, v.t.* to add to, increase: to lengthen: to supplement, make up to the required measure (often with *out*). — *n.* (*Scot.*) an addition, supplement. [O.E. *ēcan* (W.S. *īecan*); cf. **eche;** L. *augēre;* Gr. *auxanein.*]

eke² *ēk, adv.* in addition: likewise. [O.E. *ēac;* Ger. *auch,* perh. from root of **eke¹.**]

ekistics *ek-is'tiks, n.sing.* a word coined by a Greek, C. A. Doxiadis, for the science or study of human settlements. — *adj.* **ekis'tic.** — *n.* **ekistician** (-*tish'ən*). [From Mod. Gr. *oikistikē* — Gr. *oikistikos,* of or relating to settlement — *oikizein,* to settle, colonise — *oikos,* a house.]

ekka *ek'ə, n.* a small one-horse carriage. [Hindi — *ekkā,* one — Sans. *eka.*]

eklogite. See **eclogite.**

ekuele *ā-kwā'lā*, **ekpwele** *ek-pwā'lā*, *ns.* the standard monetary unit of Equatorial Guinea: — *pls.* **ekue'le, ekpwe'les.** [Native name.]

el¹ *el*, *n.* the twelfth letter of the alphabet (L, l): anything of that shape: a wing giving a building the shape of the letter L (*U.S.*).

el² *el*, (*U.S. coll.*) *n.* an elevated railroad.

e-la *ē'-lä'*, *n.* the highest note in old church music, E, the fourth space in the treble, sung to the syllable *la* in the highest hexachord: the highest pitch of anything. — *n.* **e-la-mi** (*ē'-lä'-mē'*) E, the third space in the bass ('in bass') or the first line in the treble ('in alt'), sung to *la* in the first and fourth hexachords respectively, and *mi* in the second and fifth.

elaborate *i-lab'ər-āt*, *v.t.* to produce by labour: to work out in detail: to build up from raw or comparatively simple materials: to add detail to. — *v.i.* to become elaborate: (with **on** or **upon**) to add detail, more information, etc. to a bare account. — *adj.* (*i-lab'ər-it*) wrought with labour: done with fullness and exactness: highly detailed: complicated. — *adv.* **elab'orately.** — *ns.* **elab'orateness; elabora'tion** the act of elaborating: refinement: the process by which substances are built up in the bodies of animals or plants. — *adj.* **elab'o-rātive** (or *-rā-*). — *ns.* **elab'orātor** one who elaborates; **elab'orātory** (*obs.*) a laboratory. [L. *ēlabōrāre, -ātum* — *ē*, from, *labōrāre* — *labor*, labour.]

Elaeagnus *el-i-ag'nəs*, *n.* the oleaster genus, giving name to the fam. **Elaeagnā'ceae.** [Gr. *elaiagnos*, goat willow.]

Elaeis *el-ē'is*, *n.* the oil-palm genus. [Gr. *elaion*, olive oil.]

elaeolite *el-ē'ō-līt*, *n.* a greasy-looking nepheline. [Gr. *elaion*, olive oil, *lithos*, stone.]

élan *ā-län'*, *ā-lā*, *n.* impetuosity, dash. — **élan vital** (*ā-lā vē-tal*) the creative force responsible for the growth and evolution of organisms (*Bergson*). [Fr.]

elance *i-läns'*, *v.t.* to throw as a lance. [Fr. *élancer*.]

eland *ē'lənd*, *n.* a S. African antelope, resembling the elk in having a protuberance on the larynx. [Du., — Ger. *Elend* (now *Elen*) — Lith. *élnis*, elk.]

elanet *el'ə-net*, *n.* a kite of the genus **Elanus.** [Gr. *elanos*, a kite.]

elaphine *el'ə-fīn*, *adj.* like or belonging to a red deer. [Gr. *elaphos*, stag.]

Elaps *ē'laps*, *n.* an American genus of snakes, otherwise **Micrurus** — coral-snake: applied by others to a South African genus, otherwise **Homorelaps** — garter-snake. [A form of **ellops.**]

elapse *i-laps'*, *v.i.* to slip or glide away: to pass silently, as time. — *n.* passing. [L. *ēlāpsus, ēlābī* — *ē*, from, *lābī, lāpsus*, to slide.]

elasmobranch *i-laz'mō-brangk*, or *-las'*, *n.* any member of the **Elasmobranch'iī**, a class of fishes including sharks and skates, having a cartilaginous skeleton and plate-like gills. [Gr. *elasmos*, a beaten-metal plate, *branchia*, gills.]

elastic *i-las'tik*, or *-läs'*, *adj.* having a tendency to recover the original form or size: springy: able to recover quickly a former state or condition after a shock (*fig.*): flexible: capable of stretching to include much (*lit.* and *fig.*): made of elastic. — *n.* a string or ribbon with rubber strands. — *ns.* **elas'tance** the reciprocal of the capacity of a condenser, from its electromechanical analogy with a spring; **elas'tase** an enzyme found in the pancreatic juice, decomposes elastin. — *adv.* **elas'-tically.** — *v.t.* **elas'ticate** to make elastic: — *p.adj.* **elas'ticated.** — *v.t.* **elas'ticise, -ize** (*-ti-sīz*) to make elastic. — *ns.* **elasticity** (*el-* or *ēl-əs-tis'*) power of returning to original form or size: springiness: power to recover from depression; **elas'ticness; elas'tin** a protein, chief constituent of elastic tissue; **elas'tomer** any rubber-like substance. — *adj.* **elastomeric** (*-mer'*). — **elastic band** a loop of thin rubber; **elastic collision, scattering** see under **collide**; **elastic limit** the greatest stress a material can be subjected to without permanent deformation; **elastic tissue** tissue having fibres

with elastic quality, occurring esp. in ligaments and tendons. [Late Gr. *elastikos* — *elaunein*, to drive.]

Elastoplast® *i-last'ō-pläst, -plast*, *n.* a dressing for a wound, consisting of gauze on a backing of adhesive tape.

elate *i-lāt'*, *adj.* (*rare*) lifted up: puffed up with success: exalted. — *v.t.* to raise or exalt (*obs.*): to make exultant or proud. — *adv.* **elāt'edly.** — *ns.* **elāt'edness; elā'tion** pride resulting from success: exaltation, high spirits. — *adj.* **ē'lative** (*gram.*) denoting, as in Finnish, place 'from which'. — *n.* the elative case. [L. *ēlātus*, used as pa.p. of *efferre* — *ē*, from, *lātus*, carried.]

elater *el'ə-tər*, *n.* an elastic filament aiding spore-dispersal in certain fungi, in liverworts and in horse-tails: a skipjack beetle. — *ns.* **elatē'rium** a substance contained in the juice of the fruit of the squirting cucumber, yielding the purgative **elat'erin; elaterite** (*i-lat'ər-īt*) elastic bitumen, a rubber-like mineral resin. [Gr. *elatēr*, driver — *elaunein*, to drive.]

elbow *el'bō*, *n.* the joint where the arm bows or bends: the corresponding joint in vertebrates: the part of a sleeve which covers the elbow: any sharp turn or bend. — *v.t.* to push with the elbow, to jostle. — **el'bow-chair** an armchair; **el'bow-grease** (*humorously*) vigorous rubbing: hard work; **el'bow-room** room to extend the elbows: space enough for moving or acting: freedom and scope. — **at one's elbow** close at hand; **bend, crook,** or **lift the elbow** to drink alcoholic liquor, esp. too much; **out at elbow** with coat ragged at the elbows; **up to the elbows** completely engrossed. [O.E. *elnboga*; see **ell**, and **bow¹** *n.* and *v.t.*]

elchi, eltchi, elchee *el'chē, -chi*, *ns.* an ambassador. [Turk. *ĭlchī*.]

eld *eld*, (*arch.*) *n.* age: old age, senility: former times, antiquity. [O.E. *eldo*.]

elder¹ *eld'ər*, *n.* a shrub or tree (*Sambucus*) of the Caprifoliaceae, with pinnate leaves, small flowers (the corolla wheel-shaped) and three-seeded fruits. — **eld'erberry** the acidulous purple-black drupaceous fruit of the elder; **eld'er-gun** a popgun made from elder by extracting the pith; **eld'erberry wine** a wine made from elderberries; **elder-flower water** a distilled water made from the flowers. [O.E. *ellærn*.]

elder² *eld'ər*, *adj.* older: having lived a longer time: prior in origin. — *n.* one who is older: an ancestor: one advanced to office on account of age: one of a class of office-bearers in the Presbyterian Church (*presbyter* of the New Testament). — *n.* **eld'erliness.** — *adj.* **eld'erly** somewhat old: bordering on old age. — *n.* (with *the*) elderly people. — *n.* **eld'ership** the state of being older: the office of an elder. — *adj.* **eld'est** oldest. — **Elder Brethren** the governing members of Trinity House; **elder** or **eldest hand** the player on the dealer's left, who leads in card-playing; **elders' hours** respectable hours — usually not after 10 p.m.; **elder statesman** a retired statesman consulted by the government: any administrator of age and experience: (in *pl.*, with *caps.*) a reactionary group of retired statesmen who exercised a power behind the throne in Japan. [O.E. *eldra* (W.S. *ieldra, yldra*), compar.; *eldesta* (*ield-esta*), superl. of *ald* (*eald*), old.]

eldin, elding *el'din(g)*, (*Scot.*) **eilding** *ēl'ding*, (*North.*) *ns.* fuel. [O.N. *elding* — *eldr*, fire.]

El Dorado, Eldorado *el-də-rä'dō*, the golden land (or city) imagined by the Spanish conquerors of America: any place where wealth is easily to be made. [Sp. *el*, the, *dorado*, pa.p of *dorar*, to gild — 'the gilded man', the king of the legendary city of Manoa who smeared himself with gold-dust; afterwards transferred to the city itself.]

eldritch *el'(d)rich*, (*Scot.*) *adj.* weird: uncanny. [Perh. connected with **elf**.]

Eleatic *el-i-at'ik*, *adj.* belonging to *Elea*, a Greek city of Lower Italy, or to the school of philosophers connected with it, including Xenophanes, Parmenides, and Zeno. — *n.* one belonging to this school.

elecampane *el-i-kam-pān'*, *n.* a composite plant (*Inula* *helenium*) formerly much cultivated for its medicinal root: a sweetmeat flavoured with an extract from the root. [L. *enula campāna,* field, or Campanian, inula.]

elect *i-lekt', v.t.* to choose (in preference): to select for any office or purpose: to select by vote. — *adj.* chosen: taken by preference from among others: chosen for an office but not yet in it (almost always after the noun): chosen by God for salvation (*theol.*). — *n.* one chosen or set apart. — *n.* **electabil'ity.** — *adj.* **elect'able.** — *n.* **elec'tion** (*-shən*) the act of electing or choosing: the public choice of a person for office, usually by the votes of a constituent body: freewill: the exercise of God's sovereign will in the predetermination of certain persons to salvation (*theol.*): the elected in this way (*B.*). — *v.i.* **electioneer'** to labour to secure the election of a candidate. — *n.* **electioneer'er.** — *n.* and *adj.* **electioneer'ing.** — *adj.* **elect'ive** pertaining to, dependent on, or exerting the power of choice: optional (*U.S.*). — *n.* (*U.S.*) an optional subject of study. — *adv.* **elect'ively.** — *ns.* **electiv'ity** (*ē-, e-*); **elect'or** one who elects: one who has a vote at an election: in U.S. a member of the **electoral college**: the title formerly belonging to those princes and archbishops of the German empire who had the right to elect the Emperor: — *fem.* **elect'ress, elect'oress.** — *adjs.* **elect'oral, electō'rial** (*ē-, e-*) pertaining to elections or to electors: consisting of electors. — *ns.* **elect'orāte** the dignity or the territory of an elector: the body of electors: **elect'orship.** — **electoral college** in U.S., the body of people who elect the President and Vice-President, themselves elected by popular vote: any body of electors with a similar function; **electoral vote** (*U.S.*) the vote of the members of the electoral college. [L. *ēligĕre, ēlectum* — *ē,* from, *legĕre,* to choose.]

Electra complex *i-lek'trə kom'pleks,* (*psych.*) the attachment of a daughter to her father, with hostility to her mother. [Greek story of *Electra,* who helped to avenge her mother's murder of her father.]

electret *i-lek'trit,* (*elect.*) *n.* a permanently polarised (piece of) dielectric material. [*Electr*icity and magn*et.*]

electric *i-lek'trik, adj.* pertaining to electricity: charged with or capable of being charged with electricity: producing or produced by, conveying, operated by, or making use of electricity: thrilling (*fig.*): producing a sudden startling effect. — *n.* a non-conductor of electricity, as amber, glass, etc., capable of being electrified by friction. — *adj.* **elec'trical.** — *adv.* **elec'trically.** — *ns.* **electrician** (*el-ik-trish'ən*) one who studies, or is versed in, the science of electricity: one who makes, instals, or repairs electrical apparatus; **electricity** (*el-ik-tris'i-ti*) the attractive power of amber and other substances when rubbed: an imaginary fluid supposed to explain this and related phenomena: the manifestation of a form of energy associated with separation or movement of charged particles, as electrons and protons: the science that deals with this: a feeling of excitement. — *adj.* **elec'trifiable.** — *n.* **electrificā'tion.** — *v.t.* **elec'trify** to communicate electricity to, to charge with electricity: to excite suddenly: to astonish: to adapt to electricity as the motive power: — *pr.p.* **elec'trifying;** *pa.t.* and *pa.p.* **elec'trified.** — *n.* **electrisā'tion, -z-.** — *v.t.* **elec'trise, -ize** to electrify. — **electric arc** a luminous space between electrodes when a current passes across; **electric battery** a group of cells connected in series or in parallel for generating an electric current by chemical action; **electric blanket** a blanket heated by electric current; **electric blue** a steely blue colour; **electric calamine** the mineral hemimorphite, which becomes positively electrified at one end, negatively at the other, when its temperature rises, and *vice versa* as it cools; **electric chair** the seat on which a condemned criminal is put to death by electricity; **electric eel** a cyprinoid fish, *Electrophorus electricus,* of South America, shaped like an eel, and able to give powerful electric shocks by means of an electric organ in its long tail; **electric eye** a photo-electric cell: a miniature cathode ray tube; **electric fence** a wire fence

electrically charged; **electric field** a region in which attracting or repelling forces are exerted on any electric charge present; **electric fire, heater, radiator** an apparatus using an electric current, for heating a room; **electric furnace** an apparatus for getting very high temperatures by means of an electric current; **electric guitar** one with an electrical amplifying device; **electric hare** a dummy animal electrically worked to draw on racing greyhounds; **electric motor** any device for converting electrical energy into mechanical energy; **electric organ** an organ in which the sound is produced by electrical devices instead of wind (*mus.*): in certain fishes, a structure that generates, stores and discharges electricity (*zool.*); **electric ray** the fish Torpedo; **electric seal** dyed rabbit or hare skin; **electric storm** a violent disturbance in the electric condition of the atmosphere; **electric torch** a portable electric light. [L. *ēlectrum* — Gr. *ēlektron,* amber, in which electricity was first observed.]

electrify. See **electric.**

electro- *i-lek'trō, el-ik-tro',* in composition, electric, electrolytic. — *n.* **elec'tro** (*coll.*) short for **electroplate** and **electrotype:** — *pl.* **elec'tros.** — *n.sing.* **electroacous'tics** the technology of converting acoustic energy into electrical energy and vice versa. — *adj.* **electroacous'tic.** — *n.* **elec'troanal'ysis** separation by electrolysis. — *adj.* **elec'troanalyt'ical.** — *ns.* **elec'trobiol'ogist; elec'trobio'logy** the science of the electrical phenomena in living organisms: an old name for hypnotism; **elec'trocar'diogram** a photographic record of the electrical variations that occur during contraction of the muscle of the heart; **elec'trocar'diograph** a galvanometer used for making such records; **elec'trocardiog'raphy** the study of electric currents produced during muscular activity of the heart; **elec'trocement'** cement made in an electric furnace, by adding lime to molten slag. — *adjs.* **elec'trochem'ic, -al.** — *ns.* **elec'trochem'ist; elec'trochem'istry** the study of the relation between electricity and chemical change. — *adj.* **elec'tro-convuls'ive** (**electro-convulsive therapy** shock-therapy — abbrev. **ECT**). — *n.* **elec'troculture** the cultivation of plants under stimulus of electricity. — *v.t.* **elec'trocute** to inflict a death penalty by means of electricity: to kill by electricity. — *ns.* **electrocū'tion; elec'trōde** (Gr. *hodos,* way) a conductor by which a current of electricity enters or leaves an electrolytic cell, gas discharge tube, or thermionic valve; **elec'trodeposi'tion** deposition of a layer of metal by electrolysis. — *n. sing.* **elec'trodynam'ics** the study of electricity in motion, or of the interaction of currents and currents, or currents and magnets. — *ns.* **elec'trodynamom'eter** an instrument for measuring currents by the attraction or repulsion between current-bearing coils; **elec'troenceph'alogram** (*-sef', -kef'*) a record made by an **elec'troenceph'alograph,** an instrument recording small electrical impulses produced by the brain; **elec'troencephalog'raphy: elec'troextrac'tion, elec'trowinn'ing** recovery of a metal from its salts, by passing an electric current through a solution; **elec'trogen** a molecule which emits electrons when it is illuminated; **electrogen'esis** the production of electricity, esp. in living cells, etc. — *adj.* **electrogen'ic** producing electricity: of, or capable of, electrogenesis. — *ns.* **elec'trogild'ing** electroplating with gold; **elec'trograph** a recording electrometer; **electrog'raphy.** — **electrohydraulic forming** shaping a piece of metal with a die by means of a shock wave in water set up by discharge of energy between immersed electrodes. — *n. sing.* **elec'trokinet'ics** the branch of science that treats of distribution of currents. — *ns.* **electrolier** (*-lēr'*) an electric-light fixture resembling a chandelier; **electrol'ogy** the science of electricity: electrotherapy; **elec'troluminesc'ence** luminescence produced by the application of an electric field to a dielectric phosphor. — *v.t.* **elec'trolyse, -lyze** (*-līz*) to break up by electric means: to subject to electrolysis. — *ns.* **electrolysis** (*-trol'i-sis;* Gr. *lysis,* loosing) decomposition by electric current, with migration of ions shown by changes at the electrodes: term used for the removal of hair by applying an electrically charged needle to the follicle; **elec′trolyte** (-*līt*) a substance that admits of electrolysis. — *adj.* **electrolytic** (-*lit′ik*). — *adv.* **electrolyt′ically**. — *n.* **elec′tromag′net** a piece of soft iron, etc., rendered magnetic by a current of electricity passing through a coil of wire wound round it. — *adj.* **elec′tromagnet′ic** (**electromagnetic theory** Clerk Maxwell's theory explaining light in terms of electromagnetic waves; **electromagnetic wave** a travelling disturbance in space produced by the acceleration of an electric charge, comprising an electric field and a magnetic field at right angles to each other, both moving at the same velocity in a direction normal to the plane of the two fields). — *n.* **elec′tromag′netism** a branch of science which treats of the relation of electricity to magnetism. — *adj.* **electromechan′ical** pertaining to any mechanical process or device involving the use of electricity: pertaining to electromechanics. — *n. sing.* **elec′tromechan′ics** the mechanics of the electric circuit. — *n.* **elec′tromer** a substance showing electromerism. — *adj.* **electromer′ic**. — *n.* **electrom′erism** a form of tautomerism caused by a redistribution of electrons among the atoms of a molecule or group. — *adj.* **elec′trometallur′gical**. — *ns.* **elec′tromet′allurgist** (or -*al′*); **electromet′allurgy** (or -*al′*) industrial working of metals by means of electricity; **electrŏm′eter** an instrument for measuring difference of electric potential. — *adjs.* **electromet′ric, -al**. — *n.* **electrom′etry** the science of electrical measurements. — *adjs.* **electromō′tive** pertaining to the motion of electricity or the laws governing it (**electromotive force** difference of potential or the force generated by this, being the force of an electric current — also called **electromō′tance**). — *ns.* **electromō′tor** an apparatus for applying electricity as a motive power; **elec′tromy′ograph** instrument for recording voltages produced by muscular contraction; **elec′tromyog′raphy** the study of electric currents set up in muscles by their working. — *adj.* **elec′troneg′ative** carrying a negative charge: tending to form negative ions. — *ns.* **elec′tronegativ′ity** an electronegative state: the power of e.g. an atom to attract electrons. **electrophorē′sis** (Gr. *phoreein*, to bear) migration of suspended particles, as protein macromolecules, under the influence of an electric field. — *adjs.* **electro-op′tic, -al**. — *n.sing.* **electro-op′tics** the study of the effects that an electric field has on light crossing it. — *n.* **electro-osmo′sis** movement of liquid, under an applied electric field, through a fine tube or membrane. — *n.* **elec′trophile** an electrophilic substance. — *adjs.* **electrophil′ic** having or involving an affinity for electrons, i.e. negative charge, electron-seeking; **electrophoretic** (-*et′ik*) pertaining to electrophoresis. — *ns.* **electrŏph′orus** an instrument for obtaining statical electricity by means of induction; **elec′trophotog′raphy** photography by means of electric rather than chemical processes, as in xerography. — *adjs.* **elec′trophotograph′ic; electrophysiolog′ical**. — *ns.* **elec′trophysiol′ogist; elec′trophysiol′ogy** the study of electric phenomena of living organisms. — *adj.* **elec′trophysiolog′ical**. — *v.t.* **elec′troplate** to plate or cover, esp. with silver, by electrolysis. — *n.* electroplated ware. — *ns.* **elec′troplater; elec′troplating**. — *adjs.* **elec′tropō′lar** having, as an electrical conductor, one end or surface positive and the other negative; **electropos′itive** carrying a positive charge: tending to form positive ions. — *n.* **elec′troscope** an instrument for detecting the presence of electricity in a body and the nature of it. — *adj.* **electroscop′ic**. — *ns.* **elec′troshock** an electric shock; **elec′trosonde** a sonde for measuring atmospheric electricity. — *adj.* **elec′trostat′ic**. — *ns. sing.* **elec′trostat′ics** the branch of science which treats of electricity at rest; **elec′trotech′nics** (also **elec′trotechnol′ogy**) electric technology; **electrotherapeu′tics** (also **electrother′apy**) treatment of disease by electricity. — *adjs.* **elec′trotherm′al, elec′trotherm′ic** pertaining to electricity and heat, or heat obtained electrically. —

n. sing. **elec′trotherm′ics**. — *ns.* **elec′trotherm′y; elec′trotint** a printing block produced by drawing with varnish on a metal plate, and depositing metal electrically on the parts not covered. — *adj.* **electroton′ic**. — *ns.* **electrot′onus** the state of a nerve subjected to a steady discharge of electricity; **elec′trotype** a printing plate made by electrolytically coating a mould with copper: a facsimile of a coin made by this process. — Also *adj.* — *n.* **elec′trotyper** one who makes electrotypes. — *adj.* **electrotȳp′ic**. — *ns.* **elec′trotypist; elec′trotȳpy; elec′trovalency** union within a chemical compound achieved by transfer of electrons, the resulting ions being held together by electrostatic attraction — cf. *covalency*. — *adj.* **elec′trovalent**. — *n.* **electrowinning** see **electroextraction**. [Gr. *ēlektro*, combining form of *ēlektron*; see **electron**.]

electron *i-lek′tron, n.* a natural alloy of gold and silver used by the ancients (also Latinised as **elec′trum**): a minute particle charged with electricity, or a unit charge having inertia, normally forming part of an atom but capable of isolation as in cathode rays. — *adj.* **electronic** (*el-, il-, ēl-ik-tron′ik*) of or pertaining to electronics: worked or produced by devices made according to the principles of electronics: concerned with, or working with, such devices. — *adv.* **electron′ically**. — *n.sing.* **electron′ics** the science and technology of the conduction of electricity in a vacuum, a gas, or a semiconductor: the devices, etc. based thereon. — **electron camera** any device that converts an optical image into a corresponding electric current directly by electronic means; **electron gun** the assembly of electrodes in a cathode ray tube which produces the electron beam; **electronic brain** any electronic computer; **electronic flash** an extremely intense and brief flash for high-speed photography produced by passing an electric charge through a gas-filled tube, or the apparatus for producing it; **electronic mail** the sending and receiving of messages by any electronic means; **electronic mailbox** a section of a central computer's memory reserved for a particular individual, into which messages can be directed; **electronic music** music made by arranging sounds previously generated in the laboratory and recorded on tape (cf. **musique concrète**); **electronic organ** (*mus.*) an organ in which the sound is produced electronically; **electronic piano** a kind of synthesiser; **electron micrograph** a photograph obtained by substituting a photographic plate for the fluorescent viewing screen of an electron microscope; **electron microscope** a microscope that makes use of a beam of electrons instead of light; **electron optics** the study of the effects of electric and magnetic fields on the direction of beams of electrons; **electron pair** a duplet: an electron and a positron; **electron probe** an X-ray device that bombards the specimen under examination with a very narrow beam of electrons, allowing non-destructive analysis; **electron shell** a group of electrons surrounding a nucleus of an atom and having adjacent energy levels; **electron telescope** an optical instrument with electronic image converter used with a normal telescope; **electron tube** an electronic device in which the electron conduction is in a vacuum or gas inside a gas-tight enclosure — including a thermionic valve; **elec′tron-volt** a unit of energy equal to that acquired by an electron when accelerated by a potential of one volt. — **electron ring accelerator** an accelerator in which an intense ring of circulating electrons, being accelerated, can carry along and accelerate protons or stripped ions. [Gr. *ēlektron*, amber.]

electronegative, electronegativity. See **electro-**.
electronic, etc. See **electron**.
electrophoresis … to … electrovalent. See **electro-**.
electrum. See **electron**.
electuary *i-lek′tū-ər-i, n.* a medicine mixed with honey or the like. [L.L. *ēlectuārium*, perh. — Gr. *ekleikton* — *ekleichein*, to lick up.]
eleemosynary *el-ē, el-i-ē-moz′i-nər-i,* or *-mos′, adj.* relat-

ing to charity or almsgiving: dependent on charity: of the nature of alms. [Gr. *eleēmosynē*, alms — *eleos*, pity; see **alms**.] .

elegant *el'i-gənt, adj.* pleasing to good or fastidious taste: very careful or ornate in dress: graceful in form and movement: refined and luxurious: (of style) polished: (of apparatus or work in science or mathematics) simple and effective: excellent (*slang*). — *ns.* **el'egance, el'egancy** the state or quality of being elegant: the finest propriety of manners (*arch.*): refinement : an exemplification of elegance. — *adv.* **el'egantly.** [Fr., — L. *ēlegāns, -antis* — *ē,* from, and root of *legĕre,* to choose.]

elegit *i-lē'jit, ā-lā'git,* (*law*) *n.* a writ of execution, abolished in England in 1956, whereby a debtor's property and lands could be delivered to the plaintiff until the debt was satisfied by profits, rents, etc. [L., he has chosen, — *eligere,* to chose.]

elegy *el'i-ji, n.* a song of mourning: a funeral-song: a poem of serious, pensive, or reflective mood: a poem written in elegiac metre. — *adj.* **elegī'ac** belonging to elegy: mournful: used in elegies, esp. applied to classical verse in couplets of hexameter and pentameter lines (**elegiac couplets**), or two stanzas of four iambic pentameters rhyming *abab* (**elegiac stanzas**). — *n.* elegiac verse. — *adj.* **elegī'acal.** — *ns.* **elegiast** (*e-lē'ji-ast;* Goldsmith), **el'egist** a writer of elegies. — *v.i.* **el'egise, -ize** to write elegiacally. — *v.t.* to write an elegy on. [L. *elegīa* — Gr. *elegeiā* — *elegos,* a lament.]

element *el'ə-mənt, n.* a first principle: one of the essential parts of anything: an ingredient: the proper medium, habitat or sphere of any thing or being: any one of the four substances, fire, air, earth, and water, supposed by the ancients to be the foundation of everything: (in *pl.*) the rudiments of learning: (usu. *pl.*) the bread and wine used in the Eucharist: a substance that cannot be resolved by chemical means into simpler substances (*chem.*): a member or unit of a structure: a resistance wire in an electric heater: an electrode: a determining fact or condition in a problem: the sky: a celestial sphere: (in *pl.*) the weather, the powers of nature. — *adj.* **elemental** (*-ment'l*) pertaining to the elements: belonging to or produced by or inhabiting the elements. — *n.* an elemental spirit: a nature spirit: a disembodied spirit. — *n.* **element'alism** the worship of elemental spirits: the theory which resolves the divinities of antiquity into the elemental powers. — *adv.* **element'ally.** — *adj.* **element'ary** of a single element: primary: rudimentary: simple: uncompounded: pertaining to the elements: treating of first principles. — **elemental spirits** beings in mediaeval belief who presided over the four elements, living in and ruling them; **elementary particle** any of a number of particles, e.g. electron, proton, neutron, neutrino, kaon, or pion, so-called because supposed indivisible. — **elements of an orbit** the data mathematically necessary to determine it; **in one's element** in the surroundings most natural or pleasing to one. [L. *elementum,* pl. *elementa,* first principles.]

elemi *el'im-i, n.* a fragrant resinous substance obtained from various tropical trees, esp. a species of Canarium. [Perh. Ar.]

elench *i-lengk'* (*obs.*), **elenchus** *i-lengk'əs* (*pl.* **elench'ī**) *ns.* refutation: a sophism. — *adj.* **elenc'tic** pertaining to argument, cross-examining, refuting. [L., — Gr. *elenchos* — *elenchein,* refute.]

elephant *el'i-fənt, n.* a Proboscidean (*Elephas*) of several fossil and two surviving species, the largest living land mammal, having a very thick skin, a trunk, and ivory tusks: a size of paper before metrication. — *n.* **elephantī'asis** (Gr. *elephantīāsis*) a disease chiefly of tropical climates, consisting of an overgrowth of the skin and connective tissue usually of the legs and scrotum. — *adjs.* **elephant'ine** pertaining to an elephant: like an elephant: very large or ungainly: (of a memory) capacious and reliable; **elephant'oid** elephant-like. — **elephant folio** a folio of the largest size; **elephant grass** a

kind of reed-mace, *Typha elephantum*; **elephant gun** a large-calibre rifle designed for killing elephants or other large animals; **elephant seal** the largest of the seals, the male measuring about 20 feet in length; **el'ephant's-ears'** or **-ear'** begonia: applied also to other large-leaved plants such as bergenias and species of Colocasia; **el'ephant's-foot** Hottentot bread, a plant (*Testudinaria elephantipes*) of the yam family, whose root-stock resembles an elephant's foot, eaten by the Hottentots: a tropical composite plant, Elephantopus, from the shape of its radical leaves; **elephant shrew** any member of the African family Macroscelidae, long-nosed, long-legged Insectivora, agile jumpers over loose sand. — **pink elephants** hallucinations caused by over-indulgence in alcoholic drink; **white elephant** anything that gives more trouble than it is worth — a (so-called) white elephant being an honourable but onerous gift of the kings of Siam to a courtier they wished to ruin: an unwanted possession, often given away to a jumble sale: something which proves to be useless. [Remodelled after Lat. from M.E. *olifaunt* — O.F. *olifant,* or poss. O.E. *olfend,* camel — L. *elephantus, elephās* — Gr. *elephās, -antos.*]

Eleusinian *el-ū-sin'i-ən, adj.* relating to *Eleusis* in Attica. — **eleusinian mysteries** the mysteries of Demeter celebrated there.

eleutherian *el-ū-thē'ri-ən, adj.* freedom-giving. — *n.* **eleu'therarch** (*-thər-ärk*; Gr. *archos,* chief; *Shelley*) the chief of a feigned society of **eleu'therī.** — *n.* **eleutherococ'cus** a creeping shrub found in Siberia, from which a drug is prepared that apparently increases stamina and concentration. — *adj.* **eleutherodac'tyl** (Gr. *daktylos,* toe) (of birds) having the hind-toe free. — *n.* **eleutheroma'nia** a manic desire for freedom. [Gr. *eleutheros,* free.]

elevate *el'i-vāt, v.t.* to raise to a higher position: to raise in mind and feelings: to exhilarate. — *adjs.* **el'evate, -d** raised: lofty: exhilarated, esp. by liquor. — *ns.* **elevā'tion** the act of elevating or raising, or the state of being raised: exaltation: an elevated place: a rising ground: height: a representation of the flat side of a building, drawn with mathematical accuracy, but without any attention to effect (*archit.*): angular height above the horizon: an angle made by a line with the plane of the horizon: a leap with apparent suspension in the air (*ballet*): the lifting up (of the Host) in view of the people; **el'evator** a person or thing that lifts up: a lift or machine for raising grain, etc., to a higher floor: a lift (*U.S.*): a storehouse for grain: a muscle raising a part of the body: movable control surface or surfaces at the tail of an aeroplane by which it is made to climb or dive. — *adj.* **el'evatory** able or tending to raise. — *n.* **elevon** (*el'ə-vən*) a wing flap on delta-wing or tailless aircraft acting both as an *elev*ator and as an *ail*eron. — **elevated (railroad)** a railway borne on pillars or trestles over a roadway, as in some American towns (familiarly **el,** or **L**). [L. *ēlevāre, -ātum* — *ē,* from, *levāre,* to raise — *levis,* light; see **light².**]

eleven *i-lev'n, n.* the cardinal number next above ten: a team of eleven (cricket, association football, etc.): the eleventh hour after noon or midnight. — *adj.* of the number eleven. — *n.* (usu. *n.pl.,* sometimes *n.sing.*) **elev'ens, elev'enses** (*coll.*) an eleven o'clock snack: morning coffee or the like. — *adj.* **elev'enth** next after the tenth: equal to one of eleven equal parts. — *n.* an eleventh part: an octave and a fourth (*mus.*). — *adv.* **elev'enthly.** — **eleven and twenty long** (*Shak.*) exactly right (the score aimed at in the game of one-and-thirty); **eleventh hour** the very last moment, referring to Matt. xx. 6, 9 (*adj.* **elev'enth-hour'**). — **eleven-plus (examination)** (*formerly*) a school examination taken by pupils about the age of eleven to determine to which type of secondary education (academic, non-academic, or technical) they were to proceed: this or any similar system of selection, still operated by a few local education authorities in Britain. [O.E. *en(d)le(o)fan;* cf. Goth. *ainlif,* perh. (ten and) *one left,* from the root of L. *linquĕre,* Gr. *leipein,* to leave.]

elevon. See **elevate.**

elf *elf, n.* in European folklore, a supernatural being, generally of human form but diminutive size, sometimes more malignant than a fairy: a fairy: a dwarf: a tricky, froward, or fairylike being, esp. a child: — *pl.* **elves** *(elvz).* — *v.t. (Shak.)* to entangle (hair). — *n.* **elf'hood.** — *adj.* **elf'in** small, with delicate frame: small, mischievous and charming: pertaining to a good-natured elf. — *n.* a little elf: a child. — *adjs.* **elf'ish, elv'an, elv'ish** elf-like, mischievous: tricky: distraught: froward. — **elf'-arrow, -bolt** an elf-shot; **elf'-child** a changeling, or a child supposed to have been left by elves in place of one stolen by them; **elf'land** the land of the elves or fairies; **elf'locks** *(Shak.)* locks of hair clotted together, supposedly by elves. — *v.t.* **elf'-shoot** to shoot with an elf-arrow, bewitch. — **elf'-shot** a prehistoric flint or stone arrow-head, supposed to be used by elves: sickness attributed to it. — *adj.* shot with an elf-arrow: bewitched. [O.E. *ælf;* cf. O.N. *álfr,* Sw. *elf.*]

eliad. See **œillade.**

Elian *ē'li-ən, adj.* of, or like the work of, Charles Lamb, who wrote under the name of *Elia.* — *n.* a devotee or imitator of Lamb.

elicit *i-, ē-, e-lis'it, v.t.* to draw forth: to evoke. — *ns.* **elicitā'tion; elic'itor.** [L. *ēlicĕre, ēlicitum.*]

elide *ē-, i-līd', v.t.* to rebut *(arch.):* to cut off, as a syllable: to suppress, abridge. — *n.* **elision** *(i-lizh'ən)* the suppression of a vowel or syllable: an omission. [L. *ēlīdĕre, ēlīsum — ē,* from, *laedĕre,* to strike.]

eligible *el'i-ji-bl, adj.* fit or worthy to be chosen: legally qualified for election or appointment: desirable. — *n. (coll.)* a person or thing eligible. — *n.* **eligibil'ity.** — *adv.* **el'igibly.** [Fr., — L. *ēligĕre;* see **elect.**]

eliminate *i-, ē-, e-lim'in-āt, v.t.* to thrust out *(arch.):* to remove, cancel, get rid of: to expel waste matter. — *adjs.* **elim'inable; elim'inant** *(med.)* causing elimination of waste or morbid matter. — *n.* an eliminating agent. — *n.* **eliminā'tion.** — *adj.* **elim'inative.** — *n.* **elim'inātor** one who or that which eliminates; esp. a device for substituting an electric main for a battery in a wireless receiving set. — *adj.* **elim'inatory.** [L. *ēlimināre, -ātum — ē,* from, *līmen, -inis,* a threshold.]

clision. See **elide.**

élite, elite *i-, e-, ā-lēt', n.* a chosen or select part, the pick or flower of anything (in this sense, sometimes used as *pl.*): a size of typewriter type allowing twelve letters to the inch. — Also *adj.* — *n.* **élit'ism, elit'ism** (belief in) government by an élite: consciousness of belonging to an élite: the favouring or creation of an élite. — *adj.* **élit'ist, elit'ist** favouring, creating, etc. an élite. — Also *n.* [Fr. *élite —* L. *ēlecta (pars,* a part, understood); see **elect.**]

elixir *i-, e-liks'ər, n.* a liquor once supposed to have the power of indefinitely prolonging life **(elixir of life),** or of transmuting metals: the quintessence of anything: a substance which invigorates: a panacea: a nostrum: a strong tincture: a compound tincture. [L.L., — Ar. *al-iksīr,* the philosopher's stone, from *al-,* the, *iksīr,* prob. from Late Gr. *xērion,* a desiccative powder for wounds — Gr. *xēros,* dry.]

Elizabethan *i-, e-liz-ə-bē'thən, adj.* pertaining to a Queen *Elizabeth* or her reign, esp. to the first Queen Elizabeth (1533–1603) or her reign (1558–1603) — of dress, manners, literature, etc. — *n.* a person, esp. poet or dramatist, of that age. — *n.* **Elizabeth'anism.** — **Elizabethan architecture** the mixed style that sprang up on the decline of Gothic, marked by Tudor bow-windows and turrets decorated with classic cornices and pilasters, long galleries, enormous square windows, large apartments, plaster ceilings wrought into compartments, etc.

elk *elk, n.* a deer of northern Europe and Asia, identical or close akin with the moose of N. America, the largest of all living deer: the wapiti *(U.S.* and *Can.).* — **elkhorn fern** a fern of the genus *Platycerium,* tropical epiphytic ferns, with large leaf like an elk's horn; **elk'hound** a large strong Norwegian breed of dog with thick coat and curled tail. — **Irish elk** a giant deer now extinct, known from the remains found in the Pleistocene, esp. of Ireland. [Poss. O.E. *elh* (W.S. *eolh).*]

ell¹ *el, n.* a varying measure of length originally taken from the arm: a cloth measure equal to 1¼ yd *(obs.).* — **ell'wand** a measuring rod. — **give him an inch and he'll take an ell** a concession will encourage the taking of liberties. [O.E. *eln;* Du. *el,* Ger. *Elle,* L. *ulna,* Gr. *ōlenē,* elbow.]

ell² *el.* Same as **el².**

ellagic *e-laj'ik, adj.* pertaining to gall-nuts, applied to an acid, $C_{14}H_6O_8$. [Fr. *galle,* gall, spelt backwards.]

ellipse *i-, e-lips', (geom.) n.* a figure produced by the section of one branch of a right circular cone by a plane passing obliquely and failing to meet the other branch. — *ns.* **ellip'sis** a figure of syntax by which a word or words are left out and implied *(gram.):* mark(s) indicating ellipsis *(print.):* — *pl.* **ellip'sēs; ellip'sograph** an instrument for describing ellipses; **ellip'soid** *(geom.)* a surface (or the enclosed solid) of which every plane section is an ellipse or a circle. — *adjs.* **ellipsoi'dal; ellip'tic, -al** pertaining to an ellipse: oval: having a part understood: concise, compendious: obscure, dubious: *(loosely)* circumlocutary: slightly acute at each end, rather narrow, and broadest in the middle *(bot.):* pertaining to ellipsis: — *adv.* **ellip'tically.** — *n.* **ellipticity** *(el-ip-tis'i-ti)* deviation from the form of a circle or sphere: of the earth, the difference between the equatorial and polar diameters. — **elliptic geometry, space** Riemannian geometry, space. [L. *ellipsis —* Gr. *elleipsis — elleipein,* to fall short — *en,* in, *leipein,* to leave.]

ellops *el'ops, (obs.) n.* a kind of snake *(Milt.):* a kind of sturgeon (also **el'ops):** a sea-serpent *(Goldsmith).* [Gr. *ellops,* also *elops, elaps,* perh. mute, perh. scaly, also an unknown fish, and an unknown snake; cf. **Elaps, elops.**]

elm *elm, n.* a tree (Ulmus) with serrated leaves unequal at the base, and small flowers in clusters appearing before the leaves: its timber (also **elm'wood).** — *adj.* of elm. — *adjs.* **elm'en** *(obs.)* made of elm; **elm'y** abounding with elms. [O.E. *elm;* Ger. *Ulme,* L. *ulmus.*]

El Niño *el nē'nyō* a warm current affecting the Peruvian coast every ten or so years. [Sp., the child, short for *El Niño de Navidad,* the Christ Child, from the arrival of the current at Christmas.]

Elo *el'o, adj.* denoting a scale on which the ability of chess-players is assessed, devised by Arpad *Elo,* 20th-cent. U.S. professor of physics. — **Elo ratings; Elo scale.**

elocution *el-ə-kū'shən, n.* the art of effective speaking, more esp. of public speaking, regarding solely the utterance or delivery: eloquence *(obs.).* — *v.i.* **el'ocute** *(often facet.)* to declaim. — *adjs.* **elocū'tionary; eloc'ūtory** *(rare).* — *n.* **elocū'tionist** one versed in or practising elocution: a teacher of elocution: a reciter. [L. *ēlocūtiō, -ōnis, ēloquī, -cūtus — ē,* from *loquī,* to speak.]

Elodea *e-lō'di-ə, n.* an American genus of Hydrocharitaceae, to which the Canadian waterweed belongs. — Also called **Helodea, Anacharis,** and **Phyllotria.** [Gr. *helōdēs,* marshy, marsh-dwelling — *helos,* marsh, *eidos,* form.]

éloge *ā-lōzh', elogium* *(obs.) ē-lō'ji-əm,* **elogy** *(obs.) el'ə-ji, ns.* a funeral oration: a panegyric *(obs.).* — *n.* **el'ogist** *(obs.)* one who delivers an éloge. [Fr. *éloge,* and its source L. *ēlogium,* a short statement, an inscription on a tomb, perh. confused with **eulogy.**]

Elohim *e-lō'him, n.* a Hebrew name for God. — *n.* **Elō'hist** the writer or writers of the Elohistic passages of the Old Testament. — *adj.* **Elōhist'ic** relating to Elohim — said of those passages in the Old Testament in which the name Elohim is used instead of Yahweh (Jehovah). [Heb. pl. of *Eloah —* explained by Delitzsch as a plural of intensity.]

eloin, eloign *e-loin', (arch.) v.t.* to convey to a distance:

to separate and remove. — *ns.* **eloiner, eloigner; eloin'-ment, eloign'ment.** [O.Fr. *esloigner* (Fr. *éloigner*) — L.L. *ēlongāre*; see **elongate**.]

elongate *ē'long-gāt, i-long', v.t.* to make longer: to extend. — *v.i.* to grow longer. — *adjs.* **elongate, -d.** — *n.* **elonga'tion** the act of lengthening out: distance (*obs.*): the moon's or a planet's angular distance from the sun. [L.L. *ēlongāre, -ātum* — *ē,* from, *longus,* long.]

elope *e-, i-lōp', v.i.* to escape privately, esp. with a lover (usu. with marital intentions): to run away, bolt. — *ns.* **elope'ment; elō'per.** [Cf. O.Du. *ontlōpen,* Ger. *entlaufen,* to run away.]

elops *el'ops, n.* see **ellops:** (with *cap.*) a genus of fish (fam. *Elopidae*) akin to the tarpon. [See **ellops.**]

eloquent *el'ə-kwənt, adj.* having eloquence: persuasive: strongly expressive. — *n.* **el'oquence** the power, art, or practice of uttering meaning in correct, appropriate, expressive, and fluent language: the art of such language: persuasive speech. — *adv.* **el'oquently.** [L. *ēloquēns, -entis,* pr.p. of *ēloquī.*]

elpee *el-pē', (coll.) n.* a long-playing record, a phonetic representation of the abbrev. **LP.**

Elsan® *el'san, n.* a type of portable lavatory in which chemicals are used to kill bacteria and destroy the smell. [*E.L.* Jackson, the manufacturer, and *san*(itation).]

else *els, adj.* (or *adv.*) other (in addition or instead). — *adv.* otherwise: besides: except that mentioned. — *advs.* **elsewhere'** in or to another place; **elsewhith'er; else'wise** in a different manner: otherwise. [O.E. *elles,* otherwise, orig. gen. of *el,* other; cf. O.H.G. *alles* or *elles,* L. *alius,* Gr. *allos,* other.]

elsin *el'sin,* **elshin** *el'shin, (Scot.) ns.* an awl. [From O.Du. *elssene* (mod. *els*); cf. **awl.**]

elt *elt, (dial.) n.* a young sow. [Cf. **yelt, gilt**².]

eltchi. Same as **elchi.**

eluant, eluate. See **elution.**

elucidate *ē-, i-lū'si-dāt,* or *-lōō', v.t.* to make lucid or clear: to throw light upon: to illustrate. — *n.* **elucida'tion.** — *adjs.* **elu'cidative, elu'cidatory** making clear: explanatory. — *n.* **elu'cidator.** [L.L. *ēlūcidāre, -ātum* — *ē-,* intens., and *lūcidus,* clear.]

elucubration. Obs. form of **lucubration.** [L. *ē-,* intens.]

elude *ē-, i-lūd'* or *-lōōd', v.t.* to escape by stratagem: to baffle: (of a fact, etc.) to fail to be discovered, remembered, etc. — *n.* **elu'der.** — *adj.* **elu'dible.** — *n.* **elu'sion** (*-zhən*) act of eluding: evasion. — *adj.* **elu'sive** (*-ziv, -siv*) practising elusion: deceptive. — *adv.* **elu'sively.** — *n.* **elu'soriness.** — *adj.* **elu'sory** tending to elude or cheat: evasive: deceitful. [L. *ēlūdĕre, ēlūsum* — *ē,* from, *lūdĕre,* to play.]

Elul *e'ləl* or *-lōōl, n.* the 12th month of the Jewish civil year, and 6th of the ecclesiastical. [Heb., — *âlal,* to reap.]

elution *ē-, i-lōō'shən, -lū', (chem.) n.* purification or separation by washing. — *ns.* **el'uant, eluent** a liquid used for elution; **el'uate** liquid obtained by eluting. — *v.t.* **elute'.** — *n.* **elu'tor** a vessel for elution. [L. *ēlūtiō, -ōnis,* washing — *ēluĕre, ēlūtum* — *ē,* from, *luĕre,* to wash.]

elutriate *ē-, i-lōō'tri-āt, -lū', v.t.* to separate by washing into coarser and finer portions. — *ns.* **elutria'tion; elu'triator** an apparatus for elutriating. [L. *ēlutriāre, -ātum,* to wash out, *ēluĕre* — *ē,* from, *luĕre,* to wash.]

eluvium *i-, ē-lōō'vi-əm,* or *-lū', n.* an accumulation of rock debris formed on the spot or moved by wind only, as loess. — *adj.* **elu'vial.** [Formed on the analogy of *alluvium, diluvium*; L. *ē,* from, *luĕre,* to wash.]

elvan¹ *elv'ən, n.* a granular felspathic dyke rock, composed of quartz and orthoclase. — Also **elv'anite.** [Cornish miners' name; prob. Cornish *elven,* spark.]

elvan², **elves, elvish.** See under **elf.**

elver *el'vər, n.* a young eel. [*eelfare* see **eel.**]

Elysium *ē-, i-, e-liz(h)'i-əm, n.* among the Greeks, the abode of the blessed dead (*myth.*): any delightful place. — *adj.* **Elys'ian.** [L., — Gr. *elysion* (*pedion*), the Elysian (plain).]

elytrum *el'it-rəm, n.* a beetle's forewing modified to form a case for the hind-wing: a dorsal plate in certain worms. — Also **el'ytron:** — *pl.* **el'ytra.** — *adjs.* **el'ytral; elyt'riform; elytrigerous** (*-trij'ər-əs*). [Latinised from Gr. *ĕlўtron,* a sheath.]

Elzevir *el'zi-vēr, -vər, adj.* published by the Elzevirs, a celebrated family of printers at Amsterdam, Leyden, and other places in Holland, whose small neat editions were chiefly published between 1592 and 1681: pertaining to the type used in their 12mo and 16mo editions of the Latin classics. — *n.* a special form of printing types.

em *em, n.* the thirteenth letter of the alphabet (M, m): the unit of measurement (12-point lower-case 'm') used in spacing material and in estimating dimensions of pages (*print.*; see also **quadrat**).

em- *em-, pfx.* a form of **en-** used before *b, m* or *p.*

'em *əm, pron.* them: to them. [Orig. the unstressed form of *hem,* dat. and accus. pl. of **he** (O.E. *him, heom,* dat. pl.); but now used coll. as if an abbreviation of **them.**]

emaciate *i-mā'shi-āt, -si, v.t.* to make meagre or lean: to deprive of flesh: to waste. — *v.i.* to become lean: to waste away. — *adjs.* **emā'ciate, -d.** — *n.* **emāciā'tion** the condition of becoming emaciated or lean: leanness. [L. *ēmaciāre, -ātum* — *ē-,* intens., *maciāre,* to make lean — *maciēs,* leanness.]

emanate *em'ə-nāt, v.i.* to flow out of or from anything: to proceed from some source: to arise. — *adj.* **em'anant** flowing out. — *ns.* **emana'tion** a flowing out from a source, as the universe considered as issuing from the essence of God: the *generation* of the Son and the *procession* of the Spirit, as distinct from the origination of created beings: that which issues or proceeds from some source: a radioactive gas given off by radium, thorium and actinium — radon; **em'anatist.** — *adjs.* **em'anative, em'anatory, emanā'tional.** [L. *ēmānāre, -ātum* — *ē,* out from, *mānāre,* to flow.]

emancipate *e-, i-man'si-pāt, v.t.* to set free from restraint or bondage or disability of any kind. — *ns.* **emancipā'tion** the act of setting free from bondage or disability of any kind: the state of being set free: **emancipā'tionist** an advocate of the emancipation of slaves; **eman'-cipātor.** — *adj.* **emancipa'tory.** — *n.* **eman'cipist** (*hist.*) a convict who has served his time of punishment in a penal colony. [L. *ēmancipāre, -ātum* — *ē,* away from, *mancipāre,* to transfer property — *manceps, -cipis,* one who gets property, from *manus,* the hand, *capĕre,* to take.]

emarginate *ē-mär'jin-āt, v.t.* to take away the margin of. — *adj.* depressed and notched instead of pointed at the tip, as a leaf (*bot.*): having all the edges of the primitive form crossed by a face (*min.*): having the margin broken by a notch or segment of a circle (*zool.*). — *n.* **emargina'tion.** [L. *ēmargināre, -ātum* — *ē,* out, *margināre,* to provide with a margin — *margō,* margin.]

emasculate *i-, ē-mas'kū-lāt, v.t.* to deprive of the properties of a male: to castrate: to deprive of masculine vigour: to render effeminate: to lessen or take away the power, force or effectiveness of (*fig.*). — *adj.* emasculated. — *ns.* **emasculā'tion; emas'culātor.** — *adj.* **emas'culatory** (*-lə-tər-i*). [L.L. *ēmasculāre, -ātum* — *ē,* from, *masculus,* dim. of *mās,* a male.]

embace. See **embase.**

embail *im-, em-bāl', (obs.) v.t.* to encircle: to hoop in: — *pa.p., Spens.,* **embayld'.** [Pfx. **em-** (**en-** (1a)).]

embale *im-, em-bāl', v.t.* to make up, as into a bale: to bind up: to enclose. [Fr. *emballer* — *em-* (L. *in*), in, *balle,* a bale.]

emball *em-böl', v.t.* to ensphere. — *n.* **emball'ing** (*Shak.*) the receiving of the ball (of sovereignty). [Pfx. **em-** (**en-** (1a)).]

embalm *im-, em-bäm', v.t.* to preserve from decay by aromatic drugs, as a dead body: to preserve with fragrance: to preserve unchanged but lifeless: to impregnate with balm, perfume. — *ns.* **embalm'er; em-**

balm'ing, embalm'ment. [Fr. *embaumer*, from *em-*, in, and *baume*; see **balm**.]
embank *im-, em-bangk'*, *v.t.* to enclose or defend with a bank or dike. — *ns.* **embank'er**; **embank'ment** the act of embanking: a bank or mound made to keep water within certain limits: a mound constructed so as to carry a level road or railway over a low-lying place. [Pfx. **em- (en-** (1a)).]
embar *im-, em-bär'*, *v.t.* to shut in: to hinder or stop (*arch.*): (*Milt.* **imbar'**) to put under embargo (*arch.*): — *pr.p.* **embarr'ing**; *pa.t.* and *pa.p.* **embarred'**. — *n.* **embarr'ing.** — Also **imbar'**. [Pfx. **em- (en-** (1a)).]
embarcation. Same as **embarkation.**
embargo *em-bär'gō*, *n.* a temporary order from the Admiralty to prevent the arrival or departure of ships: a stoppage of trade for a short time by authority: a prohibition, ban: — *pl.* **embar'goes.** — *v.t.* to lay an embargo on: to seize: — *pr.p.* **embar'gōing**; *pa.t.* and *pa.p.* **embar'goed** (*-gōd*). — *n.* **embarque'ment** (*Shak.*) a placing under embargo. [Sp., — *embargar*, to impede, to restrain — Sp. pfx. *em-*, in, L.L. (and Sp.) *barra*, a bar.]
embark *im-, em-bärk'*, *v.t.* to put on board ship: to engage, invest, in any affair. — *v.i.* to go on board ship: to engage in (with *on, in*). — *n.* **embarka'tion** (*em-*) a putting or going on board: that which is embarked: a vessel (*obs.*). — *adjs.* **embarked'; embark'ing.** — *n.* **embark'ment.** [Fr. *embarquer*, from *em-*, in, *barque*, bark.]
embarquement. See **embargo.**
embarras de (du) choix *ã-ba-ra dǝ (dü) shwa*, (Fr.) embarrassment in choice, a perplexing number of things to choose from; **embarras de(s) richesses** (*dǝ (dã) rē-shes*) a perplexing amount of wealth or of abundance of any kind.
embarrass *im-, em-bar'ǝs*, *v.t.* to encumber: to involve in difficulty, esp. in money matters: to put out of countenance, disconcert: to perplex. — *adj.* **embarr'assed** perplexed: constrained: out of countenance: disconcerted. — *n.* **embarr'assment** the state of feeling embarrassed: something which causes one to feel embarrassed: difficulties in money matters: a perplexing amount (see **embarras de choix**, etc.). [Fr. *embarrasser — em-*, in, *barre*, L.L. *barra*, bar.]
embase, imbase (*Spens.* **embace**) *im-bās'*, *v.t.* to lower: to bring down: to degrade: to debase: — *pa.p.* and *pa.t.* **embased'**; (*Spens.*) **embaste'.** — *adj.* **embased'.** — *n.* **embase'ment.** [Pfx. **em- (en-** (1b) and **base**, or Fr. *bas*.]
embassy *em'bǝ-si*, *n.* the charge or function of an ambassador: the person or body of persons sent on an undertaking: an ambassador's residence. — *n.* **em'bassade** (*Shak.*) an embassy. — *adv.* (*Spens. -bas'*) on an embassy. — *ns.* **embassador** (*-bas'*; *obs.*) an ambassador; **em'bassage** embassy: the sending or business of an embassy. [See **ambassador.**]
embaste. See **embase.**
embathe, imbathe *im-hādh'*, *v.t.* to bathe: to immerse: to bedew. [Pfx. **em- (en-** (1c)).]
embattle[1] *im-bat'l*, *v.t.* to furnish with battlements. — *adj.* **embatt'led** furnished with battlements: having the outline like a battlement (*her.*). — *n.* **embatt'lement** battlement. [Pfx. **em- (en-** (1c)) and O.Fr. *bataillier*, to embattle; see **battlement.**]
embattle[2] *im-bat'l*, *v.t.* to range in order of battle: to arm (*Spens.*). — *adj.* **embatt'led** arranged for battle: involved in battle (also *fig.*). [O.Fr. *embataillier — em-*, in, *bataille*, battle.]
embay[1] *im-bā'* *v.t.* to enclose in a bay: to land-lock. — *n.* **embay'ment** a bay. [Pfx. **em- (en-** (1a)).]
embay[2] *em-bā'*, (*Spens.*) *v.t.* to bathe, steep, imbue. [Fr. *em-*, in, and apparently *baigner*; see **bagnio**.]
embayld. See **embail.**
embed, imbed *im-bed'*, *v.t.* to place in a mass of matter (also *fig.*): to lay, as in a bed. — *n.* **embed'ment** the act of embedding: the state of being embedded. [Pfx. **em- (en-** (1a)).]

embellish *im-bel'ish*, *v.t.* to make beautiful with ornaments: to decorate: to make graceful: to illustrate pictorially, as a book: to add interesting and possibly untruthful details to (an account, narrative, etc.). — *n.* **embell'isher.** — *adv.* **embell'ishingly.** — *n.* **embell'ishment** the act of embellishing or adorning: a decoration: ornament. [Fr. *embellir, embellissant — em-*, in, *bel* (*beau*) beautiful.]
ember *em'bǝr*, *n.* a piece of live coal or wood: (the following definitions chiefly in *pl.*) red-hot ashes: smouldering remains of a fire, or (*fig.*) of love, passion, etc. [O.E. *æmerge*; O.N. *eimyrja*.]
Ember-days *em'bǝr-dāz*, *n.pl.* the three Fast-days (Wednesday, Friday, Saturday) in each quarter, following the first Sunday in Lent, Whitsunday, Holy Cross Day (Sept. 14th), and St Lucia's Day (Dec. 13th). — **Em'ber-week** the week in which they occur. [O.E. *ymbryne*, a circuit — *ymb* round (cf. Ger. *um*, L. *ambi-*), and *ryne*, a running, from *rinnan*, to run.]
ember-goose *em'bǝr-gōōs*, *n.* the great northern diver. [Norw. *emmer*; Ger. *Imber*.]
embezzle *im-bez'l*, *v.t.* to appropriate fraudulently (now only what has been entrusted): to impair (*obs.*). — *ns.* **embezz'lement** fraudulent appropriation of property entrusted to one; **embezz'ler.** [Anglo-Fr. *embesiler*, to make away with; perh. influenced by **imbecile** (q.v.).]
embitter, imbitter *im-bit'ǝr*, *v.t.* to make bitter or more bitter: to make more bitterly hostile. — *adj.* **embitt'ered** soured: rendered misanthropical, cynical, or disappointed. — *n.* **embitt'erer.** — *n.* and *adj.* **embitt'ering.** — *n.* **embitt'erment.** [Pfx. **em- (en-** (1b)).]
emblaze[1] *im-blāz'*, *v.t.* to light up: to set aflame. [Pfx. **em- (en-** (1b)).]
emblaze[2] *im-blāz'*, *v.t.* to describe or depict heraldically: to celebrate: to adorn heraldically. [Pfx. **em- (en-** (1c)).]
emblazon *im-blā'zn*, *v.t.* in heraldry, to adorn with figures: to depict heraldically: to celebrate. — *ns.* **emblā'zoner**; **emblā'zonment** an emblazoning; **emblā'zonry** the art of emblazoning or adorning: devices on shields. [Pfx. **em- (en-** (1c)).]
emblem *em'blǝm*, *n.* a picture representing to the mind something different from itself: a symbolic device or badge: a type or symbol: an inlaid ornament (*Milt.*). — *v.t.* to symbolise. — *n.* **emblema** (*em-blē'mǝ*) an inlaid ornament: — *pl.* **emblē'mata.** — *adjs.* **emblemat'ic, -al** pertaining to or containing emblems: symbolical: representing (with *of*). — *adv.* **emblemat'ically.** — *vs.t.* **emblematise, -ize** (*-blem'ǝ-tīz*), **em'blemise, -ize** to represent by an emblem. — *n.* **emblem'atist** a writer or inventor of emblems. [L., — Gr. *emblēma, -atos*, a thing inserted — *en*, in, and the root of *ballein*, to throw.]
emblements *em'bli-mǝnts*, *n.pl.* crops raised by the labour of the cultivator, but not tree-fruits or grass. [O.Fr. *emblaer*, to sow with corn — L.L. *imbladāre — in*, in, *bladum*, wheat.]
emblic *em'blik*, *n.* an East Indian tree (*Phyllanthus emblica*) of the spurge family: its fruit, used for tanning. — Also **emblic myrobalan.** [Ar. *amlaj* — Pers. *amleh*.]
embloom *im-blōōm'*, *v.t.* to cover with bloom. [Pfx. **em- (en-** (1a)).]
emblossom *im-blos'ǝm*, *v.t.* to cover with blossom. [Pfx. **em- (en-** (1a)).]
embody, imbody *im-bod'i*, *v.t.* to form into a body: to make corporeal: to make tangible: to express (in words, in tangible form, etc.): to make part of a body, to incorporate: to organise. — *v.i.* to unite in a body or mass: to become corporeal, carnal, or sensual: — *pr.p.* **embod'ying**; *pa.t.* and *pa.p.* **embod'ied.** — *adj.* **embod'ied.** — *n.* **embod'iment** the act of embodying: the state of being embodied: that in which something is embodied. [Pfx. **em- (en-** (1a)).]
embog *im-bog'*, *v.t.* to bog. [Pfx. **em- (en-** (1c)).]
embogue *im-bōg'*, *v.i.* to disembogue.
emboil *em-, im-boil'*, (*obs.*) *v.i.* (*Spens.*) to burn with

anger. — *v.t.* to cause to burn with anger: to irritate. [Pfx. **em- (en-** (1c)).]

emboîtement *ă-bwät-mä′, n.* encasement. — **emboîtement theory** the abandoned theory of old embryologists that the egg contained the germs of all future descendants, box within box. [Fr.]

embolden *im-bōld′n, v.t.* to make bold or courageous: to give the necessary courage for some action: to set in bold type (*typography*). — *n.* **embold′ener.** [Pfx. **em- (en-** (1b)).]

embolism *em′bol-izm, -bəl-, n.* an intercalation of days in the calendar to correct error: an intercalated prayer for deliverance from evil coming after the Lord's Prayer: the presence of one or more obstructing clots, etc. in the blood vessels (*med.*). — *adjs.* **embolic (-bol′)** relating to an embolus or an emboly; **embolis′mal; embolis′mic.** — *ns.* **em′bolus** a clot obstructing a blood-vessel; **em′boly** an invagination. — **embolismic year** see **year.** [Late Gr. *embolismos,* intercalation, Gr. *embolos,* a stopper, *embolē,* insertion, ramming — *emballein,* to throw in.]

embonpoint *ã-bõ-pwẽ′, adj.* stout, plump, full in figure: well-fed. — *n.* stoutness, plumpness, well-fed condition. [Fr., — *en bon point,* in good form.]

emborder, imborder *im-, em-bŏrd′ər, (Milt.) v.t.* to set as a border: to border. [Pfx. **em- (en-** (1c)).]

emboscata *em-bos-kä′tə, -kä′tə, n.* an erroneous form of It. *imboscata,* or Sp. *emboscada,* an ambuscade.

embosom, imbosom *im-bŏoz′əm, v.t.* to take into the bosom: to receive into the affections: to implant in the bosom or mind: to enclose or surround. [Pfx. **em- (en-** (1a)).]

emboss¹ *im-bos′, v.t.* to cover with bosses: to raise bosses on: to raise in relief: to ornament with raised work. — *adj.* **embossed′** formed or covered with bosses: raised, standing out in relief: having a protuberance in the centre (*bot.*). — *ns.* **emboss′er; emboss′ment** a prominence like a boss: raised work. [Pfx. **em- (en-** (1a)).]

emboss², imboss *im-bos′, imbosk -bosk′ (obs.) vs.i.* to take to the depths of a wood. — *vs.t.* to drive to extremity: to make to foam at the mouth: — *pa.p.* **embossed′,** *Milt.* **embost′.** [O.Fr. *embosquer, em-* (L. *in,* in), *bosc,* a wood; see **ambush.**]

emboss³ *em-bos′, (Spens.) v.t.* to clothe: to wrap: to enclose. [Origin obscure.]

embouchure *ä-bŏo-shür′, n.* the mouth of a river: the mouthpiece of a wind instrument: the disposition of the mouth in playing a wind instrument. [Fr., — *emboucher,* to put to the mouth, to discharge — *en,* in, *bouche,* a mouth.]

embound *em-bownd′, (Shak.) v.t.* to enclose. [Pfx. **em- (en-** (1a)).]

embourgeoise *im-bŏor′zhwäz, ã-bŏor-zhwaz′, v.t.* to cause to become bourgeois or middle-class: — *pr.p.* **embour′-geoising;** *pa.t.* **embour′geoised.** — *n.* **embourgeoisement** (*im-bŏor′zhwäz-mənt, ã-bŏor-zhwaz-mä*). [Fr. *em-bourgeoiser;* see **bourgeois.**]

embow *em-bow′, em-bō′, (arch.) v.t.* to bend: to arch or vault: to ensphere. — *adj.* **embowed′** bent. [Pfx. **em- (en-** (1a)).]

embowel *im-bow′əl, v.t.* to enclose (*obs.*): to disembowel, to remove the entrails from: to enclose in, or (*Spens.*) thrust into, the bowels (*obs.*): — *pr.p.* **embow′elling;** *pa.t.* and *pa.p.* **embow′elled.** — *n.* **embow′elment.** [Pfx. **em- (en-** (1a)).]

embower, imbower *im-bow′ər, v.t.* to place in a bower: to shelter, as with trees. — *v.i.* to take or give shelter. — *n.* **embow′erment.** [Pfx. **em- (en-** (la)).]

embox *im-boks′, v.t.* to set in a box. [Pfx. **em- (en- (**1a)).]

embrace¹ *im-brās′, v.t.* to take in the arms: to press to the bosom with affection: to take eagerly or willingly: to comprise: to admit, adopt, or receive. — *v.i.* to join in an embrace: — *pr.p.* **embrac′ing;** *pa.t.* and *pa.p.* **embraced′.** — *n.* an embracing: fond pressure in the arms: (in *pl.*) sexual intercourse (*arch.*). — *ns.* **em-brace′ment; embrac′er.** — *adjs.* **embrac′ing; embrac′ive.**

— *adv.* **embrac′ingly.** — *n.* **embrac′ingness.** [O.Fr. *embracer* (Fr. *embrasser*) — L. *in,* in, into, *brā(c)chium,* an arm; see **brace.**]

embrace² *em-brās′, (Spens.) v.t.* to brace, to fasten, or bind. [Pfx. **em- (en-** (1a)).]

embracer, embraceor, embrasor *em-brā′sər, (law) n.* one who seeks to influence jurors by corrupt means to deliver a partial verdict. — *n.* **embrac′ery** the offence of an embracer. [O.Fr. *embraceor,* from *embraser,* to set on fire.]

embraid *em-brād′, (Spens.) v.t.* to braid. [Pfx. **em- (en-** (1c)).]

embranchment *im-bränch′mənt, -sh-, n.* a branching off, as an arm of a river, a spur of a mountain, etc. [Fr. *embranchement.*]

embrangle, imbrangle *im-brang′gl, v.t.* to confuse, per-plex. — *n.* **embran′glement.** [Pfx. **em- (en-** (1a)).]

embrasor. See **embracer.**

embrasure¹ *em-brās′yər, (Shak.) n.* embrace. [Pfx. **em- (en-** (1a)).]

embrasure² *im-brā′zhər, (archit.) n.* an internally splayed recess of a door or window: the slant of such a recess: an opening in a wall for cannon. — Also **embrā′zure.** [Fr., — O.Fr. *embraser,* to slope the sides of a window — *em-* (— L. *in*), *braser,* to skew.]

embrave *em-brāv′, v.t.* to make showy, to decorate (*Spens.*): to inspire with bravery. [Pfx. **em- (en-** (1b)).]

embread *em-brēd′, (Spens.) v.t.* to embraid. [Pfx. **em- (en-** (1c)).]

embreathe *em-brēdh′, v.t.* to breathe into: to breathe in. [Pfx. **em- (en-** (1a)).]

embrewe (*Spens.*). See **imbrue.**

embrittle *im-brit′əl, v.t.* and *v.i.* to make or become brittle. — *n.* **embrit′tlement.** [Pfx. **em (en-(**1b)).]

embrocate *em′brō-kāt, v.t.* to moisten and rub, as with a lotion. — *n.* **embrōcā′tion** the act of embrocating: the lotion used. [L.L. *embrocāre, -ātum,* from Gr. *em-brochē,* a lotion — *embrechein,* to soak, embrocate — *en-,* in, into, *brechein,* to wet.]

embroglio. See **imbroglio.**

embroider *im-broid′ər, v.t.* to ornament with designs in needlework: to add ornament or fictitious detail to. — *ns.* **embroid′erer; embroid′ery** the art of producing ornamental designs in needlework on textile fabrics, etc.: ornamental needlework: variegation or diversity: artificial or elaborate ornamentation: embellishment: exaggeration or invented detail. [M.E. *embrouderie* — O.Fr. *embroder;* confused with or influenced by O.E. *bregdan,* to weave, braid.]

embroil *im-broil′, v.t.* to involve in a broil, or in perplexity (with): to entangle: to distract: to throw into confu-sion. — *n.* **embroil′ment** a state of perplexity or con-fusion: disturbance. [Fr. *embrouiller* — pfx. *em-,* and *brouiller,* to break out.]

embrown, imbrown *im-brown′, v.t.* to make brown: to darken, obscure. — *adj.* **embrown′ing.** [Pfx. **em- (en-** (1b)).]

embrue. Same as **imbrue.**

embrute. Same as **imbrute.**

embryo *em′bri-ō,* also (*arch.*) **embryon** *em′bri-on, ns.* a young animal or plant in its earliest stages of devel-opment: the beginning of anything: — *pls.* **em′bryos, em′bryons.** — Also *adj.* — *ns.* **embryogen′esis, embryo-geny** (*-oj′i-ni*) the formation and development of the embryo. — *adjs.* **embryolog′ic, -al.** — *ns.* **embryol′ogist; embryol′ogy** the science of the formation and devel-opment of the embryo. — *adjs.* **em′bryonal; em′bry-onate, -d; embryon′ic, embryot′ic** of or relating to anything in an imperfect or incomplete state: rudimen-tary. — *ns.* **embryot′omy** (Gr. *tomē,* a cut) the division of a foetus to effect removal; **embryulcia** (*-ul′shi-ə;* Gr. *holkē,* dragging) forcible extraction of a foetus. — **em′bryo-sac** the megaspore of a flowering plant, one of the cells of the nucellus. [L.L., — Gr. *embryon* — *en,* in, *bryein,* to swell.]

embus *im-bus′, v.t.* to put (esp. troops) into a bus. — *v.i.*

to mount a bus: — *pr.p.* **embuss'ing;** *pa.t.* and *pa.p.* **embussed'.** [Pfx. **em- (en-** (1a)).]

embusqué *ã-bü-skā*, (Fr.) *adj.* in ambush. — *n.* a slacker, shirker: one who evades military service.

embusy *em-biz'i*, (*Spens.*) *v.t.* to occupy, make busy. [Pfx. **em- (en-** (1b)).]

emcee *em-sē'*, (*coll.*) *n.* a master of ceremonies, a phonetic representation of the abbrev. **MC.** — *v.i.* and *v.t.* to act as a master of ceremonies (for).

eme *ēm*, (*obs.*) *n.* an uncle. [O.E. *ēam*; Du. *oom*.]

emeer. See **emir.**

emend *ē-mend'*, *v.t.* to remove faults or blemishes from (now *rare*): to make alterations in with a view to improving (a text). — *adj.* **ēmend'able** that may be emended. — *n.pl.* **ēmend'als** funds set apart for repairs in the accounts of the Inner Temple. — *v.t.* **ē'mendate** to correct errors. — *ns.* **ēmendā'tion** the removal of an error or fault: correction; **ē'mendātor** a corrector of errors in writings: one who corrects or improves. — *adj.* **ēmen'datory** mending or contributing to correction. [L. *ēmendāre, -ātum* — *ē*, from, *mendum*, a fault.]

emerald *em'ər-əld*, (*Spens.* **emeraude**) *n.* a very highly esteemed gemstone, a beautiful velvety green variety of beryl: (also **emerald green**) its colour. — **em'erald= copp'er** dioptase; **em'erald-cut** in gemstones, a multi-faceted flat-topped rectangular cut; **Emerald Isle** Ireland, from its greenness; **emerald type** (*print.*) a small size of type. [O.Fr. *esmeralde* — L. *smaragdus* — Gr. *smaragdos*.]

emerge *i-, ē-mûrj'*, *v.i.* to rise out of anything: to issue or come forth: to reappear after being concealed: to come into view: to come into being in the course of evolution: to crop up. — *ns.* **emer'gence** the act of emerging: a sudden appearance: an emergency (*obs.*): in botany, an outgrowth of subepidermic tissue along with epidermic — an appendage more complex in structure than a hair; **emer'gency** emergence (*obs.*): an unexpected occurrence, requiring immediate action: pressing necessity: a substitute in reserve. — Also *adj.* — *adj.* **emer'gent** emerging: suddenly appearing: arising unexpectedly: urgent: coming into being in the course of evolution: (of a state) having recently become independent. — *adv.* **emer'gently.** — *adj.* **emer'ging** developing: becoming important. — *adj.* **emersed** (*ē-mûrst'*; *bot.*) rising above the surface of water (as leaves). — *n.* **emer'sion** (*-shən*) the act of emerging: the reappearance of a heavenly body after eclipse or occultation (*astron.*). — **emergency exit** an exit to be used only in an emergency, e.g. fire. — **state of emergency** a situation in which a government suspends the normal constitution in order to deal with an emergency such as a natural disaster or civil disorder. [L. *ēmergēre, ēmersum* — *ē*, out of, *mergēre*, to plunge.]

emeritus *i-, ē-mer'i-təs*, *adj.* (often following a noun) honourably discharged from the performance of public duty, esp. denoting a retired professor. — *n.* one who has been honourably discharged from public duties: — *pl.* **emer'itī.** [L. *ēmeritus*, having served one's time — *ēmererī*, to earn — *ē-*, sig. completeness, and *merērī*, to deserve.]

emerods *em'ə-rodz*, (*B.*) *n.pl.* now **haemorrhoids:** representations of them in gold, used as charms.

emersed, emersion. See **emerge.**

emery *em'ər-i*, *n.* a very hard mineral, a variety of corundum, used as powder for polishing, etc. — *v.t.* to rub or coat with emery. — **em'ery-bag** a bag of emery-powder for cleaning and sharpening needles; **em'ery-board** a small flat strip of wood or card coated with emery-powder, used in manicure; **em'ery-cloth, -paper** cloth, paper, covered with emery-powder for polishing; **em'ery-pow'der** ground emery; **em'ery-wheel** a wheel coated with emery for polishing. [O.Fr. *esmeril, emeril* — L.L. *smericulum* — Gr. *smēris, smŷris*.]

emetic *i-met'ik*, *adj.* causing vomiting. — *n.* a medicine that causes vomiting. — *n.* **emesis** (*em'i-sis*) vomiting.

— *adj.* **emet'ical.** — *adv.* **emet'ically.** — *n.* **em'etin, -ine** the alkaloid forming the active principle of ipecacuanha root, violently emetic. [Gr. *emetikos* — *emeein*, to vomit.]

emeu. See **emu.**

émeute *ā-møt'*, sometimes *i-mūt'*, *n.* a popular rising or uproar. [Fr.]

emicate *em'i-kāt*, *v.i.* to sparkle. — *adj.* **em'icant** sparkling: flashing. — *n.* **emicā'tion.** [L. *ēmicāre, -ātum*.]

emiction *i-mik'shən*, *n.* the discharging of urine. — *adj.* **emic'tory** promoting the flow of urine. [L. *ēmingēre, ēmictum* — *ē*, from, *mingēre*, to urinate.]

emigrate *em'i-grāt*, *v.i.* and *v.t.* to remove from one country (or state) to another as a place of abode. — *adj.* **em'igrant** emigrating or having emigrated. — *n.* one who emigrates. — *n.* **emigrā'tion.** — *adj.* **emigrā'-tional.** — *n.* **emigrā'tionist** an advocate or promoter of emigration. — *adj.* **em'igrātory.** — *n.* **émigré** (*ā-mē-grā'*) a royalist who quitted France during the Revolution: an (esp. political) emigrant. [L. *ēmīgrāre, ēmīgrāre, -ātum* — *ē*, from, *migrāre*, to remove.]

éminence grise *ā-mē-näs grēz*, (Fr.) one exercising power in the background, as Cardinal Richelieu's private secretary and *alter ego* Père Joseph, nicknamed *l'Éminence Grise* ('the Grey Eminence').

eminent *em'i-nənt*, *adj.* rising above others: conspicuous: distinguished: exalted in rank or office. — *ns.* **em'inence** a part eminent or rising above the rest: a rising ground: a ridge or knob: height: distinction: a title given in 1631 to cardinals, till then styled Most Illustrious: advantage, upper hand (*Shak.*); **em'inency.** — *adj.* **eminen'tial** (*-shəl*; *obs.*). — *adv.* **em'inently.** — **eminent domain** the right by which the supreme authority in a state may compel a proprietor to part with what is his own for the public use. [L. *ēminēns, -entis*, pr.p. of *ēminēre* — *ē*, from, *minēre*, to project.]

emir *ā-mēr'*, sometimes *ē'mər*, *n.* a title given in the East and in N. Africa to all independent chieftains, and also (perh. improperly) to all the supposed descendants of Mohammed through his daughter Fatima. — *n.* **emir'-ate** the office, jurisdiction, or state of an emir. — Also **ameer, amir** (*a-mēr', ə-*), **emeer.** [Ar. *amīr*, ruler.]

Emi-Scanner® *em'i-skan-ər*, *n.* a machine which produces X-ray pictures of the head or body with the assistance of a computer. [**EMI** — see List of Abbreviations.]

emit *i-, ē-mit'*, *v.t.* to send out: to throw or give out: to issue: to utter (a declaration): — *pr.p.* **emitt'ing;** *pa.t.* and *pa.p.* **emitt'ed.** — *n.* **emissary** (*em'is-ər-i*) one sent out on a mission, esp. an underhand or secret mission: a spy: an underground outlet, esp. of a lake. — *adj.* that is sent forth: outgoing. — *adj.* **emiss'ile** protrusible. — *n.* **emission** (*-mish'ən*) the act of emitting: that which is issued at one time: the discharge of semen: the release of electrons from parent atoms on absorption of energy exceeding the average. — *adj.* **emiss'ive** emitting, sending out. — *n.* **emissiv'ity** (*ē-*) the property or power of emitting or radiating. — **emission theory** the corpuscular theory. [L. *ēmittēre, ēmissum* — *ē*, out of, *mittēre*, to send.]

emma *em'ə*, *n.* (*formerly*) a signallers' name for the letter *m*.

Emmanuel, Immanuel *i-man'ū-əl, -el*, *n.* the symbolical name of the child announced by Isaiah (Isa. vii. 14), and applied to Jesus as the Messiah in Matt. i. 23. [Gr. *Emmanouēl* — Heb. *'Immānūēl* — *'im*, with, *ānū*, us, *ēl*, God.]

emmarble *i-mär'bl*, *v.t.* to turn to marble: to represent in marble: to adorn with marble. [Pfx. **em- (en-** (1b)).]

emmenagogue *em-ēn'ə-gog*, or *-en'*, *n.* medicine intended to restore, or to bring on, the menses. — Also *adj.* — *adj.* **emmenagogic** (*-goj'ik*). — *n.* **emmenol'ogy** the study of menstruation. [Gr. *emmēna*, menses (— *mēn*, a month), and *agōgos*, drawing forth.]

Emmental, -thal, Emmentaler, -thaler *em'ən-täl, -ər*, *ns.* and *adjs.* applied to a Swiss cheese, like Gruyère, made in the Emmental or Emme valley.

emmer *em'ər, n.* a species of wheat, *Triticum dicoccum.* [Ger. dial.]

emmesh. Same as **enmesh.**

emmet *em'it,* (*arch.* and *dial.*) *n.* the ant: in Cornwall, a tourist. [O.E. *æmete.*]

emmetropia *em-e-trō'pi-ə, n.* the normal condition of the refractive media of the eye. — *n.* **emm'etrope** an emmetropic person. — *adj.* **emmetropic** (*-trop'ik*). [Gr. *en,* in, *metron,* measure, *ops,* the eye.]

emmew, immew *i-mū',* **enmew** *in-mū', vs.t.* to confine, mew up. — But in *Shak.* app. for **enew.** [Pfx. **em-** (**en-** (1a)).]

emmove *e-mōōv',* (*Spens.*) *v.t.* to move, to excite.

Emmy *em'i, n.* a television trophy, corresponding to the cinema Oscar, awarded by the American Academy of Television Arts and Sciences: — *pl.* **Em'mys, Em'mies.** [Ety. dub.]

emollient *i-mol'yənt, adj.* softening: making supple. — *n.* a softening application, as poultices, fomentations, etc. (*med.*). — *n.* **emollesc'ence** incipient fusion. — *v.t.* **emoll'iate** to soften: to render effeminate. — *n.* **emolli'tion** the act of softening or relaxing. [L. *ēmollīre,* *ēmollītum* — *ē,* intens., *mollīre,* to soften — *mollis,* soft.]

emolument *i-mol'ū-mənt, n.* advantage (*obs.*): (often in *pl.* profit arising from employment, as salary or fees. — *adjs.* **emolumen'tal; emolumen'tary.** [L. *ēmolimentum,* prob. from *ēmolēre,* to grind out — *ē,* and *molēre,* to grind, rather than from *ēmolīrī* to work out, *molīrī,* to toil.]

emong, emonges, emongest, emongst. Obs. forms of **among, amongst.**

emotion *i-mō'shən, n.* a moving of the feelings: agitation of mind: one of the three groups of the phenomena of the mind — feeling, distinguished from cognition and will (*phil.*). — *v.i.* **emote** (*i-mōt'*) to show or express exaggerated emotion. — *adjs.* **emō'tionable; emō'tional.** — *n.* **emō'tionalism** a tendency to emotional excitement (also **emotional'ity**): the habit of working on the emotions: the indulgence of superficial emotion. — *adv.* **emō'tionally.** — *adjs.* **emō'tionless; emō'tive** (*-tiv*) pertaining to the emotions: emotional: tending to arouse emotion. — *v.t.* **emove** (*i-mōōv'*) to affect with emotion. [L. *ēmōtiō, -ōnis* — *ēmovēre, -mōtum,* to stir up.]

empacket *im-pak'it,* (*Scott*) *v.t.* to pack up. [Pfx. **em-** (**en-** (1c)).]

empaestic *em-pē'stik, adj.* pertaining to the art of embossing: stamped, inlaid. [Gr. *empaiein,* to emboss.]

empaire (*Spens.*). See **impair**[1].

empale *em-pāl', v.t.* to impale: to surround with a border (*Spens.*). [**impale.**]

empanel *im-pan'əl, v.t.* to enter on a panel: — *pr.p.* **empan'elling;** *pa.t.* and *pa.p.* **empan'elled.** — *n.* **empan'elment.** — Also **impanel, impannel.** [Pfx. **em-** (**en-** (1a)).]

empanoply *im-pan'o-pli, v.t.* to invest in full armour. [Pfx. **em-** (**en-** (1a)).]

emparadise (*Milt.*), **empare** (*Spens.*), **emparlaunce** (*Spens.*), **empart** (*Spens.*), **empassionate** (*Spens.*), **empassioned** (*Spens.*). See **imparadise,** etc.

empathy *em'pə-thi, n.* the power of entering into another's personality and imaginatively experiencing his experiences: the power of entering into the feeling or spirit of something (esp. a work of art) and so appreciating it fully. — *adjs.* **empathet'ic; empath'ic.** — *v.i.* **em'pathise, -ize.** [Gr. *en,* in, *pathos,* feeling.]

empatron *em-pā'trən,* (*Shak.*) *v.t.* to patronise. [Pfx. **em-** (**en-** (1c)).]

empayre (*Spens.*). See **impair**[1].

empeach (*Spens.*). See **impeach.**

empennage *em-pen'ij, ã-pen-äzh', n.* an aeroplane's tail as a unit, including elevator, rudder, and fin. [Fr., feathering of an arrow — L. *penna,* feather, wing.]

empeople *im-pē'pl,* (*obs.*) *v.t.* to fill with people: to form into a people or community. [Pfx. **em-** (**en-** (1a)).]

emperce. See **empierce.**

emperish *im-per'ish,* (*Spens.,* etc.) *v.t.* to impair. [Perh.

(irregularly) — Fr. *empirer;* cf. **impair**[1].]

emperor *em'pər-ər, n.* the head of an empire: a high title of sovereignty: before metrication, a paper size (48 × 72 in.): — *fem.* **em'press.** — *v.t.* **em'perise, -ize** (*obs.*) to play the emperor. — *ns.* **em'perorship; em'pery** (esp. *poet.*) empire, power. — **emperor moth** except the death's-head, the largest British moth, its expanse of wings being about three inches; **emperor penguin** the largest of the penguins. [O.Fr. *emperere* — L. *imperātor,* a commander (fem. *imperātrix*) — *imperāre,* to command.]

Empfindung *emp-fin'dōong,* (Ger.) *n.* sensation, feeling.

emphasis *em'fə-sis, n.* the use of language to imply more than is said (*obs.*): forcible or impressive expression: an insistent or vigorous way of attributing importance or thrusting upon attention: stress: accent: prominence: — *pl.* **em'phases** (*-sēz*). — *v.t.* **em'phasise, -ize** to make emphatic: to lay stress on. — *adjs.* **emphat'ic** (*im-, em-fat'ik*), **-al** expressed or expressing with emphasis: stressed forcibly: impressive: strongly marked. — *adv.* **emphat'ically.** — *n.* **emphat'icalness.** [Gr. *emphasis,* image, outward appearance, significance, implied meaning — *en,* in, *phainein,* to show.]

emphlysis *em'fli-sis, n.* a vesicular eruption. — *pl.* **em'physes.** [Gr. *en,* in, *phlȳsis,* eruption — *phlȳein,* to bubble, break out.]

emphractic *em-frak'tik, adj.* stopping the pores of the skin. — *n.* a substance with this property. [Gr. *emphraktikos,* obstructive — *en,* in, *phrassein,* to stop.]

emphysema *em-fis-ē'mə,* (*med.*) *n.* an unnatural distension of a part of the body with air: distension of the lung, with breathing difficulties, etc. — *adj.* **emphysē'matous.** — *n.* **emphysē'mic** a sufferer from emphysema. [Gr. *emphȳsēma* — *emphȳsaein,* to inflate.]

emphyteusis *em-fit-ū'sis, n.* in Roman law, a perpetual right in a piece of land, for which a yearly sum was paid to the proprietor. — *adj.* **emphyteu'tic.** [Gr., — *emphyteuein,* to implant.]

empiecement *em-pēs'mənt, n.* an insertion in a garment. [Fr. *empiècement.*]

empierce, emperce *em-pērs',* (*Spens.*) *v.t.* to pierce. [Pfx. **em-** (**en-** (1c)).]

empight *em-pīt',* (*Spens.*) *adj.* fixed. [**pitch**[2].]

empire *em'pīr, n.* (*loosely*) a widespreading dominion, or group of states, etc., under the same sovereign power — not always an emperor: supreme control or dominion: the government or office of an emperor: the time of its duration: a large industrial organisation embracing many firms: a country whose sovereign owes no allegiance to another (*hist.*). — *adj.* (usu. with *cap.*) relating to or in the style of, esp. of dress or furniture, the first French Empire (1804–14). — **em'pire-building** the practice or policy of increasing one's power or authority. — Also *adj.* — **em'pire-builder; Empire Day** formerly, a public holiday celebrated on (or near) 24th May (Queen Victoria's birthday): **Empire gown** a gown with low neckline and high waist such as was worn during the first French Empire. [Fr., — L. *imperium.*]

empiric *em-pir'ik,* formerly *em', adj.* empirical. — *n.* one who makes trials or experiments: one whose knowledge is got from experience only: a quack. — *adj.* **empir'ical** resting on trial or experiment: known or knowing only by experience. — *adv.* **empir'ically.** — *ns.* **empir'icism** (*-sizm*) the system which, rejecting all *a priori* knowledge, rests solely on experience and induction (*phil.*): the dependence of a physician on his experience alone without a regular medical education: the practice of medicine without a regular education: quackery; **empir'icist** (*-sist*) one who practises empiricism. — *adj.* **empiricūt'ic** (*Shak.* **empirick qutique;** modelled on *therapeutic; obs.*) empirical. — **empirical formula** (*chem.*) a formula showing in simplest form the ratio of atoms in a molecule, not the absolute number. [Fr., — L. *empīricus* — Gr. *empeirikos* — *en,* in, *peira,* a trial.]

emplacement *im-plās'mənt, n.* the act of placing: a gun-platform (*mil.*). — *v.t.* **emplace'** (back-formation) to put in or provide with an emplacement. [Fr. *emplacement.*]

emplane *im-plān'*, *v.t.* to put or take on an aeroplane. — *v.i.* to mount an aeroplane. [Pfx. **em- (en-** (1a)) and **plane²**.]

emplaster *em-pläs'tər*, *n.* and *v.* same as **plaster**. — *adj.* **emplastic** (-*plas'*) glutinous: adhesive. — *n.* a medicine that stops the pores. — *ns.* **emplas'tron** (Gr.), **emplas'trum** (L.) a medicated plaster. [Gr. *emplastron.*]

emplecton *em-plek'ton*, (*arch.*) *n.* ashlar masonry filled up with rubble. — Also (L.) **emplec'tum**. [Gr. *emplekton* — *en*, in, *plekein*, to weave.]

emplonge (*Spens.*). See **implunge**.

employ *im-ploi'*, *v.t.* to occupy the time or attention of: to use as a means or agent: to give work to. — *n.* employment. — *adj.* **employ'able** fit, able, to be employed. — *adj.* **employed'** having employment, in a job. — *ns.* **employ'ee** (or *em-ploi-ē'*) a person employed: **employ'er; employ'ment** the act of employing: that which engages or occupies: occupation. — **employment agency** an agency which finds work for the unemployed and employees for vacant positions; **Employment Service Agency** a government agency run by the Department of Employment, which finds work for the unemployed, pays out unemployment benefit, etc. (formerly called *employment exchange, Labour Exchange*). [Fr. *employer* — L. *implicāre*, to enfold — *in*, in, and *plicāre*, to fold; cf. **imply, implicate**.]

emplume *im-plŏŏm'*, *v.t.* to furnish with a plume. [Pfx. **em- (en-** (1a)).]

empoison *im-poi'zn*, *v.t.* to put poison into: to poison (*obs.*): to embitter, corrupt. — *adj.* **empoi'soned**. — *n.* **empoi'sonment**. [Pfx. **em- (en-** (1a)).]

empolder. See **impolder**.

emporium *em-pō'ri-əm*, *-pö'*, *n.* a commercial or trading centre or mart: a big shop: — *pl.* **empō'ria, empō'riums**. [L., — Gr. *empŏrion*, a trading station — *empŏros*, a wayfarer, trader — *en*, in, *poros*, a way.]

empoverish. Obs. form of **impoverish**.

empower *im-pow'ər*, *v.t.* to authorise. [Pfx. **em- (en-** (1a)).]

empress. See **emperor**.

empressement *ã-pres-mã*, (Fr.) *n.* demonstrative warmth of manner. — *adj.* **empressé** (-*pres-ā*; Fr.) eager, enthusiastic.

emprise *em-prīz'*, (*arch.*) *n.* an enterprise: a hazardous undertaking. [O.Fr. *emprise* — pa.p. fem. of *emprendre* — L. *in*, in, *praehendĕre*, to take.]

emption *emp'shən*, *n.* the act of buying, purchase. — *adj.* **emp'tional**. [L. *emptiō, -ōnis* — *emĕre*, to buy.]

empty *emp'ti*, *adj.* having nothing within: unoccupied: unfurnished: without effect: unsatisfactory: wanting substance: meaningless: empty-headed: hungry (*coll.*): devoid (of; *Shak.* with *in*). — *v.t.* to make empty: to deprive of contents: to remove from a receptacle. — *v.i.* to become empty: to discharge: — *pr.p.* **emp'tying**; *pa.t.* and *pa.p.* **emp'tied**. — *n.* an empty bottle, box, sack, etc.: — *pl.* **emp'ties**. — *n.* **emp'tier**. — *adv.* **emp'tily**. — *ns.* **emp'tiness** the state of being empty: want of substance: unsatisfactoriness: inanity; **emp'tying**. — *adjs.* **emp'ty-hand'ed** bringing or taking away nothing or no gift; **emp'ty-head'ed** frivolous. [O.E. *æmetig* — *æmetta*, leisure, rest; the *p* is excrescent.]

emptysis *emp'ti-sis*, *n.* spitting, esp. of blood. [Gr. *emptysis*, spitting — *en*, in, *ptyein*, to spit.]

empurple *im-pûr'pl*, *v.t.* to dye or tinge purple. [Pfx. **em- (en-** (1b)).]

Empusa *em-pū'zə*, *n.* a goblin or spectre sent by Hecate (also without *cap.*; also **empuse'**): (one of) a genus of fungi parasitic upon houseflies and other insects. [Gr. *Empousa.*]

empyema *em-pī-ē'mə*, or *-pi-*, *n.* a collection of pus in any cavity, esp. the pleura. — *n.* **empyesis** (-*ē'sis*) pustulous eruption. [Gr. *empyēma, empyēsis* — *en*, in, *pyon*, pus.]

empyreal *em-pir-ē'əl*, (Milt., Pope, *em-pir'i-əl*) *adj.*

formed of pure fire or light: pertaining to the highest and purest region of heaven: sublime. — *adj.* **empyre'an** empyreal. — *n.* the highest heaven, where the pure element of fire was supposed to subsist: the heavens. [Gr. *empyros*, fiery — *en*, in, *pyr*, fire.]

empyreuma *em-pir-ū'mə*, *n.* the burned smell and acrid taste that come when vegetable or animal substances are burned: — *pl.* **empyreu'mata**. — *adjs.* **empyreumat'ic, -al**. — *v.t.* **empyreu'matise, -ize**. [Gr. *empȳreuma, -atos*, embers — *en*, in *pȳr*, fire.]

emu, emeu *ē'mū*, *n.* a flightless, fast-running Australian bird, *Dromaius novaehollandiae*, largest of living birds after the ostrich. — **emu wren** a small Australian bird (*Stipiturus*), with tail-feathers like emu feathers in structure. [Port. *ema*, an ostrich.]

emulate *em'ū-lāt*, *v.t.* to strive to equal or excel (esp. what or one whom one admires): to rival successfully: (*loosely*) to imitate. — *adj.* (*Shak.*) ambitious, eager to rival. — *n.* **emulā'tion** the act of emulating or attempting to equal or excel: rivalry: competition: contest: jealous rivalry (*obs.*). — *adj.* **em'ulātive** inclined to emulation, rivalry, or competition. — *n.* **em'ulātor**: — *fem.* **em'ulātress** (*obs.*). — *v.t.* **em'ule** (*Southey*) to emulate. — *adj.* **em'ulous** eager to emulate: desirous of like excellence with another: engaged in competition or rivalry. — *adv.* **em'ulously**. — *n.* **em'ulousness**. [L. *aemulārī, -ātus* — *aemulus*, emulous.]

emulge *i-mulj'*, (*arch.*) *v.t.* to milk or drain out. — *n.* **emul'gence**. — *adj.* **emul'gent** (*med.*) acting as a drain for. [See **emulsion**.]

emulsion *i-mul'shən*, *n.* a colloidal suspension of one liquid in another: a light-sensitive coating on photographic plates: a liquid mixture containing globules of fat (as milk), or of resinous or bituminous material. — *ns.* **emulsificā'tion; emul'sifier** apparatus for preparing emulsions: a chemical which forms or preserves an emulsion, esp. one used as a food-additive to prevent the constituents of processed foods separating out. — *v.t.* **emul'sify**. — *n.* **emul'sin** an enzyme got from bitter almonds. — *v.t.* **emul'sionise, -ize**. — *adj.* **emul'sive**. — *ns.* **emul'soid** a colloid easily dispersed, giving a suspension readily formed again after coagulation; **emul'sor** an emulsifying apparatus. — **emulsifying agent** a substance whose presence in small quantities stabilises an emulsion; **emulsion paint** a water-thinnable paint made from a pigmented emulsion of a resin in water. [L. *ēmulgēre, ēmulsum*, to milk out — *ē*, from, and *mulgēre*, to milk.]

emunctory *i-*, or *ē-mungk'tər-i*, *adj.* conveying waste: pertaining to nose-blowing. — *n.* any organ or passage of the body that carries off waste: an excretory duct. — *v.t.* **emunge** (*i-munj'*; *obs.*) to clean. [L. *ēmunctōrium*, a pair of snuffers, a means of cleansing, *ēmungĕre, ēmunctum*, to blow the nose, to cleanse.]

emure *i-mūr'*, (*Shak.*) *v.t.* and *n.* a variant of **immure**. [Pfx. **em- (en-** (1a)).]

Emys *em'is*, *n.* a genus of freshwater and marsh terrapins: (without *cap.*) any member of the genus: — *pl.* **em'ydes**. [Gr. *emys, -ydos*.]

en *en*, *n.* the fourteenth letter of the alphabet (N, n): half of an em (*print.*; see also **quadrat**).

en- *en-*, *in-*, *pfx.* (1) in words derived from L. through Fr., (a) used to form verbs with the sense of *in, into, upon*; (b) used to form verbs with the sense *cause to be*; (c) used intensively or almost meaninglessly; (2) in words derived from Gr. used to form verbs with the sense of *in*.

enable *in-ā'bl*, *v.t.* to make able: to give power, strength, or authority to: to make possible. — *n.* **enab'ler**. — **enabling act, bill, resolution** one giving or proposing to give power to act. [Pfx. **en-** (1b).]

enact *in-akt'*, *v.t.* to perform: to act the part of: to establish by law. — *n.* (*Shak.*) an enactment. — *adjs.* **enact'ing; enact'ive**. — *ns.* **enac'tion** (-*shən*), **enact'ment** the passing of a bill into law: that which is enacted: a law; **enact'or** one who practices or performs anything:

one who forms decrees or establishes laws; **enac'ture** (*Shak.*) fulfilment. [Pfx. **en-** (1b), **act.**]

enallage *en-al'ə-jē*, (*gram.*) *n.* the exchange of one case, mood, tense, etc., for another. [Gr. *enallagē — en*, in, and *allassein*, to change.]

enamel *in-am'əl, n.* vitrified coating applied to a metal or other surface and fired: any glossy enamel-like surface or coating, esp. that of the teeth: a work of art in enamel: a paint giving an enamel-like finish. — *v.t.* to coat with or paint in enamel: to form a glossy surface on, like enamel: — *pr.p.* **enam'elling**; *pa.t.* and *pa.p.* **enam'elled.** — *ns.* **enam'eller, enam'ellist; enam'elling.** [O.Fr. *enameler — en*, in, *esmail*, enamel; see **smelt²**, **melt.**]

en ami *ā-na-mē*, (Fr.) as a friend.

enamour, in U.S. **enamor**, *in-am'ər, v.t.* to inflame with love: to charm. — *n.* **enamorado** (*en-äm-ō-rä'dō*; *obs.*; *Sp.*) a lover: — *pl.* **enamorad'os.** — *adjs.* **enam'oured; enam'ouring.** — **enamoured of** in love with: keen on. [O.Fr. *enamourer* — pfx. *en-, amour* — L. *amor, -ōris*, love.]

enantiodromia *en-an-ti-ō-drō'mi-ə, n.* the process by which something becomes or is superseded by its opposite, esp. the adopting of values, beliefs, etc. opposite to those previously held: the interaction of such opposing values, beliefs, etc. — *adjs.* **enantiōdrom'iacal, -drōmī'-acal; enantiōdrō'mic.** [Gr., — *enantios*, opposite, *dromos*, running.]

enantiomer *en-an'ti-ō-mər, n.* an enantiomorph. — *adj.* **enantiomeric.** [Gr. *enantios*, opposite, *meros*, part.]

enantiomorph *en-an'ti-ō-mörf, n.* a shape or object (as a crystal, a molecule) exactly similar to another except that right and left are interchanged, each being a mirror-image of the other. — *adjs.* **enantiomorph'ic; enantiomorph'ous.** — *ns.* **enantiomorph'ism; enantio-morph'y.** [Gr. *enantios*, opposite, *morphē*, shape.]

enantiopathy *en-an-ti-op'ə-thi, n.* allopathy. [Gr. *enan-tios*, opposite, *pathos*, suffering.]

enantiosis *en-an-ti-ō'sis*, (*rhet.*) *n.* the expression of an idea by negation of its contrary (litotes), or by substi-tution of the contrary (antiphrasis, irony). [Gr. *enantiōsis*, contradiction.]

enantiostyly *en-an-ti-ō-stī'li*, (*bot.*) *n.* a dimorphous con-dition in which the style projects at one side or the other in different flowers. — *adj.* **enantiostȳ'lous.** [Gr. *enantios*, opposite, *stȳlos*, a column.]

enantiotropy *en-an-ti-o'trə-pi, n.* the existence in a sub-stance of two crystal forms, one stable above, the other below, at a transition temperature. — *adj.* **enantiōtro'pic.** [Gr. *enantios*, opposite, *tropos*, turn, habit.]

enarch. See **inarch.**

enarched *en-ärcht'*, (her.) *adj.* arched: like an arch. [Pfx. **en-** (1b).]

enarm *en-ärm', v.t.* to arm (*obs.*): to lard (*obs.*). — *adj.* **enarmed** (*her.*) having horns, hoofs, etc., of a different colour from the body. [Pfx. **en-** (1b).]

enarration *ē-nə-rā'shən*, (*arch.*) *n.* exposition: detailed narration. [L. *ēnarrātiō, -ōnis* — *ē-*, out, *narrāre*, to relate.]

en arrière *ā-na-ryer*, (Fr.) behind, in the rear.

enarthrosis *en-är-thrō'sis*, (*anat.*) *n.* a ball-and-socket joint. — *adj.* **enarthrō'dial.** [Gr. *enarthrōsis — en*, in, *arthron*, a joint.]

enate *ē'nāt, adj.* growing out. — *n.* **enā'tion** an outgrowth. [L. *ē-*, from, *nātus*, born.]

en attendant *ā-na-tā-dā*, (Fr.) in the meantime, while waiting.

enaunter *en-ön'tər, en-än'tər,* (*obs.*) *conj.* lest by chance. [Contr. from *in a(d)venture.*]

en avant *ā-na-vā*, (Fr.) forward.

en badinant *ā ba-dē-nā*, (Fr.) roguishly, banteringly.

en beau *ā bō*, (Fr.) (of manner of showing person, etc., in a picture) in flattering style, as fair or handsome.

en bloc *ā blok*, (Fr.) as one unit, wholesale.

en brochette *ā bro-shet*, (Fr.) (of food) on a skewer.

en brosse *ā bros*, (of hair) cut short and standing up stiffly. [Fr., like a brush.]

en caballo *ān kä-bä'lyō*, (Sp.) on horseback.

en cabochon. See **cabochon.**

encaenia *en-sē'ni-ə, n.* the annual commemoration of founders and benefactors at Oxford, held in June. [L., — Gr. *enkainia* (pl.), a feast of dedication — *en*, in, *kainos*, new.]

encage, (*obs.*) **incage** *in-kāj', v.t.* to shut up in a cage. [Pfx. **en-** (1a).]

encalm *in-käm',* (*obs.*) *v.t.* to becalm. [Pfx. **en-** (1b).]

encamp *in-kamp', v.t.* to form into a camp: to lodge in a camp. — *v.i.* to pitch tents: to make, or stay in, a camp. — *n.* **encamp'ment** the act of encamping: the place where a camper or company is encamped: a camp. [Pfx. **en-** (1b).]

encanthis *en-kan'this, n.* a small tumour of the inner angle of the eye. [Gr. *enkanthis — en*, in, *kanthos*, a canthus.]

encapsulate *in-kap'sūl-āt, v.t.* to enclose in a capsule: to capture the essence of, to describe succinctly but sufficiently. — *n.* **encapsulā'tion.** [Pfx. **en-** (1a).]

encarnalise, -ize *in-kär'nəl-īz, v.t.* to embody: to make carnal. [Pfx. **en-** (1b).]

encarpus *en-kär'pəs, n.* a festoon of fruit ornamenting a frieze. [Gr. *enkarpa* (neut. pl.) — *en*, in, *karpos*, fruit.]

encase, incase *in-kās', v.t.* to enclose in a case: to sur-round, cover: to line. — *n.* **encase'ment, incase'ment** the act of encasing: an enclosing substance: a covering: a lining. [Pfx. **en-** (1a).]

encash *in-kash', v.t.* to convert into cash. — *n.* **encash'-ment.** [Pfx. **en-** (1b).]

encaustic *en-kös'tik, adj.* having the colours burned in: of or pertaining to encaustic. — *n.* an ancient method of painting in melted wax. — **encaustic tile** a decorative glazed and fired tile, having patterns of different coloured clays inlaid in it and burnt with it. [Gr. *enkaustikos — enkaiein*, to burn in — *en*, in, *kaiein*, to burn.]

en cavalier *ā ka-va-lyā*, (Fr.) in a cavalier manner.

encave *en-kāv',* (*Shak.*) *v.t.* to hide. [Fr. *encaver*, to put in a cellar — *en*, in, *cave*, cellar.]

enceinte¹ *ā-sēt',* (*fort.*) *n.* an enclosure, generally the whole area of a fortified place. [Fr., — *enceindre*, to surround — L. *in*, in, *cingĕre, cinctum*, to gird.]

enceinte² *ā-sēt', adj.* pregnant, with child. [Fr., — L. *incincta*, girt about or ungirt.]

Encephalartos *en-sef-əl-är'tos, n.* the Kaffir-bread genus of cycads. [Gr. *enkephalos*, within the head, palm-cabbage, *artos*, bread.]

encephalon *en-sef'əl-on*, or *-kef', n.* the brain. — *adj.* **encephalic** (*-al'ik*) belonging to the head or brain. — *n.* **encephalin(e)** (*-sef'ə-lin*) a rarer spelling of **enkepha-lin(e)** (q.v.). — *adj.* **encephalit'ic** pertaining to en-cephalitis. — *ns.* **encephali'tis** inflammation of the brain; **enceph'alocele** (*-əl-ō-sēl*; Gr. *kēlē*, tumour) a protrusion of a portion of the brain through the skull, where the bones are incomplete in infancy; **enceph'-alogram, enceph'alograph** an X-ray photograph of the brain; **encephalog'raphy** radiography of the brain, its cavities having been filled with air or dye injected into the space around the spinal cord. — *adj.* **enceph'aloid** resembling the matter of the brain. — *ns.* **encephalop'-athy** degenerative brain disease; **encephalot'omy** (Gr. *tomē*, a cut) dissection of the brain. — *adj.* **enceph'alous** cephalous. — **encephalitis lethar'gica** (*-ji-kə*) an acute disease marked by profound physical and mental lethargy — popularly called *sleeping-sickness*, better *sleepy-sickness*. [Gr. *enkephalos — en*, in, *kephalē*, head.]

enchafe *en-chāf',* (*obs.*) *v.t.* to make warm: to irritate. [Earlier *enchaufe, eschaufe* — O.Fr. *eschauffer* — *es-* (L. *ex*), *chauffer*; see **chafe.**]

enchain *in-chān', v.t.* to put in chains: to hold fast (*fig.*): to link together (*obs.*). — *n.* **enchain'ment** the act of enchaining: the state of being enchained. [Fr. *en-chaîner — en*, in, *chaîne*, chain — L. *catēna.*]

enchant *in-chänt', v.t.* to act on by songs or rhymed

formulas of sorcery: to cast a spell upon: to compel by enchantment: to charm: to delight in a high degree. — *adj.* **enchant′ed** under the power of enchantment: delighted: possessed by witches or spirits. — *n.* **enchant′er** one who enchants: a sorcerer or magician: one who charms or delights: — *fem.* **enchant′ress.** — *adj.* **enchant′ing.** — *adv.* **enchant′ingly** with the force of enchantment: in a manner to charm or delight. — *n.* **enchant′ment** the act of enchanting: the use of magic arts: an enchanted state: that which enchants. — **enchanter's nightshade** a plant (*Circaea lutetiana*) of the evening-primrose family, growing in shady places — the name transferred apparently from another plant (perhaps mandrake, or swallow-wort) for no apparent reason.   [Fr. *enchanter* — L. *incantāre*, to sing a magic formula over — *in*, on, *cantāre*, to sing.]

encharge *in-chärj′*, *v.t.* to enjoin (*obs.*): to entrust. [O.Fr. *encharger*; see **charge.**]

encharm *in-chärm′*, (*obs.*) *v.t.* to cast a spell on: to charm. [Pfx. **en-** (1c).]

enchase *in-chās′*, *v.t.* to fix in a border or setting: to enshrine (*obs.*): to enclose (*obs.*): to enshrine in verse (*obs.*): to insert, let in: to set with jewels: to engrave: to adorn with raised, or embossed work: prob. to fewter (*Spens.*). — *n.* (*Spens.*) enchasing. — *adj.* **enchased′.**   [Fr. *enchâsser* — *en*, in, *châsse*, shrine, setting — L. *capsa*, a case; see **case¹**, **chase³**; **chase²** is a contraction.]

encheason *en-chē′zn*, (*Spens.*) *n.* a reason, cause, or occasion.   [O.Fr. *encheson* — *encheoir*, to fall in; influenced by L. *occāsiō, -ōnis*, occasion.]

encheer *in-chēr′*, (*arch.*) *v.t.* to cheer, comfort.   [Pfx. **en-** (1c).]

enchilada *en-chi-läd′ə*, *n.* a Mexican dish consisting of a rolled stuffed tortilla cooked with a chilli-flavoured sauce.   [Amer. Sp. — Sp. *enchilar*, to season with chilli.]

enchiridion, encheiridion *en(g)-kī-rid′i-on*, *n.* a book to be carried in the hand for reference: a manual.   [Gr. *encheiridion* — *en*, in, *cheir*, hand.]

enchondroma *en-kon-drō′mə*, (*path.*) *n.* an abnormal cartilaginous growth: - *pl.* **-mas, -mata** (*-tə*).   [Gr. *en*, in, *chondros*, cartilage.]

enchorial *en-kō′ri-əl*, *-kö′*, *adj.* belonging to or used in a country (*rare*): used by the people, esp. (in ancient Egypt) demotic. — Also **enchoric** (*-kor′*).   [Gr. *enchōrios* — *en*, in, and *chōrā*, a place, country.]

encincture *in-singk′chər*, *v.t.* to girdle. — *n.* a girdling: an enclosure.   [Pfx. **en-** (1a).]

encipher *in-sī′fər*, *v.t.* to put into cipher.   [Pfx. **en-** (1a).]

encircle *in-sûrk′l*, *v.t.* to enclose in a circle: to pass round. — *ns.* **encirc′ling; encir′clement.**   [Pfx. **en-** (1a).]

en clair *ä kler*, (Fr.) not in cipher.

enclasp *in-kläsp′*, *v.t.* to clasp.   [Pfx. **en-** (1c).]

enclave *en′klāv*, also *en-klāv′*, or *ä-kläv′*, *n.* a piece of territory entirely enclosed within foreign territory: an enclosure. — *v.t.* to surround.   [Fr., — L.L. *inclāvāre* — L. *in*, and *clāvis*, a key.]

enclitic *en-klit′ik*, *adj.* inclined: (of a word, esp. a particle) without accent, behaving as if not a separate word or, in ancient Greek, transferring its accent to the preceding word (*gram.*). — *n.* (*gram.*) a word or particle which always follows another word and which is enclitic to it. — *n.* **enclisis** (*eng′klis-is*). — *adv.* **enclit′ically.**   [Gr. *enklitikos* — *en*, in, *klīnein*, to lean.]

encloister *in-klois′tər*, (*obs.*) *v.t.* to immure.   [Pfx. **en-** (1a).]

enclose, inclose *in-klōz′*, *v.t.* to close or shut in: to confine: to surround: to put within, esp. of something sent within a letter or within its envelope: to seclude: to fence, esp. used of waste land. — *ns.* **enclos′er, inclos′er; enclosure, inclosure** (*-klō′zhər*) the act of enclosing: the state of being enclosed: that which is enclosed, esp. in a letter: a space fenced off: that which encloses: a barrier: the framing of a window. — **enclosed order** a religious order leading an entirely contemplative life,

not going out into the world to work.   [Pfx. **en-** (1a) and **close²**.]

enclothe *in-klōdh′*, *v.t.* to clothe.   [Pfx. **en-** (1a).]

encloud *in-klowd′*, *v.t.* to cover with clouds.   [Pfx. **en-** (1a).]

encode *in-kōd′*, *v.t.* to encipher: to record in a form other than plain written or printed text: to convert an idea or message into words, or translate (something) into a foreign language (*ling.*).   [Pfx. **en-** (1a).]

encoignure *ã-kwa-nür′*, *-nūr′*, *n.* a piece of, esp. ornamental, furniture, e.g. a cupboard or cabinet, made to fit into a corner.   [Fr., — *encoigner*, to fit into a corner — *en*, in, *coin*, a corner.]

encolour *in-kul′ər*, *v.t.* to colour, tinge.   [Pfx. **en-** (1b).]

encolpion *en-kol′pi-on*, *n.* a reliquary, cross, etc., worn on the breast. — Also (Latinised) **encol′pium.**   [Gr., — *en*, in, on, *kolpos*, bosom.]

encolure *en(g)′kol-ūr′*, (*Browning*) *n.* a horse's mane.   [Fr., horse's neck.]

encomienda *ān-kō-mē-ān′da*, (Sp.) *n.* a commandery. — *n.* **encomendero** (Sp.; *ān-kō-mān-dā′rō*) its commander: — *pl.* **encomender′os.**

encomium *en-kō′mi-əm*, also **encō′mion** (*-on*) *ns.* high commendation: a eulogy: — *pl.* **encō′miums, encō′mia.** — *n.* **encō′miast** one who utters or writes encomiums: a praiser. — *adjs.* **encomias′tic, -al** bestowing praise. — *adv.* **encomias′tically.**   [L., — Gr. *enkōmion*, a song of praise — *en*, in, *kōmos*, festivity.]

encompass *in-kum′pəs*, *v.t.* to surround or enclose: to go round (*obs.*): to bring about. — *n.* **encom′passment.**   [Pfx. **en-** (1a).]

encore *ã-, ong-kōr′, -kör′, interj.* calling for repetition of a performance, or an additional item. — *n.* a call of encore: an item given in response to such a call. — *v.t.* to call encore to.   [Fr., again, still.]

encounter *in-kown′tər*, *v.t.* to meet face to face, esp. unexpectedly: to meet in a contest: to oppose. — *n.* a meeting unexpectedly: an interview: a fight: a manner of meeting or accosting (*Shak.*). — **encounter group** a group which meets with a view to establishing greater self-awareness and greater understanding of others by indulging in unrestrained verbal and physical confrontation and contact.   [O.Fr. *encontrer* — L. *in*, in, *contrā*, against.]

encourage *en-kur′ij*, *v.t.* to put courage in: to inspire with spirit or hope: to incite: to patronise: to cherish. — *ns.* **encour′agement** the act of encouraging: that which encourages; **encour′ager.** — *n. and adj.* **encour′aging.** — *adv.* **encour′agingly.**   [O.Fr. *encoragier* (Fr. *encourager*) — pfx. *en-*, *corage*, courage.]

encradle *en-krā′dl*, (*Spens.*) *v.t.* to lay in a cradle.   [Pfx. **en-** (1a).]

encraty *en′krə-ti*, *n.* self-control. — *ns.* **En′cratism** the doctrine of the Encratites; **En′cratite** one of a heretical sect in the early church who abstained from marriage, and from flesh and wine.   [Gr. *enkrateia*, self-control — *en*, in, *kratos*, strength.]

encrease. Obs. form of **increase.**

encrimson *en-krim′zn*, *v.t.* to tinge with a crimson colour. — *adj.* **encrim′soned.**   [Pfx. **en-** (1b).]

encrinite *en(g)′kri-nīt*, *n.* a fossil crinoid: a crinoid. — *adjs.* **en′crinal; encrin′ic; encrinī′tal; encrinitic** (*-it′ik*).   [Gr. *en*, in, *krinon*, a lily.]

encroach *in-krōch′*, *v.i.* to seize on the rights of others: to intrude beyond boundaries: to extend into the territory, sphere, etc., of others. — *n.* **encroach′er.** — *adv.* **encroach′ingly.** — *n.* **encroach′ment** an act of encroaching: that which is taken by encroaching.   [O.Fr. *encrochier*, to seize — *en-* and *croc*, a hook.]

en croupe *ã krōōp*, (Fr.) on the crupper, on a pillion.

en croûte. See **croûte.**

encrust, incrust *in-krust′*, *v.t.* to cover with a crust or hard coating: to form a crust on the surface of. — *v.i.* to form a crust. — *ns.* **encrust′ment; encrustā′tion** (*en-*; usu. **incrustā′tion** *in-*) the act of encrusting: a crust or layer of anything: an inlaying of marble, mosaic, etc.   [L. *incrustāre, -ātum* — *in*, on, *crusta*, crust.]

encryption *in- krip'shən, n.* the putting of messages or information into code. — *v.t.* **encrypt'.** — *adj.* **encrypt'ed.** [See crypt-.]

en cuerpo *ān kwār'pō,* (Sp.) in close-fitting dress: without a cloak or coat: in undress, e.g. in one's shirt-sleeves: sometimes erroneously for stark naked, the Spanish for which is **en cueros** (*kwār'ōs*). — Also **in cuerpo, in querpo.**

encumber *in-kum'bər, v.t.* to impede the motion of: to hamper: to embarrass: to burden: to load with debts. — *ns.* **encum'berment** the act of encumbering: the state of being encumbered; **encum'brance** that which encumbers or hinders: a legal claim on an estate: one dependent on another, esp. a child; **encum'brancer.** [O.Fr. *encombrer,* from en-, and *combrer*; see **cumber.**]

encurtain *in-kûr'tin, v.t.* to curtain, to veil. [Pfx. **en-** (1a).]

encyclical *en-sīk'lik-l,* or *-sik',* adj. sent round to many persons or places. — *n.* a letter addressed by the Pope to all his bishops. — Also **encyc'lic.** [Gr. *enkyklios* — *en,* in, *kyklos,* a circle.]

encyclopaedia, encyclopedia *en-sī-klō-pē'di-ə, n.* the circle of human knowledge: a work containing information on every department, or on a particular department, of knowledge, generally alphabetically arranged: esp. (with *cap.*) that by Diderot, D'Alembert, and others. — *adjs.* **encyclopae'dian** embracing the whole circle of learning; **encyclopae'dic, -al** pertaining to an encyclopaedia: all-comprehensive: full of information. — *ns.* **encyclopae'dism** comprehensive knowledge: the rationalistic attitude of the French Encyclopaedists; **encyclopae'dist** the compiler, or one who assists in the compilation, of an encyclopaedia: esp. (*Encyclopédiste*) a writer for the French *Encyclopédie* (1751–65). [False Gr. *enkyklopaideiā,* a wrong reading for *enkyklios paideiā,* general education (opposed to professional or special); *enkyklios,* circular, recurring, everyday — *en,* in, *kyklos,* circle; *paideiā,* education — *pais, paidos,* a child.]

encyst *en-sist', v.t.* or *v.i.* to enclose or become enclosed in a cyst or vesicle. — *ns.* **encystā'tion; encyst'ment.** — *adj.* **encyst'ed.** [Pfx. **en-** (1a).]

end *end, n.* the last point or portion: termination or close: death: consequence: an object aimed at: a fragment, odd piece: half a unit length of cloth: a warp thread: a waxed thread ending in a bristle (*shoemaker's end*): part of a game played from one end (of the bowling-green, archery-ground, etc.): an outer district: a region: a cottage room (*Scot.*). — *v.t.* to bring to an end: to destroy. — *v.i.* to come to an end: to cease: to be at the end. — *adj.* **end'ed** brought to an end: having ends. — *n.* **end'ing** a termination: a conclusion: death: extremity: that which is at the end: the terminal syllable or portion of a word, esp. an inflection (*gram.*). — *adj.* concluding: finishing: completing: dying. — *adj.* **end'less** without end: returning upon itself: everlasting: incessant: objectless. — *adv.* **end'lessly.** — *n.* **end'lessness.** — *adv.* **end'long** (*Scot.* **end'lang**) lengthwise (*arch.*): continuously (*arch.*): straight on (*arch.*): on end. — *prep.* (*obs.*) along. — *adj.* (*rare*) set on end. — *adj.* **end'most** farthest. — *advs.* **end'ways, end'wise** on end: with the end forward. — **end'-all** that which ends all (see also **be-all and end-all** under **be**); **end'game** the final stage of a game of chess or certain other games: one's manner of playing the endgame; **endless chain** a chain whose ends are joined; **endless gearing, screw, worm** an arrangement for producing slow motion in machinery, consisting of a screw whose thread gears into a wheel with skew teeth; **end man** the man at the end of a row of performers, etc. — *adv.* and *adj.* **end'-on'** in the direction in which the end points. — **end organ** a specialised sensory or motor structure at a nerve-end; **end'-paper** a paper at the beginning or end of a book, pasted to the binding and leaving an additional fly-leaf; **end'-product** the final product of a series of operations; **end'-reader** one who peeps at the end of a novel to see the outcome; **end result** the final

result or outcome; **end'ship** (*obs.*) a village. — *adj.* **end'-stopped** having a pause at the end of each line (of verse). — **end use** the final use to which a manufactured article is put. — *n.* **end'-user** the person, company, etc. who will be the recipient of a product being sold: (usu. **end-user certificate**) in international trade, documentation naming the end-user of a product being sold, required e.g. in the exporting of arms. — **all ends up** completely: convincingly; **at a loose end, at loose ends** with nothing to do; in a state of uncertainty or confusion as to one's course of action; **at an end** terminated: discontinued: exhausted; **at one's wit's end** see **wit²**; **at the end of one's tether** without further resource; **be the end of** to cause the death of (often a coll. exaggeration); **end for end** with the position of the ends reversed; **end up** to arrive or find oneself eventually or finally: to finish (with, by): to become in the end; **get hold of the wrong end of the stick** to misunderstand blunderingly; **in the end** after all: at last; **keep one's end up** to maintain one's part: to be content to keep one's wicket standing without trying to score; **loose end** (often in *pl.*) an unsettled matter; **make both ends meet** to live within one's income (both ends meaning both ends of the year); **no end** (*coll.*) very much; **on end** erect: at a stretch; **the end** the last straw: the limit; **the end of the road** the point beyond which one can no longer continue or survive. [O.E. *ende*; cf. Ger. *Ende,* Dan. *ende,* Goth. *andeis*; Sans. *anta.*]

endamage *in-dam'ij, v.t.* to damage. — *n.* **endam'agement** damage, injury, loss. [Pfx. **en-** (1b).]

endamoeba. See **entamoeba.**

endanger *in-dān'jər, v.t.* to place in danger: to expose to loss or injury. — *ns.* **endan'gerer; endan'germent** hazard, peril. [Pfx. **en-** (1b).]

endarch *end'ärk, (bot.) adj.* having the protoxylem on the inner edge. [Gr. *endō,* within, *archē,* origin.]

endart, indart *in-därt', (Shak.) v.t.* to dart in. [Pfx. **en-** (1a).]

endear *in-dēr', v.t.* to make dear or more dear: to bind as in gratitude (*Shak.*). — *adjs.* **endeared'** beloved; **endear'ing** making dear: arousing affection: expressing love (*arch.*). — *adv.* **endear'ingly.** — *ns.* **endear'ingness; endear'ment** the act of endearing: the state of being endeared: that which excites or increases affection: a caress or utterance of love. [Pfx. **en-** (1b).]

endeavour *in-dev'ər, v.i.* to strive: to attempt. — *n.* an exertion of power towards some object: attempt or trial. — *n.* **endeav'ourment** (*Spens.*) endeavour. — **do one's endeavour** (*arch.*) to do one's utmost. [From such phrases as to *put oneself in devoir* (Fr. *se mettre en devoir*), to make it one's duty, do what one can, — Fr. *en,* in, *devoir,* duty.]

endecagon. A faulty form for **hendecagon.**

endeictic *en-dīk'tik, adj.* showing, exhibiting, demonstrating. — *n.* **endeix'is** an indication. [Gr. *endeiktikos.*]

endemic *en-dem'ik, adj.* prevalent or regularly found in a people or a district: confined to a particular area (*biol.*). — *n.* a disease constantly or generally present in a place. — *adjs.* **endemial** (*-dē'mi-əl*), **endem'ical.** — *adv.* **endem'ically.** — *ns.* **endemicity** (*-is'i-ti*), **en'demism** the state of being endemic; **endemiol'ogy** (*-dem-,* or *-dēm-*) the scientific study of endemic diseases. [Gr. *endēmios* — *en,* in, and *dēmos,* a people, a district.]

endenizen *en-den'i-zn, v.t.* to naturalise, to make a denizen. [Pfx. **en-** (1b).]

endermic, -al *en-dûrm'ik, -l, adjs.* through or applied directly to the skin — also **endermat'ic.** — *n.* **en'deron** the corium, derma, or true skin. [Gr. *en,* in, *derma,* and *deros,* skin.]

endew *en-dū', (obs.) v.t.* see **endue**: to endow (*Spens.*).

endiron. Same as **andiron.**

endite. Obs. form of **indict, indite.**

endive *en'div, -dīv, n.* a salad plant (*Cichorium endivia*) of the chicory genus: loosely, chicory. [Fr., — L. *intubus.*]

endlong. See **end.**

endo- *en'dō-, en-do'-,* in composition, inside, often interchanging with **ento-** and opp. to **ecto-, exo-**. — *n.* **en'doblast** (Gr. *blastos*, a shoot, bud) the inner cell-layer of a gastrula, the hypoblast. — *adjs.* **endocar'diac, endocar'dial** within the heart. — *ns.* **endocardī'tis** inflammation of the endocardium, esp. over the valves; **endocar'dium** (Gr. *kardiā*, heart) the lining membrane of the heart; **en'docarp** (Gr. *karpos*, fruit; *bot.*) a differentiated innermost layer of the pericarp, usu. hard, as a plum stone. — *adjs.* **endochylous** (*en-dok'i-ləs*; Gr. *chȳlos*, juice; *bot.*) having internal water-storing cells; **endocrī'nal; en'docrine** (or *-krin*; Gr. *krīnein*, to separate; *physiol.*) secreting internally: applied esp. to certain glands that pour secretions into the blood (also *n.*); **endocrinic** (*-krin'ik*). — *n.* **endocrinol'ogy** the science of the discharge of ductless glands. — *adj.* **endocritic** (*-krit'ik*) endocrine. — *n.* **en'doderm** (Gr. *derma*, skin) the inner layer of cells in a gastrula: the tissues derived from that layer. — *adjs.* **endoderm'al, endoderm'ic**. — *ns.* **endoderm'is** a close-set sheath, one cell thick, enclosing the central cylinder in plants; **en'dodyne** same as **autodyne**. — *adjs.* **endogamic** (*-gam'ik*), **endogamous** (*-dog'ə-məs*). — *ns.* **endogamy** (*en-dog'əm-i*; Gr. *gamos*, marriage) the custom forbidding marriage outside one's own group: inbreeding: pollination between two flowers on the same plant: the union of female gametes; **en'dogen** (*-jen*; Gr. *genēs*, born; *obs.*) any plant, including the monocotyledons, regarded as growing from within. — *adjs.* **endogen'ic** pertaining to the processes of change within the earth; **endogenous** (*en-doj'i-nəs*) increasing by internal growth: formed within: (of depression) with no external cause. — *ns.* **endog'eny; en'dolymph** the fluid within the membranous labyrinth of the ear. — *adj.* **endomēt'rial**. — *ns.* **endometrī'tis** inflammation of the endometrium; **endomētriō'sis** (a condition caused by) the presence of active endometrial tissue where it should not be, esp. when affecting other organs of the pelvic cavity; **endomēt'rium** (Gr. *mētra*, womb) the mucous membrane lining the cavity of the uterus; **endomix'is** (Gr. *mixis*, mingling) in Protozoa, a nuclear reorganisation without conjugation; **en'domorph** (Gr. *morphē*, form) a mineral enclosed within another mineral, the latter being termed a perimorph: a person of rounded build. — *adj.* **endomorph'ic**. — *ns.* **endomorph'y; endopar'asite** an internal parasite. — *adj.* **endophagous** (*en-dof'ə-gəs*). — *n.* **endoph'agy** (*-ə-ji*; Gr. *phagein*, aorist, to eat) cannibalism within the family or tribe: eating away from within. — *adj.* **endophyllous** (*-fil'əs*; Gr. *phyllon*, a leaf; *bot.*) being or formed within a sheathing leaf: living inside a leaf. — *n.* **endophyte** (*en'dō-fīt*; Gr. *phyton*, a plant) a plant living within another, whether parasitically or not. — *adj.* **endophytic** (*-fit'ik*). — *n.* **en'doplasm** the inner portion of the cytoplasm of a cell. — *adjs.* **endoplas'-mic, endoplas'tic**. — *ns.* **endopleura** (*-ploo'rə*; Gr. *pleurā*, a side; *bot.*) the inner seed coat; **endopodite** (*en-dop'ə-dīt*; Gr. *pous, podos*, a foot) the inner branch of a crustacean's leg; **endoradiosonde'** an electronic device put within the body to send out information about a bodily function such as, e.g. digestion (see **radiosonde** under **radio-**). — *adj.* **endorhizal** (*-rī'zl*; Gr. *rhiza*, root; *bot.*) having the radicle of the embryo enclosed within a sheath, as in monocotyledons: hence monocotyledonous. — *ns.* **en'dosarc** (Gr. *sarx, sarkos*, flesh) endoplasm; **en'doscope** (Gr. *skopeein*, to look) an instrument for viewing the cavities of internal organs. — *adj.* **endoscopic** (*-skop'ik*). — *n.* **endoscopy** (*en-dos'-kə-pi*). — *adj.* **endoskel'etal**. — *ns.* **endoskel'eton** internal skeleton or framework of the body; **endosmō'-sis** osmosis inwards, i.e. towards the solution. — Also **en'dosmose** (*-mōs*); **endosmōm'eter** an instrument for measuring endosmotic action. — *adj.* **endosmomet'ric; endosmōt'ic** pertaining to or of the nature of endosmosis. — *adv.* **endosmot'ically**. — *n.* **en'dosperm** (Gr. *sperma*, seed) in a seed, nutritive tissue formed from the embryo-sac. — *adj.* **endosper'mic**. — *n.* **en'dospore** (Gr. *sporos*, seed) the innermost layer of a spore-wall:

a spore formed within a mother-cell. — *adj.* **endos'teal** (Gr. *osteon*, bone) within a bone. — *ns.* **endos'teum** (*anat.*) the internal periosteum; **endosym'biont** an organism living within the body of its symbiotic host. — *adjs.* **endosymbiot'ic; endothē'lial**. — *n.* **endothēlium** the layer of cell tissue on the internal surfaces of blood-vessels, lymphatics, etc.: — *pl.* **endothēlia**. — *adjs.* **endotherm'ic** (Gr. *thermē*, heat) accompanied by, characterised by, or formed with absorption of heat; **endotroph'ic** (Gr. *trophē*, food) of a mycorrhiza, occurring mainly within the root of the plant it feeds. — *n.* **endozō'on** (Gr. *zōion*, animal) an entozoon: — *pl.* **endozō'a**. — *adj.* **endozō'ic** entozoic, having seeds dispersed by animals that swallow them (*bot.*). [Gr. *endon*, or *endō*, within.]

endorphin *en-dör'fin, n.* any of a group of opiate-like substances produced by the brain and the pituitary gland with pain-killing, etc. properties similar to morphine. [**endo-** and **morphine.**]

endorse¹, indorse *in-dörs', v.t.* to write on the back of (esp. one's signature, a note of contents, a record of an offence): to assign by writing on the back of: to give one's sanction to: to express approbation of: to do so as a form of advertising, usu. in return for money: to lay on the back to load (*arch.*). — *adj.* **endors'able**. — *ns.* **endorsee'** (*en-*) the person to whom a bill, etc., is assigned by endorsement; **endorse'ment** the act of endorsing: that which is written on the back: a sanction: a record of a motoring offence on a driving licence: an additional clause on a policy altering the coverage in some way (*insurance*); **endors'er**. — **endorse out** (*S.Afr.*) to order (a person) to leave a place because he lacks official permission to be there. [See **endoss**; changed under the influence of L.L. *indorsāre — in*, on, *dorsum*, the back.]

endorse² *en-dörs', (her.) n.* a vertical band or stripe on a shield, one-fourth or one-eighth of the width of a pale. — *adj.* **endorsed'** (of a pale) with an endorse on each side of it: (of wings) thrown back. [Origin obscure.]

endosarc... to ... endospore. See **endo-**.

endoss *en-dos', (obs.) v.t.* to endorse: to inscribe (*Spens.*). [M.E. *endosse* — O.Fr. *endosser*.]

endosteal... to ... endotrophic. See **endo-**.

endow *in-dow', v.t.* to give a dowry or marriage portion to: to settle a permanent provision on: to provide permanent means of support for: to enrich with any gift or faculty: to present. — *adj.* **endowed'** having (a gift, faculty, etc.) (with *with*). — *ns.* **endow'er; endow'-ment** the act of endowing: that which is settled on any person or institution: a quality or faculty bestowed on anyone. — **endowment assurance, insurance** a form of insurance providing for the payment of a certain sum at a certain date or at death if earlier. [Fr. *en* (— L. *in*), *douer*, to endow — L. *dōtāre — dōs, dōtis*, a dowry.]

endozoon, etc. See **endo-**.

endue, indue (*Spens.*, etc., endow, indew), *in-dū', v.t.* to take into the stomach, as a hawk (*obs.*): to digest (*obs.*): to take in, digest mentally (*Spens.*): to bring to (*Shak.*): to put on, as clothes: to invest with: to clothe: to supply. [O.Fr. *enduire* — L. *indūcěre — in*, into, *dūcěre*, to lead, influenced by *induěre*, to put on.]

endungeon *in-dun'jən, v.t.* to shut up in a dungeon or the like. [Pfx. **en-** (1a).]

endure *in-dūr', v.t.* to harden (*Spens.*): to remain firm under: to bear without sinking: to tolerate. — *v.i.* to remain firm: to last. — *adj.* **endur'able** that can be endured or borne: lasting. — *ns.* **endur'ableness**. — *adv.* **endur'ably**. — *ns.* **endur'ance** the state or power of enduring or bearing: a suffering patiently without sinking: patience: continuance: duration(*obs.*): lasting quality: maximum performance under given conditions: captivity (*obs.*); **endur'er**. — *adj.* **endur'ing** lasting. — *adv.* **endur'ingly**. [O.Fr. *endurer* — L. *indūrāre — in*, in, *dūrus*, hard.]

ene. Same as **e'en** (**even²**).

en effet *ã-ne-fe, (Fr.)* in effect: in fact.

For other sounds see detailed chart of pronunciation.

enema *en'i-mə, n.* a fluid injected into the rectum: the process of injecting such a fluid: — *pl.* **en'emas, ene'mata.** [Gr. *enĕma, -atos* — *enienai*, to send in — *en*, in, and *hienai*, to send.]

enemy[1] *en'i-mi, n.* one who hates or dislikes, or who is hated or disliked: a foe: a hostile force: something which is harmful to or which acts against (*fig.*). — *adj.* hostile. — **how goes the enemy?** (*coll.*) what time is it?; **the enemy, the old enemy** the Devil; **the last enemy** death. [O.Fr. *enemi* (Fr. *ennemi*) — L. *inimīcus* — *in-*, neg., *amīcus*, a friend.]

enemy[2]. A dial. form of **anemone.**

energid. See **energy.**

energumen *en-ər-gū'mən, n.* one possessed: a demoniac. [L.L. *energūmenus* — Gr. *energoumenos* — *energeein* — *en*, in, *ergon*, work.]

energy *en'ər-ji, n.* the power of doing work: the power exerted: vigorous activity: vigour: forcefulness: the capacity of a material body or of radiation to do work (*phys.*). — *adjs.* **energet'ic, -al** having, requiring, or showing energy: active: forcible: effective. — *adv.* **energet'ically.** — *n. sing.* **energet'ics** the science of the general laws of energy: the production and use of energy, e.g. in animals. — *adj.* **ener'gic** (*in-ûr'jik*) exhibiting energy. — *n.* **ener'gid** a protoplasmic unit: a cell with or without a cell-wall. — *v.t.* **en'ergise, -ize** to give strength or active force to: to stimulate to activity. — *v.i.* to act with force. — **energy gap** the amount by which energy requirements exceed the energy supply. — **conservation of energy** see **conservation.** [Gr. *energeia* — *en*, in, *ergon*, work.]

enervate *en'ər-vāt*, still sometimes *i-nûr'*, *v.t.* to deprive of nerve, strength, or courage: to weaken. — *adj.* weakened: spiritless. — *adjs.* **en'ervating, en'ervative.** — *n.* **enervā'tion.** — *v.t.* **enerve'** (*obs.*) to enervate. [L. *ēnervāre, -ātum* — *ē*, out of, *nervus*, a nerve.]

enew *e-nū'*, *v.t.* in falconry, to drive or (*refl.*) plunge into water. [O.Fr. *enewer* — *en*, in, O.Fr. *ewe* (Fr. *eau*), water.]

enface *in-fās'*, *v.t.* to stamp or print on the face of a document, bill, etc. — *n.* **enface'ment.** [Pfx. **en-** (1a).]

en face *ã fas*, (Fr.) in front: opposite: straight in the face: facing forward.

en famille *ã fa-mē-y'*, (Fr.) amongst the family, as at a family gathering, at home, without ceremony.

enfant *ã-fã*, (Fr.) *n.* a child. — **enfant de la maison** (*də la me-zõ*) a child of the house, quite at home; **enfant de son siècle** (*də sõ sye-kl'*) a child of his century — one who reflects the spirit of his time; **enfant gâté** (*gã-tā*) a spoilt child (fem. **gâtée**); **enfants perdus** (*ã-fã per-dü*) lit. lost children: forlorn hope, shock troops; **enfant terrible** (*te-rē-bl'*) a precocious child whose sayings embarrass his elders: a person whose behaviour, etc. is indiscreet, embarrassing to his associates, or (*loosely*) unconventional; **enfant trouvé** (*trōō-vā*) a foundling.

enfeeble *in-fē'bl*, *v.t.* to make feeble: to weaken. — *n.* **enfee'blement** weakening: weakness. [Pfx. **en-** (1b).]

enfelon *en-fel'ən*, (*Spens.*) *v.t.* to make fierce. [Pfx. **en-** (1b).]

enfeoff *in-fef'*, *en-fēf'*, *v.t.* to give a fief to: to invest with a possession in fee: to give up as a fief: to surrender. — *n.* **enfeoff'ment** the act of enfeoffing: the deed which invests with the fee of an estate. [O.Fr. *enfeffer* — *en-*, and *fief;* see **fief, feoff.**]

enfested *en-fest'id*, (*Spens.*) *adj.* embittered. [Perh. for **infest**, hostile, or **enfestered.**]

enfestered *en-fest'ərd, adj.* festered. [Pfx. **en-** (1b).]

en fête *ã fet*, (Fr.) in festivity: keeping, dressed for, etc. a holiday.

enfetter *en-fet'ər*, (*Shak.*) *v.t.* to bind in fetters. [Pfx. **en-** (1c).]

enfierce *en-fērs'*, (*Spens.*) *v.t.* to make fierce. [Pfx. **en-** (1b).]

enfilade *en-fi-lād'*, *n.* a number of things arranged as if threaded on a string: a series of rooms with the doors in line affording a continuous passage: a vista: a fire that rakes a line or position from end to end (*mil.*): a

situation or a body open from end to end. — *v.t.* to rake, or be in position to rake, with shot through the whole length of a line. — Also *adj.* — *adj.* **enfiled** (*en-fīld'; her.*) thrust through like a sword. [Fr. *enfiler* — *en* (L. *in*), and *fil* — L. *fīlum*, a thread; see **file,** a line or wire.]

enfire *en-fīr'*, (*Spens.*) *v.t.* to set on fire, inflame.

enfix. See **infix.**

enflesh *in-flesh'*, *v.t.* to turn into flesh. [Pfx. **en-** (1b).]

enflower *in-flow'ər*, *v.t.* to cover with flowers. [Pfx. **en-** (1a).]

enfold, infold *in-fōld'*, *v.t.* to wrap up: to encompass. — *n.* **enfold'ment** the act of enfolding: that which enfolds. [Pfx. **en-** (1a).]

enforce *in-fōrs', -förs'*, *v.t.* to gain by force: to give force to: to put in force: to give effect to: to urge: to impress: to drive: to compel: to apply force to. — *v.i.* (*Spens.*) to strive. — *adj.* **enforce'able.** — *adv.* **enforce'dly** by violence, not by choice. — *n.* **enforce'ment** the act of enforcing: compulsion: a giving effect to: that which enforces. — **enforcement notice** (*law*) an order served on one who has breached town-planning regulations; **enforcement officer; enforcement work.** [O.Fr. *enforcer* — *en* (L. *in*), and *force.*]

enforest *in-for'əst*, *v.t.* to turn into forest. [Pfx. **en-** (1b).]

enform (*Spens.*). Same as **inform**[1].

enfouldered *en-fōl'dərd*, (*Spens.*) *adj.* charged with or like lightning. [Pfx. **en-** (1c) and O.Fr. *fouldre* (Fr. *foudre*) — L. *fulgur*, lightning.]

enframe *in-frām'*, *v.t.* to put in a frame. [Pfx. **en-** (1a).]

enfranchise, -ize *in-fran'chīz, -shīz*, *v.t.* to set free: to give a franchise or political privileges to. — *n.* **enfran'chisement** (*-chiz-, -shiz-*) the act of enfranchising: liberation: admission to civil or political privileges. [O.Fr. *enfranchir* — *en*, and *franc*, free; see **franchise.**]

enfree *en-frē'*, **enfreedom** *en-frē'dəm*, (*Shak.*) *vs.t.* to set free: to give freedom to. [Pfx. **en-** (1b).]

enfreeze *en-frēz'*, *v.t.* to freeze: to turn to ice: — *pa.p.* (*Spens.*) **enfrōs'en.** [Pfx. **en-** (1c).]

eng *eng*, (*phon.*) *n.* the symbol ŋ, representing the sound of English *ng.* — Also **agma.** [From the sound.]

engage *in-gāj'*, *v.t.* to pledge (*obs.*): to bind by a gage or pledge: to render liable (*obs.*): to secure for service: to enlist: to win over, attract: to betroth: to bespeak, reserve: to hold or occupy: to enter into contest: to fasten (*archit.*): to interlock: to entangle (*arch.*). — *v.i.* to pledge one's word: to become bound: to take part: to occupy or busy oneself: to enter into conflict. — *adj.* **engaged'** pledged: promised, esp. in marriage: greatly interested: taken, booked, or bespoke: occupied: partly built or sunk into, or so appearing (*archit.*): geared together, interlocked: of literature or writer, committed (cf. **engagé**). — *ns.* **engage'ment** the act of engaging: the state of being engaged: that which engages: betrothal: promise: appointment: employment: a fight or battle: commitment (cf. **engagé**); **engāg'er** one who engages in any sense: (with *cap.*; *hist.*) an adherent of the *Engagement* of 1647, a secret treaty between Charles I and Scottish Commissioners. — *adj.* **engāg'ing** winning: attractive. — *adv.* **engāg'ingly.** — *n.* **engāg'ingness.** — **engage'ment-ring** a ring given in token of betrothal, esp. by the man to the woman. — **engage for** to answer for. [Fr. *engager* — *en gage*, in pledge; see **gage.**]

engagé *ã-ga-zhã'*, *adj.* committed to a point of view, or to social or political action. — *n.* **engagement** (*ã-gazh-mã*; sometimes *in-gāj'mənt*) commitment. [Fr.]

engaol *en-jāl'*, (*Shak.*) *v.t.* to put in gaol. [Pfx. **en-** (1a).]

en garçon *ã gar-sõ*, (Fr.) like a bachelor: in bachelor style.

en garde *ã gärd*, (Fr.) in fencing, a warning to assume a defensive position in readiness for an attack.

engarland *in-gär'lənd*, *v.t.* to put a garland round. [Pfx. **en-** (1a).]

engarrison *in-gar'i-sn*, *v.t.* to establish as a garrison. [Pfx. **en-** (1b).]

engender *in-jen'dər*, *v.t.* to beget: to bear: to breed: to sow

the seeds of: to produce. — *v.i.* to be caused or produced. — *ns.* **engen′drure, engen′dure** the act of engendering: generation. [Fr. *engendrer* — L. *ingenerāre* — *in,* and *generāre,* to generate.]
Enghalskrug *eng′hals-krook,* (Ger.) *n.* a type of beer jug. [Ger. *eng,* narrow, *Hals,* neck, *Krug,* jug.]
engild *en-gild′,* (*Shak.*) *v.t.* to gild. [Pfx. **en-** (1c).]
engine *en′jin, n.* a mechanical contrivance, esp. a complex piece of machinery in which power is applied to do work: a locomotive: a military machine: an instrument of torture (*obs.*): anything used to effect a purpose: a device, contrivance, wile (*obs.*): a snare (*obs.*): a person used as a tool (*arch.*): (see also **ingine**) ability, ingenuity, genius, turn of mind (*obs.*). — *v.t.* to equip with an engine or engines: to contrive (*obs.*). — *n.* **engineer′** one who designs or makes, or puts to practical use, engines or machinery of any type, including electrical: one who designs or constructs public works, such as roads, railways, sewers, bridges, harbours, canals, etc.: one who constructs or manages military fortifications, etc. (*hist.*), or engines (*obs.*): a soldier of a division of an army called Engineers, concerned with entrenching, road-making, etc.: an officer who manages a ship's engines: an engine-driver (esp. *U.S.*): one who does public work requiring little skill (*U.S.; facet.*): one who plots (*obs.*), or who contrives to bring about (with *of*). — *v.i.* to act as engineer. — *v.t.* to arrange, contrive: to manoeuvre, guide: to produce by engineering. — *ns.* **engineer′ing** the art or profession of an engineer: extended to apply to certain techniques or processes not connected with the work of engineers, as *protein engineering;* **en′giner** (*Shak.*) engineer; **enginery** (*en′jin-ri*) the art of managing engines: engines collectively: machinery. — **en′gine-driver** a workman who controls an engine, esp. a railway locomotive; **engineer′s chain** a chain 50 or 100 feet long, made up of one-foot links: a unit of length, 100 feet; **en′gine-fitter** one who fits together the parts of an engine; **en′gine-man** one who drives an engine; **en′gine-room** the room in a vessel in which the engines are; **en′gine-turning** a kind of ornament made by a rose-engine, as on the backs of watches, etc. [O.Fr. *engin* — L. *ingenium,* skill; see **ingenious.**]
engird *in-gûrd′, v.t.* to gird round: to encircle: — *pa.p.* and *pa.t.* **engirt′.** — *v.t.* **engir′dle.** [Pfx. **en-** (1a).]
English *ing′glish, adj.* belonging to *England* or its inhabitants: of or relating to English. — *n.* the English people (as *pl.*): a Germanic language spoken in the British Isles, U.S.A., most parts of the British Commonwealth, etc.: 14-point type: side (*U.S.; billiards.*). — *v.t.* to translate into English (*arch.* or *rare*): to make English: to impart a side to (*U.S.; billiards*). — *n.* **Eng′lander** an Englishman. — *adj.* **Eng′lified** like the English of England in speech or ways: Southroun in speech, esp. affectedly so (*Scot.*). — *ns.* **Eng′lisher** a translator into English: an Englishman (*Scot.*); **Englishism** (*U.S. rare*) an expression or idiom originating in or found only in the English of England or Britain: a custom or practice peculiar to England: great admiration or enthusiasm for England and its customs, etc.; **Eng′lishman** a native or naturalised inhabitant of England: — *fem.* **Eng′lishwoman; Eng′lishry** the fact of being an Englishman: in Ireland, the population of English descent. — **Basic English** see **base; Early English** often means Early Middle English: (*archit.*) see **early; English breakfast** a cooked breakfast, usu. consisting of several dishes or courses (cf. *continental breakfast*); **English disease** the British disease; **English flute** the recorder; **English horn** the cor anglais; **English sickness** same as **English disease; English sweat** (*hist.*) the sweating sickness (see **sweat**). — **in plain English** in clear, simple language; **little Englander** an opponent of British imperialism and empire-building; **Middle English** from about 1100 or 1150 A.D. till about 1500; **Modern English** from about 1500 onwards; **Old English** a kind of type — black-letter: the English language down to about 1100 or 1150 A.D.

(formerly, and still popularly, *Anglo-Saxon*); **presentment of Englishry** the offering of proof that a person murdered belonged to the English race, to escape the fine levied on the hundred or township for the murder of a Norman; **Young England** see **young.** [O.E. *Englisc* — *Engle,* Angles.]
englobe *in-glōb′, v.t.* to enclose as in a globe: to form into a globe. [Pfx. **en-** (1a,b).]
engloom *in-gloom′, v.t.* to make gloomy. [Pfx. **en-** (1b).]
englut *in-glut′, v.t.* to glut, to fill: to swallow: — *pr.p.* **englutt′ing;** *pa.t.* and *pa.p.* **englutt′ed.** [Pfx. **en-** (1c).]
engobe *en-gōb′, n.* a slip applied to ceramics before the glaze e.g. to mask their natural colour. [Fr.]
engore *in-gōr′, -gör′, v.t.* to gore (*Spens.*): to pierce (*obs.*): to wound (*obs.*): to make gory. [Pfx. **en-** (1c).]
engorge *in-görj′, v.t.* to devour (*Spens.*): to glut. — *v.i.* (*Milt.*), to feed voraciously. — *adj.* **engorged′** filled to excess (with blood, etc.). — *n.* **engorge′ment** the act of swallowing greedily: congestion as with blood (*med.*). [Pfx. **en-** (1c).]
engouement, engoûment *ä-goo-mä′, n.* excessive fondness: infatuation. [Fr.]
engouled *en-goold′,* (*her.*) *adj.* of bends, crosses, etc., having ends that enter the mouths of animals. [Fr. *engoulée* — *en,* in, O.Fr. *goule* (Fr. *gueule*), a beast's mouth.]
engrace *in-grās′, v.t.* to put grace into. [Pfx. **en-** (1a).]
engraff. An obsolete form of **engraft.**
engraft *in-gräft′, v.t.* to graft: to insert: to join on (to something already existing): to fix deeply: to cuckold (*obs.*). — *ns.* **engraftā′tion** (*en-*) the act of engrafting; **engraft′ment** engrafting: the thing engrafted: a scion. — Also (*obs.*) **ingraft′,** etc. [Pfx. **en-** (1a).]
engrail *in-grāl′, v.t.* to border with little semicircular indents (*her.*): to make rough (*arch.*). — *v.i.* to form an edging or border: to run in indented lines. — *n.* **engrail′ment** the ring of dots round the edge of a medal: indentation in curved lines (*her.*). [O.Fr. *engresler* (Fr. *engrêler*) — *gresle,* slender — L. *gracilis.*]
engrain, ingrain *in-grān′, v.t.* to dye of a fast or lasting colour: to dye in the raw state: to infix deeply. — *adj.* **engrained′,** more often **ingrained′** (or *in′*), dyed in grain: deeply coloured or permeated: inveterate (e.g. *engrained laziness*): thorough-going (*fig.*). — *n.* **engrain′er.** [Orig. to dye in grain, i.e., with grain; see **grain.**]
engram *en′gram,* less often **engramma** *en-gram′ə, ns.* a permanent impression made by a stimulus or experience: a stimulus impression supposed to be inheritable: a memory trace. — *adj.* **engrammat′ic.** [Ger. *Engramm* — Gr. *en,* in, *gramma,* that which is written.]
en grande tenue *ä gräd tə-nü,* (Fr.) in full dress.
en grand seigneur *ä grä sen-yœr,* (Fr.) like a great lord.
engrasp *en-gräsp′,* (*Spens.*) *v.t.* to grasp. [Pfx. **en-** (1c).]
engrave[1] *in-grāv′, v.t.* to cut with a graver on wood, steel, etc.: to cut into: to impress deeply: to form or represent by engraving: — *pa.p.* **engraved′, engrāv′en.** — *ns.* **engrāv′er; engrāv′ery** (*obs.*) the art of the engraver; **engrāv′ing** the act or art of cutting or incising designs on metal, wood, etc., for the purpose of printing impressions from them — in metal, the lines to be printed are sunk or incised; in wood, the lines to be printed appear in relief, the wood between them being cut away: an impression taken from an engraved plate: a print. [Pfx. **en-** (1a) and **grave**[1].]
engrave[2] *in-grāv′, v.t.* to deposit in the grave. [Pfx. **en-** (1a).]
engrenage *ä-grə-näzh,* (Fr.) *n.* gearing (also *fig.*): a series of events, decisions, etc., each of which leads inevitably to further ones: the taking of such or decisions as moves towards some goal, thus avoiding the necessity of discussing the desirability of the goal itself.
engrieve *en-grēv′,* (*Spens.*) *v.t.* to grieve. [Pfx. **en-** (1c).]
engroove, ingroove *in-groov′, v.t.* to cut a groove or furrow in: to fit into a groove. [Pfx. **en-** (1a).]
engross *in-grōs′, v.t.* to buy up wholesale or completely: to monopolise: to take wholly to oneself: to absorb the whole attention or powers of: to copy in a large

hand or in distinct characters: to write in legal form: to name in a list or document (*obs.*): to make thick (*Spens.*): to fatten (*Shak.*). — *adj.* **engrossed'**. — *n.* **engross'er**. — *adj.* **engross'ing** monopolising: absorbing. — *n.* **engross'ment** buying up wholesale: that which has been engrossed: a fair copy. — **engrossing a deed** writing it out in full and regular form for signature. [Fr. *en gros* — L. *in*, in, *grossus*, large; see **gross**.]

enguard *en-gärd'*, (*Shak.*) *v.t.* to guard or defend. [Pfx. **en-** (1c).]

engulf, ingulf *in-gulf'*, *v.t.* to swallow up wholly, as in a gulf: to cause to be swallowed in a gulf. — Also (*obs.*) **engulph', ingulph'**. — *n.* **engulf'ment**. [Pfx. **en-** (1a).]

engyscope *en'ji-skōp*, (*obs.*) *n.* a microscope, esp. a kind of reflecting microscope. — Erroneously **en'giscope**. [Gr. *engys*, near, *skopeein*, to view.]

enhalo *in-hā'lō*, *v.t.* to surround with a halo. [Pfx. **en-** (1a).]

enhance *in-häns'*, *v.t.* to lift (*obs.*): to raise in value: to heighten: to intensify: to add to, increase: to make more important: to improve. — *v.i.* to increase: to rise in value. — *n.* **enhance'ment**. — *adj.* **enhanc'ive**. — **enhanced radiation weapon** a neutron bomb. [A.Fr. *enhauncer*, prob. from O.Fr. *enhaucer* — L. *in*, and *altus*, high; cf. **hance**.]

enharmonic, -al *en-här-mon'ik*, *-l*, *adjs.* pertaining to music constructed on a scale containing intervals less than a semitone: pertaining to that scale of music current among the Greeks in which an interval of 2½ tones was divided into two quarter tones and a major third: distinguishing between those tones that are identified in equal temperament. — *adv.* **enharmon'ically**. — **enharmonic modulation** for instruments of equal temperament, change of notation without change of tone. [Gr. *enharmonikos* — *en*, in, *harmoniā*, harmony.]

enhearse. See **inhearse**.

enhearten *in-härt'n*, *v.t.* to encourage: to cheer. [Pfx. **en-** (1b).]

enhunger *en-hung'gər*, *v.t.* to make hungry. [Pfx. **en-** (1b).]

enhydros *en-hī'dros*, *n.* a chalcedony nodule with water or other liquid in a cavity. — *n.* **enhy'drite** a mineral with fluid inclusions. — *adjs.* **enhydrit'ic, enhy'drous**. [Gr. *enydros*, containing water — *en*, in, *hydōr*, water.]

enhypostasia *en-hī-pō-stā'zi-ə*, *n.* substantial or personal existence: personality not existing independently but by union with another, as the human nature of Christ was said to be dependent on his divine nature. — *adj.* **enhypostatic** (*-stat'ik*). — *v.t.* **enhypostatise, -ize** (*-pos'-tə-tīz*). [Gr. *en*, in, and *hypostasis*; see **hypostasis**.]

eniac *en'i-ak*, *n.* an American pioneer electronic computer, — in full, *electronic numerical integrator and calculator*.

enigma *in-ig'mə*, *n.* a statement with a hidden meaning to be guessed: anything very obscure: a mysterious person or situation: a riddle. — *adjs.* **enigmat'ic, -al** (*en-*) relating to, containing, or resembling an enigma: obscure: puzzling. — *adv.* **enigmat'ically**. — *v.t.* **enig'matise, -ize** to express enigmatically or symbolically. — *ns.* **enig'matist** one who concocts or deals in riddles: one who expresses himself riddlingly; **enigmatog'raphy** the composition of enigmas. [L. *aenigma* — Gr. *ainigma* — *ainissesthai*, to speak darkly — *ainos*, a fable.]

enisle, inisle *in-īl'*, *v.t.* to put on, or make into, an island: to isolate. [Pfx. **en-** (1a, b).]

enjambment, enjambement *in-jam(b)'mənt, ä-zhäb-mä'*, *ns.* in verse, the continuation of the sense without a pause beyond the end of the line. — *v.t. and v.i.* **enjamb** (*in-jam'*). [Fr. *enjambement* — *enjamber*, to stride, encroach — *en*, in, *jambe*, leg.]

enjoin *in-join'*, *v.t.* to lay upon, as an order: to order or direct with authority or urgency: (*law* and *U.S.*) to forbid, to prohibit by *injunction*. — *ns.* **enjoin'er; enjoin'ment**. [Fr. *enjoindre* — L. *injungĕre* — *in*, and *jungĕre*, to join.]

enjoy *in-joi'*, *v.t.* to joy or delight in: to feel or perceive with pleasure: to possess or use with satisfaction or delight: to have the use of: (usu. of a man) to have sexual intercourse with (*arch.*). — *adj.* **enjoy'able** capable of being enjoyed: giving pleasure, delightful. — *n.* **enjoy'ableness**. — *adv.* **enjoy'ably**. — *ns.* **enjoy'er; enjoy'ment** the state or condition of enjoying: the satisfactory possession or use of anything: pleasure: happiness. — **enjoy oneself** to feel pleasure, have a pleasant time. [O.Fr. *enjoier*, to give joy to — *en* (L. *in*), *joie*, joy; or O.Fr. *enjoir*, to enjoy — *en*, and *joir* — L. *gaudēre*, to rejoice.]

enkephalin(e) *en-kef'ə-lin*, *n.* a chemical found in small quantities in the brain, which relieves pain and can now be produced synthetically. [Gr. *en*, in, *kephalē*, head.]

enkernel *in-kûr'nl*, *v.t.* to enclose in a kernel. [Pfx. **en-** (1a).]

enkindle *in-kin'dl*, *v.t.* to kindle or set on fire: to inflame: to rouse. — *adj.* **enkin'dled**. [Pfx. **en-** (1c).]

enlace *in-lās'*, *v.t.* to encircle: to embrace: to entwine: to entangle: to cover with a network or with lace: to interlace. — *n.* **enlace'ment**. — Also **inlace'**. [Pfx. **en-** (1c).]

en l'air *ä ler*, (Fr.) in the air: being discussed or expected: without reality.

enlard *in-lärd'*, (*Shak.*) *v.t.* to grease, to baste. [Pfx. **en-** (1a).]

enlarge *in-lärj'* (*Spens.* **enlarg'en**) *v.t.* to make wider: to increase in size or quantity: to expand: to amplify: to reproduce on a larger scale (esp. of a photograph): to set free. — *v.i.* to grow large or larger: to be diffuse in speaking or writing: to expatiate. — *adj.* **enlarged'**. — *adv.* **enlar'gedly**. — *ns.* **enlar'gedness; enlarge'ment** the act of enlarging: the state of being enlarged: increase: extension: diffuseness of speech or writing: a photograph reproduced on a larger scale: a setting at large: release; **enlarg'er**. [O.Fr. *enlarger* — *en* (L. *in*), *large*, large.]

enlevement *in-lēv'mənt*, *n.* (esp. *Scots law*) the abduction of a woman or child. — Also (as Fr.) **enlèvement** (*ä-lev-mä*). — *adj.* **enlevé** (Fr.; *ä-lə-vä*) carried away, kidnapped.

enlight *in-līt'*, (*arch.*) *v.t.* to shed light on: to light up, kindle. — *v.t.* **enlight'en** to lighten or shed light on (*arch.*): to give light to (*arch.*): to make clear to the mind (*obs.*): to impart knowledge or information to: to elevate by knowledge or religion: to free from prejudice and superstition. — *n.* **enlight'enment** the act of enlightening: the state of being enlightened: (usu. with *cap.*) the spirit of the French philosophers of the 18th century, with a belief in reason and human progress and a questioning of tradition and authority. [O.E. *inlīhtan* — *in*, in, *līhtan*, to light; or independently formed later.]

enlink *in-lingk'*, *v.t.* to connect closely. [Pfx. **en-** (1c).]

enlist *in-list'*, *v.t.* to enrol: to engage as a soldier, etc.: to employ in advancing an object. — *v.i.* to engage in public service, esp. as a soldier: to enter heartily into a cause. — *n.* **enlist'ment** the act of enlisting: the state of being enlisted. — **enlisted man** (*U.S.*) a member of the armed forces below the rank of warrant officer, other than a cadet or midshipman. [Pfx. **en-** (1a).]

enliven *in-līv'n*, *v.t.* to put life into: to excite or make active: to make sprightly or cheerful: to animate. — *ns.* **enliv'ener; enliv'enment**. [Pfx. **en-** (1b).]

enlock *in-lok'*, *v.t.* to lock up: to enclose. [Pfx. **en-** (1a).]

enlumine *en-lōō'min*, (*Spens.*) *v.t.* Same as **illumine**.

en masse *ä mas*, (Fr.) in a body: all together.

enmesh, inmesh *in-mesh'*, **emmesh, immesh** *em-(m)esh', im-(m)esh'*, *vs.t.* to catch in a mesh or net: to entangle. [Pfx. **en-** (1a).]

enmew. See **emmew**.

en militaire *ä mē-lē-ter*, (Fr.) as a military man.

enmity *en'mi-ti*, *n.* the quality of being an enemy: unfriendliness: ill-will: hostility. [O.Fr. *enemistié* — L. *inimīcus*; see **enemy**.]

enmossed *in-most'*, *adj.* covered with moss. [Pfx. **en-** (1a).]

enmove *en-mōōv'*, (*Spens.*) *v.t.* Same as **emmove.**

ennea- *en'i-ə-*, in composition, nine. — *n.* **ennead** (*en'i-ad;* Gr. *enneas, -ados*) the number nine: a set of nine things. — *adj.* **ennead'ic.** — *n.* **enn'eagon** (*-ə-gon;* Gr. *gōniā,* angle) a polygon with nine angles. — *adj.* **enneagonal** (*-ag'ən-l*). — *n.* **enneahē'dron** a solid figure with nine faces. — *adj.* **enneahē'dral.** — *n.pl.* **Ennean'dria** (Gr. *anēr, andros,* man, male) the ninth Linnaean class of plants, with nine stamens. — *adjs.* **ennean'drian; ennean'drous; enn'eastyle** (Gr. *stȳlos,* column) having nine columns. [Gr. *ennea,* nine.]

ennoble *i-nō'bl*, *v.t.* to make noble: to elevate, distinguish: to raise to nobility. — *n.* **ennō'blement** the act of making noble: that which ennobles. [Fr. *ennoblir* — Fr. *en* (L. *in*), and *noble.*]

ennui *ä-nwē'*, *on'wē, on-wē', n.* a feeling of weariness or languor: boredom: the occasion of ennui. — *v.t.* (found mostly as *pa.p.*) to weary: to bore: — *pr.p.* **ennuying;** *pa.t.* and *pa.p.* **ennuied, ennuyed.** — *adj.* **ennuyé** (Fr.; *-yā*) bored. [Fr., distress — O.Fr. *anoi* — L. *in odiō,* as in *odiō habeō,* I hold in hatred, i.e. I am tired of; see **annoy.**]

enodal *ē-nō'dl, adj.* without nodes.

enomoty *e-nom'o-ti, n.* a band of sworn soldiers, esp. the smallest Spartan subdivision. [Gr. *enōmotiā — en,* in *omnynai,* to swear.]

enormous *i-nör'məs,* (*obs.*) **enorm'** *adjs.* abounding, exceeding the normal, esp. in a bad sense (*arch.*): immense: huge: outrageous (*arch.*): atrocious (*arch.*): considerable, very much, a great deal of (*coll.*). — *n.* **enor'mity** a great crime: great wickedness: outrage: iniquity: abnormality (*obs.*): hugeness. — *adv.* **enor'mously.** — *n.* **enor'mousness.** [L. *ēnormis — ē,* out of, *norma,* rule.]

enosis *en'ō-sis, en-ō'sis, n.* union, the aim and rallying-cry of the Greek Cypriot movement for union with Greece: — *pl.* **-ses.** [Gr. (anc. and mod.) *henosis — heis, henos,* one.]

enough *i-nuf', adj.* as much as need be: sufficient: giving content: satisfying want. — *adv.* sufficiently: quite: fairly: tolerably: used in phrases which stress or admit the state of something, as in *oddly enough, fair enough.* — *n.* sufficience: as much as satisfies desire or want: a sufficient degree or extent. [O.E. *genōh* (nom., neut. accus., and adv., for earlier *genōg*); Goth. *ganōhs;* Ger. *genug;* O.N. *gnōgr.*]

enounce *i-* or *ē-nowns', v.t.* to enunciate: to proclaim: to utter or articulate. [Fr. *énoncer* — L. *ēnuntiāre.*]

enow[1] *i-now', (arch.) adj.* and *adv.* enough: formerly used as plural of enough. [O.E. *genōg* (*genōh*), with *g* preserved in inflective forms; cf. **enough.**]

enow[2] *ē-noō', adv.* (*Scot.* and *dial.*) a moment ago: presently. [Prob. **even now.**]

en pantoufles *ä pä-tōō-fl', (Fr.) lit.,* in slippers: unconstrained, at one's ease.

en papillote *ä pa-pē-yot, (Fr.)* (of food) cooked and served in an envelope of oiled paper or foil.

en passant *ä-pa-sä, (Fr.)* in passing: by the way: applied in chess to the taking of a pawn that has just moved two squares as if it had moved only one.

en pension *ä-pä-sy̅, (Fr.)* at a fixed rate for board and lodging.

en plein air *ä ple-ner, (Fr.)* in the open air.

en plein jour *ä plē zhōōr, (Fr.)* in broad daylight.

en poste *ä post, (Fr.)* of a diplomat, resident at a place in an official capacity.

en prince *ä prẽs, (Fr.)* in princely style.

en principe *ä prē-sēp, (Fr.)* in principle.

enprint *en'print, n.* an enlarged photographic print, esp. 5 × 3½ in. ['*E*nvelope-size print' and '*en*larged print' have both been suggested as origins.]

en prise *ä prēz, (Fr.)* (of a pawn in chess) exposed to capture.

en pure perte *ä pür pert, (Fr.)* to mere loss, to no purpose.

en queue *ä kø, (Fr.)* like a tail: in a string or line: (of hair) in a queue.

enquire. See **inquire.**

enrace *en-rās', (Spens.) v.t.* to implant. [Pfx. **en-** (1a).]

enrage *in-rāj', v.t.* to make angry. — *adj.* **enraged'** angered: furious. — *n.* **enrage'ment** the act of enraging: the state of being enraged: rapture (*Spens.*). [O.Fr. *enrager — en* (L. *in*), and *rage,* rage.]

enragé *ä-rä-zhä, (Fr.; hist.) n.* any of a group of revolutionaries during the French Revolution in favour of proto-socialist economic reform rather than political reform as a means of alleviating the distress of the populace. [Fr., violently angry, crazy.]

enranckle *in-rang'kl, (Spens.) v.t.* to enrage. [Pfx. **en-** (1b).]

enrange *en-rānj', enraunge* **en-rönj', (Spens.) vs.t.* to arrange: to rove over. [Pfx. **en-** (1c).]

enrank *en-rangk', (Shak.) v.t.* to place in order. [Pfx. **en-** (1a).]

en rappel *ä ra-pel, (Fr.)* of a method of descent in mountaineering using a rope which is easily pulled free after descent. [Fr., — *rappel,* recall.]

en rapport *ä ra-pör, (Fr.)* in direct relation: in close touch or sympathy.

enrapture *in-rap'chər, v.t.* to put in rapture or ecstasy: to transport with pleasure or delight. — *adjs.* **enrap'tured, enrapt'** in ecstasy. [Pfx. **en-** (1a).]

enraunge. See **enrange.**

enravish *en-rav'ish, v.t.* to enrapture. [Pfx. **en-** (1c).]

enregiment *in-rej'(i)-mənt, v.t.* to form into a regiment. [Pfx. **en-** (1b).]

enregister *in-rej'is-tər, v.t.* to register: to enrol: to record: to put on record as ratified. [Pfx. **en-** (1c).]

en règle *ä re-gl', (Fr.)* in due order: according to rule.

en retraite *ä rə-tret, (Fr.)* in retirement: on half-pay.

en revanche *ä rə-väsh, (Fr.)* in return or requital.

enrheum *en-rōōm', (obs.) v.t.* to give a cold to , cause to catch a cold. — *adj.* (*arch.*) **enrheumed'.** [O.Fr. *enrheumer* — *en* (see **en-**(1b)) and Gr. *rheuma* (see **rheum**).]

enrich *in-rich', v.t.* to make rich: to fertilise: to adorn: to enhance: to increase the proportion of some valuable substance in: to increase the proportion of one or more particular isotopes in a mixture of the isotopes of an element, e.g. to raise the proportion of fissile nuclei above that for natural uranium in reactor fuel. — *n.* **enrich'ment** the act of enriching: that which enriches: ornamentation. [Pfx. **en-** (1b).]

enridged *en-rij'id, (Shak.) adj.* formed into ridges. [Pfx. **en-** (1b).]

enring *in-ring', v.t.* to encircle: to put a ring on. [Pfx. **en-** (1a).]

enriven *en-riv'n, (Spens.) adj.* torn. [Pfx. **en-** (1c).]

enrobe *in-rōb', v.t.* to dress, clothe, or invest. [Pfx. **en-** (1c).]

enrol, enroll *in-rōl', v.t.* (*arch.* or *U.S.*) to insert in a roll, list or register: to enter in a list as pupil, member, etc.: to enlist: to record: to put in writing: to form into a roll (*Spens.*): to enwrap (*Spens.*). — *v.i.* to enrol oneself: — *pr.p.* **enroll'ing;** *pa.t.* and *pa.p.* **enrolled'.** — *ns.* **enroll'er; enrol(l)'ment** the act of enrolling: that in which anything is enrolled: a register. [O.Fr. *enroller* (Fr. *enrôler*) — *en,* and *rolle,* roll.]

enroot *in-rōōt', v.t.* to fix by the root: to implant firmly: to entangle, as root by root (*Shak.*). [Pfx. **en-** (1c).]

enrough *in-ruf', (arch.) v.t.* to make rough. [Pfx. **en-** (1b).]

enround *en-rownd', (Shak.) v.t.* to surround. [Pfx. **en-** (1a).]

en route *ä rōōt, (Fr.)* on the road, on the way: let us go: march.

ens *enz, n.* an entity, as opp. to an attribute: — *pl.* **entia** (*en'shi-ə*). — **ens per accidens** (*enz pər ak'si-dənz, per a-ki-dāns'*) that which exists only as an accident of a substance (an **ens per se** (*sē, sā*)); **ens rationis** (*rā-shi-ō'nis, ra-ti-ō'*) an entity of reason, existing purely in the mind — opp. to **ens reale** (*rē-ā'lē, re-ä'le*) which exists actually or potentially outside of the mind. [L.L. *ēns*, pr.p. from L. *esse*, to be.]

ensample *en-säm'pl*, (*arch.*) *n.* example. — *v.t.* to give an example of. [O.Fr. *essample*; see **example**.]

ensanguine *in-sang'gwin*, *v.t.* to stain or cover with blood. — *adjs.* **ensan'guinated** (esp. *facet.*), **ensan'guined** bloody. [Fr. pfx. *en-*, in, L. *sanguis, -inis*, blood.]

ensate *en'sāt*, *adj.* sword-shaped. [L. *ēnsis*, sword.]

enschedule *en-shed'ūl*, (*Shak.*) *v.t.* to insert in a schedule. [Pfx. **en-** (1a).]

ensconce *in-skons'*, *v.t.* to cover or protect as with a sconce or earthwork (*obs.*): to hide safely: to settle comfortably. [Pfx. **en-** (1a).]

enseal *en-sēl'*, (*arch.*) *v.t.* to put one's seal to: to seal up. [Pfx. **en-** (1c).]

enseam¹ *en-sēm'*, *v.t.* to mark as with a seam. [Pfx. **en-** (1c), and **seam²**.]

enseam² *en-sēm'*, *v.t.* to grease (*obs.*): to defile (*Shak.*): to free from superfluous fat (*obs.*). [Pfx. **en-** (1c), and **seam¹**.]

enseam³ *en-sēm'*, (*obs.*) *v.t.* to contain: to introduce to company. [Der. obscure; cf. M.E. *in same, in seme*, O.E. *ætsomne, tosomne*, together, O.N. *semja*, to put together.]

ensear *en-sēr'*, (*Shak.*) *v.t.* to dry up. [Pfx. **en-** (1b), and **sear²**.]

ensemble *ä-sä-bl'*, *n.* all parts of a thing taken together: the union of performers in a concerted number (*mus.*): the group of musicians so combining: the combined effect of the performance: a costume consisting of several (matching) garments: a group of supporting dancers, corps de ballet. — Also *adj.* — **tout ensemble** (*tōō-tä-*) general appearance or effect. [Fr. *ensemble*, together — L. *in*, in, *simul*, at the same time.]

ensepulchre *en-sep'əl-kər*, *v.t.* to put in a sepulchre. [Pfx. **en-** (1a).]

ensew (*Spens.*). Same as **ensue**.

ensheathe, ensheath, insheathe *in-shēdh'*, *v.t.* to enclose as a sheath. [Pfx. **en-** (1a).]

enshell. Same as **inshell**. — *adj.* **enshield'** (*Shak.*), prob. **enshelled** or **inshelled**.

enshelter *en-shel'tər*, (*Shak.*) *v.t.* to put in shelter. [Pfx. **en-** (1a).]

enshield¹ *en-shēld'*, *v.t.* to shield or protect. [Pfx. **en-** (1c).]

enshield². See **enshell**.

enshrine *en-shrīn'*, *v.t.* to enclose in or as in a shrine. [Pfx. **en-** (1a).]

enshroud *en-shrowd'*, *v.t.* to cover up: to cover with a shroud. [Pfx. **en-** (1a).]

ensiform *en'si-förm*, *adj.* sword-shaped. [L. *ēnsis*, a sword, *fōrma*, form.]

ensign *en'sin, -sīn*, *n.* a badge, sign, or mark: a sign or flag, distinguishing a nation or a regiment (see also under **blue, red, white**): one who carries the colours: until 1871, the officer of lowest commissioned rank in the British infantry: an officer of lowest commissioned rank (*U.S. navy*). — *v.t.* (*-sīn'*) to mark with a badge or sign, in heraldry, with one placed above. — *ns.* **en'signcy, en'signship** the rank or commission of an ensign in the army. [O.Fr. *enseigne* — L. *īnsignia*, pl. of *īnsigne*, a distinctive mark — *in*, and *signum*, a mark.]

ensilage *en'sil-ij*, *n.* the storing of green fodder in pits or silos. — *vs.t.* **ensile** (*en-sīl'*, or *en'sīl*), **en'silage** to store by ensilage. [Fr., — Sp. *en*, in, and *silo* — L. *sīrus* — Gr. *sīros, sīros, seiros*, pit for corn.]

ensky *en-skī'*, (*Shak.*) *v.t.* to place in the sky. [Pfx. **en-** (1a).]

enslave *in-slāv'*, *v.t.* to reduce to slavery: to subject to a dominating influence. — *adj.* **enslaved'**. — *ns.* **enslave'ment** act of enslaving: state of being enslaved: slavery: bondage; **enslav'er**. [Pfx. **en-** (1b).]

ensnare *in-snār'*, *v.t.* to catch in a snare: to entrap: to entangle. [Pfx. **en-** (1a).]

ensnarl *en-snärl'*, (*Spens.*) *v.t.* to entangle. [Pfx. **en-** (1a).]

ensorcell *in-sör'səl, -sör'*, *v.t.* to bewitch. [O.Fr. *ensorceler* — *en*, and *sorcier*, a sorcerer.]

ensoul, insoul *in-sōl'*, *v.t.* to join with the soul: to animate as a soul. [Pfx. **en-** (1b).]

en spectacle *ä spek-ta-kl'*, (Fr.) as a spectacle.

ensphere, insphere *in-sfēr'*, *v.t.* to enclose or place in a sphere: to give a spherical form to: — *pa.p.* (*Milt.*) **insphear'd**. [Pfx. **en-** (1a).]

enstamp *in-stamp'*, *v.t.* to mark as with a stamp. [Pfx. **en-** (1c).]

enstatite *en'stət-īt*, *n.* a rock-forming mineral, an orthorhombic pyroxene, magnesium silicate. [Gr. *enstatēs*, adversary, from its refractory character.]

ensteep *en-stēp'*, (*Shak.*) *v.t.* to steep: to lay under water. [Pfx. **en-** (1c).]

enstructured *en-struk'chərd*, *adj.* incorporated into, made part of, the structure of something. [Pfx. **en-** (1a) and **structure**.]

enstyle *in-stīl'*, (*arch.*) *v.t.* to style, call. [Pfx. **en-** (1c).]

ensue *in-sū'*, *v.i.* to follow, to come after: to result (with *from*). — *v.t.* (*B., arch.*) to follow after: — *pr.p.* **ensū'ing**; *pa.t.* and *pa.p.* **ensūed'**. [O.Fr. *ensuir* (Fr. *ensuivre*) — L. *in*, after, L.L. *sequēre* — L. *sequī*, to follow.]

en suite *ä swēt*, (Fr.) in succession or connected series: forming a unit, or a set (not in Fr.). — *n.* (*Austr.*) an en suite bathroom.

ensure *in-shōōr'*, *v.t.* to make sure: to make safe: to betroth (*obs.*): to insure (*obs.*). — *n.* **ensur'er**. [See **insure**.]

enswathe, inswathe *in-swādh'*, *v.t.* to wrap. — *n.* **enswathe'ment**. [Pfx. **en-** (1c).]

ensweep *in-swēp'*, (*arch.*) *v.t.* to sweep over. [Pfx. **en-** (1c).]

ent-. See **ento-**.

entablature *en-tab'lə-chər*, *n.* in classic architecture, that part which surmounts the columns and rests upon the capitals: an engine framework upon columns. [It. *intavolatura* — *in*, in, *tavola* — L. *tabula*, a table.]

entablement *in-tā'bl-mənt*, *n.* a platform above the dado on a pedestal, on which a statue rests: an entablature. [Fr.]

entail¹, entayle *en-tāl'*, (*obs.*) *v.t.* and *v.i.* to carve. — *n.* cut, fashion. [O.Fr. *entailler* — L.L. *intaleāre* — *in*, into, *taleāre*, to cut.]

entail² *in-tāl'*, *v.t.* to settle on a series of heirs, so that the immediate possessor may not dispose of the estate: to bring on as an inevitable consequence. — *n.* the settlement of an entailed estate: an estate entailed: the transmission, or the rule of descent, of an estate. — *ns.* **entail'er; entail'ment** the act of entailing: the state of being entailed. [Pfx. **en-** (1a), and **tail²**.]

entame *en-tām'*, (*Shak.*) *v.t.* to tame. [Pfx. **en-**(1c).]

entamoeba *en-tə-mē'bə*, *n.* any amoeba of the genus *Entamoeba*, one of the species of which causes amoebic dysentery in man. — Also **endamoe'ba**. [**ento-, endo-** and **amoeba**.]

entangle *in-tang'gl*, *v.t.* to twist into a tangle, or so as not to be easily separated: to involve in complications or in an embarrassing or a compromising situation: to perplex: to ensnare. — *n.* **entang'lement** a confused state: perplexity: a tangled obstacle: a tangle: the condition of being entangled: an entangling connection. [Pfx. **en-** (1c).]

entasis *en'tə-sis*, (*archit.*) *n.* the slightly swelling outline of the shaft of a column or the like, used to counteract the illusion of concavity that an absolutely straight column would produce. [Gr. *entasis* — *en*, in, *tasis*, a stretch.]

entayle. See **entail¹**.

entelechy *en-tel'ə-ki*, (*philos.*) *n.* actuality: distinctness of realised existence: a vital principle supposed by vitalists to direct processes in an organism towards realisation of a certain end. [Gr. *entelecheia* — *en*, in, *telos*, perfection, end, *echein*, to have.]

entellus *en-tel'əs*, *n.* the hanuman monkey of India. [App. from *Entellus* the old Sicilian in *Aeneid*, book

V, from its old-mannish look.]

entender, intender *in-tend'ər*, (*obs.*) *v.t.* to make tender: to weaken. [Pfx. **en-** (1b).]

entente *ä-tät*, *n.* an understanding: a friendly agreement or relationship between states — as the **entente cordiale** (*kör-dē-äl'*) between Britain and France (1904). [Fr.]

enter *en'tər*, *v.i.* to go or come in: to penetrate: to come upon the stage: to take possession: to become a member: to put down one's name (as competitor, candidate, etc.): to become a party or participator. — *v.t.* to come or go into: to penetrate: to join or engage in: to begin: to put into: to enrol or record: to admit: to inscribe or cause to be inscribed: to register (as a vessel leaving a port, a horse for a race, a pupil for a school, etc.): to insert a record of: to initiate: to become a member of: to take possession of: to obtain right of preemption to by recording one's name in a land office, etc. (*U.S.*). — *n.* (*Shak.*) ingoing. — *adj.* **en'terable.** — *n.* **en'terer.** — *n.* and *adj.* **en'tering.** — **enter a protest** to write it in the books: thence simply, to protest; **enter into** to become a party to: to be interested in: to participate actively or heartily in: to understand sympathetically: to take up the discussion of: to be part of; **enter on, upon** to begin: to engage in. [Fr. *entrer* — L. *intrāre*, to go into, related to *inter*, between.]

enter-. Form of **inter-**, orig. through Fr. *entre*, between, etc.

enterchaunge *en-tər-chönj'.* An obs. form of **interchange.**

enterdeale (*Spens.*). See **interdeal.**

enter(o)- *en'tər(-ō)-*, in composition, intestine. — *adjs.* **en'teral** pertaining to, within, or by way of, the intestine; **en'terate** having an alimentary canal. — *n.* **enterec'tomy** (Gr. *ektomē*, a cutting out) surgical removal of part of the bowel. — *adj.* **enteric** (*en-ter'ik*) pertaining to the intestines: possessing an alimentary canal. — *n.* short for **enteric fever,** typhoid fever, an infectious disease due to a bacillus, characterised by fever, rose-red rash, enlargement of the spleen and ulceration of the intestines. — *ns.* **enteri'tis** inflammation of the intestines, esp. the small intestine; **en'terocele** (*-sēl*; Gr. *kēlē*, tumour) a hernia containing intestine; **enterocentesis** (*-sen-tē'sis*; Gr. *kentēsis*, pricking) operative puncturing of the intestine; **en'terolith** (Gr. *lithos*, stone) a concretion of organic matter with lime, bismuth or magnesium salts formed in the intestine; **Enteromor'pha** (Gr. *morphē*, form) a genus of green seaweeds of tubular form; **en'teron** in coelenterates, the body-cavity: in higher animals, the gut or alimentary canal: — *pl.* **en'tera.** — **en'teropneust** any animal of the **Enteropneus'ta** (gut-breathers; Gr. *pneein*, to breathe), the Hemichordata, or a division of them including Balanaglossus; **enteroptos'is** downward displacement of the intestines; **enteros'tomy** (Gr. *stoma*, mouth) surgical formation of an opening in the intestine; **enterot'omy** incision of the intestinal wall; **enterotox'in** an intestinal toxin which causes food poisoning; **enterovi'rus** any of several viruses occurring in and infecting the intestine. [Gr. *enteron*, gut.]

enterprise *en'tər-prīz*, *n.* an undertaking: a bold or dangerous undertaking: readiness, initiative, and daring in undertaking: a business concern. — *v.t.* to undertake. — *n.* **en'terpriser** an adventurer (*arch.*): an entrepreneur. — *adj.* **en'terprising** forward in undertaking: adventurous: full of initiative. — *adj.* **en'terprisingly.** — **enterprise zone** any of a number of sites in depressed areas in which industrial and commercial renewal is encouraged by the government by financial and other incentives. [O.Fr. *entreprise*, pa.p. of *entreprendre* — *entre*, between (L. *inter*), and *prendre* — L. *praehendĕre*, to seize.]

entertain *en-tər-tān'*, *v.t.* to maintain, keep up (*obs.*): to take on (as servant, etc.) (*obs.*): to treat (*obs.*): to receive (*obs.*): to provide lodging or refreshment for: to treat hospitably: to hold the attention or thoughts of: to hold the attention of pleasurably: to amuse: to receive and take into consideration: to keep or hold in the mind: to meet or experience (*Spens.*). — *n.* (*Spens.*;

Shak.) entertainment. — *n.* **entertain'er** one who gives or offers entertainment in any sense: one who gives amusing performances professionally. — *adj.* **entertain'ing** affording entertainment: amusing. — Also *n.* — *adv.* **entertain'ingly.** — *n.* **entertain'ment** the act of entertaining: the reception of and provision for guests: hospitality at table: that which entertains: the provisions of the table (*arch.*): a banquet (*arch.*): amusement: a performance or show intended to give pleasure. [Fr. *entretenir* — L. *inter*, among, *tenēre*, to hold.]

entertake *en-tər-tāk'*, (*Spens.*) *v.t.* to receive.

entertissued. See **intertissued.**

entête *ä-te-tā*, (Fr.) *adj.* infatuated: opinionative: — *fem.* **entêtée.**

enthalpy *en-thal'pi*, *en'thəl-pi*, *n.* the heat content of a substance per unit mass, defined as $h = u + pv$ ($u =$ internal energy, $p =$ pressure, and $v =$ volume). [Gr. *enthalpein*, to warm in.]

enthetic *en-thet'ik*, *adj.* (of diseases, etc.) introduced from without. [Gr. *enthetikos* — *entithenai*, to put in.]

enthrall, enthral *in-thröl'*, *v.t.* to bring into thraldom or bondage: to hold in thrall: to hold spellbound: — *pr.p.* **enthrall'ing;** *pa.t.* and *pa.p.* **enthralled'.** — *ns.* **enthral'dom** the condition of being enthralled; **enthral'ment** the act of enthralling: slavery. — Also (*obs.*) **inthrall', inthral'.** [Pfx. **en-** (1a).]

enthrone *in-thrōn'*, *v.t.* to place on a throne: to exalt to the seat of royalty: to install as bishop: to exalt. — *ns.* **enthrōne'ment, enthrōnisā'tion, -z-** the act of enthroning or of being enthroned. — *v.t.* **enthrō'nise, -ize** (or *en'* to enthrone, as a bishop: to exalt. [Pfx. **en-** (1a).]

enthusiasm *in-, en-thū'zi-azm*, or *-thōō'*, *n.* possession by a god, inspiration, or religious exaltation (*obs.*): religious extravagance (*obs.*): intense interest: passionate zeal. — *v.t.* and *v.i.* **enthuse'** (back-formation) to make, be, become, or appear enthusiastic. — *n.* **enthu'siast** one filled with enthusiasm. — *adjs.* **enthusias'tic, -al** filled with enthusiasm: zealous: ardent. — *adv.* **enthusias'tically.** [Gr. *enthousiasmos*, a god-inspired zeal — *enthousiazein*, to be inspired by a god — *en*, in, *theos*, a god.]

enthymeme *en'thi-mēm*, *n.* an argument of probability only (*rhet.*): a syllogism in which one premise is suppressed (*logic*). — *adj.* **enthymemat'ical.** [Gr. *enthȳmēma*, a consideration — *enthȳmeesthai*, to consider — *en*, in, *thȳmos*, the mind.]

entia. See **ens.**

entice *in-tīs'*, *v.t.* to induce by exciting hope or desire: to tempt: to lead astray. — *adj.* **entice'able.** — *ns.* **entice'ment** the act of enticing: that which entices or tempts: allurement; **entic'er.** — *n.* and *adj.* **entic'ing.** — *adv.* **entic'ingly.** [O.Fr. *enticier*, provoke; prob. related to L. *titiō*, a brand.]

entire *in-tīr'*, *adj.* whole: complete: unmingled: intact: unimpaired: untired (*Spens.*): not castrated (esp. of a horse): with untoothed and unlobed margin (*biol.*): inner, inward (*Spens.*): genuine (*arch.*). — *adv.* within (*arch.*): sincerely (*arch.*). — *n.* the whole: completeness: a stallion: porter or stout as delivered from the brewery. — *adv.* **entire'ly.** — *ns.* **entire'ness, entī'rety** completeness: the whole. — **in its entirety** in its completeness: (considered, taken, etc.) as a whole. [O.Fr. *entier* — L. *integer*, whole, from *in-*, not, and root of *tangĕre*, to touch; in some senses showing confusion with **interior.**]

entitle *en-tī'tl*, *v.t.* to give a title to: to style: to give a right or claim to. — *n.* **entī'tlement** that to which one has a right or claim. [O.Fr. *entiteler* — L.L. *intitulāre* — *in*, in, *titulus*, title.]

entity *en'ti-ti*, *n.* being, existence: something with objective reality: an abstraction or archetypal conception. [L.L. *entitās, -ātis* — *ēns*; see **ens.**]

ento- *en'tō-*, *en-to'*, **ent-** *ent-*, in composition, inside, often interchanging with **endo-** and opp. to **ecto-, exo-.** — *ns.* **en'toblast** (Gr. *blastos*, shoot, bud) endoderm: a cell nucleolus; **en'toderm** endoderm. — *adj.* **entophytal**

(-fī'tl). — n. **en'tophyte** (-fīt; Gr. *phyton*, plant) an endophyte. — *adjs.* **entophytic** (-fit'ik), **entophytous** (en-tof'i-təs or en-tō-fī'təs); **entop'ic** developed, etc., in the usual place; **entoplas'tral.** — n. **entoplas'tron** the unpaired plate behind the epiplastra in a turtle's plastron. — *adj.* **entopt'ic** (Gr. *ōps, ōpos,* eye) within the eyeball: pertaining to the visibility to the eye of objects within itself. — *n.sing.* **entop'tics** the study of such appearances. — *adj.* **ento'tic** (Gr. *ous, ōtos,* ear) of the interior of the ear. — n. **entozō'on** (Gr. *zōion,* an animal) an animal living parasitically within the body of its host: — *pl.* **entozō'a.** — *adjs.* **entozō'al; entozō'ic.** [Gr. *entos,* within.]

entoil in-toil', *v.t.* to entangle or ensnare. — n. **entoil'ment.** [Pfx. **en-** (1a).]

entomb in-tōōm', *v.t.* to place in a tomb: to bury. — n. **entomb'ment** burial. [O.Fr. *entoumber* — *en,* in, *tombe,* a tomb.]

entomic en-tom'ik, *adj.* pertaining to insects. — *adj.* **entomolog'ical** (-loj'). — *adv.* **entomolog'ically.** — *v.i.* **entomol'ogise, -ize.** — *ns.* **entomol'ogist** one learned in entomology; **entomol'ogy** (-ə-ji) the science of insects. — *adj.* **entomoph'agous** (-fə-gəs; Gr. *phagein,* to eat — aorist) insectivorous. — n. **entomoph'agy** (-fə-ji) the practice of eating insects. — *adj.* **entomoph'ilous** (Gr. *phileein,* to love) specially adapted for pollination by insects. — n. **entomoph'ily** pollination by insects: adaptation to pollination by insects. [Gr. *entoma,* insects — *entomos,* cut up — *en,* in, *tomē,* a cut.]

Entomostraca en-tō-mos'trə-kə, *n.pl.* a general name for the lower orders of Crustacea — *Phyllopods, Ostracods, Copepods,* and *Cirripedes.* — n. and *adj.* **entomos'tracan.** — *adj.* **entomos'tracous.** [Gr. *entomos,* cut up — *en,* in, *tomē,* a cut, *ostrakon,* a shell.]

entophyte... to ... **entotic.** See **ento-**.

entourage ä-tōō-räzh', *n.* surroundings: followers, attendants. [Fr., — *entourer,* to surround — *en,* in, *tour,* a circuit.]

en tout cas ä-tōō-kä', a parasol that can be used as an umbrella. — **En-Tout-Cas®** a hard tennis court that can be used in all weathers. [Fr., in any case.]

entozoon, etc. See **ento-**.

entr'acte ä-trakt', *n.* the interval between acts in a play: a piece of music or other performance between acts. [Fr., — *entre,* between, *acte,* act.]

entrail en-trāl', (*Spens.*) *v.t.* to interlace, entwine. — n. twisting, entanglement. [O.Fr. *entreillier* — *en,* and *treille,* trelliswork.]

entrails en'trālz, (*Spens.* **entralles** en'trölz), *n.pl.* the internal parts of an animal's body, the bowels: the inside of anything: the seat of the emotions (*obs.*): — *sing.* (rare) **entrail** (*Spens.* **entrall** en-tröl'). [O.Fr. *entraille* — L.L. *intrālia* — *inter,* within.]

entrain[1] in-trān', *v.t.* to put into a railway train, esp. used by troops. — *v.i.* to get into a train: to take a train. — n. **entrain'ment.** [Pfx. **en-** (1a).]

entrain[2] in-trān', *v.t.* to draw after (*arch.*): to transport one substance, e.g. small liquid particles, in another, e.g. a vapour: to suspend bubbles or particles in a moving fluid. — n. **entrain'ment.** [Fr. *entraîner.*]

entrain[3] ä-trẽ, (Fr.) *n.* liveliness, spirit. — n. **entraînement** (ä-tren-mä' enthusiasm.

en train ä trẽ, (Fr.) in progress.

entrall(es). See **entrails.**

entrammel in-tram'l, *v.t.* to trammel, fetter. [Pfx. **en-** (1c).]

entrance[1] en'trəns, *n.* an act of entering: a coming upon the stage: the power or right to enter: a place of entering: a door: the beginning (*arch.*). — n. **en'trant** one who, or that which, enters. — **entrance fee** the money paid on entering a society, club, etc. [Fr. *entrer* — L. *intrāre,* to enter.]

entrance[2] in-, en-träns', *v.t.* to put into a trance: to fill with rapturous delight. — n. **entrance'ment** a state of trance or of excessive joy. — *adj.* **entranc'ing** charming, transporting. [Pfx. **en-** (1a).]

entrap in-trap', *v.t.* to catch, as in a trap: to ensnare: to

entangle. — *ns.* **entrap'ment** the act of entrapping: the state of being entrapped: the act of luring a person into the commission of a crime so that he may be arrested and prosecuted; **entrapp'er.** [O.Fr. *entraper* — *en,* in, *trappe,* a trap.]

en travesti ä tra-ves-tē, (Fr.) (esp. of a female dancer or actress) wearing the clothes of the opposite sex.

entreasure in-trezh'ər, (*arch.*) *v.t.* to lay up, as in a treasury. [Pfx. **en-** (1a).]

entreat in-trēt', *v.t.* to ask earnestly: to beseech: to beg for: to induce (*obs.*): to treat, deal with, behave towards (*obs.*): to occupy oneself with (*Spens.*): to pass, spend (time) (*Shak.*). — *v.i.* to beseech, ask. — *adjs.* **entreat'-able** (*obs.*); **intreat'full** (*Spens.*); **entreat'ing.** — *adv.* **entreating'ly.** — *adj.* **entreat'ive** (*obs.*). — *ns.* **entreat'ment** the act of entreating: treatment (*obs.*): perhaps discourse, verbal intercourse, or favours as objects of entreaty (*Shak.*); **entreat'y** the act of entreating: earnest prayer. — Also (*Spens.*) **intreat',** etc. [O.Fr. *entraiter* — *en,* and *traiter,* to treat.]

entrechat ä-tr-shä', (*ballet*) *n.* a leap during which a dancer beats his heels together. [Fr., — It. *intrecciata,* plaited, complicated (caper).]

entrecôte ä'tr'kōt, *n.* a steak cut from between two ribs. — Also *adj.* [Fr.]

entrée ä', on'trā, *n.* entry, freedom of access, admittance: introduction, means of access: a dish served at dinner between the chief courses i.e. between fish and roast or as a substitute, also (esp. U.S.) a main course, and (esp. *Austr.*) a starter: an introduction or prelude (*mus.*): the act of entering, a formal entrance, or music for it. — **entrée dish** a dish, usually silver, with a cover, suitable for an entrée. [Fr.]

entremets ä'trə-mä, -me, *n.* any dainty served at table between the chief courses — formerly **entremes, entremesse.** [O.Fr. *entremes* — *entre,* between, *mes* (Fr. *mets*), dish.]

entrench, intrench in-trench', -trensh', *v.t.* to dig a trench around: to fortify with a ditch and parapet: to establish in a strong position: to establish or fix firmly because of an unwillingness to change or in such a way that change is difficult or impossible: to cut into, wound (*Spens.*). — *v.i.* to encroach. — n. **entrench'ment, intrench'ment** a defensive earthwork of trenches and parapets: any protection: an encroachment (*obs.*). — **entrenched provisions** in the constitution of South Africa, provisions specially safeguarded by being made subject to amendment or repeal only by exceptional procedure. [Pfx. **en-** (1c).]

entre nous ä-tr' nōō, (Fr.) between ourselves.

entrepôt, entrepôt ä'trə-pō, *n.* a storehouse: a bonded warehouse: a seaport through which exports and imports pass, esp. one from which imports are re-exported without duty being charged on them. [Fr.]

entrepreneur ä-trə-prə-nœr', *n.* one who undertakes an enterprise esp. a commercial one, often at personal financial risk: a contractor or employer: an organiser of musical or other entertainments: — *fem.* **entrepreneuse** (-nœz'). — *adj.* **entrepreneur'ial** (-nœr'i-əl, -nū', -nōō'). — *ns.* **entrepreneur'ialism; entrepreneur'-ship.** [Fr.]

entresol en'tər-sol, or ä'tr'-sol, *n.* a low storey between two main storeys of a building, generally between the ground floor and the first floor. [Fr., — *entre,* between, *sol,* the ground.]

entrez ä-trā, (Fr. *imper.*) come in.

entrism, etc. See **entryism** under **entry.**

entrold, another reading **introld,** in-trōld', (*Spens.*) apparently a past participle, meaning unknown — enrolled, in the sense of encircled, has been conjectured.

entropion, -um en-trō'pi-on, -əm, *ns.* inversion of the edge of the eyelid. [Gr. *en,* in, *tropē,* turning.]

entropy en'trə-pi, (*phys.*) *n.* a measure of unavailable energy, energy still existing but lost for purpose of doing work because it exists as the internal motion of molecules: a measure of the disorder of a system: a measure of heat content, regarded as increased in a reversible change by the ratio of heat taken in to absolute temperature. [Gr. *en*, in, *trope*, turning, intended to represent 'transformation content'.]

entrust, intrust *in-trust'*, *v.t.* to give in trust: to commit as a trust: to charge trustingly. — *n.* **entrust'ment.** [Pfx. **en-** (1c).]

entry *en'tri*, *n.* the act of entering in any sense: a coming upon the stage: the coming in of an instrument or performer: entrance: a narrow lane between houses (*dial.*): a lobby or vestibule: a hostel (*obs.*): the act of committing to writing in a record: the thing so written: a list of competitors: a young hound, or hounds collectively old enough to begin training: a taking possession (*law*). — *ns.* **en'tryism, en'trism** the practice of joining a political body in sufficient numbers to swing its policy, specif. of Trotskyists, etc. in branches of the Labour Party. — *ns.* and *adjs.* **en'tryist, en'trist.** — **entry fee** entrance fee. — **card of entry** (*bridge,etc.*) a card to bring in one's hand with; **port of entry** see **port⁴.** [Fr. *entrée* — *entrer* — L. *intrāre*, to go into.]

Entryphone® *en'tri-fōn*, *n.* a telephonic device at the entrance to e.g. a block of flats, etc. allowing communication between individual occupiers and visitors.

entwine *in-twīn'*, *v.t.* to interlace: to weave. — Also **intwine'.** [Pfx. **en-** (1c).]

entwist *in-twist'*, *v.t.* to twist round. — Also **intwist'.** [Pfx. **en-** (1c).]

enucleate *in-ū'kli-āt*, *v.t.* to deprive of a kernel or nucleus: to explain: to extract, e.g. a tumour, swelling, etc. (*surg.*). — *adj.* without a nucleus. — *n.* **enucleā'tion.** [L. *ēnucleāre* — *ē*, from, *nucleus*, a kernel.]

enumerate *i-nū'mər-āt*, *v.t.* to count the number of: to name over. — *n.* **enūmerā'tion** the act of numbering: a detailed account: a summing-up (*rhet.*). — *adj.* **enū'merative.** — *n.* **enū'merātor** one who enumerates. [L. *ē*, from, *numerāre*, *-ātum*, to number.]

enunciate *i-nun's(h)i-āt*, *v.t.* to state formally: to pronounce distinctly: to utter. — *adj.* **enun'ciable** (*-shi-* or *-si-*) capable of being enunciated. — *n.* **enunciation** (*i-nun-si-ā'shən*) the act of enunciating: the manner of uttering or pronouncing: a distinct statement or declaration: the words in which a proposition is expressed. — *adjs.* **enun'ciative** (*-si-ā-, -syā-, -sh(y)ā-*, or *-shə-*), **enun'ciatory** containing enunciation or utterance: declarative. — *n.* **enun'ciātor** one who enunciates. [L. *ēnunciāre, -ātum* — *ē*, from, *nuntiāre*, to tell — *nuntius*, a messenger.]

enure. See **inure¹.**

enuresis *en-ū-rē'sis*, *n.* incontinence of urine. — *adj.* and *n.* **enūret'ic.** [Gr. *en*, in, *ourēsis*, urination.]

envassal *en-vas'əl*, (*obs.*) *v.t.* to reduce to vassalage. [Pfx. **en-** (1c).]

envault *en-völt'*, (*obs.*) *v.t.* to enclose in a vault. [Pfx. **en-** (1a).]

enveigle. See **inveigle.**

envelop *in-vel'əp*, **en-**, *v.t.* to cover by wrapping: to surround entirely: to hide. — *n.* **envelope** (*en'vəl-ōp*) that which envelops, wraps, or covers: a cover for a letter (in this sense sometimes but quite unnecessarily pronounced *on'*, *ä'* in imitation of French): one of the coverings of a flower — calyx or corolla (*bot.*): the gas-bag of a balloon or airship: the locus of ultimate intersections of a series of curves (*math.*): the outer containing vessel of a discharge tube (*electronics*): the curve connecting the peaks of successive cycles of a modulated carrier wave (*telecomm.*). — *adj.* **envel'oped** (*her.*) entwined, as with serpents, laurels, etc. — *n.* **envel'opment** a wrapping or covering on all sides. [O.Fr. *enveloper*; origin obscure.]

envenom *in-ven'əm*, *v.t.* to put venom into: to poison: to taint with bitterness or malice. — *adj.* **enven'omed.** [O.Fr. *envenimer* — *en*, and *venim*, venom.]

en ventre sa mère *ã vã-tr' sa mer*, (*law* Fr.) in his mother's womb.

en vérité *ã vā-rē-tā*, (Fr.) in truth.

envermeil *en-vûr'mil*, (*Milt.*) *v.t.* to dye red, to give a red colour to. [O.Fr. *envermeiller* — *en*, in, *vermeil*, red, vermilion.]

en ville *ã vēl*, (Fr.) in town: not at home.

environ *in-vī'rən*, *v.t.* to surround: to encircle. — *n.* **envī'ronment** a surrounding: external conditions influencing development or growth of people, animals or plants: living or working conditions. — *adj.* **environment'al.** — *ns.* **environment'alism** the belief that environment rather than heredity is the main influence on a person's behaviour and development (*psych.*): concern about the environment and its preservation from the effects of pollution, etc.; **environment'alist** one who advocates environmentalism (*psych.*): one who is concerned with the protection of the environment, esp. from pollution. — *n. sing.* **environics** (*en-vī-ron'iks*) the study of methods of influencing behaviour by controlling environmental factors. — *n.pl.* **environs** (*in-vī'rənz*, or *en'vi-*) the places that environ: the outskirts of a city: neighbourhood. — **environmental health officer** a person appointed to investigate and prevent hazards such as pollution, lack of hygiene, etc. which might affect the health of the general public. [Fr. *environner* — *environ*, around — *virer*, to turn round; cf. **veer.**]

envisage *in-viz'ij*, *v.t.* to face (*arch.*): to consider: to present to view or to mental view: to visualise: to see, suggest or expect as a possible or likely future target, result, etc. — *n.* **envis'agement.** [Fr. *envisager* — *en*, and *visage*, the face.]

envision *in-vizh'ən*, *v.t.* to see as in a vision: to visualise: to envisage. [Pfx. **en-** (1c).]

envoy¹ *en'voi*, *n.* a messenger, esp. one sent to transact business with a foreign government: a diplomatic minister of the second order. — *n.* **en'voyship.** [Fr. *envoyé* — pa.p. of *envoyer*, to send.]

envoy², envoi *en'voi*, *n.* the concluding part of a poem or a book: the author's final words, esp. now the short stanza concluding a poem written in certain archaic metrical forms. [O.Fr. *envoye* — *envoiier*, to send — *en voie*, on the way — L. *in*, on, *via*, a way.]

envy *en'vi*, *n.* ill-will, hostility (*obs.*): a feeling of chagrin at the good looks, qualities, fortune, etc., of another: an object or person contemplated with grudging or emulous feeling. — *v.t.* (formerly *in-vī'*) to feel vexation at (*obs.*): to feel envy towards, or on account of: to grudge (*obs.*): to desire with emulation or rivalry: — *pr.p.* **en'vying;** *pa.t.* and *pa.p.* **en'vied.** — *adj.* **en'viable** that is to be envied. — *n.* **en'viableness.** — *adv.* **en'viably.** — *n.* **en'vier** one who envies. — *adj.* **en'vious** feeling envy: directed by envy: enviable (*Spens.*). — *adv.* **en'viously.** — *ns.* **en'viousness; en'vying** (*B.*) jealousy, ill-will. [Fr. *envie* — L. *invidia* — *invidēre*, to look askance at, to envy — *in*, on, *vidēre*, to look.]

enwall, inwall *in-wöl'*, *v.t.* to enclose within a wall. [Pfx. **en-** (1a).]

enwallow *en-wol'ō*, (*Spens.*) *v.t.* to roll about wallowingly. [Pfx. **en-** (1c).]

enwheel *en-{h}wēl'*, (*Shak.*) *v.t.* to encircle. [Pfx. **en-** (1a).]

enwind, inwind *in-wīnd'*, *v.t.* to wind about, enwrap. [Pfx. **en-** (1a).]

enwomb *en-wōōm'*, *v.t.* to make pregnant (*Spens.*): to conceive or have in the womb (*Shak.*): to contain. [Pfx. **en-** (1a).]

enwrap, inwrap *in-rap'*, *v.t.* to cover by wrapping: to enfold: to engross. — *n.* **enwrap'ment.** — *adj.* and *n.* **enwrapp'ing.** [Pfx. **en-** (1a).]

enwreathe, inwreathe *in-rēdh'*, *v.t.* to wreathe: to envelop: to encircle, as with a wreath. [Pfx. **en-** (1a).]

Enzed *en-zed'*, (*Austr.* and *N.Z. coll.*) *n.* New Zealand: (also **Enzedd'er**) a New Zealander. [The abbrev. **NZ** phonetically represented.]

enzian *ent'si-ən*, *n.* a type of schnapps flavoured with gentian roots, drunk in the Tyrol. [Ger. *Enzian*, gentian.]

enzone *in-zōn'*, *v.t.* to engirdle: to enclose as with a zone. [Pfx. **en-** (1a).]

enzootic *en-zō-ot'ik*, *adj.* of animal diseases, prevalent in a particular district or at a particular season. — *n.* a disease of this character. [Gr. *en,* in, *zōion,* animal, in imitation of *endemic.*]

enzyme *en'zīm, n.* any one of a large class of protein substances produced by living cells which, usu. in the presence of other substances, e.g. of coenzymes, act as catalysts in biochemical reactions. — *adjs.* **enzymat'ic, enzym'ic.** — *ns.* **enzymol'ogist; enzymol'ogy** the scientific study of enzymes. [Gr. *en,* in, *zȳmē,* leaven.]

E O *ē'ō', n.* a mid-18th-century gambling game, depending on a ball falling into slots marked either **E** or **O.**

eoan *ē-ō'ən, adj.* of or pertaining to dawn. [L. — Gr. *ēōs,* dawn.]

Eoanthropus *ē-ō-an-thrō'pəs, n.* a once-supposed very early form of man represented by parts of a skull found at Piltdown, Sussex (1912); in 1953 a hoax was exposed and the mandible shown to be an ape's. [Gr. *ēōs,* dawn, *anthrōpos,* man.]

Eocene *ē'ō-sēn,* (*geol.*) *adj.* belonging to the oldest division of the Tertiary formation. — *n.* the Eocene system, period, or strata. [Gr. *ēōs,* daybreak, *kainos,* new — from the very small proportion of living species of molluscs among its fossils.]

Eohippus *ē-ō-hip'-əs, n.* the oldest known horselike animal, an Eocene fossil. [Gr. *ēōs,* dawn, *hippos,* horse.]

EOKA *ā-ō'kə, n.* a secret Greek Cypriot combatant organisation contending for the union of Cyprus with Greece. [Gr. *Ethnikē Organōsis Kypriākou Agōnos,* National Organisation of the Cypriot Struggle.]

Eolian, Eolic. Same as **Aeolian, Aeolic.**

éolienne *ā-ol-yen', n.* dress material of fine silk and wool. [Fr.]

eolipile. Same as **aeolipile.**

eolith *ē'ō-lith, n.* a very early roughly-broken stone implement, or one naturally formed but assumed to have been used by man. — *adj.* **eolith'ic.** [Gr. *ēōs,* dawn, *lithos,* stone.]

eon. See **aeon.**

eonism *ē'ə-nizm,* (*psychiatry*) *n.* adoption by a male of female dress and manner. [Chevalier d'*Éon,* Fr. diplomat (d. 1810), who chose female dress as a disguise.]

eo nomine *ē'ō nom'i-nē, e'ō nom'i-ne,* (L.) by that name, on that claim.

eorl. Obs. form of **earl.**

eosin *ē'ō-sin, n.* a red dyestuff, $C_{20}H_8Br_4O_5$. — *adj.* **eosin'ophil** (Gr. *philos,* loving) readily staining with eosin. — *n.* a type of white blood cell, so called because it is easily stained by eosin. — *n.* **eosinophil'ia** the condition of being eosinophil: the condition in which there is an abnormally large number of eosinophils in the blood. — *adjs.* **eosinophil'ic, eosinoph'ilous** eosinophil: pertaining to eosinophils or eosinophilia. [Gr. *ēōs,* dawn.]

eothen *ē-ō'then,* (*arch.*) *adv.* from the east — the name given by Kinglake to his book of travel in the East (1844). [Gr. *eōthen,* lit. from morn, at earliest dawn.]

Eozoon *ē-ō-zō'on, n.* a once supposed fossil organism in the Archaean system of Canada, which would have been the oldest known living thing, or the banded arrangement of calcite and serpentine at that time supposed to be its remains. — *adj.* **Eozō'ic.** [Gr. *ēōs,* dawn, and *zōion,* an animal.]

ep-. See **epi-.**

Epacris *ep-ak'ris, ep'ə-kris, n.* a chiefly Australian genus of heath-like plants, giving name to the fam. **Epacrida'ceae,** close akin to the heaths: (without *cap.*) a plant of this genus. — *n.* **epac'rid** (or *ep'*) any member of the genus, or of the family. [Gr. *epi,* upon, *akris,* a summit.]

epact *ē'pakt, n.* the moon's age at the beginning of the year: the excess of the calendar month or solar year over the lunar. [Fr. *épacte* — Gr. *epaktos,* brought on — *epi,* on, *agein,* to bring.]

epaenetic *ep-ə-net'ik,* **epainetic** *ep-ī-net'ik,* (*arch.*) *adjs.* eulogistic. [Gr. *epainetikos* — *epainein,* to praise.]

epagoge *ep-ə-gō'gē, -jē,* (*log.*) *n.* induction. — *adj.* **epa-**

gog'ic. [Gr. *epagōgē* — *epi,* on, *agōgē,* leading.]

epagomenal *ep-ə-gom'ə-nəl, adj.* (esp. of days) intercalary. [Gr. *epagomenos* — *epi,* upon, in, *agein,* to bring.]

epainetic. See **epaenetic.**

epanadiplosis *ep-a-nə-di-plō'sis,* (*rhet.*) *n.* a figure by which a sentence begins and ends with the same word, as in Phil. iv. 4 (Authorised Version): — *pl.* **-ō'sēs.** [Gr.]

epanalepsis *ep-a-nə-lep'sis,* (*rhet.*) *n.* repetition or resumption, as in 1 Cor. xi. 18 and 20 (esp. Authorised Version): — *pl.* **-sēs.** [Gr.]

epanaphora *ep-ə-naf'o-rə.* Same as **anaphora.**

epanodos *ep-an'o-dos,* (*rhet.*) *n.* recapitulation of the chief points in a discourse. [Gr. *epanodos.*]

epanorthosis *ep-an-ör-thō'sis,* (*rhet.*) *n.* the retracting of a statement in order to correct or intensify it, as *For Britain's guid! for her destruction!:* — *pl.* **-ō'sēs.** [Gr.]

eparch *ep'ärk, n.* the governor of a modern Greek province: a metropolitan. — *ns.* **ep'archate, ep'archy** the province, territory or diocese of an eparch. [Gr. *eparchos* — *epi,* upon, *archē,* dominion.]

épatant *ā-pa-tã,* (Fr.) *adj.* wonderful, marvellous.

epaule *e-pöl', n.* the shoulder of a bastion. — *n.* **epaule'-ment** a side-work of a battery or earthwork to protect it from a flanking fire: a particular placing of a dancer's shoulders, one forward, one back (*ballet*). [Fr. *épaule,* shoulder — L. *spatula.*]

epaulet, epaulette *ep'əl-et, n.* a shoulder-piece: a badge of a military or naval officer (now disused in the British army): an ornament on the shoulder of a lady's dress. [Fr. *épaulette* — *épaule,* the shoulder.]

epaxial *ep-aks'i-əl, adj.* above the axis. [Gr. *epi,* on, over, and **axis.**]

epedaphic *ep-ə-daf'ik, adj.* pertaining to atmospheric conditions. [Gr. *epi,* above, *edaphos,* ground.]

épée *ā-pā', n.* a sharp-pointed, narrow-bladed sword, without a cutting edge, used for duelling, and, with a button on the point, for fencing practice. [Fr.]

Epeira *ep-īr'ə, n.* a genus of spiders, the type of the **Epeir'idae,** including the common garden spider: (without *cap.*) a spider of this genus. — *n.* **epeir'id** a member of the family. [Perh. Gr. *epi,* on, *eirein,* to string.]

epeirogenesis *ep-ī-rō-jen'i-sis,* (*geol.*) *n.* continent-building. — Also **epeirogeny** (*-roj'i-ni*). — *adjs.* **epeirogen'ic, epeirogenetic** (*-jin-et'ik*). [Gr. *ēpeiros,* mainland, *genesis,* formation.]

epencephalon *ep-en-sef'ə-lon,* or *-kef', n.* the cerebellum. — *adj.* **epencephalic** (*-si-fal'ik,* or *-ki-*). [Gr. *epi,* on, *enkephalon,* brain.]

epenthesis *e-pen'thə-sis, n.* the insertion of a sound within a word: — *pl.* **-thesēs.** — *adj.* **epenthetic** (*-thet'ik*). [Gr.]

epeolatry *ep-i-ol'ə-tri, n.* worship of words. [Gr. *epos,* word, *latreiā,* worship.]

éperdu (*fem.* **éperdue**) *ā-per-dü,* (Fr.) *adj.* distracted. — **éperdument amoureux** (*fem.* **amoureuse**)(*ā-per-dü-mã a-mōō-rø* (*-røz*)) desperately in love.

epergne *i-pûrn', n.* a branched ornamental centre-piece for the table. [Fr. *épargne* (saving), as used in phrases *taille* or *gravure d'épargne,* metal or etching with parts left in relief.]

epexegesis *ep-eks-i-jē'sis, n.* the addition of words to make the sense more clear: — *pl.* **-gēsēs.** — *adjs.* **epexeget'ic** (*-jet'ik*), **-al.** — *adv.* **epexeget'ically.** [Gr. *epexēgēsis* — *epi,* in addition, *exēgeesthai,* to explain.]

epha, ephah *ē'fə, n.* a Hebrew measure for dry goods. [Heb.; prob. of Egyptian origin.]

ephebe *ef-ēb',* **ephebus, -os** *-əs, n.* in ancient Greece, a young male citizen from 18 to 20 years of age: — *pl.* **ephē'bī.** — *adj.* **ephēb'ic** pertaining to an ephebe: pertaining to the adult period in the life-history of an individual (*biol.*). — *n.* **ephēbophilia** (*-fil'*) sexual desire for youths or adolescents. [L. *ephēbus* — Gr. *ephēbos* — *epi,* upon, *hēbē,* early manhood.]

Ephedra *ef'ed-rə, ef-ēd'rə, ef-ed'rə, n.* sea-grape, a genus of jointed, all but leafless desert plants of the Gnetaceae: (without *cap.*) a plant of this genus. — *n.*

eph′edrine (or *ef-ed′rin*) an alkaloid got from Ephedra or produced synthetically, used in treating hay fever, asthma, etc. [Gr. *ephedrā*, horsetail.]

ephelis *e-fē′lis, (med.) n.* a freckle: a coloured patch on the skin: — pl. **ephelides** (*e-fel′i-dēz, -fēl′*). [L., — Gr.]

Ephemera *ef-em′ər-ə,* or *-ēm′, n.* a genus of insects whose adult life is very short, the mayflies: (without *cap.*) an insect of this genus: (without *cap.*) that which lasts a short time (but see also **ephemeron** below): — pl. **ephem′eras** or **ephem′erae**. — adj. **ephem′eral** existing only for a day: short-lived: fleeting. — n. anything very short-lived. — ns. **ephemeral′ity**; **ephem′erid** an insect of the mayfly family, **Ephemer′idae** (*-mer′i-dē*; order Plectuptera or **Ephemerop′tera**). — adj. **ephemerid′ian**. — ns. **ephem′eris** an account of daily transactions (*arch.*): a journal (*arch.*): an astronomical almanac tabulating the daily positions of the sun, moon, planets and certain stars, etc.: — pl. **ephemerides** (*ef-e-mer′i-dēz*); **ephem′erist** one who studies the daily motions of the planets: a student or collector of ephemera; **ephem′-eron** an insect that lives only for a day: (usu. in *pl.*) an object of limited worth or usefulness, having no lasting value: anything ephemeral: — pl. **ephem′era**. — adj. **ephem′erous**. — **ephemeris time** time measured by orbital movement of earth, moon and planets, differing from mean solar time in that it allows for irregularities due to variations in rate of rotation of the earth; an ephemeris second has the same value as had the mean universal second for the 19th cent. [Gr. *ephēmeros*, living a day — *epi*, for, *hēmerā*, a day.]

Ephesian *ef-ē′zi-ən, -ē′zhən, adj.* of or pertaining to *Ephesus*. — n. an inhabitant of Ephesus: a jolly companion (*Shak.*).

ephialtes *ef-i-al′tēz, (arch.) n.* an incubus: a nightmare: — pl. **-tes**. [Gr. *ephialtēs*.]

ephod *ef′od, n.* a kind of linen surplice worn by the Jewish priests: a surplice, generally. [Heb. *ēphōd — āphad,* to put on.]

ephor *ef′ör, ef′ər, n.* a class of magistrates whose office apparently originated at Sparta, being peculiar to the Doric states. — n. **eph′oralty**. [Gr. *epi*, upon, and root of *horaein*, to see.]

epi- *ep-i-* (or **ep-** *ep-* before a vowel or *h*), *pfx.* above, over, upon, on, as *epidermis*: in addition, after, as *epiphenomenon, epirrhema*. [Gr. *epi*, on, over.]

epiblast *ep′i-blāst, n.* the outer germinal layer of an embryo. — adj. **epiblast′ic**. [Gr. *epi*, upon, *blastos*, a germ, shoot.]

epic *ep′ik, adj.* applied to a long narrative poem that relates heroic events in an elevated style: characteristic of an epic poem: impressive: large-scale. — n. an epic poem: epic poetry as a genre: a story comparable to that of an epic poem, esp. a long adventure novel or film: an epic poet (*obs.*). — adj. **ep′ical**. — adv. **ep′ically**. — ns. **ep′icism** (*-sizm*); **ep′icist**. — **epic dialect** Homer's Greek; **epic theatre** the theatre of epic drama, episodic drama with alienation (q.v.), narrative passages, etc. [Gr. *epikos — epos*, a word.]

epicalyx *ep-i-kāl′iks,* or *-kal′, n.* an apparent accessory calyx outside of the true calyx, composed of bracts or of fused stipules of sepals. [Gr. *epi*, on, and **calyx**.]

epicanthus *ep-i-kan′thəs, n.* a fold of skin over the inner canthus of the eye, characteristic of the Mongolian race. — adj. **epican′thic**. [Gr. *epi*, on, and **canthus**.]

epicarp *ep′i-kärp, (bot.) n.* the outermost layer of the pericarp or fruit. [Gr. *epi*, upon, *karpos*, fruit.]

epicede *ep′i-sēd,* **epicedium** *ep-i-sē′di-əm* or *-dī′, ns.* a funeral ode: — pls. **ep′icedes, epicē′dia**. — adjs. **epicē′-dial, epicē′dian** elegiac. [L. *epicēdīum* — Gr. *epikēdeion* — *epi*, upon, *kēdos*, care.]

epicene *ep′i-sēn, adj.* common to both sexes: having characteristics of both sexes, or neither: effeminate: of common gender (*gram.*): sometimes restricted to those words that have one grammatical gender though used for both sexes. — Also *n.* [Gr. *epi*, upon, *koinos*, common.]

epicentre *ep′i-sen-tər, n.* that point on the earth's surface directly over the point of origin of an earthquake. — Also *fig.* — adj. **epicen′tral**. [Gr. *epi*, upon, over, *kentron*, a point.]

epicheirema *ep-i-kī-rē′mə, n.* a syllogism confirmed in its major or minor premise, or both, by an incidental proposition. [Gr. *epicheirēma*, attempt, an attempted proof short of demonstrating — *epi*, upon, *cheir*, hand.]

épicier *ā-pē-syā,* (Fr.) *n.* a grocer.

epicism, epicist. See **epic**.

epiclesis *ep-i-klē′sis, n.* in the Eastern church, an invocation of the Holy Spirit at the consecration of the elements (bread and wine): — pl. **epiclēsēs**. [Gr. *epiklēsis*, invocation — *epikalein*, to summon.]

epicondyle *ep-i-kon′dīl, -dil, n.* the upper or proximal part of the condyle of the humerus or femur. — n. **epicondylitis** (*-dil-ī′tis*) inflammation of an epicondyle: inflammation of the tissues beside the epicondyle of the humerus. [Pfx. **epi-**, and **condyle**.]

epicotyl *ep-i-kot′il, n.* the stem of an embryo plant or seedling between the cotyledons and the next leaf. [Gr. *epi*, over, and **cotyledon**.]

epicritic *ep-i-krit′ik, adj.* (of certain sensory nerve fibres in the skin) able to discriminate accurately between small degrees of sensation. [Gr. *epikritikos*, determining — *epi*, on, *krīnein*, to judge.]

epicure *ep′i-kūr, n.* an Epicurean (*obs.*): one given to sensual enjoyment (*obs.*): a person of refined and fastidious taste, esp. in food, wine, etc. — adj. **Epicurē′an** pertaining to *Epicurus* (341–270 B.C.), the Greek philosopher, who taught an atomic materialism in physics and hedonism in ethics, misrepresented by opponents as brutish sensuality: (without *cap.*) given to luxury, esp. refined luxury. — n. a follower of Epicurus: (without *cap.*) a hedonist, an epicure. — n. **Epicurē′anism** the doctrines of Epicurus: attachment to these doctrines: epicurism. — v.i. **ep′icurise, -ize** (*arch.*) to play the epicure: to profess the philosophy of Epicurus. — n. **ep′icurism** pursuit of pleasure: fastidiousness in luxury: (also *ep-i-kūr′izm*; *arch.*) Epicureanism. [L. *Epicūrus* — Gr. *Epikouros*.]

epicuticle *ep-i-kū′ti-kəl, (biol.) n.* the waxy outermost layer of an insect's cuticle. — adj. **epicutic′ular**. [Pfx. **epi-**, and **cuticle**.]

epicycle *ep′i-sī-kl, n.* a circle whose centre is carried round the circumference of another circle. — adj. **epicy′clic**. — n. **epicy′cloid** a curve described by a point on the circumference of a circle rolling on the outside of the circumference of another circle. — adj. **epicycloi′dal**. [Gr. *epi*, upon, *kyklos*, a circle.]

epideictic, -al *ep-i-dīk′tik, -əl, adjs.* done for show or display. [Gr. *epi*, upon, *deiknynai*, to show.]

epidemic *ep-i-dem′ik, adj.* affecting a community at a certain time: prevalent. — n. a disease that attacks great numbers in one place, at one time, and itself travels from place to place: a widespread outbreak. — adj. **epidem′ical**. — adv. **epidem′ically**. — n. **epidemic′-ity**. — adj. **epidemiolog′ical** pertaining to epidemiology. — ns. **epidemiol′ogy** the science of epidemics; **epidēmiol′ogist**. [Gr. *epidēmos*, general — *epi*, among, *dēmos*, the people.]

Epidendrum *ep-i-den′drəm, n.* a genus of chiefly epiphytic orchids of diverse type: (without *cap.*; also **epiden′-drone**) an orchid of this genus. [Gr. *epi*, upon, *dendron*, tree.]

epidermis *ep-i-dûr′mis, n.* scarf-skin or cuticle, forming an external covering of a protective nature for the true skin or corium (*zool.*): an outer sheath of close-set cells, usually one deep (*bot.*). — adjs. **epider′mal; epider′mic; epiderm′oid**. — n. **Epidermophyton** (*-mof′i-tən*) a genus of dermatophytes, a cause of athlete's foot. — **epidermolysis bullosa** (*-mol′i-sis bōō-lō′sə*; Gr. *lysis*, loosening, Modern L. *bulla*, blister) a mutilating and incapacitating hereditary skin disease in which the skin, on slight contact, readily becomes covered with blisters: — abbrev. **E B.** [Gr. *epidermis*

— *epi*, upon, *derma*, the skin.]

epidiascope *ep-i-dī'ə-skōp, n.* a lantern for projecting images of objects whether opaque or transparent. [Gr. *epi*, upon, *dia*, through, *skopeein*, to look at.]

epididymis *ep-i-did'i-mis, n.* a mass of sperm-carrying tubes at the back of the testis: — *pl.* **epidid'ymides** (*-mi-dēz, -dī-dim'-*). [Gr., — *epi*, on, *didymos*, a testicle, twin.]

epidiorite *ep-i-dī'ə-rīt, n.* a dioritic or gabbroitic rock more or less metamorphosed, the pyroxene being changed to amphibole. [Gr. *epi*, after, and **diorite**.]

epidote *ep'i-dōt, n.* a greenish mineral, silicate of calcium, aluminium, and iron. — *n.* **epidosite** (*ep-id'ə-sīt* a rock composed of epidote and quartz. — *adj.* **epidotic** (*-dot'*). — *n.* **epidotisā'tion, -z-.** — *adj.* **epid'otised, -ized** changed into epidote. [Gr. *epididonai*, to give in addition, superadd, from the great length of the base of the crystal.]

epidural *ep-i-dūr'əl, adj.* situated on, or administered outside, the lowest portion of the spinal canal. — *n.* short for **epidural anaesthetic,** the epidural injection of an anaesthetic, esp. in childbirth. — **epidural anaesthesia** loss of painful sensation in the lower part of the body produced by injecting an anaesthetic into the lowest portion of the spinal canal. [Gr. *epi*, upon, and **dura (mater).**]

epifocal *ep-i-fō'kl, adj.* epicentral.

epigaeal, epigeal *ep-i-jē'əl,* **epigae'ous, epige'ous** *-əs,* **epigae'an, epige'an** *-ən, adjs.* growing or living close to the ground: with cotyledons above ground. [Gr. *epigaios, epigeios* — *epi*, on, *gaia, gē*, earth.]

epigamic *ep-i-gam'ik, adj.* attractive to the opposite sex. [Gr. *epigamos*, marriageable — *epi*, upon, *gamos*, marriage.]

epigastrium *ep-i-gas'tri-əm, n.* the part of the abdomen extending from the sternum towards the navel — the pit of the stomach. — *adj.* **epigas'tric.** [Gr. *epi*, upon, *gastēr*, the stomach.]

epigeal, etc. See **epigaeal.**

epigene *ep'i-jēn,* (*geol.*) *adj.* acting or taking place at the earth's surface. [Fr. *épigène* — Gr. *epigenēs*, born after.]

epigenesis *ep-i-jen'i-sis, n.* the theory, now universally accepted, that the development of an embryo consists of the gradual production and organisation of parts, as opposed to the theory of preformation, which supposed that the future animal or plant was already present complete, although in miniature, in the germ. — *ns.* **epigen'esist; epigenet'icist.** — *adj.* **epigenet'ic** pertaining to epigenesis: (of minerals) formed subsequently to the enclosing rock. — *n. sing.* **epigenet'ics** the science which studies the causes at work in development. [Gr. *epi*, upon, after, *genesis*, formation.]

epiglottis *ep-i-glot'is, n.* a cartilaginous flap over the glottis. — *adj.* **epiglott'ic.** [Gr. *epiglōttis* — *epi*, over, *glōttis*, glottis.]

epigon *ep'i-gon,* **epigone** *ep'i-gōn, ns.* one of a later generation: — *pls.* **ep'igons, ep'igones** (*-gōnz*), (often with *cap.*) **epig'onī** sons (esp. of the Seven against Thebes), or successors (esp. of Alexander): undistinguished descendants of the great. [Gr. *epi*, after, *gonē*, birth.]

epigram *ep'i-gram, n.* any concise and pointed or sarcastic saying: a short poem expressing an ingenious thought with point, usually satirical. — *adjs.* **epigrammatic** (*-grəm-at'ik*), **-al** relating to or dealing in epigrams: like an epigram: concise and pointed. — *adv.* **epigrammat'ically.** — *v.t.* **epigramm'atise, -ize** to make an epigram on. — *n.* **epigramm'atist** one who writes epigrams. [Through Fr. and L., from Gr. *epigramma* — *epi*, upon, *gramma*, a writing — *graphein*, to write.]

epigraph *ep'i-gräf, n.* an inscription, esp. on a building: a citation or motto at the beginning of a book or its part. — *v.t.* to provide with an epigraph. — *ns.* **epigrapher** (*ep-ig'rə-fər*), **epig'raphist.** — *adj.* **epigraphic** (*-graf'ik*). — *n.* **epig'raphy.** [Gr. *epigraphē* — *epi*, upon, *graphein*, to write.]

epigynous *e-pij'i-nəs,* (*bot.*) *adj.* growing upon the top of the ovary: having calyx, corolla, and stamens inserted on the top of an inferior ovary. — *n.* **epig'yny.** [Gr. *epi*, upon, *gynē*, woman, female.]

epilate *ep'i-lāt, v.t.* to remove (hair) by any means. — *ns.* **epilā'tion; ep'ilator.** [Fr. *épiler* — L. *ex*, from, *pilus*, hair.]

epilepsy *ep'i-lep-si, n.* a chronic functional disease of the nervous system, manifested by recurring attacks of sudden insensibility or impairment of consciousness, commonly accompanied by peculiar convulsive seizures. — *n.* **epilep'tic** an epileptic patient. — *adjs.* **epilep'tic, -al.** [Gr. *epilēpsiā* — *epi*, upon, and root of *lambanein*, to seize.]

epilimnion *ep-i-lim'ni-ən, n.* the upper, warm layer of water in a lake. [Gr. *epi*, upon, *limnion*, dim. of *limnē*, a lake.]

epilobium *ep-i-lōb'i-əm, n.* a willow-herb, a plant of the genus **Epilobium.** [Gr. *epi*, upon, *lobos*, a pod, from the position of the petals.]

epilogue *ep'i-log, n.* the concluding section of a book, etc.: a short poem or speech at the end of a play: the speaker thereof: the conclusion of a radio or TV programme. — *adjs.* **epilogic** (*-loj'ik*), **epilogistic** (*-jis'*). — *vs.i.* **epilogise, -ize** (*ep-il'ə-jīz,* or *ep'*), **epiloguise, -ize** (*-gīz*) to speak or write an epilogue. [Fr., — L. *epilogus* — Gr. *epilogos*, conclusion — *epi*, upon, *legein*, to speak.]

epimeletic *ep-i-mel-et'ik,* (*animal behaviour*) *adj.* of a type of social behaviour covering the care of the young by the parents, or other individuals of the same species, e.g. worker bees.

epimer *ep'i-mər, n.* an isomeric compound, differing from its corresponding isomer only in the relative positions of an attached hydrogen and hydroxyl. — *adj.* **epimeric** (*-mer'ik* having the characteristics or relationship of epimers. [*epi-* and iso*mer*.]

epinasty *ep'i-nas-ti,* (*bot.*) *n.* down-curving of an organ, caused by a more active growth on its upper side. — opp. to *hyponasty.* — *adj.* **epinas'tic.** — *adv.* **epinas'tically.** [Gr. *epi*, upon, *nastos*, pressed close.]

epinephrine *ep-i-nef'rin, -rēn, n.* adrenaline. [Gr. *epi,* upon, *nephros,* kidney.]

epinikion *ep-i-nik'i-ən,* **epinicion** *ep-i-nis(h)'i-ən, ns.* a song of victory: an ode in honour of a victor or winner. — *adjs.* **epinik'ian, epinic'ian.** [Gr. *epinīkion* — *epi*, on, after, *nīkē*, victory.]

epinosic *ep-i-nos'ik, adj.* unhealthy: unwholesome. [Gr. *epi-*, and *nosos*, disease.]

epipetalous *ep-i-pet'ə-ləs,* (*bot.*) *adj.* inserted or growing on a petal or petals.

Epiphany *e-pif'ə-ni, n.* a church festival celebrated on 6 Jan., in commemoration of the manifestation of Christ to the wise men of the East: the manifestation of a god: a usu. sudden revelation or insight into the nature, essence or meaning of something. — *adj.* **epiphanic** (*-fan'*). [Gr. *epiphaneia*, appearance — *epi*, to, *phainein*, to show.]

epiphenomenon *ep-i-fin-om'ən-ən, n.* an accompanying phenomenon, a fortuitous, less important, or irrelevant, by-product: something appearing after, a secondary symptom of a disease (*path.*): — *pl.* **epiphenom'ena.** — *n.* **epiphenom'enalism** interpretation of mind as an epiphenomenon upon the physical. — *n.* and *adj.* **epiphenom'enalist.** [Gr. *epi*, after, *phaino-menon*, neut. pr.p. pass. of *phainein*, to show.]

epiphonema *ep-i-fō-nē'mə,* (*rhet.*) *n.* an exclamation: a phrase or reflection added as a finishing touch. [Gr. *epiphōnēma*.]

epiphragm *ep'i-fram, n.* the disc with which certain molluscs close the aperture of their shell. [Gr. *epiphragma*, covering — *epiphrassein*, to obstruct.]

epiphyllous *ep-i-fil'əs,* (*bot.*) *adj.* growing upon a leaf, esp. on its upper surface. [Gr. *epi*, upon, *phyllon*, a leaf.]

epiphysis *ep-if'i-sis, n.* any portion of a bone having its own centre of ossification: the pineal gland (*epiphysis cerebri*): an ossicle of Aristotle's lantern in a sea-urchin: an upgrowth around the hilum of a seed: — *pl.* **epiph´ysēs.** [Gr., excrescence.]

epiphyte *ep´i-fīt, n.* a plant growing on another plant, without being parasitic: a vegetable parasite on the surface of an animal (*path.*). — *adjs.* **epiphyt´al, epiphytic** (*-fit´ik*), **-al.** — *n.* **ep´iphytism** (or *-fīt´* the condition of being epiphytic: a similar relation among animals. [Gr. *epi*, upon, *phyton*, a plant.]

epiplastron *ep-i-plăs´tron, n.* the anterior lateral one of the (nine) pieces forming the plastron of a turtle: — *pl.* **epiplas´tra.** — *adj.* **epiplas´tral.**

epiploon *e-pip´lō-on, n.* the great omentum. — *adj.* **epiplō´ic.** [Gr. *epiploon* — *epipleein*, to float on.]

epipolism *ep-ip´o-lizm, n.* fluorescence. — *adj.* **epipol´ic.** [Gr. *epipolē*, surface.]

epirrhema *ep-i-rē´mə, n.* in Greek comedy the address of the Coryphaeus to the audience after the parabasis. — *adj.* **epirrhēmat´ic.** [Gr. — *epi*, on, after, *rhēma*, word.]

episcopacy *e-pis´kə-pəs-i, n.* church government by bishops: the office of a bishop: a bishop's period of office: the bishops, as a class. — *adj.* **epis´copal** governed by bishops: belonging to or vested in bishops. — *adj.* **episcopā´lian** belonging to bishops, or government by bishops, or to an episcopal church. — *n.* one who belongs to an episcopal (especially Anglican) church. — *ns.* **episcopā´lianism, epis´copalism** episcopalian government and doctrine. — *adv.* **epis´copally.** — *ns.* **epis´copant** (*Milt.*) a holder of a bishopric; **epis´copate** a bishopric: the office of a bishop: a bishop's period of office: the order of bishops. — *v.i.* (*Milt.*) to act as a bishop. — *v.t.* **epis´copise, -ize** to make a bishop of: to make episcopalian. — *v.i.* to play the bishop (also *v.t.* with *it*). — *n.* **epis´copy** (*Milt.*) survey, superintendence. [Gr. *episkopos*, an overseer.]

episcope *ep´i-skōp, n.* a lantern for projecting images of opaque objects. [Gr. *epi*, on, over, *skopeein*, to look.]

episemon *ep-i-sē´mon, n.* a badge or characteristic device: one of three obsolete Greek letters used as numerals — ç or Ϲ, vau or digamma (6); Ϙ, koppa (90); and Ϡ, san, sampi (900). — *adj.* **episēmat´ic** (*zool.*) serving for recognition. [Gr. *episēmon*, a badge — *epi*, on, *sēma*, a sign.]

episepalous *ep-i-sep´əl-əs, adj.* growing or inserted upon a sepal or sepals.

episiotomy *ep-iz-i-ot´ə-mi, n.* an incision made in the perinaeum to facilitate delivery of a foetus. [Gr. *epision*, pubic region, and **-tomy.**]

episode *ep´i-sōd, n.* a story introduced into a narrative or poem to give variety: an interesting incident: a passage affording relief from the principal subject (*mus.*): an incident or period detachable from a novel, play, etc.: a part of a radio or television serial which is broadcast at one time. — *adjs.* **ep´isōdal, episō´dial, episodic** (*-sod´*), **episŏd´ical** pertaining to or contained in an episode: brought in as a digression: abounding in episodes: (only **episodic(al)**) sporadic, occurring at intervals. — *adv.* **episŏd´ically** by way of episode: incidentally. [Gr. *epeisodion* — *epi*, upon, *eisodos*, a coming in.]

episome *ep´i-sōm, n.* a genetically active particle found esp. in bacteria, able to exist and multiply either independently or integrated in a chromosome. [Pfx. **epi-**, and **-some,** — Gr. *sōma*, body.]

epispastic *ep-i-spas´tik, adj.* blistering. — *n.* a blistering agent. [Gr. *epispastikos* — *epi*, upon, *spaein*, to draw.]

episperm *ep´i-spûrm, n.* the outer seed-coat. [Gr. *epi*, upon, and *sperma*, seed.]

epispore *ep´i-spōr, -spör, n.* the outermost layer of a spore-wall. [Pfx. **epi-**, and **spore.**]

epistasis *i-pis´tə-sis, n.* the suppression by a gene of another non-allelomorphic gene: the arrest of a discharge or secretion: — *pl.* **-stasēs.** — *adj.* **epistatic** (*ep-i-stat´ik*). [Gr., stopping, — *epi*, on, *stasis*, stoppage.]

epistaxis *ep-i-stak´sis, n.* bleeding from the nose. [Gr. *epistazein*, to shed in drops.]

epistemology *ep-is-tə-mol´ə-ji, n.* the theory of knowledge. — *adj.* **epistē´mic** relating to knowledge, epistemology or epistemics. — *n.sing.* **epistē´mics** the scientific study of knowledge, its acquisition and its communication. — *adj.* **epistemological** (*-ə-loj´*). — *n.* **epistemol´ogist.** [Gr. *epistēmē*, knowledge, *logos*, discourse.]

episternum *ep-i-stûr´nəm, n.* the interclavicle: the epiplastron: the presternum of mammals. — *adj.* **epister´nal.**

epistilbite *ep-i-stil´bīt, n.* a zeolite close akin to stilbite. [Gr. *epi*, on, after, in addition to, and **stilbite.**]

epistle *i-pis´l, n.* a writing sent to one, a letter: esp. a letter to an individual or church from an apostle, as the Epistles of Paul: the extract from one of the apostolical epistles read as part of the communion service: a verse composition in letter form. — *v.t.* (*Milt.*) to preface. — *ns.* **epistler** (*-pis´*, or *-pist´*), **epistoler** (*i-pist´ə-lər*) a letter-writer: one who reads the liturgical epistle in the communion service; **epistolā´rian** a letter-writer. — *n.* **epis´tolary** a book containing the Epistles, used for readings in church. — *adjs.* **epistolā´rian, epis´tolary, epis´tolatory, epistolic** (*ep-is-tol´ik*), **-al** pertaining to or consisting of epistles or letters: suitable to an epistle: contained in letters. — *ns.* **epis´toler** the reader of the Epistle in church: a letter-writer; **epis´tolet** a short letter. — *v.i.* **epis´tolise, -ize** to write a letter. — *ns.* **epis´tolist** a writer of letters; **epistolog´raphy** letter-writing. — **epistle side** of a church, the south side, opp. to *gospel side.* [O.Fr., — L. *epistola* — Gr. *epistolē* — *epi*, on the occasion of, *stellein*, to send.]

epistrophe *e-pis´trə-fē, n.* ending of successive clauses with the same word, as in 2 Cor. xi. 22 (A.V.; *rhet.*): a refrain in music. [Gr. *epistrophē*, a return — *epi*, upon, *strephein*, to turn.]

epistyle *ep´i-stīl, n.* an architrave. [Gr. *epi*, upon, *stȳlos*, a pillar.]

epitaph *ep´i-täf, n.* a tombstone inscription: a composition in the form of a tombstone inscription. — *v.t.* to compose an epitaph upon. — *ns.* **epitapher** (*ep´i-täf-ər*), **ep´itaphist** a composer of epitaphs. — *adjs* **epitaph´ian; epitaph´ic.** [Gr. *epitaphion* — *epi*, upon, *taphos*, a tomb.]

epitasis *e-pit´ə-sis, n.* the main action of a Greek drama leading to the catastrophe — opp. to *protasis:* — *pl.* **epit´asēs.**

epitaxy *ep´i-tak-si, n.* the growth of a thin layer of crystals on another crystal so that they have the same structure. — *adj.* **epitax´ial.** [Gr. *epi*, on, *taxis*, arrangement.]

epithalamium, epithalamion *ep-i-thə-lā´mi-əm, -on, ns.* a song or poem in celebration of a marriage: — *pl.* **epithalā´mia.** — *adj.* **epithalām´ic.** [L. *epithalamium*, Gr. *epithalamion* — *epi*, upon, *thalamos*, a bride-chamber.]

epithelium *ep-i-thē´li-əm, n.* the cell-tissue that invests the outer surface of the body and the mucous membranes connected with it, and also the closed cavities of the body. — *adj.* **epithē´lial.** — *n.* **epithēliō´ma** carcinoma of the skin. — *adj.* **epithēliō´matous.** [Mod. L., — Gr., *epi*, upon, *thēlē*, nipple.]

epithem *ep´i-them, n.* a soft external application (*med.*): a group of cells exuding water in some leaves (*bot.*). — Also **epithema** (*ep-i-thē´mə, ep-ith´i-mə*): — *pl.* **ep´ithems, epithe´mata.** [Gr. *epithema, epithēma, -atos* — *epi*, on, *tithenai*, to place.]

epithermal *ep-i-thûr´məl, adj.* having energy just above the energy of thermal agitation.

epithesis *ep-ith´i-sis, n.* a paragoge. [Gr., setting on.]

epithet *ep´i-thet, n.* an adjective expressing some real quality of the thing to which it is applied: a descriptive term: a term, expression (*Shak.*). — *v.t.* to term. — *adj.* **epithet´ic** pertaining to an epithet: abounding with epithets. — *n.* **epith´eton** (*Shak.* **apath´aton**) an epithet. [Gr. *epitheton*, neut. of *epithetos*, added — *epi*, on, *tithenai*, to place.]

epithymetic *ep-i-thim-et´ik, adj.* pertaining to desire. [Gr. *epi*, upon, *thȳmos*, the soul.]

epitome *i-pit´ə-mē, n.* an abridgment or short summary

of anything, as of a book: an embodiment in little: a typical example: a personification. — *adjs* **epitomic** (*ep-i-tom'ik*), **-al.** — *v.t.* **epit'omise, -ize** to make an epitome of: to shorten: to condense: to typify: to personify. — *ns.* **epit'omiser, -z-, epit'omist** one who abridges. — **in epitome** on a small scale. [Gr. *epi*, upon, *tomē*, a cut.]

epitonic *ep-i-ton'ik, adj.* overstrained. [Gr. *epitonos* — *epi*, upon, *teinein*, to stretch.]

epitrachelion *ep-i-tra-kē'li-ən, n.* an Orthodox priest's or bishop's stole. [Gr., on the neck — *epi*, upon, *trachēlos*, neck.]

epitrite *ep'i-trīt*, (*pros.*) *n.* a foot made up of three long syllables and one short. [Gr. *epitritos* — *epi*, in addition to, *tritos*, third.]

epitrochoid *ep-i-trō'koid, n.* a curve like an epicycloid, but generated by any point on a radius. [Gr. *epi*, on, *trochos*, wheel.]

epizeuxis *ep-i-zūk'sis*, (*rhet.*) *n.* the immediate repetition of a word for emphasis. [Gr., joining on.]

eplzoon *ep-i-zō'on, n.* an animal that lives on the surface of another animal, whether parasitically or commensally: — *pl.* **epizō'a.** — *adj.* and *n.* **epizō'an.** — *adjs.* **epizō'ic** dwelling upon an animal: having seeds dispersed by animals; **epizootic** (*ep-i-zō-ot'ik*) pertaining to epizoa: containing fossil remains, as subsequent to the appearance of life (*geol.; obs.*): affecting animals as an epidemic does mankind. — *n.* an epizootic disease. — *n.sing.* **epizōot'ics** the science or study of epidemic animal diseases. [Gr. *epi*, upon, *zōion*, an animal.]

epoch *ēp'ok, ēp'ohh, ep'ok, n.* a point of time fixed or made remarkable by some great event from which dates are reckoned: the particular time, used as a point of reference, at which the data had the values in question (*astron.*): a planet's heliocentric longitude at the epoch (*astron.*): a precise date: a time from which a new state of things dates: an age, geological, historical, or other. — Also (*arch.*) **ep'ocha.** — *adj.* **epochal** (*ep'ok-l*). — **ep'och-mǎking** important enough to be considered as beginning a new age; **ep'och-marking.** [Gr. *epochē* — *epechein*, to stop, take up a position — *epi*, upon, *echein*, to hold.]

epode *ep'ōd, n.* a kind of lyric poem invented by Archilochus, in which a longer verse is followed by a shorter one: the last part of a lyric ode, sung after the strophe and antistrophe. — *adj.* **epodic** (*-od'ik*). [Gr. *epōidos* — *epi*, on, *ōidē*, an ode.]

eponychium *ep-o-nik'i-əm, n.* a narrow band of cuticle over the base of a nail. [Gr. *epi*, on, *onyx, onychos*, nail.]

eponym *ep'ə-nim, n.* one who gives his name to something: a hero invented to account for the name of a place or people: a character who gives a play, etc., its title: a distinguishing title. — *adj.* **eponymous** (*i-pon'i-məs*). [Gr. *epōnymos*, eponymous — *epi*, upon, to, *onyma, onoma*, a name.]

epopee *ep'o-pē*, **epopoeia** *ep-o-pē'yə, ns.* epic poetry: an epic poem. [Gr. *epopoiiā* — *epos*, a word, an epic poem, *poieein*, to make.]

epopt *ep'opt, n.* one initiated into the Eleusinian mysteries. [Gr. *epoptēs* — *epi*, upon, and root *op-*, to see.]

epos *ep'os, n.* the elementary stage of epic poetry: an epic poem: a series of events such as are treated in epic poetry: — *pl.* **ep'oses.** [Gr. *epos*, a word.]

epoxy *e-pok'si, adj.* containing oxygen bound to two other atoms, often carbon, which are already attached in some way. — *n.* an epoxy resin. — *n.* **epox'ide** an epoxy compound. — **epoxy** (or **epoxide**) **resins** synthetic polymers used as structural plastics, surface coatings, adhesives and for encapsulating and embedding electronic components.

épris, *fem.* **éprise**, *ā-prē, -prēz*, (Fr.) *adj.* captivated, smitten.

éprouvette *ā-prōō-vet', n.* an apparatus for testing the strength of gunpowder. [Fr. *éprouver*, to try.]

epsilon *ep-sī'lən, ep'si-lon, n.* fifth letter (E, ε) of the Greek

alphabet, short e: as a numeral ε′ = 5, ,ε = 5000. [Gr. *e psīlon*, bare or mere e.]

epsomite *ep'səm-īt, n.* a mineral, hydrated magnesium sulphate (MgSO₄·7H₂O). — **Epsom salt(s)** a purgative medicine of like composition, originally got from the springs at Epsom, in Surrey — used also in dyeing, etc.

Epstein-Barr virus *ep'stīn-bär' vi'rəs*, a virus which causes glandular fever and which is thought to be associated with various human cancers. [M.A. *Epstein* and Y.M. *Barr*, British virologists, who first isolated it in 1964.]

épuisé, *fem.* **épuisée**, *ā-pwē-zā*, (Fr.) *adj.* worn out.

epulation *ep-ū-lā'shən, n.* feasting. — *adj.* **ep'ulary.** [L. *epulātiō, epulāris*, — *epulāri, -ātus*, to feast.]

epulis *e-pū'lis, n.* a tumour of the gums, either benign or malignant, and growing from the periosteum of the jaw. [Gr. *epi*, upon, *oulon*, gum.]

epulotic *ep-ū-lot'ik, adj.* cicatrising. — *n.* a cicatrising medicament. [Gr. *epoulōtikos* — *epi*, upon, *oulē*, a scar.]

epurate *ep'ū-rāt, v.t.* to purify. — *n.* **epurā'tion.** [Fr. *épurer*.]

epyllion *e-pil'i-ən, n.* a poem with some resemblance to an epic but shorter. [Gr.; dim. of *epos*, word.]

Epyornis. A spelling of **Aepyornis.**

equable *ek'wə-bl, adj.* even, uniform: smooth: without great variations or extremes: of even temper. — *ns.* **equabil'ity, e'quableness.** — *adv.* **e'quably.** [L. *aequābilis* — *aequāre* — *aequus*, equal.]

equal *ē'kwəl, adj.* identical in quantity: of the same value: adequate: in just proportion: fit: equable: uniform: equitable: evenly balanced: just: equally developed on each side (*bot.*). — *n.* one of the same age, rank, etc.: equality (*Spens.*). — *v.t.* to be, or to make, equal to: to reach the same level as (*bot.*): — *pr.p.* **e'qualling;** *pa.t.* and *pa.p.* **e'qualled.** — *n.* **equalisā'tion, -z-** the act of making equal: the state of being equalised. — *v.t.* **e'qualise, -ize** to make equal or uniform: to equal (*obs.*). — *v.i.* to become equal: to make one's score equal to one's opponent's. — *n.* **equalī'ser, -z-** a person or thing that equalises: a score that makes both sides alike. — *adj.* **equalitār'ian** (*-kwol-*) of or pertaining to the equality of mankind. — *n.* one who believes in or favours political and social equality of mankind. — *ns.* **equalitā'rianism; equality** (*ē-kwol'i-ti*) the condition of being equal: sameness: evenness. — *adv.* **equally** (*ē'kwə-li*). — *ns.* **e'qualness** equality: equability; **ē'quant** in Ptolemy's astronomical system, (a circle centred on) a point on the line on which the earth and the centre of a given planet's deferent stand, used to reconcile observed planetary motions with the hypothesis of uniform planetary velocity. — *adj.* (*crystal.*) of a crystal's habit (q.v.) in which its diameter is equal, or nearly so, in all directions. — *v.t.* **equate'** to reduce to an average or to a common standard of comparison: to state as equal: to regard as equal. — *v.i.* to be, or be regarded, treated, etc. as, equal. — *n.* **equā'tion** the act of making equal: a statement of the equality of two quantities: reduction to a common standard: correction to compensate for an error, irregularity, or discrepancy: the quantity added for this purpose: a formula expressing a chemical action and the proportions of the substances involved. — **equal opportunities** in employment, etc., the avoidance of any discrimination between applicants, etc. on the grounds of sex, race, etc.; **equal(s) sign** the symbol =, which indicates that two (numerical) values are equal; **equal temperament** see **temperament.** — **equal to the occasion** fit or able to cope with an emergency; **equation of time** mean solar time minus apparent solar time, or the right ascension of the true sun minus that of the mean sun; **personal equation** a correction to be applied to the reading of an instrument on account of the observer's tendency to read too high, too low, etc.: any tendency to error or prejudice due to personal characteristics for which allowance must be made. [L. *aequālis*, equal, *aequāre*, *-ātum*, to make equal — *aequus*, equal.]

equanimity *e-kwə-nim'i-ti*, *ē-*, *n.* evenness of mind or temper. — *adj.* **equanimous** (*i-kwan'i-məs*). — *adv.* **equan'imously.** [L. *aequanimitās* — *aequus*, equal, *animus*, the mind.]

equate, equation. See **equal.**

equator *i-kwā'tər*, *n.* an imaginary great circle passing round the middle of the globe and equidistant from N. and S. poles: the corresponding great circle of another body: the imaginary great circle in which the plane of the earth's equator intersects the celestial sphere (so called because day and night are equal when the sun reaches it): the middle belt or line of any globular or nearly globular body that has some sort of polarity. — *adj.* **equatorial** (*ek-wə-tō'ri-əl*, *-tö'*, or *ēk-*) of, pertaining to, of the nature of, or in the neighbourhood of, an equator. — *n.* a telescope mounted on an axis, capable of moving parallel to the equator and so following a star in any part of its diurnal course. — *adv.* **equato'rially** so as to have motion or direction parallel to the equator. [See **equal.**]

equerry *ek'wə-ri*, *ik-wer'i*, *n.* princely stables (*obs.*): an officer thereof: an official in attendance upon a prince or personage. [Fr. *écurie* — L.L. *scūria*, a stable.]

equestrian *i-kwes'tri-ən*, *adj.* pertaining to horsemanship, or to the Roman order of *equitēs* or knights: on horseback. — *n.* a horseman: a performer on horseback: — *fem.* (sham Fr.) **equestrienne'.** — *n.* **eques'trianism** horsemanship. [L. *equester*, *equestris* — *eques* a horseman — *equus*, a horse.]

equi- *ē-kwi-*, a prefix meaning equal, from L. *aequus.* — *adj.* **equian'gular** having equal angles (**equiangular spiral** a curve whose radius vector makes a constant angle with the tangent — the *logarithmic spiral*). — *n.* **equiangular'ity.** — *n.* and *v.t.* **equibal'ance** equipoise. — *adj.* **equidiff'erent** having equal differences. — *n.* **equidis'tance.** — *adj.* **equidis'tant** equally distant. — *adv.* **equidis'tantly.** — *adj.* **equilat'eral** (L. *latus*, *-eris*, side) having all sides equal. — *n.* **equimul'tiple** a number multiplied by the same number as another. — *adjs.* **equipo'tent** of equal power; **equipoten'tial** of equal power, capability, potential, or potentiality, **equiprob'-able** equal in degree of probability. — *n.* **equiprobabil'-ity.** — *adj.* **e'quivalve** having valves alike in size and form.

Equidae *ek'wi-dē*, *n.pl.* a family of ungulate mammals consisting of the genus **Eq'uus** (horse, ass, zebra) and various fossil forms. [L. *equus*, horse.]

equidifferent... to ... equilateral. See **equi-.**

equilibrium *ēk-*, *ek-wi-lib'ri-əm*, *n.* balance: the state of even balance: a state in which opposing forces or tendencies neutralise each other. — *v.t.* and *v.i.* **equi-librate** (*ēk-wi-līb'rāt*, or *-lib'rāt*, or *-kwil'*) to balance: to counterpoise. — *ns.* **equilibrā'tion**; **equil'ibrator** (or *-līb'*) a balancing or stability device, esp. an aeroplane fin; **equil'ibrist** (or *lib'*, or *-līb'*) one who does balancing tricks; **equilib'rity.** [L. *aequilībrium* — *aequus*, equal, *lībra*, balance.]

equimultiple. See **equi-.**

equine *e'*, *ē'kwīn*, **equinal** *e-*, *ē-kwīn'əl*, *adjs.* pertaining to, or of the nature of, a horse or horses. — *ns.* **equinia** (*i-*, *ē-kwin'i-ə*) glanders; **equin'ity** equine nature. — **equine infectious anaemia** another name for **swamp fever.** [L. *equīnus* — *equus*, a horse.]

equinox *ek'*, *ēk'wi-noks*, *n.* the time when the sun crosses the equator, making the night equal in length to the day, about 21 March and 23 Sept.: an equinoctial point. — *adj.* **equinoc'tial** pertaining to the equinoxes, the time of the equinoxes, or to the regions about the equator. — *n.* the celestial equator or **equinoctial line.** — *adv.* **equinoc'tially** in the direction of the equinox. — **equinoctial gales** high gales popularly supposed to prevail about the times of the equinoxes — the belief is unsupported by observation; **equinoctial point** either of the two points in the heavens where the equinoctial line cuts the ecliptic; **equinoctial year** see **year.** [L.

aequus, equal, *nox*, *noctis*, night.]

equip *i-kwip'*, *v.t.* to fit out: to furnish with everything needed: — *pr.p.* **equipp'ing**; *pa.t.* and *pa.p.* **equipped'.** — *n.* **equipage** (*ek'wi-pāj*) that with which one is equipped (*arch.*): apparatus required for any operation, e.g. making tea (*arch.*): a carriage and attendants: retinue. — *v.t.* (*obs.*) to equip. — *n.* **equip'ment** the act of equipping: the state of being equipped: things used in equipping or furnishing: outfit. [Fr. *équiper*, prob. — O.N. *skipa*, to set in order, *skip*, a ship; partly influenced by confusion with L. *equus*, horse.]

équipe *ā-kēp*, (Fr.) *n.* in motor-racing and other sport, a team.

equipoise *ek'wi-poiz*, *n.* a state of balance: a counterpoise. — *v.t.* to balance: to counterpoise. [L. *aequus*, equal, and **poise.**]

equipollent *ē-*, *e-kwi-pol'ənt*, *adj.* having equal power or force: equivalent. — *n.* an equivalent. — *ns.* **equipoll'-ence**, **equipoll'ency.** [L. *aequus*, equal, *pollēns*, *pollentis*, pr.p. of *pollēre*, to be strong, able.]

equiponderate *ē-*, *e-kwi-pon'dər-āt*, *v.i.* to be equal in weight: to balance. — *adj.* equal in weight. — *n.* **equipon'derance.** — *adj.* **equipon'derant.** [L. *aequus*, equal, *pondus*, *ponderis*, weight.]

equipotent... to ... equiprobability. See **equi-.**

Equisetum *ek-wi-sē'təm*, *n.* the only surviving genus of the family **Equisetā'ceae**, constituting the **Equisetī'nae** or **Equisetā'les**, a class of pteridophytes, stiff herbaceous plants with almost leafless articulated and whorled stems and branches: (without *cap.*) a plant of this genus — also **horsetail.** — *adjs.* **equisetā'ceous; equisēt'ic; equisēt'iform.** [L. *equus*, a horse, *sēta*, a bristle.]

equitation *ek-wi-tā'shən*, *n.* the art of riding on horseback. — *adj.* **eq'uitant** riding: straddling, overlapping: of leaves, folded lengthwise over succeeding leaves. [L. *equitāre*, to ride — *equus*, a horse.]

equity *ek'wi-ti*, *n.* right as founded on the laws of nature: moral justice, of which laws are the imperfect expression: the spirit of justice which enables us to interpret laws rightly: fairness: an equitable right: the value of property in excess of any charges upon it (*U.S.*): (in *pl.*) ordinary shares: (with *cap.*) British actors' trade union. — *adj.* **eq'uitable** possessing or showing or in accordance with equity: held or exercised in equity. — *n.* **eq'uitableness.** – *adv.* **eq'uitably.** [O.Fr. *equité* — L. *aequitās*, *-ātis* — *aequus*, equal.]

equivalent *i-kwiv'ə-lənt*, *adj.* equal in value, power, meaning, etc.: interchangeable: of like combining value (*chem.*). — *n.* a thing equivalent: an equivalent weight (*chem.*). — *ns.* **equiv'alence, equiv'alency.** — *adv.* **equiv'-alently.** — **equivalent weight** (*chem.*) that weight which displaces or combines with or otherwise represents a standard unit — atomic weight, or atomic weight divided by valence. [Fr., — L. *aequus*, equal, *valēns*, *valentis*, pr.p. of *valēre*, to be worth.]

equivalve. See **equi-.**

equivocal *i-kwiv'ə-kl*, *adj.* capable of meaning two or more things: of doubtful meaning: capable of a double explanation: suspicious: questionable. — *adv.* **equiv'-ocally.** — *ns.* **equivocal'ity; equiv'ocalness.** — *v.i.* **equiv'-ocāte** to use equivocal or doubtful words in order to mislead. — *ns.* **equivocā'tion; equiv'ocātor.** — *adj.* **equiv'ocatory** containing or characterised by equivocation. — *n.* **equivoke, equivoque** (*ek'wi-vōk*) an equivocal expression: equivocation: a quibble: a pun. [L. *aequus*, equal, and *vōx*, *vōcis*, the voice, a word.]

Equus. See **Equidae.**

er *ûr*, *interj.* expressing hesitation.

-er¹ *-ər*, *suff.* marks the agent (person or thing), designating persons according to occupation (e.g. writ*er*), or place of abode (e.g. London*er*) (O.E. *-ere*); some similar words, e.g. groc*er*, offic*er*, are from Fr. *-ier* (L. *-arius*).

-er² *-ər*, *suff.* marks the comparative degree of adjectives (long*er*) and some adverbs (fast*er*). [O.E. *-ra* (*adj.*), *-or* (*adv.*).]

era *ē'rə, n.* a series of years reckoned from a particular point, or that point itself: an important date: an age: a main division of geological time. — *n.* **ē'rathem** the stratigraphical unit of rock strata corresponding to a geological era. [L.L. *aera*, a number, orig. counters, pieces of copper used in counting, pl. of *aes*, copper.]

eradiate *i-, ē-rā'di-āt, v.t.* and *v.i.* to shoot out like a ray of light. — *n.* **eradiā'tion.** [L. *ē-*, from, *radius*, a ray.]

eradicate *i-rad'i-kāt, v.t.* to pull up by the roots: to root out: to extirpate. — *adj.* **erad'icable.** — *adj.* **erad'icāted** rooted up: of a tree, or part of a tree, torn up by the roots (*her.*). — *n.* **eradicā'tion** the act of eradicating: the state of being eradicated. — *adj.* **erad'icātive** serving to eradicate or drive thoroughly away. — *n.* **erad'icātor.** [L. *ērādīcāre, -ātum*, to root out — *ē*, from, *rādīx, -īcis*, a root.]

erase *i-rāz', v.t.* to rub or scrape out: to efface: to destroy: to replace the data of a storage area with characters representing zero (*comput.*). — *adj.* **erā'sable.** — *adj.* **erased'** rubbed out: effaced: torn off, so as to leave jagged edges (*her.*). — *ns.* **erā'ser** one who, or that which, erases, as *ink-eraser*; **erā'sion** (*-zhən*), **erase'ment, era'sure** (*-zhər*) the act of erasing: a rubbing out: scraping away: the place where something written has been rubbed out. [L. *ērādēre — ē*, from, *rādēre, rāsum*, to scrape.]

Erastian *e-ras'ti-ən, -tyən, n.* a follower of Thomas *Erastus* (1524–83), a Swiss physician, who denied the church the right to inflict excommunication and disciplinary penalties: one who would subordinate the church jurisdiction to the state — a position not held by Erastus at all. — *adj.* relating to the Erastians or their doctrines. — *n.* **Eras'tianism** control of the church by the state.

erathem. See **era**.

Erato *er'ə-tō, n.* the Muse of amatory lyric poetry. [Gr. *Eratō*.]

erbium *ûr'bi-əm, n.* a rare metal (at. numb. 68; symbol **Er**), found in gadolinite, at Ytter*by*, near Stockholm. — *n.* **er'bia** erbium oxide.

Erdgeist *ārt'gīst,* (Ger.) *n.* earth-spirit.

ere[1] *ār, adv., prep.* and *conj.* before. — *advs.* **erelong', ere long** before long: soon; **erenow', ere now** before this time; **erewhile'** formerly: sometime before. [O.E. *ǣr*; cf. Du. *eer.*]

ere[2]. Same as **ear**[2].

Erebus *er'i-bəs, (myth.) n.* the dark and gloomy cavern between earth and Hades: the lower world, hell. [L., — Gr. *Erebos.*]

erect *i-rekt', adj.* upright: directed upward: right end up, not decumbent: not decumbent (*bot.*): turgid and raised (*zool.*). — *v.t.* to set upright: to set erect: to set at right angles: to raise: to build: to exalt: to establish. — *adj.* **erect'ed.** — *ns.* **erect'er, erect'or** one who, or that which, erects or raises: a muscle which assists in erecting a part or an organ: an attachment to a compound microscope for making the image erect instead of inverted. — *adj.* **erect'ile** (*-īl*) that may be erected. — *ns.* **erectility** (*e-, ē-rek-til'i-ti*); **erec'tion** the act of erecting: the state of being erected: exaltation: anything erected: a building of any kind: an enlarging and hardening of the penis usu. in response to sexual stimulation. — *adj.* **erect'ive** tending to erect. — *adv.* **erect'ly.** — *n.* **erect'ness.** [L. *ērigēre, ērēctum*, to set upright — *ē*, from, *regēre*, to direct.]

eremacausis *er-i-mə-kö'sis,* (*chem.*) *n.* very slow oxidation. [Gr. *ērema*, quietly, slowly, *kausis*, burning — *kaiein*, to burn.]

eremic *e-rē'mik, adj.* belonging to deserts. [Gr. *erēmikos — erēmiā*, desert, solitude.]

eremite *er'i-mīt, n.* a recluse who lives apart, esp. from religious motives: a hermit. — *adjs.* **eremī'tal; eremitic** (*-mit'ik*), **-al.** — *n.* **er'emitism.** [L.L. *erēmīta* — Gr. *erēmītēs — erēmos*, desert.]

e re nata *ē rē nā'tə, ā rā nā'ta,* (L.L.) from the circumstances arisen, according to the exigencies of the case.

erepsin *e-rep'sin, n.* an enzyme of the small intestine,

acting upon casein, gelatine, etc. [L. *ēripēre, ēreptum — ē*, from, *rapēre*, to snatch.]

erethism *er'e-thizm, n.* excitement or stimulation of an organ: abnormal irritability. — *adjs.* **erethis'mic; erethis'tic; erethit'ic.** [Gr. *erethismos.*]

Erewhon *er'e-(h)won, n.* the imaginary country of Samuel Butler's satirical Utopian romances *Erewhon* (1872) and *Erewhon Revisited* (1901). — *n.* and *adj.* **Erewhō'nian.** [Formed from *nowhere* spelt backwards.]

erf *ûrf, (S. Afr.) n.* a garden plot or small piece of ground: — *pl.* **er'ven.** [Du.; cf. O.E. *erfe*, inheritance.]

erg *ûrg, n.* the unit of work in the centimetre-gramme-second system — that is, the quantity of work done when the point of operation of a force of one dyne is allowed to move one centimetre in the direction of the force. — *ns.* **er'gogram** a record by ergograph; **er'gograph** an instrument for measuring and recording muscular work; **ergom'eter** an instrument for measuring work done. — *adj.* **ergonom'ic.** — *adv.* **ergonom'ically.** — *n.sing.* **ergonom'ics** the study of man in relation to his working environment: the adaptation of machines and general conditions to fit the individual so that he may work at maximum efficiency. — *ns.* **ergon'omist; ergopho'bia** morbid dislike of work. — **erg'-nine', erg'-ten',** etc., an erg multiplied by ten to the power of nine, ten, etc. [Gr. *ergon*, work.]

ergates *ûr'gə-tēz,* **ergate** *ûr'gāt, ns.* a worker ant, an undeveloped female. — *ns.* **ergatan'dromorph** (Gr. *andromorphos*, of male form) an ant combining characters of males and workers; **ergataner** (*ûr-gə-tā'nər, -tä'nər*; Gr. *anēr*, man) a worker-like wingless male ant; **ergatogyne** (*-jī'nē*; Gr. *gynē*, woman) a worker-like wingless female ant. — *adj.* **er'gatoid** worker-like, wingless but sexually perfect. — *n.* **er'gatomorph** an ergatoid ant. — *adj.* **ergatomorph'ic.** [Gr. *ergatēs*, workman — *ergon*, work.]

ergo *ûr'gō* (*log.*) *adv.* therefore, used to introduce the conclusion of a syllogism. — *v.i.* **er'gotise, -ize** to wrangle (see also **ergot**). [L. *ergō*, therefore.]

ergodic *ər-god'ik, adj.* pertaining to the probability that in a system any state will occur again. — *n.* **ergodic'ity** (*-dis'*). [Gr. *ergon*, work, *hodos*, way.]

ergogram, ergonomics, etc. See **erg**.

ergon *ûr'gən, er'gon,* (Gr.) *n.* work, business.

ergosterol. See **ergot**.

ergot *ûr'got, n.* a disease of grasses (esp. rye) and sedges due to *Claviceps purpurea*: a seed so diseased. — *n.* **ergos'terol** an unsaturated sterol got from ergot. — *v.t.* **er'gotise, -ize** to affect with ergot or with ergotism (see also **ergo**). — *n.* **er'gotism** poisoning caused by eating bread made of rye diseased with ergot. [Fr.]

eric *er'ik, n.* the blood-fine paid by a murderer to his victim's family in old Irish law. — Also **er'iach, er'ick.** [Ir. *eiric*.]

Erica *er'i-kə, n.* the heath genus: (without *cap.*) a member of the genus. — *adjs.* **ericaceous** (*er-i-kā'shəs*) belonging to plants of the genus Erica, or its family **Ericā'ceae:** heathlike; **er'icoid** with heatherlike leaves. [L., — Gr. *ereikē*, heath.]

Erigeron *e-rij'ə-ron, n.* the flea-bane genus of composites: (without *cap.*) a member of the genus. [Gr. *ērigerōn*, groundsel — *ēri*, early, *gerōn*, old.]

eringo. Same as **eryngo**.

erinite *er'i-nīt, n.* a basic arsenate of copper found in Cornwall and Ireland. [*Erin*, Ireland.]

Erinys *e-rī'nis, n.* a Fury: — *pl.* **Erinyes** (*e-rin'i-ēz*). [Gr. *Erīnȳs,* pl. *Erīnȳes.*]

erio- *er-i-ō-, -o-,* in composition, wool, fibre. — *ns.* **Eriocaulon** (*-ō-kö'lon;* Gr. *kaulos*, stalk) the pipewort genus, giving name to the **Eriocaul(on)ā'ceae,** a family of monocotyledons, akin to the Bromelias; **Eriōden'dron** (Gr. *dendron*, tree) the silk-cotton genus of trees; **eriometer** (*-om'ət-ər;* Gr. *metron*, measure) an optical instrument for measuring small diameters, of fibres, etc.; **er'ionite** a mineral which occurs in white wool-like crystals; **Eriophorum** (*-of'ər-əm;* Gr. *phoros*, carrying) the cotton-grass or cotton-sedge genus: (without *cap*.) a member of the genus. — *adj.* **eriophorous** (*-of'ər-əs*) very cottony. [Gr. *erion*, wool.]

eristic, -al *er-is'tik, -l, adjs.* of or pertaining to controversy or disputatious reasoning. [Gr. *eristikos* — *eris*, strife.]

erk *ûrk, (airmen's slang) n.* an aircraftsman. [From *airk*, for aircraftsman.]

erl-king *ûrl'-king, n.* for German *Erlkönig*, which was a mistranslation (alder-king) of the Danish *ellerkonge* (from *elverkonge*, king of the elves).

ermelin *ûr'mə-lin, n.* arch. for **ermine**.

ermine *ûr'min, n.* the stoat: a white fur, the stoat's winter coat in northern lands, used for the robes of judges and magistrates with the black tail-tip (or an imitation) attached. — *adj.* **er'mined** adorned with ermine. [O.Fr. *ermine* (Fr. *hermine*), perh. from L. (*mūs*) *Armēnius*, lit. (mouse) of Armenia, whence it was brought to Rome; but acc. to some from O.H.G. *harmîn* (Ger. *Hermelin*), ermine-fur.]

ern. An old spelling (*Milt.*) of **earn**.

erne[1] *ûrn, n.* the eagle. [O.E. *earn*; cf. O.N. *örn*, Du. *arend*.]

erne[2] *ûrn, (Spens.).* Same as **yearn**[1].

Ernie *ûr'ni, n.* the electronic machine which picks, by methods that allow full scope for chance, numbers to be used as winning numbers on premium bonds. [Abbreviation of *electronic random number indicator* equipment.]

erode *i-, e-rōd', v.t.* to eat away, wear away: to form by wearing away. — Also *v.i.* — *adjs.* **erō'ded, erose** (*-rōs'*) irregularly notched as if bitten. — *adj.* and *n.* **erō'dent** caustic. — *n.* **erosion** (*-rō'zhən*) eating away, wearing down: the denuding action of weathering, water, ice, wind, etc. (*geol.*). — *adj.* **erosive** (*-rō'ziv*). [L. *ē*, from, *rōdĕre, rōsum*, to gnaw.]

Erodium *e-rō'di-əm, n.* the stork's-bill genus of the geranium family: (without *cap.*) a plant of the genus. [Gr. *erōdios*, a heron.]

erogenic, erogenous. See **Eros**.

Eros *ēr'os* (prop. in Gr. *erōs*), *er'os, n.* the Greek love-god, identified by the Romans with Cupid: a minor planet discovered in 1898, notable for its near approach to the earth. — *adjs.* **erotic** (*e-rot'ik*), **-al** pertaining to sexual love: amatory: amorous. — *n.* (**erotic**) an amatory poem or composition. — *n.pl.* **erot'ica** erotic literature. — *ns.* **erot'icism** (*-sizm*) amorous temperament or habit: erotism; **erot'icist; er'otism** sexual desire: the manifestations of sex in its widest application. — *adjs.* **erotogenic** (*er-ət-ō-jen'ik*), **erotogenous** (*-oj'*), less correctly **erogen'ic, erog'enous**, productive of erotic desire or gratification. — *ns.* **erōtomā'nia** morbid sexual passion; **erōtomā'niac; erōtophōbia** fear of or aversion to any form of sexual involvement. [Gr. *Erōs, -ōtos*.]

erose, erosion, erosive. See **erode**.

erustrate *ē-ros'trāt, (bot.) adj.* beakless. [L. *ē*, from, *rōstrum*, a beak.]

erotema *er-ō-tē'mə*, **eroteme** *er'ō-tēm*, **erotesis** *er-ō-tē'sis, ns.* a rhetorical question. — *adj.* **erotetic** (*-tet'ik*) interrogatory. [Gr. *erōtēma, erōtēsis* — *erōtaein*, to question.]

erotic, erotism, erotogenic, etc. See **Eros**.

err *ûr, v.i.* to wander (*arch.*): to wander from the right way (*arch.*): to go astray (*arch.*): to miss the mark: to be inaccurate: to make a mistake: to sin: — *pr.p.* **erring** (*ûr'ing* or *er'ing*); *pa.t.* and *pa.p.* **erred** (*ûrd*). — *adjs.* **err'able** (*er'; obs.*) capable of erring; **errant** (*er'ənt*) wandering: roving: quixotic: thorough (*obs.*; cf. **arrant**): erring. — *n.* a knight-errant. — *adv.* **err'antly.** — *n.* **err'antry** an errant or wandering state: a rambling about like a knight-errant. — *adj.* **erra'tic** wandering: having no certain course: not stationary: irregular, capricious, irregular or unpredictable in behaviour. — *n.* a wanderer: an erratic block or boulder. — *adj.* **errat'ical.** — *adv.* **errat'ically.** — *n.* **errā'tum** an error in writing or printing, esp. one noted in a list in a book

(*pl.* **errā'ta**). — *adj.* **err'ing** wandering (*arch.*): straying from the truth or right conduct. — *n.* wandering (*arch.*): straying (*arch.*): making mistakes. — *adv.* **err'ingly.** — *adj.* **erroneous** (*i-rō'ni-əs*) erring: full of error: wrong: mistaken: wandering, straying (*arch.*). — *adv.* **errō'neously.** — *ns.* **errō'neousness; error** (*er'ər*) wandering, winding course (*arch.*): deviation from the right way (*arch.*): mistaken opinion: difference between a quantity obtained by observation and the true value: a blunder or mistake: wrong-doing; **err'orist.** — **erratic block** a mass of rock transported by ice and deposited at a distance. [L. *errāre*, to stray; cog. with Ger. *irren*, and *irre*, astray.]

errand *er'ənd, n.* a verbal message (*arch.*): a mission (*arch.*): a commission to say or do something usually involving a short journey: (in *pl.*) marketing (*dial.*). — **err'and-boy, -girl.** — **a fool's errand, a sleeveless errand** a futile journey; **make an errand** to invent a reason for going; **once'-, yince'-, ance'-errand** (*Scot.*) for the express purpose and nothing else; **run errands** to be sent to convey messages or perform small pieces of business. [O.E. *ærende*; O.N. *eyrindi*; prob. conn. with Goth. *āirus*, O.N. *ārr*, a messenger.]

errant, erratic, erratum. See under **err**.

errhine *er'īn, adj.* and *n.* sternutatory. [Gr. *errīnon* — *en*, in, *rhīs, rhīnos*, the nose.]

erroneous, error. See under **err**.

ers *ûrs, n.* the bitter vetch. [Fr., — L. *ervum*.]

ersatz *er'zats, ûr'-, er-zats', n.* a substitute: a supplementary reserve from which waste can be made good (*mil.*). — *adj.* substitute: fake. [Ger.]

Erse *ers, ûrs, n.* the name given by Lowland Scots to the language of the people of the West Highlands, as being of Irish origin: now sometimes used for Irish Gaelic, as opposed to Scottish Gaelic. [Variant of **Irish**.]

erst *ûrst, adv.* at first: formerly. — *adv.* **erst'while, erstwhile'** formerly. — *adj.* former. [O.E. *ærest*, superl. of *ær*; see **ere**.]

erubescent *er-ōō-bes'ənt, adj.* growing red: blushing. — *ns.* **erubesc'ence, erubesc'ency; erubesc'ite** the mineral bornite. [L. *ērubēscĕre*, to grow red; see **rubescent, ruby**.]

Eruca *i-rōō'kə, n.* a genus of herbs of the family Cruciferae. — **erucic acid** (*i-rōō'sik*) a crystalline fatty acid found in rape-seed, wallflower seed and mustard seed, used in some edible oils. [L. *ērūca*, rocket (see **rocket**[2]); see also **eruciform**.]

eruciform *e-rōō'si-förm, adj.* like a caterpillar. [L. *ērūca*, caterpillar, *förma*, form.]

eruct *i-rukt'*, **eructate** *-āt, vs.t.* to belch out, as wind from the stomach (also *v.i.*; also *fig.*): of a volcano, to emit (fumes and ash or lava). — *n.* **eructā'tion** (*ē-*). [L. *ēructāre, -ātum* — *ē*, from, *ructāre*, to belch forth.]

erudite *er'ōō-dīt, -ū-, adj.* learned. — *n.* a learned person. — *adv.* **er'uditely.** — *n.* **erudi'tion** the state of being learned: knowledge gained by study: learning, esp. in literature. [L. *ērudītus* — *ērudīre, ērudītum*, to free from rudeness — *ē*, from, *rudis*, rude.]

erupt *i-rupt', v.i.* to break out or through, as a volcano, a tooth from the gum, a rash on the skin. — Also *v.t.* — *n.* **erup'tion** a breaking or bursting forth: that which bursts forth: a breaking out of spots on the skin: the action of a volcano. — *adjs.* **erup'tional; erupt'ive** breaking forth: attended by or producing eruption: produced by eruption. — *n.* **erupt'iveness.** [L. *ērumpĕre, ēruptum* — *ē*, from, *rumpĕre*, to break.]

ervalenta, revalenta. See **revalenta**.

erven. See **erf**.

eryngo *e-ring'gō, n.* the candied root of sea-holly: the plant itself, a superficially thistle-like umbellifer: — *pl.* **eryn'gos, -goes.** — *n.* **Eryn'gium** (*-ji-əm*) a genus of bristly plants including the sea-holly (fam. Umbelliferae: (without *cap.*) a plant of the genus. [Gr. *ēryngos*.]

Erysimum *er-is'i-məm, n.* the treacle-mustard genus of Cruciferae. [Latinised from Gr. *ĕrysīmon*, hedge-mustard.]

For other sounds see detailed chart of pronunciation.

erysipelas *er-i-sip'i-ləs, n.* an inflammatory disease, generally in the face, marked by a bright redness of the skin. — *adj.* **erysipelatous** (*-el'ə-təs*). [Gr.; prob. — root of *erythros*, red, *pella*, skin.]

erythema *er-i-thē'mə, n.* redness of the skin. — *adjs.* **erythemal** (*er-ith'*); **erythemat'ic; erythem'atous**. [Gr. *erythēma* — *erythainein*, to redden — *erythros*, red.]

erythr(o)- *er-ith-r(ō)-*, in composition, red. — *ns.* **Erythrī'na** the kaffir-boom genus of Papilionaceae, tropical and subtropical trees with brilliant red flowers: (without *cap.*) a plant of this genus; **eryth'rism** red colouring, esp. exceptional or abnormal; **eryth'rīte** a reddish hydrous arsenate of cobalt. — *adj.* **erythrĭt'ic**. — *ns.* **eryth'roblast** (*-bläst*; Gr. *blastos*, a sprout) a cell in bone marrow that develops into an erythrocyte; **eryth'rocyte** (Gr. *kytos*, case) a red blood corpuscle; **Erythroleukae'mia** a malignant disorder of the blood characterised by an abnormal presence of erythroblasts and myeloblasts in the blood; **erythromycin** (*-mī'sin*; Gr. *mȳkēs*, fungus) an antibiotic similar to penicillin; **erythrophō'bia** a fear of blushing: a neurotic tendency to blush: an aversion to red; **erythropoiesis** (*-poi-ēs'is*; Gr. *poiēsis*, making) formation of red blood cells. [Gr. *erythros*, red.]

Erziehungsroman *er-tsē'ōōngs-rō-män'* (Ger.). Same as **Bildungsroman**.

es *es, n.* the nineteenth letter of the alphabet (S, s): anything of that shape. — Also **ess**.

escadrille *es-kə-dril', n.* a French squadron of aircraft: a flotilla. [Fr., flotilla.]

escalade *es-kə-lād', n.* the scaling of the walls of a fortress by means of ladders. — Also **escalā'dō** (for Sp. *escalada*): — *pl.* **escalā'does**. — *v.t.* to scale: to mount and enter by means of ladders. — *v.i.* **es'calate** to ascend, descend, on an escalator: to increase rapidly in scale or intensity. — Also *v.t.* — *n.* **escalā'tion**. — *n.* **es'calātor** a moving staircase. — *adj.* **es'calātory**. — **escalator clause** a clause in an agreement allowing for adjustment up or down according to change in circumstances, as in cost of material in a work contract or in cost of living in a wage agreement. [Fr., — Sp. *escalada* — *escala*, a ladder — L. *scāla*.]

escalier *es-ka-lyā*, (Fr.) *n.* staircase. — **escalier dérobé** (*dā-ro-bā*) private staircase.

Escallonia *es-kal-ōn'i-ə, n.* a South American genus of shrubs of the Saxifrage family: (without *cap.*) a plant of this genus. [Discovered by *Escallon*, an 18th-cent. Spanish traveller.]

escallop *is-kal'əp, n.* a variant of **scallop**. — *adj.* **escall'oped** (*her.*) covered with scallop-shells.

escalop. A variant of **escallop** or **scallop** except in heraldry.

escalope *es'ka-lop, n.* a boneless slice of meat, cut thin and often beaten out still thinner. [Fr.]

escamotage *es-ka-mo-täzh,* (Fr.) *n.* juggling.

escape *is-kāp', v.t.* to free oneself from: to pass out of danger from: to evade, elude. — *v.i.* to come off or come through in safety: to emerge into or gain freedom: to flee: to slip out: to issue: to leak. — *n.* act of escaping: a means of escaping: flight: flight from reality: an outlet: a leakage: an accidental or inadvertent emission: an outburst: a sally: a prank (*obs.*): a venial offence (*obs.*): a transgression (*obs.*): a person or thing that has escaped, esp. a garden plant maintaining itself wild. — *adj.* of literature, providing escape from reality: of a clause in an agreement, defining the conditions under which a party is relieved of obligation. — *adj.* **escap'able**. — *ns.* **escapade** (*es-kə-pād'*) an escape (*arch.*): a mischievous adventure; **escapado** (*-ä'dō*) an escaped evil-doer: an escapade (Sp. *escapada*): — *pl.* **escapā'does; escapee'** one who has escaped, e.g. from prison. — *adj.* **escape'less**. — *ns.* **escape'ment** an escape: part of a timepiece connecting the wheelwork with the pendulum or balance, and allowing a tooth to escape at each vibration: the clearance in a pianoforte between the string and the hammer after it has struck the string, while the key is held down; **escāp'er; escāp'ism; escāp'ist** one who seeks escape, esp. from reality. — Also *adj.* — *ns.* **escapol'ogist; escapol'ogy** the study of methods of escape from any sort of constraint or confinement and the putting into practice of these methods: (*loosely*) escapism. — **escape hatch** an emergency means of escape from ship, submarine, etc.; **escape mechanism** (*psych.*) a mental process by which one evades the unpleasant; **escape road** a short track leading off a road on a steep hill, sharp bend, etc., for vehicles going out of control; **escape valve** a valve to let steam, etc., escape when wanted; **escape velocity** (*phys.*) the minimum velocity needed to escape from the gravitation field of a body; **escape wheel** the wheel that the pallets act upon in a clock. [O.Fr. *escaper* (Fr. *échapper*) — L.L. *ex cappā*, (lit.) out of one's cape or cloak.]

escargot *es-kar-gō,* (Fr.) *n.* an edible snail.

escarmouche *e-skär'mōōsh,* (*obs.*) *n.* a skirmish. [Fr.]

escarole *es-ka-rōl, -rŏl, n.* a broad-leaved, non-curly endive. [Fr.]

escarp *is-kärp', v.t.* to make into a scarp or sudden slope. — *n.* a scarp or steep slope: the side of the ditch next the rampart (*fort.*). — *n.* **escarp'ment** the precipitous side of a hill or rock: escarp. [Fr. *escarper*, to cut steeply, from root of **scarp**.]

eschalot. See **shallot**.

eschar *es'kär, n.* a slough or portion of dead or disorganised tissue, esp. an artificial slough produced by caustics. — *adj.* **escharot'ic** tending to form an eschar: caustic. — *n.* a caustic substance. [L., — Gr. *eschara*, a hearth, mark of a burn.]

eschatology *es-kə-tol'ə-ji,* (*theol.*) *n.* the doctrine of the last or final things, as death, judgment, the state after death. — *adjs.* **eschatolog'ic, -al**. — *n.* **eschatol'ogist**. [Gr. *eschatos*, last, *logos*, a discourse.]

escheat *is-chēt', n.* property that falls to the feudal lord or to the state for want of an heir, or by forfeiture: plunder, gain (*obs.*; *Spens.* **excheat'**). — *v.t.* to confiscate. — *v.i.* to fall to the lord of the manor or the state. — *adj.* **escheat'able**. — *ns.* **escheat'age; escheat'ment; escheat'or** an official who watched over escheats. [O.Fr. *eschete* — *escheoir* (Fr. *échoir*) — L. *ex*, from, *cadĕre*, to fall.]

Escherichia *esh-ə-rik'i-ə, n.* a genus of rod-shaped, gram-negative bacteria of the fam. *Enterobacteriaceae*. — **Escherichia coli** the type species of this genus, occurring naturally in the intestines of vertebrates, and sometimes pathogenic. [T. *Escherich* (d. 1911), Ger. physician.]

eschew *is-chōō', v.t.* to shun: to flee from (*obs.*): to abstain from. [O.Fr. *eschever*; cog. with Ger. *scheuen*, to shun.]

Eschscholtzia *e-sholt'si-ə, n.* a genus of Papaveraceae, including the Californian poppy, a showy garden annual: (without *cap.*) a plant of the genus. [J. F. von *Eschscholtz*, a member of the expedition that discovered the poppy in 1821.]

esclandre *es-klä-dr', n.* notoriety: any unpleasantness. [Fr., — L. *scandalum*.]

escolar *es-kō-lär', n.* an Atlantic and Southern fish of spectacled appearance. [Sp., scholar.]

escopette *es-kō-pet',* (*U.S.*) *n.* a carbine. [Sp. *escopeta*.]

escort *es'kört, n.* a person or persons, ship or ships, etc., accompanying another or others for protection, guidance, or merely courtesy: an armed guard: a police officer accompanying a person under arrest to prevent escape: a man who accompanies a woman on an evening out: a person, usu. of the opposite sex, hired to accompany one to entertainments, etc.: a member of an aircraft, etc., crew whose duty is to look after children travelling alone: attendance. — Also used as *adj.* — *v.t.* **escort'** to attend as escort. — *n.* **escort'age**. — **escort agency** one which provides people to act as hired escorts; **escort carrier** a small aircraft-carrier used for escorting naval convoys or in support of military landings. [Fr. *escorte* — It. *scorta* — *scorgere*, to guide — L. *ex*, out, *corrigĕre*, to set right.]

escot *es-kot'*, (*Shak.*) *v.t.* to pay for, to maintain. [O.Fr. *escoter, escot*, a tax; of Gmc. origin; cf. scot[1], shot[2].]

escribano *ä-skrē-bä'nō*, (Sp.) *n.* a notary: — *pl.* escriba'nos.

escribe *ē-skrīb'*, *v.t.* to describe (e.g. a triangle) so as to touch one side externally, the others (produced) internally. [L. *ē*, out, *scrībere*, write.]

escritoire *es-krē-twär'*, *n.* a writing-desk. — *adj.* escritō'rial (or *-ör*). [Fr. *escritoire* — L.L. *scrīptōrium* — L. *scrībĕre, scrīptum*, to write.]

escroc *es-krō*, (Fr.) *n.* a swindler.

escroll, escrol *es-krōl'*, *n.* an escrow: a scroll (*her.*). — *n.* escrow (*es-krō'*) a deed in the hands of a third party, to take effect when a condition is fulfilled. [A.Fr. *escroele, escroe*; see scroll, scrow.]

escuage *es'kū-ij*, *n.* scutage. [A.Fr.; see scutage.]

escudo *es-kōō'dō*, *n.* the Portuguese unit of currency: a coin representing this: form., a coin or currency unit of various values in other countries: — *pl.* escu'dos. [Port. and Sp., shield.]

Esculapian. See Aesculapian.

esculent *es'kū-lənt*, *adj.* eatable: fit to be used for food by man. — *n.* something that is eatable. [L. *esculentus*, eatable — *esca*, food — *edĕre*, to eat.]

escutcheon *es-kuch'ən*, *n.* a shield on which a coat of arms is represented: a family shield: the part of a vessel's stern bearing her name: a shield-shaped object or ornament, etc., as a shield over a keyhole. — *adj.* escutch'eoned having an escutcheon. — a blot on the escutcheon a stain on one's good name; escutcheon of pretence an escutcheon placed with the arms of an heiress in the centre of her husband's coat. [O.Fr. *escuchon* — L. *scūtum*, a shield.]

-ese *-ēz, suff.* denoting a relationship with a country or region, as in *Japanese, Maltese*, or the literary style, jargon, etc. of a particular group, as in *journalese, officialese*.

esemplastic *es-əm-plas'tik, adj.* unifying. — *n.* esemplasy (*es-em'plə-si*) the unifying power of imagination. [Gr. *es*, into, *hen* (neut.), one, *plastikos*, moulding.]

esile *ā'sil*, (*obs.*). Same as eisel(l).

esker, eskar *esk'ər*, (*geol.*) *n.* a kame, or ridge of gravel and sand laid down by a subglacial stream or one which issues from a retreating glacier. [Ir. *eiscir*, a ridge.]

Eskimo *es'ki-mō*, *n.* and *adj.* one of a people inhabiting arctic America with its islands, Greenland, and the nearest Asiatic coast (the Eskimos themselves prefer to be called *Inuit*): their language: — *pl.* Es'kimo, -s. — Eskimo dog one of a breed of powerful dogs, with a double coat of hair, widely distributed in the Arctic regions, and indispensable for drawing sledges; Eskimo roll (*canoeing*) a complete roll-over under water. [Prob. from an Indian word meaning eaters of raw flesh.]

Esky® *es'ki*, (*Austr.*) *n.* (also without *cap.*) a portable insulated container for keeping drinks, etc. cool. [Prob. from Eskimo.]

esloin, esloyne *es-loin'* (*obs.*). Same as eloin.

esne *ez'ni*, (*hist.*) *n.* a domestic slave in O.E. times. [O.E.]

esnecy *es'nə-si*, (*obs.*) *n.* the eldest daughter's right of first choice in dividing an inheritance. [O.Fr. *ainsneece* (Fr. *aînesse*).]

esophagus. U.S. spelling of oesophagus.

esoteric *es-ō-ter'ik, adj.* inner: secret: mysterious: taught to a select few — opp. to *exoteric* (*philos.*). — *n.pl.* esoter'ica esoteric objects, etc. — *adv.* esoter'ically. — *ns.* esoter'icism (*-i-sizm*), esoterism (*es-ot'ər-izm*) the holding of esoteric opinions; es'otery secret doctrine. — esoteric Buddhism theosophy. [Gr. *esōterikos* — *esōterō*, compar. of *esō, eisō*, within.]

espada *es-pä'dha*, (Sp.) *n.* a sword: a swordfish: a matador.

espadrille *es-pə-dril'*, *n.* a rope-soled shoe. [Fr., — Prov. *espardillo* — *espart*, esparto.]

espagnole (sauce) *es-pan-yol'* (*sōs*), a brown sauce

flavoured with tomatoes and sherry. — Also (Fr.) sauce espagnole (*sōs es-pan-yol*). [Fr., Spanish (sauce).]

espagnolette *es-pan-yō-let'*, *n.* the fastening of a French window. [Fr., dim. of *espagnol*, Spanish.]

espalier *es-pal'yər*, *n.* a lattice-work of wood to train trees on: a fruit-tree trained on stakes: a row of trees so trained (*obs.*). — *v.t.* to train as an espalier. [Fr., — It. *spalliera* a support for the shoulders — *spalla*, a shoulder; cf. epaulet.]

esparto *es-pär'tō*, *n.* a strong grass (*Stipa tenacissima*, and others) grown in Spain, N. Africa, etc., and used for making paper, baskets, cordage, etc.: — *pl.* espar'tos. [Sp., — L. *spartum* — Gr. *sparton*, a kind of rope.]

especial *is-pesh'l, adj.* special: particular: principal: distinguished. — *adv.* espec'ially. — in especial in particular. [O.Fr., — L. *speciālis* — *speciēs*, species.]

esperance *es'pər-əns*, (*Shak.*) *n.* hope. [Fr. *espérance* — L. *spērāre*, to hope.]

Esperanto *es-pər-an'tō*, *n.* an international language devised by Dr Zamenhof, published 1887. — Also *adj.* — *n.* Esperan'tist a speaker of Esperanto. [Inventor's pseudonym, the hoping one.]

espial. See espy.

espiègle *es-pē-eg'l, adj.* roguish, frolicsome: arch. — *n.* espièg'lerie roguishness: frolicsomeness. [Fr., — Ger. *Eulenspiegel*; see owl.]

espionage *es-pyon-äzh', es'pi-ə-nij, es-pī'ə-nij, n.* spying: use of spies. [Fr. *espionner* — *espion*, spy.]

esplanade *es-plə-nād'*, *n.* a level space between a citadel and the first houses of the town: any level space for walking or driving in, esp. by the sea. [Fr., — Sp. *esplanada* — L. *explānāre* — *ex*, out, *plānus*, flat.]

espouse *is-powz', v.t.* to give or take in marriage or betrothal: to take upon oneself or embrace, as a cause. — *ns.* espous'al the act of espousing or betrothing: the taking upon oneself, as a cause: (*pl.*) a contract or mutual promise of marriage: a wedding: a formal betrothal; espous'er. [O.Fr. *espouser* (Fr. *épouser*) — L. *spōnsāre*, to betroth — *spondēre, spōnsum*, to vow.]

espresso *es-pres'ō*, *n.* a form of coffee-making machine giving high extraction under pressure: coffee so made: — *pl.* espress'os. — Also *adj.*, esp. of a type of coffee bar or the coffee. [It., pressed.]

esprit *es-prē*, (Fr.) *n.* wit, liveliness. — esprit de corps (*es-prē də kor*) regard for the honour of the body to which one belongs: loyalty of a member to the whole; esprit de l'escalier (*də-les-kal-yā*; by some, incorrectly, d'escalier) thinking of an apt or witty retort after the opportunity of making it is past: the retort itself; esprit fort (*for*) a free-thinker. [Fr. *esprit*, spirit, *de*, of, *corps*, body, *escalier*, staircase, *fort*, strong.]

esprit follet *es-prē fo-le*, (Fr.) mischievous goblin.

espumoso *es-pōō-mō'sō* (Sp.) *n.* a sparkling wine: — *pl.* -os.

espy *es-pī', v.t.* to watch: to see at a distance: to catch sight of: to observe: to discover unexpectedly: — *pr.p.* espy'ing; *pa.t.* and *pa.p.* espied'; *3rd pers. sing.* espies'. — *n.* espi'al the act of espying: observation. [O.Fr. *espier*; see spy.]

-esque *-esk, suff.* in the style or manner of, similar to, as *Kiplingesque*.

Esquimau *es'ki-mō*, a French spelling of Eskimo: — *pl.* Esquimaux (*es'ki-mōz*).

esquire *es-kwīr'*, sometimes *es', n.* orig. a squire or shield-bearer: an attendant on a knight (*arch.*): a landed proprietor: a title of dignity next below a knight: a gentleman acting as escort: a general title of respect in addressing letters (usu. abbrev. esq.). [O.Fr. *esquier* (Fr. *écuyer*) — L. *scūtārius* — *scūtum*, a shield.]

esquisse *es-kēs*, (Fr.) *n.* a sketch, outline.

ess *es*, see es. — collar of esses a chain of links (also written SS) in the form of the letter S, worn by various dignitaries.

essay *es'ā*, *n.* an attempt: a tentative effort: a first draft (*arch.*): a trial (*arch.*): an experiment (*arch.*): a written composition less elaborate than a treatise. — *v.t.* **essay'** to try: to attempt: to make experiment of (*arch.*): — *pr.p.* **essay'ing;** *pa.t.* and *pa.p.* **essayed'.** — *ns.* **essay'er; ess'ayist** one who essays: a writer of essays; **essayette'** a little essay. — *adjs.* **ess'ayish; essayis'tic.** [O.Fr. *essai* — L. *exagium,* weighing — *exagĕre,* to try, examine.]

esse *es'i, n.* actual existence: essence. — **in esse** in existence, opposed to *in posse,* in potentiality. [L. *esse,* to be.]

essence *es'ǝns, n.* the inner distinctive nature of anything: the qualities which make any object what it is: a being: an alcoholic solution of a volatile or essential oil: a perfume of such composition: the extracted virtues of any drug: a liquid having the properties of the substance from which it is got: (also **Essen'cia**) a particularly fine variety of Tokay wine. — *adj.* **essential** (*is-, es-en'shl*) relating to, constituting, or containing the essence: necessary to the existence of a thing: indispensable or important in the highest degree: highly rectified: pure: of e.g. disease, having no known cause. — *n.* something necessary: a leading principle. — *ns.* **essen'tialism** an educational theory that concentrates on teaching basic skills: a philosophical doctrine that distinguishes between the essence of material objects and their existence or appearance; **essen'tialist; essentiality** (*is-en-shi-al'i-ti*) the quality of being essential; an essential quality or element. — *adv.* **essen'tially.** — *n.* **essen'tialness.** — **essential minerals** those whose presence is considered necessary to entitle a rock to the name it bears — opp. to *accessory* minerals; **essential oils** oils forming the odorous principles of plants, also called *ethereal oils, volatile oils;* **essential organs** (*bot.*) stamens and carpels. — **in essence** basically, fundamentally; **of the essence** of the utmost importance. [Fr., — L. *essentia* — *essēns, -entis,* assumed pr.p. of *esse,* to be.]

Essene *es-ēn', es'ēn, n.* one of a small religious fraternity among the ancient Jews leading retired ascetic lives and holding property in common. — *n.* **Ess'enism.** [Gr. *essēnos;* origin doubtful.]

essive *es'iv,* (*gram.*) *adj.* denoting a state of being. — *n.* the essive case. [Finn. *essivi* — L. *esse,* to be.]

essoin, essoyne *es-oin', n.* an excuse for not appearing in court (*law*): an excuse (*Spens.*). — *n.* **essoin'er.** [O.Fr. *essoine* (Fr. *exoine*), *es* — L. *ex,* out of, *soin,* care.]

essonite *es'ǝn-īt,* **hessonite** *hes'ǝn-īt, n.* cinnamon-stone. [Gr. *hēssōn,* inferior (i.e. in hardness, to hyacinth which it resembles).]

-est *-ǝst, suff.* marks the superlative degree of adjectives (long*est*) and some adverbs (fast*est*). [O.E. *-est, -ost.*]

establish *is-, es-tab'lish, v.t.* to settle or fix: to set up: to place in fixed position, possession, or power: to make good: to confirm (*arch.*): to prove: to ordain: to found: to set up in business: to institute by law as the recognised state church, and to recognise officially. — *adj.* **estab'lished** fixed: ratified: instituted by law and backed by the state. — *ns.* **estab'lisher; estab'lishment** the act of establishing: a fixed state: that which is established: a permanent civil or military force: permanent staff: one's residence, household, and style of living: a business: a settlement: the church established by law: (with *cap.; derog.*) the class in a community, or in a field of activity, who hold power, usu. because they are linked socially, and who are usu. considered to have conservative opinions and conventional values. — *adj.* pertaining to an establishment or the Establishment. — *adj.* **establishmentär'ian** maintaining the principle of church establishment: favouring or upholding the Establishment. — Also *n.* [O.Fr. *establir,* pr.p. *establissant* — L. *stabilīre* — *stabilis,* firm — *stāre,* to stand.]

estacade *es-tǝ-kād', n.* a dike of piles in a morass, river, etc., against an enemy. [Fr., — Sp. *estacada.*]

estafette *es-tǝ-fet', n.* a military courier or express. [Fr., — It. *staffetta* — *staffa,* stirrup; cf. O.H.G. *stapho,* a step.]

estaminet *es-tam'ē-nā, n.* a small bar or café. [Fr.]

estancia *es-tän'syǝ, n.* a Spanish-American cattle-estate. — *n.* **estanciero** (*-syā'rō*) a farmer: — *pl.* **estancie'ros.** [Sp., station — L. *stāre,* to stand.]

estate *is-, es-tāt', n.* state (*arch.*): rank: worldly condition: total possessions: property, esp. landed: a landed property, esp. of some size: a piece of land built over either privately or by a local authority, with dwellinghouses (**housing estate**) or factories (**trading** or **industrial estate**): a piece of land given over to the cultivation of a particular crop: an order or class of men in the body politic: a chair or canopy of state, or a dais (*obs.*): an estate car (see below). — *v.t.* to give an estate to (*arch.*): to bestow upon (*arch.*). — **estate agent** the manager of landed property: an intermediary in the sale of landed property. — *adj.* **estate'-bott'led** of wine, bottled on the estate where it has been made. — **estate car** a car designed to carry passengers and goods, usu. with a large area behind the seats for luggage, etc., and a rear door; **estate duty** death duty; **estates'man** (*N. of England*) a statesman. — **man's estate** the state of manhood; **personal estate** see **person; real estate** see **real[1]; the estates of the realm** are three — Lords Spiritual, Lords Temporal, and Commons: often misused for the legislature — king, lords, and commons. — The ancient parliament of Scotland consisted of the king and the **three estates** — viz.: (1) archbishops, bishops, abbots, and mitred priors; (2) the barons and the commissioners of shires and stewartries; (3) the commissioners from the royal burghs; — in France, the nobles, clergy, and **third estate** (*tiers état*) remained separate down to 1780; **the fourth estate** (*coll.*) the press. [O.Fr. *estat* (Fr. *état*) — L. *status,* a state.]

esteem *is-, es-tēm', v.t.* to set a high estimate or value on: to regard with respect or friendship: to consider or think. — *n.* high estimation or value: favourable regard: estimation of worth. — *adjs.* **esteemed'** respected: in commercial correspondence, a colourless complimentary word; **es'timable** that can be estimated or valued: worthy of esteem: deserving our good opinion. — *adv.* **es'timably.** — *v.t.* **estimate** (*es'ti-māt*) to judge of the worth of: to ascertain how much is present of: to calculate. — *n.* (*-mit*) reputation (*Shak.*): a valuing in the mind: judgment or opinion of the worth or size of anything: a rough calculation: a preliminary statement of the probable cost of a proposed undertaking: estimation. — *n.* **estimā'tion** an act of estimating: a reckoning of value: esteem, honour: importance (*arch.*): conjecture. — *adj.* **es'timātive.** — *n.* **es'timātor.** — **hold in estimation** to esteem highly; **the estimates** accounts laid before parliament, etc., showing the probable expenditure for the year. [Fr. *estimer* — L. *aestimāre.*]

ester *es'tǝr, n.* a compound formed by the condensation of an alcohol and an acid, with elimination of water. — *n.* **esterificā'tion** (*-ter-*). — *v.t.* **ester'ify** (or *es'*). [Named by Leopold Gmelin (1788–1853), prob. — E*ss*ig, vinegar, Ä*th*er, ether.]

Esth. See **Est(h)onian.**

esthesia, esthesiogen, etc. U.S. spellings of **aesthesia,** etc.

Est(h)onian *es-t(h)ō'ni-ǝn, adj.* pertaining to *Est(h)onia,* a Baltic republic, till 1918 a province of Russia, incorporated in 1940 as a republic of the U.S.S.R. — *n.* a native or citizen thereof: its language. — *n.* **Esth** an Esthonian of the original Finnish stock.

estimate, estimation. See **esteem.**

estipulate. See **exstipulate.**

estival, etc. U.S. spelling of **aestival,** etc.

estoc *es-tok', n.* a short sword. [Fr.]

estoile *es-twäl',* (*her.*) *n.* a star with wavy points. [O.Fr. *estoile* (Fr. *étoile*), a star.]

Estonian. See **Est(h)onian.**

estop *es-top', v.t.* to stop or bar (*arch.*): to hinder, preclude (*law*): — *pr.p.* **estopp'ing;** *pa.t.* and *pa.p.* **estopped'.** — *ns.* **estopp'age** the state of being estopped; **estopp'el** a conclusive admission, which cannot be denied by the party whom it affects. [O.Fr. *estoper* — *estoupe* —

L. *stuppa*, flax; see **stop, stuff.**]

estover *es-tō'vər, n.* a right to necessaries allowed by law, as wood to a tenant for necessary repairs, etc. — **common of estovers** the right of taking necessary wood from another's estate for household use and the making of implements of industry. [O.Fr. *estover*, to be necessary, necessaries.]

estrade *es-träd', n.* a low platform. [Fr., — Sp. *estrado.*]

estramazone. Same as **stramazon.**

estrange *is-trānj', v.t.* to cut off, remove: to alienate, esp. from friendship: to divert from original use or possessor. — *adj.* **estranged'** alienated: disaffected. — *ns.* **estrang'edness; estrange'ment; estrang'er.** [O.Fr. *estranger* (Fr. *étranger*) — L. *extrāneāre* — *extrāneus*; see **strange.**]

estrang(h)elo *es-trang'gə-lō, n.* a cursive form of the old Syriac alphabet. — Also *adj.* [Syriac, perh. — Gr. *strongylos*, round.]

estrapade *es-tra-pād', n.* a horse's attempt to throw its rider. [Fr.]

estray *es-strā', n.* a beast found within a manor or lordship, wandering from its owner. — *v.i.* to stray. [See **astray.**]

estreat *es-trēt', (law) n.* a true extract, copy, or note of some original writing or record, esp. of fines and amercements to be levied by bailiffs or other officers. — *v.t.* to extract from the records of a court, as a forfeited recognisance: to levy, exact. [O.Fr. *estraite* — L. *extrahĕre* — *ex*, from, *trahĕre* to draw; see **extract.**]

estrepe *es'trēp, (law) v.t.* to commit waste (as a tenant) on lands, e.g. cutting down trees, etc. — *n.* **estrepe'ment.** [M.Fr. *estreper* — L. *exstirpāre*, to root out.]

estrich *es'trich,* **estridge** *es'trij, (obs.) ns.* the ostrich.

Estrildidae *e-stril'di-dē,* a family of oscinine birds, the weaver-finches. — *adj.* and *n.* **estril'did.** [From *astrilda,* specific name of a particular species in Linnaeus's classification.]

estro *es'trō,* (It.) *n.* enthusiasm, height of poetic inspiration.

estrogen, estrum, etc. U.S. spellings of **oestrogen, oestrum,** etc.

estuary *es'tū-ər-i, n.* the wide lower tidal part of a river. — *adjs.* **estūarial** (*-ā'ri-əl*); **estūa'rian; es'tūarine** (*-ə-rīn*). [L. *aestuārium* — *aestus*, burning, boiling, commotion, tide.]

esurient *es-ū'ri-ənt, adj.* hungry: rapacious. — *n.* **esū'rience, esū'riency** greedy hunger: needy rapacity. [L. *ēsuriēns, -entis,* pr.p. of *ēsurīre,* to be hungry — desiderative of *edĕre,* to eat.]

eta[1] *ē'tə, ā'tə, n.* the seventh letter of the Greek alphabet, long e (H, η): as a numeral η' = 8, ͵η = 8000. — *n.* **etacism** (*ā'tə-sizm*) pronunciation of eta as close e (in this dictionary represented in the respelling as *ā*) — opposed to *itacism.* [Gr. *ēta.*]

eta[2] *ā'tə, n.* (also with *cap.*) esp. form., a member of the lowest Japanese class, which did work considered menial or degrading. [Jap.]

etaerio *et-ē'ri-ō, (bot.) n.* an aggregated fruit, a group of achenes or drupels. — *pl.* **etae'rios.** [Fr. *étairion* — Gr. *hetaireiā,* association.]

étage *ā-täzh,* (Fr.) *n.* a floor, storey (**bel étage** (q.v.) is not a French usage).

étagère *ā-ta-zher,* (Fr.) *n.* an ornamental stand of shelves for bric-à-brac, etc.

étalage *ā-ta-läzh,* (Fr.) *n.* a display, esp. of goods in a shop window.

et alia (alii) *et ā'li-ə, a'li-a (ā'li-ī, a'li-ē),* (L.) and other things (people); abbrev. **et al.**

etalon *āt'əl-on, n.* an interferometer consisting of an air film enclosed between half-silvered plane-parallel glass or quartz plates. [Fr., — M.Fr. *estalon,* standard of weights and measures — O.Fr. *estal,* place.]

étape *ā-tap,* (Fr.) *n.* a storehouse: a halting-place: a day's march: rations: forage.

état *ā-ta,* (Fr.) *n.* state, rank. — *n.* **étatisme** (*ā-ta-tēzm'*) extreme state control over the individual citizen. —

adj. and *n.* **étatiste** (*-tēst*). — **état-major** (*ma-zhor*) the staff of an army, regiment, etc.

États-Généraux *ā-ta zhā-nā-rō,* (Fr.) *n.pl.* the States-General.

et cetera *et set'ər-ə,* usually written **etc.** or **&c.,** a Latin phrase meaning 'and the rest': and so on. — *n.* something in addition, which can easily be understood.

etch *ech, v.t.* and *v.i.* to design on metal, glass, etc. by eating out the lines with an acid: to eat away, corrode. — *ns.* **etch'ant** an acid or corrosive used in etching; **etch'er** one who etches; **etch'ing** the act or art of etching or engraving: the impression from an etched plate. — **etching ground** the coating of wax or varnish on a plate prepared for etching; **etching needle** a fine-pointed steel instrument used in etching. [Ger. *ätzen,* to corrode by acid; from same root as Ger. *essen;* see **eat.**]

eten, ettin *et'ən, (arch.) n.* a giant. [O.E. *eten, eoten;* O.N. *jötunn.*]

etepimeletic *et-ep-i-mel-et'ik, (animal behaviour) adj.* of a type of social behaviour shown by young animals to elicit epimeletic behaviour.

eternal *i-, ē-tûr'nl, adj.* without beginning or end of existence: everlasting: ceaseless: unchangeable: seemingly endless, occurring again and again (*coll.*). — (*arch.*) **eterne'.** — *vs.t.* **eter'nalise, -ize, eter'nise, -ize** (or *ē'tər-nīz*) to make eternal: to immortalise with fame. — *n.* **eter'nalist** one who thinks that matter has existed from eternity. — *adv.* **eter'nally.** — *n.* **eter'nity** eternal duration: the state or time after death. — **eternal triangle** a sexual relationship, full of tension and conflict, between two men and a woman or two women and a man; **eternity ring** a ring set all round with stones, emblematic of everlasting continuity. — **The Eternal** an appellation of God; **the Eternal City** Rome; **the eternal feminine** the spiritualising and purifying influence of women in social and literary matters (see **das Ewig-Weibliche** in Quotations from Foreign Languages); **the eternities** the eternal reality or truth. [Fr. *éternel* — L. *aeternus* — *aevum,* an age.]

etesian *e-tē'zh(y)ən, -zyən, adj.* periodical: blowing at stated seasons, as certain winds, esp. the north-west winds of summer in the Aegean. [L. *etēsius* — Gr. *etēsios,* annual — *etos,* a year.]

eth, edh *edh, n.* a letter (Ð ð), a barred D, used in Old English, without distinction from thorn, for voiced or voiceless th, in Icelandic and by phoneticians set apart for the voiced sound, thorn standing for the voiceless.

ethal *ē'thal.* Same as **cetyl alcohol.**

ethambutol *eth-am'bū-tol, n.* a drug used in the treatment of tuberculosis. [*ethylene, amine, butanol.*]

ethane *eth'ān, ēth', n.* a colourless, odourless hydrocarbon ($H_3C \cdot CH_3$) of the methane series. — *n.* **eth'anol** ethyl alcohol. — *n.pl.* **ethanol'amines** derivatives of ethanol used in detergents and cosmetics. [**ether.**]

ethe. See **eath.**

ethene. See under **ethyl.**

Etheostoma *e-thi-os'to-mə, n.* a genus of small American freshwater fishes akin to perch. — *adj.* **etheos'tomine.** [Gr. *ētheein,* to sift, *stoma,* mouth.]

ether *ē'thər, n.* the clear, upper air: a medium, not matter, assumed in 19th cent. to fill all space and transmit electromagnetic waves — (in these senses also **aether**): (specif. **ethyl ether** or **diethyl ether**) a colourless, transparent, volatile liquid ($C_2H_5 \cdot O \cdot C_2H_5$) of fragrant odour and a fiery, passing to a cooling, taste, used as a solvent, an anaesthetic, and in the preparation of explosives: extended to the class of compounds in which two alkyl groups are united with an oxygen atom. — *adj.* **ethe'real, ethe'rial** consisting of ether: heavenly: airy: spirit-like. — *n.* **ethērealisā'tion, -z-.** — *v.t.* **ethe'realise, -ize** to convert into ether, or the fluid ether: to render spirit-like. — *n.* **ethereal'ity.** — *adv.* **ethe'really.** — *adjs.* **ethe'reous** (*Milt.*), **etheric** (*ē-ther'ik*), **-al** ethereal. — *ns.* **etherificā'tion** (*-ther-*); **ethe'rion** a very light gas once supposed to exist in air; **ethērisā'tion, -z-.** — *v.t.* **e'thērise, -ize** to convert into ether: to stupefy with ether. — *ns.* **e′thĕrism** the condition induced by using ether: addiction to the taking of ether; **e′thĕrist** one who takes or who administers ether; **ethĕromā′nia** addiction to the taking of ether; **etheromā′niac.** — **ethereal oils** essential oils. [L. *aethēr* — Gr. *aithēr*, the heavens — *aithein*, to light up.]

ethercap. See **ettercap.**

ethic *eth′ik*, (now *rare*) *adj.* ethical. — *n.* (more commonly *n.sing.* **eth′ics**) the science of morals, that branch of philosophy which is concerned with human character and conduct: a system of morals, rules of behaviour: a treatise on morals. — *adj.* **eth′ical** relating to morals, the science of ethics, professional standards of conduct: relating to, or in accord with, approved moral behaviour: denoting a proprietary pharmaceutical not advertised to the general public (also *n.*).. — *ns.* **ethical′ity, ethicalness.** — *adj.* **eth′ically.** — *v.t.* **eth′icise, -ize** (*-sīz*) to make ethical: to treat as ethical. — *ns.* **eth′icism** the tendency to moralise or ethicise: great interest in ethics or passion for ethical ideals; **eth′icist** one versed in ethics: one who detaches ethics from religion. — **eth′ico-** in composition, ethical or of ethics. — **ethical,** or **ethic, dative** a dative implying an indirect interest in the matter, used to give a livelier tone to the sentence (e.g. *He could swear me as fluently as any bargee*); **ethical genitive** a genitive implying interest (e.g. *talking as usual about his Roman heating system*; see **your**); **situation ethics** ethics based on the proposition that no conduct is good or bad in itself and that one must determine what is right or wrong in each situation as it arises. [Gr. *ēthikos* — *ēthos*, custom, character.]

Ethiopian *ē-thi-ō′pi-ən, adj.* pertaining to Ethiopia or its natives: pertaining to the countries south of Egypt inhabited by Negro races: Negro (*arch.*). — *n.* a native of Ethiopia: a Negro (*arch.*). — *n.* (*arch.*) **Ē′thiop** (*-op*). — *adj.* **Ethiŏp′ic** belonging to Ethiopia, to the Ethiopian church, or to a group of Semitic languages including Ge′ez, Amharic, Tigre. — *n.* the Ge′ez language. — *n.* **ē′thiŏps** in old chemistry, a name given to various, dull, dingy, or black compounds. — Also **Aethiopian,** etc. — **Ethiopian pepper** see **Negro pepper** under **pepper; Ethiopian region** a biological region consisting of Africa and Arabia south of the Tropic of Cancer. [Gr. *Aithiops* — *aithein*, to burn, *ops, ōps*, face.]

ethmoid *eth′moid, adj.* like a sieve. — *adj.* **ethmoid′al.** — **ethmoid bone** one of the bones forming the anterior part of the brain-case. [Gr. *ēthmos*, a sieve, and *eidos*, form.]

ethnic, -al *eth′nik, -əl, adjs.* concerning nations or races: pertaining to gentiles or the heathen: pertaining to the customs, dress, food, etc. of a particular racial group or cult: belonging or pertaining to a particular racial group: foreign: exotic: between or involving different racial groups. — *ns.* **eth′narch** (*-närk;* Gr. *archos,* leader) a ruler or governor of a people; **eth′narchy; eth′nic** a gentile, a heathen (*obs.*): a member of a racial or cultural minority group. — *adv.* **eth′nically.** — *ns.* **eth′nicism** (*-sizm*) (*obs.*) heathenism: gentile religion; **ethni′city** (*-si-ti*). — *adj.* **ethnobotan′ical.** — *ns.* **ethnobot′anist; ethnobot′any** (the study of) traditional plant-lore, plant classification, plant use, etc. — *adj.* **ethnocen′tric.** — *adv.* **ethnocen′trically.** — *ns.* **ethnocen′trism** belief in the superiority of one's own cultural group or society and corresponding dislike or misunderstanding of other such groups; **eth′nocide** (*-sīd;* L. *caedēre*, to kill) the extermination of a racial or cultural group; **ethnog′rapher.** — *adjs.* **ethnograph′ic, -al** pertaining to ethnography: of objects useful in the study of ethnography. — *n.pl.* **ethnograph′ica** (a collection of) ethnographic objects: (*loosely*) exotica. — *ns.* **ethnog′raphy** the scientific description of the races of the earth; **eth′nolinguist.** — *adj.* **ethnolinguist′ic.** — *n.sing.* **ethnolinguist′ics** the study of the relationship between language and cultural behaviour. — *adj.* **ethnolog′ical.** — *adv.* **ethnolog′ically.** — *ns.* **ethnol′ogist; ethnol′ogy** the science that treats of the varieties of the human race: cultural anthropology; **ethnomusicol′ogist** one who makes a study of the music and/or musical instruments of primitive peoples in relation to their cultures; **ethnomusicol′ogy.** [Gr. *ethnos,* a nation.]

et hoc (or **id**) **genus omne** *et hok* (*id*) *jē′nəs om′nē, gen′ŏŏs om′ne,* (L.) and all that sort of thing.

ethos *ē′thos, n.* the distinctive habitual character and disposition of an individual, group, race, etc.: moral significance. — *adjs.* **etholog′ic, -al.** — *ns.* **ethol′ogist; ethol′ogy** the science of character: bionomics: the scientific study of the function and evolution of animal behaviour patterns. [Gr. *ēthos,* custom, character.]

ethyl *eth′il, ēth′īl, n.* the base (C_2H_5) of common alcohol, ether, etc.: (with *cap.* in U.S. trademark) an anti-knock compound containing lead tetraethyl $Pb(C_2H_5)_4$: petrol using the compound. — *n.* **eth′ylamine** (*-ə-mīn*) a substance ($NH_2C_2H_5$) resembling ammonia, with one atom of hydrogen replaced by ethyl. — *v.t.* **eth′ylate** to introduce an ethyl group into (a molecule). — *n.* **eth′ylene** (also **eth′ene**) olefiant gas, heavy carburetted hydrogen (C_2H_4). — **ethyl alcohol** ordinary alcohol; **ethylene glycol** a thick liquid alcohol used as an antifreeze. [**ether,** and Gr. *hȳlē,* matter.]

ethyne *eth′īn, ēth′, n.* acetylene.

etiolate *ē′ti-o-lāt, v.t.* to cause to grow pale with long whitish internodes and small yellow leaves for want of light, to blanch (*bot.*): to make pale. — *v.i.* to become pale. — *adj.* **etiolat′ed.** — *ns.* **etiolā′tion; e′tiolin** a yellow pigment found in etiolated plants. [Fr. *étioler* to become pale, to grow into stubble, *éteule,* stubble — L. *stipula,* a stalk, straw.]

etiology. U.S. spelling of **aetiology.**

etiquette *et′i-ket,* or *-ket′, n.* forms of ceremony or decorum: ceremony: the conventional laws of courtesy observed between members of the same profession, players, etc. [Fr. *étiquette;* see **ticket.**]

etna *et′nə, n.* a vessel for heating liquids in a saucer of burning alcohol. — *adjs.* **Aetne′an, Etne′an** of, pertaining to, resembling, or characteristic of, the volcano Etna. [L. *Aetna* — Gr. *Aitnē.*]

étoile *ā-twal,* (Fr.) *n.* a star: a star-shaped object.

Eton *ē′tn, n.* a town opposite Windsor with an old public school: (in *pl.*) an Eton suit. — *n.* **Etonian** (*ē-tōn′i-ən*) one educated at *Eton* College. — Also *adj.* — **Eton collar** a boy's broad starched turned-down collar: a like-shaped collar to a woman's jumper, etc.; **Eton crop** a fashion of cutting ladies' hair short and sleeking it; **Eton jacket** a boy's black dress-coat, untailed; **Eton suit** an Eton jacket with waistcoat and trousers in keeping.

étourdi, *fem.* **étourdie** *ā-tŏŏr-dē,* (Fr.) *adj.* thoughtless, foolish, light-minded. — *n.* **étourderie** (*ā-tŏŏr-drē*) heedlessness, stupid blundering.

étranger, *fem.* **étrangère,** *ā-trä-zhā, -zher,* (Fr.) *adj.* foreign. — *n.* a foreigner.

étrenne (*usu. in pl.* **étrennes**) *ā-tren,* (Fr.) *n.* New Year's gift.

étrier *ā-trē-yā′, n.* a small rope ladder of 1–4 rungs used as a climbing aid by mountaineers. [Fr., stirrup.]

Etruria *i-trŏŏ′ri-ə, n.* an ancient state of Italy north of the Tiber: part of Hanley, Stoke-on-Trent, where Josiah Wedgwood made *Etruria* ware. — *n. and adj.* **Etru′rian.** — *adj.* **Etruscan** (*i-trus′kən*) Etrurian. — *n.* a native of Etruria: the language of the Etruscans, of undetermined affinities. — *ns.* **Etruscol′ogist; Etruscol′ogy.** [L. *Etrūria, Etrūscus.*]

et sequens *et sē′kwənz, se-kwäns′,* (L.) and that which follows; **et sequentes** (*si-kwen′tēz, se-kwen′tās*), *neut.* **et sequentia** (*si-kwen′shi-ə, se-kwen′ti-a*), and those that follow.

et sic de ceteris *et sik dē set′ə-ris, et sēk dā kā′te-rēs,* (L.L.) and so about the rest.

et sic de similibus *et sik dē si-mil′i-bəs, et sēk dā si-mil′i-bŏŏs,* (L.) and so of the like.

ettercap *et'ər-kap*, **ethercap** *edh'ər-kap*, *ns.* Scots forms of **attercop.**

ettin. See **eten.**

ettle *et'l*, (*Scot.*) *v.t.* to purpose, intend: to aim: to aspire. — *n.* purpose, intent. [O.N. *ætla*, to think.]

étude *ā-tüd'*, (*mus.*) *n.* a composition intended either to train or to test the player's technical skill. [Fr., study.]

étui, etwee *ā-twē'*, *et-wē'*, *ns.* a small case for holding small articles. [Fr. *étui*, a case, sheath.]

etymon *et'i-mon*, *n.* the true origin of a word: an original root: the genuine or literal sense of a word (*rare*): — *pl.* **et'yma, et'ymons.** — *adjs.* **etym'ic; etymolog'ical.** — *adv.* **etymolog'ically.** — *ns.* **etymolog'icon, -cum** an etymological dictionary. — *v.i.* **etymol'ogise, -ize** to inquire into or discuss etymology. — *v.t.* to trace or propound an etymology for. — *ns.* **etymol'ogist; etymol'ogy** the science or investigation of the derivation and original signification of words: an etymon. [Neut. of Gr. *etymos*, true.]

etypic, -al *ē-tip'ik, -əl, adjs.* unconformable to type. [L. *ē*, from, Gr. *typos*, type.]

Eubacteriales *ū-bak-tē-ri-ā'lēz*, *n.pl.* an order of Schizomycetes, nonfilamentous, unbranched bacteria. — *n.* **eubactē'rium** a member of the Eubacteriales: any typical bacterium: — *pl.* **eubactē'ria.** [Gr. *eu*, well, and **bacteria.**]

eucaine, eucain *ū-kā'in, -kā'īn, -kān', n.* a safer substitute for cocaine as a local anaesthetic. [Gr. *eu*, well, and **cocaine.**]

Eucalyptus *ū-kə-lip'təs, n.* a large characteristically Australian genus of the myrtle family, forest trees, some gigantic, and mallee-shrubs, with leathery often glaucous leaves turned edgewise to the sun, many yielding timber, and some oils and gum: (without *cap.*) a tree or shrub of this genus: (without *cap.*) eucalyptus oil: — *pl.* **eucalyp'tuses, eucalyp'tī.** — *ns.* **eu'calypt** a eucalyptus; **eucalyp'tol, eucalyp'tole** cineol, a constituent of the various oils got from eucalyptus leaves. [Latinised from Gr. *eu*, well, *kalyptos*, covered.]

eucaryon, eucaryot(e), -otic. Same as **eukaryon,** etc.

Eucharis *ū'kər-is, ū-kar'is, n.* a genus of S. American bulbous plants with fragrant white flowers: (without *cap.*) a plant of this genus. [Gr., charming — *eu*, well, *charis*, grace.]

Eucharist *ū'kə-rist, n.* the sacrament of the Lord's Supper: the elements of the sacrament. — *adjs.* **Eucharist'ic, -al.** [Gr. *eucharistiā*, thanksgiving — *eu*, well, and *charizesthai*, to show favour — *charis*, grace, thanks.]

euchlorine *ū-klō'rēn, -klör', n.* a very explosive green-coloured gas, a mixture of chlorine with chlorine peroxide. — *adj.* **euchlō'ric.** [Gr. *eu*, well, *chlōros*, green.]

euchologion *ū-ko-lō'ji-on, n.* a formulary of prayers, primarily that of the Greek Church. — Also **euchology** (*-kol'ə-ji*). [Gr. *euchologion* — *euchē*, a prayer, *logos* — *legein*, to speak.]

euchre *ū'kər, n.* an American card game for two, three, or four persons, with the 32, 28, or 24 highest cards of the pack — if a player fails to make three tricks he is *euchred*, and his adversary scores against him. — *v.t.* to score over, as above: to outwit. [Ety. unknown.]

euclase *ū'klās, n.* a hydrated beryllium aluminium silicate occurring in pale-green transparent crystals. [Fr., — Gr. *eu*, well, *klasis*, breaking.]

Euclidean *ū-klid'i-ən, ū-kli-dē'ən, adj.* pertaining to Euclid, a geometrician of Alexandria *c.* 300 B.C., or to space according to his assumptions. — **Euclidean geometry** a geometry based on the postulates of Euclid.

eucrite *ū'krīt, n.* a gabbroitic rock composed of lime-feldspar, pyroxenes, and olivine. — *adj.* **eucritic** (*-krit'-ik*). [Gr. *eu*, well, *kritos*, distinguished.]

eucyclic *ū-sī'klik, (bot.) adj.* having the same number of floral leaves in each whorl. [Gr. *eu*, well, *kyklos*, wheel.]

eudaemonism, eudemonism *ū-dē'mən-izm, n.* a system of ethics that makes happiness the test of rectitude — whether *egoistic*, as Hobbes's, or *altruistic*, as Mill's. — *adj.* **eud(a)emon'ic** conducive to happiness. — *n. sing.* **eud(a)emon'ics.** — *ns.* **eud(a)e'monist; eud(a)e'-mony,** **eud(a)emō'nia** happiness, well-being: in Aristotelian philosophy, a full, active life governed by reason. [Gr. *eudaimoniā*, happiness — *eu*, well, *daimōn*, a spirit.]

eudialyte *ū-dī'ə-līt, n.* a silicate of zirconium, sodium, calcium and iron, occurring in Greenland, easily dissolved by acids. [Gr. *eu*, well, *dialyein*, to dissolve.]

eudiometer *ū-di-om'i-tər, n.* an apparatus for gas analysis, a graduated tube holding the gas over mercury, usually with wires for sparking — early used for testing the air at different times. [Gr. *eudios*, clear, fine (as weather), *metron*, measure.]

euge *ū'jē, interj.* well! well done! [Gr. *euge*.]

Eugenia *ū-jē'ni-ə, n.* the clove genus of the myrtle family. — *n.* **eugenol** (*ū'jin-ol*) the chief constituent of oil of cloves (C₁₀H₁₂O₂) — also **eugenic** (*-jen'*) **acid.** [Named after Prince *Eugene* of Savoy (1663–1736).]

eugenic[1] *ū-jen'ik, adj.* pertaining to race improvement by judicious mating and helping the better stock to prevail. — *adv.* **eugen'ically.** — *n. sing.* **eugen'ics** the science of race improvement. — *ns.* **eu'genism** (*-jin-*); **eu'genist; eugen'ecist, eugen'icist.** [Gr. *eugenēs*, of good stock.]

eugenic[2]. See **eugenol** under **Eugenia.**

eugh, eughen, ewghen. Obs. spellings (*Spens., Shak.*) of **yew, yewen.**

Euglena *ū-glē'nə, n.* a genus of aquatic unicellular organisms of the order **Euglenoidī'na** or (*bot.*) **Euglenā'les,** with a single flagellum and reddish eyespots. [Gr. *eu*, well, *glēnē*, eyeball.]

Eugubine *ū'gū-bin, -bīn, adj.* pertaining to the ancient town of *Eugubium* or *Iguvium* (mod. *Gubbio*), or to its famous seven tablets of bronze, the chief monument of the ancient Umbrian tongue.

euharmonic *ū-här-mon'ik, adj.* in just intonation. [Gr. *eu*, well, *harmoniā*, harmony.]

Euhemerism *ū-hē'mə-rizm, n.* the system which explains mythology as growing out of real history, its deities as merely magnified men. — *v.t.* and *v.i.* **euhē'merise, -ize.** — *n.* and *adj.* **euhē'merist.** — *adj.* **euhemeris'tic.** — *adv.* **euhemeris'tically.** [From *Euhēmerus*, Gr. *Euēmeros*, a 4th-cent. (B.C.) Sicilian philosopher.]

euk, ewk *ūk.* See **yuke.**

eukaryon *ū-kar'i-ən, (biol.) n.* the highly organised cell nucleus, surrounded by a membrane, characteristic of higher organisms (cf. *prokaryon*). — *n.* **eukar'yot(e)** (*-ōt, -ət*) an organism whose cells have such nuclei. — Also *adj.* — *adj.* **eukaryot'ic.** — Also **eucaryon,** etc. [Gr. *eu*, well, *karyon*, kernel.]

eulachon *ū'lə-kən, n.* the North Pacific candle-fish, so oily that it is dried for use as a candle. — Also **oolakan, oulakan, -chon, ulicon, -chon, -kon.** [Chinook jargon, *ulâkân*.]

eulogium *ū-lō'ji-əm,* **eulogy** *ū'lə-ji, ns.* praise: a speech or writing in praise: a funeral oration: — *pls.* **eulō'gia, -iums, eu'logies.** — *v.t.* **eu'logise, -ize** to extol. — *n.* **eu'logist** one who extols another. — *adj.* **eulogist'ic** full of praise. — *adv.* **eulogist'ically.** [L.L. *eulogium* — Gr. *eulogion* (classical *eulogiā*) — *eu*, well, *logos*, a speaking.]

eumelanin *ū-mel'ə-nin, n.* any melanin pigment of darker type. [*eu-*, good, most typical — Gr. *eu*, well.]

Eumenides *ū-men'i-dēz, n.pl.* euphemistic name for the Erinyes or Furies. [Gr. *Eumenidĕs*, gracious ones — *eu*, well, *menos*, disposition.]

eumerism *ū'mər-izm, (biol.) n.* aggregation of similar parts. [Gr. *eu*, well, *meros*, part.]

Eumycetes *ū-mī-sē'tēz, n.pl.* the higher fungi, Ascomycetes and Basidiomycetes. [Gr. *eu*, well, and **mycetes.**]

eunuch *ū'nək, n.* a castrated man, esp. one in charge of a harem, or a high-voiced singer: an ineffectual person, one lacking in some way in force or power (*fig.*). —

v.t. **eun'uchise, -ize** (*lit.* and *fig.*). — *ns.* **eu'nuchism** the condition of being a eunuch; **eu'nuchoidism** a condition in which there is some deficiency of sexual development and in which certain female sex characteristics, e.g. high voice, are often present. — *n.* and *adj.* **eu'nuchoid.** [Gr. *eunouchos* — *eunē,* bed, *echein,* to have (charge of).]

euoi. See **evoe.**

Euonymus *ū-on'i-məs, n.* the spindle-tree and burning bush genus of Celastraceae: (without *cap.*) a plant of this genus. — *n.* **euon'ymin** an extract of bark of burning bush. [Gr. *euōnymos,* spindle-tree.]

euouae. See **evovae.**

eupad *ū'pad, n.* an antiseptic powder containing hypochlorous acid. [*E*dinburgh *U*niversity *P*athology *D*epartment, where it originated.]

eupatrid *ū-pat'rid, n.* a member of the aristocracy in ancient Greek states. [Gr. *eupatridēs* — *eu,* well, *patēr,* father.]

eupepsy *ū-pep'si,* **eupepsia** *-ə, ns.* good digestion — opp. to *dyspepsia.* — *adj.* **eupep'tic** pertaining to good digestion: cheerful (*fig.*). — *n.* **eupepticity** (*-tis'i-ti*). [Gr. *eupepsiā,* digestibility — *eu,* well, *pepsis,* digestion — *peptein,* to digest.]

Euphausia *ū-fö'zi-ə, n.* a genus of shrimplike malacostracan crustaceans of the family **Euphausiidae** (*-ī'i-dē*) order **Euphausiacea** (*-ā'si-ə*) common in plankton. — *n.* **euphausia'cean.** — *adjs.* and *ns.* **euphaus'iid, euphaus'id** (a creature) belonging to the Euphausiidae or to the Euphausiacea. [Gr. *eu,* well, *phainein,* to show; *ousiā,* substance.]

euphemism *ū'fim-izm, n.* a figure of rhetoric by which an unpleasant or offensive thing is designated by a milder term: such a term. — *v.t.* **eu'phemise, -ize** to express by a euphemism. — *v.i.* to use euphemistic terms. — *adj.* **euphemist'ic.** — *adv.* **euphemist'ically.** [Gr. *euphēmismos* — *euphēmizein,* to speak words of good omen — *eu,* well, *phanai,* to speak.]

euphenics *ū-fen'iks, n. sing.* the science concerned with the physical improvement of human beings by modifying their development after birth (cf. *eugenics*). [By analogy, from *eugenics* and *phenotype* (Gr. *eu,* well, *phainein,* to show).]

euphobia *ū-fō'bi-ə, n.* a fear of good news. [Gr. *eu,* well, *phobos,* fear.]

euphony *ū'fə-ni, n.* an agreeable sound: a pleasing, easy pronunciation — also (*obs.*) **euphonia** (*-fō'*). — *n.* **eu'phon** a form of glass harmonica invented by Chladni in 1790. — *adjs.* **euphonic** (*-fon'*), **-al, euphō'nious** agreeable in sound. — *adv.* **euphō'niously.** — *v.t.* **eu'phonise, -ize** to make euphonious. — *n.* **euphō'nium** the bass saxhorn; the euphon. [Gr. *euphōniā* — *eu,* well, *phōnē,* sound.]

Euphorbia *ū-för'bi-ə, n.* the spurge genus of plants, giving name to the **Euphorbiā'ceae,** an isolated family of archichlamydeous dicotyledons: (without *cap.*) a plant of this genus. — *adj.* **euphorbiā'ceous.** — *n.* **euphor'bium** a gum resin got from some spurges. [*Euphorbos,* Greek physician to Juba, king of Mauritania.]

euphoria *ū-fō'ri-ə, fō',* **euphory** *ū'fə-ri, ns.* an exaggerated feeling of well-being, esp. irrational or groundless. — *adj.* **euphor'iant** inducing euphoria. — *n.* a drug which does this. — *adj.* **euphoric** (*-for'*). [Gr. *euphōriā.*]

euphrasy *ū'frə-si, -zi,* (*bot.*) *n.* eyebright (*Euphrasia*) once thought good for disorders of the eyes. [Gr. *euphrāsiā,* delight — *euphrainein,* to cheer — *eu,* well, *phrēn,* the mind.]

euphroe *ū'frō,* (*naut.*) *n.* the wooden block through which the lines of a crowfoot are rove. — Also **ū'phroe.** [Du. *juffrouw* — *jong,* young, *vrouw,* woman.]

Euphrosyne *ū-froz'i-nē,* or *-fros', n.* one of the three Charites or Graces. [Gr. *Euphrosynē* — *euphrōn,* cheerful.]

Euphuism *ū'fū-izm, n.* the affected and bombastic literary style brought into vogue by John Lyly's romance *Euphues* (1579–80): (without *cap.*) a high-flown expression in this style. — *v.i.* **eu'phuise, -ize.** — *n.*

eu'phuist. — *adj.* **euphuist'ic.** — *adv.* **euphuist'ically.** [Gr. *euphyēs,* graceful, goodly.]

Eur(o)- *ū'r(ō)-,* in composition, European (and): of or pertaining to the European Common Market: of or pertaining to Europe. — *adj.* **Euraf'rican** pertaining to Europe and Africa, or Europe and North Africa, jointly: of a human race common to Europe and North Africa, the Mediterranean race: of mixed European and African parentage or descent. — *n.* a person of Eurafrican race in either sense. — *adj.* **Eurā'sian** of mixed European and Asian parentage or descent: of, or pertaining to, Europe and Asia (*Eurasia*) taken as one continent. — *n.* a person of mixed European and Asian parentage. — *ns.* **Eurat'om** the European Atomic Energy Community (1958), an association for joint peaceful development of nuclear energy; **Eu'ro= Amer'ican; Eu'robond** a borrowing in Eurocurrency by a company from subscribers, which may or may not be marketable and for which the rate and life may be either fixed or variable. — *adj.* **Eurocent'ric** Europocentric. — *ns.* **Eur'ocheque** a special type of cheque drawn on the user's own bank which may be cashed in banks and used for making purchases in any of a number of European, and non-European, countries; **Eurocomm'unism** the theory of communism professed by Communist parties in Western Europe, more pragmatic than the Soviet theory and asserting independence of it; **Eurocomm'unist; Eu'rocrat** an official concerned with the administration of any organisation within the Common Market; **Eurocracy** (*ū-rok'rə-si*). — *adj.* **Eurocrat'ic.** — *ns.* **Eu'rocurrency** the currency of any of the countries of the Common Market; **Eu'ro-doll'ars** U.S. dollars deposited in European banks to facilitate financing of trade; **Eu'romarket, Eu'romart** the European Common Market: one of the West European stock exchanges; **Eu'ro-MP** a member of the European Parliament; **Eu'ronet** an information network linking various European databanks; **Eu'rovision** the European television network.

Euraquilo *ū-rak'wi-lō, n.* See **Euroclydon.**

eureka, rarely **heureka,** (*h*)*ū-rē'kə, interj.* announcing a discovery. — *n.* a brilliant discovery. [Gr. *heurēka,* I have found, perf. tense of *heuriskein,* to find, the cry of Archimedes when he thought of a method of detecting the adulteration of the gold for Hiero's crown.]

eurhythmy, eurythmy *ū-rith'mi,* or *-ridh', n.* rhythmical movement or order: harmony of proportion: (usu. with *cap.*) an artistic, therapeutic and educational system based on rhythmic body movement correlated to poetry, music, etc., created by Rudolf Steiner (1861–1925). — *adj.* **eurhyth'mic.** — *n. sing.* **eurhyth'mics** the art or system of rhythmic movement expounded by E. Jaques-Dalcroze (1865–1950). — *n.* **eurhyth'mist.** [Gr. *eurythmiā* — *eu,* well, *rhythmos,* rhythm.]

euripus *ū-rī'pəs, n.* an arm of the sea with strong currents, spec. that between Euboea and Boeotia: a ditch round the arena in a Roman amphitheatre. [L., — Gr. *eurīpos.*]

euro *ū'rō, n.* a wallaroo: — *pl.* **eu'ros.** [Native name.]

Euro-. See **Eur-.**

Euroclydon *ū-rok'li-don, n.* the tempestuous wind by which St Paul's ship was wrecked (Acts xxvii. 14). [Gr. *Euroklydōn,* as if — *Euros,* east wind, *klydōn,* a wave; supposed to be a wrong reading for *Eurakylōn,* L. *Euraquilō* — *Eurus* (Gr. *Euros*) and *Aquilō,* north wind.]

European *ū-rō-pē'ən, adj.* belonging to Europe. — *n.* a native of Europe: a member of the white race of man characteristic of Europe: a Europeanist. — *v.t.* **europē'anise, -ize** to assimilate to European character or ways: to integrate into the Common Market. — *ns.* **Europē'anism; Europē'anist** one who favours the Common Market and seeks to uphold or develop it. — **European Commission** a body composed of members from all the Common Market countries, which develops and submits policy proposals to the European Parliament; **European (Economic) Community** the (European) Common Market (see **common**); **European Parliament** the legislative assembly of the Common Market; **European plan** (*U.S.*) in hotels, the system of charging for lodgings and service without including meals. — See also **American plan**. [Gr. *Eurōpē*.]

europium *ū-rō'pi-əm, n.* a metal of the rare earths (at. numb. 63; symbol Eu), discovered spectroscopically by Demarçay in 1896. [**Europe**.]

Europocentric *ū-rōp-ō-sent'rik,* **Eurocentric** *ū-rō-sent'rik, adjs.* centred, or concentrating, on Europe or its civilisation. [**Europe** and **centric** (see **centre**).]

Eurus *ū'rəs, n.* the south-east wind. [L., — Gr. *Euros.*]

Eurypharynx *ū-ri-far'ingks, n.* the pelican-fish genus. [Gr. *eurys,* wide, *pharynx,* pharynx.]

Eurypterus *ū-rip'tər-əs, n.* a genus of Eurypterida. — *n.* **euryp'terid** any member of the Eurypterida. — *n.pl.* **Eurypterida** (*-ter'i-də*) a Palaeozoic fossil order of Arachnida, scorpion-like aquatic animals, sometimes over six feet long, with the last (sixth) pair of appendages expanded. — *adj.* **euryp'teroid** like or of the Eurypterida. — *n.* a eurypterid. [Gr. *eurys,* wide, *pteron,* wing.]

eurytherm *ū'ri-thûrm, n.* an organism which tolerates a wide variation in temperature. — *adjs.* **eurytherm'al, -ic, -ous.** [Gr. *eurys,* wide, *therme,* heat.]

eurythmy. Usu. American spelling of **eurhythmy.**

Eusebian *ū-sē'bi-ən, adj.* pertaining to *Eusebius* of Caesarea, father of ecclesiastical history (died 340), or to the Arian *Eusebius* of Nicomedia (died 342).

Euskarian *ūs-kā'ri-ən, adj.* Basque. [Basque *Euskara,* the Basque language.]

eusol *ū'sol, n.* an antiseptic solution got by treating eupad with water. [*E*dinburgh *U*niversity *sol*ution of *l*ime.]

eusporangiate *ū-spor-an'ji-āt, (bot.) adj.* of a group of ferns, having each sporangium derived from a group of cells — opp. to *leptosporangiate.* [Gr. *eu,* well, and **sporangium**.]

Eustachian *ū-stā'ki-ən, adj.* pertaining to the Italian physician Bartolommeo *Eustachio* (died 1574). — **Eustachian tube** the tube leading from the middle ear to the pharynx; **Eustachian valve** the rudimentary valve at the entrance of the inferior vena cava in the heart.

eustacy, eustasy *ū'stə-si, n.* changes in world shoreline level, prob. caused by rise or fall of the sea-level and not by subsidence or elevation of the land. — *adj.* **eustat'ic.** [Gr. *eu,* well, *stasis,* standing, *statikos,* causing to stand.]

eustyle *ū'stīl, adj.* with columns spaced at about two diameters and a quarter. — *n.* a colonnade or building so proportioned. [Gr. *eustylos,* well intercolumniated — *eu,* well, *stylos,* column.]

eutaxy *ū'tak-si, n.* good order. — *n.* **eutax'ite** a volcanic rock with banded structure. — *adj.* **eutaxit'ic** having such a structure. [Gr. *eu,* well, *taxis,* arrangement.]

eutectic, eutectoid. See **eutexia.**

Euterpe *ū-tûr'pē, n.* the Muse of music and lyric poetry: a genus of palms. — *adj.* **Euter'pean** pertaining to Euterpe, or to music. [Gr. *Euterpē* — *eu,* well, *terpein,* to delight.]

eutexia *ū-tek'si-ə, n.* the property of being easily melted. — *n.* **eutec'tic** a mixture in such proportions that the melting-point (or freezing-point) is a minimum, the constituents melting (or freezing) simultaneously. — *adj.* of maximum fusibility: pertaining to a eutectic. — *n.* **eutec'toid** an alloy similar to a eutectic but involving formation of two or three constituents from another solid constituent. — Also *adj.* — **eutectic point** the temperature at which a eutectic melts or freezes. [Gr. *eutēktos,* easily melted — *eu,* well, *tēkein,* to melt.]

euthanasia *ū-thən-ā'zi-ə, n.* an easy mode of death: the act or practice of putting painlessly to death, esp. in cases of incurable suffering. — Also **euthanasy** (*-than'-ə-si*). — *n.* **euthanā'siast** a supporter of, or believer in, euthanasia. [Gr. *euthanasiā* — *eu,* well, *thanatos,* death.]

euthenics *ū-then'iks, n. sing.* the science concerned with the improvement of living conditions. — *n.* **euthen'ist.** [Gr. *euthēneein,* to flourish.]

Eutheria *ū-thē'ri-ə, n.pl.* the placental mammals. — *n.,* *adj.* **euthē'rian.** [Gr. *eu,* well, *thēr,* a beast.]

Euthyneura *ū-thi-nū'rə, n.pl.* a subclass of gasteropods in which the visceral nerve-loop is not twisted. [Gr. *euthys,* straight, *neuron,* nerve.]

eutrapelia *ū-trə-pē'li-ə, (obs.)* **eutrapely** *ū-trap'ə-li, ns.* wit, ease and urbanity of conversation. [Gr. *eutrapelia* — *eutrapelos,* pleasant in conversation.]

eutrophy *ū'trə-fi, n.* healthy nutrition: the state (of a body of water) of being eutrophic. — *adj.* **eutrophic** (*ū-trof'-ik*) pertaining to healthy nutrition: (of a body of water) over-rich in nutrients either naturally or as a result of artificial pollutants, and hence having a too-abundant growth of water-plants and animals. — *n.* **eutrophicā'tion.** [Gr. *eutrophiā.*]

eutropy *ū'trə-pi, n.* regular variation of the crystalline form of a series of compounds with the atomic number of the element. — *adjs.* **eutropic** (*-trop'ik*) according to eutropy: turning sun-wise (*bot.*); **eu'tropous.** [Gr. *eu,* well, *tropos,* a turn.]

Eutychian *ū-tik'i-ən, adj.* of or pertaining to the doctrine of *Eutyches,* a 5th-cent. archimandrite of Constantinople, who held that Christ's human nature was merged in the divine. — *n.* a follower of Eutyches.

euxenite *ūks'ə-nīt, n.* a mineral, niobate and titanate of yttrium, erbium, cerium, and uranium. [Gr. *euxenos,* hospitable, as containing many rare elements.]

evacuate *i-, ē-vak'ū-āt, v.t.* to throw out the contents of: to discharge: to withdraw: to remove, as from a place of danger: to clear out troops, inhabitants, etc., from: to nullify (*law*). — *v.i.* to move away (from a place of danger): to void excrement. — *adj.* and *n.* **evac'uant** purgative. — *n.* **evacuā'tion** an act of evacuating: withdrawal, removal: that which is discharged. — *adj.* **evac'uative.** — *ns.* **evac'uātor; evac'uee** a person removed in an evacuation. [L. *ē,* from, *vacuāre, -ātum,* to empty — *vacuus,* empty.]

evade *i-, ē-vād', v.i.* to escape, slip away (*rare*). — *v.t.* to escape or avoid artfully: to shirk: to baffle, elude. — *adj.* **evā'dable.** [L. *ēvādĕre* — *ē,* from *vādĕre,* to go.]

evagation *ē-, or e-vag-ā'shən, n.* wandering: a digression. [L. *ēvagārī* — *ē,* from, *vagārī,* wander.]

evaginate *i-, ē-vaj'i-nāt, v.t.* to turn outside in: to evert: to remove from a sheath. — *adj.* without a sheath. — *n.* **evaginā'tion.** [L. *ēvāgīnāre, -ātum,* to unsheathe — *ē,* from, *vāgīna,* a sheath.]

evaluate *i-, ē-val'ū-āt, v.t.* to determine the value of. — *n.* **evaluā'tion.** — *adj.* **eval'uative** tending, serving, to evaluate. [Fr. *évaluer.*]

evanescent *ev-ən-es'ənt, adj.* fleeting: vanishing. — *v.i.* **evanesce'** to fade away. — *n.* **evanesc'ence.** — *adv.* **evanesc'ently.** [L. *ēvānēscēns, -entis* — *ē, vānēscĕre,* to vanish — *vānus,* empty.]

evangel *i-van'jəl, n.* good news (*poet.*): gospel: a doctrine set up as a saving principle, esp. in morals or politics. — *ns.* **evangeliar** (*ev-ən-jel'*), **evangelia'rion, evangeliā'rium, evangel'iary** a book of passages from the Gospels to be used at mass or in other services. — *adjs.* **evangelical** (*ev-* or *ēv-ən-jel'ik-əl*), (*arch.*) **evangel'ic** of or pertaining to the Gospel: relating to the four Gospels: according to the doctrine of the Gospel: maintaining the teaching of the Gospel: Protestant: of the school that insists especially on the total depravity of unregenerate human nature, the justification of the sinner by faith alone, the free offer of the Gospel to all, and the plenary inspiration and exclusive authority of the Bible: active and ardent in one's advocacy of some principle or cause. — *ns.* **evangel'ical** one who belongs to the evangelical school; **evangel'icalism.** — *adv.* **evangel'ically.** — *ns.* **evangel'icalness; evangel'icism** (*-sizm*) evangelical principles; **evangelīsā'tion, -z-** (*i-van-jəl-*) the act of proclaiming the Gospel: Christianisation. — *v.t.* **evan'gelise, -ize** to make acquainted with the Gospel: to Christianise. — *v.i.* to preach the

Gospel from place to place: to try to persuade others to support some principle or cause. — *ns.* **evan'gelism** evangelising: evangelicalism; **evan'gelist** one who evangelises: (with *cap.*) an author of a Gospel, especially one of the canonical Gospels: an assistant of the apostles: one who is authorised to preach but who is without a fixed charge: an itinerant preacher: a lay missionary in the Catholic Apostolic Church, a minister of the third grade: an active and ardent advocate of some principle or cause; **evangelis'tary** a book of the Gospels, or of passages from them to be read at divine service: a table of such passages — also **evangelistā'rion.** — *adj.* **evangelis'tic** tending or intended to evangelise. — *n.* **evan'gely** (*obs.*) the Gospel. — **Evangelical Union** see **Morisonian.** [L. *evangelicus* — Gr. *euangelikos* — *eu,* well, *angellein,* to bring news.]

evanish *i-van'ish, v.i.* to vanish: to die away. — *ns.* **evan'ishment; evanition** (*ev-ə-nish'ən*). [O.Fr. *evanir, evaniss-* — L. *ex,* from, *vānus,* empty; cf. **evanesce.**]

evaporate *i-vap'ər-āt, v.i.* to fly off in vapour: to pass into an invisible state: to depart, vanish. — *v.t.* to convert into vapour: to dry by evaporation: to sublimate (a metal) in order to deposit as a film. — *adj.* **evap'orable** able to be evaporated or converted into vapour. — *n.* **evaporā'tion** the act of evaporating or passing off in steam or gas: the process by which a substance changes into the state of vapour. — *adj.* **evap'orative.** — *ns.* **evap'orator; evaporim'eter** an instrument for measuring rate of evaporation; **evap'orite** a sedimentary rock formed by evaporation of salt water; **evap'orograph** a device giving direct or photographic images of objects in darkness by focusing infra-red radiations from them on to an oil-film, which evaporates in proportion to the amount of radiation, leaving an image. — **evaporated milk** milk thickened by evaporation, unsweetened. [L. *ē,* from, *vapōrāre, -ātum* — *vapor,* vapour.]

evapotranspiration *i-vap-ō-tran-spə-rā'shən, n.* the return of water into the atmosphere as vapour, by evaporation (from soil, water bodies, etc.) and transpiration (from plants): the total amount converted by this process. [**evaporate** and **transpiration.**]

evasion *i-vā'zhən, n.* the act of evading or eluding: an attempt to escape the force of an argument or accusation: an excuse. — *adjs.* **evasible** (*i-vā'zi-bl*) capable of being evaded; **evā'sive** (*-siv*) that evades or seeks to evade: elusive: not straightforward: shuffling. — *adv.* **evā'sively.** — *n.* **evā'siveness.** — **take evasive action** to move or act in such a way as to avoid an object or consequence. [L. *ēvādēre, ēvāsum;* see **evade.**]

eve. See **even².**

evection *i-, ē-vek'shən, (astron.) n.* a lunar inequality, the combined effect of the irregularity of the motion of the perigee and alternate increase and decrease of the eccentricity of the moon's orbit. [L. *ēvectiō, -ōnis* — *ē,* from, *vehēre, vectum,* to carry.]

evejar. See under **even².**

even¹ *ēv'n, ēvn, adj.* flat: level: smooth: uniform: in a straight line or plane: straightforward (*Shak.*): balanced: equal: on an equality: exact: divisible by 2 without a remainder: denoted by such a number. — *v.t.* to make even or smooth: to put on an equality: to liken: to equal: to act up to (*Shak.*). — *v.i.* to become even. — *adv.* exactly: nearly: indeed: so much as: still: extreme as the case may be, nevertheless. — *adv.* (also **e'en**) **ev'enly.** — *ns.* **ev'enness; ev'ens** even money. — *adj., adv.* quits. — **even chance** an equal probability (of success or failure, etc.); **ev'en-Chris'tian** (*obs.*) fellow-Christian; **even date** the same date. — *adj.* **ev'en-down** straight-down (of rain): downright, honest. — *adv.* thoroughly. — *adj.* **ev'en-hand'ed** impartial: just. — *n.* **ev'en-hand'edness.** — *adj.* **ev'en-mind'ed** having an even or calm mind: equable; **ev'en-tem'pered** of an equable temperament, calm. — **even money** an equal sum bet on each side. — **be even with** to be revenged on (also **get even with**): to be quits with; **even-even nuclei** nuclei in which there are an even

number of protons and also of neutrons; **even-odd nuclei** nuclei in which there are an even number of protons and an odd number of neutrons; **even now** a very little while ago (*arch.*): after all that has happened; **even on** (*Scot.*) without intermission; **even out** to become even; **even so** nevertheless; **even up on** to requite, come square with; **on an even keel** balanced, not tilting to one side or the other (also *fig.*). [O.E. *efen;* Du. *even,* Ger. *eben.*]

even² *ēv'n, n.* evening (*poet.*): eve (*obs.* or *dial.*) — also **e'en** (*ēn*). — *ns.* **eve** (*ēv*) evening (*poet.*): the night, or the whole day, before a festival: the time just preceding an event; **evening** (*ēv'ning*) the close of the daytime: the decline or end of life: an evening party, gathering or entertainment: an evening newspaper. — *adv.* **eve'nings** (*U.S.*) in the evening. — **eve'jar** (*dial.*) the nightjar; **ev'enfall** early evening, twilight; **evening class** a class held in the evenings, usu. for those who work during the day; **eve'ning-dress** the dress conventionally appropriated to social functions in the evening; **evening primrose** a N. American plant (Oenothera) with pale yellow flowers that open in the evening; **eve'ning-star** a planet, usu. Venus or Mercury, seen in the west setting soon after the sun; **ev'ensong** evening prayer, the Anglican form appointed to be said or sung at evening: the time proper for such; **ev'entide** the time of evening, evening; **eventide home** a home for old people. [O.E. *ǣfen, ǣfnung.*]

événement *ā-ven-mā,* (Fr.) *n.* an event, happening: specif. a political strike or demonstration.

event *i-vent', n.* that which happens: result: any incident or occurrence: contingency: an item in a programme of sports: a horse-riding competition, often over three days (**three-day event**), consisting of three sections — dressage, cross-country riding and show-jumping: fortune or fate (*obs.*): an organised activity at a particular venue, e.g. for sales promotion, fund-raising, etc. — *n.* **event'er** a horse trained to take part in events: the rider of such a horse, as *three-day eventer.* — *adj.* **event'ful** full of events: momentous. — *n.* **event'ing** taking part in riding events. — *adj.* **event'ual** happening as a consequence: final. — *v.i.* **event'ualise, -ize** to come to pass: to come into being. — *n.* **eventual'ity** a contingency: propensity to take notice of events, changes, or facts (*phrenology*). — *adv.* **event'ually** finally: at length. — *v.i.* **event'uate** to turn out. — **event horizon** the boundary of a black hole. — **at all events, in any event** no matter what happens; **in the event** as things turn(ed) out; **in the event of, that** in the case of: if. [L. *ēventus* — *ēvenīre,* to come out, happen — *ē,* from, *venīre,* to come.]

eventration *ē-ven-trā'shən, n.* the act of opening the belly: protrusion of an organ from the abdomen. [Fr. *éventration* — L. *ē,* from, *venter,* belly.]

ever *ev'ər, adv.* always: eternally: at all times: continually: at any time: on record (as *the biggest ever,* the biggest that ever was or happened): in any degree: at all: in the world: very, extremely (*slang,* orig. *U.S.;* used as part of an interjection or statement, as *was I ever hungry,* I was very hungry). — As a suffix, giving complete generality to relative adverbs and pronouns. — *adj.* **ev'ergreen** in leaf throughout the year: always fresh and green: unfading: never failing, retaining one's, or its, vigour, freshness, popularity, interest, etc. for ever. — *n.* a tree or shrub that is green throughout the year. — *adj.* **everlast'ing** endless: perpetual: unceasing: eternal: wearisomely long-continued. — *n.* eternity: a flower (of *Helichrysum, Antennaria,* or other genus) that may be kept for years without much change of appearance: a very durable cloth. — *adv.* **everlast'ingly.** — *n.* **everlast'ingness.** — *adj.* **ev'er-liv'ing** (*Shak.*) immortal: deathless. — *adv.* **evermore'** (or *ev'*) for all time to come (also **for evermore**): ever: unceasingly. — **ever and anon** from time to time; **ever so** to any extent: to a very great extent; **ever such a** (*coll.*) a very; **for ever** to all eternity: for a long time (*coll.*). [O.E. *ǣfre.*]

Everest *ev'ə-rəst, n.* the name of the highest mountain in the world, in the Himalayas: anything difficult to accomplish, the height of ambition (*fig.*). — **Everest pack** a light aluminium frame, carried on the back, with camping equipment strapped to it.

everglade *ev'ər-glād, n.* a large shallow lake or marsh: (with *cap.*; chiefly in *pl.*) such a marsh in southern Florida, enclosing thousands of islets covered with dense thickets. [Perh. **ever,** and **glade.**]

evert *ē-,* or *i-vûrt', v.t.* to turn inside out: to turn outwards. — *adj.* **ever'sible.** — *n.* **ever'sion.** [L. *ēvertĕre* — *ē,* from, *vertĕre, versum,* to turn.]

every *ev'ri, adj.* each of a number: all taken separately. — *prons.* **ev'erybody, ev'eryone** every person. — *adj.* **ev'eryday** of or belonging to every day, daily: common, usual: pertaining to weekdays, not Sunday. — Also *n.* — *ns.* **ev'erydayness; Ev'eryman** the hero of an old morality play, representing mankind, everybody, anybody. — *adv.* **ev'eryplace** (*U.S.*) everywhere. — *pron.* **ev'erything** all things taken singly: all. — *advs.* **ev'eryway** in every way or respect; **ev'erywhen, ev'erywhence, ev'erywhither** (*all rare*); **ev'erywhere** in every place. — **every bit, whit** the whole: quite; **every here and there** all over dispersedly; **every last** every; **every man Jack, every mother's son** every one without exception; **every now and then,** or **again,** at intervals; **every other** every second or alternate; **every so often** at intervals; **every which way** (*U.S.*) every way: in disorder; **have everything** (*coll.*) to be well endowed with possessions, attractiveness, etc. [O.E. *æfre,* ever, and *ælc,* each.]

evet *ev'it, n.* Same as **eft**[1].

evhoe. See **evoe.**

evict *i-, ē-vikt', v.t.* to dispossess by law: to expel. — *ns.* **evic'tion** the act of evicting from house or lands: the dispossession of one person by another having a better title of property in land; **evic'tor.** [L. *ēvictus,* pa.p. of *ēvincĕre,* to overcome.]

evident *ev'i-dənt, adj.* that can be seen: clear to the mind: obvious. — *n.* that which serves as evidence. — *n.* **ev'idence** that which makes evident: means of proving an unknown or disputed fact: support for a belief: indication: information in a law case: testimony: a witness or witnesses collectively. — *v.t.* to render evident: to attest, prove: to indicate. — *adjs.* **evidential** (-*den'shəl*), **eviden'tiary** furnishing evidence: tending to prove. — *advs.* **eviden'tially; ev'idently** visibly (*N.T.*): obviously: manifestly. — **in evidence** received by the court as competent evidence: plainly visible, conspicuous — a hack writer's phrase adopted from the Fr. *en évidence;* **turn King's (Queen's) evidence,** (*U.S.*) **turn State's evidence** to give evidence against an accomplice in a crime. [L. *ēvidēns, -entis* — *ē,* from, *vidēre,* to see.]

evil *ē'v(i)l, adj.* wicked: bad: mischievous: disagreeable: unfortunate. — *adv.* in an evil manner: badly. — *n.* that which produces unhappiness or calamity: harm: wickedness: depravity: sin. — *adv.* **evilly** (*ē'vil-i*) in an evil manner: not well. — *n.* **e'vilness** the state of being evil: wickedness. — **e'vil-doer** one who does evil; **evil eye** a supposed power to cause harm by a look. — *adj.* **e'vil-fā'voured** having a repulsive appearance: ugly. — **e'vil-fā'vouredness** (*B.*) ugliness: deformity. — *adj.* **e'vil-mind'ed** inclined to evil: malicious: wicked. — **e'vil-speak'ing** the speaking of evil: slander. — *adjs.* **e'vil-starred'** (*Tenn.*) born under the influence of an unpropitious star, unfortunate; **e'vil-tem'pered** bad-tempered, unpleasant, spiteful. — **e'vil-work'er** one who works or does evil. — **the evil one** the devil; **speak evil of** to slander. [O.E. *yfel;* Du. *euvel;* Ger. *übel;* cf. **ill.**]

evince *i-vins', v.t.* to overcome, overpower (*arch.*): to prove beyond doubt: to show clearly: to make evident: to give indication of. — *n.* **evince'ment.** — *adj.* **evinc'ible.** — *adv.* **evinc'ibly.** — *adj.* **evinc'ive** tending to evince, prove, or demonstrate. [L. *ēvincĕre,* to vanquish — *ē,* intens., *vincĕre,* to overcome.]

Evipan® *ev'i-pan, n.* the proprietary name of a drug, hexobarbitone sodium, used intravenously and intra-

muscularly as a basic anaesthetic.

evirate *ē'* or *e'vir-āt, v.t.* to castrate: to render weak or unmanly. [L. *ēvirāre* — *ē,* from, *vir,* a man.]

eviscerate *ē-* or *i-vis'ər-āt, v.t.* to tear out the viscera or bowels of: to gut. — *n.* **eviscerā'tion.** [L. *ē,* from, *viscera,* the bowels.]

evite *i-vīt', v.t.* to avoid. — *adj.* **evitable** (*ev'it-ə-bl*). — *v.t.* **ev'itate** (*Shak.*) to avoid. — *n.* **evitā'tion** the act of shunning. [L. *ēvitāre, -ātum* — *ē,* from, *vītāre,* to shun.]

eviternal *ēv-i-tûr'nl, adj.* eternal. — *adv.* **eviter'nally.** — *n.* **eviter'nity.** [L. *aeviternus;* see **eternal.**]

evocation, etc. See **evoke.**

evoe, evhoe, evohe, euoi *ē-vē', ē-vō'i, ū-oi', interjs.* expressing Bacchic frenzy. [L. *eu(h)oe* — Gr. *euoi, eu hoi.*]

evoke *i-vōk', v.t.* to call out: to draw out or bring forth: to call up or awaken in the mind. — *v.t.* **evocate** (*ev'ō-kāt*) to evoke: to call up from the dead. — *n.* **evocā'tion.** — *adjs.* **evocative** (*i-vok'ə-tiv*) **evoc'atory.** — *n.* **evoc'ativeness.** [L. *ēvocāre* — *ē,* from, and *vocāre,* to call.]

évolué *ā-vol-ü-ā', n.* a member of a primitive group of people who has been educated to the standards of a more advanced civilisation. — Also *adj.* [Fr., developed.]

evolution *ēv-, ev-ə-lōō'shən, n.* the act of unrolling or unfolding: the giving off (of heat, etc.): gradual working out or development: a series of things unfolded: the doctrine according to which higher forms of life have gradually arisen out of lower: the extraction of roots (*math.*): (usu. in *pl.*) orderly movements as of a body of troops, flock of birds, etc. — *n.* **ev'olute** (*math.*) an original curve from which another curve (the *involute*) is described by the end of a thread gradually unwound from the former. — *adj.* rolled back. — *v.t.* and *v.i.* to develop by evolution. — *adjs.* **evolu'tional, evolu'tionary** of or pertaining to evolution. — *ns.* **evolu'tionism** the doctrine of evolution; **evolu'tionist** one skilled in evolutions or military movements: one who believes in evolution as a principle in science. — *adj.* **ev'olutive.** [L. *ēvolūtiō, -ōnis,* — *ēvolvĕre;* see **evolve.**]

evolve *i-,* or *ē-volv', v.t.* to unroll: to disclose: to develop: to give off (heat, etc.): to unravel. — *v.i.* to disclose itself: to result. — *adj.* **evolv'able** that can be drawn out. — *n.* **evolve'ment.** — *adj.* **evolv'ent.** [L. *ēvolvĕre* — *ē-,* from, *volvĕre, volūtum,* to roll.]

evovae *i-vō'vē* **euouae** *ū-ōō'ē, (mus.) ns.* names for a Gregorian cadence, got from 'secuLorum (formerly written SECVLORVM) Amen' in the doxology 'Gloria Patri'.

evulgate *ē-,* or *e-vul'gāt, v.t.* to divulge: to publish. [L. *ēvulgāre, -ātum* — *ē,* out, *vulgus,* the people.]

evulse *i-, ē-vuls', v.t.* to pluck out. — *n.* **evul'sion.** [L. *ēvellĕre, ēvulsum* — *ē,* from, *vellĕre, vulsum,* to pluck.]

evzone *ev'zōn, n.* a soldier in an élite Greek infantry regiment. [Mod. Gr. *euzōnos* — Gr., girt for action — *eu,* well, *zōnē,* girdle.]

ewe *ū, n.* a female sheep. — **ewe'-cheese** cheese made from the milk of ewes; **ewe'-lamb** a female lamb: a poor man's one possession, one's dearest possession — used in reference to 2 Sam. xii; **ewe'-milk; ewe'-neck** of horses, a thin hollow neck. — *adj.* **ewe'-necked.** [O.E. *ēowu;* cf. L. *ovis,* Gr. *oïs,* Sans. *avi,* a sheep.]

ewer *ū'ər, n.* a large water jug with a wide spout. [Through Fr. from L. *aquārium* (neut. of *aquārius,* of water) — *aqua,* water.]

ewest *ū'ist, (Scot.) adj.* or *adv.* near. [App. from O.E. *on nēaweste,* in the neighbourhood, wrongly divided as *on ewest.*]

ewftes *ūfts, (Spens.) n.pl.* efts. [See **eft**[1].]

ewghen. An old spelling of **yewen.**

ewhow *ā'(h)wow', (Scot.) interj.* expressing deploration.

Ewigkeit *ā'vihh-kīt, n.* eternity. [Ger.]

ewk. See **yuke.**

ewt. See **newt.**

For other sounds see detailed chart of pronunciation.

ex¹ *eks, n.* the twenty-fourth letter of the alphabet (X, x).

ex² *eks, prep.* direct from, as *ex works, ex warehouse* (*commerce*): without, as *ex dividend,* without the next dividend: used when stating the former name of a ship. [L., out of, from.]

ex- *eks-, pfx.* former but surviving, as **ex-emperor**: formerly employed, etc. by. — *n.* **ex** (*coll.*) one who is no longer what he or she was, esp. a person's former husband or wife: — *pl.* **ex's, exes.**

ex **abundantia** *a-bən-dan'shi-ə, a-bōon-dan'ti-ä* (L.) out of abundance. — **ex abundanti cautela** (*-dan'tī kö-tē'lə, -dan'tē kow-tā'lä*) from excessive caution.

ex **accidenti** *eks ak-si-den'tī, a-ki-den'tē* (L.L.) accidentally, as opposed to essentially.

exacerbate *iks-,* or *igz-as'ər-bāt, v.t.* to embitter: to provoke: to render more violent or severe, as a disease. — *ns.* **exacerbā'tion, exacerbesc'ence** increase of irritation or violence, esp. the increase of a fever or disease: embitterment. [L. *exacerbāre, -ātum* — *ex,* and *acerbāre,* from *acerbus,* bitter.]

exact *igz-akt', v.t.* to force out: to compel payment of: to demand and obtain: to extort: to require as indispensable. — *v.i.* to practise extortion. — *adj.* precise: rigorous: accurate: absolutely correct: finished: consummate: strict. — *adj.* **exact'ing** compelling full payment: unreasonable in making demands: demanding much. — *ns.* **exac'tion** the act of exacting or demanding strictly: an oppressive demand: that which is exacted, as excessive work or tribute; **exact'itude** exactness: correctness. — *adv.* **exact'ly.** — *ns.* **exact'ment; exact'ness** the quality of being exact: accuracy; **exact'or, -er** one who exacts: an extortioner: one who claims rights, often too strictly: — *fem.* **exact'ress.** — **exact sciences** the mathematical sciences, whose results are precise or quantitative. — **not exactly** not altogether: not at all (*coll., iron.*). [L. *exigĕre, exāctum,* to demand, to weigh strictly — *ex,* from, *agĕre,* to drive.]

ex **aequo** *eks ē'kwō, ī',* (L.L.) equally, equitably.

exaggerate *igz-aj'ər-āt, v.t.* to magnify unduly: to overstate: to represent too strongly: to intensify. — *v.i.* to speak hyperbolically, to overstate the case. — *n.* **exaggerā'tion** extravagant representation: a statement in excess of the truth. — *adjs.* **exagg'erative, exagg'eratory** containing exaggeration or tending to exaggerate. — *n.* **exagg'erātor.** [L. *exaggerāre, -ātum* — *ex-, aggerāre,* to heap up — *agger,* a heap.]

exalbuminous *eks-al-bū'min-əs,* (*bot.*) *adj.* without albumen.

exalt *igz-ölt', v.t.* to set aloft: to elate or fill with the joy of success: to extol: to refine or subtilise (*old chem.*). — *n.* **exaltā'tion** (*egz-öl-*) elevation in rank or dignity: high estate: elation: a planet's position of greatest influence (*astrol.*): a flight (of larks) (*arch.*). — *adj.* **exalt'ed** elevated: lofty: dignified. — *n.* **exalt'edness.** [L. *exaltāre* — *ex-, altus,* high.]

exam. Short for **examination.**

examine *igz-am'in, v.t.* to test: to inquire into: to question: to look closely into: to inspect. — *n.* **exā'men** examination. — *adj.* **exam'inable.** — *ns.* **exam'inant** an examiner: one who is being examined; **exam'inate** one who is examined; **examinā'tion** careful search or inquiry: close inspection: trial: a test of capacity and knowledge, familiarly contracted to **exam':** formal interrogation in court of a witness or accused person (*law*); **examinee'** one under examination; **exam'iner, exam'inātor** one who examines; **exam'inership.** — *adj.* **exam'ining.** — **examinā'tion-in-chief** (*law*) questioning of one's own witness (cf. **cross-examination**). — *v.t.* **exam'ine-in-chief.** [Fr. *examiner* — L. *exāmināre* — *exāmen,* the tongue of a balance.]

example *igz-äm'pl, n.* a specimen: an illustration: a copy of a book: a person or thing to be imitated or not to be imitated: a pattern: a warning: an instance. — *v.t.* (*rare*) to exemplify: to instance. — *n.* **exam'plar** (*arch.*) an exemplar. — **for example** for instance: as an illustration; **make an example of** to punish severely as a

warning to others. [O.Fr., — L. *exemplum* — *eximĕre,* to take out — *ex,* out of, *emĕre, emptum,* to take.]

exanimate *egz-, igz-an'i-māt, adj.* lifeless: spiritless: depressed. — *n.* **exanimā'tion.** [L. *exanimātus—ex,* from, *anima,* breath.]

ex **animo** *eks an'i-mō,* (L.) from the mind, earnestly.

ex **ante** *eks an'ti,* based on prediction and extrapolation. [L., from before.]

exanthem *eks-an'thəm,* **exanthema** *eks-an-thē'mə, ns.* a skin eruption, esp. accompanied by fever: a disease so characterised: — *pl.* **exan'thems, exanthē'mata.** — *adjs.* **exanthēmat'ic; exanthē'matous.** [Gr. *exanthēma, -atos* — *ex-,* out, *antheein,* to blossom.]

exarate *eks'ər-āt, adj.* containing grooves or furrows: said of pupae in which the wings and legs are free. — *n.* **exara'tion** (*rare*) the act of writing: composition. [L. *exarātus* — *exarāre,* to plough up, to trace letters on a tablet.]

exarch¹ *eks'ärk, n.* a Byzantine provincial governor, esp. of Italy: a metropolitan (*Orthodox Church*): a bishop of rank between a patriarch and a metropolitan (*Orthodox Church*): the head of the Bulgarian church: an ecclesiastical inspector: a legate. — *ns.* **exarch'ate** (or *eks'*), **ex'archy** the office, jurisdiction or province of an exarch; **exarch'ist** (or *eks'*) a supporter of the Bulgarian exarch. [Gr. *exarchos,* leader.]

exarch² *eks'ärk,* (*bot.*) *adj.* having the protoxylem on the outer edge. [Gr. *ex-,* out, *archē,* beginning, origin.]

exasperate *igz-äs'pər-āt, v.t.* to make rough, harsh (*obs.*): to make more grievous or painful: to make very angry: to irritate in a high degree. — *adj.* irritated: rough with hard points (*bot.*). — *adjs.* **exas'perāting; exas'perātive.** — *ns.* **exasperā'tion; exas'perātor.** [L. *ex-,* intens., *asperāre,* to make rough — *asper,* rough.]

ex **auctoritate mihi commissa** *eks ök-to-ri-tā'tē mī'hī kə-mis'ə, owk-tō-ri-tä'te mi'hi ko-mi'sa,* (L.) by the authority entrusted to me.

Excalibur *eks-kal'ib-ər, n.* the name of King Arthur's sword. [O.Fr. *Escalibor* for Caliburn; cf. *Caladbolg,* a famous sword in Irish legend.]

excambion *eks-kam'bi-on,* (Scots law) *n.* exchange of lands — also **excam'bium.** — *v.t.* **excamb'** to exchange. [L.L. *excambiāre;* cf. **cambist, cambium, exchange.**]

excarnate *eks-kär'nāt, v.t.* to remove the flesh from. — *n.* **excarna'tion.** [L.L. *excarnāre, -ātum,* — L. *ex,* from, *carō, carnis,* flesh.]

ex **cathedra** *eks kə-thē'drə,* or *eks kath'ə-dra,* (L.L.) from the chair of office, esp. the Pope's throne in the Consistory, or a professor's chair: hence authoritatively, judicially. — *adj.* **ex-cathe'dra** spoken with, or as if with, authority: implying authoritativeness.

excaudate *eks-kö'dāt,* (*zool.*) *adj.* having no tail. [L. *ex-,*without, *cauda,* tail.]

excavate *eks'kə-vāt, v.t.* to hollow or scoop out: to dig out: to lay bare by digging. — *ns.* **excavā'tion** the act of excavating: a hollow or cavity made by excavating: an archaeological site, a dig; **ex'cavātor** one who excavates: a machine used for excavating. [L. *excavāre* — *ex-,* out, *cavus,* hollow.]

exceed *ik-sēd', v.t.* to go beyond the limit or measure of: to surpass or excel. — *v.i.* to go beyond a given or proper limit (*arch.*): to be intemperate (*arch.*): to be outstanding. — *adj.* **exceed'ing** surpassing: excessive: projecting beyond a neighbouring member (*bot.*). — Also *adv.* (*arch.*) exceedingly. — *adv.* **exceed'ingly** very much: greatly. [L. *ex-,* beyond, *cēdĕre, cēssum,* to go.]

excel *ik-sel', v.t.* to be superior to: to surpass: to exceed (*Milt.*). — *v.i.* to have good qualities in a high degree: to perform very meritorious actions: to be superior: — *pr.p.* **excell'ing;** *pa.t.* and *pa.p.* **excelled'.** — *ns.* **excellence** (*eks'ə-ləns*), **exc'ellency** great merit: any excellent quality: worth: greatness: (usu. **Exc'ellency**) a title of honour given to persons high in rank or office. — *adj.* **exc'ellent** surpassing others in some good quality: of great virtue, worth, etc.: good in a high degree. — *adv.* **exc'ellently.** — *interj.* **excel'sior** (L. *compar. adj.*, taller, loftier) higher still (after Longfellow). — *n.* (sometimes with *cap.*; orig. *U.S.*) a trade name for wood shavings for packing. [L. *excellēre* — *ex-*, out, up, *celsus*, high.]

excellence *ek-se-lăs*, (Fr.) *n.* excellence. — **par excellence** eminently, by way of ideal.

excentric. Same as **eccentric.**

except *ik-sept'*, *v.t.* to take out, or leave out: to exclude. — *v.i.* to object (usually with *to* or *against*). — *prep.* leaving out: excluding: but. — *conj.* (*arch.*) unless. — *adj.* and *n.* **except'ant.** — *prep.* **except'ing** with the exception of, except. — *n.* **excep'tion** the act of excepting: that which is excepted: exclusion: objection: offence. — *adj.* **excep'tionable** objectionable. — *adv.* **excep'tionably.** — *adj.* **excep'tional** unusual (esp. in a good sense). — *adv.* **excep'tionally.** — *adjs.* **excep'tious** (*arch.*) disposed to take exception; **excep'tive** including, making, or being an exception; **except'less** (*Shak.*) making no exception, usual. — *n.* **excep'tor.** — **take exception** to object (to); **the exception proves the rule** the existence of an exception to a supposed rule proves the general truth of the rule (often used in argument when no such conclusion is justified); this saying is a distorted translation of a part of a legal Latin phrase meaning 'the making of an exception proves that the rule holds in cases not excepted'. [L. *excipĕre*, *exceptum* — *ex*, from, *capĕre*, to take.]

exceptis excipiendis *ik-sep'tis ik-sip-i-en'dis, eks-kep'tēs eks-ki-pi-en'dēs*, (L.L.) excepting what is to be excepted: with proper exceptions.

excerpt *ek'sûrpt*, or *ek-sûrpt'*, *n.* a passage selected from a book, opera, etc., an extract. — *v.t.* **excerpt'** to select: to extract. — *ns.* **excerpt'ing; excerp'tion; excerp'tor.** [L. *excerptum*, pa.p. of *excerpĕre* — *ex*, from, *carpĕre*, to pick.]

excerpta *ik-sûrp'tə, eks-kerp'ta*, (L.; *pl.* of **excerp'tum** -*təm*, -*tōom*), *n.pl.* extracts, selections.

excess *ik-ses'*, *n.* a going beyond what is usual or proper: intemperance: that which exceeds: the degree or amount by which one thing exceeds another: usury (*Shak.*). — *adj.* in excess. — *adj.* **excess'ive** beyond what is usual or right: immoderate: extreme. — *adv.* excessively. — *adv.* **excess'ively.** — *n.* **excess'iveness.** — **excess fare** payment for distance travelled beyond, or in a class superior to, that allowed by the ticket; **excess baggage, luggage** luggage above the weight allowed free; **excess postage** payment due when insufficient stamps have been put on a letter or packet. — **carry to excess** to do too much; **excess profits tax** a tax on profits in excess of those for a specified base period or over a rate adopted as a reasonable return on capital; **in excess of** more than. [L. *excessus* — *excēdĕre, excēssum*, to go beyond.]

exchange *iks-chānj'*, *v.t.* to give or give up in return for something else: to receive in return for something else (*obs.*): to give and take mutually: to barter: to change (*obs.*). — *v.i.* to pass by exchange of office with another. — *n.* the giving and taking of one thing for another: barter: the thing exchanged: process by which accounts between distant parties are settled by bills instead of money: money-changing business: exchanging currency of one country for that of another: the difference between the value of money in different places: a stock exchange: the building where merchants, etc., meet for business: a central office where telephone lines are connected: a bar-room (*arch. U.S. slang*): in chess, the taking by both players of a piece in consecutive moves: see **employment exchange.** — *n.* **exchangeabil'ity.** — *adj.* **exchange'able** that may be exchanged. — *n.* **exchan'ger** one who exchanges or practises exchange: a money-changer, a banker (*B.*). — **exchange control** the official control of a country's foreign exchange settlements so as to conserve its holding of foreign currency; **exchange rate** (or **rate of exchange**) the ratio at which one currency can be exchanged for another; **exchange student, teacher** a

student or teacher spending some time at a school in a foreign country while one from that country attends his school. — **exchange words, blows** to quarrel verbally or physically; **force the exchange** in chess, to play so as to force one's opponent to take one piece for another; **win** (or **lose**) **the exchange** in chess, to gain (or lose) a superior piece in exchange for an inferior. [O.Fr. *eschangier* (Fr. *échanger*) — L.L. *excambiāre* — L. *ex*, from, L.L. *cambiāre*, to barter.]

excheat *eks-chēt'*, (*Spens.*) *n.* Same as **escheat.**

exchequer *iks-chek'ər*, *n.* a department of state having charge of revenue, so named from the chequered cloth which covered the table, and on which the accounts were reckoned: the Court of Exchequer: a national treasury: one's funds, finances, purse. — *v.t.* to proceed against in the Court of Exchequer. — **exchequer bill** a bill issued at the Exchequer, as security for money advanced to the government. — **Chancellor of the Exchequer** see **chancellor; Court of Exchequer** in England originally a revenue court developed out of the judicial branch of the Exchequer, acquired a general common-law jurisdiction by a legal fiction, became a division of the High Court of Justice in 1875, and is now merged in the King's (Queen's) Bench Division: in Scotland a revenue court, abolished in 1886, its jurisdiction transferred to the Court of Session. [See **chequer, check, chess.**]

excide *ek-sīd'*, *v.t.* to cut off. [L. *excīdĕre* — *ex*, from, *caedĕre*, to cut.]

excipient *ek-sip'i-ənt*, *n.* a substance mixed with a medicine to give it consistence, or used as a vehicle for its administration. [L. *excipiēns, -entis*, pr.p. of *excipĕre*, to take out, receive — *ex*, from, *capĕre*, to take.]

excise[1] *ek'sīz* or *-sīz'*, *n.* a tax on certain home commodities, and on licences for certain trades: the department in the civil administration concerned with this tax. — Also *adj.* — *v.t.* to subject to excise duty. — *adj.* **excīs'able** liable to excise duty. — **excise law** (*U.S.*) a liquor law, licensing law; **ex'ciseman** (or *-sīz'*) an officer charged with collecting the excise. [M.Du. *excijs* — O.Fr. *acceis*, tax — L.L. *accensāre*, to tax — *ad*, to, and *cēnsus*, a tax.]

excise[2] *ek-sīz'*, *v.t.* to cut off or out. — *n.* **excision** (*ek-sizh'ən*) a cutting out or off of any kind: extirpation. [L. *excīdĕre*, to cut out — *ex*, from, *caedĕre*, to cut.]

excite *ik-sīt'*, *v.t.* to call into activity: to stir up: to rouse: to energise: to produce electric or magnetic activity in: to sensitise: to stir emotionally: to raise (a nucleus, atom, molecule, etc.) to an excited state. — *n.* **excitabil'ity.** — *adj.* **excit'able** capable of being excited: responsive to stimulus: easily excited. — *ns.* **excit'ableness; excitancy** (*ek'si-tən-si*), excitant property; **excitant** (*ek'si-* or *ek-sī'*) that which excites or rouses the vital activity of the body: a stimulant: the electrolyte in an electric cell. — *adj.* exciting: stimulating. — *n.* **excitā'tion** (*ek-si-*) the act of exciting: means of excitement: a state of excitement. — *adjs.* **excīt'ative, excit'atory** tending to excite. — *adj.* **excit'ed** agitated: roused emotionally: in a state of great activity: having energy higher than that of the ground, or normal, state. — *ns.* **excite'ment** agitation: that which excites; **excit'er** one who or that which excites: an auxiliary machine supplying current for another machine: a sparking apparatus for producing electric waves. — *adj.* **excit'ing** tending to excite: stirring, thrilling. — *ns.* **excīt'on** (or *ek'si-ton*) a bound pair comprising an electron and a hole; **excī'tor** exciter: an afferent nerve stimulating a part. [Fr. *exciter* — L. *excitāre, -ātum* — *exciēre* — *ex-*, out, *ciēre*, to set in motion.]

exclaim *iks-klām'*, *v.t.* and *v.i.* to cry out: to utter or speak vehemently. — *n.* an exclamation, outcry. — *n.* **exclamation** (*eks-klə-mā'shən*) vehement utterance: outcry: an uttered expression of surprise and the like: the mark expressing this (!) (also **exclamation mark**): an interjection. — *adjs.* **exclamative** (*eks-klam'ə-tiv*), **exclam'-**

atory containing or expressing exclamation. [Fr. *exclamer* — L. *exclāmāre, -ātum* — *ex-*, out, *clāmāre*, to shout.]

exclaustration *eks-klös-trä'shən, n.* the return of a religious to the outside world on release from his or her vows. [L. *ex*, out, *claustrum,* an enclosed place.]

exclave *eks'klāv, n.* a part of a country, province, etc., disjoined from the main part, being enclosed in foreign territory. [See **enclave.**]

exclosure *eks-klō'zhər, n.* an area shut off from intrusion. [L. *ex-*, from, and **close**[1].]

exclude *iks-klōōd', v.t.* to shut out: to thrust out: to hinder from entrance: to omit: to hinder from participation: to except: to hatch. — *adj.* **exclud'ed** (*bot.*) exserted. — *ns.* **excludee'** one who is excluded; **exclu'sion** (-*zhən*) a shutting or putting out: ejection: exception; **exclu'sionism; exclu'sionist** one who excludes, or would exclude, another from a privilege. — *adj.* **exclu'sive** (-*siv*) able or tending to exclude: incompatible: debarring from participation: of the nature of monopoly: socially inaccessible or aloof: sole: not to be had elsewhere or from another: select, fashionable: without taking into account: not included. — *n.* one of a number who exclude others from their society: an exclusive product: a newspaper story published by one paper only. — *adv.* **exclu'sively.** — *ns.* **exclu'siveness; exclu'sivism** the practice of being exclusive; **exclu'sivist; exclusiv'ity.** — *adj.* **exclu'sory** exclusive. — **exclusion order** an order prohibiting the presence in, or entry to, Britain of any person known to be concerned in acts of terrorism; **exclusion principle** a fundamental law of quantum mechanics that no two particles of a group called fermions can exist in identical quantum states; **Exclusive Brethren** see **Close Brethren; exclusive dealing** the act of abstaining deliberately from any business or other transactions with persons of opposite political or other convictions to one's own — a euphemism for *boycotting;* **exclusive zone** territorial waters within a certain limit from which foreign exploitation is totally banned. — **law of excluded middle** (*log.*) that everything is either A or not-A; **to the exclusion of** so as to exclude. [L. *exclūdĕre, -clūsum* — *ex-*, out, *claudĕre*, to shut.]

excogitate *eks-koj'i-tāt, v.t.* to discover by thinking: to think out earnestly or laboriously. — *n.* **excogitā'tion** laborious thinking: invention: contrivance. — *adj.* **excog'itative.** [L. *excōgitāre, -ātum* — *ex-*, out, *cōgitāre*, to think.]

excommunicate *eks-kəm-ūn'i-kāt, v.t.* to put out of or expel from the communion of the church: to deprive of church privileges. — *adjs.* **excommun'icable; excommun'icate** (-*kit, -kāt*) excommunicated. — Also *n.* — *ns.* **excommunicā'tion** the act of expelling from the communion of a church; **excommun'ion** (*Milt.*). — *adj.* **excommun'icatory** of or pertaining to excommunication. [From L.L. *excommūnicāre* — L. *ex, commūnis*, common.]

ex concessis (or **concesso**) *eks kən-se'sis* (*kən-se'sō*), *konkā'sēs* (*kon-kā'sō*), (L.L.) from what has been conceded.

ex consequenti *eks kon-si-kwen'tī, -se-kwen'tē,* (L.L.) by way of consequence.

ex converso. Same as **e converso.**

excoriate *eks-kō'ri-āt, -kō'ri-, v.t.* to strip the skin from: to criticise severely (*fig.*). — *n.* **excoriā'tion** the act of excoriating: the state of being excoriated. [L. *excoriāre, -ātum* — *ex*, from, *corium*, the skin.]

excorticate *eks-kör'ti-kāt, v.t.* to strip the bark off. — *n.* **excorticā'tion.** [L. *ex*, from, *cortex, -icis*, bark.]

excrement[1] *eks'kri-mənt, n.* dregs: useless matter discharged from the animal alimentary, etc. system, now esp. dung. — *adjs.* **excremental** (-*ment'l*); **excrementitial** (-*tish'l*), **excrementi'tious** pertaining to or containing excrement. [L. *excrēmentum* — *excernĕre* — *ex-*, out, *cernĕre*, to sift.]

excrement[2] *eks'kri-mənt,* (*Shak.*) *n.* an outgrowth, a moustache. — *adj.* **excremental** (-*ment'l*). [L. *excrēmentum* — *ex-*, out, *crēscĕre*, to grow.]

excrementa *eks-kri-men'tə, -kre-men'ta* (L. *pl.* of **excrementum** *-təm, -tōōm*), *n.pl.* refuse matter.

excrescence *iks-kres'əns, n.* an outgrowth or projection, esp. abnormal, grotesque, or offensive: a wart or tumour: a superfluous part: outbreak. — *n.* **excresc'ency** the state of being excrescent: excrescence. — *adjs.* **excresc'ent** growing out: superfluous: of a sound or letter, added to a word for euphony, etc., without etymological justification; **excrescential** (*eks-kri-sen'shl*). [L. *excrēscĕre* — *ex-*, out, *crēscĕre*, to grow.]

excrete *eks-krēt', v.t.* to separate and discharge: to eject. — *n.pl.* **excrē'ta** matters discharged from the animal body. — *n.* **excrē'tion** the excreting of matter from an organism: that which is excreted. — *adjs.* **excrē'tive** able to excrete: concerned with excretion; **excrē'tory** (or *eks'kri-tər-i*) having the quality of excreting. — *n.* a duct that helps to receive and excrete matter. [L. *ex*, from, *cernĕre, crētum*, to separate.]

excruciate *iks-krōō'shi-āt, v.t.* to torture: to rack: to inflict severe pain: to irritate greatly. — *adj.* **excru'ciating** extremely painful: racking: torturing: agonising: intensely irritating. — *adv.* **excru'ciatingly.** — *n.* **excruciā'tion** torture: vexation. [L. *excruciāre*, to torture — *ex-*, out, *cruciāre, -ātum*, to crucify — *crux, crucis*, a cross.]

excubant *eks'kū-bənt, adj.* on guard. [L. *excubāns, -antis*, pr.p. of *excubāre*, to sleep out, lie on guard — *ex, cubāre*, to lie.]

excudit *eks-kū'dit, -kōō',* (L.) (he, she) struck, hammered, forged, printed (this).

exculpate *eks'kul-pāt,* also *-kul', v.t.* to clear from the charge of a fault or crime: to absolve: to vindicate. — *adj.* **excul'pable.** — *n.* **exculpā'tion.** — *adj.* **excul'patory** tending to free from the charge of fault or crime. [L. *ex*, from, *culpa*, a fault.]

ex curia *eks kū'ri-ə, kōō'ri-ä,* (L.) out of court.

excurrent *eks-kur'ənt, adj.* having the main stem reaching to the top: having the midrib reaching beyond the lamina: flowing outwards: carrying an outgoing current. [L. *ex*, from, *currēns, -entis*, pr.p. of *currĕre*, to run.]

excursion *iks-kûr'shən, n.* a going forth: a raid: a sally: a deviation: an escapade: a pleasure trip: a company or collection of people on a pleasure outing: a wandering from the main subject: a digression. — Also *v.i.* — *vs.i.* **excurse'** to digress; **excur'sionise, -ize** to go on an excursion. — *n.* **excur'sionist** one who goes on a pleasure trip. — *adj.* **excur'sive** rambling: deviating. — *adv.* **excur'sively.** — *ns.* **excur'siveness; excur'sus** a dissertation on some particular matter appended to a book or chapter; — *pl.* **excur'suses.** — **excursion fare** a special cheap fare allowed on certain journeys by public transport; **excursion ticket; excursion train** a special train, usually with reduced fares, for persons making an excursion. [L. *ex-*, out, *currĕre, cursum*, to run.]

excuse *iks-kūz', v.t.* to free from blame or guilt: to exonerate: to pass over, overlook: to pardon or condone (in small matters): to free from an obligation: to release, dispense with: to allow to absent oneself: to seek to extenuate or justify: to make an apology or ask pardon for. — *v.i.* to make excuse. — *n.* (*iks-kūs'*) a plea offered in extenuation: indulgence. — *adj.* **excūsable** (*iks-kūz'ə-bl*). — *n.* **excūs'ableness.** — *adv.* **excūs'ably.** — *n.* **excūs'al.** — *adj.* **excūs'atory** making or containing excuse: apologetic. — *n.* **excus'er.** — *adj.* **excusive** (*eks-kūs'iv*). — **be excused** (*euphemism*) to go to the lavatory to relieve oneself; **excuse** (*iks-kūs'*) **for** a very poor example of; **excuse me** an expression used as an apology for any slight or apparent impropriety, or for controverting a statement that has been made; **excuse-me (dance)** a dance during which one may change partners; **excuse oneself** to ask permission and then leave: to explain and seek pardon (*for* a misdeed). [L. *excūsāre* — *ex*, from, *causa*, a cause, accusation.]

ex debito justitiae *eks deb'i-tō jəs-tish'i-ē, dā'bi-tō ūs-ti'ti-ī,* (L.L.) from what is due to justice.

ex delicto *eks di-lik'tō, dā-lik'tō*, (L.L.) owing to a crime.
ex-directory *eks-dī-rek'tə-ri, -di-, adj.* of a telephone number, not listed in a directory: of a person, having such a number. [**ex²**, **directory** (see **direct**).]
ex div., ex-div *eks('-)div'*. Short for **ex dividend** (see **ex²**).
ex dono *eks dō'nō*, (L.) by gift, as a present from.
exeat *eks'i-at, n.* formal leave of absence, esp. for a student to be out of college for more than one night. [L., let him go out: 3rd pers. sing. pres. subj. of *exīre*.]
execrate *eks'i-krāt, v.t.* to curse: to denounce evil against: to denounce: to detest. — *adj.* **ex'ecrable** deserving execration: detestable: accursed: very bad, of low quality. — *adv.* **ex'ecrably.** — *n.* **execrā'tion** the act of execrating: a curse pronounced: that which is execrated. — *adj.* **ex'ecrātive** of or belonging to execration. — *adv.* **ex'ecrātively.** — *adj.* **ex'ecrātory.** [L. *exsecrārī, -ātus*, to curse — *ex*, from, *sacer*, sacred.]
execute *eks'i-kūt, v.t.* to perform: to give effect to: to carry into effect: to put to use, bring into action: to put to death by law: to run through (a program, etc.) using computer language (*comput.*). — *adj.* **execūtable** (*eks'i-kūt-ə-bl, ek-sek'ūt-ə-bl*) that can be executed. — *ns.* **execūtancy** (*eg-zek'*) technique in music; **execūtant** (*eg-zek'*) one who executes or performs: a technically accomplished performer of music; **execūter** (*eks'*); **execū'tion** the act of, or skill in, executing or performing: accomplishment: completion: carrying into effect the sentence of a court of law: the warrant for so doing: the infliction of capital punishment; **execū'tioner** one who executes, esp. one who inflicts capital punishment. — *adj.* **executive** (*eg-zek'ū-tiv*) designed or fitted to execute or perform: concerned with performance, administration, or management: active: qualifying for or pertaining to the execution of the law: administrative: for the use of business executives: hence (*loosely*) expensive, sophisticated. — *n.* the power or authority in government that carries the laws into effect: the persons who administer the government or an organisation: a person in an executive position in government or business: the head of an executive, as president, governor, mayor, etc. (*U.S.*; also **chief executive**). — *adv.* **exec'ūtively.** — *n.* **execūtor** (*eg-zek'*) one who executes or performs: a person appointed to see a will carried into effect: — *fem.* **exec'ūtrix** (*pl.* **-trixes** or **executrī'cēs**); also **exec'utress.** — *adj.* **execūtō'rial.** — *n.* **exec'ūtorship.** — *adj.* **exec'ūtory** executing official duties: designed to be carried into effect. — *n.* **exec'ūtry** executorship: moveable or heritable estate and effects (*Scots law*). — **executive program** (*comput.*) a program which controls the use of a computer and of other programs; **executive session** (*U.S.*) a meeting of the Senate for executive business, usu. held in private: hence, any meeting in private. [L. *exsequī, exsecūtus* — *ex*, out, *sequī*, to follow.]
exedra *eks'i-drə, eks-ed'rə, n.* a portico, hall, or vestibule: a seated room: a raised platform with steps, in the open air: an apse, recess, niche — also **exhedra:** — *pl.* **ex(h)edrae.** [Gr. *exedrā — ex-*, out, *hedrā*, seat.]
exeem, exeme *eks-ēm', (obs. Scot.) v.t.* to release, exempt. [L. *eximēre — ex*, from, *emēre*, to take.]
exegesis *eks-i-jē'sis, n.* interpretation, esp. Biblical. — *ns.* **ex'egēte, exegē'tist** one who interprets or expounds. — *adjs.* **exegetic** (*-jet'ik*), **-al**, pertaining to exegesis: explanatory. — *adv.* **exegēt'ically.** — *n. sing.* **exegēt'ics** the science of exegesis. [Gr. *exēgēsis — exēgeesthai*, to explain — *ex-*, out, *hēgeesthai*, to guide.]
exeme. See **exeem.**
exempla. See **exemplum.**
exemplar *egz-em'plər, -plär, n.* a person or thing to be imitated: the ideal model of an artist: a type: an example: a copy of a book. — *adv.* **exem'plarily.** — *ns.* **exem'plariness; exemplarity** (*-plar'*) exemplariness: exemplary conduct. — *adj.* **exem'plary** worthy of imitation or notice: serving as model, specimen, illustration, or warning. — **exemplary damages** (*law*) damages in excess of the value needed to compensate the plaintiff, awarded as a punishment to the offender.

[L. *exemplar — exemplum*, example.]
exemple *eg-zäpl'*, (Fr.) *n.* example, model. — **par exemple** for example.
exemplify *igz-em'pli-fī, v.t.* to illustrate by example: to make an attested copy of: to prove by an attested copy: — *pr.p.* **exem'plifying;** *pa.t.* and *pa.p.* **exem'plified.** — *adj.* **exem'plifiable.** — *n.* **exemplificā'tion** the act of exemplifying: that which exemplifies: an attested copy or transcript. [L. *exemplum*, example, *facěre*, to make.]
exempli gratia *ig-zem'plī grä'shi-ə, eks-em'plē grä'ti-ä*, (L.) by way of example, for instance — often abbreviated **e.g.**
exemplum *ig-zem'pləm, n.* an example: a short story, or anecdote pointing a moral: — *pl.* **exem'pla** (*-plə*). [L., example.]
exempt *igz-empt', -emt', v.t.* to set apart (*Milt.*): to free, or grant immunity (from). — *adj.* taken out: not liable: of goods and services, carrying no value-added tax, but on which tax charged by suppliers, etc. cannot be reclaimed. — *n.* one who is exempt: an officer who commanded in absence of his superiors, exempted on this account from ordinary duties (*hist.*). — *n.* **exemp'tion** the act of exempting: the state of being exempt: freedom from any service, duty, burden, etc.: immunity. [Fr., — L. *eximěre, exemptum — ex*, from, *eměre*, to buy.]
exenterate *eks-en'tər-āt, v.t.* to disembowel. — *adj.* (*-it*) disembowelled. — *n.* **exenterā'tion.** [L. *exenterāre* — Gr. *exenterizein — ex*, from, and *enteron*, intestine.]
exequatur *eks-i-kwä'tər, n.* an official recognition of a consul or commercial agent given by the government of the country in which he is to be. [L. *exequātur*, let him execute — the opening word.]
exequy *eks'i-kwi* (usu. in *pl.* **exequies** *-kwiz*), *n.* a funeral procession: funeral rites. — *adj.* **exequial** (*eks-ē'kwi-əl*). [L. *exequiae — ex*, from, *sequī*, to follow.]
exercise *eks'ər-sīz, n.* a putting in practice: exertion of the body for health or amusement or acquisition of skill: a similar exertion of the mind: a task designed or prescribed for these purposes: a written school task: a study in music: a set of problems, passages for translation, etc., in a text-book: an academical disputation: accomplishment (*Shak.*): (in *pl.*) military drill or manoeuvres: a ceremony or formal proceeding (*U.S.*): an act of worship or devotion: a discourse, the discussion of a passage of Scripture, giving the coherence of text and context, etc. (the *addition* giving the doctrinal propositions, etc.): a meeting of a presbytery for this purpose: hence formerly the presbytery itself. — *v.t.* to train by use: to improve by practice: to give exercise to: to trouble: to put in practice: to use: to wield. — *v.i.* to take exercise: to drill. — *adj.* **ex'ercisable.** — *n.* **ex'erciser** one who or that which exercises: a device, usu. with elasticated cords, to help in exercising the muscles. — **ex'ercise-book** a book for writing school exercises in. — **the object of the exercise** the purpose of a particular operation or activity. [O.Fr. *exercice* — L. *exercitium* — L. *exercēre, -citum*, pfx. *ex-*, and *arcēre*, to shut up, restrain.]
exercitation *egz-ûr-sit-ā'shən, n.* putting into practice: employment: exercise: a discourse. [L. *exercitātiō, -ōnis — exercēre*, to exercise.]
exergue *eks' or eks-ûrg', n.* a part on the reverse of a coin, below the main device, often filled up by the date, etc. — *adj.* **exer'gual.** [Fr., — Gr. *ex*, out of, *ergon*, work.]
exert *igz-ûrt', v.t.* to put forth (*obs.*): to bring into active operation: to do or perform (*obs.*). — *n.* **exer'tion** a bringing into active operation: striving: activity. — *adj.* **exert'ive** having the power or tendency to exert: using exertion. [L. *exserĕre, exsertum — ex*, from, *serĕre*, to put together.]
exes *eks'əz, n.pl.* a slang abbreviation of **expenses**: see also **ex** under **ex-.**
exeunt *eks'i-unt, -ōont*, (L.) (they) go out, leave the stage. — **exeunt omnes** (*om'nēz, -nās*) all go out. [See **exit.**]

exfoliate *eks-fō'li-āt, v.t.* (of skin, bark, rocks, etc.) to shed in flakes: to remove in flakes. — *v.i.* to come off in flakes: to separate into layers. — *n.* **exfolia'tion.** — *adj.* **exfo'liative.** — *n.* **exfo'liātor** an exfoliating agent. — **exfoliative cytology** the study for diagnostic purposes of cells shed from internal body surfaces. [L. *exfoliāre, -ātum*, to strip of leaves — *ex*, from, *folium*, a leaf.]

ex gratia *eks grā'shi-ə, grä'ti-ä,* (L.) as an act of grace: as a favour, not out of obligation, and with no acceptance of liability (as *ex gratia payment*).

exhale[1] *eks-hāl', egz-āl', v.t.* to breathe forth: to emit or send out as vapour, smell, etc.: to cause or allow to evaporate: to emit through a membrane. — *v.i.* to breathe out: to rise or come off as a vapour, smell, emanation: to evaporate: to ooze out. — *adjs.* **exhāl'able; exhāl'ant** exhaling: emitting vapour or liquid. — *n.* an organ or vessel that emits vapour or liquid. — *n.* **exhalation** (*eks-, egz-ə-lā'shən*) the act or process of exhaling: evaporation: that which is exhaled, vapour, effluvium, emanation: a mist: a meteoric phenomenon, a meteor (*arch.*). [L. *exhālāre — ex*, from, *hālāre, -ātum*, to breathe.]

exhale[2] *eks-hāl', (Shak.) v.t.* to hale or draw out. [Pfx. **ex-**, and **hale**[2].]

exhaust *igz-öst', v.t.* to draw off: to draw out the whole of: to use the whole strength of: to use up: to empty: to wear or tire out: to treat of or develop completely. — *v.i.* of exhaust gases in an engine, to be emitted. — *n.* an outward current, or means of producing it: the exit of used working fluid from the cylinder of an engine: the period of discharge of the fluid: the fluid so escaping (**exhaust'-gas, -steam**). — *adj.* **exhaust'ed** drawn out: emptied: consumed: tired out. — *n.* **exhaust'er** he who or that which exhausts. — *adj.* **exhaust'ible** that may be exhausted. — *n.* **exhaustion** (*-öst'yən*) the act of exhausting or consuming: the state of being exhausted: extreme fatigue. — *adjs.* **exhaust'ive** tending to exhaust: investigating all parts or possibilities; **exhaust'less** that cannot be exhausted. — **exhaust'-pipe', -valve'** the pipe, valve, through which exhaust gases pass out. [L. *exhaurīre, exhaustum — ex*, from, *haurīre*, to draw.]

exhedra. See **exedra.**

exheredate *eks-her'i-dāt, (rare) v.t.* to disinherit. — *n.* **exherēdā'tion.** [L. *exhērēdāre — ex*, out, *hērēs, -ēdis*, heir.]

exhibit *igz-ib'it, v.t.* to hold forth or present to view: to present formally or publicly: to show: to give as a remedy (*med.; arch.*). — *n.* a document or object produced in court to be used as evidence (*law*): something exhibited: an article at an exhibition. — *ns.* **exhib'iter; exhibition** (*eks-i-bish'ən*) presentation to view: display: showing off: a public show, esp. of works of art, manufactures, etc.: that which is exhibited: a public performance at the end of a school year: a grant or gift: an allowance towards support, esp. to scholars in a university: administration of a remedy (*arch.*); **exhibi'tioner** one who enjoys an exhibition at a university; **exhibi'tionism** extravagant behaviour aimed at drawing attention to self: perversion involving public exposure of one's sexual organs (*psychiatry*); **exhibi'tionist.** — *adj.* **exhibitionist'ic.** — *adv.* **-ist'ically.** — *adj.* **exhib'itive** (*igz-*) serving for exhibition: representative. — *n.* **exhibitor** (*igz-ib'i-tər*). — *adj.* **exhib'itory** exhibiting. — **make an exhibition of oneself** to behave foolishly, exciting ridicule. [L. *exhibēre, -itum — ex-*, out, *habēre, -itum*, to have.]

exhilarate *igz-il'ə-rāt, v.t.* to make hilarious or merry: to raise the spirits of: to enliven: to cheer. — *adj.* **exhil'arant** exhilarating: exciting joy, mirth, or pleasure. — *n.* an exhilarating medicine. — *adj.* **exhil'arāting** cheering: gladdening. — *adv.* **exhil'arātingly.** — *n.* **exhilarā'tion** the state of being exhilarated: joyousness. — *adjs.* **exhil'arātive, exhil'aratory.** [L. *exhilarāre, -ātum — ex-*, intens., *hilaris*, cheerful.]

exhort *ig-zört', v.t.* to urge strongly and earnestly: to counsel. — *n.* **exhortā'tion** (*eks-* or *egz-*) the act of exhorting: language intended to exhort: counsel: a religious discourse. — *adjs.* **exhort'ative, exhort'atory** (*igz-*) tending to exhort or advise. — *n.* **exhort'er** one who exhorts: in some churches a layman appointed to give religious exhortation. [L. *exhortārī, -ātus — ex-* intens., *hortārī*, to urge.]

exhume *eks-hūm', ig-zūm', v.t.* to take out of the ground or place of burial: to disinter: to bring to light. — Also **exhumate** (*eks'hūm-āt*). — *ns.* **exhumā'tion** (*eks-*); **exhum'er.** [L. *ex*, out of, *humus*, the ground.]

ex hypothesi *eks hī-poth'ə-sī,* (L.L.) from the hypothesis.

exies *ek'sāz, (Scot.) n.pl.* a fit, as of hysterics, ague. [**access.**]

exigent *eks'i-jənt, adj.* pressing: urgent: exacting: demanding immediate attention or action. — *n.* extremity (*obs.*): the last strait, the end of all (*Shak.*): a needed amount (*Browning*). — *adj.* **exigeant** (*egz-ē-zhä,* Fr.) exacting — *fem.* **exigeante** (*-zhät*). — *ns.* **ex'igence, ex'igency** (or *ij'*) pressing necessity: emergency: distress. [L. *exigēns, -entis* — pr.p. of *exigēre* — pfx. *ex-, agēre*, to drive.]

exigible *eks'i-jib-l, adj.* liable to be exacted. [See **exact.**]

exiguous *egz-, eks-ig'ū-əs, adj.* scanty: slender. — *ns.* **exigū'ity** (*eks-*); **exig'ūousness.** [L. *exiguus — exigēre*, to weight strictly; see **exact.**]

exile *eks', or egz'īl, n.* enforced or regretted absence from one's country or home: banishment: (with *cap.*) the captivity of the Jews in Babylon (in these senses formerly *egz-īl'*): one who is in exile: a banished person. — *v.t.* (formerly *egz-īl'*) to expel from one's country, to banish. — *n.* **ex'ilement** banishment. — *adjs.* **exilic** (*egz-il'ik,* or *eks-*), **exil'ian** pertaining to exile, esp. that of the Jews in Babylon. [O.Fr. *exil* — L. *exsilium*, banishment — *ex*, out of, and root of *salīre*, to leap; affected by L. *exsul*, an exile.]

exility *egz-, eks-il'i-ti, (obs.) n.* slenderness, smallness: refinement. [L. *exīlitās, -ātis — exīlis*, slender.]

eximious *eg-zim'i-əs, (arch.) adj.* excellent, distinguished. [L. *eximius — eximēre — ex*, from, *emēre*, to take.]

ex improviso *eks im-prə-vī'zō, im-prō-vē'sō, -wē',* (L.) unexpectedly.

exine *eks'in, -īn.* See **extine.** [L. *ex*, out of.]

exist *igz-ist', v.i.* to have an actual being: to live: to occur: to continue to live, esp. in unfavourable circumstances. — *n.* **exist'ence** the state of existing or being: livelihood: life: anything that exists: being. — *adjs.* **exist'ent** having being: at present existing; **existential** (*eks-is-ten'shəl*). — *ns.* **existen'tialism** a term covering a number of related doctrines denying objective universal values and holding that a person must create values for himself through action and by living each moment to the full; **existen'tialist.** [L. *existere, exsistere*, to stand forth — *ex-*, out, *sistere*, to stand.]

exit *ek'sit, eg'zit, n.* the departure of a player from the stage: any departure: a passage out: a way of departure: death: a place on a motorway where vehicles can leave by a slip road: the last instruction of a subroutine (*comput.*): — *pl.* **ex'its.** — *v.i.* to make an exit: to die: to lose the lead deliberately (*cards*): — *pa.p.* and *pa.t.* **ex'ited.** — *n.* **ex'itance** (*phys.*) the amount per unit area of light or other radiation emitted from a surface. [Partly from the L. stage direction *exit*, goes out (in pl. *exeunt*, go out) — *exīre*, to go out — *ex-*, out, and *īre, itum*, to go; partly — L. *exitus*, a way out.]

ex-libris *eks-lī'bris, -li', n.* a book plate. — *ns.* **ex-li'brism; ex-li'brist** a collector or student of book plates. [L. *ex lībrīs*, from the books (of so-and-so).]

ex mero motu *eks mē'rō mō'tū, me'rō mō'tōō,* (L.) from his own impulse: of his, its, own accord.

ex natura rei *eks na-tū'rə rē'ī, na-tōō'ra re'ē,* (L.L.) from the nature of the case; **ex natura rerum** (*rē'rəm, rā'rōōm*) from the nature of things.

ex nihilo *eks nī'hi-lō, ni',* (L.) out of nothing, as *creation ex nihilo.*

exo- *eks'ō-, eks-ō',* in composition, outside, often opp. to **endo-, ento-** (see also **ecto-**). — *adj.* **exobiolog'ical.**

— *ns.* **exobiol′ogy** the study of (possible) extra-terrestrial life; **exobiol′ogist; ex′ocarp** (Gr. *karpos*, fruit) the epicarp of a fruit. — *adj.* **ex′ocrine** (Gr. *krīnein*, to separate; *physiol.*) of glands, secreting through a duct. — *n.* an exocrine gland. — *ns.* **exocytō′sis** (*biol.*) the discharge from cell of particles too large to diffuse throught the wall; **ex′oderm** exodermis: ectoderm. — *adj.* **exoderm′al.** — *ns.* **exoder′mis** (Gr. *dermis*, skin) the outer cortex layer of a root; **exoen′zyme** an enzyme that functions outside the cell producing it. — *adj.* **exoergic** (-*ûr′jik*; Gr. *ergon*, work; *nuc.*) of a process in which energy is liberated. — *n.* **exog′amy** (Gr. *gamos*, marriage) the practice of marrying only outside of one's own group: union of gametes not closely related (*biol.*). — *adjs.* **exogam′ic; exog′amous.** — *n.* **ex′ogen** (*obs.*) a dicotyledon — so called because its stem thickens by layers growing on the outside of the wood. — *adjs.* **exogenet′ic** (*med.*) not genetic, not caused by genetic factors; **exog′enous** growing by successive additions to the outside: developing externally: having an external origin. — *ns.* **ex′onym** (Gr. *onoma*, a name) a name for a town, country, etc., in a foreign language; **exoph′agy** (Gr. *phagein*, to eat) the custom among cannibals of eating only the flesh of persons not of their own kin. — *adjs.* **exoph′agous.** — *ns.* **ex′oplasm** ectoplasm; **exop′odite, ex′opod** (Gr. *pous, podos*, foot) the outer branch of a crustacean limb. — *adj.* **exopod′itic.** — *n.* **exoskel′eton** a hard supporting or protective structure secreted externally by the ectoderm. — *adj.* **exoskel′etal.** — *n.* **ex′osphere** (Gr. *sphaira*, sphere) the outermost layer of the earth's atmosphere: the boundary of the earth's atmosphere and interplanetary space. — *adjs.* **exospher′ic, -al.** — *n.* **ex′ospore** (Gr. *sporos*, a seed) the outer layer of a spore wall: a spore formed by abstriction, not within a mother-cell. — *adjs.* **exospor′al; exospor′ous; exother′mal, exother′mic** (Gr. *thermē*, heat; *chem.*) involving evolution of heat. — *n.* **exothermi′city.** — *adj.* **exotox′ic.** — *n.* **exotox′in** a toxin produced by a micro-organism and secreted into the surrounding medium. [Gr. *exō*, outside.]

Exocet® *eks′ə-set, n.* a subsonic tactical missile, launched from ship, plane or submarine and travelling at low altitude. [Fr., — L. *Exocoetus volitans*, the flying fish.]

exode *ek′sōd, n.* the concluding part of a Greek drama: a farce or afterpiece. [Gr. *exōdion.*]

exodus *eks′ə-dəs, n.* a going out, esp. that of the Israelites from Egypt: (with *cap.*) the second book of the Old Testament. *adj.* **exodic** (-*od′*). — *n.* **ex′odist** one who goes out: an emigrant. [L., — Gr. *exodos* — *ex-*, out, *hodos*, a way.]

ex officio *eks o-fish′i-ō, -fik′,* (L.) by virtue of his office.

exomis *eks-ō′mis, n.* a one-sleeved or (in Rome) sleeveless garment — (*Browning*) **exo′mion.** [Gr. *exōmis* — *ex-*, out, *ōmos*, shoulder.]

exon[1] *eks′on, n.* an officer of the Yeomen of the Guard. [App. intended to express the pronunciation of Fr. *exempt*; see **exempt**.]

exon[2] *eks′on,* (*biol.*) *n.* any segment of a gene which consists of codons: — opp. of *intron.* [L. *ex*, out of, and Gr. neut. suff. -*on*.]

exonerate *igz-on′ər-āt, v.t.* to free from the burden of blame or obligation: to acquit. — *n.* **exonerā′tion** the act of exonerating. — *adj.* **exon′erative** freeing from a burden or obligation. [L. *exonerāre, -ātum,* — *ex,* from, *onus, oneris,* burden.]

ex opere operato, ex opere operantis. See **opus**.

exophthalmia, -mos, -mus *eks-of-thal′mi-ə, -məs, ns.* a protrusion of the eyeballs. — *adj.* **exophthal′mic.** [Gr. *ex,* out, *ophthalmos,* eye.]

exorable *eks′ər-ə-bl, adj.* capable of being moved by entreaty. — *ns.* **exorabil′ity; exorā′tion** (*obs.*) entreaty. [L. *exōrāre* — pfx. *ex-* in the sense of thoroughly, *ōrāre,* to entreat.]

exorbitant *igz-ör′bi-tənt, adj.* going beyond the usual limits: excessive. — *ns.* **exor′bitance, exor′bitancy** great

excess. — *adv.* **exor′bitantly.** — *v.i.* **exor′bitate** (*obs.*) to stray. [L. *exorbitāns, -antis,* pr.p. of *exorbitāre* — *ex,* out of, *orbita,* a track — *orbis,* a circle.]

exorcise, -ize *eks′ör-sīz, v.t.* to adjure by some holy name: to call forth or drive away, as a spirit: to deliver from the influence of an evil spirit. — *ns.* **ex′orcism** (-*sizm*) the act of exorcising or expelling evil spirits by certain ceremonies: a formula for exorcising; **ex′orcist** one who exorcises or pretends to expel evil spirits by adjuration (also **ex′orcīser, -z-**): the third of the minor orders (*R.C. Church*). [L.L. from Gr. *exorkizein* — *ex-,* out, *horkos,* an oath.]

exordium *egz-ör′di-əm, n.* the introductory part of a discourse or composition: — *pl.* **exor′diums, -ia.** — *adj.* **exor′dial** pertaining to the exordium: introductory. [L., — *exordīrī* — *ex,* out of, *ordīrī,* to begin.]

exosmosis *eks-os-mō′sis, eks-oz-, n.* osmosis outwards, i.e. away from the solution — also **ex′osmose** (-*mōs*). — *adj.* **exosmotic** (-*mot′ik*). [Gr. *ex-,* out, and **osmosis.**]

exostosis *eks-os-tō′sis,* (*anat.*) *n.* morbid enlargement of a bone: — *pl.* **exostō′ses** (-*sēz*). [Gr. *exostōsis* — *ex-,* out, *osteon,* a bone.]

exoteric *eks-ō-ter′ik, adj.* external: fit to be communicated to the public or multitude — opp. to *esoteric.* — *adj.* **exoter′ical.** — *adv.* **exoter′ically.** — *n.* **exoter′icism** (-*sizm*). [Gr. *exōterikos* — *exōterō,* comp. of *exō,* outside.]

exotic *igz-ot′ik, adj.* introduced from a foreign country: alien: foreign-looking: outlandish: romantically strange, or rich and showy, or glamorous: pertaining to strip-tease or belly-dancing. — *n.* anything of foreign origin: something not native to a country, as a plant, a word, a custom: an exotic dancer. — *n.pl.* **exot′ica** exotic objects: theatrical or musical items with an unusual theme or with a foreign flavour. — *n.* **exot′icism** (-*sizm*). [Gr. *exōtikos* — *exō,* outside.]

expand *iks-pand′, v.t.* to spread out: to lay open: to enlarge in bulk or surface: to develop, or bring out in fuller detail: to express at length, as in terms of a series, or without contractions. — *v.i.* to become opened: to increase in volume: to enlarge: to spread: to become communicative (*fig.*): to speak or write more fully (on). — *adj.* **expand′able.** — *ns.* **expand′er, -or** an electronic device which increases the range of amplitude variations in a transmission system; **expanse** (-*pans′*) a wide extent: a stretch: the amount of spread or stretch: the firmament; **expansibil′ity.** — *adj.* **expans′ible** capable of being expanded. — *adv.* **expans′ibly.** — *adj.* **expans′ile** (-*īl*) capable of expansion. — *n.* **expan′sion** the act of expanding: the state of being expanded: enlargement: that which is expanded: amount of expanding: territorial extension: immensity: extension. — *adjs.* **expan′sional; expan′sionary** tending to expansion. — *ns.* **expan′sionism; expan′sionist** one who favours territorial or currency expansion. — Also *adj.* — *adj.* **expans′ive** widely extended: diffusive: causing expansion: worked by expansion: effusive: talkative, communicative: marked by excessive feeling of well-being and delusions of self-importance (*psychiatry*). — *adv.* **expans′ively.** — *ns.* **expans′iveness; expansiv′ity** (*eks-*). — **expanded metal** steel, etc., stretched to form a mesh, used for reinforcing concrete, etc.; **expanded plastic foam** plastic; **expanding universe** (*astron.*) the theory that the whole universe is constantly expanding and the galaxies moving away from each other; **expansion board, card** (*comput.*) a printed circuit board which can be inserted into an **expansion slot** (a connector in a computer which allows extra facilities to be added temporarily or permanently); **expansion bolt** a bolt that expands within a hole, crack, etc., thus providing a firm support, e.g. in mountaineering; **expansion joint** (*eng.*) a gap left at a joint between e.g. lengths of rail or sections of concrete, to allow for heat expansion. [L. *expandĕre* — *ex-,* out, *pandĕre, pānsum,* to spread.]

ex parte *eks pär′tē, pär′te, adj.* on one side only: partial:

prejudiced. [L. *ex*, from, *parte*, abl. of *pars, partis*, party, side.]

expat *eks'pat, n.* short for **expatriate.**

expatiate *eks-pā'shi-āt, v.i.* to walk about: to range at large (usu. *fig.*): to enlarge in discourse, argument, or writing. — *n.* **expatiā'tion.** — *adjs.* **expā'tiative, expā'tiatory** expansive. — *n.* **expā'tiātor.** [L. *exspatiārī, -ātus — ex*, out of, *spatiārī*, to roam — *spatium*, space.]

expatriate *eks-pā'tri-āt, -pa', v.t.* to send out of one's country: to banish, exile (oneself or another): to deprive of citizenship. — Also *adj.* (*-tri-ət*). — *n.* an exile, voluntary or compulsory: one who lives abroad permanently, for financial or other reasons: one working abroad for a period. — *n.* **expatriā'tion** the act of expatriating: exile, voluntary or compulsory. [L.L. *expatriāre, -ātum — ex*, out of, *patria*, fatherland.]

expect *iks-pekt', v.t.* to await (*obs.*): to look forward to as likely to come or happen, or as due: to suppose. — *v.i.* (*obs.*) to wait. — *n.* (*Shak.*) expectation. — *adj.* **expect'able.** — *adv.* **expect'ably.** — *ns.* **expect'ance, expect'ancy** the act or state of expecting: that which is expected: hope. — *adj.* **expect'ant** looking or waiting for something: in expectation: not yet but expecting to be: pregnant. — *n.* one who expects: one who is looking or waiting for some benefit or office. — *adv.* **expect'antly.** — *ns.* **expectā'tion** (*eks-*) the act or state of expecting: the prospect of future good: that which is or may fairly be expected: the degree of probability: the value of something expected: (in *pl.*) prospect of fortune or profit by a will. — *adj.* **expect'ative** giving rise to expectation: reversionary. — *n.* an expectancy: an anticipatory grant of a benefice not yet vacant. — *adj.* **expect'ed.** — *adv.* **expect'edly.** — *n.* **expect'er.** *n.* and *adj.* **expect'ing.** — *adv.* **expect'ingly** in a state of expectation. — **Expectation Week** the period between Ascension Day and Whit Sunday — commemorating the Apostles' expectation of the Comforter. — **be expecting** (*coll.*) to be pregnant; **life expectancy, expectation of life** the average length of time that one may expect to live. [L. *expectāre, -ātum — ex*, out, *spectāre*, to look, freq. of *specēre*, to see.]

expectorate *eks-pek'tə-rāt, v.t.* to expel from the breast or lungs by coughing, etc.: to spit forth. — *v.i.* to discharge or eject phlegm from the throat: to spit. — *adj.* **expec'torant** tending to promote expectoration. — *n.* a medicine that promotes expectoration. — *n.* **expectorā'tion** the act of expectorating: that which is expectorated: spittle. — *adj.* **expec'torātive** having the quality of promoting expectoration. [L. *expectorāre, -ātum — ex*, from, *pectus, pectoris*, breast.]

expedient *iks-pē'di-ənt, adj.* suitable: advisable: expeditious (*Shak.*). — *n.* that which serves to promote: means suitable to an end: contrivance, shift. — *ns.* **expē'dience** haste, despatch (*Shak.*): enterprise (*Shak.*): expediency; **expē'diency** fitness: desirableness: conduciveness to the need of the moment: that which is opportune: self-interest. — *adj.* **expēdien'tial** (*-en'shl*). — *adv.* **expē'diently.** [L. *expediēns, -entis*, pr.p. of *expedīre*; see **expedite.**]

expeditate *eks-ped'it-āt, v.t.* to deprive of three claws or of the ball of the foot. — *n.* **expeditā'tion.** [L.L. *expeditāre, -ātum — ex*, from, *pēs, pedis*, foot.]

expedite *eks'pi-dīt, v.t.* to free from impediments: to hasten: to send forth: to despatch. — *adj.* (*obs.*) free from impediment: unencumbered: quick: prompt. — *adv.* **ex'peditely.** — *n.* **expedition** (*-di'shən*) speed: promptness: an organised journey to attain some object, as hunting, warfare, exploration, etc.: the party undertaking such a journey. — *adjs.* **expedi'tionary** belonging to an expedition: of the nature of an expedition; **expedi'tious** characterised by expedition or rapidity: speedy: prompt. — *adv.* **expedi'tiously.** — *n.* **expedi'tiousness.** — *adj.* **exped'itive.** [L. *expedīre, -ītum — ex*, from, *pēs, pedis*, a foot.]

expel *iks-pel', v.t.* to drive out: to eject: to discharge in disgrace (from school, etc.): to banish: to keep off (*Shak.*): — *pr.p.* **expell'ing**; *pa.t.* and *pa.p.* **expelled'.**

— *adj.* and *n.* **expell'ant, -ent.** — *n.* **expellee'** one who is expelled. [L. *expellĕre, expulsum — ex*, from, *pellĕre*, to drive.]

expend *iks-pend', v.t.* to lay out: to employ or consume in any way: to spend. — *adj.* **expend'able** that may be expended, esp. that may be sacrificed to achieve some end. — Also *n.* — *ns.* **expendabil'ity; expen'der; expend'iture** the act of expending: that which is expended: the process of using up: money spent; **expense** (*-pens'*) expenditure: outlay: cost: (in *pl.*) money out of pocket, or an allowance therefor: (in *pl.*; *Scots law*) costs in a lawsuit. — *adj.* **expens'ive** causing or requiring much expense: costly: lavish. — *adv.* **expens'ively.** — *n.* **expens'iveness.** — **expense(s) account** a statement of outlay incurred in carrying out a business commission (often with the implication that the account may be made to cover a great deal). — **at the expense of** to the cost, detriment of (often **at someone's**, etc. **expense**): with the loss or sacrifice of; **be at the expense of** to pay the cost of. [L. *expendĕre — ex-*, out, *pendĕre, pēnsum*, to weigh.]

experience *iks-pē'ri-əns, n.* test, trial, experiment (*obs.*): practical acquaintance with any matter gained by trial: long and varied observation, personal or general: wisdom derived from the changes and trials of life: the passing through any event or course of events by which one is affected: an event so passed through: anything received by the mind, as sensation, perception, or knowledge. — *v.t.* to have practical acquaintance with: to prove or know by use: to have experience of: to feel, suffer, undergo. — *adj.* **expē'rienced** taught by experience: having much experience: practised, knowledgeable, in sexual matters (*facet.*): skilful: wise. — *adjs.* **expē'rienceless** having little or no experience; **experien'tial** (*-en'shl*) pertaining to or derived from experience. — *ns.* **expērien'tialism** the doctrine that all knowledge comes from experience; **expērien'tialist.** — *adv.* **expērien'tially.** — **experience meeting** one for the relating of religious experiences. [Fr. *expérience* and L. *experientia*, from *experīrī — ex-*, intens., and old verb *perīrī*, to try.]

experiment *iks-per'i-mənt, n.* experience (*obs.*): a trial: something done to test a theory, or to discover something unknown. — *v.i.* (also *-ment'*) to make experiment or trial: to search by trial. — *v.t.* (*obs.*) to make trial of. — *adj.* **experiment'al** experienced, having experience (*obs.*): pertaining to experiment: based on or proceeding by experiment: trying out new styles or techniques: tentative. — *v.i.* **experiment'alise, -ize.** — *ns.* **experiment'alism** reliance on experiment; **experiment'alist; exper'imenter** (or *-ment'*), **exper'imentist** one who makes experiments. — *adv.* **experiment'ally.** — *n.* **experimentā'tion.** — *adjs.* **experiment'ative; exper'imented** experienced (*obs.*): practised. [L. *experīmentum*, from *experīrī*, to try thoroughly; see **experience.**]

experimentum crucis *iks-per-i-men'təm krōō'sis, eks-pe-ri-men'tōōm krōō'kis* (L.) a crucial test.

expert *eks'pûrt, adj.* taught by practice: having a familiar knowledge: having a facility of performance (with *at* or *in*): skilful, adroit (with *at* or *in*). — *v.t.* (*Spens.*) to experience. — *ns.* **ex'pert** one who is skilled in any art or science: a specialist: a scientific or professional witness; **expertise** (*-ēz'*) expert knowledge: expertness: expert appraisal, valuation. — *v.i.* and *v.t.* **ex'pertise, -ize** (*-īz*) to give an expert opinion (on). — *adv.* **ex'pertly.** — *n.* **ex'pertness.** — **expert system** (*comput.*) a program based on specialist knowledge and using artificial intelligence techniques, which can make decisions or solve problems intelligently. [Fr., — L. *expertus — experīrī*, to try thoroughly; see **experience.**]

expiate *eks'pi-āt, v.t.* to make complete atonement for: to make satisfaction or reparation for. — *adj.* (*Shak.*) expired, at an end. — *adj.* **ex'piable** capable of being expiated, atoned for, or done away. — *ns.* **expiā'tion** the act of expiating: the means by which atonement is made: atonement; **ex'piātor.** — *adj.* **ex'piatory** (*-ə-*, or

-*ā-tər-i*). [L. *expiāre, -ātum* — *ex-*, intens., *piāre*, to appease, atone for.]

expire *iks-, eks-pīr', v.t.* to breathe out: to emit: to bring to an end (*Spens.*). — *v.i.* to breathe out: to die: to come to an end: to lapse: to become invalid by lapse of time: to fulfil a term (*Spens.*). — *adj.* **expī'rable** that may expire or come to an end. — *ns.* **expī'rant** one expiring; **expirā'tion** (*eks-pi-* or *-pī-*) the act of breathing out: death (*obs.*): end: that which is expired. — *adj.* **expī'ratory** pertaining to expiration, or the emission of the breath. — *adjs.* **expired'** dead: extinct: lapsed: obsolete; **expī'ring** dying: pertaining to or uttered at the time of dying. — *n.* **expī'ry** the end or termination, esp. by lapse of time: expiration. [Fr. *expirer* — L. *ex*, from; *spīrāre, -ātum*, to breathe.]

expiscate *eks-pis'kāt*, (*Scot.*) *v.t.* to find out by skilful means or by strict examination. — *n.* **expiscā'tion.** — *adj.* **expis'cātory.** [L. *expiscārī, expiscātus* — *ex*, from, *piscārī*, to fish — *piscis*, a fish.]

explain *iks-plān', v.t.* to make plain or intelligible: to unfold and illustrate the meaning of: to expound: to account for. — *v.i.* to give an explanation. — *adj.* **explain'able.** — *ns.* **explain'er; explana'tion** (*eks-plə-nā'shən*) the act of explaining or clearing from obscurity: that which explains or clears up: the meaning or sense given to anything: a mutual clearing up of matters. — *adv.* **explan'atorily** (*iks-plan'ə-tər-i-li*). — *adjs.* **explan'atory, explan'ative** serving to explain or clear up: containing explanations. — **explain away** to modify the force of by explanation, generally in a bad sense. [L. *explānāre* — *ex-*, out, *plānāre*, to level — *plānus*, flat, plain.]

explantation *eks-plän-tā'shən, n.* the culture in an artificial medium of a part or organ removed from a living individual. — *n.* and *v.t.* **explant'.** [L. *explantāre* — *ex-*, out, *plantāre*, to plant.]

expletive *eks-, iks-plē'tiv,* or *eks'pli-tiv, adj.* filling out: added merely to fill up. — *n.* a word inserted to fill up a sentence or line of verse: a meaningless word serving a grammatical purpose only: anything present merely to fill a gap: a meaningless oath: a swear-word of any kind. — *adj.* **explē'tory** (also *eks'pli-*) serving to fill up: expletive: supplementary. [L. *explētivus* — *ex*, out, *plēre*, to fill.]

explicate *eks'pli-kāt, v.t.* to unfold, develop: to lay open or explain the meaning of. — *adj.* **explic'able** (older *eks'*) capable of being explicated or explained. — *n.* **explicā'tion** the act of explicating or explaining: explanation. — *adjs.* **explic'ative, explic'atory** (older *eks'*) serving to explicate or explain. — *n.* **ex'plicātor.** [L. *explicāre, explicātum* or *explicitum* — *ex*, out, *plicāre*, to fold.]

explication de texte *eks-plē-ka-syõ də tekst,* a method of literary criticism based on a detailed analysis of the text of the work. [Fr., lit. explication of (the) text.]

explicit¹ *iks-plis'it, adj.* not implied merely, but distinctly stated: plain in language: outspoken: clear: unreserved. — *adv.* **explic'itly.** — *n.* **explic'itness.** [See **explicate.**]

explicit² *eks'pli-sit, n.* a conclusion. [From the mediaeval custom of writing *explicit* at the end of a book or section: originally apparently for L. *explicitum est,* is completed: later taken to be 3rd sing. pres. indic., and supplied with a plural *expliciunt*; see **explicate.**]

explode *iks-plōd', v.t.* to cry down, hoot off, as an actor (*arch.*): to bring into disrepute, and reject: to cause to blow up. — *v.i.* to burst with a loud report: to burst out, break forth suddenly: (of population, to increase suddenly and rapidly. — *adj.* **explō'ded** blown up: (of a theory, etc.) rejected because proved false: (of a drawing or diagram of a machine, building, organism, etc.) showing the internal structure and separate parts and their relationship. — *n.* **explō'der.** — *adj.* **explō'sible** liable to explode. — *n.* **explō'sion** (*-zhən*) the act of exploding: a sudden violent burst with a loud report: an outburst: breaking out of feelings, etc.: a great and rapid increase or expansion, as *population explosion:*

release of breath after stoppage in articulating a stop consonant in certain positions. — *adj.* **explō'sive** (*-siv, -ziv*) liable to or causing explosion: worked, set in place, etc., by an explosion: bursting out with violence and noise. — *n.* something that will explode: a stop consonant pronounced with explosion. — *adv.* **explō'sively.** — *n.* **explō'siveness.** — **exploding star** a star that flares up, such as a nova or supernova; **explosion shot** a golf stroke to send a ball forcibly out of a bunker; **explosion welding** welding metals with very different melting points by means of pressure produced by an explosion; **explosive bolt** a bolt that can be blown out of position because it contains a small explosive charge; **explosive rivet** a rivet fixed in inaccessible places by detonation of a small charge in its end. [L. *explōdĕre, explōsum* — *ex*, from, *plaudĕre*, to clap the hands.]

exploit *eks'ploit, n.* a deed or achievement, esp. an heroic one: a feat. — *v.t.* (*iks-ploit'*) to work, make available: to turn to use: to make gain out of or at the expense of. — *adj.* **exploit'able.** — *ns.* **exploit'age; exploitā'tion** (*eks-*) the act of successfully applying industry to any object, as the working of mines, etc.: the setting-up and getting into production of an oil-field, mine, etc.: the act of using for selfish purposes; **exploit'er.** — *adjs.* **exploit'ive; exploit'ative.** [O.Fr. *exploit* — L. *explicitum*, unfolded; see **explicate.**]

explore *iks-plōr',* or *-plör', v.t.* and *v.i.* to search or travel through for the purpose of discovery: to examine thoroughly. — *ns.* **explorā'tion** (*eks-*) the act of searching, or searching for (something), thoroughly: travel for the sake of discovery: examination of a region's geology, etc., in a search for mineral resources; **explorā'tionist** a scientist engaged in mineral exploration. — *adjs.* **explor'ative, explor'atory** (*-or-*) serving to explore or investigate: searching out. — *n.* **explor'er.** — *adj.* **explor'ing.** [Fr., — L. *explōrāre, -ātum,* to search out.]

explosion. See **explode.**

expo *eks'pō, n.* an exhibition or public showing: — *pl.* **ex'pos.** [*expo*sition.]

exponent *eks-pō'nənt, adj.* setting forth: expounding. — *n.* an expounder (of): an interpreter of an art by performance: an example, illustration, type (of): a symbol showing what power a quantity is raised to, an index (*math.*). — *adj.* **exponential** (*eks-pō-nen'shl*) pertaining to or involving exponents. — *n.* an exponential function. — *adv.* **exponen'tially.** — **exponential curve** a curve expressed by an exponential equation; **exponential equation** one in which the variable occurs in the exponent of one or more terms; **exponential function** a quantity with a variable exponent, esp. e^x, where e is the base of natural logarithms; **exponential series** a series in which exponential quantities are developed; **exponential theorem** gives a value of any number in terms of its natural logarithm, and from it can at once be derived a series determining the logarithm. [L. *expōnēns, -entis,* setting forth — *ex-*, out, *pōnĕre*, to place.]

exponible *eks-pō'ni-bl, adj.* able to be, or requiring to be, explained. [L. *expōnĕre*; see **exponent.**]

export *eks-pört', -pört', v.t.* to carry or send out of a country, as goods in commerce. — *n.* **ex'port** the act of exporting: that which is exported: a commodity which is or may be sent from one country to another in traffic: a type of strong brown beer. — *adj.* **export'able.** — *ns.* **exportabil'ity; exportā'tion; export'er.** — **export reject** a manufactured article that is flawed in some way and so not passed for export, often sold at a reduced price on the home market. — **invisible exports** such items in a national trade balance as money spent by tourists from abroad, etc. — opp. to **visible exports** goods sold abroad by traders. [L. *exportāre, -ātum* — *ex-*, out of, *portāre*, to carry.]

expose *iks-pōz', v.t.* to lay forth to view: to deprive of cover, protection, or shelter: to make bare: to abandon (an infant): to submit (to an influence, as light, weather): to put up (for sale): to explain (*arch.*): to disclose: to show up. — *n.* (*U.S.*) exposé. — *ns.* **expōs'al** exposure: exposition; **exposé** (*eks-pō'zā*) an exposing: a shameful showing up: an article or programme exposing crime, scandal, etc., to public notice: a formal statement or exposition. — *adj.* **exposed'** unprotected: shelterless. — *ns.* **expōs'edness** the state of being exposed; **expōs'er; exposure** (*-pō'zhər, -zhyər*) the act of laying open or bare: subjection to an influence: the act of allowing access of light (*phot.*): duration of such access: the act of showing up an evil: a state of being laid bare: openness to danger: a shelterless state: position with regard to the sun, influence of climate, etc.: appearance in public, esp. on television. — **exposure meter** (*phot.*) an instrument, now often incorporated in the camera, for measuring the light falling on or reflected from a subject. — **expose oneself** to expose one's sexual organs in public.   [Fr. *exposer* — L. *ex-*, out, and *pausāre*, to rest, confused with *expōnĕre*, to expose; see **exponent, exposition**, and cf. **pose**[1], **compose, repose**, etc.]

exposition *eks-pō-zish'ən, n.* the act of exposing: a setting out to public view: the abandonment of a child: a public exhibition: the act of expounding: explanation: commentary: an expository discourse: the enunciation of themes in a composition: that part of a sonata, fugue, etc., in which themes are presented. — *adj.* **expositive** (*-poz'*) serving to expose or explain: explanatory: exegetical. — *n.* **expos'itor** one who, or that which, expounds: an interpreter: — *fem.* **expos'itress**. — *adj.* **expos'itory** serving to explain: explanatory. — *n.* **exposture** (*-pos'chər; Shak.*) exposure.   [L. *expositiō, -ōnis, expositor, -ōris* — *expōnĕre, expositum,* to expose, set forth; see **expound**.]

ex post facto *eks pōst fak'tō,* (L.; *lit.* from what is done or enacted after) retrospective: retrospectively.

expostulate *iks-post'ū-lāt, v.i.* to remonstrate: to discuss (*Shak.*): to claim (*Milt.*). — *n.* **expostulā'tion**. — *adjs.* **expost'ūlātive** (or *-ə-tiv*), **expost'ūlatory** (*-ā-* or *-ə-tər-i*) containing expostulation. — *n.* **expost'ūlator**.   [L. *expostulāre, -ātum* — *ex,* intens., *postulāre,* to demand.]

exposture. See **exposition**.
exposure. See **expose**.

expound *iks-pownd', v.t.* to expose, or lay open the meaning of: to explain: to interpret: to explain in a certain way. — *n.* **expound'er**.   [O.Fr. *espondre* — L. *expōnĕre* — *ex-*, out, *pōnĕre,* to place.]

express *iks-pres', v.t.* to press or force out: to emit: to represent or make known by a likeness, words, signs, symbols, etc.: to put into words: to symbolise: to state explicitly: to reveal: to designate: to despatch. — *adj.* clearly brought out: exactly representing: directly stated: explicit: clear: intended or sent for a particular purpose: expeditious. — *adv.* with haste: specially: by express train or messenger: by express. — *n.* a messenger or conveyance sent on a special errand: a special message: a regular and quick conveyance: a system for the speedy transmission of messages or goods: an express train: an express messenger. — *n.* **express'age** the system of carrying by express: the charge for doing so. — *adj.* **express'ible**. — *ns.* **expression** (*-presh'ən*) the act of forcing out by pressure: the act, or mode, or power, of representing or giving utterance: representation or revelation by language, art, the features, etc.: the manner in which anything is expressed: a word, phrase: a symbol: intonation: due indication of feeling in performance of music: the effect which a gene produces (*biol.*). — *adj.* **express'ional** of, or pertaining to, expression. — *n.* **express'ionism** (often with *cap.*) in literature and painting, a revolt against impressionism, turning away from the representation of external reality to the expression of the artist's emotions and reactions to experience. — *n.* and *adj.* **express'ionist**. — *adjs.* **expressionis'tic; express'ionless; express'ive** serving to express or indicate: full of expression: vividly representing (with *of*): emphatic: significant. — *adv.*

express'ively. — *ns.* **express'iveness; expressiv'ity** the quality of being able to express: the extent to which a gene produces an effect (*biol.*). — *adv.* **express'ly** explicitly: for the express purpose: definitely. — *ns.* **express'man; express'ness; expressure** (*eks-presh'ər*) pressing out: expression (*Shak.*): representation (*Shak.*). — **express agency, company** one that undertakes speedy transmission of goods; **express delivery** immediate delivery by special messenger: delivery by express agency; **express fee** a fee for express delivery; **expression mark** a direction written on a piece of music (usu. in Italian); **expression stop** a stop in a harmonium by which the performer can regulate the air to produce expression; **express letter, packet, parcel** one sent by special messenger; **express messenger** a special messenger; **express rifle** a rifle for big game at short range, with heavy charge of powder and light bullet; **express train** a railway-train which travels at high speed and with few stops; **express'way** a road for fast motor traffic, with dual-carriageway and no crossings on the same level. — **express oneself** to give expression to one's thoughts, ideas and opinions.   [L. *exprimĕre, expressum* — *ex,* from, *premĕre, pressum,* to press; partly through Fr. *exprès,* etc.]

expressis verbis *eks-pre'sis vûr'bis, eks-pre'sēs wer'bēs,* (L.) in express terms.

expresso *eks-pres'ō, n.* and *adj.* Same as **espresso**.

exprobrate *eks'prō-brāt,* (*arch.*) *v.t.* to reproach with: to upbraid. — *n.* **exprobrā'tion**. — *adjs.* **exprō'brative; exprō'bratory**.   [L. *exprobrāre, -ātum* — pfx. *ex-*, indicating source, *probrum,* disgrace.]

ex professo *eks prə-fe'sō, pro-,* (L.) avowedly.

expromission *eks-pro-mish'ən, n.* the intervention of a new debtor, substituted for the former one, who is consequently discharged by the creditor. — *n.* **expromissor** (*-mis'ər*).   [L. *exprōmittĕre, -missum,* to promise to pay — *ex-,* intens., *prōmittĕre,* to promise.]

expropriate *iks-prō'pri-āt, v.t.* to dispossess. — *adj.* **exprō'priable**. — *ns.* **expropriā'tion; exprō'priator**.   [L. *expropriāre, -ātum* — *ex,* from, *proprium,* property.]

ex propriis *eks prō'pri-is, prō'prē-ēs* (*pro'*), (L.) from one's own resources.

ex proprio motu *eks prō'pri-ō mō'tū, pro'pri-ō mō'toŏ,* (L.L.) of his own accord.

expugn *iks-pūn', v.t.* to take by storm: to storm: to overcome. — *adj.* **expugnable** (*-pug'* or *-pū'nəbl*) capable of being taken or vanquished. — *n.* **expugnā'tion** (*-pug-*).   [L. *expugnāre.*]

expulse *iks-puls', (obs.) v.t.* to expel forcibly, eject. — *n.* **expul'sion** the act of expelling: banishment. — *adj.* **expul'sive** able or serving to expel.   [L. *expulsāre,* freq. of *expellĕre;* see **expel**.]

expunge *iks-punj', v.t.* to wipe out: to efface: to mark for deletion. — Also **expunct** (*iks-pungkt', arch.*). — *ns.* **expunc'tion** (*-pungk'shən*); **expun'ger**.   [L. *expungĕre, -punctum* to mark for deletion by a row of dots — *ex-,* out, *pungĕre,* to prick.]

expurgate *eks'pûr-gāt,* also *-pûr', v.t.* to purge out or render pure: to purify from anything supposed to be offensive, noxious, or erroneous. — *ns.* **expurgā'tion** the act of expurgating or purifying: the removal of anything hurtful or evil: bowdlerising: exculpation; **expurgator** (*eks'pûr-gā-tər,* or *eks-pûr'gə-tər*) one who expurgates or purifies. — *adjs.* **expurgato'rial** (*-gə-tō'-ri-əl, -tō'*), **expur'gatory** pertaining to expurgation: tending to expurgate or purify. — *v.t.* **expurge** (*-pûrj'*) to purify, expurgate.   [L. *expurgāre, -ātum* — *ex-,* out, *purgāre,* to purge.]

exquisite *eks'kwiz-it,* also *-kwiz', adj.* far-fetched (*Shak.*): abstruse (*obs.*): delicious: of consummate excellence: compelling the highest admiration: of delicate perception or close discrimination: not easily satisfied: fastidious: exceeding, extreme, as pain or pleasure. — *n.* one exquisitely nice or fastidious in dress: a fop. — *adv.* **ex'quisitely**. — *n.* **ex'quisiteness**.   [L. *exquīsītus* — *ex,* out, *quaerĕre,* to seek.]

ex quocunque capite *eks kwō-kun'kwi, -koŏn'kwe, kap'it-ē,*

-e, (L.) from whatever source.

ex re nata (L.). Same as **e re nata**.

exsanguinous *iks-sang'gwin-əs, adj.* without blood: anaemic — also **exsang'uine, -d, exsanguin'eous.** — *v.t.* **exsang'uinate** (*med.*) to drain of blood. — *ns.* **exsanguinā'tion; exsanguin'ity.** [L. *ex-*, without, *sanguis, -inis*, blood.]

exscind *ik-sind', v.t.* to cut off. [L. *ex*, from, *scindĕre*, to cut.]

exsect *ik-sekt', v.t.* to cut out. — *n.* **exsec'tion.** [L. *ex*, from, *secāre, sectum*, to cut.]

exsert *ik-sûrt', v.t.* to protrude. — *adj.* **exsert'ed** projecting. — *adj.* **exser'tile** (*-tīl, U.S. -til*). — *n.* **exser'tion.** [L. *exserĕre, -sertum*; see **exert**.]

ex-service *eks-sûr'vis, adj.* formerly in one of the fighting services. — *n.* **ex-ser'viceman.**

exsiccate *ek'si-kāt, v.t.* to dry up. — *adj.* **exsicc'ant.** — *n.* **exsiccā'tion.** — *adj.* **exsicc'ative** (or *-āt'*). — *n.* **ex'siccātor** a drying agent or apparatus. [L. *exsiccare — ex-, siccus*, dry.]

exstipulate *iks-tip'ū-lāt*, (*bot.*) *adj.* without stipules. — Also **estip'ulate.**

exsuccous *ik-suk'əs, adj.* sapless. [L. *exsuccus — ex-, succus*, juice.]

exsufflicate *ik-suf'li-kāt, adj.* puffed out (*Shak.*). — *v.t.* **exsuff'late** to blow away: to exorcise by blowing away. — *n.* **exsufflā'tion** expiration: forced expiration: exorcism by blowing. [L. *ex-*, out, and *sufflāre*, to blow out — *sub*, under, *flāre*, to blow.]

ex tacito *eks ta'si-tō, ta'ki-tō*, (L.) silently.

extant *iks-tant', eks'tənt, adj.* standing out, or above the rest (*arch.*): still standing or existing. [L. *extāns, -antis — ex-*, out, *stāre*, to stand.]

extasy, extatic. Obs. forms of **ecstasy, ecstatic.**

extempore *iks-tem'pə-ri, adv.* on the spur of the moment: without preparation: suddenly. — *adj.* sudden: rising at the moment: without help of manuscript: composed and delivered or performed impromptu. — *n.* an impromptu. — *adj.* **extem'poral.** — *n.* **extemporaneity** (*-ə-nē'i-ti*). — *adj.* **extemporā'neous.** — *adv.* **extemporā'neously.** — *n.* **extemporā'neousness.** — *adv.* **extem'porarily.** — *n.* **extem'porariness.** — *adj.* **extem'porary** done on the spur of the moment: hastily prepared: speaking extempore: done without preparation: off-hand. — *n.* **extemporisā'tion, -z-.** — *v.t.* **extem'porise, -ize** to speak, or compose and play, extempore or without previous preparation: to discourse without notes: to speak off-hand. [L. *ex*, out of, and *tempore*, abl. of *tempus*, time.]

extend *iks-tend', v.t.* to stretch out: to prolong in any direction: to enlarge: to expand: to widen: to unfold: to straighten out: to hold out: to offer, accord: to exert to the full: to seize (*law, Shak.*): to value, assess. — *v.i.* to stretch, reach: to be continued in length or breadth. — *n.* **extendabil'ity.** — *adjs.* **extend'able; extend'ant** (*her.*) displayed; **extend'ed** occupying space: having extension: stretched out: extensive. — *adv.* **extend'edly.** — *ns.* **extend'er** one who or that which extends: a university extension lecture: a substance added to paint to give body, or to food to give extra bulk; **extendibil'ity.** — *adjs.* **extend'ible; extense** (*-tens'*; *obs.*) extensive. — *n.* **extensibil'ity.** — *adjs.* **extens'ible, extensile** (*eks-ten'sīl, -sil*) that may be extended. — *n.* **extension** (*iks-, eks-ten'shən*) an act of extending: condition of being extended: an added piece: a wing or annex of a house: the property of occupying space: the extent of the application of a term or the number of objects included under it — opp. to *intension* (*logic*): a word or words added to subject, predicate, or object (*gram.*): an additional telephone using the same line as the main one. — *adj.* **exten'sional.** — *adv.* **exten'sionally.** — *ns.* **exten'sionalism, extensional'ity; exten'sionist** an advocate of extension: a university extension lecturer or student; **exten'sity** massiveness or spatial quality in sensation from which perception of extension is derived. — *adj.* **extens'ive** large: widespread: comprehensive: (*eks-*) pertaining to extension: seeking

or deriving a comparatively small crop cheaply from a wide area — opp. to *intensive*. — *adv.* **extens'ively.** — *ns.* **extens'iveness; extensom'eter, extensim'eter** (*eks-*) an instrument for measuring small strains in metal; **exten'sor** a muscle that extends or straightens any part of the body; **extent'** the space or degree to which a thing is extended: bulk: compass: scope: degree or amount (as *to some extent*): a stretch or extended space: a valuation of property: a writ directing the sheriff to seize the property of a debtor, for the recovery of debts of record due to the Crown (*law*): seizure (*Shak.*): attack (*Shak.*): an act of extending (justice, courtesy, etc.) (*Shak.*). — *adj.* stretched out. — **extended family** a social unit comprising not only a couple and their children but other relatives, e.g. aunts, uncles, grandparents; **extended play** of a gramophone record, giving longer reproduction because of a closer groove and the use of a larger part of its surface area. — **university extension** the enlargement of the aim of a university, in providing instruction for those unable to become regular students. [L. *extendĕre, extentum*, or *extēnsum — ex-*, out, *tendĕre*, to stretch.]

extenuate *iks-ten'ū-āt, v.t.* to lessen: to underrate: to weaken the force of: to palliate. — *n.* and *adj.* **exten'ūāting** palliating. — *adv.* **exten'ūātingly.** — *n.* **extenūā'tion** the act of representing anything as less wrong or criminal than it seems: palliation: mitigation. — *adjs.* **exten'ūātive, exten'ūātory** tending to extenuate: palliative. — *n.* **exten'ūātor.** [L. *extenuāre, -ātum — ex-*, intens., *tenuis*, thin.]

exterior *eks-tē'ri-ər, adj.* outer: outward, external: on or from the outside: foreign. — *n.* the outside, outer surface: outward form or deportment: appearance: a representation of an outdoor scene: an outer part (esp. in *pl.*). — *v.t.* **extēr'iorise, -ize** to externalise: to bring an internal part temporarily outside the body (*surg.*). — *ns.* **exteriorisā'tion, -z-; extēriority** (*-or'i-ti*). — *adv.* **extē'riorly** outwardly. — **exterior angle** (*math.*) the angle between any side produced and the adjacent side (not produced) of a polygon. [L. *exterior*, compar. of *exter, exterus*, outward — *ex*, from.]

exterminate *iks-tûr'mi-nāt, v.t.* to drive out (*obs.*): to destroy utterly: to put an end to: to root out. — *adj.* **exter'minable** that can be exterminated: illimitable (*Shelley*). — *n.* **exterminā'tion** complete destruction or extirpation. — *adjs.* **exter'minātive, exter'minatory** serving or tending to exterminate. — *n.* **exter'minātor.** — *v.t.* **exter'mine** (*Shak.*) to exterminate. [L. *extermināre, -ātum*, to drive beyond the boundary — *ex*, out of, *terminus*, boundary.]

external *eks-tûr'nəl, adj.* exterior: lying outside: outward: belonging to the world of outward things: that may be seen: not innate or intrinsic: accidental: foreign. — *n.* exterior: (in *pl.*) the outward parts: (in *pl.*) outward or non-essential forms and ceremonies: (in *pl.*) outward circumstances or appearances. — *adj.* **extern'**, **externe** external, outward. — *n.* a non-resident, as a day-scholar, an out-patient, non-resident physician or surgeon. — *n.* **externalisā'tion, -z-.** — *v.t.* **exter'nalise, -ize** to give form or apparent reality to: to give external expression to: to extravert (one's personality): to ascribe to causes outside oneself: to regard as consisting of externals only. — *ns.* **exter'nalism** undue regard to mere externals or non-essential outward forms, esp. of religion; **exter'nalist; externality** (*-nal'i-ti*) external character: superficiality: undue regard to externals. — *adv.* **exter'nally.** — *n.* **externat** (*eks-ter-nä*; Fr.) a day-school. — **external examiner** an examiner from another seat of learning who has had no part in teaching the examinees; **external student** one examined (for an **external degree**) by a university in which he has not studied. — **external-combustion engine** one in which the fuel is burned outside the working cylinder. [L. *externus*, outward — *exter*, outside.]

exteroceptor *eks'tər-ō-sep-tər*, (*zool.*) *n.* a sensory organ, e.g. the eye, receiving impressions from outside the body. — *adj.* **exterocep'tive.** [L. *exterus*, exterior, and re*ceptor.*]

exterritorial *eks-ter-i-tō'ri-əl, -tō'.* Same as **extraterritorial.**

extinct *iks-tingkt', adj.* put out: extinguished: no longer existing: dead. — *adj.* **extinct'ed** (*Shak.*) extinguished. — *n.* **extinc'tion** extinguishing, quenching or wiping out: destruction: suppression: the cutting off of polarised light at certain angles when a section of doubly refracting mineral is rotated between crossed nicols: the absorbing by the earth's atmosphere of a planet's or star's light (*astron.*): the inhibition of a conditioned reflex (*psychol.*). — *adj.* **extinct'ive** tending to extinguish. — *n.* **extinct'ure** (*Shak.*) extinction. [L. *ex(s)tinctum*; see **extinguish.**]

extine *eks'tin, -tēn, -tīn,* (*bot.*) *n.* the outer membrane of a pollen-grain or spore. — Also **ex'ine.** [From the root of L. *exter, extimus,* outer, outmost.]

extinguish *iks-ting'gwish, v.t.* to quench, put out: to render extinct: to put an end to: to destroy, annihilate: to obscure by superior splendour: to pay off (a debt) (*law*). — *v.i.* to die out. — *adj.* **exting'uishable.** — *ns.* **exting'uishant** a substance used to extinguish fires; **exting'uisher** one who, or that which, extinguishes: a small hollow conical instrument for putting out a candle, etc.: a device for putting out fire: a conical structure resembling a candle extinguisher; **exting'-uishment** the act of extinguishing: putting an end to a right by consolidation or union (*law*). [L. *ex(s)tinguĕre, ex(s)tinctum — ex-,* out, *stinguĕre,* to quench.]

extirpate *eks'tər-pāt, v.t.* to root out: to destroy totally: to remove surgically: to exterminate — (*Spens., Shak.*) **extirp** (*eks-tûrp'*). — *adj.* **extirpable** (*eks-tûrp'ə-bl*). — *ns.* **extirpā'tion** extermination: total destruction; **ex'tirpātor** one who extirpates: an implement for weeding. — *adjs.* **ex'tirpative; extirpatory** (*ekstûrp'ə-tər-i*). [L. *exstirpāre, -ātum — ex,* out, and *stirps,* a stock, root.]

extol *iks-tōl', -tol', v.t.* to lift up (*Spens.*): to praise highly: — *pr.p.* **extoll'ing;** *pa.t.* and *pa.p.* **extolled',** *Spens.* **extold'.** — *ns.* **extoll'er; extol'ment** the act of extolling: the state of being extolled. [L. *extollĕre — ex-,* up, *tollĕre,* to lift or raise.]

extort *iks-tört', v.t.* to wring out: to gain or draw out by compulsion or violence. — *adj.* extorted: wrongfully obtained. — *adj.* **extors'ive** serving or tending to extort. — *adv.* **extors'ively.** — *n.* **extortion** (*-tör'shən*) illegal or oppressive exaction: that which is extorted. — *adjs.* **extor'tionary** pertaining to or implying extortion; **extor'tionate** oppressive: exacting, demanding too much. — *adv.* **extor'tionately.** — *ns.* **extor'tioner, extor'tionist** one who practises extortion. — *adj.* **extort'ive.** [L. *extorquēre, extortum — ex-,* out, *torquēre,* to twist.]

extra[1] *eks'trə, adj.* beyond or more than the usual or the necessary: extraordinary: additional. — *adv.* unusually. — *n.* what is extra or additional, as an item above and beyond the ordinary school curriculum, something over and above the usual course or charge in a bill, etc.: a special edition of a newspaper containing later news: a run scored at cricket from a bye, leg-bye, wide, or no-ball (not hit): a film actor temporarily engaged for a minor part, as to be one of a crowd. — *adj.* **ex'tra-condensed'** (*print.*) extremely narrow in proportion to the height. — **extra cover** in cricket, a fielding position between cover point and mid off, or the player in this position. **ext'ra-spec'ial** much out of the way. — *n.* a special late edition of an evening newspaper called for by some news of great importance. — **extra jam, marmalade,** under EEC regulations, jam, marmalade containing a considerably higher percentage (by weight) of fruit than that in ordinary jam or marmalade; **extra time** additional time allowed at the end of a match because of time lost through injury, or for other reason. [Prob. contracted from **extraordinary.**]

extra[2] *eks'trə, eks'trä,* (L.) *prep.* outside. — **extra modum** (*mō'dəm, mo'dōōm*) beyond measure, extravagant;

extra muros (*mū'rōs, mōō'rōs*) beyond the walls.

extra- *eks'tra-, -trə-, pfx.* outside. — *adjs.* **ex'tra-ax'illary** not in the axil of a leaf; **ex'tracanon'ical** not part of the canon of the Bible; **ex'tracell'ular** outside the cell-walls; **ex'tracorpor'eal** outside the body; **extra= curric'ular** of a subject or activity, outside and additional to the regular academic course; **ex'tradō'tal** not forming part of the dowry; **ex'traflo'ral** not in a flower; **ex'traforā'neous** out-door. — *v.t.* **ex'tra-ill'ustrate** (or *-lus'*) to grangerise. — **ex'tra-illustrā'tion.** — *adj.* **ex'tragalac'tic** outside the Milky Way; **ex'trajudi'cial** not made in court, beyond the usual course of legal proceeding. — *adv.* **ex'trajudi'cially.** — *adjs.* **ex'tralim'-ital** not found within a given faunal area: lying outside a prescribed area — also **ex'tralim'itary; ex'tramar'ital** (of relations, etc.) outside marriage, though properly confined to marriage; **ex'tramet'rical** in excess of the recognised number of syllables in the line; **ex'tramun'-dane** beyond the material world; **ex'tramū'ral** without or beyond the walls: connected with a university but not under its direct control; **ex'tranu'clear** outside the nucleus (of a cell or an atom); **ex'tra-parō'chial** beyond the limits of a parish; **ex'tra-phys'ical** not subject to physical laws; **ex'tra-profess'ional** not belonging to a particular profession: outside the usual limits of professional duty or practice; **ex'tra-provin'cial** outside the limits of a particular province; **ex'tra-reg'ular** unlimited by rules; **ex'tra-sensory** outside the ordinary senses as in clairvoyant and telepathic perception (**extra= sensory perception** the ability to perceive without the normal senses (cf. **sixth sense**)); **ex'tra-sō'lar** beyond the solar system; **ex'tra-terres'trial** outside, or from outside, the earth; **ex'traterrito'rial** outside a territory or territorial jurisdiction — also **exterritor'ial.** — *n.* **ex'traterritorial'ity** the privilege of being outside the jurisdiction of the country one is in. — Also **exterritorial'ity.** — *adjs.* **ex'tratrop'ical** outside the tropics; **ex'tra-ū'terine** outside the uterus; **ex'travas'cular** outside the vascular system or a vessel: not vascular; **ex'travehic'ūlar** situated, used, or happening, outside a spacecraft. [L. *extrā,* outside.]

extract *iks-, eks-trakt', v.t.* to draw out by force or otherwise: to choose out or select: to find out: to derive: to extort: to take a copy of (*Scots law*): to copy passages from: to publish passages from: to withdraw by chemical or physical means from containing or combined matter: to exhaust or treat by extraction. — *adj.* (*obs.* except *Scots law*) extracted: derived. — *n.* **extract** (*eks'*) anything drawn from a substance by heat, distillation, solvents, etc., as an essence: a passage taken from a book or writing: wool from rags from which cotton has been chemically removed. — *adjs.* **extract'able** (also **extract'ible**). — *ns.* **extractabil'ity; extract'ant** (*chem.*) a solvent used for extraction; **extrac'tion** the act of extracting: derivation from a stock or family: birth: lineage: that which is extracted. — *adj.* **extract'ive** tending or serving to extract: of the nature of an extract (**extractive matter** the soluble portions of any drug). — *n.* an extract. — *n.* **extract'or** he who, or that which, extracts. — **extractor (fan)** an electric fan which extracts air, gas, etc., from a room or building. — **extract the root of a quantity** to find its root by a mathematical process. [L. *extrahĕre, extractum — ex,* from, *trahĕre,* to draw.]

extradition *eks-trə-dish'ən, n.* a delivering up of accused persons by one government to another. — *adj.* **extraditable** (*-dīt'əbl*). — *v.t.* **ex'tradite** to hand over for trial or punishment to a foreign government. [L. *ex,* from, *trāditiō, -ōnis — trādĕre, trāditum,* to deliver up.]

extrados *eks-trā'dos, n.* the convex surface of an arch: the external curve of the voussoirs. [Fr., — L. *extrā,* outside, Fr. *dos,* back.]

extrait *eks-tre,* (Fr.) *n.* extract.

extraneous *eks-trān'yəs, adj.* external: foreign: not belonging to or dependent on a thing: not essential. — *ns.* **extraneity** (*-trə-nē'i-ti*), **extrān'eousness.** — *adv.*

extrān′eously. [L. *extrāneus*, external, *extrā*, outside.]

extraordinary *eks-trörd′-i-nə-ri, -in-ri,* or *eks-trə-örd′,* or *iks-trörd′, adj.* beyond ordinary: not usual or regular: remarkable, wonderful: special or supernumerary, as 'physician extraordinary' in a royal household, and 'extraordinary professor' in a German university, both being inferior to the ordinary official. — *n.pl.* **extraord′inaries** things that exceed the usual order, kind, or method. — *adv.* **extraord′inarily.** — *n.* **extraord′inariness.** — **extraordinary ray** in double refraction, the ray that does not obey the ordinary law of refraction. [L. *extraordinārius* — *extrā,* outside, *ordō, -inis,* order.]

extrapolate *iks-trap′ō-lāt, -ə-lāt, eks′, v.t.* to estimate from observed tendencies the value of (any variable) outside the limits between which values are known: to infer, conjecture from what is known: to project into a new area of experience or activity. — Also *v.i.* — *n.* **extrapolā′tion.** — *adjs.* **extrap′olātive, extrap′olatory.** — *n.* **extrap′olātor.** [L. *extrā,* and **interpolate.**]

extraught *iks-tröt′,* (*Shak.*) *pa.p.* of **extract.**

extravagant *iks-trav′ə-gənt, adj.* wandering beyond bounds (*arch.*): irregular: unrestrained: excessive: profuse in expenses: wasteful. — *ns.* **extrav′agance** excess: lavish expenditure: digression (*Milt.*); **extrav′agancy** vagrancy (*Shak.*): extravagance. — *adv.* **extrav′agantly.** — *v.i.* (*arch.*) **extrav′agate** to wander: to exceed proper bounds. [L. *extrā,* beyond, *vagāns, -antis,* pr.p. of *vagārī,* to wander.]

extravaganza *iks-trav-ə-gan′zə, n.* an extravagant or eccentric musical, dramatic, or literary production: extravagant conduct or speech. [It. (*e*)*stravaganza.*]

extravasate *iks-trav′ə-sāt, v.t.* to let, or force (blood or other fluid) out of the proper vessels: to pour out (lava). — *adj.* extravasated. — *n.* **extravasā′tion** the act of extravasating: the escape of any of the fluids of the living body from their proper vessels. [L. *extrā,* out of, *vās,* a vessel.]

extravert, extrovert *eks′trə-* or *-trō-vûrt, vs.t.* to turn outward or outside in: to make manifest. — *n.* (*eks′*) a person interested mainly in the world external to himself — opp. to *introvert.* — Also *adj.* — *ns.* **extraver′sion, extrover′sion.** [L. *extrā,* outside, *vertěre,* to turn; the *extro-* forms by analogy with **introvert.**]

extreat *eks-trēt′,* (*Spens.*) *n.* extraction. [**estreat.**]

extreme *iks-trēm′* (*arch. eks′*), *adj.* outermost: most remote: last: highest in degree: greatest: most violent: of opinions, etc., not moderate, going to great lengths: stringent: — *superl., rare,* **extrēm′est;** *compar., rare,* **extrēm′er.** — *n.* the utmost point or verge: end: utmost or the highest limit or degree: (in *pl., obs.*) great necessity. — *adv.* **extreme′ly.** — *ns.* **extrē′mism; extrē′mist** one ready to go to extremes: a holder of extreme opinions: an advocate of extreme action; **extremity** (*-trem′i-ti*) the utmost limit: the highest degree: greatest necessity or distress: extreme condition: an end: hand or foot. — **extreme unction** see **unction.** — **extremely high frequency** see **frequency; go to extremes** to go too far: to use extreme measures; **in the extreme** in the last, highest degree: extremely; **the last extremity** the utmost pitch of misfortune: death. [O.Fr. *extreme* — L. *extrēmus,* superl. of *exter, exterus,* on the outside.]

extricate *eks′tri-kāt, v.t.* to free from entanglements or perplexities: to disentangle: to set free. — *adj.* **ex′tricable.** — *n.* **extricā′tion** disentanglement: the act of setting free. [L. *extricāre, -ātum* — *ex,* from, *trīcae,* hindrances.]

extrinsic *iks-trin′sik, adj.* external: not contained in or belonging to a body: foreign: not essential: of a muscle, running from the trunk to limb or girdle — opp. to *intrinsic.* — *adj.* **extrin′sical.** — *n.* **extrinsical′ity.** — *adv.* **extrin′sically.** [Fr. *extrinsèque* — L. *extrīnsecus* — *exter,* outside, suff. *-in, secus,* beside.]

extrorse *iks-trörs′, adj.* turned outward: (of an anther) opening towards the outside of the flower. [Fr., — L. *extrorsus* — *extrā,* outside, *versus,* turned.]

extrovert, extroversion. Same as **extravert,** etc.

extrude *iks-trōōd′, v.t.* to force or urge out: to expel: to protrude: to make rods, tubes, etc. by extrusion. — *v.i.* to protrude. — *ns.* **extrud′er; extrusion** (*-trōō′zhən*) the act of extruding, thrusting, or throwing out: expulsion: rocks formed by the cooling of magma or lava: the operation of producing rods, tubes, etc., of metal or plastic by forcing suitable material through a die by means of a ram. — *adjs.* **extrusive** (*-trōō′siv*); **extru′sory** (*-sər-i*). [L. *extrūdēre, extrūsum* — *ex-,* out, *trūdēre,* to thrust.]

exuberant *eg-, ig-zū′bər-ənt, -zōō′, adj.* luxuriant: overflowing: abounding: in high spirits: lavish. — *ns.* **exu′berance, exu′berancy** the quality of being exuberant: luxuriance, an overflowing quantity: redundancy: outburst. — *adv.* **exu′berantly.** — *v.i.* **exu′berate** (*rare*) to be exuberant: to grow profusely. [L. *exūberāns, -antis,* pr.p. of *exūberāre* — *ex-,* intens., *über,* rich.]

exude *igz-, iks-ūd′, v.t.* to discharge by sweating: to discharge through pores or incisions. — *v.i.* to flow out of a body through the pores: to ooze out. — *ns.* **exudate** (*eks′*) exuded matter; **exudā′tion** (*eks-*) the act of exuding or discharging through pores: that which is exuded. — *adj.* **exūd′ative.** [L. *exūdāre* — *ex,* from, *sūdāre,* to sweat.]

exul *ek′sul,* (*Spens.*) *n.* an exile. [L. *ex*(*s*)*ul.*]

exulcerate *igz-ul′sər-āt, v.t.* to exasperate, afflict as with an ulcer. — *n.* **exulcerā′tion** ulceration: exasperation. [L. *exulcerāre, -ātum* — *ex-,* intens., *ulcerāre,* to ulcerate.]

exult *igz-ult′, v.i.* to rejoice exceedingly: to triumph. — *ns.* **exult′ance, exult′ancy** exultation: triumph. — *adj.* **exult′ant** exulting: triumphant. — *adv.* **exult′antly.** — *n.* **exultā′tion** (*egz-*) triumphant delight: transport. — *adv.* **exult′ingly.** [L. *ex*(*s*)*ultāre, -ātum,* from *ex*(*s*)*ilīre* — *ex-,* out or up, *salīre,* to leap.]

exurb *eks′ûrb,* (orig. *U.S.*) *n.* a residential area, esp. a prosperous one, outside the suburbs of a town. — *adj.* **exur′ban.** — *n.* and *adj.* **exur′banite.** — *n.* **exur′bia** exurbs collectively. [L. *ex-,* outside, and sub*urbia.*]

ex utraque parte *eks ū-trā′kwi pär′tē, ōō-trä′kwe pär′te* (L.) on either side.

exuviae *igz-, iks-ū′vi-ē, n.pl.* cast-off skins, shells, or other coverings of animals: fossil remains of animals (*geol.*). — *adj.* **exū′vial.** — *v.i.* **exū′viate** to shed, cast off, for a new covering or condition. — *n.* **exuviā′tion** the act of exuviating. [L., *exuěre,* to draw off.]

ex voto *eks vō′tō, wō′,* (L.) according to one's prayer, by reason of a vow: votive. — *n.* a votive offering.

eyalet *ä-yä′let, n.* a division of Turkey — a *vilayet.* [Turk., — Ar. *iyālah.*]

eyas *ī′əs, n.* an unfledged hawk. — *adj.* (*Spens.*) unfledged. — **ey′as-mus′ket** an unfledged male hawk: a child (*Shak.*). [*An eyas* for *a nyas* — Fr. *niais* — L. *nīdus,* nest.]

eye[1] *ī,* (*obs.*) *n.* a brood, esp. of pheasants. [*An eye* for *a nye* — O.Fr. *ni* — L. *nīdus,* nest.]

eye[2] *ī, n.* the organ of sight or vision: more narrowly the globe or movable part of it: the power of seeing: sight: a tinge, suffusion (*Shak.*): regard: aim: keenness of perception: anything resembling an eye, as an eye-spot: a central spot: the hole of a needle: the aperture for inserting the bias in a bowl: a round aperture: a mine entrance: a spring of water: a wire loop or ring for a hook: a round hole or window: the seed-bud of a potato: a spot on an egg: a spectacle lens: the central calm area of a cyclone: (in *pl.*) the foremost part of a ship's bows, the hawse-holes: — *pl.* **eyes;** *arch.* **eyne** (*īn*); *Scot.* **een** (*ēn*). — *v.t.* to look on: to observe narrowly. — *v.i.* (*Shak.*) to appear: — *pr.p.* **eye′ing** or **ey′ing;** *pa.t.* and *pa.p.* **eyed** (*īd*). — *adj.* **eyed** having eyes: spotted as if with eyes. — *n.* **eye′ful** as much as the eye can take in: something worth looking at, a fascinating sight or an attractive woman (*slang*). — *adj.* (*dial.*) slightly: careful, having an eye. — *adj.* **eye′less** without eyes or sight: deprived of eyes: blind. — *n.* **eyelet** see separate entry. — **eye′ball** the ball or globe of the eye. — *v.t.* (*coll.*) to face someone eyeball to eyeball, to confront: to examine closely. — *adj.* (of a measurement) by eye only, not exact. — **eye bank** see **bank³; eye'-bath** a cup that can be held in the orbit to bathe the eye; **eye'-beam** a glance of the eye; **eye'-black** mascara; **eye'bolt** a bolt, with an eye instead of the normal head, used for lifting purposes on heavy machines, etc.; **eye'bright** a little plant of the genus Euphrasia (fam. Scrophulariaceae) formerly used as a remedy for eye diseases; **eye'brow** the hairy arch above the eye. — *v.t.* to provide with artificial eyebrows. — *adj.* **eye'browless** without eyebrows. — **eye'-catcher** a part of a building designed specially to catch a person's eye (*archit.*): a striking person, esp. an attractive woman. — *adj.* **eye'-catching** striking. — **eye contact** a direct look between two people; **eye'-cup** an eye-bath: an eye-piece; **eye'-drop** (*Shak.*) a tear: (in *pl.* without hyphen) a medicine for the eye administered in the form of drops; **eye'-flap** a blinker on a horse's bridle; **eye'-glance** a quick look; **eye'glass** a glass to assist the sight, esp. one held on the bridge of the nose by a spring: an eye-piece: the lens of the eye (*Shak.*); **eye'-hole** an eyelet: an eye-socket: a peep-hole; **eye'-hook** a hook on a ring at the end of a rope or chain; **eye'lash** the row, or one, of the hairs that edge the eyelid. — *adjs.* **eye-leg'ible** (of headings, etc. on microfilm or microprint) able to be read by the naked eye; **eye'-lev'el** at the same height above ground as the average person's eyes. — **eye'lid** the lid or cover of the eye: the portion of movable skin by means of which the eye is opened or closed; **eye'liner** a kind of cosmetic used for drawing a line along the edge of the eyelid in order to emphasise the eye; **eye lotion; eye muscle** a muscle controlling the eye or a part of it: a long muscle running down the back beside the spine; **eye'-opener** something that opens the eyes literally or figuratively, a startling enlightenment: a drink, esp. in the morning (*coll.*); **eye'-piece** the lens or combination of lenses at the eye end of an optical instrument; **eye'-pit** the socket of the eye; **eye'-rhyme** a would-be rhyme between words that are spelt as if they rhymed but do not; **eye'-salve** salve or ointment for the eyes; **eye'-servant** one who does his duty only when under the eye of his master; **eye'-service** service so performed: formal worship; **eye'shade** a piece of stiff, usu. tinted transparent, material, worn like the peak of a cap to protect the eyes from the sun or other bright light; **eye'-shadow** a coloured cosmetic for the eyelids; **eye'-shot** the reach or range of sight of the eye: a glance; **eye'sight** power of seeing: view: observation; **eye socket** either of the two recesses in the skull in which the eyeballs are situated, the orbit; **eye'sore** anything that is offensive to look at; **eye'-splice** a kind of eye or loop formed by splicing the end of a rope into itself; **eye'-spot** a spot like an eye: a rudimentary organ of vision. — *adj.* **eye'-spott'ed** (*Spens.*) marked with spots like eyes. — **eye'stalk** a stalk on the dorsal surface of the head of many Crustacea, bearing an eye; **eye'strain** tiredness of irritation of the eyes; **eye'-string** the muscle that raises the eyelid; **eye'-tooth** a canine tooth, esp. in the upper jaw, below the eye; **eye'-wash** a lotion for the eye: humbug: deception; **eye'-water** water flowing from the eye: a lotion for the eyes; **eye'-wink** (*Shak.*) a rapid lowering and raising of the eyelid: a glance: the time of a wink; **eye'-wit'ness** one who sees a thing done. — **all my eye** (*slang*) humbug; **be all eyes** to give all attention; **be a sheet in the wind's eye** to be intoxicated; **clap, lay, set, eyes on** (*coll.*) to see; **cry one's eyes out** see **cry; cut one's eye-teeth** to cease to be a child: to become shrewd; **eyeball to eyeball** (of discussion, confrontation, diplomacy) at close quarters, dealing with matters very frankly and firmly (also **eye to eye**); **electric eye** see **electric; eye for eye** *lex talionis* (Exod. xxi. 24); **eye of day** the sun; **eyes down** the start of a bingo game, or of any non-physical contest; **eye up** (*slang*) to consider the sexual attractiveness of; **get (keep) one's eye in** to become (remain) proficient; **give an eye to** to attend to; **glad, green eye** see **glad, green¹; have an eye to** to contemplate: to have regard to: to incline towards; **have one's eye on** to keep in mind: to consider acquisitively; **hit one in the eye** to be obvious; **in eye** in sight; **in one's mind's eye** in imagination; **in the eyes of** in the estimation, opinion, of; **in the wind's eye** against the wind; **keep one's** (or **an**) **eye on** to observe closely: to watch; **keep one's eye(s) skinned, peeled (for)** to be keenly watchful; **make a person open his eyes** to cause him astonishment; **make eyes at** to look at in an amorous way, to ogle; **mind your eye** (*slang*) take care; **my eye!** a mild asseveration; **naked eye** see **naked; one in the eye** a rebuff; **open a person's eyes** to make him see: to show him something of which he is ignorant; **pick the eyes out of** (*Austr. coll.*) to choose and take the best parts of; **pipe,** or **put a finger in, the eye** to weep; **private eye** see **private; put a person's eye out** to blind him: to supplant him in favour; **raise an eyebrow** to be mildly surprised, shocked or doubtful; **see eye to eye** from Isa. lii. 8, but used in the sense of to think alike; **see with half an eye** to see without difficulty; **shut one's eyes to** to ignore; **throw, make, sheep's eyes at** to ogle; **turn a blind eye on** to feign not to see, wink at; **under the eye of** under the observation of; **up to the eyes, eyebrows** deeply involved (in); **with, having, an eye to** considering.   [O.E. *ēage*; cf. Goth. *augo*, Ger. *Auge*, Du. *oog*, O.N. *auga*.]

eyelet *ī'lit, n.* a small eye or hole to receive a lace or cord, as in garments, sails, etc.: a small hole for seeing through (also **eye'let-hole**): a little eye. — *v.t.* to make eyelets in.   [O.Fr. *oillet* — L. *oculus*, influenced by **eye.**]

eyeliad, eyliad. See **oeillade.**

Eyeti, Eyetie, Eytie *ī'tī,* (*slang*) *n.* an Italian.

eyne *īn,* (*arch.*) *n.pl.* eyes.   [O.E. *ēagan.*]

eyot *āt.* Same as **ait¹.**

eyra *ī'rə, n.* a South American wild cat.   [Guaraní.]

eyre *ār,* (*hist.*) *n.* a journey or circuit: a court of itinerant justices in the late 12th and 13th cents.   [O.Fr. *eire,* journey, from L. *iter,* a way, a journey — *īre, itum,* to go.]

eyrie, eyry (also **aerie, aery, ayrie**) *ā'ri, ē'ri, ī'ri, ns.* the nest of a bird of prey, esp. an eagle: a house or stronghold perched on some high or steep place: any high or inaccessible place: the brood in the nest, or a stock of children (*Shak.*).   [O.Fr. *aire*; origin unknown.]

F

F, f *ef, n.* the sixth letter in the English and Latin alphabets, derived from the Greek digamma — its sound a labiodental fricative formed by bringing the lower lip into contact with the upper teeth: the fourth note of the natural diatonic scale of C (*mus.*): as a mediaeval Roman numeral F = 40; F̄ = 40,000: F is used as a contraction for Fahrenheit: F₁, F₂ (*genetics*) first and second filial generations: ff in mediaeval script was used instead of a capital F. — **F′-clef** a clef marking F, the fourth line in the bass, the bass-clef; **f′-hole** either of a pair of holes in the belly of a violin, etc., shaped like an italic *f*; **f′-number** (*phot.*) the ratio of the focal length to the true diameter of a lens. — **the three F's** free sale, fixity of tenure, fair rent.

fa *fä, n.* the fourth note in the sol-fa notation — also anglicised in spelling as **fah**. [See **Aretinian**.]

fa' *fö;* **fa'ard, faurd** *färd, förd.* Scots for **fall; favoured.**

fab *fab, (slang) adj.* excellent, marvellous. [Contr. of **fabulous**.]

fabaceous *fə-bāsh'əs, adj.* bean-like. [L. *faba,* a bean.]

Fabergé *fa-ber-zhā, fab-ər-jā′, n.* delicate gold and enamel ware made in Russia in the 19th and early 20th centuries. [Peter Carl *Fabergé* (1846–1920).]

Fabian *fā′bi-ən, adj.* delaying, avoiding battle, cautious, practising the policy of delay: favouring the gradual introduction and spread of Socialism. — *n.* a member or supporter of the *Fabian Society* (founded 1884) for this purpose. — *ns.* **Fā′bianism; Fā′bianist.** [From Q. *Fabius* Maximus, surnamed Cunctator (delayer), from the masterly tactics with which he wore out the strength of Hannibal, whom he dared not meet in battle.]

fable *fā′bl, n.* a narrative in which things irrational, and sometimes inanimate, are, for the purpose of moral instruction, made to act and speak with human interests and passions: any tale in literary form, not necessarily probable in its incidents, intended to instruct or amuse: the plot or series of events in an epic or dramatic poem (*arch.*): a fiction or myth: a ridiculous story, an old wives' tale: a falsehood: subject of common talk. — *v.i.* to tell fictitious tales: to tell falsehoods (*obs.*). — *v.t.* to feign: to invent: to relate as if true. — *adj.* **fā′bled** mythical: renowned in story: feigned. — *n.* **fā′bler** a writer or narrator of fictions. — *n.* and *adj.* **fā′bling.** — *adj.* **fabular** (*fab′ū-lər*). — *v.i.* **fab′ulise, -ize** to write fables, or to speak in fables. — *ns.* **fab′ulist** one who invents fables; **fabulos′ity.** — *adj.* **fab′ulous** feigned, false: related in fable: celebrated in story: immense, amazing: excellent (*coll.*). — *adv.* **fab′ulously.** — *n.* **fab′ulousness.** [Fr. *fable,* and L. *fābula,* — *fārī,* to speak.]

fabliau *fab′li-ō, n.* a metrical tale after the type of those, usually coarsely humorous in quality, produced in France in the 12th and 13th centuries: — *pl.* **fabliaux** (*fab′li-ōz*) (Fr., — dim. of *fable.*]

fabric *fab′rik, n.* the act of constructing: texture: anything framed by art and labour: a building: buildings, stonework, etc.: manufactured cloth: any system of connected parts: framework (also *fig.*). — *v.t.* (*Milt.*) to construct. — *n.* **fab′ricant** (*arch.*) a manufacturer. — *v.t.* **fab′ricate** to put together by art and labour: to manufacture: to produce: to devise falsely. — *n.* **fabricā′tion** construction: manufacture: that which is fabricated or invented: a story: a falsehood. — *adj.* **fab′ricative.** — *n.* **fab′ricator.** [L. *fābrica,* fabric — *fāber,* a worker in hard materials: partly through Fr. *fabrique.*]

fabular, fabulous, etc. See **fable.**

faburden *fa′bər-dən, n.* harmony in thirds and sixths: an early kind of counterpoint: an undersong: a refrain: in 4-part harmonisation of a hymn, having the tune in the tenor: a descant. [Fr. *faux-bourdon* — *faux,* false, *bourdon,* bourdon.]

façade, facade *fa-säd′, n.* the exterior front or face of a building: the appearance presented to the world, esp. if showy and with little behind it (*fig.*). [Fr., — *face,* after It. *facciata,* the front of a building — *faccia,* the face.]

face *fās, n.* the front part of the head, including forehead, eyes, nose, mouth, cheeks, and chin: the outside form or appearance: front or surface of anything: a flat surface of a solid geometrical figure, crystal, etc.: the striking surface of a golf-club, etc.: the edge of a cutting-tool, etc.: the front or upper surface, or that usually presented: the exposed surface in a cliff, mine, or quarry: a principal cleavage-plane: the dial of a watch, etc.: the printed surface of a playing-card: a style of letter (*print.*): special appearance or expression of the countenance: aspect, look, configuration: command of facial expression and bearing: boldness, effrontery: a grimace: presence: anger or favour (*B.*). — *v.t.* to meet in the face or in front: to stand opposite to or looking towards: to confront: to stand up to: to brave: to resist: to put an additional face or surface on: to cover in front: to trim. — *v.i.* (often with *on, to, towards*) to direct or turn the face: to take or have a direction: to show a face, esp. bold or false (*obs.*). — *adjs.* **faced** having a face: having the outer surface dressed: with the front covered with another material; **face′less** without a face: (of person(s) concerned in some action) with identity concealed: robot-like, esp. of bureaucratic officials who allow no degree of personality to intrude on their decision-making processes. — *n.* **fac′er** one who faces something: one who puts on a false show (*obs*): a bold-faced person (*obs.*): a tool for smoothing or facing a surface: a severe blow on the face (*slang*): an affront (*coll.*): anything that staggers one (*coll.*). — *adj.* **facial** (*fā′shl*) of or relating to the face: for the face. — *n.* a beauty treatment to the face (*coll.*). — *adv.* **fa′cially.** — *n.* **fac′ing** a covering in front for ornament or protection. — **face′-ache** neuralgia in the nerves of the face: an ugly person (*slang;* usu. used as a mild or facet. insult); **face′-card** a playing-card bearing a face (king, queen or knave); **face′-cloth, -flann′el** a cloth laid over the face of a corpse or living person: a cloth used in washing the face; **face′-cream** a cosmetic cream for the face; **face′-fung′us** (*coll.*) a moustache or beard; **face′-guard, -mask** a kind of mask to guard or protect the face. — *v.t.* **face′-hard′en** to case-harden. — **face′-lift** renovating process, esp. one applied to the outside of a building (also *fig.*): face-lifting; **face′-lifting** an operation aiming at smoothing and firming the face; **face′man, face′-worker** a miner who works at the coal-face, as opposed to elsewhere in or at the mine; **face′-mask** a face-guard; **face′-off** in ice-hockey, etc., the dropping of the puck between two players to start the game: a confrontation (*fig.*); **face pack** a creamy cosmetic mixture put on to the face for a certain time; **face′-plate** a disc on which a piece of wood, etc. can be fixed for turning on a lathe: a protective plate in front of a piece of machinery: a flat transparent panel on the front of a protective helmet; **face′-powder** a cosmetic powder for the face; **face′-saver** a course of action that saves one's face (see below); **face′-saving** saving one's face (see below). — Also *adj.* — **face value** the value as stated on the face of a coin, etc.: the apparent value of anything, which may not be the same as its real value; **facial angle** in craniometry, the angle formed by lines drawn from the middle of the forehead to the upper jaw above the incisor teeth and from the opening of the ear to the opening of the nose. — **face down** to abash by stern looks: to confront and make concede; **face out** to carry off by bold looks: to face down; **face the music** (*slang*) to accept the unpleasant consequences at their worst: to brave a trying situation, hostile reception, etc.; **face to face** opposite: in actual presence: in confrontation (*adj.* **face'-to-face'**); **face up to** to face, stand up to: to recognise (fact, facts) and prepare to endure or act bravely; **fly in the face of** to set oneself directly against; **have two faces** to be two-faced (see **two**); **in the face of** in defiance of, despite; **look (someone) in the face** to look at without shame or embarrassment; **lose face** to lose prestige; **loss of face** humiliation, loss of dignity; **make, pull, faces at** to distort one's face into exaggerated expressions in order to amuse, annoy, etc.; **on the face of it** on its own showing: as is palpably plain: at first glance; **pull a long face** to look dismal; **put a good, brave face on (it)** to assume a bold or contented bearing (as regards something); **put one's face on** (*coll.*) to apply cosmetics to the face; **right face! left face! right about face!** words of command, on which the soldiers turn to the side specified; **run one's face** (*obs. slang*) to obtain things on credit by sheer impudence; **save one's face** to avoid humiliation or appearance of climbing down; **set one's face against** to oppose strenuously; **show one's face** to appear; **to one's face** in one's presence, openly. [Fr. *face* — L. *faciēs*, form, face; perh. from *facĕre*, to make.]

facet *fas'it*, *n.* a small surface, as of a crystal: an aspect or view: a small flat area on e.g. a bone (*anat.*). — *v.t.* to cut a facet upon, or cover with facets. — *adj.* **fac'eted** having or formed into facets. [Fr. *facette*, dim. of *face*, face.]

facetious *fə-sē'shəs*, *adj.* witty, humorous, jocose: waggish: would-be funny: pertaining to facetiae. — Also **facete** (-*sēt'*; *arch.*). — *n.pl.* **face'tiae** (-*shi-ē*) witty or humorous sayings or writings: a bookseller's term for improper books — of all degrees of indecency. — *adv.* **face'tiously.** — *n.* **face'tiousness.** [L. *facētia* — *facētus*, merry, witty.]

facia *fas(h)i-ə.* Same as **fascia.**

facies *fā'shi-ēz*, *n.* general aspect, esp. of plant, animal or geological species or formations: facial appearance or expression, esp. when characteristic of a disease or condition: — *pl.* **fā'cies.** [L. *faciēs*, face.]

facile *fas'īl*, or -*il*, *adj.* affable (*obs.*): easily persuaded: yielding: in Scots law, mentally weak, short of idiocy but so as to be easily persuaded to actions prejudicial to oneself: easy of accomplishment: easy: working with ease: fluent (usu. depreciatory). — *adv.* **fac'ilely.** — *n.* **fac'ileness.** — *v.t.* **facilitāte** (*fə-sil'*) to make easy or easier. — *n.* **facilitā'tion.** — *adj.* **facil'itātive.** — *ns.* **facil'itātor; facil'ity** ease in performance or action: fluency: easiness to be persuaded: pliancy: affability (*obs.*): a condition of being facile (*Scots law*): (esp. in *pl.* **facil'ities**) means or opportunities that render anything readily possible: anything specially arranged or constructed to provide recreation, a service, etc.: an agreed amount of money made available for borrowing (*econ.*). [Fr., — L. *facilis*, easy — *facĕre*, to do.]

facile princeps *fas'i-lē prin'seps, fa'ki-le prin'keps*, (L.) obviously pre-eminent. — *n.* an easy first.

facinorous *fa-, fə-sin'ə-rəs*, (*arch.*) *adj.* atrociously wicked. — Also **facinē'rious** (*Shak.*). — *n.* **facin'orousness.** [L. *facinorōsus* — *facinus*, a crime — *facĕre*, to do.]

façon de parler *fa-sɔ̃ də par-lā*, (Fr.) way of speaking, a mere form of words.

façonné *fa-so-nā, fas-ə-nā', fas', n.* fabric with self-coloured pattern of small figures woven into it: the pattern on such a fabric. — Also *adj.* [Fr., pa.p. of *façonner*, to work, fashion.]

facsimile *fak-sim'i-li*, *n.* an exact copy, as of handwriting, a coin, etc.: accurate reproduction: facsimile telegraph: (also **facsimile transmission**) a system for transmitting

documents in which a document is scanned electronically and the resulting analogue or digital signals are sent to a receiver which produces an exact copy of the document: — *pl.* **facsim'iles.** — *adj.* exactly corresponding. — *v.t.* to make a facsimile of, to reproduce: — *pr.p.* **facsim'ileing;** *pa.t.* and *pa.p.* **facsim'iled.** — *n.* **facsim'ilist.** — **facsimile edition** an edition of a book, etc., that is an exact reproduction of an earlier edition; **facsimile telegraph** the transmission of a still picture over a telegraph circuit and its reproduction. [L. *fac,* imper. of *facĕre,* to make, *simile,* neut. of *similis,* like.]

fact *fakt*, *n.* a deed, act, or anything done (*arch.*): anything that comes to pass: a truth: truth: reality, or a real state of things, as distinguished from a mere statement or belief: an assertion of fact: a crime committed (*obs.* except in **after, before the fact**). — *adj.* **fact'ual** pertaining to facts: actual. — *ns.* **factual'ity; fact'ualness; fact'um** a thing done, a deed. — *adj.* **fact'-finding** appointed to ascertain, directed towards ascertaining, all the facts of a situation. — **fact sheet** a paper setting out briefly information relevant to a particular subject. — **as a matter of fact** in reality; **facts of life** the details of reproduction, esp. human reproduction: the realities of a situation; **in fact, in point of fact** indeed; **the fact of the matter** the plain truth about the subject in question. [L. *factum*, neut. pa.p. of *facĕre*, to do.]

faction¹ *fak'shən*, *n.* a company of persons associated or acting together, mostly used in a bad sense: a contentious party in a state or society: dissension. — *adj.* **fac'tional.** — *ns.* **fac'tionalism; fac'tionalist; fac'tionary** a member of a faction; **fac'tionist.** — *adj.* **fac'tious** turbulent: given to faction: proceeding from party spirit: seditious. — *adv.* **fac'tiously.** — *n.* **fac'tiousness.** [L. *factiō, -ōnis* — *facĕre*, to do.]

faction² *fak'shən*, *n.* a play, programme, piece of writing, etc., that is a mixture of fact and fiction — also called **drama documentary, news fiction.** [*fact*, fiction.]

factitious *fak-tish'əs*, *adj.* artificial: made: produced by artificial conditions. — *adv.* **facti'tiously.** — *n.* **facti'tiousness.** — *adjs.* **fac'titive** causative: of a verb, which can take both a direct object and a complement; **fac'tive** making. [L. *factīcius, factitīvus* — *facĕre*, to make.]

factoid *fak'toid*, *n.* an unprovable statement which has achieved unquestioning acceptance by frequent repetition. [*fact*, and **-oid**.]

factor *fak'tər*, *n.* a doer or transactor of business for another: one who buys and sells goods for others, on commission: an agent managing heritable estates for another (*Scot.*): in math., one of two or more quantities which, when multiplied together, result in the given quantity — e.g. 6 and 4 are factors of 24: an element in the composition of anything, or in bringing about a certain result: a fact, etc. which has to be taken into account or which affects the course of events: in heredity, a gene or the like. — *v.i.* to work, act, etc. as a factor. — *adj.* **fac'torable.** — *ns.* **factorabil'ity; fac'torage** the fees or commission of a factor. — *adj.* **factō'rial** of or pertaining to a factor. — *n.* the product of all whole numbers from a given number down to one. — *n.* **fac'toring** the work of a factor: the business of buying up trade debts, or lending money on the security of these. — *v.t.* **fac'torise, -ize** to resolve into factors: to warn not to pay or give up goods (*U.S.*): to attach (effects of a debtor in the hands of another — e.g. of his heir). — *ns.* **factorisā'tion, -z-; fac'torship; fac'tory** a place where goods are manufactured: a trading settlement in another country. — **factor 8, factor VIII** one of the proteins which form the clotting agent in blood, absent in haemophiliacs; **factory farm** one carrying out **factory farming,** farming by methods of feeding and housing animals in which everything is subordinated to achieving maximum production, rapid growth, and qualities in demand on the market; **fac'tory-ship** a whaling-ship on which whales are processed: a ship which freezes or otherwise processes the catch of a fishing fleet. — **factory-gate price, charge** the price of goods calculated by the seller exclusive of freight charges to the buyer; **judicial factor** a person appointed by the Court to manage the estate of a person under some incapacity; **safety factor** see **safe.** [L. *facĕre*, to do.]

factotum *fak-tō'təm, n.* a person employed to do all kinds of work for another: — *pl.* **facto'tums.** [L.L., — L. *fac,* imper. of *facĕre,* to do, *tōtum,* all.]

factum. See **fact.**

facture *fak'chər, n.* the act or the result of making, workmanship. [L. *factūra — facĕre,* to make.]

facula *fak'ū-lə, n.* a spot brighter than the rest of the surface, sometimes seen on the sun's disc: — *pl.* **fac'ulae** (*-lē*). — *adj.* **fac'ular.** [L. *facula,* dim. of *fax,* torch.]

faculty *fak'əl-ti, n.* facility or power to act: any particular ability or aptitude: an original power of the mind: any physical capability or function: personal quality or endowment: right, authority, or privilege to act: licence: a department of learning at a university, or the professors and lecturers constituting it: the members of a profession: executive ability. — *adj.* **fac'ultative** optional: incidental: of or pertaining to a faculty: conferring privilege, permission or authority: able to live under different conditions (*zool.*). — *adv.* **fac'ultatively.** — **Court of Faculties** a court established by Henry VIII, whereby authority is given to the Archbishop of Canterbury to grant dispensations and faculties; **Faculty of Advocates** the Scottish college of advocates. [Fr. *faculté* — L. *facultās, -ātis — facilis,* easy.]

facundity *fə-kun'di-ti, n.* eloquence. [L. *fācunditās, -ātis.*]

fad *fad, n.* a weak or transient hobby, crotchet, or craze: any unimportant belief or practice intemperately urged. — *n.* **fadd'iness.** — *adj.* **fadd'ish.** — *ns.* **fadd'ishness, fadd'ism; fadd'ist** one who is a slave to some fad. — *adj.* **fadd'y.** [Ety. unknown.]

fadaise. See **fade².**

faddle *fad'l,* (*dial.*) *v.i.* to trifle. — *n.* nonsense, trifling — usually in **fiddle-faddle.**

fade¹ *fād, v.i.* to lose strength, freshness, loudness, brightness, or colour gradually: to grow pale, dull, or faint: to die away: to disappear. — *v.t.* to cause to fade: to cause to change gradually in distinctness (as *fade out, fade in*): to impart a fade to (*golf*). — *n.* a fading: a slight, delayed (often deliberate) slice (*golf*). — *adj.* (*arch.*) faded, weak. — *adj.* **fā'dable.** — *adv.* **fā'dedly.** — *n.* **fā'dedness.** — *adj.* **fāde'less** unfading: not liable to fade. — *adv.* **fāde'lessly.** — *n.* and *adj.* **fād'ing.** — *adj.* **fā'dy** wearing away. — **fade'-away** a gradual disappearance. — **fade down** (of sound or light) to fade out (*n.* **fade'-down**); **fade in** in films, radio, television, etc., to introduce (sound, a picture) gradually, bringing it up to full volume or clarity (*n.* **fade'-in**); **fade out** in films, radio, television, etc., to cause (sound, a picture) to disappear gradually (*n.* **fade'-out**); **fade up** (of sound or light) to fade in (*n.* **fade'-up**). [O.Fr. *fader — fade* — L. *vapidum,* acc. to Gaston Paris.]

fade² *fad,* (Fr.) *adj.* insipid, colourless. — *ns.* **fadaise** (*fa-dez*) a silly saying: twaddle; **fadeur** (*fa-dœr*) dullness.

fadge *faj,* (*arch.*) *v.i.* to agree, hit it off: to succeed, turn out. [Ety. dub.; not conn. with O.E. *fēgan,* to join.]

fading *fā'ding, n.* an old dance, probably Irish: the burden of a song (*Shak.*). [Origin unknown.]

fado *fä'dōō, n.* a type of Portuguese folk song or dance: — *pl.* **fad'os.** [Port., fate — L. *fātum.*]

faeces *fē'sēz, n.pl.* sediment after infusion or distillation: dregs: excrement. — *adj.* **faecal** (*fē'kl*). [L., pl. of *faex, faecis,* dregs, grounds.]

faerie, faery *fā'(ə)ri,* (*arch.*) *n.* the world of fairies, fairyland: a fairy. — Also *adj.* [A variant of **fairy.**]

faex populi *fēks pop'ū-lī, fīks po'pōō-lē,* (L.) dregs of the people, the mob.

faff *faf,* (*coll.*) *v.i.* to dither, fumble (usu. with *about*). [Origin obscure.]

fag¹ *fag, v.i.* to become weary or tired out: to work hard: to be a fag. — *v.t.* to weary: to use as a fag: — *pr.p.* **fagg'ing;** *pa.t.* and *pa.p.* **fagged.** — *n.* a schoolboy forced to do menial offices for another: a tiresome piece of work: drudgery: orig. an inferior cigarette (for *fag-end; slang*): hence any cigarette (*slang*). — *n.* **fagg'ery** drudgery: fagging. — *n.* and *adj.* **fagg'ing.** — **fag'-end** the end of a web of cloth that hangs loose: the untwisted end of a rope: the end, refuse or meaner part of a thing: the stump of a cigar or cigarette (*slang*). — **fagged out** very tired, exhausted; **fag out** to field, as a fag, in cricket. [Ety. dub.; perh. a corr. of **flag¹,** to droop (q.v.).]

fag². See **faggot.**

faggot, fagot *fag'ət, n.* a bundle of sticks for fuel, fascines, etc.: a stick: anything like a faggot: a bundle of pieces of iron or steel cut off into suitable lengths for welding: a soldier numbered on the muster-roll, but not really existing (*hist.*): a voter who has obtained his vote expressly for party purposes, on a spurious or sham qualification (*hist.*): a roll of internal organs, etc., of a pig mixed with bread and savoury herbs: derogatory term for an old woman: a male homosexual (also **fag;** *slang,* orig. *U.S.*). — *adj.* got up for a purpose, as in *faggot vote.* — *v.t.* to tie together. — *n.* **fagg'oting, fag'oting** a kind of embroidery in which some of the cross-threads are drawn together in the middle. — **burn one's faggot** to recant a heresy. [Fr. *fagot,* a bundle of sticks.]

Fagin *fā'gin, n.* a person who trains young thieves, receives stolen goods, etc. [Character in Dickens' novel *Oliver Twist.*]

fagotto *fəg-ot'ō, n.* a bassoon: — *pl.* **fagott'i** (*-ē*). — *n.* **fagott'ist** one who plays on the bassoon. [It.]

Fagus *fā'gəs, n.* the beech genus of trees, giving name to the fam. **Fagā'ceae.** — *adj.* **fagā'ceous.** [L. *fāgus,* beech; cf. Gr. *phēgos,* oak, O.E. *bōc,* beech.]

fah. See **fa.**

fahlband *fäl'bänt, n.* in crystalline rocks, a pale band rich in metals; **fahl'erz** (*-erts*) tetrahedrite: also tennantite; **fahl'ore** (*-ōr, -ör*) tetrahedrite or tennantite. [Ger. *fahl,* dun-coloured, *Band,* band, *Erz,* ore, and Eng. **ore.**]

Fahrenheit *fa', fä'rən-hīt, adj.,* of a thermometer or thermometer scale, having the freezing-point of water marked at 32, and the boiling-point at 212, degrees (to convert °F into °C, subtract 32, and take 5/9 of remainder). [Named from the inventor, Gabriel D. *Fahrenheit* (1686–1736).]

faible *feb'l, n.* a foible (of which it is a variant): the part of a foil blade between the middle and the point — the weak part. [Fr., weak.]

faience, faïence *fä-yäs, n.* glazed coloured earthenware. [Fr.; prob. from *Faenza* in Italy.]

faik *fāk,* (*Scot.*) *v.i.* and *v.t.* to abate: to excuse.

faikes. See **fakes.**

fail¹ *fāl,* (*Scot.*) *n.* a turf, sod. — **fail'-dike** a turf wall. [Perh. Gael. *fàl,* a sod.]

fail² *fāl, v.i.* to fall short or be wanting (with *in*): to fall away: to decay: to die: to prove deficient under trial, examination, pressure, etc.: to miss achievement: to be disappointed or baffled: to become insolvent or bankrupt. — *v.t.* to be wanting to: not to be sufficient for: to leave undone, omit: to disappoint or desert: to deceive (*Spens.*): to declare deficient after examination. — *n.* failure, esp. in an examination. — *adj.* **failed** that has failed: decayed, worn out: bankrupt. — *n.* **fail'ing** a fault, weakness: a foible: failure. — *adj.* that fails. — *prep.* in default of. — *n.* **fail'ure** a falling short, or cessation: lack of success: omission: decay: bankruptcy: an unsuccessful person. — *adj.* **fail'-safe** of a mechanism, incorporated in a system to ensure that there will be no accident if the system does not operate properly: of a system, designed to revert to a safe condition in the event of failure. — Also *fig.*

fail of to come short of accomplishing (a purpose); **fail safe** to revert to a safe condition in the event of failure; **without fail** for certain. [O.Fr. *faillir* — L. *fallĕre*, to deceive; cf. Du. *feilen*, Ger. *fehlen*, O.N. *feila*.]

faille *fāl, fīl, fä-y'*, *n.* a soft, closely-woven silk or rayon fabric with transverse ribs. [Fr.]

fain¹ *fān*, (*arch.* and *poet.*) *adj.* glad or joyful: eager (with *to*): content for want of better: compelled: wont (*Spens.*). — *v.t.* (*Spens.*) to delight in: to desire. — *adv.* gladly. — *adv.* **fain'ly** gladly. — *n.* **fain'ness** eagerness. [O.E. *fægen*, joyful: cf. O.N. *feginn*, glad.]

fain², **faine** *fān*, (*Spens.*) *v.t.* Same as **feign**.

fainéant *fen'ā-ā, adj.* and *n.* do-nothing, applied esp. to the later Merovingian kings of France, mere puppets, whose mayors of the palace governed the country. — *ns.* **fai'néance** (-*ās*), **fai'neancy** (-*ən-si*), **fainéantise** (-*tēz'*). [Fr., as if — *faire*, to do, *néant*, nothing; really — O.Fr. *faignant*, pr.p. of *faindre*, to skulk.]

fains *fānz*, (*school slang*) *interj.* a plea for exemption or a truce. — Also **fain'ites** and **fains I**. [Form of **fen².**]

faint *fānt*, *adj.* wanting in strength (*arch.*): dim: lacking distinctness: not bright or forcible: weak in spirit (*arch.*): lacking courage (*arch.*): done in a feeble way: inclined to faint: sickly-smelling, oppressive (*arch.*). — *v.i.* to become feeble or weak (*arch.*): to lose strength, colour, etc. (*arch.*): to swoon: to fade or decay (*arch.*): to vanish (*arch.*): to lose courage or spirit (*arch.*). — *v.t.* (*rare*) to render faint. — *n.* a swoon. — *adj.* **faint'ed** (*Milt.*) exhausted. — *n.* and *adj.* **faint'ing**. — *adj.* **faint'ish** slightly faint. — *n.* **faint'ishness**. — *adv.* **faint'ly**. — *n.* **faint'ness** want of strength: feebleness of colour, light, etc.: dejection. — *n.pl.* **faints** impure spirit that comes over at the beginning and end of distillation (also **feints**). — *adj.* **faint'y** faintish. — *adj.* **faint'-heart** (also *n.*), **faint'-heart'ed** spiritless: timorous. — *adv.* **faint'-heart'edly**. — **faint'-heart'edness**. [O.Fr. *feint*, feigned — L. *fingĕre*, to feign.]

fair¹ *fār*, *adj.* bright: clear: clean: free from blemish: pure: pleasing to the eye: beautiful: of a light hue: free from rain, fine, dry: unobstructed: open: smoothly curving: prosperous: impartial: just: equitable: good, pleasing: plausible: civil: specious: reasonable: likely: favourable: pretty good: passable: out-and-out, veritable (*dial.*): a general expression of commendation or courtesy (as *fair sir*; *arch.*). — *n.* that which is fair: a woman (*arch.*): beauty (*Shak.*). — *v.t.* to make fair. — *v.i.* to clear up, as the weather from rain. — *adv.* in a fair manner (in all senses): full, square, directly (e.g. *hit fair in the centre*): quite (*dial.*). — *n.* **fair'ing** adjustment or testing of curves in ship-building: means of reducing head-resistance in an aeroplane. — *adj.* **fair'ish** somewhat fair: pretty well: pretty drunk (*dial.*). — *adv.* **fair'ly** beautifully (*arch.*): neatly (*arch.*): justly: reasonably: plainly: gently (*obs.*): fully, quite: tolerably. — *n.* **fair'ness**. — *adjs.* **fair'-and-square'** honest (also *adv.*); **fair'-bod'ing** (*Shak.*) auspicious. — **fair copy** a clean copy after correction; **fair'-deal'ing**. — *adj.* **fair'= faced** with a light complexion: beautiful: specious. — **fair field** just conditions; **fair game** an object for justifiable attack or ridicule. — *adj.* **fair'-haired**, **fair'= headed** having light-coloured hair. — **Fair Isle** type of design used in knitwear, named from a Shetland island; **fair'-lead(er)** a ring, (set of) hole(s), etc., or more elaborate device, for guiding rope, etc., so as to reduce friction. — *adj.* **fair'-minded** judging fairly. — **fair play** honest dealing: justice. — *adjs.* **fair'-seem'ing** appearing fair; **fair'-spok'en** bland and civil in language and address. — **fair trade** euphemism for smuggling: a mild form of the protective system, in which the basis of economic policy is supposed to be reciprocity or free-trade only with such nations as grant similar privileges — also used adverbally; **fair'way** the navigable channel or usual course of vessels in a river, etc.: in golf, the smooth turf between tee and putting-green, distinguished from the uncut rough and from hazards. — *adj.* **fair'-weath'er** suitable only for, or found only in, fair weather or (esp. of friends or supporters)

favourable circumstances. — **bid fair** see **bid**; **fair (be)fall** (*arch.*) good luck to; **fair do's** (*dōōz* — *pl.* of **do**; *coll.*) an expression appealing for, or agreeing to, fair play, strict honesty, etc.; **fair enough** expressing acceptance, though not necessarily full agreement; **in a fair way** to see **way**; **in all fairness** being scrupulously fair; **keep fair with** to keep on amicable terms with; **speak fair** see **speak**; **stand fair with** to be in the good graces of; **the fair**, **the fair sex** the female sex. [O.E. *fæger*.]

fair² *fār*, *n.* a great periodical market for one kind of merchandise, or for the general sales and purchases of a district, with or without amusements: often reduced to a collection of shows, swing-boats, etc.: charity bazaar: trade show. — *n.* **fair'ing** a present given at or from a fair: any complimentary gift. — **fair'-day**; **fair'-ground**. — **a day after the fair**, behind the fair too late; **get one's fairing** (*Scot.*) to get one's deserts. [O.Fr. *feire* — L. *fēria*, holiday.]

fairnitic(k)le, **fairny-**. See **fern**.

fairy *fār'i, n.* an imaginary being, generally of diminutive and graceful human form, capable of kindly or unkindly acts towards man: fairy-folk: fairyland: an enchantress: a creature of overpowering charm: a male homosexual. — *adj.* like a fairy, fanciful, whimsical, delicate. — *adv.* **fair'ily**. — *ns.* **fair'ydom**; **fair'yhood**; **fair'yism**. — *adj.* and *adv.* **fair'ylike** like fairies or like something in fairyland: very delicate and charming. — **fair'y-beads** joints of the stems of fossil crinoids; **fair'y-butt'er** a name applied in northern England to certain gelatinous fungi; **fai'ry-cy'cle** a child's bicycle; **fair'y-god'mother** a benefactress such as Cinderella had; **fair'yland** the country of the fairies; **fairy light** (usu. in *pl.*) a tiny coloured light used as decoration; **fair'y-mon'ey, fairy gold** money given by fairies, which changes into withered leaves, slate, stones, etc.: money that comes unsought: illusory riches; **fair'y-ring** a ring of darker-coloured grass due to outward spread of a fungus (as the fairy-ring champignon, *Marasmius oreades*), attributed to the dancing of fairies; **fair'y= stone'** a fossil sea-urchin: a concretion; **fairy tale** a story about fairies or other supernatural beings: a folk-tale: a romantic tale: an incredible tale: euphemistically, a lie: a marvel. — *adj.* **fair'y-tale** beautiful, fortunate, etc., as in a fairy tale. [O.Fr. *faerie*, enchantment — *fae* (mod. *fée*); see **faerie**, **fay¹**.]

fait accompli *fe-ta-kõ-plē*, (Fr.) an accomplished fact, a thing already done.

faites vos jeux *fet võ zhø*, (Fr.) place your stakes! (e.g. in roulette).

faith *fāth*, *n.* trust or confidence: belief in the statement of another: belief in the truth of revealed religion: confidence and trust in God: the living reception of religious belief: that which is believed: any system of religious belief, esp. the religion one considers true: fidelity to promises: honesty: word or honour pledged: faithfulness. — *interj.* (*arch.*) by my faith: indeed. — *v.t.* (*fādh*; *Shak.*) to believe. — *adj.* **faith'ful** full of faith, believing: firm in adherence to promises, duty, friendship, love, etc.: loyal: constant: conformable to truth: worthy of belief: true: exact. — *adv.* **faith'fully** with confidence: with fidelity: with sincerity: with scrupulous exactitude: solemnly (*coll.*): a meaningless word used in concluding a letter. — *n.* **faith'fulness**. — *adj.* **faith'less** without faith or belief: not believing, esp. in God or Christianity: not adhering to promises, duty, etc.: inconstant: adulterous: untrustworthy: delusive. — *adv.* **faith'lessly**. — *ns.* **faith'lessness**; **faith'worthi-ness** trustworthiness. — *adj.* **faith'worthy** worthy of faith or belief. — **faith'-heal'er**; **faith'-heal'ing** or **-cure** a system of belief based on James v. 15, that sickness may be cured without medical advice or appliances, if the prayer of Christians be accompanied in the sufferer by true faith: cure by suggestion. — **bad faith** treachery: the breaking of a promise; **Father of the faithful** Abraham: the caliph; **in good faith** with honesty and sincerity: acting honestly; **keep faith** to act honestly, according to one's promise (with); **the Faithful** believers, esp. Muslims: (without *cap.*) adherents, supporters, etc. (*coll.*). [M.E. *feith, feyth* — O.Fr. *feid* — L. *fidēs* — *fīdĕre*, to trust.]

faitor *fā'tər*, (*obs.*) *n.* an impostor. — Often **fai'tour**. [O.Fr. *faitor* — L. *factor, -ōris*, doer.]

faix *fāks*, (*dial.*) *interj.* faith. [Prob. short for *faykins*; see **fay²**.]

fake¹ *fāk*, *v.t.* to fold, coil. — *n.* a coil or rope, etc. [M. E. *faken*; cf. Scot. *faik*, fold.]

fake² *fāk*, *v.t.* to rob or attack: to filch: to doctor, cook, or counterfeit. — *n.* a swindle, dodge, sham: a faked article — also **fake'ment**. — *adj.* false, counterfeit. — *ns.* **fak'er; fak'ery**. [Prob. the earlier *feak, feague*, Ger. *fegen*, to furbish up.]

fakes, faikes *fāks*, *n.pl.* thin-bedded shaly or micaceous sandstone or sandy shale.

fakir *fä-kēr'*, or *fā'kər*, *n.* religious (esp. Muslim) mendicant, ascetic, or wonder-worker in India, etc. — *n.* **fakir'ism** (or *fā'*). [Ar. *faqīr*, a poor man.]

fa-la *fä-lä'*, *n.* an old kind of madrigal. — **fa la (la,** etc.) syllables used as a refrain.

falafel. See **felafel.**

falaj *fal'aj*, *n.* a water channel, specif. one forming part of the ancient irrigation system of Oman: — *pl.* **aflaj'.** [Ar., stream.]

Falange *fä-läng'hhā* (Sp.), also *fə-lanj', fä'*, *n.* a Spanish fascist group. — *ns.* **Falangism** (*fə-lan'jizm*) (also without *cap.*); **Falan'gist** (also without *cap.*). [Sp., — Gr. *phalanx*, phalanx (q.v.).]

Falasha *fə-lä'shə*, *n.* one of a community of black Ethiopian Jews. [Amharic, immigrant.]

falbala *fal'bə-lə*, *n.* a trimming or flounce: a furbelow. [Ety. dub.; cf. **furbelow.**]

falcade *fal-kād'*, *n.* the motion of a horse when he throws himself on his haunches in a very quick curvet. [Fr., — L. *falcāta* (fem.) bent.]

falcate, -d *fal'kāt, -id, adjs.* bent like a sickle. — *ns.* **falcā'tion; fal'cula** a falcate claw. — *adjs.* **falciform** (*fal'si-förm*) sickle-shaped; **fal'cūlate.** [L. *falx, falcis*, a sickle.]

falces. See **falx.**

falchion *föl'shən, -chən, n.* a short, broad sword, bent somewhat like a sickle. [O.Fr. *fauchon*, through L.L., from L. *falx*, a sickle.]

falciform. See **falcate.**

falcon *föl'kən, fö'kən, n.* any of the long-winged birds of prey of the genus *Falco* or its kindred: a bird of prey of a kind trained to the pursuit of game: by falconers confined to the female esp. peregrine falcon (cf. **tercel**): a kind of cannon. — *ns.* **fal'coner** one who sports with, or who breeds and trains, falcons or hawks for taking wild-fowl; **fal'conet** a small field-gun in use till the 16th century. — *adj.* **fal'conine.** — *n.* **fal'conry** the art or practice of training, or hunting with, falcons. — *adj.* **fal'con-eyed** keen-eyed. — **fal'con-gen'til, -gen'tle** the female of the peregrine falcon. [O.Fr. *faucon* — L.L. *falcō, -ōnis*.]

falcula, etc. See **falcate.**

faldage *föld'ij, fald'ij,* (*hist.*) *n.* the right of the lord of a manor of folding his tenant's sheep in his own fields for the sake of the manure: a fee paid in commutation therefor. [Law L. *faldāgium* — O.E. *fald*, fold.]

falderal *fal'dər-al',* *n.* a meaningless refrain in songs: any kind of flimsy trifle — also **folderol** (*fol'dər-ol'*) and **fal de rol.** — **falderal it** to sing unmeaning sounds.

faldetta *fäl-det'ə, n.* a Maltese woman's combined hood and cape. [It.]

faldstool *föld'stōōl, n.* a folding or camp stool: a coronation stool: a bishop's armless seat: a small desk in churches in England, at which the litany is to be sung or said. — *n.* **fald'istory** (*obs.*) a bishop's seat within the chancel. [L.L. *faldistolium, faldistorium* — O.H.G. *faldstuol* — *faldan* (Ger. *falten*), to fold, *stuol* (Ger. *Stuhl*), stool.]

Falernian *fa-lûr'ni-ən, adj.* pertaining to a district (*Falernus ager*) in Campania, famous of old for its wine.

fall¹ *föl, v.i.* to descend, esp. to descend freely and involuntarily by force of gravity: to drop: to drop prostrate: to throw oneself down: to be dropped in birth: to collapse: to become lower literally or figuratively (in position, degree, intensity, value, pitch, etc.): to die away: to subside: to abate: to ebb: to decline: to sink: (of the face) to relax into an expression of dismay: to flow downwards: to slope or incline down: to hang, dangle, or trail down: to be cast or shed: to drop dead or as if dead, esp. in fight: to be overthrown: to come to ruin: to lose power, station, virtue or repute: to be degraded: to be taken or captured: to become a victim: to yield to temptation: to pass into any state or action, to become, to begin to be (as *fall asleep, fall in love, fall a-weeping*): to rush: to become involved: to betake oneself: to come to be: to befall: to come about: to come by chance or as if by chance: to come in due course: to occur: to chance, light: to issue: to come forth: to appertain: to be apportioned, assigned: to come as one's share, lot, duty, etc.: to take position or arrangement: to find place: to be disposed: to impinge: to lapse: to terminate: to revert. — *v.t.* to cause to fall (*arch.* or *U.S.*): to let fall (*arch.*): to get (as what befalls one) (*obs.; Burns*): — *pr.p.* **fall'ing;** *pa.t.* **fell;** *pa.p.* **fallen** (*fö'lən*). — *n.* the act, manner, occasion, or time of falling or of felling: descent by gravity, a dropping down: that which falls: as much as comes down at one time: onset: overthrow: descent from a better to a worse position: slope or declivity: descent of water: a cascade: length of drop, amount of descent: decrease in value: a sinking of the voice: a cadence: the time when the leaves fall, autumn (chiefly *U.S.*): a bout of wrestling: the passing of a city or stronghold to the enemy: a lapse into sin, esp. that of Adam and Eve — 'the Fall (of Man)': a falling band, a hanging fringe, flap, or ornament: a lot (*arch.*): a lowering or hoisting rope. — *adj.* **fall'en** having fallen: killed, esp. in battle: overthrown: seduced: in a degraded state, ruined. — *n.* **fall'ing.** — *adj.* **fall'-back** used as a retreat, or second alternative. — Also *n.* — **fallen star** a gelatinous mass of a blue-green alga (Nostoc, etc.) once popularly thought of meteoric origin; **fall-in** see **fall in** below; **falling band** a seventeenth-century collar of fine material turned down on the shoulders; **fall'ing-off'** decline; **falling sickness** epilepsy; **falling star** a meteor; **falling stone** a portion of an exploded meteor; **fall'-out** by-product, side benefit (*coll.*): a deposit of radioactive dust from a nuclear explosion or plant: the aftermath of any explosive occurrence or situation (*fig.*): see **fall out** below; **fall'=trap** a trap that operates by a fall. — **fall about** to laugh hysterically, to collapse (with laughter); **fall across** (*arch.*) to meet by chance; **fall among** to find oneself in the midst of; **fall apart** to disintegrate: to fail: to collapse, go to pieces; **fall away** to decline gradually: to languish: to grow lean: to revolt or apostatise; **fall back** to retreat, give way; **fall back, fall edge** (*obs.*) no matter what may happen; **fall back upon** to have recourse to an expedient or resource in reserve; **fall behind** to lag: to be outstripped: to get in arrears; **fall between two stools** to be neither one thing nor the other: to succeed in neither of two alternatives; **fall down on** (*coll.*) to fail in; **fall flat** to fail completely, have no effect; **fall flat on one's face** to come to grief, to fail dismally; **fall for** (*coll.*) to become enamoured of: to be taken in by (a trick, etc.); **fall foul of** see **foul; fall in** to (cause to) take places in ranks (*mil.; n.* **fall'-in'**): to become hollowed: to revert: to cave in, collapse; **fall in with** to concur or agree with: to comply with: to meet by chance; **fall off** to become detached and drop: to deteriorate: to die away, to perish: to revolt or apostatise: to draw back; **fall on** to begin eagerly: to make an attack: to meet (*arch.*); **fall on one's feet** to come well out of a difficulty: to gain any unexpected good fortune; **fall out** to quarrel: to happen or befall: to turn out: to (cause to) quit ranks (*mil.; n.* **fall'-out'**); **fall over** to tumble, trip up: to go over to the enemy

(*Shak.*): to go to sleep (*Scot.*); **fall over backwards** see **backwards** under **back; fall over oneself** (*coll.*) to put oneself about, to be in great haste or eagerness (to do something); **fall short** to turn out to be short or insufficient: to become used up: to fail to attain or reach what is aimed at (with *of*); **fall through** to fail, come to nothing; **fall to** to begin hastily and eagerly: to apply oneself to: to begin to eat; **fall upon** to attack: to rush against: to devolve upon: to chance upon; **try a fall** to take a bout at wrestling. [O.E. *fallan* (W.S. *feallan*); Ger. *fallen*; prob. conn. with L. *fallĕre*, to deceive.]

fall² *föl, n.* a trap. — **fall'-guy, fall guy** a dupe, easy victim: a scapegoat. [O.E. *fealle* — *feallan*, to fall.]

fall³ *föl, n.* the cry given when a whale is sighted, or harpooned: the chase of a whale. — **loose fall** the losing of a whale. [Perh. from the north-eastern Scottish pronunciation of **whale**.]

fallacy *fal'ə-si, n.* something fallacious: deceptive appearance: an apparently genuine but really illogical argument: deception, deceitfulness (*obs.*): a wrong but prevalent notion. — *adj.* **fallacious** (*fə-lā'shəs*) of the nature of fallacy: deceptive: misleading: not well founded: causing disappointment: delusive. — *adv.* **fallā'ciously**. — *n.* **fallā'ciousness**. [L. *fallācia* — *fallāx*, deceptive — *fallĕre*, to deceive.]

fallal *fal-al', n.* a streamer of ribbon: any trifling ornament. — *adj.* (*obs.*) foppish, trifling. — *n.* **fallal'ery**. — *adv.* **fallal'ishly**.

fallible *fal'i-bl, adj.* liable to error or mistake. — *ns.* **fall'ibilism** in philosophy, the doctrine that knowledge gained empirically can never be certain; **fall'ibilist**. — Also *adj.* — *n.* **fallibil'ity** liability to err. — *adv.* **fall'ibly**. [L. *fallibilis* — *fallĕre*, to deceive.]

Fallopian *fə-lō'pi-ən, adj.* relating to the Italian anatomist Gabriele *Fallopio* (1523–62). — **Fallopian tubes** two tubes or ducts through which the ova pass from the ovary to the uterus, perhaps discovered by him.

fallow¹ *fal'ō, adj.* left untilled or unsown for a time. — *n.* land that has lain a year or more untilled or unsown after having been ploughed. — *v.t.* to plough without seeding. — *n.* **fall'owness**. — **fall'ow-chat, fall'ow-finch** the wheatear. — **green fallow** fallow where land is cleaned by a green crop, as turnips. [O.E. *fealgian*, to fallow; *fealh*, fallow land.]

fallow² *fal'ō, adj.* brownish-yellow. — **fallow deer** a yellowish-brownish deer smaller than the red deer, with broad flat antlers. [O.E. *falu* (*fealu*); cf. Ger. *fahl*, O.N. *fölr*.]

false *föls, adj.* wrong: erroneous: deceptive or deceiving: untruthful: unfaithful: untrue: not genuine or real, counterfeit: improperly so called: artificial, as opposed to natural, of teeth, etc.: incorrect, not according to rule: out of tune. — *adv.* incorrectly: untruly: dishonestly: faithlessly. — *n.* (*obs.*) falsehood: untruth. — *v.t.* (*obs.*) to deceive, be false to: to feign: to falsify. — *n.* **false'hood** the state or quality of being false: want of truth: deceitfulness (*obs.*): false appearance (*obs.*): an untrue statement: the act of lying: a lie. — *adv.* **false'ly**. — *ns.* **false'ness; fals'er** a falsifier, counterfeiter (*obs.*): a deceiver, a liar (*Spens.*); **fal'sie(s)** pad(s) of rubber or other material inserted into a brassière to enlarge or improve the shape of the breasts. — *adj.* **fals'ish** somewhat false. — *ns.* **fals'ism** a self-evident falsity; **fals'ity** quality of being false: a false assertion. — **false acacia** Robinia; **false alarm** a warning without danger. — *adj.* **false-bedd'ed**. — **false bedding** (*geol.*) irregular lamination running obliquely to the general stratification, due to deposition in banks by varying currents; **false bottom** a partition cutting off a space between it and the true bottom; **false card** the card played to deceive. — *v.i.* **false-card'**. — **false conception** a uterine growth consisting of some degenerate mass instead of a foetus; **false dawn** deceptive appearance simulating dawn. — Also *fig.* — **false face** a mask. — *adj.* **false'-faced** (*Shak.*) hypocritical. — **false gallop** (*arch.*) a canter. — *adj.* **false'-heart'ed** treacherous, deceitful.

— **false hem** a strip of fabric added to the bottom of a garment, etc. in order to deepen the hem; **false imprisonment** illegal detention by force or influence; **false leg** a proleg; **false pregnancy** pseudocyesis (see under **pseud-**); **false pretences** deception; **false quantity** pronunciation or use of a long vowel as short or short as long; **false relation** (*mus.*) occurrence in different parts together or in succession of a tone and a chromatic derivative; **false rib** one that does not reach the breastbone; **false shame** shame for that which is not shameful; **false teeth** artificial teeth, dentures; **false'-work** a temporary framework used to support a building, etc. during construction. — **play someone false** to act falsely or treacherously to a person; **put in a false position** to bring any one into a position in which he must be misunderstood. [O.Fr. *fals* (mod. *faux*) — L. *falsus*, pa.p. of *fallĕre*, to deceive.]

falsetto *föl-set'ō, n.* usu. in a man, forced voice of range or register above the natural: one who uses such a voice: false or strained sentiment: — *pl.* **falsett'os**. — *adj.* and *adv.* in falsetto. [It. *falsetto*, dim. of *falso*, false.]

falsi crimen *fal-sī krī'mən, fal'sē krē'men*, (L.L.) the crime of falsification, esp. forgery.

falsidical *föl-sid'i-kəl, (rare) adj.* conveying a meaning that is false. [L. *falsus*, and *dicĕre*, to say.]

falsify *föls'i-fī, v.t.* to forge or counterfeit: to tamper with: to misrepresent: to prove or declare to be false: to be false to (*obs.*): to feign (*obs.*). — *v.i.* (*obs.*) to lie: — *pr.p.* **fals'ifying;** *pa.t.* and *pa.p.* **fals'ified.** — *adj.* **fals'ifiable.** — *ns.* **falsifiabil'ity; falsifica'tion; fals'ifier.** [Fr. *falsifier* — L.L. *falsificāre* — L. *falsus*, false, *facĕre*, to make.]

falsish, falsism, falsity. See false.

Falstaffian *föl-stäf'i-ən*, or *-staf'*, *adj.* like or pertaining to Shakespeare's *Falstaff* — corpulent, jovial, humorous, dissolute, and irrepressibly impudent.

faltboat, foldboat *fölt'bōt*, or *folt'*, *föld'bōt, ns.* a small collapsible boat of rubberised sailcloth. [Ger. *Faltboot*, folding boat.]

falter *föl'tər, v.i.* to stumble: to go unsteadily: to hesitate in speech as if taken aback: to flinch: to waver: to flag: to fail. — *v.t.* to utter falteringly. — *n.* unsteadiness. — *n.* and *adj.* **fal'tering.** — *adv.* **fal'teringly.** [Prob. a freq. of M.E. *falden*, to fold; conn. with *fault* (in which the *l* is late) is not possible.]

falx *falks, n.* a sickle-shaped part or process, as of the dura mater: — *pl.* **falces** (*fal'sēz*). [L., a sickle.]

fame *fām, n.* public report or rumour (*arch.*): renown or celebrity, chiefly in a good sense. — *v.t.* to report: to make famous. — *adjs.* **famed** renowned; **fame'less** without renown. — **fama clamo'sa** (*Scot.*) any notorious rumour ascribing immoral conduct to a minister or office-bearer in a church; **house of ill fame** a brothel. [Fr., — L. *fāma*, report, rumour, fame, from *fārī*, to speak; cf. Gr. *phēmē*, from *phanai*, to say.]

familial. See **family**.

familiar *fə-mil'yər, adj.* well acquainted or intimate: in the manner of an intimate: free: unceremonious: having a thorough knowledge: well known or understood: private, domestic: common, everyday. — *n.* one well or long acquainted: a spirit or demon supposed to attend a person at call: a member of a pope's or bishop's household: the officer of the Inquisition who arrested the suspected. — *v.t.* **famil'iarise, -ize** to make thoroughly acquainted with: to make easy by practice or study. — *n.* **familiarity** (*-i-ar'i-ti*) intimate acquaintanceship: freedom from constraint: any unusual or unwarrantable freedom in act or speech toward another, act of licence — usu. in *pl.* — *adv.* **famil'iarly.** [O.Fr. *familier* — L. *familiāris*, from *familia*, a family.]

famille jaune, noire *fam-ē zhōn, nwär*, Chinese porcelain in which the background of the design is respectively yellow, black; **famille rose, verte** (*rōz, vert*) Chinese porcelain with design in which pink, green, is prominent. [Fr., family, yellow, black, pink, green.]

family *fam'i-li, n.* the household, or all those who live in one house (as parents, children, servants): parents and their children: the children alone: the descendants of one common progenitor: race: honourable or noble descent: a group of people related to one another, or otherwise connected: a group of animals, plants, languages, etc., more comprehensive than a genus: a collection of curves in the equations of which different values are given to the parameter(s) (*math.*). — *adj.* of or concerning the family: belonging to or specially for a family: suitable for the whole family, or for children as well as parents. — *adjs.* **famil'ial** (*fəm-*) characteristic of a family; **famil'iar** see above. — *ns.* **familism** (*fam'*) the family feeling: (with *cap.*) the principles of the Familists; **Fam'ilist** one of the 16th-cent. mystical sect known as the Family of Love, which based religion upon love independently of faith. — *adj.* **familis'tic.** — **family allowance** an allowance formerly paid by the state for the support of children, now replaced by child benefit; **family baker, butcher,** etc. small retailer who supplies families, not merely institutions; **family Bible** a large Bible for family worship, with a page for recording family events; **family circle** the members of the family taken collectively: one of the galleries in a theatre; **family coach** a large carriage able to carry a whole family: a parlour game; **family doctor** a general practitioner; **family grouping** same as **vertical grouping; family man** a man with a family: a domesticated man: a man dedicated to, and who enjoys sharing activities with, his wife and children; **family name** surname; **family planning** regulating the number and spacing of children, e.g. by using contraceptives; **family tree** a diagram showing the branching of a family. — **family (fruit) tree** a fruit tree bearing different varieties of the same fruit grafted on to it; **family income supplement** a payment by the state to a family whose income from employment is below a certain level; **in a family way** in a familiar informal manner; **in the family way** pregnant; **official family** (*U.S.*) the cabinet. [L. *familia — famulus*, a servant.]

famine *fam'in, n.* extreme general scarcity of food: scarcity of anything: hunger: starvation. [Fr., — L. *famēs*, hunger.]

famish *fam'ish, v.t.* to starve. — *v.i.* (*arch.*) to die of or suffer extreme hunger or thirst. — *n.* **fam'ishment** starvation. — **be famished, famishing** to feel very hungry. [Obs. *fame*, to starve — L. *famēs*, hunger.]

famous *fā'məs, adj.* renowned: noted: excellent (*coll.*). — *v.t.* (*arch.*) to make famous. — *adv.* **fā'mously.** — *n.* **fā'mousness.** [O.Fr., — L. *fāmōsus — fāma*, fame.]

famulus *fam'ū-ləs, n.* a private secretary or factotum: an attendant, esp. on a magician or scholar. [L., a servant.]

fan[1] *fan, n.* a basket formerly used for winnowing corn by throwing it in the wind: any instrument for winnowing: a broad, flat instrument esp. used by women to cool themselves — typically in or spreading into the shape of a sector of a circle: any fan-shaped structure, as a deposit of alluvium: anything spreading in a fan shape, e.g. a bird's wing or tail: a small sail to keep a windmill to the wind: a whale's tail-fluke: a propeller screw or propeller blade: a rotating ventilating or blowing apparatus. — *v.t.* to winnow: to move by a fan or the like: to direct a current of air upon: to cool or to kindle with, or as with, a fan: to fire (a non-automatic gun) by pulling back and releasing the hammer with the other hand. — *v.i.* to move like a fan: to flutter: to spread out like a fan: — *pr.p.* **fann'ing;** *pa.t.* and *pa.p.* **fanned.** — *n.* **fann'er** a fanning apparatus for winnowing, ventilation, etc. — *n.pl.* **fann'ings** the siftings of tea. — *adv.* **fan'-wise** in the manner of a fan. — **fan dance** a solo dance in the nude (or nearly so) in which the performer attempts concealment (or nearly so) by tantalising manipulation of a fan or fans or bunch of ostrich plumes. — *adj.* **fan'fold** (of paper) in a continuous strip, scored or perforated so as to fall flat in sections, used for computer print-out. — **fan'-jet'** (a plane with) an engine in which air is taken in

through a fan and some of it, bypassing compressors, combustion chamber and turbines, mixes with the jet formed by the rest; **fan'light** a window resembling in form an open fan; **fan palm** any palm with palmate leaves, esp. palmetto. — *adj.* **fan'-shaped** forming a sector of a circle. — **fan'tail** a tail shaped like a fan: a variety of domestic pigeon with tail feathers spread out like a fan: a member of various other classes of fantailed birds such as the Australian genus of flycatchers *Rhipidura*: an artificially bred goldfish with double anal and caudal fins: a feature having parts radiating from a centre (*archit.*). — Also *adj.* (also **fan'tailed**). — **fan tracery, fan vaulting** (*archit.*) tracery rising from a capital or a corbel, and diverging like the folds of a fan over the surface of a vault; **fan wheel** a wheel with fans on its rim for producing a current of air. — **fan out** to fan, spread as a fan from a centre. [O.E. *fann*, from L. *vannus*, a basket for winnowing; cf. Fr. *van*.]

fan[2] *fan, n.* a devotee or enthusiastic follower of some sport or hobby or public favourite. — *ns.* **fan'dom; fan'zine** (*-zēn*) a magazine for enthusiasts, esp. of science fiction or pop-music. — **fan club** a group united by devotion to a celebrity; **fan mail** letters from devotees to a celebrity. [From **fanatic.**]

Fanagalo *fan'ə-gə-lō, n.* a South African pidgin language, a mixture of Zulu, Afrikaans and English.

fanal *fā'nəl,* (*arch.*) *n.* a lighthouse, a beacon. [Fr., — Gr. *phanos*, a lantern, *phainein*, to show.]

Fanariot. See **Phanariot.**

fanatic *fə-nat'ik* (by some *fan'ə-tik*), *adj.* extravagantly or unreasonably zealous, esp. in religion: excessively enthusiastic. — *n.* a person frantically or excessively enthusiastic, esp. on religious subjects. — *adj.* **fanat'ical** fanatic: extravagant (*Shak.*). — *adv.* **fanat'ically.** — *v.t.* **fanat'icise, -ize** (*-i-sīz*) to make fanatical. — *v.i.* to act as a fanatic. — *n.* **fanat'icism** (*-sizm*) wild and excessive religious or other enthusiasm. [L. *fānāticus*, belonging to a temple, inspired by a god, *fānum*, a temple.]

fan-cricket. Same as **fen-cricket** under **fen**[1].

fancy *fan'si, n.* that faculty of the mind by which it recalls, represents, or makes to appear past images or impressions — imagination, esp. of a lower, passive, or more trivial kind: an image or representation thus formed in the mind: an unreasonable lightly-formed or capricious opinion: a whim: a fantasia: capricious inclination or liking: taste: love (*Shak.*). — *adj.* pleasing to, or guided by, or originating in fancy or caprice: fantastic: capriciously departing from the ordinary, the simple, or the plain: ornate: (of flowers) parti-coloured: (of gems, esp. diamonds) of a colour other than the normal one. — *v.t.* to picture in the mind: to imagine: to be inclined to believe: to have a liking for: to be pleased with: to breed or cultivate, with a view to development of conventionally accepted points: — *pr.p.* **fan'cying;** *pa.t.* and *pa.p.* **fan'cied.** — *interj.* (also **fancy that!**) exclamation of surprise. — *adj.* **fan'cied** formed or conceived by the fancy: imagined: favoured. — *n.* **fan'cier** one who fancies: one who has a liking for anything and is supposed to be a judge of it: a breeder for points. — *adj.* **fan'ciful** guided or created by fancy: imaginative: whimsical: wild: unreal. — *adv.* **fan'-cifully.** — *n.* **fan'cifulness.** — *adj.* **fan'ciless** destitute of fancy. — **fancy bread** bread other than plain bread; **fancy cake** a cake decorated with icing, filled with cream, etc.; **Fancy Dan** a stylish rather than effective performer; **fancy dress** dress arranged according to the wearer's fancy, to represent some character; **fancy dress ball, fancy ball** a ball at which fancy dress is worn; **fancy fair** a special sale of fancy articles for some charitable purpose. — *adj.* **fancy-free'** free from the power of love. — **fancy goods** fabrics of variegated rather than simple pattern, applied generally to articles of show and ornament; **fancy man** a woman's lover (*derog.*): a pimp; **fancy monger** (*Shak.*) one who concerns himself with love. — *adj.* **fan'cy-sick** (*Shak.*)

love-sick. — **fancy stitch** a more intricate and decorative stitch than *plain stitch*; **fancy woman** a mistress: a prostitute; **fan′cywork** ornamental needlework. — **fancy oneself** to think too highly of oneself; **the fancy** sporting characters generally, esp. pugilists: pugilism: enthusiasts for a particular sport or pastime; **tickle, take someone's fancy** to attract someone mildly in some way. [Contracted from **fantasy**.]

fand[1] *fand*, (*Scot.*) *pa.t.* of **find**.

fand[2] *fand*, **fond** *fond*, (*obs.*) *vs.i.* to try, attempt: to proceed: — *pa.t.* and *pa.p.* **fand′ed, fond′ed** or (*Spens.*) **fond**. [O.E. *fandian*.]

fandangle *fan-dang′gl*, *n.* elaborate ornament: nonsense. [Perh. from **fandango**.]

fandango *fan-dang′gō*, *n.* an old Spanish dance for two or its music in 3-4 time, with castanets: a gathering for dancing, a ball (*U.S. dial.*): — *pl.* **fandang′os.** [Sp.]

fane[1] *fān*, (*obs.*) *n.* a flag: a weathercock. [O.E. *fana*, flag; cf. Ger. *Fahne*; cf. **vane** and L. *pannus*, a cloth.]

fane[2] *fān*, *n.* a temple. [L. *fānum*.]

fanfare *fan′fär*, *n.* a flourish of trumpets or bugles: a parade of enthusiasm: an elaborate style of bookbinding. — *v.t.* to herald or acclaim with a fanfare. — *ns.* **fanfarade** (*fan-fǝr-ād′*) a fanfare; **fan′faron** one who uses bravado: a blusterer, braggart; **fanfarō′na** (*Scott*; Sp. *fanfarrona*, trumpery) a gold chain; **fanfaronade′** vain boasting: bluster: ostentation. — *v.i.* to bluster. [Fr., perh. from the sound.]

fang *fang*, *n.* the tooth of a wolf, dog, etc.: a claw or talon (*obs.*): the venom-tooth of a serpent: the embedded part of a tooth, etc.: a tang (of a tool): a prong: a grip, catch (*Shak.*): grip or power of suction in a pump (*Scot.*). — *v.t.* (*obs.*; *Shak.* **phang**) to seize upon, catch: to prime a pump. — *adjs.* **fanged** having fangs or anything resembling them; **fang′less**. [O.E. *fang*, from the same root as *fōn*, to seize.]

fangle *fang′gl*, *n.* (*Milt.*; *Bunyan*) fancy. — *v.t.* (*Milt.*) to fabricate, trick out. — *adj.* **fang′led** (*Shak.*) foppish. [Mistaken back-formation from **newfangle(d)**.]

fango *fang′gō*, *n.* a clay or mud from thermal springs in Italy, esp. at Battaglio, used in treatment of gout, rheumatism, etc.: — *pl.* **fang′os**. [It., mud — Gmc.]

fanion *fan′yǝn*, *n.* a small flag, esp. for surveying. — *n.* **fan′on** a cloth for handling holy vessels or offertory bread: a maniple: a short cape worn by the Pope when celebrating High Mass. [O.Fr. *fanion, fanon* — L.L. *fanō, -ōnis*, banner, napkin — O.H.G. *fano*; cf. **fane**[1], **vane**.]

fank[1] *fangk*, (*Scot.*) *n.* a coil: a noose: a tangle. — *v.t.* **fank′le** to entangle. — *n.* a tangle, muddle. [Conn. with **fang**.]

fank[2] *fangk*, (*Scot.*) *n.* a sheep fold. [Gael. *fang*.]

fannel, fannell *fan′ǝl*, *n.* a maniple. [L.L. *fanonellus, fanula*, dims. of *fanō*; see **fanion**.]

fanny *fan′i*, (*slang*) *n.* buttocks (chiefly *U.S.*): the female genitals (*vulg.*).

Fanny Adams *fan′i ad′ǝmz*, (*slang*) tinned mutton. — **sweet Fanny Adams, sweet FA** (*slang*, in Services a euphemism) nothing at all. [From a girl murdered and cut up *c.* 1812.]

fanon. See **fanion**.

fantad. See **fantod**.

fan-tan *fan′tan*, *n.* a Chinese gambling game. [Chin.]

fantasia *fan-tä′zi-ǝ, -tä′, -zhǝ*, or *-tǝ-zē′ǝ*, *n.* a musical or other composition not governed by the ordinary rules of form. [It., — Gr. *phantasiā*; see **fantasy**.]

fantasy, phantasy *fan′tǝ-si, -zi*, *n.* fancy: imagination: mental image: love (*obs.*): caprice: fantasia: a story, film, etc., not based on realistic characters or setting: preoccupation with thoughts associated with unobtainable desires. — *v.t.* (*arch.*) to fancy, conceive mentally. — *adj.* **fan′tasied** filled with fancies. — *v.t.* and *v.i.* **fan′tasise, -ize** to indulge in gratifying fantasies: to have whimsical notions. — *ns.* **fan′tasist** a person who creates or indulges in fantasies; **fan′tasm** same as **phantasm**. — *adj.* **fantasque** (*-task′*) fantastic. — *n.* fantasy. — *ns.* **fan′tast** a person of fantastic ideas;

fantas′tic (*obs.*) one who is fantastical: a dandy, a fop. — *adjs.* **fantas′tic, -al** fanciful: not real: capricious: whimsical: wild: foppish (*obs.*): (not **-al**) incredible: (not **-al**) excellent (*slang*). — *adv.* **fantas′tically**. — *ns.* **fantastical′ity, fantas′ticalness**. — *v.t.* and *v.i.* **fantas′ticate** to fantasise over something: to give fantastic or whimsical treatment to. — *ns.* **fantastica′tion; fantas′ticism** (*-sizm*); **fantas′tico** (*Shak.*; *It.*) a fantastic: — *pl.* **fantas′ticoes; fan′tastry**. [O.Fr. *fantasie* — through L. from Gr. *phantasiā* — *phantazein*, to make visible; cf. **fancy, fantasia**.]

fanteeg. See **fantod**.

Fanti, Fantee *fan′tē*, *n.* a Ghanaian people: their language. — **go Fanti** (*Kipling, G. K. Chesterton*) to adopt the ways of the natives.

fantigue. See **fantod**.

fantoccini *fan-to-chē′nē, n.pl.* marionettes: a marionette show. [It., *pl.* of *fantoccino*, dim. of *fantoccio*, a puppet — *fante*, a boy — L. *īnfāns, -antis*.]

fantod *fan′tod*, **fantad** *-täd*, (*slang*) *ns.* a fidgety fussy person, esp. a ship's officer: (usu. in *pl.*) fidgets. — *n.* **fantigue, fanteeg** (*fan-tēg′*) anxiety, agitation.

fantom. Same as **phantom**.

fantoosh *fan-tōōsh′*, (*Scot.*) *adj.* fashionable: pretentious, showy. [Poss. conn. with Eng. dial. *fanty-sheeny*, fussy, showy, — It. *fantoccino*, marionette.]

fanzine. See **fan**[2].

fap *fap*, (*Shak.*) *adj.* fuddled, drunk.

faquir *fäk-ēr′*, *n.* Same as **fakir**.

far *fär*, *adj.* remote: more distant of two (in *Shak.* as *compar.*): (of an animal) off, right-hand (i.e. the side remote from one leading it): advanced (*obs.*). — *adv.* to, at, or over a great distance or advanced stage: remotely: in a great degree: very much: long (*obs.*). — *v.t.* (*dial.*) to remove to a distance. — *adv.* **far′most** most distant or remote. — *n.* **far′ness** the state of being far: remoteness, distance. — *adj.* **far′away** distant: abstracted, absent-minded. — *n.* the distant. — **far-away′ness; far cry** a long distance; **Far East** China, Korea, Japan, etc.: often also the countries from Burma to Indonesia and the Philippines and, as used by some, the countries of the Indian subcontinent. — *adjs.* **far′-fetched′** (*obs.* **far′fet**) fetched or brought from a remote place (*arch.*): forced, unnatural; **far′-flung** thrown far and wide: extensive. — *adv.* **far′-forth** (*Spens.*) far. — **Far North** the Arctic regions. — *adj.* and *adv.* **far′-off** in the distance. — *adj.* **far′-out** of jazz or its addicts, more up to date than 'cool': intellectual: satisfying; **far′-reach′ing** having wide validity, scope, or influence; **far′-see′ing** prescient; **far′-sight′ed** seeing far: having defective eyesight for near objects: prescient; **far′-sought** sought for at a distance. — **Far South** the Antarctic regions. — *adj.* **far′-spent** far advanced. — **Far West** (*esp.* formerly) the Great Plains, Rocky Mountains and Pacific side of North America: (now usu.) the area between the Rockies and the Pacific. — **as far as** to the extent that: up to (a particular place); **by far** in a very great degree; **far and away** by a great deal; **far and near, far and wide** everywhere, all about; **far between** at wide intervals: rare; **far be it** God forbid; **far from it** on the contrary; **go too far** to go beyond reasonable limits, esp. of tact or behaviour; **I'll see you far** (or **farther**) **first** I will not do it by any means; **in so far as** to the extent that. — See also **farther**. [O.E. *feor(r)*; Du. *ver*; O.N. *fiarre*.]

farad *far′ǝd*, *n.* a unit of electrical capacitance, the capacitance of a capacitor between the plates of which appears a difference of potential of one volt when it is charged by one coulomb of electricity. — *n.* **far′aday** a unit used in electrolysis, equal to 96 500 coulombs. — *adj.* **faradic** (*-ad′ik*) pertaining to Faraday, esp. in connection with induced currents. — *n.* **faradisā′tion**, **-z-**. — *v.t.* **far′adise, -ize** (*med.*) to stimulate by induced currents. — *n.* **far′adism** treatment by induced currents. [From Michael *Faraday* (1791–1867).]

farand, farrand, farrant *far′ǝnd, fär′, -ǝnt*, (*Scot.*) *adjs.* having a certain appearance or manner, esp. in such compound forms as *auld-farand*, old-fashioned, quaint, precocious, sagacious; *fair-farand*, goodly, specious. [M.E. *farand*, comely. Origin obscure; prob. pr.p. of **fare**.]

farandine, farrandine *far'ən-dēn*, **ferrandine** *fer'*, (*obs.*) *ns.* a cloth or a dress of silk with wool or hair. [Fr. *ferrandine*.]

farandole *far-ən-dōl'*, *n.* a Provençal dance performed in a long string: music for it, in 6-8 time. [Prov. *farandoula*.]

farborough *fär'bər-ə*, *n.* Goodman Dull's pronunciation of **thirdborough** (*Love's Lab. Lost* I, i. 182). — Another reading, **tharborough**.

farce *färs*, *v.t.* to cram: to stuff, fill with stuffing: to swell out (*Shak.*). — *n.* stuffing, force-meat: comedy of extravagant humour, buffoonery, and improbability: ridiculous or empty show: a hollow formality. — *n.* **farceur** (*fär-sœr'*; Fr.) a joker, buffoon: one who writes or acts in farces: — *fem.* **farceuse** (*-sœz'*). — *adjs.* **farci** (*fär-sē*; Fr.) stuffed; **far'cical**. — *n.* **farcical'ity** farcical quality. — *adv.* **far'cically**. — *v.t.* **far'cify** to turn into a farce. — *n.* **farc'ing** stuffing. [Fr. *farce*, stuffing, from L. *farcīre*, to stuff; the connecting links of meaning seem to be interpolation, theatrical gag, buffoonery; cf. **farse**.]

farcy *fär'si*, *n.* chronic glanders. — Also (*obs.*) **far'cin**. — *adj.* **far'cied**. — **far'cy-bud** a swollen lymphatic gland, as in farcy. [Fr. *farcin* — L.L. *farcīminum*.]

fard *färd*, *n.* white paint for the face. — *v.t.* to paint with fard: to gloss over: to trick out. [Fr., of Gmc. origin.]

fardage *fär'dij*, (*naut. obs.*) *n.* dunnage. [Fr.]

fardel[1] *fär'dl*, (*obs.*) *n.* a fourth part. [O.E. *fēortha dǣl*, fourth deal.]

fardel[2] *fär'dl*, *n.* a pack: anything cumbersome or irksome: the manyplies or omasum. — **far'del-bag** the omasum. — *adj.* **far'del-bound** constipated, esp. of cattle and sheep, by the retention of food in the omasum. [O.Fr. *fardel* (Fr. *fardeau*), dim. of *farde*, a burden, possibly — Ar. *fardah*, a package.]

farden, farding *fär'dən* (*obs.* or *dial.*). Same as **farthing**.

fare *fär*, *v.i.* to travel: to get on or succeed: to happen well or ill to: to be in any particular state, to be, to go on: to be fed. — *n.* (*orig. Spens.*) a course or passage: the price of passage: a passenger (or passengers): food or provisions for the table. — *interj.* **farewell'** may you fare well!, a parting wish for safety or success: good-bye. — *adj.* (*fär'wel*) parting: valedictory: final. [O.E. *faran*: Ger. *fahren*.]

farfet. See **far-fetched.**

farina *fə-rī'nə*, *fə-rē'nə*, *n.* ground corn: meal: starch: pollen: a mealy powder. — *adjs.* **farinaceous** (*far-i-nā'shəs*) mealy: consisting of cereals; **far'inose** (*-i-nōs*) yielding farina. [L. *farīna* — *fär*, corn.]

Faringee. See **Feringhi.**

farl(e) *färl*, (*Scot.*) *n.* the quarter of a round cake of flour or oatmeal: a cake. [**fardel**[1].]

farm *färm*, *n.* a fixed payment (*obs.*): a lease (*Spens.*): a fixed payment in composition of taxes, etc. (*hist.*): the letting out of revenue to one who collects it in exchange for a fixed sum (*hist.*): a tract of land (originally one leased or rented) used for cultivation and pasturage, along with a house and other necessary buildings: farmhouse: farmstead: a piece of land or water used for breeding animals (as *fox-, oyster-farm*): a place for treatment and disposal (*sewage-farm*): a place where e.g. children are handed over to be taken care of. — *adj.* of, belonging to, appropriate to, a farm. — *v.t.* to grant or receive the revenues of for a fixed sum: to rent to or from another: to cultivate: to use as farm: to arrange for maintenance of at fixed price. — *v.i.* to practise the business of farmer. — *n.* **farm'er** one who farms land: the tenant of a farm: one who receives taxes, etc., for fixed payment: — *fem.* **far'meress**. — *ns.* **farm'ery** buildings of a farm; **farm'ing** business of cultivating land. — **farmer general** one of those who, in France before the Revolution, leased the public revenues; **farmer's lung** a lung disease caused by the spores of actinomycetes which develop in hay baled while it is still damp; **farm'house** the farmer's house attached to a farm; **farm'-hand, -labourer** one who works on a farm. — *adj.* **farm'-in** (*econ.*) acquired by farming into (q.v. below) a company. — *n.pl.* **farm'-offices** outbuildings on a farm. — **farm'-place, farm'-stead, farm steading** farmhouse with buildings belonging to it — *Scot.* **farm'-toun** (*-tōōn*); **farm'yard** yard or enclosure surrounded by farm buildings. — **farm into** to take shares in a company or concern (usu. of a company obtaining an interest in another); **farm out** to board out for fixed payment: to give, e.g. work for which one has made oneself responsible, to others to carry out. [L.L. *firma*, a fixed payment — L. *firmus*, firm.]

farmost. See **far.**

farnesol *fär'ni-sol*, *n.* an alcohol, $C_{15}H_{25}OH$, found in various essential oils and used in perfumes. [From *Acacia farnesiana*, after Odoardo *Farnese*, 16th-cent. Italian cardinal.]

faro *fär'ō*, *n.* a game of chance played by betting on the order of appearance of certain cards. [Perh. from *Pharaoh*; reason unknown.]

farouche *fə-rōōsh'*, *fa-*, *adj.* shy, ill at ease: sullen and unsociable: socially inexperienced and lacking polish. [Fr., wild, shy, savage.]

farrago *fə-rä'gō*, *fä-rä'gō*, *n.* a confused mass of objects or persons (*obs.*): a disordered mixture: — *pl.* **farrag'-oes**. — *adj.* **farraginous** (*fə-rāj'in-əs, -raj'*) miscellaneous, jumbled. [L. *farrāgō, -inis*, mixed fodder — *fär*, grain.]

farrand, farrant. See **farand.**

farrandine. See **farandine.**

farren *far'ən*, (*dial.*) *n.* a division of land: a right of common. [Origin uncertain.]

farrier *far'i-ər*, *n.* one who shoes horses: one who cures horses' diseases: one in charge of cavalry horses. — *n.* **farr'iery** the farrier's art: veterinary surgery. [O.Fr. *ferrier* — L. *ferrum*, iron.]

farrow[1] *far'ō*, *n.* a litter of pigs. — *v.i.* or *v.t.* to bring forth (pigs). [O.E. *fearh*, a pig; Ger. (dim.) *Ferkel*; L. *porcus*.]

farrow[2] *far'ō*, *adj.* not with calf for the time being. [Ety. dub.; with *farrow cow* cf. Flem. *verwekoe, varwekoe*.]

farruca *fa-rōō'ka*, (Sp.) *n.* a Spanish gypsy dance with abrupt variations of tempo and mood.

farse *färs*, *n.* an explanation of the Latin epistle in the vernacular. — *v.t.* to extend by interpolation. [**farce.**]

Farsi *fär'sē*, *n.* Modern Persian, an Indo-European language and the official spoken language of Iran. [*Fars* ('Persia'), province of S.W. Iran.]

fart *färt*, (*vulg.*) *v.i.* to break wind from the anus. — Also *n.* [O.E. (assumed) *feortan*; cf. Gr. *perdesthai*.]

farthel *fär'dhəl*, (*Scot.*) *n.* Same as **farl(e).**

farther *fär'dhər*, **far'thermore, far'thermost, far'thest.** Same as **further**, etc., and sometimes preferred where the notion of distance is more prominent. [A variant (M.E. *ferther*) of **further**[1] that came to be thought a compar. of **far.**]

farthing *fär'dhing*, *n.* a fourth part (*obs.*): the fourth of a pre-1971 penny (from Jan. 1961, not legal tender): anything very small: the Gr. *assarion* (L. *as*) and also *kodrantēs* (L. *quadrāns*), fourth of an *as* (*B.*). — *adj.* **far'thingless.** — *n.* **far'thingsworth** as much as a farthing will buy. — **far'thingland** a varying area of land. [O.E. *fēorthing*, a fourth part — *fēortha*, fourth, and suff. *-ing*.]

farthingale *fär'dhing-gāl*, *n.* a kind of crinoline of whalebone for distending women's dress. [O.Fr. *verdugale* — Sp. *verdugado*, hooped, *verdugo*, rod.]

fasces *fas'ēz*, *n.pl.* the bundle of rods, with or without an axe, borne before an ancient Roman magistrate of high grade. [L. *fascēs*, pl. of *fascis*, bundle.]

Fasching *fa'shing*, (Ger.) *n.* (Shrovetide) carnival.

fascia *fā'shi-ə*, *n.* a band, fillet (*obs.*): a broad flat band, as in an architrave, or over a shop-front (*archit.*): a board in like position, commonly bearing the shop-keeper's name: (also **fasc′ia-board**) the instrument-board of a motor-car: any bandlike structure: (*fash′i-ə*) connective tissue ensheathing a muscle (*zool.*). — *adjs.* **fasc′ial; fasc′iate, fasc′iated.** — *ns.* **fasciā′tion** (*bot.*) union of a number of parts side by side in a flat plate; **fasciola** (*fə-sī′ō-lə*), **fasciole** (*fas′i-ōl*) a band of colour. [L. *fascia*, band, bandage.]

fascicle *fas′i-kl, n.* a bundle or bunch, esp. a bunched tuft of branches, roots, fibres, etc.: a part of a book issued in parts. — Also **fasc′icule, fascic′ulus:** — *pl.* **fascic′ulī.** — *adjs.* **fasc′icled, fascic′ular, fascic′ulate, -d.** [L. *fasciculus*, dim. of *fascis*, bundle.]

fascinate *fas′i-nāt, v.t.* to bewitch, enchant, cast the evil eye upon (*obs.*): to control by the eye like a snake: to entangle the attention of: to charm: to captivate. — *adj.* **fasc′inating** charming, delightful: binding the attention. — *n.* **fascinā′tion** the act of charming: power to harm, control, allure, or render helpless by looks or spells: state of being fascinated; **fasc′inātor** one who fascinates: a woman's light, soft head-covering. [L. *fascināre, -ātum*; perh. allied to Gr. *baskainein*, to bewitch.]

fascine *fas-ēn′, n.* a brushwood faggot, used to fill ditches, protect a shore, etc. [Fr., — L. *fascīna — fascis*, a bundle.]

fascio *fä′shō, n.* an organised political group or club: — *pl.* **fasci** (*fä′shē*). — *ns.* **Fascism** (*fash′izm*; It. **Fascismo** *fä-shēz′mō*) the authoritarian form of government in Italy from 1922–1943, characterised by extreme nationalism, militarism, anti-communism and restrictions on individual freedom: (also without *cap.*) the methods, doctrines, etc. of fascists or the Fascists; **Fasc′ist** (It. **Fascista** *fä-shēs′tə*) a member of the ruling party in Italy from 1922–1943, or a similar party elsewhere: (also without *cap.*) an exponent or supporter of Fascism, or (loosely) anyone with extreme right-wing, nationalistic, etc. views or methods: — *pl.* **Fasc′ists** (It. **Fascis′ti** *-tē*). — *adjs.* **fasc′ist, fascis′tic.** [It. *fascio*, bundle, group, with a hint of **fasces** (q.v.).]

fasciole. See **fascia.**

fash *fash,* (*Scot.*) *v.t.* to trouble, annoy. — *v.i.* to be vexed: to take trouble or pains: to annoy. — *n.* pains, trouble: annoyance. — *n.* **fash′ery.** — *adj.* **fashious** (*fash′əs*) troublesome, vexatious. — *n.* **fash′iousness.** — **never fash your thumb** take no trouble in the matter. [O.Fr. *fascher* (Fr. *fâcher*) — L. *fastīdium*, disgust.]

fashion *fash′n, n.* the make or cut of a thing: form or pattern: vogue: prevailing mode or shape of dress or that imposed by those whose lead is accepted: a prevailing custom: manner: genteel society: appearance. — *v.t.* to make: to mould according to a pattern: to suit or adapt. — *adj.* **fash′ionable** according to prevailing fashion: prevailing or in use at any period: observant of the fashion in dress or living: moving in high society: patronised by people of fashion. — *n.* a person of fashion. — *n.* **fash′ionableness.** — *adv.* **fash′ionably.** — *ns.* **fash′ioner; fash′ionist.** — **fashion house** an establishment in which fashionable clothes are designed, made and sold; **fashion jewellery** costume jewellery. — *adjs.* **fash′ionmongering, fash′ionmonging** (*Shak.*) behaving like a fop. — **fash′ion-plate** a pictorial representation of the latest style of dress: a very smartly dressed person (*fig.*). — **after** or **in a fashion** in a way: to a certain extent; **in fashion** currently favoured: fashionable; **in the fashion** in accordance with the prevailing style of dress, etc; **out of fashion** old-fashioned: unfashionable. [O.Fr. *fachon* — L. *factiō, -ōnis — facĕre*, to make.]

fashions *fash′ənz,* (*Shak.*) *n.pl.* for **farcin**, farcy.

fashious, etc. See **fash.**

fast¹ *fäst, adj.* firm: fixed: steadfast: fortified: (of sleep) sound: (of colours) not liable to fade or run. — Also in combination, as *handfast, bedfast, lockfast, colour-fast.* — *adv.* firmly, unflinchingly: soundly or sound (asleep): close: near. — *adv.* **fast′ly** (*Shak.*) firmly. — *n.* **fast′ness** fixedness: a stronghold, fortress, castle. —

fast′-and-loose′ a cheating game practised at fairs, the dupe being invited to put a stick in the loop of a coiled belt so that it cannot be pulled away — called also *prick-the-garter.* — *adj.* **fast′-hand′ed** close-fisted. — **fast by** close to, close by; **play fast and loose** (from the cheating game) to be unreliable, shifty: to behave without sense of moral obligation. [O.E. *fæst*; Ger. *fest.*]

fast² *fäst, adj.* quick: rapid: before time (as a clock): promoting fast play: for fast-moving traffic, as in *fast lane:* seeking excitement: rash: dissolute. — *adv.* swiftly: in rapid succession: extravagantly. — *adj.* **fast′ish** somewhat fast. — *n.* **fast′ness.** — **fast′back** a car whose roof slopes smoothly down towards the rear, giving a streamlined effect: a particular breed of pig; **fast food(s)** kinds of food, e.g. hamburgers, chips, etc., which can be prepared and served quickly; **fast neutron** a neutron of very high energy, usu. over 10 000 electron volts; **fast reactor** a nuclear reactor using fast neutrons, and little or no moderator. — *v.t.* **fast′-talk** to persuade with rapid, plausible talk. — **fast worker** one who gains his ends quickly and easily, esp. by unscrupulous means. — **a fast buck** (*slang*) money quickly and easily obtained; **fast and furious** rapidly and vigorously; **fast-breeder reactor** a nuclear reactor using fast neutrons which produces at least as much fissionable material as it uses; **fast forward** in a cassette player, the operation of winding a tape quickly forward; **pull a fast one** to gain an advantage by trickery. [A special use of **fast¹** derived from Scand. sense of urgent.]

fast³ *fäst, v.i.* to keep from food: to go hungry: to abstain from food in whole or part, as a religious duty. — *n.* abstinence from food: special abstinence enjoined by the church: the day or time of fasting. — *ns.* **fast′er** one who fasts; **fast′ing** religious abstinence. — **fast= day** a day of religious fasting: a day for humiliation and prayer, esp. before communion; **Fast′ens** short for **Fastens-eve** (*Scot.* **Fasten-e′en** and **Fastern′s-e′en**), **Fastens Tuesday** Shrove Tuesday (O.E. *fæstenes*, gen. of *fæsten*, fast). [O.E. *fæstan*, to fast; Ger. *fasten.*]

fast⁴ *fäst* (*Spens.*) a spelling of **faced.**

fasten *fäs′n, v.t.* to make fast or firm: to fix securely: to attach. — *v.i.* to admit of being fastened: to remain stationary: to fix: to lay hold: to make assault. — *ns.* **fastener** (*fäs′nər*) a clip, catch, or other means of fastening; **fas′tening** (*fäs′ning*) that which fastens. — **fasten on** to direct (one's eyes) on: to seize on, e.g. a fact: to fix the blame, responsibility for, on (a person) (*slang*). [**fast¹.**]

fasti *fas′tī,* L. *fäs′tē, n.pl.* those days among the ancient Romans on which it was lawful to transact legal or public business — opp. to *nefasti:* an enumeration of the days of the year, a calendar: annals. [L.]

fastidious *fas-tid′i-əs, adj.* affecting superior taste: over-nice: difficult to please: exacting in taste: nicely critical. — *adv.* **fastid′iously.** — *n.* **fastid′iousness.** [L. *fastīdiōsus — fastīdium*, loathing.]

fastigiate *fas-tij′i-āt, adj.* pointed, sloping to a point or edge: with branches more or less erect and parallel (*bot.*): conical. — *adj.* **fastig′iated.** — *n.* **fastig′ium** the apex of a building: gable-end: pediment. [L. *fastīgium*, a gable-end, roof.]

fastuous *fas′tū-əs,* (*arch.*) *adj.* haughty: ostentatious. [L. *fastuōsus — fastus*, arrogance.]

fat¹ *fat, adj.* plump, fleshy: well filled out: thick, full-bodied (as of printing types): corpulent: obese: having much, or of the nature of, adipose tissue or the substance it contains: oily: fruitful or profitable: rich in some important constituent: gross: fulsome: — *compar.* **fatt′er;** *superl.* **fatt′est.** — *n.* a substance found in adipose tissue: solid animal or vegetable oil: any member of a group of naturally occurring substances consisting of the glycerides of higher fatty acids, e.g. palmitic acid, stearic acid, oleic acid (*chem.*): the richest part of anything: a piece of work offering more than usual profit for effort: a passage that enables an actor or musician to show what he can do: inclination to corpulency: a fat animal: money (*slang*). — *adv.* in golf, striking the ground before the ball. — *v.t.* to make fat. — *v.i.* to grow fat: — *pr.p.* **fatt'ing;** *pa.t.* and *pa.p.* **fatt'ed.** — *n.* **fat'ling** a young animal fattened for slaughter. — *adj.* small and fat. — *adv.* **fat'ly** grossly: lumberingly. — *n.* **fat'ness** quality or state of being fat: fullness of flesh: richness: fertility: that which makes fertile. — *adj.* **fatt'ed (fatted calf** the not always approved fare for the returned prodigal — Luke xv. 23, etc.). — *v.t.* **fatt'en** to make fat or fleshy: to make fertile. — *v.i.* to grow fat. — *ns.* **fatt'ener; fatt'ening** (also *adj.*); **fatt'iness.** — *adjs.* **fatt'ish** somewhat fat; **fatt'y** containing fat: having qualities of fat. — *n.* a fat person. — *adj.* **fat'brained** (*Shak.*) stupid — **fat cat** (*U.S. slang*) a wealthy, prosperous person. — *adjs.* **fat'-cat; fat'-face, -d** having a fat or broad face. — **fat'-head** a dullard. — *adj.* **fat'-head'ed.** — **fat'-hen** any one of various thick-leaved plants, esp. of the goose-foot family. — *adj.* **fat'-kidney'd** (*Shak.*). — **fat'-lute** a mixture of pipe-clay and linseed-oil, for filling joints, etc.; **fat mouse** any of several kinds of mouse of the genus *Steatomys*, found in dry regions of Africa, that store fat and are eaten as a delicacy; **fat stock, fat'stock** livestock fattened for market. — *adj.* **fat'-tailed** having much fat in the tail, as certain Asiatic and African sheep. — **fatty acids** acids which with glycerine form fats; **fatty degeneration** morbid deposition of fat; **fatty heart,** etc., fatty degeneration of the heart, etc. — *adj.* **fat'-witted** dull, stupid. — **a fat lot** (*slang*) not much; **the fat is in the fire** a critical act has precipitated the trouble. [O.E. *fætt,* fatted.]

fat² *fat, n.* a vessel for holding liquids: a vat: a dry measure of nine bushels. [See **vat.**]

fatal, fatalism, etc. See **fate.**

fata Morgana *fä'tə mör-gä'nə,* a striking kind of mirage seen most often in the Strait of Messina. [Supposed to be caused by the fairy (It. *fata*) *Morgana* of Arthurian romance.]

fate *fāt, n.* inevitable destiny or necessity: appointed lot: destined term of life: ill-fortune: doom: final issue: (in *pl.*; with *cap.*) the three goddesses of fate, Clotho, Lachesis, and Atropos, who determine the birth, life, and death of men — the **fatal sisters.** — *adj.* **fāt'al** belonging to or appointed by fate: announcing fate: causing ruin or death: mortal: calamitous. — *ns.* **fāt'alism** the doctrine that all events are subject to fate, and happen by unavoidable necessity: acceptance of this doctrine: lack of effort in the face of threatened difficulty or disaster; **fāt'alist** one who believes in fatalism. — *adj.* **fātalist'ic** belong to or partaking of fatalism. — *n.* **fatality** (*fə-tal'i-ti*) the state of being fatal or unavoidable: the decree of fate: fixed tendency to disaster or death: mortality: a fatal occurrence: a person who has been killed, esp. in an accident, etc. — *adv.* **fāt'ally.** — *adjs.* **fāt'ed** doomed: destined: invested with the power of destiny (*Shak.*): enchanted (*Dryden*); **fate'ful** charged with fate. — *adv.* **fate'fully.** — *n.* **fate'fulness.** [L. *fātum,* a prediction — *fātus,* spoken — *fārī,* to speak.]

father *fä'dhər, n.* a male parent: an ancestor or forefather: a fatherly protector: a contriver or originator: a title of respect applied to a venerable man, to confessors, monks, priests, etc.: a member of certain fraternities: (usu. in *pl.*) a member of a ruling body, as *conscript fathers, city fathers:* the oldest member, or member of longest standing, of a profession or body: one of a group of ecclesiastical writers of the early centuries, usually ending with Ambrose, Jerome, and Augustine: (with *cap.*) the first person of the Trinity. — *v.t.* to adopt: to ascribe to one as his offspring or production. — *n.* **fa'therhood** state or fact of being a father: fatherly authority (*arch.*). — *adj.* **fa'therless** destitute of a living father: without a known author. — *ns.* **fa'therlessness; fa'therliness.** — *adj.* **fa'therly** like a father: paternal. — *n.* **fa'thership.** — **Father Christmas** same as **Santa Claus; fa'ther-figure** a senior person of experience and authority looked on as a trusted leader or protector;

fa'ther-in-law the father of one's husband or wife: step-father (*arch.*): — *pl.* **fa'thers-in-law; fa'therland** native land, esp. Germany (*Vaterland*): the country of one's ancestors; **fa'ther-lash'er** a name applied to two bullheads found on the British coasts; **Father's Day** a day on which fathers are honoured, the third Sunday in June, the tradition being of U.S. origin, dating from the early 20th cent.. — **be gathered to one's fathers** (*B.*) to die and be buried; **Holy Father** the Pope; **the father and mother of** see under **mother.** [O.E. *fæder;* Ger. *Vater,* L. *pater,* Gr. *patēr.*]

fathom *fadh'əm, n.* originally, the reach of the out-stretched arms: now, a nautical measure, six feet: penetration of mind: a timber measure, 216 cubic feet: — *pl.* **fath'om, fath'oms.** — *v.t.* to measure or encom-pass with outstretched arms (*arch.*): to try the depth of: to comprehend or get to the bottom of. — *adjs.* **fath'omable; fath'omless.** — *n.* **fathom'eter** a sonic depth measurer. — **fath'om-line** a sailor's line and lead for taking soundings. [O.E. *fæthm;* Du. *vadem,* Ger. *Faden.*]

fatidical *fā-, fə-tid'i-kl, adj.* having power to foretell future events: prophetical. — *adv.* **fatid'ically.** [L. *fātidicus* — *fātum,* fate, *dīcere,* to tell.]

fatigue *fə-tēg', n.* weariness from labour of body or of mind: toil: lessened power of response to stimulus, resulting from activity: failure under repeated stress as in metal: fatigue-duty (sometimes allotted as a punishment): (in *pl.*) military overalls. — *v.t.* to reduce to weariness: to exhaust the strength or power of recovery of: — *pr.p.* **fatigu'ing;** *pa.t.* and *pa.p.* **fatigued'.** — *adj.* **fatig(u)able** (*fat'ig-ə-bl*) capable of being fa-tigued: easily fatigued. — *n.* **fat'ig(u)ableness.** — *adj.* **fatigate** (*fat'i-gāt; Shak.*) fatigued. — *v.t.* (*obs.*) to fatigue. — *adv.* **fatigu'ingly.** — **fatigue'-dress** working dress; **fatigue'-duty** the part of a soldier's work distinct from the use of arms; **fatigue'-party.** [Fr. *fatigue* — L. *fatīgāre,* to weary.]

Fatimid *fat'i-mid, n.* a descendant of Mohammed's daughter, *Fatima,* and his cousin, Ali, esp. one of a dynasty ruling parts of northern Africa from 909 to 1171. — Also *adj.*

fatiscent *fā-, fə-tis'ənt, adj.* gaping with cracks. — *n.* **fatis'cence.** [L. *fatīscēns, -entis,* pr.p. of *fatīscere,* to gape.]

fatso *fat'sō,* (*derog. slang*) *n.* a fat person: — *pl.* **fat'so(e)s.** [**fat¹.**]

fattrels *fat'rəlz, fät', (Scot.) n.pl.* ends of ribbon. [O.Fr. *fatraille,* trumpery.]

fatuous *fat'ū-əs, adj.* silly: imbecile. — *adj.* **fatū'itous.** — *ns.* **fatū'ity, fat'ūousness** unconscious stupidity: imbe-cility. — **fatuous fire** ignis fatuus, will-o'-the-wisp. [L. *fatuus.*]

faubourg *fō-boōr, (Fr.) n.* a suburb just beyond the walls or a district recently included within a city.

fauces *fö'sēz, n.pl.* the upper part of the throat, from the root of the tongue to the entrance of the gullet: the throat of a flower. — *adjs.* **fau'cal (-kl)** of, produced, in the fauces, as certain Semitic guttural sounds; **faucial** (*fö'shl*) of the fauces. [L. *faucēs.*]

faucet *fö'sit, n.* a pipe inserted in a barrel to draw liquid: a tap (*U.S.*). [Fr. *fausset.*]

fauchion, fauchon *fö'shən, -chən, ns.* obsolete forms of **falchion.**

faucial. See **fauces.**

faugh *fö, interj.* expressing disgust.

faulchion, faulchin. Obsolete forms of **falchion.**

fault *fölt, formerly föt, n.* a failing: error: blemish: imperfection: a slight offence: a dislocation of strata or veins (*geol.*): a stroke in which the player fails to serve the ball properly or into the proper place (*tennis*): culpability for that which has happened amiss. — *v.i.* to fall short (*obs.*): to be faulty: to commit a fault. — *v.t.* to find fault with: to find flaw(s) in: to cause a fault in (*geol.*). — *adj.* **fault'ful** (*Shak.*) full of faults or crimes. — *adv.* **fault'ily.** — *n.* **fault'iness.** — *adj.* **fault'less** without fault or defect. — *adv.* **fault'lessly.**

— *n.* **fault′lessness.** — *adj.* **fault′y** imperfect, defective: guilty of a fault: blamable. — **fault′-finder; fault′=finding** criticism, captiousness: detection and investigation of faults and malfunctions in electronic equipment; **find′-fault** see **find; fault plane** (*geol.*) a usu. uncurved surface of rock strata where a fault has occurred. — **at fault** (of dogs) unable to find the scent: at a loss: to blame: guilty; **find fault** to carp, be critical: (with *with*) to censure for some defect; **in fault** (*arch.*) to blame; **to a fault** excessively. [O.Fr. *faute, falte* — L. *fallěre*, to deceive.]

fauna *fö′nə, n.* the assemblage of animals of a region or period: a list or account thereof: — *pl.* **faun′as, faun′ae** (*-ē*). — *n.* **faun** a Roman rural deity, protector of shepherds. — *adj.* **faun′al.** — *n.* **faun′ist** one who studies faunas. — *adj.* **faunist′ic.** [L. *Fauna, Faunus,* tutelary deities of shepherds — *favēre, fautum,* to favour.]

faurd. See **fa′.**

Faustian *fow′sti-ən, adj.* in the manner of *Faust* who, in German legend, made a bargain with the devil to gain limitless knowledge in exchange for his soul. — Also without *cap.*

faute de mieux *fōt də myø,* (Fr.) for want of better.

fauteuil *fō-tœ-y′,* also *fō′til, n.* an armchair, esp. a president's chair: the seat of one of the forty members of the French Academy: a theatre stall. [Fr.]

fautor *fö′tər, n.* a favourer: a patron: an abettor, [L. *fautor — favēre,* to favour.]

Fauve, Fauvist *föv, föv′ist, ns.* one of a group of painters at the beginning of the 20th century, including Matisse, who viewed a painting as essentially a two-dimensional decoration in colour, not necessarily imitative of nature. — *n.* **Fauv′ism.** [Fr. *fauve,* wild beast.]

fauvette *fö-vet′, n.* a warbler. [Fr.]

faux *fō,* (Fr.) *adj.* false. — **faux ami** (*fōz a-mē*) a word in a foreign language that does not mean what it appears to, e.g. in Italian, *pretendere* does not mean 'to pretend'. — *n.* and *adj.* **faux-naïf** (*fō-na-ēf*) (a person) seeming or pretending to be simple and unsophisticated. — **faux pas** (*fō pä*) a false step: a mistake, blunder.

fauxbourdon *fō-bōōr-dɔ̄.* Same as **faburden.**

favela *fä-vä′lə, n.* in Brazil, a shanty town. [Port.]

favel, favell *fä′vəl,* (*obs.*) *adj.* light-brown: chestnut. — *n.* (with *cap.*) a name for a chestnut horse, esp. as proverbial for cunning, from the deceitful but much-courted horse *Fauvel* in the O. Fr. *Roman de Fauvel;* hence **curry favell** (see **curry**²), from O. Fr. *estriller, toucher Fauvel.*

faveolate *fa-vē′ō-lāt, adj.* honeycombed. [L. *favus,* honeycomb.]

favism *fä′vizm, n.* an acute type of anaemia in which haemolysis is precipitated by contact with broad beans (by ingestion or pollen-inhalation), the original lesion being an enzyme deficiency in the red blood cells. [L. *fava,* broad bean, and *-ism.*]

Favonian *fə-vō′ni-ən, adj.* pertaining to the west wind, favourable. [L. *Favōnius,* the west wind.]

favour, or (esp. *U.S.*) **favor,** *fä′vər, n.* countenance: good-will: a kind deed: an act of grace or lenity: indulgence: partiality: advantage: a concession of amorous indulgence: a knot of ribbons worn at a wedding, election, etc.: a thing given or worn as a token of favour: appearance, face (*arch.*): a letter or written communication (*commercial jargon*): an attraction or grace (*Shak.*): an object of favour (*Milt.*). — *v.t.* to regard with goodwill: to be on the side of: to treat indulgently: to give support to: to afford advantage to: to resemble (*coll.*): to choose to wear, etc. — *adj.* **fa′vourable** friendly: propitious: conducive: advantageous: satisfactory, promising. — *n.* **fa′vourableness.** — *adv.* **fa′vourably.** — *adj.* **fa′voured** enjoying favour or preference: wearing favours: having a certain appearance, featured — as in *ill-favoured, well-favoured.* — *ns.* **fa′vouredness; fa′vourer; fa′vourite** (*-it*) a person or thing regarded with marked preference: one unduly

loved and indulged, esp. by a king: one expected to win: a kind of curl of the hair, affected by ladies of the 18th century. — *adj.* esteemed, preferred. — *n.* **fa′vouritism** inclination to partiality: preference shown to favourites. — *adj.* **fä′vourless** without favour: not favouring (*Spens.*). — **curry favour** see **curry**², and **favel; favours to come** favours still expected; **in favour of** for: on the side of: for the advantage of; **in (out of) favour** (not) approved of. [O.Fr., — L. *favor — favēre,* to favour, befriend.]

favus *fäv′əs, n.* a fungal skin disease, chiefly of the scalp, giving a honeycombed appearance. — *adjs.* **favose** (*fə-vōs′, fä′vōs*) honeycombed; **fä′vous** like a honeycomb: relating to favus. [L. *favus,* a honeycomb.]

favrile *fəv-rēl′, fäv′rəl, n.* a type of iridescent glassware developed in America at the turn of the 20th century by L. C. Tiffany. (*Orig.* trademark, — *obs. fabrile,* pertaining to a craftsman.]

faw *fö, n.* a gypsy. [From the surname *Faa.*]

fawn¹ *fön, n.* a young deer, esp. a fallow deer: its colour, light yellowish brown. — *adj.* resembling a fawn in colour. — *v.t.* and *v.i.* to bring forth (a fawn). [O.Fr. *faon,* through L.L. from L. *fētus,* offspring.]

fawn² *fön, v.i.* to cringe, to flatter in a servile way (with *upon*). — *n.* (*rare*) a servile cringe or bow: mean flattery. — *n.* **fawn′er** one who flatters to gain favour. — *n.* and *adj.* **fawn′ing.** — *adv.* **fawn′ingly.** — *n.* **fawn′ingness.** [A variant of **fain**¹ — O.E. *fægen,* glad.]

fax *faks,* a shortening of **facsimile** as in **fax machine,** a machine that scans a document, etc. electronically and transfers the information to a receiving machine by a telephone line: a copy so produced. — Also *v.t.*

fay¹ *fā, n.* a fairy. [O.Fr. *fae* — L.L. *fāta;* see **fate.**]

fay² *fā,* (*Shak.*) *n.* faith. [O.Fr. *fei.*]

fay³. Same as **fey**¹.

fay⁴ *fā, v.t., v.i.* to fit, unite closely. — **fay′ing-face** prepared surface of contact. [O.E. *fēgan;* Ger. *fügen.*]

fay⁵, **fey** *fā,* (*dial.*) *v.t.* to clean out, as a ditch. [O.N. *fægja,* to cleanse.]

fayalite *fä′ə-līt, fä-yäl′īt, n.* iron-olivine, a silicate of iron found in slag and occurring naturally. [*Fayal,* in the Azores, where it was found, probably in ballast.]

fayence. Same as **faience.**

fayne *fān,* (*Spens.*) *v.t.* same as **feign.**

faze *fāz.* See **feeze.**

feague *fēg,* (*obs.*) *v.t.* to whip: to perplex. [Cf. Du. *vegen,* Ger. *fegen.*]

feal¹ *fēl,* (*obs.*) *adj.* loyal, faithful. [O.Fr. *feal* — L. *fidēlis.*]

feal² *fēl,* (*dial.*) *v.t.* to conceal. [O.N. *fela.*]

feal³ *fēl.* Same as **fail**¹.

fealty *fē′əl-ti,* or *fēl′ti, n.* the vassal's obligation of fidelity to his feudal lord (*hist.*): loyalty. [O.Fr. *fealte* — L. *fidēlitās, -tātis,* — *fidēlis,* faithful — *fīdĕre,* to trust.]

fear *fēr, n.* a painful emotion excited by danger: apprehension of danger or pain: alarm: solicitude: an object of alarm: that which causes alarm: reverence (*B.*): piety towards God: risk. — *v.t.* to regard with fear: to expect with alarm: to be regretfully inclined to think: to be anxious or in fear about (*obs.*): to stand in awe of (*B.*): to venerate (*B.*): to terrify (*obs.*): to make afraid (*obs.*). — *v.i.* to be afraid: (with *for*) to suspect some danger to: to be in doubt. — *adjs.* **feared** (*fērd; arch.* and *Scot.*) afraid; **fear′ful** timorous: exciting intense fear: terrible: loosely, very great, very bad. — *adv.* **fear′fully.** — *n.* **fear′fulness.** — *adj.* **fear′less** without fear: daring: brave. — *adv.* **fear′lessly.** — *n.* **fear′lessness.** — *adj.* **fear′some** causing fear, frightful. — *adv.* **fear′somely.** — **fear′nought** dreadnought cloth. — **for fear** in case, lest; **no fear** (*interj.; slang*) definitely not. [O.E. *fær,* fear, *færan,* to terrify.]

feare. Same as **fere**¹.

feasible *fē′zi-bl, adj.* practicable, possible: (loosely) probable, likely. — *ns.* **feas′ibleness, feasibil′ity.** — *adv.* **feas′ibly.** — **feasibility study** an investigation to determine whether a particular project, system, etc. is desirable, practicable, etc. [Fr. *faisable,* that can be done — *faire, faisant* — L. *facĕre*, to do.]

feast *fēst, n.* a day of unusual solemnity or joy: a festival in commemoration of some event — *movable,* of varying date, as Easter; *immovable,* at a fixed date, as Christmas: a rich and abundant repast: rich enjoyment: festivity. — *v.i.* to hold a feast: to eat sumptuously (with *on*): to receive intense delight. — *v.t.* to entertain sumptuously: to delight. — *n.* **feast'er.** — *adj.* **feast'ful** festive, joyful, luxurious. — *n.* **feast'ing.** — **feast'-day; feast'-rite** a rite or custom observed at feasts. — *adj.* **feast'-won** (*Shak.*) won or bribed by feasting. — **Feast of Dedication** see **dedicate; Feast of Fools, Feast of Asses** mediaeval festivals held between Christmas and Epiphany, in which a mock bishop was enthroned in church, a burlesque mass was said, and an ass driven round in triumph; **Feast of Lots** purim; **Feast of Tabernacles** see **tabernacle; Feast of Weeks** see **week.** [O.Fr. *feste* (Fr. *fête*) — L. *fēstum,* a holiday, *fēstus,* solemn, festal.]

feat *fēt, n.* act, deed (*obs.*): a deed manifesting extraordinary strength, skill, or courage, an exploit, achievement: art, skill (*Spens.*). — *v.t.* (*Shak.*) perh., to fashion, to make feat or neat. — *adj.* (*Shak.*) neat, deft. — *adv.* (*Shak.*) **feat'ly** neatly: dexterously. [Fr. *fait* — L. *factum* — *facĕre,* to do: cf. **fact.**]

feateous, -ly. See **featous.**

feather *fedh'ər, n.* one of the growths that form the covering of a bird: a featherlike appearance, ornament or flaw: the feathered end of an arrow: plumage: condition: birds collectively: anything light or trifling: a projecting longitudinal rib or strip: a wedge: a formation of hair, e.g. on the legs of certain breeds of dog or horse: the act of feathering an oar: a foamy wave or wave-crest, esp. that caused by a submarine's periscope. — *v.t.* to furnish or adorn with a feather or feathers: to move edgewise (as an oar, to lessen air-resistance), or to make a propeller-blade, etc., rotate in such a way as to lessen resistance. — *v.i.* to take the appearance of a feather: to quiver the tail. — *adj.* **feath'ered** covered or fitted with feathers, or anything featherlike: like the flight of a feathered animal, swift: smoothed as with feathers. — *ns.* **feath'eriness; feath'ering** plumage: the addition of a feather or feathers: a featherlike appearance: an arrangement of small arcs separated by cusps, within an arch (*archit.*). — *adj.* **feath'ery** pertaining to, resembling, or covered with feathers or appearance of feathers. — **feath'er-bed** a mattress filled with feathers. — *v.t.* to pamper. — **feath'er-board'ing** same as **weather-boarding; feath'er-bonn'et** a Highland soldier's feather-covered head-dress; **feath'er-brain, feath'er-head, feath'er-pate** (*arch.*) a frivolous person; **feath'er-dust'er** a brush of feathers, used for dusting; **feath'er-edge** an edge of a board or plank thinner than the other edge; **feath'er-grass** a perennial grass (*Stipa*) with feathery awns; **feath'er-palm** any palm with pinnate leaves; **feath'er-star** a crinoid; **feath'er-stitch** one of a series of stitches making a zigzag line; **feath'erweight** lightest weight that may be carried by a racing-horse: boxer (over 8 st. 6 lb., amateur 7 lb., and not over 9 st.), wrestler, etc., below a lightweight: anyone of small moment. — **a feather in one's cap** an achievement of which one can be proud; **birds of a feather** persons of like character; **feather one's nest** to accumulate wealth for oneself while serving others in a position of trust; **in full** or **high feather** greatly elated or in high spirits; **make the feathers fly** to throw into confusion by a sudden attack; **show the white feather** to show signs of cowardice — a white feather in a gamecock's tail being considered as a sign of degeneracy. [O.E. *fether;* Ger. *Feder;* L. *penna,* Gr. *pteron.*]

featous *fēt'əs,* **feat'eous** *-i-əs,* **feat'uous** *-ū-əs,* (*arch.*) *adjs.* shapely: well-made: handsome: dexterous: neat. — *adv.* **feat'eously** (*Spens.*) dexterously, neatly. [O.Fr. *fetis* — L. *factīcius* — *facĕre,* to make; cf. **factitious.**]

feature *fē'chər, n.* form, outward appearance: beauty (*obs.*): shape, phantom (*arch.*): cast of face: an element

or prominent trait of anything: a characteristic: a part of the body, esp. of the face: (*pl.*) the face: a non-news article in a newspaper: anything offered as a special attraction or distinctive characteristic. — Also *adj.* — *v.t.* to have features resembling (*coll.*): to be a feature of: to make a feature of: to present prominently. — *adjs.* **feat'ured** with features well marked; **feat'ureless** destitute of distinct features; **feat'urely** (*arch.*) handsome. — **feature film** a long cinematograph film forming the basis of a programme. — *adj.* **feat'ure= length** (of films) of the same length as a feature film. — **feature programme** a radio or TV programme that reconstructs dramatically the life of a prominent person, or an important event, or gives a dramatic picture of an employment or activity. [O.Fr. *faiture* — L. *factura* — *facĕre,* to make.]

feblesse. See **feeble.**

febrile *fēb', feb'rīl,* or *-ril, adj.* of or like fever: feverish. — *ns.* **febricity** (*fi-bris'i-ti*) feverishness; **febricula** (*fi-brik'ū-lə*), **febricule** (*feb'*) a slight short fever. — *adjs.* **febrifacient** (*fē-bri-fā'shənt;* L. *faciēns, -entis,* making) producing fever; **febrif'ic** (*fi-*) febrifacient: feverish; **febrifugal** (*fi-brif'ū-gl, feb-ri-fū'gl;* L. *fugāre,* to drive off). — *ns.* **febrifuge** (*feb'* or *fēb'ri-fūj*) that which drives off fever; **febril'ity.** [L. *febris,* fever.]

Febronianism *feb-rō'ni-ən-izm, n.* a system of doctrine antagonistic to the claims of the Pope and asserting the independence of national churches, propounded in 1763 by Johann Nikolaus von Hontheim under the pseudonym Justinus Febronius.

February *feb'rōō-ər-i, n.* the second month of the year. [L. *Februārius* (*mēnsis*), the month of expiation, *februa,* the feast of expiation.]

feces, fecal. Same as **faeces, faecal.**

fecht *fehht,* **fechter** *-ər,* Scots forms of **fight, fighter.**

fecial. See **fetial.**

fecit *fē'sit, fā'kit,* (L.) (he or she) made or executed (this).

feck *fek,* (*Scot.*) *n.* purport (*obs.*): substance (*obs.*): efficacy: quantity, number: the bulk. — *adj.* **feck'less** spiritless: helpless: futile. — *adv.* **feck'lessly.** — *n.* **feck'lessness.** — *adv.* (*arch.*) **feck'ly** mostly: nearly. [Aphetic for **effect.**]

fecula *fek'ū-lə, n.* starch got as a sediment: sediment, dregs. — *ns.* **fec'ulence, fec'ulency.** — *adj.* **fec'ulent** containing or consisting of faeces or sediment: foul: turbid. [L. *faecula,* dim. of *faex,* dregs.]

fecund *fek'und, fek'und, -ənd, adj.* fruitful: fertile: prolific. — *v.t.* **fec'undāte** to make fruitful: to impregnate. — *ns.* **fecundā'tion; fecundity** (*fi-kund'i-ti*) fruitfulness: prolificness. [L. *fēcundus,* fruitful.]

fed *fed, pa.t.* and *pa.p.* of **feed¹.**

Fed *fed,* (*U.S. slang*) *n.* a Federal (agent), i.e. an agent of the Federal Bureau of Investigation. — Also without *cap.* [Contr. of **Federal.**]

fedarie, foedarie *fē'dər-i,* **federarie, -ary** *fed'ər-ər-i, ns.* Shakespearian words for a confederate, accomplice. [L. *foedus, -eris,* treaty; moulded on **feudary.**]

fedayee *fə-dä'yē, n.* Arab commando, esp. one involved in the conflict against Israel: — *pl.* **feda'yeen.** [Ar. *fidā'ī.*]

fedelini *fed-e-lē'nē, n.* vermicelli. [It.]

federal *fed'ər-əl, adj.* pertaining to or consisting of a treaty or covenant: confederated, founded upon mutual agreement: of a union or government in which several states, while independent in home affairs, combine for national or general purposes, as in the United States (in the American Civil War, *Federal* was the name applied to the states of the North which defended the Union against the *Confederate* separatists of the South). — *n.* a supporter of federation: a Unionist soldier in the American Civil War. — *ns.* **fed'eracy; federalisā'tion, -z-.** — *v.t.* **fed'eralise, -ize.** — *ns.* **fed'- eralism** the principles or cause maintained by federalists; **fed'eralist** a supporter of a federal constitution or union; **fed'erary** (*Shak.;* see **fedarie**). — *v.t.* and *v.i.* **fed'erate** to join in league or federation. — *adj.* united by league: confederated. — *n.* **federā'tion** the act of uniting in league: a federal union. — *adj.* **fed'erātive** united in league. — **federal** (or **covenant**) **theology** that first worked out by Cocceius (1603–69), based on the idea of two covenants between God and man — of Works and of Grace (see **covenant**). — **Federal Bureau of Investigation** in the U.S., a bureau or subdivision of the Department of Justice that investigates crimes, such as smuggling and espionage, that are the concern of the federal government. [L. *foedus, foederis,* a treaty, akin to *fīdĕre,* to trust.]

federarie, federary. See **fedarie.**

fedora *fi-dō'rǝ, -dö',* *n.* a felt hat dented lengthwise, orig. with curled brim. [*Fédora,* a play by Sardou.]

fee *fē, n.* cattle, livestock (*obs.*): property (*obs.*): money (*obs.*): the price paid for services, as to a lawyer or physician: recompense, wages: the sum exacted for any special privilege: a grant of land for feudal service (*hist.*): feudal tenure: service (*obs.*): fee simple: inheritance (*obs.*): possession (*obs.*): ownership (*obs.*). — *v.t.* to pay a fee to: to hire (*Scot.*): — *pr.p.* **fee'ing;** *pa.t.* and *pa.p.* **feed** or **fee'd.** — **fee'-farm** (*Shak.*) tenure by fee simple at a fixed rent without services; **fee'-grief** (*Shak.*) a private grief; **fee'ing-mar'ket** (*Scot.*) a fair or market at which farm-servants are hired for the year or half-year following; **fee simple** unconditional inheritance; **fee tail** an entailed estate, which may descend only to a certain class of heirs. — **base fee** qualified fee, a freehold estate of inheritance to which a qualification is annexed; **conditional fee** a fee granted on condition, or limited to particular heirs: the estate of a mortgagee of land, possession of which is conditional on payment; **great fee** the holding of a tenant of the Crown. [Partly O.E. *feoh,* cattle, property; Ger. *Vieh,* O.N. *fē;* allied to L. *pecus,* cattle, *pecūnia,* money; partly A.Fr. *fee,* probably ultimately Gmc. and of the same origin.]

fée *fā,* (Fr.) *n.* a fairy. — *n.* **féerie** (*fā-rē*) fairyland: an extravaganza (*theat.*).

feeble *fē'bl, adj.* very weak: forceless: vacillating: faint. — *v.t.* (*Spens.*) to make feeble. — *ns.* **fee'bleness; fe'blesse** (*Spens.*). — *adj.* **fee'blish** — *adv.* **fee'bly.** — *adj.* **fee'ble-mind'ed** weak-minded to the extent of being unable to compete with others or to manage one's affairs with ordinary prudence: irresolute. — *adv.* **fee'ble-mind'edly.** — **fee'ble-mind'edness.** [O.Fr. *foible,* for *floible* — L. *flēbilis,* lamentable, from *flēre,* to weep.]

feed¹ *fēd, v.t.* to give, furnish, or administer food to: to nourish: to furnish with necessary material: to foster: to give as food or as material to be used progressively: to furnish (an actor) with cues or opportunities for achieving an effect: in football, to pass the ball to. — *v.i.* to take food: to nourish oneself by eating (with *on*): — *pr.p.* **feed'ing;** *pa.t.* and *pa.p.* **fed.** — *n.* an allowance of provender, esp. to cattle: fodder: feeding: pasture: a plentiful meal: material supplied progressively for any operation: the means, channel, motion or rate of such supply: rate of progress of a tool: a theatrical feeder. — *n.* **feed'er** one who feeds: an actor who feeds another: that which supplies (water, electricity, ore, paper, etc.): a tributary: an overhead or underground cable, of large current-carrying capacity, used to transmit electric power between generating stations, substations and feeding points: a feeding-bottle: a bib: one who fattens cattle: a shepherd (*obs.*): a dependant, a servant (*arch.*). — *adj.* secondary, subsidiary, tributary. — *n.* **feed'ing** act of eating: that which is eaten: pasture: the placing of the sheets of paper in position for a printing or ruling machine. — **feed'back** return of part of the output of a system to the input as a means towards improved quality or self-correction of error; used also in speaking of biological, etc., self-adjusting systems: response or reaction providing useful information or guidelines for further development: in a public address system, etc., the returning of some of the sound output back to the microphone, producing a whistle or howl; **feed'-head**

a cistern that supplies water to a boiler; **feed'-heat'er** an apparatus for heating water for a boiler; **feed'ing-bottle** a bottle for supplying liquid food to an infant; **feeding point** (*elect.*) the junction point between a feeder and distribution system; **feed'-line** a line fed to an actor: a cue; **feed'lot** a unit in which cattle are kept indoors and made to put on weight rapidly by means of processed and blended feed supplied to them automatically; **feed'-pipe** a pipe for supplying liquid, as water to a boiler or cistern; **feed'-pump** a force-pump for supplying a boiler with water; **feed'stock** raw material used in an industrial process; **feed'stuff** any type of food for animals, esp. cattle, pigs, sheep, etc.; **feed'-water** water supplied to a boiler, etc. — **fed to the (back) teeth** (*slang*) fed up; **fed up** (*slang*) sated: jaded: nauseated: bored: (with *with*) tired of, annoyed by; **feed one's face** (*slang*) to eat heartily; **off one's feed** without appetite, disinclined to eat. [O.E. *fēdan,* to feed.]

feed² *fēd, pa.t.* and *pa.p.* of **fee.**

fee-faw-fum *fē'-fö'-fum', fee'-fī'-fŏ'-fum' interjs.* expressive of bloodthirstiness, in fairy tales, etc. — *n.* words, etc. intended to terrify. [From *Jack the Giantkiller.*]

feel *fēl, v.t.* to perceive by the touch: to try by touch: to be conscious of: to be keenly sensible of: to have an inward persuasion of: to experience. — *v.i.* to know by the touch: to have the emotions excited: to produce a certain sensation when touched, as to feel hard or hot: — *pr.p.* **feel'ing;** *pa.t.* and *pa.p.* **felt.** — *n.* the sensation of touch: an instinct, touch, knack. — *ns.* **feel'er** one who feels: a remark cautiously dropped, or any indirect stratagem, to sound the opinions of others: a tentacle: a jointed organ in the head of insects, etc., possessed of a delicate sense — an antenna; **feel'ing** the sense of touch: perception of objects by touch: consciousness of pleasure or pain: tenderness: emotion: sensibility, susceptibility, sentimentality: opinion as resulting from emotion: (in *pl.*) the affections or passions. — *adj.* expressive of great sensibility or tenderness: easily or strongly affected by emotion: sympathetic: compassionate: pitying: deeply felt. — *adj.* **feel'ingly.** — *adv.* **feel'ingly.** — **bad feeling** animosity: ill-feeling; **feel after** (*B.*) to search for; **feelings (are) running high** (there is) a general feeling of anger, emotion, etc.; **feel one's feet** to accustom oneself to a new situation, job, etc.; **feel someone (up)** (*coll.*) to caress someone's genitals; **good feeling** kindly feeling: amicable relations. [O.E. *fēlan,* to feel; Ger. *fühlen;* prob. akin to L. *palpāri,* to stroke.]

feer¹. Same as **fere¹.**

feer² *fēr, (Scot.) v.i.* to draw the first furrow in ploughing, to mark out the rigs. — *n.* **feer'in(g)** a first guiding furrow. [Perh. O.E. *fȳrian,* to make a furrow — *furh,* furrow.]

féerie. See **fée.**

feese See **feeze.**

feet *fēt, pl.* of **foot.** — *adj.* **feet'less** footless. See also **foot.**

feeze, feese, pheese, pheeze, phese *fēz, v.t.* to drive, drive off (*obs.*): to settle the business of (*Shak.*): to beat (*obs.*): to worry, perturb, discompose. — Also **faze, phase** (*fāz*). — *n.* a rush (*dial.*): a rub (*obs.*): perturbation. [O.E. *fēsian,* to drive away.]

fegary *fi-gā'ri, n.* a variant of **vagary.**

fegs *fegz, interj.* in faith, truly. [See **fay²**, **faith** and **faix.**]

Fehm(gericht). Same as **Vehm(gericht).**

feign (*Spens.* **fain, faine, fayne**) *fān, v.t.* to fashion (*obs.*): to invent: to imagine falsely (*obs.*): to assume fictitiously: to imagine (*arch.*): to make a show or pretence of, to counterfeit, simulate: to dissemble (*Spens.*). — *adj.* **feigned** pretended: simulating: imagined (*arch.*): fictitious. — *adv.* **feign'edly.** — *ns.* **feign'edness; feign'-ing.** [Fr. *feindre,* pr.p. *feignant,* to feign — L. *fingĕre, fictum,* to form.]

feint¹ *fānt, n.* a false appearance: a pretence: a mock-assault: a deceptive movement in fencing, boxing, etc. — *v.i.* to make a feint. [Fr. *feinte,* see above.]

feint² *fānt, adj.* a printers' or stationers' spelling of **faint.**

— *n.pl.* **feints** same as **faints.**

feis *fesh, n.* an ancient Irish assembly for the proclamation of laws and the holding of artistic, intellectual and sports competitions: an Irish festival on the ancient model, including sports events, folk music and dancing: — *pl.* **feiseanna** (*fesh'ə-nə*). [Ir., festival, assembly.]

feisty *fī'sti,* (*coll.,* orig. *U.S.*) *adj.* excitable, irritable, touchy: spirited. [From old U.S. dial. *fist,* a small aggressive dog — M.E. *fisten,* to break wind.]

felafel, falafel, *fə-lä'fəl, n.* a deep-fried ball of ground chick-peas, with onions, peppers, etc. and spices. [Ar. *falāfil.*]

feldgrau *felt'grow, n.* and *adj.* field-grey, the colour of German military uniforms. [Ger. *Feld,* field, *grau,* grey.]

feldsher *fel(d)'shər, n.* (in Russia and parts of Eastern Europe), a partly trained person who practises medicine: one who assists a doctor, esp. on the battlefield. [Russ. *fel'dsher* — Ger. *Feldscher,* army surgeon.]

feldspar *fel(d)'spär,* **felspar** *fel'spär, ns.* any member of the most important group of rock-forming minerals, anhydrous silicates of aluminium along with potassium (as *orthoclase, microcline*), sodium, calcium, or both (the *plagioclases*), or sodium and barium (*hyalophane*) — also (*obs.*) **feld'spath.** — *adj.* **fel(d)spathic** (-*spath'ik*). — *n.* **fel(d)'spathoid** any mineral of a group chemically akin to feldspar, including nepheline, leucite, sodalite, etc. [Swed. *feldtspat,* a name given in 1740 by D. Tilas — Sw. *feldt* or *fält,* field, *spat,* spar, apparently because of the abundance of feldspar in tilled fields of S.W. Finland: confused with Ger. *Fels,* rock.]

Félibre *fā-lē'br', n.* a member of the **Félibrige** (-*brēzh'*), a Provençal literary brotherhood, founded in 1854 by Joseph Roumanille (1818–91) and six others. [Prov., perh. doctors of the law.]

feliciter *fi-lis'i-tər, fā-lē'ki-ter,* (L.) *adv.* happily: successfully.

felicity *fi-lis'i-ti, n.* happiness: delight: a blessing: a happy event: a happiness of expression. — *v.t.* **felic'itate** to express joy or pleasure to: to congratulate. — *n.* **felicita'tion** the act of congratulating. — *adjs.* **felicif'ic** producing happiness; **felic'itous** happy: prosperous: delightful: appropriate. — *adv.* **felic'itously.** [O.Fr. *felicité* — L. *fēlīcitās, -ātis,* from *felix, -icis,* happy.]

feline *fē'līn, adj.* pertaining to the cat or the cat kind: like a cat. — *n.* any animal of the cat tribe. — *ns.* **felinity** (*fi-lin'i-ti*); **Fē'lis** the cat genus, typical of the family **Fē'lidae** and sub-family **Fēlī'nae.** [L. *fēlīnus* — *fēlēs,* a cat.]

fell¹ *fel, n.* a hill: an upland tract of waste, pasture, or moorland. — **fell'-walking (-running)** the pastime (sport) of walking (running) over fells; **fell'-walker (-runner).** [O.N. *fjall;* Dan. *fjeld.*]

fell² *fel, pa.t.* of **fall.**

fell³ *fel, v.t.* to cause to fall: to knock down: to bring to the ground: to cut down: to prostrate (as by illness; *dial.*): to stitch down with an overturned edge. — *n.* a quantity felled at a time: a falling of lambs: a felled seam. — *adj.* **fell'able.** — *n.* **fell'er.** [O.E. *fælla(n), fella(n)* (W.S. *fiellan*), causative of *fallan* (*feallan*), to fall.]

fell⁴ *fel, n.* a skin: a membrane: covering of rough hair. — **fell'monger** one who prepares skins for the tanner. [O.E. *fell;* cf. Ger. *Fell,* L. *pellis,* Gr. *pella.*]

fell⁵ *fell,* (*Spens.*) *n.* gall, bitterness. [L. *fel.*]

fell⁶ *fel, adj.* cruel: fierce: dire: ruthless: deadly: keen: doughty: pungent (*Scot.*): great, mighty (*Scot.*). — *adv.* in a fell manner: very (*Scot.*): very much (*Scot.*). — *n.* **fell'ness.** — *adv.* **felly** (*fel'li*). — *adj.* **fell-lurk'ing** (*Shak.*) lurking with treacherous purpose. [O.Fr. *fel,* cruel — L.L. *fellō, -ōnis;* see **felon.**]

fella(h). See **fellow.**

fellah *fel'ə, n.* a peasant, esp. in Egypt: — *pl.* **fell'ahs, fellahîn** (-*hēn'*). [Ar. *fellāh,* tiller.]

fellatio *fe-lā'shi-ō, n.* oral stimulation of the male genitalia: — *pl.* **fellā'tios.** — Also **fellā'tion.** — *v.t.* **fellāte'** to perform fellation on. [L.—*fellātus, pa.p.* of *fellāre,* to suck.]

feller. See **fell³, fellow.**

felloe. See **felly¹.**

fellow *fel'ō, n.* an associate: a companion and equal: one of a pair, a mate: a counterpart: the like: a member of a university who enjoys a fellowship: a member of a scientific or other society: a man generally: a worthless or contemptible person. — Also (*coll.*) **fella(h), feller.** — *adj.* **fell'owly** (*Shak.*) companionable. — *n.* **fell'owship** the state of being a fellow or partner: friendly intercourse: communion: an association: an endowment in a college for the support of graduates called Fellows: the position and income of a fellow: reckoning of proportional division of profit and loss among partners. — **fell'ow-cit'izen** one belonging to the same city; **fell'ow-comm'oner** at Cambridge and elsewhere, one of a privileged class of undergraduates, dining at the Fellows' table; **fell'ow-coun'tryman** a man of the same country; **fell'ow-crea'ture** one of the same creation, a creature like oneself; **fell'ow-feel'ing** feeling of common interest: sympathy; **fell'ow-heir** a joint-heir; **fell'ow-man'** one who shares humanity with oneself; **fell'ow-mem'ber** a member of the same body; **fell'ow-serv'ant** one who has the same master; **fell'ow-towns'man** a dweller in the same town; **fell'ow-trav'eller** one who travels in the same railway carriage, bus, etc., or along the same route: derogatory term for one who, though not a party member, takes the same political road, a sympathiser (trans. of Russ. word). — **good fellowship** companionableness; **right hand of fellowship** the right hand given esp. by one minister or elder to another at an ordination in some churches. [M.E. *felawe* — O.N. *fēlagi,* a partner in goods, from *fē* (O.E. *feoh;* Ger. *Vieh*), cattle, property, and root *lag-,* a laying together, a law. Cf. **fee, law, lay.**]

felly¹ *fel'i,* **felloe** *fel'i, fel'ō, ns.* a curved piece in the circumference of a wheel: the circular rim of the wheel. [O.E. *felg;* Ger. *Felge.*]

felly². See **fell⁶.**

felo de se *fē'lō dē sē, fe'lō də sē,* (Anglo-L.) a suicide, lit. felon of himself.

felon¹ *fel'ən, n.* one guilty of felony: a wicked person (*obs.*). — *adj.* (*arch.*) wicked or cruel: fell: fierce: mighty. — *adj.* **felonious** (*fi-lō'ni-əs*) wicked (*arch.*): depraved (*arch.*): pertaining to felony. — *adv.* **felō'niously.** — *n.* **felō'niousness** the quality of being felonious. — *adj.* **fel'onous** (*Spens.*) fell. — *ns.* **fel'onry** a body of felons; **fel'ony** orig. a crime punished by total forfeiture of lands, etc.: a grave crime, formerly classed legally as one more serious than a misdemeanour. [O.Fr., — L.L. *fellō, -ōnis,* a traitor.]

felon² *fel'ən, n.* an inflamed sore. [Perh. **felon¹.**]

felsite *fel'sīt, n.* a fine-grained intimate mixture of quartz and orthoclase: a devitrified acid igneous rock, characterised by felsitic structure. — *adj.* **felsitic** (-*sit'ik*) consisting of a fine patchy mosaic of quartz and feldspar. [**feldspar.**]

felspar. See **feldspar.**

felstone *fel'stōn, n.* felsite — an old-fashioned name. [Ger. *Felsstein,* partly anglicised.]

felt¹ *felt, pa.t.* and *pa.p.* of **feel.**

felt² *felt, n.* a fabric formed without weaving, using the natural tendency of the fibres of wool and certain kinds of hair to interlace and cling together. — *v.t.* to make into felt: to cover with felt. — *v.i.* to become felted or matted. — *v.t.* **felt'er** to mat together like felt. — *n.* **felt'ing** the art or process of making felt or of matting fibres together: the felt itself. — **felt-tip(ped) pen, felt pen** a pen with a nib of felt or similar fibrous substance. [O.E. *felt;* cf. Du. *vilt,* Ger. *Filz.*]

felucca *fe-luk'ə, n.* a small merchant-vessel used in the Mediterranean, with two masts, lateen sails, and often a rudder at each end. [It. *feluca;* cf. Ar. *falūkah.*]

felwort *fel'wûrt, n.* a gentian. [O.E. *feldwyrt — feld,* field, *wyrt,* wort.]

female *fē'māl, n.* a woman or girl (sometimes used derogatorily): any animal or plant of the same sex as a woman. — *adj.* of the sex that produces young or eggs, fructifications or seeds: for, belonging to, characteristic of, or fancifully attributed to that sex: womanish (*Shak.*): of the sex characterised by relatively large gametes (*biol.*): of parts of mechanism, hollow and adapted to receive a counterpart (*mach.*). — Also (*Milt.*) **fe'māl.** — *ns.* **fē'māleness, femality** (*fē-mal'i-ti*). — **female circumcision** the cutting or cutting off of all or part of the clitoris; **female screw** a cylindrical hole with a thread or groove cut on the inward surface. [Fr. *femelle* — L. *fēmella,* a girl, dim. of *fēmina,* woman; the second syllable influenced by association with **male.**]

feme *fem, fēm, (law) n.* a woman. — **feme covert** (*kuv'ərt*) a married woman; **feme sole** a spinster, widow, or married woman legally in the position of an unmarried. [O.Fr. *feme.*]

femerall *fem'ər-əl, n.* an outlet for smoke in a roof. [O.Fr. *fumeraille* — L. *fūmus,* smoke.]

femetary. See **fumitory.**

feminal *fem'in-əl, adj.* female: feminine. — *ns.* **feminality** (*-al'i-ti*), **feminē'ity, feminil'ity, fem'inineness, femin'ity** femaleness: the quality of being female, feminine, womanly or womanish. — *adj.* **fem'inine** (*-in*) female: characteristic of, peculiar or appropriate to, woman or the female sex: womanish: of that gender to which words denoting females, and in some languages various associated classes of words, belong (*gram.*). — *n.* the female sex or nature: a word of feminine gender. — *adv.* **fem'ininely.** — *ns.* **fem'ininism** an idiom or expression characteristic of woman: addiction to feminine ways; **feminin'ity** the quality of being feminine; **feminīsā'tion, -z-.** — *v.t.* and *v.i.* **fem'inise, -ize** to make or become feminine. — *ns.* **fem'inism** advocacy of women's rights, of the movement for the advancement and emancipation of women; **fem'inist** an advocate or favourer of feminism: a student of women. — *adj.* **feminist'ic.** — **feminine caesura** one which does not immediately follow the ictus; **feminine ending** (*Fr. pros.*) ending of a line in mute *e* (the French feminine suffix): ending in one unstressed syllable; **feminine rhyme** a rhyme on a feminine ending. [L. *fēmina,* woman, dim. *fēminīna.*]

femiter *fem'i-tər.* See **fumitory.**

femme *fam, (Fr.) n.* a woman, wife. — **femme de chambre** (*də shā-br'*) a lady's-maid: a chambermaid; **femme du monde** (*dü mɔ̃d*) a woman of the world: a society woman; **femme fatale** (*fa-tal*) an irresistibly attractive woman who brings difficulties or disaster on men: a siren; **femme incomprise** (*ɛ̃-kɔ̃-prēz*) a woman misunderstood or unappreciated; **femme savante** (*sa-vāt*) a learned woman, a blue-stocking. See also **feme.**

femto- *fem'tō-, pfx.* a thousand million millionth (10^{-15}).

femur *fē'mər, n.* the thigh-bone: the third segment of an insect's leg: — *pl.* **fē'murs, fēmora** (*fem'ər-ə*). — *adj.* **femoral** (*fem'*) belonging to the thigh. — **femoral artery** the main artery of the thigh. [L. *fēmur, -ŏris,* thigh.]

fen¹ *fen, n.* low marshy land often, or partially, covered with water: a morass or bog. — *adjs.* **fenn'ish; fenn'y.** — **fen'-berry** the cranberry; **fen'-crick'et** the mole-cricket; **fen'-fire** the will-o'-the-wisp; **fen'land; fen'man** a dweller in fen country. — *adj.* **fen'-sucked** (*Shak.*) drawn out of bogs. [O.E. *fenn;* O.N. *fen.*]

fen² *fen, v.t.* used only as a prohibitory exclamation in boys' games, to bar an action, right or privilege. [Cf. **fend¹;** or perhaps from **feign.**]

fen³ *fen, n.* a Chinese monetary unit, $\frac{1}{100}$ of a yuan: a coin of this value. [Chin.]

fence *fens, n.* a barrier, esp. of wood or of wood and wire for enclosing, bounding or protecting land: the art of fencing: defence: a receiver of stolen goods (*thieves' slang*): a place where stolen goods are received (*thieves' slang*). — *v.t.* to enclose with a fence: to fortify: to

shield: to keep off. — *v.i.* to guard: to practise fencing: to be a receiver or purchaser of stolen goods: to answer or dispute evasively: to leap fences. — *adjs.* **fenced** enclosed with a fence; **fence'less** without fence or enclosure, open. — *n.* **fenc'er** one who makes or repairs fences: one who practises fencing with a sword, etc: a horse trained to jump fences in steeplechasing. — *adj.* **fenc'ible** capable of being fenced or defended. — *n.* (*hist.*) a militiaman or volunteer enlisted at a crisis. — *adj.* **fenc'ing** defending or guarding. — *n.* the act of erecting a fence: material for fences: fences collectively: the leaping of fences: receiving stolen goods (*thieves' slang*): the act, art or sport of attack and defence with a sword, foil or the like. — **fence'-lizard** a small American lizard (*Sceloporus*); **fence-mending** see **mend one's fences** below; **fence month** close season; **fenc'ing= master** one who teaches fencing. — **fence the tables** in the ancient usage of Scotland, to debar the unworthy from partaking in communion; **mend one's fences** to improve or restore one's relations, reputation, or popularity, esp. in politics (*n.* and *adj.* **fence'-mending**); **sit on the fence** to avoid committing oneself: to remain neutral; **sunk fence** a ditch or water-course. [Aphetic from **defence.**]

fend¹ *fend, v.t.* to ward off: to shut out: to defend. — *v.i.* to offer resistance: to provide. — *n.* self-support, the shift one makes for oneself. — *adj.* **fend'y** (*Scot.*) resourceful: thrifty. [Aphetic for **defend.**]

fend² *fend, (Milt.).* Same as **fiend.**

fender *fend'ər, n.* a guard before a hearth to confine the ashes: a protection for a ship's side against piers, etc., consisting of a bundle of rope, etc.: any structure serving as a guard against contact or impact. — **fend'er-stool** a long stool placed beside a fireside fender. [**fend¹.**]

fenestella *fen-is-tel'ə, n.* a small window or window-like opening: a niche containing the piscina: (with *cap.*) a Palaeozoic genus of lace-like Polyzoa. [L., dim. of *fenestra,* a window.]

fenestra *fi-nes'trə, n.* a window or other wall-opening: a perforation: a translucent spot. — *n.* **fenes'tral** a window with some translucent material instead of glass. — *adj.* of or like a window: perforated: with translucent spots. — *adjs.* **fenestrate** (*fen'is-trit, fi-nes'- trit, -trāt*), **-d** having windows or appearance of windows: pierced: perforated: having translucent spots. — *n.* **fenestrā'tion** the arrangement of windows in a building: the fact of being fenestrate: perforation: the operation of making an artificial fenestra when the fenestra ovalis has been clogged by growth of bone. — **fenestra ovalis, rotunda** the oval and round windows, two membrane-covered openings between the middle and the internal ear. [L.]

Fenian *fē'nyən, n.* a member of an association of Irishmen founded in New York in 1857 for the overthrow of the English government in Ireland: a (esp. Irish) Catholic (*offensive*). — *adj.* belonging to the legendary *fiann,* or to the modern Fenians: Catholic (*offensive*). — *n.* **Fē'nianism.** [Old Ir. *Féne,* one of the names of the ancient population of Ireland, confused in modern times with *fiann,* the militia of Finn and other ancient Irish kings.]

fenitar *fen'i-tər.* See **fumitory.**

fenks *fengks,* **finks** *fingks, ns.* the refuse of whale-blubber. [Origin unknown.]

fennec *fen'ək, n.* a little African fox with large ears. [Ar. *fenek.*]

fennel *fen'əl, n.* a yellow-flowered umbelliferous plant of the genus *Foeniculum,* allied to dill, but distinguished by the cylindrical, strongly-ribbed fruit, the seeds and leaves being used for seasoning. — **fenn'el-flower** Nigella. — **dwarf, Florence, French, sweet fennel** see **finocchio; giant fennel** an umbelliferous plant, *Ferula communis.* [O.E. *finul* — L. *fēniculum, fēnuc(u)lum,* fennel — *fēnum,* hay.]

fennish, fenny. See **fen¹.**

fent *fent, n.* a slit, crack: a remnant or odd, short, or damaged piece of cloth (*N. Eng.*). — **fent′-merchant.** [O.Fr. *fente* — L. *findĕre*, to cleave.]

fenugreek *fen′ū-grēk, n.* a plant (*Trigonella foenum-graecum*), allied to melilot. [L. *fēnum graecum*, Greek hay.]

feod, feodal, feodary. Same as **feud²**, **feudal, feudary.**

feoff *fef, fēf, n.* a fief. — *v.t.* to grant possession of a fief or property in land. — *ns.* **feoffee′** the person invested with the fief; **feoff′er, feoff′or** he who grants the fief; **feoff′ment** the gift of a fief. [O.Fr. *feoffer* or *fiefer* — O.Fr. *fief.* See **fee.**]

feracious *fi-rā′shəs, adj.* fruitful. — *n.* **feracity** (*fi-ras′i-ti*; *rare*). [L. *ferāx, -ācis* — *ferre*, to bear.]

ferae naturae *fē′rē nə-tū′rē, fe′rīna-tōō′rī*, (L.) (of animals) wild, undomesticated.

feral¹ *fē′rəl, fer′əl, adj.* wild: untamed: uncultivated: run wild: brutish. — *adjs.* **fer′alised, -ized** run wild from domestication; **ferine** (*-rīn, -rin*) pertaining to or like a wild beast: wild: brutish. — *n.* **ferity** (*fer′i-ti*) wildness: uncultivated state: savagery. [L. *fera*, a wild beast.]

feral² *fē′rəl, adj.* deadly: funereal. [L. *ferālis.*]

fer-de-lance *fer′də-läs, n.* the lance-headed or yellow viper of tropical America. [Fr., lance-head (*lit.* iron).]

fere¹, feare, feer, fiere, pheere *fēr*, (*arch.*) *n.* a companion: a mate: a spouse: an equal. — **in fere** or (*adv.*) **yfere′** together, in company. [O.E. *gefēra*, companion, *gefēre*, company.]

fere² *fēr*, (*Scot.*) *adj.* able, sound. [O.E. *fēre.*]

feretory *fer′i-tər-i, n.* a shrine for relics carried in processions. [L. *feretrum* — Gr. *pheretron*, bier, litter — *pherein*, to bear.]

ferial *fē′ri-əl, adj.* pertaining to holidays: belonging to any day of the week which is neither a fast nor a festival. [L. *fēria*, a holiday.]

ferine, ferity. See **feral¹.**

Feringhi, Feringhee *fer-ing′gē, n.* an Indian name for a European. — Also **Farin′gee.** [Frank.]

ferly *fûr′li, adj.* fearful: sudden: singular. — *n.* (*Scot.*; *fär′li*) a wonder. — *v.i.* to wonder. [O.E. *fǣrlic*, sudden; cf. Ger. *gefährlich*, dangerous.]

ferm *fûrm, n.* a farm: lodging (*Spens.*). [Variant of **farm.**]

fermata *fûr-mä′tə*, (*mus.*) *n.* a pause. [It.]

ferment *fûr′mənt, n.* a substance that excites fermentation: internal motion amongst the parts of a fluid: agitation: tumult. — *v.t.* **ferment** (*-ment′*) to excite fermentation in: to work up, excite. — *v.i.* to rise and swell by the action of fermentation: to work, used of wine, etc.: to be in excited action: to work in the mind, as emotions. — *n.* **fermentabil′ity.** — *adj.* **ferment′able** capable of fermentation. — *n.* **fermentā′tion** the act or process of fermenting: a slow decomposition process of organic substances induced by micro-organisms, or by complex nitrogenous organic substances (*enzymes*) of vegetable or animal origin, usually accompanied by evolution of heat and gas, e.g. alcoholic fermentation of sugar and starch, and lactic fermentation: restless action of the mind or feelings. — *adj.* **ferment′ative** causing or consisting in fermentation. — *n.* **ferment′ativeness.** — *adjs.* **ferment′ed; fermentesc′ible** capable of being fermented; **fermentitious** (*-ish′əs*); **ferment′ive.** [Fr., — L. *fermentum*, for *fervimentum* — *fervēre*, to boil.]

fermi *fûr′mi, n.* a unit equal to 10^{-5} angstrom or 10^{-15} m. — *ns.* **fer′mion** one of a group of subatomic particles, such as protons, electrons and neutrons, having half-integral spin and obeying the exclusion principle; **fer′mium** the element (symbol Fm) of atomic number 100. [Italian physicist Enrico *Fermi* (1901–54).]

fern *fûrn, n.* one of the class of higher or vascular cryptogamous plants, Filices, many species of which have feather-like leaves. — *n.* **fern′ery** a place for rearing ferns; **fern′ing** (of cervical mucus, etc.) a tendency to a feathery or fern-like appearance. — *adj.* **fern′y.** — **fern′-ally** (or *-al′*) a pteridophyte other than a fern; **fern′bird** a small brown-and-white New Zealand bird, *Bowdleria punctata*, akin to the warblers, which is found in swamps and marshy scrub and which has somewhat fern-like tail feathers; **fern land** in New Zealand, land covered or formerly covered by bracken; **fern′-owl** the night-jar: the short-eared owl; **fern′-seed** the spores of ferns, once held to confer invisibility; **fern′shaw** a thicket of ferns; **fern′tic(k)le** (*obs.* or *dial.*) also **ferni-, fairni-, ferny-, fairny-** (*Scot.*) a freckle. — *adj.* **fern′tic(k)led.** [O.E. *fearn*; Ger. *Farn.*]

ferocious *fə-rō′shəs, adj.* savage, fierce: cruel. — *adv.* **ferō′ciously.** — *ns.* **ferō′ciousness; ferocity** (*-ros′i-ti*) savage cruelty of disposition: untamed fierceness. [L. *ferōx, ferōcis*, wild — *ferus*, wild.]

ferrandine. See **farandine.**

ferrate *fer′āt, n.* a salt of ferric acid. — *adjs.* **ferr′eous** pertaining to, containing, or like iron; **ferr′ic** of iron: of trivalent iron (**ferr′ic acid** a hypothetical acid H_2FeO_4) (*chem.*); **ferrif′erous** bearing or yielding iron. — *n.* **ferr′ite** a form of pure iron: any of a number of new magnetic materials (generally mixtures of iron oxide with one or more other metals) which are also electric insulators. — *adjs.* **ferrit′ic** consisting mainly of ferrite; **ferr′ous** of bivalent iron: loosely, containing iron. — **ferricy′anide** a salt of hydroferricyanic acid; **ferricyan′ogen** the trivalent radical, $Fe(CN)_6$, of the ferricyanides; **ferr′o-all′oy** (or *-oi′*) an alloy of iron and some other metal; **ferr′o-chro′mium** (or **ferr′o-chrome′**), **ferr′o-mang′anese, ferr′o-molyb′denum, ferr′o-nick′el** an alloy of iron with much chromium, etc. (as the case may be); **ferr′o-con′crete** reinforced concrete; **ferrocy′anide** a salt of hydroferrocyanic acid; **ferrocyan′ogen** the quadrivalent radical, $Fe(CN)_6$, of the ferrocyanides. — *adj.* **ferroelec′tric** exhibiting electric polarisation. — **ferrog′raphy** the technique of studying wear in machinery by measuring magnetically the ferrous content of lubricants, the results being shown by **ferr′ograms.** — *adjs.* **ferromagnēs′ian** containing iron and magnesium; **ferromagnet′ic** strongly magnetic: formerly, paramagnetic. — **ferr′o-print** a photograph made by means of iron salts; **ferropruss′iate** ferrocyanide. — *adj.* **ferrosoferr′ic** combining ferrous and ferric. — **ferr′otype** an old form of photograph upon a film on an iron plate. [L. *ferrum*, iron.]

ferrel. See **ferrule.**

ferret¹ *fer′it, n.* narrow silk or cotton ribbon. — Also *adj.* [It. *fioretto*, dim. — L. *flōs, flōris*, flower.]

ferret² *fer′it, n.* a half-tamed albino variety of the polecat, employed in unearthing rabbits. — *v.t.* to drive out of a hiding-place: to search out persistently. — *v.t., v.i.* to hunt with a ferret: — *pr.p.* **ferr′eting;** *pa.p.* **ferr′eted.** — *n.* **ferr′eter** one who ferrets. — *adj.* **ferr′ety** like a ferret. [O.Fr. *furet*, a ferret, dim. — L.L. *fūrō, -ōnis*, ferret, robber — L. *fūr*, a thief.]

ferriage. See under **ferry.**

Ferris wheel *fe′ris (h)wēl*, (*orig. U.S.*) an amusement device, a large upright wheel having seats suspended on the circumference which remain horizontal while the wheel rotates. [G. W. G. *Ferris*, American engineer.]

ferro-alloy, etc. See **ferrate.**

ferron(n)ière *fer-on-yer′, n.* a jewel held on the forehead by a chain, as in Leonardo da Vinci′s ′La Belle Ferronnière′. [Fr. *ferronnière*, fem. of *ferronnier*, ironmonger.]

ferruginous *fe-, fə-rōō′jin-əs, adj.* of the colour of iron-rust: impregnated with iron. — Also **ferrugin′eous** (*fer-*). — *n.* **ferru′go** (*-gō*) rust disease of plants. [L. *ferrūgō, -inis*, iron-rust — *ferrum.*]

ferrule *fer′ōōl, -əl, n.* a metal band, ring or cap on a stick, etc. — Also **ferr′el** (*Scot.* **virl**). [O.Fr. *virole* — L. *viriola*, a bracelet.]

ferry *fer′i, v.t.* to carry or convey (often over a water, etc., in a boat, ship or aircraft): to deliver (an aircraft coming from a factory) under its own power. — *v.i.* to cross by ferry: — *pr.p.* **ferr′ying;** *pa.t.* and *pa.p.* **ferr′ied.** — *n.* a place or route of carriage over water: the right of conveying passengers: a ferry-boat. — *n.*

ferr'iage provision for ferrying: the fare paid for it. — **ferr'y-boat; ferr'y-house** a ferryman's house: a place of shelter or refreshment at a ferry; **ferr'yman.** [O.E. *ferian*, to convey, *faran*, to go; Ger. *Fähre*, a ferry — *fahren*, to go, to carry.]

fertile *fûr'tīl, U.S. -təl, adj.* able to bear or produce abundantly: rich in resources: inventive: fertilising: capable of breeding, hatching, or germinating. — *adv.* **fer'tilely.** — *n.* **fertilisation, -z-** (*-ti-lī-zā'shən*) the act or process of fertilising. — *v.t.* **fer'tilise, -ize** to make fertile or fruitful: to enrich: to impregnate: to pollinate. — *ns.* **fer'tiliser, -z-** one who, or that which, fertilises; **fertility** (*-til'i-ti*) fruitfulness: richness: abundance. — **Fertile Crescent** a crescent-shaped region stretching from Armenia to Arabia, formerly fertile but now mainly desert, considered to be the cradle of civilisation; **fertile material** an isotope (as uranium-238) that can be readily transformed into fissionable material; **fertility drug** a drug given to apparently infertile women to induce ovulation. [Fr., — L. *fertilis* — *ferre*, to bear.]

ferule *fer'ool, n.* a cane or rod used for punishment. — *n.* **fer'ula** a ferule: a staff of command: (with *cap.*) the giant fennel genus. — *adj.* **ferulā'ceous** like a cane, reed, or Ferula. [L. *ferula*, a giant fennel — *ferīre*, to strike.]

fervent *fûr'vənt, adj.* hot: ardent: zealous: warm in feeling. — *n.* **fer'vency** heat: eagerness: emotional warmth. — *adv.* **fer'vently.** — *adjs.* **fervescent** (*-ves'ənt*) growing hot; **fer'vid** very hot: having burning desire or emotion: glowing: zealous. — *n.* **fervid'ity.** — *adv.* **fer'vidly.** — *ns.* **fer'vidness; Fervidor'** Thermidor; **fer'vour** heat: heat of emotion: zeal. — *adj.* **fer'vorous.** [L. *fervēre*, to boil, *fervēscēre, fervidus*.]

Fescennine *fes'ə-nīn, -nin, adj.* scurrilous. — **Fescennine verses** rude extempore verses, generally in Saturnian measure, in which the parties rallied and ridiculed one another. [The Etruscan town of *Fescennium*.]

fescue *fes'kū, n.* any one of the grasses, nearly allied to the brome-grasses, of the genus *Festuca*, which includes many pasture and fodder grasses: a pointer used in teaching. [O.Fr. *festu* — L. *festūca*, a straw.]

fesse, fess *fes*, (*her.*) *n.* one of the ordinaries — a horizontal band over the middle of an escutcheon, usually one-third of the whole. — *adv.* **fess(e)'-wise.** — **fesse'-point** the centre of an escutcheon. [Fr. *fasce* — L. *fascia*, a band.]

fest *fest, n.* (usu. in composition) a party or gathering, esp. for a particular activity, e.g. *songfest*. [Ger. *Fest*, festival.]

festa *fes'ta*, (It.) *n.* holiday: festival : saint's day.

festal *fes'tl, adj.* pertaining to a feast or holiday: joyous: gay. — *n.* a festivity. — *adv.* **fes'tally.** — *ns.* **festil'ogy, festol'ogy** a treatise on ecclesiastical festivals. [See **feast.**]

fester *fes'tər, v.i.* to become corrupt or malignant: to suppurate: to be idle (*coll.*). — *v.t.* to cause to fester or rankle. — *n.* a wound discharging corrupt matter. [O.Fr. *festre* — L. *fistula*, an ulcer.]

festilogy. See **festal.**

festinate *fes'ti-nāt, v.t.* to accelerate. — *adj.* (*Shak.*) hurried, hasty. — *adv.* **fes'tinately** (*Shak.*). — *n.* **festinā'tion.** [L. *festīnāre, -ātum*, to hurry.]

festive *fes'tiv, adj.* festal: mirthful. — *n.* **fes'tival** a joyful or honorific celebration: a feast: a season or series of performances of music, plays, or the like. — *adv.* **fes'tively.** — *n.* **festiv'ity** social mirth: joyfulness: gaiety: (in *pl.*) joyful celebrations. — *adj.* **fes'tivous** (or *-tī'*) festive. [L. *festīvus — festus.*]

festology. See **festal.**

festoon *fes-tōōn', n.* a garland suspended between two points: an ornament like a garland (*archit.*). — *v.t.* to adorn, hang, or connect with festoons. — *v.i.* to hang in festoons. — *n.* **festoon'ery** festoons collectively. — **festoon'-blind** a window-blind consisting of cloth gathered into rows of festoons running across its width. [Fr. *feston*, app. conn. with L. *festum*, a festival.]

festschrift *fest'shrift, n.* a festival publication, commonly a collection of learned papers or the like, presented by their authors and published in honour of some person. [Ger., festival writing.]

fet *fet, v.t.* obsolete form of **fetch**[1].

feta *fet'ə, n.* a white low-fat cheese originating in Greece and the Middle East, traditionally made from goat's or ewe's milk but now sometimes with cow's milk. — Also **fett'a.** [Mod. Gr. *pheta*, a slice (i.e. of cheese) — It. *fetta.*]

fetal. See **foetus.**

fetch[1] *fech, v.t.* to bring: to go and get: to obtain as its price: to cause to come: to call forth: to recall from a swoon: to draw (as blood, breath): to achieve the gaining over of, to take: to derive: to strike: to perform, make, take, utter (as a leap, a sigh, a circuit): to achieve: to reach or attain. — *v.i.* to make one's way: to arrive: to be effective. — *n.* the act of bringing: the distance travelled by a wind or wave without obstruction: a stratagem. — *adj.* **fetch'ing** fascinating, charming. — **fetch a compass, circuit** to go round in a wide curve; **fetch and carry** to perform humble services for another; **fetch a pump** to pour water in so as to make it draw; **fetch off** to bring out of danger or difficulty: to make away with (*Shak.*): to fleece (*Shak.*); **fetch out** to draw forth, develop; **fetch up** to recover: to come to a stop: to bring up, rear (*U.S.*): to vomit (*slang*). [O.E. *feccan*, app. an altered form of *fetian*, to fetch; cf. Ger. *fassen*, to seize.]

fetch[2] *fech, n.* the apparition, double, or wraith of a living person. — **fetch'-can'dle** a nocturnal light, supposed to portend a death. [Ety. unknown.]

fête *fet, fāt, n.* a festival: a holiday: the festival of the saint whose name one bears. — *v.t.* to entertain at a feast: to honour with festivities. — **fête champêtre** (*shā-pe-tr'*) a rural festival, garden party; **Fête-Dieu** (*dyø*) Corpus Christi; **fête galante** (*ga-lãt*) a painting depicting the amusements of elegantly attired groups in a pastoral setting, associated mainly with the French painter Jean Antoine Watteau (1684–1721). [Fr.]

fetial *fē'shəl, adj.* pertaining to the Roman *fētiālēs*, a priestly college of heralds: heraldic, ambassadorial. — Also **fē'cial.**

fetich, fetiche, etc. See **fetish.**

feticide. See **foetus.**

fetid *fē'tid,* or *fet'id, adj.* stinking: having a strong offensive smell. — *ns.* **fē'tidness, fē'tor.** — Less justifiable spellings are **foetid, foetor.** [L. *fētidus, fētor — fētēre*, to stink.]

fetish, fetich, fetiche *fe'tish, fē'tish, n.* an object believed to procure for its owner the services of a spirit lodged within it: an inanimate object to which a pathological sexual attachment is formed: such an attachment: a person who is the object of an obsessive fixation: a fixation: something regarded with irrational reverence. — *v.t.* **fet'ishise, fet'ichise, -ize** to make a fetish of (a person). — *ns.* **fet'ishism, fet'ichism** the worship of a fetish: a belief in charms: pathological attachment of sexual interest to an inanimate object; **fet'ishist, fet'ichist.** — *adjs.* **fetishist'ic, fetichis'tic.** [Fr. *fétiche* — Port. *feitiço*, magic: a name given by the Portuguese to the gods of W. Africa — Port. *feitiço*, artificial — L. *factīcius — facěre*, to make.]

fetlock *fet'lok, n.* a tuft of hair that grows above a horse's hoof: the part where this hair grows. — *adj.* **fet'locked** having a fetlock: tied by the fetlock. [History obscure; long felt as a compound of **foot** and **lock**[2] (of hair); cf. Ger. *Fissloch*.]

fetoscopy. See **foetoscopy.**

fett, *fet, v.t.* obsolete form of **fetch**[1].

fetta. See **feta.**

fetter *fet'ər, n.* (usu. in *pl.*) a chain or shackle for the feet: (usu. in *pl.*) anything that restrains. — *v.t.* to put fetters on: to restrain. — *adj.* **fett'erless.** — **fett'erlock** (*her.*) a shackle for a horse, as a charge. [O.E. *feter*; conn. with *fōt*, foot.]

fettle *fet'l, v.t.* to make ready, set in order, arrange: to tidy up (*dial.*): to line (a furnace). — *v.i.* to potter fussily about. — *n.* condition, trim, form: lining for a furnace. — *ns.* **fett′ler; fett′ling.** [Prob. O.E. *fetel*, a belt.]

fettuc(c)ine, fettucini *fet-ōō-chē′nā, -nē, ns.* tagliatelle. [It.]

fetus. See **foetus.**

fetwa *fet′wä, n.* a Muslim legal decision. [Ar.]

feu *fū*, (*Scot.*) *n.* a tenure where the vassal, in place of military services, makes a return in grain or in money: a right to the use of land, houses, etc., in perpetuity, for a stipulated annual payment (**feu′-dū′ty**): a piece of land held in feu. — *v.t.* to vest in one who undertakes to pay the feu-duty. — *n.* **feu′ar** one who holds real estate in consideration of payment of feu-duty. — *adj.* **feud′al** pertaining to a feu. [O.Fr. *feu;* see **fee.**]

feu (*pl.* **feux**) **d′artifice** *fø dar-tē-fēs,* (Fr.) fireworks; **feu de joie** (*də zhwä*) a bonfire: (in English, *not* in French) a firing of guns in token of joy.

feud[1] *fūd, n.* a war waged by private individuals, families, or clans against one another on their own account: a bloody strife: a persistent state of private enmity. — Also *v.i.* — *n.* and *adj.* **feud′ing.** — **right of feud** the right to protect oneself and one's kinsmen, and punish injuries. [O.Fr. *faide, feide* — L.L. *faida* — O.H.G. *fēhida;* vowel change unexplained; see **foe.**]

feud[2]**, feod** *fūd, n.* a fief or land held on condition of service. — *adj.* **feud′al, feod′al** pertaining to feuds or fiefs: belonging to feudalism. — *n.* **feudalīsā′tion, -z-.** — *v.t.* **feud′alise, -ize.** — *ns.* **feud′alism** the feudal system or its principles: a class-conscious social or political system resembling the mediaeval feudal system; **feud′alist; feudal′ity** the state of being feudal: the feudal system. — *adv.* **feud′ally.** — *adjs.* **feud′ary, feod′ary, feud′atory** holding lands or power by a feudal tenure. — Also *ns.* — *n.* **feud′ist** a writer on feuds: one versed in the laws of feudal tenure. — **feudal system** the system by which vassals held lands from lords-superior on condition of military service. [L.L. *feudum;* see **fee.**]

feudal. See **feu** and **feud**[2]**.**

feuilleté *fœy-tā,* (Fr.) *n.* puff-pastry.

feuilleton *fœy-tõ, n.* in French and other newspapers, a part ruled off the bottom of a page for a serial story, critical article, etc.: a contribution of such a kind. — *ns.* **feu′illetonism** (*-tən-izm*); **feu′illetonist.** [Fr. dim. of *feuillet*, a leaf — L. *folium.*]

feutre. Same as **fewter.**

fever *fē′vər, n.* disease (esp. infectious) marked by great bodily heat and quickening of pulse: extreme excitement of the passions, agitation: a painful degree of anxiety. — *v.t.* to put into a fever. — *v.i.* to become fevered. — *adjs.* **fē′vered** affected with fever: excited; **fē′verish** slightly fevered: indicating fever: restlessly excited: morbidly eager. — *adv.* **fē′verishly.** — *n.* **fē′verishness.** — *adj.* **fē′verous** feverish: marked by sudden changes: apt to cause fever. — **fē′verfew** (O.E. *fēferfūge*) a composite perennial *Matricaria* (or *Chrysanthemum*) *parthenium*, closely allied to camomile, so called from its supposed power as a febrifuge; **fē′ver-heat** the heat of fever: an excessive degree of excitement; **fever pitch** a state of great excitement, agitation; **fever therapy** cure by inducement of fever; **fe′ver-tree** a southern African tree of the genus *Acacia* usu. found in swampy, mosquito-infested places, and hence regarded (esp. formerly) as an indicator of malarious spots to be avoided and by some even thought to be itself a cause of malaria: any of various species of trees, such as the Australian *Eucalyptus globulus* or the American *Pinckneya pubens*, which yield substances useful in the treatment of fevers. [O.E. *fēfor* — L. *febris.*]

few *fū, adj.* small in number: not many. — *n.* **few′ness** smallness of number: few words, brevity (*Shak.*). — **a few** a small number (of) — used as a noun, or virtually a compound adjective; also facetiously as an *adv.*, a little; **a good few, quite a few** (*coll.*) a considerable

number; **in few** in a few words, briefly; **some few** an inconsiderable number; **the few** the minority. [O.E. *fēa*, pl. *fēawe;* cf. L. *paucus*, small.]

fewmet. Same as **fumet.**

fewter, feutre *fū′tər, n.* (*obs.*) a spear-rest. — *v.t.* (*Spens.*) to set in rest. [O.Fr. *feutre*, felt, a felt-lined socket.]

fewtrils *fū′trilz,* (*dial.*) *n.pl.* little things, trifles. [See **fattrels.**]

fey[1]**, fay, fie** *fā, adj.* doomed, fated soon to die, under the shadow of a sudden or violent death — imagined to be marked by extravagantly high spirits (chiefly Scot.): foreseeing the future, esp. calamity (chiefly Scot.): eccentric, slightly mad: supernatural: fairy-like: elfin. [M.E. *fay, fey* — O.E. *fǣge*, doomed; cf. Du. *veeg*, about to die.]

fey[2]**.** See **fay**[5]**.**

fez *fez, n.* a red brimless truncated conical cap of wool or felt, with black tassel, worn in Egypt, formerly in Turkey — the *tarboosh:* — *pl.* **fezz′es, fez′es.** — *adj.* **fezzed** (*fezd*). [From *Fez* in Morocco.]

fiacre *fē-ak′r′, n.* a hackney-coach: a cab. [Fr., from the Hôtel de St *Fiacre* in Paris, where first used.]

fiancé, fem. fiancée, *fē-ä′sā, n.* one betrothed: — *n.pl.* **fiançailles** (*fē-ä-sī-y′*) betrothal. [Fr.]

fianchetto *fyäng-ket′to,* (*chess*) *n.* the early movement of a knight's pawn to develop a bishop on a long diagonal: — *pl.* **fianchet′ti** (*-tē*). — Also *v.t.* [It., dim. of *fianco*, flank.]

Fianna Fáil *fē′an-ä foil,* the Irish republican party. [Ir., militia of Fál (a stone monument at Tara, hence Ireland); cf. **Fenian.**]

fiar *fē′ər,* (*Scots law*) *n.* the owner of the fee-simple of a property (in contrast to a *life-renter* of the property). [**fee.**]

fiars *fē′ərz,* (*Scot.*) *n.pl.* the prices of grain legally *struck* or fixed for the year at the *Fiars* Court, so as to regulate the payment of stipend, rent, and prices not expressly agreed upon — usu. **fiars prices.** [O.Fr. *feor, fuer*, fixed price, standard — L. *forum*, market.]

fiasco *fē-as′kō, n.* a flask, bottle: a failure in a musical performance: a complete failure of any kind: — *pl.* **fias′cos, fias′coes.** [It. *fiasco*, bottle, perh. from L. *vasculum*, a little vessel, *vas*, a vessel.]

fiat *fī′at,* L. *fē′ät, n.* a formal or solemn command: a short order or warrant of a judge for making out or allowing processes, letters-patent, etc. (*Spens.* **fiaunt′**). — *v.t.* to sanction. — **fiat money, currency** (esp. *U.S.*) money (paper or coin) made legal tender and assigned a value by government decree, with a commodity value lower than its face value, not convertible into other specie of equivalent value, and generally with a lower purchasing power than nominally equivalent specie. [L. *fiat* (*fiant*), let it (them) be done, 3rd pers. sing. (plur.) pres. subj. of *fīěrī*, serving as passive of *facěre*, to do.]

fib[1] *fib, n.* something said falsely: a not very serious lie. — *v.i.* to tell a fib or lie: to speak falsely: — *pr.p.* **fibb′ing;** *pa.p.* **fibbed.** — *ns.* **fibb′er** one who fibs; **fibb′ery** (*rare*) the habit of fibbing; **fib′ster** a fibber. [Perh. **fable.**]

fib[2] *fib, v.t.* to punch: to pummel: — *pa.t.* and *pa.p.* **fibbed;** *pr.p.* **fibb′ing.** [Ety. unknown.]

fiber. See **fibre.**

Fibonacci numbers, sequence, series *fē-bō-nä′chē num′-bərz, sē′kwəns, sē′rēz,* a series of numbers in which each term is the sum of the preceding two terms. [Leonardo (*Fibonacci*) of Pisa (1170–1230).]

fibre, fiber *fī′bər, n.* any fine thread-like object, of animal, vegetable, or mineral origin, natural or synthetic: a structure or material composed of fibres: texture: stamina. — *adjs.* **fī′bred** having fibre; **fī′breless** without fibre, strength, or nerve; **fī′briform** fibre-like. — *ns.* **fī′bril** a small fibre: a root-hair: a minute thread-like structure such as the longitudinal contractile elements of a muscle-fibre; **fibrill′a** a fibril filament (*pl.* **fibrill′ae** *-ē*). — *adjs.* **fī′brillar, fī′brillary, fī′brillate, -d** pertaining to, of the nature of, or having fibrils or fibrous structure. — *v.i.* **fi′brillate** to undergo fibrillation. — *n.* **fibrilla′tion** the production or formation of fibrils or fibres: a mass of fibrils: a twitching of muscle fibres: uncoordinated contraction of muscle-fibres in the heart (*med.*). — *adjs.* **fi′brillose** having, or covered with, small fibres or the appearance of small fibres; **fi′brillous** pertaining to or having small fibres. — *ns.* **fi′brin** an insoluble protein precipitated as a network of fibres when blood coagulates; **fibrin′ogen** (*-jɘn*) a protein that forms fibrin; **fibrinol′ysin** an enzyme in the blood which causes breakdown of fibrin in blood clots: a drug having the same effect. — *adj.* **fi′brinous** of or like fibrin. — *n.* **fi′brō** (*Austr.*) a wall-board of a compressed asbestos and cement mixture (also **fi′brocement′®**): a house constructed of such material: — *pl.* **fi′bros.** — Also *adj.* (also **fi′brocement′®**). — *n.* **fi′broblast** a cell in connective tissue from which fibrous tissue is formed. — *adj.* **fibroblast′ic.** — *ns.* **fibrocar′tilage** cartilage with embedded fibres; **fibrocement** see **fibro** above; **fi′brocyte** a normally inactive fibroblast which proliferates following tissue damage. — *adj.* **fi′broid** of a fibrous character. — *n.* a fibrous tumour. — *ns.* **fibroin** (*fī′brō-in*) the chief chemical constituent of silk; **fi′broline** (*-lēn*) a yarn of flax, hemp, and jute waste, used with linen or cotton for backs of carpets, etc.; **fi′brolite** a fibrous variety of the mineral sillimanite; **fibrō′ma** a tumour composed of fibrous tissue: — *pl.* **fibrō′mata, fibrō′mas.** — *v.i.* **fibrose** (*fī-brōs′*) to form fibrous tissue. — *adj.* **fibrose** (*fī′brōs*) fibrous. — *ns.* **fibro′sis** a morbid growth of fibrous tissue; **fibrosī′tis** inflammation (esp. rheumatic) of fibrous tissue. — *adjs.* **fibrōt′ic** pertaining to fibrosis; **fi′brous** composed of or like fibres; **fibrovas′cular** composed of fibres and conducting elements. — **fi′breboard** a building-board made from compressed fibrous materials; **fi′breglass** a synthetic fibre made of extremely fine filaments of molten glass, used in textile manufacture, in heat and sound insulation, and in reinforced plastics; **fibre optics** technique using fibre optic(s) bundles (as *adj.* usu. **fibre optic**). — **fibre optic(s) bundle** a bundle of extremely thin flexible glass fibres suitably coated, used in optical instruments to transmit maximum light, and images of maximum clarity, and designed, because of their flexibility, for seeing into otherwise inaccessible places. [Fr., — L. *fibra*, thread, fibre.]

fibster. See **fib¹**.

fibula *fib′ū-lɘ, n.* a brooch: the outer of the two bones from the knee to the ankle. — *adj.* **fib′ular.** [L. *fibula*, brooch.]

fiche *fēsh, n.* a card or strip of film containing miniaturised data. — Also short for **microfiche.** [Fr., a slip of paper, etc.]

fichu *fi′shōō, fē-shü, n.* a three-cornered cape worn over the shoulders, the ends crossed upon the bosom: a triangular piece of muslin, etc., for the neck. [Fr.]

fickle *fik′l, adj.* inconstant: changeable. — *v.t.* (*Scot.*) to perplex, puzzle. — *n.* **fick′leness.** [O.E. *ficol; gefic,* fraud.]

fico *fē′kō, (Shak.) n.* a fig, as a type of insignificance, a whit: a motion of contempt by placing the thumb between two fingers: — *pl.* **fic′os.** [It., fig.]

fictile *fik′tīl, -til, adj.* used or fashioned by the potter: plastic. [L. *fictilis* — *fingĕre,* to form or fashion.]

fiction *fik′shɘn, n.* a feigned or false story: a falsehood: romance: the novel, story-telling as a branch of literature: a supposition of law that a thing is true, which is either certainly not true, or at least is as probably false as true. — *adj.* **fic′tional.** — *v.t.* **fic′tionalise, -ize** to give a fictional character to (a narrative dealing with real facts). — *adj.* **fic′tionalised, -z-.** — *n.* **fic′tionist** a writer of fiction. — *adj.* **fictitious** (*-tish′ɘs*) of the nature of fiction: imaginary: not real: feigned. — *adv.* **ficti′tiously.** — *adj.* **fic′tive** fictitious, imaginative. — *n.* **fic′tor** (*obs.*) one who makes images of clay, etc. [Fr., — L. *fictiō, -ōnis* — *fictus,* pa.p. of *fingĕre,* to form, fashion.]

fid *fid, n.* a conical pin of hard wood, used by sailors to open the strands of rope in splicing: a square bar, with a shoulder, used to support the weight of the topmast or top-gallant mast. [Origin unknown.]

fiddious *fid′i-ɘs, (Shak.) v.t.* app., to treat as Coriolanus treated *Aufidius.*

fiddle *fid′l, n.* the violin (*coll.*): a similar instrument with raised bridge and fingerboard: extended to like instruments as *bass fiddle*: a violin-player: a device to keep dishes from sliding off a table at sea: a swindle, esp. petty (*slang*). — *v.t.* and *v.i.* to play on a fiddle. — *v.t.* to swindle: to falsify. — *v.i.* to be busy over trifles, to trifle. — *n.* **fidd′ler** one who fiddles: (also **fiddler crab**) a small crab of the genus *Uca* or *Gelasimus,* from the attitude of its enlarged claw). — *adjs.* **fidd′ling** trifling, busy about trifles; **fidd′ly** requiring much dexterity: time-consuming: awkward. — **fidd′le-back** the fiddle-shaped back of a chair or front of a chasuble; **fidd′le-back** a wavy grain found in some woods commonly used for the manufacture of violins, and also in woods used for other purposes. — Also *adj.* — **fiddle block** (*naut.*) a block having two sheaves of different diameters one above the other; **fidd′le-bow** a bow strung with horsehair, with which the strings of the fiddle are set vibrating. — *interj.* **fiddle-de-dee′** nonsense! — *v.i.* **fidd′le-fadd′le** to trifle, to dally. — *n.* trifling talk or behaviour. — *adj.* fussy, trifling. — *interj.* nonsense!. — **fidd′le-fadd′ler.** — *adj.* **fidd′le-fadd′ling.** — **fidd′le-head** an ornament at a ship's bow, over the cutwater, consisting of a scroll turning aft or inward; **fiddle pattern** that of spoons and forks with handles shaped like violins (*adj.* **fidd′le-pattern**); **fiddler's green** the sailors' heaven; **fiddler's money** small coins, as sixpences; **fidd′lestick** a violin bow: derisively, a mere nothing or anything. — *interj.* **fidd′lestick(s)** nonsense! — **fidd′le-string** a string for a fiddle; **fidd′lewood** a tropical American tree (*Citharexylum*; fam. Verbenaceae) yielding valuable hard wood. — **a face like a fiddle** a long or dismal face; **as fit as a fiddle** in the best of condition; **play first** or **second fiddle** to act as a first-violin or a second-violin player in an orchestra: to take a leading, or a subordinate, part in anything; **Scotch fiddle** scabies (from the motion of the fingers against the palm). [O.E. *fithele;* Ger. *Fiedel;* see **viol.**]

fiddley *fid′li, n.* iron framework round a hatchway opening. [Origin obscure.]

fide et amore *fī′dē et a-mō′rē, fī′dā et a-mō′re,* (L.) by faith and love; **fide et fiducia** (*fi-dū′shi-ɘ, fi-dōō′ki-ä*) by faith and confidence; **fide et fortitudine** (*for-ti-tū′di-nē, for-ti-tōō′di-ne*) by faith and fortitude; **fidei defensor** (*fi′dē-ī di-fen′sor, fi-dā′ē dā-fen′sor*) defender of the faith; **fide non armis** (*non är′mis, ar′mēs*) by faith, not arms; **fides et justitia** (*fī′dēz et jus-tish′i-ɘ, fi′dāz et ūs-ti′ti-a*) fidelity and justice; **fides implicita** (*im-plis′i-tɘ, im-plik′i-tä*) implicit, unquestioning faith; **fides Punica** (*pū-ni-kɘ, pōō′ni-ka*) Punic faith: treachery.

fideism *fē′dā-izm, n.* the doctrine that knowledge depends on faith rather than reason. — *adj.* **fideist′ic.** [L. *fīdĕre,* to trust.]

fidelity *fi-del′i-ti, n.* faithfulness: faithfulness to a husband or wife: honesty: firm adherence: exactitude in reproduction. [L. *fidēlitās, -ātis* — *fidēlis,* faithful — *fīdĕre,* to trust.]

fidget *fij′it, v.i.* to be unable to rest: to move about uneasily: — *pr.p.* **fidg′eting;** *pa.t.* and *pa.p.* **fidg′eted.** — *n.* one who fidgets: irregular motion: restlessness: (in *pl.*) general nervous restlessness with a desire of changing postion. — *v.i.* **fidge** (*dial.*) to move about restlessly: to be eager. — *n.* **fidg′etiness.** — *adj.* **fidg′ety** restless: uneasy. [Perh. related to **fike.**]

fidibus *fid′i-bɘs, n.* a paper spill for lighting a pipe, etc. [Ger.]

Fido *fī′dō, n.* a method of dispersing airfield fog by burning petrol. [*Fog Investigation Dispersal Operation.*]

fi donc! *fē dõ,* (Fr.) for shame!

fiducial *fi-dū′sh(y)ɘl, adj.* serving as a basis of reckoning: showing confidence or reliance: of the nature of trust.

— *adv.* **fidū'cially.** — *adj.* **fidū'ciary** of the nature of a trust: depending upon public confidence: held in trust. — *n.* one who holds anything in trust: one who depends for salvation on faith without works, an antinomian (*obs. theol.*). [L. *fidūcia*, confidence — *fīdere*, to trust.]

fidus et audax *fī'dəs et ö'daks, fī'dŏŏs et ow'däks*, (L.) faithful and bold.

fie[1] *fī, interj.* denoting disapprobation or disgust, real or feigned. — **fie upon** an expression of disapprobation of the thing named. [Cf. Fr. *fi*; L. *fī*; O.N. *fȳ, fei*; Ger. *pfuī*.]

fie[2]. See **fey**[1].

fief *fēf, n.* land held in fee or on condition of military service. [Fr., — L.L. *feudum*; see **fee, feoff**.]

field *fēld, n.* country or open country in general: a piece of ground enclosed for tillage or pasture or sport: the range of any series of actions or energies: speciality: an area of knowledge, interest, etc.: a region of space in which forces are at work (*phys.*): the locality of a battle: the battle itself: a wide expanse: area visible to an observer at one time (e.g. in a microscope): one of the two interlaced sets of scanning lines making up the picture (*TV*): one scanning of a field from top to bottom and back (*TV*): a region yielding a mineral etc.: the surface of a shield (*her.*): the background of a coin, flag, etc.: those taking part in a hunt: the entries collectively against which a contestant has to compete: all parties not individually excepted (as *to bet on the field* in a horse-race): disposition of fielders: a system or collection of elements upon which binary operations of addition, subtraction, multiplication, and division can be performed except that division by 0 is excluded (*math.*): a set of characters comprising a unit of information (*comput.*). — *v.t.* at cricket and baseball, to catch or stop and return to the fixed place: to handle skilfully (esp. questions): to put into the field for play, military action, or (*fig.*) other form of contest. — *v.i.* to stand in position for catching or stopping the ball in cricket. — *adj.* **field'ed** (*Shak.*) encamped. — *ns.* **field'er** one who fields; **field'ing** the acting in the field at cricket as distinguished from batting. — *advs.* **field'ward, -wards** towards the fields. — **field ambulance** a medical unit on the field of battle; **field allowance** a small extra payment to officers on active service; **field artillery** mobile ordnance for active operations in the field; **field battery** a battery of field artillery; **field bed** a camp or trestle bedstead: a bed in the open air; **field book** a book used in surveying fields, etc.; **field'boots** knee-length boots; **field botany, field geology,** etc., botany, geology, etc., pursued in the open air; **field capacity** the water-retaining capacity of soil; **field club** a club of field naturalists. — *n.pl.* **field colours** small flags used for marking the position for companies and regiments, also any regimental headquarters' flags. — **field'-cor'net** the magistrate of a township (*S. Afr. hist.*): rank equivalent to lieutenant, *assistant field-cornet* equal to second-lieutenant (*S. Afr. mil.*); **field day** a day when troops are drawn out for instruction in field exercises: any day of unusual activity or success; **field'-dew** (*Shak.*); **fielded panel** a panel, sometimes subdivided into smaller panels, raised above or recessed into the surrounding woodwork; **field event** an athletic event other than a race; **field'fare** (ety. dub.) a species of thrush, having a reddish-yellow throat and breast spotted with black; **field glass(es)** a binocular telescope for use in the field or open air; **field goal** (*U.S. football, basketball*) a goal scored from normal play; **field gray, field grey** a grey (*Feldgrau*) adopted for uniforms in the German army in 1st World War: a German soldier so clad; **field gun** a light cannon mounted on a carriage; **field hand** an outdoor farm labourer; **field hockey** (*U.S.*) hockey played on grass (as opposed to ice hockey); **field hospital** a temporary hospital near the scene of battle; **field ice** ice formed in the polar seas in large surfaces, distinguished from icebergs; **field kitchen** portable cooking equipment for troops, or the place where it is set up; **field lark** an American bird (*Sturnella*) of the Iceteridae, not a lark; **field marshal** an army officer of highest rank; **field meeting** a conventicle; **field'mouse** a name for various species of mouse and vole that live in the fields; **field naturalist** one who studies natural history out of doors; **field night** a night marked by some important gathering, discussion, etc. — *n.pl.* **field notes** data noted in the field, to be worked up later. — **field officer** a military officer above the rank of captain, and below that of general; **field'piece** a cannon or piece of artillery used in the field of battle; **field preacher** an open-air preacher; **field preaching.** — *adj.* **field'-sequen'tial** (*TV*) relating to the association of individual primary colours with successive fields. — **fields'man** a fielder. — *n.pl.* **field sports** sports of the field, as hunting, racing, etc. — **field'stone** (chiefly *U.S.*) stone used for building as taken from a field; **field train** a department of the Royal Artillery responsible for the safety and supply of ammunition during war; **field trial** a test in practice, as distinct from one under laboratory conditions; **field trip** an expedition (esp. by students) to observe and study something at its location; **field'work** farm work in fields: work (scientific surveying, etc.) in the field, opposed to laboratory, office, etc.: (often in *pl.*) a temporary fortification thrown up by troops in the field, either for protection or to cover an attack upon a stronghold; **field'worker** a practical research worker. — **field-emission microscope** a microscope in which a very strong electric field is applied to a metal point and movement of atoms at the point is seen on a fluorescent screen; **field-ion microscope** a modification, with greater resolving power, of the field-emission microscope, in which ions of a gas (usu. helium) which is adsorbing on the metal point are repelled and produce the image on the screen; used in conjunction with an instrument such as a mass spectrometer to identify the atoms, it is known as an **atom-probe-field=ion microscope; field of view, vision** what is visible at one moment; **keep the field** to keep the campaign open: to maintain one's ground; **take the field** to assemble on a playing-field: to begin warlike operations. [O.E. *feld*; cf. Du. *veld*, the open country, Ger. *Feld*.]

fiend *fēnd, n.* a devil: one actuated by the most intense wickedness or hate: an addict: a devotee. — *adj.* **fiend'ish** like a fiend: devilishly cruel. — *n.* **fiend'-ishness,** — *adj.* **fiend'-like** like a fiend: fiendish. [O.E. *fēond,* enemy, orig. pr.p. of *fēon,* to hate; Ger. *Feind,* Du. *vijand.*]

fient *fēnt, fint,* (*Scot.*) *n.* fiend, devil: often used, like *devil* in English, as an emphatic negative (e.g. *fient ane,* devil a one, not one). [See **fiend.**]

fierce *fērs, adj.* savage: ferocious: violent. — *adv.* **fierce'ly.** — *n.* **fierce'ness.** [O.Fr. *fers* (Fr. *fier*) — L. *ferus,* wild, savage.]

fiere. See **fere**[1].

fieri facias *fī'ə-rī fā'shi-as, fē'e-rē fak'i-äs,* (L.L.) cause to be done — the name of a writ commanding the sheriff to distrain the defendant's goods.

fiery *fīr'i, adj.* like or consisting of fire: ardent: impetuous: irritable: of ground in games, dry, hard, fast. — *adv.* **fier'ily.** — *n.* **fier'iness.** — **fiery cross** a charred cross dipped in blood, formerly carried round in the Scottish Highlands as a call to arms. [**fire**.]

fiesta *fē-es'tə, n.* saint's day: holiday: festivity. [Sp.]

fife *fīf, n.* a smaller variety of the flute. — *v.i.* to play on the fife. — *n.* **fif'er** a fife-player. — **fife'-ma'jor** (*obs.*) the chief fifer in a regiment; **fife rail** the rail round the mainmast, where a fifer sat at heaving of the anchor. [Ger. *Pfeife,* pipe, or Fr. *fifre,* fifer, both — L. *pīpāre,* to cheep.]

Fifish *fīf'ish, adj.* cranky: queer: like a **Fif'er,** or inhabitant of *Fife,* Scotland.

fifteen *fif'tēn,* or *fif-tēn', adj.* and *n.* five and ten: a set, group, or team of fifteen (as formerly the Court of Session). — *n.* **fifteen'er** a verse of fifteen syllables. — *adj.* **fifteenth'** (or *fif'*) last of fifteen: next after the fourteenth: equal to one of fifteen equal parts. — *n.* a fifteenth part: a person or thing in fifteenth position: a double octave (*mus.*): an organ stop sounding two octaves above the diapason. — *adv.* **fifteenth'ly. — the Fifteen** the Jacobite rebellion of 1715.   [O.E. *fíftēne*; see **five, ten.**]

fifth *fifth, adj.* last of five: next after the fourth: equal to one of five equal parts. — *n.* one of five equal parts: a person or thing in fifth position: an interval of four (conventionally called five) diatonic degrees (*mus.*): a tone at that interval from another: a combination of two tones separated by that interval. — *adv.* **fifth'ly** in the fifth place. — **Fifth Amendment** an amendment to the U.S. constitution which allows a person on trial not to testify against himself and forbids a second trial if a person has been acquitted in a first; **fifth column** sympathisers among the enemy, awaiting their time (expression used by a Spanish insurgent general when four columns were advancing upon Madrid); **fifth columnist** (*kol'əm-ist*); **fifth generation** (*comput.*) the type of computer being developed in the 1980s and expected to come into use in the 1990s, incorporating aspects of artificial intelligence (*adj.* **fifth'-genera′tion**); **Fifth'-mon′archism; Fifth'-mon′archist. — Fifth-monarchy men** an extreme sect at the time of the Puritan revolution, who looked for a new reign of Christ on earth in succession to Daniel's four great monarchies of Antichrist.   [O.E. *fífta*, assimilated to other ordinals in *-th.*]

fifty *fif'ti, adj.* and *n.* five tens or five times ten. — *n.pl.* **fif'ties** the numbers fifty to fifty-nine: the years so numbered (of a life or century): a range of temperatures from fifty to just less than sixty degrees. — *adj.* **fif'tieth** last of fifty: next after the forty-ninth: equal to one of fifty equal parts. — *n.* a fiftieth part: a person or thing in fiftieth position. — *adj.* **fif'tyish** apparently about fifty years old. — *n.* and *adj.* and *adv.* **fif'ty-fif'ty** half-and-half: fifty per cent. of each of two things: share and share alike. — **fifty-pence, -penny piece** in Britain, a coin worth 50 pence.   [O.E. *fíftig — fíf,* five, and *-tig,* the suff. *-ty.*]

fig¹ *fig, n.* the fig-tree (Ficus, of the mulberry family), or its fruit, growing in warm climates: a thing of little or no consequence: piles (*obs.*). — *v.t.* (*Shak.*) to insult by putting the thumb between the fingers. — **fig'-bird** any Australian oriole (genus *Sphecotheres*) feeding on figs, etc.; **fig'-leaf** the leaf of the fig-tree: a representation of such a leaf for veiling the private parts of a statue or picture: any scanty clothing (from Gen. iii. 7): any prudish evasion: a makeshift: something intended to conceal the reality of actions or motives, esp. political or international; **fig'-pecker** beccafico; **fig'-tree** the tree which produces figs; **fig'wort** any species of Scrophularia: pilewort.   [Fr. *figue* — L. *ficus,* a fig, fig-tree.]

fig² *fig, (coll.) n.* figure: dress: form. — *v.t.* to dress, get up (with *out*): (of a horse) to display in an artificially lively condition (with *out* or *up*): — *pr.p.* **figg'ing;** *pa.t.* and *pa.p.* **figged.** — *n.* **figg'ery** dressy ornament. — **in full fig** in full dress, array.   [Perh. **figure.**]

fight *fīt, v.i.* to strive: to contend in war or in single combat. — *v.t.* to engage in conflict with: to contend against: to maintain or contend for by combat, action at law, or otherwise: to manipulate in fight: to achieve by struggle: to cause to fight: — *pr.p.* **fight'ing;** *pa.t.* and *pa.p.* **fought** (*föt*). — *n.* a struggle: a combat: a strong disagreement: a battle or engagement: fighting spirit: inclination to fight: a screen to cover the men in a naval fight (*Shak.*). — *adj.* **fight'able** able to be fought. — *n.* **fight'er** one who fights: a boxer: an aircraft engaged in war. — *adj.* **fight'ing** engaged in, eager for, or fit for war or strife. — *n.* the act of fighting or contending. — **fighting chance** a chance of success given supreme effort; **fighting cock** a gamecock: a pugnacious fellow; **fighting fish** (*Betta pugnax*) a small freshwater fish of Thailand, kept for its extraordinary readiness for fighting, bets being laid on the issue. —

fight back to retaliate: to counter-attack (*n.* **fight′(-)back**); **fighting drunk** drunk and very aggressive; **fighting fit** in good condition; **fight it out** to struggle on until the end; **fight off** to resist, repel; **fight shy of** to avoid from mistrust; **fight to the finish, to the ropes, to the last ditch** to fight until completely exhausted; **live like fighting cocks** to get the best of meat and drink.   [O.E. *fehtan* (W.S. *feohtan*); Ger. *fechten.*]

figment *fig'mənt, n.* a fabrication or invention.   [L. *figmentum — fingĕre,* to form.]

figo *fē′gō, (Shak.) n.* a fico: — *pl.* **fig'os.**   [O.Sp.]

figuline *fig'ū-līn, -lin, adj.* of earthenware: fictile. — *n.* an earthen vessel.   [L. *figulīnus — figulus,* potter.]

figure *fig'ər, (U.S.* and *dial.) -yər,* (old-fashioned) *fig'ūr, n.* the form of anything in outline: appearance: a shape: a geometrical form: a diagram: a horoscope (*Shak.*): a design: an illustration: bodily shape: a human form or representation of it: a personality, personage, character: an impressive, noticeable, important, ludicrous, or grotesque person: a character denoting a number: amount: value or price: a deviation from the ordinary mode of expression (*rhet.*): the form of a syllogism with respect to the position of the middle term (*log.*): a group of notes felt as a unit (*mus.*): a series of steps or movements in a dance or in skating: a type or emblem. — *v.t.* to form or shape (*obs.*): to make an image of: to represent: to mark with figures or designs: to imagine: to reckon, to work out (often with *out*): to symbolise (*arch.*): to foreshow (*obs.*): to note by figures. — *v.i.* to make figures: to appear as a figure, make an appearance or show: to follow as a logical consequence, be expected (*coll.*). — *n.* **figūrabil'ity** the quality of being figurable. — *adjs.* **fig'ūrable; fig'ūral** represented by figure. — *n.* **figurant, figurante** (*fig'ūrənt;* It. *fēg-ōō-rän'tä*) a ballet dancer, one of those who form a background for the solo dancers. — *adj.* **fig'ūrate** of a certain determinate form: florid (*mus.*). — *n.* **figūrā'tion** act of giving figure or form: representation by or in figures or shapes, esp. significant, typical or emblematic, figures: a figure of this kind: ornamentation with a design: florid treatment (*mus.*). — *adj.* **fig'ūrative** representing by, containing, or abounding in figures of speech (*rhet.*): metaphorical: representing a figure: emblematic, symbolic: of a style of painting, sculpture, etc. characterised by the realistic depiction of people, objects, etc. (as opp. to *abstract* art). — *adv.* **fig'ūratively.** — *n.* **fig'ūrativeness.** — *adj.* **fig'ured** (*-ərd*) having a figure: marked or adorned with figures: delineated in a figure: in the form of figures. — *ns.* **fig'ūrine** (*-ēn, -ēn'*) a small carved or moulded figure; **fig'urist** one who uses or interprets by figures. — **figurate numbers** a series of numbers such that if each be subtracted from the next, and the series so formed be treated in the same way, by a continuation of the process equal differences will ultimately be obtained; **fig'ure-cast'er** (*obs.*) an astrologer; **fig'ure=cast'ing** the art of preparing casts of animal or other forms; **fig'ure-dance** a dance consisting of elaborate figures; **figured bass** a bass with numerals added to indicate chords; **fig'urehead** the figure or bust under the bowsprit of a ship: a nominal head. — *adj.* nominal, but lacking real power. — **fig'ure-skater; fig'ure-skating** skating in prescribed patterns on ice; **fig'ure=weav'ing** the weaving of figured fancy fabrics; **fig'urework** counting, calculation using numbers. — **cut a figure** to make a conspicuous appearance; **figure of speech** any of various devices (such as simile or metaphor) for using words in such a way as to make a striking effect; **figure on** to count upon: to plan (*U.S.*).   [Fr., — L. *figūra — fingĕre,* to form.]

fike *fīk, (Scot.) v.i.* to fidget restlessly. — *n.* restlessness: any vexatious requirement or detail in work: a pernickety exacting person. — *n.* **fik'ery** fuss. — *adjs.* **fik'ish, fīk'y.**   [Prob. O.N. *fīkja.*]

fil. See **fill².**

filabeg. See **filibeg.**

filaceous. See **file¹.**

filacer *fil'ə-sər, n.* formerly an officer who filed writs. — Also **fil'azer.** [O.Fr. *filacier* — *filace*, a file for papers — apparently L. *filum*, a thread.]

filagree. Same as **filigree.**

filament *fil'ə-mənt, n.* a slender or threadlike object: a fibre: the stalk of a stamen (*bot.*): a chain of cells: a thread of high resistance in an incandescent lamp or thermionic valve (*elec.*). — *adjs.* **filamentary** (-*ment'ə-ri*) like a filament; **filament'ous** threadlike. [L. *filum*, a thread.]

filander *fil-and'ər, n.* a threadlike intestinal worm in hawks: (in *pl.*) the disease it causes. [O.Fr. *filandre* — L. *filum*, thread.]

filar. See **file¹.**

Filaria *fi-lā'ri-ə, n.* a genus of nematode worms of the fam. *Filarioidea* introduced into the blood by mosquitoes: (without *cap.*) any worm of the genus. — *adj.* **filā'rial.** — *n.* **filariasis** (-*lə-rī'ə-sis*) a disease due to the presence of filaria in the blood. [L. *filum*, thread.]

filasse *fil-as', n.* vegetable fibre ready for manufacture. [Fr., — L. *filum*, thread.]

filature *fil'ə-chər, n.* the reeling of silk, or the place where it is done. — *n.* **fil'atory** a machine for forming or spinning threads. [Fr., — L. *filum*, a thread.]

filazer. Same as **filacer.**

filbert *fil'bərt, n.* the nut of the cultivated hazel —(*obs.*) **fil'berd.** [Prob. from St *Philibert*, whose day fell in the nutting season, Aug. 22 (O.S.).]

filch *filch, v.t.* to steal: to pilfer. — *n.* **filch'er** a thief. — *n.* and *adj.* **filch'ing.** — *adv.* **filch'ingly.** [Ety. unknown.]

file¹ *fīl, n.* a thread (*obs.*): a line or wire on which papers are strung: any contrivance for keeping papers in order: a collection of papers arranged for reference: a collection of data in any form: a roll or list (*Shak.*): a line of soldiers, chessboard squares, etc., ranged one behind another: a small body of soldiers. — *v.t.* to put upon a file: to arrange in an orderly way: to put on record: to bring before a court: to deposit, lodge. — *v.i.* to march in file. — *adjs.* **filaceous** (*fil-ā'shəs*) composed of threads; **filar** (*fī'lər*) having threads or wires. — *n.* **fil'er** one who or that which files: a filing-cabinet (*coll.*). — *adjs.* **filiform** (*fil'*) threadlike; **filipen'dulous** (*fil-*) hanging by or strung on a thread. — *ns.* **filoplume** (*fil'*) a slender hairlike feather; **filopō'dium** (*fil-*) a thread-like pseudopodium consisting of ectoplasm: — *pl.* **filopō'dia.** — *adj.* **filose** (*fī'lōs*) threadlike: having a threadlike end. — **file copy** a copy filed for reference: an editor's copy of a book in which errors, possible changes, etc., are noted; **file'-lead'er** the person at the head of a file; **filing cabinet** a cabinet for storing files. — **file off** to wheel off at right angles to the first direction; **file with** (*arch.*) to rank with, to be equal to; **on file** on record, catalogued; **single file, Indian file** one behind another. [L. *filum*, a thread.]

file² *fīl, n.* an instrument with sharp-edged furrows for smoothing or rasping metals, etc.: a small metal or emery-paper instrument for smoothing fingernails: a shrewd, cunning person, a deep fellow: a pickpocket (*obs.*). — *v.t.* to cut or smooth with, or as with, a file: to polish, improve, esp. of a literary style. — *adj.* **filed** polished, smooth. — *ns.* **fil'er** one who files; (usu. in *pl.*) **fil'ing** a particle rubbed off with a file. — **file'-cutter** a maker of files; **file'-fish** a fish of Balistes or kindred genus, the skin granulated like a file. [O.E. *fȳl* (W.S. *fēol*); Ger. *Feile;* Du. *vijl.*]

file³ *fīl,* (*Shak.; Scot.*) *v.t.* to defile, pollute. [O.E. *gefylan;* cf. **foul.**]

filemot *fil'i-mot, adj.* of a dead-leaf colour — *n.* the colour itself. — Also **philamot, philomot.** [Fr. *feuillemorte,* dead leaf.]

filet *fē-le* (Fr.) *n.* undercut of beef, tenderloin: a kind of lace consisting of embroidery on a square-mesh net.

filet mignon *fē-le mē-nyõ,* (Fr.) a small cut of beef from the thin end of an undercut.

filfot. See **fylfot.**

filial *fil'i-əl, adj.* pertaining to or becoming a son or daughter: bearing the relation of a child. — *adv.* **fil'ially.** [Fr., — L.L. *filiālis* — L. *filius,* a son.]

filiate, filiation. Same as **affiliate, affiliation.**

filibeg, filabeg, fillibeg, phil(l)abeg, phil(l)ibeg *fil'i-beg, n.* the kilt, the dress or petticoat reaching nearly to the knees, worn by the Highlanders of Scotland. [Gael. *feileadhbeag* — *feileadh,* plait, fold, *beag,* little.]

filibuster *fil'i-bus-tər, n.* a piratical adventurer, buccaneer: a military adventurer, one who makes unauthorised war: one who obstructs legislation by speeches, motions, etc.: obstruction in a legislative body. — *v.i.* to act as a filibuster. — *ns.* **filibus'terer; filibus'tering; filibus'terism.** — *adj.* **filibus'terous.** [Sp. *filibustero,* through Fr. *flibustier, fribustier,* from Du. *vrijbuiter* (cf. Eng. **freebooter** (under **free**), Ger. *Freibeuter*), from *vrij,* free, *buit,* booty.]

Filices *fil'i-sēz, n.pl.* the ferns: esp. the true (homosporous leptosporangiate) ferns. — *ns.pl.* **Filicales** (-*kā'lēz*), **Filicineae** (-*sin'i-ē*) the ferns, leptosporangiate and eusporangiate, with or without water-ferns. — *adj.* **filicin'ean.** [L. *filix, -icis,* fern.]

filicide *fil'i-sīd, n.* the murder of one's own child: one who murders his child. [L. *filius, filia,* son, daughter; *caedere,* to kill.]

filiform. See **file¹.**

filigree *fil'i-grē, n.* a kind of ornamental metallic lacework of gold and silver, twisted into convoluted forms, united and partly consolidated by soldering: a delicate structure resembling this (also **fil'agree;** earlier forms, **fil'igrain, fil'igrane**). — *adj.* **fil'igreed** ornamented with filigree. [Fr. *filigrane* — It. *filigrana* — L. *filum,* thread, *grānum,* a grain.]

filing. See **file².**

filiopietistic *fi-li-ō-pī-ə-tis'tik, adj.* marked by an excess of filial piety, or excessive veneration of one's ancestors. [See **filial** and **piety.**]

filioque *fil-i-ō'kwi, n.* the clause inserted into the Nicene Creed at Toledo in 589, which asserts that the Holy Ghost proceeds from the Son, as well as from the Father — not accepted by the Eastern Church. [L., and from the one.]

filipendulous. See **file¹.**

Filipino *fil-i-pē'nō, n.* a native of the *Philippine* Islands: — *pl.* **Filipi'nos.** — *fem.* **Filipi'na.** — Also *adj.* [Sp.]

filius nullius *fil'i-əs nul'i-əs, fē'li-ōōs nōō'li-ōōs,* (L.) son of nobody, a bastard; **filius populi** *po'pū-lī, po'pōō-lē,* son of the people; **filius terrae** *te're, te'rī,* son of the soil, one of mean birth.

fill¹ *fil, v.t.* to make full: to put into until all the space is occupied: to supply abundantly: to satisfy: to glut: to perform the duties of: to supply (a vacant office): to adulterate (of soap, cotton fabrics, etc.): to put amalgam, gold, etc. into (a cavity in a tooth): to fulfil, carry out (esp. *U.S.*): to make up (a prescription) (*U.S.*). — *v.i.* to become full: to become satiated. — *n.* as much as fills or satisfies: a full supply: the fullest extent: a single charge of anything: anything used to fill. — *ns.* **fill'er** he who, or that which, fills: a vessel for conveying a liquid into a bottle: a substance added to various materials to impart desired qualities; **fill'ing** anything used to fill up, stop a hole, to complete, etc., as amalgam, etc. in a tooth, the woof in weaving: (in *pl.*) the quantity of new whisky spirit that a blender puts into store for maturation in e.g. a year, or the output of a distillery supplied for such purposes. — **filler cap** a device for closing the filling pipe of a petrol tank in a motor vehicle; **filling station** a roadside installation where petrol and oil are sold to motorists. — **fill in** to occupy (time): to add what is necessary to complete, e.g. a form: to act as a temporary substitute (for; *coll.*); **fill out** to make or become more substantial, larger, fuller: to complete (a form, etc.); **fill someone in** (*coll.*) to give someone detailed information about a situation: to thrash, beat up someone (*slang*): to murder someone (*slang*); **fill the bill** to be adequate; **fill up** to fill, or be filled, by addition of more; **fill up with** to stuff with (*lit.* and *fig.*); **have one's fill of** to have enough of, esp. something unpleasant or tiresome.   [O.E. *fyllan — full*, full.]

fill², **fil** *fil*, (*Shak.*) *n.* a thill or shaft. — **fill'-horse, p(h)il'horse** (*Shak.*) a thill-horse.   [See **thill¹**.]

fille *fē-y'*, (Fr.) *n.* girl: daughter. — **fille de chambre** (*də shā-br'*) a chambermaid; **fille de joie** (*zhwä*) a prostitute; **fille d'honneur** (*do-nœr*) a maid of honour.

fillet *fil'ət*, *n.* a narrow piece of wood, metal, etc.: a band for the hair: meat or fish boned and rolled: a piece of meat without bone, esp. the fleshy part of the thigh or the undercut of the sirloin: a boned whole, or thick boneless slice of, fish: a small space or band used along with mouldings (*archit.*). — *v.t.* to bind or adorn with a fillet: to make into fillets: to bone: — *pr.p.* **fill'eting**; *pa.t.* and *pa.p.* **fill'eted**. — **fillet weld** a weld at the junction of two parts at right angles to each other, a fillet of welding material being laid down in the angle created by the intersection of the surfaces of the parts.   [Fr. *filet*, dim. of *fil*, from L. *fīlum*, a thread.]

fillibeg. See **filibeg**.

fillip *fil'ip*, *v.t.* to strike with the fingernail released from the ball of the thumb with a sudden jerk: to incite, stimulate: — *pr.p.* **fill'iping**; *pa.t.* and *pa.p.* **fill'iped**. — *n.* a jerk of the finger from the thumb: a stimulus.   [A form of **flip**.]

fillipeen. U.S. form of **philop(o)ena**.

fillister *fil'is-tər*, *n.* a kind of rabbeting plane.   [Origin unknown.]

filly *fil'i*, *n.* a young mare: a lively, wanton girl.   [Dim. of **foal**; prob. from O.N.]

film *film*, *n.* a thin skin or membrane: a thin layer or coating: a pellicle: a very slender thread: a mistiness: a thin sheet of usu. plastic-based material used for wrapping: a coating of a sensitive substance for taking a photograph: a sheet or ribbon of celluloid or the like prepared with such a coating for ordinary photographs or for instantaneous photographs for projection by cinematograph: a motion picture, or connected series of motion pictures setting forth a story, etc.: (in *pl.*) the cinema. — *v.t.* to cover with a film: to photograph, record on film: to make a motion picture of: to adapt and enact for the cinema. — *v.i.* to become covered with a film. — *adj.* **film'able** suitable for making a film of. — *ns.* **film'dom, film'land** the cinematic industry. — *adj.* **film'ic** pertaining to the cinema. — *n.* **filmi'ness**. — *adj.* **film'ish** savouring of the cinema. — *n.* **filmog'raphy** a list of the films of a particular actor or director. — *adj.* **film'y** composed of or like a film: covered with a film: gauzy: clouded. — **film badge** a badge containing sensitive film worn by those risking exposure to radioactivity to detect and usu. indicate the amount of exposure; **film colour** a vague textureless area of colour, as the sky or that seen with closed eyes, as opposed to colour seen on the surface of an object; **film fan** a devotee of the cinema; **film'goer; film noir** (*nwär*) a bleak or pessimistic film; **film set** the scenery, furniture, etc. arranged for the scene of a film. — *v.t.* **film'set** to set by a process of typesetting (*printing*). — **film'setting** typesetting by exposing type on to film which is then transferred to printing plates; **film star** a favourite cinema performer; **film'-strip** a film consisting of a series of stills to be shown separately and consecutively; **filmy ferns** a family of ferns with very thin leaves, the Hymenophyllaceae. — **sheet film** film in same sizes as photographic plates and superseding plates.   [O.E. *filmen*, conn. with *fell*, skin.]

Filofax® *fī'lə-faks*, *n.* a small, loose-leaf filing system containing a diary and a selection of information, e.g. addresses, maps, indexes, to assist the user to organise his time, business, etc.

filoplume, filopodium, filose. See **file¹**.

filoselle *fil-ō-sel'*, *n.* coarse floss silk.   [It. *filosello* — L.L. *folexellus*, cocoon; infl. by It. *filo*, thread.]

fils *fēs*, (Fr.) *n.* son: (following a name) junior.

filter *fil'tər*, *n.* an apparatus for purifying a fluid of solid matter by pouring it through porous material: a device

for wholly or partly eliminating undesirable frequencies from light or electric currents: at a road junction an auxiliary traffic light in the form of a green arrow which allows one lane of traffic to move while the main stream is held up. — *v.t.* to pass through a filter: to separate by a filter (esp. with *out*). — *v.i.* to pass through a filter: to percolate: to pass gradually and dispersedly through obstacles: to join gradually a stream of traffic: of a lane of traffic, to move in the direction specified by the filter: to become known gradually (*fig.*). — *adj.* **fil'terable, fil'trable** able to pass through a filter (see **filter-passer** below): capable of being filtered. — *n.* **filt(e)rabil'ity**. — *v.t.* and *v.i.* **fil'trate** to filter or percolate. — *n.* a filtered liquid. — *n.* **filtrā'tion** act or process of filtering. — **fil'ter-bed** a bed of sand, gravel, clinker, etc., used for filtering water or sewage; **fil'ter-paper** porous paper for use in filtering; **fil'ter-passer, filterable virus** terms used formerly for virus in sense of submicroscopic disease agent; **fil'ter-tip'** a cigarette with a filter at the mouth end.   [O.Fr. *filtre* — L.L. *filtrum*, felt.]

filth *filth*, *n.* foul matter: anything that defiles, physically or morally: obscenity: (with *the*) the police (*slang*). — *adv.* **filth'ily**. — *n.* **filth'iness**. — *adj.* **filth'y** foul: unclean: impure.   [O.E. *fȳlth — fūl*, foul.]

filtre (Fr.). See **café filtre**.

fimble *fim'bl*, *n.* the male plant of hemp, weaker and shorter in fibre than **carl-hemp**.   [Du. *femel*, female.]

fimbria *fim'bri-ə*, *n.* a fringing filament. — *adj.* **fim'briate** fringed: having a narrow border (*her*). — *v.t.* **fim'briate** to fringe: to hem. — *adj.* **fim'briated**. — *n.* **fimbria'tion**.   [L. *fimbriae*, fibres, fringe.]

fimicolous *fim-ik'ə-ləs*, *adj.* growing on dung.   [L. *fimus*, dung, *colĕre*, to inhabit.]

fin¹ *fin*, *n.* an organ by which an aquatic animal steers, balances, or swims: a fixed vertical surface on the tail of an aeroplane: a portion of a mechanism like a fish's fin in shape or purpose: a thin projecting edge or plate: hand, arm (*slang*). — *n.* **finn'er** finback. — *adjs.* **fin'less; finned** having fins; **finn'y** finned. — **fin'back, fin'-whale** a rorqual. — *adj.* **fin'-foot'ed** web-footed: with fringed toes. — **fin'-ray** a horny rod supporting a fin. — *adj.* **fin'-toed'** having lobate or fringed toes.   [O.E. *finn*; L. *pinna*, a feather, a fin.]

fin² *fin*, (U.S. *slang*), *n.* a five-dollar bill.   [Yiddish *finf*, five.]

finable. See **fine²**.

finagle *fi-nā'gəl*, *v.t.* to wangle: to obtain by guile or swindling: to cheat (a person; usu. with *out of*). — Also *v.i.* and *n.*   [Eng. dial. *fainaigue*, cheat, shirk.]

final *fī'nl*, *adj.* last: decisive, conclusive: respecting the end or motive: of a judgment ready for execution. — *n.* the last of a series (as the letters of a word, games in a contest, examinations in a curriculum, etc.): in the old church modes, the keynote or tonic, the lowest note in the authentic modes, a fourth above it in the plagal. — *v.t.* **fī'nalise, -ize** to put the finishing touches to: to put an end to completely. — *ns.* **fī'nalism** teleology, interpretation in terms of purpose: belief that an end has been reached; **fī'nalist** teleologist: one who reaches the final stage in a competition: one who believes that finality has been reached; **finality** (-al'i-ti) state of being final: completeness or conclusiveness: the principle of final cause: that which is final. — *adv.* **fī'nally**. — **final cause** see **cause**.   [Fr., — L. *fīnālis — fīnis*, an end.]

finale *fi-nä'lā, -li*, *n.* the end: the last movement in a musical composition: the concluding number of an opera or the like.   [It. *finale*, final — L. *fīnālis*.]

finance *fī-, fi-nans', fī'*, *n.* money affairs or revenue, esp. of a ruler or state: public money: the art of managing or administering the public money: (in *pl.*) money resources. — *v.t.* to manage financially: to furnish with money. — *v.i.* to engage in money business. — *adj.* **finan'cial** (-shəl) pertaining to finance. — *n.* **finan'cialist** a financier. — *adv.* **finan'cially**. — *n.* **finan'cier** (-si-ər; U.S. *fin-an-sēr'*) one skilled in finance; one who administers the public revenue. — *v.i.* and *v.t.* (*-sēr'*) to finance: to swindle. — **finance company, house** a company specialising in lending money against collateral, esp. to finance hire-purchase agreements; **financial year** any annual period for which accounts are made up: the annual period ending April 5th, functioning as the income-tax year, over which the Government's financial policies and estimates are made: the annual period ending, for many public bodies, on March 31st. [Fr., — O.Fr. *finer*, to settle — L. *finis*, an end.]

finback. See **fin**[1].

finch *finch, -sh, n.* a name applied to many passerine birds, esp. to those of the genus *Fringilla* or family Fringillidae — bullfinch, chaffinch, goldfinch, etc. — *adj.* **finched** finch-backed. — *adj.* **finch'-backed** striped or spotted on the back. [O.E. *finc*; Ger. *Fink*.]

find *find, v.t.* to come upon or meet with: to discover or arrive at: to come to perceive: to experience: to supply: to determine after judicial inquiry: to succeed in getting: to manage to reach, hit, land on, etc. — *v.i.* to come upon game: — *pr.p.* **find'ing**; *pa.t.* and *pa.p.* **found**. — *n.* an act of finding: something found, esp. of value or interest. — *ns.* **find'er** one who finds: a small telescope attached to a larger one, or a lens attached to a camera, to facilitate the directing of it upon the object required; **find'ing** act of one who finds: that which is found: a judicial verdict: (*pl.*) the appliances which some workmen have to supply, esp. of shoemakers — everything save leather: (*pl.*) accessories such as buttons and zips (*U.S.*). — **find'-fault** (*Shak.*) one who finds fault with another. — **finders keepers** (*coll.*) those who find something are entitled to keep it; **find someone in** to supply someone with; **find one's account in** to find satisfactory profit or advantage in; **find one's feet** to become able to stand, able to cope readily with new conditions; **find oneself** to feel, as regards health, happiness, etc.: to come to terms with oneself: to discover one's true vocation and interests; **find out** to discover, to detect. [O.E. *findan*; Ger. *finden*.]

fin de siècle *fẽ də sye-kl'*, (Fr.) the end of the (19th) century, or of an era: characteristic of the ideas, etc., of that time: decadent.

findon-haddock, findram. See **finnan**.

fine[1] *fīn, adj.* excellent (often ironically): beautiful: fair: not coarse or heavy: consisting of small particles: subtle: thin, slender: sharp: keen: exquisite: nice: delicate: sensitive: over-refined: over-elaborate: pretentious: showy: splendid: striking or remarkable: egregious: pure: refined: containing so many parts of pure metal out of twenty-four (as 22 carats, or ounces, fine, 22/24 gold or silver), or out of a thousand. — *v.t.* to make fine: to refine: to purify: to change by imperceptible degrees. — *adj.* and *adv.* at a more acute angle with the line of flight of the ball (as *fine leg*): (of a billiards, etc. stroke) making very slight contact. — *adv.* well, well enough (*coll*) narrowly: with little to spare. — *adj.* **fine'ish** (also **fin'ish**) somewhat fine. — *adv.* **fine'ly**. — *ns.* **fine'ness** state, fact, or degree of being fine: state of subdivision: of gold or silver, number of parts in a thousand; **fin'er** a refiner; **fin'ery** splendour: showy adornments: a place where anything is fined or refined: a furnace for making iron malleable. — *n.pl.* **fines** material (ore, coal, etc.) in a fine state of division separated out by screening; **fin'ing** process of refining or purifying: a clarifying agent (often in *pl.*). — **fine arts** see under **art**; **fine chemicals** chemicals produced in small quantities usu. of high purity, as opposed to **heavy chemicals**. — *v.t.* **fine'-draw** to draw or sew up so finely that no rent is seen: to draw out finely or too finely. — *adj.* **fine'-drawn**. — **fine gentleman, lady** an idle person, usu. ostentatiously fashionable, sometimes refined; **fine metal** comparatively pure cuprous sulphide got from *coarse metal*. —*adjs.* **fine'=spoken** using fine phrases; **fine'-spun** finely spun out: over-subtle. — **fine-tooth(ed) comb, fine comb** a comb

with slender teeth set close together. — *v.t.* **fine-tune'** to make delicate adjustments to. — **fine-tun'ing; fine writing** literary matter or style pretentiously ornate; **fin'ing-pot** a vessel used in refining. — **cut it fine** to do something with little time, space to spare; **go over, through with a fine-tooth(ed) comb** to investigate very thoroughly. [Fr. *fin*, prob. a back-formation from L. *finītus*, finished, pa.p. of *finīre*, to finish — *finis*, an end.]

fine[2] *fīn, n.* end, conclusion (*obs.* except in phrase *in fine*): a final settlement: a fee paid on some particular occasion: a fictitious suit as a means of conveying property or barring an entail: a composition by money payment: a money penalty. — *v.t.* to bring to an end (*Shak.*): to impose a fine on: to punish by fine: to pledge or pawn (*Shak.*). — *adjs.* **fin'able** liable to a fine; **fine'less** (*Shak.*) endless. — **foot of fine** see **foot**. [L. *finis*, an end.]

fine[3] *fẽn, n.* ordinary French brandy. — **fine Champagne** (*shã-pany'*) brandy distilled from wine made from grapes grown in the Champagne area of France. [Fr.]

fineer[1] *fi-nēr'*, an old form of **veneer** (*n.* and *v.t.*).

fineer[2] *fi-nēr'* (*obs.*), *v.i.* to get goods on credit by fraudulent artifice. [Prob. Du.; cf. **finance**.]

Fine Gael *fẽ'nə gāl*, (*lit.* United Ireland) the moderate party led orig. by W. T. Cosgrave.

fines herbes *fẽn-zerb*, (Fr.) (*cook.*) a mixture of herbs used as a garnish or, chopped, as a seasoning.

finesse *fi-nes', n.* subtlety of contrivance: artifice: skill, expertise: an endeavour by a player holding a higher card to take the trick with a lower, risking loss. — *v.t.* and *v.i.* to play in finesse. — *v.i.* to use artifice. — *ns.* **finess'er; finess'ing**. [Fr.]

fingan *fin-gän', n.* a small coffee-cup without a handle — used with a zarf. — Also **finjan** (*-jän'*). [Egyptian *fingān*, Ar. *finjān*.]

finger *fing'gər, n.* one of the five terminal parts of the hand, or of the four other than the thumb: anything shaped like a finger: the part of a glove that covers a finger: a finger-breadth: touch: agency (esp. of God): share, interest: (in *pl.*) grip, control. — *v.t.* to handle or perform with the fingers: to pilfer: to toy or meddle with: to make or indicate choice of fingers in performing (*mus.*): to indicate, identify a guilty person (*slang*). — *v.i.* to use or move the fingers. — *adj.* **fing'ered** having fingers, or anything like fingers, or indication of fingering. — *n.* **fing'ering** act or manner of touching with the fingers: the choice of fingers as in playing a musical instrument: the indication thereof. — *adj.* **fing'erless**. — *n.* **fing'erling** a very diminutive being or thing: a fish no bigger than a finger, esp. a salmon parr or young trout less than a year old. — **fing'er= al'phabet** a deaf and dumb alphabet; **fing'er-and-toe'** a disease of turnips in which the taproot branches: another turnip disease, anbury; **fing'erboard** the part of a violin, etc., against which the strings are stopped by the fingers; **fing'erbowl, -glass** a bowl for water to cleanse the fingers at table, **fing'er('s)-breadth** the breadth of a finger, a digit, ¾ of an inch; **finger buffet** a buffet consising of **finger foods**, food (such as sandwiches) which may be eaten with the fingers as opp. to a knife and fork; **fing'er('s)-end'; fing'er-grass** grass of genus Digitaria, with fingerlike spikes; **fing'erguard** the quillons of a sword-handle; **fing'erhold** a grasp by the fingers: something by which the fingers can hold (also *fig.*); **fing'erhole** a hole in a wind instrument closed by the finger to modify the pitch; **fing'ermark** a mark, esp. a soil, made by the finger; **fing'ernail; fing'er-paint** a somewhat thick gelatinous paint used esp. by children and applied with the hands and fingers rather than with a brush. — Also *v.t.* — **fing'er= painting; fing'erplate** a plate to protect a door from dirty fingers; **fing'er-point'er** a reprover; **fing'er-point'- ing; fing'erpost** a post with a finger pointing the way; **fing'erprint** an impression of the ridges of the finger-tip: an accurate and unique identification feature or profile produced by chemical analysis, genetic analysis, etc. (*fig.*): the basic features (*fig.*). — *v.t.* to take the fingerprints of (also *fig.*). — **fing′erprinting** (also *fig.*); **fing′erstall** a covering for protecting the finger; **fing′ertip**. — **a finger in the pie** a share in the doing of anything (often said of vexatious meddling); **be all fingers and thumbs, have one's fingers all thumbs,** etc. see under **thumb; burn one's fingers, get one's fingers burnt** see **burn; cross one's fingers** see **cross; get, pull the** or **one's finger out** (*coll.*) to start working hard or doing one's job properly or efficiently; **have at one's finger(s)-ends, fingertips** to be master of (a subject); **lay, put a finger on** to touch; **not lift a finger** to take no action; **point the finger at** to call attention to in reproof; **put, lay one's finger on** to indicate, comprehend and express, or recall, precisely; **to one's fingertips** completely: in all respects; **twist someone round one's little finger** see **little**.   [O.E. *finger*.]

fingering *fing′gər-ing, n.* a woollen yarn of two or more strands, used in hand-knitting, orig. esp. for stockings. [Perh. *fin grain,* tine grain.]

finial *fin′i-əl, n.* the bunch of foliage, etc. on the top of a pinnacle, gable, spire, etc.   [L. *finis,* end.]

finical *fin′i-kl, adj.* affectedly or excessively precise in trifles: nice: foppish. — *n.* **finicality** (*-kal′i-ti*) the state of being finical: something finical. — *adv.* **fin′ically.** — *ns.* **fin′icalness, fin′icking** fussiness and fastidiousness. — *adjs.* **fin′icking, fin′icky, fin′ikin** particular about trifles: (**finicky**) (of a job) intricate, tricky, fiddly, requiring attention to small details, delicate manipulations, etc.   [Prob. conn. with *fine*[1].]

fining. See **fine**[1].

finis *fi′nis, fī′, n.* the end: conclusion: — *pl.* **-nēs.**   [L. *finis.*]

finish *fin′ish, v.t.* to end: to complete the making of: to perfect: to give the last touches to: to complete the education of, esp. for life in society: to complete the course of a race: to put an end to, to destroy. — Also *v.i.* — *n.* that which finishes or completes: the end of a race, hunt, etc.: the last touch, elaboration, polish: the last coat of plaster or paint: (applied to cattle and sheep) the amount of flesh and fat on an animal. — *adj.* **fin′ished** brought to an end or to completion: complete: consummate: perfect. — *n.* **fin′isher** one who finishes: one who completes or perfects, esp. in crafts. — *n.* and *adj.* **fin′ishing.** — **finishing post** the post marking the end of a race; **finishing school** an establishment where some girls complete their education, with emphasis on social refinements, etc. rather than academic achievement; **finishing touches, strokes** the last minor improvements needed to achieve perfection. — **finish up** to finish: to end up, be or become in the end.   [Fr. *finir, finissant* — L. *finīre,* to end.]

finite *fī′nīt, adj.* having an end or limit: subject to limitations or conditions (opp. to *infinite*). — *adv.* **fī′nitely.** — *ns.* **finiteness, finitude** (*fin′i-tūd, fīn′*). — **finite verb** a verb limited by person, number, tense, mood, opp. to infinitive, gerund, participle.   [L. *finītus,* pa.p. of *finīre,* to limit.]

finjan. See **fingan.**

fink *fingk,* (*slang*) *n.* a strike-breaker: an informer: loosely, an unpleasant person. — Also *v.i.* (often with *on*).   [Origin uncertain.]

finks. Same as **fenks.**

Finn *fin, n.* a member of a people dwelling in Finland and adjacent regions: more generally, a member of the group of peoples to which the Finns proper belong. — *ns.* **Fin′lander** a native or citizen of Finland; **Finlandīsā′tion, -z-** in relations with the Soviet Union, a policy of accommodation rather than confrontation. — *adjs.* **Finn′ic** pertaining to the Finns or the Finno-Ugrians; **Finn′ish** pertaining to the Finns, or to Finland, or its language. — *n.* the Finno-Ugrian language of Finland. — *adjs.* **Finno-Ugrian, Finno-Ugric** (*fin′ō-ū′gri-ən, -ōō′gri-ən, -grik*) belonging to the north-western group of Ural-Altaic languages and peoples — Finnish, Estonian, Lapp, Cheremiss, Mordvin,

Zyrian, Votyak, etc. — Also **U′gro-Finn′ic.**   [O.E. *finnas,* Finns.]

finnac(k). See **finnock.**

finnan *fin′ən, obs.* **findram** *fin′rəm, ns.* a kind of smoked haddock, probably named from Findon, Kincardineshire, not from the Findhorn river. — Also **finn′an-, fin′don-hadd′ock.**

finnesko, finnsko, finsko *fin′(e)-skō, ns.* a reindeer-skin boot with the hair on: — *pl.* **finn′eskō,** etc.   [Norw. *finnsko* — Finn, Lapp, *sko,* shoe.]

finnock, finnack, finnac *fin′ək, n.* a young sea-trout. [Gael. *fionnag — fionn,* white.]

fino *fē′nō, n.* a dry sherry: — *pl.* **fi′nos.**   [Sp., fine, excellent.]

finoc(c)hio, finnochio *fin-ok′i-ō, n.* a dwarf variety of fennel, *Foeniculum* (*vulgare*) *dulce,* the leaf stalks of which are used in stews, salads, etc. — Also called **dwarf, Florence, French** or **sweet fennel.**   [It., fennel.]

finsko. See **finnesko.**

fiord, fjord *fyōr(d), fyör(d), n.* a long, narrow, rock-bound inlet.   [Norw. *fjord.*]

fiorin *fī′ə-rin, n.* a variety of creeping bent-grass (*Agrostis stolonifera*).   [Ir. *fiorthán.*]

fioritura *fyor-i-tōō′rə* (*mus.*) *n.* a florid embellishment: — *pl.* **fioriture** (*-rā*).   [It., flowering — L. *flōs, flōris.*]

fippence *fip′əns, n.* A shortened form of **fivepence.**

fipple *fip′l, n.* the under-lip (*dial.*): an arrangement of a block, and a sharp edge against which it directs the wind, in the recorder, etc. — **fipp′le-flute′** a flute with a fipple, a recorder or flageolet.   [Cf. O.N. *flipi,* a horse's lip.]

fir *fûr, n.* the name of several conifers, esp. of the genera Abies and Picea, resinous trees, valuable for their timber. — *adj.* **firr′y** abounding in firs: of fir. — **fir′-cone; fir′-tree; fir′-wood.**   [O.E. *fyrh*; cf. Ger. *Föhre.*]

fire *fīr, n.* a once-supposed substance reckoned one of the four elements: the heat and light of burning: a mass of burning matter, as of fuel in a grate: flame or incandescence: a conflagration: firing: fuel: a heating apparatus: heat or light due to other causes than burning: lightning (*poet.*): volcanic or plutonic heat: great heat: the heat of fever or inflammation: glowing appearance: a sparkle of light: discharge of fire-arms (also *fig.*): enthusiasm: ardour: passion: spirited vigour or animation: refraction of light in a gemstone. — *v.t.* to ignite: to cause to explode: to expose to heat: to bake: to cauterise (*farriery*): to fuel: to affect as if by fire: to discharge: to drive out: to dismiss (from employment, etc.): to inflame: to animate: to rouse to passion of any kind. — *v.i.* to take fire: to shoot with firearms: to become inflamed: to break out in anger: of a car, engine, etc., to start. — *adjs.* **fired** affected, or having the appearance of having been affected, with fire: baked: ignited: kindled: discharged; **fire′less.** — *ns.* **fir′er** one who fires, in any sense; **fir′ing** ignition: discharge of guns, etc.: simultaneous ringing of a peal of bells: fuelling: firewood: fuel: cautery: injury by overheating: subjection to heat. — **fire′-alarm** an apparatus for giving warning of fire: a warning of fire; **fire′arm** a weapon discharged by explosion (usu. in *pl.*); **fire′-arrow** a dart or arrow carrying a combustible; **fire′-back** a red-backed Sumatran pheasant: the back wall of a fireplace: an ornamental plate of iron so placed; **fire′ball** a bolide: ball-lightning: an incendiary or illuminating projectile: the luminous sphere of hot gases at the centre of a nuclear explosion; **fire′-balloon′** a balloon carrying fire and raised by the heating and rarefaction of air: a balloon discharging fireworks in the air; **fire′-bar** a bar of a fire-grate: a heating element in an electric radiator; **fire′-bas′ket** a portable firegrate; **fire′-bird** the Baltimore oriole, or other bird of orange and red plumage; **fire blanket** a blanket of non-inflammable material for extinguishing small fires; **fire′-blast** a blight of hops, due to a mite, giving a scorched appearance; **fire′-blight** a bacterial disease of fruit-trees, giving a scorched appearance; **fire′-bomb**

an incendiary bomb; **fire'-bombing; fire'-bote** (*hist.*) a tenant's right to cut wood for fuel; **fire box** a chamber for the fire in a steam-engine, etc.; **fire'brand** a burning piece of wood: one who foments strife; **fire'brat** a small insect found in bakehouses; **fire'-break** a strip of land kept clear to stop the spread of a fire (also *fig.*); **fire'brick** a brick refractory to fire, used for furnace-linings, grates etc.; **fire'-brigade** a body of firemen; **fire'-bucket** a bucket containing sand or water for putting out fires; **fire'bug** an incendiary; **fire'-clay** a clay poor in lime and iron, suitable for making refractory pottery and firebricks; **fire'-control'** a system of controlling the whole gunfire of a ship from one centre; **fire'-cracker** a device for making a noise, a cylinder of paper or cardboard containing an explosive and a fuse; **fire'crest** or **fire-crested wren** a bird close akin to the goldcrest, a kinglet; **fire'damp** a combustible gas given off by coal, etc., chiefly methane; **fire'dog** an andiron; **fire'-drake** a fire-breathing dragon: a luminous phenomenon: a kind of firework; **fire'-drill** a primitive instrument for getting fire by twirling a stick: practice in putting out or escaping from fire; **fire'-eater** a juggler who seems to eat fire: a seeker of quarrels; **fire'-edge** (*dial.*) a cutting edge hardened by fire: crispness in a newly baked cake: first eagerness; **fire'-engine** an engine or pump for extinguishing fires; **fire'-escape** a fixed or movable way of escape from a burning building; **fire'-extinguisher** a contrivance for ejecting agents, e.g. water or a chemical, to put out fires. — *adj.* **fire'-eyed** (*Shak.*) having fiery eyes. — **fire'-fighter** a fireman; **fire'-fighting; fire'-flag** (*Coleridge*), **fire'-flaught** (*Swinburne*) a flash of fire, lightning, etc.; **fire'float** a boat or raft used in harbours for extinguishing fires; **fire'fly** an insect, generally a beetle, that emits light by night; **fire'-grate** a grating to hold a fire; **fire'guard** a protective wire-frame or railing in front of a fireplace; **fire'-hook** a hook formerly used to tear down burning buildings; **fire'-hose** a hose for extinguishing fires; **fire'house** a house with a fireplace, a dwelling-house; **fire'-insurance** insurance against loss by fire; **fire'-irons** fireside implements — poker, tongs, shovel — not necessarily of iron; **fire'light** the light of a domestic fire; **fire'lighter** a piece of readily inflammable material or other means of lighting a fire; **fire'lock** a gun discharged by a lock with flint and steel; **fire'man** one whose function is to assist in putting out fires and rescuing those in danger: a stoker: a train driver's assistant (stoker on steam engine): one who attends to conditions of safety in a mine: one who explodes charges; **fire'mark** a metal plate formerly placed by insurance companies to mark an insured building; **fire'-marshal** (*U.S.*), **fire'-master** the head of a fire brigade. — *adj.* **fire'-new** new from the fire: brand-new. — **fire'-office** a fire insurance office; **fire'-o'pal** a flame-coloured variety of opal; **fire'pan** a metal vessel for holding fire; **fire'place** the place in a house appropriated to the fire, as the opening of a chimney into a room; **fire'-plough** (*U.S. -plow*; *archaeol.*) a stick rubbed in a wooden groove to make fire; **fire'-plug** a hydrant for use against fires; **fire'-policy** a written instrument of insurance against fire; **fire'pot** (*hist.*) an earthen pot full of combustibles, used as a missile; **fire'-power** (*mil.*) the weight of missiles that can be fired with effect in a given time. — *adj.* **fire'proof** proof against fire: incombustible. — *v.t.* to render fireproof. — **fire'proofing; fire'-raiser** an incendiary; **fire'-raising** arson. — *adjs.* **fire'-resist'ant, fire'-resist'ing** immune to effects of fire up to a required degree. — **fire'-risk**. — *adj.* **fire'-robed** (*Shak.*) robed in fire. — **fire'screen** a screen for intercepting the heat of a fire; **fire'ship** a ship carrying combustibles sent among the enemy's ships; **fire'-shovel** a shovel for the side of the fireplace: the hearth: home. — *adj.* domestic: familiar. — **fire station** a place where fire-engines, firemen, etc. are kept in readiness to attend a fire; **fire'-step, fir'ing-step** a ledge on which soldiers stand to fire over a parapet: a banquette; **fire'-stick** a primitive implement for getting

fire by friction; **fire'stone** a rock, esp. a sandstone, that stands much heat without injury; **fire'-storm** a huge blaze (esp. a result of heavy bombing) which fans its own flames by creating its own draught (also *fig.*); **fire'thorn** pyracantha; **fire'-trap** a building, etc. inadequately provided with fire exits and fire-escapes; **fire'-tube** a tube through which fire passes; **fire'-walk, -ing** the (religious) ceremony of walking barefoot over hot stones, ashes, etc.; **fire'-walker; fire'-warden** (*U.S.*) an official charged with prevention and extinction of fires; **fire'-watcher** one who watches against fire; **fire'-watching; fire'-water** ardent spirits; **fire'weed** the rosebay willow-herb, which springs up after forest, etc., fires; **fire'woman** a female fire-fighter; **fire'wood** wood for fuel; **fire'work** a combustible or explosive composition used in warfare, or a projectile carrying it (*obs.*): a contrivance for producing sparks, jets, flares, or glowing pictorial designs in fire for amusement: (now only in *pl.*) a display of these: (in *pl.*) a florid technical display in music, talk, etc.: (in *pl.*) a display of temper; **fire'worm** a glow-worm: a firefly; **fire'-worship** of fire: loosely, homage to fire (as among Parsees) as a symbol of deity but not itself a god; **fire'-worshipper; firing line** area or troops within range of the enemy for practical purposes; **firing party** a detachment told off to fire over a grave or shoot a condemned prisoner; **firing pin** a pin that strikes the detonator and explodes the cartridge in a rifle; **firing point** the temperature at which an inflammable oil takes fire spontaneously; **firing squad** a firing party, a detachment told off to shoot a condemned prisoner. — **catch, take fire** to become ignited: to become aroused about something; **fire and brimstone** hell — an exclamation of wrath or extreme irritation; **fire and sword** military devastation; **fire away** (usu. *imper.*; *coll.*) to go ahead: to begin; **fire in one's belly** ardour, passion,in speaking etc.: drive, ambition; **fire off** to discharge: to ask, utter in rapid succession; **fire out** (*Shak.*) to expel; **fire up** to start a fire: to fly into a passion; **go on fire** (*Scot.* or *Ir.*) to catch fire; **hang fire** see **hang; on fire** in a state of fiery combustion; **play with fire** to expose oneself to unnecessary risk: to treat lightly a situation which could prove dangerous; **St Anthony's fire** see **Anthony; St Elmo's fire** see **Saint; set on fire, set fire to** to ignite; **under fire** exposed to the enemy's fire: exposed to criticism. [O.E. *fȳr*; Ger. *Feuer*; Gr. *pȳr*.]

firk *fûrk, v.t.* to drive: to rouse: to whip or beat (*Shak.*). [O.E. *fercian*, to conduct.]

firkin *fûr'kin, n.* a measure equal to the fourth part of a barrel (*brewing*): 9 gallons (*brewing*): 56 lb. of butter. [With dim. suff. -*kin*, from Old Du. *vierde*, fourth.]

firlot *fûr'lət, n.* an old Scottish dry measure, the fourth part of a boll. [Earlier *ferthelot*; cf. O.N. *fiŏrthe hlotr*, fourth lot.]

firm[1] *fûrm, adj.* fixed: compact: strong: not easily moved or disturbed: unshaken: resolute: decided: (of prices, commodities, markets, etc.) steady, stable (*commerce*). — Also *adv.* — *v.t.* to make firm. — *v.i.* to become firm: to become stable or rise slightly (*commerce*). — *adj.* **firm'less** wavering. — *adv.* **firm'ly.** — *n.* **firm'ness.** — **firm'ware** (*comput.*) a set of software or similar instructions forming a more or less permanent and unerasable part of the computer's memory. — **firm down** to make (ground, etc.) firm or firmer; **firm up** (of prices, etc.) to firm (*commerce*): to make (a promise, etc.) firm or firmer. [O.Fr. *ferme* — L. *firmus*.]

firm[2] *fûrm, n.* the title under which a company transacts business: a business house or partnership. [It. *firma*, from L. *firmus*; see **farm.**]

firmament *fûr'mə-mənt, n.* the solid sphere in which the stars were thought to be fixed: the sky. — *adj.* **firmamental** (-*ment'l*). [L. *firmāmentum* — *firmus*, firm.]

firman *fûr'man*, or *fer-män', n.* a decree. [Pers. *fermān.*]

firmer (chisel) *fûr'mər (chiz'l)* a carpenter's or woodworker's wood-cutting chisel. [Fr. *fermoir*, an alteration of *formoir*, — *former*, to form.]

firn *firn*, or *fûrn*, *n.* snow on high glaciers while still granular. [Ger. *firn*, of last year; cf. obs. Eng. *fern*, former.]

firring. Same as **furring.**

first *fûrst*, *adj.* foremost: in front of or before all others: most eminent: chief: referring to the speaker or writer (*gram.*). — *n.* one who or that which is first or of the first class: a place in the first class: an academic degree of the first class: first gear. — *adv.* before anything or anyone else: for the first time. — *n.* **first'ling** the first produce or offspring, esp. of animals. — *adv.* **first'ly** in the first place. — **first'-aid'** treatment of a wounded or sick person before the doctor's arrival; **first'-aid'er.** — *adjs.* **first'-begott'en** begotten first: eldest; **first'-born** born first. — *n.* the first in the order of birth: the eldest child. — *adj.* **first'-class'** of the first class, rank, or quality. — **first'-day** Sunday; **first floor** (*adj.* **first'= floor**) see **floor**; **first'-foot'** (*Scot.*) the first person to enter a house after the beginning of the new year. — *v.t.* to visit as first-foot. — *v.i.* to go around making visits as first-foot. — **first'-foot'er; first'-fruit(s)'** the fruits first gathered in a season: first products or effects of anything: payment such as annates to a superior; **first gear** see **gear**. — *adj.* **first'-hand** obtained directly, or in order to obtain (information, etc.) directly, without an intermediary. — *adv.* **first-hand'**. — **first lady** the wife of the chief executive of a city, state, or country, esp. of the president of the U.S.A., or any woman chosen by him to carry out official duties as hostess, etc. (*U.S.*; often with *caps.*): a prominent or leading woman in any field, profession, etc.; **first lieutenant** in the Royal Navy, the executive officer, not necessarily a lieutenant, of a ship or naval establishment; **first light** the time when daylight first appears in the morning; **first name** Christian name, or the name that comes first in full name; **first'-night'** the first night of a performance; **first'-night'er** one who habitually goes to the theatre on first-nights; **first'-offend'er** one convicted for the first time. — *adjs.* **first'-past-the= post'** denoting or relating to a system of voting in which each voter casts only one vote, the candidate receiving the most votes being declared the winner; **first'-rate** of highest rate or excellence: pre-eminent in quality, size, or estimation. — *n.* a warship so rated. — *adv.* **first-rate'** excellently. — **first school** a school catering for those aged five to eight, nine or ten; **first strike** a pre-emptive disarming attack on an enemy, intended to destroy their nuclear weapons before they can be brought into use (*adj.* **first'-strike'**). — *adj.* **first'-time** immediate: carrying out an action, e.g. the purchase of a house, for the first time. — **first water** the first or highest quality, purest lustre — of diamonds and pearls (also *fig.*). — **at first** at the beginning, in the early stages, etc.; **first-class mail, post** mail sent at a higher rate to obtain quicker delivery; **first-day cover** an envelope with stamps postmarked on their first day of issue; **first degree burns, murder** see **degree; not know the first thing about** to know nothing about; **(the) first thing** before doing anything else. [O.E. *fyrst*, superl.; cf. *fore*, before.]

firth[1] *fûrth*, *n.* an arm of the sea, esp. a river-mouth. — Also **frith** (*frith*). [O.N. *fiörthr*; Norw. *fjord*.]

firth[2]. See **frith**[3].

fisc, fisk *fisk*, *n.* the state treasury: the public revenue: one's purse. — *adj.* **fisc'al** pertaining to the public treasury or revenue. — *n.* a treasurer (*obs.*): a public prosecutor, chief law officer of the crown (in the Holy Roman Empire (*hist.*): in Scotland, an officer who prosecutes in criminal cases in local and inferior courts — in full, **procurator-fiscal.** — **fiscal drag** the means by which the inland revenue automatically benefits from any increase in earned income without any actual increase in taxation rates; **fiscal year** (esp. *U.S.*) same as financial year. — **the fiscal question** free trade or protection. [L. *fiscus*, a basket, a purse.]

fisgig. See **fizgig.**

fish[1] *fish*, *n.* a vertebrate that lives in water and breathes through gills: loosely, any exclusively aquatic animal: fish flesh: a person, as in *queer fish:* a fish-dive: — *pl.* **fish** or **fish'es.** — *v.i.* to catch or try to catch or obtain fish, or anything that may be likened to a fish (as seals, sponges, coral, compliments, information, husbands, often with *for*): to serve the purpose of fishing. — *v.t.* to catch and bring out of water: to bring up or out from a deep or hidden place, obscurity or the like: to elicit (with *out*): to practice the fisher's craft in: to ransack: to hoist the flukes of. — *adj.* **fish'able.** — *ns.* **fish'er** one who fishes for sport or gain: an inappropriate name for the pekan or wood-shock; **fish'ery** the business of catching fish: a place for catching fish: right of fishing. — *adj.* **fish'ful** abounding in fish. — *v.t.* **fish'ify** (*Shak.*) to turn to fish. — *n.* **fish'iness.** — *adj.* **fish'ing** used in fishing. — *n.* the art or practice of catching fish: a fishing-ground or stretch of water where one fishes. — *adj.* **fish'y** consisting of fish: like a fish: abounding in fish: dubious, as a story: equivocal, unsafe. — **fish'ball, cake** a ball or cake of chopped fish and mashed potatoes, fried. — *adj.* **fish'-bell'ied** swelled out downward like the belly of a fish. — **fish'-bone; fish'-carv'er, fish'-trowel** a large flat implement for carving fish at table; **fish'-creel** an angler's basket: a fishwife's basket; **fish'-day** a day on which fish is eaten instead of meat; **fish('-dive')** (*slang*) a ballerina's leap on to a partner's outstretched arms; **fish eagle** a fish-eating eagle, *Haliaetus vocifer*, of central and southern Africa; **fish eaters** a knife and fork for eating fish with; **fish'erman** a fisher; **fisherman's luck** getting wet and catching no fish; **fisherman's ring** a signet ring, with the device of St Peter fishing, used in signing papal briefs; **fish'eye** (*slang*) an unfriendly, suspicious stare; **fish'eye lens** (*phot.*) an ultrawide-angle lens covering up to 180°; **fish'-fag** a woman who sells fish; **fish'-farm; fish'-farmer; fish'-farming** rearing fish in ponds or tanks; **fish'-fing'er** a fairly small oblong cake of fish coated in batter or bread-crumbs; **fish'-garth** an enclosure on a river for the preserving or taking of fish (also **fish'-weir**); **fish'-glue** isinglass, or any other glue made from the skins, air-bladders, etc. of fish; **fish'-god** a deity in form wholly or partly like a fish, like the Philistine Dagon; **fish'-guano** fishmanure; **fish'-guts; fish'-gutter; fish'-gutting; fish'= hatch'ery** a station for artificial rearing of fish; **fish'= hawk** osprey; **fish'-hook** a barbed hook for catching fish; **fish'ing-frog** the angler-fish; **fish'ing-ground** an area of water, esp. of the sea, where fish are caught; **fish'ing-line** a fine strong thread used (e.g. with a rod, hooks, etc.) to catch fish; **fish'ing-rod** a long slender rod to which a line is fastened for angling; **fish'ing= tack'le** tackle — nets, lines, etc. — used in fishing; **fish'-kett'le** a long oval dish for boiling fish; **fish'-knife** a knife with a broad, blunt-edged, usu. decorated blade for eating fish with: a broad-bladed knife for cutting and serving fish with; **fish'-ladd'er, fish'-way** an arrangement of steps and shelters for enabling a fish to ascend a fall, etc.; **fish'-louse** a copepod or other crustacean parasitic on fishes; **fish'-manure'** fish used as a fertiliser; **fish'-meal** dried fish ground to meal: (*Shak.*) a meal of fish: abstemious diet; **fish'monger** a dealer in fish. — *adj.* **fish'-net** woven as a fine net. — **fish'-oil** oil got from fishes and other marine animals; **fish'-packing** the process of canning fish; **fish'-pond** a pond in which fish are kept — formerly also **fish'-stew; fish'-sales'man** one who receives consignments of fish for sale by auction to retail dealers; **fish'-sauce** sauce proper to be eaten with fish; **fish'-scrap** fish or fishskins from which oil or glue has been extracted; **fish'skin** the skin of a fish: (also **fish'skin disease**) ichthyosis; **fish'-slice** a flat implement for carving fish at table: a broad, flat implement for turning fish, etc., in the frying-pan; **fish'-spear** a spear or dart for striking fish; **fish'-stew** a fish-pond; **fish stick** (*U.S.*) a fishfinger; **fish'-strainer** a metal colander for taking fish from a boiler. — *adj.* **fish'-tail** shaped like the tail of a fish. — *v.i.* to swing the tail of an aircraft from side to side to reduce speed while gliding downward; **fish'-torpē'do** a self-propelling torpedo; **fish'-way** a fish-ladder; **fish'-weir** a fish-garth; **fish'wife, fish'=woman** a woman who carries fish about for sale; **fish'yback** (*U.S.*) transportation of freight containers and trailers by ship or barge. — **a fish out of water** a person in an unaccustomed, unsuitable situation which makes him ill at ease; **big fish** (*slang*) an important or leading person; **drink like a fish** to drink to excess; **fish in troubled waters** to take advantage of disturbed times to further one's own interests; **have other fish to fry** to have something else to do or attend to; **make fish of one and flesh (or fowl) of another** to make invidious distinctions; **neither fish nor flesh (nor good red herring)** or **neither fish, flesh, nor fowl** neither one thing nor another; **odd fish** or **queer fish** a person of odd habits, or of a nature with which one is not in sympathy; **pretty kettle of fish** see **kettle**.   [O.E. *fisc*; Ger. *Fisch*; O.N. *fiskr*; L. *piscis*; Gael. *iasg*.]

fish² *fish, n.* a piece of wood placed alongside another to strengthen it (*naut.*): a counter for games. — *v.t.* to strengthen with a fish or fish-plate. — **fish'-joint** a joining by fish-plates; **fish'-plate** an iron plate used in pairs to join railway rails.   [Prob. Fr. *fiche*, peg, mark.]

fishgig. See **fizgig**.

fisk¹ *fisk*, (*obs.*) *v.i.* to frisk: to gad.   [Prob. a freq. of O.E. *fȳsan*, to hurry, or of *fȳsian*, to feeze.]

fisk². See **fisc**.

fisnomie *fiz'no-mi*, (*Shak.*) *n.* physiognomy.

fissile *fis'īl, -il, adj.* readily split: capable of nuclear fission. — *ns.* **fissility** (*-il'*) cleavableness; **fission** (*fish'-ən*) a cleaving: reproduction by dividing: the splitting of the nucleus of an atom into two roughly equal parts accompanied by great release of energy. — *adjs.* **fiss'ionable** capable of nuclear fission; **fiss'ive**. — *n.* **fissure** (*fish'ər*) an act of cleaving: a narrow opening — chasm, cleft, groove: a sulcus, esp. one of the furrows on the surface of the brain, as the longitudinal fissure separating the hemispheres. — *v.t.* to crack, cleave, divide. — *adj.* **fiss'ured** cleft, divided. — *adjs.* **fissicos'tate** (L. *costa*, rib) with divided ribs; **fissiling'-ual** (L. *lingua*, tongue) with cloven tongue. — *ns.* **fissip'arism** (L. *parĕre*, bring forth), **fissipar'ity**. — *adj.* **fissip'arous** reproducing by fission. — *adv.* **fissip'-arously**. — *adjs.* **fiss'ipěd, fiss'ipēde** (L. *pēs, pedis*, foot) with digits separate. — *n.* an animal with digits separate. — *adj.* **fissiros'tral** (L. *rōstrum*, beak) with deep-cleft or gaping beak. — **fission bomb** a bomb deriving its energy from atomic fission; **fission fungus** a bacterium; **fission reactor** a nuclear reactor in which nuclear fission takes place; **fission spectrum** the wide range of elements and isotopes formed in fission.   [L. *findĕre, fissum*, to cleave.]

fissle *fis'l*, (*Scot.*) *v.i.* to rustle.   [Imitative.]

fissure, fissured. See **fissile**.

fist *fist, n.* the closed or clenched hand: handwriting (*coll.*): an index (*print.*). — *v.t.* to strike or grip with the fist. — *ns.* **fist'ful** a handful; **fistiana** (*-ā'nə, -ā'nə*, *facet.*) anecdotes about boxing and boxers. — *adjs.* **fist'ic, -al** (*facet.*) pugilistic. — *n.* **fist'mele** (*-mēl*; **meal¹** in sense of *measure*) the breadth of a fist with the thumb extended, esp. as used as the measure of the correct distance between the string and the handle of a braced bow. — *adj.* **fist'y**. — **fist'icuff** a blow with the fist: (in *pl.*) boxing: (in *pl.*) a fight with fists; **fist'-law** the law of brute force. — **make a good, a reasonable, not a bad,** etc. **fist of** to do (something) fairly well, not badly, etc.   [O.E. *fȳst*; Ger. *Faust*.]

fistula *fist'ū-lə, n.* a narrow passage or duct: an artificially made opening (*med.*): a long narrow pipe-like ulcer (*path.*): a tube through which the wine of the eucharist was once sucked from the chalice — also *calamus*: — *pl.* **fist'ulae** (*-lē*), **fist'ulas**. — *adjs.* **fist'ular, fist'ulose, fist'ulous**.   [L. *fistula*, a pipe.]

fit¹ *fit, adj.* suitable: in suitable condition: meeting required standards: of suitable ability: convenient: be-

fitting: well trained and ready: in good condition: in good health. — *n.* success in fitting: adjustment and correspondence in shape and size: a thing (esp. a garment) that fits. — *v.t.* to make suitable or able: to alter or make so as to be in adjustment: to adjust: to piece together: to be suitable or becoming for: to be of such size and shape as to adjust closely to: to be in agreement or correspondence with: to furnish, supply: to drive by fits (*Shak.*). — *v.i.* to be suitable or becoming: to go into place with accurate adjustment to space: to be of such size and shape as to be able to do so: — *pr.p.* **fitt'ing**; *pa.t.* and *pa.p.* **fitt'ed**. — *adv.* **fit'ly** (*compar.* **fit'lier**; *superl.* **fit'liest**). — *ns.* **fit'ment** due (*Shak.*): something fitted to an end (*Shak.*): an article of furniture or equipment: a fitting; **fit'ness**. — *adj.* **fitt'ed** (of a cover, clothing, etc.) made, cut, sewn, etc. to fit exactly: (of a cupboard, etc.) constructed to fit a particular space and attached to, or built into, the wall of a room: (of a room) fully furnished with (matching) fitted cupboards, etc. — *n.* **fitt'er** he who, or that which fits or makes fit: one who fits on clothes: one who assembles the parts of a machine, etc. — *adj.* **fitt'ing** fit: appropriate. — *n.* anything used in fitting up, esp., in *pl.*, equipment accessories: a fixture: the work of a fitter: the act or time of trying on an article of clothing so that it can be adjusted to fit the wearer. — *adv.* **fitt'ingly**. — **fit'-out** outfit; **fitt'ing-out** a supply of things fit and necessary; **fitt'ing-shop** a shop in which pieces of machinery are fitted together; **fit'-up** temporary, improvised stage and properties (*theat.*): a frame-up, esp. by the police (*slang*). — **fit in** to find enough room or time for someone or something: to be, or cause to be, in harmony (with); **fit on** to try on: to try on a garment upon; **fit out** to furnish, equip; **fit up** to provide with fittings: to frame (*slang*).   [Origin obscure.]

fit² *fit, n.* a crisis (*obs.*): the approach of death (*Spens.*): a painful experience (*Spens.*): an attack of illness, esp. epilepsy: a convulsion or paroxysm: an access, temporary attack, or outburst of anything, as laughter: a sudden effort or motion: a mood or passing humour. — *v.t.* (*Shak.*), to wrench, cause to start, as by a fit. — *adj.* **fit'ful** marked by sudden impulses: capriciously intermittent: spasmodic. — *adv.* **fit'fully**. — *n.* **fit'-fulness**. — **fit of the face** a grimace; **fits and starts** spasmodic and irregular bursts of activity; **throw a fit** see under **throw¹**.   [O.E. *fitt*, a struggle.]

fit³ *fit, (arch.) n.* a song: a division of a poem, a canto: a strain. — Also **fitt, fitte, fytte**.   [O.E. *fitt*, a song.]

fitch¹ *fich, n.* vetch: in Isa. xxviii. 25, black cummin (*Nigella sativa*): in Ezek. iv. 9, spelt. [**vetch**.]

fitch² *fich, n.* a polecat: polecat fur: a paint-brush of polecat-hair: a small hog's-hair brush. — *ns.* **fitch'et, fitchew** (*fich'ōō*) the polecat or its fur.   [M.Du. *visse* and O.Fr. *fissle, fissau*, from the root of Du. *visse*, nasty.]

fitché, fitchée *fich'ā, (her.) adj.* cut to a point. — Also **fitch'y**.   [Fr. *fiché*, pa.p. of *ficher*, to fix.]

fitt, fitte. See **fit³**.

fitz- *fits-, pfx.* son of; used in England, esp. of the illegitimate sons of kings and princes, as *Fitzclarence*, etc.   [A.Fr. *fiz* (Fr. *fils*) — L. *fīlius*.]

five *fīv, n.* four and one: a symbol (5, v, etc.) representing that number: a group of five: a score of five points, strokes, etc.: a card with five pips: an article of the size so numbered: the fifth hour after midnight or midday: the age of five years. — *adj.* of the number five: five years old. — *adj.* and *adv.* **five'fold** in five divisions: five times as much: folded in five thicknesses. — *n.* **fiv'er** (*coll.*) a five-pound note: a five-dollar note (*U.S.*). — **Five Articles, Five Points** statements of the distinctive doctrines of the Arminians and Calvinists respectively — the former promulgated in 1610, the latter sustained by the Synod of Dort in 1619 (see **Calvinism**); **five'-a-side'** a form of association football played by five men on each side, instead of eleven. — Also *adj.* — *adj.* **five'-bar** having five bars. — **five-eighth'** (*Rugby*

football) a stand-off (*Austr.* and *N. Z.*): (**second five=eighth** an inside centre, a player positioned on the outside of the five-eighth (*N. Z.*); **five'finger(s)** a name for various plants (cinquefoil, oxlip, etc.): a starfish. — *adj.* **five'-finger** for five fingers, as a piano exercise. — **Five Nations** a confederacy of five northern Iroquoian Indian tribes. — *adj.* **five'-parted** in five parts: divided into five nearly to the base. — **five'pence.** — *adj.* **five'penny.** — **five'pins** a game with five 'pins', resembling ninepins and tenpins (*adj.* **five'pin** as in *fivepin bowling alley*). — *adj.* **five'-square** (*B.*) regularly pentagonal. — **five'-stones** the game of dibs or jacks played with five stones. — **bunch of fives** (*slang*) the fist; **five-day week** a week, five days of which are working days; **five-o'clock shadow** (*coll.*) the new growth of hair that becomes noticeable on a man's shaven face in the late afternoon; **five-pence, -penny piece** in Britain, a coin worth 5 pence (also **five'penny= piece'**). [O.E. *fíf*; Ger. *fünf*; Goth. *fimf*; W. *pump*; L. *quinque*; Gr. *pente, pempe*; Sans. *pañca*.]
fives[1] *fīvz*, (*Shak.*) *n.* Same as **vives.**
fives[2] *fīvz, n.pl.* a ball game played with the (gloved) hand (or a bat) in a walled court. [Origin obscure.]
fix *fiks, v.t.* to make firm or fast: to establish: to drive in: to settle: to make or keep permanent, solid, rigid, steady, or motionless: to fasten or attach: to put to rights, mend: to arrange, attend to (a matter; sometimes by means of trickery): to prepare: to prevent from causing further trouble (*slang*): to get even with (*slang*): to chastise (*slang*). — *v.i.* to settle or remain permanently: to become firm, stable or permanent. — *n.* a difficulty (*coll.*): a dilemma (*coll.*): the position of an aircraft as calculated from instrument readings: the establishment of one's position by any means: a shot of heroin or other drug (*slang*). — *adj.* **fix'able** capable of being fixed. — *v.t.* **fix'āte** to fix, make stable: to direct (the eyes) upon an object: to arrest the emotional development of (*psych.*). — *ns.* **fixā'tion** the act of fixing, or state of being fixed: steadiness, firmness: state in which a body does not evaporate: conversion of atmospheric nitrogen into a combined form: emotional arrest of personality, instinctive forces maintaining their earlier channels of gratification: loosely, an abnormal attachment, or an obsession; **fix'ātive** a fixing agent; **fix'āture** a gummy preparation for fixing the hair. — *adj.* **fixed** settled: not apt to evaporate: steadily directed: fast, lasting, permanent: not varying or subject to alteration: substantively for fixed stars (*Par. Lost* III, 481). — *adv.* **fix'edly.** — *ns.* **fix'edness; fix'er; fix'ing** the act or process of making fixed: arrangement: (in *pl.*) adjuncts, trimmings: (in *pl.*) equipment; **fix'ity** fixedness. — *adj.* **fix'ive.** — *ns.* **fix'ture** fixing: a movable that has become fastened to land or to a house: a fixed article of furniture: a thing or person permanently established in a place: a fixed or appointed time or event, as a horse-race; **fix'ure** (*Shak.*) stability, position, firmness. — **fixed air** the name given by Dr Joseph Black in 1756 to what in 1784 was named by Lavoisier carbonic acid; **fixed capital** see **capital; fixed charges** overheads such as interest payments, allowance for depreciation, and fixed costs, which do not vary with the volume of business done; **fixed costs** overheads such as rent and rates which do not vary with the volume of business done; **fixed idea** a monomania; **fixed income** one which does not increase or decrease, such as income from a fixed-interest investment. — *adj.* **fixed'-in'terest** having an invariable rate of interest. — **fixed odds** a betting method whereby a stated amount per unit stake is offered for a certain result or combination of results; **fixed oils** those which, on the application of heat, do not volatilise without decomposition. — *adj.* **fixed'=pen'alty** of or relating to an offence, such as illegal parking, the penalty for which is invariable and obligatory, e.g. a fine which may be imposed and paid without the offender appearing in court. — **fixed satellite** a geostationary satellite; **fixed stars** stars

which appear always to occupy the same position in the heavens — opp. to *planets.* — **fixed-wheel bicycle** a bicycle in which the pedals are so connected to the back wheel that free-wheeling is impossible, and on which only the front wheel has a conventional brake; **fixed-wing aircraft** an aircraft in which the wings are attached to the fuselage, as opposed to e.g. a helicopter with rotating 'wings' or propellers; **fix on** to single out, decide for; **fix up** to arrange or make arrangements for: to settle: to put to rights, attend to. [L. *fīgĕre, fīxus*, to fix, prob. through L.L. *fīxāre.*]
fizgig, fisgig *fiz'gig, n.* a giddy girl: a firework of damp powder: a gimcrack, a crotchet: a harpoon (also **fish'gig**): (**fiz'gig**; also **fizz'gig**) a police informer (*Austr. slang*). [**gig.**]
fizz, fiz *fiz, v.i.* to make a hissing or sputtering sound: (also **be fizzing**) to be very angry (*coll.*): — *pr.p.* **fizz'ing**; *pa.t.* and *pa.p.* **fizzed.** — *n.* a sputtering sound: a frothy drink, esp. champagne. — *n.* **fizz'er** that which fizzes: anything excellent (*coll.*): a very fast ball. — *n.* and *adj.* **fizz'ing.** — *v.i.* **fizz'le** to hiss or sputter: to go out with a sputtering sound (often with *out*): to come to nothing, be a fiasco, fail (often with *out*). — *n.* an abortive effort. — *adj.* **fizz'y.** [Formed from the sound.]
fizzen, fizzenless. See **foison.**
fjord. Same as **fiord.**
flabbergast *flab'ər-gäst*, (*coll.*) *v.t.* to stun, confound. [Prob. conn. with **flabby** and **gast**, to astonish.]
flabby *flab'i, adj.* soft, yielding: hanging loose. — *ns.* **flab** (*coll.*) excess body fat; **flabb'iness.** [**flap.**]
flabellum *fla-bel'əm, n.* a fan, anciently used to drive away flies from the chalice during the celebration of the eucharist: a fan-like structure (*biol.*). — *adj.* **flabell'ate** fan-shaped. — *n.* **flabellation** (*flab-ə-lā'shən*) the action of fanning. — *adj.* **flabell'iform.** [L., a fan.]
flaccid *flak'sid, fla'sid, adj.* limp: flabby: lax: easily yielding to pressure: soft and weak: clammy. — *adv.* **flac'cidly.** — *ns.* **flac'cidness, flaccid'ity.** [L. *flaccidus* — *flaccus*, flabby.]
flack *flak*, (*U.S. slang*) *n.* a person who handles publicity and public relations: a press agent. [Origin uncertain; possibly from **flak.**]
flacker *flak'ər*, (*dial.*) *v.i.* to flap, flutter. [Cf. O.E. *flacor*, fluttering.]
flacket *flak'it, n.* a flask, bottle. [O.Fr. *flasquet.*]
flacon *flak-5', n.* a scent-bottle, etc. [Fr.]
flaff *flaf*, (*Scot.*) *v.i.* to flap: to pant. — *n.* a flutter of the wings: a puff. — *v.i.* **flaff'er** to flutter. [Imit.]
flag[1] *flag, v.i.* to droop: to flap feebly: to grow languid or spiritless: — *pr.p.* **flagg'ing**; *pa.t.* and *pa.p.* **flagged.** — *n.* **flagg'iness.** — *adj.* **flagg'y** limp, drooping: flabby. [Perh. O.Fr. *flac* — L. *flaccus*; prob. influenced by imit. forms as **flap.**]
flag[2] *flag, n.* an iris: reed-grass (*B.*). — *n.* **flagg'iness.** — *adj.* **flagg'y** abounding in flags. — **flag'-basket** a reed basket for tools; **flag'-worm** a worm or grub bred among flags or reeds. [Ety. obscure; cf. Du. *flag.*]
flag[3] *flag, n.* a piece usually of bunting with a design, used as an emblem for military or naval purposes, signalling, decoration, display, propaganda, etc.: a conspicuous sign to mark a position, e.g. of a golf-hole, or convey information, as that a taxi is disengaged: a flagship: a bushy tail. — *v.i.* to indicate, inform by flag-signals. — *v.t.* to decorate with flags: to inform by flag-signals: to mark (e.g. a passage or item in a book) for attention, by means of a bookmark, pen or pencil mark, etc.: to indicate or code (material on computer tape, etc.) so that particular items or classes of data may be found or extracted. — *adj.* **flagg'y** like a banner: spreading. — **flag'-cap'tain** the captain of a flagship; **flag'-day** a day on which collectors levy contributions to a fund in exchange for small flags as badges to secure immunity for the rest of the day: in U.S. the 14th of June, anniversary of the adoption of the Stars and Stripes; **flag'-lieuten'ant** an officer in a flagship, corresponding to an aide-de-camp in the

army; **flag'-off'icer** a naval officer privileged to carry a flag denoting his rank — admiral, vice-admiral, rear-admiral, or commodore; **flag'ship** the ship carrying an admiral and flying his flag: anything of a similar level of importance or pre-eminence (*fig.*); **flag'pole, flag'staff, flag'stick** a pole, etc., for displaying a flag; **flag'-wagging** signalling by flag: aggressive patriotism or imperialism (also **flag'-waving**); **flag'-waver. — black, red, white, yellow flag** see **black, red, white, yellow; dip the flag** to lower the flag and then hoist it — a token of respect; **flag down** to signal (e.g. a car) to stop; **flag of convenience** a foreign flag under which a shipping company registers its tonnage to avoid taxation or other burdens at home; **flag of distress** a flag displayed as a signal of distress — usually upside down or at half-mast; **flag of truce** a white flag displayed during war when some pacific communication is desired; **show, carry, the flag** to put in an appearance, or otherwise ensure that one, or the nation, firm, etc. one represents, is not overlooked; **strike** or **lower the flag** to pull down the flag as a token of relinquishment of command, respect, submission, or surrender. [Origin unknown; cf. Dan. *flag*; Du. *vlag*, Ger. *Flagge*.]

flag⁴ *flag, n.* a stone that separates in slabs: a flat paving-stone. — *v.t.* to pave with flagstones. — *n.* **flagg'ing** flagstones: a pavement thereof. — *adj.* **flagg'y. — flag'stone.** [O.N. *flaga*, a slab.]

flagellum *fla-jel'əm, n.* a scourge: a long runner (*bot.*): a long cilium or whip-like appendage (*biol.*): — *pl.* **flagell'a. — *n.pl.* Flagellata** (*flaj-ə-lā'tə*) unicellular organisms with flagella. — *v.t.* **flag'ellate** to scourge. — *n.* any member of the Flagellata. — *adj.* having a flagellum or flagella. — *adjs.* **flag'ellated; flag'ellant** scourging. — *n.* one who scourges, esp. himself in religious discipline. — *ns.* **flag'ellantism; flagellā'tion; flag'ellātor.** — *adjs.* **flag'ellatory; flagellif'erous; flagell'iform.** — *n.* **flagellōmā'nia** enthusiasm for beating and flogging. — *n.* and *adj.* **fla'gellōmā'niac.** [L. *flagellum*, dim. of *flagrum*, a whip.]

flageolet¹ *flaj-ō-let', flaj', n.* a small fipple-flute. [Fr., dim. of O.Fr. *flageol, flajol*, a pipe; not L. *flauta*, flute.]

flageolet² *flaj-ō-let', n.* a variety of kidney bean. [Corr. of Fr. *fageolet*; L. *faseolus*.]

flagitate *flaj'i-tāt, v.t.* to entreat, importune. — *n.* **flagitā'tion.** [L. *flagitāre, -ātum.*]

flagitious *flə-jish'əs, adj.* grossly wicked: guilty of enormous crimes. — *adv.* **flagi'tiously.** — *n.* **flagi'tiousness.** [L. *flāgitiōsus — flāgitium,* a disgraceful act — *flagrāre,* to burn.]

flagon *flag'ən, n.* a large, esp. wide, bottle: a liquor-jug. [Fr. *flacon* — *flascon* — L.L. *flascō, -ōnis*; see **flask**.]

flagrant *flā'grənt, adj.* burning or raging (*arch.*): notorious: outrageous, conspicuous. — *ns.* **flā'grance, flā'grancy.** — *adv.* **flā'grantly.** [L. *flagrāns, -antis,* pr.p. of *flagrāre,* to burn.]

flagrante bello *flə-gran'tē be'lō, fla-gran'te,* (L.) while war is raging; **flagrante delicto** *di-lik'tō, dā-lik'tō,* in the very act (lit. 'while the crime is blazing').

flail *flāl, n.* an implement for threshing corn, consisting of a wooden bar (the *swingle*) hinged or tied to a handle: a mediaeval weapon with spiked iron swingle. — *v.t.* to strike with, or as if with, a flail. — Also *v.i.* [O.E. *fligel,* influenced by O.Fr. *flaiel,* prob. from L. *flagellum,* a scourge.]

flair *flār, n.* intuitive discernment: faculty for nosing out: popularly and loosely, a natural aptitude. [Fr., sense of smell — *flairer,* to smell — L.L. *flagrāre* — L. *fragrāre,* to emit a smell.]

flak *flak, n.* anti-aircraft protection, missiles, or fragments (*mil. slang*): adverse criticism: heated disagreement, dissension. — **flak jacket** a heavy protective jacket reinforced with metal. [Initials of Ger. *Flieger-* (or *Flug-*) *abwehrkanone,* anti-aircraft cannon.]

flake¹ *flāk, n.* a small flat scale or layer: a very small loose mass, as of snow: a spark or detached flame: a flash (*Spens.*). — *v.t.* to form into flakes. — *v.i.* to come off in flakes. — *n.* **flak'iness.** — *adj.* **flak'y** formed of, or tending to form, flakes: crazy, eccentric (*U.S. coll.*). — **flake'-white** the purest white lead for painting, made in the form of scales or plates. — **flake out** to collapse from weariness or illness. [Perh. conn. with O.N. *flōke,* flock of wool; O.H.G. *floccho.*]

flake² *flāk, n.* a movable hurdle for fencing: a stage hung over a ship's side for caulking, etc. (*naut.*): a frame or rack. [Cf. O.N. *flake*; Du. *vlaak.*]

flake³. Same as **fake¹.**

flam¹ *flam, n.* a whim (*arch.*): an idle fancy (*arch.*): a falsehood. — *v.t.* to deceive: to get, manage, etc. by deception. [Perh. **flim-flam** or **flamfew.**]

flam². Same as **flawn.**

flambé *fläm'bā, flä-bā, adj.* of a Chinese ceramic glaze, dense and iridescent with streaky colour effect (usu. red and blue) produced by irregular application or uneven firing: decorated with such a glaze: (also **flambéed** *fläm'bād*) in cookery, prepared or served with a dressing of flaming liquor, usu. brandy. [Fr., pa.p. of *flamber,* to flame, singe.]

flambeau *flam'bō, n.* a flaming torch: — *pl.* **flam'beaux** or **-beaus** (*-bōz*). [Fr., — O.Fr. *flambe* — L. *flamma.*]

flamboyant *flam-boi'ənt, adj.* late French Gothic (15th–16th cent.) with flame-like tracery (*archit.*): of wavy form: gorgeously coloured: (of person, style, action, etc.) ostentatious, colourful. — *n.* (also **flamboy'ante**) a tropical tree of the Caesalpinia family (*Poinciana regia*) with flame-coloured flowers. — *ns.* **flamboy'ance, flamboy'ancy.** — *adv.* **flamboy'antly.** — **flamboy'ant(e)-tree.** [Fr., pr.p. of *flamboyer,* to blaze.]

flame *flām, n.* a gaseous matter undergoing combustion: the gleam or blaze of a fire: rage: ardour of temper: vigour of thought: warmth of affection: love or its object. — *v.i.* to burn as flame: to break out in passion. — *v.t.* to set aflame. — *adjs.* **flamed** (*Spens.*) inflamed; **flame'less.** — *n.* **flame'let** a small flame. — *adj.* **flam'ing** brilliantly red: gaudy: violent: furious: flagrant: often used intensively or to express irritation, etc. (*coll.*). — *adv.* **flam'ingly.** — *n.* **flammabil'ity.** — *adjs.* **flamm'able** inflammable; **flammif'erous** producing flame; **flam'y** pertaining to, or like, flame. — *adj.* **flame'-coloured** of the colour of flame, bright reddish-yellow. — **flame'-leaf** Poinciana; **flame'-thrower** an apparatus for throwing jets of flame in warfare; **flame'-tree** a thick-stemmed Australian tree, *Brachychiton acerifolium,* with glossy leaves and scarlet bell-shaped flowers: applied to various other trees — the flamboyant-tree (q.v.), the yellow-flowered *Acacia farnesiana* of S.W. U.S.A., the scarlet-flowered *Butea frondosa* of India and Burma, and the *Nuytsia floribunda* of western Australia which has orange flowers. [O.Fr. *flambe* — L. *flamma.*]

flamen *flā'mən, n.* in ancient Rome a priest of one particular god. — *adj.* **flamin'ical.** [L. *flāmen, -inis.*]

flamenco *flä-meng'kō, n.* a type of emotionally intense gypsy song, or the dance performed to it, from Andalusia: — *pl.* **flamen'cos.** [Sp., Flemish, gypsy.]

flamfew *flam'fū, n.* a fantastic trifle. [Fr. *fanfelue.*]

Flamingant *flä-mē-gä', n.* one who favours the Flemish language or Flemish nationalism. [Fr.]

flamingo *flə-ming'gō, n.* a tropical or subtropical bird of a pink or bright-red colour, with long legs and neck: — *pl.* **flaming'o(e)s.** [Sp. *flamengo* (now *flamenco*).]

flamm. See **flawn.**

flammability, flammable. See **flame.**

Flammenwerfer *fläm'ən-ver-fər,* (Ger.) *n.* a flame-thrower.

flammiferous. See **flame.**

flammule *flam'ūl, n.* a little flame, as in a picture of a Japanese god. — *adj.* **flamm'ūlated** ruddy. — *n.* **flammūlā'tion** flamelike marking. [L. *flammula,* dim. of *flamma,* flame.]

flan *flan, n.* a flat open tart. [See **flawn.**]

flanch¹ *flanch, flänch, -sh, n.* a flange: an ordinary formed on each side of a shield by the segment of a circle (*her.*).

— adj. **flanched** charged with a pair of flanches. [Prob. related to **flank**.]

flanch² *flanch, flänch, -sh,* **flaunch** *flönch, -sh, v.i.* to widen, esp. outwards or upwards, to flare (often with *out*). — *v.t.* to cause to slope in towards the top (often with *up*). — *n.* **fla(u)nch'ing** the action or state of the verb: **(flaunching)** a sloping piece of cement e.g. round the base of a chimney-pot. [Ety. obscure.]

flanconade *flang-kə-nād', (fencing) n.* a thrust in the flank or side. [Fr., from *flanc,* the side.]

flâneur *flä-nœr', n.* one who saunters about, a stroller. — *n.* **flânerie** *(flän-rē)* idling. [Fr. *flâner,* to lounge.]

flange *flanj, n.* a projecting or raised edge or flank, as of a wheel or of a rail. — *v.i.* to widen out. — *v.t.* to put a flange on. — *adj.* **flanged.** [Perh. conn. with **flank**.]

flank *flangk, n.* the side of an animal from the ribs to the thigh: the side or wing of anything, esp. of an army or fleet: a body of soldiers on the right or left extremity. — *v.t.* to be on, pass round, attack, threaten, or protect the flank of. — *n.* **flank'er** a fortification that commands the flank of an assailing force: one of the two outside men of the second row of the scrum (also **flank forward, wing forward;** *Rugby football*). — *v.t.* *(obs.)* to defend by flankers: to attack sideways. — **do, pull, work a flanker** *(slang,* orig. *mil.)* to trick, deceive, cheat, etc. someone. [Fr. *flanc.*]

flannel *flan'əl, n.* a light woollen textile used for clothing: the garment itself: a piece of this or other cloth used for washing or rubbing, now esp. a piece of towelling for washing the face, a face-cloth: flattery, soft-soap, words intended to hide one's ignorance, true opinions, etc. *(coll.):* (in *pl.*) trousers, esp. of flannel or a similar cloth. — *v.t.* to wrap in flannel: to rub with a flannel: to flatter, to soft-soap, to utter flannel *(coll.;* also *v.i.*). — *n.* **flannelette'** a cotton imitation of flannel. — *adjs.* **flann'elled; flann'elly.** — *n.* **flann'en** *(obs.* or *dial.*) flannel. — **flann'elboard, flann'elgraph** a board covered with flannel or felt, and letters, pictures, etc., backed with material which will stick when pressed against the board; **flann'el-flower** an Australian perennial plant with daisy-like flowers. [Poss. O.Fr. *flaine,* blanket, or Welsh *gwlanen — gwlan,* wool.]

flap *flap, n.* the blow or motion of a broad loose object: anything broad and flexible hanging loose, as material covering an opening: skin or flesh detached from the underlying part for covering and growing over the end of an amputated limb: a fluster, a panic *(coll.):* any surface attached to the wing of an aircraft which can be adjusted in flight to alter the lift as a whole: an 'r' sound produced by a single light tap of the tongue against the alveolar ridge or uvula *(phon.).* — *v.t.* to beat or move with a flap: to fluster. — *v.i.* to move, as wings: to hang like a flap: to get into a panic or fluster: — *pr.p.* **flapp'ing;** *pa.t.* and *pa.p.* **flapped.** — *adj.* **flapp'able** not unflappable, easily perturbed, agitated, irritated, flustered, etc. — *ns.* **flapp'er** one who or that which flaps: a flipper: a young wild duck or partridge: a girl nearing womanhood *(obs. slang):* in the 1920s, a flighty young girl *(slang);* **flapp'erhood.** — *adjs.* **flapp'erish; flapp'ing** moving with or like a flap: (of or pertaining to races, animals, etc.) not subject to Jockey Club or National Hunt Committee regulations *(horse-racing)* or not registered under the National Greyhound Racing Club *(greyhound racing).* — *n.* the action of the verb: racing at flapping meetings *(horse-racing, greyhound racing).* — **flap'doodle** the food of fools: gross flattery, etc.: nonsense; **flap'-dragon** a game in which small edibles, such as raisins, are snatched from burning brandy, and swallowed. — *adj.* **flap'-eared** *(Shak.).* — **flap'jack** a kind of broad, flat pancake *(Shak.* and *U.S.):* an apple-puff *(dial.):* a biscuit made with rolled oats and syrup: a flat face-powder compact. — *adj.* **flap'-mouthed.** — **flap'track, flapping track** a track for flapping. [Prob. imit.]

flare *flār, v.i.* to spread: to wave: to widen out bell-wise: to burn with a glaring, unsteady light: to glitter, flash: to blaze up, lit. or in anger (with *up*). — *v.t.* to display

glaringly: to dispose of (superfluous gas or oil) by means of a flare (with *off; chem engineering.*). — *n.* a widening out, as in the bell of a horn, a bowl, a skirt: an unsteady glare: an unshaded flame: a sudden blaze: a torch: a signalling light: (the flame or light produced by) a device composed of combustible material, activated to give warning, illumination, etc.: a device for the safe disposal of superfluous gas, oil, etc. by burning in the open *(chem. engineering).* — *adj.* **flār'ing.** — *adv.* **flā'ringly.** — *adj.* **flā'ry.** — **flare'-path** a path lit up to enable an aircraft to land or take off when natural visibility is insufficient; **flare stack** *(chem. engineering)* a tall chimney with an automatic igniter at the top, for the safe disposal of superfluous gas, etc.; **flare star** a star, usu. a red dwarf, which has a periodical sudden and unpredictable increase in brightness; **flare'-up** a sudden bursting into flame: a sudden outbreak of violence, anger, etc. [Poss. conn. with Norw. *flara,* to blaze.]

flaser *flä'zər, n.* irregular streaky lenticular structure developed in metamorphic rocks. [Ger., streak.]

flash¹ *flash, n.* a momentary gleam of light: a sudden, short-lived flare or flame: (the momentary illumination from) a flash-bulb *(phot.):* a sudden burst, as of merriment: a moment, an instant: a sudden rush of water: a board for deepening or directing a stream of water: a bright garter or ribbon worn on the hose with knickerbockers or kilt, a small portion showing below the knee: a distinctive mark on a uniform: a sticker or overprinted label on a piece of merchandise advertising a reduction in price, etc.: thieves' slang: a brief news dispatch by telegraph: in a film, a scene inserted by way of explanation or comment, especially a scene of the past, a flash-back: vulgar ostentation *(coll.):* a thin piece of metal at the sides of a forging, or a similar extrusion in other materials: excess material forced out of a mould. — *adj.* showy: vulgar: pertaining to the criminal class and its speech: fashionable *(arch.).* — *v.i.* to break forth, as a sudden light *(lit.* and *fig.):* to give forth flashes of light: to sparkle brilliantly: to blaze out: to break out into intellectual brilliancy: to burst out into violence: to move like a flash: to expose oneself indecently *(slang).* — *v.t.* to cause to flash: to expand, as blown glass, into a disc: to send by some startling or sudden means: to show briefly. — *n.* **flash'er** one who or that which flashes: a device for turning off and on lights as advertising, warning, etc. signs: the signs themselves: on a vehicle, a direction indicator: a person given to indecent exposure *(slang).* — *adv.* **flash'ily.** — *ns.* **flash'iness; flash'ing** the act of blazing: a sudden burst, as of water: (a method of producing) irregular colouring of bricks (by periodically stopping air supply in burning them, or other means): a strip put over a junction to make it watertight: the practice of indecently exposing oneself *(slang).* — *adj.* emitting flashes: sparkling. — *adj.* **flash'y** dazzling for a moment: showy but empty: vapid *(Milt.):* gaudy: tawdry. — **flash'-back, -forward** in a film, a scene of the past, future, inserted as comment or explanation: an echo of the past, vision of the future; **flash blindness** blindness caused by the flash of the explosion of a powerful bomb, etc.; **flash'-board** one of a set of boards set up at the sides of a water-channel to deepen it; **flash'-bulb** an oxygen-filled electric bulb in which aluminium or other foil or filament may be fired to provide a brilliant flash, esp. for illuminating a photographic subject; **flash burn** one sustained as the result of exposure to a flash of intense heat, e.g. from a nuclear explosion; **flash card** a card on which a picture or word is printed or written, to be shown briefly to a child as an aid to learning: one of a set of large brightly-coloured cards each held up by an individual in e.g. a sports stadium and together forming a picture or message; **flash'cube** a plastic cube containing four flash-bulbs, rotated as the film is wound on; **flash fire** a sudden, extensive (increase in) conflagration caused e.g. by flash-over; **flash flood** a sudden, severe, brief flood caused by a heavy rainstorm; **flash flooding; flash'-gun** device holding and firing a flash-bulb; **flash'-house** a brothel; **flash'light** a light that flashes periodically: a sudden light used to take photographs: an electric torch; **flash'-over** an electric discharge over the surface of an insulator (*elec. engineering*): instant combustion of material that has reached a high temperature (in a burning building, etc.) as soon as oxygen reaches it; **flash'-point** the temperature at which a liquid gives off enough inflammable vapour to flash when a light is applied to it: a point in the development of a tense situation when violent action takes place: a place in the world where an outbreak of hostilities may occur at any time as a result of tension. — **flash in the pan** see **pan; news'flash** brief preliminary dispatch about news just becoming known. [Prob. imit.; cf. Sw. dial. *flasa*, to blaze.]

flash² *flash*, (*obs.* or *dial.*) *n.* a pool, pond, marshy place. [Onomatopoeic; perh. infl. by Fr. *flache*, a hollow, pool.]

flask *fläsk, n.* a narrow-necked vessel for holding liquids: a bottle: a usu. flat pocket-bottle: a horn or metal vessel for carrying powder. — *n.* **flask'et** a vessel in which viands are served: a basket (*Spens.*). [O.E. *flasce;* Ger. *Flasche;* prob. from L.L. *flascō* — L. *vasculum,* a flask.]

flat *flat, adj.* smooth: level: wanting points of prominence or interest: monotonous: uniform: fixed, unvarying: vapid, no longer brisk or sparkling: defeated: failing of effect: dejected: downright, out-and-out, sheer: (of feet) having little or no arch: (of shoes) not having a raised heel: relatively low (*mus.*): below the right pitch (*mus.*): having flats in the key-signature (*mus.*): voiced (*phon.*): (of a battery) dead, unable to generate. — *n.* a level part: a plain: a tract covered by shallow water: something broad: a storey or floor of a house, esp. one, or part of one, used as a separate residence: the floor of a particular compartment (*naut.*): a flat piece of scenery slid or lowered on to the stage: an insipid passage: a simpleton, a dupe (*coll.*): a character (♭) that lowers a note a semitone (*mus.*): a note so lowered (*mus.*): a punctured tyre. — *adv.* in or to a flat position: evenly: too low in pitch: without qualification: exactly (used in giving time taken for e.g. a race). — *n.* **flat'let** a small flat of two or three rooms. — *advs.* **flat'ling, flat'lings, flat'long** (*Spens., Shak.*) with the flat side: flat side on: not edgewise: prostrate; **flat'ly.** — *n.* **flat'ness.** — *adj.* **flatt'ed** made flat: divided into flats. — *v.t.* **flatt'en** to make flat: to knock to the ground: to knock out: to amaze. — *v.i.* to become flat. — *n.* **flatt'ing** painting leaving a non-glossy finish. — *adj.* **flatt'ish** somewhat flat. — *adj.* or *adv.* **flat'ways, flat'wise** with or on the flat side. — **flat'back** a pottery figure with a flat back, designed to stand on a mantelpiece, etc. and so be viewed only from the front; **flat'boat** large flat-bottomed boat for floating goods downstream. — *adj.* **flat broke** (*coll.*) having no money whatsoever. — **flat'-cap** low-crowned cap worn by London citizens in 16th and 17th centuries: a London citizen or apprentice; **flat'-earth'er** one who maintains that the earth is flat; **flat'fish** marine fish that habitually lies on one side, with unsymmetrical flat body — flounder, turbot, etc.; **flat'-foot** condition in which arch of instep is flattened in a policeman (*slang*). — *adj.* **flat'-footed** having flat feet: resolute (*U.S.*): ponderous: unimaginative: uninspired: unprepared (*U.S.*). — **flat'=footedness.** — *adj.* **flat'head** having an artifically flattened head, as some American Indians (also *n.;* usu. with *cap.*). — *n.* (*U.S. slang*) a simpleton: any of various species of edible platycephalous fish of the Pacific and Indian Oceans; **flat'iron** an iron for smoothing cloth; **flat'mate** a person with whom one shares a flat; **flat'-race** a race over open or clear ground; **flat rate** a fixed uniform rate; **flat spin** rotation about a horizontal axis: confused excitement; **flat tyre** a punctured tyre: a dull and spiritless person (*U.S.*); **flat'ware** domestic cutlery: plates and saucers; **flat'worm** a tape-

worm or other member of the Platyhelminthes. — **flatten out** to bring an aeroplane into a horizontal position; **flat out** at full speed: using every effort; **that's flat** I tell you plainly; **the flat** the horse flat-racing season. [O.N. *flatr,* flat.]

flatter *flat'ər, v.t.* to treat with insincere praise and servile attentions: to please with false hopes or undue praise: to overpraise: to represent over-favourably: to coax: to please with belief: to gratify. — *n.* **flatt'erer.** — *adj.* **flatt'ering.** — *adv.* **flatt'eringly.** — *adj.* **flatt'erous** (*arch.*) flattering. — *adv.* **flatt'erously** (*arch.*). — *n.* **flatt'ery** exaggerated or insincere praise. [Conn. with O.Fr. *flater* (Fr. *flatter);* Gmc.; cf. O.N. *flathra.*]

flatus *flā'təs, n.* a puff of wind: a blast: a breath: gas generated in the stomach or intestines. — *ns.* **flatulence** (*flat'ū-ləns*), **flat'ulency** distension of stomach or bowels by gases formed during digestion: windiness: emptiness of utterance. — *adj.* **flat'ulent.** — *adv.* **flat'ulently.** — *adj.* **flat'uous.** [L. *flātus, -ūs,* a blowing — *flāre,* to blow.]

flaught¹ *flöt* (*Scot. flöhht*), *n.* a flight, a flapping. — *n.* **flaugh'ter** a fluttering motion. — *v.i.* to flutter, flicker. [Related to **flight.**]

flaught² *flöt* (*Scot. flöhht*), *n.* a flake: a hide: a gust: a flash: a spark: a turf. — *v.t.* to pare, skin, card. — *v.i.* **flaugh'ter** to cut turfs, etc. — *n.* a paring of turf. [Cf. **flake¹, flaw¹, flay¹.**]

flaunch. A variant of **flanch².**

flaune. See **flawn.**

flaunt *flönt, v.i.* to wave in the wind: to move ostentatiously: to carry a gaudy or saucy appearance. — *v.t.* to display ostentatiously. — *n.* (*Shak.*) anything displayed for show. — *n.* **flaunt'er.** — *adjs.* **flaunt'ing, flaunt'y.** — *adv.* **flaunt'ingly.** [Prob. Scand.]

flautist *flöt'ist, n.* a flute player. [It. *flautista.*]

flavescent *flə-,* *flā-ves'ənt, adj.* yellowish or turning yellow. [L. *flāvēscēns, -entis,* pr.p. of *flāvēscĕre,* to become yellow — *flāvus,* yellow.]

Flavian *flāv'i-ən, adj.* of or pertaining to *Flavius* Vespasian and his sons Titus and Domitian, the Flavian emperors of Rome (A.D. 69–96).

flavin *flā'vin,* **flavine** *flā'vēn, ns.* a yellow dye made from quercitron bark: any of various antiseptic substances, of which acriflavine is one. — *n.* **flavone** (*flā'vōn*) a crystalline compound occurring in certain plants, e.g. primroses: any of a class of yellow pigments derived from this. [L. *flāvus,* yellow.]

flavour *flā'vər, n.* that quality of anything which affects the smell or taste: a smack or relish: characteristic quality or atmosphere (*fig.*): in particle physics, any of the five, or probably six, types of quark. — *v.t.* to impart flavour to. — *adj.* **flā'vorous.** — *n.* **flā'vouring** any substance used to give a flavour. — *adjs.* **flā'vourless; flā'voursome.** — **flavour of the week, month,** etc. the favourite person or thing at a given time. [O.Fr. *flaur;* prob. influenced by **savour.**]

flaw¹ *flö, n.* a gust of wind: a sudden rush: an outburst of passion: uproar. [Cf. Du. *vlaag,* Sw. *flaga.*]

flaw² *flö, n.* a flake, fragment, splinter (*Shak.*): a break, a crack: a defect. — *v.t.* to crack or break. — *adjs.* **flawed; flaw'less; flaw'y.** [O.N. *flaga,* a slab.]

flawn, flaune *flön, flam, flamm* *flam,* (*arch.*) *ns.* a custard: a pancake. [O.Fr. *flaon* — L.L. *fladō, -ōnis,* — O.H.G. *flado.*]

flax *flaks, n.* the fibres of the plant Linum, which are woven into linen cloth: the plant itself. — *adjs.* **flax'en** made of or resembling flax: light yellow; **flax'y** like flax: of a light colour. — **flax'-bush, flax'-lil'y** a New Zealand plant (*Phormium*) of the lily family, yielding a valuable fibre, **New Zealand flax; flax'-comb** a toothed instrument or hackle for cleaning the fibres of flax; **flax'-dresser** one who prepares flax for the spinner by the successive processes of rippling, retting, grassing, breaking, and scutching; **flax'-mill** a mill for working flax into linen; **flax'-seed** linseed; **flax'-wench** a female who spins flax. — **purging flax** a small wild species of flax (*Linum catharticum*). [O.E. *flæx* (W.S. *fleax*); Ger. *Flachs*.]

flay[1] *flā, v.t.* to strip off the skin from: to flog: to subject to savage criticism: — *pr.p.* **flay′ing**; *pa.t.* and *pa.p.* **flayed**. — *n.* **flay′er**. — **flay′-flint** a skinflint. [O.E. *flēan*; O.N. *flā*, to skin.]

flay[2]. See **fley**.

flea *flē, n.* any of an order of wingless, very agile, blood-sucking insects. — *adj.* **flea′some**. — **flea′-bag** (*slang*) a sleeping-bag: a distasteful place, esp. used of lodgings; **flea′-bane** a name for various composite plants (Erigeron, Pulicaria, etc.) whose strong smell is said to drive away fleas; **flea′-beetle** a jumping beetle that infests various vegetables, e.g. turnips, cabbages; **flea′-bite** the bite of a flea: a small mark caused by the bite: a trifle (*fig.*). — *adj.* **flea′-bitten** bitten by fleas: mean (*fig.*): having small reddish spots on a lighter ground, esp. of horses. — **flea′-circus** a show of performing fleas; **flea market** (*coll.*) a shop, etc. selling second-hand goods, orig. esp. clothes; **flea′-pit** a public building, e.g. a cinema, supposedly infested with vermin. — **a flea in one's ear** a stinging rebuff. [O.E. *flēah*; cf. Ger. *Floh*, Du. *vloo*.]

fleam *flēm, n.* an instrument for bleeding cattle. [O.Fr. *flieme* (Fr. *flamme*) — Gr. *phlebotomon*, a lancet — *phleps, phlebos*, a vein, and *tomē*, a cut.]

flèche *flesh, n.* a spire: a slender spire rising from the intersection of the nave and transepts in some large churches: a parapet with two faces forming a salient angle at the foot of a glacis (*fort.*): a point on a backgammon board. [Fr., arrow.]

fléchette, flechette *flā-shet′, n.* a steel dart dropped or thrown from an aeroplane, esp. in World War I: a dart fired from a gun. [Fr., dart, dim. of *flèche*, arrow.]

fleck *flek, n.* a spot or speckle: a little bit of a thing. — *vs.t.* **fleck, fleck′er** to spot: to streak. — *adjs.* **flecked** spotted, dappled; **fleck′less** without spot. [O.N. *flekkr*, a spot; Ger. *Fleck*, Du. *vlek*.]

flection. A less acceptable spelling of **flexion**.

fled *fled, pa.t.* and *pa.p.* of **flee**.

fledge *flej, v.t.* to furnish with feathers or wings. — *v.i.* to acquire feathers for flying. — *adj.* (*Milt.*) **fledged**. — *n.* **fledg′ling** (*rarely* **fledge′ling**) a bird just fledged: a very immature or inexperienced person (also *fig.*). — *adj.* **fledg′y** (*Keats*) feathery. [M.E. *fligge, flegge* — an assumed O.E. (Kentish) *flecge*; cf. O.E. *unflycge*, unfledged; see **fly**.]

flee[1] *flē, v.i.* to run away, as from danger: to disappear. — *v.t.* to keep at a distance from: to run away from, leave hurriedly: — *pr.p.* **flee′ing**; *pa.t.* and *pa.p.* **fled**. — *n.* **flē′er**. [O.E. *flēon*; Ger. *fliehen*; not akin to *fly*, but influenced by it, the *f* representing an earlier *th*.]

flee[2] *flē, n.* and *v.i.* a Scots form of **fly**.

fleece *flēs, n.* a sheep's coat of wool: the wool shorn from a sheep at one time: anything like a fleece. — *v.t.* to shear: to plunder: to charge (a person) exorbitantly: to cover, as with wool. — *adjs.* **fleeced** having a fleece; **fleece′less**. — *n.* **fleec′er** one who strips, plunders or charges exorbitantly. — *adj.* **fleec′y** woolly: like a fleece. — **fleece′-wool** that cut from a sheep at any of its clippings subsequent to its first, or yearling, clipping. [O.E. *flēos*; Du. *vlies*, Ger. *Fliess*, now *Vlies*.]

fleech *flēch*, (*Scot.*) *v.t.* and *v.i.* to flatter, coax, beg. — *ns.* **fleech′ing, fleech′ment** [Origin obscure.]

fleer *flēr, v.i.* to make wry faces in contempt: to leer. — *v.t.* to mock. — *n.* mockery. — *n.* **fleer′er**. — *n.* and *adj.* **fleer′ing**. — *adv.* **fleer′ingly**. [Cf. Norw. *flira*, Sw. *flissa* to titter.]

fleet[1] *flēt, n.* a number of ships (birds, aircraft, motor-cars, etc.) in company or otherwise associated: a navy: a division of a navy under an admiral. [O.E. *flēot*, a ship — *flēotan*, to float; conn. with Du. *vloot*, Ger. *Flotte*.]

fleet[2] *flēt, adj.* swift: nimble: transient. — *adjs.* **fleet′-foot** (*Shak.*) fleet or swift of foot; **fleet′ly**. — *n.* **fleet′ness**. [Prob. O.N. *fliōtr*, swift; but ult. cog. with succeeding word.]

fleet[3] *flēt, v.i.* to float (*obs.*): to flow (*Spens.*): to flit, pass swiftly. — *v.t.* (*Shak.*) to make to pass quickly. — *adj.* (*dial.*) shallow. — *adj.* **fleet′ing** passing quickly: temporary. — *adv.* **fleet′ingly**. [O.E. *flēotan*, to float.]

fleet[4] *flēt, n.* a shallow creek, bay, brook or drain, as in North*fleet*, *Fleet*-ditch, etc. — **Fleet Prison** or **the Fleet** a London gaol down to 1842, near the Fleet river, long a place of confinement for debtors — clandestine marriages were solemnised here down to 1754 by **Fleet parsons**, broken-down clergymen confined for debt; **Fleet Street** journalism or its ways and traditions, from the street near the Fleet with many newspaper offices. [O.E. *flēot*, an inlet.]

fleg *fleg*, (*Scot.*) *n.* a fright. — *v.t.* to frighten. [O.E. *flecgan*, to put to flight.]

fleme *flēm*, (*Scot.*) *v.t.* to put to flight: — *pa.t.* and *pa.p.* **flēm′it**. [O.E. *flieman*.]

Flemish *flem′ish, adj.* of or belonging to the Flemings, or Flanders. — *n.* the Flemings as a people: one of the two languages of Belgium, virtually identical with Dutch. — *v.t.* (without *cap.*; *naut.*) to flemish down. — *n.* **Flem′ing** a native of Flanders: a Flemish-speaking Belgian. — **Flemish bond** a bricklayer's bond of alternate headers and stretchers in every course; **Flemish coil** (*naut.*) a flat coil of rope with the end in the centre; **flemish down** (*naut.*) to stow (a rope) in a Flemish coil; **Flemish school** a school of painting formed by the brothers Van Eyck, reaching its height in Rubens, Vandyck, and Teniers; **Flemish stitch** a stitch used in making certain kinds of point-lace. [Du. *Vlaamsch*.]

flench *flench*, **flense** *flens*, **flinch** *flinch, vs.t.* to cut up the blubber of, as a whale: to flay. [Dan. *flense*.]

flesh *flesh, n.* muscular tissue: all the living substance of the body of similar composition to muscle: the soft substance that covers the bones of animals: animal food: the bodies of beasts and (sometimes) birds, not fish: the body, not the soul: animals, or animal nature: human bodily nature: mankind: kindred: bodily appetites: the soft substance of fruit, esp. the part fit to be eaten. — *v.t.* to reward with flesh: to train to an appetite for flesh, as dogs for hunting: to inure: to glut: to use upon flesh, as a sword: to use for the first time: to gratify with fleshly indulgence: to put flesh upon: to scrape flesh from. — *adj.* **fleshed** (*flesht*) having flesh: fat. — *ns.* **flesh′er** an instrument for scraping hides: a butcher (esp. *Scot.*); **flesh′hood** (*Mrs Browning*) the state of being in the flesh; **flesh′iness**. — *n.pl.* **flesh′ings** actors' flesh-coloured tights. — *adj.* **flesh′less** without flesh: lean. — *ns.* **flesh′liness; flesh′ling** a sensualist. — *adj.* **flesh′ly** corporeal: carnal: not spiritual. — Also *adv.* — *n.* **flesh′ment** (*Shak.*) the act of fleshing or initiating: excitement arising from success. — *adj.* **flesh′y** fat: pulpy: plump. — **flesh′-broth** broth made by boiling flesh; **flesh′-brush** a brush used for rubbing the skin to excite circulation; **flesh′-colour** the normal colour of the skin of a European; **flesh′-eater**; **flesh′-fly** a fly (esp. Sarcophaga) whose larvae feed on flesh; **flesh′-hook** a hook for drawing flesh from a pot; **flesh′-market**; **flesh′-meat** flesh of animals used for food; **flesh′-monger** one who deals in flesh: a whoremonger (*Shak.*): a procurer, a pimp, a slave-dealer; **flesh′-pot** a pot or vessel in which flesh is cooked: abundance of flesh: (usu. in *pl.*) high living; **flesh′= pottery** sumptuous living; **flesh′-tint** a tint or colour that represents the human body; **flesh′worm** a worm or maggot that feeds on flesh; **flesh′-wound** a wound not reaching beyond the flesh. — **an arm of flesh** human strength or help; **flesh and blood** bodily or human nature; **flesh out** to give substance to, elaborate on (an idea, etc.); **in flesh** in good condition: fat; **in the flesh** in bodily life, alive: incarnate: in person, actually present; **make someone's flesh creep** to arouse a feeling of horror in someone; **one flesh** united in marriage; **one's own flesh and blood** one's own kindred; **proud= flesh** see **proud**. [O.E. *flǣsc*; cog. forms in all Gmc. languages; Ger. *Fleisch*, etc.]

fletch *flech, v.t.* to feather. — *n.* **fletch′er** one who makes

fletton 543 **flip**

arrows. [Fr. *flèche*, an arrow, O.Fr. *flecher*, a fletcher.]

fletton *fle'tən, n.* a type of brick made near *Fletton* in Cambridgeshire, of a mottled yellow and pink colour, with sharp arrises.

fleur-de-lis, -lys *flær-də-lē', -lēs', n.* the iris: an ornament and heraldic bearing of disputed origin (an iris, three lilies, etc.), borne by the kings of France: — *pl.* **fleurs-de-lis, fleurs-de-lys** (*flær-*). — Also **flower(-)delice, flower-de-luce, flower(-)dcluce.** *ns.* **fleuret** (*flŏŏr'ət*) an ornament like a small flower (also **fleurette** *flæ-ret'*): (*-et'*) a fencing foil; **fleuron** (*flæ-rɔ̃*) a flower-like ornament, in architecture, printing, etc. — *adj.* **fleury** (*flŏŏ'ri*) having fleurs-de-lis — also **flo'ry.** — **fleur de coin** (*kwɛ̃*) mint condition of a coin. [Fr.; *lis,* being O.Fr. *liz* — L. *lilium,* lily.]

flew[1] *flŏŏ, pa.t.* of **fly**; coll. used for **fled** (*pa.t.*).

flew[2] *flŏŏ, n.* a dog's pendulous chop (usu. in *pl.*). — *adj.* **flewed** (*Shak.*). [Ety. unknown.]

flew[3]. See **flue**[3].

flex *fleks, v.t.* and *v.i.* to bend. — *n.* a bending: a flexible cord or line, esp. of insulated wire. — *n.* **flexibil'ity.** — *adj.* **flex'ible** easily bent: pliant: docile. — *n.* **flex'ibleness.** — *adv.* **flex'ibly.** — *n.pl.* **flex'ihours** hours of working under flexitime. — *adj.* **flex'ile** (*-īl, -əl*) flexible. — *ns.* **flexion** (*flek'shən*) a bend: a fold: the action of a flexor muscle: inflexion (*gram.*); **flex'itime, Flex'-time**® a system of flexible working hours in which an agreed total of hours may be worked at times to suit the worker, often with the proviso that each day certain hours (**core times**) are included; **flexog'raphy** (Gr. *graphein,* to write) (printed matter, esp. on plastic, produced by) a method of rotary printing using flexible rubber plates and spirit-based inks; **flex'or** a muscle that bends a joint, as opposed to *extensor.* — *adjs.* **flex'ūose, flex'ūous** full of windings and turnings: undulating; **flexural** (*flek'shər-əl*). — *n.* **flex'ure** a bend or turning: the curving of a line or surface (*math.*): the bending of loaded beams: obsequious bowing (*Shak.*). — **flexible disc** (*comput.*) a floppy disc. — **flex one's muscles** to cause the muscles of one's arms, shoulders, etc. to contract, in order to display them, test them as a preliminary to a trial of strength, etc. (often *fig.*). [L. *flectĕre, flexum,* to bend.]

fley, flay *flā, v.t.* (*Scot.*) to cause to flee: to frighten. — *v.i.* to be frightened. [M.E. *flayen* — O.E. *flēgan* (as in compound *āflēgan, āflīegan,* to put to flight); cf. O.N. *fleyja,* Goth. *flaugjan.*]

flibbertigibbet *flib'ər-ti-jib'it, n.* a flighty person: an imp. [Poss. imit. of meaningless chatter.]

flic *flēk,* (Fr.; *slang*) *n.* a policeman.

flichter *flihh'tər,* (*Scot.*) *n.* a flutter. — *v.t.* and *v.i.* to flutter, quiver.

flick[1] *flik, v.t.* to strike lightly, as with a lash or a finger-nail. — *n.* a stroke of this kind. — **flick'-knife** a knife the blade of which springs out on pressure of a button in the handle. — **flick through** to turn the pages of (a book, etc.) idly, or in order to get a rough impression of it. [Echoic.]

flick[2] *flik,* (*slang*) *n.* a cinematograph film: (*pl.*) a cinematograph performance. [**flicker**[1].]

flicker[1] *flik'ər, v.i.* to flutter and move the wings, as a bird: to burn unsteadily, as a flame. — *n.* an act of flickering, a flickering movement or light. — *adv.* **flick'eringly.** — **flick'ertail** (*U.S.*) a ground-squirrel. [O.E. *flicorian;* imit.]

flicker[2] *flik'ər, n.* an American woodpecker. [Echoic.]

flier, flies. See under **fly.**

flight[1] *flīt, n.* a passing through the air: a soaring: distance flown: a sally or digression, e.g. of imagination, fancy: a series of steps: a flock of birds flying together: the birds produced in the same season: a volley: a long-distance arrow (*Shak.*): the power of flying: the art or the act of flying with wings or in an aeroplane or other machine: a unit of the air-force answering to a platoon in the army: a regular air journey, numbered and at a fixed time: a line of hurdles across a race-track. — *v.t.*

to cause (birds) to fly up: to shoot (wildfowl) in flight: to put a feather in (an arrow): to impart a deceptive trajectory to (a cricket ball). — *v.i.* of birds, to rise or migrate in a flock. — *adj.* **flight'ed** (*Milt.*) flying. — *adv.* **flight'ily.** — *n.* **flight'iness.** — *adjs.* **flight'less** without power of flying; **flight'y** swift (*Shak.*): fanciful: changeable: giddy-minded. — **flight crew** the members of an aircraft crew whose responsibility is operation and navigation; **flight'-deck** the deck of an aircraft-carrier where the planes take off or land: the compartment for the crew in an aircraft; **flight'-feather** a quill of a bird's wing; **flight'-lieuten'ant** an Air Force officer of rank corresponding to naval lieutenant or army captain; **flight path** the course (to be) taken by an aircraft, spacecraft, etc.; **flight plan** a statement of the proposed schedule of an aircraft flight; **flight'-recorder** a device which records on tape or wire information about the functioning of an aircraft and its systems. — **flight of fancy** an instance of rather free speculation or indulgence in imagination; **in the first, top, flight** in the highest class. [O.E. *flyht* — *flēogan,* to fly.]

flight[2] *flīt, n.* an act of fleeing. — **take (to) flight** to flee: to disappear quickly (*fig.*). [Assumed O.E. *flyht;* cf. *flēon,* to flee.]

flim-flam *flim'flam, n.* a trick, deception: idle, meaningless talk: nonsense. [Cf. **flam.**]

flimp *flimp,* (*slang*) *v.t.* to rob while a confederate hustles. [Cf. West Flem., *flimpe,* knock, rob.]

flimsy *flim'zi, adj.* thin: without solidity, strength, or reason: weak. — *n.* transfer-paper: a bank-note (*slang*): reporters' copy written on thin paper: a carbon copy on thin paper. — *adv.* **flim'sily** in a flimsy manner. — *n.* **flim'siness.** [First in 18th century; prob. suggested by **film.**]

flinch[1] *flinch, -sh, v.i.* to shrink back, from pain, fear, etc.: to fail. — *n.* **flinch'er.** — *n.* and *adj.* **flinch'ing.** — *adv.* **flinch'ingly.** [Prob. conn. with M.E. *fleechen,* O.Fr. *flechir,* L. *flectĕre,* to bend.]

flinch[2]. Same as **flench.**

flinder *flin'dər, n.* a splinter or small fragment — usually in *pl.* [Norw. *flindra,* a splinter.]

Flindersia *flin-dûr'si-ə, n.* an Australian genus of valuable trees of the *Rutaceae:* (without *cap.*) any tree of this genus. — **Flinders grass** a native pasture grass of Australia. [From the explorer, Matthew *Flinders,* 1774–1814.]

fling *fling, v.t.* to throw, cast, toss: to dart: to send forth: to send suddenly: to cause to fall. — *v.i.* to throw the body about: to kick out: to dash or rush, throw oneself impetuously: to throw missiles: — *pr.p.* **fling'ing;** *pa.t.* and *pa.p.* **flung.** — *n.* a cast or throw: a try: a passing attack: a jibe: a taunt: complete freedom, full enjoyment of pleasure: a lively Scottish country-dance. — *n.* **fling'er.** — **fling mud at** see **mud; fling out** to break out in impetuous plain-speaking; **fling to the winds** see **wind**[1]**; full fling** at the utmost speed, recklessly. [Cf. O.N. *flengja;* Sw. *flänga.*]

flint *flint, n.* a hard mineral, a variety of quartz, from which fire is readily struck with steel: a concretion of silica: a piece of flint, esp. one used for striking fire, or one manufactured into an implement before (or after) the use of metals: anything proverbially hard: a tailor or other worker demanding full union rates of pay (opp. to *dung,* one submitting to low rates; *obs. slang*). — *adj.* made of flint: hard. — *v.t.* **flint'ify** to turn to flint. — *adv.* **flint'ily.** — *n.* **flint'iness.** — *adj.* **flint'y** consisting of, abounding in, or like flint: hard: cruel: obdurate. — **flint'-glass** a very fine and pure lead glass, originally made of calcined flints. — *adjs.* **flint'-heart, -ed** (*Shak.*) having a hard heart. — **flint'-knapp'er** one who flakes or chips flints; **flint'-knapp'ing; flint'lock** a gunlock or gun with a flint. [O.E. *flint;* Dan. *flint;* Gr. *plinthos,* a brick.]

flip *flip, v.t.* and *v.i.* to fillip: to flick: to flap. — *n.* a fillip: a flick: a hot drink of beer and spirits sweetened, or similar concoction: a trip in an aeroplane, a pleasure-flight (*coll.*). — *adj.* flippant: pert, over-smart. — *n.*

For other sounds see detailed chart of pronunciation.

flipp'er a limb adapted for swimming: a hand (*coll.*): a rubber foot-covering imitating an animal's flipper, worn by swimmers, divers, etc. — *adj.* and *adv.* **flipp'ing** (*coll.*) nasty, unpleasant: often used intensively or meaninglessly. — **flip'-dog** an iron for heating flip. — *adv.* **flip'-flap', flip'-flop'** with repeated flapping. — *n.* a coster's dance: a form of somersault: a cracker: the sound of regular footfalls: a flighty woman: a revolving apparatus for public amusement. — **flip'flop** orig., and still in U.S. and in computing, a bistable pair of valves, transistors or circuit elements, two stable states being switched by pulses: in Britain, a similar circuit with one stable state temporarily achieved by pulse: a type of flimsy sandal, esp. one held on the foot by a thong between the toes; **flip'-side** the side of a gramophone record carrying the song, etc., of lesser importance, the reverse of the side on whose merits the record is expected to sell. — *adj.* **flip'-top** having a hinged lid which can be flipped up. — *n.* a flip-top pack. — *adj.* **flipp'erty-flopp'erty** loose, dangling. — **flip one's lid** (*slang*) to go mad. [Cf. **fillip, flap.**]

flippant *flip'ənt, adj.* pert and frivolous of speech: showing disrespectful levity: nimble (*obs.*): playful (*obs.*). — *ns.* **flipp'ancy, flipp'antness** pert fluency of speech: pertness: levity. — *adv.* **flipp'antly.** [Cf. **flip**, and O.N. *fleipa*, to prattle.]

flirt *flûrt, v.t.* to jerk: to move about quickly like a fan, to flick, rap. — *v.i.* to trifle with love: to play at courtship (with *with*): to move briskly about. — *n.* a pert, giddy girl: one who coquets for amusement, usually a woman. — *n.* **flirtā'tion** the act of flirting: a light-hearted and short-lived amorous attachment. — *adj.* **flirtā'tious** (*coll.*) given to flirting. — *n.* **flirt'ing.** — *adv.* **flirt'ingly.** — *adjs.* **flirt'ish** betokening a flirt; **flirt'y** flirting, flirtatious. — **flirt'-gill** (*-jil; Shak.*) a pert or wanton woman. — **flirt with** to treat (death, danger, etc.) lightly, by indulging in dare-devil behaviour, etc.: to entertain thoughts of adopting (an idea, etc.) or joining (a movement, etc.). [Origin obscure; perhaps conn. with Fr. *fleureter*, to talk sweet nothings.]

flisk *flisk, (Scot.) v.i.* to skip or caper about: to be restive. — *n.* a whim. — *adj.* **flisk'y.** [Onomatopoeic.]

flit[1] *flit, v.i.* to move about lightly: to fly silently or quickly: to be unsteady or easily moved: to change one's abode (*Scot.*): to do this stealthily in order to avoid creditors, etc. — *v.t.* to remove, transfer: — *pr.p.* **flitt'ing;** *pa.t.* and *pa.p.* **flitt'ed,** *Spens.* **flitt.** — *n.* **flitt'ing.** [O.N. *flytja;* Sw. *flytta.*]

flit[2], **flitt** *flit,* (*obs.*) *adj.* fleet: fleeting: light. [**fleet.**]

flitch *flich, n.* the side of a hog salted and cured. [O.E. *flicce;* O.N. *flikki.*]

flite. Same as **flyte.**

flitt. See **flit**[1,2].

flitter[1] *flit'ər, v.i.* to flutter. — **flitt'er-mouse** a bat. [**flit**[1].]

flitter[2] *flit'ər, n.* (usu. in *pl.*, sometimes collectively in *sing.*) a fragment, tatter, strip. [Conn. with **flitter**[1].]

flittern *flit'ərn,* (*dial.*) *n.* an oak sapling.

flivver *fliv'ər,* (*slang*) *n.* a failure: a small cheap motor-car or aeroplane: a small destroyer. [Origin uncertain.]

flix[1] *fliks, n.* fur, beaver-down. [Origin uncertain.]

flix[2] *fliks.* An old form of **flux.** — **flix'-weed** a species of hedge-mustard, possibly so called from its use in treating the bloody flux.

float *flōt, v.i.* to be supported on or suspended in a fluid: to be buoyed up: to move lightly, supported by a fluid: to seem to move in such a way: to be free from the usual attachment: to drift about aimlessly: to flow (*Milt.*): to be flooded (*Spens., Pope*): in weaving, to pass threads without interweaving with them: to use a float: (of a currency) to be free to fluctuate in value in international exchange (*econ.*). — *v.t.* to cause to float: to cover with liquid: to convey on floats: to levitate: to separate by flotation: to smooth: to pare off (as turf): to launch (e.g. scheme): to circulate (e.g. rumour): to offer for sale (stocks, etc.) to raise capital: to launch (a company) by drawing up various docu-

ments and raising cash by selling shares: to negotiate (a loan). — *n.* state of floating (*Keats,* etc.): a wave (*lit.* and *fig.; obs.*): a contrivance for floating or for keeping something afloat, as a raft, the cork or quill of a fishing-line, the ball of a ball-cock, etc.: a blade in a paddle-wheel or water-wheel: a tool for smoothing: a plasterer's trowel: a low cart for carrying cattle, milk, etc., or decorated as an exhibit in a street parade, etc.: a footlight or the footlights collectively: money in hand for a purpose such as to give change to customers, to provide for expenses. — *adj.* **float'able.** — *ns.* **float'age, flō'tage** buoyancy: that which floats: the part of a ship above the water-line; **float'ant** an agent that causes something to float; **floatā'tion** same as **flotation; floatel** see **flotel; float'er** one who or that which floats: a person who is a vagrant, or who drifts from job to job or allegiance to allegiance: a blunder (*slang*): a floating policy (*U.S.*): a meat pie floating in pea soup (*Austr.*): a dark speck that appears to float before one's eyes, caused by dead cells and fragments of cells in the lens and vitreous humour. — *adj.* **float'ing** that floats, in any sense: not fixed: fluctuating: circulating: not clearly committed to one side or the other (*politics*). — *n.* action of the verb: the spreading of plaster on the surface of walls. — *adv.* **float'ingly.** — *adj.* **float'y.** — **float'-board** a board of an undershot water-wheel or a paddle-wheel; **float glass** glass hardened floating on the surface of a liquid; **float grass, floating grass** floating meadow-grass (*Glyceria fluitans*); **floating battery** a vessel or hulk heavily armed, used in the defence of harbours or in attacks on marine fortresses; **floating bridge** a bridge supported on pontoons; **floating capital** goods, money, etc.: capital not permanently invested; **floating charge** (*law* and *econ.*) a fluctuating borrowing facility secured on the total assets of a company; **floating crane** a large crane carried on a pontoon, used in docks; **floating currency** a national (unit of) currency whose value is allowed to fluctuate freely in the international trading market; **floating debt** unfunded debt, short-term government loan; **floating dock** a floating structure that can be sunk by admitting water to its air chambers, and raised again carrying a vessel to be repaired; **floating island** a floating aggregation of driftwood, or a mass of vegetation buoyed up from the bottom by marsh gas, or the like; **floating kidney** an abnormally mobile kidney; **floating light** a light-ship; **floating policy** an insurance policy covering movable property irrespective of its location; **floating rib** see **rib; floating vote** the votes of electors who are not permanently attached to any one political party; **floating voter; float plane** a seaplane; **float'-stone** a porous sponge-like variety of silica, so light as to float for a while on water: a bricklayer's smoothing tool. — **floating-point notation** (*comput.*) the expressing of numbers in the general form $\pm a \times b^n$ (e.g. $2\cdot3 \times 10^5$); **floating-point number** (*comput.*) a number so expressed; **floating-point operation** (*comput.*) the addition, subtraction, multiplication, or division of two floating-point numbers. [O.E. *flotian*, to float; O.N. *flota.*]

floccus *flok'əs, n.* a tuft of woolly hair: a tuft, esp. at the end of a tail: the covering of unfledged birds: — *pl.* **flocci** *flok'sī.* — *n.* **floccillā'tion** (*flok-si-*) fitful plucking at the bed-clothes by a delirious patient; **floc'cinau'cini'hilipil'ificā'tion** (*facet.*) setting at little or no value (from the Latin genitives *floccī, naucī,* at a trifle, *nihilī,* at nothing, *pilī,* at a hair, and *facĕre,* to make). — *adjs.* **flocc'ose** (or *-ōs'*) woolly; **flocc'ular; flocc'ulate.** — *v.t.* and *v.i.* **flocc'ulate** to aggregate in tufts, flakes or cloudy masses. — *ns.* **flocculā'tion; flocc'ule** a flocculus; **flocc'ulence** flocculated condition. — *adj.* **flocc'ulent** woolly: flaky: flocculated. — *n.* **flocc'ulus** a small flock, tuft, or flake: a small outgrowth of the cerebellum: a light or dark patch on the sun's surface, usu. near sunspots, caused by calcium or hydrogen vapour: — *pl.* **flocculi** (*flok'ū-lī*). [L. *floccus,* a lock, a trifle; dim. *flocculus.*]

flock[1] *flok, n.* a company of animals, as sheep, birds, etc.: a company generally: a church congregation, considered as the charge of a minister. — *v.i.* to gather or go in flocks or in crowds. — **flock′-mas′ter** an owner or overseer of a flock. [O.E. *flocc,* a flock, a company; O.N. *flokkr.*]

flock[2] *flok, n.* a lock of wool: a tuft: cloth refuse, waste wool (also in *pl.*): a woolly-looking precipitate (also in *pl.*): fine particles of wool or other fibre applied to cloth to give a raised velvety surface or pattern. — **flock′-bed** a bed stuffed with wool; **flock′-pa′per** a wallpaper dusted over with flock. [O.Fr. *floc* — L. *floccus,* a lock of wool.]

floe *flō, n.* a field of floating ice. [Prob. Norw. *flo,* layer — O.N. *flō.*]

flog *flog, v.t.* to beat or strike: to lash: to chastise with blows: to sell, sometimes illicitly (*slang*). — *v.i.* and *v.t.* to move, progress, toilingly: — *pr.p.* **flogg′ing;** *pa.t.* and *pa.p.* **flogged.** — *n.* **flogg′ing.** [Late; prob. an abbrev. of **flagellate.**]

flong *flong, n.* papier-mâché for stereotyping. [Fr. *flan.*]

flood *flud, n.* a great flow of water: an inundation: a deluge: a condition of abnormally great flow in a river: a river or other water (*poet.*): the rise of the tide: any great inflow or outflow, as of light, tears, visitors: a floodlight (*coll.*). — *v.t.* to overflow: to inundate: to supply in excessive quantity. — *v.i.* to overflow: to bleed profusely, as after parturition. — *adj.* **flood′ed.** — *n.* **flood′ing.** — **flood′gate** a gate for allowing or stopping the flow of water, a sluice or lock-gate; **flood lamp** a floodlight; **flood′light** lighting of a large area or surface by illumination from lamps situated at some distance (also **floodlighting**): a floodlight lamp. — Also *v.t.*: — *pa.t.* and *pa.p.* **flood′lighted, flood′lit.** — **floodlight projector** housing and support for a floodlight lamp with a reflector for directing the light into a suitable beam; **flood′mark** the mark or line to which the tide or a flood has risen; **flood′-plain** an extensive level area beside a river formed of deposits of sediment brought downstream and spread by the river in flood; **flood′tide** the rising tide; **flood′wall** a wall built as protection against floods; **flood′water; flood′way** an artificial passage for floodwater. — **the Flood** Noah's deluge. [O.E. *flōd,* Du. *vloed,* Ger. *Flut;* cf. **flow**[2].]

floor *flōr, flör, n.* the lower supporting surface of a room, etc.: a platform: rooms in a building on the same level: a bottom surface: that on which anything rests or any operation is performed: a levelled area: the ground (*coll.*): the part of a legislative assembly where members sit and speak: the (part of a hall, etc. accommodating) members of the public at a meeting, etc.: the part of an exchange on which dealers operate: a lower limit of prices, etc.: a quantity of grain spread out to germinate. — *v.t.* to furnish with a floor: to throw or place on the floor: to vanquish, stump (*coll.*). — *adj.* **floored.** — *ns.* **floor′er** a knock-down blow: a decisive retort, etc.: an examination question one cannot answer; **floor′ing** material for floors: a platform. — **floor′board** one of the narrow boards making up a floor; **floor′cloth** a covering for floors, esp. of linoleum or the like: a cloth for washing floors; **floor′head** the upper end of a floor timber; **flooring saw** saw curved towards the toe with extra teeth on the back above the toe, used for cutting along the cracks between floorboards, etc.; **floor plan** a diagram showing the layout of rooms, etc. on one storey of a building; **floor price** a fixed lowest limit to the possible price of something; **floor show** a performance on the floor of a ballroom, dining-room, etc., not on a platform; **floor timber** a timber placed immediately across a ship's keel, on which her bottom is framed; **floor′walker** supervisor of a section of a large store, who attends to customers' complaints, etc. — **first floor** the floor in a house above the ground floor, the second storey: in U.S. usu. the ground floor. — Also *adj.* — **cross the floor** (of a member of parliament, etc.) to change one's allegiance from one party to another; **hold the floor** to dominate

a meeting by much speaking: to speak boringly much; **take the floor** to rise to address a meeting, or to take part in a dance. [O.E. *flōr;* Du. *vloer,* a flat surface, Ger. *Flur,* flat land; W. *llawr.*]

floosie *flōō′zi, n.* an attractive young woman esp. of loose morals: a prostitute, esp. a slovenly one. — Also **floosy, -zy, -zie.** [Origin uncertain.]

flop[1] *flop, n.* a limp, heavy, flapping movement, fall, or sound: a collapse: a fiasco: a failure. — *adv.* with a flop. — *v.t.* and *v.i.* to move with a flop: to drop heavily: to change over in nature or politics (*U.S.*). — *v.i.* to collapse: to fail dismally. — *adv.* **flopp′ily.** — *n.* **flopp′iness.** — *adj.* **flopp′y.** — *n.* (*comput.*) a floppy disc. — **flop′house** (orig. *U.S.*) a cheap hotel: a doss-house; **floppy disc** (*comput.*) a storage device in the form of a thin, bendable disc. [A form of **flap.**]

flop[2] *flop, (comput.) n.* a floating-point operation (q.v.).

flor *flör, n.* a yeasty growth which is allowed to form on the surface of sherry wines after fermentation and which gives them a nutty taste. [Sp., flower, mould, — L.*flōs, flōris,* a flower.]

flora *flō′rə, flö′, n.* the assemblage of vegetable species of a region, or age: a list or descriptive enumeration of these: — *pl.* **flo′ras, flo′rae.** — *adj.* **flo′ral** pertaining to the goddess Flora, to floras, or to flowers. — *adv.* **flo′rally.** — *ns.* **Floréal** (Fr.; *flō-rā-äl′*) the 8th month of the French revolutionary calendar, about 20th April — 20th May; **florescence** (*flor-es′əns*) a bursting into flower: time of flowering (*bot.*). — *adj.* **floresc′ent** bursting into flowers. — *n.* **floret** (*flor′it*) a small flower: a single flower in a close-packed inflorescence. — *adjs.* **flo′riated, flo′reated** decorated with floral ornament. — *n.* **floribunda** (*flor-, flör-, flör-i-bun′də*) a plant, esp. a rose, whose flowers grow in clusters. — *adj.* **floricul′tural** (*flōr-, flör-*). — *ns.* **flor′iculture** the culture of flowers or plants; **floricul′turist.** — *adj.* **flôr′id** abounding in flowers (*obs.*): flowery: bright in colour: flushed with red: characterised by flowers of rhetoric, melodic figures, or other ornament: overadorned: richly ornamental. — *n.* **flôrid′ity.** — *adv.* **flôr′idly.** — *n.* **flôr′idness.** — *adjs.* **florif′erous** bearing or producing flowers; **flo′riform** flower-shaped. — *ns.* **flôr′igen** (*-i-jən;* Gr. *gennaein,* to produce) a postulated flower-forming hormone; **florilegium** (*-lē′ji-əm;* L. *legĕre,* to gather) an anthology or collection of choice extracts: — *pl.* **florilē′gia;** **flôr′ist** a cultivator or seller of flowers: (*flō′, flö′rist*) a student of flowers or of floras. — *adj.* **flôrist′ic.** — *adv.* **flôrist′ically.** — *n.sing.* **flôrist′ics** the study of floras. — *n.* **flôr′istry** the art of cultivating or selling flowers. — *adj.* **flo′ry** fleury: showy, conceited (*Scott*). — **floral diagram** a figure showing the arrangement of the parts of a flower in ground-plan. [L. *Flōra,* goddess of flowers; *flōs, flōris,* a flower.]

floreat *flō′rē-at, flö′rā-at,* (L.) may (it) flourish.

Florentine *flor′ən-tīn, adj.* pertaining to *Florence* in Tuscany. — *n.* a native or inhabitant thereof: (without *cap.*) a durable silk textile fabric — also **flor′ence:** a pie with no crust beneath the meat: (also without *cap.*) a biscuit consisting of dried fruit and nuts on a chocolate base. — **Florence flask** a long-necked round flask; **Florentine iris** see **orris**[1]. [L. *Flōrentīnus* — *Flōrentia.*]

florescent, floret, florid, etc. See **flora.**

Florideae *flor-id′i-ē,* (*bot.*) *n.pl.* a large subclass of the Rhodophyceae or red seaweeds. — *n.* and *adj.* **florid′ean.** — *adj.* **florid′eous.** [L. *flōridus,* florid.]

florin *flor′in, n.* orig. a Florentine gold coin with a lily stamped on one side, first struck in the 13th century: an English silver or cupro-nickel coin worth one-tenth of a pound first minted in 1849 (a **double florin** was coined in 1887): in Holland, the gulden. [Fr., from It. *fiorino* — *fiore,* a lily — L. *flōs, flōris.*]

florist, etc. See **flora.**

floruit *flo′rū-it, flö′rōō-, flor′ū-, -ōō-, n.* period during which a person flourished or guiding date indicating when he or she was alive. [L., 3rd pers. sing. perf.

indic. of *flōrēre*, to flourish.]

flory. See **flora, fleur-de-lis.**

floscule *flos'kūl, n.* a floret. — *adjs.* **flos'cūlar, flos'cūlous.** [L. *flōsculus*, dim. of *flōs*, a flower.]

floss *flos, n.* the rough outside of the silkworm's cocoon, and other waste of silk manufacture: fine silk in spun strands not twisted together, used in embroidery and tooth-cleaning: any loose downy or silky plant substance: fluff — also **flosh.** — *adj.* **floss'y** made of, like, or pertaining to floss: showy, overdressed (*slang*). — **floss silk, flox silk.** [Prob. O.Fr. *flosche*, down: or from some Gmc. word cog. with **fleece;** cf. O.N. *flos*, nap.]

flota *flō'tə, n.* a commercial fleet: formerly the fleet which annually conveyed the produce of America to Spain. [Sp.]

flote *flōt, n.* (*obs.*) a wave. — *n.* **flō'tage** see **floatage.** — *adj.* **flō'tant** (*her.*) floating in air or in water. — *n.* **flotā'tion** the act of floating: the science of floating bodies: the act of starting a business, esp. a limited liability company by drawing up various documents and raising capital by selling shares: (also **froth flotation**) a method of separating ore from gangue by forming a froth, the ore particles clinging to the bubbles. — **plane** or **line of flotation** the plane or line in which the horizontal surface of a fluid cuts a body floating in it. [See **float.**]

flotel, floatel *flō-tel', n.* a platform or boat containing the sleeping accommodation and eating, leisure, etc. facilities for workers on oil-rigs. [**float, hotel.**]

flotilla *flo-til'ə, n.* a fleet of small ships. [Sp., dim. of *flota*, a fleet.]

flotsam *flot'səm, n.* goods lost by shipwreck and found floating on the sea (see **jetsam**). [Anglo-Fr. *floteson* (Fr. *flottaison*) — O.Fr. *floter*, to float.]

flounce[1] *flowns, v.i.* to move abruptly or impatiently. — *n.* an impatient fling, flop, or movement. — *adv.* with a flounce. [Prob. cog. with Norw. *flunsa*, to hurry, Sw. dial. *flunsa*, to plunge.]

flounce[2] *flowns, n.* a hanging strip sewn to the skirt of a dress by its upper edge. — *v.t.* to furnish with flounces. — *n.* **floun'cing** material for flounces. [See **frounce**[1].]

flounder[1] *flown'dər, v.i.* to struggle with violent and awkward motion: to stumble helplessly in thinking or speaking. — *n.* an act of floundering. [Prob. an onomatopoeic blending of the sound and sense of earlier words like **founder, blunder.**]

flounder[2] *flown'dər, n.* a name given to a number of species of flatfish of the family Pleuronectidae — in Europe *Platichthys flesus*, in America certain species of *Pseudopleuronectes, Limanda*, etc. [Anglo-Fr. *floundre*, O.Fr. *flondre*, most prob. of Scand. origin; cf. O.N. *flythra*; Sw. *flundra*.]

flour *flowr, n.* the finely-ground meal of wheat or other grain: the fine soft powder of any substance. — *v.t.* to reduce into or sprinkle with flour. — *v.i.* of mercury, to break up into fine globules in the amalgamation process. — *adj.* **flour'y** covered with flour: like flour. — **flour bolt** a machine for bolting flour; **flour mill** a mill for making flour. [Same word as **flower.**]

flourish *flur'ish, v.i.* to bloom (*obs.* and *Scot.*): to grow luxuriantly: to thrive: to be in full vigour: to be prosperous: to use copious and flowery language: to move in fantastic figures: to display ostentatiously: to play or sing ostentatious passages, or ostentatiously (*mus.*): to play a fanfare: to make ornamental strokes with the pen: to show off. — *v.t.* to adorn with flourishes or ornaments: to make fair (*Shak.*): to brandish in show or triumph or exuberance of spirits. — *n.* decoration (*obs.*): showy splendour: a figure made by a bold stroke of the pen: the waving of a weapon or other thing: a parade of words: a showy, fantastic, or highly ornamental passage of music: a mass of blossom of a fruit-tree (*dial.*). — *adjs.* **flour'ished** decorated with flourishes; **flour'ishing** thriving: prosperous: making a show. — *adv.* **flour'ishingly.** — *adj.* **flour'ishy** abounding in flourishes. — **flourishing thread**

thread used in fancywork. — **flourish of trumpets** a fanfare heralding great persons: any ostentatious introduction. [O.Fr. *florir, floriss-* — L. *flōs, flōris*, flower.]

flouse *flows*, (*dial.*) *v.t.* and *v.i.* to splash. — Also **floush** (*flowsh*). [Cf. **flush**[1].]

flout *flowt, v.t.* to jeer at: to mock: to treat with contempt: to reject, defy (orders, etc.). — *v.i.* to jeer. — *n.* a jeer. — *adv.* **flout'ingly.** — **flout'ingstock** (*Shak.*) an object for flouting. [Prob. a specialised use of *floute*, M.E. form of **flute,** to play on the flute; so with Du. *fluiten*.]

flow[1] *flō, v.i.* to run, as water: to move or change form like a fluid: to rise or come in, as the tide: to move in a stream: to glide smoothly: to abound, run over: to run in smooth lines: to stream or hang loose and waving: to melt (*obs.*). — *v.t.* to cover with water: — *pa.t.* and *pa.p.* **flowed;** *pa.p.*, *Shak., Milt.*, **flown** (*flōn*). — *n.* a stream or current: movement of, or like that of, a fluid: that which flows or has flowed: mode of flowing: the setting in of the tide: copious fluency. — *n.* **flow'age** act of flowing: state of being flooded. — *adj.* **flow'ing** moving, as a fluid: fluent: smooth and continuous: falling in folds or in waves. — *adv.* **flow'ingly.** — *n.* **flow'ingness.** — **flow chart** a flow sheet: a chart pictorially representing the nature and sequence of operations to be carried out in a computer programme or any other activity; **flow'meter** a device for measuring, or giving an output signal proportional to, the rate of flow of a fluid in a pipe; **flow'-on** (*Austr.*) the process by which a wage or salary increase awarded to one group of workers results in a similar increase for other workers: such an increase; **flow sheet** a chart showing the successive stages of an industrial process. [O.E. *flōwan*.]

flow[2] *flō, flow*, (*Scot.*) *n.* a morass: a flat, moist tract of land: a quicksand: a moorland pool: a sea basin or sound. [Cf. Icel. *flōi*, a marshy moor; Norw. dial. *floe*, pool in a swamp; O.N. *flōa*, to flood.]

flower *flow('ə)r, n.* a growth comprising the reproductive organs of seed plants: the blossom of a plant: the flowering state: a flowering plant, esp. one valued for its blossoms: the prime of life: the best of anything: the person or thing most distinguished: the embodiment of perfection: a figure of speech: ornament of style: (in *pl.*) menstrual discharge (*obs.*): (in *pl.*) a sublimate (as **flowers of sulphur**): (in *pl.*) applied to some fungous growths, as **flowers of tan,** a slime-fungus on tan-bark. — *v.t.* to adorn with figures of flowers. — *v.i.* to blossom: to flourish. — *n.* **flower'age** flowers collectively: flowering state. — *adj.* **flower'ed** decorated with figures of flowers: fleury. — *ns.* **flower'er** a plant that flowers: embroiderer of floral figures; **flower'et** a little flower: a floret; **flower'iness.** — *n.* and *adj.* **flower'ing.** — *adjs.* **flower'less; flower'y** full of, or adorned with, flowers: highly embellished, florid. — **flower'-bed** a garden bed for flowers; **flower'-bell** a blossom shaped like a bell; **flower'-bud** a bud with the unopened flower; **flower child** one of the Flower People; **flower'-clock** a collection of flowers so arranged that the time of day is indicated by their times of opening and closing; **flower-de-leuce, flower(-)deluce** (*-di-lōōs'*), **-delice** (*-di-lēs', -līs', -del'is*) old names for the iris, or for the **fleur-de-lis; flower'-garden; flower'-girl** a girl or woman who sells flowers in the street; **flower'-head** a close inflorescence in which all the florets are sessile on the receptacle; **flowering rush** a monocotyledonous plant (*Butomus*), with large linear three-edged leaves and an umbel of rose-coloured flowers; **Flower People** (also without *cap.*) colourfully dressed adherents of a cult arising in the mid nineteen-sixties which rejected materialism and advocated universal love; **flower'pot** a pot in which a plant is grown; **Flower Power** (also without *cap.*) the movement of the Flower People; **flower'-serv'ice** a church service where offerings of flowers are made; **flower'-show** an exhibition of flowers; **flower'-stalk** the stem that supports the flower. — *adj.* **flower'y-kir'tled** (*Milt.*). — **flower**

of Jove a campion with heads of purple or scarlet flowers, and leaves silky-white with hairs; **the flowery land** China. [O.Fr. *flour* (Fr. *fleur*) — L. *flōs, flōris*, a flower.]

flown *flōn, pa.p.* of **fly**; old *pa.p.* of **flow¹**. — **flown cover** (*philately*) an envelope which has been carried by air over at least part of its delivery route.

flox silk. Same as **floss silk.**

flu, flue *flōō, n.* shortened form of **influenza.**

fluate *flōō´āt, (obs.) n.* a fluoride.

flub *flub, (U.S. slang) v.t.* to botch, fail at. — *v.i.* to perform badly: to blunder: — *pr.p.* **flubb´ing;** *pa.t.* and *pa.p.* **flubbed.** — *n.* a blunder. [Ety. unknown.]

fluctuate *fluk´tū-āt, v.i.* to move like a wave: to go up and down or to and fro: to vary this way and that. — *v.t.* to throw into fluctuation. — *adjs.* **fluc´tuant; fluc´tuating.** — *n.* **fluctua´tion** rise and fall: motion to and fro: wavelike motion: alternate variation. [L. *fluctuāre, -ātum* — *fluctus*, a wave — *fluĕre*, to flow.]

flue¹ *flōō, n.* a pipe for conveying hot air, smoke, flame, etc.: a small chimney: a flue pipe (*mus.*): the opening by which the air escapes from the foot of a flue pipe. — *v.t.* **flue´-cure** to cure (tobacco) by heat introduced through flues. — *adj.* **flue´-cured.** — **flue pipe** a pipe, esp. in an organ, in which the sound is produced by air impinging upon an edge; **flue´work** in an organ, the flue pipes collectively. [Origin uncertain.]

flue² *flōō, n.* light fluff, such as collects in unswept places: soft down or fur. — *adj.* **flu´ey.** [Origin doubtful.]

flue³, flew *flōō, (dial.) adj.* shallow, flat: flared: splayed. [Origin uncertain.]

flue⁴. Same as **flu.**

fluellin *flōō-el´in, n.* a name given to various speedwells (esp. *Veronica serpyllifolia* and *V. officinalis*) and toadflaxes (esp. *Linaria elatine* and *L. spuria*). [W. *llysiau Llewelyn,* Llewelyn's herbs.]

fluent *flōō´ənt, adj.* ready in the use of words: voluble: marked by copiousness: smooth, easy, graceful. — *n.* (*math.*) the variable quantity in fluxions. — *ns.* **flu´ence** (*Milt.*), **flu´ency, flu´entness.** — *adv.* **flu´ently.** [L. *fluēns, fluentis,* pr.p. of *fluĕre,* to flow.]

fluey. See **flue².**

fluff *fluf, n.* a soft down from cotton, etc.: anything downy: a fault in performing (a play, piece of music, etc.): a duffed stroke at golf, etc.: a girl (*coll.*). — *v.t.* to make fluffy. — *v.t.* and *v.i.* to bungle, in sport, musical or dramatic performance, etc. — *n.* **fluff´iness.** — *adj.* **fluff´y.** [Perh. conn. with **flue².**]

flügel, flugel *flü´hhəl, flōō´gl, ns.* a grand piano. — **flü´gelhorn, flu´gelhorn** a hunting-horn, a kind of keyed bugle; **flugelman** (*flōō´gl-man*) same as **fugleman.** [Ger., wing.]

fluid *flōō´id, adj.* that flows: unsolidified: likely to, tending to change: easily changed. — *n.* a substance whose particles can move about with freedom — a liquid or gas. — *adjs.* **flu´idal; fluid´ic.** — *n. sing.* **fluid´ics** the science and technology of using a flow of liquid or gas for certain operations in place of a flow of electrons. — *vs.t.* **fluid´ify; flu´idise, -ize** to make fluid: to cause (fine particles) to move as a fluid, e.g. by suspending them in a current of air or gas: to fill with a specified fluid. — *ns.* **fluidisa´tion, -z-; fluid´ity, flu´idness.** — **fluid drive** a system of transmitting power smoothly through the medium of the change in momentum of a fluid, usu. oil. [L. *fluidus,* fluid — *fluĕre,* to flow.]

fluke¹ *flōōk, n.* a flounder: a trematode worm, esp. that which causes liver-rot in sheep, so called because like a miniature flounder (also **fluke´-worm**): a variety of kidney potato. [O.E. *flōc,* a plaice; cf. O.N. *flōke.*]

fluke² *flōōk, n.* the barb of an anchor: a barb: a lobe of a whale's tail. — *adj.* **fluk´y.** [Prob. a transferred use of the foregoing.]

fluke³ *flōōk, n.* an accidental success. — *v.t.* to make, score, etc. by a fluke. — *adj.* **fluk´(e)y.** [Origin unknown.]

flume *flōōm, n.* an artificial channel for water to be applied to some industrial purpose: a ravine occupied

by a stream (*U.S.*). — **be** or **go up the flume** to come to grief, to be done for. [O.Fr. *flum* — L. *flūmen,* a river — *fluĕre,* to flow.]

flummery *flum´ər-i, n.* an acid jelly made from the husks of oats, the Scots sowens: blancmange: anything insipid: empty compliment, humbug, pretentiousness. [W. *llymru* — *llymrig,* harsh, raw — *llym,* sharp, severe.]

flummox *flum´əks, (coll.) v.t.* to perplex. [Ety. unknown.]

flump *flump, (coll.) v.t.* to throw down heavily. — *v.i.* to move with a flop or thud. — *n.* the dull sound so produced. [Imit.]

flung *flung, pa.t.* and *pa.p.* of **fling.**

flunk *flungk, (slang) v.i.* to fail in an examination: to be dismissed from college, etc. for such failure (with *out*). — Also *v.t.* and *n.* [Perh. combined **flinch¹, funk¹.**]

flunkey, flunky *flung´ki, n.* a livery servant: a footman: a mean cringer. — *n.* **flun´keydom.** — *adj.* **flun´keyish.** — *n.* **flun´keyism.** [Perh. orig. *flanker,* one who runs alongside.]

Fluon® *flōō´on, n.* tradename for **polytetrafluoroethylene.**

fluor *flōō´ər, -ör, n.* fluorite. — *v.i.* **fluoresce** (*-ər-es´*). — *ns.* **fluorescein** (*-es´ē-in*) a fluorescent dyestuff, $C_{20}H_{12}O_5$; **fluoresc´ence** the property of some substances (e.g. fluor) of emitting, when exposed to radiation, rays of greater wavelength than those received. — *adjs.* **fluoresc´ent; fluoric** (*-or´ik*). — *vs.t.* **flu´oridate, -idise, -ize** to add a fluoride to (a water or milk supply). — *ns.* **fluorida´tion; flu´oride** a compound of fluorine with another element or radical; **fluorimeter** see **fluorometer.** — *v.t.* **flu´orinate** to introduce fluorine into a chemical compound. — *ns.* **fluorina´tion; flu´orine** (*-ēn*) an element (at. numb. 9; symbol F), a pale greenish-yellow gas; **fluorite** (*flōō´ər-īt*) a mineral, calcium fluoride, commonly purple, also green, colourless, etc., crystallising in cubes and octahedra, found abundantly in Derbyshire. Its coloured varieties may fluoresce strongly in ultraviolet light; **flu´orocarbon** any of a series of compounds of fluorine and carbon (corresponding to the hydrocarbons) highly resistant to heat and chemical action; **fluorom´eter, fluorim´eter** an instrument for measuring intensity of fluorescence. — *adjs.* **fluoromet´ric, fluorimet´ric.** — *n.* **flu´oroscope** an instrument for X-ray examination by means of a fluorescent screen. — *adj.* **fluoroscōp´ic.** — **fluoros´copy; fluoro´sis** chronic poisoning by fluorine; **flu´orotype** (*obs.*) photography by means of fluorides; **flu´orspar** fluorite. — **fluorescent lighting** brighter lighting obtained for the same consumption of electricity, by using fluorescent material to convert ultraviolet radiation in the electric lamp into visible light. [L. *fluor,* flow, from its use as a flux.]

Fluothane® *flōō´ō-thān,* proprietary name for **halothane.**

flurry *flur´i, n.* a sudden blast or gust: agitation: bustle: the death-agony of the whale: a fluttering assemblage of things, as snowflakes. — *v.t.* to agitate, to confuse: — *pr.p.* **flurr´ying;** *pa.t., pa.p.* **flurr´ied.** — *v.t.* **flurr** (*flûr*) to scatter. — *v.i.* to fly up. [Prob. onomatopoeic, suggested by **flaw¹, hurry,** etc.]

flush¹ *flush, n.* a sudden flow: a flow of blood to the skin, causing redness: a suffusion of colour, esp. red: a sudden growth: a renewal of growth: a rush of feeling: a puddle (*obs.*): a watery place about a spring, etc. (*obs.*): bloom, freshness, vigour: abundance. — *v.i.* to glow: to become red in the face: to flow swiftly, suddenly, or copiously. — *v.t.* to cleanse by a copious flow of water: to clear by a blast of air: to cause to glow: to elate, excite the spirits of. — *adj.* overflowing: abounding: well supplied, as with money: in full bloom (*Shak.*): flushed. — *adj.* **flushed** suffused with ruddy colour: excited. — *ns.* **flush´er** one who flushes sewers; **flush´ing; flush´ness.** — *adj.* **flush´y** reddish. — **flush´-box** a tank for flushing a water-closet. — **in the, one's, first flush** young, youthful; **in the first flush of** in the early stages (of something), when one is at a peak of vigour, excitement, etc. [Prob. next word influenced by **flash, blush.**]

flush² *flush, v.i.* to start up like an alarmed bird. — *v.t.* to rouse and cause to start off: to force from concealment (with *out*). — *n.* the act of starting: a bird, or a flock of birds, so started (*Spens.*). [Prob. onomatopoeic; suggested by **fly, flutter, rush¹.**]

flush³ *flush, v.t.* to make even: to fill up to the level of a surface (often with *up*). — *adj.* having the surface in one plane with the adjacent surface (with *with*): of a deck, having the same level throughout the ship's length. — Also *adv.* [Prob. related to **flush¹.**]

flush⁴ *flush, n.* in card-playing, a hand in which all the cards or a specified number are of the same suit. — *adj.* in poker, consisting of cards all of the same suit. — **busted flush** in poker, a flush that is never completed: something that has to be abandoned as a failure (*fig.*); **straight flush** in poker, a sequence of five cards of the same suit (**royal flush,** if headed by ace). [Prob. Fr. *flux* — L. *fluxus,* flow; influenced by **flush¹.**]

fluster *flus'tər, n.* hurrying: flurry: heat (*obs.*): confused agitation. — *v.t.* to make hot and flurried: to fuddle with drink: to confuse. — *v.i.* to bustle: to be agitated or fuddled. — *n.* **flus'terment.** — *adj.* **flus'tery** confused. — *v.t.* **flus'trate** to fluster. — *n.* **flustrā'tion.** [O.N. *flaustr,* hurry.]

Flustra *flus'trə, n.* one of the commonest genera of marine Polyzoa. [Ety. unknown.]

flute *flōōt, n.* a wind instrument, esp. either of two types consisting of a wooden or metal tube with holes stopped by the finger-tips or by keys, the one type blown from the end through a fipple, the other (also called **transverse flute**) held horizontally and played by directing the breath across a mouth-hole: in organ-building, a stop with stopped wooden pipes, having a flute-like tone: a longitudinal groove, as on a pillar: a tall and narrow wine-glass: a shuttle in tapestry-weaving, etc. — *v.i.* to play the flute: to make fluty sounds. — *v.t.* to play or sing in soft flute-like tones: to form flutes or grooves in. — *adj.* **flut'ed** ornamented with flutes, channels, or grooves. — *ns.* **flut'er; flutina** (*-tē'*) a kind of accordion; **flut'ing** flute-playing or similar sounds: longitudinal furrowing; **flut'ist.** — *adj.* **flut'y** in tone like a flute. — **flûte-à-bec** (*flüt-ä-bek;* Fr.) a fipple-flute; **flute'-bird** a piping crow; **flute'mouth** fish (*Fistularia*) akin to the sticklebacks. [O.Fr. *fleûte;* ety. dubious.]

flutter *flut'ər, v.i.* to move about nervously, aimlessly, or with bustle: of a bird, to flap wings: of a flag, etc., to flap in the air: to vibrate, e.g. of a pulse, to beat irregularly: to be in agitation or in uncertainty: to be frivolous (*obs.*): to toss a coin (*arch.*). — *v.t.* to throw into disorder: to move in quick motions. — *n.* quick, irregular motion: agitation: confusion: a gambling transaction (*coll.*): a small speculation (*coll.*): in wind-instrument playing, rapid movement of the tongue as for a rolled 'r' (also **flutt'er-tongu'ing**): in sound reproduction, undesirable variation in pitch or loudness: abnormal oscillation of a part of an aircraft. [O.E. *flotorian,* to float about, from the root of *flēotan,* to float.]

fluvial *flōō'vi-əl, adj.* of or belonging to rivers. — *n.* **flu'vialist** one stressing rivers in explanation of phenomena. — *adjs.* **fluviat'ic, flu'viatile** (*-tīl, -til*) belonging to or formed by rivers. — *adj.* **fluvio-glā'cial** pertaining to glacial rivers. [L. *fluviālis* — *fluvius,* a river, *fluĕre,* to flow.]

flux *fluks, n.* act of flowing: a flow of matter: a state of flow or continuous change: a discharge generally from a mucous membrane: matter discharged: excrement: an easily fused substance, esp. one added to another to make it more fusible: the rate of flow of mass, volume, or energy (*phys.*). — *v.t.* to melt. — *v.i.* to flow: to fuse. — *n.* **fluxion** (*fluk'shən*) a flowing or discharge: excessive flow of blood or fluid to any organ (*med.*): a difference or variation: the rate of change of a continuously varying quantity (*math.*): (in *pl.*) the

name given by Newton to that branch of mathematics which with a different notation (developed by Leibniz) is known as the differential and integral calculus. — *adjs.* **flux'ional, flux'ionary** (*arch.*) variable: inconstant. — *n.* **flux'ionist** one skilled in fluxions. — *adj.* **flux'ive** (*Shak.*) flowing with tears. — **flux density** (*nuc.*) the number of photons (or particles) passing through unit area normal to a beam, or the energy of the radiation passing through this area. — **in a state of flux** in an unsettled, undetermined state. [O.Fr., — L. *fluxus* — *fluĕre,* to flow.]

fly *flī, v.i.* to move through the air, esp. on wings or in aircraft: to operate an aircraft: to move swiftly: to hurry: to pass quickly: to flee: to burst quickly or suddenly: to flutter. — *v.t.* to avoid, flee from: to cause to fly, as a kite, aircraft, etc.: to conduct or transport by air: to cross or pass by flying: — *pr.p.* **fly'ing;** *pa.t.* **flew** (*flōō*); *pa.p.* **flown** (*flōn*); *3rd sing. pres. indic.* **flies.** — *n.* any insect of the *Diptera:* often so widely used, esp. in composition — e.g. *butterfly, dragonfly, mayfly* — as to be virtually equivalent to insect: a fish-hook dressed in imitation of a fly: (collectively) an insect pest: a familiar spirit (*arch.*): an attendant parasite (*obs.*): a flight: a flap, esp. a tent-door: a flap of material covering, e.g. trouser opening: the trouser fastener, e.g. zip: the free end of a flag, or the like: a fast stagecoach: a light vehicle on hire, at first drawn by a man, later by a horse: a flywheel: (in *pl.*) the large space above the proscenium in a theatre, from which the scenes, etc., are controlled: — *pl.* **flies.** — *adj.* (*slang*) wideawake, knowing: surreptitious, sly. — *ns.* **flier, flyer** (*flī'ər*) one who flies or flees: an airman: an object, e.g. train, moving at top speed: a financial speculation (*slang*): part of a machine with rapid motion: a rectangular step in stairs: a flying leap (*coll.*): a handbill. — *adj.* **fly'able** (of weather) in which it is safe to fly: (of an aircraft) able to be, or fit to be, flown. — *n.* **fly'ing.** — *adj.* that flies or can fly: moving, or passing, very rapidly: organised for speedy action or transfer to any location as the need arises: (of a visit) very brief. — **fly agaric** a poisonous type of toadstool, *Amanita muscaria,* used in the production of flypaper and having hallucinogenic properties; **fly ash** a fine ash from the pulverised fuel burned in power stations, used in brick-making and as a partial substitute for cement in concrete. — *adj.* **fly'away** streaming: flighty: (of hair) too fine to hold a style for long. — **fly'bane** poison for flies: a name for various plants so used; **fly'belt** a belt of country infested by tsetse fly. — *adj.* **fly'-bitten** marked as by the bite of flies. — **fly'blow** the egg of a fly. — *adj.* **fly'-blown** tainted with flies' eggs or maggots (also *fig.*). — **fly'boat** a long, narrow, swift boat used on canals; **fly'book** a case like a book for holding fishing-flies; **fly'-by** a flight, at low altitude or close range, past a place, or body in space, for observation; **fly'-by-night** one who gads about at night: an absconding debtor: an irresponsible person. — *adj.* irresponsible, esp. in business matters: unreliable: transitory. — **fly'catcher** name for various birds that catch flies on the wing; **fly'-dressing** fly-tying; **fly'-dumping** unauthorised disposal of waste materials. — *v.i.* **fly'-fish'** to fish using artificial flies as lure. — **fly'-fisher; fly'-fishing; fly'-flap** device for driving away flies; **fly'-flapp'er; fly'-half'** (*Rugby*) a stand-off half; **flying bedstead** a testing framework resembling a bedstead in shape, that can be raised vertically from the ground by a jet engine; **flying boat** a seaplane with boat body; **flying bomb** a bomb in the form of a jet-propelled aeroplane; **flying bridge** a ferry-boat moving under the combined forces of the stream and the resistance of a long cable: a pontoon bridge: the highest bridge of a ship; **flying buttress** an arch-formed prop; **flying camp, flying column** a body of troops for rapid motion from one place to another. — *n.pl.* **flying colours** flags unfurled: triumphant success. — **Flying Corps** the precursor (1912–18) of the Royal Air Force; **flying doctor** a doctor, esp. orig. in the remote parts of

Australia, who can be called by radio, etc., and who flies to visit patients; **Flying Dutchman** a black spectral Dutch ship, or its captain, condemned to sweep the seas around the Cape of Good Hope for ever; **flying fish** a fish that can leap from the water and sustain itself in the air for a short time by its long pectoral fins, as if flying; **flying fox** a large frugivorous bat; **flying jib** in a vessel with more than one jib, the one set furthest forward; **flying leap** one made from a running start; **flying lemur** an animal (not in fact a lemur) of the genera Cynocephalus or Galeopithecus of the islands of SE Asia, whose fore and hind limbs are connected by a fold of skin — included in the Insectivora or made a separate order Dermoptera; **flying lizard** a dragon lizard; **flying machine** a power-driven aircraft; **flying officer** an officer in the Air Force of rank answering to sub-lieutenant in the navy and lieutenant in the army (formerly called **observer**); **flying party** a small body of soldiers, equipped for rapid movements, used to harass an enemy; **flying phalanger** a general name for animals akin to the phalangers with a parachute of skin between fore and hind legs; **flying pickets** mobile pickets available for reinforcing the body of local pickets during a strike; **flying saucer** a disc-like flying object reported to have been seen by sundry persons; **flying shore** a horizontal baulk or shore; **flying shot** a shot at something in motion; **flying squad** a body of police, etc. with special training, available for duty where the need arises, or one organised for fast action or movement; **flying squid** a squid with broad lateral fins by which it can spring high out of the water; **flying squirrel** a name for several kinds of squirrels with a parachute of skin between the fore and hind legs: also applied to a flying pha-langer; **flying start** in a race, a start given after the competitors are in motion: an initial advantage: a promising start; **flying wing** an arrow-head-shaped aircraft designed to minimise drag at very high speeds; **fly'-kick** a kick made while running; **fly'leaf** a blank leaf at the beginning or end of a book; **fly line** a line for angling with an artificial fly; **fly'maker** one who ties artificial flies for angling; **fly'-man** one who works the ropes in theatre flies: one who drives a fly; **fly orchis** an orchid (*Ophrys muscifera* or *insectifera*) with a flylike flower; **fly'over** a processional flight of aircraft (*U.S.*): a road or railway-line carried over the top of another one at an intersection; **fly'paper** a sticky or poisonous paper for destroying flies; **fly'-past** a cere-monial flight analogous to a march past: a fly-by in space; **flypost'ing** the practice of affixing bills illegally; **fly powder** a powder used for killing flies; **fly rail** a flap that turns out to support the leaf of a table; **fly rod** a light flexible rod used in fly-fishing, usually in three pieces — butt, second-joint, and tip; **fly'-sheet** a piece of canvas that can be fitted to the roof of a tent to give additional protection: a handbill. — *adj.* **fly'-slow** (*Shak.*; doubtful reading and sense) slow-flying. — **fly'-speck** a small spot of flies' excrement; **fly'-spray** (an aerosol containing) an insecticide; **fly'-tipping** tly dumping; **fly'trap** a trap to catch flies: a plant that traps flies, esp. the American dog bane, and Venus's flytrap (*bot.*); **fly'-tying** making artificial flies for an-gling; **fly'-under** a road or railway-line carried under another one at an intersection; **fly'way** a migration route used by birds; **fly'weight** a boxer of eight stone or less; **fly'wheel** a large wheel with a heavy rim applied to machinery to equalise the effect of the driving effort. — **a fly in the ointment** some slight flaw which corrupts a thing of value (Eccles. x. 1): a minor disadvantage in otherwise favourable circumstances; **a fly on the wall** the invisible observer that one would like to be on certain occasions; **fly a kite** see **kite-flying**; **fly at, upon** to attack suddenly; **fly high** to aim high, be ambitious; **fly in the face of** to insult: to oppose, defy: to be at variance with; **fly off the handle** (*slang*) to lose one's temper; **fly open** to open suddenly or violently; **fly out** to break out in a rage; **let fly** to attack: to throw or

send off; **like flies** (dying, etc.) in vast numbers with as little resistance as insects; **make the feathers fly** see **feather; no flies on** no want of alertness in.   [O.E. *flēogan*, to fly, pa.t. *flēah*; *flēoge*, fly, insect; Ger. *fliegen, Fliege*.]

flype *flīp*, *v.t.* to strip back: to turn partly outside in. [Prob. Scand.; cf. Dan. *flip*, a flap.]

Flysch, flysch *flish*, *n.* a great Alpine mass of Cretaceous and Lower Tertiary sandstone with shales.   [Swiss Ger.]

flyte, flite *flīt*, (*Scot.*) *v.i.* to scold, to brawl. — *ns.* **flyte, flyt'ing** a scolding-match, esp. as a poetical exhibition. [O.E. *flītan*, to strive; Ger. *befleissen*.]

foal *fōl*, *n.* the young of the horse family. — *v.i.* and *v.t.* to bring forth (a foal). — **foal'foot** coltsfoot. — **in foal, with foal** (of a mare) pregnant.   [O.E. *fola*; Ger. *Fohlen*, Gr. *pōlos*; L. *pullus*.]

foam *fōm*, *n.* bubbles on surface of liquor: a suspension of gas in a liquid: sea (*poet.*): frothy saliva or perspi-ration: any of many light, cellular materials, rigid or flexible, produced by aerating a liquid, then solidifying it. — *v.i.* to gather or produce foam: to come in foam. — *v.t.* to pour out in foam: to fill or cover with foam. — *adv.* **foam'ily.** — *n.* **foam'iness.** — *n.* and *adj.* **foam'ing.** — *adv.* **foam'ingly.** — *adjs.* **foam'less; foam'y** frothy. — **foam glass** glass in a form full of tiny air-cells through admixture of carbon under heat, used in insulation, filling lifebelts, etc.; **foam** or **foamed plastics** cellular plastics, soft and flexible like sponges, or rigid, with excellent heat-insulation properties; **foam rubber** rubber in cellular form, used chiefly in upholstery. — **foam at the mouth** to produce frothy saliva: to be extremely angry (*coll.*).   [O.E. *fām*; Ger. *Feim*, prob. akin to L. *spūma*.]

fob[1] *fob*, *n.* (*arch.*) a trick. — *v.t.* (*arch.* except with *off*) to cheat: to give as genuine: to put off: to foist, palm. [Cf. Ger. *foppen*, to jeer.]

fob[2] *fob*, *n.* a small watch pocket in a waistcoat or the waistband of trousers: a chain attaching a watch to a waistcoat, etc.: a decoration hanging from such a chain: a decorative tab on a key-ring. — **fob'-watch.** — *v.t.* to pocket.   [Perh. conn. with L. Ger. *fobke*, little pocket, H.Ger. dial. *fuppe*, pocket.]

focal, focimeter. See **focus.**

fo'c'sle *fōk'sl*, contr. form of **forecastle.**

focus *fō'kəs*, *n.* in geometry, a fixed point such that the distances of a point on a conic section from it and from the directrix have a constant ratio: in optics, a point in which rays converge after reflection or refrac-tion, or from which (*virtual focus*) they seem to diverge: any central point: the point or region of greatest activity: the point of origin (as of an earthquake): the position, or condition, of sharp definition of an image: — *pl.* **foci** (*fō'sī*), **fo'cuses.** — *v.t.* to bring to a focus: to adjust to focus: to adjust so as to get a sharp image of: to concentrate: — *pr.p.* **fo'cusing**; *pa.t.* and *pa.p.* **fo'cused**; some double the *s.* — *adj.* **fō'cal** of or belonging to a focus. — *n.* **focalisā'tion, -z-.** — *v.t.* **fō'calise, -ize** to focus. — *adv.* **fō'cally.** — *n.* **focimeter** (*fō-sim'i-tər*) apparatus to help in focusing. — **focal infection** a localised bacterial infection, as of a gland, etc.; **focal point** (*optics*) focus; **focusing cloth** a cloth thrown over a photographic camera and the operator's head and shoulders to exclude extraneous light in focusing. — **conjugate foci** two points such that each is focus for rays proceeding from the other; **focal-plane shutter** a camera shutter in the form of a blind with a slot, which is pulled rapidly across, and as close as is practicable to, the film or plate, speed being varied by adjusting the width of the slot; **in focus** placed or adjusted so as to secure distinct vision, or a sharp, definite image; **principal focus** the focus for rays par-allel to the axis.   [L. *focus*, a hearth.]

fodder *fod'ər*, *n.* food supplied to cattle: food (*slang*). — *v.t.* to supply with fodder. — *ns.* **fodd'erer; fodd'ering.** [O.E. *fōdor*; Ger. *Futter*; cf. **food**[1], **feed**[1].]

foe *fō*, *n.* an enemy: — *pl.* **foes;** *Spens.* **fone, foen** (*fōn*).

— **foe′man** an enemy in war (*pl.* **foe′men**). [M.E. *foo* — O.E. *fāh*, *fā* (adj.) and *gefā* (noun).]

foedarie. See **fedarie.**

foederatus *fed-ə-rā′təs*, *foi-de-rä′tōos* (*pl.* **foederati** *-rä′tī*, *-rä′tē*; L.) a (conquered) ally of Rome: an auxiliary soldier fighting for the Romans.

foehn. See **föhn.**

foetid, foetor. See **fetid, fetor.**

foetus, the usual but etymologically unsatisfactory form of **fetus** *fē′təs, n.* the young animal in the egg or in the womb, after its parts are distinctly formed. — *adj.* **foe′tal, fē′tal.** — *n.* **foe′ticide, fē′ticide** destruction of a foetus. — *adj.* **foeticī′dal, fē-.** — *n.* **foetos′copy, fetos′-copy** taking a sample of foetal blood from the placenta, by inserting a hollow needle through the abdomen into the uterus, for diagnosis of blood disorders. [L. *fētus,* offspring.]

fog¹ *fog, n.* a thick mist: watery vapour condensed about dust particles in drops: cloudy obscurity: confusion, bewilderment: a blurred patch on a negative, print, or transparency (*phot.*). — *v.t.* to shroud in fog: to obscure: to confuse: to produce fog on (*phot.*). — *v.i.* to become coated, clouded, blurred, confused: to be affected by fog (*phot.*). — *adj.* **fogged** (*fogd*) clouded, obscured: bewildered. — *ns.* **fogg′er, fog′man** one who sets railway fog-signals. — *adv.* **fogg′ily.** — *n.* **fogg′-iness.** — *adjs.* **fogg′y** misty: damp: fogged: clouded in mind: stupid; **fog′less** without fog, clear. — **fog′-bank** a dense mass of fog like a bank of land; **fog′-bell** a bell rung by waves or wind to warn sailors in fog. — *adj.* **fog′bound** impeded by fog. — **fog′-bow** a whitish arch like a rainbow, seen in fogs; **fog′-dog** a whitish spot seen near the horizon in fog; **fog′horn** a horn used as a warning signal by or to ships in foggy weather: a siren: a big bellowing voice; **fog′-lamp** a lamp, esp. on a vehicle, used to improve visibility in fog; **fog′-signal** a detonating cap or other audible warning used in fog; **fog′-smoke** fog. — **not have the foggiest** not to have the least idea. [Origin obscure; perh. conn. with next word; perh. with Dan. *fog,* as in *snee-fog,* thick falling snow.]

fog² *fog,* **foggage** *fog′ij, ns.* grass that grows after the hay is cut: moss (*Scot.*). — *v.i.* to become covered with fog. — *adj.* **fogg′y.** [Origin unknown; W. *ffwg,* dry grass, is borrowed from English.]

fogash *fog′osh, n.* the pike-perch. [Hung. *fogas.*]

fogey. See **fogy.**

fogle *fōg′əl,* (*slang*) *n.* a silk handkerchief. [Origin obscure.]

fogy, fogey *fō′gi, n.* a dull old fellow (also **old fog(e)y**): one with antiquated notions. — *adj.* **fō′gram** anti-quated. — *n.* a fogy. — *ns.* **fō′gramite; fogram′ity; fō′gydom.** — *adj.* **fō′gyish.** — *n.* **fō′gyism.** — **young fog(e)y** a young person who adopts old-fashioned opinions, appearance, etc. [Prob. from **foggy,** moss-grown.]

foh, pho (*pl.* **phos**) , **phoh** *fō, interj.* expressing disgust or contempt.

föhn, foehn *fœn,* **n.** a hot dry wind blowing down a mountain valley in the Alps. [Ger., — Romansch *favugn* — Lat. *Favōnius,* the west wind.]

foible *foi′bl, n.* a weakness: a penchant: a failing: a faible. [O.Fr. *foible,* weak; cf. **faible, feeble.**]

foie gras *fwä-grä,* (Fr.) fat liver (of goose) made into *pâté de foie gras* (or *foies gras*) (*pä-tä də*).

foil¹ *foil, v.t.* to defeat: to baffle: to frustrate: to beat down or trample with the feet (*obs.*): in hunting, to destroy a trail by crossing. — *n.* a check, repulse, frustration (*obs.*): an incomplete fall in wrestling: a blunt fencing sword with a button on the point. — **put on the foil** to overcome, bring to naught. [O.Fr. *fuler,* to stamp or crush — L. *fullō,* a fuller of cloth.]

foil² *foil, n.* a leaf or thin plate of metal, as tinfoil: a mercury coating on a mirror: metal-coated paper: a thin leaf of metal put under a precious stone to show it to advantage: anything that serves to set off something else: a small arc in tracery: an aerofoil or

hydrofoil. — *adj.* **foiled.** — *n.* **foil′ing.** [O.Fr. *foil* (Fr. *feuille*) — L. *folium,* a leaf.]

foin *foin, v.i.* to thrust with a sword or spear. — *n.* a thrust with a sword or spear. — *adj.* **foin′ingly.** [O.Fr. *foine* — L. *fuscĭna,* a trident.]

foison *foi′zn, n.* plenty (*arch.*): plentiful yield (*arch.*): strength, vitality, essential virtue (*Scot.*; also **fushion, fusion** *fōōzh′ən, fizh′ən, fizz′en*). — *adj.* **foi′sonless** weak, feeble (*Scot.*; also **fush′ionless, fu′sionless, fizz′-enless**). [O.Fr., — L. *fūsĭō, -ōnis — fundĕre, fūsum,* to pour forth.]

foist *foist, v.t.* to bring in by stealth: to insert wrongfully (*in* or *into* the thing affected): to pass off *on* or *upon* the person affected). — *n.* **foist′er.** [Prob. Du. dial. *vuisten,* to take in hand; *vuist,* fist.]

folacin *fō′lə-sin, n.* folic acid.

fold¹ *fōld, n.* a doubling of anything upon itself: a crease: the concavity of anything folded: a part laid over on another. — *v.t.* to lay in folds, double over: to enclose in a fold or folds, to wrap up: to embrace. — *v.i.* to become folded: to be capable of folding: to yield (*obs.*): (of a business, etc.) to collapse, cease functioning (also with *up*; *coll.*). — *suff.* **-fold** (with numerals), times, as in **ten′fold.** — *adj.* **fold′able.** — *n.* **fold′er** the person or thing that folds: a flat knife-like instrument used in folding paper: a folding case for loose papers: a folded circular. — *adj.* **fold′ing** that folds, or that can be folded. — *n.* a fold or plait: the bending of strata, usu. as the result of compression (*geol.*). — *adj.* **fold′away** which can be folded and put away. — **foldboat** see **faltboat; folded mountains** mountains produced by folding processes; **fold′ing-door′** a door consisting of two parts hung on opposite jambs; **fold′ing-machine** a mechanism that automatically folds printed sheets; **folding money** (*coll.*) paper money. — *adj., n.* **fold′-out** (a large page, e.g. containing a diagram) folded to fit into a book, and to be unfolded for inspection (also **gate′fold**). — **fold in** to mix in carefully and gradually (*cook.*). [O.E. *faldan* (W.S. *fealdan*), to fold; Ger. *falten.*]

fold² *fōld, n.* an enclosure for protecting domestic animals, esp. sheep: a flock of sheep: a church (*fig.*): the Christian Church (*fig.*). — *v.t.* to confine in a fold. — *n.* **fold′ing.** [O.E. *falod, fald,* a fold, stall.]

folderol. See **falderal.**

foliage, foliar, foliate, etc. See **folium.**

folic acid *fō′lik* (*fo′lik*) *as′id,* an acid in the vitamin B complex, found in leaves, liver, etc., or a similar acid which cures some of the symptoms of pernicious anaemia (see **pterin**). — *adj.* **fo′late** deficient in folic acid. [See **folium.**]

folie *fo-lē,* (Fr.) *n.* madness, insanity: folly. — **folie à deux** (*a də*) a form of mental illness in which two people, generally close to one another, share the same delusion; **folie de doute** (*də dōōt*) mental illness characterised by inability to make decisions, however trifling; **folie de grandeur** (*grã-dœr*) delusions of grandeur.

folio *fō′li-ō, n.* a leaf (two pages) of a book: a sheet of paper once folded: a book of such sheets: the size of such a book: one of several sizes of paper adapted for folding once into well-proportioned leaves: a page in an account-book, or two opposite pages numbered as one (*book-k.*): a certain number of words taken as a basis for computing the length of a document (*law*): a page number in a book (*print.*): a wrapper for loose papers: — *pl.* **fō′lios.** — *adj.* consisting of paper only once folded: of the size of a folio. — *v.t.* to number the leaves or the pages of: to mark off the end of every folio of, in law copying: — *pr.p.* **fō′lioing;** *pa.t.* and *pa.p.* **fō′lioed.** — **in folio** in sheets folded once: in the form of a folio. [L. *in foliō,* on leaf (so-and-so), used in references; L. *folium,* a leaf, a sheet of paper.]

folium *fō′li-əm, n.* a leaf, lamina, or lamella: — *pl.* **fō′lia.** — *adj.* **fōliāceous** (*-ā′shəs*) leaflike: like a foliage leaf: leaf-bearing: laminated. — *n.* **fō′liage** leaves collectively: a mass of leaves: plant forms in art. — *adjs.* **fō′liaged** having foliage: worked like foliage; **fō′liar**

pertaining to leaves: resembling leaves. — *v.t.* **fo′liate** orig., to beat into a leaf: to cover with leaf-metal: to number the leaves (not pages) of. — *v.i.* to split into laminae: of a plant, to grow leaves. — *adj.* **fo′liated** beaten into a thin leaf: decorated with leaf ornaments or foils: consisting of layers or laminae. — *ns.* **foliā′tion** the leafing, esp. of plants: the act of beating a metal into a thin plate, or of spreading foil over a piece of glass to form a mirror: the numbering of leaves in a book: the alternation of more or less parallel layers or folia of different mineralogical nature, of which the crystalline schists are composed (*geol.*): decoration with cusps, lobes, or foliated tracery (*archit.*); **fo′liature** foliation; **fo′liole** a leaflet of a compound leaf (*bot.*): a small leaflike structure. — *adjs.* **fo′liolate, fo′liolose** composed of or pertaining to leaflets; **fo′liose** leafy: leaflike. — **foliage leaf** an ordinary leaf, not a petal, bract, etc.; **foliage plant** one grown for the beauty of its foliage; **foliar feed** a plant food applied in solution to the leaves. [L. *folium*, a leaf; cf. **blade**; Gr. *phyllon*.]

folk *fōk, n.* people, collectively or distributively: a nation or people: the people, commons (*arch.*): those of one's own family, relations (*coll.*): now generally used as a pl. (either **folk** or **folks**) to mean people in general. — *adj.* handed down by tradition of the people (found also in **folk-art, folk-craft, folk-medicine, folk-music,** etc.). — *adj.* **folk′sy** (chiefly *U.S.*) everyday: friendly: sociable: of ordinary people: (artificially) traditional in style. — *n.* **folk′siness.** — **folk′-dance** a dance handed down by tradition of the people; **Folketing** (Dan.; *fōl′kə-ting*) the lower house of the Danish parliament or Rigsdag; **folk′-etymol′ogy** popular unscientific attempts at etymology. — *adj.* **folk′-free** having the rights of a freeman. — **folk′land** (O.E. *folcland*) in old English times, probably land held by folk-right, opposed to *bōcland* (bookland); **folk′lore** the ancient observances and customs, the notions, beliefs, traditions, superstitions, and prejudices of the common people: the study of these observances, etc. — the science of the survival of archaic belief and custom in modern ages (a name suggested by W. J. Thoms in 1846). — *adj.* **folk′lōric.** — **folk′lōrist** one who studies folklore; **folk-mem′ory** a memory of an event that survives in a community through many generations: power of remembering as attributed to a community; **folk′moot** an assembly of the people among the Old English; **folk′-right** the common law or right of the people; **folk′rock** a form of popular music which adapts folk melodies to the rhythm of rock music; **folk′-sing′er; folk′-song** any song or ballad originating among the people and traditionally handed down by them: a modern song composed in the same idiom; **folk′-speech** the dialect of the common people of a country, in which ancient idioms are embedded; **folk′-tale** a popular story handed down by oral tradition from a more or less remote antiquity; **folk′-tune** a tune handed down among the people; **folk′way** a traditional way of thinking, feeling, or acting, followed unreflectingly by a social group; **folk′-weave** a loosely woven fabric. [O.E. *folc*; O.N. *folk*; Ger. *Volk*.]

follicle *fol′i-kl, n.* a fruit formed from a single carpel containing several seeds, splitting along the ventral suture only (*bot.*): a Graafian follicle (*zool.*): any small saclike structure, as the pit surrounding a hair-root (*zool.*). — *adjs.* **follic′ulated, follic′ular, follic′ulose, follic′ulous.** [L. *folliculus,* dim. of *follis,* a wind-bag.]

follow *fol′ō, v.t.* to go after or behind: to keep along the line of: to come after, succeed: to pursue: to attend: to imitate: to obey: to adopt, as an opinion: to keep the eye or mind fixed on: to grasp or understand the whole course or sequence of: to result from, as an effect from a cause: to strive to obtain (*B.*). — *v.i.* to come after: to result: to be the logical conclusion. — *n.* a stroke that causes the ball to follow the one it has struck (*billiards*; commonly **follow-through′**): a second helping. — *ns.* **foll′ower** one who comes after: a copier: a disciple: a retainer, an attendant: a servant-girl's

sweetheart: a part of a machine driven by another part; **foll′owing** a body of supporters. — *adj.* coming next after: to be next mentioned: of a wind, blowing in the same direction as a boat, aircraft, etc., is travelling. — *prep.* after. — **foll′ow-board** in moulding, the board on which the pattern is laid; **follow-my-lead′er** a game in which all have to mimic whatever the leader does; **follow-on′, -through′** an act of following on or through. — **follow home** to follow to the point aimed at, heart of the matter; **follow on** to continue endeavours (*B.*): in cricket, to take a second innings immediately after the first, as compulsory result of being short in number of runs: to follow immediately (*coll.*): to start where another left off (*coll.*); **follow out** to carry out (e.g. instructions): to follow to the end or conclusion; **follow suit** in card-playing, to play a card of the same suit as the one which was led: to do what another has done; **follow through** to complete the swing of a stroke after hitting the ball: to carry any course of action to its conclusion; **follow up** to pursue an advantage closely: to pursue a question that has been started (*n.* **foll′ow-up**). [O.E. *folgian, fylgan;* Ger. *folgen.*]

folly *fol′i, n.* silliness or weakness of mind: a foolish thing: sin (*obs.*): a monument of folly, as a great useless structure, or one left unfinished, having been begun without a reckoning of the cost. — *v.i.* (*arch.*) to act with folly. [O.Fr. *folie* — *fol,* foolish.]

Fomalhaut *fō′məl-howt, -höt, -ə-löt, n.* a first-magnitude star in the constellation of the Southern Fish. [Ar. *fam-al-hūt,* the whale's mouth.]

foment *fō-ment′, v.t.* to apply a warm lotion to: to cherish with heat (*obs.*): to foster (usu. evil). — *ns.* **fomentā′tion** the application of a warm lotion (extended sometimes to a dry or cold application): the lotion so applied: instigation; **fomen′ter.** [L. *fōmentum* for *fovimentum* — *fovēre,* to warm.]

fomes *fō′mēz, n.* a substance capable of carrying infection: — *pl.* **fomites** (*fō′mi-tēz*). [L. *fōmes, -ĭtis,* touchwood.]

fon *fon,* (*obs.*) *n.* a fool. — *v.i.* (*obs.*) to be foolish, play the fool. — *v.t.* (*obs.*) to befool: to toy with. — *adv.* (*obs.*) **fon′ly** foolishly. [See **fond**[1].]

fonctionnaire *fõk-syo-ner,* (Fr.) *n.* an official: a civil servant.

fond[1] *fond, adj.* foolishly tender and loving (*arch.*): credulous, foolishly hopeful (*arch.*): weakly indulgent: prizing highly (with *of*): very affectionate: kindly disposed: foolish. — *v.i.* to dote. — *v.t.* **fond′le** to handle with fondness: to caress. — *ns.* **fond′ler; fond′ling** a pet: a fool (*obs.*). — *adv.* **fond′ly.** — *n.* **fond′ness.** [Pa.p. of **fon** — M.E. *fonnen,* to act foolishly, *fon,* a fool.]

fond[2] (*Spens.*), *pa.t.* of **fand**[2] and *pa.t.* and *pa.p.* of **find.**

fond[3] *fõ,* (Fr.) *n.* basis, foundation, background.

fonda *fon′dä,* (Sp.) *n.* a tavern.

fondant *fon′dənt, n.* a soft sweetmeat, made with flavoured sugar and water, that melts in the mouth. [Fr., — *fondre,* to melt — L. *fundēre.*]

fondle, fonds. See **fond**[1].

fonds *fõ,* (Fr.) *n.* landed property: capital: money: fund (*lit.* and *fig.*).

fondue *fon′dōō, fõ-dü, n.* a sauce made from cheese and wine, etc., and which is eaten by dipping pieces of bread, etc., in the mixture (also **Swiss fondue**): a dish consisting of small cubes of meat cooked at the table on forks in hot oil and served with piquant sauces (also **fondue bourguignonne,** *bōōr-gē-nyon*): a soufflé with bread or biscuit crumbs. [Fr., — fem. pa.p. of *fondre,* to melt.]

fone. See **foe.**

fons et origo *fons et o-rī′gō, -rē′,* (L.) the source and origin.

font[1] *font, n.* a vessel for baptismal water: a fount, fountain (*poet.*). — *adj.* **font′al** pertaining to a font or origin. — *n.* **font′let** a little font. — **font name** baptismal name; **font′-stone** a baptismal font of stone. [O.E. *font* — L. *fōns, fontis,* a fountain.]

font[2] *font.* See **fount**[1].

fontanelle, fontanel *fon-tə-nel', n.* a gap between the bones of the skull of a young animal: an opening for discharge. [Fr. dim., — L. *fōns, fontis,* fountain.]

fontange *fɔ-tãzh', n.* a tall head-dress worn in the 17th and 18th centuries. [Fr., from *Fontanges,* the territorial title of one of Louis XIV's mistresses.]

Fontarabian *fon-tə-rā'bi-ən, adj.* pertaining to *Fontarabia* or *Fuenterrabia* at the west end of the Pyrenees (confused by Milton with Roncesvalles).

fonticulus *fon-tik'ū-ləs, n.* the depression just over the top of the breast-bone. [L. *fonticulus,* dim. of *fōns,* fountain.]

Fontinalis *fon-tin-ā'lis, n.* a genus of aquatic mosses allied to *Hypnum:* (without *cap.*) any moss of this genus. [L. *fontinālis,* of a spring — *fōns.*]

food[1] *fōōd, n.* what one feeds on: that which, being digested, nourishes the body: whatever sustains or promotes growth (also *fig.*): substances elaborated by the plant from raw materials taken in (*bot.*). — *adj.* **food'ful** able to supply food abundantly. — *n.* **food'ie** (*coll.*) one greatly (even excessively) interested in the preparation and consumption of good food. — *adj.* **food'less** without food. — **food canal** the alimentary canal; **food'-card** a card entitling its holder to obtain his quota of rationed food-stuffs; **food chain** a series of organisms connected by the fact that each forms food for the next higher organism in the series; **food'-controll'er** an official who controls the storing, sale, and distribution of food in time of emergency; **food'-fish** an edible fish; **food poisoning** gastrointestinal disorder caused by the ingestion of foods naturally toxic to the system or of foods made toxic by contamination with bacteria or chemicals; **food processor** an electrical appliance for cutting, blending, mincing, etc. food; **food'stuff** a substance used as food; **food values** the relative nourishing power of foods. — **food conversion ratio** the ratio of the weight of foodstuff a cow, pig, chicken, etc. consumes, to its own bodyweight. [O.E. *fōda;* Goth. *fōdeins,* Sw. *fōda.*]

food[2] *fōōd,* Spens. for **feud**[1].

fool[1] *fōōl, n.* one wanting in wisdom, judgment or sense: a person of weak mind: a jester: a tool or victim, as of untoward circumstances, a dupe: a vague term of endearment (*obs.*): one with a weakness for (with *for*). — *v.t.* to deceive: to make to appear foolish: to get by fooling. — *v.i.* to play the fool: to trifle. — *adj.* (*Scot.* and *U.S.*) foolish. — *ns.* **fool'ery** an act of folly: habitual folly: fooling; **fool'ing** playing the fool: acting the jester: vein of jesting: trifling. — *adj.* **fool'ish** weak in intellect: wanting discretion: unwise: ridiculous: marked with folly: paltry. — *adv.* **fool'ishly.** — *n.* **fool'ishness.** — *adjs.* **fool'begged** (*Shak.*) perh., foolish enough to be begged for a fool (in allusion to the custom of seeking the administration of a lunatic's estate for one's own advantage); **fool'-born** (*Shak.*) born of a fool or of folly; **fool'-happ'y** happy or lucky without contrivance or judgment. — **fool'hard'iness** (*Spens.* foolhardise, -ize; -īz' or -härd'). — *adjs.* **fool'-hardy** foolishly bold: rash or incautious; **fool'ish-witt'y** (*Shak.*) wise in folly and foolish in wisdom; **fool'proof** not liable to sustain or inflict injury by wrong usage: infallible. — **fool's cap** a jester's head-dress, usu. having a cockscomb hood with bells; **fool's errand** a silly or fruitless enterprise: search for what cannot be found; **fool's gold** iron pyrites; **fool's mate** (*chess*) the simplest of the mates (in two moves each); **fool's paradise** a state of happiness based on fictitious hopes or expectations; **fool's parsley** a poisonous umbelliferous plant (*Aethusa cynapium*) that a great enough fool might take for parsley. — **All Fool's Day** see **all**; **fool around** to waste time: to trifle: to trifle with someone's affections; **fool away** to squander to no purpose or profit; **fool with** to meddle with officiously; **make a fool of** to bring a person into ridicule: to disappoint; **nobody's fool** a sensible person; **play, act the fool** to behave as a fool: to sport. [O.Fr. *fol* (Fr. *fou*) — L. *follis,* a wind-bag.]

fool[2] *fōōl, n.* a purée of fruit scalded or stewed, mixed with cream or custard and sugar, as *gooseberry fool.* [Prob. a use of preceding suggested by *trifle.*]

foolscap *fōōl'skap, n.* a long folio writing- or printing-paper, generally 17 × 13 ½ in., originally bearing the watermark of a *fool's cap* and bells.

foot *fōōt, n.* the part of its body on which an animal stands or walks: a muscular development of the ventral surface in molluscs: the absorbent and attaching organ of a young sporophyte (*bot.*): the part on which a thing stands: the base: the lower or less dignified end: a measure = 12 in., orig., the length of a man's foot: the corresponding square or cubic unit (sq. ft. 144 sq. inches; cu. ft. 1728 cu. inches): foot-soldiers: a division of a line of poetry: a manner of walking: a part of a sewing machine that holds the fabric still under the needle: — *pl.* **feet;** also, as a measure, **foot;** in some compounds and in sense of dregs, or footlights, **foots.** — *v.t.* and *v.i.* to dance: to walk: to sum up. — *v.t.* to kick: to pay: to add a foot to: to grasp with the foot: — *pr.p.* **foot'ing;** *pa.t.* and *pa.p.* **foot'ed.** — *n.* **foot'age** measurement or payment by the foot: length of organ pipe giving the lowest note: an amount (i.e. length) of cinema film. — *adj.* **foot'ed** provided with a foot or feet: having gained a football (*Shak.*). — *suff.* **-foot'ed** having a specified number of feet: having a specified manner of walking. — *ns.* **foot'er** (*slang*) football; **-foot'er** (in *comp.*) something of a particular length in feet, usu. a boat (e.g. *he sails a twenty-four-footer*); **foot'ing** place for the foot to rest on: standing: terms: installation: an installation fee or treat: foundation: lower part: position: settlement: track: tread: dance: plain cotton lace. — *adj.* **foot'less** without feet: very drunk (*coll.*). — **foot'ball** a large ball for kicking about in sport: a game played with this ball: a bargaining-point, point of controversy, etc. (*fig.*); **foot'baller, foot'ballist** a football player; **foot'bar** the bar controlled by the pilot's feet, for operating the rudder in aircraft; **foot'-bath** act of bathing the feet: a vessel for this purpose; **foot'board** a support for the foot in a carriage or elsewhere: the footplate of a locomotive engine; **foot'boy** an attendant in livery; **foot brake** a brake operated by the foot; **foot'breadth** the breadth of a foot; **foot'bridge** a bridge for foot-passengers; **foot'-candle** a former unit of illumination, equivalent to one lumen per square foot (= 10·764 lux); **foot'cloth** a sumpter-cloth reaching to the feet of the horse; **foot'fall** the sound of setting the foot down; **foot'fault** (*lawn tennis*) an overstepping of the line in serving. — Also *v.t.* and *v.i.* — **foot'gear** shoes and stockings. — *n.pl.* **foot'guards** guards that serve on foot. — **foot'hill** a minor elevation below a higher mountain or range (usually in *pl.*); **foot'hold** a place to fix the foot in: a grip: a firm starting position; **foot'-jaw** a maxilliped; **foot'-lam'bert** a former unit of luminance, equivalent to one lumen per square foot; **foot'-land-'raker** (*Shak.*) a footpad; **foot'-licker** a fawning, slavish flatterer; **foot'light** one of a row of lights along the front of the stage: (in *pl.*) the theatre as a profession. — *adj.* **foot'loose** free, unhampered. — **foot'man** one who goes on foot: a servant or attendant in livery: a foot-soldier: a servant running before a coach or rider: a low stand for fireside utensils (*pl.* **foot'men**); **foot'mark** see **foot'-print**; **foot'muff** muff for keeping the feet warm; **foot'note** a note of reference or comment at the foot of a page; **foot'pace** a walking pace: a dais; **foot'pad** a highwayman on foot; **foot'page** a boy attendant; **foot'-pass'enger** one who goes on foot; **foot'path** a way for foot-passengers only: a side pavement; **foot'plate** a platform for **foot'platemen** (*sing.* -man), train driver and assistant (on steam locomotive, stoker); **foot'post** a post or messenger that travels on foot; **foot'-pound** the energy needed to raise a mass of one pound through the height of one foot; **foot'print** the mark left on the ground or floor by a person's or animal's foot (also **foot'mark**): the area surrounding an airport, or the part of an aircraft's flight path, in which the noise level is liable to be above a certain level: the area covered by the down-driven blast of air which supports a hovercraft: the area on a floor, desk, etc., occupied by a computer or part of one: the area covered by the beam of a direct broadcast satellite; **foot'-pump** a pump held or operated by the foot; **foot'-race** a race on foot; **foot'-racing; foot'rest** a support for the foot; **foot'-rope** a rope stretching along under a ship's yard for the men to stand on when furling the sails: the rope to which the lower edge of a sail is attached; **foot'rot** ulceration of the coronary band, or other affection of the feet in sheep or cattle; **foot'rule** a rule or measure a foot in length or measured off in feet. — *v.i.* **foot'slog** to march, tramp. — **foot'slogger; foot'slogging; foot'-soldier** a soldier serving on foot. — *adj.* **foot'sore** having sore or tender feet, as by much walking. — **foot'stalk** (*bot.*) the stalk or petiole of a leaf; **foot'-stall** a side-saddle stirrup; **foot'step** a tread: a footfall: a footprint: a raised step for ascending or descending: (in *pl., fig.*) course, example; **foot'stool** a stool for placing one's feet on when sitting. — *adj.* **foot'stooled.** — **foot'-ton** a unit of work or energy equal to the work done in raising one ton one foot against normal gravity; **foot'-warmer** a contrivance for keeping the feet warm; **foot'way** a path for passengers on foot: a mine shaft with ladders; **foot'wear** a collective term for boots, shoes, socks, etc.; **foot'work** use or management of the feet, as in games. — *adj.* **foot'worn** worn by many feet: footsore. — **a foot in the door** a first step towards a usu. difficult desired end; **at the feet of** in submission, homage, supplication, or devotion to, under the spell of; **cover the feet** (*B.*) to defecate; **drag one's feet** see **drag**. — *adj.* **eight'-foot** (*mus.*) having the pitch of an open organ-pipe eight feet long, or having that pitch for the lowest note. — **foot-and-mouth disease** a contagious disease of cloven-footed animals, characterised by vesicular eruption, esp. in the mouth and in the clefts of the feet; **foot it** to walk: to dance; **foot of fine** the bottom part (preserved in the records) of a tripartite indenture in case of a fine of land; **foot the bill** to pay up; **have one foot in the grave** to be not far from death; **have one's feet on the ground** to act habitually with practical good sense; **my foot!** *interj.* expressing disbelief, usu. contemptuous; **on foot** walking or running: in activity or being; **play footsie** (*coll.*) to rub one's foot or leg against another person's, usu. with amorous intentions; **put a,** or **one's, foot wrong** (usu. in *neg.*) to make a mistake, blunder; **put one's best foot forward** to make one's best effort; **put one's foot down** to take a firm decision, usu. against something; **put one's foot in it** to spoil anything by some indiscretion; **set foot in (on)** to enter; **set on foot** to originate; **the ball is at his feet** he has nothing to do but seize his opportunity; **the footlights** the theatre as a profession; **the wrong foot** disadvantageous position or circumstances, as **catch on the wrong foot** to catch unprepared, **get off on the wrong foot** to make a bad beginning. [O.E. *fōt*, pl. *fēt*; Ger. *Fuss*, L. *pēs, pedis*, Gr. *pous, podos*, Sans. *pad*.]

footle *fōōt'l, v.i.* to trifle, to show foolish incompetence, to bungle. — *n.* silly nonsense. — *n.* and *adj.* **foot'ling** [Origin obscure.]

footra. See **fouter**.

footsie. See **play footsie** under **foot**.

footy *fōōt'i,* (*dial.*) *adj.* mean. [Origin obscure.]

foo yung, yong. See **fu yung**.

foozle *fōōz'l,* (*coll.*) *n.* a tedious fellow: a bungled stroke at golf, etc. — *v.i.* to fool away one's time. — *v.i.* and *v.t.* to bungle. — *n.* **fooz'ler.** — *n.* and *adj.* **fooz'ling.** [Cf. Ger. dial. *fuseln*, to work badly, to potter.]

fop *fop, n.* an affected dandy. — *ns.* **fop'ling** a vain affected person; **fopp'ery** vanity in dress or manners: affectation: folly. — *adj.* **fopp'ish** vain and showy in dress: affectedly refined in manners. — *adv.* **fopp'ishly.** — *n.* **fopp'ishness.** [Cf. Ger. *foppen*, to hoax.]

for *för, far, prep.* in the place of: in favour of: on account of: in the direction of: having as goal or intention: with

respect to: in respect of: by reason of: appropriate or adapted to, or in reference to: beneficial to: in quest of: notwithstanding, in spite of: in recompense of: during: in the character of: to the extent of. — *conj.* because. — **as for** as far as concerns; **for all (that)** notwithstanding; **for that** (*obs.*) because; **for to** (*arch.* or *dial*) in order to: to; **for why** (*obs.*) why: because; **nothing for it but (to)** no other possible course but (to); **to be (in) for it** to have something unpleasant impending; **what is he for a man?** (*obs.*) what kind of man is he? [O.E. *for*.]

for- *för-, far-, pfx.* (1) in words derived from O.E., used to form verbs with the senses: (a) away, off; (b) against; (c) thoroughly, utterly: intensive; (d) exhaustion; (e) destruction. (2) used in words derived from O.E. to form adjs. with superlative force. (3) a contraction of *fore-*. (4) in words derived from L. *forīs*, outside, *forās*, forth, out. No longer a living prefix.

fora. See **forum**.

forage *for'ij, n.* fodder, or food for horses and cattle: provisions: the act of foraging. — *v.i.* to go about and forcibly carry off food for horses and cattle: to rummage about for what one wants. — *v.t.* to plunder. — *n.* **for'ager.** — **for'age-cap** the undress cap worn by infantry soldiers. [Fr. *fourrage*, O.Fr. *feurre*, fodder, of Gmc. origin; cf. **fodder**.]

foramen *fō-rā'mən, fö-, n.* a small opening: — *pl.* **foramina** (*-ram'i-nə*). — *adjs.* **foram'inal; foram'inated, foram'inous** pierced with small holes: porous. — *n.* **foraminifer** (*for-ə-min'i-fər*) any member of the **Foraminif'era** (*-am-*, or *-ām-*) an order of rhizopods with a shell usu. perforated by pores (*foramina*; L. *ferre*, to bear). — *adjs.* **foraminif'eral, foraminif'erous.** — **forāmen magnum** the great hole in the occipital bone through which the spinal cord joins the medulla oblongata. [L. *forāmen — forāre*, to pierce.]

forane *for-ān', adj.* a form of **foreign,** outlying, rural, as in **vicar-forane** (q.v.).

forasmuch *för-, far-əz-much', conj.* because, since (with *as*).

foray *for'ā, n.* a raid: a venture, attempt. — *v.t.* and *v.i.* to raid: to forage. — *n.* **for'ayer.** [Ety. obscure, but ult. identical with **forage** (q.v.).]

forhad(e). See **forbid.**

forbear[1] *för-, far-bār', v.i.* to keep oneself in check: to abstain. — *v.t.* to abstain from: to avoid voluntarily: to spare, to withhold: to give up (*obs*) :— *pa.t.* **forbore'**; *pa.p.* **forborne'.** — *n.* **forbear'ance** exercise of patience: command of temper: clemency. — *adjs.* **forbear'ant, forbear'ing** long-suffering: patient. — *adv.* **forbear'ingly.** [O.E. *forberan*, pa.t. *forbær*, pa.p. *forboren*; see pfx. **for-** (1a), and **bear.**]

forbear[2] *för'bār.* Same as **forebear.**

forbid *fər-, för-bid', v.t.* to prohibit: to command not to: — *pa.t.* **forbade** *-bad'*, by some *-bād'*, or **forbad'**; *pa.p.* **forbidd'en.** — *ns.* **forbidd'al, forbidd'ance** prohibition: command or edict against a thing. — *adj.* **forbidd'en** prohibited: unlawful: not permitted, esp. in certain scientific rules: (of a combination of symbols) not in an operating code, i.e., revealing a fault (*comput.*). — *adv.* **forbidd'enly** (*Shak.*) in a forbidden or unlawful manner. — *ns.* **forbidd'er; forbidd'ing.** — *adj.* uninviting: sinister: unprepossessing: threatening or formidable in look. — *adv.* **forbidd'ingly.** — *ns.* **forbidd'ingness; forbode** (*för-bōd'; arch.*) prohibition. — **forbidden degrees** see **degree; forbidden fruit** that forbidden to Adam (Gen. ii. 17): anything tempting and prohibited: (or *Adam's apple*) a name fancifully given to the fruit of various species of Citrus, esp. to one having tooth-marks on its rind. — **over God's forbode** (*arch.*) God forbid. [O.E. *forbēodan*, pa.t. *forbēad*, pa.p. *forboden*; see pfx. **for-** (1a), and **bid**; cf. Ger. *verbieten*.]

forbore, forborne. See **forbear**[1].

forby, forbye, *Spens.* **foreby,** *fər-bī', adv.* and *prep.* near (*obs.*): past (*obs.*): by (*obs.*): besides (*Scot.*). [**for,** *adv.,* **by.**]

forçat *för'sä, n.* in France, a convict condemned to hard labour. [Fr.]

force¹ *förs, förs, n.* strength, power, energy: efficacy: validity: influence: vehemence: violence: coercion: a group of men assembled for collective action (as *police force*), (in *pl.*; sometimes with *cap.*) navy, army, air force: an armament: any cause which changes the direction or speed of the motion of a portion of matter. — *v.t.* to draw or push by main strength: to thrust: to compel: to constrain: to overcome the resistance of by force: to do violence to: to achieve or bring about by force: to ravish: to take by violence: to strain: to cause to grow or ripen rapidly (*hort.*): to work up to a high pitch: to induce to play in a particular way (*cards*): to cause the playing of (*cards*): to strengthen (*Shak.*): to attribute importance to (*obs.*). — *v.i.* to strive (*obs.*): to make way by force: to care (*obs.*). — *adj.* **forced** accomplished by great effort, as a forced march: strained, excessive, unnatural: artificially produced. — *adv.* **forc'edly.** — *n.* **forc'edness** the state of being forced: constraint: unnatural or undue distortion. — *adj.* **force'ful** full of force or might: energetic: driven or acting with power. — *adv.* **force'fully.** — *n.* **force'fulness.** — *adj.* **force'less** weak. — *n.* **forc'er** the person or thing that forces, esp. the piston of a force-pump. — *adj.* **forc'ible** having force: done by force. — *ns.* **forc'ibleness, forcibil'ity.** — *adv.* **forc'ibly.** — **forced labour** compulsory hard labour. — *v.t.* **force'-feed** to feed (a person or animal) forcibly, usu. by the mouth: — *pa.t., pa.p.* **force'-fed.** — **force'-feed'ing.** — *v.i.* **force'-land** to make a forced landing. — **forced landing** (*aero.*) a landing at a place where no landing was orig. planned, necessary because of some mishap; **force'-pump, forc'ing-pump** a pump that delivers liquid under pressure greater than its suction pressure: a pump for cleaning out pipes by blowing air through; **forcible detainer,** and **entry,** detaining property or forcing an entry into it by violence or intimidation; **forcible feeble** a weak man with show of valour (in allusion to Francis Feeble in 2 Hen. IV, III, ii. 180); **forc'ing-house** a hothouse for forcing plants, or a place for hastening the growth of animals; **forc'ing-pit** a frame sunk in the ground over a hotbed for forcing plants. — **force and fear** (*Scot.*) that amount of constraint or compulsion which is enough to annul an engagement or obligation entered into under its influence; **force the pace** to bring and keep the speed up to a high pitch by emulation; **in force** operative, legally binding: in great numbers. [Fr., — L.L. *fortia* — L. *fortis*, strong.]

force² *förs, förs,* **foss** *fos, ns.* a waterfall. [O.N. *fors.*]

force³ *förs, förs,* (*cook.*) *v.t.* to stuff, as fowl. — **force'meat** meat chopped fine and highly seasoned, used as a stuffing or alone. [For **farce.**]

force de frappe *fors də frap,* (Fr.) a strike force, esp. a nuclear one. — **force majeure** (*mä-zhœr*) superior power: an unforeseeable or uncontrollable course of events, excusing one from fulfilling a contract (*legal*).

forceps *för'seps, n.* a pincer-like instrument or organ for holding, lifting, or removing: — *pl.* **for'ceps** also **for'cepses, for'cipēs** (*-si-pēz*) — *adj.* **for'cipāte(d)** formed and opening like a forceps. — *n.* **forcipā'tion** torture by pinching with forceps. [L., — *formus,* hot, *capēre,* to hold.]

forcible, etc. See **force¹.**

ford *förd, förd, n.* a place where water may be crossed by wading. — *v.t.* to wade across. — *adj.* **ford'able.** [O.E. *ford-faran,* to go; cf. Ger. *furt-fahren,* Gr. *poros,* L. *portus,* and **fare, ferry, far.**]

fordo *för-, fər-dōō', (arch.) v.t.* to destroy: to ruin: to overcome: to exhaust: — *pr.p.* **fordo'ing;** *pa.t.* **fordid';** *pa.p.* **fordone** *-dun'.* — *adj.* **fordone'** exhausted. — **from fordonne** (*Spens.*) from being fordone. [O.E. *fordōn;* Ger. *vertun,* to consume.]

fore *för, för, adj.* in front: former, previous (*obs.*). — *adv.* at or towards the front: previously. — *n.* the front: the foremast. — *interj.* (*golf*) a warning cry to anybody in the way of the ball. — *adj.* **foremost** (*för'möst, för';*

double superl. — O.E. *forma,* first, superl. of *fore,* and superl. suffix *-st*) first in place: most advanced: first in rank and dignity. — *adj.* and *adv.* **fore'-and-aft'** lengthwise of a ship: without square sails. — **fore-and-aft'er** a vessel of fore-and-aft rig: a hat peaked before and behind; **fore'bitt** one of the bitts at the foremast; **fore'bitter** a ballad sung at the forebitts. — **at the fore** displayed on the foremast (of a flag); **fore-and-aft sail** any sail not set on yards and lying fore-and-aft when untrimmed; **to the fore** at hand: in being, alive (*Scot.*): (loosely) prominent. [O.E. *fore,* radically the same as **for,** prep.]

fore- *för, för-, pfx.* before: beforehand: in front. — *vs.t.* **fore-admon'ish** to admonish beforehand; **fore-advise'** to advise beforehand. — *n.* **fore'arm** the part of the arm between the elbow and the wrist. — *v.t.* **forearm'** to arm or prepare beforehand. — *n.* **forebear, forbear** (*för'bār, för';* orig. *Scot.*) an ancestor (from **be** and suff. **-er**). — *v.t.* **forebode'** to prognosticate: to have a premonition of (esp. of evil). — *ns.* **forebode'ment** feeling of coming evil; **forebod'er; forebod'ing** a boding or perception beforehand: apprehension of coming evil. — *adv.* **forebod'ingly.** — *ns.* **fore'-body** the part in front of the mainmast; **fore'-brace** a rope attached to the fore yard-arm, for changing the position of the foresail; **fore'-brain** the front part of the brain, the prosencephalon. — *prep.* **foreby'** (*Spens.*) same as **forby.** — *ns.* **fore'cabin** a cabin in a ship's forepart; **fore'-caddy** a caddy posted where he may see where the balls go; **fore'car** a small car carrying a passenger in front of a motor-cycle; **fore'carriage** the front part of a carriage, with arrangement for independent movement of the fore-wheels. — *v.t.* **fore'cast** to contrive or reckon beforehand: to foresee: to predict. — *v.i.* to form schemes beforehand: — *pa.t.* and *pa.p.* **fore'cast** sometimes **fore'casted.** — *ns.* **fore'cast** a previous contrivance: foresight: a prediction: a weather forecast (q.v.); **fore'caster; forecastle, fo'c'sle** (*fōk'sl,* sometimes *för'käs-l, för'*) a short raised deck at the fore-end of a vessel: the forepart of the ship under the maindeck, the quarters of the crew. — *adjs.* **forechos'en** chosen beforehand; **fore-ci'ted** quoted before or above. — *ns.* **fore'cloth** a cloth that hangs over the front of an altar, an antependium; **fore'course** a foresail; **fore'court** a court in front of a building: an outer court: the front area of a garage or filling-station, where the petrol pumps are situated: the part of a tennis-court between the net and the service line. — *v.t.* **foredate'** to date before the true time. — *ns.* **fore'-day** (*Scot.*) forenoon; **fore'deck** the forepart of a deck or ship. — *v.t.* **foredoom'** to doom beforehand. — *ns.* **fore'-edge** the outer edge of a book, furthest from the back — placed outward in a mediaeval library; **fore'-end** the early or fore part of anything; **fore'father** an ancestor. — *v.t.* **forefeel'** to feel beforehand. — *adv.* **forefeel'ingly.** — *adj.* **forefelt'.** — *ns.* **fore'finger** the finger next to the thumb; **fore'foot** one of the anterior feet of a quadruped: the foremost end of the keel, whereon rests the stem (*naut.*): — *pl.* **fore'feet; fore'front** the front or foremost part; **fore'gleam** a glimpse into the future. — *v.t.* and *v.i.* **forego'** to go before, precede: chiefly in its *pr.p.* **forego'ing** (or *för', för'*) and *pa.p.* **foregone'** (or *för', för'*); *pa.t.* **forewent'** (*rare*); formerly also *pa.p.* — See also **forgo.** — *ns.* **forego'er** (or *för', för'*); **forego'ing.** — *adj.* **fore'gone** (**foregone conclusion** a conclusion come to before examination of the evidence: an obvious or inevitable conclusion or result). — *ns.* **foregone'-ness; fore'ground** the part of a picture or field of view nearest the observer's eye, as opp. to the *background* (also *fig.*); **fore'gut** the front section of the digestive tract of an embryo or an invertebrate animal; **fore'-hammer** a sledge-hammer; **fore'hand** the front position or its occupant: the upper hand, advantage, preference: the part of a horse that is in front of its rider: the part of the court to the right of a right-handed player or to the left of a left-handed player (*tennis*): a stroke played forehand (*tennis*). — *adj.* done beforehand: anticipating, of anticipation (*Shak.*): with the palm in front — opp. to *backhand*: (of an arrow; *Shak.*) for shooting point-blank. — *adv.* with hand in fore-hand position. — *adj.* **fore′handed** forehand, as of payment for goods before delivery, or for services before rendered: seasonable: well off (*U.S.*): shapely in the foreparts. — *ns.* **forehead** (*for′id, -ed, för′hed, för′hed*) the forepart of the head above the eyes, the brow: confidence, audacity; **fore′-horse** the foremost horse of a team. — *v.t.* **forejudge′** to judge before hearing the facts and proof: see **forjudge**. — *ns.* **forejudg′(e)ment; fore′king** (*Tenn.*) a preceding king. — *v.t.* **foreknow′** (*för-, för-*) to know beforehand: to foresee. — *adj.* **foreknow′ing.** — *adv.* **foreknow′ingly.** — *n.* **foreknowledge** (*-nol′ij*). — *adj.* **foreknown′.** — *n.* **fore′-land** a point of land running forward into the sea, a headland: a front region. — *vs.t.* **forelay′** to contrive antecedently: to lay wait for in ambush: to hinder; **forelay′** *pa.t.* of **forelie**. — *n.* **fore′leg** a front leg. — *vs.t.* **forelend′, forlend′** (*arch.*) to grant or resign beforehand: — *pa.p.* and *pa.t., Spens.,* **forelent′, forlent′; forelie′** to lie before: — *pa.t., Spens.,* **forelay′; forelift′** (*Spens.*) to raise in front. — *ns.* **fore′limb; fore′lock** the lock of hair on the forehead (**pull, touch, tug the forelock** to raise one's hand to the forehead in sign of respect, subservience, etc.; **take time by the forelock** to seize an opportunity betimes): a cotter-pin; **fore′man** the first or chief man, one appointed to preside over, or act as spokesman for, others: an overseer: — *pl.* **fore′men; fore′mast** the mast that is forward, or next the bow of a ship; **fore′mastman** any sailor below the rank of petty officer. — *v.t.* **foremean′** (*arch.*) to intend beforehand. — *adj.* **fore′men′tioned** mentioned before in a writing or discourse. — *n.* **fore′name** the first or Christian name. — *adj.* **fore′named** mentioned before. — *ns.* **fore′night** (*Scot.*) the early part of the night before bedtime, the evening; **forenoon** (*för-nōōn′, för-, för′nōōn, för′*) chiefly *Scot.* and *Ir.*) the morning: the part of the day before midday, as opposed to early morning. — *adj.* (*för′, för′*) pertaining to this time. — *n.* **fore′-no′tice** notice of anything in advance of the time. — *v.t.* **fore′ordain′** to arrange beforehand: to predestinate. — *ns.* **foreordina′tion; fore′part** the front: the early part. — *adj.* **fore′past** bygone. — *ns.* **fore′paw** a front paw; **fore′pay′ment** payment beforehand; **fore′-peak** the contracted part of a ship's hold, close to the bow. — *v.t.* **foreplan′** to plan beforehand. — *n.* **fore′play** sexual stimulation before intercourse. — *v.t.* **forepoint′** to foreshadow. — *adj.* **fore-quo′ted** quoted or cited before. — *v.t.* **foreran′** *pa.t.* of **forerun**. — *n.* **fore′-rank** the front rank. — *v.i.* **forereach′** (*naut.*) to glide ahead, esp. when going in stays (with *on*). — *v.t.* to sail beyond. — *v.t.* **foreread′** to foretell: — *pa.t.* **foreread** (*-ed′*). — *n.* **fore′reading.** — *adj.* **fore-reci′ted** (*Shak.*) recited or named before. — *v.t.* **forerun′** to run or come before: to precede. — *n.* **fore′runner** a runner or messenger sent before, a precursor: a prognostic. — *adj.* **fore′said** already mentioned (see also **foresay**). — *n.* **foresail** (*för′sl, för′, -sāl*) the chief and lowest square sail on the foremast: a triangular sail on the forestay. — *v.t.* **foresay′** to predict or foretell: to ordain (*Shak.*): see **forsay**. — *v.t.* and *v.i.* **foresee′** to see or know beforehand: — *pa.t.* **foresaw′;** *pa.p.* **foreseen′.** — *adjs.* **foresee′able; foresee′ing.** — *adv.* **foresee′ingly.** — *v.t.* **foreshad′ow** to shadow or typify beforehand: to give, or have, some indication of in advance. — *n.* **foreshad′owing.** — *v.t.* **foreshew** see **foreshow**. — *ns.* **fore′ship** the forepart of a ship; **fore′shock** an earth tremor preceding an earthquake; **fore′shore** the space between high and low water marks. — *v.t.* **foreshort′en** to draw or cause to appear as if shortened, by per-spective. — *n.* **foreshort′ening.** — *v.t.* **foreshow, fore-shew** (*för-shō′, för-, arch.*) to show or represent before-hand: to predict: — *pa.t.* **foreshowcd, foreshewed** -shōd′; *pa.p.* **foreshown, foreshewn** -shōn′, also *Spens.* **fore-shewed′.** — *ns.* **fore′side** the front side: outward ap-pearance (*Spens.*); **fore′sight** act or power of foresee-

ing: wise forethought, prudence: the sight on the muzzle of a gun: a forward reading of a levelling staff. — *adjs.* **fore′sighted; fore′sightful; fore′sightless.** — *v.t.* **foresig′nify** (*arch.*) to betoken beforehand: to fore-show: to typify. — *ns.* **fore′skin** the skin that covers the glans penis, the prepuce; **fore′skirt** (*Shak.*) the loose part of a coat before. — *vs.t.* **forespeak′** to predict: to engage beforehand (*Scot.*): see **forspeak; forespend′** to spend beforehand: — *pa.p.* **forespent′.** — See also **forspend**. — *ns.* **fore-spurr′er** (*Shak.*) one who rides before; **fore′stair** (*Scot.*) an outside stair in front of a house. — *v.t.* **forestall** (*för-stöl′, för-*; O.E. *foresteall*, ambush, lit. a place taken beforehand — *steall*, stand, station) to buy up before reaching the market, so as to sell again at higher prices: to anticipate: to hinder by anticipating: to bar. — *ns.* **forestall′er; forestall′ing; forestal′ment; fore′stay** a rope reaching from the fore-mast-head to the bowsprit end to support the mast. — *v.t.* **foretaste′** to taste before possession: to antici-pate: to taste before another. — *n.* **fore′taste** a taste beforehand: anticipation. — *vs.t.* **foreteach′** (*arch.*) to teach beforehand: — *pa.t.* and *pa.p.* **foretaught′; fore-tell′** to tell before: to prophesy. — *v.i.* to utter prophecy: — *pa.t.* and *pa.p.* **foretold′.** — *n.* **foretell′er.** — *v.t.* **forethink′** to anticipate in the mind: to have prescience of: — *pa.t.* and *pa.p.* **forethought′.** — *ns.* **forethink′er; fore′thought** thought or care for the future: anticipa-tion: thinking beforehand. — *adj.* **forethought′ful.** — *ns.* **fore′time** past time; **fore′token** a token or sign beforehand. — *v.t.* **foretō′ken** to signify beforehand. — *n.* and *adj.* **foretō′kening.** — *ns.* **fore′tooth** a tooth in the forepart of the mouth: — *pl.* **fore′teeth; fore′top** the platform at the head of the foremast (*naut.*): the forepart of the crown of the head (*obs.*): a lock (usu. upright) over the forehead: an appendage to a shoe (*obs.*); **foretop′mast** the mast erected at the head of the foremast, at the top of which is the **fore′top-gall′ant=mast.** — *adj.* **forevouched′** (*Shak.*) affirmed or told before. — *n.* **fore′ward** (*arch.*) an advance guard: the front (*Shak.*). — *v.t.* **forewarn′** to warn beforehand: to give previous notice: see **forwarn**. — *n.* **forewarn′ing.** — *v.t.* **foreweigh′** (*arch.*) to estimate beforehand. — **forewent′** *pa.t.* (*Spens., pa.p.*) of **forego** (see also **forgo**). — *ns.* **fore′-wheel** one of the pair of front wheels of a wheeled vehicle; **fore′wind** a favourable wind; **fore′wing** either of an insect's front pair of wings; **fore′woman** a woman overseer, a headwoman, a spokeswoman for a group (e.g. for a jury): — *pl.* **fore′women; fore′word** a preface. [O.E. *fore*; Ger. *vor*.]

foreanent. See **fornent**.

foreclose *för-klōz′, för-, v.t.* to preclude: to prevent: to stop: to bar the right of redeeming. — *n.* **foreclosure** (*-klō′zhər*) a foreclosing: the process by which a mort-gagor, failing to repay the money lent on the security of an estate, is compelled to forfeit his right to redeem the estate (*law*). [O.Fr. *forclos*, pa.p. of *forclore*, to exclude — L. *forīs*, outside, and *claudēre, clausum*, to shut.]

fore-damned *för-dam′ned,* (*obs.*) *adj.* utterly damned (or poss. damned beforehand). [Pfx. **for-** (1c), (or poss. **fore-**).]

foregather. See **forgather**.

forego[1]. See **fore-**.

forego[2]. See **forgo**.

forehent. See **forhent**.

foreign *for′in, adj.* belonging to another country: from abroad: pertaining to, characteristic of or situated in another country: alien: extraneous: not belonging: unconnected: not appropriate. — *ns.* **for′eigner** a na-tive of another country; **for′eignism** a mannerism, turn of phrase, etc., typical of a foreigner; **for′eignness** the quality of being foreign: want of relation to something: remoteness. — **foreign aid** financial or other aid given by richer to poorer countries; **foreign bill, draft** a bill, draft, payable in a different country, state, etc. from that in which it was drawn. — *adj.* **for′eign-built′** built in a foreign country. — **foreign correspondent** a newspaper correspondent in a foreign country in order to report its news, etc.; **foreign exchange** the exchange, conversion, etc. of foreign currencies; **foreign legion** an army unit consisting of aliens: (*caps*.) a former French army unit, consisting of soldiers of all nationalities, serving outside France; **Foreign Office** government department dealing with foreign affairs. [O.Fr. *forain* — L.L. *forāneus* — L. *forās*, out of doors.]

forejudge[1]. See **fore-**.

forejudge[2]. See **forjudge**.

forel *for'əl, n.* a kind of parchment for covering books. [O.Fr. *forrel*, dim. of *forre, fuerre*, sheath.]

forensic *fə-ren'sik, adj.* belonging to courts of law, held by · the Romans in the forum: used in law pleading: appropriate to, or adapted to, argument: loosely, of or pertaining to sciences or scientists connected with legal investigations. — *n.* **forensical'ity.** — *adv.* **foren'sically.** — *n. sing.* **foren'sics** the art or study of public debate. — **forensic medicine** medical jurisprudence, the application of medical knowledge to the elucidation of doubtful questions in a court of justice. [L. *forēnsis* — *forum*, market-place, forum.]

forensis strepitum *for-en'sis strep'it-əm, -ōōm,* (L.) the clamour of the forum.

foresay[1]. See **fore-**.

foresay[2], **foreslack, foreslow.** See **forsay**, etc.

forespeak[1], **forespend**[1]. See **fore-**.

forespeak[2], **forespend**[2]. See **forspeak, forspend.**

forest *for'ist, n.* a large uncultivated tract of land covered with trees and underwood: woody ground and rude pasture: a preserve for big game: a royal preserve for hunting, governed by a special code called the **forest law**: any area resembling a forest in being covered with tree-like objects. — *adj.* pertaining to a forest: silvan: rustic. — *v.t.* to cover with trees. — *n.* **for'estage** an ancient service paid by foresters to the king: the right of foresters. — *adj.* **for'estal, foresteal** (*fər-est'i-əl*). — *n.* **foresta'tion** afforestation. — *adj.* **for'ested.** — *n.* **for'ester** one who has charge of a forest: one who has care of growing trees: a member of the Ancient Order of Foresters or similar friendly society: an inhabitant of a forest: a large kangaroo (*Austr.*). — *adj.* **for'estine.** — *n.* **for'estry** the art of planting, tending, and managing forests: forest country: an extent of trees. — *adjs.* **for'est-born** (*Shak.*) born in a forest; **for'est-bred.** — **for'est-fly** a dipterous insect (*Hippobosca equina*) that annoys horses; **Forest Marble** a Middle Jurassic fissile limestone of which typical beds are found in Wychwood Forest, Oxfordshire; **for'est-oak** a species of Casuarina; **for'est-tree** a large forest tree, esp. a timber-tree, that grows in forests. [O.Fr. *forest* (Fr. *forêt*) — L.L. *forestis* (*silva*), the outside wood, as opposed to the *parcus* (park) or walled-in wood — L. *forīs*, out of doors.]

forever *fər-ev'ər, adv.* for ever, for all time to come: eternally: everlastingly: continually. — *n.* an endless or indefinite length of time. — *adv.* **forev'ermore'** for ever hereafter.

forewarn[1]. See **fore-**.

forewarn[2]. See **forwarn.**

forfair *fər-fār', v.i.* to perish, decay (*obs.*). — *adj.* (*Scot.*) **forfairn'** worn out: exhausted. [O.E. *forfaran.*]

forfeit *för'fit, n.* that to which a right is lost: a penalty for a crime, or breach of some condition: a fine: something deposited and redeemable by a sportive fine or penalty, esp. in *pl.*, a game of this kind. — *adj.* forfeited. — *v.t.* to lose the right to by some fault or crime: to confiscate (*arch.*): to penalise by forfeiture: loosely, to give up voluntarily. — *adj.* **for'feitable.** — *ns.* **for'feiter** (*Shak.*) one who incurs punishment by forfeiting his bond; **for'feiture** act of forfeiting: state of being forfeited: the thing forfeited. — Also (*obs.*) **forfault,** etc., by association with **fault.** [O.Fr. *forfait* — L.L. *forisfactum* — L. *forīs*, outside, *facĕre*, to make.]

forfend *fər-fend', (arch.) v.t.* to ward off, avert. [Pfx. **for-** (1a), and **fend**[1].]

forfex *för'feks, n.* a pair of scissors, or pincers: the pincers of an earwig, etc. — *adj.* **for'ficate** deeply forked, esp. of certain birds' tails. — *n.* **Forfic'ula** the common genus of earwigs. — *adj.* **forfic'ulate** like scissors. [L. *forfex, -icis,* shears, pincers.]

forfoughten *fər-fö'tən* (*Scot.* **forfoughen** *fər-fohh'ən,* **forfeuchen** *-fühh'*), (*dial.*) *adj.* exhausted. [Pfx. **for-** (1c).]

forgat. See **forget.**

forgather, foregather *fər-gadh'ər, v.i.* to meet, esp. by chance: to fraternise. [Pfx. **for-** (1c).]

forgave. See **forgive.**

forge[1] *förj, förj, n.* the workshop of a workman in iron, etc.: a furnace, esp. one in which iron is heated: a smithy: a place where anything is shaped or made. — *v.t.* to form by heating and hammering, by heating and pressure, or by pressure alone (in the last case, often **cold forge**): to form: to make falsely: to fabricate: to counterfeit for purposes of fraud: to form by great pressure, electricity, or explosion. — *v.i.* to commit forgery. — *adj.* **forge'able.** *ns.* **forg'er** one who forges; **forg'ery** fraudulently making or altering anything, esp. a writing: that which is forged or counterfeited: deceit (*obs.*). — *adj.* **forg'etive** (*Shak.*) creative. — *n.* **forg'ing** a piece of metal shaped by hammering: act of one who forges. — **forge'man.** [O.Fr. *forge* — L. *fabrica* — *faber*, a workman.]

forge[2] *förj, förj, v.i.* to move steadily on (usu. with *ahead*). [Origin obscure.]

forge[3] *förj, förj, v.i.* in a horse, to click the hind shoe against the fore. [Origin obscure.]

forget *fər-get', v.t.* to lose or put away from the memory: to fail to remember or think of: to leave behind accidentally: to neglect: — *pr.p.* **forgett'ing;** *pa.t.* **forgot'** (*arch.* **forgat'**); *pa.p.* **forgott'en** (also, now *rare*, in *U.S.*, but otherwise *arch.* **forgot'**). — *adj.* **forget'ful** apt to forget: inattentive. — *adv.* **forget'fully.** — *n.* **forget'fulness.** — *adj.* **forgett'able.** — *ns.* **forgett'er; forgett'ery** (*coll. facet.*) a capacity for forgetting: a bad memory. — *n.* and *adj.* **forgett'ing.** — *adv.* **forgett'ingly.** — *adj.* **forgott'en.** — *n.* **forgott'enness.** — **forget'-me-not** any plant of the genus Myosotis, regarded as an emblem of loving remembrance. — **forget it** (*coll.*; esp. in *imper.*) used to state that there is no need to offer apologies, thanks, etc., or to say or do anything further about a particular matter; **forget oneself** to lose one's self-control or dignity, to descend to words and deeds unworthy of oneself. [O.E. *forgetan (forgietan)* — pfx. *for-,* away, *getan (gietan),* to get.]

forgive *fər-giv', v.t.* to pardon: to overlook: to remit a debt or offence (*Shak.*): to give up (*Spens.*). — *v.i.* to be merciful or forgiving: — *pa.t.* **forgave',** *pa.p.* **forgiv'en.** — *adj.* **forgiv'able** capable of being forgiven. — *n.* **forgive'ness** pardon: remission: a disposition to pardon. — *adj.* **forgiv'ing** ready to pardon: merciful: compassionate. [O.E. *forgiefan* — pfx. *for-,* away, *giefan,* to give; cf. Ger. *vergeben.*]

forgo, forego *för-, för-, fər-gö', v.t.* to leave: to give up: to relinquish: to do without: to forbear the use or advantage of: to forfeit (*arch.*). — *v.i.* to go or pass away: — *pr.p.* **for(e)go'ing;** *pa.p.* **for(e)gone';** *pa.t.* **for(e)went'.** — See also **forego.** [O.E. *forgān,* to pass by, abstain from — pfx. *for-,* away, *gān,* to go.]

forgot, forgotten. See **forget.**

forhaile *för-hāl' (Spens.) v.t.* to distract. [Pfx. **for-** (1a).]

forhent, forehent *för-hent', v.t.* to overtake: to seize: — *pa.p., Spens.,* **forhent'.** [Pfx. **for-** (1c).]

forhow *för-how', v.t.* to despise (*obs.*): (also **forhoo(ie)** *fər-hōō'(ē)), vs.t.* to desert or abandon (*Scot.*). [O.E. *forhogian,* pfx. *for-,* away, *hogian,* to care.]

forinsec *fər-in'sek, adj.* (of feudal service) due to the lord's superior: external: alien: foreign: alien: extrinsic. — *adj.* **forin'secal** (*obs.*) foreign: alien: extrinsic. [L. *forīnsecus,* from without — *forīs,* out of doors, *secus,* following]

forint *for'int, n.* the monetary unit of Hungary since 1946. [Hung., — It. *fiorino, florin.*]

forisfamiliate *för, for-is-fə-mil'i-āt, (law) v.t.* to emancipate from paternal authority: (of a father) to put (a

son) in possession of land which is accepted as the whole portion of the father's property. — *v.i.* (of a son) to renounce one's title to a further share. — *n.* **forisfamiliā'tion.** [L.L. *forīsfamiliāre, -ātum* — L. *forīs,* out of doors, *familia,* a family.]
forjeskit *fɔr-jes'kit,* **forjaskit** *-jas',* (*Scot.*) *adj.* tired out. [Pfx. **for-** (1c); cf. **disjaskit.**]
forjudge, forejudge *fōr-juj', fōr-,* (*law*) *v.t.* to deprive of a right, object, etc. by a judgment. [O.Fr. *forjugier* — *fors,* — L. *foris,* out, and *jugier* (Fr. *juger*), to judge.]
fork *fōrk, n.* a pronged instrument: anything that divides into prongs or branches: a branch or prong: the space or angle between branches, esp. on a tree or between the legs: a confluent, tributary, or branch of a river: one of the branches into which a road divides: a bifurcation: a place of bifurcation: a barbed arrow-head: the part of a bicycle to which a wheel is attached: the appearance of a flash of lightning: the bottom of a sump in a mine: a simultaneous attack on two pieces by one piece (*chess*). — *v.i.* to branch: to follow a branch road. — *v.t.* to form as a fork: to move with a fork: to stab with a fork: to menace (two pieces) simultaneously (*chess*): to pump dry. — *adj.* **forked** shaped like a fork. — *adv.* **fork'edly.** — *ns.* **fork'edness; fork'er; fork'iness.** — *adj.* **fork'y.** — **fork'-chuck** a forked lathe-centre in wood-turning; **fork'head** an arrow-head (*Spens.*): the forked end of a rod; **fork'it= tail, fork'y-tail** (*dial.*) an earwig; **fork lunch(eon), sup- per,** etc., a buffet-type meal eaten with a fork; **fork'tail** a name for various fishes and birds, as the kite. — *adj.* **fork'-tailed.** — **fork-lift truck** a power-driven truck with an arrangement of steel prongs which can lift, raise up high, and carry heavy packages and stack them where required (often used with a pallet); **fork out, over, up** (*slang*) to hand or pay over, esp. unwill- ingly. [O.E. *forca* — L. *furca.*]
forlana *fōr-lä'nɔ,* **furlana** *fōōr-, ns.* a Venetian dance in 6-8 time. [It. *Furlana,* Friulian.]
forlend. See **forelend.**
forlorn *fɔr-lörn', adj.* quite lost: forsaken: neglected: wretched. — *n.* (*Shak.*) a forsaken person: a forlorn hope. — orig. *pa.p.* of the *obs.* **forlese** (*fɔr-lēz'*) *v.t.* to lose: to forsake (*pa.t.* and *pa.p., Spens.* **forlore** *-lōr', -lör').* — *adv.* **forlorn'ly.** — *n.* **forlorn'ness.** [O.E. *forloren,* pa.p. of *forlēosan,* to lose — pfx. *for-,* away, and *lēosan,* to lose; Ger. *verloren,* pa.p. of *verlieren,* to lose.]
forlorn hope *fɔr-lörn' hōp'* a body of soldiers selected for some service of uncommon danger: a desperate enter- prise of last resort: a vain or faint hope (from associ- ation with hope = expectation). [Du. *verloren hoop,* lost troop.]
form *fōrm, n.* shape: a mould: something that holds, shapes, e.g. a piece of formwork: a species: a pattern: a mode of being: a mode of arrangement: order: regularity: system, as of government: beauty (*obs.*): style and arrangement: structural unity in music, literature, etc.: a prescribed set of words or course of action: ceremony: behaviour: condition of fitness or efficiency: a schedule to be filled in with details: a specimen document for imitation: the inherent nature of an object (*phil.*): that which the mind itself con- tributes as the condition of knowing: that in which the essence of a thing consists: a complete set of crystal faces similar with respect to the symmetry of the crystal (*crystal.*): type from which an impression is to be taken arranged and secured in a chase — *U.K.* usu. **forme** (*print.*): a long seat, a bench: a school class: the bed of a hare, shaped by the animal's body: a criminal record (*slang*): the condition of fitness of e.g. horse, athlete: a record of past performance of an athlete, horse, etc.: (*coll.*; with *the*) the correct procedure in an operation: (*coll.*; with *the*) the situation, position. — *v.t.* to give form or shape to: to bring into being: to make: to contrive: to conceive in the mind: to go to make up: to constitute: to establish. — *v.i.* to assume a form. — *adjs.* **form'able; form'al** according to form

or established mode: relating to form: ceremonious, punctilious, methodical: having the form only: sane (*Shak.*): having the power of making a thing what it is: essential: proper. — *n.* **formalīsā'tion, -z-.** — *v.t.* **form'alise, -ize** to make formal: to make official or valid: to make precise, give a clear statement of. — *v.i.* to be formal. — *ns.* **form'alism** excessive observance of form or conventional usage, esp. in religion: stiffness of manner: in art, concentration on form or technique at the expense of social or moral content; **form'alist** one having exaggerated regard to rules or established usages: one who practises formalism in art. — Also *adj.* — *adj.* **formalist'ic.** — *n.* **formal'ity** the precise observance of forms or ceremonies: a matter of form: a ceremonious observance: established order: sacrifice of substance to form. — *adv.* **form'ally.** — *n.* **form'ant** a component of a speech sound determining its quality: a determinative. — *v.i.* **formate'** to join, or fly, in formation (of aircraft): to form (*obs.*): to state pre- cisely, formulate (*obs.*). — *n.* **formā'tion** a making or producing: a structure: an arrangement of e.g. troops, aircraft, players: a stratigraphical group of strata (*geol.*): a plant community (*bot.*). — *adjs.* **formā'tional; form'ative** giving form, determining, moulding: capable of development: growing: serving to form words by derivation or inflection, not radical (*gram.*). — *n.* (*gram.*) a derivative (*old*): a formative element: any grammatical element from which words and sen- tences are constructed. — *adj.* **formed.** — *ns.* **form'er; form'ing.** — *adj.* **form'less.** — *adv.* **form'lessly.** — *n.* **form'lessness.** — **formal logic** see **logic; formal verdict** (*law*) one in which the jury follows the judge's direc- tions: in Scotland, in a fatal accident inquiry, a finding of death by misadventure with no apportioning of blame; **form class** (*linguistics*) a class of forms (words and phrases) that will fit into the same position in a construction; **form critic; form criticism** biblical criti- cism that classifies parts of scripture according to literary form and relates literary forms to historical background: **form genus** a group of species with similar morphological characters, but which are not certainly known to be related in descent; **form horse** in horse- racing the favourite, the expected winner (also *fig.*); **form letter** a letter with a fixed form and contents, used esp. when writing to a number of people about the same or essentially similar matters; **form master, mis- tress, teacher** esp. in a secondary school, the teacher who is responsible for the administration, welfare, etc. of a form; **form'work** shuttering to contain concrete. — **good** or **bad form** according to good or recognised social usage, or the opposite. [L. *fōrma,* shape.]
-form *fōrm,* in composition, having a specified form or number of forms. [L. *fōrma,* form.]
formaldehyde, formalin. See under **formic.**
formaliter *fōr-mal'i-tɔr, -ter,* (L.L.) *adv.* formally, in respect of the formal element.
format *fōr'mat, fōr'mä, n.* of books, etc., the size, form, shape in which they are issued: the style, arrangement and contents of e.g. a radio or television programme: (the description of) the way data is, or is to be, arranged in a file, on a card, disc, tape, etc. (*comput.*). — *v.t.* to arrange a book, etc., into a specific format: to arrange data for use on a disc, tape, etc. (*comput.*): to prepare a disc, etc., for use by dividing it into sectors: — *pr.p.* **form'atting;** *pa.t.* and *pa.p.* **form'atted.** — *n.* **form'atter** a program for formatting a disc, tape, etc. [Fr.]
forme (*print.*). See **form.**
former *fōrm'ɔr, adj.* (*comp.* of **fore**) before in time: past: first mentioned (of two): beforehand, first (of two) (*Shak.*). — *adv.* **form'erly** in former times: heretofore. [Formed late on analogy of M.E. *formest,* foremost, by adding comp. suff. *-er* to base of O.E. *forma,* first, itself superlative.]
formic *fōr'mik, adj.* pertaining to ants. — *ns.* **formal'- dehyde** a formic aldehyde, formalin; **for'malin, for'mol** (*-mol, -mōl*) a formic aldehyde used as an antiseptic, germicide, or preservative; **for'mate** a salt of formic

acid. — Also **for'miate.** — *adj.* **for'micant** crawling like
an ant: very small and unequal, of a pulse. — *ns.*
formicā'rium (*pl.* **-ria**), **for'micary** an ant-hill, ants'
nest, or colony. — *adj.* **for'micate** resembling an ant.
— *n.* **formicā'tion** a sensation like that of ants creeping
on the skin. — **formic acid** a fatty acid H·CO·OH,
found in ants and nettles. [L. *formīca,* an ant.]
Formica® *för-mī'kə, n.* any of a number of plastic laminates used to provide hard, heat-resistant, easily-
cleaned surfaces.
formidable *för'mid-ə-bl,* by some *-mid',* *adj.* causing fear:
inspiring awe: redoubtable. — *ns.* **formidabil'ity; for'-**
midableness. — *adv.* **for'midably.** [Fr., — L. *formīd-*
ābilis — formīdō, fear.]
formol. See under **formic.**
formula *förm'ū-lə, n.* a prescribed form: a formal statement of doctrines: a recipe: a milk mixture used as
baby food: a statement of joint aims or principles
worked out for practical purposes by diplomats of
divergent interests: a solution or answer worked out
by different sides in a dispute, etc.: a technical specification governing cars entered for certain motor-
racing events: a general expression for solving problems (*math.*): a set of symbols expressing the composition of a body (*chem.*): a list of ingredients of a patent
medicine: — *pl.* **formulae** (*förm'ū-lē*), **form'ūlas.** —
adjs. **formulaic** (*-lā'ik*); **form'ular, formūlaris'tic.** — *v.t.*
form'ūlarise, -ize. — *ns.* **formūlarīsā'tion, -z-, formūlā'-**
tion; form'ūlary a formula: a book of formulae or
precedents. — *adj.* prescribed: ritual. — *vs.t.* **form'-**
ūlate, form'ūlise, -ize to reduce to or express in a
formula: to state or express in a clear or definite form.
— *ns.* **form'ūlism** excessive use of, or dependence on,
formulae; **form'ūlist.** [L. *förmula,* dim. of *förma.*]
fornent *fər-nent'*, (*Scot.*) *adv.* and *prep.* right opposite to.
— Also **foreanent', fornenst'.** [**fore, anent.**]
fornicate[1] *för'ni-kāt, adj.* arched: arching over (*bot.*). —
n. **fornicā'tion.** [L. *fornicātus—fornix,* a vault, arch.]
fornicate[2] *för'ni-kāt, v.i.* to commit fornication. — *ns.*
fornicā'tion voluntary sexual intercourse of the unmarried, sometimes extended to cases where only one
of the pair concerned is unmarried: adultery (*B.*), or
idolatry (*fig.*); **for'nicător; for'nicātress.** [L. *fornicārī,*
-ātus — fornix, a vault, brothel.]
fornix *för'niks, n.* something resembling an arch: an
arched formation of the brain. — *adj.* **forn'ical.** [L.]
forpine *för-pīn', v.i.* (*Spens.*) to waste away. [Pfx. **for-**
(1c).]
forpit, forpet *för-pət,* (*Scot.*) *n.* a fourth part (now of a
peck). [**fourth part.**]
forrad *for'əd,* (*dial.*), **forrit** *for'ət, för'it,* (*Scot.*) *adv.* forms
of **forward** — *comp.* **forr'ader.**
forray *for-ā', n.* and *v.t.* Spenser's form of **foray.**
forren (*Milt.*). Same as **foreign.**
forsake *fər-sāk', för-, v.t.* to desert: to abandon: — *pr.p.*
forsāk'ing; *pa.t.* **forsook';** *pa.p.* **forsāk'en.** — *adj.* **for-**
sāk'en. — *adv.* **forsāk'enly.** — *ns.* **forsāk'enness; for-**
sāk'ing abandonment. [O.E. *forsacan—for-,* away,
sacan, to strive.]
forsay, foresay *för-sā', v.t.* to forbid (*obs.*): to renounce
(*Spens.*): to banish (*Spens.*). [O.E. *forsecgan—for-,*
against, *secgan,* to say.]
forset-seller. See **fosset-seller.**
forslack, foreslack *för-slak', v.i.* (*obs.*) to be or become
slack or neglectful. — *v.t.* (*Spens.*) to injure by slack-
ness. [Pfx. **for-** (1c).]
forslow, forsloe, foreslow *för-slō', v.t.* (*Spens.*) to delay.
— *v.i.* (*Shak.*) to delay. [O.E. *forslāwian — for,*
intensive, *slāwian,* to be slow.]
forsooth *fər-sōōth', för-, adv.* in truth: certainly (now only
ironically). [**for sooth.**]
forspeak, forespeak *fər-spēk', för-, v.t.* to forbid (*obs.*): to
speak against (*Shak.*): to bewitch (*Scot.*). [Pfx. **for-**
(1b).]
forspend, forespend *fər-spend', v.t.* to wear out physically:
to exhaust (resources): — *pa.t.* and *pa.p.* **forspent'.**
[Pfx. **for-** (1c).]

forswatt *för-swöt', (Spens.) adj.* covered with sweat.
[Pfx. **for-** (1c) and *swat,* old pa.p. of **sweat.**]
forswear *fər-swār', för-, v.t.* to deny or renounce upon
oath. — *v.i.* to swear falsely: — *pa.t.* **forswore';** *pa.p.*
forsworn'. — *adj.* **forsworn'** perjured, having forsworn
oneself. — *n.* **forsworn'ness.** — **forswear oneself** to
swear falsely. [Pfx. **for-** (1b).]
forswink *fər-swingk', för-, v.t.* to exhaust by labour. —
adj. **forswunk'** (*Spens.* **forswonck'**) overworked. [Pfx.
for- (1b), O.E. *swincan,* to labour.]
Forsythia *för-sī'thi-ə, -si', n.* a genus of oleaceous shrubs
with flowers like jasmine: (without *cap.*) a plant of this
genus. [After William *Forsyth* (1737–1804),
botanist.]
fort *fört, fört, n.* a small fortress: (in N. America) an
outlying trading-station. — *v.t.* to fortify. — **hold the**
fort to take temporary charge. [Fr., — L. *fortis,*
strong.]
fortalice *fört'ə-lis, n.* a fortress: a small outwork of a
fortification. [L.L. *fortalitia* — L. *fortis.*]
forte[1] *fört,* now usu. for the first meaning *fört'i, n.* that
in which one excels: the upper half of a sword or foil
blade — the strong part. [Fr. *fort,* strong.]
forte[2] *för'ti,* (*mus.*) *adj.* and *adv.* loud: — *superl.* **fortis'-**
simo, *double superl.* **fortissis'simo** as loud as possible.
— *n.* a loud passage in music. — *n.* **fortepia'no** the
18th-century name for an early type of piano. — *adj.*
and *adv.* loud with immediate relapse into softness.
[It.]
forth *förth, förth, adv.* forward: onward: out: into the
open: in continuation: abroad. — *prep.* (*Shak.*) out of,
forth from. — *v.i.* (*obs.*) **forthcome'** to come forth. —
adj. **forthcom'ing** just coming forth: about to appear:
approaching: at hand, ready to be produced: (of a
person) friendly, communicative. — *ns.* **forth'going** a
going forth; **forth'-putting** the action of putting forth:
undue forwardness (*U.S.*). — *adj.* (*U.S.*) forward. —
adv. **forth'right** (or *-rīt'*) straightforward: at once. —
n. (*Shak.*) a straight path. — *adj.* straightforward:
downright. — *adv.* **forth'rightly.** — *n.* **forth'rightness.**
— *adv.* **forthwith** (*-with', -widh',* or *förth'*) immediately.
— **and so forth** and so on. [O.E. *forth—fore,* before;
Du. *voort,* Ger. *fort.*]
forthink *fər-thingk', v.t.* (*Spens.*) to be sorry for, regret:
to rethink. — *v.i.* (*dial.*) to change one's mind. [From
O.E. *forthencan — O.E. for-* and *thencan,* to think,
thyncan, to seem.]
forthy *för-dhī', (Spens.) adv.* therefore: for that. [O.E.
forthȳ — for, and *thȳ,* instrumental case of *thæt,* that.]
forties, fortieth. See **forty.**
fortify *för'ti-fī, v.t.* to strengthen with forts, etc., against
attack: to invigorate: to confirm: to strengthen (esp.
certain wines) by adding alcohol: to enrich (a food)
by adding e.g. vitamins. — *v.i.* to put up fortifications:
— *pr.p.* **for'tifying;** *pa.t.* and *pa.p.* **for'tified.** — *adj.*
for'tifiable. — *ns.* **fortificā'tion** the art of strengthening
a military position by means of defensive works: (often
in *pl.*) the work so constructed: that which fortifies;
for'tifier. [Fr. *fortifier* — L.L. *fortificāre — fortis,*
strong, *facĕre,* to make.]
fortilage *för'ti-lāj, för', (Spens.) n.* a variant of **fortalice.**
fortis *för'tis,* (*phon.*) *adj.* of a consonant, articulated with
relatively great muscular effort and pressure of breath
(opp. to *lenis*). — Also *n.*: — *pl.* **förtēs.** [L., strong.]
fortissimo. See **forte.**
fortiter et recte *för'ti-tər et rek'tē, for'ti-ter et rek'te* (L.)
bravely and uprightly.
fortitude *för'ti-tūd,* in *U.S. -tōōd, n.* courage in endurance:
strength (*obs.*). — *adj.* **fortitū'dinous.** [L. *fortitūdō,*
-inis — fortis, strong.]
fortlet *fört'lət, fört', n.* a little fort.
fortnight *fört'nīt, n.* two weeks or fourteen days. — *adj.*
and *adv.* **fort'nightly** once a fortnight. — *n.* a magazine,
etc. appearing fortnightly. [O.E. *fēowertȳne niht,*
fourteen nights.]
Fortran *för'tran, n.* a problem-orientated computer lan-

guage widely used in scientific work. [*Formula translation*.]

fortress *för′trəs, för′, n.* a fortified place: a defence. — *v.t.* (*Shak.*) to guard. [O.Fr. *forteresse*, another form of *fortelesce* (see **fortalice**).]

fortuitous *för-tū′i-təs,* in *U.S. -tōō′, adj.* happening by chance: fortunate. — *ns.* **fortū′itism** belief in evolution by fortuitous variation; **fortū′itist.** — *adv.* **fortū′itously.** — *ns.* **fortū′itousness, fortū′ity.** [L. *fortuïtus.*]

fortune *för′chən, n.* whatever comes by lot or chance: luck: the arbitrary ordering of events: the lot that falls to one in life: a prediction of one's future: success: a great accumulation of wealth: a large amount of money: an heiress (*obs.*). — *v.i.* (*obs.*) to befall. — *v.t.* (*obs.*) to determine the fortune of. — *adj.* **for′tunate** happening by good fortune: lucky: auspicious: felicitous. — *adv.* **for′tunately** in a fortunate way, by good luck: I'm glad to say, happy to report. — *n.* **for′tunateness.** — *adjs.* **for′tuned** supplied by fortune; **for′tuneless** without a fortune: luckless. — *v.t.* (*Spens.*) **for′tunize** to make fortunate or happy. — **for′tune book** a book for use in fortune-telling; **fortune cookie** (*U.S.*) dough wrapped and cooked around a piece of paper which has a (supposed) fortune or a maxim on it, served esp. in Chinese homes and restaurants; **for′tune-hunter** one who hunts for a wealthy marriage. — *v.i.* **for′tune-tell** (back-formation). — **for′tune-teller** one who professes to foretell one's fortune; **for′tune-telling.** — **a small fortune** quite a large fortune. [Fr., — L. *fortūna.*]

forty *för′ti, adj.* and *n.* four times ten. — *n.* (*cap.* with *the*) the French Academy. — *n.pl.* **for′ties** the numbers forty to forty-nine: the years so numbered (of life, a century): a range of temperature from forty to just less than fifty degrees: (*cap.* with *the*) the sea area lying between NE Scotland and SW Norway, with a minimum depth of 40 fathoms. — *adj.* **for′tieth** the last of forty: next after the thirty-ninth: equal to one of forty equal parts. — *n.* one of forty equal parts: a person or thing in fortieth position. — *adj.* **for′tyish** apparently about forty years old. — **for′ty-five′** a micro-grooved disc record played at a speed of 45 revolutions per minute: (*cap.* with *the*) the Jacobite rebellion of 1745; **for′ty-nin′er** a gold-seeker in the 1849 rush in California; **forty winks** a short nap, esp. after dinner. — **roaring forties** the tract of stormy west winds south of 40°S latitude (occasionally also in the Atlantic north of 40°N). [O.E. *fēowertig* — *fēower*, four, *-tig*, ten (as suffix).]

forum *fö′rəm, fö′, n.* a market-place, esp. that in Rome where public business was transacted and justice dispensed: the courts of law as opposed to Parliament: a meeting to discuss topics of public concern: a publication, regular meeting, etc., serving as a medium for debate: — *pl.* **fo′rums, fo′ra.** [L. *forum*, akin to *forās*, out of doors.]

forwander *fər-won′dər, v.i.* to wander till wearied (*arch.*): to stray far (*Spens.*). — *adj.* **forwan′dered** strayed. [Pfx. **for-** (1d).]

forward *för′wərd, adj.* near or at the forepart: in advance: well advanced: too ready: presumptuous: officious: earnest (*arch.*): early ripe. — *v.t.* to help on: to send on. — *advs.* **for′ward, for′wards** towards what is in front: onward: progressively. — *adv.* **forward** (*for′-əd*) towards, in, the front part of a ship. — *ns.* **for′ward** in football, etc., a player in the front line; **for′warder; for′warding** the act of sending forward merchandise, etc. — *adv.* **for′wardly.** — *n.* **for′wardness. forward delivery** delivery of goods at a future date. — *adj.* **for′ward-looking** having regard to the future: progressive. — **forward market** a market in which commodities, etc., are contracted to be bought and sold at a future date at an agreed price (**forward price**); **forward pass** (*Rugby*) an illegal pass in which the ball is thrown forward towards the opponents' goal-line. [O.E. *foreward* (W.S. *foreweard*) — *fore*, and *-ward* (*-weard*)

sig. direction; the *s* of *forwards* is a gen. ending (cf. Ger. *vorwärts*).]

forwarn, forewarn *fər-, för-wörn′, v.t.* to forbid. [Pfx. **for-** (1b), against, and **warn.**]

forwaste *för-wāst′,* (*Spens.*) *v.t.* to waste utterly. [Pfx. **for-** (1c).]

forweary *fər-, för-wē′ri,* (*Spens.*) *v.t.* to weary out. [Pfx. **for-** (1c).]

forwent *fər-, för-went′.* See **forgo.**

forwhy *för-(h)wī′,* (*arch.*) *conj.* because. — *adv.* why. [**for,** and **why.**]

forworn *fər-wörn′, -wörn′,* (*Spens.*) *adj.* much worn. [Pfx. **for-** (1c).]

forzando, forzato. See **sforzando.**

Fosbury flop *foz′bə-ri flop,* a method of high-jumping in which the athlete goes over the bar horizontally on his back. [R. *Fosbury* (b. 1947), U.S. athlete.]

foss[1], fosse *fos, n.* a ditch, moat, trench, or canal. — *adj.* **fossed.** — *n.* **fossette′** a small hollow. — **Foss(e) Way** the Roman road that runs between Exeter and Lincoln: (without *cap.*) any of the British Roman roads having a fosse on either side. [Fr. *fosse* — L. *fossa* — *fodēre, fossum,* to dig.]

foss[2]. See **force[2].**

fossa[1] *fos′ə,* (*anat.*) *n.* a pit or depression: — *pl.* **foss′ae** (*-ē*). — *n.* **foss′ula** a small depression or groove. — *adj.* **foss′ulate.** [L., a ditch.]

fossa[2] *fos′ə,* **foussa** *fōōs′ə, ns.* a Madagascan animal (*Cryptoprocta ferox*) more or less akin to the civets: (**Fossa**) a genus of Madagascan civets. [Malagasy.]

fosse. See **foss[1].**

fosset-seller *fos′it-sel′ər,* (*Shak.*) *n.* apparently one who sells faucets. — Another reading **for′set-seller.** [*fosset, forset,* obs. forms of **faucet.**]

fossette. See **foss[1].**

fossick *fos′ik,* (*Austr.*) *v.i.* to search for gold, on the surface or in abandoned workings: to rummage. — *v.t.* to dig out. — *ns.* **foss′icker; foss′icking.** [Perh. conn. with Eng. dial. *fossick,* a troublesome person.]

fossil *fos′l,* or *-il, n.* a rock or mineral substance dug from the earth (*obs.*): a relic or trace of a former living thing preserved in the rocks (*geol.*): an antiquated, out-of-date, or unchanging person or thing (*fig.*). — *adj.* dug out of the earth: in the condition of a fossil: antiquated. — *adj.* **fossilif′erous** bearing or containing fossils. — *n.* **fossilisā′tion, -z-.** — *v.t.* **fossil′lise, -ize** to convert into a fossil (also *fig.*). — *v.i.* to become fossil: to look for fossils (*coll.*). — *adj.* **foss′il-fired** of a power station, etc., burning fossil fuel. — **fossil fuel** coal, oil, etc., produced in the earth by process of fossilisation; **fossil water** water which has been trapped in an underground reservoir since a previous geological age. [Fr. *fossile* — L. *fossilis* — *fodēre,* to dig.]

fossor *fos′or, n.* a grave-digger. — *adj.* **fossorial** (*-ō′ri-əl, -ō′; zool.*) adapted for digging. [L. *fossor* — *fodēre,* to dig.]

fossula, fossulate. See **fossa[1].**

foster[1] *fos′tər, v.t.* to bring up or nurse, esp. a child not one's own: to put a child into the care of one not its parent: to treat, e.g. the elderly, in a similar fashion: to encourage: to promote: to cherish. — *v.i.* to care for a child or elderly person in a foster-home. — *adj.* of or concerned with fostering. — *ns.* **fos′terage** the act or custom of fostering or nursing: the condition or relation of foster-child: the care of a foster-child: the act of encouraging or cultivating; **fos′terer, fos′-tress; fos′tering; fos′terling** a foster-child. — **fos′ter-brother** a male child nursed or brought up with a child or children of different parents; **fos′ter-child** a child nursed or brought up by one who is not its parent; **fos′ter-daughter; fos′ter-father** one who brings up a child in place of its father; **fos′ter-home; fos′ter-mother** one who brings up a child not her own: an apparatus for rearing chickens; **fos′ter-nurse; fos′ter-parent; fos′ter-sister; fos′ter-son.** [O.E. *fōstrian,* to nourish, *fōster,* food.]

foster[2] *fos′tər,* (*Spens.*) *n.* a forester.

fother[1] *fodh'ər, v.t.* to cover (a sail, etc.) with yarn and oakum, as stopping for a leak. [Perh. Du. *voederen* (mod. *voeren*), or L.G. *fodern,* to line.]

fother[2] *fodh'ər, n.* a load, quantity (*dial.*): a cart-load (*dial.*): a definite weight — of lead, 19½ cwt. [O.E. *fōther*; Ger. *Fuder.*]

fother[3] *fodh'ər,* dial. variant of **fodder.**

Fothergilla *fo-dhər-gil'ə, n.* a genus of North American deciduous shrubs of the witch hazel family (*Hamamelis*): (without *cap.*) any plant of the genus (also called witch-alder). [Dr John *Fothergill,* 18th-century British physician and botanist.]

fou[1] *foō,* (*Scot.*) *adj.* full: drunk.

fou[2] *foō* (*obs. Scot.*) *n.* a bushel. [Perh. **full.**]

fouat, fouet *foō'ət,* (*Scot.*) *n.* the house-leek.

Foucault current. Same as **eddy current.**

foud *fowd, n.* a bailiff or magistrate in Orkney and Shetland. — *n.* foud'rie his jurisdiction. [O.N. *fōgeti*; Ger. *Vogt*; from L. *vocātus* — *vocāre,* to call.]

foudroyant *foō-droi'ənt, -drwä'yã, adj.* thundering: dazzling: sudden and overwhelming. [Fr., pr.p. of *foudroyer* — *foudre,* lightning.]

fouet. See fouat.

fouetté *fwe'tā, n.* ballet-step in which the foot makes a whip-like movement. [Fr.]

fougade *foō-gäd'*, fougasse *foō-gäs', (mil.) ns.* a piece of improvised artillery, a small pit charged with powder or shells and loaded with stones. [Fr.]

fought *föt, pa.t.* and *pa.p.*, foughten *föt'n,* old *pa.p.*, of **fight.**

foughty *fow'ti, foō'ti, (dial.) adj.* musty: mouldy: tainted. [O.E. *fūht,* moist.]

foul *fowl, adj.* filthy: dirty: disfigured: untidy: loathsome: obscene: impure: shameful: gross: in bad condition: stormy: unfavourable: unfair: of little worth: choked up: entangled: full of errors (*print.*): ugly (*Shak.*): bad (*coll.*). — *v.t.* to make foul: to collide with, come in accidental contact with: to obstruct. — *v.i.* to collide. — *n.* the act of fouling: any breach of the rules in games or contests. — *adv.* in a foul manner: unfairly. — *adv.* foul'ly. — *n.* foul'ness. — foul'-brood a bacterial disease of bee larvae; foul'-fish fish during the spawning season; foul'mart see foumart. — *adjs.* foul=mouthed, foul'-spok'en addicted to the use of foul or profane language. — foul'-mouth'edness; foul play unfair action in any game or contest: dishonest dealing generally: violence or murder; foul'-up see foul up. — claim a foul to assert that a rule has been broken, and claim the penalty; fall foul of to come against: to clash with: to assail; foul (be)fall (*obs.*) bad luck to; foul up to befoul, make dirty: to (cause to) be or become blocked or entangled: to spoil (*coll.*): to cause to fail or break down (*coll.*): to bungle, make a mistake in (*coll.*) (*n.* foul'-up); make foul water (*naut.*) to come into such shallow water that the keel raises the mud. [O.E. *fūl*; Ger. *faul,* Goth. *fūls.*]

foulard *foō-lärd', -lär', n.* a soft untwilled silk fabric: a silk handkerchief. [Fr.]

foulder *fowl'dər,* (*Spens.*) *v.i.* to thunder. [O.Fr. *fouldre* — L. *fulgur,* lightning.]

foulé *foō'lā,* (Fr.) *n.* fulled cloth, esp. a light woollen smooth-surfaced dress material.

foumart *foō'märt, -mərt, n.* a polecat. [M.E. *fulmard* — O.E. *fūl,* foul, *mearth,* a marten.]

found[1] *pa.t.* and *pa.p.* of **find.** — *n.* found'ling a little child found deserted. — all found see all; found money money gain got for nothing; found object a natural or man-made object displayed as a work of art, either exactly as found or touched up ('composed').

found[2] *fownd, v.t.* to lay the bottom or foundation of: to establish on a basis: to originate: to endow. — *v.i.* to rely (with *on*). — *n.* founda'tion the act of founding: (often in *pl.*) the base of a building: the groundwork or basis: a permanent fund for a benevolent purpose or for some special object: a cosmetic preparation used as a base for facial make-up: a priming substance applied to a canvas or board as a base for oil-painting.

— *adj.* founda'tional. — *ns.* founda'tioner one supported from the funds or foundation of an institution; found'er one who founds, establishes or originates: an endower: — *fem.* found'ress. — foundation course an introductory course of study; foundation garment a woman's undergarment for supporting or controlling the figure; founda'tion-mus'lin, -net gummed fabrics used for stiffening dresses and bonnets; founda'tion-stone one of the stones forming the foundation of a building, esp. a stone laid with public ceremony; founda'tion-stop any organ stop whose sounds are those belonging to the keys, or differing by whole octaves only: a fundamental flue stop; found'er-mem-ber one of those members of a society who were instrumental in its foundation; founders' shares same as deferred shares; founding father one who forms or establishes an institution, organisation, etc. [Fr. *fonder* — L. *fundāre, -ātum,* to found — *fundus,* the bottom.]

found[3] *fownd, v.t.* to merit: to make by melting and allowing to harden in a mould (esp. metals): to cast. — *ns.* found'er; found'ing; found'ry the art of founding or casting: a place where founding is carried on: articles produced by founding. [Fr. *fondre* — L. *fundēre, fūsum,* to pour.]

founder *fownd'ər, v.i.* (of a building) to subside: to collapse in ruins (also *fig.*): to go to the bottom: (of a ship) to fill with water and sink: to stumble: to go lame: to stick in mud. — *v.t.* to cause to founder. — *n.* a collapse: laminitis. — *adj.* found'erous causing to founder. [O.Fr. *fondrer,* to fall in — *fond* — L. *fundus,* bottom.]

fount[1] *fownt,* font, (*print.*) *n.* a complete assortment of types of one sort, with all that is necessary for printing in that kind of letter. — Also (esp. in U.S.) font. [Fr. *fonte* — *fondre* — L. *fundēre,* to cast.]

fount[2] *fownt, n.* a spring of water: a source. — *adj.* fount'ful (*poet.*) full of springs. [L. *fōns, fontis.*]

fountain *fownt'in, n.* a spring of water, a jet: a structure for supplying drinking water or other liquid: an ornamental structure with jets, spouts, and basins of water: a reservoir from which oil, ink, etc., flows, as in a lamp, a pen: the source. — *v.i.* to spring up or gush, as from a fountain. — *adj.* fount'ainless. — fount'ain-head the head or source: the beginning; fount'ain-pen' a pen with a reservoir for ink. [Fr. *fontaine* — L.L. *fontāna* — L. *fōns, fontis,* a spring.]

four *fōr, för, n.* the cardinal number next above three: a symbol representing that number: a set of four things or persons (leaves, oarsmen, etc.): a four-oar boat: a four-cylinder engine or car: a shoe or other article of a size denoted by 4: a card with four pips: a score of four points, tricks, strokes, etc.: the fourth hour after midday or midnight: (in *pl.*; *dial.*) a snack taken at 4 o'clock (also fours'es): the age of four years. — *adj.* of the number four: four years old. — *adj.* and *adv.* four'fold in four divisions: folded in four thicknesses: four times as much. — *ns.* four'foldness; four'some a group of four: anything in which four act together, esp. a game of golf (two against two, partners playing the same ball) or a reel — also *adj.* — four'-ale' ale sold at fourpence a quart (*obs.*): cheap ale. — *adj.* four'-ball (*golf*) played two against two with four balls, best ball counting. — four'-by-two' the piece of cloth in a rifle pull-through: an army biscuit. — *adjs.* four'-col'our (*photog.*) involving or using four colours (red, blue, yellow, black) as primary; four'-dimen'-sional having four dimensions, esp. length, breadth and depth, with the addition of time. — *n. sing.* four'-eyes the fish *Anableps* (also four-eyed fish): a person wearing spectacles (*slang*). — *adj.* four'-figure running into four figures: to four places of decimals. — four'-flush' four cards of the same suit in a five-card poker hand. — *v.i.* to bluff with a four-flush: to bluff. — *adj.* bluffing: not genuine. — four'-flush'er. — *adjs.* four'-foot measuring four feet (four-foot way in railways, space of 4 ft 8½ in. (1·435 m.) between rails):

having the pitch of an open organ pipe four feet long, or having that pitch for its lowest note; **four′-foot′ed** having four feet; **four′-hand′ed** having four hands: played by four players (*cards*); **four′-horse** drawn by four horses. — **four′-hours** (*Scot. fowr′ōōrz*) a refreshment about four o'clock. — *adj.* **four′-inched** (*Shak.*) four inches wide. — **four′-in-hand** a coach drawn by four horses, two by two, driven by one person: the team drawing it: a necktie tied with a flat slip-knot, with dangling ends. Also *adj.* and *adv.* — *adjs.* **four′-leaved, four′-leafed, four′-leaf; four′-legged′.** — **four′-oar** a boat rowed with four oars; **four′-o′clock** a brightly coloured flowering plant *Mirabilis jalapa*, also known as the marvel of Peru: a similar red-flowered plant *M. laevis* found in California: the friar-bird; **four′-pack** (*coll.*) four cans of drink packaged together and sold as a single item. — *adjs.* **four′-part, four-part′ed** in four parts: divided into four nearly to the base. — **four′pence** the value of four pennies; **four′-penny** an old silver coin worth fourpence. — *adj.* sold or offered for fourpence. — **four′-post′er** a large bed with four curtain posts; **four′-pound′er** a gun that throws a four-pound shot: a four-pound loaf. — *adjs.* **four′score** eighty; **four′scorth** (*obs.*) eightieth. — **four′-seat′er** a vehicle seated for four. — *adjs.* **four′-square′** (also *adv.*) square: presenting a firm bold front: frank, honest, forthright; **four′-wheel** acting on or by means of four wheels; **four′-wheeled.** — **four′-wheel′er** a cab or other vehicle with four wheels. — **four-eyed fish** see **four-eyes; four-function calculator** an electronic calculator which can add, subtract, multiply and divide; **four-letter word** any of a number of vulgar short words, esp. of four letters, referring to sex or excrement; **fourpenny one** (*slang*) a blow, punch; **four-stroke cycle** in an internal-combustion engine, a recurring series of four strokes of the piston — an out-stroke drawing the mixed gases into the cylinder, an in-stroke compressing them, an out-stroke impelled by their explosion and working the engine, and an in-stroke driving out the burnt gas; **on all fours** on four feet, or hands and feet or hands and knees: analogous, strictly comparable; **the Four Freedoms** the four essential human freedoms as proclaimed by President Franklin D. Roosevelt in 1941 — freedom of speech, freedom of worship, freedom from want, freedom from fear; **the four hundred** (*U.S.*) the exclusive social set; **the four seas** see **sea.** [O.E. *fēower*; Ger. *vier*.]

fourchette *fōōr-shet′, n.* anything forked: a forked piece between glove fingers, uniting the front and back parts: a combination of the card next above and that next below the one just played: the furcula, or wishbone, of a bird: an animal's web foot: part of the external female genitals, a membrane at the posterior junction of the labia minora. [Fr., dim. of *fourche* — L. *furca*, fork.]

Fourcroya *fōōr-kroi′ə.* Same as **Furcraea.**

fourgon *fōōr-gɔ̃′, n.* a baggage-wagon. [Fr.]

Fourierism *fōō′ri-ər-izm, n.* the socialistic system of F. M. Charles *Fourier* (1772–1837), in which society is reorganised into small cooperative communities, or *phalanges*, allowing free development to human talent and emotions. — *adj.* **Fourieris′tic.**

fou rire *fōō rēr,* (Fr.) wild laughter, helpless giggling.

fourteen *fōr-, fōr-tēn′,* or *fōr′, fōr′tēn, n.* and *adj.* four and ten. — *n.* **fourteen′er** a verse line of fourteen syllables. — *adj.* **four′teenth** (or *-tēnth′*) last of fourteen: next after the thirteenth: equal to one of fourteen equal parts. — *n.* a fourteenth part: a person or thing in fourteenth position. — *adv.* **fourteenth′ly.** [O.E. *fēowertēne* (*-tīene*); see **four** and **ten.**]

fourth *fōrth, fōrth, adj.* last of four: next after the third: equal to one of four equal parts. — *n.* one of four equal parts: a person or thing in fourth position: an interval of three (conventionally called four) diatonic degrees: a tone at that interval from another: a combination of two tones separated by that interval. — *adv.* **fourth′ly.** — **fourth dimension** that of time, as

opposed to the three spatial dimensions: that which is beyond ordinary experience. — *adj.* **fourth′-dimen′-sional.** — **fourth estate** a group of people other than the lords, commons and clergy, who influence a country's politics: the press. — *adj.* **fourth′-rate** of the fourth order: inferior. — **fourth wall** an idea of the naturalistic theatre, that the open front of the stage-set represents as solid a wall as the other three sides; **Fourth World** the poorest and least developed of the poor countries of the world: the poorest people in the developed countries. [O.E. *fēowertha, fēortha.*]

foussa. See **fossa².**

fouter, foutre *fōō′tər,* **footra** (*Shak.*), **foutra** (*Shak.*), - *trə, ns.* a fig (as a type of worthlessness): a worthless despicable fellow (*Scot.*). [O.E. *foutre* — L. *futuĕre*, to copulate with.]

fouth, fowth *fōōth,* (*Scot.*) *n.* abundance. [**full,** suff. *-th.*]

fovea *fō′vi-ə,* (*anat.*) *n.* a depression or pit: — *pl.* **fō′veae** (*-ē*). — *adjs.* **fō′veal** of or like a fovea: of the fovea centralis; **fō′veate** pitted. — *n.* **fovē′ola** a small depression — also **fō′veole.** — **fovea centralis** (*sen-trä′lis, trä′*) a fovea in the centre of the back of the retina, the place where vision is sharpest. [L. *fŏvea.*]

fowl *fowl, n.* a bird: a bird of the poultry kind, a cock or hen: the flesh of fowl: — *pl.* **fowls, fowl.** — *v.i.* to kill or try to kill wildfowl. — *ns.* **fowl′er** one who takes wildfowl; **fowl′ing.** — **fowl′ing-net** a net for catching birds; **fowl′ing-piece** a light gun for small-shot, used in fowling; **fowl′-pest** an acute contagious virus disease of birds (**fowl′-plague**): another similar disease, Newcastle disease. [O.E. *fugol*; Ger. *Vogel.*]

fowth. See **fouth.**

fox *foks, n.* an animal akin to the dog having upright ears and a long bushy tail: — *fem.* **vix′en:** extended to other animals, as black-fox (pekan), flying-fox: anyone notorious for cunning: a kind of sword (*obs.*). — *v.t.* (*coll.*) to baffle, deceive, cheat. — *v.i.* (*coll.*) to act cunningly: to cheat. — *v.i.* and *v.t.* (of paper) to discolour, showing brownish marks. — *adj.* **foxed** of books, discoloured: drunk: baffled. — *ns.* **fox′iness** craftiness: decay: a harsh, sour taste: spotted state as in books; **fox′ing** the act of one who foxes; **fox′ship** (*Shak.*) the character of a fox, craftiness. — *adj.* **fox′y** of foxes: fox-like: cunning: reddish brown: (esp. *U.S.*; *slang*) sexually attractive. — **fox′-bat** a flying-fox, a fruit-bat; **fox′berry** the bearberry: the cowberry; **fox′-brush** the tail of a fox; **fox′-earth** a fox's burrow; **fox′-e′vil** alopecia; **fox′glove** a plant (Digitalis) with flowers like glove-fingers; **fox′-grape** an American grape (*Vitis labrusca*; also *V. rotundifolia*); **fox′hole** a fox's earth: a small entrenchment (*mil.*); **fox′hound** a hound used for chasing foxes; **fox′-hunt; fox′-hunter; fox′-mark** a brownish mark on paper that has foxed; **fox′-hunting; fox′shark** a large long-tailed shark, the thresher; **fox′-tail** a fox's brush: a genus (Alopecurus) of grasses, with head like a fox's tail; **fox′-terr′ier** a kind of terrier trained to unearth foxes; **fox′-trap; fox′-trot** a horse's pace with short steps, as in changing from trotting to walking: (fox′trot) a shuffling dance to syncopated music. — *v.i.* to dance the foxtrot: — *pr.p.* **fox′trotting;** *pa.t.* and *pa.p* **fox′trotted.** — **fox and geese** a game played with pieces on a board, where the object is for certain pieces called the geese to surround or corner one called the fox or prevent him from passing. [O.E. *fox*; Ger. *Fuchs.*]

foy¹ *foi,* (*Spens.*) *n.* allegiance. [Fr. *foi,* faith.]

foy² *foi,* (*dial.*) *n.* a parting entertainment or gift. [Du. *fooi.*]

foyer *foi′ā, foi′ər* (Fr. *fwä-yā*), *n.* in theatres, a public room opening on the lobby. [Fr., — L. *focus,* hearth.]

foyle, foyne. Spenserian spellings of **foil¹,²,** **foin.**

fozy *fō′zi,* (*Scot.*) *adj.* spongy: wanting in freshness: fat: dull-witted. — *n.* **fō′ziness** softness: want of spirit. [Cf. Du. *voos,* spongy.]

fra *frä,* (It.) *n.* brother, friar.

frab *frab,* (*dial.*) *v.t.* to worry. — *adj.* **frabb′it** peevish.

frabjous *frab'jəs, adj.* perh. joyous: surpassing. — *adv.*
frab'jously. [Invented by Lewis Carroll.]
fracas *frak'ä, frä-kä', n.* uproar: a noisy quarrel: — *pl.*
fracas (*-käz.*) [Fr., — It. *fracasso — fracassare*, to
make an uproar.]
frack *frak, fräk*, (*Scot.*) *adj.* prompt: eager: lusty. [O.E.
fræc, frec.]
fract *frakt, v.t.* to break: to violate (*Shak.*). — *adj.* **fract'ed**
broken: violated: having a part displaced, as if broken
(*her.*). — *n.* **frac'tion** (*-shən*) a fragment or small piece:
any part of a unit (*arith.*; see **decimal** and **vulgar, proper**
and **improper**): a breach of amity (*Shak.*): a portion
separated by fractionation, e.g. a mixture of hydrocarbons with similar boiling-points got by fractional
distillation in a refinery: the breaking of the bread in
the Eucharist: a group of Communists acting as a unit
within a larger non-Communist body: a faction or
schismatic group within the Communist party. — *adj.*
frac'tional belonging to a fraction or fractions: of the
nature of a fraction. — *n.* **fractionalīsā'tion, -z-.** — *v.t.*
frac'tionalise, -ize to break up into parts. — *ns.* **frac'-
tionalism** the state of consisting of discrete units: the
action of forming a fraction within the Communist
party; **frac'tionalist** a breaker-up of political unity. —
adv. **frac'tionally.** — *adj.* **frac'tionary** fractional: fragmentary. — *v.t.* **frac'tionate** to break up into smaller
units: to separate the components of by distillation or
otherwise. — *ns.* **fractionā'tion; frac'tionātor** a plant
for carrying out fractional distillation. — *n.* **frac-
tionīsā'tion, -z-.** — *v.t.* **frac'tionise, -ize** to break up
into fractions. — *n.* **frac'tionlet** a small fraction. —
adj. **frac'tious** ready to quarrel: cross. — *adv.* **frac'-
tiously.** — *ns.* **frac'tiousness; fractog'raphy** the microscopic study of fractures in metal surfaces; **frac'ture**
(*-chər*) breaking: the breach or part broken: the surface
of breaking, other than cleavage: the breaking of a
bone. — *v.t.* and *v.i.* to break through: to crack. —
fractional distillation a distillation process for the
separation of the various constituents of liquid mixtures by means of their different boiling points. —
Colles fracture see **Colles; comminuted fracture** a fracture in which the bone is splintered; **compound fracture**
the breaking of a bone, communicating with a co-existing skin wound; **greenstick fracture** a fracture where
the bone is partly broken, partly bent, occurring esp.
in limbs of children; **impacted fracture** a fracture in
which the ends of bone are driven into each other;
simple fracture a fracture of bone without wound in
the skin. [L. *frangěre, frāctum*, to break (partly
through Fr.).]
frae. See **fro.**
fraenum. Same as **frenum.**
Fragaria *frə-gā'ri-ə, n.* the strawberry genus. [L.
frāgum, the strawberry.]
fragile *fraj'īl*, in U.S. *-əl, adj.* easily broken: frail: delicate.
— *adv.* **fra'gilely.** — *ns.* **fragility** (*frə-jil'*), **fra'gileness**
the state of being fragile. [Fr., — L. *fragilis —
frangěre, frāctum.*]
fragment *frag'mənt, n.* a piece broken off: a usu. small
piece of something broken or smashed: an unfinished
portion. — *v.t.* and *v.i.* (*frag-ment'*) to break into
fragments. — *adj.* **fragmental** (*-ment'*; also *frag'mən-
təl*) composed of fragments of older rocks: in fragments. — *adv.* **frag'mentarily.** — *n.* **frag'mentariness.**
— *adjs.* **frag'mentary, fragment'ed** consisting of fragments: broken: in fragments: existing or operating in
separate parts, not forming a harmonious unity. — *n.*
fragmentā'tion division into fragments: cell division
without mitosis (*biol.*). — **fragmentation bomb, grenade**
one which shatters into small destructive fragments on
explosion. [L. *fragmentum — frangěre, frāctum*, to
break.]
fragor *frā'gör, n.* a crash. [L. *frăgor.*]
fragrant *frā'grənt, adj.* sweet-scented. — *ns.* **fra'grance**
(also **fra'grancy**) pleasantness of smell: sweet or pleasant influence (*fig.*). — *v.t.* to perfume, give a fragrance
to. — *adv.* **fra'grantly.** — *n.* **fra'grantness.** [L.

frāgrāns, -antis, pr.p. of *frāgrāre*, to smell.]
fraîcheur *fre-shœr*, (Fr.) *n.* freshness, coolness.
frail[1] *frāl, adj.* very easily shattered: feeble and infirm
(esp. *Scot.*): decrepit: morally weak: unchaste (*euph.*):
tender (*Spens.*). — *n.* (*slang*) a woman. — *adj.* **frail'ish**
somewhat frail. — *adv.* **frail'ly.** — *ns.* **frail'ness, frail'ty**
(*Spens.* **fra'iltee**) weakness: infirmity. [O.Fr. *fraile*
— L. *fragilis*, fragile.]
frail[2] *frāl, n.* a rush: a rush-basket. [O.Fr. *frayel.*]
fraim. See **fremd.**
fraise[1] *frāz, n.* a horizontal or nearly horizontal palisade
(*fort.*): a tool for enlarging a drillhole: a 16th-cent.
ruff. — *v.t.* to fence with a fraise. [Fr.]
fraise[2] *frāz*, (*dial.*) *n.* commotion.
fraise[3] *frāz.* See **froise.**
Fraktur *fräk-tōōr', n.* a German black-letter type-face.
[Ger., — L. *frāctūra*, breaking.]
framboesia *fram-bē'zi-ə, n.* yaws. [Fr. *framboise*, raspberry.]
frame *frām, v.t.* to form: to shape: to put together: to
plan, adjust, or adapt: to contrive or devise: to concoct:
to bring about: to articulate: to direct (one's steps): to
set about: to enclose in a frame or border: to make
victim of a frame-up. — *v.i.* to make one's way: to
resort: to pretend (*dial.*): to make a move: to give
promise of progress or success: to contrive (*B.*). — *n.*
the body: a putting together of parts: a structure: a
case made to enclose, border or support anything: the
skeleton of anything: the rigid part of a bicycle: a
structure on which embroidery is worked: a stocking-
making machine: a loom (*obs.*): a structure on which
bees build a honeycomb: in gardening, a structure for
cultivation or sheltering of plants: state (of mind),
mood: act of devising (*Shak.*): unit picture in cinema
film: (*formerly*) the British term for field (*TV*): the
total TV picture: a triangular support in which the
balls are grouped for the break (*snooker*, etc.): the balls
so grouped (*snooker*, etc.): in the jargon of certain
games, a definite part of a game, a game, or a definite
number of games. — *ns.* **fram'er** one who forms or
constructs: one who makes frames for pictures, etc.;
one who devises: one who formulates (e.g. law); **fram'-
ing** the act of constructing: a frame or setting. —
frame'-breaker (*hist.*) one who broke stocking-frames
on their introduction; **frame'-house** a house consisting
of a skeleton of timber, with boards or shingles laid
on; **frame'-maker** a maker of picture-frames; **frame'-
saw** a thin saw stretched in a frame; **frame'-up** a
trumped-up affair, esp. a false criminal charge against
an innocent person: a staged or preconcerted event;
frame'work the work that forms the frame: the skeleton
or outline of anything. — **frame of reference** a set of
axes with reference to which the position of a point,
etc., is described (*lit.*): the structure of standards,
arising from the individual's experience, and continually developing, to which he refers, in all cases from
the simplest to the most complicated, when judging or
evaluating (*fig.*). [O.E. *framian*, to be helpful, *fram*,
forward.]
frampold *fram'pōld, -pəld*, (*obs.*) *adj.* peevish, cross-
grained: fiery. — Also **fram'pal** (*Scott*). — *n.* **fram'pler**
(*Scott*) a brawler. [Ety. obscure.]
franc *frangk, n.* a coin forming since 1795 the unit of the
French monetary system (**new**, or **heavy, franc** introduced 1960 — 'new' dropped 1963): the unit also in
Belgium, Switzerland, etc. [O.Fr. *franc*, from the
legend *Francorum rex* on the first coins.]
franchise[1] *fran'chīz, -shīz, n.* liberty: a privilege or exemption by prescription or grant: the right of voting, esp.
for an M.P.: voting qualification: a commercial concession by which a retailer is granted by a company
the generally exclusive right of retailing its goods or
providing its services in a specified area, with use of
the company's expertise, marketing, trademark, etc.:
a similar concession granted by a public authority to
a broadcasting company: a percentage below which
the underwriter incurs no responsibility (*insurance*). —

v.t. (*obs.*) to enfranchise. — *ns.* **franchisee'** one to whom a franchise is granted; **fran'chisement** (-*chiz*-, -*shiz*-; *obs.*) liberation; **fran'chiser** a voter: a firm, etc. which grants a commercial concession. [O.Fr., — *franc*, free.]

franchise² *frä-shēz*, (Fr.) *n.* candour, frankness.

Franciscan *fran-sis'kən*, *adj.* belonging to the order of mendicant friars in the R.C. Church, founded by St *Francis* of Assisi (1182 1226). — *n.* a friar of this order. [L. *Franciscus*, Francis.]

francium *fran'si-əm*, *n.* the chemical element of atomic number 87, symbol Fr, discovered by a Frenchwoman, Mlle Perey. [**France.**]

franco *fräng'kō*, (It.) *adj.* and *adv.* post-free: franked.

Franco- *frangk'ō-*, in composition, French: French and, as **Fran'co-Ger'man, Fran'co-Russ'ian,** etc. — *ns.* **Francomā'nia, -phil(e), -phobe, -phobia** (also without *cap.*) same as **Gallomania,** etc.; see under **Gallic.** — *adj.* **Franc'ophone** (also without *cap.*) French-speaking (used e.g. of Africans for whom French is a second mother-tongue or French-speaking Canadians).

francolin *frang'kō-lin*, *n.* a (bird of the) genus (*Francolinus*) of partridges. [Fr.]

franc-tireur *frä tē-rœr*, (Fr.) *n.* a sniper: a guerrillero.

frangible *fran'ji-bl*, *adj.* easily broken. — *n.* **frangibil'ity.** [L. *frangĕre*, to break; see **fract.**]

frangipani *fran-ji-pä'nē*, *n.* the red jasmine or other species of *Plumeria*, tropical American apocynaceous shrubs with scented flowers: a perfume from or in imitation of red jasmine: (also **frangipane** *fran'ji-pān*) a pastry-cake filled with cream, almonds, and sugar. [From the name of the inventor of the perfume *Frangipani*.]

Franglais *frä-gle*, *n.* French with many English words and forms. [Fr. *Français* and An*glais*.]

franion *fran'yən*, *n.* a paramour (*obs.*): a boon-companion (*obs.*): a loose woman (*Spens.*). [Ety. dub.]

Frank *frangk*, *n.* a German of a confederation in Franconia of which a branch conquered Gaul in the 5th century, and founded France: in the East, a Western European. — *adj.* **Frank'ish.** [See **frank¹.**]

frank¹ *frangk*, *adj.* free, open: liberal (*obs.*): open or candid in expression: unrestrained (*obs.*): unmistakable, true (*med.*; as **frank pus, asthma**). — *v.t.* to sign so as to ensure free carriage: to send thus signed: to mark by means of a **frank'ing-machine** to show that postage has been paid. — *n.* the signature of a person who had the right to frank a letter: a franked cover. — *adv.* **frank'ly** to be frank: in a frank manner. — *n.* **frank'ness.** — **frank'-fee** tenure in fee-simple; **frank'= pledge** a mutual suretyship by which the members of a tithing were made responsible for one another; **frank'-ten'ement** freehold. [O.Fr. *franc* — L.L. *francus*; O.H.G. *Franko*, Frank, hence a free man.]

frank² *frangk*, (*Shak.*) *n.* a pig-sty. — *v.t.* to shut up in a sty: to cram, to fatten. [O.Fr. *franc*.]

frankalmoign *frangk'al-moin*, (*Eng. law*) *n.* a form of land-tenure in which no obligations were enforced except religious ones, as praying, etc. [O.Fr. *franc*, free, *almoigne*, alms.]

Frankenia *frang-kē'ni-ə*, *n.* the sea-heath genus, constituting a family **Frankeniā'ceae,** akin to the tamarisk family. [Named after John *Frankenius* (1590–1661), Swedish physician and botanist.]

Frankenstein *frangk'ən-stīn*, *n.* the hero of Mrs. Shelley's romance so named, who by his skill forms an animate creature like a man, only to his own torment: hence, by confusion, any creation that brings disaster to its author.

Frankfurter *frangk'fûr-tər*, -*foor-tər*, (often without *cap.*) *n.* a small smoked sausage. [Short for Ger. *Frankfurter Wurst*, Frankfurt sausage.]

frankincense *frangk'in-sens*, *n.* olibanum, a sweet-smelling resin from Arabia, used as incense: spruce resin. — **herb frankincense** laser. [O.Fr. *franc encens*, pure incense.]

franklin *frangk'lin*, (*hist.*) *n.* an English freeholder, free

from feudal servitude to a subject-superior. [L.L. *francus;* see **frank¹.**]

franklinite *frangk'lin-īt*, *n.* a zinc-manganese spinel, mined at *Franklin Forge*, New Jersey.

frantic *fran'tik*, *adj.* mad, furious: wild. — *advs.* **fran'tically, fran'ticly** (*Shak.*). — *n.* **fran'ticness** the state of being frantic. — *adj.* **fran'tic-mad** raving mad. [O.Fr. *frenetique* — L. *phrenēticus* — Gr. *phrenētikos*, mad — *phrēn*, the mind; see **frenetic, frenzy.**]

franzy *fran'zi*, (*dial.*) *adj.* cross: peevish. [Variant of **frenzy.**]

frap *frap*, *v.t.* to strike (now *dial.*): to secure by many turns of a lashing (*naut.*): — *pr.p* **frapp'ing;** *pa.t.* and *pa.p.* **frapped'.** [Fr. *frapper*, to strike.]

frappant *fra-pä*, (Fr.) *adj.* striking: affecting.

frappé *fra'pā*, *p. adj.* iced: artificially cooled: — *fem.* **frapp'ee.** [Fr., *pa.p.* of *frapper*, to strike.]

frass *fras*, *n.* excrement or other refuse of boring larvae. [Ger., — *fressen*, to eat; cf. **fret¹.**]

fratch *frach*, (*dial.*) *n.* a quarrel or brawl. — *adjs.* **fratch'ety, fratch'y; fratch'ing.** [Perh. imit.]

frate *frä'tā*, (It.) *n.* a friar, a mendicant Franciscan: — *pl.* **fra'ti** (-*tē*).

frater¹ *frä'tər*, *n.* a refectory: sometimes applied in error to a monastic common-room or to a chapter-house (by confusion with next word). — Also **fra'ter-house, frā'try.** [O.Fr. *fraitur* for *refreitor* — L.L. *refectōrium.*]

frater² *frä'tər*, *n.* a friar: a comrade. — *n.* **Fratercula** (*fra-tûr'kū-lə*) the puffin genus. — *adj.* **fraternal** (*frə-tûr'nl*) belonging to a brother or brethren: brotherly: of twins, dizygotic. — *adv.* **frater'nally.** — *n.* **fraternīsā'tion, -z-** (*frat-*) the associating as brethren. — *v.i.* **frat'ernise, -ize** to associate as brothers: to seek brotherly fellowship: to come into friendly association (with). — *ns.* **frat'erniser, -z-; frater'nity** the state of being brethren: a brotherhood: a society formed on a principle of brotherhood: an American college association: any set of people with something in common; **fratry** (*frā'ri*), **frāt'ery** a fraternity: a convent of friars (see also foregoing article). [L. *frāter*, a brother; cf. **brother,** Gr. *phrātēr*, a clansman, Sans. *bhrātr*.]

fratricide *frat'ri-sīd*, or *frāt'*, *n.* one who kills his brother: the murder of a brother. — *adj.* **fratrici'dal.** [Fr., — L. *frāter, frātris, caedĕre*, to kill.]

frau, Frau *frow*, *n.* a woman: a wife: Mrs. — *n.* **fräulein, Fräulein** (*froi'līn*) an unmarried woman: often applied to a German governess: Miss. [Ger.]

fraud *fröd*, *n.* deceit: imposture: criminal deception done with the intention of gaining an advantage: a snare (*Milt.*): a deceptive trick: a cheat, swindler (*coll.*): a fraudulent production. — *adj.* **fraud'ful** deceptive. — *adv.* **fraud'fully.** — *ns.* **frauds'man** one involved in criminal fraud; **fraud'ster** a swindler; **fraud'ulence, fraud'ulency.** — *adj.* **fraud'ulent** using fraud. — *adv.* **fraud'ulently.** — **fraudulent bankruptcy** a bankruptcy in which the insolvent is accessory, by concealment or otherwise, to the diminution of the funds divisible among his creditors. [O.Fr. *fraude* — L. *fraus*, fraud.]

Frauendienst *frow'ən-dēnst*, (Ger.) *n.* courtly love.

fraught *fröt*, (*obs.*) *n.* a load, cargo: the freight of a ship. — *v.t.* (*obs.*) to fill store. — *v.i.* (*Shak.*) to form the freight of a vessel. — *adj.* freighted, laden (*obs.*): filled (with): having or causing (esp. something bad or undesirable e.g. danger; with *with*): feeling or making anxious or distressed, tension-filled. — *n.* **fraught'age, fraut'age** (*Shak.*) loading, cargo. [Prob. Old Du. *vracht.* Cf. **freight.**]

fräulein. See **frau.**

Fraunhofer's lines *frown'hō-fərz līnz.* See **line².**

fraus pia *frös pī'ə, frows pē'a*, (L.) a pious fraud.

Fraxinus *frak'si-nəs*, *n.* the ash genus. — **Fraxinell'a** dittany (from its ashlike leaves). [L.]

fray¹ *frä*, *n.* an affray: a brawl. — *v.t.* to frighten. [Aphetic from **affray.**]

fray² *frä*, *v.t.* to wear off by rubbing: to ravel out the end or edge of: to cause a strain on (e.g. nerves, temper, etc.). — *v.i.* to become frayed: to rub off the velvet from the new antlers. — *n.* **fray'ing** the action of the verb: frayed-off material. [Fr. *frayer* — L. *fricāre*, to rub.]

frazil *frăz'il, frā'zil, n.* ground-ice: ice in small spikes and plates in rapid streams. [Canadian Fr. *frasil*; prob. Fr. *fraisil*, cinders.]

frazzle *fraz'l, v.t.* to fray, wear out. — *n.* the state of being worn out: a shred. — **burnt,** etc. **to a frazzle** completely burnt, etc. [Origin unknown.]

freak¹ *frēk, n.* a caprice: sport: an abnormal production of nature, a monstrosity: an eccentric: a weirdly unconventional person: one who is wildly enthusiastic about something (usu. in composition, as in *film-freak, football-freak, Jesus freak*). — *adj.* capricious: unusual. — *ns.* **freak'iness, freak'ishness.** — *adjs.* **freak'ish, freak'ful, freak'y** apt to change the mind suddenly: unusual, odd. — *adv.* **freak'ishly.** — **freak'-out** (*slang*) a (drug-induced) hallucinatory or (*loosely*) wildly exciting, unconventional experience or occurrence (*v.t.* **freak (out)).** — **phone freak(ing)** see **phon.** [A late word; cf. O.E. *frīcian,* to dance.]

freak² *frēk, v.t.* to spot or streak (*Milt.*): to variegate (*Milt.*). — *n.* a streak of colour. [Perh. the same as the foregoing.]

freckle *frek'l, v.t.* to spot: to colour with spots. — *n.* a yellowish or brownish-yellow spot on the skin, esp. of fair-haired persons: any small spot. — *n.* **freck'ling** a little spot. — *adjs.* **freck'ly, freck'led** full of freckles. [O.N. *freknur* (pl.), Dan. *fregne.*]

fredaine *frɔ-den,* (Fr.) *n.* an escapade, prank.

free *frē, adj.* not bound: at liberty: not under arbitrary government: not strict, or bound by rules: not literal: unimpeded: unconstrained: readily cut, separated or wrought: ready (esp. in phrase *free to confess*): guiltless: frank: lavish: uncombined: unattached: exempt (with *from*): not suffering from or encumbered with (with *of* or *from*): having a franchise (with *of*): without payment: bold: indecent: — *compar.* **freer** *frē'ɔr; superl.* **freest** *frē'ist.* — *adv.* freely: without payment: without obstruction. — *v.t.* to set at liberty: to deliver from what confines: to rid (with *from, of*): — *pr.p.* **free'ing;** *pa.t.* and *pa.p.* **freed.** — *in composition* free from, as in *trouble-free.* — *n.* **free'bie** (orig. *U.S.; slang;* also **freebee**) something supplied free of charge. — Also *adj.* — *n.* **free'dom** liberty: frankness: outspokenness: unhampered boldness: separation: privileges connected with a city (often granted as an honour merely): improper familiarity: licence. — *adv.* **free'ly.** — *ns.* **free'ness; freer** (*frē'ɔr*) a liberator. — **free agency** the state or power of acting freely, or without necessity or constraint upon the will; **free agent; free'-and-eas'y** an informal public-house club. — *adj.* informal in manners, without ceremonious restraint. — *adj.* **free'-arm** with unsupported arm. — **free association** a technique in psychoanalysis based either on the first association called forth by each of a series of words or on a train of thought suggested by a single word; **free atom** an unattached atom assumed to exist briefly during certain chemical reactions; **free'-bench** a widow's right to dower out of her husband's lands; **free'-board** the distance between water-line and deck: a strip of land outside a fence, or a right thereto; **free'booter** one who roves about freely in search of booty (Du. *vrijbuiter*); **free'bootery.** — *adj.* and *n.* **free'booting.** — **free'booty.** — *adj.* **free'born** born free. — **Free Church** that branch of the Presbyterians in Scotland which left the Established Church in the Disruption of 1843: the small minority thereof who refused to combine with the United Presbyterians in the **United Free Church** (see under **presbyter**): in England, a Nonconformist church generally; **free'-cit'y** a city constituting a state in itself; **free companion** a member of a **free company,** or mediaeval band of mercenaries ready for any service; **free'-cost** freedom from charges; **free'-diver, -diving** skin-diver, -diving; **freed'man** a man who has been a

slave and has been freed: — *pl.* **freed'men;** *fem.* **freed'woman;** *pl.* **freed'women; freedom fighter** one who fights in an armed movement for the liberation of a nation, etc. from a government considered unjust, tyrannical, etc.: **free enterprise** the conduct of business without interference from the state; **free-fall'** the motion of an unpropelled body in a gravitational field, as that of a spacecraft in orbit: the part of a parachute jump before the parachute opens. — *adj.* of or pertaining to free-fall or to a parachute jump which is partly a free-fall. — *v.i.* to fall with one's parachute kept closed. — **free= fall'ing; free fight** a confused or promiscuous fight; **free'-fish'er** one who has a right to take fish in certain waters; **free flight** the flight of a rocket, etc. when its motor is no longer producing thrust; **Free'fone®** a British Telecom service allowing callers e.g. to a business or organisation to make their calls free of charge, the charges being paid by the business or organisation concerned; **free'-food'er** an opponent of taxes on food. — *adj.* **free'-foot'ed** (*Shak.*) not restrained in movement. — **free'-for-all** a contest open to anybody: a free fight. — Also *adj.* — *adj.* **free gift** something given free with a product as an incentive to buy. — **free'-hand** executed by the unguided hand. — **free hand** complete freedom of action. — *adj.* **free'-hand'ed** open-handed: liberal. — **free'-hand'ed= ness.** — *adj.* **free'-heart'ed** open-hearted: liberal. — **free'-heart'edness; free'hold** a property held by fee simple, fee tail, or for life: the holding of property in any of such ways. — Also *adj.* — **free'holder** one who possesses a freehold; **free house** a public-house that is not tied to a particular supplier; **free kick** (*football*) a kick allowed without interference, as a penalty against the opposing side for infringing the rules; **free-la'bour** voluntary, not slave, labour; **free'-lance** one of the mercenary knights and men-at-arms who after the Crusades wandered about Europe: an unattached politician, etc.: any one who works for himself, employed or paid by others only for particular, usu. short-term, assignments (also **free'lancer**). — Also *adj., adv.* and *v.i.* — **free list** the list of persons admitted without payment to a theatre, etc., or of those to whom a book, etc., is sent; **free'-liv'er** one who freely indulges his appetite for eating and drinking: a glutton. — *v.i.* **free'load** (esp. *U.S.; coll.*) to eat at someone else's expense: to sponge: to gain from others' efforts. — *n.* a free meal. — **free'loader.** — *n.* and *adj.* **free'loading.** — **free love** the claim to freedom in sexual relations, unshackled by marriage or obligation to aliment; **free'-lov'er** one who advocates, or is thought to advocate, free love, e.g. (with *cap.*) a Perfectionist (q.v.); **free'man** a man who is free or enjoys liberty: one who holds a particular franchise or privilege: — *pl.* **free'-men;** *fem.* **free'woman;** *pl.* **free'women; free'mā'son** in the Middle Ages, a stone-mason of a superior grade: (often with *cap.*) a member of a secret fraternity, united in lodges for social enjoyment and mutual assistance. — *adj.* **freemason'ic.** — **freemā'sonry** (also with *cap.*) the institutions, practices, etc. of freemasons: instinctive understanding and sympathy. — *adj.* **free'-mind'ed** with a mind free or unperplexed: without a load of care. — **free'-port** a port open on equal terms to all traders: a free-trade zone adjacent to a port, allowing duty-free import and re-export of goods; **Free'post®** a Royal Mail service which allows inquirers or potential customers to write to a business or organisation free of charge, the postage costs being paid by the business or organisation concerned; **free radical** a group of atoms containing at least one unpaired electron existing briefly during certain chemical reactions. — *adjs.* **free'-range'** (of poultry) allowed some freedom to move about: (of eggs) laid by free-range hens; **free= reed** (*mus.*) having a reed that does not touch the side of the aperture. — **free'-rid'er** (*coll.*) one who enjoys benefits obtained for workers by a trade union without being a member of that trade union; **free'-school** a school where no tuition fees are exacted. — *v.i.*

free′-select (*Austr.*) to take up crown-land under a scheme making land available for small farms. — **free′-selec′tion** the process of doing so: the land so taken; **free′-selec′tor** (also **selec′tion, selec′tor**); **free′-sheet** a newspaper distributed free; **free′-shot** (Ger. *Freischütz*) a legendary hunter and marksman who gets a number of bullets (*Freikugeln*) from the devil, six of which always hit the mark, while the seventh remains at the devil's disposal; **free skating** competitive figure-skating in which the skater selects movements from an officially approved list of jumps, spins, etc. — *adj.* **free′-soil** in favour of free territory, opposed to slavery. — **free-soil′er.** — *adj.* **free′-space** of a radio, etc., able to operate only where there is **free space**, i.e. where the radio waves are not affected by surrounding objects such as buildings, hills, etc. — **free speech** the right to express one's opinions freely in public. — *adj.* **free′-spōk′en** accustomed to speak without reserve. — **free′-spōk′enness.** — *adj.* **free′-stand′ing** not supported by or attached to anything else. — **Free States** in America, before the Civil War of 1861–65, those of the United States in which slavery did not exist, as opposed to *Slave States*; **free′stone** any easily wrought building stone without tendency to split in layers: a freestone fruit. — *adj.* (of a type of peach, etc.) having a stone from which the pulp easily separates — opp. to *clingstone.* — *adj.* **free′style** of a (e.g. swimming or skiing) race or competition, in which a competitor is free to choose which style or method to use or which movements to perform: of wrestling, all-in: of a competitor, taking part in free-style competitions, etc. — *ns.* **free′style** freestyle competitions; **free′styler** a competitor in such competitions. — *adj.* **free′-swimm′ing** swimming about, not attached. — **free′thinker** one who rejects authority in religion: a rationalist. — *n.* and *adj.* **free′-thinking.** — **free′-thought.** — *adj.* **free′=tongued** free-spoken. — **free′-trade** free or unrestricted trade: free interchange of commodities without protective duties; **free′-trad′er** one who practises or advocates this: a smuggler: a smuggling vessel; **free verse** verse defying the usual conventions as to regularity of metre, rhyme, length of lines, etc.: rhythmic prose arranged as irregular verses; **free′-vers′er** a writer of free verse, a verslibrist; **free vote** a vote left to individual choice, free from party discipline; **free′way** a toll-free road for high-speed traffic (*U.S.*): a motorway (*S. Afr.*); **free′-wheel′** the mechanism of a bicycle by which the hind-wheel may be temporarily disconnected and set free from the driving-gear. — *v.i.* to cycle with wheel so disconnected: (of motor vehicle or its driver) to coast: to move, act, live, without restraint or concern (*fig.*). — **free′-wheel′ing; free′-will′** freedom of the will from restraint: liberty of choice: the power of self-determination. — *adj.* **free′-will** spontaneous: voluntary. — **freewoman** see **freeman; Free World** the collective name used of themselves by non-communist countries. — **free collective bargaining** collective bargaining (q.v.) without government-imposed or other restrictions; **for free** (*coll.*) given without desire for payment or other return; **free on board (f.o.b.)** delivered on a vessel or other conveyance without charge; **it's a free country** (*coll.*) their is no objection to or law against the carrying-out of whatever action has been proposed; **make free with** to be familiar with, to take liberties with: to help oneself liberally to; **make so free as to** to venture to. [O.E. *frēo*; Ger. *frei*; O.N. *frī*.]

freebie. See under **free.**

freemartin *frē′mär-tin, n.* a calf (twin with a bull) with internal male organs and external and rudimentary internal female: a similar animal of another species. [Ety. unknown; perh. conn. with Ir. *mart*, a heifer.]

Freesia *frē′zi-ə,* a South African genus of the iris family, scented greenhouse plants: (without *cap.*) a plant of this genus. [After F. H.T. *Freese*, German physician, or H. Th. *Frees*, German physician, or according to some, E. M. *Fries*, Swedish botanist.]

freet, freety. See **freit.**

freeze *frēz, v.i.* to become ice: to become solid by fall of temperature: to be at a temperature at which water would freeze: to be very cold: to become motionless, stiff, attached, or stopped by, or as if by, cold. — *v.t.* to cause to freeze: to fix: to stabilise: to prevent the use of or dealings in: to stop at, not develop beyond, a particular state or stage: to put a temporary stop to: to stop (a moving film) at a particular frame: to preserve (esp. food) by freezing and storing below freezing-point: to anaesthetise (a part of the body): — *pr.p.* **freez′ing;** *pa.t.* **frōze,** (*Milt.*) **freez′d;** *pa.p.* **frōz′en;** *obs.* or *dial.* **frōze, frōre, frōrn.** — *n.* a frost: a stoppage. — *adj.* **freez′able.** — *ns.* **freez′er** a freezing apparatus: anything that freezes: a special compartment in a refrigerator designed to freeze fresh foods: a deep-freeze; **freez′ing.** — *adj.* very cold. — *v.t.* **freeze′-dry′.** — **freeze′-dry′ing** evaporation to dryness in a vacuum for preservation or storage of a substance, e.g. an antibiotic; **freeze′-frame** a frame of a cinematographic film repeated, or a frame of a video film held, to give a still picture; **freeze′-up** in U.S. and Canada, the period when ice forms on lakes, etc., at onset of winter; **freez′ing-down** lowering of the body temperature; **freez′ing-mixture** a mixture, as of pounded ice and salt, producing cold enough to freeze a liquid by the rapid absorption of heat; **freez′ing-point** the temperature at which a liquid solidifies — that of water being 32° Fahrenheit, 0° Celsius (centigrade). — **freeze down** to lower the body temperature in preparation for heart and other operations; **freeze out** (*coll.*) to oblige to leave: to exclude. [O.E. *frēosan,* pa.p. *froren*; Du. *vreizen,* Ger. *frieren.*]

freight *frāt, n.* the lading or cargo, esp. of a ship: the charge for transporting goods by water or land. — *v.t.* to load (esp. a ship): to hire, let out. — *adj.* (*obs.*) freighted: fraught. — *ns.* **freight′age** money paid for freight; **freight′er** one who freights a vessel: a cargo-carrying boat, etc.: a transporting agent (*U.S.*). — **freight′-car** (*U.S.*) a luggage van: a goods van or wagon; **freight′liner** a train having specially designed containers and rolling-stock and used for rapid transport of goods. — Also *adj.* — **freight′shed** a goods shed or warehouse; **freight′-train** a goods train. [Prob. Old Du. *vrecht,* a form of *vracht.*]

freit, freet *frēt,* (*Scot.*) *n.* an omen. — *adj.* **freit′y, freet′y** superstitious. [O.N. *frētt,* news.]

fremd *fremd, frāmd,* **fremit** *frem′it, frām′it,* **fraim** *frām,* (*Scot.*) *adjs.* foreign: strange: not akin: estranged, cold, unfriendly. — *n.* a stranger: strange folk, other than kindred. — *Spens.* **frenne** (*fren*). [O.E. *fremde*; cf. Ger. *fremd.*]

fremescent *frəm-es′ənt,* (*rare*) *adj.* growling, muttering. — *n.* **fremesc′ence.** [L. *fremēre,* to growl.]

fremit. See **fremd.**

fremitus *frem′i-təs, n.* a palpable vibration, as of the walls of the chest. [L., a murmur.]

frena. See **frenum.**

French *french, -sh, adj.* belonging to *France* or its people: originating in France (sometimes without *cap.*). — *n.* the people of France: the language of France, also an official language in Belgium, Switzerland, Canada and other countries. — *n.* **Frenchifica′tion.** — *v.t.* **French′ify** to make French or Frenchlike: to infect with the manner of the French. — *n.* **French′iness.** — *adj.* **French′y** with an exaggerated French manner. — *n.* a contemptuous name for a Frenchman. — **French bean** the common kidney-bean (*Phaseolus vulgaris*) eaten, pods and all, as a table vegetable; **French berry** the berry of species of buckthorn, used in dyeing yellow. — *adj.* **French′-Canā′dian** of the French-speaking part of Canada. — *n.* a French-Canadian person: the French language of Canada; **French chalk** soapstone; **French cricket** an esp. children's game resembling cricket, in which the batsman's legs serve as the wicket; **French curve** a thin plate with the outlines of various curves on it, used for drawing curves; **French dressing** a salad dressing consisting of oil and vinegar or lemon juice, and usu. seasoning; **French fry** (*pl.* **French fries**), **French fried potato** a potato-chip; **French heel** a way of turning the heel in knitting: a high curved heel for ladies' shoes; **French horn** the orchestral horn; **French kiss** a kiss in which the tongue is inserted into one's partner's mouth; **French knickers** a type of wide-legged knickers; **French leave** see **take French leave** below; **French letter** (*slang*) a condom; **French loaf** crusty bread baked in long narrow shape with tapered ends; **French'man:** — *pl.* **French'men;** *fem.* **French'woman:** — *pl.* **French'women; French pitch** (*mus.*) a standard pitch established by the French government in 1859, and later widely adopted — 435 cycles per second at 15°C for A (see **international concert pitch**); **French pleat** see **French roll; French plum** a prune, a dried plum; **French polish** a varnish for furniture, consisting chiefly of shellac dissolved in spirit. — *v.t.* **French'-pol'ish** to treat with French polish. — **French-pol'isher; French-pol'-ishing; French pox** (*obs.*) syphilis; **French roll, pleat** a hairstyle in which the hair is formed into a vertical roll at the back of the head; **French roof** a modified mansard roof — really American; **French sash, window** a doorlike window; **French seam** seam stitched on right side then on wrong side to cover raw edges; **French stick** a very narrow French loaf; **French toast** bread dipped in egg (and milk) and fried; **French window** see **French sash; Frenchwoman** see **Frenchman.** — **Free** (from 1942 **Fighting**) **French** continuers under General de Gaulle of resistance to Germany in World War II after the French capitulation of 1940; **pardon, excuse my French** (*coll.*) pardon my bad language; **take French leave** to depart without notice or permission: to disappear suspiciously. [O.E. *Frencisc* — L. *Francus* — O.H.G. *Franko*.]

frenetic, phrenetic *fri-net'ik,* formerly *fren',* adj. delirious: frantic: frenzied: mad: distracted. — *n.* a madman. — adj. **frenet'ical, phrenet'ical.** — *adv.* **frenet'ically, phrenet'ically.** [O.Fr. *frénétique* — L. *phreneticus* — late Gr. *phrenētikos* — Gr. *phrenītis,* delirium — *phrēn,* heart, mind; see **phrenesiac.**]

frenne *fren,* (*Spens.*). See **fremd.**

frenum, fraenum *frē'nəm, n.* a ligament restraining the motion of a part of the body: — *pl.* **fr(a)e'na.** [L. *frēnum,* a bridle.]

frenzy *fren'zi, n.* a violent excitement: a paroxysm of madness. — *v.t.* to drive to frenzy. — *adjs.* **fren'zical, fren'zied.** [O.Fr. *frenesie* — L. and late Gr. *phrenēsis* — Gr. *phrenītis;* see **frenetic.**]

Freon® *frē'on, n.* any of a family of chemicals containing fluorine, used as refrigerants, etc. (also without *cap.*); — **Fre'on-12',** dichlorodifluoromethane (CF_2Cl_2), widely used in household refrigerators.

frequent *frē'kwənt, adj.* coming or occurring often: crowded: addicted (*Shak.*). — *v.t.* (*fri-kwent'*) to visit often: to associate with: to resort to: to crowd. — *ns.* **frē'quence** a crowd, an assembly (*Milt.*): frequency; **frē'quency** resort (*obs.*): commonness of recurrence: the number of vibrations, cycles, or other recurrences in unit time (in ascending order, high, very high, ultra-high, extremely high, super-high frequency); **frēquentā'tion** the act of visiting often. — *adj.* **frequentative** (*fri-kwent'ə-tiv; gram.*) denoting the frequent repetition of an action. — *n.* (*gram.*) a verb expressing this repetition. — *n.* **frequent'er.** — *adv.* **frē'quently.** — *n.* **frē'quentness.** — **frequency modulation** modulation in radio transmission by varying the frequency of the carrier wave, giving greater fidelity than amplitude modulation and almost freedom from atmospherics; **high frequency** a radio frequency of between 3 and 30 megahertz; **low frequency** a radio frequency of between 30 and 300 kilohertz. [L. *frequēns, frequentis;* conn. with *farcīre,* to stuff.]

frère *frer,* (Fr.) *n.* a brother.

frescade *fres-kād', n.* a cool walk. [Fr., — It. *frescata.*]

fresco *fres'kō, n.* a mode of painting upon walls covered with damp freshly-laid plaster (*true fresco*), or partly-dried plaster (*dry fresco* or *fresco secco*): a picture so

painted: — *pl.* **fres'coes, fres'cos.** — *v.t.* to paint in fresco. — *adj.* **fres'coed** (*-kōd*). — *ns.* **frescoer** (*fres'kō-ər*); **fres'coing; fres'coist.** [It. *fresco,* fresh.]

fresh *fresh, adj.* in a state of activity and health: in new condition: not stale, faded or soiled: new, recently added: raw, inexperienced: in youthful bloom: cool, invigorating: brisk: amorously over-free (*slang*): without salt: not preserved by pickling, drying, salting, etc.: not frosty, thawing (*Scot.*): cheeky, pert. — *adv.* freshly: afresh: newly. — *n.* time of freshness: a small stream of fresh water (*Shak.*): a thaw, open weather (*Scot.*). — *v.t.* to freshen. — *v.t.* **fresh'en** to make fresh: to take the saltness from. — *v.i.* to grow fresh — *v.t.* and *v.i.* to make (oneself) fresh by washing, etc. (often with *up*). — *ns.* **fresh'ener; fresh'er** a student in his or her first year, a freshman; **fresh'erdom; fresh'et** a stream of fresh water: a flood. — *adj.* **fresh'ish.** — *adv.* **fresh'ly** with freshness: newly: anew. — *n.* **fresh'ness.** — *adj.* **fresh'-blown** newly blown, as a flower. — *ns.* **fresh'man** a newcomer: a student in his first year; **fresh'manship.** — *adjs.* **fresh'-new** (*Shak.*) quite new; **fresh'-run** newly come up from the sea, as a salmon; **fresh'water** of or pertaining to water not salt: accustomed to sail only on fresh water. — **freshwater college** (*U.S.*) a provincial, esp. unsophisticated, college. [O.E. *fersc;* cf. Ger. *frisch.*]

fret¹ *fret, v.t.* to eat into: to corrode: to wear away by rubbing: to rub, chafe: to ripple, disturb: to vex, to irritate. — *v.i.* to wear away: to vex oneself: to worry: to chafe: of a liquid, to work, ferment (*dial.*): — *pr.p.* **frett'ing;** *pa.t.* and *pa.p.* **frett'ed.** — *n.* agitation of the surface of a liquid: irritation: worry: a worn or eroded spot: sea fret. — *adj.* **fret'ful** peevish. — *adv.* **fret'fully.** — *n.* **fret'fulness.** — *adj.* **frett'ing** vexing. — *n.* peevishness. [O.E. *fretan,* to gnaw — pfx. *for-,* intens., and *etan,* to eat; Ger. *fressen.*]

fret² *fret, v.t.* to ornament with interlaced work: to variegate: — *pr.p.* **frett'ing;** *pa.t.* and *pa.p.* **frett'ed.** — *n.* ornamental network: a type of decoration originating in ancient Greece, for a cornice, border, etc., consisting of lines meeting usu. at right angles, the pattern being repeated to form a continuous band (also called **grecque, (Greek) key (pattern), meander)** bendlets, dexter and sinister, interlaced with a mascle (*her.*). — *adjs.* **frett'ed, frett'y** ornamented with frets. — **fret'saw** a saw with a narrow blade and fine teeth, used for fretwork, scrollwork, etc.; **fret'work** ornamental work consisting of a combination of frets: perforated woodwork. [O.Fr. *freter,* to adorn with interlaced work, *frete,* trelliswork; prob. influenced by or confused with O.E. *frætwa,* ornament.]

fret³ *fret, n.* any of the wooden or metal ridges on the fingerboard of a guitar or other instrument on to which the strings are pressed in producing the various notes. — *v.t.* to furnish with frets: — *pr.p.* **frett'ing;** *pa.t.* and *pa.p.* **frett'ed.** [Prob. same as the above.]

Freudian *froid'i-ən, adj.* pertaining to Sigmund *Freud* (1856–1939), his theory of the libido, or his method of psychoanalysis. — *n.* a follower of Freud. — **Freudian slip** an error or unintentional action, esp. a slip of the tongue, supposed to reveal an unconscious thought.

friable *frī'ə-bl, adj.* apt to crumble: easily reduced to powder. — *ns.* **fri'ableness, friabil'ity.** [Fr.,—L. *friābilis* — *friāre, friātum,* to crumble.]

friand *frē-ã,* (Fr.) *adj.* dainty, delicate: — *fem.* **friande** (*frē-ãd*). — *n.* an epicure.

friar *frī'ər, n.* a member of one of the mendicant monastic orders in the R.C. Church — the Franciscans (*Friars Minor* or *Grey Friars*), Dominicans (*Friars Preachers,* or *Black Friars*), Carmelites (*White Friars*), Augustinians (*Austin Friars*), and others: a pale patch on a printed page. — *adj.* **fri'arly** like a friar. — *n.* **fri'ary** a convent of friars. — **fri'arbird** an Australian honeyeater with featherless head; **friar's balsam** a tincture of benzoin, storax, tolu and aloes; **friar's cap** wolf's-bane; **friar's cowl** wake-robin; **friar's lantern** the will-o'-the-wisp. [O.Fr. *frere* — L. *frāter*, a brother.]

fribble *frib'l*, *v.i.* to trifle. — *n.* a trifler. — *n.* **fribb'ler.** — *adjs.* **fribb'ling, fribb'lish** trifling. [Onomatopoeic; prob. influenced by **frivol.**]

fricadel. See **frikkadel.**

fricandeau *frik-ən-dō'*, or *frik'*, *n.* a thick slice of veal, etc., larded: — *pl.* **fricandeaux** (*-dōz*). [Fr.]

fricassee *frik-ə-sē'*, *n.* a dish of fowl, rabbit, etc. cut into pieces served in sauce. — *v.t.* to dress as a fricassee: — *pr.p.* **fricassee'ing;** *pa.t.* and *pa.p.* **fricasseed'.** [Fr. *fricassée*; origin unknown.]

fricative. See **friction.**

fricht. See **fright.**

friction *frik'shon*, *n.* rubbing: a force acting in the tangent plane of two bodies, when one slides or rolls upon another, in direction opposite to that of the movement (*statics*): disagreement, jarring. — *adj.* **fric'ative** produced by friction: pertaining to, being, a fricative. — *n.* a consonant produced by the breath being forced through a narrow opening. — *adjs.* **fric'tional; fric'-tionless.** — **friction welding** welding in which the necessary heat is produced by means of friction, e.g. by rotating one part and forcing the parts together. [L. *fricāre, frictum,* to rub.]

Friday *frī'di*, *n.* the sixth day of the week. — **Black Friday** Good Friday, from the black vestments of the clergy and altar in the Western Church: any Friday marked by a great calamity; **Good Friday** the Friday before Easter, kept in commemoration of the Crucifixion; **Holy Friday** Friday in an Ember-week — also **Golden Friday** sometimes put for Good Friday itself; **Man, Girl, Person, Friday** see **man, girl, person.** — **Friday (afternoon) car** (*coll.*) a new car with many faults in it, supposedly built on a Friday (afternoon) when workers' concentration is poor. [O.E. *Frīgedæg,* day of (the goddess) Frīg.]

fridge[1] *frij,* (*coll.*) *n.* short for **refrigerator.** — **fridge'-freez'er** a refrigerator and a deep-freeze constructed as a single unit of furniture.

fridge[2] *frij,* (*Sterne*) *v.t.* to rub, fray. [Prob. imit.]

fried. See **fry.**

friend *frend, n.* one loving or attached to another: an intimate acquaintance: a favourer, wellwisher, supporter: one of a society so named: a relative (*Scot.*): a lover (*obs.* or *euph.*). — *v.t.* to befriend. — *adj.* **friend'ed** (*arch.*) supplied with friends. — *n.* **friend'ing** (*Shak.*) friendliness. — *adj.* **friend'less** without friends: destitute. — *n.* **friend'lessness.** — *adv.* **friend'lily.** — *n.* **friend'liness.** — *adj.* **friend'ly** like a friend: having the disposition of a friend: favourable: amicable: of a football match, etc., played for amusement rather than competitively (also *n.*): pertaining to the Friends or Quakers: able to handle small variations in the input format and/or enabling the easy correction of input errors (*comput.*). — **-friendly** in composition, compatible with, helpful to, in sympathy with. — *n.* **friend'ship** attachment from mutual esteem: friendly assistance. — **friendly lead** (*arch.*) an entertainment for the benefit of one in need; **friendly society** a benefit society, an association for relief in sickness, old age, widowhood, by provident insurance. — **be friends with** to be on good terms with, well disposed towards; **have a friend at court** to have a friend in a position where his influence is likely to prove useful; **Religious Society of Friends** the proper designation of a sect of Christians better known as Quakers. [O.E. *frēond* (orig. a pr.p.; cf. *frēon,* to love); Ger. *Freund.*]

frier[1] *frī'ər,* (*Milt.*) *n.* a friar.

frier[2], fries. See **fry.**

Friesian. See **Frisian.**

frieze[1] *frēz, n.* a rough, heavy woollen cloth. — *adj.* **friezed** napped. [Fr. *frise.*]

frieze[2] *frēz,* (*archit.*) *n.* the part of the entablature between the architrave and cornice, often ornamented with figures: a decorated band along the top of a room wall. — *v.t.* to put a frieze on. [O.Fr. *frise*; It. *fregio*; perh. L. *Phrygium* (*opus*), Phrygian (work).]

frig[1] *frig,* (*vulg.*) *v.i.* and *v.t.* to masturbate: loosely, to have sexual intercourse with: (often with *about*) to potter about: (with *off*) to go away: — *pr.p.* **frigg'ing;** *pa.t.* and *pa.p.* **frigged.** — *n.* masturbation. — *n.* **frigg'ing** masturbation: pottering about. — *adj.* and *adv.* as an intensive, to a great extent, very: often used as a colourless descriptive. [Late M.E. *friggen* — L. *fricāre,* to rub.]

frig[2] *frij,* (*coll.*) *n.* short for **refrigerator.**

frigate *frig'it, n.* formerly a vessel in the class next to ships of the line: now denoting an escort vessel. — *n.* **frigatoon'** a small Venetian vessel with square stern and two masts. — **frigate bird** a large tropical sea-bird (*Fregata*) with very long wings. [O.Fr. *fregate* — It. *fregata*; ety. dub.]

frigger *frig'ər, n.* a glass ornament.

fright *frīt, n.* sudden fear: terror: a figure of grotesque or ridiculous appearance (*coll.*). — *vs.t.* **fright** (now *rare,* except as Scot. **fricht** *frihht*), **fright'en** to make afraid: to alarm: to drive by fear. — *adj.* **fright'ened.** — *n.pl.* **fright'eners** (*slang*; also in *sing.*) something intended to frighten, esp. for criminal purposes. — *adj.* **fright'-ening.** — *adv.* **fright'eningly.** — *adj.* **fright'ful** terrible: horrible: unpleasant (*coll.*): great (*coll.*). — *adv.* **fright'-fully** dreadfully: very (*coll.*). — *n.* **fright'fulness** the quality of being frightful: terrorism. — *adj.* **fright'some** frightful: feeling fright. — **put the frighteners on someone** (*slang*) to frighten someone into (not) doing something, esp. for criminal purposes; **take fright** to become afraid. [O.E. *fyrhto*; cf. Ger. *Furcht,* fear.]

frigid *frij'id, adj.* frozen or stiffened with cold: cold: chillingly stiff: without spirit or feeling: unanimated: leaving the imagination untouched: of a woman, sexually unresponsive. — *n.* **frigid'ity** coldness: coldness of affection: want of animation: sexual unresponsiveness. — *adv.* **frig'idly.** — *n.* **frig'idness.** — **frigid zones** the parts of the earth's surface within the polar circles. [L. *frīgidus* — *frīgēre,* to be cold — *frīgus,* cold.]

frigidarium *frij-i-dār'i-əm, frig-i-dār'i-ōōm,* (L.) *n.* the cooling room of Roman public baths, often with a swimming-bath.

frigorific *frig-ər-if'ik, adj.* causing cold: freezing. — *n.* **frigorif'ico** (Sp.) a slaughtering and meat-freezing establishment: — *pl.* **frigorif'icos.** [L. *frīgus, -oris,* cold, *facĕre,* to make.]

frigot *frig'ət,* (*Spens.*) *n.* Same as **frigate.**

frijol, frijole *frē'hhōl, frē-hhōl', n.* the kidney-bean, or any species of Phaseolus: — *pl.* **frijoles** (*-les*). [Sp. *frijol, frijol, fréjol.*]

frikkadel, fricadel *frik'ə-del,* (S. Afr.) *n.* a fried ball of minced meat. [Afrik. — Fr.; cf. **fricandeau.**]

frill *fril, v.i.* (*arch.*) to ruffle, as a hawk its feathers, when shivering. — *v.t.* to furnish with a frill. — *n.* a ruffle: a ruffled or crimped edging: superfluous ornament: (in *pl.*) affected airs. — *n.pl.* **frill'ies** light and pretty women's underwear. — *n.* **frill'ing.** — *adj.* **frill'y.** — **frilled lizard** a large Australian lizard (Chlamydosaurus) with an erectile frill about its neck. — **without frills** (in a manner, form, etc. which is) straightforward, clear, without posturing, with no superfluous additions, etc. [Origin unknown.]

Frimaire *frē-mār', n.* the third month of the French revolutionary calendar, about Nov. 21–Dec. 20. [Fr. *frimas,* hoar-frost.]

fringe *frinj, n.* a border of loose threads: hair falling over the brow: a border: anything bordering on or additional to an activity. — *v.t.* to adorn with a fringe: to border. — *adj.* bordering, or just outside, the recognised or orthodox form, group, etc. as in *fringe medicine, fringe banks*: less important or popular, as in *fringe sports.* — *adjs.* **fringed; fringe'less; fring'y** ornamented with fringes. — **fringe benefit** something in addition to wages or salary that forms part of the regular remuneration from one's employment; **fringe'-dweller** (*Austr.*) one, esp. an Aborigine, who lives, usu. in poverty and squalor, on the edge of a town or community; **fringe tree** a large American shrub (*Chio-*

nanthus virginica) of the olive family, whose very numerous snow-white flowers have long narrow corolla-segments. — **lunatic fringe** any, usu. small, group of fanatics or extremists within a political party, pressure group, etc. [O.Fr. *frenge* — L. *fimbriae*, threads, akin to *fibra*, a fibre.]

fringillaceous *frin-ji-lā'shəs, adj.* pertaining to the finches or **Fringill'idae.** — *adjs.* **fringill'id, fringill'iform, fringill'ine.** [L. *fringilla*, a finch.]

fripon *frē-pɔ̃,* (Fr.) *n.* knave, scamp. — *n.* **friponnerie** (*frē-pon-ə-rē*) knavery.

frippery *frip'ər-i, n.* cast-off clothes (*obs.*): an old-clothes shop, or the old-clothes trade (*obs.*): tawdry finery: foppish triviality: useless trifles. — *adj.* useless: trifling. — *ns.* **fripp'er, fripp'erer** (*arch.*) an old-clothes dealer. [O.Fr. *freperie* — *frepe*, a rag.]

fris *frish,* **friska** *frish'kö, ns.* the quick movement of a csárdás. [Hung.]

Frisbee® *friz'bi, n.* a plastic saucer-shaped disc which can be made to skim through the air, used in various catching-games, etc.

frisette *frē-zet,* (Fr.) *n.* a fringe of curls on the forehead. — *ns.* **friseur** (*frē-zœr*) a hairdresser; **frisure** (*frē-zür*) a mode of curling.

Frisian *friz'i-ən, n.* a native of *Friesland:* the Low German language of Friesland. — *adj.* of Friesland, its people, or their language. — *adj.* **Friesian** (*frēz'*) Frisian, esp. of a heavy breed of dairy-cattle. — *n.* a Frisian: a Friesian bull or cow. — *adjs.* **Fries'ic, Fries'ish.**

frisk *frisk, v.i.* to gambol: to leap playfully. — *v.t.* to search (a person or pockets) (*slang*): to search for radioactive radiation by contamination meter. — *n.* a frolicsome movement. — *n.* **frisk'er.** — *adj.* **frisk'ful** brisk, lively. — *adv.* **frisk'ily.** — *n.* **frisk'iness.** — and *adj.* **frisk'ing.** — *adv.* **frisk'ingly.** — *adj.* **frisk'y** lively: jumping with gaiety: frolicsome. [O.Fr. *frisque.*]

friska. See **fris.**

frisket *frisk'it,* (*print.*) *n.* the light frame between the tympan and the forme, to hold in place the sheet to be printed. [Fr. *frisquette.*]

frisson *frē-sɔ̃, n.* a shiver: a shudder: a thrill. [Fr.]

frist *frist,* (*obs.*) *n.* delay, respite. — *v.t.* to postpone: to grant time, as for payment. [O.E. *first,* time, respite.]

frisure. See **frisette.**

frit[1] *frit, n.* the mixed materials for making glass, pottery glazes, etc. — *v.t.* to fuse partially: — *pr.p.* **fritt'ing;** *pa.t.* and *pa.p.* **fritt'ed.** — **frit porcelain** an artificial soft-paste English porcelain (from its vitreous nature). [Fr. *fritte* — It. *fritta* — L. *frīgĕre, frīctum,* to roast.]

frit[2] *frit, n.* a small fly destructive to wheat and other cereal crops. — Also **frit'fly.** [Ety. unknown.]

frith[1]. See **firth[1].**

frith[2] *frith,* (*obs.* or *hist.*) *n.* peace: sanctuary. — **frith'borh** (*-borhh*) a surety for keeping the peace, frankpledge; **frith'gild** a union of neighbours pledged to one another for the preservation of peace; **frith'soken** sanctuary, asylum (O.E. *frithsōcn*); **frith'stool** a chair of sanctuary, placed near the altar in a church — as at Hexham and Beverley (O.E. *frithstōl*). [O.E. *frith,* peace; Ger. *Friede.*]

frith[3], firth *frith, fúrth, ns.* wooded country: brushwood: underwood. [O.E. (*ge)fyrhthe.*]

fritillary *frit'il-ər-i,* or *-il', n.* a member of the genus (*Fritillaria*) of the lily family, the best-known species with chequered purple flowers: a name for several butterflies of similar pattern. [L. *fritillus,* a dice-box.]

fritter[1] *frit'ər, n.* a piece of fruit, etc., fried in batter. [O.Fr. *friture* — L. *frīgĕre, frīctum,* to fry.]

fritter[2] *frit'ər, n.* a fragment. — *v.t.* to break into fragments: to squander piecemeal. — *n.* **fritt'erer** one who wastes time. [Perh. O.Fr. *freture* — L. *frāctūra* — *frangĕre, frāctum,* to break.]

fritto misto *frē'tō mēs'tō,* (It.) a mixed dish of fried food.

friture *frē-tür,* (Fr.) *n.* a dish of fried food: a fritter.

fritz *frits:* **on the fritz** (*U.S. coll.*) out of order. [Origin unknown.]

frivolous *friv'ə-ləs, adj.* trifling: silly. — *v.t.* and *v.i.* **friv'ol** (back-formation) to trifle. — *n.* **frivolity** (*-ol'*) a trifling habit or nature: levity. — *adv.* **friv'olously.** — *n.* **friv'olousness.** [L. *frīvolus.*]

frize. Obs. form of **freeze, frieze.**

frizz, friz *friz, v.t.* to curl tightly. — *n.* a curl: frizzed hair. — *adjs.* **frizzed** having the hair crisped into frizzes; **frizz'y.** [O.Fr. *friser,* to curl; perh. conn. with **frieze[1].**]

frizzante *frē-dzan'tā,* (It.) *adj.* of wine, sparkling.

frizzle[1] *friz'l, v.t.* to form in small short curls. — *v.i.* to go into curls. — *n.* a curl: frizzled hair. — *adj.* **frizz'ly.** [Related to **frizz** and **frieze[1].**]

frizzle[2] *friz'l, v.t.* and *v.i.* to fry: to scorch. [Perhaps onomatopoeic adaptation of **fry,** from sputtering noise.]

fro *frō, prep.* (*obs.* except in Scots form **frae** *frā*) from. — *adv.* away, only used in **to and fro** (see **to**). [O.N. *frā.*]

frock *frok, n.* a monk's wide-sleeved garment: a frock-coat: a smock-frock: a sailor's jersey: a woman's or child's dress: an undress regimental coat: a wearer of a frock (*obs.*). — *v.t.* to furnish with a frock: to invest with priestly office. — *adj.* **frocked** clothed in a frock. — *n.* **frock'ing** cloth suitable for frocks, coarse jean. — *adj.* **frock'less.** — **frock'-coat** a double-breasted full-skirted coat for men. [O.Fr. *froc,* a monk's frock — L.L. *frocus* — L. *floccus,* a flock of wool; or from L.L. *hrocus* — O.H.G. *hroch* (Ger. *Rock*), a coat.]

Froebelian *frœ-bēl'i-ən, adj.* pertaining to Friedrich Froebel, German educationist (1782–1852), or to his system (**Froebel system**) of kindergarten schools. — *n.* **Froe'belism.**

frog[1] *frog, n.* a tailless web-footed amphibian, esp. one of the genus Rana, more agile than a toad: a swelling in the throat: (with *cap.*) a contemptuous name for a Frenchman: on a railway, a structure in the rails allowing passage across or to another track: a depression made in the face(s) of a brick: the block by which the hair is attached to the heel of a violin, etc. bow. — *n.* **frogg'ery** frogs collectively: a place where frogs abound or are kept. — *adj.* **frogg'y** froglike: having or abounding in frogs. — *n.* (with *cap.*) a contemptuous name for a Frenchman. — *ns.* **frog'let, frog'ling** a little frog. — **frog'bit** a small aquatic plant (*Hydrocharis morsus-ranae*), allied to the water-soldier, but with floating leaves; **frog'-eater** one who eats frogs: a Frenchman; **frog'-fish** a name for various fishes, esp. the angler; **frog'-hopper** a froth-fly; **frog'man** an underwater swimmer fitted with webbed froglike feet. — *v.t.* **frog'-march** (sometimes **frog's'-march**) to carry a refractory or drunken prisoner, etc. face downwards between four men, each holding a limb: now usually, to seize from behind and force forwards while holding firmly by the arms or clothing: sometimes, to propel backwards between two people, each holding an arm. — *n.* the act or process of frog-marching. — **frog'mouth** any bird of the mopoke family or subfamily (Australian and S. Asian) akin to or included in the goatsuckers; **frog's'-mouth** antirrhinum, snapdragon; **frog'-spit** cuckoo-spit. — **a frog in the, one's, throat** hoarseness. [O.E. *frogga;* also *frox;* cog. with O.N. *froskr;* Ger. *Frosch.*]

frog[2] *frog, n.* a V-shaped band of horn on the underside of a horse's hoof. [Perh. same as **frog[1].** Gr. *batrachos* means frog in both senses — also influenced by It. *forchetta,* dim. of fork.]

frog[3] *frog, n.* an ornamental fastening or tasselled or braided button: an attachment to a belt for carrying a weapon. — *adj.* **frogged** having ornamental stripes or workings of braid or lace, mostly on the breast of a coat. — *n.* **frogg'ing.** [Perh. Port. *froco* — L. *floccus,* a flock, lock.]

froise *froiz,* **fraise** *frāz, ns.* a thick pancake, often with slices of bacon. [Origin unknown.]

frolic *frol'ik, adj.* (*arch.*) merry: pranky. — *n.* gaiety: a prank: a gambol: a merrymaking. — *v.i.* to play wild pranks or merry tricks: to gambol: — *pr.p.* **frol'icking.**

pa.t. and *pa.p.* **frol′icked.** — *adj.* **frol′icsome** gay: sportive. — *adv.* **frol′icsomely.** — *n.* **frol′icsomeness.** [Du. *vrolijk*, merry; cf. Ger. *fröhlich*, joyful, gay.]

from *from, frəm, prep.* out of: away, to or at a greater distance relatively to: springing out of: beginning at: apart relatively to: by reason of.   [O.E. *fram, from;* akin to Goth. *fram,* O.N. *frā.*]

fromenty. See **frumenty.**

frond *frond, n.* a leaf, esp. of a palm or fern: a leaflike thallus, or a leaflike organ of obscure morphological nature. — *n.* **frond′age** fronds collectively. — *adjs.* **frond′ed** having fronds; **frond′ent** leafy. — *n.* **frondesc′ence** the development of leaves. — *adjs.* **frondesc′ent** leaflike: leafy: springing into leaf; **frondif′erous** bearing or producing fronds; **frond′ose** leaflike: leafy.   [L. *frōns, frondis,* a leaf.]

Fronde *frönd, frɔ̃d, n.* the opposition to Mazarin and the court in France during Louis XIV′s minority. — *n.* **frondeur** (*frön-dûr′, frɔ̃-dœr*) a member of the Fronde: an irreconcilable, a dissident.   [Fr., sling — L. *funda,* sling.]

front *frunt, n.* the forehead (*poet.*): the face, appearance: the forepart of anything: the side presented to view: the face of a building, esp. the principal face: the part facing the sea or other water: a seaside promenade: the foremost line: the scene of hostilities: the direction in which troops are facing when lined up (*mil.*): a combined face presented against opponents: a group of people, organisations or parties having the same or broadly similar (esp. political or revolutionary) outlook and aims, who act together against opponents, as in *popular front* (q.v.): a set of false curls for the forehead: the breast of a man′s shirt, a dickey: the middle part of the tongue: the auditorium of a theatre: the bounding surface between two masses of air of different density and temperature (*meteor.*): the apparent or nominal leader behind whom the really powerful man works anonymously (also **front man**): something acting as a cover or disguise for secret or disreputable activities: boldness: impudence. — *adj.* of, relating to, in, the front: articulated with the front of the tongue. — *v.t.* to stand in front of or opposite: to face towards: to meet, or to oppose, face to face: to add a front to: to serve as a front to: to change into or towards a front sound: to act as the front man of: to act as the compère or frontman of: to stand, perform, etc. in front of or at the front of, as e.g. the singer with a band. — *v.i.* to be foremost (*Shak.*): to face: to act as a front for someone else or as a cover for something secret or illicit. — *ns.* **front′age** the front part of a building: extent of front: ground in front; **front′ager** (*law*) a person who owns or occupies property along a road, river or shore. — *adj.* **front′al** (*frunt′l,* also *front′l*) of or belonging to the front, or the forehead: pertaining to a front (*meteor.*). — *n.* the façade of a building: something worn on the forehead or face: a pediment over a door or window (*obs.*): a hanging of silk, satin, etc., embroidered for an altar — now usually covering only the top, the *superfrontal* — formerly covering the whole of the front, corresponding to the *antependium.* — *adjs.* **front′ed** formed with a front: changed into or towards a front sound; **front′less** lacking a front: void of shame or modesty (*arch.*). — *adv.* **front′lessly.** — *ns.* **front′let** a band worn on the forehead; **frontogen′esis** (*meteor.*; Gr. *genesis,* generation) the formation or intensification of a front; **frontol′ysis** (*-is-is; meteor.*; Gr. *lysis,* dissolution) the weakening or disappearance of a front. — *advs.* **front′-ward(s)** towards the front; **front′ways, -wise** with face or front forward. — *adj.* **front′-bench** sitting on a front bench, as a minister, or an opposition member of the standing. — *ns.* **front′-bench′er; front door; front line** the battle positions closest to the enemy: the most active, exposed or dangerous position or rôle in any activity or situation, esp. a conflict (*fig.*). — *adj.* **front′-line** of or relating to the front line: of or relating to a state bordering on another state in which there is

an armed conflict, and often involved in that conflict. — **front′man** the person who appears on television as presenter of a programme, esp. a documentary programme; **front man** see **front** *n.* above. — *adjs.* **front= of-house** see **front of the house** below; **front′-page** suitable for the front page of a newspaper: important. — *v.t.* to print a story on the front page of a newspaper. — *adj.* **front′-rank** of foremost importance. — **front′= ranker; front′-runner** in a race, one who runs best while leading the field or one who sets the pace for the rest of the runners: one who or that which is most popular, most likely to succeed, etc., esp. in some kind of competition. — **come to the front** to become noticeable: to attain an important position; **front-end computer, processor** a subsidiary computer which receives and processes data before passing it to a more powerful computer for further processing; **front-end loaded; front-end loading** the taking of a large part of the total costs and commission of an investment or insurance policy out of the early payments or profits made: any similar weighting of borrowing, deduction, etc. towards the early stages of a financial transaction or accounting period; **front-end system** that part of a computerised printing system which receives the matter to be printed and provides the input to the typesetter; **front of the house** in a theatre, the collective activities such as box-office and programme selling carried on in direct contact with the public (*adj.* **front′-of-house′**); **front-wheel drive** a system in which the driving power is transmitted to the front wheels of a vehicle as opp. to the rear wheels; **in front (of)** before.   [L. *frōns, frontis,* the forehead.]

frontier *frunt′* or *front′ēr, -yər,* or *-ēr′, n.* the border of a country: the border of settled country, esp. in U.S. the advancing limit of the West pioneered in the 19th cent.: an outwork (*Shak.*): (in *pl.*) the extreme limit of knowledge and attainment in a particular discipline or line of inquiry. — *adj.* belonging to a frontier: bordering. — *v.t.* (*Spens.*) to border. — **front′iersman** (or *-tērz′*) a dweller on a frontier.   [O.Fr. *frontier* — L. *frōns, frontis.*]

frontispiece *frunt′is-pēs* (or *front′*), *n.* the principal face of a building (*archit.*): a figure or engraving at the front of a book. — *v.t.* to put as a frontispiece: to furnish with one.   [Fr. *frontispice* — L.L. *frontispicium* — *frōns, frontis,* forehead, and *specēre, spicēre,* to see; not connected with **piece.**]

fronton *frun′tən,* (*archit.*) *n.* a pediment. — Also **frontoon** (*-tōōn′*).   [Fr., — It. *frontone.*]

frore (*obs., dial.* or *poet.*) *frōr, frör,* also (*obs.* or *dial.*) **froren, frorne, frorn** *frōr′ən, frörn,* adjs. frozen, frosty. — *adj.* **frō′ry** (*Spens.*) frozen.   [O.E. *froren,* pa.p. of *frēosan,* to freeze.]

frost *frost, n.* a state of freezing: temperature at or below the freezing-point of water: frozen dew, or *hoar-frost:* a disappointment, a failure (*slang*): coldness of manner or relations. — *v.t.* to affect with frost: to cover with hoar-frost: to make like hoar-frost: to sharpen (the points of a horse′s shoe) that it may not slip on ice. — *v.i.* to assume a frost-like appearance. — *adj.* **frost′ed** covered by frost: having a frost-like appearance (as a cake or Christmas card by sprinkling, glass by roughening): injured by frost. — *adv.* **frost′ily.** — *ns.* **frost′iness; frost′ing** coating with hoar-frost: material or treatment to give appearance of hoar-frost: icing (esp. *U.S.*). — *adjs.* **frost′less** free from frost; **frost′y** producing, attended with, covered with, frost: chill: frost-like. — **frost′bite** injury, sometimes ending in mortification, in a part of the body by exposure to cold. — *v.t.* to affect with frost. — *adjs.* **frost′bitten** bitten or affected by frost (also *fig.*); **frost′bound** bound or confined by frost. — **frost′-nail** a projecting nail in a horse-shoe serving as an ice-calk. — *v.t.* to furnish with frost-nails. — **frost′-smoke** a vapour frozen in the atmosphere, and having a smoke-like appearance; **frost′work** tracery wrought by frost, as on windows: work resembling frost tracery, etc.   [O.E. *frost, forst*

— *frēosan*; cf. Ger. *Frost*.]

froth *froth, n.* foam: chatter (*fig.*): something frivolous or trivial. — *v.t.* to cause froth on. — *v.i.* to throw up froth. — *n.* **froth'ery** mere froth. — *adv.* **froth'ily**. — *n.* **froth'iness**. — *adjs.* **froth'less; froth'y** full of or like froth or foam: empty: unsubstantial. — **froth'-blower** (*slang*) a beer-drinker; **froth flotation** see **flotation** at **flote; froth'-fly, froth'-hopper**, any insect of the family Cercopidae, whose larvae live surrounded by froth (cuckoo-spit) on plants. — *adj.* **froth-fo'my** (*Spens.*) foaming. [O.N. *frotha;* Dan. *fraade*.]

frottage *fro-täzh', n.* rubbing: the use of rubbing(s) to obtain texture effect(s) in a work of art: a work of art made by this means: a type of sexual activity in which sexual pleasure, and often orgasm, is obtained by rubbing against someone or something (*psych.*). — *n.* **frotteur** (*fro-tœr'; psych.*) one who practises frottage. [Fr.]

frou-frou *frōō'frōō, n.* the rustling of silk: elaborate trimmings, as frills, etc.: fussy decoration. [Fr.]

froughy. Same as **frowy**.

frounce[1] *frowns, (obs.) v.t.* to plait: to curl: to wrinkle up. — *v.i.* to wrinkle: to frown. — *n.* a wrinkle, a plait or curl: affected ornament. [O.Fr. *froncier;* see **flounce**[2].]

frounce[2] *frowns, (obs.) n.* a disease of the mouth in hawks. [Origin unknown.]

frow *frow, n.* a Dutchwoman. [Du. *vrouw*.]

froward *frō'ərd, (arch.) adj.* turned away: self-willed: perverse: unreasonable (opp. to *toward*). — *adv.* (*Spens.*) in an averse direction. — *prep.* (also **fro'wards**) in a direction away from. — *adv.* **fro'wardly**. — *n.* **fro'wardness**. [**fro**, and suffix. *-ward*.]

frown *frown, v.i.* to wrinkle the brow as in anger: to look angry, gloomy, threatening: to show disapprobation. — *v.t.* to express, send, or force by a frown. — *n.* a wrinkling or contraction of the brow in displeasure, etc.: a stern look. — *adj.* **frown'ing** gloomy: disapproving: threatening. — *adv.* **frown'ingly**. — **frown on, upon** to disapprove of. [From O.Fr. *froignier* (Fr. *refrogner*), to knit the brow; origin unknown.]

frowst *frowst, v.i.* to luxuriate in hot stuffiness and stupefaction. — *n.* hot stuffy fustiness: a spell of frowsting. — *ns.* **frowst'er; frowst'iness**. — *adj.* **frowst'y** fusty: close-smelling: ill-smelling. [Origin unknown.]

frowy, froughy (*Spens.* **frowie**) *frō'i, frow'i, adj.* musty, rancid (*Spens.*): of timber, soft and brittle (*dial.*). [Prob. O.E. *thrōh*, rancidity.]

frowzy, frowsy *frow'zi, (dial.) adj.* fusty: stuffy: offensive: unkempt. [Origin unknown.]

frozen *frōz'n, pa.p.* of **freeze**. — *adj.* preserved by keeping at a low temperature: very cold: stiff and unfriendly. — **frozen shoulder** a shoulder joint which has become stiff owing to enforced immobilisation, or to injury to the joint or its surrounding tissue.

fructed *fruk'tid, adj.* (*her.*) bearing fruit. — *adj.* **fructif'erous** bearing fruit. — *n.* **fructifica'tion** fruit-production: a structure that contains spores or seeds (*bot.*). — *v.t.* **fruc'tify** to make fruitful: to fertilise. — *v.i.* to bear fruit. — *adj.* **fructiv'orous** (L. *vorāre*, to devour) frugivorous. — *ns.* **fruc'tose** fruit sugar or laevulose; **fruc'tuary** one enjoying the fruits of anything. — *v.i.* **fruc'tuate** to come to fruit: to fructify. — *n.* **fructuā'tion** coming to fruit, bearing of fruit. — *adj.* **fruc'tuous** fruitful. [L. *frūctus*, fruit.]

Fructidor *frük-tē-dör, n.* the twelfth month in the French revolutionary calendar, about Aug. 18–Sept. 16. [Fr., — L. *frūctus*, fruit, Gr. *dōron*, a gift.]

frugal *frōō'gl, adj.* economical in the use of means: sparing: spare: thrifty. — *ns.* **fru'galist** one who is frugal; **frugality** (*-gal'*) economy: thrift. — *adv.* **fru'gally**. [L. *frūgālis — frūx, frūgis*, fruit.]

frugiferous *frōō-jif'ə-rəs, adj.* (L. *ferre*, to bear) fruit-bearing. — *adj.* **frugiv'orous** (L. *vorāre*, to eat) feeding on fruits or seeds. [L. *frūx, frūgis*, fruit.]

fruit (*obs.* **fruict**) *frōōt, n.* the produce of the earth, which supplies the wants of men and animals: an edible part

of a plant, generally sweet, acid, and juicy, esp. a part that contains the seed, but sometimes extended to include other parts (e.g. the leaf-stalk in rhubarb): in bot., a fructification, esp. the structure that develops from the ovary and its contents after fertilisation, sometimes including also structures formed from other parts of the flower or axis: the offspring of animals: (often in *pl.*) product, effect, advantage: a male homosexual (*slang*, esp. *U.S.*). — *v.i.* to produce fruit. — *ns.* **fruit'age** fruit collectively: fruits; **fruitä'rian** one who lives on fruit. — Also *adj.* — *adj.* **fruit'ed** having produced fruit. — *ns.* **fruit'er** a fruiterer (now *dial.*): a tree, etc. as a producer of fruit, as in *good fruiter*: a fruit-grower; **fruit'erer** one who deals in fruit: — *fem.* **fruit'eress; fruit'ery** a place for storing fruit: fruitage. — *adj.* **fruit'ful** productive. — *adv.* **fruit'fully**. — *ns.* **fruit'fulness; fruit'ing** the process of bearing, or coming into, fruit. — *adj.* **fruit'less** barren: without profit: useless: in vain. — *n.* **fruit'let** a small fruit: one of the small fruit-like parts that forms an aggregate or multiple fruit. — *adv.* **fruit'lessly**. — *n.* **fruit'lessness**. — *adj.* **fruit'y** like, or tasting like, fruit: rich: (of a voice) mellow, resonant: salacious, saucy, smutty: crazy (*U.S. slang*): male homosexual (*slang*, esp. *U.S.*). — **fruit'-bat** any bat of the suborder Megacheiroptera, large fruit-eating bats of the Old World; **fruit'-bud** a bud that produces fruit; **fruit'-cake** a cake containing raisins, etc.: a slightly mad person (*coll.*); **fruit cocktail** a fruit salad, esp. one of small, usu. diced, pieces of fruit; **fruit'-fly** an insect of genus Drosophila; **fruit'-knife** a knife with a blade of silver, etc., for cutting fruit; **fruit'-machine** a coin-operated gaming machine in which chance must bring pictures of different fruits, etc. together in a certain combination to give a win; **fruit salad** a mixture of pieces of fruit, fresh or preserved; **fruit'-tree** a tree yielding edible fruit; **fruit'wood** the wood of a fruit-tree (also *adj.*). — **bush fruits** small fruits growing on woody bushes; **first-fruits** see **first, annat; small, soft fruit(s)** strawberries, currants, etc. [O.Fr. *fruit, fruict* — L. *frūctus — fruī, frūctus*, to enjoy.]

fruition *frōō-ish'ən, n.* enjoyment: maturation, fulfilment, completion: use or possession, esp. accompanied with pleasure: now often used for *fruiting* (q.v. under **fruit**). — *adj.* **fru'itive**. [O.Fr. *fruition* — L. *fruī*, to enjoy.]

frumentation *frōō-mən-tā'shən, n.* a largess of grain bestowed on the starving or turbulent people in ancient Rome. — *adjs.* **frumentā'ceous** made of or resembling wheat or other grain; **frumentā'rious** pertaining to corn. [L. *frūmentātiō, -ōnis — frūmentārī*, to provide with corn — *frūmentum*, corn.]

frumenty *frōō'mən-ti, n.* hulled wheat boiled in milk, sometimes flavoured with spices, eggs, rum, etc. — Also **frō'menty, fur'menty, fur'mety, fur'mity** (*fûr'*). [O.Fr. *frumentee — frument* — L. *frūmentum*.]

frump *frump, n.* a dowdy woman: a flout or snub (*obs.*). — *v.t.* (*obs.*) to snub. — *adjs.* **frump'ish, frump'y** ill-dressed, dowdy.

frumple *frum'pl, (dial.) v.t.* to wrinkle.

frush[1] *frush, v.t.* (*Shak.*) to break or bruise. — *adj.* (*Scot.*) brittle: crumbly. — *n.* (*Scot.*) a crash: splinters. [O.Fr. *froissier*, to bruise — L. *frustum*, fragment.]

frush[2] *frush, n.* (*dial.*) the frog of a horse's foot: a disease in that part of a horse's foot. [Origin uncertain; cf. O.E. *forsc*, frog (animal); see **frog**[2].]

frust *frust, n.* (*Sterne*) a fragment. — *ns.* **frust'ule** the siliceous two-valved shell of a diatom, with its contents; **frust'um** a slice of a solid body: the part of a cone or pyramid between the base and a parallel plane, or between two planes: — *pl.* **frust'ums** or **frust'a**. [L. *frustum*, a bit.]

frustrate *frus-trāt', frus'trāt, v.t.* to make vain or of no effect: to bring to naught: to balk: to thwart. — *adj.* (*frus'*) vain, ineffectual: balked. — *adj.* **frustrated** thwarted: having a sense of discouragement and dissatisfaction. — *n.* **frustrā'tion**. — **frustrated export** an article orig. intended for export which for some reason has to be offered for sale on the home market. [L. *frustrāri*.]

frutex *frōō'teks*, *n.* a shrub: — *pl.* **fru'tices** (*-ti-sēz*). — *adj.* **fru'ticose** shrubby. [L. *frutex, -icis*, shrub.]

frutify *frōō'ti-fī*, (*Shak.*) *v.t.* Launcelot Gobbo's blunder for **notify** or **specify**.

fry¹ *frī*, *v.t.* to cook in oil or fat in a pan: to burn or scorch (often *fig.*): to torture with heat (*obs.*). — *v.i.* to undergo frying: to foam (*Spens.*): — *pr.p.* **fry'ing**; *pa.t.* and *pa.p.* **fried**; *3rd pers. pres. indic.* **fries**. — *n.* a dish of anything fried, esp. the offal of a pig, lamb, etc. — *n.* **fri'er** (**fry'er**) one who fries (esp. fish): a vessel for frying: a fish suitable for frying. — *n.* and *adj.* **fry'ing**. — **fried'cake** (*U.S.*) a cake fried in deep fat: a doughnut; **fry'ing-pan** a flat pan for frying with; **fry'-up** (*coll.*) mixed fried foods, or the frying of these. — **fry in one's fat** suffer the consequences of one's behaviour; **out of the frying-pan into the fire** out of one evil into a greater. [Fr. *frire* — L. *frīgĕre*; cf. Gr. *phrygein*.]

fry² *frī*, *n.* young, collectively: a swarm of young, esp. of fishes just spawned: young salmon in their second year: a number of small things. — **small fry** small things collectively, persons or things of little importance. [O.N. *friō*, seed; Dan. and Sw. *fro*.]

fub *fub*, *v.t.* (*arch.*) to put off: to fob. — *n.* **fubb'ery** (*obs.*) a deception. — **fub off** (*Shak.*) to put off or evade by a trick or a lie. [See **fob**.]

fubby *fub'i*, **fubsy** *fub'zi*, (*dial.*) *adjs.* chubby: squat. [Ety. dub.]

fuchsia *fū'shə*, *n.* any plant of a S. American genus (**Fuchsia**) of the evening primrose family, with long pendulous flowers: a reddish-purple colour. — Also *adj.* — *n.* **fuchsine** (*fōōks'ēn*) the dyestuff magenta, a green solid, purplish-red in solution (from its colour, similar to that of the flower). [Named after Leonard *Fuchs*, a German botanist, 1501–66.]

fuchsite *fōōks'īt*, *n.* a brilliant green chromium mica. [J. N. von *Fuchs* (1774–1856), German mineralogist.]

fuci. See **fucus**.

fuck *fuk* (old word, long taboo: all words, meanings, still *vulg.*) *v.i.* to have sexual intercourse: (with *about* or *around*) to play around, act foolishly: (with *off*) to go away. — *v.t.* to have sexual intercourse with (usu. of a male): (with *about* or *around*) to deal inconsiderately with: (with *up*) to botch, damage or break (*n.* **fuck'-up**). — *n.* an act of sexual intercourse: a person, esp. female, considered as a (good, poor, etc.) partner in sexual intercourse: something of very little value: used in various phrases expressing displeasure, emphasis, etc.: a term of abuse, a fucker. — *interj.* an expression of displeasure, etc. (often with an object, as in *fuck him!*). — *p. adj.* **fucked** exhausted. — *ns.* **fuck'er** one who fucks: a term of abuse: a fellow; a person; **fuck'ing** sexual intercourse. — *adj.* expressing scorn or disapprobation: often used as a meaningless qualification. — *adv.* very, to a great extent. — **(sweet) fuck all** nothing at all. [Ety. dub.; perh. Ger. *ficken*, to strike, to copulate with.]

fucus *fū'kəs*, *n.* paint for the face, cosmetic (*obs.*): (with *cap.*) the bladder-wrack genus of seaweeds, the type genus of the family *Fucaceae*: any plant of this genus: — *pl.* **fū'ci** (*-sī*), **fū'cuses**. — *adj.* **fū'coid** like, pertaining to, or containing bladder-wrack, or seaweed, or seaweed-like markings. — *n.* a marking like a fossil seaweed: a seaweed of the genus Fucus. — *adjs.* **fūcoid'al**; **fū'cused** painted. [L. *fūcus*, orchil, rouge; Gr. *phȳkos*.]

fud *fud*, (*Scot.*) *n.* a rabbit's or hare's tail: the buttocks.

fuddle *fud'l*, *v.t.* to stupefy, as with drink: to confuse. — *v.i.* to drink to excess or habitually: — *pr.p.* **fudd'ling**; *pa.t.* and *pa.p.* **fudd'led**. — *n.* intoxicating drink (*obs.*): intoxication: a drinking bout: confusion. — *n.* **fudd'ler** a drunkard. — *n.* and *adj.* **fudd'ling** tippling. — **fudd'le-cap** (*obs.*) a hard drinker. [Origin obscure.]

fuddy-duddy *fud'i-dud-i*, *n.* an old fogy, stick-in-the-mud: a carper. — *adj.* old-fogyish: old-fashioned: stuffy: prim: censorious. [Origin unknown.]

fudge¹ *fuj*, *n.* stuff: nonsense: humbug: a soft sweetmeat. — *interj.* bosh. [Origin obscure.]

fudge² *fuj*, *n.* an inserted patch in a newspaper, or space reserved for it. — *v.i.* to fadge (*arch.*): to cheat: to fail: to dodge. — *v.t.* to patch up: to fake: to distort: to dodge: to obscure, cover up. [Variant of **fadge**.]

Fuehrer. Same as **Führer**.

fuel *fū'əl*, *n.* material for a fire: something that maintains or intensifies emotion, etc. (*fig.*): food, as maintaining bodily processes: fissile material for a nuclear reactor. — *v.t.* to furnish with fuel: to incite, encourage or stimulate (esp. anger, hate, violence, etc.). — *v.i.* to take or get fuel: — *pr.p.* **fu'elling**; *pa.t.* and *pa.p.* **fu'elled**. — *n.* **fu'eller**. — **fu'el-cell'** a cell generating electricity for an external circuit as part of a chemical reaction between an electrolyte and a combustible gas or vapour supplied from outside the cell (the reaction taking place at more or less ordinary temperatures). — *adj.* **fu'el-injec'ted** having **fu'el-injec'tion**, a system of operating an internal-combustion engine in which vaporised liquid fuel is introduced under pressure directly into the combustion chamber, so dispensing with a carburettor. — **add fuel to the fire(s)** to make an angry person angrier, a heated discussion more heated, etc. [O.Fr. *fowaille* — L.L. *focāle* — L. *focus*, a fireplace.]

fuero *fwā'rō*, *n.* a code or body of law or privileges, esp. in the Basque provinces, a constitution: — *pl.* **fue'ros**. [Sp., — L. *forum*.]

fuff *fuf*, (*Scot.*) *n.* a puff: the spitting of a cat: a burst of anger. — *v.t.* and *v.i.* to puff: to spit as a cat. — *adj.* **fuff'y** light and soft. [Imit.]

fug *fug*, *n.* a very hot close, often smoky, state of atmosphere: one who fugs: dusty fluff. — *v.i.* to sit or revel in a fug. — *v.t.* to cause a fug in. — *adj.* **fugg'y**. [Origin unknown.]

fugacious *fū-gā'shəs*, *adj.* apt to flee away: fleeting: readily shed. — *ns.* **fugā'ciousness**, **fugacity** (*-gas'*). [L. *fugāx, -ācis* — *fugĕre*, to flee.]

fugal, fugato, fughetta. See **fugue**.

fugitive *fū'ji-tiv*, *adj.* apt to flee away: fleeing: fleeting: evanescent: occasional, written for some passing occasion. — *n.* one who flees or has fled: one hard to be caught: an exile. — *ns.* **fū'gie** (*Scot.*) a cock that will not fight: a runaway; **fūgitā'tion** (*Scots law*) absconding from justice: sentence of outlawry. — *adv.* **fū'gitively**. — *n.* **fū'gitiveness**. — **fū'gie-warr'ant** (*Scot.*) a warrant to apprehend a debtor supposed to be about to abscond, prob. from the phrase *in meditatione fugae*. [L. *fugitīvus* — *fugĕre*, to flee.]

fugleman *fū'gl-mən*, *n.* a soldier who stands before a company at drill as an example: a ringleader, mouthpiece of others. — *v.i.* **fū'gle** (*Carlyle*) to act like a fugleman. [Ger. *Flügelmann*, the leader of a file — *Flügel*, a wing, *Mann*, man.]

fugue *fūg*, *n.* in mus. a form of composition in which the subject is given out by one part and immediately taken up by a second (in *answer*), during which the first part supplies an accompaniment or counter-subject, and so on: a form of amnesia which is a flight from reality. — *adj.* **fū'gal**. — *adv.* **fū'gally**. — *adj.* and *adv.* **fugato** (*fū-gä'tō*, It. *fōō-gä'tō*) in the manner of a fugue without being strictly a fugue. — Also *n.*: — *pl.* **fuga'tos**. — *ns.* **fughetta** (*fū-get'ə*, It. *fōō-get'ta*) a short fugue; **fuguist** (*fūg'ist*) one who writes or plays fugues. [Fr., — It. *fuga* — L. *fuga*, flight.]

Führer *fū'rər*, Ger. *fü'rər*, *n.* the title taken by Hitler as dictator of Nazi Germany. [Ger., leader, guide.]

fulcrum *ful'krəm*, *fōōl'*, *n.* the prop or fixed point on which a lever moves (*mech.*): a support: a means to an end (*fig.*): — *pl.* **ful'crums**, **ful'cra**. — *adj.* **ful'crate** supported with fulcrums. [L. *fulcrum*, a prop — *fulcīre*, to prop.]

fulfil *fōōl-fil'*, *v.t.* to fill full (*arch.*): to complete: to accomplish: to carry into effect: to bring to consummation: to develop and realise the potential of: — *pr.p.* **fulfil'ling**; *pa.t.* and *pa.p.* **fulfilled'**. — *ns.* **fulfil'er**;

fulfill'ing, fulfil'ment full performance: completion: accomplishment. [O.E. *fullfyllan—full*, full, *fyllan*, to fill.]

fulgent *ful'jənt, adj.* shining: bright. — *n.* **ful'gency.** — *adv.* **ful'gently.** — *adj.* **ful'gid** flashing. — *ns.* **ful'gor, ful'gour** (*-gör, -gər*) splendour. — *adj.* **ful'gorous** flashing. [L. *fulgēns, -entis*, pr.p. of *fulgēre*, to shine, *fulgidus*, shining, *fulgor*, brightness.]

fulgurate *ful'gū-rāt, v.i.* to flash as lightning. — *adjs.* **ful'gūral** pertaining to lightning; **ful'gūrant** flashing like lightning. — *ns.* **fulgūrā'tion** flashing: in assaying, the sudden and final brightening of the fused globule: the destruction of tissue, esp. tumours, by electric sparks (*med.*); **ful'gūrite** a tube of vitrified sand formed by lightning. — *adj.* **ful'gūrous** resembling lightning. [L. *fulgur*, lightning.]

fulham *fool'əm, n.* a die loaded at the corner. — Also **full'am, full'an.** [Prob. the place-name *Fulham*.]

fuliginous *fū-lij'i-nəs, adj.* sooty: dusky. — *n.* **fūliginos'ity.** — *adv.* **fūlig'inously.** [L. *fūligō, -īnis*, soot.]

full[1] *fool, adj.* holding all that can be contained: having no empty space: replete: abundantly supplied or furnished: abounding: copious: filling: containing the whole matter: complete: perfect: maximum: strong: clear: intense: swelled or rounded: protuberant: having excess of material: at the height of development or end of course: (with *of*) unable to think or talk of anything but: drunk (*coll.*): — *compar.* **full'er**; *superl.* **full'est.** — *n.* the completest extent, as of the moon: the highest degree: the whole: the time of full moon. — *v.t.* to make with gathers or puckers. — *v.i.* to become full. — *adv.* quite: thoroughly, veritably: directly. — *adj.* **full'ish** inclined to fullness. — *n.* **full'ness, ful'ness** the state of being full: the moment of fulfilment: plenty, wealth (*Shak.*). — *adv.* **full'y** completely: entirely: quite. — *adjs.* **full'-a'corned** (*Shak.*) full-fed with acorns; **full'-aged** having reached majority. — **full back** see **back; full blast** full operation. — *adv.* **full'-blast** with maximum energy and fluency. — **full'-blood** an individual of pure blood. — *adjs.* **full'-blood'ed** having a full supply of blood: vigorous: thoroughbred, of unmixed descent: related through both parents; **full'-blown** fully expanded, as a flower: beyond the first freshness of youth: fully qualified or admitted: puffed out to fullness; **full'-bod'ied** with much body or substance; **full'-bore** (of a firearm) of larger calibre than small-bore. — **full'-bottom** a full-bottomed wig. — *adjs.* **full'-bott'omed** having a full or large bottom, as a wig; **full'-bound** with the boards covered as well as the back. — **full brother, full sister** son, daughter, of the same parents. — *adj.* **full'-charged** fully loaded (*lit.* and *fig.*). — *adv.* **full'-cir'cle** round in a complete revolution. — **full'-cock'** the position of a gun cock drawn fully back, or of a tap fully open. — *adv.* in that position. — *adj.* **full'-cocked'.** — **full cousin** the son or daughter of an uncle or aunt, first cousin. — *adjs.* **full'-cream'** (of milk) not skimmed: made with unskimmed milk; **full'-dress** in or requiring the dress (**full dress**) worn on occasions of state or ceremony; **full-dress debate** a set debate of some importance in which the leaders take part. — *adjs.* **full'-eyed** with large prominent eyes; **full'-face, full'-faced** having a full or broad face: (of type) bold-faced: showing the face in direct front view; **full'-fash'ioned, full'y-fash'ioned** of garments, esp. stockings, conforming to the body contour; **full'-fed** fed to plumpness or satiety; **full'-fledged', full'y-fledged'** completely fledged: having attained full membership; **full'-fraught** (*Shak.*) fully charged, equipped, endowed, all-round; **full'-front'al** of the front view of a completely naked man or woman (also **full'-front'**): with no detail left unrevealed (*fig.*); **full'-grown** grown to full size. — **full hand** full house. — *adjs.* **full'-hand'ed** bearing something valuable, as a gift; **full'-heart'ed** full of heart or courage: fraught with emotion; **full'-hot** (*Shak.*) heated to the utmost. — **full house** a performance at which every seat is taken (*theat.*): three cards of a kind and a pair (*poker*): also

full hand). — *adj.* **full'-length'** extending the whole length. — *n.* a portrait showing the whole length. — *adv.* stretched to the full extent. — *adj.* **full'-manned** (*Shak.*) having a full crew. — **full moon** the moon with its whole disc illuminated, when opposite the sun: the time when the moon is full. — *adj.* **full'-mouthed** having a full set of teeth: having food in plenty: loud: sonorous. — **full nelson** a nelson. — *adj.* **full'-orbed** having the orb or disc fully illuminated, as the full moon: round. — **full organ** the organ, or great organ, with all or most of the stops in use. — *adjs.* **full'-out** at full power: total; **full'-page** occupying a whole page. — *advs.* **full'-pelt', full'-speed', full'-split', full-tilt'** with highest speed and impetus. — **full pitch** in cricket, a ball which does not or would not pitch before passing or hitting the batsman's wicket — also **full toss.** — *adj.* **full'-rigged'** having three or more masts square-rigged. — *adv.* **full'-sail'.** — *adjs.* **full'-sailed** having all sails set: having sails filled with wind: advancing with speed and momentum; **full'-scale** of the same size as the original: involving full power or maximum effort. — **full score** a complete musical score with a staff for every part; **full sister** see **full brother.** — *advs.* **full-speed, full-split** see **full-pelt.** — **full stop** a point marking the end of a sentence: an end, a halt. — *adjs.* **full'-summed** complete in all its parts; **full'-throat'ed, full'-voiced** singing with the whole power of the voice. — *adv.* **full-tilt** see **full-pelt.** — **full time** the end of a football, rugby, etc. match. — *adj.* **full'-time** occupied during or extending over the whole working day, week, etc. — **full'-tim'er; full toss** see **full pitch.** — *adjs.* **full-voiced** see **full-throated; full'-winged** (*Shak.*) having wide, strong wings; **full'y-fash'ioned** full-fashioned; **fully-fledged** full-fledged. — **at the full** at the height, as of one's good fortune, etc.; **full and by** closehauled to the wind; **full-line forcing** the supplying of a particular product by a company to a customer only on condition that the customer takes the whole range of the company's product; **full of oneself** having a (too) high opinion of one's own importance, etc. (also **full of one's own importance**), too much the subject of one's own conversation; **full of years** old, aged: at a good old age; **full up** full to the limit; sated, wearied (*slang*); **in full** without reduction; **in full cry** in chase together, giving tongue; **in full rig** with maximum number of masts and sails; **in full swing** at the height of activity; **in the fullness of time** at the due or destined time; **to the full** in full measure, completely. [O.E. *full*; Goth. *fulls*, O.N. *fullr*, Ger. *voll*.]

full[2] *fool, v.t.* to scour and beat, as a means of finishing or cleansing woollens: to scour and thicken in a mill. — *ns.* **full'age** the charge for fulling cloth; **full'er** one who fulls cloth. — **fuller's earth** an earthy hydrous aluminium silicate, capable of absorbing grease: a division of the English Jurassic; **full'er's-herb'** soapwort; **full'ing-mill** a mill in which woollen cloth is fulled. [O.Fr. *fuler* (see **foil**[1]) and O.E. *fullere*, fuller, both — L. *fullō*, a cloth-fuller.]

fullam, fullan. See **fulham.**

fulmar *fool'mär, -mər, n.* a gull-like bird of the petrel family. [Perh. O.N. *fūll*, foul, *mār*, gull.]

fulminate *ful'min-āt, v.i.* to thunder or make a loud noise: to detonate: to issue decrees with violence, or threats: to inveigh: to flash. — *v.t.* to cause to explode: to send forth, as a denunciation: to denounce. — *n.* a salt of fulminic acid (often dangerously detonating). — *adj.* **ful'minant** fulminating: developing suddenly (*path.*). — *n.* a thunderbolt: an explosive. — *adj.* **ful'mināting** detonating. — *n.* **fulminā'tion** an act of thundering, denouncing, or detonating: a denunciation. — *adj.* **ful'minatory.** — *v.t.* and *v.i.* **fulmine** (*ful'min; Spens., Milt.*) to fulminate. — *adjs.* **fulmin'eous, ful'minous** pertaining to thunder and lightning. — **fulminating gold** a green powder made from auric oxide and ammonium hydroxide; **fulminating mercury** mercuric fulminate; **fulminating silver** a black solid made from silver oxide and ammonium hydroxide; **fulmin'ic acid**

an acid isomeric with cyanic acid.   [L. *fulmināre,*
-ātum — fulmen, -inis, lightning — *fulgēre,* to shine.]
fulness. See **full**[1].
fulsome *fool'səm, adj.* copious (*obs.*): cloying or causing
surfeit: nauseous: offensive: gross: rank: disgustingly
fawning. — *adv.* **ful'somely.** — *n.* **ful'someness.**   [**full,**
and affix *-some*.]
fulvous *ful'vəs, adj.* dull yellow: tawny. — *adj.* **ful'vid.**
[L. *fulvus,* tawny.]
fum. See **fung.**
fumado *fū-mä'dō, n.* a smoked fish, esp. a pilchard: —
pl. **fumä'do(e)s.**   [Sp., smoked — L. *fūmāre,* to
smoke.]
Fumaria *fū-mä'ri-ə, n.* the fumitory genus, giving name
to the **Fumariä'ceae,** a family akin to the poppies. —
fumaric (*fū-mar'ik*) **acid** an acid isomeric with maleic
acid, found in Fumaria and other plants.   [L. *fūmus;*
see **fumitory.**]
fumarole *fūm'ə-rōl, n.* a hole emitting gases in a volcano
or volcanic region. — Also **fum'erole.**   [Fr. *fumerolle*
or It. *fumaruola* — L. *fūmus,* smoke.]
fumatorium, fumatory. See **fume.**
fumble *fum'bl, v.i.* to grope about awkwardly: to make
bungling or unsuccessful attempts: to mumble. — *v.t.*
to handle, manage, or effect awkwardly or bunglingly:
to huddle (*arch.*): to mumble. — *n.* **fum'bler.** — *adv.*
fum'blingly.   [Cf. Du. *fommelen,* to fumble; Dan.
famle; O.N. *fālma,* to grope about.]
fume *fūm, n.* smoke or vapour, often odorous (often in
pl.): any volatile matter: heat of mind, rage, fretful
excitement: a passionate person (*arch.*): anything unsubstantial, vain conceit. — *v.i.* to smoke: to throw
off vapour: to come off or pass in fumes: to be in a
rage. — *v.t.* to treat with fumes: to give off: to offer
incense to. — *ns.* **fūm'age** hearth-money; **fumatō'rium**
(*pl.* **-riums, -ria**), **fūm'atory** a place for smoking or
fumigation; **fūmos'ity** (*arch.*) a fuming condition: an
exhalation: breath stinking of food or drink. — *adjs.*
fūm'ous, fūm'y. — **fume'-cham'ber, -cup'board** a case
for laboratory operations that give off fumes; **fumed
oak** oak darkened by ammonia fumes. — **fuming
sulphuric acid** see **oleum** under **oleate.**   [L. *fūmus,*
smoke.]
fumet[1], **fewmet** *fū'mit,* (*arch.,* usu. in *pl.*) *n.* the dung of
deer, hares, etc.   [Appar. Anglo-Fr., — L. *fimāre,* to
dung.]
fumet[2], **fumette** *fū-met', n.* the scent of game when high.
[Fr. *fumet.*]
fumetto *foo-met'to,* (It.) *n.* a cartoon or comic-strip: a
balloon in a cartoon: — *pl.* **-ti** (*-tē*).
fumigate *fūm'i-gāt, v.t.* to expose to fumes, esp. for
purposes of disinfecting, or destroying pests: to perfume (*arch.*). — *ns.* **fūm'igant** a source of fumes, esp.
a substance used for fumigation; **fūmigā'tion; fūm'-**
igator a fumigating apparatus. — *adj.* **fūm'igatory.**
[L. *fūmigāre, -ātum.*]
fumitory *fūm'i-tər-i, n.* a plant of the genus Fumaria. —
Also (*Shak.*) **fem'iter** or **fen'itar, fem'etary.**   [O.Fr.
fume-terre, lit. earth-smoke — L. *fūmus,* smoke, *terra,*
earth; so called because its rapid growth was thought
to resemble the dispersal of smoke.]
fun *fun, n.* a hoax, trick (*obs.*): merriment: sport: a source
of merriment or amusement. — *v.t.* (*obs.*) to trick. —
v.i. to make sport: — *pr.p.* **funn'ing.** — *adj.* providing
amusement; enjoyable, full of fun. — **fun'fair** a fair
with side-shows and other amusements; **fun fur** an
artificial or inexpensive (sometimes dyed) fur, esp. for
casual wear; **fun park** an outdoor place of entertainment with various amusements. — **fun run** a long-
distance race, not usually covering the full distance of
a marathon, undertaken for amusement rather than
serious athletic competition; **all the fun of the fair** all
the amusements of the occasion; **be great fun** to be
very amusing; **in fun** as a joke, not seriously; **like fun**
(*coll.*) rapidly: not at all; **make fun of, poke fun at** to
ridicule.   [Prob. a form of obs. *fon,* to befool.]
funambulist *fū-nam'bū-list, n.* a rope-walker or rope-

dancer. — *v.i.* **fūnam'būlate.** — *ns.* **fūnambūlā'tion;**
fūnam'būlātor. — *adj.* **fūnam'būlatory.**   [L. *fūnambu-*
lus, a rope walker — *fūnis,* rope, *ambulāre,* to walk.]
function *fung(k)'shən, n.* the doing of a thing: performance (*obs.*): activity (*obs.*): an activity appropriate to
any person or thing: duty peculiar to any office:
faculty, exercise of faculty: the peculiar office of
anything: a profession (*obs.*): a solemn service: a
ceremony: a social gathering: in math., a variable so
connected with another that for any value of the one
there is a corresponding value for the other: a correspondence between two sets of variables such that each
member of one set can be related to one particular
member of the other set: an event, etc. dependent on
some other factor or factors: the technical term in
physiology for the vital activity of an organ, tissue, or
cell: the part played by a linguistic form in a construction, or by a form or form class in constructions in
general (*linguistics*). — *v.i.* to perform a function: to
act: to operate: to work. — *adj.* **func'tional** pertaining
to or performed by functions: of disease, characterised
by impairment of function, not of organs: designed
with special regard to purpose and practical use:
serving a function. — *ns.* **func'tionalism** the theory or
practice of adapting method, form, materials, etc.,
primarily with regard to the purpose in hand; **func'-**
tionalist. — *adv.* **func'tionally.** — *n.* **func'tionary** one
who discharges any duty: one who holds an office. —
v.i. **func'tionate** to perform a function. — *adj.* **func'-**
tionless having no function. — **function word** (*linguis-*
tics) a word, such as an article or auxiliary, which has
little or no meaning apart from the grammatical
concept it expresses.   [O.Fr., — L. *functiō, -ōnis* —
fungī, functus, to perform.]
functus officio *fungk'təs of-ish'i-ō, foongk'toos of-ik'i-ō,*
(L.) having fulfilled an office, out of office: no longer
having official power to act: (of a power) that can no
longer be exercised.
fund *fund, n.* a sum of money on which some enterprise
is founded or expense supported: a supply or source
of money: a store laid up: a supply: (in *pl.*) permanent
government debts paying interest: (in *pl.*) money available to an organisation, for a project, etc., or (*coll.*:
usu. *facet.*) available to an individual. — *v.t.* to form
into a stock charged with interest: to place in a fund:
to provide (an organisation, project, etc.) with money.
— *adj.* **fund'able** capable of being converted into a fund
or into bonds: capable of being funded. — *adj.* **fund'ed**
invested in public funds: existing in the form of bonds.
— *ns.* **fund'er** one who provides money for a project,
etc., a financial backer; **fund'ing.** — *adj.* **fund'less**
destitute of supplies or money. — **fund'-holder** one who
has money in the public funds. — *n.* and *adj.* **fund'=**
raising (for the purpose of) the raising of money for
an organisation, project, etc.   [L. *fundus,* the bottom.]
fundamental *fun-də-men'tl, adj.* basal: serving as foundation: essential: primary: important. — *n.* that which
serves as a groundwork: an essential: the root of a
chord or of a system of harmonics (*mus.*). — *ns.*
fund'ament (*-mənt*) the lower part or seat of the body;
fundamen'talism belief in the literal truth of the Bible,
against evolution, etc.; **fundamen'talist** one who professes this belief or (*fig.*) other, e.g. political, beliefs
considered fundamental. — Also *adj.* — *n.* **fundamen-**
tal'ity. — *adv.* **fundamen'tally.** — **fundamental particle**
same as **elementary particle; fundamental unit** any of a
number of arbitrarily defined units in a system of
measurement, such as metre, second, candela, from
which the other quantities in the system are derived.
[L. *fundāmentum,* foundation, *fundāre,* to found.]
fundamentum relationis *fun-də-men'təm ri-lä-shi-ōn'is,*
foon-dä-men'toom re-lä-ti-ōn'is, (L.L.) the ground of
relation, principle of, or the nature of, the connection.
fundi *foon'dē* (*S.Afr.*) *n.* an expert.   [Nguni (S.Afr.
language) *umfundisi,* a teacher.]
fundus *fun'dəs, n.* the bottom of anything: the rounded

bottom of a hollow organ (*anat.*): — *pl.* fun′di (-ī). [L.]

funèbre *fü-ne-br'*, (Fr.) *adj.* mournful.

funebr(i)al. See funeral.

funeral *fū′nər-əl*, *n.* disposal of the dead, with any ceremonies or observances connected therewith: a procession to the place of burial or cremation, etc.: death (*Spens., Shak.*): tomb (*Spens.*). — *adj.* pertaining to the disposal of the dead. — *adjs.* fūnē′bral, fūnē′brial funereal; fū′nerary pertaining to or suiting a funeral; fūnē′real pertaining to a funeral: dismal: mournful. — funeral director an undertaker; funeral home (*U.S.*) an undertaker's place of business with facilities for funerals; funeral parlour a room that can be hired for funeral ceremonies: a funeral home. — your, my, etc. funeral your, my, etc. affair, or look-out.   [L.L. *fūnerālis* and L. *fūnerārius, fŭnebris, fŭnĕreus* — L. *fūnus, fŭnĕris*, a funeral procession.]

funest *fū-nest'*, *adj.* deadly: lamentable.   [Fr., — L. *fūnestus*, destructive.]

fung *fung*, fum *fum*, *ns.* a fabulous Chinese bird, sometimes called phoenix.   [Chin. *fung, fêng*.]

fungibles *fun′ji-blz*, (*law*) *n.pl.* movable effects which are consumed by use, and which are estimated by weight, number, and measure.   [L.L. *fungibilis* — L. *fungī*, to perform; see function.]

fungus *fung′gəs*, *n.* a plant of one of the lowest groups, thallophytes without chlorophyll, including mushrooms, toadstools, mould, etc.: proud-flesh formed on wounds: — *pl.* fungi (*fun′jī, -ji, -gī*), fung′uses. — *adjs.* fung′al pertaining to fungus; fungicīd′al fungi-destroying: pertaining to a fungicide. — *n.* fungicide (*fun′ji-sīd*) a substance which kills fungi. — *adjs.* fungiform (*fun′ji-förm*) mushroom-shaped; fung′oid (-*goid*), -al fungus-like: of the nature of a fungus. — *n.* fungos′ity the quality of being fungous. — *adj.* fung′ous of or like fungus: soft: spongy: growing suddenly: ephemeral. — fung′us-gall a malformation in a plant caused by a fungal attack.   [L. *fungus*, a mushroom, cf. Gr. *sphongos, spongos*, a sponge.]

funicle *fū′ni-kl*, *n.* a small cord or ligature: a fibre: the stalk of an ovule (*bot.*). — *adjs.* fūnic′ular; fūnic′ulate. — *n.* fūnic′ulus the umbilical cord: a funicle. — funicular railway a cable-railway.   [L. *fūniculus*, dim. of *fūnis*, a rope.]

funk¹ *fungk*, (*coll.*) *n.* a state of fear: panic: shrinking or shirking from loss of courage: one who funks. — *v.i.* to flinch: to draw back or hold back in fear. — *v.t.* to balk at or shirk from fear. — *n.* funk′iness. — *adj.* funk′y. — funk′hole (*slang*, orig. *mil.*) a place of refuge, dug-out: a place to which one can retreat for shelter, etc. (*fig.*): a job that enables one to avoid military service. — blue funk see blue¹.   [Poss. Flem. *fonck*.]

funk² *fungk*, *n.* touchwood: a spark.   [Cf. Du. *vonk*.]

funk³ *fungk*, *v.t.* to stifle with smoke. — *v.i.* to smoke and/or cause a strong unpleasant smell. — *n.* a strong, unpleasant smell, esp. of smoke (*obs.* or *U.S. dial.*): funky music (*slang*). — *adj.* funk′y with a strong, musty, or bad smell (*U.S. dial.*): of jazz, pop music, etc., unsophisticated, earthy, and soulful, like early blues music in style, emotion, etc. (*slang*): in the latest fashion, with it (*slang*): kinky (*slang*): odd, quaint (*slang*).   [Ety. dub.]

Funkia *fungk′i-ə*, *n.* the former name of an E. Asiatic genus allied to the day-lilies, now Hosta: (without *cap.*) a plant of this genus.   [From the German botanist, H. C. *Funck*, 1771–1839.]

funnel *fun′l*, *n.* a vessel, usually a cone ending in a tube, for pouring fluids into bottles, etc.: a passage for the escape of smoke, etc. — *v.t.* to pour, pass, transfer, etc. through, or as if through, a funnel. — *adj.* funn′elled with a funnel: funnel-shaped. — funn′el-net a net shaped like a funnel; funn′el-web (spider) a venemous spider (genus *Atrax*) of eastern Australia which constructs a tube-shaped or funnel-shaped lair. [Prob. through Fr. or Port. from L. *infundibulum* — *fundĕre*, to pour.]

funnel² *fun′l*, (*dial.*) *n.* the offspring of a stallion and a she-ass.   [Origin unknown.]

funny¹ *fun′i*, *adj.* full of fun: droll: amusing, mirth-provoking: queer, odd (*coll.*). — *n.* a joke (*coll.*): (in *pl.*) comic strips, or the comic section of a newspaper (*U.S.*). — *adv.* funn′ily. — *n.* funn′iness. — funny bone the bone at the elbow with the comparatively unprotected ulnar nerve which, when struck, shoots a tingling sensation down the forearm to the fingers (a punning translation of L. *humerus*); funny business tricks, deception (*slang*): amusing behaviour, joke-telling, etc. (*coll.*); funny farm (*slang*) a mental hospital or asylum; funny ha-ha funny meaning 'amusing' (opp. to *funny peculiar*); funny man (*coll.*) a comedian; funny money (*coll.*) any currency or unit of account considered in some way less real or solid than 'ordinary' money, or a sum of money similarly regarded as in some way unreal; funny paper (*U.S.*) the comic section of a newspaper; funny peculiar funny meaning 'queer, odd' (opp. to *funny ha-ha*); funny stuff funny business. [fun.]

funny² *fun′i*, *n.* a light racing-boat, with a pair of sculls. [Perh. from the foregoing.]

Funtumia *fun-tū′mi-ə*, *n.* an African genus of apocynaceous trees, yielding a type of rubber.   [From a Ghanaian name.]

fur¹ *für*, *n.* the thick, soft, fine hair of certain animals: the skin with this hair attached: a garment of fur: furred animals (opp. to *feather*): a patched or tufted tincture (*her.*): a coating on the tongue: a crust in boilers, etc.: a strengthening piece nailed to a rafter. — *v.t.* to clothe, cover, coat, trim or line with fur: to coat. — *v.i.* to become coated: — *pr.p.* furr′ing; *pa.t.* and *pa.p.* furred. — *adj.* furred. — *ns.* furr′ier a dealer or worker in furs; furr′iery furs in general: trade in furs; furr′ing fur trimmings: a coating on the tongue: (also firr′ing) strips of wood fastened to joists, etc.: a lining to a wall to carry lath, provide an air-space, etc. — *adj.* furr′y consisting of, like, covered with, or dressed in fur. — fur fabric a fabric with a fur-like pile; fur′-seal a sea-bear, an eared seal with close fur under its long hairs.   [O.Fr. *forrer* (Fr. *fourrer*), to line, encase — *forre, fuerre*, sheath.]

fur², furr *für*, (*Scot.*) *n.* a form of furrow.

furacious *fū-rā′shəs*, *adj.* thievish. — *ns.* fūrā′ciousness, fūracity (-*ras′i-ti*).   [L. *fūrāx, -ācis* — *für*, thief.]

fural, furan(e). See under furfur.

furbelow *fûr′bi-lō*, *n.* a plaited border or flounce: a superfluous ornament. — *v.t.* to flounce.   [Fr., It., and Sp. *falbala*; of unknown origin.]

furbish *fûr′bish*, *v.t.* to purify or polish: to rub up until bright: to renovate. — *n.* fur′bisher.   [O.Fr. *fourbir, fourbiss-*, from O.H.G. *furban*, to purify.]

furcate, furcated *fûr′kāt, -kit, -kā-tid*, *adjs.* forked. — *adj.* fur′cal. — *n.* furcā′tion. — *adj.* furciferous (-*sif′*) bearing a forked appendage: rascally (*facet.*; in allusion to the *furca* or yoke of criminals). — *n.* fur′cula the united clavicles of a bird — the wishbone. — *adj.* fur′cular furcate: shaped like a fork.   [L. *furca*, fork.]

Furcraea *fûr-krē′ə*, Fourcroya *foor-kroi′ə*, *ns.* a tropical American genus of plants akin to Agave, yielding Mauritius hemp.   [After A. F. de *Fourcroy* (1755–1800), French chemist.]

furder *fûr′dər*, an obs. form (*Milt.*) of further¹.

fureur *fü-rær*, (Fr.) *n.* extravagant admiration.

furfur *fûr′für, -fər* (Browning, furfair), *n.* dandruff, scurf. — *n.* fūr′an (-*an* or *-an'*) a colourless, liquid, heterocyclic compound, C_4H_4O, got from wood-tar or synthesised, and used in tanning and nylon production (also fur′furan -*fū-* or *-fə-*): any of a group of heterocyclic compounds derived from furan. — Also fūr′ane (-*ān*). — *adj.* furfuraceous (*fûr-fū-rā′shəs*) branny: scaly: scurfy. — *ns.* furfural (*fûr′fū-ral, -fə-ral*), in full furfural′dehyde, also called fūr′al, fur′fūrol(e), fūr′ol(e), a liquid ($C_4H_3O·CHO$) got by heating bran with dilute sulphuric acid; furfuran see furan above. — *adj.* fur-

furous (*fūr'fū-rəs*, *-fə-rəs*) furfuraceous. [L. *furfur*, bran.]

furibund *fū'ri-bund*, *adj.* raging. [L. *furibundus* — *furia*, rage.]

furioso *fōō-ri-ō'sō*, *fū-*, *n.* a furious person, madman: — *pl.* **furiō'sōs**. — *adj.* and *adv.* (*mus.*) with fury. [It.; cf. **furious**.]

furious. See **fury**.

furl *fûrl*, *v.t.* to roll up. [Perh. **fardel**[2].]

furlana *fōōr-lä'nə*. Same as **forlana**.

furlong *fûr'long*, *n.* 40 poles, one-eighth of a mile. [O.E. *furlang* — *furh*, furrow, *lang*, long.]

furlough *fûr'lō*, *n.* leave of absence. — *v.t.* to grant furlough to. [Du. *verlof*; cf. Ger. *Verlaub*.]

furmenty, furmety, furmity. See **frumenty**.

furnace *fûr'nis*, *n.* an enclosed structure in which great heat is produced: a time or place of grievous affliction or torment. — *v.t.* to exhale like a furnace: to subject to the heat of a furnace. [O.Fr. *fornais* — L. *fornāx*, *-ācis* — *fornus*, an oven.]

furniment *fûr'ni-mənt*, (*Spens.*) *n.* furnishing.

furnish *fûr'nish*, *v.t.* to fit up or supply completely, or with what is necessary: to supply, provide: to equip. — *adj.* **fur'nished** equipped: stocked with furniture. — *n.* **fur'nisher**. — *n.pl.* **fur'nishings** fittings of any kind, esp. articles of furniture, etc., within a house: any incidental part (*Shak.*). — *n.* **fur'nishment**. [O.Fr. *furnir, furniss-*; of Gmc. origin; cf. O.H.G. *frummen*, to further.]

furniture *fûr'ni-chər*, *n.* movables, either for use or ornament, with which a house is equipped: equipment (*Shak.*): the trappings of a horse: decorations (*Shak.*): the necessary appliances in some arts: accessories: metal fittings for doors and windows: the piece of wood or metal put round pages of type to make margins and fasten the matter in the chase (*print.*). — **furniture van** a long, high-sided van for transporting furniture, etc., e.g. when changing one's abode. [Fr. *fourniture*.]

furol(e). See under **furfur**.

furor *fū'ror*, *n.* fury: excitement, enthusiasm. — **furor loquendi** (*fū'ror lok-wen'dī, fōō'ror lok-wen'dē*) a rage for speaking; **furor poeticus** (*pō-et'ik-əs, po-āt-ik-ōōs*) poetic frenzy; **furor scribendi** (*skri-ben'dī, skrē-ben'dē*) a rage for writing. [L.]

furore *fū'ror, -rör, fōō-rör'ā*, *n.* a craze: wild enthusiasm: wild excitement. [It.]

furphy *fûr'fi*, (*Austr.*) *n.* a water cart: a rumour, false report. [John *Furphy*, an Australian water cart manufacturer.]

furr *fûr*. A Scot. form of **furrow**.

furrier, furring. See **fur**[1].

furrow *fur'ō*, *n.* the trench made by a plough: a groove: a wrinkle. — *v.t.* to form furrows in: to groove: to wrinkle. — *adj.* **fu̱rr'owy**. — **furr'ow-weed** (*Shak.*) a weed of ploughed land. [O.E. *furh*; cf. Ger. *Furche*, L. *porca*, ridge.]

furry. See **fur**[1].

furth *fûrth*, (*Scot.*) *adv.* forth: outside of. — **furthcom'ing** (*Scots law*) an action brought by an arrester against the arrestee and the common debtor after an arrestment in order that the arrested money or property be delivered to the arrester. — **furth of** outside: beyond the bounds of. [Variant of **forth**.]

further[1] *fûr'dhər*, *adv.* at or to a greater distance or degree: in addition. — *adj.* more distant: additional, more, other. — *adv.* **fur'thermore** in addition to what has been said, moreover, besides. — *adj.* **fur'thermost** most remote. — *adv.* **fur'thest** at or to the greatest distance. — *adj.* most distant. — **further education** post-school education other than at university, polytechnic, etc.; **further outlook** (*meteor.*) a general forecast given for a longer or more distant period than that covered by a more detailed forecast. — **see someone further** to see someone hanged, or the like. [O.E. *furthor* (adv.), *furthra* (adj.) — *fore* or *forth* with compar. suffix *-ther*.]

further[2] *fûr'dhər*, *v.t.* to help forward, promote. — *ns.*

furtherance a helping forward; **fur'therer** a promoter, advancer. — *adj.* **fur'thersome** helpful: advantageous: rash. [O.E. *fyrthran*.]

furtive *fûr'tiv*, *adj.* stealthy: secret. — *adv.* **fur'tively**. — *n.* **fur'tiveness**. [L. *fûrtîvus* — *fûr*, a thief.]

furuncle *fū'rung-kl*, *n.* a boil. — *adjs.* **fūrun'cular, fūrun'cūlous**. — *n.* **fūruncūlō'sis** the condition of having many boils: a highly infectious disease of salmon and related fish. [L. *fûrunculus*, lit. a little thief.]

fury *fū'ri*, *n.* rage: violent passion: madness: (with *cap.*; *myth.*) any one of the three goddesses of vengeance, the Erinyes, or euphemistically Eumenides — Tisiphone, Alecto, and Megaera (in *Milt.* a Fate): hence a passionate, violent woman. — *adj.* **furious** (*fū'ri-əs*) full of fury: violent. — *n.* **fūrios'ity** madness. — *adv.* **fū'riously**. — *n.* **fū'riousness**. — **fast and furious** see **fast**[2]; **like fury** (*coll.*) furiously. [Fr. *furie* — L. *furia* — *furēre*, to be angry.]

furze *fûrz*, *n.* whin or gorse. — *adj.* **furz'y** overgrown with furze. [O.E. *fyrs*.]

fusain *fū-zān'*, *n.* an important constituent of coal, resembling charcoal and consisting of plant remains from which the volatiles have been eliminated (also *fū'zān*): artists' fine charcoal: a drawing done with this. [Fr., the spindle-tree, or charcoal made from it.]

fusarole, fusarol *fū'sə-rōl*, or *-zə-*, (*archit.*) *n.* an astragal moulding. [Fr. *fusarolle* — It. *fusaruolo*, spindle-whorl — L. *fûsus*, spindle.]

fuscous *fus'kəs*, *adj.* brown: dingy. — Also (*Lamb*) **fusc**. [L. *fuscus*.]

fuse[1] *fūz*, *v.t.* to melt: to liquefy by heat: to join by, or as if by, melting together: to cause to fail by melting of a fuse (*elect.*). — *v.i.* to be melted: to be reduced to a liquid: to melt together: to blend, unite: of electric appliance, to fail by melting of a fuse. — *n.* a bit of fusible metal, with its mounting, inserted as a safeguard in an electric circuit. — *n.* **fūsibil'ity** the degree of ease with which a substance can be fused. — *adjs.* **fūs'ible** able to be fused or easily fused; **fū'sil** (*fū'zil*; *Milt.*) cast: fusible: molten. — Also **fūsile** (*fū'zil, -sīl, -zil*). — *ns.* **fū'sion** (*-zhən*) melting: the state of fluidity from heat: a close union of things, as if melted together: coalition (*U.S.*): nuclear fusion (q.v.); **fū'sionism** a policy that favours union or coalition; **fū'sionist**. — **fuse box** a box containing the switches and fuses for the leads of an electrical system; **fusible metal** an alloy of bismuth, lead, and tin (sometimes with mercury or cadmium) that melts at temperatures of 60° to 180°C; **fū'sing-point** melting-point; **fusion bomb** one deriving its energy from fusion of atomic nuclei, as the hydrogen bomb; **fusion music** music in which two or more different styles are combined; **fusion reactor** a nuclear reactor operating by nuclear fusion. [L. *fundēre*, *fūsum*, to melt.]

fuse[2] *fūz*, *n.* a train of combustible material in waterproof covering, used with a detonator to initiate an explosion. — Also, esp. *U.S.*, **fuze**. [It. *fuso* — L. *fūsus*, a spindle.]

fusee[1], **fuzee** *fū-zē'*, *n.* the spindle in a watch or clock on which the chain is wound: a match with long, oval head for outdoor use: a fuse for firing explosives. [O.Fr. *fusée*, a spindleful — L. *fūsus*, a spindle.]

fusee[2]. Same as **fusil**[2].

fuselage *fū'zil-ij*, or *fū-zə-läzh'*, *n.* the body of an aeroplane. [Fr. *fuseler*, to shape like a spindle — L. *fūsus*, spindle.]

fusel-oil *fū'zl-oil*, *n.* a nauseous oil in spirits distilled from potatoes, grain, etc. [Ger. *Fusel*, bad spirits.]

fushion, fushionless. See **foison**.

fusidic acid *fū-sid'ik a'sid*, an antibiotic steroid, $C_{31}H_{48}O_6$. [From the fungus *Fusidium coccineum*, from which it was first isolated.]

fusiform *fū'zi-förm*, *adj.* spindle-shaped. [L. *fūsus*, spindle, *fōrma*, shape.]

fusil[1] *fū'zil*, (*her.*) *n.* an elongated rhomboidal figure. [O.Fr. *fusel* — L. *fûsus*, a spindle.]

fusil[2] *fū'zil*, *n.* a flintlock musket. — *ns.* **fusilier'**, **fusileer'**

formerly a soldier armed with a fusil, now simply a historical title borne by a few regiments; **fusillade** (-*ād′*) simultaneous or continuous discharge of firearms: anything assaulting one in similar way (*lit., fig.*); **fusillā′tion** death by shooting. [O.Fr. *fuisil*, a flint-musket, same as It. *focile* — L.L. *focile*, steel (to strike fire with), dim. of L. *focus*, a fireplace.]

fusil[3], **fusile**. See under **fuse**[1].

fusion[1], **fusionless**. See **foison**.

fusion[2]. See **fuse**[1].

fuss *fus, n.* a bustle: flurry: commotion, esp. over trifles: petty ostentatious activity or attentions. — *v.i.* to be in a fuss, agitate about trifles. — *v.t.* to agitate, flurry. — *n.* **fuss′er**. — *adv.* **fuss′ily**. — *n.* **fuss′iness**. — *adj.* **fuss′y** given to making a fuss: finicky: requiring careful attention: overtrimmed. — **fuss′-pot**, (*U.S.*) **fuss′-budget** one who fusses. — **make a fuss of** to give much (genuinely or apparently) affectionate or amicable attention to. [Origin obscure.]

fuss-ball. See **fuzz**.

fust *fust, n.* a mouldy or musty smell: the shaft of a column. — *v.i.* to mould: to smell mouldy: to taste of the cask. — *ns.* **fustilā′rian, fustil(l)ir′ian** (*Shak.*) a term of abuse; **fust′ilugs** (*obs.*) a gross overgrown person, esp. a woman. — *adv.* **fust′ily**. — *n.* **fust′iness**. — *adj.* **fust′y** smelling of the cask: musty: stale: stuffy: wanting in freshness. [O.Fr. *fust* (Fr. *fût*), cask — L. *fūstis*, a cudgel.]

fustanella *fus-tə-nel′ə, n.* a white kilt worn by Greek and Albanian men. [Mod. Gr. *phoustanella*, dim. of *phoustani*, Albanian *fustan* — It. *fustagno*, fustian.]

fustet *fus′tət, n.* Venetian sumach (*Rhus cotinus*), or its wood, source of the dye called young fustic. [Fr., — Prov. *fustet* — Ar. *fustuq*; see **fustic**.]

fustian *fus′chən, n.* a kind of coarse, twilled cotton fabric including moleskin, velveteen, corduroy, etc.: a pompous and unnatural style of writing or speaking: bombast: a liquor made of white wine with yolk of eggs, lemon, spices, etc. — *adj.* made of fustian: bombastic. — *v.i.* **fust′ianise, -ize** (*Holmes*) to write bombastically. — *n.* **fust′ianist** one who writes bombast. [O.Fr. *fustaigne* (Fr. *futaine*) — It. *fustagno* — L.L. *fustāneum*, prob. from *El-Fustāt* (Old Cairo) where it may have been made.]

fustic *fus′tik, n.* formerly, fustet (now called **young fustic**): now, the wood of a tropical American tree (*Chlorophora tinctoria*), yielding a yellow dye (also **old fustic**). — Also **fus′toc**. [Fr. *fustoc* — Sp. *fustoc* — Ar. *fustuq* — Gr. *pistakē*, pistachio.]

fustigate *fus′ti-gāt, v.t.* to cudgel. — *n.* **fustigā′tion**. [L. *fūstīgāre, -ātum* — *fūstis*, a stick.]

fustilugs, fustily, fusty, etc. See **fust**.

fustoc. See **fustic**.

Fusus *fū′səs, n.* a genus of gasteropods, allied to whelks —the spindle-shells. [L. *fūsus*, spindle.]

futchel *fuch′əl, n.* a piece of timber lengthwise of a carriage, supporting the splinter-bar and the pole.

futhork, futhorc, futhark *foo′thōrk, -thärk, ns.* the Runic alphabet. [From the first six letters, *f, u, þ* (*th*), *o* or *a, r, k.*]

futile *fū′tīl, U.S.* -*təl, adj.* ineffectual: trifling: tattling (*obs.*). — *adv.* **fu′tilely**. — *ns.* **futilitā′rian** one who gives himself to profitless pursuits: one who believes all to be futile; **futil′ity** uselessness. [L. *fūtilis*, leaky, futile — *fundĕre*, to pour.]

futon *foo′ton, n.* a Japanese floor-mattress used as a bed. [Jap.]

futtock *fut′ək, n.* one of the crooked timbers of a wooden ship. — **futt′ock-plate** an iron plate with dead-eyes, for the topmast or topgallant rigging. — *n.pl.* **futt′ock= shrouds** short pieces of rope or chain securing the futtock-plates to a band round a lower mast. [Perh. for **foot-hook**.]

future *fū′chər, adj.* about to be: that is to come: expressive of time to come (*gram.*). — *n.* time to come: life, fate or condition in time to come: prospects, likelihood of future success: the future tense (*gram.*): (in *pl.*) goods bought and sold to be delivered at a future time. — *adj.* **fut′ureless** without prospects. — *ns.* **fut′urism** (*art*) a movement claiming to anticipate or point the way for the future, esp. a 20th-century revolt against tradition; **fut′urist** one whose chief interests are in what is to come: a believer in futurism. — *adj.* **futurist′ic**. — *ns.* **futurit′ion** future existence: accomplishment: futurity; **futurity** (*fū-tū′ri-ti*) time to come: an event, or state of being, yet to come. — *adj.* **futurolog′ical**. — *ns.* **futurol′ogist; futurol′ogy** the science and study of sociological and technological developments, values, and trends, with a view to planning for the future. — *adj.* **fu′ture-per′fect** (*gram.*) expressive of action viewed as past in reference to an assumed future time. — *n.* the future-perfect tense: a verb in that tense. [Fr. *futur* — L. *futūrus*, used as fut.p. of *esse*, to be.]

fu yung *foo yoong*, a Chinese omelette-like dish with bean sprouts, onion, meat, etc. — Also **foo yung, foo yong** (*yong*). [Chin., hibiscus.]

fuze *fūz, n.* a device used to cause a bomb, shell, mine, rocket, etc., to detonate. — Often, esp. *U.K.*, **fuse**. [**fuse**[2].]

fuzee. See **fusee**[1].

fuzz *fuz, n.* light fine particles or fibres, as dust: fluff: blurr: police (*slang*). — *v.i.* to disintegrate in fuzz. — *adv.* **fuzz′ily**. — *n.* **fuzz′iness**. — *adj.* **fuzz′y** covered with fuzz: fluffy: with many small tight curls: blurred. — **fuzz′-ball, fuss′-ball** a puff-ball. — *adj.* **fuzz′y= haired′**. — **fuzz′y-wuzz′y** a Sudanese soldier (*old coll.*, esp. *mil.*): a coloured native of any of various countries, esp. if fuzzy-haired (*slang*). [Origin doubtful.]

fuzzle *fuz′l*, (*dial.*) *v.t.* to fuddle.

fy *fī, interj.* Same as **fie**[1].

fyke[1]. Same as **fike**.

fyke[2] *fīk*, (*U.S.*) *n.* a bag-net. [Du. *fuik*.]

fyle. A Spenserian form of **file**[1,2].

fylfot, filfot *fil′fot, n.* a swastika, esp. one turned counter-clockwise. [Prob. from misunderstanding of a manuscript, *fylfot* = fill-foot, really meaning a device for filling the foot of a painted window.]

fynbos *fān′bos*, (Afrik.) *n.* (an area of) low shrubs. [Afrik. — Dutch *fijn*, fine, delicate, *bosch*, bush.]

fyrd *fūrd, fērd, n.* the militia of Old English times. [O.E. *fyrd*, army.]

fytte. See **fit**[3].

G

G, g *jē, n.* the seventh letter of our alphabet, and of the Roman; originally a form of C, inserted in the place of the disused Z, its ordinary sound (as in Latin) a voiced guttural stop, but in some words in English the same as J: the fifth note of the diatonic scale of C major — also *sol* (*mus.*): the scale or key having that note for its tonic (*mus.*): a symbol (*g*) for acceleration due to gravity (see **gravity**): a symbol (*G*) for the constant of gravitation (see **gravity**): as a mediaeval Roman numeral G = 400, Ḡ = 400 000: symbol for general intelligence. — **G′-agents** highly effective poisonous gases for poss. military use; **G′-clef** a clef, the treble clef, on the second line of the treble stave, marking G; **G′-man** (*U.S.*) an agent of the Federal Bureau of Investigation (for Government-man); **G′-string** same as **gee-string**; **g′-suit** a close-fitting suit with cells that inflate to prevent flow of blood away from the head, worn by airmen as a defence against blackout due to high acceleration and resultant great increase in weight (*g* for acceleration of gravity).

gab¹ *gab,* (*coll.*) *v.i.* to chatter, prate. — *n.* idle or fluent talk: the mouth. — *n.* **gabb′er** a chatterer. — *adj.* **gabb′y** garrulous. — **gab′fest** (*slang*; chiefly *U.S.*) a gathering characterised by much talk or gossip: a prolonged conversation, discussion, etc. — **gift of the gab** a talent (or propensity) for talking. [Origin doubtful; possibly variant of **gob**¹.]

gab² *gab,* (*obs.*) *n.* mockery: a jest: a vaunt. — *v.i.* to brag. [O.Fr. *gabber,* to mock.]

gab³ *gab, n.* a Scots form of **gob**¹.

gabardine. See **gaberdine.**

gabbart *gab′ərt,* (esp. *Scot.*) *n.* a barge. — Also **gabb′ard.** [Fr. *gabare* — Prov. and It. *gabarra.*]

gabble *gab′l, v.i.* to talk inarticulately: to chatter: to cackle like geese. — *ns.* **gabb′le** gabbling; **gabb′ler; gabb′ling, gabb′lement.** [Perh. freq. of **gab**¹, perh. M.Du. *gabbelen* — imit.]

gabbro *gab′rō, n.* a coarsely crystalline igneous rock composed of labradorite or similar plagioclase and pyroxene, often with olivine and magnetite: — *pl.* **gabb′ros.** — *adjs.* **gabbro′ic, gabbroitic** (*-it′ik*); **gabb′roid** resembling gabbro. [It.]

gabelle *gab-el′, n.* a tax, esp. formerly in France, on salt. — *n.* **gabell′er** a collector of gabelle. [Fr. *gabelle* — L.L. *gabella, gablum*; of Gmc. origin.]

gaberdine, gabardine *gab′ər-dēn, n.* a loose cloak, esp. a Jew's (*hist.*): a closely woven twill fabric, esp. of cotton and wool: a coat of this material. [O.Fr. *gauvardine*; perh. M H.G. *wallevart,* pilgrimage, whence also Sp. *gabardina,* etc.]

gaberlunzie *gab-ər-lün′i, -yi,* later *-lun′zi,* (*Scot.*) *n.* a beggar's pouch: a strolling beggar, orig. a bluegown.

gabfest. See **gab**¹.

gabion *gā′bi-ən, n.* a wickerwork or wire basket of earth or stones used for embankment work, etc. in fortification and engineering: a small curiosity (*Scott*). — *ns.* (*fort.*) **gā′bionade** a work formed of gabions; **gā′bionage** gabions collectively. — *adj.* **gā′bioned** furnished with gabions. [Fr., — It. *gabbione,* a large cage — *gabbia* — L. *cavea,* a cage.]

gable *gā′bl,* (*archit.*) *n.* the triangular part of an exterior wall of a building between the top of the side-walls and the slopes on the roof — (*Scot.*) **gā′vel.** — *adj.* **gā′bled.** — *n.* **gā′blet** (*dim.*) a small gable over a niche, buttress, tabernacle, etc. — **gā′ble-end** the end-wall of a building on the side where there is a gable; **gā′ble=win′dow** a window in a gable-end: a window with its upper part shaped like a gable. [The northern form *gavel* is prob. O.N. *gafl*; Sw. *gafvel,* Dan. *gavl*; the

southern form *gable* is prob. through O.Fr. *gable,* from O.N. *gafl.*]

gabnash *gab′nash,* (*Scot.*) *n.* prattle: chatter: a pert prattler. [Cf. **nashgab.**]

gaby *gā′bi,* (*dial.*) *n.* a simpleton. [Origin unknown.]

gad¹ *gad, n.* a metal spike or pointed bar (*obs.*): a miner's wedge or chisel: a spear (*obs.*; also **gade, gaid** *gād*): a stylus (*Shak.*): a rod or stick (*obs.*): a goad (*dial.*): the bar across a Scottish condemned cell, on which the iron ring ran which fastened the shackles (*hist.*). — *n.* **gad′ling** (*obs.*) one of the spikes on the knuckles of a gauntlet. — **upon the gad** (*Shak.*) upon the spur of the moment. [O.N. *gaddr,* a spike; confused with O.E. *gād*; see **goad.**]

gad² *gad, interj.* a minced form of **God.** — *interj.* (*arch.*) **gadzooks′** an obs. minced oath (app. for *God's hooks*; see **gadso**).

gad³ *gad, v.i.* to rush here and there in a wayward uncontrolled manner (*obs.*): to wander about, often restlessly, idly or in pursuit of pleasure (often with *about*): to straggle: — *pr.p.* **gadd′ing**; *pa.t.* and *pa.p.* **gadd′ed.** — *n.* wandering, gadding about. — *n.* **gadd′er.** — **gad′about** one who wanders restlessly from place to place. [Prob. back-formation from **gadling**¹; or from **gadfly.**]

Gadarene *gad′ə-rēn, adj.* indicative of mass panic and headlong flight towards disaster. [From the swine of *Gadara,* Matt. viii. 28.]

gade. See **gad**¹ and **Gadus.**

gadfly *gad′flī, n.* a blood-sucking fly (Tabanus) that distresses cattle: sometimes applied to a botfly: a mischievous gadabout: someone who provokes and irritates, esp. deliberately. [**gad**¹ or O.E. *gād* (see **goad**) and **fly.**]

gadge *gaj,* (*Browning*) *n.* an instrument of torture.

gadget *gaj′it, n.* any small ingenious device; a what-d'ye-call-it. — *ns.* **gadgeteer′** one who delights in gadgets; **gad′getry** gadgets: the making of gadgets. [Origin obscure.]

gadgie, gadje *gaj′i,* **gaudgie, gauje** *gö′ji,* (*dial.*; usu. *derog.*) *ns.* a fellow. [Orig. variants of **gorgio.**]

Gadhel *gad′əl, n.* a Gael, a Celt of the branch to which the Irish, the Scottish Highlanders, and the Manx belong. — *adj.* **Gadhelic** (*-el′ik, -ēl′ik,* or *gad′*). — *n.* the Q-Celtic language of this group. — See also **Gael, Goidel.** [Ir. *Gaedheal* (pl. *Gaedhil*).]

gadi *gäd′ē, gud′ē, n.* an Indian throne. [Marathi *gādī,* Bengali *gadī.*]

gadje. See **gadgie.**

gadling¹ *gad′ling,* (*obs.*) *n.* a vagabond. [O.E. *gædeling,* orig. companion.]

gadling² See **gad**¹.

gadoid. See under **Gadus.**

gadolinite *gad′ə-lin-īt, n.* a silicate of yttrium, beryllium, and iron. — *n.* **gadolin′ium** a metal of the rare earths (symbol Gd; at. numb. 64). [From the Finnish chemist *Gadolin* (1760–1852).]

gadroon *gə-drōōn′, n.* a boss-like ornament, used in series in plate, etc., to form a cable or bead. — *adj.* **gadrooned′.** — *n.* **gadroon′ing.** [Fr. *godron.*]

gadsman *gadz′mən,* (*Scot.*) *n.* one who drives horses at the plough. [**gad**¹, or O.E. *gād* (see **goad**), and **man.**]

gadso *gad′sō,* (*arch.*) *interj.* expressing surprise: — *pl.* **gad′sos.** [It. *cazzo,* the penis, assimilated to **gad**².]

Gadus *gā′dəs, n.* the cod genus, typical of the family **Gadidae** (*gad′i-dē*). — *ns.* **gāde, gad′oid** a fish of the family. — *adj.* **gad′oid** codlike. [Latinised from Gr. *gados,* the hake or similar fish.]

gadwall *gad'wöl, n.* a northern freshwater duck. [Origin unknown.]

gadzooks. See **gad²**.

gae¹ *gā,* a Scots form of **go:** — *pr.p.* **gaun;** *pa.t.* **gaed;** *pa.p.* **gane.**

gae². See **gie**.

Gaea *gī'ə, jē'ə,* **Gaia** *gī'ə, gā'ə,* **Ge** *gā, jē, n.* in Greek mythology the goddess or personification of Earth, mother of Uranus and (by him) of Oceanus, Cronus and the Titans: (**Gaia**) Earth apprehended as a living entity within the Solar System. [Gr.]

Gaekwar, Gaikwar, Guicowar *gīk'wär, n.* the title given to the ruler of the former Indian state of Baroda. [Marathi *gāekwār,* cowherd.]

Gael *gāl, n.* one whose language is Gadhelic, esp. a Scottish Highlander. — *adj.* **Gaelic** (*gāl'ik, gal'ik*) pertaining to the Gaels: pertaining to sports, such as shinty and hurling, played especially in, or originating in, Ireland and the Scottish Highlands. — *n.* Gadhelic, the language of Ireland and (now *esp*) that of the Scottish Highlands. — *v.t.* **gael'icise, -ize** (*-sīz*) — *n.* **gael'icism** (*-sizm*). — **Gaelic coffee** same as **Irish coffee; Gaelic football** a form of football, played mainly in Ireland, between teams of 15 players using a round ball which may be kicked, bounced or punched, but not thrown or run with. — See also **Goidel.** [Scottish Gael. *Gaidheal.*]

Gaeltacht *gāl'tähht, n.* the Irish-speaking districts of Ireland. [Ir. *gaedhealtacht.*]

gaff¹ *gaf, n.* a hook used esp. for landing large fish: the spar to which the head of a fore-and-aft sail is bent (*naut.*). — *v.t.* to hook or bind by means of a gaff. — *adj.* **gaff'-rigged** (of a vessel) having a gaff. — **gaff'-sail** a sail attached to the gaff; **gaff'-topsail** a small sail, the head of which is extended on a small gaff which hoists on the top mast, and the foot on the lower gaff. [Fr. *gaffe.*]

gaff² *gaf,* (*slang*) *n.* a low theatre: a fair. [Origin obscure.]

gaff³. See **gaffe.**

gaff⁴ *gaf,* (*slang*) *v.i.* to gamble. — *ns.* **gaff'er; gaff'ing.** [Origin obscure.]

gaff⁵ *gaf,* (*slang*) *n.* humbug, nonsense. — **blow the gaff** to disclose a secret, to blab. [Prob. connected with **gab²** or **gaff³;** cf. O.E. *gegaf-spræc,* scurrility.]

gaffe, rarely **gaff,** *gaf, n.* a blunder. [Fr. *gaffe.*]

gaffer¹ *gaf'ər, n.* originally a word of respect applied to an old man, now familiar (*fem.* **gammer**): the foreman of a squad of workmen: (orig. *U.S.*) the senior electrician responsible for the lighting in a television or film studio. [**grandfather,** or **godfather.**]

gaffer², **gaffing.** See **gaff⁴.**

gag¹ *gag, v.t.* to stop the mouth of forcibly: to silence: to prevent free expression by (the press, etc.): to choke up. — *v.i.* to choke: to retch: — *pr.p.* **gagg'ing;** *pa.t.* and *pa.p.* **gagged.** — *n.* something put into the mouth or over it to enforce silence (also *fig.*), or to distend jaws during an operation: the closure applied in a debate: a nauseous mouthful, boiled fat beef (*Lamb*). — *n.* **gagg'er** one who gags. — **gag'-bit** a powerful bit used in breaking horses. [Prob. imitative of sound made in choking.]

gag² *gag,* (*slang*) *v.t.* to deceive. — *v.i.* to practise imposture. — *n.* a made-up story, lie. [Possibly **gag¹.**]

gag³ *gag,* (*coll.*) *n.* an actor's interpolation into his part: a joke: a hoax. — *v.i.* to introduce a gag: to joke. — *v.t.* to introduce a gag into. — *n.* **gag'ster** (*coll.*) one who tells jokes, a comedian. — **gag'man** one who writes gags: a gagster. [Possibly **gag¹.**]

gaga *gä'gä,* (*slang*) *adj.* fatuous: in senile dotage. [Fr.]

gagaku *gä-gä'kōō, gä'gä-, n.* a type of Japanese classical music played mainly on ceremonial occasions at the Japanese court. [Jap. — *ga,* graceful, noble, *gaku,* music.]

gage¹ *gāj, n.* a pledge: something thrown down as a challenge, as a glove. — *v.t.* to bind by pledge or security: to offer as a guarantee: to stake, wager.

[O.Fr. *guage;* Gmc.; see **wage, wed.**]

gage². See **gauge.**

gage³ *gāj.* Same as **greengage.**

G-agent. See under **G.**

gaggle *gag'l, n.* a flock of geese: a group, usu. of people. — *v.i.* to cackle. — *n.* **gagg'ling** cackling. — *adj.* garrulous. [Prob. imit.]

gag-tooth *gag'-tōōth, n.* a projecting tooth. — *adj.* **gag'-toothed.**

gahnite *gän'īt, n.* a zinc spinel. [J. G. *Gahn* (1745–1818), Swedish chemist.]

Gaia. See **Gaea.**

gaid. See **gad¹.**

Gaidhealtachd *gä'yal-tähht, n.* the Gaelic-speaking districts of Scotland. [Gael.]

gaiety, gaily. See **gay.**

Gaikwar. See **Gaekwar.**

gaillard(e) *gal'yərd.* Obs. forms of **galliard.**

gain¹ *gān, v.t.* to obtain to one's advantage: to earn: to win: to be successful in: to increase (speed, weight): to draw to one's own party: to reach. — *v.i.* to profit: to become or appear better, to progress: (of clock, etc.) to go fast by so much in a given time. — *n.* that which is gained: profit: an instance of gaining, a win: ratio of actual power delivered to that which would be delivered if an amplifier were not used (*telecomm.*): ratio of output and input voltages (*telecomm.*): (or **gain'-control**) volume control in amplifier, receiving set (*telecomm.*). — *adj.* **gain'able.** — *n.* **gain'er.** — *adj.* **gain'ful** lucrative: profitable: engaged in for pay, paid. — *adv.* **gain'fully.** — *n.* **gain'fulness.** — *n.pl.* **gain'ings.** — *adj.* **gain'less.** — *n.* **gain'lessness.** — **gain ground** see **ground²; gain on, upon** to overtake by degrees: to increase one's advantage against: to encroach on. [O.Fr. *gain, gaain, gaigner, gaaignier,* from Gmc., as in O.H.G. *weidenen,* to graze, to seek forage, *weida,* pasture.]

gain² *gān,* (*dial.*) *adj.* near, straight: convenient. [O.N. *gegn.*]

gaingiving *gān'giv-ing,* (*Shak.*) *n.* misgiving.

gainly *gān'li,* (*dial.*) *adj.* shapely: comely: graceful. [**gain².**]

gainsay *gān-sā', gān'sā, v.t.* to contradict: to deny: to dispute: — *pr.p.* **gainsay'ing** (or *gān'*); *pa.t.* and *pa.p.* **gainsaid** (*gān-sād', -sed',* or *gān'*); *3rd pers. sing. pres. indic.* **gainsays** (*-sāz*) — *n.* **gain'say** (or *-sā'*) denial. — *ns.* **gainsay'er** (*B.*) an opposer; **gainsay'ing.** [O.E. *gegn,* against, and **say.**]

gainst, 'gainst *genst.* A poetic abbreviation of **against.**

gainstrive *gān-strīv',* (*obs.*) *v.t.* to strive against. — *v.i.* to resist.

gair *gār,* (*Scot.*) *n.* a gore (of cloth or land). [See **gore².**]

gairfowl. Same as **garefowl.**

gait¹ *gāt, n.* way of walking: a horse's pace. — *adj.* **gait'ed** having a particular gait. [**gate².**]

gait² *gāt,* (*dial.*) *n.* a sheaf of corn set on end.

gait³, gaitt (*Scott*) spellings of **get,** a child, **gyte².**

gaiter *gāt'ər, n.* a covering for the ankle, fitting down upon the shoe. [Fr. *guêtre.*]

gajo. See **gorgio.**

gal¹ *gal,* dial. for **girl.**

gal² *gal,* (*phys.*) *n.* an unit of acceleration, one centimetre per second per second. [*Gal*ileo; see **Galilean¹.**]

gala *gä'lə, gā', n.* a festivity: a sporting occasion. — **ga'la-dress** gay costume for a gala day. [Fr. *gala,* show — It. *gala,* finery.]

galabi(y)ah. See **gal(l)abi(y)a(h).**

galactic *gə-lak'tik, adj.* pertaining to or obtained from milk: pertaining to a galaxy or galaxies (see **Galaxy**). — *ns.* **galac'tagogue** (*-tə-gog;* Gr. *agōgos,* bringing) a medicine that promotes secretion of milk; **galactom'-eter** (Gr. *metron,* measure) an instrument for finding the specific gravity of milk. — *adjs.* **galactoph'orous** (Gr. *phoros,* bringing) milk-carrying; **galactopoiet'ic** (Gr. *poiētikos,* productive) milk-producing. — *ns.* **galactorrhoea** (*-rē'ə;* Gr. *rhoiā,* a flow) a too abundant flow of milk; **galac'tose** a sugar, ($C_6H_{12}O_6$), got by hydrolysis from lactose; **galactosaemia** (-sēm'i-ə) the presence of galactose in the blood. [Gr. *gala, galaktos*, milk.]

galage *gəl-āj'*. An obs. form of **galosh** (*n.*).

Galago *gä-lä'gō, n.* a genus of large-eared, long-tailed nocturnal African lemurs.

galah *gə-lä', n.* an Australian cockatoo with pink underparts: a fool. [Aboriginal.]

Galam butter *gä-läm' but'ər*, shea butter. [*Galam*, a district on the Senegal.]

galanga, galangal. See **galingale**.

galant *gə-länt', adj.* of a musical style, current in the 18th cent., characterised by lightness, elegance and technical accomplishment. [Fr.]

galantine *gal'ən-tēn, -tin, n.* a dish of poultry, veal, etc., served cold in jelly. [Fr.; see **gelatine**.]

galanty show *gəl-an'ti shō*, a shadow pantomime. [Prob. It. *galanti*, pl. of *galante*; see **gallant**.]

galapago *gə-lap'ə-gō, n.* a tortoise: — *pl.* **galap'agos**. [Sp.]

galatea *gal-ə-tē'ə, n.* a cotton fabric usu. with coloured stripe. [19th cent. H.M.S. *Galatea*.]

Galaxy *gal'ək-si, n.* the Milky way, the luminous band of stars stretching across the heavens: (without *cap.*) any similar system or 'universe': (without *cap.*) a splendid assemblage. [Through Fr. and L., from Gr. *galaxias — gala, -aktos*, milk.]

galbanum *gal'bə-nəm, n.* a gum-resin got from Eastern species of Ferula. [L., — Gr. *chalbanē*, prob. an Eastern word.]

galdragon *gal'drə-gən*, (*Scott*) *n.* an obs. Shetland word for a sorceress, witch. [O.N. *galdra-kona — galdr*, crowing, incantation, witchcraft, *kuna*, woman.]

gale[1] *gāl, n.* a strong wind between a stiff breeze and a hurricane: in old poetic diction, a gentle wind: a wafted smell: an outburst. [Origin obscure.]

gale[2] *gāl, n.* (usu. **sweet'-gale**) bog-myrtle. [Prob. O.E. *gagel*; cf. Ger. *Gagel*.]

gale[3] *gāl, n.* a periodic payment of rent: a mining licence: the piece of land for which the licence is granted. [Perh. **gavel**[2].]

galea *gal'i-ə, gāl'i-ə*, (*biol.*) *n.* a helmet-shaped structure. — *adjs.* **gal'eate, -d.** [L. *galea*, a skin helmet.]

galena *gə-lē'nə, n.* lead-glance, native sulphide of lead. — Also **galē'nite.** — *adj.* **galē'noid.** [L. *galēna*, lead-ore.]

galengale. See **galingale**.

Galenic *gə-len'ik, adj.* pertaining to *Galen* (*Galēnos*), the 2nd-cent. Greek physician, or to his methods and theories. — *adj.* **Galen'ical.** — *n.* a remedy such as Galen prescribed, a vegetable simple. — *ns.* **Galenism** (*gā'lən-izm*); **Gā'lenist.**

galenite, galenoid. See **galena**.

Galeopithecus *gä-li-ō-pi-thē'kəs, -pith', n.* the so-called flying-lemur. — *adjs.* **galeopithē'cine** (-*sīn*), **galeopithē'-coid.** [Gr. *galeē*, weasel, marten, *pithēkos*, ape.]

galère *ga-ler', n.* a group of (esp. undesirable) people: an unpleasant situation. [Fr., lit. galley.]

Galilean[1] *gal-i-lē'ən, adj.* of or pertaining to *Galileo*, the great Italian mathematician (1564–1642).

Galilean[2] *gal-i-lē'ən, adj.* of or pertaining to *Galilee* (L. *Galilaea*, Gr. *Galilaiā*), one of the Roman divisions of Palestine. — *n.* a native of Galilee: a Christian.

galilee *gal'i-lē*, (*archit.*) *n.* a porch or chapel at the west end of some churches, in which penitents were placed, and where ecclesiastics met women who had business with them. — **galilee porch** a galilee in direct communication with the exterior. [Perh. suggested by Mark xvi. 7, or Matt. iv. 15.]

galimatias *gal-i-mā'shi-əs, -mat'i-äs, n.* nonsense: any confused mixture of unlike things. [Fr.]

galingale *gal'ing-gāl, n.* the aromatic rootstock of certain E. Indian plants of the ginger family (Alpinia and Kaempferia), formerly much used like ginger: the rootstock of a sedge (*Cyperus longus*), of ancient medicinal repute: also the whole plant. — Also **gal'-angal** (*gal'ən-gal*), **gal'engale, galang'a.** [O.Fr. *galin-*

gal — Ar. *khalanjān* — Chin. *ko-liang-kiang* — *Ko*, a district near Canton, *liang*, mild, and *kiang*, ginger.]

galiongee *gal-yən-jē', n.* a Turkish sailor. [Turk. *qālyūnjī*, deriv. of *qālyūn* — It. *galeone*, galleon.]

galiot. See **galliot.**

galipot *gal'i-pot, n.* the turpentine that exudes from the cluster-pine. [Fr.]

gall[1] *göl, n.* bile, the greenish-yellow fluid secreted from the liver: bitterness: malignity: assurance, presumption. — *adj.* **gall'-less** without gall: mild: free from rancour. — **gall'-bladder** a reservoir for the bile; **gall'-duct** a tube for conveying bile or gall; **gall'(-)sickness** (*S.Afr.*) a tick-borne disease affecting the livers of cattle, sheep and goats (Du. *galziekte*); **gall'-stone** a concretion in the gall-bladder or biliary ducts. [O.E. *galla, gealla*, gall; cf. Ger. *Galle*, Gr. *cholē*, L. *fel*.]

gall[2] *göl, n.* an abnormal growth on a plant owing to attack by a parasite (fungus, insect, etc.). — *n.* **gallate** (*gal'āt*) a salt of gallic acid. — **gall-fly** (*göl'-*), **gall'-wasp** an insect of the hymenopterous family Cynipidae that causes galls by depositing its eggs in plants; **gallic acid** (*gal'ik*) a crystalline substance obtained from gall-nuts, etc. — used in making ink; **gall-midge** (*göl'-*) a Cecidomyia or kindred gall-making midge; **gall'-nut** a nutlike gall produced on an oak by a gall-wasp, used esp. formerly for making ink. [Fr. *galle* — L. *galla*, oak-apple.]

gall[3] *göl, n.* a painful swelling, esp. in a horse: a sore due to chafing: a state or cause of irritation: a chafed place: a bare place (*arch.*): a flaw (*arch.*): a fault or a dyke (*mining*). — *v.t.* to fret or hurt by rubbing: to irritate. — *v.i.* to become chafed: to scoff (*Shak.*). — *adj.* **gall'ing** irritating. — *adv.* **gall'ingly.** [O.E. *galla, gealla*, a sore place.]

gal(l)abi(y)a(h), -bea(h), -bi(y)eh, etc., *gal-ä'bi-ya, -bē'a, n.* a loose-fitting cloak worn esp. by Arabs: a djellaba. [See **djellaba**.]

gallant *gal'ənt, adj.* brave: noble: gay, splendid, magnificent (*rare*): attentive (esp. formally or obsequiously) to ladies: amorous (sometimes *gə-lant'* in the last two senses). — *n.* a gay, dashing person: a man (*arch.*; woman *obs.*) of fashion: a lover (also *gə-lant'* in this sense). — *adv.* **gall'antly.** — *ns.* **gall'antness; gall'antry** bravery: intrepidity: attention or devotion to ladies, often in a bad sense, amorous intrigue: gallants collectively (*Shak.*). — **the honourable and gallant member** a mode of referring in parliament to a member who is an officer in the fighting services. [Fr. *galant* — O.Fr. *gale*, a merrymaking; prob. Gmc.; cf. **gala**.]

galleass *gal'i-as*, (*Shak.*) *n.* a vessel of the same construction as a galley, but larger and heavier. — Also **gall'iass.** [O.Fr. *galeace* — It. *galeazza*, augmentative from *galea*, galley.]

galleon *gal'i-ən, n.* a large vessel with lofty stem and stern, mostly used formerly by Spaniards for carrying treasure. [Sp. *galeón*; cf. **galley**.]

gallery *gal'ə-ri, n.* a covered walk: a long balcony: a long passage: an upper floor of seats, esp. in a theatre, the highest: the occupants of the gallery: a body of spectators: a room for the exhibition of works of art: an underground passage, drift, or level. — *v.t.* to tunnel. — *adj.* **gall'eried** furnished with, or arranged like, a gallery. — *n.* **gall'eryite** one who frequents the gallery in the theatre. — **play to the gallery** to play for the applause of the least cultured. [O.Fr. *galerie* (It. *galleria*).]

gallet *gal'ət, n.* a small pebble or stone chip. — *v.t.* to fill in mortar joints with gallets: — *pr.p.* **gall'eting; *pa.t.*** and *pa.p.* **gall'eted.** [Fr. *galet*, a pebble — O.Fr. *gal*.]

galley *gal'i, n.* a long, low-built ship with one deck, propelled by oars and sails: a Greek or Roman warship: a large open rowing-boat: the cooking place on board ship: a flat oblong tray for type that has been set up (*print.*): a galley-proof (*print.*). — **gall'ey-foist** (*obs.*) a state barge; **gall'ey-proof** an impression taken from type on a galley, a slip-proof: in photocomposition, an early proof before make-up; **gall′ey-slave** one condemned to work as a slave at the oar of a galley: a drudge; **gall′ey-worm** a myriapod. [O.Fr. *galie, galee* — L.L. *galea*.]

galley-west *gal-i-west′*, (*U.S. slang*) *adv.* into confusion or unconsciousness.

galliambic *gal-i-am′bik, adj.* in or of a metre (◡◡–◡–◡––|◡◡–◡◡◡–) said to have been used by the Phrygian priests of Cybele, best known from the *Attis* of Catullus. — *n.pl.* **galliam′bics** galliambic verses. [Gr. *galliambikos* — *Gallos*, a priest of Cybele, *iambos*, an iamb.]

galliard *gal′yərd, adj.* (*arch.*) brisk, lively. — *n.* a spirited dance for two, in triple time, common in the 16th and 17th centuries: a gay fellow (*arch.*). — *n.* **gall′iardise** (*arch.; -ēz, -īz*) gaiety: a merry trick. [O.Fr. *gaillard*.]

galliass. See **galleass.**

galli-bagger, -beggar, etc. See **gally.**

gallic. See **gall².**

Gallic *gal′ik, adj.* and *n.* Gaulish. — *adj.* **Gall′ican** of or pertaining to France: esp. pertaining to the Roman Catholic Church in France, regarded as national and more or less independent. — *n.* one holding Gallican doctrines. — *n.* **Gall′icanism** the spirit of nationalism within the French Church — as opposed to *Ultramontanism,* or the absolute subjection of everything to the personal authority of the pope. — *adv.* **Gallice** (*gal′i-sē;* L. *gal′i-kā*) in French. — (all the following also without *cap.*) *v.t.* and *v.i.* **Gall′icise, -ize** to assimilate or conform to French habits, etc. — *ns.* **Gall′icism** an expression or idiom peculiar to French occurring as a use in another language; **Gallomā′nia** a mania for French ways; **Gall′ophil(e)** one who is friendly to France; **Gall′ophobe** one who dislikes or fears France or what is French; **Gallophō′bia.** [L. *Gallus,* a Gaul; *Gallicus,* Gaulish.]

galligaskins *gal-i-gas′kinz, n.pl.* wide hose or breeches worn in 16th and 17th centuries: leggings. [O.Fr. *garguesque* — It. *grechesco,* Greekish — L. *graecus,* Greek.]

gallimaufry *gal-i-mö′fri,* (*Shak.*) *n.* any inconsistent or absurd medley: a miscellaneous gathering. [Fr. *galimafrée,* a ragout, hash.]

gallinaceous *gal-in-ā′shəs, adj.* akin to the domestic fowl. [L. *gallīna,* a hen — *gallus,* a cock.]

gallinazo *gal-i-nä′zō, n.* a turkey-buzzard or other vulture: — *pl.* **gallina′zos.** [Sp., — *gallina* — L. *gallīna,* hen.]

gallinule *gal′i-nūl, n.* a water-hen. [L. *gallīnula,* a chicken — *gallīna,* a hen.]

Gallio *gal′i-ō, n.* one who keeps himself free from trouble and responsibility: — *pl.* **Gall′ios.** [From *Gallio,* Acts xviii. 12–17.]

galliot, galiot *gal′i-ət, n.* a small galley: an old Dutch cargo-boat. [Fr. *galiote* — L.L. *galea,* galley.]

gallipot *gal′i-pot, n.* a small glazed pot, esp. for medicine. [Prob. a **pot** brought in **galleys.**]

gallise, -ize *gal′īz, v.t.* in wine-making, to bring to standard proportions by adding water and sugar to inferior must. — Also **gall′isise, -ize.** [Ger. *gallisieren,* from the name of the inventor, Dr. L. *Gall.*]

gallium *gal′i-əm, n.* a metallic element (symbol Ga; atomic number 31), as gallium arsenide an important semiconductor. [L. *gallus,* a cock, from the discoverer's name, *Lecoq* de Boisbaudran, or *Gallia,* Gaul, France, his country.]

gallivant *gal-i-vant′, v.i.* to spend time frivolously, esp. in flirting: to gad about. [Perh. **gallant.**]

gallivat *gal′i-vat, n.* a large two-masted Malay boat. [Port. *galeota;* see **galliot.**]

galliwasp *gal′i-wosp, n.* a W. Indian lizard.

galloglass, gallowglass *gal′ō-glas, n.* a soldier or armed retainer of a chief in ancient Ireland and other Celtic countries. [Ir. *gallóglach* — *gall,* foreign, *óglach,* soldier.]

gallon *gal′ən, n.* a unit of capacity, in Britain equal to 4·546 litres (277·4 cubic inches), also called **imperial**

gallon, in the U.S. equal to 3·785 litres (231 cubic inches). — *n.* **gall′onage** an amount in gallons: the rate of use in gallons. [O.N.Fr. *galun, galon* (O.Fr. *jalon*).]

galloon¹ *gə-lōōn′, n.* a kind of lace: a narrow tape-like trimming or binding material, sometimes made with gold or silver thread. — *adj.* **gallooned′** adorned with galloon. [Fr. *galon, galonner;* prob. cog. with **gallant.**]

galloon² *gə-lōōn′, n.* a variant of **galleon.**

gallop *gal′əp, v.i.* to go at a gallop: to ride a galloping animal: to move very fast. — *v.t.* to cause to gallop. — *n.* the fastest pace of a horse, etc., at each stride of which all four feet are off the ground: a ride at a gallop: a fast pace (*fig.*): a track for galloping. — *n.* **gall′oper** one who, or that which, gallops: an aide-de-camp (*mil.*): (esp. in *pl.*) a fairground merry-go-round wth wooden horses that rise and fall in the imitation of galloping. — *adj.* **gall′oping** proceeding at a gallop: advancing rapidly, as *galloping consumption* (*fig.*). — **Canterbury gallop** a moderate gallop of a horse (see **canter**). [O.Fr. *galoper, galop;* prob. Gmc.; cf. **wallop.**]

gallopade *gal-əp-ād′, n.* a quick kind of dance: the music appropriate to it: a sidewise gallop. — *v.i.* to move briskly: to perform a gallopade. [Fr.]

Gallophil(e), Gallophobe, etc. See **Gallic.**

Gallovidian *gal-ō-vid′i-ən, adj.* belonging to Galloway. — *n.* a native thereof. [*Gallovidia,* Latinised from Welsh *Gallwyddel.*]

gallow *ga′lō,* (*Shak.*) *v.t.* to frighten. [O.E. *āgǣlwan,* to frighten, to astonish.]

Galloway *gal′ō-wā, n.* a small strong horse, 13–15 hands high: a breed of large black hornless cattle, orig. from *Galloway* in Scotland.

Gallowegian. See **Galwegian.**

gallowglass. See **galloglass.**

gallows *gal′ōz,* or (old-fashioned) *gal′əs, n.sing.* (orig. *pl.*) wooden frame for hanging criminals: one who deserves the gallows (*Shak.*): the look of one destined to hang (*Shak.*): any contrivance with posts and crossbeam for suspending things: a rest for the tympan of a hand printing-press: the main frame of a beam-engine: one of a pair of trouser braces: — *pl.* (really double *pl.*) **gal(l)′owses** (used by *Shak.*, in first sense above; used *Scot.* and *dial.,* with various spellings — **gall′uses,** etc. — for trouser braces). — *adj.* (often **gall′us**) deserving the gallows: villainous (*Scot.* and *dial.*): mischievous, wild, unmanageable (*Scot.* and *dial.*): impudent, saucy, tiresome (*Scot.* and *dial.*): plucky, daring (*Scot.* and *dial.*): perky, spirited, sprightly (*Scot.* and *dial.*): in some dialects, a mere intensive. — *adv.* (often **gall′us**) (*dial.*) damnably, confoundedly. — *n.* **gall′owsness** (*slang*) recklessness. — **gall′ows-bird** one who deserves hanging or has been hanged; **gall′ows-foot.** — *adj.* **gall′ows-free** free from the danger of hanging. — **gall′ows-lee** the place of hanging; **gall′ows-maker.** — *adj.* **gall′ows-ripe′** ready for the gallows. — **gall′ows-tree′** a gallows. — **cheat the gallows** to deserve but escape hanging. [M.E. *galwes* (pl.) — O.E. *galga;* Ger. *Galgen.*]

gallumph. See **galumph.**

Gallup poll *gal′əp pōl,* a method of gauging public opinion by questioning suitably distributed sample individuals, devised by George Horace *Gallup* (b. 1901).

gallus *gal′əs.* An old, Scot. or dial. spelling of **gallows.**

gally *gal′i,* (*dial.*) *v.i.* to scare, daze. — **gall′y-bagg′er, -begg′ar, -crow** (also **galli-**) a scarecrow. [**gallow.**]

galoche. See **galosh.**

galoot *gə-lōōt′,* (*slang*) *n.* a soldier: a marine: a clumsy fellow.

galop *gal′əp, gə-lop′, n.* a lively dance or dance-tune in double time. — *v.i.* to dance a galop. [Fr.; cf. **gallop.**]

galopin *gal′ə-pin, n.* an errand boy (*Scott*): a kitchen boy (*obs.*). [Fr.]

galore *gə-lōr′, -lör′, adv.* in abundance. [Ir. *go,* adverbialising participle, *leōr,* sufficient.]

galosh, golosh, galoche *gə-losh'*, *n.* a rustic shoe, sandal, or clog (*obs.*): a piece running round a shoe or boot above the sole: an overshoe. — *v.t.* to furnish with a galosh. [Fr. *galoche* — prob. L.L. *gallicula*, small Gaulish shoe.]

galowses. Same as gallowses.

galravage, -itch. See gilravage.

Galtonia *gŏl-tō'ni-ə*, *gal-*, *n.* a genus of bulbous plants of the lily family, found in Southern Africa: (without *cap.*) a plant of this genus, esp. *G. candicans*, the Cape hyacinth. [Named after Sir Francis *Galton* (1822–1911), British scientist.]

galumph, gallumph *gə-lumf'*, *v.i.* to stride along exultantly: to bound about in an unco-ordinated, noisy way. — *n.* galum'pher. [A coinage of Lewis Carroll.]

galut(h) *gä-loōt'*, *gō'ləs*, *n.* (often *cap.*) forced exile of Jews, esp. (diaspora) from Palestine. [Heb. *gālūth*, exile.]

galvanism *gal'vən-izm*, *n.* current electricity (*obs.*): medical treatment by electric currents. — *adj.* galvanic (*-van'*) of, producing, produced by, galvanism (*obs.*): also *fig.* — *n.* galvanīsā'tion, *-z-*. — *v.t.* gal'vanise, -ize to subject to action of an electric current: to stimulate to spasmodic action by, or as if by, an electric shock: to confer a false vitality upon: to coat with metal by an electric current: to coat with zinc without using a current. — *ns.* gal'vaniser, -z-; gal'vanist; galvanom'eter an instrument for measuring electric currents; galvanom'etry. — *adj.* galvanoplas'tic (*obs.*). — *ns.* galvanoplas'ty (*obs.*) electrodeposition; galvan'oscope an instrument for detecting electric currents. — galvanic battery, cell (*obs.*) an electric battery, cell; galvanic belt (*obs.*) a belt supposed to benefit the wearer by producing an electric current; galvanised iron iron coated with zinc. [From Luigi *Galvani*, of Bologna, the discoverer (1737–98).]

Galwegian *gal-wē'ji-ən*, *adj.* belonging to Galloway in Scotland (also Gallowē'gian), or of Galway in Ireland. — *n.* a native of either place. [On the analogy of *Norwegian*.]

gam[1] *gam*, *n.* a school of whales: social intercourse or visit at sea (*U.S. old*). — *v.i.* to associate in a gam. — *v.t.* (*U.S. old*; specif. of whalers) to call on, exchange courtesies with. [Ety. dub.]

gam[2] *gam*, (*Scot.*) *n.* a tooth or tusk: the mouth.

gam[3]. See gamb.

-gam- -*gam-*, gamo- *gam'ō-*, *gam-o'*, in composition, (of) marriage: (of) union: (of) reproduction or fertilisation. — *n.* gamogen'esis sexual reproduction. — *adjs.* gamopet'alous with petals united; gamophyll'ous with perianth leaves united; gamosep'alous with sepals united; gamotrop'ic. — *n.* gamot'ropism the tendency of gametes to attract each other. — -gamous having a stated number of spouses, as *bigamous*: pertaining to a stated means of fertilization or reproduction, as *allogamous*; -gamy marriage, or supposed marriage, to a stated number of spouses: a stated means of fertilization or reproduction. [Gr. *gamos*, marriage.]

gama-grass *gä'mə-gräs*, *n.* a tall N. American forage grass (*Tripsacum dactyloides*). [Perh. Sp. *grama*.]

gamash *gəm-ash'*, *n.* a kind of legging. — Also gramash' (*Scott*), gramoche' (*-osh'*; *Scott*). [Fr. (now *dial.*) *gamache*, Prov. *garamacha*, apparently from *Ghadames*, famous for leather.]

gamb *gamb*, *n.* (*her.*) a beast's whole foreleg. — *n.* gam (*slang*) a human leg. [L.L. *gamba*, a leg.]

gamba *gam'bə*, *n.* short for viola da gamba: an organ-stop of string-like quality. — *n.* gam'bist a gamba-player.

gambado[1] *gam-bā'dō*, *n.* a leather covering or boot attached to a saddle: — *pl.* gambā'does, -os. [It. *gamba*, leg.]

gambado[2] *gam-bā'dō*, *n.* a bound or spring of a horse: a fantastic movement, a caper: — *pl.* gambā'does, -os. [Sp. *gambada*; cf. gambol.]

gambeson *gam'bi-sən*, *n.* an ancient leather or quilted cloth coat worn under the habergeon. [O.Fr., — O.H.G. *wamba*, belly.]

gambet *gam'bit*, *n.* the redshank. [It. *gambetta*, ruff, *gambetta fosca*, spotted redshank.]

gambier, gambir *gam'bēr*, *n.* an astringent substance prepared from the leaves of *Uncaria gambir*, a rubiaceous climbing shrub of the East Indies, used in tanning and dyeing. [Malay.]

gambist. See gamba.

gambit *gam'bit*, *n.* the (offer of a) sacrifice of a piece for the sake of an advantage in timing or position in the opening stages of a game (gam'bit-pawn', -piece' one so offered; *chess*): an initial move in anything, esp. one with an element of trickery (*fig.*). — *v.t.* to sacrifice or offer for sacrifice in a gambit (*chess*). [Sp. *gambito* — It. *gambetto*, a tripping up — *gamba*, leg.]

gamble *gam'bl*, *v.i.* to play for money, esp. for high stakes: to engage in wild financial speculations: to take great risks for the sake of possible advantage. — *v.t.* to squander or lose by staking: to take a chance (with *on*). — *n.* a transaction depending on chance. — *ns.* gam'bler one who gambles, esp. one who makes it his business; gam'bling. — gam'bling-house, -hell a house kept for the accommodation of people who play at games of hazard for money. [Freq. of game[1].]

gamboge *gam-boōzh'*, *-bōj'*, *-boōj'*, *n.* a yellow gum-resin, chiefly got from *Garcinia morella*, used as a pigment and in medicine. — *adjs.* gambogian (*-bōj'*, *-boōj'*), gambogic (*-bōj'*). [From *Cambodia*, whence it was brought about 1600.]

gambol *gam'bl*, *v.i.* to leap: to frisk in sport: — *pr.p.* gam'bolling; *pa.t.* and *pa.p.* gam'bolled. — *n.* a frisk: a frolic. [Formerly *gambold* — O.Fr. *gambade* — It. *gambata*, a kick — L.L. *gamba*, leg.]

gambrel *gam'brəl*, *n.* the hock of a horse: a crooked stick for hanging a carcass, etc. — gambrel roof a mansard roof. [O.Fr. *gamberel*; cf. Fr. *gambier*, a hooked stick; connection with cambrel obscure.]

gambroon *gam-broōn'*, *n.* a twilled cloth of worsted and cotton, or linen. [Prob. *Gambrun*, in Persia.]

game[1] *gām*, *n.* sport of any kind: (in *pl.*) athletic sports: a contest for recreation: a competitive amusement according to a system of rules: the state of a game: manner of playing a game: form in playing: the requisite number of points to be gained to win a game: jest, sport, trick: any object of pursuit: scheme or method of seeking an end, or the policy that would be most likely to attain it: business, activity, operation: fighting spirit (*arch.*): gallantry (*Shak.*): (usu. the game) prostitution (*slang*): thieving (*slang*): the spoil of the chase: wild animals hunted by sportsmen: the flesh of such animals: a flock of swans (formerly of other animals) kept for pleasure. — *adj.* of or belonging to animals hunted as game: having the spirit of a fighting cock (*coll.*): plucky, courageous (*coll.*): having the necessary spirit and willingness for some act (*coll.*). — *v.i.* to gamble. — *adv.* game'ly. — *n.* game'ness. — *adj.* game'some playful. — *ns.* game'someness; game'ster a gambler: a lewd person (*Shak.*): a maker of sport (*Shak.*). — *adj.* game'sy keen on sports. — *n.* gam'ing gambling. — *adj.* gā'my having the flavour of game, esp. that kept till tainted: savouring of scandal, sensational: spirited, plucky (*coll.*). — game'-bag a bag for holding a sportsman's game; game ball see game point; game'-bird a bird hunted for sport; game call (*bridge*) a bid (and contract) which, if successful, will win a game; game'-chick'en, game'-cock a cock of a breed trained to fight; game chips thinly-cut (usu. disc-shaped) potato chips served with game; game'-dealer; game fish any freshwater fish of the salmon family except the grayling (opp. to *coarse fish*); game fishing; game'keeper one who has the care of game (also *fig.*); game laws laws relating to the protection of game; game licence a licence to kill, or to sell, game; game plan the strategy or tactics used by a football team, etc.: any carefully devised strategy; game point, game ball the stage at which the next point wins the game; game preserve a tract of land stocked with game preserved for sport or with protected wild animals;

game preserver one who preserves game on his land; **games'manship** (*facet.* — Stephen Potter) the art of winning games by talk or conduct aimed at putting one's opponent off; **games theory** (*math.*) the theory concerned with analysing the choices and strategies available in a game or other conflict in order to choose the optimum course of action; **game tenant** one who rents the privilege of shooting or fishing over a particular area; **game warden** a person who looks after game, esp. in a game preserve; **gam'ing-house** a gambling-house; **gam'ing-ta'ble** a table used for gambling. — **big game** the larger animals hunted; **die game** to keep up courage to the last; **give the game away** to disclose a secret; **have a game with, make game of** to make sport of, to ridicule; **off one's game** playing badly; **on one's game** playing well; **on the game** earning one's living as a prostitute; **play a waiting game** see **wait**; **play the game** to act in a fair, sportsmanlike, straightforward manner; **red game** grouse; **round game** a game, as at cards, in which the number of players is not fixed; **the game is not worth the candle** see **candle; the game is up** the game is started: the scheme has failed.   [O.E. *gamen*, play; O.N. *gaman*, Dan. *gammen*.]

game² *gām, adj.* lame.   [Origin obscure.]

gamelan *gam'ə-lan, n.* an instrument resembling a xylophone: an orchestra of S.E. Asia consisting of percussion (chiefly), wind, and stringed instruments.   [Javanese.]

gamete *gam'ēt, gam-ēt', n.* a sexual reproductive cell — an egg-cell or sperm-cell. — *adjs.* **gam'etal** (or *-ēt'*), **gametic** (*-et'* or *-ēt'*). — *ns.* **gametangium** (*gam-it-an'ji-əm*) a cell or organ in which gametes are formed: — *pl.* **gametan'gia; gametogen'esis** the formation of gametes; **gamē'tophyte** (or *gam'; Gr. phyton*, plant) in alternation of generations, a plant of the sexual generation, producing gametes.   [Gr. *gametēs*, husband, *gametē*, wife — *gameein*, to marry.]

Gamgee tissue *gam'jē tish'ōō, -ū, tis'ū,* (sometimes without *cap.*) a type of wound-dressing consisting of cotton-wool between two layers of gauze.   [After its inventor, J. S. *Gamgee* (1828–1886), English surgeon.]

gamic *gam'ik, adj.* sexual: sexually produced.   [Gr. *gamikos — gamos*, marriage.]

gamin *gam'in, ga-mē̃, n.* a street urchin, a precocious and mischievous imp of the pavement: — *fem.* **gamine** (*-mēn'*) a girl of a pert, boyish, impish appearance and disposition. — *adj.* boyish or impish. — *n.* **gaminerie** (*gam'in-ri, gam-ēn-(ə-)rē*).   [Fr.]

gamma, *gam'ə, n.* the third letter of the Greek alphabet (Γ, γ = G, g): as a numeral γ' = 3, ͵γ = 3000: in classification, the third or one of the third grade, (one of) the grade below beta. — *ns.* **gammad'ion, gammā'tion** (*-ti-on*) a figure composed of capital gammas, esp. a swastika. — **gamma camera** a device which detects gamma radiation and which is used to produce images of parts of the body into which radioactive material has been introduced; **gamma globulin** any of a group of globulins occurring in blood plasma which contain antibodies that protect against various diseases; **gamma rays** a penetrating radiation given off by radium and other radioactive substances.   [Gr.]

gamme *gam, n.* a musical scale: range, spectrum, gamut.   [Fr., — Gr. *gamma*; cf. **gamut**.]

gammer *gam'ər, n.* an old woman (*masc.* **gaffer**).   [**grandmother**, or **godmother**.]

gammerstang *gam'ər-stang,* (*dial.*) *n.* a tall, awkward person, esp. a woman: a wanton girl.   [Perh. **gammer** and **stang¹**.]

Gammexane® *gam-eks'ān, n.* a powerful insecticide.   [γ-hexachlorocyclo*hexane*.]

gammock *gam'ək,* (*dial.*) *n.* a frolic, fun. — *v.i.* to frolic, to lark.

gammon¹ *gam'ən, n.* backgammon (*arch.*): a double game at backgammon, won by bearing all one's men before one's opponent bears any: patter, chatter, esp. that of a thief's confederate to divert attention (*slang*): nonsense, humbug. — *v.t.* to defeat by a gammon at

backgammon: to hoax, impose upon. — *v.i.* to talk gammon: to feign. — *ns.* **gamm'oner; gamm'oning.**   [Prob. O.E. *gamen*, a game.]

gammon² *gam'ən, n.* the ham of a hog, esp. when cured, now usually with the adjacent parts of the side.   [O.N.Fr. *gambon, gambe,* leg.]

gammon³ *gam'ən,* (*naut.*) *n.* the lashing of the bowsprit. — *v.t.* to lash (the bowsprit).

gammy *gam'i,* (*dial.*) *adj.* lame: maimed.   [Cf. **game².**]

gamo-, -gamous. See **-gam-.**

gamp *gamp,* (*coll.*) *n.* a large, untidy umbrella: an umbrella. — *adj.* **gamp'ish** bulging.   [From Mrs Sarah *Gamp,* in Dickens's *Martin Chuzzlewit.*]

gamut *gam'ət, n.* the note G on the first line of the bass stave (*hist. mus.*): Guido of Arezzo's scale of six overlapping hexachords, reaching from that note up to E in the fourth space of the treble (*hist. mus.*): any recognised scale or range of notes: the whole compass of a voice or instrument: the full extent of anything.   [From *gamma,* the Gr. letter G, adopted when it was required to name a note added below the A with which the old scale began, and *ut,* the Aretinian (q.v.) syllable.]

gamy. See **game¹.**

-gamy. See **-gam-.**

gan *gan, pa.t.* of **gin⁵.**

ganch, gaunch *gänsh, -ch, gönsh, -ch, v.t.* to impale: to lacerate. — *n.* impaling apparatus: a wound from a boar's tusk.   [O.Fr. *gancher* — It. *gancio,* a hook.]

gander *gan'dər, n.* the male of the goose: a simpleton: a man living apart from his wife (*U.S. arch.*). — *n.* **gan'derism.** — **gan'der-moon, -month** the month of a wife's lying-in (*U.S. dial.*); **gan'der-mooner** a husband during his gander-moon (*U.S. dial.*). — **take a gander at** (*slang*) to take a look at.   [O.E. *ganra, gandra;* Du. and L.G. *gander.*]

gandy dancer *gan'di dän'sər,* (*U.S. coll.*) a railway labourer: any manual labourer: an itinerant or seasonal labourer.   [Prob. from the *Gandy* Manufacturing Company, which made tools used by railway workmen.]

gane *gān, pa.p.* of **gae¹.**

Ganesa *gən-ā'sha, n.* the elephant-headed Hindu god of wisdom and success.

gang¹ *gang, n.* a band of roughs or criminals: a number of persons or animals (esp. elk) associating together: a number of labourers working together: a set of boys who habitually play together: a set of tools, etc., used together. — *v.t.* and *v.i.* to associate in a gang or gangs. — *v.t.* to adjust in co-ordination. — *ns.* **ganger** (*gang'-ər*) the foreman of a gang of labourers; **gang'ing; gang'ster** a member of a gang of roughs or criminals; **gang'sterdom; gang'sterism.** — **gang'-bang** (*slang*) successive sexual intercourse with one, usu. unwilling, female by a group of males; **gang'land, gang'sterland** the domain of gangsters, the world of (esp. organised) crime; **gang mill** a sawmill with gang saws; **gang'-rape'** a number of successive rapes committed by members of a group on one victim on one occasion. — *v.t.* **gang'-rape.** — **gang saw** a saw fitted in a frame with others; **gangs'man** the foreman of a gang. — **Gang of Four** a term applied to a group of four of Chairman Mao's leading advisers after their political downfall (also without *caps.*; sometimes *facet.*) any similar group in politics, etc.; **gang punch** (*comput.*) to punch (the same information) in a number of cards, or (a number of cards) with the same information; **gang up on** to make a concerted attack on; **gang up with** to join in the (doubtful) activities of.   [O.E. *gang* (Dan. *gang,* Ger. *Gang*) — *gangan,* to go.]

gang² *gang, v.i.* and *v.t.* (*Scot.*) to go: — *pr.p.* **gang'ing** (*rare*); *pa.p.* and *pa.t.* not in use. — *n.* (*Scot.*) the range of pasture allowed to cattle. — *ns.* **gang'er** a walker (*Scot.*): a fast horse (*dial.*); **gang'rel** (*Scot.*) vagrant: a child beginning to walk. — Also *adj.* — **gang'board** (*naut.*) a gang-way, plank, or platform for walking on; **gang'-bye** (*Scot.*) the go-by; **Gang Days** (*obs. Scot.*)

Rogation Days; **gang'plank** a long, narrow, portable platform providing access to and from a ship. — *adj.* **gang'-there-out** (*arch. Scot.*) vagrant. — **gang'way** (O.E. *gangweg*) a passage into, out of, or through any place, esp. a ship: a way between rows of seats, esp. the cross-passage about halfway down the House of Commons (ministers and ex-ministers with their immediate followers sitting *above the gangway*). — *interj.* make way: make room to pass. [O.E. *gangan*, to go.] **gang³**. See **gangue.**

gangling *gang'gling, adj.* loosely-built, lanky. — Also **gangly** (*gang'gli*). [Orig. Scot. and Eng. dialect; O.E. *gangan*, to go.]

ganglion *gang'gli-ən, n.* a tumour in a tendon sheath: a nerve-centre: — *pl.* **gang'lia, gang'lions.** — *adjs.* **gang'liar, ganglionic** (*-on'ik*) pertaining to a ganglion; **gang'liate, -d** provided with ganglion or ganglia; **gang'liform.** [Gr.]

gangrel. See **gang².**

gangrene *gang'grēn, n.* death of part of the body: the first stage in mortification. — *v.t.* to mortify: to cause gangrene in. — *v.i.* to become gangrenous. — *adj.* **gangrenous** (*gang'grin-əs*) mortified. [Gr. *gangraina*, gangrene.]

gangue, gang *gang, n.* rock in which ores are embedded. [Fr., — Ger. *Gang* a vein.]

gangway. See **gang².**

ganister, gannister *gan'is-tər, n.* a hard, close-grained siliceous stone, found in the Lower Coal Measures of N. England. [Origin unknown.]

ganja *gän'jə, n.* an intoxicating preparation, the female flowering tops of Indian hemp, i.e. marijuana. [Hind. *gājā.*]

gannet *gan'ət, n.* a large white sea-bird of the family Sulidae, with black-tipped wings: a greedy person (*coll.*). — See also **solan.** — *n.* **gann'etry** a breeding-place of gannets. [O.E. *ganot*, a sea-fowl; Du. *gent.*]

gannister. See **ganister.**

ganoid *gan'oid, adj.* (of fish scales) having a glistening outer layer over bone: (of fishes) belonging to an order **Ganoid'ei** (*-i-ī*) in some classifications, variously defined, having commonly such scales, including many fossil forms. — *n.* a ganoid fish. — *n.* **ganoin** (*gan'ō-in*) a calcareous substance, forming an enamel-like layer on ganoid scales. [Gr. *ganos*, brightness, *eidos*, appearance.]

gant, gaunt *gänt, gönt,* (*Scot.*) *vs.i.* to yawn. — *ns.* a yawn. [Prob. freq. of O.E. *gānian*, to yawn.]

gantlet. Same as **gauntlet¹,².**

gantline *gant'līn,* (*naut.*) *n.* a rope used in a single-block hoist. [Variation of **girt** or **girth²** and **line².**]

gantlope *gant'lōp.* See **gauntlet².**

gantry *gan'tri, n.* a stand for barrels: the shelving, racks, etc. in which drinks are displayed in a bar: a platform or bridge for a travelling-crane, railway signals, etc. — Also (in first sense) **gauntry** (*gön'tri*) **gaun'tree.** — **gantry crane** a crane in bridge form with vertical members running on parallel tracks. [Perh. O.Fr. *gantier* — L. *cantērius*, a trellis — Gr. *kanthēlios*, a pack-ass.]

Ganymede *gan'i-mēd, n.* a cupbearer, pot-boy, from *Ganymēdēs*, the beautiful youth who succeeded Hebe as cupbearer to Zeus: a catamite (*arch.*).

gaol, etc. See **jail,** etc.

gap *gap, n.* an opening or breach: a cleft: a passage: a notch or pass in a mountain-ridge: a breach of continuity: an unfilled space, a lack: a divergence, disparity. — *v.t.* to notch: to make a gap in. — *adj.* **gapp'y** full of gaps. — **gap site** a piece of land in a built-up area lying empty because the building which once stood on it has been demolished. — *adj.* **gap'-toothed** with teeth set wide apart. [O.N. *gap.*]

gape *gāp, v.i.* to open the mouth wide: to yawn: to stare with open mouth: to be wide open: to bawl (*Shak.*). — *n.* act of gaping: the extent to which the mouth can be opened: the angle of the mouth: a wide opening, parting, fissure, chasm, or failure to meet: in a fish-

hook, the width between the point and the shank: (in *pl.*) a yawning fit: (in *pl.*) a disease of birds of which gaping is a symptom, caused by a thread-worm, *Syngamus,* or **gape'worm,** in the windpipe and bronchial tubes. — *n.* **gā'per** one who gapes: a mollusc (*Mya*) with shell gaping at each end: a sea-perch (*Serranus*): an easy catch (*cricket*). — *n.* and *adj.* **gā'ping.** — *adv.* **gā'pingly.** — **gape'seed** (*dial.*) an imaginary commodity that the gaping starer is supposed to be seeking or sowing: hence, the act of staring open-mouthed, or the object stared at. [O.N. *gapa,* to open the mouth; Ger. *gaffen,* to stare.]

gapó *gä-pō', n.* riverside forest periodically flooded: — *pl.* **gapós'.** [Port. (*i*)*gapó* — Tupí *igapó, ygapó.*]

gar¹. See **garfish.**

gar² *gär,* (chiefly *Scot.*) *v.t.* to cause, to compel: — *pa.t.* and *pa.p.* **garred, gart** (*Scot.*). — Also (*Spens.*) **garre.** [Norse *ger*(*v*)*a,* to make; cf. **yare.**]

garage *gar'äzh, gə-räzh', gar'ij, n.* a building where motor-vehicles are housed or tended. — *v.t.* to put into or keep in a garage. — *n.* **gar'aging** accommodation for cars, etc. — **garage sale** a sale of various items held on the seller's premises, esp. in his garage. [Fr., — *garer,* to secure; cf. **ware³.**]

garam masala *gar'əm məs-ä'lə,* a spice mixture used in making curry.

Garamond *gar'ə-mənd, n.* a form of type-face like that designed by Claude *Garamond* (d. 1561).

Garand rifle *gar'ənd* or *gə-rand' rī'fl,* a semi-automatic, gas-operated, clip-fed, .30 calibre, U.S. army rifle; also called **M1.** [After U.S. inventor J. C. *Garand,* (1888–1974).]

garb¹ *gärb, n.* external appearance (*obs.*): fashion of dress: dress: semblance, appearance (*fig.*). — *v.t.* to clothe, array. [It. *garbo,* grace; of Gmc. origin; cf. **gear.**]

garb², garbe *gärb,* (*her.*) *n.* a sheaf. [O.Fr. *garbe*; of Gmc. origin.]

garbage *gär'bij, n.* refuse, as animal offal: any worthless matter: household food and other refuse. — *ns.* **gar'bo** (*Austr. coll.*) a dustman: — *pl.* **gar'bos; garbol'ogist** (*usu. facet.*) a dustman. — **gar'bageman** (*U.S.*) a dustman; **garbage can** (*U.S.*) a bin for food-waste, etc. [Of doubtful origin.]

garbanzo *gär-ban'zō, n.* a chick-pea: — *pl.* **-zos.** [Sp.]

garble *gär'bl, v.t.* to cleanse, sift (*arch.*): to select what may serve one's own purpose from, esp. in a bad sense (*arch.*): to misrepresent or falsify by suppression and selection: to mangle, mutilate. — *ns.* **gar'bler; gar'bling.** [It. *garbellare* — Ar. *ghirbál,* a sieve, perh. — L.L. *cribellum,* dim. of *cribrum,* a sieve.]

garbo. See **garbage.**

garboard *gär'bōrd, -börd, n.* the first range of planks or plates laid on a ship's bottom next to the keel. — Also **garboard strake.** [Du. *gaarboord.*]

garboil *gär'boil,* (*Shak.*) *n.* disorder, uproar. [O.Fr. *garbouil* — It. *garbuglio,* conn. with L. *bullīre,* to boil.]

garbologist. See **garbage.**

Garcinia *gär-sin'i-ə, n.* a tropical genus of Guttiferae, trees yielding gamboge, kokum butter, and mangosteen. [After the French botanist Laurent *Garcin.*]

garçon *gär-sɔ̃, n.* a boy: a male servant, esp. a waiter in a restaurant. [Fr.]

garda *gör'də, n.* an Irish policeman or guard: — *pl.* **gardai** (*gör'də-ē*). — **Garda Siochana** (*shē'hhə-nə;* lit. guard of peace. — Ir. *síocháin,* peace) the Irish police force. [Ir. *gárda.*]

gardant (*her.*). Same as **guardant** (see under **guard**).

garden *gär'dən, n.* a piece of ground on which flowers, etc., are cultivated: a pleasant spot: a fertile region: (in *pl.*) used in street-names. — *adj.* of, used in, grown in, a garden or gardens. — *v.i.* to cultivate or work in a garden. — *ns.* **gar'dener** one who gardens, or is skilled in gardening: one employed to tend a garden; **gar'dening** the laying out and cultivation of gardens. — **garden centre** an establishment where plants, gardening equipment, etc. are sold; **garden city, suburb, village** a model town, suburb, village, laid out with broad roads, trees, and much garden ground between the houses; **gardener's garters** variegated garden ribbon-grass; **gar′den-glass** a bell-glass for covering plants; **gar′den-house** a summerhouse (*Shak.*): a house in a garden: a house kept for sensual indulgence (*obs.*); **garden party** a social gathering held in the garden of a house; **garden patch; garden path; garden stuff** garden produce for the table. — **everything in the garden is lovely** all is, or appears to be, well; **hanging garden** a garden formed in terraces rising one above another; **lead someone up the garden (path)** to draw someone on insensibly, to mislead someone; **market garden** a garden in which vegetables, fruits, etc., are raised for sale; **market gardener; philosophers of the garden** followers of Epicurus, who taught in a garden.   [O.Fr. *gardin* (Fr. *jardin*); from Gmc.; cf. **yard², garth.**]

Gardenia gär-dē′ni-ə, *n.* a genus of the madder family, Old World tropical and sub-tropical trees and shrubs with fragrant, usu. white flowers of a waxy appearance: (without *cap.*) a member of the genus.   [Named from the American botanist Dr Alex. *Garden* (*c.* 1730–91).]

garderobe gärd′rōb, (*hist.*) *n.* a wardrobe or its contents: an armoury: a private room: a privy.   [Fr.; cf. **wardrobe.**]

gardyloo gär′di-lōō, *interj.* the old warning cry in Edinburgh before throwing slops out of the window into the street. — *n.* the slops so thrown, or the act of throwing.   [Recorded in this form by Smollett; supposed to be would-be Fr. *gare de l'eau* for *gare l'eau*, beware of the water; Sterne has *garde d'eau* (*Sent. Journey*), for Paris.]

gare gär, (*Scot.*) *adj.* greedy, miserly.   [O.N. *gerr*; cf. **yare.**]

garefowl gär′fowl, *n.* the great auk.   [O.N. *geirfugl.*]

garfish gär′fish, *n.* a pike-like fish (*Belone*) with long slender beaked head: the bony pike, an American ganoid river-fish (*Lepidosteus*): any of various similar Australian fish. — Also **gar, gar′pike.**   [O.E. *gār*, spear.]

garganey gär′gə-ni, *n.* a bird akin to the teal, the summer teal.   [It. *garganello.*]

Gargantuan gär-gan′tū-ən, *adj.* like or worthy of Rabelais's hero *Gargantua*, a giant of vast appetite: enormous, prodigious (without *cap.*). — *ns.* **Gargan′tuism; Gargan′tuist.**

gargarism gär′gə-rizm, (*obs.*) *n.* a gargle — *v.t.* and *v.i.* **gar′garise, -ize.**

garget gär′git, *n.* inflammation of the throat or udder in cows, swine, etc.: (also **garget plant**) pokeweed (*U.S.*).

gargle gär′gl, *v.t.* and *v.i.* to wash (the throat) preventing the liquid from going down by expelling air against it. — *n.* a liquid for washing the throat.   [O.Fr. *gargouiller* — *gargouille*, the throat.]

gargoyle gär′goil, *n.* a projecting spout, usually grotesquely carved, from a roof-gutter: any grotesque figure or person. — Also **gur′goyle.** — *n.* **gar′goylism** (*med.*) a rare condition characterised by grotesque physical deformity and severe mental disablement.   [O.Fr. *gargouille* — L.L. *gurgulio*, throat.]

garial. See **gavial.**

garibaldi gar-i-böl′di, *-bal′di, n.* a woman's loose blouse, an imitation of the red shirts worn by followers of the Italian patriot *Garibaldi* (1807–1882). — **Garibaldi biscuit** a biscuit with a layer of currants.

garigue. See **garrigue.**

garish¹ gär′ish, *adj.* showy; gaudy: glaring. — *adv.* **gar′-ishly.** — *n.* **gar′ishness.**   [Formerly also *gaurish, gawrish*, perh. — *obs. guare*, to stare, perh. a freq. of *obs. gaw*, to stare; cf. O.N. *gā*, to heed.]

garish². See **guarish.**

garjan. See **gurjun.**

garland gär′lənd, *n.* a crown (*obs.*): a wreath of flowers or leaves: a book of selections in prose or poetry: ornament, glory (*Spens.; Shak.*). — *v.t.* to deck with a garland. — *n.* **gar′landage** (*Tenn.*) a decoration of garlands. — *adj.* **gar′landless.** — *n.* **gar′landry** garlands

collectively.   [O.Fr. *garlande.*]

garlic gär′lik, *n.* a bulbous liliaceous plant (*Allium sativum*) having a pungent taste and very strong smell: extended to others of the genus, as **wild garlic** (ramsons). — *adj.* **gar′licky** like garlic. — **gar′lic-mus′tard** a tall cruciferous hedge plant (*Sisymbium alliaria*) with garlicky smell.   [O.E. *gārlēac* — *gār*, a spear, *lēac*, a leek.]

garment gär′mənt, *n.* any article of clothing. — *v.t.* to clothe as with a garment. — *adjs.* **gar′mented; gar′-mentless.** — *n.* **gar′menture** clothing.   [O.Fr. *garniment* — *garnir*, to furnish.]

garner gär′nər, *n.* a granary: a store of anything. — *v.t.* to store. — *v.i.* (*Tenn.*) to accumulate.   [O.Fr. *gernier* (Fr. *grenier*) — L. *grānārium* (usu. in pl.), a granary.]

garnet¹ gär′nit, *n.* a mineral, in some varieties a precious stone, generally red, crystallising in dodecahedra and icositetrahedra, an orthosilicate of a bivalent and a tervalent metal. — *adj.* **garnetif′erous.** — **gar′net-paper** abrasive paper similar to glass-paper; **gar′net-rock** a rock composed of garnet with hornblende and magnetite.   [O.Fr. *grenat* — L.L. *grānātum*, pomegranate; or L.L. *grānum*, grain, cochineal, red dye.]

garnet² gär′nit, *n.* a hoisting tackle.   [Origin obscure.]

garnet³ gär′nit, *n.* a T-shaped hinge.   [Possibly O.Fr. *carne* — L. *cardō, īnis*, hinge.]

garni. See **garnish.**

garnierite gär′ni-ər-īt, *n.* a green hydrated nickel, magnesium silicate.   [Jules *Garnier*, who discovered it in New Caledonia.]

garnish gär′nish, *v.t.* to adorn: to furnish: to add herbs, etc., to a dish for flavour or decoration: to garnishee. — *n.* a gift of money, esp. that formerly paid to fellow-prisoners on entering prison or sometimes by workmen on starting a new job: something placed round a principal dish at table, whether for embellishment or relish: decoration, embellishment. — *adj.* **garni** (*gär-nē*) garnished. — *n.* **gar′nishee** a person warned not to pay money owed to another, because the latter is indebted to the garnisher who gives the warning. — *v.t.* to attach in this way: to serve with a garnishment. — *ns.* **garnishee′ment; gar′nisher** one who garnishes; **gar′nishing; gar′nishment** that which garnishes or embellishes: ornament: a garnisheement; **gar′nishry** adornment; **gar′niture** that which garnishes or embellishes: trimming: apparel: ornamentation, esp. set of ornaments, e.g. vases: set of armour.   [O.Fr. *garniss-*, stem of *garnir*, to furnish (old form *warnir*), from a Gmc. root seen in O.E. *warnian*, Ger. *warnen*; cf. **warn¹.**]

garotte. See **garrotte.**

garpike. See **garfish.**

garran. Same as **garron.**

garre. See **gar².**

garret gar′it, *n.* a turret or watch-tower (*obs.*): a room just under the roof of a house. — *adj.* **garr′eted** provided with garrets: lodged in a garret. — *n.* **gar-reteer′** (*arch.*) one who lives in a garret, esp. a poor author. — **garr′et-master** a cabinet-maker, locksmith, etc., working on his own account for the dealers.   [O.Fr. *garite*, a place of safety, *guarir, warir*, to preserve (Fr. *guérir*), from the Gmc. root seen in **ware¹.**]

garrigue, garigue ga-rēg′, *n.* uncultivated open scrubland of the Mediterranean region: the scrub growing on it.   [Fr. — Prov. *garriga*, stony ground.]

garrison gar′i-sn, *n.* a supply of soldiers for guarding a fortress: a fortified place. — *v.t.* to furnish with troops: to defend by fortresses manned with troops. — **garrison town** a town in which a garrison is stationed.   [O.Fr. *garison* — *garir, guerir*, to furnish; Gmc.; see **garret.**]

garron, garran gar′ən, *n.* a small horse.   [Ir. *gearran.*]

garrot¹ gar′ət, *n.* a name for various ducks.   [Fr.]

garrot² gar′ət, (*surg.*) *n.* a tourniquet.   [Fr.]

garrotte, garotte, (*U.S.*) **garrote** gä-rot′, gə-rot′, *n.* a Spanish mode of putting criminals to death: the ap-

paratus for the purpose — originally a string round the throat tightened by twisting a stick, later a brass collar tightened by a screw, whose point enters the spinal marrow. — *v.t.* to execute by the garrotte: suddenly to render insensible by semi-strangulation in order to rob: - *pr.p.* **garrott'ing, garott'ing;** *pa.t.* and *pa.p.* **garrott'ed, garott'ed.** — *ns.* **gar(r)ott'er; gar-(r)ott'ing.** [Sp. *garotte;* cf. Fr. *garrot,* a stick.]
garrulous *gar'ōō-ləs, -ə-, -ū-, adj.* talkative: loquacious. — *n.* **garrulity** (-ōō'li-ti, or -ū') loquacity. — *adv.* **garr'ulously.** — *n.* **garr'ulousness.** [L. *garrulus—garrīre,* to chatter.]
garrya *gar'i-ə, n.* a North American ornamental catkin-bearing evergreen shrub of the genus **Garrya.** [Named after N. *Garry* (1781–1856) of the Hudson's Bay Company.]
garryowen *ga-ri-ō'ən,* (*Rugby football*) *n.* a high kick forward together with a rush towards the landing-place of the ball. [Named after the *Garryowen* Rugby Club in Limerick.]
gart. See **gar²**.
garter *gär'tər, n.* a band used to support a stocking: (with *cap.*) (the badge of) the highest order of knighthood in Great Britain. — *v.t.* to put a garter on: to support, bind, decorate, or surround with a garter. — **gar'ter-snake** in N. America, any snake of the genus Eutaenia, non-venomous, longitudinally striped: in S. Africa applied to two venomous snakes, with black and red rings (see **Elaps**); **gar'ter-stitch** a plain stitch in knitting: horizontally ribbed knitting made by using plain stitches only. — **Garter King-of-Arms** the chief herald of the Order of the Garter. [O.Fr. *gartier* (Fr. *jarretière*) — O.Fr. *garet* (Fr. *jarret*), ham of the leg, prob. Celt., as Bret. *gar,* shank of the leg.]
garth *gärth, n.* an enclosure or yard: a garden: a weir in a river for catching fish. [O.N. *garthr,* a court; cf. **yard², garden.**]
garuda *gur'ōō-dä, n.* (also with *cap.*) a Hindu demigod, part man, part bird. [Sans.]
garum *gā'rəm, n.* a thick sauce prepared from pickled fish, very popular amongst the ancient Romans. [L., — Gr. *garos, garon.*]
garvie *gär'vi,* (*Scot.*) *n.* a sprat. — Also **gar'vock.** [Gael. *garbhag* is perh. from Scots.]
gas *gas, n.* a substance in a condition in which it has no definite boundaries or fixed volume, but will fill any space: often restricted to such a substance above its critical temperature: a substance or mixture which is in this state in ordinary terrestrial conditions: esp. coal-gas, or other gas for lighting or heating, or one used for attack in warfare: gaslight: laughing gas (see **laughing**): empty, boastful, frothy, garrulous, or pert talk (*coll.*): something delightful, impressive, exciting (*coll.*): short for gasoline (petrol) (*U.S.*): — *pl.* **gas'es.** — *v.t.* to supply, attack, poison, light, inflate, or treat with gas: to deceive, impose on by talking gas (*U.S. old*). — *v.i.* to emit gas: to talk gas: — *pr.p.* **gass'ing;** *pa.t.* and *pa.p.* **gassed.** — *ns.* **gasalier', gaselier', gasolier'** a hanging frame with branches for gas-jets (formed on false analogy after *chandelier*); **gasē'ity.** — *adj.* **gaseous** (*gāz', gās', gas', gaz'i-əs, gā'shəs, gash'əs*) in a state of gas: of gas. — *ns.* **gas'eousness; gasificā'tion** conversion into gas. — *adj.* **gas'iform.** — *v.t.* **gas'ify** to convert into gas. — *ns.* **gas'ifier; gas'ogene** see **gazogene; gas'ohol, gas'ahol** a mixture of 8 or 9 parts petrol and 1 or 2 parts alcohol, used as a fuel; **gas'olene, -oline** (-ə-lēn) a low-boiling petroleum distillate: the ordinary name for petrol (*U.S.*); **gasom'eter** a storage tank for gas. — *adjs.* **gasomet'ric, -al** pertaining to the measurement of gas. — *ns.* **gasom'etry; gassi'ness; gass'ing** poisoning by gas: idle talking. — *adj.* **gass'y** full of gas: abounding in or emitting gas: gaseous: given to vain and boastful talk (*slang*). — **gas'-bag** a bag for holding gas, esp. in a balloon or airship: a talkative person (*coll.*); **gas black** soot produced by burning natural gas; **gas'-bottle** a steel cylinder for holding compressed gas; **gas'-bracket** a gas pipe projecting

from the wall of a room for lighting purposes; **gas'-buoy** a floating buoy carrying a supply of gas to light a lamp fixed on it; **gas'-burn'er** the perforated part of a gas-fitting where the gas issues and is burned; **gas cap** gas found in the highest part of oil-containing rock; **gas'-car'bon** a hard dense carbon deposited in coal-gas retorts; **gas'-cen'trifuge** a centrifuge for separating gases; **gas chamber, oven** an enclosed place designed for killing by means of gas; **gas chromatography** a widely used form of chromatography in which a gas is passed down the column which contains the mixture to be separated and a solvent; **gas'-coal'** any coal suitable for making gas: cannel coal; **gas'-coke'** coke made in gas retorts; **gas'-condens'er** an apparatus for freeing coal-gas from tar; **gas'-cook'er** a cooking-stove using gas as fuel. — *adj.* **gas'-cooled** cooled by a flow of gas. — **gas'-en'gine** an engine worked by the explosion of gas; **gas'-escape'** a leakage of gas; **gas'field** a region in which natural gas occurs. — *adj.* **gas'-filled** filled with gas. — **gas'-fire'** a heating-stove in which gas is burned. — *adj.* **gas'-fired'** fuelled, or heated, by gas(es). — **gas'-fitter** one who fits up the pipes, etc. for gas appliances; **gas'-fittings** gas-pipes, etc., for lighting and heating by gas. — **gas'-fur'nace** a furnace of which the fuel is gas; **gas gangrene** gangrene resulting from infection of a wound by certain bacteria which form gases in the flesh; **gas'-globe** a glass used to enclose and shade a gaslight; **gas gun** a gun in which gas is the fuel or propellant; **gas'-guzzler** (*U.S. coll.*) a car that consumes large amounts of petrol. — *adj.* **gas'-guzzling** (*coll.*; esp. *U.S.*) consuming large amounts of petrol. — **gas'-heat'er** any heating apparatus in which gas is used; **gas'-hel'met** a gas-mask in the form of a helmet completely covering the head; **gas'-holder** a large vessel for storing gas: a gasometer; **gas'-jar** a jar for collecting and holding a gas in chemical experiments; **gas'-jet** a jet of gas: a gas-flame: a burner; **gas'-lamp** a lamp that burns gas; **gas'light** light produced by combustion of gas: a gas jet, burner, or lamp. — *adj.* of, concerned with, for use by, gaslight. — **gas'-lime** lime that has been used in purifying gas; **gas'-liquor** a solution of ammonia and ammonium salts got in gas-making. — *adj.* **gas'lit** lighted by gas. — **gas'-main** a principal gas-pipe from the gas-works; **gas'man** a man employed in gas-making, in repairing or installing gas fittings, or in the reading of meters; **gas'-man'tle** a gauze covering, chemically prepared, enclosing a gas-jet, and becoming incandescent when heated; **gas'-mask** a respiratory device (covering nose, mouth, and eyes) as a protection against poisonous gases; **gas'-mē'ter** an instrument for measuring gas consumed; **gas'-mo'tor** a gas-engine; **gas oil** a petroleum distillate, intermediate between kerosine and lubricating oil, used as (esp. heating) fuel; **gas oven** a gas-cooker: see **gas chamber; gas'-pipe** a pipe for conveying gas; **gas'-plant** dittany (see **burning-bush**); **gas'-po'ker** a gas-jet that can be inserted among fuel to kindle a fire; **gas'-retort** a closed heated chamber in which gas is made; **gas'-ring** a hollow ring with perforations serving as gas-jets; **gas'-shell'** a shell that gives off a poisonous gas or vapour on bursting; **gas'-stove** an apparatus in which coal-gas is used for heating or cooking; **gas'-tank** a reservoir for coal-gas; **gas'-tap; gas'-tar** coal-tar. — *adj.* **gas'-tight** impervious to gas. — **gas'-trap** a trap in a drain to prevent escape of foul gas; **gas'-turbine** a machine consisting of a combustion chamber, to which air is supplied by a compressor and in which the air is heated at constant pressure, and a turbine driven by the hot expanding gases; **gas'-water** water through which coal-gas has been passed in scrubbing: gas-, or ammoniacal, liquor; **gas'-well** a boring from which natural gas issues; **gas'-works** a factory where gas is made. — **gas and gaiters** nonsense; **gas-discharge tube** any tube in which an electric discharge takes place through a gas; **ideal gas** see under **idea; natural gas** see **natural; step on the gas** (i.e. gasoline) to press the accelerator pedal of a motor-car:

to speed up. [A word invented by J. B. van Helmont (1577–1644); suggested by Gr. *chaos*.]

gasahol, gasalier. See under **gas.**

Gascon *gas'kən, n.* a native of Gascony: (without *cap.*) a boaster. — *adj.* of Gascony. — *n.* **gasconade'** boasting talk. — *v.i.* to boast extravagantly. — *ns.* **gasconād'er; gas'conism** boastfulness. [Fr.]

gaseity, gaselier, gaseous. See under **gas.**

gash[1] *gash, v.t.* to cut deeply into. — *n.* a deep, open cut. [Formerly *garse* — O.Fr. *garser*, to scarify — L.L. *garsa*, scarification, possibly — Gr. *charassein*, to scratch.]

gash[2] *gash,* (*Scot.*) *adj.* talkative. — *v.i.* to tattle.

gash[3] *gash,* (chiefly *Scot.*) *adj.* ghastly, hideous. — Also **gash'ful, gash'ly.** — *n.* **gash'liness.** — *adv.* **gash'ly.** [Perh. **ghastful, ghastly.**]

gash[4] *gash, adj.* spare, extra (*slang*). — *n.* rubbish, waste (*naut. slang*).

gasification, gasify, etc. See under **gas.**

gasket *gas'kit, n.* a canvas band used to bind the sails to the yards when furled (*naut.*): a strip of tow, etc., for packing a piston, etc.: a layer of packing material, esp. a flat sheet of asbestos compound, sometimes between thin copper sheets, used for making gas-tight joints between engine cylinders and heads, etc. — Also **gas'kin.** [Cf. Fr. *garcette*, It. *gaschetta*; ety. dub.]

gaskins *gas'kinz,* (*Shak.*) *n.* Same as **galligaskins.**

gasohol, gasolene, gasoline, gasolier, gasometer, etc. See under **gas.**

gasp *gäsp, v.i.* to gape for breath: to catch the breath: to desire eagerly. — *v.t.* to breathe: to utter with gasps. — *n.* the act of gasping. — *ns.* **gasp'er** one who gasps: a cheap cigarette (*slang*); **gasp'iness.** — *n.* and *adj.* **gasp'ing.** — *adv.* **gasp'ingly.** — *adj.* **gasp'y.** — **the last gasp** the point of death. [O.N. *geispa*, to yawn; cf. *geip*, idle talk.]

gaspereau *gas'pə-rō* (*Can.*) *n.* the alewife (q.v.), a type of herring. [Fr. *gasparot*, a kind of herring.]

gast *gäst, v.t.* (*Shak.*) to make aghast, to frighten or terrify. — *adj.* **gastfull** (*Spens.*; see **ghastful**). — *n.* **gast'ness(e)** (*obs.*; *Shak.*) dread. [O.E. *gǣstan*; cf. **aghast.**]

Gastarbeiter *gast'ar-bī-tər, n.* a migrant worker, esp. one who does menial work. [Ger., lit. guest-worker.]

gastero-, gastro-, gastr- *gas'tə-rō-, gas'tr(ō)-, -tro'-,* in composition, belly. — *n.pl.* **Gasteromycetes** (*gas'tar-ō-mī-sē'tez;* Gr. *mykētēs,* pl. of *mykēs,* mushroom) an order of fungi — Basidiomycetes with fructification closed till the spores ripen — puffballs, stinkhorns, etc. — *n.* **gas'teropod, gas'tropod** (Gr. *pous, podos,* foot) any member of the **Gast(e)rop'oda,** a class of asymmetrical molluscs in which the foot is broad and flat, the mantle undivided, the shell in one piece, usually conical — limpets, whelks, snails, slugs, etc. — *adj.* **gast(e)rop'odous.** — *ns.* **gastraea** (*gas-trē'ə*) Haeckel's hypothetical ancestor of the Metazoa, like a gastrula; **gastraeum** (*gas-trē'əm*) the under surface of the body, esp. in birds; **gastralgia** (*gas-tral'ji-ə;* Gr. *algos,* pain) pain in the stomach. — *adj.* **gastral'gic.** — *n.* **gastrectomy** (*gas-trek'tə-mi;* Gr. *ek,* out, *tomē,* cutting) surgical removal of the stomach, or part of it. — *adj.* **gas'tric** belonging to the stomach. — *ns.* **gas'trin** a hormone which stimulates production of gastric juice; **gastrī'tis** inflammation of the stomach; **gastrocnemius** (*gas-trok-nē'mi-əs;* Gr. *knēmē,* lower leg) the muscle that bulges the calf of the leg: — *pl.* **-miī.** — *adj.* **gastroenter'ic** gastrointestinal. — *ns.* **gastroenterī'tis** inflammation of the lining of the stomach and intestines; **gastroenterol'ogist; gastroenterol'ogy** (*med.*) the study of the stomach and intestines. — *adj.* **gastrointest'inal** (or *-īn'l*) of, relating to, consisting of, the stomach and intestines. — *n.* **gastrol'oger.** — *adj.* **gastrolog'ical.** — *ns.* **gastrol'ogy** cookery, good eating; **gastromancy** (*gas'trō-man-si;* Gr. *manteiā,* sooth-saying) divination by sounds from the belly, i.e. ventriloquism: divination by large-bellied glasses; **gastronome** (*gas'trə-nōm;* Gr. *nomos,* law), **gastronomer** (*-tron'ə-*

mər) an epicure. — *adjs.* **gastronomic** (*-nom'ik*), **-al.** — *ns.* **gastron'omist; gastron'omy** the art or science of good eating; **gas'troscope** an instrument for inspecting the interior of the stomach; **gas'trosoph** (Gr. *sophos,* wise) one skilled in matters of eating; **gastros'opher; gastros'ophy; gastros'tomy** (Gr. *stoma,* mouth) the making of an opening to introduce food into the stomach; **gastrot'omy** (Gr. *tomē,* a cut) the operation of cutting open the stomach or abdomen; **gastrula** (*gas'trōō-lə*) an embryo at the stage in which it forms a two-layered cup by the invagination of its wall; **gastrulā'tion** formation of a gastrula. — **gastric fever** typhoid; **gastric juice** the acid liquid secreted by the stomach for digestion. [Gr. *gastēr,* belly.]

Gasthaus, Gasthof *gast'hows, -hōf,* (*Ger.*) *ns.* a hotel, guest-house.

gastr(o)-. See **gastero-.**

gat[1] *gat,* (*slang*) *n.* a gun, revolver. [**gatling-gun.**]

gat[2] *gat* (*B.*) *pa.t.* of **get.**

gat[3] *gat, n.* an opening between sandbanks: a strait. [Perh. O.N.]

gat[4] *gät, n.* in Indian music, the second and usu. final section of a raga. — Also **gath.** [Sans. *gāth.*]

gate[1] *gāt, n.* a passage into a city, enclosure, or any large building: a narrow opening or defile: a frame for closing an entrance: an entrance, passage, or channel: an obstacle consisting of two posts, markers, etc. between which competitors in a slalom, etc. must pass: at an airport, any of the numbered exits from which to board an aircraft: the people who pay to see a game, hence, the number attending: the total amount of money paid for entrance (also **gate'-money**): electronic circuit which passes impressed signals when permitted by another independent source of similar signals: the location of a film in a projector, printer or camera when it is being acted on or scanned: an H-shaped series of slots for controlling the movement of a gear-lever in a gear-box. — *v.t.* to supply with a gate: to punish (students or school-children) by imposing a curfew on or by confining to school precincts for a time. — *adjs.* **gāt'ed** having a gate or gates (often in composition, as **hun'dred-gated**): punished by gating; **gate'less.** — *n.* **gāt'ing.** — *v.i.* and *v.t.* **gate'crash** to enter without paying or invitation. — **gate'crasher; gate'-fine** the fine imposed upon the gated for disobedience; **gate'fold** an oversize folded leaf in a book, etc., a fold-out; **gate'-house** (*archit.*) a building over or at a gate; **gate'-keeper, gate'-man** one who watches over the opening and shutting of a gate. — *adjs.* **gate'= legged, gate'leg** of a table, having a hinged and framed leg that can swing in to let down a leaf. — **gate net** a net hung across a gateway for catching hares; **gate'= post** a post from which a gate is hung or against which it shuts; **gate'-tower** a tower beside or over a gate; **gate'-vein** the great abdominal vein; **gate'way** the way through a gate: a structure at a gate: any entrance. — **break gates** at Oxford and Cambridge, to enter college after the prescribed hour; **gate of justice** a gate as of a city, temple, etc., where a sovereign or judge sat to dispense justice; **ivory gate, gate of horn** (or in *Spenser* **silver**) in Greek legend and poetical imagery, the gates through which false and true dreams respectively come; **stand in the gate** (*B.*) to occupy a position of defence. [O.E. *geat,* a way; Du. *gat,* O.N. *gat.*]

gate[2] *gāt,* (*Scot.* and *North. dial.*) *n.* a way, path, street (often in street-names, as *Cowgate, Kirkgate*): manner of doing. See also **gait**[1] . [O.N. *gata;* Dan. *gade,* Ger. *Gasse.*]

gate[3] *gāt,* (*Spens.*) *n.* a Northern form of **goat.**

-gate *gāt,* (*facet.*) *suff.* attached to the name of a person or place to denote (on the analogy of **Watergate** (q.v.)) a scandal connected with that person or place.

gâteau *gat'ō, gä-tō, n.* a rich cake, filled with cream, decorated with icing, etc.: — *pl.* **gateaus** (*gat'ōz*), **gâteaux** (*gat'ōz, gä-tō*). [Fr.]

gather *gadh'ər, v.t.* to collect: to assemble: to amass: to cull: to pick up: to draw together: in sewing, to draw into puckers by passing a thread through: to learn by inference: to have increase in (e.g. speed). — *v.i.* to assemble or muster: to increase: to suppurate: to make way (*naut.*): to arrange signatures of a book in correct sequence for binding. — *n.* a plait or fold in cloth, made by drawing threads through: (*pl.*) that part of the dress which is gathered or drawn in. — *ns.* **gath'erer** one who collects, amasses, assembles, or culls: a workman who collects molten glass on the end of a rod preparatory to blowing; **gath'ering** the action of one who gathers: a crowd or assembly: a narrowing: a number of leaves of paper folded one within another: the assembling of the sheets of a book: a suppurating swelling. — **gath'ering-coal, -peat** a coal, peat, put into a fire, to keep it alive till morning; **gath'ering-cry** a summons to assemble for war; **gath'ering-ground** catchment area. — **gather breath** to recover wind; **gather ground** to gain ground; **gather oneself together** to collect all one's powers, like one about to leap; **gather to a head** to ripen: to come into a state of preparation for action or effect; **gather way** to get headway by sail or steam so as to answer the helm. [O.E. *gaderian, gæderian*; (*tō*)*gædere*, together; *geador*, together, *gæd*, fellowship.]

gatling-gun *gat'ling-gun, n.* a machine-gun invented by R. J. *Gatling* about 1861.

gau *gow, n.* a district. — *n.* **gauleiter** (*gow'lī-tər*) a chief official of a district under the Nazi régime: an over-bearing wielder of petty authority. [Ger. *Gau*, district, *Leiter*, leader.]

gauche *gōsh, adj.* clumsy: tactless. — *n.* **gaucherie** (*gōsh'ə-rē, -rē'*) clumsiness: (an instance of) social awkwardness. [Fr., left.]

Gaucher's disease *gō'shāz diz-ēz'*, a rare hereditary disease characterised by the accumulation of certain fats in the liver and spleen. [P. *Gaucher* (1854–1918), French physician.]

gaucho *gow'chō, n.* a cowboy of the pampas, usually of mixed Spanish and Indian descent: (in *pl.*) women's knee-length culottes: — *pl.* **gau'chos.** — *adj.* **gauches'co** of a type of Spanish poetry inspired by the life, language and customs of the gauchos. [Sp.]

gaucie, gaucy, gawcy, gawsy *gö'si,* (*Scot.*) *adj.* portly, jolly. [Origin unknown.]

gaud *göd, n.* a large ornamental bead on a rosary (*obs.*): a prank (*obs.*): an ornament: a piece of finery: showy ceremony: festivity (*obs.*). — *v.i.* (*obs.*) to make merry. — *v.t.* to adorn with gauds (*obs.*): to paint, as the cheeks (*Shak.*). — *ns.* **gaudeā'mus** (in Scotland *gow-di-ä'mōōs*; L., let us be glad; opening word of a students' song) a joyful celebration among students; **gaud'ery** finery. — *adv.* **gaud'ily.** — *ns.* **gaud'iness; gaud'y** an entertainment or feast, esp. in an English college. — *adj.* showy: gay: vulgarly bright. — **gaud'y-day; gaud'y-night.** [In part app. — O.Fr. *gaudir* — L. *gaudēre*, to be glad, *gaudium*, joy; in part directly from L.]

gaudeamus igitur *gö-di-ām'əs ij'i-tər, gow-de-äm'ōōs ig'i-tōōr,* (L.) let us therefore rejoice.

gaudgie. See **gadgie.**

gaudium certaminis *gö'di-əm sûr-tam'in-is, gow'di-ōōm ker-täm'in-is,* (L.) joy of combat.

gaudy. See **gaud.**

gaudy-green *gö'di-grēn,* (*obs.*) *n.* and *adj.* yellowish green. [O.Fr. *gaude*, weld, dyer's-rocket.]

gaufer, gaufre. See **gofer.**

gauge, also **gage,** *gāj, n.* a measuring apparatus: a standard of measure: a means of limitation or adjustment to a standard: a measurement, as the diameter of a wire, calibre of a tube, width of a row of slates: the distance between a pair of wheels or rails: a means of estimate: relative position of a ship (in this sense usu. **gage;** see **lee¹, weather**). — *v.t.* to measure: to estimate: to adjust to a standard. — *v.i.* to measure the contents of casks. — *adj.* **gauge'able** capable of being gauged. — *ns.* **gaug'er** one who gauges: an excise man; **gaug'ing** the measuring of casks holding excisable liquors. —

gauge'-glass a tube to show height of water; **gaug'ing-rod** an instrument for measuring the contents of casks. — *adjs.* **broad'-, narr'ow-gauge** in railroad construction greater or less than standard gauge, in Britain 56½ inches (1·435 metres). [O.Fr. *gauge* (Fr. *jauge*).]

gauje. See **gadgie.**

Gaul *göl, n.* a name of ancient France: an inhabitant of Gaul. — *adj.* **Gaul'ish.** — *n.* the Celtic (Brythonic) language of the Gauls. [Fr. *Gaule* — L. *Gallia, Gallus;* perh. conn. with O.E. *wealh*, foreign.]

gauleiter. See **gau.**

Gaullist *göl'ist, n.* a follower of the French soldier and statesman General Charles A. J. M. de *Gaulle* (President of the Fifth Republic 1958–69). — *n.* **Gaull'ism** principles and policies of Gaullists.

Gault *gölt, n.* a series of beds of clay and marl between the Upper and the Lower Greensand; **gault** brick earth: a brick of gault clay. — *n.* **gault'er** one who digs gault. [Origin obscure.]

Gaultheria *göl-thē'ri-ə, n.* a genus of evergreen aromatic plants of the heath family, including the American wintergreen and salal: (without *cap.*) a plant of this genus. [From the Swedish–Canadian botanist Hughes *Gaulthier.*]

gaum¹ *göm,* **gorm** *görm, vs.t.* to smear: to daub: to clog: to handle clumsily (*obs.*). — *ns.* a smear: a daub: a shiny lustre as on new varnish: stickiness: a sticky mass. — *adjs.* **gaum'y, gorm'y** dauby. [Ety. dub., perh. variant of **gum².**]

gaum² *göm,* **gorm** *görm,* (*dial.*) *ns.* notice, heed, regard, attention: understanding. — *vs.t.* to pay attention to, to heed: to understand. — *adjs.* **gaum'less, gorm'less** clumsy: stupid, witless. [O.N. *gaumr,* heed, attention.]

gaun *gö n.* Scots for **going** (see **gae¹**).

gaunch. See **ganch.**

gaunt¹. See **gant.**

gaunt² *gönt, adj.* thin: of a pinched appearance: grim. — *adv.* **gaunt'ly.** — *n.* **gaunt'ness.** [Origin obscure.]

gauntlet¹ *gönt'lit, n.* the iron glove of armour, formerly thrown down in challenge and taken up in acceptance: a long glove covering the wrist: an extension of a glove covering the wrist. — *adj.* **gaunt'leted** wearing a gauntlet or gauntlets. — **gaunt'let-guard** a guard of a sword or dagger, protecting the hand very thoroughly. — **throw down, take up, the gauntlet** to give, to accept a challenge. [Fr. *gantelet,* dim. of *gant,* glove, of Gmc. origin; cf. Sw. *vante,* a mitten, glove, O.N. *vöttr,* a glove, Dan. *vante.*]

gauntlet² *gönt'lit,* **gantlope** *gant'lōp, ns.* the military (or naval) punishment of having to run through a lane of soldiers (or sailors) who strike one as one passes. — **run the gauntlet** to undergo the punishment of the gauntlet: to expose oneself to hostile treatment. [Sw. *gatlopp — gata,* lane (cf. **gate²**), *lopp,* course (cf. **leap**); confused with **gauntlet¹.**]

gauntree, gauntry. See **gantry.**

gaup, gauper, gaupus. See **gawp.**

gaur *gowr, n.* a species of ox inhabiting some of the mountain jungles of India. [Hindustani.]

gauss *gows, n.* the C.G.S. unit of magnetic flux density (formerly used for other magnetic units). — *adj.* **Gauss'ian** (also without *cap.*) of or due to Johann Karl Friedrich *Gauss* (1777–1855), German mathematician and physicist. — **Gaussian distribution** (*statistics*) normal distribution (q.v.).

gauze *göz, n.* a thin, transparent fabric: material slight and open like gauze. — *n.* **gauz'iness.** — *adj.* **gauz'y.** — **gauze'-tree** the lace-bark. — *adj.* **gauze'-winged** having gauzy wings. [Fr. *gaze,* dubiously referred to *Gaza* in Palestine.]

gavage *gä-väzh', n.* feeding by stomach-tube: cramming of poultry. [Fr. *gaver — gave,* bird's crop.]

gave *gāv, pa.t.* of **give.**

gavel¹ *gä'vl,* a dial. form of **gable.**

gavel² *gav'l,* (*hist.*) *n.* tribute or rent. — **gav'elkind** a tenure long prevailing in Kent by which lands descended from the father to all sons (or, failing sons, to all daughters) in equal portions, and not by primogeniture; **gav′elman** a tenant holding land in gavelkind. [O.E. *gafol*, tribute; conn. with *giefan*, to give.]

gavel[3] *gav′l, n.* a mallet: a chairman's hammer.

gavelock *gav′ə-lək, n.* a javelin: a crow-bar. [O.E. *gafeluc*.]

gavial *gā′vi-əl,* **garial, gharial** *gur′i-əl, ns.* an Indian crocodile (*Gavialis*) with very long slender muzzle. [Hindi *ghariyāl,* crocodile.]

gavotte *gä-vot′, n.* a dance, somewhat like a country-dance, originally a dance of the *Gavots,* people of the French Upper Alps (also *fig.*): the music for such a dance in common time, often occurring in suites.

gawcy. Same as **gaucie.**

gawd *göd,* (*Shak.*) *n.* same as **gaud.**

gawk *gök, n.* an awkward or ungainly person, esp. from tallness, shyness, or simplicity: one who stares and gapes. — *v.i.* to stare and gape. — *ns.* **gawker; gawk′-ihood; gawk′iness.** — *adj.* **gawk′y** awkward: ungainly. — *n.* a tall awkward person: a gawk. [Ety. obscure: prob. not Fr. *gauche,* left.]

gawp, gaup *göp,* (*coll.*) *v.i.* to gape in astonishment. — *ns.* **gawp′er, gaup′er; gaup′us, gawp′us** a silly person. [From obs. *galp;* cog. with **yelp.**]

gawsy. Same as **gaucie.**

gay *gā, adj.* lively: bright: sportive, merry: dissipated: of loose life, whorish: showy: spotted (*dial.*): in modern use, homosexual (*orig. prison slang*): great, considerable (*Scot.*; usu. **gey** *gī*); often by hendiadys instead of an adv., as *gey and easy,* easy enough: unduly familiar (*U.S.*): pertaining to or frequented by homosexuals (as *gay bar*): — *compar.* **gay′er;** *superl.* **gay′est.** — *adv.* (*Scot.*; **gey**) rather, fairly, considerably. — *n.* a gallant (*obs.*): a homosexual. — *n.* **gai′ety** gayness (but not used in sense of homosexuality). — *adv.* **gai′ly.** — *n.* **gay′ness.** — *adj.* **gay′some** gladsome. — **gay deceiver** a libertine: (in *pl.*) a foam-padded brassière (*slang*); **gay liberation** the freeing of homosexuals from social disadvantages and prejudice; **gay science** a rendering of *gai saber,* the Provençal name for the art of poetry. [O.Fr. *gai* — perh. O.H.G. *wâhi,* pretty.]

gayal, gyal *gī′al, n.* an Indian domesticated ox, akin to the gaur, with curved horns. [Hindi.]

Gay-Lussac's law. See **law**[1].

gay-you *gī′ū, gā′ū, n.* a narrow flat-bottomed Vietnamese boat with outrigger and masts. [Vietnamese *ghe hâu.*]

gazal. See **ghazal.**

gaze *gāz, v.i.* to look fixedly. — *n.* a fixed look: the object gazed at. —(*Spens.*) **gaze′ment** (*Spens.*) looking intently. — *n.* **gā′zer.** — *adj.* **gā′zy** affording a wide prospect: given to gazing. — **gaze′-hound** a hound that pursues by sight; **gaz′ing-stock** one exposed to public view, generally unpleasantly. — **at gaze** in the attitude of gazing. [Prob. cog. with obs. *gaw,* to stare; cf. O.N. *gā,* to heed; Sw. dial. *gasa,* to stare.]

gazebo *gə-zē′bō, n.* a belvedere: — *pl.* **gazē′bos, gazē′boes.** [A connection with **gaze** has been suggested, but is far from certain.]

gazelle, gazel *gə-zel′, n.* a small antelope (*Gazella dorcas*) of N. Africa and S.W. Asia, with large eyes, or kindred species. [Fr., — Ar. *ghazāl,* a wild goat.]

gazette *gə-zet′, n.* a newspaper: (with *cap.*) an official newspaper containing lists of government appointments, legal notices, despatches, etc. — *v.t.* to publish or mention in a gazette: — *pr.p.* **gazett′ing;** *pa.t.* and *pa.p.* **gazett′ed.** — *n.* **gazetteer′** (*gaz-*) a geographical dictionary: orig., a writer for a gazette, an official journalist. — *v.t.* to describe in gazetteers. — *adj.* **gazetteer′ish.** — **gazetted officer** one of a higher grade who is listed in an official gazette. — **appear, have one's name in the Gazette** to be mentioned in one of the official newspapers, esp. of bankrupts. [Fr., — It. *gazzetta,* a small coin; or from It. *gazzetta,* dim. of *gazza,* magpie.]

gazogene *gaz′ə-jēn,* **gasogene** *gas′, ns.* an apparatus for

making aerated waters. [Fr. *gazogène* — *gaz,* gas, Gr. suff. *-genēs* — root of *gennaein,* to generate.]

gazon, gazoon *gə-zōōn′, n.* a sod in fortification: used erron. by Hogg for a compact body of men. [Fr., turf.]

gazoo, gazooka. See **kazoo.**

gazpacho *gas-päch′ō, gəz-, n.* a spicy Spanish vegetable soup, served cold: — *pl.* **gazpach′os.** [Sp.]

gazump *gə-zump′, v.t.* and *v.i.* to raise the price of property, etc., after accepting an offer from (a buyer), but before the contract has been signed. [Prob. Yiddish *gezumph,* to swindle.]

gazy. See **gaze.**

G-clef. See under **G.**

Ge. See **Gaea.**

geal *jēl, v.t.* and *v.i.* to congeal. [Fr. *geler.*]

gealous, gealousy. Spenser's spellings of **jealous, jealousy.**

gean *gēn, n.* the European wild cherry. [O.Fr. *guigne.*]

geanticline *jē-an′ti-klīn, n.* an anticline on a great scale. — *adj.* **geanticli′nal.** [Gr. *gē,* earth, and **anticline.**]

gear *gēr, n.* equipment: accoutrements: tackle: clothes, esp. (*coll.*) young people's modern clothes: armour: harness: apparatus: a set of tools or a mechanism for some particular purpose: household stuff: possessions: stuff: matter: affair, business, doings (often contemptuous): any moving part or system of parts for transmitting motion, e.g. levers, gear-wheels: connection by means of such parts: the actual gear ratio in use, or the gear-wheels involved in transmitting that ratio, in an automobile gear-box, e.g. first gear (low gear), fourth gear (high gear): working connection: working order: the diameter in inches of a wheel whose circumference equals the distance a bicycle would go for one turn of the pedals. — *v.t.* to harness: to put in gear, as machinery: to connect in gear: to make to work in accordance with requirements of (a project or a larger organisation; *fig.*; with *to*). — *v.i.* to be in gear. — *adj.* (*slang*) unusually good, or (later) very up to date. — *adj.* **geared.** — *n.* **gear′ing** harness: working implements: means of transmission of motion, esp. a train of toothed wheels and pinions: in a company's capital, the ratio of ordinary shares to shares with fixed interest (*econ.*). — *adj.* **gear′less.** — **gear′-box, gear′box** the box containing the apparatus for changing gear; **gear′-case** a protective case for the gearing of a bicycle, etc.; **gear′-change, gear′change** a change of gear: the mechanism with which one changes gear; **gear′-lever, -shift, -stick** a device for selecting or engaging and disengaging gears; **gear′-ratio** the ratio of the driving to the driven members of a gear mechanism; **gear′-wheel** a wheel with teeth or cogs which impart or transmit motion by acting on a similar wheel or a chain. — *adjs.* **high′-gear, low′-gear** geared to give a high or a low number of revolutions of the driven part relatively to the driving part — also *ns.* — **change gear** to select a higher or lower gear; **gear down, up** to make the speed of the driven part lower, higher, than that of the driving part; **multiplying gearing** a combination of cog-wheels for imparting motion from wheels of larger to wheels of smaller diameter, by which the rate of revolution is increased; **straight gear** the name given when the planes of motion are parallel — opposed to **bevelled gear** (see **bevel**); **three-speed gear, two-speed gear, variable gear** a contrivance for changing gear at will; see also **synchromesh.** [M.E. *gere,* prob. O.N. *gervi;* cf. O.E. *gearwe,* O.H.G. *garawi;* **yare, gar**[2].]

geare. Spens. for **gear, jeer.**

geason *gē′zn,* (*obs.*) *adj.* rare (*Spens.*): out of the way: wonderful. [O.E. *gǣne, gēsne,* wanting, barren.]

geat *jēt, n.* the hole in a mould through which the metal is poured in casting. [**jet.**]

gebur *gə-bōōr′, yə-bōōr′,* (*hist.*) *n.* a tenant-farmer. [O.E. *gebūr.*]

geck *gek,* (*Scot.*) *n.* a dupe: object of scorn: a derisive gesture: scorn. — *v.t.* to mock. — *v.i.* to scoff: to toss the head: to show disdain. [Prob. L.G. *geck;* Du. *gek,* Ger. *Geck.*]

gecko *gek'ō, n.* any lizard of the genus **Gecko** or the subclass **Gecko'nēs**, mostly thick-bodied, dull-coloured animals with adhesive toes and vertebrae concave at both ends: — *pl.* **geck'os, geck'oes.** [Malay *gēkoq*; imit. of its cry.]

ged *ged, (dial.) n.* the pike or luce. [O.N. *gedda.*]

gee¹ *jē, n.* the seventh letter of the alphabet (G, g).

gee² *gē, (dial.) n.* a fit of perversity.

gee³ *jē, v.i.* of horses, to move to the right or to move on. — *n.* **gee'-gee** a child's word for a horse. — **gee up** to proceed faster, chiefly used as a command to horses (also **gee hup**): to encourage, stimulate, buck up.

gee⁴ *jē, (dial.) v.i.* to go, to suit, to get on well.

gee⁵ *jē, n.* a radio-navigation system in which three ground stations A (master), B and C (slave), give for AB and AC two sets of intersecting hyperbolas which, charted, give an equipped aircraft its geographical position over a few hundred miles' range from A. [Ground *electronics engineering.*]

gee⁶ *jē, (U.S.) interj.* expressing surprise, sarcasm, enthusiasm, etc.: sometimes used only for emphasis — **gee whiz** *interj.* expressing surprise, admiration, etc. [Perh. **Jesus.**]

geebung *jē'bung, n.* an Australian proteaceous tree (*Persoonia*) or its fruit. [Aboriginal.]

geese, *pl.* of **goose.**

gee-string *jē'string, n.* a string or strip worn round the waist supporting a strip worn between the legs or this strip itself, or both, or any similar covering for the genitals. — Also **G-string.** [Origin obscure.]

Geëz *gē-ez', gē'ez, gēz, Giz gēz, ns.* the ancient language of Ethiopia, a Semitic tongue closely related to Arabic.

geezer *gēz'ər, (slang) n.* a queer elderly person: a man. [**guiser.**]

gefilte, gefüllte fish *gə-fil'tə fish,* a cooked mixture of fish, eggs, breadcrumbs and seasoning served as balls or cakes or stuffed into a fish. [Yiddish, lit. filled fish.]

gefuffle *gə-fuf'l.* Form of **carfuffle.**

gefüllte fish. See **gefilte fish.**

gegenschein *gā'gən-shīn, n.* a glow of zodiacal light seen opposite the sun. [Ger.]

Gehenna *gi-hen'ə, n.* the valley of Hinnom, near Jerusalem, in which the Israelites sacrificed their children to Moloch, and to which, at a later time, the refuse of the city was conveyed to be slowly burned: hence hell (*N.T.*): a place of torment. [Hcb. *Ge-hinnōm,* valley of Hinnom.]

Geiger (-Müller) counter *gī'gər (mül'ər) kown'tər,* an instrument for detecting and measuring radioactivity by registering electrical output pulses caused by ionisation of particles in a gas-filled tube. [*Geiger* and *Müller,* German physicists.]

geisha *gā'sha, n.* a Japanese girl trained to provide entertainment (as conversation, performance of dances, etc.) for men: — *pl.* **gei'sha, gei'shas.** [Jap.]

Geissler tube *gīs'lər tūb, (chem.)* a gas-filled discharge-tube, characterised by a capillary section for concentrated illumination. [Heinrich *Geissler* (1814–1879), the inventor.]

geist *gīst, n.* spirit, any inspiring or dominating principle. [Ger.]

geit. Same as **get,** a child, **gyte²**.

geitonogamy *gī-tən-og'ə-mi, n.* pollination from another flower on the same plant. — *adj.* **geitonog'amous.** [Gr. *geiton,* neighbour, *gamos,* marriage.]

gel¹ *jel, n.* a jelly-like apparently solid colloidal solution: a (sheet of) transparent substance used in theatre and photographic lighting to produce light of different colours (short for **gelatine**). — *v.i.* to form a gel: to come together, to begin to work, take shape (*coll.*; also **jell**): — *pr.p.* **gell'ing;** *pa.t.* and *pa.p.* **gelled.** — *n.* **gelā'tion** see separate article. [**gelatine.**]

gel² *gel, n.* a facet. rendering of an upper-class pronunciation of **girl.**

gelada *jel'ə-də, gel', ji-läd'ə, gi-, n.* an Ethiopian baboon, with a long mane. [Poss. from Ar. *qilādah,* collar, mane.]

gelastic *jel-as'tik, adj.* pertaining to or provoking laughter. [Gr. *gelastikos — gelaein,* to laugh.]

gelati. See **gelato.**

gelatine, gelatin *jel'ə-tēn, -tin, ns.* colourless, odourless, and tasteless glue, prepared from albuminous substances, e.g. bones and hides, used for food-stuffs, photographic films, glues, etc. — *vs.t.* **gelatinate** (*ji-lat'i-nāt*), **gelat'inise, -ize** to make into gelatine or jelly: to coat with gelatine or jelly. — *vs.i.* to be converted into gelatine or jelly. — *ns.* **gelatinā'tion, gelatinisā'tion, -z-; gelat'iniser, -z-; gelat'inoid** a substance resembling gelatine. — Also *adj.* — *adj.* **gelat'inous** resembling or formed into jelly. — **blasting gelatine** a violently explosive rubbery substance composed of nitroglycerine and nitrocotton. [Fr., — It. *gelatina, gelata,* jelly — L. *gelāre,* to freeze.]

gelation *jel-ā'shən, n.* a solidification by cooling: formation of a gel from a sol. [Partly L. *gelātiō, -ōnis — gelāre,* to freeze; partly **gel¹**.]

gelato *je-lä'tō, (Austr.) n.* a type of whipped ice-cream made from cream, milk and/or water and flavoured with fruit or nuts: — *pl.* **-ti (-tē).** [It.]

geld¹ *geld, (hist.) n.* a tax. — *v.t.* to tax. [O.E. *geld, gyld,* payment; O.N. *giald,* money: cf. **yield.**]

geld² *geld, v.t.* to emasculate, castrate: to spay: to deprive of anything essential, to enfeeble, to deprive: to expurgate: — *pa.t.* and *pa.p.* **geld'ed, gelt** (*arch.* or *dial.*). — *ns.* **geld'er; geld'ing** act of castrating: a castrated animal, esp. a horse. [O.N. *gelda;* Dan. *gilde.*]

gelder(s)-rose. Same as **guelder-rose.**

gelid *jel'id, adj.* icy cold: cold. — *adv.* **gel'idly.** — *ns.* **gel'idness, gelid'ity.** [L. *gelidus — gelū,* frost.]

gelignite *jel'ig-nīt, n.* a powerful explosive used in mining, made from nitroglycerine, nitrocotton, potassium nitrate, and wood-pulp. [**gelatine** and L. *ignis,* fire.]

gelliflowre (*Spens.*). Same as **gillyflower.**

gelly *jel'i, (Spens.) adj.* jellied.

gelosy (*Spens.*). Same as **jealousy.**

gelsemium *jel-sē'mi-əm, n.* the so-called yellow or Carolina jasmine, an American climbing-plant of the Loganiaceae. — *ns.* **gel'semine** (-*səm-ēn*) and **gelseminine** (-*sem'*) two alkaloids yielded by its rhizome and rootlets. [It. *gelsomino,* jasmine.]

gelt¹ *gelt, (arch.* or *dial.) pa.t.* and *pa.p.* of **geld²**.

gelt² *gelt, (Spens.) n.* a madman. [Ir. *geilt.*]

gelt³ *gelt, (slang) n.* money: profit. [Ger. *Geld,* Du. *geld.*]

gelt⁴ *gelt,* an obsolete erroneous form of **geld¹**: (*Spens.*) apparently for **gilt¹**.

gem *jem, n.* any precious stone, esp. when cut: a person or thing regarded as extremely admirable or flawless: a size of type smaller than diamond (*print.*): a bud (*obs.*). — *v.t.* (*obs.*) to bud: to adorn with gems: to bespangle: — *pr.p.* **gemm'ing;** *pa.t.* and *pa.p.* **gemmed.** — *v.t.* **gemm'ate** (*arch.*) to deck with gems. — *adj.* **gemm'eous** (-*i-əs*) pertaining to gems: like a gem. — *n.* **gemm'ery** (*arch.*) gems generally. — *adj.* **gem(m)olog'ical.** — *ns.* **gem(m)ol'ogist** one with special knowledge of gems; **gem(m)ol'ogy** the science of gems. — *adj.* **gemm'y** full of gems: brilliant. — **gem'-cutting** the art of cutting and polishing precious stones; **gem'-engraving** the art of engraving figures on gems; **gem'stone.** [O.E. *gim;* O.H.G. *gimma —* L. *gemma,* a bud; later remodelled on L. or reintroduced.]

Gemara *gə-mä'rə, n.* the second part of the Talmud, consisting of commentary and complement to the first part, the Mishnah. [Aramaic, completion.]

gematria *gə-mä'tri-ə, n.* a cabbalistic method of interpreting the Hebrew Scriptures by interchanging words whose letters have the same numerical value when added. [Rabbinical Heb. *gēmatriyā —* Gr. *geōmetriā,* geometry.]

Gemeinschaft *gə-mīn'shäft, (Ger.) n.* a social group held together by ties such as friendship, kinship, etc.

gemel *jem'əl, n.* a twin (*obs.*): a gimmal: a hinge (*obs.*): a pair of bars placed close together (*her.*). — **gem'el-ring** same as **gimmal ring.** [O.Fr. *gemel* (Fr. *jumeau*) —

L. *gemellus*, dim. of *geminus*, twin.]
geminate *jem'in-āt*, *v.t.* to double. — *adj.* (*bot.*) in pairs. — *n.* **geminā'tion** a doubling. — *n.pl.* **Gemini** (*jem'i-nī*) the twins, a constellation containing the two bright stars Castor and Pollux: the third sign of the zodiac: one born under this sign. — *n.* **Gem'inid** a meteor of a swarm whose radiant is in the constellation Gemini. — *adj.* **gem'inous** (*bot.*) double, in pairs. — *n.* **gem'iny** (*Shak.*) a pair, esp. of eyes. — *interj.* (perh. a separate word) expressing surprise — spelt also **gemini** (*obs.*), **gemony** (*obs.*) and (the sole current form), **jiminy.** [L. *geminus*, twin.]
gemma *jem'ə*, *n.* a plant bud, esp. a leaf-bud (*rare*): a small multicellular body produced vegetatively, capable of separating and becoming a new individual (*bot.*): a bud or protuberance from the body that becomes a new individual (*zool.*): — *pl.* **gemm'ae** (*-ē*). — *adjs.* **gemmā'ceous** bud-like: relating to gemmae; **gemm'ate** having or reproducing by buds or gemmae. — *v.t.* see under **gem.** — *v.i.* to reproduce by gemmae. — *n.* **gemmā'tion** budding or gemma-formation. — *adjs.* **gemm'ative** pertaining to gemmation; **gemmif'erous** bearing gemmae; **gemmip'arous** reproducing by gemmae. — *ns.* **gemmūlā'tion** formation of gemmules; **gemm'ule** Darwin's hypothetical particle produced by each part of the body, as a vehicle of heredity: a plumule (*obs.*): an internal bud in sponges. — **gemm'a-cup** a liverwort cupule. [L. *gemma*, a bud.]
gemman *jem'ən*, *n.* a corr. of gentleman: — *pl.* **gemmen** (*jem'ən*). [**gentleman.**]
gemmate, gemmation, etc. See **gem, gemma.**
gemmeous, gemmery. See **gem.**
gemmiferous, gemmiparous. See **gemma.**
gem(m)ologist, etc. See **gem.**
gemmule, gemmulation. See **gemma.**
gemmy[1]. See **gem.**
gemmy[2]. See **jemmy[2].**
gemony. See **geminate.**
gemot *gə-mōt'*, *yə-mōt'*, (*hist.*) *n.* a meeting or assembly. [O.E. *gemōt*; cf. **moot.**]
gemsbok *hhemz'bok* (S. Afr.), *gemz'bok*, *n.* (*Oryx gazella*) S. African antelope, about the size of a stag, with long straight horns. [Du., male chamois — Ger. *Gemsbock.*]
gemütlich *gə-müt'lēhh*, (Ger.) *adj.* amiable: comfortable: cosy. — *n.* **Gemütlichkeit** (*-kīt*) kindness: comfort: cosiness.
gen *jen*, (*slang*) *n.* general information: the low-down or inside information. — **gen up** to learn (with *on*): — *pa.t.* **genned up.**
-gen *-jən*, **-gene** *-jēn*, in composition used to denote (1) producing or produced, as in *oxygen, phosgene* (*chem.*); (2) growth, as in *endogen* (*bot.*). [Gr. *-genēs*, born.]
gena *jē'nə*, *n.* the cheek or side of the head. — *adj.* **gē'nal.** [L. *gĕna.*]
genappe *jə-nap'*, *n.* a smooth worsted yarn used with silk in fringes, braid, etc. [*Genappe* in Belgium.]
gendarme *zhã'därm*, *n.* originally man-at-arms, horseman in full armour: since the French Revolution one of a corps of French military police: a similar policeman elsewhere: a rock-pillar on a mountain: — *pl.* **gen'darmes** occasionally **gens'darmes.** — *n.* **gendarm'erie** (*-ə-rē*) an armed police force: a police station or barracks. [Fr. *gendarme*, sing. from pl. *gens d'armes*, men-at-arms — *gens*, people, *de*, of, *armes*, arms.]
gender[1] *jen'dər*, *n.* kind (*obs.*): a distinction of words roughly answering to sex (*gram.*): loosely or jocularly, sex. — *adj.* **gen'derless** not having or indicating gender: not indicating differences in sex, suitable for either sex. [Fr. *genre* — L. *genus*, kind.]
gender[2] *jen'dər*, (*arch.*) *v.t.* to beget: to generate. — *v.i.* to copulate. [Fr. *gendrer* — L. *generāre.*]
gene *jēn*, (*biol.*) *n.* one of the units of DNA, arranged in linear fashion on the chromosomes, responsible for passing on specific characteristics from parents to offspring. — *adj.* **gĕn'ic** of or relating to a gene. — *ns.* **genom(e)** (*jē'nōm*) the full set of chromosomes of an

individual: the total number of genes in such a set; **gĕn'otype** genetic or factorial constitution of an individual: group of individuals all of which possess the same genetic constitution. — *adj.* **gĕnotypic** (*-tip'ik*). — *adv.* **gĕnotyp'ically.** — *n.* **genotȳpic'ity.** — **gene flow** the passing of genes to succeeding generations. [Ger. *Gen* — Gr. *-genēs*, born.]
gêne *zhen*, (Fr.) *n.* embarrassment. — Also **gene.** **-gene.** See **-gen.**
genealogy *jē-ni-al'ə-ji*, or *jen'i-*, *n.* history of the descent of families: the pedigree of a particular person or family. — *adjs.* **genealogical** (*-ə-loj'i-kl*), **genealog'ic.** — *adv.* **genealog'ically.** — *v.i.* **geneal'ogise, -ize** to investigate or treat of genealogy. — *n.* **geneal'ogist** one who studies or traces genealogies or descents. — **genealogical tree** a table of descent in the form of a tree with branches. [Gr. *geneālogiā* — *geneā*, race, *logos*, discourse.]
genera, *pl.* of **genus.**
generable. See **generate.**
general *jen'ə-rəl*, *adj.* relating to a genus or whole class: including various species: not special: not restricted or specialised: relating to the whole or to all or most: universal: nearly universal: common: prevalent: widespread: public: vague: (after an official title, etc.) chief, of highest rank, at the head of a department (as *director-general, postmaster-general*): socially accessible and familiar with all (*obs.*). — *adv.* (*Shak.*) generally. — *n.* the total: the most part, majority: an officer who is head over a whole department: a general officer: the chief commander of an army in service: one skilled in leadership, tactics, management: in the R.C. Church, the head of a religious order, responsible only to the Pope: the head of the Salvation Army: a general servant: the public, the vulgar (*Shak.*). — *v.t.* to act as general of. — *n.* **generā'lē** (L. *gen-er-ä'le*) general principles, esp. in *pl.* **generā'lia.** — *adj.* **gen'eralisable, -z-.** — *n.* **generalisā'tion, -z-.** — *v.t.* **gen'eralise, -ize** to make general: to include under a general term: to reduce to a general form: to comprehend as a particular case within a wider concept, proposition, definition, etc.: to represent or endow with the common characters of a group without the special characters of any one member: to bring to general use or knowledge: to infer inductively. — *v.i.* to make general statements: to form general concepts: to depict general character: to reason inductively. — *ns.* **generaliss'imo** (It. *superl.*) supreme commander of a great or combined force; **gen'eralist** one whose knowledge and skills are not restricted to one particular field: opp. of *specialist*; **general'ity.** — *adv.* **gen'erally** in a general or collective manner or sense: in most cases: upon the whole. — *n.* **gen'eralship** the position of a military commander: the art of manipulating armies: tactical management and leadership. — **General Assembly** see **assemble; general delivery** (*U.S.*) poste restante; **general election** an election of all the members of a body at once; **general epistles** see **catholic; general line** the party line; **general officer** an officer above rank of colonel; **general post** formerly, dispatch of mail to all parts, opp. to local *twopenny* or *penny post:* the first morning delivery of letters: a general change of positions, etc. (from a parlour game); **general practice** the work of a **general practitioner** (abbrev. **G.P.**), a doctor who treats patients for most illnesses or complaints, referring other cases to specialists; **general principle** a principle to which there are no exceptions within its range of application. — *adj.* **gen'eral-purpose** generally useful, not restricted to a particular function. — **general servant** one whose duties embrace domestic work of every kind; **general staff** military officers who advise senior officers on policy, administration, etc.; **General Synod** see **synod.** — **General Certificate of Education** in secondary education in England and Wales, a certificate obtainable at Ordinary, Advanced, and Scholarship levels for proficiency in one or more subjects; **general post office** formerly, an office receiv-

ing letters for the general post: the head post office of a town or district; **in general** as a generalisation: mostly, as a general rule. [O.Fr. — L. *generālis* — *genus*.]

generant. See **generate**.

generate *jen'ər-āt, v.t.* to produce: to bring into life or being: to evolve: to originate: to trace out (*geom.*). — *adj.* **gen'erable** that may be generated or produced. — *ns.* **gen'erant** a begetter, producer, parent (*arch.*): a line, point, or figure that traces out another figure by its motion (*geom.*); **generā'tion** production or originating: a single stage in natural descent: the people of the same age or period: descendants removed by the same number of steps from a common ancestor: the ordinary time interval between the births of successive generations — usu. reckoned at 30 or 33 years: off-spring, progeny, race: any of a series of files, each one an amended and updated version of the previous one (*comput.*): (in *pl.*) genealogy, history (*B.*): any of a number of stages, levels, or series, generally in which each stage, etc. is seen as a development of or improve-ment on the preceding one; **generā'tionism** traducian-ism. — *adj.* **gen'erative** having the power of, or con-cerned with, generating or producing. — *n.* **gen'erātor** a begetter or producer: an apparatus for producing gases, etc.: an apparatus for turning mechanical into electrical energy: a fundamental tone (*mus.*): — *fem.* **gen'erātrix** a mother: a generator: a generant (*geom.*): — *pl.* **gen'erātrices** (*-tri-sēz*). — **generating station** a plant where electricity is generated; **generation gap** a lack of communication and understanding between one generation and the next; **generative grammar** (*linguistics*) a description of language as a finite set of grammatical rules able to generate an infinite number of grammatical sentences. — **alternation of generations** see **alternate; motion generative** (*Shak.*) a male puppet: or perh. one who is a mere puppet so far as engendering is concerned; **spontaneous generation** the origination of living from non-living matter. [L. *generāre, -ātum* — *genus*, a kind.]

generic, -al, generically. See **genus**.

generous *jen'ə-rəs, adj.* of a noble nature: courageous (*obs.*): liberal: bountiful: invigorating in its nature, as wine: nobly born (*obs.*): ample. — *adv.* **gen'erously**. — *ns.* **gen'erousness, generos'ity** nobleness or liberality of nature: nobility of birth (*arch.*). [L. *generōsus*, of noble birth — *genus*, birth.]

genesis *jen'i-sis, n.* generation, creation, or production: (with *cap.*) the first book of the Bible: — *pl.* **gen'esēs**. — *adjs.* **Genesiac** (*ji-nē'si-ak*), **-al, Genesitic** (*jenə-sit'ik*) pertaining to Genesis. [Gr.]

genet[1]. See **jennet**.

genet[2], **genette** *jen'it, ji-net', ns.* a carnivorous animal (genus *Genetta*) allied to the civet: its fur, or an imitation. [Fr. *genette* — Sp. *gineta* — Ar. *jarnait*.]

genethliac *ji-neth'li-ak, adj.* relating to a birthday or to the casting of nativities. — *n.* a caster of nativities: a genethliacon. — *adj.* **genethliacal** (*jen-ith-lī'ə-kl*). — *adv.* **genethlī'acally**. — *n.* **genethlī'acon** a birthday ode. — *adjs.* **genethlialog'ic, -al**. — *n.* **gencthlial'ogy** (Gr. *genethliǎlogiǎ*) the art of casting nativities. [Gr. *genethlē*, birth.]

genetic, -al *ji-net'ik, -əl, adjs.* pertaining to origin or to genes. — *adv.* **genet'ically**. — *n.* **genet'icist** (*-i-sist*) a student of genetics. — *n. sing.* **genet'ics** the branch of biology dealing with heredity and variation: inherited characteristics of an organism: origin: development. — *adj.* **genetotrophic** (*-trof'ik*; Gr. *trophē*, nourish-ment) denoting deficiency diseases which have an underlying genetic, and a direct nutritional, cause and which are treatable by dietary means. — **genetic code** the system by which genes pass on instructions that ensure transmission of hereditary characters; **genetic counselling** advice, based on chromosomal and amni-otic fluid investigation, etc., given to prospective par-ents on possible heritable defects in their children; **genetic engineering** a biological science whose aims

include the control of hereditary defects by the modi-fication or elimination of certain genes, and the mass production of useful biological substances (e.g. in-sulin) by the transplanting of genes; **genetic fingerprint** the particular DNA configuration exclusive to an individual human or animal or its offspring; **genetic fingerprinting** the identification of genetic fingerprints (e.g. in forensic science, to identify or eliminate a specific individual); **genetic manipulation** the alteration of natural genetic processes, usu. for the purposes of research; **genetic spiral** the line through insertions of successive leaves on a stem. [**genesis**.]

genetrix. See **genitor**.

genette. See **genet**[2].

geneva *ji-nē'və, n.* a spirit distilled from grain and flavoured with juniper berries, made chiefly in the Netherlands. — Also called **Hollands**; see **gin**[1]. — *n.* **genevrette** (*jen-əv-ret'*) a wine made from wild fruits flavoured with juniper-berries. [O.Du. *genever*, O.Fr. *genevre* — L. *jūniperus*, juniper; confused with town of *Geneva*.]

Genevan *ji-nē'vən, adj.* pertaining to *Geneva*. — *n.* an inhabitant of Geneva: an adherent of Genevan or Calvinistic theology. — *adj.* and *n.* **Genevese** (*jen'i-vēz*). — *n.* **Genē'vanism** Calvinism. — **Geneva bands** the two strips of white linen hanging down from the neck of some clerical robes; **Geneva Bible** a version of the Bible, long popular, produced by English exiles at Geneva in 1560; **Geneva Convention** an international agreement of 1865 providing for the neutrality of hospitals, and the security of sanitary officers, naval and military chaplains; **Geneva cross** a red cross on a white ground displayed for protection in war of per-sons serving in hospitals, etc.; **Geneva gown** the dark, long preaching gown of the early Geneva reformers, and still the common form of pulpit-gown among Presbyterians; **Genevan theology** so called from Calvin's residence in Geneva and the establishment of his doctrines there.

genevrette. See **geneva**.

genial[1] *jē'ni-əl, adj.* pertaining to marriage and generation (*arch.*): favouring growth: cheering: kindly: sympa-thetic: healthful. — *v.t.* **gē'nialise, -ize** to impart ge-niality to. — *ns.* **geniality** (*-al'i-ti*), **gē'nialness**. — *adv.* **gē'nially**. [L. *geniālis* — *genius*, the tutelary spirit.]

genial[2] *jə-nī'əl, adj.* of or pertaining to the chin. [Gr. *geneion*, chin — *genys*, under jaw.]

genic. See **gene**.

geniculate, -d *jə-nik'ū-lāt, -id, adjs.* bent like a knee: jointed: knotted. — *v.t.* **genic'ulate** to form joints in. — *adv.* **genic'ulately**. — *n.* **geniculā'tion**. [L. *genicu-lātus* — *geniculum*, a little knee — *genū*, the knee.]

genie *jē'ni, n.* a jinnee (see **jinn**). [Fr. *génie* — L. *genius*, adopted because of its similarity to the Arabic word.]

genii. See **genius**.

genipap *jen'i-pap, n.* a large West Indian tree (*Genipa americana*; Rubiaceae): its orange-sized, wine-flavoured fruit. — Also **gen'ip**. [From Tupí.]

Genista *jə-nis'tə, n.* a genus of shrubby, papilionaceous plants, with simple leaves and yellow flowers — green-weed and petty whin: (without *cap.*) a plant of this genus. [L. *genista*, broom.]

genital *jen'i-təl, adj.* belonging to generation or the act of producing. — *n.pl.* **gen'itals** (also **genitā'lia**) the organs of generation, esp. external. — *adjs.* **genital'ic; genito-ūr'inary** pertaining to genital and urinary or-gans or functions. [L. *genitālis* — *gignĕre, genitum*, to beget.]

genitive *jen'i-tiv, adj.* pertaining to generation (*obs.*): of or belonging to case expressing origin, possession, or similar relation (*gram.*). — *n.* (*gram.*) the genitive case: a word in the genitive case. — *adj.* **geniti'val**. — *advs.* **geniti'vally, gen'itively**. [L. *genitīvus* (— *gignĕre, genitum*, to beget) for Gr. *genikē* (*ptōsis*), properly, generic (case) — *genos*, a class.]

genitor *jen'i-tər, n.* a father: a parent: a progenitor: —

fem. **gen'etrix, gen'itrix.** — *n.* **gen'iture** engendering: birth. [L.]

genius *jēn'yəs,* or *jē'ni-əs, n.* the special inborn faculty of any individual: special taste or natural disposition: consummate intellectual, creative, or other power, more exalted than talent: one so endowed: a good or evil spirit, supposed to preside over every person, place, and thing, and esp. to preside over a man's destiny from his birth: a person who exerts a power, influence (whether good or bad) over another: prevailing spirit or tendency: type or generic exemplification: — *pl.* **ge'niuses;** in sense of spirit, **genii** (*jē'ni-ī*). [L. *genius* — *gignĕre, genitum,* to beget.]

genius loci *jē'ni-əs lō'sī, gen'i-ōos lo'kē,* (L.) the spirit of the place.

genizah *gə-nēz'ə, n.* a room adjoining a synagogue for the safe-keeping of old or damaged books, documents or valuables. [Heb.]

gennet. See **jennet.**

genoa, Genoa *jen'ō-ə, jə-nō'ə,* (*naut.*) *n.* a large jib which overlaps the mainsail. **Genoa cake** a rich cake containing fruit, with almonds on the top. [*Genoa* in Italy.]

genocide *jen'ō-sīd, n.* deliberate extermination of a race or other group: one who exterminates, or approves extermination of, a race, etc. — *adj.* **genoci'dal.** [Gr. *genos,* race, and L. *caedĕre,* to kill.]

Genoese *jen'ō-ēz,* or *-ēz',* **Genovese** *-vēz, adjs.* relating to Genoa. — *ns.* an inhabitant, citizen, or native of Genoa: — *pls.* **Genoese, Genovese.** [L. *Genua,* It. *Genova,* Genoa.]

genom(e), genotype, etc. See **gene.**

genouillère *zhə-nōō-yer, n.* the knee-piece in armour. [Fr.]

genre *zhã-r', n.* kind: a literary or artistic type or style: a style of painting scenes from familiar or rustic life. — Also *adj.* [Fr., — L. *genus.*]

Genro *gen-rō', n.* the Japanese Elder Statesmen. [Jap.]

gens¹ *jenz* (L. *gãns), n.* in ancient Rome, a clan including several families descended from a common ancestor: tribe: — *pl.* **gen'tēs.** — *adj.* **gen'tile** (q.v.). — **gens togata** the toga-wearing nation, i.e. the Romans. [L. *gēns, gentis.*]

gens² *zhã,* (Fr.) *n.pl.* people. — **gens de bien** (*də byē*) honest, respectable people; **gens de condition** (*də kɔ̃-dēs-yɔ̃*) people of rank; **gens d'église** (*dā-glēz*) churchmen; **gens de lettres** (*də letr'*) men of letters; **gens de loi** (*də lwa*) lawyers; **gens de guerre** (*də ger*) military men; **gens de peu** (*də pø*) people of humble condition; **gens du monde** (*dü mɔ̃d*) people of fashion.

gent¹ *jent,* (*Spens.*) *adj.* noble: gentle. [O.Fr., — L. *genitus,* born.]

gent² *jent, n.* short for **gentleman:** one who apes the gentleman: — *pl.* **gents.** — *n.* **gents'** men's public lavatory.

genteel *jen-tēl', adj.* well-bred: graceful in manners or in form: fashionable: now used mainly with mocking reference to a standard of obsolete snobbery or false refinement. — *adj.* **genteel'ish.** — *n.* **genteel'ism** a would-be refined substitute for the right word or phrase. — *adv.* **genteel'ly.** — *n.* **genteel'ness.** [Fr. *gentil* — L. *gentīlis;* see **gentle.**]

gentes. See **gens¹.**

gentian *jen'shən, n.* any plant of the genus *Gentiana,* herbs, usually blue-flowered, abounding chiefly in alpine regions, typical of the family **Gentianā'ceae** (sympetalous dicotyledons with corolla twisted in bud and unilocular ovary): the root and rhizome of the yellow gentian used as a tonic and stomachic. — *adj.* **gentianā'ceous.** — *n.* **gentianell'a** a name for several species of gentian, esp. *Gentiana acaulis,* with deep-blue flowers. — **gentian violet** in the British pharmacopoeia, crystal violet: sometimes, methyl violet: sometimes, a mixture of the two. [L. *gentiāna,* acc. to Pliny from *Gentius,* king of Illyria, who introduced it in medicine (2nd cent. B.C.).]

Gentile, gentile *jen'tīl, n.* anyone not a Jew (*B.*), or not a Christian (now *rare*), or not a Mormon. — *adjs.* **gen'tile** of or belonging to a *gens* or clan: belonging to the Gentiles: denoting a race or country (*gram.*); **gentilic** (*-til'ik*) tribal; **gen'tilish** heathenish. — *n.* **gen'tilism** (*-til-,* or *-til-*) paganism. — *adjs.* **gentilitial** (*jen-ti-lish'l*), **gentili'tian, gentili'tious** pertaining to a gens. [L. *gentīlis* — *gēns,* a nation, clan.]

gentilesse, gentility, etc. See **gentle.**

gentilhomme *zhã-tē-yom,* (Fr.) *n.* a nobleman: a gentleman.

gentle *jen'tl, adj.* well-born (*arch.*): mild and refined in manners: mild in disposition or action: amiable: soothing: moderate: gradual. — *v.t.* to ennoble (*arch.*): to make gentle: to handle gently. — *n.* one well born (*arch.*): a trained falcon: hence a peregrine falcon (*masc.* **ter'cel-gen'tle;** *fem.* **fal'con-gen'tle**): a soft maggot used as bait in angling. — *n.* **gentilesse** (*-til-es'*) quality of being gentle, courtesy. — *v.t.* **gen'tilise, -ize** to raise to the class of gentleman. — *n.* **gentil'ity** good birth or extraction: good breeding: politeness of manners: genteel people: marks of gentility — *ns.* **gen'tlehood** position or character attaching to gentle birth; **gen'tleness; gen'tlenesse** (*obs.*) same as **gentilesse.** — *adv.* **gent'ly.** — **gentle craft** shoemaking: angling. — *n.pl.* **gen'tlefolk** people of good family. — *adj.* **gen'tle-heart'ed** having a gentle or kind disposition. — **gen'tleman** a man of good birth or high social standing: one who without a title bears a coat of arms (*hist.*): more generally every man above the rank of yeoman, including the nobility (*hist.*): a man of refined manners: a well-to-do man of no occupation: a man of good feeling and instincts, courteous and honourable: a polite term used for man in general: a body-servant (*Shak.*): — *pl.* **gen'tlemen** — also a word of address: — *fem.* **gen'tlewoman** a personal attendant on a lady of rank (*hist.*): a woman of quality, or of good breeding, a lady (*old-fashioned*): — *pl.* **gen'tlewomen.** — *adj.* **gen'tlewomanly** like, or characteristic of, a refined and well-bred woman. — *n.* **gen'tlewomanliness.** — **Gen'tleman-at-arms** a member of the royal bodyguard, instituted in 1509, and now composed of military officers of service and distinction only; **gen'tleman-cadet'** a student in a military college; **gen'tleman-comm'oner** (*formerly*) at Oxford and Cambridge, undergraduate with special privileges; **gentleman farmer** a landowner who lives on his estate superintending the cultivation of his own soil: a farmer who deputes the work of his farm to a farm manager and other staff; **gen'tlemanhood, gen'tlemanship** the condition or character of a gentleman. — *adjs.* **gen'tlemanlike** like or characteristic of a gentleman; **gen'tlemanly** befitting a gentleman: well-bred, refined, generous. — **gen'tlemanliness; gentleman's (-men's) agreement** an agreement resting on honour, not on formal contract; **gentleman's gentleman** a valet; **Gentleman's Relish®** a savoury paste for spreading on sandwiches, etc.; **gentleman usher** (*pl.* **gentleman ushers**) a gentleman who serves as an usher at court, or as an attendant on a person of rank; **gentle reader** courteous reader, an old-fashioned phrase common in the prefaces of books; **gentlewoman,** etc. see after **gentleman.** — **Gentleman of the Chapel Royal** a lay singer who assists the priests in the choral service of the royal chapel. [O.Fr. (Fr.) *gentil* — L. *gentīlis,* belonging to the same *gens* or clan, later, well-bred; see **genteel.**]

Gentoo *jen'tōo, jen-tōo', n.* Telugu, a Telugu-speaker, a pagan of India, a Hindu (*hist.*): (without *cap.*) a Falkland Island penguin. — Also *adj.* [Port. *gentio,* a Gentile.]

gentry *jen'tri, n.* the class of people next below the rank of nobility: people of a particular, esp. an inferior, stamp (*coll.*): rank by birth: the rank of gentleman: good manners and courtesy (*Shak.*). — *ns.* **gen'trice** (*-tris; arch.*) gentle birth: good breeding; **gentrificā'tion** the move of middle-class people into a formerly working-class area with the consequent change in the character of the area: the modernising of old, badly-equipped property, usu. with a view to increasing its value. — *v.t.* **gen'trify.** [O.Fr. *genterise, gentelise,* formed from adj. *gentil,* gentle.]

genty *jen'ti, (Scot.) adj.* neat, dainty: graceful.

genu *jen'ōō, jen'ū (anat.) n.* the knee: a knee-like bend or structure. [L., knee.]

genuflect *jen'ū-flekt, v.i.* to bend the knee in worship or respect. — *n.* **genüflex'ion** (also **genüflec'tion**). [L. *genū,* the knee, *flectĕre, flexum,* to bend.]

genuine *jen'ū-in, adj.* natural: native: not spurious: real: pure: sincere. — *adv.* **gen'uinely.** — *n.* **gen'uineness.** [L. *genuīnus* — *gignĕre,* to beget.]

genus *jē'nəs, n.* a taxonomic group of lower rank than a family, consisting of closely related species, in extreme cases of one species only (*biol.*): a class of objects comprehending several subordinate species (*log.*): — *pl.* **genera** (*jen'ə-rə*), **gē'nuses.** — *adjs.* **generic, -al** (*ji-ner'ik, -əl*) general, applicable to any member of a group or class: (**generic**; of a drug, etc.) not patented or sold as a proprietary brand (also *n.*). — *adv.* **gener'ically.** — **generic name** (*biol.*) the name of the genus, placed first in naming the species, thus *Equus caballus* (horse), *Equus asinus* (ass), *Equus zebra,* etc., are species of the genus Equus, and Equus is the generic name. [L. *gĕnus, generis,* birth; cog. with Gr. *genos.*]

geo, gio *gyō, (Orkney, Shetland) n.* a gully, creek: — *pl.* **geos, gios.** [O.N. *gjā.*]

geo- *jē'ō,* in composition, of the earth. [Gr. *gē,* the earth.]

geocarpy *jē-ō-kär'pi, n.* the production, or ripening, of fruit underground. — *adj.* **geocarp'ic.** [Gr. *gē,* earth, *karpos,* fruit.]

geocentric *jē-ō-sen'trik, adj.* having the earth for centre: as viewed or reckoned from the centre of the earth (*astron.*): taking life on earth as the basis for evaluation. — Also **geocen'trical.** — *adv.* **geocen'trically.** — *n.* **geocen'tricism** (*-sizm*) belief that the earth is the centre of the universe. [Gr. *gē,* the earth, *kentron,* point, centre.]

geochemistry *jē-ō-kem'is-tri, n.* the chemistry of the crust of the earth. — *adj.* **geochem'ical.** — *adv.* **geochem'ically.** — *n.* **geochem'ist.** [geo-.]

geochronology *jē-ō-kron-ol'ə-ji, n.* the science of measuring geological time. — *adj.* **geochronolog'ical.** — *n.* **geochronol'ogist.** [geo-.]

geode *jē'ōd, n.* (a rock or stone having) a druse, i.c. a cavity lined with crystals that have grown inwards (*geol.*): a rounded hollow nodule of ironstone (*mining*). — *adj.* **geŏd'ic.** [Fr. *géode* — Gr. *geōdēs,* earthy — *gē,* earth, *eidos,* form.]

geodesy *jē-od'i-si, n.* earth measurement on a large scale: surveying with allowance for the earth's curvature. — Also *n. sing.* **geodetics** (*jē-ō-det'iks*). — *adjs.* **geodesic** (*jē-ō-des'ik, -dē'sik*), **-al** pertaining to or determined by geodesy. — *n.* **geod'esist** one skilled in geodesy. — *adjs.* **geodet'ic, -al** geodesic. — *adv.* **geodet'ically.** — **geodesic dome** a light strong dome made by combining a grid of triangular or other straightline elements with a section of a sphere; **geodesic** or **geodetic (line)** the shortest line on a surface between two points on it; **geodetic surveying** geodesy, surveying large areas with allowance for the earth's curvature. [Gr. *geōdaisiā* — *gē,* the earth, *daisis,* division.]

geodimeter *jē-ō-di'mi-tər, n.* an instrument which measures distances by means of a beam of light, calculating on the basis of the speed of light. [Orig. trademark.]

geodynamics *jē-ō-dī-nam'iks, n. sing.* the study of the dynamic processes and forces within the earth. — *adjs.* **geodynam'ic(al).** [geo-.]

geogeny. See geogony.

geognosy *jē-og'nə-si, n.* knowledge of the general structure, condition, and materials of the earth. — Also (*rare*) **geognosis** (*jē-əg-nō'sis*). — *n.* **gē'ognost.** — *adjs.* **gēognostic** (*-nos'tik*), **-al.** — *adv.* **gēognost'ically.** [Fr. *géognosie* — Gr. *gē,* the earth, *gnōsis,* knowledge.]

geogony *jē-og'ə-ni, n.* the science or theory of the formation of the earth. — Also **geogeny** (*-oj'*). — *adj.*

geogonic (*jē-ō-gon'ik*). [Gr. *gē,* the earth, *gonē,* generation.]

geography *jē-og'rə-fi, n.* the science of the surface of the earth and its inhabitants: a book containing a description of the earth. — *n.* **geog'rapher.** — *adjs.* **geographic** (*jē-ō-graf'ik*), **-al.** — *adv.* **geograph'ically.** — **geographical distribution** see distribution; **geographical mile** see mile. — **physical, political geography** see physic, politic. [Gr. *geōgraphiā* — *gē,* earth, *graphein,* to write.]

geoid *jē'oid, n.* the figure of the earth's mean sea-level surface assumed to be continued across the land, approximately an oblate ellipsoid of revolution. — *adj.* **geoid'al.** [Gr. *geōdēs, geoeidēs,* earth-like — *gē,* earth, *eidos,* form.]

geolatry *jē-ol'ə-tri, n.* earth-worship. [Gr. *gē,* earth, *latreiā,* worship.]

geology *jē-ol'ə-ji, n.* the science relating to the history and development of the earth's crust, with its successive floras and faunas. — *ns.* **geologian** (*jē-ə-lō'ji-ən*), **geŏl'ogist, geŏl'oger.** — *adjs.* **geologic** (*-loj'ik*), **-al.** — *adv.* **geolog'ically.** — *v.i.* **geol'ogise, -ize** to work at geology in the field. — *v.t.* to investigate the geology of. — **geological time** time before written history, divided into epochs each of which saw the formation of one of the great rock systems. — **dynamical geology** the study of the work of natural agents in shaping the earth's crust — wind, frost, rivers, volcanic action, etc.; **structural geology** the study of the arrangement and structure of rock masses. [Fr. *géologie* — Gr. *gē,* earth, *logos,* a discourse.]

geomagnetism *jē-ō-mag'nət-izm, n.* terrestrial magnetism: the study of this. — *adj.* **geomagnet'ic.** — *n.* **geomag'netist.** [geo-.]

geomancy *jē'ō-man-si, n.* divination by figures of or on earth. — *n.* **gē'omancer.** — *adj.* **geoman'tic.** [Gr. *gē,* earth, *manteiā,* divination.]

geomedicine *jē-ō-med'sin, n.* the study of diseases as influenced by geographical environment. — *adj.* **geomed'ical.** [geo-.]

geometry *jē-om'i-tri, n.* that part of mathematics which treats the properties of points, lines, surfaces and solids, either under classical Euclidean assumptions, or (in the case of *elliptic, hyperbolic,* etc., *geometry*) involving postulates not all of which are identical with Euclid's: any study of a mathematical system in which figures undergo transformations, concerned with discussion of those properties of the figures which remain constant: a textbook of geometry. — *ns.* **geom'eter** a geometrician: a geometrid; **geometrician** (*-me-trish'ən*) one skilled in geometry. — *adjs.* **geometric** (*-met'*), **-al** relating to or according to geometry: consisting of or using simple figures such as geometry deals with. — *adv.* **geomet'rically.** — *ns.* **geom'etrid** any moth of the family or superfamily **Geomet'ridae** whose caterpillars are loopers; **geometrīsā'tion, -z-.** — *v.t.* and *v.i.* **geom'etrise, -ize** to work geometrically: to show in geometric form. — *n.* **geom'etrist.** — **geometrical progression** a series of quantities each of which has the same ratio to its predecessor; **geometric mean** see mean[2]. [Gr. *geōmetriā* — *gē,* earth, *metron,* a measure.]

geomorphogeny *jē-ō-mör-foj'ən-i, n.* the scientific study of the origins and development of land forms. — *adj.* **geomorphogē'nic.** — *n.* **geomorphog'enist.** [geo-.]

geomorphology *jē-ō-mör-fol'ə-ji, n.* the (study of the) morphology and development of land forms, including those under the sea. — *adjs.* **geomorpholog'ic, -al.** — *adv.* **geomorpholog'ically.** — *n.* **geomorphol'ogist.** [geo-.]

Geomys *jē'ō-mis, n.* the typical genus of **Geomyidae** (*-mī'i-dē*), the pouched rats. — *adj.* **geomy'oid.** [Gr. *gē,* earth, *mȳs,* mouse.]

geophagy *jē-of'ə-ji, n.* earth-eating. — Also **geoph'agism.** — *n.* **geoph'agist.** — *adj.* **geoph'agous** (*-gəs*). [Gr. *gē,* earth, *phagein,* to eat.]

geophilous *jē-of'il-əs, adj.* living in or on the ground: geocarpic: having a short stem with leaves at ground-level. — *adj.* **geophil'ic.** [Gr. *gē*, earth, *phileein*, to love.]

geophone *jē'ə-fōn, n.* (usu. in *pl.*) a device for detecting sound-waves, shock-waves, etc. in the ground. [Gr. *gē*, earth, *phōnē*, voice, sound.]

geophysics *gē-ō-fiz'iks, n. sing.* the physics of the earth. — *adj.* **geophys'ical.** — *n.* **geophys'icist** (*-i-sist*). [geo-.]

geophyte *jē'ō-fīt, n.* a plant that survives the winter by subterranean buds. — *adj.* **geophytic** (*-fit'ik*). [Gr. *gē*, earth, *phyton*, plant.]

geopolitics *jē-ō-pol'it-iks, n. sing.* a science concerned with problems of states, such as frontiers, as affected by their geographical environment: the special combination of geographical and political considerations in a particular state: a Nazi doctrine justifying expansion by necessity for Lebensraum, etc. — *adv.* **geopolit'ically.** — *adj.* **geopolit'ical.** — *n.* **geopoliti'cian.** [Ger. *Geopolitik*; see geo-.]

geoponic, -al *jē-ō-pon'ik, -əl, adjs.* agricultural, — *n sing.* **geopon'ics** the science of agriculture. [Gr. *geōponikos* — *gē*, earth, *ponos*, labour.]

geordie *jör'di, n.* a guinea, from the figure of St *George*: a safety-lamp for miners invented by *George* Stephenson: a coal-pitman: a collier-boat: (usu. with *cap.*) a native of Tyneside. — *adj.* pertaining to Tyneside.

George *jörj, n.* a jewelled figure of St *George* slaying the dragon, worn by Knights of the Garter: the automatic pilot of an aircraft. — **George Cross** an award for outstanding courage or heroism given in cases where a purely military honour is not applicable — instituted during World War II; **George Medal** an award for gallantry given to civilians and members of the armed forces. — **St George's cross** the Greek cross of England, red on a white ground.

georgette *jör-jet', n.* a thin silk fabric. [Named after a milliner.]

Georgian *jör'ji-ən, adj.* relating to or contemporary with any of the various *Georges*, kings of Great Britain: relating to or following Henry *George*, Lloyd *George*, or other of the name: belonging to *Georgia* (*Gurjestan, Gruzia*) in the Caucasus, its people, language, etc.: of or pertaining to the American State of *Georgia*. — Also *n.* — **Georgian planet** Uranus, named after George III by its discoverer, Sir William Herschel.

georgic *jör'jik, adj.* relating to agriculture or rustic affairs. — *n.* a poem on husbandry. [L. *geōrgicus* — Gr. *geōrgikos* — *geōrgiā*, agriculture — *gē*, earth, *ergon*, work.]

geoscience *jē'ō-sī-əns, n.* any of the scientific disciplines, such as geology or geomorphology, which deal with the earth, or all of these collectively. — *adj.* **geoscientif'ic.** [geo-.]

geosphere *jē'ō-sfēr, n.* the solid part of the earth, distinguished from *atmosphere* and *hydrosphere.* [Gr. *gē*, earth, *sphaira*, sphere.]

geostatic *jē-ō-stat'ik, adj.* capable of sustaining the pressure of earth from all sides. — *n. sing.* **geostat'ics** the statics of rigid bodies. [Gr. *gē*, the earth, *statikos*, causing to stand.]

geostationary *jē-ō-stā'shən-ə-ri, adj.* of a satellite, etc., orbiting the earth in time with the earth's own rotation, i.e. circling it once every 24 hours, so remaining above the same spot on the earth's surface. [geo-.]

geostrophic *jē-ō-strof'ik, adj.* of a virtual force used to account for the change in direction of the wind relative to the surface of the earth arising from the earth's rotation: of a wind whose direction and force are partly determined by the earth's rotation. [Gr. *gē*, earth, *strophē*, a turn.]

geosynchronous *jē-ō-sing'krə-nəs, adj.* of a satellite, etc., geostationary. [geo-.]

geosyncline *jē-ō-sin'klīn, n.* a syncline on a great scale. — *adj.* **geosyncli'nal.** [geo-.]

geotaxis *jē-ō-taks'is, n.* response of an organism to the stimulus of gravity. — *adjs.* **geotact'ic, -al.** — *adv.* **geotact'ically.** [Gr. *gē*, earth, *taxis*, arrangement.]

geotechnics *jē-ō-tek'niks, n.sing.* the application of scientific and engineering principles to the solution of civil engineering, and other, problems created by the nature and constitution of the earth's crust. — *adjs.* **geotech'nic, -al.** — *n.* **geotechnol'ogy** the application of science and technology to the extraction and use of the earth's natural resources. — *adj.* **geotechnolog'ical.** [geo-.]

geotectonic *jē-ō-tek-ton'ik, adj.* relating to the structure of rock masses. — *n. sing.* **geotecton'ics** structural geology. [Gr. *gē*, earth, *tektōn*, a builder.]

geothermic *jē-ō-thûr'mik, geothermal -əl, adjs.* pertaining to or heated by the internal heat of the earth. — *n.* **geothermom'eter** an instrument for measuring subterranean temperatures. — **geothermal energy** energy extracted from the earth's natural heat, i.e. from hot springs and certain kinds of rock. [Gr. *gē*, earth, *thermē*, heat.]

geotropism *jē-ot'rop-izm, (bot.) n.* geotaxis (positive downwards, negative upwards). — *adj.* **geotrop'ic.** — *adv.* **geotrop'ically.** [Gr. *gē*, earth, *tropos*, a turning.]

gerah *gē'rä, (B.) n.* the smallest Hebrew weight and coin, 1/20 of a shekel. [Heb. *gērāh*.]

geraniol. See geranium.

geranium *ji-rān'yəm, n.* a plant of the genus **Geranium** with seed-vessels like a crane's bill, typical of the family **Geraniaceae** (*-i-ā'si-ē*): (*loosely*) any cultivated plant of the genus *Pelargonium.* — *n.* **gerā'niol** an alcohol ($C_{10}H_{18}O$) forming a constituent of many of the esters used in perfumery. [L., — Gr. *geranion* — *geranos*, a crane.]

gerbe *jûrb, n.* a wheat-sheaf (*her.*): a fountain or firework resembling a wheat-sheaf. [Fr. *gerbe*; cf. garb[2].]

Gerbera *gûr'bə-rə, jûr', n.* a genus of composite plants of S. Africa, etc: (without *cap.*) a plant of this genus. [T. *Gerber*, German naturalist.]

gerbil *jûr'bil, n.* a small desert-dwelling rodent capable of causing great damage to crops but often kept as a pet. — Also **jer'bil** and (esp. formerly) **ger'bille.** [Fr. *gerbille*.]

gere (*Spens.*). Same as gear.

gerent *jē'rənt, jer', n.* a controller, ruler. [L. *gerēns, -entis,* pr.p. of *gerĕre,* to manage.]

gerenuk *ge'rə-nook, n.* a long-legged, long-necked antelope of East Africa, *Litocranius walleri.* [From the Somali name.]

gerfalcon, gyrfalcon, jerfalcon *jûr'fö(l)-kn, n.* a large northern falcon. [O.Fr. *gerfaucon* — L.L. *gyrofalcō,* most prob. O.H.G. *gîr,* a vulture (Ger. *Geier*); see falcon.]

geriatrics *jer-i-at'riks, n. sing.* medical care of the old. — *adj.* **geriat'ric.** — *n.* (*coll.*) an old person. — *ns.* **geriatrician** (*-ə-trish'ən*), **geriatrist** (*-at'rist*); **geriatry** (*jer-ī'ə-tri*) care of the old, old people's welfare. [Gr. *gēras,* old age, *iātros,* physician.]

gerle (*Spens.*). Same as girl.

germ *jûrm, n.* a rudimentary form of a living thing, whether plant or animal: a plant ovary (*obs.*): a shoot: that from which anything springs, the origin or beginning: a first principle: that from which a disease springs: a micro-organism, esp. a malign one. — *v.i.* to put forth buds, sprout. — *ns.* **ger'men, ger'min** (*Shak.* **ger'main, ger'maine**) a rudiment: a shoot: the ovary in a flower (*obs.*); **germ'icide** that which kills germs. — *adjs.* **germici'dal; germ'inable** that can be germinated; **germ'inal** pertaining to a germ or rudiment: in germ, or (*fig.*) earliest stage of development: seminal (*fig.*); **germ'inant** sprouting: budding: capable of developing. — *v.i.* **germ'inate** to begin to grow (esp. of a seed or spore). — *v.t.* to cause to sprout. — *n.* **germinā'tion.** — *adj.* **germ'inative** — **germ'-cell** a sperm or ovum, a gamete or cell from which it springs; **germ'-lay'er** a primary layer in an embryo — ectoderm, mesoderm, or endoderm; **germ'-plasm** that part of the nuclear protoplasmic material which, according to early theories of inheritance, is the vehicle of heredity, and maintains its continuity from generation to generation; **germ theory** the theory that all living organisms can be produced only from living organisms, by the growth and development of germ-cells: the theory that micro-organisms cause all infectious diseases; **germ warfare** warfare in which bacteria are used as weapons. [Partly through Fr. *germe*, from L. *germen, -inis*, a sprout, bud, germ *germināre, -ātum*, to sprout.]

germain(e) (*Shak*.). See **germ**.

german *jûr'mən, adj.* of the first degree: full (see **brother, cousin**): closely allied. — *n.* a full brother or sister: a near relative. — *adj.* **germane** (*-mān'*) nearly related (to): relevant, appropriate (to). — *adv.* **germane'ly.** — *n.* **germane'ness.** [O.Fr. *germain* — L. *germānus.*]

German *jûr'mən, n.* a native or citizen of *Germany*, or one of the same linguistic or ethnological stock (*pl.* **Ger'mans**): the German language, esp. High German. — *adj.* of or from Germany, or the Germans: German-speaking. — *adjs.* **Germanesque'** marked by German characteristics; **Germanic** (*-man'ik*) of Germany: of the linguistic family to which German, English, Norwegian, etc., belong — Teutonic. — *n.* an extinct Indo-European tongue which differentiated into **East Germanic** (Gothic and other extinct languages), **North Germanic** or Scandinavian (Norwegian, Danish, Swedish, Icelandic) and **West Germanic** (English, Frisian, Dutch, Low German, High German). — *adv.* **German'ically.** — *v.t.* **Ger'manīse, -ize** to make German. — *v.i.* to become German: to adopt German ways. — *n.* **Germanisā'tion, -z-.** — *adj.* **Ger'manish** somewhat German. — *ns.* **Ger'manism** a German idiom: German ideas and ways; **Ger'manist** one learned in German philology or other matters relating to Germany. — *adj.* **Germanis'tic** pertaining to the study of German. — *ns.* **German'ophil** a lover of the Germans and things German, now usu. **German'ophile; Germanophil'ia; German'ophobe** one who fears or hates the Germans and things German. — **Ger'man-band'** street-musicians, orig. from Germany; **German flute** the ordinary modern flute; **German measles** rubella; **German Ocean** (*arch.*) the North Sea; **German silver** an alloy of copper, nickel, and zinc, white like silver, and first made in Germany; **German sixth** a chord with major third, perfect fifth, and augmented sixth. — **German shepherd (police) dog** see **Alsatian; High German** the speech, originally of High or Southern Germany, the literary language throughout Germany; **Low German** Platt-Deutsch, the language of Low or Northern Germany: formerly applied to all the West Germanic dialects except High German. [L. *Germānus*, German.]

germander *jər-man'dər, n.* a labiate herb (*Teucrium*) with aromatic, bitter, and stomachic properties. — **germander speedwell** a bright blue-flowered veronica (*V. chamaedrys*). [L.L. *germandra* — Late Gr. *chamandrya* — Gr. *chamaidrȳs* — *chamai*, on the ground, *drȳs*, oak.]

germane. See **german**.

Germanice *jûr-man'i-sē*, *ger-man'ik-e*, (L.) *adv.* in German.

germanium *jər-mā'ni-əm, n.* a metallic element (Ge; atomic number 32), much used in diodes, transistors and rectifiers for its properties as a semiconductor. [Discovered in 1885 by C. Winkler, a *German*.]

germen, germicide. See **germ**.

germin, germinal, germinate, etc. See **germ**.

Germinal *zher-mē-nal', n.* the seventh month of the French revolutionary calendar, about 21st March to 19th April. [See **germ**.]

gerne *gûrn*, (*Spens*.) *v.i.* to grin or gape. [**grin**[1].]

gerontic *ger-* or *jer-on'tik*, (*biol.*) *adj.* pertaining to the senescent period in the life-history of an individual. — *n.* **gerontoc'racy** government by old men. — *adjs.* **gerontocrat'ic; gerontolog'ical.** — *ns.* **gerontol'ogist; gerontol'ogy** scientific study of the processes of growing old; **geron'tophil(e)** (*-fīl, -fīl*) one who experiences **gerontophilia** (*-fīl'i-ə*), sexual feeling towards old people; **geron'tophobe** (*-fōb*) one who experiences

gerontophō'bia, an irrational fear of old people and old age; **gerontotherapeut'ics** the science of medical treatment of the diseases of old age. [Gr. *gerōn, -ontos*, old man.]

geropiga *jer-ō-pē'gə, n.* a mixture of grape-juice, brandy, etc., used to doctor port-wine. [Port.]

Gerry. See **Jerry.**

gerrymander *jer'i-man-dər*, also *ger', v.t.* to rearrange (voting districts) in the interests of a particular party or candidate: to manipulate (facts, arguments, etc.) so as to reach undue conclusions. — *n.* an arrangement of the above nature. [Formed from the name of Governor Elbridge *Gerry* (1744–1814) and sala*mander*, from the likeness to that animal of the gerrymandered map of Massachusetts in 1811.]

gerund *jer'ənd, n.* a part of a Latin verb with the value of a verbal noun, as *amandum*, loving: in English, a noun with the ending *-ing* formed from a verb and having some of the qualities of a verb, as the possibility of governing an object, etc.; often preceded by a possessive (e.g. *My leaving her was unwise*). — *adjs.* **gerundial** (*ji-rund'i-əl*), **gerundival** (*jer-ən-dī'vl*), **gerundive** (*ji-rund'iv*). — *n.* **gerund'ive** a Latin verbal adjective expressing necessity, as *amandus, -a, -um*, deserving or requiring to be loved. — **ger'und-grind'er** a pedantic teacher. [L. *gerundium* — *gerĕre*, to bear.]

Gesellschaft *gə-zel'shäft*, (Ger.) *n.* an association of people, e.g. a commercial company, united by individual commitment to a common cause.

Gesneria *jes-nē'ri-ə, n.* a tropical America genus typical of the **Gesneria'ceae**, a family close akin to the Scrophulariaceae: (without *cap.*) a plant of this genus. [Named after Konrad von *Gesner* (1516–65), Swiss botanist and scholar.]

gessamine (*Milt.*). Same as **jasmine.**

gesse (*Spens.*). Same as **guess**[1].

gesso *jes'ō, n.* plaster of Paris: a plaster surface prepared as a ground for painting: — *pl.* **gess'oes.** [It., — L. *gypsum*; see **gypsum**.]

gest[1] *jest*, (*Shak.*) *n.* time fixed for a stay in a place. [O.Fr. *giste*, a stopping-place.]

gest[2], **geste** *jest, n.* an exploit: a tale of adventure, a romance. [O.Fr. *geste* — L. *gesta*, things done — *gerĕre, gestum*, to bear, behave; cf. **jest**.]

gest[3], **geste** *jest, n.* bearing: gesture. — *adj.* **gest'ic.** [Fr. *geste* — L. *gestus* — *gerĕre, gestum*, to bear, behave.]

gestalt *gə-shtält', n.* form, shape, pattern: organised whole or unit. — **Gestalt psychology** revolt from the atomistic outlook of the orthodox school, starts with the organised whole as something more than the sum of the parts into which it can be logically analysed. [Ger.]

gestant. See **gestate.**

Gestapo *gə-stä'pō, n.* the Nazi secret police in Germany. [From Ger. *Geheime Staatspolizei*, secret state police.]

gestate *jes-tāt', v.t.* to carry in the womb during the period from conception to birth: to conceive and develop slowly in the mind. — *v.i.* to be in the process of gestating. — *adj.* **ges'tant** laden (also *fig.*). — *n.* **gestation** (*jes-tā'shən*) being carried in a vehicle, a boat, etc. (*arch.*): the process of gestating (*biol.* and *fig.*). — *adjs.* **gestā'tional, gest'ative** of carriage, esp. in the womb; **gestatō'rial, ges'tatory** pertaining to carrying (*arch.*). — **gestatorial chair** a ceremonial chair on which the pope is carried in procession. [L. *gestāre, -ātum*, to carry — *gerĕre*, to bear.]

gesticulate *jes-tik'ū-lāt, v.i.* to make vigorous gestures. — *ns.* **gesticulā'tion; gestic'ulātor.** — *adjs.* **gestic'ulative, gestic'ulatory.** [L. *gesticulāri, -ātus* — *gesticulus*, dim. of *gestus*, gesture — *gerĕre*, to carry, behave.]

gesture *jes'chər, n.* a posture, or movement of the body (*obs.*): an action, esp. of the hands, expressive of sentiment or passion or intended to show inclination or disposition: the use of such movements: an action dictated by courtesy or diplomacy, or by a desire to impress: behaviour (*Shak.*). — *v.i.* to make a gesture or gestures. — *v.t.* to express by gesture(s). — *adj.*

ges'tural. [L.L. *gestūra* — L. *gestus*, from L. *gerĕre*, to carry, behave.]

Gesundheit *gə-zōōnt'hīt*, (Ger.) *interj.* your health (said to someone who has just sneezed). — **auf Ihre Gesundheit** (*owf ē'rə*; said to a drinking companion) here's to your health.

get *get, v.t.* to obtain: to acquire: to procure: to receive: to attain: to come to have: to catch: to grasp or take the meaning of: to learn: to commit to memory: to hit: to descry: to make out: to succeed in coming into touch or communication with (e.g. a wireless station): to worst, have the better of, gain a decisive advantage over: to baffle: to irritate: to grip emotionally, take, captivate, hit the taste of exactly: to induce: to cause to be, go, or become: to betake: to beget: to attack or injure, esp. in revenge (*coll.*). — *v.i.* to arrive, to bring or put oneself (in any place, position, or state): to become: to become richer: to clear out: — *pr.p.* **gett'ing;** *pa.t.* **got,** *obs.* **gat;** *pa.p.* **got,** *arch.,* Scot., and *U.S.* **gott'en.** — *n.* that which is got (*obs.*): output (*obs.*): offspring: (also **gait(t), geit** (*get*); see also **git,** and **gyte²**) a child, brat (Scot. contemptuously): begetting (*obs.*). — *adj.* **gett'able.** — *n.* **gett'er** one who, or that which evacuates: a material used, when evaporated by high-frequency induction currents, for evacuation of gas left in vacuum valves after sealing during manufacture. — *v.t.* to evacuate (a valve) using a getter. — *v.i.* to use a getter. — *ns.* **gett'ering** evacuation using a getter; **gett'ing** a gaining: anything gained: procreation. — *adj.* **get-at'-able** easily accessible. — **get'away** an escape: a start: breaking cover; **get'-out** (*coll.*) a way of escape or avoidance. — Also *adj.* — *adj.* **get'-rich'-quick'** (*coll.*) wanting, or leading to, easy prosperity. — **get'-together** a social gathering: an informal conference; **get'-up** (style of) equipment, outfit, make-up; **get'-up-and-go'** (*coll.*) energy. — **get about, around** to travel, go visiting: to be mobile and active; **get across** (*coll.*) communicate successfully; **get ahead** to make progress, advance; **get along** to get on (see below); **get around** see **get about; get at** to reach, attain: to poke fun at (*slang*): to mean: to attack verbally: to influence by underhand or unlawful means; **get away with (something)** to pull something off: to carry a thing through successfully or with impunity; **get back at** to have one's revenge on; **get by** to succeed in passing: to elude notice and come off with impunity, manage satisfactorily, be sufficiently good (*coll.*); **get down** to alight: to depress (*coll.*); **get down to** set to work on, tackle seriously; **get in** to (manage to) enter: to gather: to send for: to manage: to be elected; **get in on** (*coll.*) to join in, become a participant in; **get off** to escape: to learn: to gain the affection of or have a sexual encounter with, someone of the opposite sex (with *with; coll.*); **get on** to proceed, advance: to prosper: to agree, consort harmoniously: to fare; **get one's own back** (*coll.*) to have one's revenge (on); **get out** to produce: to extricate oneself (with *of*): to take oneself off; **get over** to surmount: to recover from: to make an impression on an audience; **get (something) over with** to accomplish (an unpleasant task, etc.) as quickly as possible; **get round** to circumvent: to persuade, talk over; **get round to** to bring oneself to do (something); **get there** (*slang*) to achieve one's object, succeed; **get through** to finish: to reach a destination: to receive approval, or to obtain it for (something): to be put in telephonic communication: to communicate with, reach the comprehension of (with *to*); **get together** to meet for social intercourse or discussion; **get up** to arise: to ascend: to arrange: to prepare: to learn up for an occasion: to commit to memory; **have got** (*coll.*) to have; **tell someone where he gets off** (*coll.*) to deal summarily or dismissively with someone; **have got to** to be obliged to. [O.N. *geta,* cog. with O.E. *-gietan* (in compounds).]

geta *gā'tə, n.* a Japanese wooden sandal with a thong between the big toe and the other toes: — *pl.* **ge'ta** or **ge'tas.** [Jap.]

Geum *jē'əm, n.* the avens genus of the rose family: (without *cap.*) a plant of this genus. [L.]

gewgaw *gū'gö, n.* a toy: a bauble. — *adj.* showy without value. [Origin unknown.]

gey (*Scot.*). See **gay.** — *adv.* **geyan** (*gī'ən*) for **gey and.**

geyser *gā', gē'* or *gī'zər, n.* a spring that spouts hot water into the air: (usu. *gē'*) apparatus for heating water as it is drawn. — *n.* **gey'serite** sinter. [*Geysir,* a geyser in Iceland — Icel. *geysa,* O.N. *göysa,* to gush.]

Ghanaian *gä-nā'yən, -nä', adj.* of or pertaining to Ghana. — *n.* a native or citizen of Ghana.

gharial. Same as **gavial, garial.**

gharri, gharry *ga'ri, n.* esp. in India, a wheeled vehicle, generally for hire. [Hind. *gārī,* a cart.]

ghast *gäst, v.t.* (*Shak.*) to strike aghast: to affright. — *adj.* **ghast'ful** (*Spens.* **ghastfull;** *arch.*) dreary, dismal. — *adv.* **ghast'fully** frightfully. — *n.* **ghast'liness.** — *adj.* **ghast'ly** death-like: hideous: deplorable (*coll.*). — Also *adv.* (*arch.*). — *n.* **ghast'ness** (*Shak.* **gastness** q.v.). [O.E. *gǣstan;* cf. **gast.**]

ghat, ghaut *göt, n.* in India, a mountain-pass: a landing-stair: a place of cremation (*burning ghat*). [Hindi *ghāt,* descent.]

ghazal *gaz'al, n.* a Persian and Arabic verse-form, of not more than 18 couplets, the first two lines and the even-numbered lines thereafter rhyming together, mainly amatory and bacchanalian. — Also **gazal, ghazel.** [Ar. *ghazal.*]

ghazi *gä'zē, n.* a veteran Muslim warrior: a slayer of infidels: a high Turkish title. [Ar. *ghāzi,* fighting.]

Gheber, Ghebre. Same as **Guebre.**

ghee, ghi *gē, ghē, n.* clarified butter, esp. buffalo butter. [Hind. *ghī.*]

gherao *ge-row', n.* in India, the surrounding or trapping of a person (e.g. an employer) in a room, building, etc. until he or she meets one's demands: — *pl.* **gheraos'.** — Also *v.t.* [Hindi, siege, — *gherna,* to surround, besiege.]

gherkin *gûr'kin, n.* a small cucumber used for pickling. [From an earlier form of Du. *augurk(je),* a gherkin; app. from Slavonic.]

ghesse (*Spens.*). Same as **guess¹:** — *pa.t.* and *pa.p.* **ghest, ghessed.**

ghetto *get'ō, n.* the Jews' quarter in an Italian or other city, to which they used to be confined: a quarter, esp. poor, inhabited by any racial, or other identifiable group: — *pl.* **ghett'o(e)s.** — *v.t.* **ghett'oïse, -ize** to make into a ghetto. — **ghett'o-blaster** (*coll.*) a usu. fairly large portable radio and cassette-recorder unit with built-in speakers. [It. *ghetto,* foundry, one having previously occupied the site of the Venetian Jewish ghetto.]

ghi. See **ghee.**

Ghibelline, Ghibeline *gib'ə-lēn, -līn, -lin, n.* one of a party in mediaeval Italy, orig. supporters of Hohenstaufen emperors against Guelfs and pope. [It. *Ghibellino,* app. — *Waiblingen,* a Hohenstaufen town.]

ghilgai. See **gilgai.**

ghillie. Same as **gillie.**

ghost *gōst, n.* a spirit: the soul of a man: a spirit appearing after death: a dead body (*Shak.*): one who does another's work for him, as writing speeches or the like: a faint or false appearance: a semblance: a duplicated image due to additional reception of a delayed similar signal which has covered a longer path (*TV*). — *v.t.* (*arch.*) to haunt as a ghost. — *v.i.* and *v.t.* to do another's work, esp. to write (speeches, memoirs, etc.) for him. — *adj.* **ghost'-like.** — *n.* **ghost'liness.** — *adjs.* **ghost'ly** spiritual: religious: pertaining to apparitions: ghost-like: faint; **ghost'y.** — **ghost gum** an Australian tree, *Eucalyptus papuana,* with smooth white bark; **ghost'-moth** a moth (*Hepialus humuli*), the male of ghostly white appearance, the caterpillar destructive to hop-gardens; **ghost'-story** a story in which ghosts figure; **ghost town** one which once flourished owing to some natural resource in the vicinity but which is now deserted since the natural resource has been exhausted; **ghost'-word** a word that has originated in the blunder of a scribe or printer. — *v.i.* and *v.t.* **ghost'-write** to write for another as a ghost. — **ghost'-writer.** — **give up the ghost** (*B.*) to die; **Holy Ghost** the Holy Spirit, the third person in the Christian Trinity; **not to have a ghost (of a chance)** not to have the least chance of success. [O.E. *gāst*; Ger. *Geist*; the *h* from Caxton (Flemish *gheest*).]

ghoul *gōōl*, now often *gowl*, *n.* an Eastern demon that preys on the dead: a gruesome fiend: a person of gruesome or revolting habits or tastes. — *adj.* **ghoul'-ish.** — *adv.* **ghoul'ishly.** — *n.* **ghoul'ishness.** [Ar. *ghūl*.]

ghubar numeral. Same as **gobar numeral.**

ghyll *gil.* See **gill**[4].

gi. See **gi(e).**

giambeux (*Spens.*) for **jambeaux.** See under **jamb.**

giant *jī'ənt*, *n.* a huge mythical being of more or less human form: a person of abnormally great stature: anything much above the usual size of its kind: a person of much greater powers than his fellows: — *fem.* **gī'antess.** — *adj.* **gigantic.** — *ns.* **gī'anthood** the quality or character of a giant: the race of giants; **gī'antism** the occurrence of giants: gigantism. — *adj.* **gī'antly** giant-like. — *ns.* **gī'antry** giants collectively: giant stories or mythology; **gī'antship.** — **gi'ant-killer** one who defeats a far superior opponent; **gi'ant-killing; giant panda** see **panda; gi'ant-powder** a kind of dynamite. — *adj.* **gi'ant-rude** (*Shak.*) enormously rude or uncivil. — **giant's-kett'le** a great pot-hole believed to have been formed by subglacial water; **giant star** (*astron.*) a star of great brightness and low mean density; **giant('s) stride** a gymnastic apparatus enabling one to take great strides around a pole. [O.Fr. *geant* (Fr. *géant*) — L. *gĭgās* — Gr. *gĭgās, gigantos.*]

giaour *jowr*, *n.* an infidel, a term applied by the Turks to all who are not of their own religion. [Through Turk. — Pers. *gaur*; see **Guebre.**]

gib[1] *jib, gib*, *n.* a wedge-shaped piece of metal holding another in place, etc. — *v.t.* to fasten with a gib. [Origin obscure.]

gib[2] *gib*, *n.* a tom-cat, esp. one castrated: a term of reproach. — Also **gib'-cat** (*Shak.*). [From the name *Gilbert.*]

gibber[1] *jib'ər*, *v.i.* to utter senseless or inarticulate sounds. [Imit.]

gibber[2] *gib'ər*, (*Austr.*) *n.* a stone: a boulder. [Aboriginal.]

Gibberella *jib-ər-el'ə*, *n.* a genus of fungi found esp. on grasses — e.g. wheat scab. — *n.* **gibberell'in** any of several plant-growth regulators produced by a fungus of the genus. — **gibberellic** (*-el'ik*) **acid** an acid having similar effects.

gibberish *gib'ər-ish*, or *jib'*, *n.* rapid, gabbling talk: unmeaning words. — *adj.* **unmeaning.** [Imit.]

gibbet *jib'it*, *n.* a gallows, esp. one on which criminals were suspended after execution: the projecting beam of a crane. — *v.t.* to expose on, or as on, a gibbet. [O.Fr. *gibet*, a stick; origin unknown.]

gibble-gabble *gib'l-gab'l*, *n.* senseless chatter. [**gabble.**]

gibbon *gib'ən*, *n.* an E. Indian anthropoid ape (of several species) with very long arms. [Origin unknown.]

gibbous *gib'əs*, *adj.* hump-backed: humped: unequally convex on two sides, as the moon between half and full. — Also **gibb'ose.** — *ns.* **gibbos'ity, gibb'ousness.** — *adv.* **gibb'ously.** [L. *gibbōsus* — *gibbus*, a hump.]

gibbsite *gib'zīt*, *n.* hydroxide of aluminium, $Al(OH)_3$, an important constituent of bauxite. [From George *Gibbs*, American mineralogist, died 1833.]

gibe, jibe *jīb*, *v.i.* to scoff: to flout. — *v.t.* to scoff at: to taunt. — *n.* a flout: a taunt. — *n.* **gī'ber, jī'ber.** — *adv.* **gī'bingly.** [Origin obscure.]

gibel *gib'əl*, *n.* the Prussian carp, without barbules.

Gibeonite *gib'i-ən-īt*, *n.* a slave's slave — from Josh. ix.

giblets *jib'lits*, *n.pl.* the internal eatable parts of a fowl, etc.: entrails. — *adj.* **gib'let** made of giblets. [O.Fr. *gibelet*; origin uncertain.]

Gibraltarian *jib-röl-tā'ri-ən*, *n.* and *adj.* (an inhabitant) of Gibraltar. — **Gibraltar board**® (*N.Z.*) a type of plasterboard.

gibus *jī'bəs*, *n.* an opera-hat. [Fr.]

gid *gid*, *n.* sturdy, a disease of sheep. [**giddy.**]

giddy *gid'i*, *adj.* unsteady, dizzy: causing giddiness: whirling: light-headed: flighty. — Also *v.i.* and *v.t.* — *adv.* **gidd'ily.** — *n.* **gidd'iness.** — *adjs.* **gidd'y-head'ed** thoughtless, wanting reflection; **gidd'y-paced** (*Shak.*) moving irregularly. — **play the giddy goat** to act the fool. [O.E. *gidig, gydig*, insane, possessed by a god.]

Gideon *gid'i-ən*, *n.* a member of an organisation of Christian businessmen, founded in the United States in 1899, best known for putting Bibles (**Gideon Bibles**) in hotel rooms, etc. [Named after *Gideon*, the judge of Israel (Judges vi. ff).]

gidgee, gidjee *gi'jē*, (*Austr.*) *n.* a small acacia tree, the foliage of which at times emits an unpleasant odour. [Aboriginal.]

gie *gē*, *vb.* a Scots form of **give**[1]: — *pa.t.* **gied** (*gēd*), **gae** (*gā*); *pa.p.* **gien** (*gēn*).

gi(e) *gē*, *n.* judo or karate costume. [Jap. *ki*, clothing.]

gien. See **gie.**

gier-eagle *jēr'ē'gl*, (*B.*) *n.* a vulture. [Du. *gier*.]

gif *gif*, *conj.* an obsolete form (except in Scots) of **if.**

giff-gaff *gif'-gaf'*, (*Scot.*) *n.* give and take. [**give**[1].]

gift *gift*, *n.* a thing given: a bribe (*arch.*): a quality bestowed by nature: the act of giving: something easily obtained, understood, etc. — *v.t.* to endow, esp. with any power or faculty: to present. — *adj.* **gift'ed** highly endowed by nature with talents, abilities, etc.: esp. of a child, exceptionally clever. — *adv.* **gift'edly.** — *n.* **gift'edness.** — **gift'-book** a book suitable or intended for presentation; **gift horse** a horse given as a present; **gift'-shop** a shop selling articles suitable for presents; **gift token** see **token.** — *v.t.* **gift'-wrap** to wrap (a present) in coloured paper, with ribbons, etc. — **look a gift horse in the mouth** to criticise a gift (orig. to look at a gift horse's teeth to tell its age). [See **give**[1].]

gig[1] *gig*, *n.* a whip-top (*obs.*): a flighty girl (*obs.*): a light, two-wheeled carriage: a long, light boat: a machine for raising the nap on cloth (in full, **gig mill**): a fishgig (see under **fizgig**): sport, fun (*dial.*). — *v.t.* and *v.i.* **gigg'it** (*arch. U.S.*) to convey or move rapidly. — **gig'-lamps** (*slang*) spectacles; **gig'man** one who drives or keeps a gig: a narrow middle-class philistine (*Carlyle*). — *n.* **gigman'ity.** [M.E. *gigge*, a whirling thing (cf. **whirligig**); origin obscure.]

gig[2] *gig*, (*slang*) *n.* an engagement, esp. of a band or pop-group for one performance only. — *v.t.* to play a gig: — *pa.t.* **gigged.** [Ety. unknown.]

giga. See **gigue.**

giga- *gī'gə, gig'ə, jī'gə, jig'ə, pfx.* meaning ten to the ninth power (10^9). — **gi'ga-elec'tron-volt** a unit equal to a thousand million electron-volts; **gi'gahertz; gi'gawatt.** [Gr. *gigas*, giant.]

gigantic *jī-gan'tik, adj.* of, like or characteristic of a giant: huge. — Also **gigantē'an.** — *adj.* **gigantesque'** befitting or suggestive of a giant. — *adv.* **gigan'tically.** — *ns.* **gigan'ticide** the act of killing a giant; **gigant'ism** hugeness, of a business concern, etc.: excessive overgrowth, usually owing to overactivity of the pituitary gland; **gigantol'ogy** giant-lore; **gigantom'achy** (*-ki*), **gigantomachia** (*-tō-māk'i-ə*) a war of giants, esp. against the gods (Gr. *machē*, fight). [L. *gigas, gigantis*, Gr. *gigās, -antos*, a giant.]

giggle *gig'l*, *v.i.* to laugh with short catches of the breath, or in a silly manner. — *n.* a laugh of this kind: something unimportant and silly (*slang*). — *ns.* **gigg'ler; gigg'ling.** — *adjs.* **gigg'lesome, gigg'ly.** [Echoic.]

giglet, giglot *gig'lit, -lət*, *n.* a giddy girl: a wanton (*arch.*). — *adj.* (*Shak.*) inconstant. [Perh. conn. with **gig**[1]; later associated with **giggle.**]

gigolo *jig'ō-lō*, *n.* a professional male dancing partner: a young man living at the expense of an older woman: — *pl.* **gig'olos.** [Fr.]

gigot *jig'ət*, *n.* a leg of mutton, etc.: a leg-of-mutton sleeve. [Fr.]

gigue *zhēg*, (*mus.*) *n.* a lively dance-form in triple time, common in old suites. — Also (It.) **giga** (*jē'ga*). [Fr.; cf. **jig.**]

gila *hhē'lə* (in full **gila monster**) *n.* either of the two *Heloderma* species, the only venomous lizards known. [*Gila* River, Arizona.]

gilbert *gil'bərt*, *n.* the C.G.S. unit of magnetomotive force. [From the English physician and physicist William *Gilbert* (1540–1603).]

Gilbertian *gil'bûrt'i-ən*, *adj.* whimsically or paradoxically humorous. [Sir W. S. *Gilbert* (1836–1911), librettist, playwright, poet, etc.]

Gilbertine *gil'bûrt-īn*, *-in*, *n.* a member of the order of canons and nuns founded (*c.* 1148) by St *Gilbert* of Sempringham. — Also *adj.*

gilcup. See **gilt**¹.

gild¹ *gild*, *v.t.* to cover or overlay with gold or with any goldlike substance: to smear with blood (*obs.*): to flush (*obs.*): to furnish with gold: to gloss over, give a specious appearance to: to adorn with lustre: — *pr.p.* **gild'ing;** *pa.t.* and *pa.p.* **gild'ed** or **gilt.** — *ns.* **gild'er** one who coats articles with gold; **gild'ing** act or trade of a gilder: gold or imitation thereof laid on a surface. — **Gilded Chamber** the House of Lords; **gilded spurs** an emblem of knighthood; **gilded youth** rich young people of fashion. — **gild the lily** to embellish to an unnecessary extent; **gild the pill** to make a disagreeable thing seem less so. [O.E. *gyldan* — *gold*; see **gold**¹.]

gild². See **guild.**

gilder¹. See **guilder.**

gilder². See **gild**¹.

gilden, gylden *gil'dən*, (*obs.*) orig. *adj.* golden, adopted later (as *Spens.*) as a *pa.p.* of **gild**¹. [O.E. *gylden.*]

gilet *zhē-lā*, *n.* a waistcoat: in a woman's dress, a front part shaped like a waistcoat: in ballet dress, a bodice shaped like a waistcoat. [Fr.]

gilgai, ghilgai *gil'gī*, (*Austr.*) *ns.* a saucer-shaped depression forming a natural reservoir. [Aboriginal.]

gilgie, jilgie *jil'gi*, (*Austr.*) *n.* a yabby. [Aboriginal.]

gill¹ *gil*, *n.* an organ for breathing in water: the flesh under the jaw: the wattle below the bill of a fowl: one of the radiating plates under a mushroom or toadstool cap: a projecting rib of a heating surface. — *v.t.* to gut (fish): to catch (fish) by the gills in a net. — **gill cover** a fold of skin, usu. with bony plates, protecting the gills; **gill net** a type of fishing-net in which fish are caught by their gills; **gill pouch** one of a pair of outgrowths on the wall of the pharynx, found in cyclostomes and present at the embryonic stage in all vertebrates, developing, in fish, into openings (**gill slits**) containing the gills. [Cf. Dan. *giælle;* Sw. *gäl.*]

gill² *jil*, *n.* a small measure, having various values; in recent times = ¹/₄ pint. — **gill'-house** (*obs.*) a dram-shop. [O.Fr. *gelle.*]

gill³ *jil*, *n.* a girl (also **jill**) (*obs.*): a female ferret, (also **jill**): ground ivy (*dial.*): beer with an infusion of ground ivy (also **gill ale, gill beer**) (*obs.*). — *n.* **gillet** (*Scot.*) a skittish, flighty, or loose young woman (also **jillet**). — **gill'flirt** (*arch.*) a wanton girl (also **jill'flirt**). [*Gillian* or *Juliana* (from *Julius*), a woman's name.]

gill⁴, **ghyll** *gil*, *n.* a small ravine, a wooded glen: a brook. [O.N. *gil.*]

gill⁵ *jil*, *n.* a two- or four-wheeled cart for conveying timber. — Also **jill.** [Origin uncertain.]

gillaroo *gil-ə-rōō'*, *n.* an Irish trout with thickened muscular stomach. [Ir. *giolla ruadh*, red lad.]

gillet. See **gill**³.

gillie, ghillie, gilly *gil'i*, *n.* a Highland chief's attendant (*hist.*): an attendant on or guide of hunting and fishing sportsmen. — *v.i.* to act as gillie. — **gillie-wet'foot** (*obs.*), **-white-foot** (*obs.*) a barefoot Highland lad, esp. a messenger or chief's attendant. [Gael. *gille*, a lad, Ir. *giolla.*]

gillion *jil'yən, gil'*, *n.* in Britain, a thousand millions, 10⁹, equivalent of a U.S. billion. [**giga-** and **million.**]

gillravage, -itch. See **gilravage.**

gilly. See **gillie.**

gillyflower *jil'i-flowr* (*Shak.* **gillyvor** *-vər*), *n.* a flower that smells like cloves, esp. **clove-gillyflower, stock-gillyflower** (see **clove**⁴, **stock**¹). [O.Fr. *girofle* — Gr. *karyophyllon*, the clove-tree — *karyon*, a nut, *phyllon*, a leaf.]

gilpy, gilpey *gil'pi*, (*Scot.*) *n.* a boisterous girl or (formerly) boy.

gilravage, gillravage, galravage, -itch *gəl-rav'ij, -ich*, or *rāv'*, (*Scot.*) *ns.* a noisy frolic: riotous merrymaking. — *v.i.* to behave riotously. — *n.* **gilrav'ager.**

gilt¹ *gilt, pa.t.* and *pa.p.* of **gild**¹. — *adj.* gilded: gold-coloured. — *n.* gilding: money (*Shak.*). — **gilt'cup, gil'cup** a buttercup. — *adj.* **gilt'-edged** having the edges gilt: of the highest quality (**gilt-edged securities** those stocks whose interest is considered perfectly safe). — *ns.* **gilt'-edged, gilts.** — **gilt'-head** a name for several fishes, esp. a sparoid fish with a half-moon-shaped gold spot between the eyes; **gilt'-tail** a yellow-tipped worm (*Dendrobaena subrubicunda*) of old dung-hills. — *adj.* **gilt'wood** made of wood and covered with gilt.

gilt² *gilt*, (*dial.*) *n.* a young sow (in various conditions locally). [O.N. *gyltr*; cf. O.E. *gilte.*]

gimbal *jim'bl*, *n.* a gimmal (*obs.*): (in *pl.*) a contrivance with self-aligning bearings for keeping e.g. hanging objects, nautical instruments, etc., horizontal (*sing.* in composition, as **gimbal ring**). [See **gemel.**]

gimcrack, jimcrack *jim'krak*, *n.* a dodge, trick: a trivial mechanism: a trumpery knick-knack: a paltry, ill-made, flimsy article. — *adj.* trumpery, shoddy. — *n.* **gimcrack'ery.** [M.E. *gibecrake*, poss. inlay.]

gimlet *gim'lit*, *n.* a small tool for boring holes by turning it by hand: half a glass of whisky, gin, or vodka, and lime-juice. — *v.t.* to pierce as with a gimlet: to turn like a gimlet. — *adj.* **gim'let-eyed** very sharp-sighted. [O.Fr. *guimbelet*, from Gmc.; cf. **wimble**¹.]

gimmal *jim'l*, *n.* a ring (also **gimmal ring**) that can be divided into two (or three) rings: a joint or part in a piece of mechanism (also **gimm'er;** *Shak.* **gimm'or**). — *adj.* **gimm'alled** (*Shak.* **jymold**) jointed, hinged. [See **gemel.**]

gimme *gi'mi*, (*slang*) contracted form of *give me.* — *n.* (*coll.*) in golf, a short putt that one is willing to take as played by one's opponent: (usu. in *pl.*, as *the gimmes*) avarice (*U.S. slang*).

gimmer¹ *gim'ər*, (*Scot.*) *n.* a young ewe: (*contemptuously*) a woman. [O.N. *gymbr*; cf. Sw. *gimmer*, Dan. *gimmer.*]

gimmer². See **gimmal.**

gimmick *gim'ik*, *n.* a secret device for performing a trick: a device (often peculiar to the person adopting it) to catch attention, publicity: an ingenious mechanical device. — *n.* **gimm'ickry** gimmicks in quantity: use of gimmick(s). — *adj.* **gimm'icky** pertaining to a gimmick: (*loosely*) of little worth, importance. [Origin unknown.]

gimmor (*Shak.*). See **gimmal.**

gimp¹ *gimp*, *n.* a yarn with a hard core: a trimming thereof: a fishing-line bound with wire: a coarse thread in lace-making. — *v.t.* to make or furnish with gimp. — Also **guimp(e), gymp.** [Fr. *guimpe*, app. from O.H.G. *wimpal*; cf. **wimple**; perhaps confused with Fr. *guipure*; see **guipure.**]

gimp² *jimp*, (*rare*) *v.t.* to scallop, notch: to corrugate.

gin¹ *jin*, *n.* geneva: a spirit distilled from grain or malt and flavoured with juniper berries or other aromatic substances, made chiefly in Britain and the U.S. — **gin'-fizz** a drink of gin, lemon-juice, effervescing water, etc.; **gin'-palace** (*derog.*) a showily pretentious public house; **gin'shop; gin'-sling** a cold gin and water, sweetened and flavoured. — **gin and it** gin and *I*talian vermouth. [Contr. from **geneva.**]

gin² *jin*, *n.* a scheme, artifice, contrivance (*Spens.*): a snare or trap: a machine, esp. one for hoisting: a cotton-gin: an instrument of torture (*Spens.*). — *v.t.* to trap or snare: to clear of seeds by a cotton-gin: — *pr.p.* **ginn'ing;** *pa.t.* and *pa.p.* **ginned.** — *ns.* **ginn'er** one who gins cotton; **ginn'ery, gin'house** a place where cotton is ginned. — **gin trap** a powerful spring trap fitted with teeth. [**engine.**]

gin[3] *jin, n.* an Australian Aboriginal woman. [Aboriginal.]

gin[4] *jin, n.* a type of rummy in which a player whose unmatched cards count ten or less may stop the game. — Also **gin rummy.** [Origin uncertain.]

gin[5] *gin, (arch.) v.t.* and *v.i.* to begin: — *pa.t.* **gan,** used poetically in the sense of *did.* [Aphetic from O.E. *beginnan* or *onginnan,* to begin.]

gin[6] *gin, (Scot.) prep.* by (the time of). [M.E. *gain,* app. — O.N. *gegn,* against.]

gin[7] *gin, (Scot.) conj.* if. [Perh. pa.p. of *give* as a substitute for **gif**; perh. from **gin**[6].]

ging *ging, (obs.) n.* a gang or company. See **gang**[1].

gingal, gingall. See **jingal.**

gingelly. See **gingili.**

ginger *jin'jər, n.* the root-stock of *Zingiber officinale,* or other species of the genus (family Zingiberaceae) with a hot taste, used as a condiment or stomachic: ginger beer: stimulation: mettle. — *adj.* sandy, reddish. — *v.t.* to put ginger into: to make spirited, to enliven (often with *up*). — *adjs.* **gin'gerous** (*Dickens*) sandy, reddish; **gin'gery** of or like ginger: sandy in colour. — **gingerade'**, **ginger ale** an aerated drink flavoured with ginger; **ginger beer** an effervescent drink made with fermenting ginger; **ginger cordial** a cordial made of ginger, lemonpeel, raisins, water, and sometimes spirits; **ginger group** a group within e.g. a political party seeking to inspire the rest with its own enthusiasm and activity; **ginger nut** a small thick gingersnap; **ginger pop** weak ginger beer (*coll.*); **gin'gersnap** a gingerbread biscuit; **ginger wine** liquor made by the fermentation of sugar and water, and flavoured with various spices, chiefly ginger. — **ginger beer plant** a symbiotic association of a yeast and a bacterium, by which ginger beer can be prepared, also called *Californian bees.* [M.E. *gingivere* — O.Fr. *gengibre* — L.L. *gingiber* — L. *zingiber* — Gr. *zingiberis* — Prâkrit — Sans. *śṛnga,* horn, *vera,* body; Malayalam *inchiver*.]

gingerbread *jin'jər-bred, n.* a cake flavoured with treacle and usually ginger. — *adj.* of ornamental work, cheap and tawdry. — **take the gilt off the gingerbread** to destroy the glamour. [O.Fr. *gingimbrat* — L.L. *gingiber*; see **ginger**; confused with **bread.**]

gingerly *jin'jər-li, adv.* with soft steps: with extreme wariness and delicate gentleness. — Also *adj.* [Possibly O.Fr. *gensor,* compar. of *gent*; see **gent**[1].]

gingham *ging'əm, n.* a kind of cotton cloth, woven from coloured yarns into stripes or checks: an umbrella (*coll.*). [Fr. *guingan,* orig. from Malay *ginggang,* striped.]

gingili, gingelly, jinjili *jin'ji-li, n.* a species of sesame: an oil got from its seeds. [Hind. *jinjalī,* prob. — Ar. *juljulān*.]

gingival *jin-jī'vl, adj.* pertaining to the gums. — *ns.* **gingivec'tomy** the cutting back of inflamed or excess gum; **gingivī'tis** inflammation of the gums. [L. *gingīva,* gum.]

gingko. See **ginkgo.**

gingle. Same as **jingle.**

ginglymus *jing'gli-məs* (or *ging'-*), *n.* a joint that permits movement in one plane only: — *pl.* **ging'lymī.** — *adj.* **ging'limoid.** [Latinised from Gr. *ginglymos*.]

gink *gingk, (slang) n.* a fellow. [Origin unknown.]

ginkgo *gingk'gō, n.* the maidenhair tree, holy in Japan, perhaps still wild in China, forming by itself an order (**Ginkgoä'les**) of Gymnosperms. — Also **ging'ko**: — *pl.* **gink'goes, gink'koes.** [Jap. *ginkyo* — Chin. *yin,* silver, *hing,* apricot.]

ginn. See **jinn.**

ginnel *gin'əl, (N. dial.) n.* a narrow alley or path between high walls or buildings. [A voiced form of **kennel**[2].]

ginseng *jin'seng, n.* a plant of the araliaceous genus Panax, cultivated esp. in the Far East: its root, believed to have important restorative and curative properties.

[Chin. *jên-shên,* perh. image of man.]

gio. See **geo.**

giocoso *jok-ō'sō, (mus.) adj.* played in a lively or humorous manner. [It.]

Giorgi system *jör'jē sis'tim,* see **metre-kilogram(me)- second system.** [After Giovanni *Giorgi,* Italian physicist, d. 1950.]

gip *jip, n.* Same as **gyp**[1,3].

gippo, gyppo *jip'ō, (offensive) n.* an Egyptian, esp. a native Egyptian soldier: — *pl.* **gipp'os, gypp'os.** — Also **gipp'y, gypp'ie, gypp'y.** — **gippy** (or **gyppy**) **tummy** (*coll.*) diarrhoea, thought of as a hazard of holidaying in hot countries. [*Egypt.*]

gippy. See **gippo.**

gipsen *jip'sən, (Spens.) n.* an obs. form of **gypsy.**

gipsy. See **gypsy.**

giraffe *ji-räf', n.* the cameleopard, an African ruminant with remarkably long neck and forelegs. — *adjs.* **giraff'id, giraff'ine, giraffoid.** [Ar. *zarâfah*.]

girandole *jir'ən-dōl,* **girandola** *-and'ə-lə, ns.* a branched chandelier or similar structure: a pendant, etc., with small jewels attached around it: a rotating firework: a number of linked mines (*mil.*). [Fr., — It. *girandola* — *girare* — L. *gȳrāre,* to turn round — *gȳrus* — Gr. *gȳros,* a circle.]

girasol, girasole *jir'ə-sol, -sōl, ns.* a fire-opal or other stone that seems to send a firelike glow from within in certain lights: the plant heliotrope (*obs.*): the sunflower (*obs.*). [It., — *girare* (see **girandole**) and *sole* — L. *sōl,* the sun.]

gird[1] *gûrd, (N. dial.) v.i.* to gibe, jeer (with *at*). — *v.t.* (*obs.*) to taunt. — *n.* (*arch.*) a taunt, dig, gibe. [Origin obscure; not from O.E. *gyrd, gierd,* rod.]

gird[2] *gird, (Scot.) n.* a hoop. — Also **girr** (*gir*). [A form of **girth**[1].]

gird[3] *gûrd, v.t.* to bind round: to make fast by a belt or girdle: to encompass: to surround: to clothe, furnish: — *pa.t.* and *pa.p.* **gird'ed** and **girt.** — *ns.* **gird'er** a great beam, simple or built up, of wood, iron, or steel, to take a lateral stress, e.g. to support a floor, wall, roadway of a bridge: a strip of strengthening tissue (*bot.*); **gird'ing** that which girds. — **girder bridge** a bridge whose load is sustained by girders resting on supports. — **gird oneself** to tuck up loose garments under the girdle: to brace the mind for any trial or effort: see also **loin.** [O.E. *gyrdan*; cf. Ger. *gürten*.]

girdle[1] *gûrd'l, n.* a waist-belt: a cord worn about the waist by a monk, etc.: anything that encloses like a belt: a woman's lightweight, close-fitting undergarment, a form of corset, reaching from waist to thigh: a bony arch to which a limb is attached: a worm's clitellum: a ring-shaped cut around a tree: the rim of a brilliant-cut gem. — *v.t.* to bind, as with a girdle: to enclose: to cut a ring round (a tree, etc.): to cut a circular outline around (a gemstone). — *adj.* **gird'led.** — *n.* **gird'ler** one who or that which girdles: a maker of girdles. — **girdle'stead** (*arch.*) the waist. [O.E. *gyrdel* — *gyrdan,* to gird.]

girdle[2]. See **griddle.**

girkin *gûr'kin, n.* Same as **gherkin.**

girl *gûrl, n.* a female child: a daughter: a young unmarried woman: a woman irrespective of age: a sweetheart (*coll.*): a maid servant. — *n.* **girl'hood** the state or time of being a girl. — *adj.* **girl'ie, girl'y** (of magazines, photographs etc.) showing nude or scantily clad young women. — Also *n.* — *adj.* **girl'ish** of or like a girl. — *adv.* **girl'ishly.** — *n.* **girl'ishness.** — **Girl Friday** a young woman who acts as secretary or personal assistant in a business office; **girl'friend** sweetheart, or girl who is often one's companion: (**girl friend**) a girl's young female friend; **Girl Guide** a member of an organisation for girls, analogous to the (Boy) Scouts' Association (also **Guide**); **Girl Scout** a member of a similar American organisation. — **old girl** a female former pupil: a kindly disrespectful mode of address or reference to a female of any age or species. [M.E. *gerle, girle, gurle,* boy or girl, perhaps related to L.G. *gör, göre,* child.]

girlond. Obsolete form of **garland.** — In Spens. *Faerie Queene*, IV, x. 51, 9, *girlonds* may be a misprint for *guardians* (or *guerdons*).

girn *girn*, (*dial.*) *v.i.* to grin, snarl: to grimace, make a grotesque face: to complain peevishly. — *n.* an act or manner of girning. — *adj.* **girn′ie** ill-tempered.   [**grin.**]

girnel *gir′nl*, (*Scot.*) *n.* a granary (*obs.*): a meal chest. [Variant of **garner.**]

giro *jī′rō*, *n.* (also with *cap.*) a banking system by which money can be transferred direct from the account of one holder to that of another person (or to those of others): — *pl.* **gī′ros.** [Ger., transfer — Gr. *gyros*, ring.]

giron. See **gyron.**

Girondist *ji-rond′ist*, *n.* a member of the moderate republican party during the French Revolution, so called because its earliest leaders were deputies for the *Gironde* department. — Also **Giron′din.** — *n.* **Giron′-dism.**

girosol. Same as **girasol.**

girr. See **gird²**.

girt *gûrt*, *pa.p.* of **gird³** in all senses: of a ship, moored so taut by her cables to two oppositely placed anchors as to be prevented from swinging to the wind or tide. — *v.t.* to gird: to girth. — *v.i.* to girth.

girth¹. See **grith.**

girth² *gûrth*, *n.* belly-band of a saddle: circumferential measure of thickness. — *v.t.* to put a girth on: to measure the girth of. — *v.i.* to measure in girth. — Also **girt.** — **girth′line** or **girt′line** a gantline. [O.N. *gjörth*.]

gisarme *jē-zärm′*, *zhē-*, *gē-*, (*hist.*) *n.* a type of long-staffed battle-axe carried by foot-soldiers. [O.Fr. *guisarme*, prob. O.H.G. *getan*, to weed, *īsarn*, iron.]

gism. See **jism.**

gismo, gizmo *giz′mō*, (*coll.*) *n.* gadget, thingumajig: — *pl.* **gis′mos, giz′mos.** [Origin unknown.]

gist *jist*, *n.* the main point or pith of a matter. [O.Fr. *gist* (Fr. *gît*) — O.Fr. *gesir* (Fr. *gésir*), to lie — L. *jacēre*.]

git *git*, (*slang*) *n.* a person, used contemptuously: a fool: a bastard. — See also **get.** [**get,** offspring, brat.]

gitano *jē-tän′ō*, *hhē-*, (Sp.) *n.* a male gypsy: — *pl.* **gitan′os:** — *fem.* **gitan′a.**

gite, gîte *zhēt*, *n.* a resting-place (*arch.*): in France (simple holiday accommodation in) a farmhouse, cottage, etc.. [Fr. *gîte* — O.Fr. *giste*; see **gest¹**.]

gittern *git′ərn*, *n.* a kind of guitar, a cithern. — *v.i.* to play on the gittern.   [O.Fr. *guiterne*, conn. Gr. *kitharā*; see **cithern, guitar, zither.**]

giust *just*, (Spens., Scott) *n.*, *v.i.* Same as **joust.**

giusto *jōōs′tō*, (*mus.*) *adj.* suitable: regular: strict. [It., — L. *jūstus*, just.]

give¹ *giv*, *v.t.* to bestow: to impart: to yield: to grant: to donate: to permit: to afford: to furnish: to pay or render, as thanks: to pronounce, as a decision: to show, as a result: to apply, as oneself: to allow or admit. — *v.i.* to yield to pressure: to begin to melt: to grow soft: to open, or give an opening or view, to lead (with *upon, on, into,* a gallicism): — *pr.p.* **giv′ing;** *pa.t.* **gāve;** *pa.p.* **given** (*giv′n*). — *n.* yielding: elasticity. — *adj.* **giv′en** bestowed: specified: addicted, disposed: granted: admitted. — *ns.* **giv′enness; giv′er** one who or that which gives or bestows; **giv′ing** the act of bestowing: the thing given. — *adj.* that gives. — **give′away** a betrayal, revelation, esp. if unintentional: something given free with the aim of increasing sales; **given name** the name bestowed upon the individual, not that of the family —the first or Christian name, distinguished from the *surname.* — **give and take** reciprocity in concession: mutually compensatory variations: fair exchange of repartee; **give away** to give for nothing: to betray: to bestow ceremonially (as a bride); **give-away programme** a theatrical or other programme in which members of the audience seek to gain prizes; **give birth to** to bring forth: to originate; **give chase** to pursue; **give ear** to listen (to); **give forth** to emit: to publish: to expatiate (*coll.*); **give ground, place** to give way, yield; **give in to** (*obs.* **give into**) to yield to; **give it to one** (*coll.*) to scold or beat anybody severely; **give line, head, rein** etc., to give more liberty or scope — the metaphors from angling and driving; **give me** I would choose if I had the choice; **give off** to emit (e.g. a smell); **give oneself away** to betray one's secret unawares; **give out** to report: to emit: to run short: to relinquish (*Shak.*): to distribute to individuals; **give over** to transfer: to cease (N. *dial.*); **give the lie to** to charge openly with false-hood; **give tongue** to bark: to utter, expound (with *to*); **give up** to abandon: to surrender: to desist from; **give way** to fall back, to yield, to withdraw: to break, snap, collapse, under strain: to begin rowing — usually as a command to a crew: to allow traffic in a direction crossing one's path to proceed first.   [O.E. *gefan* (W.S. *giefan*), the back *g* prob. owing to Scand. influence; O.N. *gefa*, Sw. *gifva*, Dan. *give*, Goth. *giban*, Ger. *geben*.]

give². Same as **gyve.**

Giz. Same as **Geëz.**

gizmo. See **gismo.**

gizz, jiz *jiz*, (*Scot.*) *n.* a wig.   [Origin unknown.]

gizzard *giz′ərd*, *n.* a muscular stomach, esp. the second stomach of a bird. — **stick in someone's gizzard** to be more than someone can accept or tolerate.   [M.E. *giser* — O.Fr. *guiser*, supposed to be — L. *gigeria* (pl.), cooked entrails of poultry.]

gizzen *giz′n*, (*Scot.*) *v.i.* to shrink from dryness so as to leak: to wither. — *adj.* leaky: shrivelled.   [O.N. *gisna.*]

gju. See **gue.**

glabella *glə-bel′ə*, *n.* the part of the forehead between the eyebrows and just above their level: — *pl.* **glabell′ae** (*-bel′ē*). — *adj.* **glabell′ar.**   [L. *glaber*, bald, smooth.]

glabrous *glā′brəs*, **glabrate** *glā′brāt*, *-brət*, *adjs.* hairless. [L. *glaber*.]

glacé *gla′sā*, *adj.* frozen, or with ice: iced with sugar: candied: glossy, lustrous, esp. of a thin silk material or kid leather. — *v.t.* to ice with sugar: to candy: — *pres.p.* **glac′éing;** *pa.t.* and *pa.p.* **glac′éed.**   [Fr.]

glacial *glās′yəl*, *glā′si-əl*, or *-shəl*, *adj.* icy: frozen: readily or ordinarily solidified (as **glacial acetic acid** practically pure acetic acid): pertaining to ice or its action: of progress, ponderously slow, like that of a glacier. — *n.*a glacial period, an ice-age. — *ns.* **glā′cialist, glaciol′ogist** one who studies the geological action of ice. — *v.t.* **glaciate** (*glās′*, *glāsh′*) to polish by ice action: to subject to the action of land-ice: to freeze. — *n.* **glaciā′tion.** — *adj.* **glaciolog′ical.** — *n.* **glaciol′ogy** the study of the geological nature, distribution, and action of ice. — **Glacial Period** the Ice Age, or any ice age. [L. *glaciālis*, icy, *glaciāre*, *-ātum*, to freeze — *glaciēs*, ice.]

glacier *glas′yər* or *-i-ər*, *glās′yər* or *glā′shər*, *n.* a mass of ice, fed by snow on a mountain, slowly creeping downhill to where it melts or breaks up into icebergs. [Fr., — *glace*, ice — L. *glaciēs*, ice.]

glaciology. See **glacial.**

glacis *gläs-ē*, *glas′is*, *glās′is*, *n.* a gentle slope, esp. in fortification: — *pl.* **glacis** (*gläs-ē, glas′iz, glās′iz*), **glac′-ises.**   [Fr., orig. a slippery place — L. *glaciēs*, ice.]

glad¹ *glad*, *adj.* pleased: cheerful: bright: giving pleasure. — *v.t.* (*arch.*) to make glad: — *pr.p.* **gladd′ing;** *pa.t.* and *pa.p.* **gladd′ed.** — *v.t.* **gladd′en** to make glad: to cheer. — *adj.* **glad′ful** (Spens.). — *n.* **glad′fulness.** — *adv.* **glad′ly.** — *n.* **glad′ness.** — *adj.* **glad′some** (*arch.*) glad: joyous: gay. — *adv.* **glad′somely.** — *n.* **glad′-someness.** — **glad eye** (*slang*) an ogle; **glad hand** (*U.S.*) the hand of welcome or of fulsome greeting. — *v.* (**glad′-hand**) to extend the glad hand to. — **glad′-hand′er** (*U.S.*) one out to make up to all and sundry (esp. of a vote-seeking politician); **glad rags** (*coll.*) best clothes, dress clothes. — **glad of** glad to have: glad because of; **the glad and sorry** (*facet.*) the hire-purchase system.   [O.E. *glæd*; Ger. *glatt*, smooth, O.N. *glathr*, bright, Dan. *glad.*]

glad, gladdie *glad, glad'i* (*coll.*) *ns.* short forms for gladiolus.

gladdon *glad'ən,* (*dial.*) *n.* an iris. [Origin obscure.]

glade *glād, n.* an open space in a wood. — *adj.* **glā'dy** having glades. [Ety. obscure; poss. conn. with **glad**.]

gladiole, gladiolus. See **gladius**.

gladius *glad'i-əs, glād', n.* a sword (*rare*): a cuttlefish pen. — *adj.* **gladiate** (*glad', glād'*) sword-shaped. — *n.* **gladiator** (*glad'i-ā-tər*) in ancient Rome, a professional combatant with men or beasts in the arena. — *adjs.* **gladiatorial** (-ə-tō'ri-əl), **gladiatō'rian** (*obs.*), **glad'iatory** (*obs.*). — *ns.* **glad'iatorship; glad'iole, gladiolus** (*gladi-ō'ləs,* rarely *glə-dī'o-ləs*) any plant of a genus (*Gladiolus*) of the Iris family, with sword-shaped leaves: the middle part of the sternum: — *pl.* **glad'ioles, gladiō'lī, gladiō'luses.** [L. *glădius,* sword, dim. *glădĭŏlus; glădiator,* a gladiator.]

Gladstonian *glad-stō'ni-ən, adj.* pertaining to W. E. *Gladstone* (1809–98), four times prime minister. — *n.* a follower of Gladstone. — **Gladstone bag** a travelling bag or small portmanteau, opening out flat, named in his honour; **Gladstone sherry** cheap sherry (referring to reduction in duty, 1860).

glady. See **glade**.

Glagolitic *glag-ō-lit'ik, adj.* of or pertaining to Glagol, an ancient Slavonic alphabet, apparently derived from the cursive Greek of the 9th century. [Old Slav. *glagolu,* a word.]

glaik *glāk, n.* (*obs. Scot.;* usu. in *pl.*), a flash: dazzling: mocking deception: a trick: a puzzle-game. — *adjs.* (*Scot.*) **glaik'it, glaik'et** giddy: foolish. — *n.* (*Scot.*) **glaik'itness** levity. — **fling the glaiks in folk's een** (*obs. Scot.*) to throw dust in people's eyes, dazzle. [Origin obscure.]

glair *glār, n.* the clear part of an egg used as varnish: any viscous, transparent substance. — *v.t.* to varnish with white of eggs. — *adjs.* **glair'y, glair'eous** (*arch.*), **glār'eous** (*arch.*). — *n.* **glair'in** organic matter in mineral waters. [Fr. *glaire,* perh. — L.L. *clāra* (*ōvī*), white (of egg) — L. *clārus,* clear.]

glaive *glāv,* (*obs.*) *n.* a sword: a spear: a long-shafted weapon like a halberd, its edge on the outer curve: a pronged fish-spear (*dial.*; — also **gleave** *glēv*) — *adj.* **glaived.** [O.Fr. *glaive.*]

glamour, in U.S. **glamor,** *glam'ər, n.* the supposed influence of a charm on the eyes, making them see things as fairer than they are (*arch.*): fascination: enchantment: witchery (*arch.*): groomed beauty and studied charm. — *v.t.* to enchant, betwitch, cast a spell over. — *adjs.* **glam** (*slang*) glamorous; **glam'orous** full of glamour: bewitching, alluring. — *n.* **glamorīsā'tion, -z-.** — *v.t.* **glamor'ise, -ize** to make glamorous: to romanticise. — *adv.* **glam'orously.** — **glamour boy, girl** (*coll.*) a man or woman considered to be very glamorous (often *derog.*); **glam'ourpuss** a glamourous person, esp. female. [**gramary.**]

glance[1] *gläns, v.i.* to fly (off) obliquely on striking: to make a passing allusion, esp. unfavourable (with *at*): to dart a reflected ray: to flash: to snatch a momentary view (with *at*). — *v.t.* (*arch.*) to cause to glance: to direct glancingly: to deflect: to glance at. — *n.* an oblique impact or movement: a stroke by which the ball is allowed to glance off an upright bat to fine leg (*cricket*): a passing allusion, esp. satirical: a sudden shoot of reflected light: a darting of the eye: a momentary look. — *n. and adj.* **glanc'ing.** — *adv.* **glanc'ingly.** — **at a glance** immediately, at a first look. [M.E. *glenten,* poss. nasalised form of *glace,* to glance, — O.Fr. *glacier,* to slip, slide.]

glance[2] *gläns, n.* a black or grey mineral with metallic lustre, usually a sulphide, selenide, or telluride, e.g. redruthite or **copper-glance,** galena or **lead-glance,** argentite or **silver-glance.** — **glance'-coal** anthracite. [Ger. *Glanz,* glance, lustre.]

gland[1] *gland, n.* a secreting structure in plant or animal. — *adjs.* **glandif'erous** bearing acorns or nuts; **glan'diform** resembling a gland: acorn-shaped; **gland'ūlar,**

gland'ūlous containing, consisting of, or pertaining to glands. — *advs.* **gland'ūlarly, gland'ūlously.** — *n.* **glan'dūle** a small gland. — *adj.* **glandūlif'erous.** — *n.* **glans** (*glanz*) an acorn or similar fruit: a glandular structure (**glans clitoris, penis** the extremity of the clitoris, penis): — *pl.* **gland'es** (-*ēz*). — **glandular fever** infectious mononucleosis, a disease characterised by slight fever, enlargement of glands, and increase in the white cells of the blood. [L. *glāns, glandis,* an acorn.]

gland[2] *gland, n.* a device for preventing leakage at a point where a rotating or reciprocating shaft emerges from a vessel containing fluid under pressure: a sleeve or nut used to compress the packing in a stuffing-box (q.v.). [Origin unknown.]

glanders *gland'ərz, n. sing.* a malignant, contagious, and fatal disease of the horse and ass (and man), showing itself esp. on the mucous membrane of the nose, upon the lungs, and on the lymphatic system. — *adjs.* **gland'ered, gland'erous** affected with glanders. [O.Fr. *glandre,* a gland.]

glandiferous, glandular, etc., **glans.** See **gland[1]**.

glare *glār, n.* an oppressive or unrelieved dazzling light (also *fig.*): overpowering lustre (*arch.*): cheap or showy brilliance: a glassy or icy surface (*U.S.*): a fierce stare. — *adj.* (*U.S.*) glassy (of ice). — *v.i.* to emit a hard, fierce, dazzling light: to be obtrusively noticeable, to shine dazzlingly: to stare fiercely. — *v.t.* to send forth or express with a glare. — *adj.* **glar'ing** bright and dazzling: flagrant. — *adv.* **glar'ingly.** — *n.* **glar'ingness.** — *adj.* **glar'y** glaring: shining harshly. [M.E. *glāren,* to shine; cf. **glass,** O.E. *glær,* amber, L. Ger. *glaren,* to glow.]

glareous *glā'ri-əs, adj.* gravelly: growing on gravel. — *adj.* **glā'real** growing on dry exposed ground. See also **glair.** [L. *glārea,* gravel.]

glasnost *glas', glaz'nost, n.* the policy of openness and forthrightness followed by the Soviet government, initiated by Premier Mikhail Gorbachev. [Russ., speaking aloud.]

glass *gläs, n.* a hard, amorphous, brittle substance, a bad conductor of electricity, usually transparent, made by fusing together one or more of the oxides of silicon, boron, or phosphorus with certain basic oxides (e.g. sodium, magnesium, calcium, potassium), and cooling the product rapidly to prevent crystallisation: an article made of or with glass, esp. a drinking-vessel, a mirror, a lens, the cover of a watch-face, a weatherglass, a telescope, etc.: the quantity of liquid a glass holds: any fused substance like glass, with a vitreous fracture: a rock, or portion of rock, without crystalline structure: (*pl.*) spectacles. — *adj.* made of glass. — *v.t.* to glaze: to polish highly: to put in, under, or behind glass: to furnish with glass: to reflect in glass. — *adj.* **glass'en** (*arch.*) of or like glass. — *n.* **glass'ful** as much as a glass will hold: — *pl.* **glass'fuls.** — *v.t.* and *v.i.* **glass'ify** to (cause to) become (like) glass. — *adv.* **glass'ily.** — *ns.* **glassine** (-*ēn'*) a transparent paper, used for book-covers; **glass'iness.** — *adj.* **glass'y** like glass: of eyes, expressionless. — *ns.* **glass'-blower; glass'-blowing** the process of making glassware by inflating a viscid mass; **glass chin** or **glass jaw** a chin or jaw exceptionally vulnerable to punches, used chiefly of boxers; **glass'-cloth** a cloth for drying glasses: a material woven from glass threads: a polishing cloth covered with powdered glass; **glass'-coach** (*obs.*) a coach (esp. one for hire) having glazed windows; **glass'-crab** the transparent larva of the spiny lobster; **glass'-cutter** a tool for cutting sheets of glass: one who does cut-glass work; **glass'-cutting** the act or process of cutting, shaping, and ornamenting the surface of glass; **glass eye** an artificial eye made of glass: (*pl.*) spectacles (*obs.*): a form of blindness in horses. — *adj.* **glass'-faced** (*Shak.*) reflecting the sentiments of another, as in a mirror. — **glass fibre** glass melted and then drawn out into extremely fine fibres, which are later to be spun, woven, etc. (also **fibreglass**); **glass'-gall** a scum formed on fused glass. — *adj.* **glass'-gaz'ing** (*Shak.*) addicted to looking in a mirror; **glass'-grinding** the ornamenting of glass by rubbing with sand, emery, etc.; **glass harmonica** the musical glasses (see **harmonica**); **glass'-house** a glass factory: a house made of glass or largely of glass, esp. a greenhouse: military detention barracks (from one with a glass roof at Aldershot; *slang*). — *adj.* **glass'like**. — **glass jaw** see **glass chin; glass'man** a maker or seller of glass: a beggar hawking glass as a pretext (*arch.*); **glass'-painting** the art of producing pictures on glass by means of staining it chemically; **glass'-paper** paper coated with finely pounded glass, used like sand-paper; **glass'-rope** a silicious sponge (Hyalonema) with a long anchoring tuft; **glass'-snake** a legless lizard (*Ophisaurus*) with brittle tail; **glass'-soap** manganese dioxide or other substance used by glass-makers to remove colouring from glass; **glass'ware** articles made of glass; **glass wool** glass spun into woolly fibres; **glass'work** furnishings or articles made of glass: (usu. in *pl.*) a glass factory; **glass'worker; glass'wort** a name for plants of the genera Salicornia and Salsola yielding soda, once used in making glass. — *adj.* **glass'yheaded** (*Tenn.*) shiny-pated. — **live in a glass house** to be open to attack or retort; **musical glasses** see **harmonica; water**, or **soluble, glass** sodium or potassium silicate. [O.E. *glæs*.]

Glassite *gläs'īt, n.* a Sandemanian, or follower of John *Glas* (1695–1773), deposed in 1730 from the ministry of the Church of Scotland for maintaining that a congregation with its eldership is, in its discipline, subject to no jurisdiction but that of Jesus Christ.

Glaswegian *glas-, gläs-wēj'(y)ən, n.* a native or citizen of Glasgow. — Also *adj.* [Modelled on *Norwegian*.]

glauberite *glö'bər-īt, n.* a greyish-white mineral, sodium calcium sulphate, found chiefly in rock-salt, named after the German chemist Johann Rudolf *Glauber* (1604–68). — **Glauber('s) salt** (*glow'bər, glö'bər*) hydrated sodium sulphate, discovered by him.

glaucescence, etc. See **glaucous**.

glaucoma *glö-kō'mə, n.* an insidious disease of the eye, marked by increased tension within the eyeball and growing dimness of vision. — *adj.* **glaucomatous** (*-kōm'ə-təs, -kom'*). [Gr. *glaukōma*, cataract; see **glaucous**.]

glauconite *glök'ə-nīt, n.* a mineral now forming in the sea, a hydrated potassium iron and aluminium silicate, which gives a green colour to some of the beds of the Greensand. — *adj.* **glauconitic** (*-nit'ik*). — *n.* **glauconītīsā'tion, -z-** conversion into glauconite. [Gr. *glaukos*, bluish-green.]

glaucous *glö'kəs, adj.* sea-green: greyish-blue: covered with a fine greenish or bluish bloom (*bot.*). — *n.* **glaucescence** (*-ses'əns*). — *adj.* **glaucesc'ent** somewhat glaucous. [L. *glaucus* — Gr. *glaukos*, bluish-green or grey (orig. gleaming).]

Glaucus *glö'kəs, n.* a genus of translucent blue nudibranch gasteropods of warm seas. [Gr. *glaukos*, bluish-green.]

glaum *glöm*, (*Scot.*) *v.i.* to clutch (with *at*).

glaur *glör*, (*Scot.*) *n.* mire. — *adj.* **glaur'y**. [Origin unknown.]

Glaux *glöks, n.* the generic name of sea-milkwort or black saltwort, a fleshy seaside plant of the primrose family, with pink sepals and no petals, once used in soda-making. [Gr. *glaux*, wart-cress.]

glaze *glāz, v.t.* to furnish or set with glass: to cover with a thin surface of glass or something glassy: to cover with a layer of thin semi-transparent colour: to give a glassy surface to. — *n.* the glassy coating put upon pottery: a thin coat of semi-transparent colour: any shining exterior. — *v.i.* to become glassy. — *adj.* **glazed; glä'zen** (*arch.*) glassy: glazed. — *ns.* **glä'zer** a workman who glazes pottery, paper, etc.: **glä'zier** (*-zyər*) one who sets glass in window-frames, etc.; **glä'zing** the act or art of setting glass: the art of covering with a vitreous substance: semi-transparent colours put thinly over others to modify the effect

(*paint.*). — *adj.* **glä'zy**. [M.E. *glasen* — *glas*, glass; see **glass**.]

gleam *glēm, v.i.* to glow or shine, usu. not very brightly. — *v.t.* to flash. — *n.* a faint or moderate glow: a small stream of light: a beam: brightness: often used fig. as *a gleam of hope, a gleam of understanding*. — *n.* and *adj.* **gleam'ing**. — *adj.* **gleam'y** casting gleams or rays of light. [O.E. *glǣm*, gleam, brightness; see **glimmer[1]**.]

glean *glēn, v.t.* to gather in handfuls after the reapers: to collect (what is thinly scattered, neglected, or over-looked): to learn by laboriously scraping together pieces of information. — *v.i.* to gather the corn left by a reaper or anything that has been left by others: to gather facts bit by bit. — *n.* that which is gleaned: the act of gleaning. — *ns.* **glean'er; glean'ing**. [O.Fr. *glener* (Fr. *glaner*), through L.L. *glenāre*; origin unknown.]

gleave. See **glaive**.

glebe *glēb, n.* the soil (*arch.*): a clod (*arch.*): a field (*arch.*): the land attached to a parish church. — *adjs.* **glē'bous, glē'by** (*arch.*) cloddy, turfy. — **glebe'-house** a manse. [L. *glēba*, a clod.]

glede *glēd, gled* gled, (*B.*) *ns.* the common kite. [O.E. *glida*, from *glīdan*, to glide.]

gledge *glej*, (*Scot.*) *v.i.* to squint: to cast an eye around: to look cunningly. — *n.* a knowing look: a side-glance: a glimpse. [Cf. **gley[1]**.]

glee[1] *glē, n.* joy: mirth and gaiety: impish enjoyment: a song or catch in parts, strictly one without an accompaniment (*mus.*): app. glitter (proverbially coupled with *gold*; *Spens.*). — *adjs.* **glee'ful, glee'some** merry. — **glee club** (chiefly *U.S.*) a club for singing glees, part-songs, etc.; **glee'maiden** (*obs.*) a female minstrel; **glee'man** (*obs.*) a minstrel. [O.E. *glēo, glīw*, mirth; O.N. *glȳ*.]

glee[2]. See **gley[1]**.

gleed[1] *glēd, (dial.) n.* a hot coal or burning ember. [O.E. *glēd*; cf. Du. *gloed*, Ger. *Glut*, Sw. *glöd*.]

gleed[2]. See **gley[1]**.

gleek[1] *glēk*, (*obs.*) *n.* a jest or gibe, a trick. — *v.i.* to gibe (with *at*): to jest. — *v.t.* to play a trick upon. [Cf.**glaik**.]

gleek[2] *glēk*, (*hist.*) *n.* a game at cards for three, each having twelve, and eight being left for the stock. [O.Fr. *glic, ghelicque*, possibly — M.Du. *ghelic*, alike.]

gleet *glēt, n.* a viscous, transparent discharge from a mucous surface. — *v.t.* to discharge gleet. — *adj.* **gleet'y**. [O.Fr. *glette, glecte*, a flux.]

gleg *gleg*, (*Scot.*) *adj.* clever: apt: alert: keen. [O.N. *gleggr*, clever; cf. O.E. *glēaw*, wise, Ger. *glau*, clear.]

glei. See **gley[2]**.

Gleichschaltung *glīhh'shäl-tōong, n.* elimination of all opposition, enforcement of strict conformity, in politics, culture, etc. [Ger., co-ordination — *gleich*, like, *schalten*, to govern.]

glen *glen, n.* a narrow valley with a stream, often with trees: a depression, usu. of some extent, between hills. [Gael. *gleann*; cf. W. *glyn*.]

glendoveer *glen-dō-vēr', (Southey) n.* a heavenly spirit. [Fr. *grandouver*.]

glengarry *glen-gar'i, n.* a Highlander's cap of thick-milled woollen, generally rising to a point in front, with ribbons hanging down behind. [*Glengarry* in Inverness-shire.]

Glenlivet® *glen-liv'it, n.* proprietary name for a noted whisky. [*Glenlivet*, a valley in Banffshire.]

glenoid, -al *glē'noid, -əl, adjs.* socket-shaped: slightly cupped. — Also *n.* [Gr. *glēnoeidēs* — *glēnē*, a socket.]

glent *glent, v.t., v.i.,* and *n.* an earlier form of **glint**.

gley[1] *glī, glē,* **glee** *glē* (*Scot.*) *v.i.* to squint. — *adjs.* **gleyed, gleed** squint-eyed. [Origin obscure; cf. **gledge**.]

gley[2], glei *glā, n.* a bluish-grey sticky clay found under some types of very damp soil. [Russ. *gley*, clay.]

glia *glī'ə, glē'ə, n.* neuroglia. — *adj.* **gli'al**. — *ns.* **gli'adin, gli'adine** prolamine, a protein in gluten. — *n.* **gliō'ma** a tumour of the neuroglia in the brain and spinal cord:

— _pl._ **gliŏ'mata, gliŏ'mas.** — _adj._ **gliŏ'matous.** — _ns._ **gliomatō'sis** diffuse overgrowth of neuroglia in the brain or spinal chord; **gliŏ'sis** excessive growth of fibrous tissue in the neuroglia. [Gr. _gliā,_ glue.]

glib[1] _glib, adj._ smooth (_arch._): slippery (_arch._): easy: facile: fluent and plausible. — _adv._ (_arch._) glibly. — _v.t._ (_arch._) to make glib. — _adj._ **glibb'ery** (_obs._) slippery. — _adv._ **glib'ly.** — _n._ **glib'ness.** [Cf. Du. _glibberig,_ slippery.]

glib[2] _glib,_ (_Spens._) _n._ a bush of hair over the eyes. [Ir.]

glib[3] _glib,_ (_Shak._) _v.t._ to castrate. [Cf. **lib**[1].]

glidder _glid'ər,_ (_dial._) _adj._ slippery. — Also **glid** (_Scot._), **glidd'ery.** [O.E. _glidder._]

glide _glīd, v.i._ to slide smoothly and easily: to flow gently: to pass smoothly or stealthily: to travel through the air without expenditure of power: to travel by glider: to play a glide stroke. — _n._ act of gliding: a transitional sound produced in passing from one position to another (_phon._): a glance stroke (_cricket_): a smooth and sliding dance-step: an inclined plane or slide: stretch of shallow gliding water. — _ns._ **glīd'er** one who, or that which, glides: an aircraft like an aeroplane without engine (a _powered glider_ has a small engine): a hydroplane; **glīd'ing** the action of the verb in any sense: the sport of flying in a glider. — _adv._ **glīd'ingly.** — **glide slope, path** the slope along which aircraft are assumed to come in for landing, marked out, e.g. by a radio beam. [O.E. _glīdan,_ to slip; Ger. _gleiten._]

gliff _glif,_ (_Scot._) _n._ a fright, a scare: a glimpse or other transient experience: a moment. — Also **glift.** — _n._ **gliff'ing** a moment. [Ety. dub.]

glike _glīk,_ (_Shak._) _n._ Same as **gleek**[1].

glim _glim, n._ a glimpse (_Scot._): a scrap (_Scot._): a light (_slang_): an eye (_slang_). [Cf. **gleam, glimmer;** and Ger. _Glimm,_ a spark.]

glimmer[1] _glim'ər, v.i._ to burn or appear faintly. — _ns._ a faint light: feeble rays of light: an inkling, faint perception; **glimm'ering** a glimmer: an inkling. — _adv._ **glimm'eringly.** — _adj._ **glimm'ery.** — **glimm'er-gowk** (_Tenn._) an owl. [M.E. _glemern,_ freq. from root of **gleam.**]

glimmer[2] _glim'ər, n._ mica. [Ger.]

glimpse _glimps, n._ a short gleam (_arch._): a passing appearance: a momentary view. — _v.i._ (_arch._) to glimmer: to appear by glimpses. — _v.t._ to get a glimpse of. [M.E. _glymsen,_ to glimpse.]

glint _glint, v.i._ to flash with a glittering light. — _v.t._ to reflect. — _n._ a gleam. [Earlier _glent;_ prob. Scand.]

glioma, etc. See **glia.**

Glires _glī'rēz, n.pl._ a division of mammals including the typical rodents (e.g. the genus _Glis,_ Old World dormice), etc. [L. _glis, glīris,_ dormouse.]

glisk _glisk,_ (_Scot._) _n._ a glimpse. [Perh. from the same root as O.E. _glisian,_ to shine.]

glissade _glēs-äd', v.i._ to slide or glide down. — _n._ act of sliding down a slope: a gliding movement in dancing. [Fr.]

glissando _glēs-än'dō, n._ the effect produced by sliding the finger along keyboard or strings: a similar effect on the trombone, etc.: — _pl._ **glissan'dos.** — Also _adj._ and _adv._ [19th-cent. It., formed from Fr. _glissant,_ sliding.]

glisten _glis'n, v.i._ to shine, as light reflected from a wet or oily surface. — _n._ gleam. [M.E. _glistnen_ — O.E. _glisnian,_ to shine; cf. Du. _glinsteren._]

glister _glis'tər,_ (_arch._) _v.i._ to sparkle, glitter. — _adj._ **glis'tering.** — _adv._ **glis'teringly.** [M.E. _glistren;_ cf. **glisten,** and Du. _glisteren._]

glit _glit, n._ sticky, slimy or greasy material: gleet. [**gleet.**]

glitch _glich, n._ an instance of imperfect functioning in a spacecraft, as, e.g. a minute change in voltage on a line.

glitter _glit'ər, v.i._ to sparkle with light: to be splendid: to be showy. — _n._ sparkle: showiness. — _adj._ **glitt'erand** (_Spens._) glittering. — _n._ and _adj._ **glitt'ering.** — _adv._ **glitt'eringly.** — _adj._ **glitt'ery.** [M.E. _gliteren;_ cf. O.N. _glitra,_ Ger. _glitzern._]

glitterati _glit-ər-ä'tē, n.pl._ the society lions of the day —

famous, fashionable, rich and articulate people.

glittery. See **glitter.**

glitzy _glits'i,_ (_U.S. coll._) _adj._ showy, garish, gaudy: glittering. — _n._ **glitz** (a back-formation) showiness, garishness. [Perh. from Ger. _glitzern,_ to glitter.]

gloaming _glōm'ing, n._ twilight, dusk. [Apparently from a short-vowelled derivative of O.E. _glōmung — glōm,_ twilight.]

gloat _glōt, v.i._ to eye with intense, usu. malicious, satisfaction (esp. with _over_): generally, to exult (over). — _n._ an act of gloating. — _adv._ **gloat'ingly.** [Perh. O.N. _glotta,_ to grin.]

glob _glob,_ (_coll._) _n._ a roundish drop, dollop, etc. of a (semi-)liquid substance. [Uncertain, poss. **globe** and **blob.**]

globe _glōb, n._ a ball: a round body, a sphere: the earth: a sphere representing the earth (terrestrial globe), or one representing the heavens (celestial globe): an orb, emblem of sovereignty: a lamp glass: a nearly spherical glass vessel: a group (_obs._). — _v.t., v.i._ to form into a globe. — _adj._ **glōb'al** spherical: world-wide: affecting, or taking into consideration, the whole world or all peoples: comprehensive. — _ns._ **glōbalisā'tion, -z-.** — _v.t._ **glō'balise, -ize** to make global. — _adv._ **glōb'ally.** — _adjs._ **glōb'ate, -d** globe-shaped; **glōbed** globe-shaped: having a globe. — _n._ **glōb'in** the protein constituent of haemoglobin, a histone. — _adjs._ **glōb'oid, glōbose'** (or _glōb'_) globate. — _ns._ a globosity. — _n._ **glōbos'ity** (something having) the quality of being globate. — _adjs._ **glōb'ous; glōbular** (_glob'ū-lər_) spherical. — _n._ **globularity** (_glob-ū-lar'i-ti_). — _adv._ **glōb'ūlarly.** — _ns._ **glōb'ūle** a little globe or round particle: a drop: a small pill; **glōb'ūlet; glōb'ūlin** any one of a class of proteins soluble in dilute salt solutions but not in pure water; **glōb'ūlite** a minute spheroidal crystallite occurring esp. in glassy rocks. — _adjs._ **glōbulif'erous** producing or having globules; **glōb'ūlous; glōb'y** (_Milt._) round. — **global village** the world, in reference to its apparent smallness due to improved communications, and the way in which changes in one area are likely to affect the rest of the world; **globe'-fish** any fish of the families _Diodontidae_ and _Tetrodontidae,_ capable of blowing itself up into a globe; **globe'flower** a ranunculaceous plant (_Trollius_) with a globe of large showy sepals enclosing the small inconspicuous petals; **globe'-thistle** see **Echinops; globe'-trotter** one who goes sightseeing about the world; **globe'-trotting; globular cluster** (_astron._) symmetrical clusters into which many thousands of stars are gathered. [L. _globus._]

Globigerina _glob-i-jə-rī'nə, n._ a genus of foraminifers with calcareous shells of globose chambers in a spiral: (without _cap._) (the shell of) a member of this genus: — _pl._ **globigerinae** (-_ī'nē_). — **globigerina ooze** a deep-sea deposit of globigerina shells. [L. _globus,_ globe, _gerĕre,_ to carry.]

globin, globoid, globule, etc. See **globe.**

glockenspiel _glok'ən-shpēl, n._ an orchestral instrument consisting of a set of bells or bars struck by hammers, with or (more usually) without a keyboard. [Ger. _Glocke,_ bell, _Spiel,_ play.]

glode _glōd,_ (_Spens._) _pa.t._ of **glide.**

glogg _glog, n._ a Swedish hot spiced drink, of wines, spirit, and fruit, often served at Christmas. [Sw. _glögg._]

gloire _glwär,_ (_Fr._) _n._ glory.

glom[1] _glom,_ (_U.S. slang_) _v.t._ to snatch: to steal: — _pr.p._ **glomm'ing;** _pa.t._ and _pa.p._ **glommed.** — **glom on to** to appropriate: to catch on to. [Variant of esp. Scot. dial. _glaum,_ to grab, — Gael. _glàm,_ to sieze, devour.]

glom[2] _glom,_ (_U.S. slang_) _v.t._ to look at, to eye: — _pr.p._ **glomm'ing;** _pa.t._ and _pa.p._ **glommed.** [Origin uncertain.]

glomerate _glom'ər-āt, v.t._ (_rare_) to gather into a ball. — _adj._ balled: clustered in heads. — _n._ **glomerā'tion.** — _adjs._ **glomer'ular** of a glomerulus; **glomer'ūlate** of a glomerule. — _ns._ **glom'erule** (-_ōōl_) (_bot._) a little ball of spores: a cluster of short-stalked flowers; **glomer'ūlus** (_anat._) a cluster or mass of small organisms, esp. of capillaries in the kidneys: — *pl.* **glomer'ūlī.** [L. *glomerāre, -ātum* — *glomus, glomeris,* a clew of yarn.]

glonoin *glo-nō'in,* (*chem.*) *n.* a name for nitroglycerine, as used in medicine. [*glycerine, O* (oxygen), *NO₃* (nitric anhydride).]

gloom *glōōm, n.* partial darkness: cloudiness: a dark place: heaviness of mind: hopelessness: sullenness: a scowl, sullen look (*Scot.*). — *v.i.* to be or look sullen or dejected: to be or become cloudy, dark or obscure: to scowl: to dusk (*arch.*). — *v.t.* (*arch.*) to fill with gloom. — *adj.* **gloom'ful.** — *adv.* **gloom'ily.** — *n.* **gloom'iness.** — *adj.* **gloom'ing** (*Spens.*) shining obscurely. — *n.* twilight: gloaming: scowling. — *adj.* **gloom'y** dim or obscure: dimly lighted: depressed in spirits: dismal. [M.E. *gloumbe;* see **glum.**]

gloria¹ *glō', glō'ri-ə, n.* an aureole: a halo: a type of very closely-woven fabric, usu. of a mixture of silk or nylon and wool or cotton, often used for umbrellas. [L.]

gloria² *glō'ri-a, glō'ri-ə,* (L.) *n.* glory: any doxology beginning with the word "Gloria". — **gloria in excelsis** (*in ek-, ik-sel'sis, eks-chel'sis, eks-kel'sēs*) glory (to God) on high; **gloria Patri** (*pat'rī, 'ri, pät'rē*) glory (be) to the Father.

glorify *glō', glō'ri-fī, v.t.* to make glorious: to cast glory upon: to honour: to worship: to exalt to glory or happiness: to ascribe honour to: to ascribe great charm, beauty, etc., to, usually to a markedly exaggerated extent: to add undeserved prestige to, esp. *under* a euphemistic or overblown title. — *pr.p.* **glō'rifying;** *pa.t.* and *pa.p.* **glō'rified.** — *n.* **glorificā'tion** an act of glorifying: a doxology: riotous festivity (*coll.*). [L. *glōria,* glory, *facěre,* to make.]

glory *glō', glō'ri, n.* renown: exalted or triumphant honour: the occasion of praise: an object of supreme pride: splendour, beauty: resplendent brightness: summit of attainment, prosperity or gratification: in religious symbolism, a combination of the nimbus and the aureola, but often erroneously used for the nimbus: a burst of sunlight: a ring or glow of light about the moon, the Brocken spectre, or other object or phenomenon: boastful or self-gratulatory spirit (*obs.*): the presence of God: the manifestation of God to the blessed in heaven: a representation of the heavens opened: heaven. — *v.i.* to boast (*obs.*): to exult proudly: to rejoice. — *v.t.* (*obs.*) to glorify: — *pr.p.* **glō'rying;** *pa.t.* and *pa.p.* **glō'ried.** — *interj.* expressing surprise. — *ns.* **glō'riole** a halo or glory; **Gloriō'sa** a tropical genus of leaf-climbers of the lily family: (without *cap.*) a plant of this genus. — *adj.* **glō'rious** noble: splendid: conferring renown: elated, tipsy (*coll.*): boastful (*obs.*). — *adv.* **glō'riously.** — *n.* **glō'riousness.** — **Glorious Twelfth** see **twelfth;** **glo'rybox** (*Austr.*) a box in which a young woman keeps her trousseau, etc. — a bottom drawer; **glo'ry-pea'** the papilionaceous genus *Clianthus,* consisting of Sturt's desert-pea (in Australia) and the parrot-bill (in New Zealand). — **glory be** a devout ascription of Glory to God: hence, an ejaculation of exultation: an interj. expressing surprise; **glory of the snow** the plant Chionodoxa; **Old Glory** the Stars and Stripes. [O.Fr. *glorie* and L. *glōria.*]

glory-hole *glō', glō'ri-hōl, n.* a glass-maker's supplementary furnace: a hole for viewing the inside of a furnace: a nook or receptacle for miscellaneous odds and ends: a steward's room on a ship: a hiding-place: an excavation. [Perh. M.E. *glory,* to defile, or **glaury,** or **glory,** and **hole.**]

gloss¹ *glos, n.* brightness or lustre, as from a polished surface: external show. — *v.t.* to give a superficial lustre to: to render plausible: to palliate. — *n.* **gloss'er.** — *adv.* **gloss'ily.** — *n.* **gloss'iness.** — *adj.* **gloss'y** smooth and shining: highly polished. — *n.* (*coll.*) a glossy magazine. — **gloss paint** paint containing varnish, giving a hard, shiny finish; **glossy magazine** a magazine of the lusher type, usually printed on glossy paper, and abounding in illustrations and advertisements. — **gloss over** to explain away, render more acceptable. [Cf. O.N. *glossi,* blaze, *glōa,* to glow; see **glass.**]

gloss² *glos, n.* a marginal or interlinear explanation, e.g. of an obscure or unusual word: an explanation: a sophistical explanation: a collection of explanations of words. — *v.t.* to give a gloss on: to explain away. — *v.i.* to comment or make explanatory remarks. — *n.* **gloss'a** (*anat.*) the tongue: in insects, one of an inner pair of lobes in the labium. — *adjs.* **gloss'al; glossā'rial** relating to a glossary: containing explanation. — *adv.* **glossā'rially.** — *ns.* **gloss'arist** (*-ə-rist*) a writer of a gloss or of a glossary; **gloss'ary** a collection of glosses: a partial dictionary for a special purpose; **glossā'tor gloss'er** a writer of glosses or comments, a commentator; **glossec'tomy** surgical removal of the tongue; **gloss'eme** (*linguistics*) a unit or feature of a language that in itself carries significance and cannot be further analysed into meaningful units; **Gloss'ic** a phonetic alphabet devised by A. J. Ellis (1814–90); **Glossī'na** the tsetse fly genus: (without *cap.*) an insect of this genus; **glossī'tis** inflammation of the tongue; **glossodynia** (*-ō-din'i-ə;* Gr. *odynē,* pain) pain in the tongue; **glossog'rapher.** — *adj.* **glossograph'ical.** — *ns.* **glossog'raphy** the writing of glosses or comments; **glossolā'lia** (Gr. *laleein,* to talk) the 'gift of tongues', abnormal utterance under religious emotion. — *adj.* **glossolog'ical.** — *ns.* **glossol'ogist; glossol'ogy** (*obs.*) comparative philology (also **glottol'ogy**): terminology; **glottochronol'ogy** a statistical study of vocabulary to determine the degree of relationship between particular languages and the chronology of their independent development. [Gr. *glōssa, glōtta,* tongue, a word requiring explanation.]

glottis *glot'is, n.* the opening of the larynx or entrance to the windpipe: — *pl.* **glott'ises, glott'ides** (*-i-dēz*). — *adjs.* **glott'al** of the glottis; **glott'ic** pertaining to the glottis or to the tongue: linguistic. — *adj.* **glottid'ean.** — **glottal stop** a consonant sound produced by closing and suddenly opening the glottis, occurring as a phoneme in some languages, e.g. Arabic, and as a feature of others, and sometimes heard as a substitute for *t* in English. [Gr. *glōttis* — *glōtta,* the tongue.]

glottochronology, glottology. See under **gloss².**

glout *glowt,* (*arch.*) *v.i.* to be sulky. — *n.* a sulky look, the sulks. [Perh. a variant of **gloat.**]

glove *gluv, n.* a covering for the hand, with a sheath for each finger: a boxing-glove. — *v.t.* to cover with, or as with, a glove. — *adj.* **gloved.** — *n.* **glov'er** one who makes or sells gloves. — **glove box** a closed compartment in which radioactive or toxic material may be manipulated by the use of gloves attached to the walls; **glove compartment** a small compartment in the front of a car, usu. part of the dashboard, in which gloves, etc. can be kept; **glove'-fight** (*arch.*) a boxing-match in which the hands are gloved; **glove'-money** (*hist.*) a gratuity given to servants, officers of a court, etc.; **glove puppet** a puppet worn on the hand like a glove and manipulated by the fingers; **glove'-shield** (*hist.*) a shield worn by a knight on the left-hand gauntlet to parry blows; **glove'-stretcher** a scissors-shaped instrument for stretching the fingers of gloves. — **the gloves are off** (*coll.*) now the fight, argument, etc. is about to begin. [O.E. *glōf,* perh. conn. with **loof².**]

glow *glō, v.i.* to shine with an intense heat: to burn without flame: to emit a steady light: to flush: to tingle with bodily warmth or with emotion: to be ardent. — *n.* a shining with heat: a luminous appearance: a feeling of warmth: brightness of colour: warmth of feeling. — *adj.* **glow'ing.** — *adv.* **glow'ingly.** — **glow discharge** a luminous electrical discharge in gas at low pressure; **glow'lamp** an incandescent lamp, usually electric; **glow plug** an electric plug fitted in a diesel engine, that can be switched on to re-ignite the flame in a gas turbine automatically; **glow'-worm** a beetle, genus *Lampyris noctiluca,* whose larvae and wingless females are luminous. [O.E. *glōwan,* to glow; Ger. *glühen,* O.N. *glōa,* to glow.]

glower *glow'ər, glowr, v.i.* to stare frowningly: to scowl. — *n.* a fierce or threatening stare. [Origin obscure.]

Gloxinia *glok-sin'i-ǝ, n.* a tropical American genus of Gesneriaceae, with bright bell-shaped flowers: (without *cap.*) generally applied to the allied Sinningia. [*Gloxin,* a German botanist.]

gloze *glōz, (arch.) v.i.* to flatter: to comment. — *v.t.* to make glosses on, explain: to palliate by specious explanation: to flatter: to deceive with smooth words. — *n.* **glō'zing** flattery, deceit. — **gloze over** to explain away speciously. [O.Fr. *glose* — L. *glōssa* — Gr. *glōssa;* see **gloss**[2].]

glucagon *glōō'kǝ-gon, n.* a polypeptide hormone secreted by the pancreas which accelerates glycogen breakdown in the liver, so increasing blood glucose levels. [Gr. *glykys,* sweet.]

glucinum *glōō-sī'nǝm,* also **glucinium** *glōō-sin'i-ǝm, ns.* former names for beryllium. — *n.* **glucī'na** beryllia. [Gr. *glykys,* sweet, from the taste of its salts.]

glucocorticoid *glōō-kō-kör'ti-koid, n.* any of a group of steroid hormones which affect glucose metabolism. [Gr. *glykys,* sweet, and **corticoid**.]

gluconeogenesis *glōō-kō-nē-ō-jen'ǝ-sis, n.* the conversion of non-carbohydrate substances, e.g. amino-acids, into glucose. — *adj.* **gluconeogen'ic.** [Gr. *glykys,* sweet, **neo-, genesis**.]

glucoprotein. See **glycoprotein**.

glucose *glōō'kōs, n.* grape-sugar or dextrose. — *adj.* **glucos'ic** *(kos').* — *ns.* **glu'coside** any of the vegetable products making up a large group of the glycosides, which, on treatment with acids or alkalis, yield glucose or kindred substance; **glucosū'ria** glycosuria. — *adj.* **glucosū'ric.** [Gr. *glykys,* sweet.]

glue *glōō, n.* an impure gelatine got by boiling animal refuse, used as an adhesive: any of several synthetic substances used as adhesives. — *v.t.* to join with, or as with, glue or other adhesive: — *pr.p.* **glu'ing;** *pa.t.* and *pa.p.* **glued.** — *n.* **glu'er** one who cements with glue. — *adj.* **glu'ey** containing glue: sticky: viscous. — *n.* **glu'eyness.** — *adj.* **glu'ish** *(obs.)* having the nature of glue. — **glue ear** a condition of the ear where middle ear fluid fails to drain down the Eustachian tube, collecting instead behind the eardrum and causing deafness, infection and discharge; **glue'-pot** a vessel for melting or holding glue: a sticky place; **glue'-sniffer** a person who inhales the fumes of certain types of glue to achieve hallucinatory effects, etc.; **glue'-sniffing** the practice, sometimes fatal, of doing this. — **marine glue** not a glue, but a composition of rubber, shellac, and oil, that resists sea-water. [Fr. *glu* — L.L. *glus, glūtis.*]

glug *glug, n.* a word representing the sound of liquid being poured from a bottle, down one's throat, etc. — *v.i.* to flow making this sound: — *pr.p.* **glugg'ing;** *pa.t.* and *pa.p.* **glugged.** [Imit.]

glühwein, Glühwein *glü'vīn, n.* hot, sweetened, spiced red wine, mulled wine as prepared in Germany, Austria, etc. [Ger., — *glühen,* to glow, *Wein,* wine.]

glum *glum, adj.* sullen: gloomy. — *adv.* **glum'ly.** — *n.* **glum'ness.** — *adj.* **glump'ish** *(arch.)* glum. — *n.pl.* **glumps** *(arch.)* the sulks. — *adj.* **glump'y** *(arch.)* sulky. [M.E. *glombe, glome,* to frown.]

glume *glōōm, n.* an outer sterile bract which, alone or with others, encloses the spikelet in grasses and sedges. — *adj.* **glumā'ceous** like a glume, thin, brownish and papery. — *n.* **glumell'a** a palea. — *adj.* **glumif'erous** having glumes. — *n.pl.* **Glumiflō'rae** an order of monocotyledons consisting of grasses and sedges. [L. *glūma,* husk — *glūbĕre,* to peel.]

glumpish, etc. See **glum**.

gluon *glōō'on, n.* the name given to a hypothetical particle thought of as passing between quarks and so signifying the force that holds them together. [**glue**.]

glut *glut, v.t.* to gorge: to feed to satiety: to saturate: — *pr.p.* **glutt'ing;** *pa.t.* and *pa.p.* **glutt'ed.** — *n.* a glutting: a surfeit: an oversupply. [L. *gluttīre,* to swallow.]

glutaeus, gluteus *glōō-tē'ǝs, n.* any of three muscles of the buttock and hip: — *pl.* **glutae'ī, glutē'ī.** — *adj.* **glutae'al, glutē'al.** [Gr. *gloutos,* the rump.]

gluten *glōō'tǝn, n.* the nitrogenous part of the flour of wheat and other grains, insoluble in water. — *ns.* **glu'tamate** a salt of glutamic acid; **glutam'inase** an enzyme used in cancer treatment; **glu'tamine** *(-min, -mīn)* an amino acid found in proteins; **glu'telin** any of various simple proteins, found in cereals and soluble only in dilute acids and alkalis. — *adjs.* **glu'tenous** containing, made from, etc. gluten; **glu'tinous** gluey: tenacious: sticky. — *adv.* **glu'tinously.** — **glutam'ic** or **glutamin'ic acid** an important amino-acid, HOOC·CH₂·CH₂·CH(NH₂)·COOH. [L. *glūten, -inis,* glue; cf. **glue**.]

glutton[1] *glut'n, n.* one who eats to excess: one who is extremely eager (for something, e.g. hard work). — *v.i.* **glutt'onise, -ize** to eat to excess. — *adjs.* **glutt'onous, glutt'onish** given to, or consisting in, gluttony. — *adv.* **glutt'onously.** — *n.* **glutt'ony** excess in eating. — **glutton for punishment** one who seems indefatigable in seeking and performing strenuous or unpleasant work, etc. [Fr. *glouton* — L. *glūtō, -ōnis* — *glūtīre, gluttīre,* to devour.]

glutton[2] *glut'n, n.* a N. European carnivore *(Gulo gulo)* of the Mustelidae, 2–3 ft. long, having dark, shaggy fur: a related animal *(Gulo luscus)* of N. America, the wolverine. [Trans. of Ger. *Vielfrass,* lit. large feeder, a pop. imitation of Norw. *fjeldfross,* lit. mountain-cat.]

glycerine, glycerin *glis'ǝ-rēn, -in,* **glycerol** *-ol, ns.* a trihydric alcohol, a colourless, viscid, neutral inodorous fluid, of a sweet taste, soluble in water and alcohol. — *adj.* **glycer'ic.** — *ns.* **glyc'eride** an ester of glycerol; **gly'ceryl** a radical of which glycerine is the hydroxide. — **glyceryl trinitrate** same as **nitroglycerine.** [Gr. *glykeros,* sweet — *glykys.*]

glycin, glycine *glis'in, glī'sin, -sēn, -sēn', ns.* amino-acetic acid or glycocoll, CH₂(NH₂)·COOH, a sweetish colourless crystalline solid first prepared from glue. [Gr. *glykys,* sweet.]

glycocoll *glik'ō-kol,* or *glīk', n.* glycin. [Gr. *glykys,* sweet, *kolla,* glue.]

glycogen *glik'ō-jǝn,* or *glīk', n.* animal starch, a starch found in the liver, yielding glucose on hydrolysis. — *n.* **glycogen'esis** the synthesis of glycogen: the synthesis of sugar from glycogen. — *adj.* **glycogenet'ic.** — *adj.* **glycogen'ic.** [Gr. *glykys,* sweet, and the root of *gennaein,* to produce.]

glycol *glik'ol, glīk'ol, n.* the type of a class of compounds with two hydroxyl groups on adjacent carbon atoms, and so intermediate between alcohol and glycerine. — *adj.* **glycol(l)'ic.** [From *glycerine* and *alcohol.*]

glycolysis *glī-kol'i-sis, n.* the breaking down of glucose into acids, with the release of energy. — *adj.* **glycolyt'ic.** [*glyco*se and **-lysis**.]

glyconic *glī-kon'ik, (Greek pros.) adj.* consisting of four feet — one a dactyl, the others trochees. — *n.* a glyconic verse. [The Greek poet *Glycon.*]

glycoprotein *glī-kō-prō'tēn,* **glucoprotein** *glōō-kō-, ns.* any of the compounds formed by the conjugation of a protein with a substance containing a carbohydrate group other than a nucleic acid. [Gr. *glykys,* sweet, and **protein**.]

glycose *glī'kōs, n.* glucose. — *n.* **gly'coside** any of a group of compounds derived from monosaccharides, yielding, on hydrolysis, a sugar and usu. a non-carbohydrate. — *adj.* **glycosid'ic.** — *n.* **glycosū'ria** (Gr. *ouron,* urine) the presence of sugar in the urine. — *adj.* **glycosū'ric.** [Gr. *glykys,* sweet.]

glycosyl *glī'kǝ-sil, (biochemistry) n.* a radical derived from glucose. — *v.t.* **glycos'ylate** — *n.* **glycosylā'tion** the process that attaches sugar to proteins to make glycoproteins.

glyph *glif, n. (archit.)* an ornamental channel or fluting, usually vertical: a sculptured mark. — *adj.* **glyph'ic** carved. — *ns.* **glyph'ograph** a plate formed by glyphography; **glyphog'rapher.** — *adj.* **glyphograph'ic.** — *n.* **glyphog'raphy** a process of taking a raised copy of an engraved plate by electrotype. [Gr. *glyphē* — *glyphein,* to carve.]

glyptal resins *glip'təl rez'inz*, almost colourless, tacky, adhesive resins made by heating glycerol or other polyhydric alcohol with a polybasic acid, used as bonding materials for mica, and (modified) in the paint and varnish trades.

glyptic *glip'tik, adj.* pertaining to carving, esp. gem-carving. — *n.sing.* **glyp'tics** the art of gem-engraving. — *adj.* **glyptograph'ic.** — *ns.* **glyptog'raphy** the art of engraving on precious stones; **glyptothē'ca** (Gr. *thēke*, receptacle) a place for keeping sculpture. [Gr. *glyptos*, carved.]

Glyptodon *glip'tō-don, n.* an extinct genus of S. American mammals of the Edentata, with fluted teeth. — *n.* **glyp'todont** a mammal of this genus. [Gr. *glyptos*, carved, *odous, odontos*, tooth.]

gmelinite *(g)mel'in-īt, (min.) n.* a sodium aluminium zeolite. [After C. G. *Gmelin* (1792–1860), German chemist.]

gnamma hole *nam'ə hōl, (Austr.)* a rock hollow in a desert area, perh. containing water. [Aboriginal.]

Gnaphalium *na-fā'li-əm, n.* the cudweed genus of composites. [Latinised from Gr. *gnaphallion*, cotton-weed.]

gnar¹ *när, v.i.* to snarl or growl. — Also **gnarr, knar, gnarl.** [Onomatopoeic; cf. O.E. *gnyrran*, to grind the teeth, creak, Ger. *knurren*, Dan. *knurre*, to growl.]

gnar². See **knar¹.**

gnarl¹, knarl *närl, n.* a lump or knot in a tree. — *adjs.* **gnarled, gnarl'y** knotty: contorted: rugged, weather-beaten: ill-natured, bad tempered. [After Shakespeare's *gnarled* for **knurled.**]

gnarl², gnarr. See **gnar¹.**

gnash *nash, v.t.* and *v.i.* to strike (the teeth) together in rage or pain: to bite with a snap or clash of the teeth. — *n.* a snap of the teeth. — *n.* **gnash'er** one who, or that which, gnashes: (usu. in *pl.*) a tooth *(facet.).* — *adv.* **gnash'ingly.** [M.E. *gnasten*; prob. from O.N., ultimately onomatopoeic.]

gnat *nat, n.* any small fly of the family Culicidae, of which the females are commonly bloodsuckers: a mosquito: extended to other small insects. — *n.* **gnat'ling** a little gnat: an insignificant person. — **gnat'catcher** any of the insectivorous American songbirds of the genus *Polioptila.* [O.E. *gnæt.*]

gnathic *nath'ik,* **gnathal** *nath', nā'thəl, adjs.* of the jaws. — *n.* **gnath'ite** (or *nă'*) in arthropods, an appendage used as a jaw. — *n.pl.* **Gnathobdell'ida** (Gr. *bdella,* leech) an order of leeches with (usu.) jaws but no proboscis. — **-gnathous** adjective combining form. [Gr. *gnathos,* jaw.]

gnathonic, -al *na-thon'ik, -əl, adjs.* flattering. — *adv.* **gnathon'ically.** [From *Gnathō,* a character in Terence's *Eunuchus* — Gr. *gnathos,* jaw.]

gnaw *nö, v.t.* and *v.i.* (with *at*) to bite with a scraping or mumbling movement: to wear away: to bite in agony or rage: to distress persistently (*fig.*): — *pa.t.* **gnawed;** *pa.p.* **gnawed, gnawn.** — *n.* **gnaw'er** one who gnaws: a rodent. [O.E. *gnagan*; cf. **nag²**; Du. *knagen,* Mod. Icel. *naga.*]

gneiss *nīs, n.* coarse-grained foliated metamorphic rock, usually composed of quartz, feldspar, and mica. — *adjs.* **gneiss'ic, gneissit'ic** of the nature of gneiss; **gneiss'-oid** like gneiss; **gneiss'ose** having the structure of gneiss. [Ger. *Gneis.*]

Gnetum *nē'təm, n.* a tropical genus of trees and shrubs constituting with Ephedra and Welwitschia the family **Gnetā'ceae** and order **Gnetā'lēs,** gymnosperms differing from conifers in having a perianth, vessels in secondary wood, and no resin canals. [Said to be from *gnemon,* a name used in the island of Ternate.]

gnocchi *no'kē, nö'kē, nyök'kē, n.* a dish of small dumplings made from flour, semolina, or potatoes, sometimes with the addition of cheese, and served with a sauce. [It.]

gnome¹ *nōm, nō'mē, n.* a pithy and sententious saying, generally in verse, embodying some moral sentiment or precept: — *pl.* **gnomes** *(nōmz, nō'mēz),* **gnomae**

(nō'mē). — *adj.* **gnō'mic** relating to, characterised by, gnomes: of writers, expressing themselves in gnomes. — *n.* **gnō'mist** a writer of gnomes. — **gnomic aorist** *(gram.)* a past tense of the Greek verb, used in proverbs, etc., for what once happened and is generally true. [Gr. *gnōmē,* an opinion, maxim.]

gnome² *nōm, n.* a sprite guarding the inner parts of the earth and its treasures: a dwarf or goblin. — *adj.* **gnōm'ish. — the gnomes of Europe, Zürich,** etc., the big bankers. [Paracelsus's Latin *gnomus.*]

gnomon *nō'mon, n.* the pin of a dial, whose shadow points to the hour: an upright rod for taking the sun's altitude by its shadow: an index or indicator: jocularly, the nose *(obs.):* that which remains of a parallelogram when a similar parallelogram within one of its angles is taken away *(geom.):* a geometrical figure which, added to or subtracted from another, gives a figure similar to the original one. — *adjs.* **gnomonic, -al** *(-mon')* pertaining to a gnomon or to the art of gnomonics. — *adv.* **gnomon'ically.** — *n. sing.* **gnomon'-ics** the art of measuring time by the sundial. — *n.* **gnomonol'ogy** a treatise on gnomonics. [Gr. *gnōmōn,* a gnomon, a carpenter's square — *gnōnai* (aorist), to know.]

gnosis *nō'sis, n.* knowledge, esp. spiritual: — *pl.* **gnō'sēs.** — **-gnō'sis** *(-(g)nō'sis)* in composition, knowledge, recognition: — *pl.* **-gnō'sēs.** — adjective and adverb combining forms **-gnos'tic, -gnos'tically.** — *ns.* **gnōse-ol'ogy, gnōsiol'ogy** the philosophy of knowledge. — *adj.* **gnos'tic** *(nos')* having knowledge: knowing, shrewd: (with *cap.*) pertaining to Gnosticism. — *n.* (with *cap.*) an adherent of Gnosticism. — *adj.* **gnos'-tical** having knowledge. — *adv.* **gnos'tically.** — *v.i.* **Gnos'ticise, -ize** to profess, believe in, Gnosticism. — *n.* **Gnos'ticism** the eclectic doctrines of the Gnostics, whose philosophy, esp. in early Christian times, taught the redemption of the spirit from matter by spiritual knowledge, and believed creation to be a process of emanation from the original essence or Godhead. [Gr. *gnōsis* knowledge, adj. *gnōstikos — gignōskein,* to know.]

gnotobiology *nō-tō-bī-ol'ə-ji, n.* study of life under germ-free conditions. — *adj.* **gnotobiolog'ical.** — *ns.* **gnoto-biō'sis** condition of being germ-free, or germ-free and then inoculated with known micro-organisms; **gnoto-biote** *(-bī'ōt)* a gnotobiotic animal. — *adj.* **gnotobiot'ic** in the condition of gnotobiosis. — *adv.* **gnotobiot'-ically.** — *n. sing.* **gnotobiot'ics** the study of gnotobiotic animals. [Gr. *gnōtos,* known.]

gnu *noō, nū, n.* a large African antelope (*Connochaetes* or *Catoblepas*), superficially like a horse or buffalo: — *pl.* **gnu, gnus.** — Also called **wildebeest.** [From Hottentot.]

go¹ *gō, v.i.* to pass from one place to another: to be in motion: (of a path, etc.) to lead or give access (to): to proceed: to run (in words or notes): (of verse) to flow smoothly: to walk *(obs.):* to depart: to work, to be in operation: to sound (as a bell, gun): to take a direction: to extend: (with *to*) to attend habitually (school, church, etc.): (of a rumour, etc.) to be current: to be valid, hold true: to be reckoned, to be regarded (as): to be known (*by* or *under* a name): to be on the whole or ordinarily: to tend, serve as a means: to be or continue in a particular state (as in fear, in rags): to elapse: to be sold: to be spent, consumed: to move, act, in a way shown or specified: to be assigned or awarded (to): to harmonise (as colours): to die: (with *by,* (*up*)*on*) to be directed by, to act according to: (with *on*) to become chargeable to (an account, etc.): (with *to*) to subject oneself (to expense, trouble, etc.): to be pregnant (usu. with *with*): to become, or become as if: to change to a new system, as *go decimal, go metric:* to happen in a particular way: to turn out: to fare: to contribute (to, towards, a whole, purpose or result): to be contained: to be able to pass: to give way. — *v.t.* to pass through or over *(obs.* except with cognate obj., or *road,* etc.): to stake, bet: to call, bid, declare: —

pr.p. **gō′ing**, *pa.p.* **gone** (*gon*) (see separate articles); *pa.t.* **went** (supplied from **wend**); *3rd sing. pres. ind.* **goes.** — *n.* a going: affair, matter (*coll.*): (with *the*) current fashion (*coll.*): success (*coll.*): energy, activity (*coll.*): a bargain, deal (*coll.*): a spell, turn, bout (*coll.*): a portion supplied at one time (*coll.*): an attempt (*coll.*): failure to play (*cribbage*): a score for an opponent's failure to play (*cribbage*): — *pl.* **goes.** — *adj.* ready: in perfect condition. — *interj.* (called to start race, etc.) begin! — *n.* **gō′er.** — *adj.* **gō′ey** (*coll.*) enterprising, go-ahead. — *n.* **gō′ing** see separate article. — *adj.* **go′-ahead** dashing, energetic: enterprisingly progressive. — *n.* permission to proceed. — *adj.* **go′-as-you-please** not limited by rules: informal. — **go′-between** an intermediary; **go′-by** escape by artifice: evasion: any intentional disregard, as in *give* (*someone*) *the go-by*: in coursing, the act of passing by or ahead in motion; **go′-cart** a wheeled apparatus for teaching children to walk: a form of child's carriage: same as **go-kart;** **go′-down** a cutting in the bank of a stream allowing animals to get to the water; **go′-gett′er** (*coll.*) forceful aggressive person who sets about getting what he wants. — *adj.* **go′-gett′ing** forcefully ambitious. — **go′-kart** a low racing vehicle consisting of a frame with wheels, engine, and steering gear (now usu. **kart**); **go′-off** (*coll.*) start; **go′-slow′** see **go slow** below. — *adj.* **go-to-meeting** see under **Sunday.** — **all systems go** everything in the spacecraft operating as it should: everything in readiness; **all the go** (*coll.*) very fashionable; **a pretty go** (*coll., iron.*) an awkward turn of events; **at one go** in a single attempt or effort, simultaneously; **from the word go** from the very beginning; **give it a go** (*coll.*) to try, make an attempt at something; **go about** to pass from place to place: to busy oneself with: to seek, endeavour to (with *pr.p.*): (of rumour, etc.) to circulate: (of a ship) to change course; **go about one's business** to attend to one's own affairs: to be off; **go abroad** to go to a foreign country or out of doors: (of rumour, etc.) to circulate; **go against** to turn out unfavourably for: to be repugnant to: to be in conflict with; **go ahead** to proceed at once; **go along with** to agree with, support; **go along with you!** (*coll.*) none of that!; **go and** (*coll.*) to be so stupid or unfortunate as to (e.g. hurt oneself): to go in order to (do something); **go aside** to err (*arch.*): to withdraw, retire; **go at** to attack vigorously; **go back on** to betray, fail to keep (promise, etc.); **go bail** to give security (for); **go down** to sink, decline: to deteriorate: to be swallowed, believed, or accepted (esp. with pleasure): to fail to fulfil one's contract (*bridge*): to leave a university; **go down on** (*vulg.*) to perform fellatio or cunnilingus on; **go down the drain** (*coll.*) to be wasted: to become valueless; **go down with** (*coll.*) to contract (an illness); **go Dutch** see **Dutch; go far** to go a long way (*lit.* and *fig.*): to achieve success; **go for** to assail: to set out to secure: to go to get or fetch: to be attracted by: to be true of; **go for nothing** to have no value; **go halves** to share equally between two; **go hang** (*slang*) to be forgotten, neglected: to be no longer of concern; **go hard (with)** to prove difficult or unfortunate (for); **go in** to enter: (of church, school, scholars, etc.) to assemble regularly (*coll.*): (of sun, moon) to become concealed behind cloud: to take the batting (*cricket*); **go in and out** to come and go freely; **go in for** to make a practice of: to take up as a career or special interest: to take part in (a competition, etc.); **go into** to enter: to examine thoroughly, investigate: to adopt as a profession, etc.; **go in unto** (*B.*) to have sexual intercourse with; **go in with** to enter into partnership with: to join, combine with; **go it** to act in a striking or dashing manner — often in *imper.* by way of encouragement; **go it alone** to undertake a usu. difficult or dangerous task alone: to manage by oneself; **go live** (*līv*) (*coll.*) of a radio station, automation equipment, etc., to go into operation; **go native** to assimilate oneself to an alien culture or to the way of life of a foreign country (usu. less advanced than one's own); **go off** to leave: to die

(*Shak.*): to explode: to deteriorate: to proceed to an expected conclusion: to cease to like or be fond of (a person, etc.) (*coll.*): to cease to operate; **go off with** to go away with: to remove, take away (*coll.*); **go on** to continue, to proceed: an exclamation expressing disbelief (*coll.*): to behave, conduct oneself (*coll.*): to talk at length (*coll.*): to take the bowling, begin to bowl (*cricket*): to be capable of being fitted on to: to appear on stage: to fare: to begin to function: to proceed from (as in *nothing to go on*); **go one better** in some card games, to take a bet and increase the stake (also **go better**): to excel: to cap a performance; **go one's own way** to act independently; **go one's way** to depart; **go out** to become extinguished: to become unfashionable: to mingle in society; **go over** to pass in review: to recall: to revise; **go over to** to transfer allegiance to; **go places** to travel widely: to go so far in personal advancement; **go round** to be enough for all; **go slow** (of workers) deliberately to restrict output or effort in order to obtain concessions from employers (*adj.* and *n.* **go′-slow′**); **go slow with** to be sparing with; **go steady** to court (with *with*); **go the whole hog** see **whole; go through** to perform to the end, often perfunctorily: to examine in order: to undergo; **go through fire and water** to undertake any trouble or risks (from the usage in ancient ordeals); **go through with** to carry out; **go to** (*arch.*) come now (a kind of interjection, like the L. *agedum*, the Gr. *age nyn*); **go to pieces** see **piece; go to the country** see **country; go to the wall** see **wall; go under** to become submerged, overwhelmed, or ruined: to die (*arch.*); **go up** to ascend: to be erected: to be destroyed by fire or explosion: to increase (as e.g. price): to enter a university; **go with** to accompany: to agree with: accord with: to court; **go without** suffer the want of; **go without saying** to be self-evident (a Gallicism; Fr. *cela va sans dire*); **great go** at Cambridge University, a degree examination, contrasted with **little go** (last held in 1961), a preliminary examination; **have a go** to make an attempt: (of a member of the public) to tackle a criminal; **have something going for one** to enjoy the advantage of something; **I could go** (*coll.*) I should enjoy (usu. food or drink); **let go** see **let**[1]; **no go** not possible: futile: in vain; **no-go area** a part of a city, etc. to which normal access is prevented by the erection of barricades, esp. by local militants, a paramilitary group, etc.; **on the go** very active; **to be going on with** (*coll.*) for the moment, in the meantime. [O.E. *gān*, to go; cf. Ger. *gehen*, Du. *gaan*.]

go[2] *gō, n.* a Japanese game for two, played with black and white stones (or counters) on a board, the object being to capture opponent's stones and be in control of the larger part of the board. [Jap.]

goa *gō′ə, n.* a grey-brown gazelle of Tibet, with backward-curving horns. [Tibetan *dgoba*.]

Goa *gō′ə, n.* Union Territory in west of India. — *adj.* **Gō′an** of Goa or its people. — *n.* a native of Goa. — *adj.* **Goanese** (*gō-ə-nēz′*) Goan. — *n.* a Goan: the people of Goa. — **Goa bean** a papilionaceous plant (*Psophocarpus*) of tropical Asia and Africa, grown for its beans and root: its bean; **Goa butter** kokum butter; **Goa powder** araroba.

goad *gōd, n.* a sharp-pointed stick, often tipped with iron, for driving oxen: a stimulus. — *v.t.* to drive with a goad: to urge forward: to incite. — *ns.* **goads′man, goad′ster** one who uses a goad. [O.E. *gād.*]

goaf[1] *gōf,* (*dial.*) *n.* a rick in a barn. [O.N. *gólf,* floor.]

goaf[2] *gōf,* (*mining*) *n.* the space left by the extraction of a coal-seam, into which waste is packed. [Origin obscure.]

goal (*Milt.* **gole**) *gōl, n.* a limit, boundary (*obs.*): a competition, race (*obs.*): the finishing point of a race: the winning-post or a similar marker: sometimes used for the starting-post (*obs.*): a pillar marking the turning-point in a Roman chariot race: the target in archery (*obs.*): the structure or station into which the ball is driven in some games: the sending of the ball between the goalposts or over the crossbar: a score for doing so: an end or aim. — *v.t.* (*Rugby football*) to convert (a try) into a goal. — *adj.* **goal'less** with no goals scored: without goals in life, unambitious. — **goal'keeper** a player charged with defence of the goal (*coll.* **goal'ie**); **goal'-kick** (*soccer*) a free kick awarded to a defending player when an opponent has sent the ball over the goal-line but not between the posts; **goal'kicker** a player who kicks a goal, or does a goal-kick; **goal'-kicking**; **goal'-line** the boundary marking each end of the field, on which the goals are situated; **goal'mouth** the space between the goalposts and immediately in front of the goal; **goal'post** one of the upright posts at the goal; **goal'-tender** in some games, esp. ice-hockey, a goalkeeper; **goal'-tending**. — **change, move, shift the goalposts** to alter the rules of a game, conditions of an agreement, etc. after proceedings have begun, or the agreement has been enterd into. [Origin obscure.]

Goan, Goanese. See **Goa.**

goanna *gō-an'ə, n.* in Australia, any large monitor lizard. [**iguana.**]

goary. Milton's spelling of **gory.**

goat *gōt, n.* a ruminant (*Capra*) allied to the sheep: a lecher: a foolish person: (in *pl.*) the wicked (*B.*): (with *cap.*) the zodiacal sign or the constellation Capricorn. — *adj.* **goat'ish** resembling a goat, esp. in smell: lustful: foolish. — *ns.* **goat'ishness; goat'ling** a young goat in its second year. — *adj.* **goat'y.** — **goat'-ant'elope** a goatlike antelope, or animal intermediate between goat and antelope, as the chamois, the goral; **goat'-fig** the wild fig; **goat'fish** red mullet; **goat'-god** Pan; **goat'-herd** one who tends goats; **goat'-moth** a large moth whose larva, feeding on willow-wood, etc., exudes a goatlike smell; **goat'-sall'ow, -will'ow** the great sallow (*Salix caprea*); **goat's'-beard** a composite plant of the genus *Tragopogon*, John-go-to-bed-at-noon: a herbaceous perennial of the genus *Aruncus sylvester*; **goat's'-hair** cirrus clouds; **goat's'-rue** a papilionaceous border and fodder plant, *Galega officinalis*; **goat'skin** the skin of the goat: leather, or a wine-skin, made from it; **goat'sucker** the nightjar, a bird akin to the swift falsely thought to suck goats; **goat's'-thorn** an Astragalus shrub; **goat'weed** goutweed. — **get one's goat** to enrage one; **play** (or **act**) **the** (**giddy**) **goat** see **giddy.** [O.E. *gāt*; Ger. *Geiss*, Du. *geit*.]

goatee *gō-tē', n.* a tuft on the chin, resembling a goat's beard. — *adj.* **goateed'.** [**goat** and *-ee*, suff. of uncertain meaning.]

gob[1] *gob, n.* the mouth (*slang*): a mouthful, lump (*dial.*): a space left in a mine by extraction of coal: waste packed into it. — **gob'-stop'per** a very large hard round sweet for prolonged sucking. [O.Fr. *gobe*, mouthful, lump; cf. Gael. *gob*, mouth; perh. partly from **goaf**[2].]

gob[2] *gob,* (*U.S. slang*) *n.* a sailor in U.S. Navy. [Origin obscure.]

gobang *gō-bang', n.* a game played on a board of 256 squares, with fifty counters, the object being to get five in a row. — Also **gomoku** (*go-mō'kōō*). [Jap. *goban.*]

gobar numeral *gō'bär nū'mər-əl,* any of a set of numerals forming the stage between ancient Hindu numerals and present-day Arabic numerals. [Ar. *ghubār,* sanded board.]

gobbeline *gob'ə-lēn,* (*Spens.*) *n.* Same as **goblin.**

gobbet *gob'it, n.* a mouthful: a lump to be swallowed: a clot: a lump, esp. of flesh hacked or vomited: an extract, esp. for translation or comment. [O.Fr. *gobet,* dim. of *gobe;* see **gob**[1].]

gobble *gob'l, v.t.* to swallow in lumps: to swallow hastily (often with *up*): to play with a gobble (*golf*): to fellate (*vulg.*). — *v.i.* to eat greedily: to make a noise in the throat, as a turkey-cock. — *n.* (*golf*) a rapid straight putt so strongly played that if the ball had not gone into the hole, it would have gone a good way past. — *n.* **gobb'ler** a turkey-cock. [O.Fr. *gober,* to devour.]

gobbledegook, gobbledygook *gob-əl-di-gōōk',* (orig. *U.S. slang*) *n.* official jargon: rubbish, nonsense. [Imit. of pompous utterance.]

gobbo *gob'bō,* (It.) *n.* a hunchback: a hunchbacked figure: — *pl.* **gob'bi** (*-bē*).

Gobelin, Gobelins *gōb'ə-lin, -linz, gob'(ə)-,* *go-blẽ', n.* a rich French tapestry. — Also *adj.* [From the *Gobelins,* a famous family of French dyers settled in Paris as early as the 15th century.]

gobe-mouches *gob-mōōsh,* (Fr.) *n.* a fly-catcher (bird): an insectivorous plant: a credulous person.

gobioid. See **goby.**

goblet *gob'lit, n.* a large drinking-cup, properly one without a handle: a kind of saucepan (*Scot.*). [O.Fr. *gobelet,* dim. of *gobel,* of doubtful origin.]

goblin *gob'lin, n.* a frightful sprite: a bogy or bogle. [O.Fr. *gobelin* — L.L. *gobelīnus,* perh. — *cobālus* — Gr. *kobalos,* a mischievous spirit.]

gobo *gō'bō,* (chiefly *U.S.*) *n.* a device used to protect a camera lens from light: a device for preventing unwanted sound from reaching a microphone: — *pl.* **gō'boes, gō'bos.** [Origin obscure.]

gobony *gob-ō'ni.* Same as **compony.**

goburra *gō-bûr'ə.* Same as **kookaburra.**

goby *gō'bi, n.* any fish of the genus Gobius or the family **Gobi'idae** small fishes with ventral fins forming a sucker. — *adj.* **gō'bioid.** [L. *gōbius* — Gr. *kōbios,* a fish of the gudgeon kind.]

god *god, n.* a superhuman being, an object of worship: (with *cap.*) the Supreme Being of monotheist religions, the Creator: an idol: an object of excessive devotion: a man of outstandingly fine physique: (usu. in *pl.*) an occupant of the gallery (*theat.*): (*pl.*) the gallery (*theat.*): — *fem.* **godd'ess.** — *v.t.* (*Spens., Shak.*) to deify: — *pa.t.* **godd'ed.** — *ns.* **godd'ess-ship** state or quality of a goddess; **god'head** (M.E. *-hēd, -hēde,* variant of *-hōd*) state of being a god: divine nature: (*cap.* with *the*) God; **god'hood** (O.E. *-hād,* M.E. *-hōd*) position or state of being divine: a deity (*obs.*). — *adj.* **god'less** without a god: living without God. — *adv.* **god'lessly.** — *n.* **god'lessness.** — *adj.* **god'like** like a god: divine. — *adv.* (*arch.*) **god'lily.** — *ns.* **god'liness; god'ling** (*Dryden*) a little god. — *adj.* **god'ly** like God in character: pious: according to God's laws. — Also *adv.* (*arch.*). — *n.* **god'ship** the rank or character of a god: a divinity. — *adj.* and *adv.* **god'ward** towards God. — *adv.* **god'wards.** — *interj.* **God'-a-mercy!** (*arch.*) thank God: many thanks to. — *n.* (*obs.*) an expression of thanks. — *adj.* **god-aw'ful** (*coll.*) very bad: unpleasant, distasteful. — **god'child** a person to whom one is a godparent. — *adjs.* (*coll.*) **godd'am(n), god'damned** damned, accursed, hateful: utter, complete. — Also *adv.* — **god'daughter** a female godchild; **god'father** a male godparent: a sponsor (*fig.*): one who pays the bill (*slang*): the head of a criminal organisation, esp. the mafia (*coll.*). — *adjs.* **God'-fearing** reverencing God; **god'-forgotten, god'-forsaken** (or with *cap.*) remote, miserable, behind the times; **God'-gift'ed; God'-given.** — **god'mother** a female godparent; **god'parent** one who at baptism, guarantees a child's religious education; **God's acre** a burial-ground (imitated from Ger. *Gottesacker*); **god'-send** a very welcome piece of good fortune; **God slot** (*coll.*) a regular spot during the week's, day's, etc. broadcasting reserved for religious exhortation, exposition or discussion; **god'-smith** (*Dryden*) a maker of idols; **god'son** a male godchild; **god'speed** (also with *cap.*) a wish for good fortune, expressed at parting; **God's truth** an absolute truth — an emphatic asseveration. — **for God's sake** an expression of urgent entreaty: (as *interj.*) expressing, e.g. annoyance, disgust; **God knows** God is my, his, etc., witness that: (*flippantly*) it is beyond human understanding; **God's (own) country** a particularly well-favoured (esp. scenically beautiful) region: one's homeland or native region (esp. *U.S.*); **God willing** if circumstances permit; **household gods** among the Romans, the special gods presiding over the family: anything bound up with home interests. [O.E. *god;* Ger. *Gott,* Goth. *guth,* Du. *god;* all from a Gmc. root *guth-,* God, and quite distinct from *good.*]

god day *god dā,* (*Spens.*) for **good-day.**
god-den *god-en',* a dial. variant of **good-even.**
Gödel's theorem *gø'dəlz thē'ə-rəm* the theorem first demonstrated by Kurt Gödel, Austrian mathematician, in 1931, that in logic and mathematics there must be true statements that cannot be proved or disproved within the system, also that there can be no proof of the consistency of such a system from within itself.
godet *gō'dā, -det',* n. a triangular piece of cloth inserted in a skirt, etc., e.g. to make a flare. [Fr.]
Godetia *gō-dē'sh*(*y*)*ə, gə-,* n. an American genus closely akin to the evening primrose: (without *cap.*) a plant of this genus. [C. H. *Godet,* Swiss botanist.]
godown *gō-down',* n. a warehouse, or a storeroom, in the East. [Malay *gudang.*]
godroon *gō-drōōn', gə-.* Same as **gadroon.**
godso. Same as **gadso.**
godwit *god'wit,* n. a bird (*Limosa*) of the plover family, with long slightly up-curved bill and long slender legs, with a great part of the tibia bare. [Origin obscure.]
goe[1] *gō,* (*Spens.*). Same as **go, gone.**
goe[2] an earlier variant of **geo** (gully, creek).
goel *gō'el, -āl,* n. the avenger of blood among the Hebrews, the nearest relative, whose duty it was to hunt down the murderer. [Heb.]
goer, goes. See **go**[1].
goethite, göthite *gø'tīt* n. a mineral, hydrated ferric oxide. [Named in honour of the poet *Goethe.*]
goety *gō'ə-ti,* n. black magic. — *adj.* **goetic** (*-et'*). [Gr. *goēteiā,* witchcraft.]
gofer[1], **gopher, gaufer, gaufre** *gō'* or *gō'fər,* n. a wafer with pattern in crossed lines. [Fr. *gaufre,* honeycomb.]
gofer[2] *go'fər,* (*U.S. slang*) n. an office worker who is given errands to run by other members of the staff. [Alteration of *go for.*]
goff *gof,* an arch. variant of **golf.**
goffer *gōf'ər, gof', gōf',* v.t. to plait, crimp. — *n.* **goff'ering** plaits or ruffles, or the process of making them: indented tooling on the edge of a book. [O.Fr. *gauffrer* — *goffre,* a wafer.]
gog *gog,* n. obs. for **God** (in oaths).
Gog and Magog *gog' ənd mā'gog,* the nations represented in the Apocalypse as the forces of Satan at Armageddon (*Rev.* xx. 8): the last two survivors of a mythical race of giants inhabiting ancient Britain.
goggle *gog'l,* v.i. to strain or roll the eyes: (of the eyes) to protrude. — *v.t.* to turn about (the eyes). — *adj.* (of the eyes) rolling: staring: prominent. — *n.* a stare or affected rolling of the eyes: (*pl.*) spectacles with projecting eye-tubes: (*pl.*) protective spectacles: (*pl.*) spectacles, esp. with round lenses (*coll.*): the eyes (*coll.*). — *adj.* **gogg'led** wearing goggles. — *ns.* **gogg'ler** a person with goggle eyes (*coll.*): an eye (*slang*): an assiduous television-viewer (*coll.*); **gogg'ling.** — Also *adj.* — *adj.* **gogg'ly.** — **gogg'le-box** (*coll.*) a television-set. — *adj.* **gogg'le-eyed** having bulging, staring, or rolling eyes. — Also *adv.* [Poss. related to Ir. and Gael. *gog,* to nod.]
goglet *gog'lit,* n. a water-cooler. [Port. *gorgoleta.*]
go-go, gogo *gō'gō,* used loosely as *adj.* active, alert to seize opportunities. — **go-go dancer, girl** a girl who gyrates to a musical accompaniment in night-clubs or discothèques. [à gogo influenced by English go.]
Goidel *goi'dəl,* n. a Gael in the general sense (**Gadhel** (*q.v.*) now has the same meaning). — *adj.* **Goidelic** (*-del'*) Gadhelic. [O.Ir. *Góidel.*]
going[1] *gō'ing,* n. the act of moving: departure: course of life (*B.*): condition of the ground for, e.g., walking, racing: progress: gait (*obs.*). — *adj.* (for earlier **a-go'-ing**) in motion or activity: about, to be had: in existence: current. — **going concern** a business in actual activity (esp. successfully); **going forth** (*B.*) an outlet, exit; **going-o'ver** a thorough check, examination: a complete treatment: a beating; **go'ings-on'** behaviour, activities, now esp. if open to censure; **go'ings-out'** (*obs.*) expenditure. — **be hard, heavy, tough,** etc. **going** to prove difficult to do, etc.; **going-away dress,** etc. that

worn by a bride when leaving on the honeymoon. [**go**[1].]
going[2] *gō'ing, pr.p.* of **go**[1], in any sense: about or intending (to). — **going on** (**for**) approaching (an age or time); **going strong** in full activity, flourishing.
goitre, in U.S. also **goiter,** *goi'tər,* n. morbid enlargement of the thyroid gland, producing a swelling in front of the throat, sometimes accompanied by exophthalmus. — *adjs.* **goi'tred; goi'trous.** [Fr. *goître* — L. *guttur,* the throat.]
go-kart. See under **go**[1].
Golconda *gol-kon'də,* n. a rich source of wealth. [Ruined city near Hyderabad, India, once famous for diamond-cutting.]
gold[1] *gōld,* n. a heavy yellow element (Au; atomic number 79), one of the precious metals, used for coin, etc.: articles made of it: money in the form of gold coins: a standard of money value which varies with the price of the metal: the gold standard: riches: anything very precious: the centre of an archery target: a gold medal: yellow, the colour of gold. — *adj.* made of or like gold. — *adj.* **gold'en** of gold: of the colour of gold: bright, shining like gold: most valuable: happy: most favourable: of outstanding excellence. — *v.t.* (*rare*) to gild, make golden. — *v.i.* (*rare*) to become golden in colour. — *adv.* **gold'enly.** — *adjs.* **gold'ish** somewhat golden; **gold'less; gold'y** somewhat like gold. — **gold'-beater** one whose trade is to beat gold into gold-leaf; **gold-beater's skin** the outer coat of the caecum of an ox, used for separating sheets of gold being beaten into gold leaf; **gold'-beating; gold'-bee'tle** (*U.S.*) a beetle of the family *Chrysomelidae* or of the *Cassididae*; **gold'-brick'** a block of gold or (orig. *U.S. slang*) of pretended gold, hence a sham or swindle. — Also *v.t.* — **gold'-bug** (*U.S.*) a gold beetle: a plutocrat: one who favours a gold standard; **gold certificate, note** (*U.S.*) formerly, a U.S. treasury note issued on gold reserves; **gold'-cloth'** cloth of gold; **gold'crest** a golden-crested bird of the genus *Regulus* (also **golden-crested wren**); **gold'-digger** one who digs for gold, esp. a placer-miner: a woman who treats a man chiefly as a source of material gain; **gold'-digging; gold disc** a long-playing record that has sold 250 000 copies (500 000 in the U.S.) or a single that has sold 500,000 (one million in U.S.); **gold'-dust** gold in fine particles, as found in some rivers; **golden age** an imaginary past time of innocence and happiness: any time of highest achievement; **gold'-enberry** the Cape gooseberry; **golden bough** the bough plucked by Aeneas before visiting the underworld: **golden bowler** dismissal from the Army followed by a job in Whitehall; **golden boy, girl** a young man, woman, of outstanding talents, good looks, etc. likely to win renown; **golden bull** (L. *bulla aurea*) an edict issued by the Emperor Charles IV in 1356, mainly for the purpose of settling the law of imperial elections; **golden calf** see **calf**[1]; **golden chain** laburnum. — *adj.* **gold'encrest'ed.** — **Golden Delicious** a kind of sweet eating-apple; **gold(en) disc** a gold replica of a recording that has sold 1 million copies, presented to the composer, performer, etc.; **gold-end'-man** (*obs.*) a dealer in **gold'-ends'** (*arch.*), broken remnants of gold; **golden eagle** the common eagle, from a slight golden gleam about the head and neck; **gold'en-eye** a northern sea-duck (*Clangula*): the lace-wing fly; **golden fleece** in Greek mythology, the fleece of the ram Chrysomallus, the recovery of which was the object of the famous expedition of the Argonauts — it gave its name to a celebrated order of knighthood in Austria and Spain, founded in 1429; **golden girl** see **golden boy; golden goose** the fabled layer of golden eggs, killed by its over-greedy owner: a source of profit (*fig.*; also **the goose that lays the golden eggs**); **golden handshake** (*coll.*) a large sum given to an employee or member forced to leave a firm, etc.; **golden hello** (*coll.*) a large sum given to a new employee as an inducement to join a firm; **Golden Horde** the Kipchaks, a Turkic people, whose empire was founded in central and southern

Russia by Batu in the 13th century; **golden jubilee** a fiftieth anniversary; **Golden Legend** (L. *Legenda Aurea*) a celebrated mediaeval collection of saints' lives, by Jacobus de Voragine (1230–98); **golden mean** the middle way between extremes: moderation; **golden mole** a bronze-coloured S. African insectivore (*Chrysochloris*) superficially like a mole; **golden number** a number marking the position of a year in the Metonic Cycle of nineteen years; **golden oldie** (*coll.*) a song, recording, motion picture, etc. issued some considerable time ago and still popular; **golden opportunity** a very favourable one; **golden parachute** (*coll.*) an unusually lavish cash payment to a senior member of a firm on his dismissal; **golden pheasant** a golden-crested Chinese pheasant; **golden plover** a plover with yellow-speckled feathers; **golden rectangle** one in which the ratio of width to length is the same as that of length to the sum of width and length; **gold'enrod** any plant of the composite genus *Solidago*, with rodlike stems and yellow heads crowded along the branches; **golden rose** a rose of wrought gold, blessed by the Pope on the 4th Sunday in Lent; **golden rule** the precept that one should do as one would be done by: a rule of the first importance, a guiding principle; **golden salmon** the S. American dorado; **golden saxifrage** a greenish-yellow plant (*Chrysoplenium*) of the saxifrage family; **golden scoop** a system (judged to be illegal) according to which winners in bingo games in separate clubs can qualify for prizes offered by a large group of clubs acting together; **gold'en-seal** a N. American ranunculaceous plant, *Hydrastis canadensis*: its yellow rhizome, used in medicine; **golden section** division of a line so that one segment is to the other as that to the whole; **golden syrup** see **syrup**; **golden thistle, tulip** top award respectively in film-making, advertising; **golden wattle** any of various kinds of yellow-flowered Australian acacia, esp. *Acacia pycnantha*; **golden wedding** see **wed**; **gold= exchange standard** a monetary system by which a country whose government is not on the gold standard is linked in its exchange rate to another's who is; **gold'eye** a N. American freshwater fish (*Hyodon*); **gold'-fe'ver** a mania for seeking gold; **gold'field** a gold-producing region; **gold'finch** a beautiful finch, black, red, yellow and white, fond of eating thistle seeds; **gold'finny** same as **gold'sinny; gold'fish** a Chinese and Japanese freshwater fish closely allied to the carp, golden or (*silverfish*) pale in its domesticated state, brownish when wild; **goldfish bowl** a glass aquarium for goldfish: a situation entirely lacking in privacy; **gold'-foil'** gold beaten into thin sheets, but not as thin as gold-leaf: **gold'ilocks** a golden-haired person: a species of buttercup, *Ranunculus auricomus*; **gold ink** a writing fluid in which gold or an imitation is in suspension; **gold'-lace'** lace made from gold-thread. — *adj.* **gold'-laced.** — **gold'-leaf'** gold beaten extremely thin; **gold medal** in athletics competitions, etc., the medal awarded as first prize; **gold'-mine** a mine producing gold: a source of great profit; **gold'-miner; gold note** see **gold certificate; gold'-of-pleas'ure** a cruciferous plant of the genus *Camelina*; **gold paint** bronze powders mixed with transparent varnish or amyl acetate; **gold'= plate'** vessels and utensils of gold collectively: metal esp. silver, plated with gold. — *v.t.* to coat (another metal) with gold. — **gold point** (*finance*) in international transactions, an exchange rate at which it is advisable to export (**gold export point**) or import (**gold import point**) gold bullion rather than settle by bills of exchange; **gold record** a gold disc (q.v. above); **gold reserve** the gold held by a central bank, etc., to cover and support all its dealings; **gold'-rush** a rush of prospectors to a new goldfield; **gold'sinny** a kind of wrasse, the corkwing; **gold'size** an adhesive, of various kinds, used to attach gold-leaf to a surface; **gold'smith** a worker in gold and silver; **goldsmith beetle** a beetle with wing-covers of a gold colour; **gold'smithry, -ery; gold'spink** (*Scot.*, also **gowd'spink**) the goldfinch; **gold standard** a monetary standard or system according to

which the unit of currency has a precise value in gold; **gold'stick** a colonel of Life Guards who carries a gilded wand before the sovereign; **gold'stone** see **aventurine; gold'-thread'** gold-wire used in weaving: silk wound with gilded wire: a European ranunculaceous plant (*Coptis*) with yellow roots; **gold'-washer** one who obtains gold from sand and gravel by washing: a cradle or other implement for washing gold; **gold'-wasp** any wasp of a family (*Chrysididae*) with brilliant metallic colouring and telescopic abdomen, whose larvae feed on those of wasps and bees — cuckoo-fly or ruby-tail, ruby-wasp; **gold'-wire'** wire made of or covered with gold. — **as good as gold** behaving in an exemplary manner (usu. of children); **on, off, the gold standard** using or not using, gold as standard. [O.E. *gold*, O.N. *gull*, Ger. *Gold*, Goth. *gulth*.]

gold² *gōld, n.* the marigold (*obs.*): the corn-marigold (*dial.*). — Also (*Scot.*) **gool, gule** (*gōōl*), (*Spens.*) **goold** (*gōōld*). [O.E. *golde*, apparently related to **gold¹, gollan, gowan**; cf. **marigold.**]

goldarn *gol'därn*, (*U.S.*) *adj., adv.* a euphemistic alteration of **goddamn**.

Goldbach's conjecture *gōld'bahhs kən-jek'chər*, (*math.*) the theory that every even number greater than 2 is the sum of two prime numbers. [After C. *Goldbach*, 18th-cent. German mathematician.]

gole. Milton's spelling of **goal.**

golem *gō'lem, -ləm, n.* in Jewish folklore, a human image brought to life: a robot: a dolt. [Yiddish *goylem* — Heb. *gōlem*, a shapeless thing, an embryo.]

golf *golf* (sometimes *gof*, or (*Scot.*) *gowf*), *n.* a game played with a club or set of clubs over a prepared stretch of land, the aim being to propel a small ball into a series of holes. — *v.i.* to play golf. — *ns.* **golf'er; golfia'na** (*-i-ä'nə*) a collector's or dealer's term for items of golfing interest; **golf'ing.** — **golf'-bag** a bag for carrying golf-clubs; **golf'-ball** a small ball used in golf: in certain typewriters, etc. a small detachable metal sphere or hemisphere with the type characters moulded on to its surface; **golf'-club** a club used in golf: a golfing society; **golf'-course, golf'-links** the ground on which golf is played. [Origin uncertain; Du. *kolf*, a club, has been suggested.]

Golgi bodies *gol'jē bod'iz*, easily stained bodies around the centrosome in animal cells, studied by Camillo *Golgi* (1843–1926).

Golgotha *gol'gə-thə, n.* a burial-ground: a charnel-house: a place littered with bones. [See under **Calvary.**]

goliard *gō'li-ärd*, or *-lyərd, n.* a disreputable vagrant mediaeval cleric given to revelry, buffoonery, and satirical Latin versifying, follower of an imaginary Bishop Golias. — *adj.* **goliardic** (*-ärd'ik*). — *ns.* **gō'liardy, goliard'ery.** — *v.i.* **gō'lias** (*Tenn.*) to play Golias. [O.Fr., glutton — L. *gŭla*, gluttony.]

Goliath *gō-lī'əth, gə-, n.* a giant. — *v.i.* **golī'athise, -ize** to play Goliath, exaggerate extravagantly. — **goliath beetle** a tropical beetle (*Goliathus*) reaching four inches in length; **goliath frog** the largest kind of frog, living in central and west Africa. [From *Goliath*, the Philistine giant in 1 Sam. xvii.]

gollan, golland *gol'ən(d)*, **gowland** *gow'lənd, ns.* a northern name for various yellow flowers (marigold, cornmarigold, globeflower, etc.). [Perh. conn. with **gold²**; see **gowan.**]

gollar *gol'ər*, (*Scot.*) *n.* a loud inarticulate gurgling sound: a thick or guttural bawl. — Also *v.i.* [Imitative.]

golliwog. Same as **gollywog.**

gollop *gol'əp, v.t.* and *v.i.* to gulp greedily or hastily. [Perh. **gulp.**]

golly¹ *gol'i, interj.* expressing surprise. [Thought to be orig. a Negro modification of **God.**]

golly². A short form of **gollywog.**

gollywog, golliwog *gol'i-wog, n.* a fantastical doll with black face, staring eyes, and bristling hair: a person who has fuzzy hair or is in some way grotesque. [*Golliwogg*, a doll in certain U.S. children's books, the

fāte; fär; hûr; mīne; mōte; för; mūte; mōōn; fŏŏt; dhen (then); *el'ə-mənt* (element)

first of which, by Florence Upton, was published in 1895.]

goloe-shoes. A spelling of **galoshes.**

golomynka *go-lo-ming'kə, n.* a very oily fish found in Lake Baikal, resembling the gobies. [Russ.]

golosh. Same as **galosh.**

golp, golpe *golp, (her.) n.* a roundel purpure. [Perh. — Sp. *golpe,* bruise.]

goluptious *gol-up'shəs,* **goloptious** *-op', (jocular) adjs.* delicious: voluptuous.

gombeen *gom'bēn', (Ir.) n.* usury. — **gombeen'-man** a grasping usurer. [Ir. *gaimbín.*]

gombo, gombro. Same as **gumbo.**

gomeril, gomeral *gom'ər-əl, (Scot.) n.* a simpleton: a dunderhead. [Origin obscure.]

gomoku. See **gobang.**

gompa *gom'pə, n.* a Buddhist temple or monastery in Tibet. [Tibetan *gömpa,* a place of seclusion, a hermitage.]

gomphosis *gom-fō'sis, n.* an immovable articulation, as of the teeth in the jaw. [Gr. *gomphōsis* — *gomphos,* a bolt.]

gomuti *gō-mōō'ti, n.* a palm, *Arenga saccharifera:* the black fibre it yields. — Also **gomu'to** (*pl.* **gomu'tos**). [Malay *gumuti.*]

gon *gon, (geom.) n.* a grade. [Gr. *gonia,* angle.]

-gon *-gon, -gən,* in composition, having a certain number of angles as in *hexagon, polygon.* [Gr. *gōniā,* angle.]

gonad *gon'ad, (biol.) n.* an organ that produces sex-cells. — *adjs.* **gonadial** (*-ā'di-əl*), **gonadic** (*-ad'*); **gonadotrop(h)'ic** stimulating the gonads. — *n.* **gonadotrop(h)'in** a substance that does this, used as a drug to promote fertility. [Gr. *gonē,* generation.]

gondelay. See **gondola.**

gondola *gon'də-lə, n.* a long, narrow boat used chiefly on the canals of Venice: a lighter (*U.S.*): a flat railway wagon (*U.S.*): the car of an airship: the car of a balloon: a car resembling this suspended from an earth-supported structure: a (free-standing) shelved unit for displaying goods in a supermarket, etc. — (*Spens.*) **gon'delay.** — *n.* **gondolier** (*-lēr*) one who rows a gondola. [Venetian dialect; origin obscure.]

Gondwanaland *gond-wä'nä-land, n.* an ancient continent held to have connected India with S. Africa, S. America, Antarctica and Australia from Carboniferous times to Jurassic. [*Gondwana* district in India, i.e. forest of the Gonds.]

gone *gon, pa.p. of* **go¹,** in an advanced stage: lost, passed beyond help: departed: dead: weak, faint, feeling a sinking sensation: pregnant (with specified time, e.g. *six months gone*): wide of the mark, of an arrow: enamoured of (with *on; slang*): in an exalted state (*slang*). — *ns.* **gone'ness** a sinking sensation; **gon'er** (*slang*) one dead or ruined beyond recovery: a thing beyond hope of recovery. — **gone goose, gosling** (*coll.*) a hopeless case. — **gone under** ruined beyond recovery.

gonfalon *gon'fə-lon, n.* an ensign or standard with streamers. — *ns.* **gonfalonier** (*-ēr'*) one who bears a gonfalon: the chief magistrate in some mediaeval Italian republics; **gon'fanon** a gonfalon: a pennon. [It. *gonfalone* and O.Fr. *gonfanon* — O.H.G. *gundfano* — *gund,* battle, *fano* (Ger. *Fahne*), a flag; cf. O.E. *gūthfana.*]

gong *gong, n.* a metal disc, usu. rimmed, that sounds when struck or rubbed with a drumstick: an instrument of call, esp. to meals: a steel spiral for striking in a clock: a flat bell sounded by a hammer: medal (*slang*). — *v.t.* to call upon to stop by sounding a gong. — *n.* **gong'ster** one who gongs. — **gong'-stick.** [Malay.]

Gongorism *gong'gor-izm, n.* a florid, inverted, and pedantic style of writing, introduced by the Spanish poet Luis de Góngora y Argote (1561–1627), some of whose distinctive features reappeared in Euphuism. — *n.* **Gong'orist** — *adj.* **Gongoris'tic.**

gonia. See **gonion.**

goniatite *gō'ni-ə-tīt, n.* a fossil cephalopod of a group

with comparatively simple angular septa. — *n.* and *adj.* **goniati'toid.** [Gr. *gōniā,* an angle.]

gonidium *gon-id'i-əm, n.* an algal cell in a lichen: — *pl.* **gonid'ia.** — *adjs.* **gonid'ial, gonid'ic.** [Gr. *gonē,* generation, seed.]

gonimoblast *gon'i-mō-bläst, n.* in the red seaweeds, a spore-bearing filament that springs from the fertilised carpogonium. [Gr. *gonimos,* productive, *blastos,* a shoot.]

goniometer *gōn-, gon-i-om'i-tər, n.* an instrument for measuring angles, esp. between crystal-faces: a direction-finding apparatus. — *adjs.* **goniometric** (*-ə-met'rik*), **-al.** — *adv.* **goniomet'rically.** — *n.* **goniom'etry.** [Gr. *gōniā,* an angle, *metron,* measure.]

gonion *gō'ni-ən, (anat.) n.* the point of the angle either side of the lower jaw: — *pl.* **gō'nia** (*-i-ə*). [Gr. *gō'nia,* angle.]

gonk® *gongk, n.* a cushion-like soft toy, usu. with arms and legs. [Nonsense word.]

gonna *gon'ə,* (esp. *U.S.*) a coll. contraction of **going to.**

gonococcus *gon-ō-kok'əs, n.* the bacterium that causes gonorrhoea: — *pl.* **gonococci** (*-kok'sī*). — *adjs.* **gonococc'al, gonococcic** (*-kok'sik*); **gonococc'oid.** [Gr. *gonos,* seed, *kokkos,* a berry.]

gonocyte *gon'ō-sīt, n.* an oocyte or spermatocyte. [Gr. *gonos,* seed, *kytos,* a vessel.]

gonophore *gon'ə-fōr, -för, n.* a prolongation of the axis bearing stamens or carpels (*bot.*): a reproductive zooid of a hydrozoan, answering to a medusa but remaining fixed (*zool.*). [Gr. *gonos,* seed, *phoreein,* to bear.]

gonorrhoea *gon-ō-rē'ə, n.* a contagious infection of the mucous membrane of the genital tract. — *adjs.* **gonorrhoe'al, -ic.** — *U.S.* **gonorrhē'a, gonorrhē'al, -ic.** [Gr. *gonorroiă* — *gonos,* seed, *rheein,* to flow, from a mistaken notion of its nature.]

goo *gōō, (slang) n.* a sticky substance: sentimentality. — *adj.* **goo'ey.** [Origin unknown.]

goober *gōō'bər, n.* (also **goober pea**) peanut. [African.]

good *good, adj.* having suitable or desirable qualities: promoting health, welfare, or happiness: virtuous: pious: kind: benevolent: well-behaved: not troublesome: of repute: doughty: worthy: commendable: suitable: adequate: thorough: competent: sufficient: valid: sound: serviceable: beneficial: genuine: pleasing: favourable: ample, moderately estimated: considerable, as in *a good deal, a good mind*: to be counted on: — *compar.* **bett'er;** *superl.* **best.** — *n.* the end of ethics: that which is good: prosperity: welfare: advantage: temporal or spiritual: benefit: avail: virtue: possessions (*arch.*): (usu. in *pl.*) movable property, chattels, merchandise, freight. — *interj.* well: right: be it so. — *adv.* well. — *n.* **good'iness** weak, priggish, or canting goodness. — *adj.* **good'ish** pretty good, of fair quality or quantity. — *n.* **good'liness.** — *adv.* **good'ly** (*Spens*) graciously: excellently, kindly. — *adj.* comely: good-looking: fine: excellent: ample: — *compar.* **good'lier;** *superl.* **good'liest.** — *ns.* **good'lyhead, good'lihead** (*Spens.*) goodness; **good'ness** virtue: excellence: benevolence: substituted for God in certain expressions, as *for goodness sake,* and as *interj.* — *n.* **good'y** short for **goodwife** (*arch.*): (usu. in *pl.*) a delicacy or sweetmeat: (usu. in *pl.*) something pleasant or desirable (usu. *facet.*): the hero of a book, motion picture, etc. (*coll.*): a goody-goody. — *interj.* expressing pleasure. — *adj.* **goody-goody.** — *adj.* **good'y-good'y** mawkishly good: weakly benevolent or pious. — Also *n.* — *n.* and *interj.* **good afternoon** a salutation on meeting or parting in the afternoon. — **good'-breed'ing** polite manners formed by a good bringing-up; **good-broth'er, -fath'er, -moth'er, -sis'ter, -son'** (*Scot.;* also **gude-**) a brother-in-law, father-in-law, etc. — *n.* or *interj.* **good-bye'** for *God be with you:* farewell, a form of address at parting. — *adjs.* **good'-cheap** (*arch.*) cheap (lit. good-bargain); **good-condi'tioned** in a good state. — **good-dame'** (*obs.* Scot.; also **gude-dame'** *güd-, gid-*) a grandmother. — *ns.* or *interjs.* **good-day'** a common salutation at meeting or parting; **good-den'** (*arch.;* from *good-e'en*), **good=**

e'en' (*arch*.), **good-e'ven** (*arch*.), **good-eve'ning** a salutation on meeting or parting in the evening. — *adj.* **good'faced** (*Shak*.) having a handsome face. — **good'-fell'ow** a jolly or boon companion: a reveller; **good'-fell'owship** merry or pleasant company: conviviality; **good folk** good people. — *adj.* **good'-for-nothing** worthless, useless. — *n.* an idle or worthless person. — **Good Friday** see under **Friday.** — *interjs.* **good grief!** an exclamation of surprise or dismay; **good heavens!** an exclamation of surprise. — **good'-hu'mour** cheerful, tolerant mood or disposition. — *adj.* **good'-hu'moured.** — *adv.* **good'-hu'mouredly.** — **good'-hu'mouredness; good'-King-Hen'ry** a goosefoot used in cooking and sometimes grown as a pot-herb. — *interj.* **good-lack'** (*arch*.) an expression of surprise or pity (prob. a variation of *good Lord*, under the influence of **alack**). — *adj.* **good'-look'ing** handsome, attractive. — **good'-look'er** (*coll*.); **good looks** attractive appearance; **good'-man** (*arch*.) a yeoman: (usu. with *cap*.) formerly prefixed to name of a man of yeoman's rank (*fem.* **good'wife**): (*good-man'*, chiefly *Scot*.; also **gude-**) a householder or husband (*fem.* **goodwife'**) or euphemistically the devil; **goodman's croft** a patch once left untilled in Scotland to avert the malice of the devil from the crop. — *ns.* and *interjs.* **good-morn'ing** or (*arch*.) **good-morr'ow** a salutation at meeting or parting early in the day. — **good'-na'ture** natural goodness and mildness of disposition. — *adj.* **good'-na'tured.** — *adv.* **good'-na'turedly.** — **good'-na'turedness.** — *n.* and *interj.* **goodnight'** a common salutation on parting at night or well on in the day. — *interjs.* **good'-now** (*arch*.) an exclamation of wonder, surprise, or entreaty; **good'-o, good'-oh** expressing pleasure. — *adv.* well: thoroughly. — **good offices** mediation; **good people, good folk** the fairies (euphemistically); **good sailor** a person not liable to seasickness; **good Samaritan** see **Samaritan; goods'-engine** an engine used for drawing goods-trains; **good'-sense** sound judgment; **goodsire',** also **gudesire'** (*güd-, gid-*; *obs. Scot*.) and **gutcher** (*gut'shər*; (*Scot*.) a grandfather. — *adj.* **good'-sized'** (fairly) large. — *n.* and *interj.* **good'-speed'** (*arch*.) a contraction of *I wish you good speed* (i.e. success). — **goods'-train** a train of goods wagons. — *adj.* **good'-tem'pered** possessing a good temper. — **Good Templar** a member of a temperance society, modelled on the Freemasons. — *adj.* **good'time** pleasure-seeking. — **good turn** something done for someone in a kind and helpful spirit or manner; **goodwife'** (or **good'**; *arch*.) the *fem.* of **goodman; good'will'** benevolence: well-wishing: the established custom or popularity of any business or trade — often appearing as one of its assets, with a marketable money value. — *adjs.* **good'will,** (*Scot*.) **good-will'y** well-wishing: expressive of goodwill. — **good works** acts of charity. — **as good as** the same as, no less than: virtually; **be as good as one's word** to fulfil one's promise; **for good (and all)** permanently: irrevocably; **good and** (*coll*.) very; **goodies and baddies** characters in a drama regarded respectively as definitely good and definitely bad; **good for anything** ready for any kind of work; **good for you** *interj.* expressing approval (*Austr. coll.* **good on you**); **good neighbour policy** a U.S. policy from 1931 for co-operation in all fields between all the countries of North, South, and Central America; **goods and chattels** see **chattel; in somone's good books** in favour with someone; **make good** to fulfil, perform: to compensate: to come to success, esp. unexpectedly: to do well, redeeming a false start: to repair: to justify; **no good** useless: unavailing: worthless; **not, hardly** etc., **good enough** not sufficiently good: mean, unfair, very different from what was expected or promised; **stand good** to be lastingly good: to remain; **the Good Book** the Bible; **the goods** (*slang*) the real thing: that which is required, promised, etc.; **think good** to be disposed, to be willing; **to the good** for the best: on the credit or advantage side. [O.E. *gōd*; Du. *goed*, Ger. *gut*, O.N. *gōthr*, Goth. *gōths*.]

goodyear, -s *gŏŏd'yēr(z)*, (*Shak*.) *ns.* the devil, the plague, or the like — a meaningless imprecation. [Of obscure origin. Perh. orig. 'as I hope for a *good year*'.]

gooey. See **goo.**

goof *gŏŏf, n.* a stupid or awkward person. — *v.i.* to make a blunder. — *adv.* **goof'ily.** — *n.* **goof'iness.** — *adj.* **goof'y.** — **goof'ball** (*slang*) a barbiturate pill used as an exhilarant. [Perh. Fr. *goffe*.]

googly *gŏŏg'li,* (*cricket*) *n.* an off-breaking ball with an apparent leg-break action on the part of a right-arm bowler to a right-handed batsman, or conversely for a left-arm bowler. — Also *adj.* — *v.i.* **goog'le** to behave or bowl in such a manner. [Ety. dub.]

googol *gŏŏ'gol, n.* 1 followed by a hundred zeros, 10^{100}. — *n.* **goo'golplex** 1 followed by a googol of zeros, 10 to the power of a googol. [Coined by F. Kasner, mathematician.]

gook *gŏŏk,* (*slang*) *n.* one of Asiatic race, esp. a Japanese, Korean or Vietnamese soldier: esp. in Rhodesia, a guerrilla or terrorist. [Origin uncertain.]

gool, goold. See **gold**[2].

gooly, gooley, goolie *gŏŏ'li, n.* a small stone (*Austr. coll.*): (in *pl*.) testicles (*vulg*.). [Perh. Hind. *goli*, a bullet, ball.]

goon *gŏŏn, n.* a hired thug (*U.S. slang*): a stupid person. [After 'Alice the *Goon*', a character created by American cartoonist E.C. Segar (1894–1938).]

gooney(-bird) *gŏŏ'nē (-bûrd), n.* an albatross. [Prob. dial., simpleton — obs. *gony*.]

goop *gŏŏp, n.* a fool: a fatuous person: a rude, ill-mannered person (*U.S*.). — *adj.* **goop'y.** [Cf. **goof.**]

goor, Goorkha, gooroo. Alternative spellings of **gur, Gurkha, guru.**

goosander *gŏŏs-an'dər, n.* a large duck of the merganser genus. [Perh. **goose,** and O.N. *önd*, pl. *ander*, duck.]

goose *gŏŏs, n.* any one of a group of birds of the duck family, intermediate between ducks and swans: a domesticated member of the group, descended mainly from the grey-lag: the female of such a bird: — *masc.* **gander:** a tailor's smoothing-iron, from the likeness of the handle to the neck of a goose: a stupid, silly person: a game of chance once common in England, in which the players moved counters on a board, with right to a double move on reaching a picture of a goose: — *pl.* **geese** (*gēs,*) or, of tailor's goose, **goos'es.** — *v.t.* (*slang*) to hiss off the stage: to prod (someone) between the buttocks: to goad into action. — *ns.* **goos'ery** a place for keeping geese: stupidity; **goos'(e)y** a goose: a blockhead. — *adj.* like a goose: affected with goose-flesh. — **goose-barnacle** see **barnacle**[1]; **goose'-cap** a silly person; **goose'-club** a combination for saving to buy geese for Christmas, or to raffle for a goose; **goose'-egg** the egg of a goose: a zero score (*U.S*.); **goose'-fish** (*U.S*.) the angler-fish; **goose'flesh** a condition of the skin, like that of a plucked goose or other fowl: the bristling feeling in the skin due to erection of hairs through cold, horror, etc.; **goose'-flower** the pelican-flower, a gigantic Aristolochia; **goose'foot** any plant of the genus (Chenopodium) of the beet family, from the shape of the leaf: also applied to any member of the family Chenopodiaceae: — *pl.* **goose'foots; goose'-girl** a girl who herds geese; **goosegog, goosegob** see under **gooseberry; goose'-grass** cleavers: silverweed; **goose'herd** one who herds geese; **goose'-neck** a hook, bracket, pipe, etc., bent like a goose's neck; **goose'-pimples** goose-flesh; **goose'-quill** one of the quills or large wing-feathers of a goose, esp. one used as a pen; **goose'-skin** goose-flesh, horripilation; **goose'-step** (*mil*.) a method of marching (resembling a goose's walk) with knees stiff and soles brought flat on the ground. — Also *v.i.* — **goose'-wing** one of the clews or lower corners of a ship's mainsail or foresail when the middle part is furled or tied up to the yard. — *adj.* **goose'-winged** having only one clew set: in fore-and-aft rigged vessels, having the mainsail on one side and the foresail on the other, so as to sail wing-and-wing. — **the goose that lays the golden eggs** see **golden goose**

under **gold**[1]. [O.E. *gōs* (pl. *gēs*); O.N. *gās*, Ger. *Gans*, L. *anser* (for *hanser*), Gr. *chēn*.]

gooseberry gŏŏz′bə-ri, gŏŏs′-, *n.* the fruit of the **gooseberry-bush** (*Ribes grossularia*), a prickly shrub of the saxifrage family: a fermented effervescing drink (also **goose′berry-wine**) made from gooseberries: an imitation champagne: an unwanted third person. — **goose′-berry-cat′erpillar** a creamy looper with orange spots and black dots, feeding on gooseberry leaves, the larva of the **goose′berry-moth′** or magpie moth (*Abraxas grossulariata*) a yellow-bodied moth with black-spotted white wings; **goose′berry-fool′** see **fool**[2]; **goose′-berry-stone′** grossular; **goose′gog, goose′gob** (*coll.* and *dial.*) a gooseberry. — **Cape gooseberry** or **gooseberry tomato** see **cape**[2]; **Chinese gooseberry** a sub-tropical vine, *Actinidia chinensis*, with brown, hairy, edible fruit; **Coromandel gooseberry** carambola (q.v.). [Perh. **goose** and **berry**[1]; or *goose* may be from M.H.G. *krus* (Gr. *kraus*, crisp, curled); cf. O.Fr. *groisele*, *grosele*, gooseberry, Scot. *grossart*.]

gopak gō′pak, *n.* a folk-dance from the Ukraine. [From Russ.]

gopher[1] gō′fər, *n.* a name in America applied to various burrowing animals — the pouched rat, the ground squirrel, the land tortoise of the Southern States, and a burrowing snake. — *v.i.* to burrow: to mine in a small way. [Perh. Fr. *gaufre*, honeycomb.]

gopher[2] gō′fər, *n.* a kind of wood, generally supposed to be cypress (*B.*): yellow-wood (Cladastris) (*U.S.*). [Heb.]

gopher[3]. See **gofer**.

gopura gō′pŏŏ-rə, **gopuram** gō′pŏŏ-rəm, *ns.* in Southern India, a pyramidal tower over the gateway of a temple. [Sans. *gopura*.]

goral gō′rəl, gō′, *n.* a Himalayan goat-antelope.

goramy, gourami, gurami gō′, gō′, gōō′rə-mi, or -rä′mi, *ns.* a large freshwater food-fish (*Osphromenus olfax*) of the Eastern Archipelago. [Malay *gurāmī*.]

gor-belly gör′bel-i, *n.* a big belly: a big-bellied person. — *adj.* (*Shak.*) **gor′-bellied**. [Perh. O.E. *gor*, filth, and **belly**.]

gorblim(e)y gö-blī′mi, (*Cockney*) *interj.* for *God blind me.*

gorcock gör′kok, *n.* the red grouse cock. [Origin obscure.]

gorcrow gör′krō, *n.* the carrion-crow. [O.E. *gor*, filth, and **crow**.]

Gordian görd′yən, *adj.* pertaining to *Gordium* the capital, or *Gordius* the king, of ancient Phrygia, or to the intricate knot he tied: intricate: difficult. — *v.t.* (*Keats*) to tie up, knot. — *n.* **Gor′dius** a genus of hairworms. — **cut the Gordian knot** to overcome a difficulty by violent measures as Alexander cut the knot with his sword.

gore[1] gōr, gör, *n.* filth (*obs.*): clotted blood: blood. — *adv.* **gor′ily**. — *adj.* gore′y like gore: covered with gore: bloody. — **gore′-blood** (*Spens.*); **gory dew** a dark-red slimy film sometimes seen on damp walls, etc., a simple form of vegetable life, *Porphyridium cruentum.* [O.E. *gor*, filth, dung; O.N. *gor*, cud, slime.]

gore[2] gōr, gör, *n.* a triangular piece of land: a triangular piece let into a garment to widen it: a skirt (*obs.*): a sector of a curved surface. — *v.t.* to shape like or furnish with gores: to pierce with anything pointed, as a spear or horns. — *n.* **gor′ing** an angular, tapering, or obliquely-cut piece. — *adj.* forming a gore. [O.E. *gāra*, a pointed triangular piece of land, and *gār*, a spear.]

gorge görj, *n.* the throat: a ravine: the entrance to an outwork (*fort.*): a hawk's crop: the maw: the contents of the stomach: a gluttonous feed: a fish-catching device, to be swallowed by the fish. — *v.t.* to swallow greedily: to glut. — *v.i.* to feed gluttonously. — *adj.* **gorged** having a gorge or throat: glutted: having a crown or coronet about the neck (*her.*). — *n.* **gorg′et** a piece of armour for the throat: a metal badge formerly worn on the breast by army officers: a wimple: a neck ornament. — **have one's gorge rise to** be filled with loathing; **heave the gorge** to retch. [O.Fr.]

gorgeous gör′jəs, *adj.* showy: splendid: magnificent: loosely, pleasant, good, etc. — *adv.* **gor′geously**. — *n.* **gor′geousness**. [O.Fr. *gorgias*, gaudy.]

gorgerin gör′jə-rin, (*archit.*) *n.* same as **necking**. [Fr. *gorge*, throat.]

gorget. See **gorge**.

gorgia gör′jə, *n.* an improvised virtuoso passage in 16th- and 17th-cent. singing. [Obs. It. *gorgia*, throat.]

gorgio gör′jō, gör′ji-ō, *n.* one who is not a gipsy. — Also **gajo** gö′jō: — *pls.* -s. [Romany.]

Gorgon gör′gən, *n.* one of three fabled female monsters (Stheno, Euryale, and Medusa), of horrible and petrifying aspect, winged, with hissing serpents for hair: (*usu.* without *cap.*) anybody, esp. a woman, very ugly or formidable. — Also *adj.* — *adj.* **gorgō′nian**. — *n.* **gorgoneion** (-ī′on) a mask of the gorgon: — *pl.* **gorgonei′a**. — *v.t.* **gor′gonise, -ize** to turn to stone. [Gr. *Gorgō*, pl. *-ŏnĕs* — *gorgos*, grim.]

Gorgonia gör-gō′ni-ə, *n.* a genus of sea-fans or horny corals. — *adj.* **gorgo′nian**. — *n.* a horny coral. [L. *gorgōnia*, coral — *Gorgō*, Gorgon (from hardening in the air).]

Gorgonzola gör-gən-zō′lə, *n.* a blue cheese of cow's milk. [From *Gorgonzola*, a small Italian town near Milan.]

gorilla gor-il′ə, *n.* a great African ape, the largest anthropoid: a thug (*slang*). — *adjs.* **gorill′ian, gorill′ine**. [Gr. *Gorillai* (pl.), reported by Hanno the Carthaginian as a tribe of hairy women; supposed to be an African word.]

goring. See **gore**[2].

gorm, gormless, etc. See **gaum**[1,2].

gormand gör′mənd, *n.* older form of **gourmand**. — *v.i.* **gor′mandise, -ize** to eat hastily or voraciously. — *n.* **gor′mandise** (-dīz) gourmandise: gluttony: gormandising. — *ns.* **gor′mandīser, -z-; gor′mandising, -z-; gor′mandism** gluttony. [See **gourmand**.]

gorse görs, *n.* furze or whin, a prickly papilionaceous shrub (Ulex). — Also **gosse** (*Shak.*). — *adj.* **gors′y**. [O.E. *gorst*.]

gorsedd gör′sedh, *n.* a meeting of bards and druids. [W., throne.]

gorsoon. See **gossoon**.

gory. See **gore**[1].

gosh gosh, (*coll.*) *interj.* for **God**.

goshawk gos′hök, *n.* a short-winged hawk, once used for hunting wild-geese and other fowl, not having a toothed bill like the falcons proper. [O.E. *gōshafoc* — *gōs*, goose, *hafoc*, hawk.]

Goshen gō′shən, *n.* a happy place of light and plenty. [From the abode of the Israelites during the plague of darkness in Egypt, Exod. x. 23.]

goslarite gos′lər-īt, *n.* a mineral, hydrated zinc sulphate, found at *Goslar* in the Harz Mts.

gosling goz′ling, *n.* a young goose. — *n.* **gos′let** an Eastern dwarf goose (*Nettapus*). [O.E. *gōs*, goose, double dim. *-l-ing*.]

gospel gos′pəl, *n.* the teaching of Christ: a narrative of the life of Christ, esp. one of those included in the New Testament, Matthew, Mark, Luke, and John: the principles set forth therein: the stated portion of these read at service: any strongly advocated principle or system: absolute truth (*coll.*): a type of ardently religious jazz music (esp. songs) originating amongst the black population of the southern U.S. — *v.t.* (*Shak.*) to instruct in the gospel. — *v.t.* **gos′pel(l)ise, -ize** to evangelise: to square with the gospel. — *n.* **gos′peller** a preacher: an evangelist: a Wycliffite, Protestant, or Puritan (often in derision): one who reads the gospel in church. — **gospel side** the north side or gospeller's side of the altar. [O.E. *godspel(l)*, a translation of L. *evangelium* — *gōd*, good (with shortened vowel being understood as *God*, God) and *spel(l)*, story.]

Gosplan gos′plan, *n.* the Russian state economic planning department. [Russ., *Gos*udarstvennaya *plan*ovaya Comissiya.]

gospodar. See **hospodar.**

Goss *gos, n.* white china vessels and trinkets bearing the crest of a town, etc., much sold as holiday mementos. [From W. H. *Goss* (1833–1906), manufacturer, of Stoke-on-Trent.]

gossamer *gos'ə-mər, n.* very fine spider-threads that float in the air or form webs on bushes in fine weather: any very thin material. — *adj.* light, flimsy. — *adj.* **goss'-amery** like gossamer: flimsy. [M.E. *gossomer*; perh. goose-summer, a St Martin's summer, when geese are in season and gossamer abounds; cf. Ger. *Sommerfäden,* summer-threads, also *Mädchensommer,* maiden-summer.]

gossan, gozzan *gos', goz'ən, ns.* decomposed rock, largely quartz impregnated with iron compounds, at the outcrop of a vein esp. of metallic sulphides. [Cornish miner's term; origin unknown.]

gosse *gos,* (*Shak.*) *n.* a form of **gorse.**

gossip *gos'ip, n.* a sponsor at baptism (in relation to child, parent, or other sponsor) (*arch.*); a woman friend who comes at a birth (*arch.*): a familiar friend (*arch.*; *Spens.*). **goss'ib**): one who goes about telling and hearing news, or idle, malicious, and scandalous tales: idle talk: tittle-tattle: scandalous rumours: easy familiar writing. — *v.i.* to run about telling idle or malicious tales: to talk much: to chat. — *v.t.* (*Shak.*) to stand godfather to: — *pa.t.* **goss'iped.** — *n.* and *adj.* **goss'iping.** — *n.* **goss'ipry.** — *adj.* **goss'ipy.** — **gossip column** the newspaper column written by a gossip-writer; **gossip columnist; goss'ip-monger** a person who spreads gossip and rumours; **goss'ip-writer** a journalist who writes articles about the lives and loves of well-known people. [O.E. *godsibb,* godfather, one who is **sib in God,** spiritually related.]

gossoon, gorsoon *go-, gör-sōōn', ns.* a boy or boy-servant. [Anglo-Ir., — Fr. *garçon,* boy.]

Gossypium *go-sip'i-əm,* a tropical genus of the mallow family, yielding cotton. — *adj.* **goss'ypine** cottony. — *n.* **goss'ypol** a poisonous principle in cotton-seed. [L. *gossypion.*]

got. See under **get.**

Goth *goth, n.* one of an ancient Germanic nation, originally settled on the southern coasts of the Baltic, migrating to Dacia in the 3rd century, and later founding kingdoms in Italy, southern France, and Spain: a rude or uncivilised person, a barbarian. — *adj.* **Goth'ic** of the Goths or their language: barbarous: romantic: denoting the 12th- —16th-cent. style of architecture in churches, etc., with high-pointed arches, clustered columns, etc. (applied in reproach at time of the Renaissance): generally, the style, related to this, favoured in all the fine arts during this time: black-letter (*print.*): a square-cut type without serifs (*U.S.*): orig. applied to 18th-cent. tales, novels, of mystery with gloomy sinister backgrounds, now denoting psychological horror-tales (also **Gothick**): lurid, extravagantly macabre, grotesque (*slang*). — *n.* language of the Goths, an East Germanic tongue: Gothic architecture. — *n.* and *adj.* **Goth'ick** (denoting) a style of architecture, c. 1720–1840, in which the Gothic style of the middle ages was imitated: (of 18th-cent. and modern tales, etc.) Gothic. — *v.t.* **goth'icise, -ize** (*-sīz*) to make Gothic. — *n.* **Goth'icism** (*-sizm*) a Gothic idiom or style of building: rudeness of manners. — **Gothic revival** the more serious revival of the Gothic style of architecture which followed the Gothick. [The native names *Gutans* (sing. *Guta*) and *Gutōs* (sing. *Guts*), and *Gutthiuda,* people of the Goths; Latinised as *Gothī, Gotthī*; Gr. *Gothoi, Gotthoi*; O.E. *Gotan* (sing. *Gota*).]

Gothamite *gōt', got'əm-īt, n.* a simpleton: a wiseacre: (*goth', gōth'*) a New Yorker (*U.S.*). — **Goth'amist** (*gōt', got'*) a simpleton. [From *Gotham,* a village in Nottinghamshire, with which name are connected many of the simpleton stories of immemorial antiquity.]

Gothic, Gothick, etc. See **Goth.**

göthite. See **goethite.**

gotta *got'ə,* a coll. contraction of **got to.**

gotten. See under **get.**

Götterdämmerung *gœ-tər-dem'ə-rŏŏng,* (*Ger. myth.*) *n.* lit. the twilight of the gods, the ultimate defeat of the gods by evil.

gouache *gōō-äsh, gōō',* (chiefly *U.S.*) *gäsh, n.* watercolour painting with opaque colours, mixed with water, honey, and gum, presenting a matt surface: work painted according to this method. [Fr.]

Gouda *gow'də, n.* a kind of mild cheese from *Gouda* in the Netherlands.

gouge¹ *gowj,* also *gōōj, n.* a chisel with a hollow blade for cutting grooves or holes. — *v.t.* to scoop out, as with a gouge: to force out, as the eye with the thumb. [O.Fr., — L.L. *gubia,* a kind of chisel.]

gouge² *gōōj,* (*Scott*) *n.* a wench. [O.Fr.]

gougère *gōō-jer', n.* a kind of choux pastry, the dough of which has been mixed with grated cheese prior to baking. [Fr.]

goujeers an editor's would-be improvement upon **goodyear** (q.v.) from a spurious Fr. *goujère,* the French disease.

goujons *gōō-zhŏ, n.pl* small strips of fish coated in flour and deep-fried. [Fr.]

gouk. See **gowk.**

goulash *gōō'lash, n.* a stew of beef, vegetables, esp. onions, and paprika: a re-deal of cards that have been arranged in suits and order of value, so many (as e.g. 5) cards at a time (*bridge*). [Hung. *gulyás* (*hús*) herdsman (meat).]

Goura *gow'rə, n.* a New Guinea genus of beautifully crested, ground-loving pigeons. [From a native name.]

gourami. See **goramy.**

gourd *gōōrd, görd, görd, n.* a large hard-rinded fleshy fruit characteristic of the cucumber family: the rind of one used as a bottle, cup, etc.: a gourd-bearing plant. — **gourd'-worm** a fluke-worm resembling a gourd-seed, esp. the liver-fluke. [O.Fr. *gourde,* contr. from *cougourde* — L. *cucurbita,* a gourd.]

gourde *gōōrd, n.* the monetary unit of Haiti, consisting of 100 centimes. [Fr. fem. of *gourd* — L. *gurdus,* dull, stupid.]

gourds *gördz, görz, gōōrdz, n.pl.* a kind of false dice. [Cf. O.Fr. *gourd,* swindle.]

gourdy *görd'i, görd', gōōrd', adj.* swollen in the legs (of a horse). — *n.* **gourd'iness.** [O.Fr. *gourdi,* swollen.]

gourmand *gōōr'mənd, -mä, n.* one who eats greedily: a glutton: a lover of good fare. — *adj.* voracious: gluttonous. — *ns.* **gourmandise** (*gōōr'mən-dīz, gōōr-mä-dēz*) skill, or indulgence, in good eating: voracious greed (*Spens.*); **gour'mandism.** [Fr.; cf. **gormand.**]

gourmet *gōōr'mä, -me, n.* an epicure, originally one with a delicate taste in wines. [Fr., a wine-merchant's assistant.]

goustrous *gows'trəs,* (*Scot.*) *adj.* boisterous, rude.

gousty *gows'ti,* (*Scot.*) *adj.* dreary: desolate: empty.

gout¹ *gowt, n.* a drop, spot (*arch.*): a disease in which excess of uric acid in the blood is deposited as urates in the joints, etc., with swelling esp. of the great toe: a kindred disease of poultry: a swelling of the stalk in wheat and other grasses. — *n.* **gout'iness.** — *adj.* **gout'y** relating to gout: diseased with or subject to gout. — **gout'fly** a fly (*Chlorops*) whose larvae cause gout by boring in wheat, etc.; **gout'weed, -wort** bishopweed or goatweed (*Aegopodium podagraria*), an umbelliferous weed, long supposed to be good for gout. [O.Fr. *goutte* — L. *gutta,* a drop, the disease supposed to be caused by a defluxion of humours.]

gout² *gōō, n.* taste: relish. [Fr. *goût* — L. *gustus,* taste.]

goutte *gōōt,* (Fr.) *n.* a drop (of liquid); **goutte à goutte** drop by drop.

gouvernante *gōō-ver-nãt, n.* a female ruler (*obs.*): a house-keeper: a duenna: a governess. [Fr.]

gov. See governor under govern.

govern *guv'ərn, v.t.* to direct: to control: to rule with authority: to determine: to determine the case of (*gram.*): to require as the case of a noun or pronoun. — *v.i.* to exercise authority: to administer the laws. — *adj.* gov'ernable. — *ns.* gov'ernall (*Spens.*) government; gov'ernance government: control: direction: behaviour (*obs.*); gov'ernante (*obs.*) a gouvernante; gov'erness a female governor (*arch.; fig. Milt.*): a lady who has charge of the instruction of the young at home or in school (nursery governess one having charge of young children only, tending as well as teaching them). — *v.i.* to act as governess. — *v.t.* to be governess to. — *adjs.* gov'ernessy like a governess, esp. prim; gov'erning having control. — *n.* government (*guv'ər(n)-mənt*) a ruling or managing: control: system of governing: the body of persons authorised to administer the laws, or to govern a state: tenure of office of one who governs: an administrative division (*arch.*): territory (*arch.*): the power of one word in determining the case of another (*gram.*): conduct (*Shak.*). — *adj.* of or pursued by government. — *adj.* governmental (*-ment'l*) pertaining to government. — *ns.* gov'ernor a real or titular ruler, esp. of a state, province, colony: the head of an institution or a member of its ruling body: the commander of a fortress: a tutor (*arch.*): (usu. *guv'nər*) a father, chief, or master, applied more generally in kindly, usually ironically respectful, address (sometimes shortened to gov guv) (*slang*): a regulator, or contrivance for maintaining uniform velocity with a varying resistance (*mach.*): a pilot (*B.*); gov'ernorship. — governess car, cart a light low two-wheeled vehicle with face-to-face seats at the side; gov'erning-bod'y a board in whom is vested the authority to supervise and regulate the affairs of an establishment or of a particular field of activity; governmental atonement see Grotian; gov'ernor-gen'eral orig. the supreme governor of a country, etc., with deputy governors under him: the representative of the British crown in Commonwealth countries which recognise the monarchy as head of state: — *pl.* gov'ernors-gen'eral; gov'ernor= gen'eralship. [O.Fr. *governer* — L. *gubernāre* — Gr. *kybernaein*, to steer.]

gowan *gow'ən*, (*Scot.*) *n.* the wild daisy: the oxeye daisy (also horse'-gow'an). — *adjs.* gow'aned; gow'any. — luck'engow'an the globe-flower. [Apparently a form of gollan(d).]

gowd, gowdspink. Scots form of gold[1], goldspink.

gowf *gowf*, (*Scot.*) *v.t.* to strike, cuff. — *v.i.* to golf. — *n.* golf. — *n.* gowf'er golfer. — gowf'-ba' golf-ball. [See golf.]

gowk, gouk *gowk*, (*Scot.*) *n.* a cuckoo: a fool: an April fool. [O.N. *gaukr*; O.E. *gēac*.]

gowl *gowl*, (*Scot.*) *v.i.* to cry or howl. [O.N. *gaula*.]

gowland. See gollan.

gown *gown, n.* a loose flowing outer garment: a woman's dress: an academic, clerical, or official robe: the members of a university as opposed to the townspeople (see under town). — *v.t.* and *v.i.* to dress in a gown. — *v.t.* to invest or furnish with a gown. — *adj.* gowned. — gown'boy a school foundationer, wearing a gown; gown'man, gowns'man one who wears a gown, as a divine or lawyer, and esp. a member of an English university: a civilian (*arch.*). [O.Fr. *goune* — L.L. *gunna*; origin unknown.]

gowpen *gowp'ən*, (*Scot.*) *n.* the hollow of the two hands held together: a double handful (now usu. *pl.*). — *n.* gow'penful. [O.N. *gaupn.*]

goy *goi, n.* a non-Jew, Gentile: — *pl.* goy'im. — *adjs.* goy'ish, goyisch (*goi'ish*). [Heb., (non-Jewish) nation.]

gozzan. See gossan.

Graafian *grä'fi-ən, adj.* pertaining to the Dutch anatomist Regnier de *Graaf* (1641–73) who discovered the Graafian follicles in which the ova are contained in the ovary of higher vertebrates.

graal. See grail[3].

grab[1] *grab, n.* an Eastern coasting vessel. [Ar. *ghurāb.*]

grab[2] *grab, v.t.* to seize or grasp suddenly: to lay hands on: to impress or interest (*slang*). — *v.i.* to clutch: — *pr.p.* grabb'ing; *pa.t.* and *pa.p.* grabbed. — *n.* a sudden grasp or clutch: unscrupulous seizure: a double scoop hinged like a pair of jaws: a simple card-game depending upon prompt claiming. — *n.* grabb'er one who grabs: an avaricious person. — grab'-bag a bag or other receptacle for miscellaneous articles: one from which gifts are drawn (*U.S.*). — Also *fig.* — grabbing crane an excavator consisting of a crane and a large grab, so hinged as to scoop into the earth as it is lifted. — how does that grab you? (*slang*) what's your reaction to that?; up for grabs (*slang*) (ready) for the taking, for sale, etc. [Cf. Sw. *grabba*, to grasp.]

grabble *grab'l, v.t.* and *v.i.* to grope: to scramble: to struggle with (somebody or something). — *n.* grabb'-ler. [Freq. of grab[2].]

graben *grä'bən, n.* same as a rift valley. [Ger. ditch.]

Grace *grās, n.* an automatic telephone system whereby all calls, trunk as well as local, can be dialled directly by subscribers. [group routing and charging equipment.]

grace *grās, n.* easy elegance in form or manner: what adorns and commends to favour: a grace note (*mus.*): favour: kindness: pardon (*arch.*): the undeserved mercy of God: divine influence: eternal life or salvation: a short prayer before or after a meal: an act or decree of the governing body of an English university: a ceremonious title in addressing a duke, an archbishop, or formerly a king: a short period of time in hand before a deadline is reached (see days of grace below): (in *pl.*) favour, friendship (with *good*): (*cap.* in *pl.*) the three sister goddesses in whom beauty was deified (the Greek Charites), Euphrosyne, Aglaia, Thalia (*myth.*). — *v.t.* to mark with favour: to adorn. — *adjs.* graced (*Shak.*) favoured, endowed with grace or graces, virtuous, chaste; grace'ful elegant and easy: marked by propriety or fitness, becoming: having or conferring grace, in any sense. — *adv.* grace'fully. — *n.* grace'-fulness. — *adj.* grace'less wanting grace or excellence: without mercy or favour (*obs.*): depraved (*arch.*): indecorous. — *adv.* grace'lessly. — *n.* grace'lessness. — *ns.* graciosity (*grā-shi-os'i-ti*) graciousness; gracioso (*grā-shi-ō'sō*; Sp. *grä-thyō'sō*) a favourite (*obs.*): a clown in Spanish comedy: — *pl.* -os. — *adj.* gracious (*grā'shəs*) abounding in grace or kindness: proceeding from divine favour (*obs.*): acceptable: affable: becoming in demeanour: favourable (*arch.*). — *n.* used as substitute for God. — *adv.* gra'ciously. — *n.* grā'-ciousness. — *adj.* grace'-and-fa'vour (of a residence) belonging to the British sovereign and granted rent-free to a person of importance (also with *caps.*). — grace cup a cup or health drunk at the end of a feast; grace note (*mus.*) a note introduced as an embellishment, not being essential to the harmony or melody; gracious living (living in) conditions of ease, plenty, and good taste. — days of grace (three) days allowed for the payment of a note or bill of exchange after it falls due; fall from grace to backslide, to lapse from the state of grace and salvation or from favour; good gracious, gracious me exclamations of surprise; saving grace (*Christian theology*) divine grace so bestowed as to lead to salvation: a compensating virtue or quality; take heart of grace to pluck up courage (orig. of 'of grace' uncertain); with (a) good, bad, grace in amiable, ungracious, fashion; year of grace year of Christian era, A.D. [Fr. *grâce* — L. *grātia*, favour — *grātus*, agreeable.]

grâce à Dieu *gräs a dyø*, (Fr.) thanks to God.

gracile *gras'īl, -il, adj.* slender: gracefully slight in form. — *n.* gracil'ity. [L. *gracilis*, slender.]

gracious, gracioso, etc. See grace.

grackle, grakle *grak'l, n.* a myna (hill myna) or kindred bird: an American 'blackbird' of the family Icteridae. [L. *grāculus*, jackdaw.]

gradate, etc. See grade.

graddan *grad'ən*, (*Scot.*) *n.* parched grain. — *v.t.* to parch in the husk. [Gael. *gradan*.]

grade *grād, n.* a degree or step in quality, rank, or dignity: a stage of advancement: rank: a yearly stage in education (*U.S.*): a pupil's mark of proficiency (*U.S.*): (in *pl.*, with *the*) the elementary school (*U.S.*): position in a scale: a class, or position in a class, according to value: position in an ablaut series (*philol.*): one-hundredth part of a right angle (*math.*): gradient or slope: an inclined or level stretch of road or railway (*U.S.*): a class of animals produced by crossing a breed with one purer. — *v.t.* to arrange according to grade: to assign a grade to: to adjust the gradients of. — *v.i.* to shade off. — *adj.* of improved stock. — *adj.* **grā'dable** able to be graded: of or relating to a word depending on a standard, e.g. *clever, narrow* (*linguistics;* also *n.*). — *v.t.* and *v.i.* **gradate** (*grə-dāt'*) to shade off imperceptibly. — *adv.* **grādā'tim** (L. *grä-dä'tim*) step by step. — *n.* **grādā'tion** a degree or step: a rising step by step: progress from one degree or state to another: position attained: state of being arranged in ranks: a diatonic succession of chords (*mus.*): a gradual shading off: ablaut (*philol.*). — *adj.* **gradā'tional.** — *adv.* **gradā'tionally.** — *adjs.* **gradā'tioned** formed by gradations or stages; **gradatory** (*grad'ət-ə-ri*) proceeding step by step: adapted for walking. — *n.* **grād'er** one who, or that which, grades: a machine used to create a flat surface for road-building. — *adj.* **gradient** (*grā'di-ənt, -dyənt*) rising or falling by degrees: walking. — *n.* the degree of slope as compared with the horizontal: rate of change in any quantity with distance, e.g. in barometer readings: an incline. — *ns.* **grād'ienter** a surveyor's instrument for determining grades; **gradin, gradine** (*grā'din, grə-dēn'*) a rising tier of seats, as in an amphitheatre: a raised step or ledge behind an altar; **gradino** (*grä-dē'nō*: It.) a decoration for an altar gradin: — *pl.* **-ini** (*-nē*); **gradiometer** (*grā-di-om'ə-tər*) a magnetometer for measuring the gradient of a magnetic field, etc. — *adj.* **gradual** (*grad'ū-əl*) advancing by grades or degrees: gentle and slow (of a slope). — *n.* in the R.C. Church, the portion of the mass between the epistle and the gospel, formerly always sung from the steps of the altar: the book containing such anthems — also **grail.** — *ns.* **grad'ūalism** the principle, policy, or phenomenon, of proceeding by degrees; **grad'ūalist.** — *adjs.* **grad'ūalist; gradūalis'tic.** — *n.* **gradūal'ity.** — *adv.* **grad'ūally.** — *n.* **grad'ūand** one about to receive a university degree. — *v.t.* **gradūate** to divide into regular intervals: to mark with degrees: to proportion: to confer a degree upon (*U.S.*): to admit to a university degree (*arch.*). — *v.i.* to pass by grades: to receive a university degree. — *n.* one who has obtained a university degree: one who has completed a course in any educational or training institution (*U.S.*). — *adj.* **grad'ūated** marked with degrees, as a thermometer. — *ns.* **grad'ūateship; gradūā'tion** division into proportionate or regular sections, for measurement, etc.: a mark or all the marks made for this purpose: the gaining or (*U.S.*) conferring of a university degree: the ceremony marking this; **grad'ūator** an instrument for dividing lines at regular intervals; **grā'dus** a dictionary of Greek or Latin prosody — from *Gradus ad Parnassum* a step, or stairs, to Parnassus. — **grade crossing** (*U.S.*) a level crossing; **graded post** in British schools, a post with some special responsibility, and so extra payment; **grade school** (*U.S.*) elementary school; **grade separation** (*U.S.*) a crossing at which one road, etc., is an underpass or an overpass. — **at grade** (*U.S.*) on the same level; **make the grade** orig. to succeed in climbing a steep hill: to overcome obstacles: to succeed: to be up to standard. [L. *gradus,* a step — *gradī,* to step.]

gradely *grād'li,* (*dial.*) *adj.* decent: proper: fit: fine. — *adv.* properly: readily: very. — Also **graith'ly.** [See **graith.**]

Gradgrind *grad'grīnd, n.* one who regulates all human things by rule and compass and the mechanical application of statistics, allowing nothing for sentiment, emotion, and individuality. [From Thomas *Gradgrind* in Dickens's *Hard Times.*]

gradient, etc., gradin, etc., gradual, etc., graduate, etc. See **grade.**

Graeae, Graiae *grī'ī,* (*Gr. myth*) *n.pl.* three sea-goddesses, sisters of the Gorgons, having the form of old women who shared between them a single eye and a single tooth. [Gr. *graia,* old woman.]

Graecise, -ize *grē'sīz, v.t.* to make Greek: to hellenise. — *v.i.* to become Greek: to conform to Greek ways or idioms: to use the Greek language. — *n.* **Grae'cism** a Greek idiom: the Greek spirit: a following of the Greeks. — *adj.* **Graeco-Ro'man** (*grē'kō-*) of or pertaining to both Greece and Rome, esp. the art of Greece under Roman domination: applied to a mode of wrestling imagined to be that of the Greeks and Romans. — Also **Grē'cise, -ize,** etc. [L. *Graecus* — Gr. *Graikos,* Greek; *graikizein,* to speak Greek.]

Graf *gräf, n.* a count, earl: — *fem.* **Gräfin** (*grä'fin*). [Ger.]

graff¹ *gräf,* (*Scot.*) *n.* a variant of **grave¹.**

graff² *gräf, n.* and *vb.* an older form of **graft¹.**

graffito *gräf-fē'tō, n.* a mural scribbling or drawing, as by schoolboys and idlers at Pompeii, Rome, and other ancient cities (*ant.*): sgraffito. — *n.pl.* or, *loosely, n. sing.* **graffi'ti** (*-tē*) scribblings or drawings, often indecent, found on public buildings, in lavatories, etc. [It., — Gr. *graphein,* to write.]

graft¹ *gräft, n.* a small piece of a plant or animal inserted in another individual or another part so as to come into organic union: the act of inserting a part in this way: the place of junction of stock and scion: the double plant composed of stock and scion: a sucker, branch, plant (*obs.*). — *v.t.* to insert a graft in: to insert as a graft: to cuckoldise (*obs.*). — *v.i.* to insert grafts. — *ns.* **graft'er; graft'ing.** — **graft hybrid** a hybrid form produced, as some have believed, by grafting: a patchwork compound of two species propagated from the junction of tissues in a graft, each part retaining the specific character proper to the cells from which it arose. [From older **graff** — O.Fr. *graffe* (Fr. *greffe*) — L. *graphium* — Gr. *graphion, grapheion,* a style, pencil — *graphein,* to write.]

graft² *gräft, n.* a ditch, excavation (*dial.*): a spade's depth: a ditching spade: hard work (*slang*): a criminal's special branch of practice (*slang*): illicit profit by corrupt means, esp. in public life (*slang*): corruption in official life (*slang*). — *v.i.* to dig (*dial.*): to work hard (*slang*): to engage in graft or corrupt practices (*slang*). — *n.* **graft'er.** [Cf. O.N. *gröftr,* digging: the slang uses of corruption in public life, etc., may belong to **graft¹.**]

grafted. see **grufted.**

graham flour *grā'əm flowr,* (mainly *U.S.*) a type of wheat flour similar to whole-wheat flour. — **graham bread, crackers** a type of bread, crackers, made with graham flour. [After S. *Graham* (1794–1851), U.S. dietician.]

Graiae. See **Graeae.**

grail¹ *grāl, n.* gravel. — Also (*Spens.*) **graile, grayle.** [Perh. **gravel;** or O.Fr. *graile* (Fr. *grêle*), hail — L. *gracilis,* slender.]

grail². See **gradual** under **grade.**

grail³ *grāl, n.* (often **holy grail;** often with *caps.*) in mediaeval legend, the platter (sometimes supposed to be a cup) used by Christ at the Last Supper, in which Joseph of Arimathaea caught his blood, said to have been brought by Joseph to Glastonbury, and the object of quests by King Arthur's Knights: a cherished ambition or goal. — Also **graal, grayle.** [O.Fr. *graal* or *grael,* a flat dish — L.L. *gradalis,* a flat dish, ultimately from Gr. *kratēr,* a bowl.]

grain¹ *grān, n.* a single small hard seed: corn, in general: a hard particle: a very small quantity: the smallest British weight (the average weight of a seed of corn) = ¹/₇₀₀₀ of a pound avoirdupois: (in *pl.*) refuse malt after brewing or distilling: the arrangement, size and direction of the particles, fibres, or plates of stone, wood, etc.: texture: a granular surface: dried bodies of kermes or of cochineal insects, once thought to be seeds: the red dye made from these: any fast dye — to *dye in grain* is to dye deeply, also to *dye in the wool*: dye in general: innate quality or character: the particles in a photographic emulsion which go to compose the photograph. — *v.t.* to form into grains, cause to granulate: to paint in imitation of grain: to dye in grain: in tanning, to take the hair off. — *n.* **grain'age** duties on grain. — *adj.* **grained** granulated: subjected to graining: having a grain: rough: furrowed. — *ns.* **grain'er** one who grains: a paint-brush for graining; **grain'ing** specif., painting to imitate the grain of wood: a process in tanning in which the grain of the leather is raised. — *adj.* **grain'y** having grains or kernels: having large grains, so indistinct (*phot.*). — **grain alcohol** alcohol made by the fermentation of grain. — **against the grain** against the fibre of the wood — hence against the natural temper or inclination; **grains of Paradise** the aromatic and pungent seeds of an African Amomum; **in grain** in substance, in essence; **take with a grain of salt** see **salt**[1] (L. *cum grānō salis*). [Fr. *grain*, collective *graine* — L. *grānum*, seed and *grāna*, orig. pl.; akin to **corn**[1].]

grain[2] *grān*, *n.* a branch, prong, fork (*dial.*): (in *pl.*, used as *sing.*) a kind of harpoon. [O.N. *grein*.]

graine *grān*, *n.* silkworm eggs. [Fr.]

graining[1] *grān'ing*, *n.* (in Lancashire) dace — once thought a different species. [Origin unknown.]

graining[2], **grainy**, etc. See **grain**[1].

graip *grāp*, (*Scot.*) *n.* a three- or four-pronged fork used for lifting dung or digging potatoes. [A form of **grope**; cf. Sw. *grep*, Dan. *greb*.]

graith *grāth*, (*Scot.*) *n.* apparatus: equipment. — *v.t.* to make ready, to dress. — *adj.* and *adv.* **graith'ly** an older form of **gradely**. [O.N. *greithr*, ready; cf. O.E. *geræde*, ready.]

grakle. See **grackle.**

Grallae *gral'ē*, **Grallatores** *-ə-tō'rēz*, *-tō'*, *ns.pl.* in old classifications, an order of wading birds. — *adj.* **grallatō'rial.** [L. *grallātor*, a stilt-walker — *grallae*, stilts — *gradus*, a step.]

gralloch *gral'əhh*, *n.* a deer's entrails. — *v.t.* to disembowel (deer). [Gael. *grealach*.]

gram[1] *gram*, **grame** *grām*, (*obs.*) *n.* anger: grief, trouble. [O.E. *grama*, anger.]

gram[2] *gram*, *n.* chick-pea: pulse generally. — **black gram** see **urd.** [Port. *grão* (sometimes *gram*) — L. *grānum*, a grain.]

gram[3], **gramme** *gram*, *n.* a unit of mass in the metric system — formerly that of a cubic centimetre of water at 4°C, now a thousandth part of the International Prototype Kilogram (see **kilogram**). — **gram'-at'om**, **gram'-atom'ic weight**, **gram'-mol'ecule**, **gram'-molec'ular weight** the quantity of an element, a compound, whose mass in grams is equal to its atomic weight, molecular weight (a now discarded concept —see **mole**[1]); **gram'-equiv'alent (weight)** the quantity of a substance whose mass in grams is equal to its equivalent weight. [Fr. *gramme* — L. *gramma* - - Gr. *gramma*, a letter, a small weight.]

gram[4] *grām*, *n.* an Indian village. [Hindi.]

-gram -*gram*, in composition, something written or drawn to form a record. [Gr. *gramma*, letter.]

grama (grass) *grä'mə* (*gräs*), *n.* an American pasture grass (*Bouteloua*) with spikelets ranged unilaterally. [Sp., — L. *grāmen*, grass.]

gramary, gramarye *gram'ə-ri*, (*arch.*) *n.* magic: enchantment. [M.E. *gramery*, skill in grammar, hence magic; see **grammar, glamour**.]

gramash. See **gamash.**

grame. See **gram**[1].

gramercy *grə-mûr'si*, (*arch.*) *interj.* great thanks. — *n.* thanks. [O.Fr. *grant merci*, great thanks.]

gramicidin *gram-i-sī'din*, *n.* an antibiotic obtained from certain bacteria, used against Gram-positive bacteria. — Also **gramicidin D.** — *adjs.* **Gram'-neg'ative** (also **gram-**) losing a stain of methyl violet and iodine on treatment with alcohol; **Gram'-pos'itive** (also **gram-**) retaining the stain. [H. J. C. *Gram*, deviser of the method, and L. *caedĕre*, to kill.]

Gramineae *grə-*, *gra-*, *grā-min'i-ē*, *n.pl.* the grass family. — *adjs.* **graminā'ceous** (*grā-*, *gra-*), **gramin'eous**; **graminiv'orous** (*gra-*) feeding on grass, cereals, etc. [L. *grāmen*, *grāminis*, grass.]

grammalogue *gram'ə-log*, *n.* a word represented by a single sign: a sign for a word in shorthand. [Gr. *gramma*, a letter, *logos*, a word.]

grammar *gram'ər*, *n.* the science of language, from the points of view of pronunciation, inflexion, syntax, and historic development: the art of the right use of language by grammatical rules: a book that teaches these subjects: any elementary work. — *n.* **grammā'rian** one versed in grammar, a teacher of or writer on grammar. — *adjs.* **grammat'ic, -al** belonging to, or according to the rules of, grammar. — *adv.* **grammat'ically.** — *n.* **grammat'icaster** (*arch.*; see **-aster**) a piddling grammarian. — *v.t.* **grammat'icise, -ize** (*-sīz*) to make grammatical. — *v.i.* to act the grammarian. — *ns.* **grammat'icism** (*rare*) a point of grammar; **gramm'-atist** a strict grammarian. — **grammar school** orig. a school in which grammar, esp. Latin grammar, was taught: now a secondary school in which academic subjects predominate; **grammatical meaning** the functional significance of a word, etc. within the grammatical framework of a particular sentence, etc. [Gr. *gramma*, *-atos*, a letter; partly through O.Fr. *gramaire*.]

gramme. See **gram**[3].

Grammy *gram'i*, (*U.S.*) *n.* an award, corresponding to the cinema Oscar, awarded by the National Academy of Recording Arts and Sciences. [From *gramo*phone.]

Gram-negative. See **gramicidin.**

gramoche *gra-mosh'.* See **gamash.**

gramophone *gram'ə-fōn*, *n.* (with *cap.*, ® in U.S.) an instrument (invented by E. Berliner, 1887) for reproducing sounds by means of a needle moving along the grooves of a revolving disc, a record-player: (*loosely*) any record-player (now used *facet.* or *arch.*). — *adj.* **gramophonic** (*-fon'ik*). — *adv.* **gramophon'ically.** — *ns.* **gramophonist** (*gram-of'ə-nist*, *gram'ə-fōn-ist*); **gramoph'ony.** [Ill-formed from Gr. *gramma*, letter, record, *phōnē*, sound.]

Gram-positive. See **gramicidin.**

grampus *gram'pəs*, *n.* a popular name for many whales, esp. the killer: technically, Risso's dolphin (*Grampus griseus*): one who puffs. [16th century *graundepose*, earlier *grapays* — O.Fr. *graspeis* — L. *crassus*, fat, *piscis*, fish, confused with Fr. *grand*, big.]

gran[1] *gran*, (It.) *adj.* great. — **gran turismo** (*too-rēz'mō*) (a motor car) designed for touring in luxury and at high speed (term sometimes used loosely). — Abbrev. **GT.**

gran[2] *gran*, (*coll.*) *n.* short for **granny.**

granadilla *gran-ə-dil'ə*, **grenadilla** *gren'*, *ns.* the edible, oblong, fleshy fruit of *Passiflora quadrangularis*, a tropical American passion-flower: the edible fruit of various other passion-flowers. — **granadilla tree** the cocus-wood tree. [Sp.]

granary *gran'ə-ri*, *n.* a storehouse for grain or threshed corn: a rich grain-growing region. — *adj.* (of bread) containing whole grains of wheat. [L. *grānārium* — *grānum.*]

grand[1] *grand*, *adj.* pre-eminent: supreme: chief: main: exalted: magnificent: dignified: sublime: imposing: would-be-imposing: on a great scale: in complete form: in full proportions: very good (*coll.*): (in composition) of the second degree of parentage or descent, as grandchild, granddaughter, grandfather, grandmother, grandson, etc. — *n.* a grand piano: a thousand dollars, pounds (*slang*). — *ns.* **grandee'** from the 13th century a noble of the most highly privileged class in the kingdom of Castile, the members of the royal family being included: a man of high rank or station; **grandee'ship; grandeur** (*grand'yər*) vastness: splendour of appearance: loftiness of thought or deportment; **grandil'oquence.** — *adj.* **grandil'oquent** (L. *loquens, -entis,* speaking) speaking, or expressed, bombastically — (*arch.*) **grandil'oquous.** — *adv.* **grandil'oquently.** — *adj.* **gran'diose** grand or imposing: bombastic. — *adv.* **gran'diosely.** — *n.* **grandios'ity.** — *adv.* **grand'ly.** — *n.* **grand'ness.** — **grand'(d)ad** old man: a grandfather; **grand'(d)addy** (*coll.*) a grandfather: a person or thing considered the oldest, biggest, first, etc. of its kind; **gran'dam** (*arch.*), **grann'am** (*arch.*) an old dame or woman: a grandmother; **grand'-aunt** a great-aunt; **grand'child** a son's or daughter's child; **grand'daughter** a son's or daughter's daughter. — *adj.* **grand'-du'cal.** — **grand duke** a title of sovereignty over a **grand duchy,** first created by the Pope in 1569 for the rulers of Florence and Tuscany, assumed by certain German and Russian imperial princes (*fem.* **grand duchess**); **grand'father** a father's or mother's father. — *adj.* **grand'fatherly** like a grandfather, kindly. — **grandfather clause** a qualifying clause within a piece of legislation exempting those already involved in the activity with which the legislation deals; **grandfather('s) clock** an old-fashioned clock (longcase clock) standing on the ground — larger than a **grandmother('s) clock; grand juror** member of a **grand jury,** a special jury in the U.S. and until 1933 in Britain which decides whether there is sufficient evidence to put an accused person on trial; **grand larceny** see **larceny; grand'mam(m)a, grand'ma** a grandmother; **grand march** processional opening of a ball; **grand'mas'ter** orig. the title given to a chess-player winning a great international tournament, now given generally to unusually skilled players: any such player; **Grand Master** the head of a religious order of knighthood (Hospitallers, Templars, and Teutonic Knights), or of the Freemasons, etc.; **grand'mother** a father's or mother's mother. — *adj.* **grand'motherly** like a grandmother: over-anxious, fussy. — **Grand Mufti** the head of the Muslim community in Jerusalem: the former head of the state religion in Turkey; **Grand National** a steeplechase held annually at Aintree in Liverpool; **grand'-neph'ew** a great-nephew; **grand'-niece** a great-niece; **grand opera** see **opera**[1]; **grand'papa, grand'pa** a grandfather; **grand'parent** a grandfather or grandmother; **grand piano** a large harp-shaped piano, with horizontal strings; **grand'sire** a grandfather (*arch.*): any ancestor (*arch.*): a method of ringing changes on bells; **grand slam** the winning of every trick at bridge: in sports such as tennis, golf, etc., the winning of all major championships in a season; **grand'son** a son's or daughter's son; **grand'stand** an elevated erection on a racecourse, etc., affording a good view. — *v.i.* (*U.S. coll.*) to show off. — **grandstand finish** a close and rousing finish to a sporting contest: a supreme effort to win at the close of a sporting contest; **grand style** a style adapted to lofty or sublime subjects; **grand total** the sum of all subordinate sums; **Grand Tour** see **tour; grand touring** same as **gran turismo; grand'-un'cle** a great-uncle. — **delusions of grandeur** a mistaken belief in one's importance; **grand old man** (*coll.*) a person commanding great respect and veneration. [Fr. *grand* — L. *grandis,* great.]

grand² *grä,* (Fr.) *adj.* great. — **grand amateur** (*da-ma-tœr*) a collector of beautiful objects on a large scale; **grand atelier** (*dat-əl-yä*) a top-ranking fashion house; **grand coup** (*koō*) a successful stroke: in bridge or whist the trumping of a trick that could have been trumped by the winner's partner; **grand cru** (*krü*) of a wine, from a famous vineyard or group of vineyards; **Grand Guignol** see **Guignol; grand luxe** (*lüks*) great luxury; **grand mal** (*mal*) a violently convulsive form of epilepsy (see **petit mal**); **grand merci** (*mer-sē*) many thanks; **grand monde** (*mɔ̃d*) high society; **grand prix** (*prē*) chief prize: (*cap.*) any of several international motor races: any competition of similar importance in other sports (orig. *Grand Prix de Paris,* a famous horse race): — *pl.* **grands prix; grand seigneur** (*sen-yœr*) a dignified

aristocratic gentleman or noble (now usu. *ironic*); **(le) Grand Siècle** (*syekl'*) the great century, i.e., the Classical age of French literature during the reign of Louis XIV.

grandad, grandam. See **grand**[1].

grande *gräd,* (Fr.) *adj. fem.* of **grand**[2]. — **grande amoureuse** (*a-moō-rœz*) a woman greatly involved in love affairs; **(la) Grande Armée** (*ar-mā*) the great army, i.e. that led by Napoleon to invade Russia in 1812; **grande cocotte** (*ko-kot*) a high-class prostitute, usu. one kept by a rich lover; **grande dame** (*däm*) a great and aristocratic lady, or a socially important and very dignified one (now, as *grand seigneur,* often *ironic*); **grande école** (*ā-kol*) a French technical college with military connections; **grande entrée** (*ã-trā*) admission to Court, etc., on occasions of state; **grande marque** (*märk*) of motor cars, etc., a famous make; **grande passion** (*pas-yɔ̃*) a serious love affair or intense attachment; **grande tenue** (*tə-nü*) full dress, esp. military, etc.; **grande toilette** (*twa-let*) full dress, esp. women's evening dress; **grande vedette** (*və-det*) a leading film or theatre star.

grandee, grandeur, grandiloquence, etc., **grandiose,** etc. See **grand**[1].

Grandisonian *gran-di-sō'ni-ən, adj.* like the novelist Richardson's hero, Sir Charles *Grandison,* beneficent, polite, and chivalrous.

granfer *gran'fər,* (*dial.*) *n.* contr. of **grandfather.**

grange *grānj, n.* a granary (*Milt.*): a farmhouse with its stables and other buildings: a country house (*obs.*): an abiding place (*Spens.*): a lodge of the order of Patrons of Husbandry (*U.S.*). — *n.* **gran'ger** the keeper of a grange: a member of a grange. [O.Fr. *grange,* barn — L.L. *granea* — L. *granum,* grain.]

Grangerism *grān'jər-izm, n.* the practice of cutting plates and title-pages out of many books to illustrate one book. — *n.* **grangerisā'tion, -z-.** — *v.t.* **gran'gerise, -ize** to practise Grangerism on. [From James *Granger* (1716–76), whose *Biographical History of England* (1769) included blank pages for illustrations.]

granite *gran'it, n.* a coarse-grained igneous crystalline rock, composed of quartz, feldspar, and mica: a curling-stone. — *adj.* of granite: hard like granite. — *adj.* **granit'ic** pertaining to, consisting of, or like granite. — *n.* **granitificā'tion.** — *adj.* **granit'iform.** — *ns.* **gran'itite** muscovite granite; **granitisā'tion, -z-.** — *v.t.* **gran'itise, -ize.** — *adj.* **gran'itoid** of the form of or resembling granite. — *n.* **granodī'orite** a rock resembling diorite but containing quartz. — *adj.* **granolith'ic** (Gr. *lithos,* stone) composed of cement and granite chips. — Also *n.* — *n.* **gran'ophyre** (*-fir;* with *-phyre* after *porphyry*) a quartz-porphyry with graphic intergrowth of quartz and orthoclase for groundmass. — *adj.* **granophyric** (*-fir'ik, -fīr'ik*). — **graniteware** (*gran'it-wär*) a kind of speckled pottery resembling granite: a type of enamelled ironware. [It. *granito,* granite, lit. grained — L. *granum,* grain.]

granivorous *gran-iv'ər-əs, adj.* grain-eating: feeding on seeds. — *n.* **gran'ivore.** [L. *granum,* grain, *vorāre,* to devour.]

grannam. See **grand**[1].

granny, -ie *gran'i, n.* a grandmother: an old woman: an old-womanish person: a revolving cap on a chimneypot. — **granny bonds** a former name of index-linked National Savings certificates, before 1981 only available to people over 50 years old; **granny flat, annexe** a self-contained flat, bungalow, etc., built on to, as part of, or close to, a house, for a grandmother or other elderly relative; **granny knot** a knot like a reef knot, but unsymmetrical, apt to slip or jam; **Granny Smith** a crisp, green, flavoursome, Australasian variety of apple (After Maria Ann *Smith* of New South Wales, the first cultivator of this variety). [**grannam** (under **grand**[1]).]

granolithic, etc. See **granite.**

grant *gränt, v.t.* to bestow: to admit as true: to concede. — *v.i.* (*Shak.*) to consent. — *n.* a bestowing: something bestowed, an allowance: a gift: conveyance of property by deed (*Eng. law*). — *adj.* **grant′able.** — *pa.p.* or *conj.* **grant′ed** (often with *that*) (it is) admitted, accepted. — *ns.* **grantee′** (*law*) the person to whom a grant, gift, or conveyance is made; **grant′er, grant′or** (*law*) the person by whom a grant or conveyance is made. — **grant′-in-aid′** an official money grant for a particular purpose, esp. from the government to a lesser department for its programme or to ensure high standards; **grant of arms** a furnishing of a heraldic achievement to a petitioner by a king-of-arms, in exchange for a fee. — **take for granted** to presuppose, assume, esp. tacitly or unconsciously: to treat casually, without respect. [O.Fr. *graanter, craanter, creanter,* to promise — L. *crēdĕre,* to believe.]

Granth *grunt,* **Granth Sahib** *grunt sä′ib, n.* the holy book of the Sikhs (also **Adi′-Granth**). — *n.* **Gran′thi** (-*ē*) the guardian of the Granth Sahib and of the gurdwara. [Hindi *granth,* a book.]

granule *gran′ūl, n.* a little grain: a fine particle. — *adjs.* **gran′ular, gran′ūlary** (*arch.*), **gran′ūlose, gran′ūlous** consisting of or like grains or granules: containing or marked by the presence of grains or granules. — *n.* **granular′ity.** — *adv.* **gran′ūlarly.** — *v.t.* **gran′ūlate** to form or break into grains or small masses: to make rough on the surface. — *v.i.* to be formed into grains. — *adj.* **granular:** having the surface covered with small elevations. — *n.* **granūlā′tion** act of forming into grains, esp. of metals by pouring them through a sieve into water while hot: a granulated texture: (*specif.*) applied decoration made up of grains of metal (esp. gold): (in *pl.*) granulation tissue (q.v.). — *adj.* **gran′ūlative.** — *ns.* **gran′ūlātor, -er.** — *adjs.* **granūlif′erous; gran′ūliform.** — *n.* **gran′ūlite** a schistose but sometimes massive aggregate of quartz and feldspar with garnets: a granular-textured metamorphic rock. — *adj.* **granūlit′ic** of the texture of granulite. — *ns.* **granūlītīsā′tion, -z-** reduction of the components of a rock to crystalline grains by regional metamorphism; **gran′ūlōcyte** a blood cell of the leucocyte division. — *adj.* **granūlocȳt′ic.** — *n.* **granūlō′ma** a localised collection of granulation tissue occurring in certain chronic infections, e.g. tuberculosis and syphilis: — *pl.* **granūlō′mas, granūlō′mata.** — *adj.* **granūlō′matous.** — **granulated sugar** white sugar in fairly coarse grains; **granulation tissue** a new formation of connective tissue which grows in small rounded masses in a wound or on an ulcerated surface, and tends to leave a white scar. [L. *grānulum,* dim. of *grānum,* grain.]

grape[1] *grāp, v.i.* a Scottish form of **grope.**

grape[2] *grāp, n.* the fruit of the grapevine: a mangy tumour on the legs of horses: grapeshot. — *adj.* **grape′less** without the flavour of the grape, said of wine. — *n.* **grā′pery** a place where grapes are grown. — *adj.* **grā′p(e)y** made of or like grapes. — **grape′fruit** a fine variety of the shaddock, the pompelmoose, so called because it grows in large bunches like grapes; **grape hyacinth** (*Muscari*) a near ally to the hyacinths, with clusters of small grapelike flowers; **grape′-louse** the Phylloxera; **grape′seed** the seed of the vine; **grape′seed-oil** an oil expressed from it; **grape′shot** shot that scatters; **grape′stone** the pip of the grape; **grape sugar** glucose or dextrose; **grape′tree** a tropical American tree (*Coccoloba uvifera*) of the dock family, or its edible fruit; **grape′vine** *Vitis vinifera* or other species of *Vitis:* the bush telegraph: rumour (from its far-stretching branches). — **sea-grape** see **Ephedra; sour grapes** things decried because they cannot be attained (from Aesop's fable of the fox and the grapes); **the grape** (usu. *facet.*) wine. [O.Fr. *grape, grappe,* a cluster of grapes — *grape,* a hook; orig. Gmc.]

graph *gräf, n.* a symbolic diagram: a drawing depicting the relationship between two or more variables. — *v.t.* to plot on a graph. — **-graph** used as a terminal in many compounds to denote an agent that writes, records, etc., as *telegraph, seismograph,* or the thing written, as in *autograph,* etc.; **-graphy** used as a terminal in compounds to denote either a particular style

of writing, drawing, etc., as *photography, lithography,* or a method of arranging and recording data within a particular discipline as *seismography, biography.* — *n.* **grapheme** (*graf′ēm*) a letter of an alphabet: all the letters or combinations of letters together that may be used to express one phoneme. — *adj.* **graphēm′ic.** — *adv.* **graphēm′ically.** — *n. sing.* **graphēm′ics** the study of systems of representing speech sounds in writing. — *adjs.* **graphic** (*graf′ik*), **-al** pertaining to writing, describing, delineating, or diagrammatic representation: picturesquely described or describing: vivid. — *ns.* **graph′ic** a painting, print, or illustration or diagram; **graph′icacy** accurate understanding and use of visual information. — *advs.* **graph′ically; graph′icly.** — *n.* **graph′icness.** — *n. sing.* **graph′ics** graphic means of presenting, or means of reproducing, informational material: the art or science of mathematical drawing, and of calculating stresses, etc., by geometrical methods. — *ns.* **Graph′is** a genus of lichens, with fructifications like writing; **graph′ite** a mineral, commonly called blacklead or plumbago, though composed of carbon. — *adjs.* **graphĭt′ic; graph′itoid.** — *n.* **graphitīsā′tion, -z-.** — *v.t.* **graph′itise, -ize** to convert wholly or partly into graphite. — *ns.* **graph′ium** stylus; **graphol′ogy** the art of estimating character, etc., from handwriting. — *adjs.* **grapholog′ic, -al.** — *ns.* **graphol′ogist; graphoman′ia** obsession with writing; **graphopho′bia** fear of writing; **-graphy** in composition, see above. — **graphic arts** painting, drawing, engraving, as opposed to music, sculpture, etc.; **graphic formula** a chemical formula in which the symbols for single atoms are joined by lines representing valency bonds; **graphic granite** a granite with markings like Hebrew characters, owing to intergrowth of quartz and feldspar; **graph paper** squared paper suitable for drawing graphs. [Gr. *graphē,* a writing — *graphein,* to write.]

graple. See **grapple.**

grapnel *grap′nəl, n.* a small anchor with several claws or arms: a grappling-iron: a hooking or grasping instrument. [Dim. of O.Fr. *grapin* — *grape,* a hook; of Gmc. origin.]

grappa *gra′pə, n.* a brandy, orig. Italian, made from residue from a wine-press. [It., grape stalk.]

grapple *grap′l, n.* an instrument for hooking or holding: a grasp, grip, hold, or clutch: a state of being held or clutched. — *v.t.* to seize: to lay fast hold of. — *v.i.* to contend in close fight (also *fig.*). — Also (*Spens.*) **graple.** — *n.* **graplement** (*Spens.*) a close fight. — **grapp′le-plant′** a S. African plant (*Harpagophytum procumbens*) of the sesame family, with strongly hooked fruits; **grapp′ling-i′ron, -hook** an instrument for grappling: a large grapnel for seizing hostile ships in naval engagements. [Cf. O.Fr. *grappil* — *grape,* a hook.]

graptolite *grap′tə-līt, n.* one of a group of fossil Hydrozoa with one or two rows of hydrothecae on a simple or branched polypary — characteristic Silurian fossils like writing upon shales. — *adj.* **graptolit′ic.** [Gr. *graptos,* written — *graphein,* to write, *lithos,* stone.]

grasp *gräsp, v.t.* to seize and hold: to take eagerly: to comprehend. — *v.i.* to endeavour to seize (with *at, after*): to seize or accept eagerly (with *at*). — *n.* grip: power of seizing: mental power of apprehension. — *adj.* **grasp′able.** — *n.* **grasp′er.** — *adj.* **grasp′ing** seizing: avaricious. — *adj.* **grasp′ingly.** — *n.* **grasp′ingness.** — *adj.* **grasp′less** feeble, relaxed. — **grasp the nettle** see **nettle**[1]. [M.E. *graspen, grapsen,* from the root of *grāpian,* to grope.]

grass[1] *gräs, n.* common herbage: any plant of the monocotyledonous family Gramineae, the most important to man in the vegetable kingdom, with long, narrow leaves and tubular stems, including wheat and other cereals, reeds (but not sedges), bamboo, sugar-cane: pasture grasses: pasturage: time of grass, spring or summer: the surface of a mine: an informer (*slang*): temporary or casual work in a printing office: marijuana (*slang*). — *v.t.* to cover with grass: to feed with grass: to bring to the grass or ground: to inform (on) (*slang*). — *v.i.* to inform (on) (*slang*): to do temporary or casual work (*print.*). — *ns.* **grass'er** (*print.*) an extra or temporary worker; **grass'iness; grass'ing** bleaching by exposure on grass. — *adj.* **grass'y** covered with or resembling grass, green. — **grass'-box** a receptacle attached to some lawn-mowers to catch the grass cuttings; **grass carp** a breed of fish, native to the South China Sea, imported into other areas to control various kinds of weed which it eats in great quantities; **grass cloth** a name for various coarse cloths (rarely made of grass), esp. rami; **grass'cloth plant** rami; **grass court** a grass-covered tennis-court; **grass'-cutter** a mowing machine: in India, one who provides provender for baggage cattle (perh. really Hindustani *ghāskatā*). — *adjs.* **grass'-green** green with grass: green as grass; **grass'-grown** grown over with grass. — **grass'hook** another name for **sickle**[1]; **grass'hopper** a name for various saltatorial, orthopterous insects akin to locusts and crickets, that lurk among grass and chirp by rubbing their wing-covers; **grasshopper mind** a mind which is desultory or unable to concentrate on any one object for long; **grasshopper warbler** a songbird (*Locustella naevia*) whose song resembles a grasshopper's stridulation; **grass'land** permanent pasture; **grass'-moth** a small light-coloured moth that frequents grass, a veneer-moth; **grass'-oil** a name for several volatile oils derived from widely different plants, some of them grasses; **grass'-plot** a plot of grassy ground; **grass'-roots'** (orig. *U.S.*) the rural areas of a country: the ordinary people, the rank and file in a country, political party, etc., thought of as voters: foundation, basis, origin, primary aim or meaning. — Also *adj.* — **grass sickness** a disease of the bowels affecting horses; **grass'-snake** the harmless common ringed snake; **grass style** a form of Chinese calligraphy in which the shapes of words are greatly simplified for artistic effect; **grass'-tree** an Australian plant (*Xanthorrhoea*) of the lily family, with shrubby stems, tufts of long wiry foliage at the summit, and a tall flower-stalk, with a dense cylindrical spike of small flowers; **grass'-wid'ow** a wife temporarily separated from or deserted by her husband: — *masc.* **grass'-wid'ower; grass'wrack** eel-grass. — **go, be put out, to grass** to be turned out to pasture, esp. of a horse too old to work: to go into retirement, to rusticate: to fall violently (of a pugilist); **grass of Parnassus** see **Parnassus; hear the grass grow** to have exceptionally acute hearing: to be exceptionally alert; **let the grass grow under one's feet** to loiter, linger, and so lose opportunity. [O.E. *gærs, græs*; O.N., Du., and Goth. *gras*, Ger. *Gras*; prob. allied to **green**[1] and **grow**.]

grass[2] *gräs, n.* for **sparr'ow-grass**, a corruption of **asparagus**.

grassum *gräs'əm,* (*Scots law*) *n.* a lump sum paid by persons who take a lease of landed property — in England, 'premium' and 'fine'. [O.E. *gærsum*, treasure, rich gift, etc.]

graste *grāst,* (*Spens.*) pa.p. of **grace**.

grat. See **greet**[2].

grate[1] *grāt, n.* a framework of bars with interstices, esp. one for holding a fire or for looking through a door, etc.: a cage: a grid. — *adj.* **grāt'ed** having a grating. — *ns.* **graticulation** (*gra-* or *grə-tik-ū-lā'shən*) the division of a design into squares for convenience in making an enlarged or diminished copy; **graticule** (*grat'i-kūl*) a ruled grating for identification of points in a map, the field of a telescope, etc.; **grāt'ing** the bars of a grate: a perforated cover for a drain or the like: a partition or frame of bars: a surface ruled closely with fine lines to give a diffraction spectrum. [L.L. *grāta*, a grate — L. *crātis*, a hurdle; see **crate**.]

grate[2] *grāt, v.t.* to rub hard or wear away with anything rough: to irritate or jar on, or fret into anger or sorrow (*arch.*): to grind (the teeth): to emit or utter jarringly. — *v.i.* to make a harsh sound: to jar, rasp (on, against): to fret, irritate (usually with *on, upon*). — *n.* **grāt'er** an

instrument with a rough surface for rubbing down to small particles. — *adj.* **grāt'ing** rubbing harshly: harsh: irritating. — *adv.* **grāt'ingly.** [O.Fr. *grater*, through L.L., from O.H.G. *chrazzōn* (Ger. *kratzen*), to scratch, akin to Sw. *kratta*.]

grateful *grāt'f(ōō)l, adj.* causing pleasure: acceptable: thankful: having a due sense of benefits: expressing gratitude. — *adv.* **grate'fully.** — *ns.* **grate'fulness; gratificā'tion** (*grat-*) a pleasing or indulging: that which gratifies: delight, feeling of satisfaction: a recompense, tip, or bribe (*arch.*); **grat'ifier.** — *v.t.* **grat'ify** to do what is agreeable to: to please: to satisfy: to indulge: — *pr.p.* **grat'ifying;** *pa.t.* and *pa.p.* **grat'ified.** — *adj.* **grat'ifying** — *adv.* **grat'ifyingly.** [O.Fr. *grat* — L. *grātus*, pleasing, thankful.]

graticule, etc. See **grate**[1].

gratillity *grə-til'i-ti,* (*Shak.*) *n.* a small gratuity.

gratin. See **au gratin.**

gratis *grā', grä'tis, adv.* for nothing: without payment or recompense. — **gratis dictum** (*dik'təm, -tōōm*) mere assertion. [L. *grātis,* contr. of *grātiīs,* abl. pl. of *grātia,* favour — *grātus.*]

gratitude *grat'i-tūd, n.* warm and friendly feeling towards a benefactor: thankfulness. [Fr., — L.L. *grātitūdō* — L. *grātus.*]

grattoir *grat-wär,* (*archaeol.*) *n.* a scraper. [Fr.]

gratuity *grə-tū'i-ti, n.* a present: an acknowledgment of service, usu. pecuniary: a tip: a bounty: a payment to a soldier, etc., on discharge. — *adj.* **gratū'itous** done or given for nothing: voluntary: benefiting one party only (*law*): without reason, ground, or proof: uncalled for. — *adv.* **gratū'itously.** [Fr. *gratuité* — L.L. *grātuitās, -ātis* — L. *grātus.*]

gratulate *grat'ū-lāt,* (*arch.*) *v.t.* to congratulate: to welcome: to express joy at. — *adj.* (*Shak.*) gratifying. — *adj.* **grat'ulant** congratulatory. — *n.* **gratulā'tion** congratulation. — *adj.* **grat'ulatory** congratulatory.

graupel *grow'pəl, n.* frozen rain or snowflakes. [Ger. *graupeln,* to sleet.]

gravamen *grəv-ā'men, n.* grievance: the substantial or chief ground of complaint or accusation: a statement of abuses, grievances, etc. in the Church sent by the Lower to the Upper House of Convocation: — *pl.* **gravā'mina.** [L. *gravāmen* — *gravis,* heavy.]

grave[1] *grāv, v.t.* to dig (*obs.*): to engrave on hard substance: to fix deeply (e.g. on the mind): to bury (*obs.*). — *v.i.* to engrave: — *pa.p.* **graved** or **grav'en.** — *n.* a pit dug out, esp. one to bury the dead in: any place of burial: the abode of the dead (*B.*): death, destruction (*fig.*): a deadly place. — *adj.* **grave'less** (*Shak.*). — *ns.* **grāv'er** an engraver: a burin; **grāv'ing.** — *n.pl.* **grave'=clothes** the clothes in which the dead are buried. — **grave'-digger; grave'-maker** (*Shak.*) a grave-digger; **grave'stone** a stone placed as a memorial at a grave; **grave'-wax** (*arch.*) adipocere; **grave'yard** a burial-ground. — **with one foot in the grave** on the brink of death. [O.E. *grafan,* to dig, *græf,* a cave, grave, trench; Du. *graven,* Ger. *graben.*]

grave[2] *grāv, v.t.* to clean (by burning, etc.) and pay with tar (a wooden ship's bottom). — **grav'ing-dock** a dry-dock for cleaning and repair of ships. [Perh. Fr. *grave, grève,* beach.]

grave[3] *grāv, adj.* of importance: serious: not gay or showy: sedate: solemn: weighty: calling for anxiety: low in pitch. — *n.* (also *gräv*) grave accent. — *adv.* **grave'ly.** — *n.* **grave'ness.** — **grave accent** (*U.K. gräv*) a mark (`) originally indicating a pitch falling somewhat, or failing to rise, now used for various purposes. [Fr., — L. *gravis.*]

grave[4] *grāv, n.* a count, prefect, a person holding office (now only in compounds, as *landgrave, margrave, burgrave*). [Du. *graaf,* Ger. *Graf.*]

gravel *grav'l, n.* an assemblage of small rounded stones: small collections of gravelly matter in the kidneys or bladder. — *v.t.* to cover with gravel: to run aground on gravel (*obs.*): to puzzle, perplex: to irritate (*coll.*): — *pr.p.* **grav'elling;** *pa.t.* and *pa.p.* **grav'elled.** — *adj.*

grav'elly of, full, or like, gravel: (of sound) harsh. — *adjs.* **grav'el-blind'** (*Shak.* **high'-grav'el-blind'**) after Shakespeare, punningly, in a state somewhere between sand-blind and stone-blind. — **grav'el-pit** a pit from which gravel is dug. — *adj.* **grav'el-voiced'** harsh-voiced. — **grav'el-walk'** a footpath covered with gravel. [O.Fr. *gravele* (Fr. *gravier*); prob. Celt., as in Bret. *grouan*, sand, W. *gro*, pebbles.]

graven *grāv'n, pa.p.* of **grave**[1]. — **graven image** an idol: a solemn person.

graveolent *grav-ē'ō-lənt,* or *grav'i-, adj.* rank-smelling. [L. *graveolēns, -entis* — *gravis*, heavy, *olēns*, pr.p. of *olēre*, to smell.]

Graves *gräv, n.* a white, or red, table wine from the Graves district in the Gironde department of France.

graves. Same as **greaves**.

Graves' disease *grāvz' di-zēz',* exophthalmic goitre. [After R. J. *Graves*, 19th.-cent. Irish physician.]

Gravettian *grə-vet'i-ən, adj.* (*archaeol.*) relating to the Upper Palaeolithic culture of La *Gravette* in S.W. France, characterised by the narrow pointed blades with blunted back edges that were found there.

gravid *grav'id, adj.* pregnant. — *n.* **gravid'ity.** [L. *gravidus* — *gravis*, heavy.]

gravimeter *grə-vim'i-tər, n.* an instrument for measuring variations in gravity at points on the earth's surface. — *adjs.* **gravimetric** (*grav-i-met'rik*), **-al** pertaining to measurement by weight. — *n.* **gravim'etry.** — **gravimetric(al) analysis** the chemical analysis of materials by the separation of the constituents and their estimation by weight. [L. *gravis*, heavy, Gr. *metron*, measure.]

gravity *grav'i-ti, n.* weightiness: gravitational attraction or acceleration: graveness: lowness of pitch. — *n.* **grav'itas** (*-äs*) seriousness: weight, importance. — *v.i.* **grav'itāte** to be acted on by gravity: to tend towards the earth or other body: to be attracted, or move, by force of gravitation: to sink or settle down: to be strongly attracted or move (towards; *fig.*). — *n.* **gravitā'tion** act of gravitating: the force of attraction between bodies, this being directly proportional to the product of the masses and inversely to the square of the distances (the Newtonian *constant of gravitation* (symbol *G*) is 6.67×10^{-11} MKS units). — *adj.* **gravitā'tional.** — *adv.* **gravitā'tionally.** — *adj.* **grav'itātive.** — *ns.* **gravitom'eter** an instrument for measuring specific gravities; **grav'iton** a hypothetical quantum of gravitational field energy. — **gravitational field** that region of space in which appreciable gravitational force exists; **gravity cell** an electric cell having electrolytes of different specific gravities, so that they form separate layers; **gravity platform** a drilling platform, used in the oil industry, made from concrete and steel, the weight of which enables it to hold its position on the seabed; **gravity wave** liquid surface waves controlled by gravity and not by surface tension: hypothetical progressive energy-carrying waves whose existence was postulated by Einstein in 1916. — **acceleration due to gravity** (symbol *g*) the acceleration of a body falling freely under the action of gravity in a vacuum, about 32·174 feet or 9·8 metres per second per second; **specific gravity** see **specify**. [L. *gravitās, -ātis* — *gravis*, heavy.]

gravure *grə-vūr', n.* any process of making an intaglio printing plate, including photogravure: the plate, or an impression from it. [Fr., engraving.]

gravy *grāv'i, n.* the juices from meat while cooking: money, profit, or pleasure, unexpected or in excess of what one might expect (*coll.*): graft (*slang*). — **grav'y-boat** a vessel for gravy; **grav'y-soup** soup like gravy, made from fresh meat; **gravy train** (*coll.*) a position in which one can have excessive profits or advantages in contrast to other people. [Perh. *gravé*, a copyist's mistake for O.Fr. *grané* — *grain*, a cookery ingredient.]

gray[1]. Same as **grey**. — *n.* **gray'ling** a silvery-grey fish (*Thymallus*) of the salmon family, with a smaller mouth and teeth, and larger scales: a grey butterfly of

the Satyridae. — **gray'fly** (*Milt.*) an unknown insect.

gray[2] *grā, n.* the SI unit of absorbed dose of ionising radiation, equivalent to one joule per kilogram (or 100 rads); symbol Gy. [Louis H. *Gray* (1905–65), British radiobiologist.]

grayle. See **grail**[1,3].

graywacke. Same as **greywacke**.

graze[1] *grāz, v.t.* to eat or feed on (growing grass or pasture): to feed or supply with grass. — *v.i.* to eat grass: to supply grass. — *ns.* **grāz'er** an animal that grazes; **grāz'ier** one who pastures cattle and rears them for the market; **grāz'ing** the act of feeding on grass: the feeding or raising of cattle. [O.E. *grasian* — *græs*, grass.]

graze[2] *grāz, v.t.* to pass lightly along the surface of. — *n.* a passing touch or scratch. [Ety. dub.; perhaps only a special use of **graze** above; perh. from *rase* (Fr. *raser*), the *g* due to the analogy of *grate*.]

grazioso *grä-tsē-ō'sō,* (*mus.*) *adj.* and *adv.* graceful, gracefully. [It.]

grease *grēs, n.* a soft thick animal fat: oily matter of any kind: condition of fatness: an inflammation in the heels of a horse, marked by swelling, etc. — *v.t.* (in U.K. usu. pron. *grēz*) to smear with grease: to lubricate: to bribe (*slang*): to facilitate. — *n.* **greaser** (*grēz'ər,* or *grēs'ər*) one who greases: a ship's engineer: a Mexican or a Sp. American (*U.S.; offensive*). — *adv.* **greas'ily.** — *n.* **greas'iness.** — *adj.* **greas'y** (in U.K. usu. *grēz'i*) of or like grease or oil: smeared with grease: having a slippery coating: fatty: oily: obscene: unctuous or ingratiating. — **grease cup** a lubricating device which stores grease and feeds it into a bearing; **grease'-gun** a lubricating pump. — *n. sing.* **grease'-heels** grease in horses. — **grease'-mon'key** (*slang*) a mechanic; **grease paint** a tallowy composition used by actors in making up. — *adj.* **grease'-proof** resistant or impermeable to grease. — **grease'wood** a name for various oily American shrubs of the goosefoot family; **greasy spoon** (*slang*) a cheap, shabby, often grubby cafe. — **grease someone's palm** see **palm**[1]; **grease the wheels** (*fig.*) to make things go smoothly; **hart of grease** a fat hart. [O.Fr. *gresse*, fatness, *gras*, fat — L. *crassus*.]

great *grāt, adj.* big: large: of a high degree of magnitude of any kind: capital (of letters; *arch.*): elevated in power, rank, station, etc.: pre-eminent in genius: highly gifted: chief: sublime: weighty: outstanding: pregnant, teeming (*arch.*): swelling with emotion: much addicted or given to, or excelling in the thing in question: favourite: habitual: in high favour or intimacy: in a high degree: on a large scale: excellent (*coll.,* often *ironic*): in composition indicating one degree more remote in the direct line of descent (as **great'-grand'-father, great'-grand'son** and similarly **great'-great=grandfather** and so indefinitely). — *n.* bulk, mass (*obs.*): whole (*obs.*): wholesale (*obs.*): one who has achieved renown: used collectively for those who have achieved renown. — *adv.* (*coll.*) very well. — *v.t.* **great'en** to make great or greater. — *v.i.* to become great. — *adj.* **great'er** compar. of great: (with geographical names) in an extended sense (as *Greater London*). — *adv.* **great'ly.** — *n.* **great'ness.** — *n.pl.* **Greats** the final honour School of Literae Humaniores (*Classical Greats*) or of Modern Philosophy (*Modern Greats*) at Oxford. — **great ape** any of the larger anthropoid apes — the chimpanzee, gibbon, gorilla, orang-utan; **great auk** a large, flightless auk once common in North Atlantic areas, now extinct; **great'-aunt** a grandparent's sister. — *adj.* **great'-bellied** (*Shak.*) pregnant. — **Great Britain** England, Scotland and Wales; **great circle** see **circle**; **great'coat** an overcoat; **Great Dane** a large close-haired dog; **great'-grand'child** the child of a grandchild; **great'-grand'father, -grand'mother** the father (mother) of a grandparent; **great gross** a unit of quantity equal to 12 gross. — *adj.* **great'-hearted** having a great or noble heart: high-spirited: magnanimous. — **great'-heart'edness; great'-nephew, -niece** a brother's or sister's grandson, granddaughter; **great**

primer see **primer; great schism** great Eastern schism, Western schism — see **schism; great Scot(t)** exclamation of surprise; **Great Sea** the Mediterranean; **great tit** a kind of tit (see **tit³**), *Parus major*, with yellow, black and white markings; **great toe** see **toe; great⸗uncle** a grandparent's brother: **Great War** term applied esp. to war of 1914–18; **great year** (*astron.*) the length of time (about 25 800 years) it takes for the equinoctial points to make a complete revolution. — **Great White Way** a nickname for Broadway in New York: any brightly-lit street with theatres, etc.; **the greatest** (*slang*) a wonderful, marvellous person or thing; **the great unwashed** a contemptuous term for the populace. [O.E. *great*; Du. *groot*, Ger. *gross*.]

greave¹ *grēv*, (*obs.*) *n.* a thicket.   [O.E. *græfa, græfe*; cf. **grove.**]

greave². Same as **grieve**¹,².

greave³ *grēv, n.* armour for the leg below the knee. [O.Fr. *greve*, shin, greave.]

greaves *grēvz*, **graves** *grāvz, ns.pl.* dregs of melted tallow. [L.G. *groven*; cf. Ger. *Griebe*, greaves; O.E. *grēofa*, pot.]

grebe *grēb, n.* a short-winged almost tailless freshwater diving bird (*Podiceps*).   [Fr. *grèbe*.]

grece. See **gree².**

Grecian *grēsh'(y)ən, adj.* Greek. — *n.* a Greek: one well versed in the Greek language and literature: a hellenising Jew (*B.*): a senior boy of Christ's Hospital: an Irish labourer newly in England (*old slang*). — **Grecian bend** a mode of walking with a slight bend forward, at one time affected by a few women who fondly thought to imitate the pose of a figure such as the Venus of Milo; **Grecian nose** a straight nose which forms a continuous line with the forehead.   [L. *Graecia*, Greece — Gr. *Graikos*, Greek.]

grecian. See **gree².**

Grecise, -ize, Grecism, Greco-Roman. See **Graecise, -ize,** etc.

grecque *grek, n.* a Greek fret.   [Fr. (*fem.*), Greek.]

gree¹ *grē, n.* (*Spens.*) good-will, favour. — *v.i.* (*Shak., Scot.*) to agree.   [O.Fr. *gré* — L. *grātus*, pleasing; the vb. may be from O.Fr. *gréer* or aphetic from **agree.**]

gree² *grē, n.* degree, rank (*obs.*): a step (*obs.*): superiority (*dial.*): victory (*dial.*): prize (*dial.*). — *n.* **grece** (*grēs, obs.* or *dial.*; from the Fr. pl.) a flight of steps: a step: a degree. — Also spelt **grees, grese, greece, greese, grice, griece, gris, grise, grize** (*grees'ing, gress'ing* and even **grē'cian,** are obs. forms). — *adj.* **grieced** (*her.*) having steps.   [O.Fr. *gré* — L. *gradus*; see **grade.**]

greedy *grēd'i, adj.* having a voracious appetite: inordinately desirous of increasing one's own share: covetous: eagerly desirous. — *n.* **greed** an eager desire or longing: covetousness. — *adv.* **greed'ily.** — *n.* **greed'iness.** — **greedy guts** (*slang*) a glutton.   [O.E. *grædig*; Du. *gretig.*]

greegree. See **grisgris.**

Greek *grēk, adj.* of Greece, its people, or its language. — *n.* a native or citizen of Greece, of a Greek state, or of a colony elsewhere of a Greek state: the language of Greece: a member of the Greek Church: a hellenising Jew (*B.*): a cunning rogue, a merry fellow (*arch.*): an Irishman (*old slang*): any language of which one is ignorant, jargon, anything unintelligible. — *n.* **Greek'dom** the Greek world: a Greek community. — *adjs.* **Greek'ish; Greek'less** without knowledge of Greek. — *n.* **Greek'ling** a contemptible Greek. — **Greek architecture** that developed in ancient Greece (Corinthian, Doric, Ionic); **Greek Church** the church that follows the ancient rite of the East and accepts the first seven councils, rejecting papal supremacy — (*Greek*) **Orthodox** or *Eastern* Church; **Greek cross** an upright cross with arms of equal length; **Greek fire** a composition that took fire when wetted, used in war, long a secret of the Byzantine Greeks; **Greek gift** a treacherous gift (from Virgil's *Aeneid*, ii, 49); **Greek key (pattern)** a fret pattern; **Greek nose** a Grecian nose. — **Greek(-)letter society** in U.S. universities, a social, professional or

honorary fraternity or sorority, using a combination of Greek letters as a title, as Phi Beta Kappa; **the Greek calends** never, the Greeks having no calends.   [O.E. *Grēcas, Crēcas,* Greeks, or L. *Graecus* — Gr. *Graikos,* Greek.]

green¹ *grēn, adj.* of the colour usual in leaves, between blue and yellow in the spectrum: growing: vigorous: hale: new: young: unripe: fresh: undried: raw: incompletely prepared: immature: unseasoned: inexperienced: jealous: easily imposed on: relating to currency values expressing EEC farm prices, e.g. *green pound, green franc, green rate,* etc.: concerned with care of the environment esp. as a political issue. — *n.* the colour of green things: this colour as a symbol of the Irish republic: a grassy plot, esp. that common to a village or town, or for bowling, or bleaching, drying of clothes: a golf-course: the prepared ground (*putting-green*) round a golf-hole: a member of the Green Party, an environmentalist: a green pigment: (*pl.*) fresh leaves: (*pl.*) green vegetables for food, esp. of the cabbage kind: (*pl.*) money (*slang*): (*pl.*) sexual intercourse (*slang*): (*pl.*) low-grade marijuana (*slang*): (*pl.* cap.) a political party at Constantinople, under Justinian, opposed to the Blues. — *v.t.* and *v.i.* to make or become green: to introduce trees and parks into urban areas. — *ns.* **green'ery** green plants or boughs: verdure; **green'ing** a becoming or making green: a kind of apple green when ripe. — *adj.* **green'ish.** — *ns.* **green'ishness; green'let** any bird of the American family Vireonidae. — *adv.* **green'ly** immaturely, unskilfully. — *ns.* **green'ness; greenth** greenness, verdure. — *adj.* **green'y.** — **green algae** or **seaweeds** the Chlorophyceae; **green'back** an American note (often printed in green on the back), first issued in 1862: a plant condition in which fruits remain green around the stalk; **green'-bag** a lawyer's bag: a lawyer (*old slang*); **green ban** (*Austr.*) the refusal of trade unions to work on environmentally and socially objectionable projects; **green belt** a strip of open land surrounding a town; **Green Beret** (*coll.*) a British or American commando; **green'-bone** a garfish: a viviparous blenny; **green'bottle** a metallic green fly (*Lucilia*); **green card** motorists' international insurance document: a card issued by the Manpower Services Commission certifying that the holder is registered disabled under the terms of the Disabled Persons (Employment) Act 1944, and is thus entitled to certain assistance in gaining and carrying out paid work; **green'cloth** a gaming-table: a department of the royal household chiefly concerned with the commissariat — from the green cloth on the table round which its officials sat; **green corn** same as **sweet-corn; green crop** a crop of green vegetables, as grasses, turnips, etc.; **green dragon** a European aroid (*Dracunculus*): dragon-root (*U.S.*); **green'-drake** a mayfly; **green earth** any green earthy mineral used as a pigment, usu. a silicate of iron. — *adjs.* **green'ery-yall'ery** in or favouring greens and yellows, hence decadently aesthetic; **green'-eyed** having green eyes: jealous (**the green-eyed monster** jealousy). — **greenfield site** a site, separate from existing developments, which is to be developed for the first time; **green'finch, green linnet** a finch of a green colour, with some grey; **green fingers** (or **thumb**) a knack of making plants grow well; **green flash** or **ray** a flash of green light sometimes seen at the moment of sunrise or sunset; **green'fly** a plant-louse or aphis; **green gland** one of a pair of glands on the head of certain crustaceans; **Green Goddess** a type of fire-engine used in civil emergencies, etc.; **green goose** a young goose: a simpleton; **green gown** (*arch.*) a roll on the grass (sometimes but not always understood to imply loss of virginity); **green'grocer** a dealer in fresh vegetables: a large green cicada (*Austr.*); **green'hand** an inferior sailor; **green'heart** bebeeru (*Nectandra rodiei*), a S. American tree of the laurel family with very hard wood; **green'horn** a raw, inexperienced youth; **green'house** a glasshouse for plants, esp. one with little or no artificial heating: the cockpit of an

fāte; fär; hûr; mīne; mōte; för; mūte; mōōn; fŏŏt; dhen (then); *el'ə-mənt* (element)

aircraft — from the transparent sides (*airmen's slang*); **greenhouse effect** the progressive warming-up of the earth's surface due to the blanketing effect of man-made carbon dioxide in the atmosphere; **Green** or **Emerald Isle** Ireland; **green'-keeper** one who has the care of a golf-course or bowling-green; **green leek** any of various Australian parrots with green plumage; **green light** a traffic signal indicating that vehicles may advance: permission to go ahead; **green'mail** a form of business blackmail whereby a company buys a stategically significant block of shares in another company, sufficient to threaten takeover and thus to force the parent company to buy back the shares at a premium; **green manuring** growing one crop (**green manure**) and digging it under to fertilise its successor; **green monkcy** a West African long-tailed monkey, *Cercopithecus sabaeus* (**green monkey disease** a sometimes fatal virus disease with fever and haemorrhaging, orig. identified among technicians handling green monkeys in Marburg, Germany (also *Marburg disease*)); **green paper** a statement of proposed government policy, intended as a basis for parliamentary discussion; **Green Party** a party principally concerned with resource conservation and the decentralisation of political and economic power; **green plover** the lapwing; **green pound** the agreed value of the pound used to express EEC farm prices in sterling; **green revolution** agricultural advances in developing countries; **green road, way** a grassy country track used by walkers; **green'room** the retiring-room of actors in a theatre, which originally had the walls coloured green; **green'sand** a sandstone containing much glauconite: (*cap.*) two divisions (Lower and Upper) of the Cretaceous system, separated by the Gault; **green'shank** a large sandpiper with long, somewhat greenish legs; **green sickness** chlorosis; **green snake** a harmless colubrine snake common in southern U.S.; **greenstick fracture** see **fract**; **green'stone** nephrite: a vague name for any compost basic or intermediate igneous rock; **green'stuff** green vegetables, esp. of the cabbage kind; **green'sward** sward or turf green with grass; **green tea** see **tea**; **green turtle** a tropical and suh-tropical sea turtle (*Chelonia mydas*) with a greenish shell (see **turtle**[2]); **green vitriol** ferrous sulphate; **green'weed** a name given to certain half-shrubby species of Genista; **green'wood** a leafy wood or forest. — Also *adj.* — **green woodpecker** a kind of European woodpecker with green and red plumage. — **Green Cross Code** a code of road-safety rules for children issued in 1971; **something green in one's eye** a sign that one is gullible. [O.E. *grēne*; Ger. *grün*, Du. *groen*, green; O.N. *grænn*.]

green[2], **grein** *grēn*, (*Scot.*) *v.i.* to long, yearn. [Cf. O.N. *girna*.]

greengage *grēn'gāj*, *n.* a green and very sweet variety of plum. [Said to be named from Sir W. *Gage* of Hengrave Hall, near Bury St Edmunds, before 1725.]

Greenland seal *grēn'lənd sēl*, the harp-seal, found in arctic and north Atlantic waters. — **Greenland whale** the arctic right-whale, *Balaena mysticetus*. [*Greenland*, in the Arctic Ocean.]

greenockite *grēn'ək-īt*, *n.* a rare mineral, cadmium sulphide, discovered by Lord *Greenock* (1783–1859).

Greenwich (Mean) Time *grin'ij, gren', -ich* (*mēn*) *tīm* mean solar time for the meridian of *Greenwich*.

grees(e), **greesing**. See **gree**[2].

greet[1] *grēt*, *v.t.* to accost with salutation or kind wishes: to send kind wishes to: to congratulate (*obs.*): to offer congratulations on (*Spens.*): to meet, receive: to become evident to. — *v.i.* (*obs.*) to meet and salute: — *pr.p.* **greet'ing**; *pa.t.* and *pa.p.* **greet'ed.** — *n.* **greet'ing** expression of kindness or joy: salutation. [O.E. *grētan*, to greet, to meet; Du. *groeten*, Ger. *grüssen*, to salute.]

greet[2] *grēt*, (*Scot.*; *Spens.* **greete**) *v.i.* to weep (*pa.t.*, *Scot.*, **grat**; *pa.p.*, *Scot.*, **grutt'en**). — *n.* weeping: a spell of weeping. — **greeting meeting** the last meeting of a

town-council before an election. [O.E. (Anglian) *grētan*; Goth. *grētan*.]

greffier *gref'yā*, *n.* a registrar: a notary. [Fr.]

gregale *grā-gä'lä*, *n.* a north-east wind in the Mediterranean. [It., — L. *graecus*, Greek.]

gregarious *gri-gā'ri-əs*, *adj.* associating in flocks and herds: growing together but not matted (*bot.*): fond of the company of others (*fig.*). — *adj.* **gregā'rian** of the common rank. — *ns.* **gregā'rianism** gregariousness; **Gregarina** (*greg-ə-rī'nə*) a genus of Protozoa, typical of the **Gregarinida** (*-rin'*), a group of parasites; **greg'a-rine** (*-rīn, -rin*) a member of the Gregarinida. — *adv.* **gregā'riously.** — *n.* **gregā'riousness.** [L. *gregārius—grex, gregis*, a flock.]

gregatim *gri-gā'tim*, *gre-gä'tim*, (L.) *adv.* in flocks.

grège. See **greige**.

grego *grā'gō, grē'gō*, *n.* a Levantine hooded jacket or cloak: an overcoat: — *pl.* **gre'gos.** [Port. *grego* or other deriv. of L. *graecus*, Greek.]

Gregorian *gri-gō'ri-ən, -gö'*, *adj.* belonging to or established by *Gregory* — as the Gregorian chant or tones, introduced by Pope Gregory I (6th cent.), the calendar, reformed by Gregory XIII (1582), the reflecting telescope of James Gregory (1638–75), a wig attributed to a barber Gregory. — *n.* follower of any Gregory: member of an 18th-century English brotherhood. — *n.* **gregory** (*greg'ər-i*; *coll.*), **Gregory's mixture** or **powder** a laxative powder of rhubarb, magnesia and ginger, compounded by Dr James *Gregory* (1753–1821), great-grandson of aforementioned James.

greige *grāzh*, *adj.* of cloth, undyed: of a greyish-beige colour. — Also **grège.** [Fr. (*soie*) *grège*, raw silk.]

grein. See **green**[2].

greisen *grī'zən*, *n.* a rock composed of quartz and mica, often with topaz, formed from granite by fluorine exhalations. — *n.* **greisenīsā'tion, -z-.** — *v.t.* **greis'enise, -ize.** [Ger.]

greisly (*Spens.*, *Milt.*). Same as **grisly**.

gremial *grē'mi-əl*, *adj.* pertaining to the lap or bosom: intimate: resident: in full membership. — *n.* a full or resident member: a cloth laid on a bishop's knees to keep his vestments clean from oil at ordinations. [L. *gremium*, the lap.]

gremlin *grem'lin*, *n.* orig. a goblin accused of vexing airmen, causing mechanical trouble to aircraft: an imaginary mischievous agency. [Origin uncertain.]

gren *gren*, (*Spens.*) *v.i.* Same as **grin**[1].

grenade *gri-nād'*, *n.* a small bomb thrown by the hand or shot from a rifle: a glass projectile containing chemicals for putting out fires, testing drains, dispensing poison-gas or tear-gas, etc. — *ns.* **grenadier** (*gren-ə-dēr'*) orig. a soldier who threw grenades: then, a member of the first company of every battalion of foot: now used as the title (Grenadier Guards) of part of the Guards Division of infantry: any of various African weaver-birds with red and black plumage: a deep-sea fish of the *Macrouridae* family; **grenadine** (*-dēn'*) a pomegranate (or other) syrup: slices of veal or poultry fillets. [Fr., — Sp. *granada*, pomegranate — L. *grānātus*, full of seeds (*grāna*).]

grenadilla. Same as **granadilla**.

grenadine[1]. See under **grenade**.

grenadine[2] *gren'ə-dēn*, *n.* a thin silk or mixed fabric. [Fr., perh. *Granada*.]

Grenzgänger *grents'geng-ər*, (Ger.) *n.* one who crosses a national or political border, esp. from the communist countries to the West: — *pl.* **Grenz'gänger.**

grese. See **gree**[2].

Gresham's law. See **law**[1].

gressing. See **gree**.

gressorial *gres-ō', -ö'ri-əl*, (*zool.*) *adj.* adapted for walking. — Also **gresso'rious.** [L. *gressus*, pa.p. of *gradī*, to walk.]

greve. A variant of **greave**[1,3].

grew[1] *grōō*, *pa.t.* of **grow**.

grew[2]. See under **gruesome**.

grew[3] *grōō*, **grewhound** *grōō'hownd*, (*dial.*) *ns.* a grey-

hound. [By confusion with obs. *Grew*, Greek.]
grex venalium *greks ven-āl'iəm, wen-āl'i-ōōm,* (L.) the herd of hirelings.
grey, gray *grā, adj.* of a mixture of black and white with little or no hue: dull: dismal: neutral: anonymous: intermediate in character, condition, etc.: grey-haired, old, mature. — *n.* a grey colour: a grey or greyish animal, esp. a horse: a badger (*obs.*): a middle-aged or old person (*slang*). — *v.t.* to make grey or dull. — *v.i.* to become grey or dull. — *adj.* **grey'ish** somewhat grey. — *adv.* **grey'ly.** — *n.* **grey'ness.** — **grey area** an area relatively high in unemployment but not classed as a development area (q.v.): an area between two extremes, having (mingled) characteristics of both of them: a situation in which there are no clear-cut distinctions; **grey'beard** one whose beard is grey: an old man: a stoneware jar for liquor, a bellarmine; **grey'-coat** one who wears a grey coat, esp. a pupil in certain schools: a Confederate soldier. — Also *adj.* — *adj.* **grey'-coat'ed.** — **grey eminence** see **eminence grise.** — *adj.* **grey'-eycd.** — **grey'-fish** a dogfish: a young coalfish; **Grey Friar** (also without *caps.*) a Franciscan; **grey'-goose** the common wild goose (*Anser anser*). — *adjs.* **grey'-haired, grey'-headed.** — **grey'hen** the female of the blackcock; **grey'-lag** the grey-goose (perhaps from its lateness in migrating) — also **grey-lag goose; grey mare** see **mare; grey market** the unofficial and often secret, but not necessarily illegal, selling of goods, etc. alongside or in addition to an official or open market; **grey matter** the ashen-grey active part of the brain and spinal cord; **grey'-out** a mild or less severe blackout; **grey owl** the tawny owl; **grey parrot** a red-tailed grey African parrot; **grey squirrel** a N. American squirrel naturalised in Britain; **grey-weth'er** a block of sandstone or quartzite, a relic of denudation, looking at a distance like a grazing sheep; **grey wolf** the N. American timber wolf. — **grey-goose quill, shaft, wing** an arrow; **the Greys** the Scots Greys (see **Scots**). [O.E. *græg*; cf. Ger. *grau*.]
greyhound *grā'hownd, n.* a tall and slender dog with great speed and keen sight. [O.E. *grīghund* (cf. O.N. *greyhundr* — *grey*, bitch), *hund*, dog.]
greywacke *grā-wak'i, n.* an indurated sedimentary rock composed of grains (round or angular) and splinters of quartz, feldspar, slate, etc., in a hard matrix. — **greywack'e-slate'** a fine-grained fissile greywacke. [Ger. *Grauwacke*, party translated, partly adopted.]
gribble *grib'l, n.* a small marine isopod (genus *Limnoria*) that bores into timber under water. [Perh. — *grub*.]
grice[1] *grīs,* (*dial.*) *n.* a little pig: — *pl.* **grices, grice.** — Also **gryce.** [O.N. *grīss*.]
grice[2]. See **gree**[2].
gricer *grī'sər, n.* a train-spotter or railway enthusiast. — **grī'cing.** [Origin uncertain.]
grid. See **gridiron.**
griddle *grid'l, n.* a flat iron plate for baking cakes. — Also (*Scot.*) **gird'le** (*gûr'dl, gir'dl*). — **griddle car** a coach on a train where simple cooked meals can be obtained. [Anglo-Fr. *gridil*, from a dim. of L. *crātis*, a hurdle.]
gride, gryde *grīd, v.t.* and *v.i.* to pierce: to cut, esp. with a grating sound: to graze: to grate. — *n.* a harsh grating sound. [**gird**.]
gridelin *grid'ə-lin, n.* and *adj.* violet-grey. [Fr. *gris de lin*, grey of flax.]
gridiron *grid'ī-ərn, n.* a frame of iron bars for broiling over a fire: a frame to support a ship during repairs: a network: a football field (*U.S.*). — *v.t.* to cover with parallel bars or lines. — *n.* **grid** (back formation) a grating: a gridiron: a framework: a network: a network of power transmission lines: a perforated screen or spiral of wire between the filament and the plate of a thermionic valve: a grated luggage-carrier on a motorcar: a network of lines for finding places on a map, or for other purpose: framework above a theatre stage from which scenery and lights may be suspended. — **grid'lock** (*U.S.*) a traffic jam. [M.E. *gredire*, a grid-

dle; from the same source as **griddle,** but the term. *-ire* became confused with M.E. *ire*, iron.]
griece, grieced. See **gree**[2].
grief *grēf, n.* sorrow: distress: great mourning: affliction: bodily pain (*Shak.*): cause of sorrow. — *adjs.* **grief'ful** full of grief; **grief'less.** — *adjs.* **grief'-shot** pierced with grief (*Shak.*); **grief'-stricken** crushed with sorrow. — **come to grief** to meet with reverse, disaster, mishap. [O.Fr., — L. *gravis*, heavy.]
griesie, griesy, griesly. Spenserian forms of **grisy** (see under **gris, grise**), **grisly.**
grieve[1] *grēv, v.t.* to cause grief or pain of mind to: to make sorrowful: to vex: to inflict bodily pain on or do bodily harm to (*obs.*): to show grief for (*poet.*). — *v.i.* to feel grief: to mourn. — *ns.* **griev'ance** cause or source of grief: ground of complaint: condition felt to be oppressive or wrongful: distress: burden: hardship: injury (*obs.*): grief; **griev'er.** — *adv.* **griev'ingly.** — *adj.* **griev'ous** causing grief: burdensome: painful: severe: hurtful. — *adv.* **griev'ously.** — *n.* **griev'ousness.** [O.Fr. *grever* — L. *gravāre* — *gravis*, heavy.]
grieve[2] *grēv, n.* a farm overseer (*Scot.*): a governor or sheriff (*hist.*). [O.Northumbrian *græfa* (W.S. *gerēfa*); cf. **reeve**.]
griff, griffe *grif, n.* a claw: a clawlike architectural ornament: a mulatto, or person of mixed Negro and mulatto or Negro and American Indian blood: a steep narrow valley (*dial.*). [Fr. *griffe*.]
griffin, griffon, gryfon, gryphon *grif'in, -ən, ns.* an imaginary animal with lion's body and eagle's beak and wings: a newcomer in the East, a novice: a pony never before entered for a race: a watchful guardian, esp. over a young woman, a duenna (*obs.*): a tip, a signal or warning. — *adj.* **griff'inish.** — *n.* **griff'inism.** — **griffon vulture** a European vulture, *Gyps fulvus.* [Fr. *griffon* — L. *grȳphus* — Gr. *gryps*, a bird, probably the *lämmergeier*, a griffin — *grȳpos*, hook-nosed.]
griffon *grif'ən, n.* a dog like a coarse-haired terrier. — **Brussels griffon** a toy dog with a rather snub nose. [Prob. from **griffin.**]
grift *grift,* (*U.S.*) *v.i.* to swindle. — Also *n.* — *n.* **grif'ter** a con man, swindler. [Perh. from **graft**[2].]
grig *grig, n.* a cricket: a grasshopper: a small, lively eel, the sand-eel: a small, lively person. — *v.t.* to tease, irritate. — *v.i.* to fish for grigs (eels). — **merry as a grig** very merry and lively. [Origin obscure.]
gri(-)gri. See **grisgris.**
grike *grīk, n.* a fissure in limestone rock formed or widened by the dissolvent effect of rain: a deep valley, ravine. — Also **gryke.** [O.N. *kriki*, a crack.]
grill[1] *gril, v.t.* to broil on a gridiron, etc. by radiant heat: to scallop: to torment: to cross-examine harassingly. — *v.i.* to undergo grilling. — *n.* a grating: a gridiron: the part of a cooker on which meat, etc. is grilled: a grill-room: a grilled dish: an act of grilling. — *ns.* **grillade'** anything grilled; **grill'age** a foundation of crossbeams on marshy grounds. — *adj.* **grilled** embossed with small rectangular indentations as those on certain late 19th-century postage stamps of the United States and Peru. — *n.* **grill'ing.** — **grill'-room** part of a restaurant where beefsteaks, etc., are served grilled to order. — **mixed grill** a dish of several grilled meats usu. with mushrooms, tomatoes, etc. [Fr. *griller* — *gril*, a gridiron, from a dim. of L. *crātis*, a grate.]
grill[2], **grille** *gril, n.* a lattice or grating, or screen, or openwork of metal, generally used to enclose or protect a window, shrine, etc.: a grating in a convent or jail door, etc.: in real tennis, a square opening in the corner of an end wall of the court. [Fr.; see **grill**[1].]
grilse *grils, n.* a young salmon on its first return from salt water. [Origin unknown.]
grim *grim, adj.* forbidding: ferocious: ghastly: sullen: repellent: stern: unyielding: unpleasant. — *adv.* **grim'ly.** — *n.* **grim'ness.** — *adj.* **grim'looked** (*Shak.*) having a grim or dismal aspect. [O.E. *grim(m)*; Ger. *grimmig* — Grimm, fury, Du. *grimmig*, O.N. *grimmr.*]

grimace *gri-mās'*, *n.* a distortion of the face, in jest, etc.: a smirk. — *v.i.* to make grimaces. [Fr.]

grimalkin *gri-mal'kin, -möl'kin, n.* an old cat: a cat generally. [grey and **Malkin**, a dim. of *Maud*.]

grime *grīm, n.* sooty or coaly dirt: ingrained dirt. — *v.t.* to soil deeply. — *adv.* **grīm'ily.** — *n.* **grīm'iness.** — *adj.* **grīm'y.** [Cf. Flem. *grijm*.]

Grimm's law. See **law¹**.

grimoire *grē-mwär', n.* a magician's book for calling up spirits. [Fr.; cf. **gramary**.]

grin¹ *grin, v.i.* to set the teeth together and withdraw the lips in pain, derision, etc.: to give a broad smile. — *v.t.* to set (the teeth) in a grin (*obs.*): to express by grinning: — *pr.p.* **grinn'ing;** *pa.t.* and *pa.p.* **grinned.** — *n.* act of grinning. — *n.* **grinn'er.** [O.E. *grennian*; O.N. *grenja*, Ger. *greinen*, Du. *grijnen*, to grumble, Scot. **girn**; allied to **groan**.]

grin² *grin, (dial.) n.* a snare or trap. — Also *v.t.* [O.E. *grīn*.]

grind¹ *grind, (Spens.) pa.t.* of **grin¹**.

grind² *grīnd, v.t.* to reduce to powder by friction or crushing: to wear down, sharpen, smooth or roughen by friction: to rub together: to force (in, into; *lit.* and *fig.*): to produce by great effort, or by working a crank (with *out*): to oppress or harass: to work by a crank. — *v.i.* to be moved or rubbed together: to jar or grate: to drudge at any tedious task: to read hard: — *pr.p.* **grīnd'ing;** *pa.t.* **ground** (*grownd*), (*obs.*) **grind'ed;** *pa.p.* **ground,** (*obs.*) **ground'en.** — *n.* the act, sound, or jar of grinding: drudgery: laborious study for a special examination, etc.: a student who gives all his time to study. — *ns.* **grind'er** one who, or that which, grinds: a tooth that grinds food: a coach or crammer of students for examination: a hard-working student; **grind'ery** a place, where knives, etc., are ground: shoemakers' materials; **grind'ing** act or process of the verb to grind: reducing to powder. — *adj.* for grinding: wearing down: very severe: extortionate: (of sound) harsh: giving a harsh sound. — *adj.* (*arch.*) **ground'en** sharpened. — **grind'stone** a circular revolving stone for grinding or sharpening tools; **ground glass** glass obscured by grinding, sandblast, or etching. — **grind the face(s) of** to oppress as by taxation; **grind to a halt** to move more and more slowly until finally coming to a standstill (*lit.* and *fig.*); **keep one's nose to the grindstone** to subject one to severe continuous toil or punishment; **take a grinder** (*Dickens*) to put the left thumb to the nose and to work a visionary coffee-mill round it with the right hand — a gesture of derision. [O.E. *grindan*.]

gringo *gring'gō, n.* in Spanish-speaking America, one whose language is not Spanish: — *pl.* **grin'gos.** [Sp., gibberish, prob. — *Griego*, Greek.]

griot *grē-ō', n.* in parts of Africa, a tribal teller of legends and history, a poet, singer and musician. [Fr., of uncertain origin.]

grip¹ *grip, n.* a small ditch, gutter, or trench, a drain. — *v.t.* to trench. — Also **gripe** (*grīp*). [O.E. *grȳpe*, cf. L.G. *gruppe, grüppe*.]

grip² *grip, n.* a grasp or firm hold, esp. with the hand or mind: strength of grasp: the handle or part by which anything is grasped: a mode of grasping: a particular mode of grasping hands for mutual recognition: a gripsack, travelling bag (orig. *U.S.*): a holding or clutching device, e.g. a clasp for the hair: power: pinch of distress: mastery: power of holding the mind or commanding the emotions: gripe: grippe: a stagehand who moves scenery, etc., or a member of a camera crew responsible for manoeuvring the camera. — *v.t.* to take or maintain fast hold of: to hold fast the attention or interest of: to command the emotions of. — Also *v.i.* — *pr.p.* **gripp'ing;** *pa.t.* and *pa.p.* **gripped** (*gript*). — *n.* **gripp'er** one who, that which, grips: a clutch: a claw. — *adj.* **gripp'le** (*Spens.* **grip'le**) gripping, grasping: greedy. — *n.* a grip. — *adj.* **gripp'y** (*Scot.*) inclining to avarice: having grip. — **grip'sack** (*U.S.*) a bag for travel. — **come, get to grips (with)** to tackle at

close quarters, or (*fig.*) seriously and energetically. [O.E. *gripe*, grasp, *gripa*, handful.]

gripe¹ *grīp, v.t.* to grasp: to seize and hold fast: to squeeze: to afflict: to oppress: to give pain to the bowels of. — *v.i.* to clutch: to keep on complaining (*coll.*). — *n.* fast hold: grasp: forcible retention: a usurer (*slang*): a grumble (*coll.*): lashing for a boat on deck: pain: (esp. in *pl.*) severe spasmodic pain in the intestines. — *n.* **grīp'er.** — *adj.* **grīp'ing** avaricious: of a pain, seizing acutely. — *adv.* **grīp'ingly.** — **gripe'-water, Gripe Water®** a carminative solution given to infants to relieve colic and minor stomach ailments. [O.E. *grīpan* (*grāp, gripen*); O.N. *grīpa*, Ger. *greifen*, Du. *grijpen*.]

gripe², **grype** *grīp, (arch.) n.* a griffin: vulture. — **gripe's egg** a cup like a large egg. [Gr. *gryps*.]

gripe³. Same as **grip¹**.

griple. See **grip**.

grippe *grēp, n.* influenza. [Fr., — *gripper*, to seize.]

gripple. See **grip²**.

Griqua *grēk'wä, n.* one of a people of Griqualand, South Africa: one of a mixed Hottentot and European race (Hottentot prevailing).

gris¹ *gris,* **grise** *grīs, adjs.* (*obs.*) grey. — *ns.* (*arch.*) a grey fur. — *adjs.* **griseous** (*griz', gris'i-əs*) grey: blue-grey or pearl-grey; **grisy** (*Spens.* **griesie, gryesy;** all *grī'zi*) grey (*obs.*). [Fr.]

gris². See **gree²**.

grise³. See **gris¹**.

grisaille *grē-zāl', -zä'ē, n.* a style of painting on walls or ceilings, in greyish tints in imitation of bas-reliefs: a similar style of painting on pottery, enamel, glass: a work in this style. — Also *adj.* [Fr., — *gris*, grey.]

gris-amber *gris'-am'bər, (obs.) n.* ambergris. — *adj.* **gris= amb'er-steam'd'** (*Milt.*) flavoured by steam from melted ambergris.

grise¹ *grīz, (obs.) v.t.* to shudder at: to affright. — *v.i.* to shudder. — *adj.* **grī'sy** (*Spens.* **griesy, grysie**) grim: horrible: grisly. [From the verb of which O.E. *āgrīsan* is a compound; cf. **agrise**.]

grise². See **gree²**.

Griselda *griz-el'də, n.* a woman of excessive meekness and patience, from the heroine of an old tale retold by Boccaccio, Petrarch, and Chaucer.

grisely. See **grisly**.

griseofulvin *griz-i-ō-fōōl'vin, (med.) n.* oral antibiotic used as treatment for fungus infections. [Isolated from the fungus *Penicillium griseofulvin dierckx*; L. *griseus*, grey, *fulvus*, reddish yellow.]

grisette *gri-zet', n.* a gay young working-class French-woman. [Fr. *grisette*, a grey gown, which used to be worn by that class — *gris*, grey.]

grisgris, grigri, greegree (also **gris-gris,** etc.) *grē'grē, n.* African charm, amulet, or spell. [Fr.; prob. of African origin.]

griskin *gris'kin, (dial.) n.* lean from a loin of pork. [**grice¹**.]

grisled *griz'ld.* Same as **grizzled**.

grisly *griz'li, adj.* frightful, ghastly (*Spens.,* *Milt.* **greisly;** *Spens.* **griesly, grisely, grysely, gryesly**). — Also *adv.* (*rare*). — *n.* **gris'liness.** [O.E. *grislic*; cf. **grise**.]

grison *griz'ən, grīz'ən, -on, n.* a large grey S. American weasel: a grey S. American monkey. [Fr., — *gris*, grey.]

grist *grist, n.* corn for grinding, or ground: corn for grinding, or ground, at one time: malt for one brewing: supply, portion, quantity (*U.S.*): a measure of the thickness of rope or yarn: profit (*fig.*). — **grist'-mill** a mill for grinding grain. — **(bring) grist to the mill** (to be) a source of profit. [O.E. *grīst*; cf. **grind²**.]

gristle *gris'l, n.* cartilage. — *n.* **grist'liness.** — *adj.* **grist'ly.** [O.E. *gristle*.]

grisy. See **grise¹, gris¹**.

grit¹ *grit, n.* gravel (*obs.*): small hard particles of sand, stone, etc.: small woody bodies in a pear: a coarse sandstone, often with angular grains: texture of stone: firmness of character, spirit. — *v.t.* and *v.i.* to grind:

to grate: to spread with grit. — *ns.* **gritt′er; gritt′iness.**
— *adj.* **gritt′y** having or containing hard particles: of
the nature of grit: grating: determined, plucky. — **grit**
blasting a process used in preparation for metal spraying which cleans the surface and gives it the roughness
required to retain the sprayed metal particles; **grit′-**
stone. [O.E. *grēot*; Ger. *Griess*, gravel.]
grit² *grit*, a Scottish form of **great**: — *compar.* **gritt′er;**
superl. **gritt′est.**
grith *grith*, **girth** *girth*, (*hist.*) *ns.* sanctuary, asylum. —
grith′-stool a seat in which a fugitive was in sanctuary.
[O.E. *grith*.]
grits *grits*, *n.pl.* coarsely ground grain, esp. oats or in
U.S. hominy: a boiled dish of this. [O.E. *grytta*; cf.
groats.]
grivet *griv′it*, *n.* a north-east African guenon monkey.
[Fr.; origin unknown.]
grize. See **gree²**.
grizzle¹ *griz′l*, *n.* a grey colour. — *adjs.* **grizz′led** grey, or
mixed with grey; **grizz′ly** of a grey colour. — *n.* the
grizzly bear (*Ursus horribilis*) of the Rocky Mountains.
[M.E. *grisel* — Fr. *gris*, grey.]
grizzle² *griz′l*, *v.i.* to grumble: to whimper: to fret. — *n.*
a bout of grizzling. — *n.* **grizz′ler.** [Origin unknown.]
groan *grōn*, *v.i.* to utter a deep rumbling or voiced sound
as in distress or disapprobation: to be afflicted (*fig.*).
— *n.* a deep moan: a grinding rumble. — *n.* **groan′er.**
— *adj.* **groan′ful** (*arch.*; Spens. **grone′full**). — *n.* and
adj. **groan′ing.** — **groaning board** a table weighed down
with very generous supplies of food. [O.E. *grānian*.]
groat *grōt* (formerly *grŏt*), *n.* an English silver coin, worth
fourpence (4d) — after 1662 coined only as Maundy
money — the silver fourpenny-piece, coined 1836–56,
was not officially called a groat: a very small sum,
proverbially. — *n.* **groats′worth.** [O.L.G. *grote*, or
Du. *groot*, lit, great, i.e. thick.]
groats *grōts*, *n.pl.* the grain of oats deprived of the husks.
[O.E. *grotan* (pl.).]
Grobian *grō′bi-ən*, *n.* a boorish rude sloven. — *n.* **Gro′-**
bianism. [Ger. *Grobianus*, a character in German
satire of the 15th and 16th centuries — *grob*, coarse.]
grocer *grōs′ər*, *n.* a dealer in staple foods, general household supplies. — *ns.* **gro′cery** the trade or business of
a grocer: (usu. in *pl.*) articles sold by grocers: **a grocer's**
shop or food and liquor shop (*U.S.*); **groceté′ria** a
self-service grocery store. [Earlier *grosser*, a wholesale dealer; O.Fr. *grossier* — L.L. *grossārius* — *grossus*;
cf. **gross.**]
grockle *grok′l*, (*dial.*) *n.* a tourist. [Origin unknown.]
grog *grog*, *n.* a mixture of spirits and water: (an) alcoholic
drink, esp. beer (*Austr. coll.*): bricks or waste from a
clayworks broken down and added to clay to be used
for brick manufacture. — *v.i.* to drink grog. — *v.t.* to
extract the spirit from the wood of empty spirit-casks
by soaking with hot water. — *ns.* **grogg′ery** (*U.S.*; *old*)
a low public-house; **grogg′iness** state of being groggy.
— *adj.* **grogg′y** affected by grog, partially intoxicated
(*arch.*): dazed, unsteady from illness or exhaustion:
weak and staggering from blows (*boxing*): applied to
a horse that bears wholly on his heels in trotting. —
grog′-blossom a redness of the nose due to drinking;
grog′-shop a dram-shop. [From Old *Grog*, the nickname (apparently from his *grogram* cloak) of Admiral
Vernon, who in 1740 ordered that rum (until 1970
officially issued to sailors) should be mixed with
water.]
grogram *grog′rəm*, *n.* a kind of coarse cloth of silk and
mohair. [O.Fr. *gros grain*, coarse grain.]
groin¹ *groin*, *n.* the fold between the belly and the thigh:
the line of intersection of two vaults, also a rib along
the intersection (*archit.*). — *v.t.* to form into groins,
to build in groins. — *adj.* **groined.** — *n.* **groin′ing.** —
groin′-cen′tring the centring of timber during construction. [Early forms *grind*, *grine*, perh. — O.E. *grynde*,
abyss.]
groin². U.S. spelling of **groyne** (q.v.).
groin³ *groin*, (*obs.*) *v.i.* to grunt, to growl: to grumble.

[O.Fr. *grogner* — L. *grunnīre*, to grunt.]
Grolier *grō′lyā*, *n.* a book or a binding from the library
of the French bibliophile Jean *Grolier* (1479–1565). —
adj. **Grolieresque** (*grō-lyər-esk′*) after the style of
Grolier's bindings, with geometrical or arabesque
figures and leaf-sprays in gold lines.
groma *grōm′ə*, *n.* surveying instrument used by the
Romans, in which plumblines suspended from the
arms of a horizontal cruciform frame were used to
construct right angles. [L. *grōma*, a surveyor's pole,
measuring rod.]
gromet, grommet. Same as **grummet¹**.
gromwell *grom′wəl*, *n.* any plant of the genus *Lithosper-*
mum: the oyster-plant (*Mertensia*) — both of the
borage family. [O.Fr. *gromil*.]
grone. Obs. form of **groan.**
groof. See under **grovelling.**
groo-groo. See **gru-gru.**
grooly *grōōl′i*, (*slang*) *adj.* gruesome. [*grue*some and
gris*ly*.]
groom *grōōm*, *grŏŏm*, *n.* a boy, young man, esp. a servant
(*obs.*): one who has the charge of horses: a title of
several household officers (groom of the stole, grooms-
in-waiting): a bridegroom. — *v.t.* to tend, esp. a horse:
to smarten: to prepare for political office, stardom, or
success in any sphere. — **grooms′man** the attendant on
a bridegroom. [Origin obscure; cf. Du. *grom*, fry,
offspring, O.Fr. *gromet*, boy (see **gourmet, grummet²**);
encroaching on O.E. *guma* (as in bride*groom*), a man.]
groove *grōōv*, *n.* a furrow, or long hollow, such as is cut
with a tool: the track cut into the surface of a gramophone record along which the needle of the gramophone moves: a set routine: an exalted mood, one's
highest form (*jazz slang*). — *v.t.* to grave or cut a
groove or furrow in. — *v.i.* (*slang*) to experience great
pleasure: to be groovy. — *adj.* **groov′y** (also **in the**
groove; *jazz slang*) in top form, or in perfect condition:
up to date in style: generally, pleasant, delightful:
following a set routine. [Prob. Du. *groef, groeve*, a
furrow; cog. with Ger. *Grube*, a pit, O.N. *grōf*, Eng.
grave¹.]
grope *grōp*, *v.i.* to search, feel about, as if blind or in the
dark. — *v.t.* to search by feeling (one's way): to fondle
(someone) lasciviously (*coll.*). — *adv.* **grop′ingly.**
[O.E. *grāpian*; allied to **grab²**, **gripe¹**.]
groper. Same as **grouper.**
grosbeak *grōs′bēk*, *n.* formerly, the hawfinch, or other
finch of the same subfamily, with thick, heavy, seed-
crushing bill: now usu. applied to various more or less
related birds, as the cardinal and the rose-breasted
grosbeak. [Fr. *grosbec* — *gros*, thick, *bec*, beak.]
groschen *grō′shən*, *n.* an Austrian coin, a 100th part of a
schilling: a small silver coin current in the north of
Germany from the 13th to the late 19th century,
varying in value between 1/24 and 1/36 of a thaler: a
ten-pfennig piece. [Ger.]
groser *grō′zər*, **grosert, grossart** *-zərt*, **groset** *-zit*, (*Scot.*)
ns. a gooseberry. [Fr. *groseille*.]
grosgrain *grō′grān*, *n.* a heavy corded silk used especially
for ribbons and hat bands. [Fr.]
gros point *grō point*, a large cross-stitch: embroidery
composed of this stitch. [Fr.]
gross *grōs*, *adj.* coarse: rough: dense: palpable: flagrant,
glaring: extreme: shameful: whole: coarse in mind:
stupid: sensual: obscene: total, including everything:
of a horse, naturally large-girthed, as opposed to
overweight (*racing*). — *n.* the main bulk: the whole
taken together, sum total (revived from *obs.*): twelve
dozen: the total profit: — *pl.* **gross.** — *v.t.* to make as
total profit. — *adv.* **gross′ly.** — *n.* **gross′ness.** — **great**
gross a dozen gross; **gross domestic product** the gross
national product less income from foreign investments; **gross national product** the total value of all
goods and services produced by a country in a specified
period (usu. annually); **gross up** to convert a net figure
into a gross one for the purpose of tax calculation,

etc.; **in gross** in bulk, wholesale. [Fr. *gros* — L. *grossus*, thick.]

grossart. See **groser.**

grossièreté *gros-yer-tā*, (Fr.) *n.* grossness, rudeness, coarseness.

grossular *gros'ū-lər*, **grossularite** *-īt*, *ns.* gooseberry-stone, a lime alumina garnet, often green. [Fr. *groseille*, gooseberry, Latinised as *grossulāria*.]

grot *grot*, (*poet.*) *n.* a grotto.

grotesque *grō-tesk'*, *adj.* extravagantly formed: fantastic: ludicrous, absurd. — *n.* extravagant ornament, containing animals, plants, etc., in fantastic or incongruous forms (*art*): a bizarre figure or object. — *adv.* **grotesque'ly.** — *ns.* **grotesque'ness; grotesqu'ery, grotesqu'erie.** [Fr. *grotesque* — It. *grottesca* — *grotta*, a grotto.]

Grotian *grō'shi-ən*, *adj.* of or pertaining to Hugo *Grotius*, L. name of Huig van *Groot* (1583–1645), founder of the science of international law. — **Grotian theory** the theory that man is essentially a social being, and that the principles of justice are of perpetual obligation and in harmony with his nature.— **Grotian** or **governmental (theory of the) Atonement** the theory that Christ paid the penalty of human sin in order that God might for His sake forgive sinners while preserving the law that punishment should follow sin.

grotto *grot'ō*, *n.* a cave: an imitation cave, usu. fantastic: — *pl.* **grott'oes, grott'os.** — **grott'o-work.** [It. *grotta* (Fr. *grotte*) — L. *crypta* — Gr. *kryptē*, a crypt, vault.]

grotty *grot'i*, (*slang*) *adj.* ugly, in bad condition, or useless. [**grotesque.**]

grouch *growch*, *v.i.* to grumble. — *n.* a grumbling: sulks: a grumbler. — *adv.* **grouch'ily.** — *n.* **grouch'iness.** — *adj.* **grouch'y.** [See **grutch, grudge.**]

grouf. See under **grovelling.**

ground[1], **grounden.** See **grind**[2].

ground[2] *grownd*, *n.* bottom, esp. sea-bottom (*arch.*): the solid land underlying an area of water (*naut.*): the solid surface of the earth: a portion of the earth's surface: land: soil: the floor, etc.: earth (*elect.*): position: field or place of action: that on which something is raised (*lit.* or *fig.*): foundation: sufficient reason: the surface on which the work is represented (*art*): a first coat of paint: surrounding rock (*mining*): the space behind the popping-crease with which the batsman must be in touch by bat or person if he is not to be stumped or run out (*cricket*): (*pl.*) an area of land attached to or surrounding a building: (*pl.*) dregs or sediment: (*pl.*) basis of justification. — *v.t.* to fix on a foundation or principle: to put or rest on the ground: to cause to run aground: to instruct in first principles: to cover with a layer of plaster, etc., as a basis for painting: to coat with a composition, as a surface to be etched: to put to earth (*elect.*): to keep on the ground, prevent from flying: to attach to the ground-staff (*aero.*). — *v.i.* to come to the ground: to strike the bottom and remain fixed. — *n.* **ground'age** a charge on a ship in port. — *adj.* **ground'ed.** — *adv.* **ground'edly** on good grounds. — *ns.* **ground'er** a ball that keeps low; **ground'ing** foundation: sound general knowledge of a subject: the background of embroidery, etc.: act or process of preparing or laying a ground: act of laying or of running aground. — *adj.* **ground'less** without ground, foundation, or reason. — *adv.* **ground'lessly.** — *ns.* **ground'lessness; ground'ling** a fish that keeps near the bottom of the water, esp. the spinous loach: formerly a spectator in the pit of a theatre — hence one of the common herd. — *adj.* (*Lamb*) base. — **ground'-ang'ling** fishing without a float, with a weight placed a few inches from the hook — bottom-fishing; **ground annual** (*Scots law*) an annual payment forming a burden on land; **ground'-ash** a sapling of ash: a stick made of an ash sapling; **ground'bait** bait dropped to the bottom to bring fish to the neighbourhood (also *fig.*); **ground'-bass** a bass part constantly repeated with varying melody and harmony (*mus.*); **ground'-beetle** any beetle of the Carabidae, a family akin to the tiger-beetles;

ground'breaking (esp. *U.S.*) the breaking of ground at the beginning of a construction project. — *adj.* innovative, breaking new ground. — **ground'burst** the explosion of a bomb on the ground (as opposed to in the air); **ground'-cherry** any of the European dwarf cherries: any of several plants of the genus Physalis, also called husk-tomato, Cape gooseberry, etc.: the fruit of these plants; **ground'-control** control, by information radioed from a ground installation, of aircraft observed by radar; **ground cover** low plants and shrubs growing among the trees in a forest: various low herbaceous plants used to cover an area instead of grass; **ground crew** see **ground staff; ground'-cuckoo** a name for several ground-running birds akin to the cuckoo, as the chaparral cock, the coucal; **ground'-dove, -pigeon** various small American pigeons of terrestrial habits; **ground effect** the extra aerodynamic lift, exploited by hovercraft, etc. and affecting aircraft flying near the ground, caused by the cushion of trapped air beneath the vehicle; **ground'-elder** goutweed; **ground'-feed'er** a fish that feeds at the bottom; **ground floor, storey** the floor on or near a level with the ground; **ground frost** a temperature of 0° C or less registered on a horizontal thermometer in contact with the shorn grass tips of a turf surface; **ground game** hares, rabbits, etc., as distinguished from winged game; **ground'-hog** the woodchuck: the aardvark; **ground'-hold** (*Spens.* and *naut.*) ground-tackle; **ground ice** the ice formed at the bottom; **ground'-ivy** a British labiate creeping-plant (*Nepeta*) whose leaves when the edges curl become ivy-like; **gr(o)und mail** (*Scot.*) payment for right of burial; **ground'mass** the fine-grained part of an igneous rock, glassy or minutely crystalline, in which the larger crystals are embedded; **ground moraine** a mass of mud, sand, and stones dragged along under a glacier or ice-sheet; **ground'-nut** the peanut or monkey-nut (Arachis): the earth-nut; **ground'-oak** a sapling of oak: various species of *Teucrium*; **ground'-off'icer** one who has charge of the grounds of an estate; **ground'-plan** plan of the horizontal section of the lowest or ground storey of a building: first plan, general outline; **ground'plot** the plot of ground on which a building stands: method of calculating the position of an aircraft by relating the ground speed and time on course to the starting position; **ground'prox** a device, fitted to large passenger aircraft, which warns the pilot when altitude falls below a given level (*ground prox*imity warning system); **ground'-rent** rent paid to a landlord for the use of the ground for a specified term, usually in England ninety-nine years; **ground'-robin** the chewink, or towhee; **ground rule** a basic rule of procedure: a modifying (sports) rule for a particular place or circumstance; **ground'sel, ground'sell, ground'sill** the lowest timber of a structure; **ground'sheet** a waterproof sheet spread on the ground by campers, etc.; **ground'-sloth** a heavy extinct ground-going sloth; **grounds'man, ground'man** a man charged with the care of a cricket-ground or a sports-field: an aerodrome mechanic; **ground'speed** (*aero.*) speed of an aircraft relative to the ground; **ground'-squirr'el** the chipmunk or hackee; **ground staff** aircraft mechanics, etc., whose work is on the ground (also **ground crew**): paid staff of players (*cricket*): people employed to look after a sports-field; **ground'-state** the state of a nuclear system, atoms, etc., when at their lowest (or normal) energy; **ground stroke** in tennis, a return played after the ball has bounced; **ground swell** a broad, deep undulation of the ocean caused by a distant gale or earthquake: a movement, as of public or political opinion or feeling, which is evident although the cause or leader is not known; **ground tackle** tackle for securing a vessel at anchor. — *adj.* **ground'-to-air'** (of a missile) aimed and fired from the ground at a target in the air. — **ground'-water** water naturally in the subsoil; **ground'work** that which forms the ground or foundation of anything: the basis: the essential part: the first principle; **ground'-ze'ro** the point on the ground directly under the explosion of a nuclear weapon in the air. — **break ground** to begin working untouched ground: to take the first step in any project; **break new ground** to be innovative; **cut, take the ground from under someone, someone's feet** to anticipate someone's arguments or actions and destroy their force; **down to the ground** see **down**[3]; **fall to the ground** to come to nothing; **gain ground** to advance: to become more widely influential: to spread; **give ground** to fall back, retreat (*lit.* and *fig.*); **hold** or **stand one's ground** to stand firm; **(let in) on the ground floor** (to admit) on the same terms as the original promoters, or at the start (of a business venture, etc.); **lose ground** to fall back: to decline in influence, etc.; **off the ground** started, under way; **on one's own ground** in circumstances with which one is familiar; **run to ground** to hunt out, track down; **shift one's ground** to change one's standpoint in a situation or argument; **to ground** into hiding. [O.E. *grund*; cog. with Ger. *Grund*, O.N. *grunnr*.]

groundsel[1] *grown(d)'sl*, *n.* a very common yellow-flowered composite weed of waste ground (*Senecio vulgaris*). [O.E. *gundeswilge*, appar. — *gund*, pus, *swelgan*, to swallow, from its use in poultices, influenced by *grund*, ground.]

groundsel[2], **groundsell**, **groundsill**. See **ground**[2].

group *grōōp*, *n.* a number of persons or things together: a number of individual things related in some definite way differentiating them from others: a clique, school, section of a party: a scientific classification: a combination of figures forming a harmonious whole (*art*): a system of elements having a binary operation that is associative, an identity element for the operation, and an inverse for every element (*math.*): a division in the Scout organisation: a pop-group. — *v.t.* to form into a group or groups. — *v.i.* to fall into harmonious combination. — *ns.* **group'age** the collection of objects or people into a group or groups; **group'er** a member of the Oxford society; **group'ie**, **group'y** (*slang*) a (usu. female) fan who follows pop-groups, or other celebrities, wherever they appear, often in the hope of having sexual relations with them; **group'ing** the act of disposing and arranging figures in a group (*art*); **group'ist** an adherent of a group. — Also *adj.* — *ns.* **group'let** (often *derog.*) a small group, a clique or faction; **group'uscule** (-*əs-kūl*; from Fr.; often *derog.*) a grouplet. — **group'-captain** an air-force officer answering to a colonel or naval captain; **group dynamics** the interaction of human behaviour within a small social group; **group insurance** insurance issued on a number of people under a single policy; **group marriage** a hypothetical primitive relation by which every man of a group is husband to every woman of a group; **group practice** a medical practice in which several doctors work together as partners; **group sex** sexual activity in which several people take part simultaneously; **group theory** (*math.*) the investigation of the properties of groups; **group therapy** therapy in which a small group of people with the same psychological or physical problems discuss their difficulties under the chairmanship of, e.g., a doctor. — **pop group** see **pop**[2]. [Fr. *groupe* — It. *groppo*, a bunch, knot — Gmc.; cf. Ger. *Kropf*, protuberance.]

grouper *grōōp'ər* (*Amer.* and *Brit.*), **groper** *grōp'ər* (*Austr.*), *ns.* names given to many fishes, esp. various kinds resembling bass. [Port. *garoupa*.]

grouse[1] *grows*, *n.* the heathcock or moorfowl (*Lagopus scoticus*; the *red grouse*), a plump bird with a short curved bill, short legs, and feathered feet, found on Scottish moors and hills and in certain other parts of Britain: extended to other birds of the family Tetraonidae, incl. the *black grouse* or blackcock, the *willow-grouse* and various birds of North America: — *pl.* **grouse**. — **grouse'-disease'** a nematode infection of grouse; **grouse moor** a tract of moorland on which grouse live, breed, and are shot for sport. [Origin uncertain.]

grouse[2] *grows*, *v.i.* to grumble. — *n.* a grumble. — *n.* **grous'er**. [Cf. **grutch**.]

grouse[3] *grows*, (*Austr. coll.*) *adj.* very good. [Origin unknown.]

grout[1] *growt*, *n.* coarse meal: the sediment of liquor: lees: a thin coarse mortar: a fine plaster for finishing ceilings. — *v.t.* to fill and finish with grout. — *n.* **grout'ing** filling up or finishing with grout: the material so used. — *adj.* **grout'y** thick, muddy: sulky. [O.E. *grūt*, coarse meal: or perh. in part Fr. *grouter*, to grout.]

grout[2] *growt*, *v.i.* to root or grub with the snout. [Perh. conn. with O.E. *grēot*, grit.]

grove *grōv*, *n.* a wood of small size, generally of a pleasant or ornamental character: an avenue of trees: often used (quite fancifully) in street-names: an erroneous translation of *Asherah*, the wooden image of the goddess Ashtoreth, also of Heb. *eshel*, tamarisk, in Gen. xxi. 33 (*B.*): a lodge of a benefit society called Druids. [O.E. *grāf*, possibly tamarisk.]

grovelling *gruv'*, *grov'(ə-)ling*, *adv.* and *adj.* prone: facedown: later felt to be the pr.p. or verbal noun of the new *v.i.* **grov'el**, to crawl on the earth, esp. in abject fear, etc.: to be base or abject: — *pa.t.* and *pa.p.* **grov'elled**. — *n.* **grov'eller**. — *n.* **groof**, **grouf** (*grōōf*; *Scot.*) the front of the body. [M.E. *groveling*, *grofling*, prone — O.N. *grūfa*, and suff. -*ling*.]

grow *grō*, *v.i.* to have life: to have a habitat: to become enlarged by a natural process: to advance towards maturity: to increase in size: to develop: to become greater in any way: to extend: to pass from one state to another: to become. — *v.t.* to cause or allow to grow: to produce: to cultivate: (in *pass.*) to cover with growth: — *pa.t.* **grew** (*grōō*); *pa.p.* **grown** (*grōn*). — *n.* **grow'er**. — *n.* and *adj.* **grow'ing**. — *n.* **growth** a growing: gradual increase: progress, development: that which has grown: a morbid formation: increase in value (**growth-orientated** providing increased capital rather than high interest). — Also *adj.* — *n.* **growth'ist** one who is committed to or who is an advocate of growth, esp. economic. — Also *adj.* — **grow'-bag**, **grow'ing-bag** a large plastic bag containing compost in which seeds can be germinated and plants grown to full size; **grow'ing-pains'** neuralgic pains in young persons (also *fig.*); **grow'ing-point** (*bot.*) the meristem at the apex of an axis, where active cell-division occurs and differentiation of tissues begins; **grown'-up** an adult. — Also *adj.* — **growth industry** an industry or branch of industry which is developing and expanding (also *fig.*); **growth promoter** any of various substances which promote growth in plants, such as cytokinin: any of various hormonal substances used to boost the fattening of livestock. — **grow on, upon** to gain a greater hold on: to gain in the estimation of; **grow out of** to issue from, result from: to pass beyond in development: to become too big for; **grow to** to advance to, come to: of milk, to stick to the pan and develop a bad taste in heating (so prob. Shak. *Merch. of Ven.*, II, ii.); **grow together** to become united by growth; **grow up** to advance in growth, become full-grown, mature, or adult: to spring up. [O.E. *grōwan*; O.N. *grōa*.]

growl *growl* *v.i.* to utter a deep rough murmuring sound like a dog: to grumble surlily. — *v.t.* to utter or express by growling. — *n.* a murmuring, snarling sound, as of an angry dog: a surly grumble. — *ns.* **growl'er** one who growls: a N. American river fish, the large-mouthed black bass, so named from the sound it emits: a small iceberg: a four-wheeled horse-drawn cab (*slang*): a jug or pitcher used for carrying beer (*Amer.*); **growl'ery** a retreat for times of ill-humour; **growl'ing.** — *adv.* **growl'ingly.** — *adj.* **growl'y.** [Cf. Du. *grollen*, to grumble: allied to Gr. *gryllizein*, to grunt.]

grown, **growth**. See **grow**.

groyne *groin*, *n.* breakwater, of wood or other material, to check erosion and sand-drifting. [Prob. O.Fr. *groign*, snout — L. *grunnīre*, to grunt, but perh. the same as **groin**[1].]

grub *grub*, *v.i.* to dig, work, or search in the dirt (with *about* or *around*): to be occupied meanly (with *about* or *around*): to eat (*slang*). — *v.t.* to dig or root out of the ground (generally followed by *up* or *out*): to dig up the surface of (ground) to clear it for agriculture, etc.: to supply with victuals (*slang*): — *pr.p.* **grubb′ing;** *pa.t.* and *pa.p.* **grubbed.** — *n.* an insect larva, esp. one thick and soft: food (*coll.*): a ball bowled along the ground (*cricket*). — *n.* **grubb′er** he who, or that which, grubs: an implement for grubbing or stirring the soil: a grub (*cricket*): a grub-kick. — *adj.* **grubb′y** dirty: infested with grubs. — **grub′-kick** (*Rugby football*) a kick where the ball moves along the ground; **grub′=screw** a small headless screw; **grub′-shop** (*coll.*) a restaurant; **grub′-stake** (*U.S.*) outfit, provisions, etc., given to a prospector for a share in finds. — *v.t.* to provide with such. — **Grub Street** a former name of Milton Street, Moorfields, London, once inhabited by booksellers' hacks and shabby writers generally: applied adjectivally to any mean literary production. [M.E. *grobe*; origin uncertain.]

grubble *grub′l,* a variant of **grabble.**

grudge *gruj, v.t.* to murmur at (*obs.*): to look upon with envy: to give or allow unwillingly (something to a person): to be loth (to do). — *v.i.* to murmur, to show discontent (*obs.*). — *n.* secret enmity or envy: an old cause of quarrel. — *adj.* **grudge′ful** (*Spens.*). — *n.* and *adj.* **grudg′ing.** — *adv.* **grudg′ingly.** — **grudge a thought** (*Shak.*) to thank with ill-will. [**grutch.**]

grue. See **gruesome.**

gruel *grōō′al, n.* a thin food made by boiling oatmeal in water: punishment, severe treatment (*coll.*). — *v.t.* to subject to severe or exhausting experience. — *n.* and *adj.* **gru′elling.** [O.Fr. *gruel* (Fr. *gruau*), groats — L.L. *grūtellum,* dim. of *grūtum,* meal, of Gmc. origin; cf. O.E. *grūt.*]

gruesome *grōō′sam, adj.* horrible: grisly: macabre. — *n.* **grue, grew** (*Scot.*) a creeping of the flesh: a shiver: a shudder: a pellicle of ice. — *v.i.* **grue, grew** (*Scot.*) to shudder: to feel the flesh creep: to creep (as the flesh): to curdle (as the blood). — *adv.* **grue′somely.** — *n.* **grue′someness.** [Cf. Du. *gruwzaam,* Ger. *grausam.*]

gruff *gruf, adj.* rough, or abrupt in manner or sound. — *adj.* **gruff′ish.** — *adv.* **gruff′ly.** — *n.* **gruff′ness.** [Du. *grof;* cog. with Sw. *grof,* Ger. *grob,* coarse.]

grufted *gruft′id,* (*dial.*) *adj.* dirty, begrimed. – Also **grafted.** [Dial. *gruft,* particles of soil.]

gru-gru, groo-groo *grōō′grōō, n.* a name for several tropical American palms akin to the coconut palm, yielding oil-nuts: an edible weevil grub (also **gru-gru worm**) found in their pith.

grum *grum, adj.* morose: surly: deep in the throat, as a sound. — *adv.* **grum′ly.** — *n.* **grum′ness.** [Cf. Dan. *grum.*]

grumble *grum′bl, v.i.* to murmur with discontent: to express discontent: to mutter, mumble, murmur: to growl: to rumble. — *n.* the act of grumbling: an instance of grumbling: a cause of grumbling. — *ns.* **grum′bler; Grumbleto′nian** one of the country party as opposed to the court party, after 1689. — *n.* and *adj.* **grum′bling.** — *adv.* **grum′blingly.** — *adj.* **grum′bly** inclined to grumble. [Cf. Du. *grommelen,* freq. of *grommen,* to mutter; Ger. *grummeln.*]

grume *grōōm, n.* a thick fluid: a clot. — *adjs.* **grum′ous, grum′ose** composed of grains. [O.Fr. *grume,* a bunch — L. *grūmus,* a little heap.]

grummet[1]**, grommet, gromet** *grum′it, n.* a ring of rope or metal: a hole edged with rope: a washer of hemp and red-lead putty, paint or some other substance: a metal ring lining an eyelet: an eyelet: a washer to protect or insulate electrical wire passing through a hole: (usu. **grommet**) a small tube passed through the eardrum to drain the middle ear. — *n.* **grumm′et-hole.** [Perh. 15th-cent. Fr. *grom(m)ette* (Fr. *gourmette*), curb of a bridle.]

grummet[2] *grum′it, n.* a cabin-boy. [O.Fr. *gromet;* see **gourmet.**]

grumose, -ous. See **grume.**

grumph *grumf,* (*Scot.*) *n.* a grunt. — *v.i.* to grunt. — *n.* **grumph′ie** (*Scot.*) a swine. [Imit.]

grumpy *grum′pi, adj.* surly. — *adv.* **grum′pily.** — *n.* **grump′iness.** [Obs. *grump,* snub, sulkiness.]

grund mail. See **gr(o)und mail** under **mail**[2].

Grundyism *grun′di-izm, n.* conventional prudery, from the question 'But what will Mrs *Grundy* say?' in Thomas Morton's play, *Speed the Plough* (1798).

grungy *grun′ji,* (*slang*) *adj.* dirty, messy: unattractive, unappealing. [Prob. imit. coinage.]

grunion *grun′yan, n.* a small Californian sea-fish which spawns on shore. [Prob. Sp. *gruñon,* grunter.]

grunt *grunt, v.i.* to make a sound like a pig. — *v.t.* to utter with a grunt. — *n.* a sound made by a pig: a similar sound: a fish (*Haemulon,* etc.) of a family akin to the snappers, that grunts when taken from the sea. — *n.* **grunt′er** one who grunts: a pig: a grunting fish of various kinds. — *n.* and *adj.* **grunt′ing.** — *adv.* **grunt′ingly.** — *v.i.* **grunt′le** to grunt, keep grunting. — *n.* a grunt: a snout. [O.E. *grunnettan,* freq. of *grunian.*]

gruntled *grun′tald,* (*facet.*) *adj.* happy, pleased, in good humour. [Back-formation from **disgruntled.**]

gruppetto *grōō-pet′ō,* (*mus.*) *n.* a turn: — *pl.* **gruppett′i** (*-ē*). [It., a small group.]

grutch *gruch,* (*Spens.*) *v.t.* or *v.i.* to grudge. — *n.* a grudge. [O.Fr. *groucher, grocher, gruchier,* to grumble.]

grutten. See **greet**[2].

Gruyère *grü′* or *grōō′yer,* or *-yer′, n.* a whole-milk cheese, made at *Gruyère* (Switzerland) and elsewhere.

gryce; gryde; gryfon, gryphon; gryke; grype; gryesly; grysely; gryesy; grysie. See **grice**[1]**; gride; griffin; grike; gripe**[2]**; grisly; gris**[1]**; grise**[1] .

grypt *gript,* (*Spens.*) prob. for **griped** or **gripped** in the sense of bitten, pierced.

grysbok *hhräs′bok* (*S.Afr.*), *grīs′bok, n.* a small S. African antelope, ruddy chestnut with white hairs. [Du., *greybuck* — *grys,* grey, and *bok,* a buck.]

G-string. Same as **gee-string.**

g-suit. See under **G.**

gu. See **gue.**

guacamole *gwa-ka-mō′li, n.* a dish of mashed avocado with tomatoes, onions and seasoning. [Amer. Sp. — Nahuatl *ahuacamolli* — *ahuacatl,* avocado, *molli,* sauce.]

guacharo *gwä′chä-rō, n.* the oil-bird, a S. American nocturnal frugivorous bird (*Steatornis*) allied to the goatsuckers: — *pl.* **gua′charos.** [Sp. *guácharo.*]

guaco *gwä′kō, n.* a tropical American name for plants reputed antidotes against snakebite, esp. species of *Mikania* (climbing composites), and of *Aristolochia*: the medicinal substance got from them: — *pl.* **gua′cos.** [Amer. Sp.]

Guaiacum *gwī′a-kam, n.* a tropical American genus of trees of the bean-caper family, yielding lignum-vitae: (without *cap.*) their greenish resin, used in medicine: (without *cap.*) a tree of this, or a related, genus. [Sp. *guayaco,* from a Haitian word.]

guan *gwän, n.* a large noisy American arboreal game-bird.

guana *gwä′nä, n.* any large lizard. [For **iguana.**]

guanaco *gwä-nä′kō, n.* a wild llama. — Also **huana′co** (*wä-*): — *pls.* **guana′co(s), huana′co(s).** [Quechua *huanaco.*]

guanazolo *gwä-nä-zō′lō, n.* a synthetic substance (amino-hydroxy-triazolo-pyrimidine) closely resembling guanine, used experimentally in controlling cancer by the starving of tumours.

guanin(e). See **guano.**

guano *gwä′nō, n.* the dung of sea-fowl, used as manure: artificially produced fertiliser, esp. made from fish: — *pl.* **gua′nos.** — *adj.* **guanif′erous.** — *n.* **gua′nin(e)** (*-nin, -nēn*) a yellowish-white, amorphous substance, found in guano, liver, pancreas, and other organs of animals, and germ cells of plants — a constituent of nucleic acids. [Sp. *guano, huano* — Peruv. *huanu,* dung.]

guar *gwär, n.* a legume grown for forage and for its seeds which yield **guar gum.**

guaraná *gwä-rä-nä'*, *n.* a Brazilian liana (*Paullinia cupana*; Sapindaceae): a paste of its seeds (**guaraná bread**): a drink or drug made therefrom. [Tupí.]

Guaraní *gwä-rä-nē'*, *n.* an Indian of a group of tribes of southern Brazil and Paraguay (*pl.* **Guaraní**): their language, cognate with Tupí: (**guarani**, *pl.* **guaranies**) the monetary unit of Paraguay. — Also *adj.*

guarantee *gar-ən-tē'*, *n.* a person who makes a contract to see performed what another has undertaken: such a contract: surety or warrant: one responsible for the performance of some action, the truth of some statement, etc. — *v.t.* to undertake as surety for another: to secure: to engage, undertake: — *pr.p.* **guarantee'ing**; *pa.t.* and *pa.p.* **guaranteed'**. — *ns.* **guar'antor** (or -*tör'*) one who makes a guaranty; **guar'anty** a securing, guaranteeing: a written undertaking to be responsible: a person who guarantees: a security. — *v.t.* to guarantee. — **guarantee association, company, society** a joint-stock company on the insurance principle, which becomes security for the integrity of employees, e.g. cashiers [Anglo-Fr. *garantie* — *garant*, warrant and prob. Sp. *garante*; see **warrant**[1].]

guard *gärd*, *v.t.* to ward, watch, or take care of: to protect from danger or attack: to escort: to protect the edge of, as by an ornamental border: to furnish with guards: to trim (*lit., fig.*; *Shak.*). — *v.i.* to watch: to be wary. — *n.* ward, keeping: protection: watch: that which guards from danger: a man or body of men stationed to watch, protect, or keep in custody: one in charge of stage-coach or railway train: state of caution: posture of defence: the position in which a batsman grounds his bat in facing the bowling (*cricket*): a trimming, or a stripe (*obs.*): part of a sword hilt: a watch-chain: a cricketer's pad: in a book, a strip for attachment of a plate, map, or additional leaf: (*pl.*) household troops (Foot, Horse, and Life Guards). — *adj.* **guard'able**. — *n.* **guard'age** (*Shak.*) wardship. — *adj.* **guard'ant, gardant** (*her.*) having the face turned towards the beholder. — *n.* (*Shak.*) protector. — *adj.* **guard'ed** wary: cautious: uttered with caution: trimmed, or striped (*obs.*). — *adv.* **guard'edly**. — *ns.* **guard'edness; guardee'** (*coll.*) a guardsman; **guard'ian** one who guards or takes care: one who has the care of the person, property, and rights of another (e.g. a minor; *law*): a member of a board (in England till 1930) administering the poor laws. — *adj.* **protecting**. — *n.* **guard'ianship**. — *adj.* **guard'less** without a guard: defenceless. — **guard'-book** a blank book with guards; **guard'-cell** (*bot.*) one of the lips of a stoma; **guard dog** a watch-dog; **guard hair** one of the long coarse hairs which form the outer fur of certain mammals; **guard'-house, guard'-room** a house or room for the accommodation of a guard of soldiers, where defaulters are confined; **guardian angel** an angel supposed to watch over a particular person: a person specially devoted to the interests of another; **guard'-rail** a rail on a ship, train, etc., or beside a road, acting as a safety barrier: an additional rail fitted to a railway track to improve a train's stability; **guard'-ring** a keeper, or finger-ring that serves to keep another from slipping off; **guard'-ship** a ship of war that superintends marine affairs in a harbour and protects it: guardianship (*Swift*); **guards'man** a soldier of the guards; **guard's van** on a railway train, the van in which the guard travels. — **guard of honour** see **honour; mount guard** to go on guard; **on** or **off one's guard** on (or not on) the alert for possible danger: wary about what one says or does (or the reverse); **run the guard** to get past a guard or sentinel without detection. [O.Fr. *garder* — O.H.G. *warten*; O.E. *weardian*, mod. Eng. **ward**.]

guarish, garish *gär'ish*, (*Spens.*) *v.t.* to heal. [O.Fr. *guarir* (Fr. *guérir*), to heal.]

guava *gwä'və*, *n.* a small tropical American myrtaceous tree (*Psidium*): its yellow, pear-shaped fruit, often made into jelly. [Sp. *guayaba*, guava fruit; of S. Amer. origin.]

guayule *gwä-ū'lā*, *n.* a Mexican composite plant (*Parthe-*

nium argentatum): the rubber yielded by it. [Sp.; of Nahuatl origin.]

gub, gubbah *gub, gub'ə*, *ns.* a white man. [Aboriginal term.]

gubbins *gub'inz*, (*coll.*) *n.sing.* a trivial object: a device, gadget. — *n.sing* or *pl.* rubbish. [From obs. *gobbon*, portion, perh. conn. with **gobbet**.]

gubernator *gū'bər-nā-tər*, *n.* a governor. — *n.* **guberna'tion** control, rule. — *adj.* **gubernatorial** (-*nə-tö'ri-əl*, -*tö'*). [L. *gubernātor*, a steersman.]

guck *guk*, (esp. *U.S.*, *slang*) *n.* slimy, gooey muck: anything unpleasant or unappealing. — *adj.* **guck'y** slimy, gooey, mucky: slushy, sloppy, sentimental. [Prob. *goo* or *gunk* and *muck*.]

guddle *gud'l*, (*Scot.*) *v.t.* and *v.i.* to fish with the hands by groping under the stones or banks of a stream. — *v.i.* to dabble in, play messily with, something liquid. — *n.* a mess, muddle, confusion. [Origin uncertain.]

gude, guld *gūd, gid*, Scottish forms of **good**. — **gudeman, gudesire** see under **good**.

gudgeon[1] *guj'ən*, *n.* an easily caught small carp-like freshwater fish (*Gobio*): a person easily cheated. — *adj.* foolish. — *v.t.* to impose on, cheat. [O.Fr. *goujon* — L. *gōbiō*, -*ōnis*, a kind of fish — Gr. *kōbios*; see **goby**.]

gudgeon[2] *guj'ən*, *n.* the bearing of a shaft, esp. when made of a separate piece: a metallic journal piece let into the end of a wooden shaft: a pin. [O.Fr. *goujon*, the pin of a pulley.]

gue, gu, gju *gōō, gū*, *ns.* a rude kind of violin used in Shetland. [O.N. *gigja*.]

Guebre, Gueber *gä'bər, gē'bər*, *n.* a Zoroastrian in Iran. [Fr. *guébre* — Pers. *gabr*; see **giaour**.]

guelder-rose *gel'dər-rōz*, *n.* a Viburnum with large white balls of flowers. [From *Geldern* or from *Gelderland*.]

Guelf, Guelph *gwelf*, *n.* one of a papal and popular party in mediaeval Italy, opposed to the Ghibellines and the emperors. — *adj.* **Guelf'ic** pertaining to the Guelf family or party. [*Guelfo*, Italian form of the German family name *Welf*, said to have been the war-cry of Henry the Lion at the battle of Weinsberg (1140) against the Emperor Conrad III.]

guenon *gen'ən, gə-nõ*, *n.* any species of the genus Cercopithecus, long-tailed African monkeys. [Fr.]

guerdon *gûr'dən*, *n.* a reward or recompense. — *v.t.* to reward. [O.Fr. *guerdon, gueredon* (It. *guidardone*) — L.L. *widerdonum* — O.H.G. *widarlōn* (O.E. *witherlēan*) — *widar*, against, and *lōn*, reward; or more prob. the latter part of the word is from L. *dōnum*, a gift.]

guereza *ger'ə-zə*, *n.* a large, long-haired, black-and-white African monkey, with a bushy tail: any species of the same genus (*Colobus*). [App. of Somali origin.]

guerilla. See **guerrilla**.

guéridon *gä-rē-dõ, ger'i-dən*, *n.* a small ornate table or stand. [Fr.]

guernsey *gûrn'zi*, *n.* (sometimes with *cap.*) a close-fitting knitted upper garment, worn by sailors: (with *cap.*) one of a breed of dairy cattle from *Guernsey*, in the Channel Islands: (with *cap.*) Channel Island patois derived from Norman-French. — *adj.* (sometimes with *cap.*) in the style of a guernsey. — **Guernsey lily** a Nerine (q.v.).

guerra al cuchillo *gä'rä äl kōō-chē'lyō*, (Sp.) war to the knife.

guerre à mort *ger a mor*, (Fr.) war to the death; **guerre à outrance** (*ōō-träs*) war to the uttermost, to the bitter end.

guerrilla, guerilla *gər-il'ə*, *n.* harassing an army by small bands: petty warfare: loosely, one who takes part in such warfare (properly **guerrillero** -*yā'ro*, *pl.* **guerriller'os**). — Also *adj.* — **guerrilla strike** a sudden and brief industrial strike. [Sp. *guerrilla*, dim. of *guerra*, war — O.H.G. *werra*; cf. **war**; Fr. *guerre*.]

guess[1] *ges*, *v.t.* to think, believe, suppose (*arch.* and *U.S.*): to judge upon inadequate knowledge or none at all: to conjecture: to hit on or solve by conjecture. — *v.i.* to make a conjecture or conjectures. — *n.* judgment

fāte; fär; hûr; mīne; mōte; för; mūte; mōōn; fŏŏt; dhen (then); *el'ə-mənt* (element)

or opinion without sufficient evidence or grounds: a random surmise: a riddle, conundrum (*Scot.*). — *adj.* **guess′able.** — *n.* **guess′er.** — *n.* and *adj.* **guess′ing.** — *adv.* **guess′ingly.** — *n.* **guess′timate** (orig. *facet.*) an estimate based on very little knowledge. — **guess′-work** the process or result of guessing. — **anybody's guess** purely a matter of individual conjecture. [M.E. *gessen*; cog. with Du. *gissen*; Dan. *gisse*, mod. Icel. *giska, gizka*, for *gitska — geta*, to get, think; see **get, forget.**]
guess². See **othergates.**
guest *gest, n.* a visitor received and entertained gratuitously or for payment: an animal inhabiting or breeding in another's nest. — *adj.* and *n.* (an artist, conductor, etc.) not a regular member of a company, etc., or not regularly appearing on a programme, but taking part on a special occasion. — *v.i.* to be a guest artist, etc. — *v.t.* to have as a guest artist on a show. — *v.i.* **guest′en** (*Scott*) to stay as a guest. — *adv.* **guest′wise** in the manner or capacity of a guest. — **guest′-chamber** (*B.*), **guest′-room** a room for the accommodation of a guest; **guest′-house** a hospice: a boarding-house; **guest′= night** a night when non-members of a society are entertained; **guest′-rope** a rope hanging over the side of a vessel to aid other vessels drawing alongside, etc.; **guest′-worker** a Gastarbeiter (q.v.). [O.E. (Anglian) *gest* (W.S. *giest*), perh. influenced by O.N.; allied to Du. *gast* and Ger. *Gast*, L. *hostis*, stranger, enemy.]
Gueux *gø, n.pl.* the name assumed by the confederation (1565) of nobles and others to resist the introduction of the Inquisition into the Low Countries by Philip II of Spain. [Fr., beggars.]
guff *guf, n.* nonsense, humbug (*coll.*): a smell, stink (*Scot.*). [Perh. imit.; cf. Norwegian *gufs*, a puff.]
guffaw *guf-ö′, v.i.* to laugh loudly. — *n.* a loud laugh. [From the sound.]
guggle *gug′l, v.i.* to gurgle. — *n.* a gurgle. [Cf. **gurgle.**]
guichet *gē′shä, n.* a small opening in a wall, door, etc.: a ticket-office window. [Fr.; cf. **wicket.**]
Guicowar. See **Gaekwar.**
guid. See **gude.**
guide *gīd, v.t.* to lead, conduct, or direct: to regulate: to influence. — *n.* he who, or that which, guides: one who conducts travellers, tourists, mountaineers, etc.: one who directs another in his course of life: a soldier or other employed to obtain information for an army: a Girl Guide (see **girl**): a guide-book: anything serving to direct, show the way, determine direction of motion or course of conduct. — *adj.* **guid′able.** — *ns.* **guid′age** guidance; **guid′ance** direction: leadership; **guid′er** one who guides: a device for guiding: a captain or lieutenant in the Girl Guides. — *adj.* **guide′less.** — *n.* **guide′ship.** — *n.* and *adj.* **guid′ing.** — *n.* **guid′on** a pennant, usu. with a rounded fly, carried by certain cavalry companies or mounted batteries: the officer bearing it. — **guide′-book** a book of information for tourists; **guided missile** a jet- or rocket-propelled projectile carrying a warhead and electronically directed to its target for the whole or part of the way by remote control; **guide dog** a dog trained to lead blind persons; **guide′line** a line drawn, or a rope, etc., fixed, to act as a guide: an indication of course that should be followed, or of what future policy will be (*fig.*); **guide′= post** a post to guide the traveller; **guide′-rail** an additional rail to keep rolling-stock on the rails at a bend; **guide′-rope** a rope for guiding the movement of a thing hoisted or hauled; **guiding light, star** a person or thing adopted as a guide or model. [O.Fr. *guider*; perh. from a Gmc. root, as in O.E. *witan*, to know, *wīs*, wise, Ger. *weisen*, to show, conn. with **wit, wise.**]
Guignol *gē-nyol, n.* the chief puppet in French puppet shows. — **Grand** (*grä*) **Guignol** a small theatre in Paris that specialised in short plays of horror: horror plays of this type: (without *caps.*) something intended to horrify people. [Name originated in Lyons in 18th century; said to be that of a local 'character'.]
guild, gild *gild, n.* an association for mutual aid: a

corporation: a mediaeval association providing for masses for the dead, maintenance of common interests, mutual support and protection (*hist.*): meetingplace of a guild (*obs.*; *Spens.* **gyeld**): a group of plants distinguished by their way of life (e.g. saprophytes, or parasites). — *n.* **guild′ry** (*Scot.*) the corporation of a royal burgh: membership thereof. — **guild′-brother** a fellow-member of a guild; **guild′hall** the hall of a guild: a town-hall; **Guild Socialism** a form of socialism that would make trade unions or guilds the authority for industrial matters. [O.E. *gield*, influenced by O.N. *gildi*.]
guilder, gilder *gild′ər, n.* an old Dutch and German gold coin: a modern Dutch gulden: a coin vaguely (*Shak.*). [Du. *gulden.*]
guile *gīl, n.* wile, jugglery: cunning: deceit. — *v.t.* (*Spens.*) to beguile. — *adjs.* **guiled** armed with deceit: treacherous; **guile′ful** crafty: deceitful. — *adv.* **guile′fully.** — *n.* **guile′fulness.** — *adj.* **guile′less** without deceit: artless. — *adv.* **guile′lessly.** — *ns.* **guile′lessness; guil′er, guyl′er** (*Spens.*) a deceiver. [O.Fr. *guile*, deceit, perh. Gmc.; cf. **wile.**]
Guillain-Barré syndrome *gē-yɛ̃′ba-rā′ sin′drōm,* an acute polyneuritis causing weakness or paralysis of the limbs. [Georges *Guillain* and Jean *Barré*, French neurologists.]
guillemot *gil′i-mot, n.* a diving bird (*Uria*) of the auk family. [Fr., dim. of *Guillaume*, William, perh. suggested by Bret. *gwelan*, gull.]
guilloche *gi-lōsh′, n.* an ornament formed of interlacing curved bands enclosing circles. — *v.t.* to decorate with intersecting curved lines. [Fr., a guilloching tool; said to be named from one *Guillot.*]
guillotine *gil′ə-tēn, -tēn′, gē′yə-, n.* an instrument for beheading by descent of a heavy oblique blade — adopted during the French Revolution, and named after Joseph Ignace *Guillotin* (1738–1814), a physician, who first proposed its adoption: a machine for cutting paper, straw, etc.: a surgical instrument for cutting the tonsils: a specially drastic rule or closure for shortening discussion. — *v.t.* to behead, crop, or cut short by guillotine.
guilt¹ *gilt, n.* the state of having done wrong: sin, sinfulness: the state of having broken a law: liability to a penalty. — *adv.* **guilt′ily.** — *n.* **guilt′iness.** — *adj.* **guilt′less** free from crime: innocent. — *adv.* **guilt′lessly.** — *n.* **guilt′lessness.** — *adj.* **guilt′y** justly chargeable: wicked: involving, indicating, burdened with, or pertaining to guilt. — *adv.* **guilt′y-like** (*Shak.*) guiltily. — **guilt complex** a mental preoccupation with one's (real or imagined) guilt; **guilty party** a person, organisation, etc. that is guilty. — **guilty of,** (*Shak.*) **to** having committed (evil or injudicious act): to blame for (a happening; *arch.*): (sometimes in *B.*) deserving of (*obs.*). [Orig. a payment or fine for an offence; O.E. *gylt.*]
guilt² (*Spens.*). Same as **gilt¹.**
guimbard *gim′bärd, n.* a Jew's-harp. [Perh. from Prov. *guimbardo*, a kind of dance — *guimba*, to leap, gambol.]
guimp, guimpe. See **gimp¹.**
guinea *gin′i, n.* an obsolete English gold coin first made of gold brought from *Guinea*, in Africa: its value, finally 21s. — *adj.* priced at a guinea. — **guin′ea-corn** durra (*Sorghum vulgare*): pearl millet (*Pennisetum typhoideum*), a cereal; **guin′ea-fowl** an African bird (*Numida*) of the pheasant family, dark-grey with white spots; **guin′ea-grass** a tall African grass of the millet genus (*Panicum*); **guin′ea-hen** a guinea-fowl: formerly, a turkey: a courtesan (*Shak.*); **guin′ea-pig** a small S. American rodent, the cavy: a fainéant compan′ director (*slang*): a person used as the subject of ə experiment — as the cavy commonly is in the labo tory; **guin′ea-worm** a very slender threadlike paras nematode worm (Filaria) common in tropical Af
guipure *gē-poor′, n.* a kind of lace having no grou mesh, the pattern sections fixed by interlacing th

a species of gimp. [Fr. *guipure* — O.Fr. *guiper*, prob. Gmc.; cf. Goth. *weipan*, to weave.]

guiro *gwē'rō, n.* a notched gourd used as a percussion instrument in Latin America: — *pl.* **gui'ros.** [Sp., gourd.]

guise *gīz, n.* manner, behaviour: custom: external appearance: dress. — *v.t.* (*arch.*) to dress. — *v.i.* to act as a guiser. — *ns.* **guis'er, guis'ard, guizer** (both chiefly *Scot.*) a person in disguise: a Christmas (or now usu. Hallowe'en and, in Shetland, Up-Helly-Aa) mummer. [O.Fr. *guise*; cf. O.H.G. *wīsa* (Ger. *Weise*), a way, guise, O.E. *wīse*, way, *wīs*, wise.]

guitar *gi-tär', n.* a fretted musical instrument, now six-stringed — like the lute, but flat-backed. — *n.* **guitar'ist.** [Fr. *guitare* — L. *cithara* — Gr. *kitharā*; see **cithara.**]

guizer. See **guiser.**

Gujarat(h)i, Gujerat(h)i *gōōj-ə-rä'tē, n.* an Indic language spoken in the region and state of *Gujarat* in north-western India. [Hind. — Sans. *Gurjara*, Gujarat.]

gula *gū'lə, n.* the upper part of the throat: in some insects a plate on the under side of the head. — *adj.* **gū'lar.** [L. *gŭla*, throat.]

gulag *gōō'lag, n.* one of the system of esp. political prisons and forced labour camps in the Soviet Union (also *fig.*). [Russ. acronym, popularised by A. Solzhenitsyn, Russ. author (1918–), in *The Gulag Archipelago*.]

gulch *gulch, gulsh, n.* (*U.S.*) a ravine or narrow rocky valley, a gully. — *v.t.* (*dial.*) to swallow greedily. [Origin doubtful.]

gulden *gōōl'dən, n.* a gold or silver coin in Germany in the Middle Ages: the old unit of account in Austria (before 1892): a Dutch coin, the guilder or florin. [Ger., lit. golden.]

gule (*Scot.*). See **gold².**

gules *gūlz, (her.) n.* a red colour, marked in engraved figures by vertical lines. — *adj.* **gū'ly** (*obs.*). [O.Fr. *gueules*, perh. — L. *gŭla*, the throat.]

gulf (*arch.* **gulph**) *gulf, n.* an indentation in the coast: a deep place: an abyss: a whirlpool: anything insatiable: a wide separation, e.g. between opponents' viewpoints: in Oxford and Cambridge examinations, the place of those candidates for honours who are allowed a pass without honours. — *v.t.* to engulf. — *v.i.* to flow like a gulf. — *adj.* **gulf'y** full of gulfs or whirlpools. — **gulf'-weed** a large olive-brown seaweed (*Sargassum*) that floats unattached in great 'meadows' at the branching of the Gulf Stream and elsewhere in tropical oceans. [O.Fr. *golfe* — Late Gr. *kolphos* — Gr. *kolpos*, the bosom.]

gull¹ *gul, n.* a sea-mew, a sea-bird of the family Laridae, esp. of the genus *Larus*. — *n.* **gull'ery** a place where gulls breed. — *adj.* **gull'-wing** (of a motor-car door) opening upwards: (of an aircraft wing) having an upward-sloping short inner section and a long horizontal outer section. [Prob. W. *gwylan*.]

gull² *gul*, (*Shak.*) *n.* an unfledged bird. [Perh. O.N. *gulr*, yellow.]

gull³ *gul, n.* a dupe: an easily duped person: a hoax (*obs.*). — *v.t.* to beguile, hoax. — *ns.* **gull'er; gull'ery** (*arch.*) deception; **gullibil'ity.** — *adjs.* **gull'ible** easily deceived (also **gull'able**); **gull'ish.** — **gull'-catcher** (*Shak.*) a cheat. [Perh. from **gull¹** or **gull².**]

Gullah *gu'lə, gōō', n.* a member of a Negro people living in islands and coastal districts of south-east United States: their language, a creolised English.

gullet *gul'it, n.* the passage in the neck by which food is taken into the stomach: the throat: a narrow trench, passage, water channel, or ravine. [O.Fr. *goulet*, dim. of *goule* (Fr. *gueule*) — L. *gŭla*, the throat.]

gully¹, gulley *gul'i*, (*Scot.*) *n.* a big knife.

gully², gulley *gul'i, n.* a channel worn by running water, as on a mountain-side: a ravine: a ditch: a grooved rail, as for a tramway: the position between point and slips (*cricket*). — *pl.* **gull'ies, gull'eys.** — *v.t.* to wear a gully or channel in. — *adj.* **gull'ied.** — **gull'y-hole** a passage by which a gutter discharges into a drain;

gull'y-hunt'er one who picks up things from gutters. [Prob. **gullet.**]

gulosity *gū-los'i-ti, n.* gluttony. [L. *gŭlōsus*, gluttonous — *gulō*, glutton — *gŭla*, throat.]

gulp *gulp, v.t.* to swallow spasmodically or in large draughts. — *v.i.* to make a swallowing movement. — *n.* a spasmodic or copious swallow: a movement as if of swallowing: a quantity swallowed at once: capacity for gulping. — *n.* **gulp'er.** [Cf. Du. *gulpen, gulp.*]

gulph. See **gulf.**

guly. See **gules.**

gum¹ *gum, n.* the firm fleshy tissue that surrounds the bases of the teeth: insolence (*old slang*). — *v.t.* (*U.S.*) to deepen and widen the gaps between the teeth of (a saw) to make it last longer. — *adj.* **gumm'y** toothless. — **gum'boil** a small abscess on the gum; **gum'shield** a soft pad worn by boxers to protect the teeth and gums. [O.E. *gōma*, palate; O.N. *gōmr*, Ger. *Gaumen*, palate.]

gum² *gum, n.* a substance that collects in or exudes from certain plants, and hardens on the surface, dissolves or swells in water, but does not dissolve in alcohol or ether: a plant gum or similar substance used as an adhesive, a stiffener, or for other purpose: any gumlike or sticky substance: chewing-gum: a gumdrop (q.v.): a gum tree: gummosis: a rubber overshoe (*U.S.*): a beehive, orig. one made from a hollow gum tree (*U.S.*): a humbug (*arch. U.S.*). — *v.t.* to smear, coat, treat, or unite with gum: to humbug (*arch. U.S.*). — *v.i.* to become gummy: to exude gum: — *pr.p.* **gumm'ing;** *pa.t.* and *pa.p.* **gummed.** — *n.* **gumm'a** a syphilitic tumour: — *pl.* **gumm'ata.** — *adjs.* **gumm'atous; gummif'erous** producing gum. — *ns.* **gumm'iness; gumm'ing** act of fastening with gum: application of gum in solution to a lithographic stone: gummosis: becoming gummy; **gumm'ite** a hydrated oxide of uranium and lead; **gummo'sis** pathological conversion of cell walls into gum; **gummos'ity** gumminess. — *adjs.* **gumm'ous, gumm'y** consisting of or resembling gum: producing or covered with gum. — **gum ammoniac, ammoniacum** a gum resin, inspissated juice of a Persian umbelliferous plant (*Dorema*), used in medicine and manufactures: that of an African species of *Ferula*; **gum arabic** a gum obtained from various acacias; **gum benjamin** see **benjamin²**; **gum'boot** a rubber boot; **gum'-digger** (*N.Z.*) one who digs up fossilised kauri-gum; **gum dragon, tragacanth** tragacanth; **gum'drop** a gelatinous type of sweet containing gum arabic; **gum elastic** rubber; **gum juniper** sandarac; **gum'nut** the woody fruit of the eucalyptus; **gum resin** a resin mixed with gum; **gum'shoe** (*U.S.*) a rubber overshoe: a shoe with rubber sole: a detective or policeman (*slang*). — Also *v.i.* (*slang*) to snoop, pry. — **gum tree** a tree that exudes gum, or gum resin, kino, etc., esp. a eucalyptus tree, or an American tree of the cornel family (*Nyssa*). — **gum up the works** (*coll.*) to make (e.g. a machine, a scheme) unworkable; **up a gum tree** in straits (from the opossum's refuge). [O.Fr. *gomme* — L. *gummi* — Gr. *kommi*; prob. — Egyptian *kemai*.]

gum³ *gum, n.* material that gathers in the corner of the eye. — **gum rash** red-gum. [Perh. O.E. *gund*, matter, pus.]

gum⁴ *gum, n.* used in oaths for **God.**

gumbo *gum'bō, n.* the okra or its mucilaginous pods: a soup of which okra is an ingredient: a dish of okra pods seasoned: a fruit conserve: in central U.S. a fine soil which becomes sticky or soapy when wet: a Negro patois in Louisiana, etc.: — *pl.* **gum'bos.** [Angolan Negro (ki)*ngombo*.]

gump¹ *gump*, (*Scot.*) *v.t.* and *v.i.* to guddle.

gump² *gump*, (*dial.*) *n.* a foolish person.

gumphion *gum'fi-ən*, (*obs. Scot.*) *n.* a funeral banner. [gonfanon.]

gumple-foisted *gum'pl-foist'id*, (*Scott*) *adj.* sulky. [*gumps*, sulks (**gump²**); the second element appears in other words as *-faced, -feist,* etc.]

gumption *gum(p)'shən, n.* sense: shrewdness: commonsense: art of preparing colours. — *adj.* **gump'tious.**

[Poss. conn. with O.N. *gaumr*, heed.]

gun *gun*, *n.* a tubular weapon from which projectiles are discharged, usually by explosion: a cannon, rifle, revolver, etc.: a device for spraying, squirting, or otherwise propelling material: a signal by gun: one who carries a gun, a member of a shooting-party: a professional killer (*U.S. slang*): the throttle of an aircraft: the accelerator of a car: an expert or champion, esp. in shearing (*Austr. coll.*). — *v.t.* to shoot: to shoot at: to provide with guns: to open the throttle of, to increase speed (*coll.*; also **give the gun**): to rev up (the engine of a stationary car) noisily (*coll.*). — *v.i.* to shoot: to go shooting. — *adj.* (*Austr.*) expert, pre-eminent. — *ns.* **gunn′age** the number of guns carried by a ship of war; **gunn′er** one who works a gun: a private in the Artillery: a branch officer in charge of naval ordnance (*naut.*); **gunn′ery** the art of managing guns, or the science of artillery; **gunn′ing**. — **gun barrel** the tube of a gun; **gun′boat** a small vessel of light draught, fitted to carry one or more guns; **gunboat diplomacy** show or threat of (orig. naval) force in international negotiation; **gun carriage** a carriage on which a cannon is mounted; **gun′cotton** an explosive prepared by saturating cotton with nitric and sulphuric acids; **gun deck** a deck in old warships carrying guns below the main deck (earlier below spar deck); **gun dog** dog trained to work with a shooting-party; **gun′fight** fight involving two or more people with guns, esp. in old American West. — Also *v.i.* — **gun′fighter; gun′fire** the firing of guns: the hour at which the morning or evening gun is fired: an early cup of tea; **gun′flint** a piece of flint fitted to the hammer of a flintlock musket; **gun′layer** one who sets the sights of a ship's gun; **gun′-lock** the mechanism in some guns by which the charge is exploded; **gun′maker; gun′man** a man who carries a gun, esp. an armed criminal; **gun′metal** an alloy of copper and tin in the proportion of about 9 to 1, once used in making cannon: any of various metals used in imitation thereof: any of various colours with a metallic sheen; **gun moll** (*slang*) a woman who associates with criminals: a gunman's moll; **gun′play** the use of guns, esp. in a fight or display of skill; **gun′port** a porthole or similar opening for a gun; **gun′powder** an explosive mixture of saltpetre, sulphur, and charcoal; **gun′room** a room where guns are kept: on board ship, orig. the gunner's apartment, now a mess-room for junior officers; **gun′runner; gun′running** smuggling guns into a country; **gun′ship** an armed ship, helicopter, etc.; **gun′shot** the shot fired from a gun: the distance to which shot can be thrown from a gun. — *adj.* caused by the shot of a gun. — *adj.* **gun′-shy** frightened by guns. — **gun′slinger** (*coll.*) a gunfighter; **gun′smith** a smith or workman who makes or repairs guns or small arms; **gun′stick** a ramrod; **gun′stock** the piece on which the barrel of a gun is fixed; **gun′stone** (*Shak.*) a stone shot. — **as sure as a gun** quite sure, certainly; **at gunpoint** under, or using, the threat of injury from a gun; **beat the gun** to jump the gun (see **jump**); **blow great guns** to blow tempestuously — of wind; **great gun** a cannon (*obs.*): a person of great importance (*coll.*; also **big gun**); **gun for** to seek, try to obtain: to seek to ruin; **kiss the gunner's daughter** to be tied to a gun for a flogging; **son of a gun** a soldier's bastard (*obs.*): a rogue, rascal (*slang*): used as an affectionate greeting: also *interj.* (*U.S.*); **spike someone's guns** see **spike²**; **stand, stick, to one's guns** to maintain one's position staunchly. [M.E. *gonne*, poss. from the woman's name *Gunhild*.]

gundy *gun′di*, (*Scot.*) *n.* a sweetmeat made of treacle and spices. [Perh. variant of **candy**.]

gunge *gunj*, (*coll.*) *n.* any dirty, messy, or sticky substance. — *adj.* **gun′gy**. [Perh. a combination of **goo** and **sponge**.]

gung-ho *gung-hō′*, (*U.S. slang*) *adj.* (excessively or irrationally) enthusiastic, eager, zealous. [Chin. *kung*, work, *ho*, together.]

gunite *gun′īt*, *n.* a finely-graded cement concrete (a mixture of cement and sand) sprayed into position under air pressure by a cement gun. [Orig. trademark.]

gunk *gungk*, (*coll.*) *n.* unpleasant, dirty, sticky material, or semi-solid usu. valueless residue from a chemical process. [Orig. trademark of a grease-solvent.]

gunnage. See **gun**.

gunnel¹ *gun′l*, *n.* See **gunwale**.

gunnel² *gun′l*, the butter-fish (*Centronotus*), a small long coast fish of the blenny family. [Origin unknown.]

Gunnera *gun′ər-ə*, *n.* a genus of gigantic-leaved herbs of the mare's-tail family: (without *cap.*) a plant of the genus. [After J. E. *Gunner* (1718–73), Norwegian botanist.]

gunnery. See **gun**.

gunny *gun′i*, *n.* a strong coarse jute fabric. [Hindi *ganī*, *gonī*, sacking — Sans. *gonī*, a sack.]

gunsel *gun′səl*, (*U.S. slang*) *n.* a stupid or inexperienced youth: a catamite: a gunman. [Yiddish *genzel*, gosling — M.H.G. *gensel*, dim. of *gans*, goose; *gunman* meaning influenced by **gun**.]

gunter *gun′tər*, *n.* a Gunter's scale: a rig with topmast sliding on rings (from its resemblance to a sliding variety of Gunter's scale). — **Gunter's chain** a surveyor's chain of 100 links, 66 feet long (10 chains = 1 furlong; 10 sq. chains = 1 acre); **Gunter's scale** a scale graduated in several lines for numbers, logarithmic sines, etc., so arranged that trigonometrical problems can be roughly solved by use of a pair of compasses, or in another form by sliding. [From the inventor, Edmund *Gunter* (1581–1626), astronomer.]

gunwale, gunnel *gun′l*, *n.* the *wale* or upper edge of a ship's side next to the bulwarks, so called because the upper *guns* were pointed from it.

gunyah *gun′yə*, (*Austr.*) *n.* an Australian Aborigine's hut: a roughly-made shelter in the bush. [Aboriginal.]

Günz *günts*, *n.* the first (Pliocene) stage of glaciation in the Alps. — *adjs.* **Günz, Günz′ian.** [From a Bavarian tributary of the Danube.]

gup¹ *gup*, (*obs.*) *interj.* expressing remonstrance or derision. [Prob. **go up.**]

gup² *gup*, (*slang*) *n.* gossip: prattle. [Urdu *gap*.]

guppy *gup′i*, *n.* a small West Indian fish (*Lebistes*) that multiplies very rapidly and feeds on mosquito larvae; also called *millions*. [From R. J. L. *Guppy*, who sent it to the British Museum.]

gur, goor *gûr, gōōr*, *n.* an unrefined sweet cane sugar. [Hindi, coarse sugar — Sans. *guda*.]

gurami. Same as **goramy**.

gurdwara *gûr′dwär-ə*, *n.* a Sikh place of worship. [Punjabi *gurduārā* — Sans. *guru*, teacher, *dvāra*, door.]

gurge *gûrj*, (*Milt.*) *n.* a whirlpool. [L. *gurges*.]

gurgitation *gûr-ji-tā′shən*, *n.* surging. [L. *gurges*, *-itis*, whirlpool.]

gurgle *gûr′gl*, *v.i.* to flow in an irregular noisy current: to make a bubbling sound. — *n.* the sound of gurgling. [Cf. It. *gorgogliare*.]

gurgoyle. See **gargoyle**.

gurjun *gûr′jun*, *n.* an East Indian dipterocarp yielding timber and a balsamic liquid used against leprosy. — Also **gar′jan**. [Hind. *garjan*.]

Gurkha, Goorkha *gōōr′kə, gûr′kə*, *n.* one of the dominant people of Nepal, a broad-chested fighting race claiming Hindu origin, but Mongolised, from whom regiments in the British and Indian armies were formed.

gurl *gûrl*, (*Scot.*) *n.* a growl. — *v.i.* to growl. — *adj.* **gur′ly** grim: lowering: rough: surly. [Cf. **growl**.]

gurlet *gûr′lit*, *n.* a pickaxe with a head pointed at one end, bladed at the other.

Gurmukhi *gōōr′mōō-kē*, *n.* the script in which the sacred texts of the Sikhs are written, which is used also for modern secular writing and printing. [Punjabi *Gurmukhī*, lit. from the mouth of the *guru* or teacher.]

gurn *gûrn*, (*dial.*). A variant of **girn**.

gurnard *gûr′nərd*, **gurnet** *-nit*, *ns.* a fish (*Trigla*; of many species) with large angular head and three finger-like walking rays in front of the pectoral fin. [O.Fr.

gornard, related to Fr. *grogner*, to grunt — L. *grunnīre*, to grunt; from the sound they emit when taken.]

gurney *gúr'ni*, (*U.S.*) *n.* a wheeled stretcher or cart. [Origin uncertain; perh. from the personal name.]

gurrah *gur'ə*, *n.* a coarse Indian muslin. [Hind. *gārhā*, thick.]

gurry *gur'i*, *n.* whale offal: fish offal. [Origin unknown.]

guru, gooroo *gōō'rōō*, *gōō'*, *n.* a spiritual teacher: (often *facet.*) a revered instructor, mentor or pundit. — *ns.* **gu'rudom, gu'ruism, gu'ruship** the state of being a guru. [Hind. *gurū* — Sans. *guru*, venerable.]

gush *gush*, *v.i.* to flow out with violence or copiously: to be effusive, or highly sentimental. — *v.t.* to pour forth copiously. — *n.* that which flows out: a violent issue of a fluid: sentimentality, effusiveness. — *n.* **gush'er** one who gushes: an oil-well that does not have to be pumped. — *adj.* **gush'ing.** — *adv.* **gush'ingly.** — *adj.* **gush'y** effusively sentimental. [M.E. *gosshe, gusche*; the connection, if any, with O.N. *gusa, gjōsa*, Du. *gudsen*, is not clear.]

gusla *gōōs'lə*, **gusle** -*le*, **gusli** -*lē*, *ns.* a one-stringed Balkan musical instrument: a Russian instrument with several strings. — *n.* **guslar'** a performer on it. [Bulg. *gusla*, Serb. *gusle*, Russ. *gusli*.]

gusset *gus'it*, *n.* the piece of chainmail covering a join in armour, as at the armpit: an angular piece inserted in a garment to strengthen or enlarge some part of it or give freedom of movement. — *v.t.* to make with a gusset: to insert a gusset into. [O.Fr. *gousset* — *gousse*, pod, husk.]

gust¹ *gust*, *n.* a sudden blast of wind: a violent burst of passion. — *v.i.* to blow in gusts. — *adjs.* **gust'ful, gust'y** stormy: irritable. — *n.* **gust'iness.** — **gust'-lock** a mechanism on an aeroplane which prevents damage to the elevators by gusts of wind when the aeroplane is stationary. [O.N. *gustr*, blast.]

gust² *gust*, *n.* sense of pleasure of tasting (*arch.*): relish (*arch.*): gratification (*arch.*): taste experience (*obs.*): flavour (*arch.*). — *adj.* and *n.* **gust'able** (*arch.*). — *n.* **gustā'tion** the act of tasting: the sense of taste. — *adjs.* **gust'ative, gust'atory** of or pertaining to the sense of taste; **gust'ful** (*arch.*) savoury: enjoyable. — *adj.* **gust'y** (*Scot.*) savoury: appetisingly flavoured. [L. *gustus*, taste; cf. Gr. *geuein*, to make to taste.]

gusto *gus'tō*, *n.* exuberant enjoyment, zest. [It. — L. *gustus*, taste.]

gut *gut*, *n.* the alimentary canal: sheep's or other intestines or silkworm's glands prepared for violin- strings, etc.: a narrow passage: a strait: a channel: a lane: the belly, paunch (*slang*): (in *pl.*) the viscera: (in *pl.*) the inner or essential parts: (in *pl.*) stamina, toughness of character, tenacity, staying power, endurance, forcefulness (*coll.*). — *adj.* (*coll.*) of feelings or reactions, strong, deeply personal: of issues, etc., having immediate impact, arousing strong feelings. — *v.t.* to take out the guts of: to remove the contents of: to reduce to a shell (by burning, dismantling, plundering, etc.): to extract what is essential from: — *pr.p.* **gutt'ing;** *pa.t.* and *pa.p.* **gutt'ed.** — *adj.* **gut'less** cowardly, lacking strength of character. — *n.* **guts'iness** (*Scot.* and *slang*). — *adj.* **guts'y** gluttonous (*Scot.*): having pluck or nerve (*slang*): lusty, passionate (*slang*). — *n.* **gutt'er.** — *v.t.* and *v.i.* **gutt'le** to eat greedily. — *n.* **gut'zer** (*Austr.* and *N.Z.*) a heavy fall. — **gutbucket** (*gut'buk-it*) a rhythmically simple, raucous, earthy and emotional style of playing jazz; **gut'-scrap'er** (*facet.*) a fiddler. — **hate someone's guts** (*slang*) to have a violent dislike for someone; **have someone's guts (for garters)** (*slang*) to hurt or defeat someone — usu. used as a threat; **have had a gutful (of)** (*slang*) to be thoroughly fed up with, have had as much as, or more than, one is prepared to tolerate; **work, sweat, slog one's guts out** (*slang*) to work extremely hard. [O.E. *guttas* (pl.); cf. *geotan*, to pour; dial. Eng. *gut*, Ger. *Gosse*, a drain.]

gutcher. See **goodsire** under **good.**

gutta¹ *gut'ə*, *n.* a drop: a small drop-like ornament on the underside of a mutule or a regula of the Doric

entablature: a small vacuole: a small round colour-spot (*zool.*): — *pl.* **gutt'ae** (-*ē*). — *adjs.* **gutt'ate, -d** containing drops: spotted. — *n.* **guttā'tion** exudation of drops of liquid from an uninjured part of a plant (whence *v.i.* **gutt'ate**). — *n.pl.* **Guttif'erae** a family of archichlamydeous dicotyledons with abundant oil-glands and passages, and entire exstipulate opposite leaves, including mangosteen, mammee-apple, and, according to some, St John's wort. — *adj.* **guttif'erous** exuding drops: of the Guttiferae. — **gutta serena** amaurosis. [L. *gutta*, drop.]

gutta² *gut'ə*, *n.* the coagulated latex of sapotaceous and other trees, esp. gutta-percha: a hydrocarbon (empirically $C_{10}H_{16}$) found in gutta-percha: a solid gutta-percha golf-ball, used in the 19th century — (*coll.*) **gutt'y.** — **gutt'a-percha** (-*pûr'chə*) a substance like rubber, but harder and not extensible, got chiefly from the latex of Malaysian trees of the Sapotaceae (*Palaquium, Payena*, etc.). — Also *adj.* [Malay *getah*, gum, *percha*, a tree producing it.]

guttate, etc. See **gutta¹.**

gutter *gut'ər*, *n.* a channel for conveying away water, esp. at the roadside or at the eaves of a roof: a furrow, groove: a grooved piece, used to separate pages of type in a forme (*print.*): in philately, the blank strip separating the two halves of a sheet of stamps: (sometimes in *pl.*) the space comprising the fore-edges of pages lying together internally in a forme (*print.*): according to some, the inner margins between two facing pages (*print.*): slum-life, social degradation, or sordidness: (in *pl.*) mud, dirt (*Scot.*). — *v.t.* to cut or form into small hollows. — *v.i.* to become hollowed: to trickle: to run down in drops, as a candle: (of flame) to be blown downwards, or threaten to go out. — *n.* **gutt'-ering** gutters collectively: material for gutters. — **gutt'-erblood** (*Scot.*) a low-born person; **gutter broadcasting, gutter (press) journalism** sensationalistic reporting; **gutt'er-man, -mer'chant** a pavement-side seller of cheap trifles; **gutter pair** a pair of stamps separated by the gutter; **gutter press** that part of the press which specializes in sensationalistic journalism; **gutt'er-snipe** a street urchin: a neglected child from a slum area. [O.Fr. *goutiere* — *goute* — L. *gutta*, a drop.]

guttiferous, Guttiferae. See under **gutta¹.**

guttle. See **gut.**

guttural *gut'ər-əl*, *adj.* pertaining to the throat: formed in the throat: throaty in sound. — *n.* a sound pronounced in the throat or (loosely) by the back part of the tongue (*phon.*): a letter representing such a sound. — *v.t.* **gutt'uralise, -ize** to sound gutturally: to make guttural. — *adv.* **gutt'urally.** [L. *guttur*, the throat.]

gutzer. See **gut.**

guy¹ *gī*, *n.* a rope, rod, etc., used to steady anything, or hold it in position. — *v.t.* to keep in position by a guy. — **guy'-rope.** [O.Fr. *guis, guie*; Sp. *guia*, a guide.]

guy² *gī*, *n.* an effigy of *Guy* Fawkes, dressed up grotesquely on the anniversary of the Gunpowder Plot (5 Nov.): an odd figure: a fellow (*coll.*): a joke, lark (*slang*): flight, decamping (*slang*). — *v.t.* to turn to ridicule, make fun of. — *v.i.* to decamp.

guyle(r). A Spenserian forms of **guile(r).**

guyot *gē'ō*, *n.* a flat-topped submarine mountain. [A. H. *Guyot*, Swiss-born Amer. geologist.]

guyse. A Spenserian form of **guise.**

guzzle *guz'l*, *v.t.* and *v.i.* to swallow (esp. liquor, in Scotland food) greedily. — *n.* a bout of guzzling. — *n.* **guzz'ler.** [Perh. conn. with Fr. *gosier*, throat.]

gwyniad, gwiniad *gwin'i-ad*, *n.* a whitefish (*Coregonus pennanti*), found in Bala Lake. [W. *gwyniad* — *gwyn*, white.]

gyal. See **gayal.**

gybe *jīb*, *v.i.* (of a sail) to swing over from one side to the other: to alter course in this way. — *v.t.* to cause to gybe. — *n.* a gybing. — **gybe mark** a marker on a yacht-race course indicating a turning-point at which yachts must gybe. [Origin obscure; see **jib.**]

gyeld. A Spenserian form of **guild(hall).**

gylden. See **gilden.**

gym *jim, n.* and *adj.* a familiar shortening of **gymnasium, gymnastic, gymnastics.** — **gym shoe** a plimsoll; **gym slip, tunic** a belted pinafore dress worn by schoolgirls.

gymbal. Same as **gimbal.**

gymkhana *jim-kä'nə, n.* a public place for athletic games, etc.: a meeting for such sports: now esp., a meeting for equestrian sports. [Hindi *gend-khāna* (ball-house), racket-court, remodelled on *gym*nastics.]

gymmal. Same as **gimmal.**

gymnasium *jim-nā'zi-əm, n.* a place, hall, building, or school for gymnastics: orig. a public place or building where the Greek youths exercised themselves, with running and wrestling grounds, baths, and halls for conversation: (usu. *gim-nä'zi-ōōm*) a (German) secondary school: — *pl.* **gymnā'siums, -ia,** for continental schools **gymnasien** (*gim-nä'zi-ən*). — *adj.* **gymnā'sial.** — *ns.* **gymnā'siarch** (*-ärk*; Gr. *archos*, chief) head of a gymnasium; **gymnā'siast** a pupil in a gymnasium: a gymnast. — *adj.* **gymnā'sic.** — *ns.* **gym'nast** (*-nast*) one skilled in gymnastics; **gymnas'tic** a system of training by exercise: (in *pl.* used as *sing.*) exercises devised to strengthen the body: (in *pl.*) feats or tricks of agility. — *adjs.* **gymnas'tic, -al** pertaining to athletic exercises: athletic, vigorous. — *adv.* **gymnas'tically.** [Latinised from Gr. *gymnasion* — *gymnos*, naked.]

gymnic *jim'nik,* (*Milt.*) *adj.* gymnastic. [Gr. *gymnikos* — *gymnos*, naked.]

gymn(o)- *gim'n(ō)-, jim'n(ō)'-, -no',* in composition, esp. of biol. terms, naked. — *adj.* **gymnorhi'nal** (Gr. *rhīs, rhīnos,* nose) with unfeathered nostrils. — *ns.* **gym'-nosoph, gymnos'ophist** (Gr. *sophos,* wise) an ancient Hindu philosopher who wore little or no clothing, and lived solitarily in mystical contemplation; **gymnos'ophy; gym'nosperm** (Gr. *sperma,* seed) any of the lower or primitive group of seed-plants whose seeds are not enclosed in any ovary. — *adj.* **gymnosper'mous.** [Gr. *gymnos,* naked.]

gymp. Same as **gimp**[1,2].

(-)gyn-. See **gynaeco-.**

gynae, gyny *gī'ni.* A coll. shortening of **gynaecology, gynaecological.**

gynaeceum *gīn-, jīn-, jin-ē-sē'əm, n.* women's quarters in a house: the female organs of a flower (*bot.*). [Gr. *gynaikeion,* women's quarters.]

gynaeco-, in U.S. **gyneco-,** *gīn-, jīn-, gin-, jin-ē'kō-,* or *-i-ko'-,* **gyno-,** *-ō-* or, *-o',* **(-)gyn-** in composition, woman, female. — *n.* **gyn(aec)o'cracy** (Gr: *kratos,* power) government by women or a woman: a country with such a government. — *adjs.* **gyn(aec)ocrat'ic; gyn'aecoid** woman-like; **gynaecolog'ical.** — *ns.* **gynaecol'ogist; gynaecol'ogy** branch of medicine treating of women's diseases; **gynaecomas'tia, gynaeco-mas'ty** abnormal enlargement of the male breast; **gyn'aecomast; gynand'rism, gynandry** (Gr. *anēr, andros,* man, male) hermaphroditism. — *adj.* **gynan'drous** hermaphroditic: with stamen concrescent with the carpels, as in orchids. — *n.* **gynan'dromorph** (Gr. *morphē,* form) an animal combining male and female secondary characters. — *adjs.* **gynandromorph'ic, gy-nandromorph'ous.** — *ns.* **gynandromorph'ism, gynan'-dromorphy.** — *adj.* **gynodioe'cious** having herm-aphrodite and female flowers on different plants. — *ns.* **gynodioe'cism; gyn(o)ecium** (*jin-, jīn-ē'si-əm*) U.S. spellings of **gynaeceum.** — *adj.* **gynomonoe'cious** hav-ing hermaphrodite and female flowers on the same plant. — *ns.* **gynomonoe'cism; gynophō'bia** fear of women; **gyn'ophore** (Gr. *phoros,* carrying) an elonga-tion of the receptacle of a flower carrying carpels only; **gynostē'mium** (Gr. *stēma,* stamen) a united gynaeceum and androecium, as the column of an orchid. [Gr. *gynē, -aikos,* woman.]

gynn(e)y. Shakespearian spellings of **guinea(-hen).**

gyno-. See **gynaeco-.**

gyny. See **gynae.**

gyp[1] *jip, n.* a college servant at Cambridge and Durham.

[Perh. **gypsy;** or perh. obs. *gippo,* a short jacket, a varlet — obs. Fr. *jupeau.*]

gyp[2] *jip,* (*slang*) *n.* a swindle: a cheat. — *v.t.* to swindle: — *pr.p.* **gypp'ing;** *pa.t.* and *pa.p.* **gypped.**

gyp[3] *jip,* (*slang*) *n.* pain, torture. — **give someone gyp** to cause someone pain. [**gee up.**]

gyppie, gyppo, gyppy. See **gippo.**

gypseous, gypsiferous. See **gypsum.**

Gypsophila *jip-sof'i-lə, n.* a genus of hardy perennials akin to the pinks, but of more chickweed-like aspect: (without *cap.*) a plant of this genus. [Gr. *gypsos,* chalk, *phileein,* to love.]

gypsum *jip'səm, gip'səm, n.* a soft mineral, hydrated calcium sulphate, source of plaster of Paris and other plasters. — *adjs.* **gyp'seous; gypsif'erous** producing or containing gypsum. — **gypsum block** a building block (usu. hollow) made of a gypsum plaster; **(gypsum) plasterboard** a building board consisting of a core of gypsum or anhydrous gypsum plaster between two sheets of paper. [L., — Gr. *gypsos,* chalk.]

gypsy, gipsy *jip'si, n.* a Romany, a member of a wandering people of Indian origin: a cunning rogue: a dark-skinned person. — *adj.* of the gypsies: out-of-door: unconventional: operating independently or illegally (*U.S. coll.*). — *v.i.* to live like a gypsy, camp out, or picnic. — *ns.* **gyp'sydom, gyp'syism.** — **gypsy moth** a kind of tussock-moth; **gyp'sywort** a labiate plant (*Lycopus*) with which gypsies were reputed to stain their skin. [**Egyptian,** because once thought to have come from Egypt.]

gyre *jīr, n.* a ring, circle: a circular or spiral turn or movement. — *v.t.* and *v.i.* (in Lewis Carroll pro-nounced *gīr*) to spin round, gyrate. — *adjs.* **gyr'al; gyr'ant.** — *adv.* **gyr'ally.** — *v.i.* **gyrate'** to revolve, spin, whirl. — *adj.* **gyr'ate** curved around in a coil. — *n.* **gyrā'tion** a whirling motion: a whirl or twist (also *fig.*): a whorl. — *adjs.* **gyrā'tional; gyr'ātory** revolving: spinning round: of traffic, revolving in one-way lines. — *n.* **gy'rō** a gyrocompass: a gyroscope: — *pl.* **gy'ros.** — *adjs.* **gyroid'al** spiral: rotatory; **gyr'ose** having a folded surface: marked with wavy lines or ridges; **gyr'ous.** — *n.* **gyr'us** a convoluted ridge between two grooves: a convolution of the brain. — *ns.* **gyrocar** (*jī'rō-*) a monorail car balanced by a gyroscope; **gyro-com'pass** a compass which indicates direction by the freely moving axis of a rapidly spinning wheel — owing to the earth's rotation, the axis assuming and main-taining a north and south direction; **gyr'odyne** a rotorcraft in which the rotor(s) are power-driven for take-off, landing, etc., but unpowered for cruising flight. — *adj.* **gyromagnet'ic** pertaining to magnetic properties of rotating electric charges. — *ns.* **gyromag'-netism; gyr'omancy** (Gr. *manteiā,* divination) divina-tion by walking in a circle and falling from giddiness; **gyr'oplane, gyrocop'ter** a rotorcraft with unpowered rotor(s) on a vertical axis, e.g. an *autogiro;* **gyr'oscope** an apparatus in which a heavy flywheel or top rotates at high speed, the turning movement resisting change of direction of axis, used as a toy, an educational device, a compass, etc. — *adj.* **gyroscōp'ic.** — *ns.* **gyrostabilisā'tion, -z-; gyrostā'biliser, -z-** a gyroscopic device for countering the roll of a ship, etc.; **gyr'ostat** a gyroscope fixed in a rigid case. — *adj.* **gyrostat'ic.** — *n.sing.* **gyrostat'ics** the science of rotating bodies. — *n.* **gyr'ovague** (L. *gyrovagus:* — *pl. gyrovagi*) a wandering monk of the Middle Ages. — **gyromagnetic compass** a compass used in aircraft in which, in order to eliminate errors caused by changes of course and speed (greater in an aircraft than in a ship), a gyroscope is combined with a magnet system. [L. *gȳrus* — Gr. *gȳros,* a circle, ring.]

gyre-carline *gīr'-kär'lin,* (*Scot.*) *n.* a witch. [O.N. *gȳgr,* a witch, ogress, and **carline.**]

gyrfalcon. See **gerfalcon.**

gyron, giron *jī'ron,* (*her.*) *n.* two lines drawn from the edge of the escutcheon and meeting at right angles in the fesse-point. — *adj.* **gyronn'y.** [Fr. *giron,* older *geron*; O.H.G. *gêro*; cf. **gore**[2].]

gyrose, gyrous, gyrus. See **gyre.**

gyte[1] *gīt*, (*Scot.*) *adj.* crazy, mad.

gyte[2] *gīt*, (*Scot.*) *n.* a child: a first-year boy at Edinburgh High School or Academy. — Also **gait, geit.** [**get,** offspring.]

gytrash *gī'trash*, (*dial.*) *n.* a ghost.

gyve *jīv*, earlier *gīv*, *v.t.* to fetter. — *n.* a shackle: a fetter. [M.E. *gives, gyves.*]

H

H, h *āch*, sometimes spelt out **aitch**, *n.* the eighth letter in our alphabet, representing in Old English a guttural sound, gradually softened down to a spirant, and now often silent: in German notation = B natural (*mus.*): in mediaeval Roman notation = 200, H̄ = 200 000. — **H'-beam** a metal girder H-shaped in section; **H'-bomb** (H for *h*ydrogen) hydrogen bomb.

ha *hä, interj.* denoting various emotions or responses, e.g. surprise, joy, exultation, dismay, enquiry, scepticism, encouragement, hesitation, and when repeated, laughter. [Spontaneous utterance.]

ha'[1] *hā, hə,* a shortened form of have.

ha'[2] *hö, n.* Scots form of **hall.**

haaf *häf, (Orkney* and *Shetland) n.* a deep-sea fishing-ground. — **haaf'-fish'ing.** [O.N. *haf,* sea.]

haanepoot. See **hanepoot.**

haar *här, (East Coast) n.* a raw sea-mist. [O.N. *hārr,* hoary; M. Du. *hare,* bitter cold; Fris. *harig,* misty; cf. **hoar.**]

habanera *(h)ä-bä-nā'rə, n.* a Cuban Negro dance or dance-tune in 2-4 time. [*Habana* or Havana, in Cuba.]

habdabs *hab'dabz, (coll.) n.pl.* a state of extreme nervousness. — Also **ab'dabs.** — **screaming habdabs** *(coll.)* a bad case of this involving hysterical crying. [Origin uncertain.]

habeas corpus *hā'bi-əs kör'pəs,* a writ to a jailer to produce a prisoner in person, and to state the reasons of detention. [L., lit. have the body (*ad subjiciendum,* to be brought up before the judge).]

haberdasher *hab'ər-dash-ər, n.* a seller of small-wares, as ribbons, tape, etc.: a men's outfitter *(U.S.).* — *n.* **hab'erdashery** (or -*dash'*) a haberdasher's goods, business, or shop. [O.Fr. *hapertas*; origin unknown.]

haberdine *hab'ər-dēn, -dīn, -din, n.* dried salt cod. [Old Du. *abberdaen,* also *labberdaen*; prob. from Le *Labourd,* or *Lapurdum,* Bayonne.]

habergeon *hab'ər-jən (Milt. hab'ür'ji-on), n.* a sleeveless mail-coat, orig. lighter than a hauberk. [O.Fr. *haubergeon,* dim. of *hauberc.*]

habile *hab'il, adj.* fit, suitable *(obs.)*: competent *(obs.)*: dexterous, adroit *(rare).* [M.E. variant of **able,** later associated more closely with Fr. *habile,* L. *habilis.*]

habiliment *hə-bil'i-mənt, n.* attire (esp. in *pl.*). — *adjs.* **hab'ilable** *(Carlyle),* capable of being clothed; **habil'atory** of clothes or dressing. [Fr. *habiller,* to dress — L. *habilis,* fit, ready - - *habēre.*]

habilitate *hə-bil'i-tāt, v.t.* to qualify: to equip or finance (as a mine): to attire. — *v.i.* to qualify, esp. as a German university lecturer (Ger. *habilitieren*). — *ns.* **habilitā'tion; habil'itātor.** [L.L. *habilitāre,* to enable — L. *habilis,* able.]

habit *hab'it, n.* ordinary course of behaviour: tendency to perform certain actions: custom: accustomedness: familiarity: bodily constitution: characteristic mode of development: the geometric form taken by a crystal *(crystal.)*: outward appearance: dress, esp. official or customary: a garment, esp. a riding-habit: an addiction to a drug, etc. — *v.t.* to dress: to inhabit *(arch.)*. — *adj.* **hab'itable** that may be dwelt in. — *ns.* **habitabil'ity, hab'itableness.** — *adv.* **hab'itably.** — *ns.* **hab'itant** an inhabitant: (*ab-ē-tã*; Fr.) a native of esp. Canada or Louisiana of French descent (*pl.* in this sense sometimes **habitans**); **habitā'tion** act of inhabiting: a dwelling or residence: a lodge of a society. — *adj.* **habitā'tional.** — *n.* **hab'itaunce** *(Spens.)* dwelling-place. — *adjs.* **hab'ited** clothed; **habit'ual** customary: usual: confirmed by habit. — *n.* one who has a habit: a habitual drunkard, drug-taker, frequenter, etc. — *adv.* **habit'-**

ūally. — *n.* **habit'ūalness.** — *v.t.* **habit'ūāte** to accustom: to settle (in), or to frequent *(arch.).* — *ns.* **habitūā'tion** act of accustoming: process of becoming accustomed: acquired tolerance for a drug, which thereby loses its effect: development of psychological, without physical, dependence on a drug; **hab'itūde** constitution: characteristic condition: habit: relation *(obs.)*: familiar acquaintance *(obs.).* — *adj.* **habitū'dinal.** — *ns.* **habitué** *(hab-it'ū-ā*; Fr. *a-bē-tü-ā*) a habitual frequenter; **hab'itus** physical type, esp. as predisposing to disease *(med.)*: characteristic appearance, manner of growth, etc., of a plant or animal. — **hab'it-cloth** a light broadcloth. — *adj.* **hab'it-forming** of a drug, such as a taker will find it difficult or impossible to give up using. — **hab'it-maker** a maker of riding-habits. — **habit and repute** *(Scots law)* public knowledge that affords strong and generally conclusive evidence of fact. [L. *habitus,* state, dress — *habitāre,* to dwell.]

habitat *hab'i-tat, n.* the normal abode or locality of an animal or plant *(biol.)*: the physical environment of any community: the place where a person or thing can usually be found: a capsule on the sea bed, in which men can live for a prolonged period and from which they can explore their surroundings, the capsule being at the same pressure as the water around it. [L., (it) dwells.]

habitation, habitual, etc. See **habit.**

hable *hā'bl, (Spens.) adj.* Same as **able.**

haboob *hä-bōōb', n.* a sand-storm. [Ar. *habūb.*]

háček *hä'chek, n.* in Slavonic languages, the diacritic (˘) placed over a letter to modify its sound. [Czech.]

hachis *(h)ä-shē, n.* hash. [Fr.]

hachure *hash'ūr, ä-shür, n.* a hill-shading line on a map. — *v.t.* to shade with hachures. [Fr.]

hacienda *as-i-en'də, (Sp. Amer.) n.* a landed estate: a ranch or farm: a main dwelling-house on an estate: a country house: a stock-rearing, manufacturing or mining establishment in the country. [Sp., — L. *facienda,* things to be done.]

hack[1] *hak, v.t.* to cut with rough blows: to chop or mangle: to notch: to roughen with a hammer: to kick the shins of: to put up with, bear *(slang).* — *v.i.* to slash, chop: to cough: to use a computer with great skill: to gain unauthorised access to other computers. — *n.* act of hacking: gash: a notch: chap in the skin: a kick on the shin: a mattock or pick. — *ns.* **hack'er** a skilled and enthusiastic computer operator, esp. an amateur: an operator who uses his skill to break into commercial or government computer systems; **hack'ing.** — *adj.* short and interrupted, as a broken, troublesome cough. — **hack'-log** a chopping-block; **hack'-saw** a saw for metals. — **hack someone off** *(slang)* to make someone thoroughly fed up, disgusted. [Assumed O.E. *haccian,* found in composition *tō-haccian*; cf. Du. *hakken,* Ger. *hacken.*]

hack[2] *hak, n.* a horse (or formerly, still in U.S., a vehicle) kept for hire, esp. a poor one: an ordinary riding-horse: any person overworked on hire: a literary or journalistic drudge: anything hackneyed *(obs.)*. — *adj.* hired: mercenary: hackneyed. — *v.t.* to make a hack of: to use as a hack: to hackney. — *v.i.* to work as a hack: to journey on horseback. — *n.* **hackette'** *(slang)* a woman journalist. — **hack'ing-jacket, -coat** a waisted jacket with slits in the skirt and flapped pockets on a slant; **hack'-work** literary drudgery for publishers. [**hackney.**]

hack[3] *hak, n.* a grating or rack, as for feeding cattle: a rack on which food is placed for a hawk: a bank for drying bricks. [O.E. *hæce, hæc*, grating, hatch; cf. **hatch¹** and **heck¹**.]

hack⁴ *hak*, (*Shak.*) *v.i.* meaning unknown — poss. to take to the highway (or the street), or to have spurs hacked off.

hackamore *hak'ə-mōr, -mör, n.* a halter used esp. in breaking in foals, consisting of a single length of rope with a loop to serve instead of a bridle. [Sp. *jáquima*.]

hackberry *hak'ber-i, n.* the hagberry: an American tree (*Celtis occidentalis*) allied to the elm. [See **hagberry**.]

hackbolt *hak'bōlt, n.* the greater shearwater. — Also **hag'bolt, hag'den, hag'don, hag'down** (*hag'dən*). [Origin obscure.]

hackbut *hak'but*, **hagbut** *hag', ns.* an arquebus. — *n.* **hackbuteer'**. [O.Fr. *haquebute*, from O.Du. *hakebus*; see **arquebus**.]

hackee *hak'ē, n.* the chipmunk. [Imit. of its cry.]

hackery *hak'ər-i, n.* an Indian bullock-cart. [Perh. Bengali *hãkārī*, shouting.]

hackle *hak'l, n.* a comb for flax or hemp: a cock's neck feather; this worn as a decoration in a cap, etc.: (in *pl.*) the hair of a dog's neck: (in *pl.*) hair, whiskers: an angler's fly made of a cock's hackle, or its frayed-out part. — *v.t.* to dress with a hackle. — *n.* **hack'ler**. — *adj.* **hack'ly** rough and broken, as if hacked or chopped: jagged and rough (*min.*). — **make one's hackles rise** to make one angry. [Cf. **hatchel, heckle;** Du. *hekel;* Ger. *Hechel;* perh. partly from O.E. *hacele, hæcele*, cloak, vestment.]

hacklet *hak'lit*, **haglet** *hag', ns.* prob. the shearwater: the kittiwake. [Origin unknown.]

hackmatack *hak'mə-tak, n.* an American larch. [Indian word.]

hackney *hak'ni, n.* a horse for general use, esp. for hire: a horse with a high-stepping action, bred to draw light carriages: a person hired for drudgery (*obs.*). — *v.t.* to carry in a hackney-coach: to use overmuch: to make commonplace. — *adjs.* **hack'ney** let out for hire; **hack'neyed** devoted to common use: trite: dulled by overmuch use. — **hack'ney-carriage, -coach** a vehicle let out for hire; **hack'ney-coach'man; hack'neyman** one who keeps hackney horses. [O.Fr. *haquenée*, an ambling nag; poss. — *Hackney* in East London, where horses were pastured.]

hac lege *hak lē'jē, lā'ge*, (L.) with this law, under this condition.

hacqueton. Same as **acton.**

had¹ *had, pa.t.* and *pa.p.* of **have.**

had² *häd, höd, hud*, a Scots form of **hold¹**: — *pa.p.* **hadden** (*häd'n, hud'n*).

hadal. See **Hades.**

haddock *had'ək, n.* a sea-fish (*Melanogrammus aeglefinus*) of the cod family — (*Scot.*) **hadd'ie.** [M.E. *haddok;* ety. unknown.]

hade *hād*, (*min.*) *n.* the angle between the plane of a fault, etc., and a vertical plane. — *v.i.* to incline from the vertical. [Origin obscure.]

Hades *hā'dēz, n.* the underworld: the abode of the dead: hell. — *adj.* **hā'dal** forming, belonging to, the levels of the ocean deeper than 6000 metres. [Gr. *Aidēs, Haidēs*, the god of the underworld: the abode of the dead.]

hadith *had'ith, hä-dēth', n.* (often with *cap.*) the body of traditions about Mohammed, supplementary to the Koran. [Ar. *hadīth*.]

had-I-wist *had-ī-wist', (obs.) n.* vain regret: remorse. [had I wist.]

hadj, haj, hajj *häj, n.* a Muslim pilgrimage to Mecca. — *n.* **hadj'i, haj'i, hajj'i** (*-ē, -i*) one who has performed a hadj: a Christian who has visited Jerusalem. [Ar. *hajj*, effort, pilgrimage.]

hadn't *had'ənt*, for **had not.**

hadrome *had'rōm, (bot.) n.* xylem. [Gr. *hadros*, thick.]

hadron *had'ron, n.* one of a class of subatomic particles, including baryons and mesons. — *adj.* **hadron'ic.** [Gr. *hadros*, heavy, *-on* as in **proton**, etc.]

hadrosaur *had'rə-sör, n.* the name of a group of herbiv-

orous, bird-hipped, Cretaceous dinosaurs of the ornithopod class, having webbed hands and feet, a duckbill-shaped jaw and a bony crest. [Gr. *hadros*, thick, *sauros*, a lizard.]

hadst. See **have.**

hae *hā*, a form of **have**, esp. Scots.

haecceity *hek-sē'i-ti, hēk-, n.* Duns Scotus's word for that element of existence on which individuality depends, hereness-and-nowness. [Lit. thisness, L. *haec*.]

haem- *hēm-, hem-*, **haemat-, haemo-** (in U.S. **hem-, hemat-, hemo-**) in composition, blood. — *n.* **haem** (also **hem, heme**) the pigment combined with the protein (globin) in haemoglobin. — *adj.* **haemal, hemal** (*hē'məl*) of the blood or blood-vessels: ventral — opp. to *neural*. — *ns.* **Haeman'thus** (Gr. *anthos*, flower) blood-flower, a S. African amaryllid; **haematem'esis** (Gr. *emesis*, vomiting) vomiting of blood from the stomach. — *adj.* **haemat'ic** pertaining to blood. — *n* **hae'matin** a brown substance containing ferric iron obtainable from oxyhaemoglobin or from dried blood. — *adj.* **haematin'ic** having the effect of increasing the haemoglobin or of stimulating production of red blood cells. — *n.* a substance having this effect. — *ns.* **hae'matite** a valuable iron ore, Fe_2O_3, often blood-red, with red streak; **hae'matoblast** (Gr. *blastos*, a germ) a blood platelet. — *adj.* **hae'matoid** bloodlike. — *ns.* **hae'matocele** (Gr. *kēlē* a tumour) a cavity containing blood; **hae'matocrit** a graduated capillary tube in which the blood is centrifuged, to determine the ratio, by volume, of blood cells to plasma (Gr. *kritēs*, judge); **haematogen'-esis** blood formation. — *adj.* **haematogenous** (*-oj'in-əs*) producing blood: produced by, or arising in, the blood: spread through the bloodstream. — *ns.* **haematol'ogist; haematol'ogy** the study of blood; **haematol'ysis** haemolysis; **haematō'ma** a swelling composed of blood effused into connective tissue; **haematopoiesis** (*-poi-ē'sis;* Gr. *poieein*, to make) the formation of blood; **haematō'sis** the formation of blood: conversion of venous into arterial blood; **haematox'ylin** a dye got from logwood; **Haematox'ylon** (Gr. *xylon*, wood) the logwood genus; **haematū'ria** (Gr. *ouron*, urine) presence of blood in the urine. — *adj.* **haem'ic** haematic. — *ns.* **hae'min** the chloride of haematin; **haemoco'nia** (Gr. *koniā*, dust) blood-dust, small colourless granules in the blood; **haemocy'anin** (Gr. *kyanos*, blue) a blue respiratory pigment with functions similar to haemoglobin, in the blood of Crustacea and Mollusca; **hae'mocyte** a blood cell, esp. a red one; **haemodial'ysis** the purifying of the blood (in e.g. cases of kidney failure) by circulating it through an apparatus containing a semi-permeable membrane that blocks the passage of waste products (Gr. *dia*, through, *lysis*, dissolution); **haemoglō'bin** (L. *globus*, a ball) the red oxygen-carrying pigment in the red blood-corpuscles; **haemol'ysis** (Gr. *lysis*, dissolution) breaking up of red blood-corpuscles. — *adj.* **haemolyt'ic** pertaining to haemolysis. — *ns.* **hae'mony** (prob. Gr. *haimōnios*, blood-red) a plant with sovereign properties against magic, etc., in Milton's *Comus;* **haemophil'ia** (Gr. *phileein*, to like) a constitutional tendency to excessive bleeding when any blood-vessel is even slightly injured; **haemophil'iac** one who suffers from haemophilia; **haemop'tysis** (Gr. *ptysis*, a spitting) spitting of blood from the lungs; **haemorrhage** (*hem'ər-ij;* Gr. *haimorrhagiā* — *rhēgnynai*, to burst) a discharge of blood from the blood-vessels: a steady and persistent draining away (*fig.*). — Also *v.i.* — *adj.* **haemorrhagic** (*-raj'*). — *n.* **haemorrhoid** (*hem'ər-oid;* Gr. *haimorrhois, -idos* — *rheein*, to flow) dilatation of a vein about the anus — usu. in *pl.*, piles. — *adj.* **haemorrhoid'al.** — *ns.* **haemos'tasis** stoppage of bleeding or the flow of the blood; **hae'mostat** an instrument for stopping bleeding. — *n.* and *adj.* **haemostat'ic** (Gr. *statikos*, or hypothetical *states*, causing to stand) styptic. [Gr. *haima, -atos*, blood.]

haet, ha'it, hate *hāt, (Scot.) n.* a whit. [From the phrase *deil ha' it*, devil have it.]

haff *haf, n.* a lagoon separated from the sea by a long sandbar. [Ger. *Haff,* bay.]

haffet, haffit *haf', häf'it, (Scot.) n.* the side of the head: the temple: locks of hair on the temple. [**half-head;** cf. O.E. *healf-hēafod,* the sinciput.]

hafflin *häf'lin (Scot.).* Same as **halfling** (see under **half**).

hafnium *haf'ni-əm, n.* an element (Hf; at. numb. 72) discovered in 1922 by Profs. Coster and Hevesy of Copenhagen. [L. *Hafnia,* Copenhagen.]

haft *häft, n.* a handle: a winged leaf-stalk. — *v.t.* to set in a haft: to establish firmly. [O.E. *hæft;* Ger. *Heft.*]

hag¹ *hag, n.* an ugly old woman, originally a witch: one of the round-mouths, allied to the lamprey (also **hag'fish**). — *adjs.* **hagg'ed** haglike: haggard; **hagg'ish.** — *adv.* **hagg'ishly.** — *adj.* **hag'-ridden** ridden by witches, as a horse: troubled by nightmare: obsessed: troubled. — *v.t.* **hag'-ride.** — **hag'-seed** a witch's offspring; **hag'-ta'per** the great mullein; **hag'-weed** the common broom-plant — a broomstick being a witch's supposed mode of transport. [Perh. O.E. *hægtesse,* a witch; cf. Ger. *Hexe.*]

hag² *hag, (Scot.) v.t.* and *v.i.* to hack, hew. [O.N. *höggva.*]

hag³, hagg *hag, (Scot.) n.* any broken ground in a moss or bog: a place from which peat has been dug: a pool or hole in a bog: a relatively high and firm place in a bog: the rough overhanging edge of a peat-hole or stream-bank: brushwood to be cut down. [O.N. *högg,* a gash, ravine, a cutting of trees.]

hagberry *hag'ber-i,* **hackberry** *hak',* *ns.* the bird-cherry: the American hackberry. [Cf. O.N. *heggr,* bird-cherry.]

hagbolt, hagden, hagdon, hagdown. See **hackbolt.**

hagbut. See **hackbut.**

hagg. See **hag³.**

Haggada *hä-gä'də, n.* a free Rabbinical homiletical commentary on the whole Old Testament, forming, with the Halachah, the Midrash: the Passover ritual. — Also **Hagga'dah, Aga'dah.** — *adjs.* **Haggad'ic, Haggadist'ic.** — *n.* **Hagga'dist.** [Heb.]

haggard *hag'ərd, n.* an untamed hawk, or one caught when adult, esp. a female. — *adj.* untamed: intractable: lean: hollow-eyed, gaunt, from weariness, hunger, etc. — *adv.* **hagg'ardly.** — *n.* **hagg'ardness.** [O.Fr. *hagard.*]

haggis *hag'is, n.* a Scottish dish made of the heart, lungs, and liver of a sheep, calf, etc., chopped up with suet, onions, oatmeal, etc., seasoned and boiled in a sheep's stomach-bag or a substitute. [Ety. unknown.]

haggle *hag'l, v.t.* to cut unskilfully: to mangle. — *v.i.* to bargain contentiously or wranglingly: to stick at trifles: to cavil. — *n.* **hagg'ler.** [Freq. of **hag²,** at least in part.]

hagi- *hag'i-* (sometimes *haj'i-*) in composition, holy: saint. — *ns.* **hag'iarchy** rule or order of saints or holy persons; **hagioc'racy** government by holy ones. — *n.pl.* **Hagiog'rapha** those books which with the Law and the Prophets make up the Old Testament. — *n.* **hagiog'rapher** a writer of the Hagiographa: a sacred writer: a writer of saints' lives. — *adjs.* **hagiograph'ic, -al.** — *ns.* **hagiog'raphist; hagiog'raphy** a biography of a saint: a biography which over-praises its subject; **hagiol'ater** a worshipper of saints; **hagiol'atry** (Gr. *latreiā,* worship). — *adjs.* **hagiolog'ic, -al.** — *ns.* **hagiol'ogist** a writer of, or one versed in, saints' legends; **hagiol'ogy; hag'ioscope** a squint in a church, giving a view of the high altar. — *adj.* **hagioscop'ic.** [Gr. *hagios,* holy.]

haglet. Same as **hacklet.**

hah *hä, interj.* Same as **ha.**

ha-ha¹ *hä-hä, interj.* in representation of a laugh. — *n.* the sound of laughter. — *v.i.* to laugh. — *interj.* **ha-ha'** an expression of triumph, e.g. on discovering something. [Imit.]

ha-ha² *hä'hä,* **haw-haw** *hö'hö, ns.* a ditch or vertical drop e.g. between a garden and surrounding parkland, forming a barrier without interrupting the view. [Fr. *haha.*]

hahnium *hä'ni-əm, n.* an artificially-produced transuranic element (Ha; at. numb. 105). [Otto *Hahn* (1879–1968), Ger. physicist.]

haick. See **haik¹.**

haiduk, heyduck *hī'dook, n.* a brigand: a guerrilla warrior: a liveried servant. [Hung. *hajduk,* pl. of *hajdú.*]

haik¹, haick, haique, hyke *hīk, n.* an oblong cloth worn by Arabs on head and body. [Ar. *hayk.*]

haik². See **heck¹.**

haikai. See **haiku.**

Haikh *hīhh, n.* and *adj.* Armenian. [Armenian.]

haiku *hī'koo, n.* a Japanese poem in three lines of 5, 7, 5 syllables, usu. comical, developed in the 17th cent., incorporating a word or phrase that symbolises one of the seasons. — Also **haikai** (*hī'kī*) orig. a linked series of haiku forming one poem (short for *haikai no renga,* linked comic verse), and **hokku** (*hö'koo*) orig. the first half-line of a linked series of haiku. [From Jap.]

hail¹ *hāl, n.* health (*obs.*): a call from a distance: a greeting: earshot. — *adj.* (*obs.*) sound, hale. — *v.t.* to greet: to address, accost: to call to from a distance: to summon to stop or come. — *interj.* of greeting or salutation. — *n.* **hail'er.** — *adj.* **hail'-fellow(-well-met')** readily friendly and familiar. — Also *n.* and *adv.* — **hail Mary** (a recital of) the English version of the ave Maria. — **hail from** to belong to, come from (a particular place). [O.N. *heill,* health, (*adj.*) sound; cf. **hale¹, heal¹.**]

hail² *hāl, n.* frozen rain or grains of ice falling from the clouds: a shower, bombardment, of missiles, abuse, etc. — *v.i.* and *v.t.* to shower hail: to shower vigorously or abundantly. — *adj.* **hail'y.** — **hail'shot** small shot that scatters like hail; **hail'stone** a ball of hail; **hail'storm.** [O.E. *hægl (hagol);* Ger. *Hagel.*]

hail³ *hāl, (Scot.) n.* in ball-games, a goal: a score. — *v.t.* to score (a goal): to put into the goal. [App. from **hail¹,** from the shout with which the player claimed a goal.]

hain *hān, (Scot.) v.t.* to save, preserve: to spare. — *adj.* **hained.** — *n.* **hain'ing** an enclosure. [O.N. *hegna,* to enclose, protect; cf. Sw. *hägna;* Dan. *hegne.*]

hainch *hänsh, hänch,* Scots form of **haunch¹.**

haique. See **haik¹.**

hair *hār, n.* a filament growing from the skin of an animal: an outgrowth of the epidermis of a plant: a fibre: a mass or aggregate of hairs, esp. that covering the human head: anything very small and fine: a hair's-breadth: type or character (*obs.*): a locking spring or other safety contrivance in a firearm. — *v.t.* to free from hair: to furnish with hair. — *adj.* **haired** usu. in composition, having hair (of a specified type, length, etc.). — *n.* **hair'iness.** — *adj.* **hair'less** having no hair: very angry (*slang*): desperate (*slang*). — *n.* **hair'lessness.** — *adjs.* **hair'like; hair'y** of or like hair: covered with hair: dangerous, risky (*coll.*). — **hair'-ball** a concretion of hair in the stomach; **hair'-band** a band, usu. of or incorporating elastic material, worn over the hair to confine it or as an ornament; **hair'bell** same as **harebell.** — *adj.* **hair'-brained** same as **hare-brained.** — **hair'-breadth** see **hair's-breadth; hair'-brush** a brush for the hair; **hair'cloth** cloth made wholly or partly of hair; **hair'cut** a cutting of the hair or the style in which this is done; **hair'-do** (*coll.*) process or style of hairdressing: — *pl.* **hair'-dos; hair'dresser** one whose occupation is the cutting, colouring, arranging, etc. of hair: a barber; **hair'dressing** a lotion, etc. for the hair: the art or occupation of a hairdresser; **hair'-dryer, -drier** any of various types of hand-held or other apparatus producing a stream of warm air for drying the hair; **hair'-eel** a hair-worm; **hair'-grass** a genus (*Aira*) of coarse grasses (perh. only a modification of the generic name); **hair'-grip** a short, narrow band of metal, bent double, worn in the hair, to keep it in place; **hair'line** a line made of hair: a very fine line in writing, type, etc.: a finely striped cloth: the edge of the hair on the forehead. — *adj.* (of e.g. a crack) very thin: also *fig.* — **hair'-net** a net for confining a woman's hair; **hair'-oil**

a scented oil for dressing the hair; **hair'-pen'cil** a fine paint-brush; **hair'-piece** a length of false hair, or a wig covering only part of the head; **hair'pin** a bent wire or the like used for fastening up the hair. — *adj.* narrowly U-shaped, as a bend on a road. — **hair'-powd'er** powdered starch formerly dusted on the hair or wig; **hair'-rais'er** a tale of terror. — *adj.* **hair'-rais'ing.** — **hair-restor'er** a preparation claiming to make hair grow on bald places; **hair'-seal** a sea-lion, or eared seal with coarse hair only; **hair'-shirt** a penitent's garment of haircloth: an intimate or secret affliction (*fig.*); **hair's'-breadth, hair'breadth** the breadth of a hair: a minute distance. — *adj.* (of an escape, etc.) extremely narrow; **hair'-slide** a hinged clasp, often decorative, worn in the hair esp. by young girls; **hair'-space** the thinnest metal space used by compositors; **hair'-splitt'-er** a maker of over-fine distinctions; **hair'-splitt'ing; hair'-spray** lacquer sprayed on the hair to hold it in place; **hair'spring** a slender spring regulating a watch balance; **hair'streak** a butterfly (Thecla, etc.) with fine white band under the wing; **hair'-stroke** a hairline in penmanship; **hair'style** a particular way of cutting and arranging the hair; **hair'stylist; hair'-tail** a fish of the family Trichiuridae, with whiplike tail; **hair'-trigg'er** a trigger, responding to very light pressure, that releases the hair of a gun. — *adj.* having a hair-trigger: responding to the slightest stimulus. — **hair'-wave** a wavelike appearance artificially given to hair; **hair'=waver, hair'-waving; hair'-work** work done or something made with hair, esp. human; **hair'-worm** a worm, like a horse-hair, which when young lives in the bodies of insects. — **against the hair** (*arch.*) against the grain: contrary to inclination; **a hair of the dog that bit him** a smaller dose of that which caused the trouble: a morning glass after a night's debauch — a homoeo-pathic dose; **by the short hairs** in a powerless position, at one's mercy; **get in someone's hair** (*coll.*) to become a source of irritation to someone; **keep one's hair on** (*coll.*) to keep calm; **let one's hair down** to forget reserve and speak or behave freely; **lose one's hair** to grow angry; **make someone's hair curl** to shock someone extremely; **make someone's hair stand on end** to frighten or astonish someone greatly; **not turn a hair** (of a horse) to show no sweat: not to be ruffled or disturbed; **put up the hair** to dress the hair up on the head instead of wearing it hanging — once the mark of passage from girlhood to womanhood; **split hairs** to make superfine distinctions; **tear one's hair** to display frenzied grief or (*coll.*) great irritation; **to a hair, to the turn of a hair** exactly, with perfect nicety. [O.E. *hær*, Ger. *Haar*, Du. and Dan. *haar*, etc.; vowel perh. influenced by Fr. *haire*, a hair-shirt.]

hairst *hārst*, a Scottish form of **harvest.** — **hairst-rig'** a harvest-field, or a section of it, formerly cut in com-petition.

ha'it. See **haet.**

haith *hāth*, (*Scot.*) *interj.* by my faith. [**faith.**]

haj, haji, hajj, hajji. See **hadj, hadji.**

haka *hä'kä, n.* a Maori ceremonial war-dance: a similar dance performed by New Zealanders, e.g. before a rugby game. [Maori.]

hakam *häk'äm, n.* a sage: a rabbinical commentator, esp. one during the first two cents. A.D. [Heb. *hākhām*, wise.]

hake¹ *hāk, n.* a gadoid fish resembling the cod. [Prob. Scand.; cf. Norw. *hake-fisk*, lit. hook-fish.]

hake². See **heck¹.**

Hakenkreuz *hä'kən-kroits, n.* the swastika. [Ger., hook-cross.]

hakim¹ *hä-kēm', n.* a physician. [Ar. *hakīm*.]

hakim² *hä'kim, n.* a judge, governor, or official in Paki-stan. [Ar. *hakim*.]

Halachah, Halakah, Halacha *hä-lä'hhä, -kä, n.* the legal element in the Midrash. — *adj.* **Halach'ic.** [Heb., — *hālak*, to walk.]

halal *häl-äl', v.t.* to slaughter according to Muslim law. — *n.* an animal that may lawfully be eaten as so

slaughtered. — Also *adj.* [Ar. *halāl*, lawful.]

halation *hə-, ha-lā'shən, n.* blurring in a photograph by reflection and dispersion of light: a bright area around a bright spot on a fluorescent screen. [**halo.**]

halavah. See **halva(h).**

halberd *hal'bərd, n.* an axe-like weapon with a hook or pick on its back, and a long shaft, used in the 15th and 16th centuries, in the 18th century denoting the rank of sergeant. — Also **hal'bert.** — *n.* **halberdier** (*-dēr'*) one armed with a halberd. [O.Fr. *halebard* — M.H.G. *helmbarde* (Ger. *Hellebarde*) — *Halm*, stalk, or *Helm*, helmet, O.H.G. *barta* (Ger. *Barte*), axe.]

Halbstarker *halp'shtärk'ər,* (Ger.) *n.* a juvenile delin-quent.

halcyon *hal'si-ən, n.* the kingfisher, once believed to make a floating nest on the sea, which remained calm during hatching. — *adj.* calm: peaceful: happy. — **halcyon days** a time of peace and happiness. [L. *halcyōn* — Gr. *alkyōn*, fancifully changed to *halkyōn* as if from *hals*, sea, *kyōn*, conceiving.]

hale¹ *hāl, adj.* healthy: robust: sound of body: whole (*Scot.*; also *n.*, with definite article). — *n.* **hayle** (*Spens.*) welfare. — *n.* **hale'ness.** — **hale and hearty** in good health. [Northern, from O.E. *hāl*; see **whole**; cf. **hail¹, heal¹.**]

hale² *hāl, v.t.* to drag. [O.Fr. *haler*; Germanic in origin.]

haler *hä'lər, n.* a coin of Czechoslovakia, worth 1/100 of a koruna. — Also **heller** (*hel'ər*). [See **heller.**]

half *häf, n.* one of two equal parts: a half-year, term: a half-back: a halved hole in golf: half a pint, usu. of beer (*coll.*): — *pl.* **halves** (*hävz*). — *adj.* having or consisting of one of two equal parts: being in part: incomplete, as measures. — *adv.* to the extent of one-half: in part: imperfectly. — *adj.* **half'en** (*Spens.*) half. — *adv.* **half'endeale** (*Spens.*) half. — *ns.* **half'lin, half'ling** (*Scot.*) half-grown person, between boy and man: half a silver penny. — *adj.* half-grown. — *adv.* **half'lin(g)s** (*Scot.*) half: partially. — *adj.* half-grown. — **half'-adder** (*comput.*) a circuit having two inputs and outputs, which can add two binary digits and give the sum and the carry digit; **half'-and-half** a mixture of two things in equal proportions, esp. beer or porter and ale. — *adj.* and *adv.* in the proportion of one to one, or approximately: in part one thing, in part another. — **half'-ape** a lemur; **half'-back** in football, a player or position directly behind the forwards — in Rugby (*scrum* half and *stand-off* half), a link between forwards and three-quarters. — *adj.* **half'-baked'** un-derdone: incomplete: crude: immature: half-witted. — *v.t.* **half'-baptise', -ize** to baptise privately and hastily. — **half'-beak** a fish (Hyporhynchus, etc.) with spear-like under-jaw; **half'-bind'ing** a bookbinding with only backs and corners of leather or the like; **half'-blood** relation between those who have only one parent in common: a half-breed. — *adj.* **half'-blood'ed.** — **half'=blue'** at university, a substitute for a full blue, or the colours awarded him or her; **half'-board** a manoeuvre by which a sailing-ship gains distance to windward by luffing up into the wind (*naut.*): in hotels, etc., the providing of bed, breakfast and one main meal per day, demi-pension; **half'-boot** a boot reaching halfway to the knee. — *adjs.* **half'-bound** bound in half-binding; **half'-bred** poorly bred or trained: mongrel. — **half'=breed** one of mixed breed (esp. a mixture of white and coloured races); **half'-brother, half'-sister** a brother or sister by one parent only; **half'-cap** (*Shak.*) a cap only partly taken off, a slight salute; **half'-caste** a half-breed, esp. a Eurasian. — *adj.* **half'-checked** (*Shak.*) with reins attached halfway up the side-piece of the bit, giving little leverage. — **half'-cheek** (*Shak.*) a face in profile; **half'-close** (*mus.*) an imperfect cadence; **half'-cock'** the position of the cock of a gun drawn back halfway and retained by the first notch (**at half-cock** only partially prepared): a stroke made by playing neither forward nor back (*cricket*). — *adv.* in that position. — *adj.* **half'-cocked'.** — **half'-crown'** a coin worth **half'-a=**

crown′ or two shillings and sixpence, from 1970 no longer legal tender: a sum of money equivalent to this (also *adj.*); **half′-day′** a holiday of half a working day. — *adj.* **half′-dead′** (*coll.*) very weary, exhausted. — **half′-doll′ar** an American coin worth 50 cents (also *adj.*). — *adj.* **half′-done** p**a**rtly done: partly cooked. — **half′-door** the lower part of a divided door. — *n.* and *adj.* **half′-doz′en** six. — *adjs.* **half′-dū′plex** (*comput., teleg.*, etc.) allowing communication or transmission in both directions, but not simultaneously; **halfe′= hors′y** (*Spens.*) of the Centaurs, partly of the nature of horses; **half′-ever′green** having foliage that persists during part of winter: tending to be evergreen in mild areas but deciduous where the climate is more rigorous. — **half′-face** profile. — *adjs.* **half′-faced** (*Shak.*) showing only part of the face: thin-faced; **half′-frame** of a photograph, taking up half the normal area of a frame; **half′-hard′y** able to grow in the open air except in winter; **half′-heart′ed** lacking in zeal. — *adv.* **half′= heart′edly.** — **half′-heart′edness; half′-hitch** a simple knot tied around an object; **half′-hol′iday** half of a working day for recreation; **half′-hour′** a period of 30 minutes. — Also *adj.* — *adj., adv.* **half-hour′ly** at intervals of 30 minutes. — **half-hunter** see **hunter; half′-in′teger** a number formed by the division of an odd integer by two. — *adj.* **half′-in′tegral.** — **half′= kir′tle** a kind of jacket worn by women in 16th and 17th cent.; **half′-landing** small landing at the bend of a staircase; **half′-leath′er** a half-binding for a book, with leather on back and corners; **half′-length** portrait showing the upper part of the body. — *adj.* of half the whole or ordinary length. — **half′-life** the period of time in which activity of a radioactive substance falls to half its original value; **half′-light** dim light: twilight; **half′-loaf′** a loaf of half the standard weight; **half marathon** a foot-race just over half the length of a marathon (13 miles 352 yards, 21·243 km); **half′-mast′** the position of a flag partly lowered, in respect for the dead or in signal of distress. — Also *adv.* and *v.t.* — **half′-meas′ure** (often in *pl.*) any means inadequate for the end proposed; **half′-mil′er** a runner specialising in races of half a mile; **half′-moon′** the moon at the quarters when half the disc is illuminated: anything semicircular; **half′-mourn′ing** mourning attire less than deep or full mourning: the condition of having one black eye (*slang*); **half nelson** see **nelson; half′-note** (*mus.; U.S.*) a minim; **half′-one′** (*golf*) a handicap of one stroke every second hole (see also **half past one** below); **half′-pay′** reduced pay, as of an officer not on active service. — *adj.* **half′-pay** on half-pay. — **half-penny** (*hāp′ni*) a coin worth half a penny, withdrawn from circulation in 1985: its value: anything very small (*Shak.*): — *pl.* **halfpence** (*hā′pəns*), also **halfpennies** (*hāp′niz*). — *adj.* valued at a halfpenny. — **halfpenny-worth** (*hāp′ni-wûrth* —also **hap′orth** *hāp′ərth*) as much as is sold for a halfpenny or is worth a halfpenny; **half′-pike** a short-shafted pike: a spontoon; **half′-pint** (*slang*) a very small person; **half′-plate** see **plate; half′= pound** half a pound. — *adj.* weighing half a pound. — **half′-pound′er** a fish or other thing weighing half a pound: a gun that throws a half-pound shot; **half′= price′** a charge reduced to half. — *adj.* and *adv.* at half the usual price. — **half′-round′** a semicircle. — *adj.* (*Milt.*) semicircular. — **half′-roy′al** a kind of millboard. — *adj.* and *adv.* **half′-seas-o′ver** halfway across the sea: half-drunk. — **half′-shell** one shell or valve of a bivalve; **half′-shift′** a position of the hand in violin-playing giving notes a semitone above the open-string position; **half′-sole** the part of a shoe-sole from the instep to the toe; **half′-sove′reign** a gold coin worth **half′-a-sove′-reign** or ten shillings. — *adj.* **half′-starved′** very inadequately fed. — **half′-step** (*mus.; U.S.*) a semitone; **half′-sword** fighting within half a sword's length: close fight; **half′-term′** (a holiday taken at) the mid point of an academic term; **half′-text** handwriting half the size of text. — Also *adj.* — **half′-tide** the stage midway between flood and ebb. — *adj.* uncovered at half-tide.

— *adj.* **half′-tim′bered** built of a timber frame, with spaces filled in. — **half′-time′** half of full or whole time: the middle of the whole time: a short break halfway through a game (*sport*): in industry, half the time usually worked. — *adj.* **half′-time** at or for half-time. — **half′-tim′er** one who works half the full time; **half′-tint** intermediate tone, between light and dark; **half′-ti′tle** a short title preceding the title page or before a section of a book. — *adj.* **half′-tone** representing light and shade photographically by dots of different sizes. — *n.* (*mus.*) a semitone. — **half′-track** a motor vehicle with wheels in front and caterpillar tracks behind. — Also *adj.* — **half′-truth** a belief containing an element of truth: a statement conveying only part of the truth; **half′-voll′ey** see **volley.** — *adv.* **halfway′** (sometimes *häf′wā*) midway: at half the distance: imperfectly: slightly, barely (*coll.*). — *adj.* **half′way** equidistant from two points. — **halfway house** an inn, etc. situated midway between two towns, points on a journey, etc.: a midway point or state: a centre offering accommodation and rehabilitation to e.g. released prisoners, persons recovering from mental illness, etc.; **half′-wit** a would-be wit (*obs.*): an idiot. — *adj.* **half′-witt′ed** mentally defective. — **half′-year** half of a year, six months. — *adj.* **half′-year′ly** occurring or appearing every half-year. — *adv.* twice a year. — *n.* a half-yearly publication. — **by half** by a long way; **by halves** incompletely: half-heartedly; **cry halves** to claim half; **go halves** to share equally; **half past one, two,** etc., **half after one, two,** etc. (*U.S.*), **half one, two,** etc. (*coll.*) thirty minutes after one o'clock, two o'clock, etc.; **how the other half lives** (*facet.*) other (esp. richer or poorer) people's way of life; **not half** (*slang*) not moderately: not even half: not at all: very much, exceedingly; **one's other** or **better half** one's spouse. [O.E. (Anglian) *half* (W.S. *healf*), side, half; cf. Ger. *halb*; Dan. *halv*.]

halfa, alfa *(h)al′fə, ns.* N. African esparto. [Ar. *halfā.*]

halfpace *häf′pās, n.* a landing or broad step: a raised part of a floor. [O.Fr. *halt* (Fr. *haut*), high, *pas*, step.]

halibut *hal′i-bət, n.* a large flatfish, more elongated than flounder or turbot. — Also **hol′ibut.** [App. **holy butt** as much eaten on holy days; see **holy, butt⁵**; cf. Du. *heilbot*, Ger. *Heilbutt.*]

halicore *hal-ik′o-rē, n.* the dugong. [Gr. *hals*, sea, *korē*, girl.]

halide *hal′īd, n.* a compound of a halogen with a metal or radical — a chloride, bromide, etc. [Gr. *hals*, salt.]

halidom *hal′i-dəm,* (*arch.*) *n.* holiness: a holy place or thing — esp. in an oath. [O.E. *hāligdōm* — *hālig*, holy.]

halieutic *hal-i-ū′tik, adj.* pertaining to fishing. — *n. sing.* **halieu′tics** the art of fishing: a treatise thereon. [Gr. *halieutikos* — *halieus*, fisher — *hals*, sea.]

halimot(e) *hal′i-mōt, n.* an erroneous form of **hall-moot** (as if a holy or church court).

Haliotis *hal-i-ō′tis, n.* ear-shell or ormer, a genus of gasteropods with ear-shaped shell with perforations, belonging to the family **Haliōt′idae:** (without *cap.*) a member of the genus: — *pl.* **haliō′tis.** [Gr. *hals*, sea, *ous, ōtos*, ear.]

halite *hal′īt, n.* rock-salt. [Gr. *hals*, salt.]

halitus *hal′i-təs, n.* a vapour. — *n.* **halitō′sis** foul breath. — *adj.* **hal′itous** vaporous. [L.]

hall *höl, n.* the main room in a great house: a building containing such a room: a manor-house: the main building of a college: in some cases the college itself: an unendowed college: a licensed residence for students: a college dining-room: hence, the dinner itself: a place for special professional education, or the conferring of diplomas, licences, etc.: the headquarters of a guild, society, etc.: a servants' dining-room and sitting-room (*servants' hall*): a building or large chamber for meetings, concerts, exhibitions, etc.: a large room entered immediately by the front door of a house: a passage or lobby at the entrance of a house: a clear space (*arch.*). — **hall′-bed′room** (*U.S.*) a bedroom partitioned off at the end of an entrance-hall;

hall'-door front-door; **hall'mark** the authorised stamp impressed on gold, silver or platinum articles at Goldsmiths' Hall or other place of assaying, indicating date, maker, fineness of metal, etc.: any mark of authenticity or good quality. — *v.t.* to stamp with such a mark. — **hall'-moot** the court of the lord of a manor: the court of a guild; **hall'stand** a tall piece of furniture on which hats, coats and umbrellas can be left; **hall'way** an entrance hall. — **a hall, a hall** (*arch.*) a cry at a masque for room for the dance, etc.; **bachelor's hall** a place free from the restraining presence of a wife; **Liberty Hall** a place where everyone may do as he pleases; **the halls** music-halls. [O.E. *hall* (*heall*); Du. *hal*, O.N. *höll*, etc.]

hallal. Same as **halal**.

hallali *hal'ə-lē*, *n.* a bugle-call.

hallaloo *hal-ə-lōō'*, (*Fielding*) *n.* halloo.

hallan *häl'ən*, (*Scot.*) *n.* a partition or screen between the door and fireplace in a cottage. — **hallan-shak'er** (or -*shak'ər*) a sturdy beggar. [Perh. **hall**.]

hälleflinta *hel'ə-flin-tə*, *n.* a very compact rock composed of minute particles of quartz and feldspar. [Sw., hornstone.]

hallelujah, halleluiah *hal-ə-lōō'yə*, *n.* and *interj.* the exclamation 'Praise Jehovah': a song of praise to God: a musical composition based on the word. — Also **alleluia**. [Heb. *hallelū*, praise ye, and *Jāh*, Jehovah.]

halliard. See **halyard**.

halling *hal'ing, höl'ing, n.* a Norwegian country dance in 2-4 time, or its tune. [Perh. *Hallingdal*, N.W. of Oslo.]

hallion, hallian, hallyon *hal'yən*, *n.* a lout: a lazy rascal. [Origin unknown.]

hallo, halloa *hə-lö', hu-lö', interj.* expressing surprise, discovery, becoming aware: used also in greeting, accosting, calling attention. — *n.* a call of hallo: — *pl.* **hallō(e)s', halloas'.** — *v.i.* to call hallo. — Also **hello, hullo.** [Imit.]

halloo *hə-lōō', n.* a cry to urge on a chase or to call attention. — *v.i.* to cry dogs on: to raise an outcry. — *v.t.* to encourage with halloos: to hunt with halloos. — **don't halloo till you're out of the wood** keep quiet till you are sure you are safe. [Imit.]

hallow *hal'ō, v.t.* to make holy: to consecrate (*arch.*): to reverence. — *n.* (*obs.*) a saint. — *ns.* **Hallowe'en'** (esp. *Scot.*) the eve of, or the evening before, All Hallows; **Hall'owmas** the feat of All Hallows or All Saints, 1st November. [O.E. *hālgian*, to hallow, *hālga*, a saint — *hālig*, holy.]

halloysite *hal-oiz'īt, n.* a clayey mineral, a hydrated aluminium silicate. [Omalius d'*Halloy* (1783–1875), Belgian geologist.]

Hallstatt *häl'shtät, adj.* relating to a European culture transitional between Bronze Age and Iron Age. [From finds at *Hallstatt* in upper Austria.]

hallucinate *hə-lōō'sin-āt, hə-lū', v.t.* to affect with hallucination. — *v.i.* to experience hallucination. — *n.* **hallucinā'tion** a perception without objective reality: loosely, delusion. — *adjs.* **hallu'cinative, hallu'cinatory.** — *n.* **hallu'cinogen** a drug producing hallucinatory sensations. — *adj.* **hallucinogen'ic** causing hallucinations. — *n.* **hallucino'sis** a mental disorder characterised by the repeated occurrence of hallucinations. [L. *hallūcinārī* (better *ālūcinārī*), -*ātus*, to wander in the mind.]

hallux *hal'uks, n.* the innermost digit of the hind-limb: the great toe: a bird's hind-toe: — *pl.* **halluces** (-*ū'sēz*). [Wrong form of L. (*h*)*allex*, -*īcis*.]

hallyon. See **hallion**.

halm *häm.* Same as **haulm**.

halma *hal'mə, n.* in the Greek pentathlon, a long jump with weights in the hands (*hist.*): a game played on a board of 256 squares, in which the men move by jumps. [Gr., a jump.]

halo *hā'lō, n.* a ring of light or colour, esp. one round the sun or moon caused by refraction by ice-crystals: in paintings, etc. such a ring round the head of a holy person: an ideal or sentimental glory or glamour attaching to anything: — *pl.* **hā'loes, hā'los.** — *v.t.* to surround with a halo (*lit.* and *fig.*): — *pa.p.* **hā'loed, hā'lo'd.** — **halo effect** (*psych.*) the tendency to judge a person (well or ill) on the basis of one or only a few characteristics. [Gr. *halōs*, a threshing-floor, disc, halo.]

halobiont, etc., **halogen**, etc. See **haloid**.

haloid *hal'oid, n.* a halide. — *adj.* having the composition of a halide. — *n.* **halobiont** (*hal-ō-bī'ont*) an organism living or growing in a saline habitat. — *adjs.* **halobion'tic; halobiotic** (-*bī-ot'ik*) living in the sea. — *ns.* **hal'ocarbon** (*chem.*) a compound consisting of carbon and one or more halogens; **halogen** (*hal'ə-jen*) any one of certain elements in the seventh group of the periodic table, fluorine, chlorine, bromine, iodine, and astatine (the first four defined in the 19th cent. as forming salts by direct union with metals; astatine discovered in 1940). — *v.t.* **halogenate** (-*oj'*) to combine with a halogen. — *adjs.* **halog'enous; hal'ophile** (-*fil*, -*fīl*), **haloph'ilous** tolerant of salt: capable of living in salt water. — *ns.* **haloph'ily** adaptation to life in the presence of much salt; **hal'ophobe** (*bot.*) a plant that cannot survive in salty soil; **halophyte** (*hal'ō-fīt*) a plant adapted to life in soil or water containing much salt. — *adj.* **halophytic** (-*fit'*). — *n.* **hal'ōthane** a general, inhalation anaesthetic known proprietarily as Fluothane. [Gr. *hals*, salt.]

Haloragis *hal-ə-rā'jis, n.* sea-berry, an Australasian genus of plants giving name to the family **Haloragidā'ceae,** a reduced offshoot of the evening primrose family, including mare's-tail and water milfoil. [Gr. *hals*, sea, *rhāx*, *rhāgos*, a berry.]

halothane. See **haloid**.

halse¹ *höls, Scot.* and *Northern* **hause, hawse** *hös*, (*obs.* or *dial.*) *ns.* the neck: the throat: a pass, defile, or connecting ridge. — *v.t.* to embrace: — *pa.t.* **halsed,** (*Spens.*) **haulst.** — **hause'-bane** (*Scot.*) collar-bone; **hause'-lock** (*Scot.*) the wool of a sheep's neck. [O.E. *hals* (*heals*), neck; Ger. *Hals*.]

halse² *häls, hös,* (*obs.*) *v.t.* to salute, greet. [O.E. *halsian*.]

halser *höz'ər, n.* Same as **hawser.**

halt¹ *hölt, v.i.* to come to a standstill: to make a temporary stop. — *v.t.* to cause to stop. — *n.* a standstill: a stopping-place: a railway station not fully equipped. — **call a halt (to)** to stop, put an end (to). [Ger. *Halt,* stoppage.]

halt² *hölt, v.i.* to be lame, to limp (*arch.*): to walk unsteadily: to vacillate: to proceed lamely or imperfectly, to be at fault, as in logic, rhythm, etc. — *adj.* (*arch.*) lame, crippled, limping. — *n.* a limp (*arch.*): foot-rot (*dial.*): an impediment in speech (*Scot.*). — *n.* and *adj.* **halt'ing.** — *adv.* **halt'ingly.** [O.E. *halt* (*healt*); Dan. *halt.*]

halter *hölt'ər, n.* a rope for holding and leading an animal, or for hanging criminals: a woman's backless bodice held in place by straps round the neck and across the back. — *v.t.* to put a halter on. — **halter neck** a neckline on a dress, etc. in the style of a halter. — *adj.* **halt'er-necked.** [O.E. *hælftre;* Ger. *Halfter.*]

halteres *hal-tēr'ēz, n.pl.* the rudimentary hind-wings of flies. [Gr. *haltēres,* dumb-bells held by jumpers — *hallesthai,* to jump.]

halva(h), halavah *häl'və, n.* a sweetmeat, orig. Turkish, containing sesame seeds, honey, etc. [Yiddish *halva;* ult. from Ar.]

halve *häv, v.t.* to divide in half: to reduce by half: in golf, to draw: in carpentry, to join by cutting away half the thickness of each. — *n.* **halv'er** one who halves: a half-share. — *interj.* **halv'ers** used in claiming half a find. [half.]

halyard, halliard *hal'yərd, n.* a rope or purchase for hoisting or lowering a sail, yard, or flag. [For *halier* — **hale,** by association with **yard¹**.]

ham¹ *ham, n.* the back of the thigh or hock: the thigh of an animal, esp. of a hog salted and dried. — *adj.*

hamm'y. — *adjs.* **ham'-fist'ed, ham'-hand'ed** clumsy. [O.E. *hamm*; cf. dial. Ger. *hamme*.]

ham² *ham,* (*coll.*) *n.* an actor who rants and overacts: overacting: a part that lends itself to this: an inexpert boxer: an amateur, esp. an amateur radio operator. — *adj.* given to overacting or ranting: amateur: clumsy, coarse, inexpert. — *v.i.* and *v.t.* to overact. — *adj.* **hamm'y.** — *adv.* **hamm'ily.** [Prob. **hamfatter.**]

hamadryad *ham-ə-drī'ad, n.* a wood-nymph who died with the tree in which she dwelt: a large poisonous Indian snake, *Naja hamadryas*: a large baboon of Abyssinia: — *pl.* **hamadry'ads, hamadry'ades** (*-ēz*). [Gr. *hamadryas* — *hama,* together, *drȳs,* (oak) tree.]

hamal. See **hammal.**

Hamamelis *ham-ə-mē'lis, n.* the American witch-hazel genus, giving name to a family, **Hamamelida'ceae,** akin to the planes. [Gr. *hamamēlis,* medlar — *hama,* together with, *mēlon,* an apple.]

hamarthritis *ham-är-thrī'tis, n.* gout in all the joints. [Gr. *hama,* together, *arthrītis,* gout.]

hamartia *ha-mär'tē-ə, n.* in a literary work, the flaw or defect in the character of the hero which leads to his downfall (orig. and esp. in ancient Greek tragedy; see Aristotle's *Poetics*). — *n.* **hamartiol'ogy** that section of theology which treats of sin. [Gr. *hamartiā,* failure, error of judgment, sin.]

hamate *hā'māt, adj.* hooked. [L. *hāmātus* — *hāmus,* hook.]

hamble *ham'bl, v.t.* to mutilate, make useless for hunting (by cutting the balls of a dog's feet). — *v.i.* to limp, to stumble (*dial.*). [O.E. *hamelian.*]

Hamburg, Hamburgh *ham-bûrg, b(ə)-rə, ns.* a black variety of grape (often *black Hamburg*): a small blue-legged domestic fowl. — *n.* **ham'burg(h)er** Hamburg steak, finely chopped meat: (a bread roll containing) this meat shaped into a round flat cake and fried: a large sausage. [*Hamburg* in Germany.]

hame¹ *hām, n.* one of the two curved bars of a draught-horse's collar. [Cf. Du. *haam,* L.G. *ham.*]

hame² *hām,* Scots form of **home.** — *adv.* **hame'with** homewards.

hamesucken *hām'suk-n,* (*Scots law*) *n.* the assaulting of a man in his own house. [O.E. *hāmsōcn* — *ham,* home, *sōcn,* seeking, attack; cf. Ger. *Heimsuchung,* affliction.]

hamfatter *ham'fat-ər, n.* a third-rate minstrel, variety artist, actor. — *v.t.* and *v.i.* to act badly or ineffectively. [Perh. from an old Negro minstrel song, The *Hamfat* Man.]

Hamiltonian *ham-il-tō'ni-ən, adj.* pertaining to James *Hamilton* (1769–1829), or his method of teaching languages without grammar, to the philosopher Sir William *Hamilton* (1788–1856), to Sir William Rowan *Hamilton* (1805–65), Irish mathematician, or other of the name.

Hamite *ham'īt, n.* a descendant or supposed descendant of *Ham,* son of Noah: a member of a dark-brown long-headed race of N.E. Africa (Galla, Hadendoa, etc.), sometimes understood more widely to cover much of N. Africa: a speaker of any language of a N. African family distantly related to Semitic (ancient Egyptian, Berber, etc.). — *adj.* **Hamitic** (*-it'ik*).

hamlet *ham'lit, n.* a cluster of houses in the country: a small village. [O.Fr. *hamelet,* dim. of *hamel* (Fr. *hameau*), from Gmc.; cf. **home.**]

hammal, hamal *hum-äl', n.* an Eastern porter. [Ar. *hammāl.*]

hammam *hum-äm', hum'um, ham'am, n.* an Oriental bathing establishment, a Turkish bath. — Also **humm'-aum, humm'um.** [Ar. *hammām.*]

hammer *ham'ər, n.* a tool for beating metal, breaking rock, driving nails, or the like: a striking-piece in the mechanism of a clock, piano, etc.: the apparatus that causes explosion of the charge in a firearm: the mallet with which an auctioneer announces that an article is sold: a small bone of the ear, the malleus: a metal ball weighing about 7 kg, attached to a long handle of flexible wire, for throwing in competition (*athletics*):

a trouncer. — *v.t.* to beat, drive, shape, or fashion with or as with a hammer: to contrive by intellectual labour, to excogitate (with *out*): to arrive at (a conclusion) or settle (differences) after much argument (with *out*): to trounce or criticise severely: to teach by frequent and energetic reiteration (with *in* or *into*): to declare a defaulter on the Stock Exchange: to beat down the price of (a stock), to depress (a market). — *v.i.* to use a hammer: to make a noise as of a hammer: to persevere pertinaciously (with *away*). — *n.* **hamm'erer.** — *n.* and *adj.* **hamm'ering.** — *adj.* **hamm'erless.** — **hamm'er-beam** a horizontal piece of timber in place of a tie-beam at or near the feet of a pair of rafters; **hamm'er-brace** a curved brace supporting a hammer-beam; **hammer drill** a rock drill in which the piston is independent and strikes blows against the boring part; **hamm'erhead** a shark with hammer-shaped head (also **hamm'er-fish, hamm'er-head'ed shark**): the umbrette (also Du. **hamm'erkop**). — *adj.* **hamm'er-head'ed** with a head shaped like a hammer: dull in intellect, stupid. — **hamm'erlock** a hold in wrestling in which opponent's arm is twisted upwards behind his back; **hamm'erman** one who wields a hammer, as a blacksmith, goldsmith, etc.; **hamm'er-pond** an artificial pond at a water-mill; **hamm'er-toe** a condition in which a toe is permanently bent upwards at the base and doubled down upon itself. — **bring to the hammer** to sell, or cause to sell, by auction; (**come**) **under the hammer** (come up for sale) by auction; **hammer and sickle** crossed hammer and sickle emblem of the Soviet Union, or of Communism; **hammer and tongs** with great noise and violence; **hammer home** to impress (a fact) strongly and effectively on someone. [O.E. *hamor;* Ger. *Hammer,* O.N. *hamar* .]

hammercloth *ham'ər-kloth, n.* a cloth covering a coach-box. [Origin unknown.]

Hammerklavier *ham-ər-kla-vēr',* (Ger.) *n.* pianoforte.

hammerkop. See **hammer.**

hammock *ham'ək, n.* a cloth or netting hung by the ends, for use as a bed or couch. [Sp. *hamaca,* from Carib.]

Hammond organ® *ham'ənd ör'gən,* orig., a two-manual organ, with tones electromagnetically generated by means of rotating wheels controlled by the keys: a two-manual digital organ. [Invented by L. *Hammond,* 20th.-cent. U.S. mechanical engineer.]

hamose *hā'mōs, adj.* hooked — also **hā'mous.** — *adjs.* **hamular** (*ham'ū-lər*) like a small hook; **häm'ūlate** tipped with a small hook. — *n.* **häm'ūlus** a small hook or hook-like process: — *pl.* **ham'uli** (*-lī*). [L. *hāmus,* hook.]

hamper¹ *ham'pər, v.t.* to impede: to distort: to curtail. — *n.* a shackle: that which impedes: essential but somewhat cumbrous equipment on a vessel (*naut.*). [First, about 1350, in Northern writers; cf. O.N. and Mod. Icel. *hemja,* to restrain, Ger. *hemmen.*]

hamper² *ham'pər, n.* a large basket, usu. with a cover. — *v.t.* to give a hamper to, to bribe. — *ns.* **han'ap** an ornate mediaeval drinking goblet, often having a cover; **han'aper** a case for a hanap: a receptacle for treasure, paper, etc.: a former department of Chancery. [O.Fr. *hanapier* — *hanap,* drinking-cup; cf. O.H.G. *knapf;* O.E. *hnæpp,* a bowl.]

hampster. See **hamster.**

hamshackle *ham'shak-l, v.t.* to shackle by tying head to foreleg: to fetter, restrain. [**shackle;** otherwise obscure.]

hamster, hampster *ham'stər, n.* a rodent (Cricetus) with cheek-pouches reaching almost to the shoulders. [Ger.]

hamstring *ham'string, n.* the great tendon at the back of the knee or hock of the hindleg. — *v.t.* to lame by cutting the hamstring: to make powerless: — *pa.t.* and *pa.p.* **ham'stringed, ham'strung.** [ham, string¹.]

hamular, etc. See **hamose.**

hamza, hamzah *häm'zä, ham'zə, n.* in Arabic, the sign used to represent the glottal stop. [Ar. *hamzah,* a compression.]

han *han*, an old *pl.* (*Spens.*) of **have**.
Han *han*, *n.* and *n.pl.* (a member of) the native Chinese people, as opposed to Mongols, Manchus, etc. [Chin.]
hanap, hanaper. See **hamper**[2].
hance *häns, hans, n.* a curved rise from a lower to a higher part (*naut.*): the arc of smaller radius at the springing of an elliptical or many-centred arch (*archit.*). — Also **haunch.** [O.Fr. *hauce, haulce*, rise: cf. **enhance**.]
hanch[1] *hänsh*, (*Scot.*) *v.i.* and *v.t.* to snap (at) with the jaws. [Older Fr. *hancher*.]
hanch[2]. See **haunch**[1].
hand *hand*, *n.* in man the extremity of the arm below the wrist: any corresponding member in the higher vertebrates: the forefoot of a quadruped: the extremity of the hind-limb when it is prehensile: a pointer or index: a measure of four inches: a division of a bunch of bananas: side, direction, quarter: a worker, esp. in a factory or a ship: a performer: a doer, author, or producer: instrumentality: influence: share in performance: power or manner of performing: style: skill: handiwork: touch: stroke: control: (often *pl.*) keeping, custody: possession: assistance: style of handwriting: sign-manual: pledge: consent to or promise of marriage, or fulfilment of such promise: feel, handle (of a textile): the set of cards held by a player at one deal: the play of a single deal of cards: loosely, a game of cards: a turn, round, or innings in a game: in various games, (possession of) service: a round of applause: (in *pl.*) skill in handling a horse's reins. — *v.t.* to lay hands on, set hand to, manipulate, handle (*obs.*): to join hands with (*rare*): to pass with the hand: to lead, escort, or help, esp. in entering a carriage: to transfer or deliver (often with *over*). — **hand-** in composition, by hand, or direct bodily operation (as **hand'-held, hand'-knitt'ed, hand'made, hand'-painted, hand'-sewn, hand'-weed'ed**): for the hands (as **hand'-lotion, hand'-towel**): operated by hand (as **hand'-punch**): held in the hand (as **hand'-bask'et**). — *adj.* **hand'ed** having hands: with hands joined (*Milt.*). — **-hand'ed** in composition, using one hand in preference to the other, as *left-handed*: having a hand or hands as stated, as *one-handed, neat-handed*. — **-hand'edness** noun combining form. — *ns.* **hand'edness** the tendency to use one hand rather than the other: inherent asymmetry in particles, etc., e.g. causing twisting in one direction (*phys.*); **hand'er** one who hands: a blow on the hand. — **-hander** in composition, a blow, etc. with the hand or hands as stated, as *right-hander, back-hander*: a play with a specified number of characters, as *two-hander*. — *n.* **hand'ful** enough to fill the hand: a small number or quantity: a charge that taxes one's powers: — *pl.* **hand'fuls.** — *adv.* **hand'ily.** — *n.* **hand'iness.** — *adjs.* **hand'less** without hands: awkward; **hand'y** dexterous: ready to the hand: convenient: near. — **hand'bag** a bag for small articles, carried in the hand by women: a light travelling-bag; **hand'-ball** a game between goals in which the ball is struck with the palm of the hand: (**hand'ball**) a game similar to fives in which a ball is struck with the gloved hand against a wall or walls (usu. four); **hand'-barrow** wheelless barrow, carried by handles: handcart; **hand'bell** small bell with a handle, rung by hand; **hand'bill** a light pruning-hook: a bill or loose sheet bearing an announcement; **hand'book** a manual: a bookmaker's book of bets (*U.S.*); **hand'=brake** a brake applied by hand-operated lever; **hand(s)'=breadth** the breadth of a hand; **hand'car** (*U.S.*) a workman's vehicle driven by hand on a railway; **hand'-cart** a light cart drawn by hand; **hand'clap** a clap of the hands; **hand'clasp** (*U.S.*) a handshake; **hand'craft** handicraft; **hand'cuff** (esp. in *pl.*) a shackle locked upon the wrist. — *v.t.* to put handcuffs on. — **hand'fast** (*arch.*) a firm grip: custody: a handle (*dial.*): a contract, esp. a betrothal. — *adj.* (*arch.*) bound: espoused: tight-gripping. — *v.t.* (*arch.*) to betroth: to join by handfasting. — **hand'fasting** (*arch.*) betrothal: probationary marriage: private marriage; **hand'-feeding** feed-

ing of animals or machinery by hand; **hand'-gall'op** an easy gallop, restrained by the bridle-hand; **hand'-glass** a glass or glazed frame to protect plants: a mirror or a lens with a handle; **hand'-grenade'** a grenade to be thrown by hand; **hand'grip** a grasp with the hand: something for the hand to grasp: (in *pl.*) close struggle; **hand'-gun** a gun which can be held and fired in one hand; **hand'hold** a hold by the hand: a place or part that can be held by the hand; **hand'-horn** an early form of horn without valves. — *n.pl.* **hand'icuffs** fisticuffs. — **hand'-in** (*badminton*, etc.) the player who is serving. — *n.* and *adj.* **hand'-knit** (a garment) knitted by hand. — *v.t.* **hand'-knit'.** — **hand'-line** a fishing-line without a rod. — *v.i.* to fish with such a line. — **hand'list** a list without detail, for handy reference; **hand'-loom** a hand-worked weaving loom. — *adj.* **hand'made.** — **hand'maid, hand'maiden** a female servant. — *adj.* **hand'=me-down'** ready-made, usually cheap: second-hand. — *n.* a cheap ready-made or second-hand garment. — **hand'-mill** a quern: a coffee-mill, pepper-mill, etc., worked by hand; **hand'-off** act or manner of pushing off an opponent in Rugby football; **hand'-org'an** a barrel-organ; **hand'out** a portion handed out, esp. to the needy: an issue: a prepared statement issued to the press: a usu. free leaflet containing information, propaganda, etc.; **hand'-out** a player whose side is receiving the service: the situation when the first player on the serving side loses his service; **hand'over** a transfer, handing over; **hand'-pa'per** paper with a hand for watermark. — *v.t.* **hand'-pick** to pick by hand: to select carefully for a particular purpose. — **hand'play** dealing of blows; **hand'-post** a finger-post; **hand'-press** a printing or other press worked by hand; **hand'-prom'ise** (*Irish*) formerly a solemn form of betrothal; **hand puppet** a glove puppet; **hand'rail** a rail to hold for safety, support, etc., as on stairs. — *adv.* **hand'-runn'ing** (*dial.*) consecutively. — **hand'saw** a saw worked by hand, specif. with a handle at one end: perh. **heronshaw** (*Shak.*); **hand'-screen** a screen against fire or sun, held in the hand; **hand'-screw** a clamp: a jack for raising weights; **hand'set** on a telephone, the part held by the hand, containing the mouthpiece and earpiece; **hand'-shake** a shaking of hands in greeting, etc. (also **hand'-shaking**): a golden handshake or the like: an exchange of signals (on a separate line) between two or more devices which synchronises them in readiness for the transfer of data (*comput.*); **hand'shaking** (*comput.*) the process of performing a handshake. — *adjs.* **hands'-off'** not touching with the hands: operated by remote control: that cannot be touched: not interfering; **hands'-on'** operated by hand: involving practical rather than theoretical knowledge, experience, method of working, etc.: of museums, etc., with exhibits that can be handled. — **hand'spike** a bar used as a lever; **hand'spring** a cartwheel or somersault with hands on the ground; **hand'staff** a staff-like handle, as of a flail: a staff as a weapon: a javelin: — *pl.* **hand'staves, hand'staffs; hand'stand** act of balancing one's body on the palms of one's hands with one's trunk and legs in the air; **hands'turn, hand's turn** (usu. with a negative) a single or least act of work; **hand'work** work done by hand. — *adj.* **hand'worked** made, done by hand. — **hand'writing** writing, script: style of writing: individual style discernible in one's actions. — *adjs.* **hand'written** written by hand, not typed or printed; **hand'wrought** handworked. — **hand'yman** a man for odd jobs: a bluejacket. — **at any hand, in any hand** (*Shak.*) at any rate, in any case; **at first hand** directly from the source; **at hand** conveniently near: within easy reach: near in time: at the beginning (*Shak.*); **at the hand(s) of** by the act of; **bear a hand** to take part, lend aid; **bloody** or **red hand** the arms of Ulster, a sinister hand erect couped at the wrist gules, borne by baronets in a canton or inescutcheon; **by hand** by use of the hands, or tools worked by the hand, not by machinery or other indirect means: by personal delivery, not by post; **by the strong hand** by force; **change hands** to pass to other ownership or keeping; **come to hand** to arrive: to be received; **come to one's hand** to be found easy: to come to close quarters; **for one's own hand** to one's own account; **get one's hand in** to get control of the play so as to turn one's cards to good use: to get into the way or knack; **good hands** a trustworthy source: good keeping: care of those who may be trusted to treat one well; **hand and foot** orig. with respect to hands and feet: with assiduous attention; **hand and** (or **in**) **glove** on very intimate terms: in close co-operation; **hand down** or **on** to transmit in succession or by tradition; **hand in hand** with hands mutually clasped: with one person holding the hand of another: in close association: conjointly (adj. **hand'-in-hand'**); **hand it to someone** (slang) to admit his superiority, esp. as shown by his success in a difficult matter; **hand of God** unforeseen and unavoidable accident, as lightning, tempest; **hand out** to distribute, pass by hand to individuals (see also **handout**); **hand over** to transfer: to relinquish possession of; **hand over hand** by passing the hands alternately one before or above another, as in climbing a rope or swimming with a certain stroke: progressively: with steady and rapid gain (also **hand over fist**) ; **hand over head** headlong; **hands down** with utter ease (as in winning a race); **hands off** keep off: do not touch or strike; **hands up** hold the hands above the head in surrender; **hand to hand** at close quarters (adj. **hand'-to-hand'**); **hand to mouth** with provision for immediate needs only (adj. **hand'-to-mouth'**); **handwriting on the wall** see write; **have one's hands full** to be preoccupied, very busy; **hold hands** see hold; **in hand** as present payment: in preparation: under control: of a ball that has to be played from balk (billiards); **keep one's hand in** see keep; **lay hands on** to seize: to obtain or find: to subject physically to rough treatment: to bless or to ordain by touching with the hand(s) — also to **lay on hands; laying on of hands** the touch of a bishop or presbyters in ordination; **lend a hand** to give assistance; **off one's hands** no longer under one's responsible charge; **old hand** see old; **on all hands, every hand** on all sides, by everybody; **on hand** ready, available: in one's possession; **on one's hands** under one's care or responsibility: remaining as a burden or encumbrance; **on the one hand ... on the other hand** phrases used to introduce opposing points in an argument, etc.; **out of hand** at once, immediately, without premeditation: out of control; **poor hand** an unskilful one; **set** or **put one's hand to** to engage in, undertake: to sign; **shake hands** see shake; **show of hands** a vote by holding up hands; **show one's hand** to expose one's purpose; **sit on one's hands** to take no action; **slow handclap** slow rhythmic clapping showing disapproval; **stand one's hand** (slang) to pay for a drink for another; **take in hand** to undertake: to take charge of in order to educate, etc.; **take off someone's hands** to relieve someone of; **throw in one's hand** to give up a venture or plan; **tie someone's hands** to render someone powerless; **to** (**one's**) **hand** in readiness; **try one's hand at** to attempt: test one's prowess at; **under one's hand** with one's proper signature attached; **upper hand** mastery; **wash one's hands (of)** to disclaim responsibility (for) (Matt. xxvii, 24). [O.E. hand; in all Gmc. tongues, perh. rel. to Goth. hinthan, to seize.]

handicap hand'i-kap, v.t. to impose special disadvantages or impediments upon, in order to offset advantages and make a better contest: to place at a disadvantage (fig.). — n. any contest so adjusted, or the condition imposed: amount added to or subtracted from one's score in stroke competitions (golf): a disadvantage (fig.). — adj. **hand'icapped** suffering from some disability or disadvantage. — n. **hand'icapper** one who handicaps. [App. hand i' cap, from the drawing from a cap in an old lottery game.]

handicraft hand'i-kräft, n. a manual craft or trade. — n. **hand'icraftsman** a man skilled in a manual art: — fem. **hand'icraftswoman.** [O.E. handcræft — hand, cræft, craft, assimilated to **handiwork.**]

handiwork, handywork hand'i-wûrk, n. work done by the hands, performance generally: work of skill or wisdom: creation: doing. [O.E. handgewerc — hand and gewerc (geweorc), work.]

handjar, hanjar han'jär, n. a Persian dagger. — Also **khanjar.** [Pers. and Ar. khanjar.]

handkerchief hang'kər-chif, -chēf, n. a cloth or paper for wiping the nose, etc.: a neckerchief: — pl. **hand'-kerchiefs** sometimes **hand'kerchieves.** — Also (now illit.) **hand'kercher.** — **throw the handkerchief** to summon to pursuit, call upon to take one's turn — as in children's games and royal harems. [**hand, kerchief.**]

handle hand'l, v.t. to hold, move about, feel freely, with the hand: to make familiar by frequent touching: to manage: to discuss: to deal with, treat: to cope with: to pass through one's hands: to trade or do business in. — v.i. to respond to control (in a specified way). — n. a part by which a thing is held: anything affording an advantage or pretext to an opponent: feel, as of a textile: one's name (slang). — adj. **hand'led** having a handle. — ns. **hand'ler** one who handles: a pugilist's trainer or second: one who trains, holds, controls, incites, or shows off an animal at a show, fight, etc.: one who trains and uses a dog or other animal which works for the police or an armed service; **hand'ling.** — **hand'lebar** the steering-bar of a cycle, or one half of it. — **a handle to one's name** a title; **fly off the handle** see fly; **handlebar moustache** a wide, thick moustache with curved ends thought to resemble handlebars. [O.E. handle, handlian — hand.]

hand of glory hand əv glō'ri, glö', a charm made originally of mandrake root, afterwards of a murderer's hand from the gallows. [A translation of Fr. main de gloire — O.Fr. mandegloire, mandrake — mandragore.]

handsel, hansel han(d)'səl, n. an inaugural gift, e.g. a present on Handsel Monday, a coin put in the pocket of a new coat, or the like: an inauguration or beginning, as the first money taken, earnest-money, a first instalment, the first use of anything: app. payment, penalty (Spens.). — v.t. to give a handsel to: to inaugurate: to make a beginning on: to cut off, kill (Chatterton, from a blundering reading of a dictionary explanation, 'to cut off a first slice'): — pr.p. **han(d)'-selling;** pa.p. and pa.t. **han(d)selled.** — **Handsel Monday** (Scot.) the first Monday after New Year's Day, when handsels were given. [O.E. handselen, hand-gift, giving; or O.N. handsal.]

handsome han'səm, adj. convenient, handy (obs.): suitable, becoming, gracious (arch.): good-looking: well-proportioned: dignified: liberal or noble: generous: ample. — adv. **hand'somely.** — n. **hand'someness.** [hand and suff. -some; cf. Du. handzaam.]

handy. See hand.

handy-dandy hand'i-dand'i, n. a children's game of guessing which hand a thing is in. — interj. (Shak.) the formula used in the game. [hand.]

handywork. See handiwork.

hanepoot hän'ə-pōt, (S.Afr.) n. a kind of grape. — Also **haanepoot, honeypot.** [Du. haane-poot — haan, cock, poot, foot.]

hang hang, v.t. to support from above against gravity: to suspend: to decorate with pictures, tapestry, etc., as a wall: to put to death by suspending by the neck: to suspend (meat and game) until mature: to cause to be brought to justice: to fix, to fit (a door, etc.): to fasten, to stick (wallpaper, etc.): to exhibit (works of art): to prevent (a jury) from coming to a decision: (in the imper. and pass.) a euphemism for damn. — v.i. to be suspended, so as to allow of free lateral motion: to be put to death by hanging: to be brought to justice: to weigh down, to oppress (with on and over): to cling (with on followed by to): to drape well: to be exhibited: to be undecided: to be in suspense: to hover: to impend: to linger: to hold back: to depend (on): to have things hanging: to remain in close attention (with on): — pa.t. and pa.p. **hanged** (by the neck) or **hung** (in all senses). — n. action or mode of hanging: principle of connection, plan: knack of using: meaning: a declivity: a slackening of motion: a hanging mass: euphemistically, a damn. — *n.* **hangabil'ity.** — *adj.* **hang'able** liable to be hanged: punishable by hanging. — *n.* **hang'er** one who hangs: that on which anything is hung: a wood on a hillside (O.E. *hangra*): a short sword. — *adj.* **hang'ing** suspending: suspended: drooping: downcast: deserving or involving death by hanging. — *n.* death by the halter: (esp. in *pl.*) that which is hung, as drapery. — *adj.* **hung** (of an election, etc.) not decisive, producing no viable majority for any one party: (of a parliament) resulting from such an election. — **hang'-bird** a Baltimore oriole (from its pensile nest); **hang'dog** a low fellow. — *adj.* with a sneaking, cowed look. — **hang'er-on'** one who hangs on or sticks to a person or place: an importunate acquaintance: a dependant; **hang'fire** delay in explosion; **hang'-gliding** a sport in which one glides from a cliff-top, etc. hanging in a harness from a large kite; **hang'-glider** this apparatus, or the person using it; **hanging buttress** a buttress supported by a corbel or the like; **hanging committee** a committee which chooses the works of art to be shown in an exhibition; **hanging garden** see **garden**; **hanging matter** a crime leading to capital punishment: a serious matter (*coll.*); **hanging valley** a tributary valley not graded to the main valley, a product of large-scale glaciation; **hang'man** a public executioner: a word-guessing game involving the drawing of a gibbet with victim. — *adj.* rascally. — **hang'nest** a hangbird; **hang'out** a haunt; **hang'over** a survival: after-effects, esp. of drinking (see also **hung over** below); **hang'-up** (*slang*) a problem about which one may be obsessed: an inhibition (see also **hung up** below); **hung'-beef** beef cured and dried; **hung jury** a jury that fails to agree. — **get the hang of** (*coll.*) to grasp the principle or meaning of; **hang about, around** to loiter: to stay, remain, persist; **hang back** to show reluctance; **hang by a thread** to depend upon very precarious conditions (from the sword of Damocles); **hang, draw, and quarter** to hang, cut down while still alive, disembowel and cut in pieces for exposure at different places; **draw, hang, and quarter** to drag on a hurdle or otherwise to the place of execution, then hang and quarter; **hang fire** to be long in exploding or discharging: to be slow in taking effect: to hesitate; **hang in** (*slang*) to wait: to persist (also **hang in there**); **hang in the balance** to be in doubt or suspense; **hang loose** (*slang*) to do nothing: to be relaxed; **hang off** to let go: to hold off; **hang on** to wait; **hang on someone's lips** or **words** to give close, admiring attention to someone; **hang one's head** to look ashamed or sheepish; **hang out** to display, as a sign: to put outside on a clothes-line: to lodge or reside (*slang*); **hang out for** to insist on; **hang over** to project over or lean out from; **hang together** to keep united: to be consistent: to connect; **hang tough** (*U.S.*) to stay resolute or determined; **hang up** to suspend: to delay: to replace a telephone receiver, break off communication; **hang up one's hat** to take up one's abode; **hung over** suffering from a hangover; **hung up** (*coll.*) in a state of anxiety, obsessed (with *about* or on); **let it all hang out** (*coll.*) to be completely uninhibited, relaxed. [O.E. *hangian*, pa.t. *hangode*, pa.p. *hangod* (intrans.) and *hōn*, pa.t. *heng*, pa.p. *hangen* (trans.), and O.N. *hanga* and *hengja*; cf. Du. and Ger. *hangen*.]

hangar *hang'ər, hang'gär, n.* a shed for carriages, aircraft, etc. [Fr.]

hangnail *hang'nāl.* See **agnail**.

hanjar. See **handjar**.

hank *hangk, n.* a coil or skein of a specified length, varying with the type of yarn: a loop: a restraining hold (*dial.*). — *v.t.* to catch, as on a loop. — *v.i.* to catch, be entangled. [O.N. *hanki,* a hasp.]

hanker *hangk'ər, v.i.* to linger about (*dial.*): to yearn (with *after, for*). — *n.* a yearning. — *n.* **hank'ering.** [Perh. conn. with **hang**; cf. Du. *hunkeren*.]

hankie, hanky *hangk'i, n.* a coll. dim. of **handkerchief**.

hanky-panky *hangk'i-pangk'i, n.* jugglery, funny business,

underhand trickery: faintly improper (esp. sexual) behaviour. [Arbitrary.]

Hanoverian *han-ə-vē'ri-ən, adj.* pertaining to *Hanover* (Ger. *Hannover*): of the dynasty that came thence to the British throne in 1714. — *n.* a native of Hanover: a supporter of the house of Hanover, opp. to a Jacobite.

Hansa. See **Hanse**.

Hansard *han'särd, n.* the printed reports of debates in parliament, from Luke *Hansard* (1752–1828), whose descendants continued to print them down to 1889. — *v.t.* **han'sardise, -ize** to confront (someone) with his former recorded opinions.

Hanse *hans,* **Hansa** *han'sə, -zə, n.* a league, esp. one of German commercial cities. — *adjs.* **Hanse, Hansa, Hanseatic** (*han-si-at'ik*). [O.H.G. *hansa,* a band of men (M.H.G. *hanse,* merchants' guild).]

hansel. See **handsel**.

hansom *han'səm, n.* a light two-wheeled cab with driver's seat raised behind. — Also **han'som-cab**. [From the inventor, Joseph A. *Hansom* (1803–82).]

ha'n't *hänt,* a coll. contr. for **have not** or **has not**.

hantle *han'tl, hän'tl,* (*Scot.*) *n.* a good many: a good deal. [Poss. **hand** and **tale**, number.]

Hanukkah, Chanuk(k)ah *hä'nə-kə, hä-nŏŏ-kä, n.* the Jewish festival of lights commemorating the re-dedication of the temple in 165 B.C. [Heb., consecration.]

hanuman *han-ŏŏ-män', n.* a long-tailed sacred monkey of India — the entellus monkey. [*Hanumān,* Hindu monkey god.]

haoma *how'ma, n.* a drink prepared from the haoma vine, used in Zoroastrian ritual: (*cap.*) a deity, personification of haoma. [Avestan; see **soma**¹.]

hap¹ *hap, n.* chance: fortune: accident. — *v.i.* to chance, happen: — *pr.p.* **happ'ing;** *pa.t.* and *pa.p.* **happed.** — *n.* and *adj.* **hap'haz'ard** random: chance. — *adv.* at random. — *adv.* **haphaz'ardly.** — *n.* **haphaz'ardness.** — *adj.* **hap'less** unlucky: unhappy. — *adv.* **hap'lessly.** — *n.* **hap'lessness.** — *adv.* **hap'ly** by hap: perhaps: it may be. [O.N. *happ,* good luck.]

hap² *hap,* (*Scot.* and *E. Angl.*) *v.t.* to cover up: to wrap up. — *n.* a wrap. [Origin unknown.]

hapax legomenon *hap'aks le-gom'ən-on,* (Gr.) lit. said once: a word or phrase that is found once only.

ha'pence *hā'pəns,* for **halfpence**.

ha'penny *hāp'ni,* for **halfpenny**.

haphazard, hapless. See **hap**¹.

haplo- in composition, single. — *n.* **haplography** (*hap-log'rə-fi*) the inadvertent writing once of what should have been written twice. — *adj.* **hap'loid** (*biol.*) having the reduced number of chromosomes characteristic of the species, as in germ-cells (opp. to *diploid*). — *ns.* **haploid'y; haplol'ogy** omission in utterance of a sound resembling a neighbouring sound (as *idolatry* for *idololatry*). — *adj.* **haploste'monous** (Gr. *stēmōn,* thread; *bot.*) with one whorl of stamens. [Gr. *haploos,* single, simple.]

haply. See **hap**¹.

hap'orth *hā'pərth,* for **halfpennyworth**.

happen *hap'ən, v.i.* to fall out: to come to pass: to take place: to chance. — *adv.* (*N. Engl.*) perhaps. — *ns.* **happ'ening** event: a performance consisting of discrete events, in which elements from everyday life are put together in a non-realistic way, usu. demanding audience participation (*theatre*): one such event in the theatre or in other activities including those of everyday life; **happ'enstance** chance: a chance circumstance. — **happen into, on, upon** to meet or come across by chance. [**hap**¹.]

happy *hap'i, adj.* lucky: fortunate: expressing, or characterised by, content, well-being, pleasure, or good: apt: felicitous: carefree: confident: mildly intoxicated (*slang*): in combination, delighted by the possession of or use of, as *power-happy, bomb-happy* — usu. implying irresponsibility — or dazed as result of. — *v.t.* (*Shak.*) to make happy. — *adv.* **happ'ily** in a happy manner: in happiness: by chance: perhaps: I'm glad to say, luckily. — *n.* **happ′iness.** — *adj.* **happ′y-go-luck′y** easy-going: taking things as they come. — *adv.* in any way one pleases. — **happy dispatch** a euphemism for hara-kiri; **happy event** (now *facet.*) a euphemism for a birth; **happy hour** in a club, bar, etc., a time, usu. in the early evening, when drinks are sold at reduced prices; **happy hunting-ground** (also in *pl.*) the Paradise of the Red Indian: any place that one frequents, esp. to make acquisitions or to profit in any way; **happy medium** a prudent or sensible middle course.   [hap¹.]

hapteron *hap′tər-on, n.* a holdfast or attachment organ of a plant thallus. — *adj.* **haptotrop′ic** curving in response to touch, as a tendril. — *n.* **haptot′ropism.** [Gr. *haptein*, to fasten, *tropos*, turning.]

haptic *hap′tik, adj.* pertaining to the sense of touch. — *n. sing.* **hap′tics** science of studying data obtained by means of touch.   [Gr. *haptein*, to fasten.]

haqueton *hak′tən.* Same as **acton.**

hara-kiri *ha′, hä′rä-kē′rē, n.* ceremonial Japanese suicide by ripping the belly.   [Jap. *hara*, belly, *kiri*, cut.]

haram. See **harem.**

harangue *hə-rang′, n.* a loud speech addressed to a multitude: a pompous or wordy address. — *v.i.* to deliver a harangue. — *v.t.* to address by a harangue: — *pr.p.* **haranguing** (*-rang′ing*); *pa.t.* and *pa.p.* **harangued** (*-rangd′*). — *n.* **harangu′er.**   [O.Fr. *arenge, harangue* — O.H.G. *hring* (Ger. *Ring*), ring (of auditors).]

harass *har′əs,* now often *hər-as′* (similarly in derivatives), *v.t.* to distress, wear out: to annoy, pester. — *adj.* **har′assed.** — *adv.* **har′assedly.** — *n.* **har′asser.** — *n.* and *adj.* **har′assing.** — *adv.* **har′assingly.** — *n.* **har′assment.** [O.Fr. *harasser*; prob. from *harer*, to incite a dog.]

harbinger *här′bin-jər, n.* a host (*obs.*): one sent before to provide lodging (*obs.*): a forerunner, pioneer. — *v.t.* to precede as harbinger.   [M.E. *herbergeour*; see **harbour.**]

harbour (in U.S. **harbor**) *här′bər, n.* a refuge or shelter: a shelter, natural or artificial, for ships: a haven. — *v.t.* to lodge, shelter, entertain, or give asylum to: to trace to its lair. — *v.i.* to take shelter. — *ns.* **har′bourage** place of shelter: entertainment; **har′bourer.** — *adj.* **har′bourless.** — **har′bour-bar′** a sandbank at a harbour's mouth. — *n.pl.* **har′bour-dues** charges for the use of a harbour. — **har′bour-light′** a guiding light into a harbour; **har′bour-master** an officer who has charge of a harbour; **harbour seal** a small seal, *Phoca vitulina,* found in Atlantic waters. — **harbour of refuge** a harbour constructed to give shelter to ships: protection in distress.   [M.E. *herberwe* — O.E. *herebeorg* — *here,* army, *beorg,* protection; cf. Ger. *Herberge,* O.N. *herbergi.*]

hard¹ *härd, adj.* not easily penetrated or broken: unyielding to pressure: firm, solid: difficult to scratch (*min.*): difficult: strenuous: laborious: vigorous: bodily fit: coarse and scanty: stingy, niggardly: difficult to bear: difficult to please: unfeeling: insensitive: severe: rigorous: stiff: constrained: intractable: obdurate: troublesome: (of coal) anthracitic: (of water) difficult to lather owing to calcium or magnesium salt in solution: harsh: brilliant and glaring: over-sharply defined: lacking in finer shades: used as a classification of pencil-leads to indicate durability in quality and faintness in use: (of drink) (very) alcoholic: (of drug) habit-forming: (of news) definite, substantiated: (of letters) representing a guttural, not a sibilant, sound: voiceless (*obs. phon.*): (of radiation) penetrating. — *n.* hardship: hard state: hard ground: a firm beach or foreshore: hard labour. — *adv.* with urgency, vigour, etc.: earnestly, forcibly: uneasily: in excess: severely: to the full extent (as **hard aport**): with difficulty: harshly: close, near, as in **hard by.** — *v.t.* **hard′en** to make hard or harder or hardy: to make firm: to strengthen: to confirm in wickedness: to make insensitive. — *v.i.* to become hard or harder, *lit.* or *fig.* — *adj.* **hard′ened** made hard: unfeeling: obdurate. — *ns.* **hard′ener; hard′ening** the act or fact of making or becoming hard: a substance added to

harden anything: sclerosis. — *adj.* **hard′ish** somewhat hard. — *adv.* **hard′ly** with difficulty: scarcely, not quite: severely, harshly. — *ns.* **hard′ness** quality of being hard: power of, and resistance to, scratching (*min.*); **hard′ship** a thing, or conditions, hard to bear: privation: an instance of hard treatment (*obs.*). — *adv.* **hard′-a-lee′** close to the lee-side, etc. — *adj.* **hard′-and-fast′** rigidly laid down and adhered to. — **hard′-and-fast′ness; hard′back** a book with rigid covers. — Also *adj.* — *adj.* **hard′backed.** — **hard′bake** almond toffee; **hard′beam** the hornbeam. — *adjs.* **hard′-billed** having a hard bill or beak; **hard′-bitt′en** given to hard biting, tough in fight: ruthless, callous. — **hard′board** a compressed fibreboard. — *adj.* **hard′-boiled** boiled until solid: callous or cynical: practical. — **hard case** a person difficult to deal with or reform; **hard cash** specie: ready money; **hard cheese** (chiefly as *interj.*; *slang*) bad luck; **hard coal** anthracite; **hard copy** (*comput.*) output legible to the human reader, as distinct from coded material. — *adj.* **hard′-cop′y.** — **hard′core** rubble, etc., used under foundations of road; **hard core** a durable, unyielding central part: something very resistant to change, as, e.g. the most loyal or the most die-hard members of a group. — *adj.* **hard′-core** pertaining to a hard core: blatant: of pornography, explicit, very obscene. — **hard court** a tennis court laid with asphalt, concrete, etc. — *adj.* **hard′-cured** thoroughly cured, as fish, by drying in the sun. — **hard currency** metallic money: a currency with a high exchange value and not subject to depreciation: a currency backed by bullion; **hard disc** (*comput.*) a metal disc with a magnetic coating, in a sealed container, usually having a higher recording density than a floppy disc. — *adj.* **hard′-drawn** of wire, etc., drawn when cold to give the required thickness. — **hard drinker** one who drinks persistently and excessively. — *adjs.* **hard′-earned** earned with toil or difficulty; **hard edge** of a style of abstract painting using bright areas of colour with sharply defined edges. — **hard′face** a soullessly relentless person; **hard facts** undeniable, stubborn facts. — *adjs.* **hard′-fav′oured, hard′-feat′ured** of hard, coarse, or forbidding features. — **hard′-fav′ouredness; hard′-feat′uredness; hard feelings** hostility, resentment; **hard′-fern** the northern fern (*Lomaria* or *Blechnum*). — *adjs.* **hard′-fist′ed** having hard or strong fists or hands: close-fisted: niggardly; **hard′-fought** sorely contested; **hard′-got, hard′-gotten** obtained with difficulty; **hard′-grained** having a close firm grain: forbidding. — **hard′grass** cocksfoot or other coarse grass; **hard′hack** an American Spiraea. — *adj.* **hard′-hand′ed** having hard hands: rough: severe. — **hard hat** a bowler-hat: a protective helmet worn by building workers: an obstinately conservative person; **hard′head** knapweed: a fish of various kinds (gurnard, menhaden, fatherlasher). — *adjs.* **hard′-head′ed** shrewd; **hard′-heart′ed** unfeeling: cruel. — *adv.* **hard′-heart′edly.** — **hard′-heart′edness.** — *adjs.* **hard′-hit′** seriously hurt as by a loss of money: deeply smitten with love; **hard′-hitt′ing** duly condemnatory, pulling no punches. — **hard labour** physical labour as an additional punishment to imprisonment, abolished in 1948; **hard landing** one made by a spacecraft, etc. in which the craft is destroyed on impact. — *adj.* **hard′line** of an attitude or policy (**hard line**), definite and uncompromising: having such an attitude or policy. — **hard′lin′er; hard lines** a hard lot: bad luck (usu. as *interj.*); **hard man** (*coll.*) a criminal specialising in acts of violence; **hard′-metal** sintered tungsten carbide, used for the tip of high-speed cutting tools; **hard money** coin. — *adjs.* **hard′mouthed** with mouth insensible to the bit: not easily managed; **hard′nosed** (*coll.*) tough, unsentimental. — **hard on** (*slang*) an erection of the penis; **hard pad** once considered to be a neurotropic virus disease of dogs, now recognised as a symptom of distemper; **hard′-pan** a hard layer often underlying the superficial soil: the lowest level; **hard′-parts** the skeletal material in an organism. — *adjs.* **hard′-paste** (of porcelain) made of china-clay and altered granite; **hard'-pressed, hard'-pushed** in difficulties; **hard'-rid'ing** strenuously riding. — **hard rock** a form of rock and roll, usu. structurally and rhythmically simple and highly amplified; **hard roe** see **roe**[1]; **hard rubber** ebonite. — adjs. **hard'-ruled** (Shak.) ruled with difficulty; **hard'-run** greatly pressed. — **hard sauce** sauce made with butter and sugar, and flavoured with rum or other liquor; **hard science** any of the physical or natural sciences. — adj. **hard'-sec'tored** (comput.) of a floppy disc, formatted by a set of holes punched near the hub of the disc, each hole marking the start of a sector. — **hard sell** aggressive and insistent method of promoting, advertising or selling. — adjs. **hard'-set** beset by difficulty: rigid: obstinate; **hard'shell** having a hard shell: rigidly orthodox: uncompromising. — **hard shoulder** a surfaced strip forming the outer edge of a motorway, used when stopping in an emergency; **hard'-stand'ing** a hard (concrete, etc.) surface on which cars, aircraft, etc., may be parked; **hard stuff** (slang) spirituous liquor: important information; **hard swearing** persistent and reckless swearing (by a witness): (often) perjury; **hard'tack** ship-biscuit; **hard'top** a rigid roof on a motor-car: a motor-car with such a roof. — adjs. **hard'-up'** short of money, or of anything else; **hard'-vis'aged** of a hard, coarse, or forbidding visage. — **hard'ware** goods made of the baser metals, such as iron or copper: mechanical equipment including war equipment: mechanical, electrical or electronic components of a computer (compare software); **hard'-wareman.** — adj. **hard'-wear'ing** lasting well in use, durable. — **hard wheat** wheat having a hard kernel with a high gluten content. — adjs. **hard'-wired** (comput.) having or being a circuit built in, whose function therefore cannot be altered; **hard'-won** won with toil and difficulty. — **hard'wood** timber of deciduous trees, whose comparatively slow growth produces compact hard wood; **hard words** words that give difficulty to a half-educated reader: harsh words: angry words. — adj. **hard'work'ing** diligent, industrious. — **be hard going** see **going**[1]; **die hard** to die only after a desperate struggle for life: to survive obstinately: to die impenitent (obs.); **go hard but** will not easily fail that; **go hard with** turn out ill for; **hard as nails** very hard: callous: tough; **hard at it** working hard, very busy; **hard done by** badly treated; **harden off** to accustom (a plant) to outdoor conditions by gradually increasing exposure; **hard-luck story** a person's account of his own bad luck and suffering, usu. intended to gain sympathy; **hard of hearing** pretty deaf; **hard on the heels of** following immediately after; **hard put to it** in great straits or difficulty; **hold hard** to stop; **Mohs's scale of hardness** a series of minerals each of which will scratch the one before it: (1) talc, (2) gypsum, (3) calcite, (4) fluorite, (5) apatite, (6) orthoclase, (7) quartz, (8) topaz, (9) corundum, (10) diamond; **put the hard word on** (Austr.) to ask, particularly for a loan or, esp. sexual, favour; **the hard way** through personal endeavour or salutary experience. [O.E. hard (heard); Du. hard, Ger. hart, Goth. hardus; allied to Gr. kratys, strong.]

hard[2] härd, (Spens. and Scot.) for **heard.**

hardoke här'dok, (Shak., King Lear, folio) n. perhaps burdock. — The quartos have **hor'dock.** [Prob. O.E. hār, hoary, and **dock**[1].]

hards härdz, **hurds** hûrdz, ns.pl. coarse or refuse flax or hemp: tarred rags used as torches (Scott). — ns. **hard'en, herd'en, hurd'en** a coarse fabric made from hards. [O.E. heordan.]

hardy härd'i, adj. daring, brave, resolute: confident: impudent: able to bear cold, exposure, or fatigue. — ns. **hard'ihead** (arch.), **hard'ihood** boldness: audacity: robustness (rare). — adv. **hard'ily.** — ns. **hard'iment** (arch.) hardihood: a deed of hardihood; **hard'iness.** — **hardy annual** an annual plant which can survive frosts: a story or topic of conversation which comes up regularly. [O.Fr. hardi — O.H.G. hartjan, to make hard.]

hare här, n. a common very timid and very swift mammal

of the order Rodentia or in some classifications the order Lagomorpha (esp. of the genus Lepus), in appearance like, but larger than, a rabbit. — v.i. (slang) to run like a hare, hasten. — adj. **har'ish** somewhat like a hare. — **hare'-and-hounds'** a paper-chase; **hare'-bell** the Scottish bluebell (Campanula rotundifolia). — adjs. **hare'-brained,** sometimes **hair'-brained,** giddy: heedless: headlong; **hare'-foot** swift of foot. — **hare'-lip** a fissured upper lip like that of a hare. — adj. **hare'-lipped.** — **hare's'-ear** an umbelliferous plant (Bupleurum, various species) with yellow flowers; **hare's'=foot** (tre'foil) a clover with long soft fluffy heads; **hare-stane** see **hoar-stone** under **hoar.** — **first catch your hare** make sure you have a thing first before you think what to do with it — from a direction in Mrs Glasse's cookery-book, where catch was a misprint for case, skin; **hold (run) with the hare and run (hunt) with the hounds** to play a double game, to be with both sides at once; **raise, start a hare** to introduce an irrelevant topic, line of inquiry, etc. [O.E. hara; Du. haas, Dan. hare, Ger. Hase.]

hareem. Same as **harem.**

Hare Krishna hä'rä krish'nə the chant used by members of a sect of the Hindu religion called Krishna Consciousness: the sect itself: a member of the sect. [Hindi hare, O god!, Krishna, an incarnation of the god Vishnu.]

hareld har'ld, n. the long-tailed duck, Clangula hyemalis. [Mod. Icel. havella — hav, sea.]

harem hä'rəm, hä-rēm', n. women's quarters in a Muslim house: a set of wives and concubines: any Muslim sacred place. — Also **haram', hareem', harim** (-ēm'). — **harem skirt** an early 20th-century divided skirt in imitation of Turkish trousers. [Ar. harīm, haram, anything forbidden — harama, to forbid.]

harewood här'wŏŏd, n. stained sycamore wood, used for making furniture. [Ger. dial. Ehre — L. acer, maple.]

haricot har'i-kō, -kot, n. a kind of ragout or stew of mutton and beans or other vegetables: (also **haricot bean**) the kidney-bean or French bean (plant or seed). [Fr. haricot.]

harigal(d)s har'i-glz, (Scot.) n.pl. viscera.

Harijan ha'rē-jən, n. one of the caste of untouchables, the name proposed by Gandhi. [Sans. Hari, a name of Vishnu, and jana, person.]

hari-kari här'ē-kär'ē, an incorrect form of **hara-kiri.**

harim. See **harem.**

hariolate har'i-ō-lāt, v.i. to divine. — n. **hariolā'tion.** [L. hariolārī, -ātus.]

harish. See **hare.**

hark härk, v.i. to listen: to listen (to; also with at): to go (away, forward, etc.): to go in quest, or to follow (with after). — v.t. to listen to (arch.). — n. a whisper (Scot.). — **hark'-back** a going back again (lit. and fig.). — **hark away, back, forward** cries to urge hounds and hunters; **hark back** to revert (to an earlier topic, etc.). [See **hearken.**]

harken här'kən, v.i. Same as **hearken.**

harl[1] härl, **herl** hûrl, ns. a fibre of flax, etc.: a barb of a feather, esp. one used in making an artificial fly for angling. [M.E. herle — L.G.]

harl[2] härl, (Scot.) v.t. to drag along the ground: to roughcast. — v.i. to drag oneself: to troll for fish. — n. act of dragging: a small quantity, a scraping of anything: a haul: roughcast. — n. **har'ling.**

Harleian här-lē'ən, här'li-ən, adj. pertaining to Robert Harley, Earl of Oxford (1661–1724), and his son Edward, or the library collected by them. — **Harley Street** in London, a favourite abode of consultant or specialist physicians and surgeons, hence symbolically.

harlequin här'lə-kwin, n. a pantomime character, in tight spangled dress, with visor and magic wand: a buffoon: a breed of small spotted dogs. — adj. brightly-coloured: variegated. — v.i. to play the harlequin. — n. **harlequināde'** part of a pantomime in which the harlequin plays a chief part. — **harlequin duck** a variegated northern sea-duck, Histrionicus histrioni-

cus. [Fr. *harlequin, arlequin* (It. *arlecchino*), prob. the same as O.Fr. *Hellequin,* a devil in mediaeval legend, perh. of Gmc. origin.]

harlot *här′lət, n.* a general term of opprobrium applied to man or woman (*obs.*): a whore: a prostitute. — *adj.* lewd: base. — *n.* **har′lotry** prostitution: unchastity: meretriciousness: a harlot (*obs.*). — *adj.* (*obs.*) base, foul. [O.Fr. *herlot, arlot,* base fellow; ety. dub.]

harm *härm, n.* injury: moral wrong. — *v.t.* to injure. — *adj.* **harm′ful** hurtful. — *adv.* **harm′fully.** — *n.* **harm′-fulness.** — *adj.* **harm′less** not injurious, innocent: unharmed. — *adv.* **harm′lessly.** — *n.* **harm′lessness.** — **harm′doing.** — **out of harm's way** in a safe place. [O.E. *herm* (*hearm*); Ger. *Harm.*]

harmala *här′mä-lə, n.* the so-called African or Syrian rue (*Peganum harmala*) of the bean caper family. — Also **har′mel.** — *ns.* **har′malin(e), har′min(e)** alkaloids derived from its seeds. [Gr., from Semitic; cf. Ar. *harmil.*]

harman *här′mən,* (*old thieves' slang*) *n.* a constable: (in *pl.*) the stocks. — **har′man-beck** a constable. [Origin obscure; see **beak.**]

harmattan *här-mä-tan′, här-mat′ən, n.* a dry, dusty N.E. wind from the desert in W. Africa. [Fanti *harmata.*]

harmel, harmin(e). See **harmala.**

harmonic *här-mon′ik, adj.* in harmony: in harmonious proportion: pertaining to harmony: musical: concordant: in accordance with the physical relations of sounds in harmony or bodies emitting such sounds (*math.*). — *n.* a component whose frequency is an integral multiple of the fundamental frequency: an overtone: a flutelike sound produced on a violin, etc., by lightly touching a string at a node and bowing: one of the components of what the ear hears as a single sound: (see also **harmonics** below). — *n.* **harmon′ica** the musical glasses, an instrument consisting of water-filled drinking-glasses (or revolving glass basins in Benjamin Franklin's mechanised version) touched on the rim with a wet finger: an instrument composed of a sound-box and hanging strips of glass or metal, struck by a hammer: a mouth-organ. — *adj.* **harmon′-ical.** — *adv.* **harmon′ically.** — *ns.* **harmon′ichord** a keyboard instrument of violin tone, in which the strings are rubbed by rosined wheels; **harmon′icon** a harmonica: an orchestrion: a pyrophone (*chemical harmonicon*). — *n.sing.* **harmon′ics** musical acoustics. — *adj.* **harmonious** (-*mō′ni-əs*) in, having, or producing harmony: in agreement: justly proportioned: concordant: congruous. — *adv.* **harmōn′iously.** — *ns.* **harmōn′iousness; harmoniphon(e)** (-*mon′i-fon,* -*fōn*) a keyboard wind instrument with reeds; **harmonisation, -z-** (*här-mən-ī-zā′shən,* or -*i*-) any action of the verb *harmonise:* in the EEC, the progressive introduction of norms and standards applicable in all EEC countries. — *v.i.* **har′monise, -ize** to be in harmony: to sing in harmony: to agree: to be compatible. — *v.t.* to bring into harmony: to reconcile: to provide parts to (*mus.*). — *ns.* **har′moniser, -z-; har′monist** one skilled in harmony (in theory or composition): a reconciler: one who seeks to reconcile apparent inconsistencies: (*cap.*) a member of a Second Adventist celibate sect (also **Har′monite**) founded by George Rapp (d. 1847), from its settlement at *Harmony,* Pennsylvania. — *adj.* **harmonist′ic.** — *ns.* **harmōn′ium** a reed-organ, esp. one in which the air is forced (not drawn) through the reeds; **harmōn′iumist; harmonogram** (-*mon′*) a curve drawn by a harmonograph; **harmon′ograph** an instrument for tracing curves representing vibrations; **harmonom′eter** an instrument for measuring the harmonic relations of sounds; **harmony** (*här′mən-i*) a fitting together of parts so as to form a connected whole: agreement in relation: in art, a normal and satisfying state of completeness and order in the relations of things to each other: a simultaneous and successive combination of accordant sounds (*mus.*): the whole chordal structure of a piece, as distinguished from its melody or its rhythm (*mus.*): concord: music in general: a

collation of parallel passages to demonstrate agreement — e.g. of Gospels. — **harmonic conjugates** two points dividing a line internally and externally in the same ratio; **harmonic division** division by such conjugates; **harmonic mean** the middle term of three in harmonic progression; **harmonic minor** a minor scale with minor sixth and major seventh, ascending and descending; **harmonic motion** the motion along a diameter of a circle of the foot of a perpendicular from a point moving uniformly round the circumference; **harmonic pencil** (*math.*) a pencil of four rays that divides a transversal harmonically; **harmonic progression** a series of numbers whose reciprocals are in arithmetical progression, such numbers being proportional to the lengths of strings that sound harmonics; **harmonic proportion** the relation of successive numbers in harmonic progression; **harmonic range** a set of four points in a straight line such that two of them divide the line between the other two internally and externally in the same ratio; **harmonic receiver** a receiver for electric waves, in harmony with the impulses producing them; **harmonic triad** (*mus.*) the common chord. — **harmony of the spheres** see **sphere; pre-established harmony** the divinely established relation, according to Leibniz, between body and mind — the movements of monads and the succession of ideas being in constant agreement like two clocks. [Gr. *harmoniā* — *harmos,* a joint fitting.]

harmony. See **harmonic.**

harmost *här′most, n.* a Spartan governor of a subject city or province. — *n.* **har′mosty** the office of harmost. [Gr. *harmostēs.*]

harmotome *här′mə-tōm, n.* a zeolite, hydrated silicate of aluminium and barium. [Gr. *harmos,* joint, *tomē,* a cut.]

harn *härn, n.* a coarse linen fabric. [See **harden** under **hards.**]

harness *här′nis, n.* tackle: gear: equipment, esp. now of a draught animal: armour for man or horse (*arch.*): an arrangement of straps, etc., for attaching a piece of equipment to the body, as a parachute harness, a baby's leading-strings, a seat belt, etc.: the wiring system of a car, etc. when built separately for installing as a unit. — *v.t.* to equip with armour: to put harness on: to attach by harness: to control and make use of. — **har′ness-cask** (*naut.*) a cask for salt meat for daily use; **harnessed antelope** any antelope of the striped genus Tragelaphus; **har′ness-mak′er; harness racing** trotting or pacing races between specially bred horses harnessed to sulkies; **har′ness-room.** — **in harness** occupied in the routine of one's daily work, not on holiday or retired. [O.Fr. *harneis,* armour.]

harns *härnz,* (*Scot.*) *n.pl.* brains. — **harn′-pan** brain-pan. [O.E. *hærn,* prob. — O.N. *hjarne;* cf. Ger. *Hirn;* Gr. *krānion.*]

haro. See **harrow².**

haroset(h), charoset(h) *ha-rō′set, -seth, hha-, n.* in Judaism, a mixture of finely chopped apples, nuts, spices, etc. mixed with wine, and eaten with bitter herbs at the Passover meal, and symbolising the clay from which the Israelites made bricks in Egypt. [Heb. — *charsit,* clay.]

harp *härp, n.* a musical instrument played by plucking strings stretched from a curved neck to an inclined sound-board: a harmonica, mouth-organ (*coll.*). — *v.i.* to play on the harp: to dwell tediously (on). — *v.t.* to render on or to the harp: to lead, call, or bring by playing the harp: to give voice to (*arch.*): to guess at (*obs.*). — *ns.* **harp′er, harp′ist** a player on the harp. — *n.pl.* **harp′ings** (*naut.*) the foreparts of the wales at the bow. — **harp′-seal** the Greenland seal, a grey animal with dark bands curved like an old harp; **harp′-shell** a genus (*Harpa*) of gasteropods with ribs suggesting harp-strings. — **harp on about** (*coll.*) to dwell tediously or repeatedly on; **harp on one string** to dwell constantly on one topic. [O.E. *hearpe;* Ger. *Harfe.*]

harpoon *här-pōōn′, n.* a barbed dart, esp. for killing

whales. — *v.t.* to strike with a harpoon. — *ns.* **harpoon'er, harpooneer'.** — **harpoon'-gun.** [Fr. *harpon,* a clamp — L. *harpa* — Gr. *harpē,* sickle.]

harpsichord *härp'si-körd, n.* a keyboard instrument in which the strings are twitched by quills or leather points. [O.Fr. *harpechorde;* see **harp, chord.**]

harpy *här'pi, n.* a rapacious and filthy monster, part woman, part bird (*myth.*): a large South American eagle (also **har'py-ea'gle**): a rapacious woman. [Gr. *harpyia,* lit. snatcher, in Homer a personification of the storm-wind — *harpazein,* to seize.]

harquebus, harquebuse, harquebuss *här'kwi-bus, n.* Same as **arquebus.**

harridan *har'i-dən, n.* a vixenish old woman. [Prob. O.Fr. *haridelle,* a lean horse, a jade.]

harrier[1] *har'i-ər, n.* a medium-sized keen-scented dog for hunting hares: a cross-country runner. [**hare,** or **harry.**]

harrier[2]. See **harry.**

Harrovian *har-ō'vi-ən, adj.* pertaining to *Harrow.* — *n.* one educated at Harrow school.

harrow[1] *har'ō, n.* a spiked frame or other contrivance for smoothing and pulverising land and covering seeds. — *v.t.* to draw a harrow over: to tear or harass. — *adj.* **harr'owing** acutely distressing. — *adv.* **harr'owingly.** — **harrowing** or **harrying of hell** Christ's delivery of the souls of patriarchs and prophets. [M.E. *harwe.*]

harrow[2], **haro** (*pl.* **haros**) *har'ō, har-ō', interj.* alas (*arch.*): out upon it (*arch.*): in the Channel Islands a cry announcing a claim to legal redress. [O.Fr. *haro, harou;* not an appeal to *Rou* or Rollo.]

harrumph *hə-rumf', v.i.* to make a noise as of clearing the throat, usu. implying pomposity: to disapprove. [Imit.]

harry *har'i, v.t.* to plunder: to ravage: to destroy: to harass: — *pr.p.* **harr'ying;** *pa.t.* and *pa.p.* **harr'ied.** — *n.* **harr'ier** one who, or that which, harries: a kind of hawk (*Circus*) that preys on small animals. — **harrying of hell** see **harrow**[1]. [O.E. *hergian* — *here,* army; Ger. *Heer.*]

harsh *härsh, adj.* rough: jarring on the senses or feelings: rigorous. — *v.t.* **harsh'en.** — *adv.* **harsh'ly.** — *n.* **harsh'ness.** [M.E. *harsk,* a Northern word; cf. Sw. *härsk* and Dan. *harsk,* rancid, Ger. *harsch,* hard.]

harslet. See **haslet.**

hart[1] *härt, n.* a male deer (esp. red deer) esp. over five years old, when the crown or surroyal antler begins to appear: — *fem.* **hind.** — **harts'horn** the antler of the red deer: a solution of ammonia in water, orig. a decoction of the shavings of hart's horn (*spirit of hartshorn*); **hart's'-tongue** a fern (*Scolopendrium vulgare*) with strap-shaped leaves. [O.E. *heort.*]

hart[2] (*Spens.*) for **heart.**

hartal *här'tal, hûr'täl, (India) n.* a stoppage of work in protest or boycott. [Hindi *hartāl.*]

hartebeest *här'tə-bēst (Afrik.* **hartbees** *härt'bēs), ns.* a large South African antelope. — **bastard hartebeest** the sassaby. [S.Afr.Du., hart-beast.]

hartely, harten, hartlesse, (*Spens.*) for **heartly, hearten, heartless.**

hartie-hale. See under **heart.**

harum-scarum *hā'rəm-skā'rəm, adj.* flighty: rash. — *n.* a giddy, rash person. [Prob. from obs. *hare,* to harass, and **scare.**]

haruspex *ha-rus'peks, n.* one (among the Etruscans) who foretold events from inspection of entrails of animals: — *pl.* **harus'pices** (*-pi-sēz*). — *ns.* **haruspication** (*-kā'shən*), **harus'picy** (*-si*). — *adjs.* **harus'pical, harus'picate.** — *v.i.* **harus'picate.** [L., perh. from an Etruscan word and L. *specĕre,* to view.]

harvest *har'vist, n.* autumn (*obs.* and *dial.*): the time of gathering in crops: crops gathered in: fruits: the product of any labour or act. — *v.t.* to reap and gather in. — *v.i.* to gather a crop. — *n.* **har'vester** a reaper: a reaping-machine: any member of the Opiliones, a class of Arachnida with very long legs (also **har'vestman,**

harvest spider). — **har'vest-bug, -louse, -mite, -tick** a minute larval form of mites of species *Trombiculidae* and *Tetranychidae* abundant in late summer, a very troublesome biter; **har'vest-feast; har'vest-fes'tival** a church service of thanksgiving for the harvest; **har'vest-field; har'vest-fly** in U.S., a cicada of various kinds; **har'vest-goose** a goose eaten at a harvest-home feast; **har'vest-home** (a celebration of) the bringing home of the harvest; **harvest lady, harvest lord** the head reapers at the harvest; **har'vestman** a harvester; **harvest moon** the full moon nearest the autumnal equinox, rising nearly at the same hour for several days; **harvest mouse** a very small mouse that nests in the stalks of corn; **harvest queen** the corn-maiden: the harvest lady; **harvest spider** a harvester. [O.E. *hærfest;* Ger. *Herbst,* Du. *herfst.*]

Harvey Smith *här'vi smith',* a V-sign (q.v.) with palm inwards, signifying derision or contempt. — Also **Harvey Smith salute, wave,** etc. [From the showjumper *Harvey Smith,* who once made such a gesture.]

has *haz.* See **have.** — **has'-been** a person or thing no longer as popular, influential, useful, etc. as before: — *pl.* **has'-beens.**

hash[1] *hash, v.t.* to hack: to mince: to chop small. — *n.* that which is hashed: a mixed dish of meat and vegetables in small pieces: a mixture and preparation of old matter: a mess: a stupid fellow (*Scot.*). — *adj.* **hash'y.** — **settle someone's hash** (*slang*) to silence or subdue someone. [Fr. *hacher* — *hache,* hatchet.]

hash[2] *hash,* (*slang*) *n.* short for **hashish.**

hashish, hasheesh *hash'ish, -ēsh, n.* leaves, shoots, or resin of hemp, smoked, or swallowed, as an intoxicant. [Ar. *hashīsh.*]

Hasid *has'id, hhäs'id, n.* a very pious Jew: a member of any of a number of extremely devout and often mystical Jewish sects existing at various times throughout history: — *pl.* **Hasidim** (*has'id-im, hhä-sē'dim*). — Also **Hass'id, Chas(s)'id.** — *adjs.* **Has(s)id'ic, Chas(s)id'ic; Has'idist.** — *n.* **Has(s)'idism, Chas(s)'idism.** [Heb. *hāsid,* (one who is) pious.]

hask *hask, (Spens.) n.* a fish-basket. [Cf. **hassock.**]

haslet *häz'lit,* also *häs', häs',* **harslet** *härs', ns.* edible entrails, esp. of a hog. [O.Fr. *hastelet,* roast meat — *haste,* spit — L. *hasta,* a spear.]

hasp *häsp, n.* a clasp: a slotted part that receives a staple, as for a padlock: a fourth part of a spindle (*dial.*): a skein of yarn (*dial.*). — *v.t.* to fasten with a hasp. [O.E. *hæpse;* Ger. *Haspe,* Dan. *haspe.*]

hassar *has'ər, n.* a South American nest-building land-walking catfish (in the American sense). [Amer. Indian origin.]

Hassid, Hassidic, etc. See **Hasid.**

hassle *has'l, (coll.) v.t.* to harass, annoy persistently. — *v.i.* to be involved in a struggle or argument. — *n.* bother, fuss: a difficulty, problem: something requiring trouble or effort: a struggle: an argument. [Ety. dub.]

hassock *has'ək, n.* a tuft or tussock of grass, rushes, etc.: a stuffed stool: in Kent, a soft calcareous sandstone. — *adj.* **hass'ocky.** [O.E. *hassuc.*]

hast *hast.* See **have.**

hasta *äs'tä, (Sp.) prep.* and *conj.* until. — **hasta la vista** (*lä vē'stä*) until we meet again; **hasta luego** (*lŏō-ā'gō*) see you later; **hasta mañana** (*män-yän'ä*) see you to-morrow; — all three common terms of farewell.

hastate, -d *hast'āt, -id, adjs.* spear-shaped: with basal lobes turned outward (*bot.*). [L. *hastātus* — *hasta,* spear.]

haste *hāst, n.* urgency calling for speed: hurry: inconsiderate speed. — *vs.t.* **haste, hasten** (*hās'n*) to put to speed: to hurry on: to drive forward. — *vs.i.* to move with speed: to hurry: (**hasten**) to (wish to) do immediately (as in *I hasten to say that ...*). — *n.* **hastener** (*hās'n-ər*). — *adv.* **hastily** (*hāst'i-li*). — *n.* **hast'iness** hurry: rashness: irritability. — *n.pl.* **hast'ings** (*dial.*) early fruit or vegetables, esp. peas. — *adj.* **hast'y** speedy: quick: rash:

eager: irritable. — **hasty pudding** flour, milk, or oatmeal and water porridge. — *adj.* **hast′y-witt′ed** (*obs.*) rash. — **make haste** to hasten. [O.Fr. *haste* (Fr. *hâte*), from Gmc.; cf. O.E. *hǣst*, Du. *haast*, Ger. *Hast*.]

hat *hat, n.* a covering for the head, often with crown and brim: the dignity of cardinal, from former red hat: a salutation by lifting the hat (*Scot.* or *obs.*). — *v.t.* to provide with or cover with a hat: to lift one's hat to (*arch.*). — *v.i.* (*Austr.*) to work alone: — *pa.t.* and *pa.p.* **hatt′ed.** — *n.* **hat′ful** as much as will fill a hat: — *pl.* **hatfuls.** — *adj.* **hat′less.** — *n.* **hat′lessness.** — *adj.* **hatt′ed** provided or covered with a hat. — *ns.* **hatt′er** a maker or seller of hats: a miner or other who works by himself, one whose 'hat covers his family' (*Austr.*); **hatt′ing;** **hatt′ock** (*arch. Scot.*) a little hat. — **hat′band** a ribbon round a hat; **hat′box; hat′brush; hat′guard** a string for keeping a hat from being blown away; **hat′peg** a peg for hanging a hat on; **hat′pin** a long pin for fastening a hat to the hair; **hat′-plant** the sola plant, used for making topees; **hat′rack** a set of hatpegs; **hat′stand** a piece of furniture with hatpegs; **hat trick** a conjurer's trick with a hat: the taking of three wickets by consecutive balls (deserving a new hat) in cricket, or corresponding feat (as three goals) in other games: three successes in any activity. — **a bad hat** (*slang*) a rascal; **hang up one's hat** see **hang; hats off to** all honour to; **horse and hattock!** to horse! (signal of witches or fairies); **mad as a hatter** quite mad (poss. from the odd behaviour of some hatters due to mental and physical disorders caused by the mercury in the chemicals used in the making of felt hats); **my hat!** an exclamation of surprise; **pass, send, round the hat** to take up a collection, solicit contributions; **take off one's hat to** to acknowledge in admiration (*fig.*): to praise; **talk through one's hat** to talk wildly or at random; **throw one's hat into the ring** see **ring¹; under one's hat** in confidence; **wear several hats, another hat,** etc. to act in several capacities, another capacity, etc. [O.E. *hæt;* Dan. *hat.*]

hatch¹ *hach, n.* a half-door: a small gate (*dial.*): the covering of a hatchway: a hatchway. — *v.t.* to close as with a hatch. — **hatch′back** (a car with) a sloping rear door which opens upwards; **hatch boat** a kind of half-decked fishing-boat; **hatch′way** an opening in a deck, floor, wall, or roof. — **down the hatch** (*coll.*) said when about to drink something, esp. an alcoholic beverage; **under hatches** below deck, esp. in confinement: hidden, out of sight: in servitude or depressed state: dead. [O.E. *hæcc, hæc,* grating, half-gate, hatch; cf. **hack³, heck¹;** Du. *hek,* gate.]

hatch² *hach, v.t.* to bring out from the egg: to breed: to originate, develop or concoct. — *v.i.* to bring young from the egg: to come from the egg: to develop into young. — *n.* act of hatching: brood hatched. — *ns.* **hatch′er; hatch′ery** a place for artificial hatching, esp. of fish eggs; **hatch′ling** a bird or reptile newly hatched. — **count one's chickens before they are hatched** to depend too securely on some uncertain future event; **hatches, matches, and dispatches** (*coll.*) newspaper announcements of births, marriages, and deaths. [Early M.E. *hacchen,* from an assumed O.E. *hæccean.*]

hatch³ *hach, v.t.* to mark with fine lines, incisions, or inlaid or applied strips. — *n.* **hatch′ing** shading in fine lines. [O.Fr. *hacher,* to chop.]

hatchel *hach′əl, n.* and *vb.* Same as **hackle.**

hatchet *hach′it, n.* a small axe for one hand. — *adj.* **hatch′ety** like a hatchet. — *adj.* **hatch′et-faced** having a narrow face with a profile like a hatchet. — **hatchet job** (*coll.*) the (attempted) destruction of a person's reputation or standing: a severely critical attack: a severe reduction; **hatchet man** (*coll.*) a gunman: a militant journalist: one who does shady jobs for a politician or political party: a person who destroys or attempts to destroy another's reputation or standing. — **bury the hatchet** to end war (from a habit of North American Indians). [Fr. *hachette* — *hacher,* to chop.]

hatchettite *hach′it-īt, n.* mountain tallow, a natural waxy

hydrocarbon. [After Charles *Hatchett* (d. 1847), English chemist.]

hatchment *hach′mənt, n.* the arms of a deceased person within a black lozenge-shaped frame, formerly placed on the front of his house. [**achievement.**]

hate¹ *hāt, v.t.* to dislike intensely. — *n.* extreme dislike: hatred: object of hatred. — *adjs.* **hāt′able, hate′able** deserving to be hated; **hate′ful** exciting hate: odious: detestable: feeling or manifesting hate. — *adv.* **hate′fully.** — *n.* **hate′fulness.** — *adj.* **hate′less** — *ns.* **hate′lessness; hāt′er; hate′rent** (*Scot.*) hatred. — *adj.* **hate′worthy.** — *n.* **hāt′red** extreme dislike: enmity: malignity. — **hate′-monger** one who foments hatred. [O.E. *hete,* hate, *hatian,* to hate; Ger. *Hasz.*]

hate². Same as **haet.**

hath. See **have.**

hatha yoga. See **yoga.**

hatter¹. See **hat.**

hatter² *hat′ər, v.t.* to trouble, annoy (*arch.*): to batter (*dial.*).

Hatteria *hat-ē′ri-ə, n.* Sphenodon. [Origin unknown.]

hatti-sherif *ha′ti-she-rēf′,* (*hist.*) *n.* a decree signed by the Sultan of Turkey. [Pers. *khatt-i-sharīf,* noble writing, from Ar.]

hattock. See **hat.**

hauberk *hö′bərk, n.* a long coat of chain-mail sometimes ending in short trousers: originally armour for the neck. [O.Fr. *hauberc* — O.H.G. *halsberg* — *hals,* neck, *bergan,* to protect.]

haud *höd, n.* and *vb.* a Scottish form of **hold:** — *pa.p.* **hudd′en.**

haugh *höhh, hähh,* (esp. in place-names) *hö, hä,* (*Scot.*) *n.* a riverside meadow or flat. [O.E. *halh* (W.S. *healh*), corner.]

haughty *hö′ti, adj.* proud: arrogant: contemptuous: bold (*arch.*): high (*Spens.*). — *adjs.* **haught, hault, haut** (*höt; Shak., Spens., Milt.*) haughty: exalted. — *adv.* **haught′ily.** — *n.* **haught′iness.** [O.Fr. *halt, haut,* high — L. *altus,* high.]

haul *höl, v.t.* to drag: to pull with violence or effort: to transport (*U.S.*). — *v.i.* to tug, to try to draw something: to alter a ship's course: to change direction. — *n.* act of pulling, or of pulling in: contents of hauled-in net: a take, gain, loot: a hauled load: distance hauled. — *ns.* **haul′age** act of hauling: transport, esp. heavy road transport: charge for hauling; **haul′er; haulier** (*höl′yər;* this form is used esp. for a man who conveys coal from the workings to the foot of the shaft, or for one who engages in road haulage business). — **haul over the coals** see **coal; haul round** or **off** to turn a ship's course away from an object; **haul up** to come or bring to rest after hauling: to call to account. [A variant of **hale².**]

hauld *höld, n.* a Scottish form of **hold¹,** as in the *dial.* phrase *out of house and hauld,* homeless.

haulm, halm *höm, häm, ns.* straw, esp. of gathered plants: a strawy stem: a culm: straw or stems of plants collectively. [O.E. *halm (healm*).]

haulst. See **halse¹.**

hault. See **haughty.**

haunch¹ *hönch, hönsh,* also (old-fashioned) **hanch** *hänsh, ns.* the expansion of the body at and near the pelvis: the hip with buttock: the leg and loin of venison, etc.: the side or flank of an arch between the crown and the springing: the rear (*Shak.*): a jerked underhand throw (*dial.*). — *v.t.* to throw with an underhand movement (*dial.*). — **haunch bone** the innominate bone. [O.Fr. *hanche,* prob. of Gmc. origin; cf. O.H.G. *anchâ,* leg.]

haunch². See **hance.**

haunt *hönt, v.t.* to frequent: to associate much with: to intrude upon continually: to inhabit or visit (as a ghost): to cling, or keep recurring, to the memory of. — *v.i.* to be much about, to visit frequently (with *about,* etc.). — *n.* place much resorted to: resort, habit of frequenting (*Shak.*): a ghost (*U.S. dial.*). — *adj.* **haunt′ed** frequented, infested, esp. by ghosts or apparitions: obsessed: worried. — *n.* **haunt′er.** — *n.* and *adj.* **haunt′ing.** — *adv.* **haunt′ingly.** [O.Fr. *hanter.*]

haurient, hauriant *hö′ri-ənt*, (*her.*) *adj.* rising as if to breathe. [L. *hauriēns, -entis,* pr.p. of *haurīre,* to draw up, drink.]

Hausa *how′sə, -zə, n.* a Negroid people living mainly in N. Nigeria: a member of this people: their language, widely used in commerce throughout W. Africa.

hause. See **halse**[1].

hausfrau *hows′frow, n.* a housewife, esp. a woman exclusively interested in domestic matters. [Ger.]

haussmannise, -ize *hows′mən-īz, v.t.* to open out, generally rebuild, as Baron *Haussmann,* as prefect of the Seine (1853–70), did Paris. — *n.* **haussmannīsā′tion, -z-.**

haustellum *hös-tel′əm, n.* a sucking proboscis or its sucking end, as in flies: — *pl.* **haustell′a.** — *adj.* **haus′tellate** having a haustellum. — *n.* **haustō′rium** the part by which a parasitic plant fixes itself and derives nourishment from its host: — *pl.* **haustō′ria.** [L. *haurīre, haustum,* draw up, drink.]

haut[1]. See **haughty.**

haut[2] *ō,* (Fr.) *adj.* high. — **haut monde** (*mɔ̃d*) high society; **haut pas** (*pä*) a dais; **haut relief** (*rə-lyef*) high relief; **haut ton** (*tɔ̃*) high fashion. — **de haut en bas** (*də ō tä bä*) downwards, or from top to bottom (*lit.*): with an air of superiority, contemptuously.

hautboy (*h*)*ō′boi, n.* arch. name for **oboe:** a large kind of strawberry (also **haut′bois**). [Fr. *hautbois* — *haut,* high, *bois,* wood.]

haute *ōt,* (Fr.) *adj.* fem. of **haut.** — **haute bourgeoisie** (*bōōr-zhwä-zē*) the richer, more influential part of the middle class; **haute couture** (*kōō-tür*) fashionable, expensive dress designing and dressmaking; **haute cuisine** (*kwē-zēn*) cookery of a very high standard; **haute école** (*ā-kol*) horsemanship of the most difficult kind; **haute époque** (*ā-pok*) in relation to architecture, furniture, etc., the period during which Louis XIV, XV and XVI reigned in France; **haute politique** (*po-lē-tēk*) the higher reaches of politics; **haute vulgarisation** (*vül-gar-ēz-as-yɔ̃*) popularisation of scholarly subjects.

hauteur *ō′tər, ō-tœr, n.* haughtiness: arrogance. [Fr.]

haüyne *hö′in, hä′win, n.* a blue mineral, in composition like nosean, with calcium. [After the French mineralogist René J. *Haüy* (1743–1822).]

Havana *hə-van′ə, n.* a fine quality of cigar, made in *Havana* or Cuba generally.

have *hav, v.t.* to hold: to keep: to possess: to own: to hold in control: to bear: to be in a special relation to (analogous to, if short of, ownership; e.g. *to have a son, an assistant, no government*): to be characterised by: to be in enjoyment of: to experience: to know: to entertain in the mind: to grasp the meaning or point of: to have received as information: to put, assert, or express: to suffer, endure, tolerate: to hold or esteem: to cause or allow to be: to convey, take, cause to go: to accept, take: to remove (with *off, out*): to cause to be removed: to get: to obtain: to give birth to: to get the better of, hold at a disadvantage or in one's power in a dilemma: to take in, deceive: to entertain in one's home (with *back, in, round,* etc.: *coll.*): to ask to do a job in one's house, etc. (with *in, round,* etc.: *coll.*): as an auxiliary verb, used with the *pa.p.* in forming the perfect tenses: — *2nd pers. sing.* **hast;** *3rd* **has,** arch. **hath;** *pl.* **have;** *pres. subj.* **have;** *pa.t.* and *pa.p.* **had,** *2nd pers. pa.t.* **hadst;** *pa.subj.* **had;** *pr.p.* **hav′ing.** — *n.* one who has possessions: — *pl.* **haves.** — *ns.* **hav′er** one who has or possesses, a holder: the person in whose custody a document is (*Scots law*); **hav′ing** act of possessing: possession, estate: (esp. in *pl.* **hāv′ingz**) behaviour, good manners (*Scot.*). — *adj.* greedy. — **have-at′-him** (*Shak.*) a thrust; **have′-not** one who lacks possessions: — *pl.* **have′-nots; have-on′** a deception, a hoax: a piece of humbug or chaff. — **had as good** (*arch.*) might as well; **had as lief** (*arch.*) would as willingly; **had better, best** would do best to; **had like** see **like**[1]; **have at** (let me) attack: here goes; **had rather** would prefer; **have done** see **do**[1]; **have had it** (*coll.*) to be ruined:

to have missed one's opportunities: to be doomed, beyond hope: to have been killed: (also **have had that**) not to be going to get or do (something); **have it** to prevail: to exceed in any way: to get punishment, unpleasant consequences; **have (it) away** see **have it off (with); have it coming (to one)** (*coll.*) to deserve the bad luck, punishment, etc. that one is getting or will get; **have it in for (someone)** to have a grudge against (someone); **have it in one** to have the courage or ability (to do something); **have it off, away (with), have off, away** (*slang*) to have sexual intercourse (with); **have it out** to discuss or express explicitly and exhaustively; **have on** to wear: to take in, hoax, chaff: to have as an engagement or appointment; **have to** to be obliged to; **have to be** (*coll.*) to surely be; **have to do with** see **do**[1]; **have up** to call to account before a court of justice, etc.; **have what it takes** to have the necessary qualities or capabilities to do something; **have with you** (*arch.*) I am ready to go with you; **I have it!** I have found the answer (to a problem, etc.); **let (someone) have it** to attack (someone) with words, blows, etc.; **not be having any (of that)** to be unwilling to accept, tolerate, etc. the thing proposed or mentioned. [O.E. *habban,* pa.t. *hæfde,* pa.p. *gehæfd;* Ger. *haben,* Dan. *have.*]

havelock *hav′lək, n.* a white cover for a military cap, with a flap over the neck. [From Gen. Henry *Havelock,* 1795–1857.]

haven *hā′vn, n.* an inlet affording shelter to ships: a harbour: any place of retreat or asylum. — *v.t.* to shelter. — *adj.* **hā′vened.** [O.E. *hæfen;* Du. *haven,* Ger. *Hafen.*]

haveour. See **haviour.**

haver[1] *hāv′ər, v.i.* to talk nonsense, or foolishly (*Scot.* and *Northern*): to waver, to be slow or hesitant in making a decision. — *n.* (usu. in *pl.: Scot.* and *Northern*) foolish talk: nonsense. — *ns.* **hav′erel** (*Scot.* and *Northern*) a foolish person; **haver′ings** (*Scot.* and *Northern*) havers.

haver[2] *hav′ər, n.* (*Northern*) oats: the wild oat (grass). — *n.* **hav′ersack** a bag worn over one shoulder for carrying provisions, etc. (orig. horse's oats) on a journey. [O.N. (pl.) *hafrar;* cf. Ger. *Hafer, Haber,* oats.]

haversine *hav′ər-sīn, n.* half the *versine.*

havildar *hav′il-där, n.* an Indian sergeant. [Pers. *hawāl-dār.*]

haviour, haveour *hāv′yər, n.* possession (*obs.*): behaviour (*Spens.*). [Partly O.Fr. *aveir,* possession, partly **behaviour.**]

havoc *hav′ək, n.* general destruction: devastation. — *v.t.* to lay waste: — *pr.p.* **hav′ocking;** *pa.t.* and *pa.p.* **hav′ocked.** — *interj.* an ancient war-cry, signal for plunder. — **play havoc with** see **play.** [A.Fr. *havok* — O.Fr. *havot,* plunder; prob. Gmc.]

haw[1] *hö, n.* a hedge (*hist.*): an enclosure (*hist.*): a messuage (*hist.*): the fruit of the hawthorn. — **haw′buck** a bumpkin; **haw′finch** the common grosbeak (*Coccothraustes coccothraustes*); **haw′thorn** a small tree of the rose family, much used for hedges. [O.E. *haga,* a yard or enclosure, a haw; Du. *haag,* a hedge, Ger. *Hag,* a hedge, O.N. *hagi,* a field.]

haw[2] *hö, v.i.* to speak with hesitation or drawl, natural or affected. — *adj.* **haw′-haw′** affectedly superior in enunciation. — *n.* a hesitation or affectation of superiority in speech: loud vulgar laughter. — *v.i.* to guffaw, to laugh boisterously. [Imit.]

haw[3] *hö, n.* the nictitating membrane: a disease of the nictitating membrane. [Origin unknown.]

Hawaiian *ha-wī′(y)ən, adj.* pertaining to *Hawaii,* to its citizens, or to its language. — Also *n.* — **Hawaiian goose** the nene (q.v.); **Hawaiian guitar** a guitar, usu. held horizontally, on which the required notes and esp. glissandos are produced by sliding a metal bar or similar object along the strings while plucking.

haw-haw. See **ha-ha**[2], **haw**[2].

hawk[1] *hök, n.* a name given to many birds of prey of the family Accipitridae (akin to the falcons) which includes the eagles and buzzards, esp. to those of the sparrow-hawk and goshawk genus (Accipiter): in the

U.S., applied also to some falcons: (in *pl.*) all members of the Accipitridae (*biol.*): a predatory or a keen-sighted person: a hawk-moth: in politics, industrial relations, etc., a person who advocates war, aggressiveness or confrontation rather than peace and conciliation (opp. to *dove*). — *v.t.* and *v.i.* to hunt with trained hawks: to hunt on the wing. — *ns.* **hawk′er; hawk′ing** falconry. — *adj.* practising falconry: hawk-like, keen (*Shak.*). — *adj.* **hawk′ish.** — *adv.* **hawk′ishly.** — *n.* **hawk′ishness.** — *adj.* **hawk′-beaked, -billed** with a beak, or nose, like a hawk's bill. — **hawk′bell** a small bell attached to a hawk's leg; **hawk′bit** a plant (Leontodon) close akin to the dandelion. — *adj.* **hawk′-eyed** sharp-sighted. — **hawk′-moth** any member of the Sphinx family, heavy moths with hovering flight. — *adj.* **hawk′-nosed** hook-beaked. — **hawks′beard** a plant (*Crepis*) very like hawkweed; **hawks′bill** a hawk-beaked turtle; **hawk′weed** a genus (Hieracium) of yellow-headed ligulate-flowered composites. — **know a hawk from a handsaw** (prob. for *heronshaw*) to be able to judge between things pretty well. [O.E. *hafoc*; Du. *havik*, Ger. *Habicht*, O.N. *haukr*.]

hawk² *hök*, *v.t.* to force up from the throat. — *v.i.* to clear the throat noisily. — *n.* the act of doing so. [Prob. imit.]

hawk³. See **hawker.**

hawk⁴ *hök*, *n.* a plasterer's slab with handle below. [Origin uncertain; a connection with **hawk¹** has been suggested, because of how the slab is held.]

hawked *hökt*, (*Scot.* **hawk′it**) *adjs.* streaked: white-faced. — *n.* **hawk′ey, hawk′ie** a cow with white-striped face.

hawker *hök′ər*, *n.* one who goes about offering goods for sale: now confined to one who uses a beast of burden or vehicle (distinguished from a pedlar, who carries his wares bodily). — *v.t.* **hawk** to convey about for sale: to cry for sale. [Cf. L.G. and Ger. *Höker*, Du. *heuker*.]

hawkey. See **hockey², hawked.**

hawkie, hawkit. See **hawked.**

hawm *höm*, (*dial.*) *v.i.* to lounge about. [Ety. dub.]

hawse¹ *höz*, *n.* part of a vessel's bow in which the hawseholes are cut. — **hawse′hole** a hole for a ship's cable; **hawse′pipe** a tubular casting, fitted to a ship's bows, through which the anchor chain or cable passes. [O.N. *hāls*, neck.]

hawse². See **halse¹.**

hawser *hö′zər*, *n.* a small cable, a large rope used in warping: a hawser-laid rope. — *adj.* **haw′ser-laid** composed of strands with a left-handed twist twisted together to the right hand. [O.Fr. *haucier, haulser*, to raise — L.L. *altiāre* — L. *altus*, high.]

hawthorn. See **haw¹.**

hay¹ *hā*, *n.* grass, etc., cut down and dried for fodder or destined for that purpose. — *v.t.* and *v.i.* to make hay. — *ns.* **hay′ing** the making or harvesting of hay; **hay′sel** the hay season (O.E. *sǽl*, season). — **hay′band** a rope of twisted hay; **hay′box** an airtight box of hay used to continue the cooking of dishes already begun; **hay′cock** a conical pile of hay in the field; **hay fever** irritation by pollen of the nose, throat, etc., with sneezing and headache — also **hay asthma; hay′field** a field where hay is made; **hay′fork** a long-handled fork used in turning and lifting hay; **hay knife** a broad knife with a handle set crosswise at one end, used for cutting hay from a stack; **hay′loft** a loft in which hay is kept; **hay′maker** one who makes hay: a wild swinging blow (*slang*): (in *pl.*) a kind of country-dance; **hay′making; hay′mow** a rick of hay: a mass of hay stored in a barn; **hay′rick** a haystack; **hay′seed** grass seed dropped from hay: a rustic (*coll.*); **hay′stack; hay′wire** wire for binding hay. — *adj.* (*slang*), tangled: crazy: all amiss. — Also *adv.* — **hit the hay** (*slang*) to go to bed; **make hay** to toss and turn cut grass: to throw things into confusion (with *of*); **make hay while the sun shines** to seize an opportunity while it lasts. [O.E. *hīeg, hīg, hēg*; Ger. *Heu*, Du. *hooi*; O.N. *hey*.]

hay² *hā*, (*arch.*) *n.* a hedge, fence. — **hay′-bote** hedge-bote;

hay′ward one who had charge of fences and enclosures and prevented cattle from breaking through: one who herded the common cattle of a town. [O.E. *hege — haga*, a hedge.]

hay³ *hā*, (*obs.*) *interj.* used on hitting in fencing. — *n.* (*Shak.*) a hit or home-thrust. [It. *hai*, thou hast (it) — *avere* — L. *habēre*, to have.]

hay⁴. See **hey².**

hayle (*Spens.*). See **hale¹.**

hazard *haz′ərd*, *n.* an old dicing game: chance: accident: risk: the thing risked: the pocketing of the object ball (*winning* hazard), of the player's own ball after contact (*losing* hazard; *billiards*): the side of the court into which the ball is served (*court tennis*): any difficulty on golf links — bunker, long grass, road, water, whins, etc.: anything which might cause an accident, create danger, etc. — *v.t.* to expose to chance: to risk: to venture: to venture to say or utter: to jeopardise. — *adj.* **haz′ardable.** — *n.* **haz′ardize** (*Spens.*) hazard. — *adj.* **haz′ardous** dangerous: perilous: uncertain. — *adv.* **haz′ardously.** — *ns.* **haz′ardousness; haz′ardry** (*Spens.*) playing at games of hazard or chance: rashness. [O.Fr. *hasard*; prob. through the Sp. from Ar. *al zār*, the die; according to William of Tyre from *Hasart*, a castle in Syria, where the game was invented during the Crusades.]

haze¹ *hāz*, *n.* vapour or mist, often shining and obscuring vision: mistiness: lack of definition or precision. — *v.t.* to make hazy. — *v.i.* to form a haze. — *adv.* **hā′zily.** — *n.* **hā′ziness.** — *adj.* **hā′zy** thick with haze: ill-defined: not clear: confused (of the mind). [App. not O.E. *hasu, haswe*, grey.]

haze² *hāz*, *v.t.* to vex with needless or excessive tasks, rough treatment, practical jokes: to rag: to bully. — *ns.* **hā′zer; hā′zing.** [O.Fr. *haser*, to annoy.]

hazel *hā′zl*, *n.* a tree (Corylus) of the birch family: its wood. — *adj.* of hazel: light-brown, like a hazelnut. — *adj.* **hā′zelly.** — **hazel grouse, hen** the ruffed grouse; **hā′zelnut** the edible nut of the hazel-tree. [O.E. *hæsel*; Ger. *Hasel*, O.N. *hasl*, L. *corulus, corylus*.]

he *hē* (or when unemphatic *hi, ē, i*), *nom.* (irregularly, in *dial.*, or ungrammatically *accus.* or *dat.*) *masc. pron.* of *3rd pers.* the male (or thing spoken of as if male) named before, indicated, or understood: — *pl.* **they.** — *n.* a male: — *pl.* **hēs.** — *adj.* male (esp. in composition). — **he′-man** a man of exaggerated or extreme virility, or what some women take to be virility. [O.E. *hē, he.*]

head *hed*, *n.* the uppermost or foremost part of an animal's body: the brain: the understanding: self-possession: a chief or leader: a headmaster, principal: the place of honour or command: the front or top of anything: a rounded or enlarged end or top: a capitulum: a mass of leaves, flowers, hair, etc.: a head-dress or dressing for the head (*arch.*): a headache (*coll.*): the peg-box and scroll of a violin, etc.: the membrane of a drum: the essential part of an apparatus: in a bicycle, the tube in which the front-fork is socketed: an individual animal or person as one of a group: a title, heading: a topic or chief point of a discourse: a source: energy of a fluid owing to height, velocity, and pressure: strength (*arch.*): insurrectionary force (*arch.*): the highest point of anything: culmination: a cape: a froth on liquor poured out: point of suppuration: headway: a head's length or height: a mine tunnel: (in *pl.*) the obverse of a coin: one who takes hallucinogenic drugs (*slang*; often in composition, as in **acid-head**): (often in *pl.*) a ship's toilet (*naut. slang*): an electromagnetic device in tape recorders, etc. for converting electrical signals into the recorded form or vice versa, or erasing recorded material. — *adj.* of, pertaining to, the head: for the head: chief, principal: at, or coming from, the front. — *v.t.* to remove the head or top from: to behead (*obs.*): to supply with a head, top, or heading: to be the head, or at the head of (also **head up**): (with *off*) to get ahead of and turn: to go round the head of: to face: to meet in the face: to cause to face or front: to strike with the head. — *v.i.* to form a head: to face, front: to shape one's course, make (for). — *adj.* **head′ed** (usu. in composition) having a head: come to a head (*Shak.*). — *n.* **head′er** one who or a machine which removes heads from or supplies heads for casks, etc.: a dive head foremost: a brick or stone at right angles to the wall surface: the act of heading a ball: a heading at the top of a microfiche, etc., readable with the naked eye: an optional piece of coded information preceding a collection of data, giving certain details about the data (*comput.*): a card attached to the top of a dump-bin giving information such as the name(s) and author(s) of the book(s) displayed. — *adv.* **head′ily.** — *ns.* **head′iness; head′ing** action of the verb *head* in any sense: a part forming a head: a small passage to be enlarged into a tunnel: words placed at the head of a chapter, paragraph, etc. — *adj.* **head′less.** — *adv.* **head′long** with the head foremost or first: without thought, rashly: precipitately. — *adj.* rash: precipitate: precipitous. — *adj.* **head′most** most advanced or forward. — *n.* **head′ship** the position or office of head or chief. — *adj.* **head′y** affecting the brain: intoxicating: inflamed: rash: violent: exciting. — **head′ache** a pain in the head: a source of worry (*coll.*). — *adj.* **head′achy.** — **head′band** a band or fillet for the head: a band round the top of trousers, etc.: the band at each end of a book: a thin slip of iron on the tympan of a printing-press; **head′-banger** (*coll.*) one who is crazy, foolish, fanatical, etc.; **head′board** an often ornamental board or panel at the head of a bed; **head′-boom** a jib-boom or a flying jib-boom; **head′borough** (*hist.*) the head of a frank-pledge, tithing, or decennary: a petty constable; **head boy** the senior boy in a school; **head-bummer** see under **bum²**; **head′case** (*coll.*) one who is mad; **head-centre** see **centre**; **head′chair** a high-backed chair with headrest; **head′cheese** (*U.S.*) brawn; **head′cloth** a kerchief worn instead of a hat; **head cold** a cold which affects parts of the sufferer's head, as the eyes or nasal passages; **head count** (*coll.*) a count of people, bodies, etc.; **head′-crash** (*comput.*) the accidental contact of a computer head with the surface of a hard disc in a disc drive, damaging the disc and wiping out the data stored on it; **head′-dress** a covering for the head: a mode of dressing the hair (*arch.*); **head′fast** a mooring rope at the bows of a ship; **head′frame** the structure over a mine-shaft supporting the winding machinery; **head′gear** gear, covering, or ornament of the head: apparatus at the head of a mine-shaft; **head girl** the senior girl in a school; **head′-hugger** a woman's close-fitting headgear of kerchief type. — *v.i.* **head′hunt** (*coll.*) to (attempt to) deprive a political opponent of power and influence (*U.S.*): (also *v.t.*) to seek out and recruit (executives, etc.) for a business or organisation, esp. to do so professionally as e.g. a management consultant. — **head′hunter; head′hunting** the practice of collecting human heads: the action of the verb *headhunt* (*coll.*); **head′land** a point of land running out into the sea: a cape: the border of a field where the plough turns, ploughed separately afterwards; **head′-light, head′lamp** a light on the front of a vehicle; **head′line** line at the top of a page containing title, folio, etc.: title in a newspaper, caption: a news item given very briefly (*radio, TV*): (in *pl.*) the sails and ropes next the yards. — *v.t.* to give as a headline, mention in a headline: to publicise. — *v.i.* to be a headliner. — **head′liner** one whose name is made most prominent in a bill or programme; **head′lock** a wrestling hold made by putting one's arm round one's opponent's head and tightening the grip by interlocking the fingers of both hands. — *adj.* **head′-lugged** (*Shak.*) dragged by the head. — **head′man** a chief, a leader; **head′mark** a peculiar characteristic; **headmas′ter** the principal master of a school; **headmis′tress; head money** a poll tax: prize money by head of prisoners: a reward for a proscribed outlaw's head; **head′note** a note placed at the head of a chapter or page, esp. a condensed statement of points of law involved introductory to

the report of a legal decision: a tone produced in the head register (*mus.*). — *adj.* and *adv.* **head′-on′** head to head, esp. (of a collision) with the front of one vehicle, etc. hitting the front of another, or (*rarely*) a stationary object: with head pointing directly forward: directly opposed. — **head′phone** (usu. in *pl.*) a telephone receiver worn in pairs on a headband, esp. for wireless listening: a hairdressing of similar form; **head′-piece** a helmet: a hat: head, skull (*arch.; Spens.* **head′-peace**): a brain: a man of intelligence: a top part: a decorative engraving at the beginning of a book, chapter, etc. (*print.*). — *adj.* **headquar′tered** having one's headquarters (in a specified place). — *n.pl.* and *n.sing.* **headquar′ters** the quarters or residence of a commander-in-chief or general: a central or chief office, etc. — **head′race** the race leading to a water-wheel; **head′rail** one of the rails at a ship's head; **head′reach** the distance made to windward in tacking. — *v.i.* to shoot ahead, in tacking. — **head register** (*mus.*) high register: of the voice in which nose and head cavities vibrate sympathetically: (in male voice) falsetto; **head rent** rent payable to the freeholder; **head′rest** a support for the head: (also **head restraint**) a cushion fitted to the top of a car, etc. seat to prevent the head jerking back in a collision; **head-rhyme** alliteration; **head′rig** (*Scot.*) a headland in a ploughed field; **head′ring** a palm-leaf hair ornament worn by S. African native men after marriage; **head′room** uninterrupted space below a ceiling, bridge, etc.: space overhead; **head′rope** a rope for tying or leading an animal; **head′scarf** a scarf worn over the head, a headsquare: — *pl.* **-scarves; head sea** a sea running directly against a ship's course; **head′set** a set of headphones, often with a microphone attached; **head′shake** a significant shake of the head; **head′shrinker** a headhunter who shrinks the heads of his victims: a psychiatrist (*coll.*). **heads′man** an executioner who cuts off heads; **head′-square** a square cloth worn as a covering for the head; **head′stall** the part of a bridle round the head: a choir-stall with back to choir-screen (*obs.*); **head start** boost or advantage intended to overcome a disadvantage or give a better chance of success; **head′-sta′tion** the dwelling-house, etc., on an Australian sheep or cattle station; **head′stick** (*print.*) formerly a straight piece of furniture placed at the head of a form, between the chase and the type; **head′stock** (*mach.*) a device for supporting the end or head of a member or part; **head′stone** the principal stone of a building: cornerstone: gravestone; **head′-stream** a head-water: a high tributary: the stream forming the highest or remotest source. — *adj.* **head′strong** obstinately self-willed. — **head′-teach′er** a headmaster or headmistress; **head′-tire** (*obs.*) a head-dress; **head voice** tones in the head register; **head waiter** a person placed over the waiters of a restaurant or hotel; **head-wat′er** the highest part of a stream, before receiving affluents; **head′way** motion ahead, esp. of a ship: progress: the time interval or distance between buses, trains, etc. travelling on the same route in the same direction; **head wind** a directly opposing wind; **head′word** a word serving as a heading: a word under which others are grouped, as in a dictionary; **head′work** mental work; **head′work′er.** — **above, over, one's head** beyond one's comprehension; **bring, come to a head** to cause to reach a climax or crisis; **eat one's head off** see **eat**; **get, take, it into one's head** to conceive the, esp. wrong or foolish, notion (that); **give head** (*vulg.*) to perform oral sex; **give a horse his head** to let him go as he chooses (now also *fig.* **give someone his head**); **go by the head** (*naut.*) to sink head foremost; **go over someone's head** to take a problem, complaint, etc. directly to a person more senior than someone; **go to one's head** to disturb one's sobriety or good sense; **have a head on one's shoulders** to have ability and balance; **have one's head screwed on the right way** to behave sensibly; **head and shoulders** very much, as if taller by a head and shoulders: violently (*arch.*); **head first, foremost** with the head first; **head**

off to get ahead of so as to turn back: to deflect from path or intention; **heads or tails** an invitation to guess how a coin will fall; **head over heels, headlong** as in a somersault: completely; **hit the headlines** to get prominent notice in the press; **hold up one's head** see hold[1]; **keep, lose, one's head** to keep, lose, one's self-possession; **keep one's head above water** see water; **lay, put, heads together** to confer and co-operate; **off, out of, one's head** crazy; **off the top of one's head** see top[1]; **on one's (own) head be it** one must, or will, accept responsibility for any unpleasant or undesirable consequences of one's actions; **out of one's (own) head** spontaneously: of one's own invention; **over head and ears** deeply submerged or engrossed; **over one's head** see above one's head; **put heads together** see lay heads together; **show one's head** to allow oneself to be seen; **take it into one's head** see get it into one's head; **turn one's head** see turn. [O.E. *hēafod;* cf. Du. *hoofd,* Ger. *Haupt.*]
-head. See **-hood.**
heal[1] *hēl, v.t.* to make whole and healthy: to cure: to restore to soundness: to remedy, amend. — *v.i.* to grow sound. — *n.* (*arch.* and *Scot.*) health: soundness: welfare. — *adj.* **heal'able.** — *n.* **heal'er.** — *n.* and *adj.* **heal'ing.** — *adv.* **heal'ingly.** — *adj.* **heal'some** (*Scot.*) wholesome. — **heal'-all** allheal. [O.E. *hǣlan* (vb.), *hǣlu* (n.). — *hāl,* whole; cf. Ger. *heil,* Du. *heel;* O.N. *heill;* hail[1], hale[1], whole.]
heal[2]. See **hele.**
heald *hēld,* the same as **heddle.** — Also an old form of **heel**[2].
health *helth, n.* sound bodily or mental condition: soundness: condition of wholesomeness: well-being: state with respect to soundness: a toast. — *adj.* **health'ful** enjoying, indicating, or conducive to health. — *adv.* **health'fully.** — *n.* **heath'fulness.** — *adv.* **health'ily.** — *n.* **health'iness.** — *adj.* **health'less.** — *n.* **health'lessness.** — *adjs.* **health'some** healthy, wholesome; **health'y** in good health: morally or spiritually wholesome: conducive to or indicative of good health. — **health camp** (*N.Z.*) a camp intended to improve the physical and emotional condition of children who attend it; **health centre** centre for clinical and administrative health welfare work; **health farm** a place, usu. in the country, where one goes to improve one's health by dieting, exercise, etc.; **health food** food thought to be particularly good for one's health, esp. that grown, prepared, etc. without artificial fertilisers, chemical additives, etc.; **health resort** a place noted for its health-giving conditions, esp. climatic; **health stamp** (*N.Z.*) a stamp, part of the cost of which goes to supporting health camps; **health visitor** a nurse concerned mainly with health education and advice and preventive medicine rather than the treatment of disease, who visits esp. mothers with young children and the elderly in their own homes. [O.E. *hǣlth — hāl,* whole.]
heame *hēm,* (*Spens.*) *adv.* for **home.**
heap *hēp, n.* a mass of things resting one above another: a mound: a company (*Shak.*): a great number, a great deal (often in *pl.*), a collection: an old dilapidated motor car: a ruin (*B.*). — *v.t.* to throw in a heap: to amass: to load with a heap or heaps: to pile high, or above the rim or brim. — *adj.* **heap'ing** (*U.S.;* of a spoonful, etc.) heaped. — *adv.* **heaps** (*coll.*) very much. — *adj.* **heap'y** full of heaps. — **heap'stead** the buildings and works around a mine-shaft. — **knock, strike all of a heap** to confound utterly. [O.E. *hēap;* cf. O.N. *hōpr,* Ger. *Haufe,* Du. *hoop.*]
hear *hēr, v.t.* to perceive by the ear: to accede to: to listen to: to listen to in trial of ability to repeat: to try judicially: to be informed: to be a hearer of: to be called (*Milt.,* a Latinism). — *v.i.* to have or exercise the sense of hearing: to listen: to have news (of or from): to be spoken of (*Spens.,* a Graecism) — *pa.t.* and *pa.p.* **heard** (*hûrd*). — *adj.* **heard** (*hûrd*). — *ns.* **hear'er; hear'ing** power or act of perceiving sound: opportunity to be heard: audience: audition: judicial investigation and listening to evidence and arguments, esp. without a

jury: earshot: news: a scolding (*dial.*). — **hear'ing-aid** any device, electrical or other, for enabling the deaf to hear or to hear better; **hear'say** common talk: report: rumour. — *adj.* of the nature of, or based on, report given by others. — **hear, hear!** an exclamation of approval from the hearers of a speech; **hear out** to listen (to someone) until he has said all he wishes to say; **hear tell of** to hear someone speak of; **hear things** see **thing; will not hear of** will not allow, tolerate. [O.E. (Anglian) *hēran* (W.S. *hīeran, hȳran*); Du. *hooren,* O.N. *heyra,* Ger. *hören,* Goth. *hausjan.*]
heard, heare, *her,* **hearie,** (*Spens.*) forms of **herd, hair, hairy.**
hearken *härk'n, v.i.* to hear attentively: to listen. — *v.t.* to listen to, pay attention to, heed (*poet.*): to seek by enquiry (*obs.*). — *n.* **heark'ener.** [O.E. *hercnian* (*heorcnian*); cf. **hark, hear;** Ger. *horchen.*]
hearse, (*Spens.*) **herse,** *hûrs, n.* orig. a canopy or frame over a bier, designed to hold candles: a funeral service (*Spens.*): a bier (*obs.*): a car for carrying the dead. — *v.t.* to put on or in a hearse. — *adjs.* **hearse'-like, hears'y.** — **hearse'-cloth** a pall. [O.Fr. *herse* (It. *erpice*) — L. *hirpex, -icis,* a harrow.]
heart *härt, n.* the organ that circulates the blood: the stomach (*obs.*): the innermost part: the core: the chief or vital part: the breast, bosom: the (imagined) seat of the affections, understanding, and thought, as opposed to the head, the seat of reason: courage: inmost feelings or convictions: vigour: spirit: cordiality: compassion: a term of endearment or encouragement: a heart-shaped figure or object: a playing-card with heart-shaped pips: the centre of cabbage, lettuce, etc.: a diseased state of the heart. — *v.t.* to hearten (*arch.*): to fill up a centre space with rubble (*building*). — *v.i.* to form a compact head or inner mass, as a lettuce. — *adjs.* **hart'ie-hale** (*Spens.*) good for the heart, healthy; **heart'ed** having a heart, esp. of a specified kind (*hard-hearted,* etc.): seated or fixed in the heart, laid up in the heart. — *v.t.* **heart'en** to encourage, stimulate: to add strength to. — *v.i.* to take courage. — *n.* **heart'ikin** (*obs.*) a little heart (in an old minced oath). — *adv.* **heart'ily.** — *n.* **heart'iness.** — *adj.* **heart'less** without heart, courage, or feeling: callous. — *adv.* **heart'lessly.** — *ns.* **heart'lessness; heart'let** a little heart, a nucleus; **heart'ling** (*Shak.*) little heart, used in a minced oath (*ods heartlings,* God's heart). — *adv.* **heart'ly,** (*Spens.*) **harte'ly,** heartily. — *adjs.* **heart'some** exhilarating: merry; **heart'y** full of heart: heartfelt: sincere: cordial: robust: lusty: enthusiastic: unrestrained: in, or indicating, good spirits, appetite, or condition: sound: in good heart. — *n.* a hearty fellow, esp. a sailor: a student who goes in for sports, distinguished from an *aesthete.* — **heart'ache** sorrow: anguish; **heart attack** a sudden failure of the heart to function correctly, often causing death; **heart'-beat** a pulsation of the heart: a throb; **heart'-block** a condition in which the ventricle does not keep time with the auricle; **heart('s)'-blood** blood of the heart: life, essence; **heart'-bond** in masonry, a bond in which two headers meet in the middle of a wall and one header overlaps them; **heart'break** a crushing sorrow or grief. — *v.t.* (*Burns*) to break the heart of. — **heart'breaker** a flirt: a curl, lovelock. — *adjs.* **heart'breaking; heart'broken.** — **heart'burn** a burning, acrid feeling in throat or breast, cardialgia; **heart'burning** discontent: secret grudging; **heart cam** a heart-shaped cam in a stopwatch, etc.; **heart cockle, heart shell** a mollusc (*Isocardia*) or its shell, like a cockle coiled at the bosses. — *adj.* **heart'-dear** (*Shak.*) dear to the heart, sincerely beloved. — **heart disease** any morbid condition of the heart. — *adj.* **heart'-eas'ing** giving peace to the mind. — **heart'-failure** stoppage or inadequate functioning of the heart: shock producing faintness. — *adjs.* **heart'-felt** felt deeply: sincere; **heart'-free** having the affections disengaged. — **heart'-grief** deep-seated affliction; **heart'-heav'iness** depression of spirits; **heart'land** an area of a country that is centrally situated and/or

vitally important; **heart murmur** an abnormal sound from the heart indicating a structural or functional abnormality; **heartpea** see **heartseed**; **heart'-quake** trembling, fear. — adj. **heart'-rending** agonising. — **heart'-rot** decay in the hearts of trees, caused by various fungi; **heart'-searching** examination of one's feelings; **heart's'(-)ease** the pansy; **heart'seed** or **heart'-pea** balloon-vine, from the heart-shaped scar left by the seed; **heart'-ser'vice** sincere devotion, as opp. to eye-service. — adj. **heart'-shaped** shaped like the conventional representation of the human heart. — **heart shell** see **heart cockle**. — adj. **heart'-sick** despondent. — **heart'-sick'ness**. — adj. **heart'-sore** sore at heart: caused by soreness of heart (Shak.). — n. grief: a cause of grief (Spens.). — **heart'-spoon** (dial.) the depression in the breastbone: the breastbone: the pit of the stomach. — adj. **heart'-stirr'ing** rousing: exhilarating. — v.t. **heart'-strike** (arch.) to strike to the heart: to dismay: to drive into the heart: — pa.p. **heart'-stricken, heart'-struck** (obs. **-strook**). — **heart'-string** orig. a nerve or tendon imagined to brace and sustain the heart: (in pl.) affections; **heart'-throb** (slang) a sentimental emotion for one of the opposite sex: the person causing it. — adj. **heart'-to-heart** candid, intimate, and unreserved. — n. a conversation of this sort. — **heart'-ur'chin** a sea-urchin of the Spatangoidea, typically heart-shaped. — adj. **heart'warming** emotionally moving: gratifying, pleasing. — **heart'water** a fatal tick-borne viral disease of cattle, sheep and goats, with accumulation of fluid in the pericardium and pleural cavity. — adj. **heart'-whole** whole at heart: sincere: with affections disengaged: undismayed: out-and-out. — **heart'wood** the duramen or hard inner wood of a tree. — **after one's own heart** exactly to one's own liking; **at heart** in real character: substantially; **break one's heart** to die of, or be broken down by, grief or disappointment; **break someone's heart** to cause deep grief to someone; **by heart** by rote: in the memory; **cross one's heart** to emphasise the truth of a statement; **cry one's heart out** see **cry**; **dear, near, to one's heart** which one feels a warm interest in or concern for; **eat one's heart out** see **eat**; **find it in one's heart** to be able to bring oneself; **from the bottom of one's heart** most sincerely; **have a change of heart** to alter one's former opinion or viewpoint; **have a heart** (usu. in imper.) to show pity or kindness; **have at heart** to cherish as a matter of deep interest; **have one's heart in it** (often in neg.) to have enthusiasm for what one is doing; **have one's heart in one's boots** to feel a sinking of the heart; **have one's heart in one's mouth** to be in trepidation; **have one's heart in the right place** to be basically decent, generous; **have one's heart set on** to desire earnestly; **have the heart** (usu. in neg.) to have the courage or resolution (to do something unpleasant); **heart and hand, heart and soul** with complete heartiness: with complete devotion to a cause; **heart-lung machine** a machine used in chest surgery to take over for a time the functions of the heart and lungs; **heart of heart(s)** the inmost feelings or convictions: deepest affections; **heart of oak** heartwood of the oak-tree: a brave, resolute heart; **in good heart** in sound or fertile condition: in good spirits or courage; **lay, take, to heart** to store up in the mind for future guidance: to be deeply moved by something; **lose heart** to become discouraged; **lose one's heart to** to fall in love with; **set one's heart on, upon** to come to desire earnestly; **set someone's heart at rest** to render easy in mind; **speak to the heart** (B.) to comfort, encourage; **take heart** to be encouraged; **take heart of grace** see **grace**; **take to heart** to lay to heart: to come to feel in earnest; **take to one's heart** to form an affection for; **to one's heart's content** as much as one wishes; **wear one's heart on one's sleeve** to show the feelings openly; **with all one's heart** most willingly. [O.E. heorte; cf. Du. hart, Ger. Herz; L. cor, cordis; Gr. kardiā.]

hearth härth, n. the part of the floor on which the fire is made: the fireside: the house itself: the home circle: the lowest part of a blast-furnace: a brazier, chafing-dish, or fire-box. — **hearth'-brush** a brush for sweeping the hearth; **hearth'-mon'ey, -penn'y, -tax** a tax on hearths; **hearth'-rug** a rug laid over the hearth-stone or in front of the hearth or fireplace; **hearth'-stone** a stone forming a hearth: a soft stone used for whitening hearths, doorsteps, etc. [O.E. heorth; Du. haard, Ger. Herd.]

heast, heaste hēst (Spens.) n. Same as **hest**.

heat hēt, n. that which excites the sensation of warmth: sensation of warmth, esp. in a high degree: degree of hotness: exposure to intense heat: a high temperature: the hottest time: redness of the skin: vehemence, passion: sexual excitement in animals, or its period, esp. in the female, corresponding to rut in the male: a single course in a race: a division of a contest from which the winner goes on to a final test: animation: pressure intended to coerce (coll.): period of intensive search, esp. by the police for a criminal after a crime has taken place (coll.): trouble (orig. with the police; coll.). — v.t. to make hot: to agitate: perh., to run over, as in a race (Shak.). — v.i. to become hot. — adj. **heat'ed**. — n. **heat'er** one who, or that which, heats: apparatus for heating a room or building: means of heating a flatiron, etc.: a gun, pistol (esp. U.S.; slang). — n. and adj. **heat'ing**. — **heat'-ap'oplexy** sunstroke; **heat barrier** difficulties caused by a thin envelope of hot air which develops round aircraft at high speeds and occasions structural and other problems; **heat death** the final state of the universe (if it is a closed system) predicted by the Second Law of Thermodynamics, in which heat and energy are uniformly distributed throughout the substance of the universe; **heat engine** an engine that transforms heat into mechanical work; **heat'er-shield** a triangular shield, like the heater of a flatiron; **heat exchanger** device for transferring heat from one fluid to another; **heat pump** a device (on the refrigerator principle) for drawing heat from water, air, or the earth, and giving it out to warm, e.g. a room. — adj. **heat'-resistant**. — **heat shield** an object or substance designed to protect against excessive heat, esp. that which protects a spacecraft re-entering the earth's atmosphere; **heat sink** something into which unwanted heat can be shot; **heat'spot** an area of skin with nerve-ends sensitive to heat: a spot or blotch on the skin caused by heat: a freckle; **heat'stroke** exhaustion, illness, or prostration due to exposure to heat: sunstroke; **heat unit** amount of heat required to raise a pound of water 1 degree F in temperature (British thermal unit; mean value, the 180th part of heat required to raise temperature from 32°F to 212°F, being equal to 1055·06 joules); **heat wave** heated state of atmosphere passing from one locality to another: a hot spell. — **in heat, on heat** of a female animal, ready to mate; **latent heat** the heat required to change solid to liquid, or liquid to gas, without change of temperature; **mechanical equivalent of heat** the energy required to produce one heat unit; **specific heat** see **specify**; **take the heat out of** to lessen the vehemence, intensity of emotion, or acrimony of (a situation, etc.); **turn on the heat** (slang) to use brutal treatment, mental or physical, esp. in order to coerce. [O.E. hǣtu, heat; hāt, hot; Ger. Hitze.]

heath hēth, n. barren open country, esp. covered with ericaceous and other low shrubs: any shrub of genus Erica, sometimes extended to Calluna (heather) and others of the family Ericaceae: a butterfly of the Satyridae. — adj. **heath'y** abounding with heath. — **heath bell** heather bell: harebell; **heath'bird, heath'-fowl** the black grouse; **heath'cock** the male black grouse; **heath'-hen** the grey-hen or female black grouse: an extinct American bird akin to the prairie-chicken; **heath'-poult** the black grouse, esp. the female or young. [O.E. hǣth; Ger. Heide, Goth. haithi, a waste.]

heathen hē'dhn, n. one who belongs to a people of some lower form of religion, esp. polytheistic, or of no religion: any person neither Christian nor Jewish (*arch.*): a pagan: one who is ignorant or unmindful of religion: an uncivilised person (*coll.*): — *pl.* **hea′then** (collectively), **hea′thens** (individually). — *adj.* pagan: irreligious. — *ns.* **hea′thendom, hea′thenesse** (*arch.*) heathenism: the condition of a heathen: those regions of the world where heathenism prevails. — *v.t.* **hea′thenise, -ize** to make heathen or heathenish. — *adj.* **hea′thenish** relating to the heathen: rude: uncivilised: cruel. — *adv.* **hea′thenishly.** — *ns.* **hea′thenishness; hea′thenism** any religious system of the heathens: paganism: barbarism; **hea′thenry** heathenism: heathendom.   [O.E. *hǣthen;* Du. *heiden.*]

heather *hedh′ər, n.* ling, a common low shrub (*Calluna vulgaris*) of the heath family: sometimes extended to the heaths (Erica): an assemblage of heather plants. — *adj.* of the purple colour of (red) heather: composed of or from heather. — *adj.* **heath′ery.** – **heather ale** a famous liquor traditionally brewed in Scotland from the bells of heather — a lost art; **heather bell** the flower of the cross-leaved heath (*Erica tetralix*) or of the common heath (*Erica cinerea*); **heath′er-mix′ture** a woollen fabric speckled in colours like heather. — **set the heather on fire** to create a disturbance or a sensation; **take to the heather** to become an outlaw.   [Older Scots *hadder;* origin unknown; prob. influenced by **heath.**]

heather-bleat, heather-bleater *hedh′ər-blēt′, -ər,* (*Scot.*) *ns.* a snipe. — Also **heather-bluiter, -blutter** (*-blüt′, -blut′*). [O.E. *haefer-blǣte* — *hǣfer,* goat, *blǣtan,* to bleat, from its cry; influenced by **heather;** cf. also Scots *bluiter,* bittern.]

Heath(-)Robinson *hēth′rob′in-sən,* used adjectivally to describe an over-ingenious, ridiculously complicated or elaborate mechanical contrivance. — *adjs.* **Heath′= Robinsonesque′, Heath′-Robinsō′nian, Heath′-Rob′insonish.**   [*Heath Robinson* (1872–1944), an artist who drew such contraptions.]

heaume *hōm,* (*arch.*) *n.* a massive helmet.   [Fr.]

heave *hēv, v.t.* to lift up, esp. with great effort: to throw: to haul: to swell or puff out: to force from the breast (as a sigh): in mining, to displace (as a vein). — *v.i.* to be raised: to rise like waves: to retch: to strive or strain to lift or move something: to move into a certain position, orig. of a ship, now also *fig.:* — *pa.t.* and *pa.p.* **heaved,** (*naut.*) **hōve;** *pa.p.* in sense of swollen, **hōv′en.** — *n.* an effort upward: a throw: a swelling: an effort to vomit: a sigh (*Shak.*): horizontal displacement (*mining*): the lifting up of soil and rocks e.g. because of the freezing of water below the surface of the ground: in space flight, motion perpendicular to the surge (q.v.): (in *pl.*) broken wind in horses. — *ns.* **heav′er; heav′ing.** — **heave′-off′ering, heave′-shoul′der** (*B.*) an offering, an animal's shoulder, elevated in sacrifice. — **give, get the heave-ho** (*coll.*) to dismiss, reject, or snub, be dismissed, rejected, or snubbed; **heave ho!** an orig. sailors' call to exertion, as in heaving the anchor; **heave in sight** to come into view; **heave the lead** to take a sounding with a lead, to determine the depth of water (*naut.*); **heave the log** to cast the log into the water in order to ascertain the ship's speed; **heave to** to bring a vessel to a standstill, to make her lie to.   [O.E. *hebban,* pa.t. *hōf,* pa.p. *hafen;* Ger. *heben.*]

heaven *hev′n, hevn, n.* the vault of sky overhanging the earth (commonly in *pl.*): the upper regions of the air: a very great and indefinite height: any one of the concentric revolving spheres imagined by the old astronomers: (often *cap.*) the dwelling-place of God or the gods, and the blessed: (often *cap.*) the Deity as inhabiting heaven: supreme happiness. — *interj.* (in *pl.*) expressing surprise, disbelief, dismay, etc. — *n.* **heavenliness** (*hev′n-*). — *adj.* **heavenly** (*hev′n-*) of or inhabiting heaven: of or from God or the angels or saints: celestial: pure: supremely blessed: excellent (*coll.*). — *adv.* divinely, exceedingly (*arch.*): by the influence of heaven (*Milt.*). — *adj.* **heav′enward.** — *advs.* **heav′enward, heav′enwards.** — *adjs.* **heav′en-born**

descended from heaven; **heav′en-bred** (*Shak.*) bred or produced in heaven; **heav′en-direct′ed** pointing to the sky: divinely guided; **heaven-fallen** (*hevn-föln′;* Milt.) fallen from heaven; **heaven-gift′ed** bestowed by heaven; **heav′en-kiss′ing** (*Shak.*) as it were, touching the sky. — **heavenly bodies** the sun, moon, planets, comets, stars, etc.; **heavenly host** a multitude of angels. — *adj.* **heav′enly-mind′ed** with mind set upon heavenly things: pure. — **heav′enly-mind′edness.** — *adj.* **heav′en-sent** sent by heaven: very timely. — **good heavens, heavens above** expressing surprise, disbelief, dismay, etc.; **heaven forbid,** (*arch.*) **forfend** may it not happen (that); **heaven knows** God knows (q.v.); **heaven of heavens** (*B.*) the highest heavens, abode of God; **in the seventh heaven** in a state of the most exalted happiness — from the Cabbalists, who divided the heavens into seven in an ascending scale of happiness up to the abode of God; **move heaven and earth** to do everything possible; **the heavens opened** there was a very heavy shower of rain; **tree of heaven** ailanto.   [O.E. *heofon.*]

Heaviside layer. See **Kennelly-Heaviside layer.**

heavy *hev′i, adj.* weighty: ponderous: laden: abounding: of high specific gravity: not easy to bear: grievous: oppressive: grave: dull, lacking brightness and interest: wanting in sprightliness: pedantic: pompous: laborious: sad: in low spirits: drowsy: with great momentum: deep-toned: massive: thick: not easily digested: doughy: impeding the feet in walking: (of the ground) very wet and soft (*horse-racing,* etc.): heavy-armed (*mil.*): strong, as liquor: dark with clouds: gloomy: pertaining to grave or serious roles (*theat.*): of newspapers, serious, highbrow: tense, emotional, strained (*slang*): serious, important (*slang*): (of a market) with falling prices (*commerce*): — *compar.* **heav′ier;** *superl.* **heav′iest.** — *adv.* heavily. — *n.* the villain on stage or screen: a large, strong man employed for purposes of a violent and often criminal nature (*slang*): in Scotland, a type of beer similar to, but not as strong as, export: anything particularly large or heavy. — *adv.* **heav′ily.** — *n.* **heav′iness.** — *adjs.* **heav′ier-than-air′** of greater specific gravity than air, not sustained by a gasbag; **heav′y-armed** bearing heavy armour or arms. — **heavy breather; heavy breathing** loud and laboured breathing due to exertion, excitement, etc., or esp. sexual arousal, sometimes associated with anonymous obscene telephone calls; **heavy chemicals** those produced on a large scale for use in industry (e.g. sulphuric acid and sodium carbonate) (*opp.* to *fine chemicals*). — *adjs.* **heav′y-duty** made to withstand very hard wear or use; **heav′y-hand′ed** clumsy, awkward: oppressive; **heav′y= head′ed** having a heavy or large head: dull: stupid: drowsy; **heav′y-heart′ed** weighted down with grief. — **heavy hydrogen** deuterium: also tritium; **heavy industry** see **industry.** — *adj.* **heav′y-lad′en** with a heavy burden. — **heavy metal** a metal of high specific gravity, usu. above 5: guns or shot of large size: great influence or power: a person to be reckoned with: a particularly loud, simple and repetitive form of hard rock (*mus.*); **heavy particle** a baryon; **heavy rock** hard rock (*mus.*); **heavy spar** barytes; **heavy water** water in which deuterium takes the place of ordinary hydrogen, or a mixture of this and ordinary water; **heav′yweight** a person or thing well above the average weight: someone important or very influential (*coll.*): one in the heaviest class (*sport*): in boxing **light-heavyweight** over 11 st. 6 lb. and not over 12 st. 7 lb., amateur 11 st. 11 lb. and 12 st. 10 lb. **heavyweight** any weight above these; **heavy wet** (*slang*) a drink of strong ale or ale and porter mixed. — **be heavily into** (*coll.*) to be keen on or an enthusiastic practitioner of; **be heavy going** see **going¹; heavy marching order** the condition of troops fully equipped for field service; **the heavies** the heavy cavalry (*mil.*): those who play heavy parts (*theat.*): the more serious, highbrow, newspapers, journals, etc. (*coll.*): (shares in) the heavy industries.   [O.E. *hefig* — *hebban,* to heave; O.H.G. *hebîg.*]

hebdomad *heb′dō-mad, n.* a set of seven: a week: in some

Gnostic systems, a group of superhuman beings. — *adj.* **hebdomadal** (*-dom'ə-dl*) weekly. — *adv.* **hebdom'adally.** — *n.* **hebdom'adar, -er** in Scottish Universities, a senior member appointed weekly for the supervision of student discipline. — *adj.* **hebdom'adary** weekly. — *n.* a member of a chapter or convent taking weekly turn to officiate. — **hebdomadal council** an administrative board of Oxford University, meeting weekly. [Gr. *hebdomas, -ados,* a set of seven, a week — *hepta,* seven.]

Hebe *hē'bē, n.* a daughter of Zeus and Hera, cup-bearer of Olympus, a personification of youth: a genus of shrubby plants of the family Scrophulariaceae, in some classifications included in the genus *Veronica:* (without *cap.*) a member of the genus. — *n.* **hebephrenia** (*hē-bi-frē'ni-ə*) a form of insanity beginning in late childhood, arresting intellectual development, and ending in complete dementia. — *adjs.* and *ns.* **hebephrē'niac, hebephrenic** (*-fren'ik*). [Gr. *hēbē,* youth, puberty (*Hēbē,* the goddess), *phrēn,* mind.]

heben *heb'n, n., adj.* Obs. form of **ebony.**

hebenon *heb'ə-non,* **hebona** *-nə,* (*Shak.*) *ns.* something with a poisonous juice. [Perh. **ebony** or **henbane,** or Ger. *Eibenbaum,* yew-tree.]

hebetate *heb'i-tāt, v.t.* to dull or blunt. — *v.i.* to become dull. — *adj.* dull: blunt: soft-pointed. — *adj.* **heb'etant** making dull. — *ns.* **hebetā'tion, heb'etude; hebetūdinos'ity.** — *adj.* **hebetū'dinous.** [L. *hebetāre, -ātum — hebes, -etis,* blunt.]

hebona. See **hebenon.**

Hebrew *hē'brōō, n.* a Jew: — *fem.* **Hē'brewess** (*B.*): the Semitic language of the Hebrews: unintelligible speech (*coll.*). — *adj.* of the Hebrews or their language. — *adjs.* **Hebraic** (*hē-brā'ik*), **-al** relating to the Hebrews or to their language. — *adv.* **Hebrā'ically** after the manner of the Hebrew language: from right to left. — *n.* **Hebrā'icism.** — *v.t.* **Hē'brāise, -īze** to make Hebrew. — *v.i.* to use a Hebrew idiom: to conform or incline to Hebrew ways or ideals. — *ns.* **Hē'brāiser, -z-; Hē'brāism** a Hebrew idiom; **Hē'brāist** one skilled in Hebrew. — *adjs.* **Hebrāist'ic, -al** of or like Hebrew. — *adv.* **Hebrāist'ically.** — *n.* **Hē'brewism.** — **Hebrew year** see **year.** [O.Fr. *Ebreu* and L. *Hēbraeus* — Gr. *Hēbraios* — Aramaic *'ebrai* (Heb. *'ibrī*), lit. one from the other side (of the Euphrates).]

Hebridean *heb-ri-dē'ən,* **Hebridian** *-rid'i-ən, adjs.* of the Hebrides (*heb'ri-dēz*). — *n.* a native of the Hebrides. — *adj.* **He'brid** (*rare*). [Due to a misprint of L. *Hebūdēs* — Gr. *Heboudai.*]

Hecate *hek'ə-tē, Shak.* **Hecat(e)** *hek'ət, ns.* a mysterious goddess, in Hesiod having power over earth, heaven, and sea — afterwards identified with Artemis, Persephone, and other goddesses: in Shakespeare, etc., the chief or goddess of witches. [Gr. *Hekatē.*]

hecatomb *hek'ə-tom, -tōm* (sometimes *-tōōm*), *n.* a great public sacrifice: any large number of victims. [Gr. *hekatombē — hekaton,* a hundred, *bous,* an ox.]

hech *hehh,* (*Scot.*) *interj.* an exclamation of surprise, weariness, etc.

hecht *hehht.* Scottish form of the verb **hight.**

heck[1] *hek,* **haik, hake** *hāk,* (*dial.*) *ns.* the lower part of a door: an inner door: a grating, esp. in rivers or streams: a rack for animal fodder: a rack or frame for drying cheese, etc.: a piece of spinning machinery, for guiding the yarn to the reels. — **heck and manger** rack and manger. [O.E. *hec* (*hæc*), grating, hatch; cf. **hack**[3], **hatch**[1]; Du. *hek,* gate.]

heck[2] *hek, n.* and *interj.* euphemistic for **hell.**

heckelphone *hek'l-fōn, n.* an instrument of the oboe family, invented by W. *Heckel* (1856–1909), between the cor anglais and the bassoon in pitch.

heckle *hek'l, v.i.* to comb out, of flax or hemp fibres: (orig. *Scot.*) to ply with embarrassing questions, or shout or jeer abusively or disruptively at (as at an election hustings or public lecture). — *n.* a hackle. — *ns.* **heck'ler; heck'ling.** [Cf. **hackle, hatchel.**]

hecogenin *hek'ō-jen-in, jen'-, hek-oj'ən-in, n.* a chemical obtained from various plants, e.g. *Hechtia texensis,* and esp. from sisal waste, used in the manufacture of cortisone, etc. [*Hec*(htia texensis), and suffs. *-gen* and *-in.*]

hectare. See under **hecto-.**

hectic *hek'tik, adj.* pertaining to the constitution or habit of body: affected with hectic fever: feverish, agitated, rushed (*coll.*): flushed (*Shelley*). — *n.* a hectic fever: a consumptive: a flush. — *adj.* **hec'tical.** — *adv.* **hec'tically.** — **hectic fever** fever occurring in connection with certain wasting diseases of long duration. [Gr. *hektikos,* habitual — *hexis,* habit.]

hecto- *hek'tō,* **hect-** in composition (esp. in the metric system) 100 times. — *ns.* **hectare** (*hek'tär, -tār*) 100 ares or 10,000 sq. metres; **hec'togram(me)** 100 grammes; **hec'tograph** a gelatine pad for printing copies. — *v.t.* to reproduce in this way. — *adj.* **hectograph'ic.** — *ns.* **hec'tolitre** 100 litres; **hec'tometre** 100 metres; **hec'tostere** 100 cubic metres or steres. [Fr. contraction of Gr. *hekaton,* a hundred.]

hector *hek'tər, n.* a bully, a blusterer. — *v.t.* to treat insolently: to annoy. — *v.i.* to play the bully: to bluster. — *ns.* **hec'torer; hec'toring** (also *adj.*); **hec'torism.** — *adj.* **hec'torly.** — *n.* **hec'torship.** [Gr. *Hektōr,* the Trojan hero.]

he'd *hēd,* a contraction of **he had** or **he would.**

heddle *hed'l, n.* a series of vertical cords or wires, each having in the middle a loop (**hedd'le-eye**) to receive a warp-thread, and passing round and between parallel bars. — *v.t.* to draw through heddle-eyes. — Also **heald.** [An assumed O.E. *hefedl,* earlier form of *hefeld.*]

Hedera *hed'ər-ə, n.* the ivy genus of the Aralia family. — *adjs.* **hed'eral; hed'erated** ivy-crowned. [L.]

hedge *hej, n.* a close row of bushes or small trees serving as a fence: a barrier, protection (*fig.*): an act of hedging: something bought as, or which acts as, a protection against financial loss. — *v.t.* to enclose with a hedge: to obstruct: to surround: to guard: to protect oneself from loss on, by compensatory transactions, e.g. bets on the other side. — *v.i.* to make hedges: to shuffle, be evasive, as in argument: to be shifty: to buy or sell something as a financial hedge. — *adj.* living in or frequenting hedges: wayside: used by, or only fit for, vagrants: low: debased. — *ns.* **hedg'er** one who hedges or dresses hedges; **hedg'ing** the work of a hedger: the action of the verb hedge. — *adj.* **hedg'y.** — **hedge'-accen'tor** the hedge-sparrow; **hedge'bill, hedg'ing-bill** a bill for dressing hedges. — *adj.* **hedge'-born** born under a hedge, low-born. — **hedge'-bote** a tenant's right to cut wood for repairing hedges or fences; **hedge'-creep'er** a sneaking rogue; **hedge'hog** a small prickly-backed insectivorous animal that lives in hedges and bushes, and has a snout like a hog: a prickly fruit, or prickly-fruited plant: one whose manners keep others at a distance: an offensive person: a small, strongly fortified, defensive position. — *v.i.* **hedge'-hop** (*airmen's slang*) to fly low as if hopping over hedges. — **hedge'-hyss'op** a plant (*Gratiola*) of the figwort family; **hedge'-mar'riage** a clandestine marriage; **hedge'-mus'tard** a tall stiff cruciferous roadside weed (*Sisymbrium officinale*) with small yellow flowers, or kindred species; **hedge'-pars'ley** an umbelliferous roadside weed (*Torilis* or *Caucalis*) with leaves somewhat like parsley; **hedge'-par'son, hedge'-priest** a disreputable, vagrant, or illiterate parson or priest; **hedge'pig** a hedgehog; **hedge'row** a line of hedge, often with trees; **hedge'-school** an open-air school, common in Ireland in 17th and 18th centuries during the ban on Catholic education: a mean school; **hedge'-schoolmaster; hedge'-sparrow,** formerly also **hedge'-warbler,** the dunnock (*Prunella modularis*), a small bird that frequents hedges, superficially like a sparrow but with a more slender bill; **hedge'-wri'ter** a Grub Street author. [O.E. *hecg;* Du. *hegge,* Ger. *Hecke.*]

hedonism *hē'dən-izm, n.* in ethics, the doctrine that pleasure is the highest good: the pursuit of pleasure: a life style devoted to pleasure-seeking. — *adjs.* **hĕdonic** (-*don'*), **hĕdonist'ic.** — *n. sing.* **hĕdon'ics** that part of ethics or of psychology that treats of pleasure. — *n.* **hē'donist.** [Gr. *hēdonē*, pleasure.]

hedyphane *hed'i-fān, n.* a white variety of green lead ore, arsenate, phosphate, and chloride of lead and calcium with barium. [Gr. *hēdys*, sweet, pleasant, and the root of *phainein*, to show.]

heebie (or **heeby**) **-jeebies** *hē'bi-jē'biz, n.pl.* (with *the*; *slang*) a fit of nerves: irritation or depression: the creeps. [A coinage.]

heed *hēd, v.t.* to observe: to look after: to attend to. — *v.i.* to mind, care. — *n.* notice: caution: attention. — *adj.* **heed'ful** attentive: cautious. — *adv.* **heed'fully.** — *ns.* **heed'fulness; heed'iness.** — *adj.* **heed'less.** — *adv.* **heed'lessly.** — *n.* **heed'lessness.** — *adj.* **heed'y** (*Spens.*) heedful, careful. [O.E. *hēdan*; Du. *hoeden*, Ger. *hüten.*]

heehaw *hē'hö, v.i.* to bray. — *n.* a bray. [Imit.]

heel¹ *hēl, n.* the hind part of the foot below the ankle: the whole foot (esp. of beasts): the covering or support of the heel: a spur: the hinder part of anything, as a violin bow: a heel-like bend, as on a golf-club: a knob: the top, bottom, or end of a loaf or a cheese: a cad (*slang*). — *v.t.* to execute or perform with the heel: to strike with the heel: to furnish with a heel: to arm with a spur, as a fighting cock: to seize by the heels: to tie by the heels: to follow at the heels of: to supply with a weapon, money, etc. — *v.i.* to follow well (of a dog): to move one's heels to a dance rhythm: to kick the ball backwards out of the scrum with the heel (*Rugby football*). — *adj.* **heeled** provided with a heel, shod: (often in composition, as **well-heeled**) comfortably supplied with money, etc. — *ns.* **heel'er** one who heels, in any sense: one who follows at heel, as an unscrupulously faithful follower of a party boss: a dog which herds livestock by following and barking at their heels (*Austr.*); **heel'ing** a heel-piece (*Spens.*): the act of making or attaching a heel. — **heel'-ball** a black waxy composition for blacking the edges of heels and soles of shoes and boots, and for taking rubbings; **heel'-piece** a piece or cover for the heel; **heel'-tap** a layer of material in a shoe-heel: a small quantity of liquor left in the glass after drinking. — **Achilles' heel** see under **Achillean; at, on, upon the heels of** following close behind; **back on one's heels** driven back by an opponent: on the defensive; **bring to heel** to cause to come to heel; **come to heel** to come in behind: to obey or follow like a dog: to submit to authority; **cool** or **kick one's heels** to be kept waiting for some time; **dig in one's heels** to behave stubbornly; **down at heel** having the heels of one's shoes trodden down: slovenly: in poor circumstances; **heel and toe** with strict walking pace, as opposed to running; **heel in** see **hele; heel of Achilles** see under **Achillean; heels o'er gowdy** (*Scot.*), **heels over head** (*arch.*) upside down; **kick up one's heels** to frisk; **lay, set, clap, by the heels** to fetter: to put in confinement; **out at heel** having one's heels showing through holes in the socks or stockings: shabby; **set (one) back on one's heels** to surprise, astonish one; **show a clean pair of heels** to run off; **take to one's heels** to flee; **tread on someone's heels** to come crowding behind; **trip up someone's heels** to trip up or overthrow; **turn on, upon, one's heel** to turn sharply round, to turn back or away; **two for his heels** in cribbage, a score for turning up the knave; **under the heel** crushed, tyrannised over; **walk to heel** (of a dog) to walk at one's heels, under control. [O.E. *hēla*; Du. *hiel.*]

heel² *hēl, v.i.* to incline: to lean on one side, as a ship. — *v.t.* to tilt. [Earlier *heeld, hield*; O.E. *hieldan*, to slope; cf. Du. *hellen.*]

heel³. Same as **hele.**

heeze *hēz,* (*Scot.*) *v.t.* a form of **hoise.** — *n.* a lift: a heave upward. — *n.* **heez'ie** a lift.

heft¹ *heft, n.* heaving (*obs.*): retching (*Shak.*): weight (*U.S.*): the greater part (*arch.*). — *v.t.* to lift: to try the weight of. — *adj.* **heft'y** rather heavy: muscular: size-

able: vigorous: violent: abundant. — *adv.* very. [**heave.**]

heft², hefte (*Spens.*), obsolete forms of **heaved.**

heft³ *heft* (*Scot.*) *v.t.* to restrain: to retain (milk or urine). [Cf. O.N. *hefta*, to bind.]

heft⁴ *heft, n.* a number of sheets fastened together: an instalment of a serial publication. [Ger.]

heft⁵ *heft.* A Scots form of **haft.**

Hegelian *hā-gēl'i-ən, adj.* of or pertaining to Wilhelm Friedrich *Hegel* (1770–1831) or his philosophy. — *n.* a follower of Hegel. — *n.* **Hegel'ianism.**

hegemony *hi-gem'ən-i,* or *hē-,* or *-jem',* *hej'i-,* or *-g-,* or *hē-, n.* leadership: preponderant influence, esp. of one state over others. — *adjs.* **hegemō'nial, hegemōn'ic, -al.** — *ns.* **hegem'onism; hegem'onist.** [Gr. *hēgemoniā* — *hēgemōn,* leader — *hēgeesthai,* to lead.]

hegira, hejira, hejra, hijra(h) *hej', hij'(i)-rə, hi-jī'rə, ns.* the flight of Mohammed from Mecca, A.D. 622, from which is dated the Muslim era: any flight. [Ar. *hijrah,* flight, *hajara,* to leave.]

he-he *hē-hē, interj.* representing a high-pitched or gleeful laugh. — *n.* such a laugh. — *v.i.* to laugh so. [Imit.]

heid *hēd,* (*Scot.*) *n.* a head. [See **head.**]

heifer *hef'ər, n.* a young cow. [O.E. *hēahfore, hēahfru, -fre;* lit. prob. high-goer — *faran* to go.]

heigh *hā* (or *hī*), *interj.* a cry of enquiry, encouragement, or exultation — also **hey, ha.** — *interj.* **heigh'-ho** an exclamation expressive of weariness. — *n.* (*Scot.* also **heich-how** *hēhh'-how'*) routine: familiar jog-trot. [Imit.]

height *hīt, n.* the condition of being high: degree of highness: distance upwards: angle of elevation: that which is elevated: a hill: a high place: elevation in rank or excellence: utmost degree. — *v.t.* and *v.i.* **height'en** to make or become higher: to make or become brighter or more conspicuous, or (*fig.*) stronger or more intense: to elate (*obs.*). — **height of land** a watershed, esp. if not a range of hills; **height to paper** the standard height of type, blocks, etc., from foot to face (approx. 0·918 in.). [From **highth** — O.E. *hīehtho, hēahthu* — *hēah,* high.]

heil! *hīl,* (Ger.) *interj.* hail!

Heimweh *hīm'vā,* (Ger.) *n.* home-sickness.

heinous *hā'nəs,* sometimes *hē'nəs, adj.* wicked in a high degree, odious, atrocious. — *adv.* **hei'nously.** — *n.* **hei'nousness.** [O.Fr. *haïnos* (Fr. *haineux*) — *haïr,* to hate.]

heir *ār, n.* in law, one who actually succeeds to property, title, etc., on the death of its previous holder: popularly, one entitled to succeed when the present possessor dies: a child, esp. a first-born son: a successor to a position, e.g. of leadership: inheritor of qualities, or of social conditions, or the past generally. — *v.t.* (*dial.*) to inherit. — *ns.* **heir'dom, heir'ship; heir'ess** a female heir: a woman who has succeeded or is likely to succeed to a considerable fortune. — *adj.* **heir'less** without an heir. — **heir'-appa'rent** the one by law acknowledged to be heir, no matter who may subsequently be born: a person expected to succeed the leader of a party, etc. (*fig.*); **heir'-at-law'** an heir by legal right; **heir'-by= cus'tom** one whose right as heir is determined by customary modes of descent, as gavelkind, etc.; **heir'-loom** any piece of furniture or personal property which descends to the heir-at-law by special custom: any object which is passed down through a family from generation to generation; **heir'-por'tioner** (*Scots law*) a joint-heiress or her representative; **heir'-presump'tive** one who will be heir if no nearer relative should be born (also *fig.*). — **fall heir to** to inherit (also *fig.*). [O.Fr. *heir* — L. *hērēs* (vulgar accus. *hērem*), an heir.]

heist *hīst,* (*slang*) *v.t.* to steal or rob in a heist. — *n.* a robbing or theft, esp. an armed hold-up, or a particularly clever or spectacular theft: one who robs or steals. — *n.* **heist'er.** [Variant of **hoist.**]

hejab *hi-jab', he-jäb', n.* a covering for a Muslim woman's head and face, sometimes reaching the ground. [Ar. and Pers.]

hejira, hejra. See **hegira.**

Hel *hel, n.* in Northern mythology, the goddess of the dead, sister of the wolf Fenrir, and daughter of Loki.

helcoid *hel'koid, adj.* ulcerous. [Gr. *helkos*, an ulcer.]

held *pa.t.* and *pa.p.* of **hold**[1].

Heldentenor *held'ən-ten'ər, held'ən-te-nōr', n.* (a man with) a powerful tenor voice, particularly suitable for heroic roles in, esp. Wagnerian, operas: — *pl.* **-ten'ors, -tenöre** (*-te-nø'rə*). [Ger., hero tenor — *Held*, hero.]

hele, heel, heal *hēl, v.t.* (*Spens.*; now *dial.*) to hide, conceal: to cover. — **hele in** (*dial.*) to cover the roots of temporarily with earth. [O.E. *helian* from *hellan* (weak vb.) blended with *helan* (strong), both meaning to hide; Ger. *hehlen*; L. *celāre*; Gr. *kalyptein*.]

heli- *hel-i-*, in composition, helicopter (as in *ns.* **hel'ibus; hel'idrome; hel'iman; hel'ipilot; hel'iport,** etc.). — *ns.* **hel'icopter** (Gr. *pteron*, wing) a flying-machine sustained by a power-driven screw or screws revolving on a vertical axis. — *v.t.* to take or carry by helicopter. — *ns.* **hel'ipad** a landing-place for a helicopter; **hel'iscoop** a net let down from a helicopter to rescue persons in difficulty; **hel'istop** a landing-place for a helicopter. [Gr. *helix, -ikos*, screw.]

heliac *hē'li-ak*, **heliacal** *hē-lī'ək-əl, adjs.* solar: coincident with that of the sun, or as nearly as could be observed. — *adv.* **helī'acally.** — **heliacal rising** the emergence of a star from the light of the sun; **heliacal setting** its disappearance in it. [Gr. *hēliakos* — *hēlios*, the sun.]

Helianthemum *hē-li-anth'ə-məm, n.* the rock-rose genus. [Gr. *hēlios*, sun, *anthemon*, flower.]

Helianthus *hē-li-an'thəs, n.* the sunflower genus. [Gr. *hēlios*, sun, *anthos*, flower.]

helical, etc. See **helix.**

Helichrysum *he-li-krī'zəm, n.* a genus of composite plants, the flowers of which keep their colour and shape when dried: (without *cap.*) a plant of this genus. [Gr. *hēlix*, spiral, *chrysos*, gold.]

Heliconian *hel-i-kō'ni-ən, adj.* pertaining to *Helicon* (Gr. *Helikōn*), a mountain-range in Boeotia, favourite seat of the Muses, by some modern poets made a fountain.

helicopter. See **heli-.**

helictite *hel'ik-tīt, n.* a twisted, branching stalactite. [Gr. *heliktos*, twisted, and **stalactite**.]

helio- *hē'li-ō-, hē-li-o'-*, in composition, sun. — *adj.* **heliocentric** (*-sen'trik*; Gr. *kentron*, centre; *astron.*) referred to the sun as centre. — *adv.* **heliocen'trically.** — *n.* **he'liochrome** (*-krōm*; Gr. *chrōma*, colour) a photograph in natural colours. — *adj.* **heliochrō'mic.** — *ns.* **he'liochrōmy; he'liograph** (Gr. *graphē*, a drawing) an apparatus for signalling by flashing the sun's rays: an engraving obtained photographically: an apparatus for photographing the sun: an instrument for measuring intensity of sunlight. — *v.t.* and *v.i.* to communicate by heliograph. — *n.* **heliog'rapher.** — *adjs.* **heliograph'ic, -al.** — *adv.* **heliograph'ically.** — *ns.* **heliog'raphy; heliogravure** (*-grəv-ūr', -grāv'yər*; Fr. *héliogravure*) photo-engraving; **heliol'ater** a sun-worshipper. — *adj.* **heliol'atrous.** — *ns.* **heliol'atry** (Gr. *latreiā*, worship) sun-worship; **heliol'ogy** the science of the sun; **heliom'eter** an instrument for measuring angular distances, as the sun's diameter. — *adjs.* **heliomet'ric, -al; helioph'ilous** (Gr. *phileein*, to love) fond of the sun; **heliopho'bic** (Gr. *phobos*, fear) fearing or shunning sunlight. — *ns.* **he'liophyte** (Gr. *phyton*, a plant) a plant that can live in full exposure to sunlight; **heliosciophyte** (*hē-li-ō-sī'ō-fīt*; Gr. *skiā*, shadow) a plant that can live in shade but does better in the sun; **he'lioscope** (*-skōp*; Gr. *skopeein*, to look at) an apparatus for observing the sun without injury to the eye. — *adj.* **helioscopic** (*-skop'ik*). — *ns.* **heliō'sis** (Gr. *hēliōsis*) (over-)exposure to the sun: spotting of leaves by raindrops or greenhouse glass flaws, etc., acting as burning-glasses; **he'liostat** (Gr. *statos*, fixed) an instrument on the principle of the coelostat by means of which a beam of sunlight is reflected in an invariable direction, for study of the sun or for signalling; **heliotax'is** (Gr. *taxis*, arrangement) response of an organism to the stimulus of the sun's rays; **heliother'apy** (Gr. *therapeiā*, healing) medical treatment by exposure to the sun's rays; **heliotrope** (*hē'li-ō-trōp, hel'i-ō-trōp*; Gr. *hēliotropion*) any plant of the genus Heliotropium of the borage family, many species with fragrant flowers, esp. the *Peruvian heliotrope*, with small fragrant lilac-blue flowers: the colour of its flowers: a kind of perfume imitating that of the flower: a bloodstone (*min.*): a surveyor's heliograph. — *adjs.* **heliotropic** (*-trop'ik*), **-al.** — *adv.* **heliotrop'ically.** — *ns.* **heliot'ropin** piperonal; **heliotropism** (*-ot'rə-pizm*), **heliōt'ropy** the tendency of stem and leaves to bend towards (*positive heliotropism*), and roots from (*negative heliotropism*), the light; **he'liotype** (Gr. *typos*, impression) a photograph by heliotypy. — *adj.* **heliotypic** (*-tip'ik*). — *n.* **he'liotypy** (*-tī-pi*) a photo-mechanical process in which the gelatine relief is itself used to print from. — *n.pl.* **Heliozō'a** (Gr. *zōion*, an animal) sun-animalcules, an order of Protozoa, spherical with radiating processes of living matter. — *adj.* and *n.* **heliozō'an.** — *adj.* **heliozō'ic.** [Gr. *hēlios*, the sun.]

heliodor *hēl'i-ə-dōr, -dör, n.* a variety of clear yellow beryl occurring in S.W. Africa. [Ger.]

heliograph, etc. See **helio-.**

helispheric, -al. See **helix.**

helium *hē'li-əm, n.* an element (He; at. numb. 2), a very light inert gas, discovered (1868) by Lockyer in the sun's atmosphere, isolated (1895) by Ramsay from cleveite, and found in certain natural gases. — **helium speech** distorted speech of persons in a helium atmosphere. — **liquid helium** helium in liquid form (below 4·22K), which has remarkable qualities, undergoing a striking change at 2·19K (see **superfluidity**). [Gr. *hēlios*, sun.]

helix *hē'liks, n.* a screw-shaped coil: in math., a curve on a developable surface (esp. a right circular cylinder) which becomes a straight line when the surface is unrolled into a plane — distinguished from a *spiral*, which is a plane curve: the rim of the ear (*anat.*): a small volute or twist in the capital of a Corinthian column (*archit.*): a screw-propeller: (*cap.; zool.*) a genus of molluscs including the best-known land-snails: — *pl.* **hē'lixes** or **helices** (*hel'i-sēz*). — *adj.* **helical** (*hel'ik-əl*). — *adv.* **hel'ically.** — *n.pl.* **Helicidae** (*-is'i-dē*) a large family of terrestrial, air-breathing gasteropods, including the common snails. — *n.* **hel'icograph** a drawing instrument for describing spirals on a plane. — *adjs.* **hel'icoid, -al** like a helix, screw-shaped; **helispher'ic, -al** loxodromic. — **helicoid cyme** a bostryx. [Gr. *hēlix*, a spiral — *helissein*, to turn round.]

Hell *hel, n.* the place of the dead in general: the place or state of punishment of the wicked after death: the abode of evil spirits: the powers of Hell: (the following meanings without *cap.*) any place of vice or misery: a place of turmoil: (a state of) supreme misery or discomfort: anything causing misery, pain or destruction: ruin, havoc: commotion, uproar: severe censure or chastisement: used in various coll. phrases expressing displeasure, emphasis, etc. (as *what in hell?, get the hell out of here, I wish to hell he'd go away*): a gambling-house: a space under a tailor's board, or other receptacle for waste: the den in certain games. — *interj.* expressing displeasure or emphasis. — *v.i.* to live or act in a wild or dissolute fashion (usu. with *around*). — *ns.* **hell'er** an obstreperous troublesome person; **hellion** (*hel'yən*) a troublesome, mischievous child: one given to diabolical conduct. — *adj.* **hell'ish** pertaining to or like hell: very bad, severe, etc.: often used to express displeasure (*coll.*). — *adv.* **hell'ish(ly)** in the manner of hell: often used intensively (*coll.*). — *n.* **hell'ishness.** — *adj.* (*coll.*) **hell'uva, hell'ova** (**hell of a**) great, terrific. — *adv.* very. — *adj.* and *adv.* **hell'ward** towards hell. — *adv.* **hell'wards.** — **hell'bender** a large American salamander: a reckless or debauched person. — *adj.* **hell'-bent** (with *on*) recklessly determined. — *adv.* with reckless determination. — *adjs.* **hell'-black** (*Shak.*) black as hell; **hell'-born** born in hell: of hellish origin; **hell'-bred.** — **hell'-box** a receptacle for broken type; **hell'-broth** (*Shak.*) a composition boiled up for malignant purposes; **hell'-cat** a malignant hag; **hell'-fire** the fire of hell: punishment in hell; **hell'-gate** the entrance into hell. — *adj.* **hell'-hat'ed** (*Shak.*) hated or abhorred as hell. — **hell'-hole** the pit of hell; **hell'hound** a hound of hell: an agent of hell; **hell'-kite** (*Shak.*) a kite of infernal breed; **hell's angel** (often *cap.*) a member of any gang of young motor-cyclists who indulge in violent or antisocial behaviour. — *interjs.* **hell's bells, teeth,** etc. expressions of irritation, surprise, etc. — **all hell breaks, is let loose** there is chaos or uproar; **as hell** absolutely: very; **beat, kick, knock,** etc. **(the) hell out of** to beat, etc. severely; **come hell or high water** no matter what difficulties may be encountered; **for the hell of it** for fun or adventure; **give someone hell** to punish, castigate, rebuke someone severely: to cause someone pain or misery; **hell for leather** at a furious pace; **hell to pay** serious trouble, unpleasant consequences; **like hell** very much, very hard, very fast, etc.: (also **the hell, hell**) used to express strong disagreement or refusal, as in *like hell I will!*; *the hell I will!*; *will I hell!*); **not have a cat in hell's chance** see **cat**¹; **not have a hope in hell** to have no hope at all; **play hell with** see **play; to raise hell** see **raise**¹; **to hell with** an expression of angry disagreement with, intention to ignore, etc. (someone or something); **what the hell** it does not matter. [O.E. *hel, hell*; O.N. *hel,* Ger. *Hölle*; cf. **Hel.**]

hell *hel, v.t.* obs. form of **hele.** — *n.* (*dial.*) **hell'ier** a slater: a tiler: a thatcher. [See **hele.**]

he'll *hēl,* contraction for **he will** and **he shall.**

Helladic *hel-ad'ik, adj.* Greek: of the Greek mainland Bronze Age, answering roughly to Minoan. [Gr. *Helladikos,* Greek — *Hellas,* Greece.]

hellbender. See **Hell.**

hellebore *hel'i-bōr, -bör, n.* any plant of the genus Helleborus, of the buttercup family (as *black hellebore* or Christmas rose, *stinking hellebore, green hellebore*): any plant of the genus Veratrum of the lily family (*American, false,* or *white hellebore,* known also as Indian poke or itchweed): the winter aconite (*winter hellebore*): the rhizome and roots of these prepared as a drug. — *n.* **hell'eborine** (*-īn, -in*) an orchid of the genus Epipactis. [Gr. *helleboros.*]

Hellene *hel'ēn, n.* a Greek. — *adj.* **Hellēn'ic** (or *-en'*) Greek. — *v.i.* **hell'enise, -ize** (*-in-īz*; often with *cap.*) to conform, or tend to conform, to Greek usages. — *v.t.* to make Greek. — *ns.* **Hell'enism** a Greek idiom: the Greek spirit: Greek nationality: conformity to Greek ways, esp. in language; **Hell'enist** one skilled in the Greek language: one who adopted Greek ways and language, esp. a Jew. — *adjs* **Hellenist'ic, -al** pertaining to the Hellenists: pertaining to the Greeks, the Greek language and Greek culture, affected by foreign influences after the time of Alexander. — *adv.* **Hellenist'ically.** [Gr. *Hellēn,* a Greek; also the son of Deucalion.]

heller¹ *hel'ər, n.* a small coin probably first made at *Hall* in Swabia, formerly used in Austria (worth a hundredth part of a crown) and Germany (worth half a pfennig), and still in use in Czechoslovakia (see **haler**).

heller². See **Hell.**

hellgrammite, hellgramite *hel'grə-mīt, n.* a large American neuropterous larva, used as bait by bass-fishers. [Origin unknown.]

hellicat *hel'i-kat,* (*Scot.*) *adj.* giddy-headed: flighty. — *n.* a wicked creature. [Origin obscure.]

hellier. See **hell.**

hellion, etc. See **Hell.**

hello. Same as **hallo.**

helm *helm, n.* steering apparatus. — *v.t.* to direct, steer. — *adj.* **helm'less.** — **helms'man** a steersman. [O.E. *helma*; O.N. *hjálm,* a rudder, Ger. *Helm,* a handle.]

helmet *hel'mit,* (*arch.* or *poet.*) **helm** *ns.* a covering of armour for the head: any similar covering for the head: anything resembling a helmet, as a cloud on a mountain top, the top of a guinea-fowl's head, the hooded

upper lip of certain flowers. — *adjs.* **hel'meted,** (*arch.* or *poet.*) **helmed.** — **hel'met-shell** a gasteropod of the genus Cassis, having a thick heavy shell with bold ridges. [O.E. *helm*; Ger. *Helm*; cf. **hele.**]

helminth *hel'minth, n.* a worm. — *n.* **helminthī'asis** infestation with worms. — *adjs.* **helmin'thic; helmin'thoid** worm-shaped; **helmintholog'ic, -al.** — *ns.* **helminthol'-ogist; helminthol'ogy** the study of worms, esp. parasitic. — *adj.* **helminth'ous** infested with worms. [Gr. *helmins, -inthos,* a worm.]

Helodea. Same as **Elodea.**

helot *hel'ət, n.* one of a class of serfs among the ancient Spartans, deliberately humiliated and liable to massacre (*hist.*): a serf (*hist.*): a plant or animal living symbiotically with another in a subject relationship (*biol.*). — *ns.* **hel'otage** the state of a helot; **hel'otism; hel'otry** the whole body of the helots: any class of slaves. [Gr. *Heilōtēs,* also *Heilōs, -ōtos.*]

help *help, v.t.* to contribute towards the success of, aid, or assist: to give means for doing anything: to relieve the wants of: to provide or supply with a portion: to deal out: to remedy: to mitigate: to prevent, to keep from. — *v.i.* to give assistance: to contribute: — *pa.t.* **helped,** *arch.* **hōlp;** *pa.p.* **helped,** *arch.* **hōlp'en.** — *n.* means or strength given to another for a purpose: assistance: relief: one who assists: a hired servant, esp. domestic: an employee. — *adj.* **help'able.** — *n.* **help'er** one who helps: an assistant: an assistant minister (*arch.*). — *adj.* **help'ful** giving help: useful. — *n.* **help'fulness.** — *adj.* **help'ing** giving help or support. — *n.* a portion served at a meal. — *adj.* **help'less** without ability to do things for oneself: wanting assistance: destitute of (*obs.*): giving no help (*Shak.*): that cannot be helped (*Spens.*). — *adv.* **help'lessly.** — *n.* **help'-lessness.** — **helping hand** assistance: a long-handled device used for reaching and gripping objects that one cannot reach by hand; **help'line** an often free telephone line by means of which people with some problem or other may contact advisers who will help them deal with it; **help'mate** a modification of **help'meet,** itself formed from the phrase in Gen. ii. 18, 'an help meet for him', *specif.* a wife. — **cannot help (be helped)** cannot avoid (be avoided); **help off with** to aid in taking off, disposing or getting rid of; **help on with** to help to put on; **help oneself (to)** to take for oneself without waiting for offer or authority; **help out** to eke out: to supplement: to assist; **more than one can help** (illogically but idiomatically) more than is necessary; **so help me (God)** a form of solemn oath: on my word. [O.E. *helpan,* pa.t. *healp* (pl. *hulpon*), pa.p. *holpen*; O.N. *hjálpa*; Ger. *helfen.*]

helter-skelter *hel'tər-skel'tər, adv.* in a confused hurry: tumultuously. — *n.* a confused medley: disorderly motion: a fair-ground spiral slide. — *adj.* confused. — *n.* **hel'ter-skel'teriness.** [Imit.]

helve *helv, n.* the handle of an axe or similar tool. — *v.t.* to furnish with a helve. — **helve'-hamm'er** a triphammer. [O.E. *helfe* (*hielfe*), a handle.]

Helvetic *hel-vet'ik,* **Helvetian** *hel-vē'shən, adjs.* Swiss. — *n.* **helvē'tium** a superseded name for astatine. — **Helvetic Confessions** two confessions of faith drawn up by the Swiss theologians in 1536 and 1566. [L. *Helvētia,* Switzerland.]

hem¹ *hem, n.* an edge or border: a border doubled down and sewed. — *v.t.* to form a hem on: to edge: — *pr.p.* **hemm'ing;** *pa.t.* and *pa.p.* **hemmed.** — **hem'-line** the height or level of the hem of a dress, skirt, etc.; **hem'-stitch** the ornamental finishing of the inner side of a hem, made by pulling out several threads adjoining it and drawing together in groups the cross-threads by successive stitches. — *v.t.* to embroider with such stitches. — **hem in** to surround. [O.E. *hemm,* a border.]

hem² *hem, hm, n.* and *interj.* a sort of half-cough to draw attention. — *v.i.* to utter the sound *hem*: — *pr.p.* **hemm'ing;** *pa.t.* and *pa.p.* **hemmed.** [Sound of clearing the throat.]

hem³ (*h*)*əm*, (*obs.*) them: to them. See **'em.**
hem⁴ See **haem** under **haem-.**
hem-. See **haem-.**
hemal. See **haemal** under **haem-.**
he-man. See **he.**
hematite, etc. See **haematite**, etc. under **haem-.**
hemato-. See **haemato-** under **haem-.**
heme¹ *hēm*, (*Spens.*) *adv.* Same as **home.**
heme². See **haem** under **haem-.**
hemeralopia *hem-ər-ə-lō′pi-ə, n.* day-blindness: vision requiring dim light: sometimes misapplied to night-blindness. [Gr. *hēmerā*, day, *alaos*, blind, *ōps*, eye.]
Hemerobaptist *hem-ər-ō-bap′tist, n.* a member of an ancient Jewish sect that practised daily baptism: also a Mandaean. [Gr. *hēmerā*, day, *baptistēs*, a baptiser.]
Hemerocallis *hem-ər-ō-kal′is, n.* a day-lily. [Gr. *hēmerokalles* — *hēmerā*, day, *kallos*, beauty.]
hemi- *hem′i-*, in composition, half. — *ns.* **hemial′gia** (Gr. *algos*, pain) pain confined to one side of the body; **hemianops′ia** (Gr. *an-*, priv., *opsis*, sight) blindness in half of the field of vision. — Also **hemianŏ′pia, hemiŏ′pia, hemiop′sia.** — *adjs.* **hemianop′tic, hemiop′ic.** — *n.* **hemicellulose** (-*sel′ū-lōs*) a type of polysaccharide, found in plant cell walls which can be more easily broken down than cellulose. — *ns.pl.* **Hemichordata** (-*kör-dā′tə*), **Hemichorda** (-*kör′də*) a group of worm-like marine animals with rudimentary notochord, including Balanoglossus, believed by many to represent the ancestors of the vertebrates. — *n.* **hemicrania** (-*krā′ni-ə*; Ger. *hēmikrāniā* — *krānion*, skull, head) headache confined to one side. — *adj.* **hemicrys′talline** (*petrol.*) consisting of crystals in a glassy or partly glassy groundmass. — *n.* **hem′icycle** (Gr. *kyklos*, wheel) a semicircle: a semicircular structure. — *adj.* **hemicy′clic** (*bot.*) having some parts in whorls, some in spirals. — *ns.* **hemidemisem′iquaver** (*mus.*) a note equal in time to half a demisemiquaver; **hemihē′drism, hemihē′dry** (-*dri*; Gr. *hedrā*, a seat) a property of crystals of being **hemihē′dral**, or having half the number of symmetrically arranged planes occurring on a holohedron; **hemihē′dron.** — *adj.* **hemimorph′ic** (Gr. *morphē*, form) having a polar axis, dissimilar at the two ends. — *ns.* **hemimorph′ism; hemimorph′ite** the mineral electric calamine, hydrous zinc silicate, which forms crystals whose ends are different in form and pyroelectric property; **hemiŏ′lia, hemiŏ′la** (Gr. *hēmiŏlios*, half as much again — *holos*, whole) in mediaeval music, a perfect fifth: also, a triplet. — *adj.* **hemiolic** (-*ol′*) in or based on the ratio of 3 to 2, as the paeonic foot. — *ns.* **hemionus** (*hi-mī′on-əs*), **hemione** (*hem′i-ōn*; Gr. *hēmionos*, mule — *onos*, an ass) an Asiatic wild ass, the kiang or the dziggetai; **hemipar′asite** an organism that is partly parasitic, partly independent: a saprophyte capable of living parasitically. — *adj.* **hemiparasit′ic.** — *adv.* **hemiparasit′ically.** — *n.* **hemiplegia** (-*plē′ji-ə*, or -*gi-ə*; Gr. *plēgē*, a blow) paralysis of one side only. — *adj.* **hemiplegic** (-*plej′* or -*plēj′*). — Also *n.* — *n.pl.* **Hemip′tera** (Gr. *pteron*, a wing) an order of insects, variously defined, with wings (when present) often half leathery, half membranous — the bugs, cicadas, greenfly, cochineal insect, etc. — *adjs.* **hemip′teral, hemip′teran, hemip′terous.** — *ns.* **hem′ispace** the area to one side, either left or right, of the body; **hem′isphere** (Gr. *hēmisphairion* — *sphaira*, a sphere) a half-sphere divided by a plane through the centre: half of the globe or a map of it: one of the two divisions of the cerebrum. — *adjs.* **hemispher′ic, -al.** — *n.* **hemisphē′roid** the half of a spheroid. — *adj.* **hemisphēroi′dal.** — *n.* **hemistich** (*hem′i-stik*; Gr. *hēmistichion* — *stichos*, a line) one of the two divisions of a line of verse: half a line, an incomplete or unfinished line: an epodic line or refrain. — *adj.* **hem′istichal** (or -*is′*). — *n.* **hem′itrope** (Gr. *tropos*, a turn) a form of twin crystal in which one twin is as if rotated through two right angles from the position of the other. — *adjs.* **hem′itrope, hemitropal** (*hem-it′rə-pl*), **hemitropic** (-*trop′*), **hemit′ropous.** — **Eastern and Western hemi-**

spheres the eastern and western halves of the terrestrial globe, the former including Europe, Asia and Africa; the latter, the Americas; **Northern and Southern hemispheres** the northern and southern halves of the terrestrial globe divided by the equator. [Gr. *hēmi-*, half.]
hemina *hi-mī′nə*, (*obs.*) *n.* a measure for liquids, about half a pint: a measure for corn, of varying amount. [L. — Gr. *hēmina* — *hēmi-*, half.]
hemlock *hem′lok, n.* a poisonous spotted umbelliferous plant (*Conium maculatum*): the poison got from it: extended to other umbelliferous plants, e.g. water hemlock (Cicuta): a N. American tree (hemlock spruce, Tsuga) whose branches are fancied to resemble hemlock leaves. [O.E. *hymlīce* (Kentish *hemlīc*).]
hemo-. See **haemo-** under **haem-.**
hemp *hemp, n.* a plant (*Cannabis sativa*), classified by some as belonging to the mulberry family *Moraceae* but by many now placed in a separate family *Cannabinaceae*, yielding a coarse fibre, a narcotic drug, and an oil: the fibre itself: the drug: a similar fibre got from various other plants (e.g. *Manila*, *sisal*, *sunn hemp*). — *adjs.* **hemp′en** made of hemp: pertaining to the hangman's noose or hanging (*arch.*); **hemp′y** like hemp: roguish: romping. — *n.* (*Scot.*) a rogue: a romp: a tomboy. — **hemp′-ag′rimony** a composite plant (*Eupatorium cannabinum*) with hemp-like leaves; **hempen caudle** see **caudle; hempen widow** the widow of a man who has been hanged; **hemp′-nett′le** a coarse bristly labiate weed (*Galeopsis*); **hemp′-palm** a palmetto (yielding fibre); **hemp′-seed** the oil-yielding seed of hemp, a bird's food: gallows-bird (*Shak.*). [O.E. *henep*, *hænep*; cf. Gr. *kannabis*.]
hen *hen, n.* a female domestic bird: a female domestic fowl: applied loosely to any domestic fowl: the female of certain fishes and crustaceans: (facetiously, disrespectfully, or endearingly) a woman or girl: a faint-hearted person. — *v.i.* (*Scot.*) to lose courage or resolution: to balk. — *v.t.* (*Scot.*) to challenge to an act of daring. — *adj.* female: composed of females. — *ns.* **henn′er** (*Scot.*) a challenge to an act of daring; **henn′ery** a place where fowls are kept; **henn′y** a hen-like cock. — *adj.* hen-like. — **hen′-and-chick′ens** a name for various plants, esp. a garden daisy with small heads surrounding the main head; **hen′bane** a poisonous plant (*Hyoscyamus niger*) of the nightshade family; **hen′-bit** the ivy-leaved speedwell: a species of dead-nettle; **hen′-coop** a coop for a hen; **hen′-court** an enclosure for fowls; **hen′-driv′er** a hen-harrier; **hen′-flesh** gooseflesh; **hen′-harr′ier** a bird, the common harrier. — *adj.* **hen′-heart′ed** faint-hearted: timid. — **hen′-house** a house for fowls; **hen′-huss′y** a man who meddles with women's affairs; **hen′-pad(d)′le, -paid′le** see **paddle²; hen′-party** a gathering of women only. — *v.t.* **hen′peck** to domineer over (said of a wife). — **hen′peck, henpeck′ery; hen′-pen′** (*Scot.*) fowl-house manure; **hen′-roost** a roosting-place for fowls; **hen′-run** an enclosure for fowls. — *adj.* **hen′-toed′** with toes turned in. — **hen′-wife** a woman with charge of poultry. — *adj.* **hen′-witted** brainless, silly. — **hen on a hot girdle** (chiefly *Scot.*) one who is in a jumpy or nervous state. [O.E. *henn*, fem. of *hana*, a cock; Ger. *Henne* (*Hahn*, cock).]
hence *hens, adv.* from this place: from this time onward: in the future: from this cause or reason: from this origin. — *interj.* away! begone! — *advs.* **hence′forth, hencefor′ward** from this time forth or forward. [M.E. *hennes*, formed with genitive ending from *henne* — O.E. *heonan*, from the base of **he;** Ger. *hinnen, hin,* hence: so L. *hinc,* hence — *hīc,* this.]
henchman *hench′, hensh′mən, n.* a servant: a page: a right-hand man: an active political partisan, esp. from self-interest: a thick-and-thin supporter: — *pl.* **hench′-men.** — Also **hench′person,** (*fem.*) **hench′woman.** [O.E. *hengest*, a horse (Ger. *Hengst*), and *man*; not connected with **haunch.**]
hend¹ *hend*, (*obs.*) *adj.* convenient: skilful: gracious: courteous. [App. O.E. *gehende*, handy — **hand.**]

hend[2] *hend*, (*Spens.*) *v.t.* to seize, to grasp. [O.E. *gehendan* or O.N. *henda*; cf. **hand**.]

hendecagon *hen-dek'ə-gon, n.* a plane figure of eleven angles and eleven sides. — *adj.* **hendecagonal** (*-ag'ən-l*). [Gr. *hendeka*, eleven, *gōniā*, an angle.]

hendecasyllable *hen'dek-ə-sil'ə-bl, n.* a metrical line of eleven syllables. — *adj.* **hendecasyllabic** (*-ab'ik*). [Gr. *hendeka*, eleven, *syllabē*, a syllable.]

hendiadys *hen-dī'ə-dis, n.* a rhetorical figure in which a notion, normally expressible by an adjective and a noun, is expressed by two nouns joined by *and* or another conjunction, as *clad in cloth and green* for *clad in green cloth.* [Mediaeval L. — Gr. *hen dia dyoin*, lit. one by two.]

henequen *hen'ə-kən, n.* a Mexican agave: its leaf-fibre, sisal-hemp used for cordage. — Also **hen'equin, hen'-iquin.** [Sp. *henequén, jeniquén.*]

henge[1] *henj,* (*Spens.*) *n.* axis. [**hinge.**]

henge[2] *henj, n.* a circular or oval area enclosed by a bank and internal ditch, often containing burial chambers, or a circular, oval or horseshoe-shaped construction of large upright stones or wooden posts. [Back-formation from *Stonehenge*, a famous example, in O.E *Stānhengist*, hanging stones.]

heniquin. See **henequen.**

henna *hen'ə, n.* a small Oriental shrub (*Lawsonia*) of the loosestrife family, with fragrant white flowers: a red or reddish-orange pigment made from its leaves for dyeing the nails and hair and for skin decoration. — *adj.* **hennaed** (*hen'əd*) dyed with henna. [Ar. *hinnā'*.]

hennin *hen'in, n.* a steeple-hat with a veil hanging from it worn by French women in the 15th century. [Obs. Fr.]

henotheism *hen'ō-thē-izm, n.* belief in one god, supreme or specially venerated but not the only god — a stage between polytheism and monotheism. — *n.* **henothē'-ist.** — *adj.* **henotheist'ic.** [Gr. *heis, henos*, one, *theos*, god.]

henotic *hen-ot'ik, adj.* tending to unify or reconcile. [Gr. *henōtikos* — *heis, henos*, one.]

henpeck. See **hen.**

henry *hen'ri*, (*elect.*) *n.* the unit of inductance, such that an electromotive force of one volt is induced in a circuit by current variation of one ampere per sec.: — *pl.* **hen'ries** or **hen'rys.** [Joseph *Henry*, American physicist (1797–1878).]

hent *hent,* (*obs.*) *v.t.* to grasp: to take: to snatch away, carry off: to reach: — *pa.t.* and *pa.p.* **hent.** — *n.* a grasp (*obs.*): perh. a conception, intention, perh. an opportunity (*Shak.*). [O.E. *hentan*, to seize.]

heortology *hē-ört-ol'ə-ji, n.* the study of religious feasts. — *adj.* **heortological** (*-ə-loj'i-kl*). — *n.* **heortol'ogist.** [Gr. *heortē*, a feast, *logos*, discourse.]

hep[1] *hep, n.* See **hip**[2].

hep[2] *hep,* (*slang*) *adj.* knowing, informed, well abreast of fashionable knowledge and taste, esp. in the field of jazz. — **hep'-cat, hep'ster** (*slang*), a hipster (*q.v.*). — **be, get, hep to** to be, become, informed about. [Perh. *hep*, left (command in drilling) — with ideas of being in step.]

hepar *hē'pär, n.* old name for liver-coloured compounds of sulphur. — *ns.* **heparin** (*hep'ə-rin*) complex substance formed in tissues of liver, lung, etc., that delays clotting of blood, used in medicine and surgery; **hepatec'tomy** excision of the liver. — *adj.* **hepatic** (*hi-pat'ik*) pertaining to, or acting on, the liver: pertaining to liverworts: liver-coloured. — *n.* a liverwort: a hepatic medicine. — *n.* **Hepat'ica** a genus of plants with slightly liver-like leaf once classed as a section of the Anemone genus: the common liverwort *Marchantia polymorpha*: (in *pl.*) **Hepat'icae** (*-sē*) liverworts. — *adjs.* **hepat'ical; hepatico-log'ical.** — *ns.* **hepaticol'ogist** a student of liverworts; **hepaticol'ogy; hepatisation, -z-** (*-ə-tī-zā'shən*) a liver-like solidification of tissue as of the lungs in pneumonia. — *v.t.* **hep'atise, -ize** to convert into a substance resembling liver: to impregnate with sulphuretted hydrogen (*obs.*). — *ns.* **hep'atite** a variety of barytes with

a sulphureous stink; **hepati'tis** inflammation of the liver; **hepatol'ogist** a specialist in liver diseases; **hepa-tol'ogy; hepatomeg'aly** abnormal enlargement of the liver; **hepatos'copy** divination by inspection of the livers of animals. [Gr. *hēpar, hēpatos*, liver.]

hephthemimer *hef-thi-mim'ər*, (*Gr.* and *Lat. pros.*) *n.* seven half-feet. — *adj.* **hephthemim'eral** of a caesura, occurring in the middle of the fourth foot. [Gr. *hepta*, seven, *hēmi-*, half, *meros*, part.]

Hepplewhite *hep'l-(h)wīt, adj.* belonging to a graceful school of furniture design typified by George *Hepple-white* (d. 1786), who favoured the use of curves, esp. in shield-shaped chair-backs.

hept *hept,* (*Spens.*) for **heaped.**

hepta- *hep'tə-, hep-ta'*, in composition, seven. — *ns.* **hep'tachlor** (*-klōr, klör*) a very toxic pesticide, $C_{10}H_5Cl_7$, which forms the even more toxic **heptachlor epoxide,** $C_{10}H_5Cl_7O$, in the soil and in animal and plant tissue; **hep'tachord** (Gr. *chordē*, string) in Greek music, a diatonic series of seven tones, containing five whole steps and one half-step: an instrument with seven strings: an interval of a seventh; **hep'tad** (Gr. *heptas, heptados*) a group of seven: an atom, radical, or element having a combining power of seven (*chem.*). — *adj.* **hep'taglot** (Gr. *heptaglōttos* — *glōtta*, tongue) in seven languages. — *n.* a book in seven languages. — *n.* **hep'tagon** (Gr. *heptagōnos* — *gōniā*, an angle) a plane figure with seven angles and seven sides. — *adj.* **heptag'onal.** — *n.pl.* **Heptagynia** (*-jin'i-ə*; Gr. *gynē*, woman, female) in Linnaean classification an order of plants (in various classes) having seven styles. — *adj.* **heptag'ynous.** — *n.* **Heptam'eron** (Gr. *hēmerā*, a day) a book containing the transactions of seven days, esp. the collection of stories told in seven days bearing the name of Queen Margaret of Navarre (1492–1549). — *adj.* **heptam'erous** (Gr. *meros*, part) having parts in sevens. — *n.* **heptam'eter** (Gr. *metron*, measure) a verse of seven measures or feet. — *n.pl.* **Heptan'dria** (Gr. *anēr, andros*, a man, male) a Linnaean class of plants having seven stamens. — *adj.* **heptan'drous** with seven stamens. — *n.* **hep'tane** a hydrocarbon (C_7H_{16}), seventh of the methane series. — *adj.* **heptapod'ic.** — *ns.* **heptap'ody** (Gr. *pous, podos*, foot) a verse of seven feet; **hep'tarch, hep'tarchist** ruler in a heptarchy. — *adj.* **heptar'chic.** — *n.* **heptarchy** (*hep'tar-ki*; Gr. *archē*, sovereignty) a government by seven persons: a country governed by seven: a misleading term for a once supposed system of seven English kingdoms — Wessex, Sussex, Kent, Essex, East Anglia, Mercia, and Northumbria. — *adj.* **heptasyllab'ic** seven-syllabled. — *ns.* **Hep'tateuch** (*-tūk*; Gr. *teuchos*, instrument, volume) the first seven books of the Old Testament; **heptath'lon** (Gr. *athlon*, contest) since 1984, a seven-event contest consisting of 100 metres hurdles, shot-put, javelin, high jump, long jump, 200 metres sprint and 800 metres race at the Olympic games. — *adj.* **heptaton'ic** (Gr. *tonos*, tone; *mus.*) of a scale, consisting of seven notes. [Gr. *hepta*, seven.]

her[1] *hûr, pron., gen.* (or *poss. adj.*), *dat.* and *acc.* of the *pron.* **she:** herself (*refl.*; *poet.* or *dial.*): she (*coll. nom.*). [O.E. *hire*, gen. and dat. sing. of *hēo*, she.]

her[2] *hûr,* (*obs.*; *Spens.*) *pron.* or *poss. adj.* their. [O.E. *hiera, hira, heora*, gen. pl. of **he.**]

Heraclean, Heracleian *her-ə-klē'ən, adj.* pertaining to *Heracles* (Gr. *Hēraklēs*). — *adj.* **Heracli'dan, Hera-clei'dan** pertaining to the Heracleidae or descendants of Heracles (Hercules), the aristocracy of Sparta. — *n.* **Her'aclid** one claiming such descent.

Heraclitean, Heracleitean *her-ə-klī'shē-ən, adj.* pertaining to *Heraclitus*, a Greek philosopher of the 5th century B.C., who held that all things are in a state of flux, continually entering a new state of being.

herald *her'əld, n.* in ancient times, an officer who made public proclamations and arranged ceremonies: in mediaeval times, an officer who had charge of all the etiquette of chivalry, keeping a register of the genealogies and armorial bearings of the nobles: an officer whose duty is to read proclamations, blazon the arms of the nobility, etc.: a proclaimer: a forerunner: a name given to many newspapers: the redbreasted merganser, usually **her′ald-duck**. — *v.t.* to usher in: to proclaim. — *adj.* **heraldic** (*her-, hər-al′dik*) of or relating to heralds or heraldry. — *adv.* **heral′dically**. — *ns.* **her′aldry** the art or office of a herald: the science of recording genealogies and blazoning coats of arms; **her′aldship**. [O.Fr. *herault*; of Gmc. origin.]

herb *hûrb* (old-fashioned *ûrb*), *n.* a plant with no woody stem above ground, distinguished from a tree or shrub: a plant used in medicine: an aromatic plant used in cookery. — *adj.* **herbā′ceous** pertaining to, composed of, containing, or of the nature of, herbs: like ordinary foliage leaves: usu. understood as of tall herbs that die down in winter and survive in underground parts (*hort.*). — *n.* **herb′age** herbs collectively: herbaceous vegetation covering the ground: right of pasture. — *adjs.* **herb′aged** covered with grass; **herb′al** composed of or relating to herbs: pertaining to the use of plants, e.g. medicinally. — *n.* a book containing descriptions of plants with medicinal properties, orig. of all plants. — *ns.* **herb′alism** herbal medicine, the use of (extracts of) roots, seeds, etc. for medicinal purposes; **herb′alist** one who studies, collects or sells herbs or plants: one who practises herbalism: an early botanist; **herb′ar** (*Spens.*) a herb-garden, arbour (q.v.); **herbā′rian** a herbalist; **herbārium** (a room, building, etc. for) a classified collection of preserved plants: — *pl.* **herbā′riums, herbā′ria; herb′ary** a garden of herbs. — *adj.* **herbicīd′al**. — *ns.* **herb′icide** (*-i-sīd*) a substance for killing weeds, etc., esp. a selective weedkiller; **herb′ist** a herbalist. — *n.pl.* **herbiv′ora** (*-ə-rə*) grass-eating animals, esp. ungulates. — *n.* **herb′ivore** (*-vōr, -vör*). — *adj.* **herbiv′orous** eating or living on grass or herbage. — *n.* **herbiv′ory**. — *adj.* **herb′less**. — *ns.* **herb′let, herb′elet** (*Shak.*) a small herb; **herborīsā′tion, -z-**. — *v.i.* **herb′orise, -ize** to botanise. — *n.* **herb′orist** a herbalist. — *adjs.* **herb′ous, herb′ose** abounding with herbs; **herb′y** of or pertaining to herbs. — **herb′-beer** a substitute for beer made from herbs; **herb′-benn′et** (L. *herba benedicta*, blessed herb) avens; **herb′-Chris′topher** baneberry; **herb′-garden; herb′-(of-)grace′** or **of-repent′ance** the common rue; **herb′-Par′is** a tetramerous plant (*Paris quadrifolia*) of the lily family; **herb′-Pe′ter** cowslip; **herb′-Rob′ert** stinking cranesbill (*Geranium robertianum*), a plant with small reddish-purple flowers; **herb′-tea′** a drink made from aromatic herbs; **herb′-trin′ity** the pansy. [Fr. *herbe* — L. *herba*.]

Herbartian *hər-bärt′i-ən, adj.* of Johann Friedrich *Herbart* (1776–1841), German philosopher and paedagogic psychologist.

hercogamy, herkogamy *hər-kog′ə-mi,* (*bot.*) *n.* an arrangement of the flower preventing self-pollination. — *adj.* **hercog′amous**. [Gr. *herkos*, fence, *gamos*, marriage.]

Herculean *hûr-kū-lē′ən, -kū′li-ən, adj.* of or pertaining to *Hercules* (*hûr′kū-lēz*; Greek *Hēraklēs*): (without *cap.*) extremely difficult or dangerous, as the twelve labours of Hercules: (without *cap.*) of extraordinary strength and size. — **Hercules beetle** a gigantic S. American lamellicorn beetle, *Dynastes hercules*, over 6 inches long, with a long horn on the thorax of the male and a smaller one on the head: (*loosely*) a related species, such as the *Dynastes gideon* of S.E. Asia; **Hercules' choice** toil and duty chosen in preference to ease and pleasure — from a famous story in Xenophon's *Memorabilia*; **Hercules' club** a stick of great size and weight: a West Indian tree (*Xanthoxylum*): a kind of gourd: a species of Aralia. — **Pillars of Hercules** two rocks flanking the entrance to the Mediterranean at the Strait of Gibraltar.

Hercynian *hûr-sin′i-ən, adj.* of or pertaining to the forest-covered mountain region between the Rhine and the Carpathians or the mountain chains running N.W. and S.E. between Westphalia and Moravia, of Upper

Carboniferous to Cretaceous date. — *n.* **her′cynite** black spinel, aluminate of iron. [L. *Hercynia* (*silva*), the Hercynian (forest).]

herd[1] *hûrd, n.* a company of animals, esp. large animals, that habitually keep together: a group of domestic animals, esp. cows or swine, with or without a guardian: a stock of cattle: the people regarded as a mass, as acting from contagious impulse, or merely in contempt: the rabble. — *v.i.* to associate as in herds: to live like a beast in a herd. — *v.t.* to put in a herd: to drive together. — **herd′-book** a pedigree book of cattle or pigs; **herd instinct** the instinct that urges men or animals to act upon contagious impulses or to follow the herd; **herds′man** keeper of a herd. [O.E. *heord*; Ger. *Herde*; cf. **herd**[2].]

herd[2] *hûrd, n.* a keeper of a herd or flock. — *v.t.* to tend: harbour. — *v.i.* to act as herd. — *n.* **herd′ess** (*rare*). — **herd′boy** a boy who acts as shepherd, cowherd, etc.: a cowboy; **herd′-groom** (*arch.*) a herdsman: shepherd boy; **herd′man** (*obs.*) a herdsman. [O.E. *hirde, hierde*; Ger. *Hirte*; cf. **herd**[1].]

herden *hûrd′ən.* See under **hards**.

herd grass, herd's grass (*U.S.*) *hûrd(z) gräs,* timothy: redtop. [From John *Herd,* who observed timothy in New Hampshire, 1700.]

herdic *hûr′dik, n.* a low-hung two- or four-wheeled carriage with back entrance and side seats. [From the inventor, P. *Herdic* (1824–88), of Pennsylvania.]

herdwick *hûrd′wik,* (*obs.*) *n.* a grazing ground: a breed of Lake District sheep. [**herd**[2] and **wick**[2].]

here *hēr, adv.* in this place: hither: in the present life or state: at this point or time. — *interj.* calling attention to one's presence, or to what one is going to say. — *advs.* **here′about, -s** about this place; **hereaf′ter** after this, in some future time, life, or state. — *n.* a future state: the after-life. — *advs.* **hereat′** at or by reason of this; **here′away** (*coll.*) hereabout; **hereby′** not far off: by this; **herefrom′** from this: from this place; **herein′** in this; **hereinaf′ter** afterward in this (document, etc.) — opp. to **hereinbefore′**. — *n.* **here′ness** the fact of being here. — *advs.* **hereof′** of this; **hereon′** on or upon this; **hereto′** to this: till this time (*Shak.*): for this object; **here′tofore′** before this time: formerly; **hereund′er** under this; **here′unto** (also *-un′*) to this point or time; **here′upon′** on this: immediately after this; **herewith′** with this. — **here and there** in this place, and then in that: thinly: irregularly; **here goes!** an exclamation indicating that the speaker is about to do something; **here's to** I drink the health of; **here today, gone tomorrow** a comment on the transient, ephemeral nature of things; **here we are** (*coll.*) this is what we are looking for: we have now arrived (at); **here we go again** (*coll.*) the same undesirable situation is recurring; **here you are** (*coll.*) this is what you want: this is something for you: this way; **neither here nor there** of no special importance: not relevant. [O.E. *hēr,* from base of *hē,* he; Du. and Ger. *hier,* Sw. *här.*]

heredity *hi-red′i-ti, n.* the transmission of characters to descendants: heritability. — *n.* **hereditabil′ity**. — *adj.* **hered′itable** that may be inherited. — *ns.* **heredit′ament** (*her-id-*) any property that may pass to an heir; **heredità′rian** (also **heredità′rianist**) an adherent of **heredità′rianism**, the view that heredity is the major factor in determining human and animal behaviour. — *adv.* **hered′itarily**. — *n.* **hered′itariness** the quality of being hereditary. — *adj.* **hered′itary** descending or coming by inheritance: transmitted to offspring: succeeding by inheritance: according to inheritance. — *n.* **hered′itist** a hereditarian. [L. *hērēditās, -ātis — hērēs, -ēdis,* an heir.]

Hereford *her′i-fərd, adj.* of a breed of white-faced red cattle, originating in *Hereford*shire. — Also *n.*

Herero *hə-re′rō, he′rə-rō, n.* a Bantu people of South West Africa: a member of this people: its language: — *pl.* **Hereros, Hereroes**. — *adj.* of or pertaining to the Herero or their language.

heresy *her′i-si, n.* belief contrary to the authorised teaching of one's natural religious community: an opinion opposed to the usual or conventional belief: heterodoxy. — *ns.* **heresiarch** (*he-rē′zi-ärk*) a leader in heresy; **heresiog′rapher** one who writes about heresies; **heresiog′raphy; heresiol′ogist** a student of, or writer on, heresies; **heresiol′ogy; heretic** (*her′ə-tik*) the upholder of a heresy. — *adj.* **heretical** (*hi-ret′i-kl*). — *adv.* **heret′ically.** — *v.t.* **heret′icate** to denounce as heretical. —**her′esy-hunt** vexatious pursuit of a supposed heretic; **her′esy-hunter.** [O.Fr. *heresie* — L. *haeresis* — Gr. *hairesis*, the act of taking, choice, set of principles, school of thought — *haireein*, to take.]

heriot *her′i-ət, n.* a fine due to the lord of a manor on the death of a tenant — originally his best beast or chattel. — *adj.* **her′iotable.** [O.E. *heregeatu*, a military preparation — *here*, an army, *geatwe*, equipment.]

herisson *her′i-sən, n.* a spiked beam turning on a pivot, for defence: a hedgehog (*her.*). — *adj.* **hérissé** (*her′is-ā, ā′rē-sā; her.*) bristled. [Fr.; see **urchin.**]

heritable *her′i-tə-bl, adj.* that may be inherited. — *n.* **heritabil′ity.** — *adv.* **her′itably.** — *n.* **her′itor** one who inherits: in Scotland, a landholder in a parish, liable to public burdens: — *fem.* **her′itress, her′itrix** (*pl.* **her′itrixes, heritri′cēs**). — *n.* **heritage** (*her′it-ij*) that which is inherited: inherited lot, condition of one's birth: anything transmitted from ancestors or past ages: the children (of God; *B.*). — **heritable property** (*Scots law*) real property, as opposed to movable property or chattels; **heritable security** (*Scots law*) same as English mortgage. [O.Fr. *(h)eritable, (h)eritage* — L.L. *hērēditāre*, to inherit — *hērēditas*; see **heredity.**]

herkogamy. See **hercogamy.**

herl. Same as **harl**[1].

herling, hirling *hûr′ling,* (*dial.*) *n.* a young sea-trout, a finnock.

herm, herma *hûrm, -ə, ns.* a head or bust (originally of *Hermes*) on a square base, often double-faced: — *pl.* **herms, hermae** (*-ē*).

hermandad *ûr-män-däd′, n.* a confederation of the entire burgher class of Spain for police and judicial purposes, formed in 1282, and formally legalised in 1485. [Sp., brotherhood — *hermano*, brother — L. *germānus.*]

hermaphrodite *hûr-maf′rəd-īt, n.* an animal or plant with the organs of both sexes, whether normally or abnormally: a compound of opposite qualities. — *adj.* uniting the characters of both sexes: combining opposite qualities. — *n.* **hermaph′roditism** the union of the two sexes in one body. — *adjs.* **hermaphrodit′ic, -al.** — *adv.* **hermaphrodit′ically.** — **hermaphrodite brig** a brig square-rigged forward and schooner-rigged aft. [Gr. *Hermaphrodītos*, the son of *Hermēs* and *Aphrodītē*, who grew together with the nymph Salmacis into one person.]

hermeneutic, -al *hûr-mə-nū′tik, -l, adjs.* interpreting: concerned with interpretation, esp. Scripture. — *adv.* **hermeneu′tically.** — *n. sing.* **hermeneu′tics** the science of interpretation, esp. of Scriptural exegesis. — *n.* **hermeneu′tist.** [Gr. *hermēneutikos* — *hermēneus,* an interpreter, from *Hermēs.*]

Hermes *hûr′mēz, n.* the herald of the Greek gods, patron of herdsmen, arts, eloquence, and thieves: the Egyptian Thoth, identified with the Greek Hermes: a herm. [Gr. *Hermēs*, identified by the Romans with Mercury.]

hermetic, -al *hûr-met′ik, -l, adjs.* belonging in any way to the beliefs current in the Middle Ages under the name of *Hermes*, the Thrice Great: belonging to magic or alchemy, magical: perfectly close, completely sealed: obscure, abstruse. — *adv.* **hermet′ically.** — *n.* **hermetic′ity.** — *n. sing.* **hermet′ics** the philosophy wrapped up in the **hermetic books**, esoteric science: alchemy. — **hermetically sealed** closed completely: made air-tight by melting the glass. [Mediaeval L. *hermēticus* — *Hermēs Trismegistos*, Hermes the thrice-greatest, the Greek name for the Egyptian Thoth, god of science, esp. alchemy.]

hermit *hûr′mit, n.* a solitary religious ascetic: one who lives a solitary life: a beadsman: a kind of humming-

bird: a hermit-crab. — *ns.* **her′mitage** a hermit's cell: a retired abode: a wine produced near Valence (Drôme) in France, where there was a supposed hermit's cell; **her′mitess** a female hermit. — *adj.* **hermit′ical.** — **her′mit-crab** a soft-bodied crustacean that inhabits a mollusc shell. [M.E. *eremite*, through Fr. and L. from Gr. *erēmītēs* — *erēmos*, solitary.]

hern[1] *hûrn.* Same as **heron.**

hern[2] *ûrn*, a dialect form for **hers.** [App. from **her**, on the analogy of **mine, thine.**]

hernia *hûr′ni-ə, n.* a protrusion through a weak place of part of the viscera, rupture. — *adjs.* **her′nial; her′niated.** — *ns.* **hernior′rhaphy** (Gr. *rhaphē*, stitching, suture) the surgical repair of a hernia by an operation involving suturing; **herniot′omy** (Gr. *tomē*, a cut) a cutting operation for the repair of a hernia. [L.]

hernshaw *hûrn′shö, n.* See **heronshaw.**

hero *hē′rō, n.* a man of distinguished bravery: any illustrious person: a person reverenced and idealised: the principal male figure, or the one whose career is the thread of the story, in a history or work of fiction: orig. a man of superhuman powers, a demigod: — *pl.* **hē′roes** (formerly, as *Spens.*, who never uses the singular, **hērō′ēs**, from which a singular form, **hērō′ē,** was formed); *fem.* **heroine** (*her′ō-in*). — *adj.* **heroic** (*hi-rō′ik*) befitting a hero: of or pertaining to heroes: epic: supremely courageous: using extreme or elaborate means to obtain a desired result, as the preserving of life. — *n.* a heroic verse: (in *pl.*) extravagant phrases, bombast: (in *pl.*) unduly bold behaviour. — *adj.* **herō′ical.** — *adv.* **herō′ically** (*Milt.* **herō′icly**). — *ns.* **herō′icalness; herō′icness.** — *v.t.* **hē′rōise, -ize** to treat as a hero, make a hero of: to glorify. — *ns.* **heroism** (*her′ō-izm*) the qualities of a hero: courage: boldness; **hērō′on** a temple dedicated to a hero: a temple-shaped tomb or monument; **hē′roship** the state of being a hero. — **heroic age** any semi-mythical period when heroes or demigods were represented as living among men; **heroic couplet** a pair of rhyming lines of heroic verse. — *adjs.* **herō′i-com′ic, -al** consisting of a mixture of heroic and comic: high burlesque. — **heroic poem** an epic: a compromise between epic and romance which flourished in the 16th and 17th centuries; **heroic remedy** one that may kill or cure; **heroic size** in sculpture, larger than life, but less than colossal; **heroic verse** the form of verse in which the exploits of heroes are celebrated (in classical poetry, the hexameter; in English, the iambic pentameter, esp. in couplets; in French, the alexandrine); **he′ro-worship** the worship of heroes: excessive admiration of great men, or of anybody. — Also *v.t.* [Through O.Fr. and L. from Gr. *hērōs*; akin to L. *vir*, O.E. *wer*, a man, Sans. *vīra*, a hero.]

heroin *her′ō-in, hi-rō′in, n.* a derivative of morphine used in medicine and by drug-addicts. [Said to be from Gr. *hērōs*, a hero, from its effect.]

heron *her′ən, hûrn, hern, n.* a large long-legged, long-necked wading bird (Ardea or kindred genus). — *n.* **her′onry** a place where herons breed. [O.Fr. *hairon* — O.H.G. *heigir.*]

heronshaw, heronsew, hernshaw *her′ən-* or *hern′-, hûrn′-shö, -shōō, ns.* a young heron: (esp. *dial.*) a heron. [O.Fr. *herounçel,* confounded with **shaw** (wood).]

heroon. See **hero.**

herpes *hûr′pēz, n.* a skin disease of various kinds, with spreading clusters of vesicles on an inflamed base — esp. *herpes simplex* a sexually transmitted disease, and *herpes zoster* or shingles. — *adj.* **herpetic** (*-pet′ik*) relating to or resembling herpes: creeping. [Gr. *herpēs* — *herpein*, to creep.]

Herpestes *hər-pes′tēz, n.* the ichneumon or mongoose genus. [Gr. *herpēstēs* — *herpein*, to creep.]

herpetology *hûr-pi-tol′ə-ji, n.* the study of reptiles and amphibians. — *n.* **her′petofauna** reptiles and amphibians. — *adjs.* **her′petoid** reptile-like; **herpetolog′ic, -al.** — *adv.* **herpetolog′ically.** — *n.* **herpetol′ogist.** [Ger. *herpeton*, a reptile — *herpein*, to creep.]

Herr *her, n.* lord, master, the German term of address

equivalent to sir, or (prefixed) Mr: — *pl.* **Herr'en.** — *n.* **Herrenvolk** (*her'en-fōlk*) lit. 'master race', fitted and entitled by their superior qualities to rule the world. [Ger.]

herring *her'ing, n.* a common small sea-fish (*Clupea harengus*) of great commercial value, found moving in great shoals or multitudes. — *n.* **herr'inger** (*-ing-ər*) a man or boat employed in herring fishing. — *adj.* **herr'ing-bone** like the spine of a herring, applied to a kind of masonry in which the stones slope in different directions in alternate rows, to a zigzag stitch crossed at the corners, to a crossed strutting, etc.: in skiing, of a method of climbing a slope, the skis being placed at an angle and leaving a herring-bone-like pattern in the snow. — *v.t.* to make in herring-bone work, or mark with herring-bone pattern: to climb a slope on skis by herring-bone steps. — **herr'ing-buss** (*hist.*; see **buss**[2]); **herr'ing-fish'ery; herr'ing-gull** a large white gull with black-tipped wings; **herr'ing-pond** (*facet.*) the ocean, esp. the Atlantic. — **dead as a herring** quite certainly dead — a herring out of water soon dies; **neither fish nor flesh nor good red herring** see **fish**[1]; **packed like herring (in a barrel)** very closely packed; **red herring** see **red**[1]. [O.E. *hǣring, hēring*; cf. Ger. *Hering*.]

Herrnhuter *hûrn'hōōt-ər, n.* one of the Moravians or United Brethren, so called from their settlement in 1722 at *Herrnhut* in Saxony.

herry[1]. See **hery.**

herry[2] *her'i,* (*Scot.*) *v.t.* to harry. — *ns.* **herr'iment, herr'yment** spoliation: plunder. [**harry.**]

hers *hûrz, pron.* possessive of **she** (used without a noun).

hersall *hûr'səl,* (*Spens.*) *n.* rehearsal.

herse *hûrs,* (*obs.*) *n.* a harrow: a spiked portcullis: a form of battle-array: a hearse in various senses. — *adj.* **hersed** arranged in harrow form. [**hearse.**]

herseems, herseemed. See **seem.**

herself *hûr-self', pron.* an emphatic form for **she** or **her:** in real character: reflexive for **her:** predicatively (or *n.*) one having the command of her faculties, sane, in good form or (*Scot.*) alone, by herself: the mistress of a house, owner of an estate, etc. (*Scot.*). [See **her, self.**]

hership *hûr'ship,* (*Scot.*) *n.* plundering: plunder. [O.E. *here,* army, or *hergan,* to harry; cf. O.N. *herskapr,* warfare.]

hertz *hûrts, n.* the unit of frequency, that of a periodic phenomenon of which the periodic time is one second — sometimes called **cycle per second** in U.K. — *adj.* **Hertz'ian** connected with Heinrich *Hertz* (see below). — **Hertzian waves** electromagnetic waves used in communicating information through space. [After Heinrich *Hertz* (1857–94), German physicist.]

hery, herye, herry *her'i,* (*Spens.*) *v.t.* to praise, to regard as holy. [O.E. *herian,* to praise.]

hes *hēz,* pl. of **he.** — **he's** (*hēz*) a contraction of **he is** or **he has.**

Heshvan. See **Hesvan.**

hesitate *hez'i-tāt, v.i.* to hold back or delay in making a decision: to be in doubt: to stammer. — *v.t.* (*rare*) to express or utter with hesitation. — *ns.* **hes'itance, hes'itancy, hesita'tion** wavering: doubt: stammering: delay. — *adj.* **hes'itant** hesitating. — *adv.* **hes'itātingly.** — *adj.* **hes'itātive** showing hesitation. — *n.* **hes'itātor.** — *adj.* **hes'itātory** hesitating. — **hesitā'tion-form** (*linguistics*) a sound used in speech when stammering or pausing as *er, eh, um;* **hesitation waltz** a kind of waltz into which a pause and gliding step are introduced at intervals. [L. *haesitāre, -ātum,* freq. of *haerēre, haesum,* to stick.]

hesp *hesp,* a Scots form of **hasp.**

Hesper *hes'pər,* **Hesperus** *-əs, ns.* Venus as the evening star. — *adj.* **Hesperian** (*-pē'ri-ən*) western: Italian (from the Greek point of view): Spanish (from the Roman): of the Hesperides: of the skipper butterflies. — *n.* a westerner: a skipper butterfly. — *ns.* **hes'perid** (*-pər-id*) one of the Hesperides: a skipper butterfly: — *pl.* **Hesperides** (*-per'i-dēz*) the sisters who guarded in their delightful gardens in the west the golden apples which

Hera, on her marriage with Zeus, had received from Gaea; **hesperid'ium** (*bot.*) a fruit of the orange type. — *n.pl.* **Hesperiidae** (*-ī'i-dē*) a family of moth-like butterflies, the skippers. — *n.* **Hes'peris** the dame's-violet genus of Cruciferae, generally fragrant in the evening. [Gr. *hesperos,* evening, western.]

Hessian *hes'i-ən,* sometimes *hesh'(i)ən, adj.* of or pertaining to Hesse: mercenary (from the use of Hessian mercenaries by the British against the Revolutionaries) (*U.S.*). — *n.* a native or citizen of Hesse: (without *cap.*) a cloth made of jute: short for **Hessian boot,** a kind of long boot first worn by Hessian troops. — **Hessian fly** a midge whose larva attacks wheat stems in America, once believed to have been introduced in straw for the Hessian troops. [*Hesse,* Ger. *Hessen,* in Germany.]

hessonite an amended form of **essonite.**

hest *hest,* (*arch.*) *n.* behest, command: vow. — Also (*Spens.*) **heast(e)** (*hēst*). [O.E. *hǣs,* a command — *hātan,* to command.]

hesternal *hes-tûr'nəl, adj.* of yesterday. [L. *hesternus.*]

Hesvan *hes'vän,* **Heshvan** *hesh',* or *hhes(h)' ns.* the second month of the Jewish civil year and the eighth month of the Jewish ecclesiastical year. — Also **Ches(h)'van.** [Heb.]

Hesychast *hes'i-kast, n.* one of a 14th-century quietist sect of the Greek Church. — *n.* **Hes'ychasm** their doctrines and practice. [Gr. *hēsychastēs — hēsychos,* quiet.]

het[1] *het, adj.* a Scots form of **hot**[1]. [O.E. *hāt.*]

het[2] *het,* (*Brit.* and *U.S. dial.*) *pa.p.* for **heated.** — **het up** agitated.

het[3] *het,* (*coll.*) *n.* a heterosexual. — Also *adj.*

hetaira *he-tī'rə, n.* in Greece, a woman employed in public or private entertainment, as flute-playing, dancing, etc.: a paramour: a concubine: a courtesan, esp. of a superior class: — *pl.* **hetai'rai** (*-rī*). — *ns.* **hetai'ria** (*hist.*) a club or society; **hetai'rism** concubinage: the system of society that admitted hetairai: a supposed primitive communal marriage. — *adj.* **hetairis'mic.** — *n.* **hetai'-rist.** — Also (Latinised) **hetaera** (*-tē';* L. *-tī'*), etc. [Gr. *hetairā,* fem. of *hetairos,* companion; *hetair(e)iā,* a club.]

hete. See **hight.**

heter-, hetero- *het'ər-, -ō-,* or *-o'-,* in composition, other, different: one or other (often opposed to *homo-, auto-*). — *n.* **heterauxē'sis** (Gr. *auxēsis,* growth; *bot.*) unsymmetrical growth. — *adj.* **heteroblast'ic** (Gr. *blastos,* bud, germ) derived from different kinds of cells: showing indirect development. — *n.* **het'eroblasty** heteroblastic condition. — *adj.* **heterocarp'ous** (Gr. *karpos,* fruit) bearing fruit of more than one kind. — *n.pl.* **Heterocera** (*-os'ər-ə;* Gr. *keras,* horn) a loose term for moths, distinguished from *Rhopalocera* (butterflies). — *adj.* **heterocercal** (*-sûr'kl;* Gr. *kerkos,* tail) having the vertebral column passing into the upper lobe of the tail, which is usually larger than the lower, as in sharks. — *ns.* **heterocercal'ity, het'erocercy.** — *adjs.* **heterochlamydeous** (*-klə-mid'i-əs;* Gr. *chlamys, -ydos,* mantle) having calyx and corolla distinctly different; **heterochromat'ic, heterochromous** (*-krō'məs;* Gr. *chrōma,* colour) having different or varying colours; **heterochron'ic.** — *n.* **heteroch'ronism.** — *adjs.* **heterochronist'ic; heteroch'ronous.** — *n.* **heterochrony** (*ok'rə-ni;* Gr. *chronos,* time; *biol.*) divergence from the normal time sequence in development. — *adj.* **het'-eroclite** (*-klīt;* Gr. *heteroklītos — klitos,* inflected — *klīnein,* to inflect; *gram.*) irregularly inflected: irregular: having forms belonging to different declensions. — *n.* a word irregularly inflected: anything irregular. — *adjs.* **heteroclīt'ic, heteroc'lītous.** — *n.* **heterocont** see **heterokont.** — *adj.* **heterocyclic** (*-sī'klik;* Gr. *kyklos,* wheel) having a closed chain in which the atoms are not all alike (*chem.*): having different numbers of parts in different whorls (*bot.*). — *n.* **heterodactyl** (*-dak'til;* Gr. *daktylos,* toe) a heterodactylous bird. — *adj.* **heterodactylous.** — *adjs.* **heterodac'tylous** having the first and second toes turned backwards (as trogons —

not the first and fourth as parrots); **het′erodont** (Gr. *odous, odontos,* a tooth) having different kinds of teeth; **het′erodox** (Gr. *heterodoxos — doxa,* opinion — *dokeein,* to think) holding an opinion other than or different from the one generally received, esp. in theology: heretical. — *n.* **het′erodoxy** heresy. — *adjs.* **het′erodyne** (-ō-dīn; Gr. *dynamis,* strength) in radio communication, applied to a method of imposing on a continuous wave another of slightly different length to produce beats; **heteroecious** (-ē′shəs). — *n.* **heteroecism** (-ē′sizm; Gr. *oikos,* a house) parasitism upon different hosts at different stages of the life-cycle. — *adj.* **heterog′amous.** — *ns.* **heterog′amy** (Gr. *gamos,* marriage) alternation of generations (*biol.*): reproduction by unlike gametes (*biol.*): presence of different kinds of flower (male, female, hermaphrodite, neuter, in any combination) in the same inflorescence (*bot.*); **heterogenē′ity.** — *adj.* **heterogeneous** (-jē′ni-əs; Gr. *heterogenēs — genos,* a kind) different in kind: composed of parts of different kinds — opp. to *homogeneous.* — *adv.* **heteroge′neously.** — *ns.* **heteroge′neousness; heterogenesis** (-jen′i-sis; Gr. *genesis,* generation; *biol.*) spontaneous generation: alternate generation. — *adj.* **heterogenetic** (-ji-net′ik). — *n.* **heterogeny** (-oj′ən-i) a heterogeneous assemblage: heterogenesis. — *adj.* **heterogonous** (og′ə-; Gr. *gonos,* offspring, begetting) having flowers differing in length of stamens (*bot.*): having alternation of generations (*biol.*). — *ns.* **heterog′ony; het′erograft** a graft of tissue from a member of one species to a member of another species; **het′erokont, het′erocont** (Gr. *kontos,* a punting pole) any member of the **Heterocont′ae** or yellow-green algae (e.g. the common Conferva), a class usually characterised by the pair of unequal cilia on the motile cells. — *adjs.* **heterokont′an; heterologous** (-ol′ə-gəs) not homologous: different: of different origin: abnormal. — *n.* **heterol′ogy** lack of correspondence between apparently similar structures due to different origin. — *adjs.* **heterom′erous** (Gr. *meros,* part) having different numbers of parts in different whorls (*bot.*): (of lichens) having the algal cells in a layer (*bot.*): having unlike segments (*zool.*); **heteromor′phic** (Gr. *morphē,* form) deviating in form from a given type: of different forms — also **heteromor′phous.** — *ns.* **heteromor′phism, het′eromorphy.** — *adj.* **heteron′omous** (Gr. *nomos,* law) subject to different laws: subject to outside rule or law — opp. to *autonomous.* — *ns.* **heteron′omy; het′eronym** a word of the same spelling as another but of different pronunciation and meaning. — *adjs.* (often *cap.*) **heterooousian** (het-ər-ō-ōō′si-ən, or -ow′; Gr. *ousiā,* being), **heterousian** (-ōō′, -ow′, or -ō-ōō′) of unlike essence: believing the Father and Son to be of different substance. — *ns.* (often *cap.*) a holder of such belief. — *adj.* **heterophyllous** (-fil′əs; Gr. *phyllon,* a leaf) having different kinds of foliage leaf. — *ns.* **het′erophylly; heteroplasia** (plā′z(h)i-ə, -si-ə; Gr. *plasis,* a forming) development of abnormal tissue or tissue in an abnormal place. — *adj.* **heteroplastic** (-plas′tik). — *ns.* **het′eroplasty** heteroplasia: grafting of tissue from another person; **het′eropod.** — *ns.pl.* **Heterop′oda** (Gr. *pous, podos,* foot) pelagic gasteropods in which the foot has become a swimming organ; **Heterop′tera** (Gr. *pteron,* a wing) a suborder of insects, the bugs, Hemiptera with fore and hind wings (when present) markedly different. — *adj.* **heterop′terous.** — *ns.* **heteroscian** (het-ər-osh′i-ən; Gr. *skiā,* a shadow) a dweller in a temperate zone, whose noon-shadow is always thrown one way, either north or south; **heterosex′ism** the belief that homosexuality is a perversion, used as grounds for discrimination against homosexuals; **heterosex′ist** one who discriminates against homosexuals. — Also *adj.* — *adj.* **heterosex′ūal** having, or pertaining to, sexual attraction towards the opposite sex. — Also *n.* — *ns.* **heterosexual′ity; heterō′sis** cross-fertilisation: the increased size and vigour (relative to its parents) often found in a hybrid. — *n.pl.* **Heterosō′mata** (Gr. *sōma,* pl. *sōmata,* a body) the flat-fishes. — *adjs.* **heterosō′-**

matous; heterospecif′ic (of blood or serum) belonging to different groups: derived from different species; **heterosporous** (-os′por-əs, or -pōr′, -pör′) having different kinds of asexually produced spores. — *n.* **heteros′pory.** — *adj.* **heterostroph′ic** (Gr. *strophē,* a turning) consisting of unequal strophes: coiled contrary to the usual direction. — *n.* **heteros′trophy.** — *adjs.* **het′erostyled, heterosty′lous** having styles of different length in different flowers. — *ns.* **heterostyl′ism; het′erostyly.** — *adj.* **heterotact′ic.** — *ns.* **heterotax′is, het′erotaxy** (Gr. *taxis,* arrangement) anomalous arrangement of, e.g. parts of the body, etc. — *adj.* **heterothall′ic** (Gr. *thallos,* a shoot; *bot.*) having (as certain fungi) two physiologically different types of mycelium, called plus and minus, comparable to male and female. — *ns.* **heterothall′ism, het′erothally.** — *adjs.* **heterother′mal** (Gr. *thermos,* heat) taking the temperature of the surroundings; **heterŏt′ic** pertaining to or showing heterosis. — *n.* **heterotō′pia** displacement of an organ of the body. — *adj.* **heterotŏp′ic.** — *n.* **het′erotroph** a heterotrophic organism. — *adj.* **heterotroph′ic.** — *n.* **heterot′rophy** (Gr. *trophē,* livelihood; *bot.*) dependence (immediate or ultimate) upon green plants for carbon (as in most animals, fungi, etc.). — *adjs.* **heterotyp′ic** differing from the normal condition: pertaining to the first (reductional) cell division in meiosis (*biol.*), see *homotypic*; **heterousian** see **heteroousian.** — *n.* **heterozygote** (-zī′gōt; Gr. *zygōtos,* yoked — *zygon,* yoke) a zygote or individual formed from gametes differing with respect to some pair of alternative characters (one dominant and one recessive). — *adj.* **heterozy′gous.** [Gr. *heteros,* other, one or other.]

hether, hetherward (*Spens.*). Same as **hither, hitherward.**

hetman *het′man,* (*hist.*) *n.* a Polish officer: the head or general of the Cossacks: — *pl.* **het′mans.** — *ns.* **het′manate, het′manship.** [Pol., — Ger. *Hauptmann,* captain.]

heugh, heuch *hūhh,* (*Scot.*) *n.* a crag: a ravine or steep-sided valley: a quarry-face: an excavation, esp. for coal. [O.E. *hōh,* heel; cf. **hoe**².]

heulandite *hū′lan-dīt, n.* a zeolite like stilbite. [After H. *Heuland,* an English mineralogist.]

heureka. See **eureka.**

heuristic *hū-ris′tik, adj.* serving or leading to find out: encouraging desire to find out: (of method, argument) depending on assumptions based on past experience: consisting of guided trial and error. — *n.* the art of discovery in logic: the method in education by which the pupil is set to find out things for himself: (in *pl.*) principles used in making decisions when all possibilities cannot be fully explored. — *adv.* **heuris′tically.** — *ns.* **heuret′ic** (*logic*) heuristic; **heur′ism** the heuristic method or principle in education. [Irreg. formed from Gr. *heuriskein,* to find; cf. **eureka.**]

hevea rubber *hē′vē-ə rub′ər,* rubber from the S. American tree **hevea,** *Hevea brasiliensis,* used in electrical insulators for its good electrical and mechanical properties.

hew¹ *hū, v.t.* to cut with blows: to shape, fell or sever with blows of a cutting instrument. — *v.i.* to deal blows with a cutting instrument: — *pa.t.* **hewed;** *pa.p.* **hewed** or **hewn.** — *n.* (*Spens.*) hacking. — *n.* **hew′er** one who hews. — *n.* and *adj.* **hew′ing.** — *adj.* **hewn.** [O.E. *hēawan;* Ger. *hauen.*]

hew² (*Spens.*). See **hue**¹.

hewgh *hū,* (*Shak.*) *interj.* imitating the whistling of an arrow.

hex¹ *heks, n.* a witch: a wizard: a spell: something which brings bad luck. — *v.t.* to bring misfortune, etc. to by a hex: to bewitch. — *n.* **hex′ing.** [Pennsylvania Dutch *hex* — Ger. *Hexe* (*fem.*), *Hexer* (*masc.*).]

hex² *heks, n.* coll. for *uranium hexafluoride,* a compound used in separating uranium isotopes by gaseous diffusion.

hex-, hexa- *heks-, heks′ə, heks-a′-,* in composition, six. — *ns.* **hex′achord** (-körd) a diatonic series of six notes having a semitone between the third and fourth; **hexachlo′rophene, hexachlo′rophane** (or *-ŏr′*) a bactericide, $CH_2(C_6HCl_3OH)_2$, used in antiseptic soaps, deodorants, etc. — *adj.* **hex′act** (*-akt*; Gr. *aktīs, -īnos*, ray) six-rayed. — *n.* a six-rayed sponge spicule. — *adj.* **hexactī′nal** (or *-ak′ti-nl*) six-rayed. — *n. and adj.* **hexactinell′id.** — *n.pl.* **Hexactinell′ida** a class of sponges whose spicules have three axes and therefore (unless some are suppressed) six rays. — *n.* **hexad** (*heks′ad*; Gr. *hexas, -ados*) a series of six numbers: a set of six things: an atom, element, or radical with a combining power of six units (*chem.*). — *adjs.* **hexadactyl′ic, hexadact′ylous** (Gr. *daktylos*, finger, toe) six-fingered: six-toed; **hexad′ic** pertaining to a hexad. — *ns.* **hexadec′imal** a number system much used in computer programming, having a radix of 16 (also **hexadecimal notation**); **hexaëmeron** (*heks-ə-ē′mer-on*; Gr. *hēmerā*, day) a period of six days, esp. that of the creation, according to Genesis: a history of the six days of creation; **hex′afoil** a pattern with six leaf-like lobes or sections. — Also *adj.* — *adj.* **hex′aglot** (Gr. *glŏtta*, tongue) in six languages. — *n.* **hex′agon** (Gr. *hexagōnon — gōniā*, an angle) a figure with six sides and six angles. — *adj.* **hexagonal** (*-ag′ən-l*) of the form of a hexagon: of the **hexagonal system**, a crystal system with three axes at 60° to each other and a fourth perpendicular to their plane (*crystal.*). — *adv.* **hexag′onally.** — *n.* **hex′agram** (Gr. *gramma*, figure) a figure of six lines, esp. a stellate hexagon. — *n.pl.* **Hexagynia** (*-jin′i-ə*; Gr. *gynē*, woman) a Linnaean order of plants (in various classes) having six styles. — *adjs.* **hexagyn′ian, hexagynous** (*-aj′i-nəs*); **hexahē′dral.** — *n.* **hexahē′dron** (Gr. *hĕdrā*, a base) a solid with six sides or faces, esp. a cube: — *pl.* **hexahē′drons, hexahē′dra.** — *adj.* **hexam′erous** (Gr. *meros*, part) having six parts, or parts in sixes. — *n.* **hexam′eter** (Gr. *metron*, measure) a verse of six measures or feet: in Greek and Latin verse such a line where the fifth is almost always a dactyl and the sixth a spondee or trochee, the others dactyls or spondees. — *adj.* having six metrical feet. — *adjs.* **hexamet′ric, -al.** — *v.i.* **hexam′etrise, -ize** to write hexameters. — *n.* **hexam′etrist** a writer of hexameters. — *n.pl.* **Hexan′dria** (Gr. *anēr, andros*, a man, male) a Linnaean class of plants having six stamens. — *adjs.* **hexan′drian; hexan′drous** having six stamens. — *ns.* **hexane** (*heks′ān*) a hydrocarbon (C_6H_{14}), sixth member of the methane series; **hex′apla** (Gr. *hexaplā*, contracted pl. neut. of *hexaploos*, sixfold) an edition (esp. of the Bible) in six versions. — *adjs.* **hex′aplar, hexaplār′ian, hexaplăr′ic; hex′aploid** or, of having, six times the ordinary number of chromosomes. — *n.* a hexaploid cell, individual, species, etc. — *n.* **hex′apod** (Gr. *pous, podos*, a foot) an animal with six feet. — *n.pl.* **Hexap′oda** insects. — *n.* **hexap′ody** a line or verse of six feet. — *adj.* **hexarch** (*heks′ärk*; Gr. *archē*, beginning; *bot.*) having six vascular strands. — *n.* **hexastich** (*heks′ə-stik*; Gr. *hexastichos*, adj. — *stichos*, a line) a poem or stanza of six lines. — *adjs.* **hexastichal** (*-as′tik-l*) having six lines or rows; **hexastyle** (*heks′ə-stīl*; Gr. *hexastȳlos — stȳlos*, a pillar) having six columns. — *n.* a building or portico having six columns in front. — *n.* **Hexateuch** (*heks′ə-tūk*; Gr. *teuchos*, tool, afterwards book) the first six books of the Old Testament. — *adj.* **hexateuch′al.** — *ns.* **hexylene** (*heks′i-lēn*; Gr. *hȳlē*, matter), **hex′ene** an unsaturated hydrocarbon (C_6H_{12}) of the ethylene series; **hex′ose** a sugar (of various kinds) with six carbon atoms to the molecule. — **hexagonal chess** a kind of chess played on hexagonal boards. [Gr. *hex*, six; cf. L. *sex*, and **six**.] **hexobarbitone sodium** *heks-ō-bär′bi-tōn sō′di-əm.* See **Evipan®.**

hey[1] *hā, interj.* expressive of joy or interrogation, or calling attention. — *interjs.* **hey′day** (*arch.*) expressive of frolic, exultation, or wonder; **hey′-go-mad** (*dial.*) expressing a high degree of excitement. — Also *n.*, as **like hey-go-mad** helter-skelter. — *interjs. and ns.* **hey‗pass, hey′-pres′to** a conjuror's command in passing

objects. — **hey for** now for: off we go for. [Imit.] **hey**[2]**, hay** *hā, n.* a winding country-dance. — *v.i.* to dance the hay. — *ns.* **hey′-** or **hay′-de-guy** (*-gī*), **-guise, -guyes** a hay popular in the 16th and 17th centuries. [Obs. Fr. *haye.*]

heyday *hā′dā, n.* high spirits (*arch.*): culmination or climax of vigour, prosperity, gaiety, etc.: flush or full bloom. [Origin obscure.]

heyduck. See **haiduk.**

hi *hī, interj.* calling attention: hey: hello. [Cf. **hey**[1].]

hiant *hī′ənt, adj.* gaping. [L. *hiāns, -antis*, pr.p. of *hiāre*, to gape.]

hiatus *hī-ā′təs, n.* a gap: an opening: a break in continuity, a defect: a concurrence of vowel sounds in two successive syllables (*gram.*): — *pl.* **hiā′tuses.** — **hiatus hernia** one in which a part of a viscus protrudes through a natural opening, esp. through that in the diaphragm intended for the oesophagus. [L. *hiātus, -ūs — hiāre, hiātum*, to gape.]

hibachi *hib-ä′chi, n.* a portable barbecue for cooking food out of doors: — *pl.* **-chi** or **-chis.** [Japanese *hi*, fire, *bachi*, bowl.]

hibakusha *hib-ä′kōō-shə, n.* a survivor of the 1945 atomic bombings of Hiroshima and Nagasaki: — *pl.* **hiba′-kusha.** [Japanese.]

hibernate *hī′bər-nāt, v.i.* to winter: to pass the winter in a resting state. — *ns.* **hī′bernacle** winter quarters: a hibernaculum; **hībernac′ulum** a winter retreat: a bud in Polyzoa that regenerates the colony after winter (*zool.*): a winter-bud, bulb, etc., by which a plant survives the winter (*bot.*): — *pl.* **hībernac′ula.** — *adj.* **hīber′nal** belonging to winter: wintry. — *n.* **hībernā′tion.** — **hibernation anaesthesia** freezing-down. [L. *hībernāre, -ātum — hībernus*, wintry — *hiems*, winter.]

Hibernian *hī-bûr′ni-ən, adj.* relating to Hibernia or Ireland: Irish: characteristic of Ireland. — *n.* an Irishman. — *ns.* **Hiber′nianism, Hiber′nicism** (*-sizm*) an Irish idiom or peculiarity: a bull in speech. — *adv.* **Hiber′nically.** — *v.t.* **hiber′nicise, -ize** (*-sīz*; often with *cap.*) to render Irish. — *n.* **hibernīsā′tion, -z-.** — *v.t.* **hi′bernise, -ize** to hibernicise. [L. *Hībernia*, Ireland.]

Hibiscus *hib-is′kəs, n.* a genus of malvaceous plants, mostly tropical: (without *cap.*) a plant of this genus. [L., — Gr. *ibiskos*, marsh-mallow.]

hic[1] *hik, interj.* representing a hiccup.

hic[2] *hik, hēk,* (L.) this (*demons. pron.*). — **hic et ubique** (*et ū-bī′kwē, ōō-bē′kwe*) here and everywhere; **hic jacet** (*jā′set, yä′ket*) here lies; **hic sepultus** (*sə-pul′tus, se-pōōl′tōōs*) here buried.

hiccatee, hicatee *hik-ə-tē′, n.* a West Indian freshwater tortoise. [From a native name.]

hiccup *hik′up, n.* the involuntary contraction of the diaphragm while the glottis is spasmodically closed: the sound caused by this: a temporary, and usu. minor, difficulty or setback (*fig.*). — *v.i.* to make a hiccup (*lit. and fig.*). — *v.t.* to say with a hiccup: — *pr.p.* **hicc′uping;** *pa.t. and pa.p.* **hicc′uped.** — *adj.* **hicc′upy** marked by hiccups. — Also spelt **hiccough,** etc. [Imit.; an early form was **hicket**; cf. Du. *hik*, Dan. *hik*, Bret. *hik*. The spelling *hiccough* is due to a confusion with *cough*.]

hick *hik, n.* a lout: a booby. — *adj.* pertaining to, or suggestive of, a hick: rural and uncultured. [A familiar form of *Richard.*]

hickery-pickery *hik′ər-i-pik′ər-i.* See **hiera-picra.**

hickey *hik′i, (U.S. coll.) n.* a gadget: a love-bite. [Origin obscure.]

hickory *hik′ər-i, n.* a North American genus (Carya) of the walnut family, yielding edible nuts and heavy strong tenacious wood. [Earlier *pohickery*; of Indian origin.]

hickwall *hik′wöl, (dial.) n.* the green woodpecker. [Origin obscure.]

hid, hidden. See **hide**[1].

hidage. See **hide**[3].

hidalgo *hi-dal′gō, n.* a Spanish nobleman of the lowest class: a gentleman: — *pl.* **hidal′gōs;** *fem.* **hidal′ga,** *pl.* **hidal′gas.** — *adj.* **hidal′gōish.** — *n.* **hidal′gōism.** [Sp.

hijo de algo, son of something.]

hiddenite *hid′ən-īt, n.* a green spodumene, discovered by W. E. *Hidden* (1853–1918).

hidder *hid′ər,* (*Spens.*) *n.* a young male sheep: — *fem.* **shidd′er.** [Perh. **he** and **deer.**]

hide[1] *hīd, v.t.* to conceal: to keep in concealment: to keep secret or out of sight. — *v.i.* to go into, or to stay in, concealment: — *pa.t.* **hid** (*hid*); *pa.p.* **hidden** (*hid′n*), **hid.** — *n.* a hiding-place: a concealed place from which to observe wild animals, etc. — *adj.* **hidd′en** concealed: unknown. — *adv.* **hidd′enly** in a hidden or secret manner. — *n.* **hidd′enness.** — *adj.* **hidd′enmost** most hidden. — *n.* **hid′ing** concealment: a place of concealment. — **hidden economy** see **black economy** under **black;** **hide′-and-(go-)seek′** a game in which one seeks the others, who have hidden themselves; **hide′-away** a fugitive: a place of concealment: a refuge. — *adj.* that hides away. — **hide′out** a retreat; **hid′ing-place; hid′y-hole, hid′ey-hole** (*Scot.* and *U.S.*) a hiding-place. — **hide one's head** (*coll.*) to hide, keep out of sight, from shame, etc. (usu. *fig.*). [O.E. *hȳdan;* cf. M.L.G. *hûden,* and (doubtfully) Gr. *keuthein.*]

hide[2] *hīd, n.* the skin of an animal, esp. the larger animals, sometimes used derogatorily or facetiously for human skin. — *v.t.* to flog or whip: to skin. — *n.* **hīd′ing** a thrashing. — *adj.* **hide′-bound** of animals, having the hide attached so closely to the back and ribs that it is taut, not easily moved: in trees, having the bark so close that it impedes the growth: stubborn, bigoted, obstinate. — **hide (n)or hair of** the slightest trace of (something or someone). — **on a hiding to nothing** in a situation in which one is bound to lose, in spite of all one's efforts; **tan someone's hide** (*coll.*) to whip him. [O.E. *hȳd;* Ger. *Haut,* L. *cutis.*]

hide[3] *hīd, n.* in old English law, a variable unit of area of land, enough for a household. — *n.* **hīd′age** a tax once assessed on every hide of land. [O.E. *hīd,* contracted from *hīgid;* cf. *hīwan, hīgan,* household.]

hide[4] *hīd,* (*Spens.*) *pa.t.* of **hie**[1].

hideous *hid′i-əs, adj.* frightful: horrible: ghastly: extremely ugly: huge (*obs.*). — *ns.* **hideos′ity, hid′eousness.** — *adv.* **hid′eously.** [O.Fr. *hideus, hisdos* — *hide, hisde,* dread, poss. — L. *hispidus,* rough, rude.]

hidlings, hidlins, hidling *hid′lin*(*g*)(*s*), (*Scot.*) *advs.* in secrecy. — *adjs.* secret. — *ns.* a hiding-place or hiding-places: secrecy. [**hid,** and adv. suff. *-ling.*]

hidrosis *hid-rō′sis, n.* sweating, esp. in excess. — *n.* and *adj.* **hidrotic** (*-rot′ik*) sudorific. [Gr. *hidrōs, -ōtos,* sweat.]

hie[1] *hī, v.i.* to hasten (*arch.* or *poet.*). — *v.t.* to urge (on): to pass quickly over (one's way): — *pr.p.* **hie′ing, hy′ing;** *pa.t.* and *pa.p.* **hied.** — *n.* (*obs.*) haste. [O.E. *hīgian.*]

hie[2], **high** *hī,* (*Scot.*) *n.* and *interj.* the call to a horse to turn to the left — opp. to **hup.** — *v.t.* and *v.i.* to turn to the left (of or to a horse or plough-ox).

hielaman *hē′lə-man, n.* an Australian Aboriginal narrow shield of bark or wood. [Native word *hīlaman.*]

Hieland *hēl′ən*(*d*), *-ənt, adj.* a Scots form of **Highland,** — sometimes used with pejorative meanings, e.g. foolish, clumsy, etc., esp. in *neg.,* as in **no sae Hieland** not altogether absurd: not so bad as might be. — Also **Hielan', Hielant.**

hiems *hī′emz,* (*Shak.*) *n.* winter. — *adj.* **hī′emal.** [L. *hiems.*]

Hieracium *hī-ər-ā′shi-əm, n.* the hawkweed genus of Compositae: (without *cap.*) any plant of this genus. [Latinised from Gr. *hierākion,* hawkweed — *hierāx,* hawk.]

hiera-picra *hī′ər-ə-pik′rə, n.* a purgative drug from aloes and canella bark. — Also **hick′ery-pick′ery, hig′ry= pig′ry.** [Gr. *hierā* (fem.), sacred, *pikrā* (fem.), bitter.]

hierarch *hī′ər-ärk, n.* a ruler in holy things: a chief priest: a prelate: an archangel (*Milt.*): one in a high position. — *adjs.* **hī′erarchal, -arch′ic, -al.** — *adv.* **hierarch′ically.** — *ns.* **hī′erarchism; hī′erarchy** the collective body of angels, grouped in three divisions and nine orders of different power and glory; (1) seraphim, cherubim,

thrones; (2) dominations or dominions, virtues, powers; (3) principalities, archangels, angels: each of the three main classes of angels: classification in graded subdivisions: a body or organisation classified in successively subordinate grades: (*loosely*) in an organisation so classified, the group of people who control that organisation: priestly government. [Gr. *hierarchēs* — *hieros,* sacred, *archein,* to rule.]

hieratic *hī-ər-at′ik, adj.* priestly: applying to a certain kind of ancient Egyptian writing which consisted of abridged forms of hieroglyphics; also to certain styles in art bound by religious convention. — *n.* **hīerat′ica** the finest papyrus. [L. *hierāticus* — Gr. *hierātikos* — *hieros,* sacred.]

hierocracy *hī-ər-ok′rə-si, n.* priestly government. — *n.* **hī′erocrat.** — *adj.* **hierocrat′ic.** [Gr. *hieros,* sacred, *krateein,* to rule.]

hierodule *hī′ər-ō-dūl, n.* a temple slave, esp. one engaged in religious prostitution. [Gr. *hieros,* sacred, *doulos,* a slave.]

hieroglyph *hī′ər-ō-glif, n.* a sacred character used in ancient Egyptian picture-writing or in picture-writing in general. — *v.t.* to represent by hieroglyphs. — *adjs.* **hieroglyph′ic, -al.** — *n.* **hieroglyph′ic** a hieroglyph: (in *pl.*) hieroglyphic writing: (in *pl.*) writing that is difficult to read. — *adv.* **hieroglyph′ically.** — *n.* **hieroglyphist** (*-og′*) one skilled in hieroglyphics. [Gr. *hieroglyphikon* — *hieros,* sacred, *glyphein,* to carve.]

hierogram *hī′ər-ō-gram, n.* a sacred or hieroglyphic symbol. — *n.* **hierogramm′at(e)** a writer of sacred records. — *adjs.* **hierogrammat′ic, -al.** — *ns.* **hierogramm′atist; hī′erograph** a sacred symbol; **hierog′rapher** a sacred scribe. — *adjs.* **hierograph′ic, -al** pertaining to sacred writing. — *n.* **hierog′raphy** a description of sacred things. [Gr. *hieros,* sacred, *gramma,* a character, *graphein,* to write.]

hierolatry *hī-ər-ol′ə-tri, n.* the worship of saints or sacred things. [Gr. *hieros,* sacred, *latreiā,* worship.]

hierology *hī-ər-ol′ə-ji, n.* the science of sacred matters, esp. ancient writing and Egyptian inscriptions. — *adj.* **hierologic** (*-ō-loj′ik*). — *n.* **hierol′ogist.** [Gr. *hieros,* sacred, *logos,* discourse.]

hieromancy *hī′ər-ō-man′si, n.* divination by observing the objects offered in sacrifice. [Gr. *hieros,* sacred, *manteiā,* divination.]

Hieronymic *hī-ər-on-im′ik, adj.* of or pertaining to St Jerome. — Also **Hieronym′ian.** — *n.* **Hieron′ymite** a member of any of a number of hermit orders established in the 13th and 14th centuries. [L. *Hierōnymus,* Gr. *Hierōnymos,* Jerome.]

hierophant *hī′ər-ō-fant, n.* one who shows or reveals sacred things: a priest: an expounder. — *adj.* **hierophant′ic.** [Gr. *hierophantēs* — *hieros,* sacred, *phainein,* to show.]

hierophobia *hī-ər-ō-fō′bi-ə, n.* fear of sacred objects. — *adj.* **hierophō′bic.** [Gr. *hieros,* sacred, *phobos,* fear.]

hieroscopy *hī-ər-os′kə-pi, n.* hieromancy. [Gr. *hieros,* sacred, *skopeein,* to look at.]

Hierosolymitan *hī-ə-rō-sol′i-mī-tən, adj.* of or pertaining to Jerusalem. [L. and Gr. *Hierosolyma,* Jerusalem.]

hierurgy *hī′ər-ûr-ji, n.* a sacred performance. — *adj.* **hierur′gical.** [Gr. *hierourgiā* — *hieros,* sacred, *ergon,* work.]

hi-fi, (*rare*) **Hi-Fi,** *hī′fī, n.* high-fidelity sound reproduction: equipment for this, e.g. tape-recorder, record-player, etc.: the use of such equipment, esp. as a hobby. — Also *adj.*

higgle *hig′l, v.i.* to make difficulty in bargaining: to chaffer. — Also **higg′le-hagg′le** (reduplicated variant). — *n.* **higg′ler.** — *n.* and *adj.* **higg′ling.** [Prob. a form of **haggle.**]

higgledy-piggledy *hig′l-di-pig′l-di, adv.* and *adj.* haphazard: in confusion. [Origin obscure.]

high[1] *hī, adj.* elevated: lofty: tall: far up from a base, as the ground, sea-level, low-tide, the mouth of a river, the zero of a scale, etc.: advanced in a scale, esp. the scale of nature: reaching far up: expressible by a large number: of a height specified or to be specified: of advanced degree of intensity: advanced, full (in time, e.g. *season, summer*): of a period, at its peak of development, as *High Renaissance*: of grave importance: advanced: exalted: excellent: eminent: dignified: chief: noble: haughty: arrogant: extreme in opinion: powerful: angry: loud: violent: tempestuous: acute in pitch: luxurious: elated: drunk: over-excited, nervy: under the influence of a drug: standing out: difficult, abstruse: dear: for heavy stakes: remote in time: of meat, etc., slightly tainted: pronounced with some part of the tongue much raised in the mouth (*phon.*): of latitude, far from the equator: of an angle, approaching a right angle: florid. — *adv.* at or to an elevated degree: aloft: shrilly: arrogantly: eminently: powerfully: luxuriously: dear: for heavy stakes. — *n.* that which is high: an elevated region: the highest card: a high level: the maximum, highest level: a euphoric or exhilarated frame of mind (esp. *drug-taking slang*): a high school (*coll.*). — *adj.* high′er, *compar.* of high. — *n.* High′er in Scotland, (a pass in) an examination generally taken at the end of the 5th year of secondary education, more advanced than Ordinary grade. — Also *adj.* — Also Higher grade. — *v.t.* to raise higher: to lift. — *v.i.* to ascend. — *adjs.* high′ermost (*rare*), high′est *superl.* of high; high′ish somewhat high. — *adv.* high′ly in a high degree: in a high position. — *adj.* high′most. — *ns.* high′ness the state of being high: dignity of rank: a title of honour given to princes, princesses, royal dukes, etc.; hight (*hīt*), highth (*hīth*) obsolete forms of height. — high admiral a high or chief admiral of a fleet; high altar see altar; high bailiff an officer who serves writs, etc., in certain franchises, exempt from the ordinary supervision of the sheriff; high′ball (*U.S.*) whisky and soda or the like with ice in a tall glass. — *v.i.* to go at great speed. — *v.t.* to drive very fast. — *adj.* high′-batt′led (hye-battel'd; *Shak.*) app. in command of proud battalions. — high′binder (*U.S.*) a member of a Chinese criminal secret society: a conspirator: a rowdy, ruffian, blackmailer. — *adjs.* high-blest′ (*Milt.*) supremely blest or happy; high′blood′ed of noble lineage; high′-blown swelled with wind: inflated, as with pride (*Shak.*); high′-born of noble birth. — high′boy (*U.S.*) a tallboy. — *adj.* high′-bred of noble breed, training, or family. — high′brow an intellectual. — Also *adj.* — high′-browism; high camp see camp³; high′-chair a baby or young child's tall chair, used esp. at mealtimes. — *adj.* High Church of a party within the Church of England that exalts the authority of the episcopate and the priesthood, the saving grace of sacraments, etc.: of similar views in other churches. — High-Church′ism; High-Church′man. — *adjs.* high′-class superior; high-col′oured having a strong or glaring colour: ruddy: over-vivid. — high comedy comedy set in refined sophisticated society, characterised more by witty dialogue, complex plot and good characterisation than by comical actions or situations; high command the commander-in-chief of the army together with his staff, or the equivalent senior officers of any similar force; High Commission, Commissioner see under commission; high court a supreme court; high cross a town or village cross; high day a holiday or festival: (*dā′*) broad daylight: (*hī′*) heyday (erroneously). — *adj.* befitting a festival. — *adj.* high′-dried brought to an advanced stage of dryness: of fixed and extreme opinions. — High Dutch High German: pure Dutch of Holland (opp. to former *Cape Dutch*); higher criticism see critic; higher education education beyond the level of secondary education, e.g. at a university or college; Higher grade see Higher; high′er-up one occupying an upper position; high′-explos′ive a detonating explosive (e.g. dynamite, T.N.T.) of great power and exceedingly rapid action — also *adj.*; high-falutin(g) (-*lōōt′*) bombastic discourse. — *adj.* affected: pompous. — high feather high spirits: happy trim. — *adj.* high′-fed fed highly or luxuriously: pampered. — high′-feed′ing;

high fidelity good reproduction of sound. — *adj.* high-fidel′ity. — See also hi-fi. — high′-fli′er, -fly′er a bird that flies high: one who runs into extravagance of opinion or action: an ambitious person, or one naturally equipped to reach prominence: (with *cap.*; *hist.*) a High-Churchman, or, in Scotland, an Evangelical. — *adjs.* high′-flown extravagant: elevated: turgid; high′-fly′ing extravagant in conduct or opinion. — high frequency see frequent. — *adj.* high′-gear see gear. — High German of upper or southern Germany: that form of Germanic language affected by the second consonant shift, including the literary language of Germany. — *adj.* high′-grade superior: rich in metal. — *v.t.* to steal rich ore from. — *adj.* high′-grown (*Shak.*) covered with a high growth. — high hand arbitrary arrogance. — *adj.* high′-hand′ed overbearing: arbitrary. — high′-hand′edness; high′-hat′ orig. a wearer of a top-hat: a snob or aristocrat: one who puts on airs: (high′-hat) a pair of cymbals on a stand, the upper one operated by a pedal so as to strike the lower one. — *adj.* affectedly superior. — *v.i.* to put on airs. — *v.t.* to adopt a superior attitude towards or to ignore socially. — *adjs.* high′-heart′ed full of courage; high′-heeled′ having, wearing, high heels. — High Holidays, High Holy Days the Jewish festivals of Rosh Hashanah and Yom Kippur; high′jack, -er see hijack, -er; high jinks boisterous play, jollity: an old Scottish tavern game in which persons played various parts under penalty of a forfeit; high jump (a field event consisting of) a jump for height: punishment, a severe reproof. — *adj.* high′-key of paintings and photographs, having pale tones and very little contrast. — high kick a dancer's kick high in the air, usu. with a straight leg. — *adj.* high′-kilt′ed having the skirt much kilted up: indecorous. — high′land a mountainous district, esp. (in *pl.* Highlands) the north-west of Scotland, bordered geologically by the great fault running from Dumbarton to Stonehaven, or, ethnologically, the considerably narrower area in which Gaelic is or was recently spoken. — *adj.* belonging to or characteristic of a highland, esp. (usu. with *cap.*) the Highlands, of Scotland. — High′lander, High′landman an inhabitant or native of a mountainous region, esp. the Highlands of Scotland; Highland cattle a shaggy breed with very long horns; Highland dress or costume kilt, plaid, and sporran; Highland fling a lively dance of the Scottish Highlands, danced by one person. — *adj.* high′-lev′el at a high level, esp. involving very important people. — high life the life of fashionable society: the people of this society: a blend of traditional West African music and North American jazz, popular in West Africa; high′light outstanding feature: (in *pl.*) the most brightly lighted spots: (usu. in *pl.*) a portion or patch of the hair which reflects the light or which is artificially made lighter than the rest of the hair. — *v.t.* to throw into relief by strong light: also *fig.* — high living luxurious living. — *adv.* high′-lone (*Shak.*) quite alone. — high′-low (*arch.*; often *pl.*) an ankle-high shoe fastened in front. — *adj.* high′ly-strung nervously sensitive, excitable. — high′man a loaded die: — *pl.* high′men; high mass a mass celebrated with music, ceremonies, and incense. — *adjs.* high′-mett′led high-spirited, fiery; high′-mind′ed having a high, proud, or arrogant mind (*rare*): having lofty principles and thoughts. — high′-mind′edness; high-muck-a-muck see separate entry. — *adj.* high′-necked′ of a garment, covering the shoulders and neck. — high noon exactly noon: the peak (*fig.*). — *adjs.* high′-oc′tane (of petrol) of high octane number and so of high efficiency; high′-pitched′ acute in sound, tending towards treble: steep (as a roof): lofty-toned. — high′-place (*B.*) an eminence on which idolatrous rites were performed by the Jews — hence the idols, etc., themselves. — *adj.* high′-placed having a high place: placed high. — high places positions of importance; high point the most memorable, pleasurable, successful, etc. moment or occasion: high spot; high polymer a polymer of high molecular weight. — *adjs.* **high′-pow′ered** very powerful: very forceful and efficient; **high′-press′ure** making or allowing use of steam or other gas at a pressure much above that of the atmosphere: involving intense activity; **high′-priced′** costly. — **high priest** a chief priest; **high priestess; high′-priest′hood.** — *adjs.* **high′-priest′ly; high′-prin′cipled** of high, noble, or strict principle. — **high profile** a conspicuous position. — *adjs.* **high′-pro′file** prominent, public; **high′-proof** proved to contain much alcohol: highly rectified; **high′-raised, -reared** raised aloft: elevated. — **high′-ranker.** — *adjs.* **high′-ranking** senior: eminent; **high′-reach′ing** reaching upwards: ambitious. — **high relief** bold relief, standing out well from the surface. — *adjs.* **high′-rise** (of flats, office blocks, etc.) containing a large number of storeys; **high′-risk′** vulnerable to some sort of danger: potentially dangerous. — **high′road** one of the public or chief roads: a road for general traffic; **high′-roll′er** a plunging spendthrift: one who gambles for high stakes; **high′-roll′ing; high school** a secondary school, in U.K. formerly, often a grammar school; **high seas** the open ocean; **high season** the peak tourist period. — *adjs.* **high′-** or **high′ly-sea′soned** made rich or piquant with spices or other seasoning; **high′-set** placed or pitched high. — **high shoe** (*arch.*) a boot not reaching far above the ankle. — *adj.* **high′-sight′ed** (*Shak.*) looking upwards, supercilious. — **high society** fashionable, wealthy society. — *adjs.* **high′-souled** having a high or lofty soul or spirit; **high′-sound′ing** pompous: imposing; **high′-speed** working, or suitable for working, at a great speed; **high′-spir′ited** having a high spirit or natural fire: bold: daring. — **high spirits** a happy, exhilarated frame of mind; **high spot** an outstanding feature, place, etc.; **high′-stepp′er** a horse that lifts its feet high from the ground: a person of imposing bearing or fashionable pretensions. — *adjs.* **high′-stepp′ing; high′-stom′ached** (*Shak.*) proud-spirited, lofty, obstinate. — **High Street** (sometimes without *cap.*) a common name for the main, or former main, street of a town. — *adj.* **high′-strung** (esp. *U.S.*) highly-strung. — **high table** the dons' table in a college dining-hall. — *v.i.* **high′tail** to hightail it (see below). — **high′-tap′er** hog-taper. — *adj.* **high′-tast′ed** having a strong, piquant taste or relish. — **high tea** a tea with meat, etc., as opposed to a plain tea; **high tech** a style or design of furnishing, etc. imitative of or using industrial equipment; **high technology** advanced, sophisticated technology in specialist fields, e.g. electronics, involving high investment in research and development. — *adjs.* **high′-ten′sion** high-voltage; **high′-test** (of petrol) boiling at comparatively low temperature and so of high performance. — **high tide** high water: a tide higher than usual: a great festival (*rare*); **high time** quite time (that something were done): a time of jollity; **high toby** (*thieves' slang*) see **toby.** — *adj.* **high′-toned** high in pitch: morally elevated: superior, fashionable. — **high′-top** (*Shak.*) a mast-head; **high treason** treason against the sovereign or state; **high′-up** one in high position (also *adj.*). — *adjs.* **high′-veloc′ity** (of shells) propelled at high speed with low trajectory; **high′-viced** (*Shak.*) enormously wicked; **high′-vol′tage** of or concerning a high voltage, one great enough to cause injury or damage. — **high water** the time at which the tide or other water is highest: the greatest elevation of the tide; **high′-wa′ter mark** the highest line so reached: a tide-mark; **high′way** a public road on which all have right to go: the main or usual way or course: a road, path or navigable river (*law*): see **bus** (*comput.*); **Highway Code** (the booklet containing) official rules and guidance on correct procedure for road-users; **high′wayman** a robber who attacks people on the public way; **high wire** a tightrope stretched exceptionally high above the ground; **high words** angry altercation. — *adj.* **high′wrought** wrought with exquisite skill: highly finished: elaborate: worked up, agitated. — **for the high jump** (*coll.*) about to be hanged: about to be reprimanded or chastised; **from**

on high from a high place, heaven, or (*facet.*) a position of authority; **high-alumina cement** a type of quick-hardening cement, made of bauxite and chalk or limestone, found to lose strength through time under certain conditions; **high and dry** up out of the water, stranded; **high and low** rich and poor: up and down: everywhere; **high and mighty** (*ironically*) exalted: arrogant; **high as a kite** (*coll.*) over-excited, drunk, or very much under the influence of drugs; **high-level language** a computer-programming language, e.g. Algol, Fortran (qq.v.), in which statements are written in a form similar to the user's normal language and which can be used in conjunction with a variety of computers (opp. to *low-level language*); **high life below stairs** servants' imitation of the life of their employers; **high-speed steel** an alloy that remains hard when red-hot, suitable for metal-cutting tools; **high (old) time** (*coll.*) a time of special jollity or enthusiasm; **hightail it** (*coll.*) to hurry away; **hit the high spots** to go to excess: to reach a high level; **on high** aloft: in heaven; **on one's high horse** in an attitude of fancied superiority: very much on one's dignity; **on the high ropes** (*coll.*) in an elated or highly excited mood; **running high** see under **feel.** [OE. *hēah*; Goth. *hauhs*, O.N. *hār*, Ger. *hoch*.]

high[2]. See **hie**[2].

high-muck-a-muck *hī-muk-ə-muk′*, (*U.S. coll.*) *n.* an important, pompous person. [Chinook Jargon *hiu*, plenty, *muckamuck*, food.]

hight *hīt*, *Scot.* **hecht** *hehht*, *obs.* **hete** *hēt*, *vs.t.* to command (*obs.*): to promise, assure, vow (*Scot.*): to call, name (*arch.*): to mention (*Spens.*): to commit (*Spens.*): to direct, determine, intend (*Spens.*); — *Spens.* senses not found elsewhere. — *v.i.* (*arch.*, and only in pa.t.; orig. *passive*) to be called or named, to have as a name: — *pa.t.* (*arch.*) **hight**, (*Scot.*) **hecht**, (*Spens.*) **hote;** *pa.p.* (*arch.*) **hight**, (*Scot.*) **hecht**, (*obs.*) **hō′ten.** [O.E. *hēht* (*hēt*), redup. pa.t. of *hātan* (pa.p. *hāten*) substituted for the present and for the last surviving trace of the inflected passive in English, *hātte*, is or was called; cf. Ger. *ich heisse*, I am named, from *heissen*, to call, be called, command.]

highty-tighty *hī′ti-tī′ti*. Same as **hoity-toity.**

higry-pigry *hig′ri-pig′ri*. See **hiera-picra.**

hijacker, highjacker *hī′jak-ər*, *ns.* a highwayman (*hist.*): a robber or blackmailer of rum-runners and bootleggers: one who hijacks. — *vs.t.* **hi′jack, high′jack** to stop and rob (a vehicle): to steal in transit: to force a pilot to fly (an aeroplane) to an unscheduled destination: to force the driver to take (a vehicle or train) to a destination of the hijacker's choice (also *fig.*). — Also *v.i.* [Origin obscure.]

hijinks. Same as **high jinks.**

hijra, hijrah. Same as **hegira.**

hike *hīk*, *v.t.* (usually with *up*; *coll.*) to raise up with a jerk: to increase (e.g. prices), esp. sharply and suddenly. — *v.i.* to hitch: to tramp: to go walking and camping with equipment on back: (of shirts, etc.) to move up out of place. — *n.* a walking tour, outing or march: an increase (in prices, etc.). — *n.* **hi′ker.** [Perh. **hitch.**]

hila, hilar. See **hilum.**

hilarious *hi-lā′ri-əs*, *adj.* gay: extravagantly merry: very funny. — *adv.* **hilā′riously.** — *n.* **hilarity** (*hi-lar′*) gaiety: pleasurable excitement. [L. *hilaris* — Gr. *hilaros*, cheerful.]

Hilary *hil′ər-i*, *adj.* the Spring term or session of the High Court of Justice in England: also the Spring term at Oxford and Dublin universities — from St *Hilary* of Poitiers (d. *c.* 367; festival, Jan. 13).

hilch *hilsh*, (*Scot.*) *v.i.* to hobble. — *v.t.* to lift. — *n.* a limp.

hild *hild* (*Shak.*, *Spens.*). Same as **held.**

Hildebrandism *hil′də-brand-izm*, *n.* the spirit and policy of *Hildebrand* (Pope Gregory VII, 1073–1085), unbending assertion of the power of the Church, etc. — *adj.* **Hildebrand′ic.**

hilding *hild′ing*, (*arch.*) *n.* a mean, cowardly person, a dastard: a worthless beast. — *adj.* cowardly, spiritless. [Prob. conn. with **heel²**.]

hill *hil, n.* a high mass of land, less than a mountain: a mound: an incline on a road. — *v.t.* to form into a hill: to bank up (sometimes for **hele**). — *adj.* **hilled** having hills. — *ns.* **hill′iness; hill′ock** a small hill. — *adjs.* **hill′ocky; hill′y** full of hills. — **hill′-billy** (*U.S.*) a rustic of the hill country. — Also *adj.* — **hill′-digg′er** a rifler of sepulchral barrows, etc. — *ns.pl.* **hill′folk, hill′men** people living or hiding among the hills: the Scottish sect of Cameronians: the Covenanters generally. — **hill′-fort** a fort on a hill: a prehistoric stronghold on a hill; **hill′-pasture; hill′side** the slope of a hill; **hill station** a government station in the hills esp. of Northern India; **hill′top** the summit of a hill. — **hill and dale** (*obs.*; of a gramophone record) with vertical groove undulations; **old as the hills** (*coll.*) immeasurably old; **over the hill** past one's highest point of efficiency, success, etc.: on the downgrade: past the greatest difficulty; **up hill and down dale** vigorously and persistently. [O.E. *hyll*; cf. L. *collis*, a hill, *celsus*, high.]

hillo (*arch.*). Same as **hallo.**

hilt *hilt, n.* the handle, esp. of a sword or dagger (sometimes in *pl.*). — *v.t.* to furnish with a hilt. — **up to the hilt** completely, thoroughly, to the full. [O.E. *hilt*; M.Du. *hilte*; O.H.G. *helza*; not conn. with **hold.**]

hilum *hī′ləm, n.* the scar on a seed where it joined its stalk (*bot.*): the depression or opening where ducts, vessels, etc., enter an organ (*anat.*): — *pl.* **hī′la.** — *adj.* **hī′lar.** — *n.* **hī′lus** a hilum (*anat.*): — *pl.* **hī′lī.** [L. *hīlum*, a trifle, 'that which adheres to a bean'.]

him *him, pron.* the dative and accusative (objective) case of **he:** the proper character of a person. [O.E. *him,* dat. sing. of *hē, he,* he, *hit,* it.]

Himalaya(n) *him-ə-lā′ə(n), hi-mäl′yə(n), adjs.* pertaining to the Himalaya(s), the mountain range along the border of India and Tibet.

himation *hi-mat′i-on, n.* the ancient Greek outer garment, oblong, thrown over the left shoulder, and fastened either over or under the right. [Gr.]

himseems, himseemed. See **seem.**

himself *him-self′, pron.* the emphatic form of **he, him:** in his real character: having command of his faculties: sane: in normal condition: in good form: alone, by himself (*Scot.*): the head of an institution or body of people (e.g. husband; *Scot.*): the reflexive form of **him** (*dat.* and *accus.*). [See **him, self.**]

Himyarite *him′yär-īt, n.* a member of an ancient South Arabian people. — *n.* and *adj.* **Himyaritic** (*-it′ik*). [*Himyar,* a traditional king of Yemen.]

hin *hin, n.* a Hebrew liquid measure containing about four or six English quarts. [Heb. *hīn.*]

Hinayana *hin-ə-yä′nə, n.* Theravada, one of the two main systems of practice and belief into which Buddhism split, the 'Little or Lesser Vehicle' (orig. so called derogatorily by Mahayana (q.v.) Buddhists), the form of Buddhism found in Ceylon and S.E. Asia, holding more conservatively than Mahayana Buddhism to the original teachings of the Buddha and the practices of the original Buddhist communities. — Also *adj.* [Sans. *hīna,* little, lesser, *yāna,* vehicle.]

hind¹ *hīnd, n.* the female of the red deer. — *n.* **hind′berry** the raspberry. [O.E. *hind;* Du. *hinde,* Ger. *Hinde.*]

hind² *hīnd,* (now *Scot.*) *n.* a farm-servant, with cottage on the farm, formerly bound to supply a female field-worker (*bondager*): a rustic. [O.E. *hīna, hīwna,* gen. pl. of *hīwan,* members of a household.]

hind³ *hīnd, adj.* placed in the rear: pertaining to the part behind: backward — opp. to *fore.* — *adj.* **hinder** (*hīn′dər; Scot. hin′ər*) hind: last (*Scot.;* as *this hinder nicht,* last night). — *n.pl.* **hind′erlin(g)s,** less correctly **hinderlan(d)s,** (*hin′ər-lənz; Scot.*) the buttocks. — *adjs.* **hind′ermost, hīnd′most** (superlative of **hind**) farthest behind. — *adj.* and *adv.* **hīnd′ward.** — **hīnd′-brain′** the cerebellum and medulla oblongata; **hin′der-end** (*Scot. hin′ər-en′, -end′*) the latter end: buttocks; **hīnd′foot.** — *adv.* **hīndfore′most** with the back part in the front place.

— **hīnd′-gut** the posterior part of the alimentary canal; **hīnd′head** the back of the head, the occiput; **hīnd′leg.** — *n.pl.* **hīndquar′ters** the rear parts of an animal. — **hīnd′sight** wisdom after the event: the rear sight on a gun, etc.; **hīnd′-wheel; hīnd′-wing.** [O.E. *hinder,* backwards; Goth. *hindar,* Ger. *hinter,* behind; cf. O.E. *hindan* (adv.), back; **behind.**]

hinder *hin′dər, v.t.* to keep back: to stop, or prevent, progress of. — *v.i.* to be an obstacle. — *n.* **hin′derer.** — *adv.* **hin′deringly.** — *n.* **hin′drance** act of hindering: that which hinders: prevention: obstacle. — Also **hin′derance.** [O.E. *hindrian;* Ger. *hindern.*]

hinderland *hin′dər-land,* an Anglicised form of **hinterland.** See also **hind³.**

Hindi *hin′dē, n.* a group of Indo-European languages of Northern India, including Hindustani: a recent literary form of Hindustani, with terms from Sanskrit. — Also *adj.* [Hindi *Hindī* — *Hind,* India.]

hindmost, hindward. See **hind³.**

hindrance. See **hinder.**

Hindu, Hindoo *hin doo′,* or *hin′, n.* a member of any of the races of Hindustan or India (*arch.*): a believer in a form of Brahmanism. — Also *adj.* — *v.t.* and *v.i.* **Hin′duise, -ize.** — *n.* **Hindu′ism** (or *hin′*) the religion and customs of the Hindus. [Pers. *Hindū* — *Hind,* India.]

Hindustani, Hindoostanee *hin-doo-stä′nē, n.* a form of Hindi containing elements from other languages. — Also *adj.*

hing *hing, n.* asafoetida. [Hindi *hĭg* — Sans. *hiṅgu.*]

hinge *hinj, n.* the hook or joint on which a door or lid turns: a joint as of a bivalve shell: the earth's axis (*Milt.*): a small piece of gummed paper used to attach a postage-stamp to the page of an album (also **stamp′-hinge**): a cardinal point: a principle or fact on which anything depends or turns. — *v.t.* to furnish with hinges: to bend. — *v.i.* to hang or turn as on a hinge: to depend (with *on*): — *pr.p.* **hinging** (*hinj′ing*); *pa.t.* and *pa.p.* **hinged** (*hinjd*). — *adj.* **hinge′-bound** unable to move easily on a hinge. — **hinge′-joint** (*anat.*) a joint that allows movement in one plane only. — **off the hinges** disorganised: out of gear. [Related to **hang.**]

hinny¹ *hin′i, n.* the offspring of a stallion and she-ass. [L. *hinnus* — Gr. *ginnos,* later *hinnos,* a mule.]

hinny² *hin′i, n.* a Scottish or N. Eng. variant of **honey.**

hinny³ *hin′i, v.i.* to neigh, whinny. [Fr. *hennir* — L. *hinnīre.*]

hint *hint, n.* moment, opportunity (*obs.*): a distant or indirect indication or allusion: slight mention: insinuation: a helpful suggestion, tip. — *v.t.* to intimate or indicate indirectly. — *v.i.* to give hints. — *adv.* **hint′ingly.** — **hint at** to give a hint, suggestion, or indication of. [O.E. *hentan,* to seize.]

hinterland *hint′ər-land, -länt, n.* a region lying inland from a port or centre of influence. [Ger.]

hip¹ *hip, n.* the haunch or fleshy part of the thigh: the hip-joint: in archit., the external angle formed by the sides of a roof when the end slopes backwards instead of terminating in a gable. — *v.t.* to sprain or hurt the hip of: to throw over the hip: to carry on the hip (*U.S.*): to construct with a hip (*archit.*): — *pr.p.* **hipp′ing;** *pa.t.* and *pa.p.* **hipped, hipt.** — *adj.* **hipped** having a hip or hips: of a roof, sloping at the end as well as at the sides. — *n.* **hipp′ing** (*Scot.*) a baby's napkin wrapped about the hips. — *adj.* **hipp′y** having large hips. — *n.pl.* **hip′sters** (*U.S.* **hip′-hugg′ers**) trousers (for men or women) from the hips, not the waist. — **hip′-bath** a bath to sit in; **hip′-belt** the 14th-century sword-belt, passing diagonally from waist to hip; **hip′-bone** the innominate bone; **hip′-flask** a flask carried in a hip-pocket; **hip′-gir′dle** the pelvic girdle: a hip-belt; **hip′-gout** sciatica; **hip-huggers** see **hipsters; hip′-joint** the articulation of the head of the thigh-bone with the ilium; **hip′-knob** an ornament placed on the apex of the hip of a roof or of a gable; **hip′-lock** in wrestling, a form of cross-buttock; **hip′-pock′et** a trouser pocket behind the hip; **hip′-roof′** a hipped roof. — *adj.* **hip′-**

shot having the hip out of joint. — **have, catch, on the hip** to get an advantage over someone (from wrestling); **hip-joint disease** a disease of the hip-joint with inflammation, fungus growth, caries, and dislocation. [O.E. *hype*; Goth. *hups*, Ger. *Hüfte*.]

hip² *hip*, **hep** *hep*, *ns.* the fruit of the dog-rose or other rose. [O.E. *hēope*.]

hip³, hyp *hip*, *n.* (*arch.*) hypochondria. — *v.t.* to render melancholy or annoyed: to offend. — *adjs.* **hipped** melancholy: peevish, offended, annoyed: obsessed; **hipp′ish.** [hypochondria.]

hip⁴ *hip*, *interj.* an exclamation to invoke a united cheer — **hip′-hip′-hurrah′.**

hip⁵ *hip*, *adj.* a later form of **hep²**. — *ns.* **hipp′ie, hipp′y** one of the hippies, successors of the beatniks as rebels against the values of middle-class society, who stress the importance of love, organise to some extent their own communities, and wear colourful clothes; **hippie′dom, hippy′dom** the life-style, or community, of hippies; **hipster** (*hip′stər*) one who knows and appreciates up-to-date jazz: a member of the beat generation (1950s and early 1960s).

hipp-, hippo- *hip*(-*ō*)-, or (-*o*-), in composition, a horse. — *ns.* **hipp′ophile** a lover of horses; **hipp′ophobe** a hater of horses. [Gr. *hippos*, a horse.]

hipparch *hip′ärk*, *n.* in ancient Greece, a cavalry commander. [Gr. *hipparchos*.]

Hipparion *hi-pā′ri-on*, *n.* a fossil genus of Equidae. [Gr. *hipparion*, dim. of *hippos*, a horse.]

hippeastrum *hip-i-as′trəm*, *n.* any plant of the S. American genus **Hippeastrum**, bulbous, with white or red flowers. [Gr. *hippeus*, horseman, *astron*, star.]

hippety-hoppety *hip′ə-ti-hop′ə-ti*, *adv.* hopping and skipping. — *n.* and *adv.* **hipp′ety-hop′.**

hippiatric *hip-i-at′rik*, *adj.* relating to the treatment of the diseases of horses. — *n.sing.* **hippiat′rics.** — *ns.* **hippiatrist** (*-ī′ət-rist*); **hippiatry** (*-ī′ət-ri*). [Gr. *hippiātrikos* — *hippos*, horse, *iātros*, a physician.]

hippic *hip′ik*, *adj.* relating to horses. [Gr. *hippikos* — *hippos*, horse.]

hippie, hippiedom. See **hip⁵**.

hippo *hip′ō*, *n.* a shortened form of **hippopotamus**: — *pl.* **hipp′os.**

hippo-. See **hipp-.**

hippocampus *hip-ō-kam′pəs*, *n.* a fish-tailed horse-like sea-monster (*myth.*): a genus of small fishes (family Syngnathidae) with horse-like head and neck, the sea-horse: a raised curved trace on the floor of the lateral ventricle of the brain (*anat.*): — *pl.* **hippocamp′ī.** [Gr. *hippokampos* — *hippos*, a horse, *kampos*, a sea-monster.]

Hippocastanaceae *hip-ō-kast-ə-nā′si-ē*, *n.pl.* the horse-chestnut family. [**hippo-**, Gr. *kastanon*, chestnut tree.]

hippocentaur *hip-ō-sent′ör*, *n.* Same as **centaur.** [Gr. *hippokentauros* — *hippos*, a horse, and *kentauros*.]

hippocras *hip′ō-kras*, *n.* spiced wine, formerly much used as a cordial. [M.E. *ypocras*, Hippocrates.]

Hippocratic *hip-ō-krat′ik*, *adj.* pertaining to the Greek physician *Hippocrates* (*Hippokratēs*; born about 460 B.C.). — *v.i.* **Hippocratise, -ize** (*-ok′rə-tīz*) to imitate, follow, Hippocrates. — *n.* **Hippoc′ratism.** — **Hippocratic face, look,** etc., sunken, livid appearance, e.g. near death, described by Hippocrates; **Hippocratic oath** an oath taken by a doctor binding him to observe the code of medical ethics contained in it — first drawn up (perhaps by Hippocrates) in the 4th or 5th century B.C.

Hippocrene *hip-ō-krē′nē, hip′ō-krēn*, (*myth.*) *n.* a fountain on the northern slopes of Mount Helicon, sacred to the Muses and Apollo, attributed to a kick of Pegasus. [Gr. *hippokrēnē* — *hippos*, a horse, *krēnē*, a fountain.]

hippocrepian *hip-ō-krē′pi-ən*, *adj.* horseshoe-shaped. [**hippo-**, Gr. *krēpis*, a shoe.]

hippodame *hip′ō-dām*, *n.* (*Spens.*, wrongly) the sea-horse. — *n.* **hippodamist** (*hip-od′ə-mist*) a horse-tamer. — *adj.*

hippod′amous horse-taming. [**hippo-**, Gr. *damaein*, to tame.]

hippodrome *hip′ə-drōm*, *n.* a racecourse for horses and chariots (*ant.*): a circus: a variety theatre. — *adj.* **hippodromic** (*-drom′*). [Gr. *hippodromos* — *hippos*, a horse, *dromos*, a course.]

hippogriff, hippogryph *hip′ō-grif*, *n.* a fabulous mediaeval animal, a griffin-headed winged horse. [Fr. *hippogriffe* — Gr. *hippos*, a horse, *gryps*, a griffin.]

hippology *hip-ol′ə-ji*, *n.* the study of horses. — *n.* **hippol′ogist.** [**hippo-**, Gr. *logos*, discourse.]

hippomanes *hip-om′ən-ēz*, *n.* an ancient philtre obtained from a mare or foal. [**hippo-**, Gr. *maniā*, madness.]

hippophagy *hip-of′ə-ji*, *-gi*, *n.* feeding on horse-flesh. — *n.* **hippoph′agist** an eater of horse-flesh. — *adj.* **hippoph′agous** (*-gəs*) horse-eating. [**hippo-**, Gr. *phagein* (aor.), to eat.]

hippopotamus *hip-ō-pot′ə-məs*, *n.* a large African artiodactyl ungulate of aquatic habits, with very thick skin, short legs, and a large head and muzzle: — *pl.* **-muses** or **-mī**, sometimes **-mus.** — *adjs.* **hippopotamian** (*-tām′*), **hippopotamic** (*-tam′*, also *-pot′*) like a hippopotamus, clumsy. [L., — Gr. *hippopotamos* — *hippos*, a horse, *potamos*, a river.]

hippuric *hip-ū′rik*, *adj.* denoting an acid, first obtained from the urine of horses, occurring in the urine of many animals, particularly in that of herbivores and rarely in that of human beings. [**hippo-**, Gr. *ouron*, urine.]

Hippuris *hi-pū′ris*, *n.* the mare's-tail genus of Haloragidaceae. — *n.* **hipp′ūrite** a Cretaceous fossil lamellibranch (*Hippurī′tes*) with a conical valve and a flat one. — *adj.* **hippurit′ic.** [**hippo-**, Gr. *ourā*, a tail.]

hippus *hip′əs*, *n.* clonic spasm of the iris. [Mod. L. — Gr. *hippos*, a horse.]

hippy, hippydom. See **hip¹,⁵**.

hipster, hipsters. See **hip¹,⁵**.

hipt. See **hip¹**.

hirable. See **hire.**

hircine *hûr′sīn*, *adj.* goat-like: having a strong goatish smell. — *n.* **hircosity** (*-kos′i-ti*) goatishness. — **hircocervus** (*hûr-kō-sûr′vəs*) a fabulous creature, half goat, half stag. [L. *hīrcus*, a he-goat.]

hirdy-girdy *hûr′di-gûr′di*, (*Scot.*) *adv.* in confusion or tumult.

hire *hīr*, *n.* wages for service: the price paid for the use of anything: an arrangement by which use or service is granted for payment — *v.t.* to procure the use or service of, at a price: to engage for wages: to grant temporary use of for compensation (often with *out*). — *adjs.* **hir′able, hire′able; hired.** — *n.* **hire′ling** a hired servant: a mercenary: one activated solely by material considerations. — Also *adj.* — *ns.* **hir′er** one who obtains use or service for payment: (now *Scot.* or *obs.*) one who lets out on hire; **hir′ing** the act or contract by which an article or service is hired: (also **hiring fair**) a fair or market where servants are engaged (*arch.*). — Also *adj.* — **hire car** a rented car, usu. one rented for a short period; **hire′-pur′chase** a system by which a hired article becomes the hirer's property after a stipulated number of payments. — Also *adj.* — **on hire** for hiring: for hire. [O.E. *hýr*, wages, *hýrian*, to hire.]

hirling. See **herling.**

hirple *hûr′, hir′pl*, (*Scot.*) *v.i.* to walk or run as if lame. — *n.* a limping gait.

hirrient *hir′i-ənt*, *adj.* roughly trilled. — *n.* a trilled sound. [L. *hirriēns*, *-entis*, pr.p. of *hirrīre*, to snarl.]

hirsel *hûr′, hir′sl*, (*Scot.*) *n.* a stock of sheep: a multitude: the ground occupied by a hirsel of sheep. — *v.t.* to put in different groups. [O.N. *hirzla*, safe-keeping — *hirtha*, to herd.]

hirsle *hûr′, hir′sl*, (*Scot.*) *v.i.* to slide, wriggle, or hitch on the hams: to move forward with a rustling sound. [Cf. O.N. *hrista*, to shake.]

hirstie *hirs′, hûrs′ti*, (*obs. Scot.*) *adj.* dry: barren.

hirsute *hûr′sūt*, or *hər-sūt′*, *adj.* hairy: rough: shaggy: having long, stiffish hairs (*bot.*). — *n.* **hirsute′ness.**

[L. *hirsūtus* — *hirsus, hirtus*, shaggy.]
hirudin *hir-ōōd'in, n.* a substance present in the salivary secretion of the leech which prevents blood-clotting. — *n.pl.* **Hirudinea** (*-in'i-ə*) a class of worms, the leeches. — *n.* and *adj.* **hirudin'ean.** — *adjs.* **hirud'inoid; hirud'-inous.** [L. *hirūdō, -inis*, a leech.]
hirundine *hi-run'dīn, -din, adj.* of or pertaining to the swallow. [L. *hirundō, -inis*, a swallow.]
his *hiz, pron., gen.* of **he**, or (*obs.*) of **it** (or *possessive adj.*). — **hisn, his'n** dialectal forms on the analogy of **mine, thine.** [O.E. *his*, gen. of *hē, he*, he, and of *hit*, it.]
hish *hish*, a by-form of **hiss.**
Hispanic *his-pan'ik, adj.* Spanish: of Spanish origin, e.g. Mexican. — Also *n.* — *adv.* **Hispan'ically.** — *vs.t.* **hispan'icise, -ize** (*-i-sīz*; often with *cap.*), **hispan'iolise, -ize** to render Spanish. — *n.* **hispan'icism** a Spanish phrase. [L. *Hispānia*, Spain.]
Hispano- *his-pā'nō-*, in composition, Spanish, as *Hispano-American*, Spanish-American. [L. *hispānus.*]
hispid *his'pid*, (*bot.* and *zool.*) *adj.* rough with, or having, strong hairs or bristles. — *n.* **hispid'ity.** [L. *hīspidus.*]
hiss *his, v.i.* to make a sibilant sound like that represented by the letter *s*, as a goose, snake, gas escaping from a narrow hole, a disapproving audience, etc. — *v.t.* to condemn by hissing: to drive by hissing. — *n.* a sibilant. — *n.* and *adj.* **hiss'ing.** — *adv.* **hiss'ingly.** [Imit.]
hist *hist, st, interj.* demanding silence and attention: hush: silence. — *v.t.* (*hist*) to urge or summon, as by making the sound. — *v.i.* to be silent. [Imit.]
hist-, histio-, histo- *hist-, -(i-)ō-, -o'-*, in composition, tissue: sail. — *ns.* **histaminase** (*-am'i-nās*) an enzyme which helps to break down histamine, often used in the treatment of allergies; **hist'amine** (*-ə-mēn*) a base used in medicine obtained from ergot, from histidine, etc.; present also in all tissues of the body, being liberated into the blood, e.g. when the skin is cut or burnt; **hist'idine** (*-i-dēn*) an amino-acid derived from proteins; **histiocyte** (*-i-ō-sīt'*) a macrophage. — *adjs.* **histiocyt'ic; hist'ioid, hist'oid** like ordinary tissue. — *ns.* **histiol'ogy** same as **histology; Histioph'orus, Istioph'orus** (Gr. *phoros*, bearer) a genus of sword-fishes with sail-like dorsal fin. — *adj.* **histioph'oroid.** — *ns.* **hist'oblast** a cell or group of cells, forming the primary element or unit of tissue; **histochem'istry** the chemistry of living tissues; **histocompatibil'ity** (*genetics*) the factor determining the acceptance or rejection of cells; **hist'ogen** (*bot.*) a more or less well-defined region within a plant where tissues undergo differentiation; **histogenesis** (*-jen'i-sis*) the formation or differentiation of tissues (*biol.*). — *adj.* **histogenetic** (*-ji-net'ik*). — *advs.* **histogenet'ically, histogen'ically.** — *adj.* **histogen'ic.** — *ns.* **histogeny** (*his-toj'i-ni*) histogenesis; **hist'ogram** a statistical graph in which frequency distribution is shown by means of rectangles. — *adjs.* **histolog'ic, -al.** — *adv.* **histolog'ically.** — *ns.* **histologist** (*-tol'*); **histol'ogy** the study of the minute structure of the tissues of organisms; **histol'ysis** (Gr. *lysis*, loosing) the breakdown of organic tissues. — *adj.* **histolytic** (*-ō-lit'ik*). — *adv.* **histolyt'ically.** — *ns.* **his'tone** any of a group of simple proteins, strongly basic and of quite low molecular weights present in chromosomes and believed to act as gene inhibitors; **histopathol'ogist** a pathologist who studies effects of disease on tissues of the body. — *adj.* **histopatholog'ical.** — *n.* **histopathol'ogy; histoplasmō'sis** a disease of animals and man due to infection by the fungal organism *Histoplasma capsulatum.* [Gr. *histos* and *histion*, a web.]
histie same as **hirstie.**
history *hist'ər-i, n.* an account of an event: a systematic account of the origin and progress of the world, a nation, an institution, a science, etc.: the knowledge of past events: a course of events: a life-story: an eventful life, a past of more than common interest: a drama representing historical events. — *v.t.* to record (*Shak.*). — *n.* **historian** (*his-tō'ri-ən, -tö'*) a writer of history (usu. in the sense of an expert, an authority, on). — *adjs.* **histo'riāted** decorated with elaborate

ornamental designs and figures (also **sto'riated**); **historic** (*-tor'ik*) famous or important in history; **histor'-ical** pertaining to history: containing history: derived from history: associated with history: according to history: authentic. (Formerly *historic* and *historical* were often used interchangeably.) — *adv.* **histor'ically.** — *v.t.* **histor'icise, -ize** (*-sīz*) to make, or represent as, historic. — *ns.* **histor'icism, hist'orism** a theory that all sociological phenomena are historically determined: a strong or excessive concern with, and respect for, the institutions of the past. — *n.* and *adj.* **histor'icist.** — *ns.* **historicity** (*hist-ər-is'i-ti*) historical truth or actuality; **historiette'** a short history or story. — *v.t.* **histor'ify** to record in history. — *n.* **historiog'rapher** a writer of history (esp. an official historian). — *adjs.* **historiograph'ic, -al.** — *adv.* **historiograph'ically.** — *ns.* **historiog'raphy** the art or employment of writing history; **historiol'ogy** the knowledge or study of history; **historism** see **historicism.** — **historical materialism** the Marxist theory that all historic processes and forms of society are based on economic factors; **historical method** the study of a subject in its historical development; **historical novel** a novel having as its setting a period in history and involving historical characters and events; **historical painting** the painting of historic scenes in which historic figures are introduced; **historical present** the present tense used for the past, to add life and reality to the narrative; **historical school** those, esp. in the fields of economics, legal philosophy and ethnology, who emphasise historical circumstance and evolutionary development in their researches and conclusions. — **make history** to do that which will mould the future or have to be recognised by future historians: to do something never previously accomplished. [L. *historia* — Gr. *historiā* — *histōr*, knowing.]
histrionic, -al *his-tri-on'ik, -əl, adjs.* relating to the stage or actors: stagy, theatrical: affected: melodramatic: hypocritical. — *adv.* **histrion'ically.** — *ns.* (*arch.*) **his'triō** (from L.; *pl.* **his'trios**), **his'triōn** (from Fr.) an actor; **histrion'icism, his'trionism** acting: theatricality. — *n.pl.* **histrion'ics** play-acting: stagy action or speech: insincere exhibition of emotion. [L. *histriōnicus* — *histriō*, an actor.]
hit *hit, v.t.* to strike: to reach with a blow or missile (also *fig.*): to come into forceful contact with: to knock (e.g. oneself, one's head): to inflict (a blow): to drive by a stroke: to move on to (a road), reach (a place): (of news) to be published in (*coll.*): to light upon, or attain, by chance: to imitate exactly: to suit, fit, conform to: to hurt, affect painfully (*fig.*). — *v.i.* to strike: to make a movement of striking: to come in contact: to arrive suddenly and destructively: to come, by effort or chance, luckily (upon): to suit (with) (*obs.*): (of an internal combustion engine) to ignite the air and fuel mixture in the cylinders: to inject a dose of a hard drug (*slang*): to murder (*slang*): — *pr.p.* **hitt'ing;** *pa.t.* and *pa.p.* **hit.** — *n.* an act or occasion of striking: a successful stroke or shot: a lucky chance: a surprising success: an effective remark, e.g. a sarcasm, witticism: something that pleases the public or an audience: at backgammon, a move that throws one of the opponent's men back to the entering point, or a game won after one or two men are removed from the board: a murder by a gang of criminals (*slang*): a dose of a hard drug (*slang*). — *n.* **hitt'er.** — *adjs.* **hit'-and-miss'** hitting or missing, according to circumstances; **hit'-and-run'** (e.g. of an air raid) lasting only a very short time: (of a driver) causing injury and running away without reporting the incident: (of an accident) caused by a hit-and-run driver. — **hit list** (*slang*) a list of people to be killed by gangsters or terrorists (also *fig.*); **hit'-man** (*slang*) one employed to kill or attack others (also *fig.*). — *adj.* **hit'-or-miss'** random. — **hit'-parade** a list of currently popular songs: a list of the most popular things of any kind (*fig.*). — *adj.* **hitt'y-miss'y** random, haphazard. — **a hit or a miss** a case in which either success or complete failure is possible; **hard hit** gravely

affected by some trouble, or by love; **hit a blot** to capture an exposed man in backgammon: to find a weak place; **hit at** to aim a blow, sarcasm, jibe, etc., at; **hit below the belt** see **belt**; **hit it** to find, often by chance, the right answer; **hit it off** to agree, be compatible and friendly (sometimes with *with*); **hit it up** (*slang*) to inject a drug; **hit off** to imitate or describe aptly (someone, something); **hit on** or **upon** to come upon, discover, devise: to single out; **hit out** to strike out, esp. with the fist: to attack strongly (absolute or with *at*); **hit the bottle** (*slang*) to drink excessively; **hit the ceiling** or **roof** to be seized with, express, violent anger; **hit the high spots** see **high**[1]; **hit the nail on the head** see **nail**; **hit the road** (*slang*) to leave, go away; **hit the sack, hay** (*slang*) to go to bed; **hit wicket** the act, or an instance, of striking the wicket with bat or part of the body (and thus being out) (*cricket*); **make a hit with** to become popular with: to make a good impression on. [O.E. *hyttan*, app. O.N. *hitta*, to light on, to find; Sw. *hitta*, to find, Dan. *hitte*, to hit upon.]

hitch *hich*, *v.i.* to move jerkily: to hobble or limp: to catch on an obstacle: to connect with a moving vehicle so as to be towed (orig. *U.S.*): to travel by getting lifts. — *v.t.* to jerk: to hook: to catch: to fasten: to tether: to harness to a vehicle: to make fast: to throw into place: to bring in (to verse, a story, etc.), esp. with obvious straining or effort: to obtain (a lift) in a passing vehicle. — *n.* a jerk: a limp or hobble: a catch or anything that holds: a stoppage owing to a small or passing difficulty: a species of knot by which one rope is connected with another, or to some object (*naut.*): a means of connecting a thing to be dragged: a mode or act of harnessing a horse or horses, a team, or a vehicle with horses (*U.S.*): a lift in a vehicle: a slight fault or displacement in a bed of sedimentary rock (*mining*): a recess cut in rock to support a timber (*mining*). — *n.* **hitch′er.** — *adv.* **hitch′ily.** — *adj.* **hitch′y.** — *v.i.* **hitch′-hike** to hike with the help of lifts in vehicles. — **hitch′-hike; hitch′-hiker; hitching post** a post, etc. to which a horse's reins can be tied. — **clove hitch** a type of knot by which a rope is attached to a pole, spar or rope thicker than itself; **get hitched** (*slang*) to get married; **hitch and kick** a technique in high jumping whereby the athlete springs from, kicks with, and lands on, the same foot; **hitch up** to harness a horse to a vehicle: to jerk up: to marry (*slang*); **timber hitch** a knot for tying a rope round a log, etc. for hauling. [Ety. obscure.]

hithe *hīdh*, *n.* a small haven or port, esp. a landing-place on a river. Now *obs.* except in historical use or in place names. [O.E. *hȳth*.]

hither *hidh′ər*, *adv.* to this place. — *adj.* on this side or in this direction: nearer. — *v.i.* to come — chiefly in phrase *to hither and thither*, i.e. to go to and fro. — *adj.* **hith′ermost** nearest on this side. — **hith′erside** the nearer side. — *advs.* **hith′erto** up to this time: to this point or place (*arch.*); **hith′erward(s)** (*arch.*) towards this place. — **hither and thither** to and fro: this way and that. [O.E. *hider*; Goth. *hidrē*, O.N. *hethra*.]

Hitler *hit′lər*, (*coll.*) *n.* a person similar in character to Adolf *Hitler* (1889–1945), German Nazi dictator, overbearing or despotic (also (*contemptuous*) **little Hitler**). — *n.* **Hitlerism** (*hit′lər-izm*) the principles, policy, and methods of Hitler, i.e. militant anti-Semitic nationalism, subordinating everything to the state. — *ns.* and *adjs.* **Hit′lerist, Hit′lerite.**

Hitopadesa *hē-tō-pä-dā′shə*, *n.* a collection of fables and stories in Sanskrit literature, a popular summary of the *Panchatantra*. [Sans. *Hitopadeśa*.]

Hittite *hit′īt*, *n.* one of the Khatti or Heth, an ancient people of Syria and Asia Minor: an extinct language belonging to the Anatolian group of languages and discovered from documents in cuneiform writing. — Also *adj.* [Heb. *Hitti*; Gr. *Chettaios*.]

hive *hīv*, *n.* a box or basket in which bees live and store up honey: a colony of bees: a scene of great industry: a teeming multitude or breeding-place: a hat of plaited straw shaped like an old beehive (*obs.*). — *v.t.* to collect into a hive: to lay up in store (often with *away* or *up*). — *v.i.* of bees, to enter or take possession of a hive: to take shelter together: to reside in a hive. — *adjs.* **hive′less; hive′like.** — *n.* **hīv′er** one who hives. — *adj.* and *adv.* **hive′ward.** — *adv.* **hive′wards.** — **hive′-bee** common honey-producing bee, *Apis mellifica*; **hive′=hon′ey; hive′-nest** large nest built and occupied by several pairs of birds in common. — **hive off** to withdraw as if in a swarm: to assign (work) to a subsidiary company: to divert (assets or sections of an industrial concern) to other concerns: — *n.* **hive′-off.** [O.E. *hȳf*.]

hives *hīvz*, *n.* a popular term for nettlerash and similar diseases or for laryngitis. [Origin unknown.]

hiya *hī′yə*, (*slang*) *interj.* a greeting developed from how are you.

Hizen *hē-zen′*, (also without *cap.*) *adj.* of a type of richly decorated Japanese porcelain. Also *n.* [*Hizen* province in Kyushu, Japan.]

hizz *hiz*, *v.i.* (*Shak.*) to hiss. [Echoic.]

ho, hoa, hoh *hō*, *interj.* a call to excite attention, to announce destination or direction, to express exultation, surprise, or (repeated) derision or laughter: hullo: hold: stop. — *n.* cessation: moderation: — *pl.* **hos, hoas, hohs.** — *v.i.* (*obs.*) to stop. [Cf. O.N. *hō*, Fr. *ho*.]

hoactzin. See **hoatzin.**

hoar *hōr, hör*, *adj.* white or greyish-white, esp. with age or frost: mouldy (*obs.*). — *n.* hoariness: age. — *v.i.* (*Shak.*) to become mouldy. — *v.t.* (*Shak.*) to make hoary. — *adv.* **hoar′ily.** — *n.* **hoar′iness.** — *adj.* **hoar′y** white or grey with age: ancient: covered with short, dense, whitish hairs (*bot., entom.*). — **hoar′-frost** rime or white frost, the white particles formed by the freezing of the dew; **hoar′head** a hoary-headed old man. — *adj.* **hoar′-head′ed.** — **hoar′-stone** (*Scot.* **hare′=stane**) an old hoary stone: a standing-stone or ancient boundary stone. [O.E. *hār*, hoary, grey; O.N. *hārr*.]

hoard[1] *hōrd, hörd*, *n.* a store: a hidden stock: a treasure: a place for hiding anything (*obs.*). — *v.t.* to store, esp. in excess: to treasure up: to amass and deposit in secret. — *v.i.* to store up: to collect and form a hoard. — *n.* **hoard′er.** [O.E. *hord*; O.N. *hodd*, Ger. *Hort*.]

hoard[2] *hōrd, hörd*, **hoarding** *hōrd′ing, hörd′*, *ns.* a screen of boards, esp. for enclosing a place where builders are at work, or for display of bills. [O.Fr. *hurdis* — hurt, hourt, hourd, a palisade.]

hoarhound. See **horehound.**

hoarse *hōrs, hörs*, *adj.* rough and husky: having a rough husky voice, as from a cold: harsh: discordant. — *adv.* **hoarse′ly.** — *v.t.* and *v.i.* **hoars′en.** — *n.* **hoarse′ness.** [M.E. *hors, hoors* — O.E. *hās*, inferred *hārs*.]

hoast *hōst*, (*dial.*) *n.* a cough. — *v.i.* to cough. [O.N. *hōste*; cf. O.E. *hwōsta*; Du. *hoest*.]

hoastman *hōst′man*, *n.* a member of an old merchant guild in Newcastle, with charge of coal-shipping, etc. [O.Fr. *hoste* — L. *hospes*, stranger, guest.]

hoatzin *hō-at′sin*, **hoactzin** *-akt′*, *ns.* the stink-bird (*Opisthocomus*), a S. American bird forming an order by itself, with occipital crest, great crop, peculiar sternum, and, in the tree-climbing and swimming young, clawed wings. [Nahuatl *uatsin*.]

hoax *hōks*, *n.* a deceptive trick played as a practical joke or maliciously. — Also *adj.* — *v.t.* to trick, by a practical joke or fabricated tale, for sport or maliciously. — *n.* **hoax′er.** [App. **hocus.**]

hob[1] *hob*, *n.* a hub: a surface beside a fireplace, on which anything may be laid to keep hot: the flat framework or surface on top of a gas, etc. cooker on which pots are placed to be heated: a game in which stones are thrown at coins on the end of a short stick — also the stick used: a gear-cutting tool. — **hob′nail** a nail with a thick strong head, used in horseshoes, heavy workshoes, etc. — *v.t.* to furnish with hobnails: to trample upon with hobnailed shoes. — *adj.* **hob′nailed.** [Cf. **hub.**]

hob[2] *hob*, *n.* a rustic: a lout: a fairy or brownie (as Robin

Goodfellow): a clownish fellow: a male ferret: mischief. — *adj.* **hobb'ish** clownish. — *ns.* **Hobb'inoll** a rustic (from Spenser's *Shepheards Calender*); **hob'-goblin** a mischievous fairy: a frightful apparition; **hobgob'linism, hobgob'linry.** — **play hob, raise hob** to make confusion. [For *Robert*.]

hob-a-nob, hob-and-nob. Same as **hobnob.**

Hobbesian *hobz'i-ən*, **Hobbian** *hob'i-ən*, *adjs.* relating to Thomas *Hobbes* (1588–1679) or his political philosophy. — *ns.* a follower of Hobbes. — *ns.* **Hobbes'ianism, Hobb'ianism, Hobb'ism; Hobb'ist** a Hobbian. — *adjs.* **Hobb'ist, Hobbist'ical.**

hobbit *hob'it*, *n.* one of a race of imaginary beings, half human size, hole-dwelling and hairy-footed, invented by J.R.R. Tolkien in his novel *The Hobbit* (1937). — *n.* **hobb'itry.**

hobble *hob'l*, *v.i.* to walk with short unsteady steps: to walk awkwardly: (of action, verse, speech, etc.) to move irregularly. — *v.t.* to fasten the legs of (a horse) loosely together: to hamper: to perplex. — *n.* an awkward hobbling gait: a difficulty, a scrape (*arch.*): anything used to hamper the feet of an animal, a clog or fetter. — *ns.* **hobb'ler** one who hobbles: an unlicensed pilot, a casual labourer in docks, etc.: a man who tows a canal-boat with a rope; **hobb'ling.** — *adv.* **hobb'lingly.** — **hobb'le-bush** the N. American wayfaring-tree (*Viburnum alnifolium*), a small shrub with white flowers and straggling branches that impede movement among them; **hobble skirt** a narrow skirt that hampers walking. [Cf. Du. *hobbelen, hobben,* to toss: and **hopple.**]

hobbledehoy *hob'l-di-hoi'*, *n.* an awkward youth, a stripling, neither man nor boy.—*ns.* **hobbledehoy'dom, hobbledehoy'hood, hobbledehoy'ism.** — *adj.* **hobbledehoy'ish.** [Origin obscure.]

hobbler *hob'lər*, (*obs.*) *n.* one bound to keep a hobby (horse) for military service: a horseman employed for light work, as reconnoitring, etc.: a horse. [O.Fr. *hobeler* — *hobin*, a small horse.]

hobby[1] *hob'i*, *n.* a small or smallish strong, active horse: a pacing horse: a subject on which one is constantly setting off, as in *to ride* or *to mount a hobby*(*-horse*): a favourite pursuit followed as an amusement: a hobbyhorse: an early form of bicycle. — *ns.* **hobb'yism; hobb'yist** one who rides or pursues a hobby. — *adj.* **hobb'yless.** — **hobb'y-horse** a stick or figure of a horse straddled by children: one of the chief parts played in the ancient morris-dance: the wooden horse of a merry-go-round: a rocking-horse: a dandy-horse: a loose and frivolous person, male or female (*Shak.*): a hobby. — *adj.* **hobby-hors'ical** whimsically given to a hobby. [M.E. *hobyn, hoby,* prob. *Hob,* a by-form of *Rob*. O.Fr. *hobin, hobi* (Fr. *aubin*), is from the English.]

hobby[2] *hob'i*, *n.* a small species of falcon. [O.Fr. *hobé; hobet* — L.L. *hobētus*; prob. O.Fr. *hober,* to move.]

hobday *hob'dā*, *v.t.* to cure a breathing impediment in (a horse) by surgical operation. — *adj.* **hob'dayed.** [After Sir Frederick *Hobday* (1869–1939).]

hobgoblin. See **hob**[2].

hobjob *hob'job*, (*dial.*) *n.* an odd job. — *v.i.* to do odd jobs. — *ns.* **hob'jobber; hob'jobbing.**

hobnail. See **hob**[1].

hobnob *hob'nob*, *adv.* at a venture: hit-or-miss: with alternate or mutual drinking of healths. — *v.i.* to associate or drink together familiarly: to talk informally (with): — *pr.p.* **hob'nobbing.** — *n.* a sentiment in drinking (*obs.*): mutual healthdrinking: a familiar private talk. — *adj.* **hob'nobby.** [Prob. *hab nab*, have or have not (ne have); cf. *Twelfth Night*, III, iv. 'Hob, nob, is his word; give 't or take 't'.]

hobo *hō'bō*, *n.* an itinerant workman: a tramp, esp. of the bold type: — *pl.* **ho'boes.** — *v.t.* to travel as a hobo. — *ns.* **ho'bodom, ho'boism.** [Origin unknown.]

Hobson-Jobson *hob'sən-job'sən*, *n.* festal excitement, esp. at the Moharram ceremonies: the modification of names and words introduced from foreign languages, which the popular ear assimilates to already familiar

sound, as in the case of the word Hobson-Jobson itself. [Ar. *Yā Hasan! Yā Hosain!* a typical phrase of Anglo-Indian argot at the time adopted as an alternative title for Yule and Burnell's *Glossary of Anglo-Indian Colloquial Words and Phrases* (1886).]

Hobson's choice. See **choice.**

hoc *hok, hōk,* (L.) *adj., pron.* this. — **hoc anno** (*an'ō*) in this year; **hoc genus omne** (*jēn'əs, gen'ōōs, om'ne*) all that sort; **hoc loco** (*lōk', lok'ō*) in this place; **hoc tempore** (*tem'pə-rē, -po-re*) at this time.

hock[1] *hok,* **hough** *hok* (*Scot. hohh*), *n.* joint on hindleg of a quadruped, between the knee and fetlock, and sometimes on the leg of a domestic fowl, corresponding to the ankle-joint in man: a piece of meat extending from the hock-joint upward: in man, the back part of the knee-joint: the ham. — *v.t.* to hamstring. — *n.* **hock'er.** [O.E. *hōh,* the heel.]

hock[2] *hok,* (*slang*) *v.t.* to pawn. — *n.* the state of being in pawn. — **in hock** in debt: in prison: having been pawned, in pawn (*coll.*). [Du. *hok,* prison, hovel.]

hock[3] *hok, n.* properly, the wine made at *Hochheim,* on the Main, in Germany: now applied to all white Rhine wines. [Obs. *Hockamore* — Ger. *Hochheimer.*]

hock[4] *hok, v.t.* to subject to Hock-tide customs. — *v.i.* to observe Hock-tide. — **Hock'-day** (Hock Tuesday) an old English festival held on the second Tuesday after Easter Sunday, one of the chief customs being the seizing and binding of men by women until they gave money for their liberty: (in *pl.*) Hock Tuesday and the preceding day (**Hock Monday**) on which the men seized the women in like manner; **Hock'-tide** the two Hock-days. [Origin unknown.]

hockey[1] *hok'i, n.* a ball game played with a club or stick curved at one end, a development of shinty: a hockey stick (*U.S.*): ice hockey. — Also **hook'ey.** [Prob. O.Fr. *hoquet,* a crook.]

hockey[2] *hok'i,* (*dial.*) *n.* harvest-home, the harvest-supper. — Also **hawk'ey, hork'ey.** — **hock'-cart** the cart that brings home the last load of the harvest. [Origin unknown.]

hockey[3]. See **oche.**

hocus-pocus *hō'kəs-pō'kəs, n.* a juggler (*obs.*): a juggler's trick or formula: jugglery: deception: mumbo-jumbo. — *v.i.* to juggle. — *v.t.* to play tricks on. — *v.t.* **hoc'us** to cheat: to stupefy with drink: to drug (drink): — *pr.p.* **hō'cus(s)ing;** *pa.t.* and *pa.p.* **hō'cus(s)ed.** [Sham Latin.]

hod[1] *hod, n.* a V-shaped stemmed trough for carrying bricks or mortar on the shoulder: a coal-scuttle: a pewterer's blowpipe. — **hod carrier, hod'man** a man who carries a hod: a mason's labourer. [Cf. dial. *hot, hott,* M.H.G. *hotte,* obs. Du. *hodde,* Fr. *hotte,* a basket.]

hod[2] *hod,* (*Scot.*) *v.i.* to bob: to jog. — *v.i.* **hodd'le** (*Scot.*) to waddle.

hodden *hod'n, n.* coarse, undyed homespun woollen cloth. — *adj.* of or clad in hodden: rustic. — **hodd'en-grey** hodden made of mixed black and white wool. — Also *adj.* [Origin unknown.]

hoddy-doddy. See **hodmandod.**

Hodge *hoj, n.* a countryman, rustic. [For *Roger*.]

hodgepodge *hoj'poj, n.* see **hotchpotch.** — **hodge'-pudd'ing** (*Shak.*) a pudding made of a mass of ingredients mixed together.

Hodgkin's disease *hoj'kinz diz-ēz', a* disease in which the spleen, liver and lymph nodes become enlarged, and progressive anaemia occurs. [After Thomas *Hodgkin,* 19th cent. British physician.]

hodiernal *hō-di-ûrn'əl, adj.* of or pertaining to the present day. [L. *hodiernus* — *hodiē,* to-day = *hōc diē,* on this day.]

hodja. See **khoja.**

hodmandod *hod'mən-dod, n.* a shelled snail. — *n.* **hodd'y-dodd'y** (*obs.*) a dumpy person: a duped husband: a noodle. [Cf. **dodman.**]

hodograph *hod'ə-gräf,* (*math.*) *n.* a curve whose radius vector represents the velocity of a moving point. [Gr.

hodos, a way, *graphein,* to write.]

hodometer, now usu. **odometer,** *hod-om'i-tər, od-, ns.* an instrument attached to a wheel for measuring distance travelled. — *ns.* **hodom'etry, odom'etry.** [Gr. *hodos,* a way, *metron,* a measure.]

hodoscope *hod'ə-skōp,* (*phys.*) *n.* any apparatus for tracing the paths of charged particles. [Gr. *hodos,* a way, *skopeein,* to see.]

hoe¹ *hō, n.* an instrument for scraping or digging up weeds and loosening the earth. — *v.t.* to scrape, remove, or clean with a hoe: to weed. — *v.i.* to use a hoe: — *pr.p.* **hoe'ing;** *pa.t.* and *pa.p.* **hoed.** — *n.* **hō'er.** — **hoe'-cake** (*U.S.*) a thin cake of Indian meal (originally baked on a hoe-blade); **hoe'down** (esp. *U.S.*) a country-dance, esp. a square dance: hillbilly or other music for it: a party at which such dances are performed. [O.Fr. *houe* — O.H.G. *houwâ* (Ger. *Haue*), a hoe.]

hoe² *hō, n.* a promontory or projecting ridge (now only in place-names). [O.E. *hōh,* heel; cf. **heugh.**]

Hof *hof, hôf,* (Ger.) *n.* yard: manor: court.

hog¹ *hog, n.* a general name for swine: a castrated boar: a pig reared for slaughter: a yearling sheep not yet shorn (also **hogg**): the wool from such a sheep: a yearling of other species: formerly slang for a shilling: a low filthy fellow: a greedy person: an inconsiderate boor: a person of coarse manners: a frame or brush which is hauled along a ship's bottom to clean it. — *v.t.* and *v.i.* to eat hoggishly: to arch or hump like a hog's back, esp. of the hull of a ship. — *v.t.* to cut like a hog's mane: to behave like a hog or a road-hog towards: to take or use selfishly: — *pr.p.* **hogg'ing;** *pa.t.* and *pa.p.* **hogged.** — *adj.* **hogged** (*hogd*). — *ns.* **hogg'erel** a yearling sheep; **hogg'ery** hogs collectively: hoggishness of character: coarseness; **hogg'et** a yearling sheep or colt. — *adj.* **hogg'ish.** — *adv.* **hogg'ishly.** — *ns.* **hogg'ishness; hog'hood** the nature of a hog. — **hog'-back, hog's'-back** a hill-ridge, an ancient monument, or other object, shaped like a hog's back, i.e. curving down towards the ends; **hog'-chol'era** swine-fever; **hog'-deer** a small Indian deer; **hog'-fish** a fish having bristles on the head; **hog'-frame** a frame built to resist vertical flexure; **hog'-mane** a mane clipped short or naturally short and upright. — *adj.* **hog'-maned.** — **hog'-nose** an American snake (*Heterodon;* various species); **hog'-pen** a pig-sty; **hog'-plum** a West Indian tree (*Spondias*) of the cashew family, the fruit relished by hogs; **hog'-rat** the hutia, a West Indian rodent (*Capromys*); **hog'-reeve, -con'stable** an officer whose duty was to round up stray swine; **hog'-ring'er** one who puts rings into the snouts of hogs. — *v.t.* **hog'-shouther** (*-shōō'dhər; Scot.*) to jostle with the shoulder. — **hog'-skin** leather made of the skin of swine; **hog's pudding** a hog's entrails stuffed with various ingredients. — *v.t.* **hog'tie** to tie (a person) up so as to be unable to move arms or legs (also *fig.*). — **hog'ward** (*-wörd*) a swine-herd; **hog'wash** the refuse of a kitchen, brewery, etc., given to pigs: thin worthless stuff: insincere nonsense; **hog'weed** the cow-parsnip: applied also to many other coarse plants. — **bring one's hogs to a fine market** to make a complete mess of something; **go the whole hog** see **whole; hog in armour** a boor in fine clothes; **hog it** (*slang*) to eat greedily: to live in a slovenly fashion. [O.E. *hogg.*]

hog² *hog, n.* in curling, a stone that does not pass the hog-score. — *v.t.* to play a hog. — **hog'-line, hog'-score** a line drawn across the rink short of which no stone counts. [Perh. **hog¹.**]

hog³ *hog,* (*dial.*) *n.* a mound of earth and straw in which potatoes, etc., are stored. — *v.t.* to store (potatoes, etc.) in such a heap. [Origin obscure.]

hogan¹ *hō'gən, n.* a log hut, usu. covered with earth, built by the Navaho tribe of North American Indians. [Navaho.]

hogan². See under **hogen-mogen.**

hogen-mogen *hō'gən-mō'gən,* (*obs.*) *n.* haughtiness: (usu. in *pl.*) the Dutch States General. — *adj.* high and mighty: Dutch: (of liquor) strong. — *n.* **ho'gan, ho'gen**

strong liquor. [Du. *hoog en mogend,* high and mighty.]

hogg, hoggerel, hogget, etc. See under **hog¹.**

hogger *hog'ər,* (*Scot.*) *n.* a footless stocking worn as a gaiter: a short connecting-pipe. [Origin obscure.]

hoggin, hogging *hog'in, n.* sifted gravel: a mixture containing gravel. [Origin uncertain.]

hogh. A Spenserian spelling of **hoe².**

Hogmanay *hog-mə-nā', (Scot.) n.* the last day of the year: a refection or gift begged or bestowed then. [Prob. from North Fr. dial. *hoginane* — 16th cent. *aguillanneuf* (*-l'an neuf*) a gift at the New Year.]

hogshead *hogz'hed, n.* a large cask (*Shak.*): a measure of capacity = 52½ imperial gallons, or 63 old wine gallons; *of beer* = 54 gallons; *of claret* = 46 gallons; *of tobacco* (*U.S.*) = 750 to 1200 lb. [App. **hog's,** and **head;** reason unknown.]

hogtie, hogward, hogwash, hogweed. See **hog¹.**

hoh *hō.* See **ho.**

ho-hum *hō'-hum', (coll.) adj.* dull, apathetic: boring, routine.

hoi *hoi,* (*coll.*) *interj.* used to attract attention.

hoick, hoik *hoik, n.* a jerk. — *v.t.* and *v.i.* to hitch up: (esp. of aeroplanes) to jerk upwards. [Cf. **hike.**]

hoicks *hoiks, interj.* a cry to urge hounds. — *v.t.* to urge on with cries. — *v.i.* to shout hoicks: to hark back.

hoiden. See **hoyden.**

hoi polloi *hoi'-pə-loi', (Gr.)* the many: the rabble, the vulgar.

hoise *hoiz,* (*arch.*) *v.t.* to hoist: — *pa.t.* and *pa.p.* **hoised, hoist.** — **hoist with his own petar(d)** (*Shak.*) blown up with his own explosive device, caught in his own trap. [Perh. Old Du. *hijssen,* Du. *hijschen,* to hoist.]

hoist *hoist, v.t.* to lift: to heave upwards: to raise or move with tackle: to steal (*slang*). — *n.* act of lifting: the height of a sail: that part of a flag next to the mast: a lift for heavy goods. — *n.* **hoist'er** one who, or that which, lifts: a shoplifter (*slang*). — **hoist'man** one who works a hoist; **hoist'way** a hoist shaft. [Pa.t. and pa.p. of **hoise** (q.v.).]

hoisting *hōst'ing* (*Scott*). Same as **hosting** (see **host²**).

hoity-toity *hoi'ti-toi'ti, interj.* an exclamation of surprise or disapprobation. — *adj.* giddy, noisy: huffy: superciliously haughty. [From *hoit* (*obs.*), to romp; origin uncertain.]

hoke, hokey. See **hokum.**

hokku. See **haiku.**

hokum *hō'kəm, (U.S. slang) n.* something done for the sake of applause: claptrap. — Also **hoke.** — *v.t.* **hoke** (*hōk*) to overact (a part in a play). — *adj.* **hokey** (*hōk'i*) overdone, contrived: phoney. [App. **hocus-pocus** combined with **bunkum.**]

hoky-poky, hokey-pokey *hō'ki-pō'ki, n.* hocus-pocus: a kind of ice-cream sold on the streets.

Holarctic *hol-ärk'tik, adj.* of the north temperate and Arctic biological region, including Palaearctic and Nearctic. [Gr. *holos,* whole, *arktikos,* northern — *arktos,* a bear, the Great Bear constellation.]

hold¹ *hōld, v.t.* to keep: to have: to grasp: to have in one's possession, keeping, or power: to sustain: to defend successfully: to maintain: to assert authoritatively: to think, believe: to occupy: to derive title to: to bind: to contain: to have a capacity of: to enclose: to confine: to restrain: to detain: to retain: to keep the attention of: to catch: to stop: to continue: to persist in: to celebrate, observe: to conduct: to carry on: to convoke and carry on: to esteem or consider: to aim, direct: to endure: to bet (*arch.*). — *v.i.* to grasp: to remain fixed: to be true or unfailing: to continue unbroken or unsubdued: to remain valid: to continue, to persist: to adhere: to derive right: when making a telephone call, to wait, without replacing the receiver, e.g. to be connected to a person one wants to speak to (also **hold the line**): — *pr.p.* **hōld'ing;** *pa.t.* **held;** *pa.p.* **held,** *obs.* **hōld'en.** — *n.* act or manner of holding: grip: power of gripping: tenacity: a thing held: a place of confinement: custody: stronghold: (a sign for) a pause (*mus.*):

an order to keep in reserve (a room etc.) or to suspend (operations) (*U.S.*): means of influencing. — *ns.* **hold'er; hold'ing** anything held: a farm held of a superior: hold: influence: stacking (of aircraft waiting to land): tenure (*Scots law*): the burden of a song (*Shak.*): (in *pl.*) property owned (e.g. land or investments). — **hold'-all** an accommodating receptacle for clothes, etc., e.g. a canvas wrapper; **hold'back** a check: a strap joining the breeching to the shaft of a vehicle (see also **hold back** below); **hold'erbat** (*building*) a metal collar formed of two semicircular parts which can be clamped together round a pipe, with a projecting piece for fixing to a wall; **hold'fast** that which holds fast: a long nail: a catch: a plant's fixing organ other than a root; **holding company** an industrial company that owns and controls part or all of one or more other companies, usu. without having a direct hand in production; **holding operation** a course of action designed to preserve the status quo; **holding pattern** a specific course which aircraft are instructed to follow when waiting to land; **hold'over** (*U.S.*) a leftover, relic; **hold'-up** an attack with a view to robbery: a highwayman: an act or state of holding up: a stoppage. — **get hold of** to obtain: to get in touch with; **hold against** (*coll.*) to remember as a failing or as a misdemeanour on the part of; **hold back** to restrain: to hesitate: to keep in reserve (*n.* **hold'back**); **hold by** to believe in: to act in accordance with; **hold down** to restrain: to keep (a job) by carrying out its duties efficiently, esp. in spite of difficulties; **hold forth** to put forward: to show: to speak in public, to declaim; **hold good** to remain the case; **hold hands** (of two people) to be hand in hand or clasping both of each other's hands: (of several people) each to clasp the hand of the person on either side, thus forming a line, circle, etc.; **hold hard!** stop; **hold in** to restrain, check: to restrain oneself; **hold it!** keep the position exactly!; **hold of** (*Pr. Bk.*) to regard; **hold off** to keep at a distance: to refrain (from); **hold on** to persist in something: to continue: to cling: to keep (with *to*): stop (*imper.*): wait a bit; **hold (someone) in hand** to amuse in order to gain some advantage; **hold one's own** to maintain one's position; **hold one's peace, tongue** to keep silence; **hold out** to endure, last: to continue resistance: to offer; **hold out for** to wait determinedly for something one wants or has asked for; **hold out on** (*coll.*) to keep information from; **hold over** to postpone: to keep possession of (land or a house beyond the term of agreement); **hold the line** see **hold** above; **hold the road** (of a vehicle) to remain stable and under the driver's control e.g. in wet weather, at high speeds or on bends; **hold to, hold someone to** to keep, make someone keep, (a promise), adhere to (a decision), etc.; **hold together** to remain united: to cohere; **hold up** to raise: to keep back: to endure: to bring to, or keep at, a standstill: to stop and rob: to rob by threatening assault; **hold up one's head** to face the world with self-respect; **hold water** see **water; hold with** to take sides with, support: to approve of; **no holds barred** not observing any rules of fair play (*adj.* **no'-holds-barred'**); **on hold** postponed: in abeyance. [O.E. *haldan* (W.S. *healdan*); O.H.G. *haltan*, Goth. *haldan*.]

hold² *hōld*, *n.* the interior cavity of a ship used for the cargo. [**hole¹**, with excrescent *d*.]

hole¹ *hōl*, *n.* a hollow place: a cavity: an aperture: a gap: a breach: a pit: a subterfuge: a means of escape: a difficult situation: a scrape: a place of hiding, a mean lodging, a secret room for some disreputable business: an animal's excavation or place of refuge: a miserable or contemptible place: a cavity 4¼ inches in diameter, into which golf-balls are played: the distance, or the part of the game, between tee and hole: the score for playing a hole in fewest strokes: a vacancy in an energy band, caused by removal of an electron, which moves and is equivalent to a positive charge (*electronics*). — *v.t.* to form holes in: to put, send, play into a hole. — *v.i.* to go, play, into a hole. — *adj.* **holey** (*hōl'i*) full of

holes. — *n.* and *adj.* **hol'ing.** — *adj.* **hole'-and-cor'ner** secret: underhand: in obscure places. — **hole card** in stud poker, the card dealt face down in the first round. — *adj.* **hole'-in-the-wall'** (*coll.*) small, insignificant, difficult to find. — **hol'ing-axe** a narrow axe for cutting holes in posts; **hol'ing-pick** a pick used in under-cutting coal. — **a hole in one's coat** a stain on a person's reputation; **hole in one** in golf, a shot from the tee that goes into the hole, and so completes the hole with a single stroke; **hole in the heart** imperfect separation of the left and right sides of the heart; **hole out** (*golf*) to play the ball into the hole; **hole up** (*coll.*) to go to earth, hide (also *fig.*); **in holes** full of holes; **make a hole in** (e.g. one's pocket) to use up a large amount of (e.g. money); **pick holes in** see **pick¹; toad in the hole** meat baked in batter, etc. [O.E. *hol*, a hole, cavern; Du. *hol*, Dan. *hul*, Ger. *hohl*, hollow; conn. with Gr. *koilos*, hollow.]

hole² an earlier (and etymological) spelling (*Spens.*) of **whole.** — *adj.* **hole'som(e)** wholesome.

Holi *hō'lē*, *n.* a Hindu spring festival characterised by boisterous revelry. [Hind. *holī* — Sans. *holikā*.]

holibut. See **halibut.**

holiday *hol'i-dā*, *n.* orig., a religious festival: a day or (often in *pl.*) a season of idleness and recreation: (often in *pl.*) a period of time spent away from home, for recreation. — *v.i.* to go away from home for a holiday. — *adj.* befitting a holiday: cheerful. — **holiday camp** an area, often at the seaside, with chalets, hotels, entertainments, etc., for holidaymakers; **hol'idaymaker** one on holiday away from home: a tourist. — **holiday of obligation** esp. in the Roman Catholic church, an important religious festival, on which attendance in church is obligatory. [**holy, day.**]

holism *hol'izm, hōl'izm*, *n.* the theory that the fundamental principle of the universe is the creation of wholes, i.e. complete and self-contained systems from the atom and the cell by evolution to the most complex forms of life and mind: the theory that a complex entity, system, etc., is more than merely the sum of its parts. — *n.* **hol'ist.** — *adj.* **holist'ic.** — **holistic medicine** a form of medicine which considers the whole person, physically and psychologically, rather than treating merely the diseased part. [Gr. *holos*, whole; coined by General Smuts.]

holla *hol'a*, *interj.* ho, there! attend! the usual response to *ahoy!* (*naut.*). — *n.* a loud shout. — *interj.* **holl'a= ho(a)!** [Fr. *hola* — *ho* and *là* — L. *illāc*, there.]

holland *hol'ənd*, *n.* a coarse linen fabric, unbleached or dyed brown, which is used for covering furniture, etc.: orig., a fine kind of linen first made in *Holland*. — *n.* **Holl'ander** a native or citizen of *Holland*: a Dutch ship. — *adj.* **Holl'andish.** — *n.* **Holl'ands** gin made in Holland. — **sauce hollandaise** (*sōs ol-ā-dez*; Fr.), **hollandaise sauce** (*hol-ən-dāz'* or *hol'ən-dāz sōs*) a sauce made of the yolk of an egg with melted butter and lemon juice or vinegar. [*Holland.*]

holler *hol'ər*, (*U.S.* and *dial.*) *n.* and *vb.* Same as **hollo.**

Hollerith code *hol'ər-ith kōd*, (*comput.*) a code for transforming letters and numerals into a pattern of holes, for use in punched cards. [H. *Hollerith* (1860–1929), U.S. inventor.]

hollidam. See **holy.**

hollo *hol'ō*, *n.* and *interj.* a shout of encouragement or to call attention: a loud shout: — *pl.* **holl'o(e)s.** — *v.t.* and *v.i.* to shout. [Cf. **holla, hallo.**]

holloa *hol-ō'*. Same as **hallo.**

hollow *hol'ō*, *n.* a hole: a cavity: a depression: a vacuity: a groove: a channel. — *adj.* having an empty space within or below: concave: sunken: unsound, unreal, fleeting, deceptive: insincere: muffled, as if coming from a hollow. — *v.t.* (often with *out*) to make a hole in: to make hollow: to excavate. — *adv.* completely: clean. — *adv.* **holl'owly** with a hollow sound: in a hollow or insincere manner. — *n.* **holl'owness** the state of being hollow: cavity: insincerity: treachery. — *adjs.* **holl'ow-eyed** having sunken eyes; **holl'ow-ground**

ground so as to have concave surface(s); **holl'ow=
heart'ed** having a hollow heart: faithless: treacherous.
— **holl'ow-ware, holl'oware** hollow articles of iron,
china, etc., as pots and kettles. [O.E. *holh*, a hollow
place — *hol*; see **hole**[1].]
holly *hol'i, n.* an evergreen shrub (*Ilex aquifolium*; family
Aquifoliaceae) having leathery, shining, and spinous
leaves and scarlet or yellow berries, much used for
Christmas decorations. — **holl'y-fern** a spiny-leaved
fern; **holl'y-oak** the holm-oak. [O.E. *holegn*; cf. W.
celyn, Ir. *cuileann*.]
hollyhock *hol'i-hok, n.* a plant (*Althaea*) of the mallow
family brought into Europe from the Holy Land.
[M.E. *holihoc* — *holi*, holy, and O.E. *hoc*, mallow.]
Hollywood *hol'i-wŏŏd, adj.* of or belonging to *Hollywood*,
a suburb of Los Angeles in California, a centre of the
American cinema: typical of or resembling films made
there, brash and romantic, presenting the image of an
affluent or artificial society.
holm[1] *hōm, n.* an islet, esp. in a river: rich flat land beside
a river. [O.E. *holm*; Ger. *Holm*, etc.]
holm[2] *hōm,* (*Spens.*) *n.* holly: the holm-oak. — **holm'-oak'**
the evergreen oak (*Quercus ilex*), not unlike holly.
[M.E. *holin*; see **holly.**]
Holmesian *hōm'zi-ən, adj.* relating to, in the manner of,
the detective Sherlock *Holmes*, in the stories by A.
Conan Doyle (1859–1930). — *n.* a devotee of Holmes.
holmium *hōl'mi-əm, n.* a metallic element (Ho; at. numb.
67). — *n.* **hol'mia** its oxide. — *adj.* **hol'mic.** [Mod.
L. *Holmia*, Stockholm.]
holo- *hol'ō-,* **hol-** *hol-,* in composition, whole: wholly. —
adjs. **holobenth'ic** (*zool.*) passing the whole life-cycle in
the depths of the sea; **holoblast'ic** (of egg) segmenting
completely (Gr. *blastos*, a shoot, bud). — *n.* **hol'ocaust**
(*-köst'*) a sacrifice, in which the whole of the victim
was burnt: a huge slaughter or destruction of life: (with
cap.) the mass murder of Jews by the Nazis during
World War II (Gr. *holokauston* — *kaustos*, burnt). —
adjs. **holocaus'tal, holocaus'tic.** — *n.* **Holocene** (*hol'ə-
sēn; geol.*) the most recent period of geological time,
following the Quaternary period, and approximating
to the period since the last glaciation. — *adjs.* **hol'ocrine**
producing a secretion of disintegrated cells (Gr.
krinein, to separate, decide); **holocrys'talline** wholly
crystalline in structure — without glass. — *ns.* **holoen'-
zyme** an enzyme which has a protein and non-protein
component; **hol'ogram** a photograph made without
use of a lens by means of interference between two
parts of a split laser beam, the result appearing as a
meaningless pattern until suitably illuminated, when
it shows as a 3-D image (a number of pictures can be
'stored' on the same plate or film); **hol'ograph** (*-gräf*)
a document wholly written by the person from whom
it proceeds. — Also *adj.* — *v.t.* to make a hologram
of. — *adj.* **holographic** (*-graf'ik*). — *n.* **holog'raphy** (the
technique or process of) making or using holograms.
— *adj.* **holohē'dral** (Gr. *hedrā*, base). — *ns.* **holo-
hēd'rism** (*math.*) the property of having the full number
of symmetrically arranged planes crystallographically
possible; **holohē'dron** a form possessing this property.
— *adj.* **holometabol'ic.** — *n.* **holometab'olism** of an
insect, complete metamorphosis. — *adjs.* **holometab'-
olous; holophōt'al** (Gr. *phōs, phōtos,* light). — *ns.*
hol'ophote an apparatus by which all the light from a
lighthouse is thrown in the required direction; **hol'o-
phrase** a single word expressing a sentence or phrase.
— *adj.* **holophräs'tic.** — *n.* **hol'ophȳte.** — *adj.* **holophytic**
(*-fit'ik*; Gr. *phyton,* a plant) obtaining nutriment
wholly in the manner of a green plant. — *n.* **holo-
phytism** (*-fīt'izm*). — *adj.* **holop'tic** having the eyes
meeting in front. — *n.pl.* **Holostei** (*hol-os'ti-ī*; Gr.
osteon, bone) an order of fishes including Lepidosteus.
— *adj.* **holosteric** (*-ster'ik*; Gr. *stereos,* solid) wholly
solid: having no liquids (as an aneroid barometer). —
n. **hol'otype** (*zool.*) the original type specimen from
which the description of a new species is established.
— *adjs.* **holotypic** (*-tip'ik*); **holozoic** (*-zō'ik*; Gr. *zōion,*

an animal) obtaining nutrition wholly in the manner
of an animal, i.e. from other organisms live or dead.
[Gr. *holos,* whole.]
holothurian *hol-ō-thōō'ri-ən, n.* any member of the genus
Holothu'ria or family **Holothuroid'ea,** a class of worm-
like unarmoured echinoderms — the sea-cucumbers.
— Also *adj.* [Gr. *holothourion,* a kind of sea animal.]
holozoic. See **holo-.**
holp *hōlp,* **holpen** *-ən,* old *pa.t.* and *pa.p.* of **help.**
hols *holz,* (*school slang*) *n.pl.* holidays.
holster *hōl'stər, n.* a pistol-case, on saddle or belt. — *adj.*
hol'stered. [Perh. Du. *holster,* pistol-case; cf. O.E.
heolster, hiding-place.]
holt[1] *hōlt, n.* a wood or woody hill: an orchard. [O.E.
holt, a wood; O.N. *holt,* a copse, Ger. *Holz.*]
holt[2] *hōlt, n.* a hold, grasp (*Brit.* and *U.S. dial.*): a
stronghold (*obs.*): a refuge: an otter's den. [**hold**[1].]
holus-bolus *hōl'əs-bōl'əs, adv.* all at a gulp: altogether.
[Sham L.; perh. — Eng. *whole bolus* or Gr. *holos* and
bōlos, lump, bolus.]
holy *hō'li, adj.* perfect in a moral sense: pure in heart:
religious: set apart to a sacred use: regarded with awe
(often ironically): saintly: sanctimonious. — *n.* holy
object, place, or (*obs.*) person. — *adv.* **ho'lily.** — *ns.*
ho'liness sanctity: (with *cap.*) a title of the pope and of
patriarchs in Eastern Churches; **holydam(e), hollidam**
(*Shak.*), for **halidom.** — *adj.* **ho'lier-than-thou'**
offensively sanctimonious and patronising. — *n.* such
an attitude: one who has such an attitude. — **ho'ly-ale**
(conjectured in Shak., *Pericles,* Prol., 9, for rhyme's
sake) a church festival; **Holy Alliance** a league formed
after the fall of Napoleon (1815) by the sovereigns of
Austria, Russia, and Prussia, professedly to regulate
all national and international relations in accordance
with the principles of Christian charity; **holy city**
Jerusalem: Rome: Mecca: Benares: Allahabad, etc.;
holy coat the seamless coat of Jesus, claimed to be kept
at Trier. — *adj.* **ho'ly-cru'el** (*Shak.*) cruel through
holiness. — **holy day** a religious festival (see also
holiday); **Holy Family** the infant Christ with Joseph,
Mary, etc.; **Holy Ghost, Spirit** the third person of the
Christian Trinity; **holy grail** see **grail**[3]; **holy grass** a
sweet-smelling grass sometimes strewed on church
floors on festival days; **holy Joe** (*slang*) a parson: a
pious person; **Holy Land** Palestine; **Holy Office** the
Inquisition; **Holy One** God: Christ: the one who is
holy, by way of emphasis: one separated to the service
of God; **holy orders** see **order;** **ho'ly-rood** (as a place-
name, *hol'*), Christ's cross: a cross, esp. in R.C.
churches over the entrance to the chancel (for **Holy=
rood Day** see **rood**); **Holy Roller** (*derog.*) a preacher or
follower of an extravagantly emotional religious sect;
Holy Saturday the Saturday before Easter Sunday;
Holy See the Roman Catholic bishopric of Rome, i.e.
the Pope's see; **ho'lystone** a sandstone used by seamen
for cleansing the decks, said to be named from cleaning
the decks for Sunday, or from kneeling in using it. —
v.t. to scrub with a holystone. — **holy terror** (*coll.*) a
formidable person, or one given to causing commotion
or agitation; **Holy Thursday** Maundy Thursday: Ascension Day (*rare*); **holy war** a war for the extirpation
of heresy or a rival religion: a Crusade; **holy water**
water blessed for religious uses; **Holy Week** the week
before Easter; **Holy Willie** a religious hypocrite (after
Burns's poem); **holy writ** the Scriptures; **Holy Year** in
the R.C. church, a jubilee year. — **holy of holies** the
inner chamber of the Jewish tabernacle; **Holy Roman
Empire** the official denomination of the German Empire from 962 to 1806. [O.E. *hālig,* lit. whole — *hāl,*
sound; conn. with **hail**[1], **heal**[1], **whole.**]
homage *hom'ij, n.* a vassal's acknowledgment that he is
the man of his feudal superior: anything done or
rendered as such an acknowledgment: reverence, esp.
shown by outward action: a body of vassals or tenants.
— *v.t.* to do, pay, homage to. — *n.* **hom'ager** one who
does homage. [O.Fr. *homage* — L.L. *hominăticum*
— L. *homō,* a man.]

homaloid *hom′əl-oid, n.* Euclidean space, analogous to a plane. — *adj.* **homaloid′al** flat: of the nature of a plane. [Gr. *homalos*, even, *eidos*, form.]

hombre *om′brā,* (Sp.) *n.* man.

Homburg (-hat) *hom′bûrg (-hat′), n.* a man's hat, of felt, with narrow brim and crown, dinted in at the top. [First worn at *Homburg.*]

home *hōm, n.* habitual abode, or the place felt to be such: residence of one's family: the scene of domestic life, with its emotional associations: a separate building occupied by a family (*U.S.*): one's own country: the mother-country: seat: habitat: natural or usual place of anything: the den or base in a game: the goal: the inner table in backgammon: the plate in baseball (also **home plate**): an institution affording refuge, asylum, or residence for strangers, the afflicted, poor, etc.: a private hospital: a place where cats, dogs, etc., are received and boarded: in football pools, a match won by a team playing on their own ground. — *adj.* pertaining or belonging to or being in one's own dwelling, country, or playing-ground: domestic: near the dwelling or headquarters: coming or reaching home: effective, searching: made or done at home, not in a factory, abroad, etc. — *adv.* to home: at home: to the innermost or final position: effectively. — *v.i.* to go home: to find the way home: to dwell: to be guided to a target or destination. — *v.t.* to send home: to set up in a home: to guide to a target or destination. — *adj.* **home′less** without a home. — *n.* **home′lessness.** — *adj.* **home′like** like a home: familiar: easy: comfortable. — *adv.* **home′lily** (*-li-li*). — *n.* **home′liness.** — *adj.* **home′ly** pertaining to home: familiar: plain: unpretentious: ugly (*U.S.*). — *n.* **hom′er** a pigeon of a breed that can readily be trained to find its way home from a distance: any person or animal so skilled: a stroke in itself enabling a baseball-player to make a complete circuit. — *advs.* **home′ward, home′wards.** — *adjs.* **home′ward** in the direction of home; **home′y, hom′y** home-like; **hom′ing** returning home: trained to return home: guiding home: guiding to target or destination. — Also *n.* — *adjs.* **home′-and-home′, home′-and-away′** of sports events, played alternately on one's own and one's opponents' home grounds. — **home base** (*baseball*) the plate at which the batter stands when batting and which must be touched by a runner in order to score a run; **home bird, home body** a person who likes to stay at home, whose interests are in the home. — *adjs.* **home′-born** originating at home or in the home: native, not foreign; **home′bound** homeward bound: fixed to the home; **home′-bred** bred at home: native: domestic: plain: unpolished; **home′-brewed** brewed at home or for home use (*n.* **home′-brew′**): also *fig.* — **home circuit** the south-eastern circuit of Assize with boundaries changed at various times; **home′-comer; home′-coming** arrival at home: return home. — Also *adj.* — **home counties** the counties over and into which London has extended — Middlesex, Essex, Kent, Surrey (Herts, Sussex); **home′craft** household arts: arts practised at home or concerned with home life; **home′-croft** a cottage with a small piece of land for an industrial worker to grow his own food; **home′-croft′er; home′-croft′ing; home′-defence′** defence of a country by a force of its own people within it; **Home Department** that part of government which is concerned with the maintenance of the internal peace of England — its headquarters the **Home Office,** its official head the **Home Secretary; home economics** domestic science; **home economist; home′-farm** the farm attached to and near a great house. — *adj.* **home′felt** felt in one's own breast: inward: private. — **home′-fire** the domestic hearth, with its activities and connections. — *adj.* **home′-grown** produced in one's own country, or garden. — **home-guard′** a member of a volunteer force for home-defence: a force of the kind (first in war of 1939–45, **Home Guard**); **home help** a person employed by the local authority to help the handicapped or the aged with domestic work. — *adj.* **home′-keeping** staying at home. — **home′land** native land, fatherland: mother-country: in Africa, an area reserved for Black African peoples (also **Bantustan**); **home′-life** domestic life; **home loan** a mortgage. — *adj.* **home′-made** made at home: made in one's own country: plain. — **home′-maker** a housewife; **home market** the market for goods in the country that produces them; **home movie** a motion picture made at home, usu. by an amateur; **home nurse** a district nurse; **home port** the port at which a boat is registered. — *adj.* **home′-produced′** produced within the country, not imported. — **Home Rule** self-government, as that claimed by Irish (*hist.*), Scottish, Welsh Nationalists, including a separate parliament to manage internal affairs; **home′-rul′er** an advocate of Home Rule; **home run** in baseball, a hit enabling the batter to make a complete circuit of the bases. — *adj.* **home′sick** pining for home. — **home′-sickness; home′-sig′nal** a signal at the beginning of a section of railway line showing whether or not the section is clear. — *adj.* **home′spun** spun or wrought at home: not made in foreign countries: plain: inelegant. — *n.* cloth made at home: an unpolished person (*Shak.*). — **home′stall** (*obs.*) a homestead: a farmyard; **home′stead** a dwelling-house with outhouses and enclosures immediately connected with it: a piece of public land allotted under special laws to a settler (*U.S.* and *Austr.*); **home′steader; home′steading** (orig. *U.S.*) a scheme by which people are permitted to live rent-free in or buy semi-derelict buildings and improve them with the help of Government grants, etc.; **home′-straight′, home′-stretch′** the last stretch of a racecourse (also *fig.*); **home′-thrust** in fencing, a hit that goes home where it is aimed: a pointed remark that goes home; **home′-town** the town where one's home is or was; **home′-truth** a pointed, usually unanswerable, typically wounding, statement that strikes home; **home unit** (*Austr.*) a flat or apartment; **home video** a home movie made with a video camera. — *adj.* **home′ward-bound′** bound homeward or to one's native land. — **home′-work** work or preparation to be done at home, esp. for school: paid work, esp. piece-work, done at home; **home′worker.** — **at home** in one's own house: ready to receive a visitor: feeling the ease of familiarity with a place or situation (**at-home′** a reception; **not at home** out of one's house or not receiving a visitor); **bring home to** to prove to, in such a way that there is no way of escaping the conclusion: to impress upon; **do one's homework** to prepare oneself, e.g. for a discussion by acquainting oneself with the relevant facts; **eat out of house and home** to live at the expense of another so as to ruin him; **home and dry** having arrived, achieved one's aim, etc.; **home from home** a place where one feels comfortable and at ease; **long home** the grave; **make oneself at home** to be as free and unrestrained as in one's own house; **nothing to write home about** (*coll.*) not very exciting; **pay home** to strike to the quick: to retaliate. [O.E. *hām;* Du. *heim,* Ger. *Heim,* Goth. *haims.*]

homelyn *hom′əl-in, hōm′lin, n.* the spotted ray. [Origin unknown.]

homeopathy, etc. Same as **homoeopathy,** etc., under **homo-.**

homer[1] *hō′mər, n.* a Hebrew measure of capacity, roughly 11 bushels. [Heb. *khōmer,* heap — *khāmar,* to swell up.]

homer[2]. See **home.**

Homeric *hō-mer′ik, adj.* pertaining to *Homer,* the great poet of Greece (*c.* 850 B.C.): attributed to Homer: resembling Homer or his poetry: worthy of Homer: in the heroic or epic manner. — *n.* **Homerid** (*hō′mər-id*) one of the **Homer′idae** (*-i-dē*), Chian reciters of the Homeric poems, claiming descent from him. — **Homeric laughter** loud inextinguishable laughter (see *asbestos gelōs* (Gr.), in the Appendices); **Homeric question** the question of Homer's authorship of the *Iliad* and the *Odyssey,* disputed by Wolf (1795). [Gr. *hōmērikos* — *Hōmēros,* Homer.]

homicide *hom'i-sīd, n.* manslaughter: one who kills another. — *adj.* **homicī′dal** pertaining to homicide: murderous: bloody. [L. *homicīdium*, manslaughter, and *homicīda*, a man-slayer — *homō*, a man, *caedĕre*, to kill.]

homily *hom'i-li, n.* a plain expository sermon, practical rather than doctrinal: a hortatory discourse. — *adjs.* **homilet′ic, -al.** — *n.sing.* **homilet′ics** the art of preaching. — *n.* **hom′ilist.** [Gr *homīliā,* an assembly, a lecture or sermon — *homos,* the same, *īlē,* a company.]

hominid *hom'in-id, (zool.) n.* an animal of the family **Homin′idae,** comprising man and his ancestors (also *adj.*). — *n.* and *adj.* **hom′inoid.** [L. *homō, -inis,* man.]

hominy *hom'i-ni, n.* maize hulled, or hulled and crushed: a kind of porridge made by boiling this. [Amer. Ind. origin.]

homme *om,* (Fr.) *n.* man. — **homme d'affaires** *(da-fer)* a business man: an agent, steward; **homme de bien** *(də byē)* a man of worth, a good man; **homme de lettres** *(də letr')* a man of letters; **homme d'épée** *(dā-pā)* a military man; **homme d'esprit** *(des-prē)* a man of wit; **homme d'état** *(dā-tä)* a statesman; **homme du monde** *(dü mɔ̃d)* a man of fashion; **homme moyen sensuel** *(mwa-yē sā-sü-el)* the ordinary man: the man in the street; **homme sérieux** *(sā-ryø)* a serious, earnest man.

hommock. See **hummock.**

homo *hō'mō, n.* man generically: (*cap.*; *zool.*) the human genus. — **Homo erectus** (formerly known as Pithecanthropus erectus) a name given to a type of erect hominid between Australopithecus and Homo sapiens, represented by Java man and Peking man; **Homo habilis** a name given to a much earlier hominid, thought also to walk upright; **Homo neanderthalensis** see **Neanderthal; Homo sapiens** the one existing species of man. [L. *homō, -inis,* man, human being.]

homo- *hom'ō-, hom-o'-,* in many cases alternatively pronounced *hōm-,* in composition, same. — **homoeo-, homeo-, homoio-** *hom'i-ō-, -oi'ō-, or -o'-,* like, similar. — *n.* and *adj.* **homo** *(hō'mō; slang)* short for *homosexual: — pl.* **ho′mos.** — *adj.* **homoblast′ic** (Gr. *blastos,* a germ; *zool.*) derived from similar cells: showing direct embryonic development. — *adjs.* **hom′oblasty.** — *adjs.* **homocentric** *(-sen'trik;* Gr. *homokentros — kentron,* centre, point) concentric: proceeding from or diverging to the same point: of rays, either parallel or passing through one focus (*phys.*); **homocercal** *(-sûr'kəl;* Gr. *kerkos,* tail) having the upper and lower lobes of the tail-fin alike; **homochlamydeous** *(-klə-mid'i-əs;* Gr. *chlamys, -ydos,* cloak; *bot.*) with calyx and corolla similar; **homochromat′ic** monochromatic; **homochromous** *(-krō'məs;* Gr. *chrōma,* colour) alike in colour: of the same colour. — *n.* **homochromy** *(-ok',* or *-krōm')* protective coloration. — *adjs.* **homocyclic** *(-sīk'lik;* Gr. *kyklos,* a ring; *chem.*) having a closed chain of like atoms; **homodont** *(hom'ə-dont;* Gr. *odous, odontos,* tooth) having teeth all alike; **homodyne** *(hom'ə-dīn;* Gr. *dynamis,* power; *radio telephony*) applied to the reception of waves strengthened by the imposition of a locally generated wave of the same length; **hom(o)eom′erous, homoiom′erous** (Gr. *meros,* part) composed of similar parts: of lichens, having the algal cells distributed throughout the thallus: in metameric animals, having all the somites alike — also **hom(o)eomeric** *(-mer'ik).* — *ns.* **hom(o)eom′ery; hom′(o)eomorph** (Gr. *morphē,* form) a thing similar in form to another but essentially different, esp. a different chemical substance with similar crystalline form. — *adj.* **hom(o)eomorph′ic** of, pertaining to a homoeomorph: of two geometrical figures, such that one can be converted into the other by distortion (*math.*). — *n.* **hom(o)eomorph′ism.** — *adj.* **hom(o)eomorph′ous.** — *ns.* **hom(o)eomorph′y; hom(o)eopath** *(hom'* or *hōm'i-ə-path;* Gr. *pathos,* feeling), **hom(o)eopathist** *(-op'ə-thist)* one who believes in or practises homoeopathy. — *adj.* **hom(o)eopathic** *(-path').* — *adv.* **hom(o)eopath′ically.** — *ns.* **hom(o)eopathy** *(-op'ə-thi)* the system of treating diseases by small quantities of drugs that excite symp-

toms similar to those of the disease; **hom(o)eosis** *(hom-i-ō'sis;* Gr. *homoiōsis,* a becoming like; *biol.*) assumption of the character of a corresponding member of another whorl or somite; **hom(o)eostasis** *(hom-i-os'tə-sis;* Gr. *stasis,* a standing still) the tendency for the internal environment of the body to remain constant in spite of varying external conditions: a tendency towards health, stable conditions. — *adj.* **hom(o)eostat′ic.** — *n.* **hom(o)eoteleuton** *(hom-i-ō-tel-ū'ton;* Gr. *homoioteleuton teleutē,* ending) the use, or occurrence, of similar endings. — *adjs.* **hom(o)eotherm′al, -ic, -ous** homothermous. — Also **homoi′other′mal,** etc. — *ns.* **homoerot′icism, homoerot′ism** orientation of the libido towards one of the same sex. — *adjs.* **homoerot′ic; homogamic** *(-gam'ik),* **homogamous** *(hom-og'ə-məs).* — *ns.* **homogamy** *(hom-og'ə-mi;* Gr. *gamos,* marriage) breeding of like with like: inbreeding: the condition of having all the flowers of an inflorescence sexually alike (*bot.*): simultaneous ripening of stamens and stigmas (*bot.*); **homogenate** *(-oj'ə-nāt)* a substance produced by homogenising; **homogeneity** *(hom-ō-ji-nē'i-ti)* the state or fact of being homogeneous. — *adj.* **homogeneous** *(hom-ō-jēn'i-əs,* also *hōm-, -jen';* Gr. *homogenēs — genos,* kind) of the same kind or nature: having the constituent elements similar throughout: of the same degree or dimensions in every term (*math.*). — *n.* **homogē′neousness.** — *adj.* **homogenous** *(hom-oj'ən-əs)* similar owing to common descent. — *n.* **homogenesis** *(-jen'i-sis;* Gr. *genesis,* birth; *biol.*) a mode of reproduction in which the offspring is like the parent, and passes through the same cycle of existence. — *adjs.* **homogenet′ic, -al** homogenous. — *v.t.* **homog′-enise, -ize** (or *hom'o-jən-īz*) to make homogeneous: to make (milk) more digestible by breaking up fat globules, etc.: to produce (milk) synthetically by mixing its constituents. — *ns.* **homogenisa′tion, -z-; homog′eniser, -z-; homog′eny** similarity owing to common descent; **homograft** *(hom'ō-gräft)* a graft from one individual to an unrelated member of the same species; **homograph** *(hom'ō-gräf;* Gr. *graphein,* to write) a word of the same spelling as another, but of different meaning, pronunciation or origin. — *adj.* **homoiousian** *(hom-oi-ōō'si-ən,* or *-ow';* Gr. *ousiā,* being) of similar (as distinguished from identical) essence: believing the Father and Son to be of similar essence. *n.* a holder of such belief, a semi-Arian. — *v.t.* **homol′ogate** (L.L. *homologāre, -ātum —* Gr. *homologeein,* to agree — *logos,* speech) to confirm: to approve: to consent to: to ratify. — *v.i.* to agree. — *n.* **homologā′tion** (*Scots law*) confirming and ratifying by subsequent act. — *adj.* **homological** *(-loj').* — *adv.* **homolog′ically.** — *v.t.* and *v.i.* **homol′ogise, -ize** *(-jīz).* — *adj.* **homologous** *(hom-ol'ə-gəs)* agreeing: of the same essential nature, corresponding in relative position, general structure, and descent. — *n.* **hom′ologue,** *U.S.* **hom′olog,** *(-ə-log)* that which is homologous to something else, as a man's arm, a whale's flipper, a bird's wing. — *n.pl.* **homolog(o)umena** *(hom-ol-o-gōō'mi-nə;* Gr. *homolog-oumena,* things granted, neut. pl. of pr.p. pass. (contracted) of *homologeein)* the books of the New Testament whose authenticity was universally acknowledged in the early Church — opp. of *antilegomena.* — *ns.* **homol′ogy** *(-ə-ji;* Gr. *homologos)* the quality of being homologous: affinity of structure and origin, apart from form or use; **hom′omorph** (Gr. *morphē,* form) a thing having the same form as another. — *adjs.* **homomorph′ic, homomorph′ous** alike in form, esp. if essentially different: uniform. — *ns.* **homomorph′ism; homomorphō′sis** regeneration of a lost part in the original form; **hom′onym** (Gr. *homōnymos — onyma, onoma,* name) a word having the same sound and perhaps the same spelling as another, but a different meaning and origin: a name rejected as preoccupied by another genus or species (*biol.*): a namesake. — *adjs.* **homonym′ic** pertaining to homonyms; **homon′-ymous** having the same name: having different significations and origins but the same sound: ambiguous:

homunculus

equivocal. — *adv.* **homon'ymously.** — *ns.* **homon'ymy, homonym'ity.** — *adjs.* **homoousian, homousian** (*hom-* (ō-)ōō'si-ən, or -*ow'*; Gr. *ousiā*, being) of the same essence: believing the Son to be of the same essence as the Father. — *ns.* a holder of such belief (according to the Nicene Creed). — *ns.* **hom'ophile** a homosexual; **hom'ophobe** (-*fōb*; Gr. *phobos*, fear) a person with a strong antipathy to homosexuals; **homophō'bia.** — *adj.* **homophō'bic.** — *n.* **homophone** (*hom'-ə-fōn*; — Gr. *phōnē*, sound) a character representing the same sound as another: a word pronounced alike with another but different in spelling and meaning. — *adjs.* **homophonic** (-*fon'*) sounding alike in unison: in the monodic style of music; **homophonous** (-*of'*). — *ns.* **homoph'ony; homophyly** (-*of'i-li*; Gr. *phylon*, a race; *biol.*) resemblance due to common ancestry. — *adj.* **homoplast'ic** (Gr. *plastikos*, plastic, *plasma*, a mould; *biol.*) similar in structure and development owing to parallel or convergent evolution but not descended from a common source. — *ns.* **hom'oplasmy** (-*plaz-mi*), **homop'-lasy.** — *adj.* **homopō'lar** (*chem.*) having an equal distribution of charge, as in a covalent bond. — *n.* **homopolăr'ity.** — *n.pl.* **Homoptera** (-*op'*; Gr. *pteron*, a wing) an order of insects (or suborder of Hemiptera) having wings of a uniform texture — cicadas, froghoppers, green-fly, scale-insects, etc. — *adj.* **homop'-terous.** — *n.* **Homorelaps** see **Elaps.** — *adj.* **homosex'ual** having, or pertaining to, sexual propensity to one's own sex. — Also *n.* — *ns.* **homosex'ualism; homosex'-ualist; homosexual'ity.** — *adjs.* **homosporous** (-*os'por-əs*, or -ō-spō'rəs, -spō'*; Gr. *sporos*, seed; *bot.*) having spores all of one kind; **homotax'ial, homotax'ic.** — *n.* **homotax'is** (Gr. *taxis*, arrangement; *geol.*) coincidence in order of organic succession but not necessarily in time: similarity in geological age, while not necessarily strict contemporaneity. — *adj.* **homothall'ic** (*bot.*) having only one type of mycelium (opp. to *heterothallic*). — *ns.* **homothall'ism, hom'othally.** — *adjs.* **homotherm'al, homotherm'ic, homotherm'ous** (Gr. *thermē*, heat) keeping the same temperature, warm-blooded; **homotonic** (-*ton'*), **homot'onous** (Gr. *tonos*, tone) of the same tenor or tone. — *n.* **homot'ony.** — *adjs.* **homotypal** (-*tīp'l*), **homotypic** (-*tip'ik*) conforming to normal type: (**homotypic;** *biol.*) pertaining to the second (equational) cell-division in meiosis (cf. **heterotypic**). — *ns.* **hom'-otype** (-ō-*tīp*; Gr. *typos*, type) that which has the same fundamental structure as something else; **homotypy** (*hom'ō-tī-pi*, *hom-ot'i-pi*); **homousian** see **homoousian** above; **homozygōs'is** the condition of having inherited a given genetical factor from both parents, so producing gametes of only one kind as regards that factor: genetical stability as regards a given factor; **homozy'-gote** a zygote which is formed as a result of homozygosis. — *adj.* **homozy'gous.** [Gr. *homos*, same, *homoios*, like, similar.]

homunculus *hō-mung'kū-ləs, n.* a tiny man capable of being produced artificially according to Paracelsus, endowed with magical insight and power: a dwarf, manikin: a dwarf of normal proportions (*med.*): a minute human form believed by the spermatist school of preformationists to be contained in the spermatozoon: — *pl.* -**lī.** — Also **homunc'ūle, homunc'le.** — *adj.* **homunc'ūlar.** [L., dim. of *homō*.]

homy. See **home.**

hon *hun*, (*coll.*) *n.* short for **honey** as a term of endearment.

hond *hond*, an obs. form of **hand.**

Honduras bark *hon-dūr'əs bärk*, cascara amarga.

hone¹ *hōn, n.* a smooth stone used for sharpening instruments. — *v.t.* to sharpen as on a hone. — **hone'-stone** a hone: any hard fine-grained stone suitable for honing, esp. novaculite. [O.E. *hān*; O.N. *hein*; allied to Gr. *kōnos*, a cone.]

hone² *hōn,* (*dial.*) *v.i.* to pine, moan, grieve (for, after). [Perh. Fr. *hogner*, to grumble.]

honest *on'ist, -əst, adj.* full of honour: just: fair-dealing: upright: the opposite of thievish: free from fraud: candid: truthful: ingenuous: seemly: respectable (now

only patronisingly): chaste (*arch.*): honourable. — *adv.* **hon'estly** in an honest way: in truth. — *interj.* expressing annoyance, disbelief, etc. — *n.* **hon'esty** the state of being honest: integrity: candour: a cruciferous garden-plant (*Lunaria biennis*) with shining silver or satiny white dissepiments: decorum (*obs.*): chastity (*Shak.*). — **honest broker** an impartial mediator in a dispute. — *adj.* **hon'est-to-God', hon'est-to-good'ness** genuine, out-and-out. — Also *adv.* — **honest Injun (Indian)** upon my honour; **make an honest woman of** to marry, where the woman has first been seduced. [O.Fr. *honeste* — L. *honestus* — *honor*.]

honey *hun'i, n.* a sweet, thick fluid elaborated by bees from the nectar of flowers: its colour, golden brown: nectar of flowers: anything sweet like honey: a term of endearment: anything pleasant or delightful (*coll.*): — *v.t.* to sweeten: to make agreeable. — *v.i. (Shak.*) to talk endearingly: — *pr.p.* **hon'eying;** *pa.t.* and *pa.p.* **hon'eyed** (-*id*). — *adj. (Shak.*) sweet. — *adjs.* **hon'eyed, hon'ied** covered with honey: sweet: seductive: flattering; **hon'eyless.** — **hon'ey-ant** one of several types of ant, esp. of the genus *Myrmecocystus*, that feed on honey, and store it in the worker-ants, who disgorge it as necessary; **hon'ey-badg'er** the ratel; **hon'ey-bag** an enlargement of the alimentary canal of the bee in which it carries its load of honey; **hon'ey-bear** the kinkajou, which robs the nests of wild bees: the sloth-bear: the Malayan bear; **hon'ey-bee** the hive-bee; **hon'ey-bird** a honey-guide: a honey-sucker; **hon'ey-blob** (*dial.*) a sweet yellow gooseberry; **hon'eybun, hon'eybunch** terms of endearment; **hon'ey-buzz'ard** a hawk (*Pernis apivora*) that feeds on the larvae and honey of bees, wasps, etc.; **hon'ey-cart, -wag(g)on** truck for offensive refuse; **hon'ey-chile** (*U.S. dial.*) a term of endearment; **hon'eycomb** (-*kōm*) a comb or mass of waxy cells formed by bees in which they store their honey: anything like a honeycomb: a bewildering maze of rooms, cavities, etc. — *v.t.* to make like a honeycomb: to spread into all parts of. — *adj.* **hon'eycombed** (-*kōmd*). — **hon'eycomb-moth'** a bee-moth; **hon'ey= crock** a crock or pot of honey; **hon'ey-dew** a sugar secretion from aphides or plants: ambrosia: a fine sort of tobacco moistened with molasses; **honeydew melon** a sweet-flavoured melon with smooth green or orange rind; **hon'ey-eat'er** any bird of a large Australian family, the *Meliphagidae;* **honey fungus** a kind of honey-coloured edible mushroom, *Armillaria mellea,* a parasite on the roots of trees and shrubs, which it can kill; **hon'ey-guide** a species of bird of a mainly African family (*Indicatoridae*) which guides men and ratels to honey-bees' nests by hopping from tree to tree with a peculiar cry: a marking on a flower showing the way to the nectaries; **hon'ey-lō'cust** an ornamental N. American tree (*Gleditsia*); **hon'eymoon** (*obs.* **hon'ey-month**) the first weeks after marriage, commonly spent on holiday, before settling down to the business of life: a period of (unusual) harmony at the start of a new business relationship, etc. (*fig.*). — Also *v.i.* — **hon'-eymooner; hon'ey-mouse** (*obs.*) the honey possum. — *adj.* **hon'ey-mouthed** having a honeyed mouth or speech: soft or smooth in speech. — **honey possum** a long-snouted Australian marsupial (*Tarsipes*) that feeds on honey and insects (also **phalanger**); **hon'eypot** a container for honey: anything that attracts people (*fig.*): (in *pl.*) a children's game: see also **hanepoot** (*S. Afr.*); **hon'ey-sac** a honey-bag; **hon'ey-stalk** (*Shak.*) prob. the stalk or flower of the clover; **hon'ey-stone** mellite, a very soft yellow mineral found with lignite; **hon'ey-suck'er** a honey-eater; **hon'eysuckle** a climbing shrub (*Lonicera*) with beautiful cream-coloured flowers, so named because honey is readily sucked from the flower (by long-tongued insects only): applied also to clover and many other plants. — *adj.* **hon'(e)y-suckle** and *adj.* and *n.* **hon'(e)y-seed** (*Shak.;* Henry IV part 2), the Hostess's blunders for **homicidal, homicide.** — *adjs.* **hon'ey-sweet** sweet as honey; **hon'ey-tongued** soft, pleasing, persuasive, or seductive in speech: eloquent.

— **virgin honey** honey that flows of itself from the comb; **wild honey** honey made by wild bees. [O.E. *hunig*; Ger. *Honig*; O.N. *hunang*.]

honeypot *hun'i-pot*. See **honey, hanepoot.**

hong[1] *hong, n.* a Chinese warehouse: foreign mercantile house in China: one of the multinational trading and financial companies based in Hong Kong. [Chin. *hang*, row, range.]

hong[2] *hong*, obs. form of **hang, hung.**

honied. See **honeyed** under **honey.**

Honiton *hon'i-tən*, local *hun'*, *adj.* of a kind of pillow lace with sprigs, made at *Honiton*, Devon. — Also *n.*

honk *hongk, n.* the cry of the wild goose: the noise of a motor horn. — *v.i.* to make such a sound: to vomit (*slang*). — *n.* **honk'er.** [Imit.]

honky, honkie *hongk'i*, (*derog.*, orig. *U.S.*) *n.* a white man. — Also *adj.* [Origin uncertain.]

honky-tonk *hongk'i-tongk*, (*slang*) *n.* a low drinking haunt: cheap entertainment: jangly piano music. [Ety. dub.]

honor. See **honour.**

honorand *on'ə-rand, n.* a person receiving an honour, esp. an honorary degree. [L. *honōrandus*, ger. of *honōrāre*, to honour — *honor, -ōris*, honour.]

honorarium *on-ə-rā'ri-əm, hon-, n.* a voluntary fee paid, esp. to a professional man for his services: — *pl.* **honora'ria, honorā'riums.** — *adj.* **honorary** (*on'(ə-)rə-ri*) conferring honour: holding a title or office without performing services or without reward. — *n.* an honorary fee. [L. *honōrārius, honōrārium* (*dōnum*), honorary (gift) — *honor, -ōris*, honour.]

honorific (*h*)*on-ə-rif'ik, adj.* attributing or doing honour. — *n.* an honorific form of title, address or mention. — *adj.* **honorif'ical.** — *adv.* **honorif'ically.** [L. *honōrificus* — *honor, -ōris*, honour, and *facĕre*, to do, make.]

honorificabilitudinity *hon-or-if-ik-əb-il-i-tū-din'i-ti, n.* honourableness. [L.L. *honōrificābilitūdinitās*, preserved in the abl. pl. *honōrificābilitūdinitātibus* as a superlatively long word, in *Love's Labour's Lost*, V, i. 44 and elsewhere; the gen. sing. is used by Albertino Mussato (early 14th cent.).]

honoris causa *or* **gratia** *hon-ōr'is* (*-ör'*) *kö'zə, kow'zä,* or *grā'shi-ə, grā'ti-ä,* (L.L.) as an honour, a token of respect.

honour, in U.S. **honor,** *on'ər, n.* the esteem due or paid to worth: respect: high estimation: veneration: that which rightfully attracts esteem: that which confers distinction or does credit: self-respecting integrity: a fine and scrupulous sense of what is due: chastity: virginity: distinction: exalted rank: any mark of esteem: privilege: a title or decoration: a title of respect in addressing or referring to judges, etc. (in Ireland quite generally): a prize or distinction: (in *pl.*) privileges of rank or birth: an ornament or decoration (*poet.*): (in *pl.*) civilities paid: (in *pl.*) in universities, etc., a higher grade of distinction for meritorious, advanced, or specialised work: the right to play first from the tee (*golf*): any one of four (in whist) or five (in bridge) best trumps, or an ace in a no-trump hand: (in *pl.*) a score for holding these: a group of manors held by one lord. — *v.t.* to hold in high esteem: to respect: to adorn (*obs.*): to exalt: to do honour to: to confer honour upon: to grace: to accept and pay when due. — *adj.* **hon'ourable** worthy of honour: illustrious: actuated by principles of honour: conferring honour: befitting men of exalted station: (*cap.*; written **Hon.**) prefixed to the names of various persons as a courtesy title. — *n.* **hon'ourableness** eminence: conformity to the principles of honour: fairness. — *adv.* **hon'ourably.** — *adjs.* **hon'oured; hon'ourless.** — *n.* **hon'ourer.** — *adj.* **hon'our-bound** same as **in honour bound** (below). — **hon'our-point** (*her.*) the point just above the fesse-point; **honours list** a list of people who have or are to receive a knighthood, order, etc. from the monarch for e.g. service to their community or country; **hon'-ours-man** one who has taken a university degree with honours. — **affair of honour** a duel; **birthday honours**

honours granted to mark the monarch's birthday; **Companions of Honour** an order instituted in 1917 for those who have rendered conspicuous service of national importance; **Court of Honour** a court regulating affairs of honour; **debt of honour** see **debt; do the honours** to render civilities, esp. as host; **guard of honour** a body of soldiers serving as a ceremonial escort; **guest of honour** the most important or distinguished guest (at a party, etc.); **honour bright** a kind of interjectional minor oath or appeal to honour; **honours easy** see **ease; honours of war** the privileges granted to a capitulating force of marching out with their arms, flags, etc.; **in honour bound, hon'our-bound** obliged by duty, conscience, etc. (to); **in honour of** out of respect for: celebrating; **last honours** funeral rites; **laws of honour** the conventional rules of honourable conduct, esp. in the conduct of duels; **maid of honour** a lady in the service of a queen or princess: a small almond-flavoured cake, or a kind of cheese-cake: a bridesmaid (*U.S.*); **matron of honour** a married woman in the service of a queen or princess: a married woman performing the duties of a bridesmaid; **military honours** ceremonial tokens of respect paid by troops to royalty, or at the burial of an officer, etc.; **person of honour** (*obs.*) a titled person; **point of honour** any scruple caused by a sense of duty: the obligation to demand and to receive satisfaction for an insult, esp. in the duel; **upon my honour** an appeal to one's honour in support of a statement; **word of honour** a promise which cannot be broken without disgrace. [A.Fr. (*h*)*onour* — L. *honor, honōs, -ōris.*]

hoo *hōō,* (*Shak.*) *interj.* expressing boisterous emotion. — Also **hoo-oo'.**

hooch[1] *hōōhh, interj.* a Highland dancer's shout.

hooch[2] *hōōch.* See **hootch.**

hood[1] *hōōd, n.* a flexible covering for the head and back of the neck: a covering for a hawk's head: a distinctive ornamental fold worn on the back over an academic gown: a folding roof for a carriage, etc.: a chimney-cowl: an overhanging or protective cover: the expansion of a cobra's neck: a hood-moulding: a motor-car bonnet (*U.S.*). — *v.t.* to cover with a hood: to blind. — *adjs.* **hood'ed; hood'less** having no hood. — **hooded seal** a large seal (*Cystophora cristata*) of the N. Atlantic, which has an inflatable sac over the nose region; **hood'ie-crow** the hooded crow (*Corvus cornix*); **hood'-man** (*obs.*) the person blind-folded in blindman's buff; **hood'man-blind** (*Shak.*) blindman's buff; **hood'-mould, hood'-mould'ing** an uppermost projecting moulding over a door, window, or arch. [O.E. *hōd*; Du. *hoed*, Ger. *Hut.*]

hood[2] *hōōd,* (*slang*) *n.* a hoodlum.

hood[3] *hōōd,* (*Spens.*) *n.* condition. [O.E. *hād.*]

-hood *-hōōd, n. suff.* indicating state, nature, as *hardihood, manhood* (also **-head** (*-hed*) as *Godhead*): a group of people, as *priesthood, sisterhood.* [O.E. *hād,* Ger. *-heit,* state.]

hoodlum *hōōd'ləm, n.* a rowdy, street bully: a small-time criminal or gangster.

hoodoo *hōō'dōō, n.* voodoo: a bringer of bad luck: foreboding of bad luck: bad luck: a rock-pinnacle (*geol.*). — *v.t.* to bewitch: to bring bad luck to. [App. **voodoo.**]

hoodwink *hōōd'wingk, v.t.* to blindfold: to cover up, hide (*Shak.*): to deceive, impose on. [**hood**[1], **wink.**]

hooey *hōō'i,* (*slang*) *n.* nonsense.

hoof *hōōf, n.* the horny part of the feet of certain animals, as horses, etc.: a hoofed animal: a foot (*coll.*): — *pl.* **hoofs, hooves.** — *v.t.* to strike with the hoof, to kick: to expel: (with *it*) to walk: (with *it*) to dance (*slang*). — *adj.* **hoofed.** — *n.* **hoof'er** (*slang*) a professional dancer. — *adj.* **hoof'less.** — **hoof'beat** the sound of a hoof striking esp. a hard road. — *adj.* **hoof'-bound** having a contraction of the hoof causing lameness. — **hoof'-mark, hoof'print** the mark of a hoof on the ground, etc.; **hoof'rot** foot-rot. — **on the hoof** alive (of cattle). [O.E. *hōf*; Ger. *Huf*; O.N. *hófr.*]

hoo-ha(h) *hōō'hä', (slang) n.* noisy fuss.   [Imit.]

hook *hook, n.* an object of bent form, such as would catch or hold anything: a sharply bent line: a snare: an advantageous hold: a curved instrument for cutting grain, branches, etc.: a spit of land with hooked end: a boxer's blow with bent elbow: the curve of a ball in flight (*sport*): an act of hooking: in pop-music, a catchy phrase. — *v.t.* to catch, fasten, or hold with or as with a hook: to form into or with a hook: to ensnare: to pull the ball abruptly to one's left (*golf* and *cricket*): to obtain possession of (the ball) in the scrum (*Rugby football*). — *v.i.* to bend: to be curved: to pull abruptly: to act as hooker (*Rugby*). — *pa.p.* or *adj.* **hooked** (*hookt*) physically dependent on drugs: (with *on, by*) addicted to a drug, activity, or indulgence: enthralled. — *ns.* **hook'edness; hook'er** one who hooks: one whose part it is to hook the ball (*Rugby football*): a prostitute (*slang*). — *adj.* **hook'y** full of, or pertaining to, hooks. — **hook'-climber** a climbing plant that clings to its support by means of hooks. — *adj.* **hook'-nosed.** — **hook'-pin** an iron pin with hooked head used for pinning the frame of a floor or roof together; **hook'-up** a connection: a temporary linking up of separate broadcasting stations for a special transmission; **hook'-worm** a parasitic nematode with hooks in the mouth: the disease it causes, ankylostomiasis or miner's anaemia. — **by hook or by crook** one way if not another; **hook and eye** a contrivance for fastening garments by means of a hook that catches in a loop or eye; **hook it** (*slang*) to decamp, make off; **hook, line and sinker** complete(ly); **off the hook** ready-made: out of difficulty or trouble: of a telephone handset, not on its rest, so that incoming calls cannot be received; **off the hooks** out of gear: superseded: dead; **on one's own hook** on one's own responsibility, initiative, or account; **sling** or **take one's hook** (*slang*) to get out, away, make off.   [O.E. *hōc*; Du. *hoek*.]

hookah, hooka *hook'ə, n.* the water tobacco-pipe of Arabs, Turks, etc.   [Ar. *huqqah*, bowl, casket.]

hooker[1] *hook'ər, n.* a two-masted Dutch vessel: a small fishing-smack.   [Du. *hoeker*.]

hooker[2]. See **hook**.

hookey[1], **hooky** *hook'i, (U.S.) n.* truant (in the phrase *play hookey*). — **blind hookey** a gambling card-game; **Hookey Walker** see under **walk**.

hookey[2]. See **hockey**[1].

hoolachan *hōō'lə-hhən,* **hoolican** *hōō'li-kən (Scot.) ns.* a Highland reel, esp. the reel of Tulloch.   [Gael. (*ruidhle*) *Thulachain*, the reel of Tulloch, in Strathspey.]

hooley *hōō'li,* (chiefly *Irish*) *n.* a boisterous party, usu. with singing and dancing.   [Origin unknown.]

hooligan *hōō'li-gən, n.* a street rough: a (young) violent, rude person. — *n.* **hool'iganism.**   [Said to be the name of a leader of a gang, poss. *Houlihan* or *Hooley's gang.*]

hoolock *hōō'lək, n.* a small Assamese gibbon.   [Said to be native name, *hulluk.*]

hooly *hül'i, hûl'i, (Scot.) adv.* softly, carefully. — Also *adj.* — **hooly and fairly** fair and soft, gently.   [Perh. O.N. *hōfliga,* fitly, or *hōgliga,* gently.]

hoop[1] *hōōp, n.* a ring or circular band, esp. for holding together the staves of casks, etc.: a large ring of metal, etc., for a child to trundle, for leaping through, for holding wide a skirt, or other purpose: a ring: a croquet arch. — *v.t.* to bind with hoops: to encircle. — *n.* **hoop'er** one who hoops casks: a cooper. — **hoop'-ash** a kind of ash used for making hoops: the nettle-tree (Celtis); **hooped'-pot** a drinking-pot with hoops to mark the amount each man should drink. — *interj.* **hoop'-la** orig. used at a circus when a performer jumped through a hoop. — *n.* a fairground game in which small hoops are thrown over prizes: great activity, excitement or disturbance. — **hoop'-snake** any of several harmless snakes, popularly believed to have formed themselves into a hoop and rolled over the ground. — **go through the hoop** to suffer an ordeal, undergo punishment.   [O.E. *hōp*; Du. *hoep.*]

hoop[2], **hooper, hooping-cough.** See under **whoop.**

hoopoe *hōōp'ōō, n.* a crested bird (*Upupa epops*), an occasional visitor in Britain.   [Earlier *hoop* — O.Fr. *huppe,* partly remodelled on L. *ŭpŭpa;* cf. Gr. *epops.*]

hooray[1], **hoorah.** Same as **hurrah.** — **Hooray** (or **Hoorah Henry**) a young middle- or upper-class man, esp. loudly philistine.

hooray[2], **hooroo** *hōō-rā', -rōō', (Austr.) interj.* goodbye, cheerio.

hoord. An obs. form of **hoard**[1].

hoos(e)gow *hōōs'gow, n. (U.S. slang),* a prison, jail.   [Sp. *juzgado,* tribunal, courtroom — *juzgar,* to judge — L. *jūdicāre.*]

hoosh[1] *hōōsh, interj.* used in driving away animals. — *v.t.* to drive or shoo away.   [Imit.]

hoosh[2] *hōōsh, n.* a thick soup.

hoot *hōōt, v.i.* (of an owl) to give a hollow cry: to make a sound like an owl, usually expressing hostility or scorn: to laugh loudly: to sound a motor-horn, siren, or the like. — *v.t.* to greet or drive with such sounds. — *n.* the sound of hooting: the note of an owl, motor-horn, etc.: a whit (often *two hoots*): a hilarious performance, escapade, situation, etc. (*coll.*). — *interj.* (*sing.* or *pl.; Scot.*) expressing incredulity, irritation, annoyance, etc. (also **hoot'-toot', hoots'-toots'**). — *n.* **hoot'er** one who hoots: a factory or mine siren or steam-whistle: a nose (*slang*).   [Imit., prob. immediately Scand.; cf. Sw. *hut,* begone.]

hootch, hooch *hōōch, n.* a drink made by the Indians of N.W. America from fermented dough and sugar: whisky: liquor, esp. if illicitly got or made.   [Said to be from *Hootchino,* an Alaskan tribe.]

hoot(e)nanny, hoota-, -ie *hōōt'(ə-)nan-ē, n.* thingummy (*U.S., dial.*): a party with folk-singing and sometimes dancing: an informal concert with folk music.

hoove[1] *hōōv, n.* a disease of cattle and sheep, marked by distension of the abdomen by gas — also *wind-dropsy, drum-belly.* — *adjs.* **hoov'en, hō'ven.**   [Cf. **heave.**]

hoove[2]. See **hove**[2].

Hoover® *hōō'vər, n.* a vacuum-cleaner (also without *cap.*). — *v.t.* and *v.i.* to clean with a vacuum-cleaner.

hooves. See **hoof.**

hop[1] *hop, v.i.* to leap on one leg: to move in jumps like a bird: to walk lame: to limp: to move smartly (in, out): to fly (in aircraft). — *v.t.* to cause to hop: to jump or fly over: to jump from: to board when in motion (*U.S.*). — *pr.p.* **hopp'ing;** *pa.t.* and *pa.p.* **hopped.** — *n.* a leap on one leg: a jump: a spring: a dance, dancing-party: a stage in a flying journey. — *ns.* **hopp'er** one who hops: a hopping or leaping animal, esp. (*U.S.*) a grasshopper: a jack or sticker of a piano: a shaking or conveying receiver, funnel, or trough (originally a shaking one) in which something is placed to be passed or fed, as to a mill: a barge with an opening in its bottom for discharging refuse: a vessel in which seed-corn is carried for sowing: a device which holds and passes on punched cards to a feed mechanism (*comput.*); **hopp'ing.** — **-hopping** in composition, making quick journeys between, usually by air, as in *island-hopping:* of an aircraft, skimming, as in *hedge-hopping.* — **hop-off** the start of a flight; **hop'-o'-my-thumb** (i.e. on my thumb) a pygmy. — *adj.* **hopp'ing(-)mad** (*coll.*) extremely angry. — **hop'-scotch** a game in which children hop over lines scotched or traced on the ground. — **hop it** (*slang*) to take oneself off; **hop, skip** (or **step**) **and jump** a leap on one leg, a skip, and a jump with both legs; **hop the twig** (*slang*) to escape one's creditors: to die; **on the hop** in a state of restless activity: in the act, unawares, at the very moment.   [O.E. *hoppian,* to dance; Ger. *hopfen, hüpfen.*]

hop[2] *hop, n.* a plant (*Humulus lupulus*) of the mulberry family with a long twining stalk: (in *pl.*) its bitter catkin-like fruit-clusters used for flavouring beer and in medicine: opium (*slang*): any narcotic (*slang*). — *v.t.* to mix or flavour with hops. — *v.i.* to gather hops: — *pr.p.* **hopp'ing;** *pa.t.* and *pa.p.* **hopped.** — *adj.* **hopped** impregnated with hops. — *ns.* **hopp'er, hop'-pick'er** one who picks hops: a mechanical contrivance for stripping hops from the bines; **hopp'ing** the act of gathering hops: the time of the hop harvest. — *adj.* **hopp'y** tasting of hops. — **hop'bind, hop'bine** the stalk of the hop; **hop'-bitt'ers** a drink like ginger-beer, flavoured with hops; **hop'dog** the tussock-moth caterpillar: a tool for pulling out hop-poles; **hop'-flea** a small beetle injurious to hops; **hop'-fly** a greenfly injurious to hops; **hop'-garden** a field of hops; **hop'-head** (*slang*) a drug addict; **hop'-oast** a kiln for drying hops. — *adj.* **hopped'-up** (*slang*) drugged: under an exhilarating drug: excited, agitated: artificially stimulated: made to seem exciting: given added power. — **hop'-pick'er** a hopper; **hop pillow** a pillow stuffed with hops, said to aid sleep; **hop'-pock'et** coarse sack for hops: about 1½ cwt. of hops; **hop'-pole** pole supporting hop-bine; **hop'(-)sack** sack for hops: (also **-sacking**) coarse fabric of hemp and jute, or woollen fabric with roughened surface; **hop'-tree** American rutaceous shrub (*Ptelea trifoliata*) with bitter fruit, substitute for hops; **hop'-tre'foil** a yellow clover; **hop'-vine** hop-plant: its stem; **hop'-yard** field where hops are grown. — **hop up** (*slang*) to excite, artificially stimulate: to drug. [Du. *hop*.]

hope[1] *hōp, v.i.* to cherish a desire of good with some expectation of fulfilment: to have confidence: to be hopeful. — *v.t.* to desire with belief in the possibility of fulfilment: to expect, fear (*obs.*). — *n.* a desire of some good, with a certain expectation of obtaining it: confidence: anticipation: that on which hopes are grounded: an embodiment of hope: that which is hoped for. — *adj.* **hope'ful** full of hope: having qualities which excite hope: promising good or success. — *n.* a promising young person. — *adv.* **hope'fully** in a hopeful manner: if all goes well (*coll.*). — *n.* **hope'fulness.** — *adj.* **hope'less** without hope: giving no ground to expect good or success: incurable: unhoped-for (*Spens.*). — *adv.* **hope'lessly.** — *ns.* **hope'lessness; hōp'er.** — *adv.* **hōp'ingly** (*arch.*). — **hope'-chest** (*U.S.*) a repository of things stored by a woman for her marriage—a bottom drawer. — **hope against hope** to continue to hope when there is no (longer any) reason for this hope; **it is hoped** (*coll.*) if all goes well; **no'-hop'er** (*slang*) a racehorse that is not good enough to have a chance of winning: any thing or person that has no chance of success (*fig.*): — *adj.* **no'-hope';** **some hope, what a hope, not a hope** (*iron.*) that will never happen. [O.E. *hopian* — *hopa*, hope; Du. *hopen*, Ger. *hoffen*.]

hope[2] *hōp, n.* an enclosure: the upper end of a narrow mountain-valley: a combe — common in Border place-names (usu. pron. -*ap*): an inlet. [O.E. -*hop* (in compounds), or O.N. *hóp*.]

hope[3]. See **forlorn hope.**

hoplite *hop'līt, n.* a heavy-armed Greek foot-soldier. [Gr. *hoplītēs*.]

hoplology *hop-lol'ə-ji, n.* the study of weapons. — *n.* **hoplol'ogist.** [Gr. *hoplon*, tool, weapon.]

hopple *hop'l, v.t.* to restrain by tying the feet together. — *n.* (chiefly in *pl.*) a fetter for horses, etc., when left to graze. [Cf. obs. Flem. *hoppelen*; also **hop**[1], **hobble**.]

hoppus (cubic) foot *hop'əs (kū'bik) fŏŏt,* a unit of volume for round timber. [E. *Hoppus*.]

horae canonicae *hō', hō'rē kən-on'i-kē, hō'rī kan-on'i-kī,* (L.) the canonical hours.

horal *hō'rəl, hö'rəl, adj.* relating to hours: hourly. — *adj.* **ho'rary** pertaining to an hour: noting the hours: hourly: continuing an hour. [L. *hōra*, an hour.]

Horatian *hor-ā'shən, adj.* pertaining to *Horace*, the Latin poet (65–8 B.C.), or to his manner or verse.

horde *hōrd, hörd, n.* a migratory or wandering tribe or clan: a multitude. — *v.i.* to live together as a horde: to come together to form a horde. — **Golden Horde** see **gold**[1]. [Fr., — Turk. *ordu*, camp.]

Hordeum *hör'di-əm, n.* the barley genus. — *ns.* **hordein** (*hör'di-in*) a protein found in barley grains; **hordeolum** (-*dē'*) a sty on the eyelid. [L., barley.]

hordock. See **hardoke.**

hore (*Spens.*). Same as **hoar.**

horehound, hoarhound *hōr', hör'hownd, n.* a hoary labiate plant (*Marrubium vulgare*) once popular as a remedy for coughs. — Also called **white horehound.** — **black horehound, stinking horehound** a darker-coloured kindred weed (*Ballota nigra*); **water horehound** gypsywort. [O.E. *hār,* hoar, *hūne,* horehound.]

horizon *hər-ī'zən, n.* the circle in which earth and sky seem to meet (*sensible, apparent,* or *visible horizon*): a plane through the earth's centre parallel to the sensible horizon (*rational horizon*), or the great circle in which it meets the heavens: a horizontal reflecting surface, as of mercury, used as a substitute for the horizon in taking an observation (*artificial horizon*): a stratigraphical level, characterised generally by some particular fossil or fossils (*geol.*), by a different physical property of the soil (*soil science*), or by artefacts characteristic of a particular culture or period (*archaeol.*): a level line or surface (*anat.*): the limit of one's experience or apprehension. — *adj.* **horizontal** (*hor-i-zont'l*) pertaining to the horizon: parallel to the horizon: level: near the horizon: measured in the plane of the horizon: applying equally to all members of a group, aspects of an activity, etc.: of relationships between separate groups of equal status or stage of development. — *n.* a horizontal line, position, or object: a large Tasmanian shrub, whose stem and branches ascend and then grow horizontally to form a dense mass of boughs and foliage, also **horizontal scrub.** — *n.* **horizontal'ity.** — *adv.* **horizon'tally.** — **horizontal bar** (*gymnastics*) a steel bar used for swinging and vaulting exercises. [Fr., — L., — Gr. *horīzōn* (*kyklos*), bounding (circle); *horīzōn, -ŏntos,* pr.p. of *horizein,* to bound — *horos,* a limit.]

horkey. See **hockey**[2].

horme *hör'mē* (*psych.*), *n.* goal-directed or purposive behaviour. — **hormic theory** theory stressing the importance of instinctive impulses and purposive striving. [Gr. *hormē,* animal impulse.]

hormone *hör'mōn, n.* an internal secretion which on reaching some part of a plant or animal body exercises a specific physiological action. — *adjs.* **hor'monal** (or -*mōn'*), **hormōn'ic** (or -*mōn'*). [Gr. *hormōn,* contracted pr.p. of *hormaein,* to stir up.]

horn *hörn, n.* a hard outgrowth on the head of an animal, sometimes confined to the hollow structure on an ox, sheep, goat, etc., sometimes extended to a deer's antler, the growth on a giraffe's head, on a rhinoceros's snout, etc.: a beetle's antenna: a snail's tentacle: any projection resembling a horn: a cusp: a crescent tip: an outgrowth visible only to the eye of faith on a cuckold's forehead: the material of which horns are composed, keratin: an object made of or like a horn, as a drinking vessel: a funnel-shaped mouthpiece: a wind instrument orig. made from a horn, now of brass, etc.: a sounding apparatus on motor vehicles: a Jewish symbol of strength: (*cap.*; with *the*) Cape Horn, in S. America: an erect penis (*slang*): see also **horn balance.** — *adj.* made of horn. — *v.t.* to furnish with horns, real or visionary: to dishorn: to outlaw (*obs. Scots law*): to gore: to butt or push. — *v.i.* to play or blow the horn: to butt. — *adj.* **horned** having a horn or horns: curved like a horn. — *ns.* **horn'er** one who works or deals in horns: a horn-player: a cuckold-maker (*obs.*); **horn'ful; Horn'ie** (*Scot.*) the devil, usu. represented with horns; **horn'iness; horn'ing** appearance of the moon when in its crescent form: a mock serenade with tin horns and any discordant instruments, a shivaree (*U.S. dial.*): putting to the horn (*obs. Scots law*): cuckold-making (*obs.*). — *adj.* **horn'ish** like horn: hard. — *n.* **horn'ist** a horn-player. — *adj.* **horn'less** without horns. — *n.* **horn'let** a little horn. — *adj.* **horn'y** like horn: of horn: hard: callous: sexually aroused (*slang*): lecherous, lustful (*slang*). — **horn balance** a forward extension of an aircraft control surface to assist its operation; **horn'-beak** (*dial.*) the garfish; **horn'beam** a tree (*Carpinus*) resembling a beech, with hard tough wood; **horn'bill** a bird (of family Bucerotidae) with a horny excrescence on its bill; **horn'book** (*hist.*) a first book for children, which consisted of a single leaf set in a frame, with a thin plate of transparent horn in front to preserve it; **horn'bug** (*U.S.*) a stag-beetle; **horned cairn** (*archaeol.*) a long barrow with a pair of curved projecting arms at one end, or at both; **horned horse** the gnu; **horned owl, horn owl** an owl with hornlike tufts of feathers on its head; **horned poppy** a poppy (*Glaucium*) with horned seed-vessel; **horned toad** a spiny American lizard (*Phrynosoma*): a S. American toad (*Ceratophrys*) with a bony shield on the back; **horn'fels** (*-fels*; Ger. *Fels*, rock) a compact rock composed of lime silicates produced by contact metamorphism: — *pl.* **horn'fels, horn'felses.** — *adj.* **horn'-foot'ed** hoofed. — **horn gate** gate of horn (see **gate¹**); **horn'geld** (*hist.*) cornage. — *adj.* **horn'-mad** (*arch.*) mad to the point of goring anybody: enraged like a cuckold. — **horn'-mad'ness** (*Browning*); **horn'-mak'er** (*Shak.*) a cuckold-maker; **horn mercury** native mercurous chloride or calomel; **horn'-nut** water-chestnut; **horn-pout, horned-pout** see **pout².** — *adj.* **horn'-rimmed** having rims of horn, or material resembling horn. — **horn'-rims** dark horn-rimmed spectacles; **horn silver** cerargyrite; **horn spoon** a spoon made of a sheep's horn; **horn'stone** a flinty chalcedony: hornfels; **horn'tail** a hymenopterous insect, often with a stout ovipositor; **horn'work** an outwork having angular points or horns, and composed of two demi-bastions joined by a curtain (*fort.*): work in horn: cuckoldry (*obs.*); **horn'worm** a hawkmoth caterpillar; **horn'wort** a rootless water-plant (*Ceratophyllum*) with much-divided submerged leaves that turn translucent and horny; **horn'wrack** the sea-mat. — *adj.* **horn'y-hand'ed** with hands hardened by toil. — **horn'yhead** an American cyprinoid fish with hornlike processes on its head. — **horn in** to interpose, butt in (on); **horn of plenty** see **cornucopia**: a trumpet-shaped edible fungus, *Craterellus cornucopoides*; **horns of a dilemma** see **dilemma; horns of the altar** the projections at the four corners of the Hebrew altar; **letters of horning** (*Scots law*) letters running in the sovereign's name, and passing the signet, instructing messengers-at-arms to charge the debtor to pay, on his failure a caption or warrant for his apprehension being granted; **make a spoon or spoil a horn** to attempt something at the risk of failure; **pull** or **draw in one's horns** to abate one's ardour or pretensions: to curtail or restrict one's activities, spending, etc.; **put to the horn** (*obs. Scots law*) to outlaw by three blasts of the horn at the Cross of Edinburgh. [O.E. *horn*; Scand. *horn*, Ger. *Horn*, Gael. and W. *corn*. L. *cornū*, Gr. *keras*.]

hornblende *hörn'blend*, *n.* a rock-forming mineral, one of the amphiboles, essentially silicate of calcium, magnesium and iron, generally green to black, with cleavage angle about 56°. — *adj.* **hornblend'ic.** [Ger.; cf. **horn, blende.**]

hornet *hörn'it*, *n.* a large kind of wasp. — **stir up a hornet's nest** to do something which causes a violent reaction. [O.E. *hyrnet*, app. — *horn*, horn.]

hornfels, horngeld, Hornie. See **horn.**

hornito *hör-nē'tō*, *n.* a low oven-shaped fumarole: — *pl.* **horni'tos.** [Sp., dim. of *horno* — L. *furnus*, an oven.]

hornpipe *hörn'pīp*, *n.* an old Welsh musical instrument like a clarinet, prob. sometimes with a horn mouthpiece or bell: a lively English dance, usually by one person, popular amongst sailors: a tune for the dance. [**horn, pipe¹**.]

hornswoggle *hörnz'wog-l*, (*slang*; orig. *U.S.*) *v.t.* to trick, deceive: to cheat. [Ety. unknown.]

horography *hor-og'rə-fi*, *n.* the art of constructing sundials, clocks, etc. — *n.* **horog'rapher.** [Gr. *hōrā*, an hour, *graphein*, to describe.]

horologe *hor'ə-loj*, *n.* any instrument for telling the hours. — *ns.* **horologer** (*-ol'ə-jər*), **horol'ogist** a maker of clocks, etc. — *adjs.* **horolog'ic, -al.** — *ns.* **horolog'ium** a horologe (*obs.*): (*cap.*) a southern constellation (*astron.*); **horol'ogy** the science of time measurement: the art of clock-making: the office-book of the Greek Church for the canonical hours, also **horologium.** [L. *hōrologium* — Gr. *hōrologion* — *hōrā*, an hour, *legein*, to tell.]

horometry *hor-om'it-ri*, *n.* time measurement. — *adj.* **horometrical** (*-met'*). [Gr. *hōrā*, an hour, *metron*, a measure.]

horoscope *hor'ə-skōp*, *n.* a map of the heavens at the hour or on the day of a person's birth, by which the astrologer predicted the events of his life: a representation of the heavens for this purpose: any similar prediction about the future. — *adj.* **horoscopic** (*-skop'*). — *ns.* **horoscopist** (*-os'kə-pist*) an astrologer; **horos'copy** the art of predicting the events of a person's life from his horoscope: aspect of the stars at the time of birth. [Gr. *hōroskopos* — *hōrā*, an hour, *skopeein*, to observe.]

horrendous *hor-end'əs*, (*coll.*) *adj.* dreadful: frightful: horrible. — *adv.* **horrend'ously.** [L. *horrendus*, ger. of *horrēre*, to bristle.]

horrent *hor'ənt*, *adj.* bristling. [L. *horrēns, -ntis*, pr.p. of *horrēre*, to bristle.]

horrible *hor'i-bl*, *adj.* exciting horror: dreadful: detestable (*coll.*). — *n.* **horr'ibleness.** — *adv.* **horr'ibly.** [L. *horribilis* — *horrēre*, to shudder.]

horrid *hor'id*, *adj.* shaggy, bristling, rough (*arch.* or *poet.*): horrible (*arch.*): repellent, detestable (*coll.*). — *adv.* **horr'idly.** — *n.* **horr'idness.** [L. *horridus* — *horrēre*, to bristle.]

horrify *hor'i-fī*, *v.t.* to strike with horror: — *pr.p.* **horr'ifying;** *pa.t.* and *pa.p.* **horr'ified.** — *adj.* **horrif'ic** exciting horror: frightful. — *advs.* **horrif'ically; horr'ifyingly.** [L. *horrificus* — root of *horrēre*, to shudder, *facĕre*, to make.]

horripilation *hor-i-pi-lā'shən*, *n.* a contraction of the cutaneous muscles causing erection of the hairs and goose-flesh. — *adj.* **horrip'ilant.** — *v.t.* and *v.i.* **horrip'ilate.** [L. *horripilātiō, -ōnis* — root of *horrēre*, to bristle, *pilus*, a hair.]

horrisonant *hor-is'ən-ənt*, *adj.* sounding dreadfully. — Also **horris'onous** (*arch.*). [From root of L. *horrēre*, to bristle, *sonāns, -antis*, sounding.]

horror *hor'ər*, *n.* shagginess, raggedness (*obs.*): a shuddering: intense repugnance: power of exciting such feeling: a source of such feeling: anything mildly objectionable, ridiculous, grotesque, or distasteful (*coll.*). — *adj.* of a comic (i.e. strip cartoon), film, novel, etc., having gruesome, violent, horrifying, or blood-curdling themes. — *adjs.* **horr'or-stricken, -struck.** — **the horrors** extreme depression: delirium tremens. [L. *horror*, a shudder, bristling, etc.]

hors *or*, (Fr.) *prep.* out of, outside. — **hors concours** (*kɔ-kōōr*) not in competition; **hors de combat** (*də kɔ̃-ba*) unfit to fight, disabled; **hors de saison** (*də se-zɔ̃*) out of season; **hors d'œuvre** (*pl.* **d'œuvre, d'œuvres;** *dœ-vr'*) savoury, e.g. olives, sardines, etc., to whet the appetite before a meal; **hors la loi** (*la lwa*) in outlawry, outlawed; **hors série** (*sā-rē*) excluded from a series, added later; **hors texte** (*tekst*) an illustration inset separately into a book.

horse *hörs*, *n.* a solid-hoofed ungulate (*Equus caballus*) with flowing tail and mane: any member of the genus Equus (horse, ass, zebra, etc.) or the family Equidae: a male adult of the species: (*collec.*) cavalry: a wooden frame on which soldiers used to be mounted as a punishment — also *timber-mare*: a gymnastic apparatus for vaulting, etc.: a horselike apparatus or support of various kinds (as *saw-horse, clothes-horse*): a crib or translation, a pony (*U.S. slang*): a mass of barren country interrupting a lode: heroin (*slang*): — *pl.* **horses,** sometimes **horse.** — *v.t.* to mount or set as on a horse: to provide with a horse: to sit astride: to carry on the back: (of a stallion) to cover: to urge at work tyrannically. — *v.i.* to get on horseback: to travel on horseback: to charge for work before it is done (with *it*). — *adj.* **horse'less** without a horse: mechanically driven. — *ns.* **hors'iness; hors'ing** (*arch.*) birching of a person mounted on another's back. — *adj.* **hors'y** of or pertaining to horses: horselike: devoted to horses, horse-racing, or breeding. — *adj.* **horse'-and-bugg'y** hopelessly out of date. — **horse artillery** field artillery with comparatively light guns and the gunners mounted; **horse'back** the back of a horse; **horse bean** a variety of broad bean: applied also to other beans; **horse block** a block or stage for mounting and dismounting by; **horse boat** a boat for carrying horses, or towed by a horse; **horse bot** a botfly; **horse box** a trailer or railway car designed to carry horses: a stall on shipboard: a high-sided church pew (*facet.*); **horse'= boy** a stable boy; **horse brass** a usu. brass ornament orig. for hanging on the harness of a horse; **horse'= bread** a coarse bread for feeding horses; **horse'= break'er, -tam'er** one who breaks or tames horses, or teaches them to draw or carry: a courtesan who appears on horseback (*obs.*); **horse'car** (*U.S.*) a street-car drawn by horses; **horse chestnut** a smooth, brown, bitter seed or nut, perh. so called from its coarseness contrasted with the edible chestnut: the tree that produces it (*Aesculus hippocastanum*); **horse'-cloth** a cloth for covering a horse; **horse'-collar** a stuffed collar for a draught-horse, carrying the hames; **horse'-cop'er** or (*Scot.*) **horse'-couper** (*kow', kōō'*), **horse'-deal'er** one who deals in horses; **horse'-courser** (*obs.*) a jobbing dealer in horses; **horse'-dealing**; **horse'= doc'tor** a veterinary surgeon; **horse'-drench** a dose of medicine for a horse. — *adj.* **horse'-faced** having a long horselike face. — **horse fair** a fair or market for sale of horses. — *n.pl.* and *interj.* **horse'feathers** (*U.S.*) nonsense. — **horse'flesh** the flesh of a horse: horses collectively. — *adj.* of reddish-bronze colour. — **horse-flesh ore** bornite or erubescite, from its colour; **horse'fly** the forest-fly or other large fly that stings horses; **horse'-foot** coltsfoot (*obs.*): a kingcrab; **horse'-god'-mother** (*dial.*) a fat clumsy woman; **horse'-gow'an** (*Scot.*) the ox-eye daisy. — *n.pl.* **horse guards** horse soldiers employed as guards: (*cap.*) the cavalry brigade of the British household troops, esp. the *Royal Horse Guards*, or *Blues*, a regiment raised in 1661; (*cap.*) their headquarters in Whitehall, London, once seat of the departments of the army commander-in-chief: the military authorities. — **horse'hair** a hair from a horse's mane or tail: a mass of such hairs: a fabric woven from horsehair. — *adj.* made of or stuffed with horsehair. — **horse'hide; horse hoe** a hoe drawn by horses; **horse'= knack'er** one who buys and slaughters worn-out horses; **horse latitudes** two zones of the Atlantic Ocean (about 30°N and 30°S, esp. the former) noted for long calms; **horse'laugh** a harsh, boisterous laugh; **horse'= leech** a horse-doctor (*obs.*): a large species of leech, supposed to fasten on horses: a bloodsucker (Prov. xxx. 15); **horseless carriage** (*arch.*) a motor-car; **horse'= litt'er** a litter or bed borne between two horses: bedding for horses; **horse mackerel** the scad or allied fish: the tunny: applied to various other fishes; **horse'man** a rider: one skilled in managing a horse: a mounted soldier: one who has charge of horses: a kind of carrier pigeon: a kind of land-crab; **horse'manship** the art of riding and of training and managing horses; **horse-man's word** (*Scot. hist.*) a ploughman's secret word to control horses: a magic word used against one's enemy, imparted by the devil in exchange for service in hell; **horse marine** a person quite out of his element: a member of an imaginary corps; **horse'meat** food for horses; **horse mill** a mill turned by horses; **horse'= mill'iner** (*arch.*) one who provides the trappings for horses; **horse'mint** any wild mint: the American *Monarda punctata*, or any of several other species of *Monarda*: (**sweet horsemint**) the common dittany; **horse mushroom** a large coarse mushroom; **horse mussel** a mollusc (*Modiolus*) akin to the common mussel but much bigger; **horse nail** a nail for fastening a horseshoe to the hoof; **horse opera** a Wild West film; **horse pistol** a large pistol formerly carried in a holster by horsemen; **horse'play** rough, boisterous play; **horse'pond** a pond for watering horses at; **horse'power** the power a horse

can exert, or its conventional equivalent (taken as 746 watt); **horse'-race** a race by horses; **horse'-racing** the practice of racing or running horses in matches; **horse'-radish** plant allied to scurvy-grass with a pungent root, used as a condiment; **horse'radish tree** a tree, *Moringa pterygosperma*, cultivated in tropical countries for its edible capsules and its seeds, ben-nuts, which yield oil of ben — the roots tasting like horseradish: an Australian tree, *Codonocarpus cotinifolius*, with leaves of horseradish flavour; **horse rake** a rake drawn by horses; **horse'-rider; horse'-rid'ing; horse sense** (*coll.*) plain common-sense; **horse'shoe** a shoe for horses, consisting of a curved piece of iron: anything of like shape. — *adj.* shaped like a horseshoe. — **horse'shoer** (*-shōō'ər*) one who makes or affixes horseshoes; **horse'-shoe'ing; (African) horse'-sick'ness** a serious disease of horses, due to a virus; **horse soldier** a cavalry soldier; **horse'tail** a horse's tail: a Turkish standard, marking rank by number: any plant of the genus Equisetum (scouring-rush) with hollow rush-like stems, constituting with kindred fossils a class of fern-allies, Equisetinae; **horse'-thief; horse'-trading** hard bargaining; **horse'-train'er** one who trains horses for racing, etc.; **horse'way** a road by which a horse may pass; **horse'-whip** a whip for driving horses. — *v.t.* to thrash with a horsewhip: to lash. — **horse-wom'an** a woman who rides on horseback, or who rides well. — **dark horse** see **dark; flog a dead horse** to try to work up excitement about a threadbare subject; **gift horse** see **gift; high horse** see **on one's high horse** (under **high**[1]); **hold your horses** not so fast: wait a moment; **horse and hattock** see **hat; horse around** (*slang*) to fool about; **horses for courses** phrase expressing the view that each racehorse will do best on a certain course which peculiarly suits it (also *fig.*).; **horse of a different colour** another thing altogether; **put the cart before the horse** see **cart; (straight) from the horse's mouth** from a very trustworthy source (of information); **take horse** to mount on horseback; **white horse** see **white; willing horse** a willing, obliging, worker. [O.E. *hors*; O.N. *hross*; O.H.G. *hros* (Ger. *Ross*.).]

horson (*Shak.*). Same as **whoreson** at **whore**.

horst *hörst*, (*geol.*) *n.* a block of the earth's crust that has remained in position while the ground around it has either subsided or been folded into mountains by pressure against its solid sides. [Ger.]

horsy. See **horse.**

hortative *hört'ə-tiv, adj.* inciting: encouraging: giving advice. — Also **hort'atory.** — *advs.* **hort'atively, hort'-atorily.** — *n.* **horta'tion.** [L. *hortārī, -ātus,* to incite.]

horticulture *hör'ti-kul-chər, n.* the art of gardening. — *adj.* **horticul'tural.** — *n.* **horticul'turist** one versed in the art of cultivating gardens. [L. *hortus,* a garden, *cultūra* — *colĕre,* to cultivate.]

hortus siccus *hör'təs sik'əs, hor'tōōs sik'ōōs,* (L.) a collection of dried plants: a herbarium.

Horus *hō'rəs, hör', n.* the Egyptian sun-god, son of Isis and Osiris, usu. depicted with a falcon's head. [Egypt. *hur,* hawk.]

hosanna *hō-zan'ə, n.* an exclamation of praise to God. [Gr. *hōsanna* — Heb. *hōshī 'āh nnā, hōshīā',* save, *nā,* I pray.]

hose *hōz, n.* a covering for the legs or feet: stockings: socks (*half-hose*): close-fitting breeches or drawers (*obs.*): a flexible pipe for conveying water, etc., so called from its shape: a socket for a shaft: — *pl.* **hose; hos'en** (*arch.*); in sense of pipe, *pl.* **hos'es.** — *v.t.* to provide with hose (*arch.*): to play a hose on (often with *down*). — *adj.* **hosed.** — *ns.* **hosier** (*hōzh'(y)ər, hōz'yər*) a dealer in or a maker of hosiery; **hō'siery** hose collectively: knitted goods. — **hose'man** a fireman who directs the stream of water; **hose'-net** (*Scot.*) a stocking-shaped net; **hose'pipe; hose'-reel** a large revolving drum for carrying hoses. [O.E. *hosa,* pl. *hosan,* Du. *hoos,* Ger. *Hose.*]

hospice *hos'pis, n.* a house of entertainment for strangers, esp. one kept by monks: a hostel: a home of refuge: a home for the care of the terminally ill.   [Fr., — L. *hospitium* — *hospes, -itis*, a stranger, guest.]

hospitable *hos'pit-ə-bl*, or *hos-pit'*, *adj.* kind to strangers: welcoming and generous towards guests. — *n.* **hos'pitableness** (or *-pit'*). — *adv.* **hos'pitably** (or *-pit'*). — *ns.* **hospitage** (*hos'pit-ij*; *Spens.*) that which is due from a guest; **hospitality** see under **hospital**.   [L.L. *hospitāgium* — L. *hospes, -itis*, stranger, guest.]

hospital *hos'pit-l*, *n.* a hostel for travellers (*obs.*): formerly, a charitable institution for the old or destitute, or for reception (and education) of the needy young: an institution for treatment of sick or injured: a building for any of these purposes. — *ns.* **hos'pitale** (*-āl*; *Spens.*) lodging; **hospitalisā'tion, -z-.** — *v.t.* **hos'pitalise, -ize** to send to hospital. — *ns.* **hospitality** (*-al'i-ti*) (friendly welcome and) entertainment of guests (also *fig.*); **hos'pitaller** (*U.S. -pitaler*) one of a charitable brotherhood for the care of the sick in hospitals: one of the Knights of St John (otherwise called Knights of Rhodes, and afterwards of Malta), an order which built a hospital for pilgrims at Jerusalem. — **hos'pital-ship** a ship fitted out exclusively for the treatment and transport of the sick and wounded.   [O.Fr. *hospital* — L.L. *hospitāle* — *hospes, -itis*, a guest.]

hospitium *hos-pish'i-əm*, *n.* a hospice: — *pl.* **hospi'tia**.   [L.; cf. **hospice**.]

hospodar *hos'po-där*, (*hist.*) *n.* a prince or governor, esp. of Moldavia or Wallachia. — Also **gos'podar**.   [Rum. *hospodár*, of Slav. origin.]

hoss *hos*, (esp. *U.S. coll.* and *dial.*) *n.* a horse.

host¹ *hōst*, *n.* one who entertains a stranger or guest at his house without (or with) reward (*fem.* **host'ess**): an innkeeper (*fem.* **host'ess**): one who introduces performers or participants, chairs discussions, etc. on a programme or show: the venue for (an event), usu. implying some involvement in the organisation of the event and the welcoming of the participants: an organism on which another lives as a parasite (also *fig.*): a host computer (see below). — *v.t.* to receive and entertain as one's guest: to act as, be, the host of (a show, programme, event, etc.). — *v.i.* (*Spens., Shak.*) to lodge, to be a guest. — *ns.* **host'ess** a female host: a paid female partner at a dance-hall, nightclub, etc.: a prostitute. — also *v.t.* (*obs.* and *U.S.*) and *v.i.* (*obs.*); **host'ess-ship** the character or office of a hostess. — *adj.* **host'lesse** (*Spens.*) inhospitable. — *n.* **host'ry** (*Spens.*) lodging. — **host computer** a computer attached to and in control of a multi-terminal computer system, or one attached to a multi-computer network and able e.g. to provide access to a number of databases. — **air'-hostess** one appointed to look after the comfort of the passengers in an aircraft; **lie at host** (*Shak.*) to be lodged; **reckon** or **count without one's host** to count up one's bill without reference to the landlord: to fail to take account of some important possibility, as the action of another.   [O.Fr. *hoste* — L. *hospes, hospitis*.]

host² *hōst*, *n.* an army (*arch.*): a great multitude. — *n.* **host'ing** a battle (*Milt.*): a muster, a military expedition (*Spens.*). — **a host in himself** one of great strength, skill, or resources, within himself; **heavenly host** the angels and archangels; **Lord of hosts** a favourite Hebrew term for Jehovah, considered as head of the hosts of angels, the hosts of stars, etc.   [O.Fr. *host* — L. *hostis*, an enemy.]

host³ *hōst*, *n.* a sacrificial victim (*obs.*): (often *cap.*) in the R.C. Church, the consecrated wafer of the eucharist.   [L. *hostia*, a victim.]

Hosta *hōst'ə*, *n.* a genus of decorative perennial herbaceous plants (fam. *Liliaceae*) from Asia with ribbed basal leaves and blue, white, and lilac flowers: (without *cap.*) any plant of the genus.   [After Austrian botanist N. T. *Host*.]

hostage *hos'tij*, *n.* one kept in the hands of an enemy as a pledge. — **hostages to fortune** the people and things one values most (Bacon's *Essays*: Of Marriage and Single Life): hence, things of which the loss would be

particularly painful.   [O.Fr. *hostage* (Fr. *ôtage*) — L. *obses, obsidis*, a hostage.]

hostel *hos'təl*, *n.* an inn: in some universities an extra-collegiate hall for students: a residence for students or for some class or society of persons, esp. one not run commercially: a youth hostel. — *ns.* **hos'teler, hos'teller** hospitaller (*arch.*): keeper of a hostel: one who lives in, or uses, a hostel; **hos'telling** making sojourns in youth hostels; **hos'telry** an inn.   [O.Fr. *hostel, hostellerie* — L. *hospitāle*; cf. **hospital**.]

hostess. See **host¹**.

hostile *hos'tīl*, in *U.S. -təl*, *adj.* pertaining to an enemy: showing enmity or unfriendliness, or angry opposition: resistant (to; esp. to new ideas, changes): (of place, conditions) inhospitable, harsh: engaged in hostilities: pertaining to hostilities. — *adv.* **hos'tilely.** — *n.* **hostility** (*-til'*) enmity: — *pl.* **hostil'ities** acts of warfare. — **hostile witness** (*legal*) a witness who gives evidence against the party he/she was called by.   [L. *hostīlis* — *hostis*.]

hostler *hos'lər*, (*obs.*) *os'ler*, (*obs.* and *U.S.*) *n.* an ostler.

hot¹ *hot*, *adj.* (*comp.* **hott'er**; *superl.* **hott'est**) having a high temperature: very warm: fiery: pungent: giving a feeling suggestive of heat: animated: ardent: vehement: violent: passionate: sexually excited: lustful: dangerously charged with electricity: dangerous: near the object sought: of news, fresh, exciting: of jazz, etc., music which is intensely played with complex rhythms and exciting improvisations: skilful (*coll.*): recently obtained dishonestly (*coll.*): highly radioactive (*coll.*). — *adv.* **hot**ly. — *v.t.* (*coll.*) to heat: — *pr.p.* **hott'ing**; *pa.t.* and *pa.p* **hott'ed.** — *adv.* **hot'ly.** — *ns.* **hot'ness**; **hott'ie** (*coll.*) a hot-water bottle. — *adj.* **hott'ish.** — **hot air** empty talk. — *adjs.* **hot'-air** making use of heated air: boastful, empty; **hot-air balloon** one containing air which is heated by a flame to maintain or increase altitude; **hot'-and-hot'** cooked and served up at once in hot dishes. — Also *n.* — **hot'bed** a glass-covered bed heated by a layer of fermenting manure for bringing forward plants rapidly: a place or conditions favourable to rapid growth or development, usu. of a bad kind (*fig.*); **hot blast** a blast of heated air. — *adj.* **hot'-blood'ed** having hot blood: homothermous: passionate: ardent: high-spirited: irritable. — **hot'-brain** (*arch.*) a hothead. — *adj.* **hot'-brained** (*arch.*). — **hot'-cock'les** an old game in which one with eyes covered guesses who strikes him; **hot coppers** see **copper¹**; **hot dog** a hot sausage sandwich: (**hot'-dog'**) one who performs clever manoeuvres, such as spins and turns, while skiing, surfing or skate-boarding (*coll.*; esp. *U.S.*). — *v.i.* **hot'-dog'** (*coll.*; esp. *U.S.*). — **hot'-dogg'er**; **hot'-dogging**; **hot favourite** in sports, races, etc., the most likely to win (also *fig.*); **hot flue** (*obs.*) a drying-room. — *adv.* **hot'foot** in haste (**hotfoot it** (*coll.*) to rush). — **hot gospeller** a loud, forceful proclaimer of a religious faith: a fanatical propagandist; **hot gospelling**; **hot'head** an impetuous headstrong person. — *adj.* **hot'headed.** — **hot'house** a house kept hot for the rearing of tropical or tender plants: any heated chamber or drying-room, esp. that where pottery is placed before going into the kiln: a hot-bathing establishment (*obs.*): a brothel (*Shak.*): any establishment promoting the development of skills, etc. (*fig.*). — *adj.* (*fig.*) (too) delicate, unable to exist in tough, or even normal, conditions. — **hot line** special telephone and teleprinter link with the Kremlin, orig. one from Washington: any line of speedy communication ready for an emergency. — *adj.* **hot'-liv'ered** (*Milt.*) hot-tempered. — **hot melt** (or **hot-melt glue, adhesive**) an adhesive that is applied hot and which sets as it cools; **hot metal** (*print.*) used to describe machines or methods using type made from molten metal; **hot money** funds transferred suddenly from one country to another because conditions make transfer financially advantageous. — *adj.* **hot'-mouthed** (*obs.*) of a horse, restive, as when the bit hurts. — **hot pants** women's very brief shorts: sexual desire (for) (*slang*);

hot plate the flat top surface of a stove for cooking: a similar plate, independently heated, for keeping things hot; hot'pot a dish of chopped mutton seasoned and stewed in a pot, with sliced potatoes, or similar mixture; hot potato see potato. — v.t. hot'-press to press (paper, cloth, etc.) between hot plates to produce a glossy surface. — hot rod a motor-car converted for speed by stripping off non-essentials and heightening in power; hot rodder the owner of a hot rod: a reckless youth; hot seat the electric chair (U.S. slang): any uncomfortable situation (fig.); hot shoe a socket on a camera for attaching flash apparatus. — adj. hot'-short brittle when heated. — hot'shot (esp. U.S.) a person who is (esp. showily) successful, skilful, etc. — adj. hot'-spir'ited having a fiery spirit. — hot spot an area of (too) high temperature in an engine, etc.: a region of the earth where there is evidence of isolated volcanic activity due to hot material rising through the earth's mantle: a nightclub (coll.): an area of potential trouble, esp. political (fig.): a place of very high radioactivity; hot spring a spring of water which has been heated underground, occurring esp. in volcanic regions; Hot'-spur a violent, rash man like Henry Percy (1364–1403), so nicknamed; hot stuff (slang) any person, thing, or performance that is outstandingly remarkable, excellent, vigorous, or reprehensible. — adjs. hotted-up see hot up below; hot'-tem'pered having a quick temper. — hot'-trod (Scot.) the hot pursuit in old Border forays; hot wall a wall enclosing passages for hot air, affording warmth to fruit-trees; hot war real war, not cold war; hot water (coll.) a state of trouble; hot-water bottle a container of hot water, used to warm a bed, or sometimes parts of the body; hot well a spring of hot water: in a condensing engine, a reservoir for the warm water drawn off from the condenser. — go, sell, like hot cakes to sell off or disappear promptly; have the hots for (slang) to be sexually attracted to, desire sexually; hot cross bun a bun bearing a cross, customarily eaten on Good Friday; hot on (coll.) fond of, interested in: good at, well-informed about; hot on the heels (of) (coll.) following, pursuing, closely; hot under the collar indignant, embarrassed; hot up (coll.) to increase in excitement, energy, performance, etc. (adj. hott'ed-up'); in hot pursuit pursuing at full speed; make it hot for to make it unpleasant or impossible for. [O.E. hāt; Ger. heiss. Sw. het.]

hot² hot, hote hōt, (Spens.) named: was called. [Pa.t. active and passive of hight.]

hotch hoch, (Scot.) v.t. and v.i. to hitch, jog: to fidget with eagerness. — hotch with to swarm, seethe with. [Cf. Du. hotsen, Fr. hocher.]

hotchpotch hoch'poch, hotchpot hoch'pot, hodge-podge hoj'poj, ns. a confused mass of ingredients shaken or mixed together in the same pot: a kind of mutton-broth with vegetables of many kinds: a jumble: (hotchpot) a commixture of property in order to secure an equable division amongst children. [Fr. hochepot — hocher, to shake, and pot, a pot; cf. Du. hutspot.]

hote, hoten. See hight.

hotel hō-tel' (old-fashioned ō-tel'), n. a house for the accommodation of strangers: an inn: in France, also a public office, a private townhouse, a palace. — hôtel de ville (Fr. ō-tel də vēl) a town hall; hôtel-Dieu (Fr. ō-tel-dyø) a hospital; hotelier (hō-tel'yər; Fr. hôtelier; ōt-ə-lyā) one who owns, runs a hotel; hotel'-keeper. [Fr. hôtel — L. hospitālia, guest-chambers — hospes.]

Hottentot hot'n-tot, n. one of a dwindling, nomad, pastoral, pale-brown-skinned race in S.-W. Africa (resembling Bushmen and Bantu), calling themselves khoikhoin (men of men): their language: a barbarian: a coloured person (derog.): (without cap.) a small fish pachymetopon blochii. — Also adj. — Hottentot fig the edible fruit of a Mesembrianthemum; Hottentot's bread elephant-foot; Hottentot('s) god praying mantis. [Du. imit.; the language was unintelligible to them and sounded staccato.]

hotter hot'er, (Scot.) v.i. to vibrate: to tremble: to clatter:

to totter: to jolt: to swarm. — n. vibration: commotion: swarming. [Cf. Flem. hotteren.]

hottie. See hot¹.

houdah. See howdah.

houdan hōō'dən, n. a black and white five-toed domestic fowl of a breed orig. from Houdan in Seine-et-Oise.

houf(f). See howf(f).

hough hok (Scot. hohh). See hock¹.

hound hownd, n. a dog (arch., coll.): a dog of a kind used in hunting: a pursuer in a paper-chase: a contemptible scoundrel: a hunter, tracker, or assiduous seeker of anything: an addict, devotee — often in composition. — v.t. to set on in chase: to drive by harassing. — hound'-fish a dog-fish; hounds'-berry dogwood; hounds'-foot (obs.; Ger. Hundsfott, -futt, vulva canina) a scoundrel. — adj. (Scott) scoundrelly. — hound's'-tongue a plant (Cynoglossum) of the borage family (from its leaf); hound's'-tooth a textile pattern of broken checks. — Also adj. — hound'-trailing speed competition between hounds trained to follow an aniseed trail. — Gabriel('s) hounds (coll.) the yelping noise made by flights of wild-geese, ascribed to damned souls whipped on by the angel Gabriel; master of hounds the master of a pack of hounds; ride to hounds to hunt (on horseback). [O.E. hund; Gr. kyōn, kynos, L. canis, Sans. śva.]

hour owr, n. 60 minutes, or the 24th part of the day: the time as indicated by a clock, etc.: an hour's journey, or three miles: a time or occasion: an angular unit (15°) of right ascension: (in pl.) the goddesses of the seasons and the hours (myth.): (in pl.) set times of prayer, the canonical hours, the offices or services prescribed for these, or a book containing them, often illustrated (also book of hours): (pl.) the prescribed times for doing business. — adj. hour'ly happening or done every hour: frequent. — adv. every hour: frequently. — hour'-ang'le (astron.) the angle (usu. measured as time) between the declination circle of a body observed and the observer's meridian; hour'-cir'cle a great circle passing through the celestial poles: the circle of an equatorial which shows the right ascension; hour'-glass an instrument for measuring the hours by the running of sand through a narrow neck. — adj. having the form of an hour-glass: constricted. — hour'-hand the hand which shows the hour on a clock, etc. — adj. and adv. hour'long' lasting an hour. — hour'plate a timepiece dial. — at all hours at irregular hours, esp. late hours; at the eleventh hour at the last moment (Matt. xx. 6, 9); in a good or evil hour under a fortunate, or an unfortunate, impulse — from the old belief in astrological influences; keep good hours to go to bed and to rise early: to lead a quiet and regular life; on the hour at exactly one, two, etc. o'clock. [O.Fr. hore (Fr. heure) — L. hora — Gr. hōrā.]

houri hōō'ri, how'ri, n. a nymph of the Muslim paradise: a voluptuously alluring woman. [Pers. hūrī — Ar. hūriya, a black-eyed girl.]

house hows, n. a building for dwelling in: a building in general: a dwelling-place: an inn: a public-house: a household: a family in line of descent: kindred: a trading establishment: one of the twelve divisions of the heavens in astrology: a legislative or deliberative body or its meeting-place: a convent: school boarding-house: pupils of such collectively: section of a school where no such boarding-house exists: an audience, auditorium, or performance: the workhouse (old. coll.): (the House) at Oxford, Christ Church (Aedes Christi), in London, the Stock Exchange, the Houses of Parliament: a gambling form of bingo: — pl. houses (howz'iz). — adj. domestic. — v.t. house (howz) to protect by covering: to shelter: to store: to provide houses for. — v.i. to take shelter: to reside. — n. house'ful (pl. house'fuls). — adj. house'less without a house or home: having no shelter. — n. housing (howz'ing) houses, accommodation, or shelter, or the provision thereof: a cavity into which a timber fits: anything designed to cover, protect, contain, etc.

machinery or the like: housing joint. — Also *adj.* — **house'-a'gent** one who arranges the buying, selling, and letting of houses; **house'-arrest'** confinement, under guard, to one's house, or to a hospital, etc., instead of imprisonment; **house'-boat** a barge with a deck-cabin that may serve as a dwelling-place; **house'-bote** a tenant's right to wood to repair his house. — *adj.* **house'bound** confined to one's house because of illness, young children, etc. — **house'boy** a male domestic servant, usu. African or Indian; **house'-breaker** one who breaks into and enters a house for the purpose of stealing: one whose work is demolishing old houses; **house'-breaking**. — *adj.* **house'-brok'en** house-trained. — **house'-carl** (*hist.*) member of a king's or noble's bodyguard; **house church, house group** a group of Christians meeting usu. in a house for worship, prayer, Bible study, etc., usu. in addition to Sunday church worship; **house'-coat** a woman's usu. long coat-like dressing-gown, worn at home; **house'craft** skill in domestic activities; **house'-dog** a dog kept in a house: a watch-dog; **house'-du'ty, -tax** a tax laid on inhabited houses; **house'-fac'tor** (*Scot.*) a house-agent; **house'-fa'ther** the male head of a household or community: a man in charge of children in an institution; **house'-flag** the distinguishing flag of a shipowner or shipping company; **house'-fly** the common fly universally distributed; **house group** see **house church; house guest** a guest in a private house; **house'hold** those who are held together in the same house, and compose a family. — *adj.* pertaining to the house and family: well-known to the general public, as in *household name, word.* — **house'holder** the holder or tenant of a house; **household gods** see **god, lar, penates; household suffrage** or **franchise** the right of householders to vote for members of parliament; **household troops** Guards regiments whose peculiar duty is to attend the sovereign and defend the metropolis; **household word** a familiar saying or name: — *v.i.* **house'-hunt** to look for a house to live in. — **house'-hunter; house'-hunting; house'-husband** a married man who looks after the house and family and does not have a paid job; **house'keeper** a person employed to keep house: one who has the chief care of a house: one who stays much at home: a dispenser of hospitality (*obs.*): a watch-dog (*obs.*); **house'keeping** the keeping or management of a house or of domestic affairs: the money used for this: hospitality (*obs.*): operations carried out on or within a computer programme or system to ensure the efficient functioning of the programme or system (*comput.*). — *adj.* domestic. — **house'-leek** a plant (*Sempervivum tectorum*) of the stonecrop family with succulent leaves, often growing on roofs; **house lights** (*theat.*) the lights illuminating the auditorium; **house'-line** (*naut.*) a small line of three strands, for seizings, etc.; **house'maid** a maid employed to keep a house clean, etc.; **housemaid's knee** an inflammation of the sac between the knee-cap and the skin, to which those whose work involves frequent kneeling are especially liable; **house'man** a recent graduate in medicine holding a junior resident post in a hospital; **house martin** a kind of black and white swallow with a slightly forked tail, *Delichon urbica*; **house'master** in schools, the head of a (boarding-) house, esp. in connection with a public school (*fem.* **house'mistress**); **house'-mate** one sharing a house with another; **house'-moth'er** the mother of a family, the female head of a family: a woman in charge of children in an institution; **house'parent** a man or woman in charge of children in an institution; **house'-party** a company of guests spending some days in a country-house; **house plant** a plant that can be grown indoors as decoration. — *adj.* **house'-proud** taking a pride (often an excessive and fussy pride) in the condition of one's house. — **house'-room** room or place in a house (also *fig.*); **house'-stew'ard** a steward who manages the household affairs of a great family; **house'-sur'geon** a resident surgeon in a hospital — so also **house'-physi'cian**. — *adj.* **house'-to-house** performed or conducted by calling at house after house. — **house'top** the top or roof of a house. — *adj.* **house'-trained** of animals, taught to be cleanly indoors: of human beings, well-mannered (*coll.*). — **house'-warming** an entertainment given after moving into a new house; **housewife** (*hows'wīf,* formerly *huz'if*) the mistress and manager of a house: a married woman who looks after the house and family and does not have a paid job: (*huz'if*) a pocket sewing-outfit. — *adj.* **house'-wifely.** — **housewifery** (*hows'wif-ri,* -*wīf-ri, huz'if-ri*); **house'wifeship,** (*Scot.*) -**skep; house'work** domestic work; **house'y-house'y** a game in which numbers are drawn at random and marked off on players' boards until one is clear — now usu. called **bingo; housing estate** a planned residential area, esp. one built by a local authority; **hous'ing (joint)** a joint where the end of one board fits into a groove cut across another board; **housing scheme** a plan for the designing, building, and provision of houses, esp. by a local authority: sometimes applied to an area coming under such a plan. — **bring the house down** to evoke very loud applause in a place of entertainment; **full house** see **full**[1]**; house longhorn beetle** see **long**[3]**; house of call** a house where the journeymen of a particular trade call when out of work: a house that one often visits; **house of cards** a situation, etc. that is as unstable as a pile of playing cards; **house of correction** a jail; **house of God, prayer** or **worship** a place of worship; **house of ill-fame, ill repute** a brothel; **House of Commons, Lords, Peers, Representatives** see **common, lord, peer**[1]**, represent; House of Keys** see **Keys; House, Council of States** the upper house of the Indian parliament; **House of the People** the lower house of the Indian parliament; **Inner House** the higher branch of the Court of Session, its jurisdiction chiefly appellate (**Outer House** the lower branch of the Court of Session); **keep a good house** to keep up a plentifully supplied table; **keep house** to maintain or manage an establishment; **keep open house** to give entertainment to all comers; **keep the house** to remain indoors: to take charge of the house or be on watch for the time being: to be confined to the house; **like a house on fire, afire** with astonishing rapidity; **on the house** of drinks, at the publican's expense: free, with no charge; **put, set, one's house in order** to settle one's affairs; **set up house** to start a domestic life of one's own; **the Household** the royal domestic establishment. [O.E. *hūs;* Goth, *hūs,* Ger. *Haus.*]

housel *howz'əl, n.* the eucharist: the act of taking or administering it. — *v.t.* to administer the eucharist to: — *pa.p.* **hous'elled.** — *n.* **hous'elling.** — *adj.* (*Spens.*) **hous'ling** sacramental. [O.E. *hūsel,* sacrifice.]

housing[1] *howz'ing, n.* an ornamental covering for a horse: a saddle-cloth: (in *pl.*) the trappings of a horse. [O.Fr. *houce,* a mantle, of Gmc. origin.]

housing[2]. See **house.**

hout, hout-tout, houts-touts. Same as **hoot,** etc.

Houyhnhnm (*h*)*win'əm, n.* one of the noble and rational race of horses in Swift's *Gulliver's Travels.* [Perh. **whinny.**]

Hova *huv'ə, hōv'ə, n.* one of the dominant race in Madagascar, esp. of the middle class: — *pl.* **Hov'a, Hov'as.**

hove[1] *hōv, hoōv, Scot.* **hüv,** *v.t.* to swell. — *v.i.* to swell: to rise (*Spens.*). [Perh. a form of **heave.**]

hove[2]**, hoove** *hoōv,* (*Spens.*) *v.i.* to hover: to loiter, linger. [Origin unknown.]

hove[3] *pa.t.* and *pa.p.* of **heave.**

hovel *hov'əl, huv'əl, n.* a small or wretched dwelling: a shed: a framework for a corn-stack (*dial.*). — *v.t.* to put in a hovel: to shelter: to build like a hovel or shed, as a chimney with side opening: — *pa.t., pa.p.,* **hov'elled** (*U.S.* **hov'eled**). — **hov'el-post** a post for supporting a corn-stack. [Origin doubtful.]

hoveller *hov', huv'(ə-)lər, n.* a boatman acting as an uncertificated pilot or doing any kind of occasional work on the coast: a small coasting-vessel. [Ety. dub.]

hoven[1] *hō'vən.* See **hoove**[1]**.**

hoven². See **heave**.

hover *hov'ər, huv'ər, v.i.* to remain aloft flapping the wings: to remain suspended: to linger: to move about near. — *v.t.* to brood over. — *n.* act or state of hovering: a helicopter (*U.S.*): an apparatus for keeping chicks warm: in composition, describing vessels, vehicles, or stationary objects, resting on a cushion of air, e.g. **hov'ercraft** (a craft able to move at a short distance above the surface of sea or land supported by a down-driven blast of air); **hov'er-barrow, -bus, -car, -mower, -train.** — *adv.* **hov'eringly.** — **hov'er-bed** one which supports a patient on a film of warm air; **hov'er-fly** a syrphid or other wasp-like fly that hovers and darts; **hov'erport** a port for hovercraft. [Perh. — **hove²**.]

how¹ *how, adv.* and *conj.* in what manner: to what extent: by what means: in what condition: for what reason: to what an extent, in what a degree: that. — *n.* manner, method. — *adj.* **how'-to** of books, etc. showing how to do things. — Also *n.* — **and how** (*U.S. slang*) yes, certainly: very much indeed: I should think so indeed; **how about** what do you think of: would you like (something): are you interested in (doing something); **how are you** a conventional greeting to an acquaintance: sometimes specifically referring to his or her state of health; **how come** how does that come about; **how-do-you-do** see **do¹**; **how now** what is this: why is this so; **how so** (*arch.*) how can this be so? why?; **how's that** (*how-zat'*; sometimes written **howzat;** *cricket*) the appeal of the fielding side to the umpire to give the batsman out; **how's your father** amorous frolicking: sexual intercourse: nonsense, foolish activity; **the how and the why** the manner and the cause. [O.E. *hū*, prob. an adverbial form from *hwā*, who.]

how², howe *how*, (*Scot.*) *n.* a hollow. [**hole¹**.]

how³ *how*, (*dial.*) *n.* a low hill: a tumulus or barrow. [O.N. *haugr*; cf. O.E. *hēah*, high.]

how⁴ *how, interj.* a greeting thought to have been used by North American Indians. [From Sioux, related to Dakota *háo*.]

howbeit *how-bē'it, conj.* be it how it may: notwithstanding: yet: however — (*Spens.*) **howbe'.** [**how¹**, be, it¹.]

howdah, houdah *how'dä, n.* a pavilion or seat fixed on an elephant's back. [Ar. *haudaj*.]

howdie, howdy *how'di,* (*Scot.*) *n.* a midwife. [Poss. O.E. *hold,* gracious.]

howdy *how'di, interj.* a colloquial form of the common greeting, *How do you do?.* — **how'-d'ye-do', how'dy-do'** a troublesome state of matters.

howe. See **how²**.

however *how-ev'ər, adv.* and *conj.* in whatever manner or degree: nevertheless: at all events. — *poetic abbrev.* **howe'er** (*how-ār'*). [**how¹**, ever.]

howf(f), houf(f) *howf,* (*Scot.*) *n.* a haunt, resort, often a public house. — *v.i.* to resort to a place. [Poss. O.E. *hof,* a house.]

howitzer *how'its-ər, n.* a short, squat gun, used for shelling at a steep angle, esp. in siege and trench warfare. [Ger. *Haubitze* — Czech *houfnice,* a sling.]

howk *howk,* (*Scot.*) *v.t.* and *v.i.* to dig, burrow. [Earlier *holk;* cf. L.G. *holken.*]

howker *how'kər, n.* Same as **hooker¹**.

howl *howl, v.i.* to yell or cry, as a wolf or dog: to utter a long, loud, whining sound: to wail: to roar. — *v.t.* to utter with outcry: — *pr.p.* **howl'ing;** *pa.t.* and *pa.p.* **howled.** — *n.* a loud, prolonged cry of distress: a mournful cry: a loud sound like a yell, made by the wind, a wireless receiver, etc. — *n.* **howl'er** one who howls: a S. American monkey, with prodigious power of voice: a glaring and amusing blunder (*coll.*). — *adj.* **howl'ing** filled with howlings, as of the wind, or of wild beasts: tremendous (*coll.*). — *n.* a howl. — **howl down** to drown out a speaker with angry cries. [O.Fr. *huller* — L. *ululāre,* to shriek or howl — *ulula,* an owl; cf. Ger. *heulen,* Eng. **owl**.]

Howleglass. See **owl**.

howlet *how'lit, n.* an owlet: (*Scot. hōōl'it*) an owl. [**owlet**.]

howre. An obs. form of **hour**.

howso *how'sō,* (*obs.*) *adv.* howsoever.

howsoever *how-sō-ev'ər, adv.* in what way soever: although: however. — Provincial forms are **howsomev'er** and **howsomdev'er.** [**how¹, so¹, ever;** and M.E. *sum,* as.]

howtowdie *how-tow'di,* (*Scot.*) *n.* a dish of boiled chicken. [O.Fr. *hetoudeau, estaudeau,* a young chicken prepared for eating.]

howzat. See **how's that** at **how¹**.

hox *hoks,* (*Shak.*) *v.t.* to hock or hamstring. [O.E. *hōhsinu,* hock-sinew.]

hoy¹ *hoi, n.* a large one-decked boat, commonly rigged as a sloop. [M.Du. *hoei;* Du. *heu,* Flem. *hui*.]

hoy² *hoi, interj.* ho! stop!. — *v.t.* to incite, drive on.

Hoya *hoi'ə, n.* an Australasian genus of plants of the Asclepiadaceae, including the wax flower: (without *cap.*) a plant of this genus. [Thomas *Hoy,* d. 1821, English gardener.]

hoyden, hoiden *hoi'dən, n.* a tomboy, a romp (formerly also *masc.*). — *ns.* **hoy'denhood, hoy'denism.** — *adj.* **hoy'denish.** [Perh. Du. *heiden,* a heathen, a gypsy, *heide,* heath.]

huanaco. Same as **guanaco**.

hub *hub, n.* the nave of a wheel: a mark at which quoits, etc. are cast: an important centre or focus of activity as (*facet.*) *hub of the universe, solar system* (applied (*arch.*) to Boston, U.S.A). — **hub'-brake** a brake acting on the hub of a wheel; **hub'-cap** a metal covering over the end of an axle. [Prob. a form of **hob¹**; origin unknown.]

hubble-bubble *hub'l-bub'l, n.* a bubbling sound: tattle: confusion: a crude kind of hookah. [Redup. from **bubble**.]

Hubble('s) constant *hub'l(z) kon'stənt,* (*astron.*) the constant factor in **Hubble('s) law** (that the velocity of a galaxy is proportional to its distance from us), giving the rate of increase of velocity with distance in the expanding universe. [From E. P. *Hubble* (1889–1953), U.S. astronomer.]

hubbub *hub'ub, Shak.* **whoobub** *hōōb'ub, ns.* a confused sound of many voices: riot: uproar — Also **hubb'uboo.** [App. of Irish origin.]

hubby *hub'i,* (*coll.*) *n.* a diminutive of **husband**.

hubris *hū'bris,* **hybris** *hī'bris, ns.* insolence: arrogance, such as invites disaster: overweening. — *adj.* **hubris'tic.** — *adv.* **hubris'tically.** [Gr. *hybris*.]

huck. See **huckle**.

huckaback *huk'ə-bak, n.* a coarse linen or cotton with raised surface, used for towels, etc. [Origin unknown.]

huckle *huk'l, n.* the haunch: the hip. — Also **huck.** — *adjs.* **huck'le-backed, -shoul'dered** having the back or shoulders round. — **huckle'-bone** the hip-bone: the astragalus. [Poss. conn. with **hook**.]

huckleberry *huk'l-bər-i, -ber-i, n.* a N. American shrub (*Gaylussacia*) akin to whortleberry: its fruit: extended to species of whortleberry. — *n.* **huck'leberrying.** [App. for **hurtleberry**.]

huckster *huk'stər, n.* a retailer of smallwares, a hawker or pedlar: a mean, haggling fellow. — *v.i.* to deal in small articles: to higgle meanly. — *n.* **huck'sterage; huck'steress, huck'stress; huck'stery.** [Origin obscure.]

hudden. See **haud**.

huddle *hud'l, v.t.* to hustle out of sight, hush up (*obs.*): to jumble: to hustle, bundle: to drive, draw, throw or crowd together in disorder: to put hastily: to perform perfunctorily and hastily. — *v.i.* to crowd in confusion. — *n.* a confused mass: a jumble: confusion: perfunctory haste: a gathering of the team behind their line of scrimmage so as to receive instructions, signals, etc. (*U.S.* football): a secret conference: a period of deep consideration of a problem. — *adj.* **hudd'led** jumbled:

crowded: in a heap: crouching. [Poss. conn. with **hide¹**.]

huddup *hud-up'*, (*U.S.*) *interj.* get up (to a horse).

Hudibrastic *hū-di-bras'tik, adj.* similar in style to *Hudibras*, a metrical burlesque on the Puritans by Samuel Butler (1612–80). — *n.pl.* **Hudibras'tics** verses of the form used in *Hudibras*, a burlesque cacophonous octosyllabic couplet with extravagant rhymes.

hue¹ (*Spens.* **hew**), *hū, n.* appearance: colour: tint: dye. — *adjs.* **hued** having a hue; **hue'less.** [O.E. *hīow, hēow* (W.S. *hīw, hīew*); Sw. *hy,* complexion.]

hue² *hū, n.* a shouting, clamour. — *n.* **hu'er** a pilchard fishermen's lookout man. — **hue and cry** an outcry calling upon all to pursue one who is to be made prisoner (*hist.*): a proclamation or publication to the same effect (*hist.*): the pursuit itself: a loud clamour about something. [Imit.; perh. Fr. *huer.*]

huff *huf, n.* a puff of wind (*obs.*): bluster (*obs.*): a blusterer, bully (*obs.*): a fit of anger, sulks, or offended dignity: an act of huffing in draughts. — *v.t.* to puff up (*obs.*): to hector: to give offence: (in draughts) to remove from the board for omitting capture. — *v.i.* to blow, puff, swell (*obs.*): to take offence: to bluster. — *adjs.* **huff'ish, huff'y** given to huff: touchy: ready to take offence. — *advs.* **huff'ishly, huff'ily.** — *ns.* **huff'ishness, huff'iness; huff'kin** (*local*) a type of muffin or bun. — *adj.* **huff'-cap** (*obs.*) of liquor, heady: blustering. — **huffing and puffing** loud talk, noisy objections. [Imit.]

hug *hug, v.t.* to clasp close with the arms: to cherish: to keep close to, skirt: — *pr.p.* **hugg'ing**; *pa.t.* and *pa.p.* **hugged.** — *n.* a close embrace: a particular grip in wrestling. — *adj.* **hugg'able.** — **hug'-me-tight** a closefitting knitted garment. — **hug oneself** to congratulate oneself. [Ety. obscure.]

huge *hūj, adj.* vast: enormous. — *adv.* **huge'ly.** — *n.* **huge'ness.** — *adj.* **huge'ous** (*arch.*) huge. — *adv.* **huge'ously** (*arch.*). — *n.* **huge'ousness** (*arch.*). — *adj.* **hu'gy** (*arch.*). [O.Fr. *ahuge.*]

hugger-mugger *hug'ər-mug'ər, n.* secrecy: confusion. — *adj.* secret: disorderly. — *adv.* in secrecy or disorder. [Origin obscure.]

Huguenot *hū'gə-not,* or *-nō, (hist.) n.* a French Protestant. — Also *adj.* [Fr., — earlier *eiguenot* — Ger. *Eidgenoss,* confederate, assimilated to the name *Hugues,* Hugh.]

huh *hu, interj.* expressing disgust, disbelief, enquiry, etc. [Imit.]

huia *hoo'yə, hoo'ē-ə, n.* a New Zealand bird (*Heteralocha acutirostris*) akin to the crows and starlings, now prob. extinct. [Maori; imit.]

huissier *wē-syā,* (Fr.) *n.* a doorkeeper, usher: a bailiff.

huitain *wē-tān', n.* a group of eight lines of verse. [Fr., — *huit,* eight.]

hula-hula *hoo'lə-hoo'lə, n.* a Hawaiian women's dance. — Also **hu'la.** — **hu'la-hoop** a light hoop used in the diversion of keeping the hoop in motion about the waist by a swinging movement of the hips. [Hawaiian.]

hule. Same as **ule.**

hulk *hulk, n.* an unwieldy ship: a dismantled ship: a big lubberly fellow: anything unwieldy: often by confusion, a hull: — *pl.* (with *the*) old ships formerly used as prisons. — *adjs.* **hulk'ing, hulk'y** big and clumsy. [O.E. *hulc,* cf. Gr. *holkas,* a towed ship — *helkein,* to draw.]

hull¹ *hull, n.* a husk or outer covering. — *v.t.* to separate from the hull: to husk. — *adj.* **hull'y** having husks or pods. [O.E. *hulu,* a husk, as of corn — *helan,* to cover; Ger. *Hülle,* a covering, *hehlen,* to cover.]

hull² *hul, n.* the frame or body of a ship: part of a flying-boat in contact with the water: the heavily-armoured body of a tank. — *v.t.* to pierce the hull of. — *v.i.* (*Shak.*) to float or drift, as a mere hull, to float about. — *adj.* of a ship, etc., floating and moving on the hull, as opposed to being raised on hydrofoils, etc. — *adv.* **hull'-down'** so far away that the hull is below the horizon. [Perh. same word as above, modified

in meaning by confusion with Du. *hol,* a ship's hold, or with **hulk.**]

hullabaloo *hul-ə-bə-loo', n.* an uproar. [Perh. **halloo** or possibly rhyming on Scot. *baloo,* lullaby.]

hullo *hu-lō', v., n.* and *interj.* Same as **hallo.**

Hulsean *hul'si-ən, adj.* of or pertaining to John *Hulse* (1708–90), founder of the Hulsean divinity lectures at Cambridge.

hum¹ *hum, v.i.* to make a sound like bees or that represented by *m*: to sing with closed lips without words or articulation: to pause in speaking and utter an inarticulate sound: to stammer through embarrassment: to be audibly astir: to have a strong, unpleasant smell (*slang*): to be busily active. — *v.t.* to render by humming: to applaud (*obs.*): — *pr.p.* **humm'ing**; *pa.t.* and *pa.p.* **hummed.** — *n.* the noise of bees: a murmurous sound: an inarticulate murmur: the sound of humming. — *adj.* **humm'able.** — *n.* **humm'er** a person or thing that hums, as a bee, a humming-bird, a top: one who makes things hum. — *n.* and *adj.* **humm'ing.** — **humming ale** ale that froths up well, or that makes the head hum; **humm'ing-bird** any member of the tropical family Trochilidae, very small birds of brilliant plumage and rapid flight (from the humming sound of the wings); **humm'ing-top** a top that gives a humming sound as it spins. — **hum and haw** (or **ha**) to make inarticulate sounds when at a loss: to shilly-shally; **make things hum** to set things going briskly. [Imit.; cf. Ger. *hummen, humsen.*]

hum² *hum, v.t.* to impose on: to hoax. — *n.* an imposition: a hoax. [Contr. of **humbug.**]

hum³ *hum, interj.* expressing doubt or reluctance to agree.

huma *hoo'mə, n.* a fabulous restless bird. [Pers. *humā,* phoenix.]

human *hū'mən, adj.* belonging or pertaining to or of the nature of man or mankind: having the qualities of a man or the limitations of man: humane: not invidiously superior: genial, kind. — *n.* a human being. — *adj.* **humane** (*hū-mān'*) having the feelings proper to man: kind: tender: merciful: humanising, as *humane letters,* classical, elegant, polite. — *adv.* **humane'ly.** — *n.* **humane'ness.** — *v.t.* **humanise, -ize** (*hū'mən-īz*) to render human or humane: to soften: to impart human qualities to, to make like that which is human or of mankind. — *v.i.* to become humane or civilised. — *ns.* **humanīsā'tion, -z-; hū'manist** student of polite literature: at the Renaissance, a student of Greek and Roman literature: a student of human nature: advocate of any system of humanism: a pragmatist. — Also *adj.* — *n.* **hū'manism** literary culture: any system which puts human interests and the mind of man paramount, rejecting the supernatural, belief in a god, etc.: pragmatism (*phil.*): a critical application of the logical method of pragmatism to all the sciences. — *adj.* **hūmanist'ic.** — *n.* **hū'mankind** the human species. — *adj.* **hū'manlike.** — *adv.* **hū'manly** in a human manner: by human agency: having regard to human limitations: humanely. — *ns.* **hū'manness; hū'manoid** one of the immediate kindred of man (closer than *anthropoid*): resembling, with the characteristics of, a human being. — **human being** any member of the human race: a person; **humane society** a society promoting humane behaviour, usu. to animals; **human interest** in newspaper articles, broadcasts, etc., reference to people's lives and emotions; **human nature** the nature of man: the qualities of character common to all men that differentiate them from other species: irrational, or, less than saintly, behaviour (often *facet.*); **human rights** the right each human being has to personal freedom, justice, etc. [Fr. *humain* — L. *hūmānus* — *homō,* a human being.]

humanity *hū-man'it-i, n.* the nature peculiar to a human being: humanness: humaneness: the kind feelings of man: mankind collectively: in Scottish universities, Latin language and literature: (in *pl.*) grammar, rhetoric, Latin, Greek and poetry, so called from their humanising effects. — *n.* **humanitarian** (*hū-man'i-tā'ri-*

ən) one who denies Christ's divinity, and holds him to be a mere man: a philanthropist. — *adj.* of or belonging to humanity, benevolent. — *n.* **humanitā′rianism.** [Fr. *humanité* — L. *hūmānitās* — *hūmānus* — *homō*, a man.]

humble[1] *hum′bl* (old-fashioned *um′bl*), *adj.* low: lowly: modest: unpretentious: having a low opinion of oneself or of one's claims: abased. — *v.t.* to bring down to the ground: to lower: to abase: to mortify: to degrade. — *ns.* **hum′bleness; hum′blesse** (*Spens.*). — *adj.* and *n.* **hum′bling.** — *advs.* **hum′blingly, hum′bly.** — *adj.* **hum′ble-mouthed** humble in speech. — **your humble servant** an old formula used in subscribing a letter. [Fr., — L. *humilis*, low — *humus*, the ground.]

humble[2] *hum′bl.* Same as **hummel.**

humble-bee *hum′bl-bē, n.* the bumble-bee (*Bombus*). [Perh. from *humble*, freq. of **hum**[1]; cf. Ger. *Hummel*.]

humbles see **umbles.** — **hum′ble-pie′** a pie made from the umbles of a deer. — **eat humble-pie** punningly, to humble, abase oneself, eat one's words, etc.

humbug *hum′bug, n.* an imposition under fair pretences: hollowness, pretence: one who so imposes: a lump of toffee, peppermint drop, or the like. — *v.t.* to deceive: to hoax: to cajole. — *v.i.* to potter about: — *pr.p.* **hum′bugging;** *pa.t.* and *pa.p.* **hum′bugged.** — *adj.* **hum′bugg′able.** — *ns.* **hum′bugger; hum′buggery.** [Appears about 1750; origin unknown.]

humbuzz *hum′buz,* (*dial.*) *n.* a cockchafer: a bull-roarer. [**hum**[1], **buzz**[1].]

humdinger *hum-ding′ər,* (*slang*) *n.* an exceptionally excellent person or thing: a smooth-running engine: a swift vehicle or aircraft. [Prob. **hum**[1] and **ding**[1].]

humdrum *hum′drum′, adj.* dull: droning: monotonous: commonplace. — *n.* a stupid fellow: monotony: tedious talk. [**hum**[1] and perh. **drum**[1].]

humdudgeon *hum-duj′ən, n.* an unnecessary outcry. (*Scot.*): low spirits (*dial.*) [**hum**[1] and **dudgeon**[1].]

Humean, Humian *hū′mi-ən, adj.* pertaining to David Hume, or his philosophy. — *n.* a follower of Hume. — *ns.* **Hūm′ism, Hūm′ist.**

humect *hū-mekt′, v.t.* and *v.i.* to make or become moist. — Also **humect′ate.** — *adjs.* and *ns.* **humect′ant, humect′ive.** — *n.* **humectā′tion.** [L. (*h*)*ūmectāre* — *ūmēre,* to be moist.]

humefy. See **humify**[1].

humerus *hū′mər-əs, n.* the bone of the upper arm: — *pl.* **hū′merī.** — *adj.* **hū′meral** belonging to the shoulder or the humerus. — *n.* (also **humeral veil**) an oblong vestment worn on the shoulders. [L. (*h*)*umerus,* shoulder.]

humf. See **humph**[2].

humgruffin *hum-gruf′in,* **humgruffian** *-i-ən, ns.* a terrible person. [App. **hum**[1] and **griffin**[1].]

humhum *hum′hum, n.* a kind of plain, coarse cotton cloth used in the East Indies.

Humian. See **Humean.**

humic. See under **humus**[1].

humid *hū′mid, adj.* moist: damp: rather wet. — *ns.* **humidificā′tion; humid′ifier** a device for increasing or maintaining humidity. — *v.t.* **humid′ify** to make humid. — *ns.* **humid′istat** same as **hygrostat; humid′ity** moisture: a moderate degree of wetness. — *adv.* **hu′midly.** — *ns.* **hu′midness; hum′idor** a chamber, etc., for keeping anything moist, as cigars: a contrivance for keeping the air moist. [L. (*h*)*ūmidus* — (*h*)*ūmēre,* to be moist.]

humify[1] *hū′mi-fī, v.t.* to moisten. — Also (*obs.*) **hu′mefy.** — *n.* **humificā′tion.** [L. (*h*)*ūmificāre.*]

humify[2] *hū′mi-fī, v.t.* and *v.i.* to make or turn into humus. — *n.* **humificā′tion.** [**humus**[1].]

humiliate *hū-mil′i-āt, v.t.* to humble: to mortify. — *adjs.* **humil′iant** humiliating; **humil′iāting; humil′iative; humil′iatory** (*-ə-tər-i*). — *ns.* **humiliā′tion; humil′iātor.** [L. *humiliāre, -ātum.*]

humility *hū-mil′i-ti, n.* the state or quality of being humble: lowliness of mind: modesty. [O.Fr. *humilite* — L. *humilitās* — *humilis,* low.]

Humism, Humist. See **Humean.**

humite *hū′mit, n.* an orthorhombic magnesium orthosilicate also containing magnesium hydroxide, found in impure marbles. [Sir Abraham *Hume,* 19th-century mineral collector.]

humlie. See under **hummel.**

hummaum. Same as **hammam.**

hummel *hum′l,* **humble** *hum′(b)l* (*Scot.*), *adjs.* hornless: awnless. — *n.* a hornless stag. — *v.t.* to make hummel. — *ns.* **hum′lie** (*Scot.*) a polled or hornless cow, ox, etc.: **humm′eller** (*dial.*) a machine for removing barley awns. — **hummel** (usu. **hummle**) **bonnet** a type of Scotch cap worn by Highland regiments before the introduction (1851) of the glengarry. [Cf. L.G. *hummel, hommel.*]

hummer, humming. See under **hum**[1].

hummock *hum′ək,* (*arch.*) **hommock** *hom′ək, ns.* a hillock: a pile or ridge of ice. — *adjs.* **humm′ocked, humm′ocky.** [Origin unknown: at first nautical.]

hummum. Same as **hammam.**

hummus *hum′əs, hŏŏ′məs, n.* a Middle Eastern hors d'oeuvre of puréed chick-peas and sesame oil with garlic and lemon. [Turk.]

humogen *hū′mō-jən, n.* a fertiliser composed of peat treated with a culture of nitrogen-fixing bacteria. [L. *humus,* soil, Gr. *gennaein,* to produce.]

humour, in U.S. **humor,** *hū′mər, ū′mər, n.* moisture (*arch.*): a fluid: a fluid of the animal body, esp. formerly any one of the four that in old physiology were held to determine temperament: temperament or disposition of mind: state of mind (*good, ill humour*): disposition: caprice: in Corporal Nym's vocabulary in *The Merry Wives* and *Henry V* (also as *adj.* and *v.t.,* and *adj.* **hū′moured**) a word of any meaning, down to no meaning at all (*Shak.*): a mental quality which apprehends and delights in the ludicrous and mirthful: that which causes mirth and amusement: playful fancy. — *v.t.* to go along with the humour of: to gratify by compliance. — *adj.* **hū′moral** pertaining to or proceeding from a body fluid. — *ns.* **hū′moralism** the state of being humoral: the old doctrine that diseases have their seat in the humours; **hū′moralist** one who favoured the doctrine of humoralism. — *adv.* **hū′morally.** — **hūmoresk′, hūmoresque′** a musical caprice; **hū′morist** one whose conduct and conversation are regulated by humour or caprice (*arch.*): one who studies or portrays the humours of people: one possessed of humour: a writer of comic stories. — *adjs.* **hūmoris′tic** humorous; **hū′morous** governed by humour (*arch.*): capricious (*arch.*): irregular (*arch.*): full of humour: exciting laughter. — *adv.* **hū′morously.** — *n.* **hū′morousness.** — *adjs.* **hū′mourless; hū′moursome** capricious, petulant. — *n.* **hū′moursomeness.** — **humoral immunity** an acquired immunity in which antibodies circulating in body fluids play the major part. — **comedy of humours** the comedy of Ben Jonson and his school in which the characters instead of being conceived in the round are little more than personifications of single qualities; **out of humour** out of temper, displeased. [O.Fr. *humor* (Fr. *humeur*) — L. (*h*)*ūmor* — (*h*)*ūmēre,* to be moist.]

humous. See under **humus**[1].

hump *hump, n.* a hunch on the back: a protuberance: a walk with swag on back (*Austr. obs.*): despondency (*slang*): sulks (*slang*). — *v.t.* to bend in a hump: to exert oneself (*slang*): to hurry (*slang*): to vex or annoy (*slang*): to shoulder, to carry on the back (orig. *Austr.*). — *v.i.* to put forth effort: to have sexual intercourse (also *v.t.*) (*slang*). — *adjs.* **humped** having a hump; **hump′y** full of humps or protuberances: sulky, irritable (*coll.*). — **hump′back** a back with a hump or hunch: a person with a humpback: a Pacific species of salmon: a whale with a humplike dorsal fin. — *adjs.* **hump′-back, hump′-backed** having a humpback (**humpback bridge** a bridge with a sharp rise in the middle). — **hump the bluey** (*Austr.*) to travel on foot, carrying a swag; **over the hump** past the crisis or difficulty. [Origin obscure.]

humpen, Humpen *hŏŏm′pən, n.* a type of usu. cylindrical enamelled or painted glass drinking-vessel made in

Germany from the 17th century.   [Ger.]

humph[1] *hmh, huh, hmf, interj.* expressive of reserved doubt or dissatisfaction.

humph[2], **humf** *humf, (Scot.) n.* a hump. — *v.t.* to carry (something cumbersome, heavy, or awkward). [**hump.**]

Humphrey, dine with Duke. See **dine.**

humpty *hum(p)′ti, n.* a low padded seat.   [*humpty,* hunchbacked; perh. conn. with following.]

Humpty-dumpty *hum(p)′ti-dum(p)′ti, n.* a short, squat, egg-like being of nursery folklore: a gypsy drink, ale boiled with brandy. — *adj.* short and broad.

humpy[1] *hum′pi, (Austr.) n.* an Aboriginal hut.   [Aboriginal *oompi.*]

humpy[2]. See **hump.**

humstrum *hum′strum, (now dial.) n.* a hurdy-gurdy or other musical instrument.   [**hum**[1], **strum,** with imit. effect.]

humus[1] *hūm′əs, n.* decomposed organic matter in the soil. — *adjs.* **hū′mic, hū′mous; hum′usy** having much humus. [L. *humus;* cf. Gr. *chamai,* on the ground.]

humus[2]. Same as **hummus.**

Hun *hun, n.* one of a powerful squat, swarthy, and savage nomad race of Asia who moved westwards, and under Attila (433–453) overran Europe: in U.S. formerly a Hungarian (*derog.*): a barbarian: a German (*war slang* of 1914). — *adjs.* **Hunn′ic, Hunn′ish.**   [O.E. (pl.) *Hūne, Hūnas;* L. *Hunnī;* Gr. *Ounnoi, Chounnoi.*]

hunch *hunch, hunsh, n.* a hump: a lump: a premonition: a hint: an intuitive feeling. — *v.t.* to hump, bend. — **hunch′back** one with a hunch or lump on his back. — *adj.* **hunch′backed.** — **play one's hunch** to act on one's hunch (as a gambler might).   [Origin obscure.]

hundred *hun′drəd, n.* the number ten times ten: applied also to various other numbers used in telling: a set of a hundred things: a hundred pounds, dollars, etc.: (in *pl.*) an unspecified large number: a division of a county in England orig. supposed to contain a hundred families (chiefly *hist.*): — *pl.* **hundreds** or, preceded by a numeral, **hundred.** — *adj.* to the number of a hundred: **hundredth** (*obs.* or *dial.*): also used indefinitely, very many (*coll.*). — *n.* **hun′dreder, -or** (*hist.*) the bailiff, or an inhabitant, of a hundred. — *adj., adv.,* and *n.* **hun′dredfold** folded a hundred times: in a hundred divisions: a hundred times as much. — *adj.* **hun′dredth** last of a hundred: next after the ninety-ninth: equal to one of a hundred equal parts. — *n.* one of a hundred equal parts: a person or thing in hundredth position. — *adj.* **hun′dred-per-cent′** out-and-out: thoroughgoing (**not a hundred-per-cent** not in perfect health). — **hun′dred-percent′er** (*U.S.*) an uncompromising patriot; **hun′dreds-and-thou′sands** little sweets used as an ornamental dressing; **hun′dredweight** 1/20 of a ton, or 112 lb. avoirdupois (50·80 kg.; **long hundredweight**) orig. and still in U.S., 100 lb. (**short hundredweight**) 50 kg. (**metric hundredweight**), abbrev. *cwt.* (*c* standing for L. *centum, wt.* for weight). — **Chiltern Hundreds** a district of Bucks., whose stewardship is a nominal office under the Crown, the temporary acceptance of which by a member of parliament enables him to vacate his seat; **great** or **long hundred** usually six score: sometimes some other number greater than ten tens (as of herrings, 132 or 126); **Hundred Years' War** the struggle between England and France, from 1337 down to 1453; **not a hundred miles from** at, very near; **Old Hundred** see **old; one, two,** etc. **hundred hours** one, two, etc., o'clock, from the method of writing hours and minutes 1.00, 2.00, etc.; **the Hundred Days** time between Napoleon's return from Elba and his final downfall after Waterloo (the reign lasted exactly 95 days, March 20–June 22, 1815).   [O.E. *hundred* — old form *hund,* a hundred, with the suffix *-red,* a reckoning.]

hung *pa.t.* and *pa.p.* of **hang** (q.v.).

Hungarian *hung-gā′ri-ən, adj.* pertaining to Hungary or its inhabitants. — *n.* a person of Hungarian birth, descent, or citizenship: the Magyar or Hungarian language. — **Hungary** (*hung′gə-ri*) **water** oil of rosemary distilled with alcohol (said to have been used by a queen of Hungary).   [Cf. **Ugrian.**]

hunger *hung′gər, n.* craving for food: need or lack of food: strong desire for anything. — *v.i.* to crave food: to long. — *adjs.* **hung′erful** hungry; **hung′erly** (*Shak.*) hungry. — *adv.* (*Shak.*) hungrily. — *adv.* **hung′rily.** — *adj.* **hung′ry** having eager desire for food (or anything else): greedy (with *for*): stingy, mean (*Austr.*): lean: poor. — in composition, eager for, in need of (as *land-hungry*). — *adj.* **hung′er-bitten** bitten, pained, or weakened by hunger. — **hunger march** a procession of unemployed or others in need, as a demonstration; **hunger′-marcher; hunger strike** prolonged refusal of all food by a prisoner, etc. as a form of protest, or a means to ensure release. — *v.i.* **hung′er-strike.** — **hung′er= striker.** — **go hungry** to remain without food.   [O.E. *hungor* (n.), *hyngran* (vb.); cf. Ger. *Hunger,* Du. *honger,* etc.]

hung over, hung up, etc. See under **hang.**

hunk[1] *hungk, n.* a lump: a strong or sexually attractive man (*coll.*).   [Same as **hunch.**]

hunk[2] *hungk, n.* (*U.S.*) goal or base in boys' games. — *adj.* safe, secure. — *adjs.* **hunk′y** (*U.S.*), **hunk′y-do′ry** (orig. *U.S.*) in good position or condition: all right. [Du. *honk.*]

hunker[1] *hungk′ər, (U.S.) n.* orig. a member of the conservative section of the New York Democratic party (1845–48): a conservative person.   [Origin obscure.]

hunker[2] *hungk′ər, v.i.* to squat down. — *n.pl.* **hunk′ers** the hams.   [Origin obscure; perh. conn. with O.N. *hūka,* to squat.]

hunks *hungks, n. sing.* a miserly curmudgeon.   [Ety. dub.]

hunky[1] *hungk′i, (U.S.) n.* a derogatory name for a person of East European descent, esp. an unskilled workman. [For **Hungarian.**]

hunky[2]. See **hunk**[2].

hunt *hunt, v.t.* to chase or go in quest of for prey or sport: to seek or pursue game over: to ransack: to use in the hunt: to search for: to pursue: to hound, drive: to drive away, dismiss (*Austr.*). — *v.i.* to go out in pursuit of game: to search: to oscillate or vary in speed (*mech.*): of a bell, to move its order of ringing through a set of changes (**hunt up** to be rung progressively earlier; **hunt down** to be rung progressively later). — *n.* a chase of wild animals: search: a pack of hunting hounds: an association of huntsmen: the district hunted by a pack: game killed in a hunt (*Shak.*): a huntsman (*obs.*). — *ns.* **hunt′er** one who hunts: — *fem.* **hunt′ress;** a horse used in the chase: a watch whose face is protected with a metal case (a **half-hunt′er** if that case has a small circle of glass let in); **hunt′ing** the pursuit of wild game, the chase. — Also *adj.* — **hunt ball** a ball given by the members of a hunt; **hunt′-count′er** (*Shak.*) perh. one who hunts counter (q.v.); **hunt′er-gath′erer** (*anthrop.*) a member of a society which lives by hunting and gathering fruit, etc., as opposed e.g. to cultivating crops; **hunt′er-kill′er** a surface craft or submarine designed to hunt down and destroy enemy vessels; **hunt′er's-moon′** full moon following harvest-moon; **hunt′ing-box, -lodge, -seat** a temporary abode for hunting; **hunt′ing-cap** a form of cap much worn in the hunting-field; **hunt′ing-cat** a cheetah; **hunt′ing-cog** an extra cog in one of two geared wheels, by means of which the order of contact of cogs is changed at every revolution; **hunt′ing-crop, -whip** a short whip with a crooked handle and a loop of leather at the end, used in the hunting-field; **hunt′ing-field** the scene or sphere of hunting, esp. fox-hunting: the assemblage of huntsmen; **hunt′ing-ground** a place or region for hunting (**happy hunting-ground** see **happy**); **hunt′ing-horn** a horn used in hunting, a bugle; **hunt′ing-knife, -sword** a knife or short sword used to despatch the game when caught, or to skin and cut it up; **hunt′ing-leopard** a cheetah; **hunt′ing-mass** (*hist.*) hasty and abridged mass said for impatient hunters; **hunt′ing-song** a song about hunting;

hunt'ing-spider a wolf-spider; **hunt'ing-tide** the season of hunting; **hunts'man** one who hunts: one who manages the hounds during the chase; **hunts'manship** the qualifications of a huntsman; **hunt's'-up** (*Shak.*) a tune or song intended to arouse huntsmen in the morning — hence, anything calculated to arouse; **hunt'-the=gowk** the making of an April fool: (also **hunt'iegowk**) a fool's errand, a deception, or a hoax, appropriate to the First of April. — Also *adj.* — *v.t.* to make an April fool of. — **hunt'-the-slipp'er** a game in which one in the middle of a ring tries to catch a shoe passed around by the others. — *interj.* **good hunting!** good luck! (*coll.*). — **hunt after, for** to search for; **hunt counter** to follow the scent backwards; **hunt down** to pursue to extremities: to persecute out of existence: see also at **hunt** above; **hunt out** or **up** to seek out; **hunt the letter** to affect alliteration; **hunt up** see **hunt** above. [O.E. *huntian*; prob. conn. with *hentan*, to seize.]

Hunterian *hun-tē'ri-ən, adj.* of or pertaining to the surgeon John *Hunter* (1728–93), to his anatomical collection, nucleus of the Hunterian Museum in London, or to the annual Hunterian Oration at the Royal College of Surgeons: of or pertaining to his elder brother, William *Hunter* (1718–83), anatomist and obstetrician, or his museum in Glasgow.

Huntingdonian *hun-ting-dō'ni-ən, n.* a member of the Countess of Huntingdon's Connection, a denomination of Calvinistic Methodists founded by Whitefield with Selina, Countess of *Huntingdon* (1707–91). — Also *adj.*

Huntington's chorea, disease *hunt'ing-tənz ko-rē'ə, diz-ēz',* an inherited and fatal disease, marked by progressive mental deterioration. [Dr G. *Huntington* (d.1916), who described it.]

Huon pine *hū'onpīn',* a Tasmanian conifer (*Dacrydium,* or *Lagerostrobus,* franklinii), found first on the *Huon* river.

hup *hup, v.i.* to shout hup: of a horse, to go on, to go faster: to turn to the right. — *v.t.* to turn (a horse) to the right. — *n.* a cry of 'hup'. — *interj.* (to a horse) to go faster or to turn to the right. — **neither hup nor wind** (*Scot.*) to do neither one thing nor another, be unmanageable.

hupaithric *hū-pāth'rik, adj.* hypaethral.

hurcheon *hûr'chən,* Scots form of **urchin.**

hurden. See **hards.**

hurdies *hûr'diz,* (*Scot.*) *n.pl.* the buttocks: the thighs. [Origin unknown.]

hurdle *hûr'dl, n.* a frame of twigs or sticks interlaced: a movable frame of timber or iron for gates, etc. (*agri.*): in certain races, a portable barrier over which runners jump: a rude sledge on which criminals were drawn to the gallows (*hist.*): an obstacle (*fig.*): (in *pl.*) a hurdle-race. — *v.t.* to enclose with hurdles. — *v.i.* to jump as over a hurdle: to run a hurdle-race. — *ns.* **hurd'ler** a maker of hurdles: a hurdle-racer; **hur'dling.** — **hur'dle-race** a race in which hurdles have to be cleared; **hur'dle-rac'er; hur'dle-rac'ing.** [O.E. *hyrdel;* Ger. *Hürde.*]

hurds. See **hards.**

hurdy-gurdy *hûr'di-gûr'di, n.* a musical stringed instrument, whose strings are sounded by the turning of a wheel: a barrel-organ. [Imit.]

hurl *hûrl, v.t.* to fling with violence: to wheel (*Scot.*): to convey in a wheeled vehicle (*Scot.*). — *v.i.* to dash: to travel in a wheeled vehicle (*Scot.*): to play hurley. — *n.* act of hurling: a trip or journey in a wheeled vehicle (*Scot.*). — *ns.* **hurl'er; hurl'ey, hurl'ing** a game similar to hockey, of Irish origin, played by teams of 15, with broad-bladed sticks (**hurl'eys**) and a hide-covered cork ball; **hurl'y** (*Scot.*) large two-wheeled barrow. — **hurl'-barrow** a wheelbarrow; **hurl'-bat** see **whirl-bat** under **whirl; hurl'ey-house** (*Scott*) a house in a state of disrepair; **hurl'y-hack'et** (*Scot.*) a carriage, gig: an improvised sledge: sledging. [Cf. L.G. *hurreln,* to hurl, precipitate; influenced by **hurtle** and **whirl.**]

hurly *hûr'li, n.* commotion: tumult. — *n.* **hurly-burly**

(*hûr'li-bûr'li*) tumult: confusion. — Also *adj.* and *adv.* [Perh. from **hurl.**]

Huronian *hū-rō'ni-ən,* (*geol.*) *n.* and *adj.* upper Pre-Cambrian of Canada, well exemplified north of lake *Huron.*

hurrah, hurra *hŏŏr-ä', hur-ä',* **hurray** *-ā', interjs.* an exclamation of approbation or joy. — Also *n.* and *v.i.* [Cf. Norw., Sw., Dan. *hurra,* Ger. *hurrah,* Du. *hoera.*]

hurricane *hur'i-kin, -kān, n.* a West Indian cyclonic storm of great violence: a wind of extreme violence (over 75 mph (120 km/h)): anything tempestuous (*fig.*): a social party, a rout (*obs.*): (*cap.*) a type of fighting aeroplane used in World War II. — *n.* **hurricǎ'nō** (*obs.*) a hurricane: a waterspout (*Shak.*): — *pl.* **hurricǎ'noes.** — **hurr'icane-deck** a light partial deck over the saloon of some steamers; **hurr'icane-lamp** an oil lamp encased so as to defy strong wind: also a protected electric lamp. [Sp. *huracán,* from Carib.]

hurry *hur'i, v.t.* to urge forward: to hasten. — *v.i.* to move or act with haste, esp. perturbed or impatient haste: — *pr.p.* **hurr'ying;** *pa.t.* and *pa.p.* **hurr'ied.** — *n.* a driving forward: haste: flurried or undue haste: commotion: a rush: need for haste: in mus., a tremolo passage for strings, or drum roll, in connection with an exciting situation. — *adj.* **hurr'ied.** — *adv.* **hurr'iedly.** — *n.* **hurr'iedness.** — *n.* and *adj.* **hurr'ying.** — *adv.* **hurr'yingly.** — **hurr'y-skurr'y, -scurr'y** confusion and bustle. — *adv.* confusedly. — **in a hurry** in haste, speedily: soon: willingly; **hurry up** to make haste. [Prob. imit.; cf. Old Sw. *hurra,* to whirl round.]

hurst *hûrst, n.* a wood, a grove: a sand bank. [O.E. *hyrst.*]

hurt *hûrt, v.t.* to cause pain to: to damage: to injure: to wound, as the feelings. — *v.i.* to give pain: to be the seat of pain: to be injured: — *pa.t.* and *pa.p.* **hurt.** — *n.* a wound: injury. — *adj.* injured: pained in body or mind. — *n.* **hurt'er** that which hurts: a beam, block, etc., to protect a wall from wheels: the shoulder of an axle against which the hub strikes. — *adj.* **hurt'ful** causing hurt or loss: harmful. — *adv.* **hurt'fully.** — *n.* **hurt'fulness.** — *adj.* **hurt'less** without hurt or injury, harmless. — *adv.* **hurt'lessly.** — *n.* **hurt'lessness.** [O.Fr. *hurter* (Fr. *heurter*), to knock, to run against.]

hurtle *hûrt'l, v.t.* to dash: to hurl: to brandish (*Spens.*). — *v.i.* to clash (*arch.*): to rattle: to move rapidly with a clattering sound. [Freq. of **hurt** in its original sense.]

hurtleberry. A form of **whortleberry.**

husband *huz'bənd, n.* a man to whom a woman is married: a husbandman (*obs.*): a manager: a thrifty manager. — *v.t.* to supply with a husband (*arch.*): to become, be, or act as, a husband to (*arch.*): to manage with economy: to conserve: to cultivate (*arch.*). — *n.* **hus'-bandage** allowance or commission of a ship's husband. — *adjs.* **hus'bandless; hus'bandlike; hus'bandly** frugal, thrifty, pertaining to or befitting a husband. — *n.* **hus'bandry** the business of a farmer: tillage: economical management: thrift. — **hus'bandland** (*hist.*) a manorial tenant's holding: two oxgangs; **hus'bandman** a working farmer: one who labours in tillage. — **ship's husband** an owner's agent who manages the affairs of a ship in port. [O.E. *húsbonda,* O.N. *húsbóndi* — *hús,* a house, *búandi,* inhabiting, pr.p. of O.N. *búa,* to dwell; cf. **boor, bower**[1] and Ger. *bauen,* to till.]

hush *hush, interj.* or *imper.* silence: be still. — *n.* a silence, esp. after noise: a rush of water or its sound (*dial.*): the washing away of surface soil to lay bare bedrock (*min.*). — *adj.* silent (*arch.*): quiet (*arch.*): for the purpose of concealing information (e.g. *hush money*). — *v.i.* to become silent or quiet. — *v.t.* to make quiet: to calm: to procure silence or secrecy about (sometimes with *up*): to pour in a stream (*dial.*): to wash away or to pour in order to expose bedrock (*min.*). — *n.* **hush'aby** (*-ə-bī*) a lullaby used to soothe babies to sleep. — Also *v.t.* and *interj.* — *adj.* **hushed** silent, still. — *adj.* **hush'-hush, hush'y** (*coll.*) secret. — **hush'-boat** (1920s) a mystery-ship; **hush kit** (*coll.*) a device fitted to the jet engine of an aeroplane to reduce noise; **hush puppy** (*U.S.*) a ball or balls of maize dough, deep-fried. — **hush up** to stifle, suppress: to be silent. [Imit.; cf. **hist** and **whist**[1].]

husher *hush'ər*. Form of **usher**.

husk *husk, n.* the dry, thin covering of certain fruits and seeds: a case, shell, or covering, esp. one that is worthless or coarse: (in *pl.*) refuse, waste: huskiness: bronchitis in cattle caused by parasitic nematodes: a supporting frame. — *v.t.* to remove the husk or outer integument from. — *adj.* **husked** covered with a husk: stripped of husks. — *n.* **husk'er** one who husks Indian corn, esp. at a husking-bee: apparatus (as a glove) for the same purpose. — *adv.* **husk'ily**. — *ns.* **husk'iness**; **husk'ing** the stripping of husks: a festive gathering to assist in husking Indian corn (maize) — also **husk'ing-bee**. — *adj.* **husk'y** full of husks: of the nature of husks: like a husk: dry: sturdy like a corn-husk: with a dry, almost whispering voice, as if there were husks in the throat. — *n.* (*U.S.*) a sturdy fellow. [Perh. conn. with **house**.]

husky[1] *hus'ki*. See **husk**.

husky[2] *hus'ki, n.* an Eskimo sledge-dog: an Eskimo: the Eskimo language. [App. — *Eskimo*.]

huso *hū'sō, n.* the great sturgeon: — *pl.* **hu'sos**. [O.H.G. *hûso*.]

huss *hus, n.* a dogfish of various kinds, used as food. [M.E. *husk, huske*.]

hussar *hə-, hōō-zär', n.* a soldier of a light cavalry regiment: orig. a soldier of the national cavalry of Hungary in the 15th century. [Hung. *huszar*, through Old Serb. — It. *corsaro*, a freebooter.]

hussif *hus'if*. Dial. form of **housewife**.

Hussite *hus'īt, hōōs'īt, n.* a follower of the Bohemian reformer John *Hus*, martyred in 1415.

hussy *hus'i, huz'i, n.* a pert girl: a worthless wench: a housewife (*obs.*): a hussif (*obs.*). [**housewife**.]

hustings *hus'tingz, n.sing.* the principal court of the city of London: formerly the booths where the votes were taken at an election of an M.P., or the platform from which the candidates gave their addresses: electioneering. [O.E. *hústing*, a council (used in speaking of the Danes) — O.N. *hústhing* — *hús*, a house, *thing*, an assembly.]

hustle *hus'l, v.t.* to shake or push together: to crowd with violence: to jostle: to thrust hastily: to hasten roughly: to exert pressure on: to sell (esp. aggressively): to obtain (money) illicitly (*slang*). — *v.i.* to act strenuously or aggressively: to earn money illicitly (as a prostitute; *slang*). — *n.* frenzied activity: a type of lively modern dance with a variety of steps (esp. *U.S.*). — *ns.* **hus'tler** an energetic fellow: a swindler (*slang*): a prostitute (*slang*); **hus'tling**. [Du. *hutselen*, to shake to and fro; cf. **hotchpotch**.]

huswife *hus'if*. Obs. form of **housewife**.

hut *hut, n.* a small or mean house: a small temporary dwelling or similar structure. — *v.t.* to quarter in or furnish with a hut or huts. — *v.i.* to dwell in a hut or huts: — *pr.p.* **hutt'ing**; *pa.t.* and *pa.p.* **hutt'ed**. — *ns.* **hut'ment** an encampment of huts: lodging in huts; **hutt'ing** material for making huts. — **hut'-cir'cle** (*ant.*) the remains of a prehistoric circular hut, a pit lined with stones, etc. [Fr. *hutte* — O.H.G. *hutta* (Ger. *Hütte*); cf. **hide**[1].]

hutch *huch, n.* a box, a chest: a coop for rabbits: a small, cramped house (*coll.*): a baker's kneading-trough: a trough used with some ore-dressing machines: a low wagon in which coal is drawn up out of the pit. — *v.t.* (*Milt.*) to hoard up. [Fr. *huche*, a chest — L.L. *hūtica*, a box; prob. Gmc.]

Hutchinsonian *huch-in-sōn'i-ən, n.* a follower of John *Hutchinson* (1674–1737), who held that the Hebrew Scriptures contain typically the elements of all rational philosophy, natural history, and true religion.

hutia *hōō-tē'ə, n.* the hog-rat. [Sp. *hutia*, from Taino.]

Huttonian *hut-ō'ni-ən, adj.* relating to the teaching of James *Hutton* (1726–97), esp. expounding the impor-

tance of geological agencies still at work, and the igneous origin of granite and basalt. — *n.* a follower of Hutton.

huzoor *huz-ōōr', n.* an Indian potentate, or (loosely) any person of rank or importance. [Ar. *hudūr*, the presence.]

huzza *hŏŏz-ä', huz-ä', interj.* and *n.* hurrah: a shout of joy or approbation. — *v.t.* to attend with shouts of joy. — *v.i.* to utter shouts of joy or acclamation: — *pr.p.* **huzza'ing**; *pa.t.* and *pa.p.* **huzzaed, huzza'd** (*- zäd'*). [Perh. Ger. *hussa*; cf. **hurrah**.]

huzzy *huz'i*, dial. variant of **hussy**.

hwyl *hū'il, n.* divine inspiration in oratory: emotional fervour. [W.]

hyacine *hī'ə-sīn*, (*Spens.*) *n.* hyacinth (the stone).

hyacinth *hī'ə-sinth, n.* a flower that sprang from the blood of Hyacinthus, a youth accidentally killed by Apollo (*myth.*): a bulbous genus (*Hyacinthus*) of the lily family, much cultivated: extended to others of the family, as **wild hyacinth** (the English bluebell), **grape hyacinth** (*Muscari*), **Cape hyacinth** a species of Galtonia, *G. candicans*, with white flowers: a blue stone of the ancients (perh. aquamarine): a red, brown, or yellow zircon — jacinth: cinnamon-stone: a purple colour, of various hues. — *adj.* **hyacin'thine** consisting of or resembling hyacinth: very beautiful, like Hyacinthus: of a colour variously understood as golden, purple-black, or a blue or purple of some kind. [Gr. *hyakinthos*, a species of Scilla, blue larkspur, a blue stone; cf. **jacinth**.]

Hyades *hī'ə-dēz*, **Hyads** *hī'adz, ns.pl.* a cluster of five stars in the constellation of the Bull, supposed by the ancients to bring rain when they rose with the sun. [Gr. *Hyădes, Hyădes*, explained by the ancients as from *hyein*, to rain; more prob. little pigs, *hys*, a pig.]

hyaena. See **hyena**.

hyaline *hī'ə-lin, -līn, adj.* glassy: of or like glass: clear: transparent: free from granules (*biol.*). — *n.* (*Milt.*) a glassy transparent surface. — *n.* **hyalinisā'tion, -z-**. — *v.t., v.i.* **hy'alinise, -ize** (*med.*) of tissue, to change to a firm, glassy consistency. — *n.* **hy'alite** transparent colourless opal. — *adj.* **hy'aloid** (*anat.*) hyaline, transparent. — *ns.* **hyalom'elan(e)** (*-ăn, -an*; Gr. *melās, -ānos*, black) tachylite; **hyalonē'ma** (Gr. *nēma*, thread) the glass-rope sponge; **hy'alophane** (root of Gr. *phainesthai*, to seem) a feldspar containing barium; **hy'aloplasm** the clear fluid part of protoplasm. — **hyaline degeneration** hyalinisation; **hyaloid membrane** the transparent membrane which encloses the vitreous humour of the eye. [Gr. *hyalos*, glass.]

Hyblaean *hi-blē'ən, adj.* pertaining to ancient *Hybla* in Sicily, noted for its honey.

hybrid *hī'brid, n.* an organism which is the offspring of a union between different races, species, genera or varieties: a mongrel: a word formed of elements from different languages. — *adjs.* **hy'brid, hyb'ridous** produced from different species, etc.: mongrel: of a circuit, consisting of transistors and valves: of an integrated circuit, having integrated circuit(s) and other components attached to a ceramic base. — *adj.* **hybridīs'able, -z-**. — *n.* **hybridīsā'tion, -z-**. — *v.t.* **hy'bridise, -ize** to cause to interbreed. — *v.i.* to interbreed. — *ns.* **hybridis'er, -z-;** **hy'bridism, hybrid'ity** the state of being hybrid; **hybridō'ma** a hybrid cell produced from a cancer cell and an antibody-producing cell. — **hybrid bill** a public bill which affects certain private interests; **hybrid computer** one which combines features of digital and analog computers; **hybrid vigour** heterosis. [L. *hibrida*, offspring of a tame sow and wild boar; with associations of Gr. *hybris*, insolence, overweening.]

hybris. See **hubris**.

hydathode *hī'dəth-ōd*, (*bot.*) *n.* an epidermal water-excreting organ. [Gr. *hydōr, hydatos*, water, *hodos*, way.]

hydatid *hī'də-tid, n.* a water cyst or vesicle in an animal body, esp. one containing a tapeworm larva: the larva itself: hydatid disease. — *adj.* **hydatid'iform** resembling a hydatid. — **hydatid disease** an infection, esp. of the

liver, caused by tapeworm larvae, giving rise to expanding cysts; **hydatidiform mole** (*med.*) an affection of the vascular tufts of the foetal part of the placenta whereby they become greatly enlarged. [Gr. *hydatis, -idos*, a watery vesicle — *hydōr, hydatos*, water.]
hydatoid *hī'də-toid, adj.* watery. [Gr. *hydōr, -atos*, water, *eidos*, form.]
Hydnocarpus *hid-nō-kär'pəs, n.* a genus of trees akin to the chaulmoogra, yielding an oil containing chaulmoogric acid. [Gr. *hydnon*, a truffle, *karpos*, a fruit.]
hydr-. See **hydro-**.
Hydra *hī'drə, n.* a water-monster with many heads, which when cut off were succeeded by others (*myth.*): a large southern constellation: (without *cap.*) any manifold evil: (without *cap.*) a freshwater hydrozoon of the genus *Hydra*, remarkable for power of multiplication on being cut or divided. — *adj.* **hy'dra-head'ed** difficult to root out, springing up vigorously again and again. [Gr. *hydrā* — *hydōr*, water, akin to Sans. *udra*, an otter.]
hydraemia, hydragogue, Hydrangea, etc. See **hydro-**.
hydrargyrism *hī-drär'jir-izm, n.* mercurial poisoning. — *adj.* **hydrar'gyral.** — *n.* **hydrar'gyrum** mercury. [Gr. *hydrargyros*, mercury — *argyros*, silver; *hydrargyrum* is mod. L. on analogy of *argentum*, etc., L. *hydrargyrus*.]
hydrate, hydraulic, etc. See **hydro-**.
hydrazine *hī'drə-zēn, n.* a fuming corrosive liquid, $H_2N\cdot NH_2$, a powerful reducing agent, used as a rocket fuel: any of a class of organic bases derived from it. — *n.pl.* **hy'drazides** a class of chemical compounds derived from hydrazine. — **hydrazoic** (*-zō'ik*) **acid** HN_3, a colourless, foul-smelling liquid that combines with lead and other heavy metals to produce explosive salts (azides). [From **hydr-**, **azo-**.]
hydria *hī'dri-ə, hid'ri-ə, n.* a large Greek water-vase. [Gr. *hydriā*.]
hydro *hī'drō.* Short form of **hydroelectric** or **hydropathic establishment** (see under **hydro-**): — *pl.* **hy'dros.**
hydro- *hī'drō-, -dro'-,* **hydr-** in composition, of, like, by means of, water (see also **hydrogen**). — *n.* **hydraemia,** (esp. *U.S.*) **hydremia** (*hī-drē'mi-ə;* Gr. *haima,* blood) wateriness of the blood. — *adj.* **hydragogue** (*hī'drə-gog, -gōg;* Gr. *aōgos,* bringing; *med.*) removing water or serum. — *n.* a drug with that effect. — *ns.* **Hydrangea** (*hī-drān'jə, -jyə;* Gr. *angeion,* vessel) a genus of shrubby plants of the family **Hydrangeā'ceae,** with large globular clusters of showy flowers, natives of China and Japan: (without *cap.*) a plant of this genus; **hydrant** (*hī'drənt*) a connection for attaching a hose to a water-main or a fire-plug; **hydranth** (*hī'dranth;* Gr. *anthos,* flower) a nutritive polyp in a hydroid colony; **hydrarthro'sis** (*med.*) swelling of a joint caused by the accumulation in it of watery fluid; **hy'drate** a compound containing water which is chemically combined and which can be expelled without affecting the composition of the other substance: an old word for a *hydroxide* (see under **hydrogen**). — *v.t.* to combine with water: to cause to absorb water. — *n.* **hydrā'tion.** — *adj.* **hydraulic** (*hī-dröl'ik, -drol';* Gr. *aulos,* a pipe) relating to hydraulics: conveying water: worked by water or other liquid in pipes: setting in water. — *v.t.* (*mining*) to excavate and wash out by powerful jets of water: — *pr.p.* **hydraul'icking;** *pa.t.* and *pa.p.* **hydraul'icked.** — *adv.* **hydraul'ically.** — *n.sing.* **hydraul'ics** the science of hydrodynamics in general, or its practical application to water-pipes, etc. — *n.* **hydrē'mia** mainly U.S. form of **hydraemia.** — *adj.* **hy'dric** pertaining to an abundance of moisture: see under **hydrogen.** — *adv.* **hy'drically.** — *ns.* **hydride** see under **hydrogen; hydro=ae'roplane** (in U.S. **hydro-air'plane**) a seaplane. — *adj.* **hydrobiolog'ical.** — *ns.* **hydrobiol'ogist; hydrobiol'ogy** the biology of aquatic animals and plants; **hy'drocele** (*-sēl;* Gr. *kēlē,* a swelling; *med.*) a swelling containing serous fluid, esp. in the scrotum; **hydrocell'ulose** a gelatinous material obtained by hydration of cellulose, used in paper- making, etc.; **hydrocephalus** (*-sef'ə-ləs,*

or *-kef';* Gr. *kephalē,* head) an accumulation of serous fluid within the cranial cavity, either in the subdural space or the ventricles: water in the head: dropsy of the brain. — *adjs.* **hydrocephal'ic, hydroceph'alous.** — *ns.* **Hydrocharis** (*hī-drok'ə-ris;* Gr. *charis, -itos,* grace) the frogbit genus, giving name to the **Hydrocharitā'ceae,** a family of water-plants akin to the pondweeds; **hy'drochore** (*-kōr, -kör;* Gr. *chōreein,* to make room, spread about) a plant disseminated by water. — *adj.* **hydrochoric** (*-kor'ik*). — *n.pl.* **Hydrocorall'ī'nae** an order of Hydrozoa, massive reef-builders, the millepores, etc. — *n.* and *adj.* **hydrocor'alline.** — *adj.* **hydrodynamic** (*-dīn-am'ik;* Gr. *dynamis,* power), **-al.** — *n.* **hydrodynam'icist.** — *n. sing.* **hydrodynam'ics** the science of the motions and equilibrium of a material system partly or wholly fluid (called *hydrostatics* when the system is in equilibrium, *hydrokinetics* when it is not). — *adjs.* **hydroelast'ic** see **hydroelastic suspension** below; **hydroelec'tric.** — *ns.* **hydroelectric'ity** electricity produced by means of water, esp. by water-power; **hydroextract'or** a drying-machine that works centrifugally; **hy'drofoil** a device on a boat for raising it from the water as its speed increases: a boat fitted with this device: a corresponding device on a seaplane to aid its take-off (also **hy'drovane**): a seaplane with hydrofoils; **hydrogeol'ogist; hydrogeol'ogy** the branch of geology dealing with ground water; **hy'drograph** a graph showing seasonal variations in level, force, etc., of a body of water; **hydrog'rapher** (Gr. *graphein,* to write). — *adjs.* **hydrographic** (*-graf'ik*), **-al.** — *adv.* **hydrograph'ically.** — *n.* **hydrog'raphy** the investigation of seas and other bodies of water, including charting, sounding, study of tides, currents, etc. — *adj.* **hy'droid** like a Hydra: polypoid. — *n.* a hydrozoan: a hydrozoan in its asexual generation. — *adj.* **hydrokinet'ic** pertaining to hydrokinetics: pertaining to the motion of fluids: pertaining to fluids in motion: operated or operating by the movement of fluids. — *n.sing.* **hydrokinet'ics** a branch of hydrodynamics (q.v.). — *adjs.* **hydrolog'ic, -al.** — *ns.* **hydrol'ogist; hydrol'ogy** the study of water resources in land areas of the world — (*U.S.*) esp. underground water; **hydrol'ysate** (*-i-sāt*) a substance produced by hydrolysis. — *v.t.* **hydrolyse, -yze** (*hī'drōlīz*) to subject to hydrolysis. — Also *v.i.* — *ns.* **hydrolysis** (*hī-drol'i-sis;* Gr. *lysis,* loosing) chemical decomposition or ionic dissociation caused by water; **hy'drolyte** (*-līt*) a body subjected to hydrolysis. — *adjs.* **hydrolytic** (*-lit'ik*); **hydromagnet'ic.** — *n. sing.* **hydromagnet'ics** magnetohydrodynamics. — *ns.* **hy'dromancy** (Gr. *manteiā,* divination) divination by water; **hydromā'nia** a craving for water. — *adj.* **hydromant'ic.** — *n. sing.* **hydromechan'ics** hydrodynamics. — *n.* **hydromedū'sa** a hydrozoan in its sexual generation: — *pl.* **Hydromedū'sae** the class Hydrozoa. — *adjs.* **hydromedū'san, hydromedū'soid** (also *ns.*). — *ns.* **hy'dromel** (Gr. *hydromeli — meli,* honey) a beverage made of honey and water; **hydromet'allurgy** (or *-metal'ər-ji*) the extraction of metal from ore by treatment with water or other fluids; **hydromē'teor** (Gr. *meteōron,* a meteor) any weather phenomenon depending on the moisture content of the atmosphere; **hydrometeorol'ogy; hydrom'eter** (Gr. *metron,* a measure) a float for measuring specific gravity. — *adjs.* **hydrometric** (*-met'*), **-al.** — *ns.* **hydrom'etry; Hydromys** (*hī'drō-mis;* Gr. *mȳs,* mouse) an Australasian genus of aquatic rodents; **hy'dronaut** a person trained to work in an underwater vessel, e.g. a submarine; **hydronephrō'sis** distension of the kidney with urine held up as a result of obstruction in the urinary tract. — *adj.* **hydronephrō'tic.** — *n.* **hydrop'athy** the treatment of disease by water, externally and internally. — *adj.* **hydropathic** (*hī-drō-path'ik;* Gr. *pathos,* suffering) of, for, relating to, practising, hydropathy. — *n.* (in full **hydropathic establishment;** *coll.* **hy'dro,** *pl.* **hy'dros**) a hotel (with special baths, etc.) where guests can have hydropathic treatment. — *adj.* **hydropath'ical.** — *adv.* **hydropath'ically.** — *ns.* **hydrop'athist** one who practises hydropathy; **hydrophane** (*hī'drŏ-fān*; Gr. *phānos*, bright) a translucent opal transparent in water. — *adj.* **hydrophanous** (*-drof'ən-əs*) transparent on immersion. — *n.pl.* **Hydrophidae** (*hī-drof'i-dē*; Gr. *ophis*, snake) a family of venomous sea-snakes. — *n.* **hydroph'ilite** native calcium chloride (a very hygroscopic substance). — *adjs.* **hydrophil'ic** (*chem.*) attracting water; **hydroph'ilous** water-loving: pollinated by agency of water (*bot.*). — *ns.* **hydroph'ily** (Gr. *phileein*, to love) water-pollination; **hydrophō'bia** (Gr. *phobos*, fear) horror of water: inability to swallow water owing to a contraction in the throat, a symptom of rabies: rabies itself. — *adjs.* **hydrophō'bic** (or *-fob'*) pertaining to hydrophobia: repelling water (*chem.*); **hydrophobous** (*-drof'ə-bəs*) (*obs.*). — *ns.* **hydrophobic'ity; hy'drophone** (*-fōn*; Gr. *phōnē*, voice) an apparatus for listening to sounds conveyed by water; **hy'drophyte** (*-fīt*; Gr. *phyton*, plant) a plant growing in water or in very moist conditions. — *adj.* **hydrophytic** (*-fīt'ik*). — *n.* **hydrophyton** (*hī-drof'i-ton*) the coenosarc of a hydroid colony. — *adjs.* **hydroph'ytous; hydrop'ic** (erroneously **hydrop'tic**; see **hydropsy**) dropsical: thirsty: charged or swollen with water. — *n.* **hy'droplane** a light, flat-bottomed motor-boat which, at high speed, skims along the surface of the water: (erroneously) a hydro-aeroplane or seaplane. — *v.i.* of a boat, to skim like a hydroplane: of a vehicle, to skid on a wet road. — *adj.* **hydropneumat'ic** using water and air acting together. — *n.* **hydropol'yp** a hydrozoan polyp. — *n. sing.* **hydroponics** (*hī-drō-pon'iks*; Gr. *ponos*, toil) the art or practice of growing plants in a chemical solution without soil. — *ns.* **hy'dropower** hydroelectric power; **hy'dropsy** (Gr. *hydrōps*, dropsy; *arch.*) dropsy. — *n.pl.* **Hydropterid'eae** (*-i-ē*; Gr. *pteris*, *-idos*, male-fern) the water-ferns or heterosporous ferns. — *ns.* **hy'dropult** (modelled on **catapult**) a hand force-pump; **hydroquinone** (*-kwin-ōn'*, or *kwin'*, or *-kwīn'*) quinol; **hy'droscope** (Gr. *skopeein*, to view) a kind of water-clock, a graduated tube, from which the water escaped (*hist.*): an instrument for viewing under water; **hy'droski** (*-skē*) a kind of hydrofoil used on seaplanes as a source of hydrodynamic lift, on aeroplanes to make them amphibious; **hydrosō'ma, hy'drosome** (*-sōm*; Gr. *sōma*, body) a hydroid colony: — *pl.* **hydrosō'mata, hy'drosomes.** — *adjs.* **hydrosō'mal, hydrosō'matous.** — *ns.* **hy'drospace, hydrosphere** (*hī'drō-sfēr*; Gr. *sphaira*, sphere) the water on the surface of the earth — the seas and oceans; **hy'drostat** (Gr. *-statēs*, causing to stand) a contrivance for indicating the presence of water. — *adjs.* **hydrostat'ic, hydrostat'ical.** — *adv.* **hydrostat'ically.** — *n. sing.* **hydrostat'ics** a branch of hydrodynamics (q.v.). — *adj.* **hydrotac'tic.** — *ns.* **hydrotax'is** (Gr. *taxis*, arrangement) response of an organism to the stimulus of water; **hydrothē'ca** (Gr. *thēkē*, case) the horny cup of a hydranth; **hydrother'apy, hydrotherapeu'tics** treatment of disease by the external use of water, e.g. treatment of disability by developing movement in water. — *adjs.* **hydrotherapeu'tic; hydrother'mal** pertaining to, or produced by, action of heated or superheated water, esp. in dissolving, transporting, and redepositing mineral matter. — *n.* **hydrothorax** (*-thō'*, *-thŏ'*; Gr. *thōrax*, chest) dropsy in the chest. — *adj.* **hydrotrop'ic.** — *n.* **hydrot'ropism** (Gr. *tropos*, a turn) the turning of an organ towards (*positive*) or away from (*negative*) moisture. — *adj.* **hydrous** (*-hī'drəs*; *chem.*, *min.*) containing water. — *ns.* **hydrovane** see **hydrofoil; hydrozincite** (*-zingk'īt*) basic zinc carbonate. — *n.pl.* **Hydrozō'a** (Gr. *zōion*, an animal) a class of Coelenterata, chiefly marine organisms in which alternation of generations typically occurs, the hydroid phase colonial, giving rise to the medusoid phase by budding — the zoophytes, millepores, etc.: sometimes extended to include the true jellyfishes: (without *cap.*) hydrozoans: — *n.* and *adj.* **hydrozō'an.** — *n.* **hydrozō'on** a coelenterate of the Hydrozoa: — *pl.* **hydrozō'a.** — **hydrated electron** very reactive free electron released in aqueous solutions by the action of ionising radia-

tions; **hydrated ion** ion surrounded by molecules of water which it holds in a degree of orientation; **hydraulic belt** an endless belt of absorbent material for raising water; **hydraulic brake** a brake in which the force is transmitted by means of a compressed fluid; **hydraulic jack** a lifting apparatus in which oil, etc., is pumped against a piston; **hydraulic mining** hydraulicking; **hydraulic press** a press operated by forcing water into a cylinder in which a ram or plunger works; **hydraulic ram** a device whereby the pressure head produced when a moving column of water is brought to rest is caused to deliver some of the water under pressure; **hydraulic seeding** sowing seed by spraying it, mixed with nutrients, etc., on the ground; **hydraulic suspension** a system of car suspension using hydraulic units; **hydroelastic suspension** a system of car suspension in which a fluid provides interconnection between the front and rear suspension units; **hydrostatic balance** a balance for weighing bodies in water to determine their specific gravity; **hydrostatic drive, transmission** in a vehicle, drive consisting of system transmitting power through oil, under pressure; **hydrostatic extrusion** (*metallurgy*) form of extrusion in which the metal to be shaped is preshaped to fit a die forming the lower end of a high-pressure container which is filled with a pressure-transmitting liquid; pressure is built up in the liquid by a plunger until the metal is forced through the die; **hydrostatic paradox** the principle that — disregarding molecular forces — any quantity of fluid, however small, may balance any weight, however great; **hydrostatic press** a hydraulic press; **hydrostatic transmission** see **hydrostatic drive.** [Gr. *hydōr*, water.]

hydrogen *hī'drō-jən*, *n.* a gas (symbol H, atomic number 1) which in combination with oxygen produces water, the lightest of all known substances, and very inflammable, of great importance in the moderation (slowing down) of neutrons. — *adj.* **hy'dric** of or containing hydrogen. — *n.* **hy'dride** a compound of hydrogen with an element or radical. — *adjs.* **hydriodic** (*hī-dri-od'ik*) of an acid composed of hydrogen and iodine, hydrogen iodide; **hydrobrō'mic** applied to an acid composed of hydrogen and bromine, hydrogen bromide. — *n.* **hydrocar'bon** a compound of hydrogen and carbon with nothing else, occurring notably in oil, natural gas and coal. — *adj.* **hydrochloric** (*-klor'ik*, *-klōr'*, *-klŏr'*) applied to an acid composed of hydrogen and chlorine, hydrogen chloride, still sometimes called *muriatic acid.* — *ns.* **hydrochlor'ide** a compound of hydrochloric acid with an organic base; **hydrocor'tisone** one of the corticosteroids, 17-hydroxy-corticosterone, a synthesised form of which is used to treat rheumatoid arthritis, etc.; **hy'drocracking** cracking of petroleum, etc., in the presence of hydrogen. — *adjs.* **hydrocyanic** (*-sī-an'ik*) denoting an acid (*prussic acid*) composed of hydrogen and cyanogen; **hydroferricyanic** (*-fer-i-sī-an'ik*), **hydroferrōcyan'ic** applied to two acids composed of hydrogen, iron, and cyanogen, hydroferricyanic acid, $H_3Fe(CN)_6$, having an atom of hydrogen less than hydroferrocyanic, $H_4Fe(CN)_6$; **hydrofluor'ic** applied to an acid composed of fluorine and hydrogen, hydrogen fluoride. — *n.* **hydrogasificā'tion** production of methane from coal by treatment with hydrogen at high temperature and pressure. — *v.t.* **hydrogenate** (*hī'drō-jən-āt* or *hī-droj'ən-āt*) to cause to combine with hydrogen, as in the hardening of oils by converting an olein into a stearin by addition of hydrogen in the presence of a catalyst such as nickel or palladium. — *n.* **hydrogenā'tion.** — *adj.* **hydrog'enous.** — *ns.* **hydrosul'phide** a compound formed by action of hydrogen sulphide on a hydroxide; **hydrosul'phite** a hyposulphite (esp. sodium hyposulphite). — *adj.* **hydrosulphū'ric** formed by a combination of hydrogen and sulphur. — *n.* **hydrox'ide** a chemical compound which contains one or more hydroxyl groups. — *adj.* **hydrox'y** of a compound, containing one or more hydroxyl groups (also *pfx.* **hydrox'y-**). — *ns.* **hydrox'yl** (Gr. *hylē*, matter) a compound radical consisting of one atom of oxygen and one of hydrogen: sometimes loosely applied to *hydrogen peroxide*; **hydroxyl′amine** a basic substance composed of a hydroxyl group and an amino group (NH₂OH). — **hydrogen bomb**, or *H-bomb*, a bomb in which an enormous release of energy is achieved by converting hydrogen nuclei into helium nuclei — a fusion, not fission, process started by great heat; the first H-bomb was exploded by the U.S.A. in November 1952; **hydrogen ion** an atom or molecule of hydrogen having a positive charge, esp. an atom formed in a solution of acid in water — strong acids being highly ionised and weak acids only slightly; **hydrogen peroxide** see **peroxide**; **hydrogen sulphide** a compound of hydrogen and sulphur, H₂S; **hydronium ion** a hydrated hydrogen ion, as H₃O⁺. — **heavy hydrogen** see **heavy**; **hydrogenation of coal** conversion of coal to liquid fuels by hydrogenation. [Coined by Cavendish (1766) from Gr. *hydōr*, water, and *gennaein*, to produce.]

hydyne *hī′dīn, n.* an American rocket-launching fuel.

hye (*obs.*) for **hie, high.**

hyena, hyaena *hī-ē′nə,* **hyen** *hī′en* (*Shak.*), *ns.* a carrion-feeding carnivore (genus **Hyae′na,** constituting a family **Hyae′nidae**) with long thick neck, coarse mane and sloping body. — **hyena dog** an African wild dog, blotched like a hyena; **spotted hyena** an animal (*Crocuta*) resembling a hyena, with a hysterical-sounding laugh. [L. *hyaena* — Gr. *hyaina* — *hŷs,* a pig.]

hyetal *hī′i-tl, adj.* rainy: pertaining to rain or rainfall. — *n.* **hy′etograph** a rain chart: a self-registering rain-gauge. — *adjs.* **hyetograph′ic, -al.** — *adv.* **hyetograph′ically.** — *ns.* **hyetog′raphy; hyetol′ogy** a branch of meteorology dealing with rainfall; **hyetom′eter** a rain-gauge; **hyetomet′rograph** a self-registering rain-gauge, hyetograph. [Gr. *hyetos,* rain.]

Hygeian *hī-jē′ən, adj.* relating to Hygieia or to health and its preservation. [Gr. *Hygieia,* later *Hygeia,* goddess of health, daughter of Asklēpios (Aesculapius).]

hygiene *hī′jēn, n.* the science or art of preserving health: sanitary principles. — *adj.* **hygienic** (*hī-jēn′ik*). — *adv.* **hygien′ically.** — *n. sing.* **hygien′ics** principles of hygiene. — *n.* **hygienist** (*hī′jēn-ist*) one skilled in hygiene. [Fr. *hygiène* — Gr. *hygieinē* (*technē*), hygienic (art) — *hygieia,* health, *hygiēs,* healthy.]

hygristor *hī-gris′tər, n.* an electronic component whose resistance varies with humidity. [hygro-, res*istor*.]

hygro- *hī′grō-, -gro′,* in composition, wet, moist. — *n.* **hygrochasy** (*hī-grok′ə-si;* Gr. *chasis,* a gape) dehiscence on moistening. — *adj.* **hygrochas′tic.** — *ns.* **hy′grodeik** (*-dīk;* Gr. *deiknynai,* to show) a psychrometer with an index and scale; **hy′grograph** an instrument, a development of a hygroscope, for recording the humidity of the air. — *adjs.* **hygrograph′ic, -al.** — *ns.* **hygrol′ogy** the study of the humidity of the air or other gases; **hygrom′eter** an instrument for measuring the humidity of the air or of other gases. — *adjs.* **hygrometric** (*-met′rik*), **-al** belonging to hygrometry: hygroscopic. — *n.* **hygrom′etry** measurement of the humidity of the air or of other gases. — *adjs.* **hy′grophil, hygrophilous** (*-grof′;* Gr. *phileein,* to love) moisture-loving: living where there is much moisture; **hy′grophobe** (Gr. *phobeein,* to fear) growing best where moisture is scanty. — *n.* **hy′grophyte** (*-fīt;* Gr. *phyton,* plant) a plant adapted to plentiful water-supply. — *adj.* **hygrophytic** (*-fit′ik*). — *n.* **hy′groscope** an instrument that shows, without measuring, changes in the humidity of the air. — *adjs.* **hygroscopic** (*-skop′ik*), **-al** relating to the hygroscope: readily absorbing moisture from the air: indicating or caused by absorption or loss of moisture, as some movements of plants. — *ns.* **hygroscopicity** (*-skop-is′i-ti*); **hy′grostat** an apparatus which produces constant humidity. — **hygroscopic salt** a salt, esp. calcium chloride, which absorbs moisture from other substances. [Gr. *hygros,* wet.]

hying *hī′ing, pr.p.* of **hie¹,².**

hyke *hīk, n.* See **haik¹.**

Hyksos *hik′sos, -sōs, n.* a foreign line of kings (the xv and

xvi dynasties, called the shepherd kings) who ruled Egypt for centuries. [Gr. *Hyksōs* — Egyptian *Hikukhasut,* princes of the desert, app. misunderstood as shepherd princes.]

hylding (*Spens.*). Same as **hilding.**

hyle *hī′le, n.* wood, matter. — *adj.* **hy′lic** material: corporeal. — *ns.* **hy′licism, hy′lism** materialism; **hy′licist, hy′list** (wrongly **hy′loist**); **hy′lobate** a gibbon (genus **Hylob′atēs;** from the root of Gr. *bainein,* to go); **hylogen′esis** the origin of matter. — *adj.* **hylomor′phic.** — *ns.* **hylomor′phism** (*philos.*) the doctrine that matter is the first cause of the universe; **hylop′athism** (Gr. *pathos,* feeling) the doctrine that matter is sentient; **hylop′athist.** — *adj.* **hyloph′agous** (Gr. *phagein,* to eat) wood-eating. — *ns.* **hy′lophyte** (Gr. *phyton,* plant) a woodland plant; **hy′lotheism** (Gr. *theos,* god) the doctrine that there is no God but matter and the universe; **hy′lotheist.** — *adjs.* **hylot′omous** (Gr. *tomē,* a cut) wood-cutting; **hylozō′ical, hylozoist′ic.** — *ns.* **hylozō′ism** (Gr. *zōē,* life) the doctrine that all matter is endowed with life; **hylozō′ist.** [Gr. *hȳlē,* wood, matter.]

hyleg *hī′leg, n.* the ruling planet at the hour of birth. [Origin obscure; cf. Pers. *hailāj,* nativity.]

Hymen *hī′men, n.* the god of marriage (*myth.*): marriage (*arch.*). — *adjs.* **hymenē′al, hymenē′an** (also **-ae′al, -ae′an**). — *n.* **hymenē′al** wedding hymn: (in *pl.*) nuptials (*arch.*). [Gr. wedding-cry, perh. also a god.]

hymen *hī′men, n.* a membrane: a thin membrane partially closing the virginal vagina. — *adjs.* **hy′menal** pertaining to the hymen; **hymē′nial** pertaining to the hymenium. — *n.* **hymē′nium** the spore-bearing surface in fungi. — *ns.pl.* **Hymenomycetes** (*hī-mən-ō-mī-sē′tēz*) an order of fungi with exposed hymenium from an early stage — toadstools, etc.; **Hymenophyllā′ceae** the filmy ferns. — *adj.* **hymenophyllā′ceous.** — *n.pl.* **Hymenop′tera** an order of insects with four transparent wings — ants, bees, wasps, etc. — *n.* and *adj.* **hymenop′teran.** — *adj.* **hymenop′terous.** [Gr. *hȳmēn,* membrane.]

hymn *him, n.* a song of praise. — *v.t.* to celebrate in song: to worship by hymns. — *v.i.* to sing in adoration: — *pr.p.* **hymning** (*him′ing, him′ning*); *pa.t.* and *pa.p.* **hymned** (*himd, him′nid*). — *ns.* **hym′nal, hym′nary** a hymn-book. — *adj.* **hym′nic.** — *ns.* **hym′nist; hym′nodist; hym′nody** hymns collectively: hymn-singing: hymnology; **hymnographer; hymnog′raphy** the art of writing hymns: the study of hymns; **hymnol′ogist; hymnol′ogy** the study or composition of hymns. — **hymn′-book** a book of hymns. [Gr. *hymnos.*]

hynde. A Spenserian spelling of **hind².**

hyoid *hī′oid, adj.* having the form of the Greek letter upsilon (υ), applied to a bone at the base of the tongue. [Gr. *hȳoeidēs — hȳ,* the letter upsilon, and *eidos,* form.]

hyoplastron *hī-ō-plas′tron, n.* in a turtle's plastron, a plate between the hypoplastron and the entoplastron: — *pl.* **hyoplas′tra.** — *adj.* **hyoplas′tral.** [Gr. *hȳ,* the letter upsilon.]

Hyoscyamus *hī-ō-sī′ə-məs, n.* the henbane genus. — *ns.* **hy′oscine** (*-sēn, -sən;* also called **scopolamine;** used as a truth drug, for travel sickness, etc.) and **hyoscy′amine** two poisonous alkaloids similar to atropine, got from henbane. [Gr. *hyoskyamos.*]

hyp. See **hip³.**

hypabyssal *hip-ə-bis′l,* (*petr.*) *adj.* moderately deep-seated, not quite abyssal, intermediate between plutonic and eruptive. [Gr. *hypo,* beneath.]

hypaethral *hip-ē′thrəl,* or *hīp-, adj.* roofless, open to the sky. — *n.* **hypae′thron** an open court. [Gr. *hypo,* beneath, *aithēr,* upper air, sky.]

hypalgesia *hip-al-jē′si-ə, -zi-ə,* or *hīp′, n.* diminished susceptibility to pain. — Also **hypal′gia.** — *adj.* **hypalgē′sic.** [Gr. *hypo,* under, *algēsis, algos,* pain.]

hypallage *hip-, hīp-al′ə-jē,* (*rhet.*) *n.* a figure in which the relations of words in a sentence are mutually interchanged. — *adj.* **hypallact′ic.** [Gr. *hypo,* under, *allassein,* to exchange.]

hypanthium *hip-, hīp-an′thi-əm, n.* the flat or concave receptacle of a perigynous flower.   [Gr. *hypo*, under, *anthos*, flower.]

hypate *hip'ə-tē*, (*Gr. mus.*) *n.* the lowest string of the lyre, or its tone.   [Gr. *hypatē*, highest (fem.), prob. as having the longest string.]

hype *hīp*, (*slang*) *n.* a hypodermic needle: a drug addict: something which stimulates artificially: a sales gimmick, etc.: a publicity stunt: the person or thing promoted by such a stunt: a deception. — *n.* **hyp'er** one who or that which hypes. — *adj.* over-stimulated. — **hype (up)** to inject oneself with a drug: to stimulate artificially: to promote or to advertise extravagantly. **hyped up** artificially stimulated: highly excited: artificial, fake.   [Abbrev. of **hypodermic**.]

hyper- *hī'pər-*, *hī-pûr'-*, in composition, over: excessive: more than normal. — *n.* **hyperacid'ity** excessive acidity, esp. in the stomach. — *adj.* **hyperact'ive** (*med.*) abnormally or pathologically active. — *ns.* **hyperactiv'ity; hyperacusis** (*-ə-kū'sis*; Gr. *akousis*, hearing) abnormally increased power of hearing. — *adj.* **hyperacute'**. — *ns.* **hyperacute'ness; hyperadrē'nalism** excessive activity of the adrenal gland; **hyperaemia,** in U.S. **hyperemia,** (*-ē'mi-ə*; Gr. *haima*, blood) congestion or excess of blood in any part. — *adj.* **hyperae'mic**. — *n.* **hyperaesthesia,** in U.S. **hyperesthesia,** (*-ēs-* or *-es-thē'si-ə*, *-zi-ə*; Gr. *aisthēsis*, perception) excessive sensitivity to stimuli: an abnormal extension of the bodily senses assumed to explain telepathy and clairvoyance: exaggerated aestheticism. — *adjs.* **hyperaesthē'sic, hyperaesthetic** (*-thet'ik*) overaesthetic: abnormally or morbidly sensitive. — *n.* **hyperalgē'sia** (*-si-ə*, *-zi-ə*; Gr. *algēsis*, pain) heightened sensitivity to pain. — *adj.* **hyperalgē'sic**. — *adjs.* **hyperbar'ic** having specific gravity greater than that of cerebrospinal fluid (*spinal anaesthesia*): pertaining to conditions of high atmospheric pressure with a greater concentration of oxygen than normal, as in a **hyperbaric chamber,** a chamber containing oxygen at high pressure; **hyperbat'ic**. — *adv.* **hyperbat'ically**. — *ns.* **hyper'baton** (Gr., — root of *bainein*, to go; *rhet.*) a figure by which words are transposed from their natural order; **hyper'bola** (Gr. *hyperbolē*, overshooting — *ballein*, to throw; *pl.* usu. in *-s*; *geom.*) one of the conic sections, the intersection of a plane with a cone when the plane cuts both branches of the cone; **hyperbole** (*hī-pûr'bə-lē*) a rhetorical figure which produces a vivid impression by extravagant and obvious exaggeration. — *adjs.* **hyperbol'ic, -al** of a hyperbola or hyperbole. — *adv.* **hyperbol'ically**. — *v.t.* **hyper'bolise, -ize** to represent hyperbolically. — *v.i.* to speak hyperbolically or with exaggeration. — *ns.* **hyper'bolism; hyper'boloid** a solid figure certain of whose plane sections are hyperbolas. — *adj.* **hyperborean** (*-bō'*, *-bö'*; Gr. *Hyperboreoi*, a people supposed to live in sunshine beyond the north wind — *Boreas*, the north wind) belonging to the extreme north. — *n.* an inhabitant of the extreme north. — *n.* **hypercalc(a)e'mia** abnormal rise in the calcium content of the blood. — *adj.* **hypercatalect'ic** (*pros.*) having an additional syllable or half-foot after the last complete dipody. — *ns.* **hypercatalex'is; hy'percharge** the strangeness of a particle plus its baryon number. — *v.t.* (*-chärj'*) to charge excessively, to overload. — *n.* **hypercholesterolae'mia** a condition characterised by an abnormally high level of blood cholesterol. — *adj.* **hypercon'scious** more than normally aware (of). — *n.* **hypercrit'ic** one who is overcritical: a carper. — *adjs.* **hypercrit'ic, -al**. — *adv.* **hypercrit'ically**. — *v.t.* **hypercrit'icise, -ize** (*-sīz*). — *ns.* **hypercrit'icism; hy'percube** (*math.*) a theoretical solid in four or more dimensions, all sides being equal and all angles right angles. — *adj.* **hyperdac'tyl** (Gr. *daktylos*, finger, toe). — *n.* **hyperdac'tyly** possession of more than five fingers or toes. — *adj.* **hyperdorian** (*-dō'*, *-dö'*; Gr. *hyperdōrios*; *mus.*) above the Dorian mode: applied in ancient Greek music to a mode having as its lower tetrachord the upper tetrachord of the Dorian (as: *b c d e; e f g a; b*). — *ns.* **hyperdulia** (*-dōō-lī'ə*) see

dulia; hyperem'esis (Gr. *emesis*, vomiting) excessive vomiting. — *adj.* **hyperemet'ic**. — *ns.* **hyperemia, hyperesthesia** see **hyperaemia, hyperaesthesia**. — *adjs.* **hypereutec'tic** of a compound, containing more of the minor component than an eutectic compound; **hyperfō'cal** (*phot.*) referring to the minimum distance from a lens to the point from which all objects can be focused clearly; **hyper'gamous** pertaining to **hypergamy**. — *ns.* **hypergamy** (*hī-pûr'gə-mi*; Gr. *gamos*, marriage) a custom that allows a man but forbids a woman to marry a person of lower social standing: now sometimes more generally marriage of a man with a woman of higher social rank; **hyperglyc(a)emia** (*-glī-sē'mi-ə*) abnormal rise in the sugar content of the blood. — *adjs.* **hypergolic** (*-gol'ik*) of two or more liquids, spontaneously explosive on mixing. — *ns.* **hyper(h)idrō'sis** excessive sweating; **hyperinflā'tion** (*econ.*) rapid inflation uncontrollable by normal means; **hyperinō'sis** (Gr. *īs*, *īnos*, strength, fibre) excess of fibrin in the blood. — *adjs.* **hyperinōt'ic; hyperlydian** (*-lid'i-ən*; Gr. *hyperlȳdios*) above the Lydian mode: applied in ancient Greek music to a mode having as its lower tetrachord the upper tetrachord of the Lydian (as: *g a b c; c d e f; g*). — *n.* **hy'permarket, -mart** a very large self-service store with a wide range of goods. — *adj.* **hypermet'rical** beyond or exceeding the ordinary metre of a line: having or being an additional syllable. — *n.* **hypermetrō'pia** (Gr. *metron*, measure, *ōps*, eye) long-sightedness. — Also **hyperō'pia**. — *adj.* **hypermetrōp'ic**. — *ns.* **hypernatraemia** (*-nə-trē'mi-ə*; *natrium* (see **natron**) and Gr. *haime*, blood) an abnormally high concentration of sodium chloride (salt) in the blood, esp. in infants; **hy'peron** any particle with mass greater than that of a proton or neutron; **hyperpar'asite** a parasite living on another parasite; **hyperphagia** (*-fā'ji-ə*) bulimia. — *adjs.* **hyperphrygian** (*-frij'i-ən*, *-frij'ən*; Gr. *hyperphrȳgios*) above the Phrygian: applied to a mode of ancient Greek music having as its lower tetrachord the upper tetrachord of the Phrygian (as: *a b c d; d e f g; a*); **hyperphys'ical** beyond physical laws: supernatural. — *n.* **hyperplasia** (*-plā'zi-ə*, *-zhə*; Gr. *plasis*, a forming; *path.*) overgrowth of a part due to excessive multiplication of its cells. — *adjs.* **hyperplastic** (*-plas'*); **hyperpyretic** (*-pir-et'ik*; Gr. *pyretikos*, feverish). — *ns.* **hyperpyrex'ia** abnormally high body temperature; **hypersarcō'ma, hypersarcō'sis** (Gr. *hypersarkōma, hypersarkōsis* — *sarx*, flesh; *path.*) proud or fungous flesh. — *v.t.* **hypersens'itise, -ize** to increase the sensitivity of. — *adj.* **hypersens'itive** excessively sensitive. — *ns.* **hypersens'itiveness; hypersensitivi'ity**. — *adj.* **hypersen'sual** beyond the scope of the senses. — *n.* **hypersom'nia** (L. *somnus*, sleep) a pathological tendency to sleep excessively. — *adj.* **hyperson'ic** (L. *sonus*, sound) of speeds, greater than Mach 5: of aircraft, able to fly at such speeds: of sound-waves, having a frequency greater than 1000 million Hz. — *ns.* **hyperson'ics; hy'perspace** (*math.*) space having more than three dimensions; **hypersthene** (*hī'pər-sthēn*; Gr. *sthenos*, strength, because harder than hornblende) rock-forming orthorhombic pyroxene, anhydrous silicate of magnesium and iron, generally dark green, brown, or raven-black with metallic lustre; **hypersthē'nia** (*path.*) a morbid condition marked by excessive excitement of all the vital phenomena. — *adj.* **hypersthenic** (*-sthen'ik*) of hypersthene or of hypersthenia. — *ns.* **hypersthē'nite** a rock consisting almost entirely of hypersthene: an aggregate of labradorite and hypersthene (*obs.*); **hy'perstress** excessive stress; **hyperten'sion** blood pressure higher than normal: a state of great emotional tension. — *adj.* **hyperten'sive**. — *n.* a victim of hypertension. — *adj.* **hypertherm'al**. — *ns.* **hypertherm'ia** (dangerous) overheating of the body; **hyperthyroidism** (*-thī'roid-izm*) overproduction of thyroid hormone by the thyroid gland, and the resulting condition. — *adjs.* **hyperton'ic** of muscles, having excessive tone; of a solution, having a higher osmotic pressure than a specified solution; **hypertroph'ic, -al, hyper'trophied,**

hyper′trophous (Gr. *trophē*, nourishment). — *ns.* **hyper′trophy** overnourishment: abnormal enlargement; **hyperveloc′ity** very great speed, as of nuclear particles; **hyperventilā′tion** abnormally increased speed and depth of breathing; **hypervitaminō′sis** the condition resulting from too much of any vitamin (esp. vitamin D). — **hyperbolic functions** in math., a set of six functions (sinh, cosh, tanh, etc.) analogous to the trigonometrical functions; **hyperbolic geometry** that involving the axiom that through any point in a given plane there can be drawn more than one line that does not intersect a given line; **hyperbolic logarithms** natural logarithms; **hyperbolic paraboloid** a saddle-shaped surface represented by the equation $x^2/a - y^2/b = z$; **hyperbolic spiral** a spiral of polar equation $\rho\theta = k^2$; **hyperfine structure** (*phys.*) the splitting of spectrum lines into two or more very closely spaced components. [Gr. *hyper*, over.]

Hypericum *hī-per′i-kəm, n.* the St John's wort genus of plants, giving name to a family **Hypericā′ceae.** [Gr. *hyperikon* or *hypereikos* — *hypo*, under, *ereikē*, heath.]

Hyperion *hī-pēr′i-on, n.* a Titan, son of Uranus and Ge, and father of Helios, Selene, and Eos: Helios himself, the incarnation of light and beauty: a satellite of Saturn. [Gr. *Hypēriōn.*]

hypha *hī′fə, n.* a thread of fungus mycelium: — *pl.* **hy′phae** (*-fē*). — *adj.* **hy′phal.** [Gr. *hyphē*, web.]

hyphen *hī′fən, n.* a short stroke (-) joining two syllables or words. — *v.t.* to join or separate by a hyphen. — *v.t.* **hy′phenate** to hyphen. — *adj.* hyphenated. — *n.* a hyphenated American. — *adj.* **hy′phenated** hyphened: of mixed nationality, expressed by a hyphened word, as Irish-American: of divided, or alien, national sympathies. — *n.* **hyphena′tion.** — *adj.* **phenic** (*-fen′ik*). — *v.t.* **hy′phenise, -ize.** — *ns.* **hyphenīsā′tion, -z-** hyphenation; **hy′phenism** state of being a hyphenate. [Gr. *hyphĕn* — *hypo*, under, *hen*, one.]

hypinosis *hip-i-nō′sis, n.* defect of fibrin in the blood; opposite of *hyperinosis* (under **hyper-**). [Gr. *hypo*, under, *īs, īnos*, fibre.]

hypnagogic, hypnogogic image. See under **Hypnos.**

Hypnos *hip′nos, n.* the Greek god of sleep. — *adjs.* **hypnagogic** (*-goj′ik, -gog′ik*; Gr. *agōgos*, bringing) sleep-bringing: ushering in sleep: pertaining to a state of drowsiness preceding sleep; **hyp′nic** pertaining to or inducing sleep. — *n.* a soporific. — *ns.* **hypno-anaesthē′sia** hypnotic sleep; **hyp′no-anal′ysis** analysis of a patient's psychological troubles by obtaining information from him while he is in a state of hypnosis; **hypnogen′esis, hypnogeny** (*-noj′i-ni*) production of the hypnotic state. — *adjs.* **hypnogenet′ic, hypnog′enous, hypnogen′ic** inducing the hypnotic state, or sleep; **hyp′noid, -al** like sleep: like hypnosis: esp. of a state between hypnosis and waking. — *v.t.* **hyp′noidise, -ize** to put in the hypnoidal state. — *ns.* **hypnol′ogy** the scientific study of sleep; **hyp′none** an aromatic ketone used in medicine as a hypnotic; **hypnopae′dia** learning or conditioning, by repetition of recorded sound during sleep (or semiwakefulness). — *adj.* **hypnopomp′ic** (Gr. *pompē*, a sending) dispelling sleep: pertaining to a state between sleep and wakefulness. — *ns.* **hypnō′sis** a sleeplike state in which the mind responds to external suggestion and can recover forgotten memories; **hypnotee′** a person who has been hypnotised; **hypnother′apy** the treatment of illness by hypnotism. — *adj.* **hypnot′ic** of or relating to hypnosis: soporific. — *n.* a soporific: a person subject to hypnotism or in a state of hypnosis. — *adv.* **hypnot′ically.** — *adj.* **hypnotīs′able, -z-.** — *ns.* **hypnotisabil′ity, -z-; hypnotīsā′tion, -z-.** — *v.t.* **hyp′notise, -ize** to put in a state of hypnosis: to fascinate, dazzle, overpower the mind of (*fig.*). — *ns.* **hyp′notīser, -z-; hyp′notism** the science of hypnosis: the art or practice of inducing hypnosis: hypnosis; **hyp′notist** one who hypnotises. — *adjs.* **hypnotist′ic; hyp′notoid** like hypnosis. — **hypnagogic, hypnogogic, image** hallucination experienced when falling asleep or fatigued; **hypnotic suggestion** suggestion (q.v.) made to

a person under hypnosis. [Gr. *hypnos*, sleep.]

Hypnum *hip′nəm, n.* a large genus (often divided) of mosses, with capsules on special lateral branches: (without *cap.*) any moss of this genus. [Latinised from Gr. *hypnon*, a kind of lichen.]

hypo- *hī′pō-, hip′ō,* or *-o′*, in composition, under: defective: inadequate. — *n.* **hy′po** short for **hyposulphite**, in the sense of sodium thiosulphate, used as a fixing agent (*phot.*): short for **hypodermic syringe** or **injection** (see also **hype**): — *pl.* **hy′pos.** — *adj.* short for **hypodermic**: short for **hypoglycaemic.** — *adjs.* **hypoaeolian** (*hī-pō-ē-ō′li-ən*) below the Aeolian mode: applied in old church music to a plagal mode extending from *e* to *e*, with *a* for its final; **hypoallergen′ic** specially formulated in order to minimise the risk of allergy. — *n.* **hypoblast** (*hip′, hīp′ō-bläst*; Gr. *blastos*, bud; *zool.*) the inner germ-layer of a gastrula. — *adj.* **hypoblast′ic.** — *ns.* **hypobole** (*hip-ob′ə-lē*; Gr. *hypobolē*, throwing under, suggestion — *ballein*, to throw; *rhet.*) anticipation of objections; **hypocaust** (*hip′, hīp′ō-köst*; Gr. *hypokauston* — *hypo*, under, *kaiein*, to burn) a space under a floor for heating by hot air or furnace gases, esp. in ancient Roman villas; **hy′pocentre** the point on the centre of the earth directly below the centre of explosion of a nuclear bomb; **hypochlorite** (*hī-pō-klō′rīt, -klö′*) a salt of **hypochlō′rous acid,** an acid (HClO) with less oxygen than chlorous acid; **hypochondria** (*hip-, hīp-ō-kon′dri-ə*) originally the *pl.* of **hypochondrium** (see below): morbid anxiety about health: imaginary illness: a nervous malady, often arising from indigestion, and tormenting the patient with imaginary fears (once supposed to have its seat in the abdomen) (*obs.*). — *adj.* **hypochon′driac** relating to or affected with hypochondria: melancholy. — *n.* a sufferer from hypochondria. — *adj.* **hypochondrī′acal.** — *ns.* **hypochondrī′asis, hypochondrī′acism, hypochon′driasm** hypochondria; **hypochon′driast** one suffering from hypochondria; **hypochon′drium** (Gr. *hypochondrion* — *chondros*, cartilage; *anat.*) the region of the abdomen on either side, under the costal cartilages and short ribs; **hypocist** (*hī′pō-sist*; Gr. *hypokistis* — *kistos*, cistus) an inspissated juice from fruit of *Cytinus hypocistis* (Rafflesiaceae), a plant parasitic on cistus roots; **hypocorism** (*hip-, hīp-ok′ər-izm*), **hypocorisma** (*-iz′mə*; Gr. *hypokorisma* — *hypokorizesthai*, to use child-talk — *koros*, boy, *korē*, girl) a pet-name: a diminutive or abbreviated name. — *adjs.* **hypocorist′ic, -al.** — *adv.* **hypocorist′ically.** — *n.* **hypocotyl** (*hip-, hīp-ō-kot′il*) that part of the axis of a plant which is between the cotyledons and the primary root. — *adj.* **hypocotylē′donary.** — *ns.* **hypocrisy** (*hi-pok′ri-si*; Gr. *hypokrisiā*, acting, playing a part) a feigning to be better than one is, or to be what one is not: concealment of true character or belief (not necessarily conscious): an instance or act of hypocrisy; **hypocrite** (*hip′ə-krit*; Gr. *hypokritēs*, actor) one who practises hypocrisy. — *adj.* **hypocrit′ical** (also **hypocrit′ic**) practising hypocrisy: of the nature of hypocrisy. — *adv.* **hypocrit′ically.** — *n.* **hypocycloid** (*hī-pō-sī′kloid*) a curve generated by a point on the circumference of a circle which rolls on the inside of another circle. — *adj.* **hypocycloid′al.** — *ns.* **hypoderm** (*hip′* or *hīp′ō-dûrm*), **hypoder′ma, hypoder′mis** (Gr. *derma*, skin; *bot.*) the tissue next under the epidermis. — *adjs.* **hypoderm′al; hypoderm′ic** pertaining to the hypodermis: under the epidermis: under the skin, subcutaneous, esp. of a method of injecting a drug in solution under the skin by means of a fine hollow needle to which a small syringe is attached. — *n.* **hypoder′mic** a hypodermic injection: a drug so injected: a syringe for the purpose. — *adv.* **hypoder′mically.** — *adjs.* **hypodorian** (*hī-pō-dō′ri-ən, -dō′*; Gr. *hypodōrios*) below the Dorian: applied in ancient Greek music to a mode whose upper tetrachord is the lower tetrachord of the Dorian (as: *a; b c d e; e f g a*): in old church music to a plagal mode extending from *a* to *a*, with *d* as its final; **hypoeutec′tic** of a compound, containing less of the minor component than a eutectic compound; **hypogastric** (*hīp-* or *hip-ō-gas'trik*; Gr. *gastēr*, belly) belonging to the lower median part of the abdomen. — *n.* **hypogas'trium** the hypogastric region. — *adjs.* **hypogeal, -gaeal** (*-jē'əl*), **-ge'an, -gae'an, -ge'ous, -gae'ous** (Gr. *hypogeios, -gaios* — *gē* or *gaia*, the ground; *bot.*) underground: germinating with cotyledons underground; **hypogene** (*hīp'* or *hip'ō-jēn*; Gr. *gennaein*, to engender; *geol.*) of or pertaining to rocks formed, or agencies at work, under the earth's surface, plutonic — opp. to *epigene*. — *n.* **hypogeum, hypogaeum** (*hip-, hīp-ō-jē'əm*) an underground chamber: a subterranean tomb. — *pl.* **hypoge'a, -gae'a.** — *adj.* **hypoglossal** (*hīp-* or *hip-ō-glos'əl*; Gr. *glōssa*, the tongue) under the tongue. — *ns.* **hypoglyc(a)emia** (*hī-pō-gli-sē'mi-ə*; *med.*) abnormal reduction of sugar content of the blood. — *adj.* **hypoglycae'mic.** — *n.* **hypog'nathism.** — *adjs.* **hypognathous** (*hīp-* or *hip-og'nə-thəs*) having the lower jaw or mandible protruding; **hypogynous** (*hī-poj'i-nəs*; Gr. *gynē*, a woman, female; *bot.*) growing from beneath the ovary: having the other floral parts below the ovary. — *n.* **hypog'yny.** — *adj.* **hy'poid** of a type of bevel gear in which the axes of the driving and driven shafts are at right angles but not in the same plane. — *n.* **hypolim'nion** (Gr. *limnion*, dim. of *limnē*, lake) a lower and colder layer of water in a lake. — *adj.* **hypolydian** (*hī-pō-lid'i-ən*) below the Lydian mode: applied in ancient Greek music to a mode having as its upper tetrachord the lower tetrachord of the Lydian (as: *f; g a b c; c d e f*) and in old church music to a plagal mode extending from *c* to *c* with *f* as its final. — *ns.* **hypomagnesaemia** (*hī-pō-mag-nə-zē'mi-ə*) a condition, esp. in cattle, characterised by an abnormally low level of magnesium in the blood; **hypomania** (*hip-, hīp-ō-mā'ni-ə*; *med.*) simple mania, a condition marked by overexcitability. — *adjs.* **hypomā'nic** (or *-man'ik*); **hypomixolydian** (*hī-pō-mik-sō-lid'i-ən*) applied in old church music to a mode extending from *d* to *d* with *g* as its final. — *ns.* **hyponasty** (*hīp'* or *hip'ō-nas-ti*; Gr. *nastos*, pressed close; *bot.*) increased growth on the lower side causing an upward bend — opp. to *epinasty*; **hyponi'trite** a salt or ester of **hyponi'trous acid,** a crystalline acid, H₂N₂O₂, an oxidising or reducing agent; **hyponym** (*hīp'-*; Gr. *onyma = onoma*, a name) one of a group of terms whose meanings are included in the meaning of a more general term, e.g. *spaniel* and *puppy* in the meaning of *dog*; **hypophosphite** (*hī-pō-fos'fīt*) a salt of **hypophos'phorous acid,** an acid (H₃PO₂) with less oxygen than phosphorous acid. — *adj.* **hypophrygian** (*-frij'i-ən*) below the Phrygian mode: applied in ancient Greek music to a mode having as its upper tetrachord the lower tetrachord of the Phrygian (as, *g; a b c d; d e f g*); in old church music to a plagal mode extending from *b* to *b*, with *e* for its final. — *ns.* **hypophysec'tomy** surgical removal of the pituitary gland; **hypophysis** (*hīp-, hip-of'i-sis*; Gr. *hypophysis*, an attachment underneath — *phyein*, to grow; *pl.* **-sēs**) a down-growth (*zool.*): the pituitary body of the brain: an inflated part of the pedicel under the capsule, in mosses (*bot.*): in flowering plants, a cell between the suspensor and the embryo proper; **hypopitū'itarism** under-production of growth hormones by the pituitary gland; **hypoplasia** (*-plā'zi-ə, -zhə*; Gr. *plasis*, a forming; *path.*) underdevelopment or immaturity of an organ. — *adj.* **hypoplastic** (*-plas'-*). — *ns.* **hypoplastron** (*hīp-, hip-ō-plas'tron*; *zool.*) the plate behind the hyoplastron in a turtle's plastron; **hypostasis** (*hip-, hīp-os'tə-sis*; Gr. *hypostasis* — *stasis*, setting; *pl.* **-sēs**) orig. basis, foundation: substance, essence (*metaph.*): the essence or real personal subsistence or substance of each of the three divisions of the Trinity: sediment, deposit: passive hyperaemia in a dependent part owing to sluggishness of circulation (*med.*). — *adjs.* **hypostatic** (*-stat'ik*), **-al.** — *adv.* **hypostat'ically.** — *vs.t.* **hypos'tasise, -ize, hypos'tatise, -ize** to treat as hypostasis: to personify. — *ns.* **hyp'ostress** insufficient stress; **hypostrophe** (*hip-, hīp-os'trə-fi*; Gr. *hypostrophē*, turning back) relapse

(*med.*): reversion after a parenthesis (*rhet.*). — *adj.* **hypostyle** (*hip', hīp'ō-stīl*; Gr. *stȳlos*, a pillar; *archit.*) having the roof supported by pillars. — Also *n.* — *ns.* **hyposul'phate** a dithionate; **hyposul'phite** a salt of **hyposul'phurous acid** (H₂S₂O₄; also, in older usage H₂S₂O₃). — *adjs.* **hyposulphūr'ic** dithionic; **hypotac'tic.** — *ns.* **hypotaxis** (*hip-, hīp-ō-tak'sis*; Gr. *taxis*, arrangement; *gram.*) dependent construction — opp. to *parataxis*; **hypoten'sion** low blood-pressure. — *adj.* **hypoten'sive** characterised by low blood-pressure: reducing blood-pressure. — *n.* a person with low blood-pressure. — *ns.* **hypotenuse** (*hīp-, hip-ot'ən-ūs*, or *-ūz*), **hypothenuse** (*-oth'*; Fr. *hypoténuse* — L. *hypotēnūsa* — Gr. *hypoteinousa*, fem. part., subtending or stretching under — *teinein*, to stretch) the side of a right-angled triangle opposite to the right angle; **hypothalamus** (*hip-, hīp-ō-thal'ə-məs*; L.L.; *med.*) the part of the brain which makes up the floor and part of the lateral walls of the third ventricle. — *adj.* **hypothalam'ic.** — *n.* **hypothec** (*hip-, hīp-oth'ik*; Gr. *hypothēkē*, a pledge) in Scots law, a lien or security over goods in respect of a debt due by the owner of the goods — **the whole (hale) hypothec** (*Scot.*) the whole affair, collection, concern — everything. — *adj.* **hypoth'ecary** pertaining to hypothecation or mortgage. — *v.t.* **hypoth'ecate** to place or assign as security under an arrangement: to mortgage: to hypothesise (*U.S.*). — *ns.* **hypothecā'tion; hypoth'ecātor.** — *adj.* **hypotherm'al.** — *ns.* **hypothermia** (*hip-, hīp-ō-thûr'mi-ə*; Gr. *thermē*, heat) subnormal body temperature, caused by exposure to cold or induced for purposes of heart and part of the lateral **freeze down**); **hypothesis** (*hī-poth'i-sis*; Gr. *hypothesis* — *thesis*, placing) a supposition: a proposition assumed for the sake of argument: a theory to be proved or disproved by reference to facts: a provisional explanation of anything: — *pl.* **hypoth'esēs.** — *vs.t.* and *vs.i.* **hypoth'esise, -ize, hypoth'etise, -ize.** — *adjs.* **hypothet'ic, -al.** — *adv.* **hypothet'ically.** — *adj.* **hypothy'roid** pertaining to, or affected by, hypothyroidism. — *ns.* **hypothy'roidism** insufficient activity of the thyroid gland: a condition resulting from this, cretinism, etc.; **hypoton'ia.** — *adj.* **hypoton'ic** of muscles, lacking normal tone: of a solution, having lower osmotic pressure than a specified solution. — *ns.* **hypotrochoid** (*hip-, hīp-ō-trō'koid*; Gr. *trochos*, wheel, *eidos*, form) the curve traced by a point on the radius, or radius produced, of a circle rolling within another circle; **hypotyposis** (*hip-, hīp-ō-tīp-ō'sis*; *rhet.*) vivid description of a scene; **hypoventilā'tion** abnormally decreased speed and depth of breathing; **hypoxaemia,** (*U.S.*) **hypoxemia,** (*-ē'mi-ə*) deficiency of oxygenation of the blood. — *adj.* **hypox(a)em'ic.** — *n.* **hypox'ia** deficiency of oxygen reaching the body tissues. — *adj.* **hypox'ic.** [Gr. *hypo*, under.]

hypo. See **hypo-.**

hypso- *hip'sō-*, in composition, height. — *ns.* **hypsography** (*-sog'rə-fi*; Gr. *graphein*, to write) the branch of geography dealing with the measurement and mapping of heights above sea-level: a map showing topographic relief: a method of making such a map; **hypsometry** (*hip-som'ə-tri*; Gr. *metron*, a measure) the art of measuring the heights of places on the earth's surface; **hypsom'eter** an instrument for doing this by taking the boiling point of water. — *adj.* **hypsomet'ric.** — *ns.* **hyp'sophobe** a person suffering from **hypsophobia** (*hip-sō-fō'bi-ə*; Gr. *phobos*, fear), fear of (falling from) high places; **hypsophyll** (*hip'sō-fil*; Gr. *phyllon*, leaf; *bot.*) a bract. — *adj.* **hypsophyll'ary.** [Gr. *hypsos*, height.]

hypural *hī-pū'rəl*, *adj.* situated beneath the tail. [Gr. *hypo*, under, *ourā*, tail.]

Hyrax *hī'raks*, *n.* a genus (also called Procavia) of mammals superficially like marmots but really closer akin to the ungulates, living among rocks in Africa and Syria — the daman, the dassie or rock-rabbit, the cony of the Bible — constituting the order **Hyracoid'ea:** (without *cap.*) any animal of this genus: — *pl.*

hy'raxes, hy'races (*-sēz*). — *adj.* **hy'racoid.** [Gr. *hȳrax*, a shrew.]

hyson *hī'son, n.* a very fine sort of green tea. — **hy'son-skin** the refuse of hyson tea removed by winnowing. [From Chin.]

hyssop *his'əp, n.* an aromatic labiate (*Hyssopus officinalis*) used in perfumery and folk-medicine: an unknown wall-plant used as a ceremonial sprinkler (*B.*): a holy-water sprinkler. [L. *hyssōpus, -um* — Gr. *hyssōpos, -on*; cf. Heb. *'ēzōb.*]

hyster-, hystero- *his'tər-(o-)*, in composition, womb. — *v.t.* **hysterec'tomise, -ize.** — *ns.* **hysterec'tomy** (Gr. *ektomē*, a cutting out) surgical removal of the uterus; **hysterī'tis** inflammation of the uterus; **hysterot'omy** (Gr. *tomē*, a cut) surgical incision of the uterus. [Gr. *hysterā*, the womb.]

hysteranthous *his-tər-an'thəs, adj.* having the leaves appearing after the flowers. [Gr. *hysteros*, later, *anthos*, flower.]

hysteresis *his-tə-rē'sis, n.* the retardation or lagging of an effect behind the cause of the effect: the influence of earlier treatment of a body on its subsequent reaction. — *adjs.* **hysterēs'ial, hysterĕt'ic.** — **high-hysteresis rubber** rubber with less than normal bounce. [Gr. *hysterēsis*, a deficiency, coming late — *hysteros*, later.]

hysteria *his-tē'ri-ə, n.* a psychoneurosis in which repressed complexes become split off or dissociated from the personality, forming independent units, partially or completely unrecognised by consciousness, giving rise to hypnoidal states (amnesia, somnambulisms), and manifested by various physical symptoms, such as tics, paralysis, blindness, deafness, etc., general features being an extreme degree of emotional instability and an intense craving for affection: an outbreak of wild emotionalism. — *adjs.* **hysteric** (*his-ter'ik*), **-al** pertaining to, of the nature of, or affected with, hysterics or hysteria: like hysterics: fitfully and violently emotional: (**hyster'ical**) extremely funny (*coll.*). — *n.* **hyster'ic** a hysterical person. — *adv.* **hyster'ically.** — *adj.* **hyster'icky** (*coll.*). — *n.pl.* **hyster'ics** hysteric fits: popularly, fits of uncontrollable laughter or crying, or of both alternately. — *adj.* **hysterogen'ic** inducing hysteria. — *n.* **hysterogeny** (*-oj'ə-ni*). — *adjs.* **hys'teroid, -al** like hysteria. — *n.* **hysteromān'ia** hysterical mania, often marked by erotic delusions and an excessive desire to attract attention. — **hysterical pregnancy** pseudocyesis; **hysteroid dysphoria** pathological depression typical of women. [Gr. *hysterā*, the womb, with which hysteria was formerly thought to be connected.]

hysteron-proteron *his'tər-on-prot'ər-on, n.* a figure of speech in which what would ordinarily follow comes first: an inversion. [Gr., lit. latter-former.]

hythe. Same as **hithe.**

For other sounds see detailed chart of pronunciation.

I

I¹, i ī, *n.* the ninth letter of our alphabet, answering to Greek *iōta*, has various sounds (as in *dip, mind, bird, machine*). In Roman numerals I represents one; in mathematics *i* represents the imaginary square root of −1. — **I'-beam** a metal girder I-shaped in section.

I² ī, *pron.* the nominative singular of the first personal pronoun: the word used in mentioning oneself. — *n.* the object of self-consciousness, the ego. — *pron.* **I'-and-I'** Rastafarian for **we, us.** [M.E. *ich* — O.E. *ic*; Ger. *ich*, O.N. *ek*, L. *ego*, Gr. *egō*.]

I³ ī, *adv.* same as **ay.**

i' *i, prep.* a form of **in.**

-ia *-ē'ə, -yə, suff.* used in naming (1) a pathological condition, (2) a genus of plants or animals, (3) (as L. or Gr. *neut. pl.*) a taxonomic division, (4) (as *pl.*) things pertaining to (something specified).

iaido ē-ī'dō, *n.* a Japanese form of fencing. [From Jap.]

iambus ī-am'bəs, *n.* a foot of two syllables, a short followed by a long, or an unstressed by a stressed: — *pl.* **iam'buses, iam'bī.** — Also **i'amb.** — *adj.* **iam'bic** consisting of iambuses: of the nature of an iambus: using iambic verse: satirical in verse. — *n.* an iambus: (in *pl.*) iambic verse, esp. satirical. — *adv.* **iam'bically** in the manner of an iambic. — *ns.* **iam'bist, iambog'-rapher** a writer of iambics. [L. *ïambus* — Gr. *iambos* — *iaptein*, to assail, this metre being first used by satirists.]

-iana. See **-ana.**

ianthine ī-an'thīn, *adj.* violet-coloured. [Gr. *ianthinos* — *ion*, violet, *anthos*, flower.]

Iastic ī-ast'ik, (*mus.*) *adj.* Ionian. — **Iastic mode** the Ionian, hypophrygian, or hyperdorian mode of ancient Greek music. [Gr. *Iastikos*, Ionian.]

iatric, -al ī-at'rik, *-əl, adjs.* relating to medicine or physicians. — *adj.* **iatrochem'ical.** — *ns.* **iatrochemist; iatrochem'istry** an application of chemistry to medical theory introduced by Franciscus Sylvius (1614–72) of Leyden. — *adj.* **iatrogen'ic** (of a disease or symptoms) induced in a patient by the treatment or comments of a physician. — *ns.* **iatrogenic'ity; iatrö'geny.** [Gr. *iātros, iātros*, a physician.]

Iberian ī-bē'ri-ən, *adj.* of Spain and Portugal: of Iberia (now Georgia) in the Caucasus: of the ancient inhabitants of either of these, or their later representatives: of a Mediterranean people of Neolithic culture in Britain, etc. — *n.* a member of any of these peoples. [L. *Ïbēria* — Gr. *Ïbēriā*.]

Iberis ī-bē'ris, *n.* the candytuft genus of Cruciferae. [Gr. *ïbēris*, pepperwort.]

ibex ī'beks, *n.* a large-horned mountain wild-goat: — *pl.* **i'bexes,** also **ibices** (ī'bi-sēz). [L. *ibex, -icis.*]

ibidem ib-ī'dəm, ib'i-dəm, i-bē'dem, (L.) *adv.* in the same place. — Abbrev. **ib., ibid.**

ibis ī'bis, *n.* a wading bird of the genus Threskiornis, with curved bill, akin to the spoonbills, one species worshipped by the ancient Egyptians. — See also **wood ibis.** [L. and Gr. *ïbis*, prob. Egyptian.]

-ible *-ə-bl, adj. suff.* having similar uses to those of **-able** (q.v.), esp. the passive 'capable of being'. — *n. suff.* **-ibility.** — *adv. suff.* **-ibly.** — See also **-able.** [L. *-ibilis* — *-bilis* as used with a 2nd-, 3rd- or 4th-conjugation verb.]

Iblis. See **Eblis.**

Ibo ē'bō, *n.* a Negro people of S.E. Nigeria: a member of this people: their language, widely used in southern Nigeria: — *pl.* **I'bo, I'bos.** — Also *adj.* — Also **Igbo** (ē'bō).

Ibsenism ib'sən-izm, *n.* the dramatic qualities and type of social criticism characteristic of the plays of the Norwegian dramatist, Henrik *Ibsen* (d. 1906). — *n.* **Ib'senite** a champion or follower of Ibsen.

ibuprofen ī-bū-prō'fən, *n.* a non-steroidal anti-inflammatory drug used for relieving rheumatic pain, headaches, etc. [From its full name, *iso*butyl*phen*yl *pro*pionic acid.]

Icarian ī-kā'ri-ən, i-, *adj.* of or like Icarus (ī' or i'; Gr. *Ikāros*), who flew from Crete on wings made by Daedalus partly of wax, which melted as he passed too near the sun, plunging him into the sea; see also **daedal.**

ice īs, *n.* frozen water: any substance resembling this: concreted sugar on a cake, etc.: a frozen confection of fruit-juice, etc.: ice-cream: reserve, formality: coldness of manner: diamond(s) (*slang*). — *adj.* of ice. — *v.t.* to cover with ice: to freeze: to cool with ice: to cover with concreted sugar. — *v.i.* to freeze: to become covered with ice (with *up*): — *pr.p.* **ic'ing;** *pa.t.* and *pa.p.* **iced.** — *adj.* **iced** (īst) covered with or cooled with ice: encrusted with sugar. — *n.* **i'cer** one who makes icing. — *adv.* **ic'ily.** — *ns.* **ic'iness; ic'ing** covering with or of ice or concreted sugar. — *adj.* **ic'y** composed of, abounding in, or like ice: frosty: cold: chilling: without warmth of affection. — Also *adv.* — **ice'-action** the work of land-ice in grinding the earth's surface; **ice age** (*geol.*) any time when a great part of the earth's surface has been covered with ice, esp. that in Pleistocene times; **ice'-anchor** a one-armed anchor for mooring to an ice-floe; **ice'-ā'pron** a structure on the up-stream side of a bridge pier to break or ward off floating ice; **ice'-axe** an axe used by mountain climbers to cut steps in ice; **ice'-bag** a bag filled with ice; **ice'berg** (from Scand. or Du.) a huge mass of floating ice: a cold and unemotional person (*coll.*): a type of crisp light-green lettuce (also **iceberg lettuce**); **ice'-bird** the little auk or sea-dove; **ice'blink** a gleam reflected from distant masses of ice; **ice'-blue** a very pale blue. — Also *adj.* — **ice'-boat** a boat for forcing a way through or sailing or being dragged over ice. — *adj.* **ice'-bound** bound, surrounded, or fixed in with ice. — **ice'box** the freezing compartment of a refrigerator: a refrigerator (*old U.S.*): a portable insulated box filled with ice, used for storing cold food and drink; **ice'-breaker** ship for breaking channels through ice: anything for breaking ice: anything that (*fig.*) breaks the ice (see **break¹**); **ice'-bucket** a receptacle with ice for cooling bottles of wine; **ice'-cap** a covering of ice over a convexity, as a mountain top, the polar regions of a planet. — *adj.* **ice'-cold** cold as, or like, ice. — **ice'-craft** skill in travelling over or through ice; **ice'-cream'** a sweet frozen food containing cream, or one of various substitutes, and flavouring (**ice'-cream soda** soda-water with ice-cream added); **ice'-cube** a small cube of ice used for cooling drinks, etc.; **ice dance, dancing** a form of ice-skating based on the movements of ballroom dancing; **iced water** drinking water chilled with ice; **ice'-fall** a fall of ice: a steep broken place in a glacier; **ice'-fern** a fern-like encrustation on a window in frost; **ice'-field** a large area covered with ice, esp. floating ice; **ice'-fish** the capelin; **ice'-floe** a large sheet of floating ice; **ice'-foot** a belt of ice forming round the shores in Arctic regions — also **ice'-belt, ice'-ledge.** — *adj.* **ice'-free** without ice. — **ice'-front** the front face of a glacier; **ice'-hill** a slope of ice for tobogganing; **ice'-hill'ing; ice'-hock'ey** a form of hockey played on ice with a puck by skaters; **ice'-house** a house for keeping ice in; **ice'-loll'y** a lollipop consisting of water-ice on a stick; **ice'-machine** a machine for making ice in large quantity; **ice'man** a man skilled in travelling upon ice: a dealer in ice: a man who looks after an ice-rink; **ice′pack** drifting ice packed together: a pack prepared with ice; **ice′-pan** a slab of floating ice; **ice′-pick** a tool with a pointed end used by climbers for splitting ice; **ice′plant** a plant (Mesembrianthemum) whose leaves glisten like ice in the sun; **ice′-rink** a skating rink of ice; **ice′-run** a tobogganing slide; **ice′-sheet** land-ice covering a whole region; **ice′-show** an entertainment or exhibition provided by skaters on ice; **ice′-skate** a skate for moving on ice (see **skate**[1]). — Also *v.i.* — *ns.* **ice′-skater; ice′-skating; ice′-spar** a clear glassy orthoclase; **ice′-stone** cryolite; **ice′-water** water from melted ice: iced water; **ice′-worm** a species of oligochaete stated by some to be found on glaciers in Alaska, etc.; **ice′-yacht** a ship on runners and with sails for sailing over smooth ice; **ice′-yacht′ing; icing sugar** sugar in the form of a very fine powder, for icing cakes, etc. — *adj.* **ic′y-pearl′ed** (*Milt.*) studded with pearls or spangles of ice. — **break the ice** see **break**[1]; **ice out** (*fig.*) to exclude (someone) from one's company by ignoring him; **icing on the cake** anything that is a desirable addition to something already satisfactory; **cut no ice** to count for nothing; **dry ice** solid carbon dioxide, which changes directly into vapour at -78·5° Celsius, is chiefly used for refrigeration, but is also exploited in the theatre, the dense, swirling, floor-level white cloud it produces on evaporation creating a spectacular stage-effect. — *adj.* **dry′-iced′.** — **on ice** (*fig.*) kept or waiting in readiness: postponed: certain of achievement; **put on ice** to put into abeyance, to suspend; **(skate) on thin ice** (to be) in a delicate, difficult or potentially embarrassing situation; **tip of the iceberg** the top of an iceberg, visible above the water, most of it being invisible below the surface: the small obvious part of a much larger problem, etc. (*fig.*). [O.E. *īs*; O.N. *īss*; Ger. *Eis*, Dan. *is*.]

Iceland *īs′lənd, adj.* belonging to, originating in, *Iceland*. — *n.* **Ice′lander** (or *īs-land′ər*) a native or citizen of Iceland: an Iceland falcon. — *adj.* **Icelandic** (*īs-land′ik*) of Iceland. — *n.* the modern language of the Icelanders: Old Norse. — **Ice′land-dog′** a shaggy white dog, sharp-eared, imported from Iceland; **Iceland falcon** a white gerfalcon of Iceland; **Iceland moss** a lichen of northern regions, used as a medicine and for food; **Iceland poppy** a dwarf poppy (*Papaver nudicaule*) with grey-green pinnate leaves and flowers varying from white to orange-scarlet; **Iceland spar** a transparent calcite with strong double refraction.

Iceni *ī-sē′nī, n.pl.* an ancient British tribe that, led by Queen Boudicca, rebelled against the Romans in 61 A.D.

ich[1] *ich,* (*Shak.*) *v.t.* Same as **eche**.

ich[2]. See **ch**.

ichabod *ik′ə-bod, interj.* the glory is departed. [From Heb.; see 1 Sam. iv. 21.]

I Ching *ī, ē ching,* an ancient Chinese system of divination, consisting of a set of symbols, 8 trigrams and 64 hexagrams, and the text, the *I Ching,* used to interpret them. [Chin., book of changes.]

ichneumon *ik-nū′mən, n.* any animal of the mongoose genus (*Herpestes*) of the civet family, esp. the Egyptian species that destroys crocodiles' eggs: (in full **ichneu′-mon-fly**) any insect of a large family of Hymenoptera whose larvae are parasitic in or on other insects. [Gr. *ichneumōn,* lit. tracker, *ichneuein,* to hunt after — *ichnos,* a track.]

ichnite *ik′nīt,* **ichnolite** *ik′nə-līt, ns.* a fossil footprint. — *n.* **ichnography** (*ik-nog′rə-fi*) a ground plan: the art of drawing ground plans. — *adjs.* **ichnographic** (*-nō-graf′-ik*), **-al.** — *adv.* **ichnograph′ically.** — *n.* **ichnol′ogy** footprint lore: the science of fossil footprints. [Gr. *ichnos,* a track, footprint.]

ichor *ī′kör, n.* the ethereal juice in the veins of the gods (*myth.*): a watery humour: colourless matter from an ulcer. — *adj.* **i′chorous.** [Gr. *īchōr.*]

ichthy(o)- *ik′thi-(ō-),* in composition, fish. — *adj.* **ich′thic.** — *ns.* **ichthyocoll′a** (Gr. *kolla,* glue) fish-glue: isinglass;

ichthyodor′ūlite, -dor′ylite (*-i-līt*; Gr. *dory,* a spear, *lithos,* a stone) a fossil fish-spine; **ichthyog′raphy** a description of fishes. — *adjs.* **ich′thyoid, -al** fishlike. — *n.* **ich′thyoid** a fishlike vertebrate. — *n.* **ichthyol′atry** (Gr. *latreiā,* worship) fish-worship. — *adj.* **ichthyol′atrous.** — *n.* **ich′thyolite** (Gr. *lithos,* a stone) a fossil fish. — *adjs.* **ichthyolitic** (*-lit′ik*); **ichthyolog′ical.** — *ns.* **ichthyol′ogist; ichthyol′ogy** the branch of natural history that treats of fishes; **ichthyophagist** (*-of′ə-jist*; Gr. *phagein,* to eat) a fish-eater. — *adj.* **ichthyoph′agous** (*-ə-gəs*). — *ns.* **ichthyophagy** (*-of′ə-ji*) the practice of eating fish; **ichthyop′sid, -an** (Gr. *opsis,* appearance). — *ns.pl.* **Ichthyop′sida** a group of vertebrates in Huxley's classification comprising amphibians, fishes, and fishlike vertebrates; **Ichthyopterygia** (*-op-tər-ij′i-ə*; Gr. *pterygion,* a fin, dim. of *pteryx,* wing) the Ichthyosauria. — *ns.* **Ichthyor′nis** (Gr. *ornis,* a bird) a Cretaceous fossil bird with vertebrae like those of fishes, and with teeth set in sockets; **ichthyosaur** (*ik′thi-ō-sör;* Gr. *sauros,* lizard) any member of the genus **Ichthyosaur′us** or of the order **Ichthyosaur′ia,** gigantic Mesozoic fossil fishlike marine reptiles. — *adj.* **ichthyosaur′ian.** — *n.* **ichthyō′sis** a disease in which the skin becomes hardened, thickened, and rough. — *adj.* **ichthyōt′ic.** — *n.* **ich′thys** an emblem or motto (ΙΧΘΥΣ), supposed to have a mystical connection with Jesus Christ, being the first letters of the Greek words meaning 'Jesus Christ, Son of God, Saviour'. [Gr. *ichthȳs,* fish.]

icicle *īs′i-kl, n.* a hanging, tapering piece of ice formed by the freezing of dropping water. [O.E. *īsesgicel* — *īses,* gen. of *īs,* ice, *gicel,* icicle.]

icing. See **ice**.

-icism. See **-ism**.

icker *ik′ər,* (*Scot.*) *n.* an ear of corn. [O.E. (Northumbrian) *eher, æhher* (W.S. *ēar*).]

icky *ik′i,* (*coll.*) *adj.* sickly-sweet: repulsive. [Perh. — **sickly**.]

icon, ikon *ī′kon, n.* a figure: image: a portrait, carved, painted, etc.: in the Eastern Churches a figure representing Christ, or a saint, in painting, mosaic, etc. (not sculpture): a symbol, representation: anybody or anything uncritically admired. — *adj.* **icon′ic** of images or icons: conventional in type. — *v.t.* **i′conise, -ize** to admire uncritically. — *ns.* **icon′oclasm** (Gr. *klaein,* to break) the act of breaking images: opposition to image-worship; **icon′oclast** a breaker of images: one opposed to image-worship, esp. those in the Eastern Church, from the 8th century: one who assails old cherished errors and superstitions. — *adj.* **iconoclast′ic.** — *ns.* **iconog′raphy** (Gr. *graphiā,* a writing) the art of illustration: the study, description, cataloguing, or collective representation of portraits: the study of symbols used in a particular style of painting, etc., and their meaning; **iconol′ater** an image-worshipper; **iconol′atry** (Gr. *latreiā,* worship) image-worship; **iconol′ogist; iconol′ogy** the study of icons: symbolism; **iconomachist** (*-om′ə-kist*) one who contends against the use of icons in worship; **iconom′achy** (Gr. *machē,* fight) opposition to image-worship. — *adj.* **iconomat′ic** using pictures of objects to represent not the things themselves but the sounds of their names, as in a transition stage between picture-writing and a phonetic system. — *ns.* **iconomat′icism** (*-i-sizm*); **iconom′eter** an instrument for inferring distance from size or size from distance of an object, by measuring its image: a direct photographic view-finder; **iconom′etry; iconoph′ilism** a taste for pictures, etc.; **iconoph′ilist** a connoisseur of pictures, etc.; **icon′oscope** a form of electron camera; **iconos′tasis, icon′ostas** (Gr. *eikonostasis* — *stasis,* placing) in Eastern churches, a screen shutting off the sanctuary, on which the icons are placed. — **iconic memory** the persistence of a sense impression after the disappearance of the stimulus. [L. *īcōn* — Gr. *eikōn,* an image.]

icosahedron *ī-kos-ə-hē′drən,* (*geom.*) *n.* a solid with twenty plane faces: — *pl.* **icosahē′dra.** — *adj.* **icosahē′dral.** —

n. **icositetrahē′dron** (*geom.*) a solid figure with twenty-four plane faces: — *pl.* **-dra.** [Gr. *eikosi*, twenty, *hedrā*, a seat.]

Icosandria *ī-kos-an′dri-ə, n.pl.* a Linnaean class of plants with twenty or more free stamens. — *adjs.* **icosan′drian; icosan′drous.** [Gr. *eikosi*, twenty, *anēr*, *andros*, a man (male).]

icterus *ik′tər-əs, n.* jaundice: (with *cap.*) a genus of birds with much yellow in their plumage, including the Baltimore oriole, giving name to the American family **Icteridae** (*-ter′i-dē*; hangnests, bobolinks, troupials, grackles). — *adjs.* **icteric** (*-ter′ik*), **-al** relating to or affected with jaundice. — *ns.* a medicine for jaundice. — *adjs.* **ic′terine** (*-tər-īn, -in*) of or like the family Icteridae: yellowish or marked with yellow; **icteritious** (*ik-tər-ish′əs*) jaundiced: yellow. [Gr. *ikteros*, jaundice, also a yellowish bird (acc. to Pliny the golden oriole) the sight of which cured jaundice.]

ictus *ik′təs, n.* a stroke (*med.*): rhythmical or metrical stress (*pros.*): a pulsation: — *pl.* **ic′tuses** (or L. *pl.* **ic′tūs** *-tōōs*). — *adjs.* **ic′tal; ic′tic.** [L., a blow.]

I'd *īd,* contracted from *I would,* or *I had*: also used for *I should.*

id[1] *id,* **ide** *īd, ns.* a fish of the same family as the carp, inhabiting fresh water in Northern Europe. [Sw. *id.*]

id[2] *id,* (*biol.*) *n.* in Weismann's theory, an element in a chromosome carrying all the hereditary characters. — *n.* **idant** (*ī′dənt*) an aggregation of ids: a chromosome. [Gr. *idios*, own, private; appar. suggested by **idioplasm.**]

id[3] *id,* (*psych.*) *n.* the sum total of the primitive instinctive forces in an individual subserving the pleasure-pain principle. [L. *id,* it.]

-id[1] *n.* and *adj. suff.* used in the nmes of a particular zoological or racial group, or dynastic line, as *arachnid, hominid, Fatimid.* [Gr. *idēs,* son of.]

-id[2] *n. suff.* used in names of bodies, formations, particles, etc., as *hydatid, energid*: used in the names of meteors coming from a particular constellation, as *Perseid, Orionid.* [Gr. *-is, -idos,* daughter of.]

Idaean *ī-dē′ən, adj.* of Mount Ida in Crete, or that near Troy. — **Idaean vine** the cowberry. [Gr. *īdaios* — *īdē.*]

Idalian *ī-dā′li-ən, adj.* pertaining to *Idalium* (Gr. *īdălion*), in Cyprus, or to Aphrodite, to whom it was sacred.

idant. See **id**[2].

iddy-umpty *id′i-um(p)′ti, n.* (*airmen's slang*) Morse code. [From a phrase used in India to teach morse to the native troops.]

ide. See **id**[1].

idea *ī-dē′ə, n.* an image of an external object formed by the mind: a notion, thought, impression, any product of intellectual action, of memory and imagination: plan: an archetype of the manifold varieties of existence in the universe, belonging to the supersensible world, where reality is found and where God is (*Platonic*): one of the three products of the reason (the Soul, the Universe, and God) transcending the conceptions of the understanding — *transcendental ideas,* in the functions of mind concerned with unification of existence (*Kantian*): the ideal realised, the absolute truth of which everything that exists is the expression (*Hegelian*). — *adjs.* **idē′aed, idē′a'd** provided with an idea or ideas; **idē′al** existing in idea: conceptual: existing in imagination only: highest and best conceivable: perfect, as opposed to the real, the imperfect: theoretical, conforming absolutely to theory. — *n.* the highest conception of anything, or its embodiment: a standard of perfection: that which exists in the imagination only: a subring of a ring, any member of which when multiplied by any member of the ring, whether in the subring or not, results in a member of the subring (*math.*). — *adj.* **idē′aless** devoid of ideas. — *n.* **idēalisā′tion, -z-.** — *v.t.* **idē′alise, -ize** to regard or represent as ideal. — *v.i.* to form ideals: to think or work idealistically. — *ns.* **idē′alīser, -z-; idē′alism** the doctrine that in external perceptions the objects immediately

known are ideas, that all reality is in its nature psychical: any system that considers thought or the idea as the ground either of knowledge or existence: a tendency towards the highest conceivable perfection, love for or search after the best and highest: the habit or practice of idealising: impracticality: the imaginative treatment of subjects; **idē′alist** one who holds the doctrine of idealism: one who strives after the ideal: an impractical person. — *adj.* **idēalist′ic** pertaining to idealists or to idealism. — *adv.* **idēalist′ically.** — *n.* **idēality** (*-al′i-ti*) an ideal state: ability and disposition to form ideals of beauty and perfection. — *adj.* **idē′alless** having no ideals. — *adv.* **idē′ally** in an ideal manner: in ideal circumstances: mentally. — *n.* **idē′alogue** a misspelling of **ideologue.** — *v.t.* **idē′ate** to form or have an idea of: to imagine: to preconceive. — *v.i.* to form ideas. — *adj.* produced by an idea. — *n.* the correlative or object of an idea. — *n.* **idēā′tion** the power of the mind for forming ideas: the exercise of such power. — *adjs.* **idēā′tional, idē′ative.** — *adv.* **idēā′tionally.** — **ideal gas** a hypothetical gas which obeys physical laws exactly. — **get, have, ideas** (*slang*) to become, be, overambitious: to have undesirable ideas; **have no idea** to be unaware of what is happening: to be ignorant or naive; **not my,** etc. **idea of** (*coll.*) the opposite of my, etc. conception of; **what's the big idea?** (*slang*) what's the intention, purpose? (usu. said in anger). [L. *ĭdĕa* — Gr. *ĭdĕā*; cf. *idein* (aor.), to see.]

ideal, idealise, etc. See under **idea.**

idée *ē-dā,* (Fr.) *n.* idea. — **idée fixe** (*fēks*) a fixed idea, a monomania: a recurring theme in music; **idée reçue** (*rə-sü*) accepted idea: conventional outlook.

idem *ī′dem, i′dem,* (L.) *pron.* the same. — Abbrev. **id.; idem sonans** (*sō′nanz, so′näns*) sounding the same (used of a word in a legal document which, though misspelt, can be accepted as that for which it clearly stands).

idempotent *ī′dəm-pō-tənt, i-dem′pə-tənt,* (*math.*) *adj.* and *n.* (of) a quantity which does not change value when multiplied by, added to, etc. itself. — *n.* **ī′dempotency** (or *i-dem′*). [L. *idem,* the same, **potent.**]

identic, identical. See under **identity.**

identify *ī-den′ti-fī, v.t.* to make, reckon, ascertain or prove to be the same: to ascertain or establish the identity of: to assign to a species: to bind up or associate closely: to regard, or wish to regard, (oneself) as sharing (with a person or group) interests and experiences, or (because of an emotional tie, usu. abnormal) attitudes, characteristics and behaviour. — *v.i.* to become the same: to see oneself as sharing experiences, outlook, etc. (with): — *pr.p.* **iden′tifying;** *pa.t.* and *pa.p.* **iden′tified.** — *adj.* **iden′tifiable.** — *n.* **identificā′tion** the act of identifying: the state of being identified: anything which proves one's identity: a process by which a person assumes the behaviour, ideas, etc., of someone else, particularly someone whom he admires (*psych.*). — **identification card, disc,** etc. a card, disc, etc., carried on one's person, with one's name, etc., on it; **identification parade** a group of people assembled by the police, from among whom a witness tries to identify a suspect. [L.L. *identificāre* — *idem,* the same, *facĕre,* to make.]

identikit. See **identity.**

identity *ī-den′ti-ti, n.* state of being the same: sameness: individuality: personality: who or what a person or thing is: (also **old identity**) a long-standing and well-known inhabitant of a place (*Austr.* and *N.Z. coll.*): an equation true for all values of the symbols involved (*math.*). — *adj.* **iden′tical** the very same: not different: expressing or resulting in identity. — Also **iden′tic.** — *adv.* **iden′tically.** — *ns.* **iden′ticalness, identical′ity.** — **identical twins** twins developing from one zygote; **identic note, action** (*diplomacy*) identical note, action, sent by, carried out by, two or more governments in dealing with another, others; **iden′tikit** (orig. *U.S.* Identi-Kit) a device for building up a composite portrait from a large number of different features on transparent slips (also *fig.*); **identity card, disc** a card, disc, etc., bearing the owner's or wearer's name, etc., used to establish his identity; **identity crisis** psychological confusion caused by inability to reconcile differing elements in one's personality; **identity element** (*math.*) an element (*e*) in a system of elements such that $e*x = x*e = x$, for every value of x — where * denotes a binary operation (in the ordinary number system, for addition $e = 0$, for multiplication $e = 1$). — **law** or **principle of identity** (*logic*) a law stating that A is A, that a thing is the same as itself. [L.L. *identitās*, *-ātis* — L. *idem*, the same.]

ideogram *id'i-ō-gram*, or *īd'*, **ideograph** *-gräf*, *ns.* a written character or symbol that stands not for a word or sound but for the thing itself directly. — *adjs.* **ideographic** (*-graf'ik*), **-al.** — *adv.* **ideograph'ically.** — *n.* **ideography** (*-og'rǝ-fi*). [Gr. *ĭdĕā*, idea, *gramma*, a drawing, *graphein*, to write.]

ideology *īd-*, *id-i-ol'ǝ-ji*, *n.* the science of ideas, metaphysics: abstract speculation: visionary speculation: a body of ideas, usu. political and/or economic, forming the basis of a national or sectarian policy: way of thinking. — *adjs.* **ideologic** (*-loj'*), **-al** of or pertaining to an ideology: arising from, concerned with, rival ideologies. — *n.* **ideol'ogist** one occupied with ideas or an idea: a mere theorist or visionary: a supporter of a particular ideology — also **ideologue** (*ī-dē'ō-log*). [Gr. *ĭdĕā*, idea, *logos*, discourse.]

ideophone *id'i-ō-fōn*, *n.* a word or phrase that is spoken but not written, usu. one that is only fully comprehensible in the context in which it is spoken. [Gr. *ĭdĕā*, idea, *phōnē*, sound.]

ideopraxist *id-*, *id-i-ō-prak'sist*, *n.* one who is impelled to carry out an idea. [Gr. *ĭdĕā*, idea, *prāxis*, doing.]

Ides *īdz*, *n.pl.* in ancient Rome, the 15th day of March, May, July, October, and the 13th of the other months. [Fr. *ides* — L. *īdūs* (pl.).]

id est *id est*, (L.) that is. — Abbrev. **i.e.**

idioblast *id'*, *ī'di-ǝ-bläst*, *n.* a plant cell that differs from neighbouring cells. — *adj.* **idioblast'ic.** [Gr. *idios*, own, private, *blastos*, sprout.]

idiocy. See **idiot.**

idioglossia *id-i-ō-glos'i-ǝ*, *n.* a condition in which pronunciation is so bad as to be quite unintelligible. [Gr. *idios*, own, private, *glōssa*, tongue.]

idiograph *id'i-ō-gräf*, *n.* a private mark: a trademark. — *adj.* **idiographic** (*-graf'ik*) relating to an individual or to anything unique. [Gr. *idios*, own, private, *graphein*, to write.]

idiolect *id'i-ō-lekt*, *n.* an individual's own distinctive form of speech. — *adjs.* **idiolec'tal, -tic.** [Gr. *idios*, own, *legein*, to speak.]

idiom *id'i-ǝm*, *n.* a mode of expression peculiar to a language: an expression characteristic of a particular language not logically or grammatically explicable: a form or variety of language: a dialect: a characteristic mode of artistic expression of a person, school, etc. — *adjs.* **idiomat'ic, -al.** — *adv.* **idiomat'ically.** — *ns.* **idioticon** (*-ot'i-kon*) a vocabulary of a particular dialect or district; **id'iotism** (*-ǝ-tizm*) an idiom: an idiomatic expression: idiomatic character: (see also under **idiot**). — **Idiom Neutral** an international language that is a simplified version of Volapük. [Gr. *idiōma*, *idiōtikon* — *idios*, own.]

idiomorphic *id-i-ō-mör'fik*, *adj.* having the faces belonging to its crystalline form, as a mineral that has had free room to crystallise out. [Gr. *idios*, own, *morphē*, form.]

idiopathy *id-i-op'ǝ-thi*, *n.* a state or experience peculiar to the individual: a primary disease, one not occasioned by another (*med.*). — *adj.* **idiopathic** (*-path'ik*). — *adv.* **idiopath'ically.** [Gr. *idios*, own, *pathos*, suffering.]

idiophone *id'i-ō-fōn*, (*mus.*) *n.* a percussion instrument made entirely of a naturally resonant material. [Gr. *idios*, own, *phōnē*, voice.]

idioplasm *id'i-ō-plazm*, *n.* that part of the protoplasm that determines hereditary character. [Gr. *idios*, own, private, *plasma*, mould.]

idior(r)hythmic *id-i-ō-ridh'mik*, or *-rith'*, *adj.* self-regulating: allowing each member to regulate his own life. [Gr. *idios*, own, *rhȳthmos*, order.]

idiosyncrasy *id-i-ō-sing'krǝ-si*, *n.* peculiarity of temperament or mental constitution: any characteristic of a person: hypersensitivity of an individual to a particular food, drug, etc. (*med.*). — *adjs.* **idiosyncratic** (*-krat'ik*), **-al.** [Gr. *idios*, own, *synkrāsis*, a mixing together — *syn*, together, *krāsis*, a mixing.]

idiot *id'i-ǝt*, *id'yǝt*, *n.* a person so defective in mind from birth as to be unable to protect himself against ordinary physical dangers: one afflicted with the severest grade of feeble-mindedness: a flighty fool: a blockhead: a foolish or unwise person. — *adj.* afflicted with idiocy: idiotic. — *ns.* **id'iocy** (*-ǝ-si*), (*rare*) **id'iotcy** the state of being an idiot: imbecility: folly. — *adjs.* **idiotic** (*-ot'ik*), **-al** pertaining to or like an idiot: foolish. — *adv.* **idiot'ically.** — *adj.* **id'iotish** idiotic. — *n.* **id'iotism** the state of being an idiot: see also under **idiom.** — **idiot board** a mechanical device used to prompt a speaker on television; **idiot box** (*slang*) a television set; **idiot card** a large card with words, etc., for the same purpose as an idiot board. — *adj.* **id'iot-proof** of a tool, method of working, etc., so simple that even an idiot cannot make a mistake. [Fr., — L. *idiōta* — Gr. *idiōtēs*, a private person, ordinary person, one who holds no public office or has no professional knowledge — *idios*, own, private.]

idiothermous *id-i-ō-thûr'mǝs*, *adj.* warm-blooded, i.e. having a temperature of one's own, independent of surroundings. [Gr. *idios*, own, *thermē*, heat.]

idioticon. See under **idiom.**

idiot savant *ē-dyō sa-vã*, *id'i-ǝt sav'ǝnt* a mentally retarded individual who demonstrates remarkable talent in some restricted area such as memorising or rapid calculation.

idle *ī'dl*, *adj.* vain: baseless: trifling: unemployed: averse to labour: not occupied: not in use: useless: unimportant: unedifying. — *v.t.* to spend in idleness: to cause to be idle. — *v.i.* to be idle or unoccupied: of machinery, to run without doing work. — *ns.* **i'dlehood** (*arch.*); **i'dleness**; **i'dler; i'dlesse** (*poet.*) idleness. — *adv.* **i'dly.** — *adj.* **i'dle-head'ed** foolish. — **i'dle-pulley** a pulley which rotates freely and guides, or controls the tension of, a belt; **idle time** a period or periods when a computer is able to function properly but is not being used for productive work or program testing; **i'dle-wheel** a wheel placed between two others for transferring the motion from one to the other without changing the direction; **i'dle-worms** (*coll.*) worms once jocularly supposed to be bred in the fingers of lazy maidservants. [O.E. *īdel*; Du. *ijdel*, Ger. *eitel*.]

Ido *ē'dō*, *n.* an auxiliary international language developed (since 1907) from Esperanto. — *ns.* **Id'ist, I'doist.** [Ido, offspring.]

idocrase *īd'*, *id'ō-krās*, *-krāz*, *n.* the mineral vesuvianite. [Gr. *eidos*, form, *krāsis*, mixture.]

idol *ī'dl*, *n.* a figure (*arch.*): an image, a semblance: a phantom: a counterfeit (*Spens.*): an image of a god: an object of worship: an object of love, admiration, or honour in an extreme degree: (also **Idō'lon, Idō'lum**; *pl.* **Idō'la**) a false notion or erroneous way of looking at things to which the mind is prone, classified by Bacon (*Novum Organum*, i. § 39) as *Idols of the tribe* (due to the nature of man's understanding); *Idols of the den* or *cave* (due to personal causes); *Idols of the forum* (due to the influence of words or phrases); *Idols of the theatre* (due to misconceptions of philosophic system or demonstration). — *v.t.* **i'dolise, -ize** to make an idol of. — *ns.* **i'doliser, -z-; i'dolism** idol-worship: idolising: a false notion (*Milt.*); **i'dolist** (*Milt.*) an idolater; **idoloclast** (*-dol'*) a breaker of images. [L. *īdōlum* — Gr. *eidōlon* — *eidos*, form — *idein* (aor.), to see.]

idolater *ī-dol'ǝ-tǝr*, *n.* a worshipper of idols: a great admirer: — *fem.* **idol'atress.** — *v.t.* and *v.i.* **idol'atrise, -ize** to worship as an idol: to adore. — *adj.* **idol'atrous.**

— *adv.* **idol'atrously.** — *n.* **idol'atry** the worship of an image held to be the abode of a superhuman personality: excessive love. — **(on) this side of idolatory** stopping short of excessive adulation. [Fr. *idolâtre* — Gr. *eidōlolatrēs* — *eidōlon*, idol, *latreuein*, to worship.]

idyll *id'il, īd'il, -əl, n.* a short pictorial poem, chiefly on pastoral subjects: a story, episode, or scene of happy innocence or rusticity: a work of art of like character in any medium. — Also **id'yl.** — *adjs.* **idyll'ian; idyll'ic.** — *n.* **i'dyllist.** [L. *īdyllium* — Gr. *eidyllion*, dim. of *eidos*, image.]

if *if, conj.* on condition that: provided that: in case that: supposing that: whether. — *n.* a condition: a supposition. — *adj.* **iff'y** (*coll.*) dubious, uncertain, risky. — *n.* **iff'iness.** — **as if** as it would be if; **ifs and ans** things which might have happened, but which did not; **ifs and buts** objections. [O.E. *gif*; cf. Du. *of*, O.N. *ef*.]

iff *if, (log.) conj.* used to express *if and only if.*

iffy. See **if.**

igad *i-gad'.* Same as **egad.**

igapó. Same as **gapó.**

igarapé *ē-gä-rä-pä', n.* a canoe waterway in Brazil. [Tupí.]

Igbo. See **Ibo.**

igloo *ig'lōō, n.* orig. a dome-shaped hut of snow: now usu. a dwelling of other materials: a dome-shaped place of storage or container for goods: a hollow in the snow made by a seal over its breathing hole in the ice. [Eskimo.]

ignaro *ig-nä'rō, ēn-yä'rō, n.* an ignorant person: — *pl.* **igna'roes, -ros.** [Prob. from Spenser's character (*Faerie Queene*, I, viii) whose only answer is 'He could not tell' — It. *ignaro* — L. *ignārus*, ignorant.]

Ignatian *ig-nā'shən, adj.* of or pertaining to St *Ignatius*, first-century bishop of Antioch (applied to the Epistles attributed to him): or *Ignatius* Loyola. — *n.* a Jesuit. — **Ignatius's bean** see under **Saint.**

igneous *ig'ni-əs, adj.* of or like fire: produced by solidification of the earth's internal molten magma (*geol.*). [L. *igneus*, fiery — *ignis*, fire.]

ignescent *ig-nes'ənt, adj.* emitting sparks when struck. — *n.* an ignescent substance. [L. *ignēscēns, -entis,* pr.p. of *ignēscĕre,* to catch fire.]

ignimbrite *ig'nim-brīt, n.* a hard rock formed by fusion of the volcanic fragments and dust of a nuée ardente. [L. *ignis,* fire, — *imber, imbris,* a shower of rain, and **-ite.**]

ignipotent *ig-nip'ə-tənt, (Pope) adj.* presiding over fire. [L. *ignipotens,* powerful in fire — *ignis,* fire, *potens,* powerful.]

ignis fatuus *ig'nis fat'ū-əs, fat'ōō-ōōs,* will-o'-the-wisp — the light of combustion of marsh-gas, apt to lead travellers into danger: any delusive ideal that leads one astray: — *pl.* **ignes fatui** (*ig'nēz fat'ū-ī; ig'nās fat'ōō-ē*). [L. *ignis,* fire, *fatuus,* foolish.]

ignite *ig-nīt', v.t.* to set on fire: to heat to the point at which combustion occurs. — *v.i.* to take fire. — *adj.* **ignīt'able** (also **ignīt'ible**). — *ns.* **ignītabil'ity** (**ignītibil'ity**); **ignīt'er** one who ignites: apparatus for firing an explosive or explosive mixture; **ignition** (*-nish'ən*) an act of igniting: a means of igniting: the state of being ignited: the firing system of an internal-combustion engine; **ig'nitron** (or *ig-nī'tron*) a device for conducting current in which an electrode dips into a pool of mercury and draws up an arc to start ionisation. — **ignition key** in a motor vehicle, the key which is turned to operate the ignition system. [L. *ignīre, ignītum,* to set on fire, to make red-hot — *ignis,* fire.]

ignoble *ig-nō'bl, adj.* of low birth: mean or worthless: unworthy: base: dishonourable. — *v.t.* to degrade. — *ns.* **ignōbil'ity** — **ignō'bleness.** — *adv.* **ignō'bly.** [Fr., — L. *ignōbilis* — *in-,* not, (*g*)*nōbilis,* noble.]

ignominy *ig'nə-min-i,* or *-nō-, n.* loss of good name: public disgrace: infamy — formerly (*obs.* and *Shak.*) **ig'nomy.** — *adj.* **ignomin'ious** deserving or marked with igno-

miny. — *adv.* **ignomin'iously.** [L. *ignōminia, in-,* not, (*g*)*nōmen, -inis,* name.]

ignoramus *ig-nō-rā'məs, -nə-, n.* the word formerly written by a grand jury on the back of a rejected indictment: an ignorant person, esp. one pretending to knowledge: — *pl.* **ignorā'muses.** [L. *ignōrāmus,* we are ignorant, in legal use, we ignore, take no notice, 1st pers. pl. pres. indic. of *ignōrāre.*]

ignorant *ig'nər-ənt, adj.* without knowledge, in general or particular: uninstructed: uninformed: unaware: showing, arising from, want of knowledge: discourteous, rude, ill-bred (*coll.*): keeping back knowledge (*Shak.*): unknown (*obs.*). — *n.* an ignorant person. — *n.* **ig'norance** want of knowledge — in R.C. theol. *vincible* or *wilful* ignorance is such as one may be fairly expected to overcome; *invincible* ignorance is that which one cannot help or abate: the time of ignorance, i.e. before Mohammed (*Islam*): an instance of ignorance: an act committed in ignorance. — *adv.* **ig'norantly.** [Fr., — L. *ignōrāns, -antis,* pr.p. of *ignōrāre;* see **ignore.**]

Ignorantine *ig-nō-ran'tīn, -nö-, -tin, (R.C.) n.* a member of a religious congregation of men devoted to the instruction of the poor — inaccurately applied to *Brethren of the Christian Schools.*

ignoratio elenchi *ig-nə-rā'shō il-eng'kī, ig-nō-rät'i-ō el-eng'kē,* (L.) ignoring the point in question: the fallacy of arguing to the wrong point.

ignore *ig-nōr', -nör', v.t.* wilfully to disregard: to set aside. — *adj.* **ignor'able.** — *ns.* **ignorā'tion** ignoring; **ignor'er.** [L. *ignōrāre,* not to know — *in-,* not, and the root of (*g*)*nōscĕre,* to know.]

Iguana *i-gwä'nə, n.* a genus of large thick-tongued arboreal lizards in tropical America: loosely extended to others of the same family (**Iguan'idae**): (without *cap.*) in South Africa a monitor lizard. [Sp., from Carib.]

iguanid *i-gwä'nid, n.* a lizard of the family Iguanidae. [**iguana** and **-id[1].**]

Iguanodon *i-gwä'nə-don, n.* a large, bipedal, bird-hipped, Jurassic and Cretaceous herbivorous dinosaur, with teeth like those of the iguana. [**iguana,** and Gr. *odous, odontos,* tooth.]

Iguvine *ig'ū-vīn, adj.* Eugubine.

ihram *ē-räm, ēhh'räm, n.* the scanty garb worn by Muslim pilgrims on drawing near Mecca: the holy state it betokens. [Ar. *ihrām.*]

ikat *ik'at, n.* a technique of dyeing yarn and tying it prior to weaving, resulting in a fabric with a geometric pattern of colours. [Malay-Indonesian *mengikat,* to tie.]

ikebana *ē'ke-bä'nə, n.* the Japanese art of flower arrangement. [Jap., living flowers, arranged flowers.]

ikon. Same as **icon.**

il- *il, pfx.* same as **in-,** the form used with words beginning with *l,* as in *illegible.*

ilang-ilang. Same as **ylang-ylang.**

Ilchester cheese *il'chəs-tər chēz,* Cheddar cheese with beer, spices, etc. [Ilchester, in Somerset, where it was first made.]

ileac. See **ileum, ileus.**

ileum *il', īl'i-əm, n.* the posterior part of the small intestine: — *pl.* **il'ea.** — *adj.* **il'eac, il'iac.** — *n.* **ileitis** (*il-, īl-i-ī'tis*) inflammation of the ileum. [L.L. *īleum,* L. *īlia* (pl.), the groin, flank, intestines.]

ileus *il', īl'i-əs, n.* obstruction of the intestine with severe pain, vomiting, etc.: — *pl.* **il'euses.** — Also **ileac** or **iliac passion.** — *adj.* **il'eac, il'iac.** [L. *īleos* — Gr. *īleos* or *eileos,* colic.]

ilex *ī'leks, n.* the holm-oak (*Quercus ilex*): (with *cap.*) the holly genus: — *pl.* **i'lexes, ilices** (*ī'li-sēz*). [L. *īlex,* holm-oak.]

Iliac, iliac. See **ileum, ileus, Ilium, ilium.**

Iliad *il'i-ad, -əd, n.* a Greek epic ascribed to Homer, on the siege of Troy: a long story or series of woes. [Gr. *īlias, -ados* — *īlios* or *īlion,* Ilium, Troy.]

ilices. See **ilex.**

Ilium *il'i-əm, īl', n.* Troy. — *adjs.* **Il'iac, Il'ian.** [L. *īlium* — Gr. *īlion,* Troy.]

ilium *īl', il'i-əm, n.* the bone that unites with the ischium and pubis to form the innominate bone: (in *pl.*) the flanks: — *pl.* **il'ia.** — *adj.* **il'iac.** [L. *īlium* (in classical L. only in pl. *īlia*); see **ileum.**]

ilk¹ *ilk, adj.* same. — *n.* type, kind. — **of that ilk** of that same, i.e. of the estate of the same name as the family. [O.E. *ilca,* same.]

ilk² *ilk,* (*Scot.*) *adj.* each: usu. compounded with the article as **ilk'a** (*-ə, -a*). — *n., adj., adv.* **ilk'aday** every day, every day but Sunday. [O.E. *ǣlc,* each, *ān,* one.]

I'll *īl,* a contraction of **I will** or **I shall.**

ill *il, adj.* (*compar.* **worse;** *superl.* **worst**) evil, bad: wicked: producing evil: hurtful: unfortunate: unfavourable: difficult: reprehensible: sick: diseased: incorrect: cross, as temper: grieved, distressed (*Scot.*): severe (*Scot.*). — *adv.* (*compar.* **worse;** *superl.* **worst**) badly: not well: not rightly: wrongfully: unfavourably: amiss: with hardship: with difficulty. — *n.* evil: wickedness: misfortune: harm: ailment. — *ns.* **ill'ness** sickness: disease; **illth** (*Ruskin,* etc.) the contrary of wealth or well-being. — *adv.* **illy** (*il'li; rare*) ill. — *adjs.* **ill'-advised** imprudent: ill-judged; **ill'-affect'ed** not well disposed; **ill's assort'ed** incompatible: not matching; **ill'-behaved'** behaving badly, ill-mannered. — **ill'-be'ing** the state of being poor or in bad health. — *adj.* **ill'-beseem'ing** (*Shak.*) unbecoming. — **ill'-blood', ill'-feel'ing** resentment, enmity. — *adjs.* **ill'-bod'ing** inauspicious; **ill's bred'** badly bred or educated: uncivil. — **ill'-breed'ing.** — *adjs.* **ill'-condit'ioned** in bad condition: churlish; **ill'-consid'ered** badly thought out: misconceived; **ill's deed'y** (*Scot.*) mischievous; **ill'-defined'** having no clear outline (*lit.* and *fig.*); **ill'-disposed'** unfriendly: inclined to evil; **ill'-faced** (*Spens.* **ill-faste**) ugly-faced. — **ill's fame'** disrepute (see **house**). — *adjs.* **ill'-fat'ed** unlucky; **ill'-faurd'** (*Scot.*), **ill'-fā'voured** ill-looking: deformed: ugly. — *adv.* **ill'-fā'vouredly.** — **ill'-fā'vouredness; ill's for'tune** bad luck. — *adjs.* **ill'-found'ed** without foundation (*fig.*); **ill'-got', -gott'en** procured by bad means; **ill'-haired'** (*Scot.*) cross-grained; **ill'-head'ed** (*Spens.* **-hedd'ed**) not clear in the head. — **ill'-health'** poor health; **ill'-hu'mour.** — *adjs.* **ill'-hu'moured** bad-tempered; **ill'-informed'** ignorant; **ill'-judged'** not well judged; **ill'-look'ing** having an evil look: ugly. — **ill'-luck'** bad luck. — *adjs.* **ill'-manned'** provided with too few men; **ill'-mann'ered** rude: ill-bred. **ill'-matched'** not suited to one another: not matching well. — **ill'-nā'ture.** — *adj.* **ill'-nā'tured** of a bad temper: cross: peevish. — *adv.* **ill'-nā'turedly.** — **ill'-nā'turedness.** — *adjs.* **ill'-off'** in bad circumstances; **ill'-ō'mened** having bad omens: unfortunate; **ill'-spent** spent amiss; **ill's starred'** born under the influence of an unlucky star: unlucky. — **ill'-success'** lack of success; **ill'-tem'per.** — *adjs.* **ill'-tem'pered** having a bad temper: morose: badly tempered, ill-mixed, distempered (*Shak.*); **ill'-timed'** said or done at an unsuitable time. — *v.t.* **ill-treat'** to treat ill: to abuse. — **ill-treat'ment; ill'-turn'** an act of unkindness or enmity; **ill-us'age.** — *v.t.* **ill'-use** to ill-treat. — *adjs.* **ill-used'** badly used or treated; **ill's versed'** having scanty knowledge or skill (with *in*). — **ill'-will'** unkind feeling: enmity; **ill'-wisher** one who wishes harm to another. — *adj.* **ill'-wrest'ing** misinterpreting to disadvantage. — **go ill with** to result in danger or misfortune to; **ill at ease** uneasy: embarrassed; **take it ill** to be offended; **with an ill grace** ungraciously. [O.N. *illr;* not connected with O.E. *yfel,* evil, but formerly confused with it, so that *ill* is often (esp. in Scots) to be read where *evil* is written.]

illapse *il-aps', n.* a sliding in. — *v.t.* to glide in. [L. *illābī, illāpsus* — *il-(in-),* in, *lābī,* to slip, to slide.]

illaqueate *i-lak'wi-āt, v.t.* to ensnare. — *adj.* **illaq'ueable.** — *n.* **illaquea'tion.** [L. *illaqueāre, -ātum* — *il-(in-),* into, *laqueus,* a noose.]

illation *il-ā'shən, n.* the act of inferring from premises: inference: conclusion. — *adj.* **illative** (*il'ə-tiv,* also *il-ā'tiv*) pertaining to, of the nature of, expressing, or introducing an inference: of a case in some Finno-Ugric languages expressing direction into or towards (*gram.*). — *n.* the illative case: a word in this case. — *adv.* **ill'atively** (or *-ā'*). [L. *illātiō, -ōnis* — *illātus,* used as pa.p. of *inferre,* to infer — *il-(in-),* in, *lātus,* carried.]

illaudable *il-ö'də-bl, adj.* not praiseworthy. — *adv.* **illau'dably.** [Pfx. **il-** (**in-** (2)).]

Illecebrum *il-es'i-brəm, n.* a genus of plants of one species found in Devon and Cornwall, giving name in some classifications to a family **Illecebrā'ceae,** corresponding more or less to the Paronychiaceae or Corregiolaceae of others, by others again placed in Caryophyllaceae. [Said to be from L. *illecebra,* allurement, 'as enticing the simpler into bogs and marshes'.]

illegal *il-ē'gl, adj.* contrary to law. — *v.t.* **illē'galise, -ize** to render unlawful. — *n.* **illēgality** (*-gal'i-ti*) the quality or condition of being illegal. — *adv.* **illē'gally.** [Pfx. **il-** (**in-** (2)).]

illegible *il-ej'i-bl, adj.* that cannot be read: indistinct. — *ns.* **illeg'ibleness, illegibil'ity.** — *adv.* **illeg'ibly.** [Pfx. **il-** (**in-** (2)).]

illegitimate *il-i-jit'i-mit, adj.* not according to law: not in the legal position of those born in wedlock or legitimised: not properly inferred or reasoned: not recognised by authority or good usage: (of racing) other than flat-racing. — *n.* one born out of wedlock. — *v.t.* (*-māt*) to pronounce or render illegitimate. — *n.* **illegit'imacy** (*-mə-si*). — *adv.* **illegit'imately.** — *n.* **illegitimā'tion** the act of pronouncing or rendering, or state of being, illegitimate. — **illegitimate pollination** in dimorphic flowers, pollination of long style from short stamen, or short from long. [Pfx. **il-** (**in-** (2)).]

illiad. A Shakespearian form of **oeillade.**

illiberal *il-ib'ər-əl, adj.* niggardly: mean, narrow in opinion or culture. — *v.t.* **illib'eralise, -ize.** — *n.* **illiberality** (*-al'i-ti*). — *adv.* **illib'erally.** [Pfx. **il-** (**in-** (2)).]

illicit *il-is'it, adj.* not allowable: unlawful: unlicensed. — *adv.* **illic'itly.** — *n.* **illic'itness.** — **illicit process of the major** or **minor** (*log.*) the fallacy of distributing the major or minor term in the conclusion when it is not distributed in the premise. [L. *illicitus* — *il-(in-),* not, *licitus,* pa.p. of *licēre,* to be allowed.]

illimitable *il-im'it-ə-bl, adj.* that cannot be bounded: infinite. — *n.* **illim'itableness.** — *adv.* **illim'itably.** — *n.* **illimitā'tion.** — *adj.* **illim'ited.** [Pfx. **il-** (**in-** (2)).]

illinium *il-in'i-əm, n.* a name proposed for element No. 61. — See **promethium.** [*Illinois* University, where its discovery was claimed.]

illipe *il'i-pi,* **illupi** *il-ōō'pi, n.* the mahwa tree (Sapotaceae) yielding **illipe nuts** and **oil.** [Tamil *illuppai.*]

illiquation *il-i-kwā'shən, n.* the melting of one thing into another. [Pfx. **il-** (**in-** (1)).]

illiquid *il-ik'wid, adj.* of assets, etc., not readily converted into cash: deficient in liquid assets. — *n.* **illiquid'ity.** [Pfx. **il-** (**in-** (2)).]

illision *il-izh'ən, n.* the act of striking against something. [L. *illīsiō, -ōnis* — *illīdere* — in, *laedere,* to strike.]

illite *il'īt,* (*min.*) *n.* a white or pale clay mineral found in shales and sediments, having a similar structure to the micas. [U.S. state of *Ill*inois, and *-ite.*]

illiterate *il-it'ər-it, adj.* unacquainted with literature: without book-learning: uneducated: ignorant: unable to read: of or characteristic of those who are without literary education: ignorant in a particular field or subject. — *n.* an illiterate person: one who cannot read. — *adv.* **illit'erately.** — *ns.* **illit'erateness, illit'eracy** (*-ə-si*). [Pfx. **il-** (**in-** (2)).]

illocution *il-ə-kū'shən,* (*philos.*) *n.* an act which is performed by a speaker in the actual utterance of words, as an order, a promise (cf. **perlocution**). — *adj.* **illocu'tionary.** [Pfx. **il-** (**in-** (1)).]

illogical *il-oj'i-kəl, adj.* contrary to the rules of logic: regardless or incapable of logic. — *ns.* **illog'ic, illogicality** (*-kal'i-ti*) illogicalness. — *adv.* **illog'ically.** — *n.* **illog'icalness.** [Pfx. **il-** (**in-** (2)).]

illude il-ōōd', -ŭd', v.t. to trick.   [L. illūdĕre — in, on, lūdĕre, lūsum, to play.]

illume il-ūm', -ōōm', v.t. a shortened poetic form of **illumine**. — v.t. **illum'inate** (-in-āt) to light up: to enlighten: to illustrate: to adorn with coloured lettering or illustrations: to confer power of vision upon. — adj. (-āt, -it) enlightened: pretending to enlightenment: admitted to a mystery. — n. an initiate. — adj. **illu'minable** that may be illuminated. — adj. **illu'minant** enlightening. — n. a means of lighting. — n.pl. **Illumināʹtī** (L. il-lōō-mi-nä'tē) the enlightened, a name given to various sects, and especially to a society of German Free-thinkers at the end of the 18th century: (without cap.) any who claim to have special enlightenment, esp. in philosophical or religious matters. — n. **illumināʹtion** lighting up: enlightenment: intensity of lighting up: splendour: brightness: a decorative display of lights: adorning of books with coloured lettering or illustrations: divine inspiration or instance of it: the luminous flux per unit area expressed in lux (also **illu'minance**). — adj. **illu'minative** (-ə-tiv, -ā-tiv) giving light: illustrative or explanatory. — ns. **Illumina'to, -tus** (also without cap.) one of the Illuminati; **illu'minātor**. — v.t. **illu'mine** to make luminous or bright: to enlighten: to adorn. — ns. **illu'miner** an illuminator; **illu'minism** the principles of the Illuminati: belief in or claim to an inward spiritual light; **illu'minist**.   [L. illūmināre, -ātum, in, in, upon, lūmināre, to cast light.]

illupi. Same as **illipe.**

illusion il-ōō'zhən, -ū', n. a mocking (obs.): deceptive appearance: an apparition: false conception: delusion: a false sense-impression of something actually present (psych.). — ns. **illu'sionism** the doctrine that the external world is illusory: the production of illusion, esp. the use of artistic techniques, as perspective, etc., to produce an illusion of reality; **illu'sionist** a believer in or practitioner of illusionism: one who produces illusions, a conjurer, prestidigitator. — adjs. **illu'sive** (-siv), **illu'sory** (-sər-i) deceiving by false appearances: false. — adv. **illu'sively**. — n. **illu'siveness**.   [See **illude**.]

illustrate il'əs-trāt (old-fashioned il-us'trāt), v.t. to make bright, adorn (obs.): to show in a favourable light (obs.): to give distinction or honour to (obs.): to make clear to the mind (arch.): to exemplify: to explain and adorn by pictures: to execute pictures for. — adj. (-lus'; Shak.) illustrious: renowned. — n. **illustrā'tion** the act of making lustrous or clear: lighting up (obs.): the act of explaining: that which illustrates: exemplification, example: a picture or diagram elucidating, or at least accompanying, letterpress. — adj. **ill'ustrated** (or -us') having pictorial illustrations. — n. an illustrated periodical. — adjs. **illustrā'tional**, **illustrative** (il'əs-trā-tiv or -trə-, or il-us'trə-tiv), **illus'tratory** having the quality of making clear or explaining. — adv. **ill'-ustratively** (or il-us'). — n. **ill'ustrātor**. — adj. **illus'-trious** luminous (obs.): highly distinguished: noble: conspicuous. — adv. **illus'triously**. — n. **illus'triousness**.   [L. illūstris; illūstrāre, -ātum, lūstrāre, to light up, prob. — lūx, light.]

illustrious¹, etc. See **illustrate.**

illustrious² il-us'tri-əs, (Shak.) adj. dull. Perh. for illustrous, not lustrous.

illustrissimo ēl-lōōs-trē'sē-mō, (It.) adj. most illustrious.

Illyrian il-ir'i-ən, adj. of, or pertaining to, Illyria, an ancient region to the East of the Adriatic Sea, its inhabitants, or their (prob. Indo-European) language. — Also n.

ilmenite il'mən-īt, n. a black mineral composed of iron, titanium, and oxygen.   [From the Ilmen Mountains in the Urals.]

il penseroso ēl pen-se-rō'zō, (It. pensieroso) the pensive man.

im-, n, pfx. same as **in-**, the form used with words beginning with b, m, or p, as in imbalance, immodest, implant.

I'm īm, a contraction of **I am.**

image im'ij, n. likeness: a statue: an idol: a representation in the mind, an idea: a picture or representation (not necessarily visual) in the imagination or memory: an appearance: that which very closely resembles anything: a type: a figure got from another figure by joining every point in it with a fixed point, or dropping a perpendicular from it to a fixed straight line or plane, and producing to the same distance (geom.): the figure of any object formed by rays of light reflected or refracted (real if the rays converge upon it, virtual if they appear to diverge from it) (opt.): an analogous figure formed by other rays (opt.): the element of a set which is associated with an element in a different set when one set is a functon or transformation of the other (math.): a metaphor or simile (rhet.): (**public image**) the character, attributes, of a person, institution, etc., as perceived by the general public: a favourable self-representation of a public figure, etc. — v.t. to form an image of: to form a likeness of in the mind: to mirror: to imagine: to portray: to typify: to produce a pictorial representation of (a part of the body) for diagnostic medical purposes. — adjs. **im'age-able; im'ageless** having no image. — ns. **imagery** (im'ij-ri, -ə-ri) the work of the imagination: mental pictures: figures of speech: images in general or collectively; **im'aging** image formation; **im'agism; im'agist** one of a twentieth-century school of poetry aiming at concentration, exact and simple language, and freedom of form and subject. — Also adj. — adj. **imagist'ic**. — **im'age-breaker** an iconoclast; **image converter** an instrument which converts infra-red or other invisible images into visible images; **image intensifier** an electronic device for increasing the brightness of an optical image, such as the fluoroscopic image in X-ray examinations; **image orthicon** a television camera tube which converts the images it receives into electronic impulses which are transmitted as television signals. **im'age-worship.**   [O.Fr., — L. imāgō, image; cf. imitārī, to imitate.]

imaginal. See **imago.**

imagine im-aj'in, v.t. to form an image of in the mind: to conceive: to think: to think vainly or falsely: to conjecture: to contrive or devise. — v.i. to form mental images: to exercise imagination. — adj. **imag'inable**. — n. **imag'inableness**. — adv. **imag'inably**. — adj. **imag'inary** existing only in the imagination: not real: non-existent. — n. **imaginā'tion** the act of imagining: the faculty of forming images in the mind: the artist's creative power: that which is imagined: contrivance. — adj. **imag'inative** (-ə-tiv, or -ā-tiv) full of imagination: suffused with imagination. — ns. **imag'inativeness; imag'iner; imag'ining** that which is imagined; **imag'inist** (Jane Austen) a person of active imagination and speculative temper. — **imaginary point, line,** etc., a non-existent point, etc., whose co-ordinates are **imaginary numbers, quantities,** non-existent quantities involving the square roots of negative quantities.   [O.Fr. imaginer — L. imāgināri — imāgō, an image.]

imagism, imagist. See **image.**

imago i-mā'gō, -mä', n. the last or perfect state of insect life: an image or optical counterpart of a thing: an elaborated type, founded on a parent or other, persisting in the unconscious as an influence (psych.): — pl. **imagines** (i-mā'jin-ēz, -mä'gin-, -mä'), **ima'gos, -oes.** — adj. **imaginal** (i-maj').   [L. imāgō, -inis, image.]

imam i-mäm', **imaum** i-möm', ns. the officer who leads the devotions in a mosque: (with cap.) a title for various Muslim potentates, founders, and leaders. — n. **imam'-ate**.   [Ar. imām, chief.]

Imari ē-mä'ri, (also without cap.) adj. of a type of Japanese porcelain, richly decorated in red, green and blue. — Also n.   [Imari, seaport in Japan from where such porcelain was exported.]

imaum. See **imam.**

imbalance im-bal'əns, n. a lack of balance, as between the ocular muscles or between the activities of the endocrines, or between the parts of the involuntary nervous system, or between the elements of a diet (*med.*): temporary lack of balance in a self-adjusting system: lack of balance between any two corresponding things: lack of balance in the sphere of a nation's economy or in the economics of, or trade between, two nations. [Pfx. **im-(in-** (2)).]

imbark *im-bärk', v.t.* to enclose in bark. [Pfx. **im-(in-** (1)).]

imbecile *im'bi-sēl, -sīl, -sil,* formerly *im-bi-sēl', im-bes'il,* adj. feeble (now generally in mind): fatuous. — *n.* one who is imbecile: one whose defective mental state (from birth or an early age) does not amount to idiocy, but who is incapable of managing his own affairs: loosely, a foolish, unwise or stupid person. — *adj.* **imbecilic** (*im-bi-sil'ik*). — *n.* **imbecil'ity.** [Fr. *imbécille* (now *imbécile*) — L. *imbēcillus;* perh. *in-,* not, and *bēcillus,* variant of *bacillus,* dim. of *baculus,* a stick.]

imbed. Same as **embed.**

imbibe *im-bīb', v.t.* to drink in: to absorb: to receive into the mind. — *v.i.* to drink, absorb. — *ns.* **imbīb'er; imbibition** (*im-bib-ish'ən*). [L. *imbībēre — in,* in, into, *bibēre,* to drink.]

imbosk, imboss. See **emboss²**.

imbrast (*Spens.*) for **embraced** (see **embrace¹**).

imbrex *im'breks, n.* orig. in Roman buildings, one of a series of usu. curved tiles fixed over the joins of flat tiles: — *pl.* **im'brices** (*-bri-sēz*). — *v.t.* **imbricate** (*im'bri-kāt*) to lay one overlapping another, as tiles on a roof. — *v.i.* to be so placed. — *adj.* (*-kit, -kāt*) (of fish-scales, bird-scales, layers of tissue, teeth) overlapping like roof-tiles. — *n.* **imbrica'tion.** [L. *imbrex,* a tile, *imbricāre, -ātum,* to tile — *imber,* a shower of rain.]

imbroccata *im-bro-kä'tə, n.* in fencing, a thrust. [It.]

imbroglio, embroglio *im-brōl'yō, n.* a confused mass: a tangle: an embroilment: an ordered confusion (*mus.*): — *pl.* **im-, embro'glios.** [It., confusion — *imbrogliare,* to confuse, embroil.]

imbrue *im-brōō', v.t.* to wet or moisten: to soak: to drench: to stain or dye. — Also **embrue'** (*Spens.* **embrewe'**). — *n.* **imbrue'ment.** [O.Fr. *embreuver — bevre* (Fr. *boire*) — L. *bibēre,* to drink.]

imbrute *im-brōōt', v.t.* or *v.i.* to reduce, or sink, to the state of a brute. — Also **embrute'.** [Pfx. **im-(in-** (1)).]

imbue *im-bū', v.t.* to moisten: to tinge deeply: to fill, permeate (e.g. the mind) (with *with*). [O.Fr. *imbuer* — L. *imbuēre — in,* and root of *bibēre,* to drink.]

imburse *im-bûrs', v.t.* to put in a purse or in one's purse: to pay: to repay. [Pfx. **im- (in-** (1)), and L. *bursa,* a purse.]

imide *im'īd,* (*chem.*) *n.* any of a class of organic compounds formed from ammonia or a primary amine by replacing two hydrogen atoms by a metal or acid radical. [Alteration of **amide.**]

imine *im'īn, i-mīn', n.* a highly reactive nitrogen-containing organic substance having a carbon-to-nitrogen double bond. [Alteration of **amine.**]

imipramine *i-mip'rə-mēn, n.* an anti-depressant drug also used in the treatment of enuresis. [From dimethylpropylamine.]

imitate *im'i-tāt, v.t.* to strive to be like or produce something like: to copy, not necessarily exactly: to mimic. — *n.* **imitability** (*-ə-bil'i-ti*). — *adj.* **im'itable** that may be imitated or copied: inviting or worthy of imitation (*obs.*). — *ns.* **im'itancy** the tendency to imitate; **im'itant** a counterfeit; **imita'tion** the act of imitating: that which is produced as a copy, or counterfeit: a performance in mimicry: the repeating of the same passage, or the following of a passage with a similar one in one or more of the other parts of voices (*mus.*). — *adj.* sham, counterfeit: machine-made (as lace). — *adj.* **im'itative** inclined to imitate: formed after a model: mimicking. — *adv.* **im'itatively.** — *ns.* **im'itativeness; im'itator.** [L. *imitārī, -ātus.*]

immaculate *im-ak'ū-lit, adj.* spotless: unstained: pure. — *n.* **immac'ulacy** state of being immaculate. — *adv.* **immac'ulately.** — *n.* **immac'ulateness.** — **Immaculate**

Conception the R.C. dogma that the Virgin Mary was conceived without original sin — first proclaimed as article of faith in 1854 — not the same as the Virgin Birth. [L. *immaculātus — in-,* not, *maculāre,* to spot.]

immanacle *im-(m)an'ə-kl,* (*Milt.*) *v.t.* to put in manacles, to fetter or confine. [Pfx. **im- (in-** (1)).]

immanation *im-ə-nā'shən, n.* inflow. [L. *in,* in, *mānāre, -ātum,* to flow.]

immane *im-ān', adj.* huge: cruel, savage. — *adv.* **immane'ly.** — *n.* **immanity** (*im-an'i-ti*) cruelty. [L. *immānis,* huge, savage.]

immanent *im'ə-nənt, adj.* indwelling: pervading: inherent. — *ns.* **imm'anence, imm'anency** the pervasion of the universe by the intelligent and creative principle — a fundamental conception of pantheism. — *adj.* **immanental** (*-ent'l*). — *ns.* **imm'anentism** belief in an immanent God; **imm'anentist.** [L. *in,* in, *manēre,* to remain.]

immanity. See **immane.**

immantle *im-(m)an'tl, v.t.* to envelop in a mantle. [Pfx. **im- (in-** (1)).]

Immanuel. See **Emmanuel.**

immarcescible *im-är-ses'i-bl, adj.* never-fading: imperishable. — Less correctly **immarcess'ible.** [L. *in-,* not, *marcēscēre,* to languish.]

immarginate *im-är'jin-āt, -it, adj.* without distinct margin. [Pfx. **im- (in-** (2)).]

immask *im-mäsk', (Shak.) v.t.* to mask, disguise. [Pfx. **im- (in-** (1)).]

immaterial *im-ə-tē'ri-əl, adj.* not consisting of matter: incorporeal: unimportant. — *v.t.* **immatē'rialise, -ize** to separate from matter. — *ns.* **immatē'rialism** the doctrine that there is no material substance; **immatē'rialist; immateriality** (*-al'*) the quality of being immaterial or of not consisting of matter. — *adv.* **immatē'rially.** [Pfx. **im- (in-** (2)).]

immature, immatured *im-ə-tyōōr(d)', -chōōr(d)', adjs.* not ripe: not perfect: come before the natural time: (**immature**) not fully developed (mentally, physically, etc.): (**immature**) (of behaviour, attitudes, etc.) childish. — *adv.* **immature'ly.** — *ns.* **immature'ness, immatur'ity.** [Pfx. **im- (in-** (2)).]

immeasurable *im-ezh'ər-ə-bl, adj.* that cannot be measured: very great. — *n.* **immeas'urableness.** — *adv.* **immeas'urably.** — *adj.* **immeas'ured** (*Spens.*) beyond the common measure, immeasurable. [Pfx. **im- (in-** (2)).]

immediate *im-ē'di-it, -dyət, -dyit, -jət, adj.* with nothing between: not acting by second causes: direct: present: without delay. — *n.* **immē'diacy** the state of being immediate: direct appeal to intuitive understanding. — *adv.* or *conj.* **immē'diately** (sometimes with *that*) as soon as. — *ns.* **immē'diateness; immē'diatism** immediateness: the policy of action at once, esp. (*U.S. hist.*) in abolition of slavery. [Pfx. **im- (in-** (2)).]

immedicable *im-(m)ed'i-kə-bl, adj.* incurable. [Pfx. **im- (in-** (2)).]

Immelmann turn *im'əl-mən tûrn,* (*aero.*) a manoeuvre involving a half loop and a half roll carried out to achieve greater height and reverse the direction of flight. [Named after the pilot who invented it.]

immemorial *im-i-mōr'i-əl, -mör', adj.* ancient beyond the reach of memory. — *adv.* **immemō'rially.** [Pfx. **im- (in-** (2)).]

immense *i-mens', adj.* that cannot be measured: vast in extent: very large: fine, very good (*slang*). — *adv.* **immense'ly.** — *ns.* **immense'ness; immens'ity** an extent not to be measured: infinity: greatness. [Fr., — L. *immēnsus — in-,* not, *mēnsus,* pa.p. of *metīrī,* to measure.]

immensurable *im-(m)en'shōōr-ə-bl, -syōōr-, -syər-, adj.* that cannot be measured. — *n.* **immensurabil'ity.** [Pfx. **im- (in-** (2)).]

immerge *im-(m)ûrj', v.t.* and *v.i.* to plunge in. [Pfx. **im- (in-** (1)).]

---

imb- for many words see **emb-.**

immeritous *im-mer′it-əs*, (*Milt.*) *adj.* undeserving. [L. *immeritus — in-*, not, *meritus*, deserving.]

immerse *im-(m)ûrs′*, *v.t.* to dip under the surface of a liquid: to baptise by dipping the whole body: to engage or involve deeply. — *adj.* **immersed′** (*bot.*) embedded in the tissues. — *ns.* **immer′sion** the act of immersing: the state of being immersed: deep absorption or involvement: baptism by immersing: entry into a position of invisibility as in eclipse or occultation (*astron.*): the application of liquid to a microscope object-glass: a method of teaching a foreign language by giving the learner intensive practice in a situation in which all communication is in the language concerned; **immer′sionism; immer′sionist** one who favours or practises baptism by immersion. — **immersion heater** an electrical apparatus directly immersed in the liquid, used for heating water; **immersion lens** a microscope object-glass that works with a drop of oil or water between it and the cover-glass. [See **immerge.**]

immesh. See **enmesh.**

immethodical *im-(m)i-thod′ik-əl*, *adj.* without method or order: irregular. — *adv.* **immethod′ically.** [Pfx. **im- (in-** (2)).]

immew. See **emmew.**

immigrate *im′i-grāt*, *v.i.* to migrate or remove into a country with intention of settling in it. — *ns.* **imm′igrant** one who immigrates; **immigrā′tion.** [L. *immigrāre — in*, into, *migrāre*, *-ātum*, to remove.]

imminent *im′i-nənt*, *adj.* overhanging: intent: threatening: impending. — *ns.* **imm′inence** the fact or state of being imminent: impending evil (*Shak.*); **imm′inency.** — *adv.* **imm′inently.** [L. *imminēns*, *-entis — in*, upon, *minēre*, to project, jut.]

immingle *im-(m)ing′gl*, *v.t.* and *v.i.* to mingle together, to mix. [Pfx. **im- (in-** (1)).]

immiscible *im-(m)is′i-bl*, *adj.* not capable of being mixed. — *n.* **immiscibil′ity.** [Pfx. **im- (in-** (2)).]

immiseration *im-iz-ər-ā′shən*, *n.* progressive impoverishment or degradation. — Also **immiserīsā′tion**, **-z-.** — *v.t.* **immis′erise**, **-ize.** [Pfx. **im-(in-**(1)), and *misery*.]

immit *im-(m)it′*, *v.t.* to insert: to introduce: to inject: — *pr.p.* **immitt′ing;** *pa.t.* and *pa.p.* **immitt′ed.** — *n.* **immission** (*-ish′ən*). [L. *immittĕre — in*, into, *mittĕre*, *missum*, to send.]

immitigable *im-it′i-gə-bl*, *adj.* incapable of being mitigated. — *adv.* **immit′igably.** [Pfx. **im- (in-** (2)).]

immix *im-(m)iks′*, (*Milt.*) *v.t.* to mix in: to involve in mixture. [Pfx. **im- (in-** (1)).]

immobile *im-(m)ō′bīl*, *-bēl*, in U.S. *-bil*, *adj.* immovable: not readily moved: motionless: stationary. — *n.* **immobilīsā′tion**, **-z-.** — *v.t.* **immob′ilise**, **-ize** to render immobile: to put or keep out of action or circulation. — *ns.* **immob′ilism** a political policy characterised by extreme lack of action; **immobil′ity.** [Pfx. **im- (in-** (2)).]

immoderate *im-od′ər-it*, *adj.* exceeding due bounds: extravagant: unrestrained. — *ns.* **immod′eracy, immod′erateness.** — *adv.* **immod′erately.** — *n.* **immoderā′tion** want of moderation: excess. [Pfx. **im-(in-** (2)).]

immodest *im-od′ist*, *adj.* wanting restraint: exceeding in self-assertion: impudent: wanting shame or delicacy: indecent. — *adv.* **immod′estly.** — *n.* **immod′esty.** [Pfx. **im-(in-** (2)).]

immolate *im′ō-lāt*, *im′əl-āt*, *v.t.* to offer in sacrifice: to dedicate to the church or church uses (*obs.*). — *ns.* **immolā′tion** the act of sacrificing: the state of being sacrificed: that which is offered in sacrifice; **imm′olātor.** [L. *immolāre*, *-ātum*, to sprinkle meal (on a victim), hence to sacrifice — *in*, upon, *mola*, meal.]

immoment *im-mō′mənt*, (*Shak.*) *adj.* of no value. [Pfx. **im-(in-** (2)).]

immoral *im-(m)or′əl*, *adj.* inconsistent with or disregardful of morality: sometimes esp. of sexual morality: wicked: licentious. — *ns.* **immor′alism** denial or rejection of morality; **immor′alist; immorality** (*im-or-*, *im-ər-*

al′i-ti) the quality of being immoral: an immoral act or practice. — *adv.* **immor′ally.** [Pfx. **im-(in-** (2)).]

immortal *im-ör′tl*, *adj.* exempt from death: imperishable: never to be forgotten (as a name, poem, etc.). — *n.* one who will never cease to exist: (often with *cap.*) a god, esp. of the ancient Greeks and Romans: one whose works will always retain their supremacy: one of the forty members of the French Academy. — *n.* **immortalīsā′tion**, **-z-.** — *v.t.* **immor′talise**, **-ize** to make immortal. — *n.* **immortality** (*im-ör-*, *im-ər-tal′i-ti*). — *adv.* **immor′tally.** — **the Immortal Memory** a toast in memory of the Scottish poet, Robert Burns (1759–96). [Pfx. **im-(in-** (2)).]

immortelle *im-ör-tel′*, *n.* an everlasting flower. [Fr. (*fleur*) *immortelle*, immortal (flower).]

immovable *im-ōōv′ə-bl*, *adj.* impossible to move: steadfast: unyielding: impassive: motionless: unalterable: not liable to be removed (*law*; commonly **immove′able**): real, not personal (*law*). — *n.* (*law*; usu. in *pl.* **immove′ables**) immoveable property. — *ns.* **immov′ableness, immovabil′ity.** — *adv.* **immov′ably.** [Pfx. **im-(in-** (2)).]

immune *im-ūn′*, *adj.* exempt: having a high resistance to a disease due to the formation of humoral antibodies or cellular cytotoxins in response to the presence of antigens: not liable to danger, esp. infection: free from obligation. — *n.* one who is immune. — *adj.* **immunifā′-cient** producing immunity. — *n.* **immunīsā′tion**, **-z-.** — *v.t.* **imm′unise**, **-ize** to render immune, esp. to make immune from a disease by injecting disease germs, or their poisons (either active or rendered harmless). — *n.* **immun′ity** the condition of being immune. — **immuno-** (*i-mū′no-*or *im′*) in composition, immune, immunity. — *ns.* **immunoass′ay** (or *ə-sā′*) a bioassay by immunological methods; **immunochem′istry** the chemistry of antibodies, antibody reactions, etc.; **immunocytochem′istry** the study of the chemical aspects of cellular immunity. — *ns.* **immū′nogen** same as **antigen; immunogenet′ics** the study of inherited characteristics of immunity; **immunoglō′bin** a protein (antibody) found in body fluids, capable of combining with and neutralising antigens. — *adj.* **immunolog′ical.** — *ns.* **immunol′ogist; immunol′ogy** the scientific study of immunity; **immunopathol′ogy** the study of immune factors associated with disease. — *v.t.* and *v.i.* **immunosuppress′.** — *ns.* **immunosuppress′ant** a drug which inhibits the body's rejection of e.g. transplanted organs; **immunosuppress′ion.** — *adj.* **immunosuppress′ive.** — *ns.* **immunother′apy** the treatment of disease, now esp. cancer, by antigens which stimulate the patient's own natural immunity; **immunotransfū′sion** the transfusion of blood or plasma containing in high concentration the appropriate antibodies for the infection from which the patient is suffering. — **immune body** an antibody; **immune response** the production of antibodies in the body as a defensive response to the presence of antigens; **immune system** the process within an organism whereby antigenic or foreign matter is distinguished and neutralised through antibody or cytotoxic action. [L. *immūnis — in-*, not, *mūnis*, serving.]

immure *im-ūr′*, *v.t.* to wall in: to shut up: to imprison (also *fig.*). — *n.* (*Shak.* **emure′**) an enclosing wall. — *n.* **immure′ment** imprisonment: walling up. [L. *in*, in, *mūrus*, a wall.]

immutable *im-ūt′ə-bl*, *adj.* unchangeable. — *ns.* **immūtabil′ity, immūt′ableness.** — *adv.* **immūt′ably.** [Pfx. **im-(in-** (2)).]

imp¹ *imp*, *n.* a shoot, scion, graft (*obs.*): a scion of a family (*obs.*): a young man (*obs.*): a child: a teasing or taunting mischievous child: a little devil or wicked spirit. — *v.t.* to graft, engraft (*arch.*): to engraft feathers in (to mend a wing) (*falconry*). — *adj.* **imp′ish** like or characteristic of an imp, teasingly mischievous. — *adv.* **imp′ishly.** — *n.* **imp′ishness.** [O.E. *impa* — L.L. *impotus*, a graft — Gr. *emphytos*, engrafted.]

---

imp². See under **international**.

impacable *im'pak-ə-bl*, (*Spens.*) *adj.* not to be quieted or appeased. [L. *in-*, not, *pācāre*, to quiet.]

impact *im-pakt'*, *v.t.* to press firmly together: to drive close: to strike or collide. — *ns.* **im'pact** the blow of a body in motion impinging on another body: the impulse resulting from collision: the impulse resulting from a new idea or theory: strong effect, influence; **impac'tion** the act of pressing together, or of fixing a substance tightly in a body cavity: the condition so produced; **impact'ite** a glassy type of rock formed as a result of the impact (and heat) of a meteorite on the earth's surface. — **impact parameter** (*nuc.*) the distance at which two particles which collide would have passed if no interaction had occurred between them; **impacted fracture** see **fract**; **impacted tooth** one wedged between the jawbone and another tooth and thus unable to come through the gum. [L. *impactus*, pa.p. of *impingěre*; see **impinge**.]

impaint *im-pānt'*, (*Shak.*) *v.t.* to paint, depict. [Pfx. **im-(in-** (1)).]

impair¹ *im-pār'*, (*Spens.* **empaire'**, **empare'**) *v.t.* to diminish in quantity, value, or strength: to injure: to weaken. — *v.i.* to become worse: to decay. — *n.* impairing. — *n.* **impair'ment**. [O.Fr. *empeirer* (Fr. *empirer*), from L. *im-(in-*), intensive, *pējōrāre*, to make worse — *pējor*, worse.]

impair² *im-pār'*, (*Shak.*) *adj.* perh. unsuitable, unfit, inferior. [Fr., — L. *impār* — *in-*, not, *pār*, equal.]

impala *im-pä'lə*, *n.* an African antelope (*Aepyceros melampus*). [Zulu *i-mpālaj*.]

impale *im-pāl'*, *v.t.* to shut in, esp. to fence in with stakes (*arch.*): to surround with a border (*rare*): to put to death by spitting on to a stake: to transfix: to combine palewise (*her.*). — Also **empale'**. — *n.* **impale'ment** an enclosed space (*arch.*): the act or punishment of impaling: the marshalling side by side of two escutcheons combined in one (*her.*). [Fr. *empaler* — L. *in*, in, *pālus*, a stake.]

impalpable *im-pal'pə-bl*, *adj.* not perceivable by touch: extremely fine-grained: eluding apprehension. — *n.* **impalpabil'ity**. — *adv.* **impal'pably**. [Pfx. **im-(in-** (2)).]

impaludism *im-palū'-dizm*, *n.* a disease carried by insects, affecting dwellers in marshy areas. [L. *in*, in, *palus*, *palūdis*, a marsh.]

impanation *im-pə-nā'shən*, or *-pā-*, *n.* local union of the body of Christ with the consecrated bread in the Eucharist: later specially used of Luther's consubstantiation. — *adj.* **impanate** (*im-pān'āt*, *im'pən-āt*) embodied in bread. [From L.L. *impānāre*, *-ātum* — *in*, in, *pānis*, bread.]

impanel, **impannel**. See **empanel**.

imparadise *im-par'ə-dīs*, (*Milt.*) *v.t.* to put in a paradise or state of extreme felicity: to make a paradise of. — Also **empar'adise**. [Pfx. **im-(in-** (1)).]

impar(i)- *im-par-(i-)*, in composition, unequal. — *n.* **imparity** (*im-par'i-ti*) inequality: oddness (*arith.*, *obs.*). — *adjs.* **imparipinn'ate** (*bot.*) pinnate with a terminal leaflet; **imparisyllab'ic** having a syllable more in the other cases than in the nominative. [L. *impār* — *in-*, not, *pār*, equal.]

impark *im-pärk'*, *v.t.* to enclose in, or as, a park. — *n.* **imparkā'tion**. [Pfx. **im-(in-** (1)).]

imparl *im-pärl'*, (*arch.* except *law*) *v.i.* to hold a consultation. — *v.t.* to talk over. — *n.* **imparl'ance** (*Spens.* **emparl'aunce**) parleying, conference: delay in pleading, ostensibly for amicable adjustment. [Obs. Fr. *emparler* — *em-*(L. *in-*), *parler*, to talk.]

impart *im-pärt'* (*Spens.* **empart'**) *v.t.* to bestow a part of, or share out (*arch.*): to give (something abstract): to communicate, make known. — *v.i.* to give a part (of). — *ns.* **impartā'tion**; **impart'er**; **impart'ment** (*Shak.*). [O.Fr. *empartir* — L. *impartīre* — *in*, on, *pars*, *partis*, a part.]

impartial *im-pär'shl*, *adj.* not favouring one more than another: just: partial (*Shak.*). — *ns.* **impartiality** (*-shi-*

al'i-ti), **impar'tialness**. — *adv.* **impar'tially**. [Pfx. **im-(in-** (2)).]

impartible¹ *im-pärt'i-bl*, *adj.* capable of being imparted. — *n.* **impartibil'ity**. [**impart**.]

impartible² *im-pärt'i-bl*, *adj.* not partible: indivisible. — *n.* **impartibil'ity**. [Pfx. **im-(in-** (2)).]

impassable *im-päs'ə-bl*, *adj.* not capable of being passed. — *ns.* **impassabil'ity**, **impass'ableness**. — *adv.* **impass'ably**. — *n.* **impasse** (*am-pas'*, *ē-pas*) a place from which there is no outlet: a deadlock. [Pfx. **im-(in-** (2)).]

impassible *im-pas'i-bl*, *adj.* incapable of suffering, injury, or emotion. — *ns.* **impassibil'ity**, **impass'ibleness**. — *adv.* **impass'ibly**. [Church L. *impassibilis* — *in-*, not, *patī*, *passus*, to suffer.]

impassion *im-pash'ən*, *v.t.* to move with passion: to make passionate. — *adjs.* **impass'ionate** (*Spens.* **empass'ionate**) impassioned: dispassionate; **impass'ioned** (*Spens.* **empass'ioned**) moved by or charged with passion: animated. [It. *impassionare* — L. *in*, in, *passiō*, *-ōnis*, passion.]

impassive *im-pas'iv*, *adj.* not susceptible of feeling: not showing feeling: imperturbable. — *adv.* **impass'ively**. — *ns.* **impass'iveness**, **impassiv'ity**. [Pfx. **im-(in-** (2)).]

impaste *im-pāst'*, *v.t.* to form into, or enclose in, a paste: to lay colours thick on. — *ns.* **impastation** (*im-pas-tā'shən*); **impasto** (*im-päs'tō*) in painting and pottery, the thick laying on of pigments: the paint so laid on: — *pl.* **impast'os**. — *adjs.* **impast'oed**, **impast'o'd**, **impāst'ed**. [L.L. *impastāre* — *in*, into, *pasta*, paste.]

Impatiens *im-pā'shi-enz*, *n.* the balsam genus of plants, whose ripe capsules burst at a touch: (without *cap.*) a plant of this genus. [L., impatient.]

impatient *im-pā'shənt*, *adj.* not able to endure or to wait: fretful: restless: intolerant (of). — *n.* **impā'tience**. — *adv.* **impā'tiently**. [L. *impatiēns*, *-entis*, impatient — *in*, not, *patiēns*, patient.]

impave *im-pāv'*, (*Wordsworth*) *v.t.* to depict in pavement, as mosaic. [Pfx. **im- (in-** (1)).]

impavid *im-pav'id*, (*rare*) *adj.* fearless. — *adv.* **impav'idly**. [L. *impavidus* — *im-* (*in-*), not, *pavidus*, fearing.]

impawn *im-pön'*, *v.t.* to put in pawn: to pledge: to risk. [Pfx. **im- (in-** (1)).]

impeach *im-pēch'*, (*Spens.* **empeach'** *v.t.* to hinder, impede (*obs.*): to beset (*obs.*): to impair (*obs.*): to disparage: to find fault with: to call in question: to arraign (esp. when a lower legislative house charges a high officer with grave offences before the upper house as judges): to turn king's evidence against, peach upon. — *n.* hindrance (*Spens.*): damage, injury, impairment, detriment (*Spens.*): calling in question (*Shak.*). — *adj.* **impeach'able**. — *ns.* **impeach'er**; **impeach'ment**. [O.Fr. *empech(i)er*, to hinder (Fr. *empêcher*) — L. *impedicāre*, to fetter — *in*, in, *pědīca*, fetter — *pēs*, *pědis*, foot.]

impearl *im-pûrl'*, *v.t.* to adorn with or as with pearls: to make like pearls. [Pfx. **im- (in-** (1)).]

impeccable *im-pek'ə-bl*, *adj.* not liable to sin: faultless. — *n.* one who is impeccable. — *adv.* **impecc'ably**. — *ns.* **impeccabil'ity**, **impecc'ancy**. — *adj.* **impecc'ant** without sin. [Pfx. **im- (in-** (2)).]

impecunious *im-pi-kū'ni-əs*, *-nyəs*, *adj.* without money: short of money. — *n.* **impecunios'ity**. [Pfx. **im- (in-** (2)).]

impede *im-pēd'*, *v.t.* to hinder or obstruct. — *n.* **impē'dance** hindrance: an apparent increase of resistance to an alternating current owing to induction in a circuit (*elect.*). — *n.* **impediment** (*-ped'*) obstacle: a defect preventing fluent speech. — *n.pl.* **impediment'a** (L. *impedīmenta*) military baggage: baggage generally: encumbrances. — *adjs.* **impedimen'tal**, **imped'itive** hindering. [L. *impedīre* — *in*, in, *pēs*, *pedis*, a foot.]

impel *im-pel'*, *v.t.* to urge forward: to excite to action: to instigate: — *pr.p.* **impell'ing**; *pa.t.* and *pa.p.* **impelled'**. — *adj.* **impell'ent** impelling or driving on. — *n.* an impelling agent or power. — *n.* **impell'er** one who, or that which, impels: a rotor for transmitting motion. [L. *impellěre*, *impulsum* — *in*, on, *pellěre*, to drive.]

impend *im-pend'*, *v.i.* to overhang: to threaten: to be about to happen. — *ns.* (*obs.*) **impend'ence, impend'ency.** — *adjs.* **impend'ent, impend'ing.** [L. *impendēre* — *in*, on, *pendēre*, to hang.]

impenetrable *im-pen'i-trə-bl, adj.* not to be penetrated: impervious: inscrutable: occupying space exclusively (*phys.*). — *n.* **impenetrabil'ity.** — *adv.* **impen'etrably.** [Pfx. **im- (in-** (2)).]

impenetrate *im-pen'i-trāt, v.t.* to permeate: to penetrate thoroughly. — *n.* **impenetrā'tion.** [Pfx. **im- (in-** (1)).]

impenitent *im-pen'i-tənt, adj.* not repenting. — *n.* one who does not repent: a hardened sinner. — *ns.* **impen'itence; impen'itency.** — *adv.* **impen'itently.** [Pfx. **im- (in-** (2)).]

imperative *im-per'ə-tiv, adj.* expressive of command, advice, or request: authoritative: peremptory: obligatory: urgently necessary: calling out for action. — *n.* that which is imperative: the imperative mood: a verb in the imperative mood. — *adv.* **imper'atively.** — **imperative mood** the form of a verb expressing command, advice, or request. — **categorical imperative** see under category. [L. *imperātīvus* — *imperāre*, to command — *in*, in, *parāre*, to prepare.]

imperator *im-pər-ä'tər*; L. *im-per-ä'tor, n.* a commander: a ruler: an emperor. — *adj.* **imperatorial** (*im-per-ə-tō'ri-əl, -tö'*). [L. *imperātor*, a general, later an emperor — *imperāre*, to command.]

imperceable *im'pərs-ə-bl*, (*Spens.*) *adj.* unpierceable. [Pfx. **im- (in-** (2)).]

imperceptible *im-pər-sep'ti-bl, adj.* not discernible by the senses: very small, slight or gradual. — *n.* an imperceptible thing. — *ns.* **impercep'tibleness, imperceptibil'-ity.** — *adv.* **impercep'tibly.** — *adjs.* **impercep'tive, im-percip'ient** not perceiving: having no power to perceive. [Pfx. **im- (in-** (2)).]

imperfect *im-pûr'fikt, adj.* incomplete: defective: falling short of perfection: wanting any normal part, or the full normal number of parts: incapable of being enforced (*legal*): expressing continued or habitual action in past time (*gram.*): diminished, less by a semitone (*mus.*): duple (*old mus.*). — *n.* the imperfect tense: a verb in the imperfect tense. — *adj.* **imperfect'ible** that cannot be made perfect. — *ns.* **imperfectibil'ity; imper-fection** (*-fek'shən*) the state of being imperfect: a defect. — *adj.* **imperfec'tive** denoting the aspect of the verb which indicates that the action described is in progress (*gram.*). — *advs.* **imperfec'tively** (*gram.*); **imper'fectly.** — *n.* **imper'fectness.** — **imperfect cadence** a cadence which is not resolved to the tonic key, esp. one passing from tonic to dominant chord; **imperfect fungus** a fungus of the order *Fungi Imperfecti* of which no sexual stage is known. [Pfx. **im- (in-** (2)).]

imperforate *im-pûr'fə-rit, -d -rā-tid, adjs.* not pierced through or perforated: having no opening: abnormally closed (*med.*): without perforations for tearing apart, as a sheet of postage stamps. — *adj.* **imper'forable.** — *n.* **imperforā'tion.** [Pfx. **im- (in-** (2)).]

imperial *im-pē'ri-əl, adj.* pertaining to, or of the nature of, an empire or emperor: sovereign, supreme: commanding, august: (of products, etc.) of superior quality or size. — *n.* an emperor or empress: a supporter of an emperor: a tuft of hair on lower lip (earlier than Napoleon III): a pointed dome of ogee section (*build.*): the top of a coach, carriage, or a trunk for carrying on it: a British size of paper before metrication, 22 × 30 in. (a U.S. size 23 × 33): a size of slates, 33 × 24 in. (838 × 610 mm.): an obs. Russian gold coin. — *v.t.* **impē'rialise, -ize** to make imperial. — *ns.* **impē'-rialism** the power or authority of an emperor: the policy of making or maintaining an empire: the spirit of empire; **impē'rialist** a soldier or partisan of an emperor: a believer in the policy of developing and utilising the spirit of empire. — *adj.* **impērialist'ic.** — *n.* **impēriality** (*-al'i-ti*) imperial power, right, or privilege. — *adv.* **impē'rially.** — *adj.* **impē'rious** assuming command: haughty: tyrannical: domineering: peremptory: authoritative: imperial (*obs.*). — *adv.* **impē'-**

riously. — *ns.* **impē'riousness.** — **imperial cap** a size of brown paper, 22 × 29 in. (558 × 760 mm.); **imperial city** Rome: in the older German Empire a city that owed allegiance only to the emperor, exercised suzerainty within its own bounds, and had the right of voting in the imperial diet; **Imperial Conference** a former periodical conference (orig. *Colonial Conference*) of the prime ministers and other representatives of the United Kingdom and the self-governing Dominions; **imperial measure, weight** non-metric standard of measure, weight (**imperial gallon, yard, pound**) as fixed by parliament for the United Kingdom (final act 1963); **imperial octavo** a book size, $7\frac{1}{2}$ × 11 in. in Britain, $8\frac{1}{4}$ × $11\frac{1}{2}$ in U.S.; **Imperial Parliament** the parliament of the United Kingdom; **imperial preference** (*hist.*) the favouring of trade within the British Empire by discriminating tariffs. [L. *impērium*, sovereignty.]

imperil *im-per'il, v.t.* to endanger: — *pa.p.* **imper'illed.** — *n.* **imper'ilment.** [Pfx. **im- (in-** (1))]

imperious, etc. See **imperial.**

imperishable *im-per'ish-ə-bl, adj.* indestructible: everlasting. — *ns.* **imper'ishableness, imperishabil'ity.** — *adv.* **imper'ishably.** [Pfx. **im- (in-** (2)).]

imperium *im-pēr'i-əm, -per', n.* absolute sovereignty, command: the area, or extent, of absolute sovereignty. — **imperium in imperio** (*in im-pēr'i-ō, -per'*) absolute authority within the sphere of higher authority. [L. *impērium.*]

impermanence *im-pûr'mən-əns, n.* want of permanence. — *n.* **imper'manency.** — *adj.* **imper'manent.** [Pfx. **im- (in-** (2)).]

impermeable *im-pûr'mi-ə-bl, adj.* not permitting passage, esp. of fluids: impervious. — *ns.* **impermeabil'ity, imper'meableness.** — *adv.* **imper'meably.** [Pfx. **im- (in-** (2)).]

impermissible *im-pər-mis'i-bl, adj.* not permissible. — *n.* **impermissibil'ity.** — *adv.* **impermiss'ibly.** [Pfx. **im- (in-** (2)).]

imperseverant *im-pər-sev'ər-ənt*, (*Shak.*) *adj.* perh. unseeing, wanting in power to perceive what is before one, or perh. stubborn. [Pfx. **im- (in-** (2)), and **perceive** or **persevere.**]

impersistent *im-pər-sis'tənt, adj.* not persistent: not enduring. [Pfx. **im- (in-** (2)).]

impersonal *im-pûr'sən-əl, adj.* not having personality: used only in the third person singular (in English usu. with *it* as subject) (*gram.*): without reference to any particular person: objective, uncoloured by personal feeling. — *v.t.* **imper'sonalise, -ize.** — *n.* **impersonality** (*-al'i-ti*). — *adv.* **imper'sonally.** [Pfx. **im- (in-** (2)).]

impersonate *im-pûr'sən-āt, v.t.* to invest with personality or the bodily substance of a person: to ascribe the qualities of a person to (*obs.*): to personify: to assume the person or character of, esp. on the stage. — *adj.* (*-it, -āt*) personified. — *ns.* **impersonā'tion; imper'-sonātor.** [L. *in*, in, *persōna*, person; see **personate.**]

impertinent *im-pûr'ti-nənt, adj.* not pertaining to the matter in hand: trifling: intrusive: saucy: impudent. — *n.* an impertinent person: one whose presence is interfering or intrusive. — *ns.* **imper'tinence, imper'tinency** that which is impertinent: intrusion: impudence, overforwardness: matter introduced into an affidavit, etc., not pertinent to the matter (*law*). — *adv.* **imper'tinently.** [Pfx. **im- (in-** (2)).]

imperturbable *im-pər-tûr'bə-bl, adj.* that cannot be disturbed or agitated: permanently quiet. — *n.* **imperturb-abil'ity.** — *adv.* **impertur'bably.** — *n.* **imperturbā'tion.** [L. *imperturbābilis* — *in-*, not, *perturbāre*, to disturb; see **perturb.**]

imperviable *im-pûr'vi-ə-bl*, **impervious** *im-pûr'vi-əs, adjs.* not to be penetrated: not easily influenced by ideas, arguments, etc., or moved or upset (with *to*). — *ns.* **imper'viableness, imperviabil'ity, imper'viousness.** — *adv.* **imper'viously.** [Pfx. **im- (in-** (2)).]

impeticos *im-pet'i-kos*, (*Shak.*) *v.t.* a word coined by the fool in *Twelfth Night* (II, iii) perh. meaning *impocket*,

or perh. bestow on (the wearer of) a petticoat.
impetigo *im-pi-tī'gō*, *n.* a skin disease characterised by thickly-set clusters of pustules: — *pl.* **impetigines** (*-tij'i-nēz*), **impetī'gos.** — *adj.* **impetiginous** (*-tij'*). [L. *impetigo* — *impetĕre*, to rush upon, attack.]
impetrate *im'pi-trāt*, *v.t.* to obtain by entreaty or petition. — *n.* **impetrā'tion.** — *adjs.* **im'petrative, im'petrātory.** [L. *impetrāre, -ātum* — *in*, on, *patrāre*, to bring about.]
impetus *im'pi-təs*, *n.* momentum: impulse: incentive: — *pl.* **im'petuses.** — *adj.* **impetuous** (*im-pet'ū-əs*) rushing on with impetus or violence: vehement: acting with headlong energy. — *n.* **impetuosity** (*-os'i-ti*). — *adv.* **impet'uously.** — *n.* **impet'uousness.** [L. *impetus* (pl. *impetūs*) — *in*, into, on, *petĕre*, seek.]
impi *im'pi*, *n.* a body of southern African native warriors. [Zulu.]
impictured *im-pik'chərd*, (*Spens.*) *adj.* painted. [Pfx. **im-** (**in-** (1)).]
impierceable *im-pērs'ə-bl* (*Spens.* **imperceable** *im'-pərsə-bl*), *adj.* incapable of being pierced. [Pfx. **im-** (**in-** (2)).]
impiety *im-pī'ə-ti*, *n.* want of piety or veneration. [L. *impietās, -ātis* — *in*, not; cf. **piety**.]
impignorate *im-pig'nər-āt*, *v.t.* to pledge or pawn. — *n.* **impignorā'tion.** [L. *in*, in, into, *pignus, -ōris, -ĕris*, pledge.]
impinge *im-pinj'*, *v.i.* (with *on, upon, against*) to strike: to encroach. — *v.t.* to drive, strike: — *pr.p.* **imping'ing.** — *n.* **impinge'ment.** — *adj.* **imping'ent.** [L. *impingĕre* — *in*, against, *pangĕre*, to fix, drive in.]
impious *im'pi-əs* (also, esp. U.S., *im-pī'əs*), *adj.* irreverent: wanting in veneration, as for gods, parents, etc. — *adv.* **imp'iously.** [L. *impĭus* — *im-* (*in-*), not, *pĭus*; cf. **pious**.]
impish. See **imp[1]**.
implacable *im-plak'ə-bl, -plāk'* (*Spens.* *im'*), *adj.* not to be appeased: inexorable: irreconcilable. — *ns.* **implac'-ableness, implacabil'ity.** — *adv.* **implac'ably.** [Pfx. **im-** (**in-** (2)).]
implacental *im-plə-sen'tl*, *adj.* having no placenta. [Pfx. **im-** (**in-** (2)).]
implant *im-plänt'*, *v.t.* to engraft: to plant firmly: to fix in: to insert: to instil or inculcate: to plant (ground, etc., with). — *n.* (*im'*) something implanted in body tissue, as a graft, a pellet containing a hormone, a tube containing a radioactive substance. — *n.* **implantā'tion.** [Pfx. **im-** (**in-** (1)).]
implate *im-plāt'*, *v.t.* to put a plate or covering upon: to sheathe. [Pfx. **im-** (**in-** (1)).]
implausible *im-plöz'i-bl*, *adj.* not plausible. — *n.* **implausibil'ity.** [Pfx. **im-** (**in-** (2)).]
impleach *im-plēch'*, (*Shak.*) *v.t.* to intertwine. [Pfx. **im-** (**in-** (1)).]
implead *im-plēd'*, *v.t.* to sue (a person) (*arch.*). — *n.* **implead'er.** [Pfx. **im-** (**in-** (1)).]
impledge *im-plej'*, *v.t.* to pledge. [Pfx. **im-** (**in-** (1)).]
implement *im'pli-mənt*, *n.* a piece of equipment, a requisite: a tool or instrument of labour: fulfilment (*Scots law*). — *v.t.* (often *-ment'*) to give effect to: to fulfil or perform. — *adj.* **implemen'tal** instrumental: effective. — *n.* **implementā'tion** performance, fulfilment: the various steps involved in installing and operating a computer data-processing or control system (*comput.*). [L.L. *implēmentum* — L. *in*, in, *plēre*, to fill.]
implete *im-plēt'*, *v.t.* to fill. — *adj.* replete. — *n.* **impletion** (*-plē'shən*) filling: fulness: fulfilment. [L. *implēre, -ētum* — *in*, in, *plēre*, to fill.]
implex *im'pleks*, *adj.* not simple: complicated. — *n.* (*zool.*) in Arthropoda, an in-turning of the integument for attachment of muscles. — *n.* **implexion** (*im-plek'shən*). — *adj.* **implex'ūous.** [L. *implexus* — *in*, into, *plectĕre*, to twine.]
implicate *im'pli-kāt*, *v.t.* to entwine together: to enfold: to involve: to entangle: to imply: to show to be, to have been, a participator. — *n.* a thing implied. — *adj.* (*-kit*) intertwined. — *n.* **implicā'tion** the act of implicating or implying: entanglement: that which is im-

plied. — *adj.* **im'plicātive** (or *im-plik'ə-tiv*) tending to implicate. — *adv.* **im'plicatively.** — *adj.* **implicit** (*im-plis'it*) implied: relying entirely, unquestioning: entangled, involved (*rare*). — *adv.* **implic'itly.** — *n.* **implic'itness.** [L. *implicāre, -ātum*, also *-ĭtum* — *in*, in, *plicāre, -ātum* or *-itum*, to fold.]
implied, etc. See **imply.**
implode *im-plōd'*, *v.t.* and *v.i.* to burst inwards: to sound by implosion. — *ns.* **implōd'ent** an implosive sound; **Implosion** (*-plō'zhən*) bursting inward: in the formation of voiceless stops, compression of enclosed air by simultaneous stoppage of the mouth parts and the glottis (*phon.*): inrush of air in a suction stop (*phon.*). — *adj.* **implosive** (*-plōs'iv*, or *-plōz'*). — *n.* an implosive consonant: a suction stop or (sometimes) a click. [L. *in*, in, *plōdĕre* (*plaudĕre*), to clap.]
implore *im-plōr', -plör'*, *v.t.* to ask earnestly: to entreat. — Also *v.i.* — *n.* (*Spens.*) entreaty. — *ns.* **implorā'tion;** **implor'ator** (*Shak.*) one who implores or entreats. — *adj.* **imploratory** (*-plor'ə-tə-ri*). — *n.* **implōr'er.** — *adv.* **implōr'ingly** in an imploring manner. [L. *implōrāre*, to invoke with tears — *in*, in, *plōrāre*, to weep.]
implosion, implosive. See **implode.**
implunge *im-plunj'*, *v.t.* to plunge, submerge. — Also (*Spens.*) **emplonge'.** [Pfx. **im-** (**in-** (1)).]
impluvium *im-plōō'vi-əm*, *n.* in ancient Roman houses, the square basin in the atrium that received the rain-water: — *pl.* **implu'via.** [L. *implŭvium* — *in*, in, into, *pluĕre*, to rain.]
imply *im-plī'*, *v.t.* to enfold (*Spens.*): to involve the truth or reality of: to express indirectly: to insinuate: to mean: to signify: — *pr.p.* **imply'ing;** *pa.t.* and *pa.p.* **implied'.** — *adv.* **implī'edly.** [O.Fr. *emplier* — L. *implicāre*.]
impocket *im-pok'it*, *v.t.* to put in the pocket. [Pfx. **im-** (**in-** (1)).]
impolder *im-pōl'dər*, *v.t.* to make a polder of. — Also **empol'der.** [Du. *impolderen*; see **polder.**]
impolite *im-pə-līt'*, *adj.* of unpolished manners: uncivil. — *adv.* **impolite'ly.** — *n.* **impolite'ness.** [Pfx. **im-** (**in-** (2)).]
impolitic *im-pol'i-tik*, *adj.* not politic: inexpedient. — Also (*obs.*) **impolit'ical.** — *n.* **impol'icy.** — *advs.* **impolit'ically** (*rare*); **impol'iticly.** [Pfx. **im-** (**in-** (2)).]
imponderable *im-pon'dər-ə-bl*, *adj.* not able to be weighed or estimated: without weight, immaterial: without sensible weight. — Also *n.* — *ns.* **impon'derableness, imponderabil'ity.** — *n.pl.* **impon'derables** once-supposed fluids without sensible weight, as heat, light, electricity, magnetism: factors in a situation whose influence cannot be gauged. — Also (L.) **imponder-abil'ia.** — *adj.* **impon'derous** weightless: very light. [Pfx. **im-** (**in-** (2)).]
impone *im-pōn'*, *v.t.* and *v.i.* to impose: to lay on: to stake, as a wager (*Shak.* — perh. an error for *impawn*). — *adj.* **impōn'ent** competent to impose an obligation. — *n.* one who imposes. [L. *impōnĕre* — *in*, on, *pōnĕre*, to place.]
import *im-pōrt', -pört'*, *v.t.* to bring in: to bring from abroad: to convey, as a word: to signify: to betoken: to portend: (*impers.; arch.*) to be of consequence to, also to behove. — Also *v.i.* — *n.* **im'port** (formerly *-pört', -pört'*) that which is brought from abroad: meaning: importance: tendency. — *adj.* **import'able** that may be imported or brought into a country. — *ns.* **import'ance** the fact of being important: extent of value or significance: weight, consequence: appearance of dignity: import, significance (*Shak.*): importunity (*Shak.*); **import'ancy** (*Shak.*). — *adj.* **import'ant** of great import or consequence: momentous: pompous: urgent, importunate (*Shak.*). — *adv.* **import'antly.** — *ns.* **importā'tion** the act of importing: a commodity imported; **import'er.** — *adj.* **import'less** (*Shak.*) without consequence. — **invisible imports** such items in a national trade balance as money spent by tourists abroad, etc.; opp. to **visible imports** goods bought from foreign countries by traders. [L. *im-*

portāre, -ātum — in, in, *portāre,* to carry.]
importable *im-pōrt'ə-bl, -pört',* (*Spens. im'*; *obs.*), *adj.*
unbearable: irresistible. [L. *importābilis — im- (in-),*
not, *portāre,* to bear.]
importune *im-pör-tūn', -pör', adj.* inopportune, untimely
(*obs.*): burdensome (*obs.*): importunate: urgent, resistless (*Spens.*). — *v.t.* to be troublesome to (*obs.*): to urge
or crave with troublesome application: to solicit for
immoral purposes, make improper advances to: to
import, signify (*Spens.*; wrongly). — *v.i.* to be importunate. — *ns.* **impor'tunacy** (*Shak. -tūn'*), **import'un-**
ateness. — *adj.* **impor'tunate** (*-it, -āt*) inopportune
(*obs.*): burdensome (*obs.*): troublesomely urgent: pressing: pertinacious. — *v.i.* to solicit pertinaciously. —
advs. **impor'tunately; importune'ly** (or *-pör'*). — *ns.*
importun'er; importun'ing; importun'ity. [L. *impor-*
tūnus, inconvenient — *im- (in-),* not, *portus,* a harbour;
cf. **opportune.**]
impose *im-pōz', v.t.* to place upon something: to lay on:
to enjoin: to set as a burden or task: to set up in or by
authority: to pass off unfairly: to arrange or place in
a chase, as pages of type (*print.*). — *v.i.* (with *on, upon*)
to mislead, deceive: to lay a burden, as by encroaching,
taking undue advantage of one's good nature: to act
with constraining effect. — *n.* (*Shak.*) command,
injunction. — *adj.* **impos'able** capable of being imposed
or laid on. — *n.* **impos'er.** — *adj.* **impos'ing** commanding, impressive: adapted to impress forcibly: specious:
deceptive. — *adv.* **impos'ingly.** — *n.* **impos'ingness.** —
imposing stone (*print.*) a heavy table upon which metal
type is imposed. [Fr. *imposer;* see **compose.**]
imposition *im-pəz-ish'ən, n.* a laying on: laying on of hands
in ordination: a tax, a burden: a deception: a punishment task: the assembling of pages and locking them
into a chase (*print.*). [L. *impositiō, -ōnis — in,* on,
pōnĕre, pŏsitum, to place.]
impossible *im-pos'i-bl, adj.* that cannot be: that cannot
be done or dealt with: that cannot be true: out of the
question: hopelessly unsuitable: beyond doing anything with. — *n.* a person or thing that is impossible.
— *ns.* **imposs'ibilism** belief in or advocacy of an
impracticable policy; **imposs'ibilist; impossibil'ity.**
[Pfx. **im- (in- (2)).**]
impost¹ *im'pōst, n.* a tax, esp. on imports: the weight
carried by a horse in a handicap race (*coll.*). [O.Fr.
impost (Fr. *impôt*) — L. *impōnĕre, impŏsitum,* to lay
on.]
impost² *im'pōst,* (*archit.*) *n.* the upper part of a pillar in
vaults and arches, on which the weight of the building
is laid: a horizontal block resting on uprights. [Fr.
imposte — It. *imposta* — L. *impōnĕre, impŏsitum.*]
imposter. See **impostor.**
imposthume. See **impostume.**
impostor *im-pos'tər, n.* one who assumes a false character
or personates another. — Also **impost'er.** — *n.* **impos'-**
ture (*-chər*) an imposition, fraud. [L.L., — L. *im-*
pōnĕre, impŏsitum, to impose.]
impostume, imposthume *im-pos'tūm,* (*arch.*) *n.* an abscess.
— *v.t.* and *v.i.* **impos't(h)umate.** — *n.* **impost(h)ūmā'-**
tion. — *adj.* **impos't(h)ūmed.** [O.Fr. *impostume* from
aposteme — Gr. *apostēma,* abscess — *apo,* from, and
the root of *histanai,* to set; the form due to confusion
with *posthumous,* which itself is due to confusion.]
imposture. See **impostor.**
impot *im'pot,* (*school slang*) *n.* an imposition.
impotent *im'pə-tənt, adj.* powerless: helpless: without
sexual power: without self-control (*obs.*): ungovernable (*Spens.*). — *ns.* **im'potence, im'potency.** — *adv.*
im'potently. [Pfx. **im- (in- (2)).**]
impound *im-pownd', v.t.* to confine, as in a pound: to
restrain within limits: to hold up in a reservoir: to take
legal possession of. — *adj.* **impound'able.** — *ns.* **im-**
pound'age; impound'er; impound'ment. [Pfx. **im- (in-**
(1)), and **pound².**]
impoverish *im-pov'er-ish, v.t.* to make poor (*lit.* or *fig.*).
— *n.* **impov'erishment.** [From O.Fr. *empovrir, -iss,*
— L. *in,* in, *pauper,* poor.]

impracticable *im-prak'tik-ə-bl, adj.* not able to be done:
not able to be used or traversed: unmanageable (*arch.*).
— *ns.* **impracticabil'ity, imprac'ticableness.** — *adv.*
imprac'ticably. [Pfx. **im- (in- (2)).**]
impractical *im-prak'ti-kl, adj.* unpractical. — *ns.* **imprac-**
ticality (*-kal'*); **imprac'ticalness.** [Pfx. **im- (in- (2)).**]
imprecate *im'pri-kāt, v.t.* to call down by prayer (esp.
something evil): to pray for or to: to invoke evil upon.
— *v.i.* to curse. — *n.* **imprecā'tion.** — *adj.* **im'precatory**
(*-kə-tə-ri,* or *-kā* or *kā'*). [L. *imprecāri — in,* upon,
precāri, -ātus, to pray.]
imprecise *im-pri-sīs', adj.* not precise. — *n.* **imprecis'ion.**
[Pfx. **im- (in- (2)).**]
impregn *im-prēn',* (*Milt.*) *v.t.* to impregnate. — *adj.*
impregnant (*-preg'nənt*) impregnating: impregnated
(*obs.*). — *v.t.* **im'pregnate** to make pregnant: to fecun-
date: to fill or imbue (with the particles or qualities of
another thing): to saturate (also *fig.*). — *n.* **impregnā'-**
tion. [L.L. *impraegnāre, -ātum — in,* in, *praegnāns,*
pregnant.]
impregnable *im-preg'nə-bl, adj.* that cannot be taken:
proof against attack. — *n.* **impregnabil'ity.** — *adv.*
impreg'nably. [Fr. *imprenable* — L. *in-,* not, *pren-*
dĕre, prehendĕre, to take; *g,* a freak of spelling, has
come to be pronounced.]
impregnate. See **impregn.**
impresa *im-prā'zə,* (*obs.*) *n.* an emblematic device, often
with a motto: a motto. — also **imprese** (*im'prēz,* or as
Milt. -prēz'). [It.]
impresario *im-pre-sä'ri-ō,* or *-zä', n.* the manager of an
opera company, etc.: a producer or organiser of
entertainments: a showman: — *pl.* **impresa'rios, impre-**
sa'ri (*-rē*). [It., — *impresa,* enterprise.]
imprescriptible *im-pri-skrip'ti-bl, adj.* not liable to be lost
by prescription, or lapse of time: inalienable. — *n.*
imprescriptibil'ity. [Pfx. **im- (in- (2)).**]
imprese. See **impresa.**
impress¹ *im-pres', v.t.* to press: to apply with pressure,
esp. so as to leave a mark: to mark by pressure: to
produce by pressure: to stamp or print: to fix deeply
in the mind: to affect the mind: to produce a profound
effect upon, or upon the mind of. — *v.i.* to be
impressive, make a good impression. — *ns.* **im'press**
that which is made by pressure: stamp: distinctive
mark; **impressibil'ity.** — *adj.* **impress'ible** susceptible.
— *ns.* **impression** (*im-presh'ən*) the act or result of
impressing: pressure: a difference produced in a thing
by action upon it: a single printing of a book: the effect
of anything on the mind: a profound effect on the
emotions: a vague uncertain memory or inclination to
believe: belief, generally ill-founded: an imperson-
ation; **impressionabil'ity.** — *adj.* **impress'ionable** able
to receive an impression: very susceptible to impressions. — *n.* **impress'ionism** a 19th-century movement
in painting, originating in France, aiming at the realistic representation of the play of light in nature,
purporting to render faithfully what the artist actually
saw, dispensing with the academic rules of composition and colouring (often with *cap.*): any similar
tendency in other arts. — *n.* and *adj.* **impress'ionist** an
exponent of impressionism (often with *cap.*): an entertainer who impersonates people. — *adj.* **impressionis'-**
tic. — *adv.* **impressionist'ically.** — *adj.* **impressive**
(*-pres'*) exerting or tending to exert pressure: capable
of making a deep impression on the mind: solemn. —
adv. **impress'ively.** — *ns.* **impress'iveness; impressure**
(*im-presh'ər; Shak.*) impression. — **be under the im-**
pression to think or believe without certainty. [*im-*
primĕre, -pressum — in, premĕre; see **press¹.**]
impress² *im-pres', v.t.* to force into service, esp. the public
service. — *ns.* **im'press** (*Shak. im-pres'*); **impress'ment**
the act of impressing or seizing for service, esp. in the
navy. [Pfx. **im- (in- (1)),** and **prest²;** cf. **press².**]
impress³, impresse *im'pres,* (*Shak.*) *n.* an impresa.
impress⁴. A variant of **imprest.**
imprest *im'prest, n.* earnest-money: money advanced. —

v.t. **imprest'** to advance on loan. [Pfx. **im-** (**in-** (1)) and **prest**[2].]

imprimatur *im-pri-mā'tǝr, n.* a licence or permission to print a book, etc. [L. *imprīmātur*, let it be printed, subj. pass of *imprimĕre* — *in*, on, *premĕre*, to press.]

imprimis *im-prī'mis, adv.* in the first place. [L. *imprīmis* — *in prīmīs* (abl. pl.), *in*, in, *prīmus*, first.]

imprint *im-print', v.t.* to print: to stamp: to impress: to fix in the mind. — *n.* (*im'print*) that which is imprinted: the name of the publisher, time and place of publication of a book, etc., printed usu. on the title-page: the printer's name on the back of the title-page or at the end of the book. — *n.* **imprint'ing** a learning process in young animals in which their social preferences become restricted to their own species, or a substitute for this. [Pfx. **im-** (**in-** (1)).]

imprison *im-priz'n, v.t.* to put in prison: to shut up: to confine or restrain. — *adj.* **impris'onable** liable to be, or capable of being, imprisoned: (of an offence) likely to lead to imprisonment. — *n.* **impris'onment.** [Pfx. **im-** (**in-** (1)).]

improbable *im-prob'ǝ-bl, adj.* unlikely. — *n.* **improbabil'ity.** — *adv.* **improb'ably.** [Pfx. **im-** (**in-** (2)).]

improbation *im-prō-bā'shǝn, n.* in Scots law, an action for the purpose of declaring some instrument false or forged. — *adj.* **improbative** (-*prob'ǝ-tiv*) disapproving — also **improb'atory.** [Pfx. **im-** (**in-** (2)).]

improbity *im-prōb'i-ti, -prob', n.* want of probity. [Pfx. **im-** (**in-** (2)).]

impromptu *im-promp'tū, adj.* improvised: offhand. — *adv.* without preparation: on the spur of the moment. — *n.* an extempore witticism or speech: an improvised composition: a musical composition with the character of an extemporisation. [L. *impromptū* for *in promptū* (abl.), *in*, in, *promptus*, readiness.]

improper *im-prop'ǝr, adj.* not strictly belonging: not properly so called: not suitable: unfit: unbecoming: unseemly: indecent. — *adv.* **improp'erly.** — *n.* **impröpri'ety.** — **improper fraction** a fraction not less than unity. [L. *im-* (*in-*), not, *proprius*, own.]

impropriate *im-prō'pri-āt, v.t.* to appropriate to private use: to place (ecclesiastical property) in the hands of a layman. — *adj.* (*-lt*) devolved into the hands of a layman. — *ns.* **impröpriā'tion; impröʹpriator** a layman who is in possession of a benefice or its revenues. [L.L. *impropriātus* — L. *in*, in, *proprius*, one's own.]

impropriety. See **improper.**

improve *im-prōōv', v.t.* to turn to good use (*rare*): to make use of, occupy (*U.S.; arch.*): to increase (whether good or ill) (*obs.*): to raise in value (esp. by cultivating or building): to raise in price (*obs.*): to make better. — *v.i.* to increase (*obs.*): to grow in price or value: to grow better: to make progress: to make improvements: to follow up with something better (with *on*). — *ns.* **improvabil'ity, improv'ableness.** — *adj.* **improv'able.** — *adv.* **improv'ably.** — *ns.* **improve'ment** the act of improving: a change for the better: a thing changed, or introduced in changing, for the better: a better thing substituted for or following one not so good (often with *on*); **improv'er** one who, that which, improves: worker who is in part learner: one who sets himself to the improvement of land: a pad or bustle. — *pr.p.* and *adj.* **improv'ing** tending to cause improvement: instructive: edifying: uplifting. — *adv.* **improv'ingly.** — **improve the occasion** to seize an opportunity for edification or other purpose: to draw a moral from what has happened. [A.Fr. *emprower* — O.Fr. *en prou, preu*, into profit.]

improvident *im-prov'i-dǝnt, adj.* not provident or prudent: wanting foresight: thoughtless. — *adj.* **improvided** (*im-prǝ-vī'did*) unprovided: unforeseen (*Spens.*). — *n.* **improv'idence.** — *adv.* **improv'idently.** [Pfx. **im-** (**in-** (2)).]

improvise *im-prō-, -prǝ-vīz', or im', improvisate* *im-prov'i-zāt, vs.t.* to compose and recite, or perform, without preparation: to bring about on a sudden: to make or contrive offhand or in emergency. — *v.i.* to perform extempore: to do anything offhand. (The spelling with *z* is wrong.) — *ns.* **improvīsā'tion** (or *-prov'iz-*) the act of improvising: that which is improvised; **improvisator** (*improv'iz-ā-tǝr,* or *im'prov-īz-*; It. **improvvisatore** *im-prov-vē-sä-tō'rā*); sometimes *fem.* **improv'isātrix** (It. **improvvisatrice** *-trē'chä*) one who improvises: one who composes and performs or speaks without preparation. — *adjs.* **improvisātō'rial** (*-iz-ǝ-*); **improvisatory** (*-iz'* or *-īz'*). — *n.* **improvīs'er.** [Fr. *improviser* — L. *in-*, not, *prōvīsus*, foreseen; see **provide.**]

imprudent *im-prōō'dǝnt, adj.* wanting foresight or discretion: incautious: inconsiderate. — *n.* **impru'dence.** — *adv.* **impru'dently.** [Pfx. **im-** (**in-** (2)).]

impudent *im'pū-dǝnt, adj.* wanting shame or modesty: brazen-faced: shamelessly bold: pert: insolent. — *n.* **im'pudence.** — *adv.* **im'pudently.** — *n.* **impudicity** (*-dis'i-ti*). [L. *im-* (*in-*), not, *pudēns, -entis,* pr.p. of *pudēre,* to be ashamed; and *pudīcus,* modest.]

impugn *im-pūn', v.t.* to oppose: to attack by words or arguments: to call in question. — *adj.* **impugnable** (*-pūn';* distinguished from obs. or rare **impug'nable** unassailable, from L. *in-,* not). — *ns.* **impugn'er; impugn'ment.** [L. *impugnāre* — *in,* against, *pugnāre,* to fight.]

impuissant *im-pū'is-ǝnt, -pū-is', -pwis', -pwēs', (arch.) adj.* powerless. — *n.* **impuiss'ance** (or *-pū';* arch.). [Pfx. **im-** (**in-** (2)).]

impulse *im'puls, n.* the act of impelling: the effect of an impelling force: force suddenly and momentarily communicated: a beat: a single blow, thrust, or wave: a disturbance travelling along a nerve (**nerve impulse**) or a muscle: an outside influence on the mind: a sudden inclination to act. — *n.* **impul'sion** (*-shǝn*) impelling force: instigation. — *adj.* **impuls'ive** having the power of impelling: acting or actuated by impulse: not continuous: given to acting upon impulse. — *adv.* **impuls'ively.** — *ns.* **impuls'iveness; impulsiv'ity.** — *adj.* **impuls'ory.** — **impulse buyer; impulse buying** the buying of goods on a whim rather than because of previous intent. [L. *impulsus,* pressure — *impellĕre*; see **impel.**]

impunity *im-pūn'i-ti, n.* freedom or safety from punishment or ill consequences. [L. *impūnitās, -ātis* — *in,* not, *poena,* punishment.]

impure *im-pūr', adj.* mixed with something else: defiled: unholy: unchaste: unclean materially, morally, or ceremonially. — *adv.* **impure'ly.** — *ns.* **impure'ness, impur'ity.** [Pfx. **im-** (**in-** (2)).]

impurple *im-pûr'pl.* Same as **empurple.**

impute *im-pūt', v.t.* to ascribe (usually evil): to charge: to attribute vicariously (*theol.*): to reckon (*obs.*): to impart (*obs.*). — *adj.* **imput'able** capable of being imputed or charged: open to accusation: attributable. — *ns.* **imput'ableness, imputabil'ity.** — *adv.* **imput'ably.** — *n.* **imputā'tion** the act of imputing or charging: censure: reproach: the reckoning as belonging. — *adj.* **imput'ative** imputed. — *adv.* **imput'atively.** — *n.* **imput'er.** — **imputation system, tax** a method of taxation whereby all of a company's profits (whether distributed or not) are taxed at the same rate. [Fr. *imputer* — L. *imputāre, -ātum* — *in,* in, *putāre,* to reckon.]

imshi, imshy *im'shi, (mil. slang), interj.* go away! [Ar.]

in[1] *in, prep.* expressing the relation of a thing to that which surrounds, encloses, includes, or conditions it, with respect to place, time, or circumstances, or to that which is assumed, held, maintained, or the relation of a right or possession to the person who holds or enjoys it: at: among: into: within: during: consisting of: by way of: because of: by or through: by the medium or method of: with (*obs.*): among the characteristics or possibilities of: wearing: belonging to: being a member of. — *adv.* within: not out: at home: on the spot: in or to a position within or inward: in or into office, parliament, etc.: in favour: in mutual favour: in intimacy: in fashion: in the market: in season: at the bat: as an addition: alight: in pocket. — *n.* a member of the party in office or the side that is having its innings: a re-entrant or inward turn. — *adj.* inward: proceeding inwards: that is fashionable, much in use, as **in'-crowd'**, **in'-word'**, **in'-thing'**: within a small group. — *v.t.* to take in: to enclose: to gather in harvest. — **-in** in composition, indicating a (public) gathering of a group of people in one room, building, etc., orig. as a form of protest (as in *sit-in*, *work-in*), now for any joint purpose (as in *love-in*, *teach-in*). — *adj.* and *adv.* **in'-and-in'** (of breeding) from parents that are near akin: with constant and close interaction. — *n.* a game with four dice. — *adj.* **in'-and-out'** by turns good and bad. — *adjs.* **in'-built** built in; **in'-car** existing within a car; **in'-depth** of a survey, research, etc., detailed or penetrating: thorough, comprehensive, not superficial. — **in'-fighting** fighting or bitter rivalry, between individuals or within a group, that goes on more or less secretly (see also **infighting** — separate article). — *adj.* **in'-flight** provided during an aeroplane flight. — **in'group** a social group of people having the same interests and attitudes. — *adj.* and *adv.* **in'-house'** within a particular company, establishment, etc. — **in'-joke** a joke to be fully appreciated only by members of a particular limited group; **in'-off** (*billiards*) a losing hazard; **in'-patient** one lodged, fed and treated in a hospital. — *adjs.* **in'-ser'vice** carried out while continuing with one's ordinary employment as *in-service training:* (of a machine's reliability, etc.) while the machine is operating; **in'shore** close to the shore: moving towards the shore. — **in'-store** provided within a shop. — **in'-tray** a shallow container for letters, etc., still to be dealt with. — **be in it** (*Austr. coll.*) to participate; **in as far as, in so far as, insofar as** to the extent that; **in as much as, inasmuch as** considering that; **in for** doomed to receive (esp. unpleasant consequences): involved to the extent of: entered for: (see also **go**); **in for it** in for trouble: committed to a certain course; **in it** in enjoyment of success: in the running; **in itself** intrinsically, apart from relations; **in on** (*slang*) participating in; **ins and outs** (or **outs and ins**) turning this way and that: nooks and corners: the whole details of any matter: those who repeatedly enter and leave; **in that** for the reason that; **in with** friendly with, associating much with: enjoying the favour of; **nothing in it** no truth, no importance, no difficulty in the matter: no important difference — six of one and half a dozen of the other. [O.E. *in;* Du., Ger. *in*, O.N. *ī*; W. *yn*, L. *in*, Gr. *en*. O.E. also had *innan*, within; cf. O.H.G. *inanna*, Sw. *innan*.]

in² *in*, (*Spens.*) *n.* See **inn**.

-in *-in*, (*chem.*, etc.) noun-forming *suff.* usu. indicating (1) a neutral substance such as a protein, fat or glycoside, as *albumin, stearin, insulin*, (2) certain enzymes, as *pepsin*, (3) an antibiotic or other pharmaceutical production, as *penicillin, aspirin*. [Variant of **-ine¹**.]

in- *in-, pfx.*, (1) in words derived from L. and O.E., used to form verbs with the sense in, into; sometimes used to form other parts of speech with this sense; sometimes used as an intensive or almost meaningless pfx.; (2) in words derived from L., used to form negatives.

inability *in-ə-bil'i-ti, n.* want of sufficient power: incapacity. [Pfx. **in-** (2).]

in absentia *in ab-sensh'yə, ab-sent'i-ä,* (L.) in absence.

inabstinence *in-ab'sti-nəns, n.* want of abstinence. [Pfx. **in-** (2).]

in abstracto *in ab-strak'tō,* (L.) in the abstract.

inaccessible *in-ak-ses'i-bl,* or *-ək-, adj.* not to be reached, obtained, or approached. — *ns.* **inaccessibil'ity, inaccess'ibleness.** — *adv.* **inaccess'ibly.** [Pfx. **in-** (2).]

inaccurate *in-ak'ū-rit, adj.* not accurate: incorrect: erroneous. — *n.* **inacc'uracy** (*-ə-si*) want of exactness: mistake. — *adv.* **inacc'urately.** [Pfx. **in-** (2).]

inactive *in-akt'iv, adj.* not active: inert: having no power to move: sluggish: idle: lazy: having no effect: not showing any action (*chem.*): not rotating the plane of polarised light. — *n.* **inac'tion** absence of action: idleness: rest. — *v.t.* **inact'ivate** to render inactive. — *n.* **inactiva'tion.** — *adv.* **inact'ively.** — *n.* **inactiv'ity**

inaction: inertness: idleness. [Pfx. **in-** (2).]

inadaptable *in-ə-dap'tə-bl, adj.* that cannot be adapted. — *n.* **inadaptā'tion** (*-ad-*). — *adj.* **inadap'tive.** [Pfx. **in-** (2).]

inadequate *in-ad'i-kwit, adj.* insufficient: short of what is required: incompetent. — Also *n.* — *ns.* **inad'equacy** (*-kwə-si*), **inad'equateness** insufficiency. — *adv.* **inad'equately.** [Pfx. **in-** (2).]

inadmissible *in-əd-mis'i-bl, adj.* not allowable. — *n.* **inadmissibil'ity.** — *adv.* **inadmiss'ibly.** [Pfx. **in-** (2).]

inadvertent *in-əd-vûrt'ənt, adj.* inattentive: unintentional. — *ns.* **inadvert'ence, inadvert'ency** negligence: oversight. — *adv.* **inadvert'ently.** [Pfx. **in-** (2).]

inadvisable *in-əd-vī'zə-bl, adj.* not advisable, unwise. — **unadvisable** (q.v.) was formerly preferred and still is by some. — *ns.* **inadvisabil'ity, inadvis'ableness.** [Pfx. **in-** (2).]

inaidable *in-ād'ə-bl,* (*Shak.*) *adj.* that cannot be aided. [Pfx. **in-** (2).]

inalienable *in-āl'yən-ə-bl, -i-ən-ə-bl, adj.* not capable of being transferred or removed. — *n.* **inalienabil'ity.** — *adv.* **inal'ienably.** [Pfx. **in-** (2).]

inalterable, -ability. Same as **unalterable,** etc.

inamorata *in-am-o-rä'tə, n. fem.* a woman in love or beloved: — *masc.* **inamora'to:** — *pl.* **inamora'tos.** [It. *innamorata, -to* — L.L. *inamorāre*, to cause to love — L. *in*, in, *amor*, love.]

inane *in-ān', adj.* empty, void: vacuous: senseless: characterless. — *n.* the void of space. — *adv.* **inane'ly.** — *ns.* **inane'ness; inanition** (*in-ə-nish'ən*) exhaustion from want of food; **inanity** (*in-an'i-ti*) senselessness: mental vacuity: emptiness: an insipid empty-headed utterance. [L. *inānis*.]

inanimate *in-an'i-mit, -d -māt-id, adjs.* without animation: without life: dead: spiritless: dull. — *ns.* **inan'imateness, inanimā'tion.** [Pfx. **in-** (2).]

inappeasable *in-ə-pēz'ə-bl, adj.* that cannot be appeased. [Pfx. **in-** (2).]

inappellable *in-ə-pel'ə-bl, adj.* incapable of being appealed against or challenged. [Pfx. **in-** (2); see **appeal**.]

inappetent *in-ap'i-tənt, adj.* lacking desire. — *ns.* **inapp'etence, inapp'etency.** [Pfx. **in-** (2).]

inapplicable *in-ap'lik-ə-bl, in-əp-lik', adj.* not applicable. — *n.* **inapplicabil'ity.** [Pfx. **in-** (2).]

inapposite *in-ap'ə-zit, adj.* not apposite, suitable, or pertinent. — *adv.* **inapp'ositely.** — *n.* **inapp'ositeness.** [Pfx. **in-** (2).]

inappreciable *in-ə-prē'shə-bl, -shyə-bl, adj.* too small or slight to be noticed, or to be important: priceless (*arch.*). — *n.* **inappreciation** (*-shi-ā'shən*). — *adj.* **inapprē'ciative** (*-shi-ə-tiv,* or *-shi-ā-tiv*) not valuing justly or at all. [Pfx. **in-** (2).]

inapprehensible *in-ap-ri-hen'si-bl, adj.* not apprehensible or intelligible. — *n.* **inapprehen'sion.** — *adj.* **inapprehen'sive.** [Pfx. **in-** (2).]

inapproachable *in-ə-prōch'ə-bl, adj.* unapproachable: inaccessible. — *adv.* **inapproach'ably.** [Pfx. **in-** (2).]

inappropriate *in-ə-prō'pri-it, adj.* not appropriate, not suitable. — *adv.* **inappro'priately.** — *n.* **inappro'priateness.** [Pfx. **in-** (2).]

inapt *in-apt', adj.* not apt: unfit, or unqualified. — *ns.* **inapt'itude, inapt'ness** unfitness, awkwardness. — *adv.* **inapt'ly.** [Pfx. **in-** (2).]

inarable *in-ar'ə-bl, adj.* not arable. [Pfx. **in-** (2).]

inarch *in-ärch', (rare) v.t.* to graft by uniting without separating from the original stem. — Also **enarch'.** [Pfx. **in-** (1).]

inarm *in-ärm', v.t.* to embrace. [Pfx. **in-** (1).]

inarticulate *in-är-tik'ū-lit, adj.* not jointed or hinged: not uttered with the distinct sounds of spoken language: indistinctly uttered or uttering: incapable of clear and fluent expression. — *n.* **inartic'ulacy.** — *adv.* **inartic'ulately.** — *ns.* **inartic'ulateness, inarticulā'tion** indistinctness of sounds in speaking. [Pfx. **in-** (2).]

in articulo mortis *in ärt-ik'ū-lō mör'tis, ärt-ik'ōō-lō,* (L.) at the point of death.

inartificial *in-ärt-i-fish'əl, adj.* not done by art: simple. —

adv. **inartific'ially.** [Pfx. **in-** (2).]
inartistic, -al *in-är-tis'tik, -əl, adjs.* not artistic: deficient in appreciation of art. — *adv.* **inartis'tically.** [Pfx. **in-** (2).]
inasmuch *in-az-much', -əz-.* See **in**[1].
inattentive *in-ə-ten'tiv, adj.* careless: not fixing the mind to attention: neglectful. — *ns.* **inatten'tion, inatten'-tiveness.** — *adv.* **inatten'tively.** [Pfx. **in-** (2).]
inaudible *in-öd'i-bl, adj.* not able to be heard. — *ns.* **inaudibil'ity, inaud'ibleness.** — *adv.* **inaud'ibly.** [Pfx. **in-** (2).]
inaugurate *in-ö'gūr-āt, v.t.* to induct formally into an office: to cause to begin: to make a public exhibition of for the first time. — *adj.* **inau'gural** pertaining to, or done at, an inauguration. — *n.* an inaugural address. — *ns.* **inaugurā'tion; inau'gurātor.** — *adj.* **inau'-guratory** (-ə-tər-i). [L. *inaugurāre, -ātum,* to inaugurate with taking of the auspices; see **augur.**]
inaurate *in-ö'rāt,* (*rare*) *adj.* gilded: having a golden lustre. [L. *inaurāre, -ātum,* to gild — *in,* in, on, *aurum,* gold.]
inauspicious *in-ö-spish'əs, adj.* not auspicious: ill-omened: unlucky. — *adv.* **inauspic'iously.** — *n.* **inauspic'iousness.** [Pfx. **in-** (2).]
inauthentic *in-ö-then'tik, adj.* not authentic: not genuine: untrue. [Pfx. **in-** (2).]
in banco regis *in bang'kō rē'jis, rā'gis,* (L.L.) in the King's Bench.
inbeing *in'bē-ing, n.* inherent existence: inherence: inner nature. [Pfx. **in-** (1).]
inbent *in'bent, adj.* bent inwards. [Pfx. **in-** (1).]
in-between *in-bi-twēn', adj.* intervening: intermediate. — *n.* an interval: an intermediary: any thing or person that is intermediate.
in bianco *in byang'kō, bē-äng'kō,* (It.) in blank, in white.
inboard *in'bōrd, -börd, adv.* and *adj.* within the hull or interior of a ship: toward or nearer to the centre. [Pfx. **in-** (1).]
inborn *in'börn, adj.* born in or with one: innate: implanted by nature. [Pfx. **in-** (1).]
inbreak *in'brāk,* (*rare*) *n.* a violent rush in: irruption. [Pfx. **in-** (1).]
inbreathe *in-brēdh', in'brēdh, v.t.* to breathe in. [Pfx. **in-** (1).]
inbreed *in'brēd, in-brēd', v.t.* to breed or generate within: to breed in-and-in: — *pa.p.* and *adj.* **in'bred** innate: bred in-and-in. — *n.* **in'breeding.** [Pfx. **in-** (1).]
inbring *in-bring',* (*obs.*) *v.t.* to bring in: to bring into court. — *pa.p.* and *adj.* **inbrought'.** — *n.* **in'bringing.** [Pfx. **in-** (1).]
inburning *in-bûrn'ing,* (*Spens.*) *adj.* burning within. [Pfx. **in-** (1).]
inburst *in'bûrst,* (*rare*) *n.* an irruption. [Pfx. **in-** (1).]
inby, inbye *in-bī',* (*Scot.*) *adv.* toward the interior: near: near the house: towards the coal-face (*mining*). — Also *adj.* [Pfx. **in-** (1).]
Inca *ing'kə, n.* an Indian of Peru: a member of the old royal family of Peru: a Peruvian king or emperor. — Also *adj.* [Quechua, prince.]
incage. See **encage.**
incalculable *in-kal'kū-lə-bl, adj.* not calculable or able to be reckoned: too great to calculate: unpredictable. — *ns.* **incalculabil'ity, incal'culableness.** — *adv.* **incal'cul-ably.** [Pfx. **in-** (2).]
incalescent *in-ka-les'ənt,* or *-kə-, adj.* growing warm. — *n.* **incalesc'ence.** [L. *incalēscēns, -entis,* pr.p. of *in-calēscēre* — *in,* in, *calēscēre,* inceptive of *calēre,* to be warm.]
in-calf *in-käf', adj.* pregnant (with calf). [**in**[1], **calf**[1].]
in camera. See **camera.**
incandesce *in-kan-des', v.i.* to be luminous by heat. — *n.* **incandesc'ence** a white heat. — *adj.* **incandesc'ent** white-hot. — *n.* **incandescent lamp** one whose light is pro-duced by heating something to white heat, as a filament resisting an electric current in a glow-lamp, or a mantle heated by a flame. [L. *in,* in, *candēscēre* — *candēre,* to glow.]
incantation *in-kan-tā'shən, n.* a formula of words said or

sung for purposes of enchantment: the use of spells. — *n.* **in'cantator.** — *adj.* **incan'tatory** (-tə-tə-ri). [L. *incantāre,* to sing a magical formula over.]
incapable *in-kā'pə-bl, adj.* not capable: unable to receive or take in (*obs.*): unable (with *of*): incompetent: help-lessly drunk: disqualified. — *n.* an incompetent person: one who is helplessly drunk. — *n.* **incapabil'ity.** — *adv.* **incā'pably.** [Pfx. **in-** (2).]
incapacious *in-kə-pā'shəs, adj.* not large, narrow: of small capacity. — *n.* **incapā'ciousness.** — *v.t.* **incapacitate** (-*pas'*) to disable: to make unfit (for): to disqualify legally. — *ns.* **incapacitā'tion** a disqualifying; **incapac'-ity** want of capacity: inability: disability: legal disqual-ification. [L. *incapāx, -ācis.*]
Incaparina *in-kap-ər-ē'nə, n.* a high-protein dietary sup-plement developed by the *I*nstitute of *N*utrition of *C*entral *A*merica and *P*anama. [*I.N.C.A.P* and *-arina* — Sp. *fariña,* powdered manioc — L. *farina,* flour.]
in capite *in kap'it-ē, kap'it-e,* (L.L.) in chief: holding or held immediately of the crown.
incapsulate *in-kap'sūl-āt, v.t.* to enclose as in a capsule: to enclose (a modifying element) between other ele-ments of a word. [Pfx. **in-** (1).]
incarcerate *in-kär'sər-āt, v.t.* to imprison: to confine. — *n.* **incarcerā'tion** imprisonment: obstinate constriction or strangulation (*surg.*). [L. *in,* in, *carcer,* a prison.]
incardinate *in-kär'di-nāt, v.t.* to attach as a cardinal part, as a priest to his church. — *adj.* Sir Andrew Aguecheek's blunder for *incarnate* (*Twelfth Night* V, i). [L. *in,* in, into, *cardo, -inis,* a hinge.]
incarnadine *in-kär'nə-dīn, -din, v.t.* to dye red. — *adj.* carnation-coloured: flesh-colour: blood-red. [Fr. *in-carnadin* — It. *incarnadino,* carnation, flesh-colour.]
incarnate *in-kär'nāt,* or *in', v.t.* to embody in flesh, give human form to: to personify (*fig.*). — *v.i.* to form flesh, heal. — *adj.* (-*kär'nit, -nat*) invested with flesh: per-sonified. — *n.* **incarnā'tion** (often with *cap.*) the act of embodying in flesh, esp. of Christ: an incarnate form: manifestation, visible embodiment: the process of healing, or forming new flesh (*surg.*) [L.L. *incarnāre, -ātum* — L. *in,* in, *carō, carnis,* flesh.]
incase, incasement. See **encase, encasement.**
incatenation *in-kat-i-nā'shən, n.* harnessing: chaining to-gether: linking. [L. *in, catēna,* chain.]
incautious *in-kö'shəs, adj.* not cautious or careful. — *ns.* **incau'tion, incau'tiousness.** — *adv.* **incau'tiously.** [Pfx. **in-** (2).]
incave. See **encave.**
incavo *in-kä'vō, n.* the incised part in an intaglio: — *pl.* **inca'vi** (*-vē*). [It., — L. *in, cavus,* hollow.]
incede *in-sēd',* (*rare*), *v.i.* to advance majestically. — *adv.* **incēd'ingly.** [L. *incēdēre;* see Virgil, *Aeneid* I, 46.]
incendiary *in-sen'di-ər-i, n.* one who maliciously sets fire to property: one who inflames passions or promotes strife: an incendiary bomb. — *adj.* relating to incen-diarism: adapted or used for setting buildings, etc., on fire: tending to excite strife. — *n.* **incen'diarism.** — **incendiary bomb** a bomb containing a highly in-flammable substance and designed to burst into flames on striking its objective. [L. *incendiārius* — *in-cendium* — *incendēre,* to kindle.]
incendivity *in-sen-div'i-ti, n.* the power of causing ignition. [L. *incendēre,* to set on fire.]
incense[1] *in-sens', v.t.* to kindle (*obs.*): to inflame with anger: to incite, urge. — *ns.* **incense'ment** (*Shak.*) anger; **incens'or** instigator: inciter. [O.Fr. *incenser* — L. *incendēre, incēnsum,* to kindle.]
incense[2] *in'sens, n.* material burned or volatilised to give fragrant fumes, esp. in religious rites — usu. a mixture of resins and gums, etc. (olibanum, benzoin, styrax, cascarilla bark): the fumes so obtained: any pleasant smell: homage, adulation (*fig.*). — *v.t.* to perfume or fumigate with incense: to offer incense to. — *ns.* **in'censer, in'censor** (or *-sens'*) a burner or offerer of incense: a flatterer; **in'censory** (or *-sens'*) a censer or thurible. — **in'cense-boat** a boat-shaped vessel for

For other sounds see detailed chart of pronunciation.

feeding a censer with incense. — *adj.* **in'cense-breathing** exhaling fragrance. — **in'cense-burner** a stationary vessel for burning incense. [O.Fr. *encens* — L. *incēnsum* — *incendĕre*, to set on fire.]

incentive *in-sent'iv*, *adj.* inciting, encouraging: igniting (*Milt.*). — *n.* that which incites to action. [L. *incentīvus*, striking up a tune — *incinĕre* — *in*, in, *canĕre*, to sing.]

incentre *in'sen-tər*, *n.* the centre of the inscribed circle or sphere. [Pfx. **in-** (1).]

incept *in-sept'*, *v.t.* to begin (*obs.*): to take into the body. — *v.i.* at Cambridge, to complete the taking of a master's or doctor's degree. — *n.* **incep'tion** beginning. — *adj.* **incep'tive** beginning or marking the beginning: inchoative (*gram.*). — *n.* (*gram.*) an inchoative verb. — *n.* **incep'tor.** [L. *incipĕre*, *inceptum*, to begin — *in*, in, on, *capĕre*, to take.]

incertain *in-sûr'tən*, *adj.* (*Shak.*) uncertain. — *ns.* **incer'tainty** (*Shak.*), **incer'titude.** [Pfx. **in-** (2).]

incessant *in-ses'ənt*, *adj.* uninterrupted: continual. - *n.* **incess'ancy.** — *adv.* **incess'antly** unceasingly: immediately (*obs.*). — *n.* **incess'antness.** [L. *incessāns*, *-antis* — *in-*, not, *cessāre*, to cease.]

incest *in'sest*, *n.* sexual intercourse within the prohibited degrees of kindred. — *adj.* **incest'ūous** pertaining to, or characterised by, incest; turned inward on itself, or of, or within, a small closely-knit group (*fig.*). — *adv.* **incest'uously.** — *n.* **incest'uousness.** [L. *incestum* — *in-*, not, *castus*, chaste.]

inch[1] *inch*, *insh*, *n.* the twelfth part of a foot, equal to 2·54 cm.: the amount of e.g. rainfall that will cover a surface to the depth of one inch (now measured in millimetres): the amount of atmospheric pressure needed to balance the weight of a column of mercury one inch high (now measured in millibars): proverbially, a small distance or degree: (in *pl.*) stature. — *v.t.* and *v.i.* to move by slow degrees. — *adj.* **inched** containing inches: marked with inches. — *adv.* **inch'meal** inch by inch. — **inch'= tape** a measuring tape divided into inches; **inch'-worm** a looper caterpillar. — **at an inch** (*Shak.*) ready at hand; **by inches, inch by inch** by small degrees; **every inch** entirely, thoroughly; **within an inch of** very close to; **within an inch of someone's life** to the point where there is danger of death. [O.E. *ynce*, an inch — L. *uncia*, a twelfth part; cf. **ounce**[1].]

inch[2] *insh*, (*Scot.*) *n.* an island: a low-lying meadow beside a river. [Gael. *innis*, island.]

incharitable *in-char'it-ə-bl*, (*Shak.*) *adj.* uncharitable. [Pfx. **in-** (2).]

inchase *in-chās'*. Same as **enchase.**

inchoate *in-kō'āt*, *in'kō-āt*, *adj.* only begun: unfinished, rudimentary: not established. — *v.t.* (*arch.*) (*in'*) to begin. — *adv.* **inchoately** (*-kō'*, or *in'*). — *n.* **inchoā'tion** beginning: rudimentary state. — *adj.* **inchoative** (*in-kō'-ə-tiv* or *in-kō-ā'tiv*) incipient: denoting the beginning of an action, inceptive (*gram.*). — *n.* (*gram.*) an inchoative verb. [L. *inchoāre* (for *incohāre*), *-ātum*, to begin.]

inchpin *inch'*, *insh'pin*, (*obs.*) *n.* a deer's sweetbread. [Perh. **inch**[1], **pin.**]

incident *in'si-dənt*, *adj.* falling upon something: liable to occur: naturally belonging (to): consequent. — *n.* that which happens: an event: a subordinate action: an episode: that which naturally belongs to or is consequent on something else: a minor event showing hostility and threatening more serious trouble: a brief violent action, e.g. a raid, a bomb explosion. — *n.* **in'cidence** the frequency or range of occurrence: the fact or manner of falling: bearing or onus, as of a tax: the falling of a ray on a surface: the falling of a point on a line, or a line on a plane (*geom.*). — *adj.* **incidental** (*-dent'l*) incident: striking or impinging: liable to occur: naturally attached: accompanying: concomitant: occasional, casual. — *n.* anything that occurs incidentally. — *adv.* **incident'ally** in an incidental way: (*loosely*) by the way, parenthetically, as a digression. — *n.* **incident'alness.** — **incidental music** music accompanying the action of a play; **incident centre, office, room** a temporary establishment set up near the scene of a crime, disaster, or unrest, etc., by the police or army in order to collect information and monitor the situation. — **angle of incidence** the angle between an incident ray and the normal to the surface it falls on. [L. *incĭdēns*, *-entis* — *in*, on, *cadĕre*, to fall.]

incinerate *in-sin'ər-āt*, *v.t.* to reduce to ashes. — *ns.* **incinerā'tion; incin'erātor** a furnace for consuming anything. [L. *incinerāre*, *-ātum* — *in*, in, *cinis, cineris*, ashes.]

incipient *in-sip'i-ənt*, *adj.* beginning: nascent. — *ns.* **incip'- ience, incip'iency.** — *adv.* **incip'iently.** [L. *incipiēns*, *-entis*, pr.p. of *incipĕre*, to begin.]

incipit *in-sip'-it*, *in-kip'it*, (L.) (here) begins (commonly used as an introduction in mediaeval manuscripts).

incise *in-sīz'*, *v.t.* to cut into: to cut or gash: to engrave. — *adjs.* **incised'** cut: engraved: cut to about the middle (*bot.*); **incīs'iform** shaped like an incisor tooth. — *n.* **incision** (*in-sizh'ən*) the act of cutting in, esp. (*surg.*) into the body: a cut: a gash: a notch: trenchancy. — *adj.* **incisive** (*-sīs'*) having the quality of cutting in: trenchant: acute: sarcastic. — *adv.* **inci'sively.** — *ns.* **inci'siveness; incisor** (*-sīz'ər*) a cutting or foretooth. — *adjs.* **incisorial** (*-sis-ō'ri-əl*, *-sīz-*, *-ō'*), **incisory** (*-sīs'*, *-sīz'ər-i*). — *n.* **incisure** (*-sizh'ər*) a cut, incision. [Fr. *inciser* — L. *incīdĕre*, *incīsum* — *in*, into, *caedĕre*, to cut.]

incite *in-sīt'*, *v.t.* to move to action: to instigate. — *ns.* **incitant** (*in'sit-ənt*, *in-sīt'ənt*) that which incites: a stimulant; **incitā'tion** (*-sit-*, *-sīt-*) the act of inciting or rousing: an incentive. — *adj.* and *n.* **incitative** (*-sīt'ə-tiv*). — *ns.* **incite'ment; incit'er.** — *adv.* **incit'ingly.** [Fr., — L. *incitāre* — *in*, in, *citāre*, to rouse — *ciēre*, to put in motion.]

incivil *in-siv'il*, *adj.* (*Shak.*) uncivil. — *n.* **incivil'ity** want of civility or courtesy: impoliteness: an act of discourtesy (in this sense *pl.* **incivil'ities**). [Pfx. **in-** (2).]

incivism *in'siv-izm*, *n.* neglect of duty as a citizen, conduct unbecoming a good citizen. [Fr. *incivisme*.]

inclasp *in-kläsp'*. Same as **enclasp.**

incle. See **inkle**[1].

inclement *in-klem'ənt*, *adj.* severe: stormy: harsh. — *n.* **inclem'ency.** — *adv.* **inclem'ently.** [Pfx. **in-** (2).]

incline *in-klīn'*, *v.i.* to lean forward or downward: to bow or bend: to deviate or slant: to slope: to tend: to be disposed: to have some slight desire. — *v.t.* to cause to bend downwards: to turn: to cause to deviate: to slope: to tilt: to direct: to dispose. — *n.* (*in'klīn, in-klīn'*) a slope: a sloping tunnel or shaft (*min.*). — *adj.* **inclīn'able** leaning, capable of being tilted or sloped: tending: somewhat disposed: favourably disposed. — *ns.* **inclīn'ableness; inclinā'tion** (*in-klin-*) the act of inclining: a bend or bow: a slope or tilt: a deviation: angle with the horizon or with any plane or line: tendency: disposition of mind: natural aptness: favourable disposition, preference, affection. — *adj.* **inclinā'tional.** — *n.* **inclinato'rium** the dipping-needle. — *adjs.* **inclīn'atory; inclined'** bent: sloping: oblique: having a tendency: disposed. — *n.* **inclīn'ing** inclination: side, party (*Shak.*). — *n.* **inclinom'eter** (*-klin-*) instrument for measuring slopes (clinometer), the magnetic dip (dipping-needle), or the inclination of the axis of an aeroplane. — **inclined plane** one of the mechanical powers, a slope or plane up which one can raise a weight one could not lift. [L. *inclīnāre*, to bend towards — *in*, into, *clīnāre*, to lean.]

inclip *in-klip'*, (*Shak.*) *v.t.* to embrace, enfold. [Pfx. **in-** (1).]

inclose, inclosure. See **enclose.**

include *in-klōōd'*, *v.t.* to enclose: to comprise as a part: to classify, or reckon as part: to take in: to conclude (*Shak.*). — *adj.* **includ'ed** enclosed: comprised: not protruding (*bot.*). — *prep.* (or *pr.p.* merging in *prep.*) **includ'ing** with the inclusion of. — *adj.* **includ'ible.** — *n.* **inclusion** (*-klōō'zhən*) the act of including: that which is included: a foreign body enclosed in a crystal, or the like. — *adj.* **inclusive** (*-klōō'siv*) shutting in: enclosing: comprehensive: including everything: comprehending the stated limit or extremes, including (with *of*): included (*obs.* or *loose*). — *adv.* **inclu'sively.** — **inclusion body** (*med.*) a particulate body found in the cells of tissue infected with a virus; **inclusive transcription** any phonetic transcription admitting of more than one pronunciation of the transcribed words. — **include in, out** (*coll.*) to include, exclude. [L. *inclūdĕre, inclūsum* — *in*, in, *claudĕre*, to shut.]

incoagulable *in-kō-ag'ū-lə-bl, adj.* incapable of coagulation. [Pfx. **in-** (2).]

incoercible *in-kō-ûrs'i-bl, adj.* that cannot be coerced: that cannot be liquefied by pressure. [Pfx. **in-** (2).]

incog *in-kog', adv.* an abbreviation for **incognito.**

incogitable *in-koj'i-tə-bl, adj.* unthinkable. — *ns.* **incogitabil'ity, incog'itancy.** — *adjs.* **incog'itant** unthinking: without power of thought; **incog'itātive.** [L. *in-*, not, *cōgitāre*, to think.]

incognisable, incognizable *in-kog'niz-ə-bl,* or *in-kon'iz-ə-bl, adj.* that cannot be known or distinguished. — *adj.* **incog'nisant, incog'nizant** not cognisant. — *ns.* **incog'nisance, incog'nizance** failure to recognise; **incognoscibil'ity** (*-kog-nos-i-*). — *adj.* **incognosc'ible.** [See **cognition, cognosce, recognise.**]

incognito *in-kog'ni-tō, in-kog-nē'tō, adj.* unknown, unidentified: disguised: under an assumed title. — *adv.* under an assumed name: with concealment, or feigned concealment, of identity. — *n.* a man unknown, unidentified, or disguised (*fem.* **incognita**): concealment, real or feigned: — *pl.* **incognitos.** [It., — L. *incognitus* — *in-*, not, *cognitus*, known — *cognōscĕre*, to recognise, come to know.]

incognizable, etc., **incognoscible,** etc. See **incognisable.**

incoherent *in-kō-hēr'ənt, adj.* not coherent: loose: rambling. — *ns.* **incohēr'ence, -ency.** — *adv.* **incohēr'ently.** — *n.* **incohē'sion.** — *adj.* **incohē'sive** (*-siv*). [Pfx. **in-** (2).]

incombustible *in-kəm-bust'i-bl, adj.* incapable of combustion. — *ns.* **incombustibil'ity, incombust'ibleness.** — *adv.* **incombust'ibly.** [Pfx. **in-** (2).]

income *in'kum, in'kəm, ing'kəm, n.* coming in, advent (*Shak.*): that which comes in: profit, or interest from anything: revenue: a disease coming without known cause (*Scot.*). — *n.* **incomer** (*in'kum-ər*) one who comes in: one who takes possession of a farm, house, etc., or who comes to live in a place, not having been born there. — *adj.* **in'coming** coming in: accruing: ensuing, next to follow. — *n.* the act of coming in: revenue. — **incomes policy** a government policy of curbing inflation by controlling wages; **income tax** a tax directly levied on income or on income over a certain amount. — **negative income tax** a type of Government subsidy in which low-paid workers are paid an additional sum instead of having tax deducted from their wages. [Pfx. **in-** (1).]

in commendam. See **commend.**

incommensurable *in-kəm-en'shə-rə-bl, -shōō-, adj.* having no common measure: incommensurate. — *n.* a quantity that has no common measure with another, esp. with rational numbers. — *ns.* **incommensurabil'ity, incommen'surableness.** — *adv.* **incommen'surably.** — *adj.* **incommen'surate** disproportionate: not adequate: incommensurable. — *adv.* **incommen'surately.** — *n.* **incommen'surateness.** [Pfx. **in-** (2).]

incommiscible *in-kəm-is'i-bl, adj.* that cannot be mixed together. [L. *in-*, not, *commiscĕre*, to mix.]

incommode *in-kəm-ōd', v.t.* to cause trouble or inconvenience to. — *adj.* **incommō'dious** inconvenient: (of e.g. a house) rather small: troublesome (*obs.*): unsuitable (with *to, for*; *obs.*). — *adv.* **incommō'diously.** — *ns.* **incommō'diousness; incommodity** (*-od'*) inconvenience: anything that causes inconvenience. [Fr. *incommoder* — L. *incommodāre* — *in-*, not, *commodus*, commodious.]

incommunicable *in-kəm-ūn'i-kə-bl, adj.* that cannot be communicated or imparted to others. — *ns.* **incommu-**

nicabil'ity, incommun'icableness. — *adv.* **incommun'-icably.** — *adj.* **incommun'icative** uncommunicative. — *adv.* **incommun'icatively.** — *n.* **incommun'icativeness.** [Pfx. **in-** (2).]

incommunicado *in-kəm-ūn-i-kä'dō, adj.* and *adv.* without means of communication: in solitary confinement. — Also **incomunica'do.** [Sp. *incomunicado.*]

incommutable *in-kəm-ūt'ə-bl, adj.* that cannot be commuted or exchanged. — *ns.* **incommutabil'ity, incommut'ableness.** — *adv.* **incommut'ably.** [Pfx. **in-** (2).]

incomparable *in-kom'pər-ə-bl, adj.* not admitting comparison: matchless. — *ns.* **incomparabil'ity, incom'parableness.** — *adv.* **incom'parably.** — *adj.* **incompared** (*in-kom-pār'ed; Spens.*) peerless. [Pfx. **in-** (2).]

incompatible *in-kəm-pat'i-bl, adj.* not consistent: contradictory: incapable of existing together in harmony or at all: incapable of combination, co-operation, functioning together: mutually intolerant or exclusive: irreconcilable. — *n.* a thing incompatible with another: (in *pl.*) things which cannot co-exist. — *ns.* **incompatibil'ity** the state of being incompatible: an incompatible feature, element, etc.: a difference, usu. physiological, which prevents completion of fertilisation (*bot.*): a difference in physiological properties between a host and parasite which limits the development of the latter (*bot.*); **incompat'ibleness.** — *adv.* **incompat'ibly.** [Pfx. **in-** (2).]

incompetent *in-kom'pi-tənt, adj.* wanting adequate powers: unable to function: wanting the proper legal qualifications: grossly deficient in ability for one's work. — *n.* an incompetent person. — *ns.* **incom'-petence, incom'petency.** — *adv.* **incom'petently.** [Pfx. **in-** (2).]

incomplete *in-kəm-plēt', adj.* imperfect: unfinished: wanting calyx, corolla, or both (*bot.*). — *n.pl.* **Incomplē'tae** (*-tē*) an artificial group of dicotyledons with perianth absent or incomplete, the Monochlamydeae. — *adv.* **incomplete'ly.** — *ns.* **incomplete'ness; incomplē'tion.** [Pfx. **in-** (2).]

incompliance *in-kəm-plī'əns, n.* refusal to comply: an unaccommodating disposition. — *adj.* **incomplī'ant.** [Pfx. **in-** (2).]

incomposed *in-kəm-pōzd', (Milt.) adj.* discomposed. [Pfx. **in-** (2).]

incomposite *in-kom'pəz-it, adj.* simple: ill-constructed. **incomposite numbers** prime numbers. [Pfx. **in-** (2).]

incompossible *in-kəm-pos'i-bl, (rare), adj.* incapable of co-existing. — *n.* **incompossibil'ity.** [Pfx. **in-** (2).]

incomprehensible *in-kom-pri-hens'i-bl, adj.* not capable of being understood: not to be contained within limits (*theol.*). — *ns.* **incomprehensibil'ity, incomprehens'ibleness.** — *adv.* **incomprehens'ibly.** — *n.* **incomprehen'sion** lack of comprehension. — *adj.* **incomprehens'ive** not comprehensive. — *n.* **incomprehens'iveness.** [Pfx. **in-** (2).]

incompressible *in-kəm-pres'i-bl, adj.* not to be compressed into smaller bulk. — *ns.* **incompressibil'ity, incompress'ibleness.** [Pfx. **in-** (2).]

incomputable *in-kəm-pūt'ə-bl,* or *in-kom', adj.* that cannot be computed or reckoned. [Pfx. **in-** (2).]

incomunicado. See **incommunicado.**

inconceivable *in-kən-sēv'ə-bl, adj.* that cannot be conceived by the mind: incomprehensible: involving a contradiction in terms: physically impossible: taxing belief or imagination (*coll.*). — *n.* an inconceivable thing. — *ns.* **inconceivabil'ity, inconceiv'ableness.** — *adv.* **inconceiv'ably.** [Pfx. **in-** (2).]

inconcinnity *in-kən-sin'i-ti, n.* want of congruousness or proportion. — *adj.* **inconcinn'ous.** [Pfx. **in-** (2).]

inconclusive *in-kən-klōōs'iv, adj.* not settling a point in debate, indeterminate, indecisive. — *n.* **inconclusion** (*-klōō'zhən*). — *adv.* **inconclus'ively.** — *n.* **inconclus'-iveness.** [Pfx. **in-** (2).]

incondensable *in-kən-dens'ə-bl, adj.* not condensable. [Pfx. **in-** (2).]

incondite *in-kon'dit, -dīt, adj.* not well put together, irregular, unfinished. [L. *inconditus* — *in-*, not, *condĕre, conditum*, to build.]

incongruous *in-kong'grōō-əs, adj*. inconsistent: not fitting well together, disjointed: unsuitable. — Also **incong'ruent**. — *ns.* **incongruity** (*-kong-* or *-kən-grōō'*), **incong'ruousness**. — *adv.* **incong'ruously**. [Pfx. **in-** (2).]

inconie. See **incony**.

inconnu, *fem.* **inconnue** *ē-ko-nü*, (Fr.) *n*. an unknown person.

inconscient *in-kon'sh(y)ənt, adj*. unconscious: abstracted: not controlled by, or arising from, consciousness. — *adv.* **incon'sciently**. — *adj.* **incon'scious** unconscious. [Pfx. **in-** (2).]

inconscionable *in-kon'shən-ə-bl, adj*. unconscionable. [Pfx. **in-** (2).]

inconsecutive *in-kən-sek'ū-tiv, adj*. not succeeding or proceeding in regular order. — *n.* **inconsec'utiveness**. [Pfx. **in-** (2).]

inconsequent *in-kon'si-kwənt, adj*. not following from the premises: illogical: irrelevant: disconnected: unrelated: unimportant. — *n.* **incon'sequence**. — *adj.* **inconsequential** (*-kwen'shl*) not following from the premises: of no consequence or value. — *advs.* **inconsequen'tially; incon'sequently**. [Pfx. **in-** (2).]

inconsiderable *in-kən-sid'ər-ə-bl, adj*. not worthy of notice: unimportant: of no great size. — *n.* **inconsid'erableness**. — *adv.* **inconsid'erably**. [Pfx. **in-** (2).]

inconsiderate *in-kən-sid'er-it, adj*. not considerate: thoughtless: rash, imprudent. — *adv.* **inconsid'erately**. — *ns.* **inconsid'erateness, inconsiderā'tion**. [Pfx. **in-** (2).]

inconsistent *in-kən-sist'ənt, adj*. not consistent: not suitable or agreeing: intrinsically incompatible: self-contradictory: changeable, fickle. — *ns.* **inconsist'ence, inconsist'ency**. — *adv.* **inconsist'ently**. [Pfx. **in-** (2).]

inconsolable *in-kən-sōl'ə-bl, adj*. not to be comforted. — *n.* **inconsol'ableness**. — *adv.* **inconsol'ably**. [Pfx. **in-** (2).]

inconsonant *in-kon'sən-ənt, adj*. not consonant. — *n.* **incon'sonance**. — *adv.* **incon'sonantly**. [Pfx. **in-** (2).]

inconspicuous *in-kən-spik'ū-əs, adj*. not conspicuous. — *adv.* **inconspic'uously**. — *n.* **inconspic'uousness**. [Pfx. **in-** (2).]

inconstant *in-kon'stənt, adj*. subject to change: fickle. — *n.* **incon'stancy**. — *adv.* **incon'stantly**. [Pfx. **in-** (2).]

inconsumable *in-kən-sūm'ə-bl, adj*. that cannot be consumed or wasted. — *adv.* **inconsum'ably**. [Pfx. **in-** (2).]

incontestable *in-kən-test'ə-bl, adj*. too clear to be called in question: undeniable. — *n.* **incontestabil'ity**. — *adv.* **incontest'ably**. [Pfx. **in-** (2).]

incontiguous *in-kən-tig'ū-əs, adj*. not adjoining or touching. — *adv.* **incontig'uously**. — *n.* **incontig'uousness**. [Pfx. **in-** (2).]

incontinent[1] *in-kon'ti-nənt, adj*. not restraining the passions or appetites: unchaste: unable to restrain natural discharges or evacuations (*med.*). — *ns.* **incon'tinence, incon'tinency**. — *adv.* **incon'tinently**. [L. *incontinēns, -entis* — *in*, not, *continēns*; see **continent**.]

incontinent[2] *in-kon'ti-nənt*, (*arch.*) *adv.* straightway. — Also **incon'tinently**. [Fr., — L.L. *in continenti* (*tempore*), in unbroken (time).]

incontrollable *in-kən-trōl'ə-bl, adj*. uncontrollable. — *adv.* **incontroll'ably**. [Pfx. **in-** (2).]

incontrovertible *in-kon-trə-vûrt'i-bl, adj*. too clear to be called in question. — *n.* **incontrovertibil'ity**. — *adv.* **incontrovert'ibly**. [Pfx. **in-** (2).]

in contumaciam *in kon-tū-mā'shi-əm, in kon-tōō-mä'ki-am*, (L.) as an act of contumacy.

inconvenient *in-kən-vēn'yənt, adj*. unsuitable: causing trouble or uneasiness: increasing difficulty: incommodious. — *v.t.* **inconvēn'ience** to trouble or incommode. — *ns.* **inconvēn'ience, inconvēn'iency**. — *adv.* **inconvēn'iently**. [Pfx. **in-** (2).]

inconversable *in-kən-vûrs'ə-bl, adj*. indisposed to conversation, unsocial. [Pfx. **in-** (2).]

inconversant *in-kon'vər-sənt*, (*rare*) *-kən-vûr', adj*. not

versed (with *with*, or *in*). [Pfx. **in-** (2).]

inconvertible *in-kən-vûrt'i-bl, adj*. that cannot be changed or exchanged. — *n.* **inconvertibil'ity**. — *adv.* **inconvert'ibly**. [Pfx. **in-** (2).]

inconvincible *in-kən-vin'si-bl, adj*. not capable of being convinced. [Pfx. **in-** (2).]

incony, inconie *in-kun'i*, (*Shak.*) *adj*. fine, delicate, pretty. [Origin unknown.]

inco-ordinate (also **incoor-** in both words) *in-kō-örd'(i)-nit, adj*. not co-ordinate. — *n.* **inco-ordination** (*-i-nā'shən*) want or failure of co-ordination. [Pfx. **in-** (2).]

incoronate *in-kor'ə-nāt, -nit, -d -nāt-id, adjs*. crowned. — *n.* **incoronā'tion**. [Pfx. **in-** (1).]

incorporate[1] *in-kör'pər-āt, v.t.* to form into a body: to combine into one mass, or embody: to take or put into the body: to merge: to absorb: to form into a corporation: to admit to a corporation: to incarnate. — *v.i.* to unite into one mass: to form a corporation. — *adj.* (*-it*) united in one body: constituted as an incorporation. — *adj.* **incor'porāting** (*philol.*) combining the parts of a sentence in one word. — *n.* **incorporā'tion** the act of incorporating: the state of being incorporated: the formation of a legal or political body: association: an incorporated society: an embodiment. — *adj.* **incor'porative** (*-ə-tiv, -ā-tiv*). — *n.* **incor'porātor** one who incorporates: a member, or original member, of an incorporated company (*U.S.*): a member of a university admitted to membership of another. [L. *incorporāre, -ātum* — *in*, in, into, *corpus, -oris*, body.]

incorporate[2] *in-kör'pər-it, -āt, adj*. without a body: unembodied. — *adjs.* **incor'poral(l)** (*Shak.*), **incorporeal** (*-pō', -pö'ri-əl*) not having a body: spiritual: intangible. — *ns.* **incorpo'realism, incorporē'ity, incorporeality** (*-kör-pōr, -pör-i-al'i-ti*). — *adv.* **incorpo'really**. [L. *incorporātus, incorporālis*, bodiless — *in-*, not, *corpus, -oris*, body.]

incorpse *in-körps'*, (*Shak.*) *v.t.* to incorporate. [Pfx. **in-** (1).]

incorrect *in-kər-ekt', adj*. containing faults: not accurate: not correct in manner or character: not regulated (*Shak.*). — *adv.* **incorrect'ly**. — *n.* **incorrect'ness**. [Pfx. **in-** (2).]

incorrigible *in-kor'i-ji-bl, adj*. beyond correction or reform. — Also *n.* — *ns.* **incorr'igibleness, incorrigibil'ity**. — *adv.* **incorr'igibly**. [Pfx. **in-** (2).]

incorrosible *in-kə-rō'si-bl*, **incorrodible** *in-kə-rō'di-bl, adjs*. incapable of being corroded: not readily corroded. [Pfx. **in-** (2).]

incorrupt *in-kər-upt', adj*. sound: pure: not depraved: not to be influenced by bribes. — *adj.* **incorrupt'ible** not capable of decay: that cannot be bribed: inflexibly just. — *ns.* **incorrupt'ibleness, incorruptibil'ity**. — *adv.* **incorrupt'ibly**. — *ns.* **incorrup'tion, incorrupt'ness**. — *adj.* **incorrupt'ive**. — *adv.* **incorrupt'ly**. [Pfx. **in-** (2).]

incrassate *in-kras'āt, v.t.* and *v.i.* (*obs.* except in *pharmaceutics*) to thicken. — *adjs.* **incrass'ate, -d** thickened. — *n.* **incrassā'tion**. — *adj.* **incrass'ative** (*-ə-tiv*). [L.L. *incrassāre, -ātum* — L. *in*, in, *crassus*, thick.]

increase *in-krēs', v.i.* to grow in size, number, or (*arch.*) wealth: to have a syllable more in the genitive than in the nominative (*L. gram.*). — *v.t.* to make greater in size, number, or (*arch.*) wealth. — *n.* **in'crease** growth: increment: addition to the original stock: profit: produce: progeny (*arch.*). — *adjs.* **increas'able; increase'ful** (*Shak.*) abundant of produce. — *n.* **increas'er**. — *n.* and *adj.* **increas'ing**. — *adv.* **increas'ingly**. [M.E. *encressen* — A.Fr. *encresser* — L. *incrēscĕre* — *in*, *crēscĕre*, to grow.]

increate *in-krē-āt'*, (*arch.*) *adj*. uncreated. [Pfx. **in-** (2).]

incredible *in-kred'i-bl, adj*. surpassing belief: difficult to believe in: very great: unusually good (*coll.*). — *ns.* **incredibil'ity; incred'ibleness**. — *adv.* **incred'ibly**. [Pfx. **in-** (2).]

incredulous *in-kred'ū-ləs, adj*. hard of belief, sceptical: not believing: incredible (*Shak.*). — *ns.* **incredū'lity** (*-krid-*), **incred'ulousness**. — *adv.* **incred'ulously**. [Pfx. **in-** (2).]

incremate *in'kri-māt*, (*obs.*) *v.t.* to burn: to cremate. —

n. **incremā′tion.** [Pfx. **in-** (1).]
increment *ing′* or *in′kri-mənt, n.* increase: amount of increase: an amount or thing added: the finite increase of a variable quantity (*math.*): an adding of particulars towards a climax (*rhet.*): a syllable in excess of the number of the nominative singular or the second pers. sing. present indicative (*gram.*). — *adj.* **incremental** (*-ment′l*). — **incremental plotter** (*comput.*) a device presenting computer output on paper in the form of line images, e.g. graphs; **unearned increment** any exceptional increase in the value of land, houses, etc., not due to the owner's labour or outlay. [L. *incrēmentum — incrēscĕre,* to increase.]
increscent *in-kres′ənt,* (*her.*) *adj.* (of the moon) waxing. [Pfx. **in-** (1).]
incriminate *in-krim′in-āt, v.t.* to charge with a crime or fault, to criminate: to implicate, involve in a charge. — *adj.* **incrim′inatory.** [Pfx. **in-** (1).]
incross *in′kros, n.* a plant or animal produced by crossing two inbred individuals of different lineage but of the same breed. — Also *v.t.* — *n.* **incross′bred** a plant or animal produced by crossing two inbred individuals of different breeds. — *v.t.* **incross′breed.** [Pfx. **in-** (1).]
incrust, incrustation. See **encrust, encrustation.**
incubate *in′* or *ing′kū-bāt, v.i.* to sit on eggs: to hatch: to undergo incubation: to brood, meditate (*fig.*). — *v.t.* to hatch: to foster the development of (as bacteria, etc.): to brood or ponder over (*fig.*). — *n.* **incubā′tion** the act of sitting on eggs to hatch them: hatching (natural or artificial): fostering (as of bacteria, etc.): sleeping in a holy place to obtain dreams from the gods: meditation on schemes (*fig.*): the period between infection and appearance of symptoms (*med.*). — *adjs.* **in′cubātive, in′cubātory.** — *n.* **in′cubātor** a brooding hen: an apparatus for hatching eggs by artificial heat, for rearing prematurely born children, or for developing bacteria. — *adj.* **in′cubous** (*bot.*) having the upper leaf-margin overlapping the leaf above. [L. *incubāre, -ātum* (usu. *-ītum*) — *in,* on, *cubāre,* to lie, recline.]
incubus *in′* or *ing′kū-bəs, n.* the nightmare: a devil supposed to assume a male body and have sexual intercourse with women in their sleep: any oppressive person, thing, or influence: — *pl.* **in′cubuses, in′cubi** (*-bī*). [L. *incŭbus,* nightmare — *in,* on, *cubāre,* to lie.]
incudes. See **incus.**
in cuerpo. See **en cuerpo.**
inculcate *in′kul-kāt* or *-kul′, v.t.* to instil by frequent admonitions or repetitions. — *n.* **inculcā′tion.** — *adj.* **inculc′ative** (*-ə-tiv*). — *n.* **in′culcātor.** — *adj.* **inculc′atory.** [L. *inculcāre, -ātum — in,* into, *calcāre,* to tread — *calx,* heel.]
inculpable *in-kul′pə-bl, adj.* blameless. — *adv.* **incul′pably.** [L. *inculpābilis — in-,* not, *culpābilis;* see **culpable.**]
inculpate *in′kul-pāt,* or *-kul′, v.t.* to involve in a charge or blame: to charge. — *n.* **inculpā′tion.** — *adj.* **incul′patory** (*-pə-tə-ri*). [L.L. *inculpāre, -ātum* — L. *in,* in, *culpa,* a fault.]
incult *in-kult′,* (*rare*) *adj.* uncultivated. [Pfx **in-** (2).]
incumbent *in-kum′bənt, adj.* lying or resting: weighing on something: overlying (*geol.*): leaning over (*arch.*): overhanging (*arch.*): imposed or resting as a duty: lying along a surface, as a moth's wings at rest: of a radicle, lying along the back of one cotyledon (*bot.*). — *n.* one who holds an ecclesiastical benefice, or any office. — *n.* **incum′bency** a lying or resting on something: the state or fact of being incumbent or an incumbent: a duty or obligation: the holding of an office: an ecclesiastical benefice. — *adv.* **incum′bently.** [L. *incumbēns, -entis,* pr.p. of *incumbĕre,* to lie upon.]
incunabula *in-kū-nab′ū-lə, n.pl.* books printed in early period of the art, esp. before the year 1501: the cradle, birthplace, origin of a thing: — *sing.* **incūnab′ūlum.** — Also **incūn′able** (*sing.*), **incūn′ables** (*pl.*). — *adj.* **incūnab′ūlar.** — *n.* **incūnab′ūlist** a student or collector of incunabula. [L. *incūnābŭla,* swaddling-clothes, infancy, earliest stage — *in,* in, *cūnābula,* dim. of *cūnae,* a cradle.]

incur *in-kûr′, v.t.* to become liable to: to bring upon oneself: to suffer: — *pr.p.* **incurr′ing;** *pa.t.* and *pa.p.* **incurred′.** — *adj.* **incurr′able.** — *n.* **incurr′ence.** [L. *incurrĕre, incursum — in,* into, *currĕre,* to run.]
incurable *in-kūr′ə-bl, adj.* not admitting of cure or correction. — *n.* one beyond cure. — *ns.* **incur′ableness, incurabil′ity.** — *adv.* **incur′ably.** [Pfx. **in-** (2).]
incurious *in-kū′ri-əs, adj.* not curious or inquisitive: inattentive: careless: indifferent: not fastidious, uncritical (*obs.*): not exquisite (*obs.*): deficient in interest (*arch.*). — *adv.* **incū′riously.** — *ns.* **incū′riousness, incūrios′ity.** [Pfx. **in-** (2).]
incurrent *in-kur′ənt, adj.* running in: carrying an inflowing current. [L. *in,* into, *currēns, -entis,* pr.p. of *currĕre,* to run.]
incursion *in-kûr′shən, n.* a hostile inroad: the action of running in: a sudden attack, invasion. — *adj.* **incur′sive** making inroads: aggressive: invading. [L. *incursiō, -ōnis — incurrĕre.*]
incurve *in-kûrv′, v.t.* and *v.i.* to curve: to curve inward. — *n.* **in′curve** a curve inwards: a ball that curves in, or towards the batsman (*baseball*). — *v.t.* and *v.i.* **incur′vate** (or *in′*) to bend, esp. inwards. — *adj.* curved, esp. inward — also **incur′vated.** — *ns.* **incurvā′tion** bending: bowing, kneeling, etc.: an inward bend or growth; **incur′vature** a curve or curvature, esp. inward. — *adj.* **incurved′** (or *in′*) curved: curved inward. — *n.* **incur′vity.** [L. *incurvāre,* to bend in, *incurvus,* bent.]
incus *ing′kəs, n.* one of the bones in the middle ear, so called from its fancied resemblance to an anvil: — *pl.* **incudes** (*ing-kū′dēz,* or *ing′*). — *adj.* anvil-shaped. [L. *incūs, incūdis,* an anvil; see **incuse.**]
incuse *in-kūz′, v.t.* to impress by stamping, as a coin. — *adj.* hammered. — *n.* an impression, a stamp. [L. *incūsus,* pa.p. of *incūdĕre — in,* on, *cūdĕre,* to strike: to work on the anvil.]
incut *in′kut, adj.* set in by, or as if by, cutting: esp. in printing, inserted in spaces left in the text. [**in¹,** **cut.**]
Ind *ind, īnd,* (*poet.*) *n.* India.
indaba *in-dä′bə, n.* an important tribal conference: an international Scout conference: one's affair, business (*S. Afr.; coll.*). [Zulu.]
indagate *in′də-gāt,* (*arch.*) *v.t.* to search out. — *n.* **indagā′tion.** — *adj.* **in′dagātive.** — *n.* **in′dagātor.** — *adj.* **in′dagātory.** [L. *indāgāre, -ātum,* to trace.]
indart. See **endart.**
indebted *in-det′id, adj.* being in debt: obliged by something received. — *ns.* **indebt′edness, indebt′ment.** [Pfx. **in-** (1).]
indecent *in-dē′sənt, adj.* offensive to common modesty: unbecoming: gross, obscene. — *n.* **indē′cency** the quality of being indecent: anything violating modesty or seemliness. — *adv.* **indē′cently.** — **indecent assault** an assault accompanied by indecency, but not involving rape; **indecent exposure** the offence of indecently exposing part of one's body (esp. the genitals) in public. [Pfx. **in-** (2).]
indeciduous *in-di-sid′ū-əs, adj.* not deciduous. — *adj.* **indecid′uate** not deciduate. [Pfx. **in-** (2).]
indecipherable *in-di-sī′fər-ə-bl, adj.* incapable of being deciphered. [Pfx. **in-** (2).]
indecision *in-di-sizh′ən, n.* want of decision, or resolution: hesitation. — *adj.* **indecisive** (*-sī′siv*) settling nothing, inconclusive: hesitant: uncertain, indistinct. — *adv.* **indecī′sively.** — *n.* **indecī′siveness.** [Pfx. **in-** (2).]
indeclinable *in-di-klīn′ə-bl,* (*gram.*) *adj.* not varied by inflection. — *adv.* **indeclin′ably.** [Pfx. **in-** (2).]
indecomposable *in-dē-kəm-pōz′ə-bl, adj.* that cannot be decomposed. [Pfx. **in-** (2).]
indecorous *in-dek′ə-rəs,* sometimes *-di-kō′,* or *-kō′, adj.* unseemly: violating good manners. — *adv.* **indec′orously.** — *ns.* **indec′orousness, indecō′rum** want of propriety of conduct: a breach of decorum. [L. *indecōrus.*]
indeed *in-dēd′, adv.* in fact: in truth: in reality. It emphasises an affirmation, marks a qualifying word, or clause, a concession or admission, or, used as an interj.,

it expresses surprise or interrogation, disbelief, or mere acknowledgment. [**in**[1], **deed**[1].]

indefatigable *in-di-fat'i-gə-bl, adj.* not to be wearied out: unremitting in effort. — *n.* **indefat'igableness.** — *adv.* **indefat'igably.** [Fr. (obs.), — L. *indēfatīgābilis* — *in-*, not, *dē*, from, *fatīgāre*, to tire.]

indefeasible *in-di-fēz'i-bl, adj.* not to be made void. — *n.* **indefeasibil'ity.** — *adv.* **indefeas'ibly.** [Pfx. **in-** (2).]

indefectible *in-di-fekt'i-bl, adj.* incapable of defect: unfailing. [Pfx. **in-** (2).]

indefensible *in-di-fens'i-bl, adj.* untenable, that cannot be defended (*lit.* or *fig.*): that cannot be excused or justified. — *n.* **indefensibil'ity.** — *adv.* **indefens'ibly.** [Pfx. **in-** (2).]

indefinable *in-di-fīn'ə-bl, adj.* that cannot be defined. — *adv.* **indefin'ably.** [Pfx. **in-** (2).]

indefinite *in-def'i-nit, adj.* without clearly marked outlines or limits: of a character not clearly distinguished: not precise: undetermined: not referring to a particular person or thing (*gram.*; see also **article**): not distinguishing between complete and incomplete active (as the Greek aorist): not fixed in number (*bot.*): not terminating in a flower (*bot.*): racemose or centripetal (*bot.*). — *adv.* **indef'initely.** — *n.* **indef'initeness.** [Pfx. **in-** (2).]

indehiscent *in-di-his'ənt*, (*bot.*) *adj.* not dehiscent: (of fruits) not opening when mature. — *n.* **indehisc'ence.** [Pfx. **in-** (2).]

indelible *in-del'i-bl, adj.* that cannot be blotted out or effaced: making a mark which cannot be erased. — *ns.* **indelibil'ity, indel'ibleness.** — *adv.* **indel'ibly.** [L. *indēlēbilis* — *in-*, not, *dēlēre*, to destroy: influenced by words ending in *-ible*.]

indelicate *in-del'i-kit, adj.* immodest or verging on the immodest: wanting in fineness of feeling or tact: coarse. — *n.* **indel'icacy.** — *adv.* **indel'icately.** [Pfx. **in-** (2).]

in deliciis *in dəl-is'i-ēs, dāl-ik'i-ēs*, (L.) as favourites.

indemnify *in-dem'ni-fī, v.t.* to secure (with *against*): to compensate: to free, exempt (with *from*): — *pr.p.* **indem'nifying;** *pa.t.* and *pa.p.* **indem'nified.** — *n.* **indemnification** (*-fi-kā'shən*) the act of indemnifying: the state of being indemnified: the amount paid as compensation. [L. *indemnis*, unhurt (— *in-*, not, *damnum*, loss), and *facĕre*, to make.]

indemnity *in-dem'ni-ti, n.* security from damage or loss: compensation for loss or injury: legal exemption from incurred liabilities or penalties. — **Act of Indemnity** an act or decree for the protection of public officers from any technical or legal penalties or liabilities they may have been compelled to incur. [Fr. *indemnité* — L. *indemnis*, unharmed — *damnum*, loss.]

indemonstrable *in-dem'ən-strə-bl*, or *in-di-mon', adj.* that cannot be demonstrated or proved. — *n.* **indemonstrabil'ity.** [Pfx. **in-** (2).]

indene *in'dēn, n.* a hydrocarbon (C_9H_8) got from coal-tar. [indigo.]

indent *in-dent', v.t.* to cut into zigzags: to divide along a zigzag line: to notch: to indenture, apprentice: (as a deed, contract, etc.) to draw up in exact duplicate: to begin farther in from the margin than the rest of a paragraph: to impress: to dent or dint. — *v.t.* and *v.i.* to make out a written order with counterfoil or duplicate: to order (esp. from abroad): to requisition: (of a coastline, etc.) to penetrate, form recesses. — *v.i.* to move in a zigzag course (*Shak.*): to bargain (*obs.*): to make a compact (*obs.*). — *n.* (*in'dent*, also *in-dent'*) a cut or notch: a recess like a notch: an indenture: an order for goods (esp. from abroad): an (orig. Indian) official requisition for goods: a dint. — *n.* **indentā'tion** a hollow or depression: the act of indenting or notching: notch: recess. — *adj.* **indent'ed** having indentations: serrated: zigzag. — *ns.* **indent'er** a person or thing that indents; **inden'tion** indentation: blank space at the beginning of a line; **indent'ure** the act of indenting, indentation: a deed under seal, with mutual covenants, where the edge is indented for future indentification

(*law*): a written agreement between two or more parties: a contract. — *v.t.* to bind by indentures: to indent. [Two different words fused together: (1) — L.L. *indentāre* — L. *in*, in, *dēns, dentis*, a tooth; (2) — English **in**[1] and **dint, dent.**]

independent *in-di-pend'ənt, adj.* not dependent or relying on others (with *of*): not subordinate: completely self-governing: (of a business, etc.) not affiliated or merged with a larger organisation: thinking or acting for oneself: too self-respecting to accept help: not subject to bias: having or affording a comfortable livelihood without necessity of working or help from others: not depending on another for its value, said of a quantity or function (*math.*): (with *cap.*) belonging to the Independents. — *n.* (with *cap.*) one who in ecclesiastical affairs holds that every congregation should be independent of every other and subject to no superior authority — a Congregationalist: a politician or other who commits himself to no party. — *ns.* **independ'ence** the state of being independent: a competency; **independ'ency** independence: a sovereign state: an independent income: (with *cap.*) Congregationalism. — *adv.* **independ'ently.** — **Independence Day** (see **Declaration of Independence**) a day when a country becomes self-governing or the anniversary of this event (usu. celebrated with an annual national holiday); **independent school** a public school. — **Declaration of Independence** the document (1776) proclaiming with reasons the secession of the thirteen colonies of America from the United Kingdom, reported to the Continental Congress, 4th July 1776 — observed in the U.S. as a national holiday, **Independence Day; independent clause** see **clause; Independent Labour Party** a Socialist party founded by Keir Hardie in 1893. [Pfx. **in-** (2).]

in deposito *in də-poz'it-ō, dā-pos'ēt-ō*, (L.L.) for a pledge.

indescribable *in-di-skrīb'ə-bl, adj.* that cannot be described. — *n.* (*old slang*; in *pl.*) trousers. — *n.* **indescribabil'ity.** — *adv.* **indescrib'ably.** [Pfx. **in-** (2).]

indesignate *in-dez'ig-nāt*, (*log.*) *adj.* without any indication of quantification. [Pfx. **in-** (2).]

indestructible *in-di-struk'ti-bl, adj.* that cannot be destroyed. — *ns.* **indestructibil'ity, indestruc'tibleness.** — *adv.* **indestruc'tibly.** [Pfx. **in-** (2).]

indetectable *in-di-tekt'ə-bl, adj.* not to be detected. — Also **indetect'ible.** [Pfx. **in-** (2).]

indeterminable *in-di-tûr'min-ə-bl, adj.* not to be ascertained or fixed: of argument, etc., that cannot be settled. — *n.* **indeter'minableness.** — *adv.* **indeter'-minably.** — *n.* **indeter'minacy.** — *adj.* **indeter'minate** not determinate or fixed: uncertain: having no defined or fixed value. — *adv.* **indeter'minately.** — *ns.* **indeter'-minateness, indeterminā'tion** want of determination: want of fixed direction. — *adj.* **indeter'mined** not determined: unsettled. — *ns.* **indeter'minism** the theory that denies determinism; **indeter'minist.** — **indeterminacy principle** uncertainty principle. [Pfx. **in-** (2).]

indew. A Spenserian form of **endue.**

index *in'deks, n.* the forefinger (also **in'dex-fing'er**), or the digit corresponding: a pointer or hand on a dial or scale, etc.: a moving arm, as on a surveying instrument: the gnomon of a sundial: the finger of a finger-post: a figure of a pointing hand, used to draw attention (*print.*): the nose (*old slang*): anything giving an indication: a table of contents or other preliminary matter in a book (*obs.*): hence a preface, prologue, introduction (*Shak.*; *fig.*): an alphabetical register of subjects dealt with, usu. at the end of a book, with page or folio references: a similar list of other things: a list of prohibited books: a direct, or indication of the first notes of next page or line (*mus., obs.*): a symbol denoting a power (*math.*): a number, commonly a ratio, expressing some relation (as *refractive index*, the ratio of sines of angles of incidence and refraction or *cranial index*, the breadth of skull as a percentage of its length): a numerical scale showing the relative changes in the cost of living, wages, etc., with reference to some predetermined base level: the reciprocal of intercept with parameter as unit (*crystal.*): — *pl.* of a book usu. **in'dexes;** other senses **indices** (*in'di-sēz*). — *v.t.* to provide with or place in an index: to link to an index, index-link. — *ns.* **indexā'tion, in'dexing** a system by which wages, rates of interest, etc., are directly linked (**in'dex-linked'**) to changes in the cost of living index; **in'dexer.** — *adjs.* **index'ical; in'dexless.** — **in'dex= learning** superficial knowledge got together from book indexes. — *v.t.* **in'dex-link'.** — **in'dex-link'ing** indexation; **index number** a figure showing periodic movement up or down of a variable compared with another figure (usu. 100) taken as a standard. [L. *index, indicis* — *indicāre,* to show.]

index auctorum *in'deks ök-tōr'əm, -tör', owk-tōr'ōŏm,* (L.) index of authors; **index librorum prohibitorum** (*librōr'əm, -rör', prō-hib-it-ōr'əm, -ör', lib-rōr'ōŏm prō-hib-it-ōr'ōŏm*), loosely, **index expurgatorius** (*eks-pûr-gə-tō'ri-əs, -tö', -pōōr-gä-tō'ri-ōōs*) (until 1966) a list of books prohibited to Roman Catholic readers either absolutely or until amended; **index locorum** (*lok-ōr'əm, -ör', lok-ōr'ōŏm*), **rerum** (*rē'rəm, rā'rōŏm*), **verborum** (*vûr-bōr'əm, -bör', wer-bōr'ōŏm*) index of places, things, words.

indexterity *in-deks-ter'i-ti, n.* want of dexterity. [Pfx. **in-** (2).]

Indian *in'di-ən, adj.* of or belonging to India (with various boundaries) or its native population, or to the Indies, East or West, or to the aborigines of America, or to the Indians of South Africa: made of maize. — *n.* a member of one of the races of India: form., a European long resident in India: an aboriginal of America: in South Africa, a person belonging to the Asian racial group: one who carries out orders, a worker, etc., as opposed to a leader or organiser, as in *chiefs and Indians.* — *n.* **Indianisā'tion, -z-.** — *v.t.* **In'dianise, -ize** to make Indian: to assimilate to what is Indian: to cause to be done, controlled, etc., by Indians. — *v.i.* to become Indian or like an Indian. — *adj.* **In'dic** originating or existing in India: of the Indian branch of the Indo-European languages. — *n.* **In'dianist** one who has a scholarly knowledge of Indian languages, history, etc. — **In'diaman** a large ship employed in trade with India; **Indian berry** the fruit of *Anamirta cocculus* (see **cocculus indicus** under **coccus**); **Indian bread** a Virginian fungus said to have been eaten by the Indians: maize bread; **Indian club** a bottle-shaped block of wood, swung in various motions by the arms to develop the muscles; **Indian corn** maize, so called because brought from the West Indies; **Indian cress** a garden plant (*Tropaeolum majus,* popularly nasturtium) from Peru, with orange flowers; **Indian fig** the banyan-tree: the prickly pear; **Indian file** see **file**[1]; **Indian fire** a firework used as a signal light, consisting of sulphur, realgar, and nitre; **Indian gift** a gift that is asked back or for which a return gift is expected; **Indian giver; Indian hemp** *Cannabis sativa* (*Cannabis indica* is a variety), source of drug variously known as hashish, marihuana, etc.: a species of Apocynum (*U.S.*); **Indian ink** see **ink; Indian liquorice** the jequirity or crab's-eye plant; **Indian meal** ground maize; **Indian millet** durra; **Indian pink** see under **pink**[3]; **Indian pipe** an American Monotropa with a solitary drooping flower, not unlike a tobacco-pipe; **Indian poke** an American liliaceous plant, white hellebore; **Indian red** red ochre, or native ferric oxide, formerly imported from the East as a red pigment, also made artificially; **Indian rice** see **Zizania; Indian rope-trick** the supposed Indian trick of climbing an unsupported rope; **Indian runner** a breed of domestic duck; **Indian shot** a cosmopolitan tropical plant of the genus Canna, much cultivated for its flowers; **Indian summer** (orig. in America) a period of warm, dry, calm weather in late autumn: a time of particular happiness, success, etc., towards the end of a life, era, etc. (*fig.*); **Indian tobacco** an American lobelia; **Indian turnip** an American araceous plant with a starchy tuber; **Indian wrestling** a trial of strength in which two people in sitting position with elbows touching a table

clasp hands, each trying to force the other's arm backwards; **India Office** a government office in London where till 1947 were managed the affairs of the Indian government; **India paper** a thin soft absorbent paper, of chinese or Japanese origin, used in taking the finest proofs (**India proofs**) from engraved plates: a thin tough opaque paper used for printing Bibles; **in'dia-rubb'er, India rubber** an elastic gummy substance, the inspissated juice of various tropical plants: a piece of this material, esp. one used for rubbing out pencil marks; **India shawl** a Kashmir shawl. — **East India Company** a great chartered company formed for trading with India and the E. Indies, the English Company, incorporated in 1600 and (having lost its power by 1858) dissolved in 1874; **East Indian** an inhabitant or native of the East Indies, usually applied to a Eurasian; **East Indies** the Indian subcontinent, south-east Asia, and the Malay archipelago (*hist.*): Sumatra, Borneo, Java and the other islands of Indonesia, by some, but not generally, taken to include the Philippines and New Guinea; **Red Indian** one of the aborigines of America (from the coppery-brown colour of some tribes); **West Indian** a native or an inhabitant of the West Indies; **West Indies** an archipelago stretching from Florida to Venezuela. [L. *India* — *Indus* (Gr. *Indos*), the Indus (Pers. *Hind,* Sans. *sindhu,* a river).]

Indic. See **Indian.**

indican. See **indigo.**

indicate *in'di-kāt, v.t.* to point out: to show: to give some notion of: to be a mark or token of: to give ground for inferring: to point to as suitable treatment (*med.*), also (usu. in pass.) as desirable course of action in any sphere. — *adj.* **in'dicant** indicating. — *n.* that which indicates. — *n.* **indicā'tion** the act of indicating: mark: token: suggestion of treatment: symptom. — *adj.* **indicative** (*in-dik'ə-tiv*) pointing out: giving intimation: applied to the mood of the verb that expresses matter of fact (*gram.*). — *n.* the indicative mood: a verb in the indicative mood. — *adv.* **indic'atively.** — *n.* **in'dicātor** one who or that which indicates: a pointer: a diagram showing names and directions of visible objects, as on a mountain top: a substance showing chemical condition by change of colour: a measuring contrivance with a pointer or the like: any device for exhibiting condition for the time being: (with *cap.*) a genus of birds, the honey-guides. — *adj.* **in'dicatory** (or *dik'*). — **in'dicator-di'agram** a graphical representation of the pressure and volume changes undergone by a fluid in performing a work-cycle in the cylinder of an engine on compression, the area representing, to scale, the work done during the cycle. — **indicated horsepower** of a reciprocating engine, the horsepower developed by the pressure-volume changes of the working agent within the cylinder, exceeding the useful or brake horsepower at the crankshaft by the power lost in friction and pumping. [L. *indicāre, -ātum* — *in,* in, *dicāre,* to proclaim.]

indices. See **index.**

indicia *in-dish'i-ə, in-dik'i-a,* (L.) marks, signs (*sing.* **indic'-ium**).

indict *in-dīt', v.t.* to charge with a crime formally or in writing. — *adj.* **indict'able.** — *ns.* **indictee'** one who is indicted; **indict'ment** a formal accusation: the written accusation against one who is to be tried by jury: the form under which one is put to trial at the instance of the Lord Advocate (*Scots law*). — **find an indictment** of a grand jury, to be satisfied that there is a *prima facie* case, and endorse the bill *a true bill.* [With Latinised spelling (but not pronunciation) from A.Fr. *enditer* —L. *in,* in, *dictāre,* to declare, freq. of *dicĕre,* to say.]

indiction *in-dik'shən, n.* a proclamation: a decree of the emperor, fixing land-tax valuation (*Rom. hist.*): the tax itself (*Rom. hist.*): a cycle of fifteen years, instituted by Constantine the Great for fiscal purposes, and adopted by the popes as part of their chronological system: a year bearing a number showing its place in a fifteen years' cycle, reckoning from 24th September (or other day), A.D. 312 (*Rom. hist.*). [L. *indictiō, -ōnis* — *indīcĕre*, to appoint.]

indifferent *in-dif'ər-ənt, adj.* without importance: uninteresting: of a middle quality: not very good, inferior: in poor health (*dial.*): neutral: unconcerned. — *n.* one who is indifferent or apathetic: that which is indifferent. — *ns.* **indiff'erence, indiff'erency; indiff'erentism** indifference: the doctrine that religious differences are of no moment (*theol.*): the doctrine of absolute identity — i.e. that to be in thought and to exist are one and the same thing (*metaph.*); **indiff'erentist.** — *adv.* **indiff'erently** in an indifferent manner: tolerably: passably: without distinction, impartially. [Pfx. **in-** (2).]

indigenous *in-dij'in-əs, adj.* native born: originating or produced naturally in a country — opp. to *exotic.* — *adj.* and *n.* **in'digene** (*-jēn*) native, aboriginal. — *n.* **indigenisā'tion, -z-.** — *v.t.* **indi'genise, -ize** to adapt or subject to native culture or influence: to increase the proportion of indigenous people in administration, employment, etc. — *adv.* **indig'enously.** [L. *indigena,* a native — *indu-,* in, and *gen-,* root of *gignĕre,* to produce.]

indigent *in'di-jənt, adj.* in need, esp. of means of subsistence. — *ns.* **in'digence, in'digency.** — *adv.* **in'digently.** [Fr., — L. *indigēns, -entis,* pr.p. of *indigēre* — *indu-,* in, *egēre,* to need.]

indigest *in-di-jest', adj.* not digested, shapeless. — *n.* a crude mass, disordered state of affairs. — *adj.* **indigest'ed** not digested: unarranged: not methodised. — *n.* **indigestibil'ity.** — *adj.* **indigest'ible** not digestible: not easily digested: not to be received or patiently endured. — *adv.* **indigest'ibly.** — *n.* **indigestion** (*in-di-jes'chən*) want of digestion: painful digestion. — *adj.* **indigest'ive** dyspeptic. [L. *indīgestus,* unarranged — *in,* not, *dīgerĕre,* to arrange, digest.]

indign *in-dīn', (arch.) adj.* unworthy: disgraceful. [L. *in-,* not, *dignus,* worthy.]

indignant *in-dig'nənt, adj.* feeling or showing justifiable anger (often mixed with scorn). — *n.* **indig'nance** (*arch.*) indignation: contemptuous impatience. — *adv.* **indig'nantly.** — *n.* **indigna'tion** righteous anger at injustice, etc.: feeling caused by an unjustified slight, etc., to oneself: something showing anger (*Shak.*). — *v.t.* **indig'nify** to treat insultingly (*Spens.*): to disgrace (with inadequate praise) (*obs.*). — *n.* **indig'nity** unworthiness (*obs.*): disgrace: dishonour: unmerited contemptuous treatment: incivility with contempt or insult: indignation (*Spens.*). [L. *indīgnus,* unworthy — *in-,* not, *dignus,* worthy.]

indigo *in'di-gō, n.* a violet-blue dye obtained from the leaves of the indigo plant, from woad, or synthetically: the colour of this dye: indigotin: the indigo plant, any of various species of **Indigof'era,** a tropical genus of Papilionaceae: — *pl.* **in'digos, in'digoes.** — *adj.* deep violetblue. — *ns.* **in'dican** a glucoside found in indigo leaves; **in'digotin** (or *in-dig'*), **indigo blue** the blue colouring matter of indigo got from indican by hydrolysis; **indirubin** (*in-di-rōō'bin*), **indigo red** an isomer of indigotin, got from natural indigo. — **indigo bird** an American finch, of which the male is blue. [Sp. *índico, índigo* — L. *indicum* — Gr. *Indikon,* Indian (neut. adj.).]

indirect *in-di-rekt',* or *-dī-, adj.* not direct or straight: not lineal or in direct succession: not related in the natural way, oblique: not straightforward or honest. — *adv.* **indirect'ly.** — *ns.* **indirect'ness; indirec'tion** (*Shak.*) indirect course or means, dishonest practice. — **indirect evidence** or **testimony** circumstantial or inferential evidence; **indirect object** (*gram.*) a substantival or pronominal word or phrase dependent on a verb less immediately than an accusative governed by it; **indirect speech** (L. *ōrātiō oblīqua*) speech reported with adjustment of the speaker's words to change of persons and time; **indirect tax** one collected not directly from the taxpayer but through an intermediate agent, as e.g. a

customs duty (passed on in the form of higher price); **indirect taxation.** [Pfx. **in-** (2).]

indirubin. See **indigo.**

indiscernible *in-di-sûrn'i-bl,* or *-zûrn', adj.* not discernible. — *adv.* **indiscern'ibly.** [Pfx. **in-** (2).]

indiscerptible *in-di-sûrp'ti-bl, adj.* not discerptible. — *n.* **indiscerptibil'ity.** [Pfx. **in-** (2).]

indiscipline *in-dis'i-plin, n.* want of discipline. — *adj.* **indisc'iplinable.** [Pfx. **in-** (2).]

indiscoverable *in-dis-kuv'ər-ə-bl, adj.* not discoverable. [Pfx. **in-** (2).]

indiscreet *in-dis-krēt', adj.* not discreet: imprudent: injudicious. — *adv.* **indiscreet'ly.** — *ns.* **indiscreet'ness; indiscretion** (*-kresh'ən*) want of discretion: rashness: an indiscreet act, or one seemingly indiscreet: (esp. formerly) an action breaking the moral code of society. [Pfx. **in-** (2).]

indiscrete *in-dis-krēt',* or *-dis', adj.* not separated or distinguishable in parts: homogeneous. — *adv.* **indiscrete'ly.** *n.* **indiscrete'ness.** [Pfx. **in-** (2).]

indiscriminate *in-dis-krim'i-nit, adj.* not making distinctions: promiscuous. — *adv.* **indiscrim'inately.** — *adjs.* **indiscrim'inating** undiscriminating; **indiscrim'inative** (*-ə-tiv*) not discriminative. — *n.* **indiscriminā'tion.** [Pfx. **in-** (2).]

indispensable *in-dis-pens'ə-bl, adj.* that cannot be dispensed with: absolutely necessary: of a law, etc., that cannot be set aside. — *ns.* **indispensabil'ity, indispens'ableness.** — *adv.* **indispens'ably.** [Pfx. **in-** (2).]

indispose *in-dis-pōz', v.t.* to render indisposed, averse, or unfit. — *pa.p.* and *adj.* **indisposed'** averse: slightly disordered in health. — *ns.* **indispos'edness; indisposition** (*-pə-zish'ən*) the state of being indisposed: disinclination: slight illness. [Pfx. **in-** (2).]

indisputable *in-dis-pū'tə-bl,* also *-dis', adj.* beyond dispute. — *n.* **indisput'ableness.** — *adv.* **indisput'ably.** [Pfx. **in-** (2).]

indissociable *in-dis-ō'sh(y)ə-bl, adj.* incapable of being separated. [Pfx. **in-** (2).]

indissoluble *in-dis-ol'ū-bl,* or *-dis'əl-, adj.* that cannot be broken or violated: inseparable: binding for ever. — *ns.* **indissol'ubleness, indissolubility** (*-ol-ū-bil'*). — *adv.* **indissol'ubly.** [Pfx. **in-** (2).]

indissolvable *in-di-zol'və-bl,* (*arch.*) *adj.* that cannot be dissolved. [Pfx. **in-** (2).]

indissuadable *in-dis-wād'ə-bl, adj.* not to be dissuaded. — *adv.* **indissuad'ably.** [Pfx. **in-** (2).]

indistinct *in-dis-tingkt', adj.* not plainly marked: confused: not clear to the mind: dim. — *adj.* **indistinct'ive** not constituting a distinction. — *adv.* **indistinct'ively** indiscriminately. — *n.* **indistinct'iveness.** — *adv.* **indistinct'ly.** — *ns.* **indistinct'ness; indistinc'tion** (*rare*) confusion: absence of distinction, sameness. [Pfx. **in-** (2).]

indistinguishable *in-dis-ting'gwish-ə-bl, adj.* that cannot be distinguished. — *n.* **indistin'guishableness.** — *adv.* **indistin'guishably.** [Pfx. **in-** (2).]

indistributable *in-dis-trib'ū-tə-bl, adj.* not distributable. [Pfx. **in-** (2).]

indite *in-dīt', v.t.* to compose or write: to invite (*Shak.*). — *v.i.* to compose. — *ns.* **indite'ment; indit'er.** [O.Fr. *enditer;* see **indict.**]

indium *in'di-əm, n.* a soft malleable silver-white metallic element (In; at. numb. 49). [From two indigo-coloured lines in the spectrum.]

indivertible *in-di-vûrt'i-bl, adj.* not capable of being turned aside out of a course. [Pfx. **in-** (2).]

individable *in-di-vīd'ə-bl,* (*Shak.*) *adj.* that cannot be divided. [Pfx. **in-** (2).]

individual *in-di-vid'ū-əl, adj.* not divisible without loss of identity: subsisting as one: pertaining to one only or to each one separately of a group: single, separate: inseparable (*Milt.*). — *n.* a single person, animal, plant, or thing considered as a separate member of its species or as having an independent existence: a person (*coll.*). — *n.* **individualisā'tion, -z-.** — *v.t.* **individ'ualise, -ize** to stamp with individual character: to particularise. —

ns. **individ'ualism** individual character: independent action as opposed to co-operation: that theory which opposes interference of the state in the affairs of individuals, opp. to *socialism* or *collectivism*: the theory that looks to the rights of individuals, not to the advantage of an abstraction such as the state: the doctrine that individual things alone are real: the doctrine that nothing exists but the individual self; **individ'ualist** one who thinks and acts with independence: one who advocates individualism. — Also *adj.* — *adj.* **individualist'ic.** — *n.* **individuality** (-*al'i-ti*) separate and distinct existence: oneness: distinctive character. — *adv.* **individ'ually.** — *v.t.* **individ'uate** to individualise: to give individuality to. — *adj.* undivided: inseparable: individuated. — *n.* **individuā'tion** the act or process of individuating or individualising: individual existence: essence: continued identity: the sum of the processes of individual life: synthesis into a single organic whole. — *n.* **individ'uum** an indivisible entity: an individual person or thing: a member of a species. [L. *indīviduus* — *in-*, not, *dīviduus*, divisible — *dīvidĕre*, to divide.]

indivisible *in-di-viz'i-bl*, *adj.* not divisible. — *n.* (*math.*) an indefinitely small quantity. — *ns.* **indivisibil'ity, indivis'ibleness.** — *adv.* **indivis'ibly.** [Pfx. **in-** (2).]

Indo- *in'dō-*, in composition, Indian.

Indo-Chinese *in'dō-chī-nēz'*, *adj.* of or pertaining to Indo-China, the south-eastern peninsula of Asia.

indocile *in-dō'sīl*, or *in-dos'il*, *adj.* not docile: not disposed to be instructed. — Also **indō'cible.** — *n.* **indocil'ity.** [Pfx. **in-** (2).]

indoctrinate *in-dok'trin-āt*, *v.t.* to instruct in any doctrine: to imbue with any opinion. — *ns.* **indoctrinā'tion; indoc'trinātor.** [Pfx. **in-** (1).]

Indo-European *in'dō-ū-rō-pē'ǝn*, (*philol.*) *adj.* of the family of languages, also called Indo-Germanic and sometimes Aryan, whose great branches are Aryan proper or Indian, Iranian, Armenian, Greek or Hellenic, Italic, Celtic, Tocharian, Balto-Slavonic, Albanian, Germanic, and probably Anatolian.

Indo-Germanic *in-dō-jûr-man'ik*, (*philol.*) *adj.* Indo-European.

indole *in'dōl*, *n.* a substance (C_8H_7N) related to indigo. — Also **indol.** [**indigo** and L. *oleum*, oil.]

indolent *in'dǝl-ǝnt*, *adj.* indisposed to activity: not painful (*med.*). — *ns.* **in'dolence, in'dolency.** — *adv.* **in'dolently.** [L. *in-*, not, *dolēns, -entis*, pr.p. of *dolēre*, to suffer pain.]

in Domino *in dom'i-nō*, (L.L.) in the Lord.

indomitable *in-dom'it-ǝ-bl*, *adj.* not to be overcome. — *adv.* **indom'itably.** [Pfx. **in-** (2).]

Indonesian *in-dō-nē'zi-ǝn, -zh(y)ǝn, -sh(y)ǝn*, *adj.* of the East Indian or Malay Archipelago, specif. of the Republic of Indonesia, covering much of this territory: of a short, mesocephalic black-haired, light-brown race distinguishable in the population of the East Indian Islands: of a branch of the Austronesian family of languages chiefly found in the Malay Archipelago and Islands (Malay, etc.). — *n.* an Indonesian national, a member of the race or speaker of one of the languages: the official language of the Republic of Indonesia, a form of Malay also known as Bahasa Indonesia. [Gr. *Indos*, Indian, *nēsos*, island.]

indoor *in'dōr, -dör*, *adj.* practised, used, or being within a building. — *adv.* **indoors'** inside a building. — **indoor relief** (*hist.*) support given to paupers in the workhouse or poorhouse, as opposed to *outdoor relief*, or help given them at their own homes. [Pfx. **in-** (1).]

indorse. See **endorse**[1].

Indra *in'drǝ*, *n.* the Hindu god of the firmament and of rain. [Sans.]

indraught, indraft *in'dräft*, *n.* a drawing in: an inward flow of current. [**in**[1], **draught**.]

indrawn *in'drön, in-drön'*, *adj.* drawn in. [**in**[1], **drawn**.]

indrench *in-drench', -drensh'*, (*Shak.*) *v.t.* to submerge in water. [Pfx. **in-** (1).]

Indri(s) *in'drē(s)*, *ns.* a genus of short-tailed lemurs found in Madagascar: (without *cap.*) a member of a species of these, *Indris brevicaudatus*.

indubious *in-dū'bi-ǝs*, (*arch.*) *adj.* not dubious: certain. [Pfx. **in-** (2).]

indubitable *in-dū'bit-ǝ-bl*, *adj.* that cannot be doubted: certain. — *ns.* **indūbitabil'ity; indū'bitableness.** — *adv.* **indū'bitably** without doubt, certainly. [Pfx. **in-** (2).]

induce *in-dūs'*, *v.t.* to bring in (*obs.*): to draw on: to prevail on: to bring into being: to initiate or speed up (labour) artificially, as by administering drugs (also *v.i.*) (*med.*): to cause, as an electric state, by mere proximity (*phys.*): to infer inductively (*log.*). — *v.i.* to reason or draw inferences inductively. — *ns.* **induce'ment** that which induces: persuasion (*Shak., Milt.*): incentive, motive: a statement of facts introducing other important facts (*law*); **induc'er.** — *adj.* **indu'cible.** — **induced current** (*elect.*) a current set in action by the influence of the surrounding magnetic field, or by the variation of an adjacent current. — See also **induct(ion)** below. [L. *indūcĕre, inductum* — *in*, into, *dūcĕre*, to lead.]

induciae *in-dū'si-ē*, (Scots *law*) *n. sing.* the time limit within which (after a citation) the defendant must appear in court or reply. [L. *indūciae, -tiae*, truce, delay.]

induct *in-dukt'*, *v.t.* to introduce: to put in possession, as of a benefice, to install: to enlist into military service (*U.S.*). — *ns.* **induct'ance** the property of inducing an electromotive force by variation of current in a circuit: a device having inductance. — *n.* **induc'tion** a bringing or drawing in: installation in office, benefice, etc.: a prelude: an introductory section or scene: the act of inducing (*arch.*): magnetising by proximity without contact: the production by one body of an opposite electric state in another by proximity: production of an electric current by magnetic changes in the neighbourhood: reasoning from particular cases to general conclusions (*log.*). — *adjs.* **induc'tional; induct'ive.** — *adv.* **induct'ively.** — *ns.* **inductiv'ity; induct'or.** — **induction coil** an electrical machine consisting of two coils of wire, in which every variation of the current in one induces a current in the other; **induction heating** the heating of a conductive material by means of an induced current passing through it; **induction motor** an electric motor in which currents in the primary winding set up an electromagnetic flux which induces currents in the secondary winding, interaction of these currents with the flux producing rotation; **induction port, valve** a port, valve, by which steam, or an explosive mixture, is admitted to the cylinder of an engine. — **induction by simple enumeration** logical induction by enumeration of all the cases singly. [See **induce**.]

inductile *in-duk'tīl*, or *-til*, *adj.* not ductile. — *n.* **inductility** (-*til'i-ti*). [Pfx. **in-** (2).]

indue. See **endue.**

indulge *in-dulj'*, *v.t.* to yield to the wishes of: to favour or gratify: to treat with favour or undue favour: not to restrain: to grant an indulgence to or on: to grant some measure of religious liberty to (*hist.*). — *v.i.* to gratify one's appetites freely, or permit oneself any action or expression (with *in*): to partake, esp. of alcohol (*coll.*). — *n.* **indulg'ence** gratification: excessive gratification: favourable or unduly favourable treatment: a grant of religious liberty: forbearance of present payment: in the R.C. Church, a remission, to a repentant sinner, of the temporal punishment which remains due after the sin and its eternal punishment have been remitted (*plenary* indulgences, which remit all, *partial*, which remit a portion of the temporal punishment due; *temporal*, those granted only for a time, *perpetual* or *indefinite*, those which last till revoked; *personal*, those granted to a particular person or confraternity; *local*, those gained only in a particular place): exemption of an individual from an ecclesiastical law. — Also **indulg'ency.** — *adj.* **indulg'ent** ready to gratify the wishes of others: compliant: not severe. — *adv.* **indulg'ently.** — *ns.* **indulg'er; indult'** a licence granted by the Pope, authorising something to be done which the common law of the Church does not sanction. — **Declaration of Indulgence** a name given to proclamations of Charles II and (esp.) James II declaring laws restraining religious liberty suspended by the king's will. [L. *indulgēre*, to be kind to, indulge — *in-*, in, and prob. *dulcis*, sweet.]

induline *in'dū-lin, -lēn, -līn, n.* any one of a class of coal-tar dyestuffs, giving blues, etc. [**indigo.**]

indult. See under **indulge.**

indumentum *in-dū-men'təm, n.* a general covering of hair, feathers, etc.: woolly pubescence. [L. *indūmentum*, garment — *induēre*, to put on.]

induna *in-dōō'nə, n.* a tribal councillor or leader in South Africa. [Zulu, person of rank.]

induplicate *in-dū'pli-kit, (bot.) adj.* folded inwards. — *n.* **induplicā'tion.** [Pfx. **in-** (1).]

indurate *in'dū-rāt, v.t.* and *v.i.* to harden. — Also *adj.* — *n.* **indurā'tion.** — *adj.* **in'durative.** [L. *indūrāre, -ātum* — *in-*, in, *dūrāre*, to harden.]

indusium *in-dū'zi-əm, n.* a protective membrane or scale, esp. that covering a fern sorus: an insect larva-case: — *pl.* **indu'sia.** — *adjs.* **indu'sial** containing fossil insect indusia; **indu'siate** having indusia. [L. *indūsium*, an undergarment.]

industry *in'dəs-tri, n.* the quality of being diligent: assiduity: steady application: habitual diligence: systemic economic activity: any branch of manufacture and trade, *heavy* industry relating to such basic industries as coalmining, steel-making, shipbuilding, etc., involving heavy equipment, *light* industry to smaller factory-processed goods, e.g. knitwear, glass, electronics components, etc.: all branches of manufacture and trade collectively. — *adj.* **industrial** (*-dus'*) relating to or consisting in industry. — *n.* an industrial worker: (in *pl.*) stocks and shares in industrial concerns. — *n.* **industrialisā'tion, -z-.** — *v.t.* **indus'trialise, -ize** to give an industrial character, or character of industrialism, to. — *ns.* **indus'trialism** devotion to labour or industrial pursuits: that system or condition of society in which industrial labour is the chief and most characteristic feature; **indus'trialist** one who owns, or holds a powerful position in, industrial concern(s). — *adj.* of or characterised by industry. — *adv.* **indus'trially.** — *adj.* **indus'trious** diligent or active in one's labour: laborious: diligent in a particular pursuit. — *adv.* **indus'triously.** — **industrial action** a strike or go-slow; **industrial archaeology** the study of industrial machines and buildings of the past; **industrial council** see **Whitley Council; industrial estate** a planned industrial area, with factories organised to provide varied employment; **industrial melanism** melanism (e.g. in moths) developed as response to blackening of trees, etc., by industrial pollution; **industrial relations** relations between management and workers or labour in general; **industrial revolution** the economic and social changes arising out of the change from industries carried on in the home with simple machines to industries in factories with power-driven machinery — esp. such changes (from about 1760) in Britain, the first country to be industrialised; **industrial school** (*hist.* in U.K.), a school in which some industrial art is taught: a school where neglected or delinquent children are taught mechanical arts; **industrial tribunal** a tribunal set up to hear complaints and make judgements in disputes between employers and employees on matters such as industrial relations and alleged unfair dismissal. [L. *industria,* perh. from the old word *indu,* in, within, and *struĕre,* to build up.]

induviae *in-dū'vi-ē, (bot.) n.pl.* withered leaves persistent on the stems of some plants. — *adjs.* **indū'vial; indū'viate.** [L. *induviae,* clothes.]

indwell *in-dwel', v.i.* and *v.t.* to dwell or abide in: — *pr.p.* **indwell'ing;** *pa.t.* and *pa.p.* **indwelt'.** — *n.* **in'dweller** an inhabitant. — *adj.* **in'dwelling** dwelling within, abiding permanently in the mind or soul. — *n.* residence within, or in the heart or soul. [Pfx. **in-** (1).]

-ine[1] *-īn, -in, (chem.)* noun-forming *suff.* indicating (1) a basic organic compound containing nitrogen, as an amino-acid or alkaloid, (2) a halogen, as *chlorine* and *fluorine,* (3) a mixture of compounds, as *kerosine, benzine.* [L. fem. adjectival ending *-īna.*]

-ine[2] *īn,* adjectival *suff.* meaning (1) belonging to, characteristic of, as in *elephantine,* (2) like, similar to, or being, as in *adamantine, crystalline.* [L. adjectival ending *-īnus.*]

inearth *in-ûrth', (arch.) v.t.* to inter. [Pfx. **in-** (1).]

inebriate *in-ē'bri-āt, v.t.* to make drunk, to intoxicate: to exhilarate greatly. — *adj.* (*-it, -ət*) drunk: intoxicated. — *n.* a drunk person: a drunkard. — *adj.* **inē'briant** intoxicating. — Also *n.* — *ns.* **inēbriā'tion, inebriety** (*in-ē-brī'i-ti,* or *in-i-*) drunkenness: intoxication. — *adj.* **inē'brious** drunk: causing intoxication (*obs.*). [L. *inēbriāre, -ātum* — *in,* intens., *ēbriāre,* to make drunk — *ēbrius,* drunk.]

inedible *in-ed'i-bl, adj.* not good to eat, not suitable for eating (e.g. because poisonous or indigestible). — *n.* **inedibil'ity.** [Pfx. **in-** (2).]

inedited *in-ed'it-id, adj.* not edited: unpublished. [Pfx. **in-** (2).]

ineducable *in-ed'ū-kə-bl, adj.* incapable of education. — *n.* **ineducabil'ity.** [Pfx. **in-** (2).]

ineffable *in-ef'ə-bl, adj.* that cannot be described, inexpressible. — *n.* **ineff'ableness.** — *adv.* **ineff'ably.** [L. *ineffābilis* — *in-,* not, *effābilis,* effable.]

ineffaceable *in-i-fās'ə-bl, adj.* that cannot be rubbed out. — *adv.* **inefface'ably.** [Pfx. **in-** (2).]

ineffective *in-i-fek'tiv, adj.* not effective: useless. — *adv.* **ineffec'tively.** — *n.* **ineffec'tiveness.** — *adj.* **ineffec'tual** fruitless: ineffective, weak. — *ns.* **ineffectual'ity, ineffec'tualness.** — *adv.* **ineffect'ually.** — *adj.* **inefficacious** (*in-ef-i-kā'shəs*) not having power to produce an effect, or the desired effect. — *adv.* **inefficā'ciously.** — *n.* **inefficacy** (*-ef'i-kə-si*) want of efficacy. — *n.* **inefficiency** (*in-i-fish'ən-si*). — *adj.* **ineffic'ient** not efficient. — *adv.* **ineffic'iently.** [Pfx. **in-** (2).]

inelaborate *in-il-ab'ər-it, -āt, adj.* unlaboured: simple. — *adv.* **inelab'orately.** [Pfx. **in-** (2).]

inelastic *in-i-las'tik, adj.* not elastic: incompressible. — *n.* **inelasticity** (*in-el-əs-tis'i-ti*). — **inelastic collision, scattering** see under **collide.** [Pfx. **in-** (2).]

inelegance *in-el'i-gəns, n.* want of gracefulness or refinement. — Also **inel'egancy.** — *adj.* **inel'egant.** — *adv.* **inel'egantly.** [Pfx. **in-** (2).]

ineligible *in-el'i-ji-bl, adj.* not qualified for election: not suitable for choice: not rich enough or of the right social background to be chosen as a husband: unsuitable. — Also *n.* — *n.* **ineligibil'ity.** — *adv.* **inel'igibly.** [Pfx. **in-** (2).]

ineloquent *in-el'ə-kwənt, adj.* not eloquent. — *n.* **inel'oquence.** [Pfx. **in-** (2).]

ineluctable *in-i-luk'tə-bl, adj.* not to be escaped from. [L. *inēluctābilis* — *in-,* not, *ē,* from, *luctārī,* to struggle.]

inenarrable *in-en'ər-ə-bl, in-ē-nar'ə-bl, adj.* incapable of being narrated or told. [L. *inēnarrābilis* — *in-,* not, *ē-,* out, *narrāre,* to tell.]

inept *in-ept', adj.* unfit: irrelevant and futile: fatuous: void (*law*). — *ns.* **inept'itude, inept'ness.** — *adv.* **inept'ly.** [L. *ineptus* — *in-,* not, *aptus,* apt.]

inequable *in-ek'wə-bl, -ēk', adj.* not equable, changeable. [Pfx. **in-** (2).]

inequality *in-ē-kwol'i-ti,* or *in-i-, n.* want of equality: difference: inadequacy: incompetency: unevenness: dissimilarity: an uneven place. [Pfx. **in-** (2).]

inequation *in-ə-kwā'shən, -zhən, n.* a mathematical sentence which expresses an inequality. [Pfx. **in-** (2).]

inequitable *in-ek'wi-tə-bl, adj.* unfair, unjust. — *adv.* **ineq'uitably.** — *n.* **ineq'uity** lack of equity: an unjust action. [Pfx. **in-** (2).]

ineradicable *in-i-rad'i-kə-bl, adj.* not able to be eradicated or rooted out. — *adv.* **inerad'icably.** [Pfx. **in-** (2).]

inerasable *in-i-rāz'ə-bl, adj.* impossible to erase. — Also **ineras'ible.** — *advs.* **ineras'ably, -ibly.** [Pfx. **in-** (2).]

inerm *in-ûrm', adj.* unarmed: without thorns. [L. *inermis* — *in-,* not, *arma* (pl.), arms.]

inerrable *in-er'ə-bl*, or *-ûr'*, *adj.* incapable of erring. — *adv.* **inerr'ably.** — *n.* **inerr'ancy** freedom from error. — *adj.* **inerr'ant** unerring.   [Pfx. **in-** (2).]
inert *in-ûrt'*, *adj.* without inherent power of moving, or of active resistance to motion: passive: chemically inactive: sluggish: disinclined to move or act. — *n.* **inertia** (*in-ûr'shi-ə, -shyə, -shə*) inertness: the inherent property of matter by which it continues, unless constrained, in its state of rest or uniform motion in a straight line.   *adj.* **iner'tial** of, or pertaining to, inertia. — *adv.* **inert'ly.** — *n.* **inert'ness.** — **inert gas** one of several elements whose outer electron orbits are complete, rendering them inert to all the usual chemical reactions; **inertial control guidance, navigation** an automatic gyroscopic guidance system for aircraft, missiles, etc., using data computed from acceleration and the physical properties of the earth, but dispensing with the magnetic compass and independent of ground-based radio aids; **inertia-reel seat-belt** a type of self-retracting seat-belt in which the wearer is constrained only when violent deceleration of the vehicle causes the belt to lock; **inertia selling** sending unrequested goods to householders and attempting to charge for them if they are not returned.   [L. *iners, inertis,* unskilled, idle — *in-*, not, *ars, artis,* art.]
inerudite *in-er'ū-dīt*, or *ōo-*, *adj.* not erudite: unlearned.   [Pfx. **in-** (2).]
inescapable *in-is-kā'pə-bl*, *adj.* unescapable: inevitable.   [Pfx. **in-** (2).]
inesculent *in-es'kū-lənt*, *adj.* inedible.   [Pfx. **in-** (2).]
inescutcheon *in-is-kuch'ən*, (*her.*) *n.* a single shield borne as a charge.   [**in**[1], **escutcheon**.]
in esse. See **esse.**
inessential *in-is-en'shl*, *adj.* not essential: not necessary: immaterial.   [Pfx. **in-** (2).]
inessive *in-es'iv*, (*gram.*) *adj.* denoting, as in Finnish, place in which. — *n.* the inessive case.   [L. *inesse,* to be in, on, or at.]
inestimable *in-es'tim-ə-bl*, *adj.* not able to be estimated or valued: priceless. — *adv.* **ines'timably.**   [Pfx. **in-** (2).]
inevitable *in-ev'it-ə-bl*, *adj.* not to be evaded or avoided: certain to happen: exactly right, giving the feeling that the thing could not have been other than it is. — *ns.* **inevitabil'ity; inev'itableness.** — *adv.* **inev'ltably.**   [L. *inēvītābilis* — *in-*, not, *ē*, from, *vītāre*, to avoid.]
inexact *in-ig-zakt'*, *adj.* not precisely correct or true: lax. — *ns.* **inexact'itude** lack of exactitude: an example of inexactitude; **inexact'ness.** — *adv.* **inexact'ly.**   [Pfx. **in-** (2).]
in excelsis *in ek-sel'sis, ik-, eks-, iks-chel'sis,* or *-kel'sis, -sēs,* (L.L.) on the heights: on high: in the highest degree.
inexcitable *in-ik-sīt'ə-bl*, *adj.* not excitable: from which one cannot be roused (*obs.*).   [Pfx. **in-** (2).]
inexcusable *in-ik-skūz'ə-bl*, *adj.* not justifiable: unpardonable. — *ns.* **inexcusabil'ity, inexcus'ableness.** — *adv.* **inexcus'ably.**   [Pfx. **in-** (2).]
inexecrable *in-eks'i-krə-bl*, *adj.* in Shak., *Merch. of Ven.* IV, i. 128, read by some as a misprint for *inexorable,* by some as an intensive form of *execrable.*
inexecutable *in-ig-zek'ūt-ə-bl*, or *in-ek-sek'*, or *-ik-*, or *in-eks-i-kūt'ə-bl*, *adj.* incapable of being executed. — *n.* **inexecu'tion** fact or state of not being executed.   [Pfx. **in-** (2).]
inexhausted *in-ig-zös'tid*, *adj.* (*arch.*) unexhausted, not used up or spent. — *n.* **inexhaustibil'ity.** — *adj.* **inexhaust'ible** not able to be exhausted or spent: unfailing. — *adv.* **inexhaust'ibly.** — *adj.* **inexhaust'ive** unfailing (*arch.*): not exhaustive.   [Pfx. **in-** (2).]
inexistence[1] *in-ig-zist'əns*, *n.* non-existence. — *adj.* **inexist'ent.**   [Pfx. **in-** (2).]
inexistence[2] *in-ig-zist'əns*, (*arch.*) *n.* inherence. — *adj.* **inexist'ent** indwelling.   [Pfx. **in-** (1).]
inexorable *in-eks'ər-ə-bl*, *adj.* not to be moved by entreaty: unrelenting: unyielding. — *ns.* **inex'orableness, inexorabil'ity.** — *adv.* **inex'orably.**   [L.L. *inexōrābilis*

— *in-*, not, *exōrāre* — *ex*, out of, *ōrāre,* to entreat.]
inexpansible *in-ik-span'si-bl*, *adj.* incapable of being expanded.   [Pfx. **in-** (2).]
inexpectant *in-ik-spek'tənt*, *adj.* not expecting. — *n.* **inexpec'tancy.**   [Pfx. **in-** (2).]
inexpedient *in-ik-spē'di-ənt*, *adj.* contrary to expediency: impolitic. — *ns.* **inexpe'dience, inexpe'diency.** — *adv.* **inexpe'diently.**   [Pfx. **in-** (2).]
inexpensive *in-ik-spens'iv*, *adj.* not costly: not inclined to spend much. — *adv.* **inexpens'ively.** — *n.* **inexpens'iveness.**   [Pfx. **in-** (2).]
inexperience *in-ik-spē'ri-əns*, *n.* want of experience. — *adj.* **inexpe'rienced** not having experience: unskilled or unpractised.   [Pfx. **in-** (2).]
inexpert *in-eks'pûrt*, or *in-ik-spûrt'*, *adj.* unskilled. — *n.* **inexpertness.**   [Pfx. **in-** (2).]
inexpiable *in-eks'pi-ə-bl*, *adj.* not able to be expiated or atoned for: not to be appeased. — *n.* **inex'piableness.** — *adv.* **inex'piably.**   [Pfx. **in-** (2).]
inexplicable *in-eks'pli-kə-bl, -ik-splik'*, *adj.* that cannot be disentangled (*obs.*): incapable of being explained or accounted for. — *ns.* **inexplicabil'ity, inexplicableness.** — *adv.* **inexplicably.**   [Pfx. **in-** (2).]
inexplicit *in-ik-splis'it*, *adj.* not explicit: not clear.   [Pfx. **in-** (2).]
inexpressible *in-ik-spres'i-bl*, *adj.* that cannot be expressed: unutterable: indescribable. — *n.* (in *pl.*) trousers (*arch. facet.*). — *adv.* **inexpress'ibly.** — *adj.* **inexpress'ive** inexpressible (*arch.*): unexpressive. — *n.* **inexpress'iveness.**   [Pfx. **in-** (2).]
inexpugnable *in-ik-spug'nə-bl*, *adj.* not to be taken by assault: unassailable. — *adv.* **inexpug'nably.**   [Pfx. **in-** (2).]
inexpungible *in-ik-spun'ji-bl*, *adj.* incapable of being expunged.   [Pfx. **in-** (2).]
inextended *in-ik-stend'id*, *adj.* not extended: without extension. — *n.* **inextensibil'ity.** — *adj.* **inexten'sible** that cannot be extended or stretched. — *n.* **inexten'sion.**   [Pfx. **in-** (2).]
in extenso *in ik-sten'sō*, or *ek-sten'*, (L.L.) at full length.
inextinguishable *in-ik-sting'gwish-ə-bl*, *adj.* that cannot be extinguished, quenched, or destroyed. — *adv.* **inextin'-guishably.**   [Pfx. **in-** (2).]
inextirpable *in-ik-stûrp'ə-bl*, *adj.* not able to be extirpated.   [Pfx. **in-** (2).]
in extremis *in ik-strē'mis*, or *ek-strā'mēs*, (L.L.) at the point of death: at the last gasp: in desperate circumstances.
inextricable *in-eks'tri-kə-bl, -ik-strik'*, *adj.* such as one cannot extricate oneself from (*Scott*): not able to be extricated or disentangled. — *adv.* **inex'tricably.**   [L. *inextrīcābilis.*]
infall *in'föl*, *n.* an inroad: falling in: confluence, inlet, or junction.   [**in**[1], **fall**[1].]
infallible *in-fal'i-bl*, *adj.* incapable of error: certain to succeed: inevitable. — *ns.* **infall'ibilism** the doctrine of the Pope's infallibility; **infall'ibilist; infallibil'ity.** — *adv.* **infall'ibly.** — **the doctrine of infallibility** in the R.C. Church (defined in 1870) is that the Pope, when speaking *ex cathedra,* is kept from error in all that regards faith and morals.   [Pfx. **in-** (2).]
infame *in-fām'*, *v.t.* to defame. — *adj.* **infamous** (*in'fə-məs,* formerly *in-fā'məs*) having a reputation of the worst kind: publicly branded with guilt: notoriously vile: disgraceful. — *vs.t.* **infamise, -ize** (*in'fə-mīz*), **infamonise, -ize** (*in-fam'ən-īz; Shak.*) to defame, to brand with infamy. — *adv.* **in'famously.** — *n.* **in'famy** ill repute: public disgrace: an infamous act: extreme vileness: a stigma attaching to the character of a person so as to disqualify him from being a witness (*law*).   [L. *īnfāmāre* — *in-*, not, *fāma,* fame.]
infancy. See **infant.**
infangthief *in'fang-thēf*, *n.* in old English law, the right of taking and fining a thief within the boundary of one's own jurisdiction.   [O.E. *infangenethēof* — *in*, in, the root of *fōn,* to seize, *thēof,* thief.]
infant *in'fənt*, *n.* a babe: a person under the age of legal

maturity (*Eng. law*): a noble youth (*Spens.*): an infante or infanta. — *adj.* of or belonging to infants: of or in infancy: being an infant. — *v.t* (*obs.*) to give birth to. — *n.* **in'fancy** the state or time of being an infant: childhood: the beginning of anything: want of distinct utterance (*Milt.*). — *adj.* **infantile** (*in'fən-tīl*, in U.S. -*til*, also -*fant'*) pertaining to infancy or to an infant: having characteristics of infancy: no better than that of an infant: undeveloped. — *n.* **infant'ilism** persistence of infantile characters: an utterance or trait worthy of an infant. — *adj.* **in'fantine** (*-īn*) of infancy or an infant: infant-like. — **infantile paralysis** poliomyelitis; **infant mortality (rate)** (the rate of) deaths in the first year of life; **infant school** a school for children up to about the age of seven. [L. *infāns, infantis* — *in-,* not, *fāns,* pr.p. of *fārī,* to speak; cf. Gr. *phanai.*]

infante *in-fan'tā,* (*hist.*) *n.* a prince of the blood royal of Spain or Portugal, esp. a son of the king other than the heir-apparent: — *fem.* **infant'a** a princess likewise defined: the wife of an infante. [Sp. and Port. from the root of **infant.**]

infanticide *in-fan'ti-sɪd, n.* the killing of newborn children as a social institution in some states of society; the murder of an infant by, or with consent of, a parent: the murderer of an infant. — *adj.* **infanticī'dal** (or -*fant'*). [L. *infanticīdium,* child-killing, *infanticīda,* child-killer — *infāns,* an infant, *caedĕre,* to kill.]

infantry *in'fən-ri, n.* foot-soldiers: a part of an army composed of such soldiers: infants or children collectively (*arch.*). — Also *adj.* — *n.* **in'fantryman.** [Fr. *infanterie* — It. *infanteria* — *infante,* youth, servant, foot-soldier — L. *infāns, -antis.*]

infarct *in-färkt', n.* a portion of tissue that is dying because blood supply to it has been cut off. — *n.* **infarc'tion.** [Mediaeval L. *infarctus* — *in,* in, *far(c)tus* — *farcīre,* to cram, stuff.]

infare *in'fār, n.* entrance (*obs.*): ingoing (*obs.*): a house-warming after a wedding (*Scot.* and *U.S.*). [O.E. *innfær;* cf. **in¹, fare.**]

infatuate *in-fat'ū-āt, v.t.* to turn to folly: to deprive of judgment: to inspire with foolish passion. — *adj.* **infatuated:** — *pa.p., adj.* **infat'uated** deprived of judgment: doting: besotted. — *n.* **infatuā'tion.** [L. *infatuāre, -ātum* — *in,* in, *fatuus,* foolish.]

infaust *in-föst', adj.* unlucky: ill-omened. [L. *infaustus* — *in-,* not, *faustus,* propitious.]

infeasible *in-fēz'i-bl, adj.* not feasible. — *n.* **infeasibil'ity.** [Pfx. **in-** (2).]

infect *in-fekt', v.t.* to impart some quality to: to taint, especially with disease: to introduce pathogenic micro-organisms into: to corrupt: to spread to: to affect successively. — *adj.* (*Shak.*) tainted. — *n.* **infec'tion** (*-shən*) the act of infecting: that which infects or taints: an infectious disease. — *adjs.* **infec'tious** (*-shəs*), **infec'tive** (*-tiv*) having the quality of infecting: corrupting: apt to spread. — *adv.* **infec'tiously.** — *ns.* **infec'tiousness; infect'iveness; infect'or.** — **infectious mononucleosis** glandular fever. [L. *inficĕre, infectum* — *in,* into, *facĕre,* to make.]

infecundity *in-fi-kun'di-ti, n.* want of fecundity or fertility: unfruitfulness. — *adj.* **infecund** (*-fek', -fēk'*). [Pfx. **in-** (2).]

infeft *in-feft', (Scots law) v.t.* to invest with heritable property: — *pa.p.* **infeft',** rarely **infeft'ed.** — *n.* **infeft'ment** (*Scots law*) the symbolical giving possession of land in completion of the title. [enfeoff.]

infelicitous *in-fi-lis'i-təs, adj.* not felicitous or happy: inappropriate, inapt. — *n.* **infelic'ity.** [Pfx. **in-** (2).]

infelt *in'felt, adj.* felt deeply, heartfelt. [Pfx. **in-** (1).]

infer *in-fûr', v.t.* to bring on (*Spens., Shak.*): to render (*Milt.*): to derive as a consequence: to arrive at as a logical conclusion: to conclude: (usu. of a thing or statement) to entail or involve as a consequence, to imply — a use now often condemned, but generally accepted for over four centuries: — *pr.p.* **inferr'ing;** *pa.t.* and *pa.p.* **inferred'.** — *adj.* **in'ferable** (or -*fûr';* also **inferr'able, -ible**) that may be inferred or deduced. —

n. **in'ference** that which is inferred or deduced: the act of drawing a conclusion from premises: consequence: conclusion. — *adj.* **inferential** (*-en'shl*) relating to inference: deducible or deduced by inference. — *adv.* **inferen'tially.** [L. *inferre* — *in,* into, *ferre,* to bring.]

infere *in-fēr', (obs.) adv.* for **in fere,** together. [See **fere¹.**]

inferiae *in-fē'ri-ē, ēn-fe'ri-ī,* (L.) offerings to the manes of the dead.

inferior *in-fē'ri-ər, adj.* lower in any respect: subordinate: poor or poorer in quality: somewhat below the line (*print.*): of an ovary, having the other parts above it (*bot.*): of the other parts, below the ovary (*bot.*): of a planet, revolving within the earth's orbit. — *n.* one lower in rank or station. — *n.* **inferiority** (*-or'*). — *adv.* **infe'riorly** in an inferior manner. — **inferior conjunction** conjunction when the planet is between the sun and the earth; **inferiority complex** a complex involving a suppressed sense of personal inferiority (*psych.*): (*popularly*) a feeling of inferiority. [L. *inferior,* comp. of *inferus,* low.]

infernal *in-fûr'nəl, adj.* belonging to the lower regions: resembling or suitable to hell: outrageous, very unpleasant (*coll.*). — *n.* **infernality** (*-nal'*). — *adv.* **infer'nally.** — *n.* **Infer'no** hell (*It.*) (also without *cap.*): the title and subject of one of the divisions of Dante's great poem, *La Divina Commedia*: (without *cap.*) a conflagration: — *pl.* **infer'nos.** — **infernal machine** a contrivance made to resemble some ordinary harmless object, but charged with a dangerous explosive. [L. *infernus* — *inferus.*]

infertile *in-fûr'tīl,* in U.S. -*til, adj.* not productive: barren. — *n.* **infertility** (*-til'*). [Pfx. **in-** (2).]

infest *in-fest', v.t.* to disturb: to harass: to molest: to haunt, beset, or swarm about, in a troublesome or injurious way. — *adj.* (*obs.*) hostile: troublesome. — *n.* **infesta'tion** molestation (*Milt.*): attack, or condition of being attacked, esp. by parasites. [L. *infestāre,* from *infestus,* hostile.]

infeudation *in-fū-dā'shən, n.* the putting of an estate in fee: the granting of tithes to laymen. [Pfx. **in-** (1), and **feud².**]

infibulate *in-fib'ū-lāt, v.t.* to fasten with a clasp. — *n.* **infibulā'tion** the act of confining or fastening, esp. the fastening or partial closing-up of the prepuce or the labia majora by a clasp, stitches, or the like. [Pfx. **in-** (1), and *fibula,* a clasp.]

inficete *in-fi-sēt', (rare) adj.* not facetious: rudely jesting. [L. *inficētus* — *in-,* not, *facētus,* courteous, witty.]

infidel *in'fi-dl, adj.* unbelieving: sceptical: disbelieving Christianity or whatever be the religion of the user of the word. — *n.* one who rejects Christianity, etc.: (*loosely*) one who disbelieves in any theory, etc. — *n.* **infidel'ity** lack of faith or belief: disbelief in Christianity, etc.: unfaithfulness, esp. to the marriage contract: treachery. [O.Fr. *infidèle* — L. *infidēlis* — *in-,* not, *fidēlis,* faithful — *fidēs,* faith.]

infield *in'fēld, n.* in baseball, the space enclosed within the base-lines: the part of the field near the wicket (*cricket*): the players stationed in the infield: formerly, land near the farmhouse, kept constantly manured and under tillage (also *adj.*) — opp. to *outfield* (*Scot.*). — *n.* **in'fielder** a player on the infield. [**in¹, field.**]

infighting *in'fīt-ing, n.* boxing at close quarters when blows from the shoulder cannot be given. — See also under **in¹.** [**in¹, fighting.**]

infilling *in'fil-ing, n.* filling up or in: material used to fill up or level: adding to property by building inside or alongside a house while staying within one's boundaries: infill development. — *v.t.* **in'fill** to fill in. — *n.* **in'fill** material for infilling. — **infill housing, development** new houses built between or among older ones. [**in¹, fill¹.**]

infiltrate *in'fil-trāt, -fil', v.t.* to cause to percolate: to cause to percolate into: to sift into: to permeate. — *v.i.* to permeate by degrees: to sift or filter in. — *v.t.* and *v.i.* of troops, agents, to enter (hostile area) secretly and for subversive purposes. — *v.t.* **infil'ter** to filter or sift in. — *ns.* **infiltra'tion** the process of infiltrating: gradual permeation or interpenetration: gradual accession or introduction of a new element, as of population or troops: a deposit or substance infiltrated; **in'filtrator** one who gets himself accepted as a member of a group towards which he has hostile or subversive intentions. [Pfx. **in-** (1).]

infima species *in'fi-mə spē'shēz, ēn'fi-ma spe'ki-ās,* (L.L.) the lowest species included in a genus or class.

infinite *in'fin-it,* in church singing also *in'fi-nīt, adj.* without end or limit: greater than any quantity that can be assigned (*math.*): extending to infinity: vast: in vast numbers: inexhaustible: infinitated (*log.*): (of part of a verb) not limited by person or number. — *n.* that which is not only without determinate bounds, but which cannot possibly admit of bound or limit: the Absolute, the Infinite Being or God. — *adjs.* **infin'itant** denoting merely negative attribution; **infin'itary** pertaining to infinity. — *v.t.* **infin'itate** to make infinite: to turn into a negative term (*log.*). — *adv.* **in'finitely.** — *n.* **in'finiteness.** — *adj.* (orig. ordinal numeral) **infinitesimal** (*-es'*) infinitely small: (*loosely*) extremely small. — *n.* an infinitely small quantity. — *adv.* **infinites'imally.** — *ns.* **infin'itude, infin'ity** boundlessness: an infinite quantity: an infinite distance: vastness, immensity: countless or indefinite number. — **infinite canon** (*mus.*) a canon that can be repeated indefinitely; **infinite set** (*math.*) one that can be put into a one-one correspondence with part of itself; **infinitesimal calculus** differential and integral calculus. [Pfx. **in-** (2).]

infinitive *in-fin'it-iv,* (*gram.*) *adj.* expressing, in the mood that expresses, the idea without person or number. — *n.* the infinitive mood: a verb in the infinitive mood. — *adj.* **infiniti'val.** — *adv.* **infin'itively.** [L. *infīnītīvus* — *in-,* not, *fīnīre,* to limit.]

infirm *in-fûrm', adj.* feeble: sickly: weak: frail: unstable. — *ns.* **infirma'rian** an officer in a monastery having charge of the quarters for the sick; **infirmary** (*in-fûrm'ər-i*) a hospital or place for the treatment of the sick; **infirm'ity.** — *adv.* **infirm'ly.** — *n.* **infirm'ness.** [L. *īnfirmus* — *in-,* not, *firmus,* strong.]

infix *in-fiks', v.t.* to fix in: to drive or fasten in: to set in by piercing: to insert an element within a (root) (*philol.*). Also **enfix** (*Shak.*). — *n.* **in'fix** (*philol.*) an element or affix inserted within a root or word, as *m* in the Gr. *lambanō,* from the root *lab.* [L. *īnfīxus* — *in,* in, *fīgĕre, fīxum,* to fix.]

in flagrante delicto *in flə-gran'ti di-lik'tō, flä-gran'te dā-lik'tō,* (L.) in the very act of committing the crime.

inflame *in-flām', v.t.* to cause to flame: to cause to burn: to make hot: to make red: to cause inflammation in: to arouse passions in: to excite: to exacerbate. — *v.i.* to burst into flame: to become hot, painful, red or excited: to undergo inflammation. — *adjs.* **inflam'able** (*obs.*) inflammable; **inflamed'.** — *n.* **inflâm'er.** [O.Fr. *enflammer* — L. *īnflammāre;* see next.]

inflammable *in-flam'ə-bl, adj.* that may be set on fire (see **flammable**): easily kindled or excited. — *n.* an inflammable substance. — *ns.* **inflammabil'ity; inflamm'-ableness.** — *adv.* **inflamm'ably.** — *n.* **inflammation** (*-flə-mā'shən*) the state of being in flame: heat of a part of the body, with pain, redness, and swelling: kindling of the passions. — *adj.* **inflamm'atory** tending to inflame: inflaming: exciting, tending to stir up trouble. [L. *īnflammāre* — *in,* into, *flamma,* a flame.]

inflate *in-flāt', v.t.* to well with air or gas: to puff up: to elate: to expand unduly: to increase excessively. — *v.i.* to become full of air or gas: to distend. — *adj ,* *n.* **inflat'able** (any object) that can be inflated. — *adj.* **inflat'ed** swollen or blown out: turgid: pompous: hollow, filled with air (*bot.*). — *adv.* **inflat'ingly.** — *n.* **inflation** (*in-flā'shən*) the act of inflating: the condition of being inflated: afflatus, inspiration (*rare*): turgidity of style: undue increase in quantity of money in proportion to buying power, as on an excessive issue of fiduciary money : a progressive increase in the general level of prices. — *adj.* **infla'tionary.** — *ns.*

infla'tionism the policy of inflating currency; **infla'-tionist.** — *adj.* **inflat'ive** causing inflation: tending to inflate. — *ns.* **inflat'or** one who inflates: a cycle pump; **inflat'us** (L.) inspiration. — *adj.* **infla'tion-proof** of investments, etc., protected esp. by indexation against inflation. — **infla'tion-proofing.** [L. *īnflāre, -ātum* — *in,* into, *flāre,* to blow.]

inflect *in-flekt', v.t.* to bend in: to turn from a direct line or course: to modulate, as the voice: to vary in the terminations (*gram.*). — *n.* **inflec'tion, inflex'ion** a bending or deviation: modulation of the voice: the varying in termination to express the relations of case, number, gender, person, tense, etc. (*gram.*). — *adjs.* **inflec'tional, inflex'ional; inflec'tionless, inflex'ionless; inflect'ive** subject to inflection; **inflexed'** bent inward: bent: turned. — *n.* **inflexure** (*in-flek'shər*) an inward bend or fold. [L. *īnflectĕre* — *in,* in, *flectĕre, flexum,* to bend, *flexiō, -ōnis,* a bend.]

inflexible *in-flek'si-bl, adj.* that cannot be bent: unyielding: rigid: unbending. — *ns.* **inflexibil'ity, inflex'ibleness.** — *adv.* **inflex'ibly.** [Pfx. **in-** (2).]

inflict *in-flikt', v.t.* to lay on: to impose (as punishment, pain). — *n.* **inflic'tion** the act of inflicting or imposing: that which is inflicted. — *adj.* **inflict'ive** tending or able to inflict. [L. *īnflīgĕre, īnflīctum* — *in,* against, *flīgĕre,* to strike.]

inflorescence *in-flor-es'əns, -flər-, n.* mode of branching of a flower-bearing axis: aggregate of flowers on an axis. [L. *īnflōrēscĕre,* to begin to blossom.]

inflow *in'flō, n.* the act of flowing in, influx: that which flows in. — *adj.* **in'flowing** flowing in. [Pfx. **in-** (1).]

influence *in'floo-əns, n.* inflow (*obs.*): the power or virtue supposed to flow from planets upon men and things (*astrol.*): a spiritual influx: the power of producing an effect, esp. unobtrusively: the effect of power exerted: that which has such power: a person exercising such power: ascendency, often of a secret or undue kind: exertions of friends at court, wire-pulling, and the like. — *v.t.* to have or exert influence upon: to affect. — *adj.* **in'fluent** inflowing: exerting influence. — *n.* a tributary stream. — *adj.* **influential** (*-en'shl*) of the nature of influence: having much influence: effectively active (in bringing something about). — *adv.* **influen'-tially.** [O.Fr., — L.L. *īnfluentia* — L. *in,* into, *fluĕre,* to flow.]

influenza *in-floo-en'zə, n.* an epidemic virus disease attacking esp. the upper respiratory tract. — *adj.* **in-fluen'zal.** [It., influence, influenza (as a supposed astral visitation) — L.L. *īnfluentia;* see **influence.**]

influx *in'fluks, n.* a flowing in: accession: that which flows in. — *n.* **influxion** (*in-fluk'shən*). — **influx control** in South Africa, a government control which prevents Africans entering urban areas without permits. [L. *īnfluxus* — *īnfluĕre.*]

info *in'fō,* coll. short form of **information.**

in-foal *in-fōl', adj.* pregnant (with foal). [**in¹, foal.**]

infold¹. See **enfold.**

infold² *in'fold', n.* a fold inwards. [Pfx. **in-** (1).]

inforce. Same as **enforce.**

inform¹ *in-förm', v.t.* to give form to (*obs.*): to animate or give life to: to impart a quality to: to impart knowledge to: to tell: to direct (*Milt.*). — *v.i.* to take shape or form (*Shak.*): to inspire: to give shape to: to give information, make an accusation (with *against* or *on*). — *ns.* **inform'ant** one who informs or gives intelligence; **informati'cian** one engaged in informatics. — *n. sing.* **informa'tics** information science: information technology. — *n.* **information** (*in-fər-mā'shən*) intelligence given: knowledge: an accusation given to a magistrate or court. — *adjs.* **informāt'ional; inform'-ative** having power to form: instructive; **inform'atory** instructive: giving information; **informed'** knowing, intelligent, educated. — *n.* **inform'er** one who gives information: one who informs against another: an animator. — **information retrieval** the storage, classification, and subsequent tracing of (esp. computerised) information; **information science** (the study of) the processing and communication of data, esp. by means of computerised systems; **information scientist; information technology** the (esp. computerised or electronic) technology related to the gathering, recording and communicating of information; **information theory** mathematical analysis of efficiency with which communication channels are employed. [O.Fr. *enformer* — L. *īnfōrmāre* — *in*, into, *fōrmāre*, to form, *fōrma*, form.]

inform² *in-förm'*, *adj.* without form: unformed: ill-formed. — *adj.* **inform'al** not in proper form: irregular: unceremonious: (of a vote) invalid (*Austr.*). — *n.* **informal'ity.** — *adv.* **inform'ally.** — *adj.* **informed'** unformed (*Spens.*): of stars, not included within the figures of any of the ancient constellations (*astron.*). [L. *in-*, not, *fōrma*, form; *informis*, formless, misshapen.]

in forma pauperis *in för'mə pö'pər-is, för'mä powp'er-is,* (L.) as a poor man.

informidable *in-för'mi-də-bl*, (*Milt.*) *adj.* not formidable. [Pfx. **in-** (2).]

in foro conscientiae *in fö'rō kon-shi-en'shi-ē, kōn-ski-en-ti-ī,* (L.) in the court of conscience: judged by one's own conscience.

infortune *in-för'tūn*, *n.* misfortune. [Pfx. **in-** (2).]

infra *in'frə, ēn'frä,* (L.) below: lower down on the page, or further on in the book. — **infra dignitatem** (*dig-nitā'təm, -tä'tem*) below one's dignity (colloquially sometimes **infra dig.**).

infracostal *in-frə-kos'tl, adj.* beneath the ribs. [L. *īnfrā,* below, *costa,* a rib.]

infraction *in-frak'shən, n.* violation, esp. of law: breach. — *v.t.* **infract'** to infringe. — *adjs.* **infract'** (*obs.*), **infract'ed** broken: interrupted: not in. — *n.* **infrac'tor** one who infracts. [L. *īnfringĕre, īnfrāctum* — *in,* in, *frangĕre, frāctum,* to break.]

infragrant *in-frā'grənt, adj.* not fragrant. [Pfx. **in-** (2).]

infrahuman *in-frə-hū'mən, adj.* lower than human. [L. *īnfrā,* below.]

Infralapsarian *in-frə-lap-sā'ri-ən, n.* a believer in Infralapsarianism. — Also *adj.* — *n.* **Infralapsār'ianism** the common Augustinian and Calvinist doctrine, that God for his own glory determined to create the world, to permit the fall of man, to elect some and leave the rest to punishment — distinct both from *Supralapsarianism* and *Sublapsarianism:* also used as equivalent to Sublapsarianism. [L. *īnfrā,* below, after, *lāpsus,* a fall.]

inframaxillary *in-frə-mak'si-lə-ri, adj.* situated under the jaw: belonging to the lower jaw. [L. *īnfrā,* below, *maxilla,* jaw.]

infrangible *in-fran'ji-bl, adj.* that cannot be broken: not to be violated. — *ns.* **infrangibil'ity, infran'gibleness.** [L. *in-*, not, *frangĕre,* to break.]

infraorbital *in-frə-ör'bā-tl, adj.* situated below the orbit of the eye. [L. *īnfrā,* below.]

infra-red *in'frə-red', adj.* beyond the red end of the visible spectrum: using infra-red radiation: sensitive to this radiation. [L. *īnfrā,* below.]

infrasonic *in-frə-son'ik,* (*acoustics*) *adj.* of frequencies, below the usual audible limit. — *n.* **in'frasound.** [L. *īnfrā,* below.]

infrastructure *in'frə-struk'chər, n.* inner structure, structure of component parts: a system of communications and services as backing for military, commercial, etc., operations. — *adj.* **infrastruc'tural.** [L. *īnfrā,* below.]

infrequent *in-frē'kwənt, adj.* seldom occurring: rare: uncommon. — *ns.* **infrē'quence, infrē'quency.** — *adv.* **infrē'quently.** [Pfx. **in-** (2).]

infringe *in-frinj', v.t.* to violate, esp. law: to neglect to obey. — *n.* **infringe'ment.** [L. *īnfringĕre* — *in,* in, *frangĕre,* to break.]

infructuous *in-fruk'tū-əs, adj.* not fruitful. — *adv.* **infruc'tuously.** [L. *īnfrūctuōsus* — *in-,* not, *frūctuōsus,* fruitful.]

infula *in'fū-lə, n.* a white-and-red fillet or band of woollen stuff, worn by the ancient Romans upon the forehead

in religious rites: a lappet in a mitre: — *pl.* **in'fulae** (*-ē*). [L. *īnfula.*]

infundibular *in-fun-dib'ū-lər, adj.* funnel-shaped. — Also **infundib'ulate, infundib'uliform.** [L. *īnfundibulum,* a funnel — *in,* in, *fundĕre,* to pour.]

infuriate *in-fū'ri-āt, v.t.* to enrage: to madden. — *adj.* (*-it, -āt*) enraged: mad. [L. *in,* in, *furiāre, -ātum,* to madden — *furēre,* to rave.]

infuscate *in-fus'kāt, -kit, adj.* clouded with brown. [L. *in,* in, *fuscus,* brown.]

infuse *in-fūz', v.t.* to pour in: to instil: to steep in liquor without boiling: to shed, to pour (*Shak.*): to imbue. — *v.i.* to undergo infusion. — *n.* (*Spens.*) infusion. — *n.* **infus'er** a device for making an infusion, esp. of tea. — *adj.* **infus'ible.** — *n.* **infusion** (*in-fū'zhən*) pouring in: something poured in or introduced: the pouring of water over any substance in order to extract its active qualities: a solution in water of an organic, esp. a vegetable, substance: the liquor so obtained: inspiration: instilling. — *adj.* **infusive** (*-fū'siv*) having the power of infusion, or of being infused. [L. *īnfundĕre, īnfūsum* — *in,* into, *fundĕre, fūsum,* to pour.]

infusible *in-fūz'i-bl, adj.* that cannot be fused: having a high melting-point. — *n.* **infusibili'ity.** [Pfx. **in-** (2).]

infusoria *in-fū-zō'ri-ə, -zō, -sō'ri-ə, -sō', n.pl.* orig., minute organisms found in stagnant infusions of animal or vegetable material: (with *cap.*) the Ciliophora, a class of Protozoa with cilia throughout life (Ciliata) or in early life (Suctoria). — *adjs.* **infūsō'rial, infū'sory** composed of or containing infusoria. — *n.* and *adj.* **infūsō'rian.** — *n.* **infusorial earth** diatomite. [Neut. pl. of modern L. *īnfūsorius;* see **infuse.**]

ingan *ing'ən, n.* a Scots and dial. form of **onion.**

ingate¹ *in'gāt, n.* an inlet for molten metal in founding. [**in¹, gate¹.**]

ingate² *in'gāt,* (*Spens.*) *n.* a way in: entrance: ingress. [**in¹, gate².**]

ingathering *in'gadh-ər-ing, n.* collection: securing of the fruits of the earth: harvest. — **Feast of Ingathering** see **Tabernacles, Feast of.** [Pfx. **in-** (1).]

ingeminate *in-jem'in-āt, v.t.* to reiterate: to double. — *n.* **ingeminā'tion.** [L. *ingemināre, -ātum* — *in,* in, *geminus,* twin.]

ingener *in'jən-ər,* (*Shak.*) *n.* Same as **engineer.**

ingenerate¹ *in-jen'ər-āt, v.t.* to generate or produce within. — *adj.* (*-it*) inborn: innate. [Pfx. **in-** (1).]

ingenerate² *in-jen'ər-it, -āt, adj.* not generated, self-existent. [Pfx. **in-** (2).]

ingenious *in-jē'nyəs, -ni-əs, adj.* of good natural abilities (*obs.*): skilful in invention or contriving: skilfully contrived. — *adv.* **ingē'niously.** — *ns.* **ingē'niousness** power of ready invention: facility in combining ideas: curiousness in design; **ingē'nium** bent of mind. [L. *ingenium,* mother-wit.]

ingénue *ē-zhā-nü,* (Fr.) *n.* a naïve young woman, esp. on the stage: — *masc.* **ingénu.**

ingenuity *in-ji-nū'i-ti, n.* orig., ingenuousness: (by confusion with **ingenious**) ingeniousness. [L. *ingenuitās, -ātis;* see next word.]

ingenuous *in-jen'ū-əs, adj.* free-born (*obs.*): frank: honourable: free from deception. — *adv.* **ingen'uously.** — *ns.* **ingen'uousness; ingenu'ity** (see previous word). [L. *ingenuus,* free-born, ingenuous.]

ingest *in-jest', v.t.* to take into the body. — *n.pl.* **ingest'a** materials taken into the body. — *adj.* **ingest'ible.** — *n.* **ingestion** (*in-jes'chən*). — *adj.* **ingest'ive.** [L. *ingerĕre, ingestum,* to carry in — *in, gerĕre,* to carry.]

ingine *in-jīn',* (*obs.*) *n.* ability: genius. [L. *ingenium.*]

ingle¹ *ing'gl,* (Scot. *ing'l*) *n.* a fire: fireplace. — **ing'le=cheek** the jamb of a fireplace; **ing'le-nook** a chimney-corner; **ing'le-side** a fireside. [Possibly Gael. *aingeal;* or L. *igniculus,* dim. of *ignis,* fire.]

ingle² *ing'gl,* (*obs.*) *n.* a catamite: (wrongly) a friend. [Origin obscure.]

inglobe *in-glōb',* (*Milt.*) *v.t.* to englobe, form into a sphere. [Pfx. **in-** (1).]

inglorious *in-glō'ri-əs, -glō', adj.* not glorious: unhonoured: shameful. — *adv.* **inglō′riously.** — *n.* **inglō′-riousness.** [Pfx. **in-** (2).]

ingluvies *in-gloō′vi-ēz, n.* the crop or craw of birds. — *adj.* **inglu′vial.** [L. *inglŭviēs.*]

ingo *in′gō, (Scot.) n.* an ingoing, reveal: entry into or taking on of a new tenancy: — *pl.* **in′goes.** [**in**[1], **go**[1].]

ingoes. See **ingo, ingot.**

ingoing *in′gō-ing, n.* a going in: entrance: a reveal (*Scot.*). — *adj.* going in: entering as an occupant: thorough, penetrating. [**in**[1], **go**[1].]

ingot *ing′gət, -got, n.* a mass of unwrought metal, esp. gold or silver, cast in a mould. — Also (*Spens., pl.*) **ingowes, ingoes.** [Perh. O.E. *in*, in, and the root *got*, as in *goten*, pa.p. of *gēotan*, to pour; Ger. *giessen*, Goth. *giutan*.]

ingraft. See **engraft.**

ingrain *in-grān′, v.t.* the same as **engrain.** — *adj.* (pron. *in′grān* when attributive) dyed in the yarn or thread before manufacture: deeply fixed: through and through. — *adj.* **ingrained′** (attrib. *in′grānd*). [Pfx. **in-** (1).]

ingram, ingrum *ing′rəm, (obs.) adj.* ignorant. [**ignorant.**]

ingrate *in-grāt′, in′grāt, adj.* unpleasing (*obs.*): ungrateful (*arch.*). — *n.* one who is ungrateful. — *adj.* **ingrate′ful** unthankful. [L. *ingrātus* — *in-*, not, *grātus*, pleasing, grateful.]

ingratiate *in-grā′shi-āt, v.t.* to commend to someone's grace or favour (often reflexively; followed by *with*). — *adj.* **ingra′tiating.** [L. *in*, into, *grātia*, favour.]

ingratitude *in-grat′i-tūd, n.* unthankfulness. [L.L. *in-grātitūdō* — L. *ingrātus*, unthankful.]

ingravescent *in(g)-grə-ves′ənt, (med.) adj.* becoming more severe. [L. *ingravescĕre*, to become heavier — L. *gravis*, heavy.]

ingredient *in-grē′di-ənt, n.* that which enters into a compound: a component. [L. *ingrediēns, -entis*, pr.p. of *ingredī* — *in*, into, *gradī*, to walk.]

in gremio *in grēm′, grem′i-ō, (L.L.)* in the bosom.

ingress *in′gres, n.* entrance: power, right, or means of entrance. — *n.* **ingression** (*in-gresh′ən*). — *adj.* **ingress′-ive** (of speech sounds) pronounced with inhalation rather than exhalation of breath. [L. *ingressus* — *ingredī*, to go in; see **ingredient.**]

ingroove. See **engroove.**

ingross *in-grōs′, (Shak.) v.t.* Same as **engross.**

ingrowing *in′grō-ing, adj.* growing inward: growing into the flesh: growing within. — *adj.* **in′grown.** — *n.* **in′growth** growth within or inward: a structure so formed. [Pfx. **in-** (1).]

ingrum. See **ingram.**

inguinal *ing′gwin-əl, adj.* relating to the groin. [L. *inguinālis* — *inguen, inguinis*, the groin.]

ingulf, ingulph. See **engulf.**

ingurgitate *in-gûr′ji-tāt, v.t.* to swallow up greedily, as in a gulf. — *n.* **ingurgitā′tion.** [L. *ingurgitāre, -ātum* — *in*, into, *gurges, -itis*, a whirlpool.]

inhabit *in-hab′it, v.t.* to dwell in: to occupy. — *v.i.* (*arch.*) to dwell. — *adj.* **inhab′itable** that may be inhabited (see also next word). — *ns.* **inhab′itance, inhab′itancy** the act of inhabiting: abode; **inhab′itant** one who inhabits: a resident. — *adj.* resident. — *ns.* **inhabitā′tion** the act of inhabiting: dwelling-place: population, or perh. the inhabited world (*Milt.*); **inhab′itiveness** (*phrenology*) love of locality and home; **inhab′itor** an inhabitant (*B.*): a colonist, settler (*obs.*); **inhab′itress** a female inhabitant. [L. *inhabitāre* — *in*, in, *habitāre*, to dwell.]

inhabitable *in-hab′it-ə-bl, (obs.) adj.* not habitable, uninhabitable. — See also under **inhabit.** [L. *inhabitābilis* — *in-*, not, *habitābilis.*]

inhale *in-hāl′, v.t.* and *v.i.* to breathe in: to draw in. — *adj.* **inhā′lant** inhaling: drawing in. — *ns.* **inhā′lant** an inhaling organ, structure or apparatus: a medicinal preparation to be inhaled; **inhalation** (*in-hə-lā′shən*) the act of drawing into the lungs: something to be inhaled; **inhalator** (*in′hə-lā-tər*, or *-lā′*) apparatus for enabling one to inhale a gas, etc.; **inhalatorium** (*in-hāl-ə-tō′ri-əm, -tör′*) an institution or department for administering

inhalations; **inhā′ler** one who inhales; one who habitually inhales tobacco smoke: an inhalator: a respirator or gas-mask. [L. *in*, upon, *hālāre*, to breathe (L. *inhālāre* means to breathe upon).]

inharmonious *in-här-mō′ni-əs, adj.* discordant, unmusical: disagreeing: marked by disagreement and dispeace. — *adjs.* **inharmonic** (*in-här-mon′ik*), **-al** wanting harmony: inharmonious. — *adv.* **inharmō′niously.** — *ns.* **inharmō′niousness; inharmony** (*in-här′mən-i*). [Pfx. **in-** (2).]

inhaust *in-höst′, (arch.) v.t.* to drink in. [L. *in*, in, *haurīre, haustum*, to draw.]

inhearse, inherce *in-hûrs′, (Shak.) v.t.* to enclose as in a hearse: to bury. — Also **enhearse.** [Pfx. **in-** (1).]

inhere *in-hēr′, v.i.* (with *in*) to stick, remain firm in something: to be inherent. — *ns.* **inhēr′ence, inhēr′ency** a sticking fast: existence in something else: a fixed state of being in another body or substance: the relation between a quality or attribute and its subject (*philos.*). — *adj.* **inhēr′ent** sticking fast (*arch.*): existing in and inseparable from something else: innate: natural. — *adv.* **inhēr′ently.** [L. *inhaerēre, inhaesum* — *in*, in, *haerēre*, to stick.]

inherit *in-her′it, v.t.* to make heir (*Shak.*): to be the heir of, succeed as heir (*arch.*): to get as heir: to possess by transmission from past generations: to have at second-hand from anyone (*coll.*): to have by genetic transmission from ancestors. — *v.i.* to succeed. — *adj.* **inher′-itable** same as **heritable.** — *ns.* **inher′itance** that which is or may be inherited: hereditary descent; **inher′itor** one who inherits or may inherit: an heir: — *fem.* **inher′itress, inher′itrix.** [O.Fr. *enhériter*, to put in possession as heir — L.L. *inhērēditāre*, to inherit — L. *in*, in, *hērēs, hērēdis*, an heir.]

inhesion *in-hē′zhən.* Same as **inherence.**

inhibit *in-hib′it, v.t.* to hold in or back: to keep back: to check. — *ns.* **inhibi′tion** the act of inhibiting or restraining: the state of being inhibited: prohibition: a writ from a higher court to an inferior judge to stay proceedings (*obs.*): a restraining action of the unconscious will: the blocking of a mental or psychophysical process by another set up at the same time by the same stimulus: stoppage, complete or partial, of a physical process by some nervous influence; **inhib′itor** that which inhibits: a substance that interferes with a chemical or biological process. — *adjs.* **inhib′itive; inhib′itory** prohibitory. [L. *inhibēre, -hibitum* — *in, habēre*, to have.]

inholder *in-hōld′ər, (Spens.) n.* an inhabitant. [Pfx. **in-** (1).]

inhomogeneous *in-hom-ō-jēn′i-əs, adj.* not homogeneous. — *n.* **inhomogeneity** (*-jən-ē′i-ti*). [Pfx. **in-** (2).]

inhoop *in-hoōp′, (Shak.) v.t.* to confine, as in a hoop or enclosure. [Pfx. **in-** (1).]

inhospitable *in-hos′pit-ə-bl, -pit′, adj.* affording no kindness to strangers: (of a place) barren, not offering shelter, food, etc. — *ns.* **inhos′pitableness, inhospital′ity** want of hospitality or courtesy to strangers. — *adv.* **inhosp′itably.** [Pfx. **in-** (2).]

in-house. See **in**[1].

inhuman *in-hū′mən, adj.* barbarous: cruel: unfeeling. — *n.* **inhumanity** (*in-hū-man′i-ti*) the state of being inhuman or inhumane: barbarity: cruelty. — *adv.* **inhū′-manly.** [Pfx. **in-** (2).]

inhumane *in-hū-mān′, adj.* not humane, cruel. [Pfx. **in-** (2).]

inhume *in-hūm′, v.t.* to bury in the earth. — Also **inhumate** (*in′*, or *-hūm′*). — *n.* **inhumā′tion** the act of depositing in the ground: burial. [L. *inhumāre* — *in*, in, *humus*, the ground.]

inia. See **inion.**

inimical *in-im′i-kl, adj.* unfriendly: hostile: unfavourable: opposed. — *adv.* **inim′ically.** — *ns.* **inim′icalness, inimical′ity.** — *adj.* **inimicitious** (*-sish′əs; Sterne*) unfriendly. [L. *inimīcālis* — *inimīcus*, enemy — *in-*, not, *amīcus*, friend.]

inimitable *in-im′it-ə-bl, adj.* that cannot be imitated: surpassingly excellent. — *ns.* **inimitabil′ity, inim′itable-**

ness. — *adv.* **inim′itably.** [Pfx. **in-** (2).]

inion *in′i-ən n.* the external occipital protuberance: — *pl.*
in′ia. [Gr. *īnion,* the occiput.]

iniquity *īn-ik′wi-ti, n.* want of equity or fairness (*arch.*):
injustice: wickedness: a crime: (with *cap.*) one of the
names of the Vice, the established buffoon of the old
Moralities (*hist.*). — Also (*rarely*) **iniq′uitousness.** —
adj. **iniq′uitous** unjust: scandalously unreasonable:
wicked. — *adv.* **iniq′uitously.** [Fr. *iniquité* — L.
inīquitās, -ātis — *inīquus,* unequal — *in-,* not, *aequus,*
equal.]

inisle. Same as **enisle.**

initial *in-ish′l, adj.* beginning: of, at, or serving as the
beginning: original. — *n.* the letter beginning a word,
esp. a name. — *v.t.* to put the initials of one's name
to: — *pr.p.* **init′ialling;** *pa.t.* and *pa.p.* **init′ialled.** — *v.t.*
init′ialise, -ize to designate by initial letters. — *adv.*
init′ially. — *v.t.* **initiate** (*-ish′i-āt*) to begin, start: to
introduce (to) (e.g. knowledge): to admit (into), esp.
with rites, (as to a secret society, a mystery). — *v.i.* to
perform the first act or rite. — *n.* (*-it*) one who is
initiated. — *adj.* initiated: belonging to one newly
initiated. — *n.* **initiā′tion.** — *adj.* **init′iative** (*-i-ə-tiv*)
serving to initiate: introductory. — *n.* the lead, first
step, often considered as determining the conditions
for oneself or others: the right or power of beginning:
energy and resourcefulness enabling one to act without
prompting from others: the right to originate legislation, or a constitutional method of doing so. — *n.*
init′iātor one who or that which initiates. — *adj.*
init′iatory (*-i-ə-tə-ri*) tending or serving to initiate:
introductory. — *n.* introductory rite. — **initial cell**
(*bot.*) a cell that remains meristematic and gives rise
to many daughter-cells from which permanent tissues
are formed; **initiation fee** (*U.S.*) entrance fee of a
society. — **Initial Teaching Alphabet** a 44-character
alphabet in which each character corresponds to a
single sound of English, sometimes used for the teaching of reading. [L. *initiālis* — *initium,* a beginning,
inīre, initum — *in,* into, *īre, itum,* to go.]

inject *in-jekt′, v.t.* to throw in or on (*obs.*): to force in: to
inspire or instil: to fill by injection. — *adj.* **injec′table**
able to be injected. — Also *n.* — *ns.* **injec′tion** (*-shən*)
the act of injecting or forcing in, esp. a liquid: a liquid
injected into the body with a syringe or similar instrument: a magma injected into a rock (*geol.*): see **insertion** (*space*): the spraying of oil-fuel into the cylinder
of a compression-ignition engine by an injection pump:
an amount of money added to an economy in order
to stimulate production, expansion, etc.: a mapping
function in which each element in a set corresponds
to only one element in another set (*math.*); **injec′tor**
one who injects: something used for injecting, especially an apparatus for forcing water into a boiler. —
injection moulding moulding of thermoplastics by
squirting from a heated cylinder into a water-chilled
mould. [L. *injicĕre, injectum* — *in,* into, *jacĕre,* to
throw.]

injelly *in-jel′i,* (*Tenn.*) *v.t.* to place as if in jelly. [Pfx.
in- (1).]

injoint *in-joint′,* (*Shak.*) *v.t.* to join. [Pfx. **in-** (1).]

injudicious *in-joo-dish′əs, adj.* not judicious: ill-judged. —
adv. **injudic′ial** not according to law-forms. — *advs.*
injudic′ially; injudic′iously. — *n.* **injudic′iousness.**
[Pfx. **in-** (2).]

Injun *in′jən,* (*coll.*) *n.* an American Indian. — Also *adj.*
— **honest Injun** see **honest.**

injunction *in-jungk′shən, n.* the act of enjoining or commanding: an order: a precept: an exhortation: an
inhibitory writ by which a superior court stops or
prevents some inequitable or illegal act being done —
called in Scotland an *interdict:* conjunction (*Milt.*). —
v.t. **injunct′** to prohibit, restrain by means of an
injunction. — *adj.* **injunc′tive.** — *adv.* **injunc′tively.**
[L.L. *injunctiō, -ōnis* — *in,* in, *jungĕre, junctum,* to join.]

injure *in′jər, v.t.* to wrong: to harm: to damage: to hurt.
— *ns.* **in′jurant** that which causes injury; **in′jurer.** —

adj. **injurious** (*in-joo′ri-əs*) tending to injure: wrongful:
hurtful: damaging to reputation. — *adv.* **inju′riously.**
— *ns.* **inju′riousness; injury** (*in′jər-i*) that which injures:
wrong: damage: hurt: impairment: annoyance: insult,
offence (*obs.*). — **injury benefit** in Britain, a National
Insurance weekly payment for injury sustained while
at work; **injury time** in ball games, extra time allowed
for play to compensate for time lost as a result of injury
during the game. [L. *injūria,* injury — *in-,* not, *jūs,
jūris,* law.]

injustice *in-jus′tis, n.* violation or withholding of another's rights or dues: wrong: iniquity. [Pfx. **in-** (2).]

ink *ingk, n.* a black or coloured liquid used in writing,
printing, etc.: a dark liquid ejected by cuttle-fishes, etc.
— *v.t.* to daub, cover, blacken, or colour with ink. —
ns. **ink′er** one who inks: a pad or roller for inking type,
etc.; **ink′iness** — *adj.* **ink′y** consisting of or resembling
ink: very black; blackened with ink. — **ink′-bag, -sac**
a sac in some cuttle-fishes, containing a black viscid
fluid; **ink′berry** (the fruit of) any of various N. American shrubs, esp. *Ilex glabra* of the holly family and
Phytolacca americana, pokeweed; **ink′-bottle** a bottle
for holding ink; **ink′-cap** any mushroom of the genus
Coprinus, such as the *shaggy ink-cap* (*C. comatus*);
ink′-erā′ser india-rubber treated with fine sand, used
for rubbing out ink-marks; **ink′-feed** the passage by
which the nib of a fountain-pen is fed with ink;
ink′holder a container for ink: the reservoir of a
fountain-pen; **ink′horn** (*obs.*) an ink-holder, formerly
of horn: a portable case for ink, etc. — *adj.* pedantic,
bookish. — **ink′-horn-mate** (*Shak.*) a bookish man;
ink′ing-roll′er a roller covered with a composition for
inking printing type; **ink′ing-ta′ble** a table or flat
surface used for supplying the inking-roller with ink
during the process of printing; **ink pencil** a copying-
pencil, a pencil made from a composition whose marks
when moistened look like ink and can be copied by a
printing-press; **ink′pot** an ink-bottle, or pot for dipping
a pen in; **ink′-slinger** (*slang*) a professional author: a
scribbler: a controversialist; **ink′spot** a small ink stain.
— *adj.* **ink′-stained.** — **ink′stand** a stand or tray for
ink-bottles and (usually) pens; **ink′stone** a kind of stone
containing sulphate of iron, used in making ink;
ink′well a reservoir for ink let into or standing on a
desk, etc. — **China ink, Chinese ink, Indian ink,** in U.S.
India ink (sometimes without *caps.*) a mixture of
lamp-black and size or glue, usu. kept in solid form
and rubbed down in water for use: a liquid suspension
of this; **ink-blot test** see **Rorschach test; ink in** to fill in
in ink; **invisible** or **sympathetic ink** a kind of ink that
remains invisible on the paper until it is heated;
mark′ing-ink see **mark¹; print′ing-ink** see **print; sling ink**
(*slang*) to write: to earn one's bread by writing: to
engage in controversy. [O.Fr. *enque* (Fr. *encre*) —
L.L. *encaustum,* the purple-red ink used by the later
Roman emperors — Gr. *enkauston* — *enkaiein,* to burn
in; see **encaustic.**]

inkle¹ *ingk′l,* (*obs.*) *n.* a kind of broad linen tape. — Also
inc′le. [Poss. Du. *enkel,* single.]

inkle². See **inkling.**

inkling *ingk′ling, n.* a slight hint: intimation: a dim notion
or suspicion. — *v.i.* **ink′le** to have or give a hint of.
[M.E. *inclen,* to hint at; origin unknown.]

in-kneed *in′-nēd′, adj.* bent inward at the knees: knock-
kneed. [Pfx. **in-** (1).]

inlace. Same as **enlace.**

inlaid. See **inlay.**

inland *in′land, in′lənd, n.* the interior part of a country:
the peopled part, or part near the capital (*arch.*). —
adj. remote from the sea: carried on, or produced,
within a country: confined to a country: refined,
polished (*Shak.*). — *adj.* (also *in-land′*) landward:
away from the sea: in an inland place. — *n.* **in′lander**
one who lives inland. — **inland bill** a bill of exchange
that is (designated as being) payable in the same
country, state, etc., as it is drawn; **inland navigation**
passage of boats or vessels on rivers, lakes, or canals

within a country; **inland revenue** internal revenue, derived from direct taxes such as income tax and stamp duty: (with *caps.*) the government department responsible for collecting such taxes.   [O.E. *inland*, a domain — *in* and *land*.]

in-law *in'lö, (coll.) n.* a relative by marriage, e.g. mother-in-law, brother-in-law: — *pl.* **in'-laws.**

inlay *in'lā', in-lā', v.t.* to insert, embed: to insert for preservation in a larger page, serving as margin: to ornament by laying in or inserting pieces of metal, ivory, etc.: on television, to mix images electronically, using masks: — *pr.p.* **in'lay'ing;** *pa.t.* and *pa.p.* **in'laid'.** — *n.* **in'lay** inlaying: inlaid work: material inlaid. — *adj.* **in'laid'** (or *in'lād,* or *in-lād'*) inserted by inlaying: decorated with inlay: consisting of inlay: having a pattern set into the surface. — *ns.* **inlayer** (*in'lā-ər, in-lā'ər*); **inlaying.**   [Pfx. **in-** (1).]

inlet *in'let, -lət, n.* an entrance: a passage by which anything is let in: a place of ingress: a small bay or opening in the land: a piece let in or inserted.   [**in**[1], **let**[1].]

inlier *in'lī-ər, (geol.) n.* an outcrop of older rock surrounded by younger.   [**in**[1], **lie**[2].]

in limine *in li'mi-ne, lē'mi-ne,* (L.) on the threshold.

inlock *in-lok', v.t.* Same as **enlock.**

in loco parentis *in lō'kō, lok'ō, pə-, pä-ren'tis,* (L.) in the place of a parent.

inly *in'li, adj.* inward: secret. — *adv.* inwardly: in the heart: thoroughly, entirely.   [**in**[1].]

inlying *in'lī-ing, adj.* situated inside or near a centre.   [**in**[1], **lying.**]

in malam partem *in mä'ləm pär'təm, ma'lam pär'tem,* (L.) in an unfavourable manner.

inmarriage *in'mar-ij, n.* endogamy (q.v. under **endo-**).   [Pfx. **in- (1).**]

inmate *in'māt, n.* one who lodges in the same house with another (*arch.*): one of those who live in a house, esp. one confined to an institution. — *adj.* (*obs.*) dwelling in the same place.   [**in**[1] or **inn, mate**[1].]

in medias res *in mē'di-əs rēz, mä'di-, me'di-äs räs,* (L.) into the midst of things.

in memoriam. See **memory.**

inmesh. Same as **enmesh.**

inmost. See **innermost** under **inner.**

inn *in, n.* abode (*obs.;* form. often in *pl.; Spens.* **in**): a house open to the public for lodging and entertainment of travellers: a hostel: a hotel: (*loosely*) a public-house. — *v.t.* and *v.i.* (*arch.*) to lodge, put up. — **inn'holder** (*Bacon; U.S.*), **inn'keeper** one who keeps an inn; **inn sign** a painted or otherwise decorated panel outside an inn, illustrating its name; **inn'yard** the courtyard round which an old-fashioned inn was built. — **Inns of Court** the buildings of four voluntary societies that have the exclusive right of calling to the English bar (Inner Temple, Middle Temple, Lincoln's Inn and Gray's Inn): hence the societies themselves; the **Inns of Chancery** were the buildings of minor societies, residences of junior students of law.   [O.E. *inn,* an inn, house — *in, inn,* within (adv.), from the prep. *in,* in.]

innards *in'ərdz, (coll.) n.pl.* entrails: internal parts of a mechanism: interior.   [**inwards.**]

innate *in'āt, i-nāt', adj.* inborn: natural to the mind: inherent: of an anther, attached by the base to the tip of the filament (*bot.*). — *adv.* **inn'ately** (or *-nāt'*). — *n.* **inn'ateness** (or *-nāt'*). — *adj.* **innā'tive** (*arch.*) native.   [L. *innātūs* — *in-,* in, *nāscī, nātus,* to be born.]

innavigable *in-nav'i-gə-bl, adj.* unnavigable. — *adv.* **innav'igably.**   [Pfx. **in-** (2).]

inner *in'ər, adj.* (comp. of **in**[1]) farther in: interior. — *n.* (a hit on) that part of a target between the bull's eye. — *adjs.* **inn'ermost, in'most** (superl. of **in**[1]) farthest in: most remote from the outside. — **inner bar** (*legal*) Queen's or King's counsel as a whole; **inner city** the central part of a city, esp. with regard to its special social problems, e.g. poor housing, poverty; **inner man** soul: mind: stomach (*facet.*); **inner part, voice** a voice part intermediate between the highest and the lowest;

inner space the undersea region regarded as an environment; **inner tube** the rubber tube inside a tyre, which is inflated.   [O.E. *in,* comp. *innera,* superl. *innemest* = *inne-m-est* — thus a double superlative.]

innervate *in'ər-vāt, in-ûr'vāt, v.t.* to supply with nerves or nervous stimulus. — Also **innerve'.** — *n.* **innervā'tion.**   [Pfx. **in-** (1).]

inning *in'ing, n.* ingathering, esp. of crops: (in *pl.;* in U.S. sometimes in *sing.*) a team's turn of batting in cricket, etc., or a turn of batting for both teams in baseball, etc.: hence, the time during which a person or a party is in possession of anything, a spell or turn: (in *pl.*) lands recovered from the sea. — **a good innings** a long life.   [**in**[1] or **inn.**]

innocent *in'ə-sənt, adj.* not hurtful: inoffensive: blameless: harmless: guileless: simple: ignorant of evil: imbecile (*dial.*): not legally guilty: devoid (with *of*): not malignant or cancerous (*med.*). — *n.* one free from fault: one with no knowledge of evil: a child: a simpleton: an idiot. — *ns.* **inn'ocence** harmlessness: blamelessness: guilelessness: simplicity: freedom from legal guilt; **inn'ocency** (*arch.*) the quality of being innocent. — *adv.* **inn'ocently.** — **Innocents' Day** see **Childermas.**   [O.Fr., — L. *innocēns, -entis* — *in-,* not, *nocēre,* to hurt.]

innocuous *in-ok'ū-əs, adj.* harmless. — *adv.* **innoc'uously.** — *ns.* **innoc'uousness, innocū'ity.**   [L. *innocuus* — *in-,* not, *nocuus,* hurtful — *nocēre,* to hurt.]

innominate *i-nom'i-nāt, -nit, adj.* having no name. — *adj.* **innom'inable** unnamable. — *n.* (in *pl.; obs. facet.*) trousers. — **innominate artery** the first large branch given off from the arch of the aorta; **innominate bone** (*os innōminātum*) the haunch-bone, hip-bone, formed by fusion in the adult of the ilium, ischium, and pubis; **innominate vein** one of two large veins on either side of the lower part of the neck formed by the union of the internal jugular and subclavian veins.   [L. *in-,* not, *nōmināre, -ātum,* to name.]

innovate *in'ō-vāt, in'ə-vāt, v.t.* to renew, alter (*rare*): to introduce as something new. — *v.i.* to introduce novelties: to make changes. — *ns.* **innovā'tion** the act of innovating: a thing introduced as a novelty: revolution (*Shak.*): substitution of one obligation for another (*Scots law*): a season's new growth (*bot.*); **innovā'tionist.** — *adj.* **inn'ovative.** — *n.* **inn'ovātor.** — *adj.* **inn'ovatory.**   [L. *innovāre, -ātum* — *in,* in, *novus,* new.]

innoxious *in-ok'shəs, adj.* not noxious. — *adv.* **innox'iously.** — *n.* **innox'iousness.**   [Pfx. **in-** (2).]

innuendo *in-ū-en'dō, n.* insinuation: an indirect reference or intimation: a part of a pleading in cases of libel and slander, pointing out what and who was meant: — *pl.* **innuen'do(e)s.** — *v.t.* to insinuate by innuendo: to interpret as innuendo. — *v.i.* to make insinuations.   [L. *innuendō,* by nodding at (i.e. indicating, to wit — used in old legal documents to introduce a parenthetic indication), ablative gerund of *innuēre,* to nod to, indicate — *in,* to, *nuēre,* to nod.]

Innuit, Inuit *in'ū-it, in'ōō-it, n.* the Eskimo people, esp. those of Greenland, Canada and Northern Alaska: a member of this people: their language.   [Eskimo, people, *pl.* of *inuk,* a person.]

innumerable *in-(n)ū'mər-ə-bl, adj.* that cannot be numbered: countless. — *ns.* **innūmerabil'ity; innū'merableness.** — *adv.* **innū'merably.** — *adj.* **innū'merous** (*Milt.*) without number: innumerable.   [Pfx. **in-** (2).]

innumerate *in-(n)ūm'ər-it, adj.* having no understanding of mathematics or science. — Also *n.* — *n.* **innum'eracy.**   [Coined 1959 by Sir Geoffrey Crowther (on analogy of *illiterate*) — L. *numerus,* number.]

innutrition *in-(n)ū-trish'ən, n.* want of nutrition: failure of nourishment. — *adjs.* **innū'trient** not nutrient; **innūtritious** (*-trish'əs*) not nutritious.   [Pfx. **in-** (2).]

inobedient *in-ō-bē'dyənt, adj.* disobedient. — *n.* **inobe'dience.** — *adv.* **inobe'diently.**   [Pfx. **in-** (2).]

inobservant *in-əb-zûr'vənt, adj.* unobservant: heedless. — *adj.* **inobser'vable** incapable of being observed. — *ns.*

inobser'vance lack of observance; **inobserva'tion** (-*ob*-). [Pfx. **in-** (2).]

inobtrusive *in-əb-trōō'siv, adj.* unobtrusive. — *adv.* **inobtru'sively.** — *n.* **inobtru'siveness.** [Pfx. **in-** (2).]

inoccupation *in-ok-ū-pā'shən, n.* lack of occupation. [Pfx. **in-** (2).]

inoculate *in-ok'ū-lāt, v.t.* to insert as a bud or graft: to graft: to imbue: to introduce (e.g. bacteria, a virus) into an organism: to give a mild form of (a disease) in this way: to make an inoculation in, esp. for the purpose of safeguarding against subsequent infection. — *v.i.* to practice inoculation. — *n.* **inoculabil'ity.** — *adj.* **inoc'ulable.** — *n.* **inocula'tion** the act or practice of inoculating: the insertion of the buds of one plant into another: the communication of disease by the introduction of a germ or virus, esp. that of a mild form of the disease to produce immunity: the analogous introduction of anything, e.g. nitrogen-fixing bacteria into soil, seed, a crystal into a supersaturated solution to start crystallisation. — *adjs.* **inoc'ulative** (-*ə-tiv,* or -*ā-tiv*); **inoc'ulatory** (-*ə-tər-i*). — *ns.* **inoc'ulator; inoc'ulum** material used for inoculating. [L. *inoculāre,* -*ātum* — *in,* into, and *oculus,* an eye, a bud.]

inodorous *in-ō'dər-əs, adj.* without smell. — *adv.* **ino'dorously.** — *n.* **ino'dorousness.** [Pfx. **in-** (2).]

inoffensive *in-ə-fen'siv, adj.* giving no offence: harmless. — *adv.* **inoffen'sively.** — *n.* **inoffen'siveness.** [Pfx. **in-** (2).]

inofficious *in-ə-fish'əs, adj.* disobliging (*obs.*): regardless of duty (*law*): inoperative. — *adv.* **inoffi'ciously.** — *n.* **inoffi'ciousness.** [Pfx. **in-** (2).]

inoperable *in-op'ər-ə-bl, adj.* that cannot be operated on successfully, or without undue risk (*med.*): not workable. — *ns.* **inoperabil'ity, inop'erableness.** — *adv.* **inop'erably.** — *adj.* **inop'erative** not in action: producing no effect. — *n.* **inop'erativeness.** [Pfx **in-** (2).]

inoperculate *in-o-pûr'kū-lāt, adj.* without an operculum or lid. [Pfx. **in-** (2).]

inopinate *in-op'in-āt,* (*obs.*) *adj.* unexpected. [L. *in-opīnatus.*]

inopportune *in-op'ər-tūn,* -*tūn', adj.* unseasonable in time. — *adv.* **inopp'ortunely** (or -*tūn'*). — *ns.* **inopp'ortūnist** (or -*tūn'*) one who thinks a policy inopportune; **inopportūn'ity, inopp'ortuneness** (or -*tūn'*). [Pfx. **in-** (2).]

inorb *in-örb', v.t.* to set in an orb. [Pfx. **in-** (1).]

inordinate *in-örd'(i-)nit, adj.* unrestrained: excessive: immoderate. — *ns.* **inor'dinacy, inor'dinateness.** — *adv.* **inor'dinately.** — *n.* **inordinā'tion** deviation from rule: irregularity. [L. *inordinātus* — *in-,* not, *ordināre,* -*ātum,* to arrange, regulate.]

inorganic *in-ör-gan'ik, adj.* not organic: not organised: not belonging to an organism: of accidental origin, not normally developed. — *adv.* **inorgan'ically.** — *n.* **inorganisā'tion,** -*z-* want of organisation. — *adj.* **inor'ganised,** -**ized** unorganised. — **inorganic chemistry** the chemistry of all substances but carbon compounds, generally admitting a few of these also (as oxides of carbon, carbonates). [Pfx. **in-** (2).]

inornate *in-ör-nāt',* or -*ör'nit, adj.* not ornate: simple. [Pfx. **in-** (2).]

inosculate *in-os'kū-lāt, v.t.* and *v.i.* to unite by mouths or ducts, as two vessels in an animal body: to anastomose. — *n.* **inoscula'tion.** [L. *in,* in, and *osculārī,* -*ātus,* to kiss.]

inositol *in-os'i-tol, n.* a member of the vitamin B complex, occurring in practically all plant and animal tissues. [Gr. *īs, īnos,* a sinew, muscle, and suffixes -*ite* and -*ol.*]

inotropic *in-ə-trop'ik, īn-,* (*med.*) *adj.* affecting, controlling muscular contraction, esp. in the heart. [Gr. *īs, īnos,* tendon, *tropos,* a turn.]

in pace *in pā'sē, pä'chā, pä-ke,* (L.) in peace.

in partibus infidelium *in pär'ti-bəs, in-fi-dē'li-əm, pär'-ti-bōōs ēn-fi-dā'li-ōōm,* (L.) in unbelieving countries — a phrase formerly applied to titular bishops in countries where no Catholic hierachy had been set up.

in-patient. See **in**[1].

inpayment *in'-pā'mənt, n.* the payment of money into a

bank account: the amount paid in. [**in**[1], **payment.**]

in pectore *in pek'to-rē, pek'to-re,* (L.) in secret: undisclosed: in petto.

in personam *in pər-sō'nam, per-,* against a person — used of a proceeding, etc., against a specific person (see also **in rem**).

in petto *ēn, in pet'tō,* (It.) within the breast: in one's own mind but not yet divulged.

inphase *in-fāz', adj.* in the same phase. [**in**[1], **phase**[1].]

inpouring *in'pōr-ing,* -*pör-, n.* a pouring in: addition. [**in**[1], **pouring.**]

in principio *in prin-sip'i-ō,* -*kip', (L.)* in the beginning.

in propria persona *in prō-pri-ə pûr-sō'nə, pro'pri-ä per-sō'nä,* (L.L.) in person.

in puris naturalibus *in pū'ris na-tūr-āl'i-bəs, pōō'rēs na-tōō-rāl'i-bōōs,* (L.L.) quite naked.

input *in'pŏŏt, n.* contribution (*Scot.*): amount, material, or energy, that is put in: power, or energy, or coded information, stored or for storage: information available for feeding in data. — *adj.* relating to computer input. — *v.t.* to feed into, esp. into a computer: — *pr.p.* **inputt'ing;** *pa.t.* and *pa.p.* **input'.** — *n.* **inputt'er.** — **input-output analysis** (*econ.*) a method of studying an economy as a whole by analysing the relationship between the input and output of each industry. [**in**[1], **put**[1].]

inqilab *in'ki-läb, n.* in India, Pakistan, etc., revolution. [Urdu.]

inquere *in-kwēr',* (*Spens.*) *v.i.* and *v.t.* to inquire. [**inquire.**]

in querpo. See **en cuerpo.**

inquest *in'kwest,* formerly *in-kwest', n.* the fact of inquiring: a search (*obs.*): a judicial inquiry before a jury into any matter, esp. any case of violent or sudden death: the body of men appointed to hold such an inquiry: the decision reached. [O.Fr. *enqueste* — L.L. *in-questa* — L. *inquīsīta* (*rēs*) — *inquīrere,* to inquire.]

inquietude *in-kwī'i-tūd, n.* disturbance: uneasiness. — *adj.* **inquī'et** unquiet. — *v.t.* (*rare*) to disturb. — *adv.* **inquī'etly.** [Pfx. **in-** (2).]

inquiline *in'kwi-līn, adj.* living in the abode of another. — *n.* animal so living. — *ns.* **in'quilinism, inquilin'ity.** — *adj.* **inquili'nous.** [L. *inquilīnus,* tenant, lodger — *incola,* inhabitant — *in,* in, *colēre,* to inhabit.]

inquinate *in'kwin-āt, v.t.* to defile. — *n.* **inquina'tion.** [L. *inquināre,* -*ātum.*]

inquire, enquire *in-kwīr', v.i.* to ask a question: to make an investigation. — *v.t.* to ask: to seek (*obs.*): to make an examination regarding (*obs.*): to call (*Spens.*). — *n.* (*Shak.*) inquiry. — *ns.* **inquirā'tion** (*Dickens*), **enquirā'tion** inquiry; **inquiren'do** (*law*) an authority to inquire: — *pl.* **inquiren'dos.** — *n.* **inquir'er, enquir'er.** — *adj.* **inquir'ing** given to inquiry: eager to acquire information: (of e.g. a look) expressing inquiry. — *adv.* **inquir'ingly.** — *n.* **inquir'y, enquir'y** (or *ing'kwi-ri,* esp. *U.S.*) the act of inquiring: a search for knowledge: investigation: a question. [O.Fr. *enquerre* (Fr. *enquérir*) — L. *inquīrere* — *in,* in, *quaerere, quaesītum,* to seek.]

inquisition *in-kwi-zish'ən, n.* a searching examination: an investigation: a judicial inquiry: (with *cap.*) a tribunal in the R.C. church for discovery, repression, and punishment of heresy, unbelief, etc., 'the Holy Office', now the 'Congregation for Doctrine of the Faith'. — *v.t.* (*Milt.*) to subject to inquisition. — *adjs.* **inquisit'ional** searching or vexatious in making inquiry: relating to inquisition or the Inquisition; **inquisitive** (-*kwiz'i-tiv*) eager to know: apt to ask questions, esp. about other people's affairs: curious. — *adv.* **inquis'i-tively.** — *ns.* **inquis'itiveness; inquis'itor** one who inquires, esp. with undue pertinacity or searchingness: an official inquirer: a member of the Inquisition tribunal. — *adj.* **inquisitō'rial** (or -*tör'*) pertaining to an inquisitor or inquisition: unduly pertinacious in interrogation: used of criminal proceedings in which the prosecutor is also judge, or in which the trial is

held in secret (*law*). — *adv.* **inquisito′rially.** — *ns.*
inquisito′rialness; inquis′itress an inquisitorial woman.
— *adj.* **inquisitū′rient** (*Milt.*) eager to act as inquisitor.
— **Grand Inquisitor** the chief in a court of Inquisition.
[L. *inquīsītiō, -ōnis;* see **inquire.**]

inquorate *in-kwör′it, adj.* not making up a quorum.
[Pfx. **in-** (2) and **quorum.**]

in re *in rē, rā,* (L.) in the matter (of).

in rem *in rem,* (L.) against a thing, property — used of
a proceeding, etc., against property, as the arrest of a
ship.

in rerum natura *in rē′rəm nə-tū′rə, rā′rŏŏm na-tŏŏ′rä,* (L.)
in nature: in the natural or physical world: in the order
of nature.

in rixa *in rik′sə,* (L.) in a quarrel: (said) in the heat of the
moment — a defence in cases of defamation.

inro *in′rō, n.* a small Japanese container for pills and
medicines, once part of traditional Japanese dress: —
pl. **in′rō.** [Jap., seal-box.]

inroad *in′rōd, n.* an incursion into an enemy's country: a
raid: encroachment. — **make inroads into** to make
progress with: to use up large quantities of. [**in**[1] and
road in sense of riding; cf. **raid.**]

inrush *in′rush, n.* an inward rush. — *n.* and *adj.* **in′rushing.**
[**in**[1], **rush**[1].]

in saecula saeculorum *in sek′yŏŏ-lə sek-yŏŏ-lōr′-, -lör′əm,
sī′kŏŏ-lä sī′kŏŏ-lō′rŏŏm,* (L.) for ever and ever.

insalivate *in-sal′i-vāt, v.t.* to mix with saliva. — *n.* **insali-
vā′tion.** [Pfx. **in-** (1).]

insalubrious *in-sə-lŏŏ′bri-əs, -lū′, adj.* unhealthy. — *adv.*
insalu′briously. — *n.* **insalu′brity.** [Pfx. **in-** (2).]

insalutary *in-sal′ū-tər-i, adj.* unwholesome. [Pfx. **in-**
(2).]

insane *in-sān′, adj.* not sane or of sound mind: crazy:
mad: utterly unwise: senseless: causing insanity (*Shak.*).
insane root prob. a root mentioned by Plutarch, *Life
of Antony,* perh. hemlock, henbane, or belladonna).
— *adv.* **insane′ly.** — *ns.* **insane′ness** insanity: madness;
insa′nie (*Shak.*; an emendation of the reading *infamie*)
insanity; **insanity** (*in-san′i-ti*) want of sanity: mental
disorder causing one to act against the social or legal
demands of society: madness. [L. *īnsānus.*]

insanitary *in-san′i-tər-i, adj.* not sanitary. — *ns.* **insan′i-
tariness, insanitā′tion.** [Pfx. **in-** (2).]

insatiable *in-sā′sh(y)ə-bl, adj.* that cannot be satiated or
satisfied. — *ns.* **insā′tiableness, insātiabil′ity.** — *adv.*
insā′tiably. — *adj.* **insā′tiate** not sated: insatiable. —
adv. **insā′tiately.** — *ns.* **insā′tiateness; insatiety** (*in-sə-
tī′i-ti*) unsated or insatiable state. [Pfx. **in-** (2).]

inscape *in′skāp, n.* in poetry, literature, etc., the essence,
inner nature of a person, object, etc. [Coined by
Gerard Manley Hopkins, from **in**[1] and **scape**[4].]

inscient[1] *in′sh(y)ənt, -shi-ənt,* (*arch.*) *adj.* ignorant. — *n.*
in′science. [L. *īnsciēns, -entis — in-,* not, *scīre,* to
know.]

inscient[2] *in′sh(y)ənt,* (*arch.*) *adj.* having insight or inward
knowledge. [L. *in,* in, *sciēns, -entis,* pr.p. of *scīre,* to
know.]

insconce (*Shak.*). Same as **ensconce.**

inscribe *in-skrīb′, v.t.* to engrave or otherwise mark: to
engrave or mark on: to enter in a book or roll: to
dedicate: in geom., to describe within another figure
so as either to touch all sides or faces of the bounding
figure or to have all angular points on it. — *adj.*
inscrīb′able. — *ns.* **inscrīb′er; inscription** (*in-skrip′shən*)
the act of inscribing: that which is inscribed: a dedication: a record inscribed on stone, metal, clay, etc.
— *adjs.* **inscrip′tional, inscrip′tive.** — *adv.* **inscrip′tively.**
[L. *īnscrīběre, īnscrīptum — in,* upon, *scrīběre,* to write.]

inscroll *in-skrōl′,* (*Shak.*) *v.t.* to write on a scroll.

inscrutable *in-skrŏŏt′ə-bl, adj.* that cannot be scrutinised
or searched into and understood: inexplicable. — *ns.*
inscrutabil′ity, inscrut′ableness. — *adv.* **inscrut′ably.**
[L. *īnscrūtābilis — in-,* not, *scrūtārī,* to search into.]

insculp *in-skulp′,* (*Shak.*): to engrave, to cut or carve upon
something (*Shak.*): to carve: to form by carving (*arch.*).
— *adj.* **insculpt′** engraved (*Shak.*): having depressions

in the surface (*bot.*). — *n.* **insculp′ture** anything engraved (*Shak.*): an inscription (*arch.*). — *v.t.* (*arch.*) to
carve on something. [L. *īnsculpěre — in,* in, *sculpěre,*
to carve.]

inseam[1] *in′sēm, n.* an inner seam in a shoe or garment.

inseam[2]. Same as **enseam**[3].

insect *in′sekt, n.* a word loosely used for a small invertebrate creature, esp. one with a body as if cut into, or
divided into, sections: a member of the Insecta (*zool.*):
a small, wretched, insignificant person (*fig.*). — *adj.*
of insects: like an insect: small: mean. — *n.pl.* **Insec′ta**
a subphylum of arthropods sharply divided into head,
thorax, and abdomen, with three pairs of legs attached
to the thorax, usually winged in adult life, breathing
air by means of tracheae, and commonly having a
metamorphosis in the life-history. — *ns.* **insectār′ium,
in′sectary** a vivarium for insects; **insec′ticide** (*-i-sīd*)
killing of insects: an insect-killing substance: an insect-
killer. — *adjs.* **insec′tiform; insec′tile** having the nature
of an insect. — *n.* **insec′tifuge** a substance that drives
away insects. — *n.pl.* **Insectiv′ora** an order of mammals, mostly terrestrial, insect-eating, nocturnal in
habit, and small in size — shrews, moles, hedgehogs,
etc. — *n.* **insect′ivore** a member of the Insectivora. —
adj. **insectiv′orous** living on insects. — *ns.* **insection**
(*in-sek′shən*) an incision: notch: division into segments;
insectol′ogist; insectol′ogy the study of insects. — *adj.*
in′secty abounding in insects. — **in′sect-net** a light
hand-net for catching insects; **in′sect-pow′der** powder
for stupifying and killing insects: an insecticide or
insectifuge. [L. *īnsectum,* pa.p. of *īnsecāre — in,* into,
secāre, to cut.]

insecure *in-si-kūr′, adj.* apprehensive of danger or loss:
in anxious state because not well-adjusted to life:
exposed to danger or loss: unsafe: uncertain: not fixed
or firm. — *adv.* **insecure′ly.** — *n.* **insecur′ity.** [Pfx.
in- (2).]

inseem (*Shak.*). Same as **enseam**[2].

inselberg *in′zəl-bûrg, in′səl-berg,* (*geol.*) *n.* a steep-sided
eminence arising from a plain tract, often found in the
semi-arid regions of tropical countries: — *pl.* **inselberge**
(-*gə*). [Ger., island-hill.]

inseminate *in-sem′in-āt, v.t.* to sow: to implant: to introduce: to impregnate, esp. artificially. — *ns.* **inseminā′-
tion; insem′inator.** [L. *īnsēmināre — in,* in, *sēmen,
-inis,* seed.]

insensate *in-sen′sāt, -it, adj.* without sensation, inanimate:
lacking sensibility or moral feeling: lacking in good
sense. — *adv.* **insen′sately.** — *n.* **insen′sateness.** [L.
īnsēnsātus — in-, not, *sēnsātus,* intelligent — *sēnsus,*
feeling.]

insensible *in-sen′si-bl, adj.* not having feeling: not capable
of emotion: callous: dull: unconscious: imperceptible
by the senses. — *ns.* **insensibil′ity, insen′sibleness.** —
adv. **insen′sibly.** [Pfx. **in-** (2).]

insensitive *in-sen′si-tiv, adj.* not sensitive. — *adv.* **insen′-
sitively.** — *ns.* **insen′sitiveness, insensitiv′ity.** [Pfx. **in-**
(2).]

insensuous *in-sen′sū-əs, -shŏŏ-əs, adj.* not sensuous.
[Pfx. **in-** (2).]

insentient *in-sen′sh(y)ənt, adj.* not having perception. —
ns. **insen′tience, insen′tiency.** [Pfx. **in-** (2).]

inseparable *in-sep′ər-ə-bl, adj.* that cannot be separated.
— *n.* (usu. used in *pl.*) an inseparable companion. —
ns. **insep′arableness, inseparabil′ity.** — *adv.* **insep′a-
rably.** — *adj.* **insep′arate** (*Shak.*) not separate or separable. [Pfx. **in-** (2).]

insert *in-sûrt′, v.t.* to put in: to introduce (into). — *n.*
in′sert something inserted in a proof, etc.: a paper
placed within the folds of a periodical or leaves of a
book. — *adjs.* **insert′able; insert′ed** (*bot.*) attached to
or growing out of another member. — *n.* **insert′er;
insertion** (*in-sûr′shən*) the act of inserting: the mode or
condition of being inserted: the point or place of
attachment (*zool.*): that which is inserted: lace or the
like suitable for letting into another material: the
putting of a man-made craft or satellite into orbit (also

injection). — *adj.* **inser'tional.** [L. *īnserĕre, īnsertum* — *in,* in, *serĕre,* to join.]

in-service. See **in¹.**

Insessores *in-ses-ō'rēz, -ö', n.pl.* perching birds, in old classification an order answering roughly to Passeriformes. — *adj.* **insesso'rial** of the Insessores: adapted for perching. [L. *īnsessor,* pl. *-ōrēs,* besetter (of the roads), highwayman, adopted with the meaning percher — *īnsidēre* — *in,* on, *sedēre,* to sit.]

inset *in'set, n.* something set in, an insertion or insert, a leaf or leaves inserted between the folds of other leaves: a small map or figure inserted in a spare corner of another: a piece let in: the setting in of a current. — *v.t.* **inset'** to set in, to infix or implant. [**in¹, set.**]

inseverable *in-sev'ər-ə-bl, adj.* that cannot be severed or separated. [Pfx. **in-** (2).]

inshallah *in-shä'lä, interj.* (among Muslims) if God will. [Ar. *in shā'llāh.*]

insheathe. See **ensheathe.**

inshell *in-shel', (Shak.) v.t.* to draw in or withdraw, as into a shell. [Pfx. **in-** (1).]

inshelter *in-shel'tər, v.t.* to place in shelter. [Pfx. **in-** (1).]

inship *in-ship', (Shak.) v.t.* to ship, to embark. [Pfx. **in-** (1).]

inshore *in'shōr', -shör', adv.* near or toward the shore. — *adj.* (*in'shōr, -shör*) situated, carried on, or operating, near the shore, as fishing-grounds, fishing, or fishermen.

inshrine *in-shrīn'.* Same as **enshrine.**

inside *in'sīd', in'sīd, n.* the side, space, or part within: (often in *pl.*) the entrails: inner nature: that which is not visible at first sight: a passenger in the interior part of a vehicle: (in *pl.*) the inner quires of a ream of paper. — *adj.* being within: interior: indoor: working indoors: from within: from a secret or confidential source: (of a criminal 'job') carried out by, or with the help of, someone trusted and/or employed by the victim (*coll.*). — *adv.* in or to the interior: indoors: on the inner side: in or into prison (*slang*). — *prep.* within: into: on inner side of. — *n.* **insi'der** one who is inside: inside passenger: one within a certain organisation, etc.: one possessing some particular advantage. — **in'side-car** an Irish jaunting-car in which the passengers face one another; **inside edge** see **edge; inside centre** in some games, esp. rugby, (a player in) the central position nearer the stand-off half; **inside left, right** in some games, a forward between the centre and outside; **insider dealing, trading** using information not publicly available to deal on the Stock Exchange, a criminal offence; **inside track** the inner side in a race-course: the advantage in position. — **inside of** (esp. *U.S.*) in less than, within; **inside out** with the inner side turned outwards; **know (something) inside out** (*coll.*) to know thoroughly. [**in¹, side¹.**]

insidious *in-sid'i-əs, adj.* watching an opportunity to ensnare: intended to entrap: deceptive: underhand: advancing imperceptibly: treacherous. — *adv.* **insid'iously.** — *n.* **insid'iousness.** [L. *īnsidiōsus* — *īnsidiae,* an ambush — *īnsidēre* — *in,* in, *sedēre,* to sit.]

insight¹ *in'sīt, n.* power of seeing into and understanding things: imaginative penetration: practical knowledge: enlightenment: a view into anything: awareness, often of one's own mental condition (*psych.*): the apprehension of the principle of a task, puzzle, etc. (*psych.*). — *adj.* **insight'ful.** — **insight learning** direct learning without process of trial and error. [**in¹, sight¹.**]

insight² *in'sīt, in'sihht, (Scot.) n.* household goods, furniture. — Also *adj.* [Origin unknown.]

insignia *in-sig'ni-ə, n.pl.* in U.S. treated as *sing.,* signs or badges of office, honour, membership, occupation, etc.: marks by which anything is known. — Also (*rarely*) **insigne** (*in-sig'ni*). [L., neut. pl. of *īnsignis* — *in,* in, *signum,* a mark.]

insignificant *in-sig-nif'i-kənt, adj.* destitute of meaning: without effect: unimportant: petty. — *ns.* **insignif'icance, insignif'icancy.** — *adv.* **insignif'icantly.** — *adj.*

insignif'icative not significative or expressing by external signs. [Pfx. **in-** (2).]

insincere *in-sin-sēr', adj.* not sincere. — *adv.* **insincere'ly.** — *n.* **insincerity** (*-ser'i-ti*). [Pfx. **in-** (2).]

insinew *in-sin'ū, v.i.* (*Shak.*) to be joined as with sinews. [Pfx. **in-** (1).]

insinuate *in-sin'ū-āt, v.t.* to introduce gently or artfully: to hint, esp. a fault: to work into favour. — *v.i.* to creep or flow in: to enter gently: to obtain access by flattery or stealth. — *adj.* **insin'uating.** — *adv.* **insin'u-atingly.** — *n.* **insinuā'tion.** — *adj.* **insin'uative** insinuating or stealing on the confidence: using insinuation. — *n.* **insin'uator.** — *adj.* **insin'uatory** (*-ə-tər-i*). [L. *īnsinuāre, -ātum* — *in,* in, *sinus,* a curve.]

insipid *in-sip'id, adj.* tasteless: without satisfying or definite flavour: wanting spirit or interest: dull. — *adv.* **insip'idly.** — *ns.* **insip'idness, insipid'ity.** [L.L. *īnsipidus* — L. *in-,* not, *sapidus,* well-tasted — *sapĕre,* to taste.]

insipience *in-sip'i-əns, n.* lack of wisdom. — *adj.* **insip'ient.** — *adv.* **insip'iently.** [L. *īnsipientia* — *in-,* not, *sapiēns,* wise.]

insist *in-sist', v.i.* to speak emphatically and at length: to persist in pressing: to persevere (*Milt.*). — *v.t.* to maintain persistently. — *ns.* **insist'ence, insist'ency.** — *adj.* **insist'ent** urgent: prominent: insisting: (of bird's hind-toe) touching the ground with the tip only. — *adv.* **insist'ently.** — *n.* **insist'ure** persistence: prob., uniformity of motion (*Shak.*). [L. *īnsistĕre* — *in,* upon, *sistĕre,* to stand.]

in situ *in sī'tū, si'tōō,* (L.) in the original situation.

insnare. Same as **ensnare.**

insobriety *in-sō-brī'ə-ti, n.* want of sobriety, drunkenness. [Pfx. **in-** (2).]

insociable *in-sō'shə-bl, adj.* unsociable: incompatible (*obs.*). — *n.* **insociabil'ity.** [Pfx. **in-** (2).]

insofar. See **in¹.**

insolate *in'sō-lāt, in-sō'lāt, v.t.* to expose to the sun's rays: to treat by exposure to the sun's rays. — *n.* **insolā'tion** exposure to the sun's rays: received solar radiation: injury caused by the sun. [L. *īnsōlāre, -ātum* — *in,* in, *sōl,* the sun.]

insole *in'sōl, n.* the inner sole of a boot or shoe — opp. to *outsole:* a sole of some material placed inside a shoe for warmth, dryness or comfort. [**in¹, sole¹.**]

insolent *in'səl-ənt, adj.* overbearing: insulting: rude: impudent. — *n.* **in'solence.** — *adv.* **in'solently.** [L. *īnsolēns, -entis* — *in-,* not, *solēns,* pa.p. of *solēre,* to be wont.]

insolidity *in-so-lid'i-ti, n.* want of solidity. [Pfx. **in-** (2).]

insoluble *in-sol'ū-bl, adj.* not capable of being dissolved: not to be solved or explained. — *v.t.* **insol'ubilise, -ize** to render insoluble. — *ns.* **insolubil'ity, insol'ubleness.** — *adv.* **insol'ubly.** [Pfx. **in-** (2).]

insolvable *in-solv'ə-bl, adj.* not solvable. — *n.* **insolvabil'ity.** — *adv.* **insol'vably.** [Pfx. **in-** (2).]

insolvent *in-solv'ənt, adj.* not able to pay one's debts: bankrupt: pertaining to insolvent persons. — *n.* one unable to pay his debts. — *n.* **insolv'ency** bankruptcy. [Pfx. **in-** (2).]

insomnia *in-som'ni-ə, n.* sleeplessness: prolonged inability to sleep. — *n.* **insom'niac** a person who suffers from insomnia. — *adj.* suffering from, causing, or caused by, insomnia. — *adj.* **insom'nious.** — *n.* **insom'nolence.** [L. *īnsomnis,* sleepless.]

insomuch *in-sō-much', adv.* to such a degree (with *as* or *that*): inasmuch (with *as*): so.

insooth *in-sōōth', (arch.) adv.* in sooth, indeed. [**in¹, sooth.**]

insouciant *in-sōō'si-ənt, ĕ-sōō-sē-ã, adj.* indifferent, unconcerned: heedless. — *n.* **insouciance** (*in-sōō'si-əns, ĕ-sōō-sē-ãs*). — *adv.* **insouciantly** (*in-sōō'si-ənt-li, ĕ-sōō-sē-ãt'li*). [Fr., — *in-,* not, *souciant,* pr.p. of *soucier* — L. *sollicitāre,* to disturb.]

insoul. See **ensoul.**

inspan *in-span', in'span, (esp. S. Afr.) v.t.* to yoke to a vehicle: to bring or press into service. — *v.i.* to prepare to depart: — *pr.p.* **inspann'ing;** *pa.t.* and *pa.p.* **inspanned'.** [Du. *inspannen*, to yoke — *in*, in, *spannen*, to tie.]

inspect *in-spekt'*, *v.t.* to look into: to examine: to look at narrowly, officially, or ceremonially. — *n.* **in'spect** (*obs.*) inspection. — *adv.* **inspect'ingly.** — *n.* **inspec'tion** the act of inspecting or looking into: careful or official examination. — *adjs.* **inspec'tional; inspec'tive.** — *ns.* **inspec'tor** one who inspects: an examining officer: a police officer ranking below a superintendent: an officer in any of several humane societies; **inspec'torate** a district under charge of an inspector: the office of inspector: a body of inspectors. — *adj.* **inspectõ'rial.** — *ns.* **inspec'torship** the office of inspector; **inspec'tress** a female inspector. — **inspector general** the head of an inspectorate: a military officer who conducts investigations. [L. *īnspectāre*, freq. of *īnspicĕre*, *īnspectum* — *in*, into, *specĕre*, to look.]

insphere, insphear'd. See **ensphere.**

inspire *in-spīr'*, *v.t.* to breathe or blow into (*arch.*): to breathe in or blow in (air, etc.): to draw or inhale into the lungs: to infuse into (the mind), esp. with an encouraging or exalting influence: (of divine influence, etc.) to instruct or guide: to instruct or affect with a particular emotion: to bring about, cause to occur: to animate. — *v.i.* to draw in the breath: to blow (*obs.*; Spens. **inspyre**). — *adj.* **inspīr'able** able to be inhaled. — *n.* **inspirā'tion** (*in-spər-*, *-spir-*, *-spīr-*) the act of inspiring or breathing in: a breath: instruction, dictation, or stimulation by a divinity, a genius, an idea or a passion: unacknowledged prompting by authorities: an inspired condition: an object or person that inspires: an inspired thought or idea. — *adj.* **inspirā'tional.** — *adv.* **inspirā'tionally.** — *adj.* **inspirative** (*in-spīr'ə-tiv, in'spir-ā-tiv*) tending to inspire. — *n.* **inspirator** (*in'spir-ā-tər*) an inspirer: an apparatus for injecting or drawing in vapour, liquid, etc. — *adj.* **inspiratory** (*in-spir'ə-tər-i, or in-spīr'*, or *in'spir-*) belonging to or aiding inspiration or inhalation. — *ns.* **inspirā'tionism; inspirā'tionist** one who maintains the direct inspiration of the Scriptures. — *adj.* **inspīred'** actuated or directed by divine influence: influenced by elevated feeling: prompted by superior, but not openly declared, knowledge or authority: actually authoritative: unexpectedly accurate. — *n.* **inspīr'er.** — *adv.* **inspīr'ingly.** [L. *īnspīrāre in*, in, into, *spīrāre*, to breathe.]

inspirit *in-spir'it*, *v.t.* to infuse spirit into. — *adj.* **inspir'iting.** — *adv.* **inspir'itingly.** [Pfx. **in-** (1).]

inspissate *in-spis'āt*, *v.t.* to thicken, condense. — *ns.* **inspissā'tion; in'spissātor.** [L. *in*, in, *spissāre — spissus*, thick.]

inspyre (*Spens.*). See **inspire.**

instability *in-stə-bil'i-ti*, *n.* want of steadiness. — *adj.* **insta'ble** unstable. [Pfx. **in-** (2).]

install (also **instal**) *in-stöl'*, *v.t.* to place in a stall or official seat: to place in an office or order: to invest with any charge or office with the customary ceremonies: to set up and put in use: — *pr.p.* **install'ing;** *pa.t.* and *pa.p.* **installed'.** — *ns.* **install'ant** one who installs someone in an office, etc.; **installā'tion** the act of installing or placing in an office with ceremonies: a placing in position for use: apparatus placed in position for use: the complete apparatus for electric lighting, or the like; **install'ment** a knight's stall (*Shak.*): installation (*arch.*). [L.L. *īnstallāre — in*, in, *stallum*, a stall — O.H.G. *stal* (Ger. *Stall*, Eng. **stall**[1]).]

instalment, in U.S. **-stall-,** *n.* one of a series of partial payments: a portion supplied or completed at one time, as of a serial story. [A.Fr. *estaler*, to fix, set; prob. influenced by **install.**]

instance *in'stəns*, *n.* the quality of being urgent (*arch.*): motive, cause (*arch.*): solicitation, urging: occurrence: occasion: example: evidence, proof (*Shak.*): process, suit (*law*). — *v.t.* to mention as an example. — *n.* **in'stancy** insistency: urgency: imminence. — *adj.* **in'stant** urgent (*arch.*): immediate: without delay: present, current: (esp. of food, drink) pre-prepared so that

little has to be done to it before use. — *n.* the present moment of time: any moment or point of time: the present month. — *n.* **instantaneity** (*in-stant-ə-nē'i-ti*). — *adj.* **instantaneous** (*in-stənt-ā'ni-əs*) done in an instant: momentary: occurring or acting at once or very quickly: for the instant: at a particular instant. — *adv.* **instantān'eously.** — *n.* **instantān'eousness.** — *adv.* **instanter** (*in-stan'ter*; L.) immediately. — *adj.* **instantial** (*in-stan'shl*; *rare*). — *v.t.* **instan'tiate** to be or provide an example of. — *n.* **instantiā'tion.** — *adv.* **in'stantly** at once: at this very time (*Shak.*): importunately, zealously (*B.*). — **at the instance of** at the motion or solicitation of; **court of first instance** a lower court in which a legal case is first heard, from which it may be referred to a higher court; **for instance** as an example; **in the first instance** firstly, originally; **on the instant** forthwith. [L. *īnstāns, īnstantis*, pr.p. of *īnstāre*, to be near, press upon, urge — *in*, upon, *stāre*, to stand.]

instar[1] *in-stär'*, *v.t.* to adorn with stars: to place as a star (*arch.*). [Pfx. **in-** (1).]

instar[2] *in'stär*, *n.* the form of an insect between moult and moult. [L. *īnstar*, image.]

instar omnium *in', ēn'stär, om'ni-əm, -ōom*, (L.) example of all the rest.

instate *in-stāt'*, *v.t.* to put in possession: to install. — *n.* **instate'ment.** [Pfx. **in-** (1) and **state.**]

in statu pupillari *in stāt'ū pū-pi-lā'rī, stat'ōo pōo-pi-lä're*, (L.L.) in a state of wardship; **in statu quo** (*kwō*) in the former state.

instauration *in-stör-ā'shən, n.* restoration: renewal. — *n.* **in'staurātor.** [L. *īnstaurātiō, -ōnis.*]

instead *in-sted'*, *adv.* in the stead, place, or room (of): as an alternative or substitute. [**in**[1], **stead.**]

instep *in'step, n.* the prominent arched part of the human foot near its junction with the leg: the corresponding part of a shoe, stocking, etc.: in horses, the hindleg from the ham to the pastern joint. — **in'step-rais'er** an arched device to support the instep and counteract a tendency to flat feet. [Origin obscure.]

instigate *in'sti-gāt, v.t.* to urge on, incite: to foment. — *adv.* **in'stigātingly.** — *n.* **instigā'tion** the act of inciting: impulse, esp. to evil. — *adj.* **in'stigātive.** — *n.* **in'stigātor** an inciter, generally in a bad sense. [L. *īnstigāre, -ātum.*]

instil *in-stil', v.t.* to drop in: to infuse slowly into the mind: — *pr.p.* **instill'ing;** *pa.t.* and *pa.p.* **instilled'.** — Also **instill.** — *ns.* **instillā'tion, instil'ment** the act of instilling or pouring in by drops: the act of infusing slowly into the mind: that which is instilled or infused. [L. *īnstillāre — in*, in, *stillāre*, to drop.]

instinct *in'stingkt*, formerly *in-stingkt', n.* impulse: an involuntary prompting to action: intuition: the natural impulse by which animals are guided apparently independently of reason or experience: a complex co-ordination of reflex actions which results in achievement of adaptive ends without foresight or experience. — *adj.* (*in-stingkt'*) instigated or incited: moved: animated: charged: imbued. — *adj.* **instinct'ive** prompted by instinct: involuntary: acting according to or determined by natural impulse. — *adv.* **instinc'tively.** — *n.* **instinctiv'ity** (*rare*). — *adj.* **instinc'tual** pertaining to instincts. — *adv.* **instinc'tually.** [L. *īnstinctus — īnstinguĕre*, instigate.]

institorial *in-sti-tō'ri-əl, -tö'ri-, (law) adj.* pertaining to an agent or factor. [L. *īnstitōrius — īnstitor*, an agent, broker.]

institute *in'sti-tūt, v.t.* to set up, establish: to set on foot: to order (*obs.*): to appoint: to educate (*obs.*). — *n.* anything instituted or formally established: the act of instituting (*obs.*): established law: precept or principle: an institution: a literary and philosophical society or organisation for education, research, etc.: the building in which such an organisation is housed: a foundation for further education, esp. in technical subjects: a temporary school, esp. for teachers (*U.S.*): the person first nominated as heir (distinguished from the *substitutes* who follow, failing the institute) (*Scots law*): (in

pl.) a book of precepts, principles, or rules. — *n.*
institution (*-tū'shən*) the act of instituting or establishing: that which is instituted or established: foundation: established order: enactment: a society or organisation established for some object, esp. cultural, charitable, or beneficent, or the building housing it: a custom or usage, esp. one familiar or characteristic: that which institutes or instructs (*obs.*): a system of principles or rules (*obs.*): appointment of an heir: the act by which a bishop commits a cure of souls to a priest. — *adj.* **institū'tional** pertaining to institution, institutions, or institutes: being, or of the nature of, an institution: depending on or originating in institution: characterised by the possession of institutions. — *v.t.* **institū'tionalise, -ize** to make an institution of: to confine to an institution: (usu. in *pass.*) as a result of such confinement, to cause to become apathetic and dependent on routine. — *ns.* **institū'tionalism** the system or characteristics of institutions or institution life: belief in the nature of institutions; **institū'tionalist** a writer on institutes: one who sets a high value on institutionalism. — *adv.* **institū'tionally.** — *adj.* **institū'tionary** institutional: educational (*obs.*). — *n.* **in'stitūtist** a writer of institutes or elementary rules. — *adj.* **in'stitūtive** able or tending to establish: depending on an institution. — *adv.* **institū'tively.** — *ns.* **in'stitūtor, in'stitūter** one who institutes: an instructor (*obs.*). — **institutional church** one that is active through social organisations. [L. *īnstituĕre, -ūtum — in,* in, *statuĕre,* to cause to stand — *stāre,* to stand.]
instreaming *in'strēm-ing, n.* an influx. — Also *adj.* [**in¹,** streaming.]
instress *in'stres, n.* the force or energy which sustains an inscape. — Also *v.t.* [Coined by Gerard Manley Hopkins, from **in¹** and **stress.**]
instruct *in-strukt', v.t.* to prepare (*obs.*): to inform: to teach: to direct: (of a judge) to give (a jury) guidance concerning the legal issues of a case: to order or command. — *adj.* (Milt.) instructed. — *adj.* **instruct'ible** able to be instructed. — *n.* **instruc'tion** the art of instructing or teaching: information: direction: command: an element in a computer program or language that activates a particular operation: (in *pl.*) special directions, commands. — *adjs.* **instruc'tional** relating to instruction: educational; **instruc'tive** affording instruction: conveying knowledge: denoting, as in Finnish, 'by means of' (*gram.*). — *adv.* **instruc'tively.** — *ns.* **instruc'tiveness; instruc'tor** a teacher: a college or university lecturer, below assistant professor in rank (*U.S.*): — *fem.* **instruc'tress.** [L. *īnstruĕre, īnstructum — in,* in, *struĕre,* to pile up.]
instrument *in'stroo-mənt, n.* a tool or utensil: a contrivance for producing musical sounds: a writing containing a contract: a formal record: one who, or that which, is made a means or agency: a term generally employed to denote an indicating device but also other pieces of small electrical apparatus. — *v.t.* (-*ment'*) to score for instruments: to equip with indicating, measuring, or control, etc., apparatus. — *adj.* for instruments: by means of instruments (as *instrument flight*). — *adj.* **instrumental** (-*ment'l*) acting as an instrument or means: serving to promote an object: helpful: of, for, belonging to, or produced by, musical instruments: denoting a type of learning process in which a particular response is always associated with a reinforcement, the response then intensifying (*psych.*): serving to indicate the instrument or means (*gram.*). — *n.* the instrumental case (*gram.*): a piece of music for instruments only, i.e. without a vocal part. — *ns.* **instrument'alism** a form of pragmatism associated with John Dewey; **instrument'alist** one who plays on a musical instrument; **instrumentality** (-*ment-al'i-ti*) agency. — *adv.* **instrument'ally.** — *n.* **instrumentā'tion** the use or provision of instruments: the arrangement of a composition for performance by different instruments (*mus.*). — *adj.* **instrumen'ted** equipped with electronic, etc., instruments. — **instrument flying, land-**

ing navigation of aircraft by means of instruments only, landing of aircraft by means of instruments and ground radio devices only, when visibility is poor. [L. *instrūmentum — īnstruĕre,* to instruct; see **instruct.**]
insubjection *in-səb-jek'shən, n.* want of subjection. [Pfx. **in-** (2).]
insubordinate *in-səb-örd'(i-)nit, adj.* not subordinate or submissive. — *adv.* **insubord'inately.** — *n.* **insubordinā'tion.** [Pfx. **in-** (2).]
insubstantial *in-səb-stan'shəl, adj.* not substantial: not real. — *n.* **insubstantiality** (-*shi-al'i-ti*). — *adv.* **insubstan'tially.** [Pfx. **in-** (2).]
insucken *in'suk-n,* (*Scots law; hist.*) *adj.* pertaining to a sucken. [**in¹, sucken.**]
insufferable *in-suf'ər-ə-bl, adj.* that cannot be endured: detestable. — *adv.* **insuff'erably.** [Pfx. **in-** (2).]
insufficient *in-səf-ish'ənt, adj.* inadequate: lacking (*obs.*). — *ns.* **insuffic'ience** (*rare*), **insuffic'iency.** — *adv.* **insuffic'iently.** [Pfx. **in-** (2).]
insufflate *in'suf-lāt* (or -*suf'*), *v.t.* to blow in: to breathe on. — *ns.* **insufflā'tion** the act of breathing on anything, esp. in baptism or exorcism: the act of blowing air, power, etc., into a cavity or on a surface; **in'sufflātor** an instrument for insufflation. [L. *īnsufflāre — in,* in, on, *sufflāre,* to blow.]
insula *in'sū-lə* (L. *ēn'sŏŏ-la*), *n.* a block of buildings (*Rom. ant.*): an apartment house (*Rom. ant.*): Reil's island, a small lobe of the cerebrum hidden in the fissure of Sylvius (*anat.*). — *ns.* **in'sūlance** resistance between electric conductors separated by insulating material; **in'sūlant** insulating material. — *adj.* **in'sūlar** belonging to an island: surrounded by water: standing or situated alone: narrow, prejudiced. — *ns.* **in'sūlarism, insūlarity** (-*lar'i-ti*) the state of being insular. — *adv.* **in'sūlarly.** — *v.t.* **in'sūlate** to place in a detached situation: to cut off from connection or communication: to prevent the passing of heat, sound, electricity, etc. from (a body, area, etc.) to (another): to separate, esp. from the earth, by a non-conductor (*elect.*). — *ns.* **insūlā'tion; in'sūlātor** one who, or that which, insulates: a non-conductor of electricity: a contrivance for insulating a conductor: a stand for a piano leg; **in'sūlin** an extract got from the islands or islets of Langerhans in the pancreas of animals, used for treating diabetes and also mental diseases. — **insulating board** (*build.*) fibreboard of low density used for thermal insulation and acoustical control; **insulating tape** a usu. adhesive tape made from, or impregnated with, water-resistance insulating material, used for covering joins in electrical wires, etc.; **insulin shock, reaction** a state of collapse produced by an overdose of insulin. [L. *īnsula,* island.]
insulse *in-suls', adj.* insipid: stupid. — *n.* **insul'sity** (*Milt.*) stupidity. [L. *īnsulsus — in-,* not, *salēre,* to salt.]
insult *in-sult', v.t.* to assail (*obs.*): to triumph insolently or exultantly over: to treat with indignity or contempt: to affront. — *v.i.* (*obs.*) to make an attack: to behave with boastful insolence. — *n.* **in'sult** abuse: affront: contumely: injury, damage (*med.,* esp. *U.S.*). — *adjs.* **insult'able** capable of being insulted; **insult'ant** (*rare*) insulting. — *n.* **insult'er.** — *adj.* **insult'ing.** — *adv.* **insult'ingly.** — *n.* **insult'ment** (*Shak.*) insult. [L. *īnsultāre — insilīre,* to spring at — *in,* upon, *salīre,* to leap.]
insuperable *in-sū'pər-ə-bl, -sŏŏ', adj.* that cannot be overcome or surmounted. — *ns.* **insuperabil'ity, insu'perableness.** — *adv.* **insu'perably.** [L. *īnsuperābilis — in-,* not, *superāre,* to pass over — *super,* above.]
insupportable *in-səp-ört'ə-bl, -ört', adj.* unbearable: not sustainable: (-*sup'*) irresistible (*Spens.*). — *n.* **insupport'ableness.** — *adv.* **insupport'ably.** [Pfx. **in-** (2).]
insuppressible *in-sə-pres'i-bl, adj.* not to be suppressed or concealed. — *adv.* **insuppress'ibly.** — *adj.* **insuppress'ive** (*Shak.*) insuppressible. [Pfx. **in-** (2).]
insure *in-shŏŏr', v.t.* to make sure or secure: to guarantee: to make an arrangement for the payment of a sum of money in the event of loss or injury to: to make such an arrangement for the payment of (a sum of money)

(*arch.*). — *v.i.* to effect or undertake insurance. — *n.* **insurabil′ity.** — *adj.* **insur′able** that may be insured. — *ns.* **insur′ance** the act or system of insuring: a contract of insurance, a policy: the premium paid for insuring: the sum to be received; **insur′ancer** (*obs.*); **insur′ant** an insurance policy holder; **insur′er** either party to a contract of insurance (now, strictly the insurance company). [O.Fr. *enseurer* — *en*, and *seur*, sure; see **ensure, sure**[1].]

insurgent *in-sûr′jənt, adj.* rising: rushing in: rising in revolt. — *n.* one who rises in opposition to established authority: a rebel. — *ns.* **insur′gence, insur′gency** a rising up or against: rebellion: insurrection. [L. *īnsurgēns, -entis* — *in*, upon, *surgĕre*, to rise.]

insurmountable *in-sər-mownt′ə-bl, adj.* not surmountable: that cannot be overcome. — *ns.* **insurmountabil′ity, insurmount′ableness.** — *adv.* **insurmount′ably.** [Pfx. **in-** (2).]

insurrection *in-sər-ek′shən, n.* a rising or revolt. — *adjs.* **insurrec′tional, insurrec′tionary.** — *ns.* **insurrec′tionary, insurrec′tionist; insurrec′tionism.** [L. *īnsurrēctiō, -ōnis* — *īnsurgĕre*; see **insurgent**.]

insusceptible *in-səs-ep′ti-bl, adj.* not susceptible. — Also **insuscep′tive.** — *n.* **insusceptibil′ity.** — *advs.* **insuscep′tibly, insuscep′tively.** [Pfx. **in-** (2).]

inswathe. Same as **enswathe.**

inswing *in′swing, n.* an inward swing or swerve. — *n.* **inswinger** (*in′swing-ər*) a ball bowled so as to swerve to leg (*cricket*): a ball kicked so as to swing in towards the goal or the centre of the pitch (*football*). [**in**[1], **swing**.]

intact *in-takt′, adj.* untouched: unimpaired: whole: undiminished. — *n.* **intact′ness.** [L. *intactus* — *in-*, not, *tangĕre, tactum*, to touch.]

intaglio *in-täl′yō, n.* a figure cut into any substance: a stone or gem in which the design is hollowed out — opp. to *cameo*: a countersunk die: a method of printing in which the image area is sunk into the surface of the plate — opp. to *relief*: — *pl.* **intagl′ios.** — Also *v.t.* —*adj.* **intagl′iated** incised, engraved. — See **cavo= rilievo.** [It., — *in*, into, *tagliare*, to cut — L. *tālea*, a cutting, layer.]

intake *in′tāk, n.* that which is taken in: a tract of land enclosed: an airway in a mine: a place where water is taken in: a narrowing in a pipe: decrease in width as in a stocking-leg by knitting two stitches together: the place where contraction occurs: the setting back of a wall-face: a body of people taken into an organisation, as new recruits, or new pupils at a school: the point at which fuel mixture enters the cylinder of an internal-combustion engine: a cheat or cheater (*dial.*). [**in**[1], **take**.]

Intal® *in′tal, n.* a drug (*sodium cromoglycate*) used to control asthma.

intangible *in-tan′ji-bl, adj.* not tangible or perceptible to touch: insubstantial: eluding the grasp of the mind. — *n.* something intangible, e.g. a supplementary asset such as goodwill. — *ns.* **intan′gibleness, intangibil′ity.** — *adv.* **intan′gibly.** [See **intact**.]

intarsia *in-tär′si-ə,* **intarsio** *-ō* (It. *ēn-tär-sē′ä, -ō*), *ns.* a form of decorative wood inlay work, developed in Italy during the 15th cent.: coloured geometrical patterning in knitting, reminiscent of this. — Also *adj.* [It. *intarsio.*]

integer *in′ti-jər, n.* a whole: any positive whole number, any negative whole number, or zero (*arith.*). — *adjs.* **in′tegrable** (*-grə-bl*) capable of being integrated; **in′tegral** (*-grəl*) entire or whole: not fractional: not involving fractions: relating to integrals: unimpaired: intrinsic, belonging as a part to the whole. — *n.* a whole: the whole as made up of its parts: the value of the function of a variable whose differential coefficient is known (*math.*). — *adv.* **in′tegrally.** — *ns.* **integral′ity** wholeness, integrity, completeness; **in′tegrand** an expression to be integrated. — *adj.* **in′tegrant** making part of a whole: necessary to form an integer or an entire thing. — *v.t.* **in′tegrate** to make up as a whole:

to make entire: to combine, amalgamate: to desegregate: to find the integral of (*math.*): to find the total value of. — *v.i.* to become integral: to perform integration. — *adj.* made up of parts: complete: whole. — *n.* **integrā′tion** the act or process of integrating (*math.*): unification into a whole, e.g. of diverse elements in a community, as white and coloured: the state of being integrated: the formation of a unified personality (*psych.*); **integrā′tionist** one who favours integration of a community. — Also *adj.* —*adj.* **in′tegrātive** integrating: tending to integrate. — *ns.* **in′tegrātor** one who integrates: an instrument for finding the results of integrations; **integrity** (*in-teg′ri-ti*) entireness, wholeness: the unimpaired state of anything: uprightness: honesty: purity. — **integral calculus** see **calculus; integral function** (*alg.*) a function which does not include the operation of division in any of its terms; **integrated circuit** a circuit consisting of an assembly of electronic elements in a single structure which cannot be subdivided without destroying its intended function. — **monolithic integrated circuit** an integrated circuit formed in or on a single crystal of semiconductor, usu. silicon. [L. *integer* — *in-*, not, root of *tangĕre*, to touch.]

integument *in-teg′ū-mənt, n.* an external covering: either of the two coats of an ovule (*bot.*): a covering layer of tissue, such as the skin, exoskeleton, etc. (*zool.*). — *adj.* **integumentary** (*-ment′ər-i*). [L. *integumentum* — *in*, upon, *tegĕre*, to cover.]

intellect *int′i-lekt, n.* the mind, in reference to its rational powers: the thinking principle: meaning (*Shak.*): (in *pl.*) mental powers (*arch.*). — *adj.* **in′tellected** (*Cowper*) endowed with intellect. — *n.* **intellec′tion** the act of understanding: apprehension or perception (*philos.*). — *adjs.* **intellec′tive** able to understand: produced or perceived by the understanding; **intellectual** (*-lek′tū-əl*) of or relating to the intellect: perceived or performed by the intellect: having the power of understanding: endowed with a superior intellect: appealing to, or (thought to be) intended for, intellectuals: intelligible only to a person with a superior intellect. — *n.* a person of superior intellect or enlightenment (often used to suggest doubt as to practical sagacity): intellect (*obs.*): (in *pl.*) mental powers (*arch.*): (in *pl.*) things of the intellect (*obs.*). — *v.t.* **intellect′ualise, -ize** to reason intellectually: to endow with intellect: to give an intellectual character to. — *ns.* **intellect′ualism** the doctrine that derives all knowledge from pure reason: the culture (esp. exclusive or unbalanced) of the intellect; **intellect′ualist; intellectuality** (*-al′i-ti*) intellectual power. — *adv.* **intellect′ually.** [L. *intellēctus, -ūs* — *intelligĕre, intellēctum*, to understand — *inter*, between, *legĕre*, to choose.]

intelligent *in-tel′i-jənt, adj.* having intellect: endowed with the faculty of reason: alert, bright, quick of mind: well-informed: cognisant: bringing intelligence (*obs.*): communicative (*Shak.*): capable of performing some of the functions of a computer (*automation*). — *ns.* **intell′igence** intellectual skill or knowledge: mental brightness: information communicated: news: intelligence department: a footing of mutual understanding (*rare*): a spiritual being; **intell′igencer** a spy: a newsmonger: an avenue of intelligence: a newspaper. — *adj.* **intelligential** (*-jen′shl*) pertaining to the intelligence: consisting of spiritual being. — *adv.* **intell′igently.** — *adj.* **intell′igible** that may be understood: clear: capable of being apprehended by the understanding only, not by senses (*philos.*). — *ns.* **intell′igibleness, -igibil′ity.** — *adv.* **intell′igibly.** — **intelligence department, service** a department of state or armed service for securing and interpreting information; **intelligence quotient** the ratio, commonly expressed as a percentage, of a person's mental age to his actual age (abbrev. **IQ**); **intelligence test** a test by questions and tasks to determine a person's mental capacity, or the age at which his capacity would be normal; **intelligent terminal** (*comput.*) a terminal incorporating a microprocessor, capable of performing simple tasks independently of the larger computer to which it is connected. [L. *intelligēns, -entis*, pr.p. of *intelligĕre* (see preceding entry).]

intelligentsia, intelligentzia *in-tel-i-jent'si-ə*, or *-gent'*, *n.* the intellectual or cultured classes, originally esp. in Russia. [Russ., — L. *intelligentia*.]

intelligible. See **intelligent.**

Intelsat *in'tel-sat, n.* a worldwide satellite service dealing with communications such as television exchange, business messages, etc.

intemerate *in-tem'ər-it, adj.* pure: undefiled: inviolate. — *adv.* **intem'erately.** [L. *intemerātus; in-*, not, and pa.p. of *temerāre*, to violate.]

intemperance *in-tem'pər-əns, n.* want of due restraint: excess of any kind: habitual overindulgence in intoxicating liquor. — *n.* **intem'perant** one who is intemperate. — *adj.* **intem'perate** indulging to excess in any appetite or passion: given to an immoderate use of intoxicating liquors: passionate: exceeding the usual degree: immoderate. — *adv.* **intem'perately.** — *n.* **intem'perateness.** [L. *intemperans*, intemperate.]

intempestive *in-tem-pest'iv, adj.* unseasonable: untimely. — *n.* **intempestiv'ity.** [L. *intempestīvus* — *in-*, not, *tempestās*, season — *tempus*, time.]

intenable *in-ten'ə-bl, adj.* untenable. [Pfx. **in-** (2).]

intend *in-tend', v.t.* to stretch forth (*Spens.*): to expand (*Milt.*): to strain (*obs.*): to intensify (*obs.*): to direct, turn (*Shak.*): to fix the mind upon: to design: to purpose: to mean: to designate (*Spens.*): to superintend (*arch.*). — *v.i.* to direct one's course (*Shak.*): to purpose a journey: to be in attendance (*obs.*): to attend, listen (*obs.*). — *ns.* **intend'ancy** the office, term of office, or sphere of an intendant: a body of intendants; **intend'ant** an officer who superintends some public business, a title of many public officers in France and other countries: a superintendent, director or manager. — *adj.* **intend'ed** purposed: stretched (*obs.*). — *n.* (*coll.*) betrothed. — *adv.* **intend'edly** with intention or design. — *ns.* **intend'iment** (*Spens.*) attentive consideration, understanding, meaning; **intend'ment** (*Shak.*) intention, design: meaning. [O.Fr. *entendre* — L. *intendĕre, intentum* and *intēnsum* — *in*, towards, *tendĕre*, to stretch.]

intender. See **entender.**

intenerate *in-ten'ər-āt, v.t.* to make tender: to soften. — *n.* **intenerā'tion.** [L. *in*, in, to, *tener*, tender.]

intenible *in-ten'i-bl,* (*Shak.*) *adj.* irretentive. [L. *in-*, not, *tenēre*, to hold.]

intense *in-tens', adj.* strained: concentrated, dense: extreme in degree: (of person, manner, etc.) earnestly or deeply emotional, or affecting to have deep feeling: of a photographic negative, opaque. — *v.t.* **intens'ate** (*Carlyle*) to intensify. — *adv.* **intense'ly.** — *ns.* and *adjs.* **intens'ative, intens'itive** intensive. — *ns.* **intense'ness, intens'ity; intensifica'tion** the act of intensifying; **intens'ifier.** — *v.t.* **intens'ify** to make more intense. — *v.i.* to become intense: — *pr.p.* **intens'ifying;** *pa.t.* and *pa.p.* **intens'ified.** — *n.* **intension** (*-ten'shən*) straining: intentness: intensity: intensification: the sum of the qualities implied by a general name (*logic*). — *adjs.* **inten'sional; intens'ive** concentrated, intense: strained: unremitting: relating to intensity or to intension: intensifying: intensified: giving force or emphasis (*gram.*). — *n.* an intensive word. — *adv.* **intens'ively.** — *n.* **intens'iveness.** — **-inten'sive** in composition, having, using, requiring, a great deal of something, as in **labour-intensive, capital-intensive.** — **intensive culture** getting the very most out of the soil of a limited area. — **intensive care unit** an area in a hospital where a patient's condition is carefully monitored. [See **intend.**]

intent *in-tent', adj.* having the mind bent: fixed with close attention: diligently applied. — *n.* the thing aimed at or intended: purpose, intention, design: intentness (*obs.*): meaning (*obs.*). — *n.* **intention** (*in-ten'shən*) application or direction of the mind (*obs.*): design:

purpose: application of thought to an object: a concept: a plan of treatment (*med.*): (in *pl.*) purpose with respect to marriage (*coll.*). — *adj.* **inten'tional** with intention: intended: designed: directed towards, or pertaining to the mind's capacity to direct itself towards, objects and states of affairs (*philos.*). — *n.* **intentional'ity.** — *adv.* **inten'tionally** with intention: on purpose. — *adjs.* **inten'tioned** having such and such intention; **intent'ive** (*Bacon*) attentive. — *adv.* **intent'ly** earnestly: diligently. — *n.* **intent'ness. — healing by first intention** healing of a wound by immediate union, without granulation; **by second intention** with granulation; **to all intents (and purposes)** in every important respect: virtually; **well- (or ill-) intentioned** having good (or ill) designs: meaning well (or ill); **with intent** (*law*) deliberately, with the intention of doing the harm, etc., that is or was done. [See **intend.**]

inter *in-tûr', v.t.* to bury: — *pr.p.* **interr'ing;** *pa.t.* and *pa.p.* **interred'.** — *n.* **inter'ment** burial. [Fr. *enterrer* — L.L. *interrāre* — L. *in*, into, *terra*, the earth.]

inter- *in'tər-, in-tûr', pfx.* between, among, in the midst of: mutual, reciprocal: together. [L. *inter*.]

interact *in'tər-akt, n.* an interlude: an entr'acte: the interval between acts. — *v.i.* **interact'** to act on one another. — *ns.* **interac'tant** a substance, etc., which interacts; **interaction** (*-ak'shən*) mutual action; **interac'tionism** the theory that mind and body act on each other (distinguished from *psychophysical parallelism* and *epiphenomenalism*); **interac'tionist.** — *adj.* **interac'tive** allowing, or capable of, mutual action: allowing continuous two-way communication between a computer and its user. [Pfx. **inter-**.]

inter alia *in'tər, -ter, ā'li-ə, a'li-a,* (L.) among other things; **inter alios** (*ā'li-ōs, a'li-ōs*) among other persons.

interallied *in-tər-al'īd,* or *-īd', adj.* between or among allies. [Pfx. **inter-**.]

interambulacrum *in-tər-am-bū-lā'krəm, n.* in sea-urchins, a radial band between two ambulacra: — *pl.* **interambulā'cra.** — *adj.* **interambulā'cral.** [Pfx. **inter-**.]

inter-arts *in'tər-ärts', adj.* belonging to the examination between matriculation and B.A. of London University. [For **intermediate arts.**]

interatomic *in-tər-ə-tom'ik, adj.* existing, happening, etc., between atoms. [Pfx. **inter-**.]

interbank *in'tər-bangk, adj.* between or among banks. [Pfx. **inter-**.]

interbedded *in-tər-bed'id, adj.* interstratified. — *n.* **interbedd'ing.** [Pfx. **inter-**.]

interbreed *in-tər-brēd', v.t.* and *v.i.* to breed together, esp. of different races: — *pa.t.* and *pa.p.* **interbred'.** — *n.* **interbreed'ing.** [Pfx. **inter-**.]

intercalate *in-tûr'kə-lāt, v.t.* to insert between others, as a day in a calendar: to interpolate. — *adjs.* **inter'calar** (*-lər; obs.*), **inter'calary** inserted between others. — *n.* **intercalā'tion.** — *adj.* **inter'calative** (*-lā-tiv, -lə-tiv*). [L. *intercalāre, -ātum* — *inter*, between, *calāre*, to proclaim; see **calends.**]

intercede *in-tər-sēd', v.i.* to act as peacemaker between two: to plead (for one). — *adj.* **intercēd'ent.** — *n.* **intercēd'er.** [L. *intercēdĕre, -cēssum* — *inter*, between, *cēdĕre*, to go.]

intercellular *in-tər-sel'ū-lər,* (*biol.*) *adj.* placed among cells. [Pfx. **inter-**.]

intercensal *in-tər-sen'səl, adj.* between censuses. [Irreg. formed from L. *inter* and **census.**]

intercept *in-tər-sept', v.t.* to stop and seize in passage: to cut off: to stop, alter, or interrupt, the progress of: to take or comprehend between (*math.*). — *ns.* **in'tercept** (*math.*) that part of a line that is intercepted; **intercep'ter, intercep'tor** one who or that which intercepts: a light, swift aeroplane for pursuit; **intercep'tion.** — *adj.* **intercep'tive.** [L. *intercipĕre, -ceptum* — *inter*, between, *capĕre,* to seize.]

intercession *in-tər-sesh'ən, n.* the act of interceding or pleading for another. — *adj.* **intercess'ional.** — *n.* **intercessor** (*-ses'ər*) one who intercedes: a bishop who acts during a vacancy in a see. — *adjs.* **intercessôrial**

(-ōr', -ŏr'), **intercess'ory** interceding. — **intercession of saints** prayer offered on behalf of Christians on earth by saints. [See **intercede**.]

interchain in-tər-chān', v.t. to chain together. [Pfx. **inter-**.]

interchange in-tər-chānj', v.t. to give and take mutually: to exchange. — v.i. to succeed alternately. — n. **in'terchange** mutual exchange: alternate succession: a road junction or series of junctions designed to prevent streams of traffic crossing one another. — adj. **interchange'able** that may be interchanged: following each other in alternate succession (obs.). — ns. **interchange'-ableness, interchangcabil'ity**. — adv. **interchange'ably**. — ns. **interchange'ment** (Shak.) exchange, mutual transfer; **interchang'er**. [Pfx. **inter-**.]

interchapter in'tər-chap-tər, n. an intercalary chapter in a book, not numbered in the general sequence. [Pfx. **inter-**.]

intercipient in-tər-sip'i-ənt, (obs.) adj. intercepting. — n. the person or thing that intercepts. [L. intercipiēns, -entis, pr.p. of intercipĕre; see **intercept**.]

intercity in-tər-sit'i, adj. between cities. [Pfx. **inter-**.]

interclavicular in-tər-klə-vik'ū-lər, adj. situated occurring, or pertaining to (the area) between clavicles. [Pfx. **inter-**.]

interclude in-tər-klōōd', v.t. to block: to enclose: to cut off. — n. **interclusion** (-klōō'zhən). [L. interclūdĕre — inter, between, claudĕre, to shut.]

intercollegiate in-tər-kə-lē'ji-āt, -ət, adj. between colleges. [Pfx. **inter-**.]

intercolline in-tər-kol'īn, adj. lying between hills. [Pfx. **inter-**.]

intercolonial in-tər-kə-lō'ni-əl, adj. between colonies. — adv. **intercolo'nially**. [Pfx. **inter-**.]

intercolumniation in-tər-kə-lum-ni-ā'shən, (archit.) n. the spacing of, or distance between, columns, measured in terms of the lower diameter. — adj. **intercolum'nar** placed between columns. [Pfx. **inter-**.]

intercom in'tər-kom, n. a telephone system within a building, aeroplane, tank, etc. [Internal communication.]

intercommune in-tər-kə-mūn', v.i. to commune mutually or together: to hold intercourse, have dealings. — adjs. **intercomm'unal** existing between communities; **intercommun'icable**. — v.t. and v.i. **intercommun'icate** to communicate mutually or together: to have free passage from one to another. — ns. **intercommunica'tion; intercommun'ion** mutual communion or relation, esp. between churches: the permitting of members of one denomination to receive Holy Communion in the churches of another denomination; **intercommun'ity** the state of being or having in common. — **letters of intercommuning** an ancient writ issued by the Scottish Privy Council warning persons not to harbour or have any dealings with those named, on pain of being held accessory. [Pfx. **inter-**.]

interconnect in-tər-kə-nekt', v.t. to connect mutually and intimately, or by a multitude of ways. — v.i. to be mutually connected. — n. **interconnec'tedness, interconnec'tion, interconnex'ion**. [Pfx. **inter-**.]

intercontinental in-tər-kon-ti-nen'tal, adj. between or connecting different continents. [Pfx. **inter-**.]

interconver'sion in'tər-kən-ver'shən, n. the conversion of two things or more into one another, mutual conversion. — v. (back-formation) **interconvert'** to convert (two or more things) into one another. — adj. **interconvert'ible** mutually convertible: interchangeable: exactly equivalent. [Pfx. **inter-**.]

intercostal in-tər-kost'əl, adj. between the ribs or the leaf-veins. [L. inter, between, costa, a rib.]

intercourse in'tər-kōrs, -kŏrs, n. connection by dealings: communication: commerce: communion: coition. [O.Fr. entrecours — L. intercursus, a running between — inter, between, currĕre, cursum, to run.]

intercrop in-tər-krop', v.t. and v.i. to grow or cultivate in alternate rows: — pr.p. **intercropp'ing**; pa.t. and pa.p. **intercropped'**. — n. **in'tercrop**. [Pfx. **inter-**.]

intercross in-tər-kros', v.t. and v.i. to cross and recross: to cross mutually: to place or lie crosswise: to inter-breed. — n. **in'tercross** a crossing of breeds. [Pfx. **inter-**.]

intercrural in-tər-krōōr'əl, adj. situated or pertaining to (the area) between the crura or legs. [Pfx. **inter-**.]

intercurrent in-tər-kur'ənt, adj. running between, inter-vening: supervening. — n. **intercurr'ence**. [L. inter, between, currĕre, to run.]

intercut in-tər-kut', (cinema) v.t. to alternate (contrasting shots) within a sequence by cutting. [Pfx. **inter-**.]

interdash in-tər-dash', v.t. to intersperse with dashes. [Pfx. **inter-**.]

interdeal in'tər-dēl, (arch.) n. mutual dealings: inter-course: negotiations. — Also (Spens.) **enterdeale**. — v.i. **interdeal'** (arch.) to have mutual dealings. — n. **interdeal'er**. [Pfx. **inter-**.]

interdenominational in-tər-di-nom-i-nāsh'(ə)-nl, adj. common to, with participation of, various religious de-nominations: independent of denomination. [Pfx. **inter-**.]

interdental in-tər-dent'l, adj. between the teeth: pertaining to the surfaces of the teeth where they adjoin (dentistry): pronounced with the tip of the tongue between upper and lower teeth. — adv. **interdent'ally**. [Pfx. **inter-**.]

interdepartmental in-tər-dē-pärt-ment'l, adj. between departments. — adv. **interdepartment'ally**. [Pfx. **inter-**.]

interdependence in-tər-di-pend'əns, n. mutual dependence: dependence of parts one on another. — adj. **interdepend'ent**. [Pfx. **inter-**.]

interdict in-tər-dikt', v.t. to prohibit: to forbid: to forbid communion. — n. **in'terdict** prohibition: a prohibitory decree: a prohibition of the pope restraining the clergy from performing divine service. — n. **interdic'tion** (-shən). — adjs. **interdic'tive, interdic'tory** containing interdiction: prohibitory. [L. interdīcĕre, -dictum — inter, between, dīcĕre, to say.]

interdigital in-tər-dij'i-tl, adj. between digits. — v.t. and v.i. **interdig'itate** to interlock by finger-like processes, or in the manner of the fingers of clasped hands: to interstratify or be interstratified. — n. **interdigita'tion**. [Pfx. **inter-**.]

interdine in-tər-dīn', v.i. to eat together. [Pfx. **inter-**.]

interdisciplinary in-tər-di-si-plin'ə-ri, adj. involving two or more fields of study. [Pfx. **inter-**.]

interess, interesse in'tər-es, or -es', (obs.) n. interest. — v.t. to interest: — pa.p. (Shak.) **interest'**. [A.Fr. interesse — L.L. interesse, compensation, interest — L. interesse (inf.) to concern.]

interest int'(ə)-rest, -rist, n. advantage, benefit: premium paid for the use of money: any increase: concern, importance: personal influence: a right to some advantage: claim to participate or be concerned in some way: stake: share: behalf: partisanship or side: the body of persons whose advantage is bound up in anything: regard to advantage: a state of engaged attention and curiosity: disposition towards such a state: the power of arousing it: that in which one has interest or is interested. — v.t. to concern deeply: to cause to have an interest: to engage the attention of: to awaken concern in: to excite (on behalf of another). — adj. **in'terested** having an interest or concern: affected or biased by personal considerations, self-interest, etc. — adv. **in'terestedly**. — n. **in'terestedness**. — adj. **in'teresting** (old-fashioned -est') engaging or apt to engage the attention or regard: exciting emotion or passion. — adv. **in'terestingly**. — n. **in'terestingness**. — **interest group** a number of people grouped together to further or protect a common interest. — **compound interest** see **compound**; **in an interesting condition, state, situation** old-fashioned euphemisms for pregnant; **in the interest(s) of** with a view to furthering or to helping; **make interest for** to secure favour for; **simple interest** see **simple**. [From **interess**, influenced by O.Fr. interest, L. interest, it concerns, 3rd pers. sing. pres.

ind. of *interesse* — *inter*, between, among, and *esse*, to be.]

interface *in'tər-fās, n.* a surface forming a common boundary: a meeting-point or area of contact between objects, systems, subjects, etc.: the connection or junction between two systems or two parts of the same system (*comput.*): the surface of separation between phases (*chem.*). — *v.i.* (*comput.*) to interact or operate compatibly (with). — *adj.* **interfacial** (*-fā'shl*) between plane faces: of an interface. [Pfx. **inter-**.]

interfacing *in'tər-fās-ing, n.* firm material sewn between layers of fabric to shape and stiffen a garment. [Pfx. **inter-**.]

interfascicular *in-tər-fə-sik'ū-lər, adj.* between vascular bundles. [Pfx. **inter-**.]

interfemoral *in-tər-fem'ər-əl, adj.* situated between the thighs, connecting the hind limbs. [Pfx. **inter-**.]

interfenestration *in-tər-fen-is-trā'shən, n.* spacing of windows. [L. *inter*, between, *fenestra*, a window.]

interfere *in-tər-fēr', v.i.* (of a horse) to strike a foot against the opposite leg in walking: to intervene: to come in the way: to interpose: to intermeddle: (of waves, rays of light, etc.) to act reciprocally. — *n.* **interfer'ence** the act of interfering: the effect of combining similar rays of light, etc. (*phys.*): the spoiling of a wireless or television signal by others or by natural disturbances. — *adj.* **interferential** (*-fər-en'shl*). — *n.* **interfer'er**. — *adv.* **interfer'ingly**. — *ns.* **interfer'ogram** (*phys.*) a photographic or diagrammatic record of interference; **interferom'eter** an instrument which, by observing interference fringes, makes precision measurements of, wavelengths, wave speeds, angles, distances, etc: a radio telescope (**radio interferometer**) using two or more antennas spaced at known intervals and linked to a common receiver, one of its applications being the precise determination of the position of sources of radio waves in space. — *adj.* **interferomet'ric**. — *ns.* **interferom'etry; interfer'on** any of several proteins produced naturally in the body, active against many viruses. — **interference figure** a figure observed when a crystal section is viewed between crossed nicols; **interference fringes** alternate light and dark bands seen when similar beams of light interfere. — **interfere with** to meddle in: to get in the way of, hinder: to assault sexually. [O.Fr. *entreférir* — L. *inter*, between, *ferīre*, to strike.]

interfertile *in-tər-fûr'tīl, U.S. -təl, adj.* capable of interbreeding. [Pfx. **inter-**.]

interflow *in'tər-flō, n.* intermingling. — *v.i.* **interflow'** to flow into one another or between. [Pfx. **inter-**.]

interfluent *in-tûr'flōō-ənt, adj.* flowing between or together. — Also **inter'fluous**. — *n.* **inter'fluence**. [L. *interfluēns, -entis* — *inter*, between, *fluĕre*, to flow.]

interfold *in-tər-fōld', v.t.* to fold one into the other. [Pfx. **inter-**.]

interfoliate *in-tər-fō'li-āt, v.t.* to interleave. [L. *inter*, between, *folium*, a leaf.]

interfretted *in-tər-fret'id,* (*her.*) *adj.* interlaced. [Pfx. **inter-**.]

interfrontal *in-tər-frun'tl, -fron'tl, adj.* between the frontal bones. [Pfx. **inter-**.]

interfuse *in-tər-fūz', v.t.* to pour between or through: to permeate: to fuse together: to associate. — *v.i.* to fuse together: to blend. — *n.* **interfusion** (*-fū'zhən*). [Pfx. **inter-**.]

intergalactic *in-tər-gal-ak'tik, adj.* between, or among, galaxies. [Pfx. **inter-**.]

intergatory *in-tûr'gə-tə-ri,* (*obs.*) usu. in *pl.*) *n.* a shortened form of **interrogatory**. [Pfx. **inter-**.]

interglacial *in-tər-glā'sh(y)əl,* (*geol.*) *adj.* occurring between two periods of glacial action. — *n.* a retreat of ice between glaciations. [Pfx. **inter-**.]

Interglossa *in'tər-glos'ə, n.* an international language based on well-known Greek and Latin roots, devised by Lancelot Hogben (1943). [L. *inter*, between, Gr. *glōssa*, tongue.]

intergrade *in-tər-grād', v.i.* to merge in or shade off into

something else through a series of intermediate forms. — *n.* **in'tergrade** an intermediate grade. — *n.* **intergradation** (*-grə-dā'shən*). [Pfx. **inter-**.]

intergrow *in-tər-grō', v.t.* to grow into or among each other. — *adj.* **intergrown'**. — *n.* **in'tergrowth**. [Pfx. **inter-**.]

interim *in'tər-im, n.* the time between or intervening: the meantime: (with *cap.*) in the history of the Reformation, the name given to certain edicts of the German emperor for the regulation of religious and ecclesiastical matters, till they could be decided by a general council — as the Augsburg Interim (1548), etc. — *adj.* temporary. — *adv.* (*rare*) meanwhile. [L.]

interior *in-tē'ri-ər, adj.* inner: remote from the frontier or coast: inland: situated within or further in (sometimes with *to*): devoted to mental or spiritual life. — *n.* the inside of anything: the inland part of a country: a picture of a scene within a house: home affairs of a country: inner nature or character. — *n.* **interiority** (*-or'i-ti*). — *adv.* **inter'iorly**. — **interior angle** the angle between two adjacent sides of a polygon; **interior decoration, design** the construction and furnishing of the interior of a building; **interior grate** an open grate with built-in boiler; **interior monologue** a literary representation of a person's inner thoughts and feelings before they take coherent grammatical form. — *adj.* **inter'ior-sprung'** (of a mattress, etc.) containing springs. [L., compar. of assumed *interus*, inward.]

interjacent *in-tər-jā'sənt, adj.* lying between: intervening. — *n.* **interjā'cency**. [L. *interjacēns, -entis*, pr.p. of *interjacēre* — *inter*, between, *jacēre*, to lie.]

interjaculate *in-tər-jak'ū-lāt, v.t.* to ejaculate in interruption. — *adj.* **interjac'ulatory** (*-ū-lə-tə-ri*). [L. *inter*, between, *jaculārī*, to throw.]

interject *in-tər-jekt', v.t.* to throw between: to interpose: to exclaim in interruption or parenthesis: to insert. — *v.i.* to throw oneself between. — *n.* **interjec'tion** (*-shən*) a throwing between: a word thrown in to express emotion (*gram.*). — *adjs.* **interjec'tional, interjec'tionary, interjec'tural**. — *adv.* **interjec'tionally**. [L. *inter(j)icĕre, interjectum* — *inter*, between, *jacĕre*, to throw.]

interjoin *in-tər-join',* (*Shak.*) *v.t.* to join together. [Pfx. **inter-**.]

interknit *in-tər-nit', v.t.* to knit into each other. [Pfx. **inter-**.]

interlace *in-tər-lās', v.t.* to lace, weave, or entangle together. — *v.i.* to intermix. — *n.* **interlace'ment**. — **interlaced scanning** in television, the alternate scanning of an image in two sets of alternate lines. [Pfx. **inter-**.]

interlaminate *in-tər-lam'in-āt, v.t.* to insert between layers: to arrange or apply in alternate layers. — *adj.* **interlam'inar**. — *n.* **interlaminā'tion**. [Pfx. **inter-**.]

interlard *in-tər-lärd', v.t.* to mix in, as fat with lean: to diversify by mixture. [Pfx. **inter-**.]

interlay *in-tər-lā', v.t.* to lay between: to interpose. — *n.* **in'terlay** layers of tissue, etc., placed between a printing plate and its base to achieve the correct type height or printing pressure (*print.*). [Pfx. **inter-**.]

interleave *in-tər-lēv', v.t.* to put a leaf between: to insert blank leaves in. — *n.* **in'terleaf** a leaf so inserted: — *pl.* **in'terleaves**. [Pfx. **inter-**.]

interleukin *in-tər-lū'kin, n.* a protein produced by white blood cells that plays an important part in the combating of infection.

interline[1] *in-tər-līn', v.t.* to write in alternate lines: to insert between lines: to write between the lines of. — *adj.* **interlinear** (*-lin'i-ər*) written between lines. — *ns.* **interlineation** (*-lin-i-ā'shən*), **interlin'ing**. [Pfx. **inter-**.]

interline[2] *in-tər-līn', v.t.* to supply (a part of a garment, e.g. the collar) with an additional lining to reinforce or stiffen it. — *n.* **interlin'ing**.

interlinear, interlineation. See **interline**[1].

Interlingua *in-tər-ling'gwə, n.* an international language based on the living Latin roots in European languages: (without *cap.*) any artificially devised international language. — *adj.* **interlin'gual**. — *adv.* **interlin'gually**.

[L. *inter*, between, *lingua*, tongue.]
interlink *in-tər-lingk'*, *v.t.* and *v.i.* to link together.   [Pfx. **inter-**.]
interlobular *in-tər-lob'ū-lər*, *adj.* between lobes.   [Pfx. **inter-**.]
interlocation *in-tər-lo-kā'shən*, *n.* a placing between. [Pfx. **inter-**.]
interlock *in-tər-lok'*, *v.t.* to lock or clasp together: to connect so as to work together. — *v.i.* to be locked together. — *n.* **in'terlock** an interlocked condition: synchronising mechanism.   [Pfx. **inter-**.]
interlocution *in-tər-lo-kū'shən*, *n.* conference: an intermediate decree before final decision. — *n.* **interlocutor** (*-lok'ū-tər*) one who speaks in dialogue: a judge's decree (*Scots law*). — *adj.* **interloc'utory**. — *ns.* **interloc'utress, interloc'utrice, interloc'utrix** a female interlocutor.   [L. *interlocūtiō, -ōnis* — *inter*, between, *loquī, locūtus*, to speak.]
interloper *in'tər-lō-pər*, *n.* one who trades without licence: an intruder. — *v.i.* and *v.t.* **interlope'** (or *in'*) to intrude into any matter in which one has no fair concern. [Prob. L. *inter*, between, and *lope*[1].]
interlude *in'tər-lōōd, -lūd*, *n.* a short piece introduced between the acts of the mysteries and moralities, etc., unconnected with the main theme and light in character: an early form of modern drama: a short piece of music played between the parts of a drama opera, hymn, etc.: an interval, any period of time or any happening different in character from what comes before or after. — *v.t.* and *v.i.* to interrupt, as an interlude. — *adj.* **interlu'dial**.   [L. *inter*, between, *lūdus*, play.]
interlunar *in-tər-lōō'nər, -lū'*, *adj.* belonging to the moon's monthly time of invisibility. — Also **interlu'nary**. — *n.* **interlunā'tion** (*-lōō-*) the dark time between old moon and new.   [L. *inter*, between, *lūna*, the moon.]
intermarry *in-tər-mar'i*, *v.i.* to marry, esp. of different races or groups, or of near kin: to mingle by repeated marriage: (of a couple) to marry (*legal*): to marry (with *with*; *legal*). — *n.* **intermarr'iage**.   [Pfx. **inter-**.]
intermaxilla *in-tər-maks-il'ə*, *n.* the premaxilla. — *adj.* **intermax'illary** (or *-il'*) of the intermaxilla: between the maxillaries. — *n.* the intermaxilla.   [L. *inter*, between, *maxilla*, a jawbone.]
intermeddle *in-tər-med'l*, *v.i.* to meddle: to interfere improperly. — *n.* **intermedd'ler**.   [Pfx. **inter-**.]
intermediate *in-tər-mē'dyit, -di-it*, *adj.* placed, occurring, or classified between others, extremes, limits, or stages: of igneous rocks, between acid and basic in composition: intervening. — *n.* that which is intermediate: any compound manufactured from a primary that serves as a starting material for the synthesis of some other product (*chem.*). — *v.i.* (*-di-āt*) to interpose: to act between others. — *n.* **interme'diacy** (*-ə-si*) the state of being intermediate. — *adjs.* **interme'dial** (*rare*) intermediate: intermediary; **interme'diary** acting between others: intermediate. — *n.* an intermediate agent. — *adv.* **interme'diately**. — *ns.* **intermēdiā'tion** the act of intermediating; **interme'diator**. — *adj.* **interme'diatory** (*-ə-tə-ri*). — *n.* **interme'dium** an intervening agent or instrument. — **intermediate technology** technology which combines simple, basic materials with modern sophisticated tools and methods.   [Pfx. **inter-**.]
interment. See **inter**.
intermetallic *in-tər-mə-tal'ik*, *adj.* (of an alloy) formed from two metallic elements.   [Pfx. **inter-**.]
intermezzo *in-tər-met'sō*, sometimes *-med'zō*, *n.* a short dramatic or musical entertainment as entr'acte: a short intermediate movement or the like (*mus.*): — *pl.* **intermez'zi** (*-zē*) or **-os**.   [It., — L. *intermedius*.]
intermigration *in-tər-mī-grā'shən*, *n.* reciprocal migration.   [Pfx. **inter-**.]
interminable *in-tûr'min-ə-bl*, **interminate** *in-tûr'min-āt, -it*, *adjs.* without termination or limit: boundless: endless. — *n.* **inter'minableness**. — *adv.* **inter'minably**. — **interminate decimal** a decimal fraction that runs to an infinity of places.   [Pfx. **in-** (2).]

intermingle *in-tər-ming'gl*, *v.t.* and *v.i.* to mingle or mix together.   [Pfx. **inter-**.]
intermit *in-tər-mit'*, *v.t.* and *v.i.* to stop for a time. — *v.t.* (*obs.*) to interpose. — *n.* **intermission** (*-mish'ən*) an act of intermitting: an interval: music played during a theatre or similar interval: pause: a respite: perh., occupation, recreation interposed, something to do (*Shak.*). — *adj.* **intermissive** (*-mis'iv*) coming and going: intermittent. — *ns.* **intermitt'ence; intermitt'ency**. — *adj.* **intermitt'ent** intermitting or ceasing at intervals. — *advs.* **intermitt'ently; intermitt'ingly**.   [L. *intermittĕre, -missum* — *inter*, between, *mittĕre*, to cause to go.]
intermix *in-tər-miks'*, *v.t.* and *v.i.* to mix together. — *n.* **intermix'ture** a mass formed by mixture: something added and intermixed.   [L. *intermiscēre, -mixtum* — *inter*, among, *miscēre*, to mix.]
intermodulation *in-tər-mod-ū-lā'shən*, (*electronics*) *n.* unwanted mutual interference between electronic signals, affecting the amplitude of each.   [Pfx. **inter-**.]
intermolecular *in-tər-mol-ek'ū-lər*, *adj.* between molecules.   [Pfx. **inter-**.]
intermundane *in-tər-mun'dān*, *adj.* between worlds. [Pfx. **inter-**.]
intermure *in-tər-mūr'*, (*obs.*) *v.t.* to wall in.   [L. *inter*, within, *mūrus*, a wall.]
intern *in-tûrn'*, *adj.* (*obs.* **interne**) internal. — *n.* (*in'tûrn* (also *U.S.*) or *in-tûrn'*; also **interne**) an inmate, as of a boarding-school: a resident assistant surgeon or physician in a hospital (*U.S.*). — *v.t.* (**intern'**) to send into the interior of a country: to confine within fixed bounds without permission to leave the district, camp, port, or like limits. — *ns.* **internee'** one so restricted; **intern'ment** confinement of this kind.   [Fr. *interne* — L. *internus*, inward.]
internal *in-tûr'nəl*, *adj.* in the interior: domestic as opposed to foreign: intrinsic: pertaining to the inner nature or feelings: inner: — opp. to *external*. — *n.* (in *pl.*) inner parts. — *v.t.* **inter'nalise, -ize** to assimilate (an idea, etc.) into one's personality: to withdraw (an emotion, etc.) into oneself (rather than express it). — *p. adj.* **inter'nalised, -z-**. — *n.* **internality** (*-nal'i-ti*). — *adv.* **inter'nally**. — **internal evidence** evidence afforded by the thing itself; **internal rhyme** a rhyme occurring within a line of verse; **internal student** one who has studied at the university that examines him. — **internal-combustion engine** an engine in which the fuel is burned within the working cylinder.   [L. *internus* — *inter*, within.]
international *in-tər-nash'ən-l*, *adj.* between nations or their representatives: transcending national limits: extending to several nations: pertaining to the relations between nations. — *n.* (with *cap.*) a short-lived association formed in London in 1864 to unite the working classes of all countries in efforts for their economic emancipation: (with *cap.*) a second organisation of socialists of all countries formed in 1889 as a successor to the first International — also (Fr.) **Internationale** (*ē-ter-na-syō-näl'*): (with *cap.*) a rival organisation (third International) operating from Moscow from 1919 to 1943: a game or contest between players chosen to represent different nations (*coll.*): a player who takes (or has taken) part in an international match. — *n.* **Internationale** (*ē-ter-na-syō-näl'*) an international communist song, composed in France in 1871: the second International. — *v.t.* **interna'tionalise, -ize** to make international: to put under international control. — *ns.* **interna'tionalism; interna'tionalist** one who favours the common interests, or action, of all nations: one who favours the principles of the International: one who represents his country in international contests: a specialist in international law. — *adj.* **internationalis'tic**. — *adv.* **interna'tionally**. — **international law** the law regulating the relations of states (**public international law**) or that determining what nation's law shall in any case govern the relations of private persons (**private international law**); **international master** (also with *caps.*)

(a person holding) the second highest international chess title; **international (concert) pitch** since 1939, 440 cycles per second at 20°C for A in the treble clef; **international units** internationally recognised units in terms of which pure, or impure, vitamin material can be assayed. — **International Bible Students' Association** see **Russellite; International Court of Justice** the World Court; **International Date Line** the line east and west of which the date differs — the 180th meridian with deviations; **International Development Association** an organisation founded in 1960 to lend money at low interest rates to developing countries; **international match point** a scoring unit in tournament contract bridge, often shortened to **imp** or **i.m.p.; International Monetary Fund** an organisation, established in 1945 to promote international trade through increased stabilisation of currencies, which maintains a pool of money on which member countries can draw; **International Phonetic Alphabet** the alphabet of the International Phonetic Association, a series of symbols representing human speech sounds; **international standard atmosphere** a standardised atmosphere adopted internationally for comparing aircraft performance; **international standard book number** see **standard; international system of units** see **SI international temperature scale** a scale differing slightly from the absolute (thermodynamic) scale, with fixed points ranging from −182·970° Celsius, the boiling-point of oxygen, to 1063·0° Celsius, the melting-point of gold. [Pfx. **inter-.**]

interne. See **intern.**

internecine *in-tər-nē′sīn, adj.* deadly: murderous: (*loosely*) mutually destructive: involving conflict within a group. — Also **interne′cive.** [L. *internecīnus, -īvus* — *internecāre* — *inter*, between (used intensively), *necāre*, to kill.]

internee. See **intern.**

interneural *in-tər-nū′rəl*, (*anat.*) *adj.* situated between the neural spines or spinous processes of successive vertebrae. [Pfx. **inter-.**]

internist *in-tûr′nist, n.* a specialist in internal diseases: a physician, in contrast to a surgeon. [*intern* al, and **-ist.**]

internment. See **intern.**

internode *in′tər-nōd, n.* the space between two nodes. — *adjs.* **internō′dal, internō′dial** (*obs.*). [L. *internōdium* — *inter*, between, *nōdus*, a knot.]

inter nos *in′tər, -nē′, nōs*, (L.) between ourselves.

internuncio *in-tər-nun′shi-ō, n.* a messenger between two parties: the Pope's representative at minor courts: — *pl.* **internun′cios.** — *adj.* **internun′cial** relating to an internuncio: interconnecting, as the neurone linking the afferent and efferent neurones of the central nervous system. [It. *internunzio*, Sp. *internuncio*, L. *internuntius* — *inter*, between, *nuntius*, a messenger.]

interoceanic *in-tər-ō-shi-an′ik, adj.* between oceans. [Pfx. **inter-.**]

interoceptor *in-tər-ō-sep′tər*, (*physiol.*) *n.* a sensory receptor of the viscera. — *adj.* **interocep′tive.** [*Inter*ior and *re*ceptor.]

interocular *in-tər-ok′ū-lər, adj.* between the eyes. [Pfx. **inter-.**]

interorbital *in-tər-ör′bit-əl, adj.* between the orbits. [Pfx. **inter-.**]

interosculation *in-tər-os-kū-lā′shən, n.* interconnection by, or as if by, osculation: possession of characters common to different groups: dovetailing into one another. — *adj.* **interos′culant.** — *v.t.* **interos′culate.** [Pfx. **inter-.**]

interosseous *in-tər-os′i-əs, adj.* situated between bones. — Also **inteross′eal.** [Pfx. **inter-.**]

interpage *in-tər-pāj′, v.t.* to insert on intermediate pages. [Pfx. **inter-.**]

interparietal *in-tər-pə-rī′ə-təl, adj.* situated between the right and left parietal bones of the skull. [Pfx. **inter-.**]

inter partes *in′tər, -ter, pär′tēz, pär′tãs*, (L.) between parties.

interpellation *in-tər-pel-ā′shən, n.* a question raised during the course of a debate: interruption (*obs.*): intercession (*obs.*): a summons (*obs.*). — *adj.* **interpell′ant** causing an interpellation. — *n.* one who interpellates. — *v.t.* **inter′pellate** (or *-pel′*) to question by interpellation. [Fr., — L. *interpellāre, -ātum*, to disturb by speaking — *inter*, between, *pellĕre*, to drive.]

interpenetrate *in-tər-pen′i-trāt, v.t.* to penetrate thoroughly. — *v.t.* and *v.i.* to penetrate mutually. — *adjs.* **interpen′etrable, interpen′etrant.** — *n.* **interpenetrā′tion.** — *adj.* **interpen′etrātive.** [Pfx. **inter-.**]

interpersonal *in-tər-pûr′sən-əl, adj.* between persons. — *adv.* **interper′sonally.** [Pfx. **inter-.**]

interpetiolar *in-tər-pet′i-ō-lər*, (*bot.*) *adj.* between the petioles. [Pfx. **inter-.**]

interphase *in′tər-fāz, n.* an interface (*chem.*): an interval between stages of mitosis (*biol.*). [Pfx. **inter-.**]

interphone *in′tər-fōn, n.* intercom. [Gr. *phōnē*, voice.]

interpilaster *in-tər-pil-as′tər*, (*archit.*) *n.* space between two pilasters. [Pfx. **inter-.**]

interplanetary *in-tər-plan′it-ə-ri, adj.* between planets. [Pfx. **inter-.**]

interplant *in-tər-plänt′, v.t.* to plant among another crop. [Pfx. **inter-.**]

interplay *in′tər-plā, n.* mutual action: interchange of action and reaction. [Pfx. **inter-.**]

interplead *in-tər-plēd′*, (*law*) *v.i.* to discuss adverse claims to property by bill of interpleader. — *n.* **interplead′er** one who interpleads: a form of process in the English courts, by a bill in equity, intended to protect a defendant who claims no interest in the subject matter of a suit, while at the same time he has reason to know that the plaintiff's title is disputed by some other claimant. [Pfx. **inter-.**]

interpleural *in-tər-plōō′rəl, adj.* situated between the right and left pleural cavities. [Pfx. **inter-.**]

inter pocula *in′tər, -ter, pok′ū-lə, pō′kōō-la*, (L.) over one's cups, in the course of drinking.

Interpol *in′tər-pol*, the *Inter*national Criminal *Pol*ice Commission, directed to international co-operation in the suppression of crime.

interpolable. See **interpolate.**

interpolar *in-tər-pō′lər, adj.* between or connecting the poles. [Pfx. **inter-.**]

interpolate *in-tûr′pō-lāt, -pə-lāt, v.t.* to insert unfairly, as a spurious word or passage in a book or manuscript: to tamper with, to corrupt by spurious insertions: to insert, intercalate, interject: to fill in as an intermediate term of a series (*math.*). — *adj.* **inter′polable.** — *n.* **interpolā′tion.** — *adj.* **inter′polātive.** — *n.* **inter′polātor.** [L. *interpolāre, -ātum* — *inter*, between, *polīre*, to polish.]

interpone *in-tər-pōn′*, (*Scots law*) *v.t.* to interpose. [L. *interpōnĕre.*]

interpose *in-tər-pōz′, v.t.* to place between: to thrust in: to offer, as aid or services: to put in by way of interruption. — *v.i.* to come between: to mediate: to interfere. — *ns.* **interpos′al; interpos′er; interposition** (*in-tər-poz-ish′ən*) the act of interposing: intervention: mediation: in U.S., the right of a state to oppose the federal government for encroachment on the prerogatives of the state: anything interposed. [Fr. *interposer* — L. *inter*, between, Fr. *poser*, to place; see **pose**[1].]

interpret *in-tûr′prit, v.t.* to explain the meaning of, to elucidate, unfold, show the purport of: to translate into intelligible or familiar terms. — *v.i.* to practise interpretation. — *adj.* **inter′pretable** capable of being explained. — *v.t.* and *v.i.* (*arch.*) **inter′pretate.** — *n.* **interpretā′tion** the act of interpreting: the sense given by an interpreter: the power of explaining (*obs.*): the representation of a dramatic part, performance of a piece of music, or the like, according to one's conception of it. — *adjs.* **inter′pretative** (*-āt-iv, -ət-iv*), **inter′pretive** inferred by or containing interpretation. — *adv.* **inter′pretatively.** — *ns.* **inter′preter** one who translates orally for the benefit of two or more parties speaking different languages: an expounder: a translator (*obs.*):

a machine which prints out on punched cards fed into it the data contained in the patterns of holes in the cards (*comput.*): a program which executes other programs (*comput.*; cf. **compiler**); **inter'pretership; inter'pretress** a female interpreter (sometimes **inter'pretess**). [L. *interpretārī, -ātus* — *interpres, -etis*.]

interprovincial *in-tər-prə-vin'shl, adj.* between provinces. [Pfx. **inter-**.]

interproximal *in'tər-prok'si-məl, (dentistry) adj.* pertaining to the surfaces of teeth where they adjoin. [Pfx. **inter-**.]

interpunction *in-tər-pungk'shən, n.* the insertion of points in writing. — Also **interpunctūā'tion.** — *v.t.* **interpunc'-tūate.** [Pfx. **inter-**.]

interracial *in-tər-rā'sh(y)əl, -shi-əl, adj.* between races. [Pfx. **inter-**.]

interradial *in-tər-rā'di-əl, adj.* between radii or rays: pertaining to an interradius. — *adv.* **interrā'dially.** — *n.* **interrā'dius** an interradial part: a radius midway between primary radii or perradii. [Pfx. **inter-**.]

interramal *in-tər-rā'məl, adj.* situated between the rami or branches, esp. of the lower jaw. — *n.* **interramificā'-tion** (*-ram-*) interweaving of branches. [L. *inter*, between, *rāmus*, a branch.]

interregal *in-tər-rē'gəl, adj.* between kings. [Pfx. **inter-**.]

interregnum *in-tər-reg'nəm, n.* the time between two reigns: the time between the cessation of one and the establishment of another government: any breach of continuity in order, etc.: — *pl.* **interreg'na, interreg'-nums.** — *n.* **in'terreign** (*Bacon*). [L. *inter*, between, *regnum*, rule.]

interrelation *in-tər-ri-lā'shən, n.* reciprocal relation. — *n.* **interrelā'tionship.** [Pfx. **inter-**.]

interrex *in'tər-reks, n.* one who rules during an interregnum: a regent: — *pl.* **interreges** (*-rē'jēz*). [L. *inter*, between, *rēx*, a king.]

interrogate *in-ter'ə-gāt, v.t.* to question: to examine by asking questions: of a radar set, etc., to send out signals to (a radio-beacon) in order to ascertain position. — *v.i.* to ask questions. — *adj.* **interr'ogable.** — *ns.* **interr'ogant** a questioner; **interrogatee'** one who is interrogated; **interrogā'tion** the act of interrogating: a question put: the mark placed after a question (?) (also **interrogation mark).** — *adj.* **interrogative** (*in-tər-og'ə-tiv*) denoting a question: expressed as a question. — *n.* a word used in asking a question. — *adv.* **interrog'-atively.** — *ns.* **interr'ogator; interrog'atory** a question or inquiry. — *adj.* expressing a question. [L. *inter-rogāre, -ātum* — *inter*, between, *rogāre*, to ask.]

in terrorem *in te-rōr'em* or *-rör'*, (L.) as a warning.

interrupt *in-tər-upt', v.t.* to break in between: to stop or hinder by breaking in upon: to break continuity in. — *v.i.* to make an interruption. — *adj.* **interrupted** (*obs.*): gaping apart (*Milt.*). — *adj.* **interrupt'ed** broken in continuity: irregular in spacing or size of parts (*biol.*). — *adv.* **interrupt'edly** with interruptions: irregularly. — *ns.* **interrup'ter** (also **interrup'tor**) one who interrupts: apparatus for interrupting, e.g. for breaking an electric circuit, for preventing the firing of a gun from an aircraft when the screw is in the line of fire; **interrup'tion** the act of interrupting: hindrance: temporary cessation. — *adj.* **interrup'tive** tending to interrupt. — *adv.* **interrup'tively.** — **interrupted cadence** (*mus.*) a cadence in which some other chord (often the submediant) replaces the expected tonic. [L. *inter-rumpĕre, -ruptum* — *inter*, between, *rumpĕre*, to break.]

interscapular *in-tər-ska'pū-lər, (anat.) adj.* between the shoulder-blades. [Pfx. **inter-**.]

interscholastic *in-tər-skə-las'tik, adj.* between schools. [Pfx. **inter-**.]

inter-science *in-tər-sī'əns, adj.* belonging to the examination between matriculation and B.Sc. of London University. [Pfx. **inter-**.]

interscribe *in-tər-skrīb', (obs.) v.t.* to write between. [L. *interscrībĕre* — *inter*, between, *scrībĕre*, to write.]

inter se *in'tər, -ter, sē, sā*, (L.) between themselves.

intersect *in-tər-sekt', v.t.* to cut across: to cut or cross

mutually: to divide into parts. — *v.i.* to cross each other. — *ns.* **in'tersect** a point of intersection; **intersec'-tion** intersecting: the point or line in which lines or surfaces cut each other (*geom.*): the set of elements which two or more sets have in common (*math.*): a crossroads. — *adj.* **intersec'tional.** [L. *inter*, between, *secāre, sectum*, to cut.]

interseptal *in-tər-sep'tl, adj.* between septa. [Pfx. **inter-**.]

intersert *in-tər-sûrt', v.t.* (*obs.*) to insert between other things, interpolate. — *adj.* **intersert'al** (*petr.*) having interstitial crystalline or glassy matter between feldspar laths. [L. *interserĕre, -sertum*, to interpose — *inter*, between, *serĕre*, to plant.]

interservice *in-tər-sûr'vis, adj.* between the armed forces. [Pfx. **inter-**.]

intersex *in'tər-seks, (biol.) n.* an individual developing some characters of the other sex. — *adj.* **intersex'ūal** between the sexes: intermediate between the sexes. — *n.* **intersexūal'ity.** [Pfx. **inter-**.]

intersidereal *in-tər-sī-dē'ri-əl, (rare) adj.* interstellar. [Pfx. **inter-**.]

interspace *in'tər-spās, n.* an interval. — *v.t.* (*-spās'*) to put intervals between. — *adj.* **interspatial** (*-spā'shl*). — *adv.* **interspa'tially.** [Pfx. **inter-**.]

interspecific *in-tər-spis-if'ik, adj.* between species. [Pfx. **inter-**.]

intersperse *in-tər-spûrs', v.t.* to scatter or set here and there: to diversify. — *ns.* **interspers'al** (*rare*); **interspersion** (*-spûr'shən*). [L. *interspergĕre, -spersum* — *inter*, among, *spargĕre*, to scatter.]

interspinal *in-tər-spī'nəl, adj.* between spines of the vertebrae. — Also **interspī'nous.** [Pfx. **inter-**.]

interstadial *in'tər-stā'di-əl, (geol.) adj.* belonging to an interstadial. — *n.* a retreat of ice during a glacial period, less extensive than an interglacial.

interstate *in'tər-stāt*, or *-stāt', adj.* pertaining to relations, esp. political and commercial, between states: between states. — *adv.* into or to another state. [Pfx. **inter-**.]

interstellar *in-tər-stel'ər, adj.* beyond the solar system or among the stars: in the intervals between the stars. — Also **interstell'ary.** [L. *inter*, between, *stella*, a star.]

interstice *in-tûr'stis, n.* a small space between things closely set, or between the parts which compose a body: the time interval required by canon law before receiving higher orders (*R.C.*): a space between atoms in a lattice where other atoms can be located. — *adj.* **interstitial** (*-stish'l*) occurring in interstices: pertaining to the surfaces of teeth where they adjoin (*dentistry*). — *n.* an extra atom in a crystal lattice, causing a defect. [L. *interstitium* — *inter*, between, *sistĕre, stătum*, to stand, set.]

interstratification *in-tər-strat-i-fi-kā'shən, n.* the state of lying between, or alternating with, other strata. — *adj.* **interstrat'ified.** — *v.t.* and *v.i.* **interstrat'ify.** [Pfx. **inter-**.]

intersubjective *in-tər-sub-jek'tiv, -səb-, adj.* between subjects: between points of view. — *adv.* **intersubjec'tively.** — *n.* **intersubjectiv'ity.** [Pfx. **inter-**.]

intertangle *in-tər-tang'gl, v.t.* and *v.i.* to tangle together. — *n.* **intertang'lement.** [Pfx. **inter-**.]

intertarsal *in-tər-tär'sl, adj.* between tarsal bones. [Pfx. **inter-**.]

intertentacular *in-tər-ten-tak'ū-lər, adj.* between tentacles. [Pfx. **inter-**.]

interterritorial *in-tər-ter-i-tō'ri-əl, -tö', adj.* between territories. [Pfx. **inter-**.]

intertexture *in-tər-teks'chər, n.* interwoven state. [Pfx. **inter-**.]

intertidal *in-tər-tī'dl, adj.* between low-water and high-water mark. [Pfx. **inter-**.]

intertie *in'tər-tī, n.* in roofing, etc., a short timber binding together upright posts. [Origin obscure.]

intertissued *in-tər-tish'ūd, adj.* interwoven. — Also (*Shak.*) **entertiss'ued.** [Pfx. **inter-**.]

intertraffic *in-tər-traf'ik, n.* traffic between two or more persons or places. [Pfx. **inter-**.]

intertribal *in-tər-trī'bl, adj.* between tribes. [Pfx. **inter-**.]

intertrigo *in-tər-trī'gō, n.* an inflammation of the skin from chafing or rubbing: — *pl.* **intertri'gos.** [L. *intertrīgō* — *inter*, between, *terĕre, trītum*, to rub.]

intertropical *in-tər-trop'i-kl, adj.* between the tropics. [Pfx. **inter-**.]

intertwine *in-tər-twīn', v.t.* and *v.i.* to twine or twist together. — *ns.* **in'tertwine** intertwining; **intertwine'-ment.** — *n.* and *adj.* **intertwīn'ing.** — *adj.* **intertwīn'ingly.** [Pfx. **inter-**.]

intertwist *in-tər-twist', v.t.* to twist together. — *adv.* **intertwist'ingly.** [Pfx. **inter-**.]

interunion *in-tər-ūn'yən, n.* a blending together. [Pfx. **inter-**.]

interurban *in-tər-ûr'bən, adj.* between cities. [L. *inter*, between, *urbs, urbis*, a city.]

interval *in'tər-vəl, n.* time or space between: any dividing tract in space or time: a break between lessons, acts of a play, etc.: difference of pitch between any two musical tones (*mus.*). — *n.* **in'tervāle** (*U.S. dial.*; influenced by **vale**[1]) a level tract along a river. — *adj.* **intervallic** (*-val'ik*). — *n.* **intervall'um** (*obs.*) an interval. [L. *intervallum* — *inter*, between, *vallum*, a rampart.]

intervein *in-tər-vān', v.t.* to intersect, as with veins. [Pfx. **inter-**.]

intervene *in-tər-vēn', v.i.* to come or be between: to occur between points of time: to happen so as to interrupt: to interpose: to interpose in an action to which one was not at first a party (*law*). — *v.t.* (*obs.*) to separate. — *n.* **interven'er** one who intervenes. — Also (*law*) **interven'or.** — *adj.* **intervenient** (*-vēn'yənt*) being or passing between: intervening. — *adj.* **interven'ing** coming in between. — *ns.* **intervention** (*-ven'shən*) intervening: interference: mediation: interposition: a system of removing surplus produce from the market and storing it until prices rise; **interven'tionism; interven'-tionist** one who advocates interference (also *adj.*); **interven'tor** a mediator in ecclesiastical controversies. — **intervening sequence** (*biol.*) an intron; **intervention price** the market price at which intervention occurs. [L. *inter*, between, *venīre*, to come.]

interview *in'tər-vū, n.* a mutual view or sight (*obs.*): a formal meeting: a meeting between employer, board of directors, etc., and a candidate to ascertain by questioning and discussion the latter's suitability for a post, etc.: a meeting between a journalist, or radio or TV broadcaster, and a notable person to discuss the latter's views, etc., for publication or broadcasting: an article or programme based on such a meeting. — *v.t.* to have an interview with. — *ns.* **interviewee'** one who is interviewed; **in'terviewer** one who interviews. [O.Fr. *entrevue* — *entre*, between, *voir*, to see.]

intervital *in-tər-vī'təl, adj.* between lives, between death and resurrection. [L. *inter*, between, *vīta*, life.]

inter vivos *in'tər, -ter, vīvōs, wē'wōs,* (L.; *law*) from one living person to another.

intervocalic *in-tər-vō-kal'ik, adj.* between vowels. [Pfx. **inter-**.]

intervolve *in-tər-volv', v.t.* and *v.i.* to entwine or roll up one with or within another. [L. *inter*, within, *volvĕre*, to roll.]

interwar *in-tər-wör', adj.* between wars. [Pfx. **inter-**.]

interweave *in-tər-wēv', v.t.* and *v.i.* to weave together: to intermingle. [Pfx. **inter-**.]

interwind *in-tər-wīnd', v.t.* and *v.i.* to wind together or around and among one another: — *pa.t.* and *pa.p.* **interwound** (*-wownd'*). [Pfx. **inter-**.]

interwork *in-tər-wûrk', v.t.* and *v.i.* to work together: to work into another or one another. — *adj.* **interwrought** (*-röt'*). [Pfx. **inter-**.]

interwreathe *in-tər-rēdh', v.t.* to wreathe together or into one another. [Pfx. **inter-**.]

interzone *in-tər-zōn', interzonal -zōn'əl, adjs.* between zones (as of occupied country). — *n.* **in'terzone.** [Pfx. **inter-**.]

intestate *in-tes'tāt, -tit, adj.* dying without having made a valid will: not disposed of by will. — *n.* a person who dies without making a valid will. — *n.* **intes'tacy**

(*-tə-si*) the state of one dying without having made a valid will. [L. *intestātus* — *in-*, not, *testārī, -ātus*, to make a will.]

intestine *in-tes'tin, adj.* internal: contained in the animal body (*obs.*): domestic, not foreign. — *n.* (commonly in *pl.*) a part of the digestive system, divided into the smaller intestine (comprising duodenum, jejunum, and ileum) and the greater intestine. — *adj.* **intes'tinal** (also *-tīn'*) pertaining to the intestines of an animal body. [L. *intestīnus* — *intus*, within.]

inthral, inthrall. See **enthrall.**

intil *in-til', (Scot.) prep.* into, in, or unto. [**in**[1], **till**[2].]

intima *in'tim-ə, (anat.) n.* the innermost coat or membrane of an organ or part, esp. a blood or lymphatic vessel: — *pl.* **in'timae** (*-mē*). [L., short for *tunica intima*, innermost coat.]

intimate *in'ti-mit, -māt, adj.* innermost: internal: close: deep-seated: private: personal: closely acquainted: familiar: in illicit sexual connection: encouraging informality and closer personal relations through smallness, exclusiveness. — *n.* a familiar friend: an associate. — *v.t.* (*-māt*) to hint: to announce. — *n.* **in'timacy** (*-mə-si*) the state of being intimate: close familiarity: illicit sexual intercourse. — *adv.* **in'timately.** — *ns.* **intimā'tion** indication: hint: announcement; **in'timism** a genre of French impressionist painting of the early 20th cent., based on subject-matter from everyday life. — *n.* and *adj.* **in'timist** (Fr. **intimiste** *ɛ̃-tēm-ēst*). — *n.* **intim'ity** (*arch.*) intimacy. [L. *intimāre, -ātum* — *intimus*, innermost — *intus*, within.]

intime *ɛ̃-tēm', adj.* intimate: small and cosy. [Fr.]

intimidate *in-tim'i-dāt, v.t.* to strike fear into: to influence by threats or violence. — *n.* **intimidā'tion** the act of intimidating: the use of violence or threats to influence the conduct or compel the consent of another: the state of being intimidated. — *adj.* **intim'idatory.** [L. *in*, into, *timidus*, fearful.]

intinction *in-tingk'shən, n.* an Eastern mode of administering communion by dipping the bread into the wine. [L.L. *intinctiō, -ōnis* — L. *intingĕre, intinctum*, to dip in.]

intine *in'tin, -tēn, -tīn, n.* the inner membrane of a pollen grain or spore. [L. *intus*, within.]

intire *in-tīr'.* An obsolete from of **entire.**

intitule *in-tit'ūl, v.t.* same as **entitle,** now used only to mean give a title to (a Parliamentary Act, etc.). [O.Fr. *intituler* — L. *titulus*, title.]

into *in'tŏŏ, prep.* to a position within: to a state of: used to indicate the dividend in dividing (*math.*): in contact or collision with: interested in or enthusiastic about (*slang*): to part of (*math.*). — *adj.* (*math.*) describing a mapping of one set to a second set, involving only some of the elements of the latter. — **multiply into** (*rare*) to find the product of two quantities. [**in**[1], **to.**]

intoed, in-toed *in'tōd', adj.* having the toes more or less turned inwards. [Pfx. **in-** (1).]

intolerable *in-tol'ər-ə-bl, adj.* not to be endured. — *ns.* **intolerabil'ity, intol'erableness.** — *adv.* **intol'erably.** — *ns.* **intol'erance, intolerā'tion** state of being intolerant. — *adj.* **intol'erant** not able or willing to endure: not enduring difference of opinion: persecuting. — *n.* one opposed to toleration. — *adv.* **intol'erantly.** [Pfx. **in-** (2).]

intomb *in-tŏŏm', obsolete form of* **entomb.**

intonate[1] *in'tōn-āt, (obs.) v.t.* and *v.i.* to thunder. [L. *intonāre, -ātum*, to thunder; cf. next word.]

intonate[2] *in'tōn-āt, -tən-, v.t.* and *v.i.* to intone. — *ns.* **intonā'tion** the opening phrase of any plainsong melody, sung usually either by the officiating priest alone, or by one or more selected choristers: pitching of musical notes: modulation or rise and fall in pitch of the voice: intoning; **in'tonātor** a monochord. — *v.t.* and *v.i.* **intone** (*in-tōn'*) to chant, read, or utter in musical tones, singsong, or monotone: to begin by singing the opening phrase: to utter with a particular intonation. — *n.* **intōn'er.** — *n.* and *adj.* **intōn'ing.** —

adv. **intōn'ingly.** [L.L. *intonāre, -ātum* — L. *in,* in, *tonus,* tone.]

intorsion, intortion *in-tör'shən, n.* a twist: a twine. — *adj.* **intort'ed** twisted inwards: involved. [Fr. *intorsion,* L. *intortiō, -ōnis* — *in,* in, *torquēre, tortum,* to twist.]

in toto *in tō'tō,* (L.) entirely.

intown *in'tōōn,* (*Scot.*) *adj.* infield, near the farmhouse. — **intown multure** payment to the miller by those who are compelled to have their grain ground at the mill. [**in**[1], (*Scot.*) **town.**]

intoxicate *in-toks'i-kāt, v.t.* to poison (*obs.*): to make drunk: to excite to enthusiasm or madness: to elate excessively. — *adj.* **intox'icant** intoxicating. — *n.* an intoxicating agent. — *adj.* **intox'icāting.** — *n.* **intoxicā'tion** poisoning (*med.*): the state of being drunk: high excitement or elation. [L.L. *intoxicāre, -ātum* — *in,* in, *toxicum* — Gr. *toxikon,* arrow-poison — *toxon,* a bow.]

intra *in'trə, in'trä,* (L.) within. — **intra muros** (*mū'rōs, mōō'rōs*) within the wall; **intra vires** (*vī'rēz, wē'* or *vē'rās*) within the legal power of.

intra- *in'trä-, -trə-,* in composition, within, as in **intra=abdom'inal** situated within the cavity of the abdomen; **intra-artē'rial** within an artery; **intracap'sular** lying within a capsule; **intracar'diac** within the heart; **intra-cell'ular** inside a cell; **intracrā'nial** within the cranium; **intramercū'rial** within Mercury's orbit; **intramolec'ular** within the limits of the molecule; **intramun'dane** within the world; **intramū'ral** within walls: included within the college; **intramus'cular** within a muscle: **intraparī'etal** within walls, private: situated in the parietal lobe of the brain; **intrapet'iolar** between petiole and stem; **intraterritō'rial** within a territory; **intrathē'cal** within, or introduced into, the sheath of the spinal cord or brain; **intratrop'ical** within the tropics; **intra-ur'ban** within a city; **intra-ū'terine** within the uterus; **intravē'nous** within, or introduced into, a vein or veins. [L. *intrā,* within.]

intractable *in-trakt'ə-bl, adj.* unmanageable: obstinate. — *ns.* **intractabil'ity, intract'ableness.** — *adv.* **intract'ably.** [Pfx. **in-** (2).]

intrados *in-trā'dos,* (*archit.*) *n.* the soffit or under surface of an arch. [Fr., — L. *intrā,* within, *dorsum,* the back.]

intramercurial ... to ... **intramuscular.** See **intra-.**

intransigent *in-tran'si-jənt, -trän', -zi-, adj.* refusing to come to any understanding, irreconcilable: obstinate. — *n.* one who is intransigent. — *ns.* **intran'sigence; intran'sigency; intran'sigentism; intran'sigentist** one who practices such a method of opposition. — Also **intransigeant,** etc. (Fr.). [Fr. *intransigeant* — Sp. *intransigente* — L. *in-,* not, *transigēns, -entis,* pr.p. of *transigēre,* to transact; see **transact.**]

intransitive *in-tran'si-tiv, -trän', -zi-, adj.* not passing over or indicating passing over: representing action confined to the agent, i.e. having no object (*gram.*). — *adv.* **intran'sitively.** [Pfx. **in-** (2).]

in transitu *in tran' or trän'si-tōō,* (L.) in passage, in transit.

intransmissible *in-trans-mis'i-bl, -tranz-, -tränz-, adj.* that cannot be transmitted. [Pfx. **in-** (2).]

intransmutable *in-trans-mūt'ə-bl, -tranz-, -tränz-, adj.* that cannot be changed into another substance. — *n.* **intransmutabil'ity.** [Pfx. **in-** (2).]

intrant *in'trənt, adj.* entering: penetrating. — *n.* one who enters, esp. on membership, office, or possession. [L. *intrāns, -antis* — *intrāre,* to enter.]

intraparietal ... to ... **intra-uterine.** See **intra-.**

intravasation *in-tra-və-zā'shən, n.* the entrance of extraneous matter into blood or lymph vessels. [L. *intrā,* within, *vās,* a vessel.]

intravenous. See **intra-**

intreat, etc., *in-trēt'.* Arch. for **entreat,** etc.

intrench, intrenchment. See **entrench.**

intrenchant *in-trensh'ənt, -trench', (Shak.) adj.* not able to be cut or wounded, indivisible. [Pfx. **in-** (2).]

intrepid *in-trep'id, adj.* without trepidation or fear: undaunted: brave. — *n.* **intrepid'ity** firm, unshaken courage. — *adv.* **intrep'idly.** [L. *intrepidus* — *in-,* not, *trepidus,* alarmed.]

intricate *in'tri-kit, -kāt* (also *-trik'it), adj.* involved: entangled: complex. — *ns.* **in'tricacy** (*-kə-si;* also *-trik'),* **intricateness.** — *adv.* **intricately.** [L. *intrīcātus* — *in-,* in, *trīcāre,* to make difficulties — *trīcae,* hindrances.]

intrigue *in-trēg', n.* indirect or underhand scheming or plot: a private scheme: the plot of a play or romance: a secret illicit love affair. — *v.i.* to engage in intrigue. — *v.t.* to puzzle, to fascinate (orig, a Gallicism). — *n.* **intrigu'er.** — *ns.* and *adjs.* **intrig(u)ant** (*in'tri-gunt, ē-trē-gã),* (*fem.*) **intrig(u)ante** (*in-tri-gant', ē-trēgãt*). — *adj.* **intrigu'ing.** — *adv.* **intrigu'ingly.** [Fr.; see **intricate.**]

intrince *in-trins', (Shak.) adj.* intricate. [See **intrinsicate.**]

intrinsic, -al *in-trin'sik, -əl, adjs.* inward: genuine: inherent: essential, belonging to the point at issue: (of muscles) entirely contained within the limb and girdle. — *n.* **intrinsicality** (*-al'i-ti; rare*). — *adv.* **intrin'sically.** — *n.* **intrin'sicalness** (*rare*). [Fr. *intrinsèque* — L. *intrīnsecus* — *intrā,* within, suff. *-in, secus,* following.]

intrinsicate *in-trins'i-kāt, (Shak.) adj.* intricate. [App. It. *intrinsecato,* familiar, confused with **intricate.**]

intro *in'trō, n.* contraction of **introduction,** used esp. of the opening passage of a jazz or popular music piece: — *pl.* **in'tros.**

intro- *in'trō-, in-tro'-, pfx.* within, into. [L. *intrō.*]

introduce *in-trə-dūs', v.t.* to lead or bring in: to conduct into a place: formally to make known or acquainted: to bring into notice or practice: to preface. — *n.* **introduc'er.** — *adj.* **introduc'ible.** — *n.* **introduction** (*-duk'shən*) the act of introducing: preliminary matter to a book: a preliminary passage or section leading up to a movement (*mus.*): a treatise introductory to a science or course of study. — *adj.* **introductive** (*-duk'tiv*) promoting introduction. — *adv.* **introduc'torily.** — *adj.* **introduc'tory** serving to introduce: preliminary: prefatory. [L. *intrōdūcēre, -ductum* — *intrō,* inward, *dūcēre,* to lead.]

introgression *in-trə-gresh'ən, n.* the introduction of the genes of one species into another species. [L. *intrō,* inwards, and pa.p. of *gradī,* to step.]

introit *in-trō'it, or in', -troit, n.* the anthem sung at the beginning of Mass, immediately after the *Confiteor,* and when the priest has ascended to the altar (*R.C.*): in other churches, an introductory hymn, psalm, or anthem. — *n.* **intrō'itus** an entrance to a cavity, esp. the vagina: an introit. [L. *introïtus* — *introïre* — *intrō,* inwards, *īre, ītum,* to go.]

introjection *in-trō-jek'shən, n.* the endowment of inanimate objects with the attributes of living creatures: a taking into the self of persons or things from the outer world so as to experience a oneness with them and to feel personally touched by their fate. — *v.t.* and *v.i.* **introject'.** [L. *intrō,* within, *jacēre,* to throw.]

introld. See **entrold.**

intromit *in-trō-mit', or -trə-, v.t.* to send within: to admit: to permit to enter: to insert. — *v.i.* to have dealings (*Scots law*): to interfere, esp. with the effects of another (esp. *Scots law*): — *pr.p.* **intromitt'ing;** *pa.t.* and *pa.p.* **intromitt'ed.** — *ns.* **intromission** (*-mish'ən*) a sending within: insertion: in Scots law, the assumption of authority to deal with another's property (*legal,* where the party is expressly or impliedly authorised to interfere, *vicious,* where an heir or next of kin, without any authority, interferes with a deceased person's estate): the proceeds of such interference. — *adjs.* **intromiss'ive** pertaining to intromission: intromitting; **intromitt'ent** intromitting: adapted for insertion, esp. (*zool.*) in copulation. — *n.* **intromitt'er.** [L. *intrō,* inward, *mittēre, missum,* to send.]

intron *in'tron, (biol.) n.* any of the segments of a eukaryotic gene that do not carry coded information for the synthesis of proteins (compare **exon**[2]). — Also known as **intervening sequence.** [Perh. *inter*vening sequence and **-on** as in **codon** and **exon.**]

introrse *in-trörs'*, *adj.* turned or facing inward: (of an anther) opening towards the centre of the flower. — *adv.* **introrse'ly.** [L. *introrsus*, toward the middle, inward — *intrō*, inward and *versus* — *vertĕre*, to turn.]

introspect *in-trō-spekt'*, or *-tra-*, *v.t.* to look into (esp. the mind). — *v.i.* to practise introspection. — *ns.* **introspection** (*-spek'shan*) a viewing of the inside or interior: the act of observing directly the processes of one's own mind; **introspec'tionist.** — *adj.* **introspec'tive.** [L. *intrō*, within, *specĕre*, to look at.]

introsusception *in-trō-sa-sep'shan*, *n.* intussusception. [L. *intrō*, inwards.]

introvert *in-trō-vûrt'*, or *-tra-*, *v.t.* to turn inwards: to turn in upon itself: to turn inside out: to withdraw part within the rest of. — *n.* **in'trovert** anything introverted: a person interested mainly in his own inner states and processes — opp. to *extravert*, *extrovert* (*psych.*). — *adj.* **introvers'ible.** — *n.* **introver'sion** (*-shan*). — *adjs.* **introver'sive; introver'tive.** [L. *intrō*, inwards, *vertĕre*, *versus*, to turn.]

intrude *in-trōōd'*, *v.i.* to thrust oneself in: to enter uninvited or unwelcome. — *v.t.* to force in. — *ns.* **intrud'er** one who or that which intrudes: a military aircraft which raids enemy territory alone; **intrusion** (*-trōō'zhan*) the act of intruding: encroachment: an injection of rock in a molten state among and through existing rocks: a mass so injected; **intru'sionist** one who intrudes, esp. of those who, before the Scottish Disruption of 1843, refused a parish the right of objecting to the settlement of an obnoxious minister by a patron — opp. to *non-intrusionist*. —*adj.* **intru'sive** (*-siv*) tending or apt to intrude: intruded: inserted without etymological justification: entering without welcome or right: of a rock, which has been forced while molten into cracks and fissures in other rocks. — *n.* an intrusive rock. — *adv.* **intru'sively.** — *n.* **intru'siveness.** [L. *in*, in, *trūdere*, *trūsum*, to thrust.]

intrust. A variant of **entrust.**

intubate *in'tū-bāt*, *v.t.* to insert a tube in: to treat by insertion of a tube into, e.g. the larynx (*med.*). — *n.* **intubā'tion** insertion of a tube. [L. *in*, in, *tubus*, a tube.]

intuition *in-tū-ish'an*, *n.* the power of the mind by which it immediately perceives the truth of things without reasoning or analysis: a truth so perceived, immediate knowledge in contrast with mediate. — *v.t.* and *v.i.* **intuit** (*in'tū-it*) to know intuitively. — *adj.* **intu'ited.** — *adj.* **intuitional** (*-ish'an-al*). — *ns.* **intuit'ion(al)ism** the doctrine that the perception of truth is by intuition: a philosophical system which stresses intuition and mysticism as opposed to the idea of a logical universe; **intuit'ion(al)ist.** — *adj.* **intu'itive** perceived, perceiving, by intuition: received or known by simple inspection and direct apprehension. — *adv.* **intu'itively.** — *n.* **intu'itivism.** [L. *in*, into or upon, *tuērī*, *tuitus*, to look.]

intumesce *in-tū-mes'*, *v.i.* to swell up. — *n.* **intumesc'ence.** — *adj.* **intumesc'ent.** [L. *in*, in, *tumēscĕre*, to swell.]

inturbidate *in-tûr'bi-dāt*, *v.t.* to render turbid. [L. *in*, in, *turbidāre*, *-ātum*, to trouble.]

intuse *in'tūs*, (*Spens.*) *n.* a bruise. [L. *in*, in, *tundĕre*, *tūsum*, to thump.]

intussusception *in-tas-sa-sep'shan*, *n.* the passing of part of a tube (esp. the intestine) within the adjacent part: growth by intercalation of particles. — *v.t.* **intussuscept'** to receive or take in thus. — *adjs.* **intussuscept'ed, intussuscep'tive.** [L. *intus*, within, *susceptiō*, *-ōnis* — *suscipĕre*, to take up.]

intwine, intwist. Same as **entwine, entwist.**

Inuit. See **Innuit.**

Inula *in'ū-la*, *n.* the elecampane genus of Compositae: (without *cap.*) a plant of this genus. — *ns.* **in'ulase** (*-lās*) an enzyme that forms fructose from inulin; **in'ulin** a carbohydrate got from elecampane roots. [L. *inula*, prob. — Gr. *helenion*, elecampane.]

inumbrate *in-um'brāt*, *v.t.* to cast a shadow upon: to shade. [L. *inumbrāre*, *-ātum* — *in*, on, *umbrāre*, to

shade — *umbra*, a shadow.]

inunction *in-ungk'shan*, *n.* anointing: smearing or rubbing with an ointment or liniment. [L. *inunctiō*, *-ōnis* — *inunguĕre*, to anoint — *in*, in, on, *ung(u)ĕre*, to smear.]

inundate *in'un-dāt*, formerly *in-un'dāt*, *v.t.* to flow upon or over in waves (said of water): to flood: to overwhelm (*fig.*): to fill with an overflowing abundance. — *adj.* **inun'dant** overflowing. — *n.* **inundā'tion.** [L. *inundāre*, *-ātum* — *in*, in, *undāre*, to rise in waves — *unda*, a wave.]

inurbane *in-ûr-bān'*, *adj.* not urbane. — *adv.* **inurbane'ly.** — *n.* **inurbanity** (*-ban'i-ti*). [Pfx. **in-** (2).]

inure[1] *in-ūr'*, *v.t.* to use or to exercise (*obs.*): to accustom: to habituate: to harden: to put into operation (*Spens.*, *Milt.* in the form **enure'**): to commit. — *v.i.* (*law*) to come into use or effect: to serve to one's use or benefit. — Also **enure'.** — *n.* **inure'ment** the act of inuring: the state of being inured: habituation. [Pfx. **in-** (1), and **ure**[1].]

inure[2] *in-ūr'*, (*obs.*) *v.t.* to burn in. [L. *inūrĕre* — *in*, in, *urĕre*, to burn.]

inurn *in-ûrn'*, *v.t.* to place in an urn: to entomb. [Pfx. **in-** (1).]

inusitate *in-ū'zi-tāt*, (*obs.*) *adj.* unwonted. — *n.* **inusitation** (*-ā'shan*; *obs.*) disuse. [L. *inūsitātus* — *in*, not, *ūsitātus*, familiar.]

inust *in-ust'*, (*obs.*) *adj.* burned in. — *n.* **inustion** (*inus'chan*; *obs.*) burning in: cauterisation. [L. *inūrĕre*, *inūstum*; see **inure**[2].]

in usum Delphini *in ūz'am del-fī'nī*, *ōōs'ōom del-fē'nē*, (L.) for the use of the Dauphin: toned down to suit the young person.

in utero *in ū'tar-ō*, *ōō'ter-ō*, (L.) in the womb.

inutility *in-ū-til'i-ti*, *n.* want of utility: uselessness: unprofitableness: something useless. [Pfx. **in-** (2).]

in utrumque paratus *in ū-trōōm'kwi pa-rā'tas*, *ōō-trōōm'-kwe pa-rā'tōōs*, (L.) prepared for either.

inutterable *in-ut'ar-a-bl*, *adj.* unutterable. [Pfx. **in-** (2).]

in vacuo *in vak'ū-ō*, *vak'ōō-ō*, *wak'*, (L.) in a vacuum.

invade *in-vād'*, *v.t.* to enter as an enemy: to attack: to encroach upon: to violate: to seize or fall upon: to enter: to penetrate: to come upon: to rush into. — *ns.* **invad'er; invasion** (*-vā'zhan*) the act of invading: an attack: an incursion: an attack on the rights of another: an encroachment: a violation. — *adj.* **invasive** (*-vā'siv*) making invasion: aggressive: encroaching: infringing another's rights: entering, penetrating. [L. *invādĕre*, *invāsum* — *in*, in, *vādĕre*, to go.]

invaginate *in-vaj'in-āt*, *v.t.* to ensheath: to dint inwards, push or withdraw within, introvert. — *v.i.* to be introverted: to form a hollow ingrowth. —*n.* **invaginā'tion.** [Pfx. **in-** (1), and L. *vāgīna*, a sheath.]

invalid *in-val'id*, *adj.* without validity, efficacy, weight, or cogency: having no effect: void: null. — *adj.* **invalid** (*in'va-lid*, *-lēd*) deficient in health, sick, weak: disabled: suitable for invalids. — *n.* **in'valid** (*-id*, *-ēd*, *-ēd'*) one who is weak: a sickly person: one disabled for active service, esp. a soldier or sailor. — *v.t.* **in'valid** (*-id*, *-ēd*, *-ēd'*) to make invalid or affect with disease: to enrol or discharge as an invalid. — *v.i.* (*arch.*) to become an invalid: to be discharged as an invalid. — *v.t.* **invalidate** (*-val'*) to render invalid: to make of no effect. — *ns.* **invalidā'tion; invalidhood** (*in'va-lid-hōōd*, or *-lēd-*, or *-lēd'*); **in'validing** the sending or return home, or to a more healthy climate, of those rendered incapable of active duty by wounds, sickness, etc. — *adj.* **in'validish** (*-id-*, *-ēd-*, or *-ēd'*). — *ns.* **in'validism** (*-id-*, *-ēd-*, or *-ēd'*); **invalid'ity** the state of being an invalid: lack of validity; **inval'idness** want of cogency or force. — *adv.* **inval'idly.** — **invalidity pension** a pension paid by the government to someone who has been unable to work through illness for over six months. [Pfx. **in-** (2).]

invaluable *in-val'ū-a-bl*, *adj.* that cannot have a value set upon it: priceless: valueless (*obs.*). — *adv.* **inval'uably.** [Pfx. **in-** (2).]

Invar® *in'vär*, *in-vär'*, *n.* an alloy of iron, nickel and carbon, very slightly expanded by heat, used in the

making of scientific instruments.   [From **invariable**.]
invariable *in-vā'ri-ə-bl, adj.* not variable: without alteration or change: unalterable: constantly in the same state. — *ns.* **invā'riableness, invāriabil'ity.** — *adv.* **invā'riably.** — *n.* **invā'riant** that which does not change: an expression or quantity that is unaltered by a particular procedure (*math.*). — Also *adj.* — *n.* **invar'iance** invariableness: the theory of the constancy of physical laws.   [Pfx. **in-** (2).]
invasion, invasive. See **invade.**
inveagle. Same as **inveigle.**
invecked *in-vekt', adj.* invected.
invected *in-vek'tid, (her.) adj.* having or consisting of a borderline of small convex curves (opp. to *engrailed*).   [L. *invehĕre, invectum,* to enter.]
invective *in-vek'tiv, n.* a severe or reproachful accusation brought against anyone: an attack with words: a violent utterance of censure: sarcasm or satire. — *adj.* railing: abusive: satirical. — *adv.* **invec'tively** (*Shak.*).   [See **inveigh.**]
inveigh *in-vā', v.i.* to make an attack with words: to rail: to revile.   [L. *invehĕre, invectum — in,* in, *vehĕre,* to carry.]
inveigle *in-vē'gl, in-vā'gl, v.t.* to entice: to ensnare by cajolery: to wheedle — older forms **invea'gle, envei'gle.** — *ns.* **invei'glement; invei'gler.**   [Prob. altered from A.Fr. *enveogler* (Fr. *aveugler*), to blind — L. *ab,* from, *oculus,* the eye.]
invendible *in-ven'di-bl, adj.* unsaleable. — *n.* **invendibil'ity.**   [Pfx. **in-** (2).]
invenit *in-vēn'it, in-wān'it, -vān', (L.) devised (this).
invent *in-vent', v.t.* to find (*Spens.*): to devise or contrive: to design for the first time, originate: to frame by imagination: to fabricate (something false). — *adj.* **inven'tible.** — *n.* **inven'tion** that which is invented: contrivance: a deceit: faculty or power of inventing: ability displayed by any invention or effort of the imagination: a short piece working out a single idea (*mus.*). — *adj.* **inven'tive** able to invent: ready in contrivance. — *adv.* **inven'tively.** — *ns.* **inven'tiveness; inven'tor:** — *fem.* **inven'tress.** — **Invention of the Cross** a festival observed on 3rd May in commemoration of the alleged discovery of the true cross at Jerusalem in A.D. 326 by Helena, mother of Constantine the Great.   [L. *invenīre, inventum — in,* upon, *venīre,* to come.]
inventory *in'vən-tər-i, n.* a list or schedule of articles comprised in an estate, etc.: a catalogue: stock, equipment: stock of a commodity (*U.S.*): stocktaking (*U.S.*): the total quantity of material in a nuclear reactor. — *v.t.* to make an inventory of: to amount to. — *v.i.* to sum up. — *adj.* **inventō'rial.** — *adv.* **inventō'rially.**   [L.L. *inventōrium* for L. *inventārium,* a list of things found — *invenīre,* to find.]
inveracity *in-vər-as'i-ti, n.* want of veracity: an untruth.   [Pfx. **in-** (2).]
Inverness *in-vər-nes', in'vər-nes, adj.* of or named after the town of *Inverness,* as a cloak or overcoat with cape or tippet. — Also *n.*
inverse *in'vûrs, in-vûrs', adj.* inverted: upside down: in the reverse or contrary order: opposite (opp. to *direct*): opposite in effect, as subtraction to addition, etc. (*math.*): related by inversion. — *n.* an inverted state: the result of inversion: a direct opposite: a proposition formed by immediate inference from another, its subject being the negative of the original subject (*log.*): a point so related to another point that the rectangle contained by their distances from a fixed point collinear with them is constant, or related in some analogous manner (*geom.*). — *v.t.* **inverse'** to invert. — *adv.* **inversely.** — *n.* **inver'sion** (-*shən*) the act of inverting: the state of being inverted: a change or reversal of order or position: that which is got by inverting. — *adj.* **inver'sive.** — **inverse proportion** (*math.*) a process by which one quantity decreases while another increases, their product remaining constant; **inverse ratio** the ratio of reciprocals.   [L.

inversus, pa.p. of *invertĕre, inversum — in,* in, and *vertĕre,* to turn.]
invert *in-vûrt', v.t.* to turn in or about: to turn upside down: to reverse: to change the customary order or position of: to form the inverse of: to change by placing the lowest note an octave higher (*mus.*): to modify by reversing the direction of motion: to break up (cane-sugar) into dextrose and laevulose, thereby (the laevulose prevailing) reversing the direction of rotation of polarised light (*chem.*). — *n.* **in'vert** an inverted arch: inverted sugar: a homosexual. — *n.* **in'vertase** (or -*vûr'*) an enzyme that inverts cane-sugar. — *adj.* **inver'ted** turned inwards: upside down: reversed: pronounced with tip of tongue turned up and back (as *r* in S.W. England). — *adv.* **inver'tedly.** — *ns.* **inver'ter, inver'tor; inver'tin** invertase. — **inverted arch** an arch with its curve turned downwards; **inverted commas** see **comma; inverted mordent** see **mordent; inverted snob** one who prefers (the attitudes and conventions of) the lower classes to (those of) the upper classes; **invert sugar** the mixture got by hydrolysis of cane-sugar.   [L. *invertĕre, inversum — in,* in, *vertĕre,* to turn.]
invertebrate *in-vûrt'i-brit, -brāt, adj.* without a vertebral column or backbone: weak, irresolute: characterless: formless. — *n.* a member of the Invertebrata: an indecisive person. — *n.pl.* **Invertebrā'ta** a collective name for all animals other than vertebrates.   [Pfx. **in-** (2).]
invest *in-vest', v.t.* to clothe: to envelop: to put on (*Spens.*): to clothe with insignia of office: to settle or secure: to place in office or authority (with *with* or *in*): to adorn: to surround: to block up: to lay siege to: to lay out for profit, as by buying property, shares, etc. — *v.i.* (*coll.*) to lay out money, make a purchase (with *in*). — *adj.* **inves'titive.** — *ns.* **inves'titure** investing: the ceremony of investing: in feudal and ecclesiastical history, the act of giving corporal possession of a manor, office, or benefice, accompanied by a certain ceremonial, such as the delivery of a branch, a banner, etc., to signify the authority which it is supposed to convey; **invest'ment** the act of investing: putting on: clothes (*arch.*): covering: investiture: a blockade: the act of surrounding or besieging: any placing of money to secure income or profit: that in which money is invested; **inves'tor** one who invests, esp. money. — **investment trust** see **trust.**   [L. *investīre, -ītum — in,* on, *vestīre,* to clothe.]
investigate *in-vest'i-gāt, v.t.* to search or inquire into with care and accuracy. — *v.i.* to make investigation. — *adj.* **invest'igable** able to be investigated. — *n.* **investigā'tion** the act of examining: research. — *adjs.* **invest'igative, invest'igatory.** — *n.* **invest'igator.** — **investigative journalism** journalism involving the investigation and exposure of corruption, crime, inefficiency, etc.   [L. *investīgāre, -ātum — in,* in, *vestīgāre,* to track.]
inveterate *in-vet'ər-it, adj.* firmly established by long continuance: deep-rooted, confirmed in any habit: stubborn: rootedly hostile. — *adv.* **invet'erately.** — *ns.* **invet'erateness, invet'eracy** (-*ə-si*) firmness produced by long use or continuance.   [L. *inveterātus,* stored up, long continued — *in,* in, *vetus, veteris,* old.]
invexed *in-vekst', (her.) adj.* arched: concave.   [L. *in,* in, and the root of *vehĕre,* to carry.]
inviable *in-vī'ə-bl, adj.* not viable: unable to survive. — *n.* **inviabil'ity.**   [Pfx. **in-** (2).]
invidious *in-vid'i-əs, adj.* likely to incur or provoke ill-will: likely to excite envy, enviable: offensively discriminating. — *adv.* **invid'iously.** — *n.* **invid'iousness.**   [L. *invidiōsus — invidia,* envy.]
invigilate *in-vij'i-lāt, v.t.* and *v.i.* to supervise, esp. at examinations. — *ns.* **invigilā'tion; invig'ilātor.**   [L. *in,* on, *vigilāre, -ātum,* to watch.]
invigorate *in-vig'ər-āt, v.t.* to give vigour to: to strengthen: to animate. — *ns.* **invig'orant** an invigorating agent; **invigorā'tion; invig'orātor.**   [Pfx. **in-** (1).]
invincible *in-vin'si-bl, adj.* that cannot be overcome: insuperable. — *ns.* **invin'cibleness, invincibil'ity.** — *adv.*

invin'cibly. — **invincible ignorance** see **ignorant.** — **the Invincible Doctor** William of Occam (d. *c.* 1349). [Pfx. **in-** (2).]

in vino veritas *in vī′nō ver′it-as, wē′nō wār′it-äs, vē′nō vär′it-äs,* (L.) in wine is truth.

inviolable *in-vī′ə-lə-bl, adj.* that must not be profaned: that cannot be injured. — *ns.* **inviolabil′ity, invī′o-lableness** the quality of being inviolable. — *adv.* **in-vī′olably.** — *adjs.* **invī′olate** (*-lit, -lāt*), **-d** (*-lāt-id*) not violated: unprofaned: uninjured. — *adv.* **invī′olately.** — *n.* **invī′olateness.** [Pfx. **in-** (2).]

invious *in′vi-əs,* (*rare*) *adj.* impassable: trackless. [L. *invius* — in-, not, *via,* a way.]

invis'd *in′vīzd,* (*Shak.*) *adj.* prob., unseen or inscrutable. [L. *invīsus,* unseen.]

invisible *in-viz′i-bl, adj.* incapable of being seen: unseen: relating to services rather than goods (*econ.*): not shown in regular statements, as *invisible assets* (see **export, import;** *finance*). — *n.* an invisible export, etc. — *ns.* **invisibil′ity, invis′ibleness** — *adv.* **invis′ibly.** — **Invisible Church** see **visible; invisible green** green that is almost black; **invisible ink** see **ink.** [Pfx. **in-** (2).]

invite *in-vīt′, v.t.* to ask hospitably or politely to come: to express affable willingness to receive or to have done: to be of such a kind as to encourage or tend to bring on: to offer inducement: to attract. — *n.* **in′vite** (*coll.*) an invitation. — *n.* **invitation** (*in-vi-tā′shən*) the act of inviting: an asking or solicitation: the written or verbal form with which a person is invited: the brief exhortation introducing the confession in the Anglican communion office. — *adj.* **invitatory** (*in-vīt′ə-tə-ri*) using or containing invitation. — *n.* a form of invitation to worship, esp. the antiphon to the Venite or 95th Psalm. — *ns.* **invitee′** (or *-vīt′*) one who is invited, a guest; **invite′ment** (*Lamb*) allurement, temptation; **invīt′er.** — *adj.* **invīt′ing** alluring: attractive. — *n.* (*Shak.*) invitation. — *adv.* **invīt′ingly.** — *n.* **invīt′ingness** attractiveness. [L. *invītāre, -ātum.*]

in vitro *in vīt′rō, wit′rō, vit′,* (L.) in glass: in the test tube — opp. to **in vivo.**

in vivo *in vī′vō, wē′wō, vē′vō,* (L.) in the living organism.

invocate *in′vō-kāt, v.t.* to invoke. — *n.* **invocā′tion** the act or the form of invoking or addressing in prayer or supplication: an appellation under which one is invoked: any formal invoking of the blessing or help of a god, a saint, etc.: an opening prayer in a public religious service or in the Litany: a call for inspiration from a Muse or other deity as at the beginning of a poem: an incantation or calling up of a spirit: a call or summons, esp. for evidence from another case (*law*). — *adj.* **invocatory** (*in-vok′ə-tə-ri*) making invocation. [See **invoke.**]

invoice *in′vois, n.* a letter of advice of the despatch of goods, with particulars of their price and quantity. — *v.t.* to make an invoice of. [Prob. pl. of Fr. *envoi.*]

invoke *in-vōk′, v.t.* to call upon earnestly or solemnly: to implore assistance of: to address in prayer: to conjure up: to call to help, resort to. [Fr. *invoquer* — L. *invocāre, -ātum* — *in,* on, *vocāre,* to call.]

involucre *in′və-lōō-kər, -lū-, n.* an envelope (*anat.*): a ring or crowd of bracts around a capitulum, umbel, etc. (*bot.*). — Also **involū′crum.** — *n.* **involucel** (*in-vol′ū-sel*) the group of bracts below a partial umbel. — *adjs.* **involūcell′ate** having an involucel; **involu′cral** of the nature of, pertaining to, an involucre; **involu′crate** having an involucre. [L. *involūcrum* — *involvĕre,* to involve.]

involuntary *in-vol′ən-tər-i, adj.* not voluntary: not having the power of will or choice: not under control of the will: not done voluntarily. — *adv.* **invol′untarily.** — **invol′untariness.** [Pfx. **in-** (2).]

involute *in′vol-ōōt, -ūt, adj.* involved: rolled inward at the margins (*bot.*): turned inward: closely rolled. — *n.* that which is involved or rolled inward: a curve traced by the end of a string unwinding itself from another curve (the *evolute*). — *v.t.* and *v.i.* to make or become involute. — *adj.* **in′voluted.** — *n.* **involu′tion** the action

of involving: the state of being involved or entangled: complicated grammatical construction: raising to a power (*math.*): the condition satisfied by a system of pairs of points in a straight line such that the rectangle contained by their distances from a fixed point in that line (the *centre of involution*) is constant (*geom.*): retrograde development, return to normal size (*zool.*). — *adj.* **involu′tional.** — **involutional psychosis, melancholia** a psychosis occurring in middle life, with feelings of anxiety, futility, guilt, and, in some cases, with delusions of persecution. [See **involve.**]

involve *in-volv′, v.t.* to coil: to wrap up: to envelop: to entangle: to complicate: to implicate: to comprehend: to entail or imply, bring as a consequence: to be bound up with: to concern: to raise to a power (*math.*): to make (oneself) emotionally concerned (in, with): to engage the emotional interest of. — *n.* **involve′ment.** [L. *involvĕre* — *in,* in, *volvĕre, volūtum,* to roll.]

invulnerable *in-vul′nər-ə-bl, adj.* that cannot be wounded: not vulnerable (as in bridge). — *ns.* **invulnerabil′ity, invul′nerableness.** — *adv.* **invul′nerably.** [Pfx. **in-** (2).]

invultuation *in-vul-tū-ā′shən, n.* the making or use of an image of a person for purpose of witchcraft. [L.L. *invultuātiō, -ōnis.* — L. *in,* in, *vultus,* the face.]

inwall. See **enwall.**

inward *in′wərd, adj.* placed or being within: internal: seated in the mind or soul, not perceptible to the senses: uttered as if within, or with closed mouth: confidential (*arch.*): secret, private (*arch.*). — *n.* inside (*Shak.*): interior (*obs.*): an intimate friend (*Shak.*): (in *pl.*: often *in′ərdz*) entrails (also **innards**). — *adv.* toward the interior: into the mind or thoughts. — *adv.* **in′wardly** within: in the heart: privately: toward the centre. — *n.* **in′wardness** internal state: inner meaning or significance: intimacy, familiarity (*Shak.*). — *adv.* **in′wards** same as **inward.** [O.E. *inneweard* (adv.).]

inweave *in-wēv′, v.t.* to weave in: to complicate: — *pa.t.* **inwove′;** *pa.p.* **inwo′ven** (*Milt.*), etc., **inwove′**). [Pfx. **in-** (1).]

inwick *in′wik, n.* in curling, a stroke in which the stone glances off the edge of another stone, and then slides close to the tee. — *v.i.* **inwick′** to make an inwick. [**in**[1], **wick**[4].]

inwind. See **enwind.**

inwit *in′wit,* (*obs.*) *n.* inward knowledge: conscience. [**in**[1], **wit**[2].]

inwith *in′with, in-widh′,* (*Scot.*) *prep.* and *adv.* within. [**in**[1], **with**[2].]

inwork *in-wûrk′, v.t.* and *v.i.* to work in. — *n.* **in′working** energy exerted inwardly. — *adj.* **in′wrought** (as pa.p. *in-röt′*) wrought in or among other things: adorned with figures. [Pfx. **in-** (1).]

inworn *in′wōrn, in-wōrn′, -wörn, adj.* worn or worked in, inwrought. [Pfx. **in-** (1).]

inwrap. Same as **enwrap.**

inwreathe. Same as **enwreathe.**

inyala *in-yä′lə,* **nyala** *n-yä′lə, ns.* a S. African antelope. [Bantu.]

io *ī′ō, interj.* of invocation, or expressing joy or triumph or grief. — *n.* a cry of 'Io': — *pl.* **ī′os.** [Gr. *iō.*]

iodine *ī′ə-dēn, or ī′ō-dēn,* also *-dīn, -din, n.* a halogen element (symbol I; at. numb. 53) giving a violet-coloured vapour. — *n.* **i′odate** a salt of iodic acid. — *adj.* **iodic** (*ī-od′ik*) pertaining to or caused by iodine: applied to an acid (HIO₃) and its anhydride (I₂O₅). — *n.* **i′odīde** a salt of hydriodic acid. — *v.t.* **i′odise, -ize** to treat with iodine. — *ns.* **i′odism** a morbid condition due to iodine; **iodoform** (*ī-od′, -ōd′ə-förm*) a lemon-yellow crystalline compound of iodine (CHI₃) with a saffron-like odour, used as an antiseptic. — *adjs.* **iodomet′ric** (*chem.*) measured by iodine; **iod′ophile** (*-fil, -fīl*) staining intensely with iodine; **i′odous** (of, containing, or resembling iodine. — *n.* **iod′ūret** (*obs.*) an iodide. — **iodine-131** a short-lived radioactive isotope of iodine present in fall-out, widely used in medicine. [Gr. *īoeidēs,* violet-coloured — *ion,* a violet, *eidos,* form.]

iodyrite ī-od'ir-īt, n. a mineral, silver iodide.   [**iodine, argyrite.**]

iolite ī'ō-līt, n. cordierite or dichroite, a strongly dichroic transparent gem, a silicate of aluminium, magnesium, and iron, violet-blue, grey, or yellow according to direction of view by transmitted light.   [Gr. *ion*, violet, *lithos*, stone.]

ion ī'ən, ī'on, n. an electrically charged particle formed by loss or gain by an atom of electrons, effecting by its migration the transport of electricity. — *adj.* **ionic** (ī-on'ik). — *v.t.* **ionise, -ize** (ī'ən-īz) to produce ions in: to turn into ions. — *ns.* **ionīsā'tion, -z-; ī'oniser, -z-; iŏn'omer** the product of ionic bonding action between long-chain molecules, characterised by toughness and a high degree of transparency; **i'onone** either of, or a mixture of, two isomeric ketones extracted from certain plants, with an intense odour of violets, using in making perfumes; **iŏn'opause** the region of the earth's atmosphere at the outer limit of the ionosphere; **ionophore** (ī'ə-nə-fōr) a chemical compound able to combine with an ion and enable it to pass through a cell membrane, etc.; **ionophorē'sis** electrophoresis, esp. of small ions; **iŏn'osphere** the region of the upper atmosphere that includes the highly ionised Appleton and Kennelly-Heaviside layers. — *adj.* **ionosphĕr'ic.** — *n.* **iontophorē'sis** the migration of ions into body tissue through electric currents: electrophoresis. — *adj.* **iontophorĕt'ic.** — **ion engine** a space engine in which the thrust is produced by a stream of ionised particles: **i'on-exchange** transfer of ions from a solution to a solid or another liquid, used in water-softening and many industrial processes; **ionic bond** a bond within a chemical compound achieved by transfer of electrons, the resulting ions being held together by electrostatic attraction; **ion implantation** the introduction of ions into a crystalline material by subjecting the material to bombardment with a stream of ions — an important element in the production of integrated circuits; **ionisation chamber** an instrument used to detect and measure ionising radiation, consisting of an enclosure containing electrodes between which ionised gas is formed; **ionisation potential** the energy, in electron-volts, required to detach an electron from an atom, molecule or radical; **ionising radiation** any electromagnetic or particulate radiation which can cause ionisation.   [Gr. *ĭŏn*, neut. pr.p. of *ienai*, to go.]

Ionian. See **Ionic.**

Ionic ī-on'ik, adj. relating to the Ionians, one of the main divisions of the ancient Greeks, to their dialect, to Ionia, the coastal district of Asia Minor settled by them, to a foot of two long and two short syllables (*Ionic a majore*) or two short and two long (*Ionic a minore*), to verse characterised by the use of that foot, to a style of Greek architecture characterised by the volute of its capital, to a mode of ancient Greek music (the same as the Iastic, Hypophrygian, or Hyperlydian), or to an old ecclesiastical mode extending from C to C with C for its final. — *n.* the Ionic dialect: an Ionic foot or verse: an Ionic philosopher. — *adj.* and *n.* **Ionian** (ī-ō'ni-ən) Ionic: an Ionic Greek. — *vs.t.* and *vs.i.* **Ionicise, -ize** (ī-on'i-sīz), **Ionise, -ize** (ī'ən-īz) to make or become Ionian: to use the Ionic dialect. — *ns.* **I'onism; I'onist.** — **Ionic dialect** the most important of the three main branches of the ancient Greek language (Ionic, Doric, Aeolic), the language of Homer and Herodotus, of which Attic is a development; **Ionic school** the representative philosophers of the Ionian Greeks, such as Thales, Anaximander, Heraclitus, Anaxagoras, who debated the question what was the primordial constitutive principle of the cosmic universe.   [Gr. *Iōnikos, Iōnios.*]

ionium ī-ōn'i-əm, n. a radioactive isotope of thorium.   [**ion.**]

ionomer, ionone, ionopause... **iontophoretic.** See **ion.**

iota ī-ō'tə, n. the Greek letter I, ι, answering to I: as a numeral ι' = 10, ͵ι = 10,000: a jot. — *n.* **iot'acism** excessive use of the Greek letter iota or i or of its sound: the conversion of other vowel sounds into that (Eng. *ē*) of iota, as in modern Gr. of η, υ, ει, ῃ, οι, υι.   [Gr. *iōta*, the smallest letter in the alphabet, I, ι; Heb. *yōd.*]

IOU ī-ō-ū', n. a memorandum of debt given by a borrower, requiring no stamp, but a holograph, usually dated, and addressed to the lender: any similar document.   [Pronunciation of *I owe you.*]

ipecacuanha ip-i-kak-ū-an'ə, n. a valuable medicine or the Brazilian plant (*Cephaelis* or *Uragoga*; fam. Rubiaceae) whose root produces it — used as an emetic: applied to other roots used as substitutes. — Familiarly shortened to **ipecac'.**   [Port. from Tupí.]

Ipomoea ip-ō-mē'ə, n. the jalap and morning-glory genus of the Convolvulus family: (without *cap.*) a plant of this genus.   [Gr. *īps, īpos*, a worm, *homoios*, like.]

ipse dixit ip'se dik'sit, ip'se dēk'sit, (L.) he himself said it: his mere word: a dogmatic pronouncement.

ipsilateral ip-si-lat'ə-rəl, adj. belonging to or affecting the same side of the body.   [Irreg., from L. *ipse* and **lateral.**]

ipsissima verba ip-sis'ə-mə vûr'bə, ip-sis'i-ma ver', wer'ba, (L.) the very words.

ipso facto ip'sō fak'tō, (L.) by that very fact: thereby.

ir- ir-, *pfx.* same as **in-**, form used with words beginning with *r*, as in *irradiate.*

iracund ī'rə-kund, adj. inclined to anger. — *n.* **iracund'ity.** — *adj.* **iracund'ulous** somewhat iracund.   [L. *īrācundus* — *īra*, anger.]

irade i-rä'de, n. a written decree of the Sultan of Turkey.   [Turk., — Ar. *irādah*, will.]

Iranian i-, ī-rān'i-ən, or -rän', adj. and n. Persian: (of) a branch of the Indo-European tongues including Persian. — Also **Iranic** (ī-ran'ik).   [Pers. *Īrān*, Persia.]

Iraqi i-rä'kē, n. a native of Iraq: the form of Arabic spoken in Iraq. — *adj.* pertaining to the country of Iraq, its inhabitants or language.   [Ar. *'Irāqī.*]

irascible ir-as'i-bl, or īr-, adj. susceptible of or anger: irritable. — *n.* **irascibil'ity.** — *adv.* **irasc'ibly.**   [Fr., — L. *īrāscibilis* — *īrāscī*, to be angry — *īra*, anger.]

ire īr, n. anger: rage: keen resentment. — *adjs.* **irate** (ī-rāt' or īr'āt) enraged, angry; **ire'ful** full of ire or wrath: resentful. — *advs.* **irate'ly; ire'fully.** — *n.* **ire'fulness.**   [L. *īra*, anger.]

irenic ī-rēn'ik, -ren', adj. tending to create peace: pacific. — Also **iren'ical.** — *adv.* **iren'ically.** — *ns.* **iren'icism; iren'icon** same as **eirenicon.** — *n. sing.* **iren'ics** irenical theology (opp. to *polemics*). — *n.* **irenology** (ī-rən-ol'ə-ji) the study of peace.   [Gr. *eirēnē*, peace.]

irid, irid-. See **iris.**

iris ī'ris, n. the rainbow: an appearance resembling the rainbow: the contractile curtain perforated by the pupil, and forming the coloured part of the eye: the fleur-de-lis, or flag (Iris): an iris diaphragm: — *pl.* **irides** (ī'rid-ēz, i'), **i'rises**: (with *cap.*) the Greek rainbow goddess, messenger of the gods. — *v.t.* to make iridescent: to form into a rainbow: to work an iris diaphragm. — *n.* **i'rid** the iris of the eye: any plant of the iris family. — *n.pl.* **Iridā'ceae** (i-rid-ā'si-ē, ī-) the iris family, distinguished from lilies by their inferior ovary and single whorl of stamens. — Also **Irid'eae.** — *adjs.* **Iridaceous** (i-rid-ā'shəs, ī-), **irid'eal** belonging to the Iridaceae; **i'ridal, irid'ial, irid'ian** pertaining to the rainbow or the iris of the eye: rainbow-like. — *ns.* **iridec'tomy** (ir- or īr-) surgical removal of part of the iris; **iridescence** (ir-i-des'əns) play of rainbow colours, caused by interference, as on bubbles, mother-of-pearl, some feathers. — *adjs.* **iridesc'ent, ī'risated** coloured like the rainbow: glittering with changing colours. — *adv.* **iridesc'ently.** — *adj.* **iridic** (ī-rid'ik, i-) containing or consisting of iridium: of or relating to the iris of the eye. — *n.* **iridisation, -z-** (ī-rid-īz-ā'shən, or ir-id-, or -iz-) iridescence. — *v.t.* **iridise, -ize** (īr' or ir') to make iridescent: to tip with iridium. — *ns.* **irid'ium** (īr- or ir-) a very heavy steel-grey metallic element (symbol Ir; at. numb. 77), with very high melting-point; **iridodiagnos'tics; iridol'ogy** diagnosis by examination of the iris; **īridol′ogist**; **iridosmine** (*ir-id-oz′min*, or *īr-*, or *-os′*) **iridosmium** (*ir-id-oz′mi-əm*, or *īr-*, or *-os′*) a native alloy of iridium and osmium used for pen-points, also called *osmiridium*; **iridot′omy** (*ir-* or *īr-*) surgical incision into the iris of the eye. — *v.t.* **ī′risate** to make iridescent. — *n.* **irisation** (*ī-ri-sā′-shən*). — *adjs.* **irised** (*ī′rist*) showing colours like the rainbow; **īrit′ic** having iritis: affecting the iris. — *n.* **īrīt′is** inflammation of the iris of the eye. — **iris diaphragm** an adjustable stop for a lens, giving a continuously variable hole.   [Gr. *īris, -idos*, the rainbow goddess.]

iriscope *ī′ri-skōp, n.* an instrument for exhibiting the prismatic colours.   [Gr. *īris*, and *skopeein*, to see.]

Irish *ī′rish, adj.* relating to, or produced in, or derived from, or characteristic of, Ireland: Highland Scottish (*obs.*): self-contradictory, ludicrously inconsistent (as Irish thought and speech is traditionally supposed to be). — *n.* the Celtic language of Ireland or (*obs.*) of the Scottish Highlands (Gaelic): an Irish commodity, esp. whiskey: temper, passion (*coll.*): (as *pl.*) the natives or people of Ireland. — *ns.* **I′risher** (*Scot.*, often slightly contemptuous) an Irishman; **I′rishism** (also **I′ricism** *-sizm*, a faulty form) a Hibernicism, an Irish phrase, idiom or characteristic, esp. a bull; **I′rishman**; **I′rishry** the people of Ireland collectively; **I′rishwoman**. — **Irish bridge** a ford or watersplash treated so as to be permanent; **Irish car** a jaunting car; **Irish coffee** a beverage made of sweetened coffee and Irish whiskey and topped with cream; **Irish elk** see **elk**; **Irish Guards** a regiment formed in 1900 to represent Ireland in the Foot Guards; **Irish moss** carrageen; **Irish stew** mutton, onions, and potatoes stewed with flour; **Irish terrier** a breed of dog with rough, wiry, reddish-brown coat.

irk *ûrk, v.t.* (now usu. used impersonally) to weary: to disgust: to distress: to annoy, gall. — *adj.* **irk′some** causing uneasiness (*arch.*): tedious: burdensome. — *adv.* **irk′somely**. — *n.* **irk′someness**.   [M.E. *irken.*]

iroko *i-rō′kō, n.* either of the two timber trees of the genus *Chlorophora* of central and western Africa: the hard wood of these trees, often used as a substitute for teak: — *pl.* **irō′kos**.   [Yoruba.]

iron *ī′ərn, n.* an element (symbol Fe; at. numb. 26), the most widely used of all the metals: a weapon, instrument, or utensil made of iron, as a hand-harpoon, flat-iron, branding instrument, etc.: a pistol or revolver (*slang*): a golf-club with an iron head (formerly limited to certain types): strength: a medicinal preparation of iron: (in *pl.*) fetters, chains: a theatre safety curtain (orig. short for **iron curtain**, see below): a stirrup. — *adj.* formed of iron: resembling iron: harsh, grating: stern: fast-binding: not to be broken: robust: insensitive: inflexible. — *v.t.* to smooth with a flat-iron: to arm with iron: to fetter: to smooth, clear up (with *out; fig.*). — *ns.* **i′roner** one who irons: an iron for pressing clothes; **i′roning** the act or process of smoothing with hot irons: clothes to be ironed. — *adj.* **i′rony** made, consisting of, rich in iron: like iron: hard. — **Iron Age** the age in which the ancient Greeks and Romans themselves lived, regarded by them as a third step in degeneracy from the Golden Age (*myth.*): the stage of culture of a people using iron as the material for their tools and weapons (*archaeol.*); **i′ronbark** any of several eucalyptus trees. — *adjs.* **i′ron-bound** bound with iron: rugged, as a coast; **i′ron-cased**; **i′ron-clad** clad in iron: covered or protected with iron. — *n.* a ship defended by iron plates. — **i′ron-clay** clay ironstone; **Iron Cross** a Prussian war medal instituted in 1813, revived in 1870 and 1914 and reinstated by Hitler as a German war medal in 1939; **Iron Crown** the crown of Lombardy, so named from a thin band of iron said to be made from one of the nails of the Cross; **iron curtain** the safety curtain in a theatre, orig. made of iron (*arch.*): an impenetrable barrier to observation or communication, esp. (with *caps.*) between communist Russia with its satellites and the West; **i′ron-founder** one who founds or makes castings in iron; **i′ron-**

foundry; **i′ron-glance** specular iron. — *adj.* **i′ron-gray′**, **-grey′** of a grey colour like that of iron freshly cut or broken. — *n.* this colour. — **iron hand** strict, despotic control (the iron hand is sometimes hidden in the *velvet glove*, q.v.). — *adjs.* **i′ron-hand′ed**; **i′ron-heart′ed** having a heart as hard as iron: unfeeling. — **iron horse** a worn-out circumlocution for a railway engine; **i′roning-board** a smooth board covered with cloth, on which clothes are ironed; **i′ron-liq′uor** iron acetate, a dyers' mordant; **iron lung** an apparatus consisting of a chamber that encloses a patient's chest, the air pressure within the chamber being varied rhythmically so that air is forced into and out of the lungs; **iron maiden** an old instrument of torture, consisting of a box lined with iron spikes in which a prisoner was fastened; **iron man** a man of extraordinary strength (esp. *Austr.*): (the winner of) a test of endurance at a surf carnival, comprising swimming, surfing and running events (*Austr.*): a pound note (orig. *Austr. coll.*) or a dollar (*U.S. coll.*); **i′ronmaster** a proprietor of ironworks; **i′ron-mine**; **i′ron-miner**; **i′ron-mining**; **i′ron-monger** a dealer in ironmongery (*loosely*), in household goods and equipment generally; **i′ronmongery** articles made of iron: hardware; **i′ron-mould** (earlier **-mole**, *Scot.* **-mail**; O.E. *māl*, mole, spot) a spot left on wet cloth after touching iron; **i′ron-ore**; **i′ron-pan′** a hard layer in sand or gravel, due to percolation of water precipitating iron salts; **iron pyrites** common pyrites, sulphide of iron; **iron ration** a ration of concentrated food, esp. for an extreme emergency; **i′ron-sand** sand containing particles of iron-ore: steel filings used in fireworks. — *adj.* **i′ron-sick** (*naut.*) having the iron bolts and spikes much corroded. — **I′ronside**, **I′ronsides** a nickname for a man of iron resolution (as King Edmund, Oliver Cromwell): a Puritan cavalryman: a Puritan: (in *pl.*) a name given to Cromwell's irresistible cavalry. — *adj.* **i′ron-sid′ed** having a side of, or as hard as, iron: rough: hardy. — **i′ronsmith** a worker in iron, blacksmith; **i′ronstone** any iron-ore, esp. carbonate; **i′ronware** wares or goods of iron. — *adjs.* **i′ron-willed** firmly determined; **i′ron-witt′ed** (*Shak.*) unfeeling, insensible. — **i′ronwood** timber of great hardness, and many kinds of trees producing it. — *adj.* **i′ron-word′ed** (*Tenn.*) in words as strong as iron. — **i′ronwork** the parts of a building, etc., made of iron: anything of iron, esp. artistic work: (often in *pl.*) an establishment where iron is smelted or made into heavy goods. — **rule with a rod of iron** to rule with stern severity; **strike while the iron is hot** to seize one's opportunity while the circumstances are favourable to one; **too many irons in the fire** too many things on hand at once.   [O.E. *īren* (*īsern, īsen*); Ger. *Eisen*.]

irony[1] *ī′rən-i, n.* the Socratic method of discussion by professing ignorance: conveyance of meaning (generally satirical) by words whose literal meaning is the opposite, esp. words of praise used as a criticism or condemnation: a situation or utterance (as in a tragedy) that has a significance unperceived at the time, or by the persons involved (cf. **dramatic irony** at **drama**): a condition in which one seems to be mocked by fate or the facts. — *adjs.* **ironic** (*ī-ron′ik*), **iron′ical**. — *adv.* **iron′ically**. — *v.t.* and *v.i.* **i′ronise, -ize**. — *n.* **i′ronist**.   [L. *īrōnīa* — Gr. *eirōneiā*, dissimulation — *eirōn*, a dissembler, perh. — *eirein*, to talk.]

irony[2]. See **iron**.

Iroquoian *ir-ō-kwoi′ən, adj.* of, belonging to, the *Iroquois*, a confederation of American Indian tribes: of the group of languages spoken by these tribes. — Also *n.*

irradiate *ir-ā′di-āt, v.t.* to shed light or other rays upon or into: to treat by exposure to rays: to light up: to brighten: to radiate. — *v.i.* to radiate: to shine. — *adj.* adorned with rays of light or with lustre. — *ns.* **irra′diance, irra′diancy**. — *adj.* **irra′diant** — *n.* **irradiā′tion** the act of irradiating: exposure to rays: that which is irradiated: brightness: apparent enlargement of a bright object by spreading of the excitation of the retina, or in a photograph by reflections within the emulsion: spread of a nervous impulse beyond the usual area affected: intellectual light. — *adj.* **irra'diative.** [Pfx. **ir- (in-**(1)).]

irradicate *ir-ad'i-kāt, v.t.* to fix firmly. [Pfx. **ir- (in-** (1)).]

irrational *ir-ash'ən-əl, adj.* not rational: not commensurable with natural numbers: long treated as short, or having such a syllable (indicated >; *pros.*). — *n.* an irrational being or number. — *v.t.* **irra'tionalise, -ize** to make irrational. — *ns.* **irra'tionalism** an irrational system: irrationality; **irra'tionalist.** — *adj.* **irrational-ist'ic.** — *n.* **irrational'ity.** — *adv.* **irra'tionally.** [Pfx. **ir- (in-** (2)).]

irrealisable, -izable *ir-ē-ə-līz'ə-bl, adj.* not realisable. — *n.* **irreality** (*-al'i-ti*) unreality. [Pfx. **ir- (in-** (2)).]

irrebuttable *ir-i-but'ə-bl, adj.* not to be rebutted. [Pfx. **ir- (in-** (2)).]

irreceptive *ir-i-sep'tiv, adj.* not receptive. [Pfx. **ir- (in-** (2)).]

irreciprocal *ir-i-sip'rə-kəl, adj.* not reciprocal. — **ir-reciprocity** (*ir-es-i-pros'i-ti*). [Pfx. **ir- (in-** (2)).]

irreclaimable *ir-i-klām'ə-bl, adj.* that cannot be claimed back, brought into cultivation, or reformed: incorrigible. — *ns.* **irreclaimabil'ity, irreclaim'ableness.** — *adv.* **irreclaim'ably.** [Pfx. **ir- (in-** (2)).]

irrecognisable, -izable *ir-ek-əg-nīz'ə-bl,* or *ir-ek', adj.* unrecognisable. — *n.* **irrecognition** (*-nish'ən*) lack of recognition. [Pfx. **ir- (in-** (2)).]

irreconcilable *ir-ek-ən-sīl'ə-bl,* or *ir-ek', adj.* incapable of being brought back to a state of friendship or agreement: inconsistent. — *n.* an irreconcilable opponent: an intransigent: any of two or more opinions, desires, etc. that cannot be reconciled. — *ns.* **irreconcīl'ableness, irreconcīlabil'ity.** — *adv.* **irreconcīl'ably.** — *adj.* **irrec'onciled** not reconciled, esp. (*Shak.*) with God: not brought into harmony. — *n.* **irreconcile'ment.** [Pfx. **ir- (in-** (2)).]

irrecoverable *ir-i-kuv'ər-ə-bl, adj.* irretrievable: not reclaimable: beyond recovery. — *n.* **irrecov'erableness.** — *adv.* **irrecov'erably.** [Pfx. **ir- (in-** (2)).]

irrecusable *ir-i-kū'zə-bl, adj.* that cannot be rejected. — *adv.* **irrecūs'ably.** [Fr. — L.L. *irrecūsābilis.*]

irredeemable *ir-i-dēm'ə-bl, adj.* not redeemable: not subject to be paid at the nominal value. — *ns.* **irredeem'-ableness, irredeemabil'ity.** — *n.pl.* **irredeem'ables** undated government or debenture stock. — *adv.* **irredeem'ably.** [Pfx. **ir- (in-** (2)).]

Irredentist *ir-i-den'tist, n.* one of an Italian party formed in 1878, its aims to gain or regain for Italy various regions claimed on language and other grounds: one who makes similar claims for any nation. — Also *adj.* — *n.* **Irredent'ism** the programme of the Irredentist party: the doctrine of 'redeeming' territory from foreign rule. — Often **irredentist, irredentism.** [It. (*Italia*) *irredenta,* unredeemed (Italy) — L. *in-,* not, *redemptus,* pa.p. of *redimĕre,* to redeem.]

irreducible *ir-i-dūs'i-bl, adj.* that cannot be reduced or brought from one degree, form, or state to another: not to be lessened: not to be overcome: not to be reduced by manipulation, as a hernia, etc. — *n.* **irreduc'ibleness.** — *adv.* **irreduc'ibly.** — *ns.* **irreducibil'-ity, irreductibility** (*-duk-ti-bil'i-ti*); **irreduction** (*-duk'-shən*). [Pfx. **ir- (in-** (2)).]

irreflective *ir-i-flek'tiv, adj.* not reflective. — *n.* **irreflec'-tion, irreflex'ion.** [Pfx. **ir- (in-** (2)).]

irreformable *ir-i-förm'ə-bl, adj.* not reformable: not subject to revision or improvement. — *adv.* **irreform'ably.** [Pfx. **ir- (in-** (2)).]

irrefragable *ir-ef'rə-gə-bl, adj.* that cannot be refuted: unanswerable. — *ns.* **irrefragabil'ity, irref'ragableness.** — *adv.* **irref'ragably.** — **the Irrefragable Doctor** Alexander of Hales (died 1245) who prepared a system of instruction for the schools of Christendom. [L. *irrefrāgābilis* — *in-,* not, *re-,* backwards, *frangĕre,* to break.]

irrefrangible *ir-i-fran'ji-bl, adj.* incapable of refraction. — *ns.* **irrefrangibil'ity, irrefran'gibleness.** — *adv.* **ir-refran'gibly.** [Pfx. **ir- (in-** (2)).]

irrefutable *ir-ef'ūt-ə-bl,* also *-ūt', adj.* that cannot be refuted. — *ns.* **irrefutabil'ity, irref'utableness** (or *-ūt'*). — *adv.* **irref'utably** (also *-ūt'*). [Pfx. **ir- (in-** (2)).]

irregular *ir-eg'ū-lər, adj.* not regular: not conforming to rule or to the ordinary rules: disorderly: uneven: unsymmetrical: variable: (of troops) not trained under authority of a government: (of a marriage) not celebrated by a minister after proclamation of banns or of intention to marry. — *n.* an irregular soldier. — *n.* **irregularity** (*-lar'i-ti*) a rough place or bump on an even surface: an instance of action, behaviour, etc. not conforming to rules or regulations. — *adv.* **irreg'ularly.** — *adj.* **irreg'ulous** (*Shak.*) lawless. [Pfx. **ir- (in-** (2)).]

irrelative *ir-el'ə-tiv, adj.* not relative: irrelevant. — *adj.* **irrelated** (*ir-i-lā'tid*). — *ns.* **irrela'tion, irrel'ativeness.** — *adv.* **irrel'atively.** [Pfx. **ir- (in-** (2)).]

irrelevant *ir-el'ə-vənt, adj.* not relevant. — *ns.* **irrel'evance, irrel'evancy.** — *adv.* **irrel'evantly.** [Pfx. **ir- (in-** (2)).]

irreligion, irreligionist. See **irreligious.**

irreligious *ir-i-lij'əs, adj.* destitute of religion: regardless of religion: opposed to religion: false in religion (*Shak.*): ungodly. — *adv.* **irrelig'iously.** — *ns.* **irrelig'-iousness, irrelig'ion** want of religion: hostility to or disregard of religion; **irrelig'ionist.** [Pfx. **ir- (in-** (2)).]

irremeable *ir-em'i-ə-bl,* or *-ēm', adj.* not admitting of return. — *adv.* **irrem'eably.** [L. *irremeābilis* — *in-,* not, *re-,* back, *meāre,* to go, come.]

irremediable *ir-i-mē'di-ə-bl, adj.* beyond remedy or redress. — *n.* **irremē'diableness.** — *adv.* **irremē'diably.** [Pfx. **ir- (in-** (2)).]

irremissible *ir-i-mis'i-bl, adj.* not to be remitted or forgiven. — *ns.* **irremissibil'ity, irremiss'ibleness, irremission** (*-mish'ən*). — *adj.* **irremiss'ive** unremitting. [Pfx. **ir- (in-** (2)).]

irremovable *ir-i-mōōv'ə-bl, adj.* not removable: not liable to be displaced. — *ns.* **irremovabil'ity, irremov'ableness.** — *adv.* **irremov'ably.** [Pfx. **ir- (in-** (2)).]

irrenowned *ir-i-nown'id,* (*Spens.*) *adj.* inglorious. [Pfx. **ir- (in-** (2)).]

irrepairable *ir-i-pār'ə-bl,* (*arch.*) *adj.* beyond repair. [Pfx. **ir- (in-** (2)).]

irreparable *ir-ep'ər-ə-bl, adj.* that cannot be made good or rectified: beyond repair. — *ns.* **irreparabil'ity, irrep'-arableness.** — *adv.* **irrep'arably.** [Pfx. **ir- (in-** (2)).]

irrepealable *ir-i-pēl'ə-bl, adj.* that cannot be repealed or annulled. — *ns.* **irrepealabil'ity, irrepeal'ableness.** — *adv.* **irrepeal'ably.** [Pfx. **ir- (in-** (2)).]

irreplaceable *ir-i-plās'ə-bl, adj.* whose loss cannot be made good: without possible substitute. — *adv.* **irre-place'ably.** [Pfx. **ir- (in-** (2)).]

irrepleviable *ir-i-plev'i-ə-bl,* **irreplevisable** *ir-i-plev'isə-bl,* (*legal*) *adj.* unable to be replevied. [Pfx. **ir-(in-** (2)).]

irreprehensible *ir-ep-ri-hens'i-bl, adj.* beyond blame. — *n.* **irreprehens'ibleness.** — *adv.* **irreprehens'ibly.** [Pfx. **ir- (in-** (2)).]

irrepressible *ir-i-pres'i-bl, adj.* not to be put down or kept under. — *ns.* **irrepressibil'ity, irrepress'ibleness.** — *adv.* **irrepress'ibly.** [Pfx. **ir- (in-** (2)).]

irreproachable *ir-i-prōch'ə-bl, adj.* free from blame: faultless. — *ns.* **irreproachabil'ity, irreproach'ableness.** — *adv.* **irreproach'ably.** [Pfx. **ir- (in-** (2)).]

irreproducible *ir-ē-prō-dūs'i-bl, adj.* that cannot be reproduced. [Pfx. **ir- (in-** (2)).]

irreprovable *ir-i-prōōv'ə-bl, adj.* blameless. — *n.* **irreprov'-ableness.** — *adv.* **irreprov'ably.** [Pfx. **ir- (in-** (2)).]

irresistance *ir-i-zist'əns, n.* want of resistance: passive submission. — *adj.* **irresist'ible** not to be opposed with success: resistless: overpowering: overmastering. — *ns.* **irresist'ibleness, irresistibil'ity.** — *adv.* **irresist'ibly.** [Pfx. **ir- (in-** (2)).]

irresoluble *ir-ez'əl-ū-bl,* *-ōō-bl, adj.* that cannot be resolved into parts: that cannot be solved: that cannot be loosed or got rid of (*arch.*). — *n.* **irresolubil'ity.** — *adv.* **irres'olubly.** [Pfx. **ir- (in-** (2)).]

irresolute *ir-ez'əl-ūt,* *-ōōt, adj.* not firm in purpose. — *adv.* **irres'olutely.** — *ns.* **irres'oluteness, irresolution**

(-ū́shən, -ōṓshən) want of resolution. [Pfx. **ir-** (in- (2)).]

irresolvable ir-i-zolv́ə-bl, adj. that cannot be resolved. — ns. **irresolvabil'ity, irresolv'ableness.** — adv. **irresol'v-ably.** [Pfx. **ir-** (in- (2)).]

irrespective ir-i-spek'tiv, adj. not having regard (with of). — Also adv. — adv. **irrespec'tively.** [Pfx. **ir-** (in- (2)).]

irrespirable ir-es'pir-ə-bl, or -is-pīr', adj. unfit for respiration. [Pfx. **ir-** (in- (2)).]

irresponsible ir-i-spons'i-bl, adj. not responsible: without sense of responsibility: free from feeling of responsibility, light-hearted, carefree: reprehensibly careless: done without feeling of responsibility. — ns. **irresponsibil'ity, irrespon'sibleness.** — adv. **irrespons'ibly.** — adj. **irrespons'ive** not responding: not readily responding. — adv. **irrespons'ively.** — n. **irrespons'iveness.** [Pfx. **ir-** (in- (2)).]

irrestrainable ir-i-strān'ə-bl, adj. not restrainable. [Pfx. **ir-** (in- (2)).]

irresuscitable ir-i-sus'i-tə-bl, adj. incapable of being resuscitated or revived. — adv. **irresusc'itably.** [Pfx. **ir-** (in- (2)).]

irretention ir-i-ten'shən, n. absence of retention or power to retain. — adj. **irreten'tive.** — n. **irreten'tiveness.** [Pfx. **ir-** (in- (2)).]

irretrievable ir-i-trēv'ə-bl, adj. not to be recovered; irreparable. — ns. **irretrievabil'ity, irretriev'ableness.** — adv. **irretriev'ably.** [Pfx. **ir-** (in- (2)).]

irreverent ir-ev'ər-ənt, adj. not reverent: proceeding from irreverence. — n. **irrev'erence** want of reverence or veneration, esp. for God. — adj. **irreverential** (-en'shəl). — adv. **irrev'erently.** [Pfx. **ir-** (in- (2)).]

irreversible ir-i-vûrs'i-bl, adj. not reversible: that cannot proceed in the opposite direction or in both directions: incapable of changing back: not alike both ways: that cannot be recalled or annulled: (involving damage which is) permanent (med.). — ns. **irreversibil'ity, irrevers'ibleness.** — adv. **irrevers'ibly.** [Pfx. **ir-** (in- (2)).]

irrevocable ir-ev'ək-ə-bl, adj. that cannot be recalled or revoked. — ns. **irrevocabil'ity, irrev'ocableness.** — adv. **irrev'ocably.** [Pfx. **ir-** (in- (2)).]

irrigate ir'i-gāt, v.t. to wet or moisten: to water by means of canals or watercourses: to cause a stream of liquid to flow upon. — v.i. (slang) to drink. — adj. **irr'igable.** — n. **irrigā'tion.** — adjs. **irrigā'tional, irr'igative.** — n. **irr'igātor** one who, or that which, irrigates: an appliance for washing a wound, etc. — adj. **irrig'uous** watered: wet: irrigating. [L. irrigāre, -ātum, to water, and irriguus, watering, watered — in, upon, rigāre, to wet.]

irrision ir-izh'ən, n. the act of laughing at another. — adj. **irrisory** (ir-ī'sər-i) mocking, derisive. [L. irrīsio, -ōnis — in, on, at, rīdēre, rīsum, to laugh.]

irritate[1] ir'i-tāt, v.t. to excite or stimulate: to rouse: to provoke: to make angry or fretful: to excite a painful, uncomfortable, or unhealthy condition (as heat and redness) in. — n. **irritabil'ity** the quality of being easily irritated: the peculiar susceptibility to stimuli possessed by living matter. — adj. **irr'itable** that may be irritated: easily annoyed: susceptible of excitement or irritation. — n. **irr'itableness.** — adv. **irr'itably.** — n. **irr'itancy.** — adj. **irr'itant** irritating. — n. that which causes irritation. — n. **irritā'tion** the act of irritating or exciting: anger, annoyance: stimulation: the term applied to any morbid excitement of the vital actions not amounting to inflammation, often, but not always, leading to that condition (med.). — adj. **irr'itātive** tending to irritate or excite: accompanied with or caused by irritation. — n. **ir'ritātor.** [L. irrītāre, -ātum.]

irritate[2] ir'i-tāt, (Scots law) v.t. to make void. — n. **irr'itancy.** — adj. **irr'itant** rendering void. [L. irrītāre — in-, not, ratus, valid.]

irrupt ir-upt', v.i. to break in: to make irruption. — n. **irruption** (ir-up'shən) a breaking or bursting in: a sudden invasion or incursion. — adj. **irrup'tive** rushing

suddenly in. — adv. **irrup'tively.** [L. irrumpĕre, irruptum — in, in, rumpĕre, to break.]

Irvingite ûr'ving-īt, n. a popular name for a member of the Catholic Apostolic Church. — Also adj. — n. **Ir'vingism** the doctrine and practice of the Irvingites. [From Edward Irving (1792–1834).]

is iz, used as third pers. sing. pres. indic. of **be.** [O.E. is; Ger. ist, L. est, Gr. esti, Sans, asti.]

isabel iz'ə-bel, n. and adj. dingy yellowish-grey or drab. — Also **isabell'a, isabell'ine** (-in, -īn). [Origin unknown: too early in use to be from Isabella, daughter of Philip II, who did not change her linen for three years until Ostend was taken; an etymological connection with Isabella of Castile, to whom a similar legend is ascribed, is chronologically possible but by no means certain.]

isagogic ī-sə-goj'ik, -gog'ik, adj. introductory. — n. **isagoge** (ī'sə-gō-ji, or -gō') an academic introduction to a subject. — n. sing. **isagog'ics** that part of theological study introductory to exegesis. [Gr. eisagōgē, an introduction — eis, into, agein, to lead.]

isallobar īs-, īz-al'-ə-bär, (meteor.) n. the contour line on a weather chart, signifying the location of equal changes in the barometer over a specified period. [Gr. isos, equal, allos, other, different, baros, weight.]

isapostolic īs-ap-əs-tol'ik, adj. equal to the apostles, as bishops of apostolic creation, the first preachers of Christ in a country, etc. [Gr. isos, equal, apostolikos, apostolic.]

Isatis ī'sə-tis, n. the woad genus of Cruciferae. — n. **ī'satin, -tine** a substance ($C_8H_5O_2N$) got by oxidising indigo. [Gr. isatis, woad.]

isch(a)emia is-kē'mi-ə, n. deficiency of blood in a part of the body. — adj. **isch(a)em'ic.** [Gr. ischein, to restrain, haima, blood.]

ischium is'ki-əm, n. a posterior bone of the pelvic girdle: — pl. **is'chia.** — adjs. **ischiad'ic, is'chial, ischiat'ic.** [Latinised from Gr. ischion, the hip-joint.]

ischuria is-kū'ri-ə, n. a stoppage of urine. — adj. and n. **ischuretic** (is-kū-ret'ik). [Gr. ischein, to hold, ouron, urine.]

-ise, -ize -īz, a suffix forming verbs from adjs., meaning to make, as equalise, or from nouns, as botanise, satirise. [L. -izāre, from Gr. -izein; Fr. -iser.]

isenergic īs-en-ûr'jik, adj. in physics, denoting equal energy. [Gr. isos, equal, energeia, energy.]

Isengrim i'zən-grim, **Isegrim** ī'zə-grim, n. the wolf in the beast epic of Reynard the Fox.

isentropic ī-sen-trop'ik, (phys.) adj. of equal entropy. [Gr. isos, equal, entropē, a turning about — en, in, trepein, to turn.]

-ish -ish, adj. suffix signifying somewhat, as brownish, oldish, like or similar to, sometimes implying deprecation, as outlandish, childish, or roughly, approximately, as in sixish. [O.E. -isc.]

ish ish, (Scots law) n. issue, liberty of going out: expiry. [O.Fr. issir, to go out — L. exīre — ex, out of, īre, to go.]

Ishmael ish-mā'əl, n. one like Ishmael (Gen. xvi. 12), at war with society. — n. **Ish'maelite** a descendant of Ishmael: a Bedawi Arab: an Ishmael. — adj. **Ishmaelīt'ish.**

Isiac, -al. See Isis.

Isidorian is-, iz-i-dō', -dō', -ri-ən, adj. of or pertaining to St Isidore of Seville (c. 560–636), or the collection of canons and decretals adopted by him; but esp. applying to the forged Pseudo-Isidorian or False Decretals, published (c. 845) by Isidore Mercator, and fathered upon St Isidore.

isinglass ī'zing-gläs, n. a material, mainly gelatine, got from sturgeons' air-bladders and other sources. [App. from obs. Du. huizenblas — huizen, a kind of sturgeon, blas, a bladder; Ger. Hausenblase; cf. huso.]

Isis ī'sis, n. an Egyptian goddess, wife and sister of Osiris. — adjs. **ī'siac, īsī'acal.** [Gr. īsis.]

Islam iz'läm, or is', or -läm', **Is'lamism,** ns. the Muslim religion: the whole Muslim world. — adjs. **Islamic**

(-*lam'ik*), **Islamitic** (-*lə-mit'ik*). — *v.t.* **Islam'icise, -ize** to Islamise. — *ns.* **Islam'icist** one who studies Islam, Islamic law, Islamic culture, etc.; **Islamīsā'tion, -z-.** — *v.t.* and *v.i.* **Is'lamise, -ize** to convert, (cause to) conform to Islam. — *n.* **Is'lamite.** [Ar. *islām*, surrender (to God).]

island *ī'lənd, n.* a mass of land (not a continent) surrounded with water: anything isolated, detached, or surrounded by something of a different nature, e.g. a wood among prairies, a hill in a marsh or plain, a show case or counter, a building or building-site with a clear space around it: a small raised traffic-free area in a street for pedestrians: tissue or cells detached and differing from their surroundings. — *adj.* of an island: forming an island. — *v.t.* to cause to appear like an island: to isolate: to dot as with islands. — *n.* **islander** (*ī'lənd-ər*) an inhabitant of an island. — **island-hopping** see **hop¹**; **island universe** a spiral nebula regarded as forming a separate stellar system. — **islands of Langerhans** same as **islets of Langerhans; Islands of the Blest** in Greek mythology, the abode of the blessed dead, situated somewhere in the far west; **Reil's island** see **insula.** [M.E. *iland* — O.E. *īegland, īgland, ēgland* — *īeg, īg, ēg*, island (from a root which appears in Angles-*ea*, Aldern-*ey*, etc., O.E. *ēa*, L. *aqua*, water) and *land*; the *s* is due to confusion with *isle*.]

isle *īl, n.* an island. — *v.t.* to make an isle of: to set in an isle. — *v.i.* to dwell in an isle. — *n.* **islet** (*ī'lit*) a little isle. — **isles'man** an islander, esp. an inhabitant of the Hebrides — also **isle'man.** — **Isle of Wight disease** a disease of bees caused by a mite in the spiracles, that appeared in the Isle of Wight in 1906, and spread to other regions; **islets of Langerhans** (*läng'ər-häns*) groups of epithelial cells discovered by Paul *Langerhans*, a German anatomist (1847–88), in the pancreas, producing a secretion the lack of which causes diabetes. [M.E. *ile, yle* — O.Fr. *isle* (Fr. *île*) — L. *īnsula.*]

-ism -*izm*, **-asm** - *azm*, or (with **-ic**) **-icism** -*i-sizm* suffixes forming abstract nouns signifying condition, system, as ego*ism*, de*ism*, Calvin*ism*, lacon*ism*, pleon*asm*, Anglic*ism*, wittic*ism*. [L. -*ismus*, -*asmus* — Gr. -*ismos*, -*asmos*.]

ism *izm, n.* any distinctive doctrine, theory, or practice — usually in disparagement. — *adjs.* **ismat'ic, -al, ism'y** addicted to isms or faddish theories. — *n.* **ismat'icalness.** [From the suffix -*ism*.]

Ismaili *is-mä-ē'lē,* or *is-mä'i-li, n.* one of a sect of Shiite Muslims whose imam or spiritual head is the Aga Khan. — Also *adj.* — *n.* and *adj.* **Ismailian** (*is-mä-il'i-ən*). — *n.* **Is'mailism.** — *adj.* **Ismailit'ic.**

isn't *iz'ənt, for* is not.

iso- *ī'sō-, pfx.* equal: in chem. denoting an isomeric substance — e.g. **iso-oc'tane** one of the isomers of normal octane. [Gr. *isos*, equal.]

isoagglutination *ī-sō-ə-gloō-ti-nā'shən, n.* the agglutination of red blood corpuscles within the same blood-group. — *n.* **isoagglu'tinin** an antibody that causes the agglutination of red blood corpuscles in animals of the same species from which it was derived. [Pfx. **iso-**.]

isobar *ī'sō-bär, n.* a curve running through places of equal pressure: esp. one connecting places, or their representations on a map, of equal barometric pressure (*meteor.*): (see **isobare**; *chem.*). — *adjs.* **isobaric** (-*bar'-ik*), **isobaromet'ric.** [Pfx. **iso-**, and Gr. *baros*, weight.]

isobare *ī'sō-bär, n.* either of two atoms of different chemical elements but of identical atomic mass (e.g. an isotope of titanium and an isotope of chromium both of atomic mass 50). — Also **i'sobar.** [Same as **isobar** above.]

isobase *ī'sō-bās,* (*geol.*) *n.* a contour line of equal upheaval of the land. [Pfx. **iso-**, and Gr. *basis*, step.]

isobath *ī'sō-bäth, n.* a contour line of equal depth. — *adj.* **isobath'ic.** [Pfx. **iso-**, and Gr. *bathos*, depth.]

isobilateral *ī-sō-bī-lat'ər-əl, adj.* bilaterally symmetrical with upper and under surfaces alike: symmetrical about two planes (*bot.*): having the flanks of the organ

flattened surfaces. [Pfx. **iso-**, and **bilateral.**]

isobront *ī'sō-bront, n.* a contour line marking simultaneous development of a thunderstorm. [Pfx. **iso-**, and Gr. *brontē*, thunder.]

isochasm *ī'sō-kazm, n.* a contour line of equal frequency of auroral displays. — *adj.* **isochasm'ic.** [Pfx. **iso-**, and Gr. *chasma*, a gap, expanse.]

isocheim, isochime *ī'sō-kīm, n.* a contour line of mean winter temperature. — *adjs.* and *ns.* **isocheim'al, isocheim'enal, isochī'mal.** — *adj.* **isocheim'ic.** [Pfx. **iso-**, and Gr. *cheima*, winter weather, *cheimainein,* to be stormy.]

isochor, isochore *ī'sō-kōr, -kör, n.* a curve representing variation of some quantity under conditions of constant volume. — *adj.* **isochoric** (-*kor'ik*). [Pfx. **iso-**, and Gr. *chōrā*, space.]

isochromatic *ī-sō-krō-mat'ik, adj.* having the same colour (*optics*): orthochromatic (*phot.*). [Pfx. **iso-**, and Gr. *chrōma, -atos*, colour.]

isochronal *ī-sok'rən-əl,* **isoch'ronous** -*əs, adjs.* of equal time: performed in equal times: in regular periodicity. — *advs.* **isoch'ronally, isoch'ronously.** — *n.* **i'sochrone** a line on a chart or map joining points associated with a constant time difference, e.g. in reception of radio signals. — *v.t.* **isoch'ronise, -ize.** — *n.* **isoch'ronism.** [Pfx. **iso-**, and Gr. *chronos*, time.]

isoclinal *ī-sō-klī'nəl, adj.* folded with nearly the same dip in each limb (*geol.*): in terrestrial magnetism, having the same magnetic dip. — *n.* an isoclinical line, or contour line of magnetic dip. — *n.* **ī'socline** an area of rock strata with isoclinal folds: an isoclinal. — *adj.* and *n.* **isoclinic** (-*klin'ik*) isoclinal. [Pfx. **iso-**, and Gr. *klīnein*, to bend.]

isocracy *ī-sok'rə-si, n.* (a system of government in which all people have) equal political power. — *adj.* **isocrat'ic.** [Pfx. **iso-**, Gr. *krateein*, to rule.]

isocryme *ī'sō-krīm, n.* a contour line of equal temperature during the coldest time. — *adj.* and *n.* **isocrȳm'al.** [Pfx. **iso-**, and Gr. *krȳmos*, cold.]

isocyanide *ī-sō-sī'ən-īd, n.* a salt or ester of **isocyanic acid** a hypothetical acid only known in its compounds. [Pfx. **iso-**, **cyanide.**]

isocyclic *ī'sō-sī-klik, adj.* homocyclic. [**iso-**, **cyclic.**]

Isodia *ī-sō'di-ə, n.pl.* the feast of the presentation of the Virgin in the temple at the age of three. [Gr., neut. pl. of adj. *eisodios* — *eisodos*, entrance.]

isodiametric, -al *ī-sō-dī-ə-met'rik, -əl, adjs.* of equal diameters: about as broad as long. [Pfx. **iso-**.]

isodicon *ī-sod'i-kon,* (*Gr.* Church) *n.* a troparion or short anthem sung while the Gospel is being carried through the church. [Dim. of Gr. *eisodos,* entrance.]

isodimorphism *ī-sō-dī-mörf'izm,* (*crystal.*) *n.* isomorphism between each of the two forms of a dimorphous substance and the corresponding forms of another dimorphous substance. — *adjs.* **isodimorph'ic, isodimorph'ous.** [Pfx. **iso-**.]

isodomon *ī-sod'o-mon, n.* masonry of uniform blocks in courses of equal height, the vertical joints placed over the middle of the blocks below. — Also (Latinised) **isod'omum:** — *pl.* **isod'oma.** — *adj.* **isod'omous.** [Gr., neut. of *isodomos*, equal-coursed — *isos*, equal, *domos*, a course — *demein*, to build.]

isodont *ī'sō-dont,* (*zool.*) *adj.* having all the teeth similar in size and form. — Also **isodont'al.** — *n.* an isodontal animal. [Gr. *isos*, equal, *odous, odontos*, tooth.]

isodynamic *ī-sō-dīn-am'ik,* or -*din-, adj.* of equal strength, esp. of magnetic intensity. — *n.* an isodynamic line on the earth or the map, a contour line of magnetic intensity. [Pfx. **iso-**, and Gr. *dynamis*, strength.]

isoelectric *ī-sō-i-lek'trik, adj.* having the same potential. — **isoelectric point** the pH-value at which the ionisation of an ampholyte is at a minimum. [**iso-**, **electric.**]

isoelectronic *ī-sō-el-ik-tron'ik, adj.* having an equal number of electrons, or similar electron patterns. [**iso-**, **electron.**]

Isoetes *ī-sō'ə-tēz, n.* the quillwort genus constituting a family (**Isoetā'ceae**) of pteridophytes, with short stem, a bunch of quill-shaped leaves in which the sporangia are sunk, and branching roots: (without *cap*.) a plant of this genus: — *pl.* **iso′etes.** [Gr. *isoetes*, houseleek (an evergreen) — *isos*, equal, *etos*, a year.]

isogamy *ī-sog′ə-mi*, (*biol*.) *n*. the conjugation of two gametes of similar size and form. — *n.* **isogamete** (*ī-sō-gam′ēt*, or *ēt′*). — *adjs.* **isogamet′ic, isogam′ic, isog′amous.** [Pfx. **iso-**, and Gr. *gamos*, marriage.]

isogeny *ī-soj′ə-ni, n.* likeness of origin. — *adj.* **isogenetic** (*ī-sō-ji-net′ik*), **isog′enous.** [Pfx. **iso-**, and Gr. *genos*, kind.]

isogeotherm *ī-sō-jē′ō-thûrm, n.* a subterranean contour of equal temperature. — *adjs.* **isogeotherm′al, isogeotherm′ic.** — *n.* an isogeotherm. [Pfx. **iso-**, and Gr. *gē*, the earth, *thermē*, heat — *thermos*, hot.]

isogloss *ī′sō-glos, n.* a line separating one region from another region which differs from it in a particular feature of dialect. — *adjs.* **isogloss′al, -glott′al, isoglott′ic.** [Pfx. **iso-**, and Gr. *glōssa*, tongue.]

isogonic *ī-sō-gon′ik,* **isogonal** *ī-sog′ən-əl, adjs.* of equal angles, esp. of magnetic declination. — *ns.* an isogonic line or contour line of magnetic declination. — *n.* **i′sogon** an equiangular polygon. [Pfx. **iso-**, and Gr. *gōniā*, an angle.]

isogram *ī′sō-gram, n.* a line drawn on a map or diagram showing all points which have an equal numerical value with respect to a given climatic or other variable. — See also **isopleth.** [Pfx. **iso-**, and Gr. *gramma*, a letter.]

isohel *ī′sō-hel, n.* a contour line of equal amounts of sunshine. [Pfx. **iso-**, and Gr. *hēlios*, sun.]

isohyet *ī-sō-hī′ət, n.* a contour line of equal rainfall. — *adj.* **isohy′etal.** — *n.* an isohyet. [Pfx. **iso-**, and Gr. *hyetos*, rain — *hyein*, to rain.]

isokinetic *ī-sō-kin-et′ik, adj.* (of the withdrawal of a fluid sample) accomplished without disturbance to the speed and direction of flow. [Pfx. **iso-**, and Gr. *kīneein*, to move.]

Isokontae *ī′sō-kont′ē, n.pl.* the green algae, whose zoospores have usually equal cilia. — *n.* **i′sokont.** — *adj.* and *n.* **isokont′an.** [Pfx. **iso-**, and Gr. *kontos*, a (punting) pole.]

isolate *ī′sō-lāt, v.t.* to place in a detached situation, like an island: to detach: to insulate: to separate (esp. those who might be infected) (*med*.): to seclude: to segregate: to obtain in a pure, uncombined state: a pure culture of (a micro-organism). — *n.* (*-lit, lāt*) something isolated, esp. for individual study or experiment. — Also *adj.* — *n.* **isolabil′ity.** — *adj.* **i′solable.** — *ns.* **isolā′tion; isolā′tionism** the policy of avoiding political entanglements with other countries; **isolā′tionist.** — *adj.* **i′solātive** tending towards isolation: occurring without influence from outside. — *n.* **i′solātor.** — **isolating languages** those in which each word is a bare root, not inflected or compounded. [It. *isolare* — *isola* — L. *īnsula*, an island.]

isolecithal *ī-sō-les′i-thəl, adj.* (of the ova of mammals and some other vertebrates) having the yolk distributed evenly through the protoplasm. [Pfx. **iso-**, Gr. *lekithos*, egg-yolk.]

isoleucine *ī-sō-lū′sīn, n.* an essential amino acid. [**iso-**, **leucine.**]

isoline *ī′sō-līn.* Same as **isopleth.**

isologue *ī′sō-log, n.* an organic compound with similar molecular structure to another, but containing different atoms of the same valency. — *adj.* **isŏl′ogous.** [Pfx. **iso-**, Gr. *logos*, ratio.]

isomagnetic *ī-sō-mag-net′ik, adj.* having equal magnetic induction or force. — *n.* (also **isomagnetic line**) an imaginary line joining places at which the force of the earth's magnetic field is constant. [**iso-, magnetic.**]

isomer *ī′sō-mər,* (*chem*.) *n.* a substance, radical, or ion isomeric with another: an atomic nucleus having the same atomic number and mass as another or others but a different energy state. — *n.* **i′somēre** (*zool*.) an organ or segment corresponding to or homologous with another. — *adj.* **isomeric** (*-mer′ik; chem.*) identical

in percentage composition and molecular weight but different in constitution or the mode in which the atoms are arranged: of nuclei, differing only in energy state and half-life. — *v.t.* and *v.i.* **isomerise, -ize** (*ī-som′ər-īz*) to change into an isomer. — *ns.* **isomerīsā′tion, -z-; isom′erism** the property of being isomeric: the existence of isomers. — *adj.* **isom′erous** (*bot*.) having the same number of parts (esp. in floral whorls). [Pfx. **iso-**, and Gr. *meros*, part.]

isometric, -al *ī-sō-met′rik, -əl, adjs.* having equality of measure: pertaining to isometrics: having the plane of projection equally inclined to three perpendicular axes: of the cubic system, or referable to three equal axes at right angles to one another (*crystal*.). — *n.* **isomet′ric** (also **isometric line**) a line on a graph showing variations of pressure and temperature at a constant volume. — *adv.* **isomet′rically.** — *n. sing.* **isomet′rics** a system of strengthening the muscles and tuning up the body by opposing one muscle to another or to a resistant object. — *n.* **isom′etry** equality of measure. [Pfx. **iso-**, and Gr. *metron*, measure.]

isomorph *ī′sō-mörf, n.* that which shows isomorphism. — *adj.* **isomorph′ic** showing isomorphism. — *n.* **isomorph′ism** similarity in unrelated forms (*biol*.): close similarity in crystalline form combined with similar chemical constitution (*crystal*.): a one-to-one correspondence between the elements of two or more sets and between the sums or products of the elements of one set and those of the equivalent elements of the other set or sets (*math*.). — *adjs.* **isomorph′ic, isomorph′ous.** — **isomorphous mixture** a mixed crystal or solid solution in which isomorphous substances are crystallised together by vicarious substitution. [Pfx. **iso-**, and Gr. *morphē*, form.]

isoniazid(e) *ī-sō-nī′ə-zid, -zīd, n.* a drug, a pyridine derivative, used against tuberculosis; sold under several proprietary names.

isonomy *ī-son′ə-mi, n.* equal law, rights, or privileges. — *adjs.* **isonom′ic, ison′omous.** [Gr. *isonomiā* — *isos*, equal, *nomos*, law.]

isoperimeter *ī-sō-pər-im′i-tər, n.* a figure with perimeter equal to another. — *adj.* **isoperimetrical** (*ī-sō-per-i-met′ri-kəl*). — *n.* **isoperim′etry.** [Pfx. **iso-**, and Gr. *perimetron*, circumference.]

isopleth *ī′sō-pleth, n.* an isogram, esp. one on a graph showing variations of a climatic element as a function of two variables; cf. **nomogram.** [Pfx. **iso-**, and Gr. *plēthos*, great number.]

isopod *ī′sō-pod, n.* a member of the Isopoda. — *n.pl.* **Isopoda** (*ī-sop′ə-də*) an order of Crustacea with no carapace, depressed body, sessile eyes, seven pairs of nearly equal thoracic legs, and usually lamellar uropods — woodlice, fishlice, etc. — *adjs.* **isop′odan, isop′odous.** [Pfx. **iso-**, and Gr. *pous, podos*, a foot.]

isopolity *ī-sō-pol′i-ti, n.* reciprocity of rights of citizenship in different communities. [Pfx. **iso-**, and Gr. *politeiā*, citizenship.]

isoprene *ī′sō-prēn, n.* a hydrocarbon of the terpene group, which may be polymerised into synthetic rubber. [Etymology obscure.]

isopropyl *ī-sō-prop′il, n.* the radical $(CH_3)_2CH$, derived from propane. [Pfx. **iso-**, **propane.**]

Isoptera *ī-sop′tər-ə, n.pl.* an order of insects having the two pairs of wings (when present) closely alike — the termites. — *adj.* **isop′terous.** [Pfx. **iso-**, and Gr. *pteron*, a wing.]

isorhythmic *ī-sō-ridh′mik, -rith′mik, adj.* in ancient prosody, equal in the number of time-units for thesis and arsis, as dactyl, spondee, anapaest: in mediaeval motets, having a strict scheme of repeated rhythm independent of melodic repetition. [Pfx. **iso-** and Gr. *rhythmos*, rhythm.]

isosceles *ī-sos′i-lēz,* (*geom*.) *adj.* having two equal sides, as a triangle. [Gr. *isoskelēs* — *isos*, equal, *skelos*, a leg.]

isoseismal *ī-sō-sīz′məl, n.* a curve or line connecting points at which an earthquake shock is felt with equal intensity. — *adjs.* **isoseis′mal, isoseis′mic.** [Pfx. **iso-,** and Gr. *seismos,* a shaking.]

isospin *ī′sō-spin, n.* in particle physics, a quantum number applied to members of closely related groups of particles to express and explain the theory that such particles (e.g. protons and neutrons) are in fact states of the same particle differing with regard to electric charge. — Also **isotopic spin.** [*isotopic spin.*]

isosporous *ī-sos′pər-əs,* or *ī-sō-spō′rəs, -spö′, adj.* having spores of one kind only (opp. to *heterosporous*). — *n.* **isos′pory.** [Pfx. **iso-,** and Gr. *sporos,* seed.]

isostasy *ī-sos′tə-si,* (*geol.*) *n.* a condition of equilibrium held to exist in the earth's crust, equal masses of matter underlying equal areas, whether of sea or land down to an assumed level of compensation. — *adj.* **isostatic** (*ī-sō-stat′ik*) in hydrostatic equilibrium from equality of pressure: in a state of isostasy: pertaining to isostasy. — *adv.* **isostat′ically.** [Gr. *isos,* equal, *stasis,* setting, weighing, *statikos,* pertaining to weighing.]

isostemonous *ī-sō-stēm′ən-əs, adj.* having as many stamens as petals. [Pfx. **iso-,** and Gr. *stēmōn,* a thread.]

isosteric *ī-sō-ster′ik, adj.* (of two different molecules) having the same number of atoms, and the same number and arrangement of valency electrons. [Pfx. **iso-, steric.**]

isotactic *ī-sō-tak′tik, adj.* of or concerning a polymer with its attached groups of atoms in a regular order on one side of the central chain. [Pfx. **iso-, tactic.**]

isothere *ī′sō-thēr, n.* a contour line of equal mean summer temperature. — *adj.* **isotheral** (*ī-soth′ər-əl, ī-sō-thēr′əl*). — *n.* an isothere. [Gr. *theros,* summer — *therein,* to make warm.]

isotherm *ī′sō-thûrm, n.* a contour line of equal temperature. — *adj.* **isotherm′al** at constant temperature: pertaining to isotherms. — *n.* an isothermal line, isotherm. — *adv.* **isotherm′ally.** [Pfx. **iso-,** and Gr. *thermē,* heat — *thermos,* hot.]

isotone *ī′sō-tōn, n.* one of a number of nuclides having the same number of neutrons in the nucleus with differing numbers of protons. [Pfx. **iso-,** and prob. Gr. *tonos,* tension.]

isotonic *ī-sō-ton′ik, adj.* having the same tone, tension, or osmotic pressure. — *n.* **isotonic′ity.** [Pfx. **iso-,** and Gr. *tonos,* tension, tone.]

isotope *ī′sō-tōp, n.* one of a set of chemically identical species of atom which have the same atomic number but different mass numbers; a natural element is made up of isotopes, always present in the same proportions. — *adj.* **isotopic** (*-top′ik*). — *n.* **isotopy** (*ī-sot′ə-pi*) the fact or condition of being isotopic. — **isotopic number** the excess number of neutrons over protons in a nuclide; **isotopic spin** same as **isospin.** — **stable isotope** a non-radioactive isotope found in nature. [Pfx. **iso-,** and Gr. *topos,* place (*scil.* in the periodic table).]

isotron *ī′sō-tron, n.* a device for separating isotopes by accelerating ions by means of an electric field — the velocities attained are in inverse proportion to the masses. [**iso(tope)** and suff. **-tron.**]

isotropic *ī-sō-trop′ik, adj.* having the same properties irrespective of direction: without predetermined axes (*biol.*). — Also **isotropous** (*ī-sot′rə-pəs*). — *ns.* **isot′ropism, isot′ropy.** [Pfx. **iso-,** and Gr. *tropos,* turn, direction.]

isotype *ī′sō-tīp, n.* a presentation of statistical information by a row of diagrammatic pictures each representing a particular number of instances. [Pfx. **iso-,** and Gr. *typos,* form.]

I-spy *ī′-spī′, n.* a children's game of hide-and-seek, so called from the cry when one is spied: a word-game, in which one guesses objects in view, whose names begin with a certain letter of the alphabet. [**I, spy.**]

Israeli *iz-rā′lē, n.* a citizen of the modern state of Israel. — Also *adj.* [See **Israelite.**]

Israelite *iz′ri-əl-īt, -rə-, n.* a descendant of Israel or Jacob: a Jew: one of the elect (*fig.*): a member of a Christian sect that observes the Jewish law. — *adjs.* **Israelit′ic, Israelīt′ish.** [Gr. *Israēlītēs* — *Israēl,* Heb. *Yisrāēl,*

perh. contender with God — *sara,* to fight, *El,* God.]

issei *ēs′sā′, n.* a Japanese immigrant in the U.S.A. — cf. **nisei, sanei.** [Jap., first generation.]

issue *ish′ū, -ōō, is′ū, n.* a going or flowing out: an outlet: act of sending out: that which flows or passes out: fruit of the body, children: produce, profits: a fine (*obs.*): a putting into circulation, as of banknotes: publication, as of a book: a giving out for use: a set of things put forth at one time: a single thing given out or supplied (chiefly *mil.*): ultimate result, outcome: upshot: critical determination: luck or success in conclusion (*Shak.*): an act, deed (*Shak.*): a point in dispute: a point on which a question depends: a question awaiting decision or ripe for decision: a discharge or flux (*med.*): an ulcer produced artificially. — *v.i.* (in *Spens.* usu. **issue′**) to go, flow, or come out: to proceed, as from a source: to spring: to be produced: to come to a point in fact or law (*law*): to turn out, result, terminate. — *v.t.* to send out: to put forth: to put into circulation: to publish: to give out for use: to supply (*mil. jargon*). — *adj.* **iss′uable** capable of issuing, admitting of an issue. — *adv.* **iss′uably.** — *n.* **iss′uance** the act of giving out, promulgation. — *adjs.* **iss′uant** (*her.*) issuing or coming up from another, as a charge or bearing; **iss′ueless** without issue: childless. — *n.* **iss′uer** one who issues or emits. — **at issue** in quarrel or controversy: in dispute; **feigned issue** (*law*) an issue made up for trial by agreement of the parties or by an order of court, instead of by the ordinary legal procedure; **force the issue** to hasten or compel a final decision on a matter; **general issue** (*law*) a simple denial of the whole charge, as 'Not guilty', instead of a **special issue,** an issue taken by denying a particular part of the allegations; **immaterial issue** an issue which is not decisive of any part of the litigation, as opp. to a **material issue,** one which necessarily involves some part of the rights in controversy; **join,** or **take, issue** to take an opposite position, or opposite positions, in dispute: to enter into dispute: to take up a point as basis of dispute; **side issue** a subordinate issue arising from the main business. [O.Fr. *issue* — *issir,* to go or flow out, — L. *exīre* — *ex,* out, *īre,* to go.]

-ist *-ist, suff.* denoting the person who holds a doctrine or practises an art, as Calvin*ist,* chem*ist,* novel*ist,* art*ist,* royal*ist.* [L. *-ista* — Gr. *-istēs.*]

isthmus *is(th)′məs, n.* narrow neck of land connecting two larger portions (also *fig.*): a constriction. — *adj.* **isth′-mian** pertaining to an isthmus, esp. the Isthmus of Corinth. — **Isthmian Games** games held on the Isthmus of Corinth, near the Saronic Gulf shore. [L., — Gr. *isthmos,* from root of *ienai,* to go.]

Istiophorus. Same as **Histiophorus** (see under **hist-**).

istle *ist′li,* **ixtle** *ikst′li, ns.* a valuable fibre obtained from Agave, Bromelia, and other plants. [Mexican Sp. *ixtle* — Nahuatl *ichtli.*]

it[1] *it, pron.* the neut. of **he, him** (and formerly **his**) applied to a thing without life, a lower animal, a young child, rarely (except as an antecedent or in contempt) to a man or woman: used as an impersonal, indefinite, or anticipatory or provisional subject or object, as the object of a transitive verb that is normally an intransitive, or a noun: as gen., its (*obs.* and *dial.*): in children's games, the player chosen to oppose all others: the *ne plus ultra,* that which answers exactly to what one is looking for (*coll.*): an indefinable crowning quality by which one carries it off — personal magnetism: sex-appeal (*slang*): — *gen.* **its** (*obs.* **his, it;** see also **its**); *pl.* **they, them.** [O.E. *hit,* neut. (nom. and acc.) of *hē*; Du. *het,* Goth. *hita,* this; akin to Goth. *ita,* Ger. *es,* L. *id,* Sans. *i,* pronominal root = here; the *t* is an old neuter suffix, as in *that, what,* and cognate with *d* in L. *illud, istud, quod.*]

it[2] *it, n.* short for **Italian vermouth.**

ita *ē′tə, n.* the miriti palm. [Arawak *ité.*]

itacism *ē′tə-sizm, n.* the pronunciation of Greek *ēta* as in Modern Greek, like English long *e* (opp. to *etacism*): iotacism in pronunciation of various vowels and diphthongs. [Gr. ēta, eta, η.]

itacolumite *it-ə-kol'ŭm-īt, n.* a schistose quartzite containing scales of mica, talc, and chlorite, often having a certain flexibility. [*Itacolumi* mountain, Brazil.]

itaconic acid *it-ə-kon'ik,* or *īt-, as'id* a white crystalline solid got by fermentation of sugar with Aspergillus mould, used in plastics manufacture. [Anagram of *aconitic.*]

Itala. See **Italic version.**

Italian *i-tal'yən, adj.* of or relating to *Italy* or its people or language. — *n.* a native or citizen of Italy, or person of the same race: the language of Italy. — *adj.* **Ital'ianate** Italianised. — *vs.t.* **Ital'ianate, Ital'ianise, -ize** to make Italian: to give an Italian character to. — *vs.i.* to become Italian: to play the Italian: to speak Italian: to use Italian idioms: to adopt Italian ways. — *ns.* **Italianīsā'tion, -z-; Ital'ianism, Ital'icism** (*-sizm*) an Italian idiom or habit: Italian sympathies; **Ital'ianist** one who has a scholarly knowledge of Italian: a person of Italian sympathies. — *adj.* **Ital'ic** pertaining to Italy, esp. ancient Italy: of or pertaining to Italic: (without *cap.*) of a sloping type introduced by the Italian printer Aldo Manuzio in 1501, used esp. for emphasis or other distinctive purpose, indicated in MS by single underlining. — *n.* a branch of Indo-European usu. considered to comprise Oscan, Umbrian, Latin, and related languages, but sometimes applied to either the Latin group or the Osco-Umbrian group alone: (without *cap.,* usu. in *pl.*) an italic letter. — *n.* **italicīsā'tion, -z-.** — *v.t.* **ital'icise, -ize** to put in, or mark for, italics. — *n.* **Ital'iot, Ital'iote** a Greek of ancient Italy. — Also *adj.* — **Italian architecture** the style practised by Italian architects of the 15th–17th centuries, which originated in a revival of the ancient architecture of Rome; **Italianate Englishman** an Englishman of the Renaissance, full of Italian learning and vices, proverbially equivalent to a devil incarnate; **Italian garden** a formal garden with statues; **Italian iron** a smoothing iron for fluting; **Italian sixth** a chord of a note with its major third and augmented sixth; **Italian sonnet** same as **Petrarch(i)an sonnet** (see under **sonnet**); **Italian vermouth** a sweet vermouth; **Italian warehouseman** a dealer in such groceries as macaroni, olive oil, dried fruits, etc.; **Italic version** or **It'ala** a translation of the Bible into Latin, based on the 'Old Latin' version, and made probably in the time of Augustine. [L. *Ītaliānus* and Gr. *Ītalikos* — L. *Ītalia,* Gr. *Ītaliā,* Italy.]

italic, Italic, etc. See **Italian.**

Italo- *i-tal'ō-, it'ə-lō-,* in composition, Italian.

itch *ich, n.* an irritating sensation in the skin: scabies, an eruptive disease in the skin, caused by a parasitic mite: a constant teasing desire. — *v.i.* to have an uneasy, irritating sensation in the skin: to have a constant, teasing desire. — *n.* **itch'iness.** — *adj.* **itch'y** pertaining to or affected with itch or itching. — **itching palm** a greed for gain; **itch'-mite** a mite that burrows in the skin causing itch or scabies; **itch'weed** Indian poke. — *adj.* **itch'y-palm'ed.** [O.E. *giccan,* to itch; Scot. *youk, yuck,* Ger. *jucken,* to itch.]

-ite *-īt, suff.* used to form (1) names of persons, indicating their origin, place of origin, affiliations, loyalties, etc. (e.g. *Semite, Durhamite, Jacobite, Buchmanite, Janeite*); (2) names of fossil organisms (e.g. *ammonite*); (3) names of minerals (e.g. *calcite*); (4) names of salts of acids with suff. *-ous* (e.g. *sulphite,* salt of sulphurous acid); (5) names of bodily parts (e.g. *somite*). The nouns may be used also as adjs.

item *ī'təm, adv.* likewise: also. — *n.* a separate article or particular in an enumeration: a piece of news or other matter in a newspaper. — *v.t.* to set down in enumeration: to make a note of. — *v.t.* **i'temise -ize** to give or list by items. [L. *ītem,* likewise.]

iterate *it'ər-āt, v.t.* to do again: to say again, repeat. — *ns.* **it'erance, iterā'tion** repetition. — *adjs.* **it'erant, it'erative** (*-ə-tiv* or *-ā-tiv*) repeating. — *adv.* **it'erātively.** [L. *iterāre, -ātum* — *iterum,* again.]

iterum *it'ə-rəm, -e-rŏŏm,* (L.) *adv.* again.

ithyphallus *ith-i-fal'əs, n.* an erect phallus: (with *cap.*) the stinkhorn genus of fungi. — *adj.* **ithyphall'ic** of or with an ithyphallus: pertaining to the processions in honour of Dionysos in which an ithyphallus was carried, or to the hymns sung or the metres used: shameless. [Gr. *īthyphallos* — *īthys,* straight, *phallos,* a phallus.]

itinerant *i-tin'ər-ənt,* also *ī-, adj.* making journeys from place to place: travelling. — *n.* one who travels from place to place, esp. a judge, a Methodist preacher, a strolling musician, or a peddler: a wanderer. — *ns.* **itin'eracy** (*-ə-si*), **itin'erancy.** — *adv.* **itin'erantly.** — *adj.* **itin'erary** travelling: relating to roads or journeys. — *n.* a plan or record of a journey: a road-book: a route: an itinerant. — *v.i.* **itin'erate** to travel from place to place, esp. for the purpose of judging, preaching, or lecturing. [L. *iter, itineris,* a journey.]

-itis *-ī'tis, n. suff.* denoting a disease (now inflammation), as bronch*itis:* also jocularly imputing an imaginary disease, as jazz*itis.* [Gr. *-ītis.*]

it'll *it'l,* a contraction of **it will.**

its *its,* possessive or genitive of **it**[1]. (The old form was *his, its* not being older than the end of the 16th century. *Its* does not occur in the English Bible of 1611 (inserted in 1660 in Leviticus xxv. 5) or in Spenser, rarely in Shakespeare, and is not common until the time of Dryden.) — *pron.* **itself** *it-self',* the emphatic and reflexive form of **it**. — **by itself** alone, apart; **in itself** by its own nature.

it's *its,* a contraction of **it is** or **it has.**

itsy-bitsy *it'si-bit'si,* (*coll.*) *adj.* tiny. [Prob. a childish reduplicated form of **little** influenced by **bit**[1].]

I've *īv,* a contraction of **I have.**

ivory *ī'və-ri, n.* dentine, esp. the hard white substance composing the tusks of the elephant, walrus, hippopotamus, and narwhal: an object of that material, as a billiard-ball, a piano-key, a dice: a tooth or the teeth (*slang*). — *adj.* made of, resembling, or of the colour of, ivory. — *adj.* **i'voried** made like ivory: furnished with teeth (*slang*). — *n.* **i'vorist** a worker in ivory. — **i'vory-black** a black powder, originally made from burnt ivory, but now from bone; **ivory gate** (*myth.*) see **gate**[1]; **i'vory-nut** the nut of Phytelephas or other palm, yielding **vegetable ivory** a substance like ivory; **i'vory= palm; i'vory-por'celain** a fine ware with an ivory-white glaze; **ivory tower** (*fig.*) a place of retreat from the world and one's fellows: a life-style remote from that of most ordinary people, leading to ignorance of practical concerns, problems, etc.; **i'vory-tree** the palay. — **show one's ivories** (*slang*) to show the teeth. [O.Fr. *ivurie* (Fr. *ivoire*) — L. *ebur, eboris,* ivory; Coptic *ebu,* elephant, ivory.]

ivresse *ē-vres',* (Fr.) *n.* drunkenness.

ivy *ī'vi, n.* an araliaceous evergreen plant (*Hedera helix*) that climbs by roots on trees and walls. — *adjs.* **i'vied** (also **i'vy'd**) overgrown or mantled with ivy. — **i'vy= bush** a bush or branch of ivy, esp. formerly one hung at a tavern-door, the ivy being sacred to Bacchus. — **Ivy League** a name given to eight eastern U.S. universities of particular academic and social prestige. — *adjs.* **i'vy-leaved** having five-lobed leaves like ivy (as the *ivy-leaved* toadflax); **i'vy-man'tled** ivied. — **i'vy-tod'** a bush of ivy. — **ground-ivy, poison-ivy** see **ground**[2], **poison.** [O.E. *īfig,* O.H.G. *ebah.*]

iwis, ywis *i-wis', (obs.) adv.* certainly — sometimes ignorantly written *I wis,* as if 'I know'. [M.E. *ywis, iwis* — O.E. *gewis,* certain; Ger. *gewiss* (adv.).]

ixia *ik'si-ə, n.* any plant of the iridaceous genus *Ixia,* found in Southern Africa. [Mod. Latin, from Gr. *ixos,* mistletoe, birdlime.]

ixtle. See **istle.**

Iynx. A spelling of the generic name **Jynx.**

Iyyar *ē'yär, n.* the eighth month of the Jewish year (second of the ecclesiastical year). [Heb.]

izard *iz'ərd, n.* the Pyrenean ibex. [Fr. *isard.*]

-ize. See **-ise.**

izzard *iz'ərd,* **izzet** *iz'it,* (*arch.* or *dial.*) *n.* the letter Z.

J

J, j *jā,* (*Scot.*) *jī, n.* the tenth letter in our alphabet, developed from I, specialised to denote a consonantal sound (*dzh* in English, *y* in German and other languages, *zh* in French, an open guttural in Spanish), I being retained for the vowel sound — a differentiation not general in English books till about 1630: as numeral, used in old MSS and in medical prescriptions instead of *i* final, as *vj,* six: used equally with *i* for √ − 1: J represents the mechanical equivalent of heat. — **J'-curve** (*econ.*) a small initial deterioration, decrease, etc., followed by a larger sustained improvement, increase, etc., appearing on a graph as a J-shaped curve; **J'-pen** a pen with a short broad nib.

jab *jab, v.t.* and *v.i.* to poke, stab. — *n.* a sudden thrust or stab: a short straight punch: an injection (*coll.*). [Cf. **job¹.**]

jabber *jab'ər, v.i.* to gabble or talk rapidly. — *v.t.* to utter indistinctly. — *n.* rapid indistinct speaking. — *n.* **jabb'erer.** — *n.* and *adj.* **jabb'ering.** — *adv.* **jabb'eringly.** [Imit.]

jabberwock *jab'ər-wok, n.* a fabulous monster created by Lewis Carroll in his poem *Jabberwocky:* (also **jabb'-erwocky**) nonsense, gibberish.

jabble *jab'l,* (*Scot.*) *n.* an agitation in liquid: a rippling: a quantity of liquid enough to dash about or splash. — *v.t.* and *v.i.* to splash: to ripple: to dash: to jumble (*fig.*). [Imit.]

jabers *jā'bərz, n.* in the Irish oath *be jabers* prob. for **Jesus.**

jabiru *jab'i-rōō, -rōō', n.* a large Brazilian stork: extended to other kinds. [Tupi *jabirú.*]

jaborandi *jab-ə-ran'di, jab-ö-, n.* a Brazilian drug with sialagogue and diaphoretic properties, got from the leaflets of rutaceous shrubs (Pilocarpus) and other sources. [Tupí.]

jabot *zha'bō, n.* a frill of lace, etc., worn in front of a woman's dress or on a man's shirt-front, esp. (now) as part of full Highland dress. [Fr.]

jacamar *jak'ə-mär, n.* any one of a South American family (*Galbulidae*) of long-billed insect-catching birds with reversible fourth toe and usu. metallic green or bronze plumage. [Fr., — Tupí *jacamá-ciri.*]

jaçana *zhä-sə-nä', jacana jak'ə-nə, ns.* a long-toed swamp bird of the tropics. [Port., from Tupí.]

jacaranda *jak-ə-ran'də, n.* a tropical American, etc., tree of the Bignoniaceae, with lilac-coloured flowers, fern-like leaves and hard, heavy, brown wood. [Port. and Tupí *jacarandá.*]

jacchus *jak'əs, n.* a South American marmoset (*Callithrix*). [L. *Iacchus* — Gr. *Iakchos,* Bacchus.]

jacent *jā'sənt,* (*obs.*) *adj.* lying flat: sluggish. [L. *jacēns, -entis,* pr.p. of *jacēre,* to lie.]

jacinth *jas'inth, jās', n.* originally, a blue gemstone, perhaps sapphire: a reddish-orange variety of transparent zircon — hyacinth (*min.*): a variety of garnet, topaz, quartz, or other stone (*jewellery*): a reddish-orange colour: a slaty-blue fancy pigeon. [**hyacinth.**]

jack¹ *jak, n.* (with *cap.*) a familiar form or diminutive of John: (with *cap.*) the common man (*obs.*): (with *cap.*) contemptuously, a fellow (*obs.*): (usu. with *cap.*) an ill-mannered, vulgar or boorish fellow (*obs.*): (sometimes with *cap.*) an attendant, servant or labourer: (often with *cap.*) a sailor: (with *cap.*) man, fellow, used in addressing a man whose name is unknown to the speaker (*U.S. slang*): a detective (*slang*): money (*U.S. slang*): a machine or device which orig. took the place of a servant, as a boot-jack for taking off boots, a contrivance for turning a spit (*smoke-jack, roasting-jack*), an apparatus for raising heavy weights: a winch:

a socket whose switching arrangements are such that the switch turns only when a jack plug is inserted (*telecomm.,* etc.): a figure that strikes the bell in clocks: the male of some animals: a jackass (also **jack donkey**): a jack-rabbit: a jackdaw: a young pike: in keyboard instruments, part of the action that moves the hammer or carries the quill or tangent: the key itself (*Shak.*): a contrivance for guiding threads in a loom: a saw-horse: a small flag indicating nationality, flown by a ship, usu. at the bow or the bowsprit: a leather pitcher or bottle: a knave in cards: (in *pl.*) the game of dibs: a piece used in this game: the small white ball aimed at in bowls: (with *cap.*) Jacqueminot. — *v.t.* to raise with, or as if with, a jack (with *up*): to act upon with a jack: to throw up or abandon (usu. with *in* or, formerly, *up;* *slang*): to increase (as prices) (with *up*). — *v.i.* to give up (with *up*) (*old slang*). — **Jack'-a-dan'dy** a dandy or fop, esp. if diminutive; **Jack'-a-lan'tern, Jack'-o'-lan'tern** Will-o'-the-wisp; **Jack'-a-Lent** (*Shak.*) a boy (for **Jack of Lent** a kind of puppet formerly thrown at in sport at Lent); **jack'-block** a block of pulleys used for raising and lowering topgallant-masts; **jack'boot** a large boot reaching above the knee, to protect the leg, orig. covered with iron plates and worn by cavalry: military rule, esp. when brutal (*fig.*). — *v.i.* (with *around;* also *v.t.* with *it*) to behave in an oppressive or brutally authoritarian way, to domineer, throw one's weight around. — **Jack'-by-the-hedge'** (also with *cap.*) garlic-mustard; **jack'-cross'tree** the crosstree at the head of a topgallant-mast. — *adj.* **jack easy** indifferent, not caring one way or the other. — **Jack'-fool'** a fool; **Jack Frost** frost personified; **Jack'-go-to-bed-at-noon'** the small goat's-beard; **jack'hammer** a hand-held compressed-air hammer drill for rock-drilling. — *adj.* and *adv.* **jack'-high** in bowls, as far as the jack. — **Jack'-in-off'ice** (also without *cap.*) a vexatiously self-important petty official; **Jack'-in-the-box** a figure that springs up from a box when the lid is released; **Jack'-in-the-green'** a May-Day dancer enclosed in a green shrubby framework; **Jack'-in-the-pul'pit** a N. American plant (*Arisaema triphyllum*) like cuckoo-pint: also applied to various other plants, esp. of the genus *Arisaema;* **Jack Ketch** a public hangman — from one so named under James II; **jack'-knife** a large clasp-knife: a dive in which the performer doubles up in the air and straightens out again. — *v.i.* and *v.t.* to double up as a jack-knife does: (of connected vehicles or parts) through faulty control, to form, or cause to form, an angle of 90° or less. — **Jack Nasty** a sneak: a sloven; **Jack'-of-all'-trades** one who can turn his hand to anything; **jack'-o'-lantern** a will-o'-the-wisp: a lantern made from a hollowed-out pumpkin, turnip, etc., with holes cut to resemble eyes, mouth, and nose; **jack'-pine** used for several N. American species of pine; **jack'-plane** a large strong plane used by joiners; **jack plug** (*telecomm.,* etc.) a one-pronged plug used to introduce an apparatus quickly into a circuit; **jack'pot** a poker game, played for the pot or pool (consisting of equal stakes from all the players), which must be opened by a player holding two jacks or better: a money pool in card games, competitions, etc., that can be won only on certain conditions being fulfilled and accumulates till such time as they are (see also **hit the jackpot** below): a prize-money fund: a mess, an awkward situation (*U.S. slang*); **Jack'-priest'** (in contempt) a parson; **Jack'-pudd'ing** (*arch.*) a merry-andrew, buffoon; **jack'-rabb'it** a long-eared American hare; **Jack'-raft'er** a rafter shorter than the rest, as in a hip-roof; **Jack Russell (terrier)** a breed of small terrier, introduced by *John Russell*, 19th-cent. parson; **Jack'-sauce'** (*Shak*.) an impudent fellow; **Jack'-slave** (*Shak*.) a low servant, a vulgar fellow; **jack'smith** (*obs*.) a maker of jacks for the kitchen; **jack'-snipe** a small species of snipe; **Jack Sprat** a diminutive fellow; **jack'-staff** the staff on which the jack is hoisted; **jack'-stays** ropes or strips of wood or iron stretched along the yards of a ship to bind the sails to; **Jack'-straw'**, **jack'-straw** a straw effigy: a man of straw, of no real significance: a straw or slip used in the game of **jack'-straws'** or spillikins; **Jack tar** (also without *cap*.) a sailor; **jack towel** a continuous towel passing over a roller. — **before you can say Jack Robinson** very quickly; **cheap Jack** see **cheap**; **every man Jack** one and all; **hit the jackpot** to win a jackpot: to have a big success; **poor Jack** poor-John; **steeplejack** see **steeple**; **Union Jack** (not properly a jack; see **union¹**); **yellow Jack** (*slang*) yellow fever. [App. Fr. *Jacques*, the most common name in France, hence used as a substitute for *John*, the most common name in England; really = *James* or *Jacob* — L. *Jacōbus*; but possibly partly from *Juckin, Jankin,* dim. of *John*.]

jack² *jak, n.* a mediaeval defensive coat, esp. of leather. — **jack'man** a soldier clad in a jack: a retainer. [Fr. *jaque*, perh. from *Jacques*, James.]

jack³, **jak** *jak, n.* a tree of the East Indies of the breadfruit genus (*Artocarpus*): its fruit. — **jack'-fruit; jack'-tree.** [Port. *jaca* — Malayalam *chakka*.]

jackal *jak'öl, n.* a wild, gregarious animal closely allied to the dog — erroneously supposed to act as a lion's provider or hunting scout: hence, one who does another's dirty work: a drudge: one who would share the spoil without sharing the danger. — *v.i.* to play the jackal: — *pa.p.* **jack'alled.** [Pers. *shaghāl*.]

jackanapes *jak'ə-nāps, n.* an ape or monkey (*arch*.): an impudent fellow: a coxcomb: a forward child. [Origin uncertain.]

jackaroo, jackeroo *jak-ə-rōō', (Austr*.) *n.* a newcomer, or other person, gaining experience on a sheep- or cattle-station: — *fem.* **jillaroo'.** — *v.i.* to be a jackaroo. [Aboriginal]

jackass *jak'as, n.* a he-ass: a blockhead, fool. — **laughing jackass** the kookaburra. [**jack¹,** **ass**.]

jackdaw *jak'dö, n.* a daw, a small species of crow with greyish neck. [**jack¹,** **daw².**]

jackeroo. See **jackaroo.**

jacket *jak'it, n.* a short coat: an animal's coat: skin (of potatoes): a loose paper cover: outer casing of a boiler, pipe, etc., as a steam-jacket, water-jacket: the aluminium or zirconium alloy covering of the fissile elements in a reactor. — *v.t.* to furnish or cover with a jacket: to beat (*slang*). — *adj.* **jack'eted** wearing a jacket. — **jacket potato** a potato cooked in its skin. — **dust someone's jacket** to beat someone. [O.Fr. *jaquet*, dim. of *jaque*; see **jack².**]

jacksie, jacksy *jak'si, (slang) n.* the posterior: the anus. [Perh. **jack¹.**]

Jacob *jā'kəb, n.* (also **Jacob sheep**) a kind of sheep, piebald in colour, with 2 or 4 horns, originally imported to Britain from Spain. [From Gen. xxx. 40.]

Jacobean *jak-ō-bē'ən, adj.* of or characteristic of the period of James I of England (1603–25). — **Jacobean lily** (*Sprekelia formosissima*) a Mexican bulbous plant named after St James. [L. *Jacōbus*, James.]

Jacobian *jə-kō'bi-ən, (math.) n.* the matrix or determinant formed from the first partial derivatives of several functions of several variables (also **Jacobian determinant**). [From K.G.J. *Jacobi*, 19th-cent. German mathematician.]

Jacobin *jak'ō-bin, n.* a French Dominican monk, so named from their original establishment being that of St *Jacques*, Paris: one of a society of revolutionists in France, so called from their meeting in the hall of the Jacobin convent: a demagogue: an extremist or radical, esp. in politics: a hooded pigeon. — *adjs.* **Jacobin'ic, -al.** — *v.t.* **Jac'obinise, -ize.** — *n.* **Jac'obinism** the principles of the Jacobins or French revolutionists.

[Fr., — L. *Jacōbus*, James.]

Jacobite *jak'ō-bīt, n.* an adherent of James II and his descendants: in Church history, a Syrian monophysite, named after the 6th-century monk *Jacobus* Baradaeus. — Also *adj.* — *adjs.* **Jacobit'ic, -al.** — *n.* **Jac'obītism.** [L. *Jacōbus*, James.]

Jacob's-ladder *jā'kəbz-lad'ər, n.* a ladder of ropes with wooden steps (*naut*.): a wild or garden plant (Polemonium) with ladder-like leaves: an endless chain of buckets used as an elevator. [From the *ladder* seen by *Jacob* in his dream, Gen. xxviii, 12.]

Jacob's-staff *jā'kəbz-stäf, n.* a pilgrim's staff: a staff with a cross-head used in surveying (*hist*.): a sword-cane. [Prob. from the pilgrimage to St James (L. *Jacōbus*) of Compostela.]

jacobus *jə-kō'bəs, n.* a gold coin of James I worth 20 to 25 shillings. [L. *Jacōbus*, James — Gr. *Iakōbos* — Heb. *Ya'aqōb*.]

jaconet *jak'ə-net, n.* a cotton fabric, rather stouter than muslin — different from the fabric orig. so named which was imported from *Jagannāth* (Puri) in India: a thin material with waterproof backing used for medical dressings. [See also **Juggernaut.**]

jacquard *jak'ärd, jak-ärd', (often cap.) n.* an apparatus with perforated cards for controlling the movement of the warp threads in weaving intricate designs: a fabric so woven. — **Jacq'uard-loom** a loom with jacquard. [Joseph Marie *Jacquard* (1752–1834), the inventor.]

Jacqueminot *jak'mi-nō, n.* a deep-red hybrid perpetual rose. — Also **Jacque** and **Jack.** [From General *Jacqueminot* of Paris.]

Jacquerie *zhäk'rē, n.* the revolt of the French peasants in 1358: any peasant revolt. [From *Jacques* Bonhomme, Goodman Jack, a name applied in derision to the peasants.]

jactation *jak-tā'shən, n.* act of throwing: extreme restlessness in disease: bodily agitation: boasting. [L. *jactātiō, -ōnis*, tossing, boasting — *jactāre*, to throw.]

jactitation *jak-ti-tā'shən, n.* restless tossing in illness: twitching or convulsion: tossing or bandying about (*obs*.): bragging: public assertion, esp. ostentatious and false. — **jactitation of marriage** pretence of being married to another. [L.L. *jactitātiō, -ōnis* — L. *jactitāre, -ātum*, to toss about, put about, make a display of, freq. of *jactāre*, to throw.]

jaculation *jak-ū-lā'shən, n.* the act of throwing or hurling, as a dart. — *v.t.* **jac'ulate** to dart, throw. — *n.* **jac'ulātor** a dart-thrower: an archer-fish. — *adj.* **jac'ulatory** (*-ət-ər-i*) darting or throwing out suddenly: ejaculatory. [L. *jaculārī, -ātus*, to throw as a dart — *jaculum*, a dart — *jacēre*, to throw.]

Jacuzzi® *jə-kōō'zi, n.* a type of bath or small pool equipped with a mechanism that agitates the water to provide extra invigoration: (usu. without *cap*.) a bathe in such a bath or pool.

jade¹ *jād, n.* a sorry horse: a worthless nag: a woman, esp. perverse, ill-natured, or not to be trusted, often in irony. — *v.t.* to make a jade of: to weary, dull, cloy, cause to flag, from excess or over-exposure: to play the jade with. — *v.i.* to become weary. — *adj.* **jā'ded.** — *adv.* **jā'dedly.** — *n.* **jā'dery** the tricks of a jade. — *adj.* **jā'dish.** [Origin unknown; cf. O.N. *jalda*, a mare; Scot. *yaud*.]

jade² *jād, n.* a hard ornamental stone of varying shades of green and sometimes almost white — esp. *nephrite* (silicate of calcium and magnesium) and **jade'ite** (silicate of aluminium and sodium) — once held to cure side pains. — *adj.* **jade** of jade: of the colour of jade. [Fr., — Sp. *ijada*, the flank — L. *ilia*.]

j'adoube *zha-dōōb, (Fr.) I adjust (chess; a warning that only an adjustment is intended, not a move).

Jaeger® *yā'gər, n.* woollen material used in making clothes, originally containing no vegetable fibre. [Dr Gustav *Jaeger*, the original manufacturer.]

jaeger. See **jäger.**

Jaffa *jaf'ə, n.* (also **Jaffa orange**) an orange from *Jaffa* in Israel.

jag¹ *jag, n.* a notch, slash, or dag in a garment, etc.: a ragged protrusion: a cleft or division (*bot.*): a prick (*Scot.*): an inoculation, injection (chiefly *Scot.*). — *v.t.* to cut into notches: to prick or pierce: — *pr.p.* **jagg'ing;** *pa.p.* **jagged** (*jagd*). — *adj.* **jagg'ed** notched, rough-edged, uneven. — *adv.* **jagg'edly.** — *ns.* **jagg'edness; jagg'er** a brass wheel with a notched edge for cutting cakes, etc., into ornamental forms — also **jagg'ing-i'ron.** — *adj.* **jagg'y** notched: slashed: prickly (*Scot.*). [Origin unknown.]

jag² *jag, n.* a load: a saddle-bag or other bag: a quantity: a thrill: a spree, bout of indulgence: a state of indulgence: one's fill of liquor or narcotics: a spell, fit. — *v.t.* to cart: to transport by pack-horse. — *adj.* **jagged** (*jagd*; *U.S.*) drunk. — *n.* **jagg'er** a carter: a pack-horseman: a pedlar.

Jagannath *jug-ən-üt', n.* a corrected form of **Juggernaut.**

jäger, jaeger *yā'gər, n.* a (German) huntsman: a German or Austrian rifleman or sharpshooter: an attendant upon an important or wealthy person, clad in huntsman's costume: (**jaeger**) a skua that chases and robs other gulls. [Ger., hunter — *jagen,* to hunt.]

jaggery *jag'ə-ri, n.* a coarse, dark sugar made from palm-sap or otherwise. [Hindi *jāgrī,* Sans. *śarkarā*; cf. **sugar, Saccharum.**]

jaghir, jaghire, jagir *jä-gēr', n.* the government revenues of a tract of land assigned with power to administer. — *n.* **jaghir'dar** the holder of a jaghir. [Hind. and Pers. *jāgīr.*]

jaguar *jag'wär,* or *jag'ū-är, -ər, n.* a powerful beast of prey, allied to the leopard, found in South America. [Tupí *jaguára.*]

jaguarundi, jaguarondi *jä-gwə-run'dē,* or *-ron', ns.* a South American wild cat. [Tupí — Guaraní.]

Jah *yä, jä, n.* Jehovah. — *n.* **Jah'veh** same as **Yahweh.** [Heb. *Yah.*]

jai alai *hī'(ə-)lī,* or *-lī',* a game resembling handball but played with a long curved basket strapped to the wrist. [Sp. — Basque — *jai,* festival, *alai,* merry.]

jail, gaol *jāl, n.* a prison. — *v.t.* to imprison. — *ns.* **jail'er, jail'or, gaol'er** one who has charge of a jail or of prisoners: a turnkey: — *fem.* **jail'eress,** etc. — **jail'-bait** (*slang*) a girl who is not of the legal age of consent (also *adj.*); **jail'-bird, gaol'-bird** a humorous name for one who is, has been, or should be much in jail; **jail'-break, gaol'-break** see **break jail** below; **jail'-deliv'ery, gaol'-deliv'ery** clearing of jail by sending all prisoners to trial: delivery from jail; **jail'-fē'ver, gaol'-fē'ver** typhus fever, once common in jails; **jail'house** (*U.S.*) a prison. — **break jail, gaol** to force one's way out of prison (*ns.* **jail'-break, gaol'-break**); **Commission of Jail Delivery** (*obs.* from 1972) one of the commissions issued to judges of assize and judges of the Central Criminal Court in England. [O.Fr. *gaole* (Fr. *geôle*) — L.L. *gabiola,* a cage — L. *cavea,* a cage — *cavus,* hollow.]

Jain *jīn, jān,* **Jaina** *jī'na, ns.* an adherent of an Indian religion allied to Brahmanism and Buddhism. — Also *adjs.* — *n.* **Jain'ism.** [Hind. *jina,* a deified saint.]

jak *jak, n.* Same as **jack³.**

jake¹ *jāk,* (*U.S.*) *n.* a country lout: a yokel. [Perh. from the name *Jacob.*]

jake² *jāk,* (*coll.,* orig. *U.S.,* now also *Austr.* in sense of 'fine') *adj.* honest: correct: fine, OK, first-rate.

jakes *jāks,* (*Shak.*) *n.* a privy. [Origin unknown.]

jalap *jal'ap, n.* the purgative root of an Ipomoea or *Exogonium,* first brought from *Jalapa* or Xalapa, in Mexico. — *adj.* **jalap'ic.** — *n.* **jal'apin** a glucoside resin, one of the purgative principles of jalap. — **false jalap** marvel of Peru, formerly used as a substitute.

jalop(p)y *jə-lop'i, n.* an old motor-car or aeroplane. [Origin obscure.]

jalouse *jə-lōōz',* (*Scot.*) *v.t.* to suspect. — Also **jealouse,** same root as **jealous.**

jalousie *zhal-ōō-zē',* or *zhal', n.* an outside shutter with slats. — *adj.* **jal'ousied.** [Fr., — *jalousie,* jealousy.]

jam¹ *jam, n.* a conserve of fruit boiled with sugar: good luck (*coll.*). — *v.t.* to spread with jam: to make into jam. — *adj.* **jamm'y** smeared or sticky with jam: like jam: lucky, excellent (*coll.*). — **jam'pot** a jar for jam (also **jam'jar**): a high collar, esp. a clergyman's. — **jam tomorrow** better things promised for the future that remain in the future; **want jam on it** (*coll.*) to expect or want too much. [Perh. from next.]

jam² *jam, v.t.* to press or squeeze tight: to crowd full: to block by crowding: to bring to a standstill by crowding or interlocking: to interfere with by emitting signals of similar wavelength (*radio*). — *v.i.* to become stuck, wedged, etc.: to become unworkable: to press or push (as into a confined space): in jazz, to play enthusiastically, interpolating and improvising freely: — *pr.p.* **jamm'ing;** *pa.t.* and *pa.p.* **jammed.** — *n.* a crush, squeeze: a block or stoppage due to crowding or squeezing together: a jammed mass (as of logs in a river): a jamming of radio messages: a difficult or embarrassing situation (*coll.*). — *n.* **jamm'er** one who, ot that which, jams something. — **jam'-packed** completely full, crowded, etc.; **jam session** a gathering of jazz musicians (orig. an informal one) at which jazz as described at *v.i.* is played. [Poss. onomatopoeic; conn. with **champ¹.**]

jamadar *jum'ä-där.* Same as **jemadar.**

jamahiriya(h) *ja-mä'hē-rē'ya, n.* people's state, state of proletariat. [Ar., connected with *jumhūrīya,* republic — *jumhūr,* people]

Jamaica *jə-mā'kə,* **Jamaican** *-kən, adjs.* of the island of Jamaica. — *n.* **Jamai'can** a native or inhabitant of Jamaica. — **Jamaica bark** Caribbee bark; **Jamaica cedar** bastard Barbados cedar; **Jamaica ebony** cocuswood; **Jamaica pepper** allspice; **Jamaica plum** hogplum; **Jamaica rum** slowly-fermented, full-bodied pungent rum.

jamb *jam, n.* the sidepiece or post of a door, fireplace, etc.: leg-armour (in this sense also **jambe** *jam*). — *ns.* **jambeau** (*jam'bō; obs.*) leg-armour: legging: — *pl.* **jam'beaux, jam'beux** (*Spens.* **giambeux**); **jam'ber, jam'bier** (*obs.*) leg-armour. [Fr. *jambe,* leg; cf. **gamb.**]

jambee *jam-bē', n.* an 18th-century light cane. [*Jambi* in Sumatra.]

jamber, jambier. See **jamb.**

jambiya(h) *jam-bē'yä, n.* a type of Middle Eastern curved, double-edged dagger. [Ar.]

jambo *jam'bō, interj.* an E. African salutation: — *pl.* **jam'bos.** [From Swahili.]

jambok. Same as **sjambok.**

jambolan(a). See **jambu.**

jambone *jam'bōn, n.* a lone hand in euchre, played only by agreement, in which the player lays his cards on the table and must lead one chosen by his opponent, scoring 8 points if he takes all the tricks. [Origin unknown.]

jambool. See **jambu.**

jamboree *jam-bə-rē', n.* in euchre, a lone hand of the 5 highest cards, by agreement scoring 16 points for the holder: a boisterous frolic, a spree (*slang*): a great Scout rally. [Origin uncertain.]

jambu *jum', jam'bōō, n.* the rose-apple tree or other *Eugenia.* — Also **jambul, jambool** (*jum-bōōl'*), **jam'-bolan, jambolana** (*-bō-lä'nə*). [Sans. *jambu, jambū, jambula.*]

jamdani *jäm'dä-nē, n.* a variety of Dacca muslin woven in design of flowers. [Pers. *jāmdānī.*]

james. Same as **jemmy¹.**

Jamesian *jāmz'ī-ən, adj.* relating to William *James* (1842–1910), American psychologist, or other of the name of James.

Jamesonite *jim'i-sən-īt,* or *jām'sən-īt, n.* a mineral compound of lead, antimony, and sulphur. [Robert *Jameson* (1772–1854), Scottish mineralogist.]

Jamestown-weed. See **jimson-weed.**

jammy. See **jam¹.**

jampan *jam'pan, n.* an Indian sedan-chair. — *n.* **jampanee', jampani** (*-ē'*) its bearer. [Beng. *jhāmpān.*]

jane¹ *jān, n.* a small silver Genoese coin (*Spens.*): jean

(cloth). [L.L. *Janua*, L. *Genua*, Genoa.]
jane² *jān*, (*slang*) *n.* a woman. [The name, *Jane*.]
Janeite *jān'īt*, *n.* a devotee of *Jane* Austen.
jangle *jang'gl*, *v.t.* and *v.i.* to sound with unpleasant tone, as bells. — *v.t.* to upset, irritate. — *v.i.* to wrangle or quarrel. — *n.* dissonant clanging: contention. — *ns.* **jang'ler; jang'ling.** — *adj.* **jang'ly.** [O.Fr. *jangler*.]
Janian, Janiform. See **Janus.**
janissary. See **janizary.**
janitor *jan'i-tər*, *n.* a doorkeeper: attendant or caretaker: — *fem.* **jan'itrix, jan'itress.** — *adj.* **janitorial** (-*tō'*, -*tö'*). — *n.* **jan'itorship.** [L. *jānitor* — *jānua*, a door.]
janizar *jan'i-zər-i*, *n.* a soldier of the old Turkish footguards (*c.* 1330–1826), formed originally of renegade prisoners and of a tribute of Christian children: a follower, supporter. — Also **jan'issary** (-*zər-i*, -*sər-i*), **jan'izar.** — *adj.* **janizā'rian.** — **janizary music** military music with much percussion. [Fr. *Janissaire*, supposed to be — Turk. *yeni*, new, *çeri*, soldiery.]
janker *jang'kər*, (*Scot.*) *n.* a long pole on wheels for transporting large logs suspended from it. [Origin unknown.]
jankers *jang'kərz*, (*mil. slang*) *n.pl.* defaulters. — *n.sing.* punishment: detention. [Ety. dub.]
jann *jän*, *n.pl.* the least powerful order of jinn: (*sing.*) a jinni. [Ar. *jānn*.]
jannock¹ *jan'ək*, (*dial.*) *adj.* straightforward. [Origin obscure.]
jannock² *jan'ək*, (*N. of England*) *n.* oaten bread: a cake thereof. [Origin obscure.[
Jansenism *jan'sən-izm*, *n.* a system of evangelical doctrine deduced from Augustine by Cornelius *Jansen* (1585–1638), Roman Catholic Bishop of Ypres, essentially a reaction against the ordinary Catholic dogma of the freedom of the will, maintaining that human nature is corrupt, and that Christ died only for the elect, all others being irretrievably condemned to hell. — *n.* **Jan'senist** a believer in Jansenism. — Also *adj.*
jansky *jan'ski n.* in astronomy, the unit of strength of radio-wave emission, 10^{-26} W^{-2}Hz^{-1}. [Named after Karl G. *Jansky*, the American radio engineer who first discovered radio interference coming from the stars.]
jantee. See **jaunty¹.**
janty. See **jaunty¹, jonty.**
January *jan'ū-ər-i*, *n.* the first month of the year, dedicated by the Romans to Janus. [L. *Jānuārius*.]
Janus *jā'nəs*, *n.* the ancient Italian two-faced god of doors, whose temple in Rome was closed in time of peace. — *adjs.* **Jān'iform** (wrongly **Jān'uform**) two-faced; **Jān'ian, Jān'us-faced** two-faced. [L. *Jānus*.]
Jap *jap*, (*derog.*) *n.* and *adj.* Japanese. — **Jap'-silk** a thin kind of silk.
jap. Same as **jaup.**
japan *jə-pan'*, *adj.* of Japan: japanned. — *n.* Japanese ware or work: a glossy black varnish of lacquer: japanned work. — *v.t.* to varnish with japan, esp. in imitation of Japanese work: to make black: to ordain (a clergyman) (*old slang*). — *pr.p.* **japann'ing;** *pa.t.* and *pa.p.* **japanned'.** — *adj.* **Japanese** (*jap-ə-nēz'*, or *jap'*) of Japan, of its people, or of its language. — *n.* a native or citizen of Japan: the language of Japan. — *pl.* **Japanese** (formerly **Japaneses**). — *ns.* **Japanēs'ery** Japanese decoration: a Japanese ornament: Japanese bric-à-brac; **Japanesque** (-*esk'*) a design in Japanese style. — *adjs.* **Japanesque', Japanēs'y** savouring of the Japanese. — *n.* **japann'er.** — **Japan Current** Kuroshio; **japan'-earth** or terra-japonica, gambier; **Japanese cedar** a very tall Japanese conifer (*Cryptomeria japonica*) often dwarfed by Japanese gardeners; **Japanese medlar** the loquat; **Japanese paper** a fine soft paper made from paper-mulberry bark; **Japan lacquer** Japan varnish; **Japan laurel** a shrub (*Aucuba japonica*) of the dogwood family, with spotted yellow leaves; **japanned leather** patent leather (see **patent**); **Japan varnish** a varnish got from a species of sumach (*Rhus vernicifera*), extended to various other similar varnishes;

Japan wax, tallow a fat got from the berries of species of sumach.
jape *jāp*, *v.i.* to jest, joke. — *v.t.* to mock: to seduce (*obs.*). — *n.* a jest, joke, trick. [O.Fr. *japer*, to yelp.]
Japhetic *jə-fet'ik*, (*obs.*) *adj.* of European race: Indo-European in language. [From supposed descent from *Japhet*.]
Japonic *jə-pon'ik*, *adj.* Japanese. — *n.* **japon'ica** the Japanese quince (*Chaenomeles japonica*), camellia, or other Japanese plant. [New L. *japonicus*, fem. *japonica*, Japanese.]
jar¹ *jär*, *v.i.* to make a harsh discordant sound or unpleasant vibration: to give an unpleasant shock: to grate (on): to be discordant or distasteful: to tick (*Shak.*): to clash: to quarrel: to be inconsistent. — *v.t.* to shake, as by a blow: to cause to vibrate unpleasantly: to grate on: to make dissonant. — *pr.p.* **jarr'ing;** *pa.t.* and *pa.p.* **jarred.** — *n.* a harsh sudden vibration: a dissonance: a grating sound or feeling: a tick of a clock (*Shak.*): clash of interests or opinions: dispeace, conflict. — *n.* **jarr'ing** the act of jarring: severe reproof. — Also *adj.* — *adv.* **jarr'ingly.** [Imit.]
jar² *jär*, *n.* a wide-mouthed wide vessel: as much as a jar will hold: a Leyden jar (q.v.): a drink (of an alcoholic beverage) (*coll.*). — *v.t.* to put in jars. — *n.* **jar'ful:** — *pl.* **jar'fuls.** [Fr. *jarre* or Sp. *jarra* — Ar. *jarrah*.]
jar³ *jär*, *n.* a turn, used only in the phrase *on the jar*, ajar. [Earlier *char* — O.E. *cerr*; cf. **char³, ajar.**]
jararaca or **jararaka** *jär-ər-äk'ə*, *n.* a venomous South American snake of the family *Crotalidae*. [Tupí — Guaraní.]
jardinière *zhär'dē-nyer'*, *n.* a vessel for the display of flowers, growing or cut: a dish including a mixture of diced or sliced cooked vegetables: a lappet forming part of an old head-dress. [Fr., gardener (fem.).]
jargon¹ *jär'gən*, *n.* chatter, twittering: confused talk: slang: artificial or barbarous language: the terminology of a profession, art, group, etc. — *v.i.* to twitter, chatter: to speak jargon. — *ns.* **jargoneer', jar'gonist** one who uses jargon; **jargonīsā'tion, -z-** — *v.t.* **jargonise, -ize** to express in jargon. — *v.i.* to speak jargon. [Fr. *jargon*.]
jargon². See **jargoon.**
jargonelle. See next word.
jargoon *jär'gōōn'*, **jargon** *jär'gən*, *ns.* a brilliant colourless or pale zircon. — *n.* **jargonelle'** an early pear (orig. a gritty kind). [Fr. *jargon*; prob. conn. with **zircon**.]
jark *järk*, (*cant*) *n.* a seal on a document (usu. counterfeit document): a pass, safe-conduct. — **jark'man** a swindling beggar, a begging-letter writer.
jarl *yärl*, (*hist.*) *n.* a noble, chief, earl. [O.N.; conn. with **earl**.]
jarool. See **jarul.**
jarosite *jar'ō-sīt*, *n.* a hydrous sulphate of iron and potassium forming hexagonal crystals. [From Barranco *Jaroso*, an area in Spain.]
jarrah *jar'ə*, *n.* a Western Australian timber tree, *Eucalyptus marginata*. [Aboriginal.]
jarta, yarta *yär'tə*, (*Shetland*) *n.* lit. heart, used as an endearment. — Also *adj.* — Also (*Scott*) **yar'to.** [O.N. *hjarta*, heart.]
jarul, jarool *jə-rōōl'*, *n.* the Indian bloodwood (*Lagerstroemia*), a lythraceous tree. [Beng. *jarūl*.]
jarvey, jarvie *jär'vi*, (*slang*) *n.* a hackney-coach driver: a jaunting-car driver. [Earlier *Jarvis*, poss. from St *Gervase*, whose emblem is a whip.]
jasey, jasy, jazy *jā'zi*, *n.* a wig, orig. of worsted. [**jersey**.]
Jasher, Jashar *jäsh'ər*, *n.* one of the lost books of the ancient Hebrews, quoted twice (Josh. x. 13; 2 Sam. i. 18), most probably a collection of heroic ballads.
jasmine *jas'min* or *jaz'*, **jessamine** *jes'ə-min*, *ns.* a genus (*Jasminum*) of oleaceous shrubs, many with very fragrant flowers. — **red jasmine** a tropical American shrub akin to periwinkle — frangipani (*Plumeria*). [Fr. *jasmin*, *jasemin* — Ar. *yāsmīn*, *yāsamīn* — Pers. *yāsmīn*.]
jasp *jasp* (*Spens.*), **jasper** *jas'pər*, *ns.* a precious stone

(*obs.*): an opaque quartz containing clay or iron compounds, used in jewellery or ornamentation and red, yellow, brown or green in colour: a fine hard porcelain (also **jas′perware**). — *adj.* of jasper. — *adjs.* **jaspe, jaspé** (*jasp, jas′pā*) mottled, variegated, or veined. — *n.* cotton or rayon cloth with a shaded effect used for bedspreads, curtains, etc. — *v.t.* **jasp′erise, -ize** to turn into jasper. — *adjs.* **jasp′erous, jasp′ery**. — *n.* **jas′pis** jasper. — *adjs.* **jaspid′ean, jaspid′eous**. [O.Fr. *jaspe, jaspre* — L. *iaspis, -idis*; and directly from Gr. *iaspis, -idos*, of Eastern origin.]

jasy. See **jasey**.

Jat *jät, n.* one of a tribe situated in north-west India and Pakistan. — Also *adj.* [Hindi *jāt*.]

jataka *jä′ta-ka, n.* a nativity, the birth-story of Buddha. [Sans. *jātaka* — *jāta*, born.]

jato *jä′tō*, (*aero.*) *n.* a jet-assisted take-off, using a **jato unit** consisting of one or more rocket motors, usu. jettisoned after use: — *pl.* **jā′tos**.

jaunce, jaunse, *jöns, jäns, v.i.* (*Shak.*) to prance: to cause a horse to prance. — *n.* prancing (*Shak.*): a wearisome journey (*dial.*). [Perh. from a doubtful O.Fr. *jancer*, to cause to prance.]

jaundice *jön′dis* (rarely *jän′dis*), *n.* a disease in which there is yellowing of the eyes, skin, etc., by excess of bile pigment, the patient in rare cases seeing objects as yellow: a disease showing this condition: state of taking an unfavourable, prejudiced view. — *v.t.* to affect with jaundice, in any sense. — *adj.* **jaun′diced** affected with jaundice: feeling, or showing, prejudice, distaste, or jealousy. [Fr. *jaunisse* — *jaune*, yellow — L. *galbīnus*, yellowish, *galbus*, yellow.]

jaunse. See **jaunce**.

jaunt *jönt* (also *jänt*) *v.i.* to go from place to place, formerly with fatigue, now chiefly for pleasure: to make an excursion. — *n.* an excursion: a ramble. — *adj.* **jaunt′ing** strolling: making an excursion. — **jaunt′ing-car** a low-set, two-wheeled, open vehicle used in Ireland, with side-seats usu. back to back. [Origin obscure; cf. **jaunce**.]

jauntie. See **jonty**.

jaunty[1], **janty** *jön′ti* (also *jän′ti*), *adj.* gentlemanly (formerly **jantee, jauntee**) (*obs.*): having an airy or sprightly manner approaching swagger. — *adv.* **jaunt′ily**. — *n.* **jaunt′iness**. [Fr. *gentil*.]

jaunty[2]. See **jonty**.

jaup *jöp*, or *jäp*, **jap** *jäp*, (*Scot.*) *vs.t.* and *vs.i.* to spatter: to splash. — *ns.* a splash: a spattering. [Origin unknown.]

Java *jä′va*, *adj.* of the island of Java. — *adjs.* and *ns.* **Ja′van, Javanese′**. — **Java man** formerly Pithecanthropus erectus, now generally designated Homo erectus; **Java plum** the jambolana (*Eugenia jambolana*); **Java sparrow** a kind of weaver-bird.

javel *jav′al*, (*Spens.*) *n.* a worthless fellow. [Origin unknown.]

Javel(le) water *zha-* or *zha-vel′ wö′tar*, **eau de** (*ō da*) **Javel(le)**, a solution of potassium chloride and hypochlorite used for bleaching, disinfecting, etc. [After *Javel*, former town, now part of the city of Paris.]

javelin *jav′(a)-lin, n.* a throwing-spear. — **jav′elin-man** an armed member of a sheriff's retinue or a judge's escort at assizes: a soldier armed with a javelin. [Fr. *javeline*; prob. Celt.]

jaw[1] *jö, n.* a mouth-structure for biting or chewing: one of the bones of a jaw: one of a pair of parts for gripping, crushing, cutting, grinding, etc.: (in *pl.*) a narrow entrance: talkativeness, scolding (*slang*). — *v.t.* (*slang*) to scold. — *v.i.* to talk, esp. in excess. — *adj.* **jawed** having jaws. — *n.* **jaw′ing** (*slang*) talk, esp. unrestrained, abusive, or reproving. — **jaw′bone** the bone of the jaw. — *v.t.* and *v.i.* (*U.S. slang*) to engage in jawboning, to lecture or scold. — **jaw′boning** (*U.S. slang*) governmental urging of industry to restrict wage increases, accept restraints, etc.; **jaw′-break′er** a heavy-duty rock-breaking machine with hinged jaws (also

jaw′-crush′er): a word hard to pronounce (*slang*; also **jaw′-twist′er**); **jaw′fall** a falling of the jaw (*arch.*): depression of spirits (*rare*). — *adj.* **jaw′-fallen** (*rare*) depressed in spirits: dejected. — **jaw′-foot** a foot-jaw, maxilliped; **jaw lever** an instrument for opening the mouth of a horse or cow to admit medicine; **jaw′-tooth** a molar. — **hold one's jaw** to cease from talking or scolding. [Perh. **chaw**[1], modified by Fr. *joue*, cheek.]

jaw[2] *jö*, (*Scot.*) *n.* a dash or surge of liquid: a portion of liquid so dashed. — *v.t.* and *v.i.* to pour suddenly in a body. — **jaw′box** a sink; **jaw′hole** a cesspool: an entrance to a sewer. [Origin unknown.]

jawan *ja-wän′, n.* an Indian common soldier. [Urdu *javān*.]

jawari. See **jowar**.

jawbation *jö-bā′shan, n.* for **jobation**. [Influenced by **jaw**[1]; see **Job**.]

ja wohl *ya vōl′*, (Ger.) yes indeed.

jay[1] *jā, n.* a bird of the crow family with gay plumage: a wanton woman (*arch. slang*): an indifferent actor (*arch. slang*): a stupid, awkward or easily duped fellow (*U.S. slang*). — *adj.* (*U.S. slang*) stupid, unsophisticated. — *v.i.* **jay′walk**. — **jay′walker** a careless pedestrian whom motorists are expected to avoid running down; **jay′walking**. [O.Fr. *jay*.]

jay[2] *jā, n.* tenth letter of the alphabet (J, j): an object or mark of that shape.

jazerant *jaz′a-rant*. See **jesserant**.

jazy. Same as **jasey**.

jazz *jaz, n.* any of various styles of music with a strong rhythm, syncopation, improvisation, etc., originating in American Negro folk music: an art form and also various types of popular dance music derived from it: garish colouring, lively manner, vivid quality: insincere or lying talk (*slang*): talk, in general (*slang*). — Also *adj.* — *v.t.* to impart a jazz character to (often with *up*). — *adv.* **jazz′ily**. — *n.* **jazz′iness**. — *adj.* **jazz′y**. **jazz age** the decade following World War I, esp. in America; **jazz′man** a jazz musician; **jazz′-rock′** music which is a blend of jazz and rock music. [Origin uncertain.]

jealous *jel′as, adj.* suspicious of, or incensed at, rivalry: envious: solicitous: anxiously heedful: mistrustfully vigilant: brooking no unfaithfulness. — *v.t.* **jealouse** (*ja-lōōz′*; *obs.* except *Scot.*; see **jalouse**). — *adv.* **jeal′ously**. — *ns.* **jeal′ousy, jeal′oushood** (*Shak.*), **jeal′ousness**. [O.Fr. *jalous* — L. *zēlus* — Gr. *zēlos*, emulation.]

Jeames *jēmz, n.* a flunkey. [From Thackeray's *Jeames* (James) de la Pluche.]

jean *jēn*, (esp. formerly) *jān, n.* a twilled-cotton cloth (also in *pl.*): (in *pl.*) trousers or overalls of jean: (in *pl.*) close-fitting, sometimes three-quarter length, casual trousers of jean or similar material. — *n.* **jeanette** (*ja-net′*) a light or coarse jean. — **satin jean** a smooth, glossy fustian. [O.Fr. *Janne* — L. *Genua*, Genoa.]

jeat *jet* (*obs.*). Same as **jet**[1,2].

jebel, djebel *jeb′al, n.* in Arab countries, a hill or a mountain. [Ar., mountain.]

Jebusite *jeb′ū-zīt, n.* one of a Canaanitish people, predecessors of Israelites at Jerusalem: 17th-century nickname for Roman Catholic. — *adj.* **Jebusitic** (*-zit′ik*).

Jeddart *jed′art*, **Jethart** *jedh′art, ns.* Jedburgh, in S.E. Scotland. — **Jethart justice** hanging first and trying afterwards; **Jethart staff** a sort of battle-axe with a long head. [O.E. *Gedwearde*.]

jee[1]. Same as **gee**[1,3].

jee[2] *jē*, (*Scot.*) *v.i.* to stir: to budge. — *v.t.* to disturb: to set on one side or ajar. — *n.* a displacement to the side: a condition of being ajar. — **jee** or **jow one's ginger** to bestir onself, show perturbation.

jeel *jēl*, (*Scot.*) *v.i.* to congeal: to set. — *n.* extreme cold: jelly. — *ns.* **jee′lie, jee′ly** jelly: jam. — *v.i.* to set, to jelly. — **jeely nose** (*coll.*) a bleeding nose.

jeep *jēp, n.* a light military vehicle with great freedom of movement. [From G.P., for *general purpose*; perh. with reminiscence of a comic-strip animal character.]

For other sounds see detailed chart of pronunciation.

jeepers (creepers) jē'pərz (krē'pərz), (*U.S. slang*) *interj.* expressing surprise (for *Jesus Christ.*).

jeepney jēp'ni, *n.* in the Philippines, a jitney constructed from a jeep. [*jeep* and jit*ney*.]

jeer jēr, *v.t.* to make sport of: to treat with derision. — *v.i.* (*usu.* with *at*) to scoff: to deride: to make a mock. — *n.* a railing remark: biting jest: mockery. — *n.* **jeer'er.** — *n.* and *adj.* **jeer'ing.** — *adv.* **jeer'ingly.** [Origin unknown.]

jeff¹ jef, *v.i.* to gamble with printer's quadrats thrown like dice.

jeff² jef, *n.* a rope, in circus slang.

Jeffersonian jef-ər-sōn'i-ən, *adj.* pertaining to Thomas *Jefferson* (1743–1826), U.S. President 1801–09: of the American Democratic party. — *n.* a Democrat.

jehad. See **jihad.**

Jehovah ji-hō'və, *n.* Yahweh, the Hebrew God, a name used by Christians. — *n.* **Jehō'vist** one who held that the vowel-points annexed to the word *Jehovah* in the Hebrew are the proper vowels of the word (*obs.*): a writer of passages in the Pentateuch in which the name applied to God is Yahweh, a Yahwist. — *adj.* **Jehovist'-ic.** — **Jehovah's Witnesses** a Christian fundamentalist sect which rejects all other religions and denominations, believes in the imminent end of the world, and refuses to accept civil authority where it clashes with its own principles — originally called the International Bible Students' Association (see **Russellite**). [Heb.; for *Yĕhōwāh*, i.e. *Yahweh* with the vowels of *Adōnāi*.]

Jehu jē'hū, (*coll.*) *n.* a driver, esp. a furious whip. [A reference to 2 Kings ix. 20.]

jeistiecor jēs'ti-kōr, -kōr, (*obs.*; *Scot.*) *n.* a close-fitting garment. [Fr. *juste au corps*, close-fitting to the body.]

jejune ji-jōōn', *adj.* empty: spiritless, meagre, arid: showing lack of information or experience: naïve, immature, callow. — *adv.* **jejune'ly.** — *ns.* **jejune'ness, jeju'nity; jeju'num** the part of the small intestine between the duodenum and the ileum. [L. *jejūnus*, hungry.]

Jekyll and Hyde jēk'il (or jek'il) ənd hīd, the good side and the bad side of a human being — from R.L. Stevenson, *The Strange Case of Dr Jekyll and Mr Hyde* (1886).

jelab. See **djellaba.**

jell. See **jelly¹.**

jellaba. See **djellaba.**

jelly¹ jel'i, *n.* anything gelatinous: the juice of fruit boiled with sugar: a conserve of fruit, jam (*U.S.* and formerly *Scot.*): a gelatinous preparation for the table (in U.S. **jell'o,** formerly a trademark: — *pl.* **jell'os**): a glass for jelly: a jellyfish. — *v.i.* to set as a jelly: to congeal. — *v.t.* to make into a jelly. — *v.i.* and *v.t.* **jell** to jelly: to take distinct shape (*coll.*). — *adjs.* **jell'ied** in a state of jelly: enclosed in jelly; **jell'iform.** — *v.t.* **jell'ify** to make into a jelly. — *v.i.* to become gelatinous. — **jelly baby** a kind of gelatinous sweet in the shape of a baby; **jelly bag** a bag through which fruit juice is strained for jelly; **jell'ybean** a kind of sweet in the shape of a bean with a sugar coating and jelly filling; **jell'yfish** a marine coelenterate with jelly-like body: a person who lacks firmness of purpose; **jell'ygraph** a copying appliance that uses a plate of jelly. — *v.t.* to copy by this means. — **jell'y-pan** (*Scot.*) a preserving-pan. [Fr. *gelée,* from *geler* — L. *gelāre,* to freeze; cf. **gel.**]

jelly² jel'i, *n.* a coll. shortening of **gelignite.**

jelutong jel'ŏŏ-tong, *n.* pontianac, a substitute for gutta-percha: the Bornean apocynaceous tree (*Dyera costulata*) yielding it. [Malay.]

jemadar jem'ə-där, *n.* an Indian army officer below a subahdar: an officer of police, customs, etc. — Also **jamadar** (*jum'*), **jem'idar.** [Urdu *jama'dār*.]

jemima ji-mī'mə, (*coll.*) *n.* an elastic-sided boot. [An appropriate woman's name.]

jemmy¹ jem'i, *n.* a burglar's short crowbar: a baked sheep's head (*slang*): an overcoat (*dial.*). [A form of the name *James*.]

jemmy² jem'i, (*dial.*) *adj.* neat, smart, handy. — Also

gemm'y. — *n.* **jemm'iness** neatness. [Cf. **jimp.**]

Jena glass yā'nə gläs, a special type of glass containing borates and free silica, resistant to chemical attack. [From *Jena,* Germany.]

je ne sais quoi zhə nə se kwa, an indefinable something. [Fr., I don't know what.]

Jenkins jengk'inz, (*coll.*) *n.* a society reporter: a toady.

jennet jen'it, *n.* a small Spanish horse. — Also **genn'et, gen'et.** [O.Fr. *genet* — Sp. *jinete,* a light horseman, perh. of Arab origin.]

jenneting jen'it-ing, *n.* a kind of early apple. [Prob. St John's apple — Fr. *Jeannet,* dim. of *Jean,* John; not from *June-eating.*]

Jenny jen'i, *n.* generic name for a country lass (*Scot.*): a womanish man (*Scot.*): (the following meanings usu. without *cap.*) a wren or owl regarded as female: a she-ass (also **jenny donkey**): a travelling crane: a spinning-jenny: an in-off into a middle pocket from near the cushion (*billiards*). — **Jenny-long'-legs** (*Scot.*), **Jenn'y-spinner** (*dial.*) a crane-fly; **Jenny-wren'** a wren. [From the name *Jenny*.]

jeofail jef'āl, (*obs.*) *n.* an error in pleadings, or the acknowledgment of a mistake. [A.Fr. *jeo fail,* I mistake.]

jeopardy jep'ər-di, *n.* hazard, danger: the danger of trial and punishment faced by the accused on a criminal charge (*U.S. law*). — *vs.t.* **jeop'ard** (*rare* and *U.S. arch.*), **jeop'ardise, -ize, jeop'ardy** (*rare*) to put in jeopardy. — *n.* **jeop'arder.** — *adj.* **jeop'ardous** (*obs.*) dangerous: venturesome. — *adv.* **jeop'ardously.** [Fr. *jeu parti,* a divided or even game — L.L. *jocus partītus* — L. *jocus,* a game, *partītus,* divided — *partīrī,* to divide.]

jequirity jə-kwər'i -ti, *n.* Indian liquorice (see **liquorice**): (also **jequirity bean**) its seed, otherwise crab's-eye, prayer-bead. [Origin obscure.]

jerbil. See **gerbil.**

jerboa jûr-bō'ə, *n.* a desert rodent (family *Dipodidae*) that jumps like a kangaroo. [Ar. *yarbū'.*]

jereed. See **jerid.**

jeremiad jer-i-mī'ad, *n.* a lamentation: a tale of grief: a doleful story. — *n.* **Jeremī'ah** a person who continually prophesies doom. [From *Jeremiah,* reputed author of the *Book of Lamentations.*]

jerfalcon. Same as **gerfalcon.**

Jericho jer'i-kō, *n.* a remote place, to which one is humorously consigned. [Supposed to refer to 2 Sam. x. 4, 5.]

jerid, jereed jer-ēd', *n.* a blunt Oriental javelin: a tournament in which it is used. [Ar. *jarīd.*]

jerk¹ jûrk, *n.* a stroke (*obs.*): a short movement begun and ended suddenly: a twitch: an involuntary spasmodic contraction of a muscle: a movement in physical exercises: a short burst of bird-song (*obs.*): a useless person (*slang*): in weight-lifting, a movement lifting the barbell from shoulder height to a position on outstretched arms above the head: (also **clean and jerk**) a weight-lifting competition involving such a lift (cf. **clean**). — *v.t.* to thrash (*obs.*): to throw or move with a jerk. — *v.i.* to move with a jerk: to utter abruptly. — *ns.* **jerk'er** one who jerks: a hornyhead (fish); **jerk'iness.** — *adj.* **jerk'y** moving or coming by jerks or starts, spasmodic. — **jerk off** (*vulg.*) to masturbate. [An imit. word, akin to **yerk.**]

jerk², etc. See **jerque,** etc.

jerk³ jûrk, *v.t.* to make into charqui. — *n.* charqui (also **jerked'-meat, jerk'y**). [**charqui.**]

jerkin jûr'kin, *n.* a jacket, a short coat or close waistcoat. — *n.* **jirkinet'** (*Scot.*) a woman's bodice. [Origin unknown.]

jerkinhead jûr'kin-hed, (*archit.*) *n.* the combination of a truncated gable with a lipped roof. [Perh. from **jerk¹.**]

jeroboam jer-ō-bō'əm, *n.* a very large bowl: a large bottle, esp. one for wine holding the equivalent of 6 normal bottles, or for champagne, the equivalent of 4 normal bottles. [Allusion to 1 Kings xi. 28.]

jerque, jerk *jûrk, v.t.* to search (as a vessel) for concealed or smuggled goods: to examine (as a ship's papers). — *ns.* **jerqu′er, jerk′er; jerqu′ing, jerk′ing.** [Poss. It. *cercare,* to search.]

jerrican, jerrycan *jer′i-kan, n.* a kind of petrol-can, orig. German.

Jerry, Gerry *jer′i,* (*war slang*) *n.* a German.

jerry[1] *jer′i* (*slang*) *n.* a chamber-pot. [**jeroboam.**]

jerry[2] *jer′i, n.* (*coll.*) a jerry-builder. — *adj.* hastily made of bad materials. — **jerr′y-builder** one who builds flimsy houses cheaply and hastily. — **jerr′y-building.** — *adj.* **jerr′y-built.** — **jerr′y-come-tum′ble** (*dial.*) a tumbler, circus performer; **jerr′y-shop** a low dram-shop. [Prob. the personal name.]

jerrymander. A mistaken form of **gerrymander.**

jersey *jûr′zi, n.* the finest part of wool: combed wool: a knitted woollen, etc. upper garment: a fine knitted fabric in cotton, nylon, etc.: (with *cap.*) a cow of Jersey breed. — *n.* **Jer′sian** a hybrid obtained by mating a Jersey bull and a Friesian cow. [From the island of *Jersey.*]

Jerusalem artichoke *jər-ōōs′ə-ləm är′ti-chōk,* see **artichoke; Jerusalem cross** a cross potent; **Jerusalem letters** tattooed letters on one who has made a pilgrimage to Jerusalem; **Jerusalem pony** an ass; **Jerusalem sage** a perennial plant, *Phlomis fruticosa,* found in south Europe, with dense yellow flowers.

jess *jes, n.* a short strap round the leg of a hawk. — *adj.* **jessed** having jesses on. [O.Fr. *ges* — L. *jactus,* a cast — *jacĕre,* to throw.]

jessamine. See **jasmine.**

jessamy *jes′ə-mi,* (*obs.*) *n.* jasmine: a dandy.

jessant *jes′ənt,* (*her.*) *adj.* overlying: also app. for **issuant.** [App. O.Fr. *gesant,* pr.p. of *gesir* — L. *jacēre,* to lie.]

Jesse *jes′i, n.* a genealogical tree of Christ's descent from *Jesse:* a large branched church candlestick. — **Jesse window** one showing Christ's genealogy in stained glass or carved on the mullions.

jesserant *jes′ə-rənt,* **jazerant** *jaz′,* (*hist.*) *ns.* splint armour. [O.Fr. *jaseran*(*t*), *jazeran* — Sp. *jacerina.*]

Jessie *jes′i,* (*Scot.*) *n.* (also without *cap.*) an effeminate man.

jest *jest, n.* something ludicrous: object of laughter: joke: fun: something uttered in sport. — *v.i.* to make a jest: to joke. — *v.t.* to jeer at, ridicule: to utter as a jest. — *ns.* **jestee′** (*Sterne*) the object of a jest; **jest′er** one who jests: a reciter of romances (*arch.*): a buffoon: a court-fool. — *adj.* **jest′ful** given to jesting. — *n.* and *adj.* **jest′ing.** — *adv.* **jest′ingly.** — **jest′book** a collection of funny stories; **jest′ing-stock** (*obs.*) a butt for jests. [Orig. a deed, a story, M.E. *geste* — O.Fr. *geste* — L. *gesta,* things done, doings — *gerĕre,* to do.]

Jesuit *jez′ū-it, n.* a member of the famous religious order, the Society of *Jesus,* founded in 1534 by Ignatius Loyola: (*opprobriously*) a crafty person, an intriguer, a prevaricator. — *adjs.* **Jesuit′ic, -al.** — *adv.* **Jesuit′ically.** — *ns.* **Jes′uitism, Jes′uitry** the principles and practices of or ascribed to the Jesuits. — **Jesuits′ bark** cinchona (brought to Rome by Jesuit missionaries); **Jesuits′ drops** friar's balsam.

Jesus *jē′zəs, n.* the founder of Christianity — also (in hymns, etc., esp. in the vocative) **Jesu** (*jē′zū*). [Gr. *Iēsous* (voc. and oblique cases *Iēsou*) — Heb. *Yēshūa′,* contr. of *Yehōshūa′,* Joshua.]

jésus *zhā′zü, n.* a size of paper in France, approximately super-royal. — **grand jésus** imperial size.

jet[1] *jet, n.* a rich black variety of lignite, very hard and compact, taking a high polish, used for ornaments: jet-black. — *adj.* of jet: jet-black. — *n.* **jett′iness.** — *adj.* **jett′y** of the nature of jet, or black as jet. — *adj.* **jet′-black′** black as jet. — Also *n.* [O.Fr. *jaiet* — L. and Gr. *gagātēs* — *Gagas* or *Gangai,* a town and river in Lycia, where it was obtained.]

jet[2] *jet, n.* a narrow spouting stream: a spout, nozzle or pipe emitting a stream or spray of fluid: a strutting movement (*obs.*): a jet-plane. — *v.t.* and *v.i.* to spout. — *v.i.* to jut (*obs.*): to encroach (*Shak.*): to strut (*obs.*):

to travel by jet-plane: — *pr.p.* **jett′ing;** *pa.t.* and *pa.p.* **jett′ed.** — **jet′-drive.** — *adj.* **jet′-driven** driven by the backward emission of a jet of gas, etc. — **jet′foil** a hydrofoil powered by a jet of water; **jet lag** exhaustion, discomfort, etc., resulting from the body's inability to adjust to the rapid changes of time zone necessitated by high-speed long-distance air-travel. — *adj.* **jet′-lagged.** — **jet′liner** an airliner powered by a jet engine; **jet′(-)plane** a jet-driven aeroplane. — *adj.* **jet′-propelled.** — **jet′-propulsion; jet′-setter** a member of the jet set. — *adj.* **jet′-setting** living in the style of the jet set. — **jet′(-)stream** very high winds more than 20 000 feet above the earth: the exhaust of a rocket engine. — **the jet set** moneyed social set able to spend much of their time at fashionable resorts all over the world. [O.Fr. *jetter* — L. *jactāre,* to fling.]

jet d'eau *zhe dō,* (Fr.) jet of water, e.g. in an ornamental fountain.

jeté *zhə-tā,* (*ballet*) *n.* a leap from one foot to the other in which the free leg usu. finishes extended forward, backward, or sideways. [Fr., thrown.]

Jethart. See **Jeddart.**

jeton. See **jetton.**

jetsam *jet′səm, n.* jettison (*obs.*): goods jettisoned from a ship and washed up on shore: according to some, goods from a wreck that remain under water (see **flotsam**). — Also **jet′som** (*arch.*), **jet′son** (*arch.*). — *n.* **jett′ison** the act of throwing goods overboard. — *v.t.* to throw overboard, as goods in time of danger: to abandon, reject (*fig.*). — **flotsam and jetsam** often, unclaimed odds and ends. [A.Fr. *jetteson* — L. *jactātiō, -ōnis,* a casting — *jactāre,* freq. of *jacĕre,* to cast.]

jettatura *jet-ə-tōō′rə, n.* the spell of the evil eye. [It. *iettatura,* a Neapolitan word — L. *ējectāre* — *jactāre,* freq. of *jacĕre,* to throw.]

jettison. See **jetsam.**

jetton, jeton *jet′ən, n.* a piece of stamped metal used as a counter in card-playing, casting accounts, etc. [Fr. *jeton* — *jeter,* to throw — L. *jactāre,* freq. of *jacĕre,* to throw.]

jetty *jet′i, n.* a projection: a pier. [O.Fr. *jettee,* thrown out; see **jet**[2].]

jeu *zhə,* (Fr.) *n.* a game. — **jeu de mots:** — *pl.* **jeux de mots** (*də mō*) a play on words, a pun; **jeu d'esprit:** — *pl.* **jeux d'esprit** (*des-prē*) a witticism; **jeu de paume** (*pōm*) real tennis.

jeune *zhœn,* (Fr.) *adj.* young. — **jeune amour** (*a-mōōr*) young love; **jeune fille** (*fē-y′*) a girl; **jeune premier** (*prə-myā*): — *fem.* **première** (*prə-myer*), (*theat.*) a juvenile lead.

jeunesse dorée *zhœ-nes do-rā,* (Fr.) gilded youth: luxurious, stylish, sophisticated young people.

Jew *jōō, n.* a person of Hebrew descent or religion: an Israelite: (*offensively*) a usurer, miser, etc.: — *fem.* **Jew′ess.** — *v.t.* (*offensively*) to overreach, or to cheat. — *adj.* **Jew′ish** of the Jews or their religion. — *adv.* **Jew′ishly.** — *n.* **Jew′ishness.** — **Jew′-bait′ing** the persecuting of Jews; **jew′fish** a name for several very large American and Australian fishes; **Jew's′-ear** an ear-like fungus (Auricularia) parasitic on elder and other trees; **Jew's eye** formerly, something of very high value (*Shak.* 'worth a Jewe's eye'; from the practice of torturing Jews for money); **Jew's′-frank′incense** benzoin; **Jew's-harp, Jews′-harp′, -trump′** (also without *cap.*) a small lyre-shaped instrument played against the teeth by twitching a metal tongue with the finger; **Jews′ houses, leavings** in Cornwall, remains of prehistoric miners' dwellings, mine refuse, and tin furnaces; **Jew's mallow** a yellow-flowered plant, *Kerria japonica* (fam. Rosaceae): (**Jews′ mallow**) jute, *Corchorus olitorius* (*obs.*); **Jew's′-(myr′tle** butcher's broom; **Jew's′-pitch** asphaltum; **Jew's′-stone** a large fossil sea-urchin spine; **Jews′ thorn** Christ's thorn. — **wandering Jew** see **wander.** [O.Fr. *Jueu* — L. *Jūdaeus* — Gr. *Ioudaios* — Heb. *Yehūdāh,* Judah.]

jewel *jōō′əl, n.* a precious stone: a personal ornament of precious stones, gold, etc.: a hard stone (ruby, etc.) used for pivot bearings in a watch: an imitation of a gemstone: a glass boss: anything or anyone highly valued. — *v.t.* to adorn with jewels: to fit with a jewel: — *pr.p.* **jew′elling;** *pa.t.* and *pa.p.* **jew′elled.** — *ns.* **jew′eller** one who deals in, or makes, jewels; **jewellery** (*jōō′əl-ri*), **jew′elry** jewels in general. — **jew′el-case** a casket for holding jewels; **jew′elfish** an African cichlid, *Hemichromis bimaculatus*, popular in aquaria for its bright colours; **jew′el-house** a room in the Tower of London where the crown-jewels are kept; **jeweller's rouge** finely powdered ferric oxide, used for polishing; **jew′el-weed** any plant of the genus Impatiens. **jewel in the crown** orig. (in *pl.*) any or all of the countries of the British Empire, esp. (in *sing.*) India: the best, most highly prized, most successful, etc. of a number or collection (*fig.*).   [O.Fr. *jouel* (Fr. *joyau*); either a dim. of Fr. *joie*, joy, from L. *gaudium*, joy — *gaudēre*, to rejoice — or derived through L.L. *jocāle*, from L. *jocārī*, to jest.]

Jewry *jōō′ri, n.* Judaea: a district inhabited by *Jews*: the Jewish world, community, or religion.

jezail *jez′īl, -āl′, n.* a heavy Afghan gun.   [Pers. *jazā′il*.]

Jezebel *jez′ə-bəl, n.* a shameless painted woman.   [From Ahab's wife, 2 Kings ix. 30.].

jhala *jä′lə, n.* part of the second movement of a raga. [Sans.]

jiao *jow, n.* a unit of Chinese currency, equal to 10 fen or ¹⁄₁₀ of a yuan.   [Chin.]

jib[1] *jib, n.* a triangular sail borne in front of the foremast in a ship: the boom of a crane or derrick: the underlip (*dial.*): the face: a jibbing horse: an act of jibbing: a standstill. — *v.t.* to cause to gybe. — *v.i.* (*usu.* with *at*) to gybe: (of a horse) to balk or shy: to refuse, show objection, boggle: — *pr.p.* **jibb′ing;** *pa.t.* and *pa.p.* **jibbed.** — *n.* **jibb′er** a jibbing horse. — **jib′-boom′** a boom or extension of the bowsprit, on which the jib is spread; **jib′-crane′** a crane with an inclined arm fixed to the foot of a rotating vertical post, the upper ends connected. — **the cut of one's jib** one's appearance. [Origin obscure: perh. several different words; cf. **gibbet, gybe;** the j sound stands in the way of connecting with Dan. *gibbe,* Du. *gijpen.*]

jib[2] *jib,* (*Scot.*) *v.t.* to milk closely, strip: to fleece. — *n.pl.* **jibb′ings** the last milk drawn from a cow.

jibbah *jib′ə.* See **jubbah.**

jibber[1]. Same as **gibber**[1].

jibber[2]. See **jib**[1].

jib-door *jib′-dōr, -dör, n.* a disguised door, flush with the wall.   [Origin unknown.]

jibe[1]. Same as **gybe.**

jibe[2], **jiber.** See **gibe.**

jibe[3] *jīb* (*chiefly U.S.*) *v.i.* to agree, accord (with).   [Poss. related to **chime**[1].]

jickajog. See **jig-jog.**

jiffy *jif′i,* (*coll.*) *n.* an instant (sometimes shortened to **jiff**): (with *cap.*; ®) the proprietary element in the word **Jiffybag**, a padded envelope in which to post books, etc.   [Origin unknown.]

jig *jig, n.* a jerky movement: a lively dance usu. in 6–8 time: a dance-tune of like kind — a giga or gigue: a mocking ballad (*obs.*): a jingle or piece of doggerel (*obs.*): a farcical afterpiece or interlude sung and danced to popular tunes (*obs.*): a jest (*obs.*): a contrivance of various kinds, esp. one for catching fish by jerking hooks into its body, an appliance for guiding a tool, a miner's jigger. — *v.t.* and *v.i.* to jerk: to perform as a jig. — *v.t.* to work upon with a jig: — *pr.p.* **jigg′ing;** *pa.t.* and *pa.p.* **jigged.** — *ns.* **jigamaree′, jigg′umbob** a what's-its-name: a gadget; **jigg′er** one who jigs in any sense: anything that jigs: one of many kinds of subsidiary appliances, esp. with reciprocating motion, as an oscillation transformer, an apparatus for separating ores by jolting in sieves in water, a simple potter's wheel or a template or profile used with it, a warehouse crane, the bridge or rest for the cue in billiards: a golf-club, used esp. formerly, with narrow

lofted iron head: old-fashioned sloop-rigged boat: a jigger-mast (*naut.*): a sail on a jigger-mast (*naut.*): odd person: odd or despised contrivance: a small measure for drinks. — *v.t.* to jerk or shake: to form with a jigger: to ruin (sometimes with *up*). — *v.i.* to tug or move with jerks. — *adj.* **jigg′ered** (*coll.*) exhausted. — *n.* **jigg′ing.** — *adj.* **jigg′ish.** — *v.t.* and *v.i.* **jigg′le** to move with vibratory jerks. — *n.* a jiggling movement. — **jig borer** an adjustable precision machine-tool for drilling holes; **jigg′er-mast** a four-masted ship's aftermost mast: a small mast astern; **jig′saw** a narrow reciprocating saw: a jigsaw puzzle. — *v.t.* and *v.i.* to cut with a jigsaw. — **jigsaw puzzle** a picture cut up into pieces, as by a jigsaw, to be fitted together. — **the jig is up** (*coll.*) the game is up, trick discovered, etc. [Origin obscure; Fr. *gigue* is from the English word.]

jigajig, etc. See **jig-jog.**

jigamaree. See **jig.**

jigger[1] *jig′ər, n.* a form of **chigoe.**

jigger[2]. See **jig.**

jiggered[1] *jig′ərd,* (*coll.*) *adj.* confounded.   [Origin doubtful.]

jiggered[2]. See **jig.**

jiggery-pokery *jig′ə-ri-pō′kə-ri, n.* trickery: deception.   [Cf. **joukery-pawkery.**]

jiggety-jog. See **jig-jog.**

jiggle, jiggumbob. See **jig.**

jig-jog *jig′-jog′, adv.* with a jolting, jogging motion. — *n.* a jolting motion: a jog. — Also **jick′ajog, jig′jig, jig′ajig, jig′ajog, jigg′ety-jog′.** — **jig′(-a)-jig′** (*slang,* used esp. in pidgins) sexual intercourse.   [**jig, jog.**]

jigot. Same as **gigot.**

jihad, jehad *jē-had′, n.* a holy war (for the Muslim faith): a stunt campaign.   [Ar. *jihād,* struggle.]

jilgie. See **gilgie.**

jill[1], **jillet,** etc. See **gill**[3].

jill[2]. See **gill**[5].

jillaroo. See **jackaroo.**

jilt *jilt, n.* one, esp. a woman, who encourages and then rejects a lover. — *v.t.* to discard (a lover) after encouragement.   [Possibly **jillet** or **gillet.**]

jimcrack. See **gimcrack.**

Jim Crow *jim krō,* (*derog.*) a generic name for the Negro: racial discrimination against Negroes. — **jim′-crow** a tool for bending or straightening iron rails or bars: a plane or other tool that works in both directions. — **Jim Crow car, school** etc., one for Negroes only. [From a Negro minstrel song with the refrain 'Wheel about and turn about and jump *Jim Crow'.*]

jiminy *jim′in-i.* See **geminate.**

jimjam *jim′jam, n.* a gimcrack: a gadget: an oddity: (in *pl.*) delirium tremens: (in *pl.*) the fidgets.   [Origin unknown.]

jimmy *jim′i,* (*chiefly U.S.*) *n.* a burglar's jemmy. — *v.t.* to force open, esp. with a jimmy.   [**James.**]

Jimmy *jim′i,* (*slang*) *n.* an act of urinating. — Also **Jimmy Riddle.**   [Rhyming slang for *piddle.*]

jimmy-o'goblin *jim′i-ō-gob′lin,* (*slang*) *n.* a pound sterling or Irish punt.   [Rhyming slang for *sovereign.*]

Jimmy Riddle. See **Jimmy.**

jimp *jimp,* (*Scot.*) *adj.* slender: elegant: scant. — *advs.* **jimp, jimp′ly** neatly: hardly: scant. — *n.* **jimp′ness.** — *adj.* **jimp′y** neat.   [Origin unknown.]

jimson-weed, jimpson-weed, Jamestown-weed *jim′sən-wēd, n.* thorn-apple.   [*Jamestown,* Virginia, where it established itself.]

jingal, gingall, gingal *jin(g)′göl, -göl′, n.* a large Chinese or Indian swivel-musket.   [Hind. *janjāl.*]

jingbang *jing-bang′, jing′,* (*slang*) *n.* company: collection: lot.   [Origin unknown.]

jingle *jing′gl, n.* a succession of clinking sounds: that which makes a tinkling sound, esp. a metal disc on a tambourine: a thin or paltry correspondence of sounds in verse: a verse or set of verses of such a kind: a short, simple verse, usu. with music, used to advertise a product, etc.: a covered two-wheeled vehicle. — *v.t.* and *v.i.* to sound with a jingle. — *ns.* **jing′ler; jing′let**

a ball serving as the clapper of a sleigh-bell; **jing'ling** a game in which blindfolded players within a ring try to catch a player with a bell tied to him. — *adj.* **jing'ly.** — **jing'le-jang'le** a dissonant continued jingling: a jingling trinket; **jingling Johnny** a Chinese pavilion, or musical percussion instrument. [Imit.]

jingo, Jingo *jing'gō, n.* used in the mild oaths 'By jingo!', 'By the living jingo!' (*Scot.* 'By jing!', 'By jings!'): from its occurrence in a music-hall song of 1878 that conveyed a threat against Russia, a (British) chauvinist. — *pl.* **jing'oes.** — *adjs.* **jing'o, jing'oish** chauvinist. — *ns.* **jing'oism; jing'oist.** — *adj.* **jingois'tic** characteristic of jingoism. — *adv.* **jingois'tically.** [Appears first as a conjurer's summoning call; possibly from Basque *Jinkoa, Jainko(a)*, God.]

jingo-ring *jing'gō-ring, n.* a children's game in which the players dance round one of their number singing 'Here we go round the jingo-ring'. [Conn. with **jink**.]

jinjili. See **gingili.**

jink *jingk,* (orig. *Scot.*) *v.i.* to dodge nimbly. — *v.t.* to elude: to cheat. — *n.* a quick, illusory turn. — **high jinks** see **high.** [Perh. a natural expression of the movement.]

jinker *jing'kər,* (Austr.) *n.* a sulky or other light horse-drawn passenger conveyance: a two-wheeled trailer for carrying logs. [Origin uncertain.]

jinn *jin, n.pl.* (*sing.* **jinnee, jinni, djinni, genie** (*jin-ē', jēn'i*)) a class of spirits in Muslim mythology, formed of fire, living chiefly on the mountains of Kâf which encircle the world, assuming various shapes, sometimes as men of enormous size and portentous hideousness. — Also **djinn, ginn.** The *jinn* are often called *genii* by a confusion. A plural **jinns** is sometimes erroneously used. [Ar. *jinn,* sing, *jinnī.*]

jinricksha, jinrickshaw, jinrikisha. See **ricksha.**

jinx *jingks, n.* a bringer of bad luck: an unlucky influence. — *v.t.* to bring bad luck to, put a spell on. — *adj.* **jinxed** beset with bad luck. [App. from *Jynx,* the bird being used in spells, and the name itself coming to mean 'a spell or charm'.]

jirble *jir', jŭr'bl,* (*Scot.*) *v.t.* and *v.i.* to pour splashingly or unsteadily.

jird *jûrd, n.* a N. African gerbil of the genus *Meriones.* [Berber (*u*)*gherda.*]

jirga *jēr'gə, n.* in Afghanistan, a council of tribal headmen. [Pushtu.]

jirkinet. See **jerkin.**

jism, gism *jiz'əm, **jissom** jis'əm, ns.* energy, force (*coll.,* chiefly *U.S.*): semen (*vulg.*). [Origin unknown.]

jitney *jit'ni,* (*U.S. slang*) *n.* five-cent piece: a bus or other, smaller, passenger vehicle, usu. with low fares. — *adj.* cheap: paltry. [Perh. Fr. *jeton,* counter.]

jitter *jit'ər,* (orig. *U.S.*) *v.i.* to behave in a flustered way. — *n.pl.* **jitt'ers** a flustered state. — *adj.* **jitt'ery.** — **jitt'erbug** (*U.S.*) a type of two-step to jazz music: one who dances so, the standard movements allowing of energetic improvisation: (in Britain, by misunderstanding or extension) a scaremonger, alarmist. — *v.i.* to dance a jitterbug, esp. wildly and grotesquely.

jiu-jitsu. Same as **ju-jitsu.**

jive *jīv, n.* a style of jazz music: dancing thereto: jargon (*slang*). — *v.i.* to play or dance jive: to talk jargon (*slang*). — *n.* **jī'ver.**

jiz. See **gizz.**

jizz *jiz, n.* the characteristic feature(s) of behaviour, plumage or anatomy which distinguish a bird from other species which resemble it. [Ety. uncertain.]

jo, joe *jō,* (*Scot.*) *n.* a beloved one: — *pl.* **joes.** [An old form of **joy.**]

joanna *jō-an'ə,* (*slang*) *n.* a piano. [Rhyming slang.]

joannes. See **johannes.**

Job *jōb, n.* a person of great patience — from *Job* in the *Book of Job.* — *n.* **jōbā'tion** (also **jawbā'tion**) a tedious scolding. — *v.t.* **jobe** (*jōb*) to reprimand tediously. — **Job's comforter** one who aggravates the distress of the unfortunate man he has come to comfort; **Job's news** bad news; **Job's post** the bearer of bad news; **Job's**

tears the stony involucres of an Indian grass, *Coix lachryma,* used as beads: round grains of chrysolite.

job[1] *job, n.* a sudden thrust with anything pointed, as a beak. — *v.t.* and *v.i.* to prod or peck suddenly. — *v.t.* to punch (*Austr. coll.*): — *pr.p.* **jobb'ing;** *pa.t.* and *pa.p.* **jobbed.** [App. imit.; cf. **jab.**]

job[2] *job, n.* any definite piece of work, esp. of a trifling or temporary nature: any undertaking or employment with a view to profit: an appointment or situation: state of affairs (*coll.*): a transaction in which private gain is sought under pretence of public service: an end accomplished by intrigue or wire-pulling: a criminal enterprise, esp. theft: a hired horse or carriage: a job-lot. — *adj.* employed, hired, or used by the job or for jobs: bought or sold lumped together. — *v.i.* to work at jobs: to buy and sell, as a broker: to practise jobbery. — *v.t.* to perform as a job: to put or carry through by jobbery: to deal in, as a broker: to hire or let out, esp. horses. — *ns.* **jobb'er** one who jobs: one who buys and sells, as a broker: a stock-jobber: one who turns official actions to private advantage: one who engages in a mean lucrative affair: a wholesale merchant, esp. if selling to retailers (*U.S.*): in composition with *first, second,* etc., one in, or seeking, their first, second, etc. job; **jobb'ery** jobbing: unfair means employed to secure some private end. — *adj.* **jobb'ing** working by the job. — *n.* the doing of jobs: miscellaneous printing-work: buying and selling as a broker: stock-jobbing: jobbery. — *adj.* and *n.pl.* **job'less** (people) having no job. — **job centre, Jobcentre** (also without *cap.*) a government-run employment agency where information about available jobs is displayed; **job'-lot'** a collection of odds and ends, esp. for sale as one lot: any collection of inferior quality; **job'-mas'ter** a livery-stable keeper who jobs out horses and carriages. — **a bad, good, job** a piece of work ill, or well, done: an unlucky, or lucky, fact; **have a job to** (*coll.*) to have difficulty in; **job off** to sell (goods) cheaply to get rid of them; **job of work** a task, bit of work; **job out** to divide (work) among contractors, etc.; **jobs for the boys** jobs given to or created for associates or adherents; **just the job** (*coll.*) exactly what is wanted; **odd jobs** occasional pieces of work; **on the job** at work, in activity. [Origin unknown.]

jobation, jobe. See **Job.**

jobernowl *job'ər-nōl, n.* a dull head: a stupid person. [App. Fr. *jobard,* a noodle, and **nowl, noll.**]

jobsworth *jobz'wûrth,* (*derog. slang*) *n.* a minor official, esp. one who adheres rigidly and unco-operatively to petty rules. [From 'It's more than my *job's worth* to let you...'.]

Jock *jok, n.* Jack (*Scot.*): the jack or knave in cards (*Scot.*): a yokel: a Scottish soldier (*slang*). [**Jack.**]

jock *jok, n.* a jockstrap: an athlete (*U.S. coll.*). [jock-strap.]

jockey *jok'i, n.* a man (orig. a boy) who rides in a horse-race: a horse-dealer: one who takes undue advantage in business. — *v.t.* to jostle by riding against: to manoeuvre: to trick by manoeuvring. — *v.i.* (often with *for*) to seek advantage by manoeuvring. — *ns.* **jockette'** (*facet.*) a female jockey; **jock'eyism; jock'eyship** the art or practice of a jockey. — **Jockey Club** an association for the promotion and ordering of horse-racing: a perfume composed of rose, orris, cassia, tuberose, bergamot, etc.; **jockey strap** see **jockstrap.** [Dim. of **Jock.**]

jocko *jok'ō, n.* a chimpanzee: — *pl.* **jock'os.** [Fr., from a W. African word *ncheko.*]

Jock Scott *jok skot,* (*angling*) *n.* a kind of artificial fly.

jockstrap *jok'strap, n.* genital support worn by men participating in athletics. — Also **jock, jockey strap.** [Dial. *jock,* the male organ, **strap.**]

jockteleg *jok'tə-leg,* (*Scot.*) *n.* a large clasp-knife. [The suggested *Jacques de Liège* lacks confirmation.]

joco *jō-kō',* (*Scot.*) *adj.* cheerfully complacent. [jocose.]

jocorous *jō-kō'rəs, -kö',* (*Anglo-Ir.*) *adj.* jocose. [jocose.]

jocose *jō-kōs', adj.* full of jokes: facetious: merry. — *adv.*

jocose'ly. — *ns.* **jocose'ness, jocosity** (-*kos'i-ti*) the quality of being jocose. — *adj.* **jocose'rious** half in jest, half in earnest. [L. *jocōsus* — *jocus*, a joke.]

jocular *jok'ū-lər, adj.* given to jokes: inclined to joke: of the nature of, intended as, a joke. — *n.* **jocularity** (-*lar'i-ti*). — *adj.* **joc'ularly.** — *n.* **joc'ulātor** a professional jester or minstrel. [L. *joculāris* — *jocus*.]

jocund *jŏk'und, jok'und, -ənd, adj.* mirthful: merry: cheerful: pleasant. — *ns.* **jocundity** (-*kund'i-ti*), **joc'undness.** — *adv.* **joc'undly.** [O.Fr. — L.L. *jocundus* for L. *jūcundus*, pleasant, modified by association with *jocus*.]

jodel *yō'dl.* Same as **yodel.**

jodhpurs *jod'pûrz, n.pl.* riding-breeches with a tight extension to the ankle (also **jodhpur breeches**): ankle-high boots worn with jodhpur breeches for riding (also **jodhpur boots, shoes**). [*Jodhpur* in India.]

joe¹ *jō*, **joey** *jō'i*, (*slang*) *ns.* a fourpenny bit (*Joseph* Hume, M.P., 1836): a threepenny bit: (with *cap.*) a man, fellow, esp. a soldier (*U.S.*). — *n.* **Joey** (*jō'i*) a circus clown, esp. in the English tradition (*Joseph* Grimaldi). — **Joe Miller** an old or stale jest, a jest-book; **Joe Millerism** the habit of retailing stale jests — from *Joe Miller* (1684–1738), a comedian but a notoriously dull fellow on whom a jest-book was fathered; **Joe Soap,** or merely **Joe** (*airmen's slang*), one imposed on to perform unpleasant tasks. — **not for Joe** see **Joseph.**

joe². Same as **jo.**

joey¹ *jō'i* (*Austr.*) *n.* a young animal, esp. a kangaroo. [Origin unknown.]

joey². See **joe¹.**

jog *jog, v.t.* to shake: to push with the elbow or hand: to stimulate, stir up, as the memory. — *v.i.* to move by jogs: to trudge: to run at a slow, steady pace, as a form of exercise: — *pr.p.* **jogg'ing;** *pa.t.* and *pa.p.* **jogged.** — *n.* a slight shake: a push or nudge: a spell of jogging. — *ns.* **jogg'er** one who moves slowly and heavily (*Dryden*): a person who jogs for exercise; **jogg'ing** running at a slow, steady pace, esp. for exercise. — **jog'trot** a slow jogging trot: humdrum routine. — **be jogging** to move on: to depart; **jog along** to proceed at a slow but steady pace, esp. of life, events, etc. [Perh. akin to **shog.**]

joggle¹ *jog'l, n.* a tooth, notch, or pin to prevent sliding of surfaces in contact: a joint so made. — *v.t.* to join with a joggle. [Perh. conn. with **jag¹.**]

joggle² *jog'l, v.t.* to jog or shake slightly: to jostle. — *v.i.* to shake: — *pr.p.* **jogg'ling;** *pa.t.* and *pa.p.* **jogg'led.** [App. dim. or freq. of **jog.**]

johannes *jō-(h)anēz, n.* a gold coin of *John V* of Portugal. — Also **joann'es.** — *adjs.* **Johann'ean, Johann'ine** of or pertaining to John, esp. the Apostle. [L. *Jōhannēs* from *Jōannēs* — Gr. *Iōannēs* — Heb. *Yōchānān*, John.]

Johannisberger *jō-han'is-bûrg-ər, n.* a white Rhenish wine grown at *Johannisberg* ('St John's Mountain'), near Wiesbaden.

John *jon, n.* a proper name, a diminutive of which, **Johnn'y** (also **Johnn'ie**), is sometimes used in slang for a simpleton, an empty-headed man-about-town or fellow generally: (without *cap.*) a lavatory (*slang*): a prostitute's client (*slang*). — *ns.* **Johnian** (*jōn'i-ən*) a member of St *John's* College, Cambridge; **johnn'ie, johnn'y** (*slang*) a condom. — **John'-a-dreams'** (*Shak.*) a dreamy fellow; **John a-Nokes, John a-Stiles, -Styles** fictitious persons in English law-suits, or generally; **John'-apple** a kind of apple, otherwise apple-John; **John Barleycorn** malt liquor personified; **John Bull** a generic name for an Englishman, from Arbuthnot(t)'s *History of John Bull,* 1712; **John Bullism** the typical English character, or any act or word expressive of it; **John Canoe** see separate entry; **John Chinaman** a Chinaman: the Chinese generically; **John Citizen** a typical citizen; **John Collins** an alcoholic drink based on gin; **John Company** the East India Company; **John Doe** see **Doe; John Dory** see **dory¹; John'-go-to-bed-at= noon'** the goat's-beard (from its early closing); **John Kanoo** see **John Canoe; Johnn'y-cake** a flat cake made from maize flour or wheat flour; **Johnn'y-come-late'ly** a newcomer; **Johnn'y-head'-in-air, John o'dreams** a dreamy, impractical persờn; **Johnn'y-raw** a beginner: a greenhorn; **John Thomas** (*slang*) the penis.   [L. *Jōhannēs*; see **johannes.**]

John Canoe *jon kə-nōō'*, (*West Indies*) a boisterous rhythmic dance performed esp. as part of Christmas celebrations: the celebrations themselves: any of, esp. the leader of, the dancers: the mask or head-dress of such a dancer. — Also **John Kanoo, joncanoe, junkanoo,** etc. [From a W. African language.]

Johnsonian *jon-sō'ni-ən, adj.* of, in the manner of, Dr Samuel *Johnson,* the lexicographer (1709–1784). — *ns.* **Johnsō'nianism, John'sonism** (-*sən-izm*); **John'sonese** Johnsonian style, idiom, diction, or an imitation of it — ponderous English, full of antitheses, balanced triads, and words of classical origin. — *n.pl.* **Johnsōniana** (-*ä'nə, -ā'nə*) matters, miscellaneous items, connected with Johnson.

joie de vivre *zhwa də vē-vr'*, (Fr.) joy of living: exuberance.

join *join, v.t.* to connect: to unite: to associate: to add or annex: to become a member of: to come into association with or the company of: to go to and remain with, in, or on: to draw a straight line between (*geom.*). — *v.i.* to be connected: to combine, unite: to run into one: to grow together: to be in, or come into, close contact. — *n.* a joining: a place where things have been joined: a mode of joining. — *ns.* **joind'er** (esp. *law*) joining, uniting; **join'er** one who joins or unites: a worker in wood, esp. one who makes smaller structures than a carpenter: one who joins many societies; **join'ery** the art of the joiner: joiner's work; **join'ing** the act of joining: a seam: a joint; **joint** a joining: the place where, or mode in which, two or more things join: a place where two things (esp. bones) meet with power of movement as of a hinge: a node, or place where a stem bears leaves, esp. if swollen: a segment: a piece of an animal's body as cut up for the table: the flexible hinge of cloth or leather connecting the back of a book with its sides: a crack intersecting a mass of rock (*geol.*): the place where adjacent surfaces meet: condition of adjustment at a joint (in the phrase *out of joint*): a place of resort for tramps: a low resort: a place, esp. a public house or hotel: a cigarette containing marijuana (*coll.*). — *adj.* joined, united, or combined: shared among more than one: sharing with another or others. — *v.t.* to unite by joints: to fit closely: to provide with joints or an appearance of joints: to fill the joints of: to divide into joints. — *v.i.* to fit like or by joints. — *adj.* **joint'ed** having joints: composed of segments: constricted at intervals. — *n.* **joint'er** the largest kind of plane used by a joiner: a bricklayer's tool for putting mortar in joints. — *adj.* **joint'less.** — *adv.* **joint'ly** in a joint manner: unitedly or in combination: together. — *ns.* **joint'ness; joint'ure** property settled on a woman at marriage to be enjoyed after her husband's death. — *v.t.* to settle a jointure upon. — *ns.* **joint'uress, joint'ress** a woman on whom a jointure is settled. — **join'-hand** running hand; **joint account** a bank account held in the name of two or more people, any of whom can deposit or withdraw money; **jointed cactus** a plant (*Opuntia pusilla*) of the prickly-pear genus, a serious pest in S. Africa; **joint'-fir** any plant of the family Gnetaceae; **joint'-heir** one who inherits jointly with another or others; **joint'ing-rule** a long straight-edged rule used by bricklayers for keeping their work even; **joint'-oil** synovia; **joint'-stock** stock held jointly or in company (**joint'-stock company** one in which each shareholder can transfer shares without consent of the rest); **joint'-stool** (*Shak.*) a stool made of parts inserted in each other; **joint'-ten'ancy; joint'-ten'ant** one who is owner of land or goods along with others; **joint'-worm** (*U.S.*) a hymenopterous larva that attacks grain-stalks near the first joint. — **join battle** see **battle; join in** to (begin to) take part; **join issue** to begin to dispute: to take up the contrary view or side; **join up** to enlist, esp. in participation in a general movement; **out of joint** dislocated: disordered (*fig.*); **put someone's nose out of**

joint to supplant someone in another's love or confidence: to disconcert: to rebuff; **second joint** the middle piece of a fly fishing-rod: the thigh of a fowl — opp. to the leg or drumstick, the first joint; **universal joint** a contrivance by which one part is able to move freely in all directions, as in the ball-and-socket joint. [O.Fr. *joindre* — L. *jungĕre, junctum*, to join.]

joist *joist, n.* a beam supporting the boards of a floor or the laths of a ceiling. — *v.t.* to fit with joists. [O.Fr. *giste* — *gesir* — L. *jacēre*, to lie.]

jojoba *hō-hō′bə, n.* a desert shrub of the box family, native to Mexico, Arizona and California, whose edible seeds yield a waxy oil chemically similar to spermaceti. [Mex. Sp.]

joke *jōk, n.* a jest: a witticism: anything said or done to excite a laugh: anything provocative of laughter: an absurdity. — *v.t.* to cast jokes at: to banter: to make merry with. — *v.i.* to jest: to be merry: to make sport. — *n.* **jok′er** one who jokes or jests: a fifty-third card in the pack, used at euchre, poker, etc.: an innocent-looking clause insidiously introduced to cripple the effect of a bill or document (*U.S.*): an unforeseen factor affecting a situation: a fellow (*slang*). — *adjs.* **joke′some; jō′key, jō′ky.** — *adv.* **jok′ingly** in a joking manner. — **joke′smith** a maker of jokes. — **joking apart** if I may be serious, seriously; **no joke** a serious or difficult matter. [L. *jocus*.]

jokol *yō′köl,* (*Shetland; obs.*) *adv.* yes (lit. yes carl). — Also **yo′kul.** [Shetland Norn *jo*, yes, and (inferred) *koll* — O.N. *karl*, carl.]

jole. Another form of **jowl**[1,2].

joli laide *zho-lē led,* (Fr.) a woman whose ugliness is part of her charm: — *pl.* **jol′ies laides.**

joll. Another form of **jowl**[1,2].

jolly *jol′i, adj.* merry: expressing or exciting mirth, jovial: comely, robust: used as an indefinite expression of approbation (*coll.*) — *v.t.* to make fun of: to put or keep in good humour, beguile. — *adv.* (*coll.*) very. — *n.* a marine (*slang*): a jollification (*coll.*). — *n.* **jollificā′tion** a making jolly: noisy festivity and merriment. — *v.i.* **joll′ify.** — *adv.* **joll′ily.** — *ns.* **joll′iment** (Spens.) merriment; **joll′iness, joll′ity, joll′yhead** (Spens.). — **Jolly Roger** the pirates' black flag with white skull and crossbones. [O.Fr. *jolif, joli*, very doubtfully referred to O.N. *jōl*, Yule.]

jollyboat *jol′i-bōt, n.* a ship's boat. [Origin obscure.]

jolt *jōlt, v.i.* to shake or proceed with sudden jerks. — *v.t.* to shake with a sudden shock. — *n.* a sudden jerk: a shock: a stimulating shock. — *n.* **jolt′er.** — *adv.* **jolt′ingly** in a jolting manner. — *adj.* **jolt′y.** [Ety. obscure.]

jolterhead *jōlt′ər-hed,* **jolthead** *jōlt′hed, ns.* a large clumsy head: a blockhead. [Ety. obscure.]

jomo. See **zho.**

Jonah *jō′nə, n.* a bringer of ill-luck on shipboard or elsewhere. — **Jonah word** a word with which a chronic stutterer has difficulty. [From the prophet *Jonah*.]

Jonathan *jon′ə-thən, n.* the people of the United States, collectively, or a typical specimen (*Brother Jonathan*): an American variety of apple. [Perh. from the sagacious Governor *Jonathan* Trumbull, 1710–85.]

joncanoe. See **John Canoe.**

jongleur *zhɔ̄-glær′, n.* a wandering minstrel: a mountebank. [Fr., — O.Fr. *jogleor* — L. *joculātor*; cf. **juggler.**]

jonquil *jong′kwil,* formerly *jung-kwil′, n.* a name given to certain species of narcissus with rush-like leaves. [Fr. *jonquille* — L. *juncus*, a rush.]

jonty *jon′ti,* **jaunty, jauntie, janty,** *jön′ti, jän′ti,* (*slang*) *ns.* a naval master-at-arms.

jook, etc. See **jouk.**

jor *jör, n.* the second movement of a raga. [Sans.]

joram. See **jorum.**

Jordan[1] *jor′dn, n.* a country in S.-W. Asia. — Also *adj.* — *adj.* **Jordan′ian** (*-dān′*). — *n.* a native or citizen of Jordan. [See next.]

Jordan[2] *jör′dn, n.* the great river of Palestine: death (*fig.*;

as a passage into the Promised Land, Numb. xxxiii. 51): (usu. without *cap.*) a chamber-pot (*Shak.*; according to some, from *Jordan*-bottle, a pilgrim's bottle containing *Jordan* water).

jordeloo *jör-di-lōō′.* Same as **gardyloo.**

jorum, joram *jōr′əm, jōr′, n.* a large drinking-bowl: a great drink. [Ety. unknown; poss. from *Joram* in 2 Sam. viii. 10.]

Joseph *jō′zif, n.* one whose chastity is above temptation — from the story of *Joseph* and Potiphar's wife in Gen. xxxix.: (without *cap.*) a caped overcoat worn by women in the 18th century for riding — possibly in allusion to *Joseph's* coat, Gen. xxxvii. — **not for Joseph** (or **Joe**) not on any account (prob. from the refrain of a 19th-cent. music-hall song).

josephinite *jo′zə-fēn-īt, n.* a mineral found only in *Josephine* Creek, in Oregon, U.S.A., and believed to have originated at the outer edge of the earth's core and been carried up nearly 2 000 miles to the surface.

Josephson junction *jō′zif-sən jung′shən,* (*electronics*) a junction formed from two superconducting metals separated by a thin insulating layer, allowing the unimpeded passage of a current and generating microwaves when subjected to a certain voltage. [B.D. *Josephson* (1940–), English physicist.]

josh *josh, v.t.* to ridicule: to tease. — *n.* a hoax: a derisive jest: a fool. — *n.* **josh′er.**

joskin *jos′kin, n.* a clown, yokel. [Thieves' cant.]

joss *jos, n.* a Chinese idol: luck: fate. — *n.* **joss′er** a clergyman (*Austr.*): a fellow (*slang*): a blunderer (*slang*). — **joss′-house** a temple; **joss′-stick** a stick of gum which gives off a perfume when burned, used as incense in India, China, etc. [Port. *deos*, god — L. *deus*.]

joss-block *jos′-blok,* (*dial.*) *n.* a horse-block.

jostle *jos′l,* **justle** *jus′l, vs.i.* to tilt, joust (*obs.*). — *vs.t.* and *vs.i.* to shake or jar by collision: to hustle: to elbow. — *ns.* an act of jostling. — *ns.* **jos′tlement, jos′tling.** [Freq. of **joust, just.**]

jot *jot, n.* an iota, a whit, a tittle. — *v.t.* to set down briefly: to make a memorandum of: — *pr.p.* **jott′ing;** *pa.t.* and *pa.p.* **jott′ed.** — *ns.* **jott′er** one who jots: a book or pad for rough notes; **jott′ing** a memorandum: a rough note. [L. *iōta* (read as *jōta*) — Gr *iōta*, the smallest letter in the alphabet, equivalent to *i*; Heb. *yōd*.]

jota *hho′tä, n.* a Spanish dance in triple time. [Sp.]

jotun *yō′tən,* **jötunn** *yœ′tən, ns.* a giant. [O.N. *jötunn*.]

jougs *jōōgz, jugz, n.pl.* an iron neck-ring — the old Scottish pillory. [Prob. O.Fr. *joug*, a yoke — L. *jugum*.]

jouisance, jouysaunce *jōō′is-əns,* (Spens.) *n.* joyousness. [Fr. *jouissance* — *jouir*, to enjoy — L. *gaudēre*, to rejoice.]

jouk, jook *jōōk,* (*Scot.*) *v.i.* to duck: to dodge: to bow. — *n.* an elusive duck or dodging movement: a bow. — *ns.* **jouk′ery, jook′ery, jouk′ery-pawk′ery** (*Scot.*) trickery, roguery. [Ety. obscure.]

joule[1] *jōōl, jowl, n.* orig. unit of energy, now of energy, work and heat in the MKS and SI systems, equal to work done when a force of 1 newton advances its point of application 1 metre (1 joule = 10^7 ergs). [After the physicist J. P. *Joule* (said to be pronounced *jowl*; 1818–89).]

joule[2]. See **jowl**[2].

jounce *jowns, v.t.* and *v.i.* to jolt, shake. [Ety. dub.]

jour *zhōōr* (Fr.) *n.* a day. — **jour de fête** (*də fet*) a feast day, esp. a saint's day.

journal[1] *jûr′nəl, n.* a daily register or diary: a book containing a record of each day's transactions: a newspaper published daily (or otherwise): a magazine: the transactions of any society. — *adj.* (*Shak.*) diurnal. — *n.* **journalese′** the jargon of bad journalism. — *v.i.* **jour′nalise, -ize** to write for or in a journal. — *v.t.* to enter in a journal. — *ns.* **journ′alism** the profession of conducting or writing for public journals: writing of fleeting interest or hasty character; **jour′nalist** one who writes for or conducts a newspaper or magazine: one who keeps a journal. — *adj.* **journalist'ic**. — *n.* **jour'no** (*slang*) a journalist: — *pl.* **jour'nos**. [Fr., — L. *diurnālis*; see **diurnal**.]

journal² *jûr'nəl*, (*mech.*) *n.* that part of a shaft or axle which rests in the bearings. — *v.t.* to provide with or fix as a journal. — **jour'nal-box** a box or bearing for a journal. [Origin unexplained.]

journal intime *zhōōr-nal ɛ̃-tēm* (Fr.), a diary.

journey *jûr'ni*, *n.* a day's work or travel (*obs.*): a campaign (*obs.*): any travel: tour: excursion: movement from end to end of a fixed course: the weight of finished coins delivered at one time to the Master of the Mint (also **jour'ney-weight**): a train of colliery trucks: — *pl.* **jour'neys**. — *v.i.* to travel: — *pr.p.* **jour'neying**; *pa.t.* and *pa.p.* **jour'neyed** (*-nid*). — *n.* **jour'neyer**. — *adj.* **jour'ney-bat'ed** (*Shak.*) wayworn. — **jour'neyman** one who works by the day: any hired workman: one whose apprenticeship is completed: an electrically controlled clock or dial; **jour'ney-work** work done by a journeyman or for hire: necessary, routine work. [Fr. *journée* — *jour*, a day — L. *diurnus*.]

joust, just *just* (*jōōst* and *jowst* are recent pronunciations due to the spelling), *n.* the encounter of two knights on horseback at a tournament. — *v.i.* to tilt. — *n.* **joust'er**. [O.Fr. *juste, jouste, joste* — L. *juxtā*, nigh to.]

jouysance. See **jouisance**.

Jove *jōv*, *n.* another name for the god Jupiter. — *adj.* **jovial** (*jō'vi-əl*) joyous: full of jollity and geniality: (*cap.*) of Jupiter: (*cap.*) influenced by Jupiter. — *ns.* **joviality** (*-al'i-ti*), **jō'vialness.** — *adv.* **jō'vially.** — *adj.* **Jō'vian** of the god, or the planet, Jupiter. — **by Jove** an exclamation of surprise, admiration, etc. [L. *Jovis* (in the nom. usu. *Juppiter, Jupiter*), the god Jove or Jupiter, or the planet Jupiter, an auspicious star.]

jovial, Jovian. See **Jove**.

jovysaunce. A misreading of **jouysaunce**. See **jouisance**.

jow *jow*, (*Scot.*) *v.t.* and *v.i.* to ring, toll: to rock. — *n.* a stroke of a bell. — *n.* and *adj.* **jow'ing-in'** ringing in. — **jow one's ginger** see **jee one's ginger** at **jee²**. [jowl².]

jowar *jow-är'*, **jowari, jawari, -ē**, *ns.* durra. [Hind. *jawār, jawārī.*]

jowl¹ *jowl, jōl* (obs. **jole, joll** *jōl*), *n.* the jaw: the cheek: a pendulous double chin: a dewlap: a head: the head and shoulders of a salmon, sturgeon, or ling. — *adj.* **jowled.** — *n.* **jowl'er** a heavy-jawed hound. [Prob. several different words. The development and relations of M.E. *chaul*, O.E. *ceafl*, jaw, M.E. *chol*, O.E. *ceolu, ceolur*, etc., and the modern forms with *j* are difficult to make out. Fr. *joue*, cheek, or some other word may have added to the confusion.]

jowl², **joll, jole, joule**, *jōl*, (*dial.*) *v.t.* and *v.i.* to bump: to beat: to toll. — *n.* a stroke: a knock. [Ety. obscure.]

joy *joi*, *n.* intense gladness: rapture: mirth: a cause of joy: a beloved one. — *v.i.* to rejoice: to be glad: to exult. — *v.t.* to give joy to: to enjoy (*Milt.*): — *pr.p.* **joy'ing**; *pa.t.* and *pa.p.* **joyed.** — *n.* **joy'ance** (*poet.* orig. *Spens.*) gaiety, festivity. — *adj.* **joy'ful** full of joy: feeling, expressing, or giving joy. — *adv.* **joy'fully.** — *n.* **joy'fulness.** — *adj.* **joy'less** without joy: not giving joy. — *adv.* **joy'lessly.** — *n.* **joy'lessness.** — *adj.* **joy'ous** joyful. — *adv.* **joy'ously.** — *n.* **joy'ousness.** — *v.i.* **joy'-pop** (*slang*) to take addictive drugs from time to time without forming an addiction. — **joy'-ride** (*slang*) a pleasure-drive, esp. reckless or surreptitious, often in a stolen car; **joy'-rider; joy'-riding; joy'-stick** the control-lever of an aeroplane, invalid car, video game, etc. (*slang*): a lever controlling the movement of the cursor on a VDU screen (*comput.*); **joy'-wheel** a great wheel that carries passengers high in the air in pleasuregrounds. — **no joy** (*slang*) no news, reply, information, luck. [Fr. *joie* (cf. It. *gioja*) — L. *gaudium*.]

Joycean *joi'sē-ən*, *adj.* of, or in the manner of, James Joyce (1882–1941), Irish writer. — *n.* a student or imitator of James Joyce.

juba *jōō'bə*, *n.* a Negro breakdown or rustic dance, in which the spectators clap hands, slap their thighs, and sing verses with *juba* as a refrain.

jubate *jōō'bāt*, (*zool.*, etc.) *adj.* maned. [L. *jubātus* — *juba*, mane.]

jubbah *jōōb'ə, jub'ə*, *n.* a long loose outer garment worn by Muslims. — Also **jibbah, djibbah.** [Ar. *jubbah.*]

jube¹ *jōō'bē*, *n.* a rood-loft. [L., imper. of *jubēre*, to command.]

jube² *jōōb.* A coll. shortening of **jujube**.

jubilant *jōō'bi-lənt*, *adj.* shouting for joy: uttering songs of triumph: rejoicing. — *ns.* **ju'bilance, ju'bilancy** exultation. — *adv.* **ju'bilantly.** — *v.i.* **ju'bilate** to exult, rejoice. — *ns.* **jubilate** (*jōō-bi-lä'tē, yōō-bi-lä'te*) the third Sunday after Easter, so called because the church service began on that day with the 66th Psalm, 'Jubilate Deo', etc.: also the 100th Psalm, which in the English Prayer Book is a canticle used as an alternative for the Benedictus; **jubilā'tion** a shouting for joy: the declaration of triumph: rejoicing. [L. *jūbilāre*, to shout for joy. Not conn. with *jubilee*.]

jubilee *jōō'bi-lē*, *n.* among the Jews, every fiftieth year, a year of release of slaves, cancelling of debts, return of property to its former owners, proclaimed by the sound of a trumpet: the celebration of a fiftieth anniversary — e.g. of a king's accession, a bishop's consecration, etc.: in the R.C. Church, a year (every twenty-fifth — *ordinary jubilee*) of indulgence for pilgrims and others, an *extraordinary jubilee* being specially appointed by the Pope: any season or condition of great joy and festivity: joyful shouting: exultant joy. — **jubilee clip** a metal loop with a screw fitting, placed round a tube, hose, etc., and tightened to form a watertight connection. — **silver, golden, diamond jubilee** respectively a twenty-fifth, fiftieth, sixtieth anniversary. [Fr. *jubilé* — L. *jūbilaeus* — Heb. *yōbēl*, a ram, ram's horn.]

jud *jud*, *n.* a mass of coal holed or undercut so as to be thrown down by wedges. [Origin unknown.]

Judaean, Judean *jōō-dē'ən*, *adj.* of Judaea or the Jews. — *n.* a native of Judaea: a Jew. [L. *Judaea.*]

Judaeo- *jōō-dā'ō-*, U.S. **Judeo** *jōō-dē'ō-*, in composition, Jewish, as *Judaeo-Spanish*, Jewish-Spanish, Ladino. [L. *Judaea.*]

Judaic *jōō-dā'ik*, *adj.* pertaining to the Jews. — *n.pl.* **Judā'ica** the culture of the Jews — their literature, customs, etc., esp. as described in books, articles, etc. — *adj.* **Judā'ical** Judaic. — *adv.* **Judā'ically.** — *n.* **Judāīsā'tion, -z-.** — *v.t.* **Ju'dāīse, -īze** to conform to, adopt, or practise Jewish customs or Judaism. — *ns.* **Ju'dāīser, -z-; Ju'dāīsm** the doctrines and rites of the Jews: conformity to the Jewish rites; **Ju'dāīst** one who holds the doctrines of Judaism. — *adj.* **Judāist'ic.** — *adv.* **Judāist'ically.** [L. *Jūdaicus* — *Jūda*, Judah, a son of Israel.]

Judas *jōō'dəs*, *n.* a traitor: (also without *cap.*) a Judashole: used attributively, as in *Judas goat*, denoting an animal or bird used to lure others. — *adj.* **Ju'das=coloured** red, of hair (*Judas* traditionally being redhaired). — **Ju'das-hole, Ju'das-window** (also without *caps.*) a spy-hole in a door, etc.; **Ju'das-kiss** any act of treachery under the guise of kindness (Matt. xxvi. 48, 49); **Ju'das-tree** a tree (*Cercis*) of the Caesalpinia family, with rose-coloured flowers that appear before the leaves (*Judas* having traditionally hanged himself on one): also the elder (for the same reason). [*Judas* Iscariot.]

judder *jud'ər*, *n.* a vibratory effect in singing produced by alternations of greater or less intensity of sound: aircraft or other vibration. — Also *v.i.* [Prob. **jar¹** and **shudder.**]

Judenhetze *yōō'dən-het-sə* (Ger.), *n.* Jew-baiting.

Judeo-. See **Judaeo-**.

judge *juj*, *v.i.* to exercise the office of judge: to point out or declare what is just or law: to try and decide questions of law or guiltiness, etc.: to pass sentence: to compare facts to determine the truth: to form or pass an opinion: to distinguish. — *v.t.* to hear and determine authoritatively: to sit in judgment on: to pronounce on the guilt or innocence of: to sentence: to decide the merits of: to be censorious towards: to condemn (*B*.): to decide: to award: to estimate: to form an opinion on: to conclude: to consider (to be). — *n.* one who judges: one appointed to hear and settle causes, and to try accused persons: one chosen to award prizes, to decide doubtful or disputed points in a competition, etc.: an arbitrator: one who can decide upon the merit of anything: in the Jewish history, a supreme magistrate having civil and military powers: one capable of discriminating well: (with *cap*.; in *pl*.) title of 7th book of the Old Testament. — *ns.* **judge′ship** the office of a judge; **judg′ment** (also **judge′ment**) the act of judging: the comparing of ideas to elicit truth: faculty by which this is done, the reason: opinion formed: discrimination: good taste: sentence: condemnation: doom: a misfortune regarded as sent by Providence in punishment. — *adj.* **judgment′al** (also **judgement′al**) involving judgment: apt to pass judgment. — **judge′-ad′vocate** the crown-prosecutor at a court-martial. — *adj.* **judge′-made′** based on decisions of judges (as law). — **Judges' Rules** in English law, a system of rules governing the behaviour of the police towards suspects, e.g. the cautioning of a person about to be charged; **judg′ment-day** the day of final judgment on mankind; **judg′ment-debt** a debt evidenced by legal record; **judg′ment-hall** a hall where a court of justice meets; **judg′ment-seat** the seat or bench in a court from which judgment is pronounced. — **Judge Advocate General** the civil adviser to the crown on military law, esp. courts-martial: — *pl.* **Judge Advocates General, Judge Advocate Generals; judgment of Solomon** a judgment intended to call the bluff of the false claimant — like that of Solomon in 1 Kings iii. 16–28; **judgment reserved** decision delayed after the close of a trial (in Scotland, 'avizandum made'); **judgment respited** execution of sentence delayed. [A.Fr. *juger* — L. *jūdicāre — jūs*, law, and *dīcĕre*, to say, to declare.]

Judica *jōō′di-kə, n.* Passion Sunday — from the opening words of the introit, '*Judica* me, Deus' (43rd Psalm).

judicature *jōō′di-kə-chər, n.* power of dispensing justice by legal trial: jurisdiction: the office of judge: the body of judges: a court: a system of courts. — *adj.* **ju′dicable** that may be judged or tried. — *n.* **judicā′tion** judgment. — *adj.* **ju′dicative** having power to judge. — *ns.* **ju′dicātor** one who judges; **ju′dicatory** (-*kə-tər-i*) judicature: a court. — *adj.* pertaining to a judge: distributing justice. [L. *jūdicāre, -ātum*, to judge.]

judicial *jōō-dish′əl, adj.* pertaining to a judge or court of justice: established by statute: arising from process of law: of the nature of judgment: judge-like, impartial: critical. — *adj.* **judic′ially.** — **judicial astrology** the would-be science of the influence of the planets on human affairs; **judicial combat** trial by battle; **Judicial Committee** an offshoot of the Privy Council, forming a court of appeal; **judicial murder** a death sentence which is deemed unjust although passed in accordance with legal procedure; **judicial separation** the separation of two married persons by order of the Divorce Court; **judicial trustee** (or **factor,** in Scotland) an administrator appointed by the courts to manage the estate of someone under some imperfection. [L. *jūdiciālis — jūdicium*.]

judiciary *jōō-dish′ər-i, -i-ər-i, adj.* pertaining to judgment, judges, or courts of law. — *n.* a body of judges: a system of courts. [L. *jūdiciārius*.]

judicious *jōō-dish′əs, adj.* according to sound judgment: possessing sound judgment: discreet. — *adv.* **judic′iously.** — *n.* **judic′iousness.** [Fr. *judicieux* — L. *jūdicium*.]

judo *jōō′dō, n.* a modern variety of ju-jitsu. — *n.* **judogi** (*jōō′dō-gi* or *-dō′gi*) the costume (jacket and trousers) worn by a **ju′dōist** or **judoka** (*jōō′dō-kə* or *-dō′kə*), a person who practises, or is expert in, judo. [Jap. *jiu*, gentleness, *do*, way.]

Judy *jōō′di, n.* Punch's wife in the puppet-show: a frump,

an odd-looking woman: (without *cap*.) a girl (*dial.* or *slang*). [From the name *Judith*.]

jug[1] *jug, n.* a vessel with a handle and a spout or lip for pouring liquids: a jugful. — *v.t.* to boil or stew as in a closed jar: — *pr.p.* **jugg′ing;** *pa.t.* and *pa.p.* **jugged.** — *n.* **jug′ful** as much as a jug will hold: — *pl.* **jug′fuls.** — **jug band** a band using jugs and other utensils as musical instruments; **jugged hare** hare cut in pieces and stewed with wine and other seasoning. [Origin unknown.]

jug[2] *jug, (slang) n.* prison. [Cf. **jougs.**]

jug[3] *jug, n.* a note of the nightingale. — *v.i.* to utter the sound. — Also **jug′-jug′.** [Imit.]

juga. See **jugum.**

jugal *jōō′gəl, adj.* relating to a yoke, esp. that of marriage: malar. — *n.* the malar bone. [L. *jugālis — jugum*, a yoke.]

jugate *jōō′gāt, adj.* paired (*bot*.): having the leaflets in pairs (*bot*.): joined side by side or overlapping, as heads shown on a coin, etc. [L. *jugāre, -ātum*, to join — *jugum*, a yoke.]

Jugendstil *yōō′gənd-shtēl, n.* the German term for art nouveau. [Ger. *Jugend*, youth (the name of a magazine first appearing in 1896), *Stil*, style.]

Juggernaut *jug′ər-nöt, n.* an incarnation of Vishnu, beneath the car of whose idol at Puri devotees were supposed by Europeans to immolate themselves (also **Jugannath;** *jug′u-nät,*): hence, any relentless destroying force or object of devotion and sacrifice: (without *cap*.) a very large lorry. [Sans. *Jagannātha*, lord of the world.]

juggins *jug′inz, (slang) n.* a simpleton. [Origin unknown.]

juggle *jug′l, v.i.* to perform as an entertainer (*obs*.): to amuse by sleight-of-hand, conjure — now usu. to manipulate balls or other objects with great dexterity (also *fig*.): to practise artifice or imposture: to tamper or manipulate. — *v.t.* to transform, render, put by jugglery. — *n.* a trick by sleight-of-hand: an imposture. — *ns.* **jugg′ler; jugg′lery** (-*lə-ri*) art or act of a juggler: legerdemain: trickery. — *n.* and *adj.* **jugg′ling.** — *adv.* **jugg′lingly** in a deceptive manner. [O.Fr. *jogler* — L. *joculārī*, to jest — *jocus*, a jest.]

Juglans *jōō′glanz, n.* the walnut genus, giving the name to the family **Juglandaceae** (-*glən-dā′si-ē*). — *adj.* **juglandaceous** (-*dā′shəs*). [L. *jūglāns — Jovis glāns*, Jove's acorn.]

Jugoslav. Same as **Yugoslav.**

jugular *jug′, jōō′ū-lər, adj.* pertaining to the neck. — *n.* one of the large veins on each side of the neck. — *v.t.* **jug′ūlate** to cut the throat of: to strangle, check by drastic means (*fig*.). — **go for the jugular** to attack someone at the place at which they are most vulnerable and liable to greatest harm. [L. *jugulum*, the collarbone — *jungĕre*, to join.]

jugum *jōō′gəm, n.* a pair of opposite leaves (*bot*.): in certain insects, a process on the back edge of the fore-wing that unites it to the hind-wing in flight: — *pl.* **ju′ga.** [L., yoke.]

juice *jōōs, n.* the sap of vegetables: the fluid part of animal bodies: interesting quality: piquancy: electric current, petrol vapour, or other source of power (*slang*). — *v.t.* to squeeze juice from (a fruit): (with *up*) to enliven (*U.S.*). — *adj.* **juice′less.** — *ns.* **juic′er** (esp. *U.S.*) a juice extractor; **juic′iness.** — *adj.* **juic′y.** — **juice extractor** a kitchen device for extracting the juice from fruit, etc. — **step on the juice** (*slang*) to accelerate a motor-car. [Fr. *jus*, broth, lit. mixture.]

ju-jitsu, jiu-jitsu *jōō-jit′sōō, n.* a system of fighting barehanded developed by the samurai in Japan: a system of wrestling as sport founded on it. [Jap. *jū-jutsu*.]

ju-ju, juju *jōō′jōō, n.* an object of superstitious worship in West Africa: a fetish or charm. [App. Fr. *joujou*, a toy.]

jujube *jōō′jōōb, n.* a spiny shrub or small tree (Zizyphus) of the buckthorn family: its fruit, which is dried as a sweetmeat: a lozenge made of sugar and gum in imitation of the fruit. [Fr. *jujube* or L.L. *jujuba* — Gr. *zizyphon*.]

juke *jook* (*slang*) *v.i.* to dance. — **juke'-box** a slot machine that plays gramophone records; **juke'-joint** a resort for dancing and drinking. [Gullah *juke*, disorderly — W. African *dzug*, to lead a careless life.]

julep *joo'ləp, n.* a sweet drink, often medicated: an American drink of spirits, sugar, ice, and mint (also **mint'-julep**). [Fr., — Sp. *julepe* — Ar. *julāb* — Pers. *gulāb* — *gul*, rose, *āb*, water.]

Julian *jool'yən, adj.* pertaining to *Julius* Caesar (100–44 B.C.). — **Julian year** see **year.**

julienne *joo-li-en', zhü-lyen, n.* a clear soup, with shredded vegetables: any foodstuff which has been shredded. [Fr. name.]

juliet cap *joo'i-et kap,* a round close-fitting skullcap worn by women. [Prob. *Juliet,* in Shakespeare's *Romeo and Juliet.*]

July *joo-lī',* formerly and still by some *joo'lī, n.* the seventh month of the year. [L. *Jūlius,* from Gaius Julius Caesar, who was born in it.]

July-flower. A mistaken form of **gillyflower.**

jumar *joo'mär, n.* a clip used in mountaineering, which grips the rope when weight is applied, and runs freely along the rope when the weight is taken off: a climb using these. — *v.i.* to climb using jumars. [Swiss name.]

jumart *joo'märt, -mərt, n.* the fabled offspring of a bull and a mare, or stallion and cow. [Fr.]

jumbal, jumble *jum'bl, n.* a thin, crisp, sweet cake, formerly made in the shape of a ring. [Perh. **gimmal, gimbal.**]

jumbie. See **jumby.**

jumble[1] *jum'bl, v.t.* to mix confusedly: to throw together without order: to shake up, jolt. — *v.i.* to be mixed together confusedly: to be agitated: to flounder. — *n.* a confused mixture: confusion: things sold at a jumble-sale: jolting. — *n.* **jum'bler.** — *adv.* **jum'blingly** in a confused or jumbled manner. — *adj.* **jum'bly.** — **jum'ble-sale** a sale of miscellaneous articles, rubbish, etc., often for charity. [Origin obscure.]

jumble[2]. See **jumbal.**

jumbo *jum'bō, n.* anything very big of its kind: an elephant (after a famous large one so named): a jumbo jet: — *pl.* **jum'bos.** — *adj.* huge: colossal. — *v.t.* **jum'boise, -ize** (*-bō-īz*) to enlarge (a ship) by adding a prefabricated section, e.g. amidships. — **jumbo jet** a large jet airliner. [Prob. mumbo-*jumbo*; earlier than Jumbo the elephant.]

jumbuck *jum'buk,* (*Austr.*) *n.* a sheep. [Origin unknown.]

jumby, jumbie *jum'bi, n.* a West Indian Negro's word for a ghost or evil spirit. [Congolese *zumbi*.]

jumelle *joo-mel', zhü-mel, n.* a paired or twinned article, esp. opera-glasses. [Fr., twin; cf. **gemel, gimmal.**]

jump[1] *jump, v.i.* to spring or bound: to move suddenly: to bounce: to rise suddenly: to pass discontinuously: to throb: to agree, coincide (*with*). — *v.t.* to cause or help to leap: to toss: to leap over, from, or on to: to skip over: to spring or start, as game: to risk (*Shak.*): to appropriate, as when the owner has failed to satisfy conditions or has abandoned his claim: to attack (*slang*): (of a male) to have sexual intercourse with (*vulg.*): to make up hastily, patch up (*obs.*): — *pr.p.* **jump'ing;** *pa.t.* and *pa.p.* **jumped.** — *n.* act of jumping: a bound: an obstacle to be jumped over: height or distance jumped: a sudden rise or movement: a start: (in *pl.*) convulsive movements, chorea, delirium tremens, or the like: a bounce: a discontinuity: a venture, a hazard (*Shak.*). — *adv.* (*Shak.*) exactly. — *n.* **jump'er** one who jumps: a long iron drill used in quarries, etc.: one of certain Welsh Methodists (*c.* 1760), who jumped about in worship. — *adv.* **jump'ily.** — *n.* **jump'iness.** — *adj.* **jump'y** nervy, inclined to start. — **jump'-cut** in filming, an abrupt change from one scene or subject to another, across an interval of time. — *adj.* **jumped'-up** (*coll.*) upstart. — **jump'ing-bean** the

seed of a Mexican euphorbiaceous plant (*Sebastiania*), which an enclosed larva causes to move or jump; **jump'ing-deer'** the black-tailed American deer; **jump'-ing-hare'** a South African rodent akin to the jerboa; **jump'ing-jack** a toy figure whose limbs can be moved by pulling a string; **jump'ing-mouse'** a genus (*Zapus*) of jumping rodents, American and Chinese; **jump'ing= spider** any member of the spider family *Salticidae* that leap upon their prey; **jump'-jet** a fighter plane able to land and take off vertically; **jump leads** two electrical cables for supplying power to start a car from another battery; **jump'-off** (*U.S.*) the start: starting-place: see **jump off** below; **jump'-seat** a movable carriage-seat: a carriage with a movable seat: a folding seat; **jump suit** a one-piece, trouser and jacket or blouse, garment for either sex. — **for the high jump** see **high; jump at** to accept with eagerness; **jump down someone's throat** to assail someone with violent rating; **jumping-off place** the terminus of a route: the point where one sets forth into the wilds, the unknown, etc.; **jump off** in showjumping, to compete in another, more difficult round, when two or more competitors have an equal score after the first (*n.* **jump'-off**); **jump on** to jump so as to come down heavily upon: to censure promptly and vigorously; **jump** (one's) **bail** to abscond, forfeiting one's bail; **jump ship** (*coll.*) (of a sailor) to leave one's ship while still officially employed, in service, etc.; **jump start** to start a car by pushing it and engaging the gears while it is moving (*n.* **jump'-start;** also **bump start**); **jump the gun** (i.e. the starting-gun in a race) to get off one's mark too soon, act prematurely, take an unfair advantage; **jump the queue** to get ahead of one's turn (*lit.* and *fig.*); **jump to conclusions** to form inferences prematurely; **jump to it!** hurry! [Prob. onomatopoeic.]

jump[2] *jump, n.* a short coat: (in *pl.*) stays: clothes. — *n.* **jump'er** an overall, slipped over the head: a woman's knitted upper garment, originally one loose at the waist: a pinafore dress (*U.S.*). [Perh. from Fr. *juppe,* now *jupe,* a petticoat.]

juncate (*Spens.*). A form of **junket.**

junco *jung'kō, n.* the reed-bunting (*obs.*): a North American snow-bird: — *pl.* **junc'oes, junc'os.** [Sp. *junco* — L. *juncus,* rush.]

junction *jung'shən, jungk', n.* a joining, a union or combination: place or point of union, esp. of railway lines. — **junction box** a casing for a junction of electrical wires. [L. *junctiō, -ōnis*; see **join.**]

juncture *jungk'chər, n.* a joining, a union: a critical or important point of time. [L. *junctūra*; see **join.**]

Juncus *jungk'əs, n.* the typical genus of rushes, giving name to the **Juncā'ceae,** the rush family: (without *cap.*) a plant of this genus. — *adj.* **juncā'ceous.** [L. *juncus,* a rush.]

June *joon, n.* the sixth month. — **June'berry** the fruit of the shad-bush; **June drop** a falling of immature fruit through a variety of causes, at its height around June. [L. *Jūnius.*]

juneating *joon'ēt-ing.* An erroneous form of **jenneting.**

Jungermanniales *yoong-ər-man-i-ā'lēz, n.pl.* one of the main divisions of the Hepaticae, with thallus or leafy stem, and usually capsule opening by four valves. [Ludwig *Jungermann* (1572–1653), German botanist.]

Jungian *joong'i-ən, adj.* of, according to, the theories of the Swiss psychologist, Carl Gustav *Jung* (1875–1961).

jungle *jung'gl, n.* originally waste ground: a dense tropical growth of thickets, brushwood, etc.: dense tropical forest: a jumbled assemblage of large objects: a confusing mass of, e.g. regulations: a place or situation where there is ruthless competition, or cruel struggle for survival. — *adj.* **jungli** (*jung'gli;* *Ind.*) inhabiting a jungle: wild and boorish. — *n.* an inhabitant of a jungle: an uneducated peasant. — *adj.* **jung'ly.** — **jungle fever** a severe malarial fever; **jungle fowl** the wild parent of the barndoor fowl; **jungle juice** (*slang*) alcoholic liquor, esp. of poor quality, or home-made. — *adj.* **jun'gle-green** very dark green. [Sans. *jāngala,* desert.]

junior *jōōn'yər, adj.* younger: less advanced: of lower standing. — *n.* one younger, less advanced, or of lower standing: a young person: a bridge-player on the declarer's right: an American student in his third year (of four). — *n.* **juniority** (*-i-or'i-ti*). — **junior common room** (*abbrev.* **JCR**) in some universities, a common room for the use of students, as opposed to a senior common room, for the use of staff; **junior miss** in the fashion trade, a teenage girl or young woman; **junior optime** see **optime**; **junior service** the Army; **junior soph** an undergraduate of the second year at Cambridge. [L. *jūnior*, compar. of *jŭvenis*, young.]

juniper *jōō'ni-pər, n.* an evergreen coniferous shrub (**Juniperus**) whose berries are used in making gin. [L. *jūniperus*.]

junk¹ *jungk, n.* a Chinese vessel, with high fore-castle and poop, sometimes large and three-masted. [Port. *junco*, app. — Javanese *djong*.]

junk² *jungk, n.* pieces of old cordage (*arch.*): rubbish generally: a chunk: salt meat, perh. because it becomes as hard as old rope (orig. *naut.*): nonsense (*fig.*): a narcotic (*slang*). — *v.t.* to cut into junks: to treat as junk: (esp. *U.S.*) to discard, abandon as useless. — *n.* **junk'er, junk'ie, junk'y** a narcotics addict: (**junkie** or **junky**; *loosely*) one hooked on something, an addict (*coll.* usu. in combination, as *art junkie, coffee junkie*). — *adj.* **junk'y** rubbishy: worthless. — **junk bond** a bond offering a high yield but with low security; **junk'-bottle** (*U.S.*) a thick strong bottle of green or black glass; **junk'-dealer, junk'man** a dealer in junk; **junk food** food of little nutritional value, usu. easily available and quick to prepare; **junk mail** unsolicited mail such as advertising circulars, etc.; **junk'-ring** a metal ring confining the packing of a piston; **junk'-shop** a place where junk is sold; **junk'-yard** a yard in which junk is stored or collected for sale. [Origin doubtful.]

junkanoo. See **John Canoe.**

junker¹ *yŏŏngk'ər, n.* a young German noble or squire: an overbearing, narrow-minded, reactionary aristocrat. — *ns.* **junk'erdom; junk'erism.** [Ger., — *jung*, young, *Herr*, lord.]

junker². See **junk².**

junket *junk'it, n.* a rush-basket (*dial.*): a cream cheese: any sweetmeat or delicacy (*obs.*): curds mixed with cream, sweetened and flavoured: a feast or merrymaking, a picnic, an outing, a spree. — *v.i.* to feast, banquet, take part in a convivial entertainment or spree. — *v.t.* to feast, regale, entertain: — *pr.p.* **junk'eting;** *pa.p.* **junk'eted.** — *n.* (often in *pl.*) **junk'eting** a merry feast or entertainment, picnicking. [A.Fr. *jonquette*, rush-basket — L. *juncus*, a rush.]

junkie, junky. See **junk².**

Juno *jōō'nō, n.* in Roman mythology, the wife of Jupiter, identified with the Greek Hera, special protectress of marriage and guardian of woman from birth to death: a queenly woman. — *adjs.* **Junō'nian** pertaining to Juno; **Junoesque** (*-esk'*) large, buxom, and (usu.) beautiful. [L. *Jūnō, -ōnis.*]

junta *jun'tə, hŏŏn'ta, n.* a meeting, council: a Spanish grand council of state: (in the following meanings also **jun'to,** *pl.* **jun'tos**) a body of men joined or united for some secret intrigue: a confederacy: a cabal or faction: a government formed by a usu. small group following a coup d'état. [Sp., L. *jungĕre, junctum*, to join.]

jupati *jōō'pə-tē* or *-tē', n.* a species of raphia palm. [Tupí.]

Jupiter *jōō'pi-tər, n.* the chief god among the Romans, the parallel of the Greek Zeus (also **Jove**): the largest and, next to Venus, the brightest of the planets. — **Jupiter's beard** the house-leek: a kidney-vetch: a fungus (*Hydnum barba-jovis*). [L. *Jūpiter, Juppiter*, Father (*pater*) Jove.]

jupon *jōō'pən, n.* a sleeveless jacket or close-fitting coat, extending down over the hips: a petticoat. [Fr.]

jura. See **jus.**

Jura. See **Jurassic.**

jural *jōō'rəl, adj.* pertaining to natural or positive right.

— *adv.* **ju'rally.** [L. *jūs, jūris*, law.]

jurant *jōō'rənt, adj.* taking an oath. — *n.* one who takes an oath. — *adj.* **ju'ratory** pertaining to an oath. [L. *jūrāre, -ātum*, to swear.]

Jurassic *jōō-ras'ik,* (*geol.*) *adj.* of the middle division of the Mesozoic rocks, well-developed in the *Jura* Mountains. — *n.* the Jurassic period or system. — Also **Ju'ra.**

jurat¹ *jōō'rat, n.* the official memorandum at the end of an affidavit, showing the time when and the person before whom it was sworn. [L. *jūrātum*, sworn — *jūrāre*, to swear.]

jurat² *jōō'rat, n.* a sworn officer, as a magistrate. [Fr., — L. *jūrāre, -ātum*, to swear.]

juratory. See **jurant.**

jure *jōō're, yōō're,* (L.) *adv.* by law. — **jure divino** (*di-vī'nō, dē-wē'nō*) by divine law; **jure humano** (*hū-mā'nō,*(h)*ōō-mā'nō*) by human law.

juridical *jōō-rid'ik-əl,* **jurid'ic** *adjs.* relating to the distribution of justice: pertaining to a judge: used in courts of law. — *adv.* **jurid'ically.** — **juridical days** days on which law courts are in session. [L. *jūridicus* — *jūs, jūris*, law, *dīcĕre*, to declare.]

jurisconsult *jōō'ris-kon-sult', n.* one who is consulted on the law: a lawyer who gives opinions on cases put to him: one learned in law. [L. *jūris cōnsultus* — *jūs, jūris*, law, *cōnsulĕre, cōnsultus*, to consult.]

jurisdiction *jōō-ris-dik'shən, n.* the distribution of justice: legal authority: extent of power: district over which any authority extends. — *adjs.* **jurisdic'tional, jurisdic'tive.** [L. *jūrisdictiō, -ōnis.*]

jurisprudence *jōō-ris-prōō'dəns, n.* the science or knowledge of law. — *adj.* **jurispru'dent** learned in law. — *n.* one who is learned in law. — *adj.* **jurisprudential** (*-den'shl*). — **medical jurisprudence** forensic medicine (see **forensic**). [L. *jūrisprūdentia* — *jūs, jūris*, law, *prūdentia*, knowledge.]

jurist *jōō'rist, n.* one who is versed in the science of law, esp. Roman or civil law: a student of law: a graduate in law: a lawyer (*U.S.*). — *adjs.* **jurist'ic, -al.** — *adv.* **jurist'ically.** [Fr. *juriste.*]

juris utriusque doctor *jōō'ris ū-tri-us'kwē, yōō'ris ōō-triōōs'kwe, dok'tör,* (L.) doctor both of canon and of civil law.

jury *jōō'ri, n.* a body of persons sworn to declare the truth on evidence before them: a committee of adjudicators or examiners. — *n.* **ju'ror** one who serves on a jury (also **ju'ryman,** — *pl.* **ju'rymen,** — *pl.* **ju'rywomen**). — **ju'ry-box** the place in which the jury sits during a trial; **ju'ry-pro'cess** a writ summoning a jury. — **jury of matrons** a jury of women empanelled to give a decision in a case of alleged pregnancy. [A.Fr. *juree* — *jurer* — L. *jūrāre*, to swear.]

jurymast *jōō'ri-mäst, -məst, n.* a temporary mast raised instead of one lost. — *adj.* **ju'ry-rigged** rigged in a temporary way. — **ju'ry-rudd'er** a temporary rudder for one lost. [Not *injury-mast*, but perh. O.Fr. *ajurie*, aid — L. *adjūtāre*, to aid.]

jus¹ *jus, yōōs,* (L.) *n.* law: a legal right: — *pl.* **jura** (*jōō'rə, yōō'rä*). — **jus canonicum** (*kə-non'i-kəm, ka-non'ikōōm*) canon law; **jus civile** (*si-vī'lē, kē-wē'le, -vē'*) civil law; **jus divinum** (*di-vī'nəm, di-wē'nōōm, -vē'*) divine right; **jus gentium** (*jen'shi-əm, gen'ti-ōōm*) law of nations; **jus mariti** (*ma'ri-tī, -tē*) right of a husband; **jus naturale** (*nat-ū-rā'lē, nat-ōō-rāl'e*) law of nature: common sense of justice; **jus primae noctis** (*prī'mē, prē'mī, nok'tis*) the formerly alleged right of a feudal superior to deflower a vassal's bride; **jus sanguinis** (*sang'gwi-nis*) the principle that one's nationality is that of one's natural parents; **jus soli** (*sō'lī, sō'lē*) the principle that one's nationality is that of the country in which one was born.

jus² *zhüs,* Fr. *zhü,* (*cook.*) *n.* juice: gravy. [Fr.]

jusqu'au bout *zhüs-kō bōō,* (Fr.) to the very end. — *ns.* **jusqu'auboutisme** (Fr.) the practice of pursuing an object to the last; **jusqu'auboutiste** (Fr.; also anglicised as **jusqu'about'ist**).

jussive *jus'iv, adj.* expressing command. — *n.* a grammatical form or construction expressing command. [L. *jubēre, jussum*, to command.]

just[1] *just*. Same as **joust**.

just[2] *just, adj.* righteous (*B.*): fair: impartial: according to justice: due: in accordance with facts: well-grounded: accurately true: exact: normal (*obs.*): close-fitting (*obs.*). — *adv.* precisely: exactly: so much and no more: barely: only: quite (*coll.*). — *adv.* **just'ly** in a just manner: equitably: accurately: by right. — *n.* **just'ness** equity: fittingness: exactness. — **just intonation** observance of the true mathematical theoretical pitch, without compromise or temperament. — **just about** nearly: more or less; **just about to** see **about to; just now** precisely at this moment: hence, a little while ago, or very soon; **just so** exactly, I agree: in a precise, neat manner. [Fr. *juste*, or L. *jūstus* — *jūs*, law.]

juste milieu *zhüst mēl-yø*, (Fr.) *n.* the just mean, the happy medium.

justice *jus'tis, n.* the quality of being just: integrity: impartiality: rightness: the awarding of what is due: a judge: a magistrate. — *ns.* **jus'ticer** a vindicator or administrator of justice; **jus'ticeship** the office or dignity of a justice or judge. — *adj.* **justiciable** (*jus-tish'i-ə-bl*) liable to trial. — *ns.* **justiciar** (*-tish'i-ər; hist.*) an administrator of justice: a chief-justice; **justiciary** (*-tish'i-ə-ri*) a judge: a chief-justice: jurisdiction of a justiciar or justiciary. — *adj.* pertaining to the administration of justice. — **justices' justice** the kind of justice sometimes administered by the unpaid and amateur magistracy of England. — **chief'-jus'tice** in the Commonwealth, a judge presiding over a supreme court: in the U.S., a judge who is chairman of a group of judges in a court; **do justice to** to give full advantage to: to treat fairly: to appreciate (a meal, etc.) fully (*coll.*); **European Court of Justice** an EEC institution whose function is to ensure that the laws embodied in the EEC treaties are observed, and to rule on alleged infringements; **High Court of Justice** a section of the English Supreme Court, comprising Chancery and King's (Queen's) Bench Divisions; **High Court of Justiciary** the supreme criminal court in Scotland; **Justice of the Peace** (abbrev. **JP**) a local minor magistrate commissioned to keep the peace; **Lord Chief=justice** the chief judge of the King's (or Queen's) Bench Division of the High Court of Justice; **Lord Justice=clerk** the Scottish judge ranking next to the Lord Justice-general, presiding over the Second Division of the Inner House of the Court of Session, vice-president of the High Court of Justiciary; **Lord Justice-general** the highest judge in Scotland, called also the Lord President of the Court of Session. [Fr., — L. *jūstitia*.]

justify *jus'ti-fī, v.t.* to make just: to prove or show to be just or right: to vindicate: to absolve: to punish, esp. to hang (*obs.*): to adjust by spacing (*print.*): — *pr.p.* **jus'tifying;** *pa.t.* and *pa.p.* **jus'tified.** — *adj.* **jus'tifiable** (or *-fī'*) that may be justified or defended. — *n.* **jus'tifiableness** (or *-fī'*). — *adv.* **jus'tifiably** (or *-fī'*). —

n. **justification** (*jus-ti-fi-kā'shən*) act of justifying: that which justifies: vindication: absolution: a plea of sufficient reason. — *adjs.* **jus'tificātive, justificatory** (*jus-tif'i-kə-tə-ri* or *jus'ti-fi-kā-tə-ri*, or *-kā'*) having power to justify. — *ns.* **jus'tificātor, jus'tifier** one who defends or vindicates: he who pardons and absolves from guilt and punishment. — **justifiable homicide** the killing of a person in self-defence, or to prevent an atrocious crime. — **justification by faith** the doctrine that men are justified by faith in Christ. [Fr. *justifier* and L. *jūstificāre* — *jūstus*, just, *facēre*, to make.]

justle. See **jostle.**

jut *jut, n.* a projection: a jerking movement (*obs.*). — *v.i.* to project: — *pr.p.* **jutt'ing;** *pa.t.* and *pa.p.* **jutt'ed.** — *adj.* **jutt'ing.** — *adv.* **jutt'ingly.** — **jut'-win'dow** a bay window. [A form of **jet**[2].]

jute *jōōt, n.* the fibre of *Corchorus capsularis* and *C. olitorius* (fam. Tiliaceae), plants of Bangladesh, etc., used for making sacks, mats, etc.: the plant itself. — Also *adj.* — **China jute** a species of Abutilon: its fibre. [Bengali *jhuto* — Sans. *jūṭa*, matted hair.]

Jute *jōōt, n.* a member of a Germanic people originally from Jutland, who with the Angles and Saxons invaded Britain in the 5th century. [M.Eng. — L.L. *Jutae, Jutes.*]

jutty *jut'i, n.* a projecting part of a building: a pier, a jetty. — *v.t.* (*Shak.*) to project beyond. — *v.i.* to jut. [Cf. **jetty.**]

juvenal *jōō'vən-əl,* (*Shak.*) *n.* a youth. [L. *juvenālis,* belonging to youth — *juvenis,* young.]

Juvenalian *jōōv-i-nā'li-ən, adj.* of the Roman satirist *Juvenal* (Decimus Junius Juvenalis, 1st-2nd cent. A.D.): lurid and denunciatory rather than humorous.

juvenescent *jōō-vən-es'ənt, adj.* becoming youthful. — *n.* **juvenesc'ence.** [L. *juvenēscĕre,* to grow young.]

juvenile *jōō'və-nīl, adj.* young: pertaining or suited to youth or young people: having or retaining characteristics of youth: childish. — *n.* a young person: a book written for the young: an actor who plays youthful parts. — *n.* **ju'venileness.** — *n.pl.* **juvenilia** (*-il'yə*) writings or works of one's childhood or youth. — *n.* **juvenility** (*-il'i-ti*) juvenile character. — **juvenile court** a special court for the trial of children and young persons aged under seventeen; **juvenile delinquent, juvenile offender** a young law-breaker, in Britain under the age of seventeen; **juvenile hormone** a hormone necessary to an insect in immature stages, which must be absent when it changes to adult form. [L. *juvenīlis* — *juvenis,* young.]

juxtaposition *juks-tə-pə-zish'ən, n.* a placing or being placed close together. — *v.t.* **jux'tapose** (or *-pōz'*) to place side by side. — *adj.* **juxtaposi'tional.** — **juxtaposition twin** crystals twinned as if set together face to face without interpenetration. [L. *juxtā,* near, and **position, pose**[1].]

jymold. See **gimmal.**

Jynx *jingks, n.* the wryneck genus: (without *cap.*) a wryneck. [L. *iynx* — Gr. *iynx* or *īynx*.]

K

K, k *kā, n.* the eleventh letter in our alphabet, derived from Greek kappa, representing a back voiceless stop, formed by raising the back of the tongue to the soft palate: as a mediaeval numeral, K = 250: in mathematics *k* often stands for a constant quantity: in thermometry K stands for (a degree on) the Kelvin scale: often used as a symbol for a thousand (from **kilo-**): a unit of 1024 words, bytes or bits (*comput.*). — **the five Ks** the symbols of a Sikh's spiritual and cultural allegiance to Sikhism, worn by baptised Sikhs —**kaccha, kangha, kara, kesh,** and **kirpan** (qq.v.)

ka¹ *kä, n.* in ancient Egyptian religion, the double or genius, or individuality. [Egypt.]

ka², kae *kā*, (*obs.*) *v.t.* serve (in the phrase *ka me, ka thee,* one good turn deserves another). [Origin unknown.]

ka³. See **kae¹.**

Kaaba *kä'bɔ, n.* the holy building at Mecca into which the Black Stone is built. [Ar. *ka'bah — ka'b,* cube.]

kaama *kä'mɔ, n.* the hartebeest. [Of Hottentot or Bantu origin.]

kabab. See **kebab.**

kabala. See **cabbala.**

kabaya *kä-bä'yɔ, n.* a loose tunic. [Malay, from Pers. or Ar.]

kabbala(h). See **cabbala.**

kabele. See **kebele.**

kabeljou, kabeljouw *kob', kub'l-yō, n.* a large South African fish, *Johnius hololepidotus.* [Afrik.]

kabob. See **kebab.**

kabuki *kä-boo-kē', n.* a popular Japanese dramatic form, historical, classical, eclectic, with music, in which traditionally men played both male and female roles.

Kabyle *ka-bīl', n.* one of a branch of the great Berber people of North Africa: a dialect of Berber. [Fr., — Ar. *qabū'il,* pl. of *qahīlah,* a tribe.]

kaccha *kuch'ɔ, n.* the short trousers traditionally worn by Sikhs. [Punjabi.]

kacha, kachcha. Same as **cutcha.**

kachahri, kacheri *kuch'ɔ-ri, kuch-er'i, n.* an Indian magistrate's office or courthouse. — Also **cutcherry.** [Hindi *kacahrī.*]

kachina *kɔ-chē'nɔ, n.* any of the ancestral spirits invoked by the Pueblo Indians of North America at ritual ceremonies: a dancer who impersonates the ancestral spirits at these ceremonies: — **kachina doll** a doll representing a kachina given to children by the dancers at these ceremonies. [Hopi *qachina,* supernatural.]

kack-handed. See **cack-handed.**

Kaddish *kad'ish, n.* a Jewish form of thanksgiving and prayer, used at funerals, etc. [Aramaic *qaddīsh.*]

kade. See **ked.**

kadi *kä'di, n.* Same as **cadi.**

kae¹ *kā,* (*Scot.*) *n.* a jackdaw. — Also **ka.** [Cf. M.Du. *ka,* Dan. *kaa.*]

kae². See **ka².**

Kaffir, Kaffer *kaf'ɔr, kuf'ɔr, n.* name applied to certain indigenous peoples of S. Africa including the Xhosa (*hist.*): now often used deprecatorily: any of the languages spoken by them (*hist.*): (*pl.*) S. African mining shares. — Earlier **Caffre, Kaf'ir.** — Also *adj.* — **kaff'ir-boom** (Du. *boom,* tree) the coral-tree (*Erythrina caffra*); **kaffir bread** the pith of S. African cycads (*Encephalartos*); **kaffir corn** sorghum. [**Kafir** (q.v.).]

kaffiyeh *käf-ē'ye, n.* a Bedouin shawl for the head. — Also **kuffi'(y)eh, kuf(f)i'ah, kufi'ya(h).** [Ar. *kaffīyah.*]

kafila. See **cafila.**

Kafir *käf'ɔr, n.* an infidel (*offensive*; also **Caffre**): a native of Kafiristan (in Afghanistan): a Kaffir. [Ar. *käfir,* unbeliever.]

Kafkaesque *kaf'kɔ-esk', adj.* in the style of, reminiscent of, the ideas, work, etc. of the Czech novelist Franz *Kafka* (1883–1924), esp. in his vision of man's isolated existence in a dehumanised world.

kaftan. Same as **caftan.**

kago *käg'ō, n.* a Japanese basketwork palanquin: — *pl.* **kag'os.** [Jap. *kago.*]

kagool, kagoul(e). See **cagoul(e).**

kahal *kä'hal, n.* any of the Jewish communities scattered across Europe: the local governing body of any of these communities. [Heb. *kähal,* congregation, community.]

kai *kä'ē, kī,* (*N. Zealand,* etc.) *n.* food. — *n.* **kai'kai** food: feast. — *v.t.* to eat. [Maori; also in other Polynesian languages.]

kaiak. Same as **kayak.**

kaid *kä-ēd', käd, n.* a North African chief. [Ar. *qä'īd;* cf. **alcaide.**]

kaie *kā,* an obsolete form of **key¹,².**

kaif. See **kef.**

kail¹ *kāl, n.* a ninepin: (in *pl.*) the game of ninepins: (in *pl.*) skittles. [Cf. Du. *kegel,* Ger. *Kegel,* Fr. *quille.*]

kail², kaim. See **kale, kame¹.**

kaimakam *kī-mä-käm', n.* a Turkish lieutenant-colonel or lieutenant-governor. [Turk. *kaymakam* — Ar. *qä'imaqäm.*]

kain. Same as **cain.**

kainite *kī'nīt, kā'nīt, kā'in-īt, n.* hydrous magnesium sulphate with potassium chloride, found in salt deposits, used as a fertiliser. [Ger. *Kainit* — Gr. *kainos,* new, recent.]

Kainozoic. Same as **Cainozoic.**

kaisar-i-Hind *kī'sär-i-hind', n.* title from 1876 to 1947 of the British monarch as emperor of India. [Pers. *qaysari-Hind* — L. *Caesar.*]

kaiser *kī'zɔr, n.* an emperor, esp. a German Emperor. — Also (*obs.*) **kesɔr, keasar** (*kē'zɔr*). — *ns.* **kai'serdom;** **kai'serin** the wife of a kaiser; **kai'serism; kai'sership.** — **the Kaiser's war** the war of 1914–18 (Kaiser Wilhelm II). [Ger., — L. *Caesar.*]

kajawah *kä-jä'wä, n.* a camel litter or pannier. [Pers.]

kaka *kä'kä, n.* a New Zealand parrot (*Nestor meridionalis*). — *ns.* **ka'ka-beak, -bill** the New Zealand glory-pea (*Clianthus*); **ka'kapō** the New Zealand owl-parrot, large-winged but almost flightless: — *pl.* **ka'kapōs.** [Maori *kaka,* parrot, *po,* night.]

kakemono *kak-i-mō'nō, n.* a Japanese wall-picture or calligraphic inscription on a roller: — *pl.* **kakemō'nos.** [Jap. *kake,* to hang, *mono,* thing.]

kaki *kä'kē, n.* the Japanese persimmon, or Chinese date-plum. [Jap.]

kakiemon *kä-ki-ā'mon, n.* a Japanese porcelain, first made by Sakaida *Kakiemon* in the 17th century, recognisable from its characteristic use of iron-red.

kakistocracy *kak-is-tok'rɔ-si, n.* government by the worst. [Gr. *kakistos,* superl. of *kakos,* bad, *kratos,* power.]

kakodyl. Same as **cacodyl.**

kala-azar *kä'lä-ä-zär', n.* a tropical fever, characterised by bloodlessness, and ascribed to a protozoan parasite. [Assamese *kälä,* black, *āzär,* disease.]

kalamdan *kal'am-dan, n.* a Persian writing-case. [Pers. *qalamdān* — *qalam,* a pen, *dān,* holding.]

kalamkari *kal-am-kä'rē, n.* a method of colouring and decorating by several dyeings or printings: a chintz so treated. [Pers. *qalamkārī,* writing, painting, etc. — *qalam,* pen.]

kalashnikov *kɔ-lash'ni-kof, n.* a sub-machine gun made in the U.S.S.R. [Russ.]

kale, kail *kāl, n.* a cabbage with open curled leaves:

cabbage generally: broth of which kale is a chief ingredient, and also dinner (*Scot.*). — *ns.* **kail'-pot'** (*Scot.* -**pat'**); **kail'-runt'** a cabbage stem; **kail'yard'**, -**yaird'** a cabbage-patch. — **Kailyard school** a set of Scottish sentimental story-writers (one of these, Ian Maclaren, used the title *Beside the Bonnie Brier Bush*, 1894, in allusion to the Jacobite song 'There grows a bonnie brier bush in our kailyard'). — **give someone his kale through the reek** (*Scot.*) to reprimand someone severely. [Northern form of **cole**.]

kaleidophone kə-lī'də-fōn, *n.* an instrument for exhibiting sonorous vibrations by lines of light on a screen. [Gr. *kalos*, beautiful, *eidos*, form, *phōnē*, voice.]

kaleidoscope kə-lī'də-skōp, *n.* an optical toy in which one sees an ever-changing variety of beautiful colours and forms. — *adj.* **kaleidoscopic** (-skop'ik) pertaining to a kaleidoscope: showing constant change. [Gr. *kalos*, beautiful, *eidos*, form, *skopeein*, to look.]

kalendar, kalends. Same as **calendar, calends.**

Kalevala kä'le-vä-lə, *n.* the great Finnish epic, in eight-syllabled trochaic verse (from which Longfellow's *Hiawatha* is imitated) pieced together from oral tradition by Dr. Elias Lönnrot in 1835–49. [Finnish *kaleva*, a hero, -*la*, denoting place.]

kali[1] kal'i, or kā'lī, *n.* the prickly saltwort or glasswort (*Salsola kali*): its ash (*obs.*): alkali, esp. potash (*obs.*). — *ns.* **kalinite** (kal'in-īt) native potash alum; **kā'lium** potassium. [Ar. *qili* as in root of **alkali**.]

kali[2] kä'lē, *n.* a carpet with long nap: the large carpet covering the centre of a Persian room. [Pers. *kālī*.]

Kali kä'lē, *n.* a Hindu goddess, Durga, wife of Siva, as goddess of destruction. [Sans.]

kalian käl'yän', *n.* a Persian hookah. [Pers.]

kalif. See **caliph.**

Kaliyuga käl-i-yŏŏ'gə, *n.* in Hindu mythology, the present (fourth) age of the world, of universal degeneracy. [Sans.]

Kallima kal'i-mə, *n.* an Oriental genus of butterflies, mimicking dead leaves. [Gr. *kallimos*, beautiful.]

kallitype kal'i-tīp, *n.* a photographic process in which ferric are reduced to ferrous salts. [Gr. *kallos*, beauty, *typos*, type.]

Kalmia kal'mi-ə, *n.* a genus of North American evergreen shrubs of the heath family, including the mountain laurel or calico-bush: (without *cap.*) a shrub of the genus. [From Peter *Kalm*, pupil of Linnaeus.]

Kalmuck kal'muk, *n.* a member of a Mongolian race in China and Russia: their language. — Also *adj.* — Also **Cal'muck.** [Turki and Russ.]

kalong kä'long, *n.* a large fruit-bat. [Malay *kālong*.]

kalotype. Same as **calotype.**

kalpa kal'pə, *n.* a day of Brahma, a period of 4320 million years. — Also **cal'pa.** [Sans., formation.]

kalpak käl'päk, or -päk', *n.* a triangular Turkish or Tatar felt cap. — Also **calpac, calpack.** [Turk. *qālpāq*.]

kalpis kal'pis, *n.* a water-vase. [Gr.]

kalumpit kä-lŏŏm-pēt', *n.* a Philippine tree of the myrobalan genus: its edible fruit. [Tagálog.]

kalyptra ka-lip'trə, *n.* a veil worn by Greek women. [Gr.; see also **calyptra.**]

kam, kamme, cam kam, (*Shak.*) *adj.* and *adv.* awry. [Cf. W., Gael., Ir. *cam*.]

Kama kä'mä, *n.* the god of love in the Puranas: impure desire. — Also **Cama, Ka'madeva** (-dä-vä). [Sans. *Kāma*.]

kamacite kam'ə-sīt, *n.* a variety of nickeliferous iron, found in meteorites. [Ger. *Kamacit* (*obs.*), from Gr. *kamax, kamakos*, vine-pole, shaft.]

kamala kä'mä-lä, *n.* an orange dyestuff got from the fruit-hairs of an East Indian tree of the spurge family (*Mallotus philippinensis*): the tree itself. — Also **kamela, kamila** (kä-mä'lä, -mē'lä). [Sans. *kamala*; Hind. *kamēlā, kamīlā*.]

kame[1], **kaim** kām, *n.* a comb (*Scot.*): a low irregular ridge like a cock's comb: an esker, a bank or ridge of gravel, sand, etc., associated with the glacial deposits of Scotland (*geol.*): a fortified site (*Scott*). [Northern form of **comb**[1].]

kame[2], **came** kām, *n.* a lead rod for framing a pane in a lattice or stained-glass window.

kamees ka-mēs'. Same as **camise.**

kameez kə-mēz', *n.* in S. Asia, a loose tunic with tight sleeves, worn by women. — See also **shalwar-kameez.** [Urdu *kamis* — Arab. *qamīs* (see **camise**).]

kamela. See **kamala.**

kamerad kam-ər-äd', *interj.* comrade (said to have been a German form of surrender or appeal for quarter). — *v.i.* to surrender. [Ger., — Fr. *camarade*, comrade.]

kami kä'mi, *n.* a Japanese lord, national god, demigod, or deified hero (or any of their supposed descendants, as the mikados and, formerly, the imperial family), or any natural force or power. [Jap., superior.]

kamichi kä'mē-shē, *n.* the horned screamer, a South American bird. [Fr., from Carib.]

kamik kä'mik, *n.* a knee-length sealskin boot. [Eskimo.]

kamikaze kä-mi-kä'zē, *n.* (a Japanese airman, or plane, making) a suicidal attack. — Also *adj.* (usu. *fig.*) of, or pertaining to, a kamikaze attack or someone who carries it out. [Jap., divine wind.]

kamila. See **kamala.**

kamis ka-mēs'. Same as **camise.**

kamme. See **kam.**

kampong kam'pong, kam-pong', *n.* an enclosed space: a village. [Malay.]

kamseen, kamsin. Same as **khamsin.**

kana kä'nä, *n.* Japanese syllabic writing, as distinguished from Japanese written in Chinese characters. [Jap.]

kanaka kən-ak'ä, kan'ə-kä, *n.* a South Sea Islander, esp. an indentured or forced labourer: the Hawaiian language. [Hawaiian, a man.]

Kanarese, Canarese kan-ər-ēz', *adj.* of *Kanara* in western India. — *n.* one of the people thereof: their Dravidian language, now called *Kannada*, akin to Telugu.

kandy kan'di, *n.* Same as **candy**[2].

kaneh, caneh kä'ne, *n.* a Hebrew measure of 6 cubits' length. [Heb. *qāneh*, reed, cane.]

kang kang, *n.* a large Chinese water-jar: a platform (e.g. of brick) for sleeping on that can be warmed by a fire underneath. [Chin.]

kanga, khanga kang'gə, *n.* in East Africa, a piece of cotton cloth, usually brightly decorated, wound around the body as a woman's dress. [Swahili.]

kangaroo kang-gə-rŏŏ', *n.* a large Australian herbivorous marsupial (fam. *Macropodidae*), with short forelimbs, very long hind-legs and great power of leaping: (in *pl.*: with *cap.*) the Australian national Rugby league team: (in *pl.*; *Brit. slang*) Australian mining shares. — *v.i.* (*Austr. coll.*) of a car, to move forward in jerks. — **kangaroo'-app'le** the edible fruit of a species of Solanum: the plant that yields it; **kangaroo closure** the method of allowing the chairman to decide which clauses shall be discussed and which passed or leaped over; **kangaroo court** a court operated by a mob, by prisoners in jail, by any improperly constituted body: a tribunal before which a fair trial is impossible: a comic burlesque court; **kangaroo'-grass** a valuable Australian fodder grass (*Anthistiria* or *Themeda*); **kangaroo justice** the kind of justice dispensed by a kangaroo court; **kangaroo paw** (*Austr.*) a plant of the genus *Anigozanthus*, the flower of which resembles a paw in shape; **kangaroo'-rat'** a North American rodent (*Dipodomys*) akin to the jerboa: sometimes used for rat-kangaroo; **kangaroo'-thorn'** a prickly Australian acacia (*Acacia armata*). [Aboriginal.]

kangha kung'hə, *n.* the comb traditionally worn by Sikhs in their hair. [Punjabi.]

Kannada kun'ə-də, *n.* an important Dravidian language. [Kanarese, *Kannada*.]

kans kans, *n.* an Indian grass which is allied to sugar-cane. [Hindi *kās*.]

kant. Same as **cant**[2].

kantar, cantar *kan-tär′, n.* a varying weight in Turkey, Egypt, etc., approximately a hundredweight.   [Ar. *qintār*; see **quintal**.]

kantele *kan′tə-lā, n.* a Finnish zither.   — Also **kan′tela**, [Finn. *kantele*.]

kanten *kan′tən, n.* agar-agar jelly.   [Jap.]

kantha *kän′thə, n.* an embroidered cloth quilt.   [Beng.]

Kantian *kant′i-ən, adj.* pertaining to the German philosopher Immanuel *Kant* (1724–1804) or his philosophy.   — *ns.* **Kan′tianism, Kant′ism** the doctrines or philosophy of Kant; **Kant′ist** one who is a disciple or follower of Kant.

kantikoy, canticoy *kan′ti-koi,* **cantico** (*-kō; pl.* **can′ticos**) *ns.* an American Indian religious dance: a dancing-match.   — *v.i.* to dance as an act of worship.   [From Algonquian.]

Kanuck. Same as **Canuck.**

kanzu *kan′zōō, n.* a long white garment worn by men in central East Africa.   [From Swahili.]

kaoliang *kä-ō-li-ang′, n.* sorghum grain of several varieties: a spirituous liquor made from it.   [Chin., tall grain.]

kaolin, kaoline *kā′ō-lin, n.* China clay, esp. that composed of kaolinite.   — *v.t.* and *v.i.* **ka′olinise, -ize** to turn into kaolin.   — *n.* **ka′olinite** a hydrated aluminium silicate occurring in minute monoclinic flakes, a decomposition product of feldspar, etc.   — *adj.* **kaolinit′ic.**   — *n.* **kaolinō′sis** a disease caused by inhaling kaolin dust. [From the mountain *Kao-ling* (high ridge) in China.]

kaon *kā′on, n.* one of several types of subatomic particle of smaller mass than a proton.   — See **meson**.   [*K* (pronounced *kā*) and mes*on*.]

kapellmeister *kə-pel′mīs′-tər, n.* the director of an orchestra or choir, esp. formerly of the band of a ruling prince in Germany.   [Ger. *Kapelle*, chapel, orchestra, *Meister*, master.]

kapok *kāp′, käp′ok, n.* very light, waterproof, oily fibre covering the seeds of a species of silk-cotton tree, used for stuffing pillows, life-belts, etc.   [Malay *kāpoq*.]

kappa *kap′ə, n.* the tenth (earlier eleventh) letter of the Greek alphabet (Κ, κ): as a numeral κ′ = 20, ‚κ = 20 000.]

kaput, kaputt *kə-pōōt′, adj.* (*slang*) ruined: broken: smashed.   [Ger.]

kara *kur′ə, n.* the steel bangle, signifying the unity of God, traditionally worn by Sikhs.   [Punjabi.]

karabiner *ka-rə-bēn′ər,* (*mountaineering*) *n.* a steel link with a spring clip in one side.   [Ger.]

karait *kär-īt′.* Same as **krait.**

Karaite *kā′rä-īt, n.* one of a stricter sect of Jews adhering to the literal interpretation of Scripture as against oral tradition.   — *n.* **ka′raism.**   [Heb. *qārā*, to read.]

karaka *kə-ra′kə, n.* a New Zealand tree with edible orange fruit whose seeds are poisonous until treated. [Maori.]

karakul, caracul *kär′ə-kōōl, -kōōl′, n.* (often with *cap.*) an Asiatic breed of sheep: a fur prepared from the skin of very young lambs of the Karakul or Bukhara breed, or of kids: a cloth imitating it.   [Russ. *Kara Kul*, a lake near Bukhara.]

karat. U.S. spelling of **carat.**

karate *ka-rä′ti, n.* a Japanese combative sport using blows and kicks.   — *ns.* **kara′teist; kara′teka** an expert in karate.   — **karate chop** a sharp downward blow with the side of the hand.

Karen *kə-ren′, n.* (one of) a people of eastern and southern Burma: the language of the Karens.   — Also *adj.*   — **Karenn′i** (one of) a group of eastern Karen peoples whose women stretch their necks by wearing brass collars.

karite *kar′i-ti, n.* the shea-tree.   [Native African name.]

Karling *kär′ling, n.* and *adj.* Carlovingian.   [Ger. *Karl,* Charles, and patronymic suffix *-ing*.]

karma *kur′mə, kär′mə, n.* the conception (Buddhist, etc.) of the quality of actions, including both merit and demerit, determining the future condition of all sentient beings: the theory of inevitable consequence

generally: the result of the actions of a life.   — *adj.* **kar′mic.**   [Sans. *karma*, act.]

Karmathian *kär-mä′thi-ən, n.* a member of a pantheistic socialistic Muslim sect which arose in Turkey about the close of the 9th century.   [*Karmat*, its founder.]

karmic. See **karma.**

Karoo, Karroo *kä-rōō′, n.* a high inland pastoral tableland (*S. Afr.*): a series of strata in South Africa of Permian and Trias age (*geol.*).   [Believed to be of Hottentot origin.]

kaross *kä-ros′, n.* a S. African skin blanket.   [Perh. a Hottentot modification of Du. *kuras*, cuirass.]

karri *kar′ē, n.* a Western Australian gum-tree (*Eucalyptus diversicolor*): its red timber.   [Aboriginal.]

Karroo. See **Karoo.**

karst *kärst, n.* rough limestone country with underground drainage.   [From the *Karst* district, east of the Adriatic.]

karsy. See **kazi.**

kart *kärt, n.* go-kart (q.v.).   — *n.* **kart′ing** go-kart racing.

Kartell *kär-tel′, n.* a German form of **cartel.**

kary- *ka′ri-,* **karyo-,** *ka′ri-ō-,* in composition, nucleus.   — *ns.* **karyokinesis** (*-kin-ē′sis;* Gr. *kinēsis,* movement; *biol.*) mitosis — a complicated process of division of the cell-nucleus, involving the arrangement of protoplasmic fibres in definite figures; **karyol′ogy** the study of cell-nuclei, esp. of chromosomes; **kar′yolymph** a colourless, watery fluid, occupying most of the space inside the nuclear membrane: nuclear sap; **karyol′ysis** dissolution of the nucleus by disintegration of the chromatin: gradual disappearance of the nucleus in a dead cell: liquefaction of the nuclear membrane in mitosis; **kar′yoplasm** the protoplasm of a cell-nucleus; **kar′yosome** a nucleus: a chromosome: an aggregation of chromatin: a type of nucleolus.   [Gr. *karyon*, kernel.]

karzy. See **kazi.**

kasba(h), casbah, *kaz′bä, n.* a castle or fortress in a N. African town or the area round it, esp. in Algiers.

Kashmir *kash-mēr′, n.* a region in the north-west of the Indian subcontinent: (without *cap.; obs.;* also *kash′-*) same as **cashmere.**   — *adj.* **Kashmiri** (*kash-mēr′i*) belonging to Kashmir.

kat[1], qat *kat, n.* a shrub (*Catha edulis*) of the spindle-tree family, used like tea by the Arabs and whose leaves are chewed as a drug.   [Ar. *qat*.]

kat[2], khat *kät, n.* the chief ancient Egyptian unit of weight, 1/50 lb. avoirdupois.

katabasis *kat-ab′ə-sis, n.* a going down.   — *adj.* **katabatic** (*-ə-bat′ik;* of a wind) blowing downward.   [Gr.]

katabolism, catabolism, *kat-ab′ə-lizm,* (*biol.*) *n.* the disruptive processes of chemical change in organisms — destructive metabolism, opposed to *anabolism.*   — *adj.* **katabolic** (*kat-ə-bol′ik*).   [Gr. *katabolē — kataballein,* to throw down — *kata,* down, *ballein,* to throw.]

katabothron, katavothron *kat-ə-both′ron, kat-av′oth-ron, ns.* an underground water-channel.   [Mod. Gr. *katabothron* — Gr. *kata,* down, *bothros,* hole.]

katadromous. Same as **catadromous.**

katakana *kat-ä-kä′nä, n.* a Japanese syllabary.   [Jap.]

katana *kä-tä′nä,* (Jap.) *n.* a long single-edged samurai sword, slightly curved towards the tip.

katathermometer *ka-tə-thər-mom′i-tər, n.* an alcohol thermometer for measuring the cooling power of the air.   [Gr. *kata,* down, and **thermometer**.]

katavothron. See **katabothron.**

kathak *kəth-äk′, n.* a classical dance of Northern India in which brief passages of mime alternate with rapid, rhythmic dance.   [Sans., a professional storyteller — *katha,* story.]

kathakali *käth-ə-kä′li, n.* a classical dance drama of Southern India.   [Malayalam, drama.]

katharsis, kathode. Same as **catharsis, cathode.**

kati. See **catty.**

kation. See **cation.**

katorga *kä′tər-gə,* (Russ.) *n.* penal servitude, hard labour, esp. in the labour camps of Joseph Stalin.

katti. See **catty.**

katydid *kā′ti-did*, *n.* an American insect akin to the grasshopper. [Imit. of its note.]

katzenjammer *kat′sən-jam-ər*, or *-jam′*, *n.* a hangover: a similar state of emotional distress (*fig.*): an uproar, clamour. [Ger., meaning 'cats' misery'.]

kaugh. See **kiaugh.**

kauri *kow′ri*, or **kauri-pine**, *n.* a splendid coniferous forest-tree of New Zealand (*Agathis australis*), source of **kau′ri-gum**, a resin used in making varnish. [Maori.]

kava *kä′və*, *n.* a species of pepper (*Piper methysticum*): a narcotic drink prepared from its root and stem. — Also **a′va**. [Polynesian.]

kavass *kä-väs′*, *n.* an armed attendant in Turkey. — Also **cavass**. [Ar. *qawwās*.]

kaw. See **caw.**

kay[1] *kā*, *n.* the eleventh letter of the alphabet (K, k).

kay[2]. See **quay.**

kayak *kī′ak*, *n.* an Eskimo seal-skin canoe: a canvas, fibreglass, etc. canoe built in this style. [Eskimo.]

kayle. Same as **kail**[1].

kayo(e) *kā-ō′* (*slang*). Stands for **K.O.** (knockout (q.v.)) *n.* and *v.t.*: — *pl.* **kayos′, -oes′**.

Kazak, Kazakh *kaz-äk′*, *n.* a member of a Turko-Tatar people of central Asia: the Turkic dialect spoken by Kazaks. [Russ.]

kazatzka *kəz-at′skə*, *n.* a Slavic folk-dance performed by a man and a woman. [Russ. *kazachki*, Cossack dances.]

kazi, karzy, kars(e)y *kä-zi*, (*slang*) *n.* a lavatory. [Said to be from It. *casa*, house.]

kazoo *kä-zōō′*, *n.* a would-be musical instrument, a tube with a strip of catgut, plastic, etc., that resonates to the voice. — Also **gazoo′, gazoo′ka**. [Prob. imit.]

kea *kē′ə*, *n.* a New Zealand parrot that sometimes kills sheep. [Maori.]

keasar *kēz′ər*. See **kaiser.**

keb *keb*, (*Scot.*) *v.i.* to cast a lamb prematurely. — *n.* a ewe that has cast its lamb. [Cf. Ger. *Kibbe, Kippe*, ewe.]

kebab, kabob, kabab, kebob, cabob *kə-bab′*, *-bob′*, *ns.* (also used in *pl.*) small pieces of meat cooked with vegetables, etc., esp. (from Turkish **shish kebab**) when on a skewer. [Ar. *kabab*.]

kebbie *keb′i*, (*Scot.*) *n.* a shepherd's crook: a crook-handled walking-stick.

kebbock, kebbuck *keb′ək*, (*Scot.*) *n.* a cheese. [Origin unknown; Gael. *cabag*, a cheese, may be derived from this word.]

kebele *kə-bā′lā*, *n.* a self-governing association found in towns in Ethiopia. — Also **kabe′le** (*kä-*). [From Amharic.]

keblah. See **kiblah.**

kebob. See **kebab.**

keck[1] *kek*, *v.i.* to retch, feel loathing. — *n.* a retching. [Imit.]

keck[2]. See **kex.**

keckle[1] *kek′l*, *v.t.* to protect by binding with rope or chains. — *n.* **keck′ling** rope, chains, etc., used to keckle cables or hawsers. [Origin unknown.]

keckle[2] *kek′l*, (chiefly *Scot.*) *v.i.* a form of **cackle.**

kecks, kecksy. See **kex.**

ked *ked*, **kade**, *kād*, *ns.* a wingless fly (*Melophagus ovinus*) that infests sheep. [Origin unknown.]

keddah. Same as **kheda.**

kedge[1] *kej*, *n.* a small anchor for keeping a ship steady, and for warping the ship. — *v.t.* to move by means of a kedge, to warp. — *n.* **kedg′er** a kedge. [Origin doubtful.]

kedge[2] *kej*, (*dial.*) *adj.* brisk, lively: pot-bellied. — Also **kedg′y, kidge**. [Cf. *cadgy*.]

kedgeree *kej′ə-rē*, *n.* an Indian dish of rice, cooked with butter and dal, flavoured with spice, shredded onion, etc.: a similar European dish made with fish, rice, etc. [Hind. *khichrī*.]

keech *kēch*, (*Shak.*) *n.* a lump of fat. [Perh. conn. with **cake.**]

keek *kēk*, (*Scot.*) *v.i.* to peep. — *n.* a peep. — *n.* **keek′er** one who peeps or spies: an inspector of coal: an eye: a black eye. — **keek′ing-glass** a mirror. [M.E. *kyke*; cf. Du. *kijken*, Ger. *kucken*.]

keel[1] *kēl*, *n.* the part of a ship extending along the bottom from stem to stern, and supporting the whole frame: a longitudinal member running along the under side of an airship's hull or gas-bag: the two lowest petals of a papilionaceous flower, arranged like a ship's keel (*bot.*): any narrow prominent ridge. — *v.t.* or *v.i.* to navigate: to turn keel upwards. — *n.* **keel′age** dues for a keel or ship in port. — *adj.* **keeled** keel-shaped (*bot.*): having a ridge on the back. — *v.t.* **keel′haul** to punish by hauling under the keel of a ship by ropes from the one side to the other: to rebuke severely. — **keel′-hauling.** — **on an even keel** calm(ly); **keel over** to stagger, fall over. [O.N. *kjölr*.]

keel[2] *kel*, *n.* a low flat-bottomed boat: a coal-lighter: a ship. — Also **keel′boat**. — *ns.* **keel′er, keel′man** one who works on a barge. [Du. *kiel*, ship, prob. — O.E. *cēol*, ship.]

keel[3] *kēl*, (*Shak.*) *v.t.* to cool. [O.E. *cēlan*, to chill.]

keel[4] *kēl*, (*Scot.*) *n.* red ochre, ruddle. — *v.t.* to mark with ruddle. [Origin obscure: Gael. *cíl*, ruddle, may be from this word.]

keelie *kē′li*, (*Scot.*) *n.* the kestrel or other hawk: a town rough, particularly one belonging to Glasgow and surrounding district: a boorish vulgarian. [Perh. imit.; some connect with **gillie**.]

keeling *kē′ling*, (*Scot.*) *n.* a codfish. [Origin unknown.]

keelivine, keelyvine *kē′li-vīn*, (*Scot.*) *n.* a lead pencil. [**keel**[4]; ety. otherwise unknown.]

keelson *kel′sən*, *kēl′*, **kelson** *kel′sən*, *ns.* a ship's inner keel, which binds the floor-timbers to the outer keel. [**keel**[1]; the forms in kindred languages suggest that the second syllable is equivalent either to **sill**, or to **swine**, animal names being sometimes used in similar ways.]

keelyvine. See **keelivine.**

keen[1] *kēn*, *adj.* eager: sharp, having a fine edge: piercing: acute of mind: penetrating: intense. — *v.t.* to sharpen. — *adv.* **keen′ly**. — *n.* **keen′ness**. — **keen prices** very low prices. — **keen on** (*coll.*) devoted to: fond of: much interested in: very desirous of. [O.E. *cēne*, bold, fierce, keen; Ger. *kühn*, bold; O.N. *kœnn*, expert.]

keen[2] *kēn*, *n.* a lamentation over the dead. — *v.i.* to wail over the dead. — *ns.* **keen′er** a professional mourner; **keen′ing** wailing, lamentation. [Ir. *caoine*.]

keep *kēp*, *v.t.* to reck of, care for (*obs.*): to tend: to have the care of: to guard: to maintain: to manage, conduct, run: to attend to the making of records in: to retain: to retain as one's own: to have in one's custody: to have habitually in stock for sale: to support, supply with necessaries: to have in one's service: to remain in or on: to adhere to: to continue to follow or hold to: to continue to make: to maintain hold upon: to restrain from departure, to hold back: to prevent: to reserve: to preserve in a certain state: to observe: to celebrate: to conform to the requirements of: to fulfil. — *v.i.* to care, reck (*obs.*): to remain: to continue to be or go: to be or remain in a specified condition: to remain fresh or good: to last or endure: to continue: to lodge (*obs.*): to have rooms at college (Cambridge): to refrain: to confine or restrict oneself: to keep wicket: — *pr.p.* **keep′ing**; *pa.t.* and *pa.p.* **kept** (*kept*). — *n.* care (*arch.*): a charge: condition: that which keeps or protects: subsistence: food: the innermost and strongest part of a castle, the donjon: a stronghold. — *ns.* **keep′er** one who or that which keeps, in any sense: an attendant, esp. upon the insane, or upon animals in captivity: a custodian: a gamekeeper: the title of certain officials as *Lord Keeper* (*of the Great Seal*), whose office since 1757 has been merged in that of Lord Chancellor: one who keeps a mistress (*obs.*): a wicket-keeper: the socket that receives the bolt of a lock: the armature of a magnet: a guard-ring; **keep′-**

ership office of a keeper; **keep'ing** care: preservation: reservation: retention: observance: custody: charge: maintenance, support (*Shak.*): maintenance of, or as, a mistress: just proportion: harmonious consistency. — **keep fit** a programme of physical exercises designed to keep the muscles, circulation and respiratory system in good condition; **keep'ing-room** (*dial.*) a sitting-room, parlour; **keep'net** a cone-shaped net suspended in a river, etc., in which fish caught by anglers can be kept alive; **keep'sake** something given to be kept for the sake of the giver: an annual gift-book (such as *The Keepsake* itself, 1827–56). — *adj.* (also **keep'saky**) sumptuously inane; **kept woman** a woman maintained financially by a man as his mistress. — **for keeps** as a permanent possession: for good: permanently: with serious intent: defensively (*cricket*); **how are you keeping?** how are you?; **in keeping with** consonant with; **keep an act** formerly, to hold an academical disputation; **keep an eye on, keep chapel, company, counsel, distance, hours, house, the peace, a term**, etc. see the nouns; **keep at it** to persist in anything; **keep back** to withhold: to keep down, repress; **keep body and soul together** to maintain life; **keep down** to restrain: to repress: to remain low: to set in lower-case type, avoiding capitals: to retain (food) in the stomach, not to vomit; **keep from** to abstain from: to remain away from; **keep in** to prevent from escaping: to confine in school after school hours: to conceal: to restrain; **keep in with** to maintain the confidence or friendship of someone, often with the suggestion of unworthy means; **keep off** to hinder or prevent from approaching or making an attack, etc.: to stay away or refrain from; **keep on** to continue; **keep on about** to continue talking about; **keep on at** to nag, badger (*coll.*); **keep one's breath to cool one's porridge** to hold one's peace when further talk is clearly in vain; **keep one's countenance** to avoid showing one's emotions; **keep one's hand in** to retain one's skill by practice; **keep one's head down** to avoid attracting attention to oneself; **keep one's mind on** to concentrate on; **keep one's powder dry** see **powder**; **keep someone going in something** to keep someone supplied with something; **keep tab(s) on** to keep a check on, to keep account of; **keep time** to observe rhythm accurately, or along with others: to go accurately (as a clock); **keep to** to stick closely to: to confine oneself to; **keep under** to hold down in restraint; **keep up** to retain one's strength or spirit: to support, prevent from falling: to continue, to prevent from ceasing: to maintain in good condition: to continue to be in touch (with): to keep pace (with; also *fig.*, as **keep up with the Joneses**, to keep on social equality with one's neighbours, e.g. by having possessions of like quality in like quantity): to stop (*obs.*); **keep wicket** to act as a wicket-keeper. [O.E. *cēpan.*]
keeshond *kās'hond, -nt, n.* a medium-sized dog of the spitz group once common on Dutch barges. [Du., — *kees,* terrier, *hond,* dog.]
keeve, kieve *kēv, n.* a large tub. [O.E. *cȳf,* vat.]
kef *kāf, n.* a state of dreamy repose: something, as Indian hemp, smoked to produce this. — Also **kaif** (*kīf*), **kif** (*kif, kēf*). [Ar. *kaif,* pleasure.]
keffel *kef'l,* (*dial.*) *n.* a horse, nag. [W. *ceffyl;* cf. **caple.**]
keffiyeh. Same as **kaffiyeh.**
kefir, kephir *ke'fər, n.* an effervescent drink of low alcoholic content, made from fermented cow's milk. [Native name in the Caucasus.]
kefuffle. See **carfuffle.**
keg *keg, n.* a small cask: a metal cask in which beer is kept under gas pressure. — **keg beer** any of various types of beer kept in and served from pressurised kegs. [Earlier *cag* — O.N. *kaggi.*]
keight *kīt,* (*Spens.*) *v.t.* for **caught** (*pa.t.* of **catch**).
keir. See **kier.**
keitloa *kāt'lō-ə, n.* a two-horned rhinoceros. [Tswana *kgetlwa.*]
keksye. See **kex.**
kelim. See **kilim.**

kell *kel,* (*Northern*) *n.* a woman's head-dress or hair-net: a film, network: a caul. [**caul.**]
kellaut. See **killut.**
kelly *kel'i, n.* in drilling processes, the top pipe of a rotary string of drill pipes, with which is incorporated a flexibly attached swivel through which mud is pumped to the bottom of the hole. [Origin uncertain.]
keloid, cheloid *kē'loid, n.* a hard growth of scar tissue in skin that has been injured. — *adj.* **keloid'al, cheloid'al.** [Gr. *chēlē,* claw.]
kelp *kelp, n.* any large brown seaweed, wrack: the calcined ashes of seaweed, a source of soda, iodine, etc. — Also **kilp.** — *n.* **Kel'per** (also without *cap.*) an inhabitant of the Falkland Islands. — *adj.* of or pertaining to the Falkland Islands. [M.E. *culp;* origin unknown.]
kelpie, kelpy *kel'pi, n.* a malignant water-sprite haunting fords in the form of a horse (*Scot.*): an Australian breed of sheep-dog. [Origin uncertain.]
kelson. Same as **keelson.**
kelt[1] *kelt, n.* a salmon, etc., that has just spawned. [Origin unknown.]
kelt[2] *kelt,* (*Scot.*) *n.* coarse cloth usu. made of black and white wool mixed and not dyed. — *n.* and *adj.* **kelt'er.** [Origin obscure.]
Kelt, Keltic. Same as **Celt, Celtic.**
kelter[1]. See **kilter.**
kelter[2]. See **kelt**[2].
keltie, kelty *kel'ti,* (*Scot.*) *n.* a bumper, esp. one imposed as a penalty on one who does not drain his glass completely.
Kelvin *kel'vin, adj.* applied to a thermometer scale with absolute zero for zero and centigrade degrees. — *n.* **kel'vin** (SI units) the unit of temperature (formerly 'degree Kelvin'): kilowatt-hour (*rare*). [Sir William Thomson, Lord *Kelvin* (1824–1907), physicist.]
kemb *kem,* (*obs.* and *dial.*) *v.t.* to comb. — *adj.* **kempt** (*kemt, kempt*) combed, tidy. [O.E. *cemban.*]
kembo. Same as **kimbo.**
kemp[1] *kemp, n.* the coarse, rough hairs of wool: (in *pl.*) knotty hair that will not felt. [O.N. *kampr,* beard.]
kemp[2] *kemp, n.* a champion (*arch.*): a contest in reaping or other work (*Scot.*). — *v.i.* to strive for mastery. — *ns.* **kem'per, kem'pery-man** a champion, a knight-errant; **kemp'ing.** [O.E. *cempa,* a warrior; cf. **champion.**]
kemple *kem'pl,* (*Scot.*) *n.* forty bottles of hay or straw. [Origin obscure.]
kempt. See **kemb.**
ken[1] *ken, v.t.* to cause to know, direct (*obs.*): to see and recognise at a distance (*arch.*): to know (mainly *Scot.*): — *pa.t.* and *pa.p.* **kenned, kent.** — *n.* range of sight or knowledge. — *ns.* **kenn'er; kenn'ing** range of vision: a small portion, a little bit (*Scot.*): a periphrastic formula in Old Norse or other old Germanic poetry; **ken-no** (*ken'ə; Scot.,* know not) a cheese prepared in ostensible secrecy for the gossips at a birth. — *adj.* **kent** known. — **beyond one's ken** outside the limits of one's knowledge. [O.E. *cennan,* causative of *cunnan,* and O.N. *kenna;* cf. **can**[1], **con**[2].]
ken[2] *ken,* (*slang*) *n.* a house, esp. disreputable. [Perh. Pers. *khān,* a caravanserai: or **kennel**; or conn. with preceding word.]
kenaf *kə-naf' n.* a herbaceous plant, the fibres of which can be used as a substitute for wood-pulp in paper-making. [Persian.]
Kendal-green *ken'dl-grēn, n.* green cloth for foresters made at *Kendal* in Westmorland.
kendo *ken'dō,* or *-dō', n.* Japanese art of swordsmanship practised with bamboo staves, in 18th-century-style armour, and observing strict ritual. [Jap. *kendō.*]
kennel[1] *ken'l, n.* a house for dogs: a pack of hounds: the hole of a fox, etc.: a haunt: (in *pl.*) an establishment where dogs are boarded. — *v.t.* to put or keep in a kennel. — *v.i.* to live in a kennel: — *pr.p.* **kenn'elling;** *pa.t.* and *pa.p.* **kenn'elled.** — **kenn'el-maid, kenn'el-man** an attendant upon dogs. [From an O.N. Fr. form

answering to Fr. *chenil* — L. *canīle* — *canis*, a dog.]
kennel[2] *ken'l, n.* a street gutter. [M.E. *canel* — O.N.Fr. *canel* — L. *canālis*; see **canal**.]
kennel-coal. Same as **cannel-coal.**
Kennelly-Heaviside layer *or* **region** *ken'ə-li-hev'i-sīd lā'ər, rē'jən,* a strongly ionised region of the upper atmosphere about 60 miles up, in which wireless waves are deflected. — Also **Heaviside layer; E-layer.** [From A. E. *Kennelly* and O. *Heaviside*, who inferred its existence.]
kenner. See **ken**[1].
kennet *ken'it,* (*obs.*) *n.* a small hunting dog. [O.N.Fr. *kennet,* dim. — L. *canis,* dog.]
Kennick *ken'ik, n.* the jargon of tramping tinkers.
kenning, ken-no. See **ken**[1].
kenosis *ken-ō'sis, n.* the self-limitation of the Logos in incarnation. — *adj.* **kenotic** (*-ot'ik*). — *n.* **kenot'icist** (*-i-sist*) a believer in kenosis. [Gr. *kenōsis,* emptying, from Phil. ii. 7.]
Kensington *ken'zing-tən, adj.* (of person) interested exclusively in an artificial city life and in material values. [Part of a London borough.]
kenspeckle *ken'spek-l,* (*Scot.* and *dial.*) *adj.* easily recognised: conspicuous. — Also **ken'speck.** [Appar. O.N. *kennispeki,* power of recognition.]
kent[1] *kent,* (*Scot.*) *n.* a leaping or punting pole. — *v.t.* and *v.i.* to punt or pole. [Cf. **quant.**]
kent[2]. See **ken**[1].
kent-bugle *kent'-bū'gl, n.* an obsolete key-bugle. [Supposed to be named after a Duke of Kent.]
kente cloth *ken'ti kloth,* a silk cloth made in Ghana by sewing together long narrow handwoven strips. [Origin uncertain.]
Kentish *kent'ish, adj.* of Kent. — *n.* the dialect of Kent, Essex, etc. — **Kent'ish-fire'** synchronised volleys of applause — probably from anti-Catholic demonstrations in Kent, 1828–29; **Kent'ish-man** a native of W. Kent (one born east of the Medway being a *Man of Kent*); **Kent'ish-rag'** a rough limestone in the Lower Greensand of Kent.
kentledge *kent'lij, n.* pig-iron in a ship's hold for ballast. — Also **kint'ledge.** [Origin unknown.]
Kenyapithecus *kēn'yə-pith'ə-kəs, ken'yə- n.* a lower Pliocene genus of fossil anthropoid ape: an example of this genus, first discovered by L.S.B. Leakey in Kenya in 1961. [*Kenya* and Gr. *pithēkos,* ape.]
kep *kep,* (*Scot.*) *v.t.* to catch (an approaching object): — *pa.t.* and *pa.p.* **kepp'it.** — *n.* a catch: act or opportunity of catching. [**keep.**]
kephalic *ki-fal'ik.* Same as **cephalic.**
kephir. See **kefir.**
kepi *kāp'ē, n.* a flat-topped forage-cap with a straight peak. [Fr. *képi.*]
Keplerian *kep-lē'ri-ən, adj.* pertaining to the German astronomer Johann *Kepler.* See **law**[1].
keppit. See **kep.**
kept. *pa.t.* and *pa.p.* of **keep.**
keramic *ki-ram'ik.* Same as **ceramic.**
keratin *ker'ə-tin, n.* a nitrogenous compound, the essential ingredient of horny tissue, as of horns, nails, etc. — *v.t., v.i.* **ker'atinise, -ize** to make or become horny. — *n.* **keratinisā'tion, -z-** formation of keratin: becoming horny. — *adj.* **keratinous** (*kə-rat'i-nəs*) horny. — *n.* **keratī'tis** inflammation of the cornea. — *adjs.* **keratogenous** (*-oj'i-nəs*) producing horn or keratin; **ker'atoid** resembling horn or keratin. — *n.* **ker'atō-plasty** grafting of part of a healthy cornea to replace a piece made opaque by disease, etc. — *adj.* **ker'atose** (esp. of certain sponges) having a horny skeleton. — *n.* **keratō'sis** a horny growth on or over the skin, e.g. a wart: a skin condition producing this; **keratot'omy** surgery of the cornea. [Gr. *keras, -atos,* a horn.]
keratophyre *ker'ət-ō-fīr, n.* a fine-grained soda trachyte. [Gr. *keras, -atos,* horn, and *-phyre* from **porphyry.**]
keraunograph *kə-rön'ō-gräf, n.* an instrument for recording distant thunderstorms. [Gr. *keraunos,* a thunderbolt, *graphein,* to write.]

kerb, *also* (*chiefly U.S.*) **curb** (q.v.), *kûrb, n.* a hearth fender: a kerbstone, pavement edge: a kerb market: an edging or margin of various kinds. — **kerb'-crawler** someone who drives along slowly with the intention of enticing people into his car; **kerb'-crawling; kerb drill** the safe procedure for crossing a road adopted by some pedestrians; **kerb'-market** a market in stocks operating separately from the stock-exchange, originally on the pavement; **kerb'-merchant, -trader, -vendor** one who sells on or beside the pavement; **kerb'side** (also *adj.*); **kerb'stone** a stone placed edgeways as an edging to a path or pavement. — **kerb'stone-bro'ker** one outside the stock exchange. [Fr. *courbe* — L. *curvus,* bent.]
kerchief *kûr'chif, n.* a square piece of cloth worn to cover the head, neck, etc.: a handkerchief. — *v.t.* to cover with a kerchief. — *adj.* **ker'chiefed.** [O.Fr. *cuevre-chief* (Fr. *couvrechef*) — *covrir,* to cover, *chef,* the head.]
kerf *kûrf, n.* a cut: a notch: the groove made by a saw: a cut place, face of a cut: the place where a cut is made: a quantity cut at once, as of wool, etc.: a single layer of hay, turf, etc., cut. [O.E. *cyrf,* a cut.]
kerfuffle. See **carfuffle.**
kermes *kûr'mēz, n.* the female bodies of a coccus insect (*Kermes,* or *Coccus, ilicis*), used as a red dyestuff: the oak (**kermes oak;** *Quercus coccifera*) on which they breed: a cherry-red mineral, antimony oxysulphide (also **kermes mineral, ker'mesite**). [Pers. and Ar. *qirmiz.*]
kermesse *kûr'mis, n.* a cycle-race held in an urban area. [Flem. *kermesse, kermis.*]
kermis *kûr'mis, n.* a fair in the Low Countries: in America, an indoor fair. — Also **ker'mess, kir'mess.** [Du. *kermis* — *kerk,* church, *mis,* mass.]
kern[1]. See **kirn**[1].
kern[2] *kûrn, v.i.* to granulate. [Cf. **corn**[1].]
kern[3] *kûrn,* (*print.*) *n.* part of a type that projects beyond the body and rests on an adjoining letter. — *v.t.* to give (a typeface) a kern. [Fr. *carne,* a projecting angle — L. *cardō, -inis.*]
kern[4], **kerne** *kûrn, n.* an Irish foot-soldier: a boor. — *adj.* **ker'nish.** [From Ir. — Old Gael.; see **cateran.**]
kernel *kûr'nl, n.* a seed within a hard shell: the edible part of a nut: a gland (*rare*): a nucleus: the important part of anything. — *v.i.* (*rare*) to form kernels. — *adj.* **ker'nelly** full of, or resembling, kernels. [O.E. *cyrnel* — *corn,* grain, and dim. suffix *-el;* Ger. *Kern,* a grain.]
kernicterus *kûr-nik'tər-es, n.* a condition of acute neural dysfunction linked with high levels of bilirubin in the blood. [Ger. *Kern,* nucleus, and Gr. *ikteros,* jaundice.]
kernish. See **kern**[4].
kernite *kûrn'it, n.* hydrated oxide of sodium and boron. [*Kern* Co., California, where much is mined.]
kerogen *ker'ō-jen, n.* the organic matter in oil-shale that gives oil on distillation. [Gr. *kēros,* wax, and root of *gennaein,* to generate.]
kerosine *ker'ō-sēn, n.* paraffin-oil obtained from shale or by distillation of petroleum. This spelling is now used commercially; **kerosene** is the older spelling. [Gr. *kēros,* wax.]
Kerria *ker'i-ə, n.* a plant genus comprising a single species, the Jew's mallow: (without *cap.*) any plant of this genus. [From William *Kerr,* late 18th- — early 19th-cent. English gardener.]
kersantite *kûr'sən-tīt, n.* a dyke-rock of black mica and plagioclase. [*Kersanton,* a locality in Brittany.]
kersey *kûr'zi, n.* a coarse woollen cloth. [Perh. from *Kersey* in Suffolk.]
kerseymere *kûr'zi-mēr,* or *-mēr', n.* twilled cloth of the finest wools. [For **cassimere, cashmere.**]
kerve *kûrv', v.t.* (*Spens.*) a form of **carve.**
kerygma *kə-rig'mə, n.* (preaching of) the Christian gospel, esp. in the way of the early Church. — *adj.* **kerygmat'ic.** [Gr. *kērygma,* proclamation, preaching.]
kesar *kē'zər, n.* See **kaiser.**

kesh *kāsh, n.* the uncut hair and beard traditionally worn by Sikhs. [Punjabi.]
kest *kest,* an obs. form of **cast.**
kestrel *kes'trəl, n.* a small species of falcon. [O.Fr. *cresserelle.*]
ket¹ *ket,* (*Scot.*) *n.* carrion. [O.N. *kjöt.*]
ket² *ket,* (*Scot.*) *n.* matted wool. [A.Fr. *cot.*]
keta *kē'tə, n.* a Pacific salmon, the dog-salmon. [Russ. *keta.*]
ketch¹ *kech, n.* a small two-masted vessel. [Earlier *catch,* perh. from the vb. **catch.**]
ketch² *kech,* an obs. form of **catch.**
ketchup *kech'əp, n.* a sauce made from tomatoes, mushrooms, etc. — Also **catch'up, cat'sup.** [Malay *kēchap,* perh. from Chinese.]
ketone *kē'tōn, n.* an organic compound consisting of a carbonyl group united to two like or unlike alkyl radicals. — **kēt-, kētō-** denoting a ketone compound or derivative. — *n.* **kē'tose** any of a class of monosaccharide sugars which contain a ketone group. — *n.* **ketō'sis** the excessive formation in the body of ketone or acetone bodies, due to incomplete oxidation of fats — occurs in e.g. diabetes. [Ger. *Keton,* from *Aketon,* acetone.]
kettle¹ *ket'l, n.* a vessel for heating or boiling liquids, esp. one with a spout and a lid for domestic use: a cauldron: a cavity like a kettle in rock (see **giant's-kettle**): a kettledrum (*Shak.*). — *n.* **kett'leful.** — **kett'ledrum** a musical instrument, consisting of a hollow metal hemisphere with a parchment head, tuned by screws: a large tea-party; **kett'ledrumm'er; kett'le-holder** a little cloth, etc., for lifting a hot kettle; **kett'lestitch** in bookbinding, the stitch which is made at the head and tail of each section of a book to interlock the sections. — **a kettle of fish** (cf. **kiddle**) a riverside picnic at which new-caught salmon are cooked on the spot: a situation, set of circumstances (ironically — often **a pretty kettle of fish**) an awkward mess. [O.E. *cetel*; Ger. *Kessel,* Goth. *katils*; all perh. from L. *catillus,* dim. of *catīnus,* a deep cooking-vessel.]
kettle². See **kiddle.**
kettle-pins. Same as **kittle-pins.**
Ketubah *ke-tōō-vä', n.* a formal Jewish marriage contract which couples sign before their wedding. [Heb. *kethūbhāh,* document.]
Keuper *koi'pər,* (*geol.*) *n.* the uppermost division of the Trias. — Also *adj.* [Ger. miners' term.]
kevel *kev'l.* Same as **cavel.**
kewpie doll *kū'pi dol,* a plump baby doll with a top-knot of hair. [**Cupid.**]
kex *keks, n.* a dry, often hollow, herbaceous (usu. umbelliferous) stalk: any tall umbelliferous plant. — Also **kecks,** and (false singulars) **keck, kecks'y, keks'ye.** [Origin unknown.]
key¹ *kē,* formerly *kā, n.* an instrument for locking or unlocking, winding up, turning, tuning, tightening or loosening: a wedge: a piece inserted to prevent relative motion: a tapered piece of metal for fixing the boss of a wheel, etc., to a shaft: a spanner: the middle stone of an arch: a piece of wood let into another piece crosswise to prevent warping: in musical instruments, a lever or piston-end pressed to produce the sound required: a similar part in other instruments for other purposes, as in a typewriter or calculating machine: a lever to close or break an electrical circuit: a dry winged fruit, as of ash or maple, often hanging with others in bunches: a fret pattern: preparation of a surface to take plaster, glue, or the like: a keynote (*obs.*): a system of tones definitely related to one another in a scale: an artificial system for distinguishing similar species (*biol.*): that which gives command of anything or upon which success turns: a scheme or diagram of explanation or identification: a set of answers to problems: a crib translation: that which leads to the solution of a problem: a leading principle: general tone of voice, emotion, morals, etc. — *v.t.* to lock or fasten with a key: to furnish with a key: to prepare a surface e.g.

for plastering: to give an advertisement a feature that will enable replies to it to be identified: to mark the position on the layout of something to be printed, using symbols (*print.*): to attune (with *to*): to stimulate (to a state of nervous tension and excitement), raise (in pitch or standard), increase (with *up*): to use a keyboard, type. — Also *v.i.* — *adj.* vital: essential: crucial. — *adjs.* **keyed** furnished with a key or keys: set to a particular key: in a state of tension or readiness; **key'less** without a key: not requiring a key. — **key'board** a range of keys or levers in a musical instrument, computers etc.: (in *pl.*) usu. in pop groups, musical instruments, esp. electronic, incorporating keyboards. — *v.i.* and *v.t.* to operate a device by means of a keyboard. — **key'bugle** a bugle with keys, giving a chromatic scale of two octaves. — *adj.* **key'-cold** (*Shak.*) cold as a key, lifeless. — **key'-desk** the frame enclosing keyboards, stops, etc., of an organ; **key'-fruit** a winged fruit; **key'hole** the hole in which a key of a lock is inserted; **key'hole-lim'pet** a mollusc (*Fissurella*) with perforated conical shell; **keyhole saw** a padsaw (q.v. under **pad²**); **key industry** an industry indispensable to others and essential to national economic welfare and independence; **key man** an indispensable worker, essential to the continued conduct of a business, etc.; **key money** a premium, fine, or sum additional to rent, demanded for the grant, renewal, or continuance of a tenancy; **key'note** the fundamental note or tonic: any central principle or controlling thought. — *adj.* of fundamental importance. — *v.t.* and *v.i.* to give the keynote: to put forward the central principle in an opening address at a convention. — **key pad** a device incorporating push-button controls by which a television, etc., can be operated; **key'-pin** the pivot on which a pipe-key turns: a pin serving as fulcrum for a key of an organ, etc.; **key'-plate** a keyhole escutcheon; **key punch** (*comput.*) a device operated by a keyboard, which transfers data on to punch-cards, etc.; **key'-ring** a ring for holding a bunch of keys; **key'-seat** a groove for receiving a key, to prevent one piece of machinery from turning on another; **key signature** the indication of key by marking sharps, flats or naturals where the key changes or at the beginning of a line; **key'stone** the stone at the apex of an arch: the chief element or consummation: that on which all else depends. — *v.t.* and *v.i.* to produce a **keystone effect** i.e. the distortion of a television picture in which a rectangular pattern is transformed into a trapezoidal pattern. — **key'stroke** the operation of a key on a typewriter or other machine using keys; **key'-way** a groove cut in a shaft or boss to accommodate a key; **key word** a headword: a word that encapsulates the passage in which it appears. — **have the key of the street** (*coll.*) to be locked out: to be homeless; **key in,** **into** (*comput.*) to transfer, store, etc. data by operating a keyboard; **power of the keys** the power to loose and bind, conferred by Christ on Peter (Matt. xvi. 19), and claimed by the Popes. [O.E. *cæg.*]
key². An old spelling of **quay.**
key³ *kē, n.* a low island or reef. — Also **cay.** [Sp. *cayo.*]
Keynesian *kānz'i-ən, adj.* relating to John Maynard Keynes (1883–1946) or to his economic teaching, esp. his advocacy of a measure of public control within capitalism of the unrestricted play of economic forces both national and international. — *n.* **Keynes'ianism.**
Keys *kēz, n.pl.* in full **House of Keys,** the lower house of the Manx Court of Tynwald. [App. **key¹,** not Manx *kiare-as-feed,* four-and-twenty.]
kgotla *hhö'tlə, kgot'lə, n.* an assembly of tribal elders in Botswana: the place of such assembly. [Bantu.]
khaddar *kud'ər, n.* in India, hand-spun, hand-woven cloth. — Also **khadi.** [Hind. *khādar, khādī.*]
khaki *kä'ki, adj.* dust-coloured, dull brownish or greenish yellow: militaristically imperialist (*hist.*). — *adv.* (*hist.*) with war-spirit. — *n.* a light drab cloth used for military uniforms. [Urdu and Pers. *khākī,* dusty.]
khalat *kal'ət.* Same as **killut.**

khalif. See **caliph**. — *ns.* **khalifa, khalifah** (*kä-lē'fä*) a caliph: a Senusi leader: the Mahdi's successor; **khalifat, khalifate** (*käl'i-fat, -fāt*) the caliphate. [Ar. *khalīfah*.]

khamsin *kam'sin, -sēn'*, *n.* a hot S. or S.E. wind in Egypt, blowing for about fifty days from mid-March. — Also **kamseen', kam'sin**. [Ar. *khamsīn* — *khamsūn*, fifty.]

khan[1] *kän, n.* an Eastern inn, a caravanserai. [Ar. *khan*.]

khan[2] *kän, n.* in N. Asia, a prince or chief: in Persia, a governor. — *ns.* **khan'ate** a khan's dominion or jurisdiction; **khan'um** (*-ōōm*) lady: Mrs. [Turki (and thence Pers.) *khān*, lord or prince.]

khanga. See **kanga**.

khanjar. See **handjar**.

khansama(h) *kän'sä-mä, n.* a house-steward or butler in India. [Hindi *khānsāmān* — Pers. *khān*, lord, and *sāmān*, household stores.]

kharif *kə-rēf', (India) n.* crop sown before the monsoon to ripen in autumn. [Hind. *kharīf* — Ar., gathered.]

khat. Same as **kat**[2].

Khaya *kä'yə, n.* a genus of African trees akin to mahogany: (without *cap.*) any tree of this genus. [Wolof *khaye*.]

kheda, keddah *ked'ə, n.* an enclosure for catching wild elephants: the operation of catching wild elephants. [Hindi *khedā*.]

khedive *ke-dēv', n.* the title (1867–1914) of the viceroy of Egypt. — *ns.* **khedi'va** his wife; **khedi'v(i)ate** the khedive's office or territory. — *adjs.* **khedi'v(i)al.** [Fr. *khédive* — Turk. *khidīv, hudîv* — Pers. *khidīw*, prince.]

khidmutgar *kid'mut-gär,* **khitmutgar** *kit', ns.* a tableservant. [Hind., — Pers. *khidmat*, service, and agent suffix *-gār*.]

khilafat *kil'ä-fat, kil-ä'fat, n.* caliphate. — *adj.* of an anti-British agitation among Muslims in India after Treaty of Sèvres, 1920. [Ar. *khilāfat*; cf. **caliph**.]

khilat *kil'ət.* Same as **killut**.

khilim. See **kilim**.

khitmutgar. See **khidmutgar**.

Khmer *kmür, kmer, n.* a member of a people inhabiting Cambodia: their language, the official language of Cambodia. — Also *adj.* (See **Mon-Khmer**.)

khoja, khodja *kō'ja,* also **hodja,** *hō', ns.* an Eastern title of respect: a professor or teacher. [Turk. and Pers., *khōjah, khwājah*.]

khor *kōr, kör, n.* a dry watercourse: a ravine. [Ar. *khurr, khorr*.]

khotbah, khotbeh. See **khutbah**.

khud *kud, n.* a pit, hollow: a ravine. [Hindi *khad*.]

khurta. See **kurta**.

khuskhus. Same as **cuscus**[2].

khutbah *kōōt'bä, n.* a Muslim prayer and sermon delivered in the mosques on Fridays. — Also **khot'bah, khot'beh.** [Ar.]

kiang, kyang, *kyang, ki-ang', n.* a Tibetan wild ass. [Tibetan *rkyang*.]

kia-ora *kē'ä-ö'rə, (N.Z.) interj.* good health. [Maori.]

kiaugh *kyöhh, kyähh, (Scot.) n.* care, trouble. — Also **kaugh** (*köhh, kähh*).

kibble[1] *kib'l, n.* the bucket of a draw-well. — **kibb'le-chain** the chain for drawing up a bucket. [Cf. Ger. *Kübel*.]

kibble[2] *kib'l, v.t.* to grind cereal, etc., fairly coarsely. [Origin obscure.]

kibbutz *kē-bōōts', n.* a Jewish communal agricultural settlement in Israel: — *pl.* **kibbutzim** (*kē-bōōts-ēm'*). — *n.* **kibbutz'nik** a person who lives and works on a kibbutz. [Heb.]

kibe *kīb, n.* chilblain, esp. on heel. [Cf. W. *cibwst*.]

kibitka *ki-bit'kə, n.* a Russian covered wagon or sledge: a Central Asian felt tent. [Russ.]

kibitzer *kib'it-sər, n.* onlooker (at cards, etc.) who gives unwanted advice. — *v.i.* **kib'itz.** [Yiddish.]

kiblah *kib'lä, n.* the point toward which Muslims turn in prayer. — Also **keb'lah.** [Ar. *qiblah*.]

kibosh, kybosh *kī'bosh, ki-bosh', (coll.) n.* nonsense, rot. — *v.t.* to dispose of finally. — **put the kibosh on** to kibosh. [Ety. obscure.]

kick *kik, v.t.* to hit with the foot: to put or drive by blows

with the foot: to start or work by foot on a pedal: to achieve by a kick or kicking: to free oneself from (e.g. a habit) (*slang*). — *v.i.* to thrust out the foot with violence: to show opposition or resistance: to recoil violently: to jerk violently: to move as if kicked: to be exposed to kicking, lie around (often with *about*): to flourish (usu. in *pr.p.*). — *n.* a blow or fling with the foot: the recoil of a gun: a jerk: kicking power: resistance: resilience: fashion (*arch. slang*): the depression in the bottom of a bottle: stimulus, pungency (*coll.*): thrill (*coll.*): dismissal (esp. with *the*; *slang*): sixpence (*slang*): an enthusiastic but short-lived interest: a phase of such interest. — *adj.* **kick'able.** — *n.* **kick'er** one who kicks, esp. a horse. — **kick'back** part of a sum received paid to another by confidential agreement for favours past or to come: money paid in return for protection: a strong reaction (*fig.*); **kick'-down** a method of changing gear in a car with automatic gear transmission, by pressing the accelerator pedal right down; **kick'ing-strap'** a strap behind a draught-horse's hindquarters to prevent kicking; **kick'-off** the first kick in a game of football; **kick pleat** a pleat at the back of a narrow skirt from knee-level to hem, for greater ease in walking; **kick'-start'** the starting of an engine by a treadle; **kick turn** a skiing turn through 180°; **kick'-up'** a disturbance: a dance: a depression in the bottom of a bottle. — **for kicks** for thrills; **kick about, kick around** to consider: to provisionally discuss: (of a person) to wander around doing nothing in particular: (of an object) to lie about serving no useful purpose; **kick in** (*slang*) to contribute: to die; **kick oneself** to reproach oneself; **kick one's heels** see **heel**[1]; **kick out** (*coll.*) to eject with force: to dismiss; **kick over the traces** to throw off control; **kick or strike the beam** to rise, as the lighter scale of a balance, so as to strike against the beam — hence to be of little weight or importance; **kick the bucket** see **bucket**; **kick up a dust** or **row** to create a disturbance; **kick upstairs** to promote (usu. to a less active or less powerful position). [M.E. *kiken*: origin unknown: W. *cicio*, to kick, comes from Eng.]

kickie-wickie *kik'i-wik'i, (Shak.) n.* a wife. [Altered by editors to **kicksy-wicksy**; perh. conn. with **kickshaws**.]

kickshaw *kik'shöz,* **kickshaw** *-shö, ns.* a trinket, a cheap, worthless article: a delicacy (*arch.*). [Fr. *quelque chose*, something.]

kid[1] *kid, n.* a young goat: extended to young antelope, etc.: a child or young person (*coll.*): leather of kidskin, or a substitute: a glove, shoe, or boot of kid (*arch.*). — *adj.* made of kid leather or imitation kid leather. — *v.t.* and *v.i.* to bring forth (of a goat): — *pr.p.* **kidd'ing;** *pa.t.* and *pa.p.* **kidd'ed.** — *ns.* **kidd'y** dim. of kid: a flashy thief (*thieves' slang*): — *pl.* **kidd'ies; kiddy'wink, kidd'iewink, -ie** (*facet.*) extended forms of **kiddy,** a child; **kid'ling** a young kid. — **kid'-fox** (*Shak.*) a young fox; **kid'-glove'** a glove of kid. — *adj.* as if done by one wearing kid-gloves: overnice, delicate. — **kid'-skin; kids' stuff** (*coll.*) something only suitable for children: something very easy. [O.N. *kith*: cf. Dan. *kid*; Ger. *Kitze*, a young goat.]

kid[2] *kid, n.* a small tub. [Perh. a variant of **kit**[1].]

kid[3] *kid, n.* a faggot. [Origin unknown: W. *cedys*, faggots, is prob. from Eng.]

kid[4] *kid, (coll.) v.t.* and *v.i.* to hoax: to pretend, esp. banteringly (also **kidd'y**): to tease. — *n.* a deception. — *ns.* **kidd'er; kidology** (*kid-ol'ə-ji; coll.*) the art of kidding, sometimes to gain a psychological advantage. [Perh. conn. with **kid**[1], a child.]

kidder *kid'ər,* **kiddier** *-i-ər, ns.* a forestaller: a huckster. [Origin obscure.]

Kidderminster *kid'ər-min-stər, n.* a two-ply or ingrain carpet formerly made at *Kidderminster*. — Also *adj.*

kiddle *kid'l, n.* a stake-fence set in a stream for catching fish. — Also **kid'el, kett'le.** [O.Fr. *quidel*; cf. Bret. *kidel*.]

kiddush *kid'əsh, n.* a Jewish blessing which is uttered over wine or bread on holy days.   [Heb. *qiddūsh*, sanctification.]

kiddy, etc. See **kid**[1,4].

kidel. See **kiddle**.

kidge. See **kedge**[2].

kidling. See **kid**[1].

kidnap *kid'nap*, *v.t.* to steal (a human being), often for ransom: — *pr.p.* **kid'napping**; *pa.t.* and *pa.p.* **kid'napped**. — *n.* an instance of this. — *n.* **kid'napper**. [**kid**[1], a child, **nap**[4].]

kidney *kid'ni*, *n.* one of two flattened glands that secrete urine: temperament, humour, disposition — hence, sort or kind. — **kid'ney-bean** the French bean: a red variety of runner bean; **kidney machine** an apparatus used, in cases where the kidney functions badly, to remove by dialysis harmful substances from the blood; **kid'ney-ore'** haematite in kidney-shaped masses; **kid'ney-potā'to** a kidney-shaped variety of potato; **kid'ney=stone** nephrite: a septarian nodule: a hard deposit in the kidney; **kidney vetch** any plant of the papilionaceous genus Anthyllis, including lady's fingers. [M.E. *kidenei* (pl. *kideneiren*), perh. a compound of *ei* (pl. *eiren*), egg, confused sometimes with *nere*, kidney.]

kidology. See **kid**[4].

kie-kie *kē'kē*, *n.* a New Zealand climbing plant (*Freycinetia banksii*) of the screw-pine family.   [Maori.]

kier, keir, *kēr*, *n.* a bleaching vat.   [Cf. O.N. *ker*, tub.]

kierie *kē'rē*, (*S.Afr.*) *n.* a stick.   [Prob. Hottentot.]

kieselguhr *kē'zl-gōōr*, *n.* diatomite.   [Ger., — *Kiesel*, flint, *Guhr*, fermentation.]

kieserite *kēz'ər-īt*, *n.* a mineral, hydrated magnesium sulphate (MgSO$_4$H$_2$O), a source of Epsom salts. [After D. G. *Kieser* (1779–1862) of Jena.]

kieve. See **keeve**.

kif. See **kef**.

kight (*Spens.*). Same as **kite**[1].

kike *kīk*, (*offensive slang*) *n.* and *adj.* Jew.   [Possibly from the *-ki* ending of many E. European Jewish immigrants' names in U.S. at the end of the 19th cent.]

kikumon *kik'ōō-mon*, *n.* the chrysanthemum badge of the Japanese imperial family.   [Jap. *kiku*, chrysanthemum, *mon*, badge.]

Kikuyu *ki-*, *kē-kōō'ū*, *n.* an agricultural Negro tribe of Kenya: a member thereof. — **kikuyu (grass)** an African grass (*Pennisetum clandestinum*) grown in Australia and S. America.

kild *kild*, a Spenserian form of **killed**.

kilderkin *kil'dər-kin*, *n.* a small barrel: a liquid measure of 18 gallons.   [Old Du. *kindeken, kinneken* (Scot. *kinken*), dim. of *kintal* — L.L. *quintāle*, quintal, associated with Du. *kind*, child.]

kilerg *kil'ûrg*, *n.* a thousand ergs.   [Gr. *chīlioi*, thousand, **erg**.]

kiley. Same as **kylie**.

kilfud-yoking *kil-fud'-yōk'ing*, (*Scot.*) *n.* a fireside disputation.   [Scot. *kilfuddie*, the aperture for feeding a kiln, and **yoking**.]

kilim *ki-lēm'*, *n.* a pileless woven rug traditionally made in the Middle East. — Also **kelim, khilim**.   [Turk. — Pers. *kilīm*.]

kill[1] *kil*, *v.t.* to put to death, to slay: to deprive of life: to destroy: to nullify or neutralise, to render inactive, to weaken or dilute: to reject, discard, defeat: to fascinate, overcome: to injure seriously (*Ir.*): to spoil: to muffle or still: to cause to stop (as machinery, etc.): to exhaust: to cause severe pain: to consume completely (*coll.*): to mark for cancellation (*print.*): to check (the distribution of) type (*print.*): to play (a return shot) so hard that opponent cannot play it back again (*lawn tennis*, etc.). — *v.i.* to murder, slaughter. — *n.* an act or instance of killing, destroying, etc.: prey or game killed: a ball impossible to return (*lawn tennis*, etc.). — *n.* **kill'er** one who kills: one who murders readily or habitually: a slaughterer or butcher: an instrument for killing: a neutralising agent: the grampus or other ferocious delphinid (also **killer whale**). — *adj.* **kill'ing** depriving of life: destructive: deadly, irresistible: exhausting: fascinating: irresistibly funny (*coll.*). — *n.* slaughter: a severe handling. — **kill'-court'esy** (*Shak.*) a discourteous person; **kill'cow** a butcher: a bully; **killing time** the days of the persecution of the Covenanters; **kill'joy** a spoil-sport. — *adj.* austere. — **in at the kill** (*fig.*) present at the culminating moment; **kill by inches** to kill gradually, as by torture; **kill off** to exterminate; **kill the fatted calf** to prepare an elaborate feast, etc., for a homecoming or welcome; **kill time** to occupy oneself with amusements, etc., in order to pass spare time or to relieve boredom; **kill two birds with one stone** to effect one thing by the way, or by the same means with which another thing is done; **kill up** (*Shak.*) to exterminate; **make a killing** (*coll.*) to make a lot of money, a large profit; **to kill** (*coll.*) in an irresistible manner.   [M.E. *killen* or *cullen*.]

kill[2] *kil*, (*U.S. dial.*) *n.* a stream, brook: a river: a channel (used chiefly in place-names, particularly in areas originally settled by Dutch).   [Du. *kil* from M.Du. *kille*, a channel.]

killadar *kil'ə-där*, *n.* the commandant of a fort or garrison.   [Hind. (Pers.) *qil'adär*.]

killas *kil'əs*, *n.* clay slate.   [Cornish miners' term.]

killcrop *kil'krop*, *n.* an insatiate child: a changeling. [L.G. *kilkrop*; Ger. *Kielkropf*.]

killdeer *kil'dēr*, *n.* the largest North American ringplover. — Also **kill'dee**.   [Imit.]

killick, killock *kil'ik, -ək*, *ns.* a small anchor: its fluke: in the Royal Navy, a leading seaman (from his badge, bearing the symbol of an anchor).   [Origin obscure.]

killikinick. See **kinnikinick**.

killogie *ki-lō'gi*, (*Scot.*) *n.* the space before the fireplace of a kiln.   [**kiln, logie**.]

killut *kil'ut*, *n.* in India, a robe of honour or other ceremonial present. — Also **kell'aut, khal'at, khil'at**. [Hind. and Pers. *khil'at*.]

Kilmarnock *kil-mär'nək*, *n.* a kind of closely woven broad blue cap, originally made at *Kilmarnock* in Scotland. — **Kilmarnock cowl** a kind of nightcap.

kiln *kiln, kil*, *n.* a large oven for drying, baking, or calcining corn, hops, bricks, pottery, limestone, etc. — *v.t.* to dry, fire, etc. in a kiln. — *v.t.* **kiln'-dry** to dry in a kiln: — *pa.p.* and *adj.* **kiln'-dried**. — **kiln'-hole** the mouth of a kiln.   [O.E. *cyln, cylen* — L. *culīna*, a kitchen.]

Kilner jar® *kīl'nər jär*, a glass jar with an airtight lid, used for preserving fruit and vegetables.

kilo *kēl'ō*, *n.* a shortened form of **kilogram(me)** or sometimes of other word with the prefix **kilo-**: — *pl.* **kil'os**.

kilo- *kil'ə-, kil'ō-*, *pfx.* denoting 1000 times the unit to which it is attached, e.g. **kil'obar** = 1000 bars; **kil'obit** (*comput.*) 1024 bits; **kil'obyte** (*comput.*) 1000 bytes: 2^{10} (1024) bytes; **kil'ocalorie** 1000 calories, used to measure energy content of food (see also **calorie** under **caloric**); **kil'ocycle per second** kilohertz (q.v.); **kil'ogram(me)** SI base unit of mass, the mass of a platinum-iridium cylinder at BIPM, Paris, 2·205 lb; **kil'ogram=calorie** same as **kilocalorie**; **kil'ohertz** 1000 cycles of oscillation per second, used to measure frequency of sound and radio waves; **kil'ojoule** 1000 joules, used to measure energy, work and heat; **kil'omega-** *pfx.* now replaced by **giga-**, one thousand million times; **kil'ometre** (also *-om'-*) 1000 metres, 0·6214 or about ⅝ mile; **kil'oton(ne)** a measure of explosive force equivalent to that of 1000 ton(ne)s of TNT; **kil'ovolt** 1000 volts; **kil'owatt** 1000 watts, the power dissipated by one bar of the average electric fire; **kil'owatt hour** the energy consumed by a load of one kilowatt in one hour of use (3·6 megajoules), the unit by which electricity is charged to the consumer.   [Gr. *chīlioi*, a thousand.]

kilp *kilp*. Same as **kelp**.

kilt[1] *kilt*, *n.* a man's short pleated skirt, usu. of tartan, forming part of Highland dress: any similar garment. — *v.t.* to tuck up (skirts): to truss up (*arch.*): to hang, string up (*arch.*): to pleat vertically. — *v.i.* (*arch.*) to move lightly and quickly, to trip. — *adj.* **kilt'ed** dressed in a kilt: tucked up: vertically pleated. — *n.* **kilt'y,**

kilt'ie a wearer of a kilt. [Scand.; cf. Dan. *kilte*, to tuck up; O.N. *kilting*, a skirt.]

kilt[2] *kilt*, (*Spens.* and *Ir.*, esp. hyperbolically) *pa.p.* of **kill**[1].

kilter *kil'tər*, (esp. *dial.* and *U.S.*) *n.* good condition. — Also **kelter** (*kel'tər*; *dial.*). — **out of kilter** out of order, not functioning properly. [Origin unknown.]

kimberlite *kim'bər-līt*, *n.* a mica-peridotite, an eruptive rock, the matrix of the diamonds found at *Kimberley* and elsewhere in South Africa.

kimbo *kim'bō*, *v.t.* to set akimbo: — *p.adj.* **kim'boed.**

Kimeridgian, Kimm- *kim-ə-rij'i-ən*, (*geol.*) *adj.* of the lowest division of the Upper Jurassic, named from a clay well developed at *Kimmeridge* in Dorset. — Also *n.*

kimmer. See **cummer.**

kimono *ki-mō'nō*, *n.* a loose robe with wide sleeves, fastening with a sash, an outer garment in Japan: a dressing-gown of similar form: — *pl.* **kimō'nos.** — **kimono sleeve** a magyar sleeve. [Jap.]

kin[1] *kin*, *n.* persons of the same family: relatives: relationship: affinity. — *adj.* related. — *adj.* **kin'less** without relations. — *ns.* **kinsfolk** (*kinz'fōk*) folk or people kindred or related to one another (also **kinfolk, kins'folks**); **kin'ship** relationship. — **kins'man** a man of the same kin or race as another: — *fem.* **kins'woman.** — **next of kin** the relatives (lineal or collateral) of a deceased person, among whom his personal property is distributed if he dies intestate: the person(s) most closely related to an individual by blood or marriage, or a legal ruling; **of kin** of the same kin. [O.E. *cynn*; O.N. *kyn*, Goth. *kuni*, family, race; cog. with L. *genus*, Gr. *genos*.]

kin[2] *kin*, *n.* a Japanese and Chinese weight, the catty. [Jap. *kin*, Chin. *chin*.]

-kin a noun suffix denoting a diminutive, as lamb*kin*, mani*kin*; also in proper names, as Jen*kin* (*John*), Wil*kin* (*William*). [Prob. Du. or L.G.; cf. Ger. *-chen*.]

kina[1], **kinakina.** See **quina.**

kina[2] *kē'nə*, *n.* the monetary unit of Papua New Guinea. [Native name.]

kinaesthesis, in U.S. **kinesthesis,** *kīn-ēs-thē'sis, kin-, -es-, n.* sense of movement or of muscular effort. — Also **kinaesthē'sia** (*-zi-ə, -zyə*). — *adj.* **kinaesthetic** (*-thet'ik*) pertaining to kinaesthesis. [Gr. *kīneein*, to move, *aisthēsis*, sensation.]

kinase *kī'nāz, kin'āz, n.* a biochemical agent, e.g. a metal ion or a protein, which converts a zymogen to an enzyme, and so acts as an activator. [*kinetic*, **-ase.**]

kinchin *kin'chin*, *n.* a child in thieves' slang. — **kin'chin-cove** (*obs.*) a boy; **kin'chin-lay** the robbing of children; **kin'chin-mort** (*obs.*) a girl. [Appar. Ger. *Kindchen*, little child.]

kincob *king'kəb*, *n.* a rich silk fabric embroidered with gold or silver thread, made in India. [Hind. and Pers. *kimkhāb*.]

kind[1] *kīnd*, *n.* those of kin, a race: sort or species, a particular variety: nature, the material universe (*arch.*): innate character (of a person) (*arch.*): fundamental qualities (of a thing): sex (*obs.*): produce, as distinguished from money: a eucharistic element. — *adj.* having or springing from the feelings natural for those of the same family: disposed to do good to others: benevolent. — *adv.* **kind'a** (*coll.*) shortening of **kind of** (somewhat, sort of). — *adj.* **kind'less** (*Shak.*) unnatural, destitute of kindness. — *adv.* **kind'ly** in a kind manner: a (rather peremptory) substitute for please (for the *adj.*, see sep. art.). — *n.* **kind'ness** the quality or fact of being kind: a kind act. — *adj.* **kind'-heart'ed.** — **kind'-heart'edness.** — *adj.* **kind'-spok'en** spoken kindly: given to speaking kindly. — **after (its) kind** according to (its) nature; **do one's kind** (*Shak.*) to act according to one's nature; **in a kind** (*arch.*) in a way, to some extent; **in kind** in goods instead of money: tit for tat; **kind of** (*coll.*) of a kind, somewhat, sort of, to some extent, as it were — used adjectivally and adverbially. [O.E. (*ge*)*cynde* — *cynn*, kin.]

kind[2] *kīnd* (*obs.*) *v.t.* to beget: — *Spens., pa.p.* **kynd'ed.**

kindergarten *kin'dər-gär-tn*, *n.* an infant school on Froebel's principle (1826), in which object-lessons and games figure largely. — *n.* **kindergart'ener** a teacher in a kindergarten: a pupil of a kindergarten (*U.S.*). — Also **kindergärtner** (*-gert'nər*). [Ger., — *Kinder*, children, *Garten*, garden.]

kinderspiel *kin'dər-spēl*, *n.* a children's cantata or play. [Ger., children's sport, child's play — *Kinder*, children, *Spiel*, game, play.]

kindle[1] *kin'dl*, *v.t.* to set fire to: to light: to inflame, as the passions: to provoke: to incite. — *v.i.* to take fire: to begin to be excited: to be roused. — *ns.* **kin'dler; kin'dling** the act of causing to burn: materials for starting a fire. [Cf. O.N. *kyndill*, a torch — L. *candēla*, candle.]

kindle[2] *kin'dl*, (*Shak.*) *v.t.* and *v.i.* to bring forth young. — *n.* brood, litter. — **in kindle** with young. [M.E. *kindlen*: cf. **kind**[1].]

kindly *kīnd'li*, *adj.* natural (*obs.*): orig., belonging to the kind or race: native: native-born (*arch.*): inclined to kindness: benign: genial: comfortable. — *adv.* in a kind or kindly manner (see also under **kind**[1]). — *adv.* **kind'lily** (*rare*). — *n.* **kind'liness.** — *adj.* **kind'ly-nä'tured.** — **kindly tenant** (*Scot.; obs.*) a tenant of the same stock as his landlord, or one whose family has held lands in succession, from father to son, for several generations. — **take it kindly** to feel it as a kindness; **take kindly to** (often with *neg.*) to take a favourable view of, or to adopt (a practice) with enthusiasm. [O.E. *gecyndelic*; cf. **kind**[1].]

kindred *kin'drid* (*Spens.* **kin'red**), *n.* relationship by blood, less properly, by marriage: relatives: a group of relatives, family, clan. — *adj.* akin: cognate: congenial. — *ns.* **kin'dredness; kin'dredship.** [M.E. *kinrede* — O.E. *cynn*, kin, and the suffix *-ræden*, expressing mode or state.]

kine *kīn*, (*B.*) *n.pl.* cows. [M.E. *kyen*, a doubled plural of O.E. *cū*, a cow, the plural of which is *cȳ*; cf. Scots **kye.**]

kinema, kinematograph. See **cinema, cinematograph.**

kinematics *kin-i-mat'iks*, or *kīn-*, *n. sing.* the science of motion without reference to force. — *adjs.* **kinemat'ic, -al.** [Gr. *kīnēma*, motion — *kīneein*, to move.]

kinesipathy *kin-ē-sip'ə-thi*, *n.* a mode of treating disease by muscular movements, cure by movement, exercise — also **kinesither'apy.** — *adjs.* **kinesiat'ric, kinesipath'ic.** — *ns.* **kine'sipath, kinesip'athist.** [Gr. *kīnēsis*, movement.]

kinesis *kī-nē'sis*, or *ki-*, *n.* movement, change of position, *specif.* under stimulus and with direction not precisely determined. — *n. sing.* **kinē'sics** (study of) body movements which convey information in the absence of speech. — *ns.* **kinesiol'ogist; kinesiol'ogy** scientific study of human movement, relating mechanics and anatomy. [Gr. *kīnēsis*, movement.]

kinesthesis, etc. U.S. spelling of **kinaesthesis,** etc.

kinetheodolite *kin-, kīn-i-thi-od'ə-līt, n.* an improved form of theodolite used in tracking missiles and artificial satellites.

kinetics *kī-net'iks* or *ki-*, *n. sing.* the science of the action of force in producing or changing motion. — *adjs.* **kinet'ic, -al** pertaining to motion or to kinetics: due to motion. — *ns.* **kinet'ograph** a camera for taking motion-pictures; **kinet'oscope** an early form of cinematograph: an instrument for the production of curves by combination of circular movements. — **kinetic art, sculpture** art, sculpture, in which movement (produced by air currents, or electricity, or sound, etc.) plays an essential part; **kinetic energy** energy possessed by a body by virtue of its motion. [Gr. *kīnetikos* — *kīneein*, to move.]

kinfolk. Same as **kinsfolk,** under **kin**[1].

king *king*, *n.* a hereditary chief ruler or titular head of a nation: a monarch: a queen bee (*obs.*): a playing-card having the picture of a king: the most important piece in chess: a crowned man in draughts: one who is pre-eminent among his fellows: (*cap.*; *pl.*) the title of two historical books of the Old Testament: — *fem.* **queen**. — *v.t.* to make king: to furnish with a king: to play king (with object *it*). — **king-** in composition, most important. — *n.* **king'dom** the state or attributes of a king: a monarchical state: a region that was once a monarchical state: one of the three grand divisions of natural history (animal, vegetable, mineral). — *adj.* **king'domed** (*Shak.*) constituted like a kingdom. — *n.* **king'hood** kingship: kingliness. — *adj.* **king'less**. — *ns.* **king'let** a little or petty king: the golden-crested wren; **king'lihood**. — *adj.* **king'-like**. — *ns.* **king'liness**; **king'ling** a petty king. — *adj.* **king'ly** belonging or suitable to a king: royal: king-like. — Also *adv.* — *n.* **king'ship** the state, office, or dignity of a king. — **king'-app'le** a large red variety of apple; **king'-archon** the second of the nine archons in Athens, successor to the abolished kings in religious functions; **king'-bird** an American tyrant-flycatcher; **king'-bolt, -rod** a metal rod in a roof connecting the tie-beam and the ridge; **king'-co'bra** a large Asiatic species of cobra; **king'-crab** Limulus, a curious large marine arachnoid, with convex horse-shoe-shaped buckler, the last of its race (Xiphosura); **king'craft** the art of governing, mostly in a bad sense; **king'-crow** a kind of drongo; **king'cup** the buttercup: the marsh-marigold; **king'fish** the opah: any of various fish notable for size or value (*Austr.*); **king'fisher** a European fish-eating bird with very brilliant blue-green and chestnut plumage, formerly known as the halcyon: any bird of the same family, most species of which are not fish-eating: a brilliant blue colour (also *adj.*); **king'-hit** (*Austr. slang*) a knockout blow. — Also *v.t.* — **King Log** a do-nothing king, as opp. to **King Stork**, one who devours his frog-subjects — from Aesop's fable; **king'maker** one who has the creating of kings or other high officials in his power; **king mob** the vulgar multitude; **king'-of-arms'** (sometimes **-at-arms'**) a principal herald (those of England having the designations Garter, Clarencieux, and Norroy and Ulster (includes N. Ireland), of Scotland, Lyon); **king'-penguin** a large penguin, smaller than the emperor; **king'-pin** a tall pin, or one prominently placed: a pin on which swivels an axle of the type of that of an automobile front-wheel: the most important person of a group engaged in an undertaking: the key issue; **king'post** a perpendicular beam in the frame of a roof rising from the tie-beam to the ridge; **king prawn** a large prawn, esp. of the genus *Penaeus*, found around Australia; **king'-sal'mon** the largest Pacific salmon, the quinnat; **King's Bench (Queen's Bench** in a queen's reign) formerly a court in which the king sat: now a division of the High Court of Justice; **king's bounty** see **bounty**; **king's'-chair, -cush'ion** a seat formed by two persons clasping wrists; **king's counsel** (or **queen's counsel**) an honorary rank of barristers and advocates; **king's English** (or **queen's English**) correct standard speech; **king's evidence** (or **queen's evidence**) evidence given for the Crown by a criminal against his accomplices (**turn king's evidence** to give such evidence); **king's-e'vil** a scrofulous disease formerly supposed to be healed by the touch of the king; **king's'-hood** the second stomach of a ruminant, sometimes humorously for the human stomach. — *adj.* **king'-size(d)** of large size. — **king's'-man** a royalist: a custom-house officer; **king's peace** (or **queen's peace**) orig. the peace secured by the sovereign for certain persons (as those employed on his business): the peace of the kingdom generally; **King's Proctor** (or **Queen's Proctor**) a legal officer chiefly concerned with establishing collusion in divorce cases; **King's Regulations** (or **Queen's Regulations**) the regulations governing the British Armed Forces; **King's Scout** (or **Queen's Scout**) a (Boy) Scout who has reached the highest level of proficiency, etc.; **king's'-spear** an asphodel; **king's speech** (or **queen's speech**) the sovereign's address to parliament at its opening and closing; **king's'-yell'ow** orpiment as a pigment; **king'-vul'ture** a large brilliantly-coloured

tropical American vulture; **king'wood** a beautiful Brazilian wood — also *violet-wood*: the papilionaceous tree yielding it, a species of Dalbergia. — **King Charles's head** a matter that persists in obtruding itself as did King Charles's head in the thoughts of Mr Dick in *David Copperfield*; **King Charles spaniel** see **spaniel**; **kingdom come** (*slang*) the state after death; **King James Bible** (or **Version**) the Authorised Version; **king of beasts** the lion; **king of birds** the eagle; **king of kings** a powerful monarch with other monarchs subject to him: (*cap.*) God, Christ; **king of metals** gold; **king of terrors** death; **king of the castle** (orig. from a children's game) the most important, powerful person in a group; **king of the forest** the oak; **king of the herrings** the shad: the oarfish: applied also to various other fishes, as the opah, the rabbit-fish or chimaera; **take the king's shilling** see **shilling**; **three kings of Cologne** the three Wise Men of the East, Caspar, Melchior, and Balthazar; **turn king's (queen's) evidence** see **evident**. [O.E. *cyning* — *cynn*, a tribe, with suffix *-ing*; cog. with **kin**[1].]

kingle *king'l*, (*Scot.*) *n.* very hard rock, esp. sandstone.

kinin *kī'nin*, (*biol.*) *n.* a plant hormone which promotes cell-division and is used commercially as a preservative for cut flowers: any of a group of polypeptides in the blood, causing dilation of the blood vessels and contraction of smooth muscles. [Gr. *kīn(ēsis)*, movement.]

kink[1] *kingk*, *n.* a twisted loop in a string, rope, etc.: a mental twist: a crick: a whim: an imperfection: an unusual sexual performance (*coll.*). — *v.i.* to form a kink. — *v.t.* to cause a kink in. — *n.* **kink'le** a slight kink. — *adj.* **kink'y** twisted: curly: eccentric (*coll.*): mad (*coll.*): out of the ordinary in an attractive and sophisticated way (*coll.*): homosexual, or sexually perverted (*coll.*). [Prob. Du. *kink*; but cf. Sw. and Norw. *kink*, Ger. *Kink*.]

kink[2] *kingk*, (*Scot.*) *v.i.* to cough loudly: to gasp for breath. — *n.* a convulsive cough or gasp. — **kink'-cough, kink'-ho(a)st** (*Scot.*) whooping-cough, chincough. [Northern form of **chink**[3].]

kinkajou *king'kə-jōō*, *n.* a South American animal allied to the raccoon. [App. from a North Amer. Indian word misapplied.]

kinkle, kinky. See **kink**[1].

kinnikinick *kin-i-kin-ik'*, **killikinick** *kil-*, *ns.* a mixture used by American Indians as a substitute for tobacco: a species of cornel or other plant entering into it. [From Algonquian, mixture.]

kino *kē'nō*, *n.* an astringent exudation from various tropical trees: — *pl.* **kin'os**. [App. of W. African origin.]

kinone. See **quinol**.

kinred (*Spens.*). See **kindred**.

kinsfolk, kinship, etc. See **kin**[1].

kintledge. See **kentledge**.

kiosk *kē'osk, ki-osk'*, *n.* an Eastern garden pavilion: a small roofed stall for sale of papers, sweets, etc., either out-of-doors or inside a public building: a bandstand: a public telephone box. [Turk. *köşk*, *keushk* — Pers. *kūshk*.]

kip[1] *kip*, (*Scot.*) *v.i.* to play truant. — Also *n.* in the phrase *to play the kip*, to play truant. [Origin uncertain.]

kip[2] *kip*, *n.* the skin of a young animal. — **kip'-skin** leather made from the skin of young cattle, intermediate between calfskin and cowhide. [Obs. Du., bundle of hides, is suggested.]

kip[3] *kip*, *n.* a level or slight incline at the end of an underground way, on which the tubs of coal stand till hoisted up the shaft.

kip[4] *kip*, (*slang*) *n.* a house of ill-fame: a lodging-house: a bed: a nap. — *v.i.* to go to bed: to lie. — **kip'-house** a brothel: a tramps' lodging-house. — **kip down** to go to bed. [Cf. Dan. *kippe*, a low alehouse.]

kip[5], **kipp** *kip*, (*Scot.*) *n.* anything beaked: a pointed hill. [Cf. Ger., orig. L. G., *Kippe*, point, tip.]

kip[6] *kip*, (*Austr.*) *n.* a short flat stick used to throw up pennies in the game of two-up. [Origin unknown.]

kip⁷ *kip, n.* a unit of weight equal to 1000 pounds. [*ki*lo, pound.]

kipe *kīp, (dial.) n.* an osier basket for catching pike. [O.E. *cȳpe*.]

kipp¹ *kip, n.* a form of generator for hydrogen sulphide or other gas. — Also **Kipp's apparatus.** [P. J. *Kipp* (19th cent.), Dutch founder of a firm of manufacturers of scientific apparatus.]

kipp². See **kip⁵.**

kippage *kip'ij, (Scot.) n.* a state of displeasure or anger. [Fr. *équipage;* see **equipage** under **equip.**]

kipper *kip'ər, n.* a male salmon during the spawning season after spawning: a salmon or (esp.) herring split open, seasoned, and dried: a person (often *giddy kipper; slang*). — *v.t.* to cure or preserve, as a salmon or herring. — *n.* **kipp'erer.** [Perh. O.E. *cypera,* a spawning salmon; or perh. from **kip⁵** from the beaked lower jaw of the male salmon after spawning.]

kir *kēr, n.* a drink made of white wine and blackcurrant syrup or liqueur. [F.*Kir* (1876–1968), Frenchman who is said to have invented it.]

kirbeh *kir'be, n.* a skin for holding water. [Ar. *qirba.*]

Kirbigrip®, kirby-grip, kirbigrip *kûr'bi-grip, n.* a kind of hair-grip. [From **Kirby,** the name of one of the original manufacturers.]

kiri *kir'i.* Older form of **kierie.**

kirimon *kē'ri-mon, n.* one of the two imperial crests of Japan, bearing three leaves and three flowers of Paulownia. [Jap.]

kirk *kirk, kûrk, (Scot.) n.* church, in any sense: by English Episcopalians sometimes specially applied to the Church of Scotland. — *v.t.* to church. — *ns.* **kirk'ing, kirk'in'** the first attendance of a pair after marriage, of a magistrate after election. — *adj.* and *adv.* **kirk'-ward.** — **kirk session** the lowest court in the Scottish Presbyterian church, minister(s) and elders as the governing body of a particular congregation; **kirk'ton, -town** (*Scot.*) the village in which the parish church stands; **kirkyard, -yaird** (-*yärd';* or *kirk'*) a churchyard. — **Auld Kirk** see **auld; make a kirk or** (or **and**) **a mill of it** do what you please or can with it. [A Northern Eng. form of **church.** — O.N. *kirkja* — O.E. *cirice.*]

kirmess. See **kermis.**

kirn¹ *kirn,* **kern** *kern, kûrn, (Scot.) ns.* the cutting of the last sheaf or handful of the harvest: a harvest-home. — **kirn'-ba'by, corn'-ba'by, kirn'-doll'ie, corn'-doll'ie, corn'-maiden** a dressed-up figure made of the last handful of corn cut: (esp. **corn-dollie**) any of a number of straw decorations usu. of traditional design. [Origin unknown.]

kirn² *kirn, n.* a Northern form of **churn.** — **kirn'-milk'** buttermilk.

kirpan *kər-pän', n.* a small sword or dagger, worn by Sikh men as a symbol of religious loyalty. [Punjabi.]

kirschwasser *kērsh'väs-ər, n.* a liqueur made from the wild cherry. — Also **kirsch.** [Ger., cherry water.]

kirtle *kûr'tl, (hist.) n.* a sort of gown or outer petticoat: a mantle. — *adj.* **kir'tled.** [O.E. *cyrtel;* Dan. *kjortel;* O.N. *kyrtill;* app. — L. *curtus,* short.]

kisan *kē'sän, (India) n.* a peasant. [Hindi *kisān.*]

kish *kish, n.* a solid graphite which has separated from, and floats on the top of, a molten bath of cast-iron or pig-iron which has a high carbon content. [Origin uncertain; poss. Ger. *Kies,* gravel.]

Kislev, Chislev *kis'lef,* **Kisleu** *kis'li-ōō, ns.* the third (ecclesiastically ninth) Jewish month, parts of November and December. [Heb.]

kismet *kiz'met,* or *kis', n.* fate, destiny. [Turk. *qismet* — Ar. *qisma.*]

kiss *kis, v.t.* to caress or salute with the lips: to touch gently. — *v.i.* to salute with the lips: to collide: (of billiard balls, etc.) to touch while moving. — *n.* a caress or salute with the lips: a drop of sealing-wax. — *adj.* **kiss'able.** — *n.* **kiss'er** one who kisses: the mouth (*pugilistic slang*). — **kiss'-curl** a flat, circular curl at the side of the forehead; **kiss'ing-com'fit** a perfumed comfit for sweetening the breath; **kissing cousin** a more or less distant relation with whom one is on terms familiar enough to kiss on meeting; **kiss'ing-crust** that part of the upper crust of the loaf which overhangs and touches another; **kissing gate** a gate set in a V-or U-shaped frame. — *n.pl.* **kiss'ing-strings** cap or bonnet strings tied under the chin. — **kiss'-in-the-ring'** an old game in which one kisses another after a chase round a ring of players; **kiss'-me** the wild-pansy or other plant: a short veil: a small bonnet — also **kiss'-me= quick; kiss'-off** (*slang*) a sudden, usu. offensive dismissal. — **kiss and tell** (*coll.*) to give an exposé of one's sexual adventures; **kiss hands** to kiss the sovereign's hands on acceptance of office; **kiss of death** (*coll.*) something that causes failure, destruction, etc.; **kiss off** (*slang*) to dismiss: to kill: to die; **kiss of life** a mouth-to-mouth method of restoring breathing: a means of restoring vitality or vigour (*fig.*); **kiss of peace** a kiss of greeting between the members of the early, and some branches of the modern, Church; **kiss the book** to kiss a Bible or New Testament, in England, after taking a legal oath; **kiss the gunner's daughter** to get a flogging, tied to the breech of a cannon; **kiss the rod** to submit to punishment. [O.E. *cyssan,* to kiss — *coss,* a kiss; Ger. *küssen,* Dan. *kys;* allied to **choose** and **gust².**]

kist *kist, (Scot.) n.* a chest. — *v.t.* to coffin. — **kist o' whistles** an organ. [O.E. *cist,* chest, or O.N. *kista.*]

kistvaen, cistvaen *kist'vīn, n.* a chest-shaped burial-chamber made of flat stones. [W. *cist,* chest, and *maen,* stone, *m* being aspirated.]

kit¹ *kit, n.* a small wooden tub: an outfit: a set of persons (*coll.* or *slang*): equipment: material, tools, instructions, assembled in a container for some specific purpose: the container itself. — *v.t.* (sometimes with *out*) to provide with kit. — **kit'-bag** a strong canvas bag for holding one's kit or outfit (*mil.*): a knapsack: a strong canvas grip; **kit'-boat, -car** a boat, car, put together, from standard components, by an amateur builder. [Prob. Middle Du. *kitte,* a hooped beer-can.]

kit² *kit, n.* a small pocket violin. [Origin obscure; cf. O.E. *cytere,* Gr. *kithara.*]

kit³ *kit, n.* a contraction of **kitten.** — **kit'-cat** the game of tip-cat (see also **Kitcat**).

Kitcat *kit'kat, n.* the name of a London Whig literary club, which existed from about 1688 or 1703 to about 1720, meeting for some time at the pie-shop of Christopher (*Kit*) Cat (or Catling): a portrait 36 by 28 inches in size, like those of the Kitcat Club painted by Kneller to fit their later low-ceilinged clubroom.

kitchen *kich'ən, n.* a place where food is cooked: cooking department or equipment: a tea-urn (*obs. Scot.*): anything eaten as a relish with other food (chiefly *Scot.*). — *v.t.* to regale in the cook-room (*Shak.*): to serve as relish to (*Scot.*): to make palatable (*Scot.*): to use sparingly, make to last (*Scot.*). — *ns.* **kitch'endom** the domain of the kitchen; **kitch'ener** a person employed in the kitchen: a cooking-stove; **kitchenette'** a tiny kitchen: a compact combined kitchen and pantry. — **kitchen cabinet** an informal, unelected group of advisers to a political office-holder; **kitchen Dutch, kitchen Kaffir** (*arch. S.Afr.*) a mixture of Dutch or Kaffir with English, used in speaking to native servants; **kitch'en= fee** the fat that falls from meat in roasting — the cook's perquisite; **kitch'en-fur'niture** the furniture of a kitchen: the percussion instruments of an orchestra; **kitch'en-gar'den** a garden where vegetables are cultivated for the kitchen; **kitch'en-gar'dener; kitch'en= knave** a scullion; **kitch'en-maid** a maid or servant whose work is in the kitchen; **kitch'en-midd'en** (Dan. *kjökkenmödding*) a prehistoric rubbish-heap; **kitchen physic** (*Milt.*) substantial fare; **kitch'en-range** a kitchen grate with oven, boiler, etc., attached, for cooking. — *adj.* **kitch'en-sink'** (of plays, etc.) dealing with sordid real-life situations. — **kitch'en-stuff** material used in kitchens: kitchen refuse, esp. fat from pots, etc.; **kitchen tea** in Australia, a bride's shower, the gifts being kitchen utensils, etc.; **kitchen unit** a set of up-to-date kitchen fitments; **kitch'en-wench** a kitchen-maid. [O.E. *cycene* — L. *coquīna* — *coquĕre*, to cook.]

kite[1] *kīt, n.* a rapacious bird of the hawk kind (fam. *Accipitridae*): a rapacious person: a light frame covered with paper or cloth for flying in the air: a more complicated structure built of boxes (*box-kite*), often for carrying recording instruments or a man in the air: a light and lofty sail: a rumour or suggestion given out to see how the wind blows, test public opinion, or the like: an accommodation bill, esp. a mere paper credit: an aircraft (*airmen's slang*). — *v.t.* to cause to fly like a kite: to write (a cheque) before one has sufficient money in one's bank to cover it (*slang*). — *v.i.* to fly like a kite: to rise sharply. — **kite'-balloon'** an observation-balloon designed on the principle of the kite to prevent revolving, etc.; **kite'-flying** sending up and controlling a kite: the dealing in fictitious accommodation paper to raise money: testing public opinion by circulating rumours, etc. (**fly a kite** to take part in **kite-flying**); **kite'-mark** a kite-shaped mark on goods indicating conformity in quality, size, etc., with the specifications of the British Standards Institution. [O. E. *cyta*; cf. W. *cud*, Bret. *kidel*, a hawk.]

kite[2], **kyte** *kīt*, (*Scot.*) *n.* a paunch, belly. [Ety. dub.]

kith *kith, n.* knowledge: native land: acquaintance — obs. except in **kith and kin**, friends (originally home-country) and relatives. [O.E. *cȳth* — *cunnan*, to know.]

kithara *kith'ə-rə.* Same as **cithara**. [Gr.]

kithe. Same as **kythe**.

kitling. See **kitten**.

kitsch *kich, n.* trash: work in any of the arts that is pretentious and inferior or in bad taste. — *adj.* **kitsch'y.** — *adv.* **kitsch'ily.** [Ger.]

kitten *kit'n, n.* a young cat (*dim.* **kitt'y**): sometimes the young of another animal. — *v.t.* and *v.i.* (of a cat) to bring forth. — *n.* **kit'ling** (*Scot.*) a kitten. — *adjs.* **kitt'enish, kitt'eny** frolicsome: skittish: affectedly playful. — *v.t.* and *v.i.* **kitt'le** (*Scot.*) to kitten: to come, bring into being. — **kitt'en-moth** any of the smaller kindred of the puss-moth. — **have kittens** to be in a state of excitement or anger. [M.E. *kitoun* — O.N.Fr. *caton*, dim. of *cat* — L.L. *cattus*, cat.]

kittiwake *kit'i-wāk, n.* a species of gull with long wings and rudimentary hind-toe. [Imit.]

kittle[1] *kit'l*, (orig. *Scot.*) *adj.* ticklish, intractable. — *v.t.* to tickle: to puzzle. — *adj.* **kitt'ly** (*Scot.*) easily tickled, sensitive. — **kitt'ly-bend'ers** (*Amer.*) running on thin bending ice. [Ety. obscure.].

kittle[2]. See **kitten**.

kittle-pins *kit'l-pinz, n.pl.* skittles. — Also **kett'le-pins.** [Prob. alteration of **kail**[1] (q.v.).]

kittly. See **kittle**[1].

kittul *kit-ōōl', n.* the jaggery palm (*Caryota urens*): its fibre. [Sinhalese *kitūl.*]

kitty[1] *kit'i, n.* a jail (*arch.*): a pool or fund of money held in common: the jack (*bowls*).

kitty[2]. See **kitten**.

kiwi *kē'wē, n.* the Apteryx: a New Zealander (*coll.*): a non-flying member of an airfield staff (*coll.*): a kiwi fruit. — **kiwi fruit** the edible green fruit of the Chinese gooseberry (q.v.). [Maori, from its cry.]

Klan, Klansman. See **Ku-Klux Klan.**

klang *klang*, (*mus.*) *n.* a complex tone, composed of fundamental and harmonics: timbre. — Also **clang.** — **klang'farbe** (*-fär-bə*) tone-colour, timbre. [Ger.]

klavier *klä-vēr', n.* clavier. [Ger. — Fr. *clavier.*]

klaxon *klaks'ən, n.* orig., a mechanical horn with rasping sound: (with *cap.*; ®) an electric horn.

klebsiella *kleb'zi-el-ə, n.* a genus of gram-negative rodlike bacteria, which cause various diseases in man and animals, incl. pneumonia. [E. *Klebs* (d.1913), Ger. pathologist.]

Kleenex® *klē'neks, n.* a kind of soft paper tissue used as a handkerchief.

Kleig light. Same as **Klieg light.**

Klein bottle *klīn bot'l*, (*math.*) a one-sided four-dimen-

sional surface, which in three dimensions can be represented as a surface obtained by pulling the narrow end of a tapering tube over the wall of the tube and then stretching the narrow end and joining it to the larger end. [Felix *Klein*, Ger. mathematician.]

klendusic *klen-dū'sik, adj.* of plants, able to withstand disease by means of some protective mechanism. — *n.* **klendū'sity.** [Gr. *kleidoein*, to lock up — *kleis*, a key.]

klepht *kleft, n.* a Greek or Albanian brigand. — *adj.* **klepht'ic.** — *n.* **klepht'ism.** [Mod. Gr. *klephtēs* — anc. Gr. *kleptēs*, thief — *kleptein*, to steal.]

kleptocracy *klep-tok'rə-si, n.* government by thieves, a thieves' régime: a country with such a government: a body or order of thieves. — *adj.* **kleptocrat'ic.** [Gr. *kleptēs*, thief, and **-cracy.**]

kleptomania *klep-tō-mā'ni-ə, n.* a mania for stealing: a morbid impulse to secrete things. — *n.* **kleptomā'niac.** [Gr. *kleptein*, to steal, *maniā*, madness.]

Kletterschuhe *klet'ər-shōō-ə, n.pl.* felt-soled rock-climbing boots. [Ger. — *kletter-*, climbing, *Schuh* (pl. *-e*), shoe.]

Klieg light, Kleig light *klēg līt*, a type of incandescent floodlighting lamp for film studio use. — **klieg eyes** the effect of strain on the eyes caused by the brilliance of floodlights in film production. [From *Kliegl* brothers, the inventors.]

klinker *klingk'ər, n.* a very hard paving-brick (also **clinker**). [Du.]

klinostat *klī'nō-stat, n.* a revolving stand for experimenting with growing plants. [Gr. *klīnein*, to incline, *statos*, standing.]

klipdas *klip'dus, n.* the Cape hyrax. [Du., lit. rock-badger.]

klipspringer *klip'spring-ər, n.* a small South African antelope. [Du. *klip*, rock, *springer*, jumper.]

Klondike, Klondyke *klon'dīk*, (also without *cap.*) *n.* a very rich source of wealth: a card game, a form of patience. — *v.t.* and *v.i.* to export (fresh herring) direct from Scotland to the Continent: to trans-ship (fish) at sea. — *n.* **klon'dyker.** [From the gold-rush to *Klondike* in the Yukon, in 1896, etc.]

kloof *klōōf*, (*S.Afr.*) *n.* a mountain ravine. [Du., cleft.]

kludge *kluj*, (*comput.*; *coll.*) *n.* a botched or makeshift device or program which is unreliable or inadequate in function.

klutz *kluts*, (*U.S. slang*) *n.* an idiot: an awkward, stupid person. [Ger. *Klotz*, idiot.]

klystron (*rare* **Klystron**) *klis', klīs'tron, n.* any of a number of electron tubes (amplifiers, oscillators, etc.) in which the velocity of the electron beam is modulated by an ultra-high-frequency field and subsequently imparts energy to it or other u.h.f. fields. [Gr. *klystēr*, syringe.]

knack *nak, n.* a petty contrivance: a toy: a nice trick: dexterity, adroitness. — *n.* **knack'iness.** — *adjs.* **knack'ish, knack'y** cunning, crafty. — *n.* **knack'wurst** a kind of highly seasoned sausage. [Orig. imit.; cf. Du. *knak*, a crack, Ger. *knacken*, to crack.]

knacker[1] *nak'ər, n.* anything that makes a snapping or cracking sound: (*pl.*) castanets or clappers, bones: (in *pl.*) testicles (*slang*). [Imit.]

knacker[2] *nak'ər, n.* a horse-slaughterer: one who buys and breaks up old houses, ships, etc.: a worn-out horse. — *v.t.* to castrate: to kill: to wear out, exhaust. — *adj.* **knack'ered** (*slang*) exhausted, worn out. — *n.* **knack'ery** a knacker's yard. [Origin obscure.]

knag *nag, n.* a knot in wood: a peg. — *n.* **knagg'iness.** — *adj.* **knagg'y** knotty: rugged. [Cf. Dan. *knag*, Ger. *Knagge.*]

knap[1] *nap, v.t.* to snap or break with a snapping noise: to break in pieces with blows, as stones: to pronounce with a snapping effect: to rap: to bite off, nibble: to steal: — *pr.p.* **knapp'ing;** *pa.t.* and *pa.p.* **knapped.** — *n.* **knapp'er** one who breaks stones, esp. one who breaks up flint-flakes for gun-flints. — *v.i.* **knapp'le** to nibble. — **knap'-bottle** the bladder-campion; **knapp'ing-ham-**

mer (*Scot.*) a hammer for breaking stones. [Du. *knappen*, to crack or crush.]

knap² *nap*, (*obs.* except *dial.*) *n.* a protuberance: a hillock: a hill-crest. [O.E. *cnæpp*.]

knapsack *nap'sak, n.* a case for necessaries borne on the back: a rucksack. [Du. *knappen*, to crack, eat.]

knapskull, knapscull, knapscal *nap'skəl*, (*Scot. obs.*) *n.* a kind of helmet. [Origin unknown.]

knapweed *nap'wēd, n.* a composite plant of the genus *Centaurea*, like a spineless thistle. [Earlier *knopweed*; see **knop.**]

knar¹, gnar *när, n.* a knot on a tree. — *adj.* **knarred, gnarred** gnarled, knotty. [Cf. L.G. *knarre*, Du. *knar*; also **knur.**]

knar² *när.* See **gnar¹.**

knarl. See **gnarl.**

knave *nāv, n.* orig., as in *Shak.*, a boy: a serving-boy: a false, deceitful fellow: a playing-card bearing the picture of a servant or soldier. — *ns.* **knav'ery** dishonesty; **knave'ship** (*Scot.*) a certain quantity of grain, the due of the miller's servant. — *adj.* **knav'ish** fraudulent: rascally. – *adv.* **knav'ishly.** — *n.* **knav'ishness.** — **knave'-bairn** (*Scot.*) a male child. [O.E. *cnafa, cnapa*, a boy, a youth; Ger. *Knabe, Knappe.*]

knawel *nö'əl, n.* a cornfield weed (*Scleranthus*) of the chickweed family. [Ger. *Knauel* or *Knäuel.*]

knead *nēd, v.t.* to work and press together into a mass, as flour into dough: to operate upon in massage. — *n.* **knead'er.** — **knead'ing-trough** a trough for kneading. [O.E. *cnedan*; O.N. *knotha*, Ger. *kneten*, to knead.]

knee *nē, n.* the joint between the thigh and shin bones: in a horse's foreleg, the joint answering to the wrist: in a bird the joint answering to the ankle: part of a garment covering the knee: a root upgrowth by which swamp-growing trees breathe: a piece of timber or metal like a bent knee: a genuflection (*Shak.*). — *v.t.* to kneel to (*Shak.*): to achieve by kneeling, or pass over on the knees (*Shak.*): to furnish with a knee: to press, strike or nudge with the knee: to make baggy at the knee. — *v.i.* to kneel. — *adj.* **kneed, knee'd** having knees or angular joints: baggy at the knees, as trousers; **knee'-breech'es** breeches extending to just below the knee, as in court-dress; **knee'-cap** the knee-pan: a cap or strong covering for the knees, used chiefly for horses to save their knees in case of a fall. — *v.t.* to subject to knee-capping. — **knee'-capping** a form of torture or (terrorist) punishment in which the victim is shot or otherwise injured in the knee-cap; **knee'-cords** knee-breeches of corduroy. — *adjs.* **knee'-crooking** obsequious: fawning; **knee'-deep** rising to the knees: sunk to the knees. — **knee'-drill** directed devotional exercises. — *adj.* **knee'-high** rising or reaching to the knees. — **knee'hole** the space beneath a desk or bureau for the knees when sitting; **knee'-holl'y** butcher's broom; **knee'-jerk** a reflex throwing forward of the leg when tapped below the knee-cap. — *adj.* of a reaction, automatic, unthinking, predictable. — **knee'-joint** the joint of the knee: a joint with two pieces at an angle, so as to be very tight when pressed into a straight line. — *adj.* **knee'-length** reaching to the knee. — **knee'-pan** the patella, a flat round bone on the front of the knee-joint; **knee sock** a sock reaching to just below the knee; **knee'-stop, -swell** a lever worked by the performer's knee, for regulating the wind-supply of a reed-organ, etc.; **knees'-up** (*coll.*) a riotous dance or party; **knee'-tim'ber** timber bent into a shape suitable for a knee in shipbuilding, etc.; **knee'-trib'ute** (*Milt.*) the homage of kneeling. — **bring someone to his knees** to make someone admit defeat; **give** or **offer a knee** (*Thackeray*, etc.) to act as second in a fight, it being usual for the principal to rest on the second's knee between the rounds; **on the knees of the gods** awaiting the decision of fate (after Homer). [O.E. *cnēow, cnēo*; Ger. *Knie*, L. *genu*, Gr. *gony*.]

kneel *nēl, v.i.* to rest or fall on the bended knee: — *pa.t.* and *pa.p.* **kneeled, knelt** (*nelt*). — *n.* **kneel'er** one who kneels: a flat cushion to rest the knees on while

kneeling: a hassock. [O.E. *cnēowlian.*]

Kneipe *knī'pə*, (Ger.) *n.* a tavern, a student's beer-house or drinking party.

knell *nel, n.* the stroke of a bell: the sound of a bell at a death or funeral. — *v.i.* to sound as a bell: to toll. — *v.t.* to summon as by a tolling bell. [O.E. *cnyllan*, to beat noisily; Du. and Ger. *knallen.*]

knelt *nelt, pa.t.* and *pa.p.* of **kneel.**

Knesset *knes'it, n.* the one-chamber parliament of Israel. [Heb., assembly.]

knevell. A form of **nevel.**

knew *nū, pa.t.* of **know.**

knicker. Same as **nicker³.**

knickerbocker *nik'ər-bok-ər, n.* (*cap.*) descendant of one of the original Dutch settlers of New York: (*cap.*) a New Yorker: (in *pl.*) loose breeches gathered in at the knee. — Also *n.pl.* **knick'ers, knicks** (*coll.*) knickerbockers: a woman's undergarment of similar form, covering the thigh and not always gathered in. — *adj.* **knick'ered** clad in knickers. — *interj.* **knick'ers** (*slang*) expressing outrage or disbelief. — **knickerbocker glory** a large and opulent ice-cream sundae. — **get one's knickers in a twist** (*coll.*) to become harassed, anxious, or worried. [From the wide-breeched Dutchmen in Knickerbocker's (Washington Irving's) humorous *History of New York*.]

knick-knack *nik'-nak, n.* a small, trifling ornamental or would-be ornamental article — *dim.* **knick-knack'et.** — *ns.* **knick-knack'atory** a collection of knick-knacks; **knick-knack'ery** knick-knacks collectively. — *adj.* **knick'-knacky.** — Also **nick'-nack,** etc. [A doubling of **knack.**]

knife *nīf, n.* an instrument for cutting: — *pl.* **knives** *nīvz.* — *v.t.* to cut: to convey or apply with a knife: to stab: to try to defeat by treachery e.g. within the party: — *v.i.* to cut (with *through*) or penetrate (with *into*) as if with a knife. — *adj.* **knife'less** without a knife: without use of the knife. — *n.* **knif'ing** the (criminal) act of putting a knife into someone. — **knife'-and-fork'** a trencherman. — *adj.* involving or relating to use of knife and fork. — **knife'-board** a board on which knives are cleaned: a seat running along the top of an old form of bus (*coll.*); **knife'-box** a box for keeping table cutlery in; **knife'-boy** a boy employed in cleaning knives; **knife'-edge** a sharp-edged ridge: a sharp piece of steel like a knife's edge serving as the axis of a balance, etc. (also *fig.*); **knife'-grinder** one who grinds or sharpens knives; **knife'-money** a knife-shaped bronze currency formerly used in China; **knife pleat** a narrow, flat pleat; **knife'-point** the sharp tip of a knife (**at knife-point** under threat of injury); **knife'-rest** a rest for a carving knife or fork; **knife'-switch** a switch in an electric circuit, in which the moving element consists of a flat blade which engages with fixed contacts. — **have one's knife in** to be persistently hostile or vindictive towards; **under the knife** undergoing a surgical operation; **war to the knife** unrelenting conflict. [M.E. *knif* — O.E. *cnīf.*]

knight *nīt, n.* orig. a lad, servant: one of gentle birth and bred to arms, admitted in feudal times to a certain honourable military rank: one of the rank, with the title 'Sir', next below baronets: a member of the equestrian order in ancient Rome: one devoted to the service of a lady, her 'servant' or champion: a chessman, usu. with a horse's head, that moves one square forward, backward, or to either side, and one diagonally, at each move. — *v.t.* to make a knight. — *ns.* **knight'age** knights collectively; **knight'hood** the rank, title, or status of knight: the order or fraternity of knights. — *adj.* **knight'less** (*Spens.*) unbecoming a knight. — *n.* **knight'liness.** — *adj.* **knight'ly** like a knight: befitting a knight: chivalrous: of a knight or knights. — Also *adv.* — **knight'-bach'elor** a knight not a member of any order: — *pl.* **knights'-bach'elors, knights'-bach'elor; knight'-bann'eret** a knight who carried a banner and who was superior in rank to the knight-bachelor: — *pl.* **knights'-bann'erets; knight'-**

err'ant a knight who travelled in search of adventures: a man or boy who behaves in a quixotic fashion: — *pl.* **knights'-err'ant; knight'-err'antry; knight'hood-err'-ant** (*Tenn.*) the body of knights-errant; **knight'-mar'-shal** formerly an officer who had cognisance of offences within twelve miles of the king's abode; **knight'-service** tenure by a knight on condition of military service; **knight's fee** a holding of land for which knight-service was required; **knight's progress** a series of moves in which a knight may visit every square on the chess-board; **Knights Templars** see **temple**[1]. — *The following are jocular titles used formerly* (*excluding* **knight of the shire**, *which is hist.*): — **knight of industry** a footpad, thief, or sharper; **knight of St Crispin** a shoemaker; **knight of the pestle** an apothecary; **knight of the post** (i.e. possibly the whipping-post) a professional false witness and offerer of bail; **knight of the rainbow** a flunkey (from his livery); **knight of the road** a highwayman: a commercial traveller: a tramp; **knight of the shears** a tailor; **knight of the shire** a member of parliament for a county; **knight of the spigot** a tapster, a publican; **knight of the stick** a compositor; **knight of the whip** a coachman. — **Knights of Labour** in the United States, a national labour organisation; **Knights of Malta** see **hospital**. [O.E. *cniht*, youth, servant, warrior; Ger. *Knecht* and Du. *knecht*, servant.]

Kniphofia nip-hōf'i-ə, nī-fō'fi-ə, *n.* an African genus of the lily family, otherwise called *Tritoma*, the red-hot poker or torch-lily. [Named after J. H. *Kniphof* (1704–65), German botanist.]

knish *knish, n.* in Jewish cookery, dough with a potato, meat, etc., filling, baked or fried. [Yiddish — Russ.]

knit *nit, v.t.* to form into a knot (*arch.*): to tie together (*arch.*): to intertwine: to unite into network by needles or machinery: to make by means of knitting-needles or knitting-machine: to unite closely, to draw together: to contract. — *v.i.* to interweave with needles: to grow together: — *pr.p.* **knitt'ing**; *pa.t.* and *pa.p.* **knitt'ed** or **knit**. — *n.* a style of knitting (*Shak.*): a knitted fabric or article. — *ns.* **knitt'er; knitt'ing** the work of a knitter: union, junction: the network formed by knitting. — Also *adj.* — **knitt'ing-machine'** a machine for knitting; **knitt'ing-needle** a long needle or wire used for knitting; **knit'wear** knitted clothing. — **knit one's brows** to frown. [O.E. *cnyttan* — *cnotta*, a knot.]

knitch *nich,* (*dial.*) *n.* a faggot. [O.F. *gecnycc*, bond.]

knittle *nit'l, n.* a small line made of two or three yarns twisted with the fingers (*naut.*): (in *pl.*) the halves of two yarns in a rope, twisted for pointing. [O.E. *cnyttels*, sinew, string.]

knive nīv, *v.t.* to knife. — **knives**, *pl.* of **knife.**

knob *nob, n.* a hard protuberance: a hard swelling: a round ornament or handle: the penis (*slang*). — *adj.* **knobbed** containing or set with knobs. — *ns.* **knobb'er** a stag in its second year; **knobb'iness; knobb'le** a little knob. — *adjs.* **knobb'ly, knobb'y** having, full of knobs: knotty. — **knob'-stick** a stick with knobbed head: a blackleg or scab (*slang*). — **with knobs on** (*coll.*) with interest, more so. [Cf. Low Ger. *knobbe*; **knop.**]

knobkerrie *nob'ker-i, n.* a round-headed stick used as a club and a missile by S. African natives. [**knob** and **kiri**, on the model of Afrik. *knopkierie*.]

knobble. See **knob, knubble.**

knock *nok, v.i.* to strike with something hard or heavy: to drive or be driven against something: to strike for admittance: to rap: to make a noise by, or as if by, striking: (of machinery) to rattle: (of internal-combustion engine) to give noise of detonation. — *v.t.* to strike: to drive against: to render, put, make, or achieve by blows: to impress strongly, stun, daze, confound (*slang*): to arrest (*slang*): to disparage, criticise in a carping way (*coll.*). — *n.* a sudden stroke: a rap: the noise of detonation in an internal-combustion engine: a clock (*Scot.*): a reversal, shock (*coll.*): a criticism (*coll.*). — *ns.* **knock'er** one who knocks: a hammer suspended at a door for making a knock: a goblin inhabiting a mine who points out the presence of ore

by knocks (*dial.*): a carper (*coll.*): (in *pl.*) breasts (*slang*); **knock'ing** a beating on a door: a rap: a noise as if of something that knocks: knock in an internal-combustion engine: a piece knocked off. — **knock'about** a boisterous performance with horseplay: a performer of such turns: a doer of odd jobs, esp. on a station (*Austr.*): a small yacht without bowsprit: a small motor-car suitable for doing short journeys. — *adj.* of the nature of knockabout: suitable for rough use. — **knock'-back** a set-back: a refusal of parole from prison (*slang*). — *adj.* **knock'-down** such as to overthrow: adapted for being taken to pieces: (of prices) very low. — **knock'er-up** a person employed to rouse workers in the morning; **knocking copy** advertising material which denigrates competing products; **knock'ing-shop** (*slang*) a brothel; **knock'-knee** state of being knock-kneed. — *adj.* **knock'-kneed** having knees that knock or touch in walking: weak (*fig.*). — **knock'-on'** see **knock on** and **knock-on effect** below. — *adj.* (*coll.*) causing a series of effects. — **knock'out'** the act of knocking out: a blow that knocks out: a combination among dealers at an auction: any person or thing of outstanding attraction or excellence (*coll.*; **technical knockout** see under **technical**). — *adj.* (of a competition) eliminating losers at each round. — **knockout auction** an auction where the bidders are largely swindling confederates; **knockout drops** a drug put in a drink to render the drinker unconscious; **knock'-rating** the measurement of freedom from detonation of a fuel in an internal-combustion engine in terms of the percentage of octane in an octane-heptane mixture of equivalent knock-proneness; **knock'-up'** (in tennis, etc.) practice immediately before a match. — **knock about, around** to mistreat physically: to saunter, loaf about: to travel about, roughing it and having varied experiences; **knock back** (*slang*) to drink, eat: to cost: to shock; **knock cold** to fell: to shock violently; **knock copy** to disparage a rival's wares; **knock down** to fell with a blow: to demolish: to assign with a tap of the auctioneer's hammer (to): to reduce in price: to embezzle (*U.S.*) (*adj.* **knock-down** see above); **knock-for-knock agreement, policy,** etc., an arrangement between motor insurance companies by which, after an accident involving two cars, each company settles the damage to the car it insures without considering which driver was to blame; **knock into a cocked hat** see **cock**[1]; **knock off** to stop work: to stop, discontinue: to accomplish hastily: to deduct: to steal (*slang*): to copy illegally, to pirate (*slang*): to kill (*slang*): to have sexual intercourse with (*slang*); **knock on** (*Rugby football*) to knock forward with the hand or arm (an infringement of the rules; *n.* **knock'-on'**); **knock-on effect** the effect one action or occurrence has on one or more indirectly related matters or circumstances; **knock on the head** to suppress, put an end to; **knock on wood** see **touch wood**; **knock out** to dislodge by a blow: to strike insensible or incapable of recovering in time, in boxing: to overcome, demolish: to produce, esp. quickly or roughly (*coll.*): to tire (oneself) out (*slang*): to overwhelm with amazement, admiration, etc. (*slang*); **knock sideways** to put off one's usual course; **knock the bottom out of** to make, or show to be, invalid: to make ineffectual, bring to nothing; **knock the living daylights out of** see **day**; **knock together** to get together or construct hastily; **knock under** (*arch.*) to give in, yield; **knock up** to rouse by knocking: to weary out: to be worn out: to construct or arrange hastily: to score (so many runs) (*cricket*): to make pregnant (*slang*); **up to the knocker** (*slang*) up to the required standard of excellence or fashion. [O.E. *cnocian*; perh. imit.]

knoll[1] *nōl* (*Scot.* **knowe** now), *n.* a round hillock: the top of a hill (*dial.*). [O.E. *cnol*; Ger. *Knollen*, a knob, lump.]

knoll[2] *nōl.* Arch. form of **knell.**

knop *nop,* (*arch.*) *n.* a knob: a bud: a loop: a tuft. [Cf. O.N. *knappr*; Du. *knop*, Ger. *Knopf.*]

knosp *nosp, n.* the unopened bud of a flower: an architectural ornament resembling that. [Ger. *Knospe.*]

knot¹ *not, n.* a snipe-like shore bird (*Calidris canutus*) of the sandpiper family. [Origin unknown: the connection with King Cnut is a fancy of Camden's.]

knot² *not, n.* an interlacement of parts of a cord or cords, etc., by twisting the ends about each other, and then drawing tight the loops thus formed: a piece of ribbon, lace, etc., folded or tied upon itself in some particular form, as *shoulder-knot, breast-knot*, etc.: anything like a knot in form: a bond of union: an elaborately designed flower-bed (*dial.*): a tangle (in string, hair, etc.): a difficulty: the main point or central part of a tangle, intricacy, problem, or difficulty: a complex of lines, mountains, etc.: the base of a branch buried in a later growth of wood: a node or joint in a stem, esp. of a grass: a lump: a concretion: a swelling: a knob: a boss: a bud: a hill: a clump or cluster: a measured quantity of yarn: a division of the knot-marked logline: a nautical mile per hour, used in navigation and meterology: (loosely) a nautical mile. — *v.t.* to tie in a knot: to unite closely: to make knotty: to make by knotting: to remove knots from: to cover knots in (before painting wood). — *v.i.* to form a knot or knots: to knit knots for a fringe: — *pr.p.* **knott'ing**; *pa.t.* and *pa.p.* **knott'ed**. — *adjs.* **knot'less** without knots; **knott'ed** full of, or having, knots. — *ns.* **knott'er** a person or contrivance that makes or removes knots; **knott'iness** the quality of being knotty; **knott'ing** formation or removal of knots: covering of knots before painting: material for the purpose: fancywork done by knitting threads into knots. — *adj.* **knott'y** containing knots: hard, rugged: difficult: intricate. — **knot garden** a garden with intricate formal designs of shrubs, flowerbeds, etc.; **knot'grass** a much-jointed species of Polygonum, a common weed: applied also to various grasses; **knot'-hole** a hole in wood where a knot has fallen out; **knot'weed** any of various plants of the genus *Polygonium*; **knot'work** ornamental work made with knots: carving or decoration in interlaced forms. — **at a rate of knots** (*coll.*) very fast; **bowline knot** see **bowline**; **get knotted!** (*slang*) *interj.* expressing anger, derision, defiance, etc.; **granny knot** see **granny**; **porters' knot** a shoulder-pad with loop for the forehead; **tie someone (up) in knots** to confuse, bewilder someone completely. [O.E. *cnotta*; Ger. *Knoten*, Dan. *knude*, L. *nōdus*.]

knotenschiefer *knō'tən-shē-fər, n.* spotted slate, spotted schist, slightly altered argillaceous rock spotted with little concretions. [Ger., knot slate or schist.]

knout *knōōt*, also *nowt, n.* whip formerly used as an instrument of punishment in Russia: punishment inflicted by the knout. — *v.t.* to flog. [French spelling of Russ. *knut.*]

know *nō, v.t.* to be informed of: to be assured of: to be acquainted with: to recognise: to approve (*B.*): to have sexual commerce with (*arch.*). — *v.i.* to possess knowledge: — *pr.p.* **know'ing**; *pa.t.* **knew** (*nū, U.S. nōō*); *pa.p.* **known** (*nōn.*) — *n.* knowledge (*Shak.*): possession of the relevant facts. — *adj.* **know'able** capable of being known, discovered, or understood. — *ns.* **know'ableness; know'er**. — *adj.* **know'ing** intelligent: skilful: cunning. — *adv.* **know'ingly** in a knowing manner: consciously: intentionally. — *n.* **know'ingness** the quality of being knowing or intelligent: shrewdness. — *adj.* **known** widely recognised. — **know'-all** one who thinks he knows everything; **know'-how** the faculty of knowing the right thing to do in any contingency: specialised skill; **know'-noth'ing** one who is quite ignorant: a member of the (Native) American Party (1854–56), originally secret. — *adj.* completely ignorant. — **know'=noth'ingism**. — **in the know** in possession of private information: initiated; **I wouldn't know** I am not in a position to know; **know all the answers** to be completely informed on everything, or to think one is; **know better** to be too wise, well-instructed (to do this or that); **know how many beans make five** to be sensible, aware, have

one's wits about one; **knowing to** (*obs.*) aware, informed, of; **known as** going by name of; **know the ropes** to understand the detail or procedure, as a sailor does his rigging; **know what's o'clock, know what's what** to be wide awake; **know which side one's bread is buttered on** to be fully alive to one's own interest; **what do you know?** what is the news?: a greeting or expression of incredulity; **you never know** (*coll.*) perhaps. [O.E. *cnāwan*; O.N. *knā*, L. (*g*)*nōscere*, Gr. *gignōskein*.]

knowe. See **knoll**¹.

knowledge *nol'ij, n.* assured belief: that which is known: information, instruction: enlightenment, learning: practical skill: acquaintance: cognisance (*law*): sexual intimacy (*arch.*). — *v.t.* (*obs.*) to acknowledge. — *n.* **knowledgeabil'ity**. — *adj.* **knowl'edgeable** possessing knowledge: intelligent. — *adv.* **knowl'edgeably**. — **knowledge base** (*comput.*) a collection of specialist knowledge formulated for use esp. in expert systems; **knowledge box** (*slang*) the head; **knowledge engineering** (*comput.*) the application of artificial intelligence techniques in constructing expert systems. — **to one's knowledge** so far as one knows. [M.E. *knowleche*, where *-leche* is unexplained; see **know**.]

knub, nub *nub, n.* a knob: a small lump: the waste or refuse of silk-cocoons. — *n.* **knubb'le, nubb'le** a small lump. — *adjs.* **knubb'ly, nubb'ly, knubb'y, nubby.** [Cf. Low Ger. *knubbe.*]

knubble, nubble *nub'l*, **knobble** *nob'l, vs.t.* to beat with the fists: to knock. [**knob**.]

knuckle *nuk'l, n.* projecting joint of a finger: the kneejoint of a calf or pig (*cook.*). — *v.i.* (in marbles) to touch the ground with the knuckles (usu. with *down*): to touch the forehead as a mark of respect: to yield (usu. with *down* or *under*): to bend the knuckles or knee. — *v.t.* to touch with the knuckle: to shoot (a marble) from the thumb knuckle. — **knuck'le-bone** any with a rounded end: (in *pl.*) the game of dibs; **knuck'le-bow** the curved part of a sword-guard that covers the fingers; **knuck'leduster** a metal covering for the knuckles, like a cestus, for attack or defence; **knuck'le-head** (*coll.*) idiot. — *adj.* **knuck'le-head'ed**. — **knuck'le-head'edness; knuck'le-joint** a joint where the forked end of a connecting-rod is joined by a bolt to another piece of the machinery; **knuckle sandwich** (*slang*) a blow with the fist. — **knuckle down (to)** to set oneself to hard work: see also above; **knuckle under** to yield to authority, pressure, etc.; **near the knuckle** on the verge of the indecent; **rap someone's knuckles** to reprimand someone. [M.E. *knokel*, not recorded in O.E.; cf. Du. *knokkel* (dim. of *knok*), Ger. *Knöchel*, ankle-bone, knuckle (dim. of *Knochen*, bone).]

knur, knurr, nur, nurr *nûr, n.* an excrescence on a tree: a hard ball or knot of wood. — **knur and spell** a game played with a knur, trap (*spell*), and stick, in vogue chiefly in the North of England. [M.E. *knurre*; cf. Du. *knor*, M.H.G. *knorre*, Ger. *Knorren*.]

knurl, nurl *nûrl, n.* a small excrescence, or protuberance: a ridge or bead, esp. in series, as in the milling of a screw-head: a kink: a dwarfish person (*Burns*). — *v.t.* to make knurls on, to mill. — *adj.* **knurled** (spelt **gnarled**, *Shak.*, Measure for Measure, folio 1623) covered with knurls. — *n.* **knurl'ing** mouldings or other woodwork elaborated into a series of knobs. — *adj.* **knurl'y** gnarled. [Prob. a dim. of **knur**.]

knut *knut, nut*, (*slang*). See **nut**.

KO, ko *kā'ō*, (*coll.*) *v.t.* to knock out: — *pr.p.* **KO'ing, ko'ing**; *pa.t.* and *pa.p.* **KO'd, ko'd**. — *n.* a knockout: — *pl.* **KO's, ko's**.

koa *kō'ə, n.* a Hawaiian acacia. [Hawaiian.]

koala *kō-ä'lə, n.* an Australian marsupial, like a small bear, called also **koala bear, native bear**. [Australian *kūlā*.]

koan *kō'än, n.* in Zen Buddhism, a nonsensical question given to students as a subject for meditation. [Jap., a public proposal or plan.]

kob *kob, n.* an African water-antelope. [Wolof.]

koban *kō'ban*, **kobang** *kō'bang, ns.* an obsolete Japanese oblong gold coin, rounded at the corners. [Jap. *ko-ban*.]

kobold *kō'bold, n.* in German folklore, a spirit of the mines: a domestic brownie. [Ger.]

Kodak *kō'dak, n.* a make of camera. — *v.t.* and *v.i.* to photograph with a Kodak. [The trademark name of the Eastman *Kodak* Company.]

Kodiak (bear) *kō'di-ak* (*bār*), the largest variety of brown bear, *Ursus arctos*, found in Alaska and the Aleutian Islands. [From *Kodiak* Island, Alaska.]

koff *kof, n.* a small Dutch sailing-vessel. [Du. *kof*.]

kofta *kof'tə, n.* in Indian cookery, minced and seasoned meat or vegetables, shaped into a ball and fried.

koftgar *koft'gär, n.* one who inlays steel with gold. — *n.* **koftgari** (*koft-gur-ē'*) such work — sometimes **koft'-work**. [Hind. from Pers. *koftgar*.]

kohl *kōl, n.* a fine powder of native stibnite (formerly known as antimony), black in colour, used orig. in the East to shade the area around the eyes. [Ar. *koh'l*.]

kohlrabi *kōl'rä'bi, n.* a cabbage with a turnip-shaped stem. [Ger., — It. *cavolo rapa* — L. *caulis*, cabbage, *rapa*, turnip.]

Koine *koi'nē, n.* a Greek dialect developed from Attic, in use in the Eastern Mediterranean in Hellenistic and Byzantine times: (often without *cap.*) any dialect which has spread and become the common language of a larger area. [Gr. *koinē* (*dialektos*) common (dialect).]

kokra *kok'rə, n.* the wood of an Indian tree (*Aporosa*) of the spurge family, used for making flutes, clarinets, etc.

kok-saghyz *kok'-sä'gēz, n.* a species of dandelion (*Taraxacum kok-saghyz*) from the Tien Shan, grown in Russia, etc., for rubber-making.

kokum *kō'kəm, n.* an East Indian tree (*Garcinia indica*). — **kokum butter** an edible fat got from its nuts. [Marathi *kokamb*, mangosteen.]

kola. See **cola.**

Kolarian *kō-lä'ri-ən, n.* and *adj.* Munda (language).

kolinsky *ko-lin'ski, n.* (the fur of) a species of mink, (*Mustela sibirica*), found in eastern Asia. [Russ. *kolinski*, of the Kola Peninsula.]

kolkhoz *kol-hhoz', n.* a collective or co-operative farm. [Russ. abbrev. of *kollektivnoe khozyaistvo*.]

kolo *kō'lo, n.* a Serbian dance or dance-tune: — *pl.* **kō'los.** [Serb., wheel.]

Kominform, Komintern. Alternative forms of **Cominform, Comintern.**

komissar. Same as **commissar.**

komitaji *kō-mē-tä'jē, n.* orig. a member of the Bulgarian Revolutionary Committee in Macedonia: any Balkan guerrillero. [Turk. *qomitaji*, committee-man, bandit — *qomite* — Fr. *comité*, committee.]

Kommers *kom-ers', n.* a German students' gathering. — *n.* **Kommers'buch** (*-boohh*) a songbook for such occasions. [Ger., — L. *commercium*, commerce.]

Komodo dragon or **lizard** *kə-mō'dō drag'ən, liz'ərd,* a very large monitor lizard (*Varanus komodoensis*) of some Indonesian islands. [From *Komodo* Island, Indonesia.]

Komsomol *kom'sō-mol, n.* the Communist youth organisation of Russia. [Russ. abbrev. of *Kommunisticheskii Soyuz Molodezhi*.]

kon (*Spens.*) form of **con²**: — *pa.t.* **kond.**

konfyt *kon-fīt', n.* a preserve of fruit, in syrup or candied: jam. [Afrik. — Du. *konfijt*.]

konimeter *kon-im'i-tər, n.* an instrument for measuring dust in air. — *ns.* **koniol'ogy** the study of dust in the air and its effects; **kon'iscope** an instrument for estimating the dustiness of air. [Gr. *konis*, dust, *metron*, measure, *skopeein*, to look at.]

konk. Same as **conk**[1,2].

koodoo. See **kudu.**

kook¹ *kook,* (*slang*) *n.* a person who is mad, foolish, or eccentric and amoral. — *adj.* **kook'ie, kook'y** with the qualities of a kook: (of clothes) smart and eccentric. [Prob. from **cuckoo**.]

kook². See **cook³.**

kookaburra *kook'ə-bur'ə, n.* an Australian kingfisher (*Dacelo novaeguineae*) which has a discordant laughing call, the laughing jackass. [Aboriginal.]

kookie, kooky. See **kook¹.**

koolah *koo'lə, n.* an *obs.* form of **koala.**

kop *kop,* (*S.Afr.*) *n.* a hill, generally round-topped. [Du.; lit. head.]

kopeck, copeck *kō-pek', kō'pek, n.* a Russian coin, the hundredth part of a rouble. [Russ. *kopeika*.]

kopje. Older form of **koppie.**

koppa *kop'ə, n.* a Greek letter (ϙ) between Pi and Rho in the alphabet, answering to Q, dropped by most dialects but retained as a numeral; ϙ′ = 90, ϙ = 90000. [Gr.; cf. Hebr. *qōph*.]

koppie *kop'i, n.* a low hill. [Cape Du. *kopje* — *kop*, head.]

kora¹ *kō'rə, kō', n.* the water-cock (*Gallicrex*). [Origin uncertain.]

kora² *kōr'ə, kō', n.* a West African musical instrument similar to a harp. [W. African name.]

Koran *kō-rän', kō-,* sometimes *kō'rən, kō', n.* the Muslim Scriptures. — *adj.* **Koranic** (*-rän'ik*). [Ar. *qurān*, reading.]

korfball *kōrf'böl, körf', n.* a game of Dutch origin resembling basket-ball played by teams of six men and six women a side. [Du. *korfbal* — *korf*, basket, *bal*, ball.]

korkir. Same as **corkir.**

korma *kör'mə, n.* a mild-flavoured Indian dish, meat or vegetables braised in water, stock, yoghourt or cream.

korora *kō'rō-rə, n.* the fairy penguin or little (blue) penguin (*Eudyptula minor*), smallest of all the penguins. [Maori.]

koruna *ko-roo'nə, n.* the standard monetary unit of Czechoslovakia, 100 halers.

kos, koss. Same as **coss.**

kosher *kō'shər, adj.* pure, clean, according to the Jewish ordinances — as of meat killed and prepared by Jews: legitimate, proper, genuine (*coll.*). — *n.* (a shop selling) kosher food. [Heb. *kāshēr*, right.]

kosmos. Same as **cosmos.**

koss. See **kos.**

koto *kō'tō, n.* a Japanese musical instrument consisting of a long box with thirteen silk strings: — *pl.* **kō'tos.** [Jap.]

kotow *kō-tow'.* A less common form of **kowtow.**

kottabos *kot'ə-bos.* Same as **cottabus.**

kotwal, cotwal *kōt'wäl, n.* a chief constable or magistrate of an Indian town. [Hind. *kotwāl*.]

Kotytto *kot-it'ō,* or **Kotys** *kot'is, ns.* a Thracian goddess worshipped with wild orgies. [Gr. *Kotyttō, Kotys*.]

koulan, koumiss, kourbash, kouskous. See **kulan, kumiss, kurbash, couscous.**

kow. See **cow².**

kowhai *kō'hī, -(h)wī, n.* New Zealand tree or shrub of the genus *Sophora*, with golden flowers. [Maori.]

kowtow *kow-tow', n.* the Chinese ceremony of prostration. — *v.i.* to perform that ceremony: to abase oneself before (with *to*). — Also **kōtow'.** [Chin. *k'o*, knock, *t'ou*, head.]

kraal *kräl, n.* a S. African village of huts surrounded by a fence: loosely, a single hut: a corral. — *v.t.* to pen. [Du. *kraal* — Port. *curral* — L. *currĕre*, to run.]

kraft *kräft, n.* a type of strong brown wrapping paper made from pulp treated with a sulphate solution. [Ger. *Kraft*, strength.]

krait *krīt, n.* a deadly Indian rock snake (*Bungarus caeruleus*). [Hind. *karait*.]

kraken *krä'kən, n.* a fabled sea-monster. [Norw.; the *-n* is the def. art.]

krakowiak. See **cracovienne** under **Cracovian.**

Krameria *krä-mē'ri-ə, n.* the rhatany genus of Caesalpiniaceae, or according to some, constituting a family **Krameriā'ceae**: (without *cap.*) a plant of this genus. [J. G. H. and W. H. *Kramer*, 18th-century German botanists.]

krang *krang.* Same as **kreng.**

krantz *kränts,* (*S.Afr.*) *n.* a crown of rock on a mountain-top: a precipice. — Also **krans, kranz.** [Du. *krans*, a wreath.]

kraut *krowt*, (often *cap.*; *slang*) *n.* a German. [From **sauerkraut.**]

kreasote, kreatine. Same as **creosote, creatine.**

kreese. Same as **kris.**

kremlin *krem'lin*, *n.* a citadel, esp. (with *cap.*) that of Moscow: (with *cap.*) the Russian government. — *ns.* **Kremlinol'ogist; Kremlinol'ogy** the study of the Russian government and its policies. [Russ. *kreml'*.]

kreng *kreng*, *n.* the carcass of a whale after the blubber has been removed. — Also **krang.** [Du.]

kreosote. Same as **creosote.**

kreplach *krep'lähh*, *n.pl.* small dough dumplings filled with cheese, meat, etc., usually served in soup. [Yiddish.]

kreutzer *kroit'sər*, *n.* an obs. copper coin of Austria, South Germany, etc., 100 to the florin or gulden. [Ger. *Kreuzer* — *Kreuz*, cross, because at one time stamped with a cross.]

k'ri *krē*, *n.* a marginal reading in the Hebrew Bible. [Heb. *qerē*, read (imper.).]

kriegspiel, kriegsspiel *krēg'spēl*, *n.* a war-game played on a map to train officers: a form of chess in which the players use separate boards and are allowed only limited communication through an umpire. [Ger. *Kriegsspiel* — *Krieg*, war, *Spiel*, game.]

Krilium® *kril'i-əm*, *n.* an improver of soil structure, consisting of synthetic polymers.

krill *kril*, *n.* a species of *Euphausia* (fam. *Euphausiaceae*), shrimplike animals eaten by whales, etc. [Norw. *kril*.]

krimmer *krim'ər*, *n.* tightly curled grey or black fur from a Crimean type of lamb. — Also **crimm'er.** [Ger. *Krim*, Crimea.]

kris *krēs*, *n.* a Malay dagger with wavy blade: — *pl.* **kris'es.** — *v.t.* to stab with a kris. — Also **crease, creese, kreese.** [Malay.]

Krishna *krish'nə*, *n.* a deity in later Hinduism, a form of Vishnu. — *n.* **Krish'naism** (also called **Krishna Consciousness**) belief in, worship of, Krishna. [Sans.]

kromesky *krō-mes'ki*, *krə-*, or *krō'-*, *krō'-*, *n.* a croquette fried in bacon or calf's udder. [Russ. *kromochka*.]

krone *krō'nə*, *n.* (*pl.* **kro'ner**) in Denmark and Norway, **krona** *krōō'na* (*pl.* **kro'nor**) in Sweden, and **króna** *krō'na* (*pl.* **krónur**) in Iceland, a silver coin and monetary unit equal to 100 öre. — *n.* **krone** (*krō'nə*; *pl.* **kro'nen**) a former silver coin of Austria, equal to 100 heller: in Germany a former gold coin of 10 marks. [Cf. **crown.**]

Kronos *kron'os*, *n.* a supreme god of the Greeks, son of Ouranos and Gaia, dethroned by his son Zeus.

krónur. See **krone.**

Kru, Kroo *krōō*, *n.* one of a West African people of the coast of Liberia noted as seamen. — Also *adj.* — **Kru'-** or **Kroo'-boy, -man.**

Krugerrand *krōō'gər-rand*, *n.* a South African coin containing one troy ounce of fine gold and bearing a portrait of President *Kruger.* — Also **Kruger Rand, rand, krugerrand.** [**rand**[1].]

krummhorn, krumhorn, crumhorn *krōōm'hörn*, *n.* an old double-reed wind instrument with curved end: an organ reed-stop. [Ger., curved horn.]

kryometer, etc. Same as **cryometer,** etc.

krypsis *krips'is*, *n.* the 17th cent. doctrine that Christ secretly exercised divine powers. [Gr., concealment.]

krypton, crypton *krip'ton*, *n.* an inert gas discovered in the air (where it is present in extremely small quantity) by Sir W. Ramsay in 1898 (Kr; atomic number 36), used in fluorescent lights and lasers. [Gr. *kryptein*, to hide.]

ksar *ksär*, *n.* a Miltonic form of **tsar.**

Kshatriya *kshat'ri-ya*, *n.* a member of the second or military caste among the Brahmanic Hindus. [Sans.]

k'thibh *kthēv*, *n.* a textual reading in the Hebrew Scriptures: originally a marginal note calling attention to the textual form. [Heb. *kethībh*, written.]

kuchcha. Same as **cutcha.**

Kuchen *kōōhh'ən*, (Ger.) *n.* cake.

kudos *kū'dos*, Gr. *kü'dos*, *n.* credit, fame, renown, prestige. [Gr. *kȳdos*, glory.]

kudu, koodoo *kōō'dōō*, *n.* an African antelope with long spiral horns. [From Hottentot.]

kudzu *kōōd'zōō*, *n.* an ornamental papilionaceous plant of China and Japan (*Pueraria thunbergiana*) with edible root tubers and a stem yielding a fibre. [Jap.]

kuffi(y)eh, kuf(f)iah, kufiya(h). See **kaffiyeh.**

Kufic, Cufic *kū'fik*, *adj.* of Al *Kūfa*, south of Babylon: esp. of the lettering of its coins, inscriptions, and MSS., mainly early copies of the Koran.

Kuh-horn *kōō'hörn*, *n.* an alpenhorn. [Ger.]

Ku-Klux Klan *kōō'*, *kü'kluks klan*, or **Ku-Klux** or **the Klan** a secret organisation in several Southern U.S. states after Civil War of 1861–65, to oppose Northern influence, and prevent Negroes from enjoying their rights as freemen — revived in 1916 to deal drastically with Jews, Catholics, Negroes, etc., and to preserve white Protestant supremacy. — *n.* **Klan'sman** a member of this organisation. [Gr. *kyklos*, a circle, and **clan.**]

kukri *kōōk'rē*, *n.* a sharp, curved Gurkha knife or short sword. [Hindi *kukrī*.]

kuku *kōō'kōō*, *n.* a large fruit-eating pigeon of New Zealand (*Hemiphaga novaeseelandiae*), the woodpigeon. [Maori.]

kulak *kōō-lak'*, *n.* in Tsarist times, a rich peasant: later, an exploiter. [Russ., fist.]

kulan, koulan *kōō'län*, *n.* the onager, or a nearly related wild ass of the Kirghiz Steppe. [Kirghiz.]

Kultur *kōōl-tōōr'*, *n.* culture: civilisation: a type of civilisation: sometimes used ironically. — *ns.* **Kultur'geschichte** (-*gə-shehh'tə*) history of civilisation; **Kultur'kampf** (-*kampf*) the war of culture (said by Virchow in 1873 of the conflict between Bismarck and the Catholic Church); **Kultur'kreis** (-*krīs*) an area regarded as a centre of diffusion of culture elements. [Ger.]

kumara *kōō'mə-rə*, *n.* sweet potato. [Maori.]

kumari *kōō-mar'i* (*Ind.*) *n.* Miss (title of respect).

kumiss, koumiss *kōō'mis*, *n.* fermented mares' milk. [Russ. *kumis* — Tatar *kumiz.*]

kümmel *küm'l*, *kim'l*, *kōōm'l*, *n.* a liqueur flavoured with cumin and caraway seeds. [Ger., — L. *cumīnum* — Gr. *kymīnon*, cumin.]

kumquat *kum'kwot*, *n.* a small kind of orange. [Cantonese, gold orange.]

kung fu *kung fōō*, the art of unarmed combat and self-defence developed in ancient China. [Chin., combat skill.]

kunkur or **kunkar** *kung'kûr*, *kung'kər*, *n.* a concretionary limestone in India: a laterite found in Ceylon. [Hindi *kankar*, stone.]

Kunstlied *kōōnst'lēt*, (Ger.) *n.* an art-song.

Kuomintang *kwō'min-tang*, *gwō'min-däng*, *n.* the Chinese nationalist people's party. [Chin.]

Kuo-yü *kwō'*, *gwō'yü*, *n.* lit. 'national language', a form of Mandarin taught all over China.

Kupferschiefer *kōōp'fər-shē-fər*, *n.* a shale rich in copper in the Permian of Germany. [Ger., copper shale.]

kurbash, kourbash *kōōr'bash*, *n.* a hide whip used in the East. — *v.t.* to whip with a kurbash. [Ar. *qurbāsh*.]

kurchatovium *kûr-cha-tō'vi-əm*, *n.* element 104 named by Russians (who claimed its discovery in 1966) after a Russian physicist (American name **rutherfordium**).

Kurd *kōōrd*, *kûrd*, *n.* one of the people of Kurdistan, Iranian in speech, often blond, Xenophon's *Kardouchoi.* — *adj.* and *n.* **Kurd'ish.**

kurgan *kōōr-gän'*, *n.* a sepulchral barrow. [Russ. from Tatar.]

Kurhaus *kōōr'hows*, *n.* a building in which a spa is housed. [Ger., lit. cure-house.]

Kuroshio *kōō-rō'shi-ō*, *n.* a warm current flowing north along the western edge of the Pacific. [Jap., black stream.]

kurrajong *kur'ɔ-jong*, *n.* a name for various Australian trees with fibrous bark. — Also **curr'ajong**. [Aboriginal.]

kurre (*Spens.*). Same as **cur.**

kursaal *koōr'zäl*, *n.* the reception-room of a spa. [Ger., lit. cure-saloon.]

kurta, khurta *koōr'tä*, *n.* a loose-fitting collarless shirt or tunic worn in India. [Hindi.]

kurtosis *kɔr-tō'sis*, (*statistics*) *n.* the relative degree of sharpness of the peak on a frequency-distribution curve. [Gr. *kurtōsis*, bulging, swelling — *kurtos*, curved.]

kurvey *kûr-vā'*, (*rare S.Afr.*) *v.i.* to transport goods. — *n.* **kurvey'or** transport rider. [Du. *karwei*, work — Fr. *corvée*; cf. **corvée**.]

Kushitic. Same as **Cushitic.**

kutch. Same as **cutch**[2].

kutcha. Same as **cutcha.**

kvass *kväs*, *n.* rye-beer. [Russ. *kvas*.]

kvetch *kvech*, *v.i.* to complain, whine, esp. incessantly. — *ns.* **kvetch, kvetch'er** a complainer, fault-finder. [Yiddish.]

kwacha *kwach'ɔ*, *n.* the basic unit of currency in Zambia and Malawi. [Native name, meaning 'dawn'.]

kwashiorkor *kwä-shi-ör'kör*, or *kwosh'*, *n.* a widespread nutritional disease of children in tropical and subtropical regions due to deficiency of protein. [Ghanaian name.]

kwela *kwä'la*, *n.* Zulu folk-music of jazz type. [Bantu, lift, from leaping upward in dancing to the music.]

Kwok's disease. Same as **Chinese restaurant syndrome** (under **China**).

ky. See **kye.**

kyang. See **kiang.**

kyanise, -ize *kī'ɔ-nīz*, *v.t.* to preserve from dry-rot by injecting corrosive sublimate into the pores of (wood). [From John H. *Kyan* (1774–1830).]

kyanite *kī'ɔ-nīt*, *n.* a mineral, an aluminium silicate, generally sky-blue. — Also **cyanite** (*sī'*). [Gr. *kyanos*, blue.]

kyat *kyät*, *kē-ät'*, *n.* the monetary unit of Burma.

kybosh. See **kibosh.**

kydst (*Spens.*). See **kythe.**

kye, ky *kī*, (*Scot.*) *n.pl.* cows. [See **kine.**]

kyle *kīl*, *n.* a narrow strait. [Gael. *caol.*]

kylie, kiley, kyley *kī'li*, *n.* a boomerang. [Aboriginal.]

kylin *kē'lin*, *n.* a fabulous animal figured in the decoration of Chinese pottery. [From Chinese *ch'ī lin.*]

kylix *kil'* or *kīl'iks.* Same as **cylix.**

kyllosis *kil-ō'sis*, *n.* club-foot. [Gr. *kyllōsis.*]

kyloe *kī'lō*, *n.* one of the cattle of the Hebrides. [Origin unknown.]

kymograph *kī'mō-gräf*, *n.* an instrument for recording the pressure of fluids, esp. of blood in a blood-vessel. — *n.* **ky'mogram** such a record. — *adj.* **kymographic** (*-graf'ik*). — *n.* **kymog'raphy.** [Gr. *kȳma*, a wave, *graphein*, to write.]

kynd, kynde *kīnd*, (*Spens.*) *n.*, *adj.*, and *v.t.* Same as **kind**[1,2].

kyne (*Spens.*). Same as **kine.**

kyphosis *kī-fō'sis*, *n.* a hunchbacked condition. — *adj.* **kyphotic** (*-fot'ik*). [Gr. *kyphōsis* — *kȳphos*, a hump.]

Kyrie eleison *kēr'i-e el-ā'i-son*, *kir'*, *kīr'i-e el-e-ē'son*, *el-e-ā'son*, etc., (abbrev. **Kyrie**) a form of prayer in all the ancient Greek liturgies, retained in the R.C. mass, following immediately after the introit (including both words and music): one of the responses to the commandments in the Anglican ante-communion service. [Gr. *Kyrie, eleēson*, Lord, have pity.]

kyrielle *kēr-i-el'*, *n.* a string of short lines in stanzas all ending with the same word. [Fr., litany, rigmarole, kyrielle — Gr. *Kȳrie eleēson*; see preceding.]

kyte. See **kite**[2].

kythe, kithe *kīdh*, (*Scot.*) *v.t.* to make known: —2nd pers. sing. **kydst**, in Spenser blunderingly used in the sense of knowest. — *v.i.* to show oneself, to appear. [O.E. *cȳthan*, to make known. See **uncouth.**]

For other sounds see detailed chart of pronunciation.

L

L, l *el, n.* the eleventh letter in the Roman, the twelfth in our alphabet, representing a lateral liquid sound, the breath passing the side or sides of the tongue: anything shaped like the letter: used as a sign for pound (L. *lībra*): as a Roman numeral L = 50, L̄ = 50 000: an elevated railway, or train (*U.S.*). — **L-dopa** see **dopa**.

la¹ *lä, interj.* lo! see! behold! ah! indeed!   [Cf. **lo, law⁵**.]

la² *lä, n.* the sixth note of the scale in sol-fa notation — also spelt **lah.**   [See **Aretinian.**]

laager *lä′gər,* (Afrik. form **laer,** not used in S. Afr. Eng.) *n.* in South Africa, a defensive ring of ox-wagons: any extemporised fortification: an encampment: a defensive group of people drawn together by similarity of opinion, etc. — *v t.* and *v.i.* to arrange or camp in a laager.   [Cape Du. *lager* — Ger. *Lager*, a camp; Du. *leger*; cf. **lair, layer, leaguer.**]

lab *lab, n.* a familiar contraction of **laboratory.**

labanotation *lāb-ə-nō-tā′shən, n.* the Laban system of ballet notation. — Also called **Laban system.** [Rudolf von *Laban*, who proposed it.]

labarum *lab′ə-rəm, n.* orig. a Roman military standard, the imperial standard after Constantine's conversion — with a monogram of the Greek letters XP (ChR), for Christ: a similar ecclesiastical banner borne in processions: any moral standard or guide.   [L., — Late Gr. *labaron*, origin unknown.]

labda, labdacism; labdanum. See **lambda; ladanum.**

labefactation *lab-i-fak-tā′shən,* **labefaction** *-fak′shən, ns.* a weakening decay: overthrow.   [L. *labefactātiō, -ōnis* — *labāre*, to totter, *facĕre*, to make.]

label *lā′bl, n.* an attached band or strip (*arch.*): a small slip placed on or near anything to denote its nature, contents, ownership, destination, etc.: a paper annexed to a will, as a codicil (*law*): a fillet with pendants (an eldest son's cadency mark; *her.*): a dripstone (*archit.*): a characterising or classificatory designation (*fig.*): the piece of paper at the centre of a gramophone record giving the maker's tradename and identifying the recorded material: the tradename itself (*coll.*): a manufacturer's or retailer's tradename attached to goods to identify them: a strip of material with this or other information on it: a character or set of characters indicating the start of an instruction in a program and used elsewhere in the program to refer to that instruction (*comput.*). — *v.t.* to affix a label to: to describe by or on a label: to replace an atom in (a molecule or compound) by a radioactive isotope, for the purpose of identification: — *pr.p.* **lā′belling;** *pa.t.* and *pa.p.* **lā′belled.** — **labelled atom** a tagged atom.   [O.Fr. *label*, perh. — O.H.G. *lappa* (Ger. *Lappen*), flap.]

labellum *lə-bel′əm, n.* the lower petal, morphologically usu. the upper, of an orchid: applied also to other lip-like structures in flowers: — *pl.* **labell′a.** — *adj.* **labell′oid.**   [L., dim. of *labrum*, lip.]

labial *lā′bi-əl, adj.* of or formed by the lips: sounded by impact of air on a lip-like projection, as an organ flue-pipe (*mus.*). — *n.* a sound formed by the lips. — *v.t.* **lā′bialise, -ize** to make labial: to pronounce with rounded lips. — *n.* **lā′bialism** a tendency to labialise. — *adv.* **lā′bially.** — *n.pl.* **Lābiatae** (*-ā′tē*) a family of sympetalous dicotyledons with lipped flowers, four-cornered stems, and opposite branches — the dead-nettles, mints, etc. — *adj.* **lā′biate** lipped: having a lipped corolla: belonging to the Labiatae. — *n.* any plant of the Labiatae. — *n.* **lā′bium** a lip or lip-like part: in insects the underlip, formed by the partial fusion of the second maxillae: — *pl.* **lā′bia.** — *adj.* and *n.* **lābiodent′al** (a sound) produced by the lips and teeth together, as *f* and *v.* — **labia majora (minora)** the two outer (inner) folds of skin surrounding the vaginal orifice in human females.   [L. *lăbium*, lip.]

labile *lā′bīl, -əl, adj.* unstable: apt to slip or change. — *n.* **labīl′ity.**   [L. *lābilis* — *lābī*, to slip.]

labis *lā′bis, n.* the cochlear or eucharistic spoon.   [Gr. *labis*, handle — root of *lambanein*, to take.]

labium. See **labial.**

lablab *lab′lab, n.* a tropical bean (*Dolichos lablab*) with edible pods.   [Ar. *lablāb*.]

laboratory *lə-bor′ə-tə-ri,* (esp. *U.S.*) *lab′ə-rə-tə-ri, n.* orig. a chemist's workroom: a place for experimental work or research.   [L. *lahōrāre* – *labor*, work.]

labor Improbus *lā′bör im-prō′bəs, la′bor im-pro′bŏŏs,* (L.) persistent, dogged labour.

laborious, etc. See **labour.**

labour, in U.S. **labor,** *lā′bər, n.* toil: work: bodily work: pains: duties: a task requiring hard work: effort toward the satisfaction of needs: workers collectively: supply or services of workers, esp. bodily workers: the Labour Party or its cause, principles, or interest: the outcome of toil (*arch.*): trouble taken (*arch.*): exertion of influence (*arch.*): the pangs and efforts of childbirth: heavy pitching or rolling of a ship. — *adj.* of labour or the Labour Party. — *v.i.* to undergo labour: to work: to take pains: to be oppressed: to move slowly: to be in travail: to pitch and roll heavily (*naut.*). — *v.t.* to spend labour on (*arch.*): to cultivate (*dial.*): to elaborate, work out in detail: to strain, over-elaborate. — *adj.* **laborious** (*lə-bō′, -bō′ri-əs*) involving or devoted to labour: strenuous: arduous. — *adv.* **labo′riously.** — *n.* **labo′riousness.** — *adj.* **lā′boured** cultivated (*dial.*): worked (*arch.*): bearing marks of effort in execution: strained: over-elaborated. — *ns.* **lā′bourer** one who labours: one who does work requiring little skill; **lā′bourism; lā′bourist** one who contends for the rights of workers; **Lā′bourite** a member or supporter of the Labour Party. — *adj.* **lā′boursome** (*Shak.*) laborious. — **labour camp** a penal institution where the inmates are forced to work: temporary accommodation for workers; **Labour Day** in many countries the 1st of May, a day of labour demonstrations: in U.S. (**Labor Day**), the first Monday in September; **Labour Exchange** see **employment exchange; labour force** the number of workers employed in an industry, factory, etc. — *adj.* **la′bour-intens′ive** requiring a relatively large number of workers for the capital invested (opp. of *capital-intensive*). — **Labour Party** a party aiming at securing for workers by hand or brain the fruits of their industry and equitable distribution thereof: its representatives in parliament: a local organisation of the party. — *adj.* **la′bour-sav′ing** intended to supersede or lessen labour. — **labo(u)r union** (*U.S.*) a trade union. — **hard labour** compulsory work imposed in addition to imprisonment, abolished in U.K. in 1948; **labour of love** work undertaken without hope of emolument; **labour with** to take pains to convince.   [O.Fr. *labour, labeur* — L. *labor.*]

Labrador *lab′rə-dör,* or *lab-rə-dör′, n.* a mainland region of Newfoundland and Quebec. — Also *adj.* — *n.* **lab′radorite** (or *-dör′*) a plagioclase feldspar with fine play of colours found on the Labrador coast. — **Labrador (dog, retriever)** a sporting dog about twenty-two inches in height, either black or (**yellow** or **golden Labrador**) from red to fawn in colour; **Labrador tea** a shrub of the heather family (Ledum) used in Labrador as a substitute for tea.

labrum *lā′brəm, n.* a lip: a lip-like part: — *pl.* **lā′bra.** — *n.* **lā′bret** a lip ornament. — *adj.* **lā′brose** thick-lipped.   [L. *lăbrum*, a lip.]

Labrus *lā'brəs, n.* the wrasse genus of fishes, of the family **La'bridae.** — *adjs.* and *ns.* **la'brid, la'broid** (*la', lā'*). [L. *lābrus, lābros,* a kind of fish.]

labrys *lab'ris, lāb'ris, n.* the double-headed axe, a religious symbol of ancient Crete, etc. [Gr., from Lydian; perh. conn. with **labyrinth.**]

laburnum *lə-bûr'nəm, n.* a small poisonous papilionaceous tree, a native of the Alps. [L.]

labyrinth *lab'i-rinth, n.* orig. a building with intricate passages: an arrangement of tortuous paths or alleys (usually between hedges) in which it is difficult to find the way out: a maze: a tangle of intricate ways and connections: a perplexity: the cavities of the internal ear (*anat.*). — *adjs.* **labyrinth'al, labyrinth'ian, labyrinth'ic, -al, labyrinth'ine** (-*īn,* -*in*). — *ns.* **labyrinthī'tis** inflammation of the inner ear; **labyrinth'-odont** an extinct stegocephalian amphibian of Carboniferous, Permian, and esp. Triassic times, so called from the mazy pattern of a section of the teeth (Gr. *odous, odontos,* tooth) in some. [Gr. *labyrinthos,* perh. conn. with *labrys,* the double axe; see **labrys.**]

lac¹. Same as **lakh.**

lac² *lak, n.* a dark-red transparent resin produced on the twigs of trees in the East by coccid insects (**lac insects**). — **lac'-dye, lac'-lake** scarlet colouring matters obtained from it. [Hind. *lākh* — Sans. *lākṣā,* 100 000, hence the (teeming) lac insect.]

laccolite *lak'ō-līt, n.* a mass of igneous rock that has risen in a molten condition and bulged up the overlying strata to form a dome. — Also **lacc'olith** (*-lith*). — *adjs.* **laccolitic** (*-lit'ik*), **laccolith'ic.** [Gr. *lakkos,* a reservoir, *lithos,* a stone.]

lace *lās, n.* a string for passing through holes: an ornamental fabric made by looping, knotting, plaiting, or twisting threads into definite patterns. — *v.t.* to fasten with a lace (often with *up*): to compress or pinch by lacing: to adorn with lace: to streak: to thrash: to reprimand severely (often with *into*): to intermix, as coffee with brandy, etc.: to intertwine. — *v.i.* to have lacing as mode of fastening: to practise tight-lacing. — *adj.* **laced.** — *n.* **lacet** (*lās-et'*) a kind of braidwork. — *n.* and *adj.* **lac'ing.** — *adj.* **lac'y** (also **lac'ey**) like lace. — **lace'bark** a lofty West Indian tree of the Daphne family, the inner bark like a coarse lace; **lace'-boot** a boot fastened by a lace; **laced mutton** (*Shak.*) a prostitute; **lace'-frame** a machine used in lace-making; **lace'-leaf** see **lattice-leaf** under **lattice; lace'-man** a dealer in lace; **lace'-paper** paper stamped or cut like lace; **lace'-pill'ow** a cushion held on the knees by lacemakers; **lace'-ups** boots or shoes having laces; **lace'-wing** the golden-eye, a neuropterous insect with gauzy wings and brilliant golden eyes; **lacy glass** early form of pressed glass with lacy design (also **lace glass**). [O.Fr. *las,* a noose — L. *laqueus.*]

lacerate *las'ə-rāt, v.t.* to tear: to rend: to wound: to afflict. — *adjs.* **lac'erable; lac'erant** harrowing; **lac'erate, -d** rent, torn: with edges cut into irregular segments (*bot.*). — *n.* **lacera'tion.** — *adj.* **lac'erative** tearing: having power to tear. [L. *lacerāre, -ātum,* to tear — *lacer,* torn.]

Lacerta *la-sûr'tə, n.* a genus of lizards, including the common lizard: one of the northern constellations, the Lizard. — *adj.* **lacertian** (*-sûr'shyən*) of lizards: lizard-like. — *n.pl.* **Lacertil'ia** the lizard order or suborder of reptiles. — *adjs.* **lacertil'ian; lacer'tine.** [L.]

lacet, lacey. See **lace.**

laches *lach'iz,* (*law*) *n.* negligence or undue delay, esp. such as to disentitle to remedy. [A.Fr. *lachesse.*]

Lachesis *lak'i-sis, n.* in myth, that one of the three Fates who assigned to each mortal his destiny — she spun the thread of life from the distaff held by Clotho: a genus of snakes including the bushmaster. [Gr.]

lachrymal *lak'ri-məl, adj.* of or for tears. — *n.* a tear-bottle: a bone near the tear-gland: (in *pl.*) lachrymal organs: (in *pl.*) weeping fits. — *adjs.* **lach'rymary, lach'rymatory** lachrymal: causing tears to flow. — *ns.* a tear-bottle. — *ns.* **lachrymā'tion** the secretion of tears;

lach'rymātor a substance that causes tears to flow, as tear-gas: a contrivance for letting it loose. — *adj.* **lach'rymose** shedding tears: given to weeping: lugubrious. — *adv.* **lach'rymosely.** — Also **lacrymal, lacrimal,** etc. — **lachryma Christi** (*lak'ri-mə kris'tē*; L., Christ's tear) a sweet but piquant wine from grapes grown on Vesuvius; **lachrymal duct** a duct that conveys tearwater from the inner corner of the eye to the nose; **lachrymal gland** a gland at the outer angle of the eye that secretes tears; **lachrymal urn** a tear-bottle. [From *lachryma,* a mediaeval spelling of L. *lacrima,* tear; cf. Gr. *dakry;* Eng. **tear;** Gr. *dakrȳma* may have influenced the spelling.]

lacinia *lə-sin'i-ə, n.* a long narrow lobe in a leaf, etc.: the inner lobe of the maxilla (*entom.*): — *pl.* **lacin'iae** (*-ē*). — *adjs.* **lacin'iate, -d** cut into narrow lobes, slashed. — *n.* **laciniā'tion.** [L., a lappet, tag.]

lack¹ *lak, n.* want, deficiency: a thing absent or in short supply. — *v.t.* to be without: to be short of or deficient in: to need: to miss (*obs.*). — *v.i.* (now usu. in *pr.p.*) to be wanting, absent: to be deficient: to be in want (*obs.*). — *adj.* **lack'ing.** — **lack'-all** one who is destitute; **lack'-beard; lack'-brain** (*Shak.*) a fool; **lack'land.** — Also *adj.* — **lack'-Latin** (*obs.;* often *Sir John Lack-Latin*) an ignorant priest. — *adj.* uneducated, ignorant. — *adj.* **lack'-linen** (*Shak.*) wanting linen. — **lack'-love** one who is deficient in love. — Also *adj.* — *adj.* **lack'-lus'tre** dull, without brightness, sheen or vitality. — Also *n.* [Cf. M.L.G. and Du. *lak,* blemish.]

lack² *lak, n.* See **good-lack** under **good.**

lackadaisical *lak-ə-dā'zi-kl, adj.* affectedly pensive: vapidly sentimental: listless: languishing: indolent. — *interjs.* (*arch.*) **lack'adai'sy, lack'aday.** [See **alack-a-day.**]

lacker. See **lacquer.**

lackey, lacquey *lak'i, n.* a footman or valet: a servile follower: — *pl.* **lack'eys, lacqu'eys.** — *v.t.* and *v.i.* to serve or attend as or like a footman. — **lackey moth** a moth (*Malacosoma neustria*) of the egger group with gaudily striped caterpillar, like a footman in livery. [O.Fr. *laquay* (Fr. *laquais*) — Sp. *lacayo,* a lackey; perh. Ar. *luka',* servile.]

lacmus *lak'məs, n.* Same as **litmus.**

Laconian *lə-kō'nyən, -ni-ən,* **Laconic** *lə-kon'ik, adjs.* of Laconia or Lacedaemonia, Spartan. — *adjs.* **laconic, -al** expressing or expressed in few words after the manner of the Laconians: sententiously brief. — *adv.* **lacon'ically.** — *ns.* **laconism** (*lak'*), **lacon'icism** a concise style: a short, pithy phrase. [Gr. *lakōnikos.*]

lacquer, lacker *lak'ər, n.* a solution of film-forming substances in a volatile solvent, esp. a varnish of lac and alcohol: a similar substance sprayed on the hair to hold it in place: the juice of the lacquer-tree (*Japan lacquer*) or similar product: a covering of one of these: an article, or ware, so coated. — *v.t.* to cover with lacquer: to varnish. — *ns.* **lacqu'erer; lacqu'ering** varnishing with lacquer: a coat of lacquer varnish. — **lacqu'er-tree'** a tree of the genus Rhus. [Fr. *lacre* — Port. *lacre, laca; lacrymal,* see **lac².**]

lacquey. See **lackey.**

lacrimal, etc. Variants of **lachrymal,** etc.

lacrosse *lə-, lä-kros', n.* a team game (orig. N. American) in which the ball is driven through the opponents' goal by means of a crosse. [Fr.]

lacteal *lak'ti-əl, adj.* of milk: conveying chyle. — *n.* a lymphatic conveying chyle from the intestines to the thoracic ducts. — *ns.* **lactase** (*lak'tās*) an enzyme that acts on lactose; **lac'tate** a salt of lactic acid. — *v.i.* (also *lak-tāt'*) to secrete milk. — *n.* **lactā'tion** secretion or yielding of milk: the period of suckling. — *adj.* **lac'teous** milky. — *n.* **lactesc'ence.** — *adjs.* **lactesc'ent** turning to milk: producing milky juice; **lac'tic** pertaining to milk; **lactif'erous** conveying or producing milk or milky juice; **lactif'ic** producing milk or milky juice; **lactif'luous** flowing with milk. — *n.* **lactobacill'us** any bacterium of the genus *Lactobacillus,* which converts certain carbohydrates to lactic acid. — *adj.* **lactogen'ic**

inducing lactation. — *ns.* **lactom′eter** a hydrometer for testing the relative density of milk; **lac′tone** an anhydride formed by the reaction between the hydroxyl group and the carboxyl group in a hydroxycarboxylic acid molecule; **lactoprō′tein** any protein present in milk; **lac′toscope** an instrument for measuring the purity or richness of milk; **lac′tose** milk-sugar, $C_{12}H_{22}O_{11} + H_2O$, obtained by evaporating whey. — **lactic acid** an acid obtained from milk, $CH_3CH(OH)$ COOH. [L. *lac, lactis,* milk; Gr. *gala, galaktos,* milk.]

lactoflavin *lak-tō-flā′vin, n.* an earlier name of riboflavin. [L. *lac, lactis,* milk, *flāvus,* yellow.]

Lactuca *lak-tū′kə, n.* the lettuce genus of composite plants, with milky juice. [L. *lactūca — lac, lactis,* milk.]

lacuna *lə-, la-kū′nə, n.* a gap or hiatus: an intercellular space (*biol.*): a cavity: a depression in a pitted surface: — *pl.* **lacū′nae** (*-nē*). — *adj.* **lacūn′al** lacunary. — *n.* **lacū′nar** a sunken panel or coffer in a ceiling or a soffit: a ceiling containing these: — *pl.* **lacū′nars, lacunaria** (*lak-ū-nā′ri-ə*). — Also *adj.* — *adjs.* **lacūn′ary, lacūn′ate** pertaining to, or including, lacunae; **lacū′nose** having lacunae: pitted. [L. *lacūna,* hollow, gap and *lacūnar, -āris,* a fretted ceiling.]

lacustrine *lə-kus′trīn, adj.* pertaining to lakes: dwelling in or on lakes: formed in lakes. [L. *lacus,* a lake.]

lacy. See **lace.**

lad[1] *lad, n.* a boy: a youth: a stable-man: a dashing fellow: a lover (*Scot.*). — *n.* **ladd′ie** a little lad: a boy. — **lad′s love** (*dial.*) southernwood. [M.E. *ladde,* youth, servant; origin obscure.]

lad[2]. Obs. form of **led.**

ladanum *lad′ə-nəm, n.* a resin exuded from Cistus leaves in Mediterranean countries. — Also **lab′danum.** [L. *lādanum, lēdanum —* Gr. *lādanon, lēdanon — lēdon,* the Cistus plant, prob. — Pers. *lādan.*]

ladder *lad′ər, n.* a contrivance, generally portable, with rungs between two supports, for going up and down: anything of similar form, as a run in knitwear where the breaking of a thread gives an appearance of rungs: a contrivance for enabling fish to ascend a waterfall (*fish-ladder, salmon-ladder*): means of attaining a higher status (*fig.*). — *v.t.* to furnish with a ladder: to scale with a ladder. — *v.i.* to develop a ladder. — *adjs.* **ladd′ered, ladd′ery.** — *adj.* **ladd′er-back** of a chair, having a back consisting of several horizontal bars between two uprights. [O.E. *hlæder;* Ger. *Leiter.*]

laddie. See **lad**[1].

lade[1] *lād, v.t.* to load: to burden: to put on board: to ladle or scoop: to empty, drain, as with a ladle. — *v.i.* to take cargo aboard: — *pa.t.* **lād′ed;** *pa.p.* **lād′en, lād′ed.** — *adj.* **lād′en** loaded: burdened. — *n.* **lād′ing** the act of loading: that which is loaded: cargo: freight. [O.E. *hladan,* pa.t. *hlōd;* pa.p. *hlæden, hladen,* load, draw water.]

lade[2], **laid** *lād,* Scottish forms of **load.**

lade[3] *lād, (Scot.) n.* a mill-stream. [Perh. O.E. *lād,* way, course; cf. **lode, lead**[1].]

laden. See **lade**[1].

la-di-da, lah-di-dah *lä-di-dä′, (slang), adj.* affectedly fine, esp. in speech or bearing.

Ladin *lä-dēn′, n.* a Romance tongue spoken in the upper Inn valley: a general name for the Rhaeto-Romanic languages or dialects. — Also **Ladi′no.** — *n.* **Ladinity** (*-din′i-ti*). [L. *Latīnus,* Latin.]

Ladino[1] *lä-dē′nō, n.* the old Castilian tongue: the language, Spanish mixed with Hebrew, spoken by Jews in areas near the E. Mediterranean: a Spanish-American of mixed white and Indian blood: — *pl.* **Ladin′os.** [Sp., — L. *Latīnus,* Latin.]

Ladino[2]. See **Ladin.**

ladle *lād′l, n.* a large spoon for lifting liquid: the floatboard of a mill-wheel: a long-handled pan or bucket for holding and conveying molten metal: a church collection-box on a long handle (*Scot.*). — *v.t.* to transfer or distribute with a ladle. — *n.* **lad′leful** as much as a ladle will hold: — *pl.* **lad′lefuls.** — **ladle out**

to distribute generously. [O.E. *hlædel — hladan,* to lade.]

ladrone *lə-drōn′, n.* a robber. [Sp. *ladrón —* L. *latrō, -ōnis.*]

lady (*cap.* when prefixed), *lā′di, n.* the mistress of a house: used as the feminine of **lord** and of **gentleman,** and ordinarily as a less formal substitute for **dame:** any woman of refinement of manners and instincts: a consort, a term formerly preferred to wife by some who liked to stand upon their dignity (*arch.*): a lady-love or object of chivalric devotion: a girl-friend, mistress, etc.: a size of slates, 16 × 8 inches: used also as a feminine prefix: in composition, denoting a woman who performs a certain job, etc., as *tea-lady*: — *pl.* **ladies** (*lā′diz*); old genitive **lā′dy.** — *n.* **ladies′** ladies' public lavatory. — *adj.* **lā′dyfied, lā′dified** inclined to affect the manners of a lady. — *v.t.* **lā′dyfy, lā′dify** to make a lady of: to call My Lady or Your Ladyship. — *n.* **lā′dyhood** condition, character of a lady. — *adj.* **lā′dyish** having the airs of a fine lady. — *n.* **lā′dyism** affectation of the airs of a fine lady. — *n.* **lā′dykin** an endearing dim. of **lady.** — *adj.* **lā′dylike** like a lady in manners: refined: soft, delicate: often implying want of touch with reality and sincerity — genteel. — *n.* **lā′dyship** the title of a lady. — *ns.* **ladies′ companion** a small bag used for a woman's needlework; **ladies′ fingers** see **lady′s finger(s)** below; **ladies′ gallery** a gallery in the House of Commons, once screened off by a grille; **ladies′** (or **lady′s**) **man** one fond of women's society; **lā′dybird** any member of the family Coccinellidae, little round beetles, often brightly spotted, preying on green-fly, etc. — also **lā′dybug, lā′dycow, lā′dyfly; Lady Bountiful** (also without *caps.;* often *derog.;* from a character in Farquhar's *The Beaux' Stratagem*) a rich and generous woman, often applied to one who is ostentatiously or offensively so; **lady chapel** a chapel dedicated to the Virgin Mary, usually behind the high altar, at the end of the apse; **Lady Day** 25th March, the day of the annunciation of the Virgin; **lā′dy-fern** a pretty British fern (*Athyrium filix-foemina*), with long bipinnate fronds (imagined by the old herbalists to be the female of the male-fern); **lā′dy-help** one paid to assist in housework, but treated more or less as one of the family; **lā′dy-in-wait′ing** an attendant to a lady of royal status; **lā′dy-killer** a man who is, or fancies himself, irresistible to women; **lā′dy-love** a lady or woman loved: a sweetheart; **lā′dy′s-cu′shion** the mossy saxifrage; **lā′dy′s finger, fingers** a name for many plants, esp. the kidney-vetch: gumbo, okra: a finger-shaped cake; **lā′dy′s-maid** a female attendant on a lady, esp. for the toilet; **lā′dy′s-mantle** a genus (*Alchemilla*) of rosaceous plants with small, yellowish-green flowers and leaves like folded drapery; **lā′dy′s-slipp′er** a genus (*Cypripedium*) of orchids with large slipper-like lip; **lā′dy′s-smock, lā′dy-smock** the cuckoo-flower (*Cardamine pratensis*), a cruciferous meadow-plant, with pale lilac-coloured flowers; **lā′dy′s-thist′le** the milk thistle; **lady′s** (or **ladies′**) **tresses** (*sing.* or *pl.*) an orchid of the genus *Spiranthes* with small white flowers; **lā′dy-trifles** (*Shak.*) trifles befitting a lady. — **find the lady** see **three-card trick** under **three; her, your ladyship; my lady** forms of expression used in speaking of, or to, one who has the title of Lady; **our Lady** the Virgin Mary; **(Our) Lady′s bedstraw** see **bedstraw** under **bed**[1]. [O.E. *hlǣfdige,* lit. app. the bread-kneader — *hlāf,* loaf, and a lost word from the root of **dough.**]

Laender. See **Land.**

laeotropic *lē-ō-trop′ik, adj.* turning to the left. [Gr. *laios,* left, *tropos,* a turn.]

laer. See **laager.**

laesa majestas *lē′zə mə-jes′tas, lī′sa mä-yes′täs* (L.) injured majesty, lese-majesty (q.v.).

laesie (*Spens.*) for **lazy.**

laetare *lē-tā′ri, lī-tär′e, n.* the fourth Sunday in Lent. [*Laetāre* (first word of the introit), imper. sing. of L. *laetārī,* to rejoice — *laetus,* joyful.]

laevigate a faulty spelling of **levigate.**

laevo-, levo- *lē-vō-*, in composition, on, or to, the left. [L. *laevus*, left.]

laevorotatory, levorotatory *lē-vō-rō'tə-tə-ri, -rō-tā'*, *adj.* counterclockwise: rotating the plane of polarisation of light to the left. — *n.* **laevorotā'tion.** [L. *laevus*, left, *rotāre*, to rotate.]

laevulose *lēv'ū-lōs*, or *lev'*, *n.* fructose, a laevorotatory sugar ($C_6H_{12}O_6$). — Also **levulose.** [L. *laevus*, left.]

lag¹ *lag*, *adj.* hindmost: behindhand: late: tardy. — *n.* he who, or that which, comes behind: the fag-end: (esp. in *pl.*) dregs: a retardation or falling behind: the amount by which one phenomenon is delayed behind another: delay. — *v.i.* to move or walk slowly: to loiter: to fall behind: to string (*billiards*): — *pr.p.* **lagg'ing;** *pa.t.* and *pa.p.* **lagged.** — *adj.* **lagg'ard** lagging. — *ns.* **lagg'ard, lagg'er** one who lags behind. — *n.* and *adj.* **lagg'ing.** — *adv.* **lagg'ingly.** — **lag'-end** (*Shak.*) the last or long-delayed end. — **lag of the tides** the progressive lengthening of the interval between tides as neap-tide is approached — opp. to *priming.* [Origin unknown.]

lag² *lag*, *n.* a stave: a lath: boarding: a wooden lining: a non-conducting covering: a perforated wooden strip used instead of a card in weaving. — *v.t.* to furnish with a lag or lagging. — *ns.* **lagg'er** one who insulates pipes, machinery, etc. against heat loss; **lagg'ing** boarding, as across the framework of a centre for an arch, or in a mine to prevent ore falling into a passage: a non-conducting covering for pipes, etc. to minimise loss of heat. [Prob. O.N. *lögg*, barrel-rim; cf. Sw. *lagg*, stave.]

lag³ *lag*, (*slang*) *v.t.* to steal: to carry off: to arrest: to transport or send to penal servitude. — *n.* a convict: an old convict: a term of penal servitude or transportation. [Origin unknown.]

lagan *lag'ən*, *n.* wreckage or goods at the bottom of the sea: later taken to mean such goods attached to a buoy with a view to recovery. — Also **ligan** (*lī'gən*). [O.Fr. *lagan*, perh. Scand. from the root of **lay³, lie²**; falsely associated with L. *ligāmen*, a tying.]

lagena *lə-jē'nə*, (*ant.*) *n.* a narrow-necked bottle. — *adj.* **lage'niform** flask-shaped. [L. *lagēna* — Gr. *lagȳna*.]

lager *lä'gər*, *n.* (in full **lager beer**) a light beer kept for up to six months before use. [Ger. *Lager-bier* — *Lager*, a storehouse.]

laggen, laggin *lag', läg'ən*, (*Burns*) *n.* the angle between the side and bottom of a wooden dish. — **lagg'en-gird** a hoop at the bottom of a wooden vessel. [Cf. **lag², leglin.**]

lagniappe *lan'yap*, *n.* something given beyond what is strictly required: a gratuity. [Louisiana Fr., from Amer. Sp. (Quechua *yápa*, addition).]

lagomorph *lag'o-mörf*, *n.* an animal of the order *Lagomorpha* of gnawing mammals having two pairs of upper incisors, e.g. hares, rabbits. — *adjs.* **lagomor'phic, lagomor'phous.** [Gr. *lagōs*, hare, *morphē*, form.]

lagoon *lə-gōōn'*, *n.* a shallow lake, esp. one near or communicating with the sea or a river. — Also (oldfashioned) **lagune.** — *adj.* **lagoon'al.** [It. *laguna* — L. *lacūna*.]

Lagos rubber *lä'gos rub'ər*, a high-grade rubber yielded by tropical African trees of the genus Funtumia. [*Lagos*, a state of Nigeria.]

lagrimoso *läg-ri-mō'sō*, (*mus.*) *adj.* and *adv.* plaintive(ly). [It., — L. *lacrimōsus*, tearful — *lacrima*, a tear.]

Lagting, Lagthing *läg'ting*, *n.* the upper house of the Norwegian parliament: the parliament of the Faeroe Islands (also **Løg'ting**). [Norw. *lag*, Faeroese *løg*, law, *ting* (*thing*), court, parliament.]

lagune. Same as **lagoon.**

lah. Same as **la².**

lahar *lä'här*, *n.* a mud-lava or other mud-flow.

lah-di-dah. See **la-di-da.**

laic, laical, laicise, laicity. See **lay⁶.**

laid¹ *lād*, *pa.t.* and *pa.p.* of **lay.** — *adj.* put down, prostrate: pressed down: flattened by wind and rain. — *adj.* **laid'-back, laid back** (*slang*) relaxed: easygoing: unhurried. — **laid paper** such as shows the marks of the close parallel wires on which the pulp was laid — opp. to *wove;* **laid work** in embroidery, couching of the simplest kind.

laid² *lād*, Scottish form of **load.**

laidly *lād'li*, *adj.* Northern (*Scot.*) form of **loathly.**

laigh *lähh*, *adj.* and *adv.* a Scots form of **low²**: low-lying: sunken. — *n.* a tract of low-lying or sunken land.

laik. Same as **lake⁴.**

laika *lī'kə*, *n.* any of several similar breeds of working dog, originating in Finland, small and reddish-brown.

lain *pa.p.* of **lie².**

Laingian *lang'i-ən*, *adj.* of or pertaining to the theories or practices of R. D. *Laing* (1927–   ), British psychiatrist, esp. his view that mental illness is a response to stress caused by a person's family life or by social pressures. — *n.* a supporter of Laing's theories and practices.

lair¹ *lār*, *n.* a lying-place, esp. the den or retreat of a wild beast: an enclosure for beasts: the ground for one grave in a burying-place (*Scot.*). — *v.t.* to put in a lair. — *v.i.* to lie: to go to a lair. — *n.* **lair'age** a place where cattle are housed or laired, esp. at markets and docks. [O.E. *leger*, a couch — *licgan*, to lie down; Du. *leger*, Ger. *Lager*.]

lair² *lār*, (*Scot.*) *v.t.* and *v.i.* to mire. — *n.* mire. — *adj.* **lair'y** (*Scot.*). [O.N. *leir*, mud.]

lair³ *lār*, *n.* Scots form of **lore¹.**

lair⁴ *lār*, (*Austr. slang*) *n.* a flashily dressed man. — *v.i.* **lai'rise, -ize** to act the lair. — *adj.* **lair'y.** — **laired up** dressed flashily.

laird *lārd*, (*Scot.*) *n.* a landed proprietor. — *n.* **laird'ship.** [Northern form of **lord.**]

lairy. See **lair²·⁴.**

laisse *les*, *n.* a tirade or string of verses on one rhyme. [Fr.]

laissez-aller *les'ā-al'ā*, *n.* unconstraint. — Also **laiss'er= all'er.** [Fr., let go.]

laissez-faire *les'ā-fer'*, *n.* a general principle of noninterference. — Also **laiss'er-faire'.** [Fr., let do.]

laissez-passer *les'ā-päs'ā*, *n.* pass, special passport. [Fr., let pass.]

laitance *lā'təns*, *n.* a milky accumulation of fine particles which forms on the surface of newly laid concrete if the concrete is too wet or is vibrated or tamped too much. [Fr., — *lait*, milk.]

laith *lāth*, *adj.* a Scots form of **loth.** — *adj.* **laithfu'** (*lāth'fə*) bashful.

laity. See **lay⁶.**

lake¹ *lāk*, *n.* a reddish pigment originally got from lac: a coloured substance got by combination of a dye with a metallic hydroxide: its colour: carmine. — *v.t.* and *v.i.* to make or become lake-coloured. — *adj.* **lak'y.** [**lac².**]

lake² *lāk*, *n.* a large or considerable body of water within land: a large quantity, an excess, as of wine, etc. (*econ.*). — *ns.* **lake'let** a little lake; **lak'er** a fish found in lakes: a boat for lakes: one who sails on lakes: a Lake poet: a visitor to the Lake District. — *adjs.* **lāk'ish** savouring of the Lake school; **lāk'y.** — **lake'-basin** a hollow now or once containing a lake: the area drained by a lake; **Lake District** a picturesque and mountainous region in (formerly) Cumberland, Westmorland, and Lancashire (now in Cumbria), with many lakes; **lake'= dweller; lake'-dwelling** a settlement, esp. prehistoric, built on piles in a lake; **lake herring** see **cisco; lake'= law'yer** (*U.S.*) the bowfin: the burbot; **Lake poets, Lake school** Wordsworth, Coleridge, and Southey, dwellers in the Lake District. [M.E. *lac*, either — O.E. *lacu*, stream (see next word), confused in sense with L. *lacus*, lake, or from *lacus* itself, directly or through Fr. *lac*.]

lake³ *lāk*, (*obs.*) *n.* a small stream or water channel. [O.E. *lacu.*]

lake⁴, laik *lāk*, (*N.England*) *v.i.* to sport, play: to take a holiday from work: to be unemployed. [O.E. *lācan.*]

lakh, lac *lak*, *n.* the number 100 000: 100 000 rupees. [Hind. *lākh* — Sans. *laksa*, 100 000.]

lakin *lā′kin*, (*Shak.*) *n.* a shortened form of **ladykin**, dim. of **lady**.

Lakshmi *luksh′mē*, *n.* in Hindu mythology, Vishnu's consort. [Sans.]

la-la *la′la*, *lä′lä*, *v.i.* to sing an accompaniment using syllables such as la-la. [Poss. **la²**.]

lalang *lä′läng*, *n.* a coarse grass, *Imperata arundinacea*, of the Malay archipelago. [Malay.]

laldie, laldy *lal′di*, (*Scot.*) *n.* a beating, thrashing (as punishment): vigorous action of any kind. — **get laldie** to receive a thrashing; **give it (someone) laldie** to do something (punish someone) energetically and enthusiastically. [Perh. conn. with O.E. *læl*, a whip, weal, bruise.]

Lalique glass *lal-ēk′ gläs*, ornamental glassware, esp. with bas-relief decoration of figures, flowers, etc. [Named after René *Lalique* (d. 1945), Fr. designer of jewellery and glassware.]

lallan *lal′*, *läl′ən*, *adj.* and *n.* a form of **lawland, lowland**. — *n.* **Lallans** Broad Scots: a form of Scots developed by modern Scottish writers.

lallation *lal-ā′shən*, *n.* childish speech: pronouncing of *r* like *l*. — *n.* **lall′ing** babbling. [L. *lallāre*, to sing lullaby.]

l'allegro *lä-lā′grō*, (It.) *n.* the merry, cheerful man.

lallygag, lolly- *lal′, lol′i-gag*, (*coll.*) *vs.i.* to idle, loiter: to caress, esp. publicly. [Ety. dub.]

lam¹ *lam*, *v.t.* to beat. — *n.* **lamm′ing** a thrashing. [Cf. O.E. *lemian*, to subdue, lame, O.N. *lemja*, to beat, lit. lame.]

lam² *lam*, (*U.S. slang*) *n.* escape, hurried flight, esp. from the police. — *v.i.* (with *it*, or *out*, *into*, etc.) to escape, flee. — **on the lam** escaping, running away; **take it on the lam** to make an escape, flee. [Origin uncertain, perh. from **lam¹**.]

lama *lä′mə*, *n.* a Buddhist priest in Tibet. — *ns.* **Lamaism** (*lä′mə-izm*) the religion prevailing in Tibet and Mongolia, being Buddhism corrupted by Sivaism, and by Shamanism or spirit-worship; **La′maist**. — *adj.* **lamaist′ic**. — *ns.* **la′masery** (or *lä-mä′sə-ri*), **lamaserai** (*-rī*) a Tibetan monastery. [Tibetan, *blama*, the *b* silent.]

lamantin *lä-man′tin*, *n.* the manatee. [Fr.]

Lamarckism *lä-märk′izm*, *n.* the theory of the French naturalist J. B. P. A. de Monet de *Lamarck* (1744–1829) that species have developed by the efforts of organisms to adapt themselves to new conditions — also **Lamarck′ianism**. — *adj.* and *n.* **Lamarck′ian**.

lamasery, lamaserai. See **lama**.

lamb *lam*, *n.* the young of a sheep: its flesh as a food: lambskin: one simple, innocent or gentle as a lamb. — *v.t.* and *v.i.* to bring forth as sheep: to tend at lambing. — *ns.* **lamb′er** one who tends lambing ewes: a lambing ewe; **lamb′kin, lamb′ling**, (*Scot.*) **lamb′ie** a little lamb. — *adj.* **lamb′-like** like a lamb: gentle. — **lamb′-ale** a feast at lamb-shearing; **lamb's ears, tongue** a labiate plant, *Stachys lanata*, with silver woolly leaves; **lamb′skin** the skin of a lamb dressed with the wool on: the skin of a lamb dressed as leather: a woollen cloth resembling this: a cotton cloth with raised surface and deep nap; **lamb's′-lett′uce** corn-salad; **lamb's′-tails′** hazel catkins; **lamb's tongue** see **lamb's ears**; **lamb's′-wool** fine wool, specif. wool obtained from the first shearing of a (yearling) lamb: an old English beverage composed of ale and the pulp of roasted apples, with sugar and spices. — **like a lamb to the slaughter** meekly, innocently, without resistance; **the Lamb, Lamb of God** applied to Christ, in allusion to the paschal lamb and John i. 29. [O.E. *lamb*; Ger. *Lamm*, Du. *lam*.]

lambast *lam-bast′*, *v.t.* to thrash: to reprimand severely. — Also **lambaste** (*lam-bāst′*). [Perh. **lam¹** and **baste**.]

lambda *lam′də*, also (more correctly) **labda** *lab′də*, *ns.* the Greek letter (Λ, λ) corresponding to Roman *l*: as a numeral, λ′ = 30, λ = 30000: used as a symbol for wavelength: the meeting of the sagittal and lambdoid sutures of the skull. — *ns.* **lamb′dacism, lab′dacism** a

too frequent use of words containing *l*-sounds: faulty pronunciation of the sound of *l*: a defective pronunciation of *r*, making it like *l*. — *adjs.* **lamb′doid, -al** shaped like the Greek capital Λ — applied in anatomy to the suture between the occipital and the two parietal bones of the skull. — **lambda particle** a subatomic particle, the lightest of the hyperons. [Gr. *lambda*, properly *labda* — Heb. *lāmedh*.]

lambent *lam′bənt*, *adj.* licking: moving about as if touching lightly: gliding over: flickering: softly radiant, glowing: (esp. of wit) light and brilliant. — *n.* **lam′bency** the quality of being lambent: a flicker. — *adv.* **lam′bently**. — *adj.* **lam′bitive** (*obs.*) taken by licking. — *n.* a medicine so taken. [L. *lambĕre*, to lick.]

lambert *lam′bərt*, *n.* a unit of brightness, one lumen per square centimetre. [After J. H. *Lambert* (1728–77), German scientist.]

Lambeth degree *lam′bəth di-grē′*, degree conferred by the Archbishop of Canterbury, whose palace is at *Lambeth*.

lambitive. See **lambent**.

lambkin, lambling. See **lamb**.

lamboys *lam′boiz*, (*ant.*) *n.pl.* kilted flexible steel-plates worn skirt-like from the waist. [Perh. Fr. *lambeaux*, flaps; or a blunder for *jambeaux*.]

lambrequin *lam′bər-kin*, or *-bri-kin*, *n.* a veil over a helmet: mantling: a strip of drapery over a window, doorway, from a mantelpiece, etc. [Fr.]

lame¹ *lām*, *adj.* disabled, esp. in the use of a leg: hobbling: unsatisfactory: imperfect. — *v.t.* to make lame: to cripple: to render imperfect. — *adv.* **lame′ly**. — *n.* **lame′ness**. — *adj.* **lam′ish** a little lame: hobbling. — **lame duck** see **duck³**. [O.E. *lama*, lame; Du. *lam*, Ger. *lahm*.]

lame² *lām*, *n.* a thin plate, esp. of metal, as in armour. — *n.* **lamé** (*lä′mā*) a fabric in which metal threads are interwoven. [Fr., — L. *lāmina*, a thin plate.]

lamella *lə-mel′ə*, *n.* a thin plate or layer: — *pl.* **lamell′ae** (*-ē*). — *adjs.* **lamell′ar** (or *lam′i-*); **lam′ellate** (or *-el′*), **-d**; **lamell′iform**; **lamell′oid**; **lamell′ose**. — *n.* **lamell′ibranch** (*-brangk*; L. *branchiae*, gills) any member of the **Lamellibranchiā′ta**, Pelecypoda, or bivalve molluscs, from their plate-like (nutritive) gills. — *adj.* **lamellibranch′iate**. — *n.* **lamell′icorn** (L. *cornū*, horn) a member of the **Lamellicornia**, former name for a very numerous group of beetles — the cockchafer, etc., with the ends of the antennae expanded in flattened plates. — *adj.* **lamelliros′tral** (L. *rōstrum*, beak) having transverse lamellae within the edge of the bill. [L. *lāmella*, dim. of *lāmina*.]

lament *lə-ment′*, *v.i.* to utter grief in outcries: to wail: to mourn. — *v.t.* to mourn for: to deplore. — *n.* sorrow expressed in cries: an elegy or dirge: a musical composition of like character. — *adj.* **lamentable** (*lam′ənt-ə-bl*) deserving or expressing sorrow: sad: pitiful: worthless (*coll.*). — *adv.* **lam′entably**. — *n.* **lamentā′tion** act of lamenting: audible expression of grief: wailing: (*cap.; pl.*) a book of the Old Testament traditionally attributed to Jeremiah. — *adj.* **lament′ed**. — *n.* and *adj.* **lament′ing**. — *adv.* **lament′ingly**. [L. *lāmentārī*.]

lameter, lamiter *lām′i-tər*, (*Scot.*) *n.* a cripple. [Obscurely derived from **lame¹**.]

lamia *lā′mi-ə*, *n.* in Greek and Roman mythology, a blood-sucking serpent-witch. [Gr. and L. *lāmiă*.]

lamiger, lammiger *lam′i-jər*, (*dial.*) *n.* a cripple. [Cf. **lameter**.]

lamina *lam′i-nə*, *n.* a thin plate or layer: a leaf blade: a thin plate of bone: a plate of sensitive tissue within a hoof: — *pl.* **lam′inae** (*-nē*). — *adjs.* **lam′inable** suitable for making into thin plates; **lam′inar, lam′inary** consisting of or like thin plates or layers: of or relating to a fluid, streamlined flow. — *n.* **Laminā′ria** the tangle genus of brown seaweeds, with large expanded leathery fronds. — *adj.* **laminār′ian**. — *v.t.* **lam′inarise, -ize** to make (a surface, etc.) such that a flow over it will be laminar. — *adjs.* **lam′inate, -d** in laminae or thin plates: consisting of scales or layers, over one another:

made by laminating. — *v.t.* **lam′inate** to make into a thin plate: to separate into layers: to make by putting layers together. — *n.* a laminated plastic, or other material similarly made. — *ns.* **laminā′tion** arrangement in thin layers: a thin layer; **lam′inator** one who manufactures laminates; **laminī′tis** inflammation of a horse's lamina. — **laminar flow** viscous flow: a fluid flow in which the particles move smoothly without turbulence, esp , as in aircraft, such a non-impeding flow over a streamlined surface (*phys.*); **laminated plastic** sheets of paper, canvas, linen, or silk, impregnated with a resin, dried and pressed together. [L. *lāmina*, a thin plate.]

lamington *lam′ing-tən*, (*Austr.*) *n.* a piece of sponge-cake, coated in chocolate and coconut. [From Lord *Lamington*, Governor of Queensland (1895–1901).]

lamiter. See **lameter**.

Lammas *lam′əs*, *n.* the feast of first fruits on 1st August. — **Lamm′as-tide** season of Lammas. [O.E. *hlāf-mæsse, hlāmmæsse — hlāf*, loaf, *mæsse*, feast.]

lammer *läm′, lam′ər*, (*Scot.*) *n.* amber. [Fr. *l′ambre*, the amber.]

lammergeier, lammergeyer *lam′ər-gī-ər*, *n.* the great bearded vulture of southern Europe, etc. [Ger. *Lämmergeier — Lämmer*, lambs, *Geier*, vulture.]

lammiger. See **lamiger**.

lammy, lammie *lam′i*, *n.* a thick quilted jumper worn in cold weather by sailors. [Perh. **lamb**.]

lamp[1] *lamp, n.* a vessel for burning oil with a wick, and so giving light: any structure containing a source of artificial light: any source of light: an eye (*arch.* and *slang*). — *v.i.* (*Spens.*) to shine. — *v.t.* to illumine: to supply with lamps. — *ns.* **lamp′ad** a lamp, candlestick, or torch; **lamp′adary** in the Greek Church, one who looks after the lamps and carries a lighted taper before the patriarch: a candelabrum; **lampaded′romy, lampadephor′ia** (Gr. *lampadēdromiā, lampadēphoriā*) an ancient Greek torch-race; **lamp′adist** a runner in a torch-race; **lamp′adomancy** (Gr. *manteiā*, divination) divination by flame. — *adj.* **lamp′ing** shining. — *n.* **lamp′ion** an oil lamp, often in a coloured glass pot for illuminations. — **lamp′-black** soot from a lamp, or from the burning of bodies rich in carbon (mineral oil, turpentine, tar, etc.) in a limited supply of air: a pigment made from it. — *v.t.* to blacken with lampblack. — **lamp′-burner** that part of a lamp from which the flame proceeds; **lamp′-chimney, lamp′-glass** a glass funnel placed round the flame of a lamp; **lamp′-fly** (*Browning*) perh. a glow-worm, or a firefly; **lamp′holder** a socket for an electric bulb; **lamp′hole** a shaft for lowering a lamp into a sewer; **lamp′-hour** the energy required to maintain a lamp for an hour; **lamp′light** the light shed by a lamp or lamps; **lamp′lighter** a person employed to light street-lamps: a spill or other means of lighting a lamp (*U.S.*); **lamp′post, lamp′-standard** the pillar supporting a street-lamp; **lamp′-room** a room in which miners' or other lamps are kept, tended, etc.; **lamp′shade** a structure for moderating or directing the light of a lamp; **lamp′-shell** a brachiopod, esp. Terebratula or kindred genus, from its shell like an antique lamp. — **smell of the lamp** to show signs of great elaboration or study. [Fr. *lampe*, and Gr. *lampas, -ados — lampein*, to shine.]

lamp[2] *lamp*, (*Scot.*) *v.i.* to run wild, to scamper: to go jauntily, stride along.

lampas[1] *lam′pas*, *n.* a material of silk and wool used in upholstery. [Fr.]

lampas[2], **lampasse** *lam′pas*, (*Shak.*) *n.* a swelling of the roof of the mouth in horses. [Fr. *lampas*.]

lampern *lam′pərn, n.* a river lamprey. [O.Fr. *lamprion*.]

lampion. See **lamp**[1].

lampoon *lam-pōōn′, n.* a personal satire. — *v.t.* to assail with personal satire. — *ns.* **lampoon′er; lampoon′ery; lampoon′ist.** [O.Fr. *lampon*, perh. from a drinking-song with the refrain *lampons*, let us drink.]

lamprey *lam′pri, n.* a genus (*Petromyzon*) of cyclostomes that fix themselves to the fish they prey on and to

stones, etc. by their mouths: — *pl.* **lam′preys.** [O.Fr. *lamproie* — L.L. *lamprēda, lampetra* — explained as from L. *lambēre*, to lick, *petra*, rock, but found also as *naupreda, nauprida.*]

lamprophyre *lam′prō-fīr, n.* a compact intrusive rock with phenocrysts of black mica, hornblende, etc., but not of feldspar. — *adj.* **lamprophyric** (*-fir′ik*). [Gr. *lampros*, bright, and *-phyre* from **porphyry**.]

lampuki *lam′pōō-kē, n.* a Mediterranean food-fish, the dolphin (*Coryphaena*). — Also **lam′puka.** [Maltese.]

lana *lä′nə, n.* genipap wood. [S. American word.]

lanate *lä′nāt*, **lanose** *lä′nōs, -nōz, adjs.* woolly. [L. *lānātus — lāna*, wool.]

Lancasterian *lang-kəs-tē′ri-ən, adj.* pertaining to Joseph *Lancaster* (1778–1838), or his method of teaching by means of monitors.

Lancastrian *lang-kas′tri-ən, adj.* pertaining to *Lancaster*, or Lancashire, or the dukes or house of Lancaster. — *n.* a native of Lancaster or Lancashire: an adherent of the house of Lancaster.

lance[1] *läns, n.* a cavalry weapon with a long shaft, a spearhead, and a small flag: a similar weapon for other purposes: a surgeon's lancet: a blade in a cutting tool to sever the grain in advance of the main blade: the bearer of a lance. — *v.t.* to shoot out, fling (*obs.*): to pierce, as with a lance: to open with a lancet. — *v.i.* to rush, dart, fling oneself (*obs.*). — Also **launce.** — *ns.* **lance′let** any of the narrow, translucent, backboned marine animals of the genera Amphioxus and Asymmetron; **lanc′er** a light cavalry soldier armed with a lance, or of a regiment formerly so armed: (*pl.*) a popular set of quadrilles, first in England about 1820, or its music. — *adj.* **lanc′iform** shaped like a lance. — **lance′-corporal** (formed on **lance prisado;** see below) acting corporal: the military rank between private and corporal (*army slang*, **lance′-jack**); **lance′-sergeant** a corporal acting as a sergeant; **lance′-wood** a wood of various kinds, strong and elastic, brought from Jamaica, Guyana, etc. [Fr., — L. *lancea*; Gr. *lonchē*, a lance; cf. **launch**[1].]

lance[2]. See **launce**[3].

lancegay *läns′gā*, (*obs.*) *n.* a kind of spear. [O.Fr., — *lance*, a lance, *zagaye*, a pike (as in **assegai**).]

lance-knight, -knecht. Erroneous forms of **landsknecht**.

lanceolate, -d *län′si-ə-lāt, -id, adjs.* shaped like a lance-head: lancet-shaped: tapering toward both ends and two or three times as long as broad (*bot.*). — Also **lan′ceolar.** — *adv.* **lan′ceolately.** [L. *lanceolātus — lanceola*, dim. of *lancea*, lance.]

lance prisado *läns pri-zä′dō*, **prisade** *pri-zäd′*, **pesade** *pi-zäd′*, **spcisade** *spē-zäd′*, (*obs.*) a lance-corporal. [It. *lancea spezzata*, broken lance, as if meaning an experienced soldier.]

lancet *län′sit, n.* a surgical instrument used for opening veins, abscesses, etc.: a lancet window: a lancet arch. — *adj.* shaped like a lancet, narrow and pointed. — *adj.* **lan′ceted.** — **lancet arch** high and narrow pointed arch; **lancet window** a tall, narrow, acutely arched window. [O.Fr. *lancette*, dim. of **lance**[1]; see **lance**[1].]

lanch. See **launch**[1].

lancinate *län′sin-āt, v.t.* to lacerate: to pierce. — *adj.* **lan′cinating** (of pain) shooting, darting. — *n.* **lancinā′tion** sharp, shooting pain. [L. *lancināre, -ātum*, to tear.]

land[1] *land, n.* the solid portion of the surface of the globe: a country: a district: a nation or people: a constituent part of an empire or federation: real estate: ground: soil: a group of dwellings or tenements under one roof and having a common entry (*Scot.*): in composition, domain, district frequented or dominated by, as *gangland.* — *v.t.* to set on land or on shore: to set down: to deposit, drop, or plant: to cause to arrive: to bring ashore: to capture: to secure: to attach to one's interest: to earth (*up*): to silt, to block with earth. — *v.i.* to come on land or on shore: to alight: to arrive, find oneself, end by being. — *adj.* of or on the land: land-dwelling: terrestrial. — *adj.* **land′ed** possessing land or estates: consisting in or derived from land or real estate. — *ns.* **land′er** one who, or that which, lands: a heavy blow (*coll.*): **land′ing** disembarkation: a coming to ground: alighting: putting ashore: setting down: a place for getting on shore or upon the ground: the level part of a staircase between flights of steps or at the top. — *adj.* relating to the unloading of a vessel's cargo, or to disembarking, or to alighting from the air. — *adjs.* **land′less; land′ward** lying towards the land: inland: rural (*Scot.*). — *advs.* **land′ward, -s** towards the land: in the country (*Scot.*). — **land′-agent** a person employed to let farms, collect rents, etc.: an agent or broker for buying and selling of land; **land′-army** a body of women organised for farm-work in wartime; **land bank** a bank issuing notes on the security of property; **land′-breeze** a breeze setting from the land towards the sea; **land′-bridge** (*geol.*) a connection by land allowing terrestrial plants and animals to pass from one region to another; **land′-crab** any crab that lives much or chiefly on land; **landed interest** the combined interest of the land-owning class in a community; **land′fall** an approach to land after a journey by sea or air: the land so approached; **land′fill** the disposal of refuse by burying it under the soil: refuse disposed of in this way: a place where landfill is practised; **land′filling; land′-fish** (*Shak.*) a fish on land, one who is more fish than man; **land′-flood** an overflowing of land by water: inundation; **land′force** a military force serving on land; **land′form** a feature of the landscape such as a valley or escarpment; **land′-girl** a girl who does farm-work; **land′-grabber** one who acquires land by harsh and grasping means: one who is eager to occupy land from which others have been evicted; **land′-grabbing; land grant** a grant of public land (to a college, etc.). — *v.t.* **land′-haul** to haul (e.g. a boat) overland. — **land′-herd** a herd of land animals; **land′holder** a tenant or proprietor of land. — *adj.* **land′holding.** — **land′-hunger** desire to possess land; **land′ing-beam** a radio beam by which an aircraft is guided in to land; **land′ing-carriage** the wheeled structure on which an aeroplane runs when starting or landing; **land′ing-craft** a small, low, open vessel, or vessels, for landing troops and equipment on beaches; **land′ing-field** a field that allows aircraft to land and take off safely; **land′ing-gear** wheels, floats, etc., of an aircraft used in alighting; **land′ing-ground** a piece of ground prepared for landing aircraft as required; **land′ing-net** a kind of scoop-net for landing a fish that has been hooked; **land′ing-place** a place for landing; **land′ing-ship** a ship whose forward part can be let down in order to put vehicles ashore; **land′ing-speed** the minimum speed at which an aircraft normally lands; **land′ing-stage** a platform, fixed or floating, for landing passengers or goods; **land′ing-strip** a narrow hardsurfaced runway; **land′-jobber** a speculator in land; **land′-jobbing; land′lady** a woman who has tenants or lodgers: the mistress of an inn: a hostess (*obs.*); **land′=law** (usu. *pl.*) a law concerning property in land; **Land League** an association founded in Ireland in 1879, to procure reduction of rents and to promote peasant-proprietorship — suppressed 1881; **land′-line** overland line of communication or transport. — *adj.* **land′-locked** almost or quite shut in by land: cut off from the sea. — **land′lord** a man who has tenants or lodgers: the master of an inn; **land′lordism** the authority, policy, behaviour, or united action of the landowning class: the system of land-ownership; **land′-lubber** (*naut.*; in contempt) a landsman. — *adj.* **land′-lubberly.** — **land′=man** a countryman: a landsman; **land′mark** any land-boundary mark: any conspicuous object on land marking a locality or serving as a guide: an event of outstanding moment in history, thought, etc.; **land′=mass** a large area of land unbroken by seas; **land′=measure** a system of square measure used in measuring land; **land′-measuring** determination of superficial extent of land; **land′-mine** a type of bomb laid on or near the surface of the ground, to explode when an enemy

is over it: a large bomb dropped by parachute. — *v.t.* to lay land-mines. — **land′-mining; land office** (*U.S.*) an office dealing with the sale of public land; **land′-owner** one who owns land; **land′-ownership.** — *adj.* **land′-owning.** — **land′-pilot** (*Milt.*) one skilled in finding his way by land; **land′-pirate** a highway robber: one who swindles sailors in port: a piratical publisher (*obs.*); **land′-plane** an aeroplane that rises from and alights on land. — *adj.* **land′-poor** (*U.S.*) poor through owning much unprofitable land. — **land′race** a large white Danish breed of pig; **land′rail** the corncrake; **land′-rat** a rat properly so called, not a water-rat: a thief by land, distinguished from a pirate; **land′-reeve** a land-steward's assistant; **land′-roll** a clod-crusher; **Land′-rover®** a sturdy motor-vehicle used for driving on rough ground; **land′-scrip** (*U.S.*) negotiable government certificate entitling to acquisition of public land; **land′-shark** a land-grabber: one who plunders sailors on shore: a lean breed of hog (*arch. U.S.*); **land′-ship** a land vehicle having certain properties of a ship — e.g. a tank; **land′skip** same as **landscape; land′slide** a landslip (orig. *U.S.*): a great transference of votes; **land′slip** a fall of land or rock from a hillside or cliff: a portion so fallen; **lands′man** one who lives or serves on land: one inexperienced in seafaring; **land′-spring** a shallow intermittent spring; **land′-steward** one who manages a landed estate; **land′-survey′ing** measurement and mapping of land; **land′-survey′or; land′-tax** a tax upon land; **land′-val′ue** (usu. in *pl.*) the economic value of land, a basis of taxation; **land′-waiter** a custom-house officer who attends on the landing of goods from ships; **land′wind** a wind blowing off the land; **land-yacht(ing)** see **yacht. — land of milk and honey** a land of great fertility promised to the Israelites by God: any region of great fertility; **land of Nod** the land to which Cain went after killing Abel (*O.T.*): the state of slumber (*coll.*); **land with** to encumber with (a burden, difficult situation, etc.); **see how the land lies** to find out in advance how matters stand. [O.E. *land*; Du. *land*, Ger. *Land*.]

land² *land*, (*obs.*) *n.* Same as **laund.**

land³ *land*, (*U.S.*) *n.* and *interj.* euphemism for **lord.**

Land *länt*, *n.* a state or province in Germany and Austria functioning as a unit of local government: — *pl.* **Länder,** sometimes **Laender** (*len′dər*). [Ger. *Land*, *land*.]

landamman(n) *land′am-an* (Ger. *länt′äm-än*), *n.* the chief magistrate in some Swiss cantons. [Ger. *Landammann* — *Land*, land, and *Amtmann*, bailiff — *Amt*, office, and *Mann*, man.]

landau *lan′dö*, *n.* a carriage with folding top. — *n.* **landaulet′, -ette′** a motor-car whose enclosed part can be uncovered: a small landau. [*Landau* in Germany, where it is said to have been first made.]

landdamne *land-dam′*, (*Shak.*) *v.t.* said to mean to abuse with violence (perh. a misprint for *lamdamn* or *lamedamn*).

landdros(t) *lunt′dros(t)*, (*S. Afr. hist.*) *ns.* a district magistrate or sheriff. [Du., — *land*, land, *drost*, a bailiff.]

lande *läd*, *n.* a heathy plain or sandy tract (now forested) along the coast in S.W. France. [Fr.]

landgrave *land′grāv*, *n.* a German count with jurisdiction over a territory: later a mere title: — *fem.* **landgravine** (*land′grə-vēn*). — *n.* **landgrā′viate** the territory of a landgrave. [Ger. *Landgraf* — *Land*, land, *Graf*, count.]

ländler *lent′lər*, *n.* a South German and Austrian dance, or its tune, like a slow waltz. [Ger., — *Landl*, a nickname for Upper Austria.]

land-louper *land′lowp-ər*, **landloper, land-loper** *-lōp-ər*, (now *dial.*, esp. *Scot.*) *ns.* a vagabond or vagrant. [M.Du. *landlooper* — *land*, land, *loopen*, to ramble; cf. Ger. *Landläufer*.]

landscape *land′skāp*, *n.* the appearance of that portion of land which the eye can view at once: the aspect of a country, or a picture representing it: the painting of such pictures. — *v.t.* to improve by landscape-gardening. — Also *v.i.* — *adj.* of a page, illustration, etc., wider than it is deep (*printing*). — **land'scape-gar'dening** the art of laying out grounds so as to produce the effect of a picturesque landscape; **land'-scape-mar'ble** a limestone with dendritic markings; **land'scape-paint'er, land'scapist** a painter of landscapes; **land'scape-paint'ing.** [Du. *landschap*, from *land* and *-schap*, suffix = *-ship*.]

landsknecht *länts'knehht, (hist.) n.* a mercenary footsoldier of the 16th century. [Ger., — *Lands*, gen. of *Land*, country, *Knecht*, servant, soldier.]

Landsmaal, -mål *läns'mōl, n.* a literary language based on Norwegian dialects by Ivar Aasen (1850), now called Nynorsk, new Norse. [Norw., — *land*, land, *maal*, speech.]

Landsting, Landsthing *läns'ting, n.* the upper house of the Danish Rigsdag or parliament: a Swedish provincial council. [Dan. and Sw. — *land*, land, *t(h)ing*, parliament.]

Landsturm *länt'shtōōrm, n.* a general levy in time of national emergency: the force so called out. [Ger., — *Land*, land, *Sturm*, alarm.]

Landtag *länt'tähh, n.* the legislative assembly of a German state or land: the Diet of the Holy Roman Empire, or of the German Federation: formerly the provincial assembly of Bohemia or Moravia. [Ger., — *Land*, country, *Tag*, diet, day.]

Landwehr *länt'vär, n.* an army reserve. [Ger., — *Land*, land, *Wehr*, defence.]

lane[1] *lān, n.* a narrow passage or road: a narrow street: a passage through a crowd or among obstructions: a division of a road for a single stream of traffic: a channel: a sluggish stream (*Scot.*): a prescribed course. — **lane'way** a lane. — **Red Lane** the throat, gullet. [O.E. *lane, lone.*]

lane[2] *lān, adj.* a Scottish form of **lone.** — **my lane, his lane**, etc., alone.

lang *lang, adj.* a Scottish form of **long.** — *adv.* **lang syne** (*sīn*) long since, long ago. — *n.* time long past.

langaha *läng-gä'hə, n.* a Madagascan wood snake, with a long flexible snout. [Perh. Malagasy.]

langlauf *läng'lowf, n.* cross-country skiing. [Ger. *lang*, long and *Lauf*, race, run, leap.]

Langobard *lang'gō-bärd.* See **Lombard.**

langouste *lä-gōōst', n.* the spiny lobster. — *n.* **langoustine** (*-ēn'*) the Norway lobster (see **lobster**), larger than a prawn but smaller than a lobster. [Fr.]

langrage, langridge *lang'grij, n.* shot consisting of a canister containing irregular pieces of iron, formerly used to damage sails and rigging. — Also (*obs.*) **langrel** (*lang'grəl*). [Origin unknown.]

Langshan *lang'shan, n.* a small black Chinese hen. [From a place near Shanghai.]

langspel, langspiel *läng'späl, -spēl, ns.* an old Shetland cithern. [Norw. *langspill* — *lang*, long, *spill*, play, instrument.]

language *lang'gwij, n.* human speech: a variety of speech or body of words and idioms, esp. that of a nation: mode of expression: diction: any manner of expressing thought or feeling: an artificial system of signs and symbols, with rules for forming intelligible communications, for use in e.g. a computer: a national branch of one of the religious and military orders, e.g. the Hospitallers. — *v.t.* (*arch.*) to express in language. — *adjs.* **lang'uaged** skilled or rich in or having language; **lang'uageless** (*Shak.*) speechless, silent. — **language laboratory** a room in which pupils in separate cubicles are taught a language by means of material recorded on tapes. — **bad language** swearing; **dead language** one no longer spoken, as opp. to **living language; speak the same language** to come within one's range of understanding: to have the same tastes or habit of mind. [Fr. *langage* — *langue* — L. *lingua*, the tongue.]

langue *läg, n.* language viewed as a general or abstract system, as opposed to *parole* (*linguistics*): a language

(q.v.) of a religious or military order. [Fr., — L. *lingua*, tongue.]

langued *langd, (her.) adj.* having a tongue (of this or that tincture). [Fr. *langue* — L. *lingua*, tongue.]

langue de chat *läg-də-sha', a very thin finger-shaped biscuit or piece of chocolate. [Fr., cat's tongue.]

Langue d'oc *läg dok, a collective name for the Romance dialects of southern France — the tongue of the troubadours, often used as synonymous with Provençal, one of its chief branches. The name itself survived in the province *Languedoc*, giving name to a class of wines. — *adj.* **Languedocian** (*lang-gə-dō'shi-ən*). — **Langue d'oil** (*läg do-ēl, doil*), also **Langue d'oui** (*dwē*) the Romance dialect of northern France, the language of the trouvères, the main element in modern French. [O.Fr. *langue* — L. *lingua*, tongue; *de*, of; Prov. *oc*, yes — L. *hōc*, this; O.Fr. *oil, oui*, yes — L. *hōc illud*, this (is) that, yes.]

languescent. See **languid.**

languet, languette *lang'gwet, -get, -get', n.* a tongue-like object or part. [Fr. *languette*, dim. of *langue*, tongue.]

languid *lang'gwid, adj.* slack: flagging: inert: listless: faint: relaxed: spiritless. — *adj.* **languescent** (*-gwes'ənt*) growing languid. — *adv.* **lang'uidly.** — *n.* **lang'uidness.** [L. *languidus* — *languēre*, to be weak.]

languish *lang'gwish, v.i.* to become or be languid, inert, depressed: to lose strength and animation: to pine: to flag, droop: to look languishingly. — *n.* (*Shak.*) languishing: languishment. — *adj.* **lang'uished** sunken in languor. — *ns.* **lang'uisher; lang'uishing.** — *adj.* expressive of languor, or merely sentimental emotion: lingering. — *adv.* **lang'uishingly.** — *n.* **lang'uishment** the act or state of languishing: tenderness of look. [Fr. *languiss-* (serving as part. stem of *languir*) — L. *languēscĕre* — *languēre*, to be faint.]

languor *lang'gər, n.* affliction (*obs.*): pining: languidness: listlessness: lassitude: dreamy inertia: tender softness. — *adj.* **lang'uorous** full of or expressing languor: languishing. [L. *languor*, *-ōris*.]

langur *lung-gōōr', n.* the entellus monkey or other of its genus. [Hindi *lāgūr*.]

laniard. See **lanyard.**

laniary *lā'ni-ər-i, adj.* fitted for tearing. [L. *laniārius*, of a butcher — *lanius*, a butcher.]

laniferous *lan-if'ər-əs, adj.* wool-bearing. — Also **lanigerous** (*-ij'-*). [L. *lānifer, lāniger* — *lāna*, wool, *ferre, gerĕre*, to bear.]

lank *langk, adj.* flabby: drooping: flaccid: limp: thin: (of hair) straight and flat. — *v.t. and v.i.* (*Shak.*) to make or become lank. — *n.* **lank'iness.** — *adv.* **lank'ly.** — *n.* **lank'ness.** — *adj.* **lank'y** lean, tall, and ungainly: long and limp. [O.E. *hlanc*.]

lanner *lan'ər, n.* a kind of falcon, esp. the female. — *n.* **lann'eret** the male lanner. [Fr. *lanier*, possibly — L. *laniārius*, tearing, or from *lānārius*, a weaver (a mediaeval term of reproach).]

lanolin(e) *lan'ō-lin, -lēn, n.* fat from wool, a mixture of palmitate, oleate, and stearate of cholesterol. [L. *lāna*, wool, *oleum*, oil.]

lanose. See **lanate.**

lansquenet *lans'kə-net, n.* a landsknecht: a card game. [Fr., — Ger. *Landsknecht*.]

lant[1] *lant, n.* stale urine, used in wool-scouring. [O.E. and O.N. *hland*.]

lant[2] *lant.* Same as **launce**[3].

Lantana *lan-tā'nə,* or *-tä', n.* a showy-flowered genus of shrubs of the vervain family: (without *cap.*) a shrub of this genus.

lanterloo *lant'ər-lōō, (obs.) n.* a card game, ancestral form of loo. [Fr. *lanturlu* (a meaningless refrain).]

lantern *lant'ərn, n.* a case for holding or carrying a light: the light-chamber of a lighthouse: a magic lantern: one surmounting a building, giving light and air. — *v.t.* to furnish with a lantern. — *n.* **lant'ernist** one who works a magic lantern. — **lantern fly** any insect of the homopterous family Fulgoridae, with a lantern-like proboscis, formerly thought to give out light. — *adj.*

lan'tern-jawed hollow-faced. — **lantern jaws** thin long jaws; **lantern slide** a transparent slip with a picture to be projected by a magic lantern or slide projector; **lan'tern-wheel, lan'tern-pinion** a type of cog-wheel consisting of pins fastened at each end to circular plates, somewhat like a lantern in appearance. — **lantern of the dead** a lighted tower, once common in French cemeteries. [Fr. *lanterne* — L. *lanterna* — Gr. *lamptēr* — *lampein*, to give light.]

lanthanum *lan'thə-nəm, n.* a metallic element (at. numb. 57; symbol La). — *n.pl.* **lan'thanides** the rare-earth elements. — **lanthanum glass** optical glass used for high-quality photographic lenses, etc. [Gr. *lanthanein*, to escape notice, because it lay hid in rare minerals till 1839.]

lanthorn obs. spelling of **lantern,** based on folk etymology, from the old use of horn for lanterns.

lantskip *lant'skip, (Milt.) n.* Same as **landscape.**

lanugo *lan-ū'gō, n.* down: an embryonic woolly coat of hair: — *pl.* **lanū'gos.** — *adjs.* **lanū'ginose** (*-jin-*), **lanūginous** downy: covered with fine soft hair. [L. *lānūgō*, *-inis,* down *lāna,* wool.]

lanx *langks,* (*ant.*) *n.* a platter: — *pl.* **lances** (*lan'sēz*). [L.]

lanyard, laniard *lan'yərd, n.* a short rope used as a fastening or handle (*naut.*): a cord for hanging a knife, whistle, or the like about the neck. [Fr. *lanière,* origin doubtful; confused with **yard.**]

lanzknecht an erroneous form of **landsknecht** (as if from Ger. *Lanze,* lance).

Laodicean *lā-od-i-sē'ən, adj.* lukewarm in religion, like the Christians of *Laodicea* (Rev. iii. 14–16). — *n.* **Laodice'anism.** [Gr. *Lāodikeia,* Laodicea.]

Laotian *la-ō'shən, adj.* of Laos or its people. — *n.* a native of Laos.

lap¹ *lap, v.t.* to scoop up with the tongue (often with *up*): to take in greedily or readily (*fig.*) (usu. with *up*): to wash or flow against. — *v.i* to drink by licking up: to make a sound or movement as of lapping: — *pr.p.* **lapp'ing;** *pa.t.* and *pa.p.* **lapped.** — *n.* a motion or sound of lapping: that which may be lapped: thin liquor. — *n.* and *adj.* **lapp'ing.** [O.E. *lapian*; L.G. *lappen*; L. *lambēre,* to lick; Gr. *laptein.*]

lap² *lap, n.* a flap: a lobe (of the ear): a fold: a hollow: part of a garment disposed to hold or catch: the fold of the clothes and body from waist to knees of a person sitting: place where one is nurtured (*fig.*; in phrases): a round, as of a race-course, or of anything coiled: an overlap: amount of overlap (in slating, over the next but one): in a steam-engine, the distance the valve has to move from mid position to open the steam or exhaust port: in euchre, etc., points carried over to another game: a polishing disc, cylinder, or the like: the length of material needed to go round a drum, etc.: a layer or sheet of (cotton, etc.) fibres. — *v.t.* to wrap, enfold, surround: to lay overlappingly: to polish with a lap: to unite accurately: to get or be a lap ahead of: to traverse as a lap or in laps: to hold in the lap. — *v.i.* to lie with an overlap: to extend beyond some limit. — *ns.* **lap'ful; lapp'er** one who wraps or folds: a machine that compacts scutched cotton into a fleece upon a roller called a **lap-roller.** — *n.* and *adj.* **lapp'ing.** — **lap'-board** a flat wide board resting on the lap, used by tailors and seamstresses; **lap'dog** a small dog fondled in the lap: a pet dog (also *fig.*). — *adj.* **lap'-joint'ed** having joints formed by overlapping edges. — **lap'stone** a stone held in the lap to hammer leather on; **lap'streak** a clinker-built boat. — Also *adj.* — *adj.* **lap'top** (of a computer) somewhat smaller than a desktop computer, able to be carried in a briefcase, etc. and set on one's lap. — *n.* a laptop computer. — **lap'work** lap-jointed work. — **lap of honour** a ceremonial circuit of field, track, show ring, made by the victor(s) in a contest; **the lap of luxury** luxurious conditions; **in the lap of the gods** of a situation, such that the result cannot be predicted. [O.E. *læppa,* a loosely hanging part; Ger. *Lappen,* a rag.]

lap³ *lāp* or *lap,* Scots *pa.t.* of **leap¹.**

lap⁴, lappie form. **lapje** *lap, lap'i,* (*S.Afr.*) *ns.* a rag or clout. [Afrik., — Du. *lap,* rag, patch.]

laparoscopy *lap-ər-os'kəp-i, n.* surgical examination by means of a **laparoscope** (*lap'ər-əs-kōp*), a tube-shaped optical instrument which permits examination of the internal organs from outside. [Gr. *laparā,* flank, *skopeein,* to see.]

laparotomy *lap-ə-rot'ə-mi, n.* surgical cutting of the abdominal wall. [Gr. *laparā,* flank, *tomē,* cutting.]

lapel (*obs.* **lappel**) *la-, lə-pel', n.* part of a coat folded back continuing the collar. — *adj.* **lapelled'.** [Dim. of **lap².**]

lapis *lap'is, n.* a stone (the Latin word, used in certain phrases only, as *lapis philosophicus,* the philosophers' stone, *lapis ollaris,* potstone). — *adj.* **lapidār'ian** pertaining to stones: inscribed on stones: learned in stones. — *ns.* **lap'idarist** (*-ə-rist*) an expert in gems; **lap'idary** (*-ə-ri*) a cutter of stones, esp. gem-stones: a treatise on gems (*obs.*): an expert in gems (*obs.*). — *adj.* pertaining to stones: dwelling in stone-heaps (as a kind of bee): inscribed on stone: suitable for inscription. — *v.t.* **lap'idate** (*arch.*) to pelt with stones. — *n.* **lapidā'tion** stoning. — *adj.* **lapid'eous** stony. — *n.* **lapidesc'ence** (*arch.*). — *adjs.* **lapidesc'ent** (*arch.*) becoming stone: petrifying; **lapidic'olous** (L. *colēre,* to inhabit) living under or among stones; **lapidif'ic** (*arch.*). — *n.* **lapidificā'tion** (*arch.*). — *v.t.* and *v.i.* **lapid'ify** (*arch.*) to turn into stone: — *pr.p.* **lapid'ifying;** *pa.t.* and *pa.p.* **lapid'ified.** — *n.pl.* **lapilli** (*lä-pil'lē*) small fragments (in size from a pea to a walnut) of lava ejected from a volcano (*pl.* of It. *lapil'lo*; also of L. *lapill'us*). — *adj.* **lapill'iform.** — **lapis laz'ūlī** a beautiful stone consisting of calcite and other minerals coloured ultramarine by lazurite, haüyne, and sodalite, commonly spangled with iron pyrites (see **azure, lazulite, lazurite**). — **lapis lazuli blue** a deep blue, sometimes veined with gold, used in decoration and in porcelain; **lapis lazuli ware** a pebble ware veined with gold upon blue. [L. *lapis, -idis,* a stone.]

Lapith *lap'ith, n.* one of a people of Thessaly who fought with the Centaurs: — *pl.* **-ae** or **-s.**

lapje. See **lap⁴.**

Lapp *lap,* **Lap'lander** *-lən-dər, ns.* a native or inhabitant of Lapland: one of the race or people inhabiting Lapland. — *adjs.* **Lapp, Lap'landish; Lapp'ish.** — *ns.* the language of the Lapps.

lappel. See **lapel.**

lapper. See **lopper¹.**

lappet *lap'it, n.* a little lap or flap. — *adj.* **lapp'eted.** — **lapp'et-head** (*obs.*) a head-dress with lappets; **lappet moth** a moth of the Lasiocampidae whose caterpillar has lappets on its sides. [Dim. of **lap².**]

lappie. See **lap⁴.**

lapsang (souchong) *lap'sang (soō-shong', -chong'),* (also with *caps.*) a variety of souchong tea with a smoky flavour. [Chin.]

lapse *laps, v.i.* to slip or glide: to pass by degrees: to fall away by cessation or relaxation of effort or cause: to fall from the faith: to fail in virtue or duty: to pass into disuse: to pass or fail owing to some omission or non-fulfilment: to become void. — *v.t.* to catch in a lapse (*Shak.*; perh. with associations of *lap* or *latch*): to allow to pass, fall away, or become void. — *n.* a slip: a gliding (*arch.*): passage (of time): a falling away: a failure (in virtue, attention, memory, etc.): a vertical gradient as of atmospheric temperature. — *adjs.* **laps'able** liable to lapse; **lapsed** having slipped or passed or been let slip: fallen away (esp. in the Christian Church, from the faith). — **lapse rate** (*meteor.*) rate of change in temperature in relation to height in the atmosphere. [L. *lāpsāre,* to slip, *lāpsus,* a slip — *lābi, lāpsus,* to slip.]

lapsus *lap'səs, lap'sŏos,* (L.) *n.* a slip. — **lapsus calami** (*kal'ə-mī, ka'la-mē*) a slip of the pen; **lapsus linguae** (*ling'gwē, -gwī*) a slip of the tongue; **lapsus memoriae** (*me-mōr'i-ē* or *mŏr'* or *-ri-ī*) a slip of the memory.

Laputa *lä-pū'tə, n.* a flying island in Swift's *Gulliver's Travels,* inhabited by people who engaged in ridiculous projects. — *ns*. **Lapu′tan, Lapu′tian** (*-shən*) an inhabitant of Laputa. — *adjs*. absurd: chimerical.

lapwing *lap′wing*, *n*. a bird of the plover family, the peewit. [M.E. *lappewinke* — O.E. *lǣpewince*, *hlǣpewince, hlēapewince*: modified by folk ety.]

laquearia *lak-wi-ā′ri-ə*, L. *lak-we-ä′ri-a*, *n.pl*. a panelled ceiling. [L.]

lar *lär*, *n*. the god of a house (orig. prob. a field god): — *pl*. **lares** (*lā′rēz*; L. *lä′räs*). [L. *lar*.]

larboard *lär′bōrd, -börd, läb′ərd*, (*obs*.) *n*. and *adj*. port or left. [M.E. *laddeborde*, influenced by **starboard;** origin unknown.]

larceny *lär′sə-ni*, *n*. the legal term in England and Ireland for stealing: theft. — *ns*. **lar′cener, lar′cenist** a thief. — *adj*. **lar′cenous**. — *adv*. **lar′cenously**. — **grand larceny** in England before 1827, larceny of property of the value of one shilling or more, as opposed to **petty larceny,** larceny of property less in value than one shilling; **simple larceny** as opposed to **compound larceny,** is larceny uncombined with aggravating circumstances. [O.Fr. *larrecin* (Fr. *larcin*) — L. *latrōcinium* — *latrō*, a robber.]

larch *lärch*, *n*. any tree of the coniferous genus Larix, distinguished from cedar by the deciduous leaves. — *adj*. (*rare*) **larch′en**. [Ger. *Lärche* — L. *larix, -icis*.]

lard *lärd*, *n*. the rendered fat of the hog. — *v.t*. to smear or enrich with lard: to stuff with bacon or pork: to fatten: to mix with anything: to stuff or load: to interlard, interpenetrate: to garnish, strew. — *v.i*. (*Shak*.) to be intimately mixed. — *adj*. **lardā′ceous**. — *n*. **lar′don, lardoon′** a strip of bacon used for larding. — *adj*. **lar′dy**. — **lar′dy-cake** esp. in S. England, a rich sweet cake made of bread dough, with lard, dried fruit, etc. [O.Fr., — L. *lāridum, lārdum*; cf. Gr. *lārīnos*, fat, *lāros*, pleasant to taste.]

lardalite. See **laurdalite**.

larder *lärd′ər*, *n*. a place where food is kept: stock of provisions. — *n*. **lard′erer** one in charge of a larder. [O.Fr. *lardier*, bacon-tub; see **lard**.]

lardon, lardoon, lardy. See **lard**.

lare *lär*, *n*. a Northern form of **lore**[1]; also a Spenserian form of **lair** (*pasture*).

lares et penates *lā′rēz et pe-nā′tēz, lä′rās et pe-nä′tās*, (L.) household gods: valued personal or household objects.

Largactil® *lär-gak′til*, *n*. a tranquillising drug, chlorpromazine.

large *lärj*, *adj*. great in size: extensive: bulky: broad: copious: abundant: generous: magnanimous: loftily affected or pretentious: in a great way: diffuse (*obs*.): (of language) free, licentious (*Shak*.): (of the wind) having a favouring component (*naut*.). — *adv*. before the wind (*naut*.): ostentatiously: prominently, importantly. — *n*. (*mus*.) an obsolete note, equal to two (or in 'perfect' time three) longs. — *adv*. **large′ly** in a large manner: in great measure. — *v.i*. and *v.t*. **lar′gen** (*poet*.) to enlarge. — *n*. **large′ness**. — *adj*. **larg′ish** fairly large, rather big. — *adjs*. **large′-hand′ed** having large hands: grasping (*Shak*.): profuse; **large′-heart′ed** having a large heart: of liberal disposition or comprehensive sympathies: generous; **large′-mind′ed** magnanimous: characterised by breadth of view. — **as large as life** actually, really; **at large** at liberty: at random: in general: in full: representing the whole area, not a division (*U.S*.); **large paper edition** a special edition with wider margins. [Fr., — L. *largus*, abounding.]

largess, largesse *lär-jes′, lärj′es*, *n*. a bestowal or distribution of gifts: generosity. — *n*. **largition** (*lär-jish′ən*) giving of largess. [Fr. *largesse* and L. *largītiō, -ōnis* — *largus*.]

largo *lär′gō*, (*mus*.) *adj*. broad and slow. — Also *adv*. — *n*. a movement to be so performed: — *pl*. **lar′gos**. — *adj*. **larghet′to** somewhat slow: not so slow as largo. — *n*. a somewhat slow movement: — *pl*. **larghet′tos**. [It., — L. *largus*.]

lariat *lar′i-ət*, *n*. a picketing rope, a lasso. [Sp. *la*, the, *reata*, picketing rope.]

Laridae, larine. See **Larus**.

lark[1] *lärk*, *n*. a well-known bird (*Alauda*) that flies high as it sings: extended to various similar birds. — *v.i*. to catch larks. — *adj*. **lark′-heeled** having a long hindclaw. — **lark′ing-glass** an instrument with mirrors used by bird-catchers to dazzle larks; **lark′s′-heel** the Indian cress: the larkspur; **lark′spur** any plant of the genus Delphinium, from the spurred flowers. — **get up with the lark** to rise very early in the morning. [M.E. *laverock* — O.E. *lǣwerce, lāwerce*; Ger. *Lerche*.]

lark[2] *lärk*, *n*. a frolic: a piece of mischief. — *v.i*. to frolic. — *ns*. **lark′er; lark′iness**. — *adjs*. **lark′ish; lark′y** (*coll*.). [Perh. from the preceding (cf. **skylarking**); some connect it with **lake**[4].]

larmier *lär′mi-ər*, *n*. a corona or other course serving as a drip-stone (*archit*.): a tear-pit (*zool*.). [Fr., — *larme* — L. *lacrima*, a tear.]

larn *lärn*, (*dial*. or *facet*.) *v.t*. and *v.i*. to learn: to teach. [**learn**.]

larnax *lär′naks*, *n*. a chest, coffin, etc. of ancient Greece, usually made of terracotta and frequently ornamented: — *pl*. **larnakes** (*lär′nak-ēz*). [Gr., perh. conn. with late Gr. *narnax*, a chest.]

laroid. See **Larus**.

larrigan *lar′i-gən*, *n*. a long boot made of oiled leather worn by lumbermen, etc. [Origin unknown.]

larrikin *lar′i-kin*, (*Austr*.) *n*. a rough or hooligan. — Also *adj*. — *n*. **larr′ikinism**. [Origin doubtful; a connection with 'larking about' has been suggested but remains unsubstantiated.]

larrup *lar′əp*, (*coll*.) *v.t*. to flog, thrash. [Cf. Du. *larpen*, thresh with flails.]

larum *lar′əm*, *n*. alarm: a noise giving notice of danger. — **lar′um-bell**. [**alarm**.]

Larus *lär′əs, lär′əs*, *n*. the principal genus of the gull family (**Laridae** *lar′i-dē*). — *adjs*. **lar′ine; lar′oid**. [L., — Gr. *lāros*, a bird, prob. a gull.]

larva *lär′va*, *n*. a spectre or ghost: an animal in an immature but active state markedly different from the adult, e.g. a caterpillar: — *pl*. **larvae** (*lär′vē*; L. *-vī*). — *adjs*. **lar′val; lar′vate, -d** clothed as with a mask; **larvicī′dal** destroying larvae. — *n*. **lar′vicide**. — *adjs*. **lar′viform; larvip′arous** giving birth to larvae. [L. *lārva, lārua*, a spectre, a mask.]

larvikite. See **laurvikite**.

larynx *lar′ingks*, *n*. the upper part of the windpipe: — *pl*. **larynges** (*lər′in-jēz*, or *lar-in′jēz*) or **lar′ynxes**. — *adjs*. **laryngal** (*lar-ing′gl*), **laryngeal** (*lar-in′ji-əl*). — *ns*. **laryngectomy** (*-jek′*) surgical removal of the larynx; **laryngismus** (*-jiz′məs*) spasm of the larynx. — *adj*. **laryngitic** (*-jit′ik*). — *n*. **laryngitis** (*-jī′tis*) inflammation of the larynx. — *adj*. **laryngological** (*-ing-gə-loj′*). — *ns*. **laryngol′ogist; laryngology** (*-gol′ə-ji*) the science of the larynx; **laryngophony** (*-gof′*) the sound of the voice as heard through the stethoscope applied over the larynx; **laryng′oscope** a mirror for examining the larynx and trachea. — *adj*. **laryngoscop′ic**. — *ns*. **laryngos′copist; laryngos′copy; laryng′ospasm** spasmodic closure of the larynx; **laryngot′omy** the operation of cutting into the larynx. [Gr. *larynx, -yngos*.]

lasagne *lä-zän′yə, -sän′, la-, lə-, n.pl*. flat pieces of pasta: (*sing*.) a baked dish of this with tomatoes, cheese, meat. — Also **lasagna**. [It.; sing. *lasagna*.]

lascar *las′kər, -kär*, or *las-kär′, n*. an Oriental (originally Indian) sailor or camp-follower. [Hind. and Pers. *lashkar*, army, or *lashkarī*, a soldier.]

lascivious *lə-siv′i-əs, adj*. wanton: inclining or tending to libidinousness. — *adv*. **lasciv′iously**. — *n*. **lasciv′iousness**. [L.L. *lascīviōsus* — L. *lascīvus*, playful.]

laser[1] *lās′ər, n*. silphium (*hist*.): (now) the juice of laserwort. — *ns*. **Laserpicium, Laserpitium** (*las-ər-pish′i-əm*) a genus of umbelliferous perennial herbs of Europe, Asia and North Africa; **laserwort** (*lās′ər-wûrt*) any plant of the genus, esp. herb frankincense (L. *latifolium*): also applied to species of *Ferula* and *Thapsia*. [L. *lāser*, the juice of *lāserpīcium*, the silphium plant.]

laser[2] *lāz′ər, n*. a device which amplifies an input of light, producing an extremely narrow and intense monochromatic beam. — Also *adj.* — *v.i.* **lase** (of a crystal, etc.) to be, or become, suitable for use as a laser. — *adj.* and *n.* **lā′sing.** [*Light amplification by stimulated emission of radiation.*]

lash[1] *lash, n.* the flexible part of a whip, or its terminal piece of whipcord: a scourge: an eyelash: a stroke with a whip or anything pliant: a sweep or flick: a stroke of satire. — *v.t.* to strike with, or as if with, a lash: to dash against: to drive, urge, or work by blows of anything flexible, or figuratively: to whisk or flick with a sweeping movement: to secure with a rope or cord: to scourge with sarcasm or satire: to lavish, squander (*obs.*). — *v.i.* to dash: to make a rapid sweeping movement or onset: to use the whip. — *ns.* **lash′er** one who lashes or whips: a rope for binding one thing to another; **lash′ing** act of whipping: a rope for making things fast: (colloquial, esp. in *pl.*) an abundance of anything. — **lash′-up** (*slang*) a mess, fiasco: an improvisation. — **lash out** to kick out, fling out, hit out without restraint: to spend extravagantly. [Perh. several different words, with possible connections with **latch, lash**[2] and **lacc.**]

lash[2] *lash, adj.* slow, slack (*obs.*): soft: insipid. — *n.* **lash′er** a weir: a waterfall from a weir: a pool below a weir. [M.E. *lasche*, slack — O.Fr. *lasche* (Fr. lâche, cowardly) — L. *laxus*, lax.]

lashkar *lash′kär, n.* a camp of Indian soldiers (*obs.*): a body of armed Indian tribesmen, a force. [Hind., army, camp; cf. **lascar.**]

Lasiocampidae *lā-zi-ō-kamp′i-dē*, or *lā-si-*, *n.pl.* a family of moths including eggers and lackey moths. [Gr. *lasios*, woolly, *kampē*, a caterpillar.]

lasket *las′kit, n.* a loop at the foot of a sail, to fasten an extra sail. [Perh. **latchet.**]

lasque *läsk, n.* a flat thin diamond used esp. in India. [Perh. Pers. *lashk*, a bit, piece.]

lass *las, n.* a girl: a sweetheart: a maid-servant (*Scot.*). — *ns.* (dims.) **lassie** (*las′i*) the ordinary Scots word for a girl; **lass′ock.** — *adj.* **lass′lorn** (*Shak.*) forsaken by one's mistress. [Origin obscure; the association with **lad**[1] may be accidental.]

Lassa fever *la′sə fē′vər*, an infectious tropical virus disease, often fatal, transmitted by rodents. [From *Lassa*, in Nigeria, where it was first recognised.]

lassitude *las′i-tūd, n.* faintness: weakness: weariness: languor. [L. *lassitūdō — lassus*, faint.]

lasslorn, lassock. See lass.

lasso *la-soo′, la′so, n.* a long rope with a running noose for catching wild horses, etc.: — *pl.* **lasso(e)s′** (or *las′*). — *v.t.* to catch with the lasso: — *pr.p.* **lasso′ing** (or *las′*); *pa.p.* **lassoed** (*las-ood′* or *las′*). [S. Amer. pron. of Sp. *lazo* — L. *laqueus*, a noose.]

lassu *losh′oo, n.* the slow movement of a csárdás. [Hung.]

last[1] *läst, n.* a shoemaker's model of the foot on which boots and shoes are made or repaired. — *v.t.* to fit with a last. — *n.* **last′er** one who fits the parts of shoes to lasts: a tool for doing so. [O.E. *læste*, last, *lāst*, footprint.]

last[2] *läst, v.i.* to continue, endure: to escape failure: to remain fresh, unimpaired: to hold out: to survive. — *n.* **last′er** one who has staying power: a thing that keeps well. — *adj.* **last′ing** enduring: durable. — *n.* endurance. — *adv.* **last′ingly.** — *n.* **last′ingness.** — **last out** to last as long as or longer than: to last to the end or as long as is required. [O.E. *læstan*, to follow a track, keep on, suffice, last; see foregoing word.]

last[3] *läst, n.* a load, cargo: a varying weight, generally about 4000 lb. — *n.* **last′age** the lading of a ship: room for stowing goods in a ship: a duty formerly paid for the right of carrying goods, etc. [O.E. *hlæst* — *hladan*, to lade; Ger. *Last*, O.N. *hlass*.]

last[4] *läst, adj.* latest: coming or remaining after all the others: final: immediately before the present: utmost: ending a series: most unlikely, least to be preferred. — Also *adv.* — *adv.* **last′ly** finally. — *adjs.* **last′-ditch** (of an attempt, etc.) made at the last moment or in the

last resort; **last′-gasp′** made, etc. when almost at the point of death, defeat, etc. — **last heir** the person to whom lands escheat for want of other heirs. — *adj.* **last′-minute** made, done, or given at the latest possible time. — **last post** (*mil.*) second of two bugle-calls denoting the hour of retiring for the night: farewell bugle-call at military funerals; **last rites** religious rites performed for those near death; **last straw** (the straw that breaks the camel's back) that beyond which there can be no endurance; **last word** final remark in an argument: final decision: the most up-to-date of its kind (*coll.*). — **at last** in the end; **at long last** after long delay; **breathe one's last** to die; **die in the last ditch** to fight to the bitter end; **first and last** altogether; **last thing** after doing everything else; **on one's last legs** on the verge of utter failure or exhaustion; **put the last hand to** to finish, put the finishing touch to; **see (hear) the last of** see (hear) for the last time; **the Last Day** the Day of Judgment; **the Last Supper** the supper partaken of by Christ and his disciples on the eve of the crucifixion; **the last trump** the trumpet that will sound at the Last Day (1 Cor. xv. 52); **to the last** to the end: till death. [O.E. *latost*, superl. of *læt*, slow, late.]

lat *lät, n.* in India, an isolated pillar. [Hindi *lat*.]

Latakia *lat-ä-kē′ə, n.* a Syrian tobacco from *Latakia.*

latch[1] *lach, v.t.* (*Shak.*) probably to moisten, but possibly to fasten (next word). — *n.* (*Scot.*) a mire: a boggy water-channel. — Also **letch.** [**leach**[1].]

latch[2] *lach, n.* a door catch lifted from without by a lever or string: a light door-lock, opened from without by a key. — *v.t.* (*obs.*) to seize, take, receive. — *v.t.* and *v.i.* to fasten with a latch. — *ns.* **latch′key, latch′-string** a key, string, for opening a latched door. — **latchkey child** one who regularly returns home to an empty house; **latch on to** (*coll.*) to attach oneself to: to gain comprehension of; **on the latch** not locked, but to be opened by a latch. [O.E. *læccan*, to catch.]

latchet *lach′it, (obs.) n.* a loop: a thong or lace. [O.Fr. *lachet*, a form of *lacet*, dim. of *laz*; see **lace.**]

late *lät, adj.* (*compar.* **lät′er**; *superl.* **lät′est**) slow (*dial.*): tardy: behindhand: coming, remaining, flowering, ripening, producing, etc., after the due, expected, or usual time: long delayed: far advanced towards the close: deceased: departed: out of office: former: not long past: most recent. — Also *adv.* — *adj.* **lät′ed** (*Shak.*) belated. — *adv.* **late′ly** recently. — *v.t.* and *v.i.* **lät′en** to make or grow late. — *ns.* **late′ness; lät′est** (*coll.*; with *the*) the latest news. — *adj.* and *adv.* **lät′ish.** — **late′-comer** a person who arrives late. — **at (the) latest** not later than (a stated time); **late in the day** (*fig.*) at an unreasonably late stage of development, etc.; **of late** recently. [O.E. *læt*, slow; Du. *laat*, O.N. *latr*, Ger. *lass*, weary; L. *lassus*, tired.]

lateen *lə-tēn′, adj.* applied to a triangular sail, common in the Mediterranean, the Lake of Geneva, etc. [Fr. (*voile*) *latine* — L. *Latīnus*, Latin.]

La Tène *la ten*, of a division of the Iron Age exemplified at *La Tène* near Neuchâtel in Switzerland, later than Hallstatt.

latent *lā′tənt, adj.* hid: concealed: not visible or apparent: dormant: undeveloped, but capable of development. — *ns.* **lā′tence, lā′tency.** — *adv.* **lā′tently.** — *n.* **latesc′ence.** — *adj.* **lätesc′ent** becoming latent. — **latent heat** see **heat; latent image** in photography, the invisible image produced by the action of light on the sensitive chemicals on a film, etc., which becomes visible after development; **latent period** the time between stimulus and reaction: that between contracting a disease and appearance of symptoms. [L. *latēns, -entis*, pr.p. of *latēre*, to lie hid; Gr. *lanthanein*, to be hidden.]

lateral *lat′ə-rəl, adj.* belonging to the side: (of a consonant) produced by air passing over one or both sides of the tongue (*phon.*). — *n.* a lateral part, movement, consonant, etc. — *ns.* **lateralīsā′tion, -z-** the specialised development in one or other hemisphere of the brain of the mechanisms controlling some activity or ability; **laterality** (*-ral′i-ti*) the state of belonging to the side:

physical one-sidedness, either right or left. — *adv.*
lat′erally. — **lateral line** in fishes, a line along the side
of the body, marking the position of a sensory organ;
lateral thinking thinking which seeks new ways of
looking at a problem and does not merely proceed by
logical steps from the starting-point of what is known
or believed. [L. *laterālis* — *latus*, *latĕris*, a side.]
Lateran *lat′ə-rən, adj.* pertaining to the Church of St John
Lateran at Rome, the Pope's cathedral church, on the
site of the splendid palace or basilica of Plautius
Lateranus (executed 66). — **Lateran Councils** five
general councils of the Western Church, held in the
Lateran basilica (1123, 1139, 1179, 1215, and 1512–17),
regarded by Roman Catholics as ecumenical; **Lateran
Treaty** restored the papal state (1929). [L. *Lat-
erānus.*]
laterigrade *lat′ə-ri-grād, adj.* running sideways, like a
crab. [L. *latus*, *-ĕris*, side, *gradus*, step.]
laterite *lat′ə-rīt, n.* a clay formed by weathering of rocks
in a tropical climate, composed chiefly of iron and
aluminium hydroxides. — *n.* **laterīsā′tion, -z-** conversion into laterite. [L. *later, latĕris*, a brick.]
lateritious *lat-ə-rish′əs, adj.* brick-red. [L. *laterīcius* —
later, latĕris, a brick.]
latewake *lāt′wāk, n.* a mistaken form of **lykewake.**
latex *lā′teks, (bot.) n.* the milky juice of some plants, e.g.
rubber trees: — *pl.* **lā′texes, lā′tǐcēs.** — *adj.* **laticiferous**
(*lat-i-sif′ə-rəs*) containing or conveying latex. [L.
lătex, lăticis.]
lath *läth, n.* a thin slip of wood: a substitute for such a
slip, used in slating, plastering, etc.: anything long and
thin: — *pl.* **laths** (*lädhz, läths*). — *v.t.* to cover with
laths. — *adj.* **lathen** (*läth′ən*). — *n.* **lath′ing** the act or
process of covering with laths: a covering of laths. —
adj. **lath′y** like a lath. — **lath′-splitter** one who splits
wood into laths. — **dagger of lath** the Vice's weapon
in the old morality plays. [O.E. *lætt.*]
lathe[1] *lādh, n.* a machine for turning and shaping articles
of wood, metal, etc.: the swing-frame of a loom
carrying the reed for separating the warp threads and
beating up the weft. [Origin doubtful.]
lathe[2] *lādh, n.* a division of Kent. [O.E. *læth*, a district;
O.N. *lāth*, landed property.]
lather *ladh′ər, lādh′ər, n.* a foam made with water and
soap: froth from sweat. a state of agitation (*coll.*). —
v.t. to spread over with lather: to thrash (*coll.*). — *v.i.*
to form a lather. — *adj.* **lath′ery.** [O.E. *lēathor*; O.N.
lauthr.]
lathi, lathee *lä-tē′, n.* a heavy stick. [Hind. *lāthī.*]
Lathyrus *lath′i-rəs, n.* the sweetpea genus of Papilionaceae: (without *cap.*) a plant of this genus. — *n.*
lath′yrism a disease with stiffness and paralysis of the
legs among eaters of chickling, but apparently due to
admixture of seeds of cultivated vetch. [L., — Gr.
lathyros, the chickling vetch.]
laticlave *lat′i-klāv, n.* a broad stripe on a Roman senator's
tunic. [L. *lātus*, broad, *clāvus*, a stripe.]
latifundia *lat-i-fun′di-ə, n.pl.* great landed estates. — Also
in *sing.* **latifun′dium** and as It. *pl.* **latifondi** (*lä-tē-fon′dē*).
[Pl. of L. *lātifundium* — *lātus*, wide, *fundus*, an estate.]
Latin *lat′in, adj.* pertaining to ancient Latium (esp.
Rome) or its inhabitants, or its language, or to those
languages that are descended from Latin, or to the
peoples speaking them, esp. (*popularly*) the Spanish,
Portuguese and Italians or the inhabitants of Central
and South America of Spanish, etc. extraction: of or
denoting the temperament considered characteristic of
the Latin peoples, passionate, excitable, volatile: written or spoken in Latin: Roman Catholic. — *n.* an
inhabitant of ancient Latium: the language of ancient
Latium, and esp. of Rome: a person belonging to a
Latin people: a Roman Catholic. — *adjs.* **Latian**
(*lā′shyən, -shən*) of Latium; **Lat′inate** imitating Latin
style: (of vocabulary) borrowed from Latin. — *n.*
Lat′iner one who knows Latin: an interpreter (*obs.*).
— *v.t.* **Lat′inise, -ize** to turn into or make Latin or like
to Latin. — *v.i.* to use Latin idioms or derivatives. —

ns. **Lat′inism** a Latin idiom: the use or inclination
towards use of Latin idioms, words, or ways; **Lat′inist**
one skilled in Latin; **Latin′ity** the quality of one's Latin.
— **Latin America** those parts of America where Spanish, Portuguese, and French are the official languages,
with the exception of French-speaking Canada. — *adj.*
and *n.* **Lat′in-Amer′ican.** — **Latin Church** the Church
that formerly used Latin and which recognises the
primacy of Rome — the Roman Catholic Church;
Latin cross an upright cross with the lowest limb
longest; **Latin Empire** that portion of the Byzantine
Empire seized in 1204 by the Crusaders (French and
Venetian), and overthrown by the Greeks in 1261;
Latin Kingdom the Christian kingdom of Jerusalem
ruled by French or Latin kings, and lasting from 1099
to 1187; **Latin Quarter** the educational and students'
quarter of Paris around the Sorbonne (where Latin
was spoken in the Middle Ages; Fr. *quartier latin*),
famous for its unconventional way of life; **Latin Union**
a monetary union (1865–1926) of France, Belgium,
Italy, and Switzerland, with Greece from 1868. —
classical Latin the Latin of the writers who flourished
from about 75 B.C. to about A.D 200; **dog Latin**
barbarous Latin; **Late Latin** the Latin written by
authors between A.D 200 and *c.* 600; **Low Latin**
Mediaeval, or Late and Mediaeval, Latin; **Middle** or
Mediaeval Latin the Latin of the Middle Ages between
A.D 600 and 1500; **New, Modern, Latin** Latin as written
between 1500 and the present time, mostly used as a
scientific medium; **Silver Latin** see **silver; thieves′ Latin**
thieves' cant; **Vulgar Latin** colloquial Latin, esp. that
of the period under the emperors. [L. *Latīnus*,
belonging to *Latium*, the district round Rome.]
latirostral *lat-i-ros′trəl, adj.* broad-billed. — Also **latiros′-
trate.** [L. *lātus*, broad, *rōstrum*, beak.]
latiseptate *lat-i-sep′tāt, adj.* having a broad partition.
[L. *lātus*, broad, *saeptum*, a fence (used in pl.).]
latitant *lat′i-tənt, adj.* lurking: lying in wait: hibernating:
dormant. — *n.* **lat′itancy.** — *ns.* **lat′itat** a writ based
on the supposition that the person summoned is in
hiding; **latitā′tion.** [L. *latitāre, -ātum* (3rd pers. sing.
pres. *latitat*), freq. of *latēre*, to be in hiding.]
latitude *lat′i-tūd, n.* width (now chiefly playful): a wide
extent: range: scope: allowance: breadth in interpretation: extent of signification: freedom from restraint: laxity: angular distance from the equator
(*geog.*): a place of specified angular distance from the
equator (*geog.*): angular distance from the ecliptic
(*celestial latitude; astron.*). — *adjs.* **latitūd′inal** pertaining to latitude: in the direction of latitude; **latitūdinā′-
rian** broad or liberal, esp. in religious belief: lax. — *n.*
a member of a school of liberal and philosophical
theologians within the English Church in the later half
of the 17th century: one who regards specific creeds,
methods of church government, etc., with indifference.
— *n.* **latitūdinā′rianism.** — *adj.* **latitūd′inous** broad,
wide, esp. in interpretation. [L. *lātitūdō, -inis* —
lātus, broad.]
latke *lät′kə, n.* a traditional Jewish pancake, esp. one
made with grated potato. [Yiddish, — Russ. *latka*,
a pastry.]
latration *lə-trā′shən, n.* barking. — *adj.* **latrant** (*lā′trənt*).
[L. *lātrāre, -ātum*, to bark.]
la trenise. See **trenise.**
latria *lä-trī′ə.* See **dulia.** [Gr. *latreiā* — *latreuein*, to
serve.]
latrine *lə-trēn′, n.* a lavatory, esp. in barracks, etc. [L.
lātrīna — *lavātrīna* — *lavāre*, to wash.]
latrocinium *lat-rō-sin′i-əm,* **latrociny** *lat′rō-sin-i, (obs.) ns.*
highway-robbery: Pope Leo I's name for the 'Robber-
Council' at Ephesus in 449, which upheld Eutychian-
ism. [L. *latrōcinium*, robbery.]
latron *lā′tron, n.* a robber. [L. *latrō, -ōnis*.]
-latry *-lə-tri*, in composition, worship. [Gk. *latreiā* —
latreuein to serve.]
latten *lat′ən, n.* brass or similar alloy in former use:
tin-plate: metal in thin plates. [O.Fr. *laton* (Fr.

laiton), prob. — O. Prov. — Ar. *lātūn*, copper, — Turkic; a Germanic origin for the word has also been postulated, cf. **lath.**]

latter *lat'ər, adj.* later: coming or existing after: second-mentioned of two: modern: recent: last (*Shak.*). — *adv.* **latt'erly** towards the latter end: of late. — *adj.* **latt'-ermost** last (O.E. *lætemest*). — *adjs.* **latt'er-born** (*Shak.*) younger; **latt'er-day** modern: recent. — **latter end** the final part: the end of life; **latt'ermath** aftermath; **latt'er= mint** (*Keats*) apparently a late kind of mint; **latt'er-wit** (*arch. U.S.*) a witty thought after the occasion has passed. — **Latter-day Saint** a Mormon. [O.E. *lætra*, compar. of *læt*, slow, late.]

lattice *lat'is, n.* a network of crossed laths or bars, called also **latt'ice-work:** anything of like pattern: a window with lozenge-shaped panes set in lead, called also **lattice window:** a space-lattice: the geometrically regular, three-dimensional arrangement of fissionable and non-fissionable material in an atomic pile: the regular arrangement of atoms in crystalline material: a system of lines for position-fixing overprinted on a navigational chart: a partially ordered set in which any two elements have a least upper bound and a greatest lower bound (*math.*). — *v.t.* to form into open work: to furnish with a lattice. — **latt'ice-bridge** a bridge of lattice-girders; **latt'ice-gird'er** a girder composed of upper and lower members joined by a web of crossing diagonal bars; **latt'ice-leaf** the lace-leaf or ouvirandra (*Aponogeton fenestrale*), a water-plant of Madagascar with leaves like open lattice-work. — **red lattice** (*Shak.*) the sign of an ale-house. [Fr. *lattis* — *latte*, a lath.]

latticinio *la-ti-chē'ni-ō, n.* a type of Venetian glassware containing decorative threads of milk-white glass: a piece of such glassware: the white glass itself: — *pl.* **-ni** (*-nē*). — Also *adj.* — Also **lattici'no:** — *pl.* **-ni.** [It., — L. *lacticinium*, food made with milk — *lac, lactis,* milk.]

latus rectum *lā'təs rek'təm, la'tōos rek'tōom,* a focal chord parallel to the directrix of a conic. [L. *lātus rectum,* right or perpendicular side.]

Latvian *lat'vi-ən, adj.* Lettish. — *n.* a native or citizen of Latvia or Lettland. [Lettish *Latvija,* Latvia, Lettland.]

lauch *löhh,* a Scots form of **law**[2] (*Scott*) and of **laugh,** *n.* and *vb.:* — *pa.t.* **leuch, leugh** (*lūhh*); *pa.p.* **leuch'en, leugh'en.**

laud *löd, v.t.* to praise: to celebrate. — *n.* praise: (in *pl.*) in the R.C. Church, the prayers immediately following matins. — *adj.* **laud'able** praiseworthy. — *n.* **laud'-ableness.** — *adv.* **laud'ably.** — *n.* **laudā'tion** praise: honour paid. — *adjs.* **laud'ative, laud'atory** containing praise: expressing praise. — *ns.* (*obs.*) eulogy. — *n.* **laud'er.** [L. *laudāre* — *laus, laudis,* praise.]

laudanum *löd'(ə-)nəm, n.* tincture of opium. [Coined by Paracelsus; perh. **ladanum,** transferred to a different drug.]

lauf *lowf, n.* a run in a bobsleigh contest. [Ger.]

laugh *läf, v.i.* to emit explosive inarticulate sounds of the voice, generally, with a smile, heaving of the sides, and other bodily movements, under the influence of amusement, joy, scorn, etc., or of bodily stimulus as tickling: to be amused, make merry about (with *at*): to make fun of (with *at*): to flout (with *at*): to have a cheerful appearance (*fig.*). — *v.t.* to render, put, or drive with laughter: to express by laughter: to laugh at, deride (*Spens.*). — *n.* an act or sound of laughing. — *adj.* **laugh'able** ludicrous. — *n.* **laugh'ableness.** — *adv.* **laugh'ably.** — *n.* **laugh'er** one who laughs: a breed of pigeon with laughing note. — *adj.* **laugh'ful** mirthful. — *n., adj.* **laugh'ing.** — *adv.* **laugh'ingly.** — *adj.* **laugh'-some** inclined to laugh: provocative of laughter. — *n.* **laugh'ter** the act or sound of laughing. — *adj.* **laugh'y** inclined to laugh. — **laugh'ing-gas** nitrous oxide, which may excite laughter when breathed, used as an anaesthetic, esp. in dentistry; **laughing hyena** the spotted hyena (*Crocuta crocuta*); **laughing jackass** the kookaburra; **laugh'ing-stock** an object of ridicule. — *adj.*

laugh'worthy deserving to be laughed at. — **be laughing** (*coll.*) to have no (further) problems, worries, etc.: to be in a favourable or advantageous position; **don't make me laugh** (*coll.*) an expression of scornful disbelief; **have the last laugh** to triumph finally after one or more setbacks or defeats: to have one's actions, etc. finally vindicated after being scorned; **have the laugh of** to best; **laugh and lie** (or **lay**) **down** an old card-game in which a player lays down his hand on attaining his object; **laugh in, up, one's sleeve** to laugh inwardly; **laugh in someone's face** to scorn or mock a person openly; **laugh off** to treat (injuries, etc.) as of no importance; **laugh on the wrong side of one's mouth, on the other side of one's face** to be made to feel disappointment or sorrow, esp. after boasting, etc.; **laugh someone out of court** to prevent someone getting a hearing by ridicule; **laugh to scorn** to deride or jeer at; **no laughing matter** a very serious matter. [O.E. (Anglian) *hlæhhan* (W.S. *hliehhan*); Ger. *lachen,* Goth. *hlahjan.*]

launce[1] *löns, läns* (*Spens.*). Same as **lance**[1].

launce[2] *löns, läns,* (*Spens.*) *n.* a balance. [L. *lanx, lancis,* a plate, a scale of a balance.]

launce[3], **lance** *löns, läns, n.* a sand eel (*Ammodytes*), an eel-like fish that buries itself in wet sand at ebb-tide. — Also **lant.** [Perh. conn. with **lance**[1].]

launcegaye *löns'gā, läns'gā.* Same as **lancegay.**

launch[1], **lanch** *lönch, lönsh, länch, länsh, vs.t.* to throw or hurl: to dart: to send forth: to set going: to initiate: to cause or allow to slide into water or to take off from land: to pierce (*Spens.*): to lance (*obs.*): to put (a book or other product) on the market, esp. with attendant publicity, etc.: to throw (oneself) freely, venturesomely, or enthusiastically (into some activity) (with *into*). — *v.i.* to rush, dart, plunge, fling oneself: to be launched: to take off: to throw oneself freely, venturesomely, or enthusiastically (into some activity) (with *out, into*): to begin a usu. long story, speech, etc. (with *into*). — *n.* the act or occasion of launching: a lancing (*Spens.*). — *n.* **launch'er** a device for launching, esp. for sending off a rocket. — **launch'ing-pad** a platform from which a rocket can be launched: a place, event, etc. which gives a good start to a career, etc., or at which a project, campaign, etc. is launched (*fig.*); **launch'ing-site.** — *n.pl.* **launch'ing-ways** the timbers on which a ship is launched. — **launch pad, site** same as **launching-pad, -site; launch vehicle** see **vehicle; launch window** the period of time during which the launching of a spacecraft must take place if the flight is to be successful. [O.Fr. *lanchier, lancier* (Fr. *lancer*); see **lance**[1].]

launch[2] *lönch, lönsh, länch, länsh, n.* the largest boat carried by a man-of-war: a large power-driven boat for pleasure or short runs. [Sp. *lancha,* perh. from Malay *lanchār,* swift.]

laund *lönd,* (*Shak.*) *n.* a glade: a grassy place. [O.Fr. *launde, lande;* prob. Celt.; see **lawn**[2].]

launder *lön'dər, län', n.* a washerwoman or washerman (*obs.*): a trough for conveying water. — *v.t.* to wash and iron clothes, etc.: to handle the transfer of money, goods, etc. or the movement of people in such a way that the identity or illegality of the source, the illegality of the transfer, or the identity or criminality of the people remains undetected (*coll.*). — *v.i.* to wash and iron clothes, etc.: to admit of laundering. — *ns.* **laun'derer; laun'dress** a woman who washes and irons clothes; **laun'dry** a place where clothes, etc. are washed and dressed: clothes, etc. for or from the laundry, a wash. — **laundry list** a list of items to be laundered: a list of items or matters to be achieved, produced, dealt with, prevented, etc. (*fig.*); **laun'dry-maid; laun'dry= man** a male worker in a laundry: one who runs a laundry: a man who collects and delivers laundry; **laun'dry-woman.** [M.E. *lavander* — O.Fr. *lavandier* — L. *lavandārius,* from the ger. of *lavāre,* to wash.]

launderette *lön-dər-et', **laundrette** -dret', n.* a shop where customers wash clothes in washing-machines. [Orig. trademark.]

Laundromat® *lön'drō-mat, n.* a launderette.

laura *lö'rə,* **lavra** *läv'rə, ns.* a group of recluses' cells. [Gr. *laurā* (mod. *labra,* with *b* as *v*), alley, lane, monastery.]

lauraceous. See under **Laurus.**

Laurasia *lör-ā'sh*(*y*)*ə, -zh*(*y*)*ə, n.* the ancient landmass thought to have existed in the northern hemisphere, and which subsequently split up to form N. America, Greenland, Europe and northern Asia. — *adj.* **Laurā'-sian.** [*Laurentia,* the ancient N. American landmass — the Laurentian strata of the Canadian Shield, and Eur*asia.*]

laurdalite, lardalite *lör', lär'dəl-īt, ns.* a coarse nepheline syenite. [*Laurdal* or *Lardal* in Norway.]

laureate *lö'ri-it, adj.* crowned with laurel. — *n.* one crowned with laurel: a poet laureate. — *v.t.* (*-āt*) to crown with laurel, in token of literary merit: to confer a degree upon. — *ns.* **lau'reateship; laureā'tion** crowning with laurel: graduation. — **poet laureate** (also with *caps.*) formerly one who received a degree in grammar (i.e. poetry and rhetoric) at the English universities: a poet bearing that title in the royal household or in a society: — *pl.* **poet laureates, poets laureate.** [L. *laureātus,* laurelled — *laurus,* laurel.]

laurel *lor'əl, n.* the sweet bay tree (*Laurus nobilis*), used by the ancients for making honorary wreaths: another species of Laurus found in Madeira and the Canaries: the cherry-laurel: in America any species of Rhododendron or of Kalmia: extended to various trees and shrubs of similar appearance: a crown of laurel: honours gained (often in *pl.*). — *adjs.* **lau'rel; lau'relled** crowned, adorned or covered with laurel. — **lau'rel=wa'ter** a sedative and narcotic water distilled from cherry-laurel leaves; **lauric acid** (*lör'ik*) an acid, $CH_3 \cdot (CH_2)_{10} \cdot COOH$, occurring in the berries of *Laurus nobilis,* etc.; **lauryl alcohol** (*lor'il* or *lör'*) a liquid made by the reduction of coconut oil or its fatty acids, used in the manufacture of detergents; **lauryl thiocyanate** a salt of lauryl alcohol used as a disinfectant. — **cherry=laurel, Japan laurel, spurge-laurel** see under **cherry, Japan, spurge.** — **look to one's laurels** to be careful lest one loses one's pre-eminent position; **rest on one's laurels** (sometimes said as a criticism) to be content with one's past successes and the honour they bring, without attempting any further achievements. [Fr. *laurier* — L. *laurus.*]

Laurentian *lö-ren'sh*(*y*)*ən, adj.* pertaining to *Lorenzo* or *Laurentius* de' Medici, or to the library founded by him at Florence: of or pertaining to the river St *Lawrence:* applied to a series of Pre-Cambrian rocks covering a large area in the region of the Upper Lakes of North America.

lauric. See under **laurel.**

Laurus *lö'rəs,* in the laurel genus, giving name to the family **Laurā'ceae,** leathery-leaved archichlamydeous dicotyledons. — *adj.* **laurā'ceous.** [L.]

laurustine, laurustinus *lö'rəs-tīn, -tī'nəs, ns.* a winter-flowering shrub (*Viburnum tinus*). [L. *laurus,* laurel, *tīnus,* laurustine.]

laurvikite, larvikite *lör', lär'vik-īt, ns.* a soda syenite composed mainly of feldspar with schiller structure. [*Laurvik* or *Larvik* in Norway.]

lauryl. See under **laurel.**

laus Deo *lös dē'ō, lows dā'ō,* (L.) praise to God.

lauwine *lö'win,* (Byron) *n.* an avalanche. [Ger. *La(u)wine,* perh. — *lau,* tepid.]

lav *lav,* (coll.) *n.* short for **lavatory.**

lava *lä'və, n.* matter discharged in a molten stream from a volcano or fissure, whether still molten or subsequently solidified: — *pl.* **la'vas.** — *adj.* **la'vaform** in the form of lava. [It., poss. — L. *lavāre,* to wash, or from L. *lābes,* a falling down — *lābī,* to slide, fall.]

lavabo, lavage, lavatory, etc. See **lave**[1].

lava-lava *lä'və-lä'və, n.* a rectangular piece of printed cloth worn by both sexes in Polynesia as a kind of skirt. [Samoan, clothing.]

lavallière, lavaliere *la-va-lyer', lav'ə-lēr, n.* a loosely-tied bow: a jewelled pendant worn round the neck on a chain. [After the Duchesse de *la Vallière* (1644–1710).]

lavatera *la-və-tē'rə, lə-vä'tə-rə, n.* a genus of herbs and shrubs (fam. Malvaceae) with large pink, white, or purple mallow-like flowers: (without *cap.*) a plant of the genus. [The brothers *Lavater,* 17th- and 18th-century Swiss physicians and naturalists.]

lave[1] *lāv, v.t.* and *v.i.* to wash: to bathe. — *ns.* **lavabo** (*lav-ā'bō*) in the mass, the ritual act of washing the celebrant's fingers while he says *Lavabo inter innocentes:* a monastic lavatory: a fixed basin or wash-stand: — *pl.* **lavā'bos, -boes; lavage** (*lav'ij, läv-äzh'; med.*) irrigation or washing out; **lavation** (*lav-ā'shən*) washing; **lav'atory** a place, room, fixture, or vessel for washing: a laundry: a bowl, usu. with a wooden or plastic seat and flushed by water, used for urination and defecation: a room containing a lavatory and often a wash-basin: a ritual washing: a lotion (*obs.*). — *adj.* **lavator'ial.** — *ns.* **lavement** (*lāv'*) a washing: a lavage; **lāv'er** a large vessel for washing, esp. ritual washing: the basin of a fountain (*Spens.*): an ablution (*Milt.*). — **lavatory paper** toilet-paper. [L. *lavāre, -ātum;* Gr. *louein,* to wash.]

lave[2] *lāv,* (Scot.) *n.* remainder. [O.E. *lāf;* O.N. *leif;* see **leave**[2].]

lave[3] *lāv, v.t.* to pour out: to bale. [O.E. *lafian,* to pour; fused with L. *lavāre,* to wash.]

laveer *lä-vēr',* (arch.) *v.i.* to beat to windward. [Du. *laveeren;* cf. **luff.**]

lavender *lav'ən-dər, n.* a labiate plant (*Lavandula vera*) with fragrant pale-lilac flowers, yielding a volatile oil: sprigs of it used for perfuming and preserving linen, etc.: the colour of its blossoms. — *adj.* of the colour of lavender flowers. — *v.t.* to sprinkle with lavender. — **lav'ender-cott'on** a species of Santolina; **lav'ender=wa'ter** a perfume composed of spirits of wine, essential oil of lavender, and ambergris. — **lay in lavender** to lay by carefully, with sprigs of lavender: to pawn (*coll.*); **oil of lavender** an aromatic oil distilled from lavender flowers and stems, used as a stimulant and tonic. [A.Fr. *lavendre* (Fr. *lavande*) — L.L. *lavendula,* earlier *livendula,* perh. conn. with *līvidus,* livid.]

laver[1]. See **lave**[1].

laver[2] *lāv'ər, n.* edible seaweed of various kinds, esp. Porphyra (*purple laver*) and Ulva (*green laver*). — **laver bread, laverbread** (*lā'vər* or *lä'vər bred*) a name for a food popular in Wales, the fronds of Porphyra boiled, dipped in oatmeal and fried. [L. *laver,* a kind of water-plant.]

laverock *lav'ə-rək,* Scot. *lāv'*(*ə-*)*rək,* an archaic and dialectal form of **lark**[1].

lavish *lav'ish, n.* (*obs.*) profusion: over-abundance: extravagant outpouring. — *v.t.* to expend or bestow profusely: to waste. — *adj.* bestowing profusely: prodigal: extravagant: unrestrained. — *adv.* **lav'ishly.** — *ns.* **lav'ishment; lav'ishness.** [O.Fr. *lavasse, lavache,* deluge of rain — *laver* — L. *lavāre,* to wash.]

lavolt *la-volt',* **lavolta** *-ə,* (*Shak.*) *ns.* an old dance in which there was much turning and high leaping. — *v.i.* to dance the lavolta. [It. *la volta,* the turn.]

lavra. See **laura.**

law[1] *lö, n.* a rule of action established by authority: a statute: the rules of a community or state: jurisprudence: established usage: that which is lawful: the whole body of persons connected professionally with the law: litigation: a rule or code in any department of action, as morality, art, honour, arms (including heraldry), a game: a theoretical principle educed from practice or observation: a statement or formula expressing the constant order of certain phenomena: the Mosaic code or the books containing it (*theol.*): a start (*sport*): indulgence (*obs.*). — *v.t.* to go to law with: to determine (*Burns*): to expedite (*obs.*). — *v.i.* (*obs.*) to go to law. — *adj.* **law'ful** allowed by law: rightful. — *adv.* **law'fully.** — *ns.* **law'fulness; law'ing** going to law (*arch.*): expeditation (*obs.*). — *adj.* **law'less** not subject to or controlled by law: unruly. — *adv.* **law'lessly.** — *ns.* **law'lessness; law'yer** a practitioner in the law, esp. a solicitor: one learned or skilled in law: an interpreter of the Mosaic law (*N.T.*): a brier, bramble, or other tenacious trailing or climbing plant (see also **Penang-lawyer**). — *adj.* **law'yerly.** — *adj.* **law'-abiding** obedient to the law. — **law'-agent** (*Scots law*) a solicitor; **law'-book** a book treating of law or law cases; **law'-breaker** one who violates a law; **law'-burrows** (*Scots law*) a writ requiring a person to give security against doing violence to another; **law'-calf** a book-binding in smooth, pale-brown calf; **law centre** an office, usu. in a socially deprived area, where free legal advice and assistance are given (also **neighbourhood law centre**); **law'-court** a court of justice; **law'-day** a day of open court; **lawful day** one on which business may be legally done — not a Sunday or a public holiday; **law'-giver** one who enacts or imposes laws. — *adj.* **law'-giving.** — **law Latin** Latin as used in law and legal documents, being a mixture of Latin with Old French and Latinised English words; **law'-list** an annual book of information about lawyers, courts, etc.; **Law Lord** a peer in parliament who holds or has held high legal office: in Scotland, a judge of the Court of Session; **law'-maker** a legislator; **law'-man** one of a select body with magisterial powers in some of the Danish towns of early England: (**law'man**) a sheriff or policeman (*U.S.*; now *arch.* or *facet.* exc. Texas); **law'-mer'chant** the customs that have grown up among merchants in reference to mercantile documents and business; **law'-monger** a low pettifogging lawyer; **law'-officer** a legal functionary and adviser of the government, esp. Attorney-General, Solicitor-General, or Lord Advocate; **law'-stā'tioner** one who sells parchment and other articles needed by lawyers; **law'suit** a suit or process in law; **law'-writer** a writer on law: a copier or engrosser of legal papers. — **be a law unto oneself, itself** to act in a way that does not follow established rules or conventions; **Bode's law** (*astron.*) a rule popularised by Johann *Bode* (1747–1826, German astronomer) but first announced by Johann Titius (1729–96), which states that the distances of the planets from the sun in astronomical units is found by adding 4 to the series 0, 3, 6, 12, 24, . . . and dividing the number so obtained by 10; **Boyle's,** or **Mariotte's, law** the law that, for a gas at a given temperature, pressure varies inversely as volume — announced by Robert *Boyle* in 1662, and confirmed by Mariotte (1620–84, French physicist); **Charles's law** the law that all gases have the same value for the coefficient of expansion at constant pressure, stated by J. A. C. *Charles* (Fr. physicist, 1746–1823) — also called **Gay-Lussac's law** after J. L. Gay-Lussac (1778–1850, French chemist and physicist); **go to law with** to resort to litigation against; **Gresham's law** the law, formulated by Sir Thomas *Gresham* (1519–79), that of two forms of currency the inferior or more depreciated tends to drive the other from circulation, owing to the hoarding and exportation of the better form; **Grimm's law** the law formulating certain changes undergone by Indo-European stopped consonants in Germanic, stated by Jacob *Grimm* (1785–1863); **have the law of, have the law on** (*coll.*) to enforce the law against; **Kepler's laws** three laws of planetary motion discovered by Johann *Kepler* (1571–1630) — (1) the orbits of the planets are ellipses with the sun at one focus; (2) the areas described by their *radii vectores* in equal times are equal; (3) the squares of their periodic times vary as the cubes of their mean distances from the sun; **law of averages** see **average; law of nations,** now **international law,** originally applied to those ethical principles regarded as obligatory on all communities; **law of nature** the invariable order of nature: natural law; **law of octaves** see **octave; law of the jungle** the rules for surviving, succeeding, etc. in a competitive or hostile situation by the use of force, etc.; **law of the land** the established law of a country; **laws of motion** see **motion; law of the Medes and Persians** see **Median; lay down the law** to state authoritatively or dictatorially; **Murphy's law** (*facet.*) the law which states that if anything can go wrong, it will; **Parkinson's law** see separate entry; **Sod's law** see **sod³; Snell's law** the law of refraction discovered by Willebrod *Snell* (1591-1626), a Dutch mathematician, which states that the sine of the angle of incidence divided by the sine of the angle of refraction is a constant, known as the refractive index; **take the law into one's own hands** to obtain justice, or what one considers to be justice, by one's own actions, without recourse to the law, the police, etc.; **the law** (*coll.*) the police: a policeman; **Verner's law** a law stated by Karl *Verner* in 1875, showing the effect of accent in the shifting of Indo-European stopped consonants and *s* in Germanic, and explaining the most important anomalies in the application of Grimm's law. [M.E. *lawe* — late O.E. *lagu*, of O.N. origin, from the same root as **lie², lay.**]

law² *lö,* (*obs.*) *n.* score, share of expense. — *n.* **law'ing** (*Scot.*) a tavern reckoning. [O.N. *lag*, market-price.]

law³ *lö,* (*Scot.*) *n.* a hill, esp. rounded or conical. [Northern form of **low³,** O.E. *hlāw.*]

law⁴ *lö,* (*Scot.*) *adj.* low. — *n.* and *adj.* **law'land** lowland. [Northern form of **low².**]

law⁵ *lö, interj.* expressing asseveration (*obs.*): expressing surprise (*dial.*).   [Partly for **la** or **lo,** partly **lord** (q.v.).]

lawk *lök,* **lawks** *löks,* (*dial.*) *interjs.* implying surprise. [**lord** or **lack².**]

lawn¹ *lön, n.* a sort of fine linen or cambric: extended to some cottons. — *adj.* made of lawn. — *adj.* **lawn'y.** — **lawn sleeves** wide sleeves of lawn worn by Anglican bishops.   [Prob. from *Laon,* near Rheims.]

lawn² *lön, n.* an open space between woods (*arch.*): a smooth space of ground covered with grass, generally beside a house. — *adj.* **lawn'y.** — **lawn'-mower** a machine for cutting grass on a lawn; **lawn'-par'ty** (*U.S.*) a garden-party; **lawn'-sprink'ler** a machine for watering a lawn by sprinkling; **lawn tennis** a game derived from tennis, played by one or two a side on an unwalled court (hard or of turf), the aim being to hit the ball over the net and within the court, if possible so as to prevent his return.   [**laund.**]

lawrencium *lö-ren'si-əm, n.* the name given to element 103 (symbol Lr) first produced at Berkeley, California. [Ernest O. *Lawrence* (1901–58), scientist.]

lax¹ *laks, adj.* slack: loose: soft, flabby: not strict in discipline or morals: loose in the bowels. — *adj.* **lax'ative** having the power of loosening the bowels: giving freedom (*arch.*): speaking, expressing itself, freely (*obs.*). — *n.* a purgative or aperient medicine. — *ns.* **lax'ativeness; laxā'tor** a muscle that relaxes an organ or part; **lax'ism** the view that in morals an opinion only slightly probable may be safely followed; **lax'ist** one holding loose notions of moral laws, or of their application; **lax'ity, lax'ness.** — *adv.* **lax'ly.**   [L. *laxus,* loose.]

lax² *laks, n.* a salmon (usu. one caught in Swedish or Norwegian waters).   [Revived use — O.E. *leax;* O.H.G. *lahs,* O.N. *lax;* cf. **lox².**]

lay¹ *lā, n.* a form of **lea¹,²,³.**

lay² *lā, pa.t.* of **lie².**

lay³ *lā, v.t.* to cause to lie: to place or set down: to beat down: to deliver of a child (*obs.*): to spread on a surface: to spread something on: to cover: to apply: to cause to subside: to exorcise: to put below the horizon by sailing away: to deposit: to set on the table: to wager: to put forward: to cause to be: to set: to produce and deposit: to station: to locate: to set in position: to waylay: to beset (*Shak.*): to impose: to attribute, impute: to set material in position for making: to form by setting in position and twisting (as a rope): to design, plan: to layer (*hort.*): to cause (a hedge) to grow more thickly by pressing some of the growth to the ground: to have sexual intercourse with (*slang*). — *v.i.* to produce eggs: to wager, bet: to deal blows: to lie (*arch.*, *naut.*, and *illit.*): — *pr.p.* **lay'ing;** *pa.t.* and *pa.p.* **laid.** — *n.* a situation, a lying-place: an oyster-bed: a mode of lying: a disposition, arrangement or plan: a layer: a mode of twisting: laying activity: a bet (*Shak.*): a share of profit, esp. in whaling: a field or method of operation, esp. in thieving (*slang*): an act of sexual intercourse (*slang*): a partner, usually female, in sexual intercourse (*slang*). — *n.* **layer** (*lā'ər, lār*) one who or that which lays — e.g. a hen, a bricklayer: (*lār*) a course, bed, or stratum: a distinctively coloured space between contour-lines on a map: a shoot bent down to earth in order to take root. — *v.t.* and *v.i.* to propagate by layers. — *v.t.* to put in layers. — *v.i.* to be laid flat, lodge. — *adj.* **lay'ered** in or with layers. — *ns.* **lay'ering; lay'ing** the first coat of plaster: the act or time of laying eggs: the eggs laid. — **lay'about** a lounger, loafer; **lay'away** goods on which a deposit has been paid, kept for a customer until he completes payment (as *vb.* **lay away**); **lay'back** a method of climbing a sharp-edged crack in a horizontal position. — Also *v.i.* — **lay'-by** an expansion of a roadway to allow vehicles to draw up out of the stream of traffic: — *pl.* **lay'-bys:** a deposit against future purchase (also **lay'-bye;** *S.Afr.*); **lay'-down** in card games, esp. bridge, a hand which cannot fail to take the number of tricks required to win, and which therefore is sometimes exposed to view without any play taking place: the contract made by the holder of such a hand. — Also *adj.* — **lay'er-cake** a cake built up in layers; **lay'-off** the act of laying off or period of time during which someone lays off or is laid off; **lay'-out** that which is laid out: a display: an outfit: the disposition, arrangement, plan, esp. of buildings or ground: the general appearance of a printed page: a set, unit, organisation; **lay'-shaft** an auxiliary geared shaft in a machine, esp. the secondary shaft in an automobile gear-box; **lay'stall** a place for depositing dung, rubbish, etc.; **lay'-up** the time or condition of being laid up. — **lay aboard** to run alongside, esp. in order to board; **lay about one** to deal blows vigorously or on all sides; **lay a course** to succeed in sailing to the place required without tacking; **lay aside, away** to discard: to put apart for future use (see also **layaway** above); **lay at** to endeavour to strike; **lay away** (*Scot.*, etc.) to lay eggs in out-of-the-way places; **lay bare** to make bare, disclose; **lay before** to submit to, as of plans; **lay by** to keep for future use: to dismiss: to put off; **lay by the heels** see **heel; lay down** to give up: to deposit, as a pledge: to apply, as embroidery (*arch.*): to formulate: to assert (law, rule): to store: to plant: to record: to lay on (*print.*); **lay hands on** see **hand; lay heads together** to confer together; **lay hold of,** or **on,** to seize; **lay in** to get in a supply of; **lay into** to beat thoroughly; **lay it on** to charge exorbitantly: to do anything, as to exaggerate, or to flatter, with profuseness; **lay off** to mark off: to doff: to harangue volubly: to hedge (*betting*): to discontinue work or activity: to dismiss temporarily: to cease (*coll.*); **lay on** to install a supply of: to provide: to deal blows with vigour: to arrange made-up pages in the correct order on the imposing surface (also **lay down**) (*print.*); **lay on hands** see **hand; lay oneself open to** to make oneself vulnerable to, or open to (criticism, etc.); **lay oneself out to** to make it one's professed object or practice, take great pains, to; **lay on load** (*Spens.*) to belabour; **lay on the table** see **table; lay open** to make bare, to show, expose: to cut open; **lay out** to display: to expend: to plan: to dispose according to a plan: to prepare for burial: to fell: to take measures, seek; **lay siege to** to besiege: to importune; **lay the table** to put dishes, etc. on the table in preparation for a meal; **lay to** to apply with vigour: to bring a ship to rest; **lay to heart** see **heart; lay under** to subject to; **lay up** to store up, preserve: (usu. in *pass.*) to confine to bed or one's room: to put in dock for cleaning, repairs, etc. or because no longer wanted for or fit for service; **lay upon** to wager upon; **lay wait** to

lie in wait, or in ambush; **lay waste** to devastate; **on a lay** on shares instead of wages.   [O.E. *lecgan*, to lay, causative of *licgan*, to lie; cf. O.N. *leggja*, Ger. *legen*.]

lay⁴ *lā, n.* a short narrative poem: a lyric: a song.   [O.Fr. *lai*; origin obscure.]

lay⁵ *lā* (*arch.*) *n.* law: religious faith.   [O.Fr. *lei* (Fr. *loi*) — L. *lēx, lēgis,* law.]

lay⁶ *lā, adj.* pertaining to the people: not clerical: non-professional: not trumps (*cards*). — *n.* the laity: a layman (*obs.*). — *adj.* **laic** (*lā'ik*) lay. — *n.* a layman. — *adj.* **lā'ical.** — *n.* **lāicisā'tion, -z-.** — *v.t.* **laicise, -ize** (*lā'i-sīz*) to make laical: to open to the laity. — *ns.* **lāic'ity** the state of being lay: the nature of the laity; **lā'ity** the people as distinguished from some particular profession, usu. the clerical. — **lay baptism** baptism administered by a layman; **lay brother, sister** one under vows of celibacy and obedience, who serves a religious house, but is exempt from the studies and choir duties of monks or nuns; **lay communion** the state of being in the communion of the church as a layman; **lay impropriator** an impropriator who is a layman; **lay'man** one of the laity: a non-professional man: one not an expert; **lay'person; lay reader** in the Anglican Church, a layman authorised to read part of the service; **lay sister** see **lay brother; lay vicar** a layman who is vicar-choral in an Anglican cathedral.   [O.Fr. *lai* — L. *lāicus* — Gr. *lāikos* — *lāos,* the people.]

lay-day *lā'dā, n.* one of a number of days allowed for loading and unloading of cargo. — **lay'time** the total time allowed.   [Perh. **delay** and **day, time.**]

layer. See **lay³.**

layette *lā-et', n.* a baby's complete outfit.   [Fr.]

lay-figure *lā'-fig'ər, n.* a jointed model used by painters: a living person or a fictitious character wanting in individuality. — Also (earlier) **lay'man.**   [Du. *leeman* — *led* (now *lid*), joint, *man,* man.]

laylock *lā'lək, n.* an obsolete form of **lilac.**

lazar *laz'ər, n.* one afflicted with a loathsome and pestilential disease like *Lazarus,* the beggar (Luke xvi. 20). — *n.* **Laz'arist** a member of the Roman Catholic Congregation of the Priests of the Mission, founded by St Vincent de Paul in 1624. — *adj.* or *adv.* **la'zar-like.** — **lazar house** a lazaretto.

lazaretto *laz-ə-ret'ō, n.* a hospital for infectious diseases, esp. leprosy: a place of quarantine: a place for keeping stores on a ship: — *pl.* **lazarett'os.** — Also **laz'aret.**   [It. *lazzaretto.*]

lazuli *laz'ū-lī.* See **lapis lazuli.**

lazulite *laz'ū-līt, n.* a blue mineral, hydrated phosphate of aluminium, magnesium, and iron.   [L.L. *lazulum* — Pers. *lājward;* cf. **azure, lapis lazuli, lazurite.**]

lazurite *laz'ū-rīt, n.* a blue cubic mineral, sodium aluminium silicate with some sulphur, a constituent of lapis lazuli.   [L.L. *lazur* — Pers. *lājward;* cf. **azure, lapis lazuli, lazulite.**]

lazy *lā'zi, adj.* disinclined to exertion: averse to labour: sluggish. — *v.i.* **laze** to be idle (back-formation). — *adv.* **la'zily.** — *n.* **la'ziness.** — **la'zy-bed** a bed for growing potatoes, the seed being laid on the surface and covered with earth dug out of trenches along both sides; **la'zy-bones** (*coll.*) a lazy person, an idler; **lazy eye** an apparently healthy eye having, nevertheless, impaired vision: amblyopia; **la'zy-jack** a jack constructed of compound levers pivoted together; **lazy Susan** a revolving tray with a number of separate dishes or sections for foods, intended to be placed on a dining-table, etc. — *n.pl.* **la'zy-tongs** a series of diagonal levers pivoted together at the middle and ends, capable of being extended by a movement of the scissors-like handles so as to pick up objects at a distance. — *adj.* constructed on the model of lazy-tongs.   [Origin unknown.]

lazzarone *läd-zä-rō'nā,* or *laz-ə-rō'ni, n.* a Neapolitan beggar: — *pl.* **lazzaro'ni** (*-nē*).   [It.]

lazzo *läd'dzō,* (It.) *n.* a piece of farce, or comic dialogue, in the commedia dell'arte: — *pl.* **laz'zi** (*-ē*).

lea¹ *lē, n.* open country — meadow, pasture, or arable. — Also **lay, lee, ley** (*lā, lē*). [O.E. *lēah*; dial. Ger. *lohe, loh*; perh. Flem. *-loo* in place names, as Water*loo*; confused with **lease⁴**.]

lea² *lē, adj.* and *n.* fallow: arable land under grass or pasture. — Also **lay** (*lā*), **ley** (*lē, lā*). — **lea'-rig** an unploughed rig or grass field; **ley'-farm'ing** pasturing and cropping in alternating periods. [O.E. *lǣge*, found in *lǣghrycg*, lea-rig.]

lea³ *lē,* **lay, ley** *lā, ns.* a measure of yarn — 80 yards of worsted, 120 of cotton, 300 of linen. [Perh. conn. with Fr. *lier* — L. *ligāre*, to bind.]

leach¹ *lēch, v.t.* to allow (a liquid) to percolate through something: to subject (something) to percolation so as to separate soluble constituent(s): to drain away by percolation. — *v.i.* to percolate through or out of: to pass out of by the action of a percolating liquid: to lose soluble elements by the action of a percolating liquid. — Also **letch**. — *ns.* **leach'ate** a liquid that has percolated through or out of some substance: a solution got by leaching; **leach'ing**. — *adj.* **leach'y** liable to be leached. — **leach'-trough, -tub** a trough or tub in which ashes are leached. — **bacterial leaching** the use of selected strains of bacteria to accelerate the acid leach of sulphide minerals. [O.E. *leccan*, to water, irrigate, moisten.]

leach², leachour. Spens. for **leech², lecher.**

lead¹ *lēd, v.t.* to show the way by going first: to precede: to guide by the hand: to direct: to guide: to conduct: to convey: to cart (*dial.*): to induce: to live: to cause to live or experience: to adduce (*Scots law*): to have a principal or guiding part or place in: to play as the first card of a round (*cards*). — *v.i.* to be first or among the first: to be guide or chief: to act first: to cart crops to the farmyard (often with *in*): to afford a passage (to), or (*fig.*) tend towards: of a newspaper, etc., to have as its main story, feature, etc. (with *with*): — *pa.t.* and *pa.p.* **led**. — *n.* first place: precedence: the amount by which one is ahead: direction: guidance: an indication: a precedent or example: a chief rôle: the player of a chief rôle: leadership: initiative: the act or right of playing first, or the play of him who plays first: the first player of a side (*curling*, etc.): a leash: a watercourse leading to a mill: a channel among ice: the course of a running rope from end to end: a main conductor in electrical distribution. — *adj.* chief: main: leading. — *ns.* **lead'er** one who leads or goes first: a chief: the principal first violin: the head of a party, expedition, etc.: the leading editorial article in a newspaper (also **leading article**): the principal upward-growing shoot of a tree: a horse in a front place in a team: a tendon: a translucent connection between a fishing-line and bait: a line of dots to guide the eye (*print.*): the principal wheel in any machinery: an alternative name for conductor (of orchestra, etc.) (*U.S.*); **leaderette'** a brief newspaper leader; **lead'ership** the office of leader or conductor: those acting as leaders of a particular organisation or group: ability to lead; **lead'ing** guidance: spiritual guidance: leadership: carting (crops, etc.). — *adj.* acting as leader: directing, controlling: principal: preceding. — **lead'er=ca'ble** a cable on the sea-bottom by which ships with induction-receiving apparatus can find their way into port; **lead'-in'** the part of the groove on a record before the start of the recording (also **lead-in groove**; opp. to *lead-out*): the cable connecting the transmitter or receiver to the elevated part of an aerial: the introduction to, or introductory passage of, a commercial, discussion, newspaper article, piece of music, etc. — Also *adj.* — **leading aircraft(s)man, -woman** the rank above aircraft(s)man, -woman; **leading business** the acting of the principal parts or rôles in plays (by the **leading lady** and the **leading man**); **leading case** (*law*) a case serving as a precedent; **leading counsel** counsel who takes precedence of another in conducting a case; **leading edge** the edge first met: the foremost edge of an aerofoil or propeller blade: rising amplitude portion

of a pulse signal (*telecomm.*); **leading lady, man** see **leading business; leading light** a very influential member; **leading note** the seventh tone of a major or minor scale, which leads the hearer to expect the tonic to follow; **leading question** a question so put as to suggest the desired answer; **lead'ing-strings** strings used to lead children beginning to walk: vexatious care or custody; **lead'-out** the part of the groove on a record after the recording has finished (also **lead-out groove**; opp. to **lead-in**): a wire by which electric current can enter or leave an electronic instrument. — Also *adj.* — **lead time** (orig. *U.S.*) the time between the conception or design of a product, factory, alteration, etc. and its production, completion, implementation, etc. — **lead apes in hell** see **ape**; **lead astray** to draw into a wrong course: to seduce from right conduct; **lead by the nose** to make one follow submissively; **Leader of the House of Commons, Lords,** a senior member of the government in whom rests the primary authority for initiating the business of the House; **lead in** (*Scot.*) to house the harvest; **lead in prayer** to offer up prayer in an assembly, uniting the prayers of others; **lead off** to begin or take the start in anything; **lead on** to persuade to go on, to draw on: to persuade to a foolish course: to hoax in jest; **lead out** to conduct to execution or a dance: to proceed to play out (*cards*); **leads and lags** (*commerce*) in international trade, the early payment of bills, dividends, etc. to concerns abroad, the delayed invoicing of foreign customers and delayed conversion of foreign currencies into sterling (in order to take advantage of expected changes in the rate of exchange), which have an effect on the balance of payments situation; **lead someone a dance** see **dance**; **lead the way** to go first and guide others; **lead up to** to bring about by degrees, to prepare for by steps or stages: to play in challenge to, or with a view to weakness in (*cards*). [O.E. *lǣdan*, to lead, *lād*, a way; Ger. *leiten*, to lead.]

lead² *led, n.* a heavy soft bluish-grey metal (symbol Pb; at. numb. 82): a plummet for sounding: a thin plate of lead separating lines of type: a pan or cauldron of lead, or of a kind once made of lead: a leaden frame for a window-pane: extended to blacklead: the core of coloured material in a coloured pencil: a stick of blacklead for a pencil: (*pl.*) sheets of lead for covering roofs, or a flat roof so covered. — *adj.* made of lead. — *v.t.* to cover, weight, or fit with lead: to separate the lines of with leads (*print.*). — *adjs.* **lead'ed** fitted or weighted with or set in lead: separated by leads (*print.*); **lead'en** made of lead: lead-coloured: inert: depressing: heavy: dull. — *v.t.* and *v.i.* to make or become leaden. — *adv.* **lead'enly.** — *n.* **lead'enness.** — *adjs.* **lead'less; lead'y** like lead. — **lead'-arm'ing** tallow, etc., placed in the hollow of a sounding-lead to ascertain the nature of the bottom; **lead colic** see **lead poisoning** below. — *adj.* **lead'en-stepp'ing** (*Milt.*) moving slowly. — **lead'-glance'** galena; **lead'-line** a sounding-line; **lead'-paint'** paint with red lead or white lead as base; **lead'-pencil** a blacklead pencil for writing or drawing; **lead poisoning** plumbism, poisoning by the absorption of lead into the system, its commonest form **lead colic,** or painter's colic: death by shooting (*slang*); **leads'man** a seaman who heaves the lead; **lead tree** tree of lead. — **red lead, white lead** see **red, white; swing the lead** (*naut.* and *mil. slang*) to invent specious excuses to evade duties; **tree of lead** Saturn's tree. [O.E. *lēad*; Ger. *Lot.*]

leaf *lēf, n.* one of the lateral organs developed from the stem or axis of the plant below its growing-point, esp. one of those flat green structures that perform the work of transpiration and carbon-assimilation, but also more generally any homologous structure, as a scale, a petal: the condition of having leaves: leaves collectively: anything beaten thin like a leaf: two pages of a book on opposite sides of the same paper: a broad thin part or structure, hinged, sliding, or inserted at will, as of folding doors, window-shutters, table-tops, drawbridges, etc.: — *pl.* **leaves** (*lēvz*). — *v.t.*, *v.i.* (with *through*) to turn the pages of (a book, etc.). — *v.i.* (also **leave**) to produce leaves: — *pr.p.* **leaf'ing**; *pa.p.* **leafed**. — *adj.* in the form of leaves. — *n.* **leaf'age** foliage. — *adj.* **leafed** (*lēft*) having leaves (also **leaved** *lēvd*). — *ns.* **leaf'ery** leafage; **leaf'iness**. — *adj.* **leaf'less** destitute of leaves. — *n.* **leaf'let** a little leaf: a division of a compound leaf: a single sheet of printed political, religious, advertising, etc. matter, flat or folded, or several sheets folded together. — *v.t.* to distribute leaflets to. — *v.i.* to distribute leaflets. — *pr.p.* **leaf'- leting**, less correctly **leaf'letting**; *pa.t.* and *pa.p.* **leaf'- leted**, less correctly **leaf'letted**. — *n.* **leafleteer'**. — *adj.* **leaf'-like**. — *adjs.* **leaf'y**, **leav'y** covered with or abound- ing in leaves: leaf-like. — **leaf'-base** the base of a leaf-stalk, where it joins the stem; **leaf'-bridge** a draw- bridge with rising leaves swinging on hinges; **leaf'bud** a bud producing a shoot with foliage leaves only (not flowers); **leaf'-climb'er** a plant that climbs by means of its leaves (petioles or tendrils); **leaf'-curl** a plant disease of various kinds characterised by curling of the leaves; **leaf'-cushion** a swollen leaf-base: a pulvinus that serves as a hinge for leaf movements: a raised scar marking the position of a leaf; **leaf'-cutter** an insect (ant or bee) that cuts pieces out of leaves; **leaf'-cutt'ing** a leaf used as a cutting for propagation; **leaf'-fall** the shedding of leaves: the time of the shedding of leaves, usu. autumn: premature fall of leaves; **leaf'-green** chlorophyll; **leaf'-hopper** a name for various hopping orthopterous insects that suck plant juices; **leaf'-in'sect** an orthopterous insect of family Phasmidae with wing-covers like leaves; **leaf'-met'al** metal, especially alloys imitating gold and silver, in very thin leaves, for decoration; **leaf'-mosa'ic** the arrangement of leaves so as to avoid shading one another: a name for various virus diseases of potato, tobacco, etc., in which the leaf is mottled; **leaf'-mould** earth formed from decayed leaves, used as a soil for plants. — *adj.* **leaf'-nosed** having a leaf-like structure on the nose, as certain bats. — **leaf'-roll** a potato disease; **leaf'-scar** a scar left by the fall of a leaf; **leaf'-sheath** a leaf-base more or less completely enveloping the stem; **leaf'-spring** a spring made up of narrow, curved strips of metal of increasing length; **leaf'-stalk** the petiole of a leaf; **leaf'-trace'** a branch from the vascular system of the stem destined to enter a leaf. — **take a leaf out of someone's book** see **book**; **turn over a new leaf** to begin a new and better course of conduct. [O.E. *lēaf*; Ger. *Laub*, Du. *loof*, a leaf.]

league¹ *lēg*, *n.* a nautical measure, 1/20th of a degree, 3 international nautical miles, 3·456 statute miles (5·556 km.): an old measure of length, varying from the Roman league, 1·376 mod. Eng. miles (2·215 km.), to the French, 2·764 miles (4·448 km.), and the Spanish, 4·214 miles (6·781 km.), in general, e.g. in poetry, taken to be about 3 miles (4·828 km.). [L.L. *leuga*, *leuca*, Gallic mile of 1500 Roman paces; poss. Gaulish.]

league² *lēg*, *n.* a bond or alliance: a union for mutual advantage: an association or confederacy: an associ- ation of clubs for games: a class or group. — *v.t.* and *v.i.* to join in league. — *n.* **lea'guer** a member of a league, esp. (with *cap.*) that against the Huguenots in the time of Henry III of France, the Anti-Corn-Law League, or the Irish Land League. — **league match** a match between two clubs in the same league; **league table** a table in which clubs in a league are placed according to their performances, or (*fig.*) any grouping made to reflect relative success, importance, etc. — **in league with** having made an alliance with, usu. for a bad purpose; **in the big league** (*coll.*) among the most important, powerful, etc. people, organisations, etc.; **League of Nations** an international body, under a covenant drawn up in 1919, to secure peace, justice, scrupulous observance of treaties, and international co-operation generally — superseded in 1945 by the United Nations; **not in the same league as** not of the same calibre, ability, importance, etc. as; **top, bottom,**

of the league (*fig.*) highest, lowest, in a particular field of achievement, or in quality. [Fr. *ligue* — L.L. *liga* — L. *ligāre*, to bind.]

leaguer¹ *lēg'ər*, (*arch.*) *n.* a camp, esp. of a besieging army: siege: (by confusion with **ledger**) an ambassador. — *v.t.* to beleaguer. — **lea'guer-la'dy**, **lea'guer-lass'** a female camp-follower. [Du. *leger*, a lair.]

leaguer² *lēg'ər*, (*obs.*) *n.* an old Dutch liquid measure: a large cask. [Du. *ligger*, a tun.]

leaguer³. See **league**².

leak *lēk*, *n.* a crack or hole in a vessel through which fluid may pass: passage through such an opening: urination (*slang*): a place, means, instance, of unin- tended or undesirable admission or escape (*lit.* and *fig.*): the usu. unauthorised, but sometimes only ap- parently unauthorised, divulgation of secret informa- tion: a high resistance, esp. serving as a discharging path for a condenser (*elect.*). — *adj.* (*obs.*) leaky. — *v.i.* to have a leak: to pass through a leak. — *v.t.* to cause to leak: to let out or in by, or (*fig.*) as if by, a leak: to divulge (secret information) without, or ap- parently without, authorisation, or to cause this to be done. — *ns.* **leak'age** a leaking: that which enters or escapes by leaking: an allowance for leaking; **leak'er**; **leak'iness**. — *adj.* **leak'y**. — **leak out** to find vent: (of secret information) to be divulged to the public with- out, or apparently without, authorisation; **spring a leak** to become leaky. [O.E. *hlec*, leaky; or perh. re- introduced from Du. or L.G. *lek*, leak; or O.N. *leka*, to leak.]

leal *lēl*, *adj.* true-hearted, faithful. — *n.* **lealty** (*lē'əl-ti*). — **Land o' the Leal** the home of the blessed after death — heaven. [O.Fr. *leel*, *leiel*; doublet of **loyal**.]

leam¹, **leme** *lēm*, (*arch.*) *n.* a gleam of light, a glow. — *v.i.* to shine. [O.E. *lēoma*.]

leam² *lēm*. Same as **lyam**.

lean¹ *lēn*, *v.i.* to incline: to be or become inclined to the vertical: to rest sideways against something: to bend over: to swerve: to abut: to have an inclination: to rely. — *v.t.* to cause to lean: — *pa.t.* and *pa.p.* **leaned** (*lēnd*) or **leant** (*lent*). — *n.* an act or condition of leaning: a slope: a thing to lean on (*arch.*). — *n.* and *adj.* **lean'ing**. — **lean'-to** a shed or penthouse propped against another building or wall: — *pl.* **lean'-tos**. — **lean on** (*slang*) to put pressure on, to use force on (a person); **lean over backwards** see **backwards**. [O.E. *hlēonian*, *hlinian*, and causative *hlǣnan*; Du. *leunen*.]

lean² *lēn*, *adj.* thin, wanting flesh: not fat: without fat: unproductive: unprofitable, taking extra time — a printer's word. — *n.* flesh without fat. — *adv.* **lean'ly**. — *n.* **lean'ness**. — *adj.* **lean'y** (*Spens.*) lean. — *adj.* **lean'-burn'** of, using, or pertaining to a fuel-air mixture in which the fuel component is relatively low, thus reducing the amount of fuel used and pollution pro- duced. — **lean concrete** a non-load-bearing concrete of low cement content. — *adjs.* **lean'-faced** having a thin face: slender and narrow, as letters (*print.*); **lean'= witt'ed** of little sense. [O.E. *hlǣne*; L.G. *leen*.]

leap¹ *lēp*, *v.i.* to move with bounds: to spring upward or forward: to jump: to rush with vehemence: to pass abruptly or over a wide interval. — *v.t.* to bound over: to cause to take a leap: to cover (of male animals): — *pr.p.* **leap'ing**; *pa.t.* and *pa.p.* **leaped** *lēpt*, or **leapt** *lept*. — *n.* an act of leaping: a bound: the space passed by leaping: a place of leaping: an abrupt transition: a wide gap or interval. — *n.* **leap'er** a steeplechaser: one who leaps. — **leap day** an intercalary day in the calendar (29th February); **leap'-frog** a sport in which one person in turn places his hands on the back of another stooping in front of him, and vaults over him: a method of advancing against an enemy force in which one part of an army engages with the enemy whilst the rear part advances (*mil.*). — *v.t.* and *v.i.* to jump (over) as in leap-frog (also *fig.*): to go in advance of each other alternately (*mil.*; also *fig.*): — *pr.p.* **leap'-frogging**; *pa.t.* and *pa.p.* **leap'-frogged**. — *adj.* and *n.* **leap'-frogging**. — **leap'ing-house** (*Shak.*) a brothel; **leap'ing-time**

(*Shak.*) active youth; **leap second** a second added to or subtracted from one scale of time whenever necessary, to bring that scale into harmony with another scale or with the rotation of the earth; **leap year** a year with an intercalary day (perh. because any anniversary after that day misses or leaps over a day of the week). — **by leaps and bounds** by a large amount or extent: very quickly; **leap in the dark** an act of which we cannot foresee the consequences. [O.E. *hlēapan*; cf. **lope**[1], **loup**, Ger. *laufen*, to run.]

leap[2] *lēp, n.* a basket: a wicker net. [O.E. *lēap.*]

leaprous, leaperous, leaporous, old spellings of **leprous.**

leapt. See **leap**[1].

lear[1], **leare, lere, leir** *lēr, v.t.* to teach (*arch.* and *Scot.*): to learn (*Spens.*). — *n.* that which is learned, a lesson: lore: learning (*Scot.*). [O.E. *lǣran*, to teach.]

lear[2], **leer, lehr** *lēr, n.* a glass-annealing oven. [Ety. dub.]

learn *lûrn, v.t.* to be informed: to get to know: to gain knowledge, skill, or ability in: to teach (now *illit.*). — *v.i.* to gain knowledge or skill: — *pa.t.* and *pa.p.* **learned** (*lûrnd*) or **learnt** (*lûrnt*). — *adjs.* **learn'able** that may be learned; **learned** (*lûrn'id*) having learning: versed in literature, etc.: skilful. — *adv.* **learn'edly.** — *ns.* **learn'edness; learn'er** one who learns: one who is yet in the rudiments; **learn'ing** what is learned: knowledge: scholarship: skill in languages or science. — **learning curve** a graph used in education and research to represent progress in learning; **New Learning** the awakening to classical learning in the 16th century, led (in England) by Colet, Erasmus, Warham, More, etc. [O.E. *leornian*; Ger. *lernen*; cf. O.E. *lǣran* (Ger. *lehren*), to teach.]

leary. Same as **leery** under **leer.**

lease[1] *lēs, n.* a contract letting or renting a house, farm, etc., for a term: tenure or rights under such a contract: duration of such tenure: a hold upon, or prospect of continuance of, life, enjoyment, health, etc. — *v.t.* to grant or take under lease. — *adj.* **leas'able.** — *n.* **leas'er** a lessee. — **lease'back** the selling of a building, etc. to a person or organisation from whom the seller then leases it — also **sale and leaseback; lease'hold** a tenure by lease: land, etc., so held. — *adj.* held by lease. — **lease'holder** — *n.* and *adj.* **lease'-lend'** see **lend-lease** under **lend.** [Fr. *laisser*, to leave — L. *laxāre*, to loose, *laxus*, loose.]

lease[2] *lēz, (dial.) v.i.* to glean. — *n.* **leas'ing** gleaning. [O.E. *lesan*, to gather.]

lease[3] *lēs, n.* a place or mode of separating warp threads at the ends. — **lease'-band, lease'-rod** a band, rod, above and below which the warp threads are placed. [Perh. conn. with **leash.**]

lease[4], **leaze** *lēz, (dial.) n.* pasture. [See **leasow.**]

leash *lēsh, n.* a line for holding a hawk or hound: control by a leash, or as if by a leash: a set of three, especially animals. — *v.t.* to hold by a leash: to bind. [O.Fr. *lesse* (Fr. *laisse*), a thong to hold a dog by — L. *laxus*, loose.]

leasing *lēz'ing, (dial.) n.* falsehood, lies: lying. — **leas'ing-mak'er** a speaker of seditious words; **leas'ing-mak'ing.** [O.E. *lēasung* — *lēasian*, to lie — *lēas*, false, loose; Goth. *laus*, O.H.G. *los*.]

leasow, leasowe *lē'sō, -zō, (dial.) n.* pasture. — *v.t.* and *v.i.* to pasture. [Same word as **lease**[4] — O.E. *lǣs*, a meadow, in oblique cases *lǣswe*; cf. **mead, meadow.**]

least[1] *lēst, adj.* (serving as superl. of **little**) little beyond all others: smallest. — *adv.* in the smallest or lowest degree. — *n.* the smallest amount: the lowest degree. — *advs.* **least'aways, least'ways** (*dial.*), **-wise** (*rare* or *U.S.*) at least: however — used to tone down a preceding statement. — **at least,** or **at the least** at the lowest estimate: at any rate. [O.E. *lǣst* (adj. and adv.); compar. *lǣssa* (adj.), *lǣs* (adv.); no positive.]

least[2] *lēst, (Spens.) conj.* same as **lest**[1].

leasure (*Spens.*). An obsolete spelling of **leisure.**

leat, leet *lēt, (dial.) n.* a trench for bringing water to a mill-wheel, etc. [O.E. *gelǣt.*]

leather *ledh'ər, n.* a tanned, tawed, or otherwise dressed skin: a strap or other piece of leather: the ball in certain

games: human skin (*slang*): (in *pl.*) riding breeches made from leather. — *adj.* of leather. — *v.t.* to apply leather to: to thrash (*coll.*). — *ns.* **leatherette'** cloth or paper made to look like leather; **leath'ering** (*coll.*) a thrashing. — *adjs.* **leath'ern** of or like leather; **leath'ery** resembling leather: tough. — **leath'er-back** a large variety of sea-turtle; **leath'er-cloth** a fabric coated on one face so as to resemble leather — called also **American cloth; leath'er-coat** (*Shak.*) an apple with a rough coat, the golden russet; **leath'ergoods** objects and utensils made from leather; **leath'er-head** a blockhead: an Australian friar-bird with a bare head; **leath'er-jacket** one of various fishes: a grub of the crane-fly; **leath'er-knife** a curved knife for cutting leather. — *adjs.* **leath'er-lunged** strong-lunged, able to shout vigorously; **leath'er-mouthed** (*-mowdhd*) of certain fish, having a mouth like leather, smooth, and toothless. — **leath'er-neck** a sailors' name for a soldier or marine (from the leather stock he once wore), esp. now a U.S. marine. — *adj.* **leath'er-winged** (*Spens.*) having wings like leather. — **artificial leather** any of certain plastic materials treated so as to simulate leather; **fair leather** leather not artificially coloured; **morocco leather** see **morocco; patent leather** — also **japanned** or **lacquered leather** see **patent; Russia leather** see **Russia; split leather** leather split by a machine, for trunk-covers, etc.; **white leather** tawed leather, having its natural colour. [O.E. *lether*, leather; Du. *leder*, Ger. *Leder*.]

leave[1] *lēv, n.* permission: liberty granted: a formal parting: a farewell: permission to depart or be absent: permitted absence from duty: the time of this: holidays. — **leave'-taking** bidding farewell. — **French leave** see **French; leave of absence** permission to be absent, or the (time of) permitted absence; **take leave** to assume permission; **take (one's) leave (of)** to depart (from), say farewell (to); **take leave of one's senses** to become irrational. [O.E. *lēaf*, permission, cog. with *lēof*, dear; see **lief.**]

leave[2] *lēv, v.t.* to allow, or cause, to remain: to abandon, resign: to quit or depart from: to have remaining at death: to bequeath: to refer for decision, action, etc. — *v.i.* to desist: to cease: to depart: — *pr.p.* **leav'ing;** *pa.t.* and *pa.p.* **left.** — *n.pl.* **leav'ings** things left: relics: refuse. — **leav'ing-shop** an unlicensed pawnshop. — **be left with** to have remaining; **leave a little (much) to be desired** to be slightly (very) inadequate or unsatisfactory; **leave alone** to let remain undisturbed; **leave be** to leave undisturbed; **leave behind** to forget to bring, or leave intentionally or accidentally: to go away from (also *fig.*); **leave go** (*coll.*) to let go; **leave it at that** to take no further action, make no further comment, etc.; **leave off** to desist, to terminate: to give up using; **leave out** to omit; **leave unsaid** to refrain from saying. [O.E. *lǣfan.*]

leave[3] *lēv, (Spens.) v.t.* to levy, to raise. [Fr. *lever.*]

leave[4], **leaved, leaves, leavy.** See **leaf.**

leaven *lev'n, n.* the ferment, e.g. yeast, that makes dough rise: anything that makes a general change. — *v.t.* to raise with leaven: to permeate with an influence. — *n.* **leav'ening.** — *adj.* **leav'enous** containing leaven. [Fr. *levain* — L. *levāmen* — *levāre*, to raise — *levis*, light.]

Leavisite *lē'vis-īt, n.* a follower of the English literary critic and editor F.R. *Leavis* (1895–1978). — Also *adj.*

leaze. Same as **lease**[4].

lebbek *leb'ek, n.* an Old World tropical mimosaceous timber tree (*Albizzia lebbek*). [Origin unknown.]

Lebensraum *lāb'ənz-rowm, (Ger.) n.* space inhabited by living things: room to live (and, if necessary, expand).

Lecanora *lek-ə-nō'rə, -nō', n.* a genus of lichens, including the edible manna lichen of the steppes and deserts of Asia and Africa: (without *cap.*) a lichen of this genus. [Gr. *lekanē*, a dish.]

lecher *lech'ər, n.* a man addicted to lewdness. — *v.i.* to practise lewdness. — *n.* **lech** (*lech; slang*): back-formation from *lecher*) lust, a lewd desire: a lecher. — *v.i.* to lust. — *adj.* **lech'erous** lustful: provoking lust. —

adv. **lech′erously.** — *ns.* **lech′erousness; lech′ery.** [O.Fr. *lecheor* — *lechier*, to lick; O.H.G. *leccôn*, Ger. *lecken*, Eng. **lick.**]

Lecher wires *lehh′ər wīrz*, two insulated parallel stretched wires, forming a microwave electromagnetic transmission line. [Ernst *Lecher*, Austrian physicist.]

lechwe *lēch′wē, lech′wā, n.* an African antelope, smaller than the water-buck to which it is related. [Bantu; cf. Sotho *letsa*, antelope.]

lecithin *les′i-thin, n.* a very complex substance containing phosphorus, found in yolk of egg, brain, blood, etc. [Gr. *lekithos*, egg-yolk.]

lectern *lek′tərn, n.* a reading-desk (usu. one from which the lessons are read in a church). — Also (*obs.*) **lec′turn, lett′ern.** [L.L. *lectrīnum* — *lectrum*, a pulpit — Gr. *lektron*, a couch.]

lectin *lek′tin, n.* any of a number of naturally occurring substances, usu. proteins derived from plants, which act like antibodies but are not formed in response to an antigen. [L. *lectus, pa.p.* of *legēre*, to choose, select.]

lection *lek′shən, n.* a reading: a lesson read in Church. — *n.* **lec′tionary** a book of church lessons for each day. [L. *lectiō, -ōnis* — *legĕre, lectum,* to read.]

lecturn. See **lectern.**

lectisternium *lek-ti-stûr′ni-əm, n.* an ancient Roman religious observance at which images of gods were placed on couches as at a feast. [L., — *lectus*, a couch, *sternĕre*, to spread.]

lector *lek′tör, -tər, n.* a reader, esp. in a college: an ecclesiastic in one of the minor orders, lowest in the Orthodox, next above doorkeeper in the Roman Catholic. — *ns.* **lec′torate; lec′torship; lec′tress** a female reader. — **lector benevole** (*bi-nev′ə-li, be-nev′o-le*) kind reader. [L. *lector, -ōris* — *legĕre, lectum,* to read.]

lecture *lek′chər, n.* reading (*arch.*): a lesson or period of instruction: a discourse on any subject, esp. a professorial or tutorial discourse: an expository and discursive religious discourse: an endowed lectureship, as the Bampton, Hulsean, etc.: a formal reproof. — *v.t.* to instruct by discourses: to instruct authoritatively: to reprove. — *v.i.* to give a lecture or lectures. — *ns.* **lec′turer** one who lectures: a college or university instructor of lower rank than a professor: one of a class of preachers in the Church of England, supported by voluntary contributions; **lec′tureship** the office of a lecturer: the foundation of a course of lectures. [L. *lectūra* — *legĕre, lectum,* to read.]

lecythus *les′i-thəs, n.* the Latinised form of **lekythos.** — *n.* **Lec′ythis** the monkey-pot genus of **Lecythidā′ceae,** a family of tropical trees, including Brazil-nut, cannon-ball tree, and anchovy-pear. — *adj.* **lecythidā′ceous.** [See **lekythos.**]

led *led, pa.t.* and *pa.p.* of **lead¹.** — *adj.* under leading or control, esp. of a farm or place held along with another by a non-resident. — **led captain** an obsequious attendant, a henchman; **led horse** a spare horse led by a servant: a sumpter-horse or pack-horse.

ledden *led′n,* (*Spens.*) *n.* language, dialect, speech. [O.E. *lēden, lēoden,* language — *lēode,* people, confused with *lǣden,* Latin — L. *Latīnum,* Latin.]

lederhosen *lā′dər-hōz-ən, n.pl.* short leather trousers with braces. [Ger., leather trousers.]

ledge *lej, n.* an attached strip: a raised edge (*obs.*): a shelf-like projection: a ridge or shelf of rocks: a lode. — *adj.* **ledg′y** abounding in ledges. [M.E. *legge,* prob. from the root of **lay³.**]

ledger *lej′ər,* formerly also **lidger** *lij′ər, ns.* a book that lies permanently in one place (*obs.*): a register, account book (*U.S.*): the principal book of accounts among merchants, in which the entries in all the other books are entered: a horizontal timber in scaffolding: a flat grave-slab: (also **leidger, lieger, leiger**) a resident, esp. an ambassador (*obs.*). — *adj.* resident, stationary. — *v.i.* to fish with a ledger-line. — **ledg′er-bait** fishing bait that lies on the bottom, the **ledg′er-tackle** being weighted; **ledg′er-line** a line fixed in one place (*angling*): a short line added above or below the stave where required (often **leger-line;** *mus.*). [App. from O.E. *licgan,* to lie, *lecgan,* to lay.]

Ledum *lē′dəm, n.* the Labrador tea genus of ericaceous plants: (without *cap.*) a plant of this genus. [Latinised from Gr. *lēdon,* ladanum.]

lee¹ *lē, n.* shelter: the sheltered side: the quarter toward which the wind blows: tranquillity (*obs.*). — *adj.* (opp. to *windward* or *weather*) sheltered: on or towards the sheltered side. — *adj.* **lee′ward** (also *naut. lū′ərd, loō′ərd*) pertaining to, or in, the direction towards which the wind blows. — *adv.* towards the lee. — Also *n.* — **lee′-board** a board lowered on the lee-side of a vessel, to lessen drift to leeward; **lee′-ga(u)ge** position to leeward — opp. to *weather-gage;* **lee shore** a shore on a ship's lee side; **lee side** the sheltered side; **lee tide** a tide in the same direction as the wind; **lee′way** leeward drift: room to manoeuvre, latitude. — **lee licht of the mune** (in Scottish ballads) perh. the pleasant moonlight; **make up leeway** to make up for lost time, ground, etc. [O.E. *hlēo(w),* gen. *hlēowes,* shelter; O.N. *hlē,* L.G. *lee;* see also **lew¹.**]

lee² *lē,* (*Spens.*) *n.* a river. [Poss. from the River *Lee.*]

lee³. See **lea¹, lees, lie¹.** — *n.* **leear** (*lē′ər*) Scots form of **liar.**

leech¹ *lēch, n.* the side edge of a sail. [Cf. O.N. *līk;* Dan. *lig;* Sw. *lik,* a bolt-rope.]

leech² *lēch, n.* a blood-sucking worm: a physician (*arch.*): one who attaches himself to another for personal gain. — *v.t.* to apply leeches to: to cling to like a leech: to drain. — *v.i.* (usually with *on*) to cling to. — *ns.* **leech′craft** (*arch.*) the art of medicine; **leech′dom** (*arch.*) a remedy or prescription. [O.E. *lǣce,* perh. orig. two different words.]

leechee. Same as **lychee.**

leek *lēk, n.* a vegetable (*Allium porrum*) of the onion genus — national emblem of Wales. — **eat the leek** (*Shak.* — *Henry V,* V, i.) to be compelled to take back one's words or put up with insulting treatment. [O.E. *lēac,* leek, plant; cf. **charlock, garlic, hemlock.**]

lee-lane *lē′lān′,* (*Scot.*) *n.* used only in phrases (**by**) **my, his,** etc., **lee-lane** quite alone. — Also **lee′some-lane.** [lee of obscure origin; see **lone.**]

leep¹ *lēp, v.t.* to plaster with cow dung. [Hindi *līpnā.*]

leep² *lēp,* (*dial.*) *v.t.* to boil, to scald. [Cf. O.N. and Icel. *hleypa,* to curdle — O.N. *hlaupa,* to leap.]

leer¹ *lēr, n.* a sly, sidelong, or lecherous look: complexion, colour (*Shak.*). — *v.i.* to glance sideways: to look lecherously. — *n.* and *adj.* **leer′ing.** — *adv.* **leer′ingly.** — *adj.* **leer′y** cunning: wary (with *of*). [O.E. *hlēor,* face, cheek.]

leer². Same as **lear².**

Leerie *lē′ri,* (*Scot.*) *n.* a nickname for a lamplighter — in full **Lee′rie-licht′-the-lamp.**

lees *lēz, n.pl.* sediment or dregs of liquor. — *sing.* (*rare*) **lee.** [Fr. *lie* — L.L. *lia.*]

leese *lēz,* (*Spens., Shak.*) *v.t.* to lose: — *pa.t.* **lore** (*lōr, lör*); *pa.p.* **lore, lorn** (in *Spens.,* in the sense of left). [O.E. *lēosan* (in compounds), to lose.]

leesome-lane. See **lee-lane.**

leet¹ *lēt,* (*Scot.*) *n.* a selected list of candidates for an office. — **short leet** a select list for the final choice. [Origin uncertain.]

leet² *lēt,* (*hist.*) *n.* a court-leet: its jurisdiction or district: the right to hold it. [A.Fr. *lete* or Anglo-Latin *leta,* possibly — O.E. *lǣth,* lathe (of a county).]

leet³. See **leat.**

leet⁴. See **lite¹.**

leetle *lē′tl,* an old-fashioned affectation for **little.**

leeward, leeway. See **lee¹.**

leeze. See under **lief.**

left¹ *left, pa.t.* and *pa.p.* of **leave².** — *adjs.* **left′-off** laid aside, discarded; **left′-o′ver** remaining over from a previous occasion. — *n.* a thing left over: a survival: food uneaten at a meal (usu. in *pl.*). — **left-luggage office** a room at an airport or a railway station where for a small fee one can safely leave one's luggage for a time.

left² *left, adj.* on, for, or belonging to that side, or part of the body, etc. on that side, which in man has normally the weaker and less skilful hand (opp. to *right*): on that side from the point of view of a person looking downstream, a soldier looking at the enemy, a president looking at an assembly, an actor looking at the audience: relatively liberal, democratic, progressive, innovating in politics: inclined towards socialism, communism. — *n.* the left side: the region to the left side: the left hand: a blow with the left hand: a shot on the left side or a bird so killed: a glove, shoe, etc., for the left hand or foot, etc.: the more progressive, democratic, socialist, radical or actively innovating party or wing (from its sitting in some legislatures to the president's left). — *adv.* on or towards the left. — *adj.* and *n.* left′ie, left′y (often *derog.*) (a) leftist. — *n.* left′ism the principles of the political left. — *adj.* and *n.* left′ist. — *adj.* and *adv.* left′ward towards the left: on the left side: more left-wing. — Also *n.* (*rare*). — *advs.* left′wardly, left′wards. — **Left Bank** the artistic quarter of Paris on the south bank of the Seine. — *adjs.* left′-bank; left′-footed performed with the left foot: having more skill or strength in the left foot; left′-hand on the left side: towards the left: with thread or strands turning to the left: performed with the left hand; left′-hand′ed having the left hand stronger and readier than the right: for the left hand: counterclockwise: forming a mirror-image of the normal or right-handed form: awkward: unlucky: dubious (as *a left-handed compliment*): morganatic. — *adv.* left′= hand′edly. — left′-hand′edness; left′-hand′er a blow with the left hand: a left-handed person; left′-hand′iness awkwardness; left wing the political left: the wing on the left side of an army, football pitch, etc. — *adj.* left′-wing playing on the left wing: belonging to the more leftwardly inclined section: (having opinions which are) progressive, radical, socialist, etc. — left′= wing′er a person with left-wing views or who supports the left wing of a party, etc.: a player on the left wing. — have two left feet to be clumsy or awkward, e.g. in dancing; left-hand drive a driving mechanism on the left side of a vehicle which is intended to be driven on the right-hand side of the road; left, right, and centre in, from, etc. all directions: everywhere; over the left (shoulder) (*obs. slang*) contrariwise. [M.E. *lift, left* — O.E. (Kentish) *left*, weak, worthless; cf. O.E. *lyftādl*, paralysis.]

lefte *left*, (*Spens.*) *pa.t.* lifted.

leg *leg, n.* a walking limb: the human hind-limb, or sometimes the part between knee and ankle: a long, slender support of anything, as of a table: in cricket, that part of the field, or that fielder, on or behind a line straight out from the batsman on the on side (also *adj.*): a branch or limb of anything forked or jointed, as a pair of compasses: the part of a garment that covers the leg: a backward movement of the leg in bowing (*arch.*): a swindler, esp. at a racecourse (for *blackleg*; *old slang*): a distinct part or stage of any course, e.g. of a flight: in sports, one event or part in a contest consisting of two or more parts or events. — *v.t.* and *v.i.* to walk vigorously (*v.t.* with *it*): to propel through a canal tunnel by pushing with the feet on wall or roof. — *adj.* legged (*legd, leg′id*; usu. in composition) having (a certain type, number, etc. of) legs. — *ns.* legg′er a bargeman who works: a worker or machine that makes stocking-legs; legg′iness; legg′ing an outer and extra gaiter-like covering for the lower leg; legg′ism (*arch.*), the character of a blackleg. — *adjs.* legg′y having noticeably long and lank legs; leg′less having no legs: very drunk (*coll.*). — *ns.* leg′lessness; leg′let a leg ornament. — **leg bail** see **bail¹**; leg′-break (*cricket*) a ball that breaks from the leg side towards the off side on pitching: a ball bowled to have this deviation: spin imparted to a ball to cause such a deviation; leg′-bus′iness (*slang*) ballet-dancing; leg′=

bye in cricket, a run made when the ball touches any part of the batsman's person except his hand; leg′= guard a cricketer's pad; leg′-iron a fetter for the leg; leg′-man, leg′-woman one whose share in the business of an organisation involves journeys outside the office: an assistant who runs errands or gathers information: a newspaper reporter. — *adj.* leg-of-mutt′on shaped like a leg of mutton, as a triangular sail, a sleeve tight at the wrist and full above. — leg′-pull a bantering attempt to impose on someone's credulity; leg′-puller; leg′-pulling; leg′-rest a support for the legs; leg′room space for one's legs, as in a car; leg′-show an entertainment depending mainly on the exhibition of women's legs; leg side (or the leg; *cricket*) that half of the field nearest the batsman's legs (opp. to *off side*); leg′-slip′ (*cricket*) a fielder or position on the leg side somewhat behind the batsman; leg′-spin (*cricket*) (a) leg-break; leg′-spinner (*cricket*) one who bowls leg-breaks; leg theory (*cricket*) the policy of bowling on the striker's legs with a trap of leg-side fielders: bodyline; leg′-warmers long footless socks; leg-woman see leg-man; leg′work (*coll.*) work involving much travelling, searching, etc. — a leg up a help or hoist in mounting, climbing, or generally; change the leg (of a horse) to change the gait; feel one's legs to begin to support oneself on the legs; find one's legs to become habituated, to attain ease; fine, long, short, square leg (*cricket*) fielding positions respectively fine from, far from, near to, square to, the batsman on the leg side; in high leg (*arch.*) in great excitement; leg before (wicket) in cricket, a way of being given out as penalty for stopping with the leg (or any part of the body except the hands) a straight or off-break ball that would have hit the wicket (l.b.w.); not have a leg to stand on to have no case at all; on one's last legs see last; on one's legs standing, esp. to speak; pull someone's leg to make a playful attempt to impose upon someone's credulity; shake a leg (*coll.*) to hurry up; show a leg to make an appearance: to get up; upon one's legs in an independent position.   [O.N. *leggr*, a leg; Dan. *læg*, Sw. *lägg*.]

legacy *leg′ə-si, n.* that which is left to one by will: a bequest of personal property. — *ns.* leg′atary a legatee; legatee′ one to whom a legacy is left; legator (*li-gā′tər*) a testator. — legacy duty a duty levied on legacies, varying according to degree of relationship, abolished in 1950; leg′acy-hunter one who courts those likely to leave legacies. — cumulative legacy an additional legacy to the same person; demonstrative legacy a general legacy with a particular fund named from which it is to be satisfied; general legacy a sum of money payable out of the assets generally; residuary legatee the person to whom the remainder of the property is left after all claims are discharged; specific legacy a legacy of a definite thing, as jewels, pictures, a sum of stock in the funds, etc.; substitutional legacy a second legacy to the same person instead of the first. [L. *lēgāre, -ātum*, to leave by will.]

legal *lē′gl, adj.* pertaining to, or according to, law: lawful: created by law: according to the Mosaic law or dispensation (*theol.*). — *ns.* lēgalese′ complicated legal jargon; lēgalisā′tion, -z- a process whereby something previously unlawful is made lawful. — *v.t.* lē′galise, -ize to make lawful. — *ns.* lē′galism strict adherence to law: in theol., the doctrine that salvation depends on strict adherence to the law, as distinguished from the doctrine of salvation by grace: the tendency to observe letter or form rather than spirit, or to regard things from the point of view of law; lē′galist one inclined to legalism: one versed in law. — *adj.* lēgalis′-tic. — *adv.* lēgalist′ically. — *n.* lēgality (-*gal′i-ti*). — *adv.* lē′gally. — legal aid financial assistance given to those unable to pay the full costs of legal proceedings; legal tender that which a creditor cannot refuse in payment of a debt; legal year see year. [L. *lēgālis* — *lēx, lēgis*, law.]

legate *leg′it, n.* an ambassador, esp. from the Pope: a delegate, deputy, esp. orig. a Roman general's lieutenant: the governor of a Papal province (*hist.*). — *n.* **leg′ateship.** — *adj.* **leg′atine** (-*ə-tīn*) of or relating to a legate. — *n.* **legation** (*li-gā′shən*) a diplomatic mission, body of delegates, or its official abode: the office or status of legate: a Papal province (*hist.*). [L. *lēgātus* — *lēgāre*, to send with a commission.]

legatee. See **legacy.**

legato *le-gä′tō*, (*mus.*) *adj.* and *adv.* smooth, smoothly, the notes running into each other without a break (*superl.* **legatis′simo**). — *n.* a legato passage or manner: — *pl.* **legat′os.** [It., bound, tied — L. *ligāre, -ātum*, to tie.]

legend[1] *lej′ənd, n.* a story of a saint's life: a collection of such stories: a traditional story: a body of tradition: an untrue or unhistorical story: a person having a special place in public esteem because of striking qualities or deeds, real or fictitious: the body of fact and fiction gathered round such a person: a motto, inscription, or explanatory words (with e.g. a picture): a book of readings from the Bible and saints' lives (*obs.*). — *n.* **leg′endary** a book or writer of legends. — *adj.* pertaining to, of the nature of, consisting of, or described in, legend: romantic: fabulous. — *ns.* **leg′endist** a writer of legends; **leg′endry.** [Fr. *légende* — L.L. *legenda*, to be read.]

legend[2] *lej′ənd, n.* Shak. for **legion.**

leger *lej′ər*, (*obs. cant*) *n.* one who sells short weight in charcoal: one who swindles by scamping work, using bad materials, or the like. — *n.* **leg′ering.** [Poss. Fr. *léger*, light.]

legerdemain *lej-ər-də-mān′, n.* sleight-of-hand: jugglery. — *adj.* juggling: tricky. [Lit. light of hand — Fr. *léger*, light, *de*, of, *main*, hand.]

legerity *li-jer′i-ti, n.* lightness: nimbleness. [Fr. *légèreté* — *léger*, light — assumed L.L. *leviārius* — L. *levis*, light.]

leger-line — better **ledger-line.** See **ledger.**

legge *leg*, (*Shak.*) *n.* dregs of the people. [**lag**[1].]

legger, leggism, etc. See **leg.**

leghorn *leg′hörn, li-görn′, n.* fine straw plait made in Tuscany: a hat made of it: (*li-görn′*) a small breed of domestic fowl. [*Leghorn* (It. *Legorno*, now *Livorno*, L. *Liburnus*) in Italy.]

legible *lej′i-bl, adj.* clear enough to be deciphered: easy to read: readable (*rare*). — *ns.* **leg′ibleness; legibil′ity.** — *adv.* **leg′ibly.** [L. *legibilis* — *legĕre*, to read.]

legion *lē′jən, n.* in ancient Rome, a body of three to six thousand soldiers: a military force: applied especially to several in French history: a great number. — *adj.* (*rare*) multitudinous. — *adj.* **le′gionary** of, relating to, or consisting of, a legion or legions: containing a great number. — *n.* a member of a legion. — *adj.* **le′gioned** arrayed in legions. — *n.* **lēgionnaire** (-*nār′*; Fr. *légionnaire*) a member of the British, Foreign, etc. Legion. — **American Legion** an association of U.S. war veterans; **(Royal) British Legion** an ex-servicemen's and -women's association; **Foreign Legion** a body of foreigners, esp. that in the French army organised in 1831; **Legionnaire's** or **Legionnaires' Disease** a severe, sometimes fatal, pneumonia-like disease caused by the bacterium *Legionella pneumophila* (so named after an outbreak of the disease at an American Legion convention in Philadelphia in 1976); **Legion of Honour** a French order instituted in 1802 by Napoleon I; **their name is Legion** they are beyond numbering (from Mark v. 9); **Thundering Legion** in Christian tradition a body of soldiers under Marcus Aurelius, whose prayers brought down a thunder-storm and destroyed the enemy. [L. *legiō, -ōnis* — *legĕre* to levy.]

legislate *lej′is-lāt, v.i.* to make laws. — *n.* **legislā′tion.** — *adj.* **leg′islătive** (or *-lə-tiv*) law-making: having power to make laws: pertaining to legislation. — *n.* law-making power: the law-making body. — *adv.* **leg′islatively.** — *n.* **leg′islator** a lawgiver: a member of a legislative body: — *fem.* (*rare*) **leg′islatress.** — *adj.* **legislatorial** (-*lə-tō′ri-əl, -tō′*) of or pertaining to, or of

the nature of, a legislator, legislature, or legislation. — *ns.* **leg′islatorship; leg′islature** a law-making body. [L. *lēx, lēgis*, law, *latum*, serving as supine to *ferre*, to bear.]

legist *lē′jist, n.* one skilled in the laws. [Fr. *légiste.*]

legit *lij-it′*, coll. shortening of **legitimate** *adj.*

legitim *lej′i-tim*, (*Scots law*) *n.* that which children are entitled to out of a deceased father's moveable estate — also **bairn's-part.** [L. *lēgitima* (*pars*), lawful (part) — *lēx*, law.]

legitimate *li-jit′i-mit, -māt, adj.* lawful: lawfully begotten, born in wedlock, or having the legal status of those born in wedlock: related, derived, or transmitted by birth in wedlock or subsequently legitimated: as used by believers in the theory of divine right, according to strict rule of heredity and primogeniture: logically inferred: following by natural sequence: genuine: conforming to an accepted standard: of, or pertaining to, legitimate drama (*theat.*). — *v.t.* (-*māt*) to make lawful: to give the rights of a legitimate child to. — *n.* **legit′imacy** (-*mə-si*) the fact or state of being legitimate. — *adv.* **legit′imately.** — *ns.* **legit′imateness; legitimā′tion** the act of rendering legitimate, esp. of conferring the privileges of lawful birth. — *v.t.* **legit′imise, -ize** to legitimate. — *n.* **legit′imist** one who believes in the right of royal succession according to the principle of heredity and primogeniture. — **legitimate drama** drama of permanent value: drama of typical form, normal comedy and tragedy, distinguished from opera, play with music, variety, etc. as well as cinema and television; **legitimate pollination** in heterostyled plants, pollination of long styles from long stamens, short from short. [L.L. *lēgitimāre, -ātum* — L. *lēgitimus*, lawful — *lēx*, law.]

leglin, leglan, leglen *leg′lən*, (*Scot.*) *n.* a milking-pail. — **cast a leglin girth** to have an illegitimate child. [Cf. **laggen.**]

legume *leg′ūm, li-gūm′, n.* a pod (as in pea, bean, etc.) of one carpel: a vegetable used as food. — *n.* **legū′min** a globulin got in peas, beans, etc. — *n.pl.* **Legūminō′sae** (-*sē*) an order of angiosperms characterised by the legume, including Papilionaceae, Mimosaceae, and Caesalpiniaceae. — *adj.* **legū′minous** pertaining to pulse: of or pertaining to the Leguminosae: bearing legumes. [L. *legūmen*, pulse, prob. — *legĕre*, to gather.]

lehr. See **lear**[2].

Lehrjahre *lār′yä-rə, n.* or *n.pl.* (also without *cap.*) an apprenticeship (usu. *fig.*). [Ger., — *lehren*, to teach, *Jahre*, years.]

lei[1]. See **leu.**

lei[2] *lā′ē, n.* a garland, wreath. [Hawaiian.]

Leibni(t)zian *līb-nit′si-ən, adj.* pertaining to the great German philosopher and mathematician Gottfried Wilhelm *Leibniz* (1646–1716). — *n.* **Leibni(t)z′ianism** the philosophy of Leibniz — the doctrine of primordial monads, pre-established harmony, fundamental optimism on the principle of sufficient reason.

Leicester *les′tər, adj.* of a long-woolled breed of sheep that originated in *Leicestershire*. — *n.* a sheep of that breed. — **Leicester(shire) plan** a comprehensive school system, started in Leicestershire in 1957, which avoids the use of very large schools and also makes full use of free modern methods of learning.

leidger, leiger. See **ledger.**

leiotrichous *lī-ot′ri-kəs, adj.* straight-haired. — *n.* **leiot′richy** (-*ki*) straight-hairedness. [Gr. *leios*, smooth, *thrix, trichos*, hair.]

Leipoa *lī-pō′ə, n.* a genus of Australian mound-birds: (without *cap.*) a bird of this genus. [Gr. *leipein*, to leave, forsake, and *ōon*, an egg.]

leir. See **lear**[1].

leish *lēsh*, (*Scot.*) *adj.* active, supple, athletic. [Orig. uncertain.]

Leishmania *lēsh-mān′i-ə, -man′i-ə, n.* a genus of Protozoa (fam. Trypanosomidae): (without *cap.*) any protozoon of the genus Leishmania, or any protozoon of the

Trypanosomidae in a non-flagellated form: — *pl.*
leishman'ia, -iae (*-i-ē*), **-ias.** — *ns.* **leishmaniasis** (*lēsh-mən-ī´ə-sis*), **leishmaniō´sis** any of various diseases, such as kala-azar, due to infection with Leishmania: — *pl.* **-sēs.** [Named after Sir William *Leishman* (1865–1926), who discovered the cause of kala-azar.]
leisler *līz´lər, n.* a small black bat (*Nyctalus leisleri*) named after the 19th-century zoologist T.P. *Leisler.* — Also **Leisler's bat.**
leister *lēs´tər,* (*Scot.*) *n.* a salmon-spear. — *v.t.* to spear with a leister. [O.N. *ljōstr*; Dan. *lyster.*]
leisure *lezh´ər,* (*U.S.* and old-fashioned) *lēzh´ər, n.* time free from employment: freedom from occupation: convenient opportunity. — *adj.* free from necessary business: for casual wear. — *v.i.* to have leisure. — *v.t.* to make leisurely. — *adj.* **leis´urable** leisured: leisurely. — *adv.* **leis´urably.** — *adj.* **leis´ured** having much leisure. — *adj.* and *adv.* **leis´urely** not hasty or hastily. — **leisure suit** a loose-fitting garment comprising matching top and trousers made from a soft fabric; **leisure wear** comfortable, casual clothing worn on informal occasions. — **at** (one's) **leisure** free from occupation: at one's ease or convenience. [O.Fr. *leisir* — L. *licēre,* to be permitted.]
leitmotiv *līt´mō-tēf´, n.* a theme associated with a person or a thought, recurring when the person appears on the stage or the thought becomes prominent in the action: a recurring theme (*fig.*). — Also **leitmotif.** [Ger., — *leiten,* to lead, and *Motiv,* a motif.]
lek[1] *lek, n.* a unit of Albanian currency = 100 qintars: a coin or note of this value.
lek[2] *lek, n.* the piece of ground on which the blackcocks and cock capercailzies gather to display: the season during which this displaying takes place. — *v.t.* to gather and display at a lek. — *n.* **lekk´ing.** [App. from Sw. *leka,* to play.]
leke. Spens. form of **leak** (*adj.*).
lekythos *lē´ki-thos,* (*ant.*) *n.* a narrow-necked Greek flask. [Gr. *lēkythos.*]
lem, or **LEM** *lem, n.* abbrev. for **lunar excursion module.**
leman *lem´ən,* or *lēm´,* (*arch.*) *n.* a lover: a sweetheart: a paramour: later chiefly *fem.* and in a bad sense: — *pl.* **lem´ans.** [O.E. *lēof,* lief, *mann,* man.]
leme. See **leam**[1].
lemel, limail *lē´mel, ns.* the dust and filings of metal. [M.E. *lemaille* — M.Fr. *lemaille* — O.Fr. *limer,* to file — L. *limāre,* to file.]
lemma *lem´ə, n.* a preliminary proposition (*math.*): a premise taken for granted (*math.*): a theme, argument, heading, or head-word: — *pls.* **lemm´as, lemm´ata.** [Gr. *lēmma, -atos,* from the root of *lambanein,* to take.]
lemming *lem´ing, n.* a northern rodent (*Lemmus* and other genera) near allied to voles. [Norw. *lemming.*]
Lemna *lem´nə, n.* the duckweed genus, giving name to the family **Lemnā´ceae,** free-floating spathifloral monocotyledons. [Gr. *lemna,* water starwort.]
Lemnian *lem´ni-ən, adj.* pertaining to *Lemnos* in the Aegean Sea. — **Lemnian earth** a bole from Lemnos; **Lemnian ruddle** a red ochre found in Lemnos.
lemniscate *lem-nis´kāt, n.* the locus of the foot of the perpendicular from the centre of a conic upon the tangent. [L. *lēmniscātus,* ribboned — Gr. *lēmniskos,* a ribbon, bandage.]
lemon[1] *lem´ən, n.* a pale yellow oval citrus fruit with acid pulp: the tree that bears it: a pale yellow colour: something disappointing, worthless, unattractive, unpleasant (*slang*). — *adj.* flavoured with lemon: (coloured) pale yellow. — *v.t.* to flavour with lemon. — *n.* **lemonade´** a drink (still or aerated) made with lemon juice or more or less flavoured with lemon. — *adj.* **lem´ony.** — **lemon balm** same as **balm** (*Melissa officinalis*); **lemon cheese, curd** a soft paste of lemons, eggs, and butter. — *adj.* **lem´on-coloured.** — **lemon drop** a hard lemon-flavoured sweet; **lem´on-grass** a fragrant perennial grass (*Cymbopogon* or *Andropogon*) of India, etc., smelling like lemon and yielding an essential oil; **lemon peel** the skin of lemons, candied or not; **lemon**

squash a highly concentrated lemon drink; **lemon squeezer** a small hand-press for extracting the juice of lemons; **lem´on-weed** sea-mat. — *n.* and *adj.* **lem´on=yell´ow.** — **hand someone a lemon** (*slang*) to swindle someone; **the answer is a lemon** (*coll.*) one is given an unsatisfactory answer or no answer at all. [Fr. *limon* (now the lime); cf. Pers. *līmūn;* cf. **lime**[2].]
lemon[2] *lem´ən, n.* a species of sole differing in its markings from the common sole (**lem´on-sole´,** or **sand sole**): a kind of dab resembling a sole (**lem´on-dab´, lem´on-sole´,** also called **smear-dab** or **smooth dab**). [Fr. *limande.*]
lempira *lem-pē´rə, n.* the monetary unit of Honduras, equivalent to 100 centavos. [*Lempira,* a department of Honduras named after a native chief.]
lemur *lē´mər, n.* any member of the **Lemuroidea** (*lem-ū-roid´i-ə*) or *Prosimiae,* a group of mammals akin to the monkeys, forest dwellers, mainly nocturnal in habits, common in Madagascar: an ancient Roman ghost of the dead: — *pl.* **lē´murs** (animals), **lemures** (*lem´ū-rēz;* spectres). — *n.* **Lemuria** (*li-mū´ri-ə; pl.*) an ancient Roman festival (9th, 11th, and 13th of May) when ghosts were exorcised: (*sing.*) a hypothetical vanished continent where the Indian Ocean now is, posited to explain the distribution of lemurs. — *ns.* and *adjs.* **lemurian** (*li-mū´ri-ən*), **lemurine** (*lem´ū-rīn*), **lem´uroid.** [L. *lemŭrēs,* ghosts.]
lend *lend, v.t.* to give the use of for a time: to afford, grant, or furnish, in general: to let for hire. — *v.i.* to make a loan: — *pr.p.* **lend´ing;** *pa.t.* and *pa.p.* **lent.** — *n.* (*Scot.*) a loan (often **len´**). — *ns.* **lend´er; lend´ing** the act of giving in loan: that which is lent or supplied (*Shak.*). — **lend´-lease** an arrangement authorised by Congress in 1941 by which the President could supply war materials to other countries whose defence he deemed vital to the United States. — Also *adj.* — **lend an ear** (*coll.*) to listen; **lend itself to** to be able to be used for. [O.E. *lǣnan* — *lǣn, lān,* a loan.]
lenes. See **lenis.**
leng *leng,* (*obs.*) *v.i.* to lengthen: to tarry: to long (*Spens.*). [O.E. *lengan.*]
lenger *leng´gər, adj.* and *adv.* (*Spens.*) longer. — *adj.* and *adv.* **leng´est** (*obs.*) longest. [O.E. *lengra,* compar. of *lang* (adj.), *lengest,* superl. of *lang* and of *lange* (adv.).]
length *length, n.* quality of being long: extent from end to end: the longest measure of anything: long continuance: prolixity: time occupied in uttering a vowel or syllable: the quantity of a vowel: any definite portion of a known extent: a stretch or extent: distance (chiefly *Scot.*): a suitable distance for pitching a cricket ball: the lengthwise measurement of a horse, boat, etc. (*racing*). — in composition **-length,** stretching downwards, or sometimes along, as far as, e.g. *knee-length, arm's-length.* — *v.t.* and *v.i.* **length´en** to increase, in length. — *adj.* (*obs.*) **length´ful.** — *adv.* **length´ily.** — *n.* **length´iness.** — *advs.* **length´ways, length´wise** in the direction of the length. — *adj.* **length´y** of great or tedious length: rather long. — **length´sman** someone responsible for the upkeep of a particular stretch of road or railway. — **at length** in full: fully extended: at last; **go (to) great lengths, go to all lengths, any length(s)** to do everything possible (sometimes more than is ethical) to achieve a purpose; **length of days** prolonged life. [O.E. *lengthu* — *lang,* long.]
lenient *lēn´yənt, -ni-ənt, adj.* softening (*arch.*): soothing (*arch.*): mild: merciful. — *n.* (*med. arch.*) that which softens: an emollient. — *ns.* **lē´nience, lē´niency.** — *adv.* **lē´niently.** — *v.t.* **lenify** (*len´, lēn´; arch.*) to mitigate, to assuage. — *adj.* **lenitive** (*len´*) mitigating: laxative. — *n.* any palliative: an application for easing pain (*med.*): a mild purgative (*arch.*). — *n.* **lenity** (*len´*) mildness: clemency. [L. *lēniēns, -entis,* pr.p. of *lēnīre,* to soften — *lēnis,* soft.]
Leninism *len´in-izm, n.* the political, economic and social principles and practices of the Russian revolutionary leader, *Lenin* (Vladimir Ilyich Ulyanov; 1870–1924),

esp. his theory of government by the proletariat. — *ns.* **Len′inist, Len′inite.**

lenis *lē′nis, (phon.) adj.* of a consonant, articulated with relatively little muscular effort and pressure of breath (opp. to *fortis*). — Also *n.:* — *pl.* **lē′nes** (*-ēz*). — *n.* **lenition** (*li-nish′ən*) a softening of articulation, common in Celtic languages. [L., soft.]

lenitive, lenity. See **lenient.**

leno *lē′nō, n.* a thin muslin-like fabric: — *pl.* **lē′nos.** [Perh. Fr. *linon.*]

lenocinium *lē-nō-sin′i-əm, (Scots law) n.* connivance at one's wife's adultery. [L. *lēnōcinium,* enticement — *lēnō,* a pander.]

lens *lenz, n.* a piece of transparent matter causing regular convergence or divergence of rays passing through it (*opt.*): the refracting structure (*crystalline lens*) between the crystalline and vitreous humours of the eye: a device to influence the direction of sound waves (*acoustic lens*): (*cup.*) the lentil genus: — *pl.* **lens′es.** — *n.* **lent′icel** (*-sel; bot.*) a breathing pore in bark. — *adj.* **lenticell′ate.** — *n.* **lent′icle** (*geol.*) a lenticular mass. — *adj.* **lenti′cūlar** shaped like a lens or lentil seed: double-convex. — *n.* a three-dimensional picture made up of photographs of a scene which have been taken from several different angles, split into strips, juxtaposed, and laminated with corrugated plastic, the corrugations acting as lenses to create an illusion of depth. — *adv.* **lenticˈularly.** — *adjs.* **lent′iform, lent′oid.** — **electron lens** any arrangement of electrodes designed to influence the direction of cathode rays. [L. *lēns, lentis,* lentil.]

Lent *lent, n.* spring (*obs.*): the time from Ash Wednesday to Easter observed in the Western Churches (a longer period in the Eastern Churches) as a time of fasting in commemoration of Christ's fast in the wilderness (Matt. iv. 2). — *adj.* **Lent′en** (also without *cap.*) of Lent: sparing: fleshless. — **lenten rose** a herbaceous perennial, *Helleborus orientalis,* which flowers from February to April; **lent′-lil′y** the daffodil. [O.E. *lencten,* the spring; Du. *lente,* Ger. *Lenz.*]

lent *pa.t.* and *pa.p.* of **lend.**

lentamente, lentando, lenti. See **lento.**

Lentibulariaceae *len-tib-ū-lā-ri-ā′si-ē, n.pl.* the bladderwort and butterwort family of tubifloral dicotyledons. [Origin obscure.]

lentic *len′tik, (ecology) adj.* associated with standing water: inhabiting ponds, swamps, etc. [L. *lentus,* slow.]

lenticel, lentiform, etc. See **lens.**

lentigo *len-tī′gō, n.* a freckle: (usu.) freckles: — *pl.* **lentigines** (*len-tij′i-nēz*). — *adjs.* **lentig′inose, lentig′inous** (*bot.*) minutely dotted. [L. *lentīgō, -inis,* a freckle — *lēns,* a lentil.]

lentil *len′til, n.* an annual papilionaceous plant (*Lens esculenta,* or *Ervum lens*) common near the Mediterranean: its seed used for food. [O.Fr. *lentille* — L. *lēns, lentis,* the lentil.]

lentisk *len′tisk, n.* the mastic tree. [L. *lentiscus.*]

lento *len′tō, (mus.) adj.* slow. — *adv.* slowly. — *n.* a slow passage or movement: — *pl.* **len′tos, len′ti** (*-tē*). — *adv.* **lentamen′te** (*-tā*). — *adj.* and *adv.* **lentan′do** slowing. — *adj.* and *adv.* **lentiss′imo** very slow(ly). [It., — L. *lentus,* slow.]

lentoid. See **lens.**

lentor *len′tör, (arch.) n.* sluggishness: viscidity. — *adj.* **len′tous.** [L. *lentus,* slow.]

lenvoy *len-voi′.* Same as **envoy².** [Fr. *l′* for *le,* the.]

Leo *lē′ō, n.* the Lion, a constellation between Cancer and Virgo: the 5th sign of the zodiac, in which it used to be (the constellation is now in the sign Virgo): one born under this sign. — *n.* **Lē′onid** (*-ə-nid*) a meteor of a swarm whose radiant is in the constellation Leo. — *adj.* **Lē′onine** pertaining to any of the Popes named Leo: of a kind of Latin verse, generally alternate hexameter and pentameter, rhyming at the middle and end (prob. from some unknown poet named Leo,

Leoninus, or Leonius): (without *cap.*) lionlike. [L. *leō, -ōnis,* lion.]

leone *lē-ō′nē, n.* the monetary unit of Sierra Leone, equivalent to 100 Sierra Leone cents.

leontiasis *lē-ont-ī′ə-sis, n.* a form of leprosy giving a lionlike appearance. [Gr. *leontiāsis* — *leōn, -ontos,* lion.]

leopard, *fem.* **leop′ardess,** *lep′ərd, -es, n.* a large spotted animal of the cat kind found in Africa and Asia: in America, the jaguar: a lion passant gardant (also *rarely,* **leop′ardess;** *her.*). — **leop′ard-cat** a spotted wild cat of India; **leop′ard-moth** a white moth (*Zeuzera pyrina*) with black spots on wings and body; **leop′ard′s= bane** a composite plant, *Doronicum;* **leop′ard-wood** letter-wood. — **hunting leopard** the cheetah; **snow leopard** the ounce. — **the leopard cannot change its spots** personality traits cannot be changed. [O.Fr., — L. *leopardus* — Gr. *leopardos* (for *leontopardos*) — *leōn,* lion, *pardos,* pard.]

leotard *lē′ə-tärd, n.* a skin-tight garment worn by dancers and acrobats, sleeveless or long-sleeved, legs varying from none at all to ankle-length. [Jules *Léotard,* 19th-century French trapeze artist.]

lep *lep, v.i. (dial.,* esp. *Ir.*) for **leap¹:** also *dial.* for the *pa.t.* — *pa.t.* (*Spens.*) **lepp′ed.**

leper *lep′ər, n.* leprosy (*obs.*): one affected with leprosy: a tainted person (*fig.*): an outcast. — *n.* **lep′ra** leprosy: a scurfy, mealy substance on some plants (*bot.*). — *adj.* **lep′rose** (*-rōs*) scaly: scurfy. — *ns.* **leprosā′rium** a hospital for lepers; **leprosity** (*-ros′i-ti*) scaliness; **lep′-rosy** (*-rə-si*) a name formerly widely applied to chronic skin diseases: now to one caused by a bacillus and occurring in two forms, tubercular, beginning with spots and thickenings of the skin, and anaesthetic, attacking the nerves, with loss of sensation in areas of skin: corruption (*fig.*). — *adj.* **lep′rous** of or affected with leprosy: scaly: scurfy. [O.Fr. *lepre* and Gr. *leprā* — *lepros,* scaly — *lepos,* or *lepis,* a scale, *lepein,* to peel.]

lepid *lep′id, adj.* pleasant, jocose. [L. *lepidus.*]

lepid-, lepido- *lep′id-, -ō-, -o′,* in composition, scale. — *n.* **Lepidoden′dron** (Gr. *dendron,* tree) a genus of fossil trees, mainly Carboniferous of the **Lepidodendrā′ceae,** akin to Lycopodiaceae, the stem covered with ovate leaf-scars arranged spirally. — *adj.* and *n.* **lepidoden′-droid.** — *ns.* **lepid′olite** (Gr. *lithos,* stone) a lithia mica, usu. pink; **lepidomelane′** (Gr. *melās, -ānos,* black) a black mica rich in iron, occurring in scales. — *n.pl.* **Lepidop′tera** (Gr. *pteron,* wing) an order of insects, with four wings covered with fine scales — butterflies and moths. — *ns.* **lepidop′terist** a student of butterflies and moths; **lepidopterol′ogy.** — *adj.* **lepidop′terous.** — *ns.* **Lepidosī′ren** (Gr. *Seirēn,* a Siren) an Amazon mudfish; **Lepidos′teus** (Gr. *osteon,* a bone) a genus of fishes with rhomboid scales hard like bone, the bony pike; **Lepidos′trobus** (Gr. *strobos,* twist) the fossil fructification of Lepidodendron. — *adj.* **lep′idote** (Gr. *lepidōtos*) scaly: scurfy. [Gr. *lepis, -idos,* a scale.]

leporine *lep′ə-rīn, adj.* pertaining to or resembling the hare. [L. *leporīnus* — *lepus, lepŏris,* the hare.]

lepped. See **lep.**

lepra. See **leper.**

leprechaun, leprechawn *lep′rə-hhön, n.* a little brownie, who helps Irish housewives, mends shoes, grinds meal, etc. [Prob. Old Ir. *luchorpán, lu,* small, *corpan, corp,* a body.]

leproserie, leprosery *lep′rə-sər-i, n.* a leper hospital. [Fr. *léproserie.*]

leprosy, leprous, etc. See **leper.**

-lepsy *-lep-si, (med.)* in composition, a seizing, seizure, as in *catalepsy.* — *-leptic* adjectival combining form. [Gr. *lēpsis* — *lambanein,* to seize, take.]

lepton *lep′ton, n.* the smallest ancient Greek coin, translated mite in the N.T. (*pl.* **lep′ta**): a modern Greek coin, 1/100th of a drachma (*pl.* **lep′ta**): any of a group of subatomic particles with weak interactions, electrons, negative muons, tau particles and neutrinos (opp. to **baryon**) (*pl.* **lep′tons**). — *adjs.* **lepton′ic** of or pertaining to leptons; **leptocephal′ic** (Gr. *kephalē*, head) narrow-skulled. — *n.* **leptoceph′alus** the larva of an eel. — *adj.* **leptocerc′al** (Gr. *kerkos*, tail) slender-tailed. — *n.* **leptodac′tyl** (Gr. *daktylos*, finger, toe) a bird or other animal with long slender toes. — *adj.* **leptodac′tylous** slender-toed. — *n.* **lep′tome** phloem or bast. — *adjs.* **leptophyll′ous** (*bot.*) with long slender leaves; **lep′torrhine** (Gr. *rhīs, rhīnos,* nose) narrow-nosed. — *n.* **lep′tosome** (Gr. *sōma,* body) a person with a slight, slender physical build: an asthenic. — *adjs.* **leptosō′mic, leptosomatic** (*-sə-mat′ik*). — *n.* **leptospīrō′-sis** (Gr. *speira,* a coil) a disease of animals or man caused by bacteria of the genus **Leptospī′ra.** — *adj.* **leptosporan′giate** having each sporangium derived from a single cell (opposed to *eusporangiate*). — *n.* **lep′totene** (*-tēn*) the first stage of meiotic prophase in which long, slender, single-stranded chromosomes develop. [Gr. *leptos,* neut. *lepton,* slender.]

lere. Same as **lear**[1].

Lerna *lûr′nə,* **Lerne** *lûr′nē, ns.* a swamp near Argos, supposed to be the home of the Hydra killed by Hercules. — *adjs.* **lernaean, lernean** (*lûr-nē′ən*).

les. See **lez(z).**

Lesbian *lez′bi-ən, adj.* of the island of *Lesbos,* Mitylene, or Mytilene, home of Alcaeus and Sappho: amatory, erotic: (also without *cap.*) homosexual (of women). — *n.* (also without *cap.*) a woman homosexual. — *n.* **Les′bianism** (also without *cap.*). — *adj.* **les′bic** lesbian. — **Lesbian rule** an adaptable standard, from the pliable leaden rule of Lesbian masons.

lese-majesty, leze-majesty *lēz′-maj′is-ti, n.* an offence against the sovereign power, treason. — **lese, leze,** treated as if it had verbal force, has also been used to form compounds such as **lese′-human′ity, leze′-lib′erty.** [Fr. *lèse majesté,* transl. of L. *laesa mājestās,* injured majesty — *laedĕre,* to hurt.]

lesion *lē′zhən, n.* a hurt: a morbid change in the structure of body tissue caused by disease or injury, esp. an injury or wound (*med.*). [Fr. *lésion* — L. *laesiō, -ōnis* — *laedĕre, laesum,* to hurt.]

less *les, adj.* (used as *comp.* of **little**) smaller (not now used of material things): in smaller quantity: minor: fewer (*arch.* and *coll.*): inferior, lower in estimation: younger: more (*Shak.,* with an expressed or implied negative). — *adv.* not so much: in a lower degree. — *n.* a smaller portion or quantity. — *conj.* (*Milt.*) unless (often written **'less**). — *prep.* without: with diminution of, minus. — **much less** often used by confusion for much more; **no less** (usu. *iron.*) a phrase used to express admiration; **nothing less than** (formerly) anything rather than: (now) quite as much as. [O.E. *læssa,* less, *læs* (adv.); apparently not conn. with **little**.]

-less *-les, -lis, adj. suffix* free from, lacking, as guilt*less,* god*less.* [O.E. *-lēas,* Ger. *-los,* Goth. *-laus.*]

lessee *les-ē′, les′ē, n.* one to whom a lease is granted. [**lease**[1].]

lessen *les′n, v.t.* to make less, in any sense: to lower in estimation: to disparage: to belittle. — *v.i.* to become less, shrink. [**less.**]

lesser *les′ər, adj.* less: smaller: inferior: minor. — *adv.* (*Shak.*) less. [Double comp. from **less.**]

lesson *les′n, n.* a portion of Scripture read in divine service: a spell, instalment, or prescribed portion of instruction: an exercise: a piece or performance of music (*obs.*): an instructive or warning experience or example: a severe reproof. — *v.t.* (*arch.*) to instruct: to train: to rebuke. — *n.* **less′oning.** [Fr. *leçon* — L. *lectiō, -ōnis* — *legĕre,* to read.]

lessor *les′ör, n.* one who grants a lease. [**lease**[1].]

lest[1] *lest, conj.* that not: for fear that. [M.E. *leste* — O.E. *thy̆ læs the,* the less that — *thy̆* instrum. case; see **the**[2].]

lest[2] *lest,* (*Spens.*) *v.i.* for **list**[5] to listen.

let[1] *let, v.t.* to leave (*Shak.*): to omit (*Shak.*): to allow to escape (*arch.*): to allow to go or come: to give leave or power to, to allow, permit, suffer (usu. with infin.

without *to*): to grant to a tenant or hirer: in the imper. with accus. and infin. without *to,* often used virtually as an auxiliary with imperative or optative effect: to behave so as to give an impression, make it appear (*obs.;* also *v.i.*): — *pr.p.* **lett′ing;** *pa.t.* and *pa.p.* **let.** — *n.* a letting for hire. — *adj.* **lett′able** able to be hired out, suitable for letting. — *ns.* **lett′er** one who lets, esp. on hire; **lett′ing.** — **let′-alone** (*Shak.*) absence of restraint, freedom. — *adj.* refraining from interference: leaving things to themselves. — **let′-down** an act or occasion of letting down: a disappointment; **let′-off** a festivity: an outlet: (in games) a failure to take advantage of an opportunity; **let′-out** a chance to escape, avoid keeping (an agreement, contract, etc.); **lett′er=gae′** (*Scot.*) one who lets go, a precentor; **let′-up** cessation: abatement: alleviation. — **let alone** not to mention, much less: to refrain from interference with: (*imper.*) trust (*arch.*); **let be** (*dial.* **let-a-be**) to leave undisturbed: not to mention, to say nothing of (*Scot.*); **let blood** to bleed; **let down** to allow to fall: to lower: to leave in the lurch, fail to back up at need, betray trust; **let drive** to aim a blow: to discharge a missile; **let fall** to drop; **let fly** to fling, discharge, shoot; **let go** to cease holding: to slacken (*naut.*); **let in** to allow to enter: to take in or swindle (*arch.*): to betray into or involve in (*for*) anything vexatious: to insert: to leak inwards; **let in on** (*coll.*) to allow to take part in; **let into** to admit to the knowledge of: to throw into one with; **let loose** to set free: to let go restraint, to indulge in extravagant talk or conduct; **let off** to allow to go free or without exacting all: to fire off, discharge; **let on** (*coll.*) to allow to be believed, to pretend: to betray awareness: to reveal, divulge; **let oneself go** (*coll.*) to allow one's appearance, life-style, etc., to deteriorate: to act without restraint; **let out** to allow to get free, or to become known: to strike out or kick out (*arch.*): to widen, slacken, enlarge: to put out to hire: to leak outwards; **let someone know** to inform someone; **let up** (*coll.*) to become less: to abate; **let up on** (*coll.*) to cease to have to do with; **let well alone** to let things remain as they are from fear of making them worse; **to let** available for hire. [O.E. (Anglian) *lētan* (W.S. *lǣtan*), to permit, pa.t. *lēt;* pa.p. *lǣten;* Ger. *lassen.*]

let[2] *let, v.t.* (*arch.*) to hinder: to prevent: — *pa.t.* and *pa.p.* **lett′ed, let.** — *adj.* **let** (*arch.*) obstructed. — *n.* hindrance, obstruction (*arch.*): delay (*arch.*): obstruction by the net, or other ground for cancelling a service (*lawn tennis,* etc.): a service so affected. — *n.* **lett′er.** [O.E. *lettan,* to hinder — *lǣt,* slow.]

-let *-lit, -lət, n. suffix* used to form diminutives, as brace*let,* leaf*let,* stream*let.*

letch *lech, v.t.* a variant of **leach**[1]. — *n.* (*dial.*) a boggy patch of ground. — Also **latch.** [See **leach**[1].]

lethal *lē′thəl, adj.* death-dealing: deadly: mortal. — *n.* **lethal′ity.** — *adv.* **le′thally.** — *n.* **le′thee** (*Shak.*) app. life-blood, or death; prob. with some reminiscence of Lethe (see below). — *adj.* **lethif′erous** carrying death. [L. *lēt(h)ālis* — *lēt(h)um,* death.]

lethargy *leth′ər-ji, n.* heavy unnatural slumber: torpor. — *adjs.* **lethargic** (*-är′*), **-al** pertaining to lethargy: unnaturally sleepy: torpid. — *adv.* **lethar′gically.** — *adj.* **leth′argied.** — *v.t.* **leth′argise, -ize.** [Gr. *lēthārgiā,* drowsy forgetfulness — *lēthē,* forgetfulness, *ārgos,* idle.]

Lethe *lē′thē, n.* a river of the underworld causing forgetfulness of the past to all who drank of it: oblivion. — *adjs.* **lethē′an; leth′ied** (*Shak.*). [Gr. *lēthē,* forgetfulness (*lēthēs hydōr,* the water or river of forgetfulness) — *lēthein,* a collateral form of *lanthanein,* to be hidden.]

lethee, lethiferous. See **lethal.**

Letraset® *let′rə-set, n.* a transfer lettering system of alphabets, symbols, etc. which can be stripped into position on paper, film, etc.

Lett *let, n.* a member of a people inhabiting **Lett′land** (Latvia): a native or citizen of Latvia. — *adjs.* **Lett′ic** of the group (also called *Baltic*) of languages to which

Lettish belongs, incl. Lithuanian and Old Prussian; **Lett'ish.** — *n.* language of Letts. [Ger. *Lette* — Lettish *latvis* (now *latvietis*).]

letter[1] *let'ər, n.* a conventional mark primarily used to express a sound of speech: often loosely applied to the sound itself: a written or printed message: literal meaning: printing-type: (in *pl.*) learning, literary culture. — *v.t.* to stamp letters upon: to mark with a letter or letters. — *adj.* **lett'ered** marked with letters: educated: versed in literature: literary. — *ns.* **lett'erer; lett'ering** act of impressing or marking with letters: the letters impressed: their style or mode of formation. — *adj.* **lett'erless** without letters: illiterate. — **lett'er-board** a board on which matter in type is placed for keeping or convenience in handling; **lett'er-bomb** a device inside an envelope which explodes when the envelope is opened; **lett'er-book** a book in which letters or copies of letters are kept; **lett'er-box** a box or slot for receiving mail; **lett'er-card** a card folded and gummed like a letter, with perforated margin for opening; **letter-carrier** postman: mail-carrier; **lett'er-clip** an appliance for gripping letters or papers to keep them together; **lett'er-file** arrangement for holding letters for reference; **lett'er-founder** one who casts type; **lett'erhead** a printed heading on notepaper, etc.: a piece of notepaper with such heading. — *adj.* **lett'er-perfect** (of actor, etc.) having the words of the part committed accurately to memory, word-perfect. — **lett'erpress** printed reading matter: a copying-press: a method of printing in which ink on raised surfaces is pressed on to paper. — *ns.pl.* **lett'ers-pat'ent** a writing conferring a patent or privilege, so called because written on open sheets of parchment; **letters requisitory,** or **rogatory** an instrument by which a court of one country asks that of another to take a certain evidence on its behalf. — **lett'er-stamp** an instrument for cancelling postage-stamps: a stamp for imprinting dates, etc.; **lett'er-weight** a paper-weight; **lett'er-wood** leopard-wood, a South American tree of the bread-nut genus, with dark brown mottled heart-wood; **lett'er-writer** one who writes letters, esp. for hire: a book of forms for imitation in writing letters. — **letter of credit** a letter authorising credit or cash to a certain sum to be given to the bearer; **letter of indication** a banker's letter requesting foreign bankers to accept the bearer's circular notes; **letter of marque** see **marque**[1]; **letter of the law** literal interpretation of the law; **letters of administration** see **administer; letters of credence, letters credential** a diplomat's formal document accrediting him to a foreign government; **to the letter** exactly, in every detail. [Fr. *lettre* — L. *littera, lītera*.]

letter, letting. See **let**[1,2].

lettern *let'ərn* (*obs.*). Same as **lectern**.

lettre *le-tr'*, (Fr.) *n.* a letter. — **lettre de cachet** (*də ka-she*) a letter under the royal signet: a royal warrant for arrest and imprisonment; **lettre de change** (*də shäzh*) a bill of exchange; **lettre de marque** (*də märk*) a letter of marque or of reprisal.

lettuce *let'is, n.* a composite plant (*Lactuca sativa*) with milky juice: its leaves used as a salad: extended to other (inedible) plants of the genus. — **frog's lettuce** a kind of pondweed; **lamb's lettuce** corn-salad. [Appar. from some form (perh. the pl.) of A.Fr. *letue* (Fr. *laitue*) — L. *lactūca* — *lac*, milk.]

leu *le'oo̅, n.* the monetary unit of Rumania. — Also (*rare*) **ley** (*lā*): — *pl.* **lei** (*lā*). [Rum., lion.]

leuc-, leucin-, leuk-, leuko- *lūk-, loo̅k-, lūs-, loo̅s-, lū'ko̅-, loo̅k'o̅-, -ko'-* (*-c-* and *-k-* are in most cases interchangeable, and, except in the first case, **-k-** forms have not been given below), in composition, white. — *ns.* **leucaemia, leukaemia,** (or more strictly formed) **leuchaemia** (*lū-kē'mi-ə*; Gr. *haima,* blood) a sometimes fatal cancerous disease in which too many leucocytes are accumulated in the body, associated with changes in the lymphatic system and enlargement of the spleen. — *adj.* **leucae'mic** — *ns.* **leucae'mogen** a substance that encourages the development of leucaemia; **leuc'oblast** an immature cell which will develop into a leucocyte. — *adj.* **leucocrat'ic** of igneous rocks, light in colour, due to a low content of iron and magnesium. — *n.* **leucocyte** (*-kō̅-sīt*; Gr. *kytos,* container, used as if cell) a white corpuscle of the blood or lymph. — *adj.* **leucocytic** (*-sit'ik*). — *ns.* **leucocythaemia** (*-sī-thē'mi-ə*; Gr. *haima,* blood) leucaemia; **leucocytol'ysis** (Gr. *lysis,* dissolution) breaking down of the leucocytes; **leucocytopē'nia** (Gr. *pĕniā,* poverty) poverty in leucocytes; **leucocytō'sis** the presence of an excessive number of white corpuscles in the blood; **leucoder'ma, leucoder'-mia** (Gr. *derma,* skin) a condition in which white patches, surrounded by a pigmented area, appear in the skin; **leucopē'nia** leucocytopenia; **leucoplakia** (*lū-, loo̅-kō̅-plä'ki-ə;* Gr. *plax, plakos,* a flat surface) the stage of a chronically inflamed area at which the surface becomes hard, white and smooth; **leucoplast** (*lū', loo̅'kō̅-pläst;* Gr. *plastos,* formed — *plassein,* to form; *bot.*) a starch-forming body in protoplasm (also **leucoplas'tid**); **leucopoiesis** (*lū-, loo̅-kō̅-poi-ē'sis;* Gr. *poieein,* to make) the production of white blood cells; **leucorrhoea** (*lū-, loo̅-kō̅-rē'ə;* Gr. *rhoiā* — *rheein,* to flow) an abnormal mucous or muco-purulent discharge from the vagina, the whites; **leucotomy** (*lū-, loo̅-kot'ə-mi;* Gr. *tomē,* a cutting) a surgical scission of the white association fibres between the frontal lobes of the brain and the thalamus to relieve cases of severe schizophrenia and manic-depressive psychosis; **leu'-cotome** (*-kō̅-tōm*) a needle used for the purpose. — **leu'co-base, leu'co-compound** a colourless reduction product of a dye that can be converted back to the dye by oxidation. [Gr. *leukos,* white.]

leuch, leuchen. See **lauch.**

leucin(e) *lū', loo̅'sin, -sēn, n.* a decomposition product of proteins. [Gr. *leukos,* white.]

Leuciscus *lū, loo̅-sis'kəs, n.* a genus of freshwater cyprinoid fishes, including the roach, dace, chub, minnow, etc. [Gr. *leukiskos,* white mullet.]

leucite *lū', loo̅'sīt, n.* a whitish mineral (silicate of aluminium and potassium). — *adj.* **leucitic** (*-sit'ik*). — *n.* **leucitohē'dron** the cubic icositetrahedron, simulated by typical leucite crystals. [Gr. *leukos,* white.]

leuco-. See **leuc-.**

Leucojum *lū-, loo̅-kō'jəm, n.* the snowflake genus of amaryllids. [Gr. *leukoïon,* snowdrop, etc. — *leukos,* white, *ion,* violet.]

leucoma *lū-, loo̅-kō'mə, n.* a white opacity of the cornea. [Gr. *leukōma* — *leukos.*]

leugh, leughen. See **lauch.**

leuk(o)-. Alternative form of **leuc(o)-.** See **leuc-.**

lev, lew *lef, n.* the monetary unit or franc of Bulgaria: — *pl.* **leva** (*lev'ä*). [Bulg., lion.]

Levant *li-vant', n.* the East (*obs.*): the eastern Mediterranean and its shores: (without *cap.*) the levanter wind: (without *cap.*) a kind of morocco leather. — *adj.* (without *cap.*) (*lev'ənt*) eastern. — *n.* **Levant'er** an inhabitant of the Levant: (without *cap.*) a boisterous easterly wind in the Levant. — *adj.* **Levant'ine** (or *lev'ən-tīn*) of the Levant. — *n.* (without *cap.*) a closely-woven twilled silk cloth. [Fr. *levant* or It. *levante,* east, lit. rising — L. *levāre,* to raise.]

levant *li-vant', v.i.* to decamp. — *n.* **levan'ter** one who absconds, esp. with bets unpaid. [Sp. *levantar,* to move — L. *levāre,* to raise.]

levator *le-vā'tər, -tör, n.* a muscle that raises — opp. to *depressor.* [L. *levātor,* a lifter — *levāre.*]

leve. See **lief.**

levee[1] *lev'i,* also *lev'ā, li-vē', n.* getting out of bed (*arch.*): a morning (or comparatively early) reception of visitors, esp. by a person of distinction. — *v.t.* to attend the levee of. [Fr. *levée, lever* — L. *levāre,* to raise.]

levee[2] *lev'i, li-vē', n.* a natural or artificial riverside embankment, esp. on the Lower Mississippi: a quay. [Fr. *levée,* raised; see the foregoing.]

levée en masse *lə-vā ä mas,* (Fr.). See **levy.**

level *lev'l, n.* an instrument for testing horizontality: a horizontal position: a condition of horizontality: a horizontal plane or line: a nearly horizontal surface or region with no considerable inequalities: the horizontal plane, literal or figurative, that anything occupies or reaches up to: height: a horizontal mine-gallery: the act of aiming (*Shak.*): the thing aimed at (*Spens.*): an ascertainment of relative elevation: a levelling survey: natural or appropriate position or rank: a condition of equality: a ditch or channel for drainage, esp. in flat country. — *adj.* horizontal: even, smooth: even with anything else: uniform: well-balanced, sound of judgment: in the same line or plane: filled to a level with the brim: equal in position or dignity. — *adv.* in a level manner: point-blank. — *v.t.* to make horizontal: to make flat or smooth: to lay low: to raze: to aim: to make equal: to direct: to survey by taking levels. — *v.i.* to make things level: to aim: to speak honestly, confess: to guess, estimate. — *v.t.* and *v.i.* to change in spelling or pronunciation, making one word, form, the same as another: — *pr.p.* **lev′elling;** *pa.t.* and *pa.p.* **lev′elled.** — *ns.* **lev′eller** one who levels in any sense: one who would remove all social or political inequalities, esp. (*cap.*) one of an ultra-republican party in the parliamentary army, crushed by Cromwell in 1649; **lev′elling** act of making level: change in spelling or pronunciation making one word, form, the same as another. — **level best** (*coll.*) one's utmost; **lev′el-cross′-ing** a place at which a road crosses a railway at the same level. — *adj.* **lev′el-head′ed** having sound common sense. — **lev′elling-rod, -staff** a graduated rod used in levelling; **lev′el-pegg′ing(s)** equal state of two rivals, contestants, etc. (often in the form **be level=pegging with**). — *adj.* at the same level, equal. — **find one's level** to come to equilibrium in one's natural position or rank; **level down** or **up** to lower or raise to the same level or status; **level off** to make flat or even: to reach and maintain equilibrium; **level with** (*slang*) to tell the truth; **on the level** fair: honestly speaking. [O.Fr. *livel, liveau* (Fr. *niveau*) — L. *lībella*, a plummet, dim. of *lībra*, a balance.]

level-coil *lev′l-koil,* (*arch.*) *n.* an old Christmas game in which the players changed seats: a hubbub. [Fr. *lever le cul*, to lift the buttocks.]

lever *lē′vər, n.* a bar turning on a support or fulcrum for imparting pressure or motion from a source of power to a resistance. — *v.t.* to move with a lever. — *n.* **le′verage** the mechanical power gained by the use of the lever: advantage gained for any purpose. — **le′ver-watch** a watch having a vibrating lever in the mechanism of the escapement. [O.Fr. *leveor — lever —* L. *levāre*, to raise.]

lever de rideau *lə-vā də rē-dō,* (Fr.) curtain-raiser.

leveret *lev′ə-rit, n.* a hare in its first year. [O.Fr. *levrette* (Fr. *lièvre*) — L. *lepus, lepŏris*, a hare.]

leviable. See **levy.**

leviathan *le-vī′ə-thən, n.* a water animal, in Job xli, apparently a crocodile (*B.*): a huge sea-monster: anything of huge size, esp. a ship or a man: (after Hobbes's book, 1651) the state: Satan (*obs.*). — *adj.* gigantic, formidable. [Heb. *livyāthān.*]

levigate[1] *lev′i-gāt, v.t.* to smooth: to grind to fine powder, esp. with a liquid. — *adj.* smooth. — *adj.* **lev′igable.** — *n.* **leviga′tion.** [L. *lēvigāre, -ātum — lēvis*, smooth; Gr. *leios*; akin to **level.**]

levigate[2] *lev′i-gāt, v.t.* to lighten. [L. *lĕvigāre, -ātum — lĕvis*, light.]

levin *lev′in,* (*arch.*) *n.* lightning. [M.E. *leuen(e)*, prob. — O.N.]

levirate *lēv′* or *lev′i-rāt, n.* the (ancient Hebrew and other) custom of compulsory marriage with a childless brother's widow. — *adjs.* **lev′irate, leviratical** (*-rat′i-kl*). — *n.* **levirā′tion.** [L. *lēvir*, a brother-in-law.]

Levis® *lē′vīz, n.pl.* (also without *cap.*) heavy, close-fitting denim, etc., trousers, reinforced at points of strain with copper rivets.

levitation *lev-i-tā′shən, n.* the act of rising by virtue of lightness: act of rendering light: the floating of heavy bodies in the air, according to spiritualists: raising and floating on a cushion of air. — *v.t., v.i.* **lev′itate** to (cause to) float. [On the model of *gravitate* — L. *levis*, light.]

Levite *lē′vīt, n.* a descendant of *Levi*: an inferior priest of the ancient Jewish Church: (also without *cap.*) a clergyman (*slang*). — *adjs.* **levitic** (*li-vit′ik*), **-al.** — *adv.* **levit′ically.** — *n.* **Levit′icus** the third book of the Old Testament. — **Levitical degrees** the degrees of kindred within which marriage was forbidden in Lev. xviii. 6–18.

levity *lev′it-i, n.* lightness of weight (*arch.*): lightness of temper or conduct: thoughtlessness: disposition to trifle: vain quality. [L. *levitās, -ātis — levis*, light.]

levo-. Same as **laevo-.**

levulose. Same as **laevulose.**

levy *lev′i, v.t.* to raise, collect, as an army or tax: to call for: to impose: to begin to wage: — *pr.p.* **lev′ying;** *pa.t.* and *pa.p.* **lev′ied.** — *n.* the act of levying: a contribution called for from members of an association: a tax: the amount collected: troops levied. — *adj.* **leviable** (*lev′i-ə-bl*) able to be levied or assessed. — **levy war** to make war; **levy in mass** (Fr. **levée en masse**) a levy of all able-bodied men for military service. [Fr. *levée — lever —* L. *levāre*, to raise.]

lew[1] *lū, lōō, adj.* tepid, lukewarm. [O.E. *hlēow.*]

lew[2]. See **lev.**

lewd *lōōd, lūd, adj.* ignorant (*obs.*): bare (*B.*): bad (*obs.*): lustful: unchaste. — *adv.* **lewd′ly.** — *ns.* **lewd′ness; lewds′by, lewd′ster** (*arch.*) one addicted to lewdness. [O.E. *lǣwede*, ignorant.]

lewis *lōō′is, n.* a dovetail iron tenon for lifting blocks of stone (also **lew′isson**): a freemason's son. [Ety. dub.]

Lewis gun *lōō′is gun,* a light machine-gun invented by Col. Isaac Newton *Lewis.*

Lewisian *lōō-iz′i-ən,* or *-is′, adj.* of *Lewis* in the Outer Hebrides: Pre-Cambrian (*geol.*).

lewisite[1] *lōō′is-īt, n.* a yellow cubic mineral, calcium titanium antimonate. [Named after W. J. *Lewis* (1847–1926), English mineralogist.]

lewisite[2] *lōō′is-īt, n.* a vesicant liquid, an arsine derivative, used in chemical warfare. [Named after W. L. *Lewis*, American chemist.]

lewisson. See **lewis.**

lex *leks,* (L.) *n.* law. — **lex non scripta** (*non skrip′tə, nōn skrēp′tä*) unwritten law — i.e. the common law; **lex scripta** (*skrip′tə, skrēp′tä*) statute law; **lex talionis** (*ta-li-ō′nis, tä-*) the law of talion.

lexeme *lek′sēm,* (*gram.*) *n.* a word or other essential unit of vocabulary in its most abstract sense. [*lex*icon, and *-eme*.]

lexicon *leks′i-kən, n.* a word-book or dictionary: a vocabulary of terms used in connection with a particular subject. — *adj.* **lex′ical** belonging to a lexicon: pertaining to the words of a language as distinct from its grammar and constructions. — *adv.* **lex′ically.** — *n.* **lexicographer** (*-kog′rə-fər*). — *adjs.* **lexicographic** (*-kə-graf′ik*), **-al.** — *ns.* **lexicog′raphist; lexicog′raphy** the writing and compiling of dictionaries; **lexicol′ogist; lexicol′ogy** the study of the history and meaning of words. — **lexical meaning** the meaning of the base word when not inflected. [Gr. *lexikon*, a dictionary — *lexis*, a word, *legein*, to speak.]

lexigraphy *leks-ig′rə-fi, n.* a system of writing in which each sign represents a word. — *n.* **lex′igram** a sign which represents a word. — *adjs.* **lexigraphic** (*-graf′ik*), **-al.** [Gr. *lexis*, word, *graphein*, to write.]

lexis *lek′sis, n.* the way in which a piece of writing is expressed in words, diction: the total stock of words in a language. [Gr., word.]

ley[1] *lā, lē.* Same as **lea**[1,2,3]. — **ley′-farming** see **lea**[2].

ley[2]. See **leu.**

ley[3] *lā, n.* (also **ley line**) one of the straight lines between features of the landscape, possibly pathways, or perhaps having scientific or magical significance in prehistoric times. [Var. of **lea**[1].]

Leyden jar *lā′dən jär,* a condenser for electricity, a glass jar coated inside and outside with tinfoil or other conducting material. [*Leyden* in Holland, where it was invented.]

leze-majesty, leze-liberty, etc. See **lese-majesty.**

lez(z), les, lezzy *lez, lez'i, (coll.) n.* short forms of **lesbian.**

lhasa apso *lä'sə ap'sō,* a Tibetan (breed of) small, long-haired terrier: — *pl.* **lhasa apsos.** [*Lhasa,* the capital of Tibet.]

lherzolite *lûr'zə-līt, n.* peridotite, consisting essentially of olivine with monoclinic and orthorhombic pyroxenes. [From Lake *Lherz* in the Pyrenees (Ariège).]

li *lē, n.* a Chinese unit of distance, about one-third of a mile. [Chin.]

liable *lī'ə-bl, adj.* subject to an obligation: exposed to a possibility or risk: subject (*Shak.*): responsible (for): tending (usually with *to*): apt: fitting, suitable (*Shak.*): likely (to). — *n.* **liabil'ity** state of being liable: that for which one is liable, a debt, etc. — **employers' liability** responsibility of employers to their servants for the negligence of those to whom they have delegated their authority; **limited liability** a principle of modern statute law which limits the responsibilities of shareholders in a partnership, joint-stock company, etc., by the extent of their personal interest therein. [App. — Fr. *lier* — L. *ligāre,* to bind.]

liaison *lē-ā'zn, -zō, lyez-ō, n.* union, or bond of union: connection: illicit union between the sexes: in French, the linking in pronunciation of a final (and otherwise silent) consonant to a vowel beginning the next word: effective conjunction with another unit or force (*mil.*). — *v.i.* **liaise** (*lē-āz'*; back-formation) to form a link (with): to be or get in touch (with). — **liaison officer** an officer forming a link with another unit or force. [Fr., — L. *ligātiō, -ōnis* — *ligāre,* to bind.]

liana *lē-ä'nə,* **liane** *lē-än', ns.* any climbing plant, especially any contorted woody kind festooning tropical forests. — *adj.* **lian'oid.** [Fr. *liane,* Latinised or Hispanicised as *liana,* app. — *lier* — L. *ligāre,* to bind.]

liang *lyang, n.* a Chinese ounce or tael. [Chin.]

liar. See **lie¹.**

liard *lī'ərd, adj.* grey: dapple-grey (*Scot.* **lī'art, ly'art**). — *n.* (*lyär*) an old French coin of little worth. [O.Fr. *liard, liart.*]

Lias *lī'əs,* (*geol.*) *n.* and *adj.* Lower Jurassic. — *adj.* **Liassic** (*lī-as'ik*). [A Somerset quarryman's word, app. — O.Fr. *liois* (Fr. *liais*), a kind of limestone.]

lib¹ *lib,* (now *dial.*) *v.t.* to geld. [Cf. Du. *lubben.*]

lib². See **liberate.**

libation *lī-bā'shən, li-, n.* the pouring forth of wine or other liquid in honour of a god, or (*facet.*) for other purpose: the liquid poured. — *adj.* **lī'bant** sipping: lightly touching. — *v.t.* **lī'bate** (*rare*) to make a libation to. — *adj.* **lī'batory.** [L. *lībāre, -ātum,* to pour, sip, touch; Gr. *leibein,* to pour.]

libbard *lib'ərd,* (*arch.*) *n.* same as **leopard.**

libber. See **liberate.**

libeccio *li-bet'chō, n.* the south-west wind. — Also (*Milt.*) **libecchio** (It. *li-bek'i-ō*): — *pl.* **libecc(h)'ios.** [It., — L. *Libs;* Gr. *Lips, Libos.*]

libel *lī'bl, n.* a written accusation: any malicious defamatory publication or statement: written defamation (*English law;* distinguished from *slander* or spoken defamation; in Scots law both are slander): the statement of a plaintiff's grounds of complaint. — *v.t.* to defame by libel: to satirise unfairly: to proceed against by producing a written complaint (*law*): — *pr.p.* **lī'belling;** *pa.t.* and *pa.p.* **lī'belled.** — *ns.* **lī'bellant** one who brings a libel; **libellee'** one against whom a libel is brought; **lī'beller** a defamer; **lī'belling.** — *adj.* **lī'bellous** containing a libel: defamatory. — *adv.* **lī'bellously.** [L. *lībellus,* dim. of *līber,* a book.]

liber *lī'bər, n.* bast. [L. *līber,* bast, book.]

liberal *lib'ə-rəl, adj.* befitting a freeman or a gentleman: directed towards the cultivation of the mind for its own sake, disinterested (opposed to *technical* and *professional*): generous: noble-minded: broad-minded: not bound by authority or traditional orthodoxy: looking to the general or broad sense rather than the literal: candid: free: free from restraint: licentious in speech or action (*obs.*): ample: (*cap.*) of the Liberal Party (see below). — *n.* one who advocates greater freedom in political institutions: one whose views in theology are liberal. — *n.* **liberalīsā'tion, -z-.** — *v.t.* and *v.i.* **lib'eralise, -ize** to make or become liberal, or enlightened. — *ns.* **lib'eralism** the principles of a liberal in politics or religion; **lib'eralist.** — *adj.* **liberalist'ic.** — *n.* **liberality** (*-al'i-ti*) the quality of being liberal: generosity: largeness or nobleness of mind: candour: freedom from prejudice. — *adv.* **lib'erally.** — **liberal arts** the studies that make up a liberal education: in the Middle Ages, the *trivium* and *quadrivium;* **Liberal Party** successors of the Whigs, including the Radicals, advocates of democratic reform and liberty; **Liberal Unionists** a section of the Liberal Party that opposed Gladstone's Home Rule policy (1886) and joined the Conservatives. [L. *līberālis,* befitting a freeman — *līber,* free.]

liberate *lib'ə-rāt, v.t.* to set free: to release from restraint, confinement, or bondage: to steal, appropriate (*facet.*): to give off. — *ns.* **liberā'tion** setting free, releasing: freeing, or seeking to free (a group) from social disadvantages, prejudices, injustice or abuse (*coll. abbrev.* **lib**); **liberā'tionism; liberā'tionist** one who is in favour of church disestablishment: one who supports the cause of social freedom and equality for sections of society believed to be underprivileged or discriminated against (*coll.* shortening **libb'er**); **lib'erātor.** — *adj.* **lib'eratory** (*-ə-tə-ri*) tending to liberate. — **liberated woman** one who rejects the older ideas of woman as the weaker sex, a woman's place being in the home, etc., and lives and works on equal terms with men; **liberation theology** esp. in S. America, a development of Christian doctrine that demands a commitment to social revolution whenever injustice and exploitation are thought to exist. [L. *līberāre, -ātum* — *līber,* free.]

liberty *lib'ər-ti, n.* freedom from constraint, captivity, slavery, or tyranny: freedom to do as one pleases: the unrestrained enjoyment of natural rights: power of free choice: privilege: permission: free range: leisure: disposal: the bounds within which certain privileges are enjoyed: (often in *pl.*) a limited area outside a prison in which prisoners were allowed to live (*arch.*): presumptuous or undue freedom: speech or action violating ordinary civility. — *n.* **libertā'rian** a believer in free-will: one who believes in the maximum amount of freedom of thought, behaviour, etc. — Also *adj.* — *ns.* **libertā'rianism; liber'ticide** a destroyer of liberty: destruction of liberty; **lib'ertinage** (also *-ûrt'*) debauchery; **lib'ertine** (*-tēn, -tin, -tīn*) originally, a freedman: formerly one who professed free opinions, esp. in religion: one who leads a licentious life, a rake or debauchee. — *adj.* belonging to a freedman: free: unrestrained: licentious. — *n.* **lib'ertinism.** — **lib'erty-boat** a boat for liberty-men; **liberty bodice** an undergarment like a vest formerly often worn by children; **liberty cap** a cap of liberty (q.v. under **cap¹**): a yellowish-brown conical-capped mushroom yielding the drug psilocybin; **Liberty Hall** (*coll.;* also without *cap.*) a place where one may do as one likes; **liberty horse** a circus horse that, as one of a group and without a rider, carries out movements on command; **lib'erty-man** a sailor with permission to go ashore; **liberty ship** a prefabricated all-welded cargo-ship mass-produced in the U.S.A. during World War II. — **at liberty** free: unoccupied: available; **civil liberty** freedom of an individual within the law: individual freedom as guaranteed by a country's laws; **liberty of indifference** freedom of the will; **liberty of the press** freedom to print and publish without government permission; **take liberties with** to treat with undue freedom or familiarity, or indecently: to falsify; **take the liberty** to venture, presume. [Fr. *liberté* — L. *lībertās, -ātis,* liberty: L. *lībertīnus,* a freedman — *līber,* free.]

libido *li-bē'dō, li-bī'dō, n.* vital urge, either in general or as of sexual origin (*psych.*): sexual impulse: — *pl.*

libid'os. — *adjs.* **libidinal** (-*bid'*) pertaining to the libido; **libid'inous** lustful, lascivious, lewd. — *ns.* **libid'inist** a lewd person; **libidinos'ity, libid'inousness.** — *adv.* **libid'inously.**   [L. *libīdō, -inis,* desire — *libet, lubet,* it pleases.]

libken *lib'ken,* (*old slang*) *n.* a place of abode.   [Old slang *lib,* to sleep, **ken**[2].]

libra *lī'brə,* L. *lē', n.* a Roman pound (*ant.;* used in contraction lb. for the British pound, and £ for a pound in money): (*cap.*) the Balance, a constellation between the Virgin and the Scorpion: the seventh sign of the zodiac in which it used to be (it is now in Scorpio): one born under this sign.   [L. *lībra.*]

libraire *lē-brer,* (Fr.) *n.* bookseller. — *n.* **librairie** (*lē-bre-rē*) book-trade: bookshop.

library *lī'brə-ri, n.* a collection of books: a building or room containing it: a publisher's series: also a collection of gramophone records, etc.; a collection of computer programs. — *ns.* **librā'rian** the keeper of a library; **librā'rianship.** — **library edition** an edition of a book with high-quality binding, etc. — **lending library** one from which people may take books away on loan.   [L. *lībrārium,* a bookcase — *liber,* a book.]

librate *lī'brāt, v.t.* to poise: to balance. — *v.i.* to oscillate: to be poised. — *n.* **librā'tion** balancing: a state of equipoise: a slight swinging motion. — *adjs.* **librā'tional; lī'bratory.** — **libration of the moon** a slight turning of the moon to each side alternately so that more than half of its surface is visible one time or other.   [L. *lībrāre, -ātum* — *lībra,* balance.]

libretto *li-bret'ō, n.* the text or book of words of an opera, oratorio, or ballet: — *pl.* **librett'i** (-*ē*), **librett'os.** — *n.* **librett'ist** a writer of libretti.   [It., dim. of *libro* — L. *liber,* a book.]

Librium® *lib'ri-əm, n.* proprietary name for chlordiazepoxide, a tranquilliser.

Libyan *lib'i-ən, adj.* of *Libya* in North Africa. — *n.* a native thereof.   [Gr. *Libyē,* Libya.]

lice *līs,* plural of **louse.**

licence, in U.S. **license,** *lī'səns, n.* a being allowed: leave: grant of permission, as for manufacturing a patented article, developing an area or natural resource, selling intoxicants, driving a motor vehicle, piloting an aeroplane, using a television set, keeping a dog, owning a gun: the document by which authority is conferred: excess or abuse of freedom: licentiousness, libertinage, debauchery: a departure for effect from a rule or standard in art or literature: tolerated freedom. — *v.t.* **li'cense** to grant licence to: to permit to depart, dismiss: to authorise or permit. — Also **licence.** — *adjs.* **li'censable; li'censed** holding a licence: permitted, tolerated. — *ns.* **licensee'** one to whom a licence is granted, esp. to sell alcoholic drink; **li'censer,** (chiefly *U.S.*) **li'censor** one who grants licence or permission: one authorised to license; **li'censure** act of licensing; **licentiate** (*lī-sen'-shi-āt*) among Presbyterians, a person authorised by a Presbytery to preach: a holder of an academic diploma of various kinds: in some European universities, a graduate ranking between bachelor and doctor. — *adj.* **licentious** (-*sen'shəs*) indulging in excessive freedom: given to the indulgence of the animal passions: dissolute. — *adv.* **licen'tiously.** — *n.* **licen'tiousness.** — **licence block** see **block; licensed victualler** a person licensed to sell food and esp. drink, for consumption on his premises, a publican; **license plate** (*U.S.*) a vehicle number plate. — **special licence** licence given by the Archbishop of Canterbury permitting the marriage of two specified persons without banns, and at a place and time other than those prescribed by law — loosely used in Scotland in speaking of marriage by consent registered by warrant of the sheriff.   [Fr. *licence* — L. *licentia* — *licēre,* to be allowed.]

licentia vatum *lī-sen'shyə vā'təm, li-ken'ti-ä wä'tŏŏm, vä',* (L.) poetic licence.

lich[1] *lich,* (*Spens.*) *adj.* a Southern form of **like**[1].

lich[2] *lich, n.* a body, living or dead (*obs.*). — **lich'gate, lych'gate** a roofed churchyard gate to rest the bier

under;   **lich'-owl** a screech-owl, deemed a death-portent; **lich'wake** see **lykewake; lich'way** a path by which the dead are carried to burial.   [M.E. *lich, liche* (Southern), *like* (Northern) — O.E. *līc;* Ger. *Leiche,* corpse.]

lichanos *lik'a-nos,* (*anc. Gr. mus.*) *n.* the string or the note struck by the forefinger.   [Gr. *lichanos,* forefinger, *lichanos* — *leichein,* to lick.]

lichee. Same as **lychee.**

lichen *lī'kən, lich'ən, n.* a compound plant consisting of a fungus and an alga living symbiotically, forming crusts and tufts on stones, trees, and soil: an eruption on the skin. — *adj.* **li'chened** covered with lichens. — *ns.* **li'chenin** a starch got from Iceland moss; **li'chenism** the consorting of fungus and alga as a lichen; **li'chenist, lichenol'ogist** one versed in **lichenol'ogy,** the study of lichens. — *adjs.* **li'chenoid; li'chenose, li'chenous** abounding in, or pertaining to, of the nature of, lichens, or lichen.   [L. *līchēn* — Gr. *leichēn, -ēnos.*]

lichgate, etc. See **lich**[2].

lichi. See **lychee.**

licht *lihht,* the Scots form of **light**[1,2,3].

licit *lis'it, adj.* lawful, allowable. — *adv.* **lic'itly.**   [L. *licitus.*]

lick *lik, v.t.* to pass the tongue over: to take in by the tongue: to lap: to put or render by passing the tongue over: to pass over or play upon in the manner of a tongue: to smear: to beat (*slang*). — *v.i.* (*slang*) to go at full speed. — *n.* an act of licking: a quantity licked up, or such as might be imagined to be licked up: a slight smearing or wash: a place where animals lick salt: a blow, flick (esp. *Scot.* in *pl.,* a thrashing): vigorous speed (*coll.*): a wag (*Scot.*). — *ns.* **lick'er; lick'ing** a thrashing. — **lick'er-in'** a toothed cylinder that takes in material to a carding engine; **lick'penny** that which licks up, or is a drain upon, one's money; **lick'-platter, lick'spittle** a toady; **lick'-trencher** a parasite. — **a lick and a promise** a perfunctory wash; **lick into shape** to mould into due form, from the notion that the she-bear gives form to her shapeless young by licking them; **lick one's lips** to recall or look forward with pleasure; **lick one's wounds** to retire from a defeat, failure, etc., esp. in order to try to recover one's strength, pride, etc.; **lick someone's boots** to toady; **lick the dust** to be slain: to be abjectly servile.   [O.E. *liccian;* Ger. *lecken,* L. *lingĕre,* Gr. *leichein.*]

lickerish, liquorish *lik'ər-ish, adj.* dainty: tempting: eager to taste or enjoy: lecherous. — *adv.* **lick'erishly.** — *n.* **lick'erishness.**   [Variant of **lecherous.**]

lickety-split *lik'ə-ti-split', (U.S. coll.) adv.* immediately: very quickly.   [**lick, split.**]

licorice. Another spelling (chiefly *U.S.*) for **liquorice.**

lictor *lik'tör, -tər, n.* an officer who attended a Roman magistrate, bearing the fasces.   [L. *lictor.*]

lid *lid, n.* a cover, hinged or separate, for the opening of a receptacle: the movable cover of the eye: an effective restraint (*fig.*): a hat (*slang*). — *adjs.* **lidd'ed** having a lid or lids; **lid'less.** — **flip one's lid** see **flip; put the lid on it** to end the matter: to be a culminating injustice, misfortune, etc.; **take, lift, blow the lid off** to uncover, reveal (a scandal, etc.).   [O.E. *hlid* (Du. *lid*) — *hlīdan,* to cover.]

Lide *līd,* (*obs.* or *dial.*) *n.* the month of March.   [O.E. *hlŷda,* conn. with *hlūd,* loud.]

lidger. See **ledger.**

lido *lē'dō, n.* a bathing beach: an open-air swimming-pool: — *pl.* **lid'os.**   [From the *Lido* at Venice — L. *lītus,* shore.]

lidocaine *lī'də-kān,* U.S. name for **lignocaine.**   [Acetanilid and cocaine.]

lie[1] *lī, n.* a false statement made with the intention of deceiving: anything misleading or of the nature of imposture: (with *the*) an accusation of lying. — *v.i.* to utter falsehood with an intention to deceive: to give a false impression: — *pr.p.* **ly'ing;** *pa.t.* and *pa.p.* **lied.** — (*Scot.*) **lee** (*lē*), *n.* and *v.i.* often of an unintentional false statement. — (*dial.*) **lig.** — *n.* **lī'ar** one who lies, esp. habitually. — *adj.* **ly′ing** addicted to telling lies. — *n.* the habit of telling lies. — *adv.* **ly′ingly.** — **lie detector** an instrument claimed to detect lying by recording abnormal involuntary bodily reactions in a person not telling the truth. — **give someone the lie (in his throat)** to charge someone to his face with lying; **give the lie to** to charge with lying: to prove false; **lie in one's throat** to lie shamelessly; **white lie** a minor falsehood, esp. one uttered for reasons of tact, etc. [O.E. *lyge* (noun), *lēogan* (strong vb.): Du. *liegen*, Goth. *liugan*, Ger. *lügen*, to lie.]

lie² *lī*, *v.i.* to be in a horizontal or nearly horizontal posture: to assume such a posture: to lean: to press: to be situated: to have a position or extent: to remain: to be or remain passively: to abide: to be still: to be incumbent: to depend: to consist: to be sustainable (*law*): to be imprisoned (*Shak.*): to lodge, pass the night (*arch.*): — *pr.p.* **ly′ing;** *pa.t.* **lay;** *pa.p.* **lain,** (*B.*) **lī′en** — erroneously **laid,** by confusion with **lay**³. — *n.* mode or direction of lying: slope and disposition: relative position: general situation: a spell of lying: an animal's lurking-place or favourite station: position from which a golf-ball is to be played: a layer: a railway siding. — *n.* **lī′er.** — **lie′-abed′** one who lies late. — Also *adj.* — **lie-down** see **lie down** below; **lie′-in′** a longer than usual stay in bed in the morning; **ly′ing-in′** confinement during child-birth: — *pl.* **ly′ings-in′.** — Also *adj.* — **lie along** to be extended at full length (*arch.*); **lie at someone's door** to be directly imputable to someone; **lie at someone's heart** to be an object of interest or affection to someone; **lie back** to lean back on a support: to rest after a period of hard work; **lie by** to be inactive: to keep out of the way: to lie to (*naut.*); **lie by the heels** (*arch.*) to be in prison; **lie down** to place oneself in a horizontal position, esp. in order to sleep or rest (*n.* **lie′-down′**); **lie hard** or **heavy on, upon, to** to oppress, burden; **lie in** to be in childbed: to stay in bed later than usual; **lie in one** to be in one's power; **lie in the way** to be ready, at hand: to be an obstacle; **lie in wait** to lie in ambush; **lie low** to keep quiet or hidden: to conceal one's actions or intentions; **lie of the land** (*fig.*) the current situation; **lie on, upon** to be incumbent on; **lie on one's hands** to remain unwanted, unclaimed, or unused; **lie on the oars** see **oar; lie out of** to remain without the good of, without payment of; **lie over** to be deferred to a future occasion; **lie to** to be or become nearly stationary with head to wind; **lie under** to be subject to or oppressed by; **lie up** to abstain from work: to take to or remain in bed: of a ship, to go into or be in dock; **lie with** to lodge or sleep with (*arch.*): to have sexual intercourse with: to rest with as a choice, duty, etc.; **lying-in hospital** a maternity hospital; **take it lying down** to endure without resistance or protest. [O.E. *licgan*; Ger. *liegen*; Goth. *ligan*.]

Liebig *lē′big, n.* a beef extract first prepared by the German chemist J. von *Liebig* (1803–73). — **Liebig condenser** the ordinary water-cooled glass condenser used in laboratory distillations.

lied *lēt, n.* a German lyric or song, esp. an art-song: — *pl.* **lieder** (*lē′dər*). — **lied ohne worte** (*ō′nə vör′tə*) song without words. [Ger.; cf. O.E. *lēoth*, a song.]

lief *lēf*, (*arch.*) *adj.* and *n.* beloved, dear. — *adv.* willingly. — Also *adj.* and *adv.* **lieve, leve** (*lēv*): — *compar.* **lief′er, liev′er** (*Scot.* **loor**); *superl.* **lief′est, liev′est.** — **had as lief** should like as well to; **had liefer, liever** had rather; **leeze me** (*Scot.*) for *lief is me*, an expression of affection (usu. *with on*). [O.E. *lēof*; Ger. *lieb*.]

liege *lēj, adj.* free except as within the relations of vassal and feudal lord: under a feudal tenure. — *n.* one under a feudal tenure: a vassal: a loyal vassal, subject: a lord or superior (also in this sense, **liege′-lord**). — *n.* **liege′-dom** allegiance. — *adj.* **liege′less** not subject to a superior. — *n.* **liege′man** a vassal: a subject. [O.Fr. *lige*, prob. from O.H.G. *ledic*, free, *līdan*, to depart.]

lieger. See **ledger.**

lien¹ *lē′ən, lēn,* (*law*) *n.* a right to retain possession of another's property until the owner pays a debt. [Fr., — L. *ligāmen*, tie, band.]

lien² *lī′ən,* (*B.*) *pa.p.* of **lie²**.

lien³ *lī′ən, n.* the spleen. — *adj.* **lī′enal.** [L. *liēn.*]

lientery *lī′ən-tə-ri, n.* a form of diarrhoea with liquid evacuations of undigested food. — *adj.* **lienteric** (*-ter′-ik*). [Gr. *leios*, smooth, *enteron,* an intestine.]

lier. See **lie²**.

lierne *li-ûrn′, n.* a cross-rib or branch-rib in vaulting. [Fr.]

lieu *lū, loō, n.* place, stead, chiefly in the phrase 'in lieu of'. [Fr., — L. *locus,* place.]

lieutenant *lef-, lif-, ləf-ten′ənt,* also (esp. *navy*) *le-, lə-, loō-ten′-, arch. loōt′nənt,* in U.S., *loō-, n.* one representing, or performing the work of a superior (form. also *fig.*): an officer holding the place of another in his absence: a commissioned officer in the army next below a captain, or in the navy next below a lieutenant-commander and ranking with captain in the army: one holding a place next in rank to a superior, as in the compounds **lieuten′ant-col′onel, lieuten′ant-comman-d′er, lieuten′ant-gen′eral.** — *ns.* **lieuten′ancy, lieuten′-antship,** (*Shak.*) **lieuten′antry** office or commission of a lieutenant: the body of lieutenants; **lieuten′ant-col′-onelcy; lieuten′ant-command′ership; lieuten′ant-gen′er-alship; lieuten′ant-gov′ernor** a State governor's deputy (*U.S., Austr.*): a governor subordinate to a governor-general: a governor (Isle of Man, Jersey, Guernsey); **lieuten′ant-gov′ernorship.** — **Lord Lieutenant** the title of the viceroy of Ireland (till 1922): a permanent governor of a county, head of the magistracy and the chief executive authority: — *pl.* **Lords Lieutenant, Lord Lieutenants, Lords Lieutenants.** [Fr.; see **lieu** and **tenant.**]

lieve, etc. See **lief.**

life *līf, n.* state of being alive: conscious existence: animate or vegetative existence: the sum of the activities of plants and animals: continuation or possession of such a state: continued existence, activity, or validity of anything: the period of usefulness of machinery, etc.: vitality: union of soul and body: the period between birth and death: a continued opportunity of remaining in the game: career: present state of existence: manner of living: moral conduct: animation: liveliness: appearance of being alive: a living being: living things: social state: human affairs: narrative of a life: eternal happiness: a quickening principle: that on which continued existence depends: one who imparts animation: the living form and expression, living semblance: in wines, sparkle: in cut gems, reflection: a life sentence (*coll.*): an insured person: — *pl.* **lives** (*līvz*). — *interj.* used as an oath, abbreviated from *God's life.* — *adj.* used (and in composition) for the duration of life: of life. — *adjs.* **life′ful** (*Spens.* **lyfull, lifull**) full of vital energy; **life′less** dead: insensible: without vigour: insipid: sluggish. — *adv.* **life′lessly.** — *n.* **life′lessness.** — *adjs.* **life′like** like a living person or the original; **life′some** full of life: gay, lively. — *n.* **lif′er** a person sentenced for life: a life sentence. — *adj.* **life′-and-death′** critical: determining between life and death. — *adv.* **life′-annū′ity** a sum paid to a person yearly during life; **life′-assur′ance, life′-insur′-ance** insurance providing a sum of money for a specified beneficiary in the event of the policy-holder's death, and for the policy-holder if he reaches a specified age; **life′belt** a buoyant belt for sustaining a person in the water: any aid to survival (*fig.*); **life′-blood** the blood necessary to life: that which gives strength or life: a twitching, as of the eyelid; **life′boat** a boat for saving shipwrecked persons; **life′-buoy** a float for supporting a person in the water till he can be rescued; **life class** an art class in which the students draw or paint the human body from a live model; **life′-cycle** (*biol.*) the round of changes in the life and generations of an organism, from zygote to zygote; **life′-estate′** an estate held during the life of the possessor; **life′-force′** a directing principle supposed to be immanent in living things, turning their activities to nature's own purposes. — *adj.* **life′-giving** imparting life: invigorating.

— **life′guard** a bodyguard: one employed to rescue bathers in difficulties; **Life Guards** two troops of horse, first so styled in 1685, amalgamated in 1922, forming, with the Royal Horse Guards, the Household Cavalry; **life′-his′tory** the history of a life: the succession of changes from zygote to maturity and death: the life-cycle. — *adj.* **life′hold** held for life. — **life′-in′terest** an interest lasting during a life; **life′-jack′et** a buoyant jacket, a lifebelt; **life′-line** a rope for saving or safe-guarding life: a vital line of communication. — *adj.* **life′long** lasting throughout life. — **life′manship** (*facet.* — Stephen Potter) the art of making the other fellow feel inferior, of placing oneself at an advantage; **life′= mor′tar** a mortar for throwing a line to a ship in distress; **life′-peer** a peer whose title is not hereditary; **life′-peer′age; life′-peeress** a woman who receives a peerage which cannot be handed down to heirs; **life′= preserv′er** an apparatus for saving from drowning: a club or cosh; **life raft** a raft kept on board a ship for use in an emergency. — *adj.* **life′-ren′dering** (*Shak.*) yielding up life. — **life′-rent** (*Scots law*) a right to use for life; **life′-renter** one who enjoys a life-rent: — *fem.* **life′-rentrix; life′-rock′et** a rocket for carrying a line to a ship in distress; **life′-saver** one who saves from death, esp. from drowning: one employed to rescue bathers in difficulty: something, or someone, that comes to one's aid at a critical moment (*fig.*); **life′-sav′ing.** — *adj.* designed to save life, esp. from drowning. — **life′-school** a school where artists work from living models; **life sciences** the sciences (biology, medicine, etc.) concerned with living organisms; **life sentence** a prison sentence to last for the rest of the prisoner's natural life (usu. now lasting approx. 15 years). — *adjs.* **life′-size(d)** of the size of the object represented. — **life′span** the length of time during which a person or animal normally lives, or a machine, etc., functions; **life style** way of living, i.e. one's material surroundings, attitudes, behaviour, etc.: the (characteristic) way of life of a group or individual; **life-support machine, system** a device or system of devices designed to maintain human life in adverse conditions, e.g. in space, during illness, etc.; **life′-table** a table of statistics of probability of life; **life′-tenant** the holder of a life-estate; **life′time** time during which one is alive. — *adj.* **life′-wear′y** (*Shak.*) weary of life: wretched. — **life′-work** the work to which one's life is or is to be devoted. — **bring to life** to confer life upon: to reanimate; **come to life** to become alive: to be reanimated; **for life** for the whole period of one's existence: (as if) to save one's life; **for the life of him** though it were to save his life: do what he might; **high life** fashionable society or its manner of living; **line of life** a crease in the palm in which palmists see a promise of longevity; **not on your life** (*coll.*) on no account; **see life** to see how other people live, esp. the disreputable; **take someone's life** to kill someone; **the life and soul** the one who is the chief source of merriment, etc., esp. at a party; **the life of Riley** (*rī′li*) an easy, troublefree life; **to the life** very closely like the original: exactly drawn. [O.E. *līf*; O.N. *līf*, Sw. *lif*, Du. *liif*, body, life; Ger. *Leib*, body, *leben*, to live, *Leben*, life.]

lift[1] *lift*, (*Scot.*) *n.* the air, heavens, sky. [O.E. *lyft*; Ger. *Luft*, O.N. *lopt*, Goth. *luftus*, the air.]

lift[2] *lift*, *v.t.* to bring to a higher position: to elevate: to take up: to take up for burial (*Scot.*): to increase (in value, price etc.) (*U.S.*): to elate: to take and carry away: to hold up, support: to arrest (*slang*): to steal: to plagiarise: to remove or revoke. — *v.i.* to rise. — *n.* act of lifting: lifting power: vertical distance of lifting: the component of the aerodynamic force on an aircraft acting upwards at right angles to the drag: that which is to be raised: that which assists to lift: an enclosed platform moving in a well to carry persons or goods up and down: the well in which it works: one of the layers of material in a shoe heel, esp. an extra one to increase the wearer's height: a contrivance for raising or lowering a vessel to another level of a canal:

a step in advancement: a boost to one's spirits: a feeling of elation: help on one's way by taking upon a vehicle. — *adj.* **lift′able.** — *n.* **lift′er** one who, or that which, lifts: a thief (*Shak.*). — **lift′-boy, -girl, -man** a person whose job is to operate a lift in a hotel, store, etc.; **lift′ing-bridge** a bridge whose roadway can be raised bodily; **lift′-off** the take-off of an aircraft or rocket: the moment when this occurs; **lift′-pump** any pump that is not a force-pump. — **have one's face lifted** to undergo an operation for smoothing and firming it; **lift a, one's hand (to)** to raise it in hostility. [O.N. *lypta — lopt*, the air.]

lifull. See **life.**

lig[1] *lig*, (*slang*) *v.i.* to lie about, to idle: to be a freeloader, esp. in the entertainment industry. — *ns.* **ligg′er; ligg′ing.** [Orig. dial. for **lie**[2].]

lig[2], **ligge** *lig*, (*Spens.* and *Northern dialect*) *v.i.* a form of **lie**[2]. — *infin.* and *pl.* (*Spens.*) also **ligg′en; lig** is also a dialect form of **lie**[1].

ligament *lig′ə-mənt, n.* anything that binds: the bundle of fibrous tissue joining bones or cartilages (*anat.*): a bond of union. — *adjs.* **ligamental** (*-ment′l*), **ligament′-ary, ligament′ous.** — *n.* **ligand** (*lig′ənd, lī′*) an atom, molecule, radical, or ion which forms a complex with a central atom. — *v.t.* **ligate** (*lī′gāt*) to tie up. — *ns.* **līgā′tion** act of binding: state of being bound; **ligature** (*lig′ə-chər*) anything that binds: a bandage: a tie or slur (*mus.*): a type of two or more letters (e.g. æ, ff) (*print.*): a cord for tying the blood-vessels, etc. (*med.*): impotence produced by magic. — *v.t.* to bind with a ligature. [L. *ligāre*, to bind.]

ligan; ligate, etc. See **lagan; ligament.**

liger *lī′gər, n.* cross between *li*on and female ti*ger.*

ligge, liggen. See **lig**[2].

ligger[1] *lig′ər, n.* the horizontal timber of a scaffolding: a nether millstone: a plank bridge: a coverlet for a bed: a kelt or spent salmon: a night-line with float and bait for pike-fishing. [**lig,** Northern form of **lie**[2].]

ligger[2], **ligging.** See **lig**[1].

light[1] *līt, n.* the agency by which objects are rendered visible: electromagnetic radiation capable of producing visual sensation: that from which it proceeds, as the sun, a lamp: a high degree of illumination: day: a gleam or shining from a bright source: a gleam or glow in the eye or on the face: the power of vision: an eye (*arch.*): the brighter part of a picture: means of igniting or illuminating: a lighthouse: mental or spiritual illumination (*fig.*): enlightenment: a hint, clue, help towards understanding: knowledge: open view: aspect: a conspicuous person: an aperture for admitting light: a vertical division of a window. — *adj.* not dark: bright: whitish: well lighted. — *v.t.* to give light to: to set fire to: to attend with a light. — *v.i.* to become light or bright: — *pr.p.* **light′ing;** *pa.t.* and *pa.p.* **light′ed** or **lit.** — *n.* **light′er** one who sets alight: a spill, mechanical device, or other means of igniting. — *adj.* **light′ful** full of light. — *n.* **light′ing** illumination: ignition, kindling: disposal or quality of lights. — Also *adj.* — *adjs.* **light′ish; light′less.** — *n.* **light′ness.** — *adj.* **light′some** full of light. — **light′-ball** (*hist.*) a combustible ball used to give light in warfare; **light bulb** a glass bulb containing a low-pressure gas and a metal filament, which glows when an electric current is passed through it, and is the usual method of electric lighting. — *n.pl.* **light′-dues** tolls from ships, for maintenance of light-houses. — *adj.* **light′fast** (of colour in fabric, or coloured fabric) that will not fade in the light. — **light′house** a building with a light to guide or warn ships or aircraft; **light′houseman, light(house)keep′er** the keeper of a lighthouse. — *n.* and *adj.* **light′ing-up (lighting-up time** the time of day from which vehicles must show lights). — **light meter** (*phot.*) an exposure meter; **light′-mill** a radiometer; **light′-or′gan** a keyboard instrument that gives a play of light as an organ gives sound; **light pen** (*comput.*) a pen-like photoelectric device that can enter or alter data on a visual display unit: a light-sensitive fibre-optic device shaped like a pen, used for reading bar-coded labels. — *adj.* **light'-proof** light-tight. — **light'ship** ship serving the purpose of a lighthouse; **light'-table** (*printing*) a (table incorporating a) ground-glass surface, illuminated from below, for use when working on lay-out with negatives, positives and proofs. — *adj.* **light'-tight** impervious to light. — **light time** the time taken by light to travel from a heavenly body to the observer; **light'-tower; light'-year** distance light travels in a year (about 6 000 000 000 000 miles). -- **according to one's lights** as far as one's knowledge, spiritual illumination, etc., enable one to judge; **between the lights** in the twilight; **between two lights** under cover of darkness; **bring to light** to reveal; **come to light** to be revealed; **fixed light** in lighthouses, an unchanging light; **floating light** a light at the masthead of a lightship; **hide one's light under a bushel** see **bushel; in a good, bad light** putting a favourable, unfavourable construction on something; **inner light** spiritual illumination, light divinely imparted; **in one's, the, light** between one and the source of illumination or chance of success, etc.; **in the light of** considering, taking into account; **light at the end of the tunnel** an indication that success, completion, etc. is assured, if still distant; **light of nature** intellectual perception or intuition: man's capacity of discovering truth unaided by revelation (*theol.*); **lights out** (*mil.*) bugle or trumpet call for extinction of lights: the time at which lights are turned out for the night, in a boarding-school, barracks, etc.; **light up** to light one's lamp, pipe, cigarette, etc.: to turn on the light: to make or become light or bright; **lit (up)** drunk; **northern (southern) lights** aurora borealis (australis); **see the light** to come into view or being: to be converted; **shed, throw, light on** to clarify; **stand in one's own light** to hinder one's own advantage; **strike a light** (*slang*) an exclamation expressing surprise. [M.E. *liht* — O.E. (Anglian) *leht, leht* (W.S. *leoht*); Ger. *Licht.*]

light² *lit, adj.* not heavy: of short weight: easily suffered or performed: easily digested: well risen, as bread: containing little alcohol: not heavily armed: active: not heavily burdened: unimportant: not dense or copious or intense: slight: scanty: gentle: delicate: nimble: facile: frivolous: unheeding: gay, lively: amusing: unchaste: loose, sandy: giddy, delirious: idle: worthless: delivered of a child (in *compar.*; *obs.*): falling short in the number of tricks one has contracted to make (*bridge*). — *adv.* lightly. — *v.t.* (*obs.*) to lighten (see also next article). — *v.t.* **light'en** to make lighter. — *v.i.* to become lighter. — *ns.* **light'er** a large open boat used in unloading and loading ships; **light'erage** loading, unloading and ferrrying by lighters: the payment for such service; **light'erman.** — *adj.* **light'ish.** — *adv.* **light'ly** in a light manner: slightly: easily, readily, unthinkingly (*Shak.*): not improbably (*arch.*): promptly. — *v.t.* (esp. in Scots form **lichtly** (*lihht'li*)) to slight. — *n.* **light'ness.** — *n.pl.* **lights** the lungs of an animal (as lighter than adjoining parts). — *adj.* **light'some** light, gay, lively, cheering. — *n.* **light'someness.** — *adj.* **light'-armed** armed in a manner suitable for activity. — **light engine** one without coaches or trucks attached. — *adjs.* **light'er-than-air** of aircraft, sustained by a gas-bag; **light'-faced** of type, having thin lines; **light'-fing'ered** light or active with one's fingers: thievish; **light'-foot, -ed** nimble, active; **light'-hand'ed** with light, delicate, or dexterous touch: having little in the hand: empty-handed: insufficiently manned; **light'-head'ed** giddy in the head: delirious: thoughtless: unsteady. — **light'-head'edness.** — *adj.* **light'-heart'ed** unburdened or merry of heart: free from anxiety: cheerful: inconsiderate. — *adv.* **light'-heart'edly.** — **light'-heart'edness; light-heavyweight** see under **heavy.** — *adj.* **light'-heeled** swift of foot: loose, unchaste (*obs.*). — **light'-horse'** light-armed cavalry; **light'-horse'man; light industry** see **industry; light'-in'fantry** light-armed-infantry. — *adj.* **light'-legged** swift of foot. — **light literature, music,** etc., such as calls for little mental

effort; **light-middleweight** see under **middle.** — *adj.* **light'-mind'ed** frivolous or unstable: inconsiderate. — **light'-mind'edness; light'-o'-love** a fickle or wanton woman: in *Shak.* the name of an old dance tune; **light railway** a railway of light construction. — *adj.* **light'-spir'ited** having a cheerful spirit. — **light water** normal water (H₂O) as opposed to heavy water (q.v.); **light'-weight** a man or animal between the middleweight and the featherweight, as a boxer over 9st. and not over 9st. 9lb. (amateur 7lb.): a person of little importance or influence: a light article of any kind, esp. a motor-cycle. — *adj.* light in weight: lacking substance, earnestness, solemnity, etc. (*fig.*). -- *adj.* **light'-winged** having light wings: volatile. — **lighten up** (*U.S. slang*) to relax, calm down; **make light of** to treat as of little consequence. [O.E. (Anglian) *liht* (W.S. *lioht, leoht*); Ger. *leicht*, O.N. *lettr*; L. *levis.*]

light³ *lit, v.i.* to dismount: to come down as from a horse or vehicle or from fall or flight: to alight: to settle: to rest: to come by chance: — *pr.p.* **light'ing;** *pa.t.* and *pa.p.* **light'ed** or **lit.** — Also (*Pr. Bk.*) **light'en.** — **light into** (*coll.*) to attack, with blows or words; **light out** to decamp. [O.E. *lihtan*, to dismount, lit. make light; see preceding.]

lighten¹ *lit'n, v.t.* to make light or lighter, or brighter: to illuminate. — *v.i.* to become light, lighter, or brighter: to flash as lightning. — *ns.* **light'ening** a making or becoming lighter or brighter; **light'ning** the electric flash usually followed by thunder: a revival or exhilaration supposed to precede death (*Shak.*). — *adj.* characterised by speed and suddenness. — **light'ning-arrest'er** apparatus for protecting electrical apparatus in thunderstorms; **light'ning-bug** a firefly; **light'ning-conduc'tor, -rod** a metallic rod for protecting buildings from lightning; **lightning strike** an industrial strike without warning; **light'ning-tube'** a fulgurite. [**light¹**.]

lighten². See **light²ˌ³**.
lightsome. See **light¹ˌ²**.
lignage *lin'ij* (*Spens.*). Same as **lineage.**
lign-aloes, lignaloes *lin-al'oz, lig-nal'oz*, (*B.*) *n.* aloes-wood. [L. *lignum*, wood, and *aloes*, gen. of L. and Gr. *aloe*, aloe.]
ligne *lin*, (Fr. *len-y'*), *n.* a measure of watch movement (Swiss ligne = 2·256 mm.). [Fr.]
ligneous, lignite, etc. See **lignum¹**.
lignocaine *lig'no-kan, n.* a local anaesthetic used e.g. in dentistry and also to regulate an unsteady heart-beat. [L. *lignum*, wood, and *cocaine*.]
lignum¹ *lig'nam, n.* wood. — *adj.* **lig'neous** woody: wooden. — *n.* **lignifica'tion.** — *adj.* **lig'niform** resembling wood. — *v.t.* and *v.i.* **lig'nify** to turn into wood or woody: — *pr.p.* **lig'nifying;** *pa.t.* and *pa.p.* **lig'nified.** — *n.* **lig'nin** a complicated mixture of substances deposited in thickened cell-walls of plants. — *adj.* **ligniper'dous** (L. *perdere*, to destroy) destructive of wood. — *n.* **lig'nite** (*-nit*) brown coal, a stage in the conversion of vegetable matter into coal. — *adjs.* **lignitic** (*-nit'ik*); **ligniv'orous** (L. *vorare*, to devour) feeding on wood. — *n.* **lignocell'ulose** any of several compounds of lignin and cellulose occurring in woody tissue. — **lig'num-vitae** (*vi'te*; L. *lig'noom we'ti, ve'*; wood of life) the wood of Guaiacum. [L. *lignum*, wood.]
lignum² *lig'nam*, (*Austr.*) *n.* a wiry shrub (*Muehlenbeckia cunninghamii*) or other shrub of the Polygonum family, forming dense masses in swamps and plains in Australia. — **lig'num-scrub'; lig'num-swamp'.** [For **Polygonum.**]
ligroin *lig'ro-in, n.* a petroleum fraction boiling between 80° and 120°C. [Origin unknown.]
ligule *lig'ul, n.* (*bot.*) a scale at the top of the leaf-sheath in grasses: a similar scale on a petal: a strap-shaped corolla in composite plants. — *n.* **lig'ula** a tongue-like part or organ: the anterior part of an insect's labium, or lower lip. — *adjs.* **lig'ular; lig'ulate** (*bot.*) like a strap: having ligules. — *n.pl.* **Liguliflo'rae** a division of the Compositae having all flowers ligulate. — *adjs.*

liguliflo'ral; lig'uloid. [L. *ligula*, dim. of *lingua*, a tongue.]

Liguorian *li-gwō'ri-ən, -gwō', n.* and *adj.* Redemptorist.

ligure *lig'ūr, -yər, (B.) n.* an unknown precious stone — jacinth or amber according to R.V. (New English Bible says turquoise). [Gr. *ligȳrion.*]

like[1] *līk, adj.* identical, equal, or nearly equal in any respect: similar, resembling: suiting, befitting: characteristic of: inclined, likely, probable (*dial.*). — *n.* one of the same kind: the same thing: a stroke bringing the total to the same as the other side's (*golf*): an exact resemblance. — *adv.* in the same manner: probably (*dial.*): as it were (*dial.*): as if about (*dial.*): nearly (*coll.*): to some extent (*dial.*): sometimes used meaninglessly (*dial.*). — *conj.* (*Shak.*; another reading *as*; now *illit.*) as: as if. — *prep.* in the same manner as: to the same extent as. — *v.t.* (*Shak.*) to compare, liken. — *v.i.* (*obs.*) to be or seem likely (to), come near (to). — **-like** used as an *adj.-forming suff.* with *ns.*, with the force 'resembling', 'suitable to', 'typical of', as *cat-like, lady-like*: used as an *adj.-* and *adv.-forming suff.* with *adjs.* with the force 'somewhat', 'kind of', as *stupid-like* (*coll.*). — *ns.* **like'lihood** similitude (*obs.*): semblance (*obs.*): resemblance (*obs.*): probability: promise of success or of future excellence; **like'liness** likelihood: likeness (*Spens.*). — *adj.* **like'ly** similar (*Spens.*): like the thing required: promising: probable: credible: pleasing (*dial.*): comely (*dial.*). — *adv.* probably. — *v.t.* **lik'en** to represent as like or similar: to compare. — *n.* **like'ness** resemblance: semblance: guise: one who or that which has a resemblance: a portrait. — *adv.* **like'wise** in the same or similar manner: moreover: too. — *adj.* **like'-mind'ed** having similar opinions, values, etc. — **compare like with like** to compare only such things as are genuinely comparable; **feel like** to be disposed or inclined towards; **had like** was likely, came near to; **look like** to show a likelihood of: to appear similar to; **something like a** a fine specimen, a model of what the thing should be; **such like** of that kind; **the like** (*coll.*) similar things; **the likes of (them)** people like (them). [O.E. *līc*, seen in *gelīc*; O.N. *līkr*, Du. *gelijk*, Ger. *gleich* (= *geleich*).]

like[2] *līk, v.t.* to please (*obs.*): to be pleased with: to approve: to enjoy. — *n.* a liking, chiefly in phrase 'likes and dislikes'. — *adj.* **lik(e)'able** lovable: amiable. — *ns.* **līk'er** one who likes; **līk'ing** affection, inclination: taste: satisfaction: beloved (*Milt.*): condition, plight (*obs.*). — *adj.* (*obs.*) pleasing: in good condition (also **good'-liking, well'-liking**). — **on liking** (*arch.*) on approval. [Orig. impersonal — O.E. *līcian*, to please, to be suitable — *līc*, like, suitable, like.]

like[3] *līk, (Scot.) n.* a corpse: a lykewake. — **like'wake, -walk** see **lykewake**. [Northern form of **lich**[2].]

likin *lē-kēn', n.* formerly, a Chinese transit duty. [Chin.]

lilac *lī'lək, n.* a European tree (*Syringa vulgaris*) of the olive family, with light-purple or white flowers, or other species of the genus: a light purple colour. — *adj.* of that colour. [Fr. (*obs.*; now *lilas*) and Sp., — Ar. *līlāk, līlāk* — Pers. *līlāk, nīlak*, bluish.]

lilangeni *lil-ən-gen'i, n.* the unit of currency of Swaziland: — *pl.* **emalangeni** (*em-ə-lən-gen'i*).

liliaceous, lilied, etc. See **lily**.

lill[1] *lil, (Spens.) v.t.* to loll (the tongue). [Cf. **loll**.]

lill[2] *lil, (Scot.) n.* a finger-hole of a wind instrument. [Cf. Du. *lul*.]

Lillibullero *lil-i-bōō-le'rō, -lē'rō, n.* the famous ballad in mockery of the Irish Catholics, which 'sung James II out of three kingdoms'. — Also **Lilliburlē'ro**. [From the meaningless refrain.]

Lilliputian *lil-i-pū'sh(y)ən, n.* an inhabitant of **Lill'iput** (*-put, -poot*), an imaginary country described by Swift in his *Gulliver's Travels*, inhabited by pygmies: a midget, pygmy. — *adj.* (also without *cap.*) diminutive.

Lilo® *lī'lō, n.* (also without *cap.*) an inflatable mattress, often used in camping, etc.

lilt *lilt, v.i.* to do anything briskly or adroitly, as to hop about (*dial.*): to sing or play, esp. merrily, or vaguely

and absent-mindedly, giving the swing or cadence rather than the structure of the melody: to hum. — *v.t.* to sing or play in such a manner. — *n.* a cheerful song or air: cadence, movement of a tune or the like: a springy quality, in gait, etc.: a lill, a finger-hole (*obs.*). [M.E. *lulte*; origin unknown.]

lily *lil'i, n.* any plant or flower of the genus **Lil'ium**, typical genus of **Liliā'ceae,** a family of monocotyledons differing from rushes chiefly in the large conspicuous flowers: extended to others, of the same family, of the kindred Amaryllidaceae, or unrelated: the fleur-de-lis: a person or thing of great purity or whiteness (*fig.*). — *adj.* white: pale. — *adjs.* **liliā'ceous; lil'ied** adorned with lilies: resembling lilies. — *adj.* **lil'y-liv'ered** white-livered: cowardly. — **lily pad** a leaf of a waterlily. — *adj.* **lil'y-white.** — **lily of the Nile** Richardia or Zantedeschia; **lily of the valley** Convallaria, with two long oval leaves and spikes of white bell-shaped flowers. [O.E. *lilie* — L. *līlium* — Gr. *leirion*, lily.]

lima *lē'mə, n.* (in full **Lima bean**) a bean (*Phaseolus lunatus*) akin to the French bean. — **li'ma-wood** a kind of brazil-wood. [*Lima* in Peru.]

limaces, etc. See **Limax**.

limail. See **lemel**.

limation *lī-mā'shən, n.* filing. [L. *līma*, a file.]

Limax *lī'maks, n.* the common genus of slugs, giving name to the slug family **Limā'ceae:** (without *cap.*) a slug of this genus: — *pl.* **limaces** (*lī-mā'sēz*). — *adj.* **limaceous** (*lī-mā'shəs*). — *n.* **limacel** (*lim-ə-sel'*) a slug's reduced, usually embedded, shell. — *adjs.* **limaciform** (*lim-as'*, or *lī-mās'*) slug-like; **limacine** (*lim'ə-sīn, lī', -sin*) of, resembling or relating to slugs. — *ns.* **limacol'ogist; limacol'ogy** the study of slugs; **limaçon** (*lim'ə-son*; Fr. *lē-ma-sɔ̃*) a curve whose polar equation is $r = a \cos \theta + b$. [L. *līmāx*, a slug.]

limb[1] *lim, n.* a member or organ of the body, now only an arm, leg, or wing: a prudish euphemism for leg: a projecting part: a main branch of a tree or of anything else: a member of a body of people, as 'a limb of the law': an imp, scapegrace, as 'a limb of Satan'. — *v.t.* to supply with limbs (*Milt.*): to dismember. — *adjs.* **limbed** furnished with limbs; **limb'less.** — *adv.* **limb'-meal** (*Shak.*) limb by limb. — **limb'-girdle** a bony arch with which a limb articulates. — **out on a limb** in a hazardous position on one's own (*fig.*). [O.E. *lim*; O.N. *limr*, Sw. *lem*.]

limb[2] *lim, n.* an edge or border, as of the sun, etc.: the edge of a sextant, etc.: the free or expanded part of a floral or other leaf (*bot.*). — *adjs.* **lim'bate** bordered; **lim'bous** overlapping. [L. *limbus*, a border.]

limbeck, limbec *lim'bek, (Spens., Shak.) n.* aphetic for **alembic**.

limber[1] *lim'bər, n.* the shaft of a vehicle (*dial.*): the detachable fore-part of a gun-carriage (*mil.*). — *v.t.* to attach to the limber. [Poss. Fr. *limonière*.]

limber[2] *lim'bər, adj.* pliant, flexible. — *v.t.* to make limber. — **lim'ber-neck** botulism in birds. — **limber up** to tone up the muscles in preparation for physical effort of some sort. [Origin uncertain.]

limber[3] *lim'bər, (naut.) n.* (usu. *pl.*) channel or hole on either side of the keelson for drainage. [Fr. *lumière* — L. *lumināria*, windows.]

limbic *lim'bik, adj.* of, or relating to, the **limbic system** in the brain, the hypothalamus, etc., concerned with basic emotions. [L. *limbicus* — *limbus*, border.]

Limbo, limbo *lim'bō, n.* the borderland of Hell, assigned to the unbaptised (*Limbus patrum* for the righteous who died before Christ, *Limbus infantum* for children): any unsatisfactory place of consignment or oblivion: an uncertain or intermediate state: prison: — *pl.* **Lim'bos, lim'bos.** — Also **Lim'bus** (*-bəs*). [From the Latin phrase *in limbo, in,* in, and abl. of *limbus*, border.]

limbo *lim'bō, n.* a West Indian dance in which the dancer bends backwards and passes under a bar which is progressively lowered: — *pl.* **lim'bos.** [Perh. **limber**[1].]

Limburger (cheese) *lim'bûrg-ər (chēz), n.* a white cheese from *Limburg* in Belgium, of strong taste and smell.

limburgite *lim'bər-gīt, n.* a volcanic rock composed of olivine and augite, etc., in a fine-grained or glassy groundmass. [*Limburg* in Baden, a typical locality.]

Limbus patrum, infantum. See **Limbo.**

lime¹ *līm, n.* any slimy or gluey material (*dial.*): bird-lime: the white caustic earth (calcium oxide, quicklime, caustic lime) got by calcining calcium carbonate (as limestone): calcium hydroxide (slaked lime) got by adding water to quicklime: loosely, limestone or calcium carbonate. — *adj.* of lime. — *v.t.* to cover with lime: to cement (*dial.*): to treat with lime: to manure with lime: to ensnare (also *fig.*). — *v.i.* (*Shak.*) to adulterate wine with lime. — *ns.* **līm'iness; līm'ing** the soaking of skins in limewater to remove hair: application of lime. — *adj.* **līm'y** glutinous, sticky (*dial.*): smeared with, containing, like, of the nature of, lime. — **lime'-burner** one who calcines limestone, etc., to form lime; **lime'kiln** a kiln or furnace in which calcium carbonate is calcined to lime; **lime'light** Drummond light, light produced by a blowpipe-flame directed against a block of quicklime: the glare of publicity (*fig.*). — *v.t.* (esp. *fig.*) to illuminate by limelight, to subject to the glare of limelight: — *pa.t.* and *pa.p.* **lime'lit** or **limelighted.** — **lime'pit** a lime-filled pit in which hides are steeped to remove hair; **lime'stone** a sedimentary rock of calcium carbonate, sometimes (*magnesian*) limestone) with much dolomite; **lime'-twig** a twig smeared with bird-lime: a snare; **lime'wash** a milky mixture of slaked lime and water, used for coating walls, etc.; **lime'water** a suspension of calcium hydroxide in water. [O.E. *līm*; Ger. *Leim*, glue, L. *līmus*, slime.]

lime² *līm, n.* a tropical citrus tree, *C. aurantifolia*: its small nearly globular fruit, with acid pulp: the colour of the fruit, a yellowish green. — *n.* **lime'y** (*slang*) a British sailor or ship (from the use of lime-juice on British ships to prevent scurvy): any British person. — **lime'-juice** the acid juice of the lime. [Fr., — Sp. *lima*; cf. **lemon¹**.]

lime³ *līm, n.* the linden tree (*Tilia europaea*), or other of the genus. — **lime'-tree; lime'-wood.** [*lind.*]

lime⁴, lime-hound. See **lyam.**

limen *lī'men,* (*psych.*) *n.* the threshold of consciousness: the limit below which a stimulus is not perceived. — *adj.* **liminal** (*līm', lim'in-əl*). [L. *līmen, -inis,* threshold.]

limerick *lim'ə-rik, n.* a form of humorous verse in a five-line jingle. [Said to be from a refrain formerly used, referring to *Limerick* in Ireland.]

limes *lī'mēz, lē'mes, n.* a boundary or boundary work, esp. of the Roman Empire: — *pl.* **limites** (*lī'mit-ēz, lē'mi-tās*). [L. *līmes, -itis.*]

limey. See **lime².**

limicolous *lī-mik'ə-ləs, adj.* living in mud. — *adj.* **lī'mous** (*arch.*) muddy: slimy. [L. *līmus,* mud, *colēre,* to dwell.]

limit *lim'it, n.* boundary: that which may not be passed: restriction: a predetermined price at which a broker is instructed to buy or sell (*Stock exchange*): a value, position, or figure, that can be approached indefinitely (*math.*): a prescribed time (*Shak.*): that which is bounded, a region or division: (with *the*) the unspeakable extreme of endurability (*coll.*). — *v.t.* to appoint, specify (*Shak.*): to confine within bounds: to restrict. — *adj.* **lim'itable.** — *n.* **limitā'rian** one who limits salvation to part of mankind. — *adj.* **lim'itary** (*-ə-ri*) of a boundary: placed at the boundary: confined within limits: licensed as a limiter (*hist.*). — *n.* **limitā'tion** a limiting: a disability, lack of talent: in law a specified period within which an action must be brought, etc. — *adjs.* **lim'itātive** tending to limit; **lim'ited** within limits: narrow: restricted. — *n.* a limited company. — *adv.* **lim'itedly.** — *ns.* **lim'itedness; lim'iter** the person or thing that limits or confines: a friar who had a licence to beg within certain bounds (*hist.*). — *n.* and *adj.* **lim'iting.** — *adj.* **lim'itless** having no limits: boundless: immense: infinite. — *adv.* **lim'itlessly.** — *n.*

lim'itlessness. — **limited edition** an edition, esp. of a book, of which only a certain number of copies is printed or made; **limited express** (*U.S.*) an express railway train carrying a limited number of passengers; **limited liability** see **liable; limited (liability) company** one whose owners enjoy limited liability; **limited monarchy** one in which the monarch shares the supreme power with others. — **off limits** out of bounds; **statute of limitations** an act specifying the period within which certain action must be taken; **within limits** to a limited extent. [L. *līmes, -itis,* boundary.]

limitrophe *lim'i-trōf, adj.* near the frontier: border. [L. *līmitrophus* — *līmes, -itis,* border, Gr. *trophos,* feeder.]

limma *lim'ə, n.* a pause of one mora (*pros.*): in Pythagorean music, the difference between two whole tones and a perfect fourth: applied also to other minute intervals. [Gr. *leimma,* a remnant.]

limmer *lim'ər,* (*dial.,* esp. *Scot.*) *n.* a rogue or thief: a hussy, a jade. [Origin obscure.]

limn *lim, v.t., v.i.* (*arch.*) to draw or paint, esp. in water-colours: orig. to illuminate with ornamental letters, etc.: — *pr.p.* **limning** (*lim'ing, lim'ning*). — *n.* **limner** (*lim'nər*) a painter on paper or parchment: a portrait-painter. [O.Fr. *luminer* or *enluminer* — L. *lūmināre* or *illūmināre.*]

Limnaea *lim-nē'ə, n.* a genus of pond-snails. — *n.* **limnae'id** any member of the family **Limnae'idae,** to which it belongs. — *adjs.* **limnetic** (*-net'ik*) living in fresh water; **limnolog'ical.** — *ns.* **limnol'ogist; limnol'ogy** the scientific study (embracing physical, geographical, biological, etc., characteristics) of lakes and other freshwater bodies. — *adj.* **limnoph'ilous** living in ponds or marshes. [Gr. *limnē,* a pool or marsh.]

limonite *lī'mən-īt, n.* brown iron ore, hydrated ferric oxide, a deposit in bogs and lakes (*bog-iron*) or a decomposition product in rocks. — *adj.* **limonitic** (*-it'ik*). [Gr. *leimōn,* a meadow.]

limosis *lī-mō'sis, n.* a morbidly ravenous appetite. [Gr. *līmos,* hunger.]

limous. See under **limicolous.**

Limousin *lē-moo-zē̃, n.* a breed of cattle. — *n.* **limousine** (*lim'oo-zēn*) large closed motor-car (orig. with the driver's seat outside but covered by the roof) which has a partition separating driver and passengers: loosely, any large motor-car (sometimes used ironically). [*Limousin,* a district in France.]

limp¹ *limp, adj.* wanting stiffness: flaccid: drooping: of a cloth binding for books, not stiffened by boards. [Origin obscure.]

limp² *limp, v.i.* to halt: to drag a leg: (of damaged ship, aircraft) to proceed with difficulty. — *n.* a limping gait: a halt. — *n.* and *adj.* **limp'ing.** — *adv.* **limp'ingly.** [There was an O.E. adj. *lemp-healt,* halting.]

limpet *lim'pit, n.* a gasteropod (*Patella,* etc.) with conical shell, that clings to rocks: one not easily ousted. — **limpet mine** an explosive device designed to cling to a surface, esp. one attached to a ship's hull by a magnet, etc. [O.E. *lempedu,* lamprey.]

limpid *lim'pid, adj.* clear: transparent. — *n.* **limpid'ity.** — *adv.* **lim'pidly.** — *n.* **lim'pidness.** [L. *limpidus.*]

limpkin *limp'kin, n.* an American wading bird, *Aramus guarauna,* like a rail. [From its limping gait.]

Limulus *lim'ū-ləs, n.* the king-crab genus: (without *cap.*) a crab of this genus. [L. *līmulus,* dim. of *līmus,* looking sideways.]

limy. See **lime¹.**

lin¹ *lin, v.i.* (*Spens.*) to cease, to give over. — *v.t.* (*obs.*) to cease from. [O.E. *linnan,* to cease.]

lin². See **linn.**

linac. Abbrev. for *lin*ear *ac*celerator.

linage. See under **line².**

linalool *lin-al'ō-ol, lin'ə-lool, n.* a fragrant liquid alcohol, used as an ingredient of perfume, got from oil of rosewood and other essential oils. [Mex. Sp. *lináloe,* a tree with aromatic wood — L. *lignum aloes,* lignaloes.]

linch *linch, linsh,* (*dial.*) *n.* a boundary ridge or un-

ploughed strip: a terrace or ledge. — Also **linch′et,
lynch′et.** [O.E. *hlinc*, ridge; cf. **link³.**]
linchpin *linch′, linsh′pin, n.* a pin used to keep a wheel on
its axle: a person or thing essential to a plan, organisation, etc. (*fig.*). [O.E. *lynis*, axle, and **pin.**]
Lincoln-green *lingk′ən-grēn, n.* a bright green cloth once
made at *Lincoln*: its colour.
lincomycin *lingk-ō-mī′sin, n.* an antibiotic used against
streptococcal and staphylococcal infections, produced
from the bacterium *Streptomyces lincolnensis*. [L.
*lincol*nensis and *-mycin*.]
lincrusta *lin-krus′tə, n.* a thick, embossed type of wallpaper. [L. *līnum*, flax, *crusta*, rind, on analogy of
linoleum.]
linctus *lingk′təs, n.* a syrup-like medicine: — *pl.* **linc′tuses.**
— *n.* **linc′ture.** [L. *linctus, -ūs*, a licking.]
lind *lind,* **linden** *lin′dən.* Same as **lime³.** [O.E. *lind*; cf.
O.N. *lind*, Ger. *Linde*.]
lindane *lin′dān.* Same as **Gammexane.**
lindworm *lind′wûrm,* (*myth.*) *n.* a wingless dragon.
[Adapted from Sw. and Dan. *lindorm*.]
line¹ *līn, n.* flax, its fibre, or its seed (*obs.*): heckled flax:
yarn spun from good flax: linen thread or cloth (*obs.*).
— *v.t.* to cover on the inside: to fill, stuff: to reinforce,
strengthen (esp. books): to be placed along the side
of: to serve as lining for. — *adj.* **lined** having a lining.
— *ns.* **lin′er** one who lines: that which serves as a lining:
a sleeve of metal, resistant to wear and corrosion, etc.,
fitted inside or outside a cylinder, tube, etc. (*engineering*): a sleeve for a gramophone record, or an insert
inside it, or the text printed on either (usu. **liner notes**);
lin′ing the action of one who lines: material applied to
a surface, esp. material on the inner surface of a
garment, etc.: contents: (in *pl.*) underclothing, esp.
drawers (*obs.* or *dial.*). — **line one's pocket(s)** to make
a profit, esp. dishonestly. [O.E. *līn,* flax, cognate
with or derived from L. *līnum*; cf. next word.]
line² *līn, n.* a thread, string, cord, rope, esp. one for
fishing, sounding, hanging clothes, or guidance: that
which has length without breadth or thickness (*math.*):
a long narrow mark: a streak, stroke, or narrow stripe:
draughtsmanship: a row: a row of printed or written
characters, ships, soldiers, etc.: a verse, such as is usu.
written in one row: a series or succession, as of
progeny: a service of ships, buses, etc. or a company
running them: a course, route, system: a railway or
tramway track or route: a stretch or route of telegraph,
telephone, or power wires or cables: a connection by
telephone: an order given to an agent for goods: such
goods received: trade in, or the stock on hand of, any
particular goods: a lineament: a rank: a short letter or
note: a wrinkle: a trench: limit: method: policy: a rule
or canon: (with *the*; often *cap.*) the equator: lineage:
direction: occupation: course: province or sphere of
life, interest, or taste: regular army: line of battle (see
below): an old measurement, the twelfth part of an
inch: relevant information (*coll.*): glib talk (*slang*): in
TV, the path traversed by the electron beam or scanning spot in moving once from side to side (horizontal
scanning) or from top to bottom (vertical scanning)
of the picture: a queue (*U.S.*): (usu. **the line**) the odds,
esp. on football games, set by bookmakers (*U.S.*): (the
following in *pl.*) marriage or church membership
certificate: words of an actor's part: lot in life (*rare*):
outlines: military field-works: rows of huts (*mil.*): a
school imposition: fits of bad temper (*Shak.*). — *v.t.*
to mark out with lines: to cover with lines: to put in
line: to form a line along: to give out for public singing,
as a hymn, line by line: to delineate, sketch (sometimes
verbally): to measure with a line (*arch.*). — *v.i.* to take
a place in line. — *ns.* **linage, lineage** (*līn′ij*) aligning
(*arch.*): measurement or payment by the line; **lineage**
(*lin′i-ij*), obs. forms **linage, lignage, lynage** (*līn′ij*),
ancestry. — *adj.* **lineal** (*lin′i-əl*) of or belonging to a
line or lines or one dimension: composed of lines: in
the direction of a line: in, of, or transmitted by, direct
line of descent, or legitimate descent. — *n.* **lineality**

(*-al′i-ti*). — *adv.* **lin′eally.** — *n.* **lineament** (*lin′i-ə-mənt*)
feature: distinguishing mark in the form, esp. of the
face. — *adj.* **linear** (*lin′i-ər*) of or belonging to a line:
of one dimension: consisting of, or having the form
of, lines: long and very narrow, with parallel sides:
capable of being represented on a graph by a straight
line: of a system, in which doubling the cause doubles
the effect. — *n.* **linearity** (*lin-i-ar′i-ti*). — *adv.* **lin′early.**
— *adjs.* **lin′eate, -d** marked with lines. — *n.* **line′ā′tion**
marking with lines: arrangement of or in lines. — *adjs.*
lined (*līnd*) marked with lines: having a line; **lineolate**
(*lin′i-ə-lāt*) marked with fine lines. — *ns.* **līn′er** one who
makes, marks, draws, paints, or writes lines: a paint-
brush for making lines: a line-fisher: a line-fishing
boat: a vessel or aircraft of a line: colouring matter
used to outline the eyes; **līn′ing** alignment: the making
of a line: use of a line: marking with lines. — *adj.* **līn′y,
līn′ey.** — **line abreast (ahead)** naval formation(s) in
which all the vessels are side by side (one behind the
other); **linear A** a script, essentially the same as linear
B, used with an earlier Semitic language of Crete; **linear
accelerator** apparatus in which electrons are accelerated while travelling down (a) metal tube(s), e.g. by
means of electromagnetic waves; **linear B** an ancient
script (*c.* 1400 B.C.) found in Crete, deciphered with
all but general acceptance as a form of Greek seven
centuries earlier than any previously known; **linear
equation** a multinomial equation in the first degree;
linear motor an electric motor which produces direct
thrust, without the use of gears; **linear perspective** that
part of perspective which regards only the positions,
magnitudes, and forms of the objects delineated; **linear
programming** that which enables a computer to give
an optimum result when fed with a number of unrelated variables, used in determining the most efficient
arrangement of e.g. an industrial process; **line block** a
printing block consisting of black and white only,
without gradations of tone; **line drawing** a drawing in
pen or pencil using lines only, without gradations of
tone; **line′-engrav′er; line′-engrav′ing** the process of
engraving in lines, steel or copperplate engraving: an
engraving so done; **line′-fence** (*U.S.*) a farm-boundary
fence; **line′-fish** one taken with the line rather than the
net; **line′-fish′er, -fish′erman; line′-fish′ing; line′man**
one who attends to lines of railway, telegraph, telephone, or electric-light wires, etc.; **line′-of-batt′le-ship**
a ship fit for the line of battle, battleship; **line′-out**
(*Rugby football*) method of restarting play when the
ball has gone into touch, the forwards of each team
lining up behind each other facing the touch line and
trying to catch the ball when it is thrown in; **line′-
print′er** a machine for rapid printing of computer
output, a line at a time; **line′-shooter** (*slang*) one who
shoots a line; **linesman** (*līnz′*) lineman: a soldier in a
regiment of the line: in Association football, one who
marks the spot at which the ball goes into touch: in
lawn-tennis, an official whose job is to watch a line to
see which side of it the ball falls; **line′-squall** one of a
chain of squalls occurring along a travelling line, with
rise and sudden change of wind, rise of pressure and
fall of temperature; **line′-storm** (*U.S.*) an equinoctial
storm; **line′-up′** arrangement in line: putting or coming
into line: a queue: the bill of artistes appearing in a
show. — **above the line** (of advertising) through the
media and by poster; **all along the line** at every point
(*lit.* or *fig.*); **below the line** (of advertising) by such
means as free gifts, mail shot (q.v.) to households, etc.;
bring into line to cause to conform; **down the line**
(*tennis*) of a shot, travelling parallel to and close to
the side of the court; **draw the line** see **draw; end of the
line** (*fig.*) a point beyond which it is useless or impossible to proceed; **fall into line** to conform; **Fraunhofer's
lines** dark lines crossing the spectrum — from the
Bavarian optician Joseph von *Fraunhofer* (1787–1826);
get a line on (*slang*) to get information about; **give line**
(from angling) to allow apparent freedom in order to
secure at last; **hold the line** see **hold¹; in line** in a straight

line: in agreement or harmony (*with*): in the running (with *for*): in a line of succession (with *to*); **lay it on the line** to speak out firmly and frankly; **lay, put on the line** to risk, stake (a reputation, etc.); **line of battle** arrangement in line to meet the enemy; **line of beauty (Hogarth's)** a curve like a drawn-out S; **line of sight** the straight line between the eye and the object on which it is focused (also **line of vision**): the straight line along which the eye looks, in any direction: the straight line between a transmitter and the receiving antenna (*telecomm*.); **line up** to bring into alignment: to make a stand (in support of, or against): to gather together in readiness: to secure, arrange (for a person); **one's line of country** one's field of study or interest; **on the line** (*paint*.) hanging on the level of the eyes; **on the lines of** in a (specified) manner or direction; **read between the lines** to infer what is not explicitly stated; **shoot a line** see **shoot**; **toe the line** see **toe**. [Partly from O.E. *līne*, cord (from or cognate with L. *līnum*, flax), partly through Fr. *ligne*, and partly directly from L. *līnea*; cf. preceding word.]

line³ *līn, v.t.* (esp. of a dog or wolf) to copulate with. [Fr. *ligner*.]

line⁴ *līn, n.* a form of **lind**. — **line-grove** (*Shak*.).

lineage, lineal, linear, etc. See **line²**.

lined. See **line¹,²**.

linen *lin'ən, n.* cloth made of lint or flax: underclothing, orig. of linen: articles of linen, or of other materials as cotton, rayon, etc. — **table-linen, bed-linen, body-linen**. — *adj.* of or like linen. — **lin'en-draper** a dealer in linens; **lin'en-fold, lin'en-scroll'** a decoration in mouldings like parallel folds of linen; **linen paper** paper made of flax fibres, or with a similar texture. — **wash one's dirty linen at home, in public** to keep secret, to expose, sordid family affairs. [O.E. *līnen* (adj.) — *līn*, flax; see **line¹**.]

lineolate. See **line²**.

-ling *-ling,* noun suffix denoting a diminutive as duck*ling*, hence expressing affection as dar*ling* (O.E. *dēorling*), sometimes implying deprecation, as under*ling*.

ling¹ *ling, n.* a fish (*Molva*) of the cod family. [Prob. conn. with **long³**.]

ling² *ling, n.* heather. — *adj.* **ling'y**. [O.N. *lyng*.]

ling³ *ling, n.* Scots form of **line²**. — **sting and ling** see **sting²**.

lingam *ling'gam, n.* the Hindu phallus, a symbol of Siva. — Also **ling'a**. [Sans.]

lingel, lingle *ling'gl* (chiefly *Scot*., *ling'l*), *n.* a shoemaker's waxed thread. [O.Fr. *lignoel* — a dim. from L. *līnea*.]

linger *ling'gər, v.i.* to remain long: to delay in reluctance: to tarry: to loiter: to be protracted: to remain alive, although gradually dying. — *v.t.* to prolong, protract (*Shak*.): to pass in tedium or dawdling. — *n.* **ling'erer**. — *n.* and *adj.* **ling'ering**. — *adv.* **ling'eringly**. [Freq. from O.E. *lengan*, to protract — *lang*, long.]

lingerie *lēzh-ə-rē, n.* linen goods: women's underclothing. [Fr., — *linge*, linen — L. *līnum*, flax, thread, linen.]

lingle. See **lingel**.

lingo *ling'gō, n.* language, esp. one despised or not understood: the jargon of a profession or class. — *pl.* **ling'oes**. [Prov. *lengo, lingo*, or some other form of L. *lingua*, language.]

lingoa geral *ling'gwä zher-äl'*, a trade jargon used in Brazil based on Tupi-Guarani. [Port., general language.]

lingot *ling'gət, n.* an ingot. [Fr. *lingot* — Eng. **ingot**, with the def. art. *l'*.]

lingua *ling'gwə, n.* the tongue: a tongue-like structure. — *adj.* **ling'ual** relating to the tongue: pronounced using the tongue (*linguistics*): of a tooth-surface, facing towards the tongue (*dentistry*): relating to language (*rare*). — *adv.* **ling'ually**. — *adj.* **ling'uiform** tongue-shaped. — *ns.* **ling'uist** one who has a good knowledge of languages: one who studies linguistics: in West Africa, an intermediary between chief or priest, and the people; **ling'uister** (*U.S.*) an interpreter. — Also **link'ster, ling'ster**. — *adjs.* **linguist'ic, -al** pertaining to languages or knowledge or study of languages. — *adv.*

linguist'ically. — *n.* **linguistic'ian** a student of linguistics. — *n.sing.* **linguist'ics** the scientific study of language in its widest sense, in every aspect and in all its varieties. — *ns.* **ling'uistry; lingula** (*ling'gū-lə*) a little tongue-like part: (*cap*.) a narrow-shelled genus of brachiopods: extended loosely to kindred genera, as **Lingulell'a**, the characteristic fossil of the Upper Cambrian *Lingula Flags*. — *adjs.* **ling'ular** pertaining to a lingula; **ling'ulate** tongue-shaped. — **lingua franca** (*ling'gwə frangk'ə;* It., Frankish language) a mixed Italian trade jargon used in the Levant: a language chosen as a medium of communication among speakers of different languages: any hybrid language used for the same purpose: the familiar conventions of any style in music or the arts, readily recognised and understood by devotees; **linguistic philosophy** a term loosely used to cover methods of analysis of philosophically puzzling concepts by meticulous assembly and scrutiny of the widely-varying expressions of these concepts in ordinary discourse; later extended to a systematic study of the working of language itself. — Also **linguistic analysis**. [L. *lingua* (for *dingua*), the tongue.]

linguini *ling-gwē'nē*, **linguine** *-nā, n.pl.* long thin flat pieces of pasta. [It., pl. of *linguino, linguina*, dims. of *lingua*, tongue.]

linhay, linny *lin'i*, (*dial*.) *n.* a shed, open in front. [Origin obscure.]

liniment *lin'i-mənt, n.* a thin ointment: an embrocation. [L. *linīmentum* — *linīre, linĕre*, to smear.]

linin *lī'nin, n.* a substance which forms the network of a cell nucleus. [L. *līnum*, thread, net.]

lining. See **line¹,²**.

link¹ *lingk, n.* a ring of a chain, chain-mail, etc.: anything connecting (also *fig*.): a unit in a communications system: the 1/100th part of the surveyor's chain, 7·92 inches (approx. 20 cm.): a segment or unit in a connected series: a winding of a river (*Scot*.): a cuff-link. — *v.t.* to connect. — *v.i.* to be or become connected: to go arm-in-arm. — *n.* **link'age** an act or mode of linking: the fact of being linked: a system of links: a chemical bond: product of magnetic flux by number of coils (*elect*.): a system of lines pivoted together, describing definite curves (*math*.): a tendency of certain characters to be inherited together (*biol*.). — **linked verse** a form of Japanese verse alternating three lines of respectively 3, 7, 5 syllables with two lines of 7, 7 syllables, different poets supplying succeeding verses; **link man** one who provides a connection as by passing on information, or by holding together separate items of a broadcast programme; **link'-mo'tion** reversing gear of a steam-engine: a system of pieces moving as a linkage; **link'-up** a connection, union; **link'work**. — **missing link** any point or fact needed to complete a series or a chain of argument: an intermediate form in the evolution of man from simian ancestors. [Prob. from an O.N. form cog. with O.E. *hlencan* (pl.), armour; Icel. *hlekkr*, Ger. *Gelenk*, a joint.]

link² *lingk,* (*hist*.) *n.* a torch of pitch and tow: burnt links used as blacking (*Shak*.). — **link'boy, link'man** an attendant carrying a link in dark streets. [Origin doubtful.]

link³ *lingk, n.* a bank (*obs*.): (in *pl.* often treated as *sing*.) a stretch of flat or gently undulating ground along a seashore, hence a golf-course. [O.E. *hlinc*, a ridge of land, a bank; cf. **linch**.]

link⁴ *lingk,* (*Scot*.) *v.i.* to move nimbly: to trip along briskly. [Cf. Norw. *linke*, to hobble, limp.]

linkster. See **lingua**.

linn, lin *lin, n.* a waterfall: a cascade: a pool: a deep ravine. [O.E. *hlynn*, a torrent, combined with Gael. *linne*, Ir. *linn*, W. *llyn*, pool.]

Linnaean, Linnean *lin-ē'ən, adj.* pertaining to *Linnaeus* or *Linné*, the Swedish botanist (1707–1778), or to his artificial system of classification.

linnet *lin'it, n. Linota cannabina*, a common finch, feeding on flax-seed. — **green linnet** the greenfinch. [O.Fr. *linette, linot* — *lin*, flax — L. *līnum*; cf. O.E. *līnece* or *līnete*, and **lintie**.]

linney, linny. See **linhay**.

linoleic *lin-ō-lē'ik*, **linolenic** *lin-ō-lēn'ik* (or -*len'*), **acid** *as'id*, highly unsaturated fatty acids obtained from the glycerides of certain fats and oils, as linseed oil, and constituting Vitamin F.

linoleum *lin-ō'li-əm*, *-lyəm, n.* floor-covering made by impregnating a fabric with a mixture of oxidised linseed-oil, resins, and fillers (esp. cork). — Also *adj.* — Also **lino** (*lī'nō*) (*coll.*): — *pl.* **li'nos.** — **linocut** (*lī'nō-kut*) a design cut in relief in linoleum: a print from such a block; **lino tile** a floor tile made of linoleum or a similar material. [L. *līnum*, flax, *oleum*, oil.]

Linotype® *līn'ō-tīp, n.* a machine for producing stereotyped lines: a slug or line of printing-type cast in one piece.

linsang *lin'sang, n.* a civet-like animal of Borneo and Java: applied also to kindred animals of the Himalayas, Burma, and West Africa. [Javanese *linsun*.]

linseed *lin'sēd, n.* lint or flax seed — also **lint'seed.** — **lin'seed-cake** the cake remaining when the oil is pressed out of lint or flax seed, used as a food for sheep and cattle; **lin'seed-meal** the meal of linseed, used for poultices and as a cattle-food; **lin'seed-oil** oil from flax seed. [O.E. *līn*, flax, *sǣd*, seed.]

linsey *lin'zi, n.* cloth made of linen and wool. — Also *adj.* — **lin'sey-woolsey** (-*wŏŏl'zi*) a thin coarse stuff of linen and wool mixed, or inferior wool with cotton: gibberish (*Shak.*). — *adj.* of linen and wool: neither one thing nor another. [Perh. **line**[1], **wool**, and possibly **say**[3].]

linstock *lin'stok, n.* a staff to hold a lighted match for firing cannon. — Also **lint'stock.** [Du. *lontstok* — *lont*, a match (cf. **lunt**), *stok*, a stick.]

lint *lint, n.* flax (*Scot.*): scraped linen or a cotton substitute for dressing wounds: cotton fibre (esp. *U.S.*): raw cotton. — *n.* **lin'ter** (*U.S.*) a machine for stripping off short cotton fibre from the ginned seeds: (in *pl.*) the fibre so removed. — *adj.* **lint'y.** — **lint'seed** (*Scot.*) flax seed for sowing. — *adj.* **lint'white** flaxen. [M.E. *lynt*, *lynet*, perh. — L. *linteus*, of linen — *līnum*, flax.]

lintel *lint'l, n.* a timber or stone over a doorway or window. — *adj.* **lint'elled.** [O.Fr. *lintel* (Fr. *linteau*) — a dim. of L. *līmes, -itis*, border.]

lintie *lin'ti*, **lintwhite** *lint'(h)wīt*, (now chiefly *Scot.*) *ns.* a linnet. [O.E. *linetwige*, lit. perh. flax-twitcher.]

lintseed; lintstock. See **linseed; linstock.**

lintwhite. See **lint** and **lintie.**

lion *lī'ən, n.* a large, fierce, tawny, loud-roaring animal of the cat family, the male with shaggy mane: a man of unusual courage (*fig.*): (*cap.*) the constellation or the sign Leo (*astron.*): any object of interest, esp. a famous or conspicuous person much sought after (from the lions once kept in the Tower, one of the sights of London): an old Scots coin, with a lion on the obverse, worth 74 shillings Scots (James VI): (*cap.*) a member of an international organisation of professional people's clubs (**the Lions**), with charitable, etc., aims: — *fem.* **li'oness.** — *ns.* **li'oncel, li'oncelle, li'onel** (*her.*) a small lion used as a bearing; **li'onet** a young lion. — *v.t.* **li'onise, -ize** to treat as a lion or object of interest: to go around the sights of: to show the sights to. — *n.* **li'onism** lionising: lion-like appearance in leprosy. — *adjs.* **li'on-like, li'only.** — **li'on-cub** a young lion; **li'on-heart** one with great courage. — *adj.* **li'on-heart'ed.** — **li'on-hunt'er** a hunter of lions: one who runs after celebrities; **lion's mouth** (*fig.*) a dangerous position; **lion's provider** (*arch.*) the jackal, supposed to attend upon the lion, really his hanger-on; **lion's share** the whole or greater part; **li'on-tā'mer.** — **twist the lion's tail** to harass Great Britain. [A.Fr. *liun* — L. *leō, -ōnis* — Gr. *leōn, -ontos*.]

lip *lip, n.* either of the muscular flaps in front of the teeth and surrounding the mouth: any similar structure, as each of the two divisions of a labiate corolla: the edge or rim of an orifice, cavity, or vessel: part of such a rim bent outwards like a spout: impudent talk, insolence (*slang*). — *v.t.* to touch with the lips: to kiss: to wash, overflow, or overrun the edge of: to lap or lave: to form a lip on: to edge: to turn or notch the edge of (*Scot.*): (of a golfer or shot) to get the ball to the very edge of (the hole): to utter with the lips. — *v.i.* to manage the lips in playing a wind-instrument: to lap at the brim: to have water lapping over: — *pr.p.* **lipp'ing;** *pa.t.* and *pa.p.* **lipped.** — *adj.* of the lip: formed or sounded by the lips: (in composition) from the lips only, not sincere. — *adjs.* **lip'less; lipped** (*lipt*) having a lip or lips: labiate; **lipp'y** with hanging lip: saucy (*slang*). — *adj.* **lip'-deep** insincere: immersed to the lips. — **lip'gloss** a substance applied to the lips to give them a glossy appearance. — *v.i.* **lip'-read.** — **lip'-reader; lip'-read'ing** gathering what a person says by watching the movement of the lips; **lip'-rounding** rounding of the lips, as in pronouncing *o*; **lip'salve** ointment for the lips: blandishment; **lip'-service** insincere praise or worship; professed, not real, respect or loyalty. — *adj.* **lip'-smacking** delicious, appetising. — **lip'stick** colouring for the lips in the form of a stick. — *v.t.* and *v.i.* to paint with lipstick. — **lip'-sync(h)** (*lip'sink*) the synchronisation of lip movements with already recorded sound, esp. by singers making television appearances: the synchronisation of the voice with already filmed lip-movements (in dubbing). — also *v.t.* and *v.i.* — **bite one's lip** to show annoyance or disappointment: to repress an emotion or utterance; **hang on someone's lips** to listen eagerly to all that he has to say; **in Lipsburie pinfold** (*Shak.*) perh. between the teeth; **(keep) a stiff upper lip** (to show) a face of resolution, with no yielding to emotion; **make a lip** (*Shak.*) to pout in sullenness or derision; **smack one's lips** to bring the lips together and part them with a smack, as an indication of relish. [O.E. *lippa*; Du. *lip*, Ger. *Lippe*, L. *labium*.]

lip-, lipo- *lip-, līp-(ō-)*, in composition, fat. — *ns.* **lip'ase** (-*ās, -āz*) an enzyme that breaks up fats; **lipec'tomy** (Gr. *ektomē*, a cutting out) surgical removal of fatty tissue; **lip'id**, sometimes **lip'ide** (-*īd*), any of a group of chemicals found in tissues, including fats, oils and waxes (esters of fatty acids), derivatives of these such as phospholipids (q.v.), and other substances such as steroids and terpenes; **lip'ochrome** (-*krōm*; Gr. *chrōma*, colour) a pigment of butter fat, etc. — *adj.* **lip'oid** fat-like. — *n.* a fat-like substance: a lipid. — *ns.* **lipō'ma** a fatty tumour: — *pl.* **lipō'mata; lipomatō'sis** the excessive growth of fat. — *adj.* **lipō'matous.** — *n.* **lipoprō'-tein** a water-soluble protein found in the blood, which carries cholesterol. — *adj.* **liposō'mal.** — *n.* **lip'ōsome** (Gr. *sōma*, body) a naturally occurring lipid globule in the cytoplasm of a cell: an artificial droplet of an aqueous substance surrounded by a lipid, used in the treatment of various diseases. [Gr. *lipos*, fat.]

liparite *lip'ə-rīt, n.* rhyolite. [From the *Lipari* Islands, where it occurs.]

Lipizzaner *lip-it-sä'nər, n.* a breed of horses (usu. grey or white in colour) particularly suited for displays of haute école. — Also **Lippizaner, Lippizzaner, Lippizana** (-*nə*), **Lippizzana.** [*Lipizza* (*Lippiza, Lippizza*), near Trieste, where orig. bred.]

lipogram *lip'ō-gram*, or *līp', n.* a writing, esp. in verse, from which all words are omitted which contain a particular letter. — *adj.* **lipogrammat'ic.** — *ns.* **lipogramm'atism; lipogramm'atist; lipog'raphy** accidental omission of a letter or letters in writing. [Gr. *leipein*, to leave, *gramma*, a letter, *graphein*, to write.]

lippen *lip'n*, (*Scot.*) *v.i.* to trust, rely, depend (with *to, on*). — *v.t.* to expect. — *adj.* **lipp'ening** (*Scott*) unguarded. [Origin obscure.]

Lippes loop. See **loop**[1].

lippitude *lip'i-tūd*, (*arch.*) *n.* soreness of the eyes. [L. *lippitūdō* — *lippus*, blear-eyed.]

lippy, lippie *lip'i, n.* an old Scottish dry measure, the fourth part of a peck. [Dim. from O.E. *lēap*, a basket; cf. **leap**[2].]

liquate *lik'wāt, v.t.* to melt: to subject to liquation. — *adj.* **liq'uable.** — *n.* **liqua'tion** melting: separation of metals with different melting-points. [L. *liquāre, -ātum,* to liquefy.]

liquefy *lik'wi-fī, v.t.* to make liquid. — *v.i.* to become liquid: to drink (*facet.*): — *pr.p.* **liq'uefying;** *pa.t.* and *pa.p.* **liq'uefied.** — *n.* and *adj.* **liquefacient** (*-fā'shənt*). — *n.* **liquefaction** (*-fak'shən*). — *adj.* **liq'uefiable.** — *n.* **liq'uefier.** — **liquefied petroleum gas** propane or butane under moderate pressure, used in vehicles in place of petrol or diesel oil. [L. *liquefacĕre* — *liquēre,* to be liquid, *facĕre,* to make.]

liquesce *lik-wes', v.i.* to become liquid: to merge. — *ns.* **liquesc'ence, liquesc'ency.** — *adj.* **liquesc'ent.** [L. *liquēscĕre* — *liquēre,* to be liquid.]

liqueur *lik-ūr',* or *lē-kœr', n.* an alcoholic preparation flavoured or perfumed and sweetened — as chartreuse, cherry brandy, curaçao, benedictine, kümmel, maraschino. — *v.t.* to flavour with a liqueur. — *adj.* (of brandy or whisky) that may be drunk as a liqueur. — **liqueur'-glass** a very small drinking-glass. [Fr., — L. *liquor;* see **liquor.**]

liquid *lik'wid, adj.* flowing: fluid: watery: in phys., in a state between solid and gas, in which the molecules move freely about one another but do not fly apart: clear: moist: of sound, etc., free from harshness: indisputable: unfixed: readily converted into cash. — *n.* a liquid substance: a flowing consonant sound, as *l, r.* — *v.t.* **liq'uidate** to clear up or off: to wind up (a commercial firm, etc.): to turn (assets) into cash: to dispose of: to wipe out, do away with (*slang*): to kill off (*slang*). — *v.i.* to go into liquidation. — *ns.* **liquidā'tion; liq'uidator.** — *v.t.* **liq'uidise, -ize** to render liquid: to purée (food). — *ns.* **liq'uidiser, -z-** a machine which purées foodstuffs; **liquid'ity** the state of being liquid: the condition of having liquid assets. — *adv.* **liq'uidly.** — *n.* **liq'uidness.** — **liquid crystal** a liquid which is anisotropic, like a crystal, over a definite range of temperature above its freezing point. — **go into liquidation** (of a commercial firm, etc.) to be wound up, become bankrupt; **liquid crystal display** a display, esp. in electronic calculators, based on the changes in reflectivity of a liquid crystal cell when an electric field is applied. [L. *liquidus,* liquid, clear — *liquēre,* to be clear.]

Liquidambar *lik-wid-am'bər, n.* a genus of balsamiferous trees of the family Hamamelidaceae, found in North America and Asia. [L. *liquidus,* liquid, L.L. *ambar,* amber.]

liquidus *lik'wi-dəs, n.* (also **liquidus curve, freezing-point curve**) a curve plotted on a graph showing how temperature affects the composition of a melting or solidifying mixture, above which curve the mixture is entirely liquid. [L., liquid.]

liquor *lik'ər, n.* anything liquid, esp. the product of cooking or other operation: a liquid secretion: a beverage, esp. alcoholic: strong drink: a strong solution: any prepared solution. — *v.t.* to apply liquor or a solution to: to rub with oil or grease (*Shak.*). — *v.i.* (*slang*) to drink (esp. with *up*). — **in liquor,** also **liquored** (*slang*), drunk; **liquor laws** laws controlling the sale of intoxicating drinks. [O.Fr. *licur, licour* (Fr. *liqueur*) — L. *liquor, -ōris.*]

liquorice, licorice *lik'ə-ris,* (in U.S. also *-rish*), *n.* a papilionaceous plant (*Glycyrrhiza glabra,* or other species) of Europe and Asia: its long sweet root used in medicine: an extract from the root: confectionery made from it. — **liquorice allsorts** an assortment of sweets flavoured with liquorice. — **Indian liquorice** Abrus (also *liquorice-vine*); **wild liquorice** a kind of milk-vetch (*Astragalus glycyphyllus* — also *liquorice-vetch*): rest-harrow. [A. Fr. *lycorys* — L.L. *liquirītia,* a corr. of Gr. *glykyrrīza* — *glykys,* sweet, *rhīza,* root.]

liquorish. Another spelling of **lickerish:** also used to mean inclined towards liquor.

lira *lē'rə, n.* Italian monetary unit (coins of 5, 10, etc., lire being in circulation): the monetary unit of Turkey,

equivalent to 100 piastres: — *pl.* **lire** (*lē'rā*), **lir'as.** [It., — L. *lībra,* a pound.]

Liriodendron *līr-i-ō-den'dron, n.* the tulip-tree genus: (without *cap.*) a tree of this genus. [Gr. *leirion,* a lily, *dendron,* a tree.]

liripoop *lir'i-pōōp,* (*obs.*) *n.* the long tail of a graduate's hood: a part or lesson committed to memory: a silly person. — Also **lir'ipipe** (*-pīp*). [L.L. *liripipium;* origin unknown.]

lirk *lirk,* (*Scot.*) *n.* a fold: a wrinkle. — *v.i.* to wrinkle. [Origin unknown.]

lis *lēs,* (*her.*) *n.* a fleur-de-lis: — *pl.* **lis, lisses** (*lēs'iz*). [Fr.]

Lisbon *liz'bən, n.* a light-coloured wine from Estremadura in Portugal, shipped from Lisbon.

lisk *lisk,* (*dial.*) *n.* the groin: the flank or loin. [M.E. *leske,* prob. of Scand. origin.]

lisle *līl, n.* a long-stapled, hard-twisted cotton yarn. — Also *adj.* [Old spelling of *Lille,* France.]

lisp *lisp, v.i.* to speak with the tongue against the upper teeth or gums, as in pronouncing *th* for *s* or *z:* to articulate as a child: to utter imperfectly. — *v.t.* to utter with a lisp. — *n.* the act or habit of lisping: a defect of speech by which one lisps. — *n.* **lisp'er.** — *adj.* and *n.* **lisp'ing.** — *adv.* **lisp'ingly.** [O.E. *wlisp* (adj.), stammering; Du. *lispen,* Ger. *lispeln.*]

lispound, lispund *lis'pownd, -pŏnd,* (*Orkney* and *Shetland*) *n.* a varying weight, 12 to 34 pounds. [L.G. or Du. *lispund,* for *livschpund,* Livonian (*Livonia,* former Baltic province of Russia) pound.]

lissencephalous *lis-en-sef'ə-ləs, adj.* with smooth cerebral hemispheres. [Gr. *lissos,* smooth, *enkephalon,* brain.]

lissome, lissom *lis'əm, adj.* lithesome, nimble, flexible. — *n.* **liss'om(e)ness.** [**lithesome.**]

lissotrichous *lis-ot'ri-kəs, adj.* smooth-haired. [Gr. *lissos,* smooth, *thrix, trichos,* hair.]

list[1] *list, n.* the selvage on woven textile fabrics: a border: a stripe: a strip: a ridge or furrow made with a lister (also **list'er ridge;** *arch. U.S.*): a strip cut from an edge: material composed of cut-off selvages: a boundary (*obs.*): a destination (*Shak.*): (in *pl.*) the boundary of a tilting-ground or the like, hence the ground itself, combat. — *adj.* made of strips of woollen selvage. — *v.t.* to border: to put list on: to remove the edge from: to plough with a lister (*U.S.*). — *adj.* **list'ed** enclosed for tilting or the like: fought in lists. — *n.* **list'er** (*U.S.*) a double-mould-board plough. — **enter the lists** to come forward for contest. [O.E. *līste;* Ger. *Leiste;* affected in some senses by O.Fr. *lisse* (Fr. *lice,* It. *lizza*) — L.L. *liciae,* barrier.]

list[2] *list, n.* a catalogue, roll, or enumeration. — *v.t.* to place in a list or catalogue: to enrol (as soldiers). — *v.i.* to enlist (also **'list,** as if for **enlist**). — *n.* **list'ing** a list: position in a list: a print-out of all the data stored in a file (*comput.*): an official quotation for stock so that it can be traded on the Stock Exchange. — **listed building** one officially listed as being of special architectural or historic interest, which cannot be demolished or altered without (local) government consent; **list price** the price of an article as shown in a catalogue or advertisement. — **active list** the roll of those liable for active service; **List D schools** since 1969 the name given in Scotland to community homes (formerly approved schools). [O.F. *liste,* of Gmc. origin, ultimately same word as above, from the sense of a strip of paper.]

list[3] *list, n.* a fillet (*archit.*): a division of parted hair. — *n.* **list'el** a small fillet. [It. *lista, listello;* ult. the same as **list**[1,2].]

list[4] *list, v.t.* to please (*impers., arch.*): to have pleasure in (*pers.*): to desire: to like or please: to choose: to cause to heel over (*naut.*). — *v.i.* to heel over: — *pa.t.* **list'ed, list;** *pa.p.* **list'ed;** *3rd pers. sing. pr.t.* **list, lists, listeth.** — *n.* joy (*obs.*): desire: inclination: choice: heeling over. — *adj.* **list'less** having no desire or wish: uninterested: languid. — *adv.* **list'lessly.** — *n.* **list'-lessness.** [O.E. *lystan,* impers., to please — *lust,* pleasure.]

list⁵ *list*, (*arch.* or *poet.*) *v.i.* to listen. — *v.t.* to listen to. — *adj.* **list′ful** attentive.   [O.E. *hlystan*.]

listel. See **list³.**

listen *lis′n*, *v.i.* to give ear or hearken: to follow advice. — *n.* act of listening. — *adj.* **list′enable** pleasant to listen to. — *ns.* **listener** (*lis′nər*) one who listens or hearkens; **list′enership** the estimated number of listeners to a radio broadcast. — **list′ener-in** (*pl.* **list′-eners-in**); **list′ening-in; list′ening-post** a post where men are stationed to hear what the enemy is doing: a position advantageous for the gathering of information about the affairs of another country, etc. — **listen in** to listen to a wireless broadcast: to overhear intentionally a message intended for another.   [O.E. *hlysnan*, recorded in the Northumbrian form *lysna*.]

lister. See **list¹.**

Listerism *lis′tər-izm*, *n.* antiseptic treatment of surgical wounds introduced by the English surgeon Lord *Lister* (1827–1912). — *adj.* **Listerian** (*-tē′ri-ən*) pertaining to Lister or his system. — *v.t.* **Lis′terise, -ize** to treat by Listerism.

listful. See **list⁵.**

listless. See **list⁴.**

lit. *Pa.t.* and *pa.p.* of **light¹,³.**

litany *lit′ə-ni*, *n.* a prayer of supplication, esp. in processions: an appointed form of responsive prayer in public worship in which the same thing is repeated several times: a long list or catalogue, evocative or merely boring. — **lit′any-desk, -stool** in the English Church, a movable desk at which a minister kneels, facing the altar, while he recites the litany. — **lesser litany** the common formula, 'Kyrie eleison, Christe eleison, Kyrie eleison'.   [L.L. *litanīa* — Gr. *litaneiā* — *litesthai*, to pray.]

litchi. See **lychee.**

lit. crit. Abbrev. of **literary criticism.**

lit de justice *lē də zhüs-tēs*, (Fr.). See under **bed¹.**

lite¹, lyte *līt*, (*dial.*, also **leet**, otherwise *obs.*) *n.*, *adj.*, *adv.* little.   [O.E. *lȳt*.]

lite² (*Spens.*). Same as **light³:** also as **light²** in phrase *lungs and lites.*

lite pendente *lī′tē pen-den′tē, lē′te pen-den′te*, (L.) pending the suit.

liter. American spelling of **litre.**

literacy. See **literate.**

literae, litterae, humaniores *lit′ər-ē hū-mān-i-ōr′ēz, -ōr′, lit′e-rī(h)ōō-mān-i-ōr′ās*, (L.) polite letters, the humanities, Latin and Greek: name of school and examination at Oxford University.

literal *lit′ə-rəl*, *adj.* pertaining to letters of the alphabet: of the nature of a letter: according to the letter: not figurative or metaphorical: following word for word: inclined to use or understand words in a matter-of-fact sense. — *n.* a wrong letter in printed or typed matter: a misprint of a letter. — *v.t.* **lit′eralise, -ize.** — *ns.* **lit′eraliser, -z-; lit′eralism** strict adherence to the letter: interpretation that is merely verbal: exact and unimaginative rendering (*art*); **li′teralist; literality** (*-al′i-ti*). — *adv.* **lit′erally** (often used by no means literally). — *n.* **lit′eralness.**   [L. *litterālis* — *littera* (*litera*), a letter.]

literary *lit′ər-ər-i*, *adj.* pertaining to letters of the alphabet (*obs.*): epistolary (*obs.*): pertaining to, of the nature of, versed in, or practising literature or the writing of books: bookish: of language, formal. — *adv.* **lit′erarily.** — *ns.* **lit′erariness; lit′eraryism** a bookish expression. — **literary agent** one who deals with the business affairs of an author; **literary criticism** the art of making judgments on literary works (*abbrev.* **lit. crit.**); **literary executor** one appointed to deal with unpublished material after an author's death.   [L. *literārius* — *litera* (*littera*), a letter.]

literate *lit′ər-it, -āt*, *adj.* learned: able to read and write: having a competence in or with (often in composition, as *computer-literate*). — *n.* one who is literate: an educated person without a university degree, esp. a candidate for orders, or formerly a woman holding a certificate from St Andrews University (*L.L.A.*, *Lady*

Literate in Arts). — *n.* **lit′eracy** condition of being literate. — *n.pl.* **literati** (*-ä′tē*) men of letters, the learned: — *sing.* **literā′tus** (or *-ä′*; L.), **literato** (*-ä′tō*; It.). — *adv.* **literā′tim** (L. *-ä′*) letter for letter: without the change of a letter. — *ns.* **literā′tion** the representation of sounds by letters; **lit′erātor** a dabbler in learning: a man of letters, a literary man. — *adj.* **lit′erose** affectedly or spuriously literary. — *n.* **literos′ity.**   [L. *litera, literātus, literātim, literōsus* — *litera* (*littera*), letter.]

literature *lit′(ə-)rə-chər*, *n.* the art of composition in prose and verse: the whole body of literary composition universally, or in any language, or on a given subject, etc.: literary matter: printed matter: humane learning: literary culture or knowledge. — *adj.* **lit′eratured** (*Shak.*) learned, having literary knowledge.   [L. *literātūra* — *litera* (*littera*), a letter.]

literose. See **literate.**

lith *lith*, (*arch.* and *Scot.*) *n.* a joint or segment.   [O.E. *lith*, a member; Ger. *Glied*.]

lith-, litho- *lith-, -ō-, -ə-, -o-*, in composition, stone: calculus. — *ns.* **lith′ate** (*obs.*) a urate; **lithī′asis** (Gr. *lithiāsis*) formation of calculi in the body. — *adj.* **lith′ic** pertaining to or got from stone or calculi. — *ns.* **lithist′id** any of the **Lithist′ida**, hard stony sponges; **lith′ite** a calcareous body secreted in an animal cell, esp. with a sensory function. — *adj.* **lithochromatic** (*-ə-krō-mat′ik*, or *-krə-*). — *n. sing.* **lithochromat′ics** the art or process of painting in oil upon stone and taking impressions therefrom. — *ns.* **lith′ochromy** (*-krō-mi*; Gr. *chrōma, -atos*, colour) painting on stone: chromolithography; **lith′oclast** (Gr. *klaein*, to crush) an instrument for crushing bladder-stones; **lith′ocyst** (*-ō-sist*; Gr. *kystis*, a bladder) a sac containing a lithite. — *adj.* **lithodomous** (*-od′ə-məs*; Gr. *lithodomos*, a mason — *domos*, a dwelling) living in burrows in rocks. — *n.* **Lithod′omus** the date-shell genus. — *adj.* **lithogenous** (*-oj′i-nəs*) rock-building. — *ns.* **lith′oglyph** (*-ə-glif*; Gr. *glyphein*, to carve) an engraving on stone, esp. a precious stone; **lith′ograph** (*-gräf*; Gr. *graphein*, to write) a print from stone (**lithographic stone** or **slate** a fine-grained slaty limestone), or a substitute (as zinc or aluminium), with greasy ink. — *v.t.* and *v.i.* to print so. — *n.* **lithographer** (*-og′rə-fər*). — *adjs.* **lithographic** (*-ə-graf′ik*), **-al.** — *adv.* **lithograph′ically.** — *n.* **lithog′raphy.** — *adjs.* **lith′oid, lithoid′al** like stone. — *n.* **lith′olapaxy** (Gr. *lapaxis*, evacuation) the operation of crushing stone in the bladder and working it out. — *adj.* **lithol′atrous.** — *n.* **litholatry** (*-ol′ə-tri*; Gr. *latreiā*, worship) stone-worship. — *adjs.* **litholog′ic, -al.** — *ns.* **lithol′ogist; lithol′ogy** the science of rocks as mineral masses: the department of medicine concerned with calculi; **lith′omancy** (*-man-si*; Gr. *manteiā*, divination) divination by stones; **lith′omarge** (*-ō-märj*; L. *marga*, marl) a compact china-clay. — *adj.* **lithophagous** (*-of′ə-gəs*; Gr. *phagein*, to eat) stone-swallowing: rock-boring. — *n.* **lith′ophane** (*-ō-fān*; Gr. *phainesthai*, to appear) porcelain with pictures showing through transparency. — *adj.* **lithophilous** (*-of′i-ləs*; Gr. *philos*, friend) growing, living, or sheltering among stones. — *ns.* **lithophysa** (*-ō-fī′sə*; Gr. *phȳsa*, bubble) a bladder-like spherulite (also **lith′ophyse**): — *pl.* **lithophy′sae** (*-sē*); **lith′ophyte** (*-fīt*; Gr. *phyton*, plant) a plant that grows on rocks or stones: a stony organism, as coral. — *adj.* **lithophytic** (*-fit′ik*). — *ns.* **lith′opone** (*-ō-pōn*; Gr. *ponos*, work) a white pigment of barium sulphate and zinc sulphide; **lithoprint** (*lī′thō-*) a print made by lithography; **lith′osphere** (*-ō-sfēr*; Gr. *sphaira*, sphere) the rocky crust of the earth. — *adj.* **lithospheric** (*-sfer′ik*). — *n.* **lith′otome** (*-ō-tōm*; Gr. *tomos*, cutting) an instrument for lithotomy. — *adjs.* **lithotomic** (*-tom′*), **-al.** — *n.* **lithotomist** (*-ot′əm-ist*) one who cuts for stone in the bladder. — *adj.* **lithot′omous** boring in rocks, as some molluscs. — *ns.* **lithot′omy** cutting for stone in the bladder; **lithotripsy, lith′otripter, lith′otrite,** etc. see under **lithotrity.**   [Gr. *lithos*, stone.]

litharge *lith′ärj*, *n.* lead monoxide, such as is got in

refining silver. [Fr., — Gr. *lithargyros* — *lithos*, a stone, *argyros*, silver.]
lithe¹ *līdh*, *adj.* supple, limber. — *adv.* **lithe′ly.** — *n.* **lithe′ness.** — *adj.* **lithe′some.** — *n.* **lithe′someness.** [O.E. *līthe*, soft, mild; Ger. *lind* and *gelinde*.]
lithe² *līdh*, (*obs.*) *v.i.* to listen. [O.N. *hlýtha*, to listen.]
lither *lidh′ər*, *adj.* bad (*obs.*): lazy (*obs.*): soft, yielding (*Shak.*). — *adj.* **lith′erly** mischievous. — *adv.* idly. [O.E. *lýthre*, bad; influenced by **lithe¹**.]
lithia *lith′i-ə*, *n.* oxide of lithium (from its mineral origin, unlike soda and potash). — Also *adj.* — *adj.* **lith′ic** pertaining to or got from lithium. — *n.* **lithium** (*-i-əm*) the lightest metallic element (symbol Li; at. numb. 3). [Gr. *lithos*, stone.]
litho *lī′thō*, *n.* (*pl.* **lī′thos**), *adj.* short for **lithograph, -graphic, -graphy** (see under **lith-**).
Lithospermum *lith-ō-spûr′məm*, *n.* a genus of plants of the borage family. [Gr. *lithospermon*, gromwell — *lithos*, stone, *sperma*, seed.]
lithotrity *lith-ot′ri-ti*, **lithotripsy** *lith′ō-trip-si*, *ns.* the operation of crushing a stone in the bladder, kidney or gall bladder, so that its fragments may be passed naturally from the body. — *ns.* **lith′otrite, lithotrī′tor, lithotrip′ter, -trip′tor, lithontrip′tor** a device that crushes stones by ultrasound. — *adjs.* **lithotritic** (*-trit′-ik*), **lithotrip′tic, lithontrip′tic, lithonthryp′tic.** — *ns.* a medicine producing the like result. — *v.t.* **lithot′ritise, -ize.** — *ns.* **lithot′ritist, lithotrip′tist, lithontrip′tist** one who performs the operation. [Gr. *lithōn* (gen. pl.) *thryptika*, breakers of stones; reconstructed as from Gr. *tripsis*, rubbing, or L. *trītus*, rubbing.]
Lithuanian *li-thū-ā′ni-ən*, *adj.* pertaining to the U.S.S.R. republic of *Lithuania* on the Baltic Sea, or its people, or their language. — *n.* the Lithuanian language: a native or inhabitant of Lithuania.
litigate *lit′i-gāt*, *v.t.* and *v.i.* to dispute, esp. by a lawsuit. — *adjs.* **lit′igable; lit′igant** contending at law: engaged in a lawsuit. — *n.* a person engaged in a lawsuit. — *n.* **litigā′tion.** — *adj.* **litigious** (*-ij′əs*) pertaining to litigation: inclined to engage in lawsuits: disputable: open to contention: perh. depending on results of negotiation (*Shak.*). — *adv.* **litig′iously.** — *n.* **litig′iousness.** [L. *lītigāre*, *-ātum* — *līs*, *lītis*, strife, *agěre*, to do.]
litmus *lit′məs*, *n.* a substance obtained from certain lichens, turned red by acids, blue by alkalis. — **litmus paper** a test-paper dipped in litmus solution; **litmus test** (*fig.*) an event seen as an indicator of underlying attitudes, factors, etc. [O.N. *litmosi*, herbs used in dyeing — *litr*, colour, *mosi*, moss.]
litotes *līt′* or *lit′ō-tēz*, (*rhet.*) *n.* meiosis or understatement: esp. affirmation by negation of the contrary. [Gr. *lītotēs*, simplicity — *lītos*, plain.]
litre *lē′tər*, *n.* the metric unit of capacity, orig. intended to be 1 cubic decimetre: (1901) volume of a kilogram of water at 4°C, under standard atmospheric pressure (1·000 028 cu. dm.): (1964) 1 cubic decimetre. — **-litre** in composition, denoting the capacity of the cylinders of a motor-vehicle engine (as *three-litre*). [Fr., — L.L. *lītra* — Gr. *lītrā*, a pound.]
litten. See **loot².**
litter *lit′ər*, *n.* a heap of straw, bracken, etc., esp. for animals to lie upon: materials for a bed: any scattered or confused collection of objects, esp. of little value: a state of confusion and untidiness with things strewn about: wastage, rubbish: a couch carried by men or beasts: a stretcher: a brood of animals: an occasion of birth of animals. — *v.t.* to cover or supply with litter: to scatter carelessly about: to give birth to (said of animals). — *v.i.* to produce a litter or brood: to strew rubbish, etc. untidily. — *adjs.* **litt′ered; litt′ery** in condition of litter: addicted to litter. — **litt′er-basket, -bin** a receptacle for rubbish; **litt′er-bug, -lout** one who wilfully drops litter; **litt′ermate** a fellow-member of a litter. [O.Fr. *litiere* — L.L. *lectāria* — L. *lectus*, a bed.]
litterae humaniores. See **literae humaniores.**
littérateur *lē-tā-rä-tœr′*, *n.* a literary man. [Fr.]

little *lit′l*, *adj.* small in size, extent, quantity, or significance: petty: small-minded: young: resembling or reminiscent of something else, but on a small(er) scale. — *n.* (or *adj.* with a noun understood) that which is small in quantity or extent: a small quantity: a small thing. — *adv.* in a small quantity or degree: not much. — **less, least** serve as compar. and superl. to the adv. and to some extent, along with **lesser,** to the adj. — *ns.* **litt′leness; litt′ling** (*Scot.* **litt′lin, litt′leane;** O.E. *lȳtling*) a child. — **Little Dipper,** (*U.S.*) **Little Dipper** Ursa Minor; **litt′le-ease** a confined space in which a prisoner can neither sit, stand nor lie: the pillory: the stocks; **little end** in an internal-combustion engine, the smaller end of the connecting rod; **Litt′le-end′ian** one of the Lilliputian party who opposed the *Big-endians,* maintaining that boiled eggs should be cracked at the little end; **little Englander** an opponent of British imperialism and empire-building; **little finger** the fifth and smallest digit of the hand; **little go** see **go¹; little magazine** a small high-brow magazine; **little man** a man of no importance, an underdog; **little Mary** (*J. M. Barrie*) the stomach; **little office** a short service of psalms, hymns, collects, etc.; **little people** the fairies, or a traditional race of pygmies; **little theatre** a small theatre in which experimental plays, and other plays not likely to be a great commercial success, are produced; **little toe** see **toe; little woman** (*facet.*) one's wife. — *adj.* **litt′leworth** worthless. — **by little and little, little by little** by degrees; **in little** on a small scale; **little green men** type of men imagined as originating in parts of the universe other than our earth; **make little of** to treat as of little consequence, belittle: to comprehend only slightly; **twist, wind, wrap someone round one's little finger** to control someone completely, or influence someone to a great extent. [O.E. *lȳtel.*]
littoral *lit′ər-əl*, *adj.* belonging to the seashore, to lands near the coast, the beach, the space between high and low tidemarks, or water a little below low-water mark: inhabiting the shore or shallow water in a lake or sea. — *n.* the strip of land along it. [L. *littorālis* for *lītorālis* — *lītus*, *lītoris*, shore.]
liturgy *lit′ər-ji*, *n.* the form of service or regular ritual of a church — strictly, that used in the celebration of the eucharist: in ancient Greece, personal service to the state. — *adjs.* **liturgic** (*-ûrj′ik*), **-al.** — *adv.* **litur′gically.** — *n. sing.* **litur′gics** the doctrine of liturgies. — *ns.* **liturgiol′ogist; liturgiol′ogy** the study of liturgical forms; **lit′urgist** a leader in public worship: one who adheres to, or who studies, liturgies. [Gr. *leitourgiā.*]
lituus *lit′ū-əs*, *n.* an augur's curved staff: a J-shaped Roman trumpet: a curve of similar form with the polar equation $r^2 \theta = a$. [L. *lituus.*]
live¹ *liv*, *v.i.* to have, or continue in, life, temporal, spiritual, or figurative: to last: to enjoy life: to direct one's course of life: to be supported, subsist, get a living: to escape destruction or oblivion: to dwell. — *v.t.* to spend or pass: to act in conformity to: to express by one's life, make one's life the same thing as: — *pr.p.* **liv′ing;** *pa.t.* and *pa.p.* **lived** (*livd*). — *adjs.* **liv′able, live′able** worth living, capable of being lived: habitable. — *n.* **liv′er.** — *adjs.* **liv′able(-with)** such as one could endure to live with; **live′-in′** of an employee, living at the place of work: of a sexual partner, sharing the same dwelling. — **live and let live** to give and expect toleration or forbearance; **live down** to live so as to allow to be forgotten; **live for** to attach great importance to: to long for; **live in, out** to dwell in, away from, one's place of employment; **live it up** to go on the spree: to live rather too intensely; **live on** to live by feeding upon, or with expenditure limited to; **live on air** to have no apparent means of sustenance; **live out** to survive: (of someone in domestic service) to live away from the workplace (*U.S.*); **live to** to live long enough to, come at last to; **live together** to cohabit; **live under** to be tenant to; **live up to** to rule one's life in a manner worthy of: to spend up to the scale of; **live well** to live luxuriously; **live with** to cohabit with: to accept and

adapt to as an inescapable part of one's life; **the living theatre** the live theatre. [O.E. *lifian* (W.S. *libban*).]

live[2] *līv, adj.* having life: alive, not dead: active: stirring: unquarried or unwrought: charged with energy (as by electricity, explosives or other chemicals, etc.) and still capable of discharge: burning: vivid: of the theatre, etc., concerned with living performance as distinct from filming, broadcasting, or televising: of a broadcast, made directly from the actual event, not from a recording: fully operational (*comput.*): a fishmonger's word for very fresh. — **-lived** (*-līvd*; sometimes *-livd*) in composition, having life (as *long-lived*). — *v.t.* **liv'en** to enliven. — *v.i.* to become lively. — **live'-ax'le** driving-axle; **live'-bait** a living animal as bait; **live= birth'** birth in a living condition (opposed to *still-birth*). — *adj.* **live'-born.** — **live'-box** a glass box for examining living objects under the microscope: a box for live fish; **live cartridge** one containing a bullet, opposed to a *blank* or a *spent* cartridge; **live centre** a rotating centre in the headstock of a lathe, turning with the workpiece; **live circuit** a circuit through which an electric current is flowing. — *n.pl.* **live'-feath'ers** those plucked from the living fowl. — **live load** a moving weight or variable force on a structure; **live'-oak** an American evergreen oak, with durable wood; **live'-rail, live'-wire** one carrying electric current: (**live'-wire**; *fig.*) a person of intense energy or alertness; **live shell** a shell still capable of exploding; **live steam** steam at full pressure, direct from a boiler; **live'stock** domestic animals, esp. horses, cattle, sheep, and pigs: domestic or body vermin (*slang*); **live'ware** all the people working with a computer system; **live'-weight** weight of living animals; **live'-well** the well in a fishing-boat where fish are kept alive. [**alive.**]

livelihead. See **lively.**

livelihood *līv'li-hŏŏd, n.* means of living: support. — Also (*Spens.*) **live'lod, live'lood.** [O.E. *līflād* — *līf*, life, *lād*, course.]

livelong[1] *liv'long,* also *līv'long, adj.* very long: protracted: enduring: complete, entire. [**lief,** used intensively, **long.**]

livelong[2] *liv'long, n.* the orpine, a plant difficult to kill. [**live**[1], **long**[3].]

livelood. See **livelihood.**

lively *līv'li, adj.* vital (*obs.*): lifelike: oral (*obs.*): brisk: active: sprightly: spirited: vivid. — *adv.* vivaciously: vigorously. — *n.* **live'lihead** (*obs.*) liveliness: life: living form: livelihood. — *adv.* **live'lily.** — *n.* **live'liness.** — **look lively!** make haste. [O.E. *līflic* — *līf*, life.]

liven. See **live**[2].

liver[1] *liv'ər, n.* a large gland that secretes bile, formerly regarded as seat of courage, love, etc.: its substance as food: a disordered state of the liver (*coll.*): in old chemistry a sulphide or other liver-coloured substance (*liver of sulphur,* mixture got by heating potassium carbonate with sulphur). — *adj.* **liver-colour.** — *adjs.* **-liv'ered** having a liver, as *white-livered, lily-livered,* cowardly; **liv'erish, liv'ery** suffering from disordered liver: irritable. — *n.* and *adj.* **liv'er-col'our** dark reddish brown. — *adj.* **liv'er-coloured.** — **liv'er-fluke** a trematode worm that infects the bile-ducts of sheep and other animals. — *adj.* **liv'er-grown** having a swelled liver. — **liv'er-rot** a disease caused by liver-flukes. — *n.pl.* **liver salts** mineral salts taken to cure indigestion. — **liver sausage** a rich sausage made of liver; **liver spot** a liver-coloured mark on the skin appearing in old age; **liv'er-wing** a fowl's right wing, which is cooked with the liver; **liv'erwort** (*-wûrt*) any plant of the Hepaticae, forming with the mosses the Bryophyta, some kinds having once been used medicinally in diseases of the liver; **liv'erwurst** (*-wûrst*) liver sausage. [O.E. *lifer;* Ger. *Leber,* O.N. *lifr.*]

liver[2]. See **live**[1].

liver[3] *lī'vər, n.* a fanciful bird on the arms of the city of Liverpool. [Formed from *Liverpool.*]

Liverpudlian *liv-ər-pud'li-ən, adj.* belonging to Liverpool.

— *n.* a native of Liverpool. [*Liverpool,* influenced by *puddle.*]

livery[1] *liv'ər-i, n.* a delivery or handing over (*obs.*): a dispensing or allowance of food or clothes to servants and retainers (*hist.*): the feeding, care, and stabling of a horse at a certain rate: the distinctive dress or badge of a great man's household (*hist.*): the distinctive garb of a person's servants, esp. men-servants, or of a body, e.g. a trade-guild: any characteristic garb: the distinctive decoration used for all its aircraft, etc. by an airline, etc.: a body of liverymen or of livery-servants: a livery-servant (*arch.*). — *adj.* **liv'eried** clothed in livery. — **liv'ery-com'pany** a guild of the city of London; **livery cupboard** a small cupboard used for the temporary storage of food, etc.; **liv'eryman** a man who wears a livery: a freeman of the city of London entitled to wear the livery and enjoy other privileges of his company: one who keeps or works at a livery-stable; **livery pot** a flask in which an allowance of wine was formerly given to a servant; **liv'ery-servant** a servant who wears a livery; **liv'ery-stable** a stable where horses are kept at livery and for hire. — **at livery** of a horse, kept at the owner's expense at a livery stable; **sue one's livery** (*Shak.*) to ask for the writ delivering a freehold into the possession of its heir. [A.Fr. *liveré,* lit. handed over — *livrer* — L. *līberāre,* to free.]

livery[2]. See **liver**[1].

lives *līvz, n.* plural of **life.**

livid *liv'id, adj.* black and blue: of a lead colour: discoloured: pale, ashen: extremely angry (*coll.*). — *ns.* **livid'ity, liv'idness, livor** (*lī'vər, -vör*). [L. *līvidus* — *līvēre,* to be of a lead colour.]

living *liv'ing, adj.* live: alive: having vitality: lively: in present life, existence, activity, or use. — *n.* means of subsistence: manner of life: a property: a benefice. — **living death** a life of unrelieved misery; **living fossil** an animal or a plant of a group of which most are extinct; **living memory** the memory of anybody or somebody still alive; **living rock** rock still in its natural position; **liv'ing-room** a sitting-room for all-round use; **living wage** a wage on which it is possible for a workman and his family to live fairly. [Pr.p. of **live**[1].]

Livingstone daisy *liv'ing-stən dā'zi,* a S. African annual succulent plant (*Dorotheanthus bellidiformis* or *Mesembryanthemum criniflorum*), with daisy-like flowers. [Ety. unknown.]

livor. See **livid.**

livraison *lē-vrez-ɔ̄,* (Fr.) *n.* a number of a book published in parts.

livre *lēvr', n.* an old French coin, superseded by the franc in 1795: an old French weight about 1 lb. avoirdupois. [Fr., — L. *lībra,* a pound.]

lixiviation *liks-iv-i-ā'shən, n.* leaching. — *adjs.* **lixiv'ial, lixiv'ious.** — *v.t.* **lixiv'iate.** — *n.* **lixiv'ium** lye. [L. *lixīvium,* lye.]

lizard *liz'ərd, n.* any member of the Lacertilia, an order of scaly reptiles, usually differing from snakes in having four legs, movable eyelids, and non-expansible mouths: (with *cap.*) the constellation Lacerta. — *adj.* **liz'ard-hipped** (of dinosaurs) having a pelvis slightly similar to a lizard's, the pubis extending forwards and downwards from the limb socket, saurischian. [O.Fr. *lesard* (Fr. *lézard*) — L. *lacerta.*]

'll *l.* Shortened form of **will, shall.**

llama *lä'mə, n.* a S. American transport animal of the camel family, a domesticated guanaco: its wool: cloth made thereof. [Sp., from Quechua.]

llano *lyä'nō,* or *lä'nō, n.* one of the vast steppes or plains in the northern part of South America: — *pl.* **lla'nos.** — *n.* **llanero** (*lyä-nä'rō*) an inhabitant of the llanos: — *pl.* **llaner'os.** [Sp., — L. *plānus,* plain.]

lo *lō, interj.* look: behold: — *pl.* **lōs.** [O.E. *lā.*]

loach *lōch, n.* a small river-fish of a family (*Cobitidae*) akin to the carps. [Fr. *loche.*]

load *lōd, n.* that which is carried: that which may or can be carried at one time or journey: a burden: a charge: a freight or cargo: a definite quantity, varying according to the goods: weight carried: power output of an engine, etc.: work imposed or expected: power carried by an electric circuit: a large quantity borne: a burden sustained with difficulty: that which burdens or grieves: a weight or encumbrance: weight of blows (*Spens.*): abundance (*coll.*, esp. in *pl.*). — *v.t.* to lade or burden: to charge: to put a load on or in: to put on or in anything as a load: to put film in (a camera): to put on overmuch: to weigh down: to overburden: to supply, present, or assail overwhelmingly or lavishly: to weight: to give weight or body to, by adding something: to mix with white: to lay on in masses (*painting*): to add charges to (*insurance*): (of wine) to doctor, drug, adulterate, or fortify. — *v.i.* to put or take on a load: to charge a gun: to become loaded or burdened: — *pa.t.* **load′ed**; *pa.p.* **load′ed** or (*arch.*) **load′en**. — **-load** in composition, indicating that which is being conveyed in a vehicle (as in *busload, coachload, lorryload*). — *adj.* **load′ed** rich, wealthy: under the influence of drink or drugs (*slang*): weighted in discussion in a certain direction: charged with contentious material. — *v.t.* **load′en** (*obs.* or *dial.*) to load. — *ns.* **load′er; load′ing** the act of lading: that with which anything is loaded. — *adj.* **load′-bearing** of a wall, etc., supporting a structure, carrying weight. — **loaded question** a question designed to make an unwilling answerer commit himself to some opinion, action, or course; **load factor** the ratio of an external load to the weight of an aircraft: the actual payload on an aircraft as a percentage of the maximum permissible payload: the ratio of an average load to peak load over a period; **loading coil** a coil inserted in an electric circuit to increase inductance; **loading gauge** a suspended bar that marks how high a railway truck may be loaded: the maximum horizontal and vertical space that rolling stock may safely occupy above the track; **load′-line** a line on a ship's side to mark the depth to which her cargo may be allowed to sink her; **load′master** a member of an aircrew who is in charge of the cargo; **load shedding** temporarily reducing the amount of electricity sent out by a power station. — **a load of** a quantity of something distasteful or senseless (as in *a load of rubbish, a load of tripe*); **a load off one's mind** relief from anxiety; **get a load of** (*slang*) to listen to, look at, pay attention to; **load dice** to make one side heavier than the other so as to influence their fall for purposes of cheating; **load the dice against someone** (*fig.*) to deprive someone of a fair chance of success. [O.E. *lād*, course, journey, conveyance; meaning affected by the unrelated **lade**[3]; cf. **lode, lead**[1].]

loadstar, loadstone. Same as **lodestar, lodestone.**

loaf[1] *lōf, n.* bread (formerly, still *Scot.*): a portion of bread baked in one mass, esp. of standard weight: a moulded portion of food, esp. bread or meat: a conical mass of sugar: any lump (*obs.*): a cabbage-head: the head, or brains (*slang*): — *pl.* **loaves** (*lōvz*). — *v.i.* **loaf, loave** (*lōv*) to form a head, as a cabbage. — **loaf′-bread** (*Scot.*) ordinary plain bread; **loaf′-cake** (*U.S.*) a plain cake like a loaf in form; **loaf′-sug′ar** refined sugar moulded in the form of a great cigar. — **half loaf** a loaf of half the standard weight; **loaves and fishes** temporal benefits, the main chance (John vi. 26). [O.E. *hlāf*, bread.]

loaf[2] *lōf, v.i.* to loiter or stand idly about, pass time idly. — *n.* **loaf′er** one who loafs: a casual shoe, often resembling a moccasin. — *adj.* **loaf′erish.** — *n.* and *adj.* **loaf′ing.** [Poss. — Ger. *Landläufer*, tramp, vagabond.]

Loaghtan *lohh′tən, n.* a breed of four-horned sheep with a soft brown fleece, native to the Isle of Man. [Manx *loaghtyn*, brown, poss. lit. mouse-brown, from *lugh*, mouse and *dhoan*, brown.]

loam *lōm, n.* a soil consisting of a natural mixture of clay and sand, with animal and vegetable matter: a composition basically of moist clay and sand used in making bricks. — *v.t.* to cover with loam. — *n.* **loam′iness.** — *adj.* **loam′y.** [O.E. *lām*; Ger. *Lehm*; cf. **lime**[1].]

loan[1] *lōn, (Scot.) n.* a lane: an open space for passage left between fields of corn: a place for milking cows. — Also **loan′ing.** [O.E. *lone, lane*; see **lane**[2].]

loan[2] *lōn, n.* anything lent, esp. money at interest: the act of lending: the condition of being lent: an arrangement for lending: permission to use. — *v.t.* to lend. — *adj.* **loan′able.** — **loan collection** privately-owned works of art lent by their owner for a public exhibition; **loan′-hold′er** one who holds security for a loan; **loan′-office** a public office at which loans are negotiated, received, or recorded: a pawnshop; **loan′-shark** a usurer; **loan′-sharking** the lending of money at an exorbitant rate of interest; **loan′-society** a society organised to subscribe money to be lent; **loan translation** a compound, phrase, etc. that is a literal translation of a foreign expression, as English *motorway* from German *Autobahn*, German *Fernsehen* from English *television* — also called a calque; **loan′-word** one borrowed from another language. [O.N. *lān*; cf. **lend**, O.E. *lǣnan*, Dan. *laan*.]

loast *lōst, (Spens.) pa.p.* of **loose.**

loath. Same as **loth.**

loathe *lōdh, v.t.* to dislike intensely: to feel disgust at. — *adj.* **loathed.** — *ns.* **loath′edness; loath′er.** — *adj.* **loath′ful** exciting loathing or disgust: (*Spens.* **lothefull, lothfull**) loathsome: reluctant. — *ns.* **loath′fulness; loath′ing** extreme hate or disgust: abhorrence. — *adj.* **hating.** — *adv.* **loath′ingly.** — *n.* **loath′liness.** — *adjs.* **loath′ly** (*arch.*) hideous: loathsome; **loathsome** (*lōth′, lōdh′səm*) exciting loathing or abhorrence: detestable. — *adv.* **loath′somely.** — *n.* **loath′someness.** — *adj.* **loathy** (*lōdh′i; arch.*). [O.E. *lāthian*; cf. **loth.**]

loave, loaves. See **loaf**[1].

lob *lob, n.* a lump: a clumsy person: a lout: something thick and heavy: a pollack: a lobworm: in cricket, a slow, high underhand ball: in lawn tennis, a ball high overhead, dropping near the back of the court. — *v.t.* to droop (*Shak.*): to bowl or strike as a lob: — *pa.t.* and *pa.p.* **lobbed.** — **Lob′-lie′-by-the-fire** a brownie who works by night for his bowl of cream: a Puck; **Lob's pound** (*dial.*) prison: difficulty. [Cf. Fris. and Du. *lob*.]

lobar, lobate, etc. See **lobe.**

lobby *lob′i, n.* a small hall or waiting-room: a passage serving as a common entrance to several apartments: the ante-chamber of a legislative hall: a corridor into which members pass as they vote (also **divis′ion=lobb′y**): a group of persons who campaign to persuade legislators to make regulations favouring their particular interests. — *v.t.* to seek to influence (public officials) (esp. in the lobby). — *v.i.* to frequent the lobby in order to influence members or to collect political intelligence: to conduct a campaign in order to influence public officials. — *ns.* **lobb′yer; lobb′ying; lobb′yist.** — **lobby correspondent** reporter on parliamentary affairs; **lobb′y-member** (*U.S.*) formerly, one who frequented a lobby in the interest of some cause; **lobby system** the giving of political information to lobby correspondents on condition that the source is not revealed. [L.L. *lobia* — M.H.G. *loube* (Ger. *Laube*), a portico, arbour — *Laub*, a leaf; cf. **lodge.**]

lobe *lōb, n.* a broad, esp. rounded, segmental division, branch, or projection: the soft lower part of the ear: a division of the lungs, brain, etc.: a division of a leaf. — *adjs.* **lōb′ar, lōb′ate, lōbed, lōb′ose.** — *n.* **lōbā′tion lobing.** — **lōbe′-foot** a phalarope. — *adjs.* **lōbe′-foot′ed, lō′biped** having lobate feet, i.e. with lobes along the sides of the toes, as a coot. — *ns.* **lobec′tomy** surgical excision of a lobe of any organ or gland of the body; **lobe′let, lobule** (*lob′ūl*) small lobe; **lōb′ing** division into lobes: formation of, possession of, or provision with, lobes. — *adj.* **lobiped** see **lobe-footed.** — *v.t.* **lobot′omise, -ize** to perform a lobotomy on: to render dull, bland or inoffensive (*fig.*). — *n.* **lobot′omy** surgical incision into a lobe of an organ or gland: (loosely) leucotomy. — *adjs.* **lōb′ular, -ulate(d).** — *ns.* **lōbulā′tion; lōb′ulus** a small lobe or lobe-like structure: — *pl.*

lŏb′uli (-ĭ); **lō′bus** a lobe: — *pl.* **lŏ′bī.** — **lobar pneumonia** inflammation of a whole lobe of the lungs, as distinguished from **lobular pneumonia,** which attacks the lungs in patches.   [Gr. *lobos*, lobe.]

Lobelia *lō-bē′lyə,* *n.* a genus of plants giving name to a family, **Lobeliā′ceae,** differing from Campanulaceae in having two carpels and zygomorphic flowers, twisted upside-down, including blue-flowered garden plants: (without *cap.*) a plant of this genus. — *n.* **lobeline** (*lō′bə-lēn, -lin*) a poisonous alkaloid obtained from *Lobelia inflata,* used as a respiratory stimulant and to discourage tobacco-smoking.   [Named after the botanist Matthias de *Lobel* (1538–1616).]

loblolly *lob′lol-i, n.* thick gruel, hence ship's medicine (*dial.*): a lout (*dial.*): a muddy swamp or mire (*U.S.*): a name for various American pines (also **loblolly pine**). — **lob′lolly-bay** an American tree of the tea family (*Gordonia lasianthus*), its bark used in tanning; **lob′-lolly-boy** (*obs.*) a ship-surgeon's attendant; **lob′lolly≈ tree** a name for several American leathery-leaved trees. [Perh. **lob** and **lolly**.]

lobo *lō′bō,* (*U.S.*) *n.* a timber wolf.   [Sp., wolf — L. *lupus.*]

lobose, lobotomy, etc. See **lobe.**

lobscouse *lob′skows, n.* a stew or hash with vegetables or biscuit, a sea dish. — Also **lob's course.**   [Origin obscure; cf. **lob, loblolly.**]

lobster *lob′stər, n.* a large strong-clawed edible crustacean (*Homarus*), red when boiled: extended to kindred kinds, as the **Norway lobster** (*Nephrops*), **spiny** or **rock lobster** (*Palinurus*): a British soldier (*obs. slang*). — **lob′ster-pot** a basket for trapping lobsters.   [O.E. *loppestre* — L. *locusta,* a lobster; cf. **locust.**]

lobular, lobus, etc. See **lobe.**

lobworm *lob′wûrm, n.* a lugworm: sometimes an earthworm.   [**lob, worm.**]

local *lō′kl, adj.* pertaining to position in space: of or belonging to a place: confined to a place or places. — *n.* someone or something local, as an inhabitant, a public-house, an examination, an item of news, a railway train, in U.S. a trade union branch: a place: (*lō-käl′*; erroneously **locale,** for Fr. *local*) the scene of some event. — *n.* **localīsa′tion, -z-.** — *v.t.* **lo′calise, -ize** to assign, limit, to a place. — *n.* **lo′caliser, -z-** something that localises, esp. a radio transmitter used in effecting a blind landing. — Also *adj.* as *localiser beam,* etc. — *ns.* **lo′calism** the state of being local: affection for place: provincialism; **lo′calist** someone preoccupied with local concerns; **locality** (*lō-kal′i-ti*) place: position: district. — *adv.* **lo′cally.** — *v.t.* **locate′** to place: to set in a particular position: to designate or find the place of. — *v.i.* to settle, take up one's abode (*U.S.*). — *n.* **loca′tion** act of locating: a farm: a claim or place marked off (for native occupation, etc.): position, site: site for filming outside the studio (*cinema*): a leasing on rent (*law*): a position in a memory which can hold a unit of information, e.g. a word (*comput.*): such a unit of information (*comput.*). — *adj.* **locative** (*lok′ə-tiv*) pertaining to location: denoting place where (*gram.*). — *n.* the locative case: a word in the locative case. — **local action** (*law*) a legal action relating to a specific place and which must be brought there; **local anaesthesia** anaesthesia affecting a restricted area only of the body; **local anaesthetic; local authorities** elected bodies for local government, e.g. town councils, county councils; **local call** a telephone call made to another number on the same exchange or group of exchanges; **local colour** colour of individual items as apart from general colour-scheme in a picture: faithful, characteristic details of particular scenery, manners, etc., giving verisimilitude in works of art and fiction; **local examinations** examinations of school pupils held in various local centres by universities; **local government** self-administration (in local affairs) by towns, counties, and the like, as opp. to *national* or *central government;* **local option** the right of a town or district to decide whether liquor licences shall be granted

within its bounds, or to decide whether or not to enforce (locally) permissive laws and regulations; **local preacher** a Methodist layman authorised to preach in his district; **local radio** radio (programmes) broadcast from a local station to a relatively small area, often on local themes; **local time** the time of a place as measured by the passage of the sun over the meridian passing through that place; **local veto** the power of a district to prohibit the sale of liquors in its own area. — **local education authority** the department of a local authority which administers state education; **on location** outside the studio (of filming or sound-recording). [L. *locālis* — *locus,* a place.]

locate, location, etc. See under **local.**

locellate *lō-sel′āt, adj.* divided into small compartments. [L. *locellus,* dim. of *locus,* a place.]

loch *lohh, n.* a lake: an arm of the sea. — *n.* **loch′an** (*Gael.*) a lakelet.   [Gael. *loch;* O.E. (Northumbrian) *luh.*]

Lochaber-axe *lohh-ä′bər-aks, n.* a long-handled Highland variety of halberd.   [*Lochaber* district in Inverness-shire.]

lochan. See **loch.**

lochia *lok′i-ə,* or *lōk′, n.pl.* a discharge from the uterus after childbirth. — *adj.* **lō′chial.**   [Gr. *lochia* (pl.).]

loci. Plural of **locus** (q.v.).

lock[1] *lok, n.* a fastening device, esp. one in which a bolt is moved by mechanism, with or without a key: an enclosure for raising or lowering boats: the part of a firearm by which it is discharged: a grapple in wrestling: in Rugby football, one of the two inside men in the second row of a scrum (also **lock′-for′ward**): a state of being jammed, or immovable: an assemblage of things mutually engaged: a lockful: a lock-keeper: any narrow, confined place: a lock-hospital: locking up: the full extent of the turning arc of the front wheels of a motor vehicle. — *v.t.* to fasten (door, chest, etc.) with a lock: to fasten so as to impede motion: to engage: to jam: to shut up: to close fast: to embrace closely: to furnish with locks. — *v.i.* to become fast: to unite closely: to become locked. — *ns.* **lock′age** the locks of a canal: the difference in the levels of locks: materials used for locks: water lost by use of a lock: tolls paid for passing through locks; **lock′er** box, small cupboard, properly one that may be locked; **locket** (*lok′it*) a little ornamental case usually containing a miniature or memento, and hung from the neck. — *adj.* **lock′fast** firmly fastened by locks. — *n.* **lock′ful** enough to fill a lock. — **lock′away** a long-term security. — Also *adj.* — **lock′-chain** a chain for fastening the wheels of a vehicle by tying the rims to some part which does not rotate; **lock′er-room** a room for changing clothes and for storing belongings in lockers; **lock′-gate** a gate for opening or closing a lock in a canal, river, or dock-entrance; **lock′-hos′pital** a hospital for venereal diseases (from one in Southwark, originally a lazar-house, probably an specially isolated); **lock′house** a lock-keeper's house; **lock′(ing)-nut** a nut screwed on top of another one to prevent it loosening: a nut designed to lock itself when screwed tight; **lock′-jaw** tetanus: loosely, trismus; **lock′-keeper** the attendant at a lock; **lock′man** a lock-keeper: a hangman (*Scot., obs.*): an under-sheriff, or a coroner's summoner (*Isle of Man*); **lock′out** the act of locking out, esp. used of the locking out of employees by the employer during an industrial dispute; **lock′pick** a picklock; **locks′man** a turnkey: a lock-keeper; **lock′smith** one who makes and mends locks; **lock′step** a style of marching in which each individual is as close as possible to the one immediately in front; **lock′stitch** a sewing-machine stitch formed by the locking of two threads together; **lock′-up** a place for locking up prisoners, motor-cars, etc.: a locking up. — *adj.* capable of being locked up. — **a shot in the locker** see **shot; Davy Jones's locker** see under **Davy Jones; lock away** to hide, usu. by locking up out of sight; **lock horns** to engage in combat, physical or otherwise; **lock in, out** to confine, keep out, by locking doors; **lock on (to)** of a radar beam, to track (an object) automatically; **lock, stock, and barrel** the whole: altogether; **lock up** to confine: to lock securely: to lock whatever is to be locked: to make inaccessible or unavailable (*fig.*); **under lock and key** locked up: imprisoned. [O.E. *loc.*]

lock[2] *lok, n.* a tuft or ringlet of hair, wool, etc.: a small quantity, as of hay: a quantity of meal, the perquisite of a mill-servant (*Scots law*): a lovelock (*Shak.*): (in *pl.*) dreadlocks (q.v.). [O.E. *locc*; O.N. *lokkr*, Ger. *Locke*, a lock.]

Lockian *lok'i-ən, adj.* pertaining to the philosophy of John *Locke* (1632–1704). — *ns.* **Lock'ian, Lock'ist.**

lockram *lok'rəm, n.* a coarse linen said to have been made at *Locronan* (Ronan's cell) in Brittany.

loco[1] *lō'kō, (U.S.) adj.* mad. — *n.* (also **lo'co-plant, -weed**) Astragalus or other leguminous plant: — *pl.* **lō'co(e)s.** — *adj.* **locoed** (*lō'kōd*) poisoned by loco: mad. [Sp. *loco*, mad.]

loco[2] *lō'kō.* Short for **locomotive**: — *pl.* **lō'cos.** — **lō'coman** a railway engine driver.

loco citato *lō'kō si-tä'tō, lok'ō ki-tä'tō,* (L.) in the passage cited — abbrev. **loc. cit.**

locofoco *lō-kō-fō'kō, (U.S.) n.* a friction match: (usu. *cap.*) one of the extreme section of the Democratic party of 1835, known as the Equal Rights Party: — *pl.* **lōcōfō'cos.** [Origin unknown.]

locomotive *lō-kə-mō'tiv, adj.* moving from place to place: capable of, or assisting in, locomotion. — *n.* a locomotive machine: a railway engine. — *adj.* **locomo'bile** (*-bil*) having power of changing place: self-propelling. — *n.* a locomobile vehicle. — *n.* **locomobil'ity.** — *v.i.* **lo'comote** to move from place to place (back-formation). — *ns.* **locomotion** (*-mō'shən*); **locomotiv'ity; locomo'tor.** — *adjs.* **locomo'tor, locomo'tory.** — **locomotor ataxy, ataxia** tabes dorsalis, a chronic degenerative disease of the nervous system of which want of power to co-ordinate the muscles is a characteristic symptom. [L. *lŏcus*, a place, *movēre*, *mōtum*, to move.]

locorestive *lō-kō-res'tiv, (Lamb) adj.* staying in one place. [Humorously modelled on preceding — L. *restāre*, to stay still.]

Locrian *lō'kri-ən, adj.* of *Locris* in Greece, or its people, the *Locri.* — *n.* one of the Locri. — **Locrian mode** in ancient Greek music, the same as the Hypodorian. [Gr. *Lokros*, Locrian.]

loculus *lok'ū-ləs, n.* a small compartment (*bot.*, *anat.*, *zool.*): in ancient catacombs, a small recess for holding an urn: — *pl.* **loc'uli** (*-lī*). — Also **loc'ule** (*-ūl*): — *pl.* **loc'ules.** — *n.* **loc'ulament** (*bot.*) loculus. — *adjs.* **loc'ular, loc'ulate** having loculi; **loculicidal** (*lok-ū-li-sī'dl*; L. *caedĕre*, to cut) dehiscing along the back of the carpel. [L. *loculus*, dim. of *locus*, a place.]

locum (tenens) *lō'kəm (tēn', ten'enz) n.* a deputy or substitute, esp. for a clergyman or doctor: — *pl.* **lō'cum-tenentes** (*ten-en'tēz, -tās*), **locums.** — *n.* **lō'cum-ten'ency** the holding by a temporary substitute of a post. [L. *lŏcum*, accus. of *lŏcus*, a place, *tĕnēns*, pr.p. of *tenēre*, to hold.]

locuplete *lok'ū-plēt, adj.* well-stored. [L. *locuplēs, -ētis.*]

locus *lō'kəs, lok'ōōs, n.* a place, locality, location: a passage in a writing: the position of a gene in a chromosome: the line or surface constituted by all positions of a point or line satisfying a given condition (*math.*): — *pl.* **loci** (*lō'sī, lok'ē*). — **locus classicus** (*klas'i-kəs, -kōōs*) the classical passage, the stock quotation; **locus paenitentiae** (*pē-ni-ten'shi-ē, pī-ni-ten'ti-ī*) room for penitence: time for repentance; **locus standi** (*stan'dī, -dē*) a place for standing: a right to interfere. [L. *lŏcus*, place.]

locust *lō'kəst, n.* a name for several kinds of migratory winged insects of the family *Acrididiae*, akin to grasshoppers, highly destructive to vegetation: extended to various similar insects: a devourer or devastator (*fig.*): a locust-bean: a locust-tree. — *v.i.* (*rare*) to lay waste like locusts. — *n.* **locust'a** a grass spikelet: (*cap.*) a genus of grasshoppers of the family **Locust'idae** (not usually reckoned locusts): — *pl.* **locust'ae** (*-ē*). —

lo'cust-bean' the carob-bean; **lo'cust-bird** any of several pratincoles that feed on locusts; **lo'cust-tree** the carob: the false acacia (*Robinia pseudo-acacia*): a large West Indian tree (*Hymenaea courbaril*) of the Caesalpinia family, with buttress roots, valuable wood, bark exuding animé; **lo'cust-years** years of poverty and hardship (Churchill, after Joel ii, 25). [L. *locusta*, lobster, locust; cf. **lobster.**]

locution *lok-ū'shən, n.* act or mode of speaking: expression, word, or phrase. — *adj.* **locū'tionary** of or pertaining to an utterance. — *n.* **loc'utory** a room for conversation, esp. in a monastery. [L. *loquī, locūtus,* to speak.]

lode *lōd, n.* a vein containing metallic ore: a reach of water: an open ditch. — **lodes'man** a pilot; **lode'star, load'star** the star that guides, the Pole Star — often used figuratively; **lode'stone, load'stone** a form of magnetite which exhibits polarity, behaving, when freely suspended, as a magnet: a magnet — often figuratively. [O.E. *lād,* a course; cf. **load.**]

loden *lō'dən, n.* a thick waterproof woollen cloth with a short pile: (also **loden coat**) a coat made of this cloth. [Ger.]

lodge *loj, n.* an abode, esp. if secluded, humble, small, or temporary: a house in the wilds for sportsmen: a gate-keeper's cottage: a college head's residence: a porter's room: the meeting-place of a branch of some societies, as freemasons: the branch itself: an American Indian's abode: the dwelling-place of a beaver, otter, etc.: a retreat: often, a villa (as part of its name): an accumulation (*obs.*): a loggia: a box in a theatre. — *v.t.* to furnish with a temporary dwelling: to place: to deposit: to infix: to vest: to settle: to drive to covert: to lay flat, as grain. — *v.i.* to dwell, esp. for a time, or as a lodger: to pass the night: to take covert: to come to rest in a fixed position: to lie flat, as grain. — *ns.* **lodg'er** one who lodges: one who lives in a hired room or rooms; **lodg'ing** temporary habitation: (often in *pl.*) a room or rooms hired in the house of another: harbour; **lodg'ment** (also **lodge'ment**) act of lodging, or state of being lodged: accumulation of something that remains at rest: the occupation of a position by a besieging party, and the works thrown up to maintain it (*mil.*). — **lodge'-gate'** a gate with a lodge; **lodge'-keeper; lodge'pole** a pole used in making an Amer. Indian lodge; **lodgepole pine** either of two fast-growing N. American pines (*Pinus contorta*); **lodg'ing-house** a house where lodgings are let: a house other than a hotel where travellers lodge: a house where vagrants may lodge; **lodging turn** a turn of railway work that requires sleeping away from home. [O.Fr. *loge* — O.H.G. *lauba,* shelter; cf. **lobby, loggia.**]

lodicule *lod'i-kūl, n.* a small scale in a grass flower. — Also **lodic'ula:** — *pl.* **lodic'ulae** (*-ē*). [L. *lōdĭcula,* dim. of *lōdīx, -īcis,* coverlet.]

lo'e *lōō.* Scots form of **love** (verb).

loess, löss *læs,* or *lō'is, n.* a loamy deposit of aeolian origin. [Ger. *Löss.*]

lo-fi *lō'-fī, (coll.) adj.* of sound reproduction, of low quality: loosely applied to anything shoddy or inferior. [**low**[2]; modelled on **hi-fi.**]

loft *loft, n.* upper region, sky, height (*Spens.*): a room or space immediately under a roof: a gallery in a hall or church: an upper room: an attic or upper floor, usu. unfurnished, for storage, etc. (*U.S.*): a floor or ceiling (*Spens.*): a room for pigeons: a layer (*Milt.*): a stroke that causes a golf-ball to rise: a backward slope on a golf-club head for the purpose of lofting: a lifting action. — *v.t.* to furnish with a loft (*obs.*): to put or keep in a loft (*obs.*): to strike up (*golf*): to toss: to propel high into the air or into space. — *n.* **loft'er** a golf iron for lofting. — *adv.* **loft'ily.** — *n.* **loft'iness.** — *adj.* **loft'y** very high in position, character, sentiment, manner, or diction: stately: haughty: of wool, bulky, springy, supple, and soft. — **cock of the loft** the head or chief of a set; **lofted house** (*Scot.*) a house of more than one storey. [Late O.E. *loft* — O.N. *lopt,* sky, an upper room; O.E. *lyft*, Ger. *Luft*, the air.]

log[1] *log*, *n.* short for **logarithm**. — **log tables** a book of tables setting out logarithmic values.

log[2] *lōg*, *log*, *n.* a Hebrew liquid measure, believed to be very nearly an English pint. [Heb. *lōg*.]

log[3] *log*, *n.* a bulky piece of wood: a clog or impediment: an inert or insensitive person (*fig.*): an apparatus (originally a block of wood) for ascertaining a ship's speed: a record of a ship's, or other, performance and experiences, a log-book. — *adj.* consisting of logs. — *v.t.* to cut or haul in the form of logs: to enter in a log-book, or record otherwise: to cover a distance of, according to the log: to record the name and punishment of: to punish. — *n.* **logg'at** a small log or piece of wood: a stake: (in *pl.*) old game of throwing loggats at a stake. — *adj.* **logged** (*logd*) reduced to the inactivity or helplessness of a log: waterlogged: cleared of logs. — *ns.* **logg'er** a lumberman: (also **data logger**) a device which automatically records data; **logg'ing**. — **log'-board** a hinged board for noting particulars for the log-book; **log'-book** a book containing an official record of a ship's progress and proceedings on board, or of a journey made by an aircraft or car, or of any progress: a headmaster's record of attendances, etc.: the registration documents of a motor vehicle; **log'-cab'in** a hut built of hewn or unhewn logs; **log'-canoe'** a boat made by hollowing out the trunk of a tree; **log'-chip** the quadrant-shaped board attached to a logline; **logg'erhead** a blockhead: a dunce: a round piece of timber in a whale-boat, over which the line is passed (*naut.*): a large sea-turtle (*Caretta caretta*): a round mass of iron with a long handle, heated for various purposes. — *adj.* **logg'erheaded.** — **log'-glass** a 14- or 28-second sand-glass, used with the logline to ascertain the speed of a ship; **log'-head** a blockhead; **log'-house** a log-cabin; **log'-hut'**; **log'-jam** jamming that brings floating logs to a standstill: congestion of events, etc., leading to a complete cessation of action (*fig.*): such cessation of action; **log'juice** (*slang*) bad port wine, as if coloured with logwood; **log'line** the line fastened to the log, and marked for finding the speed of a vessel; **log'-man** a man who carries logs (*Shak.*): one who cuts and removes logs; **log'-reel** a reel on which the logline is wound. — *v.t.* and *v.i.* **log'-roll.** — **log'-roller**; **log'-rolling** a gathering of people to facilitate the collection of logs after the clearing of a piece of land, or for rolling logs into a stream: the sport of trying to dislodge another person standing on the same floating log: mutual aid among politicians, etc., esp. trading in votes to secure passage of legislation; **log'-saw** a bow-saw; **log'-slate** a double slate used as a logboard; **log'wood** a tropical American tree (*Haematoxylon campechianum*) of the Caesalpinia family, exported in logs: its dark-red heartwood: an extract from it used in dyeing. — **at loggerheads** at issue, quarrelling; **log in** or **on** (*comput.*) to gain access to a mainframe system, usually by means of a code; **log out** or **off** (*comput.*) to disconnect from a mainframe system; **sleep like a log** to be very deeply asleep. [Origin obscure.]

logan *log'ən*, *n.* a rocking-stone. — Also **log'an-stone, logg'an-stone, logg'ing-stone.** [Dialect word *log*, to rock; poss. conn. with Dan. *logre*, to wag the tail.]

loganberry *lō'gən-ber-i*, *-bər-i*, *n.* a supposed hybrid between raspberry and a Pacific coast blackberry, obtained by Judge J. H. *Logan* (d. 1928).

Logania *lō-gā'ni-ə*, *n.* a genus of Australian plants giving name to the **Loganiā'ceae**, akin to the gentians. [Named after James *Logan* (1674–1751), botanist, scholar, and statesman.]

logaoedic *log-ə-ē'dik*, (*ancient prosody*) *adj.* combining dactyls with trochees. [Gr. *logos*, prose, *aoidē*, song.]

logarithm *log'ə-ridhm*, *-rithm*, *n.* the power of a fixed number (called the base of the system, usu. 10 or *e*) that equals the number in question. — *adjs.* **logarith'-mic, -al.** — *adv.* **logarith'mically.** — **logarithmic sine, cosine**, etc., the logarithm of the sine, cosine, etc.;

logarithmic spiral the path of a point travelling along a radius vector with a velocity increasing as its distance from the pole, its polar equation being $r = a^\theta$, or $\theta = k \log r$. [Gr. *logos*, ratio, reckoning, *arithmos*, number.]

loge *lozh*, *n.* a box in the theatre or opera house.

loggan-stone. See **logan.**

loggat, logger, loggerhead, etc. See **log**[3].

loggia *loj'(y)ə*, *n.* a covered open arcade: — *pl.* **loggie** (*loj'ā*), **loggias.** [It.; cf. **lodge.**]

logging-stone. See **logan.**

Loghtan, Loghtyn. Alternative spellings of **Loaghtan.**

logia *log'i-ə*, *n.pl.* sayings, esp. early collections of those attributed to Christ: — *sing.* **log'ion.** [Gr.]

logic *loj'ik*, *n.* the science and art of reasoning correctly: the science of the necessary laws of thought: the principles of any branch of knowledge: sound reasoning: individual method of reasoning: convincing and compelling force (as of facts, events): basis of operation as designed and effected in a computer, comprising **logical elements** which perform specified elementary arithmetical functions. — *adj.* **log'ical** of or according to logic: rightly reasoning: following necessarily from facts or events: of, used in, logic circuits (*comput.*). — *ns.* **logical'ity, log'icalness.** — *adv.* **log'-ically.** — *n.* **logician** (*loj-ish'ən*) one skilled in logic. — *v.i.* **log'icise, -ize** (*-sīz*) to argue. — **logical analysis** (*philos.*) analysis, the process of stating clearly what our concepts comprise and imply; **logical atomism** (*philos.*) the theory that all propositions can be analysed into simple elements; **logical designer** one engaged in the scientific construction of computers; **logical positivism** (or **empiricism**) see **positive**; **logic circuit** (*comput.*) an electronic circuit with usu. two or more inputs and one output, which performs a logical operation, e.g. *and*, *not*; **logic diagram** (*comput.*) a diagram showing logical elements and interconnections without engineering details. — **chop logic** see **chop.** [Gr. *logikē* (*technē*), logical (art) — *logos*, speech, reason.]

logie *lō'gi*, (*Scot.*) *n.* the space before a kiln fire. [Origin unknown; cf. **killogie**.]

logion. See **logia.**

logistic, -al *loj-is'tik*, *-əl*, *adjs.* pertaining to reasoning, to calculation, or to logistic(s): proportional. — *ns.* **logis'-tic** the art of calculation: sexagesimal arithmetic; **logistician** (*-tish'ən*) one skilled in logistics. — *n.sing.* or *pl.* **logis'tics** the art of movement and supply of troops: the handling of the practical detail of any large-scale enterprise or operation. — **logistics vessel** a ship designed for the transport of troops and vehicles, and for their landing directly on to beaches. [Gr. *logistikos* — *logizesthai*, to compute; influenced by Fr. *loger*, to lodge.]

loglog *log'log*, *n.* the *log*arithm of a *log*arithm. — Also **lō'log.**

logo. See **logotype.**

logodaedalus *log-ō-dē'də-ləs*, *n.* an artificer in words. — *adj.* **logodaedal'ic.** — *n.* **logodae'daly** verbal legerdemain. [Latinised from Gr. *logodaidalos* — *logos*, word, *Daidalos*, Daedalus; see **daedal.**]

logogram *log'ō-gram*, **logograph** *-gräf*, *ns.* a single sign for a word: a logogriph. [Gr. *logos*, word, *gramma*, letter, *graphein*, to write.]

logographer *log-og'rə-fər*, *n.* in Greek literature, one of the earliest annalists, esp. those before Herodotus: a professional speech-writer. — *adjs.* **logographic** (*-graf'-ik*), **-al.** — *adv.* **logograph'ically.** — *n.* **logog'raphy** a method of printing with whole words cast in a single type. [Gr. *logos*, word, *graphein*, to write.]

logogriph *log'ō-grif*, *n.* a riddle in which a word is to be found from other words made up of its letters, or from synonyms of these. [Gr. *logos*, word, *griphos*, a net, riddle.]

logomachy *log-om'ə-ki*, *n.* contention about words or in words merely. — *n.* **logom'achist.** [Gr. *logomachiā* — *logos*, word, *machē*, fight.]

logorrhoea, -rrhea *log-ō-rē'ə, n.* excessive flow of words. [Gr. *rhoiā,* flow.]

Logos *log'os, n.* in the Stoic philosophy, the active principle living in and determining the world: the Word of God incarnate (*Christian theol.*). [Gr. *logos,* word.]

logothete *log'ō-thēt, n.* a chancellor, esp. in the Byzantine Empire and in Norman Sicily. [Gr. *logothetēs,* an auditor.]

logotype *log'ō-tīp, n.* a type of a word or several letters cast in one piece: a single piece of type comprising a name and/or address, trademark, or design: an identifying symbol consisting of a simple picture or design and/or letters. — Also **log'o:** — *pl.* **log'os.** [Gr. *logos,* word, *typos,* an impression.]

Løgting. See **Lagting.**

-logy *-lo-ji, suffix* indicating science, theory: discourse, treatise. [Gr. *logos* word, reason.]

loid *loid, (slang) n.* short for **celluloid.** — *v.t.* to open (a lock) with a strip of celluloid.

loin *loin, n.* the back of a beast cut for food: (usu. in *pl.*) the reins, or the lower part of the back: (in *pl.*) generating source. — **loin'-cloth** a piece of cloth for wearing round the loins. — **gird up one's loins** to prepare for energetic action, as if by tucking up one's clothes. [O.Fr. *loigne* — L. *lumbus,* loin.]

loipe *loi'pə, n.* a track used for cross-country skiing. [Dan. *løjpe.*]

loir *loir, n.* a large European species of dormouse. [Fr. — L.L. *lis,* liris — L. *glīs, glīris.*]

loiter *loi'tər, v.i.* to proceed lingeringly: to dawdle: to linger. — *n.* **loi'terer.** — *n.* and *adj.* **loi'tering.** — *adv.* **loi'teringly.** [Du. *leuteren,* to dawdle; Ger. dial. *lottern,* to waver.]

loke *lōk, (dial.) n.* a short, narrow lane: a cul-de-sac: a private road: a grass-covered track. [M.E. — O.E. *loca,* an enclosed place.]

Loki *lō'ki, n.* an evil god in Norse mythology.

Lok Sabha *lok sä'bə,* the lower house of the Indian parliament. [Hindi *lok,* people, *sabha,* assembly.]

lokshen *lok'shən, n.pl.* noodles. — **lokshen pudding** a traditional Jewish pudding made with noodles, egg, sugar, dried fruit and cinnamon; **lokshen soup** a traditional Jewish noodle soup. [Yiddish, pl. of *loksh,* a noodle — Russ. *loksha.*]

Loligo *lō-lī'gō, n.* the typical genus of **Loliginidae** (*lol-i-jin'i-dē*) including the common squid. [L. *lōlīgō, -inis.*]

Lolium *lō'li-əm, n.* a genus of grasses including darnel and rye-grass. [L. *lōlium,* darnel, 'tares'.]

loll *lol, v.i.* to lie lazily about, to lounge, sprawl: to dangle, hang (now mainly of the tongue). — *v.t.* to let hang out. — *n.* **loll'er.** — *adv.* **loll'ingly.** — *v.i.* **loll'op** to lounge, idle: to bound clumsily along. [Perh. imit.; cf. Du. *lollen,* to sit over the fire.]

Lollard *lol'ərd, n.* a follower of Wycliffe: an idler. — *ns.* **Loll'ardy, Loll'ardry, Loll'ardism.** [M.Du. *lollaerd,* mutterer, droner — *lollen,* to mew, bawl, mutter; combined with **loller** (see **loll**).]

lollipop *lol'i-pop, n.* a sweetmeat made with sugar and treacle: a large boiled sweetmeat which has been allowed to solidify around a stick: (usu. in *pl.*) a sweetmeat in general (also *fig.*): (in *pl.*) popular works of classical music. — Also **loll'y** — as *slang,* money. — **lollipop man, woman, lady** one appointed to conduct children across a busy street, distinguished by carrying a pole with a disc on the end. [Perh. Northern dial. *lolly,* tongue.]

lollop. See **loll.**

loll-shraub, loll-shrob *lol'-shrōb', -shrob', (India) n.* claret. [Hind. *lāl sharāb* — Pers. *lāl,* red, Ar. *sharāb,* wine.]

lolly. See **lollipop.**

lollygag. See **lallygag.**

lolog. Same as **loglog.**

loma¹ *lō'mə (zool.) n.* a membranous fringe or flap. [Gr. *lōma, -atos.*]

loma² *lō'mə, (U.S.) n.* in south-western states, a hill with

a broad, flat top. [Sp., back, ridge.]

Lombard *lom'bərd, (rare) lum'bərd, n.* an inhabitant of *Lombardy* in N. Italy: (also **Langobard** *lang'gō-bärd,* **Longobard** *long'*) one of the Langobardi, or Longobardi, a Germanic tribe, which founded a kingdom in Lombardy (568), overthrown by Charlemagne (774): a banker or money-lender, so called from the number of Lombard bankers in London (*obs.*). — *adjs.* **Lom'-bard, Lombardic** (*-bärd'ik*). — **Lombard architecture** the Romanesque style of Northern Italy, superseded by the Gothic in the 13th century; **Lombardic script** a mediaeval Italian style of handwriting; **Lombard Street** the chief centre of the banking interest in London; **Lombardy poplar** a variety of black poplar with erect branches. [O.Fr. — L. *Langobardus, Longobardus.*]

lome. Spens. for **loam.**

lomentum *lō-ment'əm, n.* a pod that breaks in pieces at constrictions between the seeds: — *pl.* **loment'a.** — Also **lō'ment** (*-mənt*). — *adj.* **lomentā'ceous.** [L. *lōmentum,* bean-meal (used as a cosmetic) — *lavare, lōtum,* to wash.]

lompish. Spens. for **lumpish.**

Londoner *lun'dən-ər, n.* a native or citizen of *London.* — *adjs.* **Londonese', Londonian** (*-dō'ni-ən*), **Lon'donish, Lon'dony.** — *n.* **Londonese'** cockney speech. — *v.t.* and *v.i.* **Lon'donise, -ize.** — *n.* **Lon'donism** a mode of speech, etc., peculiar to London. — **London Clay** a Lower Eocene formation in south-eastern England; **London ivy** smoke; **London Pride** a hardy perennial saxifrage (*Saxifraga ambrosa*) — also **none-so-pretty** and *St Patrick's cabbage:* formerly applied to other plants.

lone *lōn, adj.* isolated: solitary: unfrequented, uninhabited: unmarried, or widowed. — *ns.* **lone'ness; lon'er** a lone wolf. — *adj.* **lone'some** solitary: feeling lonely. — Also *n.* — *adv.* **lone'somely.** — *n.* **lone'someness.** — **lone wolf** (*fig.*) one who prefers to act on his own and not to have close friends or confidential relationships. [alone.]

lonely *lōn'li, adj.* unaccompanied: isolated: uninhabited: unfrequented: uncomfortably conscious of being alone. — *n.* **lone'liness.** — **lonely heart** a usu. unmarried person without close friends and consequently lonely and unhappy. — *adj.* **lone'ly-heart.** [alone.]

long¹ *long, (Shak. and dial.) adj.* and *adv.* on account. [along².]

long² *long, (arch.) v.i.* to belong, pertain, be fitting. [Not found as a vb. in O.E.; perh. — *gelang,* along, beside (as if to go along with).]

long³ *long, adj.* not short: of a specified (or to be specified) length: extended in space in the direction of greatest extension: far-extending: extended in time: of extended continuance: distant in time (*rare*): of distant date: requiring much time in utterance or performance: *loosely,* accented: *loosely,* in a long syllable: numerically extensive: of more than average number (as a suit of cards): exceeding the standard value (see **dozen, hundred**): having a large holding in a commodity, etc. (*finance*): tedious: — *compar.* **longer** (*long'gər*), *obs.* **leng'er;** *superl.* **longest** (*long'gist*), *obs.* **leng'est.** — *n.* a long time: a long syllable (*pros.*): the long summer university vacation (*coll.*): an obsolete note equal to two (in 'perfect' time three) breves (*mus.*; L. *longa*): (in *pl.*) long trousers: (in *pl.*) long-dated securities. — *adv.* for, during, or by, a great extent of time: throughout the whole time: far in space (*rare*): — *compar.* and *superl.* as for *adj.* — *v.i.* to yearn. — **-long** in composition, of a specified length (as *year-long, mile-long*). — *ns.* **long'a** (*mus.*) a long; **long'ing** an eager desire, craving. — *adj.* yearning. — *adv.* **long'ingly.** — *adj.* **longish** (*long'ish, -gish*). — *adv.* **long'ly** (*Shak.*) long. — *n.* **long'ness** (*rare*). — *adj.* **long'some** long and tedious. — *advs.* **long'ways, -wise** lengthwise. — *adj.* **long'-ago'** of the far past. — *n.* the far past. — **long arm** far-reaching power; **long'boat** the largest and strongest boat of a ship: a longship; **long'bow** a bow drawn by hand — opp. to **crossbow.** — *adj.* **long'-breathed** (*bretht'*) able to continue violent exercise of the lungs for a long time. — **longcase clock** grandfather clock. — *adj.* **long'-chain** (*chem.*) having a long chain of atoms in the molecule. — **long'cloth** a cotton made in long pieces. — *ns.pl.* **long'-clothes,** (*obs.*) **-coats** long garments for a baby. — *adjs.* **long'-da'ted** of securities, due for redemption in more than fifteen years; **long'= descend'ed** of ancient lineage; **long'-dist'ance** going or extending to or over a long distance or time. — **long'-divi'sion** division in which the working is shown in full; **long dozen** thirteen. — *adj.* **long'-drawn (-out')** prolonged: unduly protracted. — **long drink** a large thirst-quenching drink (sometimes alcoholic) in a tall glass. — *adjs.* **long'-eared** with long ears or earlike feather-tufts; **long'-faced** dismal-looking. — **long face** a dismal expression; **long'-field** (*cricket*) a fielder or station near the boundary on the bowler's side; **long'= firm** a company of swindlers who get goods on pretence of being established in business, and then decamp without payment; **long'-hair** a highbrow. — Also *adj.* — *adj.* **long'-haired** highbrow: unconventional, hippy. — **long'hand** ordinary writing — opp. to *shorthand,* **long haul** a journey over a great distance: any activity requiring lengthy effort (*fig.*). — *adj.* **long'-haul.** — **long'-head** a dolichocephal. — *adj.* **long'-headed** dolichocephalous: shrewd: sagacious. — **long'-head'- edness; long home** the grave; **long hop** (*cricket*) a short-pitched, and so long-bounding, ball, easy to hit; **long'horn** an animal with long horns or antennae, as a longicorn beetle (**house longhorn beetle** a beetle whose larvae are very destructive to house timbers): a long-eared owl; **long'-house** a long communal house, esp. of American Indians; **long hundred(weight)** see **hundred; long johns** long underpants; **long jump** a jump for distance along the ground; **long'-leg** (*cricket*) a fields-man, or his station, far out behind the batsman and a little to his left. — *adj.* **long'-legged** having long legs. — **long'-legs** a crane-fly. — *adjs.* **long'-life** of food-stuffs, treated so as to prolong freshness; **long'-lived** (-livd'; also -līvd') having a long life. — **long mark** a macron; **long'-meas'ure** lineal measure: (also **long metre**) quatrains of eight-syllable lines; **long moss** a tropical American rootless epiphyte (*Tillandsia us-neoides*) of the pineapple family, resembling bunches of hair; **long'-nine'** (*obs. U.S.*) a cheap cigar; **long odds** in betting, a remote chance, unfavourable odds in terms of risk, favourable in terms of potential gain; **long'-off, long'-on** (*cricket*) the fielders in the long-field to the off and on of the batsman respectively: their position. — *adj.* **long-oil** see **oil length** under **oil.** — **long'-pig'** (from cannibal term) human flesh as food. — *adj.* **long'-playing** of a gramophone record, giving length in reproduction because of the extremely fine groove. — **long'prim'er** a size of type (about 10-point) intermediate between small pica and bourgeois; **long'= pur'ples** the early purple orchis: purple loosestrife. — *adj.* **long'-range** long in range: covering a long future time or long distance. — **long robe** see **robe.** — *n.pl.* **longs'-and-shorts'** Greek or Latin verses: masonry of alternate vertical and horizontal blocks, as in quoins and jambs. — **long sheep** a long-woolled sheep; **long'-ship** (*hist.*) a long vessel of the old Norsemen; **long shot** (a bet, entry, venture, etc., with) a remote chance of success: a shot taken at a distance from the object filmed. — *adj.* **long'-sight'ed** able to see far but not close at hand: hypermetropic: presbyopic: having fore-sight: sagacious. — **long'-sight'edness.** — *n.pl.* **long'= six'es** candles weighing six to a pound. — **long'-slip** (*cricket*) a fielder some distance behind the batsman on the off side. — *adjs.* **long'-spun** long-drawn, tedious; **long'-stand'ing** of long existence or continuance; **long'= sta'ple** having a long fibre; **long'-stay** staying perma-nently or semi-permanently, as patients in a hospital. — **long'-stop** one who stands behind the wicket-keeper to stop balls missed by him (*cricket*): a person or thing that acts as a final safeguard or check (*fig.*). — *v.i.* to field as long-stop. — *adj.* **long'-suff'ering** enduring long and patiently. — *n.* long endurance or patience. —

long suit the suit with most cards in a hand: an advantageous quality or talent (*fig.*); **long'-tail** an animal, esp. a dog, with uncut tail: a greyhound. — Also *adj.* — *adjs.* **long'-term** extending over a long time: of a policy, concerned with time ahead as distinct from the immediate present; **long'-time** enduring for a long time. — **long-togs, long Tom, long ton** see **tog, Tom, ton**[1]. — *adj.* **long'-tongued** having a long tongue: talkative, babbling. — **long vacation** a long holiday during the summer, when schools, etc., are closed; **long view** the taking into consideration of events, etc., in the distant future. — *adjs.* **long'-vis'aged** long-faced: of rueful countenance; **long'-waist'ed** having a long waist: long from the armpits to the hips. — **long'wall** a long working face in a coal-mine (**longwall system, working** a mining technique in which a seam is exposed along its length and then removed, layer by layer). — *adj.* **long'-wave** (*radio*) of, or using, wavelengths over 1000 metres. — **long whist** see **whist**[2]. — *adj.* **long'= wind'ed** long-breathed: tediously wordy and lengthy. — **long'-wind'edness.** — **a long figure** (*slang*) a high price or rate; **a long purse** abundance of money; **as long as** provided only that; **before long, ere long** soon; **draw the long bow** see **bow**[2]; **in the long run** see **run; long on** well supplied with; **make a long arm** (*coll.*) to help oneself freely at table; **make a long nose** to cock a snook or put a thumb to the nose; **no longer** not now as formerly; **not long for this world** near death; **so long!** (*coll.*) good-bye; **so long as** provided only that; **the long and the short (of it)** or (*Shak.*) **the short and the long (of it)** the sum of the matter in a few words. [O.E. *lang, long* (adj.), *lange, longe* (adv.); Ger. *lang,* O.N. *langr;* L. *longus.*]

longa *long'ga, n.* See **long**[3].

longaeval, -aevous. See **longevity.**

longan *long'gan, n.* a tree (*Nephelium longana*) akin to the lychee: its fruit. [Chin. *lung-yen,* dragon's eye.]

longanimity *long-g∂-nim'i-ti, n.* forbearance. — *adj.* **lon-ganimous** (-gan'). [L. *longanimitās, -ātis* — *longus,* long, *animus,* spirit.]

longe. Same as **lunge**[2].

longeron *lon'j∂-, lon'zh∂-ron, lõ-zh∂-rõ, n.* a longitudinal member of an aeroplane. [Fr.]

longevity *long-jev'i-ti, n.* great length of life. — *adjs.* **longaeval, -geval, longaevous, -gevous** (-jēv'). [L. *longaevitās, -ātis* — *longus,* long, *aevum,* age.]

longicaudate *lon-ji-kö'dāt,* (*zool.*) *adj.* long-tailed. [L. *longus,* long, *cauda,* tail.]

longicorn *lon'ji-körn, n.* any beetle of the family *Ceram-bycidae,* with very long antennae (the larvae feed on wood). — Also *adj.* [L. *longus,* long, *cornū,* horn.]

longinquity *lon-jingk'wi-ti, n.* remoteness. [L. *longin-quitās, -ātis* — *longus,* long.]

longipennate *lon-ji-pen'āt,* (*zool.*) *adj.* having elongate wings or feathers. [L. *longus,* long, *penna,* feather, wing.]

longitude *lon'ji-tūd, long'gi-, n.* length: arc of the equator between the meridian of a place and a standard meridian (usually that of Greenwich) expressed in degrees E. or W.: the arc of the ecliptic between a star's circle of latitude and the first point of Aries or vernal equinox, measured eastwards (*astron.*). — *adj.* **longi-tūd'inal** of or in length or longitude: lengthwise. — *adv.* **longitūd'inally.** — **longitudinal wave** (*acoustics*) a wave in which the particles are displaced in the direction of advance of the wave. [L. *longitūdō, -inis,* length — *longus,* long.]

Longobard. See **Lombard** (second meaning).

longshore *long'shōr, -shör, adj.* existing or employed along the shore. — **long'shoreman** a stevedore: one who makes a living along the shore. [**alongshore.**]

longueur *lõ-gær,* (Fr.) *n.* a tedious passage, e.g. in a book: prolixity: — often in *pl.*

Lonicera *lon-is'∂r-∂, n.* the honeysuckle genus: (without *cap.*) a honeysuckle. [A. *Lonicerus* (d.1586), Ger. botanist.]

Lonsdale belt *lonz'dāl belt,* award (see **belt**) for gaining the same boxing title three times in succession. [Lord *Lonsdale*.]

loo[1] *lōō*, (*coll.*) *n.* a lavatory. [Ety. dub.]

loo[2] *lōō*, *n.* a card game. — *v.t.* to subject to a forfeit at loo. — **loo'-table** a form of round table, orig. one for playing loo. [See **lanterloo**.]

loo[3] *lōō*, Scots form of **love** (verb).

looby *lōōb'i*, *n.* a clumsy, clownish fellow. — *adj.* clumsy, stupid. — *adv.* **loob'ily** (*obs.*). [Cf. **lob**.]

loof[1] *lōōf*. Same as **luff**.

loof[2] *lōōf*, *Scot. lüf*, *n.* the palm of the hand: — *pl.* **loofs, looves.** — *n.* **loof'ful** (*Scot. lüf'fə*) an open handful. [O.N. *lófi*.]

loofah *lōō'fə*, *n.* a tropical genus (*Luffa*) of the gourd family: the fibrous network of its fruit, used as a flesh-brush. — Also **loofa, luffa** (*luf'*). [Ar. *lūfah*.]

look *lŏŏk*, *v.i.* to direct the sight with attention: to give attention: to face: to seem: to seem to be: to have an appearance: to tend. — *v.t.* to make sure: to see to it: to ascertain by a look: to look at: to expect: to seem likely: to render by a look: to express by a look: to refer to, turn (up): to give (a look, as cognate object). — *n.* the act of looking: view: air: appearance: (in *pl.*) beauty, comeliness (also *good looks*). — *imper.* or *interj.* see: behold. — *ns.* **look'er** one who looks: an observer: one who has good looks (*coll.*); **look'ing.** — *adj.* (in composition) having the appearance of. — **look'-alike** a person who closely resembles another in personal appearance, a double; **look'er-in'** a television viewer; **look'er-on'** an onlooker: a mere spectator: — *pl.* **look'ers-on'**; **look'-in'** a chance of doing anything effectively or of sharing: a short casual call; **look'ing=for** (*B.*) expectation; **look'ing-glass** a mirror. — *adj.* topsy-turvy (alluding to *Through the Looking-Glass* (1872) by Lewis Carroll). — **look'out'** a careful watch: a place to observe from: one set to watch: prospect: concern; **look'-round** inspection; **look'-see** (*slang*) a look around. — **look after** to take care of: to seek: to expect (*B.*); **look alive** (*coll.*) to bestir oneself; **look down on** to despise; **look down one's nose** to regard with contempt; **look for** to search for: to expect; **look forward to** to anticipate with pleasure; **look here!** I say! attend to this!; **look in** to make a short call: to watch television; **look into** to inspect closely: to investigate; **look on** to regard, view, think: to be a spectator; **look out** to be watchful: to be on one's guard: to look for and select: to show, appear (*Shak.*); **look over** to examine cursorily: to overlook or pass over; **look sharp** (*coll.*) be quick about it; **look small** to appear or feel foolish and ashamed; **look to** to look at, towards: to watch: to take care of: to depend on (for): to expect (to do); **look up** to search for, refer to: to take courage: to improve, to have taken a turn for the better: to seek out and call upon, visit (*coll.*); **look up to** to feel respect or veneration for; **look you** (*arch.* and *Welsh*) observe, take notice of this; **not much to look at** (*coll.*) plain, unattractive. [O.E. *lōcian*, to look.]

loom[1] *lōōm*, *n.* a tool, implement (*obs.*): a receptacle (*Scot.*): a machine for weaving: the shaft of an oar: a flexible, non-metallic, insulating covering for electric wires. [O.E. *gelōma*, a tool.]

loom[2] *lōōm*, *v.i.* to appear indistinctly or as in a mirage, esp. in an exaggerated or magnified form: to take shape, as an impending event. — *n.* an indistinct or mirage-like appearance. [Origin obscure.]

loom[3]. Same as **loon**[2].

loon[1] *lōōn*, also (*Shak.*) **lown(e)** *lown*, *ns.* a low-born fellow (*arch.*): a rascal: a harlot: in north-east of Scotland, a boy (also **loon'ie**): a simple-minded or eccentric person (*coll.*): (in *pl.*) casual trousers that flare widely from the knees (also **loon'-pants**). [Origin unknown.]

loon[2] *lōōn*, **loom** *lōōm*, *ns.* any of an order of northern diving birds. — *n.* **loon'ing** their cry. [O.N. *lōmr*.]

loony *lōōn'i*, *n.* and *adj.* for **lunatic**. — **loon'y-bin** (*slang*) a lunatic asylum.

loop[1] *lōōp*, *n.* a doubling of a cord, chain, etc., leaving a space: an ornamental doubling in fringes: anything of like form, as an element in fingerprints: a branch of anything that returns to the main part: a set of instructions used more than once in a program (*comput.*): an aerobatic manoeuvre in which an aircraft climbs, from level flight, to describe a circle in the sky: any loop-shaped movement or manoeuvre: an intra-uterine contraceptive device shaped like a loop (also **Lippes loop**). — *v.t.* to fasten in or with a loop: to ornament with loops: to make a loop of. — *v.i.* to travel in loops. — *adj.* **looped**. — *n.* **loop'er** a geometrid caterpillar, from its mode of walking by forming the body in a loop and planting its hinder legs close behind the six 'true' legs: one who loops the loop in an aeroplane. — *n.* and *adj.* **loop'ing.** — *adj.* **loop'y** having loops: crafty (*Scot.*): slightly crazed (*slang*). — **loop'=line** a branch railway that returns to the main line. — **loop the loop** to move in a complete vertical loop or circle, head downwards at the top of the curve. [Ety. dub.]

loop[2] *lōōp*, **loophole** *lōōp'hōl*, *ns.* a slit in a wall: a means of escape or evasion. — *adj.* **looped** (*Shak.*) full of small openings. — *v.t.* **loop'hole** to make loopholes in. — **loop'-light** a small narrow window. [Perh. M.Du. *lūpen*, to peer.]

loor. See **lief**.

loord *lōōrd*, (*Spens.*) *n.* a lout. [Fr. *lourd*, heavy.]

loos (*Spens.*). See **los**.

loose *lōōs*, *adj.* slack: free: unbound: not confined: not compact: unattached: untied: not close-fitting: not tight: relaxed: inexact: indefinite: vague: not strict: unrestrained: lax: licentious: inattentive: dispersedly or openly disposed: not serried: in Rugby football, referring to all play except for the set scrums and line-outs. — *adv.* loosely. — *n.* an act or mode of loosing, esp. an arrow: the loose state: unrestraint: freedom: abandonment: an outbreak of self-indul-gence: a course or rush (*obs.*): event, upshot, end (as in *at the very loose*) (*Shak.*): loose play (*Rugby foot-ball*). — *v.t.* to make loose: to set free: to unfasten: to untie: to disconnect: to relax: to slacken: to discharge: to solve (*Spens.*). — *v.i.* to shoot: to weigh anchor (*arch.*). — *adv.* **loose'ly.** — *v.t.* **loos'en** to make loose: to relax: to make less dense: to open, as the bowels. — *v.i.* to become loose: to become less tight. — *ns.* **loos'ener** a laxative; **loose'ness** the state of being loose: diarrhoea. — *adj.* **loose'-bod'ied** flowing, loose-fitting: loose in behaviour. — **loose'-box** a part of a stable where horses are kept untied; **loose change** coins kept about one's person for small expenditures; **loose'-cover** a detachable cover, as for a chair; **loose'-cut** a disease of cereal crops caused by a parasitic fungus, *Ustilago nuda*, that reduces the grains to powder; **loose fish** one of irregular, esp. lax habits: a prostitute; **loose forward** in Rugby union football, either of the two wing forwards or the no. 8, at the back of the scrum: in Rugby league, the player at the back of the scrum; **loosehead prop** the prop forward on the left of his front row in the scrum; **loose housing** a means of housing cattle whereby the animals have access to shelter but are free to move about in straw covered yards. — *adjs.* **loose'-leaf** having a cover such that leaves may be inserted or removed; **loose'-limbed'** having supple limbs. — **at a loose end** see **end; break loose** to escape from confinement; **give a loose to** to give rein or free vent to; **let loose** to set at liberty; **loosen up** to become less shy or taciturn; **on the loose** indulging in a bout of unrestraint: freed from confinement. [O.N. *lauss*; O.E. *lēas*; see **less**.]

loosestrife *lōōs'strīf*, *n.* a plant (*Lysimachia vulgaris*) of the primrose family, or other member of the genus (as yellow pimpernel, creeping Jenny): a tall waterside plant (*Lythrum salicaria*, purple loosestrife). [In-tended as a translation of Gr. *lysimacheion*, common loosestrife (as if from *lyein*, to loose, *machē*, strife), which may be from the personal name *Lysimachos*.]

loot[1] *lōōt*, *n.* plunder: money (*slang*). — *v.t.* or *v.i.* to plunder. — *n.* **loot'er.** [Hindi *lūt*.]

loot² *lüt, lōōt,* Scots *pa.t.* of **let¹:** — *pa.p.* **loot′en, litt′en, lutt′en.**

loot³ *lōōt,* (*coll.*) *n.* abbrev. for **lieutenant.**

looves. See **loof².**

lop¹ *lop, v.i.* to hang down loosely. — *adj.* **lop′-eared** having drooping ears. — **lop′grass** (or **lop**) soft brome-grass. — *adj.* **lop′-sid′ed** ill-balanced: heavier, bigger, on one side than the other. [Perh. conn. with **lob.**]

lop² *lop, v.t.* to cut off the top or ends of, esp. of a tree: to cut away, as superfluous parts: — *pr.p.* **lopp′ing;** *pa.t.* and *pa.p.* **lopped.** — *n.* twigs of trees cut off: an act of lopping. — *ns.* **lopp′er; lopp′ing** a cutting off: that which is cut off. [O.E. *loppian.*]

lope¹ *lōp, v.i.* to leap: to run with a long stride. [O.N. *hlaupa;* cf. **leap¹, loup¹.**]

lope² *lōp,* (*Spens.*) *pa.t.* of **leap¹.**

loper *lō′pər, n.* one of usu. a pair of sliding or hinged pieces of wood, metal, etc., which act as supports for a desk top or the extended flap of a table. [Ety. unknown.]

lopho- *lŏf-ō-, lof-ō-,* in composition, crested, tufted. — *n.* **loph′obranch** (*-brangk;* Gr. *branchia,* gills) any fish of the seahorse and pipefish group, characterised by tufted gills. — Also *adj.* — *adjs.* **lophobranch′iate; loph′odont** (*-dont;* Gr. *odous, odontos,* a tooth) having transversely ridged molar teeth. — *n.* **loph′ophore** (*-fōr;* Gr. *phoros,* bearing) a ring of ciliated tentacles round the mouth of some sedentary marine animals. [Gr. *lophos,* a crest.]

lopper¹ *lop′ər* (*dial.;* Scot. **lapper** *läp′ər*), *v.i.* to curdle. — *v.t.* to curdle: to clot. — *n.* a clot: slush. — *n.* (*Scot.*) **lapp′er(ed)-milk′.** [O.N. *hlöypa,* to curdle.]

lopper², lopping. See **lop².**

loq. See **loquitur.**

loquacious *lō-kwā′shəs, adj.* talkative. — *adv.* **loquā′-ciously.** — *ns.* **loquā′ciousness, loquacity** (*-kwas′*). [L. *loquāx, -ācis* — *loquī,* to speak.]

loquat *lō′kwot, -kwat, n.* a Chinese and Japanese tree (*Eriobotrya japonica*) of the rose family: its small, yellow fruit. [Chinese *luh kwat.*]

loquitur *lok′wi-tər, -tōōr,* (L.) speaks (3rd pers. pres. indic.), used with a person's name as stage direction, etc. — Abbrev. **loq.**

lor, lor′. See **lord.**

loral, lorate. See **lore².**

loran *lō′, lö′rän, n.* a long-range radio-navigation system. [*Lo*ng-*ra*nge *n*avigation.]

lorcha *lör′chə, n.* a light vessel of European build, but rigged like a Chinese junk. [Port.]

lord (**Lord,** when prefixed), *lörd, n.* a master: a feudal superior (also **lord′-supe′rior;** *hist.*): a ruler: the proprietor of a manor (*hist.*): an owner (*arch.*): a dominant person: a husband (*arch.,* or *facet.*): a titled nobleman — duke (not prefixed), marquess, earl, viscount or (esp.) baron: a peer: by courtesy the son of a duke or marquis, or the eldest son of an earl: a bishop, esp. if a member of the House of Lords: a judge of the Court of Session: used as part of various official titles: (with *cap.*) God: (with *cap.*) Christ. — *v.t.* to make a lord (*arch.*): to address as lord: (with *it*) to play the lord, tyrannise. — *interj.* expressing surprise (*coll.* **lor, lor′, law, lordy**). — *n.* **lord′ing** (*arch.*) sir (usu. in *pl.,* gentlemen): a petty lord. — *adj.* **lord′less.** — *ns.* **lord′liness; lord′ling** a little lord: a would-be lord — also **lord′kin.** — *adj.* **lord′ly** like, becoming, or of a lord: magnificent: lavish: lofty: haughty: tyrannical. — Also *adv.* — *ns.* **lordol′atry** (*jocular*) worship of nobility; **lord′ship** state or condition of being a lord: the territory of a lord (*hist.*): dominion: authority: used in referring to, addressing, a lord (with *his, your*), or a woman sheriff or judge (with *her, your*). — **Lord Lieutenant** see **lieutenant; Lord Mayor** see **mayor; Lord Provost** see **provost; Lord's Day** Sunday; **lords ordinary** the judges forming the Outer House of the Court of Session; **Lord's Prayer** prayer Christ taught his disciples (Matt. vi. 9–13); **lords spiritual** the archbishops and bishops (and formerly mitred abbots) in the House of Lords; **Lord's Supper** holy communion; **Lord's table** the communion table; **lords temporal** the lay peers. — **drunk as a lord** extremely drunk; **House of Lords** upper house of British parliament; **live like a lord** to live in luxury; **Lord knows (who, what,** etc.) I don't know, and I question if anybody does; **Lord of Misrule** see **misrule; Lord of Session** a judge of the Court of Session; **lords and ladies** common arum; **My Lord** (*mi-lörd′, mi-lud′*) used in addressing a judge or other lord: formerly also prefixed. [M.E. *lovered, laverd* — O.E. *hlāford* — *hlāf,* bread, *ward* (W.S. *weard*), keeper, guardian.]

lordosis *lör-dō′sis, n.* abnormal curvature of the spinal column, the convexity towards the front. — *adj.* **lordot′ic** affected with, relating to lordosis. [Gr. *lordōsis* — *lordos,* bent back.]

lore¹ *lör, lör, n.* that which is learned: teaching (*arch.*): doctrine (*arch.*): learning: now esp. learning of a special, traditional, or out-of-the-way miscellaneous kind. — *n.* **lor′ing** (*Spens.*) teaching. [O.E. *lār.*]

lore² *lör, lör, n.* a thong (*obs.*): the side of the head between eye and bill (*ornithology*). — *adjs.* **lor′al; lor′ate** strap-like. [L. *lōrum,* thong.]

lore³. See **leese.**

lorel. See **losel.**

Lorelei *lör′ə-lī, n.* in Germanic legend, a siren of the Rhine who lured sailors to their death. [Ger. *Lurlei,* the name of the rock she was believed to inhabit.]

lorette *lör-et′, n.* a courtesan. [Fr., from the church of their district in Paris, Notre Dame de *Lorette.*]

lorgnette *lörn-yet′, n.* eyeglasses with a handle: an opera-glass. — *n.* **lorgnon** (*lörn′yō*) an eyeglass: eyeglasses. [Fr. *lorgner,* to look sidelong at, to ogle.]

lorica *lō-, lö-, lə-rī′kə, n.* leather corslet: the case of a protozoan, rotifer, etc.: — *pl.* **lori′cae** (*-sē*). — Also **loric** (*lō′, lö′rik*). — *v.t.* **loricate** (*lor′i-kāt*) to coat or armour protectively. — *adj.* armoured with plates or scales. — *n.* **loricā′tion.** [L. *lōrīca,* a leather corslet — *lōrum,* a thong.]

lorikeet *lor-i-kēt′, n.* a small lory. [From **lory,** on analogy of para**keet.**]

lorimer *lor′i-mər,* **loriner** *-nər, ns.* a maker of the metal parts of horse-harness. [O.Fr. *loremier, lorenier* — L. *lōrum,* a thong.]

loring. See **lore¹.**

loriot *lō′ri-ət, lö′, n.* the golden oriole. [Fr. *loriot* — *l′,* the, O.Fr. *oriol* — L. *aureolus,* dim. of *aureus,* golden — *aurum,* gold.]

loris *lō′, lö′ris, n.* the slender lemur of Sri Lanka: an East Indian lemur (*Nycticebus* or *Bradycebus tardigradus,* the *slow loris*). [Fr. *loris;* said to be from Du.]

lorn *lörn,* (*arch.*) *adj.* lost: forsaken: left (*Spens.*). [O.E. *loren,* pa.p. of *lēosan* (found in compounds), to lose; see **leese.**]

lorrell. See **losel.**

lorry *lor′i, n.* a heavily-built motor vehicle for transporting loads by road: a long wagon without sides, or with low sides. — *v.i.* (or *v.t.* with *it*) **lorr′y-hop** to proceed by help of lifts on lorries. — **lorr′y-hopping.** [Origin uncertain.]

lory *lō′, lö′ri, n.* any parrot of a family with brushlike tongues, natives of New Guinea, Australia, etc.: in South Africa a touraco. [Malay *lūrī.*]

los, loos *lōs,* (*obs.*) *n.* praise, reputation. [O.Fr., — L. *laudēs,* pl. of *laus,* praise.]

lose¹ *lōōz, v.t.* to fail to keep or get possession of: to be deprived or bereaved of: to cease to have: to cease to hear, see or understand: to mislay: to waste, as time: to miss: to be defeated in: to cause the loss of: to cause to perish: to bring to ruin. — *v.i.* to fail, to be unsuccessful: to suffer waste or loss: of a clock or watch, to go too slowly: — *pr.p.* **los′ing;** *pa.t.* and *pa.p* **lost** (*lost*). — *adj.* **los′able.** — *n.* **los′er.** — *n.* and *adj.* **los′ing.** — *adv.* **los′ingly.** — *adj.* **lost** (*lost*) parted with: no longer possessed: missing: thrown away: squandered: ruined: confused: unable to find the way (*lit.* and *fig.*). — **losing game** a game that is going against one: a game played with reversal of the usual aim; **lost**

cause a hopeless endeavour; **lost soul** a damned soul, an irredeemably evil person; **lost tribes** the tribes of Israel that never returned after deportation by Sargon of Assyria in 721 B.C. — **get lost!** (*slang*) go away and stay away!: stop annoying or interfering!; **lose face** see **face**; **lose oneself** to lose one's way: to become rapt or bewildered; **lose out** (*coll.*) to suffer loss or disadvantage: (also with *on*) to fail to acquire something desired; **lose way** of a boat, to lose speed; **lost** to insensible to. [O.E. *losian*, to be a loss; apparently influenced in sense by **leese** and in pronunciation by **loose**.]

lose[2] *lōz*, *v.t.* Spens. for **loose**. — Also **los'en**: — *pa.p.* **loast**, **los'te** (both *lōst*).

losel *lō'zl*, *lōō'zl*, **lorel** *lō'*, *lö'rəl* (*Spens.* **lozell**, **lorrell**), *ns.* a worthless fellow: a scamp. — *adj.* good-for-nothing. [Apparently from the past participle *losen*, *loren*, of **leese**.]

losh *losh*, (*Scot.*) *interj.* lord.

loss *los*, *n.* losing: diminution: default (*Shak.*): bereavement: destruction: defeat: deprivation: detriment: that which is lost. — *adj.* **loss'y** (*elect.*, *telecomm.*) dissipating energy, said of a dielectric material or of a transmission line with high attenuation. — **loss adjuster** an assessor employed by an insurance company, usu. in fire damage claims; **loss'-leader** a thing sold at a loss to attract other custom. — **at a loss** running in deficit: off the scent: at fault: nonplussed: perplexed. [O.E. *los*, influenced by **lost**.]

löss. See **loess**.

lost. See **lose**.

los'te *lōst*, a Spens. *pa.p.* of **loose**, **lose**[2].

lot *lot*, *n.* an object, as a slip of wood, a straw, drawn or thrown out from among a number in order to reach a decision by chance: decision by this method: sortilege: a prize so to be won: destiny: that which falls to any one as his fortune: a separate portion: a parcel of ground: a set: a set of things offered together for sale: the whole: a plot of ground allotted or assigned to any person or purpose, esp. for building: a turn (*obs.*): a tax or due (*hist.*; see **scot**): a large quantity or number. — *v.t.* to allot: to separate into lots: to cast lots for (*obs.*): — *pr.p.* **lott'ing**; *pa.t.* and *pa.p.* **lott'ed**. — **across lots** (*U.S.*) by short cuts; **bad lot** a person of bad moral character; **cast** or **throw in one's lot with** to share the fortunes of; **cast** or **draw lots** to draw from a set alike in appearance in order to reach a decision; **lots of** (*coll.*) many; **lots to blanks** (*Shak.*) any odds; **the lot** the entire number or amount. [O.E. *hlot*, lot — *hlēotan*, to cast lots.]

lota, lotah *lō'tä*, *n.* in India, a small brass or copper pot. [Hindi *lotā*.]

lote. See **lotus**.

loth, loath *lōth*, *adj.* hateful, repulsive, ugly (*obs.*): reluctant, unwilling. — **nothing loth** not at all unwilling. [O.E. *lāth*, hateful; cf. **loathe**.]

Lothario *lō-thä'ri-ō*, *-thā'*, *n.* a gay seducer: — *pl.* **Lothar'ios.** [From *Lothario*, in Rowe's play, *The Fair Penitent*.]

lothefull, lothfull (*Spens.*). See **loathe**.

lotic *lō'tik*, *adj.* associated with, or living in, running water. [L. *lavāre*, *lōtum*, to wash.]

lotion *lō'shən*, *n.* a washing (*obs.*): a liquid preparation for external application, medicinal or cosmetic. [L. *lōtiō*, *-ōnis*, a washing — *lavāre*, *lōtum*, to wash.]

Lotophagi. See under **lotus**.

loto. See **lottery**.

lotos. See **lotus**.

lottery *lot'ər-i*, *n.* an arrangement for distribution of prizes by lot: a matter of chance: a card game of chance. — *n.* **lott'o**, **lō'to** a game played by covering on a card each number drawn till a line of numbers is completed: — *pl.* **lott'os**, **lō'tos**. [It. *lotteria*, *lotto*, of Gmc. origin; cf. **lot**.]

lotus *lō'təs*, *n.* an Egyptian or Indian water-lily of various species of Nymphaea and Nelumbium: a tree (possibly the jujube) in North Africa, whose fruit induced in the eater a state of blissful indolence and forgetfulness: an

architectural ornament like a water-lily: (*cap.*) the bird's-foot trefoil genus. — Also **lote** (*lōt*), **lō'tos.** — **lot'us-eat'er** an eater of the lotus, one given up to indolence; **Lot'us-eat'ers, Lotophagi** (*lō-tof'ə-jī*; Gr. *phagein*, to eat) a people who ate the fruit of the lotus, among whom Ulysses lived for a time; **Lo'tus-land** the country of the Lotus-eaters; **lotus position** a seated position used in yoga, cross-legged, with each foot resting on the opposite thigh. [Latinised Gr. *lōtos*.]

louche *lōōsh*, *adj.* squinting: ambiguous: shady, sinister. — *adv.* **louche'ly.** [Fr.]

loud *lowd*, *adj.* making a great sound: noisy: obtrusive: vulgarly showy. — *advs.* **loud, loud'ly.** — *v.t.* and *v.i.* **loud'en** to make or grow louder. — *adj.* **loud'ish.** — *n.* **loud'ness.** — **loudhail'er** a portable megaphone with microphone and amplifier. — *adjs.* **loud'-lunged; loud'-mouthed.** — **loud'mouth** (*coll.*) one who talks too much or too offensively: a boaster; **loud'speak'er** an electroacoustic device which amplifies sound. — *adj.* **loud'-voiced.** [O.E. *hlūd*; Ger. *laut*; L. *inclytus*, *inclutus*, Gr. *klytos*, renowned.]

lough *lohh*, *n.* the Irish form of **loch**.

louis *lōō'i*, *n.* a French gold coin superseded in 1795 by the 20-franc piece: — *pl.* **lou'is** (*-iz*). — *n.* **lou'is-d'or'** a louis: a 20-franc piece: — *pl.* **louis-d'or** (*lōō'i-dör'*). — *adjs.* **Lou'is-Quatorze** (*-kä-törz'*) characteristic of the reign (1643–1715) of Louis XIV, as in architecture and decoration; **Lou'is-Quinze** (*-kẽz*) of that of Louis XV (1715–1774); **Lou'is-Seize** (*-sez*) of that of Louis XVI (1774–92); **Lou'is-Treize** (*-trez*) of that of Louis XIII (1610–43).

loun, lound. See **lown**[2].

lounder *lōōn'dər*, *lown'dər*, (*Scot.*) *v.t.* to beat, to bethump. — *n.* a heavy blow. — *n.* **loun'dering** a beating.

lounge *lownj*, *v.i.* to loll: to idle. — *v.t.* to idle (away). — *n.* an act, spell, or state of lounging: an idle stroll: a resort of loungers: a sitting-room in a private house: a room in a public building for sitting or waiting, often providing refreshment facilities: (also **lounge'-bar**) a more expensive and luxurious bar in a public house: a kind of sofa, esp. with back and one raised end: (also **lounge chair**) an easy chair suitable for lolling in. — *n.* **loung'er** one who lounges: a woman's long loose dress for wearing indoors: an extending chair or light bed for relaxing on — *n.* and *adj.* **loung'ing.** — *adv.* **loung'ingly.** — **lounge'-liz'ard** one who loafs with women in hotel lounges, etc.; **lounge'-suit** a man's matching jacket and trousers for (formal) everyday wear. [Origin doubtful.]

loup[1] *lowp*, (*Scot.*) *n.* a leap. — *v.i.* to leap: to dance: to flee: to burst. — *v.t.* to leap over. — *pa.t.* **loup'it**; *pa.p.* **loup'en, loup'it.** — **loup'ing-ill** a disease causing sheep to spring up in walking, due to a virus transmitted by ticks; **loup'ing-on'-stane'** a stone to mount a horse from. — *adj.* **loup'-the-dyke** runaway: flighty: wayward. [O.N. *hlaup*; cf. **lope**[1], **leap**[1].]

loup[2]. A variant (*Scott*) of **loop**[1] and (*Spens.*) of **loop**[2].

loupe *lōōp*, *n.* a small jeweller's and watchmaker's magnifying glass, worn in the eye-socket. [Fr.]

lour, lower *lowr*, *low'ər*, *v.i.* to look sullen or threatening: to scowl. — *n.* a scowl, glare: a gloomy threatening appearance. — *n.* and *adj.* **lour'ing, lower'ing.** — *adv.* **lour'ingly, lower'ingly.** — *adj.* **lour'y, lower'y.** [M.E. *louren*; cf. Du. *loeren*.]

loure *lōōr*, *n.* an old slow dance, or its tune, usu. in 6–4 time, sometimes included in suites. [Fr., bagpipe.]

louse *lows*, *n.* a wingless parasitic insect (Pediculus), with a flat body, and short legs: extended to similar animals related and unrelated (see **bird-louse, fish-louse**, etc.): a person worthy of contempt (*slang*; *pl.* **louses**): — *pl.* **lice** (*līs*). — *v.t.* (*lowz*) to remove lice from: to spoil, make a mess of (with *up*; *slang*). — *adj.* **lou'sily** (*-zi-*). — *n.* **lous'iness.** — *adj.* **lousy** (*low'zi*) infested with lice: swarming or full (with *with*; *slang*): inferior, bad, unsatisfactory (*slang*). — **louse'-wort** any plant of the genus Pedicularis, marsh-growing scrophulariaceous herbs popularly supposed to cause grazing animals to become lousy. [O.E. *lūs*, pl. *lȳs*; Ger. *Laus*.]

lout[1] (*obs*. **lowt**) *lowt, n.* a bumpkin: an awkward boor. — *v.t.* (*Shak.*) to treat with contempt, to flout. — *v.i.* to play the lout. — *adj.* **lout'ish** clownish: awkward and boorish. — *adv.* **lout'ishly.** — *n.* **lout'ishness.** [Perh. conn. with next word.]

lout[2] (*obs*. **lowt**) *lowt,* (*arch.*) *v.i.* to bow: to stoop. — *n.* a bow. [O.E. *lūtan*, to stoop.]

louvre, louver *lōō'vər, n.* a turret-like structure on a roof for escape of smoke or for ventilation: a dovecote (*obs.*): an opening or shutter with louvre-boards: a louvre-board. — *adj.* **lou'vred, lou'vered.** — **lou'vre-, lou'ver-board** a sloping slat placed across an opening; **lou'vre-, lou'ver-door, -win'dow** a door, open window crossed by a series of sloping boards. [O.Fr. *lover, lovier*; origin obscure.]

lovage *luv'ij, n.* an umbelliferous salad plant (*Levisticum officinale*) of Southern Europe akin to Angelica: a liquor made from its roots and seeds: any plant of the kindred genus *Ligusticum*, including *Scottish lovage*. [O.Fr. *luvesche* — L.L. *levisticum*, L. *ligusticum*, lit. Ligurian.]

lovat *luv'ət, n.* a greyish- or bluish-green colour, usu. in tweed or woollen cloth: cloth of this colour (also **lov'at-green'**). — Also *adj.* [From *Lovat*, in Inverness-shire.]

love *luv, n.* fondness: charity: an affection of the mind caused by that which delights: strong liking: devoted attachment to one of the opposite sex: sexual attachment: a love-affair: the object of affection: used as a term of endearment or affection: the god of love, Cupid, Eros: a kindness, a favour done (*Shak.*): the mere pleasure of playing, without stakes: in some games, no score. — *v.t.* to be fond of: to regard with affection: to delight in with exclusive affection: to regard with benevolence. — *v.i.* to have the feeling of love. — *adjs.* **lov'able, love'able** (*luv'ə-bl*) worthy of love: amiable; **love'less.** — *n.* **love'lihead** (*rare*) loveliness. — *adv.* **love'lily** (*rare*). — *n.* **love'liness.** — *adj.* **love'ly** loving, amorous (*Shak.*): exciting admiration: attractive: extremely beautiful: delightful (*coll.*). — *adv.* **lovingly** (*Spens.*): beautifully (*obs.*): delightfully, very well (*coll.*). — *n.* (*coll.*) a beautiful woman, esp. showgirl, model. — *n.* **lov'er** one who loves, esp. one in love with a person of the opposite sex (in the singular usually of the man): a paramour: one who is fond of anything: a friend (*Shak.*). — *adjs.* **lov'ered** (*Shak.*) having a lover; **lov'erless; lov'erly** (*arch.*) like a lover; **love'some** (*arch.*) lovely: loving; **love'worthy** worthy of being loved. — *n.* **lov'ey** (*coll.*) a term of endearment. — *n.* and *adj.* **lov'ing.** — *adv.* **lov'ingly.** — *n.* **lov'ingness.** — **love'-affair'** an amour honourable or dishonourable; **love'-apple** the tomato; **love'-arrow** a hair-like crystal of rutile enclosed in quartz: a calcareous dart protruded by a snail, supposed to have a sexual function; **love'bird** a small African parrot (*Agapornis*), strongly attached to its mate: extended to other kinds; **love'bite** a temporary red patch left on the skin after sucking and biting during love-making; **love'-bro'ker** (*Shak.*) a go-between in love-affairs; **love'-charm** a philtre; **love'-child** an illegitimate child; **love'-day** (*Shak.*) a day for settling disputes; **love'-drug** dagga; **love'-favour** something given to be worn in token of love; **love'-feast** the agape, or a religious feast in imitation of it; **love'-feat** an act of courtship; **love'-game** (*lawn-tennis*) a game in which the loser has not scored (poss. from Fr. *l'œuf*, egg — cf. **duck**[3] in cricket); **love'-in-a-mist'** a fennel-flower (*Nigella damascena*): a West Indian passion-flower; **love'-in-i'dleness** the pansy; **love'-juice** a concoction dropped in the eye to excite love; **love'-knot, lov'er's-knot** an intricate knot, used as a token of love; **love'-letter** a letter of courtship; **love'-lies-bleed'ing** a kind of amaranth with drooping red spike; **love'light** a lustre in the eye expressive of love; **love'lock** a long or prominent lock of hair, esp. one hanging at the ear, worn by men of fashion in the reigns of Elizabeth and James I. — *adj.* **love'lorn**

forsaken by one's love: pining for love. — **love'-lornness; love'-maker; love'-making** amorous courtship: sexual intercourse; **love'-match** a marriage for love, not money, status, etc.; **love'-monger** (*rare*) one who deals in affairs of love; **love'-nest** a place where lovers, often illicit, meet or live; **love'-potion** a philtre; **lovers' lane** a quiet path or road frequented by lovers; **love'-seat** an armchair for two; **love'-shaft** a dart of love from Cupid's bow. — *adj.* **love'sick** languishing with amorous desire. — **love'-song** a song expressive of or relating to love; **love'-story** a story whose subject-matter is romantic love; **love'-suit** (*Shak.*) courtship; **love'-token** a gift in evidence of love; **lov'ing-cup** a cup passed round at the end of a feast for all to drink from; **lov'ing-kind'ness** (*B.*) kindness full of love: tender regard: mercy. — *adj.* **lovey-dovey** (*luv'i-duv'i; coll.*) loving, sentimental. — **fall in love** to become in love (with); **for love or money** in any way whatever; **for the love of it** for the sake of it: for the pleasure of it; **for the love of Mike** (*slang*) for any sake; **in love (with)** romantically and sexually attracted, devoted (to); **make love to** to try to gain the affections of: to have sexual intercourse with; **of all loves** (*Shak.*) for any sake, by all means; **play for love** to play without stakes; **there's no love lost between them** they have no liking for each other. [O.E. *lufu*, love; Ger. *Liebe*; cf. L. *libet, lubet*, it pleases.]

Lovelace *luv'lās, n.* a well-mannered libertine. [From *Lovelace*, in Richardson's *Clarissa*.]

lover. An obsolete form of **louver** (louvre).

low[1] *lō, v.i.* to make the noise of oxen. — *n.* sound made by oxen. — *n.* **low'ing.** [O.E. *hlōwan*; Du. *loeien*.]

low[2] *lō, adj.* occupying a position far downward or not much elevated: of no great upward extension: not reaching a high level: depressed: not tall: of type or blocks, below the level of the forme surface: reaching far down: of clothes, cut so as to expose the neck (and bosom): quiet, soft, not loud: grave in pitch, as sounds produced by slow vibrations: produced with part of the tongue low in the mouth (*phon.*): in shallow relief: expressed in measurement by a small number: of numbers, small: of small value, intensity, quantity, or rank: weak in vitality or nutrition: scanty, deficient: attributing lowness: for stakes of no great value: dejected: debased: base: mean: vulgar: humble: socially depressed: little advanced in organisation or culture: of latitude, near the equator: of dates, comparatively recent (*arch.*): attaching little value to priesthood, sacraments, etc.: — *compar.* **lower** (*lō'ər*); *superl.* **lowest** (*lō'ist*), **low'ermost.** — *n.* that which is low or lowest: an area of low barometrical pressure: a low or minimum level: low gear. — *adv.* in or to a low position, state, or manner: humbly: with a low voice or sound: at low pitch: at a low price: late (*arch.*): in small quantity or to small degree. — *v.t.* **low'er** to make lower: to let down: to lessen: to dilute (*obs.*). — *v.i.* to become lower or less. — *n.* **low'ering** the act of bringing low or reducing. — *adj.* letting down: sinking: degrading. — *adj.* **low'ermost** lowest. — *n.* **low'lihead** (*arch.*) humility. — *adv.* **low'lily** (-*li-li*). — *n.* **low'liness.** — *adj.* **low'ly** humble: modest: low in stature or in organisation. — *n.* **low'ness.** — *adj.* **low'-born** of humble birth. — **low'boy** a Low-Churchman (*obs.*): a short-legged dressing-table with drawers (*U.S.*). — *adj.* **low'-bred** ill-bred: unmannerly. — **low'-brow** one who is not intellectual or makes no pretensions to intellect. — Also *adj.* — *adj.* **Low Church** of a party within the Church of England setting little value on sacerdotal claims, ecclesiastical constitutions, ordinances, and forms, holding evangelical views of theology — opp. to *High Church.* — **Low-Church'ism; Low-Church'man; low comedy** comedy of farcical situation, slapstick, low life. — *adjs.* **low'-cost'** cheap; **low'-country** lowland (**the Low Countries** Holland and Belgium); **low'-down** (*coll.*) base: dishonourable. — *n.* (*slang*) information, esp. of a confidential or damaging nature. — **low-down'er** (*obs. U.S.*) a poor white; **Low**

Dutch (*obs.*) Low German including Dutch. — *adjs.*
low'er-brack'et in a low grouping in a list; **low'er-case**
(*print.*) lit. kept in a lower case, small as distinguished
from capital; **low'er-class** pertaining to persons of the
humbler ranks. — **low'er-deck** deck immediately above
the hold: ship's crew (as opposed to officers). — Also
adj. — **lower house, chamber** the larger more representative of two legislative chambers; **lower regions** Hades,
hell. — *adjs.* **low frequency, low'-gear, Low German** see
frequency, gear, German; low'-key' in painting or
photography, in mostly dark tones or colours, with
few, if any, highlights: undramatic, understated, restrained: of a person, not easily excited, showing no
visible reaction. — **low'land** land low with respect to
higher land (also *adj.*); **low'lander** (also *cap.*) a native
of lowlands, esp. the **Lowlands** of Scotland; **Low Latin**
see **Latin; low life** sordid social circumstances: persons
of low social class. — *adjs.* **low'-life; low'-lived** (*-līvd*)
vulgar: shabby. — **low'-loader** a low sideless wagon
for very heavy loads; **low mass** mass without music
and incense. — *adjs.* **low'-mind'ed** moved by base or
gross motives: vulgar; **low'-necked** of a dress, cut low
in the neck and away from the shoulders, décolleté;
low'-paid' (of worker) receiving, (of job) rewarded by,
low wages; **low'-pitched** of sound, low in pitch: of a
roof, gentle in slope: having a low ceiling; **low'-
press'ure** employing or exerting a low degree of pressure (viz. less than 50 lb. to the sq. inch), said of steam
and steam-engines: having low barometric pressure.
— **low profile** a manner or attitude revealing very little
of one's feelings, intentions, activities, etc. — *adj.*
low-pro'file. — **low relief** same as **bas-relief.** — *adjs.*
low'-rise of buildings, having only a few storeys, in
contrast to *high-rise* (q.v.); **low'-slung'** (of vehicle, etc.)
with body close to the ground: (of building) not tall;
low'-spir'ited having the spirits low or cast down: not
lively: sad. — **low'-spir'itedness; Low Sunday** the first
Sunday after Easter, so called in contrast to the great
festival whose octave it ends. — *adj.* **low'-tar'** of
cigarettes, made of tobacco with a low tar content. —
low technology simple, unsophisticated technology
used in the production of basic commodities. — *adjs.*
low'-ten'sion using, generating or operating at a low
voltage; **low'-thought'ed** having the thoughts directed
to low pursuits. — **low tide, water** the lowest point of
the tide at ebb; **low toby** see **toby; Lowveld** (*lō'felt, -velt;*
also without *cap.*) the lower altitude areas of the
eastern Transvaal; **low'-wat'ermark** the lowest line
reached by the tide: anything marking the point of
greatest degradation, decline, etc. (*fig.*); **low wines** the
weak spirit produced from the first distillation of
substances containing alcohol. — **an all-time low** the
lowest recorded level; **in low water** short of money; **lay
low** to overthrow, fell, kill; **lie low** see **lie**[2]; **lowest, least,
common denominator** see **denominate; low-level
language** any computer-programming language that is
designed as a machine code rather than as a language
comprehensible to the user (opp. to *high-level language*); **low side window** a narrow window (or lower
part of a window) near the ground, sometimes found
in old churches, esp. in the chancel; **low-temperature
physics** study of physical phenomena at temperatures
near absolute zero. [O.N. *lāgr*, Du. *laag*, low; allied
to O.E. *licgan*, to lie.]
low[3] *lō*, (*arch.* except in place names) *n.* a hill: a tumulus.
[O.E. *hlāw*; cf. **law**[3].]
low[4], **lowe** *low*, (*Scot.*) *n.* a flame. — *v.i.* to blaze. —
low-bell (*low', lō', lōō'bel; dial.*) a small bell: a bell used
by night along with a light, to frighten birds into a
net. [O.N. *logi*; cf. Ger. *Lohe*.]
lowan *lō'ən.* Same as **mallee-bird.**
lower[1] *lowr*, **lowering, lowery.** See **lour.**
lower[2] *lō'ər.* See **low**[2].
lown[1], **lowne** *lown*, *n.* variants of **loon**[1].
lown[2], **lownd, loun, lound** *lown(d)*, (*Scot.*) *adj.* sheltered:
calm: quiet. — *adv.* quietly. — *n.* calm: quiet: shelter.
— *v.i.* to calm. [O.N. *logn* (noun).]

Lowrie *low'ri*, (*Scot.*) *n.* a nickname for the fox. — Also
Low'rie-tod, Tod-low'rie. [*Laurence.*]
lowse *lows*, (*Scot.*) *adj.* loose. — *v.t.* (*lows*, or *lowz*) to
loose: to unyoke: to redeem. — *v.i.* to unyoke the
horses: to knock off work: — *pa.t.* and *pa.p.* **lows'it.**
[See **loose.**]
lowt. See **lout**[1,2].
lox[1] *loks*, *n.* liquid oxygen, used as a rocket propellant.
— Also **lox'ygen.**
lox[2] *loks*, *n.* a kind of smoked salmon. [Yiddish *laks*,
from M.H.G. *lahs*, salmon.]
loxodrome *loks'ə-drōm*, *n.* a line on the surface of a sphere
which makes equal oblique angles with all meridians,
a rhumb-line — also **loxodromic curve, line** or **spiral.**
— *adjs.* **loxodromic** (*-drom'ik*), **-al.** — *n. sing.* **loxo-
drom'ics,** *n.* **loxod'romy** the art of sailing on rhumb-
lines. [Gr. *loxos*, oblique, *dromos*, a course.]
loxygen. See **lox**[1].
loy *loi*, *n.* a long, narrow spade with footrest on one side
of the handle.
loyal *loi'əl*, *adj.* faithful: true as a lover: firm in allegiance:
personally devoted to a sovereign or would-be
sovereign: legitimate (*Shak.*): manifesting loyalty. —
n. **loy'alist** a loyal adherent, esp. of a king or of an
established government: (also with *cap.*) in Northern
Ireland, a supporter of the British government: (also
with *cap.*) in English history, a partisan of the Stuarts:
(also with *cap.*) in the American war of Independence,
one that sided with the British. — *adv.* **loy'ally.** — *n.*
loy'alty. [Fr., — L. *lēgālis* — *lēx, lēgis*, law.]
lozell. See **losel.**
lozenge *loz'inj*, *n.* a diamond-shaped parallelogram or
rhombus: a small sweetmeat, medicated or not, originally diamond-shaped: a diamond-shaped shield for
the arms of a widow, spinster, or deceased person
(*her.*). — *n.* **loz'en** (*Scot.*) a window-pane. — *adjs.*
loz'enged divided into lozenges; **loz'engy** (*her.*) divided
into lozenge-shaped compartments. — *adj.* **loz'enge-
shaped.** [Fr. *losange* (of unknown origin).]
LP *el-pē'*, (*coll.*) *n.* a long-playing record.
LSD. See under **lysis.**
luau *lōō-ow'*, *n.* a Hawaiian dish made of coconut, taro,
octopus, etc.: a Hawaiian feast or party. [Hawaiian
lu'au.]
lubber *lub'ər*, **lubbard** *lub'ərd*, *ns.* an awkward, clumsy
fellow: a lazy, sturdy fellow. — *adj.* **lubberly.** — *adj.*
and adv. **lubb'erly.** **lubber fiend** a beneficent goblin
or drudging brownie, Lob-lie-by-the-fire; **lubber's hole**
a hole in a mast platform saving climbing round the
rim; **lubber('s) line** a line on the compass bowl marking
the position of the ship's head. [Origin doubtful.]
lubfish *lub'fish*, *n.* a kind of stockfish. [**lob.**]
lubra *lōō'brə*, (*Austr.*) *n.* an Aboriginal woman. [Abo-
riginal.]
lubricate *lōō', lū'bri-kāt*, *v.t.* to make smooth or slippery:
to supply with oil or other matter to overcome friction:
to supply with liquor: to bribe. — *adjs.* **lu'bric, -al,**
lubricious (*-brish'əs*), **lu'bricous** (*-kəs*) slippery: lewd. —
adj. **lu'bricant** lubricating. — *n.* a substance used to
reduce friction. — *n.* **lubrica'tion.** — *adj.* **lu'bricātive.**
— *ns.* **lu'bricātor; lubricity** (*-bris'i-ti*) slipperiness:
smoothness: instability: lewdness; **lubritō'rium** (chiefly
U.S.) a place in a garage or service station where motor
vehicles are lubricated. — **lubricated water** water with
certain additives which make it flow more smoothly.
[L. *lūbricus*, slippery.]
lucarne *lōō-, lū-kärn'*, *n.* a dormer-window, esp. in a
church spire. [Fr. (of unknown origin).]
luce *lōōs, lūs*, *n.* a freshwater fish, the pike. [O.Fr. *lus*
— L.L. *lūcius*.]
lucent *lōō', lū'sənt*, *adj.* shining: bright. — *n.* **lu'cency.**
[L. *lūcēns, -entis*, pr.p. of *lūcēre*, to shine — *lūx, lūcis*,
light.]
lucerne *lōō-, lū-sûrn'*, *n.* purple medick, a plant resembling
clover, also called alfalfa (esp. *U.S.*), valuable as
fodder for cattle, etc. — Also **lucern'** (*Browning*

lu'zern); formerly often **la lucerne**. [Fr. *luzerne*.]
luces. See lux.
lucid *lōō', lū'sid, adj.* shining: transparent: easily understood: intellectually bright: not darkened with madness. — *ns.* **lucid'ity, lu'cidness.** — *adv.* **lu'cidly.** — **lucid intervals** times of sanity in madness, of quietness in fever, turmoil, etc. [L. *lūcidus — lūx, lūcis,* light.]
Lucifer *lōō', lū'si-fər, n.* the planet Venus as morning-star: Satan: (without *cap.*) a match of wood tipped with a combustible substance to be ignited by friction — also **lu'cifer-match'.** — *adj.* **Lucifē'rian** pertaining to Lucifer. — *ns.* **lucif'erase** an oxidising enzyme in the luminous organs of certain animals that acts on luciferin to produce luminosity; **lucif'erin** a protein-like substance in the luminous organs of certain animals, esp. glow-worms, fire-flies. — *adj.* **lucif'erous** light-bringing: light-giving. [L. *lūcifer,* light-bringer — *lūx, lūcis,* light, *ferre,* to bring.]
lucifugous *lōō-, lū-sif'ū-gəs, adj.* shunning light. [L. *lūx, lūcis,* light, *fugĕre,* to flee.]
lucigen *lōō', lū'si-jən, n.* a lamp burning oil mixed with air in a spray. [L. *lūx, lūcis,* light, and root of L. *gignĕre, genitum,* to beget.]
Lucina *lōō-, lū-sī'nə, n.* the Roman goddess of childbirth, Juno: also Diana: hence, the moon: a midwife (*arch.*). [L. *Lūcīna,* thought by the Romans to be from *lūx, lūcis,* light, as if the bringer to light.]
Lucite® *lū'sīt, n.* a kind of solid, transparent plastic, often used instead of glass.
luck *luk, n.* fortune: good fortune: an object with which a family's fortune is supposed to be bound up. — *adv.* **luck'ily** in a lucky way: I'm glad to say, fortunately. — *n.* **luck'iness.** — *adj.* **luck'less** without good luck: unhappy. — *adv.* **luck'lessly.** — *n.* **luck'lessness.** — *adj.* **luck'y** having, attended by, portending, or bringing good luck. — **luck'-penny** a trifle returned for luck by a seller: a coin carried for luck; **luck'y-bag** a bag sold without disclosing its contents: a bag in which one may dip and draw a prize (also **luck'y-dip**): a receptacle for lost property on board a man-of-war; **lucky charm** an object which is supposed to promote good fortune; **luck'y-piece** a coin: the illegitimate child of a prosperous father (*coll.*); **lucky stone** a stone with a natural hole through it (carried for good fortune); **lucky strike** a stroke of luck. — **down on one's luck** (*coll.*) see **down³**; **push one's luck** (*coll.*) to try to make too much of an advantage, risking total failure; **touch lucky** (*coll.*) to have good luck; **tough luck** an expression of real or affected sympathy for someone's predicament; **try one's luck (at)** to attempt something; **worse luck** unfortunately. [Prob. L.G. or Du. *luk*; cf. Ger. *Glück,* prosperity.]
lucken *luk'ən, (Scot.) adj.* closed. — **luck'enbooth** a booth or shop, esp. of the type found in Edinburgh in the 18th century (**Luckenbooth brooch** a usu. silver and heart-shaped brooch, orig. sold at such a booth); **luck'engow'an** the globe-flower. [O.E. *locen,* pa.p. of *lūcan,* to lock.]
lucky¹, luckie (prefixed or vocative, **Lucky**) *luk'i, (Scot.) n.* an elderly woman: a woman who keeps an ale-house. — **luck'ie-dad** a grandfather. [Perh. from adj. **lucky**, under **luck**.]
lucky² *luk'i, (slang) n.* departure. — **cut** or **make one's lucky** (*arch.*) to bolt.
lucre *lōō', lū'kər, n.* sordid gain: riches. — *adj.* **lu'crative** (*-krə-tiv*) profitable. — *adv.* **lu'cratively.** [L. *lucrum,* gain.]
luctation *luk-tā'shən, n.* struggle. [L. *luctātiō, -ōnis.*]
lucubrate *lōō', lū'kū-brāt, v.i.* to study by lamplight: to discourse learnedly or pedantically. — *ns.* **lucūbrā'tion** study or composition protracted late into the night: a product of such study: a composition that smells of the lamp; **lu'cūbrātor.** [L. *lūcubrāre, -ātum — lūx,* light.]
luculent *lōō', lū'kū-lənt, adj.* bright: clear: convincing. — *adv.* **lu'culently.** [L. *lūculentus — lūx,* light.]
Lucullan *lōō-, lū-kul'ən, adj.* in the style of the Roman L.

Licinius *Lucullus,* famous for his banquets. — Also **Lucullē'an, Lucull'ian, Lucull'ic.**
Lucuma *lōō'kū-mə, n.* genus, mostly S. American, of sapotaceous trees with edible fruit: (without *cap.*) a tree of this genus. [Quechua.]
lucumo *lōō', lū'kū-mō, n.* an Etruscan prince and priest: — *pl.* **lu'cumos,** (L.) **lucumōn'es** (*-ēz*). [L. *lŭcŭmō,* from Etruscan.]
Lucy Stoner *lōō'si stō'nər, (U.S.)* a woman who keeps her maiden name after marriage. [From *Lucy Stone,* an American suffragist (1818–93).]
lud *lud, n.* a minced form of **lord** (trivial and forensic). — *n.* **lud'ship.**
Luddite *lud'īt, n.* one of a band of destroyers of machinery in northern England about 1812–18: hence, any opponent of technological innovation, etc. — Also *adj.* — *n.* **Ludd'ism.** [Said to be from one Ned *Ludd,* who had smashed stocking-frames at a slightly earlier date.]
ludic *lōō'dik, adj.* playful. [Fr. *ludique* — L. *ludus,* play.]
ludicrous *lōō', lū'di-krəs, adj.* sportive (*obs.*): humorous (*obs.*): adapted to excite laughter: ridiculous, absurd: laughable. — *adv.* **lu'dicrously.** — *n.* **lu'dicrousness.** [L. *lūdicrus — lūdĕre,* to play.]
ludo *lōō', lū'dō, n.* a game in which counters are moved on a board according to the fall of dice: — *pl.* **lud'os.** [L. *lūdō,* I play.]
lues *lōō', lū'ēz, n.* a pestilence: now confined to syphilis. — *adj.* **luetic** (*-et'ik*; an etymologically unjustifiable formation). [L. *lŭēs.*]
luff *luf, n.* the windward side of a ship: the act of sailing a ship close to the wind: the loof, or the after-part of a ship's bow where the planks begin to curve in towards the cut-water. — *v.i.* to turn a ship towards the wind. — *v.t.* to turn nearer to the wind: to move (the jib of a crane) in and out. — **luff'ing(-jib) crane** a jib crane with the jib hinged at its lower end to the crane structure so as to permit of alteration of its radius of action. [M.E. *luff, lof*(*f*) — O.Fr. *lof*; possibly from a conjectured M.Du. form *loef* (modern Du. *loef*).]
luffa. See **loofah.**
luffer-board *luf'ər-bōrd, -börd.* Same as **louvre-board.**
Luftwaffe *lōōft'vä-fə,* (Ger.) *n.* air force.
lug¹ *lug, v.t.* to pull: to drag heavily: to carry something heavy: of sailing-ships, to carry too much sail. — *v.i.* to pull: — *pr.p.* **lugg'ing;** *pa.t.* and *pa.p.* **lugged.** — *n.* **lugg'age** the trunks and other baggage of a traveller. — **lugg'age-carrier** a structure fixed to a bicycle, motor-car, etc., for carrying luggage; **lugg'age-van** a railway wagon for luggage. — **lug in** to introduce without any apparent connection or relevance. [Cf. Sw. *lugga,* to pull by the hair; perh. conn. with **lug⁴**.]
lug² *lug,* **lugsail** *lug'sāl, lug'sl, ns.* a square sail bent upon a yard that hangs obliquely to the mast. — *n.* **lugg'er** a small vessel with lugsails.
lug³ *lug, n.* a pole or stick: a perch or rod of land (*Spens.*). [Origin obscure.]
lug⁴ *lug, n.* the flap or lappet of a cap: the ear (*coll.*; chiefly *Scot.*): an earlike projection or appendage: a handle: a loop: a chimney corner (*Scot.*). — *adj.* **lugged** (*lugd*) having lugs or a lug. — *n.* **lugg'ie** (*Scot.*) a hooped dish with one long stave. — **lug'-chair** an easy-chair with side headrests. [Perh. conn. with **lug¹**.]
lug⁵ *lug,* **lugworm** *lug'wûrm, ns.* a sluggish worm found in the sand on the seashore, much used for bait. [Origin doubtful.]
luge *lōōzh, lüzh, n.* a light toboggan. — *v.i.* to glide on such a sledge. — *pr.p.* and *n.* **lug'ing, luge'ing.** [Swiss Fr.]
Luger® *lōō'gər,* (Ger.) *n.* a type of pistol.
luggage. See **lug¹.**
lugger. See **lug².**
luggie. See **lug⁴.**
lugsail. See **lug².**
lugubrious *lōō-gōō'bri-əs,* or *-gū', adj.* mournful: dismal. — *adv.* **lugu'briously.** [L. *lūgubris — lūgēre,* to mourn.]

lugworm. See lug[5].

Luing cattle *ling kat'l*, a breed of hardy beef cattle. [*Luing*, island off west Scotland.]

luit *lüt, lit*, **luit'en,** *Scot.* pa.ts. and *pa.ps.* of **let**[1].

luke *lōōk*, (*dial.*) *adj.* moderately warm: tepid. — *adjs.* **luke'warm** luke: half-hearted; **luke'warmish.** — *adv.* **luke'warmly.** — *ns.* **luke'warmness, luke'warmth.** [M.E. *luek, luke*; doubtful whether related to **lew**[1], or to **Du**. *leuk*.]

lull *lul, v.t.* to soothe: to compose: to quiet. — *v.i.* to become calm: to subside. — *n.* an interval of calm: a calming influence. — *n.* **lull'aby** (*-ə-bī*) a song to lull children to sleep, a cradle-song. — *v.t.* to lull to sleep. [Cf. Sw. *lulla*.]

lulu *lōō'lōō*, (*slang*) *n.* thing, person, that is outstandingly bad or good.

lum *lum*, (*Scot.*) *n.* a chimney: a chimney-pot hat (also **lum'-hat**). **-lum'-head** the top of a chimney. [Origin obscure; O.Fr. *lum*, light, and W. *llumon*, chimney, have been suggested.]

lumbago *lum-bā'gō, n.* a rheumatic affection of the muscles or fibrous tissues in the lumbar region: — *pl.* **lumbā'gos.** — *adj.* **lumbaginous** (*-baj'i-nəs*). [L. *lumbāgō*, lumbago — *lumbus*, loin.]

lumbang *lōōm-bäng', n.* the candle-nut tree or other species of Aleurites, whose nuts yield **lumbang'-oil'**. [Tagálog.]

lumbar *lum'bər, adj.* of or relating to the section of the spine between the lowest rib and the pelvis. — **lumbar puncture** the process of inserting a needle into the lower part of the spinal cord to take a specimen of cerebrospinal fluid, inject drugs, etc. [L. *lumbus*, loin.]

lumber[1] *lum'bər, n.* furniture stored away out of use: anything cumbersome or useless: timber, esp. sawn or split for use (*U.S.* and *Canada*). — *v.t.* to fill with lumber: to heap together in confusion: to cumber: to cut the timber from. — *v.i.* to work as a lumberman. — *ns.* **lum'berer** a lumberjack; **lum'bering** felling, sawing and removal of timber. — **lum'ber-camp** a lumberman's camp; **lum'berjack, lum'berman** one employed in the felling, sawing, etc., of timber; **lum'ber-jacket** a man's longish, loose-fitting, sometimes belted jacket fastened right up to the neck and usu. in bold-patterned heavy material: a woman's cardigan of like fastening; **lum'ber-mill** a sawmill; **lum'ber-room** a room for storing things not in use; **lum'ber-yard** a timber-yard. [Perhaps from **lumber**[2] or from **lumber**[3] influenced by **lumber**[2].]

lumber[2] *lum'bər*, (*arch. slang*) *n.* pawn: a pawnshop: prison. — *v.t.* to pawn: to imprison. — *n.* **lum'berer** a pawnbroker. — **lum'ber-pie'** a pie of meat or fish, with eggs. [See **Lombard**.]

lumber[3] *lum'bər, v.i.* to move heavily and clumsily: to rumble. — *n.* **lum'berer.** — *adjs.* **lum'berly, lum'bersome.** — *n.* **lum'bersomeness.** [M.E. *lomeren*, perh. a freq. formed from *lome*, a variant of **lame**[1]; but cf. dial. Sw. *lomra*, to resound.]

Lumbricus *lum-brī'kəs, n.* a very common genus of earthworms, giving name to the family **Lumbricidae** (*-bris'i-dē*) to which all British earthworms belong: (without *cap.*) a worm of this genus. — *adj.* **lum'brical** (or *-brī'*) worm-like. — *n.* (for **lumbrical muscle**), also **lumbricā'-lis** one of certain muscles of the hand and foot used in flexing the digits. — *adjs.* **lumbriciform** (*-bris'*), **lum'bricoid** (or *-brī'*) worm-like. [L. *lumbrīcus.*]

lumen *lōō', lū'men, n.* a unit of luminous flux — the light emitted in one second in a solid angle of one steradian from a point-source of uniform intensity of one candela: the cavity of a tubular organ (*anat.*): the space within the cell-wall (*bot.*): — *pl.* **lu'mina, lu'mens.** — *adjs.* **lu'menal, lu'minal** of a lumen. — *n.* **lu'minance** luminousness: of the surface radiating normally. — *adj.* **lu'minant** giving light. — *n.* an illuminant. — *ns.* **lu'minarism; lu'minarist** one who paints luminously, or with skill in lights: an impressionist or plein-airist; **lu'minary** a source of light, esp. one of the heavenly bodies: one who illustrates any subject or instructs

mankind. — Also *adj.* — *n.* **luminā'tion** a lighting up. — *v.t.* **lu'mine** (*-in*) to illumine. — *v.i.* **luminesce'** to show luminescence. — *n.* **luminescence** (*-es'əns*) emission of light otherwise than by incandescence and so at a relatively cool temperature: the light so emitted. — *adjs.* **luminesc'ent; luminif'erous** giving, yielding, being the medium of, light. — *ns.* **lu'minist** a luminarist; **luminosity** (*-os'i-ti*) luminousness: the measure of the quantity of light actually emitted by a star, irrespective of its distance. — *adj.* **lu'minous** giving light: shining: lighted: clear: lucid. — *adv.* **lu'minously.** — *n.* **lu'minousness.** — **luminous energy** energy emitted in the form of light; **luminous flux** a measure of the rate of flow of luminous energy; **luminous intensity** a measure of the amount of light radiated in a given direction from a point source; **luminous paint** a paint that glows in the dark, those that glow continuously having radioactive additives. [L. *lūmen, -inis*, light — *lūcēre*, to shine.]

luminaire *lū-min-er', n.* the British Standards Institution term for a light fitting. [Fr.]

lumme, lummy *lum'i, interj.* (Lord) love me.

lummox *lum'əks*, (*coll.*) *n.* a stupid, clumsy person. [Origin unknown.]

lummy *lum'i*, (*slang*; *Dickens*) *adj.* excellent.

lump *lump, n.* a shapeless mass: a protuberance: a swelling: a feeling as if of a swelling in the throat: a considerable quantity: the whole together: the gross: an inert, dull, good-natured, or fair-sized person: a lumpfish. — *v.t.* to throw into a confused mass: to take in the gross: to include under one head: to endure willy-nilly: to put up with: to be lumpish about: to dislike. — *v.i.* to be lumpish: to gather in a lump: to stump along. — *ns.* **lumpec'tomy** the surgical removal of a lump, caused by cancer, in the breast, esp. as opposed to removal of the entire breast; **lump'er** a labourer employed in the lading or unlading of ships: a militiaman (*dial.*): one inclined to lumping in classification — opp. to *hair-splitter*. — *adv.* **lump'ily.** — *n.* **lump'iness.** — *adjs.* **lump'ing** in a lump: heavy: bulky; **lump'ish** like a lump: heavy: gross: dull: sullen. — *adv.* **lump'ishly.** — *ns.* **lump'ishness; lump'kin** a lout. — *adj.* **lump'y** full of lumps: like a lump. — **lump'fish, lump'-sucker** a clumsy sea-fish (*Cyclopterus*) with pectoral fins transformed into a sucker; **lump'-su'gar** loaf-sugar broken in small pieces or cut in cubes; **lump sum** a single sum of money in lieu of several; **lump'y-jaw'** actinomycosis affecting the jaw in cattle. — **if you don't like it you may lump it** take it as you like, but there is no remedy; **in the lump** in gross; **take one's lumps** (*coll.*) to be reprimanded, scolded; **the lump** system of using for a particular job self-employed workmen, esp. in order to evade tax and national insurance payments. [Origin doubtful; found in various Gmc. languages.]

lumpen *lum'pən, adj.* pertaining to a dispossessed and/or degraded section of a social class, as in **lumpen proletariat** (also as one word), the very poor lowest-class down-and-outs: stupid, boorish. — *adj.* **lump'enly.** [From Ger. *Lumpen*, a rag.]

lunacy, lunar, lunate, lunatic, etc. See **lune**.

lunch *lunch, lunsh, n.* a thick slice, a lump (*dial.*): a slight repast between breakfast and midday meal: midday meal: formerly a snack at any time of day, now a light midday meal (*U.S.*). — *v.i.* to take lunch. — *v.t.* to provide lunch for. — *n.* **lunch'eon** lunch. — *v.i.* to lunch (also *v.t.*). — *ns.* **luncheonette'** (*U.S.*) a restaurant serving snacks and light meals; **lunch'er.** — **lunch box** a box or container in which one carries, esp. to one's place of work, sandwiches, etc., for one's lunch; **lunch'eon-bar** a counter where luncheons are served; **lunch'eon-basket** basket for carrying lunch, with or without cutlery, etc.; **lunch'eon-meat** a type of pre-cooked meat containing preservatives, usually served cold; **lunch(eon) voucher** a ticket or voucher given by employer to employee to be used to pay for the latter's lunch; **lunch'-hour, lunch'-time** the time of, or time set apart for, lunch: an interval allowed for lunch. [Perh.

altered from **lump;** or from Sp. *lonja,* slice of ham, etc.]
lune *lōōn, lūn, n.* anything in the shape of a half-moon: a lunule: a fit of lunacy (*Shak.*). — *ns.* **lunacy** (usu. *lōō′nə-si*) a form of insanity once believed to come with changes of the moon: insanity generally: extreme folly; **lun′anaut** same as **lunarnaut.** — *adj.* **lunar** (usu. *lōō′nər*) belonging to the moon: measured by the moon's revolutions: caused by the moon: like the moon: of silver (*old chem.*). — *n.* a lunar distance. — *ns.* **lunā′rian** an inhabitant of the moon: a student of the moon; **lu′narist** one who thinks the moon affects the weather; **lun′arnaut** an astronaut who travels, has travelled, to the moon; **lu′nary** the moonwort fern: the plant honesty. — *adj.* lunar. — *adjs.* **lu′nate, -d** crescent-shaped; **lunatic** (*lōō′nə-tik*) affected with lunacy. — *n.* a person so affected: a madman. — *ns.* **lunā′tion** a synodic month; **lunette′** a crescent-shaped ornament: a semicircular or crescent-shaped space where a vault intersects a wall or another vault, often occupied by a window or by decoration: an arched opening in a vault: a detached bastion (*fort.*): a small horseshoe: a watchglass flattened more than usual in the centre: in the R.C. Church, a moon-shaped case for the consecrated host. — *adjs.* **lunisō′lar** pertaining to the moon and sun jointly (**lunisolar calendar, lunisolar year** one divided according to the changes of the moon, but made to agree in average length with the solar year); **lunitī′dal** pertaining to the moon and its influence on the tide (**lunitidal interval** the time interval between the moon's transit and the next high tide at a particular place). — *n.* **lu′nula** a lunule: a crescent-like appearance, esp. the whitish area at the base of a nail: a Bronze Age crescent-shaped gold ornament forming part of a necklace. — *adjs.* **lu′nular; lu′nulate, -d** shaped like a small crescent (*bot.*): having crescent-shaped markings. — *n.* **lu′nule** anything in form like a small crescent: a geometrical figure bounded by two arcs of circles. — **lunar caustic** fused crystals of silver nitrate, applied to ulcers, etc.; **lunar cycle** see **metonic cycle; lunar distances** a method of finding the longitude by comparison of the observed angular distance of the moon from a star at a known local time, with the tabulated angular distance at a certain Greenwich time; **Lunar Excursion Module (LEM, lem)** module for use in the last stage of the journey to land on the moon; **lunar month** see **month; lunar theory** the *a priori* deduction of the moon's motions from the principles of gravitation; **lunar year** see **year; lunatic asylum** a former, now offensive, name for a mental hospital; **lunatic fringe** the more nonsensical, extreme-minded, or eccentric members of a community or of a movement.   [L. *lūna,* the moon — *lūcēre,* to shine.]
lung *lung, n.* a respiratory organ in animals that breathe atmospheric air: an open space in a town (*fig.*). — *adj.* **lunged.** — *n.* **lung′ful.** — **lung′-book** a breathing organ in spiders and scorpions, constructed like the leaves of a book; **lung′-fish** one of the Dipnoi, having lungs as well as gills. — *adj.* **lung′-grown** having an adhesion of the lung to the pleura. — **lung′wort** a genus (Pulmonaria) of the borage family, once thought good for lung diseases because of its spotted leaves: a lichen (*Lobaria pulmonaria*) on tree-trunks, used as a domestic remedy for lung diseases. — **iron lung** see **iron.** [O.E. *lungen.*]
lunge[1] *lunj, n.* a sudden thrust as in fencing: a forward plunge. — *v.i.* to make a lunge: to plunge forward. — *v.t.* to thrust with a lunge: — *pr.p.* **lunge′ing, lung′ing.** [Fr. *allonger,* to lengthen — L. *ad,* to, *longus,* long.]
lunge[2], **longe** *lunj, n.* a long rope used in horse-training: training with a lunge: a training-ground for horses. — *v.t.* to train or cause to go with a lunge.   [Fr. *longe* — L. *longus,* long.]
lungi *lōōn′gē, n.* a long cloth used as loin-cloth, sash, turban, etc.   [Hind. and Pers. *lungī.*]
lungie[1] *lung′i,* (*Scot.*) *n.* the guillemot.   [Norw. dial. *lomgivie.*]
lungie[2], **lunyie** *lung′i, lun′yi, ns.* Scottish forms of **loin.**

lunisolar, lunitidal, lunulate, lunule, etc. See **lune.**
lunker *lung′kər,* (*coll.,* esp. *U.S.*) *n.* a particularly large specimen of an animal, esp. a fish.   [Origin unknown.]
lunkhead *lungk′hed,* (*coll.,* esp. *U.S.*) *n.* a fool, blockhead. [Perh. a form of **lump,** and **head.**]
lunt *lunt,* (*Scot.*) *n.* a slow-match or means of setting on fire: a sudden flame, blaze: smoke. — *v.t.* to kindle: to smoke. — *v.i.* to blaze up: to emit smoke: to smoke tobacco.   [Du. *lont,* a match; cf. Ger. *Lunte.*]
lunyie. See **lungie**[2].
Lupercal *lōō′pər-kal, -kl,* or *lū′, n.* the grotto, or the festival (Feb. 15) of *Lupercus,* Roman god of fertility and flocks. — Also (*pl.*) **Lupercā′lia.**   [Perh. *lupus,* wolf, *arcēre,* to ward off.]
lupin, lupine *lōō′, lū′pin, n.* (a plant of) genus (*Lupinus*) of Papilionaceae, with flowers on long spikes: its seed.   [L. *lupīnus.*]
lupine *lōō′, lū′pin, adj.* of a wolf: like a wolf: wolfish.   [L. *lupīnus* — *lupus,* a wolf.]
luppen *lup′n,* Scots. *pa.p.* of **leap**[1].
lupulin *lōō′pū-lin, n.* a yellow powder composed of glands from hop flowers and bracts, used as a sedative. — *adjs.* **lu′puline, lupulinic** (*-lin′ik*).   [L. *lupus,* hopplant.]
lupus *lōō′, lū′pəs, n.* a chronic tuberculosis of the skin, often affecting the nose: (wth *cap.*) a constellation in the southern hemisphere (*astron.*).   [L. *lupus,* a wolf.]
lur. See **lure**[2].
lurch[1] *lûrch, n.* an old game, probably like backgammon: in various games, a situation in which one side fails to score at all, or is left far behind: a discomfiture. — *v.t.* to defeat by a lurch: to outdo so as to deprive of all chance (*Shak.*): to leave in the lurch. — **leave someone in the lurch** to leave someone in a difficult situation without help.   [O.Fr. *lourche.*]
lurch[2] *lûrch, n.* wait, ambush. — *v.i.* to lurk, prowl about. — *v.t.* to get the start of, forestall (*arch.*): to defraud, to overreach (*arch.*): to filch (*arch.*). — *n.* **lurch′er** one who lurches: a glutton (*obs.*): a dog with a distinct cross of greyhound, esp. a cross of greyhound and collie.   [Connection with **lurk** difficult; influenced apparently by foregoing.]
lurch[3] *lûrch, v.i.* to roll or pitch suddenly forward or to one side. — *n.* a sudden roll or pitch.   [Origin obscure.]
lurdan, lurdane, lurden *lûr′dən, n.* a dull, heavy, stupid or sluggish person. — Also *adj.*   [O.Fr. *lourdin,* dull — *lourd,* heavy.]
lure[1] *lōōr, lūr, n.* any enticement: bait: decoy: a bunch of feathers used to recall a hawk. — *v.t.* to entice: decoy.   [O.Fr. *loerre* (Fr. *leurre*) — M.H.G. *luoder* (Ger. *Luder*), bait.]
lure[2], **lur** *lōōr, n.* a long curved Bronze Age trumpet still used in Scandinavian countries for calling cattle, etc.   [O.N. *lūthr;* Dan. and Norw. *lur.*]
Lurex® *lū′reks, n.* (fabric made from) a plastic-coated aluminium thread.
Lurgi *lōōr′gi, adj.* pertaining to a German plant that enables coal-gas to be made from low-grade coal.
lurgy, lurgi *lûr′gi,* (esp. *facet.*) *n.* a fictitious disease. [Invented and popularised by the cast of BBC Radio's *The Goon Show* (1949–1960).]
lurid *lōō′, lū′rid, adj.* glaringly, wanly, or dingily reddishyellow or yellowish-brown: dingy brown or yellow (*bot.*): gloomily threatening: ghastly pale, wan: ghastly: melodramatically sensational: brimstony. — *adv.* **lu′ridly.** — *n.* **lu′ridness.**   [L. *lūridus.*]
lurk *lûrk, v.i.* to lie in wait: to be concealed: to skulk: to go or loaf about furtively. — *n.* a prowl: a lurkingplace: a swindling dodge. — *n.* **lurk′er.** — *n.* and *adj.* **lurk′ing.** — **lurk′ing-place.**   [Perh. freq. from **lour.**]
lurry *lur′i,* (*Milt.*) *n.* gabbled formula: confusion. [liripoop.]
luscious *lush′əs, adj.* sweet in a great degree: delightful: fulsome: voluptuous. — *adv.* **lusc′iously.** — *n.* **lusc′iousness.**   [Origin unknown; **delicious,** influenced by

lush[1], has been suggested.]

lush[1] *lush, adj.* rich and juicy: luxuriant. — *adv.* **lush'ly.** — *n.* **lush'ness.** [Perh. a form of **lash[2]**.]

lush[2] *lush, (arch. slang) n.* liquor: a drink: a drinking bout: (not *arch.*) a drinker or drunkard. — *v.t.* to ply with liquor. — *v.t.* and *v.i.* to drink. — *n.* **lush'er.** — *adj.* **lush'y** tipsy. — **lush'-house** a low public house. [Perh. from foregoing.]

Lusiad *lōō', lū'si-ad, n.,* and **Lusiads** (*-adz*) *n.pl.* a Portuguese epic by Camoens, celebrating Vasco da Gama's voyage to India by the Cape. — *n.* and *adj.* **Lusitā'nian** Portuguese. — *n.* and *adj.* **Lusita'no-Amer'-ican** Brazilian of Portuguese descent. — *pfx.* **Luso-**Portuguese. — *n.* **Lu'sophile** a lover of Portugal. [Port. *Os Lusiadas,* the Lusitanians; L. *Lūsitānia,* approximately, Portugal.]

lusk *lusk, (obs.) n.* a lazy fellow. — *adj.* lazy. — *v.i.* to skulk: to lie about lazily. — *adj.* **lusk'ish.** — *n.* **lusk'-ishness.** [Origin obscure.]

lust *lust, n.* pleasure (*Spens., Shak.*): appetite: relish: longing: eagerness to possess: sensual desire: sexual desire, now always of a degraded kind. — *v.i.* to desire eagerly (with *after, for*): to have carnal desire: to have depraved desires. — *n.* **lust'er.** — *adj.* **lust'ful** having lust: inciting to lust: sensual. — *adv.* **lust'fully.** — *n.* **lust'fulness.** — *adj. (obs.)* **lust'ick, lust'ique** (*Shak.* 'as the Dutchman says'; for Du. *lustig*) lusty, healthy, vigorous. — *ns.* **lust'ihead, lust'ihood, lust'iness.** — *adv.* **lust'ily.** — *adjs.* **lust'less** (*Spens.*) listless, feeble; **lust'y** vigorous: healthful: stout: bulky: lustful (*Milt.*): pleasing, pleasant (*obs.*). — *adjs.* **lust'-breathed** (*-brēdh'id; Shak.*) animated by lust; **lust'-di'eted** (*Shak.*) pampered by lust. [O.E. *lust,* pleasure.]

lustrate, etc. See **lustre[2]**.

lustre[1], *U.S.* **luster** *lus'tər, n.* characteristic surface appearance in reflected light: sheen: gloss: brightness: splendour: renown (*fig.*): a candlestick, vase, etc., ornamented with pendants of cut-glass: a dress material with cotton warp and woollen weft, and highly finished surface: a metallic pottery glaze. — *v.t.* to impart a lustre to. — *v.i.* to become lustrous. — *adj.* **lus'treless** — *n.* **lus'tring.** — *adj.* **lus'trous** bright: shining: luminous. — *adv.* **lus'trously.** — **lus'treware** pottery, etc. with a metallic glaze. [Fr., — L. *lūstrāre,* to shine on.]

lustre[2], **lustrum** *lus'trəm, ns.* a purification of the Roman people made every five years, after the taking of the census: a period of five years. — *pl.* **lus'tres, lus'tra, lus'trums.** — *adj.* **lus'tral.** — *v.t.* **lus'trate** to purify by sacrifice: to perambulate (*obs.*). — *n.* **lustrā'tion** purification by sacrifice: act of purifying. [L. *lūstrum,* prob. — *luĕre,* to wash, to purify.]

lustring *lus'tring, n.* a glossy silk cloth. — Also **lus'trine, lutestring** (*lōōt', lūt'string*). [Fr. *lustrine* — It. *lustrino.*]

lustrum. See **lustre[2]**.

lusty. See **lust.**

lusus naturae *lōō'səs na-tū'rē, lōō'sōōs na-tōōr'ī,* (L.) a sport or freak of nature.

lute[1] *lōōt,* or *lūt, n.* an old stringed instrument shaped like half a pear. — *v.i.* to play on the lute. — *v.t.* and *v.i.* to sound as if on a lute. — *ns.* **lut'anist, lut'enist, lut'er, lut'ist** a player on the lute; **luthier** (*lūt'i-ər*) a maker of lutes, guitars, and other stringed instruments. — **lute'string** string of lute (see also **lustring**). [O.Fr. *lut* (Fr. *luth*); like Ger. *Laute,* from Ar. *al,* the, *'ūd,* wood, the lute.]

lute[2] *lōōt, lūt, n.* clay, cement or other material used as a protective covering, an airtight stopping, or the like: a rubber packing-ring for a jar. — *v.t.* to close or coat with lute. — *n.* **lut'ing.** [L. *lutum,* mud — *luĕre,* to wash.]

lute[3] *lōōt, lūt, n.* a straight-edge for scraping off excess of clay in a brick mould. [Du. *loet.*]

luteal. See **lutein.**

lutecium. Same as **lutetium.**

lutein *lōōt'ē-in, lūt', n.* a yellow colouring-matter in yolk of egg. — *adj.* **luteal** (*lōō'ti-əl*) pertaining to (the formation of) the corpus luteum. — *n.* **luteinīsā'tion, -z-** the process of stimulation to the ovary, whereby ovulation occurs and a corpus luteum is formed. — *v.t.* and *v.i.* **lu'teinise, -ize.** — *n.* **lutĕ'olin** the yellow colouring-matter of weld or dyer's weed. — *adjs.* **lutĕ'olous** yellowish; **lu'teous** (*-i-əs*) golden-yellow; **lutescent** (*-es'ənt*) yellowish. — **luteinising hormone** a hormone that, in females, stimulates ovulation and the formation of the corpus luteum (q.v.), and in males, the production of androgen. [L. *lūteus,* yellow, *lūteum,* egg-yolk, *lūtum,* weld.]

lutenist. See **lute[1]**.

lutestring. See **lustring, lute.**

Lutetian *lū-tē'shən, adj.* Parisian. [L. *Lutetia Parīsiōrum,* the mud town of the Parisii, Paris — *lutum,* mud.]

lutetium *lōō-tē'shi-əm, lū-, n.* metallic element (Lu; at. numb. 71) first separated from ytterbium by Georges Urbain, a Parisian. [L. *Lutetia,* Paris.]

Lutheran *lōō'thər-ən, adj.* pertaining to Martin *Luther,* the great German Protestant reformer (1483–1546), or to his doctrines. — *n.* a follower of Luther. — *ns.* **Lu'ther(an)ism; Lu'therist.**

luthern *lōō', lū'thərn, n.* a dormer-window. [Prob. a variant of **lucarne.**]

luthier. See **lute[1]**.

Lutine bell *lōō-tēn', lōō', bel,* a bell recovered from the frigate *Lutine,* and rung at Lloyd's of London before certain important announcements.

lutten. See **loot[2]**.

lutz *lōōts, n.* in figure-skating, a jump (with rotation) from the back outer edge of one skate to the back outer edge of the other. [Poss. Gustave *Lussi* of Switzerland, born 1898, the first exponent.]

lux *luks, n.* a unit of illumination, one lumen per square metre: — *pl.* **lux, luxes, luces** (*lōō'sēs*). — **lux'meter** instrument for measuring illumination. [L. *lūx,* light.]

luxate *luks'āt, v.t.* to put out of joint: to displace. — *n.* **luxā'tion** a dislocation. [L. *luxāre, -ātum* — *luxus* — Gr. *loxos,* slanting.]

luxmeter. See **lux.**

luxe *lōōks, luks,* Fr. *lüks, n.* luxury. — see also **de luxe.** [Fr. — L. *luxus,* a dislocation, extravagance, luxury.]

lux mundi *luks mun'dī, lōōks mōōn'dē,* (L.) light of the world.

luxulyanite, luxul(l)ianite *luks-ūl'yən-īt, -ul', -ōōl', n.* a tourmaline granite found at *Luxulyan,* Cornwall.

luxury *luk'shə-ri,* also *lug'zhə-ri, n.* abundant provision of means of ease and pleasure: indulgence, esp. in costly pleasures: anything delightful, often expensive, but not necessary: a dainty: wantonness (*Shak.*). — *adj.* relating to or providing luxury. — *ns.* **luxuriance** (*lug-zhōō'ri-əns, -zū', -zhū',* or *luk-,* etc.), **luxu'riancy** growth in rich abundance or excess: exuberance: overgrowth: rankness. — *adj.* **luxu'riant** exuberant in growth: overabundant: profuse: erroneously, for luxurious. — *adv.* **luxu'riantly.** — *v.i.* **luxu'riate** to be luxuriant (*obs.*): to live luxuriously: to enjoy luxury: to enjoy, or revel in, free indulgence. — *n.* **luxuriā'tion.** — *adj.* **luxu'rious** of luxury: given to luxury: ministering to luxury: furnished with luxuries: softening by pleasure: luxuriant (*Milt.*): lustful (*Shak.*). — *adv.* **luxu'riously.** — *ns.* **luxu'riousness; luxurist** (*luk'shə-rist, -sū-*) one given to luxury. [O.Fr. *luxurie* — L. *luxuria,* luxury — *luxus,* excess.]

luz *luz, n.* a bone supposed by Rabbinical writers to be indestructible, probably the sacrum.

luzern. See **lucerne.**

Luzula *lōō', lū'zū-lə, n.* the wood-rush genus, with flat generally hairy leaves. [Old It. *luzziola* (mod. *lucciola*), firefly, glow-worm, from its shining capsules.]

lyam *lī'əm,* **lime, lyme** *līm, ns.* a leash: a lyam-hound. — *n.* **ly'am-hound, lime'-hound, lyme'-hound** a bloodhound. [O.Fr. *liem* (Fr. *lien*) — L. *ligāmen* — *ligāre*, to tie.]

lyart. See **liard.**

Lycaena *lī-sē'nə, n.* a genus of butterflies giving name to the family **Lycae'nidae,** usu. small and blue or coppery. [Gr. *lykaina,* she-wolf.]

lycanthropy *lī-, li-kan'thrə-pi, n.* power of changing oneself into a wolf: a kind of madness, in which the patient fancies himself to be a wolf. — *ns.* **lycanthrope** (*lī'kan-thrōp,* or *-kan'*), **lycan'thropist** a wolf-man or werewolf: one affected with lycanthropy. — *adj.* **lycanthropic** (*-throp'*). [Gr. *lykos,* a wolf, *anthrōpos,* a man.]

lycée *lē'sā, n.* a state secondary school in France. [Fr., lyceum.]

Lyceum *lī-sē'əm, n.* a gymnasium and grove beside the temple of Apollo at Athens, in whose walks Aristotle taught: (without *cap.*) a college: (without *cap.*) a place or building devoted to literary studies, lectures, etc.: (without *cap.*) an organisation for instruction by lectures (*U.S.*): (without *cap.*) a lycée: — *pl.* **lyce'ums.** [L. *Lycēum* — Gr. *Lykeion* — *Lykeios,* an epithet of Apollo (pcrh. wolf-slayer, perhaps the Lycian).]

lychee, litchi, lichee, lichi *lī'chē, lē'chē,* **leechee** *lē'chē, ns.* a Chinese fruit, a nut or berry with a fleshy aril: the tree (*Litchi chineasis;* fam. Sapindaceae) that bears it. [Chin. *li-chi.*]

lychgate. Same as **lichgate.**

Lychnic *lik'nik, n.* the first part of the vespers of the Greek Church. — *ns.* **Lychnap'sia** (Gr. *haptein,* to touch, light) a series of seven prayers in the vespers of the Greek Church; **lych'noscope** a low side window (named on the theory that it was intended to let lepers see the altar lights). [Gr. *lychnos,* a lamp.]

Lychnis *lik'nis, n.* the campion genus of the pink family: (without *cap.*) a plant of this genus. [Gr. *lychnis,* rose-campion.]

lycopod *lī'kə-pod, n.* a club-moss, any plant of the genus Lycopodium or of the Lycopodiales. — *ns.pl.* **Lycopōdiā'ceae** a homosporous family of Lycopodiales; **Lycopōdiā'lēs, Lycopodī'nae, Lycopodīn'eae** one of the main branches of the Pteridophytes, usually with dichotomously branched stems and axillary sporangia, commonly in cones. — *n.* **Lycopō'dium** the typical genus of Lycopodiaceae, club-moss, or stag's horn: (without *cap.*) a powder consisting of the spores of Lycopodium. [Gr. *lykos,* a wolf, *pous, podos,* a foot.]

Lycosa *lī-kō'sə, n.* a genus of hunting spiders, including the true tarantula, typical of the family **Lycosidae** (*-kos'i-dē*) or wolf-spiders. [Gr. *lykos,* a wolf, also a kind of spider.]

Lycra® *lī'krə, n.* (a fabric made from) a lightweight, synthetic, elastomeric fibre.

lyddite *lid'īt, n.* a powerful explosive made in Kent, composed mainly of picric acid. [Tested at *Lydd.*]

Lydford law *lid'fərd lö,* the same kind of law as that called Jeddart justice. [*Lydford* in Devon.]

Lydian *lid'i-ən, adj.* pertaining to *Lydia* in Asia Minor: of music, soft and slow, luxurious and effeminate. — *n.* native of Lydia: the language of ancient Lydia, apparently akin to Hittite. — **Lydian mode** in ancient Greek music, a mode of two tetrachords with a semitone between the two highest notes in each and a whole tone between the tetrachords (as: *c d e f; g a b c*; but reckoned downwards by the Greeks): in old church music, an authentic mode, extending from *f* to *f,* with *f* for its final; **Lydian stone** touchstone. [Gr. *Lȳdiā,* Lydia.]

lye[1] *lī, n.* a short side-branch of a railway. [See **lie**[2].]

lye[2] *lī, n.* a strong alkaline solution: a liquid used for washing: a solution got by leaching. [O.E. *lēah, lēag;* Ger. *Lauge;* allied to L. *lavāre,* to wash.]

lyfull. See **life.**

lying. See **lie**[1,2].

lykewake, likewake *līk'wāk,* **like'-, lyke'walk** *-wök,* (*Scot.;* Eng. **lichwake** *lich'*) *ns.* a watch over the dead, often with merrymaking. [O.E. *līc;* Ger. *Leiche,* a corpse, and **wake.**]

lym *lim, n.* a conjectural Shakespearian form of **lyme.**

Lymantriidae *lī-man-trī'i-dē, n.pl.* the tussock-moths, a family akin to the eggers. [Gr. *lȳmantēr,* destroyer.]

lyme, lyme-hound. See **lyam.**

lyme-grass *līm'-gräs, n.* a coarse sand-binding grass, *Elymus arenarius* or other of the genus. [Origin unknown.]

Lymeswold® *līmz'wōld, n.* a kind of mild blue full-fat soft cheese.

lymiter (*Spens.*). Same as **limiter.**

Lymnaea. An erroneous form of **Limnaea.**

lymph *limf, n.* pure water: a colourless or faintly yellowish fluid collected into the lymphatic vessels from the tissues in animal bodies, of a rather saltish taste, and with an alkaline reaction: a vaccine. — *n.* **lymphadenop'athy** (Gr. *adēn,* a gland, *pathos,* suffering) a disease of the lymph nodes. — *adj.* **lymphangial** (*-anj'əl;* Gr. *angeion,* vessel) pertaining to the lymphatic vessels. — *ns.* **lymphan'giogram, lymphangiog'raphy** same as **lymphogram, lymphography; lymphangitis** (*-an-jī'tis*) inflammation of a lymphatic vessel. — *adj.* **lymphat'ic** mad (*obs.*): pertaining to lymph: of a temperament or bodily habit once supposed to result from excess of lymph: disposed to sluggishness and flabbiness. — *n.* a vessel that conveys lymph. — *adv.* **lymphat'ically.** — *ns.* **lymph'ocyte** (*-ō-sīt*) a kind of leucocyte formed in the lymph nodes and spleen; **lymphog'raphy** radiography of the lymph glands and lymphatic system, recorded on a **lymph'ogram:** the description of the lymphatic system (prob. *obs.*). — *adj.* **lymph'oid** of, carrying, or like lymph: pertaining to the lymphatic system. — **lymph'okine** (Gr. *kinein,* to move) any of a number of substances secreted by lymphocytes activated by contact with an antigen and thought to play a part in cell-mediated immunity; **lymphō'ma** a tumour consisting of lymphoid tissue. — **lymphatic system** the network of vessels that conveys lymph to the venous system; **lymph gland, node** any of the small masses of tissue sited along the lymphatic vessels, in which lymph is purified, and lymphocytes are formed. [L. *lympha,* water; *lymphāticus,* mad.]

lymphad *lim'fad, n.* a Highland galley. [Gael. *longfhada.*]

lymphangial, lymphatic, lymphocyte, etc. See **lymph.**

lynage (*Spens.*). Same as **lineage.**

lyncean. See **lynx.**

lynch *linch, linsh, v.t.* to judge and put to death without the usual forms of law. — **lynch'-law.** [Captain William *Lynch* of Virginia.]

lynchet. See **linch.**

lynchpin. A variant of **linchpin.**

lyne (*Spens.*). Same as **line**[1] (linen).

lynx *lingks, n.* an animal of the cat family, high at the haunches, with short tail and tufted ears: — *pl.* **lynx'es:** (with *cap.*) the genus to which this cat belongs: (with *cap.*); Latin *gen.* **Lyncis** *lin'sis*) a constellation in the Northern Hemisphere. — *adjs.* **lyncean** (*lin-sē'ən*) lynx-like: sharp-sighted; **lynx'-eyed.** [L., — Gr. *lynx, lynkos.*]

lyomerous *lī-om'ə-rəs, adj.* relating to the **Lyom'erī,** soft-bodied fishes. [Gr. *lyein,* to loosen, *meros,* part.]

Lyon *lī'ən, n.* the chief herald of Scotland. — Also **Lord Lyon, Lyon King-of-arms** (or **-at-arms**). — **Lyon Court** the court over which he presides, having jurisdiction in questions of coat-armour and precedency. [From the heraldic *lion* of Scotland.]

lyophil, lyophile *lī'ō-fil, -fīl,* **lyophilic** *-fil'ik, adjs.* of a colloid, readily dispersed in a suitable medium. — *n.* **lyophilisā'tion, -z-** freeze-drying. — *v.t.* **lyoph'ilise, -ize** to dry by freezing. — *adjs.* **ly'ophobe** (*-fōb*), **lyophobic** (*-fob'*) of a colloid, not readily dispersed. [Gr. *lȳe,* separation, *phileein,* to love, *phobeein,* to fear.]

lyre *līr, n.* a musical instrument like the harp, anciently used as an accompaniment to poetry — a convex sound-chest with a pair of curved arms connected by a cross-bar, from which the strings were stretched over a bridge to a tailpiece. — *n.* **Ly'ra** one of the northern constellations. — *adjs.* **ly′rate, -d** lyre-shaped: having the terminal lobe much larger than the lateral ones (*bot.*). — *advs.* **ly′ra-way, ly′ra-wise** according to lute tablature. — *adj.* **lyric** (*lir′*) pertaining to the lyre: fitted to be sung to the lyre: of poems or their authors, expressing individual or private emotions. — *n.* a lyric poem: a song: (in *pl.*) the words of a popular song: a composer of lyric poetry (*obs.*). — *adj.* **lyrical** (*lir′*) lyric: song-like: expressive, imaginative: effusive. — *adv.* **lyr′ically.** — *ns.* **lyricism** (*lir′i-sizm*) a lyrical expression: lyrical quality; **lyr′icist** the writer of the words of a song, musical, opera, etc.: a lyric poet. — *adj.* **lyriform** (*lī′*) shaped like a lyre. — *ns.* **lyr′ism** (*līr′, lir′*) lyricism: singing; **lyrist** (*līr′* or *lir′*) a player on the lyre or harp: (*lir′*) a lyric poet. — **ly′ra-vi′ol** an obsolete instrument like a viola da gamba adapted for playing from lute tablature; **lyre′-bird** an Australian passerine bird about the size of a pheasant, the tail-feathers of the male arranged, in display, in the form of a lyre; **lyriform organs** (*zool.*) patches of chitin on the legs and other parts of spiders, believed to be olfactory in function. — **wax lyrical** to grow expressive or effusive in praise of something. [L. *lyra* — Gr. *lyrā.*]

Lysenkoism *li-sen′kō-izm, n.* the teaching of the Soviet geneticist T. D. *Lysenko* (1898–1976) that acquired characters are inheritable.

lyse, lysergic acid, lysin, etc. See **lysis.**

lysis *lī′sis, n.* the gradual abatement of a disease, as distinguished from *crisis*: breaking down as of a cell (*biol.*): the action of a lysin. — *v.t.* **lyse** (*līz*) to cause to undergo lysis. — **-lysis** (*-lis′is*) in composition, the action of breaking down, or dividing into parts. — **-lyse, -lyze** (*-līz*) verb combining form. — **-lyst** (*-list*), **-lyte** (*-līt*) noun combining forms. — **-lytic, -lytical**

(*-lit′*) adjectival combining forms. — *adjs.* **lysigenic** (*lī-* or *lī-si-jen′ik*), **lysigenet′ic, lysigenous** (*-sij′i-nəs*) caused by breaking down of cells. — *ns.* **lysim′eter** an instrument for measuring percolation of water through the soil; **lysin** (*lī′sin*) a substance that causes breakdown of cells; **ly′sine** (*-sīn, -sēn*) an amino-acid, a decomposition product of proteins; **ly′sol** a solution of cresol in soap, a poisonous disinfectant (a trademark in some countries); **ly′sosome** (Gr. *soma*, a body) any of the tiny particles present in most cells, containing enzymes that play a part in intracellular digestion; **ly′sozyme** (*-zīm*) a bacteriolytic enzyme present in some plants, animal secretions (c.g. tears), egg-white, etc. — **lysergic acid** (*lī-sûr′jik*) a substance, $C_{16}H_{16}O_2N_2$, got from ergot, causing (in the form of lysergic acid diethylamide — **LSD** or **ly′sergide**) a schizophrenic condition, with hallucinations and thought processes outside the normal range. [Gr. *lysis*, dissolution — *lyein*, to loose.]

lyssa *lis′ə, (path.) n.* rabies. [Gr., madness, rabies.]

lyte. Form of **light³** or **lite¹.**

-lyte. See **lysis.**

lythe¹ (*Spens.*). Form of **lithe¹.**

lythe² *līdh, (Scot.) n.* the pollack.

Lythrum *lith′rəm, n.* the purple loosestrife genus, giving name to a family of archichlamydeous dicotyledons, **Lythrā′ceae,** commonly hexamerous, heterostyled, with epicalyx. [Latinised from Gr. *lythron*, gore, from the colour of its flowers.]

-lytic(al). See **lysis.**

lytta *lit′ə, n.* a cartilaginous or fibrous band on the under surface of the tongue in carnivores — the worm of a dog's tongue. [Gr., Attic form of *lyssa* (see **lyssa**).]

For other sounds see detailed chart of pronunciation.

M

M, m *em, n.* the twelfth letter of the Roman, the thirteenth of our alphabet, representing a labial nasal consonant: an object or figure shaped like the letter: as a Roman numeral M = 1000; M̄ = 1 000 000: in chem. *m* = *meta-*, or *meso-*, and it is used as a symbol in chem. and other sciences, with a number of meanings: in road-classification, followed by a number, short for motorway, as *M90*: followed by a number, used to designate monetary categories, the lower the number, the more liquid the money (*econ.*). — **M1** a Garand rifle (q.v.); **M′-roof** a roof formed by the junction of two common roofs, so that its section is like the letter M; **M′-way** a written contraction of **motorway**. See also **em.**

'm *m*, a shortened form of **am**: a contraction of **madam.**

m' *m(ə)*, a shortened form of **my** as in *m'lud* (see **lud**).

M'. See **Mac.**

ma *mä, n.* a childish contraction for **mamma.**

ma'am *mäm, mam, məm, n.* a contraction of **madam**, the pronunciation *mäm* being used as a form of address to female royalty. — Also (*coll.*) **marm** (*mäm*), **mum.**

maar *mär, n.* (*geol.*) a crater that has been formed by a single explosion and so does not lie in a cone of lava. [Ger.]

Mab *mab, n.* the name of a female fairy, bringer of dreams: the queen of the fairies.

Mabinogion *mab-i-nō'gi-on, n.* a title applied to four tales in the *Red Book of Hergest*, a Welsh MS. of the 14th century: extended to the whole collection in Lady Charlotte Guest's edition and translation in 1838. [W., juvenilities.]

mac. See **mac(k)intosh.**

Mac *mak, mək,* a Gaelic prefix in names, meaning *son* (of). — Also written **Mc** and **M'.** [Gael. and Ir. *mac,* son; W. *mab,* O.W. *map.*]

macabre *ma-, mə-kä'br', -bər, adj.* gruesome: like the Dance of Death. — *adj.* **macaberesque** (*-bər-esk'*). [Fr. *macabre,* formerly also *macabré,* perh. a corr. of *Maccabee* in reference to 2 Macc. xii. 43–6, said to have been represented in mediaeval drama, or from Heb. *meqabēr,* grave-digger.]

macaco *mə-kä'kō, n.* any of various kinds of lemur: — *pl.* **maca'cos.** [Fr. *mococo.*]

Macadamia *mak-ə-dā'mi-ə, n.* an orig. Australian genus of evergreen trees (fam. Proteaceae): (without *cap.*) a tree of this genus. — **macadamia nut** (also **Queensland nut**) the edible nut of two species of macadamia, *M. ternifolia* and *M. integrifolia*: the tree bearing this nut. [John *Macadam* (1827–65), Scottish-born Australian chemist.]

macadamise, -ize *mək-ad'əm-īz, v.t.* to cover with small broken stones, so as to form a smooth, hard surface. — *ns.* **macad'am** macadamised road surface: material for macadamising; **macadamīsā'tion, -z-.** [From John Loudon *McAdam* (1756–1836).]

macahuba. See **macaw-tree.**

macaque *mə-käk', n.* a monkey of genus Macacus or Macaca, to which belong the rhesus and the Barbary ape. [Fr., — Port. *macaco,* a monkey.]

macarise, -ize *mak'ə-rīz, v.t.* to declare to be happy or blessed. — *n.* **mac'arism** a beatitude. [Gr. *makar,* happy.]

macaroni *mak-ə-rō'ni, n.* a paste of hard wheat flour pressed through perforations into long tubes, and dried: a medley: something fanciful and extravagant: in the 18th century, a dandy: a rock-hopper or crested penguin: — *pl.* **macarō'ni(e)s.** — *adj.* **macaronic** (*-ron'-ik*) in a kind of burlesque verse, intermixing modern words Latinised, or Latin words modernised, with genuine Latin — loosely, verse in mingled tongues. — *n.* (often in *pl.*) macaronic verse. — *adv.* **macaron'ically.** — **macaroni cheese** macaroni served with a cheese sauce. [It. *maccaroni* (now *maccheroni*), pl. of *maccarone,* prob. — *maccare,* to crush.]

macaroon *mak-ə-rōōn', n.* a sweet biscuit made of almonds. [Fr. *macaron* — It. *maccarone* (see above).]

macassar-oil *mə-kas'ər-oil, n.* an oil once used for the hair, got from the seeds of a sapindaceous tree *Schleichera trijuga*, or from ylang-ylang flowers, or other Eastern source. [*Macassar* or Mangkasara in Celebes.]

macaw *mə-kö', n.* any of the large, long-tailed, gaudy tropical American parrots of the genus *Ara*. [Port. *macao.*]

macaw-tree, -palm *mə-kö'trē, -päm, ns.* a South American palm (*Acrocomia*) whose nuts yield a violet-scented oil. — Also **maco'ya, macahuba** (*mä-kä-ōō'ba*). [Sp. *macoya,* from Arawak; Port. *macauba,* from Tupí.]

Maccabaean, Maccabean *mak-ə-bē'ən, adj.* pertaining to Judas *Maccabaeus*, or to his family the Hasmonaeans or *Macc'abees*, who freed the Jewish nation from the persecutions of Antiochus Epiphanes, king of Syria, about 166 B.C. (1 Macc., 2 Macc.).

macchie *mak'kyä, n.pl.* Italian form of **maquis**, a thicket.

mace[1] *mās, n.* a metal or metal-headed war-club, often spiked: a somewhat similar staff used as a mark of authority: a mace-bearer: a light, flat-headed stick formerly used in billiards: a mallet used by a currier in dressing leather. — *n.* **mā'cer** a mace-bearer: in Scotland, an usher in a law-court. — **mace'-bearer** one who carries the mace in a procession, or before men in authority. [O.Fr. *mace* (Fr. *masse*) — hypothetical L. *matea,* whence L. dim. *mateola,* a kind of tool.]

mace[2] *mās, n.* a spice which is ground from the dried layer immediately within a nutmeg drupe and outside shell and kernel. — **mace'-ale** ale flavoured with mace. [M.E. *macis* (mistakenly supposed to be a plural) — Fr.; of uncertain origin.]

Mace® *mās, n.* a type of tear gas (also **Chemical Mace**). — *v.t.* (also without *cap.*) to spray, attack, or disable with Mace.

macédoine *ma-sā-dwän', -sə-, n.* a mixture of diced vegetables or of fruit, sometimes diced, in syrup or jelly: a mixture or medley. [Fr., lit. Macedonia.]

maceranduba. Same as **massaranduba.**

macerate *mas'ər-āt, v.t.* to steep: to soften, or remove the soft parts of, by steeping: to wear down, esp. by fasting: to mortify. — *v.i.* to undergo maceration: to waste away. — *ns.* **macerā'tion; mac'erātor** one who macerates: a paper-pulping apparatus. [L. *mācerāre, -ātum,* to steep.]

machair *ma'hhər, n.* a low-lying sandy beach or boggy links affording some pasturage. [Gael.]

Machairodus *ma-kī'rə-dəs,* **Machaerodus** *-kē', ns.* the sabre-toothed tiger of prehistoric times. — *n.* and *adj.* **machair'odont.** [Gr. *machaira,* a sword, *odous, odontos,* a tooth.]

machan *ma-chän', n.* a shooting-platform up a tree. [Hindi *macān.*]

machete *ma-shet'ē, ma-chä'tā, n.* a heavy knife or cutlass used by the Cubans, etc. [Sp.]

Machiavellian *mak-i-ə-vel'yən, adj.* destitute of political morality, ruled by expediency only: crafty, perfidious in conduct, activity. — *n.* one who imitates Niccolo *Machiavelli*, statesman and writer, of Florence (1469–1527): any cunning and unprincipled statesman. — *ns.* **Machiavell'ianism, Machiavell'ism** the principles taught by Machiavelli, or conduct regulated by them: cunning statesmanship.

machicolation *ma-chik-ō-lā'shən*, (*archit.*) *n.* a space between the corbels supporting a parapet, or an opening in the floor of a projecting gallery, for dropping solids or liquids on an attacking enemy: a structure with such openings: the provision of such openings or structures. — *v.t.* **machic′olate** to provide or build with machicolations. — *adj.* **machic′olated.** [Fr. *mâchicoulis.*]

machinate *mak′i-nāt, mash′*, *v.i.* to form a plot or scheme esp. for doing harm. — *ns.* **machinā′tion** act of machinating: (often in *pl.*) an intrigue or plot; **mach′inātor** one who machinates. [L. *māchinārī, -ātus* — *māchina* — Gr. *mēchanē*, contrivance.]

machine *mə-shēn′*, *n.* any artificial means or contrivance: any instrument for the conversion of motion: an engine: a vehicle, esp. a motor-cycle: one who can do only what he is told: a contrivance by which a god might descend upon the stage: a supernatural agent employed in carrying on the action of a poem: an organised system: a political party organisation (*U.S.*; also **party machine**). — *v.t.* to use machinery for: to print, sew, or make by machinery. — *ns.* **machin′ery** machines in general: the working parts of a machine: combined means for keeping anything in action, or for producing a desired result: supernatural agents in a poem: **machin′ist** a constructor of machines: one well versed in machinery: one who works a machine. — **machine code, language** instructions for processing data, put into a form that can be directly understood and obeyed by a (specific) computer; **machine′-gun** an automatic quick-firing gun on a stable but portable mounting. — *v.t.* to shoot at with a machine-gun. — *adj.* with the speed or rhythm of a machine-gun. — **machine′-gunner; machine intelligence** computer science and allied studies. — *adj.* **machine′-made** made by machinery. — **machine′man** a man who manages the working of a machine; **machine′-pis′tol** a small submachine-gun. — *adj.* **machine′-read′able** (of data) in a form that can be directly processed by a computer. — **machine′-rul′er** an instrument for ruling lines on paper; **machine screw** a screw, usu. not more than ¼ inch in diameter, with a machine-cut thread, used with a nut, or in tapped holes in metal parts; **machine′-shop** a workshop where metal, etc., is machined to shape; **machine′-tool** a power-driven machine, as lathe, milling machine, drill, press, for shaping metal, wood, or plastic material; **machine′-work** work done by a machine. [Fr., — L. *māchina* — Gr. *mēchanē*, akin to *mēchos*, contrivance.]

machismo. See **macho.**

Mach number *mähh, mahh, num′bər*, the ratio of the air speed (i.e. speed in relation to the air) of an aircraft to the velocity of sound under the given conditions. — *n.* **mach′meter** an instrument for measuring Mach number. [Named after Ernst *Mach*, Austrian physicist and philosopher (1838–1916).]

macho *mach′ō*, *adj.* aggressively male: ostentatiously virile. — *n.* a man of this type (*pl.* **mach′os**): machismo. — *n.* **machismo** (*ma-chiz′mō, -chēz′, -kiz′, -kēz′*) the cult of male virility and masculine pride. [Sp. *macho*, male — L. *masculus.*]

machree *mə-hrē′*, (*Anglo-Ir.*) my dear, my love. [Ir. *mo chroidhe*, of my heart, *mo*, my, and gen. of *croi*, heart.]

Machtpolitik *mähht′pō-lē-tēk′*, (Ger.) *n.* power politics, esp. the doctrine that a state should use force to attain its ends.

machzor. See **mahzor.**

macintosh. See **mackintosh.**

mack[1]. Shortened form of **mac(k)intosh.**

mack[2] *mak*, (*slang*) *n.* a pimp, pander. [Shortening of obsolete **mackerel.**]

mackerel *mak′ər-əl, n.* a food fish (*Scomber*), bluish green, with wavy cross-streaks above, and silvery below: a bawd or pander (*obs.*). — **mack′erel-breeze′** a breeze that ruffles the surface of the sea and so favours

mackerel fishing; **mack′erel-guide′** the common garfish, which visits the coasts just before the mackerel; **mack′erel-midge′** a small rockling; **mack′erel-shark′** the porbeagle; **mack′erel-sky′** a sky with clouds broken into long, thin, white, parallel masses. [O.Fr. *makerel* (Fr. *maquereau*).]

mackinaw *mak′in-ö, n.* an American Indian's blanket: a short heavy woollen coat: a flat-bottomed lake-boat. [*Mackinaw*, an island between Lakes Huron and Michigan.]

mac(k)intosh *mak′in-tosh, n.* waterproof cloth: a waterproof overcoat: — *contr.* **mac(k)** (*mak*). [From Charles *Macintosh* (1766–1843), a Scottish chemist, the patentee.]

mackle *mak′l, n.* a spot or blemish in printing, by a double impression, wrinkling, etc. — *v.t.* to spot, blur. [See next.]

macle *mak′l, n.* a dark spot in a crystal: chiastolite: a twin crystal. — *adj.* **macled** (*mak′ld*) spotted. [Fr. *macle* — L. *macula*, spot.]

Macmillanite *mək-mil′ən-īt, n.* a Cameronian or Reformed Presbyterian. [From Rev. John *Macmillan* (1670–1753), who helped to form the church.]

Mâcon *mä-k̃ɔ, n.* a burgundy from Mâcon district.

maconochie *mə-kon′ə-hhi,* (*mil.*) *n.* tinned meat and vegetable stew: tinned food. [Packer's name.]

macoya. See **macaw-tree.**

macramé, macrami *mə-krä′mi, n.* a fringe or trimming of knotted thread: knotted threadwork. [App. Turk. *maqrama*, towel.]

macro- *mak-rō-, -ro-*, in composition, long, great, sometimes interchanging with *mega-*. — *ns.* **mac′rō** (*comput.*) a macroinstruction: — *pl.* **mac′ros; macro-axis** (*mak′rō-aks′is; crystal.*) the longer lateral axis. — *adj.* **macrō′bian** (Gr. *bios*, life) long-lived. — *n.pl.* **macrobiō′ta** the larger organisms in the soil. — *n.* **macrobiote** (*-bī′ōt*) a long-liver. — *adj.* **macrobiotic** (*-bī-ot′ik*) prolonging life: long-lived: (of a seed) able to remain alive in dormant state for years: relating to longevity, or to macrobiotics. — *n. sing.* **macrobiot′ics** the art or science of prolonging life: a cult partly concerned with diet, foods regarded as pure being vegetable substances grown and prepared without chemicals or processing. — *n.* **macrocar′pa** an evergreen conifer, *Cupressus macrocarpa*, planted esp. for ornamentation and as a wind-break. — *adjs.* **macrocephalic** (*-si-fal′ik*), **macrocephalous** (*-sef′ə-ləs*). — *ns.* **macrocephaly** (*-sef′ə-li*; Gr. *kephalē*, head) largeness, or abnormal largeness, of head; **mac′rocode** (*comput.*) a macroinstruction; **mac′rocopy** an enlarged copy of printed material for use by people with weak sight; **mac′rocosm** (*-kozm*; Gr. *kosmos*, world) the great world: the whole universe — opp. to *microcosm*. — *adj.* **macrocos′mic.** — *adv.* **macrocos′mically.** — *n.* **mac′rocycle** a macrocyclic organic molecule or compound. — *adj.* **macrocy′clic** being or having a ring structure with a large number of atoms. — *n.* **mac′rocyte** (*-sīt*; Gr. *kytos*, a vessel, container) an abnormally large red blood cell associated with some forms of anaemia. — *adjs.* **macrodactyl** (*-dak′til*), **macrodactylic** (*-til′ik*), **macrodactylous** (*-dak′til-əs*; Gr. *daktylos*, finger, toe) long-fingered, long-toed. — *ns.* **macrodac′tyly** condition of being macrodactylous; **macrodiag′onal** (*crystal.*) the longer lateral axis; **macrodome** (*crystal.*) a dome parallel to the macrodiagonal. — *n.sing.* **macroeconomics** (*-ēk-ən-om′iks, -ek′*) the study of economics on a large scale or of large units. — *adj.* **macroeconom′ic.** — *ns.* **macroevolū′tion** major evolutionary developments over a long period of time, such as have given rise to the taxonomic groups above the species level; **mac′rofauna, mac′roflora** animals, plants, that are visible to the naked eye; **mac′rofossil** a fosssil large enough to be seen with the naked eye; **macrogamete′** (or *-gam′ēt*) a female gamete; **mac′roinstruction** (*comput.*) an instruction written in a programming language, usu. in assembly language, which generates and is replaced by a series of microinstructions; **macrol′ogy** much talk with little to say. — *adj.* **macromolec'ular.** — *n.* **macromol'ecule** a large molecule, esp. one formed from a number of simpler molecules; **mac'ron** (U.S. *mā'*; Gr., *makros*) a straight line placed over a vowel to show it is long (as in *ē*) — opp. to *breve*, the mark of a short vowel (*ĕ*); **mac'rophage** (*-fāj*) any of the large phagocytic cells sited in the walls of blood vessels and found in connective tissue, usu. immobile but stimulated into mobility by inflammation; **macropin'akoid, mac'roprism** (*crystal.*) a pinakoid, prism, parallel to the macrodiagonal; **mac'ropod** an animal of the **Macropod'idae** (*-ē*; Gr. *pous, podos*, foot), the family of marsupials comprising the kangeroos and related animals. — *adjs.* **macrop'terous** (Gr. *pteron*, a wing) long-winged: long-finned; **macroscop'ic** visible to the naked eye — opp. to *microscopic.* — *adv.* **macroscop'ically.** — *ns.* **macrosporan'gium** (*pl.* **-ia**), **mac'rospore** same as **megasporangium, -spore; Macrozā'mia** (Gr. *zamia*, loss) a genus of Australian cycads: (without *cap.*) a plant of this genus. — *n.pl.* **Macrura** (*makrōō'rə*; Gr. *ourā*, tail) a group of decapod crustaceans including lobsters, shrimps, prawns, etc. — *adjs.* **macru'ral, macru'rous** long-tailed. [Gr. *makros*, long, also great.]

mactation *mak-tā'shən, n.* slaying, esp. of a sacrificial victim. [L. *mactātiō, -ōnis.*]

macula *mak'ū-lə, n.* a spot, as on the skin, the sun, a mineral, etc.: — *pl.* **maculae** (*-lē*). — *adj.* **mac'ular** spotted: patchy: of or pertaining to the macula lutea. — *v.t.* **mac'ulate** to spot, to defile. — *adj.* (*-lit*) spotted: soiled. — *ns.* **maculā'tion** act of spotting, a spot; **mac'ulāture** an impression taken from an engraved plate to remove the ink before inking afresh; **mac'ule** a macula: a mackle. — *adj.* **mac'ulose** spotted. — **macula lutea** (*lōō'ti-ə*; L. *luteus*, yellow) the yellow-spot (q.v.). [L. *macula*, a spot.]

mad *mad, adj.* (*compar.* **madd'er;** *superl.* **madd'est**) disordered in intellect: insane: proceeding from madness: extremely and recklessly foolish: infatuated: frantic with pain, violent passion, or appetite: furious with anger (*coll.*, orig. *U.S.*): extravagantly playful or exuberant: rabid. — *v.t.* (*Shak.*) to drive mad. — *v.i.* (*arch.*) to be mad: to act madly. — *v.t.* **madd'en** to make mad: to enrage. — *v.i.* to become mad: to act as one mad. — *adj.* **madd'ening** driving to madness: making very angry: extremely annoying. — *adv.* **madd'eningly.** — *adj.* **madd'ing** distracted, acting madly. — *adv.* **madd'ingly.** — *n.* **mad'ling** a mad person. — *adv.* **mad'ly** insanely: frantically: extremely (*coll.*). — *n.* **mad'ness.** — *adjs.* **mad'brain, mad'brained** (*Shak.*) disordered in brain or mind: rash: hot-headed; **mad'-bred** (*Shak.*) bred in madness or heat of passion. — **mad'cap** a person who acts madly: a wild, rash, hot-headed person: an exuberantly frolicsome person. — *adj.* fond of wild and reckless or extravagantly merry action. — **mad'-doc'tor** formerly, one who studied and treated diseases of mad people; **Mad Hatter** a character in Lewis Carroll's *Alice in Wonderland* given to irrational behaviour and logic-chopping (see also **hatter** under **hat**); **mad'house** formerly, a house for mad persons, an asylum: a place where there is noise, confusion, and unpredictable behaviour; **mad'man** a man who is mad: a foolish and reckless man; **mad'woman; mad'wort** a plant believed to cure canine madness — Alyssum, *Asperugo*, etc. — **go mad** to become demented; **like mad** madly, furiously; **mad as a hatter** see **hat**. [O.E. *gemǣd(e)d*; O.Sax. *gimēd*, foolish.]

madam *mad'əm, n.* a courteous form of address to a lady, esp. an elderly or a married one: (with *cap.*) the word of address to a woman in a formal letter: a woman of rank, station, or pretension: the mistress of a household (*arch.*): a formidable woman: a capricious or autocratic woman: a general term of opprobrium for a woman: a concubine (*obs.*): the woman in charge of a brothel: (with *cap.*) prefixed to a name instead of Mrs or Miss (in U.S. to distinguish mother-in-law from daughter-in-law) (*obs.*): — *pl.* **mad'ams;** in sense (2)

above, **mesdames** (*mā-däm'*). — *v.t.* to address as madam. — *n.* **madame** (*ma-däm', mad'əm;* usu. *cap.*) prefixed instead of Mrs to a French or other foreign woman's name: used also of palmists, milliners, and musicians: — *pl.* **mesdames.** [Fr. *ma*, my, *dame*, lady — L. *mea domina.*]

mad-apple *mad'-ap-l, n.* the fruit of the egg-plant: the Dead Sea apple: a gall produced by a gall-wasp (*Cynips insana*) on an oak in the East. [From some form of mod. L. *melongēna*, It. *melanzana; mālum insānum*, transl. as mad apple.]

madarosis *mad-ə-rō'sis, n.* loss of hair, esp. of the eyebrows or eyelashes. [Gr. *madarōsis* — *madaros*, bald, *madaein*, to fall off.]

madder *mad'ər, n.* a plant (*Rubia tinctorum*) whose root affords a red dye, or other species of Rubia. — **madd'er-lake** a colour mixed either with oil or water, made from madder. — **field madder** a minute lilacflowered plant (*Sherardia arvensis*) of the same family. [O.E. *mæddre, mædere;* O.N. *mathra,* Du. *mede,* later *meed, mee.*]

made *mād, pa.t.* and *pa.p.* of **make** and *adj.* — **made dish** a dish of various ingredients, often recooked; **made ground** ground formed by artificial filling in; **made man, woman** one whose prosperity is assured; **made road** one with deliberately made surface, not merely formed by traffic: a road with a metalled surface as opposed to a gravel surface. — **be made** (*coll.*) to have one's prosperity assured; **made to measure, order** made to individual requirements; **made up** put together, finished: parcelled up: dressed for a part, disguised: painted and powdered: meretricious: artificial, invented: consummate (*Shak.*).

madefy *mad'i-fī, v.t.* to moisten. — *n.* **madefac'tion.** [L. *madefacĕre, -factum* — *madēre*, to be wet.]

Madeira *mə-dē'rə, ma-dā'ra, n.* a rich wine of the sherry class produced in *Madeira.* — **Madeira cake** a variety of sponge-cake.

madeleine *mad-len', n.* a small, shell-shaped rich cake. [Fr., prob. named after *Madeleine* Paulmier, 19th-cent. French cook.]

Madelenian. Same as **Magdalenian.**

mademoiselle *mad-mwə-zel', n.* a form of address to an unmarried French or other foreign woman: (with *cap.*) prefixed to a name, Miss (*pl.* **Mesdemoiselles** *mād-*): a French governess. — Contracted to **mamselle** (*mamzel'*), *pl.* **mamselles** (*-zelz'*). [Fr. *ma*, my, and *demoiselle;* see **damsel.**]

maderise, -ize *mad'ə-rīz, v.i.* (of a white wine) to become rusty in colour and flat in taste, as a result of absorbing too much oxygen during maturation. — *n.* **maderisā'tion, -z-.** [Fr. *maderiser,* from the colour of the wine Madeira.]

madge¹ *maj, n.* a leaden hammer. [Woman's name.]

madge² *maj, n.* the barn owl: the magpie. [App. from the woman's name.]

madid *mad'id, adj.* wet, dank. [L. *madidus* — *madēre,* to be wet; akin to Gr. *madaein.*]

Madonna *mə-don'ə, n.* my lady (*Shak.*): the Virgin Mary, esp. as seen in works of art. — *adj.* **madonn'aish.** — *adv.* **madonn'awise** after the fashion of the Madonna, esp. in the arrangement of a woman's hair. — **Madonn'a-lil'y** the white lily. [It., lit. my lady — L. *mea domina.*]

madoqua *mad'ō-kwə, n.* a very small Abyssinian antelope. [Amharic *midaqua.*]

madras *mə-dräs', n.* a large, usu. bright, handkerchief worn on the head by Negroes, formerly exported from *Madras:* a fine cotton fabric: sunn.

madras(s)a(h) *ma-dras'a,* **medresseh** *mə-dres'ə, ns.* a Muslim college: a mosque school. [Ar. *madrasah.*]

madrepore *mad'ri-pōr, -pör, n.* a coral of the common reef-building type. — *adj.* **madreporic** (*-por'ik*). — *n.* **mad'reporite,** or **madreporic plate,** in echinoderms, a perforated plate serving as opening to the stone canal. [It. *madrepora* — *madre,* mother — L. *māter,* and Gr. *pōros,* a soft stone, stalactite, etc., or L. *porus,* a pore.]

madrigal *mad'ri-gəl, n.* an unaccompanied song in several parts in counterpoint (*mus.*): a lyrical poem suitable for such treatment. — *adj.* **madrigā'lian.** — *n.* **mad'-rigalist.** [It. *madrigale*, prob. from L.L. *mātricālis*, primitive, simple (— L. *mātrix*, see **matrix**), altered under the influence of It. *mandria*, a herd — L. *mandra* — Gr. *mandrā*, a stall, stable, sty, etc.]

madroño *ma-drō'nyō, n.* a handsome evergreen Arbutus tree of North California: — *pl.* **madrō'ños.** — Also **madrō'ña** (*-nyə*). [Sp. *madroño.*]

madzoon. See **matzoon.**

mae. See **mo**[1].

Maecenas *mē-sē'nas, n.* a Roman knight who befriended Virgil and Horace: any rich patron of art or literature. [L. *Maecēnās, -ātis.*]

maelstrom *māl'strom, n.* a particularly powerful whirlpool: (with *cap.*) a well-known whirlpool off the coast of Norway: a confused, disordered state of affairs: any resistless overpowering influence for destruction. [Du. (now *maalstroom*), a whirlpool.]

maenad *mē'nad, n.* a female follower of Bacchus: a woman beside herself with frenzy. — *adj.* **maenad'ic** bacchanalian: furious. [Gr. *mainas, -ados,* raving — *mainesthai,* to be mad.]

Maeonian *mē-ō'ni-ən, adj.* and *n.* Lydian. — *n.* **Maeonides** (*mē-on'i-dēz*) Homer, as a supposed native of Lydia. [Gr. *Maiŏnia,* an old name for Lydia.]

maestoso *mä-es-tō'sō, mī-stō'sō,* (*mus.*) *adj.* and *adv.* with dignity or majesty. [It.]

maestro *mī'strō, mä-es'trō, n.* a master, esp. an eminent musical composer or conductor: — *pl.* **maestros** (*mī'strōz*), **maestri** (*mä-es'trē*). [It.]

Mae West *mā west,* an airman's pneumatic life-jacket. [From its supposed resemblance, when inflated, to the figure of an American actress of that name.]

Maffia. See **Mafia.**

maffick *maf'ik, v.i.* to rejoice with hysterical boisterousness. — *ns.* **maff'icker, maff'icking.** [By back-formation from *Mafeking,* treated jocularly as a gerund or participle, from the scenes in the streets of London on the news of the relief of the town (1900).]

maffled *maf'ld,* (*coll.*) *adj.* confused in the intellect. — *n.* **maff'lin(g)** a simpleton.

Mafia, Maffia *mä'fē-ə, n.* a spirit of opposition to the law in Sicily, hence a preference for private and unofficial rather than legal justice: a secret criminal society originating in Sicily, controlling many illegal activities, e.g., gambling, narcotics, etc., in many parts of the world, and particularly active in the U.S. (also called **Cosa Nostra**): (also without *cap.*) any group considered to be like the Mafia, e.g. with regard to its criminal and unscrupulous use of power, fear, etc. to gain its ends. — *n.* **Mafioso** (*-fē-ō'sō, -zō*) a member of the Mafia (also without *cap.*): — *pl.* **Mafiosi** (*-sē, -zē*). [Sicilian Italian *mafia.*]

ma foi *ma fwa,* (Fr.) my goodness (*lit.* upon my faith).

mag[1] *mag,* (*arch. slang*) *n.* a halfpenny. — Also **maik, make** (*māk*).

mag[2] *mag,* (*dial.*) *v.i.* to chatter. — *v.t.* to tease: (*Scott* **magg**) to steal. — *n.* chatter: the magpie: the long-tailed titmouse. — *n.pl.* **mag(g)s** (*Scot.*; perh. **mag**[1]) a gratuity: the free allowance granted to some workers, esp. drinks for brewery employees. — **mags'man** a street swindler. [From the name *Margaret.*]

mag[3]. Short for **magazine** (periodical publication) (*coll.*).

magazine *mag-ə-zēn', also mag', n.* a storehouse: a place for military stores: a ship's powder-room: a compartment in a rifle for holding extra cartridges: a periodical publication or broadcast containing articles, stories, etc., by various people. — **magazine'-gun, -rifle** one from which a succession of shots can be fired without reloading. [Fr. *magasin* — It. *magazzino* — Ar. *makhāzin,* pl. of *makhzan,* a store-house.]

Magdalen, Magdalene *mag'də-lən, -lēn* (in the names of Oxford and Cambridge colleges, *mŏd'lin*) *ns.* (without *cap.*) a repentant prostitute: an institution for receiving such persons (abbrev. for *Magdalene hospital, asy-*

lum). [From Mary *Magdalene,* i.e. (Gr.) *Magdalēnē,* of Magdala (Luke viii. 2), on the assumption that she was the woman of Luke vii. 37–50.]

Magdalenian, Madelenian *ma(g)d-ə-lē'ni-ən, adjs.* belonging to an upper Palaeolithic culture that succeeded the Solutrean and preceded the Azilian. [La *Madeleine,* a cave on the Vézère.]

Magdeburg hemispheres *mag'de-bûrg hem'i-sfērz,* two hemispherical cups held together by atmospheric pressure when the air is pumped out from between them. [Invented at *Magdeburg* in Germany.]

mage *māj.* See **magus.**

Magellanic clouds *mag-el-an'ik,* or *maj-, klowdz,* two galaxies in the southern hemisphere, appearing to the naked eye like detached portions of the Milky Way, the nearest galaxies to the earth.

Magen David *mä'gän dä'vēd,* the Star of David. — Also **Mogen David** (*mō'gən dö'vid*). [Heb., shield of David.]

magenta *mə-jen'tə, n.* the dyestuff fuchsine: its colour, a reddish purple. — *adj.* reddish purple. [From its discovery about the time of the battle of *Magenta* in North Italy, 1859.]

magg. See **mag**[2].

maggot *mag'ət, n.* a legless grub, esp. of a fly: a fad or crotchet: a whimsical tune or impromptu (*obs.*). — *adj.* **magg'oty** full of maggots: crotchety: very drunk (*slang*). — *n.* **maggotorium** (*-tō', -tö'*) a place where maggots are bred for sale to fishermen. [Poss. a modification of M.E. *maddok, mathek,* dim., see **mawk.**]

maggot-pie. See **magpie.**

maggs. See **mag**[2].

magi, magian. See **magus.**

magic *maj'ik, n.* the art of producing marvellous results by compelling the aid of spirits, or by using the secret forces of nature, such as the power supposed to reside in certain objects as 'givers of life': enchantment: sorcery: art of producing illusions by legerdemain: a secret or mysterious power over the imagination or will. — *v.t.* to affect by, or as if by, magic: — *pr.p.* **mag'icking;** *pa.t.* and *pa.p.* **mag'icked.** — *adjs.* **mag'ic** pertaining to, used in, or done by, magic: causing wonderful or startling results: marvellous, exciting (*coll.*); **mag'ical** pertaining to magic: wonderful, enchanting. — *adv.* **mag'ically.** — *n.* **magician** (*mə-jish'ən*) one skilled in magic: a wizard: an enchanter: a wonder-worker. — **magic bullet** a drug, etc., which is capable of destroying bacteria, cancer cells, etc., without adversely affecting the host; **magic carpet** one that, in fairy stories, can transport people magically through the air; **magic eye** a miniature cathode ray tube in a radio receiver which helps in tuning the receiver by indicating, by means of varying areas of luminescence and shadow, the accuracy of the tuning; **magic lantern** an apparatus for projecting pictures on slides upon a screen; **magic mushroom** any of various mushrooms, e.g. *Psilocybe mexicana,* which contain a hallucinogen; **magic square** a square filled with rows of figures so arranged that the sums of all the rows will be the same, perpendicularly, horizontally or diagonally — as the square formed from the three rows 2, 7, 6; 9, 5, 1; 4, 3, 8; **magic circles, cubes, cylinders, spheres,** are similarly arranged. — **black magic** the black art, magic by means of evil spirits; **natural magic** the art of working wonders by a superior knowledge of the powers of nature: power of investing a work of art with an atmosphere of imagination: legerdemain; **sympathetic magic** magic aiming at the production of effects by mimicry, as bringing rain by libations, injuring a person by melting his image or sticking pins in it; **white magic** magic without the aid of the devil. [Gr. *magikē* (*technē*), magic (art). See **magus.**]

magilp, megilp *mə-gilp', n.* a vehicle used by oil-painters, consisting of linseed-oil and mastic varnish. [Origin unknown.]

Maginot-minded *mä'zhē-nō-mīnd'id, adj.* over-concerned

with the defensive (*mil.*): static in ideas. [From the abortive French Maginot Line fortifications (1927–35) along the German border (war minister André *Maginot*; 1877–1932).]

magister *mə-jis'tər, n.* one licensed to teach in a mediaeval university: still used in the degree titles of *Magister Artium,* etc. — *adj.* **magisterial** (*maj-is-tē'ri-əl*) pertaining or suitable to, or in the manner of, a teacher, master artist, or magistrate: of the rank of a magistrate: authoritative: dictatorial: of a magistery. — *adv.* **magistē'rially.** — *ns.* **magistē'rialness; magistē'rium** the philosopher's stone: teaching authority or function; **magistery** (*maj'is-tə-ri*) in alchemy, a transmuting agent, as the philosopher's stone: a product of transmutation: a precipitate: any sovereign remedy: magisterium; **mag'istracy** (*-trə-si*) the office or dignity of a magistrate: a body of magistrates. — *adj.* **magistral** (*mə-jis'trəl,* or *maj'is-*) of or pertaining to a master: masterly: authoritative: specially prescribed for a particular case as a medicine: effectual: guiding or determining the other positions (*fort.*). — Also *n.* — *ns.* **magistrand** (*maj'*) at Scottish universities, an arts student ready to proceed to graduation, now only at St Andrews and Aberdeen; **mag'istrate** one who has power of putting the law in force, esp. a justice of the peace, a provost, or a bailie. — *adjs.* **magistratic** (*-trat'ik*), **-al.** — *n.* **mag'istrature.** — **Magister Artium** (*mə-jis'tər är'shi-əm*) Master of Arts. [L. *magister,* master.]

Maglemosian *mag-li-mō'zi-ən,* (*archaeol.*) *adj.* of a culture represented by finds at *Maglemose* in Denmark, transitional between Palaeolithic and Neolithic.

maglev *mag'lev, adj.* of or pertaining to a railway, train, carriage, etc., operating by *magnetic lev*itation (q.v.).

magma *mag'mə, n.* a pasty or doughy mass: molten or pasty rock material: a glassy base of a rock: — *pl.* **mag'mata** (*-mə-tə*), **mag'mas.** — *adj.* **magmatic** (*-mat'ik*). [Gr. *magma, -atos,* a thick unguent.]

Magna Carta (Charta) *mag'nə kär'tə,* the Great Charter obtained from King John, 1215, the basis of English political and personal liberty: any document establishing rights. [L.]

magna cum laude *mag'nə kum lö'dē, mag'nä kōōm low'de,* (L.) with great distinction (*laus, laudis,* praise).

magnalium *mag-nā'li-əm, n.* a light, strong, easily-worked, and rust-resisting alloy of *magn*esium and *al*uminium used in aircraft construction, etc.

magnanimity *mag-nə-nim'i-ti, n.* greatness of soul: that quality of mind which raises a person above all that is mean or unjust: generosity. — *adj.* **magnanimous** (*-nan'*). — *adv.* **magnan'imously.** [L. *magnanimitās* — *magnus,* great, *animus,* mind.]

magnate *mag'nāt, -nit, n.* a noble: a man of rank or wealth, or of power. [L. *magnās, -ātis* — *magnus,* great.]

magnes *mag'nēz* (*arch.*) *n.* lodestone. — **mag'nesstone** (*Spens.*). [L. and Gr. *magnēs.*]

magnesium *mag-nē'z(h)i-əm, -z(h)yəm, -shi-əm, -shyəm, n.* a metallic element (symbol Mg; at. numb. 12) of a bright, silver-white colour, burning with a dazzling white light. — *n.* **magnē'sia** an imagined substance sought by the alchemists (*obs.*): manganese (*obs.*): a light white powder, oxide of magnesium: basic magnesium carbonate, used as a medicine. — *adj.* **magnē'sian** belonging to, containing, or resembling magnesia. — *n.* **magnesite** (*mag'nəs-īt*) native magnesium carbonate. — **Magnesian Limestone** dolomite rock: a division of the Permian of England. [From *Magnesia,* in Thessaly.]

magnet *mag'nit, n.* the lodestone (**natural magnet**): a bar or piece of steel, etc., to which the properties of the lodestone have been imparted: anything or anyone that attracts (*fig.*). — *adjs.* **magnetic** (*mag-net'ik*), **-al** pertaining to the magnet: having, or capable of acquiring, the properties of the magnet: attractive: strongly affecting others by personality: hypnotic. — *adv.* **magnet'ically.** — *n.* **magnetician** (*-ish'ən*) one

versed in magnetism. — *n.sing.* **magnet'ics** the science of magnetism. — *adj.* **magnetīs'able, -z-.** — *n.* **magnetīsā'tion, -z-.** — *v.t.* **mag'netise, -ize** to render magnetic: to attract as if by a magnet: to hypnotise. — *ns.* **mag'netīser, -z-; mag'netism** the cause of the attractive power of the magnet: the phenomena connected with magnets: the science which treats of the properties of the magnet: attraction: influence of personality; **mag'-netist** one skilled in magnetism; **mag'netite** magnetic iron ore (Fe$_3$O$_4$), called lodestone when polar; **magneto** (*mag-nē'tō;* for *magneto-electric machine*) a small generator with permanent magnet, used for ignition in an internal-combustion engine, etc.: — *pl.* **magnē'tos.** — **magneto-** in composition, magnetic: pertaining to magnetism: magneto-electric. — *adjs.* **magnē'to-elec'tric, -al** pertaining to magneto-electricity. — *ns.* **magnē'to-electric'ity** electricity produced by the action of magnets: the science thereof; **magnē'tograph** an instrument for recording the variations of the magnetic elements. — *adj.* **magnē'tohydrodynam'ic.** — *n.sing.* **magnē'tohydrodynam'ics** a branch of mathematical physics dealing with interactions between an electrically-conducting fluid (such as an ionised gas) and a magnetic field: the practical application of such interactions to producing magnetohydrodynamic power by means of a **magnetohydrodynamic generator.** — *ns.* **magnetometer** (*mag-ni-tom'i-tər*) an instrument for measuring the strength or direction of a magnetic field, esp. the earth's; **magnetom'etry.** — *adj.* **magnetomō'tive** producing a magnetic flux. — *n.* **magnē'ton** (or *mag'ni-ton*) a natural unit of magnetic moment. — *n.sing.* **magnēto-op'tics** the study of the influence of magnetism on light. — *ns.* **magnet'osphere** the region surrounding the earth or other body corresponding to its magnetic field; **magnē'to-stric'tion** (or *-net'*) the change in dimensions produced in a magnetic material, esp. nickel, when it is magnetised; **mag'netron** a vacuum tube combined with a magnetic field to deflect electrons. — **magnet (high) school** in the U.S., a school which in addition to providing a general education specialises in teaching in one particular subject area such as science, languages or performing arts. — **animal magnetism** Mesmer's name for hypnotism: power to hypnotise: according to Christian Science, the false belief that mortal mind exists (and has power to transfer thoughts): sexual power of attraction due entirely to physical attributes; **artificial magnet** a magnet made by rubbing with other magnets; **bar magnet** a magnet in the form of a bar; **horse-shoe magnet** a magnet bent like a horse-shoe; **magnetic battery** several magnets placed with their like poles together, so as to act with great force; **magnetic bottle** the containment of a plasma during thermonuclear experiments by applying a specific pattern of magnetic fields; **magnetic curves** the curves formed by iron-filings about the poles of a magnet; **magnetic disc** (*comput.*) a disc, disc file; **magnetic drum** (*comput.*) a storage device consisting of a rotating cylinder with a magnetic coating; **magnetic equator** the line round the earth where the magnetic needle remains horizontal; **magnetic field** the space over which magnetic force is felt; **magnetic fluid** a hypothetical fluid formerly assumed to explain the phenomena of magnetism; **magnetic flux** the surface integral of the product of the permeability of the medium and the magnetic field intensity perpendicular to the surface; **magnetic flux density** the product of the field intensity and the permeability of the medium; **magnetic forming** use of magnetic fields to shape metal; **magnetic induction** induced magnetisation in magnetic material: magnetic flux density; **magnetic ink** ink with magnetic quality used, e.g. in printing cheques that are to be sorted by machine; **magnetic levitation** suspension of e.g. a train above a track by means of a magnetic field; **magnetic meridian** the vertical plane through the magnetic needle; **magnetic mine** a mine sunk to the sea-bottom, detonated by a pivoted magnetic needle when a ship approaches; **magnetic** monopole see **monopole; magnetic needle** the light bar in the mariner's compass which, because it is magnetised, points always to the north; **magnetic north** the direction indicated by the magnetic needle; **magnetic poles** two nearly opposite points on the earth's surface, where the dip of the needle is 90°; **magnetic storm** a disturbance in the magnetism of the earth; **magnetic tape** flexible plastic tape, coated on one side with magnetic material, used to register for later reproduction television images, or sound, or computer data; **permanent magnet** a magnet that keeps its magnetism after the force which magnetised it has been removed; **personal magnetism** power of a personality to make itself felt and to exercise influence; **terrestrial magnetism** the magnetic properties possessed by the earth as a whole. [Through O.Fr. or L., from Gr. *magnētis* (*lithos*), Magnesian (stone), from *Magnēsiā*, in Lydia or Thessaly.]

magnifiable. See **magnify.**

magnific *mag-nif'ik*, **magnifical** -*əl*, (*arch.*) *adjs.* magnificent: exalted: pompous. — *adv.* **magnif'ically.** — *n.* **magnif'ico** (It. *adj.*) a Venetian noble: a grandee: — *pl.* **magnif'icoes.** [L. *magnificus*; cf. **magnify.**]

Magnificat *mag-nif'i-kat, n.* the song of the Virgin Mary, Luke i. 46–55, beginning in the Vulgate with this word. [L. '(my soul) doth magnify', 3rd pers. sing. pres. ind. of *magnificāre.*]

magnification. See **magnify.**

magnificence *mag-nif'i-səns, n.* well-judged liberality (*arch.*): the quality of being magnificent. — *adj.* **magnif'icent** great in deeds or in show: noble: pompous: displaying greatness of size or extent: very fine (*coll.*). — *adv.* **magnif'icently.** [L. *magnificēns, -entis*, lit. doing great things.]

magnifico. See **magnific.**

magnify *mag'ni-fī, v.t.* to make great or greater: to enlarge: to cause to appear greater: to exaggerate: to praise highly. — *v.i.* to signify (*old slang*): — *pr.p.* **mag'nifying;** *pa.t.* and *pa.p.* **mag'nified.** — *adj.* **mag'nifiable** that may be magnified. — *ns.* **magnification** (-*fi-kā'shən*) act or power of magnifying: state of being magnified: enlarged appearance or state or copy: extolling; **mag'nifier** (-*fī-ər*) one who, or that which, magnifies or enlarges, esp. a pocket-lens (**magnifying glass**): one who extols. [L. *magnificāre* — *magnus*, great, *facĕre*, to make.]

magniloquent *mag-nil'ə-kwənt, adj.* speaking in a grand or pompous style: bombastic. — *n.* **magnil'oquence.** *adv.* **magnil'oquently.** [L. *magnus*, great, *loquēns*, -*entis*, pr.p. of *loquī*, to speak.]

magnitude *mag'ni-tūd, n.* greatness: size: extent: importance: a measure of the intensity of a star's brightness (see also **of the first magnitude** below). — **absolute magnitude** see **absolute; of the first magnitude** (*astron.*) (of a star) of the first degree of brightness: of a very important, significant or catastrophic kind (*fig.*). [L. *magnitūdō* — *magnus.*]

Magnolia *mag-nōl'i-ə*, or -*yə, n.* an American and Asiatic genus of trees with beautiful foliage, and large solitary flowers, giving name to the family **Magnoliā'ceae,** with petaloid perianth and spirally arranged stamens and carpels: (without *cap.*) any tree of this genus. — *adj.* **magnoliā'ceous.** [From Pierre *Magnol* (1638–1715), a Montpellier botanist.]

Magnox® *mag'noks,* (also without *cap.*) *n.* a material consisting of any of various magnesium-based alloys containing a small amount of aluminium, from which containers for the fuel of certain nuclear reactors are made: such a container or reactor. — Also *adj.* [*mag*nesium *no* *ox*idation.]

magnum *mag'nəm, n.* a two-quart bottle or vessel: as a bottle-size of champagne or other wine, the equivalent of two ordinary bottles, containing usu. 1½ litres: two quarts of liquor: — *pl.* **mag'nums.** — **mag'num bōn'um** a large good variety, esp. of plums or potatoes: — *pl.* **mag'num bōn'ums.** [L. *magnum* (neut.), big, *bŏnum* (neut.), good.]

magnum opus *mag'nəm ōp'əs, mag'nŏŏm op'ŏŏs,* (L.) a great work, esp. of literature or learning, esp. a writer's greatest achievement or the culmination of his efforts.

Magnus effect, force *mag'nəs i-fekt', förs* the force which acts on a cylinder rotating in a stream of fluid flowing in a direction perpendicular to the cylinder's axis, the force thrusting in a direction perpendicular to both the axis and the direction of the flow. [H.G. *Magnus* (1802–1870), German scientist.]

Magog. See **Gog and Magog.**

magot *mag'ət, mä-gō', n.* the Barbary ape, a macaque, the only European monkey: a small grotesque figure, in Chinese or Japanese workmanship. [Fr.]

magot-pie. See **magpie.**

magpie *mag'pī, n.* the pie (*Pica rustica*), a black-and-white chattering bird allied to the crow: extended to other black-and-white or pied birds (in Australia, a piping crow): a chattering person: an Anglican bishop (*obs.*): a hit on the penultimate outermost division of a target: one who hoards or steals trifles (*fig.*): a halfpenny (*obs. slang*). — (*Shak.*) **mag'ot-pie, magg'ot-pie.** — **magpie moth** the moth of the gooseberry caterpillar. [*Mag, Magot,* shortened forms of *Margaret,* and **pie[1].**]

magsman. See **mag[2].**

maguey *mag'wā, mä-gā'i, n.* agave. [Sp.]

magus *mā'gəs, n.* an ancient Persian priest or member of a priestly class: an Eastern magician: a magician: (with *cap.*) one of the three wise men from the East who brought gifts to the infant Christ: — *pl.* **mā'gi** (-*jī*). — *ns.* **mage** (*māj*) a magus or sorcerer; **mage'ship.** — *adj.* **mā'gian** pertaining to the magi or to a sorcerer. — *n.* a magus: a sorcerer. — *ns.* **mā'gianism, mā'gism** the philosophy or teaching of the magi. [L., — Gr. *magos* — O.Pers. *magus.*]

Magyar *mag'yär, mod'yor, n.* one of the prevailing people of Hungary: the Finno-Ugric speech of Hungary. — *adj.* (without *cap.*) of a garment, cut with the sleeves in a piece with the rest. — *v.t.* and *v.i.* **Mag'yarise, -ize** to make or become Magyar. — *n.* **Mag'yarism** Hungarian national spirit. [Magyar.]

Mahabharata *mə-hä-bä'rə-tə, n.* one of the great epics of ancient India. [Sans.]

Mahadeva *mə-hä-dā'və, n.* Siva. [Sans. *mahat*, great, *deva*, god.]

maharaja, maharajah *mä-hä-rä'jä, mə-hä-rä'jə, n.* formerly, a great Indian prince, esp. a ruler of a state: — *fem.* **maharani, maharanee** (-*rä'nē*). [Hind., from Sans. *mahat*, great, *rājan*, king, *rānī*, queen.]

maharishi *mä-hä-rē'shi, n.* a leading instructor in the Hindu faith. [Sans. *mahat*, great, *rishi*, sage.]

mahatma *mə-hät'mä, -hat'mə, n.* one skilled in mysteries or religious secrets: an adept: a wise and holy leader. [Sans. *mahātman*, high-souled.]

Mahayana *mä-hə-yä'nə, n.* the branch of Buddhism practised esp. in China, Japan, Tibet and the Himalayas, that seeks enlightenment for all humanity, embraces many methods for attaining it, and recognises many texts as scripture. — Also *adj.* — *n.* **Mahaya'nist.** [Sans., lit. great vehicle.]

Mahdi *mä'dē, n.* the great leader of the faithful Muslims, who is to appear in the last days: a title of various insurrectionary leaders, esp. one who overthrew the Egyptian power in the Sudan in 1884–85. — *ns.* **Mah'diism, Mah'dism; Mah'diist, Mah'dist.** [Ar. *mahdīy.*]

mah-jongg *mä-jong', n.* an old Chinese table game for four, played with small painted bricks or 'tiles'. — Also **mah-jong.** [Chin., *lit.* sparrows — perh. an allusion evoked by the chattering sound of the tiles during play.]

mahlstick. See **maulstick.**

mahmal *mä'mäl, n.* the empty litter sent to Mecca in the hadj.

mahoe *mä'hō-i, n.* the whitewood tree of New Zealand. [Maori.]

mahogany *mə-hog'ə-ni, n.* a tropical American tree (*Swietenia mahogoni*) of the Meliaceae: its timber, valued for furniture-making: the colour of the timber, a dark reddish brown: a dining-table (*coll.*): gin and treacle (*obs. slang* or *dial.*): brandy and water (*obs. slang*). — Also *adj.*   [Origin unknown.]

Mahommedan, Mahometan. See **Mohammedan.**

Mahonia *mə-hō'ni-ə, n.* a pinnate-leaved genus (or section of *Berberis*) of the barberry family: (without *cap.*) a plant of this genus.   [Named after Bernard McMahon, Irish-American gardener and botanist (*d.* 1816).]

Mahoun, Mahound *mə-hown(d)', -hōōn(d)',* or *mä', n.* Mohammed, imagined in the Middle Ages to be a pagan god (*arch.*): the devil (*Scot.* mə-hōōn').

mahout *mə-howt', n.* the keeper and driver of an elephant.   [Hind. *mahāut, mahāwat.*]

Mahratta. See **Maratha.**

mahseer, mahsir *mä'sēr, n.* a large fish found in the rivers of Northern India.   [Hind. *mahāsir.*]

mahua, mahwa *mä'(h)wä, n.* a kind of butter-tree (*Bassia*, or *Illipe, latifolia*) with edible flowers. — **mahua butter** a fat got from its seeds. — Also **mowa, mowra.**   [Hindi *mahūā.*]

mahzor, machzor *muhh-zör', mähh', n.* the Jewish prayer-book used for festivals and other special occasions: — *pl.* **ma(c)hzorim** (*-ēm').*   [Heb. *mahzor*, a cycle.]

maid *mād, n.* an unmarried woman, esp. one who is young: a virgin: a female servant: a young skate. — *v.i.* to work as a maid-servant. — *n.* **maid'hood.** — *adjs.* **maid'ish; maid'less** without a maid. — *adj.* **maid'-pale** (*Shak.*) pale, like a sick girl. — **maid'-child** (*B., Shak.*) a female child; **maid'-servant** a female servant. — **maid of all work, maid'-of-all'-work** a maid who does general housework; **maid of honour** see **honour; old maid** a woman left unmarried: a card game.   [Shortened from **maiden.**]

maidan *mī-dän', n.* an open plain: an open space, an esplanade or parade-ground near a town, in Persia and India.   [Pers. *maidān.*]

maiden *mād'n, n.* a maid: a corn-maiden (*Scot.*): a washing dolly: a clothes-horse: a horse that has never won a race: (usu. with *cap.*) the name of a Scottish beheading machine similar to a guillotine (*hist.*). — *adj.* unmarried: virgin: female: pertaining to a virgin or young woman: consisting of maidens: unpolluted (*fig.*): fresh: new: unused: in the original or initial state: grown from a seed: that has never been captured, climbed, trodden, penetrated, pruned, etc.: that has never won a race (of a horse): first. — *ns.* **maid'enhead** (pron. *-hed*; M.E. suff. *-hēd(e), -hood*) virginity: the first assay, experience, or use of anything (*obs.*): the hymen; **maid'enhood** the state or time of being a maiden: maidenhead. — *adjs.* **maid'enish** (*depreciatorily*) like a maiden; **maid'enlike.** — Also *adv.* —*n.* **maid'enliness.** — *adj.* **maid'enly** maidenlike: becoming a maiden: gentle: modest. — Also *adv.* — **maiden assize** an assize at which there are no criminal cases; **maiden battle** a first contest; **maiden castle** a common (though largely unexplained) name for a prehistoric earthwork: a castle never taken; **maiden fortress** a fortress that has never been captured; **maid'enhair** a fern (*Adiantum*), with fine footstalks: extended to species of spleenwort (**maid'enhair-spleenwort**); **maid'enhair-tree** the ginkgo. — *adj.* **maid'en-meek** meek as a maiden. — **maiden name** the family name of a married woman before her marriage; **maiden over** in cricket, an over in which no runs are made; **maiden pink** a wild species of pink, *Dianthus deltoides*; **maiden speech** one's first speech, esp. in Parliament; **maiden stakes** in horse-racing, the prize in a race (**maiden race**) between horses that have not won before the date of entry. — *adj.* **maid'entongued** gentle in voice like a girl. — **maiden voyage** a first voyage; **maid'enweed** mayweed. — *adj.* **maid'enwid'owed** widowed while still a virgin.   [O.E. *mægden.*]

maidism *mä'id-izm, n.* pellagra (attributed to a maize diet).   [**maize¹.**]

maieutic *mī-* or *mä-ūt'ik, adj.* helping birth, esp. of thoughts. — *n.sing.* **maieut'ics** the Socratic art.   [Gr.

maieutikos — maia, good woman, a midwife; Socrates, son of a midwife, called himself a midwife to men's thoughts.]

maigre *mä'gər, meg'r', adj.* made without flesh: belonging to a fast-day or to a fast. — *adv.* without using flesh (*obs.*). — *n.* (also **meagre** *mē'gər*) a large Mediterranean fish (*Sciaena aquila*) noted for the sound it emits.   [Fr. *maigre*, lean — L. *macer.*]

maik *māk, n.* Same as **mag¹,** or **make³.**

maiko *mī'kō, n.* an apprentice geisha: — *pl.* **mai'ko, -kos.**   [Jap.]

mail¹ *māl, n.* defensive armour for the body, formed of steel rings or network: armour generally: protective covering of an animal. — *v.t.* to clothe in mail. — *adj.* **mailed** protected by mail. — *adj.* **mail'-clad** clad with a coat of mail. — **mailed fist** physical force.   [Fr. *maille* — L. *macula*, a spot or a mesh.]

mail² *māl, n.* a travelling bag (*obs.*): a bag for the conveyance of letters, etc.: the contents of such a bag: post (esp. for long distances): correspondence: a batch of letters, etc.: the person or the carriage by which the mail is conveyed. — *v.t.* to post: to send by post. — *adj.* **mail'able** capable of being sent by mail. — **mail'-bag** a bag in which letters are carried; **mail'-boat** a boat that carries the public mails; **mail'-box** (*U.S.*) a letter-box; **mail'-cart** a cart in which mails are carried: a small hand-cart, with long handles, for the conveyance of children; **mail'-catcher** an apparatus for catching up mail-bags by a train in motion; **mail'-coach, -car, -carriage, -drag, -gig, -van** a conveyance that carries the public mails; **mailing list** a list of the names and addresses of those to whom advertising material, information, etc. is to be posted; **mail'man** also **mail'carrier** a postman; **mail'merge** (a computer program for) the producing of a series of letters addressed to individuals by merging a file of names with a file containing the text of the letter. — Also *v.i.* — **mail order** an order for goods to be sent by post (*adj.* **mail'-ord'er**); **mail'-plane, mail'-train** one that carries the public mails; **mail shot** an item of unsolicited, usu. advertising, material sent by post.   [O.Fr. *male*, a trunk, a mail — O.H.G. *malha, malaha*, a sack.]

mail³ *māl, (Scot.) n.* payment: rent. — *ns.* **mail'er** one who pays rent: a cottager; **mail'ing** a rented farm: rent.   [Late O.E. *māl* — O.N. *māl*, speech, agreement; cf. O.E. *mǽl.*]

mail⁴, maile *māl, (obs.) n.* a halfpenny.   [A.Fr. *mayle* — assumed L.L. *metallea*; see **medal.**]

mail⁵ *māl, (Scot.) n.* a spot, esp. one caused by ironing cloth. — *v.t.* to spot.   [O.E. *māl*; see **mole².**]

mail⁶ *māl, (obs.) v.t.* to wrap up: to confine (a bird) in a handkerchief, etc. (*falconry*).   [Ety. dub., poss. as for **mail².**]

maillot *mä-yō', n.* tights for ballet-dancer, etc.: one-piece close-fitting swimsuit.   [Fr., *lit.* swaddling-clothes.]

maim *mām, v.t.* to disable: to mutilate: to lame or cripple: to render defective. — *n.* serious bodily injury: a lameness: the loss of any essential part. — *adj.* maimed, crippled. — *adj.* **maimed.** — *ns.* **maimedness** (*māmd', mā'mid-nis*); **maiming.**   [O.Fr. *mahaing.*]

main¹ *mān, n.* might: strength: the principal part: the mainland: the high sea: a great expanse (*Shak., Milt.*): a principal pipe or conductor in a branching system distributing water, gas, electricity, etc.: (*pl.*) the water, gas or electricity supply available through such a system: that which is essential: the most part: purpose (*obs.*). — *adj.* strong (*Milt.*): sheer (as in *main force*): great: extensive: important: chief, principal: first in importance or extent: leading: general. — *adv.* (*dial.*) exceedingly. — *adv.* **main'ly** chiefly, principally: much (*obs.* or *dial.*). — **main'boom** the spar that extends the foot of a fore-and-aft mainsail; **main'brace** the brace attached to the mainyard (see **splice**); **main chance** see **chance; main clause** (*gram.*) a principal clause; **main'course** mainsail; **main'-deck** the principal deck of a ship; **main'door** a door giving independent access to a house, distinguished from one opening upon a common passage: a ground-floor house in a tenement building or villa-block, entered from the front by a door of its own (*Scot.*); **main'frame** the central processing unit and storage unit of a computer: a large computer. — *adj.* (of a computer) of the large, powerful type rather than the small-scale kind. — **main'land** (*-lənd, -land*) the principal or larger land, as opposed to neighbouring islands; **main'lander; main line** a railway line between important centres: an important vein (*slang*). — *adj.* **main'line.** — *v.i.* (*slang*) to take narcotics intravenously. — **main'liner; main'lining; main'mast** (*-məst, -mäst*) the principal mast, usually second from the prow; **main'sail** (*-sl, -sāl*) the principal sail, generally attached to the mainmast; **main'sheet** the sheet or rope attached to the lower corner of the mainsail; **main'spring** the spring that gives motion to any piece of machinery, esp. that of a watch or a clock: principal motive, motivating influence (*fig.*); **main'stay** a rope stretching forward and down from the top of the mainmast: chief support; **main store** the memory or store (q.v.) of a computer; **main stream** a river with tributaries: the chief direction or trend in any historical development, including that of an art. — *adj.* **main'stream** pertaining to the main stream (*lit.* and *fig.*): of swing, coming in the line of development between early and modern (*jazz*): in accordance with what is normal or standard. — *v.t.* (esp. *U.S.*) to make mainstream: to integrate (handicapped children) into classes of normal children (*education*). — **main'top** a platform on the top of the lower mainmast; **maintop-gall'ant= mast** the mast above the maintopmast; **maintop'mast** the mast next above the lower mainmast; **maintop'sail** the sail above the mainsail, in square-rigged vessels; **main'yard** the lower yard on the mainmast. — **in the main** for the most part: on the whole; **might and main** utmost strength; **Spanish Main** see **Spanish.** [Partly O.E. *mægen*, strength, partly O.N. *meginn*, strong; influence of O.Fr. *maine, magne* (— L. *magnus*), great, is questioned.]

main² *mān, n.* a banker's shovel. [O.Fr. *main* — L. *manus*, hand.]

main³ *mān, n.* in hazard, a number (5 to 9) called before throwing the dice: a game of hazard: a cockfighting match: a set of cocks engaged in a match: a match in some other sports. [Perh. same as preceding.]

main⁴ *mān,* (*dial.; Shak.*) *v.t.* to lame, maim.

mainor, mainour, manner *mān'ər, man'ər,* (*arch.; hist.*) *ns.* act or fact, esp. of theft: that which is stolen. — **in, with, the manner** in the act: in possession of the thing stolen. [A.Fr. *meinoure, mainoure, mainoevere;* see **manoeuvre.**]

mainpernor. See **mainprise.**

mainprise *mān'prīz,* (*arch.; law*) *n.* suretyship, esp. for the appearance of a prisoner. — *n.* **mainpernor** (*-pûr'nər*) one who gives mainprise. [A.Fr. *mainprise, mainpernour* — *main,* hand, *prendre,* to take.]

mains *mānz,* (*Scot.*) *n.pl.* a home farm. [**demesne, domain.**]

maintain *mān-tān', mən-, men-, v.t.* to observe or practise: to keep in existence or in any state: to preserve from capture, loss, or deterioration: to uphold: to carry on: to keep up: to support: to make good: to support by argument: to affirm: to defend: to support in an action in which one is not oneself concerned (*law*). — *n.* **maintainabil'ity.** — *adjs.* **maintain'able; maintained'** financially supported, e.g. (of a school, etc.) from public funds. — *ns.* **maintain'er; maintenance** (*mān'tən-əns*) the act of maintaining, supporting, or defending: continuance: the means of support: defence, protection: illegal outside interference in a lawsuit, etc., in favour of one of the parties (*law*). — *v.t.* to keep in working order. — **main'tenance-man** one keeping machines, etc., in working order. — **cap of maintenance** a cap of dignity borne by or before a noble or other person of rank. [Fr. *maintenir* — L. *manū* (abl.) *tenēre,* to hold in the hand.]

maiolica. See **majolica.**

maire *mer,* (Fr.) *n.* mayor.

maise *māz.* Same as **mease¹.**

maison de ville *me-zɔ̃ də vēl,* (Fr.) a town house, residence in town.

maisonnette, maisonette *māz-on-et', mez-, n.* a small house or flat. [Fr. *maisonnette.*]

maist. See **most.**

maister *mās'tər,* (obs. and *Scot.*). Same as **master.** — *ns.* **mais'terdome** (obs.); **mais'tring** (obs.); **mais'try** (obs.).

maître (*fem.* **maîtresse**) **de ballet** *metr'* (*me-tres*) *də bal-e, ns.* one who trains dancers and takes rehearsals (formerly one who acted also as choreographer). [Fr., ballet master, mistress.]

maître d'hôtel *metr' dō-tel,* a house-steward, major domo: the manager or head-waiter of a hotel. — See also **à la maître d'hôtel.**

maize¹ *māz, n.* a staple cereal (*Zea mays*) in America, etc., with large ears (corncobs) — called also *Indian corn,* or *mealies:* the yellow colour of maize. — Also *adj.* — **water maize** *Victoria regia.* [Sp. *maíz* — from Haitian.]

maize² *māz.* Same as **mease¹.**

majesty *maj'is-ti, n.* greatness and glory of God: grandeur: dignity: elevation of manner or style: royal state: a title of monarchs (*His, Her, Your, Majesty; Their, Your, Majesties*): a representation of God (sometimes Christ) enthroned: the canopy of a hearse. — *adjs.* **majestic** (*mə-jes'tik*), **-al** having or exhibiting majesty: stately: sublime. — *adv.* **majes'tically** in a majestic manner. — *ns.* **majes'ticalness, majes'ticness** (obs.) majesty. [Fr. *majesté* — L. *mājestās, -ātis* — *mājor, mājus,* compar. of *magnus,* great.]

Majlis *māj-lis', n.* the Iranian parliament: in various Middle-Eastern countries, (appeal to) an assembly. — Also **Mejlis'.** [Pers. *majlis.*]

majolica *mə-jol'i-kə,* or *-yol',* **maiolica** *-yol', ns.* glazed or enamelled earthenware. — **majol'icaware.** [Perh. from *Majorca.*]

major *mā'jər, adj.* greater, or great, in number, quantity, size, value, importance, dignity: in boys' schools, senior: greater (than minor) by a semitone (*mus.*): involving a major third (see below; *mus.*). — *n.* a person of full legal age (in U.K., before 1970, 21 years; from 1970, 18 years): an officer in rank between a captain and lieutenant-colonel: by courtesy, a sergeant-major: anything that is major opposed to minor: a student's special subject (*U.S.*): a kind of wig (obs.). — *v.i.* to play the major, strut: to specialise in a particular subject at college (with *in; U.S.*): to specialise in a particular product, etc. (with *in, on*). — *v.t.* to channel or concentrate (one's activities, efforts, etc.) in a particular direction. — *ns.* **majorat** (*mä-zhō-rä;* Fr.) primogeniture; **majorette'** a member of a group of girls who march in parades, etc., wearing a decorative approximation to military uniform, sometimes twirling batons, playing instruments, etc.; **majority** (*mə-jor'i-ti*) pre-eminence: the greater number: the greater part, the bulk: the difference between the greater and the less number: full age (see **major** above): the office or rank of major. — Also *adj.* — *n.* **mā'jorship.** — **major axis** in conic sections, that passing through the foci; **ma'jor-dō'mō** (Sp. *mayor-domo,* L. *mājor domūs*) an official who has the general management in a large household: a general steward; **ma'jor-gen'eral** an officer in the army next in rank below a lieutenant-general; **ma'jor-gen'eralcy, major-gen'eralship; majority carrier** (*electronics*) in a semiconductor, the electrons or holes that carry most of the measured current; **majority rule** government by members, or by a body including members, of the largest ethnic group(s) in a country, as opp. to a political system which excludes them; **majority verdict** the verdict reached by the majority in a jury, as distinct from a unanimous verdict; **major key, mode, scale** one with its third a major third above the tonic; **major orders** in the R.C. Church, the higher degrees of holy orders, i.e. bishop, priest and deacon; **major premise** (*log.*) that in which the major term occurs; **major suit** (*bridge*) spades or hearts, valued more highly than diamonds or clubs; **major term** the term which is the predicate of the conclusion; **major third** (*mus.*) an interval of four semitones; **major tone** an interval of vibration ratio 8:9. — **go over to**, or **join, the majority** to die. [L. *mājor*, comp. of *magnus*.]

majoritaire *mä-zhor-ē-ter*, (Fr.) *n.* a member of a majority section of a party, esp. of socialists.

majority. See **major**.

majuscule *mə-jus′kūl*, or *maj′əs-kūl*, (*palaeog.*) *n.* a large letter whether capital or uncial. — Also *adj.* — *adj.* **majus′cular**. [L. (*littera*) *mājuscula*, somewhat larger (letter).]

mak *mäk*, Scots form of **make**. — *n.* **makar** see **maker**.

make[1] *māk*, *v.t.* to fashion, frame, construct, compose, or form: to create: to bring into being: to produce: to conclude, contract: to bring about: to perform: to force: to cause: to result in: to cause to be: to convert or turn: to appoint: to render: to represent as doing or being: to reckon: to get as result or solution: to occasion: to bring into any state or condition: to establish: (in the navy) to promote: to prepare: to shut (as a door) (*Shak.*): to shuffle (*cards*): to declare as trumps (*cards*): to obtain, gain earn: to score: to constitute: to amount to: to count for: to turn out: to be capable of turning or developing into or serving as: to arrive in sight of: to reach, succeed in reaching: to accomplish, achieve: to attempt, offer, or start: to be occupied with: to do: to cause, assure, success of: to persuade (a woman) to have sexual intercourse with one (*slang*): to have sexual intercourse with (*slang*). — *v.i.* to behave (as if), esp. in order to deceive: to proceed: to tend: to contribute: to flow: to versify (*arch.*): to be in condition for making: to matter (as *it maksna*, it does not matter; *Scot.*): — *pr.p.* **māk′ing**; *pa.t.* and *pa.p.* **māde**. — *n.* form or shape: structure, texture: build: formation: manufacture: brand: type: making: quantity made: establishment of an electric circuit or contact: trump declaration. — *adj.* **mak(e)′able**. — *ns.* **māk′er** one who makes: (*cap.*) the Creator: (*arch.*; esp. in Scots form, **makar** *mak′*, *māk′ər*) a poet: the declarer (*bridge*): a knave in cards (*obs.*): a calker's tool; **māk′ing** the act of forming (often in composition, as in *bread-making, cabinet-making*): structure: form: (in *pl.*) gains: (in *pl.*) that from which something can be made. — *adj.* **make′-and-break′** making and breaking a circuit. — **make′bate** a mischief-maker. — *v.i.* **make′-believe** see **make believe** below. — *n.* feigning (also **make′-belief**). — *adj.* feigned. — *adjs.* **make′-do** makeshift; **make-or-break** see **make or break** below. — **make′-peace** (*Shak.*) a peace-maker; **make′-ready** preparation of a letterpress sheet for printing, so as to obtain evenness of impression; **make′shift** a temporary expedient or substitute. — *adj.* of the nature of or characterised by temporary expedient. — **make′-up** the way anything is arranged, composed, or constituted, or the ingredients in its constitution: one's character, temperament, mental qualities: an actor's materials for personating a part or a woman's, esp. cosmetics, for self-beautification: the effect produced thereby: the arrangement of composed types into columns or pages (*print.*); **make′-weight** that which is thrown into a scale to make up the weight: a person or thing of little value added to supply a deficiency. — **in the making** in the process of being formed, developed, etc., or of becoming; **make account of** see **account**; **make one's day** see **day**; **make a face** to grimace, contort the features; **make a figure** to be conspicuous; **make after** to follow or pursue; **make a fool of** see **fool**; **make against** to militate, tell, against; **make a (good) meal, dinner**, etc., to dine, etc. (plentifully or heartily); **make a meal of** see **meal**[1]; **make amends** to render compensation or satisfaction; **make an ass of oneself** to behave like a fool; **make a night (day) of it** to extend an, esp. enjoyable, activity through the whole night (day); **make as if**, or (*U.S.*) **like**, or **as though** to act as if, to pretend that; **make at**

to make a hostile movement against; **make away (with)** to put out of the way, get rid of, destroy, kill; **make believe** to pretend, feign: to play at believing; **make bold** see **bold**; **make certain (of)** to find out: to put beyond doubt: to secure; **make do (with)** to manage (with the means available — usually inferior or inadequate); **make down** to refashion so as to fit a smaller person: to turn down the sheets and blankets of (*Scot.*); **make eyes at** see **eye**; **make for** to set out for, seek to reach: to favour; **make free with** see **free**; **make friends** to become friendly: to acquire friends; **make good, make light of, make little of, make love (to), make merry** see **good**, etc.; **make head or tail of** to find any sense in; **make it** to reach an objective: to succeed in a purpose: to become a success (*coll.*): to have one's way sexually (with) (*vulg.*); **make much of** to treat with fondness, to cherish, to foster: to turn to great account: to find much sense in, succeed in understanding; **make no doubt** to have no doubt, to be confident; **make nothing of** to think it no great matter, have no hesitation or difficulty: to be totally unable to understand; **make of** to construct from (as material): to understand by: to make much of, to pet (*obs.* and *Scot.*): to esteem (*obs.*); **make off** to decamp; **make off with** to run away with; **make on** (*Shak.*) to make much of; **make one's way** to proceed: to succeed; **make or break, make or mar** to be the crucial test that brings success or failure to (*adj.* **make′-or-break′**); **make or meddle with** to have to do with, interfere with; **make out** to descry: to discern: to decipher: to comprehend, understand: to prove: to seek to make it appear: to draw up: to achieve (*obs.*): to fill up: to make shift, get along somehow: to succeed: to engage in love-making (with) (*slang*); **make over** to remake, reconstruct: to transfer; **make sail** to increase the quantity of sail: to set sail; **make sure (of)** to ascertain: to put beyond doubt or risk: to secure: to feel certain: to betroth (*obs.*); **make the best of** to turn to the best advantage: to take in the best spirit; **make the most of** to use to the best advantage; **make up** to fabricate: to feign: to collect: to put together: to parcel: to put into shape: to arrange: to compose (quarrels): to become friends again (after a quarrel, etc.): to constitute: to repair: to complete, supplement: to adjust one's appearance (as an actor for a part): to apply paint and powder, etc., to the face: to put type, etc., into columns and pages: to set out and balance (accounts): to make good: to compensate: to decide (*Shak.*); **make up one's mind** to come to a decision; **make up to** to make friendly, adulatory, or amorous approaches to: to compensate; **make way** see **way**; **make with** (*coll.*, orig. *U.S.*) to start using, doing, etc. (something), to bring on or into operation; **on the make** (*coll.*) bent on self-advancement or promotion, or on finding a sexual partner. [O.E. *macian*; Ger. *machen*.]

make[2] *māk*, *n.* Same as **mag**[1].

make[3] *māk*, (*Scot.*) **maik** (*obs.* or *dial.*) *n.* a mate, consort: an equal. — *adj.* **make′less** (*obs.* or *dial.*) without a mate: matchless. [O.E. (*ge*)*mæcca*; see **match**.]

makimono *mäk-i-mō′nō*, *n.* a roll, as of silk, esp. a long picture or writing rolled up and not hung: — *pl.* **makimō′nos**. [Jap., — *maki*, roll, scroll, *mono*, thing.]

mako[1] *mä′kō*, *n.* any of several sharks of the genus *Isurus*: — *pl.* **ma′kos**. — Also **mako shark**. [Maori.]

mako[2] *mä′kō*, **mako-mako** *mä′kō-mä′kō*, *ns.* a small tree of New Zealand with red berries that turn purple as they ripen: — *pls.* **ma′kos, ma′ko-ma′kos**. — Also called **wine-berry**. [Maori.]

mal *mal*, (Fr.) *n.* pain, sickness. — **mal de mer** (*də mer*) sea-sickness; **mal du pays** (*dü pā-ē*) homesickness, nostalgia; **mal du siècle** (*dü syekl′*) depression about the state of the world; used by Sainte-Beuve (1833) and current in the 20th cent.

mal- *mal-, pfx.* bad, badly. [Fr., — L. *male*, badly.]

Malabar-rat *mal′ə-bär-rat′*, *n.* the bandicoot rat. [*Malabar* in India.]

Malacca-cane *məl-ak′ə-kān*, *n.* a brown walking-cane made from a rattan. [*Malacca*, a centre of the trade.]

malachite *mal'ə-kīt, n.* a green mineral, basic copper carbonate. [Gr. *malachē*, mallow, as of the colour of a mallow leaf.]

malacia *mal-ā'shi-ə, n.* pathological softening: perverted appetite. [Gr. *malakiā*, softness.]

malacology *mal-ə-kol'ə-ji, n.* the study of molluscs. — *adj.* **malacological** (*-kə-loj'*). — *n.* **malacol'ogist.** [Gr. *malakos*, soft, *logos*, discourse.]

malacophilous *mal-ə-kof'i-ləs,* (*bot.*) *adj.* pollinated by snails. [Gr. *malakos*, soft, *phileein*, to love.]

Malacopterygii *mal-ə-kop-tər-ij'i-ī, n.pl.* a soft-finned suborder of bony fishes — herrings, salmon, etc. — *adj.* and *n.* **malacopteryg'ian.** [Gr. *malakos*, soft, *pteryx, pterygos,* a wing, fin.]

Malacostraca *mal-ə-kos'trə-kə, n.pl.* the best-known class of crustaceans — crabs, lobsters, shrimps, prawns, etc. — *adj.* and *n.* **malacos'tracan.** — *adj.* **malacos'tracous.** [Gr. *malakos*, soft, *ostrakon,* a shell.]

maladaptation *mal-ad-ap-tā'shən, n.* faulty adaptation. — *adjs.* **maladap'ted; maladap'tive.** [Pfx. **mal-.**]

maladdress *mal-ə-dres', n.* awkwardness: clumsiness: tactlessness. [Fr. *maladresse.*]

maladjusted *mal-ə-just'id, adj.* poorly or inadequately adjusted, esp. to one's environment or circumstances. — *n.* **maladjust'ment.** [Pfx. **mal-.**]

maladministration *mal-əd-min-is-trā'shən, n.* bad management, esp. of public affairs. — *v.t.* **maladmin'ister.** [Pfx. **mal-.**]

maladroit *mal'ə-droit* (or *-droit'*), *adj.* not dexterous: unskilful: clumsy. — *adv.* **maladroit'ly.** — *n.* **maladroit'ness.** [Fr.]

malady *mal'ə-di, n.* illness: disease, either of the body or of the mind: a faulty condition. [Fr. *maladie* — *malade*, sick — L. *male habitus,* in ill condition — *male,* badly, *habitus,* pa.p. of *habēre,* to have, hold.]

mala fide *mā'lə fī'dē, ma'lä fē'dä,* (L.) in bad faith, treacherously.

Malaga *mal'ə-gə, n.* a white wine imported from *Málaga.*

Malagasy *mal-ə-gas'i, adj.* of or pertaining to Madagascar or its inhabitants. — *n.* a native of Madagascar: the language of Madagascar. — Also **Malagash'** (or *mal';* *arch.*).

malagueña *mal-ə-gān'yə, n.* a Spanish dance. [Sp., belonging to the city of Málaga.]

malaguetta *mal-ə-get'ə, n.* grains of paradise (also **malaguetta pepper**). [Origin obscure.]

malaise *mal-āz', n.* uneasiness: a feeling of discomfort or of sickness. [Fr. *malaise.*]

malakatoone. Same as **melocoton.**

malamute. See **malemute.**

malander, mallander, mallender *mal'ən-dər, n.* an eruption of the skin behind a horse's knee — often *pl.* [Fr. *malandre* — L. *malandria* (sing. or pl.).]

malapert *mal'ə-pûrt, adj.* bold: forward: saucy: impudent. — *adv.* **mal'apertly.** — *n.* **mal'apertness.** [O.Fr., unskilful — *mal* (L. *malus*), bad, *appert* for *espert* (L. *expertus;* see **expert**) but understood in English as if — Fr. *apert,* open, outspoken — L. *apertus,* open.]

malapportionment *mal-ə-pōr'shən-mənt, n.* (*U.S.*) unequal or unfair apportioning of members to a legislative body. [Pfx. **mal-.**]

malappropriate *mal-ə-prō'pri-āt, v.t.* to misuse. — *n.* **malappropriā'tion.** [Pfx. **mal-.**]

malapropism *mal'ə-prop-izm, n.* misapplication of words without mispronunciation, from Mrs *Malaprop* in Sheridan's play, *The Rivals,* who uses words *malapropos.*

malapropos *mal'a-prō-pō, mal-ə-prō-pō', adj.* out of place: unsuitable: inapt. — *adv.* inappropriately: unseasonably. [Pfx. **mal-.**]

malar *mā'lər, adj.* pertaining to the cheek. — *n.* the cheek-bone. [L. *māla,* the cheek — *mandēre,* to chew.]

malaria *mə-lā'ri-ə, n.* poisonous air arising from marshes, once believed to produce fever: miasma: the fever once attributed thereto, actually due to a protozoan parasite transmitted by mosquitoes. — *adjs.* **malā'rial, malā'-**

rian, malā'rious. — *ns.* **malā'rio'logist; malā'rio'logy** the study of malaria. [It. *mal' aria* — L. *malus,* bad, *āēr, āĕris,* air.]

malark(e)y *mə-lär'ki,* (*U.S.*) *n.* absurd talk: nonsense.

malassimilation *mal-ə-sim-i-lā'shən, n.* imperfect assimilation or nutrition. [Pfx. **mal-.**]

malate. See **malic.**

Malathion® *mal-ə-thī'on, n.* a phosphorus-containing insecticide used chiefly in the house and garden. [From diethyl *maleate.*]

malax, malaxate *mal'aks, -āt, vs.t.* to soften by kneading, rubbing or mixing. — *ns.* **mal'axage; malaxā'tion; mal'axātor.** [L.L. *malaxāre,* to soften.]

Malay, -an *mə-lā', -ən, ns.* a member of a race inhabiting Malaysia, Singapore and Indonesia (formerly known as the Malay Archipelago): the language of the Malays. — *adjs.* of the Malays, their language, or their countries. — *adj.* **Malay'sian** (*-si-ən, -zhən, -shən*) relating to the Malay Archipelago or esp. to Malaysia. — Also *n.* [Malay *malāyu.*]

Malayala(a)m *ma-lə-yä'ləm, n.* the Dravidian language of Kerala. — Also *adj.*

malconformation *mal-kon-för-mā'shən, n.* bad conformation or form. [Pfx. **mal-.**]

malcontent *mal'kən-tent, adj.* discontented, dissatisfied, esp. in political matters. — *n.* one discontented. — *adj.* **malcontent'ed.** — *adv.* **malcontent'edly.** — *n.* **malcontent'edness.** [O.Fr. *malcontent*]

mal del pinto. See **pinta**².

mal de mer. See under **mal.**

maldistribution *mal-dis-tri-bū'shən, n.* uneven, unfair, or inefficient, distribution. [Pfx. **mal-.**]

male¹ *māl,* (*Spens.*) *n.* for **mail¹.**

male² *māl, adj.* masculine: of or pertaining to the sex that begets (not bears) young, or produces relatively small gametes: staminate (*bot.*): adapted to fit into a corresponding hollow part (*mach.*). — *n.* one of the male sex: apparently, a father (*Shak.*). — **male chauvinist (pig)** (*coll. derog.*) a man who believes in the superiority of men over women and acts accordingly (*abbrev.* MCP); **male'-fern** an elegant woodland fern once fancied to be the male of the lady-fern; **male orchis** the early purple orchis (cf. **Orchis**); **male order** in architecture, the Doric order; **male rhymes** those in which stressed final syllables correspond; **male screw** see **screw.** [O.Fr. *male* — L. *masculus,* male — *mās,* a male.]

maleate. See **malic.**

Malebolge *mä-lä-bol'jä, n.* the eighth circle of Dante's Hell. [It., bad holes or pits, *lit.* pockets.]

malediction *mal-i-dik'shən, n.* cursing: a calling down of evil. — *adjs.* **maledicent** (*-dī'sənt*) cursing; **mal'edict** (*-dikt; arch.*) accursed. — *v.t.* and *v.i.* to curse. — *adjs.* **maledic'tive, maledic'tory.** [L. *maledīcĕre, -dictum* — *male,* ill, *dīcĕre,* to speak.]

malefactor *mal'i-fak-tər, n.* an evil-doer: a criminal. — *n.* **malefac'tion** (*Shak.*) a crime, an offence. — *adjs.* **malefac'tory, malefic** (*məl-ef'ik*) doing mischief: producing evil. — *adv.* **malef'ically.** — *ns.* **mal'efice** (*-i-fis; arch.*) an evil deed: enchantment; **maleficence** (*ef'i-səns*). — *adjs.* **malef'icent, maleficial** (*mal-i-fish'l; rare*) hurtful: wrong-doing. [L. *malefacĕre,* to do evil.]

maleic. See under **malic.**

malemute *mäl'ə-mūt, n.* an Eskimo dog. — Also **mal'amute.** [From a tribe on the Alaskan coast.]

malengine *mal-en'jin,* (*Spens.*) *n.* evil device: deceit. [O.Fr. *malengin* — L. *malus, -um,* bad, *ingenium,* ingenuity.]

malentendu *ma-lä-tä-dü,* (Fr.) *n.* a misunderstanding.

malevolent *mal-ev'ə-lənt, adj.* wishing evil: ill-disposed towards others: rejoicing in another's misfortune. — *n.* **malev'olence.** — *adv.* **malev'olently.** [L. *malevolēns, -entis,* ill disposed, wishing evil.]

malfeasance *mal-fē'zəns, n.* evil-doing (*rare*): the doing of what one ought not to do (*rare*): an illegal deed, esp. of an official (*law*). — *adj.* **malfea'sant.** [Fr. *malfaisance* — L. *male,* ill, *facĕre,* to do.]

malformation *mal-för-mā'shən, n.* faulty structure: deformity. — *adj.* **malformed'.** [Pfx. **mal-.**]

malfunction *mal-fungk'shən, n.* the act or fact of working imperfectly. — *v.i.* to work or function imperfectly. — *n.* **malfunc'tioning.** [Pfx. **mal-.**]

malgrado *mal-grä'dō, (obs.) prep.* in spite of. [It.]

malgre. Same as **maugre.**

malgré *mal-grā,* (Fr.) *prep.* in spite of. — **malgré lui, moi,** etc., in spite of his, my, etc., efforts: willy-nilly; **malgré tout** (*too*) nevertheless, all things considered.

mali, mallee *mä'lē, n.* one of the gardener class in India. [Hindi *mālī.*]

Malian *mä'li-ən, adj.* of or pertaining to *Mali* in W. Africa. — *n.* a native or citizen of Mali.

Malibu board *mal'i-bōō bōrd,* a long, light surfing board equipped with fins. [*Malibu,* California.]

malic *mā'lik, mal'ik, adj.* obtained from apple juice — applied to an acid ($H_6C_4O_5$) found in unripe fruits. — *ns.* **ma'late** a salt or ester of malic acid; **maleate** (*mal'i-āt*) a salt or ester of maleic acid. — *adj.* **maleic** (*mə-lē'ik*). — *n.* **malonate** (*mal'ə-nāt*) a salt or ester of malonic acid. **maleic acid** an acid, isomeric with fumaric acid, got from malic acid; **maleic hydrazide** a chemical used in retarding plant growth; **malon'ic acid** a white crystalline acid $CH_2(COOH)_2$. [L. *mālum,* an apple; Gr. *mēlon.*]

malice *mal'is, n.* ill-will: spite: disposition or intention to harm another or others: a playfully mischievous attitude of mind. — *v.t.* to have ill-will against: to wish to injure (*pa.p.* in *Spens.* **mal'ist**) — *adj.* **malicious** (*mə-lish'əs*) bearing ill-will or spite: moved by hatred or ill-will: mischievous. — *adv.* **mali'ciously.** — *n.* **mali'ciousness.** — **malice aforethought** (*law*) the predetermination to commit a crime esp. against the person, i.e. serious injury or murder. [Fr., — L. *malitia* — *malus,* bad.]

malicho *mal'i-chō, -kō, n.* mischief (Shak., *Hamlet,* III, ii, 146). [Conjectured to be for Sp. *malhecho,* mischief.]

malign *mə-līn', adj.* baleful: injurious: malignant. — *v.t.* to speak evil of, especially falsely and rancorously, to defame: to regard with malice or hatred (*obs.*): to grudge (*obs.*). — *ns.* **malign'er; malignity** (*mə-lig'ni-ti*) state or quality of being malign: great hatred, virulence: deadly quality. — *adv.* **malign'ly.** — *n.* **malign'ment.** [Fr. *malin,* fem. *maligne* — L. *malignus* for *maligenus,* of evil disposition — *malus,* bad, and *gen-,* root of *genus.*]

malignant *mə-lig'nənt, adj.* disposed to do harm: baleful: actuated by great hatred: Royalist or Cavalier (also *cap., hist.*): rebellious, disaffected (*obs.*): tending to cause death, or to go from bad to worse, esp. cancerous (*med.*). — *n.* (usu. *cap.*) a Royalist or Cavalier. — *ns.* **malig'nance, malig'nancy.** — *adv.* **malig'nantly.** [L. *malignāns, -antis,* pr.p. of *malignāre,* to act maliciously.]

Malines *mə-lēn'.* Same as **Mechlin.**

malinger *mə-ling'gər, v.i.* to feign sickness in order to avoid duty. — *ns.* **maling'erer; maling'ery** feigned sickness. [Fr. *malingre,* sickly.]

malison *mal'i-zn, -sn, (poet.) n.* a curse — opp. to *benison.* [O.Fr. *maleison;* a doublet of **malediction.**]

malist (*Spens.*). See **malice.**

malkin *mö'kin, n.* a dirty or lewd woman (Shak.): a cat (*dial.*): a mop (*dial.*): a scarecrow (*dial.*): a hare (*Scot.*). — Also **maw'kin.** [Dim. of *Matilda, Maud.*]

mall *möl,* or *mal, n.* a maul, large wooden beetle or hammer: a mallet for the old game of pall-mall: the game itself: a pall-mall alley: (from a former alley of the kind in London) a level shaded walk: a public walk: a street, area, etc., of shops, along which vehicles are not permitted. — *v.t.* to maul or beat. [See **maul** and **pall-mall.**]

mallam *mal'əm, n.* an African scribe, teacher or learned man. [Hausa.]

mallander. See **malander.**

mallard *mal'ərd, n.* a kind of wild duck common in the

northern hemisphere — the male has a shiny green head. [O.Fr. *mallart, malart;* origin obscure.]

malleate *mal'i-āt, v.t.* to hammer: to beat thin. — *adj.* **mall'eable** able to be beaten, rolled, etc., into a new shape (also *fig.*). — *ns.* **mall'eableness, malleabil'ity; malleā'tion** hammering: a hammer-mark. — *adj.* **malleiform** (*mal'ē-i-förm*) hammer-shaped. — *n.* **malleus** (*mal'i-əs*) one of the small bones of the middle ear in mammals. [L. *malleus,* a hammer.]

mallecho. An editorial emendation of **malicho** (*Shak.*).

mallee[1] *mal'ē, n.* any of many small trees of the genus Eucalyptus, esp. *E. dumosa:* a vegetation community of such trees (also **mallee scrub**): an arid area where mallee forms the predominant vegetation. — **mall'ee= bird, -fowl, -hen** an Australian mound-bird; **mallee gate** a makeshift gate. [Aboriginal.]

mallee[2]. Same as **mali.**

malleiform. See **malleate.**

mallemaroking *mal'i-mə-rō'king, n.* carousing of seamen in icebound ships. [Obs. Du. *mallemerok,* a romping woman — *mal,* foolish, *marok* — Fr. *marotte,* a favoured object.]

mallemuck *mal'i-muk, n.* the fulmar or similar bird. [Du. *mallemok* — *mal,* foolish, *mok,* gull; Ger. *Mallemuck.*]

mallender. See **malander.**

malleolus *mə-lē'ə-ləs, n.* a bony protuberance on either side of the ankle. — *adj.* **mallē'olar** (or *mal'i-*). [L. *malleolus,* dim. of *malleus,* hammer.]

mallet *mal'it, n.* a hammer with a large head, e.g. of wood: a soft-headed stick used to beat a gong, etc. (*mus.*): a long-handled hammer for playing croquet or polo. [Fr. *maillet,* dim. of *mail,* a mall.]

malleus. See **malleate.**

Mallophaga *mal-of'ə-gə, n.pl.* an order of wingless parasitic insects, bird-lice or biting-lice. — *adj.* **malloph'agous.** [Gr. *mallos,* a flock of wool, *phagein,* to eat.]

mallow *mal'ō, n.* any plant of the genus Malva, from its emollient properties or its soft downy leaves: extended to other genera of Malvaceae: a mauve colour. [O.E. *m(e)alwe* — L. *malva;* Gr. *malachē* — *malassein,* to soften.]

malm *mäm, n.* calcareous loam, earth specially good for brick: an artificial mixture of clay and chalk. [O.E. *m(e)alm (-stān),* a soft (stone).]

malmag *mal'mag, n.* the tarsier. [Philippine word.]

malmsey *mäm'zi, n.* a sort of grape: a strong and sweet wine, first made in Greece and exported from Monembasia. — Also **malvasia** (*mäl-vä-sē'ə*), **malvesie, malvoisie** (*mäl'və-zi, -voi-zi*). [L.L. *malmasia;* cf. O.Fr. *malvesie,* Fr. *malvoisie,* It. *malvasia,* Sp. *malvasia.*]

malnutrition *mal-nū-trish'ən, n.* imperfect or faulty nutrition. [Pfx. **mal-.**]

malodour *mal-ō'dər, n.* an ill smell. — *adj.* **malo'dorous.** — *n.* **malo'dorousness.** [Pfx. **mal-.**]

malo-lactic *mäl-ə-lak'tik, mal-, adj.* concerning or involving the conversion of malic acid to lactic acid in the fermentation of wine.

malonate. See **malic.**

malonic acid. See **malic.**

Malpighia *mal-pig'i-ə, n.* the Barbados cherry genus of tropical American trees, shrubs, and lianes, giving name to the family **Malpighiā'ceae** of the order *Geraniales.* — *adj.* **Malpigh'ian** applied to several structures, esp. in the kidney, investigated by Marcello *Malpighi* (1628–94).

malposition *mal-pə-zish'ən, n.* a wrong position, misplacement, chiefly *med.* [Pfx. **mal-.**]

malpractice *mal-prak'tis, n.* an evil or improper practice: professional misconduct: treatment falling short of reasonable skill or care: illegal attempt of a person in position of trust to benefit himself at others' cost. — *n.* **malpractitioner** (*-tish'ən-ər*). [Pfx. **mal-.**]

malpresentation *mal-prez-ən-tā'shən, n.* abnormal presentation in childbirth. [Pfx. **mal-.**]

mal soigné *mal swa-nyā*, (Fr.) badly groomed, unkempt.

malstick. See **maulstick.**

malt *mölt*, *n.* barley or other grain steeped in water, allowed to sprout, and dried in a kiln, used in brewing ale, etc.: malt liquor. — *v.t.* to make into malt: to treat or combine with malt. — *v.i.* to become malt: to drink malt liquor (*facet.*). — *adj.* containing or made with malt. — *n.* **malt′ase** an enzyme that produces grape-sugar from maltose. — *adj.* **malt′ed** containing or made with malt. — *ns.* **malt′ing** a building where malt is made; **malt′ose** a hard, white crystalline sugar, formed by the action of malt or diastase on starch; **malt′ster** a maltman. — *adj.* **malt′y.** — **malt′-dust** grain-sprouts produced and screened off in malt-making; **malt′=ex′tract** a fluid medicinal food made from malt; **malt′=floor** a perforated floor in the chamber of a malt-kiln, through which heat rises; **malt′-horse** a heavy horse, such as is used by brewers — hence (*Shak.*) a dull, stupid person; **malt′-house, malt′-kiln**; **malt liquor** a liquor, as ale or porter, formed from malt; **malt′-mill** a mill for grinding malt; **malt′man** one whose occupation it is to make malt; **malt tea** the liquid infusion of the mash in brewing; **malt′worm** (*Shak.*) a lover of malted liquors, a tippler. [O.E. *m(e)alt*; cf. Ger. *Malz*.]

Malta *mol′*, *möl′tə*, *adj.* of the island of Malta. — *adj.* **Maltese** (*-tēz′*) of Malta, its people, or language. — *n.* one of the people of Malta (*pl.* **Maltese**): an official language of Malta — Semitic with a strong Italian infusion. — **Malta fever** undulant fever, once common in Malta (see also **brucellosis**); **Maltese cross** the badge of the knights of Malta, a cross with two-pointed expanding limbs; **Maltese dog** a very small spaniel with long silky hair. [L. *Melita*, Gr. *Melitē*.]

maltalent *mal′tal-ənt*, (*Spens.*) *n.* ill-will. [Fr. *mal*, ill, *talent*, disposition; see **talent**[1].]

Maltese. See **Malta.**

maltha *mal′thə*, *n.* a thick mineral pitch: an ancient cement: mineral tar. [Gr.]

Malthusian *mal-thūz′i-ən*, *adj.* relating to Thomas Robert Malthus (1766–1834), or to his teaching that the increase of population tends to outstrip that of the means of living. — *n.* a disciple of Malthus. — *n.* **Malthūs′ianism.**

maltreat *mal-trēt′*, *v.t.* to use roughly or unkindly. — *n.* **maltreat′ment.** [Fr. *maltraiter* — L. *male*, ill, *tractāre*, to treat.]

Malva *mal′və*, *n.* the mallow genus, giving name to the family **Malvā′ceae**, including hollyhock, cotton, etc., akin to the lime family: (without *cap.*) a plant of this genus. — *adj.* **malvā′ceous.** [L.; cf. **mallow**.]

malvasia. Same as **malmsey.**

malversation *mal-vər-sā′shən*, *n.* misbehaviour in office as by bribery, extortion, embezzlement: corrupt administration (of funds). [Fr., — L. *male*, badly, *versārī*, *-ātus*, to occupy oneself.]

malvesie, malvoisie. Same as **malmsey.**

mal vu *mal vü*, (Fr.) looked upon with disapproval.

mam *mam*, (*dial.*) *n.* mother.

Mam *mam*, *n.* a Mayan language. [Sp. *mame*, from Amerindian.]

mama. See **mamma**[1].

mamba *mam′bə*, *n.* a large, deadly African snake (*Dendraspis*), black or green. [Kaffir *im mamba*, large snake.]

mambo *mam′bō*, *n.* a voodoo priestess: a West Indian dance, or dance-tune, like the rumba: — *pl.* **mam′bos.** — *v.i.* to dance the mambo. [Amer. Sp., prob. from Haitian.]

mamelon *mam′ə-lən*, *n.* a rounded hill or protuberance. [Fr., nipple.]

mameluco *mam-e-lōō′kō*, *n.* in Brazil, the offspring of a person of European stock and an Indian: — *pl.* **mamelu′cos.** [Port.; cf. **Mameluke**.]

Mameluke *mam′ə-lōōk*, *n.* one of a military force originally of Circassian slaves — afterwards the ruling class and sultans of Egypt: a slave, esp. white. [Ar.

mamlûk, a purchased slave — *malaka*, to possess.]

mamilla, *U.S.* **mammilla,** *mam-il′ə*, *n.* the nipple of the mammary gland: a nipple-shaped protuberance: — *pl.* **mam(m)ill′ae** (*-ē*). — *adjs.* **mam′illar, mam′illary** pertaining to the breast: nipple-shaped: studded with rounded projections; **mam′illate, mam′illated** having mamillae: nipple-shaped. — *n.* **mamillā′tion.** — *adj.* **mamill′iform.** [L. *mam(m)illa*, dim. of *mamma*.]

mamma[1], **mama** *mä-mä′* (in U.S. *mä′mə*), *n.* mother — once considered genteel, now used chiefly by young children. — *n.* **mammy** (*mam′i*) a child's word for mother: a coloured nurse (*U.S.*). — **mamm′y-wagon** in West Africa, an open-sided bus. [Repetition of *ma*, a child's natural utterance.]

mamma[2] *mam′ə*, *n.* the milk gland: the breast: — *pl.* **mamm′ae** (*-ē*). — *adjs.* **mamm′ary** of the nature of, relating to, the mammae or breasts; **mamm′ate** having breasts. — *n.* **mamm′ifer** a mammal. — *adjs.* **mammif′erous** having mammae; **mamm′iform** having the form of a breast. — *n.* **mammill′a** see **mamilla.** — *adj.* **mammogen′ic** of hormones, promoting growth of the duct and alveolar systems of the milk gland. — *ns.* **mamm′ogram** X-ray photograph of the breast; **mammog′raphy** radiological examination of the breast. [L. *mamma*.]

mammal *mam′əl*, *n.* a member of the **Mammalia** (*mə-mā′li-ə*), the class of animals that suckle their young. — *adjs.* **mammā′lian; mammalif′erous** (*geol.*) bearing remains of mammals; **mammalog′ical.** — *ns.* **mammalogist** (*-al′ə-jist*); **mammal′ogy** the scientific knowledge of mammals. [L. *mammālis*, of the breast — *mamma*, the breast.]

mammary, mammate. See **mamma**[2].

mammee *mam-ē′*, *n.* a fruit (also **mammee apple**) of the West Indies, etc., having a sweet taste and aromatic odour: the tree producing it (*Mammea americana*; family Guttiferae). — **mammee′-sapo′ta** the marmalade tree or its fruit. [Sp. *mamey*, from Haitian.]

mammer *mam′ər*, (*Shak.*) *v.i.* to hesitate, to stand muttering and in doubt. [Prob. imit.]

mammet *mam′it*, **maumet, mawmet** *möm′it*, **mommet** *mom′it*, *ns.* an idol: a puppet, a figure dressed up (*Shak.*). — *ns.* **mamm′etry, maum′etry, maw′metry** idolatry: idols collectively: Islam (*arch.*). [**Mohammed**; cf. **Mahoun(d).**]

mammifer, mammiform. See **mamma**[2].

mammilla. Same as **mamilla.**

mammock *mam′ək*, *n.* a shapeless piece, shred (also **mumm′ock**). — *v.t.* (*Shak.*) to tear to pieces, to mangle. [Origin obscure.]

mammogenic, mammography. See **mamma**[2].

mammon *mam′ən*, *n.* riches: (with *cap.*) the god of riches. — *adj.* **mamm′onish** devoted to money-getting. — *ns.* **mamm′onism** devotion to gain; **mamm′onist, mamm′onite** a person devoted to riches: a worldling. — *adj.* **mammonist′ic.** [L.L. *mam(m)ōna* — Gr. *mam(m)ōnās* — Aramaic *māmōn*, riches.]

mammoth *mam′əth*, *n.* an extinct species of elephant. — *adj.* resembling the mammoth in size: gigantic. — **mamm′oth-tree′** the Sequoia. [Former Russ. *mammot* (now *mamant* or *mamont*).]

mammy, mammy-wagon. See **mamma**[1].

mamselle. See **mademoiselle.**

man[1] *man*, *n.* a human being: mankind: a grown-up human male: a male attendant or servant: a workman, employee: a vassal: a follower: an uncommissioned soldier: one possessing a distinctively manly character: a husband, or man living as a husband with a woman: a piece used in playing chess or draughts or similar game: a cairn or rock pillar: a hill with such a man: a ship, as in *man*-of-war: a word of familiar address: formerly in the Scottish Highlands, a layman of peculiar holiness and austerity: — *pl.* **men.** — *adj.*, also in composition (as **man′-cook′**) male. — *v.t.* to furnish with a man or men: to provide with a (human) worker, operator, etc.: to strengthen or put manhood into: to accustom (a hawk) to being handled, to humans, etc.

(*falcony*): — *pr.p.* **mann'ing**; *pa.t.* and *pa.p.* **manned** (*mand*). — *n.* **man'dom** (*rare*) humanity, man collectively. — *adj.* **man'ful** having the good qualities of a man: manly: bold: courageous: vigorous: stout: noble-minded. — *adv.* **man'fully.** — *ns.* **man'fulness; man'hood** state of being a man: manly quality: human nature; **man'kind'** the human race, the mass of human beings: (*man'kind*) human males collectively. — *adj.* (*Shak.*) man-like, viragoish. — *adj.* **man'-like** having the appearance or qualities of a human being or of an adult human male. — *adv.* in the manner of a man: in a way that might be expected of a male person: manfully. — *n.* **man'liness.** — *adjs.* **man'ly** befitting a man: brave: dignified: noble: pertaining to manhood: not childish or womanish; **manned** (*mand*); **mann'ish** like or savouring of a male or grown-up man (usu. depreciatory): masculine. — *n.* **mann'ishness.** — **man'about-town'** a fashionable, sophisticated man; **man'-at-arms'** a soldier, esp. mounted and heavy-armed; **man'-body** (*Scot.*) a man; **man'-child** a male child: a boy: — *pl.* **men'-children; man'-day** a day's work of one man: — *pl.* **man'-days; man'-eater** a cannibal: a tiger or other animal that has acquired the habit of eating men: a woman given to chasing, catching and devouring men (*coll.*). — *adj.* **man'-en'tered** (*Shak.*) entered upon manhood. — **Man Friday** a factotum or servile attendant — from Robinson Crusoe's man. — *v.t.* **man'handle** to move by manpower: to handle, treat, roughly (orig. *slang*). — **man'hole** a hole large enough to admit a man, esp. to a sewer, cable-duct, or the like; **manhood suffrage** right to vote accorded to male citizens; **man'-hour** an hour's work of one man: — *pl.* **man'-hours; man'hunt** an organised search for a person, esp. one mounted by police, etc. for a criminal; **man'-jack'**, **man jack** individual man (as *every man-jack*). — *adj.* **man'-made** made by man: humanly made or originated: (of fibre, fabric, etc.) artificial, synthetic. — **man'-mill'iner** a man engaged in millinery — often in contempt; **man'-man'agement** the organisation of the work of subordinates. — *adj.* **man'-mind'ed** having the mind or qualities of a man. — **man'-of-war'**, **man'-o'-war'** a warship: a soldier (*arch.* or *facet.*): (in full **man-of-war bird**) the frigate-bird: (**Portuguese man-of-war** see **Physalia**): — *pl.* **men'-of-war'**, **men'-o'-war'**; **man'-of-war's'-man** a man who serves on board a warship; **man'-or'chis** an orchid (*Aceras anthropophora*) whose flowers are like little men; **man'pack** a package of supplies or equipment designed to be carried by one person; **man'power** the agency or energy of man in doing work: the rate at which a man can work: available resources in population or in able-bodied men; **man'-queller** (*Shak.*) a man-killer, a murderer; **man'rider, man'riding train** the formal name for a paddy (train) (q.v.); — **man'-servant** a male servant: — *pl.* **men'-servants; man'shift** the work done by one man in one shift or work period. — *adj.* **man'-size(d)** suitable for, or requiring, a man: very big (*coll.*). — **man'slaughter** the slaying of a man: unlawful homicide without malice aforethought (*law*); **man'-slayer** one who kills a man; **man'-stealer** one who steals human beings, especially to make slaves of them; **man'trap** a trap for catching trespassers: any source of potential danger; **man'-watching** the study of body language; **man'-week, man'-year** a week's, year's work of one man: — *pl.* **man'-weeks, man'-years; men'folk(s)** male people, esp. a woman's male relatives; **mens'wear** clothing for men. — **as one man** all together: unanimously; **be one's own man** to be independent, not answerable to anyone else; **be someone's man** to be exactly the person someone is seeking for a particular purpose; **man alive!** an exclamation of surprise; **man in the moon** a fancied semblance of a man seen in the moon; **man in the street** the ordinary, everyday man — Tom, Dick, or Harry; **man of business** an agent or a lawyer; **man of God** a holy man: a clergyman; **man of his hands** a man of prowess; **man of law** a lawyer; **man of letters** a scholar: a writer; **man of sin** the devil:

Antichrist; **man of straw** a person of no substance (esp. financially): one nominally, but not really, responsible: a sham opponent or argument set up for the sake of disputation; **man of the match** the most outstanding player in a cricket, football, etc. match (also *fig.*); **man of the moment** the man (most capable of) dealing with the present situation; **man of the world** one accustomed to the ways and dealings of men; **man to man** one man to another as individuals in fight or talk: frank and confidential; **old man of the sea** see **old**; **to a man** without exception.   [O.E. *mann*; Ger. *Mann*, Du. *man*.]
man². See **mun¹**.
mana *mä'nä*, (*anthrop.*) *n.* a mysterious power associated with persons and things.   [Maori.]
manacle *man'ə-kl*, *n.* a handcuff. — *v.t.* to handcuff: to shackle.   [O.Fr. *manicle* — L. *manicula*, dim. of *manica*, sleeve, glove, handcuff — *manus*, hand.]
manage *man'ij*, *n.* (*arch.*) manège — *v.t.* to train by exercise, as a horse: to handle: to wield: to conduct: to control: to administer, be at the head of: to deal tactfully with: to husband, use sparingly (*arch.*): to contrive successfully: to have time for: to be able to cope with: to manipulate: to contrive: to bring about. — *v.i.* to conduct affairs: to get on, contrive to succeed. — *n.* **manageabil'ity** the quality of being manageable. — *adj.* **man'ageable** that can be managed: governable. — *n.* **man'ageableness.** — *adv.* **man'ageably.** — *ns.* **man'agement** the art or act of managing: manner of directing or of using anything: administration: skilful treatment: a body of managers; **man'ager** one who manages: in an industrial firm or business, a person who deals with administration and with the design and marketing, etc., of the product, as opposed to its actual construction: one who organises other people's doings: a domestic contriver: a person legally appointed to manage a business, property, etc., as receiver: a party leader (*U.S.*): — *fem.* **man'ageress; man'agership.** — *adjs.* **manage'rial** of or pertaining to a manager, or to management; **man'aging** handling: controlling: administering: contriving: domineering. — **management accounting** same as **cost-accounting; management consultant** one who advises firms on the most efficient procedures applicable to particular businesses or industries.   [It. *maneggio* — L. *manus*, the hand.]
manakin *man'ə-kin*, *n.* a small tropical American bird of various species of or akin to the Cotinga family: (*erroneously*) a manikin.   [See **manikin**.]
mañana *man-yä'nə*, *män-yä'nä*, (Sp.) *n.* and *adj.* tomorrow: an unspecified time in the future.
manatee, manati *man-ə-tē'*, *n.* a sirenian (*Manatus* or *Trichechus*) of the warm parts of the Atlantic and the rivers of Brazil.   [Sp. *manatí* — Carib *manatoui*; not connected with L. *manus*, hand.]
mancando *mangk-an'dō*, (*mus.*) *adj.* and *adv.* fading away.   [It., lacking.]
manche *mänsh*, (*her.*) *n.* sleeve.   [Fr.]
Manchester *man'chis-tər*, *adj.* belonging to or made in *Manchester*, or similar to goods made in Manchester, applied esp. to cotton cloths. — **Manchester school** the followers of Bright and Cobden, advocates of free-trade and of individual freedom of action; **Manchester terrier** an English breed of small short-haired black-and-tan dog.
manchet *man'chit*, *n.* the finest bread of wheat (*obs.*): a round loaf (*arch.* or *dial.*): a loaf of manchet.   [Origin obscure.]
manchineel *manch-i-nēl'*, *n.* a tropical American tree (*Hippomane*) of the spurge family, with poisonous latex.   [Sp. *manzanilla*, dim. of *manzana*, apple.]
Manchu, Manchoo *man-chōō'*, or *man'*, *n.* one of the race from which Manchuria took its name, and which governed China from the 17th to the 20th century: their language. — *adj.* of or pertaining to Manchuria or to its inhabitants. — *n.* **Manchu'ria.** — *adj.* **Manchur'ian.**   [Manchu, pure.]
mancipation *man-si-pä'shən*, (*Rom. hist.*) *n.* a legal transfer by actual or symbolic sale. — *v.t.* **man'cipate.** —

adj. **man′cipatory** (-pə-tə-ri). [L. *mancipātiō, -ōnis* — *manus,* hand, *capĕre,* to take.]

manciple *man′si-pl, n.* a steward: a purveyor, particularly of a college or an inn of court. [O.Fr., — L. *manceps, -cipis,* a purchaser: see foregoing.]

Mancunian *man*(*g*)-*kūn′i-ən, adj.* belonging to Manchester. — *n.* a Manchester person. [Doubtful L. *Mancunium,* a Roman station in Manchester. *Mamucium* is probably right.]

mancus *mang′kəs,* (*hist.*) *n.* an old English coin or its value, thirty pence: — *pl.* **manc′uses.** [O.E. *mancus.*]

-mancy *-man-si, -mən-si,* in composition, divination. — **-mantic** adjective combining form. [Gr. *manteiā.*]

mand. Spens. for **manned.** See **man**[1].

Mandaean *man-dē′ən, n.* and *adj.* one of an ancient and surviving sect in southern Babylonia, their religion a corrupt Gnosticism, with many Jewish and Parsee elements. — Also *Mendaites, Nasoraeans, Sabians,* or (misleadingly) *Christians of St John*: the Aramaic dialect of their sacred books. — Also *adj.* [Mandaean *mandayyā,* knowledge, gnosis.]

mandala *mun′də-lə, n.,* a symbol of the universe, varying a little but having an enclosing circle, usu. images of deities, and a tendency to arrangement in fours, used as an aid to religious meditation: in the psychology of Jung, symbol of the wholeness of the self (in imperfect form shows lack of harmony in the self). [Sans. *maṇḍala.*]

mandamus *man-dā′məs, n.* a writ or command issued by a higher court to a lower: — *pl.* **mandā′muses.** [L. *mandāmus,* we command.]

mandarin *man′də-rin, -rēn, n.* a member of any of nine ranks of officials under the Chinese Empire (*hist.*): a statuette of a seated Chinese figure, often with a movable head (a *nodding mandarin*): (*cap.*) the most important form of the Chinese language: a man in office, bureaucrat: a person of standing in the literary world, often one who tends to be reactionary or pedantic or express himself *ore rotundo* (also **man′-darine**) a small kind of orange (of Chinese origin): its colour: a liqueur. — *adj.* pertaining to a mandarin: of style or language, formal and ornate. — *n.* **man′-darinate** office of mandarin: mandarins as a group. — **mandarin collar** or **neck** a high, narrow, stand-up collar the front ends of which do not quite meet; **mandarin duck** a crested Asiatic duck (*Aix galericulata*); **mandarin orange** a mandarin (mandarine). [Port. *mandarim* — Malay (from Hind.) *mantrī,* counsellor — Sans. *mantra,* counsel.]

mandate *man′dāt, n.* a charge: a command from a superior official or judge to an inferior, ordering him how to act, esp. from the Pope to a legate, etc.: a right given to a person to act in name of another: a rescript of the Pope: the sanction held to be given by the electors to an elected body, to act according to its declared policies, election manifesto, etc.: the power conferred upon a state by the League of Nations in 1919 to govern a region elsewhere: (also with *cap.*) any of the regions governed in this way (also **mandated territory**). — *v.t.* **mandate′** to assign by mandate: to invest with authority. — *ns.* **man′datary, man′datory** (-də-tə-ri) the holder of a mandate: a mandate; **mandā′tor** the giver of a mandate. — *adj.* **man′datory** containing a mandate or command: of the nature of a mandate: bestowed by mandate: compulsory: allowing no option. [L. *mandātum* — *mandāre* — *manus,* hand, *dăre,* give.]

mandible *man′di-bl, n.* a jaw or jaw-bone, esp. the lower: either part of a bird's bill: an organ performing the functions of a jaw in the lower animals, as one of the first pair of mouth appendages in insects or crustaceans. — *adjs.* **mandib′ular** relating to the jaw; **mandib′ulate, -d.** [L. *mandibula* — *mandĕre,* to chew.]

mandilion. See **mandylion.**

Mandingo *man-ding′gō, n.* an African people of the Niger valley: a member of this people: their language: — *pl.* **Manding′o, -oes, -os.** — Also *adj.*

mandioc, mandioc(c)a. See **manioc.**

mandir, mandira *mun′dər, -ä, n.* a Hindu or Jain temple. [Hind.]

mandoline, mandolin *man′də-lin, -lēn, n.* a round-backed instrument like a lute, sustained notes being played by repeated plucking. — *ns.* **mandō′la, mandō′ra** a large mandoline. [It. *mandola, mandora,* dim. *mandolino.*]

mandorla *man′dör-lə, n.* an oval panel, or a work of art filling one: the vesica piscis. [It., almond.]

mandrake *man′drāk, n.* a poisonous plant (*Mandragora*) of the potato family, subject of many strange fancies: extended to various other plants, as white bryony. — (*Shak.*) **mandragora** (-*drag′ə-rə*). [L. *mandragora* — Gr. *mandragorās.*]

mandrel, mandril *man′drəl, n.* a bar of iron fitted to a turning-lathe on which articles to be turned are fixed: the axle of a circular saw. [Fr. *mandrin.*]

mandrill *man′dril, n.* a large West African baboon with a red and blue muzzle. [Prob. **man**[1] and **drill**[2].]

manducate *man′dū-kāt, v.t.* to chew or eat. — *adj.* **man′-ducable.** — *n.* **manducā′tion.** — *adj.* **man′ducatory** (-kə-tə-ri). [L. *manducāre* — *mandĕre,* to chew.]

mandylion *man-dil′i-ən, n.* a loose outer garment worn e.g. by soldiers over their armour (also **mandil′ion**) (*hist.*): (with *cap.*) the name of a cloth supposed to bear the imprint of the face of Jesus, renowned in the Eastern Christian world as the Image of Edessa (modern Urfa in Turkey) whence it was taken to Constantinople in 944 and finally lost in the sack of 1204. [M.Fr. *mandillon,* cloak, and Late Gr. *mandylion,* cloth; cf. ultimately L. *mantel*(*l*)*um,* napkin or cloak, and L. *mantele, mantelium,* napkin.]

mane *mān, n.* long hair on the back of the neck and neighbouring parts, as in the horse and the lion: a long bushy head of hair. — *adjs.* **maned; mane′less.** — **mane′-sheet** a covering for the upper part of a horse's head. [O.E. *manu*; O.N. *mön*; Ger. *Mähne.*]

-mane *mān,* in composition, one who is very enthusiastic about a specified thing. [Gr. *maniā.*]

manège *man-ezh′, n.* the managing of horses: the art of horsemanship or of training horses: a horse's actions and paces as taught him: a riding-school. — *v.t.* to train, as a horse. [Fr.; cf. **manage.**]

maneh. Same as **mina**[1].

manes *mā′nēz,* (*Roman myth.*) *n.pl.* the spirits of the dead. [L. *mānēs.*]

manet *ma′net* (L.) remains (on the stage): — *pl.* **manent.**

maneuver. U.S. spelling of **manoeuvre.**

mangabeira *mang-ga-bā′rə, n.* a Brazilian apocynaceous rubber tree (*Hancornia speciosa*). [Port., — Tupí *mangaba.*]

mangabey *mang′gə-bā, n.* the white-eyelid monkey, any species of the mainly West African genus *Cercocebus,* esp. the sooty mangabey. [From a district in Madagascar, where, however, they are not found.]

mangal *mang-gäl′, n.* a brazier. [Turk.]

manganese *mang-gə-nēz′, mang′, n.* a hard brittle greyish-white metallic element (Mn; at. numb. 25): (originally and commercially) its dioxide (*black manganese*) or other ore. — *n.* **mang′anate** a salt of manganic acid. — *adjs.* **manganic** (-*gan′ik*) of manganese of higher valency; **manganif′erous** containing manganese. — *ns.* **Mang′anin**® an alloy of copper with manganese and some nickel; **mang′anite** a salt of manganous acid (*chem.*): a grey ore, hydrated oxide of manganous (*min.*). — *adj.* **mang′anous** of manganese of lower valency. — **manganese bronze** a bronze or brass with a little manganese; **manganese spar** rhodochrosite; **manganese steel** a very hard, shock-resistant steel containing a higher than usual percentage of manganese. [Fr. *manganèse* — It. *manganese* — L. *magnēsia.*]

mange. See **mangy.**

mangel-wurzel, mangold-wurzel *mang′gl-wûr′zl, n.* a variety of beet cultivated as cattle food. — Also **mang′el, mang′old.** [Ger. *Mangold,* beet, *Wurzel,* root.]

manger *mānj′ər, n.* a trough in which food is laid for horses and cattle. — **dog in the manger** see **dog**[1].

[O.Fr. *mangeoire* — L. *mandūcāre*, to chew, eat.]

mangetout *măzh-tōō, n.* a type of pea, the pod of which is also eaten. — Also **mangetout pea, sugar pea.** [Fr., *lit.,* eat-all.]

mangey. See **mangy.**

mangle[1] *mang'gl, v.t.* to hack to raggedness: to tear in cutting: to mutilate: to bungle (*fig.*): to distort. — *n.* **mang'ler.** [A.Fr. *mangler, mahangler,* prob. a freq. of O.Fr. *mahaigner,* to maim — *mahaing,* a hurt.]

mangle[2] *mang'gl, n.* a rolling-press for smoothing linen: a wringer. — *v.t.* to smooth with a mangle: to calender: to wring (clothes). — *n.* **mang'ler.** [Du. *mangel* — Gr. *manganon*; cf. **mangonel.**]

mango *mang'gō, n.* a tropical, orig. East Indian, tree (*Mangifera indica*) of the cashew-nut family: its fleshy fruit: a green musk-melon pickled: — *pl.* **mang'oes.** — **wild mango** an African tree of the Simarubaceae with edible fruit, oil-giving seed, and termite-resistant wood. [Port. *manga* — Malay *manggā* — Tamil *mān-kāy,* mango-fruit.]

mangold, mangold-wurzel. See **mangel-wurzel.**

mangonel *mang'gə-nel, n.* a mediaeval engine for throwing stones, etc. [O.Fr., — L.L. *mangonum* — Gr. *manganon.*]

mangosteen *mang'gə-stēn, n.* a tree, *Garcinia mangostana,* or its dark brown, orange-shaped fruit, with thick rind and delicious rose-coloured pulp. — Also **mang'ostan.** [Malay *mangustan.*]

mangouste. See **mongoose.**

mangrove *mang'grōv, n.* a tree, esp. species of Rhizophora, that grows in muddy swamps covered at high tide or on tropical coasts and estuary shores. [Origin obscure.]

mangy, mangey *mānj'i, adj.* scabby: affected with mange: shabby, seedy: mean. — *ns.* **mange** (*mānj*; a back-formation) inflammation of the skin of animals caused by mites; **mang'iness.** [Fr. *mangé,* eaten, pa.p. of *manger* — L. *mandūcāre,* to chew.]

manhandle. See **man**[1].

Manhattan *man-hat'ən, n.* an American cocktail containing vermouth, whisky, bitters, etc. [*Manhattan,* New York.]

manhole, manhood, manhunt. See **man**[1].

mania *mā'ni-ə, n.* a mental illness characterised by euphoria, excessively rapid speech and violent, destructive actions (*psychiatry*): the elated phase of manic-depressive psychosis (*psychiatry*): excessive or unreasonable desire: a craze. — **-mānia** in composition, an abnormal and obsessive desire or inclination, or, more loosely, an extreme enthusiasm, for a specified thing. — **-māniac** noun and adjective combining form. — *n.* **mā'niac** a person affected with mania: a madman. — *adj.* affected by, relating to, mania: raving mad. — *adj.* **maniacal** (*mə-nī'ə-kl*). — *adv.* **mani'acally.** — *adj.* **manic** (*man'ik*) of or affected by mania. — *adv.* **man'ically.** — **man'ic-depress'ive** one suffering from manic-depressive psychosis. — Also *adj.* — **manic-depressive psychosis** a form of mental illness characterised by phases of depression and elation, either alone or alternately, with lucid intervals. [L., — Gr. *maniā.*]

Manichaean, Manichean *man-i-kē'ən, adj.* pertaining to followers of *Mani* or *Manichaeus,* a native of Ecbatana (*c.* A.D. 216–*c.* 276), who taught that everything sprang from two chief principles, light and darkness, or good and evil. — *n.* a believer in Manichaeanism — also **Man'ichee.** — *ns.* **Manichae'anism, Man'ichaeism, Maniche'anism, Man'icheism** any belief in radical dualism.

manicure *man'i-kūr, n.* the care of hands and nails: professional treatment for the hands and nails: one who practises this. — *v.t.* to apply manicure to. — *n.* **man'icurist.** [L. *manus,* hand, *cūra,* care.]

manifest *man'i-fest, adj.* that may be easily seen by the eye or perceived by the mind. — *v.t.* to make clear or easily seen: to put beyond doubt: to reveal or declare. — *n.* an open or public statement: a list or invoice of the cargo of a ship or aeroplane to be exhibited at the custom-house: a list of passengers carried by an aeroplane. — *adj.* **manifest'able, manifest'ible** that can be manifested or clearly shown. — *n.* **manifestā'tion** act of disclosing what is dark or secret: that by which something is manifested: display: mass-meeting, procession, demonstration. — *adj.* **manifest'ative.** — *adv.* **man'ifestly.** — *n.* **man'ifestness** state of being manifest. [L. *manifestus,* prob. *manus,* the hand, *festus,* pa.p. of obs. *fendēre,* to strike, to dash against (as in *offendēre*).]

manifesto *man-i-fest'ō, n.* a public written declaration of the intentions, opinions, or motives of a sovereign or of a leader, party, or body: — *pl.* **manifest'o(e)s.** — *v.i.* (*rare*) to issue a manifesto. [It.; see **manifest.**]

manifold *man'i-fōld, adj.* various in kind or quality: many in number: having many features: performing several functions. — *n.* a pipe with several lateral outlets to others: aggregate (*math.*): a topological space or surface that is related in a particular way to Euclidean space (*math.*): a carbon-copy: manyplies (*dial.*; also in *pl.*). — *v.t.* to multiply: to make simultaneous copies of. — *n.* **man'ifolder.** — *adv.* **man'ifoldly.** — *n.* **man'ifoldness.** — **man'ifold-pa'per** thin paper for making copies; **man'ifold-writ'er** a copying apparatus. [**many,** and suff. **-fold.**]

maniform *man'i-förm, adj.* having the form of a hand. [L. *manus,* the hand, *förma,* a shape.]

manihoc. See **manioc.**

Manihot *man'i-hot, n.* a tropical American genus of the spurge family, including manioc. [**manioc.**]

manikin, mannikin *man'i-kin, n.* a dwarf: an anatomical model: a mannequin: (*erroneously*) a manakin. [Du. *manneken,* a double dim. of *man*; Eng. **man**[1].]

manil(l)a *mə-nil'ə, n.* cheroot made in *Manila*: abaca: strong paper orig. made from abaca. — **Manil(l)a hemp** abaca.

manilla *mə-nil'ə, n.* a West African bracelet, serving as money. [Sp.,—L.L. *manilia,* a bracelet—L. *manus,* the hand, or L. *monīlia* (pl. of *monīle*), necklace, influenced by *manus.*]

manille *mə-nil', n.* in ombre and quadrille, the highest card but one. [Sp. *malilla.*]

manioc *man'i-ok, n.* a plant of the Manihot genus, cassava: meal therefrom. — Also **man'dioc, mandio'c(c)a, man'ihoc.** [Tupí *mandioca.*]

maniple *man'i-pl, n.* a company of foot-soldiers in the Roman army (*hist.*): in the Western Church, a eucharistic vestment, a narrow strip worn on the left arm. — *adj. and n.* **manipular** (*mə-nip'ū-lər*). [L. *manipulus* — *manus,* the hand, *plēre,* to fill.]

maniplies. Same as **manyplies.**

manipular. See **maniple, manipulate.**

manipulate *mə-nip'ū-lāt, v.t.* to work with the hands: to handle or manage: to give a false appearance to: to turn to one's own purpose or advantage. — *n.* **manipulā'tion.** — *adjs.* **manip'ul(āt)able** capable of being manipulated; **manip'ular, manip'ulative, manip'ulatory.** — *n.* **manip'ulātor** one who manipulates: a mechanical device for handling small, remote, or radioactive objects. — See also **master-slave manipulator** under **master.** [L.L. *manipulāre, -ātum*; see **maniple.**]

Manis *mā'nis, n.* the pangolin or scaly ant-eater. [App. intended as sing. of **manes.**]

manito *man'i-tō, n.* a spirit or object of reverence among American Indians: — *pl.* **man'itos** — Also **manitou** (*-tōō*). [Algonkin.]

manjack *man'jak, n.* a West Indian boraginaceous tree (*Cordia macrophylla*): its fruit.

man-jack, mankind. See **man**[1].

manky *mang'ki,* (*dial.*) *adj.* dirty, rotten. [Origin unknown.]

manly. See **man**[1].

manna *man'ə, n.* the food miraculously provided for the Israelites in the wilderness (*B.*): delicious food for body or mind: anything advantageous falling one's way as by divine bounty: a sugary exudation from the **mann'a-ash** (*Fraxinus ornus*), **-larch (Briançon manna),** and other trees, from a species of tamarisk, from Alhagi, etc.: edible fragments of the **mann'a-li'chen** (*Lecanora*): float-grass seeds: honey-dew. — *adj.* **mannif'erous.** — *ns.* **mann'ite, mann'itol** a sweet alcohol, $C_6H_8(OH)_6$, got from manna, from seaweeds of the genus Laminaria, etc.; **mann'ose** a sugar ($C_6H_{12}O_6$) got by oxidising mannitol. — **mann'a-croup** (-*krōōp'*; Russ. *krupa*), **-groats** grains of manna-grass; **mann'a-dew** manna imagined to be solidified dew; **mann'a-grass'** an aquatic grass (*Glyceria*) with edible seeds, float-grass. [Heb. *mān hū*, what is it? or from *man*, a gift.]

mannequin *man'i-kin*, *n.* a dummy figure: a person, usu. a woman, employed to wear and display clothes. [Fr., — Du.; see **manikin.**]

manner[1] *man'ər*, *n.* the way in which anything is done: method: fashion: personal style of acting or bearing: custom: style of writing or of thought: sort (of; formerly often with omission of following *of*): style: (*pl.*) morals (*arch.*): (*pl.*) social conduct: (*pl.*) good behaviour. — *adj.* **mann'ered** having manners (esp. in compounds, as *well-* or *ill-mannered*): affected with mannerism: artificial: stilted. — *ns.* **mann'erism** a constant sameness of manner: stiltedness: a marked peculiarity or trick of style or manner, esp. in literary composition: manner or style becoming wearisome by its sameness: a late 16th-cent. art style characterised by distortion esp. of the human figure, bright harsh colours, etc.; **mann'erist** one addicted to mannerism. — *adj.* **manneris'tic.** — *adv.* **manneris'tically.** — *n.* **mann'erliness.** — *adj.* **mann'erly** showing good manners: well-behaved: not rude. — *adv.* with good manners: civilly: respectfully: without rudeness. — **all manner of** all kinds of; **by no manner of means** under no circumstances whatever; **in a manner** in a certain way; **make one's manners** (*arch.*) to salute a person on meeting by a bow, curtsy, etc.; **shark's manners** rapacity; **to the manner born** accustomed from birth. [Fr. *manière* — *main* — L. *manus*, the hand.]

manner[2] *man'ər*, *n.* Same as **mainor (in** or **with the manner).**

manniferous. See **manna.**

mannikin. See **manikin.**

manning, mannish. See **man**[1].

mannite, mannitol, mannose. See **manna.**

manoao *mä'nō-ow*, *n.* a shrub of the heath group: — *pl.* **ma'noaos.** [Maori.]

manoeuvre, in U.S. **maneuver,** *ma-nōō'vər*, or -*nū'*, *n.* a piece of dexterous management: a stratagem: a skilful and clever movement in military or naval tactics: (usu. *pl.*) a large-scale battle-training exercise of armed forces. — *v.i.* and *v.t.* to perform a manoeuvre: to manage with art: to change the position of troops or of ships: to effect or to gain by manoeuvres. — *ns.* **manoeu'vrer; manoeuvrabil'ity.** — *adj.* **manoeu'vrable.** — In U.S. **maneuverer,** etc. [Fr. *manœuvre* — L. *manū*, by hand, *opera*, work; cf. **manure.**]

manometer *man-om'i-tər*, *n.* an instrument for measuring and comparing the pressure of fluids. — *adjs.* **manometric** (*man-ō-met'rik*), **-al.** — *n.* **manom'etry.** [Gr. *manos*, rare, thin, *metron*, measure.]

ma non troppo *ma non trop'ō* (*mus.*) *adv.* but not too much. See **troppo.** [It.]

manor *man'ər*, *n.* the land belonging to a nobleman, or so much as he formerly kept for his own use: the district over which the court of the lord of the manor had authority (*hist.*): a tract of land in America for which a fee-farm rent was paid (*hist.*): a police district (*slang*). — *adj.* **manorial** (*ma-nō'ri-əl*, -*nö'*) pertaining to a manor. — **man'or-house, -seat** the house or seat belonging to a manor. [O.Fr. *manoir* — L. *manēre*, *mānsum*, to stay.]

manqué *mä-kā*, (Fr.) *adj.* having had ambition or potential, but without it being fulfilled — placed after the noun.

manred *man'red*, (*obs.*) *n.* homage: a body of vassals. — (*Scot.*) **man'rent.** [O.E. *mannrǣden*; **man**[1] and suff. -*rǣden*, expressing mode or state.]

mansard *man'särd*, *n.* a roof having the lower part steeper

than the upper. — Usually **man'sard-roof'.** [Employed by François *Mansard* or *Mansart* (1598–1666).]

manse *mans*, *n.* an ecclesiastical residence, esp. that of a parish minister of the Church of Scotland. — **son of the manse** a minister's son. [L.L. *mansus, mansa,* a dwelling — *manēre, mānsum,* to remain.]

mansion *man'shən*, *n.* abode, stay (*obs.*): a resting-place on a journey (*obs.*): a dwelling-place (*arch.*; often in *pl.*): an apartment, separate lodging in a building (*obs.*): a large house: a manor-house: a house (*astrol.*): (in *pl.*) a large building let in flats. — *n.* **man'sionary** (*Shak.* **man'sonry**) residence: mansions. — **man'sion-house** a mansion (**the Mansion House** the official residence of the Lord Mayor of London). [O.Fr., — L. *mānsiō, -ōnis* — *manēre, mānsum,* to remain, to stay.]

manslaughter. See **man**[1].

mansonry. See **mansion.**

mansuete *man'swēt*, (*arch.*) *adj.* gentle: mild: tame. — *n.* **man'suetude** (-*swi-tūd*). [L. *mānsuētus* — *manus,* hand, *suēscēre,* to accustom.]

mansworn *man'swörn,* -*swörn,* (*arch.*) *adj.* perjured. [O.E. *mānswerian* — *mān,* evil, *swerian,* to swear.]

manta *man'tə*, *n.* a blanket: a cloak: a horse-cloth: mantlet (*fort.*): (with *cap.*) a genus of gigantic rays or sea-vampires. [Sp.]

manteau, manto *man'tō, n.* (17th–18th cent.) a woman's loose gown: — *pls.* **man'teaus** (-*tōz*), **man'teaux** (-*tō,* -*tōz*), **man'toes, man'tos.** [Fr. *manteau* — L. *mantel-lum.*]

manteel *man-tēl',* (*obs.*) *n.* a soldier's cloak: a lady's cape. [Fr. *mantille* — Sp. *mantilla.*]

mantel *man'tl*, *n.* a manteltree: a mantelpiece: a mantel-shelf. — *n.* **man'telet** a mantlet. — **man'telpiece** the ornamental structure over and in front of a fireplace: a mantelshelf; **man'telshelf** the ornamental shelf over a fireplace; **man'teltree** the lintel or arch of a fireplace. [**mantle.**]

mantelet. See under **mantel, mantle.**

mantic *man'tik*, *adj.* relating to divination: prophetic. — See also **-mancy.** [Gr. *mantikos* — *mantis,* a prophet.]

manticore *man'ti-kōr,* -*kör,* **manticora** -*kō',* -*kö'rə, ns.* a fabulous compound of lion and scorpion with a human head. [L. *manticora* — Gr. *mantichōrās,* a wrong reading for *martichōrās,* from an Old Persian word for man-eater.]

mantid. See **Mantis.**

mantilla *man-til'ə, n.* a small mantle: a kind of veil covering the head and falling down upon the shoulders. [Sp.; dim. of *manta.*]

Mantis *man'tis, n.* a genus of orthopterous insects carrying their large spinous forelegs in the attitude of prayer: (without *cap.*) an insect of this or a related genus. — *n.* **man'tid** any member of the genus. — **mantis shrimp** a stomatopod crustacean with claws like the mantis. [Gr. *mantis, -eōs,* prophet.]

mantissa *man-tis'ə, n.* the fractional part of a logarithm. [L., make-weight.]

mantle *man'tl*, *n.* a cloak or loose outer garment (*arch.*): a covering: symbol of the spirit or authority (of; in allusion to Elijah, 1 Kings xix. 19 ff.): a fold of the integument of a mollusc or a brachiopod secreting the shell: the back and folded wings of a bird: a scum on a liquid (*arch.*): a hood or network of refractory material that becomes incandescent when exposed to a flame: the part of the earth immediately beneath the crust, constituting the greater part of the earth's bulk, and presumed to consist of solid heavy rock. — *v.t.* to cover: to obscure: to form a scum upon (*arch.*): to suffuse: to disguise. — *v.i.* to spread like a mantle: to develop a scum (*arch.*): to froth: to be suffused: to stretch the wings over the legs, as a hawk. — *ns.* **man'tlet, man'telet** a small cloak for women: a movable shield or screen (*fort.*); **man'tling** cloth suitable for mantles: the drapery of a coat-of-arms (*her.*). — **mantle rock** loose rock at the earth's surface. [Partly through O.E. *mentel,* partly through O.Fr. *mantel* (Fr.

manteau) — L. *mantel(l)um*.]

manto. See **manteau.**

Mantoux test *man-tōō test*, (*med.*) a test for the existence of tuberculosis in man by the injection of tuberculin into the skin. [From C. *Mantoux* (1877–1956), French physician.]

mantra *man′trə*, *n.* a Vedic hymn: a sacred text used as an incantation: extended to music having mystical effect: a word, phrase, etc., chanted or repeated inwardly in meditation. — Also **mantram**. [Sans., instrument of thought.]

mantrap. See **man**[1].

mantua *man′tū-ə*, *n.* (17th–18th cent.) a woman's loose outer gown —(*Scot.*) **mant′y.** — **man′tua-mak′er** a dressmaker. [**manteau**, confused with *Mantua*, in Italy.]

Mantuan *man′tū-ən*, *adj.* of *Mantua* in Italy. — *n.* a native or inhabitant of Mantua, esp. Virgil. — Also the name of the Latin pastoral poet Baptista *Mantuanus* (1448–1516).

manty. See **mantua.**

manual *man′ū-əl*, *adj.* of the hand, done, worked, or used by the hand, as opposed to automatic, computer-operated, etc.: working with the hands. — *n.* drill in the use of weapons, etc.: a handbook or handy compendium of a large subject or treatise: an old office-book like the modern R.C. *Rituale*: a key or keyboard played by hand: a primary feather. — *adv.* **man′ually.** — **manual alphabet** the signs for letters made by the deaf and dumb; **manual exercise** drill in handling arms. [L. *manuālis* — *manus*, the hand.]

manubrium *mā-nū′bri-əm*, *n.* any handle-like structure: the presternum or anterior part of the breast-bone in mammals: the pendent oral part of a medusa: — *pl.* **manū′bria.** — *adj.* **manū′brial.** [L. *manūbrium*, a handle.]

manufacture *man-ū-fak′chər*, *v.t.* to make, originally by hand, now usu. by machinery and on a large scale: to fabricate, concoct: to produce unintelligently in quantity. — *v.i.* to be occupied in manufactures. — *n.* the practice, act, or process of manufacturing: anything manufactured. — *n.* **manufact′ory** a factory or place where goods are manufactured. — *adj.* **manufact′ural.** — *n.* **manufact′urer** one who works in a factory (*obs.*): a person or business engaged in manufacturing: a director or manager of a firm that manufactures goods: one who makes, concocts, or invents. — *adj.* **manufact′uring** pertaining to manufactures. [Fr., — L. *manū* (abl.) by hand, *factūra*, a making, from *facĕre*, *factum*, to make.]

manuka *mä′nōō-kä*, *n.* an Australian and New Zealand tree (*Leptospermum*) of the myrtle family, with hard wood, its leaves formerly a substitute for tea. [Maori.]

manul *mä′nōōl*, *n.* a Central Asian wild cat. [Mongolian.]

manumit *man-ū-mit′*, *v.t.* to release from slavery: to set free: — *pr.p.* **manumitt′ing;** *pa.t.* and *pa.p.* **manumitt′ed.** — *n.* **manumission** (*-mish′ən*). [L. *manūmittĕre* or *manū mittĕre* or *ēmittĕre*, to send from one's hand or control — *manus*, the hand, *mittĕre*, *missum*, to send.]

manure *mən-ūr′*, formerly *man′ūr*, *v.t.* to hold, occupy (*obs.*): to manage (*obs.*): to cultivate (*obs.*): to enrich with any fertilising substance. — *n.* any substance applied to land to make it more fruitful. — *ns.* **manūr′ance** (*arch.*) cultivation; **manūr′er.** — *adj.* **manūr′ial.** — *n.* **manūr′ing.** [A.Fr. *maynoverer* (Fr. *manœuvrer*); see **manoeuvre.**]

manus *mā′nəs*, *mä′nōōs*, *n.* the hand or corresponding part of an animal. [L. *mănus*, pl. *-ūs*.]

manuscript *man′ū-skript*, *adj.* written by hand or typed, not printed. — *n.* a book or document written by hand before invention of printing: copy for a printer, in handwriting or typed: handwritten form. — Abbrev. **MS.** [L. *manū* (abl.), by hand, *scrībĕre*, *scrīptum*, to write.]

Manx *mangks*, *n.* the language of the Isle of *Man*, belonging to the Gadhelic branch of Celtic. — *adj.* pertaining to the Isle of Man or to its inhabitants. — **Manx cat** a breed of cat with only a rudimentary tail; **Manx′man:** — *fem.* **Manx′woman.**

many *men′i*, *adj.* (*compar.* **more** *mōr*, *mör*; *superl.* **most** *mōst*) consisting of a great number: numerous. — *n.* many persons: a great number (usu. with omission of *of*): company, retinue (*Spens.*; perh. for **meinie**). — *adjs.* **man′y-coloured**, **man′y-eyed** having many colours, eyes; **man′yfold** (compare **manifold**) many in number. — *adv.* many times over. — *adjs.* **man′yfold′ed** (*Spens.*) having many layers: having many folds; **man′y-head′ed** having many heads: consisting of many. — **man′y-root** Ruellia. — *adj.* **man′y-sid′ed** having many qualities or aspects: having wide interests or varied abilities. — **man′y-sid′edness.** — *adj.* **man′y-tongued′**. — **many a** many (with singular noun and verb); **many-headed beast, monster** the people (see *belua multorum capitum* in *Appendices*); **the many** the crowd. [O.E. *manig*.]

manyplies *men′i-plīz*, *n. sing.* and *pl.* the third stomach of a ruminant — the *omasum* or *psalterium*. — Also **man′iplies** and (*dial.*) **moniplies**, **monyplies** (*mon′*, *mun′*). [**many**, **ply**[1].]

manzanilla *man-zə-nil′ə*, *-nē′yə*, *n.* a very dry, light sherry. [Sp.; also meaning camomile; same root as **manchineel**.]

manzanita *man-zə-nē′tə*, *n.* bearberry of Californian species. [Sp., dim. of *manzana*, apple.]

manzello *man-zel′ō*, *n.* a musical instrument like the soprano saxophone. [Origin uncertain.]

Maoist *mow′ist*, *n.* one who adheres to the Chinese type of communism as set forth by *Mao* Tse-tung. — Also *adj.* — *n.* **Mao′ism.** — **Mao′-jacket, -suit** a jacket, suit in the style of those worn by Mao Tse-tung and his followers — common dress in modern China.

Maori *mow′ri*, *mä′ō-ri*, *n.* a member of the aboriginal people of New Zealand: the language of this people: — *pl.* **Mao′ris.** — Also *adj.* — **Maori hen** the weka; **Maoriland** New Zealand; **Maoritanga** (*mow-ri-täŋ′gə*) Maori traditions and culture. [Maori.]

maormor *mär′mōr*, *-mör*, a wrong form of **mormaor.**

map *map*, *n.* a representation in outline of the surface features of the earth, the moon, etc., or of part of it, usu. on a plane surface: a similar plan of the stars in the sky: a representation, scheme, or epitome of the disposition or state of anything: see **function** (*math.*). — *v.t.* to make a map of: to place (the elements of a set) in one-to-one correspondence with the elements of another set (*math.*): — *pr.p.* **mapp′ing;** *pa.t.* and *pa.p.* **mapped.** — *ns.* **mapp′er;** **mapp′ery** (*Shak.*) perh. working with, or making, maps, or planning out; **mapp′ist.** — **map′-measurer** an instrument for measuring distances on a map; **map′-mounter** one who mounts maps, or backs them with cloth and fixes them on rollers, etc.; **map projection** see **projection;** **map′-reading** the interpretation of what one sees in a map. — *adv.* **map′wise** in the manner of a map. — **map out** to plan, divide up, and apportion; **off the map** out of existence: negligible: of a location, remote from main thoroughfares, etc.; **on the map** to be taken into account. [L. *mappa*, a napkin, a painted cloth, orig. Punic.]

maple *mā′pl*, *n.* any tree of the genus *Acer*, from the sap of some species of which sugar and syrup can be made; its timber. — *adj.* of maple. — **maple sugar; maple syrup; maple leaf** the emblem of Canada. [O.E. *mapul*, maple.]

mappemond *map′ə-mönd*, *map-mönd′*, *n.* a map of the world (*hist.*): the world itself (*obs.*). [L.L. *mappa mundī*.]

mapstick. See **mopstick** under **mop**[1].

maquette *ma-ket′*, *n.* a small model of something to be made, esp. a model in clay or wax of a piece of sculpture. [Fr.]

maqui *mä′kē*, *n.* a Chilean evergreen shrub (*Aristotelia maqui*; fam. *Elaeocarpaceae*) whose berry yields a medicinal wine. [Araucan.]

maquillage *ma-kē-yäzh, n.* (art of using) cosmetics, make-up. [Fr.]

maquis *mä'kē', n.sing.* and *pl.* a thicket formation of shrubs, as in Corsica and on Mediterranean shores (*bot.*): (often *cap.*) French guerrilla bands (1940–45), or a member of one. — *n.* (often *cap.*) **maquisard** (*mä-kē-zär*) a member of the maquis. [Fr., — It. *macchia* — L. *macula*, mesh.]

mar *mär, v.t.* to interfere with (*obs.*): to spoil: to impair: to injure: to damage: to disfigure: — *pr.p.* **marr'ing;** *pa.t.* and *pa.p.* **marred** (*Spens.* **mard**). — *n.* **mar'dy** (*dial.*) a spoilt child: a timid or petulant cry-baby. — Also *adj.* and *v.t.* — **mar'plot** one who defeats or mars a plot by unwarranted interference. — *adj.* and *v.i.* **mar'prelate** (to inveigh) after the manner of Martin *Marprelate*, the name assumed by the author of certain anti-episcopal tracts, 1588–9. — **mar'-sport** a spoil-sport; **mar'-text** an ignorant preacher. [O.E. *merran.*]

mara *mə-rä', n.* the so-called Patagonian hare or Dolichotis.

marabou(t) *mar'ə-bōō(t), n.* an adjutant bird, esp. an African species: its feathers: a plume or trimming of its feathers: a feather necklet: a very white raw silk. [Same as next word.]

marabout *mar'ə-bōōt, n.* a Muslim hermit, esp. in N. Africa: a Muslim shrine. [Fr., — Ar. *murābit*, hermit.]

maraca *mə-rak'ə, n.* a dance-band instrument, a gourd or substitute, containing beans, beads, shot, or the like. [Carib.]

maraging *mär'ā-jing, n.* a metallurgical process by which a metal alloy is slowly cooled in the air, becoming very strong and resistant to corrosion. [From *mar*tensite and *aging*.]

marah *mä'rä, n.* bitterness: something bitter. [Heb.]

maranatha *mar-ə-nä'thə.* See **anathema.**

Maranta *mə-ran'tə, n.* the arrowroot genus of monocotyledons giving name to the family **Marantā'ceae,** akin to the banana and ginger families. [After Bartolommeo *Maranta*, 16th-cent. Italian herbalist.]

maraschino *mar-ə-skē'nō, -shē'nō, n.* a liqueur distilled from a cherry grown in Dalmatia: — *pl.* **maraschi'nos.** — **maraschino cherry** a cherry preserved in real or imitation maraschino and used for decorating cocktails, etc. [It., — *marasca, amarasca,* a sour cherry — L. *amarus,* bitter.]

marasmus *mə-raz'məs, n.* a wasting away of the body. — *adj.* **maras'mic.** — *n.* **Maras'mius** a common genus of toadstools, including the fairy-ring champignon, drying up in sunshine but recovering in damp. [Latinised — Gr. *marasmos* — *marainein,* to decay.]

Maratha, Mahratta *mə-rät'ə, n.* a member of a once dominant people of S.W. India. — *n.* **Marathi** (*mə-rät'ē*) their Sanskritic language. [Hindi *maraṭha* — Sans. *mahārāṣṭra,* great kingdom.]

Marathon *mar'ə-thon, -thən, n.* scene of the Greek victory over the Persians, 490 B.C., 22 miles from Athens: (without *cap.*) a marathon race: (without *cap.*) a test of endurance. — *adj.* (without *cap.*) of great length in time, or distance, etc.: displaying powers of endurance and stamina. — *n.* **mar'athoner.** — *adj.* and *n.* **Marathōn'ian.** — **marathon race** a long-distance footrace (usually 26 miles 385 yards — 42·195 kilometres), commemorating the tradition that a Greek ran from Marathon to Athens with news of the victory: a long-distance race in other sports, e.g. swimming. [Gr. *Marathōn.*]

Marattia *mə-rat'i-ə, n.* a genus of ferns giving name to the **Marattiā'ceae,** a tropical family of very large primitive eusporangiate ferns. [Named after G. F. *Maratti* (d. 1777), Italian botanist.]

maraud *mə-röd', v.i.* to rove in quest of plunder. — *v.t.* to harry. — *n.* raiding: plundering. — *n.* **maraud'er.** [Fr. *maraud,* rogue; origin obscure.]

maravedi *mar-ə-vā'di, n.* an obsolete Spanish copper coin of little value. [Sp. *maravedi* — Ar. *Murābitīn,* the

dynasty of the Almoravides (11th and 12th cent.).]

marble *mär'bl, n.* a granular crystalline limestone: (*loosely*) any rock of similar appearance taking a high polish: a slab, work of art, tombstone, tomb, or other object made of marble: a little hard ball (originally of marble) used by boys in play: marbling: anything hard, cold, polished, white, or otherwise like marble (*fig.*): (in *pl.*) a game played with little balls: (in *pl.*) one's wits (*coll.*). — *adj.* composed of marble: shining: unyielding: hard: insensible: marbled. — *v.t.* to stain or vein like marble. — *adj.* **mar'bled** irregularly mottled and streaked like some kinds of marble: wrought in marble: furnished with marble. — *ns.* **mar'bler; mar'bling** a marbled appearance or colouring: the act of veining or painting in imitation of marble. — *adj.* **mar'bly** like marble. — *adjs.* **mar'ble-breast'ed** hard-hearted, cruel; **mar'ble-con'stant** constant or firm as marble, immovable. — **mar'ble-cutter** one who hews marble: a machine for cutting marble; **mar'bled-white'** a butterfly of the Satyridae. — *adjs.* **mar'ble-edged** having the edges marbled, as a book; **mar'ble-heart'ed** hard-hearted, insensible. — **mar'ble-paper** paper coloured in imitation of variegated marble. — **Elgin marbles** a collection of marbles obtained chiefly from the Parthenon by Lord *Elgin* in 1811, now in the British Museum. — **have/lose (all) one's marbles** have/lose one's wits (*coll.*). [O.Fr. *marbre* — L. *marmor;* cf. Gr. *marmaros* — *marmairein,* to sparkle.]

Marburg disease. See **green monkey disease** at **green**[1].

marc *märk,* Fr. *mär, n.* fruit-refuse in wine- or oil-making: brandy made from this (also **marc brandy**). [Fr.]

Marcan *mär'kən, adj.* of the Evangelist St Mark or his gospel.

marcantant *mär'kən-tant,* (*Shak.*) *n.* a merchant. [It. *mercatante.*]

marcasite *mär'kə-sīt, n.* sulphide of iron in orthorhombic crystals (in the gem trade can be pyrite, polished steel, etc.). [L.L. *marcasīta* — Ar. *marqashīt(h)ā;* origin unknown.]

marcato *mär-kä'tō, adj.* marked: emphatic: strongly accented: — *superl.* **marcatis'simo.** — Also *adv.* [It., — *marcare,* to mark.]

Marcel, marcel *mär-sel', n.* (in full **Marcel wave**) an artificial wave imparted to hair by a hot iron, a comb, and manipulation. — *v.t.* to make a marcel in. — *adj.* **marcelled'.** [*Marcel,* a French hairdresser, the inventor (1872).]

marcella *mär-sel'ə, n.* a type of cotton or linen fabric, in twill weave. [Anglicisation of *Marseilles.*]

marcescent *mär-ses'ənt, adj.* withering without falling off. — *adj.* **marcesc'ible.** [L. *marcēscēns, -entis,* pr.p. of *marcēscĕre — marcēre,* to fade.]

Marcgravia *märk-grā'vi-ə, n.* a tropical American genus of climbing epiphytic shrubs, with pitcher-like bracts developed as nectaries, visited by humming-birds, giving name to the family **Marcgraviā'ceae,** akin to the tea family. [After Georg *Markgraf* (1610–44), German traveller.]

March *märch, n.* the third month of the year (in England until 1752 the year began on 25th March). — **March beer** strong beer brewed in March; **March hare** a hare gambolling in the breeding season, proverbially mad. [L. *Martius* (*mēnsis*), (the month) of Mars.]

march[1] *märch, n.* a boundary: border: a border district — used chiefly in *pl.* **march'es.** — *v.i.* to have a common boundary. — *n.* **march'er** an inhabitant or lord of a border district. — **march'-dyke, -dike** a boundary wall, usu. of turf; **march'man** a borderer; **march'-stone** a boundary stone; **march'-trea'son** an offence against the laws of the marches, e.g. raiding the neighbouring country in time of peace. — **Lord marcher** (*hist.*) a lord who had royal prerogative in, and jurisdiction over, lands in the marches; **riding the marches** a ceremony of riding round the bounds of a municipality. [Fr. *marche;* of Gmc. origin; cf. **mark**[1], O.E. *mearc.*]

march[2] *märch, v.i.* to walk in a markedly rhythmical military manner, or in a grave, stately, or resolute manner: to advance steadily or irresistibly. — *v.t.* to cause to march: to force to go. — *n.* a marching movement: an act of marching: distance traversed at a stretch by marching: regular advance: a piece of music fitted for marching to, or similar in character and rhythm, usu. with a trio: a move made by a chess piece. — **marching orders** orders to march: (as from employment, etc.) dismissal (*coll.*); **marching regiment** one without permanent quarters; **march past** the march of a body in front of one who reviews it. — **forced march** a march vigorously pressed forward for combative purposes; **on the march** afoot and journeying; **rogue's march** music played in derision of a person expelled; **steal a march on** to gain an advantage over, esp. in a sly or secret manner. [Fr. *marcher*, to walk, prob. — L. *marcus*, a hammer.]

Marchantia *mär-kan'shi-ə, -ti-ə, n.* a genus of liverworts with flat, lobed and branched thallus, growing in damp places, giving name to the family **Marchantiā'ceae**: (without *cap.*) a liverwort of this genus. [Named after Nicolas *Marchant* (d. 1678), French botanist.]

Märchen *mer'hhyən,* (Ger.) *n.* a story or fable, a folk-tale: — same form for *pl.*

marchioness *mär'shən-es, -is, n.* the wife of a marquis, marquess: a woman who holds a marquisate in her own right: a size of roofing slate 22 × 12 in. (55·88 × 30·48 cms.). — *n.* **marchesa** (*mär-kā'za*) It. fem. of **marchese** (*mär-kā'ze*) a marquis. [L.L. *marchiōnissa*, fem. of *marchiō, -ōnis*, a lord of the marches.]

marchpane *märch'pān, n.* until 19th cent., name of **marzipan** (q.v.). [It. *marzapane*.]

Marcionite *mär'shən-īt, n.* a follower of *Marcion* of Sinope (d. A.D. 165), who, partly under Gnostic influences, constructed an ethico-dualistic philosophy of religion. — Also *adj.* — *ns.* **Mar'cionist; Mar'cionītism.**

Marcobrunner *mär'kō-broŏn-ər, n.* a fine white wine produced in Erbach, near Wiesbaden. [From the nearby *Markbrunnen* fountain.]

Marconi® *mär-kō'ni, adj.* connected with Gugliemo *Marconi* (1874–1937), or his system of wireless telegraphy. — *v.t.* and *v.i.* (without *cap.*) to communicate by wireless telegraphy. — *n.* **marcō'nigram** a message so transmitted. — *v.t.* and *v.i.* **marcō'nigraph.**

Marco Polo sheep *mär'kō pōl'ō shēp,* a type of Asiatic wild sheep with large horns. [After the Venetian explorer.]

mard, mardy. See under **mar.**

Mardi Gras *mär-dē grä,* (Fr.) Shrove Tuesday.

mare[1] *mär, n.* the female of the horse. — **mare's'-nest** a supposed discovery that turns out to have no reality; **mare's'-tail** a tall marsh plant of the genus Hippuris: also applied to the horsetail: (in *pl.*) long straight fibres of grey cirrus cloud. — **the grey mare is the better horse** the wife rules her husband, or is the abler. [O.E. *mere*, fem. of *mearh*, a horse; cog. with Ger. *Mähre*, O.N. *merr*. W. *march*, a horse.]

mare[2] *mär,* (Shak.) *n.* the nightmare (q.v.).

mare[3] *mä'rē, ma're, n.* any of various darkish level areas in (*a*) the moon, (*b*) Mars: — *pl.* **maria** (*mä'ri-ə, ma'ri-a*). [L., sea.]

mare clausum *mä'rē klö'səm, ma're klow'soŏm,* (L.) a closed sea — a sea within the jurisdiction of one state. — **mare liberum** (*lib'ə-rəm, lē'be-roŏm*) a sea open to free navigation by ships of any nation.

Marek's disease *mä'reks diz-ēz',* a viral cancerous disease causing paralysis in poultry. [After a German veterinary surgeon.]

maremma *mär-em'ə, n.* seaside marshland: an Italian sheepdog. [It., — L. *maritima*, seaside.]

mareschal *mär'shl* (*arch.*). Same as **marshal.**

marg. See **margarine.**

margarin *mär'gər-in, n.* a mixture of palmitin and stearin once thought a compound: a glyceryl ester of margaric acid. — *ns.* **margarine** (*mär'gər-ēn*; pop. pron. *mär'-jər-ēn*; contr. **marg** *märg,* **marge** *märj*) a butterlike substance made from vegetable oils and fats, etc.; **mar'garite** a pearly-lustred mineral sometimes reck-

oned a lime-alumina mica. — *adjs.* **margaric** (*-gar'*), **margarit'ic; margaritif'erous** pearl-bearing. — **margar(it)ic acid** an acid intermediate between palmitic and stearic. [Gr. *margarītēs*, a pearl.]

margarita *mär-gə-rē'tə, n.* a cocktail of tequila and lemon juice. [From the Sp. name *Margarita*.]

margay *mär'gä, n.* a spotted S. American tiger-cat. [Fr. (or Sp.), — Tupí *mbaracaïa.*]

marge[1] *märj, n.* margin, brink. [Fr., — L. *margō, -inis.*]

marge[2]. See **margarine.**

margin *mär'jin, poet.* and *arch.* **margent** *mär'jənt, ns.* an edge, border: the blank edge on the page of a book: something allowed more than is needed: a deposit to protect a broker against loss: difference between selling and buying price. — *v.t.* to furnish with margins: to enter on the margin. — *adj.* **mar'ginal** pertaining to a margin: in or on the margin: barely sufficient. — *n.* marginal constituency. — *n.pl.* **marginā'lia** notes written on the margin. — *v.t.* **mar'ginalise, -ize** to furnish with notes: to push to the edges of society. — *ns.* **mar'ginalism** an economic theory that the value of a product depends on its value to the final consumer; **mar'ginalist; marginal'ity.** — *adv.* **mar'ginally.** — *adjs.* **mar'ginate, -d** having a well-marked border; **mar'gined.** — **marginal constituency, seat, ward** a constituency, ward that does not provide a safe seat for any of the political parties; **marginal land** less fertile land which will be brought under cultivation only if economic conditions justify it. [L. *margō, marginis;* cf. **mark**[1], **march**[1].]

margosa *mär-gō'sə, n.* the tree that yields nim-oil. [Port. *amargosa* (fem.), bitter.]

margrave *mär'grāv, n.* a German nobleman of rank equivalent to an English marquis: — *fem.* **margravine** (*mär'grə-vēn*). — *ns.* **mar'gravate, margrā'viate** the jurisdiction or dignity of a margrave. [M.Du. *markgrave* (Du. *markgraaf;* Ger. *Markgraf*) — *mark,* a border, *grave* (mod. *graaf*), a count; cf. Ger. *Graf,* O.E. *gerēfa,* Eng. **reeve**[1], **sheriff.**]

marguerite *mär-gə-rēt', n.* the ox-eye daisy or other single chrysanthemum. [Fr., daisy — Gr. *margarītēs,* pearl.]

maria. See **mare**[3].

mariachi *mar-i-ä'chi, n.* a small street band of Mexican musicians. [Mex. Sp.]

mariage de convenance *ma-rē-äzh də kõ-və-näs,* (Fr.) marriage for reasons of material advantage rather than love.

marialite *mä'ri-ə-līt, n.* a variety of scapolite rich in sodium, chlorine, and silica, poor in calcium. [*Maria* Rose vom Rath, a mineralogist's wife.]

Marian[1] *mä'ri-ən, adj.* relating to the Virgin *Mary* or to Queen Mary (Tudor or Stewart). — *n.* a devotee, follower, or defender of Mary: an English Roman Catholic of Mary Tudor's time. — *ns.* **Mariol'atry** (Gr. *latreiā,* worship) (excessive) worship of the Virgin Mary, the veneration duly paid to her being properly hyperdulia (q.v. under **dulia**); **Mariol'ater** one who practises Mariolatry. — *adj.* **Mariol'atrous.** — *ns.* **Mariol'ogist; Mariol'ogy** the study of the nature of, and doctrines and traditions concerning, the Virgin Mary. — Also **Maryol'atry, Maryol'ogy,** etc. [L. *Marīa.*]

Marian[2] *mar'i-ən, mä'ri-ən, adj.* relating to the great Roman general Gaius *Marius* (d. 86 B.C.).

mariculture *mar'i-kul-chər, n.* the cultivation of plants and animals of the sea in their own environment. [L. *mare,* sea.]

marid *mar'id, mä-rēd', n.* a jinni of the most powerful class. [Ar. *mārid, marīd.*]

marigold *mar'i-gōld, n.* a composite plant (*Calendula*) or its orange-yellow flower: extended to other yellow flowers (see **corn**[1], **marsh**). — **African, French marigold** Mexican composites (*Tagetes*). [From the Virgin *Mary* and **gold**[2].]

marigraph *mar'i-gräf, n.* a recording tide-gauge. — *n.*

mar'igram a record given by one.   [L. *mare,* sea, Gr. *graphein,* to write.]

marijuana, marihuana *ma-ri-(hh)wä′na, n.* hemp: its dried flowers and leaves smoked as an intoxicant.   [Amer. Sp.]

marimba *ma-rim′ba, n.* an African xylophone, adopted by Central Americans and jazz musicians (also **marim′-baphone**).   [African origin.]

marine *ma-rēn′, adj.* of, in, near, concerned with, or belonging to, the sea: done or used at sea: inhabiting, found in or got from the sea. — *n.* a soldier serving on shipboard: shipping, naval or mercantile, fleet: nautical service: naval affairs: a sea-piece in painting. — *ns.* **marina** (*ma-rē′na*) a yacht, etc., station, prepared with every kind of facility for a sailing holiday; **marinade** (*mar-i-nād′*) a liquor or pickle in which fish or meat is steeped before cooking, to improve the flavour, tenderise, etc. — *vs.t.* **mar′inade, mar′inate** to steep in wine, oil, herbs, etc. — *n.* **mar′iner** a sailor. — **marine acid** hydrochloric acid; **marine boiler** a steamship boiler; **marine engine** a ship's engine; **marine glue** see **glue**; **marine insurance** insurance of ships or cargoes; **marine soap** a coconut-oil soap, for washing with sea-water; **marine store** a place where old ships' materials are bought and sold; **marine stores** old ships' materials: supplies for ships; **marine trumpet** the tromba marina. — **tell that to the marines** a phrase expressive of disbelief and ridicule, from the sailor's contempt for the marine's ignorance of seamanship. [Fr., — L. *marīnus* — *mare,* sea.]

marinière *ma-ri-ni-yer′, adj.* esp. of mussels, cooked in white wine with onions and herbs.   [Fr. *à la marinière,* in the manner of the bargeman's wife.]

Marinist *ma-rē′nist, n.* a follower or imitator of the Italian poet Giambattista *Marini* (1569–1625). — *n.* **Marin′ism** his manner, full of strained conceits.

Mariolatry, Mariology, etc. See **Marian**[1].

marionette *mar-i-a-net′, n.* a puppet moved by strings. [Fr., dim. of the name *Marion,* itself a dim. of *Marie, Mary.*]

Mariotte's law. See **law**[1].

mariposa *mar-i-pō′za, n.* any of various plants of the *Calochortus* genus, with white, yellow or blue tulip-like flowers, native to N. America. — Also **mariposa lily, tulip.**   [Sp. butterfly.]

marischal. A Scots spelling of **marshal.**

marish *mar′ish,* (*obs.*) *n.* and *adj.* Same as **marsh.**

Marist *mar′ist, n.* a member of a modern R.C. congregation for teaching, preaching, and foreign missions. — *adj.* devoted to the service of the Virgin.   [Fr. *Mariste.*]

maritage *mar′it-ij,* (*hist.*) *n.* the feudal superior's right to dispose of a vassal's heiress (or heir) in marriage, or exact a fine: the fine exacted.   [L.L. *marītāgium.*]

marital *mar′i-tal, ma-rī′tal, adj.* pertaining to a husband, or to a marriage: of the nature of a marriage. — *adv.* **mar′itally** (or *ma-rī′*).   [L. *marītālis* — *marītus,* a husband.]

maritime *mar′i-tīm, adj.* pertaining to the sea: relating to sea-going or sea-trade: having a sea-coast: situated near the sea: living on the shore, littoral: having a navy and sea-trade.   [L. *maritimus* — *mare,* sea.]

Marivaudage *mä-rē-vō-däzh, n.* preciosity in writing. [Fr., from Pierre de *Marivaux* (1688–1763), French author.]

marjoram *mär′ja-ram, n.* an aromatic labiate plant (*Origanum*) used as a seasoning.   [O.Fr. *majorane*; origin doubtful.]

mark[1] *märk, n.* a boundary (*arch.*): a limit (*arch.*): a standard: a territory, esp. a border territory (*arch.*): a tract of common land belonging to a village community (*hist.*): a boundary stone, post, or the like: an object indicating position or serving as a guide: an object to be aimed at, striven for, or attained, as a butt, a goal, the jack at bowls, the pit of the stomach in boxing: a hawk's quarry (*obs.*): a suitable victim (*slang*): that which exactly suits one (*slang*): a visible

indication or sign: a symbol: a distinctive device: a brand: a set, group, or class, marked with the same brand: a type, model, issue, etc. (usu. numbered, as in *mark 1*): a stamp: a token: a substitute for a signature: a distinguishing characteristic: an impression or trace: a discoloured spot, streak, smear, or other local modification of appearance: note: distinction: noteworthiness: a point awarded for merit: a footprint: the impression of a Rugby football player's heel on the ground on making a fair catch: the starting-line in a race: a groove indicative of youth in a horse's incisor (as in *mark of mouth*): a tag on a lead-line indicating so many fathoms, feet, etc. — *v.t.* to make a mark on: to indicate: to record: to put marks on (a child's, student's, etc., written work) to show where it is correct or incorrect: to make emphatic, distinct, or prominent: to characterise in a specified way: to impress with a sign: to note: to regard: in football, hockey, etc., to remain close to (one's opponent) in order to try and prevent his obtaining or passing the ball (also *v.i.*). — *v.i.* to take particular notice. — *adj.* **marked** having marks: indicated: noticeable: prominent: emphatic: watched and suspected: doomed. — *adv.* **mark′edly** (*mär′kid-li*) noticeably. — *ns.* **mark′er** a person or tool that marks: something that marks a position, as a stationary light, a flare: one who marks the score at games, as at billiards: a counter or other device for scoring: a bookmark: a recorder of attendances: a kind of school monitor: a memorial tablet (*U.S.*): the soldier who forms the pivot round which a body of soldiers wheels; **mark′ing** the act of making a mark or marks: (esp. in *pl.*) disposition of marks. — Also *adj.* — **mark′er-bea′con, -bomb, -flag; marking gauge** a carpenter's tool for scoring a line parallel to the edge of a piece of wood. **mark′ing-ink** indelible ink, used for marking clothes; **mark′ing-nut** the fruit of an East Indian tree (*Semecarpus*) of the cashew family, yielding a black juice used in marking clothes; **mark′man** one of the community owning a mark: a marksman; **marks′man, marks′woman** one good at hitting a mark: one who shoots well; **marks′manship** skill as a marksman or markswoman; **mark′-white** (*Spens.*) the centre of a target. — **beside the mark** see under **beside; (God) bless** or **save the mark** a phrase expressing ironical astonishment or scorn, from the usage of archery; **make one's mark** to make a notable impression: to gain great influence; **mark someone's card** to give someone the information he wants; **mark down** to set down in writing: to label at a lower price or to lower the price of (*n.* **mark′-down**): to note the position of: to destine for one's own; **mark off** to lay down the lines of: to graduate: to mark as attended to, disposed of; **mark of the Beast** see under **beast; a mark on** (*arch. slang*) (one having) a preference for; **mark out** to lay out the plan or outlines of: to destine; **mark time** to move the feet alternately in the same manner as in marching, but without changing ground: to keep things going without progressing; **mark up** to raise the price of (*n.* **mark′-up**); **off the mark** well away from the start in a race; **on your mark(s)** said before a race begins to prepare the runners for the starting command or signal; **pass the mark** to pass on the badge of demerit to the next offender (as formerly in some schools); **soft mark** an easy dupe: one easy to cope with; **up to the mark** satisfactory, up to standard: fit and well.   [O.E. (Mercian) *merc* (W.S. *mearc*), a boundary, a limit; Ger. *Mark,* Goth. *marka.*]

mark[2] *märk, n.* a weight of 8 ounces (for gold and silver; *obs.*): its value in money at 20 pennies to an ounce = 13s. 4d. (*obs.*): a coin of Germany (in 1924 officially named the Reichsmark; in 1948 the Deutsche mark), of Finland (the *markka, pl. markkaa,* originally equivalent to a franc), and formerly of various countries. [O.E. *marc,* of doubtful origin.]

market *mär′kit, n.* a periodic concourse of people for the purposes of buying and selling: a building, square, or other public place used for such meetings: a shop (orig.

U.S.): a region in which there is a demand for goods: buying and selling: opportunity for buying and selling: demand: state of being on sale: bargain: sale: rate of sale: value. — *adj.* relating to buying and selling. — *v.i.* to deal at a market: to buy and sell. — *v.t.* to put on the market: — *pr.p.* **mar′keting**; *pa.t.* and *pa.p.* **mar′keted.** — *adj.* **mar′ketable** fit for the market: saleable. — *ns.* **marketabil′ity, mar′ketableness; marketeer′** one who buys or sells at a market: a supporter of Britain's entry into the Common Market; **mar′keter** one who goes to market, buys or sells at a market; **mar′keting** the act or practice of buying and selling in market. — **mar′ket-bell** (*Shak.*) a bell to give notice of the time of market; **mar′ket-cross′** a cross or similar structure anciently set up where a market was held; **mar′ket-day** the fixed day on which a market is held; **mar′ket-gar′den** a garden in which fruit and vegetables are grown for market; **mar′ket-gar′dener; mar′ket=gar′dening; mar′ket-hall, mar′ket-house** a building in which a market is held; **market leader** a company that sells more goods of a specified type than any other company: a brand of goods selling more than any other of its kind; **mar′ket-maker** since the changes of 27 October 1986, a broker-dealer on the Stock Exchange; **mar′ket-making; mar′ket-man** one who sells, buys, or works in a market; **mar′ket-place** the market-square: broadly, the world of commercial transactions; **mar′-ket-square′** the open space in a town where markets are held; **mar′ket-price′, mar′ket-val′ue** the current price; **market research** research to determine consumers' preferences and what they can afford to buy; **mar′ket-town** a town having the privilege of holding a public market; **mar′ket-woman.** — **go to market** (*Austr. coll.*) to become very angry and violent; **in the market for** desirous of buying; **on the market** available for buying: on sale. [Late O.E. *market* — O.N.Fr. *market* (Fr. *marché*, It. *mercato*), from L. *mercātus*, trade, a market — *merx*, merchandise.]

markhor *mär′kör, n.* a wild goat (*Capra falconeri*) of the mountains of Asia. [Pers. *mārkhōr.*]

markka *mär-kä′, n.* the monetary unit of Finland: — *pl.* **markkaa** or **markkas.** [Cf. **mark².**]

Markov chain *mär′kof chān* a series of events, the probability of each event of which depends on the probability of the event immediately preceding it.

marksman, markswoman. See **mark¹.**

marl¹ *märl, n.* a limy clay often used as manure: the ground (*poet.*). — *v.t.* to cover with marl. — *adj.* **mar′ly** like marl: abounding in marl. — **marl′-pit** a pit where marl is dug; **marl′stone** a Middle Lias series of argillaceous limestones with ironstones, etc. [O.Fr. *marle* (Fr. *marne*) — L.L. *margila*, a dim. of L. *marga*, marl.]

marl² *märl, v.t.* to bind with marline. [Du. *marlen*, app. a freq. of *marren*, to bind.]

marl³, marle *märl*, an obs. form of **marvel.**

marl⁴ *märl*, a dial. form of **marble.** — *adj.* mottled. — *adj.* **marled** marbled. — *n.* **marl′ing.** — *adjs.* **marl′y, mirl′y** marbled.

marlin *mär′lin, n.* a large oceanic fish of the genus *Makaira* akin to the swordfishes. [**marline-spike.**]

marline *mär′lin, n.* a small rope for winding round a larger one to keep it from wearing. — **mar′line-spike** a spike for separating the strands of a rope in splicing. — Also spelt **marlin, marlinspike.** [Du. *marling*, vbl. n. from *marlen* (see **marl²**), or *marlijn* — *marren*, and *lijn*, rope (cf. **moor², line**).]

marls. See **meril.**

marly. See **marl¹, marl⁴.**

marm. See **ma'am.**

marmalade *mär′mə-lād, n.* a jam or preserve generally made of the pulp (and rind) of oranges, originally of quinces. — **marmalade tree** a tropical American sapotaceous tree (*Vitellaria*, or *Lucuma, mammosa*) cultivated for its fruit, the **marmalade plum.** [Fr. *marmelade* — Port. *marmelada* — *marmelo*, a quince — L. *melimēlum* — Gr. *melimēlon*, a sweet apple — *meli*, honey, *mēlon*, an apple.]

marmarosis *mär-mə-rō′sis, n.* conversion of limestone into marble. — *v.t.* **mar′marise, -ize.** [Gr. *marmaros*, crystalline rock — *marmairein*, to sparkle.]

marmem alloy *mär′məm al′oi* an alloy which, under the influence of temperature changes, can be changed from one condition to another and back again. [*martensite, memory*, because the alloy 'remembers' its former condition.]

marmite *mär′mīt, mär-mēt′, n.* a metal or earthenware cooking vessel, esp. for soup. [Fr., pot or kettle.]

marmoreal *mär-mōr′i-əl, -mör′, adj.* of, or like, marble. [L. *marmor*, marble; Gr. *marmaros*; see **marmarosis.**]

marmose *mär′mōs, n.* a small South American opossum. [Fr., app. from *marmouset*; see next.]

marmoset *mär′mə-zet, n.* a very small American monkey. [Fr. *marmouset*, grotesque figure.]

marmot *mär′mət, n.* a genus of stout burrowing rodents (*Marmota* or *Arctomys*), in America called woodchuck. [It. *marmotto* — Romansch *murmont* — L. *mūs, mūris*, mouse, *mōns, montis*, mountain.]

marocain *mar′ə-kān, n.* a dress material finished with a grain surface like morocco-leather. [Fr. *maroquin*, morocco-leather; cf. **maroquin.**]

Maronian *ma-rō′ni-ən, adj.* Virgilian. [Publius Vergilius *Marō* (-*ōnis*).]

Maronite *mar′ə-nīt, n.* one of a former Monothelite sect, now Uniats, living around Lebanon. [St *Marōn*, about A.D. 400, or John *Marōn*, a patriarch of the sect in the 7th century.]

maroon¹ *mə-rōōn′, n.* a brownish crimson: a detonating firework. — *adj.* of the colour maroon. [Fr. *marron*, a chestnut — It. *marrone*, a chestnut.]

maroon² *mə-rōōn′, n.* a fugitive slave: a marooned person. — *v.t.* to put and leave ashore on a desolate island: to isolate uncomfortably. — *ns.* **maroon′er; maroon′ing.** [Fr. *marron* — Sp. *cimarrón*, wild.]

maroquin *mar-ə-kēn′, mar′ə-k(w)in, n.* goat-leather: morocco-leather. [Fr.; cf. **marocain.**]

maror *mä-rōr′, -rör′, n.* a dish of bitter herbs (esp. horseradish) eaten during the Jewish Passover, symbolising the bitterness of the Egyptian oppression of the Israelites. [Heb.]

marplot, marprelate. See **mar.**

marque¹ *märk, n.* reprisals (*obs.*): a privateer. — **lett′er(s)=of-marque′** a privateer's licence to commit acts of hostility. [Fr.]

marque² *märk, n.* a brand or make, esp. of car. [Fr.]

marquee *mär-kē′, n.* a large tent. [From **marquise**, as if *pl.*]

marquess, etc. See **marquis.**

marquetry, marqueterie *märk′i-tri, n.* work inlaid with pieces of various-coloured wood, ivory, metal, etc. [Fr. *marqueterie* — *marqueter*, to inlay — *marque*, a mark.]

marquis or (spelling used by some holders of the title) **marquess** *mär′kwis, n.* a title of nobility next below that of a duke: — *fem.* **marchioness** (*mär′shən-es, -is*). — *ns.* **mar′quisate, -quessate** the lordship of a marquis; **marquise** (*mär-kēz′*) in France, a marchioness: a style of parasol about 1850: an entrance canopy: a marquee: a ring set with gems arranged to form a pointed oval: a gem cut into the shape of a pointed oval; **mar′quisette** a woven clothing fabric, used also for curtains and mosquito nets. [O.Fr. *marchis*, assimilated later to Fr. *marquis* — L.L. *marchēnsis*, a prefect of the marches.]

marram, marrum *mar′əm, n.* a seaside grass (*Ammophila*, or *Psamma, arenaria*), a binder of sand-dunes. [O.N. *marr*, sea, *halmr*, haulm.]

Marrano *mə-rä′nō, n.* a mediaeval Spanish or Portuguese Jew converted to Christianity, esp. one overtly practising Christianity to avoid persecution but secretly adhering to Judaism: — *pl.* **Marra′nos.** [Sp., lit. pig, the meat of which is forbidden to Jews.]

marrels. See **meril.**

marriage *mar′ij, n.* the ceremony, act, or contract by which a man and woman become husband and wife:

the union of a man and woman as husband and wife: a declaration of king and queen in bezique, etc.: a close union (*fig.*). — *adj.* **marr'iageable** suitable for marriage. — *n.* **marr'iageableness.** — **marr'iage-bed** the bed of a married couple: marital intercourse: the rights and obligations of marriage; **marr'iage-bone** a merrythought; **marr'iage-broker** one who, for a fee, arranges a marriage contract; **marr'iage-con'tract** an agreement to be married: an agreement respecting property by persons about to marry; **marr'iage-fa'vour** a knot or decoration worn at a marriage; **marriage guidance** help and advice given to people with marital problems; **marr'iage-li'cence** a licence to marry without proclamation of banns in a church; **marr'iage-lines** a certificate of marriage; **marriage partner** one's husband or wife; **marr'iage-por'tion** a dowry; **marr'iage-ring'** a wedding ring; **marr'iage-sett'lement** an arrangement of property, etc., before marriage, by which something is secured to the wife or her children if the husband dies. — **marriage of convenience** a marriage (or *fig.*, a close business union, etc.) for reasons of expediency rather than affection. [O.Fr. *mariage*; see **marry¹**.]

marrons glacés *ma-rɔ̃ gla-sā*, (Fr.) chestnuts coated with sugar.

marrow¹ *mar'ō, n.* the soft tissue in the hollow parts of the bones: pith or pulp of plants (*obs.*): a vegetable marrow (see under **vegetable**): the essence or best part of anything: the inner meaning or purpose. — *adjs.* **marr'owish** of the nature of, or resembling, marrow; **marr'owless** having no marrow; **marr'owy** full of marrow: strong: forcible: pithy. — **marr'ow-bone** a bone containing marrow: (*pl.*) the knees or the bones of the knees; **marr'owfat** a rich kind of pea, called also Dutch admiral pea; **marr'ow-men** those who in the Church of Scotland supported the teaching of *The Marrow of Modern Divinity* (1645) after its republication in 1718; **marr'ow-squash** (*U.S.*) vegetable marrow. — **spinal marrow** the spinal cord. [O.E. (Anglian) *merg, mærh* (W.S. *mearg*); Ger. *Mark*.]

marrow² *mar'ō, (N. Eng. dial.) n.* a mate: a companion: a match, equal, like: one of a pair. — *v.i.* to be a marrow. — *v.t.* to be a marrow to: to couple. — *adj.* **marr'owless.** [Origin unknown.]

marrowsky *mar-ow'ski, n.* a spoonerism. — *v.i.* to utter a spoonerism. [Said to be from the name of a Polish count.]

marrum. See **marram.**

marry¹ *mar'i, v.t.* to take for husband or wife: to give in marriage: to unite in matrimony: to unite, join, put together (sometimes with *up*). — *v.i.* to take a husband or a wife: — *pr.p.* **marr'ying;** *pa.t.* and *pa.p.* **marr'ied.** — *adj.* **marr'ied.** — *n.* **marr'ier** one who marries in any sense: the sort of person likely to marry. — *n.* and *adj.* **marr'ying.** — **marry into** to become a member of (a family) by marriage; **marry off** to find a spouse for (e.g. one's son or daughter). [Fr. *marier* — L. *marītāre,* to marry, *marītus,* a husband — *mās, maris,* a male.]

marry² *mar'i, (arch.) interj.* indeed! forsooth! — **marry come up** an exclamation of defiant protest. [By *Mary*.]

Mars *märz, n.* the Roman god of war: the planet next after the earth in the order of distance from the sun: iron (*old chem.*). [L. *Mārs, Mārtis.*]

Marsala *mär-sä'lə* (It. *mär-sä'lä*), *n.* a light wine resembling sherry, from *Marsala* in Sicily.

Marseillaise *mär-sə-lāz', -sā-ez', n.* the French national anthem, in origin a revolutionary hymn composed by Rouget de Lisle in 1792, sung by the volunteers of *Marseilles* as they entered Paris, 30 July, and when they marched to the storming of the Tuileries.

marsh *märsh, n.* a tract of wet land: a morass, swamp, or fen. — *adj.* inhabiting or found in marshes. — *n.* **marsh'iness.** — *adj.* **marsh'y** of the nature of marsh: abounding in marshes. — **marsh'-fe'ver** malaria; **marsh'-gas** methane; **marsh'-harr'ier** a harrier frequenting marshes; **marsh hawk** a common N. Ameri-

can hawk with a white patch on its rump (also **hen harrier**); **marsh'land** marshy country; **marsh'lander; marsh'locks** a marsh-growing species of cinquefoil (Potentilla or Comarum) — also **marsh'-cinq'uefoil; marsh'-mall'ow, marsh'mallow** a maritime marshgrowing plant (*Althaea officinalis*) close akin to hollyhock: a gelatinous sweetmeat, originally made from its root: a person or thing excessively soft, sweet, or sentimental; **marsh'-man** a marsh-dweller; **marsh marigold** the kingcup (*Caltha palustris*), a marsh plant of the buttercup family with flowers like big buttercups; **marsh'-robin** the chewink (q.v.); **marsh'-sam'-phire** a plant of the genus *Salicornia,* glasswort; **marsh tit** the grey tit (*Parus palustris*); **marsh'-warbler** a small brown and white Eurasian warbler with a pale stripe over the eyes; **marsh'wort** a small umbelliferous marsh plant akin to celery. [O.E. *mersc, merisc,* orig. adj.: see **mere¹**.]

marshal *mär'shl, n.* a farrier (*obs.*): an officer in a royal household, originally the king's farrier, later having care of military arrangements, the regulation of ceremonies, preservation of order, points of etiquette, etc.: any official with like functions: a law-court officer with charge of prisoners: a prison-keeper: (Oxford) a proctor's attendant or bulldog: the chief officer who regulated combats in the lists (*hist.*): in France, etc., an officer of the highest military rank: a civil officer appointed to execute the process of the courts (*U.S.*): a police or fire-brigade head (*U.S.*). — *v.t.* to arrange in order: to usher: to combine in one coat of arms, or with a coat. — *v.i.* to come together in order: — *pr.p.* **mar'shalling;** *pa.t.* and *pa.p.* **mar'shalled.** — *ns.* **mar'-shalcy** the rank, office, or department of a marshal: esp. (in the form **Mar'shalsea**) till 1842 a prison in Southwark, under the marshal of the royal household; **mar'shaller; mar'shalling; mar'shalship.** — **marshalling yard** a place where railway wagons are sorted out and made up into trains. — **air-marshal,** etc. see **air; field marshal** see **field; marshal of the Royal Air Force** an officer of supreme rank in the Royal Air Force, ranking with an admiral of the fleet or a field marshal. [O.Fr. *mareschal* (Fr. *maréchal*); from O.H.G. *marah,* a horse, *schalh* (Ger. *Schalk*), a servant.]

Marsilea *mär-sil'i-ə, n.* a genus of aquatic leptosporangiate ferns, with four-lobed leaves and bean-like stalked sporocarps, giving name to a family **Marsileā'ceae.** — Also **Marsilia.** [Named after L. F. *Marsigli* (1658–1730), Italian naturalist.]

Marsipobranchii *mär'sip-ō-brangk'i-ī, n.pl.* the Cyclostomata. — *n.* **mar'sipobranch.** — *adj.* **marsipobranch'-iate.** [Gr. *marsipos,* pouch, *branchia,* gills.]

marsupium *mär-sū'pi-əm, (zool.) n.* a pouch. — *adj.* **marsū'pial** pertaining to a pouch or to the Marsupialia: of the nature of a pouch: of the Marsupialia. — *n.* a member of the Marsupialia. — *n.pl.* **Marsupiā'lia** an order of mammals co-extensive with the subclass *Metatheria,* animals whose young are born in a very imperfect state and are usually carried in a pouch by the female. [L. *marsūpium* — Gr. *marsip(p)ion, marsyp(p)ion,* a pouch.]

mart¹ *märt, n.* a place of trade. — *v.i. (Shak.)* to traffic. — *v.t. (Shak.)* to vend. [Du. *markt,* mart; cf. **market.**]

mart² *märt, (Scot.) n.* a cow or ox fattened, killed (usu. about Martinmas), and salted for winter use. [Gael. *mart,* cow, ox.]

martagon *mär'tə-gən, n.* the Turk's-cap lily. [Turk. *martagān,* a kind of turban.]

martel *mär'tl, n.* a war-hammer. — *v.i. (Spens.)* to hammer: — *pa.t.* **mar'telled.** [O.Fr. *martel.*]

martellato *mär-tel-lä'tō, (mus.) adj.* played with a hammering touch, or with short quick detached strokes of the bow. — Also *adv.* [It., hammered.]

martello *mär-tel'ō, n.* (in full **martello tower**) a circular fort for coast defence: — *pl.* **martell'os.** [From Cape *Mortella* in Corsica, where one resisted for some time a British cannonade in 1794.]

marten *mär'tən, n.* an animal (**pine-marten**) close akin to the weasels, or other species of *Mustela*. [Fr. *martre*, from the Gmc. root seen in Ger. *Marder*, and O.E. *mearth*, marten.]

martenot *mär'tən-ō, n.* an electronic musical instrument resembling a spinet in appearance, invented by the Frenchman Maurice *Martenot* (born 1898).

martensite *mär'tin-zīt, n.* a constituent of rapidly cooled steel consisting of a solid solution of carbon in iron and resulting from the decomposition of austenite at low temperatures. — *adj.* **martensitic** (*-zit'ik*). [Named after Adolph *Martens* (d. 1914), German metallurgist.]

martial *mär'shl, adj.* belonging to Mars, the god of war, or to the planet Mars: of or belonging to war, or to the army and navy: warlike. — *ns.* **mar'tialism; mar'-tialist** a soldier. — *adv.* **mar'tially.** — **martial art** any of various combative sports or methods of self-defence (usu. of oriental origin) including karate, kung fu, etc.; **martial law** exercise of arbitrary power by the supreme authority in time of emergency (war, riot, etc.), ordinary administration ceasing to operate. [Fr. *martial* — I. *mārtiālis* — *Mārs*.]

Martian *mär'shən, adj.* of Mars (god or planet): of battle. — *n.* an imagined inhabitant of Mars. [L. *Mārtius* — *Mārs*.]

martin *mar'tin, n.* a bird of the swallow genus (*Delichon* or *Chelidon*). — Also **mar'tinet** (*obs.*). [The name *Martin*.]

martinet [1] *mär-ti-net'*, or *mär', n.* a system of drill drawn up by *Martinet*, an officer of Louis XIV (*obs.*): a strict disciplinarian. — *n.* **martinet'ism.**

martinet [2]. See **martin.**

martingale *mär'tin-gāl, n.* a strap passing between a horse's forelegs, fastened to the girth and to the bit, noseband, or reins, to keep his head down: a short spar under the bowsprit: in gambling, the policy of doubling the stake on losing. [Fr., perh. from a kind of breeches worn at *Martigues* in Provence.]

Martini® *mär-tē'nē, n.* a type of vermouth made by the firm of *Martini* and Rossi: (without *cap.*) a cocktail of vermouth, gin, bitters, etc. perh. named after its inventor.

Martini (-Henry) *mär-tē'nē (-hen'ri), n.* a 19th-cent. rifle with action as designed by Frederic *Martini* and barrel by H. *Henry,* a gunsmith.

Martinmas *mär'tin-məs, n.* the mass or feast of St *Martin,* 11 Nov., a term-day in Scotland. — Also (*obs.*) **Mar'tlemas.**

martlet *märt'lit, n.* the martin: a martin or swallow without feet, used as a bearing, a crest, or a mark of cadency for a fourth son (*her.*). [From Fr. *martinet,* dim. of *martin,* martin.]

martyr *mär'tər, n.* one who by his death bears witness to his belief: one who suffers for his belief: one who suffers greatly from any cause, a victim. — *v.t.* to put to death for one's belief: to torture. — *n.* **mar'tyrdom** state of being a martyr: the sufferings or death of a martyr: torment generally. — *v.t.* **mar'tyrise, -ize** to offer as a sacrifice: to cause to suffer martyrdom: to make a martyr of: to torture. — *adj.* **martyrolog'ical.** — *ns.* **martyrol'ogist; martyrol'ogy** a history of martyrs: a discourse on martyrdom; **mar'tyry** a shrine, chapel or monument erected in memory of a martyr. [O.E., — L., — Gr., a witness.]

marvel *mär'vl, n.* a wonder: anything astonishing or wonderful: astonishment (*arch.*). — *v.i.* to wonder: to feel astonishment. — *v.t.* to wonder at (*obs.*). — *pr.p.* **mar'velling;** *pa.t.* and *pa.p.* **mar'velled.** — *adj.* **mar'-vellous** astonishing: almost or altogether beyond belief: improbable, very good, extremely pleasing (*coll.*). — *adv.* **mar'vellously.** — *n.* **mar'vellousness.** — **marvel of Peru** (*pə-rōō'*) a showy garden flower (*Mirabilis jalapa,* family Nyctaginaceae) from Mexico, open and scented in the evening. [Fr. *merveille* — L. *mīrābilis,* wonderful — *mīrārī,* to wonder.]

Marxian *märks'i-ən, adj.* pertaining to Karl *Marx* (1818–83) or his socialism, esp. as interpreted in

Russia. — *n.* a follower of Marx. — *ns.* **Marx'ianism, Marx'ism.** — *n.* and *adj.* **Marx'ist.**

marybud *mā'ri-bud, n.* a marigold bud.

Maryolatry, Maryology, etc. See **Marian** [1].

marzipan *mär-zi-pan', n.* a sweet almond paste, formerly called marchpane. [Ger., — It. *marzapane.*]

Mas. See **Mass.**

Masai *mä'sī, n.,* an African people of the highlands of Kenya and Tanzania. — Also *adj.*

mascara, mascaron. See **mask.**

mascle *mas'kl, n.* a bearing, lozenge-shaped and perforated (*her.*): a lozenge-shaped plate for scale-armour. — *adjs.* **mas'cled, mas'culy.** [App. O.Fr. *mascle* — L.L. *mascula* — L. *macula,* mesh, influenced by O.H.G. *masca,* mesh.]

mascon *mas'kon, n.* any of several mass concentrations of dense material, of uncertain origin, lying beneath the moon's surface. [*mass concentration.*]

mascot *mas'kət, n.* a talisman: a supposed bringer of good luck. [Fr. *mascotte.*]

masculine *mäs', mas'kū-lin, -lin, adj.* male (*rare*): characteristic of, peculiar to, or appropriate to, a man or the male sex: mannish: of that gender to which belong words denoting males and, in some languages, various associated classes of words (*gram.*). — *n.* the male sex or nature: a male: a word of masculine gender. — *adv.* **mas'culinely.** — *n.* **mas'culineness.** — *v.t.* **mas'culinise, -ize** to cause to develop masculine characters. — *v.i.* to develop such characters. — *ns.* **mas'culinist** an advocate of men's rights or privileges (coined in supposed imitation of *feminist*); **masculin'ity.** — **masculine ending** a stressed syllable at the end of a line (*pros.*); **masculine rhyme** a rhyme on a final stressed syllable: in French one without a final mute *e.* [Fr., — L. *masculīnus* — *masculus,* male — *mās,* a male.]

masculy. See **mascle.**

maser *māz'ər, n.* a device used to amplify long range radar and radio astronomy signals (very small when not amplified) while generating little unwanted noise within itself. — *v.i.* **mase** (a back-formation) to act as a maser by generating and amplifying microwaves. [*M*icrowave *a*mplification by *s*timulated *e*mission of *r*adiation.]

mash [1] *mash, n.* in brewing, a mixture of crushed malt and hot water: a mixture, as of bran with meal or turnips, beaten and stirred as a food for animals: any material beaten or crushed into a soft or pulpy state: crushed condition: a muddle, hash, or bungle. — *v.t.* to make into a mash: to pound down or crush: to infuse (*dial.*). — *ns.* **mash'er; mash'ing.** — *adj.* **mash'y** produced by mashing: of the nature of a mash. — **mash'-tub, -tun, -vat, mash'ing-tub** a vessel in which the mash in breweries is mixed. [O.E. *masc*(*-wyrt*), mash(-wort).]

mash [2] *mash,* (*obsolescent slang*) *v.t.* to seek to fascinate (one of the other sex): to treat as a sweetheart. — *v.i.* to flirt. — *n.* one who mashes or is mashed: a masher: mashing. — *n.* **mash'er** a fellow who dresses showily to attract the attention of silly young women: a dandy. — **mash'man** a worker, e.g. in a distillery, who helps to make the mash. — **mashed on** enamoured of. [Ety. dub.]

mashallah *mä-shä'lä, interj.* (among Muslims) what God will. [Ar. *mā shā'llāh.*]

mashie, mashy *mash'i, n.* an iron golf-club for lofting, a number five iron. — **mash'ie-nib'lick** a club between mashie and niblick, a number six iron. [Perh. Fr. *massue,* club.]

mashlam, mashlin, etc. See **maslin.**

masjid *mus'jid, n.* a mosque. [Ar.]

Mas-John. See **Mass.**

mask [1] *mäsk, n.* a covering for the face, or the upper part of it, for concealment, disguise, or protection: a false-face: a grotesque representation of a face worn in the ancient drama, or used as an architectural ornament, etc.: a fox's (or other beast's) face or head: a mould of a face: a masque: a disguise, pretence, or concealment (*fig.*): any means of screening or disguising: a screen to cover part of a sensitive surface (*phot.*): a screen used to cover parts of a surface on to the exposed parts of which an integrated circuit is to be etched. — *v.t.* to cover the face of with a mask: to hide, cloak, screen, or disguise. — *v.i.* to masquerade: to be disguised in any way. — *ns.* **mascara** (*mas-kä'rə*; Sp. *máscara*) colouring for the eyelashes; **mas'caron** (*archit.*) a grotesque face on a keystone, door-knocker, etc. — *adj.* **masked** wearing a mask: concealed: personate (*bot.*). — *n.* **mask'er** one who wears a mask: a masquerader: a device that produces a noise to mask a different auditory stimulus, used e.g. by tinnitus sufferers. — **masked'-ball** a ball in which the dancers wear masks. [Fr. *masque* — Sp. *máscara* or It. *maschera*, of doubtful origin, app. conn. in some way with L.L. *mascus, masca*, a ghost, and with Ar. *maskharah*, a jester, man in masquerade.]

mask² *mäsk*, (*Scot.*) *v.t.* .to steep, infuse. — *v.i.* to be infusing. [See **mash¹**.]

maskal(l)onge, maskinonge, maskanonge. See **muskellunge.**

maslin *mas'lin, n.* a mixed grain, esp. rye and wheat. — Also (*Scot.*) **mash'lam, mash'lim, mash'lin, mash'loch** (*-lohh*), **mash'lum.** [O.Fr. *mesteillon* — L.L. *mistiliō, -ōnis* — L. *mistus*, mixed — *miscēre*, to mix.]

masochism *maz'ə-kizm, n.* pleasure, esp. sexual pleasure, in being dominated or treated cruelly by the other sex: (*loosely*) morbid gratification in suffering pain, physical or mental. — *n.* **mas'ochist.** — *adj.* **masochist'ic.** [From the novelist Sacher-*Masoch*, who described it.]

mason *mā'sn, n.* one who cuts, prepares, and lays stones: a builder in stone: a member of the society of freemasons. — *v.t.* to build in or repair stonework, brickwork, etc. — *adjs.* **masonic** (*mə-son'ik*) relating to freemasonry; **mā'sonried** constructed of masonry. — *n.* **mā'sonry** the art, skill, or practice of a mason: the work of a mason: building-work in stone: freemasonry. — *adj.* consisting of mason-work. — **mason's mark** a device carved on stones by a mason to identify his share in the work. — **master-mason** see under **master.** [O.Fr. *masson* (Fr. *maçon*) — L.L. *maciō, -ōnis*, prob. Gmc.; cf. M.H.G. *mezzo*, a mason, whence Ger. *Steinmetz*, a stone-mason; O.H.G. *meizan*, to hew, whence Ger. *Meissel*, a chisel.]

Mason-Dixon Line *mā'sn-dik'sn līn*, the boundary between Pennsylvania and Maryland following a line surveyed between 1763 and 1767 by Charles *Mason* and Jeremiah *Dixon*, later thought of as separating the free Northern states from the slave states of the South.

masoolah, massoola, masula *mä-soo'lə, n.* a high manyoared Indian surf-boat. [Origin obscure.]

Masora, Masorah *mä-sō'rə, -sō', n.* a collection of critical notes on the text of the Old Testament. — Also **Masso'ra(h)**, **Masso'reth.** — *n.* **Mas(s)'orete** (*-rēt*) a compiler of the Masora. — *adj.* **Mas(s)oretic** (*-ret'ik*). [Heb. *māsoreth*, mod. *māsōrāh*.]

masque *mäsk, n.* a masked person: a company of maskers: a masquerade or masked ball: a form of courtly spectacle in vogue in the 16th and 17th centuries, in which masked performers danced and acted, developing into a form of drama with scenery and music: a literary composition for the purpose: a mask (*obs.*). — *n.* **masqu'er** a masker. [See **mask¹**.]

masquerade *mäsk-ər-ād', n.* an assembly of persons wearing masks, generally at a ball: disguise. — *v.i.* to wear a mask: to join in a masquerade: to go in disguise: to pretend to be (with *as*). — *n.* **masquerā'der.** [Fr. *mascarade*; see **mask¹**.]

mass¹ *mas, n.* a lump of matter: matter, material (*obs.*): a quantity: a collected or coherent body: an unbroken expanse: the aggregate: the main body: the greater part: the principal part: quantity of matter in any body, measured by its resistance to change of motion: (in *pl.*) the lower classes of the people. — *adj.* pertaining to a mass, or to large numbers or quantities, or to ordinary people as a whole. — *v.t.* to form into mass:

to bring together in masses. — *v.i.* to assemble in masses. — *adj.* **massive** (*mas'iv*) bulky: weighty: giving an impression of weight: not separated into parts or elements: without crystalline form: (*loosely*) great in quantity: on a very large scale, or of great size or power (*fig.*). — *adv.* **mass'ively.** — *ns.* **mass'iveness, mass'iness.** — *adj.* **mass'y** massive, made up of masses. — **mass defect** the difference between the sum of the masses of the neutrons and protons in a nucleus and the mass of the nucleus itself; **mass media, mass medium** see **medium; mass'-meet'ing** a large meeting for a public protest or assertion; **mass number** the atomic weight of an isotope, the number of nucleons in the nucleus; **mass observation** study of the habits, opinions, etc., of the general body of a community. — *v.t.* **mass'-produce'** to produce in great quantity by standardised process. — *adj.* **mass'-produced'.** — **mass'-produc'tion; mass radiography** taking of large numbers of chest X-ray photographs by mobile units; **mass spectrograph** an instrument by means of which a positive ray spectrum can be obtained, the images due to particles of different masses being spaced according to the masses, so that the atomic weights of the particles can be deduced; **mass spectrometer** an instrument like the mass spectrograph but measuring not the masses of particles but the relative number of particles of each mass present; **mass spectrometry.** — **in mass** as a body: all together; **in the mass** in the aggregate: as a whole: indiscriminately; **law of mass action** (*chem.*) rate of chemical change is proportional to the product of the concentrations of the reacting substances; **mass-energy equivalence** (*phys.*) the fundamental principle that mass and energy are equivalent and interconvertible. [Fr. *masse* — L. *massa*, a lump, prob. — Gr. *māza*, a barley cake — *massein*, to knead.]

mass² (often with *cap.*) *mas, mäs, n.* the celebration of the Lord's Supper or Eucharist in R.C. churches: the office for it: a musical setting of certain parts of the R.C. liturgy: a church service (*Shak.*): a church festival or feast-day, as in *Candlemas, Christmas, Martinmas,* etc. — **mass'-bell** a sacring bell; **mass'-book** the R.C. missal or service-book; **mass'priest** formerly a R.C. secular priest, as distinct from one living under a rule — later, a priest retained in chantries, etc., to say masses for the dead: a R.C. priest generally. [O.F. *mæsse* — L.L. *missa* — L. *mittĕre*, to send away, perh. from the phrase at the close of service, *ite, missa est* (*ecclesia*), go, (the congregation) is dismissed.]

Mass, Mas *mäs,* **Mess, Mes** *mes,* (*obs.*) *ns.* shortened forms of **Master.** — **Mas(s)'-John', Mes(s)'-John'** (*obs.*) a contemptuous name for a Scottish parish minister.

massa *mas'ə, n.* (*esp. Southern U.S.*) a corruption of **master.**

massacre *mas'ə-kər* (*Spens.* sometimes *-ak'*), *n.* indiscriminate slaughter, esp. with cruelty: carnage. — *v.t.* to kill with violence and cruelty: to slaughter. [Fr.; origin doubtful.]

massage *ma'säzh, mə-säzh', n.* a system of treatment for painful muscles, etc. by stroking, pressing, tapping, kneading, friction, etc. — *v.t.* to subject to massage: to present in a favourable light by devious means. — *ns.* **massa'gist, masseur** (*-sær'*, or *-sûr'*): — *fem.* **masseuse** (*-sœz'*). [Fr., from Gr. *massein*, to knead.]

massaranduba *mas-ə-ran-doo'bə, n.* the Brazilian milktree (*Mimusops elata*). — Also **masseranduba, maceranduba.** [Port. *maçaranduba*, from Tupí name.]

massé *mas'ā, n.* in billiards, a sharp stroke made with the cue vertical or nearly so. [Fr.]

masseter *mas-ē'tər, n.* a muscle that raises the under jaw. [Gr. *masētēr* (not *massētēr*), chewer — *masaesthai*, to chew.]

masseur, masseuse. See **massage.**

massicot *mas'i-kot, n.* yellow lead monoxide. [Fr.]

massif *ma-sēf', mas'if, n.* a central mountain mass: an orographic fault-block. [Fr.]

massive, massy, etc. See mass¹.
massoola. See masoolah.
Massora(h), Massorete. See Masora.
massymore *mas-i-mōr', -mör', (Scott) n.* a subterranean prison. [Perh. Sp. *mazmorra*; cf. **mattamore.**]
mast¹ *mäst, n.* a long upright pole, esp. one for carrying the sails of a ship. — *v.t.* to supply with a mast or masts. — *adjs.* mast'ed; mast'less. — mast'head the top of a mast: the name of a newspaper or periodical in the typographical form in which it normally appears, or a similar block of information regularly used as a heading. — *v.t.* to raise to the masthead: to punish by sending to the masthead. — mast'house the place where masts are made or stored. — before the mast as a common sailor (whose quarters are in the forecastle). [O.E. *mæst*; Ger. *Mast.*]
mast² *mäst, n.* the fruit of the oak, beech, chestnut, and other forest trees, on which swine feed: nuts, acorns. — *adjs.* mast'ful; mast'less; mast'y of the nature of mast: as if well fed on mast. — *adj.* mast'-fed. — mast cell a cell in connective tissue thought to produce histamine and other agents controlling the release of acid in the stomach. [O.E. *mæst*; Ger. *Mast*, whence *mästen*, to feed.]
mastaba *mas'tə-bə, n.* an ancient Egyptian tomb in which offerings were made in an outer chamber communicating with an inner one where was the figure of the dead man, with a shaft descending to the actual grave. [Ar. *mastabah*, a bench.]
mastectomy. See mastoid.
master *mäs'tər, n.* one who commands or controls: a lord or owner: a leader or ruler: a teacher: an employer: the commander of a merchant ship: formerly the navigator or sailing-master of a ship-of-war: one eminently skilled in anything, esp. art: one who has complete knowledge: a workman who has set up on his own account, or is qualified to do so: (with *cap.*) formerly prefixed to a name or designation as Mr is now, now only of a boy in this use: (usu. with *cap.*) a title of dignity or office — a degree conferred by universities, as *Master of Arts*, etc., an official of the Supreme Court, the designation of the heir apparent to certain Scottish titles, or of his son, the head of some corporations, as Balliol College, etc., of a lodge of freemasons, etc.: a husband (*dial.*): an original (film, record, etc.) from which copies are made. — *adj.* chief: controlling: predominant: of a master: of the rank of a master: original. — *v.t.* to become master of: to overcome: to gain control over: to acquire a thorough knowledge of: to become skilful in: to rule as master: to temper, to season: to treat with lye (*tanning*). — *v.i.* (*arch.*; also *v.t.* with *it*) to act the master or be a schoolmaster. — *ns.* mas'terate degree, title, or rank, of master; mas'terdom power of control: masterfulness. — *adj.* mas'terful exercising the authority or power of a master: imperious: masterly (*rare*). — *adv.* mas'terfully. — *ns.* mas'terfulness; mas'terhood; mas'tering action of verb *master*: lye. — *adj.* mas'terless without a master or owner: ungoverned: unsubdued: beyond control. — *n.* mas'terliness. — *adj.* mas'terly like a master: with the skill of a master: overbearing (*obs.*). — *adv.* with the skill of a master. — *ns.* mas'tership the condition, authority, status, office, or term of office of master: rule or dominion: superiority; mas'tery the power or authority of a master: upper hand: control: masterly skill or knowledge. — mas'ter-at-arms a ship's chief police officer; mas'ter-build'er a chief builder: one who directs or employs others; mas'ter-card the card that commands a suit; mas'ter-class the dominant class in a society: a lesson, esp. in music, given to talented students by a renowned expert; mas'ter-clock one that regulates other clocks electrically; mas'ter-hand the hand of a master: a person highly skilled; mas'ter-joint a joint of the most marked system of those by which a rock is intersected; mas'ter-key a key that opens many (different) locks, esp. all the locks in a certain building: a clue able to

guide one out of many difficulties (*fig.*); masterly inactivity the position or part of a neutral or a Fabian combatant, carried out with diplomatic skill, so as to preserve a predominant influence without risking anything; mas'ter-mar'iner the captain of a merchant-vessel or fishing-vessel; mas'ter-ma'son a freemason who has attained the third degree; mas'termind a mind, or a person having a mind, of very great ability: the person conceiving or directing a project. — *v.t.* to originate, think out, and direct. — mas'ter-pass'ion; mas'terpiece piece of work worthy of a master: one's greatest achievement; master race see Herrenvolk; mas'tersinger a Meistersinger; mas'terstroke a stroke or performance worthy of a master: superior performance: an effective, well-timed act; mas'ter-switch a switch for controlling the effect of a number of other switches or contactors; mas'ter-wheel the wheel in a machine which imparts motion to other parts: mas'ter-work work worthy of a master: masterpiece; mas'-terwort a plant (*Peucedanum*, or *Imperatoria*, *ostruthium*) akin to parsnip, once used as a pot-herb and in medicine: applied also to Astrantia, etc. — little masters a 16th–17th cent. group of followers of Dürer, notable for fine work on wood and copper; master of ceremonies, of the rolls, etc. see ceremonies, rolls, etc.; master of the horse the Roman *Magister Equitum*, an official appointed by the dictator to act next under himself: an equerry, esp. a high official of the British court; Master of the King's/Queen's Musick an honorary title conferred by the British sovereign usu. on a distinguished British composer; Master of the Temple the preacher of the Temple Church in London; master-slave manipulator a manipulator, esp. one used to handle, from behind a protective screen, radioactive material; masters of the schools at Oxford, the conductors of the first examination (*Responsions*) for the degree of B.A.; old masters a term applied collectively to the great painters about the time of the Renaissance, esp. the Italians; passed master one who has passed as a master: a qualified or accomplished master, a thorough proficient (also pastmaster). [Partly O.E. *mægester*, partly O.Fr. *maistre* (Fr. *maître*), both from L. *magister*, from root of *magnus*, great.]
mastic, mastich *mas'tik, n.* a pale yellow gum resin from the lentisk and other trees, used for varnish, cement, liquor: a tree exuding mastic, esp. the lentisk (*Pistachia lentiscus*; cashew-nut family): a bituminous or oily cement of various kinds. [Fr. *mastic* — L.L. *mastichum* — Gr. *mastichē*.]
masticate *mas'ti-kāt, v.t.* to chew: to knead mechanically, as in rubber manufacture. — *adj.* mas'ticable that may be chewed. — *ns.* mastica'tion; mas'ticātor one who masticates: a tooth or jaw (*facet.*): a machine for grinding: a machine for kneading india-rubber. — *adj.* mas'ticatory (-*kə*-*tə-ri*) chewing: adapted for chewing. — *n.* a substance chewed to increase the saliva. [L. *masticāre, -ātum*; cf. Gr. *mastax*, jaw, *mastichaein*, to grind the teeth.]
masticot. Same as massicot.
mastiff *mas'tif, n.* a thick-set and powerful variety of dog used as a watch-dog. [O.Fr. *mastin*, app. — L. *mansuētus*, tame; perh. confused with O.Fr. *mestif*, mongrel.]
Mastigophora *mas-ti-gof'ə-rə*, (*zool.*) *n.pl.* the flagellates in a wide sense. — *n.* and *adj.* mastigoph'oran. — *adjs.* mastigophoric (-*gə-for'ik*); mastigoph'orous of the Mastigophora: whip-carrying. [Gr. *mastīx, -īgos*, whip, *phoreein*, to carry.]
mastitis. See mastoid.
Mastodon *mas'tə-don, n.* a genus of extinct elephants, so named from the teat-like prominences of the molar teeth of some species: (without *cap.*) an animal of this genus. — *adj.* mastodon'tic. [Gr. *mastos*, breast, *odous, odontos*, a tooth.]
mastoid *mas'toid, adj.* like a nipple or a teat. — *n.* a process of the temporal bone behind the ear (also mastoid bone, process): mastoiditis (*coll.*). — *ns.* mas-

tect'omy surgical removal of a breast; **masti'tis** inflammation of the mammary gland. — *adj.* **mastoid'al.** — *n.* **mastoidi'tis** inflammation of the air cells of the mastoid processes. — **radical mastectomy** the surgical removal of a breast together with some pectoral muscles and lymph nodes of the armpit. [Gr. *mastos*, a nipple.]

masturbation *mas-tər-bā'shən, n.* stimulation, usually by oneself, of the sexual organs by manipulation, etc., so as to produce orgasm. — *v.i.* and *v.t.* **mas'turbate.** — *n.* **mas'turbātor.** — *adj.* **masturbat'ory.** [L. *masturbārī*.]

masty. See **mast**[2].

masu *mä'sōō, n.* a Japanese salmon (*Oncorhynchus masou*). [Jap.]

masula. See **masoolah.**

masurium *mə-sōō'ri-əm, -sū', n.* a name proposed for element No. 43 when its discovery was prematurely claimed — see **technetium.** [*Masurenland*, in East Prussia, now in N. Poland.]

mat[1] *mat, n.* a piece of fabric of sedge, rushes, straw, coarse fibre, etc., or of rubber, wire, or other material, for cleaning shoes, for covering a floor, hearth, threshold, for protection, packing, for standing, sleeping, etc., on, or for other purpose: a rug: a small piece of straw-plait, cloth, slab of cork or wood, etc., for placing under a vase, dish, or other object: a sack of matting used to cover a chest of tea, coffee, etc.: a certain weight held by such a sack: a closely interwoven or tangled mass, as of hair, of vegetation, of brushwood protecting a river-bank: a web of rope-yarn. — *v.t.* to cover with mats: to interweave: to tangle closely. — *v.i.* to become tangled in a mass: — *pr.p.* **matt'ing;** *pa.t.* and *pa.p.* **matt'ed.** — *n.* **matt'ing** mat-making: becoming matted: covering with mats: material used as mats. — **mat'grass, mat'weed** a small, tufted, rush-like moorland grass (*Nardus stricta*): marram. — **on the mat** on the carpet (*fig.*). [O.E. *matt*(*e*), *meatte* — L. *matta*, a mat; perh. of Punic origin.]

mat[2] *mat, adj.* dull or lustreless. — Also **matt, matte.** — *n.* **mat** a dull uniform finish or surface: a border of dull gold or of white or colour round a picture: a punch for roughening a surface. — *v.t.* to produce a dull surface on: to frost (glass). [Fr. *mat*; Ger. *matt*, dull; cf. **checkmate; amate**[2]**, mate**[2]**.**]

mat[3]. Abbrev. for **matrix.**

matachin *mat-ə-chēn', -shēn', (arch.) n.* a masked sword-dancer or sword-dance. [Fr. (obs.) *matachin* and Sp. *matachín*, perh. — Ar. *mutawajjihīn*, masked.]

matador, matadore *mat'ə-dör, -dör, n.* the man who kills the bull in bullfights: one of the three chief cards at ombre and quadrille: a form of dominoes. [Sp. *matador* — *matar*, to kill — L. *mactāre*, to kill, to honour by sacrifice — *mactus*, honoured.]

matamata *ma-tə-mä'tə, n.* a South American river-turtle. [Port., from Tupí *matamatá*.]

match[1] *mach, n.* a piece of inflammable material which easily takes or carries fire: a prepared cord for firing a gun, an explosive, etc.: a short stick of wood or other material tipped with an easily ignited material. — **match'box** a box for holding matches; **match'-cord** slow-match; **match'lock** the lock of a musket containing a match for firing it: a musket so fired; **match'=maker; match'stick** the wooden shaft of a match. — *adj.* very thin, like a matchstick: (of figures in a drawing, etc.) having limbs suggested by single lines. — **match'wood** touchwood: wood suitable for matches: splinters. [O.Fr. *mesche* (Fr. *mèche*); origin obscure.]

match[2] *mach, n.* that which tallies or exactly agrees with another thing: an equal: one able to cope with another: a condition of exact agreement, compatibility or close resemblance, esp. in colours: equality in contest: a compact (*obs.*): a formal contest or game: a pairing: a marriage: one to be gained in marriage. — *v.i.* to be exactly or nearly alike: to correspond: to form a union: to compete or encounter (esp. on equal terms). — *v.t.* to be equal to: to be a counterpart to: to be compatible

with, or exactly like, in colour, etc.: to be able to compete with: to find an equal or counterpart to: to pit or set against another in contest or as equal: to treat as equal: to fit in with: to suit: to join in marriage. — *adjs.* **match'able; matched.** — *n.* **match''er.** — *adjs.* **match'ing; match'less** having no match or equal: superior to all: peerless: not matching (*Spens.*). — *adv.* **match'lessly.** — *n.* **match'lessness.** — **match'board** a board with a tongue cut along one edge and a groove in the opposite edge; **matchboard'ing; match'-joint** the junction of matchboards; **match'maker** one who plans to bring about marriages: one who arranges boxing matches; **match'making; match'-play** scoring in golf according to holes won and lost rather than the number of strokes taken; **match point** the stage at which another point wins the match: the point that wins the match: a unit of scoring in bridge tournaments. — **to match** in accordance, as in colour. [O.E. *gemæcca*; cf. **make**[3].]

match-maker. See **match**[1].

matchmaker. See **match**[2].

mate[1] *māt, n.* a companion: an equal: a fellow workman: a friendly or ironic form of address: a husband or wife: an animal with which another is paired: one of a pair: a ship's officer under the captain or master: in the navy, formerly a rank to which a warrant-officer might be promoted: an assistant, deputy (as *plumber's mate*). — *v.t.* to be equal to, to rival (*arch.*): to marry: to cause (esp. animals) to copulate: to couple: to fit. — *v.i.* to claim equality (*arch.*): to marry: (usu. of animals) to copulate: to consort (*arch.*). — *adj.* **mate'less** without a mate or companion. — *n.* **mate'ship** (esp. *Austr.*) the bond between close friends. — *adj.* **māt(e)'y** (*coll.*) friendly and familiar, esp. in a studied or overdone manner. [Prob. M.L.G. *mate* or earlier Du. *maet* (now *maat*); cf. O.E. *gemetta*, a messmate, and **meat.**]

mate[2] *māt, adj.* (*arch.*) checkmated: confounded: baffled: exhausted: daunted. — *v.t.* to checkmate: to subdue (*arch.*): to baffle (*arch.*): to confound (*arch.*). — *n.* and *interj.* checkmate. [O.Fr. *mat*, checkmated; see **checkmate, mat**[2].]

mate[3], **maté** *ma'tä, n.* a South American species of holly (*Ilex paraguayensis*): an infusion of its leaves and green shoots, Paraguay tea. [Sp. *mate* — Quechua *mati*, a gourd (in which it is made).]

matelassé *mat-lä-sä, adj.* and *n.* (a jacquard fabric) having a raised pattern as if quilted. — Also **matel(l)asse.** [Fr., — *matelas*, a mattress.]

matelot. See **matlo.**

matelote *mat'ə-lōt, n.* fish stewed with wine sauce, onions, etc.: a sort of hornpipe. [Fr., — *matelot*, a sailor.]

mater *mä'tər, mā'ter, n.* mother (*slang*): either of the two membranes of the brain, outer and inner, separated by the arachnoid — the *dura mater*, or *dura*, and *pia mater*, or *pia*. [L. *māter*; cf. Gr. *mētēr*; **mother**.]

materfamilias *mä'tər-fa-mil'i-as, mā'ter-, n.* the mother of a family or household: — *pl.* strictly **matresfamil'ias** (-*trās*-), sometimes **materfamil'iases.** L. *māter*, a mother, *familiās*, old gen. of *familia*, a household.]

material *mə-tē'ri-əl, adj.* relating to matter: consisting of matter: being the substance of the thing (*Shak.*): matterful (*Shak.*): corporeal, not spiritual: bodily: physical: gross, lacking spirituality: relating to subject-matter: relevant: of serious importance, esp. of legal importance: pertaining to matter as opposed to form (*philos.*). — *n.* that out of which anything is or may be made: that which may be made use of for any purpose: one who is suitable for a specified occupation, training, etc.: a fabric. — *n.* **materialisā'tion, -z-.** — *v.t.* **matē'rialise, -ize** to render material: to cause to assume bodily form: to reduce to or regard as matter: to render materialistic. — *v.i.* to take bodily form: to become actual (*coll.*). — *ns.* **matē'rialism** the doctrine that denies the independent existence of spirit, and maintains that there is but one substance — matter: the explanation of history as the working out of economic conditions: blindness to the spiritual: exces-

sive devotion to bodily wants or financial success;
matē'rialist. — Also *adj.* — *adjs.* **materialist'ic, -al.** —
advs. **materialist'ically; matē'rially** in material manner:
in respect of matter or material conditions, or material
cause: in a considerable or important degree. — *ns.*
matē'rialness, materiality (*-al'i-ti*). — **material distinction** the distinction between individuals of the same
species; **material evidence** evidence tending to prove or
to disprove the matter under judgement; **material
fallacy** a fallacy in the matter or thought, rather than
in the logical form. — **dialectical materialism** Karl
Marx's view of history as a conflict between two
opposing forces, thesis and antithesis, which is resolved by the forming of a new force, synthesis; present
conditions are due to a class struggle between the
capitalists, whose aim is private profit, and the workers, who resist exploitation. [L. *māteriālis* — *māteria*, matter.]

materia medica *mə-tē'ri-ə med'i-kə*, substances used in
medicine: the science of their properties and use.
[L.L., medical material.]

matériel *ma-tū-ri-el', -ryel', n.* material: equipment: the
baggage and munitions of an army. [Fr.]

maternal *mə-tûr'nəl, adj.* of a mother: motherly: on the
mother's side: of the nature, or in the person, of a
mother. — *adv.* **mater'nally.** — *n.* **mater'nity** the fact
of being in the relation of mother: motherhood: maternal nature: a maternity hospital. — *adj.* of or for
women at or near the time of childbirth. [Fr. *mater-
nel* (It. *maternale*) and *maternité* — L. *māternus* —
māter, mother.]

matey. See **mate**[1].

matfelon *mat'fel-ən, n.* the greater knapweed. [O.Fr.
matefelon; cf. **mate**[2] and **felon**[2].]

math[1] *math, (dial.) n.* a mowing. [O.E. *mǣth*.]

math[2]. See **mathematics**.

mathematic, -al *math-i-mat'ik, -əl, adjs.* pertaining to, or
done by, mathematics: very accurate. — *adv.* **mathemat'ically.** — *ns.* **mathematician** (*-mə-tish'ən*) one
versed in mathematics; **mathemat'icism** the belief that
everything can be described or explained ultimately in
mathematical terms. — *n.sing.* or *pl.* **mathemat'ics**
(*coll.* **maths**, in U.S. **math**) the science of magnitude
and number, and of all their relations. — *v.i.* and *v.t.*
math'ematise, -ize to explain, formulate, or treat
(something) in mathematical terms. — Also **mathemat'icise, -ize.** — *adjs.* **mathemat'icised, -z-, math'-
ematised, -z-.** — **mathematical logic** same as **symbolic
logic.** [Gr. *mathēmatikē* (*epistēmē*, skill, knowledge)
relating to learning — *mathēma* — root of *manthanein*,
to learn.]

mathesis *mə-thē'sis* (*obs. math'i-sis*), *n.* mental discipline,
esp. mathematical. [Gr. *mathēsis*.]

maths. See **mathematic**.

Mathurin, Mathurine *math'ū-rin, -rēn, n.* a Trinitarian
canon. [Perh. from their house near St *Mathurin's*
chapel in Paris.]

matico *mä-tē'kō, n.* a Peruvian pepper shrub, used as a
styptic: — *pl.* **mati'cos.** [Sp. dim. of *Mateo*,
Matthew.]

Matilda *mə-til'də,* (*Austr.*) *n.* a swag. — **walk, waltz
Matilda** to travel around carrying one's swag.
[Woman's Christian name.]

matin *mat'in, n.* morning (*Shak.*): a morning song (*Milt.*):
(in *pl.*; often *cap.*) one of the seven canonical hours of
the R.C. Church, usually sung between midnight and
daybreak, or now by anticipation the afternoon or
evening before: (in *pl.*) the daily morning service of
the Church of England. — *adj.* of the morning: of
matins. — *adj.* **mat'inal.** — *n.* **matinée, matinee** (*mat'i-
nā, mat(-ə)-nā'*) a public entertainment or reception
usually held in the afternoon: a woman's dress for
morning wear. — **matinée coat, jacket** a baby's coat
or jacket made of wool or similar material; **matinée
idol** a handsome actor, popular esp. among women.
[Fr. *matines* (fem. pl.) — L. *mātūtīnus*, belonging to

the morning — *Mātūta*, goddess of morning, prob.
akin to *mātūrus*, early.]

matlo, matlow *mat'lō,* (*slang*) *n.* a seaman, sailor: — *pl.*
mat'los, mat'lows. — Also **matelot** (*mat'lō*). [Fr.
matelot.]

matrass *mat'rəs, n.* a long-necked chemical flask: a
hard-glass tube closed at one end. [Fr. *matras.*]

matriarchy *mā'tri-är-ki, n.* government by a mother or
by mothers: an order of society in which descent is
reckoned in the female line. — *n.* **mā'triarch** a patriarch's wife: a woman of like status to a patriarch: an
elderly woman who dominates her family or associates: an old woman of great dignity. — *adj.* **matriar'-
chal.** — *ns.* **matriar'chalism** a condition of society with
matriarchal customs: the theory of such a society;
matriar'chate the position of a matriarch: a matriarchal condition or community. [Formed on the analogy of **patriarchy** — I. *māter*, mother.]

matric. See **matriculation**.

matrice *mā'tris, mat'ris, n.* Same as **matrix**.

matricide *māt'* or *mat'ri-sīd, n.* a murderer of his (or her)
own mother: the murder of one's own mother. — *adj.*
matric'dal. [L. *mātricīda, mātricīdium* — *māter*,
mother, *caedēre*, to kill.]

matriclinic, matriclinous, etc. See **matroclinic**.

matricula *mə-trik'ū-lə, n.* a register of members, students,
etc. — *adj.* **matric'ular** pertaining to a register: contributed to the federal fund (as formerly by German
states). — *v.t.* **matric'ulate** to admit to membership by
entering one's name in a register, esp. in a college. —
v.i. to become a member of a college, university, etc.,
by being enrolled. — *n.* one admitted to membership
in a society. — *ns.* **matriculā'tion** the act of matricu-
lating: the state of being matriculated: an entrance
examination (familiarly **matric'**); **matric'ulātor.** — *adj.*
matriculā'tory. [L.L. *mātrīcula*, a register, dim. of
L. *mātrīx.*]

matrifocal *mat'ri-fō-kəl,* (*anthrop.*, etc.) *adj.* centred on
the mother: (of societies, families, etc.) in which authority and responsibility rest with the mother. — *n.*
matrifocal'ity. [L. *māter*, a mother, *fōcus*, a hearth.]

matrilineal *mat-ri-lin'i-əl,* **matrilinear** *-ər, adjs.* reckoned
through the mother or through females alone. — *adv.*
matrilin'eally. — *n.* **mat'riliny** (or *-lī'ni*). [L. *māter*,
a mother, *līnea*, a line.]

matrilocal *mat-ri-lō'kl, adj.* of a form of marriage, in
which the husband goes to live with the wife's group.
[L. *māter*, mother, *locālis* — *locus*, place.]

matrimony *mat'ri-mən-i, n.* wedlock: a card game of
chance in which one of the winning combinations is
that of king and queen: the combination of king and
queen in that and in various other games. — *adj.*
matrimonial (*-mō'ni-əl*) relating to marriage. — *adv.*
matrimo'nially. [L. *mātrimōnium* — *māter, mātris*,
mother.]

matrix *mā'triks,* or *mat'riks, n.* the womb (*anat.*): the
cavity in which anything is formed: that in which
anything is embedded, as ground-mass, gangue, intercellular substance, cementing material: the bed on
which a thing rests, as the cutis under a nail, the hollow
in a slab to receive a monumental brass: a mould: a
rectangular array of quantities or symbols (*math.*): any
rectangular array in rows and columns: — *pl.* **ma'trices**
(*-tris-ēz*, or *-iz*): by strict adherence to L. quantities it
would be *mā-trī'sēz*) or **ma'trixes.** — Abbrev. **mat.**
[L. *mātrīx, -īcis*, a breeding animal, later, the womb
— *māter*, mother.]

matroclinic *mat-rō-klin'ik,* **matroclinous** *-klī'nəs, adjs.* inherited from the mother: more like the mother than
the father. — *n.* **matroclī'ny.** — Also **matriclinic,** etc.
[L. *māter* (or Doric Gr. *mātēr*), mother, and Gr. *klīnein*,
to lean.]

matron *mā'trən, n.* a married woman: an elderly lady of
staid and sober habits: one in charge of nursing and
domestic arrangements in a hospital, school, or other
institution. — *ns.* **mā'tronage, mā'tronhood** state of
being a matron: a body of matrons. — *adj.* **mā'tronal**

pertaining or suitable to a matron: motherly: grave. — *v.t.* **mā′tronise, -ize** to render matronly: to act as matron to: to chaperon. — *v.i.* to become a matron or matronly. — *adj.* **mā′tronly** like, becoming, or belonging to a matron: elderly: sedate: plump. — *n.* **mā′tronship.** — *adj.* **ma′tron-like.** — **matron of honour** see **honour.** [Fr. *matrone* — L. *mātrōna* — *māter*, mother.]

matronymic. See **metronymic.**

matross *mə-tros′*, (*obs.*) *n.* a gunner's assistant in artillery. [Du. *matroos*, app. — Fr. *matelot*, a sailor.]

matt. Same as **mat²**.

mattamore *mat-ə-mōr′*, **-mör′** or *mat′*, *n.* a subterranean chamber. [Fr. *matamore* — Ar. *matmūrah*.]

matte¹ *mat*, *n.* a product of the smelting of sulphide ores. — Also *regulus* and *coarse metal*. [Fr.]

matte² *mat*, *adj.* Same as **mat²**.

matte³ *mat*, (*cinematography*) *n.* a kind of mask used to block out areas of the image, allowing a different image to be superimposed: an image produced in this way. [Fr.]

matted. See **mat¹**.

matter *mat′ər*, *n.* that which occupies space, and with which we become acquainted by our bodily senses: that out of which anything is made, material: subject or material of thought, speech, writing, dispute, etc.: substance (opp. to *form*): good sense (*Shak.*): anything engaging the attention: affair: subject: thing: that with which one has to do: cause or ground: thing of consequence: something that is amiss: that with which a court is concerned, something to be tried or proved: importance: an approximate amount: material for work, type set up, copy, etc. (*print.*): that which may be sent by post (*postal matter*): pus. — *v.i.* to be of importance: to signify: to form or discharge pus. — *v.t.* (*obs.*) to mind, concern oneself about. — *adjs.* **matt′erful** full of matter, pithy; **matt′erless; matt′ery** purulent: containing, discharging, or covered with pus. — *adj.* **matter′-of-fact′** adhering to literal, actual or pedestrian fact: not fanciful: prosaic. — **as a matter of fact** really; **for that matter** as for that: indeed; **matter of course** a thing occurring in natural time and order, as to be expected; **matter of form** a (mere) official procedure or conventional etiquette; **no matter** it does not matter: it makes no difference. [O.Fr. *matiere* — L. *māteria*, matter.]

Matthaean *math-ē′ən*, *adj.* of the evangelist Matthew or his gospel. [*Matthew*.]

mattie *mat′i*, (*Scot.*) *n.* a young herring with undeveloped roe. [Du. *maatjes* (*haring*) — L. Ger. *mädeken*, maiden.]

matting. See **mat¹**.

mattins. Same as **matins**, *pl.* of **matin**.

mattock *mat′ək*, *n.* a kind of pickaxe for loosening the soil, with cutting end instead of a point. [O.E. *mattuc*.]

mattoid *mat′oid*, *n.* a person on the borderline between sanity and insanity. [It. *mattoide* — *matto*, mad.]

mattress *mat′ris*, *n.* a bed made of a stuffed bag, or a substitute or supplementary structure of wire, hair, foam rubber, etc.: a mass of brushwood, etc., used to form a foundation for roads, etc., or for the walls of embankments, etc. [O.Fr. *materas* (Fr. *matelas*) — Ar. *matrah*, a place where anything is thrown.]

mature *mə-tūr′*, U.S. also **-tōōr′**, *adj.* fully developed: having the mental, emotional and social development appropriate to an adult: perfected: ripe: well thought out: due: in due time (*Milt.*): suppurating. — *v.t.* to bring to ripeness, full development or perfection: to bring to a head: to cause to suppurate. — *v.i.* to come to or approach ripeness, full development, or perfection: to become due. — *adj.* **matur′able** capable of being matured. — *v.t.* **maturate** (*mat′*) to make mature: to promote the suppuration of (*med.*). — *v.i.* (*med.*) to suppurate perfectly. — *n.* **matura′tion** a bringing or a coming to maturity: the process of suppurating fully: the final stage in the production of a germ-cell, at which the reducing division occurs. — *adjs.* **maturā′tional; matur′ative** (or *mat′*) promoting ripening: promoting suppuration. — *adv.* **mature′ly.** — *ns.* **mature′ness; matur′ity** ripeness: full development: the time of becoming due, as of a bill. [L. *mātūrus*, ripe.]

matutinal *mat-ū-tī′nl* (or *mə-tū′ti-nl*), *adj.* pertaining to the morning: happening early in the day. — Also **matutine** (*mat′ū-tīn*). [L. *mātūtīnālis, mātūtīnus*; see **matin.**]

maty. See **mate¹**.

matzo *mat′sə*, **-sō**, *n.* unleavened bread: a wafer of it: — *pl.* (with verb *sing.* or *pl.*) **mat′zoth, -zos.** — Also **mat′zoh, matza(h): —** *pls.* **mat′zot(h), matza(h)s.** [Yiddish *matse*; from Heb.]

matzoon *mät-sōōn′*, **madzoon** *mäd-zōōn′*, *ns.* a food similar to yoghurt made from fermented milk. [Armenian.]

maud *möd*, *n.* a Scottish shepherd's woollen plaid. [Origin unknown.]

maudlin *möd′lin*, *adj.* tearful (*obs.*): silly: sickly-sentimental: fuddled, half-drunk. — *n.* **maud′linism** the tearful stage of drunkenness. [M.E. *Maudelein*, through O.Fr. and L. from Gr. *Magdalēnē*, (woman) of Magdala, from the assumption that Mary Magdalene was the penitent woman of Luke vii. 38.]

maugre, maulgre *mö′gər*, also **-gri, mö(l)-grē′**, (*arch.*) *prep.* in spite of, notwithstanding: a curse upon (*Spens.*, with dative). — *adv.* in despite. — *n.* ill-will, spite (*obs.*). [O.Fr. *malgré* — L. *male grātum* — *male*, badly, *grātum*, agreeable.]

maul *möl*, *n.* a war-club or mace (*obs.*): a heavy wooden hammer or beetle, a mall: a loose scrimmage (*Rugby football*): in goal, a struggle for the ball when carried across the goal-line, but not yet touched down (*Rugby football*). — *v.t.* to beat with a maul or heavy stick: to handle roughly, batter, maltreat: to split with a maul (*U.S.*). — *v.i.* to thrust forward in a close mass, esp. in Rugby football. — *n.pl.* **maul′ers** (*slang*) hands. [**mall.**]

maulgre. See **maugre.**

maulstick *möl′stik*, *n.* a stick used by painters as a rest for the hand. — Also **mahl′stick, mal′stick.** [Du. *maalstok* — *malen*, to paint, *stok*, stick, assimilated to **stick.**]

maulvi *möl′vi*, *n.* a teacher of Islamic law, a learned man. [Urdu, *mulvī* — Arab. *maulawiyy*.]

maumet, maumetry. Same as **mammet, mammetry.**

maun *mön, män, mun*, (*Scot.*) *v.t.* must. — **maunna** (*mön′ə, mun′ə*) must not. [See **mun¹.**]

maund¹ *mönd*, (*Shak.*) *n.* a basket. [O.E. *mand*.]

maund² *mönd*, *n.* a measure of weight in India, its value varying in different places from about 25 to 85 pounds avoirdupois. [Hind. and Pers. *man*.]

maund³ *mönd*, (*obs. slang*) *v.t.* and *v.i.* to beg. — *n.* **maund′er** a beggar. — *v.i.* to beg. [Poss. Fr. *mendier*, to beg — L. *mendicāre*.]

maunder¹ *mön′dər*, *v.i.* to grumble: to mutter: to drivel: to wander idly. — *ns.* **maun′derer; maun′dering** drivelling talk. [Origin unknown.]

maunder². See **maund³**.

maundy *mön′di*, *n.* the religious ceremony of washing the feet of the poor, in commemoration of Christ's washing the disciples' feet (John xiii) — long practised by some monarchs. — **maundy money** the dole given away on **Maundy Thursday**, the day before Good Friday, by the royal almoner, usu. a silver penny for each year of sovereign's age — the small silver coins specially minted since 1662. [Fr. *mandé* — L. *mandātum*, command (John xiii. 34).]

maunna. See **maun.**

Mauretania *mör-i-tān′yə* *n.* an ancient country of N. Africa. — *adj.* **Mauretān′ian** of the country or its people. — *n.* one of its people.

Maurist *mö′rist*, *n.* a member of the reformed Benedictine Congregation of St *Maur*, settled from 1618 at the abbey of St *Maur*-sur-Loire, near Saumur, notable for its great services to learning. — Also *adj.*

Mauritius *mo-, mö-rish'əs, adj.* of the island of *Mauritius* (named after Maurice (1567–1625), Prince of Orange). — **Mauritius hemp** the fibre of an amaryllidaceous plant, *Furcraea gigantea.*

Mauser *mow'zər, n.* series of German rifles, esp. a magazine rifle of 1897. [Inventor's surname.]

mausoleum *mö-so-lē'əm, n.* a magnificent tomb or monument. — *adj.* **mausolē'an.** [L. *mausōlēum* — Gr. *Mausōleion,* the magnificent tomb of *Mausōlos* (d. 353 B.C.), satrap of Caria, erected by his widow Artemisia at Halicarnassus.]

mauther, mawther *mö'dhər, (dial.* esp. E. Anglia) *n.* a girl: a great awkward girl. — Also (esp. vocatively) **mawr, mor.** [Origin obscure.]

mauvais *mo-ve,* (Fr.) *adj.* bad, worthless: — *fem.* **mauvaise** (*-vez*). — **mauvais goût** (*gōō*) bad taste, lack of taste; **mauvaise honte** (*mo-vez ɔ̃t*) false modesty, bashfulness; **mauvais moment** (*mo-mã*) a bad, unpleasant moment — also **mauvais quart d'heure** (*kär dær*) a brief but unpleasant experience, lit. a bad quarter of an hour; **mauvais sujet** (*sü-zhã*) a worthless fellow; **mauvais ton** (*tɔ̃*) bad style, bad form.

mauve *mōv, möv, n.* a purple aniline dye: its colour, that of mallow flowers. — *adj.* of the colour of mauve. — *n.* **mauv(e)'in(e)** mauve dye. [Fr., — L. *malva,* mallow.]

maverick *mav'ər-ik, (orig. U.S.) n.* a stray animal without an owner's brand, esp. a calf: one who does not conform: anything dishonestly obtained. — *v.t.* to seize without legal claim. [From Samuel *Maverick,* a Texas cattle-raiser.]

mavin *māv'in, (U.S. slang)* an expert, a pundit. [Yiddish — Hebrew *mevin,* understanding.]

mavis *mā'vis, n.* the song-thrush (see also **thrush**[1]). [Fr. *mauvis.*]

mavourneen *mə-vōōr'nēn,* (Ir.) *n.* and *interj.* my dear one. [Ir. *mo mhurnín.*]

maw[1] *mö, n.* the stomach, esp. in the lower animals: the craw in birds: the fourth stomach in ruminants: inward parts: any insatiate gulf or receptacle (*fig.*). — *adj.* **maw'bound** (of cattle) constipated by impaction of the rumen. — **maw'-worm** a worm infesting the stomach or intestines. [O.E. *maga;* Ger. *Magen.*]

maw[2] *mö, n.* a mew or gull. [O.N. *mār.*]

maw[3] *mö, n.* an old card-game. [Origin unknown.]

mawk *mök, (now dial.) n.* a maggot. — *adj.* **mawk'ish** (orig.) maggoty: loathsome, disgusting: squeamish: insipid: sickly: sickly-sentimental, maudlin. — *adv.* **mawk'ishly.** — *n.* **mawk'ishness.** — *adj.* **mawk'y.** [O.N. *mathkr,* maggot.]

mawkin. Same as **malkin.**

mawmet, mawmetry; mawpus. See **mammet; mopus**[1].

mawr, mawther. See **mauther.**

mawseed *mö'sēd, n.* poppy seed as cage-bird food, etc. [Ger. *Mahsaat* — *Mah,* poppy.]

max *maks, (obs.) n.* gin. [Origin obscure.]

maxi- *mak'si-,* in composition, (very) large, long (abbrev. of **maximum**) as in e.g. the following: — **max'i-coat, -skirt, -dress** a coat, skirt, dress reaching the ankle; **max'i-single** a gramophone record longer than an ordinary single.

maxi *mak'si, n.* short for **maxi-coat,** etc. — *adj. (coll.)* (extra) large or long.

maxilla *mak-sil'ə, n.* a jawbone, esp. the upper: in arthropods, an appendage close behind the mouth, modified in connection with feeding: — *pl.* **maxill'ae** (*-ē*). — *adj.* **maxill'ary** (or *maks'*) pertaining to a jaw or maxilla. — *n.* a bone forming the posterior part of the upper jaw. — *ns.* **maxill'iped, -pede** (*-ped, -pēd*) in Crustacea, a jaw-foot, an appendage behind the mouth, adapted to help in passing food to the mouth; **maxill'ula** in crustaceans, a maxilla of the first pair: — *pl.* **maxill'- ūlae** (*-lē*). [L. *maxilla,* jawbone.]

maxim *maks'im, n.* a general principle, serving as a rule or guide: a pithy saying: a proverb. — *ns.* **max'imist, max'im-mong'er** maker of maxims. [Fr. *maxime* — L. *maxima* (*sententia,* or some other word), greatest

(opinion, etc.), fem., superl. of *magnus,* great.]

Maxim *maks'im, n.* often put for **Max'im-gun',** an automatic machine-gun invented by Hiram *Maxim* (1840–1916).

maxima. See **maximum.**

maxima cum laude *maks'i-ma kum löd'ē, kōōm lowd'e,* (L.) with distinction, with the greatest praise (of attainment of high standard in degree examinations).

maximal, etc. See **maximum.**

maximum *maks'i-məm, adj.* greatest. — *n.* the greatest number, quantity, or degree: the highest point reached: the value of a variable when it ceases to increase and begins to decrease (*math.*): — *pl.* **max'ima.** — opp. to **minimum.** — *adj.* **maxi'mal** of the highest or maximum value. — *n.* **max'imalist** one who makes the fullest demands: a Bolshevik: one who demands the maximum programme. — *adv.* **max'imally.** — *n.* **max'imin** in games theory, the strategy of making all decisions in such a way as to maximise the chances of incurring the minimal potential loss. — *v.t.* **max'imise, -ize** to raise to the highest degree. — *v.i.* to give greatest scope to a doctrine. — **maximum and minimum thermometer** a thermometer that shows the highest and lowest temperatures that have occurred since last adjustment. [L., superl. neut. of *magnus,* great.]

maxixe *mä-shē'shä, n.* a Brazilian dance: a tune for it. [Port.]

maxwell *maks'wəl, n.* the cgs unit of magnetic flux, equal to 10^{-8} weber. [James Clerk-*Maxwell* (1831–79), Scottish physicist.]

may[1] *mā, vb.* expressing ability, permission, freedom, possibility, contingency, chance, competence, or wish, or softening a blunt question — used with infin. without *to:* — infin. and participles obsolete: *2nd pers. sing.* **mayst, may'est;** *3rd* **may;** *pa.t.* **might** (*mīt*), *(obs.* or *dial.)* **mought** (*mowt*); *2nd pers.* **might'est, mightst.** — *adv.* **may'be** perhaps, possibly. — *n.* a possibility. — *adv.* **may'hap** (or *-hap'*) perhaps. [O.E. *mæg,* pr.t. (old pa.t.) of *magan,* to be able, pa.t. *mihte;* cog. with Goth. *magan,* Ger. *mögen.*]

may[2] *mā, n.* a maid. [Prob. O.E. *mæg,* a kinswoman.]

May *mā, n.* now the fifth month of the year (see **March**): the early or gay part of life: *(without cap.)* may-blossom. — *v.i.* (also without *cap.*) to gather may on Mayday: to participate in May sports. — *n.* **may'ing** the observance of Mayday customs. — **May'-app'le** *Podophyllum* or its egg-shaped fruit; **may'-bee'tle, may'-bug** the cockchafer; **may'-bird** the whimbrel: the bobolink; **may'-bloom', -bloss'om** the hawthorn flower; **May'day** the first day of May, given to sports and to socialist and labour demonstrations. — Also *adj.* — **May'-dew'** the dew of May, esp. that of the morning of the first day of May, said to whiten linen, and beautify faces; **may'-duke** a variety of sour cherry; **May'fair** the aristocratic West End of London, at one time scene of a fair in May; **may'flower** the hawthorn or other flower that blooms in May; **may'fly** a short-lived plectopterous insect (Ephemera) that appears in May: the caddis-fly; **May'-game** sport appropriate to Mayday: frolic generally; **May'-la'dy** the queen of the May; **May laws** Prussian laws passed in three successive Mays (1873–75) restricting the power of the Church; **may'-lil'y** the lily of the valley; **May'-lord'** a youth directing May-games: one enjoying transitory dignity; **May'-meet'ings** meetings of various religious and philanthropic societies held in London in May; **May'-morn', -morn'ing** a morning in May: youthful freshness as of May (*Shak.*); **may'pole** a pole erected for dancing round on Mayday; **May'-queen'** a young woman crowned with flowers as queen on Mayday; **May'-time** the season of May; **may tree** the hawthorn. [O.Fr. *Mai* — L. *Māius* (*mēnsis*), prob. (month) sacred to *Māia,* mother of Mercury.]

maya *mä'yə, n.* illusion. [Sans. *māyā.*]

Maya *mä'yə, n.* one of an Indian people of Central America and Southern Mexico who developed a remarkable civilisation (also **May'an**). — *adjs.* **Ma'ya,**

Ma'yan. — *ns.* **Mayol'ogist, Mayol'ogy.**

maybe. See **may**[1].

mayday *mā'dā,* the international radiotelephonic distress signal for ships and aircraft. [Fr. (*infin.*) *m'aider,* pron. *mā-dā,* help me.]

Mayday. See **May.**

mayest. See **may**[1].

mayflower, mayfly. See **May.**

mayhap. See **may**[1].

mayhem *mā'hem, mā'əm, n.* maiming: malicious damage (*legal* and *U.S.*): (*erron.*) havoc, chaos (*coll.*). [**maim.**]

Mayologist, etc. See **Maya.**

mayonnaise *mā-ə-nāz', or mā', n.* a sauce composed of the yolk of eggs, salad-oil, and vinegar or lemon-juice, seasoned: any cold dish of which it is an ingredient. [Fr.]

mayor *mā'ər, mār, n.* the chief magistrate of a city or borough in England, Ireland, etc., whether man or woman: the head of a municipal corporation. — *adj.* **may'oral.** — *ns.* **may'oralty, may'orship** the office of a mayor; **may'oress** a mayor's wife, or other lady who performs her social and ceremonial functions. — **Lord Mayor** the chief magistrate of certain English, Welsh, Irish and Australian cities and boroughs; **Mayor of the Palace** in Merovingian France, the king's majordomo or prime minister, the real ruler. [Fr. *maire* — L. *mājor,* compar. of *magnus,* great.]

maypole. See **May.**

mayst. See **may**[1].

mayster *mās'ter,* **maysterdome,** etc. Spenserian forms of **master,** etc.

mayweed *mā'wēd, n.* stinking camomile (*Anthemis cotula*): corn feverfew (*Matricaria inodora*; a scentless mayweed): applied to various similar plants. [O.E. *mægtha,* mayweed, and **weed**[1].]

mazard, mazzard *maz'ərd, n.* a head or skull (*Shak.*): a wild European cherry. [Prob. **mazer.**]

mazarine[1] *maz-ə-rēn', n.* a rich blue colour: a blue gown or stuff. — Also *adj.* — *n.* **mazarinade'** a satire or pamphlet against Cardinal *Mazarin* (1602–61). — **Mazarin(e) Bible** the first printed Bible, printed by Gutenberg and Fust about 1450, of which the Cardinal had twenty-five copies; **mazarine hood** a hood of a form said to have been worn by the Duchesse de *Mazarin.*

mazarine[2] *maz-ə-rēn', n.* a 17th-cent. deep, usu. metal, plate: a cooking and serving dish set inside a larger dish. — Also **mazarine dish, plate.** [Origin uncertain.]

Mazdaism *maz'dä-izm,* **Mazdeism** *maz'dē-izm, ns.* the religion of the ancient Persians. — *adj.* **Mazdē'an.** [See **Ormuzd.**]

maze[1] *māz, n.* bewilderment: a labyrinth: a set of intricate windings. — *v.t.* to bewilder: to confuse. — *adj.* **maze'ful** (*Spens.*). — *n.* **maze'ment.** — *adv.* **mā'zily.** — *n.* **mā'ziness.** — *adj.* **mā'zy.** [Prob. from a lost O.E. word; the compound *āmasod,* amazed, occurs.]

maze[2] *māz.* Same as **mease**[1].

mazer *mā'zər, n.* a hard wood, probably maple: a cup of maple wood (*Spens.*): a similar cup of other material. [O.Fr. *masere,* of Gmc. origin; cf. O.H.G. *masar,* O.N. *mösurr,* a maple-tree.]

mazhbi *maz'bi, n.* a Sikh of low caste. [Hindi — Arabic *mazhab,* religion or sect.]

mazout. See **mazut.**

mazuma *mə-zōō'mə,* (*slang*) *n.* money. [Yiddish.]

mazurka *mə-zōōr'kə, or -zûr', n.* a lively Polish dance: music for it, in triple time. [Pol., Masurian woman.]

mazut, mazout *mə-zōōt', n.* petroleum residue after distillation. [Russ. *mazat',* to daub, smear.]

mazzard. See **mazard.**

Mc. See **Mac.**

MC *em-sē', n.* a master of ceremonies (see **ceremony**).

McCarthyism *mə-kär'thi-izm, n.* the hunting down and removal from public employment of all suspected of Communism. — *adj.* **McCar'thyite** of, relating to, this kind of purge or any purge of dissident factions in a party, etc. [From Joseph *McCarthy* (1909–1957), U.S. politician.]

McNaghten rules *mək-nö'tn rōōlz,* (*Eng. law*) rules dating from Rex v. *McNaghten* (1843), under which mental abnormality relieves from criminal responsibility only if the person did not know what he was doing or did not know that what he was doing was wrong.

MCP. Abbrev. for **male chauvinist pig** (see **male**[2]).

me[1] *mē, mi, pers. pron.* the accusative and dative of **I.** See also **me-too.** [O.E. *mē.*]

me[2]. An anglicised spelling of **mi.**

ME. Abbrev. for **myalgic encephalomyelitis** (see **myalgia**).

meacock *mē'kok,* (*Shak.*) *adj.* timorous, effeminate, cowardly. — *n.* a milksop. [Origin unknown.]

mea culpa *mē'ə kul'pə, mā'ä kōōl'pä,* (L.) by my own fault — an acknowledgement of one's guilt or mistake.

mead[1] *mēd, n.* honey and water fermented and flavoured. [O.E. *meodu;* Ger. *Met,* W. *medd.*]

mead[2] *mēd,* (*poet.*), and **meadow** *med'ō, ns.* a level tract producing grass to be mown down: a rich pasture-ground, esp. beside a stream. — *adj.* **mead'owy.** — **mead'ow-brown'** a butterfly of the Satyridae; **meadow foxtail** a perennial grass (*Alopecurus pratensis*), common in Europe and N. Asia, and introduced into N. America; **mead'ow-grass** any grass of the genus Poa (**floating meadow-grass** manna-grass, float-grass); **mead'ow-lark'** (*U.S.*) a name for various species of birds of the genus *Sturnella* (family Icteridae); **meadow pipit** *Anthus pratensis,* a common brown and white European songbird; **mead'ow-rue'** a genus (*Thalictrum*) of the buttercup family with rue-like leaves; **mead'ow-saff'ron** *Colchicum autumnale* — also *autumn-crocus,* or *naked lady;* **mead'ow-sax'ifrage** a saxifrage (*Saxifraga granulata*) that grows on banks and dry meadows: applied also to umbelliferous plants of the genera Seseli and Silaus. [O.E. *mǣd,* in oblique cases *mǣdwe* — *māwan,* to mow; Ger. *Matte.*]

meadow-sweet *med'ō-swēt, n.* the rosaceous plant queen-of-the-meadows (*Spiraea ulmaria*), a tall fragrant plant of watery meadows. [Earlier **mead-sweet** which may be from **mead**[1] or from **mead**[2], as the obs. **mead'wort** is in O.E. *meduwyrt.*]

meagre *mē'gər, adj.* having little flesh: lean: poor: without richness or fertility: barren: scanty: without strength: jejune: maigre. — *n.* the maigre. — *adv.* **mea'grely.** — *n.* **mea'greness.** [Fr. *maigre* — L. *macer, macra, -rum,* lean; cf. Ger. *mager.*]

meal[1] *mēl, n.* the food taken at one time: the act or occasion of taking food, as a breakfast, dinner, or supper. — *n.* **meal'er** one who takes his meals at a boarding-house, lodging elsewhere. — **meals'-on-wheels** a welfare service taking cooked, usu. hot, meals to old people in need of such help; **meal ticket, meal'-ticket** a ticket that can be exchanged for a meal (esp. at reduced price): someone or something that is the source of one's expenses or income: someone who can be depended upon; **meal'-tide** (*arch.;* Scot. **meltith** *mel'tith,* a meal), **meal'-time** the time for a meal. — **make a meal of** to consume as a meal: to enjoy to the full: to treat or perform in an unnecessarily laborious or meticulous way. [O.E. *mǣl,* measure, time, portion of time; Du. *maal,* Ger. *Mahl.*]

meal[2] *mēl, n.* grain ground to powder: other material in powder: a powdery surface-covering. — *v.t.* to cover with meal: to grind into meal. — *v.i.* to yield or be plentiful in meal. — *n.* **meal'iness.** — *adj.* **meal'y** like meal, powdery: covered with meal or with something like meal: spotty: whitish. — **meal'-ark** (*Scot.*) a large chest for holding meal; **meal'-man** or **meal'-monger** one who deals in meal; **Meal Monday** the second Monday in February, a St Andrews (and formerly, Edinburgh) University holiday, originally to allow the students to go home and replenish their stock of meal; **meal'-poke** a beggar's meal-bag; **meal'-tree** the wayfaring tree, from its mealy leaves and shoots; **meal'-worm** the larva of a beetle (Tenebrio) abounding in granaries and flour-stores; **meal'y-bug** a hothouse pest, a coccus insect with a white powdery appearance. — *adj.* **meal'y-mouthed** (*-mowdhd*) smooth-tongued: over-squeamish, esp. in choice of words. — **meal'y-mouth'-edness.** [O.E. *melu, melo*; Ger. *Mehl*, Du. *meel*, meal.]

meal[3] *mēl*, (*Shak.*, in *pa.p.* **meal'd**) *v.t.* to stain, spot. [O.E. *mǣlan*.]

mealie *mēl'i, n.* (esp. in South Africa) an ear of maize: (esp. in *pl.*) maize. — Also **meal'y.** — **mealie meal** finely ground maize. [S.Afr. Du. *milie*, millet.]

mean[1] *mēn, adj.* low in rank or birth: base: sordid: low in worth or estimation: of little value or importance: poor, humble: low: inconsiderable: despicable: shabby: paltry: small-minded: ungenerous: stingy: malicious, bad-tempered: out of sorts, uncomfortable (*U.S.*): skilful, excellent (*slang*). — *n.* **mean'ie, -y** (*coll.*) an ungenerous, ungracious, small-minded, or malicious person. — *adv.* **mean'ly.** — *n.* **mean'ness.** — *adjs.* **mean'-born; mean'-spir'ited.** — **mean'-spir'itedness.** [O.E. *gǣne*; Ger. *gemein*; L. *commūnis*, common.]

mean[2] *mēn, adj.* intermediate: average: moderate (*obs.*). — *n.* that which is between or intermediate: an average amount, or value: a middle state or position: an intermediate term in a progression: meantime (*Spens.*): a middle or intermediate part (*mus.*): an instrument or medium: a mediator or intercessor (*obs.*): — *pl.* in form **means** that by whose instrumentality anything is caused or brought to pass: (treated as *sing.* or *pl.*) way to an end: (treated as *pl.*) pecuniary resources: what is required for comfortable living. — *ns.* **mean'time, mean'while** the intervening time. — *advs.* in the intervening time. — **means test** the test of private resources, determining or limiting claim to concession or allowance. — *v.t.* **means'-test.** — **mean sun** an imaginary sun moving uniformly in the equator, its position giving **mean (solar) time** (coinciding with true sun time four times a year); **mean'-tone** (*mus.*) an interval of mean value between a major and a minor second, formerly used in a system of temperament. — **arithmetic(al) mean** the sum of a number of quantities divided by their number; **by all means** certainly; **by any means** in any way; **by means** (*Spens.*) because; **by means of** with the help or use of; **by no means** certainly not; **geometric(al) mean** the *n*th root of the product of *n* quantities; **golden mean** the middle course between two extremes: a wise moderation; **harmonic mean** the reciprocal of the arithmetical mean of the reciprocals of two quantities; **in the mean** (*Spens.*) in the meantime; **mean free path** the average distance travelled by a molecule, atom, etc., between collisions; **quadratic mean** the square root of the arithmetical mean of the squares of the given quantities. [O.Fr. *meien* (Fr. *moyen*) — L. *mediānus* — *medius*, middle.]

mean[3] *mēn, v.t.* to have in mind as signification: to intend, to purpose: to destine, design: to signify. — *v.i.* (with *well, ill*) to have good, bad, intentions or disposition: (with *much, little*, etc.) to be of much, little, importance (to): — *pr.p.* **mean'ing**; *pa.t.* and *pa.p.* **meant** (*ment*). — *n.* **mean'ing** that which is in the mind or thoughts: signification: the sense intended: purpose. — *adj.* significant. — *adjs.* **mean'ingful; mean'ingless** senseless: expressionless: without significance. — *adv.* **mean'-ingly** significantly: intentionally. [O.E. *mǣnan*; Ger. *meinen*, to think.]

mean[4], **meane, mein, mene** *mēn,* (*Shak.* and *Scot.*) *v.t.* and *v.i.* to lament, to moan: to complain. [O.E. *mǣnan*; cf. **moan.**]

meander *mi-an'dər, n.* a sinuosity: a winding course: a maze: an intricate fret pattern: perplexity. — *v.i.* to wind about: to be intricate: to wander listlessly (with some reminiscence of **maunder**). — *adjs.* **mean'dered** formed into or covered with mazy passages or patterns; **mean'dering, mean'drian** (*obs.*), **mean'drous** winding. [L. *Maeander* — Gr. *Maiandros*, a winding river in Asia Minor.]

meane. See **mean**[4].

means. See **mean**[2].

meant *ment, pa.t.* and *pa.p.* of **mean**[3].

meare *mēr,* Spenser's spelling of **mere**[2,3]. — **mear'd** (*Spens.*) *pa.t.* of **mere**[3].

mease[1] *mēz,* **maze, maize, maise** *māz,* (*dial.*) *ns.* a measure of five 'hundreds' of herrings — varying from 500 to 630. [O.Fr. *meise,* receptacle for herrings; O.N. *meiss,* box, basket; O.H.G. *meisa*.]

mease[2] *mēz,* (*Scot.*) *v.t.* to assuage: to mitigate. [O.Fr. *amesir* — L. *ad,* to, *mītis,* mild.]

measles *mē'zlz, n. pl. but usu. sing. in construction* an infectious fever accompanied by eruptions of small red spots upon the skin: a disease of swine and cattle, caused by larval tapeworms: a blister or a disease of trees (*obs.*). — *n.* **mea'sle** a tapeworm larva. — *v.t.* (*arch.*) to infect with measles. — *v.i.* (*arch.*) to take measles. — *adj.* **mea'sled** measly. — *n.* **mea'sliness.** — *adj.* **mea'sly** infected with measles, or with tapeworm larvae: spotty: paltry, miserable. — **German measles** rubella. [M.E. *maseles;* cf. Du. *mazelen,* measles, O. H. G. *masala,* blister; Ger. *Masern,* measles.]

measure *mezh'ər, n.* the ascertainment of extent by comparison with a standard: a system of expressing the result of such ascertainment: the amount ascertained by comparison with a standard: that by which extent is ascertained or expressed: size: a standard or unit: a quantity by which another can be divided without remainder: an instrument for finding the extent of anything, esp. a graduated rod or tape for length, or a vessel of known content for capacity: the quantity contained in a vessel of known capacity — often a bushel: adequacy or due amount: some amount or degree, a portion: proportion: moderation: restraint: limit (*Milt.*): extent: that which is meted out to one, treatment: a means to an end: an enactment or bill: rhythm: a unit of verse — one foot or two feet: metre: strict time: a bar of music: a strain: a dance, esp. a slow and stately one: the width of a page or column, usually in *ems* (*print.*): (in *pl.*) a series of beds or strata (*geol.*). — *v.t.* to ascertain or show the dimensions or amount of (sometimes with *out* or *up*): to mark out or lay off (often with *off* or *out*): to mete (out): to proportion: to pit: to traverse: to sing or utter in measure (*Spens.*). — *v.i.* to be of the stated size: to take measurements. — *adj.* **meas'urable** that may be measured or computed: moderate: in small quantity or extent. — *n.* **meas'urableness.** — *adv.* **meas'urably.** — *adj.* **meas'ured** determined by measure: mensurable: rhythmical: with slow, heavy, steady rhythm: considered: restrained. — *adv.* **meas'uredly.** — *adj.* **meas'-ureless** boundless. — *ns.* **meas'urement** the act of measuring: the quantity found by measuring; **meas'-urer.** — *n.* and *adj.* **meas'uring.** — **measurement goods** light goods carried for charges according to bulk, not weight; **meas'uring-rod, -tape** one for measuring with; **meas'uring-worm'** a looper caterpillar. — **above,** or **beyond,** or (*arch.*) **out of, measure** to an exceedingly great degree; **be the measure of (something)** to be standard by which the quality, etc., of something may be judged; **for good measure** as something extra or above the minimum necessary; **get, have, someone's measure** to realise, know what someone's character and abilities really are, esp. having been deceived; **hard measures** harsh treatment; **in a measure, in some measure** to some degree; **made to measure** see **made; measure one's length** to fall or be thrown down at full length; **measure up** (sometimes with *to*) to reach a certain, or a required, standard, to be adequate; **measure strength** to engage in a contest; **measure swords** orig. to compare lengths of swords before a duel: to fight; **out of measure** see **above measure; short measure** less than the due and professed amount; **take measures** to adopt means to gain an end; **take someone's measure** to estimate someone's character and abilities; **tread a measure** to go through a dance; **within measure** moderately; **without measure** immoderately. [O.Fr. *mesure* — L. *mēnsūra,* a measure — *mētīrī, mēnsum,* to measure.]

meat *mēt, n.* anything eaten as food: a meal (*obs.*): the edible part of anything (now chiefly *U.S.*): the flesh of animals used as food — sometimes beef, mutton, pork, veal, etc., as opposed to poultry, fish, etc.: proleptically, game, destined prey: food for thought, substance, pith (*fig.*). — *n.* **meat'iness.** — *adjs.* **meat'less** foodless: without butcher's meat; **meat'y** full of meat (*lit.* and *fig.*); fleshly: flesh-like in taste or smell: pithy. — **meat'-ball** a ball of minced meat; **meat'-eater** one who eats butcher's meat: a carnivore; **meat'-fly** a blowfly: a flesh-fly; **meat'head** a stupid person (*U.S. slang*); **meat jelly** jelly formed from the solidified juices of cooked meat; **meat loaf** a loaf-shaped mass of chopped or minced meat, cooked and usually eaten cold; **meat'-man** a seller of butcher's meat; **meat'=mar'ket** a flesh-market; **meat'-off'ering** a Jewish sacrificial offering of fine flour or first-fruits with oil and frankincense; **meat'-paste; meat'-pie; meat'-plate** a large, esp. oval, plate on which meat is served; **meat rack** a place where young male homosexual prostitutes gather (*slang*); **meat'-safe** a receptacle for storing meat; **meat'-salesman** one who sells meat, esp. to the retail butchers; **meat'screen** a metal screen behind roasting meat, to throw back the fire's heat upon it; **meat'-tea'** a high tea with meat; **meat'-tub** a pickling-tub; **meat wagon** a police van for transporting prisoners (*slang*). — **meat and drink** (*fig.*) a required source of sustenance or invigoration. [O.E. *mete.*]

meath(e) *mēdh, n.* an obs. form of **mead**[1].

meatus *mi-ā'təs, (anat.) n.* an opening of a passage or canal: — *pl.* **mea'tuses.** — *adj.* **mea'tal.** [L. *meātus* (pl. *-ūs*) — *meāre,* to go.]

meawes. A Spenserian spelling of **mews** (*pl.* of **mew**[1]).

meazel. See **mesel.**

mebos *mā'bos,* (*S.Afr.*) *n.* salted or sugared dried apricots. [Perh. Jap. *umeboshi,* a kind of plum.]

Mecca *mek'ə, n.* the birthplace of Mohammed, a place of pilgrimage for Muslims: any outstanding place reverenced or resorted to — e.g. St. Andrews, Mecca of golf.

Meccano® *mi-kä'nō, n.* small metal plates, rods, nuts and bolts, etc., with which models can be constructed.

mechanic *mi-kun'ik, adj.* mechanical. — *n.* a handicraftsman: a skilled worker, esp. one who makes or maintains machinery: an air-mechanic: a term of contempt for one of the lower orders (*obs.*). — *adj.* **mechan'ical** pertaining to machines or mechanics: dynamical: worked or done by machinery or by mechanism: acting or done by physical, not chemical, means: machine-like: of the nature of a machine or mechanism: without intelligence or conscious will: performed simply by force of habit: reflex: skilled in mechanism: manual (*arch.*): manually employed: technical (*obs.*): mechanistic. — *n.* (*Shak.*) a mechanic. — *adv.* **mechan'ically.** — *n.pl.* **mechan'icals** the mechanical parts (*coll.*). — *n.* **mechanician** (*mek-ən-ish'ən*) a machine-maker: one skilled in the structure of machines. — *n.sing.* **mechan'ics** dynamics, the science of the action of forces on bodies, including kinetics and statics: the art or science of machine construction: the details of making or creating by manual or other process (also *n.pl.*): the system on which something works (also *n.pl.*). — *n.pl.* routine procedure(s). — *n.* **mechanisā'tion, -z-.** — *v.t.* **mech'anise, -ize** to make mechanical: to adapt to mechanical working: to provide with armoured armed vehicles. — *ns.* **mech'anism** the construction of a machine: the arrangement and action by which a result is produced: a philosophy that regards the phenomena of life as explainable by mechanical forces: the means adopted unconsciously towards a subconscious end (*psych.*); **mech'anist** a mechanician: a believer in philosophical mechanism. — *adj.* **mechanist'ic.** — *adv.* **mechanist'ically.** — **mechanical powers** the elementary forms or parts of machines — three *primary,* the lever, inclined plane, and pulley; and three *secondary,* the wheel-and-axle, the wedge, and the screw; **mechanical tissue** any tissue that gives a plant power of resisting stresses; **mechan-**

ics' institute an institution for the education of mechanics, with lectures, library, etc.; **mechanised Sikh** a Sikh who shaves and crops his hair, and does not wear a turban. [Gr. *mēchanikos* — *mēchanē,* a contrivance.]

Mechitharist. See **Mekhitarist.**

Mechlin *mek',* or *mehh'lin, adj.* produced at *Mechlin* or Malines, in Belgium. — *n.* lace made at Mechlin.

meconic *mi-kon'ik, adj.* denoting an acid obtained from poppies. — *ns.* **meconate** (*mek'ən-āt,* or *mēk'*) a salt of meconic acid; **mec'onin** a white, fusible, neutral substance ($C_{10}H_{10}O_4$) existing in opium; **mecō'nium** the first faeces of a newborn child, or of a newly emerged insect imago: opium; **Meconops'is** (Gr. *opsis,* appearance) a genus of largely Asiatic poppies: (without *cap.*) a plant of this genus: — *pl.* **meconops'ēs.** [Gr. *mēkōn,* the poppy.]

Mecoptera *mē-kop'tə-rə, n.pl.* an order of insects linking the Hymenoptera with the Trichoptera — the scorpion-flies. [Gr. *mēkos,* length, *pteron,* wing.]

medaewart *med'ē-wärt, n.* meadow-sweet (*Spens.*). [O.E. *meduwyrt;* see **meadow-sweet.**]

medal *med'l, n.* a piece of metal usu. in the form of a coin bearing some device or inscription, struck or cast usually in commemoration of an event or as a reward of merit. — *v.t.* to decorate with a medal: — *pr.p.* **med'alling;** *pa.t.* and *pa.p.* **med'alled.** — *n.* **med'alet** a small medal, esp. one bearing a representation of one or more saints, worn by Roman Catholics. — *adj.* **medallic** (*mi-dal'ik*). — *n.* **medallion** (*mi-dal'yən*) a large medal: a bas-relief of a round (sometimes a square) form: a round ornament, panel, tablet, or design of similar form. — *v.t.* to ornament, decorate, with medallions: to make in the form of a medallion. — *n.* **med'allist** one with expert knowledge of medals, or a collector of medals: a designer or maker of medals: one who has gained a medal, e.g. as a prize in sports, or for bravery. — **medal play** golf scored by strokes for the round, not by holes. [Fr. *médaille* — It. *medaglia;* through L.L. from L. *metallum,* metal.]

Medau *mā'dow, n.* a form of rhythmical exercise, mainly for women, using e.g. balls, hoops and clubs, developed by Hinrich *Medau* (1890–1974).

meddle *med'l, v.t.* and *v.i.* (*arch.*) to mix. — *v.i.* to concern oneself (with; *arch.*): to engage in fight (*Shak.*): to interfere unnecessarily, temerariously, (with, in): to tamper (with). — *n.* **medd'ler.** — *adj.* **medd'lesome** given to meddling. — *n.* **medd'lesomeness.** — *n.* and *adj.* **medd'ling.** [O.Fr. *medler,* a variant of *mesler* (Fr. *mêler*) — I..L. *misculāre* — L. *miscēre,* to mix.]

Mede. See **Median.**

medfly. See **Mediterranean fruit fly.**

media *mē'di-ə, n.* a voiced stop consonant, or a letter representing it: the middle coat of a blood-vessel: a middle primary vein of an insect's wing: — *pl.* **mē'diae** (*-ē*). — See also **medium.** [L. *media* (*littera, tunica, vena*), middle (letter, coat, vein), fem. of *medius,* middle.]

mediacy. See **mediate.**

mediaeval, medieval *med-i-ē'vl, U.S. mē-d(ē)-ē'vl, adj.* of the Middle Ages. — *ns.* **medi(a)e'valism** the spirit of the Middle Ages: devotion to mediaeval ideals; **medi(a)e'valist** one versed in the history, art, etc., of the Middle Ages: one who follows mediaeval practices. — *adv.* **medi(a)e'vally.** [L. *medius,* middle, *aevum,* age.]

medial *mē'di-əl, adj.* intermediate: occurring within a word: median: pertaining to a mean or average. — *n.* (*phon.; obs.*) a media. — *adv.* **me'dially.** [L.L. *mediālis* — L. *medius,* middle.]

median *mē'di-ən, adj.* in the middle, running through the middle: situated in the straight line or plane (*median line, plane*) that divides anything longitudinally into symmetrical halves. — *n.* a straight line joining an angular point of a triangle with the middle point of the opposite side: a middle nervure of an insect's wing: in a series of values, the value middle in position (not usu. in magnitude). [L. *mediānus* — *medius,* middle.]

Median *mē'di-ən, adj.* pertaining to *Media*, an ancient kingdom north-west of Persia, its people, or their Indo-European language (also *n.*). — *n.* **Mede** one of the people of Media, fused as a nation with the Persians about 500 B.C. — *adj.* **Me'dic.** — *v.i.* **Me'dise, -ize** to become Median, or as the Medians: to favour the Persians (called Medes by the Greeks). — *v.t.* to make Median. — *n.* **Mē'dism** the adoption of Persian interests — to a Greek, treachery. — **law of the Medes and Persians** the type of 'that which altereth not' (Dan. vi. 12). [Gr. *Mēdos*, a Mede.]

mediant *mē'di-ənt, n.* the third tone of a scale, about midway between tonic and dominant. [L.L. *mediāns, -antis,* pr.p. of *mediāre,* to be in the middle.]

mediastinum *mē-di-ə-stī'nəm, n.* a membranous septum, or a cavity, between two principal portions of an organ, esp. the folds of the pleura and the space between the right and left lungs. — *adj.* **mediastī'nal.** [Neut. of L.L. *mediastīnus,* median (in classical L. *mediastinus* is a drudge) — *medius.*]

mediate *mē'di-it, adj.* middle: intervening: indirect: related or acting through something intervening. — *v.i.* (-*āt*) to interpose between parties as a friend of each: to act as intermediary: to intercede: to be or act as a medium: to hold a mediate position. — *v.t.* to bring about, end, promote, obtain, or communicate by friendly intervention, or by intercession, or through an intermediary: to be the medium or intermediary of: to transmit, convey, pass on. — *n.* **mē'diacy** mediateness. — *adv.* **mē'diately.** — *ns.* **mē'diateness** the state of being mediate; **mediā'tion** the act of mediating or coming between: an entreaty for another; **mediatīsā'tion, -z-.** — *v.t.* **mē'diatise, -ize** to cause to act in a subordinate position or through an agent: to reduce from immediate to mediate vassal (of the empire) without loss of dignity: to annex, or to subordinate, as a smaller state to a larger neighbouring one. — *adj.* **mē'diative** (-*ə-tiv*). — *n.* **mē'diātor** one who mediates between parties at strife: — *fem.* **mē'diātress, mediā'trix:** — *pl.* **mediātrices** (-*trī'sēz*). — *adj.* **mediatō'rial.** — *adv.* **mediatō'rially.** — *n.* **mē'diatorship.** — *adj.* **mē'diatory.** [L.L. *mēdiāre, -ātum,* to be in the middle — L. *mēdius.*]

medic¹ *med'ik, adj.* medical (*poet.*). — *n.* a physician (*rare*): a medical student (*slang*). — *n.* **medicas'ter** a quack. — **medico-** combining form, relating to medicine or medical matters, as in *adjs.* **med'ico-chirur'gical** relating to both medicine and surgery; **med'ico-le'gal** relating to the application of medicine to questions of law. [L. *medicus.*]

medic². See **medick.**

Medicaid *med'i-kād,* (also without *cap.*) *n.* in the U.S., a scheme providing assistance with medical expenses for people with low incomes. [*Medical aid.*]

medical *med'i-kl, adj.* relating to the art of healing: relating to the art of the physician, distinguished from surgery. — *n.* (*coll.*) a student of medicine: a medical examination to ascertain the state of one's physical health. — *adv.* **med'ically.** — **medical certificate** a certificate from a doctor stating that a person is, or has been, unfit for work, etc., or that a person has, or has not, passed a medical examination; **medical officer** a doctor in charge of medical treatment, etc., in an armed service or other organisation. — **Medical Officer of Health** (abbrev. **MOH**) formerly, a public officer in charge of medical services in a town, etc. [L.L. *medicālis* — L. *medicus,* a physician — *medērī,* to heal.]

medicament *med-ik'ə-mənt,* or *med', n.* a substance used in curative treatment, esp. externally. — *v.t.* to treat with medicaments. — *adjs.* **medicamental** (-*ment'l*), **medicament'ary.** — *adv.* **medicament'ally.** [L. *medicāmentum* — *medicāre.*]

Medicare *med'i-kār,* (also without *cap.*) *n.* in the U.S., a scheme providing medical insurance for people aged 65 and over. [*Medical care.*]

medicaster. See **medic¹.**

medicate *med'i-kāt, v.t.* to treat with medicine: to impreg-

nate with anything medicinal: to drug, doctor, tamper with. — *adj.* **med'icable** that may be healed. — *adj.* **med'icated.** — *n.* **medicā'tion.** — *adj.* **med'icative.** [L. *medicāre, -ātum,* to heal — *medicus.*]

Medicean *med-i-sē'ən, adj.* relating to the *Medici,* a distinguished Florentine family which attained to sovereign power in the 15th century.

medicine *med'sin, -sn,* also (esp. *U.S.*) *med'i-sin, -sn, n.* any substance used (esp. internally) for the treatment or prevention of disease: a drug: the art or science of prevention and cure of disease, esp. non-surgically: remedial punishment: a charm, magic: anything of magical power: a physician (*Shak.*). — *v.t.* to treat or cure by medicine. — *adjs.* **medicinable** (*med'sin-ə-bl*) having a healing power; **medicinal** (*med-is'i-nl,* sometimes *med-i-sī'nl;* in *Shak.,* etc., *med'si-nl; Milt.* **med'cinal**) used in medicine: curative: relating to medicine: like medicine. — *adv.* **medic'inally.** — *n.* **mediciner** (*med'sin ər, med-is'i-nər; arch.*) a physician. — **med'icine-ball** a heavy ball tossed and caught for exercise; **med'icine-bott'le; med'icine-chest** a chest for keeping a selected set of medicines; **med'icine-dropp'er; med'icine-man** among savages, a witch-doctor or magician. — **a dose, taste, of one's own medicine** harsh or unpleasant treatment given, often in revenge, to one used to giving such treatment to others. [L. *medicīna* — *medicus.*]

medick, in U.S. **medic,** *med'ik, n.* any species of *Medicago,* a genus distinguished from clover by its spiral or sickle-shaped pods and short racemes — including lucerne. [L. *mēdica* — Gr. *Mēdikē* (*poā*), Median (herb), i.e. lucerne.]

medico *med'ik-ō,* (*slang*) *n.* a medical practitioner or student: — *pl.* **med'icos.** [It. *medico,* or Sp. *médico* — L. *medicus,* a physician.]

medico-. See **medic¹.**

medieval. Same as **mediaeval.**

medina *mə-dē'nə, n.* in North African cities, the ancient, native quarter. [Ar., town.]

medio- *mē'di-ō-,* (in compounds) middle. [L. *medius,* middle.]

mediocre *mē'di-ō-kər,* or -*ō', adj.* of middling goodness (usu. disparagingly). — *n.* **medioc'rity** (-*ok'*) a middling degree: a mediocre person. [Fr. *médiocre* — L. *mediocris* — *medius,* middle.]

Medise, Medism. See **Median.**

meditate *med'i-tāt, v.i.* to consider thoughtfully (with *on, upon*): to engage in contemplation, esp. religious. — *v.t.* to consider deeply, reflect upon: to revolve in the mind: to intend. — *adj.* **med'itated.** — *n.* **meditā'tion** the act of meditating: deep thought: serious continuous contemplation, esp. on a religious or spiritual theme: a meditative discourse: a meditative treatment of a literary or musical theme. — *adj.* **med'itative.** — *adv.* **med'itatively.** — *n.* **med'itativeness.** — **meditate the muse** (Latinism, after Milton) to give one's mind to composing poetry. [L. *meditārī,* prob. cog. with L. *medērī,* to heal.]

mediterranean *med-i-tə-rā'ni-ən, adj.* situated in the middle of earth or land: land-locked: (with *cap.*) of the **Mediterranean Sea** (so called from being in the middle of the land of the Old World) or its shores. — **Mediterranean fever** Malta or undulant fever; **Mediterranean fruit fly** a small black-and-white two-winged fly, orig. native to Africa but now widely distributed, the larvae of which feed on ripening fruit — (often shortened to **med'fly**); **Mediterranean race** a long-headed dark race of white men, of medium stature, inhabiting south Europe and north Africa. [L. *mediterrāneus* — *medius,* middle, *terra,* earth.]

medium *mē'di-əm, n.* the middle place or degree: a middle course: a mean (*obs.*): (in *pl.*, **mediums**) medium-dated securities; any intervening means, instrument, or agency: instrumentality: a substance through which any effect is transmitted: that through which communication is maintained: (*pl.* **media**) a channel (as newspapers, radio, television) through which information, etc. is transmitted to the public (also **mass medium**): (*pl.* usu. **media**) any material, e.g. punched cards, paper tape, on which data is recorded (*comput.*): an enveloping substance or element in which a thing exists or lives: environment: a vehicle for paint, etc.: a nutritive substance on which a culture (as of bacteria, tissue, etc.) may be fed: (*pl.* **mediums**) in spiritualism, the person through whom spirits are said to communicate with the material world: (*pl.* **mediums**) a person of supernormal sensibility: — *pl.* **mē′dia**, or **mē′diums**. — *adj.* intermediate: between fast and slow, long and short, etc.: mean, average (*obs.*): of a standard size of paper between demy and royal, now 18 in. by 23 in. — *adj.* **mediumis′tic** of or pertaining to spiritualistic mediums. — *adjs.* **me′dium-da′ted** of securities, redeemable in five to fifteen year's time; **me′dium-term** intermediate between short-term and long-term. — **medium waves** (*radio*) electromagnetic waves of between 200 and 1000 metres. — **circulating medium** money passing from hand to hand, as coin, bank notes, etc. [L. *medium*, neut. of *medius*, middle.]

medius *mē′di-əs, n.* the middle finger. [L. *medius*, middle.]

Medjidie *me-jēd′i-e, n.* a Turkish order of knighthood founded by Sultan Abdu'l *Majīd*.

medlar *med′lər, n.* a small tree (*Mespilus*, or *Pyrus, germanica*) akin to the apple: its fruit. [O.Fr. *medler, mesler* — L. *mespilum* — Gr. *mespilon*.]

medle. An old spelling (*Shak.* and *Spens.*) of **meddle.**

medley *med′li, n.* a mingled and confused mass: a miscellany: a song or piece of music made up of bits from various sources: a cloth woven from yarn of different colours: a mêlée, fight (*obs.*). — **medley relay** a race in which each team member runs a different distance or (in swimming) uses a different stroke. [O.Fr. *medler, mesler*, to mix.]

Médoc *mā-dok′, n.* a French wine produced in the district of *Médoc*, department of Gironde.

medresseh. See **madrasa.**

medulla *me-dul′ə, n.* the inner portion of an organ, hair, or tissue: bone-marrow: pith: a loose or spongy mass of hyphae: — *pl.* **medull′ae** (*-ē*), **medull′as.** — *adjs.* **medull′ar, -y** consisting of, or resembling, marrow or pith; **medull′ate** having medulla; **med′ullated** provided with a medullary sheath. — **medulla oblongā′ta** (or *-ä′tə*) that part of the brain that tapers off into the spinal cord; **medullary ray** (*bot.*) a band of cells (appearing as a ray in cross-section) cutting radially through wood and bast; **medullary sheath** a thin layer surrounding the pith (*bot.*): a whitish fatty membrane covering an axis-cylinder (*anat.*). [L. *medulla*, marrow.]

Medusa *me-dū′zə, n.* one of the three Gorgons, whose head, with snakes for hair, turned beholders into stone, but was cut off by Perseus, and placed in Athena's aegis: (without *cap.*) a jellyfish: (without *cap.*) an individual of the free-swimming sexual generation of jellyfishes and Hydrozoa: — *pl.* **medū′sae** (*-zē*), **medū′sas.** — *adj.* **medū′san.** — *n.* a medusa. — *adjs.* **medū′siform** like a jellyfish; **medū′soid** like a medusa. — *n.* a sexual hydrozoan that remains attached to the parent hydroid colony. [L. *Medūsa* — Gr. *Medousa*, the Gorgon *Medusa* (lit. ruler).]

meed *mēd, n.* wages (*arch.*): reward: what is bestowed for merit: measure, portion. [O.E. *mēd*; Ger. *Miete*.]

meek *mēk, adj.* mild and gentle of temper: submissive. — *v.t.* **meek′en** to render meek. — *v.i.* to become meek. — *adv.* **meek′ly.** — *n.* **meek′ness** the state or quality of being meek. [O.N. *mjūkr*; early mod. Du. *muik*, soft.]

meer *mēr,* an alternative spelling of **mere**[1,2,3]. — *adj.* **meered, mered** (*Shak.*) (possibly) set up as a *mere* or division, dividing: (according to some) sole, or entire.

meerkat *mēr′kat, n.* a monkey (*obs.*): a South African carnivore (*Cynictis penicillata*), akin to the ichneumon: the suricate: a ground-squirrel: a lemur. — Also **meer′cat.** [Du. *meerkat*, monkey, as if 'overseas cat',

from *meer*, sea, *kat*, cat, but perh. really an Eastern word.]

meerschaum *mēr′shəm, n.* a fine light whitish clay, sepiolite — once supposed to be a petrified sea-scum: a tobacco-pipe made of it. [Ger., — *Meer*, sea, *Schaum*, foam.]

meet[1] *mēt, adj.* fitting: qualified: even, quits (*Shak.*). — *adv.* fittingly (*Shak.*). — *adv.* **meet′ly.** — *n.* **meet′ness.** [Prob. from an O.E. (Anglian) form answering to W.S. *gemǣte* — *metan*, to measure.]

meet[2] *mēt, v.t.* to come face to face with: to come into the company of: to become acquainted with, be introduced to: to encounter in conflict: to find or experience: to refute: to be suitable to: to satisfy, as by payment: to receive, as a welcome: to cause to meet, bring into contact: to await the arrival of, keep an appointment with. — *v.i.* to come together from different points: to assemble: to come into contact: to have an encounter: to balance, come out correct: — *pa.t.* and *pa.p.* **met.** — *n.* a meeting, as of huntsmen: an assembly for racing: (*slang*) a covert pre-arranged meeting between criminals or between police and informant. — *n.* **meet′ing** a coming face to face for friendly or hostile ends: an interview: an assembly: an organised assembly for transaction of business: an assembly for religious worship, esp. (in England) of Dissenters: a place of meeting: a junction. — **meet′ing-house** a house or building where people, esp. Dissenters (particularly Quakers), meet for public worship. — **give the** (or **a**) **meeting** (*arch.*) to appoint or come to a rendezvous, for a duel or other purpose; **meet halfway** to make concessions in compromise; **meet in with, wi'** (*Scot.*) to meet with, come across; **meet the ear,** or **eye** to be readily apparent; **meet up (with)** to meet, by chance or arrangement; **meet with** to come to or upon, esp. unexpectedly: to meet, come together with, usu. for a purpose (*U.S.*): to undergo, chance to experience: to obviate (as an objection) (*Bacon*); **well met** an old complimentary greeting. [O.E. *mētan*, to meet — *mōt, gemōt*, a meeting.]

mefloquine *mef′lō-kwin, n.* an antimalarial drug.

meg(a)-, megalo- *meg(ə-)(lō-)*, in composition, very big, unusually large, on a very large scale: in names of units, a million, as *megabar, megohm, megawatt*, etc. — **megamega-** in composition, a million million (better **tera-**). — *ns.* **meg′abar; meg′abit; meg′abyte.** — *adj.* **megacephalous** (*-sef′ə-ləs*; Gr. *kephalē*, head) large-headed. — *n.pl.* **Megachelroptera** (*-kīr-op′tər-ə*) the fruit-bats. — *ns.* **meg′acurie; meg′acycle** a million cycles: a million cycles per second; **meg′adeath** death of a million people, a unit in estimating casualties in nuclear war; **meg′adyne; megafar′ad; meg′afauna** (or *-fō′nə, -fō′nə*), **meg′aflora** (or *-flō′rə, -flō′rə*) large animals, plants, visible to the naked eye; **meg′afog** a fog-signal with megaphones pointing in several directions; **meg′agauss; meg′ahertz; meg′ajoule; meg′alith** (Gr. *lithos*, stone) a huge stone, as in prehistoric monuments. — *adj.* **megalith′ic.** — *ns.* **megaloblast** an abnormally large nucleated red blood cell found in the bone-marrow of people suffering from a **megaloblastic anaemia** such as pernicious anaemia; **megalomā′nia** the delusion that one is great or powerful: a mania, or passion, for big things. — *n.* and *adj.* **megalomā′niac.** — *adj.* **megalomaniacal** (*-mə-nī′ə-kl*). — *ns.* **megalop′-olis** a wide-spreading, thickly-populated urban area; **meg′alosaur, megalosau′rus** (Gr. *sauros*, a lizard) a gigantic lizard-hipped Jurassic and Cretaceous dinosaur (*Megalosaurus*), carnivorous in mode of life. — *adj.* **megalosau′rian.** — *ns.* **meg′anewton; meg′aparsec; meg′aphone** (Gr. *phōnē*, voice) a funnel-shaped device for directing, or increasing volume of, sound. — *v.t.* and *v.i.* to communicate by megaphone. — *ns.* **meg′apode** (Gr. *pous, podos*, foot) a mound-bird; **meg′arad; meg′aron** (Gr. *megaron*) the principal hall of an ancient Greek house; **meg′ascope** (Gr. *skopeein*, to view) an instrument for projecting an enlarged image. — *adj.* **megascopic** (*-skop′ik*) enlarged: visible to the naked eye. — *ns.* **megasporangium** (*-spor-an'ji-əm*) a sporangium producing only megaspores: — *pl.* **megasporan'gia; meg'aspore** the larger of two forms of spore: a spore giving rise to a female gametophyte; **megasporophyll** (*-spor'ə-fil*) a sporophyll that carries or subtends only megasporangia; **meg'astore** very large shop, esp. of a chain-store; **meg'astructure** a very large building or construction; **Megathē'rium** (Gr. *thērion*, wild beast) a genus of gigantic extinct S. American ground-sloths; **meg'aton, -ne** (*-tun*) one million tons: a unit of explosive power equalling a million tons of TNT (**megaton bomb** a bomb of this force); **meg'a-tonnage** the total explosive capacity in megatons, -nes. — *adj.* **meg'avitamin** consisting of or relating to large doses of vitamins. — *ns.* **meg'avolt; meg'awatt** (**megawatt day** the unit of energy used in speaking of nuclear power reactors (day = 24 hours)); **meg'ohm.** [Gr. *megas*, fem. *megalē*, neut, *mega*, big.]

Megaera *mə-jē'rə, me-gī'ra, n.* one of the Furies. [L., — Gr. *Megaira*.]

megafarad, etc., **megalomania,** etc., **megasporophyll.** See under **meg(a)-.**

megass(e) *mə-gäs'.* Same as **bagasse.**

Megatherium... **megawatt.** See under **meg(a)-.**

megilp *mə-gilp'.* See **magilp.**

megohm. See under **meg(a)-.**

megrim[1] *mē'grim.* See **migraine.**

megrim[2] *mē'grim, n.* the scald-fish.

mein. See **mean**[4].

meinie, mein(e)y *mā'ni, n.* a retinue (*Shak.*): a herd. [O.Fr. *mesnie* — L. *mānsio -ōnis*, a dwelling.]

meint. See **ming.**

meiofauna *mī'ə-fö-nə, -fö-nə* or *-fö'nə, -fö'nə, n.pl.* animals less than 1mm and more than 0·1mm across. [Gr. *meion*, less, and **fauna.**]

meionite *mī'ən-īt, n.* a scapolite with less sodium and silica than marialite. [Gr. *meiōn*, less, from the short vertical axis of its crystal.]

meiosis *mī-ō'sis, n.* understatement as a figure of speech (*rhet.*): litotes: cell-division with reduction of the number of chromosomes towards the development of a reproductive cell (*biol.*): — *pl.* **meiō'ses.** — *adj.* **meiotic** (*-ot'ik*). [Gr. *meiōsis,* diminution.]

Meissen (china, porcelain, ware). Same as **Dresden.**

Meistersinger *mīs'tər-zing-ər, -sing-ər, n.* one of the burgher poets and musicians of Germany in the 14th–16th centuries, the successors of the Minnesingers: — *pl.* **Meistersinger, -s.** [Ger., master-singer.]

meith *mēth,* (*Scot.*) *n.* a landmark: a boundary. [Prob. O.N. *mith,* a fishing-bank found by landmarks.]

Mejlis. Same as **Majlis.**

me judice *mē jōō'di-sē, mā yōō'di-ke,* (L.) I being judge, in my opinion.

Mekhitarist, Mechitharist *mehh-, mek-i-tär'ist, n.* an Armenian Uniat monk of a congregation founded by *Mekhitar* (1676–1749) at Constantinople in 1701, since 1717 with headquarters near Venice. — Also *adj.*

mekometer *mə-kom'ə-tər, n.* a device for accurate measurement of distances by means of a light beam. [Gr. *mēkos,* length.]

mel *mel,* (esp. *pharmacy*) *n.* honey. [L.]

melaconite *mel-ak'ən-īt, n.* tenorite. [Gr. *melās,* black, *konis,* dust.]

melamine *mel'ə-mēn, n.* a white crystalline organic substance used in forming **melamine resins,** thermosetting plastics used as adhesives, coatings, etc. [Ger. *Melamin.*]

melampode *mel-am'pōd, mel',* (*Spens.*) *n.* the black hellebore. [Gr. *melampodion.*]

melanaemia *mel-ən-ē'mi-ə, n.* the presence of melanin in the blood. [Gr. *melās, -ānos,* black, *haima,* blood.]

melancholy *mel'ən-kol-i, -kəl-i,* formerly *mel-ang'kol-i, n.* black bile, an excess thereof, or the mental condition of temperament supposed to result therefrom (*obs.*): surliness (*obs.*): continued depression of spirits: dejection: melancholia: indulgence in thoughts of pleasing

sadness: pensiveness. — *adj.* prone to, affected by, expressive of, or causing, melancholy: depressed: pensive: deplorable. — *ns.* **melanchō'lia** a mental state characterised by dejection and misery; **melanchō'liac** a sufferer from melancholia. — Also *adj.* — *adj.* **melancholic** (*-kol'ik*) affected with, or caused by, melancholy or melancholia: dejected: mournful. — *n.* a melancholiac. — *adj.* **melanchō'lious.** [Gr. *melancholiā* — *melās, -ānos,* black, *cholē,* bile.]

Melanesian *mel-ən-ēz'i-ən, -ēz'yən, -ēzh'(y)ən, adj.* pertaining to *Melanesia,* a group of islands lying N.E. of Australia, in which the dominant race is dark-skinned. — *n.* a native, or a language, of these islands. — **Neo-Melanesian** see **neo-.** [Gr. *melās, -ānos,* black, *nēsos,* an island.]

mélange *mā-lãzh', n.* a mixture: a medley. [Fr.]

melanic *mi-lan'ik, adj.* black or dark in pigmentation. — *ns.* **melanin** (*mel'ə-nin*) the dark pigment in skin, hair, etc.; **mel'anism** more than normal development of dark colouring matter. — *adj.* **melanist'ic.** — *ns.* **mel'anite** a black garnet; **melano** (*mi-lä'nō, mel'ə-nō*; on the analogy of *albino*) a person or animal abnormally dark: — *pl.* **melanos; mel'anocyte** (*-sīt, -lan'*) an epidermal cell that can produce melanin; **melanō'ma** any skin tumour consisting of melanin-pigmented cells: (also **malignant melanoma**) a malignant tumour consisting of melanin-pigmented cells, which usually develops from a mole and metastasises rapidly: — *pl.* **melanō'mata, melanō'mas; mel'anophore** (*-för, -för*) a chromatophore containing melanin; **melanō'sis** an abnormal deposit of melanin: the associated condition of body. — *adjs.* **melanōt'ic; mel'anous** dark-complexioned. — *n.* **melanū'ria** the presence of a dark pigment in the urine. — *adj.* **melanū'ric.** — *ns.* **melaphyre** (*mel'ə-fīr*; after *porphyry*) orig. a dark porphyritic rock: applied very loosely to an altered basalt; **melatō'nin** a hormone produced by the pineal gland of mammals. [Gr. *melās, -ānos,* black.]

Melanochroi *mel-ən-ok'rō-ī,* or *-ō-krō'ī, n.pl.* a race or type of man with dark hair and pale skin — dark-haired Caucasian type. — *adjs.* **melanochrō'ic, melanochroous** (*-ok'rō-əs*). [Gr. *melās, -ānos,* black, and either *ōchros,* pale, or *chroā,* skin.]

melanterite *mi-lan'tə-rīt, n.* native copperas. [Gr. *melantēriā,* a black pigment.]

Melastomaceae *mel-ə-stō-mā's(h)i-ē, n.pl.* a tropical family of plants akin to the myrtles, very abundant in South America, characterised by the leaf-veins diverging from the base and meeting at the tip, named from the Old World genus **Melastoma** (*mi-las'tō-mə*). — *adj.* **melastomā'ceous.** [Gr. *melās,* black, *stoma,* mouth, from the fruit of some staining the lips.]

melba toast *mel'bə tōst* very thin crisp toast. — **melba sauce** a sauce for puddings, made from raspberries. [Named after Dame Nellie *Melba* (1861–1931), Australian operatic singer.]

meld[1] *meld,* (*obs.* except in cards, etc.) *v.t.* and *v.i.* to declare: to announce. — Also *n.* [O.E. *meldan,* or Ger. *melden.*]

meld[2] *meld, v.t.* and *v.i.* to merge, blend, combine. — Also *n.* [Poss. **melt** and **weld.**]

melder *mel'dər,* (*Scot.*) *n.* the quantity of meal ground at one time. [O.N. *meldr.*]

mêlée *mel'ā, n.* a fight in which the combatants are mingled together: a confused conflict: an affray. [Fr., — *mêler,* to mix; cf. **meddle, mell**[1].]

Melia *mē'li-ə, n.* a genus of trees including the nim or margosa, giving name to the family **Meliā'ceae** (mahogany, *Cedrela,* etc.). — *adj.* **meliā'ceous** (*-shəs*). [Gr. *meliā,* ash-tree (from a resemblance in leaves).]

Meliboean *mel-i-bē'ən, adj.* in poetry, amoebaean. [From *Meliboeus,* in Virgil's first eclogue.]

melic[1] *mel'ik, adj.* to be sung: lyric: strophic. [Gr. *melikos* — *melos,* song.]

melic[2] *mel'ik, n.* a grass (*Melica*) of the fescue tribe. — Also **mel'ic-grass'.** [Origin obscure.]

melicotton. See **melocoton.**

melilite *mel'i-līt, n.* a tetragonal mineral, calcium aluminium magnesium silicate, often honey-yellow. [Gr. *meli*, honey, *lithos*, stone.]

melilot *mel'i-lot, n.* a genus (*Melilotus*) of clover-like plants with racemes of white or yellow flowers and a peculiar sweet odour. [Gr. *melilōtos — meli*, honey, *lōtos*, lotus.]

melinite *mel'in-īt, n.* an explosive made from picric acid. [Fr. *mélinite* — Gr. *mēlinos*, quince yellow — *mēlon*, quince.]

meliorate *mē'li-ə-rāt, v.t.* to make better. — *v.i.* to grow better. — *n.* **meliorā'tion.** — *adj.* **mē'liorative** tending towards improvement. — *ns.* **mē'liorātor; mē'liorism** the doctrine that the world is capable of improvement, as opposed to *optimism* and *pessimism;* **mē'liorist; meliority** (*-or'i-ti*) betterness. [L.L. *meliōrāre, -ātum* — L. *melior*, better.]

meliphagous *mel-if'ə-gəs, adj.* feeding upon honey. [Gr. *meli*, honey, *phagein* (aor.), to eat.]

melisma *mel-iz'mə, n.* a song: a tune: a melodic embellishment: — *pl.* **melis'mata, melis'mas.** — *adj.* **melismatic** (*-mat'ik*) florid in melody, esp. where one syllable is sung to a number of notes. [Gr. *melisma, -matos,* a song, tune.]

mell[1] *mel, v.t.* and *v.i.* to mix, mingle. — *v.i.* to have to do (with *with*): to have intercourse: to join in fight: to be concerned: to meddle. [O.F. *meller;* cf. **meddle, medley.**]

mell[2] *mel, n.* a Northern form of **mall, maul.**

mellay *mel'ā, n.* another form of **mêlée.**

melliferous *mel-if'ə-rəs, adj.* honey-producing. — *ns.* **mellificā'tion** honey-making; **mellif'luence** (L. *fluĕre*, to flow) a flow of sweetness: a smooth sweet flow. — *adjs.* **mellif'luent, mellif'luous** flowing with honey or sweetness: smooth. — *advs.* **mellif'luently, mellif'luously.** — *n.* **mell'ite** honey-stone. — *adjs.* **mellit'ic; melliv'orous** (L. *vorāre*, to devour) eating honey. [L. *mel, mellis,* honey.]

mellow *mel'ō, adj.* soft and ripe: well matured: soft to the touch, palate, ear, etc.: genial: half-tipsy. — *v.t.* to soften by ripeness or age: to mature. — *v.i.* to become soft: to be matured, ripened: to become gentler and more tolerant. — *adv.* **mell'owly.** — *n.* **mell'owness.** — *adj.* **mell'owy** mellow. — **mellow out** (*slang*) to become relaxed or calm (esp. under the influence of drugs). [Prob. O.E. *melu*, meal, influenced by *mearu*, soft, tender.]

melocoton, melocotoon *mel-ō-kot-ōn', -ōōn', (obs.) ns.* a large kind of peach. — Also **malakatoone', melicott'on.** [Sp. *melocotón* — It. *melocotogna*, quince, peach — L.L. *mēlum cotōneum* — Gr. *mēlon Kўdōnion*, Cydonian (Cretan) apple, quince.]

melodrama *mel'ō-drä-mə,* or *-drä', n.* a play with musical accompaniment to the action and spoken dialogue, with or without songs (*obs.*): a kind of romantic and sensational drama, crude, sentimental, and conventional, with strict attention to poetic justice and happy endings — also **mel'odrame** (*-dräm*). — *adj.* **melodramat'ic** (*-drə-mat'ik*) of the nature of melodrama: overstrained: sensational. — *v.t.* **melodram'atise, -ize** to make melodramatic. — *n.* **melodramatist** (*-dram'ə-tist*) a writer of melodramas. [Gr. *melos,* a song, *drāma,* action.]

melody *mel'ə-di, n.* an air or tune: music: an agreeable succession of single musical sounds, as distinguished from *harmony.* — *n.* **melodeon, melodion** (*mi-lō'di-ən*) a small reed-organ: an improved accordion. — *adj.* **melodic** (*mi-lod'ik*). — *n.sing.* **melod'ics** the branch of music concerned with melody. — *adj.* **melō'dious** full of melody: agreeable to the ear. — *adv.* **melō'diously.** — *n.* **melō'diousness.** — *v.i.* **mel'odise, -ize** to make melody: to perform a melody. — Also *v.t.* — *n.* **mel'odist.** — **melodic minor** a minor scale with major sixth and seventh ascending and minor sixth and seventh descending. [Fr., through L.L., — Gr. *melōidiā*.]

melomania *mel-ō-mā'ni-ə, n.* a craze for music. — *n.*

melomā'niac. — *adj.* **melomanic** (*-man'*). [Gr. *melos,* song, *maniā,* madness.]

melon *mel'ən, n.* any of several juicy gourds: the plant bearing it: profits to be divided (*slang*). [Fr., — L. *mēlō, -ōnis* — Gr. *mēlon,* an apple.]

Melpomene *mel-pom'i-nē, n.* the Muse of tragedy. [Gr. *Melpomĕnē,* lit. songstress.]

melt[1] *melt, v.i.* to become liquid from the solid state, esp. by heat: to fuse: to dissolve: to stream with liquid: to lose distinct form: to blend: to shade off: to become imperceptible: to disperse, be dissipated, disappear (sometimes with *away*): to be softened emotionally. — *v.t.* to cause to melt in any sense: — *pa.t.* **melt'ed,** *arch.* **mōlt;** *pa.p.* **melt'ed,** *arch.* **mōlt'en, ymōlt'en, ymōlt'.** — *n.* the act of melting: the state of being melted: molten material: the quantity melted. — *n.* and *adj.* **melt'ing.** — *adv.* **melt'ingly.** — *n.* **melt'ingness.** — *adj.* **mōlt'en** melted: made of melted metal. — *adv.* **mōlt'enly.** — **melt'down** the process in which, due to a failure of the cooling system, the radioactive fuel in a nuclear reactor overheats, melts through its insulation, and is released into the environment; **melt'ing-point** the temperature at which a given solid begins to become liquid; **melt'ing-pot** a vessel for melting things in: a state of dissolution preparatory to shaping anew (*fig.*); **melt'-water** water running off melting ice or snow. — **molten salt reactor** one in which uranium is dissolved in a molten mixture of fluoride salts. [O.E. *meltan* (intrans. strong vb.), and *mæltan, meltan* (causative weak vb., W.S. *mieltan*); O.N. *melta,* to digest, to malt, Gr. *meldein.*]

melt[2]. See **milt.**

meltith *mel'tith,* (*Scot.*) *n.* a meal: a cow's yield at one milking. [**meal-tide.**]

melton *mel'tən, n.* a strong cloth for overcoats. [*Melton* Mowbray, in Leicestershire.]

member *mem'bər, n.* a distinct part of a whole, esp. a limb of an animal: a clause (*gram.*): one of a society: a representative in a legislative body. — *adj.* **mem'bered** having limbs. — *n.* **mem'bership** the state of being a member or one of a society: the members of a body regarded as a whole. — *adj.* **mem'bral** pertaining to the limbs rather than the trunk. — **member of parliament** a member of the House of Commons, abbrev. **MP.** [Fr. *membre* — L. *membrum.*]

membrane *mem'brān, -brin, n.* a thin flexible solid sheet or film: a thin sheet-like structure, usually fibrous, connecting other structures or covering or lining a part or organ (*biol.*): a skin of parchment. — *adjs.* **membranaceous** (*-brə-nā'shəs*), **membrān'eous** (*rare*), **mem'-branous** (*-brə-nəs*) like or of the nature of a membrane: thin, translucent, and papery (*bot.*). — **membrane bone** one formed directly from connective tissue without passing through a stage of cartilage. [L. *membrāna* — *membrum.*]

membrum virile *mem'brəm vir-ī'lē, -brōōm wir-ē'le,* (L.) the penis.

memento *mi-men'tō, n.* something kept or given as a reminder: a brown study (*obs.*): — *pl.* **memen'tos** or **-toes.** — **memento mori** (*mō'rī, mo'rē*) remember that you must die: anything to remind one of mortality. [L., imper. of *meminisse,* to remember.]

Memnon *mem'non, n.* an Ethiopian king who fought for the Trojans: a statue of Amenhotep, or Amenoph(is), III at Thebes in Egypt, thought by the Greeks to be of Memnon and to give out a musical sound at sunrise in salutation of his mother Eos (the Dawn). — *adj.* **Memnōn'ian.** [Gr. *Memnōn.*]

memo *mem'ō, n.* a contraction for **memorandum:** — *pl.* **mem'os.**

memoir *mem'wär, -wör, n.* (usu. in *pl.*) a written record set down as material for history or biography: a biographical sketch: a record of a study of some subject investigated by the writer: (in *pl.*) the transactions of a society. — *ns.* **mem'oirism** the act or art of writing memoirs; **mem'oirist** a writer of memoirs. [Fr. *mémoire* — L. *memoria,* memory — *memor,* mindful.]

memorabilia, memorable, etc. See **memory.**

memorandum *mem-ə-ran'dəm, n.* something to be remembered: a note to assist the memory: a brief note of some transaction (*law*): a summary of the state of a question (*diplomacy*): — *pl.* **memoran'dums, memoran'da.** — *n.* **memoran'dum-book** a book for keeping notes or memoranda. — **memorandum of association** a legal document required for registering a company under the Companies Act. [L., a thing to be remembered, neut. gerundive of *memorāre*, to remember.]

memory *mem'ə-ri, n.* the power of retaining and reproducing mental or sensory impressions: an impression so reproduced: a having or keeping in the mind: time within which past things can be remembered: commemoration: a religious service in commemoration: remembrance: of computers, a store (q.v.). — *n.pl.* **memorabil'ia** (from L.) things worth remembering: noteworthy points. — *n.* **memorabil'ity.** — *adj.* **mem'orable** deserving to be remembered: remarkable: easily remembered. — *n.* **mem'orableness.** — *adv.* **mem'orably.** — *adjs.* **mem'orative** (*obs.*) pertaining to memory: aiding the memory; **memorial** (*or', -or'*) serving or intended to preserve the memory of anything: done in remembrance of a person, event, etc.: pertaining to memory: remembered (*obs.*). — *n.* that which serves to keep in remembrance: a monument: a note to help the memory: a written statement of facts: a record: memory (*obs.*): (in *pl.*) historical or biographical notices. — *v.t.* **memor'ialise, -ize** to present a memorial to: to commemorate: to petition by a memorial. — *n.* **memor'ialist** one who writes, signs, or presents a memorial. — *n.* **memorīsā'tion, -z-.** — *v.t.* **mem'orise, -ize** to commit to memory: to cause to be remembered (*Shak.*): to record, celebrate (*arch.*). — *adv.* **memor'iter** (L.) from memory: by heart. — **Memorial Day** a day (Monday nearest 30th May) kept in honour of U.S. servicemen killed in war (orig. known as *Decoration Day* and kept, in most parts of U.S. on 30th May, in honour of men killed in the U.S. Civil War, 1861–65); **memo'ria tech'nica** (L.) artificial memory — a mnemonic device; **memory bank** (*comput.*) a memory or store (q.v.); **memory trace** (*psych.*) a hypothetical change in the cells of the brain caused by the taking-in of information, etc. — **a memory like a sieve** see **sieve; in living memory** within the memory of people still alive; **in memor'iam** to the memory of: in memory. [L. *memoria*, memory.]

Memphian *mem'fi-ən, adj.* relating to *Memphis*, an ancient capital of Egypt. — Also **Mem'phite** (*-fīt*), **Memphitic** (*-fit'*).

mem-sahib *mem'-sä-ib, n.* in India, a married European lady. [**ma'am** and **sahib.**]

men plural of **man.** — **menfolk(s), menswear** see under **man.**

menace *men'əs, -is, n.* a threat or threatening: a show of an intention to do harm: a threatening danger. — *v.t.* to threaten. — *v.i.* to act in a threatening manner. — *n.* **men'acer.** — *adj.* **men'acing.** — *adv.* **men'acingly.** [Fr., — L. *mināciae* (pl.), threats — *minae*, overhanging parts, threats.]

menadione *men-ə-dī'ōn, n.* vitamin K_3. [methyl *naph*-thoquinone, *-dione*, suff. denoting a compound containing two carbonyl groups.]

menage. Obsolete form of **manage.**

ménage *mā-näzh', n.* a household: the management of a house: a benefit society (*Scot.*): an arrangement for selling on instalment (*Scot.*). — **ménage à trois** (*a trwä*) a household composed of a husband and wife and the lover of one of them. [Fr., — L. *mānsiō*, dwelling.]

menagerie *mi-naj'ə-ri, n.* a collection of wild animals in cages for exhibition: the place where these are kept. [Fr. *ménagerie* — *ménage.*]

menarche *mə-när'kē, n.* the first menstruation. [Gr. *mēn*, month, *archē*, beginning.]

mend *mend, v.t.* to remove a fault from: to repair: to make better: to correct: to improve: to improve upon: to supplement (*obs.*). — *v.i.* to grow better: to reform. — *n.* a repair: a repaired place: an act of mending: (in *pl.*) amends (*arch.*). — *ns.* **mend'er; mend'ing** the act of repairing: a repair: things requiring to be mended. — **mend one's pace** to go quicker; **mend one's ways** to reform one's behaviour; **on the mend** improving, recovering. [amend.]

mendacious *men-dā'shəs, adj.* lying. — *adv.* **mendā'ciously.** — *n.* **mendacity** (*-das'i-ti*) lying: a falsehood. [L. *mendāx, -ācis,* conn. with *mentīrī,* to lie.]

mendelevium *men-de-lē', -lā'vi-əm, n.* the element (symbol Md) of atomic number 101, artificially produced in 1955 and named after the Russian D. I. *Mendeleev* (1834–1907), who developed the periodic table of elements.

Mendelian *men-dēl'i-ən, adj.* pertaining to the Austrian-German Gregor *Mendel* (1822–84), or his teaching on heredity. — *n.* a believer in Mendel's theory. — *n.* **Men'delism** (*-də-lizm*).

mendicant *men'di-kənt, adj.* begging. — *n.* a beggar: a begging friar (*hist.*). — *ns.* **men'dicancy, mendicity** (*-dis'i-ti*) the condition of a beggar: begging. [L. *mendicans, -antis,* pr.p. of *mendīcāre,* to beg — *mendīcus,* a beggar.]

mene. See **mean**[4].

meneer *mən-ē'ər, mən-ēr', (S. Afr.) n.* a form of **mynheer.**

Menevian *men-ē'vi-ən, (geol.) adj.* and *n.* Middle Cambrian. [L.L. *Menevia,* St David's, in Dyfed, Wales.]

meng, menge. See **ming.**

menhaden *men-hā'dn, n.* an oily fish (*Brevoortia tyrannus*) of the herring family, found off the east coast of the United States. [From an Indian name.]

menhir *men'hēr, n.* an ancient monumental standing stone. [Breton *men,* stone, *hir,* long.]

menial *mē'ni-əl, adj.* of or pertaining to a train of servants or work of a humiliating or servile nature: servile. — *n.* a domestic servant: one performing servile work: a person of servile disposition. [A.Fr. *menial;* cf. **meinie.**]

Ménière's disease, syndrome *mān-yerz'* or *-ē-erz' diz-ēz, sin'drōm,* a disorder characterised by attacks of dizziness, buzzing noises in the ears, and progressive deafness, due to chronic disease of the labyrinth of the ear. [P. *Ménière* (1799–1862), a French physician.]

meninx *mē'ningks, n.* any of three membranes that envelop the brain and spinal cord: — *pl.* **meninges** (*men-in'jēz*). — *adj.* **mening'eal.** — *ns.* **meningiō'ma** a tumour of the meninges of the brain and, more rarely, of the spinal cord; **meningitis** (*-jī'*) inflammation of the meninges; **meningocele** (*men-ing'gō-sēl;* Gr. *kēlē,* tumour) protrusion of the meninges through the skull. — *adjs.* **meningococc'al** (*men-ing-go-kok'l*), **meningococcic** (*-kok'sik*) caused by a meningococcus. — *n.* **meningococc'us** a coccus which causes epidemic cerebrospinal meningitis. [Gr. *mēninx, -ingos,* a membrane.]

Menippean *men-ip-ē'ən, adj.* pertaining to, or in imitation or emulation of, the Greek satirist *Menippos* (3rd cent. B.C.) of Gadara.

meniscus *men-is'kəs, n.* a crescent-shaped figure: a crescentic fibrous cartilage in a joint: a convexo-concave lens: a liquid surface curved by capillarity: — *pl.* **menis'ci** (*-kī* or *-sī;* L. *-kē*) or **menis'cuses.** — *adj.* **menis'coid** (*bot.*) watchglass-shaped. — *n.* **meniscec'tomy** (Gr. *ektomē,* cutting out) surgical removal of a meniscus cartilege. — **meniscus telescope** a telescope in which the spherical aberration of a concave spherical mirror is corrected by a meniscus lens. [Gr. *mēniskos,* dim. of *mēnē,* the moon.]

Menispermum *men-i-spûr'məm, n.* the moonseed genus, giving name to a family **Menispermā'ceae** akin to the buttercup family: (without *cap.*) a plant of this genus, esp. *Menispermum canadense.* — *adj.* **menispermā'ceous.** [Gr. *mēnē,* moon, *sperma,* seed.]

Mennonite *men'ən-īt, n.* one of a Protestant sect combining some of the distinctive characteristics of the Baptists and Friends. [From *Menno* Simons (d. 1559), their chief founder.]

menology _mē-nol'ə-ji, n._ a register or calendar of Saints' days, esp. of the Greek Church. [Late Gr. _mēnologion_ — _mēn_, month, _logos_, account.]

menominee _mi-nom'i-nē, n._ a whitefish of N. American lakes. [From an Indian tribe.]

meno mosso _mā'nō mos'sō_, _(mus.)_ not so quick. [It.]

menopause _men'ō-pöz, n._ the ending of menstruation, change of life. — _adj._ **menopaus'al** of, relating to, or experiencing, the menopause: suffering from strange moods or behaviour in middle age _(coll.)_. [Gr. _mēn_, month, _pausis_, cessation.]

menopome _men'ə-pōm, n._ the hellbender — from its persistent gill-aperture. [Gr. _menein_, to remain, _pōma_, lid.]

menorah _mə-nō'rə, -nö'rə, n._ (also with _cap._) a candelabrum with a varying number of branches, usu. seven, used in Jewish religious ceremony. [Heb. _menōrāh_.]

menorrhagia _men-ə-rā'ji-ə, n._ excessive flow of blood during menstruation [Gr. _mēn_, month, and _-rragia_ — _rhēgnynai_, to break, burst.]

menorrhoea, _(U.S._ **menorrhea)** _men-ə-rē'ə, n._ the normal flow of the menses. [Gr. _mēn_, month, _rhoiā_, flow.]

Mensa _men'sə, n._ one of the southern constellations, the Table. [L. _mēnsa_, table.]

mensal[1] _men'səl, adj._ monthly. — Also **men'sual.** [L. _mensis_, month.]

mensal[2] _men'səl, adj._ belonging to the table. [L. _mēnsa_, table.]

mensch _mensh_, _(U.S. slang)_ an honest, decent, morally-principled person. [Yiddish _mensch_, a person.]

mense _mens_, _(Scot.) n._ propriety: an ornament: credit. — _v.t._ to grace or set off (something). — _adjs._ **mense'ful** _(Scot.)_ decorous: respectable: gracious: generous; **mense'less** _(Scot.)_ graceless, uncivil. [O.N. _mennska_, humanity; cf. O.E. _menniscu_, humanity, _mennisc_, human.]

menses _men'sēz, n.pl._ the monthly discharge from the uterus. [L. _mēnsēs_, pl. of _mēnsis_, month.]

mensh _mensh_, _(coll.)_ short for **mention.**

Menshevik _men'shə-vik_, _(hist.) n._ a moderate or minority socialist in Russia — as opp. to **Bolshevik.** [Russ. _menshye_, smaller, _-(v)ik_, agent suffix.]

mens rea _menz rē'ə_, _mens rā'a_, _(law)_ a wrongful purpose: criminal intent: awareness of the wrongfulness of an act. [Modern L., guilty mind.]

menstruum _men'strōō-əm, n._ a solvent (from a fancy of the alchemists): — _pl._ **men'strua,** or **men'struums** (**menstrua** also the menses). — _adj._ **men'strual** monthly: pertaining to the menses. — _v.i._ **men'struate** to discharge the menses. — _n._ **menstrua'tion.** — _adj._ **men'struous.** [L. neut. of _mēnstruus_, monthly — _mēnsis_.]

mensual. See **mensal**[1].

Mensur _men-sōōr'_, _(Ger.) n._ a German students' duel, a form of sport: — _pl._ **Mensur'en.** [Ger., measurement (from the measured distance of the participants) — L. _mēnsūra_.]

mensurable _men'sh(y)ər-ə-bl_, or _-sūr-, adj._ measurable: having a fixed relative time-value for each note _(mus.)._ — _n._ **mensurabil'ity.** — _adj._ **mens'ural** pertaining to measure: measurable _(mus.)._ — _n._ **mensurā'tion** the act or art of finding by measurement and calculation the length, area, volume, etc., of bodies. — _adj._ **men'surātive.** [L. _mēnsūrāre_, to measure.]

ment. See **ming.**

mental[1]. See **mentum.**

mental[2] _men'tl, adj._ pertaining to the mind: done in the mind, esp. in the mind alone, without outward expression: suffering from, or provided for, or involved in the care of, disease or disturbance of the mind: mentally unbalanced _(slang)._ — _ns._ **men'talism** the process of mental action: idealism; **men'talist; mentality** _(-tal'i-ti)_ mind: mental endowment: a cast of mind: a way of thinking; **mentā'tion** mental activity. — _adv._ **men'tally.** — _n._ **menticide** _(men'ti-sīd)_ the systematic reduction of a person's mind by psychological or other pressure to a point where views formerly repugnant will be accepted. — **mental age** the age in years, etc., at which an average child would have reached the same stage of mental development as the individual under consideration; **mental cruelty** conduct in marriage, not involving physical cruelty or violence, that wounds feelings or personal dignity — in U.S., grounds for separation or divorce; **mental deficiency** mental retardation; **mental home, hospital; mental patient; mental retardation** retarded development of learning ability, whether arising from innate defect or from some other cause. [Fr., — L. _mēns, mentis_, the mind.]

menthol _men'thol, n._ a camphor got from oil of peppermint, used as a local analgesic. — _adj._ **men'tholated** containing menthol. [L. _mentha_, mint.]

menticide. See **mental**[2].

mention _men'shən, n._ a brief notice: the occurrence or introduction of name or reference. — _v.t._ to notice briefly: to remark: to name. — _adj._ **men'tionable** fit to be mentioned: worth mentioning. — **honourable mention** an award of distinction not entitling to a prize; **not to mention** to say nothing of — a parenthetical rhetorical pretence of refraining from saying all one might say. [L. _mentiō, -ōnis._]

mentonnière _men-ton-i-er'_, _(hist.) n._ a piece of armour for the chin and throat. [Fr., — _menton_, chin — L. _mentum.]_

mentor _ment'ər, -tör, n._ a wise counsellor: a tutor: a trainer. — _adj._ **mentorial** _(-tör', -tör'i-əl)._ — _ns._ **men'toring; men'torship.** [Gr. _Mentōr_, the tutor by whom (or Athena in his form) Telemachus was guided.]

mentum _men'təm, n._ the chin: the central part of the labium in insects. — _adj._ **men'tal** _(anat.)_ pertaining to the chin. [L. _mentum_, the chin.]

menu _men'ū, n._ a bill of fare: a list of subjects, options, etc. _(fig._ or _comput.)._ — _adj._ **men'u-driven** (of computer software) offering the user lists of options for movement through the system. [Fr., — L. _minūtus_, small.]

menuisier _mə-nwē-zyā_, _(Fr.) n._ a joiner.

meo periculo _mē'ō pe-rik'ū-lō_, _mā'ō pe-rēk'ōō-lō_, _(L.)_ at my own risk.

meow _mi-ow'_, _myow._ A form of **miaow.**

mepacrine _mep'ə-krēn, n._ a bitter yellow powder derived from acridine dye compounds, formerly used against malaria — also **atabrin, atebrin.**

meperidine _me-per'i-dēn, -din, n._ pethidine.

Mephistopheles _mef-is-tof'i-lēz, n._ the devil in the _Faust_ story. — Also **Mephistoph'ilis, Mephostoph'ilus,** etc.: abbrev. **Mephis'tō.** — _adjs._ **Mephistophelē'an, Mephistophē'lian, Mephistophelic** _(-fel')_ cynical, scoffing, fiendish. [Ety. unknown; prob. influenced by Gr. _mē_, not, _phōs, phōtos_, light, _philos_, loving.]

mephitis _me-fī'tis, n._ a poisonous exhalation: a foul stink. — _adjs._ **mephitic** _(-fit')_, **-al.** — _n._ **meph'itism** _(-it-izm)_ mephitic poisoning. [L. _mephītis._]

meprobamate _mep-rō-bam'āt, n._ a drug used as a muscle relaxant and as a sedative.

Mercalli scale _mər-kal'i skāl_, a scale of intensity used to measure earthquake shocks, graded from 1 (very weak) to 12 (catastrophic). [From the inventer, Giuseppe _Mercalli_ (1850–1914), Italian geologist.]

merc. See **mercenary.**

mercantile _mûr'kən-tīl, adj._ pertaining to merchants: having to do with trade: commercial: mercenary. — _ns._ **mer'cantilism; mer'cantilist.** — **mercantile agency** a means of getting information about the circumstances of merchants for those who sell to them; **mercantile law** the law relating to the dealings of merchants with each other; **mercantile marine** the ships and crews of any country employed in commerce; **mercantile system** _(economics)_ the system of encouraging exportation and restricting importation, so that more may be received than is paid away. [Fr., — It. _mercantile_ — L. _mercārī_; cf. **merchant.**]

mercaptan _mər-kap'tan, n._ a substance analogous to an alcohol, with sulphur instead of oxygen. — _n._ **mercap'-tide** a compound in which a metal takes the place of a hydrogen atom of a mercaptan. [L. _mercūrium captāns_, laying hold of mercury, from the readiness with which it forms mercury mercaptide.]

mercat *mer'kət*, a Scottish form of **market** (*n*).

Mercator *mər-kā'tor, mer-kä'tōr, n.* a Latin translation of the name of the Flemish-born German cartographer Gerhard Kremer (lit. shopkeeper; 1512–94). — **Mercator's projection** a representation of the surface of the globe in which the meridians are parallel straight lines, the parallels straight lines at right angles to these, their distances such that everywhere degrees of latitude and longitude have the same ratio to each other as on the globe itself.

mercenary *mûr'sin-ər-i, adj.* hired for money: actuated by the hope of reward: too strongly influenced by desire of gain: sold or done for money. — *n.* one who is hired: a soldier hired into foreign service (*coll.* shortened form **merc** (*mûrk*)). — *adv.* **mer'cenarily.** — *n.* **mer'cenarism** the state of being a mercenary. [L. *mercēnārius* — *mercēs*, hire.]

mercer *mûr'sər, n.* a dealer in textiles, esp. the more costly: a dealer in small wares. — *n.* **mer'cery** the trade of a mercer: the goods of a mercer. [Fr. *mercier*.]

mercerise, -ize *mûr'sər-īz, v.t.* to treat (cotton) so as to make it appear like silk. — *ns.* **mercerīsā'tion, -z-; mer'ceriser, -z-.** [From John *Mercer* (1791–1866), the inventor of the process.]

merchant *mûr'chənt, n.* a trader, esp. wholesale: a shopkeeper: a supercargo (*obs.*): a merchantman: a fellow, esp. one who specialises or behaves in some specified way (*slang*). — *adj.* commercial. — *v.i.* to trade. — *v.t.* to trade in. — *n.* **merchandise** (*-dīz*) goods bought and sold for gain: trade (*B.* and *Shak.*): dealing. — *v.t.* (also **-ize**) to traffic in (*Shak.*): to buy and sell: to plan the advertising of, selling campaign for. — Also *v.i.* (also **-ize**). — *n.* **mer'chandising, -z-.** — *adj.* **mer'chantable** fit or ready for sale: marketable. — *n.* **mer'chanting.** — *adj.* and *adv.* **mer'chantlike** (*Shak.*) like a merchant. — *n.* **mer'chantry** the business of a merchant: merchants collectively. — **merchant bank** see **bank**[3]; **mer'chantman** a trading ship: a merchant (*B.*): — *pl.* **mer'chantmen; merchant navy, service** the mercantile marine; **merchant prince** a merchant of great wealth, power, and consequence; **merchant ship** a ship that carries merchandise; **merchant tailor** a tailor who supplies the cloth for the clothes which he makes. — **speed merchant** see **speed.** [Fr. *marchand*.]

merchet *mûr'chit*, (*hist.*) *n.* a fine paid to a lord for the marriage of a daughter. [A.Fr. *merchet*; see **market**.]

merchild. See **mermaid.**

mercury *mûr'kū-ri, n.* a silvery metallic element (Hg; atomic number 80) liquid at ordinary temperatures, also called *quicksilver*: the column of mercury in a thermometer or barometer: a plant (**dog's'-mer'cury** *Mercurialis perennis*) of the spurge family: the plant Good-King-Henry: a preparation of mercury: a messenger: a common title for newspapers: mercurial character (*obs.*): (with *cap.*) the Roman god of merchandise, theft, and eloquence, messenger of the gods, identified with the Greek Hermes: (with *cap.*) the planet nearest the sun. — **mer'curate** *v.t.* to mercurialise: to convert into a compound with mercury. — *n.* **mercurā'tion.** — *adj.* **mercū'rial** containing mercury: of or like mercury: caused by mercury: (with *cap.*) of or pertaining to Mercury the god or the planet: (sometimes with *cap.*) having the qualities attributed to persons born under the planet — eloquent, etc.: active, sprightly, often changing. — *n.* a drug containing mercury: the plant mercury (*obs.*): (sometimes with *cap.*) one born under the planet (*obs.*). — *v.t.* **mercū'rialise, -ize** to treat with mercury or a drug containing mercury (*med.*): to make mercurial. — *ns.* **mercū'rialism** a morbid condition due to mercury; **mercū'rialist** (*obs.*) a believer in the medical use of mercury: a mercurial person. — *adv.* **mercū'rially.** — *adjs.* **mercū'ric** containing bivalent mercury; **mer'curous** containing univalent mercury. [L. *Mercūrius*, prob. *merx, mercis*, merchandise.]

mercy *mûr'si, n.* forbearance towards one who is in one's power: a good thing regarded as derived from God: a happy chance (*dial.*): a forgiving disposition: clemency: compassion for the unfortunate. — *interj.* an expression of thanks (now *obs.*) or surprise (for *God have mercy*). — Also **mercy on us.** — *adjs.* **mer'ciable** (*Spens.*) merciful; **mer'ciful** full of, or exercising, mercy. — *adv.* **mer'cifully.** — *n.* **mer'cifulness.** — *v.t.* **mer'cify** (*Spens.*, in *pa.p.* **mer'cifide**) to deal mercifully with, to pity. — *adj.* **mer'ciless** without mercy: unfeeling: cruel. — *adv.* **mer'cilessly.** — *ns.* **mer'cilessness.** — **mercy killing** killing, esp. painlessly, to prevent incurable suffering; **mer'cy-seat** the seat or place of mercy: the covering of the Jewish Ark of the Covenant: the throne of God. — **at the mercy of** wholly in the power of; **for mercy!** (*obs.*), **for mercy's sake!** an earnest conjuration in the form of an appeal to pity; **leave (a person) to someone's tender mercies** or **mercy** (*ironic*) to leave (a person) exposed to unpleasant treatment at someone's hands; **sisters of mercy** members of female religious communities who tend the sick, etc. [Fr. *merci*, grace — L. *mercēs, -ēdis*, the price paid, wages, later favour.]

mere[1] *mēr, n.* a pool or lake. — Also (*obs.*) **meer.** — **mere swine** (*obs.*) a porpoise: a dolphin. [O.E. *mere*, sea, lake, pool; Ger. *Meer*, Du. *meer*, L. *mare*, the sea.]

mere[2] *mēr, adj.* unmixed (*obs.*): pure (*obs.*): only what is said and nothing else, nothing more, nothing better: absolute (*obs.*). — *adv.* (*obs.*) absolutely. — *adj.* **mered, meered** see under **meer.** — *adv.* **mere'ly** purely (*obs.*): entirely (*obs.*): simply: only: without being more or better. [L. *merus*, unmixed.]

mere[3] *mēr*, (*dial.*) *n.* a boundary. — *v.t.* to bound: to mark off. — **meres'man** (*dial.*) a man appointed to ascertain boundaries; **mere'stone** (*dial.*) a boundary stone. [O.E. *gemǣre*.]

mere[4], **meri** *mer'i, n.* a war-club. [Maori.]

merel, merell. Same as **meril.**

meretricious *mer-i-trish'əs, adj.* of the nature of harlotry: characteristic or worthy of a harlot: flashy: gaudy. — *adv.* **meretric'iously.** — *n.* **meretric'iousness.** [L. *meretrīx, -īcis*, a harlot — *merēre*, to earn.]

merfolk. See **mermaid.**

merganser *mûr-gan'sər, n.* any bird of the genus *Mergus* (goosander, smew, etc.). [L. *mergus*, a diving bird, *ānser*, a goose.]

merge *mûrj, v.t.* to dip or plunge (*arch.*): to cause to be swallowed up or absorbed in something greater or superior: to cause to coalesce, combine, or amalgamate. — *v.i.* to be swallowed up, or lost: to coalesce: to lose identity in something else: to combine or amalgamate. — *ns.* **mer'gence; mer'ger** (*law*) a sinking of an estate, title, etc., in one of larger extent or of higher value: a combine, an absorption. [L. *mergĕre, mersum*.]

meri. See **mere**[4].

mericarp *mer'i-kärp, n.* a separating one-seeded part of a schizocarp, esp. half of a cremocarp. [Gr. *meros*, a part, *karpos*, fruit.]

meridian *mə-rid'i-ən, adj.* of or at midday: on the meridian: pertaining to a meridian or the sun or other body on the meridian: at culmination or highest point. — *n.* midday: a midday dram or nap (*Scot.*): an imaginary great circle through the poles of the earth, the heavens, or any spherical body or figure, or its representation on a map: in particular, that cutting the observer's horizon at the north and south points, which the sun crosses at local noon: culmination or highest point, as of success, splendour, power, etc. — *adj.* **merid'ional** pertaining to the meridian: in the direction of a meridian: midday: culminating: southern: characteristic of the south. — *n.* a southerner, esp. in France. — *n.* **meridional'ity.** — *adv.* **merid'ionally.** — **meridian altitude** the arc of a meridian between a heavenly body and the horizon; **meridian circle** a telescope mounted to revolve in the plane of the meridian; **meridian passage** the transit or passage of a heavenly body across the observer's meridian. — **magnetic meridian** see under **magnet; prime** (or **first**) **meridian** the meridian from which longitudes are measured east or west, specif. that through Greenwich. [L. *merīdiānus, merīdiōnālis* — *merīdiēs* (for *medīdiēs*), midday — *medius*, middle, *diēs*, day.]

meril, merel, merell *mer'əl, n.* a counter used in the game of merils: (in *pl.*) a rustic game played by two persons with counters on a figure marked on the ground, a board, etc., consisting of three squares, one within another, the object to get three counters in a row at the intersection of the lines joining the corners and the mid-points of the sides. — Also **marls, marr'els, mor'- als, morr'is, mir'acles.** — **fivepenny morris** the game as played with five pieces each; **ninepenny morris, nine men's morris** with nine: the figure cut in the ground for the game (*Shak.*). [O.Fr. *merel*, counter.]

merimake *mer'i-māk*, (*Spens.*) *n.* merrymaking: sport.

meringue *mə-rang', n.* a crisp cake or covering made of a mixture of sugar and white of eggs. [Fr.; origin unknown.]

merino *mə-rē'nō, n.* a sheep of a fine-woolled Spanish breed (also **merino sheep**): a fine dress fabric, originally of merino wool: a fine woollen yarn, now mixed with cotton: knitted goods of this: waste from fine worsted clothes: — *pl.* **meri'nos.** — *adj.* belonging to the merino sheep or its wool: made of merino. [Sp., a merino sheep, also a governor — L. *mājōrīnus*, greater, also (L.L.) a head-man — L. *mājor*, greater.]

merism *mer'izm*, (*biol.*) *n.* repetition of parts. — *adj.* **merist'ic.** [Gr. *meros*, part.]

meristem *mer'is-tem, n.* the formative tissue of plants, distinguished from the permanent tissues by the power its cells have of dividing and forming new cells. — *adj.* **meristematic** (*-sti-mat'ik*). [Gr. *meristos*, divisible, *merizein*, to divide — *meros*, a part.]

merit *mer'it, n.* excellence that deserves honour or reward: worth: value: desert: that which one deserves, whether reward or punishment (*arch.*): (in *pl.*, esp. in *law*) the intrinsic right or wrong. — *v.t.* to earn: to have a right to claim as a reward: to deserve. — *v.i.* (*obs.*) to acquire merit. — *ns.* **meritoc'racy** (government by) the class of persons who are in prominent positions because of their ability, real or apparent; **mer'itōcrat.** — *adjs.* **meritōcrat'ic; meritorious** (*-tōr', -tör'*) possessing merit or desert: deserving of reward, honour, or praise. — *adv.* **meritor'iously.** — *n.* **meritor'iousness.** — **order of merit** arrangement in which the best is placed first, the next best second, and so on: (*caps.*) a strictly limited British order (OM), instituted in 1902, for eminence in any field. [L. *meritum* — *merēre, -itum*, to obtain as a lot, to deserve.]

merk *merk, n.* the old Scots mark or 13s. 4d. Scots, 13⅓d. sterling. [**mark**².]

merkin *mûr'kin, n.* a hair-piece for the pubic area. [Origin uncertain.]

merle¹, merl *mûrl*, (*arch.* or *literary Scot.*) *n.* the blackbird. [Fr., — L. *merula*.]

merle² *mûrl, adj.* (of a dog, usu. a collie) with bluish-grey fur flecked or streaked with black (also **blue merle**). — Also *n.* [Cf. **marl⁴, marly, mirly**.]

merlin *mûr'lin, n.* a species of small falcon, *Falco columbarius*. [A.Fr. *merilun* — O.Fr. *esmerillon*.]

merling *mûr'ling*, (*obs.*) *n.* the whiting. [O.Fr. *merlanke* — L. *merula*, a sea-carp.]

merlon *mûr'lən*, (*fort.*) *n.* the part of a parapet between embrasures. [Fr. *merlon* — It. *merlone* — *merlo*, battlement.]

mermaid *mûr'mād, n.* a sea-woman, a woman to the waist, with fish's tail. — **mer'child; mer'folk; mer'maid'en; mer'maid's-glove'** the largest kind of British sponge; **mer'maid's-purse'** the egg-case of skate, etc.; **mer'man; mer'people.** [O.E. *mere*, lake, sea, *mægden*, maid.]

meroblastic *mer-ō-blast'ik*, (*zool.*) *adj.* undergoing or involving cleavage in part of the ovum only, as where there is much yolk. — *adv.* **meroblast'ically.** [Gr. *meros*, part, *blastos*, a shoot, bud.]

merogenesis *mer-ō-jen'i-sis*, (*biol.*) *n.* segmentation. —

adj. **merogenetic** (*-ji-net'ik*). [Gr. *meros*, part, *genesis*, production.]

merogony *mer-og'ə-ni, n.* the production of an embryo from a fertilised fragment of an ovum without a nucleus. [Gr. *meros*, part, *gonē*, birth.]

meroistic *mer-ō-ist'ik*, (*entom.*) *adj.* of an ovary, producing yolk-forming cells as well as ova. [Gr. *meros*, part, *ōion*, egg.]

merome *mer'ōm, n.* a merosome. [Gr. *meros*, part.]

Merops *mer'ops, n.* the bee-eater genus. — *n.* **merop'idan** a bird of the bee-eater family (**Mcrop'idae**). [Gr. *merops*, bee-eater.]

merosome *mer'ō-sōm, n.* one of the serial segments of which a body is composed, as the ring of a worm, a metamere, a somite. [Gr. *meros*, part, *sōma*, body.]

Merovingian *mer-ō-vin'ji-ən, adj.* pertaining to the first dynasty of Frankish kings in Gaul, founded by Clovis. — *n.* a member of this family. [L. *Merovingi* — *Merovaeus* or *Merovech*, king of the Salian Franks (448–457), grandfather of Clovis.]

merozoite *mer-ō-zō'īt*, (*zool.*) *n.* a young trophozoite resulting from the division of a schizont. [Gr. *meros*, part, *zōion*, animal.]

merpeople. See **mermaid.**

merry¹ *mer'i, adj.* pleasant (*obs.*): sportive: cheerful: noisily gay: causing laughter: enlivened by drink: lively: used as an intensifier of *hell*, as in *play merry hell with.* — *adv.* **merr'ily.** — *ns.* **merr'iment** gaiety with laughter and noise: mirth: hilarity; **merr'iness.** — **merr'y-an'drew** a quack's zany: a buffoon: one who makes sport for others; **merry dancers** the aurora; **merry England** an idealistically jovial picture of life in England in the past, esp. in Elizabethan times (as used originally, e.g. by Spenser, the phrase meant 'fair, pleasant England'); **merr'y-go-round** a revolving ring of wooden horses, etc., for riding at a funfair: a roundabout: a whirl of activity, etc. (*fig.*): any activity inclined to circularity (*fig.*); **merr'y-make** a merrymaking. — *v.i.* to make merry. — **merr'ymaker; merr'ymaking** a merry entertainment: a festival; **merr'yman** a zany: a jester: (in *pl.*; **merry men**) followers, in arms or in outlawry; **merr'y-night'** a village festival; **merr'ythought** a fowl's furcula or wishbone. — **make merry** to hold festival: to indulge in enjoyment: to turn to ridicule (with *with* or *over*); **the merry monarch** Charles II. [O.E. *myr(i)ge*.]

merry² *mer'i, n.* a gean. [Fr. *merise*.]

mersalyl *mər-sal'il, n.* a diuretic. [**mercury, salicyl**.]

merse *mûrs n.* low flat marshland. [Scots form of **marsh**.]

Mersey *mûr'zē, -zi n.* the river on which the city of Liverpool stands. — **Mersey beat, Mersey sound** popular music in the style of the Beatles and other Liverpool groups during the 1960s.

mersion *mûr'shən, n.* dipping. [L. *mersiō, -ōnis*; cf. **merge**.]

Merulius *mə-rōō'li-əs, n.* the dry-rot fungus genus.

merum sal *mer'əm, mer'ōōm sal*, (L.) pure salt, genuine Attic wit.

merveilleux *mer-ve-yə, fem.* **merveilleuse** *mer-ve-yœz*, (Fr.) *adj.* marvellous. — *n.* a fantastic extremist in fashion in France during the Directorate, the women aping classical modes.

merycism *mer'i-sizm, n.* rumination, a disease symptom in man. [Gr. *mērykismos*.]

Mes, Mes-John. See **Mass.**

mesa *mā'sə, n.* a table-shaped hill. [Sp., — L. *mēnsa*, table.]

mesail, mezail *mes', mez'āl, n.* a vizor, esp. one made in two parts. [Fr. *mézail*.]

mesal. See **mesial.**

mésalliance *mā-zal-yãs*, (Fr.) *n.* an unsuitable marriage: marriage with one of lower station.

mesaraic *mes-ə-rā'ik, adj.* mesenteric. [Gr. *mesaraikos* — *mesos*, middle, *araiā*, flank, belly.]

mesarch *mes'ärk, adj.* having the protoxylem surrounded by xylem formed later (*bot.*): originating in a moderately moist habitat (*ecology*). — **mesarch succession** an ecological succession originating in a mesic habitat. [Gr. *mesos*, middle, and *archē*, beginning.]

mesaticephalic *mes-ə-ti-sef-al'ik*, **mesaticephalous** *-sef'ə-ləs*, *adjs*. intermediate between dolichocephalic and brachycephalic. — *n*. **mesaticeph'aly**. [Gr. *mesatos*, midmost, *kephalē*, head.]

mescal *mes-kal'*, *n*. the peyote cactus, chewed or drunk in infusion as an intoxicant in Mexico: an intoxicant distilled from Agave. — *ns*. **mescalin** (*mes'kəl-in*) the principal alkaloid ($C_{11}H_{17}NO_3$) in mescal, producing hallucinations and schizophrenia; **mescal'ism** addiction to mescal. [Sp. *mescal, mezcal* — Nahuatl *mexcalli*.]

mesdames, Mesdemoiselles. See **madam, mademoiselle**.

mese *mes'ē*, (*Gr. mus*.) *n*. the middle string of the lyre: its note: the keynote. [Gr. *mesē* (*chordē*), middle (string).]

meseems. See **seem**.

mesel, meazel *mēz'l*, (*obs*.) *n*. a leper: leprosy (*Shak*.). — *adj*. leprous. — *adj*. **mes'eled**. [O.Fr. *mesel* — L. *misellus*, dim. of *miser*, wretched.]

Mesembrianthemum, conventionally **Mesembryanthemum**, *mi-zem-bri-an'thi-məm*, *n*. a genus of succulent plants (family Aizoaceae), mostly South African (Hottentot fig, ice-plant, Livingstone daisy): (without *cap*.) a plant of this genus. [Gr. *mesēmbriā*, midday — *mesos*, middle, *hēmerā*, day, and *anthemon*, a flower: some are open only about midday.]

mesencephalon *mes-en-sef'ə-lon*, *n*. the mid-brain. — *adj*. **mesencephalic** (*-si-fal'ik*). [Gr. *mesos*, middle, and **encephalon**.]

mesentery *mes'ən-tər-i*, or *mez'*, *n*. a fold of the peritoneum, keeping the intestines in place: in coelenterates, a vertical inward fold of the body wall. — *adjs*. **mesenterial** (*-tē'ri-əl*), **mesenteric** (*-ter'ik*). — *n*. **mesenteron** (*-en'tər-on*) the mid-gut. [Gr. *mesos*, middle, *enteron*, intestines.]

mesh *mesh*, *n*. the opening between the threads of a net: the threads and knots bounding the opening: a network: a trap: the engagement of geared wheels or the like. — *v.t.* to catch in a net: to provide or make with meshes: to entwine. — *v.i.* to become engaged, as gear-teeth: to become entangled. — *n*. **mesh'ing**. — *adj*. **mesh'y** formed like network. — **mesh'-work** a network, web. [Perh. M.Du. *maesche*; cf. O.E. *max*, net; Ger. *Masche*.]

meshuga, meshugga, -gge *mi-shŏŏ'gə*, (*slang*) *adj*. mad: crazy. — *n*. **meshugg'enah, -eh** a crazy person. [Yiddish, from Hebrew.]

mesial *mē'zi-əl*, *adj*. middle: facing towards the centre of the curve formed by the upper or lower teeth (*dentistry*): in or towards the median plane or line — also **mē'sal, mē'sian**. — *advs*. **mē'sally, mē'sially**. [Gr. *mesos*, middle.]

mesic[1]. See **meson**.

mesic[2] *me'zik, mē'*, *-sik*, *adj*. pertaining to, or adapted to life with, a moderate supply of moisture. [Gr. *mesos*, middle.]

mesmerise, -ize *mez'mər-īz*, *v.t.* to hypnotise: (*loosely*) to fascinate, dominate the will or fix the attention of. — *adjs*. **mesmeric** (*-mer'ik*), **-al**. — *ns*. **mesmerīsā'tion, -z-**; **mes'meriser, -z-, mes'merist; mes'merism** hypnotism as expounded, with some fanciful notions, from 1775 by Friedrich Anton or Franz *Mesmer*, a German physician (1734–1815): hypnotic influence.

mesne *mēn*, (*law*) *adj*. intermediate. [Law Fr. *mesne*, middle; cf. **mean**[2].]

mes(o)- *mes(-ō or -o), mez-, mē-*, in composition, middle. — *n*. **Mesoamer'ica** central America, between Northern Mexico and Panama. — *adj*. **Mesoamer'ican** (also without *cap*.). — *n*. **mes'oblast** (Gr. *blastos*, shoot) the middle germinal layer. — *adj*. **mesoblas'tic**. — *n*. **mes'ocarp** (Gr. *karpos*, fruit) the middle layer of a pericarp. — *adjs*. **mesocephalic** (*-si-fal'ik*), **-cephalous** (*-sef'ə-ləs*) mesaticephalic: mesencephalic. — *ns*. **mesoceph'alism, mesoceph'aly; mes'oderm** (Gr. *derma*,

skin) the mesoblast or tissues derived from it; **mesogloea** (*-glē'ə*; Gr. *gloiā*, glue) in coelenterates and sponges, a structureless gelatinous layer between ectoderm and endoderm; **mesohipp'us** one of the prehistoric group of three-toed ungulate mammals probably related to the modern horse; **mes'olite** (Gr. *lithos*, stone) a zeolite intermediate in composition between natrolite and scolecite. — *adj*. **Mesolith'ic** intermediate between Palaeolithic and Neolithic. — *ns*. **mesom'erism** (*chem*.) resonance: a type of tautomerism; **mes'omorph** (*-mörf*; Gr. *morphē*, form) a person of muscular bodily type. — *adjs*. **mesomor'phic, mesomor'phous** relating to a mesomorph: relating to an intermediate state of matter between solid and liquid (*chem*.). — *ns*. **mes'omorphy; mes'ophyll** (Gr. *phyllon*, leaf) the spongy tissue within a leaf; **mes'ophyte** (*-fīt*; Gr. *phyton*, plant) a plant intermediate between a xerophyte and a hydrophyte. — *adj*. **mesophytic** (*-fit'ik*). — *ns*. **mes'oscaphe** (*-skāf*; Gr. *skaphos*, ship) a submersible observation chamber for use at less great depths than the bathyscaphe; **mes'osphere** the region of the earth's atmosphere above the stratosphere. — *adj*. **mesothē'-lial**. — *ns*. **mesothēliō'ma** (from (**epi**)**thelium** and **-oma**) a rare malignant tumour of the lining of the chest or abdomen, sometimes caused by blue asbestos dust; **mesothē'lium** the cell tissue that forms the lining of the chest and abdomen in vertebrates and lines the body cavity in vertebrate embryos. — *adj*. **mesothoracic** (*-thō-, -thō-ras'ik*). — *n*. **mesothor'ax** the middle one of the three segments of an insect's thorax. — *n.pl*. **Mesozō'a** (Gr. *zōion*, animal) minute animals once thought intermediate between Protozoa and Metazoa, prob. Metazoa reduced by parasitism. — *adj*. **Mesozō'ic** (Gr. *zōē*, life) of the Secondary geological period, including the Triassic, Jurassic, and Cretaceous systems. [Gr. *mesos*, middle.]

meson *mēz'on, mes'on, n*. a short-lived subatomic particle of smaller mass than a proton (η-mesons, π-mesons (also called **pī'ons**), and κ-mesons, k-mesons (also called **kā'ons**); the muon, formerly classified as the μ-meson is now known to be a lepton). — *adjs*. **mes'ic, meson'ic**. — *n*. **mes'otron** (*obs*.; after *electron*) formerly a meson, then a μ-meson. — **mesic, mesonic, atom** a nucleus with an orbital meson. [Gr. *meson*, neut. of *mesos*, middle.]

mesophyll... Mesozoic. See under **mes(o)-**.

mesprise, mesprize. See **misprise**[1,2].

mesquin *mes-kē̃*, (Fr.) *adj*. mean: — *fem*. **mesquine** (*-kēn*). — *n*. **mesquinerie** (*-kēn-ə-rē*) meanness.

mesquite, mesquit *mes-kēt', mes'kēt, n*. a leguminous tree or shrub (*Prosopis*) of America, with nutritious pods. [Mex. Sp. *mezquite*.]

mess[1] *mes, n*. a dish of food, course, or meal (*arch*.): a set of usually four persons served together at a banquet (*arch*.): a set of four (*Shak*.): a number of persons who take their meals together, esp. in the fighting services: a place where a group of persons in a fighting service take their meals together: a cow's yield at one milking (*dial*.): a quantity of a specified food (*arch*. or *dial*. *U.S.*): a take or haul of fish (*U.S.*): a dish of soft, pulpy or liquid stuff: liquid, pulpy or smeary dirt: a mixture disagreeable to the sight or taste: a medley: disorder: confusion: embarrassment: a bungle. — *v.t.* to supply with a mess: to make a mess of (usu. with *up*): to muddle: to befoul. — *v.i.* to eat of a mess: to eat at a common table: to belong to a mess: to make a mess: to meddle, involve oneself (with, in) (*coll*.; esp. *U.S.*): to tangle (with) (*coll*.; esp. *U.S.*). — *adv*. **mess'ily**. — *n*. **mess'iness**. — *adj*. **mess'y** confused, untidy (also *fig*.): involving, or causing, dirt or mess: bungling. — **mess deck** (*naut*.) the crew's living-quarters on board ship: the crew's dining-hall (*U.S.*); **mess'mate** a member of the same mess: a commensal; **mess'-room; mess'-tin** a soldier's utensil serving as plate, cup, and cooking-vessel; **mess'-up** a mess, muddle, bungle, or confusion. — **mess about** or **around** (*coll*.) to potter about: to behave in a foolish or annoying way: to meddle or interfere (with): to upset, put into a state of disorder or confusion; **mess of pottage** a material advantage accepted in exchange for something of higher worth, as by Esau (Gen. xxv. 29 ff.); **mess or mell** (*Scot.*) to associate, have to do. [O.Fr. *mes* (Fr. *mets*), a dish — L. *mittĕre, missum,* to send, in L.L. to place.]

mess² *mes, n.* obs. form of **mass²**.

Mess, Mess-John. See **Mass**.

message *mes'ij, n.* any communication sent from one person to another: an errand: an official communication of a president, governor, etc., to a legislature or council: the teaching that a poet, sage, prophet, has to communicate to the world: (usu. in *pl.*) domestic shopping, a journey for the purpose, or the goods bought (*Scot.*). — *v.t.* to send as a message: to transmit as by signalling. — *v.i.* (*Dickens*) to carry a message. — *n.* **mess'enger** (-*ən-jər*) one who brings a message: one employed to carry messages and perform errands: a forerunner: a light scudding cloud preceding a storm: a small object sent along a line, as a paper up a kite string: the secretary-bird: a rope or chain connecting a cable with the capstan for heaving up the anchor: an officer who executes the summonses of the Court of Session, usu. called a **mess'enger-at-arms** (*Scots law*). — **mess'age-boy, -girl** an errand boy or girl; **mess'age-stick** (*Austr.*) a carved stick carried as identification by an aboriginal messenger; **message unit** (*U.S.*) a unit used in charging timed, e.g. long-distance, telephone calls; **messenger RNA** (*biochemistry*) a short-lived, transient form of RNA which serves to carry genetic information from the DNA of the genes to the ribosomes where the requisite proteins are made — abbrev. **m-RNA;** **mess'enger-wire** a wire supporting an overhead cable. — **get the message** (*slang*) to understand; **king's,** or **queen's, messenger** an officer who carries official despatches. [Fr., — L.L. *missāticum* — L. *mittĕre, missum,* to send.]

messan *mes'ən,* (*Scot.*) *n.* a lap-dog: a cur. [Perh. Gael. *measan.*]

Messerschmitt *mes'ər-shmit, n.* a German fighter aircraft used by the Luftwaffe in World War II, esp. the M.E.-109. [Willy *Messerschmitt* (1898–1978), aircraft designer.]

Messiah *mə-sī'ə, n.* the expected deliverer of the Jews: by Christians, applied to Jesus: a hoped-for deliverer, saviour, or champion generally — also **Messi'as.** — *adj.* **Messianic** (*mes-i-an'ik*). — *ns.* **Messi'anism** belief in a Messiah; **Messi'anist; Messi'ahship.** [Gr. *Messiās* — Aram. *m'shīhā,* Heb. *māshīah,* anointed — *māshah,* to anoint.]

Messidor *mes-i-dör', n.* the tenth month of the French revolutionary calendar, about June 19th — July 18th. [Fr., — L. *messis,* harvest, Gr. *dōron,* a gift.]

Messieurs *mes-yə, pl.* of **Monsieur;** contracted and anglicised as **Messrs** (*mes'ərz*) and used as pl. of **Mister.**

messuage *mes'wij,* (*law*) *n.* a dwelling and offices with the adjoining lands appropriated to the household: a mansion-house and grounds. [A.Fr.; poss. orig. a misreading of *mesnage;* cf. **ménage.**]

mestee *mes-tē',* **mustee** *mus-tē', ns.* the offspring of a white person and a quadroon. — *n.* **mestizo** (*mes-tē'zō;* Sp. -*thō*) a half-caste, esp. of Spanish and American Indian parentage: — *pl.* **mesti'zos;** *fem.* **mesti'za,** *pl.* **mesti'zas.** [Sp. *mestizo* — a L.L. derivative of L. *mixtus,* mixed.]

mesto *mes'tō,* (*mus.*) *adj.* sad. [It.]

met *pa.t.* and *pa.p.* of **meet².**

met. *met.* Abbrev. for **meteorology. — met'cast** a weather forecast; **met man** a weather forecaster; **Met Office** the Meteorological Office.

Met *met.* — **the Met.** (*coll.*) Metropolitan Opera, New York: London Metropolitan police: Metropolitan Railway.

met(a)- *met(ə)-,* in composition, among, with: after, later: often implies change, as *metamorphose:* beyond, above, as *metamathematics.* In *chem.* meta- indicates (1) a derivative of, or an isomer or polymer of, the substance named, or (2) an acid or hydroxide derived

from the ortho- form of the substance by loss of water molecules, or (3) a benzene substitution product in which the substituted atoms or groups are attached to two carbon atoms which are themselves separated by one carbon atom (in this sense commonly represented by *m*). — *adj.* **metacarp'al** (also *n.*). — *ns.* **metacarp'us** (Gr. *karpos,* wrist) the part of the hand (or its bones) between the wrist and the fingers, or its corresponding part, e.g. the foreleg of a horse between 'knee' and fetlock; **met'acentre** (Gr. *kentron,* point) the point of intersection of a vertical line through the centre of gravity of a body floating in equilibrium and that through the centre of gravity of the displaced liquid when the body is slightly displaced. — *adj.* **metacen'-tric.** — *ns.* **metachro'sis** (-*krō'sis;* Gr. *chrōsis,* colouring) ability to change colour in animals; **metagal'axy** the whole universe considered as a system of galaxies: any system of galaxies. — *adj.* **metagalac'tic.** — *n.* **metagen'esis** (Gr. *genesis,* generation; *biol.*) alternation of generations. — *adjs.* **metagenet'ic; metagnathous** (*met-ag'nə-thəs;* Gr. *gnathos,* jaw) of birds, having crossed mandibles: of insects, having biting jaws in the larvae, sucking in the adult state. — *ns.* **met'alanguage** a language or a system of symbols used to discuss another language or symbolic system; **metal'dehyde** a polymer of acetaldehyde. — *adj.* **metalinguis'tic** of or pertainin to (a) metalanguage or to metalinguistics. — *adv.* **metalinguis'tically.** — *ns. sing.* **metalinguis'tics** the study of the relation between a language and other features of behaviour in a particular culture, of language structure in relation to meaning, of expression or gesture accompanying spoken language, etc.; **metamathemat'ics** the logical analysis of formal mathematics, its concepts, terminology, use of symbols, etc. — *ns.* **met'amer** (Gr. *meros,* a part; *chem.*) a compound metameric with another; **met'amere** (-*mēr; zool.*) a segment, merosome, or somite. — *adj.* **metamer'ic.** — *ns.* **metam'erism** a particular form of isomerism in which different groups are attached to the same central atom (*chem.*): segmentation of the body along the primary axis, producing a series of homologous parts (*zool.*); **met'aphase** the stage of mitosis at which the chromosomes form the equatorial plate; **metaphos'-phate** a salt of metaphosphoric acid. — *adjs.* **metaphos-phor'ic** applied to an acid (HPO_3) containing a molecule less of water than orthophosphoric acid; **metapsychic, -al** (*met-ə-sī'kik, -l;* from **psychic** on the analogy of **metaphysics**). — *n. sing.* **metapsych'ics** the study of psychic phenomena beyond the limits of ordinary or orthodox psychology — 'psychical research'. — *adj.* **metapsycholog'ical.** — *ns.* **metapsy-chol'ogy** theories and theorising on psychological matters, such as the nature of the mind, which cannot be verified or falsified by experiment or reasoning; **metasil'icate** (*-i-kāt*) a salt of metasilicic acid. — *adjs.* **metasilic'ic** (*-is'ik*) applied to an acid (H_2SiO_3) containing a molecule less of water than orthosilicic acid; **metasōmat'ic.** — *ns.* **metasōm'atism** (Gr. *sōma, -atos,* body; *geol.*) metamorphism by chemical changes in minerals; **metastabil'ity** a state which appears to be chemically stable, often because of the slowness with which equilibrium is attained — said of, e.g., a supersaturated solution: a metastable state. — *adjs.* **meta-stable** (*met'ə-stā-bl*) having metastability (**metastable state** an excited state, esp. of an atom which has, however, insufficient energy to emit radiation); **meta-tarsal** (-*tär'sl*) (also *n.*). — *n.* **metatar'sus** (Gr. *tarsos,* the flat of the foot) that part of the foot, or its bones, between the tarsus and the toes. — *n.pl.* **Metatheria** (-*thē'ri-ə;* Gr. *thērion,* a wild beast) the marsupials. — *adj.* **metathoracic** (-*thö-ras'ik, -thō-*). — *n.* **metathorax** (-*thö'raks, -thō'*) the third and last segment of an insect's thorax. — *n.pl.* **Metazoa** (*met-ə-zō'ə;* also without *cap.;* Gr. *zōion,* animal) many-celled animals (opp. to single-celled *Protozoa*): — *sing.* **metazō'on.** — *adj. and n.* **metazō'an.** — *adjs.* **metazō'ic; metempiric, -al** (*met-em-pir'ik, -l*) beyond the scope of experience.

— *ns.* **metempir'icism** (*-i-sizm*); **metempir'icist.** [Gr. *meta*, among, with, beside, after.]

metabasis *met-ab'ə-sis, n.* a transition. — *adj.* **metabatic** (*met-ə-bat'ik*). [Gr. *metabasis* — *meta* (see **met(a)-**) and *bainein*, to go.]

metabolism *met-ab'əl-izm, n.* the sum total of chemical changes of living matter: metamorphosis. — *n.pl.* **Metab'ola** in some classifications, insects that undergo metamorphosis. — *adj.* **metabolic** (*-bol'ik*) exhibiting or relating to metabolism. — *v.t.* and *v.i.* **metab'olise, -ize** to subject to or be changed by metabolism. — *n.* **metab'olite** a product of metabolism. [Gr. *metabolē,* change.]

metacarpus, etc., **metacentre,** etc. See **met(a)-**.

metachronism *met-ak'ron-izm, n.* (an example of) the error of dating an event too late — opp. to *prochronism.* [Gr. *metachronios, metachronos,* anachronistic, out of date — *meta* (see **met(a)-**) and *chronos,* time.]

metachrosis, metagalaxy, etc. See **met(a)-**.

metage *mēt'ij, n.* official weighing of coal, grain, etc.: the charge for such weighing. [**mete**¹.]

metagenesis, -etic, metagnathous. See **met(a)-**.

metagrobolise, -ize *met-ə-grob'əl-īz,* **metagrabolise, -ize** *-grab', vs.t.* to mystify: to puzzle out. [Obs. Fr. *metagraboulizer* (Rabelais).]

métairie *mā-ter-ē', n.* a piece of land cultivated for a share of the produce. [Fr.; see **métayer**.]

metal *met'l, n.* an opaque elementary substance, possessing a peculiar lustre, fusibility, conductivity for heat and electricity, readiness to form positive ions, etc., such as gold, etc.: an alloy: that which behaves chemically like a true metal: courage or spirit (now spelt *mettle*): intrinsic quality: the guns of a ship-of-war: or or argent as a tincture (*her.*): molten material for glass-making: country-rock (*mining*): broken stones used for macadamised roads or as ballast for railways: (*pl.*) the rails of a railroad. — *adj.* made of metal. — *v.t.* to furnish or cover with metal: — *pr.p.* **met'alling;** *pa.t.* and *pa.p.* **met'alled.** — *adjs.* **met'alled** covered with metal, as a road; **metallic** (*mi-tal'ik*) pertaining to, or like, a metal: consisting of metal: of a colour, etc., having the lustre characteristic of metals: of a sound, like the sound produced by metal when struck. — *adv.* **metall'ically.** — *n.* **met'alliding** a high-temperature electrolytic technique for creating metal alloys on the surface of metals. — *adjs.* **metallif'erous** bearing or yielding metal; **met'alline** of, like, consisting of, or mixed with, metal. — *ns.* **met'alling** road-metal, broken stones; **metallisā'tion, -z-.** — *v.t.* **met'allise, -ize** to make metallic: to deposit thin metal films on glass or plastic. — *ns.* **met'allist** a worker in metals; — *adjs.* **metallogenet'ic** (*geol.*) relating to metallogeny; **metallogēn'ic** (or *-jen';* *geol.*) (of an element) occurring as an ore or a naturally occurring metal, as opposed to in rocks: metallogenetic (*U.S.*). — *ns.* **metallog'eny** (*geol.;* from Fr. — Gr. *genesis,* origin) (the study of) the origin and distribution of mineral deposits, esp. with regard to petrological, etc., features; **metallog'rapher.** — *adj.* **metallograph'ic.** — *ns.* **metallog'raphy** the study of the structure and constitution of metals; **met'alloid** a non-metal: an element resembling a metal in some respects, as selenium, tellurium. — *adjs.* **met'alloid, metalloid'al** pertaining to, or of the nature of, the metalloids. — *n.* **metall'ophone** an instrument like a xylophone with metal bars, the hammers being operated by hand or by means of a keyboard. — *adj.* **met'ally** suggestive of metal. — **met'al-work, -er, -ing.** [O.Fr., — L. *metallum* — Gr. *metallon,* a mine.]

metalanguage, metaldehyde. See **met(a)-**.

metalepsis *met-ə-lep'sis,* (*rhet.*) *n.* metonymy, esp. of a double, complicated, or indirect kind. — *adjs.* **metalep'tic, -al.** [Gr. *metalēpsis,* substitution.]

metalinguistics. See **met(a)-**.

metallic... metallophone. See **metal.**

metallurgy *met'əl-ûr-ji, met-al'ər-ji, n.* art and science applied to metals, including extraction from ores, refining, alloying, shaping, treating, and the study of

structure, constitution, and properties. — *adjs.* **metallur'gic, -al** pertaining to metallurgy. — *n.* **met'allurgist** (or, now more usu., *-al'*). [Gr. *metallourgeein,* to mine — *metallon,* a mine, *ergon,* work.]

metamathematics. See **met(a)-**.

metamere, metamerism. See **met(a)-**.

metamorphosis *met-ə-mör'fəs-is,* sometimes *-fōs'is, n.* change of shape, transformation: transformation of a human being to a beast, stone, tree, etc. (*folklore*): the marked change which some living beings undergo in the course of growth, as caterpillar to butterfly, tadpole to frog: — *pl.* **metamor'phoses** (*-sēz,* or *-fō'sēz*). — *adj.* **metamor'phic** showing or relating to change of form: formed by alteration of existing rocks by heat, pressure, or other processes in the earth's crust (*geol.*). — *ns.* **metamor'phism** transformation of rocks in the earth's crust (*contact metamorphism,* by contact with or neighbourhood of igneous material; *regional,* owing to general conditions over a wide region); **metamor'phist** one who believes that Christ's body merged into the Deity at the Ascension. — *v.t.* **metamor'phose** (*-fōz, -fōs*) to transform: to subject to metamorphism or metamorphosis: to develop in another form. — *v.i.* undergo metamorphosis. [Gr. *metamorphōsis* — *meta* (see **met(a)-**) and *morphē,* form.]

metanoia *met-ə-noi'ə, n.* repentance: a fundamental change in character, way of life, etc.: a spiritual conversion. [Gr. *metanoia,* a change of mind or heart, repentance.]

metaphase. See **met(a)-**.

metaphor *met'ə-fər, n.* a figure of speech by which a thing is spoken of as being that which it only resembles, as when a ferocious man is called a tiger. — *adjs.* **metaphoric** (*-for'ik*), **-al.** — *adv.* **metaphor'ically.** — *n.* **met'aphorist.** — **mixed metaphor** an expression in which two or more metaphors are confused, as *to take arms against a sea of troubles.* [Gr. *metaphorā* — *meta* (see **met(a)-**) and *pherein,* to carry.]

metaphosphoric, -phosphate. See **met(a)-**.

metaphrase *met'ə-frāz, n.* a turning of prose into verse or verse into prose: a rendering in a different style or form: an altered wording: a word for word translation — also **metaphrasis** (*-af'rə-sis*). — *n.* **met'aphrast** (*-frast*) one who produces a metaphrase. — *adj.* **metaphrast'ic.** [Gr. *metaphrasis* — *meta* (see **met(a)-**) and *phrasis,* a speaking.]

metaphysics *met-ə-fiz'iks, n. sing.* the branch of philosophy which investigates the first principles of nature and thought: ontology or the science of being: loosely and vaguely applied to anything abstruse, abstract, philosophical, subtle, transcendental, occult, supernatural, magical. — *n.* **metaphys'ic** metaphysics: philosophical groundwork. — *adj.* metaphysical. — *adj.* **metaphys'ical** pertaining to metaphysics: abstract: beyond nature or the physical: supernatural: fanciful: addicted to far-fetched conceits (applied by Johnson to Donne, Cowley, and others). — *adv.* **metaphys'ically.** — *n.* **metaphysician** (*-ish'ən*) one versed in metaphysics. [Originally applied to those writings of Aristotle which in the accepted order came after (Gr. *meta*) those dealing with natural science (*ta physika* — *physis,* nature).]

metaplasia *met-ə-plā'si-ə, n.* tissue transformation, as of cartilage into bone. — *ns.* **metaplasis** (*-ap'lə-sis*) metaplasia: the period of maturity in the life-cycle; **met'aplasm** (*-plazm*) cell-contents other than protoplasm: a change in a word by addition, dropping, or exchange of parts. — *adj.* **metaplast'ic.** [Gr. *metaplasis, metaplasmos,* a moulding afresh — *meta* (see **met(a)-**) and *plassein,* to form.]

metapsychic(s), metasilicate, etc., **metasomatic,** etc., **metastability,** etc. See **met(a)-**.

metastasis *met-as'tə-sis, n.* removal from one place to another: transition: transformation: paramorphic change in rocks: metabolism: transfer of disease from its original site to another part of the body: a secondary tumor distant from the original site of disease: — *pl.*

metas'tasēs. — *v.i.* **metas'tasise, -ize** to pass to another part of the body, as a tumour. — *adj.* **metastatic** (*-stat'ik*). [Gr. *metastasis*, change of place — *meta* (see **met(a)-**) and *stasis*, a standing.]

metatarsus, -al, Metatheria. See **met(a)-**.

metathesis *met-ath'ə-sis, n.* transposition or exchange of places, esp. between the sounds or letters of a word: — *pl.* **metath'esēs.** — *v.t.* **metath'esise, -ize** to transpose (by metathesis). — *adjs.* **metathetic** (*met-ə-thet'ik*), **-al.** [Gr., — *metatīthenai*, to transpose — *meta* (see **met(a)-**) and *tithenai*, to place.]

metathoracic, -thorax. See **met(a)-**.

métayer *mā-tā-yā'* or *mā', n.* a farmer who pays, instead of money rent, a fixed proportion of the crops. — *n.* **métayage** (*-yäzh'*, or *mā'*) this system. [Fr., — L.L. *medietārius* — L. *medietās*, half — *medius*, middle.]

Metazoa, etc. See **met(a)-**.

metcast. See **met.**

mete[1] *mēt, v.t.* to measure: to apportion (*pa.t.* **mēt'ed,** in Spens. **mott**). — *n.* measure. — **mete'stick, mete'wand, mete'yard** a measuring-rod. [O.E. *metan*; Ger. *messen.*]

mete[2] *mēt, n.* a boundary or limit. [L. *mēta*, a goal or boundary.]

metempiric, etc. See **met(a)-**.

metempsychosis *met-emp-si-kō'sis, n.* the passing of the soul after death into some other body: — *pl.* **metempsychō'sēs.** [Gr. *metempsychōsis* — *meta* (see **met(a)-**), *en*, in, *psychē*, soul.]

meteor *mē'tyər, mē'ti-ər, n.* orig., now rarely, any atmospheric phenomenon: a luminous appearance: one of numberless small bodies travelling through space, revealed to observation when they enter the earth's atmosphere as aerolites, fireballs, or shooting-stars: anything brilliant or dazzling but short-lived. — *adj.* **meteoric** (*mē-ti-or'ik*) above the earth's surface: atmospheric: influenced by weather: of or pertaining to meteors in any sense: of the nature of a meteor: transiently flashing like a meteor: rapid (*fig.*). — *adv.* **meteor'ically** in manner of a meteor. — *ns.* **me'teorist** one versed in meteors; **me'teorite** a meteor that has fallen to earth as a lump of stone or metal. — *adjs.* **meteorit'ic, meteorit'ical, me'teorital** (*-īt-l*). — *n.* **meteorit'icist.** — *n. sing.* **meteorit'ics** the science or study of meteors. — *ns.* **me'teorogram** a meteorograph record; **me'teorograph** an instrument by which several meteorological elements are recorded in combination; **me'teoroid** a meteor that has not reached the earth's atmosphere; **me'teorolite** (Gr. *lithos*, stone) a meteoric stone. — *adjs.* **meteorolog'ic, -al.** — *ns.* **meteorol'ogist; meteorol'ogy** the study of weather and climate. — *adj.* **me'teorous** (or, usu. in poetry, *mē-tē'ər-əs*) like a meteor, meteoric. — **meteor crater** a crater formed by the fall of a meteor; **meteoric iron** iron as found in meteorites; **meteoric showers** or **meteor showers, storms** showers of meteors; **meteoric stones** aerolites; **Meteorological Office** a government department issuing weather forecasts, etc.; **meteor streams** streams of dust revolving about the sun, whose intersection by the earth causes meteor showers. [Gr. *ta meteōra*, things on high — *meta* and the root of *aeirein*, to lift.]

meteorism *mē'tyər-izm, -ti-ər-, (med.) n.* excessive accumulation of gas in the intestines: tympanites. [Medical L. *meteōrismus* — Gr. *meteōrismos*, raising, being raised, up — *meteōrizein*, to lift; cf. **meteor.**]

meter[1] *mē'tər, n.* a measurer: an apparatus for measuring, esp. quantity of a fluid, or of electricity, used: a gauge or indicator: a parking meter. — *v.t.* to measure by a meter. — **meter maid, man** (*facet.*) a traffic warden. [**mete[1].**]

meter[2]. American spelling of **metre[1,2].**

-meter *-mi-tər* or *-mē-*, in composition, an instrument for measuring. — **-metric, -al** (*-met'rik, -l*) adjective combining forms. — **-met'rically** adverb combining form. — **-metry** (*-mi-tri*) noun combining form. [Gr. *metron*, measure.]

methadone *meth'ə-dōn, n.* a synthetic addictive drug

similar to morphine, longer-acting than heroin. — Also **meth'adon** (*-don*). [**di**methyl**amino-, di**phenyl, heptan**one**.]

methane *mē'thān, meth'ān, n.* marsh-gas (CH_4), the simplest hydrocarbon, found wherever the decomposition of vegetable matter is taking place under water, also in coal-mines, forming when mixed with air the deadly fire-damp. — **mēthanom'eter** (*mining*) an instrument for detecting the presence of methane in mines. [**methyl.**]

methanol *meth'ə-nol, n.* methyl alcohol, wood spirit. [**methane, -ol,** suffix — L. *oleum*, oil.]

methaqualone *meth-ə-kwā'lōn, n.* a hypnotic sedative drug ($C_{16}H_{14}N_2O$).

Methedrine® *meth'ə-drēn, n.* a former proprietary name for an amphetamine, methylamphetamine hydrochloride, a soft drug, but used by drug addicts.

metheglin *meth-eg'lin, n.* a Welsh fermented liquor made from honey. [W. *meddyglyn* — *meddyg*, medicinal (— L. *medicus*, physician), *llyn*, liquor.]

methinks *mi-thingks', methink'eth, methink' v.impers.* it seems to me: I think: — *pa.t.* **methought** (*mi-thöt'*). [O.E. *mē thyncth*, it seems to me; *thyncan*, to seem, has been confused with *thencan*, to think; cf. Ger. *dünken*, to seem, *denken*, to think.]

methionine *meth-ī'o-nēn, n.* an essential sulphur-bearing amino-acid.

method *meth'əd, n.* the mode or rule of accomplishing an end: orderly procedure: manner: orderly arrangement: methodicalness: classification: a system, rule: manner of performance: an instruction-book systematically arranged. — *adjs.* **methodic** (*mi-thod'ik*), **-al** arranged with method: disposed in a just and natural manner: observing method: formal. — *adv.* **method'ically.** — *n.* **method'icalness.** — *v.t.* **meth'odise, -ize** to reduce to method: to dispose in due order. — *ns.* **Meth'odism** the principles and practice of the Methodists; **meth'odist** one who observes method: (*cap.*) a follower of the Wesleys — a name given first to a group of students at Oxford 'for the regularity of their lives as well as studies'. — *adjs.* **Methodist'ic, -al** resembling the Methodists, esp. as viewed by opponents: strict in religious matters. — *adv.* **Methodist'ically.** — *ns.* **methodol'ogy** a system of methods and rules applicable to research or work in a given science or art: evaluation of subjects taught and principles and techniques of teaching them; **Meth'ody** a disrespectful nickname for a Methodist. — **method acting** acting as a personal living of a part, contrasted with mere technical performance (also called **the method**). [Gr. *methodos* — *meta*, after, *hodos*, a way.]

methomania *meth-ō-mā'ni-ə, n.* an intermittent morbid craving for alcohol. [Gr. *methē*, strong drink, *maniā*, madness.]

methotrexate *meth-ō-treks'āt, n.* a drug ($C_{20}H_{22}N_8O_5$) used in cancer treatment.

methought. See **methinks.**

methoxamine hydrochloride *meth-oks'ə-mēn hī-drō-klōr'īd, -klör', n.* a drug used in slowing down the action of the heart.

meths *meths, n. sing.* short for **methylated spirits.**

Methuselah *mi-thū'zə-lə, -thōō', n.* a patriarch said to have lived 969 years (Gen. v. 27): any very aged person: a very large wine-bottle (holding about $6\frac{1}{2}$ quarts): as a bottle-size of champagne, the equivalent of eight bottles.

methyl *meth'il, mē'thīl, (chem.) n.* the radical (CH_3) of wood (or methyl) alcohol ($CH_3 \cdot OH$). — *n.* **methylamine** (*-ə-mēn'*) an inflammable gas ($CH_3 \cdot NH_2$) which can be got from herring brine. — See also **dimethylamine** and **trimethylamine.** — *v.t.* **meth'ylate** to mix or impregnate with methyl alcohol: to introduce the radical CH_3 into. — *n.* a methyl alcohol derivative: a compound with a methyl group. — *ns.* **methylā'tion; methyldō'pa** an antihypertensive drug ($C_{10}H_{13}NO_4$); **meth'ylene** the hypothetical compound CH_2. — *adj.* **methyl'ic.** — **methylated spirit(s)** alcohol made unpalatable with methyl alcohol, and usually other things; **methyl chloride** a refrigerant and local anaesthetic; **methyl-propyl ether** an inhalation anaesthetic; **methyltestos′terone** (-ōn) a synthetic androgen with similar actions and functions to those of testosterone; **methyl violet** an antiseptic dye used as a stain in microscopy and formerly used as a disinfectant, a mixture of the hydrochlorides of tetra-, penta-, and hexa-methylpararosaniline: crystal violet. [Gr. *methu*, wine, *hȳlē*, wood.]

methysis *meth′i-sis*, (*path.*) *n.* drunkenness. — *adj.* **methys′tic** intoxicating. [Gr.]

metic *met′ik*, *n.* a resident alien. [Gr. *metoikos* — *meta*, indicating change, and *oikos*, a house.]

metical *met′i-kəl n.* the monetary unit of Mozambique, equal to 100 centavos. [Port. *metical*, — Ar. *mithqāl*, a measure of weight.]

meticulous *me-tik′ū-ləs*, *adj.* timid (*obs.*): scrupulously careful: (*popularly*) overcareful. — *adv.* **metic′ulously**. — *n.* **metic′ulousness**. [L. *meticulōsus*, frightened — *metus*, fear.]

métier *mā′tyā, n.* one's calling or business: that in which one is specially skilled. [Fr., — L. *ministerium*.]

metif *mā′tēf*, *n.* (sometimes with *cap.*) the offspring of a white and a quadroon. — *n.* **métis** (*mā-tēs′*; sometimes with *cap.*) a person of mixed descent, esp., in Canada, a half-breed of French and Indian parentage: — *pl.* **métis** (-*tēs′* or -*tēz′*); *fem.* **métisse′** (sometimes with *cap.*). [Fr.; cf. **mestizo**.]

Metis *mē′tis*, *n.* a Greek personification of prudence. [Gr. *mētis*.]

métis, métisse. See **metif**.

metol *mē′tol, n.* *p*-methylaminophenol sulphate, the basis of a rapid developer for photographic negatives. [From *Metol*, a trademark.]

Metonic *mi-ton′ik*, *adj.* pertaining to the Athenian astronomer *Mētōn* or his cycle (**Metonic cycle** beginning on 27th June, 432 B.C.) of 19 years after which the moon's phases recur on the same days of the year.

metonym *met′ə-nim*, *n.* a word used in a transferred sense. — *adjs.* **metonym′ic, -al**. — *adv.* **metonym′ically**. — *n.* **metonymy** (*mi-ton′i-mi*) a trope in which the name of one thing is put for that of another related to it, the effect for the cause, etc., as 'the bottle' for 'drink'. [Gr. *metōnymiā* — *meta*, indicating change, and *onyma* = *onoma*, a name.]

me-too *mē-tōō′ adj.* imitative. — *n.* a product resulting from me-tooism. — *ns.* **me-too′er** a person who imitates or adopts the policy or activity of another, for his own advantage; **me-too′ism** imitating the policy or activity which is proving successful for a rival. [Coll. interj. *me too!*]

metope[1] *met′o-pē*, also *met′ōp*, (*archit.*) *n.* the slab, plain or sculptured, between the triglyphs of a Doric frieze. [Gr. *metōpē* — *meta* and *ōpē*, an opening for a beam-end.]

metope[2] *met′ōp*, *n.* the face, forehead, frontal surface generally. — *adj.* **metopic** (*mit-op′ik*). — *ns.* **metopism** (*met′ə-pizm*) the condition of having a persistent metopic or frontal suture; **metoposcopy** (*met-ə-pos′kə-pi*; Gr. *skopeein*, to look) the study of character from the physiognomy. — *adjs.* **metoposcop′ic, -al**. — *n.* **metopos′copist**. [Gr. *metōpon*, forehead, lit. between the eyes — *meta*, and *ōps*, eye.]

metopon *met′ō-pon*, *n.* a pain-relieving drug derived from opium but less habit-forming than morphine.

metopryl *met′ō-pril*, *n.* an anaesthetic related to ether, but more powerful and less disturbing in after-effects.

metre[1] (*U.S.* **meter**) *mē′tər*, *n.* that regulated succession of certain groups of syllables (long and short, stressed and unstressed) in which poetry is usually written: verse, or poetry generally: a scheme of versification, the character of a stanza as consisting of a given number of lines composed of feet of a given number, arrangement, and kind: musical time. — *v.t.* and *v.i.* to versify. — *adjs.* **metred** (*mē′tərd*) rhythmical; **metric** (*met′rik*), **-al** pertaining to metre: in metre: consisting

of verses. — *adv.* **met′rically**. — *n.* **metrician** (*me-trish′-ən*) a metricist. — *v.t.* **met′ricise, -ize** (-*sīz*) to analyse the metre of. — *n.* **met′ricist** (-*sist*) one skilled in metres: one who writes in metre. — *n. sing.* **met′rics** the art or science of versification (also *n.* **met′ric**). — **metrifica′-tion** metrical structure: the act of making verses; **met′rifier** a versifier; **met′rist** one skilled in the use of metres: a student of metre; **metromā′nia** a mania for writing verses. — **common metre** a quatrain in eights and sixes, of four and of three iambic feet alternately — also **service metre,** from its use in the metrical psalms, etc., and **ballad metre,** from its use in old ballads; **long metre** an octosyllabic quatrain, the four lines with four feet each; **short metre** the quatrain in sixes, with the third line octosyllabic. [O.E. *mēter* and O.Fr. *metre*, both — L. *metrum* — Gr. *metron*, measurement, metre; and partly directly.]

metre[2] (*U.S.* **meter**) *mē′tər*, *n.* the fundamental unit of length in the metric system — orig. intended to be one ten-millionth of distance from pole to equator: later the distance between two marks on a platinum-iridium bar in Paris: defined more recently in terms of the wavelength in vacuo of the orange radiation of the krypton-86 atom: by British Act of Parliament (1963) 1 yard equals 0·9144 metre. — *adj.* **metric** (*met′rik*) pertaining to the metre, or to the metric system. — *v.t.* and *v.i.* **met′ricate** to convert, change to the metric system. — *n.* **metrica′tion**. — **metre-kilogram(me)=second** (contr. M.K.S. or MKS) **system** a system of scientific measurement having the metre, etc., as units of length, mass, time (with the addition of **ampere** — M.K.S.A., or more usually MKSA — forming the Giorgi system of units); **metric system** the SI or any decimal system of weights and measures; **metric ton** see **tonne**. — **go metric** to metricate. [Fr. *mètre* — Gr. *metron*, measure.]

metric[1] *met′rik*, *adj.* quantitative. — *adj.* **met′rical** pertaining to measurement. — *n. sing.* **met′rics** the theory of measurement. — *ns.* **metrol′ogist; metrol′ogy** the science of weights and measures, or of weighing and measuring. [Gr. *metron*, measure.]

metric[2]. See **metre**[1].

metric[3]. See **metre**[2].

metricate. See **metre**[2].

metrician, etc., **metrifier, metrist.** See **metre**[1].

metr(o)- in composition, of the uterus. — *ns.* **metritis** (*mə-trī′tis*) inflammation of the uterus; **metrorrhagia** (*mē-trō-rā′ji-ə, me-*; Gr. -*rragia* — *rhēgnynai*, to break, burst) bleeding from the uterus between menstrual periods. [Gr. *metra*, womb.]

métro *mā′trō*, *n.* (often with *cap.*) an underground railway, esp. the Paris subway: — *pl.* **mét′ros**. — Also **metro, Metro.** [Fr. *métro*. Abbrev. for *chemin de fer métropolitain*, metropolitan railway.]

metrology. See **metric**[1].

metromania. See **metre**[1].

metronome *met′rə-nōm, n.* an instrument with an inverted pendulum that can be set to beat so many times a minute, the loud ticking giving the right speed of performance for a piece of music. — *adj.* **metronomic** (-*nom′ik*). [Gr. *metron*, measure, *nomos*, law.]

metronymic *met-rə-nim′ik*, *adj.* derived from the name of one's mother or other female ancestor: indicating the mother: using such a system of naming. — *n.* an appellation so derived (cf. *patronymic*). — Also **matronymic** (prob. — L. *māter*, though Doric Greek is *mātēr*). [Gr. *mētēr, -tros*, mother, *onyma* = *onoma*, name.]

metropolis *mi-trop′ə-lis*, *n.* the capital of a country, county, etc.: the chief cathedral city, as Canterbury of England, or chief see of a province: the mother-city of an ancient Greek colony: a chief centre, seat or focus: the main habitat (*biol.*): — *pl.* **metrop′olises**. — *adj.* **metropolitan** (*met-rə-pol′i-tən*) of a metropolis: of the mother-church. — *n.* the bishop of a metropolis, presiding over the other bishops of a province, in the

Eastern Orthodox churches, a person ranking between an archbishop and a patriarch, in the R.C. Church and the Church of England, an archbishop. — *n.* **metropol'itanate.** — *v.t.* **metropol'itanise, -ize** to make into or like a metropolis. — *adj.* **metropolit'ical.** — **metropolitan county, district** a county or district in a heavily-populated industrial area of England, the district running more, and the county fewer, public services than other districts or counties. [Gr. *metropolis* — *mētēr*, mother, *polis*, city.]

metrorrhagia. See under **metr(o)-**.

metrostyle *met'rə-stīl, n.* a device for regulating speed in a player-piano. [Gr. *metron*, measure, *stylos*, a pillar.]

mettle *met'l, n.* temperament: ardent temperament: spirit: sprightliness: courage. — *adj.* (*Scot.*) **mettlesome.** — *adjs.* **mett'led, mett'lesome** high-spirited: ardent. — *n.* **mett'lesomeness.** — **put (someone) on his mettle** to rouse (a person) to put forth his best efforts. [**metal.**]

meu *mū, n.* baldmoney or spignel. [L. *mēum* Gr. *mēon.*]

meum et tuum *mē'əm et tū'əm, me'ōom et tōō'ōom,* (L.) mine and thine.

meunière *mən-yer', (Fr.) mø-nyer, adj.* (of food, esp. fish) coated in flour and fried in butter, then served in butter, lemon juice and herbs, esp. parsley. [Fr. *à la meunière,* in the manner of the miller's wife (from the coating of flour).]

meuse[1], muse, mews *mūs, mūz, n.* a way of escape through a hedge, etc. — *v.i.* to pass through a meuse. [O.Fr. *muce,* a place for hiding things.]

meuse[2]. See **mew[3].**

meve *mēv,* an obs. form of **move** (*vb.*).

mew[1] *mū, n.* a gull. [O.E. *mǣw;* Du. *meeuw,* O.N. *mār,* Ger. *Möwe.*]

mew[2] *mū, v.i.* to cry as a cat. — *n.* the cry of a cat. — *interj.* expressing derision. [Imit.]

mew[3] *mū, v.t.* to shed, moult, or cast: to change, as the covering or dress: to confine, as in a cage. — *v.i.* to cast the antlers or feathers: to moult. — *n.* the process of moulting: a cage for hawks, esp. while mewing a coop: a place of confinement: a retreat: a hiding-place. — *n.* **mews, meuse** (*mūz, mūs;* orig. *pl.* of **mew,** now commonly as *sing.* with new *pl.* **mews'es**) a street or yard of stabling (often converted into dwelling-houses or garages) — from the king's mews at Charing Cross when hawks were succeeded by horses. [O.Fr. *muer* — L. *mūtāre,* to change.]

mewl *mūl, v.i.* to mew: to cry feebly, as a child. [Imit.]

mews[1]. See **mew[3].**

mews[2]. See **meuse[1].**

Mexican *meks'i-kən, adj.* of Mexico and its people. — *n.* a native or citizen of Mexico: an Aztec: the Nahuatl language: a Mexican dollar: a coarse cotton cloth. — **Mexican hog** the peccary; **Mexican tea** a kind of goosefoot, used as an anthelmintic. [Sp. *Mexicano,* now *Mejicano.*]

meynt. See **ming.**

mezail. See **mesail.**

meze, mézé *mā'zā, n.* a type of appetiser or hors d'oeuvre served in Greece, Turkey, the Lebanon, etc., esp. with an aperitif before dinner. [Turk. *meze,* a snack, an appetiser.]

mezereon *me-zē'ri-ən, n.* a European shrub (*Daphne mezereum*) whose flowers appear in early spring: its extremely acrid bark, or the bark of related species, used in medicine. — Also **mezē'reum** (*-əm*). [Ar. and Pers. *māzaryūn.*]

mezuza(h) *mə-zōōz'ə, n.* a parchment scroll containing scriptural texts which is placed in a case and fixed to the doorpost by some Jewish families as a sign of their faith: — *pl.* **-zu'zahs, -zuzoth** (*-zōō-zōt'*). [Heb., (lit.) doorpost.]

mezzanine *mez'ə-nēn, n.* an entresol (*archit.*): a small low window (*archit.*): a room below the stage. — Also *adj.* [Fr., — It. *mezzanino* — *mezzano* — L. *mediānus* — *medius,* middle.]

mezza voce *met'sə vō'chā, med'zä,* (*mus.*) *adj.* and *adv.* with medium volume, tone. [It.]

mezzo *met'sō, n.* a mezzo-soprano: — *pl.* **mez'zos.**

mezzo-forte *met'sō-, med'zō-för'tā, adj.* and *adv.* rather loud. [It.]

mezzo-piano *met'sō-, med'zō-pyä'nō, -pē-ä'nō, adj.* and *adv.* rather soft. [It.]

mezzo-relievo, mezzo-rilievo *met'sō-, med'zō-ril-yä'vō, n.* a degree of relief in figures halfway between high and low relief. [It.]

mezzo-soprano *met'sō-, med'zō-sō-prä'nō, n.* a voice between soprano and contralto: low soprano: a part for such a voice: a person possessing it: — *pl.* **mez'zo= sopra'nos.** [It. *mezzo,* middle, and *soprano.*]

mezzotint *met'sō-, med'zō-tint, n.* a method of copper-plate engraving giving an even gradation of tones by roughening a plate and removing the bur for lights: an impression from a plate so produced. — Also **mezzotinto** (*-tin'tō*): — *pl.* **mezzotin'tos.** [It. *mezzo-tinto* — *mezzo,* middle, half, *tinto,* tint — L. *tingĕre, tinctum,* to dye.]

mganga *m-gang'gə, n.* in East Africa, a native doctor, a witch doctor. [Swahili.]

mho *mō, n.* formerly a unit of electric conductance, that of a body with a resistance of one ohm (now **siemens**): — *pl.* **mhos.** [**ohm** spelt backwards.]

mhorr *mör, n.* a West African gazelle. [Ar.]

mi *mē, n.* the third note of the scale in sol-fa notation — also anglicised in spelling as **me.** [See **Aretinian.**]

mia-mia *mī'ə-mī'ə, n.* a native dwelling hut. [Aboriginal.]

miaow *mi-ow', myow'.* Same as **mew[2].**

miarolitic *mi-ə-rō-lit'ik,* (*geol.*) *adj.* having irregular cavities into which the constituent minerals of the rock project with perfectly terminated crystals. [It. *miarolo,* local name of a granite.]

miasma *mi-* or *mī-az'mə, n.* an unwholesome exhalation — also **mī'asm:** — *pls.* **mias'mata, mias'mas, mī'asms.** — *adjs.* **mias'mal, miasmat'ic, mias'matous, mias'mic, mias'mous.** [Gr. *miasma, -atos,* pollution — *mi-ainein,* to stain, pollute.]

miaul *mi-öl', mi-owl', v.i.* to cry as a cat. — *n.* a mew. [Fr. *miauler;* imit.]

mica *mī'kə, n.* a rock-forming mineral (muscovite, biotite, lepidolite, etc.) with perfect basal cleavage, the laminae flexible and elastic, and usu. transparent, of various colours, used as an electric insulator and as a substitute for glass: — *pl.* **mi'cas.** — *adj.* **micaceous** (*-kā'shəs*). — *v.t.* **mi'cate** to furnish with mica. — **mi'ca-schist', -slate'** a metamorphic rock consisting of alternate folia of mica and quartz. [L. *mīca,* a crumb; use probably influenced by association with *mīcāre,* to glitter.]

Micawberish *mi-kö'bər-ish, adj.* like Wilkins *Micawber* in Dickens's *David Copperfield,* jaunty and improvident, always 'waiting for something to turn up'. — *n.* **Micaw'berism.**

mice *mīs,* plural of **mouse.**

micelle *mi-sel',* **micella** *mī-sel'ə, ns.* a group of molecular chains, a structural unit found in colloids: a hypothetical unit of living matter. — *adj.* **micell'ar.** [Dim. of L. *mīca,* crumb, grain.]

Michaelmas *mik'əl-məs, n.* the festival of St *Michael,* Sept. 29: a quarterly rent-day in England. — **Mich'aelmas= dai'sy** a wild aster: any of several garden plants of genus Aster with clusters of small purple, pink, blue, etc., flowers; **Michaelmas term** the autumn term at Oxford and Cambridge and some other universities. [**mass[2].**]

miche *mich,* (*dial.*) *v.i.* to mouch, skulk, slink: to loaf: to play truant. — *v.t.* to pilfer. — *n.* **mich'er.** — *n.* and *adj.* **mich'ing.** [Poss. same as **mooch.**]

Michurinism *mē-chōō'rin-ism, n.* Lysenkoism. [I. V. *Michurin,* Russian horticulturalist.]

mick, mickey, micky *mik'(i), ns.* an Irishman (*rather offensive*): a flask for alcohol (*mainly Can.*): a wild young bull (*Austr.*). — *adj.* **mick'ey** (*U.S. slang*) (of music, a band, etc.) Mickey Mouse. — *ns.* **mickey,**

Mickey (Finn) (*slang*) a doped drink: that which is added to the drink, usu. a stupefying drug or a strong laxative. — *vs.t.* to drug someone's drink: to trick someone. — **Mickey Mouse** an animated cartoon character created by Walt Disney, 1928. — *adj.* (*slang*) simple, easy, often derisively so: unimportant, insignificant: (of music, a band, etc.) trite, corny. — **mick′ey-taking** (*slang*). — **take the mick, mickey (micky),** or (*rarely*) **mike** (or **a mike**), **out of** (*slang*; perhaps with different origin) to annoy: to make game of. [*Michael.*]

mickle *mik′l,* (*arch.*) *adj.* much: great. — *n.* a great quantity. — *adv.* much. — *Scot.* **muck′le. — many a little** (or **pickle**) **makes a mickle** (*often absurdly* **many a mickle makes a muckle**) every little helps. [O.E. *micel, mycel.*]

micky. See **mick**.

Micmac *mik′mak, n.* an Indian tribe of eastern Canada: a member of it: its language.

mico *mē′kō, n.* a marmoset, esp. the black-tailed: — *pl.* **mi′cos.** [Port., — Carib *meku,* monkey.]

micro *mī′krō,* (*coll.*) *n.* short for **microprocessor** or **microcomputer:** — *pl.* **mi′cros.**

micr(o)- *mī-kr(ō)-, mī-kr(ə)-,* in composition, (1) (a) abnormally or extremely small: (b) using, or used in, or prepared for, microscopy: (c) dealing with minute quantities, objects or values: (d) dealing with a small area: (e) magnifying, amplifying: (f) reducing, or reduced, to minute size: (2) a millionth part, as in **mī′croampere** a millionth part of an ampere, **mi′crobar** one-millionth of a bar of pressure, **mī′crofarad, mī′crogram,** and many others. [Gr. *mikros,* little.]

microanalysis *mī-krō-ə-nal′i-sis, n.* chemical analysis of minute quantities. — *adj.* **microanalyt′ical.** [**micro-** (1c).]

microanatomy *mī-krō-ə-nat′ə-mi, n.* the study of the anatomical structures of microscopic tissues. [**micro-** (1c).]

microbalance *mī′krō-bal-əns, n.* a balance for measuring very small weights. [**micro-** (1c).]

microbarograph *mī-krō-bar′ō-gräf, n.* a barograph that records minute variations of atmospheric pressure. [**micro-** (1c).]

microbe *mī′krōb, n.* a microscopic organism, esp. a disease-causing bacterium. — *adjs.* **micro′bial, micro′-bian, micro′bic.** — *ns.* **microbiol′ogist; microbiol′ogy** the biology of microscopic or ultramicroscopic organisms, as bacteria, viruses, fungi; **mi′crobiota** the smallest soil organisms. [Fr., — Gr. *mikros,* little, *bios,* life.]

microburst *mī-krō-bûrst, n.* a sudden, violent downward rush of air usu. associated with thunderstorms. [**micro-** (1d).]

microcapsule *mī′krō-kap-sūl, n.* an extremely small, thin-walled capsule of plastic or wax, formed around liquid, powder, etc., which, when fractured, releases its contents to fulfil some purpose; such capsules have been used e.g. to make copying paper without carbon. — *n.* **microencapsulā′tion.** [**micro-** (1a).]

microcard *mī′krō-kärd, n.* a card reproducing some 200 or more pages of a book in microscopic print for later reading by enlargement. [**micro-** (1f).]

microcephalous *mī-krō-sef′ə-ləs, adj.* abnormally small-headed. — Also **microcephalic** (-*si-fal′ik*). — *ns.* **microceph′al** an abnormally small-headed person; **microceph′aly** abnormal smallness of head. [Gr. *mikros,* little, *kephalē,* head.]

Microcheiroptera, (*U.S.* **-chir-**), *mī-krō-kī-rop′tə-rə, n.pl.* bats other than fruit-bats (which are large). [**micro-** (1a), **Cheiroptera.**]

microchemistry *mī-krō-kem′is-tri, n.* chemistry dealing with very small quantities. [**micro-** (1c).]

microchip *mī′krō-chip, n.* a chip (q.v.) of silicon, etc. [**micro-** (1f).]

Microchiroptera. See **Microcheiroptera.**

microcircuit *mī′krō-sûr-kit, n.* an electronic circuit with components formed in one unit of semiconductor crystal. [**micro-** (1f).]

microcirculation *mī-krō-sûr-kū-lā′shən, n.* the circulation of blood or lymph in the finest blood-vessels or capillaries of the circulatory and lymphatic systems. [**micro-** (1a).]

microclimate *mī′krō-klī-māt, -klī-mit, n.* the climate of a small or very small area, esp. if different from that of the surrounding area. — *n.* **microclimatol′ogy** the study of a microclimate or microclimates. [**micro-** (1d).]

microcline *mī′krō-klīn, n.* an anorthic potash-feldspar with cleavage-angle differing very slightly from a right angle. [Gr. *mikros,* little, *klīnein,* to slant.]

micrococcus *mī-krō-kok′əs, n.* a rounded bacillus: — *pl.* **micrococci** (-*kok′sī*). — *adj.* **micrococc′al.** [**micro-** (1a) and Gr. *kokkos,* a grain.]

microcode *mī-krō-kōd,* (*comput.*) *n.* a microinstruction or a sequence of microinstructions. [**micro-** (1c).]

microcomponent *mī-krō-kəm-pō′nənt, n.* a minute component of e.g. a microcircuit. [**micro-** (1a).]

microcomputer *mī-krō-kəm-pū′ter, n.* a tiny computer containing a microprocessor, often used as the control unit for some instrument, tool, etc.: the microprocessor itself. [**micro-** (1f).]

microcopying *mī-krō-kop′i-ing, n.* copying on microfilm. — *n.* **mī′crocopy.** [**micro-** (1f).]

microcosm *mī′krō-kozm, n.* a little universe or world: man, who was regarded by ancient philosophers as a model or epitome of the universe. — *adjs.* **microcos′-mic, -al** pertaining to the microcosm. — *n.* **microcosmog′raphy.** — **microcosmic salt** sodium ammonium hydrogen phosphate, used as a blowpipe flux (orig. got from human urine). — **in microcosm** on a small scale, as an exact copy or representative model of a larger group, etc. [Gr. *mikros,* small, *kosmos,* world.]

microcrystalline *mī-krə-kris′təl-īn, -in, adj.* having a crystalline structure visible only under the microscope. [**micro-** (1a).]

microcyte *mī′krə-sīt, n.* a small red blood corpuscle. [**micro-** (1a), and Gr. *kytos,* a container (used as if = cell).]

microdetector *mī-krō-di-tekt′ər, n.* an instrument for detecting minute amounts of changes. — *n.* **microdetec′-tion.** [**micro-** (1c).]

microdissection *mī-krō-di-sek′shən, n.* dissection under the microscope. [**micro-** (1b).]

microdot *mī′krə-dot, n.* photograph of usu. secret material reduced to size of large dot: a small pill containing concentrated LSD (*slang*). [**micro-** (1f).]

microeconomics *mī-krō-ēk-ə-nom′iks, -ek-, n. sing.* that branch of economics dealing with individual households, firms, industries, commodities, etc. — *n.pl.* economic methods, principals, etc., applicable to an individual firm, etc. — *adj.* **microeconom′ic.** [**micro-** (1d).]

microelectronics *mī-krō-el-ik-tron′iks, -ē-lik-, n. sing.* the technology of electronic systems involving microminiaturisation, microcircuits or other microelectronic devices. — *adj.* **microelectron′ic.** [**micro-** (1f).]

microencapsulation. See **microcapsule.**

microevolution *mī-krō-ēv-ə-lōō′shən, -ev-, n.* evolutionary change taking place over a relatively short period within a species or subspecies as a result of the repeated selection of certain characteristics. [**micro-** (1c).]

microfauna *mī′krō-fö-nə,* (or -*fö′nə*) *n.* extremely small animals, usu. those invisible to the naked eye. [**micro-** (1a,b).]

microfelsitic *mī-krə-fel-sit′ik, adj.* of the cryptocrystalline texture of a quartz-felsite groundmass. [**micro-** (1a).]

microfiche *mī′krə-fēsh, n.* a sheet of microfilm suitable for filing: — *pl.* **mī′crofiche, mī′crofiches** (-*fēsh*). [**micro-** (1f), and Fr. *fiche,* slip of paper, etc.]

microfilaria *mī-krō-fi-lā′ri-ə, n.* the early larval stage of certain parasitic *Nematoda.* [**micro-** (1a).]

microfilm *mī′krə-film, n.* a photographic film for preserving a microscopic record of a document, which can be enlarged in projection. — *v.t.* to record on microfilm. [**micro-** (1f).]

microflora *mī-krō-flō-rə, -flö-rə, n.* extremely small plants, usu. those invisible to the naked eye.   [**micro-** (1a,b).]

microform *mī′krə-förm, n.* any of the media of reproduction by microphotography, as microfiche, microfilm, videotape, etc.   [**micro-** (1f).]

microfossil *mī-krō-fos-l, -il, n.* a fossil that may only be examined by means of a microscope.   [**micro-** (1a,b).]

microgamete *mī-krə-gam′ēt,* or *-ēt′, n.* the smaller, generally the male, gamete.   [**micro-** (1a).]

microgram *mī′krə-gram, n.* a micrograph — a photograph or drawing of an object under the microscope: a message typed and photographically reduced for sending by air, enlarged on receipt and printed on a card: the card concerned.   [**micro-** (1f).]

microgranite *mī-krə-gran′it, n.* a completely but minutely crystalline rock of the composition of granite. — *adj.* **microgranit′ic.**   [**micro-** (1a).]

micrograph *mī′krə-gräf, n.* a pantograph instrument for minute writing or drawing: a minute picture: a drawing or photograph of a minute object as seen through a microscope. — *n.* **micrographer** (*mī-krog′rə-fər*) one who draws or describes microscopic objects. — *adj.* **micrographic** (*mī-krə-graf′ik*) pertaining to micrography: minutely written or delineated: showing intergrowth of crystalline constituents on a microscopic scale (*geol.*). — *n.* **microg′raphy** study with the microscope: the description of microscopic objects.   [**micro-** (1f) and Gr. *graphein,* to write.]

microgroove *mī′krə-gro͞ov, n.* the fine groove of long-playing gramophone records.   [**micro-** (1a).]

microinstruction *mī′krō-in-struk-shən,* (*comput.*) *n.* a single, simple command encoding any of the individual steps, (e.g. add, compare) to be carried out by a computer.   [**micro-** (1a).]

Microlepidoptera *mī-krō-lep-id-op′tər-ə, n.pl.* small moths of various kinds.   [**micro-** (1a).]

microlight *mī′krə-līt, n.* a very light miniature aircraft.   [**micro-** (1a).]

microlite *mī′krə-līt, n.* a mineral composed of calcium, tantalum, and oxygen, occurring in very small crystals: an incipient crystal, detected under the microscope by polarised light. — *n.* **mī′crolith** a microlite: a very small stone implement of the Stone Age, usu. used with a haft. — *adjs.* **microlith′ic; microlitic** (*-lit′ik*).   [**micro-** (1a) and Gr. *lithos,* a stone.]

micrology *mī-krol′ə-ji, n.* the study of microscopic objects: the study or discussion of trivialities. — *adjs.* **micrologic** (*-loj′*), **-al.** — *adv.* **microlog′ically.** — *n.* **microl′ogist.**   [Gr. *mikros,* little, *logos,* discourse.]

micro-manipulation *mī-krō-mə-nip-ū-lā′shən, n.* the technique of using delicate instruments, as **microneedles** and **micropipettes,** to work on cells, bacteria, etc., under high magnifications, or of working with extremely small quantities in microchemistry.   [**micro-** (1b, c).]

micro-meteorite *mī-krō-mē′tē-ə-rīt, n.* a particle of meteoric dust too small to be consumed by friction in the atmosphere.   [**micro-** (1a).]

micro-meteorology *mī-krō-mē-tē-ə-rol′ə-ji, n.* the study of atmospheric conditions over a small area, and usu. to a very limited height above the ground.   [**micro-** (1d).]

micrometer *mī-krom′i-tər, n.* an instrument, often attached to a microscope or telescope, for measuring very small distances or angles: (also **micrometer gauge, micrometer calliper(s)**) an instrument which measures small widths, lengths, etc., to a high degree of accuracy. — *adjs.* **micrometric** (*mī-krə-met′rik*), **-al.** — *n.* **microm′etry** measuring with a micrometer.   [**micro-** (1c).]

micrometre. See **micron.**

micromicr(o)- *mī-krō-mī-kr(ō)-* (*obs.;* now **pico-**) in composition, a millionth of a millionth part, as in **micromicrocurie** (used in measuring the quantity of a radioactive substance present in stable material), **micromicrofarad,** etc.   [**micro-** (2).]

micromillimetre *mī-krə-mil′i-mēt-ər, n.* one millionth of a millimetre (*obs.;* now **nan′ometre**): (*erroneously*) one thousandth of a millimetre.   [**micro-** (2).]

microminiature *mī-krō-min′i(-ə)-chər, adj.* made on an extremely small scale. — *n.* **mīcrominiaturisā′tion, -z-** reduction to extremely small size of scientific or technical equipment or any part of it. — *v.t.* **mīcromin′iaturise, -ize.**   [**micro-** (1f).]

micron, mikron *mī′kron, n.* (now *obs.,* better **mī′crometre**) one millionth of a metre (denoted by μ).   [Gr. *mikron,* neut. of *mikros,* little.]

microneedle *mī-krō-nēd-l, n.* See under **micro-manipulation.**

Micronesian *mī-krə-nē′zh(y)ən, -zyən, -zi-ən, adj.* pertaining to *Micronesia,* a group of small islands in the Pacific, north of New Guinea. — *n.* a native of the group.   [Gr. *mikros,* little, *nēsos,* an island.]

micronutrient *mī-krə-nū′tri-ənt, n.* a nutritive substance required in minute quantities by a plant. — Also *adj.*   [**micro-** (1a).]

micro-organism *mī-krō-ör′gən-izm, n.* a microscopic (or ultramicroscopic) organism.   [**micro-** (1a).]

micropalaeontology *mī-krō-pal-i-ion-tol′ə-ji, n.* a branch of palaeontology dealing with microfossils. — *n.* **micropalaeontol′ogist.**   [**micro-** (1a).]

micropegmatite *mī-krə-peg′mə-tīt, n.* a micrographic intergrowth of quartz and feldspar. — *adj.* **micropegmatitic** (*-tit′ik*).   [**micro-** (1a).]

microphone *mī′krə-fōn, n.* an instrument for intensifying sounds: a sensitive instrument (pop. contracted **mike** *mīk*), similar to a telephone transmitter, for picking up sound-waves to be broadcast or amplified and translating them, e.g. by means of a diaphragm and carbon granules, into a fluctuating electric current. — *adj.* **microphonic** (*-fon′ik*).   [Gr. *mikros,* small, *phōnē,* voice.]

microphotograph *mī-krə-fōt′ə-gräf, n.* strictly, a photograph reduced to microscopic size: loosely, a photomicrograph, or photograph of an object as magnified by the microscope. — *n.* **microphotographer** (*-og′rə-fər*). — *adj.* **microphotographic** (*-ə-graf′ik*). — *n.* **microphotog′raphy.**   [**micro-** (1f).]

microphyllous *mī-krō-fil′əs,* (*bot.*) *adj.* small-leaved.   [Gr. *mikros,* little, *phyllon,* leaf.]

microphysics *mī-krə-fiz′iks, n.sing.* physics dealing with subatomic particles.   [**micro-** (1c).]

microphyte *mī′krō-fīt, n.* a microscopic plant. — *adj.* **microphyt′ic.**   [**micro-** (1b).]

micropipette *mī-krō-pip-et′, n.* See under **micro-manipulation.**

microprint *mī′krō-print, n.* a microphotograph of e.g. printed text, reproduced on paper, card, etc. — *adj.* **mī′croprinted.** — *n.* **mī′croprinting.**   [**micro-** (1f).]

microprobe *mī-krō-prōb, n.* a device that produces a very thin electron beam by means of which the chemical make-up of various compounds may be examined.   [**micro-** (1b).]

microprocessor *mī-krō-prō′ses-ər, n.* an integrated circuit on a silicon chip, or a number of these, acting as the central processing unit of a computer.   [**micro-** (1f).]

micropropagation *mī-krō-pro-pə-gā′shən, n.* propagation by growing new plants from single cells of the parent plant.   [**micro-** (1c).]

micropsia *mī-krop′si-ə, n.* a condition in which objects look smaller than usual.   [Gr. *mikros,* little, *opsis,* appearance.]

micropterous *mī-krop′tər-əs, adj.* with reduced fins or hind-wings.   [Gr. *mikros,* little, *pteron,* wing.]

micropyle *mī-krə-pīl, n.* the orifice in the coats of the ovule leading to the apex of the nucellus, through which the pollen-tube commonly enters (*bot.*): an opening by which a spermatozoon may enter an ovum (*zool.*). — *adj.* **micropy′lar.**   [Gr. *mikros,* little, *pylē,* gate.]

microscope *mī′krə-skōp, n.* an instrument for magnifying minute objects. — *adjs.* **microscopic** (*-skop′ik*), **-al** pertaining to a microscope or to microscopy: magnifying: able to see minute objects: invisible or hardly visible without the aid of a microscope: minute. — *adv.* **microscop′ically.** — *ns.* **microscopist** (*mī-kros′kop-*

ist, *mī-krə-skō'pist*); **micros'copy.** — **acoustic microscope** one in which ultrasonic waves passed through the specimen are scanned by a laser beam; **come under the microscope** to be subjected to minute examination; **compound microscope, simple microscope** microscopes with respectively two lenses and a single lens; **electron, proton, ultraviolet microscope** one using a beam of electrons, protons, or ultraviolet rays; **phase-contrast, phase-difference, microscope** see **phase; reflecting microscope** see **reflect.** [Gr. *mikros*, little, *skopeein*, to look at.]

microseism *mī'krə-sīzm, n.* a slight earth-movement detectable only instrumentally. — *adjs.* **microseis'mic, -al.** — *ns.* **microseis'mograph** an instrument for recording microseisms and distant earthquakes; **microseismom'-eter** an instrument for measuring microseisms; **microseismom'etry.** [Gr. *mikros*, little, *seismos*, earthquake.]

microsome *mī'krə-sōm, n.* a minute granule or drop in cytoplasm. — *adj.* **microsō'mal.** [Gr. *mikros*, little, *sōma*, body.]

microspore *mī'krə-spōr, -spör, n.* the smaller of two forms of spore: a spore giving rise to a male gametophyte. — *ns.* **microsporangium** (*-spör-an'ji-əm*) a sporangium producing only microspores: — *pl.* **microsporan'gia; microsporophyll** (*-spör', -spör'ə-fil*) a sporophyll that carries or subtends only microsporangia. [micro- (1a).]

microstructure *mī-krō-struk'chər*, or *mī', n.* structure, especially of metals and alloys, as revealed by the microscope. [micro- (1a, b).]

microsurgery *mī-krō-sûr'jə-ri, n.* surgery performed on cells or other very small plant or body structures, requiring the use of a microscope. — *n.* **microsur'geon.** [micro- (1b).]

microtechnology *mī-krō-tek-nol'əj-i, n.* microelectronic technology. [micro- (1f).]

microtome *mī'krə-tōm, n.* an instrument for cutting thin sections of objects for microscopic examination. — *adjs.* **microtomic, -al** (*-tom'ik, -l*). — *ns.* **microtomist** (*-krot'ə-mist*); **microt'omy.** [Gr. *mikros*, little, *tomē*, a cut.]

microtone *mī'krə-tōn,* (*mus.*) *n.* an interval less than a semitone. — *n.* **microtonal'ity.** [micro- (1a).]

microtubule *mī-krō-tū'būl, n.* any of the relatively rigid structures in the cytoplasm of many plant and animal cells. — *adj.* **microtū'bular.** [micro- (1a).]

microwave *mī'krō-wāv, n.* in radio communication, one of very short wavelength: now usu. a wave in the radiation spectrum between normal radio waves and infrared. — Also *adj.* — **microwave oven** an oven in which food is cooked by the heat produced by microwaves passing through it. [micro- (1a).]

microwire *mī'krō-wīr, n.* a very strong, very fine filament of metal or other material. [micro- (1a).]

microwriter *mī-krō-rīt-ə, n.* a hand-held five- or six-key device by means of which text can be generated on a printer or VDU. [micro- (1a).]

micrurgy *mī'krûr-ji, n.* micro-manipulation. [micro- (1b, c) and Gr. *-ourgos* (as in *metallourgos*, working a mine) — *ergon*, work.]

Micrurus. See **Elaps.**

micturition *mik-tū-rish'ən, n.* the frequent desire to pass urine: (*loosely*) the act of urinating. — *n.* **mic'tion** (*obs.*) voiding urine. — *v.i.* **mic'turate** (*irregularly formed*) to urinate. [L. *micturīre, -ītum*, desiderative of *mingĕre, mi(n)ctum*, to pass urine, *mi(n)ctiō, -ōnis*, urination.]

mid- *mid-,* in composition, the middle part of: of or in the middle of. [From **mid,** adj.; not always hyphened.]

mid[1] *mid, adj.* middle: situated between extremes: uttered with the tongue in a position between high and low (*phon.*). — *n.* the middle. — *adj.* **midd'est** (*Spens.*) middle: middlemost. — *n.* **midst** middle. — *adv.* in the middle. — *prep.* (also **'midst** as if for **amidst**) amidst. (M.E. *middes,* from gen. of **mid,** with excrescent *t,* cf. **whilst;** perh. partly a superl.). — *adj.* **mid'most**

middlemost. — *n.* the very middle. — *adv.* in the very middle. — *prep.* in the very middle of. — **mid-age'** (*Shak.*) middle age; **mid-air'** a region somewhat above the ground: the midst of a course through the air. — Also *adj.* — *adj.* **mid'-Atlan'tic** evincing both British and American characteristics. — **mid'brain** the part of the brain derived from the second brain vesicle of the embryo; **mid'day** noon. — *adj.* of, at, or pertaining to, noon. — **mid'field** the middle area of a football, etc. pitch, not close to either team's goal: the players who operate in this area, acting as links between a team's defending and attacking players; **mid'-gut** that part of the alimentary canal formed from the original gastrula cavity and lined with endoderm: also, the small intestine; **mid'-heav'en** the middle of the sky or of heaven: the meridian; **mid'-hour** the middle time: an intervening hour; **mid'iron** a heavy golf club used for long approach shots. — *adj.* **mid'land** in the middle of, or surrounded by, land: distant from the coast: inland. — *n.* the interior of a country: (*pl.*) esp. (*cap.*) the central parts of England. — **mid'-leg'** the middle of the leg. — *adv.* as high or deep as the middle of the leg. — **mid'-Lent'** the middle of Lent: the fourth Sunday in Lent; **mid-life crisis** the feeling of panic, pointlessness, etc., experienced at middle age by those who are concerned that they are no longer young; **midlitt'oral** that part of the seashore that lies between high and low neap tidemarks. — Also *adj.* — **mid'=mor'ning; mid'night** the middle of the night: twelve o'clock at night: pitch darkness. — *adj.* of or at midnight: dark as midnight. — **midnight sun** the sun visible at midnight in the polar regions; **mid'noon'** noon; **mid'-o'cean; mid-off', mid-on'** (*cricket*) a fieldsman on the *off,* or *on,* side nearly in line with the bowler: his position; **mid'-point** a point lying halfway between two other points (whether in time or space): a point lying at the centre of an area; **mid'rib** the rib along the middle of a leaf; **mid'-sea'** the open sea; **mid'-seas'on** (also *adj.*). — *adj.* **mid'ship** in the middle of a ship. — **mid'shipman** once the title of a young officer (orig. quartered *amidships*) entering the navy, thereafter a junior ranking below a sub-lieutenant, but above a naval cadet, now, since 1957, only a shore ranking during training — (by landsmen) shortened colloquially to **mid, midd'y,** jocularly **mid'shipmate.** — *adv.* **mid'ships** amidships. — **mid-sky'** the middle of the sky; **midstream'** the middle of the stream. — *adv.* in the middle of the stream. — **mid'summer** (also *-sum'*) the middle of the summer: the summer solstice, about the 21st of June; **Midsummer day** the 24th of June, a quarter-day; **midsummer madness** madness attributed to the hot sun of midsummer; **midsummer moon** a season when madness was supposed to be rife. — *adj.* **mid-Victo'rian** of or characteristic of the middle part of Queen Victoria's reign. — **mid'-term'** the middle of an academic term, term of office, etc. — Also *adj.* — **mid'way** the middle of the way or distance: a middle course: a central avenue in an American fair or exhibition. — *adj.* in the middle of the way or distance. — *adv.* halfway. — *prep.* halfway along or across. — **Mid'-week** Wednesday (cf. Ger. *Mittwoch*). — *adj.* **mid'-week** in the middle of the week. — **Mid'west** Middle West; **mid'-wick'et** a fieldsman on the on side, about midway between mid-on and square leg: his position; **mid-win'ter** the middle of winter: the winter solstice (21st or 22nd December), or the time near it. — *adj.* **mid'-year** in the middle of the (academic) year. [O.E. *midd*; cf. Ger. *Mitte,* L. *medius,* Gr. *mesos*.]

mid[2]. Short for **midshipman** (see **mid**[1]).

'mid, mid, for **amid.**

Midas *mī'das, n.* a king of Phrygia whose touch turned all to gold, and on whom Apollo bestowed ass's ears: a genus of marmosets. — **Midas's ear** a shell of the genus Auricula; **Midas touch** the ability to make money easily.

midden *mid'ən, n.* a dunghill: a refuse-heap: a kitchen-midden (*ant.*). — **midd'en-cock'; midd'enstead** a place where dung is heaped up. [Scand., as Dan. *mödding* — *mög*, dung; cf. **muck**[1].]

middle *mid'l, adj.* equally distant (in measurement or in number of steps) from the extremes: avoiding extremes, done as a compromise: intermediate: intervening: of that voice which is intermediate between active and passive, reflexive or expressing an action in some way affecting the agent (*gram.*): (*cap.*; of languages) between Old and Modern (as *Middle English, Middle High German*). — *v.t.* to place in the middle: to fold in the middle (*naut.*): to hit (the ball) with the middle of the bat (*cricket*). — *n.* the middle point, part, or position: midst: the central portion, waist: the middle voice (*gram.*): the middle term (*log.*): a middle article. — **midd'le-age'**. — *adj.* **midd'le-aged'** (*-ājd'*) between youth and old age, variously reckoned to suit the reckoner. — **middle-age(d) spread** a thickening of the body attributable to the onset of middle-age; **Middle Ages** the time between the fall of the Western Roman empire and the Renaissance (5th–15th cent.); **Middle America** the countries lying between the United States of America and Colombia, sometimes including the West Indies: the American middle-class, esp. the conservative elements of it. — *n.* and *adj.* **Midd'le-Amer'ican**. — **middle article** a newspaper article of literary or general rather than topical interest. — *adj.* **midd'le-brack'et** in a midway grouping in a list. — **midd'lebreaker** (*U.S.*) a lister. — *adj.* **midd'lebrow** midway between highbrow and lowbrow. — Also *n.* — **middle C** the C in the middle of the piano keyboard: the first line below the treble or above the bass stave; **middle class** that part of the people which comes between the aristocracy and the working-class. — Also *adj.* — **middle distance** in a picture, the middle ground. — *adj.* **midd'le-dis'tance** in athletics, of or denoting a race of 400, 800, or 1500 metres, or an athlete who takes part in such a race. — **middle ear** the part of the ear containing the malleus, incus and stapes; **midd'le-earth'** the earth, considered as placed between the upper and lower regions; **Middle East** formerly the countries from Iran to Burma: now generally used of an area including the Arabic-speaking countries around the eastern end of the Mediterranean Sea and in the Arabian Peninsula, along with Greece, Turkey, Cyprus, Iran and the greater part of N. Africa. — *adj.* **Midd'le-East'ern**. — **Midd'le-East'erner; middle eight** an eight-bar section occurring two-thirds of the way through a conventionally structured pop song and acting as a foil to the rest of the piece; **Middle English** see **English; middle game** the part of a chess game between the opening and the end game; **middle ground** the part of a picture between the foreground and background: a compromise position. — *adj.* **midd'le-in'come** having, or relating to those who have, an average income which makes them neither rich nor poor. — **Middle Kingdom** China; **midd'leman** one occupying a middle position: an intermediary, esp. between producer and consumer: in Ireland, one who rents land in large tracts, and lets it in small portions; **middle management** the junior managerial executives and senior supervisory personnel in a firm. — *adj.* **midd'lemost** nearest the middle. — **middle name** any name between a person's first name and surname: the notable quality or characteristic of a specified thing or person (*facet.*). — *adj.* **midd'le-of-the-road'** midway between extremes. — **middle passage** the voyage across the Atlantic from Africa to the West Indies on board a slave-ship; **middle school** a school for children between the ages of about 9 to 13: in some secondary schools, an administrative unit usu. comprising the third and fourth forms. — *adj.* **midd'le-sized** of average size. — **Middle States** New York, New Jersey, Pennsylvania, Delaware; **midd'le-stitch'ing** monk's-seam; **middle term** (*log.*) that term of a syllogism which appears in both premises but not in the conclusion; **middle watch** that from midnight to 4 a.m.; **midd'le-weight** a boxer (over 10 st 7 lb. and not over 11 st. 6

lb. — professional only) or jockey of intermediate weight (**light-middleweight** a boxer, amateur only, not over 11 st. 2 lb.); **Middle West** the region between the Appalachians and the Rockies, the Mississippi basin as far south as Kansas, Missouri, and the Ohio River; **midd'le-world** middle-earth. — **in the middle of** occupied with, engaged in (doing something): during: while. [O.E. *middel* (adj.); Du. *middel*, Ger. *Mittel*; see **mid**[1].]

middling *mid'ling, adj.* intermediate (*obs.*): moderate (*coll.*): indifferent: mediocre: fairly good. — *adv.* (*coll.*) fairly: fairly well. — *n.* (usu. in *pl.*) goods of a middle quality: the coarser part of ground wheat: partially concentrated ore. [Orig. Scots — **mid**[1] and suff. -ling.]

middy[1] *mid'i, n.* a colloquial short form of **midshipman**: (also **middy blouse**) a loose blouse worn, esp. formerly, by women and esp. children, having a collar with a broad flap at the back in the style of a sailor's uniform.

middy[2] *mid'i, (Austr. coll.) n.* a measure of beer, varying in amount from one place to another: the glass containing it. [Ety. dub.]

Midgard *mid'gärd, (Scand. myth.) n.* the abode of men, middle-earth. [O.N. *mithgarthr*, mid-yard.]

midge *mij, n.* a small gnat-like fly, esp. of the family Chironomidae: a very small person. — *n.* **midg'et** something very small of its kind: a very small person. [O.E. *mycg, mycge*; Ger. *Mücke*.]

Midi *mē-dē', n.* the south (of France). — *n.* **midinette** (*-net'*) a Paris work-girl or a shop-girl in the millinery or fashion trade (noticeable at lunch-hour). [Fr. *midi*, midday; *midinette* is said to be from *midi* and *dînette*, snack.]

midi- *mid'i-,* in composition, of middle size, length, etc., as **mid'i-skirt**, one reaching to about mid-calf. [**mid**[1]; cf. **mini-**.]

midi *mid'i, n.* short for **midi-skirt**.

midland, midmost, midnight, etc. See **mid**[1].

Midrash *mid'rash, n.* the Hebrew exposition of the Old Testament — its two divisions, *Haggada* and *Halachah*: — *pl.* **Midrashim** (*mid-rä'shēm*) commentaries on individual books or sections of the Old Testament. [Heb., exposition.]

midriff *mid'rif, n.* the diaphragm: the part of a woman's garment that fits over the diaphragm. [O.E. *midd*, middle, *hrif*, belly.]

midshipman, midst. See **mid**[1].

midwife *mid'wīf, n.* a woman, or (*rarely*) a man, who assists women in childbirth: *pl.* **midwives** (*mid'wīvz*). — *v.t.* (also **mid'wive**; *-wīv*) to help in bringing forth (a child) (also *fig.*): — *pr.p.* **-wīfing, -wīving**; *pa.t., pa.p.* **-wifed, -wīved**. — *n.* **mid'wifery** (*-wif-ə-ri, -wif-ri, -if-ri, -wīf'ri*) the art or practice of a midwife: assistance at childbirth: obstetrics. — **midwife toad** either of two species of small European toad, *Alytes obstetricans* and *Alytes cisternasi*, so called because the males bear the fertilised eggs on their backs until they hatch. [O.E. *mid*, with (Ger. *mit*, Gr. *meta*), *wīf*, woman.]

mien *mēn, n.* an air or look, manner, bearing (*literary*): expression of face (*obs.*). [Perh. **demean**, influenced by Fr. *mine*, of unknown origin.]

mieve *mēv, (Spens.) v.t.* Same as **move**.

miff *mif, (coll.) n.* a slight feeling or fit of resentment. — *v.t.* to put out of humour. — *v.i.* to take offence: to wither away. — *adj.* **miffed**. — *n.* **miff'iness**. — *adj.* **miff'y** ready to take offence or to wither away: touchy. — Also (*obs.*) **miff'y**. [Cf. Ger. *muffen*, to sulk.]

might[1] *mīt, pa.t.* of **may**[1]. — **might(e)st** see **may**[1]. — **might'-have-been** one who, or that which, might have been, or might have come to something.

might[2] *mīt, n.* power: ability: strength: energy or intensity of purpose or feeling. — *adj.* **might'ful** (*Shak.*) mighty: powerful. — *adv.* **might'ily**. — *n.* **might'iness** the state of being mighty: power: greatness: great amount: a title of dignity: excellency. — *adj.* **might'y** having greater power: strong: valiant: very great: important: exhibiting might: wonderful. — *adv.* (now *coll.*, usu.

with a tinge of irony except in *U.S.*) very. — **might and main** utmost strength.

mignon *mē-nyõ*, (Fr.) *adj.* small and dainty: — *fem.* **mignonne** (*mē-nyon*).

mignonette *min-yə-net'*, *n.* a sweet-scented Reseda: a fine kind of lace. [Fr. *mignonette*, fem. dim. of *mignon*, daintily small, a darling.]

migraine (from 18th cent.) *mē'grān, mī'*, **megrim** (from 14th cent.) *mē'grim, ns.* a pain affecting only one half of the head or face and usu. accompanied by nausea: a condition marked by recurring migraines: (for the fol. meanings, **megrim**) vertigo: (*pl.*) lowness of spirits: a caprice (*arch.*). — *n.* **migraineur** (*-œr'*) one who suffers migraines. — *adj.* **mi'grainous**. [Fr. *migraine* — Gr. *hēmikrāniā* — *hēmi*, half, *krānion*, skull.]

migrate *mī-grāt', v.i.* to pass from one place to another: to change one's abode to another country, college, etc.: to change habitat periodically: to move (as parasites, phagocytes, etc.) to another part of the body: to pass in a stream (as ions, particles). — *n.* **mi'grant** a person or animal that migrates or is migrating. — Also *adj.* — *adj.* **mi'gratory** (*-grə-tə-ri*) migrating or accustomed to migrate: wandering. — *ns.* **migrā'tion** a change of abode: a removal from one country or climate to another, esp. in a body: a number removing together; **migrā'tionist** one who emigrates: one who explains facts by a theory of migration; **mi'grātor**. [L. *migrāre, -ātum*; cf. *meāre*, to go.]

mihrab *mē-räb'*, or *mēhh'*, *n.* a niche or slab in a mosque marking the direction of Mecca. [Ar. *mihrāb*.]

mikado *mi-kä'dō*, *n.* a title given by foreigners to the Emperor of Japan: — *pl.* **mika'dos**. [Jap., exalted gate.]

mike[1] *mīk*, *n.* a contraction of **microphone** and **microscope**.

mike[2]. Variant of **mick**.

mikron. See **micron**.

mil *mil*, *n.* a unit (1/1000 in.) in measuring the diameter of wire: a proposed coin = £1/1000: in Cyprus, a coin of this value: in pharmacy, a millilitre: a unit of angular measurement, used esp. with artillery, equal to 1/6400 of a circle or 0.05625°. [L. *mīlle*, a thousand.]

milady, miladi *mi-lād'i*, *n.* a French-English term for an English lady of quality. [Fr. modification of **my lady**.]

milage. See **mile**.

milch *milch, milsh, adj.* giving milk. — **milch'-cow** a cow yielding milk or kept for milking: a ready source of gain or money (*fig.*). [O.E. *milce* (found in the compound *thri-milce*, May, when cows can be milked thrice a day); cf. **milk**.]

mild *mīld, adj.* gentle in temper and disposition: not sharp or bitter: acting gently: gently and pleasantly affecting the senses: soft: calm. — *n.* mild ale. — *v.t.* **mild'en** to render mild. — *v.i.* to become mild. — *adv.* **mild'ly**. — *n.* **mild'ness**. — **mild ale** formerly, new ale, without the taste that comes from keeping: now ale with less hop flavouring than pale ale. — *adj.* **mild'-spok'en** having a mild manner of speech. — **mild steel** steel with little carbon. — **put it mildly** to understate the case. [O.E. *milde*, mild; cf. Ger. *mild*, O.N. *mildr*, gracious, etc.]

mildew *mil'dū*, *n.* honey-dew (*obs.*): a disease on plants, caused by the growth of minute fungi (Erysiphe, Oidium, etc.): a similar appearance on other things or of another kind: a fungus causing the disease. — *v.t.* to taint with mildew. — *adj.* **mil'dewy**. [O.E. *meledēaw, mildēaw*, from a lost word for honey and *dēaw*, dew; influenced by *melu*, meal.]

mile *mīl*, *n.* a Roman unit of length, 1000 (double) paces (*mīlle passūs* or *passuum*; about 1611 English yards): applied to various later units, now in Britain and U.S. to one of 1760 yards or 5280 feet (1.61 km.) — *statute mile*. — *ns.* **mīl'age, mile'age** the total number of miles covered by a motor vehicle, etc.: (also **mil(e)age allowance**) travelling allowance at so much a mile: miles travelled per gallon of fuel: use, benefit (*fig. coll.*); **mī'ler** a runner of a mile race. — **mile'-castle** one of a

series of small forts placed at mile intervals along a Roman wall; **mileom'eter, mīlom'eter** an instrument that records the number of miles that a vehicle, etc. has travelled; **mile'stone** a stone or mark showing distance in miles: a stage or reckoning-point: an important event, stage, etc. (*fig.*). — **geographical** or **nautical mile** one minute of longitude measured along the equator — 6082.66 feet: in British practice, *Admiralty measured mile*, 6080 feet (1.8532 km.); *international nautical mile* — official unit in U.S. since 1954 — 6076.1033 feet, or 1.852 km; **Irish mile** (*obs.*) 2240 yards; **Scots mile** (*obs.*) about 1976 yards. [O.E. *mīl* — L. *mīlia*, pl. of *mīlle* (*passuum*) a thousand (paces).]

miles gloriosus *mē'lāz glōr-ē-ō'səs, mī'lēs, glōr-, -sōōs*, (L.) *n.* a vainglorious soldier, used as a stock character in Roman and later comedy: *pl.* **milites gloriosi** (*mē'lē-tāz glōr-ē-ō'sē, mī'li-tēz, glōr-, -sī*). [From the title and the hero of a play by Plautus.]

Milesian[1] *mi-lē'zyən, -zhyən, -zhən*, or *mī-, adj.* of *Miletus*, an Ionian Greek city of Asia Minor. — *n.* a native or citizen of Miletus. — **Milesian tales** witty voluptuous tales, from a lost book so called, by Aristides 'of Miletus' (2nd cent. B.C.). [Gr. *Mīlēsios — Mīlētos*.]

Milesian[2] *mi-lē'shyən, -shən, -zhyən, -zhən*, or *mī-, adj.* of *Milesius* or *Miledh*, a mythical king of Spain, or his sons and their followers who seized Ireland: Irish. — *n.* (usu. *jocular*) an Irishman.

milfoil *mil'foil*, *n.* yarrow or other species of Achillea: extended to other plants with finely divided leaves, as **wat'er-mil'foil** (Myriophyllum, family Haloragidaceae). [O.Fr. — L. *mīllefolium — mīlle*, a thousand, *folium*, a leaf.]

miliary *mil'i-ər-i, adj.* like a millet-seed: characterised by an eruption like millet-seeds. — *n.* **miliaria** (*mil-i-ā'ri-ə*) prickly-heat. [L. *miliārius — milium*, millet.]

milieu *mēl-yø'*, *n.* environment, setting, medium, element: — *pl.* **milieus'**, or **milieux'** (*-yø*). [Fr., middle.]

militant *mil'it-ənt, adj.* fighting: engaged in warfare: actively contending: combative: using violence: militaristic. — *n.* one who takes active part in a struggle: one who seeks to advance a cause by violence. — *n.* **mil'itancy**. — *adv.* **mil'itantly**. — *adj.* **mil'itar** (*obs.*) military. — *adv.* **mil'itarily**. — *n.* **militarīsā'tion, -z-**. — *v.t.* **mil'itarise, -ize** to reduce or convert to a military model or method: to make militaristic: to subject to military domination. — *ns.* **mil'itarism** an excess of the military spirit: domination by an army, or military class or ideals: belief in such domination: a tendency to overvalue military power or to view things from the soldier's point of view; **mil'itarist** a soldier (*Shak.*): a student of military science: one imbued with militarism. — *adjs.* **militarist'ic**; **mil'itary** pertaining to soldiers, armies, or warfare: warlike. — *n.* soldiery: the army: a soldier (*obs.*). — *v.i.* **mil'itate** to serve as a soldier (*arch.*): to contend: to have weight, tell (esp. with *against*): to fight for a cause. — **military academy** a training-college for army officer cadets; **military band** a band of brasses, woodwinds, and percussion; **military cross** a decoration (M.C.) awarded since 1914 to army officers (below major) and warrant officers; **military honours** see **honour**; **military medal** a medal awarded since 1916 to non-commissioned and warrant officers and serving men; **military police** a body of men and women functioning as a police force within the army; **military policeman, -woman**. — **church militant** see **church**. [L. *mīles, -itis*, a soldier, *mīlitāris*, military, *mīlitāre, -ātum*, to serve as a soldier.]

militaria *mil-i-tā'ri-ə, n.pl.* weapons, uniforms, and other things connected with wars past and present. [*military*, and noun suffix *-ia*; or L., things military, neut. pl. of *mīlitāris*, military.]

militarise, etc. See **militant**.

militia *mi-lish'ə*, *n.* a body of men enrolled and drilled as soldiers, but only liable to home service (transformed in 1908 into the Special Reserve; again called militia, 1921): the National Guard and its reserve (*U.S.*): a general levy: a territorial force: troops of the second line. — **milit′iaman.** [L. *mīlitia*, military service or force — *mīles*, a soldier.]

milk *milk, n.* a white liquid secreted by female mammals for the nourishment of their young: a milklike juice or preparation: lactation. — *v.t.* to squeeze or draw milk from: to supply with milk: to extract money, venom, etc., from: to extract: to manipulate as if milking a cow. — *v.i.* to yield milk. — *adj.* **milk′en** (*rare*) of or like milk. — *n.* **milk′er** one who milks cows, etc.: a machine for milking cows: a cow that gives milk. — *adv.* **milk′ily.** — *ns.* **milk′iness** cloudiness: mildness; **milk′ing** the act or art of milking (*lit.* or *fig.*): the amount of milk drawn at one time. — Also *adj.* — *adjs.* **milk′less; milk′like; milk′y** made of, full of, like, or yielding, milk: clouded: soft: gentle. — *adj.* **milk′-and-wa′ter** insipid: wishy-washy. — **milk′-bar** a shop where milk, milk-shakes, and the like are sold for drinking on the spot; **milk cap** any fungus of the large and mainly inedible genus *Lactarius*, so called because of a milky fluid that it exudes when bruised; **milk chocolate** eating chocolate made from cocoa, cocoa-butter, sugar, and condensed or dried milk; **milk′-cow** a milch-cow; **milk-denti′tion** the first set of teeth; **milk′en-way** (*Bacon*) the Milky Way; **milk′-fe′ver** a fever accompanying the secretion of milk shortly after childbirth: in cows, a condition that may occur (without fever) after calving, characterised by low sugar and calcium levels in the blood, paralysis and unconsciousness; **milk′fish** a large silvery fish (*Chanos chanos*) of the Pacific and Indian Oceans, widely used as food and often bred in fish-farms: a percoid fish (*Parascorpis typus*) of the coastal water of southern Africa: the biche-de-mer (*Austr.*); **milk′-float** a vehicle in which milk-bottles are carried; **milk′-gland** a mammary gland; **milk glass** a usu. white, but sometimes coloured, opaque glass; **milk′-house** a place for keeping milk; **milking machine** a machine for milking cows; **milking-parlour** see **parlour; milk′ing-stool** a stool on which the milker sits; **milk′ing-time; milk′-kin′ship** the bond arising from fostering; **milk′-leg** white-leg. — *adj.* **milk′=liv′ered** (*Shak.*) white-livered. — **milk′-loaf** a loaf of a sweetish kind of bread; **milk′maid** a woman who milks; **milk′man** a man who sells or delivers milk; **milk′-mo′lar** a grinding milk-tooth, shed and superseded by a premolar; **milk′-porr′idge** porridge made with milk instead of water; **milk′-pudd′ing** rice, tapioca, etc., cooked with milk; **milk′-punch** a drink made of milk, rum or whisky, sugar, and nutmeg; **milk round** a milkman's normal morning route: the periodic recruitment of undergraduates by large companies; **milk′-run** a milkman's morning round: a routine flight (*U.S. airmen's slang*); **milk′-shake** milk shaken up with a flavouring; **milk sickness** trembles: the acute trembling, vomiting and weakness occurring in humans as a result of the consumption of meat or dairy products of cattle afflicted with trembles; **milk snake** *Lampropeltis doliata*, a non-venomous, North American snake of the Colubridae family, popularly believed to milk cattle; **milk′-sop** a piece of bread sopped or soaked in milk: a soft, unadventurous, effeminate fellow; **milk stout** stout sweetened with lactose; **milk′-su′gar** lactose; **milk′-this′tle** lady's thistle (*Silybum marianum*), with white-veined leaves; **milk′-tooth** one of the first or deciduous set of teeth; **milk′-tree** a tree yielding a milklike nourishing juice, as the cow-tree of Venezuela, the massaranduba of Pará; **milk′-vetch** a plant of the genus Astragalus, cultivated as fodder and supposed to increase yield of milk; **milk′-walk** a milkman's round. — *adj.* **milk′-warm** warm as new milk. — **milk′-weed** a plant of the genus Asclepias, from its milky juice (**milk-weed butterfly** the monarch butterfly). — *adj.* **milk′-white.** — **milk′wood** any of various trees with latex; **milk′wort** a plant (Polygala) supposed by some to promote production of milk (**sea′-milkwort** Glaux); **Milky Way** the Galaxy. — **milk and honey** abundance, plenty: luxury; **milk of human kindness** (*Shak.*) compassionate nature; **milk of lime, of magne-**

sia a suspension of calcium hydroxide, magnesium hydroxide, in water; **milk of sulphur** precipitated sulphur. [O.E. (Mercian) *milc* (W.S. *meolc*), milk; Ger. *Milch*, milk; L. *mulgēre*, Gr. *amelgein*, to milk.]

mill[1] *mil, n.* a machine for grinding by crushing between hard, rough surfaces, or for more or less similar operations: a building or factory where corn is ground, or manufacture of some kind is carried on, as spinning and weaving, paper-making, sawing of timber: a snuff-box (commonly **mull**), orig. one with grinding apparatus (*Scot.*): a contest at boxing (*slang*). — *v.t.* to grind: to press, stamp, roll, cut into bars, full, furrow the edges of, or otherwise treat in a mill: to froth up: to beat severely with the fists (*slang*): to revolve in the mind. — *v.i.* to move round in a curve: to practise the business of a miller: to box (*slang*): (often with *about*, *around*; of crowd) to move in an aimless and confused manner. — *adj.* **milled** prepared by a grinding-mill or a coining-press: transversely grooved on the edge (as a coin or screw-head): treated by machinery, esp. smoothed by calendering rollers in a paper-mill. — *ns.* **mill′er** one who owns or works a mill; **mill′ing** the business of a miller: the act of passing anything through a mill: the act of fulling cloth: the process of turning and ridging the edge of a screw-head or coin: a gruelling: aimless and confused movement of a crowd; **milloc′racy** a governing class of mill-owners, or their rule; **mill′ocrat.** — **mill′-board** stout pasteboard, used esp. in binding books; **mill′dam** the dam of a millpond: a millpond: a millrace or tail-race (*Scot.*); **miller's dog** same as **tope**[3]; **mill′er's-thumb** the bull-head; **mill′-eye** the opening by which meal comes from a mill; **mill′-girl; mill′-hand** a factory worker; **mill′-horse** a horse that turns a mill; **milling machine** a machine-tool for shaping metal, with rotating cutters; **mill′-owner; mill′pond** a pond to hold water for driving a mill (proverbially smooth): the Atlantic Ocean (*facet.*); **mill′race** the current of water that turns a mill-wheel, or the channel in which it runs; **mill′rind** an iron support fitted across the hole in an upper millstone; **mill′-run** a millrace: a test of the quality or mineral content of ore or rock by milling it; **mill′=six′pence** (*Shak.*) a milled sixpence; **mill′stone** one of the two stones used in a mill for grinding corn: a very heavy burden (*fig.*); **mill′stone-grit′** a hard, gritty sandstone suitable for millstones: (*cap.*) a series of grits, sandstones, shales, underlying the British Coal Measures; **mill′-stream** the stream of water that turns a mill-wheel; **mill′tail** a tailrace; **mill′-tooth** a molar; **mill′-wheel** a waterwheel used for driving a mill; **mill′=work** the machinery of a mill: the planning and putting up of machinery in mills; **mill′wright** a wright or mechanic who builds and repairs mills. — *adj.* **run-of=the-mill** see **run.** — **gastric mill** in Malacostraca, a digestive organ, sometimes known as the stomach, provided with muscles and ossicles for trituration of food; **go, put, through the mill** to undergo, subject to, probationary hardships, suffering or experience, or severe handling; **see through a millstone** to see far into or through difficult questions. [O.E. *myln* — L.L. *molīna* — L. *mola*, a mill — *molēre*, to grind.]

mill[2] *mil, n.* the thousandth part of a dollar (not coined) (*U.S.*): a mil. [L. *mīlle*, a thousand.]

mill[3] *mil,* (*slang*) *v.t.* and *v.i.* to rob: to steal.

mille *mēl,* (Fr.) *n.* thousand. — *ns.* **millefeuille(s)** (*mēl-fœy′;* Fr. *feuille*, leaf) a layered cake made with puff-pastry; **millefleurs** (*mēl-flœr;* Fr. *fleur*, flower) a perfume prepared from many kinds of flowers: (also **mille fleurs**) a floral pattern used in tapestry, on porcelain, etc.

millefiori *mēl-e-fē-ō′rē,* (It.) *n.* ornamental glass made by fusing coloured rods together. [Thousand flowers.]

millenary *mil′in-ər-i* (also *-ēn′,* or *-en′*), *n.* a thousand: a thousand years: a thousandth anniversary: a signatory of the Millenary Petition (*hist.*): a believer in the millennium. — *adj.* consisting of a thousand, or a thousand years: pertaining to the millennium or to belief in it. — *adj.* **millenā′rian** pertaining to the millennium. — *n.* a believer in the millennium. — *ns.* **millenā′rianism, mill′enărism.** — **Millenary Petition** a petition of Puritan tendency, signed by nearly a thousand clergymen, presented to James I in 1603. [L. *mīllēnārius*, of a thousand — *mīlle*.]

millennium *mil-en′i-əm, n.* a thousand years: a thousandth anniversary, millenary: the thousand years after the second coming of Christ: (usu. *ironical*) a coming golden age: — *pl.* **millenn′ia, millenn′iums.** — *adj.* **millenn′ial.** — *ns.* **millenn′ialist** a believer in the millennium; **millenn′ianism, millenn′iarism.** [L. *mīlle*, a thousand, *annus*, a year.]

millepede. See **millipede.**

millepore *mil′i-pōr, -pör, n.* a hydrozoan coral with many pores or polyp-cells. [L. *mīlle*, a thousand, *porus* — Gr. *poros*, a passage.]

Millerian *mil-ēr′i-ən, adj.* pertaining to W. H. *Miller* (1801–80), mineralogist, or to the crystallographic notation used by him, by which a plane is represented by indices which are the reciprocals of its intercepts on the axes (expressed as fractions of the parameters). — *n.* **mill′erite** native nickel sulphide, crystallising in needles, named in his honour.

millesimal *mil-es′im-əl, adj.* thousandth: consisting of thousandth parts. — *adv.* **milles′imally.** [L. *mīllēsimus* — *mīlle*, a thousand.]

millet *mil′it, n.* a food-grain (*Panicum miliaceum*): extended to other species and genera (Setaria, Panicum, etc.). — **mill′et-grass** a tall panicled woodland grass (*Milium effusum*); **mill′et-seed.** — *adj.* of the size or appearance of seeds of millet: miliary. [Fr. *millet* — L. *milium*.]

milli- *mil′i-*, in composition, in names of units, a thousandth part. — *ns.* **mill′iampere, mill′iare** (*-är*), **mill′ibar,** etc., a thousandth part of an *ampere, are, bar*, etc. — **millimicro-** (*obs.*) in composition, nano-; **millimilli-** (*obs.*) in composition, micro-. [L. *mīlle*, a thousand.]

Millian *mil′i-ən, n.* a follower of the philosopher John Stuart *Mill* (1806–73). — Also *adj.*

milliard *mil′yärd, n.* a thousand million. [Fr., — L. *mīlle*, a thousand.]

milliary *mil′i-ər-i, adj.* pertaining to a Roman mile. — *n.* a Roman milestone. [L. *mīlliārius, -a, -um.*]

millième *mēl-yem′, n.* a coin representing one thousandth of the basic unit of currency, as in Egypt. — Also **millime** (*mē-lēm′*) in Tunisia. [Fr., — L. *mīlle*, a thousand.]

milliner *mil′in-ər, n.* orig. a dealer in goods made in *Milan* — 'fancy goods': one who makes or sells women's headgear, trimmings, etc. — *n.* **mill′inery** the articles made or sold by milliners: the industry of making them. — **horse′-mill′iner** see **horse.** [*Milaner*, a trader in Milan wares, esp. silks and ribbons.]

million *mil′yən, n.* a thousand thousands (1 000 000): a very great number: a million pounds, dollars, etc.: (in *pl.*) the guppy. — Also *adj.* — *n.* **millionaire** (*-ār′*) a man worth a million pounds, dollars, etc. (more or less): — *fem.* **millionair′ess.** — *adj.* **mill′ionary** pertaining to, or consisting of, millions. — *adj.* and *adv.* **mill′ionfold** (usu. preceded by *a* or a numeral). — *adj.* and *n.* **mill′ionth** the ten hundred thousandth. — **the million** the great body of the people generally. [Fr., — L.L. *mīlliō, -ōnis* — L. *mīlle*, a thousand.]

millipede, millepede *mil′i-pēd, n.* any myriapod of the class Chilognatha, vegetarian cylindrical animals with many joints, most of which bear two pairs of legs: a woodlouse (*rarely*). — Also **mill′iped, mill′eped** (*-ped*). [L. *mīllepeda*, a woodlouse — *mīlle*, a thousand, *pēs, pēdis*, a foot.]

mill-mountain *mil′mownt′ən, n.* purging flax (see **flax**). [Origin unknown.]

Mills bomb, grenade *milz bom, gri-nād′*, a type of handgrenade, invented by Sir William *Mills* (1856–1932).

milo *mī′lō, n.* any of several drought-resistant varieties of sorghum, orig. from Africa but introduced elsewhere, cultivated as a grain and fodder crop: — *pl.*

mī′los. — Also **milo maize.** [Sotho *maili*.]

milometer. See **mileometer.**

milor, milord *mi-lör(d)′, n.* a rich Englishman. [Fr. modification of **my lord.**]

Milquetoast *milk′tōst, n.* (also without *cap.*) a very timid, unassertive person. [From the comic-strip character Caspar *Milquetoast* created by the American cartoonist H.T. Webster *c.* 1952.]

milreis *mil′rās, n.* 1000 reis: a Port. coin superseded by the escudo: a coin of Brazil (now cruzeiro). [Port., thousand reis.]

milsey *mil′si, (Scot.) n.* a milk-strainer. [**milk,** and either **sye** or **sile.**]

milt *milt,* **melt** *melt, ns.* the spleen (also, in Jewish cookery, **miltz** *milts*): the soft roe of male fishes. — *v.t.* (of fishes) to impregnate. — *n.* **milt′er** a male fish, esp. in the breeding season. [O.E. *milte*, Ger. *Milz*, spleen.]

Miltonia *mil-tō′ni-ə, n.* a genus of tropical American orchids with brightly-coloured flowers: (without *cap.*) a plant of the genus. [After Charles Fitzwilliam, Viscount *Milton* (1786–1857), English statesman and horticulturist.]

Miltonic *mil-ton′ik, adj.* relating to *Milton* (1608–1674), or relating to his poetry, or in his manner. — *adj.* and *n.* **Miltonian** (*-tōn′i-ən*). — *n.* **Mil′tonism** (*-tən-izm*). — **Miltonic sonnet** see **sonnet.**

Miltown® *mil′town, n.* meprobamate.

miltz. See **milt.**

Milvus *mil′vəs, n.* the kite genus. — *adj.* **mil′vine.** [L. *milvus*, a kite.]

mim *mim,* (*Scot.* and *dial.*) *adj.* demure, prim. — *adj.* **mim′-mou'd** (*-mōōd*; Scots form of **mouthed**). [Imit.]

mimbar *mim′bär*, **minbar** *min′, ns.* a mosque pulpit. [Ar. *minbar.*]

mime *mīm, n.* an ancient farcical play of real life, with mimicry (esp. in its Latin form): an actor in such a farce: a play without dialogue, relying solely on movement, expression, etc.: an actor in such a play: mimicry without words: a mimic: a buffoon. — *v.t.* and *v.i.* to act as a mime: to act with mimicry: to mimic. — *ns.* **mīm′er; mimesis** (*mim-* or *mīm-ē′sis*) imitation or representation in art: the rhetorical use of a person's supposed or imaginable words: simulation of one disease by another (*med.*): mimicry (*biol.*); **mime′ster.** — *adjs.* **mimet′ic, -al** (*mim-* or *mīm-*) imitative: mimic: pertaining to, showing mimicry, mimesis or miming. — *adv.* **mimet′ically.** — *ns.* **mimetite** (*mim′i-, mīm′i-*) a mineral, lead arsenate and chloride (from its resemblance to pyromorphite); **mimic** (*mim′ik*) a mime-actor (*obs.*): one who imitates, esp. one who performs in ludicrous imitation of others' speech and gestures: an unsuccessful imitator or imitation: a plant or animal exemplifying mimicry. — *adj.* miming (*obs.*): imitative: mock or sham. — *v.t.* to imitate, esp. in ridicule or so as to incur ridicule: to ape: to produce an imitation of: to resemble deceptively: — *pr.p.* **mim′icking;** *pa.t.* and *pa.p.* **mim′icked.** — *adj.* (*obs.*) **mimical** (*mim′*). — *ns.* **mim′icker; mimicry** (*mim′*) an act of mimicking: an advantageous superficial resemblance to some other species or object (*biol.*); **mīmog′rapher** a writer of mimes; **mīmog′raphy; Mīmus** the mocking-bird genus. [Gr. *mīmos*, a mime, *mīmēsis*, imitation, *mīmētēs*, an imitator.]

mimeograph *mim′i-ō-gräf, n.* an apparatus on which handwritten or typescript sheets can be reproduced from a stencil: a copy so produced. — *v.t.* to produce a copy or copies of (something) in this way. [*Mimeograph*, formerly a trademark.]

mimer ... mimetite. See **mime.**

mimic¹, mimmick. See **minnick.**

mimic², mimicker, mimographer, Mimus, etc. See **mime.**

miminy-piminy *mim′i-ni-pim′i-ni.* Same as **niminy-piminy.**

Mimosa *mim-ō′zə, n.* the sensitive plant genus: (without *cap.*) a plant of this genus: (without *cap.*) popularly extended to *Acacia* and other genera of the **Mimosā′ceae** (*mim-* or *mīm-*) a regular-flowered family of

Leguminosae. — *adj.* **mimosā'ceous** (*mim-* or *mīm-*). [Gr. *mīmos*, a mimic.]

Mimulus *mim'ū-ləs, n.* the musk and monkey-flower genus of the figwort family: (without *cap.*) a plant of the genus. [Gr. *mīmos*, a mime, with L. dim. suffix *-ulus*, from the grinning corolla.]

mina¹ *mī'nə, n.* a Greek weight, or sum of money, 100 drachmas: a weight of money valued at fifty, or sometimes sixty, shekels (*B.*): — *pl.* **mī'nas, -nae** (*-ē*). — Also **maneh** (*mä'ne*), **mna** (*mnä*). [L. *mina* — Gr. *mnā*; cf. Heb. *māneh*.]

mina². Same as **myna**.

minacious *min-ā'shəs, adj.* threatening. — *n.* **minacity** (*-as'*). [L. *mināx, -ācis* — *minārī*, to threaten.]

Minamata disease *mi-nə-mä'tə diz-ēz'* a disease caused by eating fish contaminated by industrial waste containing mercury compounds, and characterised by a usu. permanent condition involving impairment of speech and sight, muscular weakness, paralysis, etc., and sometimes coma or death. [From *Minamata*, a town in Japan where the disease was first recognised.]

minar *min-är', n.* a tower. — *n.* **min'aret** (or *-ret'*) a mosque tower, from which the call to prayer is given. [Ar. *manār, manārat*, lighthouse — *nār*, fire.]

minatory *min'ə-tə-ri* (or *mīn'*), *adj.* threatening. [L. *minārī, -ātus*, to threaten.]

minauderie *mēn-ō-də-rē', n.* a display of affectation. [Fr.]

minbar. See **mimbar**.

mince *mins, v.t.* to cut into small pieces: to chop fine: to diminish or suppress a part of in speaking: to pronounce affectedly. — *v.i.* to walk with affected nicety: to speak affectedly: — *pr.p.* **minc'ing**; *pa.t.* and *pa.p.* **minced** (*minst*). — *n.* minced meat: mincemeat. — *n.* **minc'er** one who minces: a machine for mincing. — *adj.* **minc'ing** not speaking fully out: speaking or walking with affected nicety. — Also *n.* — *adv.* **minc'ingly**. — **minced collops** see **collop**; **mince'meat** meat chopped small — hence anything thoroughly broken or cut to pieces: a chopped mixture of raisins, peel, and other ingredients; **mince-pie'** a pie made with mincemeat, esp. in latter sense. — **make mincemeat of** to destroy utterly (esp. *fig.*); **mince matters, words** to speak of things with affected delicacy, or to soften an account unduly. [O.Fr. *mincier, minchier* — L. *minūtus*; cf. **minute¹**.]

mind *mīnd, n.* memory: commemoration (*arch.* or *R.C.*): record, mention (*obs.*): thought: judgment: opinion: purpose (*Shak., Milt.*): inclination: attention: direction of the will: the state of thought and feeling: wits, right senses, sanity: consciousness: intellect: that which thinks, knows, feels, and wills: soul: personality: a thinking or directing person. — *v.t.* to remind (*arch.* and *Scot.*): to bring to mind (*Spens.*): to remember (*Scot.*): (*refl.*) to remember (with *of*; *arch.*): to attend to: to tend, have care or oversight of: to be careful about: to beware of: to purpose (*Shak.*): to have a mind to (*dial.*): to apply oneself to: to be troubled by, object to, dislike: to notice (*obs.* or *dial.*). — *v.i.* to remember (with *of*; *dial.*): to attend: to care: to look out, take heed: to be troubled, object. — *interj.* be careful, watch out!. — *adj.* **mind'ed** inclined: disposed. — **-mind'ed** in composition, having a mind of such-and-such a kind or inclined towards this or that. — **-mind'edness** in composition, inclination. — **mind'er** one who minds a machine, child, etc.: a child left to be minded (*arch.*): a short wooden stick used by a child to propel a hoop: a bodyguard, usu. of a criminal (*slang*). — *adj.* **mind'ful** bearing in mind: taking thought or care: attentive: observant: having memory (*arch.*): inclined (*obs.*). — *adv.* **mind'fully**. — *ns.* **mind'fulness; mind'ing** (*Scot.*) a memory, something recalled: a usu. small gift, to mark an occasion or in remembrance of the giver. — *adj.* **mind'less** without mind: stupid: unmindful. — *adv.* **mind'lessly**. — *n.* **mind'lessness**. — **mind'-bender** a brain-teaser, a puzzle. — *adjs.* **mind'-bending** permanently inclining the mind

towards certain beliefs, etc.: forcing the mind to unwonted effort, teasing the brain; **mind'-blowing** (of a drug) producing a state of ecstasy: (of an exhilarating experience, etc.) producing a similar state; **mind'-boggling** astonishing: incomprehensible. — **mind'-cure, mind'-healing** the cure or healing of a diseased mind, or of bodily ailment through the mind or by the supposed influence of a mind; **mind'-curer, -healer; mind'-reader** a thought reader; **mind'-reading; mind'set** attitude of habit of mind; **mind's eye** visual imagination, mental view, contemplation. — **absence of mind** inattention to what is going on owing to absorption of the mind in other things; **bear in mind** see **bear¹**; **break one's mind** (*obs.*) to make known, confide, or divulge one's thoughts; **cast one's mind back** to think about, try to recall past events, etc.; **change one's mind** to come to a new resolution or opinion; **cross someone's mind** see **cross**; **do you mind?** an interjection expressing annoyance or disagreement; **do**, or **would, you mind?** please do: do you object?; **have a (good, great) mind** to wish or to be inclined strongly; **have a mind of one's own** to be strong-willed and independent, unwilling to be persuaded or dissuaded by others; **have half a mind** to be somewhat inclined; **if you don't mind** if you have no objection; **in two minds** wavering; **know one's own mind** to be sure of one's intentions and opinions: to be self-assured; **make up one's mind** to come to a decision; **mind one's p's and q's** to be watchfully accurate and punctilious; **mind out** (often with *for*) to beware (of), look out (for); **mind you** an expression used to introduce a qualification added to something already said; **mind your eye** (*slang*) look out; **mind your own business** this is none of your affair; **month's mind** commemoration by masses one month after death or burial: strong desire or inclination; **never mind** do not concern yourself: it does not matter: you are not to be told; **of one** (or **a**, or **the same**) **mind** agreed; **of two minds** uncertain what to think or do; **on one's mind** weighing upon one's spirit; **out of mind** forgotten: out of one's thoughts; **out of one's mind** mad; **piece of one's mind** see **piece**; **presence of mind** a state of calmness in which all the powers of the mind are on the alert and ready for action; **put in mind** to remind (of); **put out of one's mind** to think no more about, forget about; **set one's mind on** to fix a settled desire upon; **set, put one's mind to** to focus one's attention on; **speak one's mind off** to distract someone from; **time out of mind** from time immemorial; **to my,** etc. **mind** to my, etc. thinking, in my, etc. opinion: to my, etc. liking; **year's mind** a commemorative service on the anniversary of a death or burial. [O.E. *gemynd* — *munan*, to think; Dan. *minde*, memorial, L. *mēns*, the mind.]

Mindel *min'dl*, (*geol.*) *n.* the second glaciation in the Alpine region. — *adjs.* **Min'del, Mindelian** (*-dē'li-ən*). [*Mindel*, a tributary of the Danube, in Bavaria.]

Mindererus *min-dər-ē'rəs, n.* Latinised name of the German physician R. M. *Minderer* (*c.* 1570–1621). — **Mindererus spirit** ammonium acetate solution, a diaphoretic.

mine¹ *mīn, pron.*, genitive of **I**, used predicatively or absolutely, belonging to me: my people: that which belongs to me: (adjectivally, esp. before a vowel or *h* or after its noun) my (*arch.*). [O.E. *mīn*.]

mine² *mīn, n.* a place from which minerals are dug — not usually including building-stone, and legally distinguished from a quarry by being artificially lighted: a cavity in the earth (*arch.*): a burrowing animal's gallery, as an insect's in a leaf: an excavation dug under a position to give secret ingress, to subvert it, or to blow it up (*mil.*): an explosive charge therefor: a submerged or floating charge of explosives in a metal case to destroy ships: a land-mine: a rich source. — *v.t.* to excavate, tunnel, make passages in or under: to obtain by excavation: to work as a mine: to bring down or blow up by a mine: to beset with mines: to lay mines in or under. — *v.i.* to dig or work a mine or mines: to tunnel: to burrow: to lay mines: to proceed secretly, insidiously (*fig.*). — *n.* **mi′ner** one who works in a mine: a soldier who lays mines: an insect or other animal that makes galleries in the earth, leaves, etc. — *n.* and *adj.* **min′ing.** — *adj.* **min′y** pertaining to mines: like a mine. — **mine′-captain** the overseer of a mine; **mine′= detection**; **mine′-detector** an apparatus for detecting explosive mines; **mine′-field** an area beset with mines (also *fig.*); **mine′-hunter** a ship for locating mines; **mine′-layer** a ship for laying mines; **mine′-owner; min= er's anaemia** ankylostomiasis; **miner's inch** the amount of water that will flow in twenty-four hours through an opening of one square inch at a pressure of six inches of water; **miner's lamp** a lamp carried by a miner, commonly on his cap; **miner's phthisis** phthisis caused by breathing dusty air in mines; **miner's worm** the hookworm that causes ankylostomiasis; **mine′-sweeper** a vessel for removing mines; **mine′-thrower** (a transl. of Ger. **Minenwerfer** *mē′nən-ver-fər*, in soldiers' slang **minnie** *min′i*) a trench-mortar; **mine′-worker** a miner. [Fr. *mine* (noun), *miner* (verb), of doubtful origin.]

mine³ *mīn*, (*Shak.*, Merry Wives, I, iii. at end) *n.* perhaps for **mind** (disposition), or **mien.**

mineola. See **min(n)eola.**

mineral *min′ər-əl*, *n.* a substance produced by processes of inorganic nature: a substance got by mining: ore: a substance neither animal nor vegetable: a mine (*Shak.*): a poison (*Shak.*): a mineral water (in a wide sense). — *adj.* relating to minerals: having the nature of minerals: impregnated with minerals, as water: of inorganic substance or nature. — *n.* **mineralisā′tion, -z-.** — *v.t.* **min′eralise, -ize** to make into a mineral: to give the properties of a mineral to: to go looking for and examining minerals. — *ns.* **mineralīs′er, -z-** one who, that which, mineralises: an element that combines with a metal to form an ore, as sulphur: a gas or vapour that promotes the crystallising out of minerals from an igneous magma; **min′eralist** one versed in or employed about minerals. — *adj.* **mineralog′ical** pertaining to mineralogy. — *adv.* **mineralog′ically.** — *v.i.* **mineralogise, -ize** (*-al′*) to collect or study minerals. — *ns.* **mineral′ogist** one versed in mineralogy; **mineral′ogy** the science of minerals. — **mineral alkali** (*obs.*) sodium carbonate; **mineral caoutchouc** elaterite; **mineral coal** coal in the ordinary sense, distinguished from charcoal; **mineral jelly** a soft yellow substance resembling soft soap, got from the less volatile residue of petroleum; **mineral kingdom** that department of nature which comprises substances that are neither animal nor vegetable; **mineral oil** any oil of mineral origin; **mineral pitch** natural asphalt; **mineral spring, well** a spring of mineral water; **mineral tallow** a soft yellowish natural hydrocarbon; **mineral tar** pissasphalt; **mineral water** spring water impregnated with minerals: an artificial imitation thereof: loosely, an effervescent non-alcoholic beverage; **mineral wax** ozokerite; **mineral wool** a mass of fibres got by blowing steam through molten slag. [Fr. *minéral* — *miner*, to mine; cf. **mine².**]

Minerva *min-ûr′və*, *n.* the Roman goddess of wisdom, identified with the Greek Athena. — **Minerva Press** a London printing-house that issued sentimental novels about 1800. [L., prob. from root of *mēns*, the mind.]

minestrone *min-i-strōn′i*, *n.* a thick vegetable soup with pieces of pasta, etc. [It.]

minette *min-et′*, *n.* an intrusive rock of orthoclase and biotite in a close-grained ground-mass. [Fr.]

minever. See **miniver.**

ming *ming*, **meng** *meng*, **menge** *menj*, (*arch.*) *vs.t.* and *vs.i.* to mix: to unite, couple: to work up — *pa.t.* and *pa.p.* **minged, menged**, older forms **meint, meynt** (*ment, mānt*), **ment.** [O.E. *mengan*; Ger. *mengen*.]

Ming *ming*, *n.* a Chinese dynasty (1368–1643). — *adj.* of the dynasty, its time, or esp. its pottery and other art.

mingle *ming′gl*, *v.t.* and *v.i.* to mix. — *n.* a mixture: a medley. — *ns.* **ming′lement; ming′ler; ming′ling.** — *adv.* **ming′lingly.** — **ming′le-mang′le** a medley, jumble. —

adj. jumbled. — *v.t.* to confuse, jumble together. [Freq. of **ming.**]

mingy *min′ji*, (*coll.*) *adj.* niggardly. — *n.* **min′giness.** [Perh. a portmanteau-word from **mangy** or **mean¹** and **stingy.**]

mini- *min′i-*, in composition, small (abbrev. of **miniature**) as in e.g. the following (also often without hyphen): — **min′i(-)budget** a supplementary budget, produced esp. in times of fiscal emergency; **min′i-buff′et** a snack-bar on a train; **min′i-bus** a small motor bus; **min′i-cab** a small motor vehicle plying for hire; **min′i-car; min′i= computer** a computer, which may have several terminals, lying in capability between a mainframe and a microcomputer; **min′i-dress** a dress with a mini-skirt; **min′i-mo′torway** one with two lanes; **min′ipill** a low-dose oral contraceptive containing no oestrogen; **min′i-skis** short, slightly thick, skis for learners; **min′i= skirt** a skirt whose hem-line is well above the knees; **min′i-sub(′marine); Min′itrack®** a system for tracking an earth satellite or a rocket by radio signals from it to a series of ground stations. — **mini-rocket launcher** a hand-gun firing tiny rockets.

mini *min′i*, *n.* short for **mini-car, mini-computer, mini= skirt.** — *adj.* (*coll.*) small, miniature.

miniate. See **minium.**

miniature *min′i(-ə)-chər, min′yə-tūr, -tyər*, *n.* rubrication (*obs.*): manuscript illumination: a painting on a very small scale, on ivory, vellum, etc.: the art of painting in this manner: a small or reduced copy, type or breed of anything: a chess problem with few pieces or moves. — *adj.* on a small scale: minute. — *v.t.* to represent on a small scale. — *n.* **miniaturisā′tion, -z-.** — *v.t.* **min′iaturise, -ize** to make very small: to make something on a small scale. — *n.* **min′iaturist** one who paints or makes miniatures. — **in miniature** on a small scale. [It. *miniatura* — L. *minium*, red lead; meaning affected by association with L. *minor, minimus*, etc., and their derivatives.]

minibus *min′i-bəs*, *n.* a light passenger horse-drawn vehicle (*obs.*): (-*bus*) a mini-bus (q.v. under **mini-**). [L. *minor*, less, *minimus*, least, and **omnibus.**]

Minié *min′i-ā*, *adj.* invented by C. E. Minié (died 1879) — applied to a bullet and a rifle adapted to it.

minify *min′i-fī*, *v.t.* to diminish, in appearance or reality. — *n.* **minificā′tion.** [Ill-formed (after **magnify**) from L. *minor*, less.]

minikin *min′i-kin*, *n.* a little darling: a diminutive or undersized person or thing: a small sort of pin: the treble string of a lute. — *adj.* diminutive: dainty: affected: mincing. [Obs. Du. *minneken*, dim. of *minne*, love; cf. **minnesinger.**]

minim *min′im*, *n.* a least part: a note, formerly the shortest, equal to two crotchets (*mus.*): apothecaries' measure, one-sixtieth of a fluid drachm: apothecaries' weight, a grain: a short down-stroke in handwriting: a diminutive creature (*Milt.*): a friar, sister, or lay member of any of three orders founded by St Francis of Paula (1416–1507) — so called as if humbler than even the Friars Minor. — *adj.* (*rare*) extremely minute. — *adj.* **min′imal** of least, or least possible, size, amount, or degree: of the nature of a minimum: negligible. — *ns.* **min′imalism; min′imalist** a Menshevik: a person advocating a policy of the least possible action, intervention, etc.: a practitioner of minimal art; **minimisā′= tion, -z-.** — *v.t.* **min′imise, -ize** to reduce to the smallest possible amount: to make as light as possible: to estimate at the lowest possible: loosely, to lessen, diminish: loosely, to belittle. — *ns.* **min′imism** inclination to reduce a dogma to the least possible; **min′imist; min′imum** the least quantity or degree, or the smallest possible: the lowest point or value reached: in *math.*, a value of a variable at which it ceases to diminish and begins to increase — opp. of *maximum*: — *pl.* **min′ima.** — *adj.* smallest or smallest possible. — *n.* **min′imus** a being of the smallest size (*Shak.*): in boys' schools, youngest of the surname. — **minimal art** art whose practitioners reject such traditional elements as composition and interrelationship between parts of the whole; **minimising glass** a diminishing glass; **minim rest** a rest of the duration of a minim; **minimum wage** the lowest wage permitted by law or regulation for certain work: a fixed bottom limit to workers' wages in various industries. — **minimum lending rate** the minimum rate of interest (successor to the **bank-rate**, q.v., and itself abolished in 1981) charged by the Bank of England to the discount market. [L. *minimus, -a, -um*, smallest.]

miniment *min'i-mənt, n.* obs. form of **muniment**.

minimum. See **minim**.

minion *min'yən, n.* a darling, a favourite, esp. of a prince: a flatterer: a servile dependant: an old type size, approx. 7-point, between nonpareil and brevier, giving about 10½ lines to the inch (*print.*).   [Fr. *mignon, mignonne.*]

minipill. See **mini-**.

miniscule. An alternative, less acceptable spelling of **minuscule**.

minish *min'ish*, (*arch.*) *v.t.* to make little or less: to diminish.   [Fr. *menuiser*, to cut small, said of a carpenter — L. *minūtia*, smallness.]

minister *min'is-tər, n.* a servant (*arch.*): one who administers or proffers, in service or kindness: one who serves at the altar: a clergyman (not now usually, as in *Pr. Bk.*, of the Church of England): the head, or assistant to the head, of several religious orders: one transacting business for another: the responsible head of a department of state affairs: the representative of a government at a foreign court. — *v.i.* to give attentive service (to): to perform duties: to supply or do things needful: to conduce. — *v.t.* (*arch.*) to furnish, supply. — *adj.* **ministē'rial** pertaining to a minister or ministry (in any sense): on the government side: administrative: executive: instrumental: conducive. — *n.* **ministē'rialist** a supporter of the government in office. — *adv.* **ministē'rially.** — *adj.* **min'istering** attending and serving. — *n.* **ministē'rium** the body of the ordained Lutheran ministers in a district: — *pl.* **ministē'ria.** — *adj.* **min'istrant** administering: attendant. — Also *n.* — *n.* **ministrā'tion** the act of ministering or performing service: office or service of a minister. — *adj.* **min'istrative** (*-trə-tiv,* or *-trā-tiv*) serving to aid or assist: ministering. — *ns.* **min'istress** a female who ministers; **min'istry** act of ministering: service: office or duties of a minister: the clergy: the clerical profession: the body of ministers who manage the business of the country: a department of government, or the building it occupies: term of office as minister. — **Minister of State** an additional, non-Cabinet, minister in an exceptionally busy government department; **Minister of the Crown** a government minister in the Cabinet; **Minister without Portfolio** a government minister, a member of the cabinet having no specific department.   [L. *minister* — *minor*, less.]

Minitrack®. See **mini-**.

minium *min'i-əm, n.* vermilion: red lead: its colour. — *adj.* **min'iate** of the colour of minium. — *v.t.* to paint with minium: to illuminate. — *n.* **miniā'tion.**   [L. *minium*, red-lead, also cinnabar.]

miniver, minever *min'i-vər, n.* white fur, orig. a mixed or variegated fur: the ermine in winter coat.   [O.Fr. *menu*, small — L. *minūtus*, and *vair*, fur — L. *varius*, particoloured.]

minivet *min'i-vet, n.* a brightly coloured shrike-like bird (*Pericrocotus* of several species) of India, etc.   [Etymology unknown.]

mink *mingk, n.* a small animal (of several species) of the weasel kind: its fur: a coat or jacket made from its fur.   [Perh. from Sw. *mänk*.]

minke *mink'ə, n.* the lesser rorqual.   [From a Norwegian whaler, *Meincke*, who harpooned one by accident.]

Minkstone *mink'stōn, n.* a cast concrete with a very smooth finish.

min(n)eola *min-i-ō'lə, n.* a variety of citrus fruit developed from a tangerine and a grapefruit and resembling an orange, grown in the U.S. and elsewhere.   [Poss. *Mineola* in Texas.]

minnesinger *min'i-sing-ər,* Ger. *-zing-ər, n.* one of a 12th–13th cent. school of German amatory lyric poets, mostly of noble birth.   [Ger. *Minne,* love, *Singer,* singer.]

minnick *min'ik,* **minnock** *-ək,* **mimic, mimmick** *mim',* (*dial.*) *ns.* an affected person. — *v.i.* to be over-dainty in eating: to behave with affected primness. — In Shak. *Mids. N. Dr.*, III, ii. 19, by some amended to *mimic*.

minnie¹ *min'i,* (*Scot.; hypocoristic*) *n.* mother.

minnie². See **mine-thrower** under **mine²**.

minnock. See **minnick**.

minnow *min'ō, n.* a very small freshwater fish (*Phoxinus phoxinus*) close akin to chub and dace: loosely extended to other small fish: a small, unimportant person or thing (*fig.*).   [Prob. an O.E. form related to extant *myne*.]

mino *mē'nō, n.* a raincoat of hemp, etc.: — *pl.* **mi'nos**.   [Jap.]

Minoan *min-ō'ən,* mīn-, *adj.* pertaining to prehistoric Crete and its culture. — *n.* a prehistoric Cretan.   [Gr. *Mīnōs,* a legendary king of Crete.]

minor *mī'nər, adj.* lesser: inferior in importance, degree, bulk, etc.: inconsiderable: lower: smaller (than major) by a semitone (*mus.*): in boys' schools, junior: Franciscan. — *n.* a person under age: the minor term, or minor premise (*log.*): anything that is minor opposed to major. — *ns.* **minoritaire** (*mē-nor-ē-ter;* Fr.) a member of a minority section of a party, esp. of socialists; **mī'norite** a Franciscan friar: — *fem.* **mī'noress.** — *adj.* Franciscan. — *n.* **minority** (*min-* or *mīn-or'i-ti*) the condition or fact of being little or less: the state or time of being under age (also **mī'norship**): the smaller number: less than half: the party, social group, section of the population, etc., of smaller numbers: the number by which it falls short of the other party — opp. to *majority.* — *adj.* of the minority. — **minor axis** in conics, that perpendicular to the major axis; **minor canon** see **canon²**; **minority carrier** (*electronics*) in a semiconductor, the electrons or holes which carry the lesser degree of measured current; **minority group** a section of the population with a common interest, characteristic, etc., which is not common to most people; **minor key, mode, scale** one with its third a minor third above the tonic; **minor orders** the lower degrees of holy orders, i.e. porter, exorcist, lector, acolyte; **minor planet** a small planet, any one of many hundreds with orbits between those of Mars and Jupiter; **minor poet** a genuine but not great poet; **minor premise** (*log.*) that in which the minor term occurs; **minor prophets** the twelve from Hosea to Malachi in the Old Testament; **minor suit** in bridge, clubs or diamonds; **minor term** (*log.*) the term which is the subject of the conclusion; **minor third** (*mus.*) an interval of three semitones; **minor tone** an interval with a vibration ratio of 9/10.   [L. *minor,* less; cf. **minus**.]

Minorca *min-ör'kə, n.* a black variety of laying poultry of Mediterranean family.   [From the island of *Minorca,* Sp. *Menorca*.]

minorite, minority, etc. See **minor**.

Minotaur *min'* or *mīn'ə-tör, n.* the bull-headed monster in the Cretan Labyrinth, offspring of Pasiphae, wife of Minos.   [Gr. *Mīnōtauros* — *Mīnōs,* Minos, *tauros,* bull.]

minster *min'stər, n.* a monastery (*obs.*): an abbey church or priory church: often applied to a cathedral or other great church without any monastic connection.   [O.E. *mynster* — L. *monastērium,* a monastery.]

minstrel *min'strəl, n.* orig. a professional entertainer: a musician: now generally a mediaeval harper who sang or recited his own or others' poems: a poet (*poet.*): one of a troupe of entertainers with blackened faces. — *n.* **min'strelsy** (*-si*) the art or occupation of a minstrel: music: a company or body of minstrels: a collection of songs.   [O.Fr. *menestrel* — L.L. *ministeriālis* — L. *minister,* attendant.]

mint[1] *mint, n.* a place where money is coined, esp. legally: a source or place of fabrication: a vast sum of money. — *v.t.* to coin: to invent: to stamp. — *adj.* in mint condition. — *ns.* **mint′age** coining: coinage: stamp: duty for coining; **mint′er.** — **mint condition, state** the condition of a new-minted coin: perfect condition, as if unused; **mint′-man** one skilled in coining or coinage; **mint′-mark** a mark showing where a coin was minted; **mint′-master** the master of a mint: one who invents. [O.E. *mynet*, money — L. *monēta*; see **money.**]

mint[2] *mint, n.* any plant of the aromatic labiate genus Mentha, as spearmint, peppermint, pennyroyal: any labiate (*U.S.*): a sweet flavoured with mint. — *adj.* **mint′y.** — **mint′-ju′lep** see **julep; mint′-sauce′** chopped spearmint or other mint mixed with vinegar and sugar, used as a sauce for roast lamb: punningly, money. [O.E. *minte* — L. *mentha* — Gr. *minthē, mintha.*]

mint[3] *mint, (Scot.) v.t. and v.i.* to purpose: to attempt: to aim: to threaten by movement: to venture: to aspire (with *at*): to hint. — *n.* attempt: aim: threatening gesture: an incipient movement. [O.E. *myntan,* to mean.]

minuend *min′ū-end, n.* the number from which another is to be subtracted. [L. *minuendus (numerus)* — *minuěre,* to lessen.]

minuet *min-ū-et′, n.* a slow, graceful dance in triple measure, invented in Poitou about the middle of the 17th century: the music for such a dance: a sonata movement in the same form. [Fr. *menuet* — *menu,* small — L. *minūtus,* small.]

minus *mī′nəs, prep.* diminished by (*math.*): deficient in respect of, deprived of, without (*coll.*). — *adj.* negative. — *n.* a deficiency or subtraction: a negative quantity or term: the sign (also **minus sign**) of subtraction or negativity (−) opposed to *plus.* — **minus strain** (*bot.*) one of two strains in heterothallism. [L. *minus,* neut. of *minor,* less.]

minuscule *min′əs-kūl,* or *-us′, n.* a small cursive script, originated by the monks in the 7th–9th centuries: a manuscript written in it: a lower-case letter (*print.*): opposed to *majuscule.* — *adj.* very small, very unimportant. — *adj.* **minus′cular.** [L. (*littera*) *minuscula,* smallish (letter).]

minute[1] *mīn-ūt′,* or *min-ūt′, adj.* extremely small: having regard to the very small: exact. — *adv.* **minute′ly.** — *n.* **minute′ness.** [L. *minūtus,* pa.p. of *minuěre,* to lessen.]

minute[2] *min′it, n.* the sixtieth part of an hour: the sixtieth part of a degree: an indefinitely small space of time: a particular moment: a brief jotting or note: (in *pl.*) a brief summary of the proceedings of a meeting: a minute's walk, or distance traversed in a minute. — *v.t.* to make a brief jotting or note of: to record in the minutes. — *adj.* **minutely** (*min′it-li; Shak.*) happening once a minute. — **min′ute-bell** a bell sounded every minute, in mourning; **min′ute-book** a book of minutes or short notes; **min′ute-drop** a drop falling at a minute's interval; **min′ute-glass** a sand-glass that runs for a minute; **min′ute-gun** a gun discharged every minute, as a signal of distress or mourning; **min′ute-hand** the hand that indicates the minutes on a clock or watch; **min′ute-jack** (*Shak.*) time-server, or a flighty, unstable person; **min′uteman** (often *cap.*) a man ready to turn out at a minute's warning, as in the American war of independence (*hist.*): a member of an armed right-wing organisation in the U.S., formed to take prompt action against Communist activities: a three-stage intercontinental ballistic missile; **minute steak** a small thin piece of steak which can be cooked quickly; **min′ute-watch** a watch that marks minutes; **min′ute-while** (*Shak.*) a minute's time. — **up to the minute** right up to date. [Same word as foregoing.]

minutia *mi-nū′shi-ə, n.* a minute particular or detail: — *pl.* **minū′tiae** (*-ē*). — *adj.* **minū′tiose** (*-shi-ōs*). [L. *minūtia,* smallness.]

minx *mingks, n.* a pert young girl: a jade. [Poss. from **minikin;** or L.Ger. *minsk, minske,* a wench, jade,

cognate with Ger. *Mensch,* man, human being.]

minyan *min′yən, min-yan′,* (*Heb.*) *n.* the minimum number of people required by Jewish law to be present for a religious service to be held, i.e. ten male adults: — *pl.* **minyanim, minyans.** [Heb., number.]

Miocene *mī′ō-sēn,* (*geol.*) *adj.* of the Tertiary period preceding the Pliocene and having a smaller proportion of molluscan fossils of species now living. — *n.* the Miocene system, period, or strata. [Gr. *meiōn,* smaller, *kainos,* recent.]

miosis *mī-ō′sis, n.* a variant spelling of **meiosis** and of **myosis.**

mir *mēr, n.* a Russian village community (pre-1917). [Russ., world.]

Mira *mī′rə, n.* a variable star in the constellation Cetus. [L. *mīra* (fem.), wonderful.]

mirabelle *mir′ə-bel, n.* (the cherry-like fruit of) a European species of plum-tree: a colourless liqueur distilled from this fruit. [Fr.]

mirable *mīr′ə-bl, adj.* (*Shak.*) wonderful. — *n.pl.* **mirabi′lia** (*mir-* or *mīr-*) wonders. — *n.* **Mirabilis** (*mir-* or *mīr-ab′il-is*) the marvel of Peru genus: (without *cap.*) short for aqua-mirabilis. [L. *mīrābilis,* wonderful.]

miracle *mir′ə-kl, n.* a supernatural event: hyperbolically, a marvel, a wonder: a miracle play. — *adj.* **miraculous** (*-ak′ū-ləs*) of the nature of a miracle: done by supernatural power: very wonderful: able to perform miracles. — *adv.* **mirac′ulously.** — *n.* **mirac′ulousness.** — **miracle fruit** a tasteless African red berry which becomes sweet-tasting when mixed with a sour substance; **mir′acle-mong′er** one who pretends to work miracles; **miracle play** a mediaeval form of drama founded on Old or New Testament history, or the legends of the saints. [Fr., — L. *mīrāculum* — *mīrārī, -ātus,* to wonder at.]

miracles. See **meril.**

mirador *mir-ə-dōr′, -dör′, n.* a belvedere or watch-tower. [Sp.]

mirage *mi-räzh′, n.* an appearance of objects raised or depressed, erect or inverted, single or double, owing to the varying refractive index of layers of hot and cold air, the sky often simulating the appearance of water: something illusory (*fig.*). [Fr. *mirer,* to look at — L. *mīrārī,* to wonder at.]

mirbane *mûr′bān, n.* apparently meaningless word, used in **essence,** or **oil, of mirbane,** a name for nitrobenzene as used in perfumery.

mire *mīr, n.* deep mud. — *v.t.* to plunge and fix in mire: to soil with mud — *v.i.* to sink in mud. — *n.* **mir′iness.** — *adj.* **mir′y** consisting of mire: covered with mire. — **mire′-drum** the bittern; **mire′-snipe** the common snipe. [O.N. *mȳrr,* bog.]

mirepoix *mēr-pwä′, n.* sautéed vegetables used for making sauces, etc. [Prob. after the Duc de *Mirepoix,* 18th-cent. French general.]

mirific, -al *mīr-if′ik, -əl, adjs.* wonder-working: marvellous. — *adv.* **mirif′ically.** [L. *mīrificus* — *mīrus,* wonderful, *facěre,* to do.]

miriti *mi-ri-tē′, mir′i-ti, n.* any palm of the genus Mauritia. [Tupí.]

mirk, etc. Same as **murk,** etc.

mirligoes *mûr′li-gōz,* (*Scot.*) *n.pl.* dizziness.

mirliton *mûr′li-tən, mēr-lē-tõ, n.* a toy reed-pipe. [Fr.]

mirly. See **marl**[4].

mirror *mir′ər, n.* a looking-glass: a reflecting surface: a faithful representation (*fig.*): an example, good or bad. — *v.t.* to reflect an image of, as in a mirror: to furnish with a mirror. — *pr.p.* **mirr′oring;** *pa.p.* **mirr′ored.** — *adj.* and *adv.* **mirr′orwise** with interchange of left and right. — **mirr′or-im′age** an image with right and left reversed as in a mirror; **mirror machine** a device for experimentation in the controlled production of thermonuclear energy, in which gas is tossed to and fro between magnetic mirrors; **mirror nuclides** pairs of nuclides, one containing the same number of protons as the other has neutrons; **mirror symmetry** the symmetry of an object and its reflected image; **mirr′or=**

writer one who writes mirrorwise; **mirr'or-writing** writing which is like ordinary writing as seen in a mirror. [O.Fr. *mireor, mirour* — L. *mīrārī, -ātus*, to wonder at.]

mirth *mûrth, n.* merriness: pleasure: delight: noisy gaiety: jollity: laughter. — *adj.* **mirth'ful** full of mirth: causing mirth: merry: jovial. — *adv.* **mirth'fully.** — *n.* **mirth'fulness.** — *adj.* **mirth'less.** — *adv.* **mirth'lessly.** — *n.* **mirth'lessness.** [O.E. *myrgth* — *myrige*, merry.]

MIRV *mûrv, n.* a missile containing many thermonuclear warheads, able to attack separate targets. [*M*ultiple *I*ndependently *T*argeted *R*e-entry *V*ehicle.]

miry. See mire.

Mirza *mûr'zə, mēr'zə, n.* as a Persian title (after a name) Prince: (before) official or learned man. [Pers. *mirzā, mīrzā.*]

mis- *mis, pfx.* wrong, ill, e.g. *misbehave, misdeed, mislead.* [O.E. *mis-*; O.N. *mis-*, Goth. *missa-*, Ger. *miss-*; cf. **miss¹**.]

mis *mis,* (*Spens.*) *v.i.* to do amiss: to fail. [**miss¹**.]

misacceptation *mis-ak-sep-tā'shən, n.* understanding in a wrong sense. [Pfx. **mis-**.]

misadventure *mis-əd-ven'chər, n.* ill-luck: mishap: accidental killing. — *adjs.* **misadvent'ured** (*Shak.*) unfortunate: **misadvent'urous.** — *n.* **misadvent'urer.** [M.E. — O.Fr., *mesaventure.*]

misadvertence *mis-əd-vûrt'əns, n.* inadvertence. [Pfx. **mis-**.]

misadvise *mis-əd-vīz', v.t.* to advise ill. — *adj.* **misadvised'.** — *adv.* **misadvī'sedly.** — *n.* **misadvīs'edness.** [Pfx. **mis-**.]

misaim *mis-ām', v.t.* to aim ill. [Pfx. **mis-**.]

misallege *mis-ə-lej', v.t.* to allege wrongly. [Pfx. **mis-**.]

misalliance *mis-ə-lī'əns, n.* an unsuitable alliance, esp. marriage with one of a lower rank. — *adj.* **misallied'.** [Fr. *mésalliance.*]

misallot *mis-ə-lot', v.t* to allot wrongly. — *n.* **misallot'ment.** [Pfx. **mis-**.]

misandry *mis'ən-dri, n.* hatred of men. — *n.* **mis'andrist.** [Gr. *misandria* — *misandros*, hating men.]

misanthrope *mis'ən-thrōp, n.* a hater of mankind, one who distrusts everyone else — also **misanthropist** (*mis-an'throp-ist*). — *adjs.* **misanthropic, -al** (*mis-ən-throp'ik, -əl*) hating or distrusting mankind. — *adv.* **misanthrop'ically.** — *ns.* **misan'thropos** (*Shak.*) a misanthrope; **misan'thropy** hatred or distrust of mankind. [Gr. *mīsanthrōpos* — *mīseein*, to hate, *anthrōpos*, a man.]

misapply *mis-ə-plī', v.t.* to apply wrongly: to use for a wrong purpose. — *n.* **misapplicā'tion** (*-ap-*). [Pfx. **mis-**.]

misappreciate *mis-ə-prē'shi-āt, v.t.* to fail to appreciate rightly or fully. — *n.* **misappreciā'tion.** — *adj.* **misapprē'ciātive.** [Pfx. **mis-**.]

misapprehend *mis-ap-ri-hend', v.t.* to apprehend wrongly: to take or understand in a wrong sense. — *n.* **misapprehen'sion.** — *adj.* **misapprehen'sive.** — *adv.* **misapprehen'sively** by or with misapprehension or mistake. — *n.* **misapprehen'siveness.** [Pfx. **mis-**.]

misappropriate *mis-ə-prō'pri-āt, v.t.* to put to a wrong use: to take dishonestly for oneself. — *n.* **misappropriā'tion.** [Pfx. **mis-**.]

misarrange *mis-ə-rānj', v.t.* to arrange wrongly: to put in wrong order. — *n.* **misarrange'ment.** [Pfx. **mis-**.]

misarray *mis-ə-rā', n.* want of proper order. [Pfx. **mis-**.]

misassign *mis-ə-sīn', v.t.* to assign wrongly. [Pfx. **mis-**.]

misaunter *mis-ön'tər,* (*obs.*) *n.* misadventure. [O.Fr. *mesaventure,* see **aunter**.]

misavised *mis-ə-vīz'id,* (*Spens.*) *adj.* ill-advised.

misbecome *mis-bi-kum', v.t.* to be unbecoming or unsuitable to. — *adj.* **misbecom'ing.** — *n.* **misbecom'ingness.** [Pfx. **mis-**.]

misbegot, misbegotten *mis-bi-got', -got'n, adj.* unlawfully begotten (*Shak.*): monstrous. [Pfx. **mis-**, and *pa.p.* of **beget.**]

misbehave *mis-bi-hāv', v.t.* (*refl.*) and *v.i.* to behave ill or improperly. — *adj.* **misbehaved'** (*Shak.*) badly behaved: ill-bred. — *n.* **misbehav'iour.** [Pfx. **mis-**.]

misbelieve *mis-bi-lēv', v.t.* to believe wrongly or falsely. — *ns.* **misbelief'** (or *mis'*) belief in false doctrine; **misbeliev'er.** — *adj.* **misbeliev'ing.** [Pfx. **mis-**.]

misbeseem *mis-bi-sēm', v.t.* to suit ill. [Pfx. **mis-**.]

misbestow *mis-bi-stō', v.t.* to bestow improperly, or on the wrong person. — *n.* **misbestow'al.** [Pfx. **mis-**.]

misborn *mis'börn* or *mis-börn', adj.* abortive: deformed from birth: base-born. — *n.* **misbirth'** an abortion. [Pfx. **mis-**.]

miscalculate *mis-kal'kū-lāt, v.t.* and *v.i.* to calculate wrongly. — *n.* **miscalculā'tion.** [Pfx. **mis-**.]

miscall *mis-köl', v.t.* to call by a wrong name: (*Spens.*; now mainly *Scot.* — also **misca'**) to call by an ill name: to abuse or revile. [Pfx. **mis-**.]

miscarriage *mis-kar'ij, n.* an act or instance of miscarrying: failure: failure to reach the intended result or destination: ill-conduct (*obs.*): act of bringing forth prematurely, esp. of expelling a foetus between the third and seventh months. — *v.i.* **miscarr'y** to be unsuccessful: to fail of the intended effect: to bring forth before the proper time: to be born prematurely. — *v.t.* (*obs.*) to lead astray. — **miscarriage of justice** failure of the courts to do justice. [Pfx. **mis-**.]

miscast *mis-käst', v.t.* and *v.i.* to cast (in any sense) amiss or blameworthily. [Pfx. **mis-**.]

miscegenation *mis-i-jin-ā'shən, n.* mixing of race: interbreeding, intermarriage, or sexual intercourse between different races. — *v.i.* **misc'egenate** to practise miscegenation. — *v.t.* to produce by miscegenation. — *adj.* mixed in race. — *ns.* **miscegenā'tionist, misc'egenātor, miscegenist** (*mis-ej'in-ist*) one who favours or practises miscegenation; **miscegen** (*mis'i-jən*), **misc'egene** (*-jēn*), **misc'egine** (*-jin, -jīn*) an individual of mixed race. [L. *miscēre*, to mix, *genus*, race.]

miscellaneous *mis-əl-ān'i-əs, adj.* mixed or mingled: consisting of several kinds. — *adj.* **miscellanarian** (*-ən-ā'ri-ən*). — *n.* a writer of miscellanies. — *adv.* **miscellān'eously.** — *ns.* **miscellān'eousness; miscellanist** (*mis-el'ən-ist,* or *mis'əl*) a writer of miscellanies; **miscellany** (*mis-el'*, or *mis'əl-*) a mixture of various kinds: a collection of writings on different subjects or by different authors. — *n.pl.* **miscellā'nea** (L. neut. *pl.*) a miscellany. [L. *miscellāneus* — *miscēre*, to mix.]

mischallenge *mis-chal'ənj,* (*Spens.*) *n.* a wrongful challenge. [Pfx. **mis-**.]

mischance *mis-chäns', n.* ill-luck: mishap. — *v.i.* to chance wrongly: to come to ill-luck. — *adjs.* **mischance'ful; mischan'cy** (*chiefly Scot.*) unlucky: dangerous. [M.E. — O.Fr. *meschance.*]

mischanter *mis-chän'tər,* **mishanter,** *mi-shän',* (*Scot.*) *ns.* an unlucky chance, misfortune. [**aunter;** perh. influenced by *obs. mischant, meschant* — O.Fr. *mescheant* (Fr. *méchant*), unlucky, wicked.]

mischarge *mis-chärj', v.t.* to charge wrongly. — *n.* a mistake in charging. [Pfx. **mis-**.]

mischief *mis'chif, n.* an ill consequence: evil: injury: damage, hurt: the troublesome fact: a source of harm: petty misdeeds or annoyance: pestering playfulness: a mischievous person: the devil (*coll.*). — Also *v.t.* — *adj.* **mischievous** (*mis'chiv-əs; Spens.* usu. *-chēv'*) causing mischief: injurious: prone to mischief. — *adv.* **mis'chievously.** — *n.* **mis'chievousness.** — **mis'chief= maker** one who stirs up strife. — *n.* and *adj.* **mis'chief= making.** [O.Fr. *meschef,* from *mes-* (From L. *minus,* less) and *chef* — L. *caput,* the head.]

mischmetal *mish'met-l, n.* an alloy of cerium with rare-earth metals and iron, used to produce the spark in cigarette and other lighters. [Ger. *mischen,* to mix, and **metal.**]

miscible *mis'i-bl, adj.* that may be mixed. — *n.* **miscibil'ity.** [L. *miscēre,* to mix.]

misclassify *mis-klas'i-fī, v.t.* to classify wrongly. — *n.* **misclassificā'tion.** [Pfx. **mis-**.]

miscolour *mis-kul'ər, v.t.* to colour falsely: to give a wrong meaning to: to misrepresent. [Pfx. **mis-**.]

miscomprehend *mis-kom-pri-hend', v.t.* to misunderstand.

— *n.* **miscomprehen'sion.** [Pfx. **mis-**.]

miscompute *mis-kəm-pūt'*, *v.t.* to reckon wrongly. — *n.* **miscomputā'tion** (*-kom-*) wrong computation: false reckoning. [Pfx. **mis-**.]

misconceit *mis-kən-sēt'*, (*Spens.*) *n.* misconception. — *v.t.* to have wrong conception of. [Pfx. **mis-**.]

misconceive *mis-kən-sēv'*, *v.t.* and *v.i.* to conceive wrongly: to mistake: to suspect (*obs.*). — *n.* **misconcep'tion.** [Pfx. **mis-**.]

misconduct *mis-kon'dukt*, *n.* bad conduct: wrong management: adultery: behaviour, not necessarily morally reprehensible, such as would lead any reasonable employer to dismiss an employee (*legal*). — *v.t.* **misconduct** (*-kən-dukt'*). [Pfx. **mis-**.]

misconjecture *mis-kən-jek'chər*, *n.* a wrong conjecture or guess. — *v.t.* or *v.i.* to guess or conjecture wrongly. [Pfx. **mis-**.]

misconster *mis-kon'stər*, obs. form of **misconstrue.**

misconstruction *mis-kən-struk'shən*, *n.* wrong construction, construing, or interpretation: faulty construction. — *v.t.* **misconstruct'.** [Pfx. **mis-**.]

misconstrue *mis-kən-strōō'*, or *-kon'strōō*, *v.t.* to construe or to interpret wrongly. [Pfx. **mis-**.]

miscontent *mis-kən-tent'*, (*arch.*) *n.*, *adj.*, and *v.t.* discontent. — *adj.* **miscontent'ed.** — *n.* **miscontent'ment.** [Pfx. **mis-**.]

miscopy *mis-kop'i*, *v.t.* to copy wrongly or imperfectly. — *n.* an error in copying. [Pfx. **mis-**.]

miscorrect *mis-kə-rekt'*, *v.t.* to alter or mark wrongly in would-be correction. — *n.* **miscorrec'tion.** [Pfx. **mis-**.]

miscounsel *mis-kown'sl*, *v.t.* to advise wrongly. [Pfx. **mis-**.]

miscount *mis-kownt'*, *v.t.* to count wrongly: to misjudge. — *n.* a wrong counting. [Pfx. **mis-**.]

miscreant *mis'kri-ənt*, *n.* orig. a misbeliever, a heretic or infidel: a vile wretch, a detestable scoundrel. — *adj.* unbelieving (*arch.*): depraved, ill-doing. — *ns.* **mis'creance, mis'creancy, mis'creaunce** (*Spens.*) false religious belief. [O.Fr. *mescreant* — *mes-* (from L. *minus*, less) and L. *crēdēns, -entis*, pr.p. of *crēdĕre*, to believe.]

miscreate, -d *mis-krē-āt'*, *-id*, *adjs.* created amiss: deformed. — *n.* **miscreā'tion.** — *adj.* **miscreā'tive** inclining towards wrong creation. — *n.* **miscreā'tor.** [Pfx. **mis-**.]

miscreaunce. See **miscreant.**

miscredit *mis-kred'it*, *v.t.* to disbelieve. [Pfx. **mis-**.]

miscreed *mis-krēd'*, *n.* a false creed. [Pfx. **mis-**.]

miscue *mis-kū'*, *n.* at billiards, a stroke spoiled by the slipping off of the cue: a mistake. — *v.t.* to hit (a billiard ball) wrongly. — *v.i.* to make a faulty stroke (*billiards*): to answer the wrong cue, or to miss one's cue (*theat.*): to make a mistake. [Pfx. **mis-**, or **miss**[1].]

misdate *mis-dāt'*, *v.t.* to date wrongly. — *n.* a wrong date. [Pfx. **mis-**.]

misdeal *mis-dēl'*, *n.* a wrong deal, as at cards. — *v.t.* and *v.i.* to deal wrongly: to divide improperly: — *pa.t.* and *pa.p.* **misdealt** (*-delt'*). [Pfx. **mis-**.]

misdeed *mis-dēd'*, *n.* wrong-doing, an evil deed. [O.E. *misdǣd.*]

misdeem *mis-dēm'*, (*arch.*) *v.t.* and *v.i.* to think ill (of): to think or judge wrongly (of): to suspect: — *pa.p.* **misdeemed'**, (*Spens.*) **misdempt'.** — *adjs.* **misdeem'ful; misdeem'ing** misjudging: suspicious: deceiving (*Spens.*). — *n.* misjudgment: suspicion. [Pfx. **mis-**.]

misdemean *mis-di-mēn'*, *v.t.* (*refl.*) and *v.i.* to misbehave. — *ns.* **misdemean'ant** one guilty of petty crime, or misconduct; **misdemean'our**, in U.S. **misdemean'or**, bad conduct: a misdeed: formerly a legal offence of less gravity than a felony. [Pfx. **mis-**, **demean**[1].]

misdempt. See **misdeem.**

misdescribe *mis-dis-krīb'*, *v.t.* to describe wrongly. — *n.* **misdescrip'tion.** [Pfx. **mis-**.]

misdesert *mis-di-zûrt'*, (*Spens.*) *n.* ill-desert. [Pfx. **mis-**.]

misdevotion *mis-di-vō'shən*, *n.* ill-directed devotion. [Pfx. **mis-**]

misdid. See **misdo.**

misdiet *mis-dī'ət*, (*Spens.*) *n.* improper feeding. [Pfx. **mis-**.]

misdight *mis-dīt'*, (*Spens.*) *adj.* ill-arranged: in sorry plight. [Pfx. **mis-**.]

misdirect *mis-di-rekt'*, *-dī-*, *v.t.* to direct wrongly. — *n.* **misdirec'tion.** [Pfx. **mis-**.]

misdo *mis-dōō'*, *v.t.* to do wrongly or badly: to injure (*obs.*): to kill (*obs.*). — *v.i.* to act amiss: — *pa.t.* **misdid'**; *pa.p.* **misdone'**; old *infin.* (*Spens.*) **misdonne'.** — *ns.* **misdo'er; misdo'ing.** [Pfx. **mis-**.]

misdoubt *mis-dowt'*, *v.t.* to have a doubt, suspicion, misgiving, or foreboding of or about: to suspect. — *n.* suspicion: hesitation: misgiving. — *adj.* **misdoubt'ful.** [Pfx. **mis-**.]

misdraw *mis-drö'*, *v.t.* to draw or draft badly. — *n.* **misdraw'ing.** [Pfx. **mis-**.]

misdread *mis-dred'*, (*Shak.*) *n.* dread of evil to come. [Pfx. **mis-**.]

mise *mēz, mīz*, *n.* expenditure, outlay (*obs.*): in Wales and the county palatine of Chester, a payment to a new king, prince, Lord of the Marches, or earl, to secure certain privileges: the issue in a writ of right: the adjustment of a dispute by agreement (*hist.*): a stake in gambling: the lay-out of cards. — **mise(-)en(-)scène** (*mē-zä-sen*) the act, result, or art, of setting a stage scene or arranging a pictorial representation (also *fig.*). [O.Fr. *mise*, placing or setting — L. *mittĕre*, *missum*.]

misease *mis-ēz'*, (*arch.*) *n.* distress: uneasiness. [O.Fr. *mesaise.*]

miseducation *mis-ed-ū-kā'shən*, *n.* improper or hurtful education. [Pfx. **mis-**.]

misemploy *mis-im-ploi'*, *v.t.* to employ wrongly or amiss: to misuse. — *n.* **misemploy'ment.** [Pfx. **mis-**.]

misentreat *mis-in-trēt'*, *v.t.* to ill-treat. [Pfx. **mis-** and **entreat** (to treat).]

misentry *mis-en'tri*, *n.* a wrong entry. [Pfx. **mis-**.]

miser[1] *mī'zər*, *n.* a wretch (*Spens.*, *Shak.*): one who lives miserably in order to hoard wealth: a niggard. — *adj.* like a miser. — *n.* **mi'serliness.** — *adj.* **mi'serly.** [L. *miser*, wretched.]

miser[2] *mīz'ər*, *n.* a well-boring instrument. [Origin doubtful.]

miserable *miz'ə-rə-bl*, *adj.* wretched: exceedingly unhappy: causing misery: extremely poor or mean: contemptible. — *n.* a wretch: very weak tea. — *n.* **mis'erableness.** — *adv.* **mis'erably.** [Fr. *misérable* — L. *miserābilis* — *miser.*]

misère *mē-zer'*, *miz-ār'*, *n.* in card games, an undertaking to take no tricks. [Fr. *misère*, misery.]

Miserere *miz-e-rē'ri*, *mis-e-rā're*, *n.* the 50th Psalm of the Vulgate (51st in A.V.) — from its first word (*R.C.*): a musical setting of it: (without *cap.*) a misericord in a church stall. [L., 2nd pers. sing. imper. of *miserērī*, to have mercy, to pity — *miser*, wretched.]

misericord, misericorde *miz-er'i-körd*, or *miz'ər-*, or *-körd'*, *n.* mercy, forgiveness, pity (*obs.*): a relaxation of monastic rule: a room in a monastery where some relaxation of rule was allowed: a bracket on a turn-up seat in a choir-stall, allowing the infirm some support when standing, often intricately carved: a narrow-bladed dagger for killing a wounded foe. [O.Fr. *misericorde* — L. *misericordia* — *misericors, -cordis*, tender-hearted.]

miserly. See **miser**[1].

misery *miz'ər-i*, *n.* wretchedness: extreme pain: miserable conditions: misère (*cards*): avarice (*Shak.*): very unhappy experience: a doleful person (*coll.*). [O.Fr., — L. *miseria.*]

misesteem *mis-es-tēm'*, *n.* disrespect. — *v.t.* to value wrongly. — *v.t.* **mises'timate** to estimate wrongly. [Pfx. **mis-**.]

misfaith *mis-fāth'*, *n.* distrust. [Pfx. **mis-**.]

misfall *mis-föl'*, (*obs.*) *v.t.* to befall unluckily: — *pa.t.* **misfell'**; *pa.p.* **misfall'en** (*Spens.* **misfalne'**). [Pfx. **mis-**.]

misfare *mis-fār'*, (*Spens.*) *n.* misfortune. — *v.i.* to fare ill.

— *n.* **misfar'ing** (*Spens.*) wrong-doing. [O.E. *misfaran*.]

misfeasance *mis-fēz'əns*, (*law*) *n.* the doing of a lawful act in a wrongful manner, as distinguished from *malfeasance*. — *n.* **misfeas'or**. [O.Fr. *mesfaisance* — pfx. *mes-* (from L. *minus*, less) *faisance* — *faire* — L. *facĕre*, to do.]

misfeature *mis-fē'chər*, *n.* ill feature, trait, or aspect: deformity. — *adjs.* **misfeat'ured** ill-featured; **misfeat'uring** distorting the features. [Pfx. **mis-**.]

misfeign *mis-fān'*, *v.i.* to feign with bad design. [Pfx. **mis-**.]

misfile *mis-fīl'*, *v.t.* to file (information) under the wrong headings, etc. [Pfx. **mis-**.]

misfire *mis-fīr'*, *v.i.* to fail to go off, explode, or ignite, at all or at the right time: to fail to have the effect intended (*fig.*). — *n.* a failure to fire, or to achieve effect. [**miss**[1], **fire**.]

misfit *mis'fit*, *n.* a bad fit: a thing that fits badly: a person who cannot adjust himself to his social environment, or his job, etc. — *v.t.* and *v.i.* (*mis-fit'*) to fit badly. [Pfx. **mis-**.]

misform *mis-förm'*, *v.t.* to form or shape badly or improperly. — *n.* **misformā'tion**. [Pfx. **mis-**.]

misfortune *mis-för'tūn*, *n.* ill-fortune: an evil accident: calamity: an illegitimate child, or the having of one (*coll.*). — *adj.* **misfor'tuned** (*arch.*) unfortunate. [Pfx. **mis-**.]

misgive *mis-giv'*, *v.t.* to suggest apprehensions to, fill with forebodings: to give amiss. — *v.i.* to have apprehensive forebodings: to fail (*Scot.*). — *pa.t.* **misgave'**; *pa.p.* **misgiv'en**. — *n.* **misgiv'ing** mistrust: a feeling that all is not well. [Pfx. **mis-**.]

misgo *mis-gō'*, (*obs.* or *dial.*) *v.i.* to go astray or amiss: — *pa.t.* **miswent** (supplied from **miswend**); *pa.p.* **misgone** (*mis-gon'*; *obs.*, now illit., **miswent'**). [Pfx. **mis-**.]

misgotten *mis-got'n*, (*Spens.*) *adj.* ill-gotten: misbegotten. [Pfx. **mis-**.]

misgovern *mis-guv'ərn*, *v.t.* to govern badly or unjustly. — *ns.* **misgov'ernaunce** (*Spens.*) mismanagement; **misgov'ernment**; **misgov'ernor**. [Pfx. **mis-**.]

misgraff *mis-gräf*, (*Shak.*) **misgraft** *mis-gräft'*, *vs.t.* to graft unsuitably. [Pfx. **mis-**.]

misgrowth *mis-grōth'*, *n.* an irregular growth: an excrescence: a sport of nature. [Pfx. **mis-**.]

misguggle *mis-gug'l*, **mishguggle** *mish-*, (*Scot.*) *vs.t.* to bungle, mar. [Pfx. **mis-**.]

misguide *mis-gīd'*, *v.t.* to guide wrongly: to lead into error: to ill-treat (*Scot.*). — *n.* (*obs.*) misbehaviour. — *n.* **misguid'ance**. — *adj.* **misguid'ed** erring: misdirected: ill-judged. — *adv.* **misguid'edly**. — *n.* **misguid'er**. [Pfx. **mis-**.]

mishallowed *mis-hal'ōd*, (*arch.*) *adj.* consecrated to evil. [Pfx. **mis-**.]

mishandle *mis-han'dl*, *v.t.* to handle amiss or unskilfully: to maltreat. [Pfx. **mis-**.]

mishanter. Same as **mischanter**.

mishap *mis-hap'*, *mis'hap*, *n.* ill chance: unlucky accident: misfortune. — *v.i.* to happen unfortunately. — *v.i.* **mishapp'en** (*Spens.*) to happen ill. [Pfx. **mis-**.]

mishapt (*Spens.*), for **misshaped**.

mishear *mis-hēr'*, *v.t.* and *v.i.* to hear wrongly. [Pfx. **mis-**.]

mishguggle. See **misguggle**.

mishit *mis-hit'*, *v.t.* to hit faultily. — *n.* (*mis'hit*) a faulty hit. [Pfx. **mis-**.]

mishmash *mish'mash*, *n.* a hotch-potch, medley. [Redup. of **mash**[1]; cf. Ger. *Mischmasch* — *mischen* — L. *miscēre*, to mix.]

mishmee, mishmi *mish'mē*, *n.* the bitter tonic rootstock of an Assamese gold-thread (*Coptis teeta*). [Said to be Assamese *mishmītīta*.]

Mishnah, Mishna *mish'nä*, *n.* the Jewish oral law, finally redacted A.D 220: — *pl.* **Mishnayōth'**. — *adjs.* **Mishnā'ic, Mish'nic**. [Heb. *mishnāh* — *shānāh*, to repeat, teach, learn.]

misimprove *mis-im-prōōv'*, *v.t.* to turn to bad use: to make worse by would-be improvement. — *n.* **misimprove'ment**. [Pfx. **mis-**.]

misinform *mis-in-förm'*, *v.t.* to inform or tell incorrectly. — *ns.* **misinform'ant; misinformā'tion; misinform'er**. [Pfx. **mis-**.]

misinstruct *mis-in-strukt'*, *v.t.* to instruct amiss. — *n.* **misinstruc'tion** wrong instruction. [Pfx. **mis-**.]

misintelligence *mis-in-tel'i-jəns*, *n.* wrong or false information: misunderstanding: want of intelligence. [Pfx. **mis-**.]

misintend *mis-in-tend'*, (*obs.*) *v.t.* to intend or aim in malice. [Pfx. **mis-**.]

misinterpret *mis-in-tûr'prit*, *v.t.* to interpret wrongly: to explain wrongly. — *ns.* **misinterpretā'tion; misinter'preter**. [Pfx. **mis-**.]

misjoin *mis-join'*, *v.t.* to join improperly or unfitly. — *n.* **misjoin'der** (*law*) an incorrect union of parties or of causes of action in a suit. [Pfx. **mis-**.]

misjudge *mis-juj'*, *v.t.* and *v.i.* to judge wrongly. — *n.* **misjudg'ment** — also **misjudge'ment**. [Pfx. **mis-**.]

misken *mis-ken'*, (*Scot.*) *v.t.* to be, or to appear, ignorant of: to fail or refuse to recognise. [Pfx. **mis-**.]

misknow *mis-nō'*, *v.t.* to misapprehend. — *n.* **misknowledge** (*mis-nol'ij*). [Pfx. **mis-**.]

mislay *mis-lā'*, *v.t.* to place amiss: to lay in a place not remembered: to lose: — *pa.t.* and *pa.p.* **mislaid'**. [Pfx. **mis-** and **lay**[3].]

mislead *mis-lēd'*, *v.t.* to draw into error: to cause to mistake: — *pa.t.* and *pa.p.* **misled'**. — *n.* **mislead'er**. — *adj.* **mislead'ing** deceptive. — *adv.* **mislead'ingly**. [Pfx. **mis-**.]

misleared *mis-lērd'*, (*Scot.*) *adj.* mistaught: unmannerly: ill-conditioned. [Pfx. **mis-**.]

misleeke *mis-lēk'*, (*Spens.*) *v.i.* for **mislike**.

misletoe. A former spelling of **mistletoe**.

mislight *mis-līt'*, *v.t.* to lead astray by a light. [Pfx. **mis-**.]

mislike *mis-līk'*, (*arch.*) *v.t.* to dislike: to displease. — *v.i.* to disapprove. — *n.* dislike: disapprobation. — *ns.* **mislīk'er; mislīk'ing**. [Pfx. **mis-**.]

mislippen *mis-lip'n*, (*Scot.*) *v.t.* to distrust: to suspect: to disappoint, deceive: to neglect, overlook. [Pfx. **mis-**.]

mislive *mis-liv'*, *v.i.* to live a bad life. [Pfx. **mis-**.]

misluck *mis-luk'*, *n.* ill-luck. — *v.i.* to meet with bad luck, to fail. [Pfx. **mis-**.]

mismake *mis-māk'*, *v.t.* to make amiss, shape ill. — *pa.p.* and *adj.* **mismade'**. [Pfx. **mis-**.]

mismanage *mis-man'ij*, *v.t.* to conduct badly: to conduct carelessly. — *n.* **misman'agement**. [Pfx. **mis-**.]

mismanners *mis-man'ərz*, *n.pl.* bad manners. [Pfx. **mis-**.]

mismarry *mis-mar'i*, *v.t.* and *v.i.* to marry unsuitably. — *n.* **mismarri'age**. [Pfx. **mis-**.]

mismatch *mis-mach'*, *v.t.* to match unsuitably. — *n.* a bad match. — *n.* **mismatch'ment**. [Pfx. **mis-**.]

mismate *mis-māt'*, *v.t.* and *v.i.* to mate unsuitably. — *adj.* **mismat'ed**. [Pfx. **mis-**.]

mismeasure *mis-mezh'ər*, *v.t.* to measure wrongly. — *n.* **mismeas'urement**. [Pfx. **mis-**.]

mismetre *mis-mēt'ər*, *v.t.* to spoil the metre of. [Pfx. **mis-**.]

misname *mis-nām'*, *v.t.* to call by an unsuitable or wrong name. [Pfx. **mis-**.]

misnomer *mis-nō'mər*, *n.* a misnaming: a wrong or unsuitable name. — *v.t.* to misname. [O.Fr. from *mes-* (from L. *minus*, less) and *nommer* — L. *nōmināre*, to name.]

miso *mē'sō*, *n.* a paste, used for flavouring, prepared from soy beans and fermented in brine: — *pl.* **mi'sos**. [Jap.]

miso- *mis-ō-*, *mīs-ō-*, in composition, hater of, hating. — *adjs.* **misocap'nic** (Gr. *kapnos*, smoke) hating smoke, esp. that of tobacco; **mis'oclere** (-*klēr*; Gr. *kleros*, clergy; *Fuller*) hating the clergy. — *n.* **misogamist** (-*og'ə-mist*; Gr. *gamos*, marriage) a hater of marriage; **misog'amy; misogynist** (-*oj'i-nist*, -*og'*; Gr. *gynē*, a woman) a woman-hater. — *adjs.* **misogynist'ical, misog'ynous**. — *ns.* **misog'yny; misology** (-*ol'ə-ji*; Gr. *logos*, reason) hatred of reason, reasoning, or knowl-

edge; **misol'ogist; misoneism** (*-nē'izm*; Gr. *neos*, new)
hatred of novelty; **misonē'ist.** — *adj.* **misonēist'ic.**
[Gr. *mīseein*, to hate.]
misobserve *mis-ob-zûrv'*, *v.t.* and *v.i.* to fail to observe:
to observe amiss or incorrectly. — *n.* **misobserv'ance.**
[Pfx. **mis-**.]
misocapnic... to ... **misoneistic.** See **miso-**.
misorder *mis-ör'dər*, *n.* and *v.t.* disorder. [Pfx. **mis-**.]
mispersuasion *mis-pər-swā'zhən*, (*rare*) *n.* a wrong persuasion or notion: a false opinion. — *v.t.* **mispersuade'.**
[Pfx. **mis.**]
mispickel *mis'pik-əl*, *n.* arsenical pyrites, a mineral composed of iron, arsenic, and sulphur. [Ger.]
misplace *mis-plās'*, *v.t.* to put in a wrong place: to mislay:
to set on an improper object (*fig.*), or indulge in in
unsuitable circumstances (*fig.*). — *n.* **misplace'ment.**
[Pfx. **mis-**.]
misplay *mis-plā'*, *n.* a wrong play. — Also *v.t.* and *v.i.*
[Pfx. **mis-**.]
misplead *mis-plēd'*, *v.t.* and *v.i.* to plead wrongly. — *n.*
misplead'ing an error in pleading. [Pfx. **mis-**.]
misplease *mis-plēz'*, *v.t.* to displease. [Pfx. **mis-**.]
mispoint *mis-point'*, *v.t.* to punctuate wrongly. [Pfx.
mis-.]
mispraise *mis-prāz'*, *v.t.* to praise amiss: to dispraise.
[Pfx. **mis-**.]
misprint *mis-print'*, *v.t.* to print wrong. — *v.i.* to make
footprints in unusual positions. — *n.* (*mis'print, mis'-
print'*) a mistake in printing. [Pfx. **mis-**.]
misprise[1], **misprize** *mis-prīz'*, *v.t.* to scorn: to slight: to
undervalue. — *n.* (*Spens.* **mesprise, mesprize, misprize**)
scorn: slighting: failure to value. [O.Fr. *mespriser* —
pfx. *mes-* (from L. *minus*, less), L.L. *pretiāre* — L.
pretium, price, value.]
misprise[2], **misprize** *mis-prīz'*, *v.t.* to mistake. — *n.* (*Spens.*
mesprize) error. — *adj.* **misprised'** mistaken. [O.Fr.
mespris, pa.p. of *mesprendre*, to commit an offence;
cf. **misprision**[1].]
misprision[1] *mis-prizh'ən*, *n.* mistake: criminal oversight
or neglect in respect of the crime of another (*law*): any
serious offence, failure of duty — *positive* or *negative*,
according as it is maladministration or mere neglect.
— **misprision of heresy, treason,** etc., knowledge of and
failure to give information about heresy, treason, etc.
[O.Fr. *mes-* (from L. *minus*, less), L.L. *prēnsiō, -ōnis*
— L. *praehendere*, to take.]
misprision[2] *mis-prizh'ən*, *n.* failure to appreciate. [**misprise**[1], after the model of **misprision**[1].]
mispronounce *mis-prə-nowns'*, *v.t.* to pronounce incorrectly. — *n.* **mispronunciation** (*-nun-si-ā'shən*) wrong or
improper pronunciation. [Pfx. **mis-**.]
misproportion *mis-prə-pör'shən, -pōr'*, *n.* lack of due
proportion. — *adj.* **mispropor'tioned.** [Pfx. **mis-**.]
misproud *mis-prowd'*, *adj.* unduly proud. [Pfx. **mis-**.]
mispunctuate *mis-pungk'tū-āt, -pungk'chŏŏ-*, *v.t.* and *v.i.*
to punctuate wrongly. — *n.* **mispunctuā'tion.** [Pfx.
mis-.]
misquote *mis-kwōt'*, *v.t.* to quote wrongly. — *n.* **misquo-
tā'tion.** [Pfx. **mis-**.]
misrate *mis-rāt'*, *v.t.* to value wrongly. [Pfx. **mis-**.]
misread *mis-rēd'*, *v.t.* to read wrongly. — *n.* **mis'read'ing.**
[Pfx. **mis-**.]
misreckon *mis-rek'n*, *v.t.* and *v.i.* to reckon or compute
wrongly. — *n.* **misreck'oning.** [Pfx. **mis-**.]
misregard *mis-ri-gärd'*, (*Spens.*) *n.* inattention. [Pfx.
mis-.]
misrelate *mis-ri-lāt'*, *v.t.* to relate incorrectly. — *n.* **mis-
relā'tion.** — **misrelated participle** a participle which the
grammatical structure of the sentence insists on attaching to a word it is not intended to qualify (e.g.
Lost in thought, the bus passed me without stopping).
[Pfx. **mis-**.]
misremember *mis-ri-mem'bər*, *v.t.* and *v.i.* to remember
wrongly or imperfectly: to forget (*dial.*). [Pfx. **mis-**.]
misreport *mis-ri-pört', -pōrt'*, *v.t.* to report falsely, misleadingly, or wrongly: to speak ill of (*Shak.*). — *n.*
false reporting or report: ill repute (*obs.*). [Pfx. **mis-**.]

misrepresent *mis-rep-ri-zent'*, *v.t.* to represent falsely: to
give a misleading interpretation to the words or deeds
of: to be an unrepresentative representative of. — *n.*
misrepresentā'tion. [Pfx. **mis-**.]
misrule *mis-rōōl'*, *n.* disorder: bad or disorderly government. — *v.t.* and *v.i.* to govern badly. — **Lord of
Misrule** a leader of Christmas revels. [Pfx. **mis-**.]
Miss *mis*, *n.* a title prefixed to the name of an unmarried
(formerly, and now *dial.* and *U.S. illit.*, also a married)
woman or girl (at first less respectful than *Mrs*): also
prefixed to a representational title, esp. in beauty
contests, e.g. *Miss World*: (without the name) an eldest
daughter, young lady of the house (*obs.*): vocatively
used alone in displeasure, real or assumed, or to
address a waitress, female teacher, etc.: (without *cap.*)
a schoolgirl, or girl or woman with the faults attributed
to schoolgirls: a person between a child and a woman:
a kept mistress (*obs.*): — *pl.* **miss'es** — either 'the Miss
Hepburns' or 'the Misses Hepburn' may be said, but
the latter is more formal. — *n.* **miss'hood.** — *adj.*
miss'ish schoolgirlish: having the faults attributed to
schoolgirls — sentimental, insipid, namby-pamby,
squeamish, silly, etc. — *ns.* **miss'ishness; miss'y** (usu.
subservient) the little girl. — *adj.* missish. — **Miss
Nancy** (*coll.*) a very effeminate man. [Shortened
form of **mistress**.]
miss[1] *mis*, *v.t.* (or *v.i.*, *arch.*, with *of*) to fail to hit, reach,
find, meet, touch, catch, get, have, take advantage of,
observe, see: to avoid (a specified danger): to fail (to
do; *arch.*): to omit: to discover the absence of: to feel
the want of: to leave out: to do without (*Shak.*). —
v.i. to fail to hit or obtain: to fail: to go wrong (*obs.*):
to miss fire. — *n.* the fact or condition or an act or
occasion of missing: failure to hit the mark: loss: (the
source of or reason for) a feeling of loss or absence:
wrong-doing (*Shak.*). — *adjs.* **miss'able; miss'ing** not
to be found: not in the expected place: wanting: of
unascertained fate (*mil.*). — *adv.* **miss'ingly** (*Shak.*)
with sense of loss. — **missing link** a hypothetical extinct
creature thought to be intermediate between man and
the anthropoid apes: any one thing required to complete a series. — **give a miss** in billiards, to allow an
opponent to score by intentionally missing: to leave
out, omit, avoid anything; **go missing** to disappear,
esp. unexpectedly and inexplicably: to be mislaid; **miss
fire** to fail to go off or explode (cf. **misfire**); **miss one's
tip** (*slang*) to fail in one's plan or attempt; **miss out** to
omit: (with *on*) to fail to experience or benefit from;
miss stays (*naut.*) to fail in going about from one tack
to another; **miss the bus** (or **boat**) (*coll.*) to lose one's
opportunity; **near miss** see under **near**. [O.E. *missan*;
Du. *missen*, to miss.]
miss[2]. See **Miss**.
missa (also *cap.*) *mis'ə, -a*, (L.) *n.* the Mass (*R.C.*). —
missa, Missa solemnis (*sol-em'nis*) high mass.
missal *mis'l*, *n.* a book containing the complete service
for mass throughout the year. [L.L. *missāle*, from
missa, mass.]
missay *mis-sā'*, (*arch.*) *v.t.* and *v.i.* to say or speak amiss,
wrongly, falsely, or in vain: to slander: to revile: —
pa.t. and *pa.p.* **missaid** (*-sed'*). — *n.* **missay'ing.** [Pfx.
mis-.]
missee *mis-sē'*, *v.t.* and *v.i.* to see wrongly. [Pfx. **mis-**.]
misseem *mis-sēm'*, (*Spens.*) *v.t.* to misbecome. — *adj.*
misseem'ing unbecoming. — *n.* false appearance.
[Pfx. **mis-**.]
missel *mis'l, miz'l*, *n.* mistletoe (*obs.*): the missel-thrush.
— **miss'el-thrush** a large thrush fond of mistletoe
berries. — Also **miss'el-bird.** [O.E. *mistel, mistil*,
mistletoe.]
missel-tree *mis'l-trē*, *n.* a melastomaceous tree (*Bellucia
aubletii*) of northern South America, with edible
berries.
missend *mis-send'*, *v.t.* to send by mistake: to send to the
wrong person or place: — *pa.t.* and *pa.p.* **missent'.**
[Pfx. **mis-**.]
misset *mis-set'*, *v.t.* to set or place wrongly or unfitly: to

put out of humour (*Scot.*). [Pfx. **mis-**.]

misshape *mis-shāp'*, *v.t.* to shape ill: to deform. — *n.* deformity. — *adjs.* **misshap'en, misshaped'** (*Spens.* **mishapt**) ill-shaped. — *n.* **misshap'enness.** [Pfx. **mis-**.]

missheathed *mis-shēdh'id*, (*Shak.*) *adj.* wrongly sheathed. [Pfx. **mis-**.]

missile *mis'īl, mis'l, adj.* capable of being thrown or projected: pertaining to a missile. — *n.* a weapon or object for throwing by hand or shooting from a bow, gun, or other instrument, esp. a rocket-launched weapon, often nuclear-powered. — *n.* **miss'il(e)ry** (*-īl-ri, -l-ri*) missiles collectively: their design, manufacture and use. [L. *missilis* — *mittĕre, missum,* to throw].

missing. See **miss**[1].

mission *mish'ən, n.* an act of sending, esp. to perform some function: a flight with a specific purpose, as a bombing raid or a task assigned to an astronaut or astronauts: the errand or purpose for which one is sent: that for which one has been or seems to have been sent into the world, vocation: a sending out of persons on a political or diplomatic errand, for the spread of a religion, or for kindred purpose: an organisation that sends out missionaries: its activities: a station or establishment of missionaries: any particular field of missionary enterprise: the body of persons sent on a mission: an embassy: a settlement for religious, charitable, medical, or philanthropic work in a district: a religious organisation or district not fully developed as a parish: a series of special religious services conducted by a missioner. — *adj.* of a mission or missions, esp. characteristic of the old Spanish missions in California. — *v.t.* (*rare*) to commission. — *v.t.* and *v.i.* **miss'ionarise, -ize** to act as missionary (to, among, or in). — *n.* **miss'ionary** one sent upon a mission, esp. religious. — *adj.* pertaining to missions. — *n.* **miss'ioner** a missionary: a person in charge of parochial missions. — *v.t.* and *v.i.* **miss'ionise, -ize** to do missionary work (upon, in, among). — **mission architecture** the style of the old Spanish missions in California, etc.; **miss'ionary-bish'op** one having jurisdiction in an unconverted country, or in districts not yet formed into dioceses; **missionary position** in sexual intercourse, the face-to-face position with the male on top. [L. *missiō, -ōnis* — *mittĕre,* to send.]

missis, missus *mis'is, -iz, n.* (*illit., coll.*) mistress of the house: wife. [**mistress.**]

missive *mis'iv, adj.* sent: missile (*obs.*). — *n.* that which is sent, as a letter: messenger (*Shak.*): a missile (*obs.*). — *n.pl.* letters sent between two parties in which one makes an offer and the other accepts it (*Scots law*). — **letter missive** a missive, esp. from a sovereign or authority to a particular person or body, as one giving *congé d'élire.* [L.L. *missīvus* — L. *mittĕre, missum,* to send.]

misspeak *mis-spēk', v.t.* and *v.i.* to speak wrongly. [Pfx. **mis-**.]

misspell *mis-spel', v.t.* and *v.i.* to spell wrongly: — *pa.t.* and *pa.p.* **misspelt', misspelled'.** — *n.* **misspell'ing** a wrong spelling. [Pfx. **mis-**.]

misspend *mis-spend', v.t.* to spend ill: to waste or squander: — *pa.t.* and *pa.p.* **misspent'.** [Pfx. **mis-**.]

misstate *mis-stāt', v.t.* to state wrongly or falsely. — *n.* **misstate'ment.** [Pfx. **mis-**.]

misstep *mis-step', v.i.* to make a false step: to make a mistake. — *n.* a mistake in conduct, etc. [Pfx. **mis-**.]

missuit *mis-sōōt', -sūt', v.t.* to be unbecoming to. [Pfx. **mis-**.]

missummation *mis-sum-ā'shən, n.* wrong addition. [Pfx. **mis-**.]

missus. See **missis.**

mist *mist, n.* watery vapour seen in the atmosphere: cloud in contact with the ground: thin fog: rain in very fine drops: a suspension of liquid in a gas: condensed vapour on a surface: a dimness or dim appearance: anything that dims or darkens the sight or the judgment. — *v.t.* to obscure or veil with mist or as with

mist. — *v.i.* to become misty or veiled: to form a mist or vapour-cloud. — *adj.* **mist'ful** misty. — *adv.* **mist'ily.** — *ns.* **mist'iness; mist'ing** mist: the action of the verb *mist.* — *adj.* misty: hazy: dimming. — *adj.* **mist'y** full of, covered with, obscured by, mist: like mist: dim: obscure: clouded: vague: not perspicuous. — **mist'=flower** a North American hemp-agrimony, with clusters of blue or violet flowers. — **mist up, over,** of a surface, to become covered with condensed vapour; **Scotch mist** a thick wetting mist: a drizzle. [O.E. *mist,* darkness, dimness; Icel. *mistr,* Du. *mist.*]

mistake *mis-tāk', v.t.* to remove wrongfully (*obs.*): (app.) to take or come upon to his loss (*Spens.*): to understand wrongly: to take for another thing or person: to be wrong about: to think wrongly: to believe wrongly to be (*Spens.*). — *v.i.* to err in opinion or judgment: to do amiss: — *pa.t.* **mistook'**; *pa.p.* **mistak'en** also **mista'en'.** — *n.* a taking or understanding wrongly: an error: (*mis'*) a faulty shot in cinematography. — *adjs.* **mistak'able; mistak'en** understood wrongly: guilty of or under a mistake: erroneous: incorrect: ill-judged. — *adv.* **mistak'enly.** — *ns.* **mistak'enness; mistak'ing** (*Shak.*) a mistake. — **mistaken identity** an error in identifying someone. — **and no mistake** (*coll.*) assuredly; **be mistaken** to make or have made a mistake: to be misunderstood; **mistake one's man** to think too lightly of the man one has to deal with; **mistake one's way** to take the wrong road. [M.E. *mistaken* — O.N. *mistaka,* to take wrongly — *mis-,* wrongly, *taka,* to take.]

misteach *mis-tēch', v.t.* to teach wrongly: — *pa.t.* and *pa.p.* **mistaught** (*mis-töt'*). [Pfx. **mis-**.]

mistell *mis-tel', v.t.* to count, narrate, or inform, wrongly: — *pa.t.* and *pa.p.* **mistold'.** [Pfx. **mis-**.]

mistemper *mis-tem'pər,* (*obs.*) *n.* and *v.t.* disorder. — *adj.* **mistem'pered** tempered or mixed ill (*Shak.*): tempered for an evil purpose (*Shak.*). [Pfx. **mis-**.]

mister *mis'tər, n.* craft, trade, profession (*obs.*): manner, kind (*Spens.*; without *of* — what mister man, orig. = man of what class, hence what kind of man): need, necessity (*Scot.*). — *v.i.* (*Spens.*) to be necessary: to have need. — *v.t.* to need. — *n.* **mis'tery** see **mystery**[2]. [O.Fr. *mestier* (Fr. *métier*), trade — L. *ministerium,* service.]

Mister *mis'tər, n.* a title prefixed to a man's name, and to certain designations (as Mr Justice, Mr Speaker), written **Mr:** (without *cap.*) sir (*coll., illit.*). — *v.t.* **mis'ter** (*illit.*) to address as 'mister'. [**master.**]

misterm *mis-tûrm', v.t.* to name wrongly or unsuitably. [Pfx. **mis-**.]

mistery. Same as **mystery**[2].

misthink *mis-thingk', v.t.* to think ill of (*Shak.*): to think wrongly. — *v.i.* to have wicked or mistaken thoughts (*obs.*): — *pa.t.* and *pa.p.* **misthought** (*mis-thöt'*). — *n.* **misthought'** a wrong notion. [Pfx. **mis-**.]

mistico *mis'ti-kō, n.* a small Mediterranean coaster, between a xebec and a felucca: — *pl.* **mis'ticos.** [Sp. *místico,* prob. from Ar.]

mistigris *mis'ti-gris, -grē, n.* a variation of poker in which a joker or blank card can be given any value: the card so used. [Fr. *mistigri,* knave of clubs.]

mistime *mis-tīm', v.t.* to time wrongly. — *adj.* **mistimed'** unseasonable. [Pfx. **mis-**.]

mistitle *mis-tī'tl, v.t.* to call by an unsuitable title. [Pfx. **mis-**.]

mistle. Same as **mizzle**[1] or **missel.**

mistletoe *mis'l-tō,* or *miz',* n. a hemiparasitic evergreen shrubby plant (*Viscum album*) with white viscous fruits, growing on the apple, apricot, etc. (very rarely on the oak): extended to other species of its genus or family (Loranthaceae). [O.E. *misteltān* — *mistel, mistil,* mistletoe, *tān,* twig; see **missel.**]

mistold *mis-tōld', pa.t.* of **mistell.**

mistook *mis-tōōk', pa.t.* of **mistake.**

mistral *mis'tral, n.* a violent cold dry north-east wind in southern France. [Fr., — Prov. *mistral* — L. *magistrālis,* masterful, *magister,* master.]

mistranslate *mis-trans-lāt'*, *v.t.* and *v.i.* to translate incorrectly. — *n.* **mistranslā'tion.** [Pfx. **mis-.**]

mistrayned *mis-trānd'*, (*Spens.*) *pa.p.* drawn away, misled. [Pfx. **mis-**; see **train**[1].]

mistreading *mis-trēd'ing*, (*Shak.*) *n.* a false step, misdeed. [Pfx. **mis-.**]

mistreat *mis-trēt'*, *v.t.* to treat ill. — *n.* **mistreat'ment.** [Pfx. **mis-.**]

mistress *mis'tris*, *n.* (*fem.* of **master**) a woman employer of servants or head of a house or family: a woman (or anything personified as a woman) having power of ownership: a woman teacher, esp. in a school: a woman well skilled in anything: a woman loved and courted: a concubine: vocatively madam (*arch.* and *dial.*): the jack at bowls (*Shak.*): (with *cap.*; *mis'iz*; now usu. written **Mrs**; *fem.* of **Mister, Mr**) a title prefixed to the name, once of any woman or girl, now ordinarily of a married woman, sometimes also prefixed to a designation. — *adj.* principal: leading: ruling. — *v.t.* to make a mistress of, pay court to as a mistress: to address as mistress: to become or be mistress of or over: (with *it*) to play the mistress. — *adjs.* **mis'tressless; mis'tressly.** — *n.* **mis'tress-ship.** [O.Fr. *maistresse* (Fr. *maîtresse*) — L.L. *magistrissa*, fem. from L. *magister*, master.]

mistrial *mis-trī'əl*, *n.* a trial void because of error: an inconclusive trial (*U.S.*). [Pfx. **mis-.**]

mistrust *mis-trust'*, *n.* distrust. — *v.t.* to distrust: to suspect. — *v.i.* to have suspicion. — *adj.* **mistrust'ful.** — *adv.* **mistrust'fully.** — *n.* **mistrust'fulness.** — *adv.* **mistrust'ingly.** — *adj.* **mistrust'less.** [Pfx. **mis-.**]

mistryst *mis-trīst'*, (*Scot.*) *v.t.* to disappoint by not keeping an engagement. — *adj.* **mistryst'ed** disturbed, put out. [Pfx. **mis-.**]

mistune *mis-tūn'*, *v.t.* to tune wrongly or falsely: to put out of tune. [Pfx. **mis-.**]

misunderstand *mis-und-ər-stand'*, *v.t.* to take in a wrong sense: to fail to appreciate the true nature, motives, etc. of: — *pa.t.* and *pa.p.* **misunderstood'.** — *n.* **misunderstand'ing** a mistake as to meaning: a slight disagreement. — *adj.* **misunderstood'.** [Pfx. **mis-.**]

misuse *mis-ūs'*, *n.* improper use: application to a bad purpose: evil usage or behaviour (*Shak.*). — *v.t.* **misuse** (*mis-ūz'*) to use for a wrong purpose or in a wrong way: to treat ill: to speak ill of (*Shak.*): to deceive (*Shak.*): — *pa.t.* (*Spens.*) **misust** (*ūst'*). — *ns.* **misus'age** misconduct, evil practice (*Spens.*): ill-usage: wrong use; **misus'er.** [Pfx. **mis-.**]

misventure *mis-ven'chər*, *n.* a misadventure. — *adj.* **misvent'urous.** [Pfx. **mis-.**]

miswandred *mis-won'dərd*, (*Spens.*) *adj.* strayed over. [Pfx. **mis-.**]

misween *mis-wēn'*, *v.t.* and *v.i.* to judge wrongly, have a wrong opinion of (*Spens.*). [Pfx. **mis-.**]

miswend *mis-wend'*, (*Spens.*) *v.i.* to go astray or amiss: to come to grief, miscarry: — *pa.t.* and *pa.p.* **miswent'** (see **misgo**).

misword *mis-wûrd'*, *n.* (*dial.*) an angry or harsh word. — *v.t.* to word incorrectly. — *n.* **misword'ing.** [Pfx. **mis-.**]

misworship *mis-wûr'ship*, *v.t.* to worship wrongly. — *n.* worship of a wrong object. [Pfx. **mis-.**]

miswrite *mis-rīt'*, *v.t.* to write incorrectly. [Pfx. **mis-.**]

misyoke *mis-yōk'*, *v.t.* to yoke or marry unsuitably. [Pfx. **mis-.**]

mitch *mich*, (*dial.*) *v.i.* to play truant, esp. from school. [Perh. — O.Fr. *muchier, mucier*, to hide, lurk.]

mite[1] *mīt*, *n.* a very small acaridan arachnid. — *adj.* **mīticīd'al.** — *n.* **mīt'icide** (L. *caedĕre*, to kill) a poison or other agent that destroys mites. — *adj.* **mīt'y** infested with mites. [O.E. *mīte*.]

mite[2] *mīt*, *n.* orig. an old Flemish coin of very small value: used to translate the Gr. *lepton* of which two make a *kodrantēs* or 'farthing' (Mark xii. 42) (*B*): vaguely, a very small amount: a small contribution proportionate to one's means: a minute portion or fragment: a jot: a diminutive person: a small child. [M.Du. *mīte* (Du.

mijt); perh. ult. the same as the preceding.]

miter. American spelling of **mitre**[1,2].

mither. See **moider.**

Mithras *mith'ras*, **Mithra** *-rä*, *ns.* the ancient Persian light-god, whose worship became popular in the Roman Empire. — *n.* **Mithraeum** (*-rē'əm*) a grotto sacred to Mithras: — *pl.* **Mithrae'a.** — *adj.* **Mithrā'ic.** — *ns.* **Mithrā'icism, Mith'raism** (*-rä-izm*); **Mith'raist.** [L. and Gr. *Mithrās* — O.Pers. *Mithra*.]

mithridate *mith'ri-dāt*, *n.* an antidote to poison, *Mithridates* (better, *Mithradātēs*), king of Pontus (reigned *c.* 120–63 B.C.), having traditionally made himself proof against poisons. — *adj.* **Mithridatic, Mithradatic** (*-dat'-ik*) pertaining to Mithridates, esp. of his wars against Rome. — *vt.* **mithrid'atise, -ize.** — *n.* **mith'ridatism** (*-dāt-izm*) immunity to a poison acquired by taking gradually increased doses of it. — **mithridate mustard** field penny-cress (*Thlaspi arvense*); **mithridate pepperwort** field cress (*Lepidium campestre*).

miticidal, miticide. See **mite**[1].

mitigate *mit'i-gāt*, *v.t.* to mollify, appease: to make more easily borne: to lessen the severity, violence, or evil, of: to temper. — *adjs.* **mit'igable; mit'igant** mitigating. — *n.* **mitigā'tion.** — *n.* and *adj.* **mit'igātive.** — *n.* **mit'igātor.** — *adj.* **mit'igātory.** [L. *mītigāre, -ātum* — *mītis*, mild.]

mitochondrion *mīt-, mit-ō-kon'dri-ən*, *n.* an energy-producing body, thread-like to spherical in shape, present in cytoplasm: — *pl.* **mitochon'dria.** — *adj.* **mitochon'drial.** [Gr. *mitos*, thread, *chondros*, granule.]

mitosis *mī-, mi-tō'sis*, *n.* an elaborate process of cell-division involving the arrangement of protoplasmic fibres in definite figures — karyokinesis: — *pl.* **mitō'ses** (*-sēz*). — *adj.* **mitotic** (*-tot'ik*). — *adv.* **mitot'ically.** — *n.* **mit'ogen** (Gr. *gennaein*, to engender) a substance that causes cells to divide. — *adjs.* **mitogenet'ic, mitogen'ic.** [Gr. *mitos*, fibre.]

mitraille *mē'trī-y'*, *n.* small shot or projectiles sent in a shower, esp. from a mitrailleuse. — *ns.* **mitrailleur** (*-yær'*) a machine-gunner: a mitrailleuse; **mitrailleuse** (*-yæz'*) a machine-gun (orig. one having a number of barrels) that discharges a stream of small missiles. [Fr.]

mitre[1] *mī'tər*, *n.* a Greek (or later) woman's head-fillet: a girdle (*Pope*, following *Homer*): an eastern hat or turban: a high head-dress, cleft on top, worn by archbishops and bishops, and by some abbots: episcopal dignity (*fig.*): a gasteropod of the genus *Mitra* or its conical shell (**mit're-shell**): a gusset in sewing, etc. — *v.t.* to adorn with a mitre. — *adjs.* **mī'tral** of or like a mitre: of the mitral valve; **mit'riform** (*mīt'*, or *mit'*) mitre-shaped. — **mitral valve** a mitre-shaped valve of the heart; **mi'tre-wort** bishop's cap. [Fr., — Gr. *mitrā*, fillet.]

mitre[2] *mī'tər*, *n.* a joint (also **mi'tre-joint**) in which each piece is cut at an angle of 45° to its side, giving a right angle between the pieces: sometimes applied to any joint where the plane of junction bisects the angle: an angle of 45°: a gusset, a tapered insertion. — *v.t.* to join with a mitre: to turn a corner in, by cutting out a triangular piece and joining (*needlework*). — *v.i.* to meet in a mitre. — **mi'tre-wheel** a bevel-wheel having its face inclined 45° to its axis. [Prob. same as above.]

mitt *mit*, *n.* a mitten: a hand (*slang*): a padded leather glove worn in baseball. [Abbrev. of **mitten**.]

mitten *mit'n*, *n.* a kind of glove, without a separate cover for each finger: a glove for the hand and wrist, but not the fingers: a boxing-glove: dismissal (*slang*): (in *pl.*) handcuffs (*slang*). — *adj.* **mitt'ened** covered with a mitten or mittens. — **mitt'en-crab** a Chinese crab that can do damage to river banks. — **frozen mitten** (*slang*) chilly reception, the cold shoulder; **get the mitten** (*slang*) to be dismissed, esp. as a suitor. [O.Fr. *mitaine*; origin obscure.]

mittimus *mit'i-məs*, *n.* a warrant granted for sending to prison a person charged with a crime (*law*): a writ by which a record is transferred out of one court to another (*law*): dismissal, discharge (*coll.*): a nickname for a magistrate. [L., we send — *mittĕre*, to send.]

Mitty (Walter Mitty) *wŏl'tər mit'i*, a nobody who lives a life of imaginary roles as a somebody: an intrepid daydreamer. [From the hero of a short story by James Thurber.]

mitzvah *mits'və, mits-vä'*, n. a good deed: — *pl.* **-voth** (*-vōt'*), **-vahs.** [Heb., (lit.) commandment.]

miurus *mī-ū'rəs*, n. a hexameter with short penultimate syllable. [Latinised from Gr. *meiouros*, curtailed — *meiōn*, less, *ourā*, a tail.]

mix *miks*, v.t. to combine so that the parts of one thing or things of one set are diffused among those of another: to prepare or compound in like manner: to blend: to mingle: to join: to combine in one film (*cinematography*): to confound: to associate: to interbreed, cross: to involve. — *v.i.* to become, or to be capable of becoming, mixed: to be joined: to associate: to have intercourse. — *n.* a mixing, mingling: a mixture, esp. a standard mixture: a formula giving constituents and proportions: a jumble, a mess. — *adjs.* **mix'able; mixed** (*mikst*) mingled: promiscuous: of or for both sexes: miscellaneous: confused: not select: combining characters of two or more kinds: between front and back (*phon.*). — *adv.* **mix'edly** (or *mikst'li*). — *ns.* **mix'edness** (or *mikst'*); **mix'er** one who mixes: that by which or in which things are mixed: one who is easily sociable in all sorts of company: one who mixes drinks: a soft drink for adding to an alcoholic one: a troublemaker (*slang*): a device by means of which two or more input signals are combined to give a single output signal (*electronics*): one who uses such a device (*coll.*). — *adj.* **mixt** (same as **mixed**). — Also *pa.p.* and *pa.t.* — *ns.* **mix'ter-max'ter, mix'tie-max'tie, mix'ty-max'ty, mix'y-max'y** (all *Scot.*) a confused jumble. — *adjs.* and *advs.* in a confused jumble. — *ns.* **mixtion** (*miks'chən*) a mixture of amber, mastic, and asphaltum used as a mordant for gold-leaf: mixture (*obs.*); **mix'ture** (*-chər*) act of mixing: state of being mixed: the product of mixing: a product of mixing in which the ingredients retain their properties — distinguished from **compound** (*chem.*): in an organ, a compound-stop giving harmonics: a mixture of petrol vapour and air (*motoring*). — *adj.* **mix'y** mixed. — *adj.* **mixed'-abil'ity** of classes, etc. accommodating members who differ in (esp. academic) ability. — **mixed bag** any assortment of diverse people, things, characteristics, etc.; **mixed blessing** something which has both advantages and disadvantages; **mixed bud** (*bot.*) one containing young foliage leaves and also the rudiments of flowers or inflorescences; **mixed chalice** the chalice prepared for the eucharist, containing wine mixed with water; **mixed crystal** a crystal formed from two or more distinct compounds; **mixed doubles** tennis matches with a male and a female player as partners on each side; **mixed economy** a national economy of which parts are state-owned and other parts privately-owned; **mixed farming** farming of both crops and livestock; **mixed foursome** a golf match with a male and female player as partners on each side; **mixed grill** see **grill;** **mixed language** one which contains elements (e.g. vocabulary, syntax) from two or more separate languages; **mixed marriage** one between persons of different religions or races. — *adj.* **mixed'-mē'dia** of a work in the arts, combining traditional forms, e.g. acting, dance, painting, and electronic media, e.g. tape recording. — **mixed metaphor** see **metaphor; mixed number** one consisting of an integer and a fraction, e.g. 2½; **mixed train** railway train made up partly of passenger carriages and partly of goods wagons. — *adj.* **mixed'-up'** socially confused, bewildered, and ill-adjusted. — **mix-in'** a fight (*U.S.*); **mixing valve** one which mixes hot and cold water (as in a **mixer tap**); **mix'-up'** confusion: a confused jumble. — **mix it** (*slang*) to fight forcefully. to cause trouble. [L. *miscēre, mixtus*, to mix; exact relation to O.E. *miscian*, Ger. *mischen*, uncertain.]

mixen *miks'n*, n. a dunghill. [O.E. *mixen* — *mix, meox*, dung.]

mixo- *miks-ō-*, in composition, mixed. — *adjs.* **mixobarbar'ic** part barbaric, part Greek; **mixolyd'ian** (also with *cap.*) in ancient Greek music the same as hyperdorian: in old church music applied to an authentic mode extending from *g* to *g*, with *g* for its final; **mixotroph'ic** (*biol.*) combining different modes of nutrition. [Gr. *mīxis*, mixing, *misgein*, to mix.]

miz, mizz *miz*, (*coll.*) n. and adj. short for **misery, miserable.**

mizmaze *miz'māz*, n. a labyrinth: bewilderment. [**maze¹**.]

mizzen, mizen *miz'n*, n. in a three-masted vessel, the hindmost of the fore-and-aft sails: the spanker or driver. — *adj.* belonging to the mizzen: nearest the stern. — **mizz'en-course; mizz'en-mast; mizz'en-sail.** [Fr. *misaine*, foresail, foremast — It. *mezzana*, mizzensail — L.L. *mediānus*, middle — L. *medius*, middle; the development of meaning is puzzling.]

mizzle¹ *miz'l*, v.i. to rain in small drops. — *n.* fine rain. — *n.* **mizz'ling.** — *adj.* **mizz'ly.** [Cf. L.Ger. *miseln*, mist.]

mizzle² *miz'l*, (*slang*) v.i. to decamp. [Origin obscure.]

mizzle³ *miz'l*, v.t. to confuse. [Origin obscure.]

mizzonite *miz'ən-īt*, n. a scapolite richer in sodium than meionite. [Gr. *meizōn*, greater, from its longer vertical axis.]

Mjöllnir, Mjölnir *myœl'nir*, n. Thor's terrible hammer. [O.N.]

mna. See **mina¹.**

mneme *nē'mē*, n. a memory-like capacity of living matter for after-effect of stimulation of the individual or an ancestor. — *adj.* **mne'mic** pertaining to the mneme. — *ns.* **mne'mon** a hypothetical unit of memory; **mnemonic** (*ni-mon'ik*) a device, e.g. verse, to help memory: (in *pl.*, treated as *sing.*) art of assisting memory. — *adj.* pertaining to the mneme. — *adj.* **mnemon'ical.** — *ns.* **mnē'monist** a teacher or practitioner of mnemonics: one from whose memory nothing is erased; **Mnemosyne** (*nē-mos'i-nē*, or *-moz'*) the Greek Goddess of memory, mother of the Muses. — *adj.* **mnemotechnic** (*nē-mō-tek'nik*) mnemonic. — *ns.* **mnemotech'nics** mnemonics; **mnemotech'nist.** [Gr. *mnēmē*, memory, *mnēmōn*, mindful, *Mnēmosynē*, Mnemosyne.]

mo¹ *mō*, (*arch.*) adv. and adj. more. — Also **moe** (*obs.*); (*Scot.*) **mae** (*mā*) more (in number, not quantity). [O.E. *mā* (adv.); cf. **more, most.**]

mo². See **moment.**

-mo *-mō*, the final syllable of certain Latin ordinal numbers, used in composition with English cardinal numbers to denote the number of leaves in a gathering of a book; see **twelvemo, sixteenmo** under **twelve, sixteen.**

moa *mō'ə*, n. a gigantic extinct bird (Dinornis) of New Zealand. [Maori.]

Moabite *mō'ə-bīt*, n. one of the ancient people of *Moab*, living east of the lower Jordan and the Dead Sea. — *adj.* of or pertaining to Moab. — **Moabite stone** a basalt slab found (1868) at Dibon in Moab, with a long inscription in Hebrew-Phoenician letters, about the revolt of Mesha, king of Moab, against Israel (9th cent. B.C.; 2 Kgs. iii.).

moan *mōn*, n. lamentation: a lament: a complaint: a grumble (*coll.*): a low murmur of pain: a sound like a murmur of pain. — *v.t.* to lament: to bemoan: to utter with moans: to condole with (*obs.*). — *v.i.* to make or utter a moan: to grumble (*coll.*). — *n.* **moan'er.** — *adj.* **moan'ful** expressing sorrow: lamentable. — *adv.* **moan'fully.** — **moaning minnie** an air-raid siren (*war slang*): a person given to complaining (*coll.*). [Unrecorded O.E. *mān* (noun) answering to the verb *mǣnan*.]

moat *mōt*, n. a deep trench round a castle or fortified place, sometimes filled with water: a mote-hill. — *v.t.* to surround with a moat. — *adj.* **moat'ed.** [O.Fr. *mote*, mound.]

mob¹ *mob*, n. the mobile or fickle common people: the

vulgar: the rabble: a disorderly crowd: a riotous assembly: a gang: a large herd or flock (*Austr.* and *N.Z.*). — *adj.* of or relating to the Mob. — *v.t.* to attack in a disorderly crowd: to crowd around, esp. with vexatious curiosity or attentions: to drive by mob action. — *v.t.* and *v.i.* to form into a mob: — *pr.p.* **mobb′ing**; *pa.t.* and *pa.p.* **mobbed.** — *adjs.* **mobbed** crowded (*coll.*); **mobb′ish.** — *ns.* **mobile** (*mō′bi-li*; 17th cent.) the mob; **moboc′racy** (*slang*) rule or ascendency exercised by the mob; **mob′ocrat.** — *adj.* **mobocrat′ic.** — *n.* **mob′ster** gangster. — *adj.* **mob-hand′ed** in large numbers: constituting a large group. — **mob′-law** lynch-law: the will of the mob; **mobs′man** a member of a mob: a swell-mobsman (q.v.). — **the mob, the Mob** (*U.S. slang*) the Mafia: organised crime in general. [L. *mōbile* (*vulgus*), fickle (multitude); *movere*, to move.]

mob² *mob*, (*obs.*) *n.* a loose woman: a négligé dress: a mob-cap. — *v.t.* to muffle the head of. — *adj.* **mobbed** in dishabille: muffled up. — **mob′-cap** a woman's indoor morning cap with puffy crown, a broad band, and frills (*hist.*). — **mob it** (*obs.*) to go unobtrusively to an unfashionable part of the theatre. [Perh. *Mab*, for *Mabel*; but cf. O.Du. *mop*; mod. Du. *mopmuts*, a woman's nightcap.]

mobble. See **moble.**

mobby, mobbie *mob′i*, *n.* a spirituous beverage made from sweet-potatoes (*West Indies*): fruit juice for brandy-making, or brandy made therefrom (*U.S. arch.*). [Carib *mabi*.]

mobile *mō′bīl, -bēl, -bil*, *adj.* movable: able to move about: easily, speedily moved: not fixed: changing rapidly: of a liquid, characterised by great fluidity. — *n.* with *great, principal*, etc., translation of primum mobile (*obs.*): a moving or movable body or part: an artistic structure, orig. consisting of dangling forms, now sometimes having a base, in which movement is caused by air currents: short for mobile police, library, etc. — *ns.* **mobile** (*mō-bi-li*) see **mob¹**; **mobilisation, -z-** (*mō-* or *mo-bil-i-zā′shən*, or *-ī-*). — *v.t.* **mō′bilise, -ize** to make movable, mobile, or readily available: to put in readiness for service in war: to call into active service, as troops. — *v.i.* to make armed forces ready for war: to undergo mobilisation. — *n.* **mobility** (*mō-bil′i-ti*), quality of being mobile: description of the drift of ions (including electrons and holes in semiconductors) under applied electric fields, additional to thermal agitation (*electronics*): the mob (*slang*). — **mobile home** a caravan or other vehicle with sleeping, cooking, etc. facilities; **mobile police** police patrolling in vehicles; **mobile shop, library**, etc. one set up in a motor vehicle, driven to customers' homes; **mobility allowance** money paid by the government to disabled people to compensate for their travel costs. [Fr., — L. *mōbilis* — *movēre*, to move.]

Möbius strip *mœ′bē-əs strip*, (*math.*) the one-sided surface formed by joining together the two ends of a long rectangular strip, one end being twisted through 180 degrees before the join is made. [August F. *Möbius* (1790–1868), mathematician.]

moble, mobble *mob′l*, (*obs.*) *v.t.* to muffle, as in a mob. — *adj.* **mob′led** (*Shak.*) muffled: other suggestions are, richly endowed (cf. Fr. *meuble*), set in motion, violently agitated (L. *mōbilis*), or that there is no meaning at all. [Freq. of **mob²**.]

mobocracy, mobster, etc. See **mob¹.**

moccasin, mocassin *mok′ə-sin, n.* a North American Indian's shoe of deerskin or other soft leather: a shoe or slipper more or less resembling it: a venomous North American pit-viper. — **mocc′asin-flow′er** a lady's-slipper orchid. [American Indian.]

Mocha *mok′ə, mō′kə, n.* (also without *cap.*) a fine coffee: a coffee, or coffee and chocolate, flavour: a deep brown colour: a soft leather used for gloves, made from sheep- or goatskin. — **Mocha stone** a moss agate or similar stone. [Coffee and stone first brought from *Mocha*, on the Red Sea.]

mochell. Spens. for **muchel.** See under **much.**

mock *mok, v.t.* to deride: to scoff at derisively: to make sport of: to mimic in ridicule: to simulate: to defy, set at naught, tantalise, disappoint, deceive, befool, as if in mockery (*fig.*). — *v.i.* to jeer: to scoff: to speak or behave as one not in earnest. — *n.* ridicule: a bringing into ridicule: a scoff: a mockery: a thing mocked: (in *pl.*) practice examinations taken at school as a preparation for public examinations. — *adj.* sham: false: resembling, or accepted as a substitute for, the true or real. — *adj.* **mock′able** worthy of derision. — *ns.* **mock′age** (*obs.*); **mock′er; mock′ery** derision: ridicule: subject of ridicule: mimicry: imitation, esp. a contemptible or insulting imitation: false show: insulting or ludicrous futility. — *n.* and *adj.* **mock′ing.** — *adv.* **mock′ingly.** — *adj.* **mock′-hero′ic** burlesquing the heroic style. — *n.* a mock-heroic composition: (in *pl.*) mock-heroic verses: (in *pl.*) sham heroic utterances or pose. — *adj.* **mock-hero′ical.** — *adv.* **mock′-hero′ically.** — **mock′ing-bird, mock′ingbird** an American bird (*Mimus*) of the thrush family, that mimics other birds' songs and other sounds; **mock′ing-thrush** a thrasher. — *adj.* **mock′-mod′est.** — **mock′-mod′esty** sham modesty; **mock moon** a paraselene, or bright spot in the moon's halo, 22° to right or left of the moon, due to refraction from ice crystals floating vertically; **mock′-or′ange** a tall shrub (*Philadelphus*, commonly called syringa) of the saxifrage family with strong-scented flowers: a kind of cherry-laurel (*U.S.*); **mock′-priv′et** a shrub (Phillyrea) akin to privet; **mock sun** a parhelion or spot in the sun's halo; **mock′-up** a full-size dummy model: a fabrication. — Also *adj.* — **mocks the pauses** (Shak., *Ant. and Cleo.*, V, i. 2) perh. throws away the opportunities given by the pauses; **mock turtle soup** an imitation of turtle soup, made of calf's head or veal; **put the mockers on** (*slang*) to put an end to, put paid to. [O.Fr. *mocquer*; origin uncertain.]

mockado *mok-ä′dō*, (*obs.*) *n.* an inferior cloth of Flemish origin: trumpery: — *pl.* **mocka′does.** [Prob. It. *mocaiardo*, haircloth.]

mocker-nut *mok′ər-nut, n.* a kind of hickory-nut with kernel difficult to extract.

mocock *mō-kok′*, **mocuck** *mō-kuk′, ns.* an American Indian birch-bark box or basket. [Orig. Algonquian.]

mocuddum. See **muqaddam.**

mod *mod, möd, mōd, n.* a Highland literary and musical festival. [Gael. *mòd* — O.N. *mōt*; cf. **moot.**]

Mod *mod, n.* a member of a teenage faction in (originally) the 1960s distinguished by special dress (typically neat), etc., from their rivals, the Rockers.

mod. con. *mod kon, modern convenience*, any item of up-to-date plumbing, heating, etc.

mode *mōd, n.* way or manner of acting, doing, happening, or existing: kind: form: manifestation: state of being: that which exists only as a quality of substance: a mood (*gram.*): character as necessary, contingent, possible or impossible (*log.*): a mood (*log.*): actual percentage mineral composition (*petr.*): the value of greatest frequency (*statistics*): modality: fashion: that which is fashionable: fashionableness: a model of fashion (*obs.*): alamode, or a garment made of it: open-work between the solid parts of lace: the method of dividing the octave according to the position of its steps and half-steps (*mus.*): in old music, the method of time-division of notes (*perfect* into three, *imperfect* into two; *major*, division of large into longs, *minor* of long into breves). — *adj.* **modal** (*mōd′l*) relating to mode. — *ns.* **mod′alism** the doctrine first set forth by Sabellius that the Father, the Son, and the Holy Spirit are not three distinct personalities but only three different modes of manifestation; **mod′alist** one who holds this theory. — *adj.* **modalist′ic.** — *n.* **modality** (*mōd-al′i-ti*) fact or condition of being modal: mode: method, terms, style: any of the primary methods of sensation: classification of propositions as to whether true, false, necessary, possible or impossible (*log.*): the quality of being

limited by a condition (*law*). — *adv.* **mod′ally.** — *adj.* **modish** (*mōd′ish*) fashionable: affectedly, foolishly, or absurdly fashionable. — *adv.* **mod′ishly.** — *ns.* **mod′ishness; mod′ist** a follower of the fashion; **modiste** (*mō-dēst*; Fr.) a professedly fashionable dressmaker or milliner. — **Greek modes** consist each of two disjunct tetrachords with a whole tone (diazeuctic tone) between them, or two conjunct tetrachords with a whole tone above (where the prefix is *hyper-*) or below them (*hypo-*); **Gregorian, mediaeval** or **ecclesiastical modes** have the same names as Greek modes but do not correspond to them (see **authentic, plagal**; also **Aeolian, Locrian, Ionian, Dorian, Phrygian, Lydian, Mixolydian** and names under **hyper-, hypo-**); **major mode** modern mode, consisting of two steps, a half-step, three steps, and a half-step; **minor mode** a modern mode consisting of a step, a half-step, two steps, a half-step, and two steps. [L. *modus*; partly through Fr. *mode*.]
model *mod′l, n.* a plan, design (*obs.*): a preliminary solid representation, generally small, or in plastic material, to be followed in construction: something to be copied: a pattern: an imitation of something on a smaller scale: a person or thing closely resembling another: one who poses for an artist, photographer, etc.: one who exhibits clothes for a shop by wearing them: a pattern of excellence: an article of standard design or a copy of one: structural type: a medal (*obs.*): a close covering or mould (*Shak.*). — *adj.* of the nature of a model: set up for imitation: completely suitable for imitation, exemplary. — *v.t.* to form after a model: to shape: to make a model or copy of: to form in some plastic material: of a mannequin, to display (a garment) by wearing it. — *v.i.* to practise modelling: — *pr.p.* **mod′elling;** *pa.t.* and *pa.p.* **mod′elled.** — *ns.* **mod′eller; mod′elling** the act or art of making a model of something, a branch of sculpture: rendering of solid form: working as a model. [O.Fr. *modelle* — It. *modello,* dim. of *modo* — L. *modus,* a measure.]
modem *mō′dəm, -dem,* (*comput.*) *n.* an electronic device used to transmit and receive data as a frequency-modulated tone over a communications system. [*modulator, demodulator.*]
modena *mod′i-nə, n.* a shade of crimson. [*Modena* in Italy.]
moderate *mod′ə-rāt, v.t.* to keep within measure or bounds: to regulate: to reduce in intensity: to make temperate or reasonable: to pacify: to preside as moderator over or at: to decide as an arbitrator (*obs.*). — *v.i.* to become less violent or intense: to preside or act as a moderator. — *adj.* (*-rit*) kept within measure or bounds: not excessive or extreme: temperate: of middle rate, average. — *n.* one whose views are far from extreme: one of a party in the Scottish Church in the 18th century and early 19th, broad in matters of doctrine and discipline, opposed to Evangelicalism and popular rights. — *adv.* **mod′erately.** — *ns.* **mod′erateness; modera′tion** act of moderating: state of being moderated or moderate: freedom from excess: self-restraint: the process of slowing down neutrons in an atomic pile: (in *pl.*) the first public examination for B.A. at Oxford (*coll.* **mods**); **mod′eratism** moderate opinions in religion or politics; **mod′erator** one who, or that which, moderates: a president, esp. in Presbyterian church courts: formerly an officer at Oxford and Cambridge who superintended degree examinations: one of two presiding over Mathematical Tripos at Cambridge: a moderations examiner at Oxford: a person appointed to standardise the marking, etc., of school public examinations: an oil-lamp with regulated flow of oil: the material in which neutrons are slowed down in an atomic pile: — *fem.* **mod′erātrix; mod′erātorship.** — **moderate (in) a call** of a presbytery, to act with the congregation in calling the minister it has chosen. [L. *moderārī, -ātus* — *modus,* a measure.]
moderato *mod-ə-rä′tō,* (*mus.*) *adj.* and *adv.* at a moderate speed. — *n.* a movement or passage to be played at this speed. [It.]

modern *mod′ərn, adj.* of or characteristic of present or recent time: not ancient or mediaeval: in education, mainly or wholly concerned with subjects other than Greek and Latin: of a style of type with contrasting thick and thin strokes, serifs at right-angles, curves thickened in the centre (*print.*): everyday, commonplace (*Shak.*): (with *cap.*), of a language, of or near the form now spoken and written, distinguished from *Old* and *Middle*. — *n.* one living in modern times, esp. distinguished from the ancient Greeks and Romans: a modernist: a modern printing type. — *n.* **modernīsā′tion, -z-.** — *v.t.* **mod′ernise, -ize** to adapt to the present time, conditions, needs, language, or spelling. — *v.i.* to adopt modern ways. — *ns.* **mod′erniser, -z-; mod′ernism** modern usage, expression, or trait: modern spirit or character: a tendency to adjust Christian dogma to the results of science and criticism; **mod′ernist** an admirer of modern ideas, ways, literature, studies, etc.: one who favours modernism; **modernis′tic; modern′ity.** — *adv.* **mod′ernly.** — *n.* **mod′ernness.** — **modern dance** a style of dance more expressive and less stylised than classical ballet; **modern jazz** a style of jazz which evolved in the early 1940s, characterised by greater rhythmic and harmonic complexity than previously. [L.L. *modernus* — *modo,* just now, orig. abl. of *modus.*]
modest *mod′ist, adj.* restrained by a sense of seemliness: unobtrusive: unpretentious: unassuming: diffident: decent: chaste: pure and delicate, as thoughts or language: not excessive or extreme: moderate. — *adv.* **mod′estly.** — *n.* **mod′esty** the quality or fact of being modest: a slight covering for a low neck. [L. *modestus* — *modus,* a measure.]
modicum *mod′i-kəm, n.* a small quantity: a small person (*obs.*): (disrespectfully) a woman (*obs.*): — *pl.* **mod′icums.** [L. neut. of *modicus,* moderate — *modus.*]
modify *mod′i-fī, v.t.* to moderate: to determine the mode of (*philos.*): to change the form or quality of: to alter slightly: to vary: to differentiate: of a word or phrase, to limit or qualify the sense of (*gram.*): to subject to umlaut (*philol.*): to assess, decree, or award (a payment) (*Scots law*): — *pr.p.* **mod′ifying;** *pa.t.* and *pa.p.* **mod′ified.** — *adj.* **mod′ifiable.** — *n.* **modification** (*-fi-kā′shən*) act of modifying or state of being modified: result of alteration or change: changed shape or condition: a change due to environment, lasting only as long as the operative conditions (*biol.*). — *adjs.* **mod′ificative, mod′ificatory** tending to modify: causing change of form or condition. — *adj.* **mod′ified** (*-fīd*) altered by modification: homologous but developed in a different direction (*biol.*). — *n.* **mod′ifier** (*-fī-ər*) one who modifies: a modifying agent: a diacritic indicating modification, esp. umlaut. [Fr. *modifier* — L. *modificāre, -ātum* — *modus,* a measure, *facēre,* to make.]
modillion *mod-il′yən,* (*archit.*) *n.* an ornamental bracket under a Corinthian or other cornice. [It. *modiglione* — L. *modulus* — *modus,* a measure.]
modiolus *mo-dī′ə-ləs, n.* the axis of the cochlea of the ear: (with *cap.*; also **Modiola**) the horse mussel genus. — *adj.* **modī′olar.** [L. *mŏdĭŏlus,* nave of a wheel, water-wheel bucket, drinking-vessel, etc., dim of *modus.*]
modish, modist, modiste. See **mode.**
modius *mō′di-əs, mod′i-ōōs, n.* a Roman dry measure, about a peck: a cylindrical head-dress of the gods: — *pl.* **mō′dii** (*-ī*). [L. *mŏdius.*]
modiwort. A Scots form of **mouldwarp.**
mods. See under **moderate.**
modulate *mod′ū-lāt, v.t.* to regulate, adjust: to inflect: to soften: to vary the pitch or frequency of: to impress characteristics of signal wave on (carrier wave) (*radio*): to vary velocity of electrons in electron beam. — *v.i.* to pass from one state to another: to pass from one key into another using a logical progression of chords that links the two keys (*mus.*). — *n.* **modulabil′ity** the capability of being modulated. — *adjs.* **mod′ular** of or pertaining to mode or modulation, or to a module;

mod'ularised, -ized consisting of modules: produced in the form of modules: divided into modules. — *ns.* **modular'ity; modulā'tion; mod'ulātor** one who, or that which, modulates: any device for effecting modulation (*radio*): a chart used in the tonic sol-fa notation on which modulations are shown; **mod'ule** a small measure or quantity: a unit of size, used in standardised planning of buildings and design of components: a self-contained unit forming part of a spacecraft or other structure: a standard unit or part of machinery, etc. in a system: a set course forming a unit in an educational scheme: an assembly within a geometrical framework of electronic units functioning as a system: a component part of a program, complete in itself and with its own function (*comput.*): a measure, often the semidiameter of a column, for regulating proportions of other parts (*archit.*): a model, image (*Shak.*). — *adv.* **mod'ulo** (*math.*) with respect to a (specified) modulus. — *n.* **mod'ulus** a constant multiplier or coefficient (*math.*): a quantity used as a divisor to produce classes of quantities, each class distinguished by its members yielding the same remainders (*math.*): the positive square root of the sum of the squares of the real and imaginary parts of a complex number (*math.*): a quantity expressing the relation between a force and the effect produced: — *pl.* **moduli** (*mod'ū-lī*). [L. *modulārī, -ātus*, to regulate, *modulus*, dim. of *modus*, a measure.]

modus *mō'dəs, mo'dŏŏs, n.* manner, mode: the way in which anything works: a fixed payment instead of tithes: — *pl.* **mō'dī.** — **modus operandi** (*op-ər-an'dī, -an'dē*) mode of operation, way of working; **modus vivendi** (*vi-ven'dī, -dē, wē-wen'dē*) way of life or living: an arrangement or compromise by means of which those who differ may get on together for a time: such an arrangement between states or between a state and the Pope. [L. *mŏdus*, manner.]

moe *mō.* See **mo**[1], **mow**[1].

moellon *mō'ə-lon, n.* rubble in mason-work. [Fr.]

Moeso-gothic *mē-sō-goth'ik, adj.* relating to the *Goths* who settled in *Moesia.* — *n.* their language.

mofette *mō-fet', n.* an opening in the earth giving out carbon dioxide with some nitrogen and oxygen — the last stage of volcanic activity. [Fr., — It. *mofeta*, perh. L. *mephītis*, foul exhalation.]

mofussil *mō-fus'l, n.* in India, all outside the capital or great towns. — *adj.* provincial: rural. [Hind. *mufassil* — Ar. *mufassal*, distinct, separate, pa.p. of *fassala*, to separate.]

mog. See **moggy.**

Mogadon® *mog'ə-don, n.* proprietary name for nitrazepam, a drug used to treat insomnia.

Mogen David. See **Magen David.**

moggan *mog'ən, (Scot.) n.* a footless stocking. [Origin unknown.]

moggy, moggie, mog *mog'i, mog, ns.* a cat (*slang*): a pet name for a cow, etc. (*dial*). [Perh. *Maggie.*]

Mogul *mō'gul, mō-gul', n.* a Mongol or Mongolian, esp. one of the followers of Baber, the conqueror of India (1483–1530): a name applied to the best quality of playing-cards: (without *cap.*) an influential person, magnate. — *adj.* pertaining to the Mogul Empire, architecture, etc. — **Great Mogul** the title by which Europeans knew the Emperors of Delhi. [Pers. *Mughul*, properly a Mongol.]

mogul *mō'gəl, n.* a mound of hard snow forming an obstacle on a ski-slope. [Poss. — Norw. dial. *muge*, heap.]

mohair *mō'hār, n.* the long, white, fine silken hair of the Angora goat: other hair as a substitute for it: cloth made of it. [Ar. *mukhayyar*; influenced by **hair**.]

Mohammedan *mō-ham'i-dən,* **Mahommedan** *mə-hom',* **Mahometan** *mə-hom'it-ən,* **Muhammadan, Muhammedan** *mōō-ham'a-dən, -i-dən, adjs.* pertaining to Mohammed (formerly popularly rendered as Mahomet) or to his religion, Islam. — *n.* a follower of Mohammed, a Muslim: one who professes Mo-

hammedanism, Islam. — *v.t.* and *v.i.* **Mohamm'edanise, -ize,** etc., to convert to, or conform to, Mohammedanism, Islam. — *ns.* **Mohamm'edanism, Mohamm'edism,** etc., Islam, the religion of Mohammed, contained in the Koran. — See also **Mahoun, mammet.** These terms are felt to be offensive by many Muslims, who prefer **Muslim, Islam, Islamic,** etc. [Ar. *Muhammad*, the great prophet of Arabia (*c.* 570–632); lit. praised.]

Moharram, Muharram, Muharrem *mō-, mōō-hur'um, ns.* the first month of the Muslim year: a great fast in commemoration of Hasan and Hosain (grandsons of Mohammed) during its first ten days: a public procession during the fast. [Ar. *muharram*, sacred.]

Mohawk *mō'hök, n.* an Indian of an Iroquois tribe of New York State: a Mohock: (often without *cap.*) a skating movement consisting of a stroke on the edge of one skate followed by a stroke in the opposite direction on the same edge of the other skate. [From an Algonquian name.]

mohel *mō'(h)el, n.* an official Jewish circumciser. [Heb.]

Mohican *mō-hē'kən,* **Mohegan** *-gən, ns.* an Indian of a former tribe in Connecticut. — Also *adj.* [From a native name.]

Moho, Mohorovicic(ian), discontinuity *mō'hō, mō-hō-rō'-və-chich(-i-ən) dis-kon-ti-nū'i-ti,* the boundary between the rocks of the earth's crust and the different rock of the mantle. [A. *Mohorovičić*, who deduced a difference of rock nature from the behaviour of earthquake shocks.]

Mohock *mō'hok, n.* one of a band of aristocratic ruffians of early 18th-century London. [**Mohawk.**]

mohr. Same as **mhorr.**

Mohs scale *mōz skāl,* a scale of numbers from 1 to 10 (1 representing talc, 10 representing diamond) in terms of which the relative hardness of solids can be expressed. [F. *Mohs* (1773–1839), German mineralogist.]

mohur *mō'hər, n.* a former Persian and Indian gold coin, in India fifteen rupees. [Pers. *mohr.*]

moider *moi'dər,* **moither** *-dhər,* **mither** *mī'dhər, (dial.) vs.t.* to confuse: to stupefy, overcome. — *v.i.* to work hard: to wander in mind. [Dialect word; origin obscure.]

moidore *moi'dōr, -dör, n.* a disused gold coin of Portugal. [Port. *moeda d'ouro*, lit. money of gold — L. *monēta, dē, aurum.*]

moiety *moi'ə-ti, n.* half: one of two parts or divisions: a small share (*Shak.*). [O.Fr. *moite* — L. *medietās, -tātis*, middle point, later half — *medius*, middle.]

moil *moil, (arch.) v.t.* to wet: to bedaub: to defile. — *v.i.* (*dial.*) to toil: to drudge. — *n.* (*dial.* and *arch.*) a spot: a defilement: labour: trouble: turmoil. — *n.* **moil'er.** [O.Fr. *moillier* (Fr. *mouiller*) to wet — L. *mollis*, soft.]

moineau *moi'nō, n.* a small flat bastion to protect a fortification while being erected. [Fr.]

Moira *moi'ra, n.* a Fate (goddess): fate, destiny. — *pl.* **Moirai** (*-rī*). [Gr. *Moirā.*]

moire *mwär,* also *mwör, mōr, moir, n.* orig. watered mohair: now watered silk or other fabric with watered appearance (also **moire antique**). — *adj.* **moiré** (*mwär'ā, moi'rī*) watered. — *n.* a watered appearance on cloth or metal surface: sometimes for moire, the material. — **moiré effect, pattern** an optical effect, a shifting wavy pattern seen when two surfaces covered with regular lines are superimposed. [Fr., from English **mohair.**]

moist *moist, adj.* damp: humid: rainy: watery: juicy (*Shak.*). — *v.t.* (*Shak.*) to moisten. — *vs.t.* **moisten** (*mois'n*) to make moist: to wet slightly; **moist'ify** (*jocular*) to make moist. — *adv.* **moist'ly.** — *ns.* **moist'ness; moist'ure** moistness: that which makes slightly wet: liquid, esp. in small quantity. — *adj.* **moist'ureless.** — *v.t.* **moist'urise, -ize** to add or restore moisture to. — Also *v.i.* — *n.* **moist'uriser, -z-** that which moisturises, esp. a cosmetic cream which restores moisture to the skin. [O.Fr. *moiste* (Fr. *moite*), perh. — L. *mustum*, juice of grapes, new wine, perh. L. *mūcidus*, mouldy.]

moit. See **mote**[2].

moither. See **moider.**

mokaddam. See **muqaddam.**

moke *mōk*, (*slang*) *n.* a donkey: a variety performer on several instruments: a Negro (*U.S. slang*). [Origin unknown.]

moki *mō'ki*, *n.* a New Zealand sea fish belonging either to the species *Latridopsis ciliaris* or *Chironemus spectabilis* (**red moki**): (formerly) the blue cod, *Parapercis colias*. [Maori.]

moko *mō'kō*, *n.* a system of tattooing practised by the Maoris: a Maori tattoo: — *pl.* **mōkos.** [Maori.]

mol, molal, etc., **molar,** etc. See **mole**[1].

molar *mō'lər*, *adj.* used for grinding: pertaining to a grinding tooth. — *n.* a grinding tooth, or back tooth. [L. *molāris* — *mola*, a millstone — *molĕre*, to grind.]

Molasse *mō-läs'*, *n.* a series of Oligocene or Miocene sandstones and sandy marls in Switzerland, France, and Germany. [Fr.]

molasses *mo-las'iz*, *n.sing.* a thick treacle that drains from sugar. [Port. *melaço* (Fr. *mélasse*) — L.L. *mellāceum* — *mel, mellis*, honey.]

mold. See **mould**[1,2,3], **mole**[2].

moldwarp. Same as **mouldwarp.**

mole[1] *mōl*, *n.* the amount of substance that contains as many (specified) entities (e.g. atoms, molecules, ions, photons) as there are atoms in 12 grams of carbon-12 (abbrev. **mol** *mōl*): formerly defined as equal to gram-molecule. — *adj.* **mol'al** of, relating to, or containing, a mole. — *n.* **molal'ity** the concentration of a solution expressed as the number of moles of dissolved substance per thousand grams of solvent. — *adj.* **mol'ar** of, or relating to, a mole: per mole: per unit amount of substance: of, or relating to molecules: of or pertaining to mass or masses or to large masses (L. *mōles*, mass). — *ns.* **molar'ity** the concentration of a solution expressed as the number of moles of dissolved substance per litre of solution; **mole'-electronics** (also **molecular electronics**) technique of growing solid-state crystals so as to form transistors, etc., for microminiaturisation. [Ger., — *Molekül*, molecule; both words (Ger. and Eng.) ult. from L. *mōles*, mass.]

mole[2] *mōl*, *n.* a spot, esp. one caused by iron on linen (*obs.* except in Scots form **mail** and in **iron-mould**): a small spot or elevation on the skin, often coloured and hairy. — *Spens.* **mōld.** [O.E. *māl*.]

mole[3] *mōl*, *n.* a small insectivorous animal (*Talpa*) with very small eyes and soft fur, which burrows in the ground and casts up little heaps of mould: extended to kindred or similar animals: one who works in darkness or underground: a spy who successfully infiltrates a rival organisation, esp. one not engaging in espionage until firmly established and trusted: one who sees badly (*fig.*): a boring machine which makes a tunnel, e.g. for a pipeline. — **mole'cast** a molehill; **mole'catcher** one whose business it is to catch moles; **molc'-crick'et** a burrowing insect (*Gryllotalpa*) of the cricket family, with forelegs like a mole's; **mole drainer** (*agri.*) a pointed cylinder on the lower edge of a blade, which is drawn longitudinally through soil to form a drainage channel (**mole drain**). — *adj.* **mole'-eyed** having eyes like those of a mole: seeing imperfectly. — **mole'hill** a little hill or heap of earth cast up by a mole; **mole plough** a mole drainer; **mole'rat** a name for several burrowing rodents (*Spalax, Bathyergus*, etc.); **mole'-skin** the skin of a mole: mole's fur: a superior kind of fustian, double-twilled, cropped before dyeing: (in *pl.*) clothes, esp. trousers, made of this fustian; **mole'-spade** a small spade used by molecatchers. — **make a mountain out of a molehill** to magnify a trifling matter; **mole out** to seek, or elicit, bit by bit, as if by burrowing. [M.E. *molle, mulle*; cf. Du. *mol*, L.G. *mol, mul*; poss. shortened from **mouldwarp.**]

mole[4] *mōl*, *n.* a massive breakwater: an ancient Roman mausoleum. [Fr. *môle* — L. *mōles*, mass.]

mole[5] *mōl*, *n.* an abnormal fleshy mass of tissue formed in the uterus; see also **hydatidiform mole.** [L. *mola*, millstone.]

mole[6] *mō'li*, *n.* in Mexican cooking, a sauce made mainly with chilli and chocolate, served with meat dishes. [Amer. Sp.; see **guacamole.**]

molecule *mol'i-kūl*, or *mōl'*, *n.* the smallest particle of any substance that retains the properties of that substance: a gram-molecule. — *adj.* **molecular** (*mol-ek'ū-lər*). — *n.* **molecularity** (*mol-ek-ū-lar'i-ti*). — *adv.* **molec'ularly.** — **molecular biology** study of the molecules of the substances involved in the processes of life; **molecular electronics** see **mole**[1]; **molecular formula** a formula showing the number of atoms of each element in a molecule, e.g. benzene, C_6H_6; **molecular weight** a former term for relative molecular mass (q.v.) [Fr. *molécule*, — L. *mōles*, mass.]

molendinar *mol-en'din-ər*, (*pedantically facet.*) *adj.* pertaining to a mill or a miller. — *n.* a molar tooth. — *adj.* **molen'dinary** (*pedantically facet.*) relating to a mill. — *n.* a mill. [L.L. *molendīnum*, a mill — L. *molĕre*, to grind.]

molest *mə-, mō-lest'*, *v.t.* to vex: to interfere with in a troublesome or hostile way: to annoy. — *n.* annoyance. — *ns.* **molestā'tion** (*mo-, mō-*); **molest'er.** — *adj.* **molest'ful.** [Fr. *molester* — L. *molestāre* — *molestus*, troublesome.]

molimen *mō-lī'mən*, *n.* a great effort, esp. any periodic effort to discharge a natural function. — *adj.* **moliminous** (*-lim'in-əs*). [L. *mōlīmen* — *mōlīrī*, to toil — *mōles*, mass.]

moline *mō'līn, -līn'*, (*her.*) *adj.* like a millstone rind — applied to a cross with each arm ending in two outward curving branches. — *n.* a moline cross. [L. *mola*, a mill.]

Molinism[1] *mol'in-izm*, *n.* the doctrine of the 16th-cent. Spanish Jesuit Luis *Molina*, reconciling predestination and free will by God's foreknowledge, the efficacy of grace depending on the co-operation of the will. — *n.* **Mol'inist.**

Molinism[2] *mol'in-izm*, *n.* the quietism of Miguel de *Molinos* (17th cent.). — *n.* **Mol'inist.**

moll *mol*, *n.* (with *cap.*) a familiar form of *Mary*: a gangster's girl-friend: a prostitute.

mollah, molla. See **mullah.**

mollie *mol'i*. Same as **mallemaroking.**

mollify *mol'i-fī*, *v.t.* to soften: to assuage: to cause to abate: to appease. — *v.i.* to become soft: to relax in severity or opposition — *pr.p.* **moll'ifying** — *pa.t.* and *pa.p.* **moll'ified.** — *ns.* **mollification** (*-fi-kā'shən*); **moll'ifier.** [Fr. *mollifier* — L. *mollificāre* — *mollis*, soft, *facĕre*, to make.]

mollities *mol-ish'i-ēz*, (*arch.*) *n.* softness, softening. — *adj.* **mollitious** (*-ish'əs*) luxurious. [L. *mollitiēs* — *mollis*, soft.]

mollusc, mollusk *mol'əsk*, *n.* one of the **Mollusca** (*-us'kə*), a large phylum of invertebrates, without segments or limbs, usually having a mantle or fold of skin that secretes a shell — lamellibranchs, gasteropods, cephalopods, and some smaller groups: a person of inert habit. — *adjs.* **mollus'can, mollus'cous** of or belonging to the Mollusca. — *n.* **mollus'cicide** (*-ki-sīd*) an agent for destroying molluscs, e.g. snails responsible for spread of disease. — *adj.* **mollus'cicidal.** — *n.* **mollus'coid** a member of a now abandoned division of invertebrates, the **Molluscoid'ea**, Polyzoa and brachiopods. — *adj.* of the Molluscoidea: like a mollusc. [L. *molluscus*, softish — *mollis*, soft.]

Mollweide's projection *mol'vī-dəz prə-jek'shən*, an equal-area representation of the surface of the globe in which the parallels of latitude are straight lines (closer together nearer the poles) and the meridians (apart from the central one) are curved, the curvature increasing toward the marginal meridians. [K. *Mollweide* (d.1825), Ger. mathematician and astronomer.]

molly *mol'i*, *n.* (with *cap.*) dim. of *Mary*: a milksop. — *n.* **moll'ycoddle** an effeminate fellow. — *v.t.* to coddle.

—**Molly Maguire** a member of an Irish society formed in 1843 to resist government evictions, who disguised themselves as women: a member of a Pennsylvanian secret society formed to resist oppressive conditions in the mines, and crushed in 1877.

mollymawk *mol'i-mök*. Same as **mallemuck**.

Moloch *mō'lok*, *n.* a Semitic god to whom children were sacrificed (also **Mo'lech**): any cause to which dreadful sacrifice is made or destruction due: (without *cap.*) an exceedingly spiny harmless Australian lizard. — *v.t.* **mo'lochise, -ize** to sacrifice as to Moloch. [Gr. and L. *Moloch* — Heb. *Mōlek*.]

Molossian *mol-os'i-ən*, *adj.* of *Molossia* or *Molossis* in Epirus, famous in ancient times for its great dogs of mastiff kind. — *n.* **moloss'us** a metrical foot of three long syllables: — *pl.* **moloss'ī**.

Molotov cocktail *mol'ə-tof kok'tāl*, a crude form of hand-grenade consisting of a bottle with inflammable liquid, and a wick to be ignited just before the missile is thrown. [V. M. *Molotov* (1890–1986), Russian statesman.]

molt[1]. See **moult**.

molt[2], **molten**, etc. See **melt**[1].

molto *mol'tō*, (*mus.*) *adv.* very: much. [It.]

Molucca bean *mo-luk'ə bēn'*, nicker nut, bonduc.

moly *mō'li*, *n.* a magic herb given by Hermes to Odysseus as a counter-charm against the spells of Circe: a species of wild onion, *Allium moly*. [Gr. *mōly*.]

molybdenum *mol-ib'din-əm* (also *mol-ib-dē'nəm*), *n.* silvery-white metallic element (symbol Mo; atomic number 42). — *ns.* **molyb'date** a salt of molybdic acid; **molybdēn'ite** (or *-ib'dən-īt*) a mineral, molybdenum disulphide. — *adj.* **molyb'dic**. — *n.* **molybdō'sis** lead-poisoning. — *adj.* **molyb'dous**. — **molybdic acid** H_2MoO_4. [Latinised neuter — Gr. *molybdaina*, a lump of lead, a leadlike substance — *molybdos*, lead.]

mom *mom*, (*U.S. coll.*) *n.* mother. — Also **momm'a**, **momm'y**. [See **mamma**[1].]

mome[1] *mōm*, (*obs.*) *n.* a buffoon: a carper. [**Momus**.]

mome[2] *mōm*, (*Spens.*) *n.* a blockhead. [Origin obscure.]

moment *mō'mənt*, *n.* a point of time: a time so short that it may be considered as a point: a very short time (abbrev. in slang, **mo**): a second: a precise instant: the present, or the right, instant: moving cause or motive (*Shak.*): importance, consequence: an infinitesimal change in a varying quantity (*math.*, *obs.*): a stage or turning-point: an element or factor (as in *psychological moment*, rightly used): a measure of turning effect — the *moment of a force* about a point is the product of the force and the perpendicular on its line of action from the point. — *adjs.* **momentān'eous** momentary: instantaneous; **mo'mentany** (*Shak.*) momentary. — *adv.* **mo'mentarily** for a moment: every moment: at any moment. — *n.* **mo'mentariness**. — *adj.* **mo'mentary** lasting for a moment: short-lived. — *adv.* **mo'mently** every moment: for a moment. — *adj.* occurring every moment: of a moment. — *adj.* **momentous** (-*ment'*) of great consequence. — *adv.* **moment'ously**. — *ns.* **moment'ousness; moment'um** the quantity of motion in a body measured by the product of mass and velocity: force of motion gained in movement, impetus (*coll.*): — *pl.* **moment'a**. — **moment of truth** the climax of the bullfight: a moment when, suddenly and dramatically, one is face to face with stark reality — often a testing moment (*fig.*). [L. *mōmentum*, for *movimentum* — *movēre*, *mōtum*, to move.]

momma, mommy. See **mom**.

mommet. See **mammet**.

Momus *mō'məs*, *n.* the god of ridicule. [Latinised from Gr. *mōmos*, blame, reproach, personified.]

mon-. See **mon(o)-**.

mona *mō'nə*, *n.* a West African monkey, *Cercopithecus mona*. [It., Sp., or Port. *mona*, monkey.]

monachism *mon'ək-izm*, *n.* monasticism. — *adjs.* **mon'achal, mon'achist**. — *n.* **Mon'achus** the monk-seal genus. [Gr. *monachos*, solitary — *monos*, single, alone.]

monacid *mon-as'id*, **monoacid** *mon-ō-as'id*, *adjs.* having one replaceable hydrogen atom: capable of replacing one hydrogen atom of an acid. [**mon(o)-**.]

monact *mon'akt*, *adj.* one-rayed. — *adjs.* **monact'inal** (-*i-nəl* or -*ī'nəl*), **monact'ine** (-*in*). [Gr. *monos*, single, alone, *aktis*, -*inos*, a ray.]

monad *mon'ad*, *n.* the number one: a unit: an ultimate unit of being, material and psychical: a spirit: God: a hypothetical primitive living organism or unit of organic life: a flagellate of the genus Monas or akin to it: a univalent element, atom, or radical. — Also *adj.* —*adjs.* **monad'ic, -al; monad'iform** like a monad. — *ns.* **mon'adism, monadol'ogy** a theory or doctrine of monads, esp. Leibniz's; **mon'as** a monad: (with *cap.*) a genus of flagellates. [Gr. *monas*, -*ados*, a unit — *monos*, single, alone.]

monadelphous *mon-ə-del'fəs*, *adj.* of stamens, united by the filaments in one bundle: of a flower or plant, having all the stamens so united. — *n.pl.* **Monadel'phia** in Linnaeus's system, a class of plants with stamens united in one bundle. [Gr. *monos*, single, alone, *adelphos*, brother.]

monadic... to ...**monadology**. See **monad**.

monal. See **monaul**.

monandrous *mon-an'drəs*, *adj.* having or allowing one husband or male mate (at a time): having one stamen or one antheridium (*bot.*). — *n.pl.* **Monan'dria** in Linnaeus's system, a class of plants with one stamen. — *n.* **monan'dry** the condition or practice of being monandrous. [Gr. *monos*, single, alone, *anēr*, *andros*, a man, male.]

monarch[1] *mon'ərk*, *n.* a sole hereditary head of a state, whether titular or ruling: a large butterfly (*Danaus plexippus*) with orange and black wings. — *adjs.* **monarchal** (-*ärk'əl*), **monarch'ial, monarch'ic, -al**. — *ns.* **Monarch'ian** a Christian who denied the personal independent subsistence of Christ — *dynamic*, when regarding the divinity of Christ as only a power (*dynamis*) communicated to him; *modalistic*, when regarding Christ as the Father who had assumed flesh, a mere *modus* of the Godhead; **Monarch'ianism**. — *adj.* **Monarchianis'tic**. — *v.t.* **mon'archise, -ize** to rule over as a monarch: to convert into a monarchy. — *v.i.* (also *v.t.* with *it*) to play the monarch. — *ns.* **mon'-archism** the principles of monarchy: love of monarchy; **mon'archist** an advocate of monarchy: a believer in monarchy: a Monarchian. — Also *adj.* — *adj.* **monarchist'ic**. — *ns.* **Monarch'o** (*Shak.*) a foppish fantastic megalomaniac (from a crazy Italian about Elizabeth's court); **mon'archy** a kind of government of which there is a monarch: a state with monarchical government: the territory of a monarch. [Gr. *monarchēs* — *monos*, single, alone, *archein*, to rule.]

monarch[2] *mon'ärk*, (*bot.*) *adj.* having one xylem strand. [Gr. *monos*, single, alone, *archē*, origin.]

Monarda *mən-är'də*, *n.* a genus of North American aromatic herbs of the mint (Labiatae) family: (without *cap.*) a plant of this genus. [N. *Monardes* (d. 1588), Spanish botanist.]

monas. See **monad**.

monastery *mon'əs-tər-i*, -*tri*, *n.* a house for monks, or (*rarely*) nuns. — *adjs.* **monastē'rial, monastic** (-*as'tik*), **-al** pertaining to monasteries, monks, and nuns: recluse: solitary. — *n.* **monas'tic** a monk. — *adv.* **monas'tically**. — *n.* **monas'ticism** (-*sizm*) the corporate monastic life or system of living. [Late Gr. *monastērion* — *monastēs*, a monk — *monos*, single, alone.]

Monastral blue®, **green**® *mon-as'trəl blōō*, *grēn* trade-names for certain phthalocyanine pigments.

monatomic *mon-ə-tom'ik*, *adj.* consisting of one atom: having one replaceable atom or group: univalent. [**mon(o)-**.]

monaul, monal *mon'öl*, *n.* a magnificent Himalayan pheasant (*Lophophorus*). [Nepali *munāl*.]

monaural *mon-ö'rəl*, *adj.* having or using only one ear: pertaining to one ear: of a gramophone record, etc., giving the effect of sound from a single direction —

not stereophonic. [**mon**(o)-.]

monaxial *mon-aks'i-əl, adj.* having only one axis. — *adj.* **monax'on** monaxial. — *n.* a monaxonic sponge, spicule. — *adj.* **monaxon'ic.** — *n.pl.* **Monaxon'ida** an order of sponges with monaxon spicules only. [**mon**(o)-.]

monazite *mon'əz-īt,* (*min.*) *n.* a phosphate of cerium, lanthanum, neodymium, praseodymium, and usually thorium, a source of thorium. [Gr. *monazein,* to be solitary — on account of its rarity.]

monchiquite *mon'shi-kīt, n.* a fine-grained lamprophyric rock, composed of olivine and augite with little or no feldspar, in an analcite groundmass. [From the Serra de *Monchique,* in S.W. Portugal.]

mondain *mɔ̃-ɛ̃, adj.* worldly, fashionable: — *fem.* **mondaine** (*mɔ̃-den*). — *n.* a man (woman) who lives in fashionable society. [Fr., — L. *mundānus* — *mundus,* world.]

Monday *mun'di, n.* the second day of the week. — *adj.* **Mon'dayish** having the feelings normal after Sunday's activities or inactivities with the prospect of the week's work. — **Monday Club** a right-wing group of Conservatives formed in 1961, holding discussions over Monday lunch. — **black Monday, Handsel Monday, Meal Monday, Plough Monday** see **black,** etc. [O.E. *mōnandæg, mōnan,* gen. of *mōna,* moon, *dæg,* day.]

mondial *mon'di-əl, adj.* of the whole world, worldwide. [Fr. — L. *mundus,* world.]

monecious. Same as **monoecious.**

Monel metal® *mō-nel' met'l,* a nickel-base alloy with high strength and resistance to corrosion.

moner *mōn'ər,* **moneron** *mon-ēr'on, ns.* Haeckel's hypothetical simplest protozoan: — *pl.* **monēr'a.** [Gr. *monērēs,* single.]

monergism *mon'ər-jizm,* (*theol.*) *n.* the doctrine that regeneration is entirely the work of the Holy Spirit, the natural will being incapable of co-operation. [Gr. *monos,* single, alone, *ergon,* work.]

monetary *mon'* or *mun'i-tər-i, adj.* of or relating to money: consisting of money. — *ns.* **mon'etarism; mon'etarist** one who advocates an economic policy based chiefly on the control of a country's money supply; **monetīsā'tion, -z-.** — *v.t.* **mon'etise, -ize** to give the character of money to, to coin as money. — **monetary unit** the principal unit of currency of a state. [L. *monēta* (see **money**).]

moneth *munth* (*Spens.*). Same as **month.**

money *mun'i, n.* coin: pieces of stamped metal used in commerce: any currency used in the same way. wealth:—*pl.* **mon'eys, mon'ies** (*arch.* and *legal*) sums of money: money. — *adj.* **mon'eyed, mon'ied** having money: rich in money: consisting in money. — *n.* **mon'eyer** one who coins money legally (*arch.*): a capitalist (*obs.*). — *adj.* **mon'eyless** having no money. — **money'-bag** a bag for or of money: (*pl.*) a rich man; **mon'ey-bill** a bill introduced into parliament or congress for raising revenue or otherwise dealing with money. — *adj.* **mon'ey-bound** unable to move for want of money. — **money'-box** a box for collecting or saving money, usu. with a slit for insertion; **mon'ey-broker** one who carries out transactions in money for others; **mon'ey-changer** one who exchanges one currency for another; **mon'ey-grubber** a sordid accumulator of wealth. — *n.* and *adj.* **mon'ey-grubb'ing.** — **mon'ey-lender** a professional lender of money at interest; **mon'ey-lending; mon'ey-maker** one who acquires riches: anything that brings profit; **mon'ey-making** act of gaining wealth. — *adj.* lucrative, profitable. — **mon'ey-mar'ket** (the dealers in) the market for short-term loans for business, etc.; **mon'ey-or'der** an order for money deposited at one post-office, and payable at another; **mon'ey-scriv'ener** one who does financial business for clients; **mon'ey-spi'der** a small spider supposed to bring luck; **mon'ey-spinner** a money-spider: a successful speculator: anything that brings much money: **mon'ey's-worth** something as good as money: full value; **mon'ey-taker** one who receives

payments of money, esp. at an entrance-door: one who can be bribed; **mon'eywort** a round-leaved loosestrife, creeping Jenny. — **for my, our, money** if I, we, were to choose, express an opinion, etc.; **hard money** coin; **in the money** among the prize-winners (*racing,* etc.): well-off; **make money** to acquire wealth: to make a profit; **money down** money paid on the spot; **money for jam, old rope,** etc., money obtained without effort; **money of account** a monetary unit (not represented by current coins) used in keeping accounts; **money talks** the wealthy have much influence; **pot(s) of money** a large amount of money; **put money into** to invest in; **put money on** to place a bet on; **put one's money where one's mouth is** to support one's judgment by betting money; **ready money** money paid for a thing at the time at which it is bought: money ready for immediate payment. [O.Fr. *moneie* (Fr. *monnaie*) — L. *monēta,* money, a mint, *Monēta* (the reminder) being a surname of Juno, in whose temple at Rome money was coined.]

mong *mung,* (now *dial.*) *n.* a mixture: a crowd. — **mong'corn, mung'corn** maslin. [O.E. *gemang.*]

'mong, 'mongst aphetic for **among, amongst.**

monger *mung'gər, n.* (chiefly in composition) a dealer — except in a few instances, as *ironmonger,* one who traffics in a petty, or discreditable way, or in unpleasant subjects. — *ns.* **mong'ering, mong'ery.** [O.E. *mangere* — L. *mangō, -ōnis,* a furbisher, slave-dealer — Gr. *manganeuein,* to use trickery.]

Mongol *mong'gol, n.* a member of Genghis Khan's clan, or of the various populations under him: one of the people of Mongolia: their language: a member of a broad-headed, yellow-skinned, straight-haired, small-nosed human race, often with an epicanthic fold of skin (otherwise called Tungus): (often without *cap.*) a person affected by Mongolism. — *adj.* of the Mongols, Mongolia, or Mongolian. — *adj.* **Mongolian** (*mong-gō'li-ən*) of Mongolia, the Mongols, or their language. — *n.* the language of Mongolia. — *adj.* **Mongolic** (*-gol'ik*) Mongolian: of Mongolian type: of the division of the Ural-Altaic languages to which Mongolian, Buriat, and Kalmuck belong. — *v.t.* **Mong'olise, -ize** to make Mongolian. — *n.* **Mong'olism** (often without *cap.*) a congenital disease caused by chromosomal abnormality, in which there is mental deficiency and a broadening and flattening of the features, now more usu. called **Down's syndrome.** — *adj.* **Mong'oloid** of Mongolian race or type: (often without *cap.*) affected with Mongolism. — *n.* a person of Mongolian type: (often without *cap.*) a person affected by Mongolism. — **Mongoloid eye** an eye with an epicanthic fold. [Said to be from Mongol *mong,* brave.]

mongoose *mong', mung'gōōs, n.* an Indian animal of the civet family, a great slayer of snakes and rats: any other species of the genus (Herpestes), including the ichneumon: a Madagascan lemur: — *pl.* **mong'ooses.** — Also **mung'oose,** (Fr.) **mangouste'.** [Marathi *mangūs.*]

mongrel *mung'grəl, n.* an animal, esp. a dog, of a mixed breed (usu. in contempt): a person, thing, or word of mixed or indefinite origin or nature: that which is neither one thing nor another. — *adj.* mixed in breed: ill-defined. — *v.t.* **mong'relise, -ize.** — *n.* **mong'relism.** — *adj.* **mong'relly.** [Prob. from root of O.E. *mengan,* to mix.]

monial *mōn'i-əl, n.* a mullion. [O.Fr., of unknown origin.]

moni(c)ker *mon'i-kər,* (*slang;* orig. tramps') *n.* an alias, nickname, or real name.

monied, monies. See **money.**

Monilia *mon-il'i-ə, n.* a genus of fungi with conidia in branched chains: (without *cap.*) a fungus of this genus. — *n.* **moniliasis** (*-ī'ə-sis*) a disease of the mouth and digestive tract in birds, animals, and man (**thrush**²), caused by fungi of the genus *Monilia.* — *adj.* **monil'iform** like a string of beads. [L. *monīle,* a necklace.]

moniment *mon'i-mənt.* See **monument.**

moniplies *mun', mon'i-plīz.* See **manyplies.**

monism *mon'izm, n.* a philosophical theory that all being may ultimately be referred to one category; thus *idealism, pantheism, materialism* are monisms — as opposed to the dualism of matter and spirit. — *n.* **mon'ist.** — *adjs.* **monist'ic, -al.** [Gr. *monos,* single, alone.]

monition *mon-ish'ən, n.* a reminding or admonishing: warning: notice: a summons to appear and answer (*law*). — *adj.* **mon'itive** conveying admonition. — *n.* **mon'itor** one who admonishes: an adviser: a senior pupil who assists in school discipline or other pupil with a special responsibility: a back-board (*obs.*): apparatus for testing transmission in electrical communication: a person employed to monitor: a low iron-clad with revolving gun-turrets (from an American ship so named, the first of its kind, 1862): a genus (*Varanus*) of very large lizards of Africa, Asia, and Australia (from a fancy that they give warning of the presence of a crocodile): a detector for radioactivity: an instrument used in a production process to keep a variable quantity within prescribed limits by transmitting a controlling signal: a screen in a television studio showing the picture being transmitted: — *fem.* **mon'itress.** — *v.t.* to act as monitor to: to check (as the body and clothing of persons working with radioactive materials) for radioactivity: to track, or to control (an aeroplane, guided missile, etc.): to watch, check, supervise. — *v.i.* (*radio*) to tap on to a communication circuit, usu. in order to ascertain that the transmission is that desired: to listen to foreign broadcasts in order to obtain news, code messages, etc. — *adj.* **monitorial** (*-ōr', -ôr'*) relating to a monitor. — *adv.* **monito'rially.** — *n.* **mon'itorship.** — *adj.* **mon'itory** giving admonition or warning. [L. *monēre, -itum,* to remind.]

monk *mungk, n.* formerly, a hermit: a man (other than a friar, but loosely often applied to a friar also) of a religious community living together under vows: a bullfinch: an inky blotch or overinked place in print: formerly, touchwood for firing mines. — *ns.* **monk'ery** (*contemptuous*) monasticism: behaviour of monks: monks collectively; **monk'hood** the state or character of a monk. — *adj.* **monk'ish** (*depreciatory*) pertaining to a monk: like a monk: monastic. — **monk'fish** the angel fish (shark): any of several types of angler-fish; **monk's cloth** a type of heavy cotton cloth; **monk'-seal** a seal (*Monachus albiventer*) of the Black Sea, Mediterranean, and N.W. Africa, dark grey above, light underneath; **monks'hood** wolfsbane, a poisonous ranunculaceous plant (*Aconitum*) with a large hoodlike posterior sepal; **monk's rhubarb** patience-dock; **monk's'-seam** (*naut.*) a strong seam formed by overlapping two pieces and stitching on each side and down the middle — also *middle-stitching.* [O.E. *munuc* — L. *monachus* — Gr. *monachos* — *monos,* alone.]

monkey *mungk'i, n.* any mammal of the Primates except man and (usually) the anthropoid apes: an ape: a sheep (*Austr. slang*): a name of contempt, esp. for a mischievous person, also of playful endearment: the falling weight of a pile-driver: a large hammer for driving bolts: 500 pounds, or dollars (*slang*): anger (*slang*): a liquor-vessel of various kinds: — *pl.* **monk'eys.** — *v.i.* to meddle with anything, to fool. — *v.t.* to imitate as a monkey does. — *adj.* **monk'eyish.** — *n.* **monk'eyism** monkey-like behaviour. — **monk'ey-bag** a small money-bag, hung round the neck; **monk'ey-block** a small swivel-block, used to guide running rigging; **monk'ey-board** a foot-board behind a vehicle: a high-level platform on an oil-derrick; **monk'ey-boat** a narrow, half-decked river-boat; **monk'ey-bread** the baobab tree or its fruit; **monkey business** underhand dealings: mischievous behaviour; **monk'ey-en'gine** a pile-driving engine; **monk'ey-flow'er** a species of Mimulus; **monk'ey-gaff** a small gaff above the spanker gaff for the flag; **monk'ey-gland** ape's testicle, grafted experimentally on man (1920–30s) to effect rejuvenescence; **monk'ey-grass** a coarse fibre from the leaf-stalks of *Attalea funifera,* used for brooms, etc.; **monk'ey=**

hammer a drop-press with a ram, which is raised and let drop freely; **monk'ey-jacket** a close-fitting jacket; **monk'ey-jar** a water-monkey; **monk'ey-nut** the pea-nut or ground-nut (Arachis); **monkey pod** the rain-tree; **monk'ey-pot** the round-lidded outer shell of the sapucaia nut; **monk'ey-pump** a straw let through a gimlet-hole for sucking liquor from a cask; **monk'ey-puzz'le** the so-called Chile pine, *Araucaria imbricata,* with close-set prickly leaves; **monk'ey-rail** a light rail above the quarter-rail; **monk'ey-rope** a forest creeper or liana: a rope round a sailor's waist for working in a dangerous place; **monk'ey-run** a favourite place of parade and striking up of acquaintance; **monk'ey-shine** (*U.S. slang*) a monkeyish trick; **monk'ey-suit** a man's evening suit; **monk'ey-tail** a vertical scroll at the end of a hand-rail; **monk'ey-trick; monk'ey-wheel** a tackle-block over which runs a hoisting-rope; **monk'ey-wrench** a wrench with a movable jaw. — **have a monkey on one's back** to be addicted to drugs; **have, get, one's monkey up** to be angry; **make a monkey (out) of** to make a fool of; **not to give a monkey's** (*vulg. slang*) not to care, be interested, at all; **suck the monkey** to drink from a cask through an inserted tube: to drink rum, etc., from a coconut. [Perh. from M.L.G. *moneke,* conn. Sp., Port. *mono,* monkey.]

Mon-Khmer *mōn'kmer', adj.* of a group of Austroasiatic languages that includes *Mon,* spoken in Pegu (Burma), and *Khmer* in Cambodia.

mon(o)- *mon(-ō)-,* in composition, single. [Gr. *monos,* single, alone.]

mono *mon'ō,* (*coll.*) *n.* a monaural gramophone record: monaural reproduction: — *pl.* **mon'os.** — Also *adj.*

monoacid. Same as **monacid.**

monoamine *mon-ō-am'īn, -ēn, n.* an amine containing only one amino-group. [**mon(o)-**.]

monobasic *mon-ō-bā'sik, adj.* capable of reacting with one equivalent of an acid: (of an acid) having one replaceable hydrogen atom. [**mon(o)-**.]

monoblepsis *mon-ō-blep'sis, n.* a condition in which vision is more distinct when one eye only is used. [Gr. *monos,* single, *blepsis,* sight.]

monocardian *mon-ō-kär'di-ən, adj.* having an undivided heart. [Gr. *monos,* single, alone, *kardiā,* heart.]

monocarpellary *mon-ō-kär'pəl-a-ri,* or *-pel', adj.* of or with only one carpel. [**mon(o)-**.]

monocarpic *mon-ō-kärp'ik, adj.* fruiting once only. — *n.* **mon'ocarp** a monocarpic plant. — *adj.* **monocarp'ous** monocarpic: having only one ovary: producing one fruit. [Gr. *monos,* single, alone, *karpos,* fruit.]

monoceros *mo-nos'ər-os, n.* a one-horned animal: the unicorn: perhaps the swordfish, or the narwhal (*Spens.*). — *adj.* **monoc'erous.** [Gr. *monokerōs* — *monos,* single, alone, *keras,* a horn.]

monochasium *mon-ō-kā'zi-əm, n.* a cymose inflorescence in which each axis in turn produces one branch: — *pl.* **monocha'sia.** — *adj.* **monocha'sial.** [Gr. *monos,* single, alone; apparently on the analogy of **dichasium,** as if that were from Gr. *di-,* twice, and *chasis,* separation.]

monochlamydeous *mon-ō-klə-mid'i-əs,* (*bot.*) *adj.* having a one-whorled perianth. — *n.pl.* **Monochlamyd'eae** a division of the Archichlamydeae or choripetalae, usually with perianth in one whorl. [**mon(o)-**.]

monochord *mon'ō-körd, n.* an acoustical instrument with one string, sound-board and bridge: a similar instrument with more than one string and bridge: a clavichord: a tromba marina. [**mon(o)-**.]

monochroic *mon-ō-krō'ik, adj.* of one colour. [Gr. *monochroos* — *monos, chrōs,* colour.]

monochromatic *mon-ō-krō-mat'ik, adj.* of one colour or wavelength only: completely colour-blind: done in monochrome. — *ns.* **monochro'masy** complete colour-blindness; **monochro'mat, -mate** one who sees all colours as differing in brilliance only; **monochro'matism** monochromatic vision; **monochro'mator** a device capable of isolating and transmitting monochromatic or nearly monochromatic light; **mon'ochrome** representation in one colour: a picture in one colour:

black and white: monochromy; **monochro′mist** one who practises monochrome. — *adj.* done, reproduced, etc. in a single colour or hue: black and white. — **mon′ochromy** the art of monochrome. [Gr. *monochrōmatos* — *monos*, single, alone, *chrōma*, *-atos*, colour.]

monocle *mon′ə-kl*, *n.* a single eyeglass. — *adj.* **mon′ocled** wearing a monocle. [Fr. *monocle* — Gr. *monos*, L. *oculus*, eye.]

monocline *mon′ō-klīn*, (*geol.*) *n.* a fold in strata followed by resumption of the original direction. — *adj.* **monoclīn′al**. [Gr. *monos*, single, alone, *klīnein*, to cause to slope.]

monoclinic *mon′ō-klin-ik*, (*crystal.*) *adj.* referable to three unequal axes, two intersecting each other obliquely and at right angles to the third. [Gr. *monos*, single, alone, *klīnein*, to incline.]

monoclinous *mon′ō-klī-nəs* or *-klī′*, (*bot.*) *adj.* hermaphrodite. [Gr. *monos*, single, alone, *klīnē*, bed.]

monoclonal *mon-ō-klō′nəl*, *adj.* (of an antibody) derived from a single cell clone that can reproduce itself in vast quantities in the laboratory, having applications in the diagnosis and treatment of infections, etc. [**mon**(o).]

mono-compound *mon-ō-kom′pownd*, (*chem.*) *n.* a compound containing one atom or group of that which is indicated. [**mon**(o)-.]

monocoque *mon-ō-kok′*, *-kōk′*, (*aero.*) *n.* a fuselage or nacelle in which all, or nearly all, structural loads are carried by the skin: a motor vehicle structure in which body and chassis are in one and share stresses: the hull of a boat made in one piece. [Fr., lit. single shell.]

monocotyledon *mon-ō-kot-i-lē′dən n.* (often shortened to **monocot** or to the **Monocotylē′dones** (*-ēz*), or **Monocot′ylae**, one of the two great divisions of the Angiosperms, the embryos with one cotyledon, leaves commonly parallel-veined, the parts of the flower usually in threes, the vascular bundles scattered and (with exceptions) without cambium. — *adj.* **monocotylē′donous.** [**mon**(o)-.]

monocracy *mon-ok′rə-si*, *n.* government by one person. — *n.* **mon′ocrat** (*-ō-krat*). — *adj.* **monocrat′ic**. [Gr. *monos*, single, alone, *kratos*, power.]

monocrystal *mon′ō-kris-təl*, *n.* a single crystal. — *adj.* **monocrys′talline.** [**mon**(o)-.]

monocular *mon-ok′ū-lər*, *adj.* one-eyed: of, for, or with, one eye — Also **monoc′ulous.** [Gr. *monos*, single, alone, L. *oculus*, an eye.]

monoculture *mon′ō-kul-chər*, *n.* the growing of one kind of crop only, or a large area, over which it is grown. — *adj.* **monocul′tural.** [**mon**(o)-.]

monocyclic *mon-ō-sīk′lik*, *adj.* having one whorl or ring. [**mon**(o)-.]

monocyte *mon′ō-sīt*, *n.* a large phagocytic leucocyte with a single oval or kidney-shaped nucleus and clear cytoplasm. [Gr. *monos*, single, *kytos*, vessel.]

monodactylous *mon-ō-dak′ti-ləs*, *adj.* one-toed or one-fingered. [Gr. *monos*, single, alone, *daktylos*, finger, toe.]

Monodelphia *mon-ō-del′fi-ə*, *n.pl.* one of the three primary divisions of mammals, the placental mammals or Eutheria. — *adjs.* **monodel′phian**, **monodel′phic**, **monodel′phous.** [Gr. *monos*, single, alone, *delphys*, womb.]

monodic, monodist. See **monody.**

Monodon *mon′ō-don*, *n.* the narwhal. — *adj.* **mon′odont** one-tusked: of the monodon. [Gr. *monos*, single, alone, *odous*, *odontos*, tooth, tusk.]

monodrama *mon′ō-drä-mə*, *n.* a dramatic piece for a single performer. — *adj.* **monodramatic** (*-drə-mat′ik*). [**mon**(o)-.]

monody *mon′ə-di*, *n.* a mournful ode or poem in which a single mourner bewails: a song for one voice: a manner of composition in which one part or voice carries the melody, the others accompanying. — *adjs.* **monodic** (*-od′*), **-al**. — *n.* **mon′odist** one who writes monodies. [Gr. *monōidiā* — *monos*, single, alone, *ōidē*, song.]

monoecious *mon-ē′shəs*, *adj.* hermaphrodite: having separate male and female flowers on the same plant. — *n.pl.* **Monoe′cia** in the Linnaean system, a class so characterised. — *n.* **monoecism** (*-ē′sizm*). [Gr. *monos*, single, alone, *oikos*, a house.]

monofil *mon′ō-fil*, *n.* a single strand of synthetic fibre. — Also **monofil′ament.** [Gr. *monos*, single, alone, L. *fīlum*, a thread.]

monogamy *mon-og′ə-mi*, *n.* the rule, custom, or condition of marriage to one wife or husband at a time, or (now rarely) in life. — *adjs.* **monogamic** (*mon-ō-gam′ik*), **monogamous** (*-og′əm-*). — *n.* **monog′amist.** [Gr. *monos*, single, alone, *gamos*, marriage.]

monogenesis *mon-ō-jen′i-sis*, *n.* development of offspring from a parent like itself: asexual reproduction: community of origin. — *adj.* **monogenet′ic.** — *ns.* **monogenism** (*-oj′ən-izm*) the doctrine of the common descent of all living things, or of any particular group (esp. mankind) from one ancestor or pair; **monog′enist.** — *adjs.* **monogenist′ic; monog′enous.** — *n.* **monog′eny** descent from one common ancestor or pair: asexual reproduction. [**mon**(o)-.]

monoglot *mon′ō-glot*, *n.* one who knows only one language. — Also *adj.* [Gr. *monos*, single, alone, *glōtta*, tongue.]

monogony *mon-og′ən-i*, *n.* asexual reproduction. [Gr. *monos*, single, alone, *gonos*, begetting.]

monogram *mon′ə-gram*, *n.* a figure consisting of several letters interwoven or written into one. — *adj.* **monogrammatic** (*-grə-mat′ik*). [Gr. *monos*, single, alone, *gramma*, *grammatos*, a letter.]

monograph *mon′ə-gräf*, *n.* a treatise written on one particular subject or any branch of it: a systematic account. — *v.t.* to write a monograph upon. — *ns.* **monographer** (*mon-og′rə-fər*), **monog′raphist** a writer of monographs. — *adjs.* **monographic** (*-graf′*), **-al** pertaining to a monograph or a monogram: drawn in lines without colours. — *n.* **monog′raphy** (*rare*) a monograph. [Gr. *monos*, single, alone, *graphein*, to write.]

monogyny *mon-oj′i-ni*, or *-og′*, *n.* the custom, practice, or condition of having only one wife: marriage with one wife: the habit of mating with one female. — *n.pl.* **Monogynia** (*mon-ō-jin′i-ə*) in various Linnaean classes of plants an order having one style. — *adjs.* **monogyn′ian; monog′ynous** having one wife: practising monogyny: mating with one female: having one style: monogynian. [Gr. *monos*, single, alone, *gynē*, woman.]

monohull *mon′ō-hul*, *n.* a vessel with one hull, as opp. to catamaran, trimaran. [**mon**(o)-.]

monohybrid *mon-ō-hī′brid*, *n.* a cross between parents differing in one heritable character. [**mon**(o)-.]

monohydric *mon-ō-hī′drik*, *adj.* containing one hydroxyl group. [**mon**(o)-.]

monolatry *mon-ol′ə-tri*, *n.* the worship of one god without excluding belief in others. — *n.* **monol′ater.** — *adj.* **monol′atrous.** [Gr. *monos*, single, alone, *latreiā*, worship.]

monolingual *mon-ō-ling′gwəl*, *adj.* expressed in one language: speaking only one language. — *ns.* **monoling′ualism; monoling′uist.** [Gr. *monos*, single, L. *lingua*, tongue.]

monolith *mon′ō-lith*, *n.* a pillar, or column, of a single stone: anything resembling a monolith in uniformity, massiveness or intractability. — *adj.* **monolith′ic** pertaining to or resembling a monolith: of a state, an organisation, etc., massive, and undifferentiated throughout: intractable for this reason. — **monolithic integrated circuit** see **integer.** [Gr. *monos*, single, alone, *lithos*, a stone.]

monologue *mon′ə-log*, *n.* a composition put into the mouth of one person, or intended to be spoken by one person: a harangue that engrosses conversation. — *adjs.* **monologic** (*-loj′*), **-al.** — *v.i.* **monologise, -ize** (*mon-ol′ə-jīz*) to indulge in this. — Also **monol′oguise, -ize** (*-gīz*). — *ns.* **monol′ogist** one who talks in monologue (also **mon′ologuist**); **monol′ogy** the habit of doing so.   [Gr. *monos*, single, alone, *logos*, speech.]

monomachy *mon-om'ə-ki, n.* single combat: a duel. — Also **monomā'chia.**   [Gr. *monos*, single, alone, *machē*, a fight.]

monomania *mon-ō-mā'ni-ə, n.* madness confined to one subject: an unreasonable interest in any particular thing. — *n.* **monomā'niac** one affected with monomania. — *adjs.* **monomā'niac, monomaniacal** (*-mə-nī'ə-kl*).   [Gr. *monos*, single, alone, *maniā*, madness.]

monomark *mon'ō-märk, n.* a particular combination of letters, figures, etc. as a mark of identification. [**mon**(**o**)**-.**]

monomer *mon'ō-mər, n.* the simplest of any series of compounds having the same empirical formula — opp. to *polymer.* — *adj.* **monomer'ic.**   [Gr. *monos*, single, alone, *meros*, part.]

monometallic *mon-ō-mi-tal'ik, adj.* involving or using but one metal as a standard of currency. — *ns.* **monometallism** (*-met'əl-izm*); **monomet'allist.**   [**mon**(**o**)**-.**]

monometer *mon-om'i-tər,* (*pros.*) *adj.* consisting of one measure. — *n.* a verse of one measure.   [**mon**(**o**)**-,** and **meter**[1].]

monomial *mon-ō'mi-əl, n.* an algebraic expression of one term only: a name consisting of one word. — Also *adj.* [Ill-formed from Gr. *monos*, single, alone, L. *nōmen*, name.]

monomode *mon'ō-mōd, adj.* designating a very fine optical fibre (less than 10 micrometres in diameter) used in telecommunications.   [**mon**(**o**)**-**]

monomorphic *mon-ō-mör'fik, adj.* existing in one form only. — *adj.* **monomor'phous.**   [Gr. *monos*, single, alone, *morphē*, form.]

monomyarian *mon-ō-mī-ā'ri-ən, adj.* having one adductor muscle.   [Gr. *monos*, single, alone, *mȳs, myos*, muscle.]

mononuclear *mon-ō-nū'kli-ər, adj.* having a single nucleus: monocyclic. — *n.* (*med.*) **mononucleosis** (*mon-ō-nūk-li-ō'sis*) the presence in the blood of an abnormally large number of a type of leucocytes. — See also **infectious mononucleosis** under **infect.**   [**mon**(**o**)**-.**]

monopetalous *mon-ō-pet'ə-ləs,* (*bot.*) *adj.* having petals united.   [**mon**(**o**)**-.**]

monophagous *mon-of'ə-gəs, adj.* having only one kind of food. — *n.* **monoph'agy** (*-ji*) feeding on one food: eating alone.   [Gr. *monos*, single, alone, *phagein* (aor.), to eat.]

monophasic *mon-ō-fāz'ik, adj.* (of electric current) single-phase (also **mon'ophase**): having one period of rest and one of activity during the 24 hours (*biol.*).   [**mon**(**o**)**-.**]

monophobia *mon-ō-fō'bi-ə, n.* morbid dread of being alone. — *adj.* **monophō'bic.**   [**mon**(**o**)**-.**]

monophonic *mon-ō-fon'ik, adj.* homophonic: monaural (opp. to *stereophonic*). — *n.* **monoph'ony.**   [Gr. *monos*, single, alone, *phōnē*, voice, sound.]

monophthong *mon'of-thong, n.* a simple vowel sound. — *adj.* **monophthongal** (*-thong'gəl*). — *v.t.* **mon'ophthongise, -ize** (*-gīz*) to turn into a monophthong.   [Gr. *monophthongos* — *monos*, single, alone, *phthongos*, sound, vowel.]

monophyletic *mon-ō-fi-let'ik,* or *-fī-, adj.* derived from a single stock.   [Gr. *monos*, single, alone, *phȳletikos*, pertaining to a tribesman — *phȳlē*, tribe.]

monophyodont *mon-ō-fī'ō-dont, adj.* having only one set of teeth. — *n.* an animal with but one set of teeth. [Gr. *monophyēs*, of simple nature, *monos*, single, *odous, odontos*, tooth.]

Monophysite *mō-nof'i-zīt, -sīt, n.* one who holds that Christ had but one composite nature. — *adj.* **Monophysitic** (*-sit'ik, -zit'ik*). — *n.* **Monoph'ysitism.** — All words also without *cap.*   [Gr. *monos*, single, alone, *physis*, nature.]

monopitch *mon'ō-pich,* (*archit.*) *adj.* of a roof, forming a single, uniform slope.   [**mon**(**o**)**-.**]

Monoplacophora *mon-ō-plak-of'ə-rə, n.pl.* a very primitive limpet-like class of molluscs, believed, till the discovery (1952) of the living Neopilina off the W. coast of Mexico, to have been extinct since early

Silurian times.   [Gr. *monos*, single, alone, *plax, plakos*, plate, *phoros*, bearing, from the single piece of shell.]

monoplane *mon'ə-plān, n.* an aeroplane or glider with one set of planes or wings.   [**mon**(**o**)**-.**]

monoplegia *mon-ō-plē'ji-ə, n.* paralysis limited to a single part.   [Gr. *monos*, single, alone, *plēgē*, stroke.]

monopode *mon'ə-pōd, n.* a one-footed man, esp. a member of a fabled tribe with single foot large enough to be used by its owner as a sunshade (Pliny, *Naturalis Historia*): a one-footed table, etc. — *adj.* one-footed. — *adj.* **monopo'dial** pertaining to or of the nature of a monopodium. — *adv.* **monopo'dially.** — *n.* **monopo'dium** (*bot.*) an axis that continues to grow without being supplanted, as in the sympodium, by a lateral branch.   [L. *monopodius, -um* — Gr. *monos*, single, alone, and *pous, podos*, foot.]

monopole *mon'ō-pōl,* (*phys.*) *n.* (usu. **magnetic monopole**) a particle, thought to exist, that has a single magnetic charge.   [**mon**(**o**)**-.**]

monopoly *mon-op'ə-li, n.* sole power, or privilege, of dealing in anything: exclusive command or possession: that of which one has such a sole power, privilege, command, or possession: (with *cap.*; ℝ) a board-game for two or more players, their object being the acquisition of property. — *v.t.* **monop'olise, -ize** to have a monopoly of: to keep to oneself: to engross. — *ns.* **monop'oliser, -z-, monop'olist.** — *adj.* **monopolis'tic.** — **Monopolies and Mergers Commission** a body set up by the government to investigate monopolies, etc., where a monopoly is defined as 25 per cent of the market. [L. *monopōlium* — Gr. *monopōlion* — *monos*, single, alone, *pōleein*, to sell.]

monoprionidian *mon-ō-prī-ə-nid'i-ən, adj.* serrated on one side of (graptolites).   [Gr. *monos*, single, alone, *prīōn*, a saw.]

monopsony *mon-op'sə-ni, n.* a situation where only one buyer exists for the product of several sellers, or where one of several buyers is large enough to exert undue influence over the price of a product. — *n.* **monop'sonist.** — *adj.* **monopsonis'tic.**   [Gr. *monos*, single, alone, *opsonia*, a purchase — *opsonein*, to buy.]

monopteros *mon-op'tər-os,* **monopteron** *-on, ns.* a circular Greek temple with one ring of columns. — *adj.* **monop'teral.**   [Gr. *monos*, single, alone, *pteron*, a wing.]

monoptote *mon'op-tōt, n.* a word with but one case form. [Gr. *monoptōtos* — *monos*, single, alone, and *ptōtos*, fallen; cf. *ptōsis*, case (see **case**[2]).]

monorail *mon'ō-rāl, n.* a railway with carriages running astride of, or suspended from, one rail. — Also *adj.* [**mon**(**o**)**-.**]

monorchid *mon-ör'kid, adj.* having only one testicle. — *n.* **monorch'ism.**   [Faultily formed from Gr. *monorchis* — *monos*, single, alone, *orchis, -eōs*, testicle.]

monorhine *mon'ō-rīn, adj.* having one nostril. — Also **monorhin'al.**   [Gr. *monos*, single, alone, *rhīs, rhīnos*, nose.]

monorhyme *mon'ə-rīm, n.* a series or tirade of lines all rhyming together. — Also *adj.* — *adj.* **mon'orhymed.** [**mon**(**o**)**-.**]

monosaccharide *mon-ō-sak'ə-rīd, n.* a simple sugar that cannot be hydrolysed.   [**mon**(**o**)**-.**]

monosepalous *mon-ō-sep'ə-ləs,* (*bot.*) *adj.* having the sepals all united.   [**mon**(**o**)**-.**]

monosis. See **monosy.**

mono-ski *mon'ō-skē, n.* a ski on which both feet are placed. — *v.i.* to use a mono-ski. — *n.* **mon'o-skier** [**mon**(**o**)**-.**]

monosodium glutamate *mon-ō-sō'di-əm glōō'tə-māt,* a white crystalline salt which brings out the flavour of meat (*glutamate*, a salt of glutamic acid).

monostich *mon'ə-stik, n.* a poem of one line. — *adj.* **monostichous** (*-os'tik-əs*) in one line: in one row.   [Gr. *monos*, single, alone, *stichos*, row, line.]

monostrophic *mon-ə-strof'ik, adj.* not divided into strophe, antistrophe, and epode: having the same strophic or stanzaic structure throughout. — *n.pl.* **monostroph'-ics** monostrophic verses. [Gr. *monostrophikos* — *monos*, single, alone, *strophē*, a strophe.]

monostyle *mon'ō-stīl*, (*archit.*) *adj.* consisting of a single shaft. — *adj.* **monostyl'ar.** [Gr. *monos*, single, alone, *stȳlos*, a pillar.]

monosy *mon'os-i*, (*biol.*) *n.* separation of parts normally fused. — Also **monō'sis.** [Gr. *monōsis*, solitariness — *monos*, single, alone.]

monosyllable *mon-ə-sil'ə-bl*, *n.* a word of one syllable. — *adj.* **monosyllabic** (*-ab'ik*). — *n.* **monosyll'abism.** [**mon**(o)**-**.]

monosymmetric, -al *mon-ō-sim-et'rik*, *-əl*, *adjs.* having only one plane of symmetry. [**mon**(o)**-**.]

monotelephone *mon-ō-tel'i-fōn*, *n.* a telephone that trans-mits sounds of one pitch only. [**mon**(o)**-**.]

monothalamous *mon-ō-thal'ə-məs*, *adj.* single-chambered: with but one cavity: (of fruit) formed from a single flower. — Also **monothalamic** (*-am'ik*). [Gr. *monos*, single, alone, *thalamos*, a chamber.]

monothecal *mon-ō-thē'kl*, *adj.* having only one theca. — Also **monothe'cous.** [Gr. *monos*, single, alone, *thēkē*, case.]

monotheism *mon'ō-thē-izm*, *n.* the belief in only one God. — *n.* **mon'otheist.** — *adjs.* **monotheist'ic, -al.** [Gr. *monos*, single, alone, *theos*, God.]

Monotheletism *mon-ō-thel'i-tizm*, *n.* the doctrine that Christ had but one will — opp. to *Ditheletism*. — Also **Monothelism** (*mon-oth'əl-izm*), **Monothel'itism.** — *ns.* **Monoth'elēte, Monoth'elite.** — *adjs.* **Monothelēt'ic, -al.** — All words also without *cap.* [Gr. *monos*, single, alone, *thelētēs*, a willer — *thelein*, to will.]

monotint *mon'ə-tint*, *n.* drawing or painting in a single tint. [**mon**(o)**-**.]

monotocous *mon-ot'ə-kəs*, *adj.* producing single offspring at a time: fruiting once only. [Gr. *monos*, single, alone, *tokos*, birth, offspring.]

monotone *mon'ə-tōn*, *n.* a single, unvaried tone or utter-ance: a succession of sounds having the same pitch: continued or extended sameness: sameness in colour. — *adj.* in monotone: monotonic (*math.*). — *v.t.* and *v.i.* to sing, declaim, speak, utter, in monotone. — *adjs.* **monotonic** (*-ton'ik*) in monotone: of a function or sequence, having the property of either never increas-ing or never decreasing; **monotonous** (*mon-ot'ə-nəs*) uttered in one unvaried tone: marked by dull uniform-ity. — *adv.* **monot'onously.** — *ns.* **monot'onousness; monot'ony** dull uniformity of tone or sound: want of modulation in speaking or reading: irksome sameness or want of variety (*fig.*). [Gr. *monos*, single, alone, *tonos*, a tone.]

Monotremata *mon-ō-trē'mə-tə*, *n.pl.* the lowest order of Mammalia, having a single opening for the genital and digestive organs. — *adj.* **monotre'matous** — also **mon'-otreme.** — *n.* **mon'otreme** a member of the Mono-tremata. [Gr. *monos*, single, alone, *trēma*, *-atos*, a hole.]

monotroch *mon'ō-trok*, (*Scott, facet.*) *n.* a wheelbarrow. [Gr. *monos*, single, alone, *trochos*, wheel.]

Monotropa *mon-ot'rə-pə*, *n.* a genus akin to wintergreen — the bird's-nest and Indian pipe, nourished by a fungal mycorrhiza in humus. [Gr. *monotropos*, soli-tary — *monos*, single, alone, *tropos*, turn.]

monotype *mon'ə-tīp*, *n.* a sole type, a species forming a genus by itself: a single print made from a picture painted on a metal or glass plate: (with *cap.*; ℞) the name of a machine that casts and sets type, letter by letter. — Also *adj.* — *adj.* **monotypic** (*-tip'ik*). [**mon**(o)**-**.]

monovalent *mon-ō-vā'lənt, mon-ov'əl-ənt*, *adj.* univalent. — *ns.* **monova'lence, monova'lency.** [**mon**(o)**-**.]

monoxide *mon-ok'sīd*, *n.* an oxide with one oxygen atom in the molecule. [**mon**(o)**-**.]

monoxylon *mon-oks'i-lon*, *n.* a canoe made from one log. — *adj.* **monox'ylous.** [Gr., — *monos*, single, alone, *xylon*, wood.]

monozygotic *mon-ō-zī-got'ik*, *adj.* developed from one

zygote. — **monozygotic twins** twins developed from a single zygote, identical twins. [**mon**(o)**-**.]

Monroeism *mən-rō'izm*, *n.* (or **Monroe doctrine**) President Monroe's principle (1823) that Europe must refrain from intervention in the affairs of independent coun-tries in the American continents.

Monseigneur *mɔ̃-sen-yœr*, *n.* my lord: a title in France given to a person of high birth or rank, esp. to bishops, etc. (written *Mgr*): the Dauphin: — *pl.* **Messeigneurs** (*me-sen-yœr*). — *n.* **Monsieur** (*mə-syø*) sir: a title of courtesy in France = *Mr* in English (printed *M.* or in full): the eldest brother of the king of France: (without *cap.*) a Frenchman generally — arch. and illiterate or grotesque, **moun'seer** (or *-sēr'*): (without *cap.*) a French gentleman: — *pl.* **Messieurs** (Fr. *mes-yø*, written *MM.*; Eng. *mes'ərz*, written **Messrs**) and (of **monsieur**) **messieurs.** — **Monsieur de Paris** the public executioner. [Fr. *mon seigneur, sieur*, my lord — L. *meum seniōrem* (accus.), my elder.]

Monsignor *mon-sēn'yər* (It. *mon-sēn-yōr'*), **Monsignore** (*-yō'rā*) *ns.* a title conferred on prelates and on digni-taries of the papal household. — *pls.* **Monsignors** (*-sēn'*), **Monsigno'ri** (*-rē*). [It. — Fr.]

monsoon *mon-sōōn'*, *n.* a periodical wind of the Indian Ocean, S.W. from April to October, and N.E. the rest of the year: a similar wind elsewhere: in N. and W. India, the rains accompanying the S.W. monsoon. — *adj.* **monsoon'al.** — **break of the monsoon** the first onset of the monsoon rain. [Port. *monção* — Malay *mūsim* — Ar. *mausim*, a time, a season.]

mons pubis *monz pū'bis*. Same as **mons veneris:** — *pl.* **montes pubis** (*mon'tēz*). [L., hill of the pubis.]

monster *mon'stər*, *n.* anything out of the usual course of nature: a prodigy: a fabulous animal: an abnormally formed animal or plant: a grotesque animal: a gigantic animal: anything gigantic: anything horrible from ugliness or wickedness. — *adj.* gigantic, huge. — *n.* **monstrosity** (*-stros'i-ti*; *obs.* **monstruos'ity**) the state or fact of being monstrous: marked abnormality: an abnormally formed animal, plant, part, or object: anything outrageously constructed. — *adj.* **mon'strous** (*obs.* **mon'struous**) out of the common course of nature: enormous: wonderful: horrible: outrageous: prepos-terous. — *adv.* (*arch.*) exceedingly. — *adv.* **mon'-strously.** — *n.* **mon'strousness.** [Fr. *monstre* — L. *mōnstrum*, an evil omen, a monster — *monēre, moni-tum*, to warn.]

Monstera *mon-stē'rə*, *n.* a genus of tropical American evergreen plants of the family Araceae that have shining green perforated leaves and can be grown to a height of 20 feet as hothouse or indoor plants, esp. *Monstera deliciosa* (having aerial roots) and *Monstera pertusa* (the 'Swiss cheese plant'): (without *cap.*) any plant of this genus. [Mod. L., perh. because leaves thought freakish.]

monstrance *mon'strəns*, *n.* the ornamental receptacle in which the consecrated host is exposed in R.C. churches for the adoration of the people. [O.Fr., — L. *mōnstrāre*, to show.]

monstre sacré *mɔ̃-str' sak-rā*, a person (esp. in the world of theatre or cinema) whose appeal to the public is increased by his eccentricity. [Fr., sacred monster.]

mons veneris *monz ven'ə-ris*, the mound of flesh over the pubis on the female human body: — *pl.* **montes veneris** (*mon'tēz*). [L., hill of Venus.]

montage *mɔ̃-täzh'*, *n.* selection and piecing together of material for a cinematograph film with a view to effect: (act or process of making) a composite photograph: setting-up, assemblage, superimposition: a picture made partly by sticking objects on the canvas. [Fr., — *monter*, to mount.]

Montagnard *mɔ̃-tä-nyär*, *n.* one of the Mountain or the extreme democratic wing of the French Legislative Assembly (1st Oct. 1791 to 21st Sept. 1792), so called because sitting on the topmost benches. [Fr., moun-taineer.]

Montagu's harrier *mon'tə-gūz har'i-ər*, *n.* a bird of prey

(*Circus pygargus*) of the *Accipitridae* family, with long wings and tail, native to Europe. [After George *Montagu*, 18th.–19th.-cent. British naturalist.]

montane *mon'tān, adj.* mountainous: mountain-dwelling. [L. *montānus* — *mōns, montis,* a mountain.]

Montanism *mon'tən-izm, n.* a 2nd-century heresy founded by the prophet and 'Paraclete' *Montānus* of Phrygia — an ascetic reaction in favour of the old discipline and severity. — *n.* and *adj.* **Mon'tanist.** — *adj.* **Montanist'ic.**

montant *mont'ənt, n.* a vertical member in panelling or framing: in fencing, apparently an upward blow (also, as if Sp., **montant'o;** *Shak.*). [Fr., — *monter,* to rise.]

montan wax *mon'tən waks,* (*chem.*) a bituminous wax extracted under high temperature and pressure from lignite, used in candles and some polishes. [L. *montanus,* of a mountain.]

montaria *mont-ä-rē'ə, n.* in Brazil, a light canoe made of one log. [Port.]

Montbretia *mon(t)-brēsh'yə, n.* a genus of S. African iridaceous plants: (without *cap.*) a plant of this genus: (without *cap.*) a plant (*Crocosmia*) of the iris family bearing bright orange-coloured flowers: (without *cap.*) a plant of the genus Tritonia. [After a French botanist, Coquebert de *Montbret* (1780–1801).]

mont-de-piété *mɔ̃-də-pyā-tā* (Fr.), **monte di pietà** (*mon'tā dē pyā-tā';* It.) *ns.* a state pawnshop: — *pls.* **monts-de=piété** (*mɔ̃*), **monti di pietà** (*mon'tē*). [Fund (lit. mount) of pity or piety.]

monte *mon'tā, -ti, n.* a shrubby tract, a forest: a Spanish-American gambling card-game. — **three-card monte** a Mexican three-card trick. [Sp., mountain, scrub, cards remaining after a deal — L. *mōns, montis,* a mountain.]

Monte Carlo method *mon'ti kär'lō meth'əd,* (*math.*) a statistical procedure when mathematical operations are performed on random numbers. [From the casino at *Monte Carlo* and the various numerical systems tried there to win at roulette.]

monteith *mən-, mon-tēth', n.* a large 17th- or 18th-century bowl, usually of silver, fluted and scalloped, for cooling punch-glasses (said to be named from 'a fantastical Scot' who wore his cloak so scalloped): a cotton handkerchief with white spots on a coloured ground (from Glasgow manufacturers).

montem *mon'tem, n.* a former custom of Eton boys to go every third Whit-Tuesday to a hillock on the Bath road and exact 'salt-money' from passers-by, for the university expenses of the senior scholar or school captain. [L. *ad montem,* to the hill.]

montero *mon-tā'rō, n.* a huntsman: a Spanish horseman's helmet-like cap with a flap. — Also **monte'ro-cap':** — *pl.* **monte'ros.** [Sp. *montero,* a huntsman — *monte* — L. *mōns, montis,* a mountain.]

Montessorian *mon-tes-ōr'i-ən, -ör', adj.* pertaining to Dr Maria *Montessori* or her method (*c.* 1900) of education, insisting on spontaneity and freedom from restraint.

Montezuma's revenge *mon-tə-zōōm'əz ri-venj', n.* diarrhoea, esp. caused by travelling in Mexico and/or eating Mexican food. [*Montezuma II,* a 15th-cent. Mexican ruler.]

montgolfier *mon(t)-gol'fi-ər, n.* a hot-air balloon. [From the brothers *Montgolfier,* of Annonay, who sent up the first in 1783.]

month *munth, n.* the moon's period: one of the twelve conventional divisions of the year, or its length — a *calendar* month. — *n.* **month'ling** (*arch.*) a month-old child. — *adj.* **month'ly** performed in a month: done, recurring, or appearing once a month. — *n.* a monthly publication: a monthly rose: (*pl.*) the menses (*coll.*). — *adv.* once a month: in every month. — **monthly nurse** a nurse attending a woman in the first month after childbirth; **monthly rose** a rose supposed to bloom every month; **month's mind** see **mind.** — **anomalistic month** the interval between the moon's perigee passages = 27·5545 days; **lunar month** a month reckoned

by the moon: a synodic month; **a month of Sundays** see **Sunday; sidereal** or **stellar month** the time in which the moon passes round the ecliptic to the same point among the stars = 27·3217 days; **solar month** one-twelfth of a solar year; **synodic month** the period of the moon's phases = 29·5306 days; **tropical** or **periodic month** from the moon's passing the equinox till she again reaches it = 27·3216 days. [O.E. *mōnath* — *mōna,* moon.]

monticellite *mon-ti-sel'īt, n.* an orthorhombic calcium magnesium silicate. [After the Italian mineralogist Teodoro *Monticelli* (1759–1845).]

monticle. See **monticulus.**

monticolous *mon-tik'ə-ləs, adj.* mountain-dwelling. [L. *monticola,* a mountain-dweller — *mōns, montis,* mountain, *colĕre,* to inhabit.]

monticulus *mon-tik'ū-ləs, n.* a little elevation — also **mon'ticle** and **mon'ticule.** — *adjs.* **montic'ulate, montic'ulous** having small projections. [L. *monticulus,* dim. of *mōns,* mountain.]

Montilla *mon-til'ya, n.* a sherry-like white wine produced in the region of *Montilla* in S. Spain.

montmorillonite *mont-mə-ril'ə-nīt,* (*min.*) *n.* a hydrated silicate of aluminium, one of the important clay minerals and the chief constituent of bentonite and fuller's earth. [From *Montmorillon,* in France.]

montre *mɔ̃tr', n.* the visible pipes of an organ, usually the open diapason. [Fr., sample, show.]

monture *mon'tūr, mɔ̃-tür, n.* a mounting, setting, frame. [Fr.]

monument *mon'ū-mənt* (*obs.* **mon'iment**), *n.* anything that preserves the memory of a person or an event, a building, pillar, tomb, tablet, statue, etc.: any structure, natural or artificial, considered as an object of beauty or of interest as a relic of the past: a historic document or record (sometimes confused with **muniment**): a stone, post, river, etc. marking a boundary (*U.S.*): a relic, indication, or trace: a notable or enduring example: a warning token or admonition (*Spens.*): a prodigy (*Shak.*). — *v.t.* to commemorate by or on a monument. — *adj.* **monumental** (*-ment'əl*) of or relating to or of the nature of a monument, tomb, memento, or token: memorial: massive and lasting: vast: impressive: amazing: loosely, very large. — *adv.* **monument'ally.** [L. *monumentum, monimentum* — *monēre,* to remind.]

mony *mun'i, mon'i,* a Scots form of **many.**

monyplies *mun'i-plīz.* See **manyplies.**

monzonite *mon'zən-īt, n.* a coarse-grained intermediate igneous rock. — *adj.* **monzonit'ic.** [Monte *Monzoni* in the Dolomite Mountains.]

moo *mōō, v.i.* to low. — *n.* a cow's low. [Imit.]

mooch, mouch *mōōch, v.i.* to play truant (*dial.*): to go blackberrying (*dial.*): to slouch about: to skulk: to loiter, wander (about): to sponge. — *v.t.* to pilfer: to beg, cadge (*U.S.*). — *n.* the act of mooching. — *n.* **mooch'er, mouch'er.** [Perh. O.Fr. *muchier,* to hide; cf. **miche.**]

mood¹ *mōōd, n.* a form of the verb to express the mode or manner of an action or of a state of being (*gram.*): the form of the syllogism as determined by the quantity and quality of its three constituent propositions (*log.*): in mediaeval music, mode in the sense of relative time value. [**mode.**]

mood² *mōōd, n.* temporary state of the emotions or of attitude: state of gloom or sullenness: anger, heat of temper (*obs.*). — *adv.* **mood'ily.** — *n.* **mood'iness** sullenness. — *adjs.* **mood'y** indulging in moods: sullen: angry (*obs.*): faked, pretended (*prison slang*). — *n.* (*slang*) insidious, flattering talk: lies, deception. — *v.t.* (*slang*) to persuade by flattery and cajolery. **mood'y=mad** (*Shak.*) mad with anger. [O.E. *mōd,* mind; cf. Ger. *Mut,* courage.]

Moog synthesizer® *mōōg sin'thi-sīz-ər,* an electronic musical instrument with a keyboard, that can produce a wide range of sounds. [Developed by Robert *Moog,* an American engineer.]

mooi *mō'i*, (*Afrik.*) *adj.* fine — a general word of commendation. [From Du.]

mooktar *mōōk'tär*, *n.* Same as **mukhtar.**

mool *mōōl*, a Scots form of **mould**[1].

moola(h) *mōō'lə*, (*slang*) *n.* money. [Origin uncertain.]

moolah. See **mullah.**

mooly. See **muley.**

mooli *mōō'li*, *n.* a long white carrot-shaped root vegetable from East Africa, tasting similar to a radish. [Native word.]

moon *mōōn*, *n.* (often with *cap.*) the earth's satellite: a satellite: a month: anything in the shape of a moon or crescent: a crescent-shaped outwork (*fort.*). — *v.t.* to adorn with moons or crescents. — *v.i.* to wander about or gaze vacantly at anything (usu. with *around, about*): to present one's bare buttocks to public view, esp. through a vehicle window (*slang, esp. U.S.*). — *adj.* **mooned** marked with the figure of a moon. — *n.* **moon'er** one who moons about. — *adj.* **moon'ish** like the moon: variable: inconstant: **moon'less** destitute of moonlight. — *n.* **moon'let** a small earth-satellite, whether natural or man-made. — *adj.* **moon'y** of or relating to the moon: moon-like: crescent-shaped: bearing a crescent: round and shining: moonlit: inclined to moon: fatuous: tipsy (*slang*). — *n.* a noodle. — **moon'beam** a beam of light from the moon. — *adj.* **moon'blind** affected with moon-eye: blinded by the moon: nightblind: dim-sighted, purblind. — **moon boot** a bulky padded boot with a quilted fabric covering, for wearing in snow, reminiscent of a spaceman's boot; **moon'-bow** a rainbow cast by the moon; **moon'calf** a false conception or fleshy mass formed in the womb: a monster (*obs.*): a deformed creature (*obs.*): a dolt; **moon daisy** the ox-eye daisy; **moon'eye** a disease affecting horses' eyes: an American freshwater shad-like fish. — *adj.* **moon'-eyed.** — **moon'face** a full, round face — a point of beauty in the East. — *adj.* **moon'-faced.** — **moon'-fish** the opah or other silvery disc-shaped fish; **moon'-flower** the ox-eye daisy: a night-blooming plant of the Convolvulaceae, *Calonyction aculeatum*, or any of several related plants; **moon'-glade** the track of moonlight on water; **moon'-god, -goddess** a god or goddess representing or associated with the moon; **moon'-knife** a leather-worker's crescent-shaped knife; **moon'light** the light of the moon — sunlight reflected from the moon's surface: smuggled spirit. — *adj.* lighted by the moon: occurring in moonlight. — **moon'lighter** in Ireland, one who committed agrarian outrages by night about 1880: a moonshiner: one who takes work in the evening in addition to his normal day's work, esp. when the income from this is not declared for tax assessment; **moonlight flit(ting)** a removal by night, with rent unpaid; **moon'lighting.** — *adjs.* **moon'lit** lit or illumined by the moon; **moon'-loved** loved by the moon. — **moon'-mad'ness** lunacy, once thought to be connected with the moon's changes; **moon pool** (*oil industry*) the open shaft let through the hull of a deep-sea drilling vessel to accommodate the vertical pipe-line connected to the oil-well; **moon'quake** a tremor of the moon's surface. — *adj.* (*Scott*) **moon'-raised** excited or maddened by the moon. — **moon'raker** a moon-sail: a Wiltshireman (from a Gotham story); **moon'raking** the following of crazy fancies; **moon'rise** the rising of the moon; **moon'sail** a small sail, sometimes carried above the sky-scraper; **moon'scape** the physical appearance of the surface of the moon, or a representation of it; **moon'seed** a plant (*Menispermum*) with lunate seeds; **moon'set** the setting of the moon; **moon'shine** moonlight: show without reality (*fig.*): nonsense (*coll.*): a month (*Shak.*): spirits illicitly distilled or smuggled. — *adj.* lighted by the moon: made of moonlight, bodiless (*fig.*). — **moon'shiner** a smuggler or illicit distiller of spirits. — *adj.* **moon'shiny** lighted by the moon: visionary, unreal. — **moon'shot** act or process of launching an object or vehicle to orbit, or land on, the moon; **moon'stone** an opalescent orthoclase feldspar, perh.

sometimes selenite; **moon'strike** the act or process of landing a spacecraft on the surface of the moon. — *adj.* **moon'struck** (also **moon'-stricken**) affected by the moon, lunatic, crazed. — **moon'wort** a eusporangiate fern (*Botrychium lunaria*) with lunate pinnae, or other of the genus: the plant honesty (from its silvery septum). — **eggs in moonshine** an old dish, fried eggs with onions and various flavourings; **over the moon** (*coll.*) delighted. [O.E. *mōna*; cf. Ger. *Mond*, L. *mēnsis*, Gr. *men*.]

moong bean. See **mung bean.**

Moonies *mōōn'iz*, *n.pl.* a coll., often derog., term for members of the Unification Church, a sect founded in 1954 by Sun Myung *Moon*, a S. Korean: — *sing.* **Moon'ie.**

moonshee. Same as **munshi.**

Moon-type *mōōn'tīp*, *n.* a system of embossed lettering for the blind, invented by Dr William *Moon* (1847).

moop. Same as **moup.**

moor[1] *mōōr*, *n.* a wide tract of untilled ground, often covered with heath, and having a poor, peaty soil: a heath: (*Scot.*) **muir** (*mür, mär, mür*). — *adjs.* **moor'ish, moor'y** resembling a moor: sterile: marshy: boggy. — **moor'-band** a hard ferruginous layer formed under moorland soil (also **moor'-band pan, moor'-pan**); **moor'-buzz'ard** the marsh-harrier; **moor'cock, moor'fowl** red, or black, grouse; **moor'hen** water-hen: female moor-fowl; **moor'ill** (*Scot.*) a cattle disease of moorland districts, marked by haemoglobin in the urine; **moor'-land** a tract of moor: moorish country. — *adj.* of moorland. — **moor'log** a deposit of decayed woody material under a marsh, etc.; **moor'man** a dweller in moors; **moor'-pout, muir'-pout, -poot** (*-powt, -pōōt*) a young grouse. [O.E. *mōr.*]

moor[2] *mōōr*, *v.t.* to fasten by cable or anchor. — *v.i.* to make fast a ship, boat, etc.: to be made fast. — *ns.* **moor'age** condition of being moored: act of mooring: a due paid for mooring: a place for mooring; **moor'ing** act of mooring: that which serves to moor or confine a ship: (in *pl.*) the place or condition of a ship thus moored. — **moor'ing-mast.** [Prob. from an unrecorded O.E. word answering to M.Du. *mâren.*]

Moor *mōōr*, *n.* a Mauretanian: a member of the mixed Arab and Berber people of Morocco and the Barbary coast: one of the Arab and Berber conquerors and occupants of Spain from 711 to 1492: in some countries, a Muslim: a dark-coloured person generally, a Negro: — *fem.* **Moor'ess.** — *n.* **Moor'ery** a Moorish quarter. — *adj.* **Moor'ish.** [Fr. *More, Maure* — L. *Maurus*, doubtfully connected with Byzantine Gr. *mauros*, black.]

moorva. Same as **murva.**

moose *mōōs*, *n.* the American elk: a member of an American secret fraternity: — *pl.* **moose.** — **moose'yard** an area where the moose tread down the snow and spend the winter. [Algonquian *mus, moos.*]

moot *mōōt*, *n.* orig. a meeting: a deliberative or administrative assembly or court (*hist.*): its meeting-place: discussion: a law student's discussion of a hypothetical case. — *v.t.* to argue, dispute: to propose for discussion. — *v.i.* to dispute, plead. — *adj.* debatable. — *adj.* **moot'able.** — *ns.* **moot'er; moot'ing.** — **moot case** a case for discussion: a case about which there may be difference of opinion; **moot'-court** a meeting for discussion of hypothetical cases; **moot'-hall, -house** a town-hall or council chamber: a hall for moot-courts; **moot'-hill** a hill of meeting on which the moot was held (often confused with **mote-hill**); **moot'man** a law student who argues in moots; **moot point** an undecided or disputed point. [O.E. (*ge*)*mōt* (n.), *mōtian* (vb.), akin to *mētan*, to meet.]

moove. An old spelling of **move.**

mop[1] *mop*, *n.* a bunch of rags, yarn, or the like, on the end of a stick, for washing, removing dust, soaking up liquid, etc.: any similar instrument, as for cleansing a wound, polishing, etc.: a thick or bushy head of hair: an act of mopping: a hiring-fair (probably from the custom of carrying a badge of occupation; *dial*.). — *v.t.* to wipe, dab, soak up, or remove with a mop or as if with a mop: to clear away or dispose of as residue: — *pr.p.* **mopp'ing;** *pa.t.* and *pa.p.* **mopped.** — *ns.* **mopp'er; mopp'et** a rag-doll: a little woolly dog: a doll-like woman: (a term of endearment or contempt for) a little girl or child. — *adj.* **mopp'y** (*slang*) drunk. — *n.* **mop'sy** a dowdy: a slattern: a term of endearment. — **mop'board** (*U.S.*) skirting-board. — *adj.* **mop'= head'ed** having a shaggy, unkempt head of hair. — **mop'stick** the handle of a mop: a hand-rail nearly circular in section: (also **map'stick**) a rod for raising a piano damper; **mop'-up'** an action of mopping up. — **mops and brooms** half-drunk: out of sorts; **mop up** to clear away or clean up with a mop: to clear away, dispose of: to absorb (e.g. surplus credit): to capture or kill (enemy stragglers) after a victory, etc.; **Mrs Mop(p)** a cleaner, charwoman. [Possibly from O.Fr. *mappe* — L. *mappa*, a napkin; or possibly from the name *Mabel*.]

mop² *mop*, *n.* a grimace. — *v.i.* to grimace. — *n.*, *v.i.* often **mop and mow.** [Cf. Du. *moppen*, to pout.]

mopane, *mo-pä'ni*, *n.* a small S. African tree of the Leguminosae, growing in areas of low rainfall, with rough bark and racemes of small green flowers. [Bantu.]

mope *mōp*, *v.i.* to go aimlessly and listlessly: to yield to low spirits. — *v.t.* (*arch.*) to make spiritless. — *n.* a listless person: (esp. in *pl.*) moping. — *n.* **mop'er.** — *adv.* **mop'ingly.** — *adj.* **mop'ish** dull: spiritless. — *adv.* **mop'ishly.** — *ns.* **mop'ishness; mop'us** one who mopes. — *adj.* **mop'y.** [Origin obscure.]

moped *mō'ped*, *n.* a *mo*tor-assisted *ped*al cycle.

mopoke *mō'pōk*, *n.* the owl *Ninox novaeseelandiae*, of Australia and New Zealand: (*Austr.*) the tawny frog-mouth (to which the call is wrongly attributed): a silly person. — Also **mope'hawk, more'-pork.** [From the cry of the owl.]

Mopp, Mrs. See under **mop¹.**

mopper, moppy, etc. See **mop¹.**

mopus¹ *mop'əs*, **mawpus** *mö'pəs*, (*slang*) *ns.* a small coin.

mopus². See **mope.**

moquette *mō-ket'*, *n.* a carpet and soft furnishing material with a loose velvety pile, the back made of thick canvas, etc. [Fr.]

mor¹ *mör*, *mōr*, *n.* a layer of humus formed by slow decomposition in acid conditions. [Dan.]

mor². See **mauther.**

mora¹ *mō'rə*, *mö'*, *n.* delay, esp. unjustifiable (*law*): the duration of a short syllable or half that of a long (*pros.*). [L., delay.]

mora², morra *mor'ə*, *n.* the game of guessing how many fingers are held up. [It. *mora*.]

moraceous. See under **Morus.**

moraine *mo-rān'*, *n.* a continuous marginal line of débris borne on or left by a glacier: a garden imitation of this. — *adjs.* **morain'al, morain'ic.** [Fr.]

moral *mor'əl*, *adj.* of or relating to character or conduct considered as good or evil: ethical: conformed to or directed towards right, virtuous: esp. virtuous in matters of sex: capable of knowing right and wrong: subject to the moral law: supported by evidence of reason or probability — opp. to *demonstrative*: real or effective, if not apparent: moralising (*Shak.*). — *n.* in *pl.* writings on ethics: the doctrine or practice of the duties of life: moral philosophy or ethics: principles and conduct, esp. sexual: in *sing.* the practical lesson that can be drawn from anything: an exposition of such lesson by way of conclusion: a symbol: (sometimes *mor-äl'*, after Ger. *Moral* or Fr. *morale*) morality: a certainty (*slang*): an exact counterpart (*slang*): (spelt **morale** to look French and to suggest the Fr. pron. *mor-äl'* — the French word in this sense is *moral*) condition with respect to discipline and confidence, pride, fixity of purpose, faith in the cause fought for, etc. (usu. *mil.*). — *v.t.* and *v.i.* to moralise. — *ns.* **morale** *mor-äl'* (Fr. *morale*) morality: see above (*mil.*; **moral**);

moralisa'tion, -z- act of moralising, explanation in a moral sense. — *v.t.* **mor'alise, -ize** to apply to a moral purpose: to explain in a moral sense: to make moral: to furnish with matter of morality. — *v.i.* to speak or write on moral subjects: to make moral reflections. — *ns.* **mor'aliser; mor'alism** a moral maxim: moral counsel: morality as distinct from religion; **mor'alist** one who teaches morals, or who practises moral duties: a moral as distinguished from a religious man: one who prides himself on his morality. — *adj.* **moralist'ic.** — *n.* **morality** (*mor-al'i-ti*) quality of being moral: that which renders an action right or wrong: the practice of moral duties apart from religion: virtue: the doctrine of actions as right or wrong: ethics: a mediaeval allegorical drama in which virtues and vices appear as characters (also **moral'ity-play**). — *n.* **mor'aller** (*Shak.*) a moralist. — *adv.* **mor'ally** in a moral manner: in respect of morals: to all intents and purposes, practically. — **moral agent** one who acts under a knowledge of right and wrong; **moral certainty** a likelihood great enough to be acted on, although not capable of being certainly proved; **moral courage** power of facing disapprobation and ridicule; **moral defeat** a success so qualified as to count as a defeat, or to point towards defeat; **moral faculty** moral sense; **moral law** a law or rules for life and conduct, founded on what is right and wrong: the law of conscience: that part of the Old Testament which relates to moral principles, esp. the ten commandments; **moral philosophy** ethics; **Moral Rearmament** a movement succeeding the Oxford Group in 1938, advocating absolute private and public morality (abbrev. **M.R.A.**); **moral sense** that power of the mind which knows or judges actions to be right or wrong, and determines conduct accordingly: (or **moral interpretation**, etc.) tropological interpretation of e.g. the Bible, finding of secondary meaning; **moral support** the help afforded by approbation; **moral theology** ethics treated with reference to a divine source; **moral victory** a defeat in appearance, but in some important sense a real victory. [L. *mōrālis* — *mōs, mōris*, manner, custom, (esp. in *pl.*) morals.]

morale. See under **moral.**

morall (*Shak., Mids. N. Dr.*) *n.* emended by editors to **mural,** but possibly a misprint for **wall.**

morals. Same as **merils.**

morass *mə-ras'*, *n.* a tract of soft, wet ground: a marsh. — *adj.* **morass'y.** — **morass ore** bog-iron ore. [Du. *moeras* — O.Fr. *maresc*, influenced by Du. *moer*, moor.]

morat *mō'rat*, *mö'*, *n.* a drink made of honey and mulberry juice. [L.L. *mōrātum* — *mōrum*, mulberry.]

moratorium *mor-ə-tō'ri-əm, -tö'*, *n.* an emergency measure authorising the suspension of payments of debts for a given time: the period thus declared: a temporary ban on, or decreed cessation of, an activity: — *pl.* **morator'ia, morator'iums.** — *adj.* **moratory** (*mor'ə-tə-ri*) delaying: deferring. [Neut. of L.L. *mōrātōrius,* adj. from *mora*, delay.]

Moravian¹ *mo-rā'vi-ən, adj.* pertaining to *Moravia* or the Moravians. — *n.* one of the people of Moravia: one of the *Unitas Fratrum* or *United Brethren*, a small body of Protestants of extraordinary missionary energy, founded in the 15th century. — *n.* **Morā'vianism.** [L. *Moravia,* Moravia — *Morava*, the river March.]

Moravian² *mo-rā'vi-ən, adj.* of the old province or the modern county of Moray. — *n.* a Moray man. [L.L. *Moravia,* Moray.]

moray, murray, murrey, murry *mō'rā, mō-rā', mur'i, mur-ā', ns.* an eel of the family Muraenidae. [Port. *moreia* — L. *mūraena* — Gr. (*s*)*mýraina,* fem. of (*s*)*mýros,* eel.]

morbid *mör'bid, adj.* sickly: unwholesome: inclined to dwell on unwholesome or horrible thoughts: relating to, or of the nature of, disease. — *n.* **morbid'ity** sickliness: unwholesomeness: ratio of sickness. — *adv.* **mor'bidly.** — *n.* **mor'bidness.** — **morbid anatomy** the science or study of diseased organs and tissues. [L.

morbidus — *morbus*, disease.]

morbidezza *mör-bi-det'sə, n.* that quality of flesh-painting which gives the impression of life. [It.]

morbiferous, etc. See **morbus.**

morbilli *mör-bil'ī, n.pl.* measles. — *adjs.* **morbill'iform, morbill'ous.** [L.L. dim. of L. *morbus,* disease.]

morbus *mör'bəs, n.* disease (L.; used in phrases). — *adjs.* **morbif'erous** disease-bringing; **morbi'fic** disease-causing. — **morbus gallicus** the French disease, syphilis. [L.]

morceau *mör'sō, n.* a morsel: a fragment: a piece of music: a short literary composition: — *pl.* **mor'ceaux** (-sō). — **morceau de salon** (*də sä-lõ; mus.*) a drawing-room piece. [Fr.; see **morsel.**]

mordacious *mör-dā'shəs, adj.* given to biting: biting in quality (*lit.* or *fig.*). — *adv.* **mordā'ciously.** — *ns.* **mordacity** (*-das'i-ti*), **mordancy** (*mör'dən-si*). — *adj.* **mor'dant** biting: incisive: serving to fix dyes, paints, gold-leaf. — *n.* a corroding substance: any substance that combines with and fixes a dyestuff in material that cannot be dyed direct: a substance used to cause paint or gold-leaf to adhere. — *v.t.* to treat with a mordant. — *adv.* **mor'dantly.** [L. *mordēre,* to bite.]

mordent *mör'dənt,* (*mus.*) *n.* a grace in which the principal note is preceded in performance by itself and the note below (**lower mordent**) or itself and the note above (**upper,** or **inverted, mordent**): the character indicating it: sometimes extended to other graces. [Ger., — It. *mordente.*]

more[1] *mör, mör, adj.* (serving as *compar.* of **many** and **much**) in greater number or quantity: greater in size or importance (now *rare*): additional: other besides. — *adv.* to a greater degree: rather: again: longer: further: moreover. — *n.* a greater thing: something further or in addition: — *superl., adj.* and *adv.* **most** (*mōst*). — *adj.* **mo'rish, more'ish** such that one wants more. — **any more** anything additional: further; **more and more** continually increasing; **more by token** in proof of this, besides; **more or less** about: in round numbers; **no more** nothing in addition: never again: no longer in existence: dead. [O.E. *māra,* greater; as an adv. **more** has superseded **mo**[1].]

more[2] *mör, mör, n.* a root: a stump: a plant (*Spens.*). [O.E. *moru, more,* carrot, parsnip; Ger. *Möhre.*]

more[3] *mör'ē, mör'ē, mör'e* (L.), *adj.* in the manner; **more majorum** (*mə-jör'əm, -jör'əm, mä-yōr'ŏŏm*) after the manner of our (their) ancestors; **more suo** (*sū', sŏŏ'ŏ*) in his (her) own way, in characteristic fashion.

moreen *mo-rēn', n.* a stout corded fabric, woollen, cotton, or both, often watered. [Poss. conn. with **moire.**]

moreish. See **more**[1].

morel[1] *mor-el', n.* any edible discomycete fungus of the genus Morchella. [Fr. *morille;* cf. O.H.G. *morhila* (Ger. *Morchel*), a mushroom; **more**[2].]

morel[2] *mor-el', n.* a nightshade, esp. black nightshade: (also *mor'əl*) a dark-coloured horse (*obs.*). — *adj.* blackish. [L.L. *morellus,* blackish, perh. — L. *mōrum,* a mulberry, perh. Late Gr. *mauros,* black.]

morel[3] *mor-el', mor'əl, morell'o* (-ō; *pl.* **morell'os**) *ns.* a dark-red cherry, much used in cooking and for cherry brandy. [Possibly — It. *morello,* dark-coloured (see preceding); possibly — Flem. *marelle* — It. *amarella,* a dim. from L. *amārus,* bitter.]

morendo *mo-ren'dō,* (*mus.*) *adj.* and *adv.* dying away, in speed and tone. [It., dying.]

moreover *mör-ō'vər, mör-, adv.* more over or beyond what has been said: further: besides: also. [**more**[1], **over.**]

more-pork. See **mopoke.**

mores *mō', mö'rēz, mō'rās, n.pl.* customs, manners. [L. *mōs, mōris,* custom.]

Moresco *mor-es'kō, n.* a Moorish dance or morris-dance (It. *Moresca*): a Moor or Morisco: — *pl.* **Mores'coes.** — *adj.* Moorish. [It., Moorish.]

Moresque *mor-esk', adj.* in the Moorish manner. — *n.* an arabesque. [Fr., — It. *Moresco.*]

Moreton Bay *mör'tən bā, mör',* the first settlement in Queensland. — **Moreton Bay chestnut** an Australian

papilionaceous tree (*Castanospermum australe*): its chestnut-like seed; **Moreton Bay fig** an Australian fig tree (*Ficus macrophilla*).

Morgan *mör'gən, n.* any horse of an American breed developed in Vermont by Justin *Morgan* in the late 18th-cent. — light and sturdy for farm work, they are also bred for trotting races.

morganatic *mör-gən-at'ik, adj.* of, by, or of the nature of, a left-handed marriage, that is, a marriage (in some countries) between persons of unequal rank (latterly only where one is of a reigning or mediatised house), the marriage being valid, the children legitimate, but unable to inherit the higher rank, the wife (if the lower-born) not being granted the husband's title. — *adv.* **morganat'ically.** [L.L. *morganātica,* a gift from a bridegroom to his bride; cf. Ger. *Morgengabe,* O.E. *morgengifu,* a morning gift.]

morganite *mör'gə-nīt,* (*min.*) *n.* a pink or rose-coloured variety of beryl, obtained chiefly from California and Madagascar, used as a gemstone. [From J. Pierpont *Morgan,* U.S. financier.]

morgay *mör'gā, n.* the small spotted dogfish or bounce. [Cornish and Welsh *morgi* — *mör,* sea, *ci,* dog.]

morgen *mör'gən, n.* a unit of land-measurement — in Holland, S. Africa, and parts of the U.S.A., a little over two acres; in Norway, Denmark, and Prussia, about two-thirds of an acre. [Du. and Ger.; perh. *morgen,* morning, hence a morning's ploughing.]

morgenstern *mör'gən-stûrn, -shtern, n.* a morning-star (weapon). [Ger.]

Morglay *mör'glā, n.* Sir Bevis of Hampton's sword: hence, a sword. [Cf. **claymore.**]

morgue[1] *mörg, n.* a place where dead bodies are laid out for identification: a place, as in a newspaper office, where miscellaneous material for reference is kept. [Fr.]

morgue[2] *mörg, n.* hauteur. [Fr.]

moria *mō'ri-ə, mö', n.* folly. [Gr. *mōriā.*]

moribund *mor'i-bund, adj.* about to die: in a dying state. — *n.* **moribund'ity.** [L. *moribundus* — *morī,* to die.]

moriche *mor-ē'chä, n.* the miriti palm. [Carib.]

morigeration *mō-rij-ə-rā'shən, mö-, n.* deferential behaviour. — *adjs.* **morig'erate, morig'erous.** [L. *mōrigerātiō, -ōnis* — *mōs, mōris,* custom, humour, *gerere,* to bear.]

Moringa *mor-ing'gə, n.* the horse-radish tree genus, constituting a family **Moringa'ceae,** apparently linking the poppies with the Leguminosae. [Perh. Sinh. *murungā.*]

morion[1], **morrion** *mör'* or *mör'i-ən, n.* an open helmet, without visor or beaver. [Fr., prob. from Sp. *morrión* — *morra,* crown of the head.]

morion[2] *mor'i-ən, n.* black quartz. [Fr.]

Morisco *mo-ris'kō, n.* a Moor, esp. a Christianised Moor in Spain after the fall of Granada in 1492: the Moorish language (*obs.*): (without *cap.*) a morris-dance or dancer: an arabesque: — *pl.* **Moris'co(e)s.** — *adj.* Moorish. — *n.* and *adj.* **Morisk'** (*obs.*).

morish. See **more**[1].

Morisonian *mor-i-sō'ni-ən, n.* a member of the Evangelical Union, formed in 1843 by the Rev. James *Morison* (1816–93), after his separation from the United Secession Church — incorporated with the Congregational Union of Scotland in 1896. — *n.* **Morisō'nianism.**

morkin *mör'kin, n.* a beast that has died by accident. — *n.* **mor'ling, mort'ling** a sheep dead of disease: its wool. [A.Fr. *mortekine* — L. *morticīna* (fem. adj.), carrion — *mors,* death.]

mormaor *mör-mā'ər,* (*hist.*) *n.* a high steward. [Gael. *mormaer,* now *mòrmhaor* — *mòr,* great, *maor,* steward.]

Mormon *mör'mən, n.* one of a religious sect with headquarters since 1847 in Salt Lake City, polygamous till 1890, calling itself *The Church of Jesus Christ of Latter-day Saints,* founded in 1830 by Joseph Smith, whose *Book of Mormon* was given out as translated from the golden plates of *Mormon,* a prophet. — *ns.*

Mor'monism; Mor'monite.

Mormops *mör'mops, n.* a genus of repulsive-looking American leaf-nosed bats. [Gr. *mormō*, a bugbear, *ōps*, face.]

morn *mörn, (poet., dial.) n.* the first part of the day: morning. — **the morn** (*Scot.*) tomorrow; **the morn's morn** or **morning** (*Scot.*) tomorrow morning; **the morn's nicht** (*Scot.*) tomorrow night. [M.E. *morwen* — O.E. *morgen;* Ger. *Morgen.*]

mornay (sauce) *mör'nā (sōs), n.* a cream sauce with cheese flavouring. — *adj.* (placed after noun) served with this sauce. [Perh. Philippe de *Mornay,* Fr. Huguenot leader.]

morne[1] *mörn, n.* the blunt head of a jousting-lance. — *adjs.* **morné** (*mör-nā'*) of a lion rampant, without teeth or claws; **morned** (*her.*) blunted. [Fr. *morner* (pa.p. *morné*) to blunt.]

morne[2] *mörn, (arch.) adj.* dismal, gloomy, sombre. [Fr.]

morning *mörn'ing, n.* the first part of the day, until noon, or the time of the midday meal: the early part of anything: an early dram (chiefly *Scot.*): a slight repast before recognised breakfast (*dial.*). — *adj.* of the morning: taking place or being in the morning. — *adv.* **morn'ings** (*coll.* or *dial.*) in the morning. — **morn'ing-dress** dress, esp. formal dress, worn in early part of day, as opp. to *evening-dress;* **morn'ing-gift** a gift made by the husband to the wife on the morning after marriage; **morn'ing-glo'ry** a plant of the genus *Ipomoea* (esp. *Ipomoea purpurea*) or *Convolvulus,* with showy flowers of various colours; **morn'ing-gown** a gown for wearing in the morning; **morn'ing-land** the east; **morn'-ing-prayer** prayer in the morning: matins; **morn'ing-room** a sitting-room for use in the morning; **morn'ing-sick'ness** nausea and vomiting in the morning, common in the early stages of pregnancy; **morn'ing-star** a planet, esp. Venus, when it rises before the sun: a precursor: a mediaeval weapon, a spiky ball attached directly or by a chain to a handle; **morn'ing-tide** the morning time: early part; **morn'ing-watch** the watch between 4 and 8 a.m. — **morning-after pill** a contraceptive pill taken within a specified time after intercourse; **the morning after** (*coll.*) the unpleasant after-effects of a night of excessive drinking, etc. [Contr. of M.E. *morwening;* cf. **morn.**]

Moro *mör'ō, mör'ō, n.* one of any of the tribes of Muslim Malays in the Philippine Islands: — *pl.* **Moro(s).** [Sp., lit. moor, L. *Maurus.*]

morocco *mə-rok'ō, n.* a fine goat-skin leather tanned with sumac, first brought from *Morocco* (also **morocco leather**): a sheep-skin leather imitation of it: a very strong ale, anciently brewed in Westmorland: — *pl.* **morocc'os.** — *adj.* consisting of morocco. — **French morocco** an inferior kind of Levant morocco, with small grain; **Levant morocco** a fine quality of morocco, with large grain; **Persian morocco** a morocco finished on the grain side.

moron *mör'on, mör', n.* a somewhat feeble-minded person: a former category of mental retardation, describing a person with an I.Q. of 50–69, i.e. one who remains throughout life at the mental age of eight to twelve. — Also *adj.* — *adj.* **moron'ic.** [Gr. *mōros,* foolish.]

morose *mə-rōs', adj.* sour-tempered: gloomy: severe. — *adv.* **morose'ly.** — *ns.* **morose'ness; morosity** (*-os'i-ti; obs.*). [L. *mōrōsus,* peevish — *mōs, mōris,* manner.]

morph[1] *morf, (zool., etc.) n.* a variant form of an animal, etc. [Gr. *morphē,* form.]

morph[2]. See **morphic.**

-morph *-mörf,* **morph(o)-** *mör'fō-,* in composition, of a specified form, shape or structure. — **-morph'ic** adjective combining form. — **-morph'ism** noun combining form. [Gr. *morphē,* form.]

morphallaxis, morpheme, etc. See **morphic.**

Morpheus *mör'fūs, -fyəs, -fi-əs, n.* Greek god of dreams, son of Hypnos (sleep). — *adjs.* **morphē'an** (also *mör'*), **morphet'ic** (irreg. formed). [Gr. *Morpheus,* lit. moulder, shaper — *morphē,* shape.]

morphew *mör'fū, n.* a skin eruption. [It. *morfea.*]

morphia *mör'fi-ə, n.* morphine. — *ns.* **mor'phine** (*-fēn*) the principal alkaloid in opium, used as a hypnotic; **mor'-phinism** the effect of morphine on the system: the habit of taking morphine; **morphinomā'nia; morphinomā'-niac.** [Gr. *Morpheus,* god of dreams.]

morphic *mör'fik, adj.* relating to form, morphological. — *ns.* **morph** (*linguistics;* a back-formation from **mor-pheme**) the whole or a part of a spoken or written word corresponding to or representing one or more morphemes; **morphallax'is** regeneration in a changed form (Gr. *allaxis,* change); **morpheme** (*mör'fēm*) a linguistic unit that has meaning. — *adj.* **morphēm'ic.** — *n.sing.* **morphēm'ics** the study of morphemes. — *n.* **morpho-genesis** (*-fə-jen'i-sis*) the origin and development of a part, organ, or organism. — *adj.* **morphogenet'ic.** — *ns.* **morphogeny** (*-foj'i-ni*) morphogenesis; **morphogra-pher** (*-fog'rə-fər*); **morphog'raphy** descriptive morphology. — *adjs.* **morpholog'ic, -al.** — *ns.* **morphol'ogist; morphol'ogy** the science of form, esp. that of the outer form, inner structure, and development of living organisms and their parts: also of the external forms of rocks and land-features: also of the forms of words; **morphophōn'ēme** (either or any of) two or more phonemes which form variant morphs representing one morpheme (as *wife, wives*). — *adj.* **morpho-phonēm'ic.** — *n.sing.* **morphophonēm'ics.** — *n.* **morphō'-sis** morphogenesis. — *adjs.* **morphŏt'ic** pertaining to morphosis; **morphotrop'ic.** — *n.* **morphot'ropy** the effect on crystalline form of the addition or substitution of an element or radical. [Gr. *morphē,* form.]

morphine, etc. See **morphia.**

Morpho *mör'fō, n.* a tropical American genus of brilliant and gigantic butterflies, often bright blue: (without *cap.*) a butterfly of this genus: — *pl.* **morph'os.** [Gr. *Morphō,* a name of Aphrodite.]

morphogenesis, etc., **morphographer,** etc., **morphologic,** etc., **morphophoneme,** etc. See **morphic.**

morra. See **mora**[2].

morrhua *mor'ōō-ə, n.* an old generic, now specific, name of the cod (*Gadus morrhua*). [L.L. *morua.*]

morrion. See **morion**[1].

morris[1], **morrice** *mor'is,* **morr'is-dance,** *ns.* a dance, according to some of Moorish origin, which came to be associated with May games, with (latterly) Maid Marian, Robin Hood, the hobby-horse, and other characters, who had bells attached to their dress: a tune for the dance. — *v.i.* **morr'is** to perform by dancing. — *ns.* **morr'is-dancer; morr'is-pike** (*Shak.*) a Moorish pike. [**Moorish.**]

morris[2]. See **meril** (for **nine men's morris,** etc.).

Morris chair *mor'is chār,* a kind of armchair with an adjustable back. [From William *Morris,* 19th-cent. English designer and architect.]

Morrison shelter *mor'i-sən shel'tər,* a kind of portable steel air-raid shelter for use inside a house or other building, developed during World War II and named after the then Secretary of State for Home Affairs and Home Security, Herbert S. *Morrison.*

Morris-tube *mor'is-tūb, n.* a small-bore rifle-barrel inserted in the breech of a larger, for short-range practice. [R. *Morris* (d. 1891), the inventor.]

morro *mor'ō, n.* a rounded hill or headland: — *pl.* **morr'os.** [Sp.]

morrow *mor'ō, n.* the day following the present: tomorrow: the next following day: the time immediately after any event. [M.E. *morwe* for *morwen;* cf. **morn.**]

morsal. See **morsure.**

morse[1] *mörs, n.* the walrus. [Lappish *morsa,* or Finn. *mursu.*]

morse[2] *mörs, n.* the fastening of a cope. [L. *morsus,* a bite, catch.]

Morse *mörs, n.* signalling by a code in which each letter is represented by a combination of dashes and dots or long and short light-flashes, sound signals, etc., invented by Sam F. B. *Morse* (1791–1872). — Also *adj.*

morsel *mör'səl, n.* a bite or mouthful: a small piece of food: a choice piece of food, a dainty: a small piece of anything: a small person. — v.t. to divide into morsels: to apportion in small parcels. [O.Fr. morsel (Fr. morceau, It. morsello), dim. from L. morsus — mordēre, morsum, to bite.]

morsing-horn mör′sing-hörn, n. the small horn that used to hold the fine powder used for priming. [Fr. amorcer, to prime (a gun).]

morsure mörs′ūr, n. a bite. — adj. **mors′al**. [L. morsus, bite.]

mort[1] mört, n. death (obs.): a flourish sounded at the death of a buck, etc., in hunting: a sheep that has died a natural death (see also under **morkin** — **morling, mortling**): a dead body. — **mort′bell** a funeral bell; **mort′cloth** a pall; **mort′-head** a death's-head; **mort′-safe** a heavy grating used to guard a corpse against resurrectionists; **mort′-stone** a wayside stone on which the bearers lay the bier for a rest. [Fr. mort, death, dead.]

mort[2] mört, (dial.) n. a great deal. [Origin obscure.]

mort[3] mört, (cant) n. a woman: a loose woman. [Origin obscure.]

mort[4] mört, n. a salmon, 3 years old. [Origin obscure.]

mortal mör′tl, adj. liable to death: causing death: deadly: fatal: punishable with death: involving the penalty of spiritual death, as opposed to venial: to the death: implacable: human: very great (coll.): tediously long (coll.): without exception (coll.): very drunk (slang). — n. a human being. — adv. (dial. or coll.) extremely: confoundedly. — v.t. **mor′talise, -ize** to make mortal. — n. **mortality** (-tal′i-ti) condition of being mortal: death: frequency or number of deaths, esp. in proportion to population: the human race, nature, or estate. — adv. **mor′tally**. — adj. **mor′tal-star′ing** (Shak.) deadly-visaged. — **bills of mortality** see **bill**[3]. [L. mortālis — morī, to die.]

mortar mör′tər, n. a vessel in which substances are pounded with a pestle: a short piece of artillery for throwing a heavy shell, a bomb, a life-line, etc.: a mixture of cement, sand, and water. — v.t. to join or plaster with mortar: to bombard with a mortar. — **mor′tar-board** a square board, with a handle beneath, for holding mortar: a square-topped college cap. [O.E. mortere — L. mortārium, a mortar, matter pounded.]

mortgage mör′gij, n. a conditional conveyance of, or lien upon, land or other property as security for the performance of some condition (as the payment of money), becoming void on the performance of the condition: the act of conveying, or the deed effecting it: the amount of money advanced by a building society, bank, etc., on the security of one's property. — v.t. to pledge as security for a debt. — ns. **mortgagee′** one to whom a mortgage is made or given: one who gives or grants a mortgage; **mort′gagor** (-jər) one who mortgages his property. — Also (sometimes) **mort′-gager**. [O.Fr. — mort, dead, gage, a pledge.]

mortice. See **mortise**.

mortician mör-tish′ən, (U.S.) n. an undertaker. [L. mors, mortis, death.]

mortiferous mör-tif′ər-əs, adj. death-bringing: fatal. — n. **mortif′erousness**. [L. mors, mortis, death, ferre, to bring.]

mortify mör′ti-fī, v.t. to kill (obs.): to destroy the vital functions of: to deaden: to subdue by severities and penance: to vex in a humiliating way: to dispose of by mortification (Scots law). — v.i. to lose vitality: to become gangrenous: to be subdued: to practise asceticism: — pr.p. **mor′tifying**; pa.t. and pa.p. **mor′tified**. — adj. **mortif′ic** death-bringing: deadly. — n. **mortification** (mör-ti-fi-kā′shən) act of mortifying or state of being mortified: the death of part of the body: a bringing under of the passions and appetites by a severe or strict manner of living: humiliation: chagrin: that which mortifies or vexes: a bequest to some charitable institution (Scots law). — adj. **mor′tified**. — n. **mor′tifier**. — adj. and n. **mor′tifying**. [Fr. mortifier — L.L. mortificāre, to cause death to — mors, mortis, death, facĕre, to make.]

mortise, mortice mör′tis, n. a hole made in wood, stone, etc. to receive a tenon: a recess cut into a printing-plate for the insertion of type, etc. (print.): — v.t. to cut a mortise in: to join by a mortise and tenon. — n. **mor′tiser, mor′ticer**. — **mor′tise-lock, mor′tice-lock** a lock whose mechanism is covered by being sunk into the edge of a door, etc. [Fr. mortaise; ety. unknown.]

mortling. See **morkin**.

mortmain mört′mān, (law) n. the transfer of property to a corporation, which is said to be a dead hand, i.e. one that can never part with it again. — **statutes of mortmain** acts of parliament restricting or forbidding the giving of property to religious houses. [Fr. morte (fem.), dead, main — L. manus, hand.]

Morton's fork, crutch mör′tənz förk, kruch, a casuistic device for trapping everyone alike — from the practice of the 15th-cent. Archbishop of Canterbury and statesman John Morton, of exacting loans not only from the rich who could patently afford it, but also from the apparently poor, who were presumed to be saving money.

mortuary mört′ū-ər-i, adj. connected with death or burial. — n. a place for the temporary reception of the dead: a payment to the parish priest on the death of a parishioner or to a bishop or archdeacon on the death of a priest. [L. mortuārius — mortuus, dead, morī, to die.]

morula mör′ū-lə, n. a solid spherical mass of cells resulting from the cleavage of an ovum: framboesia. — adj. **mor′ular**. [L. mōrum, a mulberry.]

Morus mō′rəs, mō′, n. the mulberry genus, giving name to the family **Morā′ceae**, including fig, breadfruit, Ceará rubber. — adj. **morā′ceous**. [L. mōrus, a mulberry tree; cf. Gr. mŏrĕā.]

morwong mör′wong, mō′wong, n. an Australian and N.Z. food fish. [Aboriginal.]

Mosaic mō-zā′ik, adj. pertaining to Moses, the great Jewish lawgiver. — n. **Mō′saism**. — **Mosaic Law** the law of the Jews given by Moses at Mount Sinai.

mosaic mō-zā′ik, n. the fitting together in a design of small pieces of coloured marble, glass, etc.: a piece of work of this kind: anything of similar appearance, or composed by the piecing together of different things: a leaf-mosaic: leaf-mosaic disease (or **mosaic disease**): a hybrid with the parental characters side by side and not blended. — adj. relating to, or composed of, mosaic. — adv. **mosā′ically**. — ns. **mosā′icism** (-i-sizm) presence side by side of patches of tissue of unlike constitution; **mosā′icist** (-i-sist) a worker in mosaic. — **mosaic gold** an alloy of copper and zinc, ormolu: a stannic sulphide; **mosaic map** a composite photographic map made from aerial photographs. [Fr. mosaïque — L.L. mosaicum, mūsaicum — mūsa — Gr. mousa, a muse; cf. L.L. mūsaeum or mūsīvum (opus), mosaic (work).]

Mosasauros mō-sə-sö′rəs, n. a gigantic Cretaceous fossil pythonomorph reptile. [L. Mosa, the Maas, near which the first was found, Gr. sauros, a lizard.]

moschatel mos-kə-tel′, n. a small plant (Adoxa moschatellina), constituting in itself the Adoxaceae (by some included in the honeysuckle family), with pale-green flowers and a supposed musky smell. [Fr. moscatelle — It. moschatella — moscato, musk.]

moschiferous mos-kif′ər-əs, adj. producing musk. [L.L. moschus, Gr. moschos, musk, L. ferre, to bring.]

mose mōz, v.i. only in Shak., Taming of the Shrew, III, ii. 51 — **mose in the chine** to have glanders. [Supposed to be for mourn in the chine, perh. — Fr. morve d'eschine, glanders, running from the spine: the morbid matter of glanders was thought to come from the spine. Another suggestion is that mose is for pose, catarrh, turned into a verb.]

Moselle mō-zel′, n. white wine from the district of the river Moselle, with an aromatic flavour.

Moses basket mō′zəz bäs′kit, a portable cot for babies. [Story of Moses in the bulrushes, Exod. ii. 3.]

mosey mō′zi, (slang) v.i. to move along gently: to jog: to make off: to hurry.   [Perh. for **vamoose.**]

moshav *mō-shäv′*, *n.* an agricultural settlement in Israel: (also **moshav ovdim** *ōv-dēm′*) a joint association of privately-owned farms, on which machinery and marketing are usually operated communally: — *pl.* **moshavim** (*-shə-vēm′*), **moshvei ovdim** (*mosh-vā ′*). — **moshav shitufi** (*shi-tōō-fē′*) an agricultural association in which land and all resources are held in common, but the family unit is preserved, with its own house and garden: — *pl.* **moshavim′ shitufim′.**   [Heb., dwelling.]

moskonfyt *mos-kon′fāt*, (*S.Afr.*) *n.* a thick syrup made from grapes.   [Afrik. *mos,* must, *konfyt,* jam.]

Moslem *moz′lem, -ləm, n.* and *adj.* Same as **Muslim.**

moslings *moz′lingz, n.pl.* the thin shavings taken off by the currier in dressing skins.   [Perh. *morsellings,* as if dim. of **morsel.**]

mosque *mosk, n.* a Muslim place of worship.   [Fr. *mosquée* — It. *moschea* — Ar. *masjid* (in N. Africa pron. *masgid*) — *sajada* (*sagada*), to pray.]

mosquito *mos-kē′tō, n.* loosely, any small biting or stinging insect: any of several long-legged insects of the family *Culicidae,* the females of which have their mouth-parts adapted for bloodsucking and can therefore transmit disease incl. malaria: — *pl.* **mosqui′to(e)s.** — **mosquito canopy, curtain, net** an arrangement of netting to keep out mosquitoes; **mosquito fish** the topminnow; **mosquito hawk** the nighthawk or goatsucker; **mosqui′to-weight** a light featherweight boxer.   [Sp. dim. of *mosca,* a fly — L. *musca.*]

moss *mos, n.* a bog (now chiefly *Scots*): boggy ground or soil: any of the Musci, a class of Bryophyta, small plants with simply constructed leaves, and no woody material, attached by rhizoids, the zygote growing into a small spore-bearing capsule that grows parasitically on the parent plant: a mass of such plants: a moss-like growth, covering, or excrescence: loosely extended to plants of similar appearance to true mosses: a moss-rose. — *v.t.* to cover with moss: to clear of moss. — *v.i.* to gather moss. — *n.* **moss′iness.** — *adj.* **moss′y** overgrown or abounding with moss: like moss: boggy. — **moss′-ag′ate** chalcedony with moss-like inclusions of chlorite, manganese oxide, etc.; **moss′-back** a person of antiquated views; **moss′bluiter** (*-blüt′ər, -blit′ər; Scot.*) the bittern; **moss′-cheep′er** (*Scot.*) the titlark; **moss′-crop** (*Scot.*) cotton-grass; **moss′-flow** (*Scot.*) a watery bog; **moss green** a muted yellowy-green. — *adj.* **moss′-grown** covered with moss. — **moss′-hag′, -hagg′** (*Scot.*) a pit or slough in a bog; **moss′land** wet, peaty land; **moss′-litt′er** a loose mass of lumps of peaty material; **moss′plant** a plant of moss: the sexual generation in the life-history of a moss, on which the asexual generation is parasitic; **moss′-rose** a variety of rose having a moss-like growth on and below the calyx; **moss stitch** a knitting stitch — alternate plain and purl stitches along each row and in succeeding rows; **moss′=troop′er** one of the freebooters that used to infest the mosses of the Border. — *n.* and *adj.* **moss′-troop′ing.** — **club-moss** see **lycopod; Iceland moss** see **Iceland.**   [O.E. *mōs,* bog; Du. *mos,* Ger. *Moos,* moss, bog.]

Mössbauer effect *mæs′bow-ər if-ekt′,* (*nuc.*) a method of producing gamma rays with precise wavelengths, so that measurements can be made by gamma radiation — discovered by Rudolf Ludwig *Mössbauer,* 20th-cent. German physicist.

mossbunker *mos′bung-kər, n.* the menhaden.   [Du. *marsbanker,* the scad or horse-mackerel.]

mossie[1] *mos′i,* **mozzie** *moz′i,* (*coll.*) *ns.* short for **mosquito.**

mossie[2] *mos′i, n.* (*S. Afr.*) (also **Cape sparrow**) a common S. African sparrow, *Passer melanurus,* the male of which has a black head and curved white mark at the eye.   [Afrik., from Du. *mosje,* dim. of *mos,* sparrow.]

most *mōst, adj.* (*superl.* of **more**[1]) greatest: in greatest quantity or number. — *adv.* in the highest degree: almost (*U.S. dial.*; perhaps aphetic). — *n.* the greatest number or quantity. — *advs.* **most′ly** for the most part; **most′what** (*Spens.*) for the most part, mostly. — **at**

(the) most at the utmost computation; **for the most part** chiefly: in the main; **make the most of** see **make**[1]; **the mostest** (*facet.*) the most, the ultimate.   [The Northumbrian form *mäst* (*Scot.* **maist**) may have occurred in O.E. beside the ordinary form *mæst;* or the vowel may come from analogy with the comparative; cf. Ger. *meist.*]

-most *-mōst* in composition, indicating superlative, e.g. *hindmost, farthermost.*   [O.E. superl. suffix. *-mæst, -mest.*]

mot[1] *mot,* (*obs.*) *n.* a motto: a hunter's horn-call.   [Fr., — L. *muttum,* a murmur.]

mot[2] *mō,* (Fr.) *n.* a word: a pithy or witty saying. — **le mot juste** (*lə mō zhüst*) the word which fits the context exactly.

mot[3]. See **motte**[1].

mot[4]. See **mote**[1].

MOT *em-ō-tē′, n.* a compulsory annual check made by order of the Ministry of Transport on vehicles of more than a certain age.   Also **MOT′ test.**

mote[1] *mōt,* (*arch.*) *v.t.* may: must: —*3rd pers. sing. pres. tense* **mote;** *pa.t.* (*Spens.*) **mote, mot** (*mot*), in *pl.* **mot′en** (but see also **must**[1]). — **so mote I thee** so may I prosper (see **thee**[2]).   [O.E. *mōt,* may, *pa.t.* **mōste;** confused with **mought;** Ger. *muss,* must.]

mote[2] *mōt, n.* a particle of dust: a speck: a seed or other foreign particle in wool or cotton (Yorkshire **moit**): a stain or blemish: anything very small. — *adjs.* **mōt′ed, mote′y** (*Scot.* **motty** *mot′i*) containing a mote or motes. — **mote spoon** a perforated spoon formerly used to remove tea-leaves from a tea-cup or teapot spout, or for straining other liquids.   [O.E. *mot;* Du. *mot.*]

mote[3]. See **motte**[2].

motel *mō-tel′, n.* hotel made up of units, each accommodating a car and occupants: a hotel with accommodation and servicing facilities for cars. — *n.* **motel′ier** owner or manager of a motel.   [**mo**(tor), (**ho**)tel.]

moten. See **mote**[1].

motet, motett *mō-tet′, n.* a polyphonic choral composition, usually unaccompanied, with biblical or similar prose text: loosely, an anthem or church cantata. — *n.* **motett′ist.**   [Fr. *motet,* dim. of *mot;* cf. **mot**[2].]

motey. See **mote**[2].

moth *moth, n.* the cloth-eating larvae of the clothes-moth: the imago of the same kind: any member of the Heterocera, a popular and unscientific division of the Lepidoptera, broadly distinguished from butterflies by duller colouring, thicker body, antennae not clubbed, wings not tilted over the back in rest, and by the habit of flying by night: that which eats away gradually and silently: various kinds of insect vermin (*obs.*): a fragile, frivolous creature, readily dazzled into destruction (*fig.*): a light aeroplane: — *pl.* **moths** (*moths*) — *adjs.* **mothed** (*motht*) moth-eaten; **moth′y** full of moths: moth-eaten. — **moth′ball** a ball of naphthalene or other substance for keeping away clothes-moths. — *v.t.* to lay up in mothballs: to spray with a plastic and lay up (a ship, etc.): to lay aside temporarily, postpone work on, keep in readiness for eventual use. — *v.t.* **moth′-eat** (back formation) to prey upon, as a moth eats a garment. — *adj.* **moth′-eaten** eaten or cut by the larvae of moths (also *fig.*). — **moth′-flower** a flower pollinated by moths; **moth′-hunter** a goatsucker. — *adj.* **moth=proof** (of clothes, etc.) chemically rendered resistant to moths. — Also *v.t.* — **(put) in mothballs** (to put) temporarily in abeyance.   [O.E. *moththe, mohthe;* Ger. *Motte.*]

mother[1] *mudh′ər, n.* a female parent: a matron: that which has produced anything: the female head of a religious house or other establishment: a familiar term of address to, or prefix to the name of, an old woman: extended to an ancestress, a stepmother, mother-in-law, foster-mother: an apparatus for chicken-rearing: the womb (*obs.*): hysteria (*obs.*): short for motherfucker (*offensive slang*). — *adj.* received by birth, as it were from one's mother: being a mother: acting the part of a mother: originating: used to produce others from. — *v.t.* to give birth to: to acknowledge, to adopt, to treat as a son or daughter: to foster: to attribute the maternity or authorship of (with *on* or *upon*): to find a mother for. — *ns.* **moth'erhood** state of being a mother; **moth'ering** a rural English custom of visiting the mother church or one's parents on Mid-Lent Sunday (**Mothering Sunday**). — *adj.* **moth'erless** without a mother. — *n.* **moth'erliness.** — *adj.* **moth'erly** pertaining to, or becoming, a mother: like a mother. — **moth'er-cell'** (*biol.*) a cell that gives rise to others by division; **moth'er-church** the church from which others have sprung: a principal church; **moth'er-cit'y** one from which another was founded as a colony; **moth'er-coun'try, -land** the country of one's birth: the country from which a colony has gone out; **moth'er-craft** knowledge and skill required for care of child; **moth'er-fig'ure** an older woman who symbolises for one the qualities and authority of one's mother; **moth'er-fuck'er** (*offensive slang*) an extremely objectionable, unpleasant, etc. person or thing; **Mother Hubbard** a woman's loose flowing gown, like that proper to the nursery heroine; **moth'er-in-law** the mother of one's husband or wife: a stepmother (*obs.*): — *pl.* **moth'ers-in-law; moth'er-in-law's tongue** Sansevieria; **moth'er-liq'uor, moth'er-lye** mother-water; **mother lode** (*mining*) the main lode of any system. — *adj.* **moth'er-na'ked** naked as at birth. — **moth'er-of-mill'ions** ivy-leaved toadflax; **moth'er-of-pearl'** the nacreous internal layer of the shells in some molluscs (also *adj.*); **moth'er-right** succession in the female line: matriarchy; **Mother's Day** a day for honouring of mothers, as, in U.S., second Sunday in May; also used for Mothering Sunday; **mother's help** one employed to help a mother with domestic duties, esp. the supervision of children; **moth'er-ship** a ship having charge of torpedo-boats or small craft: a ship which provides a number of other, usu. smaller, ships with services, supplies, etc.; **moth'er's-mark, moth'er-spot** a birthmark; **mothers' meeting** a periodical meeting of mothers connected with a church; **mother's** (or **mothers'**) **ruin** (*slang*) gin; **mother superior** the head of a convent or any community of nuns; **moth'er-to-be'** a woman who is pregnant, esp. with her first child; **moth'er-tongue** native language: a language from which another has its origin; **moth'er-wa'ter** residual liquid, still containing certain chemical substances, left after others have been crystallised or precipitated from it; **moth'er-wit** native wit: common sense; **moth'erwort** a labiate (*Leonurus cardiaca*) or other plant supposed to help womb disease. — **be mother** (*facet.*) to pour the tea; **every mother's son** every man without exception; **fits of the mother** (*obs.*) hysteria; **Mother Carey's chicken, goose** the storm petrel, or similar bird; **the mother and father** (or **father and mother**) (**of**) (*coll.*) the biggest, greatest (usu. *fig.*), as in *the mother and father of an argument* (or *all arguments*). [O.E. *mōdor*; Du. *moeder*, O.N. *mōthir*, Ger. *Mutter*, Ir. and Gael. *mathair*, L. *māter*, Gr. *mētēr*, Sans. *mātr*.]

mother[2] *mudh'ər, n.* dregs: scum: a slimy mass of bacteria that oxidises alcohol into acetic acid (in full, **mother of vinegar**). — *v.i.* to become mothery. — *adj.* **moth'ery** like or containing mother. [Poss. the same as the foregoing; or poss. — Du. *modder*, mud; cf. **mud.**]

mothering, motherly. See **mother**[1].

motif *mō-tēf', n.* a theme or subject: an element in a composition, esp. a dominant element: a figure, subject, or leitmotif (*mus.*): an ornament added to a woman's garment, often symbolic. [Fr. *motif*; see **motive.**]

motile *mō'tīl*, in U.S. *-til, adj.* capable of moving spontaneously as a whole: characterised by motion: imagining most readily in terms of muscular action. — *n.* one whose imagery naturally takes the form of feelings of action. — *n.* **motility** (*-til'i-ti*). [L. *mōtus*, movement.]

motion *mō'shən, n.* the act, state, manner, of changing place: a single movement: change of posture: power

of moving or of being moved: agitation: a natural impulse: a working in the mind: a feeling: an emotion: a prompting: an instigation: a formal proposal put before a meeting: an application to a court, during a case before it, for an order or rule that something be done, esp. something incidental to the progress of the cause rather than its issue: evacuation of the intestine: a piece of mechanism: progression of a part (*mus.*): a puppet show (*obs.*): a puppet (*Shak.*): (in *pl.*) faeces. — *v.t.* to direct or indicate by a gesture: to move, propose: to make a movement indicating as one's intention (*obs.*): to give motion to. — *v.i.* to offer a proposal. — *adj.* **mō'tional.** — *n.* **mō'tionist** one who is skilled in motions. — *adj.* **mō'tionless** without motion. — **mō'tion-man** (*obs.*) a puppet-showman; **mō'tion-pic'ture** a cinematograph film; **motion sickness** same as **travel sickness.** — **angular motion** change of angle between a standard direction and a line joining the moving object and a fixed point; **go through the motions** to make a half-hearted attempt: to pretend; **laws of motion** Newton's three laws: (1) Every body continues in its state of rest, or of uniform motion in a straight line, except so far as it may be compelled by force to change that state; (2) Change of motion is proportional to force applied, and takes place in the direction of the straight line in which the force acts; (3) To every action there is always an equal and contrary reaction. [Fr. *motion* — L. *mōtiō, -ōnis* — *movēre, mōtum*, to move.]

motive *mō'tiv, adj.* causing motion: having power to cause motion: concerned with the initiation of action: moving (*obs.*). — *n.* an incitement of the will: a consideration or emotion that excites to action: a motif: a moving part of the body (*Shak.*). — *v.t.* to motivate. — *v.t.* **mo'tivate** to provide with a motive: to induce. — *n.* **motivā'tion** motivating force, incentive. — *adjs.* **motivā'tional** pertaining to motivation; **mo'tiveless.** — *n.* **mo'tivelessness.** — *adj.* **motiv'ic** of, having or concerning a musical motif. — *n.* **motiv'ity** power of moving or of producing motion. — **motivated art** art produced under the influence of drugs; **motivation(al) research** research into motivation, esp. into consumer reaction, carried out scientifically; **motive power** the energy or source of the energy by which anything is operated. [L.L. *mōtīvus* — L. *movēre, mōtum*, to move.]

motley *mot'li, adj.* particoloured: variegated: made of, or dressed in, motley: jester-like: heterogeneous. — *n.* a cloth of mixed colours (*obs.*): a particoloured garb, such as a jester wore (*obs.*): a patchwork (*obs.*): a jester (*Shak.*). — *adj.* **mot'ley-mind'ed** (*Shak.*) having a mind of heterogeneous and inconsistent contents. [Poss. from O.E. *mot*, a speck.]

motmot *mot'mot, n.* a tropical American bird (*Momotus* and related genera), akin to rollers and kingfishers, that nibbles its tail-feathers into racquet-shape. [Said to be Mexican name.]

motocross *mō'tō-kros, n.* a form of scrambling, motorcycle racing round a very rough circuit. [**motor.**]

moto perpetuo *mō'tō per-pet'oo-ō*, (It.) perpetual motion: a piece of music that goes swiftly without stop from beginning to end.

motor *mō'tər, n.* a mover: that which gives motion: a machine whereby some source of energy is used to give motion or perform work, esp. an internal-combustion engine or a machine for converting electrical into mechanical energy: a motor-car: a muscle, or a nerve, concerned in bodily movement. — *adj.* giving or transmitting motion: driven by a motor: of, for, with, relating to, motor vehicles: concerned with the transmission of impulses: initiating bodily movement: pertaining to muscular movement or the sense of muscular movement. — *v.t.* and *v.i.* to convey, traverse, or travel by a motor vehicle: to put on speed, to move fast (*coll.*). — *adjs.* **mo'torable** of roads, able to be used by motor vehicles; **moto'rial** motory. — *n.* **motorisā'tion, -z-.** — *v.t.* **mo'torise, -ize** to furnish with, or adapt to the use of, a motor or motors: to interpret or imagine in terms of motor sensation. — *ns.* **mo′torist** one who drives a motor-car, esp. for pleasure; **moto′rium** that part of the nervous system concerned in movement. — *adj.* **mo′tory** causing, conveying, imparting motion: motor. — **mo′tor-band′it** a robber who uses a motor-car; **mo′tor-bi′cycle, -bike, -boat, -bus, -car, -coach, -cy′cle, -launch, -lorr′y, -ship** one driven by a motor; **motorcade** (*mō′tər-kād*; after **cavalcade**) a procession of motor-cars; **motor caravan** a motor vehicle with living, sleeping, etc. facilities, like a caravan; **mo′tor-cy′cling; mo′tor-cyclist.** — *adj.* **mo′tor-driven** driven by a motor. — **motor generator** an electrical generator driven by an electric motor, whereby one voltage, frequency or number of phases, i.e. those of the motor, can be used to produce a different voltage, frequency or number of phases, i.e. those of the generator; **mo′tor-jet** a reciprocating engine with a fan for jet-propulsion; **mo′torman** a man who controls a motor, esp. that of a tram-car or electric train; **motor neurone** (*anat.*) a neurone conveying a voluntary or motor impulse; **motor neurone disease** a disease in which progressive damage to motor neurones leads to muscle weakness and degeneration; **mo′tor-scoo′ter** a small motor-cycle, usu. with an engine of under 225 c.c.; **mo′tor-trac′tion** the conveyance of loads, including passengers, by motor vehicles; **mo′tor-trac′tor** an internal-combustion engine for hauling loads, esp. for drawing agricultural implements; **mo′torway** a trunk road for fast-moving motor vehicles, with separate carriageways for vehicles travelling in opposite directions, and limited access and exit points. — **motorway madness** (*coll.*) reckless driving in bad conditions on motorways, esp. in fog. [L. *mōtor* — *movēre*, to move.]

motorail *mō′tō-rāl, n.* a system of carrying cars and passengers by train on certain routes. [**motor.**]

motoscafo *mō-tō-skä′fō,* (It.) *n.* a motor-boat: — *pl.* **motoscafi** (*-fē*).

motser *mot′sər,* **motza** *mot′zə,* (Austr. *coll.*) *ns.* a large amount of money, esp. the proceeds from a gambling win.

mott *mot* (Spens.), *pa.t.* of **mete[1].**

motte[1], mott, mot *mot, n.* (S.W. U.S.) a clump of trees, esp. in prairie country. [Mex. Sp. *mata*.]

motte[2] *mot,* **mote** *mōt,* (arch.) *ns.* a mound, esp. with a castle, a tumulus. — **mote′-hill.** — **motte and bailey** designating the type of castle commonly built by the Normans, with a keep built on a mound surrounded by a walled bailey. [O.Fr. *mote* (Fr. *motte*); often confused with **moot, moot-hill.**]

mottle *mot′l, v.t.* to variegate blotchily. — *n.* a blotched appearance, condition, or surface: yarns of two colours folded together. — *adj.* **mott′led.** — *n.* **mott′ling.** — *adj.* **mott′le-faced.** [Prob. from **motley.**]

motto *mot′ō, n.* a short sentence or phrase adopted as representative of a person, family, etc., or accompanying a coat of arms: a passage prefixed to a book or chapter shadowing forth its matter: a scrap of verse or prose enclosed in a cracker or accompanying a sweetmeat: — *pl.* **mott′oes** (*-ōz*). — *adj.* **mott′ō′d, mott′oed.** [It., — L. *muttum,* a murmur.]

motty. See **mote[2].**

Motu *mō′tōō, n.* a member of a group of aboriginal people of Papua New Guinea: their language, of the Malayo-Polynesian family: — *pl.* **Motu, Motus.**

motuca *mō-tōō′kə,* **mutuca** *mōō-tōō′kə, ns.* a large Brazilian biting fly of the Tabanidae. [Tupí *mutuca* (Port. *motuca*).]

motu proprio *mō′tū prō′pri-ō, mō′tōō pro′pri-ō,* (L.) of his own accord.

motza. See **motser.**

mou′, mou *mōō, n.* a Scots form of **mouth.**

mouch, moucher. Same as **mooch,** etc.

moucharaby *mōō-shar′ə-bi, n.* a balcony enclosed with lattice-work. [Fr., — Ar. *mashrabiyyah*.]

mouchard *mōō-shär,* (Fr.) *n.* a police spy.

mouchoir *mōō-shwär,* (Fr.) *n.* a pocket-handkerchief.

moudi(e)wart, -wort. Scots forms of **mouldwarp.**

moue *mōō,* (Fr.) *n.* a grimace of discontent, pout.

moufflon, mouflon, muflon *mōōf′lon, n.* a wild sheep of the mountains of Corsica, etc.: extended to large big-horned wild sheep of other kinds: — *pl.* **moufflon,** etc. or **-s.** [Fr. *mouflon* — L.L. *mufrō, -ōnis.*]

mought *mōt,* mowt (Spens. *möt*), (obs. or dial.) *pa.t.* of **may.** See also **mote[1].**

mouillé *mōō′yā, adj.* (of *l* and *n*) sounded in a liquid manner, palatalised — as *gl* in 'seraglio', *ñ* in 'señor'. [Fr. moistened.]

moujik *mōō-zhik′, mōō′zhik, n.* Same as **muzhik.**

moulage *mōōl-äzh′, n.* the making of moulds (esp. of objects of interest in criminal investigation). [Fr. — M.Fr. *mollage* — O.Fr. *mouler,* to model — *modle,* a mould — L. *modulus,* a measure.]

mould[1] (*U.S.* **mold**) *mōld, n.* loose soft earth: earth, considered as the material of which the body is formed or to which it turns: the earth of the grave: the ground, the land, the world (obs. or arch.): (in *pl.*) clods, esp. in allusion to the grave (Scot. **mouls, mools** *mōōlz*): soil rich in decayed matter. — *v.t.* to cover with soil. — *v.i.* (obs.) to moulder. — *v.i.* **mould′er** to crumble to mould: to turn to dust: to waste away gradually. — *v.t.* to turn to dust. — *adj.* **mould′y** like, or of the nature of, mould. — **mould′-board** the curved plate in a plough which turns over the soil. [O.E. *molde*; Ger. dialect *molt, molten,* Goth. *mulda.*]

mould[2] (*U.S.* **mold**) *mōld, n.* a woolly growth on bread, cheese, or other vegetable or animal matter: any one of various small fungi (Mucor, Penicillium, etc.) of different classes, forming such growths. — *v.i.* to become mouldy. — *v.t.* to cause or allow to become mouldy. — *n.* **mould′iness.** — *adj.* **mould′y** overgrown with mould: like mould: stale: musty. [M.E. *mowle*; cf. O.N. *mygla.*]

mould[3] (*U.S.* **mold**) *mōld, n.* a templet: matrix in which a cast is made: a formed surface from which an impression is taken: the foundation upon which certain manufactured articles are built up: a thing formed in a mould, esp. a jelly or blancmange: nature: form: model: a pattern: that which is or may be moulded: a set of mouldings (archit.): a wire tray used to make paper by hand. — *v.t.* to knead: to mix (obs.): to shape: to model: to form in a mould. — *adj.* **mould′able.** — *ns.* **mould′er; mould′ing** the process of shaping, esp. any soft substance: anything formed by or in a mould: an ornamental edging or band projecting from a wall or other surface, as a fillet, astragal, bead, etc.: a strip of wood that can be applied for the purpose. — **mould′-candle** a candle made in a mould, not dipped; **mould′-fac′ing** a fine powder or wash applied to the face of a mould to ensure a smooth casting; **mould′ing-board** a baker's board for kneading dough; **mould′-loft** a room in which the several parts of a ship's hull are laid off to full size from the construction drawings. — *adj.* **mould′-made** of paper, made on a machine, but having a deckle-edge like that of handmade paper. [O.Fr. *modle, molle* (Fr. *moule*) — L. *modulus,* a measure.]

mouldwarp *mōld′wörp, n.* a mole. — Also (Scot.) **mowdi(e)- (mow′di-), moudi(e)wart, -wort** (*mōō′di-wûrt*). [O.E. *molde,* mould, earth, *weorpan,* to throw; cf. O.H.G. *multwurf* (Ger. *Maulwurf*), Dan. *muldvarp.*]

moulin *mōō′lē, n.* a shaft in a glacier worn by water running down a crack. — *n.* **moulinet** (*mōō-li-net′,* or *mōō′*) a machine for bending a crossbow. [Fr. *moulin,* mill, and dim. *moulinet* — L.L. *molīnum.*]

moult (*U.S.* **molt**) *mōlt, v.i.* to cast feathers or other covering: to be shed. — *v.t.* to shed. — *n.* the act, process, condition, or time of moulting. — *adj.* **moult′en** (Shak.) having moulted. — *n.* **moult′ing.** [O.E. (*bi*)*mūtian,* to exchange — L. *mūtāre*; the *l,* first a freak of spelling, afterwards sounded.]

mound[1] *mownd, n.* a boundary-fence or hedge (obs.): a bank of earth or stone raised as a protection: a hillock: a heap. — *v.t.* to enclose with a fence or an embankment (obs.): to fortify with an embankment: to heap in a mound. — **mound'-bird** a megapode, or bird of the Australian family Megapodidae, gallinaceous birds that build large mounds as incubators; **mound'-builder** one of the Indians who in early times built great mounds in the eastern United States: a mound-bird. [Origin obscure; O.E. *mund* means guardianship.]

mound[2] *mownd, n.* a king's orb. [Fr. *monde* — L. *mundus*, the world.]

mounseer *mown'sēr*, or *-sēr'*, (*arch., illit.,* or *derisive*) *n.* for *monsieur*, a Frenchman.

mount[1] *mownt, n.* a mountain (*arch.* except **Mount**, as prefix to a name): a small hill or mound, natural or artificial: a fleshy protuberance on the hand. [O.E. *munt* and O.Fr. *mont*, both — L. *mōns, montis*, mountain.]

mount[2] *mownt, v.i.* to go up: to climb: to get upon horseback, bicycle, or the like: to extend upward: to extend backward in time: to rise in level or amount: to amount (*obs.*). — *v.t.* to climb, ascend: to get up on: to cover or copulate with: to cause to rise, to lift, raise, erect: to place upon anything high: to put on horseback, or the like: to furnish with an animal, bicycle, etc., to ride on: to fix in a setting, on a support, stand, or mount: to furnish with accessories: to put in position and state of readiness for use or exhibition: to stage: to be armed with: to carry, wear, or put on: to put into operation, carry out. — *n.* a rise: an act of mounting: manner of mounting: a step to mount by: a signal for mounting: a riding animal or cycle: that upon which a thing is placed or in which it is set for fixing, strengthening, embellishing, esp. the card surrounding a picture: the slide, cover-glass, etc., used in mounting an object for the microscope. — *adj.* **mount'ed** on horseback: furnished with horses: set on high: raised on steps, generally three, as a cross (*her.*): set up: set (also in composition). — *ns.* **mount'er; mount'ing; mount'y, mount'ie** (*coll.*) a Canadian mounted policeman. — **mount'ing-block** a block or stone to enable one to mount a horse. — **have the mount** to ride (a particular horse) in a race; **mount guard** see **guard.** [Fr. *monter*, to go up — L. *mōns, montis*, mountain.]

mountain *mownt'in, n.* a high hill: a wine made from mountain grapes: in Ireland, wild pasture land: a large quantity, excess, esp. of agricultural, dairy, etc. products bought up by an economic community to prevent a fall in prices: (*cap.*) the extreme party in the French Revolution (see **Montagnard**). — *adj.* of a mountain: growing, dwelling, etc. on or among mountains. — *adj.* **mount'ained.** — *n.* **mountaineer'** an inhabitant of mountain country: a climber of mountains: a member of the Mountain. — *v.i.* to climb mountains. — *n.* **mountaineer'ing** mountain climbing. — *adj.* **mount'-ainous** full of, characterised by, mountains: large as a mountain: huge. — **mount'ain-ash'** the rowan-tree; **mount'ain-beav'er** the sewellel; **mountain bicycle** a bicycle with a strong, heavy frame and wide tyres designed for use over rough terrain; **mount'ain-blue'** blue carbonate of copper; **mount'ain-bram'ble** the cloudberry; **mount'ain-cat'** a catamount, a wild-cat; **mount'ain-chain'** a range of mountains forming a long line; **mount'ain-cork', mount'ain-leath'er** a matted mass of a fibrous amphibole, cork-like or leathery; **mountain devil** a moloch; **mount'ain-dew'** whisky; **mount'ain-flax** amianthus; **mount'ain-everlast'ing** the cat's-foot (*Antennaria dioica*), a small woolly composite plant of the hills and seashore; **mountain goat** short for **Rocky Mountain Goat; mount'ain-hare'** a smaller species of hare, grey in summer, usually white in winter. — *adv.* and *adj.* **mount'ain-high', mount'ains-high'** high as a mountain (hyperbolically). — **mount'ain-lau'rel** kalmia; **Mountain Limestone** the lowest division of the Carboniferous in England, the Carboniferous Limestone; **mount'ain-li'on** the puma; **mount'ain-marr'ow** lithomarge; **mount'ain-meal** bergmehl; **mount'ain-rail'-way** a light narrow-gauge railway for mountainous regions, usually a rack-railway; **mountain ringlet** *Ere-bia epiphron*, a rare alpine butterfly; **mount'ain-sheep'** the bighorn of the Rocky Mountains; **mount'ain-sick'ness** sickness brought on by breathing rarefied air; **mount'ain-side** the slope of a mountain; **mount'ain-soap'** a greasy kind of halloysite; **mount'ain-tall'ow** hatchettite; **mount'ain-tea'** the American evergreen *Gaultheria procumbens*; **mount'ain-top; mount'ain-wood** a fibrous wood-like asbestos. — **Old Man of the Mountain** a popular name for the chief of the *Hashsh āshīn* (see **assassin**). [O.Fr. *montaigne* — L. *mōns, montis*, mountain. In some compounds *mountain* is used like Ger. *Berg*, as if = mine.]

mountant *mownt'ənt, n.* an adhesive paste for mounting photographs, etc.: any substance in which specimens are suspended on a microscope slide. — *adj.* (*Shak.*) rising on high. [Fr. *montant*, pr.p. of *monter*, to mount.]

mountebank *mown'ti-bangk, n.* a quack who harangues and plays the fool: a buffoon: a charlatan. — *v.t.* to win, effect, render, by mountebankery. — *v.i.* (or *v.t.* with *it*) to play the mountebank. — *ns.* **moun'tebank-ery, moun'tebanking, moun'tebankism.** [It. *montimbanco, montambanco* — *montare*, to mount, *in*, on, *banco*, bench.]

mountenance, mountenaunce *mount'ən-əns, -äns,* (*Spens.*) *n.* amount: distance. [App. O.Fr. *montance*, assimilated to **maintenance;** cf. **mount**[2], **mountant.**]

mounty, mountie. See **mount**[2].

moup, moop, *mōōp,* (*Scot.*) *v.t.* to nibble: to mumble. — *v.i.* to consort. [Origin obscure.]

mourn *mōrn, mörn,* (*rare*) *mōōrn, v.i.* to grieve: to be sorrowful: to wear mourning: to murmur as in grief. — *v.t.* to grieve for: to utter in a sorrowful manner. — *n.* **mourn'er** one who mourns: one who attends a funeral, especially a relative of the deceased: a person hired to lament or weep for the dead: a penitent at a revival meeting (*U.S.*). — *adj.* **mourn'ful** causing, suggesting, or expressing sorrow: feeling grief. — *adv.* **mourn'fully.** — *n.* **mourn'fulness.** — *adj.* **mourn'ing** grieving: lamenting. — *n.* the act of expressing grief: the dress of mourners, or other tokens of mourning — also (*Scot.*) in *pl.* — *adv.* **mourn'ingly.** — **mourn'ing-band'** a band of black material worn round the sleeve or (*hist.*) the hat, to signify that one is in mourning; **mourn'ing-bord'er** a black margin used on notepaper, etc., by those in mourning: a dirty edge on a fingernail (*coll.*); **mourn'ing-bride** the sweet scabious (*Scabiosa atropurpurea*); **mourn'ing-cloak'** an undertaker's cloak, formerly worn at a funeral: the Camberwell beauty (*U.S.*); **mourn'ing-coach'** a closed carriage for carrying mourners to a funeral; **mourn'ing-dove'** an American pigeon with plaintive note; **mourn'ing-piece** a picture intended to be a memorial of the dead; **mourn'ing-ring'** a ring worn in memory of a dead person; **mourn'ing-stuff** a lustreless black dress fabric, as crape, cashmere, etc., for making mourning clothes. — **half-mourning** see **half; in mourning** wearing black (in China, white) in token of mourning: of a ship, painted blue: with eyes blackened (*slang*). [O.E. *murnan;* O.H.G. *mornēn,* to grieve.]

mournival *mōr'ni-vəl, mör', n.* in gleek, a set of four aces, kings, etc. [Fr. *mornifle.*]

mousaka. Same as **moussaka.**

mouse *mows, n.* a little rodent animal (*Mus*) found in houses and in the fields: extended to various voles and other animals more or less like the mouse, the *flitter-*mouse, *shrew-*mouse: a device which is moved by hand over a flat surface thereby causing the cursor to move correspondingly on screen (*comput.*): a small lead weight used to balance sash windows: a term of endearment (*obs.*): a muscle (*obs.*): part of a hindleg of beef, next the round (*dial.*; also **mouse'-butt'ock** and **mouse'-piece**): a match for firing a cannon or mine (*obs.*): a knot or knob to prevent slipping (*naut.*; also **mous'ing**): a black eye, or discoloured swelling (*slang*): a timid, shy, colourless person: — *pl.* **mice** (*mīs*). — *v.i.* (*mowz*) to hunt for mice or as if for mice: to prowl.

— *v.t.* to treat or to tear as a cat does a mouse: to paw or handle amorously (*arch.*): to secure with a mouse (*naut.*). — *ns.* **mouse′kin, mous′ie** a young or little mouse; **mouser** (*mowz′er*) a cat good at catching mice: a prying person (*arch.*); **mousery** (*mows′ər-i*) a resort of mice. — *n.* and *adj.* **mousing** (*mowz′ing*). — *v.t.* **mousle** (*mowz′l*) to pull about roughly or disrespectfully. — *adj.* **mous(e)y** (*mows′i*) like a mouse in colour or smell: abounding with mice: noiseless, stealthy: of hair, limp and dull greyish-brown: of person, uninteresting, too unassertive. — **mouse′-colour** the grey colour of a mouse. — *adjs.* **mouse′-colour, -ed.** — **mouse′-deer** a chevrotain. — *adj.* **mouse′-dun** mouse-coloured. — **mouse′-ear** a name of several plants with soft leaves shaped like a mouse's ear, esp. forget-me-not: (**mouse′-ear chick′weed**) any plant of the genus Cerastium, akin to chickweed; **mouse-eared bat** a kind of bat, *Myotis myotis*, found chiefly in continental Europe and Western Asia); **mouse′-hole** a hole made or used by mice: a small hole or opening; **mouse′-hunt** (*Shak.*) a mouser; **mouse′-sight** myopia; **mouse′-tail** a small ranunculaceous plant (*Myosurus*) with a spike of seed-vessels very like the tail of a mouse; **mouse′-trap** a trap for mice: any cheese of indifferent quality. [O.E. *mūs*, pl. *mȳs*; Ger. *Maus*, L. *mūs*, Gr. *mȳs*, mouse, muscle.]

mousmee, mousmé *mōōs′mā, n.* a Japanese girl, esp. a waitress. [Jap. *musume.*]

mousquetaire *mōōs-kə-ter′, n.* a musketeer: a woman's cloak trimmed with ribbons, with large buttons, fashionable about 1855: a broad turnover linen collar worn a few years earlier. — **mousquetaire glove** a woman's glove, long-armed, loose at top, without slit lengthwise. [Fr.]

moussaka, mousaka *mōō-sä′kə, n.* a Greek dish consisting of minced meat, aubergines, tomatoes and cheese.

mousse *mōōs, n.* a a frothy dish made with whipped cream, eggs, etc., flavoured and usu. eaten cold: a cosmetic preparation, usu. a hair application, of like consistency. [Fr., moss.]

mousseline *mōōs-lēn′, n.* fine French muslin: a very thin glassware: a claret-glass made of it. — **mousseline-de-laine** (*-də-len′*) an all-wool muslin; **mousseline-de-soie** (*-də-swä′*) a silk muslin. — **mousseline sauce** a kind of sauce hollandaise made light by adding whipped cream or egg-white. [Fr.]

moust. See **must**[5].

moustache, mustache *məs-, mus-, mōōs-täsh′, n.* the hair upon the upper lip — also **mustachio** (*-tä′shō*; *pl.* **musta′chios**). — Also in *pl.* — *adj.* **moustached′, mustach′ioed; moustach′ial.** — **moustache′-cup** a cup with the top partly covered, formerly used to keep the moustache from getting wet. — **old moustache** an old soldier. [Fr. *moustache* — It. *mostaccio* — Doric Gr. *mystax, -ākos*, the upper lip, moustache.]

Mousterian *mōōs-tē′ri-ən, adj.* of an early Palaeolithic culture between Acheulean and Aurignacian. [Le *Moustier*, a cave on the Vézère which has yielded implements of this age.]

moutan *mōō′tan, n.* a tree peony. [Chin.]

mouter *mōōt′ər, a* Scots form of **multure.**

mouth *mowth, n.* the opening in the head of an animal by which it eats and utters sound: opening or entrance, as of a bottle, river, etc.: a consumer of food: a speaker: a spokesman: cry, voice, utterance: a wry face, a grimace: backchat, insolence: — *pl.* **mouths** (*mowdhz*). — *v.t.* (*mowdh*) to utter: to utter with exaggerated, affectedly pompous, or self-conscious action of the mouth: to form (words) silently by moving the lips: to declaim or spout: to take in the mouth: to feel, mumble, or mangle with the mouth: to train to the bit. — *v.i.* to declaim, rant (also *v.t.* with *it*): to apply mouths (*Shak.*): to grimace: to debouch. — *adjs.* **mouthable** (*mowdh′ə-bl*) lending itself to elocutionary utterance; **mouthed** (*mowdhd*) having a mouth. — *ns.* **mouther** (*mowdh′ər*) one who mouths; **mouth′ful** (*mowth′fəl*) as much as fills the mouth: a small quantity: a big word:

a momentous utterance (*slang*): — *pl.* **mouth′fuls.** — *adjs.* **mouth′less; mouthy** (*mowdh′i*) ranting: affectedly over-emphatic. — **mouth-breather** (*mowth′-brē′dhər*) one who habitually breathes through the mouth; **mouth′-breeder** a cichlid fish that carries its young in its mouth for protection. — *adj.* **mouth-filling** (*mowth′*) full-sounding. — **mouth′-friend** (*Shak.*) one who only professes friendship; **mouth′-harp** a mouth-organ; **mouth′-hon′our** (*Shak.*) insincere civility. — *adj.* **mouth′-made** (*Shak.*) insincere. — **mouth music** music (usually accompanying dance) sung, not played on instrument(s); **mouth′-organ** a small musical instrument encasing metallic reeds, played by the mouth — a harmonicon or harmonica: Pan-pipes; **mouth′piece** the piece of a musical instrument, tobacco-pipe, mask, etc., held to or in the mouth: a cigarette-holder: a spokesman. — *adj.* **mouth′-to-mouth** of a method of artificial respiration in which a person breathes air directly into the patient's mouth to inflate the lungs. — **mouth′wash** an antiseptic solution for cleansing the mouth and for gargling with. — *adj.* **mouth′watering** causing the release of saliva in the mouth, highly appetising. — **be all mouth** (*slang*) to be unable to support one's boastful talk with action; **by word of mouth** see **word; down in the mouth** see **down**[3]; **have a big mouth** (*coll.*) to (habitually) talk indiscreetly, loudly, or too much; **make a poor mouth** to profess poverty; **shoot one's mouth off** (*slang*) to talk freely, inaccurately, tactlessly, etc.; **shut, stop the mouth of** to silence. [O.E. *mūth*; Ger. *Mund*, Du. *mond.*]

mouton *mōō′tən, n.* a sheepskin which has been processed, sheared and dyed to resemble the fur of another animal. [Fr. *mouton*, a sheep.]

mouvementé *mōōv-mä-tā,* (Fr.) *adj.* full of movement, lively.

move *mōōv, v.t.* to cause to change place or posture: to set in motion: to impel: to excite to action: to cause (the bowels) to be evacuated: to persuade: to instigate: to arouse: to provoke: to provoke to anger (*obs.*; now *move to anger, move anger in*): to touch the feelings of: to propose formally before a meeting: to recommend. — *v.i.* to go from one place to another: to change place or posture: to walk, to carry oneself: to change residence: to make a motion as in an assembly: to bow or salute on meeting (*arch.*): to begin to act: to take action: to become active or exciting (*coll.*): to go about one's activities, live one's life, pass one's time: in chess, draughts, etc., to transfer a piece in one's turn to another square: — *pr.p.* **mov′ing;** *pa.t.* and *pa.p.* **moved.** — *n.* an act of moving: a beginning of movement: a proceeding or step: play in turn, as at chess: turn to play, in chess, draughts, etc.: advantage depending on whose turn it is to play: the manner in which a chessman, or the like, can be moved. — *adj.* **movable** (*mōōv′ə-bl*) mobile: changeable: not fixed: other than heritable (*Scots law*). — Also (esp. *law*) **move′able.** — *n.* (esp. in *pl.*) a portable piece of furniture: a piece of movable or moveable property. — *ns.* **mov′ableness** (**move′ableness**); **mov(e)abil′ity.** — *adv.* **mov′ably** (**move′ably**). — *adj.* **move′less** motionless: immovable. — *adv.* **move′lessly.** — *ns.* **move′lessness; move′ment** act or manner of moving: change of position: activity: impulse: motion of the mind, emotion: the moving parts in a mechanism, esp. the wheelwork of a clock or watch: melodic progression: accentual character: tempo or pace: a main division of an extended musical composition, with its own more or less independent structure: the suggestion of motion conveyed by a work of art: a general tendency or current of thought, opinion, taste or action, whether organised and consciously propagated or a mere drift; **mov′er; mov′ie, mov′y** (*slang*) a moving picture, a cinematograph film: a showing of such: (in *pl.*, **movies,** usu. with **the**) motion pictures in general, or the industry that provides them. — Also *adj.* — *adj.* **mov′ing** causing motion: changing position: affecting the feelings: pathetic. — *adv.* **mov′ingly.** — **movable feast** a church feast, such as Easter, whose date varies from year to year; **moving average** a sequence of values derived from an earlier sequence from which a mean was taken of each successive group of values with a constant number of members. — *adj.* **mov′ing-coil** of, or pertaining to, electrical equipment that incorporates a coil of wire so placed within a magnetic field as either to vibrate when current is passed through it, or to generate a current when vibrated. — **moving pictures** the cinematograph: cinematograph films; **moving staircase** an escalator. — **get a move on** to hurry up: to make progress; **know a move or two** to be sharp or knowing; **move heaven and earth** see **heaven**; **move house** to move to a new place of residence: to move one's possessions to such; **on the move** changing or about to change one's place: travelling: progressing. [A.Fr. *mover*, O.Fr. *movoir* (Fr. *mouvoir*) — L. *movēre*, to move. The obsolete **meve**, **mieve** represent those forms in Fr. with accented root-syllable, as *meuvent* (3rd pers. pl.).]

Moviola® *moo̅-vē-ō′lə*, *n.* a machine reproducing both the sound and picture used to facilitate film-editing. [**movie** and **pianola**.]

mow¹ *mow*, also *mō*, *n.* a wry face. — *v.i.* to make grimaces. — Also **moe** (*obs.*). — **nae mows** (*nā mowz*; *Scot.*) no laughing matter. [O.Fr. *moue*, **moe** (Fr. *moue*), or M.Du. *mouwe*, both meaning grimace.]

mow² *mow*, also *mō*, *n.* a pile of hay, corn in sheaves, pease, etc., esp. in a barn: a place for such a heap in a barn. — *v.t.* to heap in a mow: — *pr.p.* **mow′ing**; *pa.t.* and *pa.p.* **mowed** (*mowd*). — *v.i.* **mow′burn** to heat and ferment in the mow. — *adj.* **mow′burnt**. [O.E. *mūga*, heap; O.N. *mūgi*, swath, crowd, mob.]

mow³ *mō*, *v.t.* to cut down, or cut the grass upon, with a scythe or a grass-cutting machine: to cut down in great numbers: — *pr.p.* **mow′ing**; *pa.t.* **mowed** (*mōd*); *pa.p.* **mowed** or **mown** (*mōn*). — *adjs.* **mowed**, **mown**. — *ns.* **mow′er** one who mows grass, etc.: a machine with revolving blades for mowing grass; **mow′ing** the act of cutting: land from which grass is cut. — **mow′ing-machine′**. [O.E. *māwan*; Ger. *mähen*; L. *metĕre*, to reap.]

mowa *mow′sə*, **mowra** *mow′rə*. Same as **mahua**.

mowdi(e)wart, -wort. Scots forms of **mouldwarp**.

mown; mowra. See **mow³; mowa**.

moxa *mok′sə*, *n.* a cauterising cone of the leaf down of a wormwood (*Artemisia moxa*), or sunflower pith, cotton-wool, or other material. — *n.* **moxibustion** (*-bust′yən*; modelled on *combustion*) cauterisation by moxa: burning of a herbal moxa as a counter-irritant. [Jap. *mogusa*.]

moxie *mok′si*, (*U.S. slang*) *n.* courage, daring, energy. [*Moxie®*, a soft drink.]

moy *moi*, (*Shak.*) *n.* supposed by Pistol (misunderstanding a Frenchman's *moi*, me) to be the name of a coin, or possibly a measure (Fr. *muid* — L. *modius*) of corn.

moya *moi′ä*, *n.* volcanic mud. [Prob. Amer. Sp.]

Moygashel® *moi′gə-shel*, *n.* (also found without *cap.*) a type of linen manufactured in Northern Ireland. [Place name.]

moyity, moyle. Spens. for **moiety, moil**.

moyl, moyle *moil*, (*obs.*) *n.* a mule. [O.Fr. *mul, mule*.]

moz, mozz *moz*, (*Austr. slang*) *n.* a curse or jinx. — *n.* **mozz′le** luck, esp. bad luck. [Heb. *mazzāl*, luck.]

Mozarab *mō-zar′ab*, *n.* a privileged Christian Spaniard under Moorish rule. — *adj.* **Mozar′abic**. [Sp. *Mozárabe* — Ar. *musta′rib*, would-be Arab.]

Mozartian, -ean *mō-tsär′ti-ən*, *adj.* of or like (the style, etc. of) Wolfgang Amadeus *Mozart* (1756–1791), Austrian composer.

moze *mōz*, *v.t.* to gig, raise a nap on. [Origin obscure.]

mozetta *mō-tset′ə*, *n.* a short cape to which a hood may be attached, worn by popes, cardinals, bishops, abbots. — Also **mozzett′a**. [It., dim. from *mozzo*, docked.]

mozz. See **moz**.

mozzarella *mot-sə-rel′ə*, *n.* a softish Italian cheese. [It.]

mozzie. See **mossie**.

mozzle. See **moz**.

mpret *bret*, *n.* a former title of the ruler of Albania. [Albanian, — L. *imperātor*, emperor.]

mridangam, mridamgam, mridang(a) *mri-däng′gəm, mri-däng′* (*gə*) *ns.* a two-headed Indian drum, one of the heads being larger than the other. [Sans. *mṛidaṁga*.]

M-roof. See under **M**.

Mr, Mrs. See **Mister, Mistress**.

Ms. *miz*, *n.* a title substituted for **Mrs** or **Miss** before the name of a woman, to avoid distinguishing between the married and the unmarried.

MS. See **manuscript**.

mu *mū, moo̅, mü*, *n.* the Greek letter M, μ, equivalent to M: as a numeral, μ′ = 40, ‚μ = 40,000: used as a symbol for **micron** and **micro-** (2). — **mu-** (or μ-) **meson** a subatomic particle, classed formerly as the lightest type of meson, now as the heaviest type of lepton, having unit negative charge, now largely superseded by **mu′on** (*mū′* or *moo̅′*) (q.v.). [Gr. *mȳ*.]

mucate, mucedinous. See **mucus**.

much *much* (*compar.* **more**; *superl.* **most**), *adj.* in great quantity: great (*obs.*): many (*Shak.*). — *adv.* in a great degree: to a great extent: in nearly the same way: by far: in old ironical use, like the modern slang 'not much', I don't think. — *n.* a great deal: anything of importance or worth. — Also in unshortened form (*arch.*) **much′el**, *adj., adv.,* and *n.* (*Spens.* **much′ell**, **moch′ell**; Northern form **mick′le**, **muck′le**). — *adv.* (*arch.* and *jocular*) **much′ly**. — *n.* **much′ness** (*arch.*) greatness: magnitude. — **(as) much as** although, even though; **make much of** see **make¹**; **much about it** something like what it usually is; **much of a muchness** just about the same value or amount; **not up to much** (*coll.*) not very good; **too much for** more than a match for; **too much of a good thing** more than can be tolerated. [M.E. *muche, muchel* — O.E. *micel, mycel*.]

mucic, mucid, mucilage. See under **mucus**.

muck *muk*, *n.* dung: manure: wet or clinging filth: anything contemptible or worthless: dirt, debris, rubble: gold (*poet.; arch.*): rubbishy reading matter: a mess. — *v.t.* to clear of muck: to manure with muck: to befoul: to make a mess of, to bungle (with *up*). — *v.i.* (usu. with *about; coll.*) to potter: to act the fool. — *n.* **muck′er** one who mucks: a money-grubber (*obs.*): a mess: a mishap, disaster (orig. a fall in the mire): a coarse, unrefined person: a young townsman, not a student (*arch. U.S.*). — *v.t.* to hoard (*obs.*): to squander: to vitiate. — *v.i.* to come to grief: to make a muddle of anything. — *n.* **muck′iness.** — *adj.* **muck′y** nasty, filthy: of the nature of muck: like muck. — **muck′-heap** a dunghill; **muck′-midd′en**; **muck′-rake** a rake for scraping filth. — *v.i.* to seek out and expose scandals or supposed scandals, whether for worthy or unworthy motives. — **muck′-raker**; **muck′-raking**. — *v.i.* **muck′-spread** to spread manure. — **muck′spreader** an agricultural machine for spreading manure; **muck′-sweat** profuse sweat; **muck′-worm** a worm or grub that lives in muck: one who acquires money by mean devices: a miser. — **make a muck of** (*coll.*) to make dirty: to mismanage; **muck in (with)** (*coll.*) to share with: to help, participate (in). [Prob. Scand.; cf. ON. *myki*, Dan. *mög*, dung.]

muckender *muk′ən-dər*, (*obs.*) *n.* a handkerchief: a table-napkin. [Apparently from some Languedocian dialect; cf. Fr. *mouchoir*, Sp. *mocador*.]

Mucker *mook′ər*, *n.* a nickname for a member of a Königsberg sect (1835) of dualistic theosophists: (without *cap.; muk′ər*) a fanatical reformer: a hypocrite. [Ger.]

muckle *muk′l*, a Scottish form of **mickle**.

muckluck, mukluk, mucluc *muk′luk*, *n.* an Eskimo sealskin boot. [Eskimo.]

mucoid. See **mucus**.

Mucor *mū′kər*, *n.* a genus of zygomycete fungi including some of the commonest moulds, giving name to order or family **Mucorā′les** or **Mūcorin′eae:** (without *cap.*)

any mould of this genus. [L., mould.]

mucosa, mucosity. See **mucus.**

mucro *mū'krō, n.* a short stiff sharp point forming an abrupt end: — *pl.* **mūcrō'nes** (-*nēz*), **mū'cros.** — *adjs.* **mu'cronate, -d** (-*krən-āt, -id*). [L. *mūcrō, -ōnis*, a sharp point.]

mucus *mū'kəs, n.* the slimy fluid secreted by the mucous membrane of the nose or other parts. — *n.* **mu'cate** a salt of mucic acid. — *adjs.* **mucedinous** (-*sed', -sēd'*) mouldy, mildewy; **mu'cic** (-*sik*) applied to an acid got by oxidation of gums; **mu'cid** mouldy, musty; **muciferous** (-*sif'*) secreting or conveying mucus. — *n.* **mu'cigen** (-*si-jen*) a substance secreted by the cells of mucous membrane, converted into mucin. — *n.* **mu'cilage** (-*si-lij*) a gluey mixture of carbohydrates in plants: any sticky substance: gum used as an adhesive. — *adj.* **mucilaginous** (-*laj'*). — *ns.* **mucilag'inousness; mu'cin** any one of a class of albuminous substances in mucus. — *adjs.* **mucoid** (*mū'koid*) like mucus; **mucopū'rulent** of mucus and pus. — *ns.* **mucosa** (*mū-cō'sə*) the mucous membrane: — *pl.* **mucō'sae** (-*sē*). — *adj.* **mucosanguin'eous** consisting of mucus and blood. — *n.* **mucos'ity.** — *adjs.* **mu'cous** like mucus: slimy: viscous: producing mucus; **mu'culent** like mucus. — *n.* **mucoviscidō'sis** cystic fibrosis. — **mucous membrane** a lining of various tubular cavities of the body, with glands secreting mucus. [L. *mūcus*, nose mucus; cf. *mungĕre*, to wipe away.]

mud *mud, n.* wet soft earth: a mixture of earthy or clayey particles with water: a similar mixture with certain added chemicals used as a lubricant in drilling oil-wells: something worthless or contemptible. — *v.t.* to bury in mud: to clog with mud: to plaster with mud: to befoul: to make turbid: to supply with mud. — *v.i.* to hide in the mud. — *adv.* **mudd'ily.** — *n.* **mudd'iness.** — *adj.* **mudd'y** foul with mud: containing mud: covered with mud: of the nature of mud: like mud: mud-coloured: confused: stupid. — *v.t. and v.i.* to make or become muddy: — *pr.p.* **mudd'ying**; *pa.t. and pa.p.* **mudd'ied.** — **mud'-bath** a bath in mud, esp. as a remedy: an outdoor event taking place in muddy conditions (*coll.*); **mud'-boat** a board or sled for conveyance over mud-flats or swamps: a boat for carrying away dredged mud; **mud'-cat** (*U.S.*) a name given to several species of catfish; **mud'-clerk** (*obs. U.S.*) an assistant purser; **mud'-cone** a cone formed by a mud-volcano; **mud'-dauber** a wasp of the family *Specidae* that deposits its eggs in individual cells constructed of mud. — *adjs.* **mudd'y-head'ed; mudd'y-mett'led** (*Shak.*) spiritless. — **mud'-fish** a fish that burrows in mud, esp. a lung-fish; **mud'-flap** a flap fixed behind the wheels of a vehicle to prevent mud, etc., being thrown up behind; **mud'-flat** a muddy stretch submerged at high water; **mud'-guard** a screen to catch mud-splashes from a wheel; **mud hen** any of a variety of water-birds, as rails, coots, gallinules, that dwell in marshy places; **mud'-hole** a hole with mud in it: an opening for removing sediment from a boiler, etc.; **mud'-hook** (*slang*) an anchor; **mud'lark** a name for various birds that frequent mud: one who picks up a living along the banks of tidal rivers: a street-arab. — *v.i.* to work or play in mud. — **mud'-la'va** a stream of mud from a volcano; **mud'-lump'** an upstanding area of mud, often exhaling gases, as in the Mississippi delta; **mud'-minn'ow** a small fish (*Umbra*) akin to the pikes; **mud'pack** a cosmetic paste one ingredient of which is fuller's earth; **mud'-pie'** a moulded mass of mud made by children in play; **mud'-pupp'y** (*U.S.*) the axolotl: a hellbender; **mud'scow** a flat mud-boat; **mud'-skipper** a goby that can skip about on bare mud; **mud'-slinger; mud'-slinging** vilification; **mud'stone** an argillaceous rock not distinctly fissile; **mud turtle** a freshwater turtle of the genus *Kinosternon*; **mud'-volca'no** a vent that emits mud; **mud'wort** a small mud-growing scrophulaceous plant (*Limosella aquatica*). — **clear as mud** not at all clear; **his, her,** etc., **name is mud** he, she, etc., is out of favour; **mud in your eye** good health! (used as a toast); **throw,**

fling mud at to insult, to slander. [Cf. Old Low Ger. *mudde*, Du. *modder*.]

muddle *mud'l, v.t.* to render muddy: to confuse: to bungle: to mix. — *v.i.* to wallow, dabble, or grub in mud (*arch.*): to potter about: to blunder. — *n.* confusion, mess: mental confusion, bewilderment. — *n.* **mudd'lehead** a blockhead. — *adj.* **muddlehead'ed.** — *adv.* **muddlehead'edly.** — *ns.* **muddlehead'edness; mudd'ler.** — **muddle away** to squander or fritter away confusedly; **muddle through** to get through difficulties blunderingly. [Freq. of **mud.**]

mudéjar *moo-dhā'hhar,* (Sp.) *n.* a Spanish Moor, esp. one permitted to remain in Spain after the Christian reconquest: — *pl.* **mudé'jares.** (-*ās*) — *adj.* of a style of architecture characeristic of the mudéjares. — Also with *cap.* [Ar. *mudajjan*, one allowed to remain.]

mudir *moo-dēr', n.* a local governor. — *n.* **mudir'ieh, mudir'ia** a mudir's province or office. [Ar. *mudīr*.]

mudra *mə-drä', n.* any of the symbolic hand gestures in Hindu religious ceremonies and Indian dance. [Sans., lit. sign, token.]

mueddin. See **muezzin.**

munster *moon'stər, n.* a semi-soft cheese of *Munster* in N.E. France, often flavoured with caraway or aniseed.

muesli *moo'zli, mü'zli, n.* a dish of rolled oats, nuts, fruit, etc. eaten esp. as a breakfast cereal. [Swiss Ger.]

muezzin *moo-ez'in, n.* the Muslim official who calls to prayer. — Also **muedd'in.** [Ar. *mu'adhdhin*.]

muff[1] *muf, n.* a cylinder of fur or the like for keeping the hands warm: a similar contrivance for the feet, ear, etc.: a mitt (*obs.*). — *n.* **muffettee'** (*obs.*) a muffler: a woollen cuff. [Prob. from Du. *mof*; cf. Ger. *Muff*, a muff.]

muff[2] *muf, n.* one who is awkward or unskilful, esp. in sport: a duffer: a bungler: an unpractical person: one who lacks savoir-faire: a failure, esp. to hold a ball. — *v.t.* to perform awkwardly: to bungle: to miss. — *v.i.* to act clumsily, esp. in letting a ball slip out of the hands. [Poss. **muff**[1].]

muffettee. See **muff**[1].

muffin *muf'in, n.* a soft, porous cake, eaten hot, with butter: a small plate: one who dangles after a young woman: a poor ball-player. — *n.* **muffineer'** a dish for keeping muffins hot: a castor for sprinkling salt or sugar on muffins. — **muff'in-bell'** a bell rung by a muffin-man; **muff'in-cap** a round flat cap for men; **muff'in-fight', -worr'y** (*coll.*) a tea-party; **muff'in-man** one who goes round selling muffins. [Origin unknown.]

muffle[1] *muf'l, n.* the thick naked upper lip and nose, as of a ruminant. [Fr. *mufle*.]

muffle[2] *muf'l, v.t.* to envelop, for warmth, concealment, stifling of sound, etc.: to blindfold (*arch.*): to deaden or dull the sound of. — *n.* a boxing-glove (*obs.*): a means of muffling: a receptacle, oven, or compartment in which things can be heated in a furnace without contact with the fuel and its products: a muffled state: a muffled sound. — *adj.* **muff'led.** — *n.* **muff'ler** a scarf for the throat: any means of muffling: one who muffles: a silencer (*U.S.*). [App. Fr. *mouffle*, mitten.]

muflon. See **moufflon.**

mufti *muf'ti, n.* an expounder of Muslim law: the civilian dress of one who wears a uniform when on duty: plain clothes: a civilian. [Ar. *muftī*.]

mug[1] *mug, n.* a cup with more or less vertical sides: its contents. — *ns.* **mug'ful** (-*fəl*): — *pl.* **mug'fuls; mugg'er** a hawker of earthenware. — **mug'-house** (*obs.*) an alehouse; **mug'-hunter** (*games*) a pot-hunter. [Origin unknown; cf. Norw. *mugga*, Sw. *mugg*.]

mug[2] *mug,* (*coll.*) *n.* the face: the mouth. — *v.i.* (*theat.*) to grimace. — **mug'shot, mug shot** (*coll.*) a photograph of a person's face, esp. one taken for police records. [Poss. from the grotesque face on a drinking-mug.]

mug[3] *mug,* (*coll.*) *n.* a simpleton: an easy dupe. — **a mug's game** something only fools would do. [Origin unknown.]

mug[4] *mug,* (*coll.*) *n.* a sap or swot: an exam. — *v.t. and* *v.i.* (often with *up*) to study hard: to swot up. [Origin unknown.]

mug[5] *mug, n.* a woolly-faced sheep. — **mug'-ewe, -lamb, -sheep.**

mug[6] *mug,* (*slang*) *v.t., v.i.* to attack from behind, seizing by the throat: to attack suddenly with the intention of robbing. — *ns.* **mugg'er; mugg'ing.** [Perh. **mug**[2].]

mugearite *mōō-gēr'īt, n.* a dark finely crystalline basic igneous rock composed mainly of oligoclase, ortho-clasc, and olivine, with iron oxides, developed at *Mugeary* in Skye.

mugger[1] *mug'ər, n.* a broad-snouted Indian crocodile. [Hind. *magar.*]

mugger[2]. See **mug**[1,6].

muggins *mug'inz, n.* a children's card-game: a form of dominoes: a simpleton. [Ety. dub.]

Muggletonian *mug-l-tō'ni-ən, n.* a member of a sect founded by John Reeve and Lodowick *Muggleton* (1609–98), who claimed to be the two witnesses of Rev. xi. 3–6.

muggy *mug'i, adj.* foggy: close and damp, as weather: wet or mouldy, as straw. — *n.* **mugg'iness** dampness: a muggy condition. — *adj.* **mugg'ish.** [Perh. O.N. *mugga,* mist.]

mugwort *mug'wûrt, n.* a common British wormwood. [O.E. *mucgwyrt,* lit. midge-wort.]

mugwump *mug'wump, n.* an Indian chief: a person of great importance, or one who thinks himself so: one who dissociates himself from political parties, a smug Independent. [Algonquian *mugquomp,* a great man.]

Muhammedan, Muharram. See **Mohammedan, Mohar-ram.**

muid *mü-ē, n.* an old French measure of capacity: a hogshead: a dry measure for corn, etc.: (*S.Afr.; mā'id*) a sack of 3 bushels. [Fr., — L. *modius;* cf. Du. *mud.*]

muil; muir. See **mule**[2]; **moor**[1].

muist. See **must**[5].

mujahedin, mujaheddin, mujahidin *mōō'jə-həd-ēn', n.pl.* Islamic fundamentalist freedom fighters. [Ar. *mu-jāhidīn,* fighters.]

mujik. See **muzhik.**

mukhtar *mōōk'tar, n.* an Indian lawyer. [Ar. *mukhtār,* chosen.]

mukluk. See **muckluck.**

mulatto *mü-lat'o, n.* the offspring of a Negro and a person of European stock (also *adj.*): — *pl.* **mulatt'os:** — *fem.* **mulatt'a, mulatt'ress.** [Sp. *mulato,* dim. of *mulo,* mule; Fr. *mulâtre.*]

mulberry *mul'bər-i, n.* the edible multiple fruit of any tree of the genus Morus (family Moraceae): the tree bear-ing it, with leaves on which silkworms feed: extended to various fruits or plants more or less similar super-ficially or really: the colour of the fruit, dark purple. — *adj.* mulberry-coloured. — *adj.* **mul'berry-faced** having a face blotched with purple. — **mul'berry-fig** the true sycamore (sycomore), a fig-tree with leaves like those of mulberry; **Mulberry harbour** a precon-structed harbour (code name *Mulberry*) towed across the Channel for the 1944 landings in Normandy in World War II. [Prob. O.H.G. *mulberi* (Mod. Ger. *Maulbeere*) — L. *mōrum;* cf. **morus, berry.**]

mulch, mulsh *mulch, mulsh, ns.* loose material, strawy dung, etc., laid down to protect the roots of plants. — *v.t.* to cover with mulch. — *adj.* soft. [Cf. Ger. dial. *molsch,* soft, beginning to decay; O.E. *melsc.*]

Mulciber *mul'si-bər, n.* Vulcan. — *adj.* **Mulcibē'rian.** [L.]

mulct *mulkt, n.* a fine: a penalty. — *v.t.* to fine: to swindle: to deprive (with *of*): — *pa.p.* **mulct'ed, mulct.** [L. *mulcta,* a fine.]

mule[1] *mūl, n.* the offspring of the ass and horse (esp. he-ass and mare): a hybrid: a cross between a canary and another finch: a cotton-spinning machine: an obstinate person: a coin with obverse and reverse designs struck from dies of two different issues: a person who transports drugs for a dealer (*slang*). — *adj.* hybrid. — *n.* **muleteer** (*mūl-i-tēr'*) a mule-driver.

— *adj.* **mul'ish** like a mule: obstinate. — *adv.* **mul'ishly.** — *n.* **mul'ishness.** — **mule'-deer** a long-eared deer, black-tail of N. America. [O.E. *mūl* — L. *mūlus* was superseded by O.Fr. *mul* (masc.; in Mod. Fr. the dim. *mulet* is used), *mule* (fem.) — L. *mūlus, mūla.*]

mule[2] *mūl* (*Scot.* **muil** *mül*), *n.* a loose slipper. [Fr. *mule.*]

muley, mulley, mooly *mōōl'i, mūl'i, adjs.* hornless. — *ns.* a hornless cow: any cow. [Gael. *maol* or W. *moel,* bald.]

mulga *mul'gə, n.* any of several acacias, esp. *A. aneura,* typically found in arid regions of Australia: (with *the*) the outback. — **mulga wire** (*Austr.*) bush telegraph. [Native word.]

muliebrity *mū-li-eb'ri-ti, n.* womanhood. [L. *muliebri-tās, -tātis* — *mulier,* a woman.]

mull[1] *mul, n.* a muddle. — *v.t.* to bungle. [Ety. dub.]

mull[2] *mul,* (*Scot.*) *n.* a promontory. [Prob. Gael. *maol* or O.N. *mūli,* snout; cf. Ger. *Maul.*]

mull[3] *mul,* (*Scot.*) *n.* a snuff-box. [See **mill**[1].]

mull[4] *mul, n.* a soft muslin. — Also **mul'mul(l).** [Hind. *malmal.*]

mull[5] *mul, v.i.* (often with *over*) to cogitate, ponder, turn over in the mind. [Origin obscure.]

mull[6] *mul, v.t.* to crumble. [Cf. O.E. *myl,* dust.]

mull[7] *mul, v.t.* to warm, spice, and sweeten (wine, ale, etc.). — *adj.* **mulled.** — *n.* **mull'er.** [Origin obscure.]

mull[8] *mul,* (*Shak.*) *v.t.* to dull, stupefy. [Origin obscure; perh. from the mulling of wine.]

mullah, moolah, molla(h) *mul'ə, mōōl'ə, mōō'lə, mol'ə, ns.* a Muslim learned in theology and law: a Muslim schoolmaster or teacher: a fanatical preacher of war on the infidel. [Pers., Turk., Hind. *mullā* — Ar. *maulā.*]

mullein *mul'in, n.* a tall, stiff, yellow-flowered woolly plant (Verbascum) of the Scrophulariaceae — popu-larly known as *hag-taper, Adam's flannel, Aaron's rod, shepherd's club.* [A.Fr. *moleine.*]

muller *mul'ər, n.* a pulverising tool. [Perh. O.Fr. *moloir* — *moldre* (Fr. *moudre*), to grind.]

mullet[1] *mul'it, n.* a fish of the genus *Mugil,* palatable, nearly cylindrical: another fish (*Mullus*), slightly com-pressed — **red mullet.** [O.Fr. *mulet,* dim. — L. *mullus,* red mullet.]

mullet[2] *mul'it,* (*her.*) *n.* a five-pointed star — cadency mark of a son. [O.Fr. *molette,* rowel of a spur — L. *mola,* a millstone.]

mulley. See **muley.**

mulligan *mul'i-gən,* (*U.S. coll.*) *n.* a stew made from various scraps of food. [Perh. from the surname.]

mulligatawny *mul-i-gə-tö'ni, n.* an East Indian curry-soup. [Tamil *milagu-tannīr,* pepper-water.]

mulligrubs *mul'i-grubz,* (*coll.*) *n.pl.* colic: sulkiness.

mullion *mul'yən, n.* an upright division between the lights of windows, etc. — *adj.* **mull'ioned.** [Apparently from **monial.**]

mullock *mul'ək, n.* rubbish, esp. mining refuse. [From obs. or dial. *mull,* dust; cf. O.E. *myl.*]

mulloway *mul'ə-wā, n.* a large Australian food-fish, *Sci-aena antarctica.* [Origin unknown.]

mulmul(l). See **mull**[4].

mulse *muls,* (*obs.*) *n.* a drink of honey and wine or of honey and water. [L. *mulsum* — *mulsus* mixed with honey.]

mulsh. Same as **mulch.**

mult(i)-, mult-, mul-ti-, in composition, much, many. — *adjs.* **multang'ular** having many angles; **multan'imous** (L. *animus,* mind) having a many-sided mind; **mult(i)-artic'ulate** many-jointed; **multi-acc'ess** (*comput.*) de-noting a system which permits several operators work-ing at different terminals to have access to its facilities at the same time; **multi-auth'or(ed)** denoting a text which has been written by several individuals; **multi-cam'erate** (L. *camera,* chamber) having many cham-bers or cells; **multicap'itate** (L. *caput, -itis,* head) many-headed; **multicau'line** (L. *caulis,* stem) having many stems; **multicell'ular** having or made up of many cells; **multicen'tral, multicen'tric** having or proceeding from many centres; **multichann′el** having or employing several communications channels; **multicipital** (*mul-ti-sip′i-təl*; L. *caput, -itis,* head) having many heads, multicapitate. — *n.* **multicolour** (*mul′ti-kul-ər*) diversity or plurality of colour. — *adj.* many-coloured. — *adjs.* **mul′ticoloured; multicos′tate** (L. *costa,* rib) many-ribbed; **multicul′tural** of a society made up of many distinct cultural groups; **multicus′pid** having more than two cusps. — *n.* a multicuspid tooth. — *adj.* **multicus′pidate.** — *n.* **mul′ticycle** (*obs.*) a velocipede with more than three wheels: one intended to carry several men. — *adjs.* **multiden′tate** (L. *dēns, dentis,* tooth) many-toothed; **multidentic′ūlate** having many denticulations or fine teeth; **multidigitate** (*-dij′i-tāt;* L. *digitus,* finger) many-fingered; **multidimen′sional** (*math.*) of more than three dimensions; **multidisciplin′ary** involving a combination of several (academic) disciplines, methods, etc.; **mul′tifaced** many-faced; **multifac′eted** (of a gem) having many facets: having many aspects, characteristics, etc.; **multifactor′ial** involving or caused by many different factors; **mul′tifid** also **multif′idous** cleft into many lobes. — *ns.* **mul′tifil, multifil′ament** a multiple strand of synthetic fibre. — *adjs.* **multifil′-ament** composed of many filaments; **multiflo′rous** many-flowered; **mul′tifoil** having more than five foils or arcuate divisions. — *n.* a multifoil ornament — *adjs.* **multifō′liate** (L. *folium,* leaf) with many leaves; **multifō′liolate** with many leaflets; **mul′tiform** having many forms, polymorphic. — *n.* that which is multiform. — *n.* **multiform′ity.** — *adj.* **mul′tigrade** of or pertaining to a motor oil with a viscosity such as to match the properties of several grades of motor oil. — *n.* **multigrav′ida** (L. *gravida,* pregnant) a pregnant woman who has had one or more previous pregnancies: — *pl.* **multigrav′idae** or **-as.** — *n.* **mul′tihull** a sailing vessel with more than one hull. — *adjs.* **multiju′gate, multiju′gous** (L. *jugum,* yoke) consisting of many pairs of leaflets; **multilat′eral** (L. *latus, lateris,* side) many-sided: with several parties or participants. — *ns.* **multilat′eralism; multilat′eralist** one who favours multilateral action, esp. in abandoning or reducing production of nuclear weapons. — *adjs.* **multilineal** (*-lin′*), **multilin′ear** having many lines; **multilingual** (*-ling′gwəl;* L. *lingua,* tongue) in many languages: speaking several languages: (of a country, state, or society) in which several languages are spoken. — *ns.* **multilin′gualism** the ability to speak several languages; **multilin′guist** one who is multilingual. — *adjs.* **multilō′bate, mul′tilobed** many-lobed; **multilobular** (*-lob′ū-lər*), **multilob′-ulate** having many lobules; **multilocular** (*-lok′ū-lər*), **multiloc′ulate** many-chambered. — *n.* **multil′oquence** much speaking. — *adjs.* **multil′oquent, multil′oquous.** — *ns.* **multil′oquy; multimē′dia** the use of a combination of different media of communication (in e.g. entertainment, education): simultaneous presentation of several visual and/or sound entertainments. — Also *adj.* — *ns.* **multimillionaire′** one who is a millionaire several times over; **multinat′ional** a large business company which operates in several countries. — *adj.* of this type of company: multiracial (*S. Afr.*); **multinō′-mial** (*alg.*) consisting of more than two terms: relating to multinomials. — *n.* a multinomial expression. — *adjs.* **multinom′inal** having many names; **multinū′clear, multinū′cleate, -d** having several nuclei; **multinū′cleo-late** having several nucleoli. — *ns.* **multi-own′ership** ownership of property on the principle of time-sharing (q.v.); **multipa′ra** (L. *parĕre,* to bring forth) a woman who has given birth for the second or later time, or is about to do so — opp. to *primapara;* **multipar′ity** the condition of being a multipara: the condition of being multiparous. — *adjs.* **multip′arous** pertaining to a multipara: producing more than one at birth (*zool.*): giving rise to several lateral axes (*bot.*); **multipar′tite** (L. *partītus,* divided) divided into many parts: much cut up into segments. — *n.* **mul′tiped** (L. *pēs, pedis,* foot) a many-footed animal: a woodlouse (*obs.*; also **multipede** *-pēd*). — *adj.* **mul′tiphase** polyphase. — *ns.*

mul′tiplane an aeroplane with more than two sets of supporting planes; **mul′tiplex** (*telecomm.*) a system enabling two or more signals to be sent simultaneously on one communications channel. — *v.t.* to incorporate in a multiplex system. — Also *adj.* — *ns.* **mul′tiplexer; multi-ply** (*mul′ti-plī*) plywood of more than three thicknesses. — *adjs.* **multipō′lar** having several poles or axons; **multip′otent** (L. *potēns, -entis,* powerful; *Shak.*) having power to do many things. — *n.* **multipres′ence** the power of being in many places at once. — *adj.* **multipres′ent.** — *n.* **multipro′gramming** (*comput.*) a technique of handling several programs simultaneously by interleaving their execution through time-sharing. — *adjs.* **mul′tipur′pose; multirā′cial** embracing, consisting of, many races. — *n.* **multirā′cialism** the policy of recognising the rights of all in a multiracial society. — *adjs.* **multiram′ified** (L. *rāmus,* branch, *facĕre,* to make) having many branches; **multisep′tate** having many septa; **multisē′rial, multisē′riate** in many rows; **multisonant** (*mul-tis′ən-ənt;* L. *sonāns, -antis,* pr.p. of *sonāre,* to sound) having many sounds: sounding much; **multispī′ral** having many coils; **mul′ti-stage** in a series of distinct parts: of a rocket, consisting of a number of parts that fall off in series at predetermined places on its course; **mul′tistor(e)y; multisulc′ate** (L. *sulcus,* furrow) having many furrows; **multi-task′-ing** (*comput.*) of, or pertaining to, a system capable of running several processes or jobs simultaneously; **mul′ti-track** of a recording, made up of several different tracks blended together; **multituber′culate, -d** having many tubercles, as teeth. — *ns.* **multivā′lence** (or *-tiv′ə-*), **multivā′lency** (or *-tiv′ə-*). — *adjs.* **multivā′lent** (or *-tiv′ə-; chem.*) having a valency greater than one; **multivār′iate** consisting of, concerned with, many variables; **multivār′ious** differing widely. — *ns.* **multiver′-sity** a large university made of up several campuses; **multivibrā′tor** an electronic oscillating device using two transistors, the output of one providing the input of the other. — *adj.* **multiv′ious** (L. *via,* way) going many ways. — *n.* **multivit′amin** a pill containing several vitamins. — *adj.* **multiv′ocal** (L. *vōx, vōcis,* voice) of many meanings. — *n.* a word of many meanings. — *adjs.* **multivoltine** (*-vol′tīn;* It. *volta,* turn, winding) having several annual broods — of silkworm moths; **mul′ti-wall** made of three or more layers of special paper; **multocular** (*mul-tok′ū-lər;* L. *oculus,* eye) having many eyes: of a microscope, enabling several to observe an object at once; **multungulate** (*mul-tung′gū-lāt;* L. *ungula,* hoof) having the hoof divided into more than two parts. — *n.* a multungulate mammal. [L. *multus,* much.]

multangular... to ... **mult(i)articulate.** See **mult(i)-.**

multeity *mul-tē′i-ti, n.* manifoldness, very great numerousness. [L. *multus,* much, many, *-eity* as in *haecceity.*]

multi-access... to ... **multifactorial.** See **mult(i)-.**

multifarious *mul-ti-fā′ri-əs, adj.* having great diversity: made up of many parts: manifold: in many rows or ranks (*bot.*). — *adv.* **multifā′riously.** — *n.* **multifā′-riousness** the state of being multifarious: multiplied variety: the fault of improperly joining in one bill distinct and independent matters, and thereby confounding them (*law*). [L. *multifārius;* poss. from *fārī,* to speak.]

multifid... to ... **multiplane.** See **mult(i)-.**

multiple *mul′ti-pl, adj.* consisting of many elements or components, esp. of the same kind: manifold: compound: multiplied or repeated: allowing many messages to be sent over the same wire (*teleg.*). — *n.* a quantity which contains another an exact number of times: an object for display, claimed to be art but designed for reproduction in numbers industrially. — *n.* **mul′tiplet** an optical spectrum line having several components: a group of subatomic particles. — *adv.* **multiply** (*mul′ti-plī*). — *adj.* **mul′tiple-choice′** of an examination question, accompanied by several possible answers from which the correct answer is to be chosen. — **multiple cinema** a cinema which has been converted into two or more separate cinemas; **multiple fruit** a single fruit formed from several flowers in combination, as a pineapple, fig, mulberry; **multiple sclerosis** disseminated sclerosis; **multiple shop, store** one of many shops belonging to the same firm, often dispersed about the country; **multiple star** group of stars so close as to seem one. — **common multiple** number or quantity that can be divided by each of several others without a remainder; **least common multiple** the smallest number that forms a common multiple. [Fr., — L.L. *multiplus* — root of L. *plēre*, to fill.]

multiplepoinding *mul-ti-pl-pind′ing*, (*Scots law*) *n*. a process by which a person who has funds claimed by more than one, in order not to have to pay more than once, brings them all into court that one of them may establish his right.

multiplex¹ *mul′ti-pleks, adj.* multiple. [L. *multiplex* — *plicāre*, to fold.]

multiplex². See under **mult(i)-**.

multiply¹ *mul′ti-plī, v.t.* to increase the number of: to accumulate: to magnify (*obs.*): to reproduce: to obtain the product of (*math.*). — *v.i.* to become more numerous: to be augmented: to reproduce: to perform the mathematical process of multiplication: — *pr.p.* **mul′tiplying;** *pa.t.* and *pa.p.* **mul′tiplied.** — *adjs.* **mul′tipliable, mul′tiplicable** (or *-plik′*). — *n.* **mul′tiplicand** (or *-kand′*) a quantity to be multiplied by another. — *adj.* **mul′tiplicate** (or *-tip′*) consisting of more than one: in many folds. — *n.* the condition of being in many copies: one of these copies. — *n.* **multiplicā′tion** the act of multiplying or increasing in number: increase of number of parts by branching (*bot.*): the rule or operation by which quantities are multiplied. — *adj.* **mult′iplicātive** (or *-plik′ə-tiv*) tending or having power to multiply: indicating how many times (*gram.*). — *ns.* **mul′tiplicātor** (*math.*) a multiplier; **multiplicity** (*-plis′i-ti*) the state of being manifold: a great number; **mul′tiplier** one who multiplies: a quantity by which another is multiplied: a device or instrument for intensifying some effect: a geared fishing-reel for drawing in the line quickly. — **multiplication table** a tabular arrangement giving the products of pairs of numbers usually up to 12; **multiplying glass** (*obs.*) a magnifying glass: a faceted glass for multiplying reflexions. — **multiply words** to say much: to be wordy. [Fr. *multiplier* — L. *multiplicāre* — *plicāre*, to fold.]

multiply² *mul′ti-pli.* See under **multiple**.

multi-ply ... to ... **multiramified.** See under **mult(i)-**.

multiscience *mul-tish′əns, n.* knowledge of many things. [L.L. adj. *multiscius* — L. *scientia,* knowledge.]

multiseptate ... to ... **multituberculate.** See **mult(i)-**.

multitude *mul′ti-tūd, n.* the state of being many: a great number or (*rare*) quantity: a crowd: the mob. — *adjs.* **multitud′inary** (*rare*); **multitud′inous.** — *adv.* **multitud′inously.** — *n.* **multitud′inousness.** [L. *multitūdō, -inis* — *multus*.]

multivalence ... to ... **multiocular.** See **mult(i)-**.

multum *mul′təm, n.* an adulterant in brewing. [Prob. neut. of L. *multus*, much.]

multum in parvo *mul′təm, mōōl′tōōm in pär′vō, -wō,* (L.) much in little, a large amount in a small space; **multum non multa** (*non mul′tə, nōn mōōl′ta*) much, not many things.

multungulate. See **mult(i)-**.

multure *mul′tyər,* (*Scot.*) **mouter** (*mōōt′ər*) *ns.* a fee, generally in kind, for grinding grain: the right to such a fee. — *v.t.* and *v.i.* to take multure (for). — *n.* **mul′turer** (**mou′terer**) one who receives multures: a miller: one who pays multures. [O.Fr. *molture, moulture* — L. *molitūra,* a grinding.]

mum¹ *mum, adj.* silent. — *n.* silence. — *interj.* not a word. — *v.i.* (also **mumm**) to act in dumb show: to act in a mummers' play: to masquerade: — *pr.p.* **mumm′ing;** *pa.t.* and *pa.p.* **mummed.** — *ns.* **mumm′er** an actor in a folk-play, usu. at Christmas: a masquerader: an

actor; **mumm′ery** mumming: great show without reality: foolish ceremonial; **mumm′ing.** — *n.* and *interj.* **mum′-bud′get** (*obs.*) mum. — *n.* **mum′chance** a silent game with cards or dice (*obs.*): a fool (*dial.*). — *adj.* silent. — **mum's the word** not a word. [An inarticulate sound with closing of the lips; partly O.Fr. *momer,* to mum, *momeur,* mummer; cf. Du. *mommen,* to mask.]

mum² *mum, n.* a wheatmalt beer, sometimes with oat and bean meal. [Ger. *Mumme.*]

mum³ *mum,* **mummy** *mum′i, ns.* childish words for mother. — *adj.* **mum′sy** (*coll.*) maternal: homely, comfy: old-fashioned. [Cf. **mamma¹**.]

mum⁴ *mum.* See **ma'am**.

mum⁵ *mum,* (esp. *Amer.*) *n.* a short form of **chrysanthemum.**

mumble *mum′bl, v.t.* and *v.i.* to say, utter, or speak indistinctly, softly, or perfunctorily: to mouth with the lips, or as with toothless gums. — *ns.* **mum′blement** (*Carlyle*) mumbling speech; **mum′bler.** — *n.* and *adj.* **mum′bling.** — *adv.* **mum′blingly.** — **mum′ble-news** (*Shak.*) a tale-bearer. [Frequentative from **mum¹**.]

Mumbo-jumbo *mum′bō-jum′bō, n.* a god or bugbear of West Africa: (without *cap.*) any object of foolish worship or fear: mummery or hocus-pocus: — *pl.* **mum′bo-jum′bos.** [Said to be Mandingo.]

mumchance, mumm, mummer; mummia, mummify. See **mum¹; mummy¹.**

mummock *mum′ək.* See **mammock.**

mummy¹ *mum′i, n.* an embalmed or otherwise preserved dead body: the substance of such a body, formerly used medicinally: dead flesh: anything pounded to a formless mass: a bituminous drug or pigment. — *v.t.* to mummify: — *pr.p.* **mumm′ying;** *pa.t.* and *pa.p.* **mumm′ied.** — *ns.* **mumm′ia** mummy as a drug; **mummificā′tion.** — *adj.* **mumm′iform.** — *v.t.* **mumm′ify** to make into a mummy: — *pr.p.* **mumm′ifying;** *pa.t.* and *pa.p.* **mumm′ified.** — **mumm′y-case; mumm′y-cloth** cloth for wrapping a mummy: a similar fabric used as a basis for embroidery: a fabric like crape with cotton or silk warp and woollen weft; **mumm′y-wheat** a variety of wheat alleged (incredibly) to descend from grains found in Egyptian mummy-cases. [O.Fr. *mumie* — L.L. *mumia* — Ar. and Pers. *mūmiyā* — Pers. *mūm,* wax.]

mummy². See **mum³**.

mump *mump, v.t.* to mumble or mutter (*dial.*): to mumble or munch (*dial.*): to get by, or visit for the purpose of, begging or sponging (*dial.*): to cheat (*obs.*). — *v.i.* (*dial.*) to mumble: to sponge: to sulk: to mope: to grimace: to be silent (*arch.*): to play the beggar. — *n.* **mump′er** one who mumps: a beggar (*old cant*). — *adj.* **mump′ish** having mumps: dull: sullen. — *adv.* **mump′ishly.** — *n.* **mump′ishness.** — *n. sing.* **mumps** an acute infectious disease characterised by a painful swelling of the parotid gland: gloomy silence. — **mump′ing-day** St Thomas's Day, 21st Dec., when the poor used to go around begging corn, money, etc. [Cf. **mum¹** and Du. *mompen,* to cheat.]

mumpsimus *mump′si-məs, n.* an error cherished after exposure: stubborn conservatism: an antiquated person. [An ignorant priest's blunder (in an old story) for L. *sūmpsimus,* we have received, in the mass.]

mumsy. See **mum³**.

mun¹ *mun,* (*dial.*) *v.t.* must — used in pres. indic. only; 3rd pers. **mun.** — Also **maun, man.** [O.N. *mon, mun,* or *man* (inf. *monu, munu*), a preterite-present verb.]

mun² *mun, n.* a dialect form of **man¹.**

munch *munch, munsh, v.t.* and *v.i.* to chew with marked action of the jaws, esp. with a crunching noise. — *n.* **munch′er.** — **the munchies** (*slang*) an alcohol- or drug-induced craving for food. [Prob. imit.]

Munch(h)ausen *mōōn′show-zən, n.* an exaggerated, fantastical story, or its teller. — **Munch(h)ausen('s) syndrome** a syndrome in which a person feigns injury or illness in order to obtain hospital treatment. [Baron *Münchausen,* hero of a series of improbable adventure stories by R. E. Raspe (1737–94).]

Munda *mŏŏn'də, n.* any member of a group of peoples of eastern India, or speaker of their group of languages (also called Kolarian), a division of the Austroasiatic family of languages. — Also *adj.*

mundane *mun-dān', adj.* worldly: earthly: cosmic: ordinary, banal. — *adv.* **mundane'ly.** — *n.* **mundanity** (*-dan'i-ti*). [L. *mundānus* — *mundus,* the world.]

mundic *mun'dik, n.* iron pyrites. [From Cornish.]

mundify *mun'di-fī, v.t.* to cleanse, purify. — *n.* **mundificā'tion.** — *adj.* **mundif'icative.** [L.L. *mundificāre* — L. *mundus,* clean, *facĕre,* to make.]

mundungus *mun-dung'gəs, (arch.) n.* a rank-smelling tobacco. [Sp. *mondongo,* black pudding.]

mung bean *mŏŏng, mung, bēn,* a leguminous Asian plant, *Phaseolus aureus,* or its seeds, grown for forage and as a source of bean sprouts. [Hindi *mūng.*]

mungcorn. See **mong.**

mungo *mung'gō, n.* the waste produced in a woollen-mill from hard spun or felted cloth, or from tearing up old clothes, used in making cheap cloth: — *pl.* **mun'gos.** [Origin obscure.]

mungoose. Same as **mongoose.**

Munich *mū'nik, -nihh, n.* a buying off by concession. — *n.* **Mu'nichism.** [From the pact signed at *Munich* (1938) yielding the Sudetenland of Czechoslovakia to Hitler.]

municipal *mū-nis'i-pl, adj.* pertaining to home affairs: pertaining to (the government of) a borough, town or city. — *n.* **municipalisā'tion, -z-.** — *v.t.* **munic'ipalise, -ize** to erect into a municipality: to bring under municipal control or ownership. — *ns.* **munic'ipalism** concern for the interests of one's municipality: belief in municipal control; **municipality** (*-pal'i-ti*) a self-governing town: a district governed like a city: in France, a division of the country. — *adv.* **munic'ipally.** [L. *mūnicipālis* — *mūniceps, -ipis,* an inhabitant of a *mūnicipium,* a free town — *mūnia,* official duties, *capĕre,* to take.]

munificence *mū-nif'i-səns, n.* magnificent liberality in giving: bountifulness. — *adj.* **munif'icent.** — *adv.* **munif'icently.** [L. *mūnificentia* — *mūnus,* a present, *-facĕre,* to make.]

munify *mū'ni-fī, v.t.* to fortify. — *n.* **munifience** (*-nif'i-əns; Spens.*) defence, fortification. [Irregularly formed from L. *mūnīre,* to fortify, *facĕre,* to make.]

muniment *mū'ni-mənt, n.* a means of defence: a record fortifying or making good a claim: (in *pl.*) furnishings, equipment, things provided. — *v.t.* **munite'** (*Bacon*) to fortify, strengthen. — *v.t.* **munit'ion** to supply with munitions. — *ns.* **munition** (*-nish'ən;* commonly in *pl.*) fortification: defence: material used in war: weapons: military stores; **munitioneer', munit'ion-work'er** a worker engaged in making munitions: — *fem.* (*obs. coll.*) **munitionette'.** [L. *mūnīre, -ītum,* to fortify; *mūnīmentum,* fortification, later, title-deeds — *moenia,* walls.]

munnion *mun'yən.* Same as **mullion.**

Munro *mun-rō', n.* a designation orig. of Scottish (now also English, Irish and Welsh) mountains over 3000 feet: — *pl.* **Munros'.** [Orig. list made by H.T. *Munro.*]

munshi, moonshee *mŏŏn'shē, (Ind.) n.* a secretary: an interpreter: a language teacher. [Hind. *munshī* — Ar. *munshi'.*]

muntin, munting *munt'in*(*g*)*, ns.* the vertical framing piece between door panels. [**montant.**]

muntjak, muntjac *munt'jak, n.* a name for a group of small deer of the Oriental region. [From the Malay name.]

Muntz metal *munts met'l,* alpha-beta brass, 60% copper and 40% zinc. [G. F. *Muntz,* 19th-cent. English metallurgist.]

muon *mū'on, mŏŏ', n.* a lepton formerly classified as a mu- (or μ) meson. See **mu.** — *adj.* **mŭon'ic.** — *n.* **muonium** (*mū-ōn'i-əm*), an isotope of hydrogen. — **muonic atom** (*mū-on'ik*) a hydrogen-like atom, formed by the slowing-down of an energetic muon by ionisation as it traverses matter.

muqaddam, mokaddam, mocuddum *mŏŏ-kud'um, mō-, ns.* a head-man. [Ar.]

muraena, murena *mū-rē'nə, n.* a favourite food-fish of the Romans, a moray: **Muraena** the moray genus, giving name to a family of eels, **Murae'nidae.** [L. *mūraena;* see **moray.**]

murage. See **mure.**

mural *mū'rəl, adj.* of, on, attached to, or of the nature of, a wall. — *n.* a wall (in *Shak.* only a conjectural emendation (*obs.*); see **morall**): mural decoration, esp. painting. — *n.* **mur'alist** one who paints or designs murals. — **mural circle** a large graduated circle, fixed to a wall, for measuring arcs of the meridian; **mural crown** an embattled crown given among the ancient Romans to him who first mounted the wall of a besieged city; **mural painting** a painting executed, especially in distemper colours, upon the wall of a building. [L. *mūrālis* — *mūrus,* a wall.]

murder *mûr'dər, n.* the act of putting a person to death intentionally and unlawfully: excessive or reprehensible slaughter not legally murder: hyperbolically, torture, excessive toil or hardship. — *v.t.* to kill (ordinarily a person) unlawfully with malice aforethought: to slaughter: hyperbolically, to torture: to beat, defeat utterly (*coll.*): to destroy (*coll.*): to mangle in performance (*coll.*). — Also (now only *dial.*) **murther** (*-dhər*). — *n.* **mur'derer** (*obs.* or *dial.* **mur'therer**) one who murders, or is guilty of murder: a small cannon (also **mur'dering-piece**) (*obs.*): — *fem.* **mur'deress.** — *adj.* **mur'derous.** — *adv.* **mur'derously.** — **cry, scream blue murder** see **blue**[1]; **get away with murder** to do as one pleases yet escape punishment or censure; **murder will out** murder cannot remain hidden: the truth will come to light. [O.E. *morthor* — *morth,* death; Ger. *Mord,* Goth. *maurthr;* cf. L. *mors, mortis,* death.]

mure *mūr, n.* a wall (*Shak.*). — *v.t.* to wall in or up: to confine: to close. — *n.* **mur'age** a tax for the building or upkeep of town-walls. — *adj.* **mur'iform** (*bot.*) with cells arranged like bricks in a wall. [Fr. *mur* and L. *mūrus,* a wall.]

murena. See **muraena.**

Murex *mū'reks, n.* a genus of gasteropod molluscs, some of which yielded the Tyrian purple dye: (without *cap.*) a mollusc of this genus. — *pl.* **mu'rexes, mu'rices** (*-ri-sēz*). [L. *mūrex, -icis.*]

murgeon *mûr'jən, (Scot.) n.* a grimace. — *v.t.* and *v.i.* to mock with grimaces. [Origin obscure.]

muriate *mūr'i-āt, n. (arch.)* a chloride. — *adjs.* **mur'iāted** impregnated or combined with chlorine or a chloride; **muriatic** (*-at'ik*) briny: hydrochloric (not in scientific use). [L. *muria,* brine.]

muricate *mūr'i-kāt, (bot.) adj.* rough or warty with short sharp points. — Also **mur'icated.** [L. *mūricātus* — *mūrex, -icis,* a murex, a sharp stone.]

murices. See **Murex.**

Muridae *mū'ri-dē, n.pl.* the mouse family. [L. *mūs, mūris,* a mouse.]

murine *mūr'īn, -in, adj.* mouselike: of the mouse family or subfamily. — *n.* a murine animal. — **murine typhus** a mild form of typhus endemic among rats and passed to humans by fleas. [L. *mūrīnus* — *mūs, mūris,* mouse.]

murk, mirk *mûrk, (Scot.) mirk, n.* darkness (*lit., fig.*). — *adj.* dark: gloomy: obscure. — *adv.* **murk'ily.** — *n.* **murk'iness.** — *adj.* **murk'ish.** — *adjs.* **murk'some; murk'y** dark: obscure: gloomy. [O.E. *mirce* (n. and adj.), O.N. *myrkr,* Dan. and Sw. *mörk;* the forms with *i* are chiefly due to Spens. and Scottish influence.]

murl *mûrl, (Scot.) v.t.* and *v.i.* to crumble. — *adj.* **murl'y.** [Origin obscure.]

murlain, murlan, murlin *mûr'lən, (Scot.) n.* a round, narrow-mouthed basket. [Gael. *mùrlan.*]

murmur *mûr'mər, n.* a low, indistinct sound, like that of running water: an abnormal rustling sound from the heart, lungs, etc.: a glide-vowel: a muttered or subdued grumble or complaint: rumour (*Shak.*). — *v.i.* to utter a murmur: to grumble. — *v.t.* to say or utter in a murmur. — *ns.* **murmurā'tion** murmuring: a doubtful word for a flock of starlings; **mur'murer.** — *n.* and *adj.* **mur'muring.** — *adv.* **mur'muringly.** — *adj.* **mur'murous.** — *adv.* **mur'murously.** [Fr. *murmure* — L. *murmur*; cf. Gr. *mormÿrein*, to surge.]

murphy *mûr'fi, (coll.) n.* a potato: — *pl.* **mur'phies.** — **Murphy's game** a confidence trick whereby an envelope stuffed with paper is surreptitiously substituted for one full of money; **Murphy's law** same as **Sod's law.** [From the common Irish name *Murphy.*]

murra, murrha *mur'ə, n.* an unknown precious material for vases, etc., first brought to Rome by Pompey (61 B.C.) from the East, conjectured to be agate. — *adjs.* **murrhine, murrine** (*mur'īn, -in*), **myrrhine** (*mir'īn, -in*). [L. *murra*; Gr. *morria* (pl.).]

murrain *mur'in, -ən, n.* a pestilence (*obs.*): now only a cattle-plague, esp. foot-and-mouth disease. — *adj.* affected with murrain: confounded. — *adv.* confoundedly. — Also **murr'en** (*Shak., Milt.*), **murr'ion** (*Shak.*), **murr'in** (*Spens.*). — *adj.* **murr'ained.** [O.Fr. *morine,* pestilence, carcass.]

murram *mur'əm, n.* a tough, clayey gravel used as road metal in tropical Africa. [Native name.]

murray. See **moray.**

murre *mûr, n.* a guillemot: a razorbill. — *n.* **murrelet** (*mûr'lit*) a name for various small birds akin to the guillemot. [Origin obscure.]

murren. See **murrain.**

murrey[1] *mur'i, n.* and *adj.* mulberry-colour, dark purplish red. [O.Fr. *moré* — L. *mōrum,* mulberry.]

murrey[2]. See **moray.**

murrha, murr(h)ine. See **murra.**

murrin, murrion. See **murrain.**

murry. Same as **moray.**

murther, murtherer. Same as **murder, murderer.**

murva, moorva *mōōr'və, n.* bowstring hemp. [Sans. *mūrvā.*]

Musa *mū'zə, n.* the banana genus, giving name to a family **Musā'ceae,** order **Musā'les,** of (mostly) gigantic tree-like herbs. — *adj.* **musā'ceous.** [Latinised from Ar. *mauz.*]

Musak. See **Muzak.**

musang *mū-, mōō-sang', n.* a paradoxure, or kindred animal. [Malay *mūsang.*]

Musca *mus'kə, n.* the house-fly genus: a small constellation in the south, between the Crux and the Chamaeleon. — *n.* **muscatō'rium** (*Eastern Church*) a flabellum. — *adj.* **muscid** (*mus'id*) of the house-fly family **Muscidae** (*mus'i-dē*). — *n.* a member of the family. — **muscae volitantes** (*mus'ē vol-i-tan'tēz, mōōs'kī wo-li-tan'tās*; L., fluttering flies) ocular spectra like floating black spots before the eyes. [L. *musca,* a fly.]

muscadel *mus-kə-del', mus'* Same as **muscatel.**

muscadin *müs-ka-dē̃, (hist.) n.* a fop or dandy: a middle-class moderate revolutionary. [Fr.]

muscadine *mus'kə-dīn, -din, (arch.) n.* muscatel (wine, grape, or pear). [Perh. Prov. *muscat,* fem. *muscade.*]

muscardine *mus'kär-din, -dēn, -dīn, n.* a silkworm disease caused by a fungus (*Botrytis*). [Fr.]

muscarine *mus'kər-in, n.* an alkaloid poison found in certain fungi. — *adj.* **muscarin'ic** of, like, or producing effects similar to muscarine. [L. *muscarius — musca,* a fly.]

muscat *mus'kat, n.* muscatel wine: a musky grape or its vine. [Prov. *muscat.*]

muscatel *mus-kə-tel', or mus', n.* a rich spicy wine, of various kinds: a grape of musky smell or taste: the vine producing it: a raisin from the muscatel grape: a variety of pear. — Also **muscadel.** [O.Fr. *muscatel, muscadel* — Prov. *muscat,* musky.]

Muschelkalk *mōōsh'əl-kälk, n.* the middle member of the Trias in Germany, largely shelly limestone — wanting in Britain. [Ger. *Muschel,* shell, *Kalk,* lime.]

Musci *mus'ī, n.pl.* mosses, one of the two great divisions of the Bryophyta, the other being the Hepaticae or liverworts. — *n.* **muscology** (*-kol'ə-ji*) bryology. — *adjs.*

mus'coid (*-koid*), **mus'cose** moss-like. [L. *muscus,* moss.]

muscid. See **Musca.**

muscle[1] *mus'l, n.* a contractile structure by which bodily movement is effected: the tissue forming it: bodily strength: power, strength of other kinds (financial, political, etc.) (*coll.*). — *v.i.* to force one's way, thrust. — *adj.* **muscled** (*mus'ld*) having muscles. — *n.* **musc'ling,** delineation of muscles, as in a picture. — *adj.* **muscular** (*mus'kū-lər*) pertaining to a muscle: consisting of muscles: having strong muscles: brawny: strong: vigorous. — *n.* **muscularity** (*-lar'i-ti*). — *adv.* **mus'cularly.** — *ns.* **musculā'tion** muscular action: musculature; **mus'culăture** provision, disposition and system of muscles. — *adj.* **mus'culous** (*obs.*) muscular. — *adj.* **musc'le-bound** having the muscles stiff and enlarged by over-exercise. — **musc'le-man,** a man of extravagant physical development, esp. one employed as an intimidator. — Also *fig.* — **musc'le-reading** interpretation of slight involuntary muscular movements; **muscle, muscular, sense** kinaesthesis; **muscular Christianity** a vigorous combination of Christian living with devotion to athletic enjoyments, associated with Charles Kingsley (who repudiated the name); **muscular dystrophy** (*dis'trə-fi*) any of the forms of a hereditary disease in which muscles progressively deteriorate. — **muscle in** (*coll.*) to push in: to grab a share. [Fr. *muscle,* or directly — L. *musculus,* dim. of *mūs,* a mouse, muscle.]

muscle[2]. See **mussel.**

muscology, muscoid, muscose. See **Musci.**

muscone. Same as **muskone.**

muscovado *mus-kō-vä'dō, n.* unrefined sugar, after evaporating the cane-juice and draining off the molasses: — *pl.* **muscova'dos.** [Sp. *mascabado.*]

Muscovy *mus'kə-vi, (hist.) n.* the old principality of Moscow: extended to Russia in general. — *ns.* and *adjs.* **Muscovian** (*-kō'vi-ən*) Muscovite; **Mus'covite** of Muscovy: Russian: a Russian. — *n.* **mus'covite** (*min.*) common white mica, first got in Russia, a silicate of aluminium and potassium: its thin transparent plates, still used as glass — also **Muscovy glass.** — *adj.* **Muscovitic** (*-vit'ik*). — **mus'covy-duck** see **musk.** [*Moscovia,* Latinised from Russ. *Moskva,* Moscow.]

muscular. See **muscle**[1].

muse[1] *mūz, v.i.* to study in silence: to be absent-minded: to meditate. — *v.t.* to meditate on: to wonder at (*Shak.*): to say musingly. — *n.* deep thought: contemplation: a state or fit of absence of mind. — *adjs.* **mused** bemused, muzzy, fuddled; **muse'ful** meditative. — *adv.* **muse'fully.** — *n.* **mus'er.** — *n.* and *adj.* **mus'ing.** — *adv.* **mus'ingly.** [Fr. *muser,* to loiter, in O.Fr. to muse; perh. orig. to hold the muzzle (O.Fr. *muse*) in the air, as a dog that has lost the scent; perh. influenced by **Muse.**]

muse[2]. See **meuse**[1].

Muse *mūz, n.* one of the nine goddesses of the liberal arts — daughters of Zeus and Mnemosyne (**Calliope** of epic poetry; **Clio** of history; **Erato** of love poetry; **Euterpe** of music and lyric poetry; **Melpomene** of tragedy; **Polyhymnia** of sacred lyrics; **Terpsichore** of dancing; **Thalia** of comedy; **Urania** of astronomy): an inspiring goddess more vaguely imagined: poetic character: poetry or art: an inspired poet (*Milt.*). [Fr., — L. *Mūsa* — Gr. *Mousa.*]

museologist, museology. See **museum.**

muset. Same as **musit.**

musette *mū-zet', n.* an old French bagpipe: a simple pastoral melody or gavotte trio for, or in imitation of, the bagpipe: a small (esp. army) knapsack. [Fr., dim. of *muse,* a bagpipe.]

museum *mū-zē'əm, n.* orig. a temple, home or resort of the Muses: a place of study: a resort of the learned: an institution or repository for the collection, exhibition, and study of objects of artistic, scientific, historic, or educational interest: an art gallery (*U.S.*): a collection of curiosities: — *pl.* **musē'ums.** — *ns.* **museol'ogist; museol'ogy** the study of museums and their organisation. — **musē′um-piece** a specimen so fine as to be suitable for exhibition in a museum, or so old-fashioned as to be unsuitable for anything else. [L. *mūseum* — Gr. *mouseion*; see **Muse**.]

mush[1] *mush*, *n*. meal boiled in water, esp. Indian meal: anything pulpy: sloppy sentimentality (*coll.*): rubbish: background of noise from a wireless receiver: an umbrella (*slang*; see also **mushroom**). — *v.t.* to reduce to mush: to crush the spirit of, wear out (*dial.*). — *adv.* **mush′ily**. — *n.* **mush′iness**. — *adj.* **mush′y**. [Prob. **mash**[1].]

mush[2] *mush*, (*Scot.*) *v.t.* to notch or scallop the edges of. [Perh. Fr. *moucher*, to trim.]

mush[3] *mush* (*Can.* and *U.S.*) *v.i.* to travel on foot with dogs over snow. — *n.* a journey of this kind. — *interj.* and *imper.* a command to dogs to start moving or move faster. — *n.* **mush′er**. [Prob. Fr. *marcher*, to walk.]

musha *mush′ə*, (*Ir.*) *interj.* expressing surprise. [Ir. *maiseadh*.]

mushroom *mush′rŏŏm*, *n.* an edible fungus (*Agaricus*, or *Psalliota*, *campestris*, or kindred species) of toadstool form: any edible fungus: any fungus of umbrella shape whether edible or not: any fungus: an object shaped like a mushroom: a hat with drooping brim: an umbrella (*slang*): anything of rapid growth and decay (*fig.*): one who rises suddenly from a low condition (*fig.*): an upstart. — *adj.* of or like a mushroom. — *v.i.* to expand like a mushroom cap: to gather mushrooms: to increase, spread with disconcerting rapidity. — *n.* **mush′roomer**. — **mush′room-anch′or** an anchor with mushroom-shaped head; **mushroom cloud** a mushroom-shaped cloud, esp. one resulting from a nuclear explosion. [O.Fr. *mousseron*, perh. *mousse*, moss, which may be of Germanic origin.]

music *mū′zik*, *n.* the art of expression in sound, in melody, and harmony, including both composition and execution: sometimes specially of instrumental performance to the exclusion of singing: the science underlying it: a musical composition (*obs.*): the performance of musical compositions: compositions collectively: a connected series of (sweet) sounds: melody or harmony: pleasing sound: sound of definite pitch, not mere noise: a band of musicians (*arch.*): musical instruments (*obs.* or *dial.*): written or printed representation of tones, expression, etc., or of what is to be played or sung: sheets or books of parts or scores collectively: harmonious character: fun (*U.S.*). — *adj.* of or for music. — *v.i.* to perform music: — *pr.p.* **mu′sicking**. — *adj.* **mu′sical** pertaining to, of, with, or producing, music: pleasing to the ear: of definite pitch (unlike mere noise): melodious: having skill in, or aptitude or taste for, music. — *n.* a musical person, party, or performance, esp. a theatrical performance or film in which singing and usu. dancing play an important part — a successor to musical comedy with less frivolous plot. — *ns.* **musicale** (*mū-zi-käl′,* — Fr. *soirée musicale*) a social gathering with music, or the programme of music for it; **musicality** (*-al′i-ti*). — *adv.* **mu′sically**. — *ns.* **mu′sicalness**; **musician** (*mū-zish′ən*) one skilled in music: a performer or composer of music, esp. professional; **musi′cianer, mu′sicker** (*obs.* or *dial.*). — *adj.* **musi′cianly** characteristic of, or becoming, a musician. — *n.* **musi′cianship**. — *adj.* **musicolog′ical**. — *ns.* **musicol′ogist**; **musicol′ogy** academic study of music in its historical, scientific, and other aspects; **musicother′apy** the treatment of (esp. mental) illness by means of music. — **musical box** a toy that plays tunes automatically, by projections from a revolving barrel twitching a comb; **musical chairs** the game of prancing round a diminishing row of chairs and securing one when the music stops (also *fig.*); **musical comedy** a light dramatic entertainment with sentimental songs and situations held together by a minimum of plot; **musical director** the conductor of an orchestra (in a theatre, etc.); **musical flame** a flame that gives a musical tone when surrounded by an open tube;

musical glasses see **harmonica**; **musical sand** sand of nearly uniform size of grain that gives out a definite note when walked on; **mu′sic-box** a barrel-organ (*obs.*): a musical box: jocularly, a piano; **mu′sic-case, -fō′lio** a roll, portfolio, etc., for carrying sheet music; **music centre** a unit consisting of a record player, tape-recorder, and radio, with loudspeakers; **mu′sic-demy′** a size of writing-paper, 20¾ in. × 14⅜ in.; **mus′ic-dra′ma** that form of opera introduced by Wagner in which the relations of music and drama are reformed; **mu′sic-hall** orig. and still sometimes a concert-hall, usu. now a hall for variety entertainments; **mu′sic-holder** a music-case: a clip, rack, or desk for holding music during performance; **mu′sic-house** concert-hall: firm dealing in music or musical instruments; **mu′sic-master, -mistress, -teacher** a teacher of music; **mu′sic-paper** paper ruled for writing music; **mu′sic-pen** a five-channelled pen for drawing the stave; **mu′sic-rack** a rack attached to a musical instrument for holding the player's music; **mu′sic-roll′** a case for carrying music rolled up: a roll of perforated paper for mechanical piano-playing; **mu′sic-room** a room in which music is performed: a room beside the stage in which the musicians were stationed (*obs.*); **mu′sic-seller** a dealer in printed music; **mu′sic-shell** a volute shell with markings like music; **mu′sic-stand** a light adjustable desk for holding music during performance; **mu′sic-stool** a piano-stool. — **face the music** see **face**; **music of the spheres** see **spheres**; **music to one's ears** anything that one is very glad to hear; **rough music** uproar: charivari. [Fr. *musique* — L. *mūsica* — Gr. *mousikē* (*technē*) musical (art) — *Mousa*, a Muse.]

musimon *mūs′* or *mus′i-mon*, **musmon** *mus′mon*, *ns.* the moufflon. [L. *mus(i)mō, -ōnis.*]

musique concrète *mü-zēk kɔ-kret,* (Fr.) a kind of mid-20th cent. music, made up of odds and ends of recorded sound variously handled.

musit *mū′zit*, (*Shak.*) *n.* a gap in a fence or thicket through which an animal passes. [**meuse**[1].]

musive *mū′siv*, *adj.* Same as **mosaic**.

musk *musk*, *n.* a strong-smelling substance, used in perfumery, got chiefly from the male musk-deer: the odour thereof: the musk-deer: a species of Mimulus, said once to have smelt of musk. — *adj.* (or prefix to the names of many animals and plants) supposed to smell of musk. — *v.t.* to perfume with musk. — *adj.* **musked** (*muskt*) smelling, or tasting, like musk. — *adv.* **musk′ily**. — *ns.* **musk′iness**; **mus′kone** a macrocyclic ketone that gives musk its distinctive smell and is synthesised for use as an ingredient in perfumes. — *adj.* **musk′y** having the odour of musk. — **musk′-bag, -cod, -pod, -pouch, -sac** a musk-gland; **musk′-bag, -ball** a bag, ball, containing musk, as a perfuming sachet; **musk′-beet′le** a longicorn beetle that smells of attar of roses; **musk′-cat** a musk-yielding animal, usu. the musk-deer, prob. confused with the civet-cat: a scented effeminate dandy: a courtesan; **musk′-ca′vy** the hog-rat; **musk′-deer** a hornless deer (*Moschus moschiferus*) of Asia, chief source of musk; **musk′-duck** (also by confusion **muscovy-duck**) a large musky-smelling South American duck (*Cairina moschata*); **musk′-gland** a skin pit in some animals producing musk; **musk′-mall′ow** a species of mallow with faint odour of musk; **musk′-mel′on** the common melon (apparently transferred from a musky-scented kind); **musk orchid** a small musk-scented European orchid (*Herminium monorchis*); **musk′-ox** a long-haired ruminant (*Ovibos moschatus*) of northern Canada and Greenland, exhaling a strong musky smell; **musk′-pear** a fragrant variety of pear; **musk′-plant** a plant, *Mimulus moschatus;* **musk′-plum** a fragrant kind of plum; **musk′-rat** the musquash: a musk-shrew: its skin; **musk′-rose** a fragrant species of rose; **musk′-sheep** the musk-ox; **musk′-shrew** the desman: a musky-smelling Indian shrew; **musk′-thist′le** a thistle (*Carduus nutans*) with large drooping scented heads; **musk turtle** any of a group of small American turtles of the genus *Sternotherus*, esp.

Sternotherus odoratus which has particularly musky smell. [Fr. *musc* — L. *muscus*, Gr. *moschos*, prob. — Pers. *mushk*, perh. — Sans. *muṣka*, a testicle (for which the gland has been mistaken).]

muskeg *mus-keg'*, (*Can.*) *n.* swamp, bog, marsh. [Cree Indian word.]

muskellunge *mus'kə-lunj*, *n.* a large North American freshwater fish (*Esox masquinongy*) of the pike family. — Also **maskal(l)onge** (*mas'kə-lonj*), **maskinonge**, **maskanonge** (*mas'kə-nonj*). [Algonquian.]

musket *mus'kit*, *n.* a male sparrow-hawk: a military hand firearm, esp. of an old-fashioned smooth-bore kind. — *ns.* **musketeer'** a soldier armed with a musket; **musketoon'**, **musquetoon'** a short musket: a soldier armed with one; **mus'ketry** muskets collectively: practice with, or the art of using, small arms: fire of muskets: a body of troops armed with muskets. — *adj.* **mus'ket-proof** capable of resisting the force of a musket-ball. — **mus'ket-rest** a forked support for the heavy 16th-century musket; **mus'ket-shot** shot for or from a musket: the discharge of a musket: the range of a musket. [O.Fr. *mousquet*, musket, formerly a hawk — It. *moschetto*, perh. — L. *musca*, a fly.]

muskle. See **mussel.**

Muslim *muz'*, *mōoz'*, *mus'lim*, *n.* a follower of the Islamic religion, a Mohammedan. — *adj.* of, belonging to, the followers of Islam, Mohammedans. — *n.* **Mus'limism.** — Also **Mos'lem**, **Mos'lemism.** [Ar. *muslim*, pl. *muslimīn* — *salma*, to submit (to God); cf. **Mussulman, Islam.**]

muslin *muz'lin*, *n.* a fine soft cotton fabric, gauzy in appearance, but woven plain: cotton cloth for shorts, etc. (*U.S.*): womankind (*slang*): sails, canvas (*naut. slang*): a collector's name for several different moths. — *adj.* made of muslin. — *adj.* **mus'lined** clothed with muslin. — *n.* **muslinet'** a coarse kind of muslin. — **mus'lin-kale** (*Scot.*) thin broth made without meat. [Fr. *mousseline* — It. *mussolino*, from It. *Mussolo*, the town of Mosul in Mesopotamia.]

musmon. See **musimon.**

musquash *mus'kwosh*, *n.* a large aquatic American animal akin to the voles, very destructive to dams and waterways (also **musk-rat**): its fur. [From an Amer. Ind. word.]

musquetoon. See **musket.**

musrol *muz'rōl*, (*obs.*) *n.* the nose-band of a bridle. [Fr. *muserolle* — It. *museruola* — *muso*, muzzle.]

muss, musse *mus*, *n.* a scramble (*Shak.*): disturbance: confusion, disorder: confused conflict (*arch. U.S.*): a mess. — *v.t.* and *v.i.* to disarrange: to mess. — *n.* **muss'iness.** — *adj.* **muss'y** disordered. [Perh. different words; cf. **mess.**]

mussel *mus'l* (formerly also **muscle, muskle** *mus'l, mus'kl*) *n.* a marine lamellibranch shellfish of the family Mytilidae: a freshwater lamellibranch of the Unionidae: the shell of any of these: a mussel-plum. — *adj.* **muss'elled** poisoned by eating infected mussels. — **muss'el-plum** a dark purple plum not unlike a mussel-shell; **muss'el-scalp'** (*Scot.* -*scaup*) a bed of mussels; **muss'el-shell'**. [O.E. *mūs(c)le*; cf. Ger. *Muschel*, Fr. *moule*; all from L. *mūsculus*, dim. of *mūs*, mouse.]

mussitation *mus-i-tā'shən*, *n.* low muttering: speaking movement without sound. — *v.t.* **muss'itate** to mutter. [L. *mussitāre*, freq. of *mussāre*, to mutter.]

Mussulman, Musulman *mus'l-mən*, *-män'*, *n.* a Muslim: — *pl.* **Muss'ulmans**; blunderingly or facetiously **Mussulmen.** — Similarly **Muss'ulwoman.** [Pers. *musulmān* — Ar. *muslim, moslim*, Muslim.]

mussy. See **muss.**

must¹ *must*, *v.t.* am, is, are obliged physically or morally: cannot but: insist upon (with *inf.* without *to*): —used only in the present (orig. past) indic.: —3rd *pers. sing.* **must.** — *n.* an essential, a necessity: a thing that should not be missed or neglected. — Also *adj.* [Orig. pa.t. of **mote** — O.E. *mōste*, pa.t. of *mōt*; cf. Ger. *müssen.*]

must² *must*, *n.* new wine: unfermented, or only partially fermented, grape-juice or other juice or pulp for fermentation: process of fermentation. — *adj.* **must'y.** [O.E. *must* — L. *mustum* (*vīnum*) new (wine).]

must³ *must*, *n.* mustiness: mould. [App. back formation — **musty².**]

must⁴, musth *must*, *n.* dangerous frenzy in some male animals, as elephants. — *adj.* in such a state. — *adj.* **must'y** in a frenzy. [Pers. and Hind. *mast*, intoxicated.]

must⁵, muist, moust *müst, mōost*, (*obs. Scot.*) *n.* musk: hair-powder. — *v.t.* to powder. [O.Fr. *must*, a form of *musc*: see **musk.**]

mustache, mustachio. Same as **moustache.**

mustang *mus'tang*, *n.* the feralised horse of the American prairies. [Sp. *mestengo*, now *mesteño*, belonging to the *mesta* or graziers' union, combined with *mostrenco*, homeless, stray.]

mustard *mus'tərd*, *n.* any of various species of the *Sinapis* section of the genus Brassica: their (powdered) seeds: a pungent condiment prepared from the seeds: the brownish-yellow colour of the condiment. — **mus'tard-gas** the vapour from a poisonous blistering liquid, $(CH_2Cl\cdot CH_2)_2S$, got from ethylene and sulphur chloride; **mus'tard-oil** a volatile oil got from black mustard seeds; **mus'tard-plas'ter** a plaster made from black and white mustard flour, deprived of their fixed oil; **mus'-tard-tree** a name given to a shrub *Salvadora persica* (family *Salvadoraceae*, prob. akin to Oleaceae) on the theory that it is the plant referred to in the N.T., which others think is only black mustard grown tall, as it does in Palestine. — **black mustard** *Brassica nigra*; **French mustard** mustard prepared for table by adding salt, sugar, vinegar, etc.; **garlic-mustard, hedge-mustard** see **garlic, hedge**; **mustard and cress** a salad of seedlings of white mustard and garden cress; **Sarepta mustard** *Brassica juncea*; **white mustard** *Brassica alba*; **wild mustard** charlock. — **keen as mustard** (*slang*) intensely enthusiastic. [O.Fr. *mo(u)starde* (Fr. *moutarde*) — L. *mustum*, **must²** (because the condiment was prepared with must).]

mustee. Same as **mestee.**

Mustela *mus-tē'lə*, *n.* the marten genus, giving name to the family **Muste'lidae** (otters, badgers, and weasels) and the subfamily **Muṣteli'nae** (weasels and martens). — *adj.* and *n.* **mus'teline** (-*təl-īn*). [L. *mustēla*, weasel.]

muster *mus'tər*, *n.* a display, demonstration (*obs.*): an example (*arch.*): a commercial sample: an assembling or calling together, esp. of troops, as for inspection, verification, etc.: inspection: an assembly: a register: a round-up (*Austr.* and *N.Z.*): (perh. orig. a misunderstanding) a company of peacocks. — *v.t.* and *v.i.* to show forth (*obs.*): to assemble: to enroll: to number. — *v.t.* to summon up (often with *up*): (*Austr.* and *N.Z.*) to round up (livestock). — *v.i.* to pass muster. — *n.* **must'erer** (*Austr.* and *N.Z.*) one who musters (livestock). — **mus'ter-book** (*Shak.*) a book in which military forces or a ship's crew are registered; **mus'ter-file** (*Shak.*) a muster-roll; **mus'ter-master** one who has charge of the muster-roll; **mus'ter-roll** a register of the officers and men in each company, troop, regiment, ship's crew, etc.: roll-call (*naut.*). — **muster in** (*U.S.*) to enroll, receive as recruits; **muster out** (*U.S.*) to discharge from service; **pass muster** to bear examination, be well enough. [O.Fr. *mostre, moustre, monstre* — L. *mōnstrum* — *monēre*, to warn.]

musth. See **must⁴.**

musty¹. See **must².⁴.**

musty² *must'i*, *adj.* mouldy: spoiled by damp: stale in smell or taste: deteriorated from disuse.

Musulman. Same as **Mussulman.**

mutable *mū'tə-bl*, *adj.* that may be changed: subject to change: variable: inconstant, fickle. — *ns.* **mutabil'ity**, **mū'tableness.** — *adv.* **mū'tably.** — *n.* **mū'tagen** (*biol.*) a substance that produces mutations. — *adj.* **mutagen'ic.** — *v.t.* **mū'tagenise, -ize** to treat with mutagens. — *ns.* **mutagen'esis** the origin or induction of a mutation; **mutagenic'ity** the condition of being mutagenic; **mutan'dum** something to be altered: — *pl.* **mutan'da;**

mū′tant a form arising by mutation. — *v.t.* and *v.i.*
mutate′ to cause or undergo mutation. — *ns.* **mutā′tion**
change: umlaut: in Celtic languages a change of initial
consonant depending on the preceding word: in old
music a change of syllable for the same note in passing
to another hexachord: discontinuous variation or
sudden inheritable divergence from ancestral type
(*biol.*); **mutā′tionist** a believer in evolution by mutation.
— *adjs.* **mu′tative, mu′tatory** changing: mutable. — *n.*
mū′ton the smallest element of a gene capable of giving
rise to a new form by mutation. — **mutation mink** a
much valued shade of mink produced by selective
breeding; **mutation rate** the frequency of gene mutations in a given species; **mutation stop** an organ-stop
whose tones differ from those the keys indicate by an
interval other than a whole number of octaves. [L.
mūtāre, -ātum, to change — *movēre, mōtum*, to move.]
mutatis mutandis *mū-tā′tis mū-tan′dis, moō-tä′tēs*
moō-tan′dēs, (L.) with necessary changes. — **mutato**
nomine (*mū-tā′tō nom′i-nē, moō-tä′tō nōm′i-ne*) the
name being changed.
mutch *much*, (*Scot.*) *n.* a woman's close cap. [M.Du.
mutse; Du. *muts*, Ger. *Mütze*.]
mutchkin *much′kin, n.* a Scottish liquid measure, three-
fourths of an imperial, one-fourth of a Scottish pint.
[Obsolete Du. *mudseken.*]
mute¹ *mūt, adj.* dumb: silent: refusing to plead (*law*):
without vocal utterance: unpronounced or faintly
pronounced: pronounced by stoppage of the breath-
passage. — *n.* a dumb person: a silent person: one who
refuses to plead (*law*): a funeral attendant: a dumb
servant in an Eastern house: an actor with no words
to speak: a stop-consonant: a clip, pad, or other device
for subduing the sound of a musical instrument. —
v.t. to deaden the sound of with a mute: to silence. —
adj. **mut′ed** (of e.g. sound, colour) softened, not loud,
harsh, or bright. — *adv.* **mute′ly.** — *ns.* **mute′ness;**
mut′ism dumbness. — **mute swan** the common swan.
— **mute of malice** (*law*) refusing to plead. [L. *mūtus.*]
mute² *mūt, v.i.* to dung, as birds. — *n.* birds' dung: an
act of muting. [O.Fr. *mutir, esmeutir*; prob. Germanic; cf. **smelt.**]
mutessarif *moō-təs-ä′rif, n.* the head of a Turkish sanjak.
— *n.* **mutessa′rifat** his office or jurisdiction. [Turk.
mutesarif — Ar. *mutasarrif.*]
muticous *mūt′i-kəs, adj.* awnless: spineless: pointless.
[L. *muticus*, awnless.]
mutilate *mū′ti-lāt, v.t.* to maim: to remove a material part
of: to deform by slitting, boring, or removing a part.
— *adj.* mutilated. — *ns.* **mutilā′tion; mu′tilātor.** [L.
mutilāre, -ātum — *mutilus.*]
mutine *mū′tin, n.* mutiny (*obs.*): a mutineer, rebel (*Shak.*).
— *v.i.* (*Shak., Milt.*) to mutiny, rebel. — *n.* **mutineer′**
one who mutinies. — *v.i.* to mutiny. — *adj.* **mu′tinous**
disposed to mutiny: unsubmissive: of the nature of, or
expressing, mutiny. — *adv.* **mu′tinously.** — *n.* **mu′ti-**
nousness. — *n.* **mu′tiny** insurrection against constituted
authority, esp. naval or military: revolt, tumult, strife.
— *v.i.* to rise against authority, esp. in military or naval
service: — *pr.p.* **mu′tinying;** *pa.t.* and *pa.p.* **mu′tinied.**
— **Mutiny Act** an act passed by the British parliament
from year to year, to regulate the government of the
army, from 1689 down to 1879, when it was superseded. [Fr. *mutin*, riotous — L. *movēre, mōtum*, to
move.]
muton. See **mutable.**
mutoscope *mū′tō-skōp, n.* an early form of cinematograph. [L. *mūtāre*, to change, Gr. *skopeein*, to look
at.]
mutt *mut*, (*slang*, orig. *U.S.*) *n.* a blockhead: a dog, esp.
a mongrel. [Perh. for **mutton-head.**]
mutter *mut′ər, v.i.* to utter words in a low, indistinct voice:
to murmur, esp. in hostility, grumbling, mutiny, or
menace: to sound with a low rumbling. — *v.t.* to utter
indistinctly. — *n.* a murmuring (*Milt.*): indistinct
utterance: low rumbling: subdued grumbling. — *ns.*
mutterā′tion (*Richardson*) complaining; **mutt′erer.** —

n. and *adj.* **mutt′ering.** — *adv.* **mutt′eringly.** [Prob.
imit., like dial. Ger. *muttern*; L. *muttīre.*]
mutton *mut′n, n.* a sheep (*obs.* or *jocular*): sheep's flesh
as food: women as food for lust, hence a prostitute
(*obs. slang*); an em (*print.*). — *adj.* **mutt′ony.** —
mutt′on-bird an Australasian shearwater, esp. the
short-tailed, said by some to taste like mutton; **mutt′-**
on-chop a piece of mutton cut from the rib. — *adj.* (of
whiskers) shaped like a mutton-chop, i.e. broad and
rounded on the cheek, tapering to meet the hairline.
— **mutton cloth** a plain-knitted cloth (usu. cotton) of
loose texture; **mutt′on-cut′let.** — *n.pl.* **mutt′on-dum′-**
mies (*slang*) white plimsolls. — **mutt′on-fist** a coarse,
big hand: a printer's index-hand; **mutt′on-ham** a salted
leg of mutton; **mutt′on-head** a heavy, stupid person.
— *adj.* **mutt′on-head′ed** stupid. — **mutt′on-on-su′et** the
fat about the kidneys and loins of sheep; **mutt′on-**
thump′er a clumsy bookbinder. — **mutton dressed as**
lamb (*coll.*) elderly woman dressing or behaving in
style suitable to a young one; **return to our muttons**
(*coll.*) return to the subject of discussion — a playful
translation of the judge's 'Revenons à nos moutons'
in the old French farce of *Maître Pathelin*, in which
the witnesses wander from the matter in dispute, some
sheep. [O.Fr. *moton* (Fr. *mouton*), a sheep — L.L.
multō, -ōnis; perh. of Celt. origin.]
mutual *mū′tū-əl, adj.* interchanged: reciprocal: given and
received: common, joint, shared by two or more
(*Shak.*; now regarded by many as incorrect). — *n.*
mutualisā′tion, -z-. — *v.t.* **mu′tualise, -ize** to put upon
a mutual footing. — *ns.* **mu′tualism** symbiosis: theory
that mutual dependence is necessary for the welfare
of the individual and society: practice based on this;
mutuality (*-al′i-ti*). — *adv.* **mu′tually.** — **mutual friend**
(*Dickens*) a common friend; **mutual funds** (*U.S.*) unit
trusts; **mutual inductance** (*elect.*) the generation of
electromotile force in one system of conductors by a
variation of current in another system linked to the
first by magnetic flux; **mutual inductor** (*t.*) a component
consisting of two coils designed to have a definite
mutual inductance; **mutual insurance** the system of a
company in which the policy-holders are the shareholders; **mutual wall** a wall equally belonging to each
of two houses. — **mutual admiration society** a group
of persons supposed, generally satirically or humorously, to overestimate one another's and their own
merits; **mutual improvement society** a society whose
members meet to hear lectures, read essays, hold
debates, etc., in order to stimulate each other to
improve in knowledge and in public speaking. [Fr.
mutuel — L. *mūtuus* — *mūtāre*, to change.]
mutuca. See **motuca.**
mutule *mū′tūl, n.* a kind of square, flat bracket, in Doric
architecture, above each triglyph and each metope,
with guttae. [L. *mūtulus*, a mutule, modillion.]
mutuum *mū′tū-əm, n.* a bailment consisting of a loan of
goods for consumption, as corn, coal, etc., to be
returned in goods of the same amount. [L. neut. of
mūtuus, lent.]
mutuus consensus *mū′tū-əs kon-sen′səs, moō′toō-oōs kōn-*
sān′soōs, (L.) mutual consent.
muu-muu *moō′moō, n.* a simple loose dress worn chiefly
in Hawaii. [Hawaiian *mu′u mu′u.*]
mux *muks*, (*U.S.* and *dial.*) *v.t.* to spoil, botch. — *n.* a
mess. [Origin obscure.]
Muzak® *mū′zak, n.* one of the kinds of piped music (q.v.).
— Also (erroneously) **Musak.**
muzhik, moujik, mujik *moō-zhik′, moō′zhik, n.* a Russian
peasant. [Russ. *muzhik.*]
muzzle *muz′l, n.* the projecting jaws and nose of an
animal: a strap or a cage for the mouth to prevent
biting: the extreme end of a gun, etc. — *v.t.* to put a
muzzle on: to keep from hurting: to gag or silence. —
v.t. and *v.i.* to touch, thrust, or investigate with the
muzzle. — *n.* **muzz′ler** one who muzzles: a blow on the
mouth: a muzzle-loader: a direct head-wind. —
muzz′le-bag a canvas bag fixed to the muzzle of a gun

at sea, to keep out water; **muzz'le-load'er** a firearm loaded through the muzzle — opp. to *breech-loader*. — *adj.* **muzz'le-load'ing**. — **muzz'le-veloc'ity** the velocity of a projectile the moment it leaves the muzzle of a gun. [O.Fr. *musel* (Fr. *museau*) — L.L. *mūsellum*, dim. of *mūsum* or *mūsus*, beak.]

muzzy *muz'i, adj.* dazed, bewildered: tipsy: blurred: hazy. — *adv.* **muzz'ily**. — *n.* **muzz'iness**. [Origin unknown.]

mvule *mvōō'le, n.* a huge tropical African timber tree (*Chlorophora excelsa*) of the mulberry family.

M-way. See **M.**

my *mī* (sometimes *mi*), *poss. adj.* or *gen.* of *pron.* **I**, of or belonging to me. — *interj.* expressing surprise (perh. for **my word**, or **my God**). [**mine**[1] — O.E. *mīn* (gen.), of me.]

Mya *mī'ə, n.* a genus of lamellibranch molluscs, the gapers, including the American soft or long clam. [Gr. *mȳs* or *myax*, a mussel.]

myal. See **myalism.**

myalgia *mī-al'ji-ə, n.* pain in muscle. — *adj.* **myal'gic**. — **myalgic encephalomyelitis** a long-term post-viral syndrome with chronic fatigue and muscle pain on exercise (abbrev. **ME**). [Gr. *mȳs*, muscle, *algos*, pain.]

myalism *mī'əl-izm, n.* West Indian Negro witchcraft. — *adj.* **my'al**. [Prob. of West African origin.]

myall[1] *mī'öl, n.* an Australian aboriginal living traditionally. — *adj.* wild: unaccustomed to white society. [Aboriginal.]

myall[2] *mī'öl, n.* an Australian acacia of various species with hard, scented wood: the wood of such a tree. [Australian *maiāl*.]

myasthenia *mī-əs-thē'ni-ə, n.* muscular weakness or debility. — *adj.* **myasthenic** (*-then'*). — **myasthenia gravis** (*grä'vis*) a chronic progressive disease in which the (esp. facial) muscles become fatigued, with progressive muscular paralysis. [Gr. *mys*, muscle, *asthenia*.]

mycelium *mī-sē'li-əm, n.* the white thread-like mass of hyphae forming the thallus of a fungus: — *pl.* **myce'lia**. — *adj.* **myce'lial**. [Gr. *mȳkēs*, a mushroom.]

Mycenaean *mī-sē-nē'ən, adj.* of the ancient city state of *Mȳcēnae* (Gr. *Mȳkēnai*) in Argolis, Agamemnon's kingdom, or its culture culminating in the Bronze Age.

Mycetes *mī-sē'tēz, n.* the howler genus of South American monkeys. [Gr. *mȳkētēs*, bellower.]

mycetes *mī-sē'tēz, n.pl.* (*rare* except in composition) fungi. — *ns.* **mycetol'ogy** mycology; **mycetō'ma** Madura foot, a disease of foot and leg in India, caused by a fungus. — *n.pl.* **Mycetozō'a** the Myxomycetes or slime-fungi (when regarded as animals). — *n. and adj.* **mycetozō'an**. [Gr. *mȳkēs, -ētos*, pl. *mȳkētēs*, a mushroom.]

myc(o)- *mīk-, mī-kō-*, in composition, fungus: mushroom. See also terms under **mycetes**. — *ns.* **mycobactē'rium** any of several Gram-positive parasitic or saprophytic bacteria, e.g. those causing leprosy and tuberculosis; **mycodomatium** (*-dō-mā'shyəm, -shi-əm*; Gr. *domation*, a chamber) a fungus-gall: — *pl.* **mycodomā'tia**. — *adjs.* **mycologic** (*mī-kə-loj'ik*), **-al**. — *ns.* **mycologist** (*-kol'*); **mycol'ogy** the study of fungi; **mycophagist** (*mī-kof'ə-jist*; Gr. *phagein*, to eat) a toadstool-eater; **mycoph'agy**; **Mycoplas'ma** (*-plaz'mə*) a genus of pathogenic agents apparently neither viruses nor true bacteria, including the cause of so-called 'virus' pneumonia: (without *cap.*) any member of the genus: — *pl.* **-plas'mas, -plas'mata**. — *ns.* **mycorrhiza**, **mycorhiza** (*mī-kō-rī'zə*; Gr. *rhiza*, root) a fungal mycelium investing or penetrating the underground parts of a higher plant and supplying it with material from humus instead of root-hairs. — *adj.* **mycor(r)hī'zal**. — *n.* **mycosis** (*-kō'sis*) a disease due to growth of a fungus. — *adj.* **mycotic** (*-kot'ik*). — *ns.* **mycotoxicosis** (*-tok-si-kō'sis*) poisoning caused by a mycotoxin; **mycotoxin** (*-tok'sin*) any poisonous substance produced by a fungus. — *adj.* **mycotroph'ic** (*-trof'ik*; Gr. *trophē*, food) (of a plant) living in symbiosis with a fungus. [Gr. *mȳkēs, -ētos*, pl. *mȳkētēs*, a mushroom.]

mydriasis *mi-drī'ə-sis, n.* morbid dilatation of the pupil

of the eye. — *adj.* **mydriatic** (*mid-ri-at'ik*). — *n.* a drug causing the pupil to dilate. [Gr. *mydriāsis*.]

myel-, myelo- *mī-ə-l(ō)-* in composition, bone marrow, or the spinal chord. — *ns.* **my'elin** the substance forming the medullary sheath of nerve-fibres; **myelī'tis** inflammation of the spinal chord: inflammation of the bone marrow; **my'eloblast** an immature cell of bone marrow, found in the circulating blood only in diseased conditions. — *adj.* **my'eloid** like, pertaining to, of the nature of, marrow. — *ns.* **myeloma** (*-lō'mə*) a tumour of the bone marrow, or composed of cells normally present in bone marrow; **my'elon** the spinal cord. [Gr. *myelos*, marrow.]

mygale *mig'ə-lē, n.* an American bird-catching spider of the genus **Mygale**. [Gr. *mȳgalē*, a field-mouse, a shrew — *mȳs*, mouse, *galeē*, weasel.]

myiasis *mī'i-ə-sis, mī-i-ā'sis, n.* disease caused by presence of flies or their larvae. [Gr. *myia*, fly.]

Mylodon *mī'lə-don, n.* a genus of gigantic Pleistocene ground-sloths with a short, broad skull: (without *cap.*) a sloth of this genus. — *n. and adj.* **my'lodont**. — *adj.* of, relating to this genus. [Gr. *mylē*, a mill, *odous, odontos*, a tooth.]

mylohyoid *mī-lō-hī'oid, adj.* pertaining to or near the jawbone and the hyoid bone. — *n.* a muscle so placed. [Gr. *mylē*, a mill.]

mylonite *mī'lən-īt, n.* a hard compact often streaky granular rock produced by crushing. — *adj.* **mylonitic** (*-it'ik*). — *n.* **mylonītīsā'tion, -z-**. — *v.t.* **my'lonitise, -ize** to turn into mylonite. [Gr. *mylōn*, a mill.]

myna, mynah, mina *mī'nə, n.* any of various related sturnoid Asiatic birds of which the species *Gracula religiosa*, black with white spots on the wings, can be taught to imitate human speech. [Hind. *mainā*.]

mynheer *mīn-hār', Du. mən-ār', n.* my lord: Dutch for *Mr* or *sir*: a Dutchman. [Du. *mijn*, my, *heer*, lord.]

myo- *mī'ō-, mī-o'-*, in composition, muscle. — *n.* **my'oblast** a cell producing muscle-tissue. — *adjs.* **myoblast'ic; myocar'dial (myocardial infarction** destruction of the myocardium due to interruption of blood supply to the area). — *ns.* **myocardiop'athy** any non-inflammatory disease of the myocardium; **myocardī'tis** inflammation of the myocardium; **myocar'dium** the muscular substance of the heart. — *adj.* **myoelec'tric** of apparatus, etc. which uses the small electric currents produced within the body which normally cause muscular contraction and relaxation. — *ns.* **myofi'bril** one of the elongated contractile cells that make up striated muscle; **my'ogen** an albumin, soluble in water, found in muscle. — *adj.* **myogen'ic** (of contraction) arising spontaneously in a muscle, independent of nervous stimuli. — *ns.* **myoglō'bin** a protein that stores oxygen in muscle; **my'ogram** a myographic record; **my'ograph** an instrument for recording muscular contractions. — *adjs.* **myograph'ic, -al**. — *ns.* **myog'raphist; myog'raphy**. — *adjs.* **my'oid** like muscle; **myolog'ical**. — *ns.* **myol'ogist; myol'ogy** the study of muscles; **myō'ma** a tumour composed of muscular tissue; **my'osin** a protein that contributes to the process of contraction in muscles; **myosī'tis** (irregularly formed) inflammation of a muscle; **my'otube** a cylindrical cell that develops from a myoblast, representing a stage in the development of muscle fibres. [Gr. *mȳs, mȳos*, muscle.]

myomancy *mī'ō-man-si, n.* divination from the movements of mice. — *adj.* **myoman'tic**. [Gr. *mȳs*, a mouse, *manteiā*, divination.]

myopia *mī-ō'pi-ə, n.* shortness of sight. — *adj.* **myopic** (*-op'*) short-sighted (also *fig.*). — *n.* a short-sighted person. — *ns.* **my'ops** (*-ops*), **my'ope** (*-ōp*) a short-sighted person. [Gr. *myōps*, short-sighted — *myein*, to shut, *ōps*, the eye.]

myosin. See **myo-.**

myosis *mī-ō'sis, n.* abnormal contraction of the pupil of the eye. — *adjs.* **myosit'ic; myotic** (*-ot'*). — Also *n.* [Gr. *myein*, to close, blink.]

myositis. See **myo-.**

Myosotis *mī-os-ō'tis, n.* the forget-me-not genus of the borage family. — *ns.* **myosō'tis, my'osote** a plant of this genus. [Gr. *myosōtis,* madwort, (*Asperugo*), etc. — *mȳs, mȳos,* a mouse, *ous, ōtos,* an ear.]

myotube. See **myo-.**

myrbane. Same as **mirbane.**

myria- *mir'i-ə-,* in composition, ten thousand: a very large number. See **myriad, myriapod.**

myriad *mir'i-əd, n.* any immense number. — *adj.* numberless. — *adj.* and *n.* (or *adv.*) **myr'iadfold.** — *n.* and *adj.* **myr'iadth.** [Gr. *mȳrias, -ados,* ten thousand.]

myriapod *mir'i-ə-pod, n.* a member of the Myriapoda. — *n.pl.* **Myriapoda** (*-ap'ə-də*) a class of Arthropoda with many legs, centipedes and millipedes. — Also **myriopod,** etc. [Gr. *mȳriopous, -podos,* many-footed — *mȳrios,* numberless, *pous, podos,* a foot.]

Myrica *mi-rī'kə, n.* orig., the tamarisk: the sweet-gale or bog-myrtle genus, of the family **Myricā'ceae.** [Gr. *myrīkē* (*myrĭkē*), tamarisk.]

myringa *mir-ing'gə, n.* the eardrum. — *ns.* **myringitis** (*-in-jī'tis*) inflammation of the eardrum; **myringoscope** (*-ing'gə-skōp*) an instrument for viewing the eardrum; **myringotomy** (*-ing-got'əm-i*) incision of the eardrum. [L.L. *miringa* — Gr. *mēninx,* membrane.]

myriorama *mir-i-ō-rä'mə, n.* a picture composed of interchangeable parts that can be variously combined. [Gr. *mȳrios,* numberless, *horāma,* a view.]

myrioscope *mir'i-ə-skōp, n.* a variety of kaleidoscope. [Gr. *mȳrios,* numberless, *skopeein,* to view.]

Myristica *mir-* or *mīr-is'ti-kə, n.* the nutmeg genus, giving name to the family **Myristicā'ceae.** — *adjs.* **myris'tic; myristicivorous** (*-is-ti-siv'ə-rəs*) feeding upon nutmegs. — **myristic acid** a fatty acid ($C_{13}H_{27}$·COOH) got from nutmegs. [Gr. *mȳrizein,* to anoint.]

myrmecoid *mûr'mik-oid, adj.* ant-like. — *adjs.* **myrmecolog'ic, -al.** — *ns.* **myrmecol'ogist; myrmecol'ogy** the study of ants. — *adjs.* **myrmecoph'agous** feeding on ants: of the ant-bear genus **Myrmecoph'aga; myrmecoph'ilous** having a symbiotic relation with ants. — *ns.* **myr'mecophile; myrmecoph'ily.** [Gr. *myrmēx, -ēkos,* ant.]

Myrmidon *mûr'mi-dən, n.* one of a tribe of warriors who accompanied Achilles to Troy: (without *cap.*) one of a ruffianly band under a daring leader: one who carries out another's orders without fear or pity. — *adj.* **myrmidō'nian.** — **myrmidons of the law** (*facet.*) policemen, bailiffs, etc. [Gr. *Myrmidōnes* (pl.).]

myrobalan *mī-rob'ə-lən,* or *mi-, n.* the astringent fruit of certain Indian mountain species of Terminalia (Combretaceae): a variety of plum. — **emblic myrobalan** see **emblic.** [Gr. *mȳrobalanos,* bito — *myron,* an unguent, *balanos,* an acorn.]

myrrh *mûr, n.* a bitter, aromatic, transparent gum, exuded from the bark of Commiphora: sweet cicely. — *adj.* **myrrh'ic.** — *n.* **myrrh'ol** the volatile oil of myrrh. [O.E. *myrra* — L. *myrrha* — Gr. *myrrā*; an Eastern word; cf. Ar. *murr.*]

myrrhine. See under **murra.**

myrtle *mûr'tl, n.* an evergreen shrub (Myrtus) with beautiful and fragrant leaves: extended to various other plants, some near akin, others not, e.g. a kind of beech in Australia (see also under **bog, wax**). — **myr'tle-wax** wax from the candle-berry. [O.Fr. *myrtil,* dim. of *myrte* — L. *myrtus* — Gr. *myrtos.*]

Myrtus *mûr'təs,* the myrtle genus, giving name to the family **Myrtā'ceae.** — *adj.* **myrtā'ceous.** [L., — Gr. *myrtos.*]

myself *mī-self',* or *mi-self', pron.* I or me, in person (used for emphasis, almost always in apposition): me (reflexively). [**me¹, self.**]

mysophobia *mī-sō-fō'bi-ə, n.* morbid fear of contamination. [Gr. *mȳsos,* defilement, *phobos,* fear.]

mystagogue *mis'tə-gog, -gōg, n.* an initiator into religious mysteries — also **mystagō'gus.** — *adj.* **mystagog'ic** (*-goj', -gog'*), **-al.** — *n.* **mys'tagogy** (*-goj-, -gog-*). [Gr. *mystēs,* one initiated, *agōgos,* a leader.]

mystery¹ *mis'tər-i, n.* a secret doctrine: (usu. in *pl.*) in ancient religions, rites known only to the initiated, as the Eleusinian mysteries: (in *pl.*) the secrets of freemasonry, etc.: anything very obscure: that which is beyond human knowledge to explain: anything artfully made difficult: a sacrament: a miracle play (also **mys'tery-play'**): a shiftless, drifting girl (*slang*): — *pl.* **mys'teries.** — *adj.* **mystē'rious** containing mystery: having an air of mystery: obscure: secret: incomprehensible. — *adv.* **mystē'riously.** — *n.* **mystē'riousness.** — **mys'tery-man'** a conjurer: a medicine-man; **mys'tery-mong'er** a dealer in mysteries; **mys'tery-ship'** a Q-boat; **mys'tery-tour'** an excursion to a destination which remains secret until the journey's end. [L. *mystērium* — Gr. *mystērion* — *mystēs,* one initiated — *mȳeein,* to initiate — *mȳein,* to close the eyes.]

mystery², mistery *mis'tər-i, n.* office, service, duty (*obs.*): craft, art, trade (*arch.*): skill (*Shak.*): a trade guild (*hist.*). [L.L. *misterium* — L. *ministerium* — *minister,* servant; confused with *mystērium* and prob. with **maistry, mastery.**]

mystic, -al *mis'tik, -əl, adjs.* relating to mystery, the mysteries, or mysticism: mysterious: sacredly obscure or secret: involving a sacred or a secret meaning hidden from the eyes of the ordinary person, only revealed to a spiritually enlightened mind: allegorical. — *n.* **mys'tic** one who seeks or attains direct intercourse with God in elevated religious feeling or ecstasy. — *adv.* **mys'tically.** — *ns.* **mys'ticalness; mys'ticism** (*-sizm*) the habit or tendency of religious thought and feeling of those who seek direct communion with God or the divine: fogginess and unreality of thought (with suggestion of **mist**); **mystificā'tion; mys'tifier** one who or that which mystifies: a hoaxer. — *v.t.* **mys'tify** to make mysterious, obscure, or secret: to involve in mystery: to bewilder: to puzzle: to hoax: — *pr.p.* **mys'tifying;** *pa.t.* and *pa.p.* **mys'tified.** — **mystic recitation** the recitation of parts of the Greek liturgy in an inaudible voice. [L. *mysticus* — Gr. *mystikos* — *mystēs,* an initiate; cf. **mystery¹.**]

mystique *mis-tēk', mēs-tēk, n.* incommunicable spirit, gift, or quality: secret (of an art) as known to its inspired practitioners: sense of mystery, remoteness from the ordinary, and power or skill surrounding a person, activity, etc. [Fr.]

myth *mith* or (old-fashioned) *mīth, n.* an ancient traditional story of gods or heroes, esp. one offering an explanation of some fact or phenomenon: a story with a veiled meaning: mythical matter: a figment: a commonly-held belief that is untrue, or without foundation. — *adjs.* **myth'ic, -al** relating to myths: fabulous: untrue. — *adv.* **myth'ically.** — *v.t.* **myth'icise, -ize** (*-i-siz*) to make the subject of myth: to explain as myth. — *ns.* **myth'icism** (*-sizm*) theory that explains miraculous stories as myth; **myth'iciser, -z-, myth'icist.** — *v.t.* **myth'ise, -ize** to mythicise. — *ns.* **myth'ism** mythicism; **myth'ist** a maker of myths: a mythicist; **mythogen'esis** the production or origination of myths; **mythog'rapher** a writer or narrator of myths; **mythog'raphy** representation of myths in art: collection or description of myths; **mythol'oger, mytholō'gian** a mythologist. — *adjs.* **mytholog'ic, -al** relating to mythology, fabulous. — *adv.* **mytholog'ically.** — *v.t.* **mythol'ogise, -ize** to interpret or explain the mythological character of: to render mythical. — *ns.* **mythol'ogiser, -z-; mythol'ogist; mythol'ogy** a body of myths: the scientific study of myths: symbolical meaning (*obs.*). — *n.* and *adj.* **myth'omane** mythomaniac. — *n.* **mythomā'nia** (*psychiatry*) lying or exaggerating to an abnormal extent. — *n.* and *adj.* **mythomā'niac.** — *adjs.* **mythopoeic** (*mith-ō-pē'ik*; Gr. *poieein,* to make), **mythopoetic** (*-pō-et'ik*) myth-making. — *ns.* **mythopoe'ist** a myth-maker; **mythopō'et** a writer of poems on mythical subjects; **mythus** (*mith'əs*; L.), **mythos** (*mith'os*; Gr.) myth: mythology: theme, scheme of events: the characteristic or current attitudes of a culture or group, expressed symbolically (through poetry, art, drama, etc.). — **mythical theory** the theory of D. F. Strauss

(1808–74) and his school, that the Gospels are mainly a collection of myths, developed during the first two centuries, from the imagination of the followers of Jesus. — **comparative mythology** the science that investigates myths and seeks to relate those of different peoples. [Gr. *mȳthos*, talk, story, myth.]

Mytilus *mit'i-ləs, n.* the common mussel genus, giving name to the family **Mytilidae** (*mī-til'i-dē*). — *adjs.* **mytil'iform, myt'iloid.** [L. *mȳtilus, mītulus, mŭtulus.*]

myxoedema *mik-sē-dē'mə, n.* a diseased condition due to deficiency of thyroid secretion, characterised by loss of hair, increased thickness and dryness of the skin, increase in weight, slowing of mental processes, and diminution of metabolism. — Also **myxedema.** [Gr. *myxa*, mucus, *oidēma*, swelling.]

myxoma *mik-sō'mə, n.* a tumour of jelly-like substance: — *pl.* **myxō'mata.** — *adj.* **myxō'matous.** — *n.* **myxo-** **matō'sis** a contagious virus disease of rabbits. [Gr. *myxa*, mucus.]

Myxomycetes *mik-sō-mī-sē'tēz, n.pl.* slime-fungi, a class of very simple plants, by some reckoned animals (Mycetozoa) forming in the vegetative stage naked masses of protoplasm with many nuclei, creeping on wet soil, on rotten wood, etc. — *n.sing.* **myxomycete** (*-sēt'*). [Gr. *myxa*, mucus, *mykētēs*, pl. of *mykēs*, a mushroom.]

Myxophyceae *mik-sō-físh'i-ē, n.pl.* the Cyanophyceae. [Gr. *myxa*, slime, *phȳkos*, seaweed.]

myxovirus *mik'sō-vī-rəs, n.* any of a group of related viruses causing influenza, mumps, etc. [Gr. *myxa*, mucus, **virus.**]

mzungu *əm-zōōng'-gōō n.* in E. Africa, a white person. [Swahili.]

For other sounds see detailed chart of pronunciation.

N

N, n *en, n.* the fourteenth letter of our alphabet, thirteenth of the Greek, representing a point nasal consonant sound, or before *g* or *k* a back nasal (as in *sing, sink*): anything having the shape of the letter: an indefinite number, esp. in a series (*math.*): as a mediaeval numeral, N = 90, and N̄ = 90 000: a unit of measurement **(en)** = half an em (*print.*): an indefinite number, often (*coll.*) implicitly a large number. — *adj.* **nᵗʰ, nth.** — *adj.* **n′-type** (i.e. 'negative-type') of a semiconductor, having an excess of conduction electrons over mobile holes (see **hole**). — **to the nᵗʰ (nth)** to any power: hence (*coll.*) to an unlimited degree.

'n' a *coll.* shortening of **and.**

na *nä, adv.* a Scottish form of **no¹**: (*ni, nä, encliticaly; Scot.*) not.

Naafi *nä'fi, n.* an organisation for providing canteens for servicemen and service-women: one of the canteens. — Also **NAAFI.** [From the initials of *N*avy, *A*rmy, and *A*ir-*F*orce *I*nstitute(s).]

naam, nam *näm,* (*hist.; law*) *n.* distraint. [O.E. *näm,* related to *niman,* to take.]

naan. See **nan.**

naartje. Same as **nartjie.**

nab¹ *nab, v.t.* to seize, snatch: to arrest (*coll.*): — *pr.p.* **nabb′ing;** *pa.t.* and *pa.p.* **nabbed.** — *n.* **nabb′er.** [Origin obscure; cf. **nap⁴**.]

nab² *nab, n.* a hilltop: a promontory: a projection: the keeper of a door-lock. [O.N. *nabbr* or *nabbi*.]

nab³ *nab,* (*obs. slang*) *n.* the head: a hat.

Nabataean *nab-ə-tē'ən,* **Nabathaean** *-thē', ns.* and *adjs.* (one) of an ancient powerful Arab people about Petra. [Gr. *Nabat(h)aios*.]

nabk *nabk, nubk, n.* the Christ's-thorn. [Ar. *nebq*.]

nabla *nab'lə,* (*math.*) *n.* in Cartesian co-ordinates, the symbol ∇, an inverted delta, also called **del,** representing the vector operator **i**∂/∂x + **j**∂/∂y + **k**∂/∂z. [Gr. *nabla,* nebel (q.v.), from the shape.]

nabob *nä'bob, n.* a nawab (*obs.*): a European who has enriched himself in the East (*arch.*; used in Europe only): in Europe, any man of great wealth, an important person. [Hind. *nawwāb;* see **nawab**.]

nabs *nabz,* (*slang*) *n.* a personage, in such phrases as **his nabs,** himself. [Cf. **nob², nib²**.]

nacarat *nak'ə-rat, n.* a bright orange-red: a fabric so coloured. [Fr.]

nacelle *nä-sel', n.* a little boat (*obs.*): the car of a balloon: a body on an aircraft housing engine(s), etc. [Fr., — L.L. *nāvicella,* — L. *nāvis,* ship.]

nach. See **nautch.**

nache *näch, n.* the rump. [See **aitchbone**.]

Nachschlag *nähh'shlähh,* (*mus.*) *n.* a grace-note whose time is taken off the preceding note. [Ger., — *nach,* after, *Schlag,* stroke.]

nachtmaal *nähht'mäl.* Older form of **nagmaal.**

nacket *nak'it,* **nocket** *nok'it, ns.* a snack, light lunch. [Origin obscure.]

nacre *nä'kər, n.* mother-of-pearl or a shellfish yielding it. — *adj.* **nä'creous** (also **nä'crous**). — *n.* **nä'crite** a clay mineral, identical in composition to kaolinite but differing in optical characteristics and atomic structure. [Fr.; prob. of Eastern origin.]

nada *nä'də, n.* nothing: nothingness. [Sp.]

nadir *nä'dēr, -dər, n.* the point of the heavens diametrically opposite to the zenith: the lowest point of anything. [Fr., — Ar. *nadīr* (*nazīr*), opposite to.]

nae *nä, adj.* a Scots form of **no²**. — *adv.* same as **no¹,** esp. with a comparative. — **nae'body** nobody; **nae'thing** nothing.

naevus *nē'vəs,* L. *nī'vōos, n.* a birthmark: a pigmented spot or an overgrowth of small blood-vessels in the skin: — *pl.* **naevi** (*nē'vī,* L. *nī'vē*). — *obs.* **naeve** (*nēv; pl.* **naeves**). — *adj.* **nae'void.** [L.]

naff *naf,* (*slang*) *adj.* inferior, worthless: vulgar, socially crass. — *n.* an incompetent. — *adj., adv.* **naff'ing** used as an offensive qualification. — **naff off** an offensive injunction to go away. [Origin disputed; suggested derivations are: *naf,* back-slang for *fan(ny),* the female genitalia; *naff,* navel, or nothing; *naffy* (**Naafi**) generally contemptuous, specif. 'shirking'.]

nag¹ *nag, n.* a horse, esp. a small one: a riding-horse, or an inferior horse: a jade (*Shak.*). [M.E. *nagge;* origin obscure; cf. M.Du. *negge, negghe* (mod. Du. *neg, negge*).]

nag² *nag, v.t.* or *v.i.* to find fault with, urge (to do something), cause pain to, or worry, constantly: (with *at*) to worry or annoy continually: — *pr.p.* **nagg'ing;** *pa.t.* and *pa.p.* **nagged.** — *ns.* **nag, nagg'er** a scold (esp. female). — *adj.* **nagg'y.** [Cf. Norw. *nage,* to grow, rankle, Sw. *nagga,* to gnaw.]

naga *nä'gə, n.* a snake, esp. the cobra (*Ind.*): a divine snake (*Hind. myth.*). [Sans. *nāga*.]

nagana *nä-gä'nə, n.* a disease of horses and cattle caused by a trypanosome transmitted by tsetse flies. [Zulu *nakane*.]

nagapie *nahh'ə-pi,* (*S.Afr.*) *n.* the bush-baby or nocturnal lemur. [Afrik., lit. 'night-ape' (see **bush-baby**) — Du. *nacht,* night, *aap,* monkey.]

nagari *nä'gə-rē, n.* devanagari: the group of alphabets to which devanagari belongs. [Sans. *nāgarī,* town-script — *nāgaran,* town (perh. referring to a particular town); addition of *deva*-to form *devanagari* was a later development.]

nagmaal *nähh'mäl, näk', n.* (*South Africa*) a Dutch Reformed Church Sacrament, the Lord's Supper. [Earlier *nachtmaal,* night meal; from Du.]

nagor *nä'gör, n.* a West African antelope (*Redunca redunca*). [Fr., arbitrarily formed by Buffon from earlier *nanguer*.]

Nahal *na-häl', n.* an organisation of young soldiers in Israel: (without *cap.*) an agricultural settlement established and manned by such soldiers. [Heb.]

Nahuatl *nä'wät-l, n.* the language of the Aztecs. — Also *adj.*

Naia. See **Naja.**

naiad *nī'ad, nä'əd, n.* a river or spring nymph: the aquatic larva of the dragonfly, mayfly, stone-fly or damselfly: — *pl.* **nai'adēs, nai'ads.** — *n.* **Nai'as** a genus of water-plants, giving name to a family **Naiadā'ceae** akin to or including the pondweeds. [Gr. *nāias, -ados,* pl. *-adēs,* from *naein,* to flow.]

naiant *nä'ənt,* (*her.*) *adj.* swimming horizontally. [Prob. from an A.Fr. form of O.Fr. *noiant, pr.p.* — L. *natāre,* to swim.]

naïf *nä-ēf',* now usu. **naïve** *nä-ēv', adjs.* with natural or unaffected simplicity, esp. in thought, manners, or speech: artless: ingenuous. — *adv.* **naïve'ly.** — *ns.* **naïveté** (*nä-ēv'tā*), **naïvety** (*nä-ēv'ti*) natural simplicity and unreservedness of thought, manner, or speech: ingenuosity. — **naïve painting** primitive painting. — Also **naif, naive,** etc. [Fr. *naïf,* fem. *naïve* — L. *nātīvus,* native — *nāscī, nātus,* to be born.]

naik *nä'ik, n.* a lord or governor: a corporal of Indian infantry. [Urdu *nä'ik* — Sans. *nāyaka,* leader.]

nail *nāl, n.* a horny plate at the end of a finger or toe, usu. distinguished from a claw as being flattened: a claw: a small spike, usu. of metal, and with a head, used for fastening wood, etc.: a nail-shaped excrescence, esp. one at the tip of a bird's bill: a measure of length (2¼ inches). — *v.t.* to fasten, pierce (*rare* or *obs.*), or stud (*rare*) with nails: to fix: to pin down, hold fast (*fig.*): to catch or secure (*slang*). — *adj.* **nailed** having nails: fastened with nails. — *ns.* **nail′er** a maker of nails; **nail′ery** a place where nails are made; **nail′ing** making nails: fastening with nails. — **nail′-bed** that portion of the true skin on which a finger-, toe-nail rests; **nail′-biting** chewing off the ends of one's finger-nails. — *adj.* of an event or experience, which induces nail-biting (as a sign of anxiety, excitement or tension). — **nail′-bomb** an explosive device containing gelignite and packed with long nails; **nail′-brush** a brush for cleaning the nails; **nail′-file** a file for trimming finger-or toe-nails; **nail gun** an implement used to put in nails; **nail′-head** the head of a nail: an ornament shaped like it. — *adjs.* **nail′-head′(ed)** having a head suggesting that of a nail: having nail-head ornaments. — **nail′-head= spar′** calcite crystallised in a scalenohedron terminated by a rhombohedron; **nail′-hole** a hole made by or for a nail: a notch for opening a pocket-knife; **nail polish** nail-varnish; **nail′-rod** a strip of iron to be made into nails: iron in that form: strong coarse tobacco (*Austr.*): a stick of liquorice; **nail′-scissors** small scissors designed especially for trimming the finger- and toe-nails; **nail′-varnish** varnish for finger- or toe-nails. — **a nail in one's, the, coffin** any event, experience, etc. which has the effect of shortening one's life: a contributory factor in the downfall of anything; **hard as nails** in excellent physical condition: callous, unsympathetic, unsentimental; **hit the nail on the head** to touch the exact point; **nail a lie to the counter** to expose it and put it out of currency, from the old custom of shopkeepers with counterfeit coins; **nail one's colours to the mast** see **colour; on the nail** on the spot. [O.E. *nægel*; Ger. *Nagel*.]

nain *nān*, (*Scot.*) *adj.* own. — *n.* **nainsel′′, nainsell′** own self: a Highlander (from the Highlander's formerly alleged habit of referring to himself as *her nainsel′*). [*mine ain*, my own.]

nainsook *nān′sŏŏk*, *n.* a kind of muslin like jaconet. [Hind. *nainsukh* — *nain*, eye, *sukh*, pleasure.]

Nair, Nayar, *nī′ər*, *n.* a people of Kerala who were formerly a noble and military caste of the Malabar coast and who practised a peculiar system of polyandry and matriliny.

naira *nī′rə*, *n.* the standard unit of currency in Nigeria.

naissant *nās′ənt*, *adj.* nascent: rising or coming forth (*her.*). [Fr., *pr.p.* of *naître* — L. *nāscī*, *nātus*, to be born.]

naïve. See **naïf.**

Naja *nā′jə*, *-yə*, *n.* the cobra genus. — Also **Naia.** [App. Linnaeus's misreading of **naga**, or of Sinh. *naiā*, *nayā*.]

naked *nā′kid*, *adj.* without clothes: uncovered: bare: exposed: open to view: unconcealed: undisguised: evident: unarmed: defenceless: unprovided: without ornament: simple: artless: without the usual covering. — *adv.* **na′kedly.** — *n.* **na′kedness.** — **naked bed** (*obs.*) a bed in which one is (orig.) entirely naked, (later) without ordinary day clothes; **naked eye** the eye unassisted by glasses of any kind; **naked lady** the meadow-saffron. [O.E. *nacod*; Ger. *nackt*.]

naker *nā′kər*, *n.* a kettledrum. [O.Fr. *nacre* — Ar. *naqāra*.]

nala, nalla, nallah. Same as **nulla(h).**

naloxone *nal-ok′sōn*, *n.* a potent drug ($C_{19}H_{21}NO_4$) used as an antidote for various narcotics, esp. morphine. [*N-allylnoroxymorphone.*]

nam *pa.t.* of **nim.** See also **naam.**

namaste *nä′məs-ti*, *n.* in India, a traditional form of greeting, a slight bow with the palms pressed together before the chest or face. — Also **namaskar** (*nä-məs-kär′*; Sans. *kara*, doing). [Sans. *namas*, obeisance, salutation, bow, and *te*, dat. of *tuam*, you.]

namby-pamby *nam′bi-pam′bi*, *adj.* feebly wishy-washy: prettily or sentimentally childish. — *n.* namby-pamby writing or talk: a namby-pamby person: — *pl.* **nam′by= pam′bies.** — *adj.* **nam′by-pam′bical.** — *n.* **nam′by=**

pam′biness. — *adj.* **nam′by-pam′byish.** — *n.* **nam′by= pam′byism.** [Nickname given by Carey or by Swift to *Ambrose* Philips (1674–1749), whose simple odes to children were despised by 18th-century Tories.]

name *nām*, *n.* that by which a person or a thing is known or called: a designation: reputation: fame: a celebrity: family or clan: seeming or pretension without reality: authority: behalf: assumed character (of). — *v.t.* to give a name to: to mention the name of: to designate: to speak of or to call by name: to state or specify: to utter (with cognate object): to mention for a post or office: to nominate: to mention formally by name in the House of Commons as guilty of disorderly conduct: to make known the name of (someone implicated in a crime, an accomplice, etc.) to the police, etc. — *adjs.* **nam′able, name′able** capable, or worthy, of being named; **named; name′less** without a name: anonymous: undistinguished: indescribable: unspeakable. — *adv.* **name′lessly.** — *n.* **name′lessness.** — *adj.* **name′ly** (*Scot.*) famous (for). — *adv.* especially (*obs.*): by name: that is to say. — *ns.* **nam′er; nam′ing.** — **name brand** a make of an article bearing a manufacturer's distinguishing name; **name′-calling** abuse; **name′-child** a person called after one; **name′-day** the day of the saint of one's name: the day when a ticket bearing the buyer's name, etc., is given to the seller (*Stock Exchange*): the day on which a name is bestowed; **name′-dropping** trying to impress by casual mention of important or well-known persons as if they were one's friends; **name′-dropper.** — *v.i.* **name′-drop.** — **name′-part** the part that gives title to a play, title-rôle; **name′-plate** an attached plate bearing the name of occupant, owner, manufacturer, etc.: a masthead (*journalism*; *U.S.*); **name′sake** one bearing the same name as another; **name′-son** a male name-child; **name′-tape** a short piece of cloth tape attached to a garment, etc., marked with the owner's name. — *adj.* **name′worthy** worth naming: distinguished. — **call names** to bestow abuse upon; **in name** fictitiously, as an empty title; **in name of** on behalf of: by the authority of; **name after** (*U.S.* **name for**) to give (a child) the same name as another person, in honour of that person; **name the day** to fix a day, esp. for a marriage; **no names, no pack-drill** (*coll.*) mention no names, then no-one gets into trouble; **proper name** a name given to a particular person, place, or thing; **take a name in vain** to use a name lightly or profanely; **the name of the game** (*coll.*) the thing that is important or essential: the central trend or theme, what it's all about (*usu. derog.*); **you name it** this applies to whatever you mention, want, etc.; **to one's name** belonging to one. [O.E. *nama*; Ger. *Name*; L. *nōmen*.]

namma hole. Same as **gnamma hole.**

nan, naan *nän*, *n.* a type of slightly leavened bread, as baked in India and Pakistan, similar to pitta bread. [Hindi.]

nana[1]. See **nanny.**

nana[2] *nä′nə*, (orig. *Austr. slang*) an idiot, fool: the head, as in **off one's nana.** [Prob. ba*nana*.]

Nancy *nan′si*, (also without *cap.*) *n.* an effeminate young man: a homosexual — also **Nance, Nan′cy-boy, Miss Nan′cy** (also without *cap.*). — Also *adj.* [From the girl's name.]

Nancy-pretty *nan′si-prit′i*, *n.* the plant *Saxifraga umbrosa*, London Pride. [Prob. for **none so pretty.**]

NAND *nand*, (*comput.*) *n.* a logic circuit that has two or more inputs and one output, the output signal being 1 if any of its inputs is 0, and 0 if all its inputs are 1. [*not and*.]

Nandi bear *nan′di bär*, a great fierce animal reputed to live in E. Africa, perh. the spotted hyena. [From the *Nandi* Forest, Kenya.]

nandine *nan′din*, *n.* a West African palm-civet. [Prob. a native name.]

nandu, nandoo *nan′dŏŏ*, *n.* rami or China grass. [Tupí *nandú*.]

nanism *nān′* or *nan′izm*, *n.* condition of being dwarfed.

— *n.* **nanisā'tion, -z-** artificial dwarfing. [Gr. *nānos, nannos,* dwarf.]

nankeen *nan'kēn,* or *-kēn',* *n.* a buff-coloured cotton cloth first made at *Nanking* in China: (in *pl.*) clothes, esp. breeches, made of nankeen. — Also **nan'kin** (or *-kin'*).

nanny *nan'i, n.* a she-goat (also **nann'y-goat**): a children's nurse, esp. one trained to take care of children: a pet name for a grandmother. — Also **nana, nanna.** — *adj.* (*derog.*; of institutions, the state, etc.) protective to an intrusive extent. — *v.t.* to nurse: to overprotect: to supervise to the point of meddlesomeness. — *adj.* **nann'yish** overprotective. [From the woman's name.]

nano- *nān-ō-, nan-ō-,* in composition, one thousand millionth, 10^{-9}, as in **nan'ogram, nan'ometre, nan'o-second:** of microscopic size, as in **nan(n)'oplankton** very small forms of plankton. [Gr. *nānos,* a dwarf.]

Nansen passport *nan'sən päs'pört,* a passport that the League of Nations issued to stateless people. [F. *Nansen,* high commissioner for refugees with the League of Nations, 1920–22.]

Nantz *nants,* (*arch.*) *n.* brandy. [*Nantes* in France.]

naos *nā'os, n.* a temple: the inner cell of a temple. [Gr. *nāos,* temple.]

nap[1] *nap, v.i.* to take a short or casual sleep: — *pr.p.* **napp'ing;** *pa.p.* **napped.** — *n.* a short or casual sleep. — **catch someone napping** to detect someone in error that might have been avoided: to catch someone off his guard or unprepared. [O.E. *hnappian.*]

nap[2] *nap, n.* a woolly surface on cloth, now (distinguished from *pile*) such a surface raised by a finishing process, not made in the weaving: the woolly surface removed in the process: a cloth with such a surface: a downy covering or surface on anything. — *v.t.* to raise a nap on: to remove nap from. — *adj.* **nap'less** without nap, threadbare. — *n.* **napp'iness.** — *adj.* **napp'y** downy: shaggy. [M.E. *noppe;* app. — M.Du. or M.L.G. *noppe.*]

nap[3] *nap, n.* the card-game *Napoleon:* in that game a call of five: the winning of five tricks: a racing tip that professes to be a certainty — one that one may 'go nap' on. — *v.t.* to name (a particular horse) as certain to win. — **go nap** to undertake to win all five tricks: to risk all.

nap[4] *nap, v.t.* to seize: to steal. [Cf. Sw. *nappa,* Dan. and Norw. *nappe,* to catch, snatch; relation to **nab**[1] uncertain.]

napa, nappa *nap'ə, n.* a soft leather made (orig. at *Napa* in California) by a special tawing process, from sheep-skin or goatskin.

napalm *nā'päm, na', n.* a petroleum jelly, highly in-flammable, used in bombs and flame-throwers. [*naph*thenate *palm*itate.]

nape *nāp, n.* the back of the neck. [Ety. dub.]

Naperian. See **Napierian.**

napery *nāp'ə-ri,* (*arch.* and *Scot.*) *n.* linen, esp. for the table. [O.Fr. *naperie* — L.L. *napāria* — *napa,* a cloth — L. *mappa,* a napkin.]

naphtha *naf'thə* (sometimes *nap'tə*), *n.* rock-oil: a vague name for the liquid inflammable distillates from coal-tar, wood, etc., esp. the lighter and more volatile. — *n.* **naph'thalene** an ill-smelling hydrocarbon ($C_{10}H_8$) got by distillation of coal-tar, crystallising in plates, used for killing moths, etc. — *adj.* **naphthal'ic** (*naf-thal'ik*) pertaining to, or derived from, naphthalene. — *v.t.* **naph'thalise, -ize** to treat with naphtha. — *ns.* **naph'thol** a hydroxyl derivative of naphthalene ($C_{10}H_7OH$), of two kinds; **naphthyl'amine** (or *-mēn'*) an amino-derivative of thalene ($C_{10}H_7NH_2$) of two kinds, used in dyeing. [Gr. *naphtha.*]

Napierian, Naperian *nā-pē'ri-ən, adj.* pertaining to John *Napier* of Merchiston (1550–1617), or to his system of logarithms: now applied to natural logarithms, loga-rithms to the base *e,* the limit of $(1 + 1/m)^m$ when *m* approaches infinity, Napier's own base being a quan-tity depending on e^{-1}. — **Napier's bones,** or **rods** an invention of Napier's for multiplying and dividing mechanically by means of rods.

napiform *nā'pi-förm, adj.* turnip-shaped. [L. *nāpus,* a turnip.]

napkin *nap'kin, n.* a small square of linen, paper, etc., used at table for wiping the mouth and hands, or otherwise: a handkerchief (*Scot.*): a pad of disposable material or a folded square of towelling, muslin, etc. placed between a baby's legs and kept in place by a fastening at the waist, for absorbing urine and faeces (usu. shortened to **nappy** (*nap'i*)). — **nap'kin-ring** a ring in which a table-napkin is rolled. [Dim. of Fr. *nappe* — L. *mappa.*]

Naples-yellow *nā'plz-yel'ō, n.* a light-yellow pigment, lead antimoniate, originally an Italian secret.

napoleon *nə-pōl'yən,* or *-i-ən, n.* a twenty-franc gold coin issued by *Napoleon:* a French modification of the game of euchre, each player receiving five cards and playing for himself (commonly **nap**): a kind of rich iced cake: (with *cap.*) used generically in reference to *Napoleon* I, 1769–1821, Emperor of the French, to denote a person of paramount power and frightening ruthless-ness. — *adj.* **Napoleonic** (*-i-on'ik*) relating to *Napoleon* I or III, the Great or the Little. — *ns.* **Napol'eonism; Napol'eonist; napol'eonite** an orbicular diorite found in Corsica, Napoleon's native island.

napoo *nä-poo', (slang* of 1914 war) *adj.* and *interj.* no more: used up: good for nothing: dead. — *v.t.* to kill. [Fr. *il n'y en a plus,* there is no more.]

nappa. See **napa.**

nappe *nap, n.* a sheet of rock brought far forward by recumbent folding or thrusting (*geol.*): a sheet (*math.*): one of the two sheets on either side of the vertex forming a cone (*math.*). [Fr. *nappe,* tablecloth — L. *mappa.*]

napper *nap'ər, (slang) n.* the head.

nappy[1]. See **napkin.**

nappy[2] *nap'i, adj.* of liquor, having a head: heady, strong: tipsy: of a horse, nervous, jumpy, excitable. — *n.* strong ale. [Perh. from **nappy,** shaggy; see **nap**[2].]

napron *nā'prən, n.* earlier form (*Spens.*) of **apron.**

naras. See **narras.**

Narcissus *när-sis'əs, n.* the daffodil genus of the Amaryllis family: (without *cap.*) a plant of this genus, esp. *N. poeticus* (the poet's narcissus): — *pl.* **narciss'uses** or **narciss'ī:** in Greek myth., a youth who pined away for love of his own image, and was transformed into the flower. — *ns.* **narciss'ism** sensual gratification found in one's own body, whether as a normal stage of development or a pathological condition; **narciss'ist.** — *adj.* **narcissis'tic.** [L., — Gr. *Narkissos;* the con-nection with *narkē,* numbness, seems to be fanciful.]

narco-analysis, etc. See **narcotic.**

narcolepsy *när'kō-lep-si, n.* a condition marked by short attacks of irresistible drowsiness. [Gr. *narkē,* numb-ness, and *lēpsis,* seizure.]

narcotic *när-kot'ik, adj.* producing torpor, sleep, or dead-ness: affecting the central nervous system so as to produce dizziness, euphoria, loss of memory and of neuromuscular co-ordination, and eventually uncon-sciousness. — *n.* anything having a narcotic effect, e.g. a drug, alcohol, an inert gas. — *n.* **narcosis** (*-kō'sis*) drowsiness, unconsciousness or other effects to the central nervous system produced by a narcotic: — *pl.* **narco'ses** (*-sēz*). — *adv.* **narcot'ically.** — *n.* **nar'cotine** (*-kə-tēn*) one of the alkaloids in opium. — *v.t.* **nar'-cotise, -ize** to subject to the influence of a narcotic. — *ns.* **nar'cotism** the influence of narcotics; **nar'cotist.** — **nar'co-analysis** hypnoanalysis when narcotics are used in producing the hypnotic state; **nar'cocathar'sis** narco-analysis; **nar'cohypno'sis** the use of narcotics to produce hypnosis; **nar'cosyn'thesis** the bringing out of repressed emotions by narcotics so that they become freely accepted into the self; **nar'co-ther'apy** treatment of disturbed mental states by prolonged drug-induced sleep. [Gr. *narkōtikos — narkē,* numbness, torpor.]

nard *närd, n.* spikenard: an inappropriate name for matweed (*Nardus stricta*). — *v.t.* to anoint with nard. [L. *nardus* — Gr. *nardos.*]

nardoo *när-dōō′, n.* an Australian Marsilea: its sporocarps, ground into flour and used as a food by aboriginals. [Aboriginal.]

nare *när, n.* (*arch.*) a nostril, esp. a hawk's. — *n.pl.* **nār′ēs** (L.; *anat.*) nostrils. — *adjs.* **nār′ial, nār′ine** (*-īn*). — *n.* **nār′icorn** a horny termination of a bird's nostril. [L. *nāris,* pl. *-ēs,* nostril.]

narghile *när′gil-i, n.* a hookah. — Also **nargile(h), narg(h)il(l)y.** [Pers. *nārgīleh* — *nārgīl,* a coconut (from which it used to be made).]

narial, etc., **naricorn.** See **nare.**

nark *närk,* (*slang*) *n.* an informer: a police spy, as *copper's nark:* one who curries favour, a pick-thank: a spoilsport: a persistent fault-finder: an annoying or baffling circumstance: an expert. — *v.i.* to grumble. — *v.t.* and *v.i.* to watch: to spy: to annoy: to tease. — *adjs.* **nark′y** irritable; **narked** annoyed. — **nark at** to fret with persistent criticism. [Romany *nāk,* nose.]

narks, the. See **nitrogen narcosis.**

narquois *när-kwä,* (Fr.) *adj.* mocking, malicious.

narras, naras *nar′əs, n.* edible melon-like fruit of a S.-W. African long-rooted thorny cucurbitaceous shrub (*Acanthosicyos horrida*). [Hottentot *qnaras.*]

narrate *nə-* or *na-rāt′, v.t.* to tell of (a series of events): to give a running commentary on (a film, etc.). — *v.i.* to recount or relate events. — *adj.* **narrāt′able** — *n.* **narrā′tion** the act of telling: that which is told: an orderly account of a series of events. — *adj.* **narrative** (*nar′ə-tiv*) narrating: giving an account of any occurrence: inclined to narration: story-telling. — *n.* that which is narrated: a continued account of any series of occurrences: story. — *adv.* **narr′atively.** — *n.* **narrā′tor.** — *adj.* **narr′ātory** like narrative: consisting of narrative. [L. *narrāre, -ātum,* prob. — *gnārus,* knowing.]

narre *när,* (Spens.) *adv.* an old comparative of **nigh.**

narrow[1] *nar′ō, adj.* of little breadth: of small extent from side to side: closely confining: limited: contracted in mind or outlook: bigoted: not liberal: parsimonious: with little to spare: close: strict, precise: detailed: keen: (of money) denoting the more liquid kinds, e.g. in hand, or readily withdrawn from a bank account, etc.: tense (*phon.*). — *n.* a narrow part or place: (usu. in *pl.*) narrow passage, channel, or strait. — *adv.* narrowly. — *v.t.* to make narrow: to contract or confine. — *v.i.* to become narrow: to reduce the number of stitches in knitting. — *n.* **narr′owing** the act of making less in breadth: the state of being contracted: the part of anything which is made narrower. — Also *adj.* — *adv.* **narr′owly.** — *n.* **narr′owness.** — **narr′ow-boat** a canal-boat, esp. one of 7 feet (2·1 metres) or less in width, and 72 feet (about 22 metres) in length. — *v.t.* **narr′owcast.** — **narr′owcasting** cable television: the production and distribution of material on video tapes, cassettes, etc.; **narrow escape** an escape only just managed. — *adjs.* **narr′ow-gauge** of a railway, less than 4 ft 8½ in. (about 1·4 metres) in gauge; **narr′ow-mind′ed** of a narrow or illiberal mind. — **narr′ow-mind′edness; narrow seas** the seas between Great Britain and the Continent; **narrow squeak** a narrow escape. [O.E. *nearu.*]

narrow[2]. See **nary.**

Narthex *när′theks, n.* a former genus of umbelliferous plants, now included in Ferula: (without *cap.*) a western portico or vestibule in an early Christian or Oriental church or basilica, to which women and catechumens were admitted: (without *cap.*) a vestibule between the church porch and the nave. [Gr. *narthēx,* giant fennel, a cane or stalk, a casket, a narthex.]

nartjie (*orig.* **naartje**) *när′chi,* (Afrik.) *n.* a small sweet orange like the mandarin. [Prob. conn. with **orange.**]

narwhal *när′wəl, n.* a kind of whale (Monodon) with one large projecting tusk (occasionally two tusks) in the male. [Dan. *narhval;* O.N. *nāhvalr,* may be from *nār,* corpse, *hvalr,* whale, from its pallid colour.]

nary *när′i,* (*U.S.* and *dial.*) for **ne'er a** never a, not one. — Also **narrow a** (*nar′ō*).

nas *naz, näz, obs.* for **ne has** (Spens.) and for **ne was.**

nasal *nā′zl, adj.* belonging to the nose: affected by, or sounded through, the nose. — *n.* a sound uttered through the nose: a letter representing such a sound: a paired bone that forms the bridge of the nose: the nose-piece in a helmet. — *ns.* **Nasalis** (*naz-ā′lis*) the proboscis monkey genus; **nasalisation, -z-** (*nā-zə-lī-zā′shən*). — *v.i.* and *v.t.* **na′salise, -ize** to render nasal, as a sound. — *n.* **nasality** (*nā-zal′i-ti*). — *adv.* **na′sally.** — *n.* **nasion** (*nā′zi-on*) the median point of the nasofrontal suture. [L. *nāsus,* the nose.]

nasard *naz′ərd, n.* an organ mutation-stop. [Fr.]

nascent *nas′ənt, nās′ənt, adj.* coming into being. — *ns.* **nasc′ence** (*rare*), **nasc′ency.** [L. *nāscēns, -entis,* pr.p. of *nāscī, nātus,* to be born.]

naseberry *nāz′bər-i, -ber′i, n.* the sapodilla plum: the tree bearing it. — Also **neesberry** (*nēz′*), **nisberry** (*niz′*). [Sp. *néspera, níspero,* medlar tree — L. *mespilus,* medlar; cf. **medlar.**]

nashgab *nash′gab, näsh′gäb,* (Scot.) *n.* prattle: chatter: a pert chatterer. — Also **gab′nash.**

Nasik *nä′sik, n.* a town of Bombay. — Also *adj.,* esp. of an elaborate form of magic square devised there.

nasion. See **nasal.**

Naskhi. See **Neskhi.**

naso- *nā′zō-,* in composition, nose: of the nose (and something else), as *adjs.* **nasofront′al** pertaining to the nose and the frontal bone; **nasolac′rymal** pertaining to the nose and tears, as the duct that carries tears from the eye and the nose. — *n.* **nasophar′ynx** that part of the pharynx above the soft palate. [L. *nāsus,* nose.]

nastalik, nasta′liq *nas-tə-lēk′, n.* Persian cursive script, having long horizontal strokes and rounded characters. [Ar. from *naskhi,* cursive script, and *talik,* hanging.]

nastic *näs′tik, nas′, adj.* (of plant movements) not related to the direction of the stimulus. [Gr. *nastos,* close-pressed.]

Nasturtium *nas-tûr′shəm, n.* the water-cress genus of Cruciferae: (without *cap.;* in popular use) the Indian cress (*Tropaeolum majus*), a garden climber. [L. *nāsus,* nose, *torquēre,* to twist (from its pungency).]

nasty *näs′ti, adj.* disgustingly foul: nauseous: filthy: obscene: threatening: threatening danger: spiteful: ill-natured: difficult to deal with: awkward: unpleasant: objectionable. — *n.* (*coll.*) something or someone unpleasant or intractable: an obscene or sadistic film, as in *video nasty.* — *adv.* **nas′tily.** — *n.* **nas′tiness.** — **a nasty piece, bit, of work** a person very objectionable in character and conduct. [Perh. for earlier *nasky* (cf. Sw. dial. *naskug, nasket*); or perh. connected with Du. *nestig,* dirty.]

nasute *nā′zūt, -sūt,* or *-zūt′, -sūt′, adj.* keen-scented: critically discriminating: beaked. — *n.* a beaked soldier white-ant. [L. *nāsūtus* — *nāsus,* nose.]

nat *nat* (*coll.;* often with *cap.*) *n.* short for **nationalist.**

natal[1]. See **nates.**

natal[2] *nā′tl, adj.* of or connected with birth: native. — *adj.* **natalitial** (*nat-* or *nāt-ə-lish′l*) pertaining to a birthday. — *n.* **natality** (*nə-, nā-tal′i-ti*) birth: birth-rate. — **natal therapy** in psychoanalysis, the treatment of rebirthing (q.v.). [L. *nātālis* — *nāscī, nātus,* to be born.]

natale solum *na-tā′lē sō′ləm, nä-tä′le sol′ŏŏm,* (L.) native soil.

natalitial, natality. See **natal**[2].

natant *nāt′ənt, adj.* floating: swimming. — *n.* **natation** (*nat-* or *nāt-ā′shən*) swimming. — *adjs.* **nātato′rial, nā′tatory** pertaining to swimming: having the habit of swimming: adapted or used for swimming. — *n.* **nātato′rium** (*U.S.*) a swimming-pool. [L. *natāns, -antis,* pr.p. of *natāre,* freq. of *nāre,* to swim.]

natch[1] *nach,* (*dial.*) *n.* the rump. [See **aitchbone.**]

natch[2] *nach,* (*slang*) *adv.* of course, short for **naturally.**

natch[3]. See **nautch.**

nates *nā'tēz, n.pl.* the buttocks. — *adjs.* **nā'tal; nā'tiform.**
[L. *natis,* pl. *-ēs.*]
natheless(e). See **nathless.**
nathemore *nā-thə-mōr', -mör',* **nathemo** *-mō', (Spens.)*
advs. not or never the more.   [O.E. *nā thȳ mā,* never
the more (cf. following).]
nathless, natheless, nathelesse, naythles *nāth', nath', näth',*
nädh', nadh', nädh'(ə)-les, or (as *Spens.*) *-les', (arch.)*
adv. and *prep.* notwithstanding.   [O.E. *nā,* never, *thȳ,*
by that (instrum. case), *læs,* less.]
natiform. See **nates.**
nation[1] *nā'shən, n.* a body of people marked off by
common descent, language, culture, or historical tradition: the people of a state: an American Indian tribe
or federation of tribes: a set of people, animals, etc.:
a great number: an old division of students in universities: (in *pl.*) the heathen or Gentiles. — *adj.* **national**
(*nash'nəl, -ə-nəl*) pertaining to a nation or nations:
belonging or peculiar to, characteristic of, or controlled by, a nation: public: general: attached to one's
own country. — *n.* a member or fellow-member of a
nation. — *n.* **nationalīsā'tion, -z-.** — *v.t.* **nat'ionalise,**
-ize to make national: to make the property of the
nation: to bring under national management: to naturalise: to make a nation of. — *ns.* **nat'ionalism;**
nat'ionalist one who favours or strives after the unity,
independence, interests, or domination of a nation: a
member of a political party specially so called, e.g. the
Irish Nationalist party who aimed at Home Rule: an
advocate of nationalisation. — Also *adj.* — *adj.* **nationalist'ic.** — *adv.* **nationalist'ically.** — *n.* **nationality**
(*-al'it-i*) membership of, the fact or state of belonging
to, a particular nation: nationhood: a group or set
having the character of a nation: national character.
— *adv.* **nat'ionally.** — *n.* **nationhood** (*nā'*) the state or
fact of being a nation. — *adj.* **nationless** (*nā'*) without
nationality or nations. — **national air, anthem** an
official song or hymn of a nation, sung or played on
ceremonial occasions; **national call** (formerly **trunk
call**) a long-distance telephone call within the country,
not international; **national church** a church established
by law in a country; **National Convention** the sovereign
assembly in France from 21 Sept. 1792 to 26 Oct. 1795;
national debt money borrowed by the government of
a country and not yet paid back; **national grid** the grid
(q.v.) of power-lines in, or of lines on maps of, Great
Britain; **National Guard** a force which took part in the
French Revolution, first formed in 1789: organised
militia of individual States (*U.S.*); **national insurance**
a system of compulsory insurance paid for by weekly
contributions by employee and employer, and yielding
benefits to the sick, retired, unemployed, etc.; **national
park** area owned by or for the nation, set apart for
preservation and enjoyment of the beautiful or interesting; **national school** in England, formerly, a school
connected with the National Society, established in
1811, to promote elementary education; **national service** compulsory service in the armed forces; **National
Socialism** the policies of the National Socialist Party;
National Trust, National Trust for Scotalnd charitable
bodies concerned with the preservation of historic
monuments and buildings, and areas of natural beauty,
in Great Britain and Northern Ireland. — *adj.* **na'tion-
wide** covering the whole nation. — **National Health
Service** in Britain, the system under which medical,
dental, etc. treatment is available free, or at a nominal
charge, to all, paid for out of public taxation; **National
Savings Bank** a department of the Post Office with
which money may be deposited to accumulate interest;
National Socialist (German Workers') Party an extreme nationalistic fascist party in Germany, led by
Adolf Hitler.   [L. *nātiō, -ōnis* — *nāscī, nātus,* to be
born.]
nation[2] *nā'shən, (U.S. dial.) n., adj., adv., interj.* for
damnation.
native *nā'tiv, adj.* belonging naturally: innate: inherent:
natural: in a natural state: unsophisticated: occurring

in a natural station: occurring naturally as a mineral
(not manufactured), or naturally uncombined (as an
element): belonging by birth: having a right by birth:
born or originating in the place: being the place of
birth or origin: belonging to the people originally or
at the time of discovery inhabiting the country, esp.
when they are not yet fully civilised: connected by
birth: born a thrall (*obs.*): applied to Australian plants
and animals to which the name of an already known
different kind has been transferred: (of an oyster)
raised in a (British) artificial bed. — *n.* one born in
any place: (*disparagingly*) one born and long dwelling
in a place: one born under a particular planet or sign:
a member of a native race: a coloured person (*coll.
derog.; no longer common*): in South Africa, a member
of the black, Negroid race (*now considered offensive
and no longer in official use*): an indigenous species,
variety, or breed, or an individual of it: a native oyster:
a born thrall (*obs.*). — *adv.* **na'tively.** — *ns.* **na'tiveness;**
na'tivism the belief that the mind possesses some ideas
or forms of thought that are inborn and not derived
from sensation: the disposition to favour the natives
of a country in preference to immigrants; **na'tivist.** —
adj. **nativis'tic.** — *n.* **nativity** (*nə-tiv'i-ti*) the state or
fact of being born: the time, place, and manner of
birth: nationality by birth: the fact or status of being
native: the birth of Christ, hence the festival commemorating it — Christmas, or a picture representing it: a
horoscope: bondage by birth (*obs.*). — **native bear** the
koala. — *adj.* **na'tive-born** born in the country: having
a status by virtue of birth (*Scot.; obs.*). — **native cat** a
marsupial cat, a carnivorous, cat-sized white-spotted
animal of the genus Dasyurus, with a pointed snout;
native companion see **brolga; native land** the land to
which one belongs by birth; **native language** the language one acquires first, usu. that of one's native land;
native rock unquarried rock; **native speaker** one who
speaks the language in question as his native language.
— **go native** see **go; one's native heath** one's homeland,
one's own locality.   [L. *nātīvus* — *nāscī, nātus,* to be
born.]
Nato *nā'tō, n.* the North Atlantic Treaty Organisation
(see **north**).
natrium. See **natron.**
natrolite *nāt'* or *nat'rə-līt, n.* a common fibrous zeolite,
hydrated sodium aluminium silicate.   [**natron,** and
Gr. *lithos,* stone.]
natron *nā'trən, n.* a hydrated carbonate of sodium found
on some lake borders. — *n.* **na'trium** chemists' Latin
for sodium.   [Ar. *natrūn* — Gr. *nitron.*]
natter *nat'ər, v.i.* to be peevish (*N. of England*): to rattle
on in talk, esp. grumblingly: to chatter, talk much
about little (*coll.*). — Also *n.* — *adjs.* **natt'ered, natt'ery**
peevish.   [Origin obscure.]
natterjack *nat'ər-jak, n.* a toad with a yellow stripe down
the back.   [Origin unknown.]
nattier blue *nat'i-ər blōō* a soft azure.   [J. M. *Nattier* (d.
1766), French painter.]
natty *nat'i,* (*coll.*) *adj.* dapper: spruce: clever, ingenious,
deft (*dial.*). — *adv.* **natt'ily.** — *n.* **natt'iness.**   [Possibly
connected with **neat**[2].]
natura *nə-tūr'ə, na-tōō'ra,* (L.) *n.* nature. — **natura natu-
rans** (*nat'ūr-əns, na-tōō'räns*) creative nature; **natura
naturata** (*na-tūr-ā'tə, na-tōō-rä'ta*) created nature.
natural *nach'(ə)rəl, adj.* pertaining to, produced by, or
according to nature: furnished by or based on nature:
not miraculous: not the work of man: not interfered
with by man: inborn: having the feelings that may be
expected to come by nature, kindly: normal: happening in the usual course: spontaneous: not far-fetched:
not acquired: without affectation: not fictitious: physical: life-like, like nature: related by actual birth (not
adoption, etc.): hence (now rarely) legitimate: (now
usually) illegitimate: natural-born, or having the status
of the natural-born: in a state of nature, unregenerate:
of classification, according to ancestral relationships
(*biol.*): according to the usual diatonic scale, not sharp

or flat (*mus.*). — *n.* an idiot: one having a natural aptitude (for), or being an obvious choice (for): a thing assured by its very nature of success, a certainty: a tone that is neither sharp nor flat (*mus.*): a character (♮) cancelling a preceding sharp or flat (*mus.*): a white key in keyboard musical instruments. — *n.* **naturalīsā'-tion, -z-.** — *v.t.* **nat'uralise, -ize** to make natural or easy: to cause an introduced species of plant, animal, etc. to adapt to a different climate or to different conditions of life: to grant the privileges of natural-born citizens to: to adopt into the language: to admit among accepted institutions, usages, etc.: to explain naturalistically. — *v.i.* to acquire citizenship in another country: to study natural history in the field: of a plant, animal, etc., to adapt to a new environment. — *ns.* **nat'uralism** following of nature: a close following of nature without idealisation: the theory that this should be the aim of art and literature, esp. the form of realism advocated or practised by Emile Zola: a world-view that rejects the supernatural: the belief that natural religion is of itself sufficient: deism; **nat'uralist** one who studies nature, more particularly zoology and botany, esp. zoology, and esp. in the field: a dealer in live animals and articles of use and interest to students of nature, often a taxidermist: a believer in naturalism. — *adj.* **naturalist'ic** pertaining to, or in accordance with, nature, natural history, or naturalism. — *advs.* **naturalist'ically; nat'urally** in a natural manner: by nature: according to nature or one's own nature: in a life-like manner: normally: in the ordinary course: of course. — *n.* **nat'uralness.** — *adj.* **nat'ural-born** native. — **natural death** death owing to disease or old age, not violence or accident; **natural gas** gases issuing from the earth, whether from natural fissures or bored wells, applied particularly to the hydrocarbon gases associated with the production of petroleum and used as domestic or industrial fuel in place of town gas (q.v.); **natural history** originally the description of all that is in nature, now used of the sciences that deal with the earth and its productions — botany, zoology, and mineralogy, esp. field zoology; **natural law** a law of nature: the sense of right and wrong which arises from the constitution of the mind of man, as distinguished from the results of revelation or legislation; **natural logarithm** one to the base *e*; **natural magic** see **magic; natural numbers** the whole numbers 1, 2, 3, and upwards; **natural order** in botany, a category now usually called a family; **natural philosophy** the science of the physical properties of bodies: physics, or physics and dynamics; **natural religion** see **natural theology; natural resources** features, properties, etc. of the land such as minerals, an abundance of water, timber, etc. that occur naturally and can be exploited by man; **natural scale** a scale of music written without sharps or flats; **natural science** the science of nature, as distinguished from mental and moral science and from mathematics; **natural selection** evolution by the survival of the fittest with inheritance of their fitness by next generation; **natural system** a classification of plants and animals according to presumed relationship by descent, distinguished in botany from the artificial system of Linnaeus; **natural theology,** or **natural religion,** religion derived from reason without revelation; **natural wastage** (reduction of staff by) non-replacement of those who leave, e.g. through retirement; **natural year** see **year.** [L. *nātūrālis* — *nātūra*, nature.]

nature *nā'chər, n.* the power that creates and regulates the world: the power of growth: the established order of things: the cosmos: the external world, esp. as untouched by man: the qualities of anything which make it what it is: essence: being: constitution: kind or order: naturalness: normal feeling: kindliness: conformity to truth, or reality: inborn mind, character, instinct, or disposition: vital power of man, animal (*obs.*): course of life: nakedness: a primitive undomesticated condition: the strength or substance of anything. — *adjs.* **na'tured** having a certain temper or disposition (esp. in compounds, as *good-natured*); **na'turing** creative. — *ns.* **na'turism** communal nudity practised in the belief that it encourages self-respect, respect for others and a feeling of being in harmony with nature: nature-worship; **na'turist.** — *adj.* **naturist'ic.** — *n.* **nat'uropath** one who practises naturopathy. — *adj.* **naturopath'ic.** — *n.* **nāturop'athy** (also *nat-*) the promotion of health and natural healing by a system of diet, exercise, manipulation, care, and hydrotherapy: the philosophy of the system. — **na'ture-cure** the practice of, or treatment by, naturopathy; **na'ture-god'** a deity personifying some force of physical nature; **na'ture-knowl'edge, na'ture-study** a branch of school work intended to cultivate the powers of seeing and enjoying nature by the observation of natural objects, e.g. plants, animals, etc.; **na'ture-myth** a myth symbolising natural phenomena; **na'ture-printing** printing from plates that have been impressed with some natural object; **nature strip** (*Austr.*) a strip of grass, etc. bordering a road or footpath or dividing two carriageways; **na'ture-worship, na'turism** worship of the powers of nature. — **debt of nature** death; **ease,** or **relieve, nature** to evacuate the bowels; **in the nature of** of the same sort as, that amounts to. [Fr., — L. *nātūra* — *nāscī, nātus,* to be born.]

naturopath, -pathy. See **nature.**

naught *nöt, n.* nothing: a nought (q.v.): wickedness, evil (*obs.*). — *adj.* (*arch.*) good for nothing: worthless: bad: immoral: hurtful: foiled: ruined. — *adv.* ill: not at all. — **be naught** (*obs.*) keep out of the way: efface yourself: go to the devil; **bring to naught** to frustrate, baffle; **come to naught** to come to nothing, to fail; **set at naught** to treat as of no account, to despise. — Also **nought.** [O.E. *nāht, nāwiht* — *nā,* never, *wiht,* whit.]

naughty *nöt'i, adj.* worthless (*obs.*): wicked (*Shak.*): bad: ill-behaved: verging on the indecorous: now chiefly applied to children, or used playfully in feigned censure. — *n.* (*Austr. coll.*) an act of sexual intercourse. — *adv.* **naught'ily.** — *n.* **naught'iness.** — **naughty nineties** (*joc.*) the 1890s, renowned for gaiety and high living; **naughty pack** (*obs.*) a person, esp. a woman, of loose life, a 'bad lot'. [**naught.**]

naumachy *nö'mə-ki,* **naumachia** *nö-mā'ki-ə, ns.* a sea-fight, esp. one got up as a spectacle among the Romans: a place for the purpose. [Gr. *naumachiā* — *naus,* a ship, *muchē,* a fight.]

naunt *nänt,* (*arch.*) *n.* aunt. [For **mine aunt.**]

nauplius *nö'pli-əs, n.* a larval form in many Crustacea, with one eye and three pairs of appendages: — *pl.* **nau'plii (-ī).** — *adjs.* **nau'pliiform (-plē-i-), nau'plioid.** [L., a kind of shellfish — Gr. *Nauplios,* a son of Poseidon — *naus,* a ship, *pleein,* to sail.]

nausea *nö'si-ə, -shi-ə, -zhə, n.* (*orig.*) sea-sickness: a feeling of inclination to vomit: sickening disgust or loathing. — *adj.* **nau'seant** producing nausea. — *n.* a substance having this quality. — *v.i.* **nau'seate** to feel nausea or disgust. — *v.t.* to loathe: to strike with disgust. — *adj.* **nau'seating** causing nausea or (*fig.*) disgust. — *adjs.* **nau'seative** (*obs.*) inclined to or causing nausea; **nau'seous (-shəs, -shi-əs, -si-əs)** producing nausea: disgusting: loathsome. — *adv.* **nau'seously.** — *n.* **nau'seousness.** [L., — Gr. *nausiā,* sea-sickness — *naus,* a ship.]

nautch *nöch,* **nach, natch** *näch, ns.* in India, a performance of professional dancing women known as **nautch'-girls.** [Hind. *nāch,* dance.]

nautic *nöt'ik* (*rare*), **-al -əl, adjs.** of or pertaining to ships, to sailors, or to navigation. — *adv.* **nau'tically.** — *n. sing.* **nau'tics** the science of navigation. — *n.pl.* water sports. — **Nautical Almanac** a periodical book of astronomical tables specially useful to sailors; **nautical mile** see **mile.** [L. *nauticus* — Gr. *nautikos* — *nautēs,* sailor, *naus,* a ship.]

nautilus *nö-ti-ləs, n.* a tetrabranchiate cephalopod (**pearly nautilus**) of southern seas, with a chambered external shell: a Mediterranean dibranchiate cephalopod (**paper nautilus** or argonaut) wrongly believed by Aristotle to use its arms as sails: — *pl.* **nau'tiluses,** or **nau'tilī.** [L.,

— Gr. *nautilos*, a sailor, a paper nautilus — *naus*, ship.]

Navaho, Navajo, *nav'ə-hō, n.* a North American Indian people of Utah, Arizona and New Mexico; a member of this people; their language. — *pl.* **Nav'ahos, -jos.** [Sp. *Navajó*, name of a particular pueblo.]

navaid *nav'ād, n.* in a ship or aircraft, any of the electronic devices designed to aid navigation. [Formed from *navigational aid*.]

Navajo. See **Navaho.**

naval *nā'vl, adj.* pertaining to warships or a navy: nautical (*obs.*). — *n.* **nav'alism** the cult of naval supremacy or sea-power. — **Naval Brigade** a body of seamen organised to serve on land; **naval crown** a garland awarded to a Roman who had distinguished himself in a sea-fight; **naval officer** an officer in the navy: a custom-house officer of high rank (*U.S.*). [L. *nāvālis* — *nāvis*, a ship.]

navarch *nāv'ärk, n.* an admiral in ancient Greece. — *n.* **nav'archy** the office of navarch: a fleet. [Gr. *nauarchos* — *naus*, ship, *archē*, rule.]

navarho *nav'ə-rō, n.* low-frequency, long-range radio navigation system for aircraft. [*navigation*, *aid*, *rho* (ρ), a navigational symbol for distance.]

navarin *nav'ə-rin, nav-a-rē, n.* a stew of mutton or lamb, with turnip and other root vegetables. [Fr.]

nave¹ *nāv, n.* the middle or main body of a basilica, rising above the aisles: the main part of a church, generally west of the crossing, including or excluding its aisles. [L. *nāvis*, a ship.]

nave² *nāv, n.* the hub or central part of a wheel, through which the axle passes: the navel (*Shak.*). [O.E. *nafu*; cf. Du. *naaf*, Ger. *Nabe*.]

navel *nā'vl, n.* the umbilicus or depression in the centre of the abdomen: a central point: nombril (*her.*). — **na'vel-or'ange** a variety of orange with a navel-like depression, and a smaller orange enclosed; **na'vel= string** the umbilical cord; **na'velwort** pennywort (Cotyledon). [O.E. *nafela*, dim. of *nafu*, nave of a wheel.]

navette *na-vet', n.* in jewel-cutting, a pointed oval shape: a jewel cut in this shape. [Fr., shuttle, dim. of *nef*, ship.]

navew *nā'vū, n.* a rape or coleseed with carrot-shaped root: a wild Swedish turnip. [Fr. *naveau*, dim. — L. *nāpus*.]

navicert *nav'* or *nāv'i-sûrt, n.* a certificate granted by a belligerent to a neutral ship testifying that she carries no contraband of war. [**navigational certificate**.]

navicula *nav-ik'ū-lə, n.* an incense-boat: (with *cap.*) a genus of diatoms: (without *cap.*) a plant of this genus. — *adj.* **navic'ular** boat-shaped: pertaining to the navicular bone. — *n.* the navicular bone. — **navicular bone** a boat-shaped bone on the thumb side of the wrist joint, the scaphoid bone: a corresponding bone in the ankle joint; **navicular disease** inflammation of the navicular bone in horses. [L. *nāvicula*, dim. of *nāvis*, a ship.]

navigate *nav'i-gāt, v.i.* to conduct or manage a ship, aircraft, motor vehicle, etc., in sailing, flying or moving along: to find one's way and keep one's course, esp. by water or air: to sail. — *v.t.* to direct the course of: to sail, fly, etc., over, on, or through. — *n.* **navigability** (*-gə-bil'i-ti*). — *adj.* **nav'igable** that may be passed by ships, etc.: dirigible. — *ns.* **nav'igableness; naviga'tion** the act, science, or art of conducting ships or aircraft, etc., esp. the finding of position and determination of course by astronomical observations and mathematical computations: travel or traffic by water or air: a voyage (*arch.*): shipping generally: a navigable route: a canal or artificial waterway. — *adj.* **naviga'tional** pertaining to navigation. — *n.* **nav'igator** one who navigates or sails: one who directs the course of a ship, etc.: one (usu. co-driver) who describes the route to, and directs, the driver in car rally or race: an explorer by sea: a navvy: an instrumental or other aid to navigation. [L. *nāvigāre, -ātum* — *nāvis*, a ship, *agĕre*, to drive.]

navvy *nav'i, n.* a labourer — originally a labourer on a navigation or canal: a machine for digging out earth, etc. (see **steam-navvy**). — *v.i.* to work as a navvy, or like a navvy. — *v.t.* to excavate: — *pr.p.* **navv'ying;** *pa.t.* and *pa.p.* **navv'ied.** [**navigator**.]

navy *nā'vi, n.* a fleet of ships: the whole of a nation's ships-of-war: the officers and men belonging to a nation's warships. — *adj.* of, used by, such as is supplied to, the navy. — *n.* and *adj.* **na'vy-blue'** dark blue as in naval dress. — **na'vy-list'** a list of officers and ships of a navy; **na'vy-yard** (*U.S.*) a government dockyard. [O.Fr. *navie* — L. *nāvis*, a ship.]

nawab *nə-wäb', -wôb', n.* a deputy or viceroy in the Mogul empire: a Muslim prince or noble: an honorary title bestowed by the Indian government: a nabob (*rare*). [Hind. *nawwāb* — Ar. *nawwāb*, respectful pl. of *nā'ib*, deputy.]

nay *nā, adv.* no: not only so, but: yet more: in point of fact. — *n.* a denial: a vote against. — **nay'-say** a refusal. — *v.t.* to refuse: to deny. — **nay'ward** (*Shak.*) the negative side. [M.E. *nay, nai* — O.N. *nei*; Dan. *nei*; cog. with **no**.]

naya paisa. See **paisa.**

Nayar. See **Nair.**

naythles. See **nathless.**

nayword *nā'wûrd, n.* a catchword or watchword (*Shak.*): a proverbial reproach, a byword (*Shak.* **ayword**). [Origin obscure.]

Nazarene *naz'ə-rēn, n.* an inhabitant of *Nazareth*, in Galilee: a follower of Jesus of Nazareth, originally used of Christians in contempt: an early Jewish Christian: any of a group of German painters who, in the early 19th cent., tried to restore the quality of religious art. — Also **Nazarē'an, Naz'arite.**

Nazarite *naz'ə-rīt, n.* a Jewish ascetic under a vow (see Num. vi.) (also **Naz'irite**): a Nazarene. — *adj.* **Nazaritic** (*-it'ik*). — *n.* **Naz'aritism** (*-īt-izm*). [Heb. *nāzar*, to consecrate.]

naze *nāz, n.* a headland or cape. [O.E. *næs*; cf. **ness**.]

Nazi *nä'tsē, n.* and *adj.* for Ger. *Nazional-sozialist*, National Socialist, Hitlerite. — *ns.* **Naz'ism, Naz'iism.** — *v.t., v.i.* **Naz'ify.** [Ger.]

nazir *nä'zir, n.* formerly, an Indian court official who served summonses, etc.: an official of various kinds. [Ar. *nāzir*, overseer.]

Nazirite. See **Nazarite.**

ne *nē, ni,* (*obs.*) *adv.* not. — *conj.* nor. [O.E. *ne.*]

neafe, neaffe (*Shak.*). See **nieve.**

neal *nēl, v.t.* and *v.i.* an aphetic form of **anneal.**

Neanderthal *ni-an'dər-täl, adj.* of a Palaeolithic species of man whose remains were first found in 1857 in a cave in the *Neanderthal*, a valley between Düsseldorf and Elberfeld (1930, part of Wuppertal): primitive (*coll.*): extremely old-fashioned and reactionary (*coll.*). — *n.* **Nean'derthaler, Nean'derthal** (also *fig.*). — *adj.* **Nean'- derthaloid.** — All words also without *cap.*

neanic *nē-an'ik,* (*zool.*) *adj.* pertaining to the adolescent period in the life-history of an individual. [Gr. *neanikos*, youthful.]

neap *nēp, adj.* of tides, of smallest range. — *n.* a neap tide. — *v.i.* to tend towards the neap. — *adj.* **neaped** left aground between spring tides. — **neap'tide, neap tide** a tide of minimum amplitude, occurring when the sun and moon are working against each other. [O.E. *nēp*, app. meaning helpless; *nēpflōd*, neap tide.]

Neapolitan *nē-ə-pol'i-tən, adj.* of the city or the former kingdom of Naples. — *n.* a native, citizen, or inhabitant of Naples: (without *cap.*) a small rectangular chocolate. — **Neapolitan ice** ice-cream made in layers of different colours and flavours; **Neapolitan sixth** (*mus.*) a chord of the subdominant with its minor third and minor sixth; **Neapolitan violet** a scented double variety of sweet violet. [L. *Neāpolītānus* — Gr. *Neāpolis*, new town — *neos, -ā, -on*, new, *polis*, city.]

near *nēr, adv.* (*orig.*, as compar. of **nigh**) nigher, more closely, to or at a shorter distance: (now as positive) to or at no great distance: close: closely: nearly: almost:

narrowly: — new double *compar.* **near′er;** *superl.* **near′-est.** — *prep.* close to (**near′er, near′est** also are *preps.*). — *adj.* nigh: not far away in place or time: close in kin, friendship, imitation, approximation, or in any relation: close, narrow, so as barely to escape: short, as a road: stingy: of horses, vehicles, etc., left, left-hand: — *compar.* **near′er;** *superl.* **near′est.** — *v.t.* and *v.i.* to approach: to come nearer. — *adv.* **near′ly** at or within a short distance: closely: intimately: scrutinisingly, parsimoniously: almost: approximately but rather less. — *n.* **near′ness.** — **near beer** in the U.S, any of several beers containing ½ per cent alcohol or less. — *adjs.* **near′-begaun, near′-gaun** (*Scot.*) niggardly; **near′-by** neighbouring. — *adv.* (usu. **near-by′**) close at hand. — *prep.* (also **near by**) close to. — **near cut** (*old*) a short cut; **Near East** formerly, an area including the Balkans and Turkey, and sometimes also the countries to the west of Iran: now synonymous with **Middle East** (q.v.). — *adj.* **near′-hand** (*Scot.*) near. — *adv.* nearly. — *adj.* **near′-legged** (*Shak.*) of horses, walking so that the legs interfere. — **near miss** (*lit.* and *fig.*) a miss that is almost a hit; **near point** the nearest point the eye can focus; **near′side** the side of a vehicle nearer to the kerb e.g. when it is being driven, in Britain the left side: the left side of a horse or other animal, or of a team of horses. — Also *adj.* — *adj.* **near′-sight′ed** short-sighted. — *n.* **near′-sight′edness.** — **a near thing** a narrow escape; **near as a touch, as ninepence, as dammit** (*coll.*) very nearly. [O.E. *nēar,* compar. of *nēah,* nigh (*adv.*), and O.N. *nǣr,* compar. (but also used as positive) of *nā,* nigh; cf. Ger. *näher.*]

near- *nēr-,* in composition, almost, as *adj.* **near′-white′:** a substitute closely resembling, as **near′-beer** a beverage resembling beer, with a very low alcohol content, **near′-silk′** artificial silk.

Nearctic *nē-ärk′tik, adj.* of the New World part of the Holarctic region. [Gr. *neos,* new, *arktikos,* northern — *arktos,* bear, the Great Bear.]

neat[1] *nēt,* (*arch.* or *dial.*) *n.* an ox, cow, bull, etc.: — *pl.* **neat.** — **neat′-cattle; neat′-herd; neat′-house; neat′-stall; neat′s leather** leather made of the hides of neat. — **neat′s-foot oil** an oil obtained from the feet of oxen. [O.E. *nēat,* cattle, a beast — *nēotan, nīotan,* to use; cf. Scot. **nowt** from O.N. *naut.*]

neat[2] *nēt, adj.* clean (*obs.*): unmixed: undiluted: undiminished, net: clear, shining (*Spens.*): elegant: trim: tidy: finished, adroit: deft: well and concisely put: ingenious, effective, economical in effort or method. — *adv.* neatly. — *v.t.* **neat′en** to make neat, tidy. — *adv.* **neat′ly.** — *n.* **neat′ness.** — *adj.* **neat′-hand′ed** dexterous. [Fr. *net,* clean, tidy — L. *nitidus,* shining, bright — *nitēre,* to shine.]

neath, ′neath *nēth,* (*dial.* and *poet.*) *prep.* beneath. [Aphetic for **aneath,** or for **beneath.**]

neb *neb, n.* a beak or bill: the mouth (*obs.*): the nose: a nib: the sharp point of anything. — *v.i.* to bill. — *v.t.* to put a neb on. — *adj.* **nebbed** (*nebd*) having a neb. [O.E. *nebb,* beak, face; cog. with Du. *neb,* beak.]

nebbich *neb′ihh,* **nebbish, nebish** *-ish,* **nebbishe(r)** *neb′-ish-ə(r), ns.* a colourless, insignificant, incompetent person, a perpetual victim. — Also *adj.* [Yiddish.]

nebbuk, nebek, nebeck *neb′ək.* Same as **nabk.**

nebel *nē′bəl, n.* a Hebrew instrument, apparently a harp. [Heb. *nēbel.*]

nebish. See **nebbich.**

neb-neb *neb′-neb, n.* bablah pods. [Prob. African word.]

nebris *neb′ris, n.* a fawn-skin worn by Bacchus and his votaries. [Gr. *nebris.*]

nebuchadnezzar *neb-ū-kad-nez′ər, n.* a large bottle, esp. of champagne, the equivalent of 20 ordinary bottles. [*Nebuchadnezzar,* king of Babylon in 2 Kgs. 24–25, following the tradition of calling bottle-sizes after well-known Old Testament figures.]

nebula *neb′ū-lə, n.* a little cloudiness: a slight opacity of the cornea: a liquid for spraying: a faint, misty appearance in the heavens produced either by a group of stars too distant to be seen singly, or by diffused

gaseous matter: — *pl.* **neb′ulae** (*-lē*). — *adjs.* **neb′ular** pertaining to nebulae: like or of the nature of a nebula; **neb′ulé** (*-lā*), **neb′uly** (*her.*) wavy. — *ns.* **nebule** (*neb′ūl*) wavy moulding; **nebulīsā′tion, -z-.** — *v.t.* **neb′ulise, -ize** to reduce to spray. — *ns.* **nebulīs′er, -z-** spraying apparatus, atomiser; **nebu′lium** an element formerly assumed in order to explain certain lines in the spectra of gaseous nebulae — lines now known to be due to states of oxygen, and also nitrogen, not possible under earthly conditions; **nebulos′ity.** — *adj.* **neb′ulous** hazy, vague, formless (*lit., fig.*): cloudlike: like, of the nature of, or surrounded by, a nebula. — *adv.* **neb′ulously.** — *n.* **neb′ulousness.** — **nebular hypothesis** the theory of Laplace that the solar system was formed by the contraction and breaking up of a rotating nebula. [L. *nebula,* mist; cf. Gr. *nephelē,* cloud, mist.]

nécessaire *nā-ses-er,* (Fr.) *n.* a dressing-case, work-box.

necessary *nes′is-ə-ri, adj.* that must be: that cannot be otherwise: unavoidable: indispensable: enforced (*arch.*): (of agent) not free. — *n.* that which cannot be left out or done without (food, etc.) — used chiefly in *pl.*: a privy (*obs.* or *dial.*): money (*coll.*). — *n.* and *adj.* **necessā′rian.** — *n.* **necessā′rianism** the doctrine that the will is not free, but subject to causes without, which determine its action. — *adv.* **nec′essarily** (or *nes-is-e′rə-li*) as a necessary consequence: inevitably: (*loosely*) for certain. — *n.* **nec′essariness. — necessary house, place** (*obs.* or *dial.*) a privy; **necessary truths** such as cannot but be true. [L. *necessārius.*]

necessity *ni-ses′i-ti, n.* a state or quality of being necessary: that which is necessary or unavoidable: unavoidable compulsion: great need: poverty. — *n.* and *adj.* **necessitā′rian.** — *n.* **necessitā′rianism** necessarianism. — *v.t.* **necess′itate** to make necessary: to render unavoidable: to compel. — *n.* **necessitā′tion.** — *adjs.* **necess′itied** (*Shak.*) subject by need; **necess′itous** in necessity: very poor: destitute. — *adv.* **necess′itously.** — *n.* **necess′itousness.** — **natural necessity** the condition of being necessary according to the laws of nature, **logical** or **mathematical** according to those of human intelligence, **moral** according to those of moral law; **of necessity** necessarily; **works of necessity** work so necessary as to be allowable on the Sabbath. [L. *necessitās, -ātis.*]

neck *nek, n.* the part connecting head and trunk (often in allusion to the halter or the yoke; *fig.*): the flesh of that part regarded as food: anything resembling that part: the part connecting head and body of anything, e.g. a violin: the plain lower part of the capital of a column: any narrow connecting part, e.g. an isthmus: anything narrow and throatlike, as the upper part of a bottle: a plug of igneous or fragmental rock filling a volcanic vent: a col: the part of a garment on or nearest the neck: a neck's length: impudence, audacity (*slang*). — *v.t.* to strike, pull, or chop the neck of, esp. so as to kill: to catch or fasten by the neck: to embrace (*slang*): to make a neck on: to drink (*slang*). — *v.i.* (*slang*) to embrace. — *n.* **neck′atee** (*obs.*) a neckerchief. — *adj.* **necked** having a neck. — *ns.* **neck′ing** the neck of a column (*archit.*): a moulding between the capital and shaft of a column, gorgerin (*archit.*): embracing, petting (*slang*); **neck′let** a simple form of necklace: a pendant strung for the neck: a small boa or fur for the neck. — **neck′-band** the part of a shirt, etc., encircling the neck: a band worn on the neck; **neck′beef** the coarse flesh of the neck of cattle: inferior stuff; **neck′-bone** a cervical vertebra; **neck′-cloth** a piece of folded cloth worn round the neck by men as a band or cravat, the ends hanging down often of lace; **neck′erchief** a kerchief for the neck; **neck′gear** apparel for the neck; **neck′-herr′ing** (*obs.*) a heavy blow on the neck; **necking party** petting party; **neck′lace** (*-lis, -ləs*) a lace, chain, or string of beads or precious stones worn on the neck: in S. Africa, the punishment of having a petrol-soaked tyre placed round the neck and set alight, used by blacks against blacks thought to be government sympathisers (also **neck′lacing**); **neck′line** the boundary-

line of a garment at the neck; **neck'-moulding** a moulding where the capital of a column joins the shaft;
neck'-piece a piece forming, covering, or bordering a
neck; **neck'-sweet'bread** the thymus gland of veal or
lamb; **neck'tie** a band of fabric tied round the neck
under the collar and usu. hanging down in front, a tie
(esp. *U.S.*): a hangman's noose (*U.S. slang*); **neck-tie
party** (*U.S. slang*) a lynching; **neck'verse** the test of
ability to read for those who claimed benefit of clergy,
usually Psalm li. 1, success giving the privilege of being
branded on the hand instead of hanging; **neck'wear**
apparel for the neck, as ties or scarves; **neck'weed**
hemp, source of the hangman's rope (*old slang*): a kind
of speedwell, from its reputed medicinal virtue (*U.S.*).
— **get it in the neck** to be severely dealt with, hard hit;
harden the neck to grow more obstinate; **neck and crop**
completely: bodily: in a heap: summarily and unceremoniously; **neck and neck** exactly equal: side by side;
neck of the woods (*coll.*) a particular area, part of the
country; **neck or nothing** risking everything; **save one's
neck** to escape narrowly with one's life or reputation;
stick one's neck out to put oneself at risk, expose oneself
to trouble, danger, or contradiction; **talk through (the
back of) one's neck** to talk wildly or absurdly wide of
the truth; **tread on the neck of** to oppress or tyrannise
over; **up to one's neck** deeply involved, esp. in a
troublesome situation. [O.E. *hnecca*; cf. O.H.G.
hnac, also O.Ir. *cnocc*, hill.]

necro- *nek'rō-, -ro'*, in composition, dead: dead body. —
ns. **necrōbiō'sis** degeneration of living tissue; **necrog'-
rapher** an obituary writer; **necrol'ater; necrol'atry** worship of, or morbid or sentimental reverence for, the
dead, or dead bodies. — *adjs.* **necrōlog'ic, -al.** — *ns.*
necrol'ogist; necrol'ogy an obituary list; **nec'rōmancer**
a sorcerer; **nec'rōmancy** the art of revealing future
events by calling up and questioning the spirits of the
dead: enchantment. — *adjs.* **necrōman'tic, -al.** — *adv.*
necrōman'tically. — *adj.* **necroph'agous** feeding on
carrion. — *ns.* **nec'rophile** (*-fīl*) one who is morbidly
attracted to corpses; **necrophilia** (*-fil'*) necrophilism.
— *adjs.* **necrophil'iac, -phil'ic.** — *ns.* **necroph'ilism,
necroph'ily** a morbid liking for dead bodies. — *adj.*
necroph'ilous. — *n.* **necrophō'bia** a morbid horror of
corpses. — *adj.* **necroph'orous** carrying away and
burying dead bodies, as burying beetles. — *ns.* **necrop'-
olis** a cemetery: — *pl.* **-lises** (*-lis-əz*), **-leis** (*-līs*); **nec'ropsy**
(or *-rop'*) a post-mortem examination. — *adjs.*
necrōscop'ic, -al. — *ns.* **necros'copy** a post-mortem
examination, autopsy; **necrot'omy** dissection of a dead
body: the surgical excision of necrosed bone from a
living body. [Gr. *nekros*, dead body, dead.]

necrosis *nek-rō'sis, n.* death of part of the living body.
— *v.t.* and *v.i.* **necrose** (*nek-rōs'*) to affect with or
undergo necrosis. — *adj.* **necrŏt'ic.** — *v.t.* and *v.i.*
nec'rōtise, -ize to necrose. [Gr. *nekros*, dead body.]

nectar *nek'tər, n.* the name given by Homer, Hesiod,
Pindar, etc., to the beverage of the gods, giving life
and beauty: a delicious beverage: the honey of the
glands of plants. — *adjs.* **nectā'real, nectā'rean, nectā'-
reous, nec'tarous** of or like nectar; **nec'tared** imbued
with nectar: mingled, filled, or abounding with nectar.
— *n.* **nectā'reousness.** — *adjs.* **nectā'rial** of the nature
of a nectary; **nectarif'erous** producing nectar; **nec'-
tarine** (*-in*) sweet as nectar. — *n.* (*-ēn, -in*) a variety of
peach with a smooth skin. — *n.* **nec'tary** a glandular
organ that secretes nectar. — **nec'tar-guide'** a marking
that guides insects to the nectary of a flower. [Gr.
nektar; ety. dub.]

nectocalyx *nek-tō-kā'liks, n.* a hydrozoan swimming-bell:
— *pl.* **nectocā'lyces** (*-li-sēz*). [Gr. *nēktos*, swimming,
kălyx, shell, flower-cup.]

ned *ned, (chiefly Scot.; slang) n.* a young hooligan, a
disruptive adolescent. [Poss. the familiar form of
Edward; see **Ted.**]

neddy *ned'i, n.* a donkey: a fool (*coll.*): a racehorse (*Austr.
slang*). [From *Edward*.]

née *nā, adj.* (of a woman) born — used in stating a
woman's maiden name. [Fr., fem. pa.p. of *naître*, to
be born.]

need *nēd, n.* want of something which one cannot well
do without: necessity: a state that requires relief: want
of the means of living. — *v.t.* to have occasion for: to
want: to require: (used before the infinitive with *to*, or
in negative, interrogative, conditional, etc. sentences
without *to*) to require or be obliged (to do something):
(used before a verbal noun) to require (to be dealt with
in a particular way). — *v.i.* (*arch.*) to be necessary. —
ns. **needcess'ity** a dialect or illiterate combination of
need and **necessity; need'er.** — *adj.* **need'ful** full of need:
having need: needy: necessary: requisite. — *adv.* **need'-
fully.** — *n.* **need'fulness.** — *adv.* **need'ily.** — *n.* **need'-
iness.** — *adj.* **need'less** having no need (*Shak.*): not
needed: unnecessary. — *adv.* **need'lessly.** — *n.* **need'-
lessness.** — *adv.* **need'ly** (*Shak.*) necessarily. — *n.*
need'ment (*Spens.*) something needed. — *adv.* **needs** of
necessity: indispensably. — *adj.* **need'y** very poor:
necessary (*Shak.*). — *n.* **need'y-hood** (*Herrick*). —
need'-be a necessity; **need'-fire** fire produced by friction, to which a certain virtue is superstitiously attached: a beacon. — **must needs, needs must** (often
iron.) must inevitably; **the needful** (*slang*) ready money:
whatever is requisite, usu. in *do the needful* (*coll.*).
[O.E. *nēd, nīed, nyd*; Du. *nood*, Ger. *Noth* (mod. *Not*).]

needle *nēd'l, n.* a small, sharp instrument for sewing: any
similar slender, pointed instrument, as for knitting,
etching, playing gramophone records, dissection,
(hooked) for crochet: the suspended magnet of a
compass or galvanometer: a pointer on a dial: the
pointed end of a hypodermic syringe: a hypodermic
injection (*coll.*): anything sharp and pointed: a pinnacle of rock: an obelisk: a long slender crystal: a
strong beam passed through a wall as a temporary
support: a long, narrow, stiff leaf: a feeling of irritation
(*slang*): dislike, enmity (*slang*). — *adj.* (of a contest)
intensely keen and acutely critical. — *v.t.* to sew: to
pierce: to penetrate: to thread: to pass through: to
underpin with needles: to irritate, goad, heckle. — *v.i.*
to pass out and in: to sew. — *ns.* **need'leful** as much
thread as will serve conveniently for one threading of
a needle; **need'ler** a needlemaker. — *adj.* **need'ly** like
needles. — **need'le-bath** a shower-bath with very fine
strong jets; **need'le-book** a needle-case in book form;
need'le-case a case for holding needles; **need'lecord** a
cotton material with closer ribs and flatter pile than
corduroy; **need'le-craft** the art of needlework; **need'le=
fish** a pipe-fish: a garpike; **need'le-furze** the petty whin;
need'le-gun a gun in which the cartridge is exploded
by the impact of a spike; **need'le-paper** black paper
used for wrapping needles; **need'le-point** the point of
a needle: a very sharp point: point-lace made with a
needle: embroidery on canvas, done with woollen
yarns, used on chair-covers, etc. — *adj.* **need'le-point'ed**
pointed like a needle, round in section: without a barb,
as a fish-hook. — **needle time** the amount of time
allowed to a radio channel for the broadcasting of
recorded music; **need'le-tin** cassiterite in slender crystals; **need'lewoman** a woman who does needlework: a
seamstress; **need'lework** work done with a needle: the
business of a seamstress. — **get the needle** (*coll.*) to be
irritated; **give the needle to** to irritate; **look for a needle
in a haystack, bottle of hay** to engage in a hopeless
search. [O.E. *nǣdl*; Ger. *Nadel*; cog. with Ger. *nähen*,
to sew; L. *nēre*, to spin.]

neeld *nēld*, **neele** *nēl*, obsolete forms of **needle.**

neem. Same as **nim³.**

neep *nēp, (Scot.) n.* a turnip. [O.E. *nǣp* — L. *nāpus*.]

ne'er *nār, adv.* contr. of **never.** — *adj.* and *n.* **ne'er'-do-well**
(*Scot.* **-weel**) good-for-nothing.

Ne'erday *nār'dā, (chiefly Scot.) n.* New Year's Day:
(without *cap.*) a gift on New Year's Day.

neesberry. Same as **naseberry.**

neeze, neese *nēz, v.i.* and *n.* sneeze. [Cf. O.N. *hnjōsa*,
and **sneeze.**]

nef *nef, n.* a church nave (*obs.*): a mediaeval, usually shiplike, piece of plate for a great lord's napkin, table utensils, etc. [Fr. *nef*, ship, nave — L. *nāvis*.]

nefandous *ni-fan'dəs*, *adj.* abominable. [L. *nefandus*, unspeakable — *ne-*, not, *fandus*, to be spoken — *fārī*, to speak.]

nefarious *ni-fā'ri-əs*, *adj.* extremely wicked: villainous. — *adv.* **nefā'riously.** — *n.* **nefā'riousness.** — *adj.* **nefast** (*ni-fast'*) abominable. [L. *nefārius*, *nefāstus* — *nefās*, wrong, crime — *ne-*, not, *fās*, divine law, prob. from *fārī*, to speak.]

neg, **neg.** Abbrev. of **negative.**

negate *ni-gāt'*, *v.t.* to deny: to nullify: to imply the non-existence of: to make ineffective. — *ns.* **negation** (*-gā'shən*) the act of saying no: denial: a negative proposition (*log.*): something that is the opposite (of a positive quality, state, etc.): a thing characterised by the absence of qualities; **negā'tionist** one who merely denies, without offering any positive assertion. — *adj.* **negative** (*neg'ə-tiv*) denying: expressing denial, refusal, or prohibition (opp. to *affirmative*): denying the connection between a subject and a predicate (*log.*): lacking positive quality: failing to affirm: opposite, contrary to, neutralising, that which is regarded as positive: censorious (*U.S.*): defeatist: obstructive, unconstructive: less than nothing (*math.*): reckoned or measured in the opposite direction to that chosen as positive (*math.*): at relatively lower potential (*elect.*): of, having, or producing negative electricity (*elect.*; see below): having dark for light and light for dark (*opt.*, *phot.*): in complementary colours (*opt.*, *phot.*): acid (*chem.*): laevorotatory (*opt.*): having the index of refraction for the extraordinary ray less than for the ordinary in double refraction (*opt.*): in a direction away from the source of stimulus (*biol.*). — *n.* a word or statement by which something is denied: a word or grammatical form that expresses denial: a negative proposition or term: the right or act of saying no, or of refusing assent: the side of a question or the decision which denies what is affirmed: an image in which the lights and shades are reversed: a photographic plate bearing such an image: a negative quantity. — *v.t.* to prove the contrary of: to reject by vote: to veto: to reject by veto: to deny: to neutralise. — *adv.* **neg'atively.** — *ns.* **neg'ativeness; neg'ativism** the doctrine or attitude of a negationist: a tendency to do the opposite of what one is asked to do; **negativ'ity** the fact of being negative. — *adj.* **neg'atory** expressing denial. — *n.* **negatron** (*neg'ə-tron*) a negative electron, as opp. to a positron. — **negative angle** one generated by a straight line moving clockwise; **negative electricity** electricity arising from the excess of electrons; **negative income tax** see **income; negative interest** money charged on or deducted from interest on bank deposits, etc.; **negative pole** that pole of a magnet which turns to the south when the magnet swings freely; **negative proton** an antiproton; **negative sign** the sign (−, read *minus*) of subtraction. [L. *negāre*, *-ātum*, to deny.]

neglect *ni-glekt'*, *v.t.* to treat carelessly: to pass by without notice: to omit by carelessness: to fail to bestow due care upon. — *n.* disregard: slight: omission: uncaredfor state. — *adj.* **neglect'able** (*rare*) negligible. — *ns.* **neglect'edness; neglect'er.** — *adj.* **neglect'ful** careless: accustomed to omit or neglect things: slighting. — *adv.* **neglect'fully.** — *n.* **neglect'fulness.** — *adv.* **neglect'ingly** carelessly: heedlessly. — *n.* **neglection** (*-glek'shən*; *Shak.*) negligence. — *adj.* **neglect'ive** (now *rare*) neglectful. [L. *neglegĕre*, *neglectum* — *neg-* or *nec-*, not, *legĕre*, to gather.]

négligé *nā'glē-zhā*, *n.* easy undress. — *adj.* carelessly or unceremoniously dressed: careless. — *n.* **negligee** (*neg'-li-jē*, *neg'li-zhā*), **negligée** (*neg'li-zhā*) a loose gown worn by women in the 18th century: a woman's loose decorative dressing-gown of flimsy material: a necklace, usually of red coral. [Fr., neglected.]

negligence *neg'li-jəns*, *n.* the fact or quality of being negligent: want of proper care: habitual neglect: an act of carelessness or neglect (*arch.*): a slight: carelessness

about dress, manner, etc.: omission of duty, esp. such care for the interests of others as the law may require. — *adj.* **neg'ligent** neglecting: careless: inattentive: disregarding ceremony or fashion. — *adv.* **neg'ligently.** — *n.* **negligibil'ity.** — *adj.* **neg'ligible** (sometimes **neg'-ligeable**) such as may be ignored because very little or very unimportant. — *adv.* **neg'ligibly.** [L. *negligentia* for *neglegentia* — *neglegĕre*, to neglect.]

négociant *nā-gō-sē-ã*, (Fr.) *n.* a merchant, esp. a winemerchant.

negotiate *ni-gō'shi-āt*, *v.i.* to traffic: to bargain: to confer for the purpose of mutual arrangement. — *v.t.* to arrange for by agreement: to manage: to transfer or exchange for value: to cope with successfully (*coll.*). — *n.* **negotiabil'ity.** — *adj.* **nego'tiable.** — *ns.* **negotiā'-tion; nego'tiātor:** — *fem.* **nego'tiatress** (*-shyə-*), **negotiatrix** (*ni-gō'shyə-triks*, or *ni-gō-shi-ā'triks*). [L. *negōtiārī*, *-ātus* — *negōtium*, business — *neg-*, not, *ōtium*, leisure.]

Negrillo *ni-gril'ō*, *n.* an African Negrito: — *pl.* **Negrill'os.** [Sp., dim. of *negro*, black.]

Negrito *ni-grē'tō*, *n.* a member of any of a number of pygmy negroid peoples of S.-E. Asia and Africa: — *pl.* **Negri'tos.** [Sp., dim. of *negro*, black.]

negritude, négritude. See **Negro.**

Negro *nē'grō*, *n.* (formerly also without *cap.*) a member of any of the dark-skinned peoples of Africa or a person racially descended from one of these: — *pl.* **Ne'groes.** — *adj.* of or pertaining to Negroes. — *ns.* **Ne'gress** (sometimes *derog.*; formerly also without *cap.*) a Negro woman or girl; **nē'gritude** translation of French **négritude** (apparently invented by the poet Aimé Césaire) the essential quality of the Negro genius. — Also **nigritude.** — *adj.* **ne'groid** of Negro type: having physical characteristics associated with Negro races, e.g. full lips, tightly curling hair, etc. — *n.* one who is of Negro type: one who is a Negro in a broad sense only. — *adj.* **negroid'al.** — *ns.* **ne'grōism** any peculiarity of speech among Negroes, esp. in the southern U.S.: devotion to the cause of the Negroes; **ne'grophil, ne'grophile** a friend of the Negro, and a supporter of his cause; **negrophilism** (*ni-grof'*); **negroph'ilist; ne'grophobe** one who dislikes Negroes; **negropho'bia.** — **ne'gro-corn** (*W.Indies*) durra; **ne'gro-head** tobacco soaked in molasses and pressed into cakes, so called from its blackness: an inferior rubber. [Sp. *negro* — L. *niger*, *nigra*, *nigrum*, black.]

negus[1] *nē'gəs*, *n.* port or sherry with hot water, sweetened and spiced. [Said to be from Colonel *Negus*, its first maker, in Queen Anne's time.]

negus[2] *nē'gəs*, *n.* the king of Abyssinia. [Amharic.]

neif. Same as **nieve.**

neigh *nā*, *v.i.* to utter the cry of a horse. — *n.* the cry of a horse. [O.E. *hnǣgan*.]

neighbour, (*U.S.*) **neighbor**, *nā'bər*, *n.* a person who dwells near another: a person or thing that is near another: one of a pair (*Scot.*). — *adj.* (*arch.* and *U.S.*) neighbouring. — *v.t.* and *v.i.* to live or be near. — *n.* **neigh'bourhood** state of being neighbours, kindly feeling: a set of neighbours: a district, locality, esp. with reference to its inhabitants as a community: a district: a region lying near: a near position: nearness: all the points that surround a given point in a specified degree of closeness (*math.*). — *adj.* **neigh'bouring** being near: adjoining. — *n.* **neigh'bourliness.** — *adj.* **neigh'bourly** like or becoming a neighbour: friendly: social. — Also *adv.* — *adj.* **neigh'bour-stained** (*Shak.*) stained with neighbours' blood. — **good neighbours** the fairies; **in the neighbourhood of** approximately, somewhere about; **neighbourhood law centre** see under **law.** [O.E. *nēahgebūr* — *nēah*, near, *gebūr* or *būr*, a farmer.]

neist *nēst*, a dialectal form of **nighest** (*obs.*), **next.**

neither *nī'dhər*, or *nē'dhər*, *adj.* and *pron.* not either. — *conj.* not either: and not: nor yet. — *adv.* not at all: in no case. [O.E. *nāther*, *nāwther*, abbrev. of *nāhwæther* — *nā*, never, *hwæther*, whether; the vowel assimilated to **either.**]

neive. Same as **nieve.**

nek *nek,* (*S.Afr.*) *n.* a col.   [Du., neck.]

nekton *nek'ton, n.* the assemblage of actively swimming organisms in a sea, lake, etc.   [Gr. *nēkton* (neut.), swimming.]

nelis, nelies *nel'is, n.* a winter pear: — *pl.* **nel'is, nel'ies.** [Fr. *nélis.*]

nellie, nelly, not on your (*nel'i; slang*) not on any account — said to be from *not on your Nellie Duff,* rhyming with *puff,* meaning 'life'.

nelly *nel'i, n.* a large petrel.   [Perh. the woman's name.]

nelson *nel'sən, n.* a wrestling hold in which the arms are passed under both the opponent's arms from behind, and the hands joined so that pressure can be exerted with the palms on the back of his neck. — Also **full nelson.** — **half nelson** this hold applied on one side only, i.e. with one arm under one of the opponent's arms: a disabling restraint (*fig.*).   [From the proper name.]

Nelumbium *ni-lum'bi-əm,* **Nelumbo** *-bō, ns.* a genus of water-lilies including the Egyptian bean of Pythagoras, and the sacred lotus: (without *cap.*) a plant of this genus: — *pl.* **nelum'biums, nelum'bos.**   [Prob. Tamil.]

Nemathelminthes *nem-ə-thel-min'thēz, n.pl.* according to some, a group including nematodes, Nematomorpha, and Acanthocephala. — *n.sing.* **nemathel'minth.** — *adj.* **nemathelmin'thic.**   [Gr. *nēma, -atos,* a thread, *helmins, -minthos,* worm.]

nematic *nə-mat'ik,* (*chem.*) *adj.* being in, or having, a mesomorphic phase in which the atoms or molecules are arranged in parallel lines, but not in the parallel planes typical of a smectic substance.   [Gr. *nēma,* gen. *nēmatos,* a thread.]

nematocyst *nem'ət-ō-sist,* or *-at', n.* a stinging organ in jellyfishes, etc., a sac from which a stinging thread can be everted.   [Gr. *nēma, -atos,* a thread, *kystis,* a bladder.]

nematode *nem'ə-tōd, n.* a round-worm or thread-worm. — Also *adj.* — *ns.pl.* **Nematōd'a, Nematoid'ea** the nematodes. — *ns.* **nematodiri'asis** (Gr. *-iāsis,* as in *psoriasis,* etc.) a disease of young lambs caused by nematodirus larvae; **Nematodi'rus** (Gr. *deirē,* neck) a genus of parasitic nematode worms found in the intestines of mammals: (without *cap.*) a worm of this genus. — *adj.* **nem'atoid.** — *ns.* **nematol'ogist; nematol'ogy** the study of nematodes.   [Gr. *nēma, -atos,* thread, *eidos,* form.]

Nematomorpha *nem-ət-ō-mör'fə, n.pl.* the hair-worms.   [Gr. *nēma, -atos,* thread, *morphē,* form.]

nematophore *nem'ət-ō-fōr, -för, n.* a mouthless type of hydrozoan polyp that engulfs food by pseudopodia.   [Gr. *nēma, -atos,* thread, *phoros,* carrying.]

Nembutal® *nem'bū-təl, n.* proprietary name for sodium ethylmethylbutyl barbiturate, used as a sedative, hypnotic, and antispasmodic.

Nemean *nem-ē'ən, nem'i-ən, nēm'i-ən, adj.* of Nemea (Gr. *Nēmeā*), valley of Argolis, famous for its games held in the second and fourth years of each Olympiad, and for the lion slain by Herakles.

Nemertinea *nem-ər-tin'i-ə, n.pl.* a phylum of worm-like animals, mostly marine, ciliated, often brightly coloured with protrusile proboscis. — Also **Nemer'tea.** — *ns.* and *adjs.* **nemer'tean, nemer'tine, nemer'tian.**   [Gr. *Nēmertēs,* one of the nereids.]

Nemesia *nem-ē'zh(y)ə, -sh(y)ə, -si-ə, n.* a S. African genus of the figwort family, including some brightly coloured garden flowers: (without *cap.*) a plant of this genus.   [Gr. *nemesion,* a kind of catchfly.]

Nemesis *nem'i-sis,* (*myth.*) *n.* the Greek goddess of retribution: (without *cap.*) retributive justice.   [Gr. *nemesis,* retribution — *nemein,* to deal out, dispense.]

nemine contradicente *nem'ə-nē kon-trə-di-sen'tē, nā'mi-ne kon-trä-dē-ken'te,* (L.; often abbrev. **nem. con.**) without opposition: no-one speaking in opposition; **nemine dissentiente** (*di-sen-shi-en'tē, -ti-en'te*) no-one dissenting.

nemn. See **nempt.**

Nemophila *nem-of'i-lə, n.* a N. American genus of *Hydrophyllaceae,* favourite garden annuals, esp. one with blue, white-centred flowers: (without *cap.*) a plant of this genus.   [Gr. *nemos,* a glade, wooded pasture, *phileein,* to love.]

nemoral *nem'ə-rəl, adj.* of a wood or grove. — *adj.* **nem'orous** wooded.   [L. *nemus, -ŏris,* a grove.]

nempt *nemt,* (*Spens.*) named, called: — *pa.p.* of obs. vb. **nemn** to name.   [O.E. *nemnan.*]

nene *nā'nā, n.* the Hawaiian goose, a rare bird of Hawaii, having grey-brown plumage, a black face and partially-webbed feet.   [Hawaiian.]

nenuphar *nen'ū-fär, n.* a water-lily, esp. the common white or yellow: (with *cap.*) a synonym of Nuphar.   [L.L. *nenuphar* — Ar. and Pers. *nīnūfar, nīlūfar* — Sans. *nīlotpala* — *nīla,* blue, *utpala,* lotus.]

Neo *nē'ō, nā'ō, n.* an artificial language launched by an Italian, Arturo Alfandari, in 1961.

neo- *nē'ō-,* in composition, new, young, revived in a new form. — *n.* **nē'oblast** (Gr. *blastos,* a shoot, bud) in many of the lower animals such as the Annelida, any of the large amoeboid cells which play an important part in the phenomena of regeneration. — *adj.* and *n.* **Neo-Cath'olic** of, or a member of the school of, liberal Catholicism that followed Lamennais, Lacordaire and Montalembert about 1830: Anglo-Catholic with extreme leanings towards Rome. — *n.* **Neoceratodus** (*-ser-a-tō'dəs*) the name of the genus to which the barramunda belongs, now used in preference to Ceratodus. — *adj.* and *n.* **Neo-Chris'tian** of, or a believer in, a liberalised and rationalised Christianity. — *n.* **Neo-Christian'ity.** — *adjs.* **neoclass'ic, -al** belonging to a revival of classicism, or classicism as understood by those who would revive it, e.g. in the 18th century. — *ns.* **neoclass'icism** (*-i-sizm*); **neoclass'icist; neocolōn'ialism** the policy of a strong nation of obtaining control over a weaker through economic pressure, etc. — *adj.* and *n.* **Neocom'ian** (*-kō'mi-ən; geol.*; L. *Neocōmium,* Neuchâtel — Gr. *kōmē,* a village) Lower Cretaceous. — *n.* **Neo-Dar'winism** a later development of Darwinism, laying greater stress upon natural selection and denying the inheritance of acquired characters. — *ns.* and *adjs.* **Neo-Darwin'ian, Neo-Dar'winist.** — *n.* **neodymium** (*-dim'i-əm*) a metal (Nd; at. numb. 60), the chief component of the once-supposed element *didymium* (q.v.); **Neofascism** (*-fash'izm*) a movement attempting to reinstate the policies of fascism; **Neofasc'ist; Neogaea** (*-jē'ə; biol.*; Gr. *gaia,* the earth) the Neotropical region. — *adj.* **Neogae'an.** — *n.* and *adj.* **Neogene** (*-jēn'; geol.*; Gr. *neogenēs,* new-born) Miocene and Pliocene. — *n.* **neogenesis** (*-jen'ə-sis; biol.* etc.) regeneration of tissue. — *adj.* **neogenetic** (*-et'*). — *n.* and *adj.* **Neo-Goth'ic** revived Gothic of the 19th century. — *ns.* **neogramma'rian** a philologist of the 19th-century German school that introduced scientific exactitude into the study of sound change; **Neohell'enism** the modern Hellenism inspired by the ancient: the devotion to ancient Greek ideals in literature and art, esp. in the Italian Renaissance; **Neo-Impress'ionism** a style of painting which aimed at producing greater luminosity of colour by applying pure unmixed colours in small dots; **Neo-Kant'ianism** the philosophy of *Kant* as taught by his successors. — *n.* and *adj.* **Neo-Kan'tian.** — *n.* **Neo-Lamarck'ism** a modern adaptation of Lamarckism. — *n.* and *adj.* **Neo-Lamarck'ian.** — *n.* and *adj.* **Neo-Lat'in** Romance, i.e. Italian, Rhaeto-Romanic, French, Provençal, Spanish, Portuguese, and Rumanian. — *adj.* **Neolithic** (*-lith'ik*; Gr. *lithos,* a stone) of the later or more advanced Stone Age. — *ns.* **ne'olith** a Neolithic artefact; **neol'ogy** (Gr. *logos,* a word) the introduction of new words, or new senses of old words: a neologism: new doctrines, esp. German rationalism (*theol.*); **neolō'gian.** — *adjs.* **neologic** (*-loj'*), **-al.** — *adv.* **neolog'ically.** — *v.i.* **neol'ogise, -ize** to introduce new words or doctrines. — *ns.* **neol'ogism** a new word, phrase, or doctrine: the use of old words in a new sense; **neol'ogist.** — *adjs.* **neologis'-**

tic, -al. — *ns.* **Neo-Malthus′ianism** doctrine of the necessity for birth-control to control population; **Neo-Melanē′sian** a language based on English, developed in Melanesia; **neomycin** (-*mī′sin*; Gr. *mykēs,* a fungus) an antibiotic effective against certain infections, esp. infections of the skin, eyes. — *adj.* **neonāt′al** pertaining to the newly born. — *adj.* and *n.* **ne′onate** (one) newly born. — *ns.* **neonatol′ogy** the care and treatment of the newly born; **neo-Naz′i** a member or supporter of any of a number of modern movements espousing the principles of National Socialism or the like; **neo-Nazism; neonō′mianism** (Gr. *nomos,* law) the doctrine that the gospel is a new law and that faith has abrogated the old moral obedience. — *n.* and *adj.* **neonō′mian.** — *n.* **neopā′ganism** a revival of paganism, or its spirit. — *n.* and *adj.* **neopā′gan.** — *v.t.* and *v.i.* **neopā′ganise, -ize.** — *ns.* **nē′ophile** one who loves novelty and new things: one who is obsessive about keeping up to date with fashion, trends, etc.; **neophīl′ia; neophīl′iac; neophobia** (-*fō′bi-ə*; Gr. *phobos,* fear) dread of novelty; **neophyte** (*nē′ō-fīt;* Gr. *neophytos,* newly planted — *phyein,* to produce) a new convert: one newly baptised: a newly ordained priest: a novice in a religious order: a tiro or beginner. — *adj.* **neophytic** (-*fit′ik*). — *ns.* **Neopilina** (-*pil-ī′nə; Pilina,* a Palaeolithic genus of similar appearance) a genus of Monoplacophora (q.v.); **neo′plasm** (Gr. *plasma,* form, mould) a morbid new growth or formation of tissue. — *adj.* **neoplas′tic.** — *ns.* **Neo-Plas′ticism** (or **neoplasticism**) a style of abstract painting in which geometrical patterns are formed of patches of flat colour enclosed by intersecting vertical and horizontal lines (see **plastic**); **Neoplā′tonism** a combination of Platonism with Oriental elements, developed by Plotinus, Porphyry, Proclus, etc. — *adj.* **Neoplatonic** (-*plə-ton′ik*). — *ns.* **neoplā′tonist; neoprene** (*nē′ō-prēn*) an oil-resisting and heat-resisting synthetic rubber made by polymerising chloroprene; **Neopythagorē′anism** a revived Pythagoreanism of Alexandria beginning in the first century B.C. — *n.* and *adj.* **Neopythagorē′an.** — *n.* **neorē′alism** a modern form of realism in the arts and literature: particularly, an esp. Italian movement in cinematography concentrating on social themes and the realistic depiction of life, esp. of the lower classes. — *n.* and *adj.* **neorē′alist.** — *adj.* **neorealist′ic.** — *ns.* **neoteny, neoteinia** (*nē-ot′ən-i, nē-ō-tī′ni-ə;* Gr. *teinein,* to stretch) prolonged retention of larval or immature character or characters in the adult form. — *adjs.* **neotenic** (*nē-ō-ten′ik*), **-tein′ic; neot′enous; Neotrop′ical** (*biol.*) of tropical America. — *ns.* **neovī′talism** the theory or belief that complete causal explanation of vital phenomena cannot be reached without invoking some extra-material concept; **neovī′talist.** — *adj.* **Neozoic** (*nē-ō-zō′ik;* Gr. *zōikos,* of animals) later than Palaeozoic: later than Mesozoic. [Gr. *neos,* new.]

neon *nē′on, n.* a gaseous element (Ne; at. numb. 10) found in the atmosphere by Sir Wm. Ramsay (1852–1916). — **neon lamp, light** an electric discharge lamp containing neon, giving a red glow, used e.g. for advertising signs: (*loosely*) one of a variety of tubular fluorescent lamps giving light of various colours; **neon lighting.** [Neuter of Gr. *neos,* new.]

neonatal . . . to . . . **neoteny.** See **neo-**.

neoteric, -al *nē-ō-ter′ik, -əl, adjs.* of recent origin, modern. — *adv.* **neoter′ically.** — *v.i.* **neoterise, -ize** (*ni-ot′ə-rīz*). — *ns.* **neot′erism** the introduction of new things, esp. new words; **neot′erist.** [Gr. *neōterikos* — *neōteros,* compar. of *neos,* new.]

Neotropical . . . to . . . **Neozoic.** See **neo-**.

nep *nep,* **nip** *nip, ns.* catmint. [L. *nepeta.*]

nepenthe *ni-pen′thē, n.* a sorrow-lulling drink or drug (*poet.*): the plant yielding it. — *adj.* **nepen′thean.** — *n.* **Nepen′thes** (-*thēz*) nepenthe: the pitcher-plant genus, constituting a family **Nepenthā′ceae** akin to the family Sarracenia and the sundews. [Gr. *nepenthēs, -es* — pfx. *nē-,* not, *penthos,* grief.]

neper *nā′pər, nē′, n.* a unit for expressing the ratio of two currents, or two voltages, etc., the number of nepers being equal to the natural logarithm of the ratio. (Cf. **decibel, bel.**) [John *Napier;* see **Napierian.**]

nephalism *nef′ə-lizm, n.* total abstinence from alcoholic drinks. — *n.* **neph′alist.** [Gr. *nēphalios,* sober; *nēphein,* to be sober.]

nepheline *nef′ə-lēn, n.* a rock-forming mineral, silicate of sodium, potassium, and aluminium, colourless, usually crystallising in hexagonal prisms. — Also **neph′-elite.** — *n.* **neph′elinite** a basalt-like rock compound of nepheline and pyroxene, with no feldspar or olivine. — **neph′eline-bas′alt** a basalt with nepheline instead of (or in addition to) feldspar. [Gr. *nephelē,* a cloud (from the clouding effect of acid on it).]

nephelometer *nef-ə-lom′i-tər, n.* an instrument for measuring cloudiness, esp. in liquids. — *adj.* **nephelomet′ric.** — *n.* **nephelom′etry.** [Gr. *nephelē,* cloud, *metron,* measure.]

nephew *nev′ū,* or *nef′ū, n.* the son of a brother or sister: extended to a like relation by marriage: a grandson or descendant (*obs.*): a pope's or priest's son (*euph.*): — *fem.* **niece.** [(O.)Fr. *neveu* — L. *nepōs, nepōtis,* grandson; cf. O.E. *nefa,* Ger. *Neffe,* nephew.]

nepho- *nef-o-, -ō-,* in composition, cloud. — *ns.* **neph′ogram** a photograph of a cloud; **neph′ōgraph** (-*gräf*) an instrument for photographing clouds in order to determine their position; **nephology** (*nef-ol′ə-ji*) the study of clouds in meteorology. — *adjs.* **nephologic** (-*ə-loj′*), **-al.** — *ns.* **nephol′ogist; neph′ōscope** an apparatus which determines the direction and velocity of movement of clouds. [Gr. *nephos,* cloud.]

nephr(o)- *nef-r(o)-, -r(ō)-,* in composition, kidney. — *ns.* **nephralgia** (*nef-ral′ji-ə*), **nephral′gy** pain in the kidneys; **nephrec′tomy** surgical removal of a kidney. — *adj.* **neph′ric.** — *ns.* **nephrid′ium** in invertebrates and lower chordates, an organ serving the function of a kidney; **neph′rīte** the mineral jade, in the narrower sense — an old charm against kidney disease; **nephrīt′ic** (*obs.*) a medicine for the kidneys. — *adjs.* **nephrīt′ic, -al** pertaining to the kidneys, or nephritis, or jade. — *n.* **nephrī′tis** inflammation of the kidneys. — *adjs.* **neph′-roid** kidney-shaped; **nephrolog′ical.** — *ns.* **nephrol′ogist; nephrology** the science concerned with structure, functions, diseases, of the kidneys; **neph′ron** one of the filtering units of the kidney; **nephrop′athy** (Gr. *pathos,* suffering) disease of the kidneys; **neph′ropexy** (Gr. *pēxis,* fixing) fixation of a floating kidney; **nephropto′-sis** (Gr. *ptōsis,* fall) floating kidney; **nephrō′sis** a disease of the kidney characterised by non-inflammatory degeneration of the tubules. — *adj.* **nephrōt′ic.** — *n.* **nephrot′omy** incision into the kidney. [Gr. *nephros,* a kidney.]

nepionic *nep′i-on-ik, nēp′i-on-ik,* (*biol.*) *adj.* pertaining to the embryonic period in the life-history of an individual. [Gr. *nēpios,* infant.]

nepit. See **nit**[4].

ne plus ultra *nē plus ul′trə, nā ploōs ool′trä,* (L.) nothing further: the uttermost point or extreme perfection of anything.

nepotism *nep′o-tizm, n.* undue patronage to one's relations, esp. by a pope. — *adjs.* **nepotic** (*ni-pot′ik*), **nepotis′tic.** — *n.* **nep′otist.** [L. *nepōs, nepōtis,* a grandson.]

Neptune *nep′tūn, n.* the Roman sea-god, identified with the Greek Poseidon: a remote planet of the solar system, discovered in 1846. — *adj.* **Neptū′nian** pertaining to Neptune or to the sea: formed by water (*geol.*). — *n.* an inhabitant of Neptune: a Neptunist. — *ns.* **Nep′tūnist** a believer in the origin of rocks generally as chemical precipitates from the sea — opp. to *Plutonist* or *Vulcanist;* **neptū′nium** an element (Np; at. numb. 93) named as next after uranium, as Neptune is next after Uranus. — **neptunium series** a series formed by the decay of artificial radio-elements, the first member being plutonium-241 and the last bismuth-209 — neptunium-237 being the longest-lived. [L. *Neptūnus.*]

nerd, nurd *nûrd, (slang) n.* a clumsy, or foolish, or insensitive, or irritating, etc. person. [Origin unknown.]

nereid *nē'rē-id, n.* a sea-nymph, or daughter of the sea-god *Nereus* (*Gr. myth.*): a marine polychaete worm (**Nereis,** or kindred genus) superficially like a long myriapod: (with *cap.*) the smaller of the two satellites of the planet Neptune, the other being Triton. [Gr. *nēreis* or *nēreïs — Nēreus.*]

Nerine *ni-rī'nē, n.* a South African amaryllid genus, with scarlet or rose-coloured flowers, including the Guernsey lily: (without *cap.*) a plant of this genus. [L. *nērinē,* a nereid.]

Nerita *ni-rī'tə, n.* a round-shelled genus of gasteropods of warm seas. — *n.* **nerite** (*nē'rīt*) a sea-snail of the genus Nerita or its family **Nerit'idae.** — *adj.* **neritic** (*nē-rit'ik*) belonging to the shallow waters near land. — *n.* **Neritina** (*ner-it-ī'nə*) a brackish and freshwater genus akin to Nerita. [Gr. *nēreitēs, nēritēs,* a sea-snail (of various kinds).]

Nerium *nē'ri-əm, n.* the oleander genus. [Latinised from Gr. *nērion.*]

nerka *nûr'kə, n.* the sockeye salmon. [Origin unknown.]

Nernst *närnst, adj.* invented by or due to the German chemist and physicist Walter *Nernst* (1864–1941), applied esp. to an electric lamp with a filament or rod of rare-earth oxides whose conductivity is greatly increased by heating.

nero-antico *nä-rō-an-tē'kō, n.* a deep-black marble found in Roman ruins. [It., ancient black.]

neroli *ner'ə-lē, n.* an oil distilled from orange flowers — also **neroli oil.** [Said to be named from its discoverer, an Italian princess.]

Neronian *nē-rō'ni-ən, adj.* pertaining to *Nero,* Roman emperor from A.D. 54 to 68: excessively cruel and tyrannical. — *adj.* **Neronic** (*-ron'ik*). [L. *Nērō, -ōnis.*]

nerve *nûrv, n.* a sinew (now chiefly *fig.*): a bowstring (*poet.*): strength: a cord that conveys impulses between the brain or other centre and some part of the body (*anat.*): a leaf-vein or rib (*bot.*): a nervure in an insect's wing (*entom.*): a vault rib: self-possession: cool courage: impudent assurance, audacity (*coll.*): (in *pl.*) nervousness. — *v.t.* to give strength, resolution, or courage to. — *adjs.* **nerv'al** of the nerves; **ner'vate** (of a leaf) having veins: nerved. — *ns.* **nervā'tion, nerv'ature** disposition of nerves, esp. in leaves: venation. — *adjs.* **nerved** furnished with nerves; **nerve'less** without nerves or nervures: without strength: inert: slack, flabby: unnerved: without nervousness. — *ns.* **nerve'lessness; nerve'let** a little nerve: a tendril; **nerv'er** one who, or that which, nerves. — *adj.* **nerv'ine** (*-ēn, -īn*) acting on the nerves: quieting nervous excitement. — *n.* a medicine that soothes nervous excitement. — *n.* **nerv'iness.** — *adj.* **nerv'ous** having nerve: sinewy: strong, vigorous, showing strength and vigour: pertaining to the nerves: having the nerves easily excited or weak, agitated and apprehensive (often with *of*): shy: timid: in a jumpy state. — *adv.* **nerv'ously.** — *n.* **nerv'ousness.** — *adj.* **nerv'ular.** — *ns.* **nerv'ule** a small branch of a nervure; **nervūrā'tion; nerv'ure** a leaf-vein: a chitinous strut or rib supporting and strengthening an insect's wing (*entom.*): a rib of a groined vault. — *adj.* **nerv'y** nervous: cool: calling for nerve: jumpily excited or excitable. — **nerve agent** a nerve gas or similar substance; **nerve'-cell** any cell forming part of the nervous system: a neuron; **nerve'-cen'tre** an aggregation of nerve-cells from which nerves branch out: in an organisation, the centre from which control is exercised (*fig.*); **nerve'-end', -end'ing** the free end of a nerve, generally with accessory parts forming an end-organ; **nerve'-fi'bre** an axon; **nerve gas** any of a number of gases, prepared for use in war, having a deadly effect on the nervous system, esp. on nerves controlling respiration. — *adj.* **nerve'-rack'ing, -wrack'ing** distressfully straining the nerves. — **nerve, nervous, impulse** the electrical impulse passing along a nerve fibre when it has been stimulated; **nervous breakdown** a loose term

indicating nervous debility following prolonged mental or physical fatigue: a euphemism for any mental illness; **nervous system** the brain, spinal cord, and nerves collectively. — **bundle of nerves** (*coll.*) a very timid, anxious person; **get on one's nerves** to become oppressively irritating; **live on one's nerves** to be in a tense or nervous state: to be of an excitable temperament; **lose one's nerve** to lose confidence in one's ability: to become suddenly afraid; **war of nerves** see **war**[1]. [L. *nervus,* sinew; cf. Gr. *neuron.*]

nescience *nesh'i-əns, nesh'əns, nes'i-əns, -yəns, n.* want of knowledge. — *adj.* **nesc'ient.** [L. *nescientia — nescīre,* to be ignorant — *ne-,* not, *scīre,* to know.]

nesh *nesh, (dial.) adj.* soft, crumbly: tender: delicate in one's health: cowardly, afraid: lacking energy. — *n.* **nesh'ness.** [O.E. *hnesce.*]

Nesiot, Nēsiōt *nē'si-ōt, (anthrop.) n.* an Indonesian. [Gr. *nēsiōtēs,* an islander — *nēsos,* an island.]

Neskhi, Neski *nes'ki,* **Naskhi** *nas'ki, ns.* Arabic cursive handwriting. [Ar. *naskhī.*]

ness *nes, n.* a headland. [O.E. *næs, næss.*]

nest *nest, n.* a structure prepared for egg-laying, brooding, and nursing, or as a shelter: a place of retreat, resort, residence, or lodgment: a den: a comfortable residence: a group of machine-guns in a position fortified or screened by sandbags or the like: a place where anything teems, prevails, or is fostered: the occupants of a nest, as a brood, a swarm, a gang: a set of things (as boxes, tables) fitting one within another: a set of buildings, as advance factories, divided into blocks and units: an accumulation: a tangled mass. — *v.i.* to build or occupy a nest: to go bird's-nesting. — *v.t.* and *v.i.* to lodge, settle. — *n.* **nest'er** one who builds a farm or homestead on land used for grazing cattle (*U.S. hist.; derog.*): a nest-builder. — **nest'-egg** an egg, real or sham, left or put in a nest to encourage laying: something laid up as the beginning of an accumulation: money saved; **nest'ing-box** a box set up for birds to nest in; **nest'ing-place.** — **feather one's nest** see **feather.** [O.E. *nest;* Ger. *Nest,* L. *nīdus.*]

nestle *nes'l, v.i.* to nest (*arch.*): to lie or press close or snug as in a nest: to settle comfortably or half hidden. — *v.t.* to cherish, as a bird does her young: to thrust close: to provide a nesting-place for. — *n.* **nestling** (*nes'ling,* or *nest'*) a young bird in the nest. — Also *adj.* [O.E. *nestlian — nest.*]

Nestor *nes'tör, -tər, n.* an old king of Pylos, a Greek hero at Troy remarkable for eloquence, wisdom, and long life: an old counsellor: an old man: the kea parrot genus. [Gr. *Nestor.*]

Nestorian *nes-tō'ri-ən, -ō', adj.* pertaining to *Nestorius,* patriarch of Constantinople (428–31), or to his teaching, that the divinity and humanity of Christ were not united in a single self-conscious personality. — *n.* a follower of Nestorius. — *n.* **Nesto'rianism.**

net[1] *net, n.* an open fabric, knotted into meshes: a piece or bag, or a screen or structure, of such fabric used for catching fish, butterflies, etc., carrying parcels, stopping balls, retaining hair, excluding pests: a network: machine-made lace of various kinds: a snare: a difficulty: a let (*lawn-tennis*): the shape of a three-dimensional figure when laid out flat (*math.*). — *adj.* of or like net or network. — *v.t.* to form into network: to mark or cover with network: to set with nets: to fish with nets: to form by making network: to take with a net: to capture: to send into the net. — *v.i.* to form network: — *pr.p.* **nett'ing;** *pa.t.* and *pa.p.* **nett'ed.** — *n.* **net'ful** enough to fill a net. — *adj.* **nett'ed** made into a net: reticulated: caught in a net: covered with a net. — *n.* **nett'ing** the act or process of forming network: a piece of network: any network of ropes or wire. — *adj.* **nett'y** like a net. — **net'ball** a game in which the ball is thrown into a net hung from a pole; **net'-cord** a string supporting a lawn-tennis net: a shot in which the tennis-player strikes the net-cord with the ball; **net'-fish** any fish, like the herring, usually caught in nets — opp. to *trawl-fish* and *line-fish*; **net'-fish'ery** a place for net-fishing: the business of net-fishing; **net'-fishing** fishing with nets; **net game, net'-play** (in tennis, etc.) play near the net; **net'-player; net'-prac'tice** cricket practice with nets; **nett'ing-need'le** a kind of shuttle used in netting. — *adjs.* **net'-veined** having veins that branch and meet in a network; **net'-winged** having net-veined wings. — **net'work** any structure in the form of a net: a system of lines, e.g. railway lines, resembling a net: a system of units, as, e.g. buildings, agencies, groups of persons, constituting a widely spread organisation and having a common purpose: an arrangement of electrical components: a system of stations connected for broadcasting the same programme (*radio* and *TV*): a system of computer terminals and other peripheral devices that can pass information to one another. — *v.t.* to broadcast on radio or TV stations throughout the country, as opposed to a single station covering only one region. — **dance in a net** to act in imagined concealment. [O.E. *net, nett*; Du. *net*, Ger. *Netz*.]

net², nett *net, adj.* clean (*obs.*): bright (*obs.*): unmixed, pure (*obs.*): neat, trim (*rare*): clear of all charges or deductions (opp. to *gross*): of weight, not including that of packaging: lowest, subject to no further deductions. — *v.t.* to gain or produce as clear profit: — *pr.p.* **nett'ing;** *pa.t.* and *pa.p.* **nett'ed.** [**neat².**]

nete *nē'tē*, (*Gr. mus.*) *n.* the highest string or note of the lyre. [Gr. *nētē* or *neatē* (*chordē*), lit. lowest (string).]

netheless *nedh'(ə-)les, adv.* Spens. for **nathless.**

nether *nedh'ər, adj.* lower. — *n.pl.* **neth'erlings** (*Dickens*) stockings. — *adjs.* **neth'ermore** (*rare*) lower; **neth'ermost** lowest. — *advs.* **neth'erward, -s** (*rare*) downwards. — **neth'erstock** (*hist.*) a stocking. [O.E. *neothera*, adj. — *nither*, adv., from the root *ni-*, down; Ger. *nieder*, low.]

Netherlander *nedh'ər-land-ər, n.* an inhabitant of the *Netherlands* or Low Countries, now Holland, formerly also Belgium. — *adjs.* **Netherland'ic; Neth'erlandish** Dutch.

Nethinim *neth'in-im, n.pl.* the old Jewish temple servants. [Heb. *nĕthīnīm*.]

netsuke *net'skē, -skā, ne'tsŏo-ke', n.* a small Japanese carved ornament, once used to fasten small objects, e.g. a purse or pouch for tobacco, medicines, etc., to a sash — now collectors' pieces. [Jap. *ne*, root, bottom, *tsuke* — *tsukeru*, to attach.]

nett. See **net².**

nettle¹ *net'l, n.* a common weed (Urtica) with stinging hairs. — *v.t.* to sting: to sting with annoyance. — *adj.* **nett'lesome** irritable. — **nett'le-cell** a nematocyst; **nett'le-cloth** cloth of nettle-fibre: thick japanned cotton; **nett'le-fish** a jellyfish; **nett'le-rash** a rash of red or white weals with irritation like nettle-stings: urticaria; **nett'le-tree** a tree (*Celtis*) of the elm family, with nettle-shaped leaves, edible drupes, and wood good for turning: a tropical and Australian genus (*Laportea*) of the nettle family, with virulently stinging leaves. — **dead-nettle, hemp-nettle** see **dead, hemp.** — **grasp the nettle** to set about an unpleasant task, duty, etc. with firmness and resolution. [O.E. *netele*; Ger. *Nessel*.]

nettle². Same as **knittle.**

netty, network, etc. See **net¹.**

neuk *nük, nūk,* a Scots form of **nook.**

neume *nūm, n.* in mediaeval music, a succession of notes sung to one syllable: a sign giving a rough indication of rise or fall of pitch. — Also **neum.** [O.Fr., — Gr. *pneuma*, breath.]

neur- *nūr-,* **neuro-** *nū'rō-,* in composition, pertaining to a nerve-cell, to a nerve-fibre, to nerve-tissue, or to the nervous system (esp. the brain and spinal cord): pertaining to the nerves and some other system (e.g. **neurovas'cular, neuromus'cular**) concerned with, dealing with, the nervous system (e.g. **neuroanat'omist, -anat'omy; neurobiol'ogist, -biology; neurophysiol'ogy; neuropsychi'atry; neuropsychol'ogy; neuroradiol'ogy; neur'osurgeon, neurosur'gery**). — *adj.* **neu'ral** of, or

relating to, nerves: dorsal (opp. to *haemal*). — *n.* **neuralgia** (*nū-ral'jə, -jyə;* Gr. *algos,* pain) paroxysmal intermittent pain along the course of a nerve: pain of a purely nervous character. — *adj.* **neural'gic.** — *ns.* **neurasthenia** (*nū-rəs-thē'ni-ə;* Gr. *astheneia,* weakness) nervous debility; **neurasthē'niac** one suffering from neurasthenia. — *adj.* **neurasthenic** (*-then'ik,* or *-thēn'-ik*). — Also *n.* a neurastheniac. — *ns.* **neurā'tion** nervation; **neurec'tomy** the surgical excision of part of a nerve; **neurilemm'a, neurolemm'a** (Gr. *eilēma,* covering) the external sheath of a nerve-fibre; **neuril'ity** the essential character of nerve; **neur'ine** (*-ēn, -in, -īn*) a very poisonous ptomaine formed in putrefying flesh; **neur'ism** a supposed 'nerve-force' acting in evolution (cf. **bathmism**); **neur'ite** an axon or dendrite. — *adj.* **neuritic** (*-it'ik*) relating to, of the nature of, or having, neuritis. — *n.* one suffering from neuritis. — *ns.* **neurī'tis** inflammation of a nerve; **neuroanatomist, -anatomy, neurobiologist, -biology** see **neur-** above; **neur'oblast** an embryonic nerve-cell. — *adj.* **neuroen'docrine** pertaining to the nervous and endocrine systems, and to their interaction. — *ns.* **neuroendocrinol'ogy** the study of the interaction of the nervous and endocrine systems; **neuroethol'ogy** the description of features of animal behaviour in terms of the mechanisms of the nervous system; **neurofibrō'ma** a fibroma of the peripheral nerves: — *pl.* **-mas, -mata; neurofibromatō'sis** a condition characterised by the formation of neurofibromas and areas of dark pigmentation on the skin. — *adj.* **neurogen'ic** caused or stimulated by the nervous system. — *n.* **neurog'lia** (Gr. *gliā,* glue) the supporting tissue of the brain and spinal cord, etc.; **neur'ogram** same as **engram; neurohypnol'ogy, neurypnol'ogy** old names for the science of hypnotism. — *n.* and *adj.* **neurolep'tic** (a drug) which reduces nervous tension. — *n.* **neur'olinguist.** — *adj.* **neurolinguis'tic.** — *n.sing.* **neurolinguis'tics** the branch of linguistics which deals with the processing and storage of language in the brain. — *adj.* **neurolog'ical.** — *ns.* **neurol'ogist; neurol'ogy** orig. the study of the nervous system: that branch of medicine concerned with the diagnosis and treatment of diseases of the nervous system; **neurol'ysis** breaking down of nerve tissue, or exhaustion of a nerve; **neurōm'a** a tumour consisting of nerve tissue. — *adj.* **neuromuscular** see **neur-** above. — *ns.* **neu'ron, neu'rone** a nerve-cell with its processes. — *adj.* **neurōn'al.** — *n.* **neur'opath** (*-path;* Gr. *pathos,* suffering) one whose nervous system is diseased or abnormal. — *adjs.* **neuropath'ic, -al.** — *ns.* **neuropathist** (*nūr-op'ə-thist*) a specialist in nervous diseases; **neuropathol'ogy** the pathology of the nervous system; **neurop'athy** nervous disease generally; **neuropharmacol'ogist; neuropharmacol'ogy** the scientific study of the effects of drugs on the nervous system; **neurophysiology** see **neur-** above; **neur'oplasm** the protoplasm of a nerve cell; **neuropsychiatry, neuropsychology, neuroradiology** see **neur-** above; **neur'oscience** any or all of the scientific disciplines studying the nervous system and/or the mind and mental behaviour; **neurosci'entist; neuro'sis** orig., nervous activity, distinguished from or associated with mental: functional derangement through disordered nervous system, esp. without lesion of parts: mental disturbance characterised by a state of unconscious conflict, usually accompanied by anxiety and obsessional fears (also called *psychoneurosis*): (*loosely*) an obsession: — *pl.* **neurōses** (*-sēz*); **neurosurgeon, neurosurgery** see **neur-** above. — *adj.* **neurotic** (*-ot'ik*) of the nature of, characterised by, or affected by, neurosis: (*loosely*) obsessive: hypersensitive. — *n.* a person with neurosis: a medicine for nerve diseases (*arch.*). — *ns.* **neurot'icism** (*-sizm*); **neurotomy** (*-ot'ə-mi*) the surgical cutting of a nerve; **neurotox'in** a substance poisonous to nerve-tissue; **neurotransmitt'er** a chemical substance which transmits messages from one nerve-cell to another in the nervous system. — *adj.* **neurotrop'ic** having a special affinity for nerve cells. — *n.* **neurypnology** see **neurohypnology.** — **neural arch** the arch of a vertebra protecting the spinal cord; **neural plate** the part of the ectoderm of an embryo which develops into the neural tube; **neural tube** the channel formed by the closing of the edges of a fold in the ectoderm of an embryo, later developing into the spinal cord and the cerebral hemispheres. [Gr. *neuron*, a nerve.]

Neuroptera *nū-rop′tə-rə, n.pl.* a former order of insects, comprising those now placed in a superorder, **Neuropteroidea** (*nū-rop-tə-roi′di-ə*), the insects generally having four net-veined wings — alder-flies, snake-flies, lace-wings, etc. — *adj.* **neurop′terous.** — *n.* **neurop′terist** a student of the Neuropteroidea. [Gr. *neuron*, a nerve, *pteron*, a wing, *eidos*, form.]

neuston *nū′ston, n.* minute organisms on the surface of water. [Gr. neut. of *neustos*, swimming.]

neuter *nū′tər, adj.* neither one thing nor another: neutral: neither masculine nor feminine (*gram.*): neither active nor passive (*gram.*): intransitive (*gram.*): sexless: apparently sexless: sexually undeveloped: castrated: without, or without a functional, androecium or gynaeceum. — *n.* a neutral: a neuter word, plant, or animal: esp. a worker bee, ant, etc.: a castrated cat. — *v.t.* to castrate. [L. *neuter*, neither — *ne*, not, *uter*, either.]

neutral *nū′trəl, adj.* indifferent: taking no part on either side: not siding with either party: pertaining to neither party: not involved in a war or dispute: belonging to neither, esp. of two adjoining countries: of no decided character: having no decided colour: indistinct in sound: with no noticeable smell: belonging to neither of two opposites, as acid and alkaline, electrically positive and negative: neuter: without transmission of motion. — *n.* a person or nation that takes no part in a contest: a citizen or ship of a neutral state: an electric conductor ordinarily at zero potential: a position of gear in which no power is transmitted: a neuter. — *n.* **neutralisā′tion, -z-.** — *v.t.* **neu′tralise, -ize** to declare neutral: to make inert: to render of no effect: to counteract. — *ns.* **neu′traliser, -z-; neu′tralism** the policy of not entering into alliance with other nations or taking sides ideologically; **neu′tralist** one who takes or favours a neutral position (also *adj.*); **neutrality** (*-tral′i-ti*) the fact or state of being neutral: those who are neutral. — *adv.* **neu′trally.** [L. *neutrālis* — *neuter*, neither.]

neutron *nū′tron,* (*phys.*) *n.* an uncharged particle of about the same mass as the proton. — *ns.* **neutrett′o** a name suggested for a neutral meson: a type of neutrino: — *pl.* **neutrett′os; neutrino** (*-trē′nō*) an uncharged particle with zero mass when at rest: — *pl.* **neutri′nos.** — **neutron bomb** a type of nuclear bomb which destroys life by immediate intense radiation, without blast and heat effects to destroy buildings, etc.; **neutron number** the number of neutrons in the nucleus of an atom; **neutron radiography** radiography using a beam of neutrons; **neutron star** a supposed heavenly body of very small size and very great density, an almost burnt out and collapsed star, whose existence has not, however, been confirmed. [L. *neuter*, neither.]

neutrophil *nū′trō-fil, adj.* (of a cell, etc.) stainable with a neutral dye. — *n.* a neutrophil cell, etc.: a leucocyte with granular cytoplasm and a lobular nucleus. [Ger. — L. *neuter* (see **neuter**) and Gr. *philos* (see **phil-, -phil**).]

névé *nā′vā, n.* firn: the snow lying on the surface of a glacier. [Fr., — L. *nix, nivis*, snow.]

nevel *nev′əl,* (*Scot.*) *v.t.* to pound with the nieves. [**nieve.**]

never *nev′ər, adv.* not ever: at no time: in no degree: not. — *adjs.* **nev′er-end′ing; nev′er-fad′ing; nev′er-fail′ing.** — *adv.* **nev′ermore** at no future time. — **nev′er-nev′er** the hire-purchase system (*coll.*): (sometimes with *cap.*) a remote, thinly peopled or desolate area (also **never (-never) land, country** (sometimes with *caps.*)); **never= never land** (also with *caps.*) an imaginary place, imaginary conditions, too fortunate ever to exist in reality. — *advs.* **nevertheless′** notwithstanding: in spite of that; **neverthemore′** (*obs.*) none the more. — *n.* **nev′er-was′**

one who never was of any account. — **never a** no; **never so** (*arch.*) ever so. [O.E. *nǣfre* — *ne*, not, *ǣfre*, ever.]

new *nū, adj.* lately made or produced: young: fresh: not much used: having lately happened or begun to be: recent, modern: not before seen or known: only lately discovered or experienced: other than the former or preceding, different: additional: strange, unaccustomed: lately begun: beginning afresh: renewed: reformed or regenerated: restored or resumed: not of an ancient family: fresh from anything: uncultivated or only recently cultivated. — *n.* that which is new: newness. — *adv.* (often joined by hyphen to an adj.) newly: anew. — *v.t.* (*arch.*) to renew. — *v.i.* (*arch.*) to be renewed. — *adj.* **new′ish** somewhat new: nearly new. — *adv.* **new′ly** very lately: afresh (*rare*): in a new way (*rare*). — *n.* **new′ness.** — **new Australian** an immigrant to Australia; **new birth** renewal, esp. spiritual; **new blood** (a person with) fresh talent: a revitalising force. — *adjs.* **new′-blown** just come into bloom; **new′born** newly born. — **new broom** (*fig.*) see **new brooms sweep clean** under **broom; new chum** a newly-arrived and inexperienced immigrant to Australia; **New Church, New Jerusalem Church** the Swedenborgian Church. — *adj.* **new′come** recently arrived. — **new′comer** one who has lately come. — *adj.* **new′-Commonwealth** of, belonging to, members of the Commonwealth who have joined more recently than the orig. self-governing dominions. — *v.t.* **new′-create** (*Shak.*) to create anew. — **New Deal** Franklin D. Roosevelt's policies for prosperity and social improvement in the United States, 1933–40; **New Englander** a native or citizen of any of the New England states. — *adjs.* **new′-fallen** newly fallen; **newfangled** see separate article; **new= fash′ioned** made in a new way or fashion: lately come into fashion; **new′-fledged** having just got feathers; **new′-found** newly discovered or devised. — **New Jerusalem** the heavenly city (**New Jerusalem Church** see **New Church** above). — *adj.* **new′-laid** newly laid. — **New Learning** the new studies of the Renaissance; **New Left** an extreme left-wing movement among students, etc., in the 1960s; **New Light** a member of a relatively more advanced religious school — applied esp. to the party within the 18th-century Scottish Secession Church which adopted voluntaryist views of the relations of Church and State, also sometimes to the Socinianising party in the Church of Scotland in the 18th century, etc.; **new look** a change in women's fashions (1947), notably in longer and fuller skirts: a radical modification in the appearance of something. — *n.* and *adj.* **new′ly-wed** (a person who is) recently married. — *adjs.* **new′-made** recently made; **new= marr′ied** newly married. — **new maths** a method of teaching mathematics which is more concerned with basic structures and concepts than numerical drills. — *v.t.* **new′-mod′el** to model or form anew. — **new moon** the moment when the moon is directly in line between the earth and sun, and therefore invisible: the time when the waxing moon becomes visible: the narrow waxing crescent itself. — *adjs.* **new′-mown** newly mown; **new′-old** old but renewed: at once new and old. — **new poor** those who have come to think themselves poor by loss of advantages; **new rich** the recently enriched: parvenus. — *adjs.* **new′-risen** having newly risen; **new′-sad** (*Shak.*) recently made sad. — **New′-speak** a type of English described by George Orwell in his book, *Nineteen Eighty-four* (1949), developed by reducing vocabulary to such a point, and forming new words of such ugliness and so little emotive value, that literature and even thought will be impossible: (also without *cap.*) any type of language considered similar in style, etc. (esp. *pejorative*); **New Style** see **style; new town** a town planned and built by the government to aid housing conditions in near-by large cities, stimulate development, etc.; **New Wave** see **Nouvelle Vague:** a slightly later movement in jazz aiming at freedom from set patterns and styles: (also without *caps.*) any similar artistic, musical, cultural, etc. movement or grouping; **new woman** a name applied, esp. by scoffers, in the late 19th century to such women as actively sought freedom and equality with men; **New World** North and South America; **New Year** the first few days of the year. — **New Jersey tea** red-root; **New Model Army** the Parliamentary army as remodelled by Cromwell (1645); **New Red Sandstone** (*geol.*) an old name for the Permian and Trias; **New Year's Day** the first day of the year; **of new** (*arch.*) anew: of late. [O.E. *nīwe, nēowe*; Ger. *neu*, Ir. *nuadh*, L. *novus*, Gr. *neos*.]

Newcastle disease *nū'kä-səl diz-ēz'*, an acute, highly contagious viral disease of chickens and other domestic and wild birds, first recorded at *Newcastle*-upon-Tyne in 1926 — also called **fowl-pest**.

newel *nū'əl, n.* the upright column about which the steps of a circular staircase wind: an upright post at the end or corner of a stair handrail (also **newel post**). — *adj.* **new'elled.** [O.Fr. *noual* (Fr. *noyau*), fruitstone — L.L. *nucālis*, nutlike — L. *nux, nucis*, a nut.]

newell *nū'əl, (Spens.) n.* a new thing. [A combination of **novel** and **new**.]

newfangled *nū-fang'gld*, earlier **newfangle** *-gl, adjs.* unduly fond of new things: newly but superfluously devised. — *adv.* **newfang'ledly.** — *n.* **newfang'ledness, newfang'-leness.** [M.E. *newefangel* — *newe* (O.E. *nīwe*), new, *fangel*, ready to catch — *fang-*, the stem of O.E. *fōn*, to take.]

Newfoundland *nū-fownd'lənd, adj.* of *Newfoundland* (*nū'fənd-land*). — *n.* a very large, intelligent breed of dog from Newfoundland, originally black, a strong swimmer.

Newgate *nū'gāt, n.* a famous prison in London, originally housed in the *new gate* of the city, the latest building demolished in 1902–3. — **Newgate Calendar** a record of Newgate prisoners, with their crimes; **Newgate frill** or **fringe** a beard under the chin and jaw.

newmarket *nū-mär'kit*, or *nū', n.* a card game in which the stakes go to those who succeed in playing out cards whose duplicates lie on the table: a close-fitting coat, originally a riding-coat, for men or women. [*New-market*, the racing town.]

news *nūz, n.* (*orig. pl.*) tidings: a report of a recent event: something one had not heard before: matter suitable for newspaper readers: newspaper: newsprint. — *v.t.* to report. — *n.* **news'iness.** — *adj.* **news'y** full of news or gossip. — *n.* (*U.S.*) a newsboy. — **news agency** an organisation which collects material for newspapers, magazines, etc.; **news'agent** one who deals in newspapers; **news'boy, news'girl** a boy or girl who delivers or sells newspapers; **news'cast** a news broadcast or telecast; **news'caster** one who gives newscasts: an apparatus which gives a changing display of news headlines, etc.; **news'casting; news'dealer** (*U.S.*) a newsagent; **news fiction** see **faction**[2]; **newsflash** see under **flash**; **news'girl** see **newsboy**; **news'hawk, news'hound** a reporter in search of news for e.g. a newspaper; **news'letter** orig. a written or printed letter containing news sent by an agent to his subscribers — the predecessor of the newspaper: a sheet of news supplied to members of a particular group; **news'man, -woman** a bringer, collector, or writer of news: a seller of newspapers; **news'-monger** one who deals in news: one who spends much time in hearing and telling news; **news'paper** a paper published periodically for circulating news, etc.; **news'-paperdom; news'paperism; news'paper-man, -woman** a journalist; **news'print** paper for printing newspapers; **news'reader** one who reads news on radio or television; **news'reel** film showing, or a programme commenting on, news items; **news'room** a reading-room with newspapers: room, etc., where news is made ready for newspaper, newscast, etc.; **news'-sheet** a printed sheet of news, esp. an early form of newspaper; **news'-stand** a stall for the sale of newspapers; **news'-theatre** a cinema showing chiefly newsreels; **news'trade** the business of newsagents; **news'-value** interest to the general public as news; **news'-vendor** a seller of newspapers;

newswoman see **newsman.** — *adj.* **news'worthy** sufficiently interesting to be told as news. — **news'worthiness; news'-writer** a reporter or writer of news. [Late M.E. *newes*; Fr. *nouvelles*.]

newt *nūt, n.* a tailed amphibian (*Triturus, Molge*, or *Triton*) of the salamander family — formed with initial *n*, borrowed from the article **an**, from **ewt**, a form of **evet** or **eft**[1]. [O.E. *efeta, efete*.]

newton *nū'tən, n.* the SI unit of force — it is equal to the force which, acting on a mass of one kilogramme, produces an acceleration of one metre per second per second. — *adj.* **Newtonian** (*nū-tō'ni-ən*) relating to, according to, formed or discovered by, Sir Isaac *Newton* (1642–1727) — also **Newtonic** (*-ton'ik*). — **Newtonian telescope** a form of reflecting telescope; **Newton's cradle** a sophisticated toy consisting of five metal balls hanging in a frame, caused to hit against one another at speeds which vary.

next *nekst, adj.* (*superl.* of **nigh**) nearest in place, in kinship or other relation: nearest following (or preceding if explicitly stated) in time or order. — *adv.* nearest: immediately after: on the first occasion that follows: in the next place. — *prep.* (*arch.* or *dial.*) nearest to. — *adv.* **next'ly.** — *n.* **next'ness** (*rare*). — **next best**, biggest, etc., next in order after the best, biggest, etc. — *adj.* **next'-door** dwelling in or occupying the next house, shop, etc.: at or in the next house: neighbouring. — *adv.* **next-door'.** — **next friend** a person appointed, or permitted, by a court of law to act on behalf of a minor or other person under legal disability; **next Saturday**, etc., (on) the first Saturday, etc. after the present day: in Scotland often (on) the Saturday, etc. of next week. — **next door to** in the next house to: near, bordering upon, very nearly; **next of kin** see **kin**[1]; **next to** adjacent to: almost: thoroughly acquainted with (*old U.S. slang*); **next to nothing** almost nothing at all. [O.E. *nēhst* (*nīehst*), superl. of *nēh* (*nēah*), near; Ger. *nächst*.]

nexus *nek'səs, n.* a bond: a linked group. [L. *nexus*, pl. *-ūs* — *nectĕre*, to bind.]

ngaio *nī'ō, n.* a New Zealand tree with white wood: — *pl.* **ngai'os.** [Maori.]

ngwee *ng-gwē', n.* the hundredth part of a Zambian kwacha (q.v.), or a coin of this value: — *pl.* **ngwee.** [Native word, bright.]

niacin *nī'ə-sin, n.* nicotinic acid.

niaiserie *nyez-(ə-)rē*, (Fr.) *n.* simplicity, foolishness.

nib[1] *nib, n.* something small and pointed: a pen-point: a bird's bill: a peak: a projecting point or spike: a timber carriage pole: a handle on a scythe's shaft (*dial.*): (in *pl.*) crushed cocoa-beans: (in *pl.*) included particles in varnish, wool, etc. — *v.t.* to furnish with a nib: to point: to mend the nib of: to reduce to nibs. — *adj.* **nibbed** having a nib. [**neb.**]

nib[2] *nib, (slang) n.* a person of the upper classes: a person of importance or appearance of importance. — **his nibs** himself: his mightiness. [Cf. **nabs, nob**[2].]

nibble *nib'l, v.t.* to bite gently or by small bites: to eat a little at a time. — *v.i.* to bite gently: to show signs of accepting, as an offer, or of yielding, as to temptation (with *at*): to find fault. — *n.* the act of nibbling: a little bit: half a byte (*comput. rare*). — *ns.* **nibb'ler; nibb'ling.** — *adv.* **nibb'lingly.** [Origin obscure; cf. L.G. *nibbelen*, Du. *knibbelen*.]

Nibelung *nē'bəl-oŏng, n.* one of a supernatural race in Germanic mythology, guardians of a treasure wrested from them by Siegfried, the hero of the *Nibelungenlied*, an epic of *c.* 1190–1210: in the Nibelungenlied, the name Nibelungen is applied first to Siegfried's followers and subjects, and then to the Burgundians: — *pl.* **Ni'belungen.** [Ger.]

niblick *nib'lik, n.* a golf-club with a heavy head with wide face, used for lofting — a number eight or nine iron. [Origin uncertain.]

niccolite *nik'əl-īt, n.* a hexagonal mineral, nickel arsenide, also called kupfernickel, copper-nickel. [See **nickel**.]

nice *nīs, adj.* foolishly simple (*obs.*): wanton (*Shak.*): coy

(*Milt.*): over-particular: hard to please: fastidious: forming or observing very small differences: calling for very fine discrimination: done with great care and exactness, accurate: critical, hazardous (*arch.*): easily injured (*obs.*): delicate: dainty: agreeable, delightful, respectable (often used in vague commendation by those who are not nice, also sometimes ironic). — *adj.* **nice′ish** somewhat nice. — *adv.* **nice′ly.** — *ns.* **nice′ness** quality of being nice; **nicety** (*nīs′i-ti*) the quality of being nice: delicate management: exactness of treatment: degree of precision: fineness of perception or feeling: critical subtlety: a matter of delicate discrimination or adjustment: a refinement: coyness (*Spens.*, *Shak.*): fastidiousness: a delicacy. — **nice and** used almost adverbially — commendably, pleasantly; **to a nicety** with great exactness. [O.Fr. *nice*, foolish, simple — L. *nescius*, ignorant — *ne*, not, *scīre*, to know.]

Nicene *nī′sēn, adj.* pertaining to the town of *Nicaea*, in Bithynia, where an ecumenical council in 325 dealt with the Arian controversy, and another in 787 condemned the Iconoclasts. — *n.* and *adj.* **Nicaean** (*nī-sē′-ən*). — **Nicene Creed** the creed based on the results of the first Nicene Council.

niche *nich, nēsh, n.* a recess in a wall: a suitable or actual place or condition in life or public estimation or the system of nature: a place in the market not subject to the normal pressures of competition (*commerce*). — *v.t.* to place in a niche. — *adj.* **niched** placed in a niche. [Fr., — It. *nicchia*, niche, of doubtful origin.]

nicher. See **nicker¹.**

Nichrome® *nī′krōm, n.* trademark for a nickel-chromium alloy with high electrical resistance and ability to withstand high temperatures.

nick¹ *nik, n.* a notch: a score for keeping an account (*arch.*): a cut: a fraudulent dint in the bottom of a beer-can (*obs.*): the precise point aimed at: the precise moment of time: at hazard, a throw answering to a main: a prison, a police-office (*slang*): the line formed where floor and wall meet in a squash, etc. court. — *v.t.* to notch: to cut in notches (as the hair of a fool; *Shak.*): to cut off: to defraud: to mark by cutting, carve out: to cut: to snip: to score, as on a tally: to tally with (*obs.*): to hit with precision: to hit off (*obs.*): to catch in the nick of time: to catch (*slang*): to arrest (*slang*): to steal (*slang*): to rob: to cheat at hazard, to defeat by throwing a nick: at hazard, to throw the nick of: to make a cut in a horse's tail muscle, so that the tail is carried higher. — *v.i.* of breeding animals, to mate well. — *n.* **nick′er** one who, or that which, nicks: in the early 18th century, a brawler who broke windows with coppers. — **nick′stick** (*arch.*) a tally. — **in (very) good nick** (*coll.*) in (very) good health or condition; **in the nick** (now usu. **nick of time**) just in time: at the critical moment; **out of all nick** (*Shak.*) out of all reckoning, exceedingly. [Possibly connected with **nock, notch.**]

nick² *nik,* (*arch.*) *v.t.* to deny (in the phrase *to nick with nay*). [Origin unknown; possibly O.E. *ne ic*, not I.]

Nick *nik, n.* the devil, esp. **Old Nick.** — Also (*Scot.*) **Nickie-ben′.** [Apparently for *Nicholas.*]

nickar. See **nicker³.**

nickel *nik′l, n.* an element (symbol Ni; at. numb. 28), a white, magnetic, very malleable and ductile metal largely used in alloys: a 5-cent piece (of copper and nickel; *U.S.*). — *adj.* of nickel. — *v.t.* to plate with nickel: — *pr.p.* **nick′elling;** *pa.t.* and *pa.p.* **nick′elled.** — *adjs.* **nick′elic** of trivalent nickel; **nickelif′erous** containing nickel. — *n.* **nick′eline** (*obs.*) niccolite. — *v.t.* **nick′elise, -ize** to plate with nickel. — *adj.* **nick′elous** of bivalent nickel. — **nick′el-bloom** earthy annabergite; **nick′el-ochre** earthy annabergite; **nick′el-plat′ing** the plating of metals with nickel; **nick′el-sil′ver** German silver; **nick′el-steel′** a steel containing some nickel. [Ger. *Kupfer-nickel*, niccolite — *Kupfer*, copper, *Nickel*, a mischievous sprite, goblin, because the ore looked like copper-ore but yielded no copper.]

nickelodeon *nik-ə-lō′di-ən, n.* a five-cent entertainment: a juke-box. [See **nickel, odeon.**]

nicker¹ *nik′ər,* (*Scot.*) *v.i.* to neigh: to snigger. — *n.* a neigh: a snigger: a loud laugh. — Also **nicher** (*nihh′ər*).

nicker² *nik′ər,* (*arch.*) *n.* a water-monster or water-demon. [O.E. *nicor.*]

nicker³ *nik′ər, n.* a clay marble (also **knicker**): the round seed of a Caesalpinia (or Guilandina if this is considered a separate genus), used for playing marbles (also **nick′ar**). [Cf. Du. *knikker*, North Ger. *Knicker.*]

nicker⁴ *nik′ər,* (*slang*) *n.* £1.

nick-nack, etc. Same as **knick-knack,** etc.

nickname *nik′nām, n.* a name given in contempt or sportive familiarity. — *v.t.* to give a nickname to. [M.E. *neke-name*, for *eke-name*, with *n* from the indefinite article; see **an¹, eke¹, name.**]

nickum *nik′əm,* (*Scot.*) *n.* a mischievous boy.

nickumpoop. See **nincompoop.**

nicky-tam *nik′i-tam′,* (*Scot.*) *n.* a piece of string, etc., worn below the knee to keep the bottom of the trouser-leg lifted clear in dirty work or to exclude dust, etc.

nicol *nik′l, n.* a crystal of calcium carbonate so cut and cemented as to transmit only the extraordinary ray, used for polarising light. — Also **Nicol('s) prism.** [From William *Nicol* (*c.* 1768–1851) of Edinburgh, its inventor.]

nicompoop. See **nincompoop.**

nicotian *ni-kō′sh(y)ən, adj.* of tobacco. — *n.* a tobacco smoker. — *n.* **Nicotiana** (*-shi-ä′nə, -ā′nə*) the tobacco genus of Solanaceae: (*without cap.*) a plant of the genus. — *n.pl.* (*without cap.*) the literature of tobacco. — *ns.* **nicotinamide** (*-tin′*) a member of the vitamin B complex; **nicotine** (*nik′ə-tēn*) a poisonous alkaloid ($C_{10}H_{14}N_2$) got from tobacco leaves. — *adj.* **nicotinic** (*-tin′ik*). — *n.* **nic′otinism** a morbid state induced by excessive use of tobacco. — **nicotinic acid** a white crystalline substance, a member of the vitamin B complex, deficiency of which is connected with the development of pellagra. [Jean *Nicot*, who sent tobacco to Catherine de Medici.]

nicotine, etc. See **nicotian.**

nicrosilal *nik-rō′sil-əl, n.* a cast-iron alloy containing *nickel, chromium,* and *silicon*, used in high-temperature work.

nictate *nik′tāt, v.i.* to wink — also **nic′titate.** — *ns.* **nicta′tion, nictita′tion.** — **nictitating membrane** the third eyelid, developed in birds, etc., a thin movable membrane that passes over the eye. [L. *nictāre, -ātum* and its L.L. freq. *nictitāre, -ātum*, to wink.]

nid *nid,* **nide** *nīd, ns.* a pheasant's nest or brood. [L. *nīdus,* nest.]

nidal, etc. See **nidus.**

niddering, nidderling, nidering, niderling, niding. See **nithing.**

niddle-noddle *nid′l-nod′l, adj.* and *adv.* with nodding head. — *v.i.* to noddle the head: to waggle. — *v.t.* and *v.i.* **nid′-nod′** to keep nodding. [**nod.**]

nide. See **nid.**

nidget *nij′it,* (*arch.* or *illit.*) *n.* an idiot. [idiot, with *n* from the indefinite article.]

nidicolous *nid-ik′ə-ləs, adj.* (of young birds) staying long in the nest. [L. *nīdus,* a nest, *colĕre,* to inhabit.]

nidificate. See **nidify.**

nidifugous *nid-if′ū-gəs, adj.* (of young birds) leaving the nest soon after hatching. [L. *nīdus,* nest, *fugĕre,* to flee.]

nidify *nid′i-fī, v.i.* to build a nest. — Also **nidificate** (*nid′i-fi-kāt*). — *n.* **nidifica′tion.** [L. *nīdus,* nest, *facĕre,* to make.]

nidor *nī′dör, n.* a strong smell or fume, esp. of animal substances cooking or burning. — *adv.* **nī′dorous.** [L. *nīdor, -ōris.*]

nidus *nī′dəs, n.* a nest or breeding-place: a place where anything is originated, harboured, developed, or fostered: a place of lodgment or deposit: a point of infection: a nerve-centre: — *pl.* **nī′dī.** — *adjs.* **nī′dal** pertaining to a nest or nidus; **nīdament′al** nest-forming:

(of glands) secreting material for the formation of a nest or of an egg-covering. — *ns.* **nīdament'um** an egg-capsule; **nīdā'tion** renewal of the lining of the uterus; **nidūlā'tion** (*nid-*) nest-building. [L. *nīdus*, a nest.]

nie. An obsolete spelling of **nigh.**

niece *nēs, n.* orig. a granddaughter, or any female descendant: now, a brother's or sister's daughter: extended to a like relation by marriage: euphemistically, a pope's or priest's daughter: — *masc.* **nephew.** [O.Fr., — L.L. *neptia* — L. *neptis.*]

nief. See **nieve.**

niello *ni-el'ō, n.* a method of ornamenting metal by engraving, and filling up the lines with a black composition: a work so produced: an impression taken from the engraved surface before filling up: the compound used in niello-work: — *pl.* **niell'i** (-*ē*), **niell'os.** — *v.t.* to decorate with niello: — *pr.p.* **niell'oing;** *pa.t.* and *pa.p.* **niell'oed.** — *adj.* **niellāted** (*nē'*). — *n.* **niell'ist.** [It. *niello* — L.L. *nigellum*, a black enamel — L. *nigellus*, dim. of *niger*, black.]

Niersteiner *nēr's(h)tīn-ər, n.* a Rhine wine, named from *Nierstein*, near Mainz.

Nietzschean *nēch'i-ən, adj.* of Friedrich *Nietzsche* (1844–1900) or his philosophy. — *n.* a follower of Nietzsche. — *n.* **Nietzsch'eanism.**

nieve, neive *nēv*, **neif, nief** (*Shak.* **neafe, neaffe**) *nēf,* (*arch.* except *dial.*) *ns.* the fist. — *ns.* **nieve'ful** a closed handful; **nie'vie-(nie'vie-)nick'-nack** a Scottish children's pastime, a mode of assigning by lot, by guessing which hand contains something, the holder repeating a rhyme. [M.E. *nefe* — O.N. *hnefi, nefi*; cf. Sw. *näfve*, fist.]

nife *nī'fi, n.* the earth's hypothetical core of nickel and iron. [Chemical symbols *Ni* and *Fe*.]

niff *nif*, (*dial.* or *slang*) *n.* a stink. — *v.i.* to smell nasty. — *adj.* **niff'y.**

niffer *nif'ər*, (*Scot.*) *v.t.* to barter. — *v.i.* to haggle. — *n.* an exchange: hazard. [Possibly **nieve.**]

niffnaff *nif-naf'*, (*dial.*) *n.* a trifle: a diminutive person. — *v.i.* to trifle. — *adjs.* **niff-naff'y, niff'y-naff'y** fastidious.

Niflheim *niv'l-hām*, (*Scand. myth.*) *n.* a region of mist, ruled over by Hel. [O.N. *Niflheimr* — *nifl*, mist, *heimr*, home.]

nifty *nif'ti*, (*slang*) *adj.* fine: spruce: sharp, neat: smart: quick: agile. — *n.* **nift'iness.**

Nigella *nī-jel'ə, n.* a genus of ranunculaceous plants, with finely dissected leaves, and whitish, blue, or yellow flowers, often almost concealed by their leafy involucres — *Nigella damascena* is called love-in-a-mist, devil-in-a-bush, and ragged lady: (without *cap.*) a plant of the genus. [Fem. of L. *nigellus*, blackish — *niger*, black, from the black seeds.]

niger *nī'jər*, (*obs.*) *n.* a Negro. — **ni'ger-oil** an oil got from the black seeds (**ni'ger-seeds**) of an East African composite, *Guizotia abyssinica*, cultivated also in India. [L. *niger*, black.]

niggard *nig'ərd, n.* one who grudges to spend or give away: a false bottom or side in a fire-grate. — *adj.* niggardly. — *v.t.* and *v.i.* (*Shak.*) to treat or behave as a niggard. — *ns.* **nigg'ardise, -ize** (-*īz; arch.*), **nigg'-ardliness** meanness, stinginess. — *adj.* **nigg'ardly** stingy. — *adv.* stingily: grudgingly. [Origin obscure.]

nigger *nig'ər, n.* a Negro, or a member of any very dark-skinned race (*derog.* now esp. *offensive*): a black insect larva of various kinds. — *adj.* Negro: blackish brown. — *v.t.* to exhaust by overcropping: to char: to blacken. — *n.* **nigg'erdom** niggers collectively. — *adj.* **nigg'erish** — *ns.* **nigg'erism** an idiom or expression characteristic of niggers: African blood; **nigg'erling** a little nigger. — *adj.* **nigg'ery.** — **nigg'erhead** a nodule, boulder, or boss of dark-coloured rock: an American river-mussel (*Quadrula*), a source of mother-of-pearl: negrohead tobacco: a tussock in a swamp (*U.S.*). — **nigger in the wood-pile** a hidden evil influence; **work like a nigger** to toil hard. [Fr. *nègre* — Sp. *negro*; see **Negro.**]

niggle *nig'l, v.i.* to trifle, potter: to busy oneself with petty scrupulosity: to move in a fidgety or ineffective way: to gnaw: to criticise in a petty way. — *v.t.* to work, make, perform, with excessive detail: to befool. — *n.* small cramped handwriting: a minor criticism. — *ns.* **nigg'ler; nigg'ling** fussiness, finicking work: petty elaboration. — *adj.* over-elaborate: petty: fussy: cramped: persistently annoying. — *adj.* **nigg'ly.** [Cf. Norw. *nigle.*]

nigh *nī, adj.* (*obs.*) near. — *adv.* (*poet., dial.,* or *arch.*) nearly: near. — *prep.* (*poet., dial.,* or *arch.*) near to. — *v.t.* and *v.i.* (*obs.*) to approach, draw near: to touch. — *adv.* and *prep.* (*obs.*) **nigh'-hand** near hand: almost, nearly. — *adv.* **nigh'ly** (*obs.*) almost: closely: sparingly (*Spens.*). — *n.* (*obs.*) **nigh'ness.** [O.E. *nēah, nēh*; Du. *na*, Ger. *nahe.*]

night *nīt, n.* the end of the day: the time from sunset to sunrise: the dark part of the twenty-four-hour day: darkness: obscurity, ignorance, evil, affliction, or sorrow (*fig.*): death (*fig.*): the experience of a night: a night set apart for some purpose, esp. receiving visitors. — *adj.* belonging to night: occurring or done in the night: working or on duty by night. — *adj.* **night'ed** benighted: darkened, clouded (*Shak.*). — *n.* **nightie** see **nighty.** — *adj.* **night'less** having no night. — *adj.* and *adv.* **night'long** lasting all night. — *adj.* **night'ly** done or happening by night or every night: dark as night (*Shak.*). — *adv.* by night: every night. — *adv.* **nights** (orig. *gen.* of *n.*; *coll.*) at, by night. — *adj.* **night'ward** occurring towards night. — *n.* **night'y, night'ie** a night-gown. — **night air** the air at night: a peculiarly unwholesome gas, formerly imagined by some to circulate at night; **night'-ape** a bush-baby; **night'-attire'** garments worn in bed; **night'-bell** a door-bell for use at night; **night'-bird** a bird that flies or that sings at night: a person who is active or about at night; **night'-blind'ness** inability to see in a dim light, nyctalopia; **night'-brawl'er** one who raises disturbances in the night; **night'cap** a cap worn at night in bed: a drink taken before going to bed; **night'-cart** (*hist.*) a cart used to remove the contents of privies before daylight; **night'-cellar** (*arch.*) a disreputable resort or tavern, open by night; **night'-chair** a night-stool; **night'-churr** the goatsucker, so called from its cry. — *n.pl.* **night=clothes** garments worn in bed. — **night'-cloud** stratus; **night'-club** a club open between nightfall and morning for amusement or dissipation; **night'-clubbing** dining, dancing, etc., at a night-club; **night'-crawl'er** a large earthworm which comes to the surface at night, used as bait for fishing; **night'-crow** (*Shak.*) an undefined bird of ill omen that cries in the night; **night'-dog** (*Shak.*) a dog that hunts in the night; **night'dress** attire for the night, esp. a nightgown; **night'fall** the fall or beginning of the night: the close of the day: evening. — *adj.* **night'faring** travelling by night. — **night'fire** a fire burning in the night: a will-o'-the-wisp; **night=fish'ery** a mode or place of fishing by night; **night=flower** a flower that opens by night. — *adj.* **night=flow'ering.** — **night'-fly** a moth or fly that flies at night. — *adj.* **night'-fly'ing** flying by night (also *n.*). — **night'-foe** one who makes his attack by night; **night'-foss'icker** (*Austr.*) one who robs a digging by night. — *adj.* **night'-foun'dered** lost in the night. — **night'-fowl** a night-bird; **night'gear** night-clothes; **night'-glass** a spy-glass with concentrating lenses for use at night; **night'(-)gown** a loose robe for sleeping in, for men or women: a dressing-gown (*obs.*); **night'-hag** a witch supposed to be abroad at night; **night'hawk** a goatsucker: a prowler by night; **night'-her'on** a heron of nocturnal habit, of various kinds; **night'-house** (*obs.*) a tavern open during the night; **night'-hunter** one who hunts, poaches, or prowls about the streets for prey by night; **night'jar** a goatsucker; **night'-latch** a door-lock worked by a key without and a knob within; **night letter** (*U.S.*) a telegram sent overnight, and so at a cheaper rate; **night life** activity in the form of entertainments at night; **night'-light** lamp, candle that gives a subdued light all night: the faint light of the night; the light of phosphorescent sea-animals; **night′-line** a fishing-line set overnight; **night′-man** a night watchman, worker, or scavenger; **night′mare** (O.E. *mære*, M.E. *mare*, the nightmare incubus; cf. O.H.G. *mara*, incubus, O.N. *mara*, nightmare) an unpleasant dream: a dream accompanied by pressure on the breast and a feeling of powerlessness to move or speak — personified as an incubus or evil spirit: a horrifying experience (*fig.*). — *adjs.* **night′marish; night′mary** (*rare*). — **night out** a domestic, or other, servant's night of freedom to be absent: a festive night away from home, work, and restrictions; **night′-owl** an exclusively nocturnal owl: one who sits up very late; **night′-pal′sy** (*arch.*) a numbness of the legs, incidental to women; **night′piece** a picture or literary or musical description of a night-scene: a painting to be seen by artificial light; **night′-por′ter** a porter in attendance during the night; **night′-rail** (*hist.*) a loose wrap or dressing-jacket; **night′-rav′en** (*Shak.*) a bird that cries at night, supposed to be of ill-omen; **night′-rest** the repose of the night; **night′-rider** (*U.S.*) a participant in a lynching, etc.: a member of the Ku-Klux Klan; **night′-robe** a nightgown: a dressing-gown; **night′-rule** (*Shak.*) a revel at night; **night′-school** a school held at night, esp. for those at work during the day; **night′-sea′son** the nighttime; **night′-shift** a gang or group of workers that takes its turn by night: the time it is on duty: a nightdress (*arch.*); **night′shirt** a man's shirt for sleeping in; **night′-shriek** a cry in the night; **night′-side** the dark, mysterious, or gloomy side of anything; **night′-sight** power of vision by night: a sighting device on a camera, rifle, etc., to enable it to be used at night; **night′-soil** the contents of privies, cesspools, etc., generally carried away at night and sometimes used for fertiliser; **night′-spell** a charm against harm by night; **night′spot** (*coll.*) a night-club; **night′-steed** one of the horses in the chariot of Night; **night′-stick** an American policeman's truncheon; **night′-stool** a close-stool for use in a bedroom; **night′-ta′per** a night-light burning slowly. — *n.pl.* **night′-terr′ors** (*arch.*) the sudden starting from sleep in fright. — **night′-tide** night-time: a flood-tide in the night; **night′-time** the time when it is night. — *adj.* **night′-tripp′ing** (*Shak.*) tripping about in the night; **night′-wak′ing** watching in the night. — **night′-walk** a walk in the night; **night′-walk′er** (*arch.*) a somnambulist: one who walks about at night, usu. for bad purposes, esp. a prostitute. — *n. and adj.* **night′-wan′derer** one who wanders by night. — *adjs.* **night′-wan′dering; night′-war′bling** singing in the night. — **night′-watch** a watch or guard at night: one who is on watch by night: time of watch in the night; **night′-watch′man** one who is on watch by night, esp. on industrial premises and building sites: a batsman, not a high scorer, put in to defend a wicket until the close of play (*cricket*); **night′wear** clothes worn at bedtime and while sleeping; **night′-work** work done at night; **night′-work′er**. — **make a night of it** to spend the night, or a large part of it, in amusement or celebration; **of a night, of nights** in the course of a night: some time at night. [O.E. *niht*; Ger. *Nacht*, L. *nox*, Gr. *nyx*.]

nightingale[1] *nīt′ing-gāl*, *n.* a small bird of the thrush family celebrated for the rich love-song of the male heard chiefly at night: a person with a beautiful singing voice. [O.E. *nihtegale* — *niht*, night, *galan*, to sing, Ger. *Nachtigall*.]

nightingale[2] *nīt′ing-gāl*, *n.* a flannel scarf with sleeves, worn by invalids sitting up in bed. [Florence *Nightingale* (1820–1910), Crimean hospital nurse.]

nightjar, nightmare, nightpiece. See **night**.

nightshade *nīt′shād*, *n.* a name given to various plants, chiefly of the Solanaceae and chiefly poisonous or narcotic. — **deadly nightshade** belladonna; **woody nightshade** bittersweet; **black nightshade** *Solanum nigrum*; see also **enchant**. [O.E. *nihtscada*, app. — *niht*, night, *scada*, shade.]

nightshirt, nightspot, nightwear. See **night**.

nig-nog[1] *nig′-nog*, *n.* a fool: a raw recruit to army or to a civilian service. [Origin uncertain.]

nig-nog[2] *nig′-nog*, (*offensive slang*) *n.* a person of a dark-skinned race. [Reduplicated form of **nigger**.]

nigrescence *nī-* or *ni-gres′əns*, *n.* blackness: dark colouring or pigmentation: blackening. — *adjs.* **nigresc′ent** growing black or dark: blackish; **nigricant** (*nig′ri-kənt*) black: blackish. — *v.t.* **nig′rify** to blacken. — *n.* **nig′ritude** blackness. [L. *niger*, black.]

Nigritian *ni-grish′ən*, *adj.* of *Nigritia*, or Sudan, esp. Western Sudan, the home of the Negroes in the narrow sense. — *n.* a true Negro. [L. *niger*, black.]

nigritude. See **Negro, nigrescence**.

nigromancy *nig′rō-man-si*, *n.* an old form of **necromancy**, the black art. [From association with L. *niger*, black.]

nigrosine *nig′rō-sēn, -ro-sin*, *n.* a blackish coal-tar colour dye. [L. *niger*, black.]

nihil *nī′hil*, *n.* nothing. — *ns.* **ni′hilism** (*-hil-* or *-il-izm*) belief in nothing: denial of all reality, or of all objective growth of truth: extreme scepticism: nothingness: in tsarist Russia, a terrorist movement aiming at the overturn of all the existing institutions of society in order to build it up anew on different principles; **ni′hilist**. — *adj.* **nihilist′ic**. — *n.* **nihility** (*-hil′*) nothingness: a mere nothing. [L. *nihil*, nothing.]

nihil ad rem *nī′, ni′hil ad rem*, (L.) nothing to the point; **ni′hil obstat** (*ob′stat*) nothing hinders — a book censor's form of permission to print.

-nik *-nik*, in composition, a person who does, practises, advocates, etc. something, as in *beatnik, kibbutznik, peacenik*. [Russ. suffix, influenced in meaning by Yiddish suffix denoting an agent.]

Nike *nī′kē*, *n.* the Greek goddess of victory. [Gr. *nīkē*, victory.]

nikethamide *nik-eth′a-mīd*, *n.* a drug used as a heart stimulant — also **coramine**. [nicotinic acid, di*ethyl*, *amide*.]

niks-nie. See under **nix[2]**.

nil *nil*, *n.* nothing: zero. [L. *nīl*, *nīhil*, nothing.]

Nile green *nīl grēn*, a very pale green colour, thought of as the colour of the River *Nile*.

nilgai *nēl′* or *nil′gī*, **nilgau, nylghau** *-gow, -gö, ns.* a large Indian antelope, the male slaty-grey, the female tawny. [Pers. and Hind. *nīl*, blue, Hind. *gāi*, Pers. *gāw*, cow.]

nill, n'ill *nil*, (*arch.*) *v.t.* will not: refuse: — *pa.t.* (*obs.*) **nould(e), n'ould** (*nōōd*), also **nilled**. [O.E. *nylle* — *ne*, not, *willan*, to wish.]

Nilometer *nī-lom′i-tər*, *n.* a gauge for measuring the height of the *Nile*. [Gr. *neilometrion*.]

Nilot *nīl′ot*, **Nilote** *-ōt, ns.* an inhabitant of the banks of the Upper Nile: a Hamitised Negro of the Upper Nile. — *adj.* **Nilotic** (*-ot′ik*) of the Nile. [Gr. *Neilōtēs*.]

nim[1] *nim*, *v.t.* to take (*obs.*): to steal, pilfer (*arch. slang*): — *pa.t.* (*obs.*) **nam**, (*arch.*) **nimmed**. — *n.* **nimm′er**. [O.E. *niman*, to take.]

nim[2] *nim*, *n.* an old and widespread game, perh. orig. Chinese, in which two players take alternately from heaps or rows of objects (now usu. matches). [Perh. **nim[1]**.]

nim[3] *nēm*, *n.* margosa, a species of Melia, yielding **nim′-oil**. — Also **neem**. [Hind. *nīm*.]

nimbi. See **nimbus**.

nimble *nim′bl*, *adj.* light and quick in motion: active: swift. — *ns.* **nim′bleness, nim′blesse** (*Spens.*) quickness of motion either in body or mind. — *adv.* **nim′bly**. — *adjs.* **nim′ble-fing′ered** skilful with the fingers: thievish; **nimbl′e-foot′ed** swift of foot; **nim′ble-witt′ed** quick-witted. [App. O.E. *næmel, numol* — *niman*, to take; cf. Ger. *nehmen*.]

nimbus *nim′bəs*, *n.* a cloud or luminous mist investing a god or goddess: a halo: a rain-cloud: — *pl.* **nim′bī, nim′buses**. — *adjs.* **nimbed** (*nimd*); **nim′bused**. — *n.* **nimbostratus** (*-strā′, -stra′*) a low, dark-coloured layer of cloud, bringing rain. [L.]

nimiety *ni-mī′i-ti*, *n.* (*rare*) excess. — *adj.* **nimious** (*nim′i-əs; Scots law*) excessive. [L. *nimis*, too much.]

niminy-piminy *nim'i-ni-pim'i-ni, adj.* affectedly fine or delicate. — *n.* affected delicacy. [Imit.]

nimonic *ni-mon'ik, adj.* of alloys used in high-temperature work, e.g. gas turbine blades — chiefly nickel, with chromium, titanium and aluminium. [*nickel, Monel* metal.]

Nimrod *nim'rod, n.* any great hunter. [From the son of Cush, Gen. x. 8–10.]

nincompoop *nin(g)'kəm-pōōp, n.* a simpleton: a booby — earlier **nic'ompoop, nick'umpoop** — shortened to **nin'com, nin'cum** and also **poop.** [Origin unknown; not from L. *nōn compos (mentis),* not in possession (of his wits).]

nine *nīn, n.* the cardinal number next above eight: a symbol representing it (9, ix, etc.): a set of that number of things or persons (as a baseball team): a shoe or other article of a size denoted by 9: a card with nine pips: a score of nine points, tricks, etc.: the ninth hour after midday or midnight: the age of nine years: (with *cap.*; with *the*) the nine Muses. — *adj.* of the number nine: nine years old. — *adj.* and *adv.* **nine'fold** in nine divisions: nine times as much. — *adj.* **ninth** (*nīnth*) last of nine: next after the eighth: equal to one of nine equal parts. — *n.* a ninth part: a person or thing in ninth position: an octave and a second (*mus.*): a tone at that interval (*mus.*). — *adv.* **ninth'ly** in the ninth place. — **nine'-eyes** a lamprey (from its seven pairs of gill-pouches): a butterfish (from its spots). — *adjs.* **nine'-foot, -inch, -mile,** etc., measuring 9 feet, etc.; **nine'-hole** having nine holes. — **nine'holes** a game in which a ball is to be bowled into nine holes in the ground or in a board: a difficulty, fix (*U.S.*); **nine'pence** the value of nine pennies: a coin of that value: a high standard of niceness, nimbleness, etc. — *adj.* **nine'-penny** costing, offered at, or worth ninepence. — *n.* a ninepence. — **nine'-pin** a bottle-shaped pin set up with eight others for the game of **nine'pins** in which players bowl a ball at these pins (see **skittles**). — *n.* and *adj.* **nine'score** nine times twenty. — **nine worthies** see **worth¹.** — **naughty nineties** see **naughty; nine days' wonder** see **wonder; ninepenny marl** or **morris, nine men's morris** see **meril; nine points of the law** worth nine-tenths of all the points that could be raised (proverbially of possession); **to the nines** to perfection, fully, elaborately. [O.E. *nigon;* Du. *negen,* L. *novem,* Gr. *ennea,* Sans. *nava.*]

nineteen *nīn-tēn', or nīn'tēn, n.* and *adj.* nine and ten. — *n.* and *adj.* **nine'teenth** (or *-tēnth'*). — *adv.* **nineteenth'ly.** — **nineteenth hole** a golf club-house, esp. the bar or restaurant. — **nineteen to the dozen** with great volubility. [O.E. *nigontēne (-tiene);* see **nine, ten.**]

ninety *nīn'ti, n.* and *adj.* nine times ten. — *n.pl.* **nine'ties** the numbers ninety to ninety-nine: the years so numbered in a life or a century: a range of temperature from ninety to just less than one hundred degrees. — *adj.* **nine'tieth** last of ninety: next after the eighty-ninth: equal to one of ninety equal parts. — *n.* a ninetieth part: a person or thing in ninetieth position. [O.E. *nigontig (hundnigontig).*]

ninja *nin'jə, n.* (also with *cap.*) one of a body of trained assassins in feudal Japan: — *pl.* **-ja, -jas.** [Jap.]

ninny *nin'i, n.* a simpleton. — Also (*arch.* or *dial.*) **ninn'y-hammer.** [Possibly from **innocent;** poss. — It. *ninno,* child; Sp. *niño.*]

ninon *nē-nɔ̃', n.* a silk voile or other thin fabric. [Fr. *Ninon,* a woman's name.]

ninth. See **nine.**

Niobe *nī'ō-bē, n.* a daughter of Tantalus, turned into stone as she wept for her children, slain by Artemis and Apollo. — *adj.* **Niobe'an.** [Gr. *Niobē.*]

niobium *nī-ō'bi-əm, n.* a metallic element (symbol Nb; at. numb. 41) discovered in the mineral tantalite — also, but not now officially, called *columbium.* — *n.* **nī'obate** a salt of niobic acid. — *adj.* **nio'bic** (**niobic acid** hydrated niobium pentoxide). — *n.* **ni'obite** same as **columbite.** — *adj.* **nio'bous.** [See **Niobe.**]

nip¹ *nip, n.* a small quantity of spirits — also **nipp'er**

(*U.S.*). — *v.i.* to take a dram. — *n.* **nipp'erkin** a small measure of liquor. [Origin obscure.]

nip² *nip, v.t.* to pinch: to press between two surfaces: to remove or sever by pinching or biting (often with *off*): to check the growth or vigour of: to give a smarting or tingling feeling to: to concern closely and painfully (*obs.*): to reprehend sharply (*obs.*): to snatch: to steal (*coll.*): to arrest (*slang*). — *v.i.* to pinch: to smart: to go nimbly: — *pr.p.* **nipp'ing;** *pa.t.* and *pa.p.* **nipped** (*nipt*). — *n.* an act or experience of nipping: the pinch of cold: a nipping quality: pungency or bite (*Scot.*): a sharp reprehension (*obs.*): a more or less gradual thinning out of a stratum (*min.*): a short turn in a rope, the part of a rope at the place bound by the seizing or caught by jambing (*naut.*): a small piece, such as might be nipped off: a cutpurse (*old slang*). — *n.* **nipp'er** one who, or that which, nips: a chela or great claw, as of a crab: a horse's incisor, esp. of the middle four: a pickpocket or cutpurse (*slang*): a boy assistant to a costermonger, carter, etc.: a little boy or (sometimes) girl: (in *pl.*) small pincers: (in *pl.*) any of various pincer-like tools: (in *pl.*) handcuffs. — *v.t.* to seize (two ropes) together. — *adv.* **nipp'ingly.** — *adj.* **nipp'y** pungent, biting: nimble (*coll.*): niggardly: (esp. of weather) very cold, frosty. — **nip'-cheese** a stingy fellow (*slang*): a purser (*obs. naut.*). — **nip and tuck** (*U.S.*) full speed: neck and neck; **nip in** to cut in; **nip in the bud** see **bud¹.** [Prob. related to Du. *nijpen,* to pinch.]

nip³. See **nep.**

Nip. See **Nippon.**

Nipa *nē', nī'pə, n.* a low-growing East Indian palm of brackish water (*Nipa fruticans*): an alcoholic drink made from it. [Malay *nīpah.*]

nipperkin. See **nip¹.**

nipperty-tipperty *nip'ər-ti-tip'ər-ti,* (*Scot.*) *adj.* finical: mincing: fiddle-faddle.

nipple *nip'l, n.* the pap of the breast: a teat: a small projection with an orifice, esp. for regulating flow or lubricating machinery. — *v.t.* to furnish with a nipple. — **nipp'le-shield** a defence for the nipple worn by nursing women; **nipp'lewort** a tall composite weed (*Lapsana communis*) with small yellow heads, once esteemed as a cure for sore nipples. [A dim. of **neb** or **nib¹.**]

Nippon *nip-on', n.* the Japanese name of Japan. — *n.* and *adj.* **Nipp'onese.** — *n.* **Nip** (*slang*) a Japanese. [Jap. *ni,* sun, *pon* — *hon,* origin.]

nippy. See **nip².**

nipter *nip'tər, n.* the ecclesiastical ceremony of washing the feet — the same as **maundy.** [Gr. *niptēr,* a basin — *niptein,* to wash.]

nirl *nirl,* (*Scot.*) *n.* a lump: a crumb: a stunted person. — *v.t.* to stunt: to shrink or shrivel: to pinch with cold. — *adjs.* **nirled, nirl'it; nirl'y, nirl'ie** knotty: stumpy: stunted: niggardly. [Perh. **knurl;** perh. conn. Icel. *nyrfill,* niggard.]

nirvana *nir-vä'nə, n.* the cessation of individual existence — the state to which a Buddhist aspires as the best attainable: (*loosely*) a blissful state. [Sans. *nirvāna,* a blowing out.]

nis¹, n'is, nys *nis, niz,* (*obs.*) a contraction for **ne is,** is not.

nis² *nis, n.* in Scandinavian folklore, a brownie or friendly goblin: — *pl.* **nisses.** [Dan. and Sw. *nisse.*]

Nisan *nī'san, nē-sän', n.* the seventh civil, first ecclesiastical, month of the Jewish calendar (March to April) — called Abib before the Captivity. [Heb. *Nīsān.*]

nisberry. Same as **naseberry.**

nisei sanei *nē-sā', n.* a resident in the Americas born of Japanese immigrant parents — cf. **issei, sanei.** [Jap., second generation.]

nisi *nī'sī, adj.* to take effect unless, after a time, some condition referred to, be fulfilled. [The L. conj. *nisi,* unless.]

nisi prius *nī'sī prī'əs, ni'si pri'ōos,* (L.) unless previously — a name (from the first words of the writ) given to the jury sittings in civil cases.

nisse. Same as **nis²**.

Nissen *nis'ən, adj.* designed by Col. P. N. *Nissen* (1871–1930), applied to a semi-cylindrical corrugated-iron hut.

nisus *nī'səs, n.* effort: striving: impulse. [L. *nīsus,* pl. *-ūs.*]

nit¹ *nit, n.* the egg of a louse or other vermin: a young louse: a term of contempt (*Shak.* etc.). — *adj.* **nitt'y** full of nits. — **nit'-grass** a rare grass (Gastridium) with nit-like flowers; **nit'-picking** (*coll.*) petty criticism of minor details. — *v.i.* **nit'-pick.** [O.E. *hnitu;* Ger. *Niss.*]

nit² *nit,* (*coll.*) *n.* a fool. [Poss. foregoing, or an abbrev. of **nitwit.**]

nit³ *nit, n.* the unit of luminance, one candela per square metre. [L. *nitor,* brightness.]

nit⁴ *nit,* (*comput.*) *n.* a unit of information (1·44 bits) — also **nep'it.** [Napierian di*git.*]

niterie, nitery *nīt'ə-ri,* (*coll.*) *n.* a nightclub. [**night, -ery.**]

nithing *nī', ni'dhing,* (*hist.*) *n.* an infamous person: an abject coward: a traitor. — *adj.* cowardly: dastardly: niggardly — wrongly **nid(d)ering, nid(d)erling** (*nid',*) **nid'ing.** [O.N. *nīthingr* (in O.E. as *nīthing*) — *nīth,* contumely; Ger. *Neiding.*]

Nithsdale *niths'dāl, n.* an 18th-century woman's riding-hood. [From the Countess of *Nithsdale,* who contrived her husband's escape from the Tower in her clothes in 1716.]

nitid *nit'id, adj.* shining: gay. [L. *nitidus* — *nitēre,* to shine.]

Nitinol *nit'in-ol, n.* an alloy of nickel and titanium, in particular one which, when shaped and then heated to fix that shape, will after reshaping or deformation return to the original shape on reheating. [The chemical symbols *Ni* and *Ti,* and the initial letters of the U.S. *N*aval *O*rdnance *L*aboratory in Maryland where the alloy was discovered.]

niton *nī'ton, n.* a former name for radon. [L. *nitēre,* to shine.]

nitraniline. See **nitro-**.

nitrazepam *nī-trā'zi-pam, n.* a hypnotic taken for the relief of insomnia. [*Nitro-* and *-azepam* as in **diazepam.**]

nitre *nī'tər, n.* sodium carbonate (*obs.*): potassium nitrate or saltpetre (**cubic nitre** is sodium nitrate, or Chile saltpetre): a supposed nitrous substance in the air, etc. (*obs.*). — *n.* **ni'trate** a salt of nitric acid: a fertiliser — natural (potassium or sodium) or synthetic (calcium) nitrate. — *v.t.* to treat with nitric acid or a nitrate: to convert into a nitrate or nitro-compound. — *ns.* **nitratine** (*nī'trə-tin*) sodium nitrate as a mineral; **nitrā'-tion.** — *adj.* **ni'tric.** — *n.* **ni'tride** a compound of nitrogen with another element. — *v.t.* to turn into a nitride: to case-harden by heating in ammonia gas. — *ns.* **ni'triding; nitrificā'tion** treatment with nitric acid: conversion into nitrates, esp. by bacteria through the intermediate condition of nitrites. — *v.t.* and *v.i.* **ni'trify** to subject to or suffer nitrification: — *pr.p.* **ni'trifying;** *pa.t.* and *pa.p.* **ni'trified.** — *ns.* **ni'trile** (*-tril, -trēl, -trīl*) any of a group of organic cyanides (general formula R·C:N); **ni'trite** a salt of nitrous acid; **nitrom'-eter** an apparatus for estimating nitrogen or some of its compounds; **nitrosā'tion** conversion of ammonium salts into nitrites. — *adjs.* **ni'trous; ni'try** (*obs.*) applied to the air, as supposed to contain nitre (see above). — *n.* **ni'tryl** nitroxyl (see **nitro-**). — **nitric acid** HNO₃; **nitric anhydride** N₂O₅; **nitric oxide** NO; **nitrous acid** HNO₂; **nitrous anhydride** N₂O₃; **nitrous oxide** laughing gas, N₂O. [Fr., — L. *nitrum* — Gr. *nitron,* sodium carbonate; prob. of Eastern origin; cf. Egyptian *ntr(j),* Heb. *nether,* Ar. *nitrún.*]

Nitrian *nit'ri-ən, adj.* belonging to *Nitriae* (Nitriai), a region of ancient Egypt west of the Nile delta, including the Natron lakes and a great assemblage of hermit settlements. [Gr. *nitriā,* a soda pit — *nitron,* soda.]

nitride, nitrile, nitrify, etc. See **nitre.**

nitro- *nī-trō-,* in composition, indicating nitration. — *n.*

nitro-an'iline, nitran'iline any nitro-derivative of ani-line. — *n.pl.* **ni'trobactē'ria** bacteria that convert ammonium compounds into nitrites, and (esp.) those that convert nitrites into nitrates. — *ns.* **nitroben'zene** a yellow oily liquid (C₆H₅NO₂) got from benzene and nitric and concentrated sulphuric acid; **nitrocell'ulose** cellulose nitrate, used as an explosive, in lacquers, glues, etc.; **ni'tro-com'pound, ni'tro-deriv'ative** a compound in which one or more hydrogens of an aromatic or aliphatic compound are replaced by nitro-groups; **ni'trocott'on** guncotton; **nitroglyc'erine** a powerfully explosive compound produced by the action of nitric and sulphuric acids on glycerine; **ni'tro-group** the radical NO₂; **nit'rohydrochlor'ic acid** same as **aqua= regia; nitromē'thane** a liquid (CH₃NO₂) obtained from methane and used as a solvent and as rocket-fuel; **nitrosamine** (*-sə-mēn', -sa'mēn*) any of a class of neutral organic chemical compounds which cause cancer; **ni'tro-silk** an artificial silk in which fibres of cellulose nitrate are made and then turned into cellulose; **nitrō'-sō-group** the group NO; **nitrotol'uene** a nitroderivative of toluene; **nitrox'yl** the group NO₂.

nitrogen *nī'trō-jən, n.* a gaseous element (symbol N; at. numb. 7) forming nearly four-fifths of common air, a necessary constituent of every organised body, so called from its being an essential constituent of nitre. — *v.t.* **nitrogenise, -ize** (*-troj'*) to combine or supply with nitrogen. — *adj.* **nitrog'enous** of or containing nitrogen. — **nitrogen cycle** the sum total of the transformations undergone by nitrogen and nitrogenous compounds in nature — from free nitrogen back to free nitrogen; **nitrogen fixation** the bringing of free nitrogen into combination; **nitrogen mustard** any of several compounds with a molecular structure resembling that of a mustard gas, used in cancer treatments; **nitrogen narcosis** intoxicating and anaesthetic effect of too much nitrogen in the brain, experienced by divers at considerable depths — also called **rapture of the deep, depths** and (*slang*) **the narks.** [Gr. *nitron,* sodium carbonate (but taken as if meaning nitre), and the root of *gennaein,* to generate.]

nitrometer, nitrosation, nitrous, nitry, nitryl. See **nitre.**

nitrosamine, nitroxyl. See **nitro-.**

nitty. See **nit¹.**

nitty-gritty *nit'i-grit'i,* (*coll.*) *n.* the basic details, the fundamentals, esp. in phrase *get down to the nitty-gritty.* [Origin uncertain; perhaps from **grit¹.**]

nitwit *nit'wit,* (*slang*) *n.* a blockhead. — *adj.* **nit'witted.** [Poss. Ger. dial. *nit,* not, and **wit.**]

nival *nī'vəl, adj.* growing among snow. — *adj.* **niveous** (*niv'i-əs*) snowy, white. — *n.* **Nivôse** (*nē-vōz*) the 4th month of the French revolutionary calendar, about 21 Dec. to 19 Jan. [L. *nix, nivis,* snow.]

nix¹ *niks,* (*Gmc. myth.*) *n.* a water-spirit, mostly malignant: — *fem.* **nix'ie, nix'y.** [Ger. *Nix,* fem. *Nixe;* cf. **nicker².**]

nix² *niks,* (*slang*) *n.* nothing: short for 'nothing doing, you'll get no support from me': postal matter addressed amiss (*old U.S.,* usu. in *pl.*). — *n.* **nix-nie, niks-nie** (*niks'nē; S.Afr.*) nothing at all. — **nix my dolly** (*obs. slang*) never mind. [Coll. Ger. and Du. for Ger. *nichts,* nothing.]

nix³ *niks, interj.* a cry to give warning of an approaching policeman, master, etc.

nizam *ni-zäm',* or *nī-zam', n.* the title of the prince of Hyderabad in India: a Turkish soldier. [Hind. *nizām,* regulator.]

no¹ *nō, adv.* not so: not: (with *compar.*) in no degree, not at all. — *n.* a denial: a refusal: a vote or voter for the negative: — *pl.* **noes.** — *n.* **no'-no** (*coll.*) a failure, non-event: something which must not be done, said, etc.: — *pl.* **no'-nos, -no's, -noes.** — **no more** destroyed: dead: never again. [O.E. *nā* — *ne,* not, *ā,* ever; cf. **nay.**]

no² *nō, adj.* not any: not one: by no means properly called. — *adj.* **no-account'** (*U.S.*) worthless: insignificant. — **no'-ball'** (*cricket*) a ball bowled in such a way that it is disallowed by rules; **no'-fines'** concrete from which the fine aggregate (i.e. sand) has been omitted. — *adj.* **no'-good** bad, worthless. — *n.* a bad, worthless person. — **no-hope(r)** see **hope**[1]; **no'-man** one ready to say 'no'; **no'-man's-land** a waste region to which no one has a recognised claim: neutral or disputed land, esp. between entrenched hostile forces (also *fig.*); **no'-meaning** want of meaning: something said that is deficient in meaning. — *n.* and *pron.* **no'-one, no one** nobody. — *adj.* **no-non'sense** sensible, tolerating no nonsense. — **no-side'** the end of a game at Rugby football; **no'-trump', no'-trumps'** (*bridge*) a call for the playing of a hand without any trump suit. — *adj.* **no'-trump'.** — **no-trump'er** a no-trump call: a hand suitable for this: one addicted to calling no-trumps. — *advs.* **no'way, no'ways, no'wise** in no way, manner, or degree (see also below). — *adj.* **no'-win'** (of a situation) in which one is bound to lose or fail whatever one does. — **no-claims bonus, discount** a reduction in the price of an insurance policy because no claims have been made on it; **no doubt** surely; **no end, no go** see **end, go**[1]; **no joke** not a trifling matter; **no one** no single; **no time** a very short time; **no way** (*coll.*) under no circumstances, absolutely not — emphatic expression of disagreement or dissent. [O.E. *nān*, none. See **none**.]

no[3] *nō, (mod. Scot.) adv.* not. [Perh. from *nocht*; see **not**[1], **nought**.]

no[4], **nō, noh** *nō, n.* (often with *cap.*) the Japanese drama developed out of a religious dance: — *pl.* **no(h).** — Also **nō'gaku** (-gä-kōō; Jap. *gaku*, music): — *pl.* **no'gaku.** [Jap. *nō.*]

Noachian *nō-ā'ki-ən, adj.* of *Noah* or his time — also **Noachic** (-*ak'*, -*āk'*). — **Noah's ark** a child's toy in imitation of the Ark with its occupants.

nob[1] *nob, n.* head (*coll.*): the knave of turn-up suit in cribbage. — **one for his nob** a point scored for holding the nob: a blow on the head. [Perh. **knob.**]

nob[2] *nob, n.* a superior person. — *adv.* **nobb'ily.** — *n.* **nobb'iness.** — *adj.* **nobb'y** smart. [Origin obscure; cf. **nabs, nib**[2].]

nobble *nob'l, (slang) v.t.* to get hold of, esp. dishonestly: to win over, persuade, or dissuade, as by bribery or coercion: to swindle: to injure or drug (a racehorse) to prevent it from winning: to prevent from doing something: to seize. — *n.* **nobb'ler** (*slang*) one who nobbles: a finishing-stroke: a thimble-rigger's confederate: a dram of spirits. [Perh. **nab**[1].]

nobbut *nob'ət, (dial.) adv.* only. — *prep.* except. — *conj.* except that. [**no**[1,2], **but**[1].]

Nobel prize *nō-bel' prīz',* one of the annual prizes for work in physics, chemistry, medicine, literature, and the promotion of peace instituted by Alfred B. *Nobel* (1833–96), Swedish discoverer of dynamite.

nobelium *nō-bel'i-əm, -bēl', n.* the name given to a transuranic element (symbol No, at. numb. 102) in 1957 when its production at the *Nobel* Institute, Stockholm, was claimed.

nobilesse. See **noblesse.**

nobiliary. See under **nobility.**

nobility *nō-bil'i-ti, n.* the quality of being noble: high rank: dignity: excellence: greatness of mind or character: noble descent: nobles as a body. — *adj.* **nobil'iary** of nobility. — *v.t.* **nobil'itate** to ennoble. — *n.* **nobilitā'-tion.** — **nobiliary particle** a preposition forming part of a title or some names, e.g. Ger. *von*, Fr. *de*, It. *di.* [See next word.]

noble *nō'bl, adj.* illustrious: high in rank or character: of high birth: impressive: stately: generous: excellent. — *n.* a person of exalted rank: a peer: an obsolete gold coin = 6s. 8d. (33p) sterling. — *n.* **no'bleness.** — *adv.* **no'bly.** — **noble art** boxing; **noble gas** an inert gas; **no'bleman** a man who is noble or of rank: a peer: — *pl.* **no'blemen;** *fem.* **no'blewoman; noble metal** one that does not readily tarnish on exposure to air, as gold, silver, platinum (opposed to *base metal*). — *adj.* **no'ble-mind'ed.** — **no'ble-mind'edness; noble opal** precious opal, a translucent or semi-transparent bluish or yellowish white variety with brilliant play of colours; **noble rot** a mould which forms on over-ripe grapes and produces the characteristic richness of certain wines, e.g. Sauternes, Tokay; **noble savage** a romantic and idealised view of primitive man. — **most noble** the style of a duke. [Fr. *noble* — L. *(g)nōbilis* — *(g)nōscĕre,* to know.]

noblesse *nō-bles', n.* nobility: nobleness: a body of nobility. — (*Spens.*) **no'blesse, no'bilesse.** — **noblesse oblige** (*ō-blēzh*) rank imposes obligations. [Fr.]

nobody *nō'bə-di, n.* no person: no-one: a person of no account. — **nobody's business** (*slang*) a thing nobody could hope to deal with or nobody troubles about. — **like nobody's business** very energetically or intensively. [**no**[2], **body**.]

nocake *nō'kāk, n.* meal made of parched Indian corn. [Amer. Ind. word *nookik*, etc.]

nocent *nō'sənt, (rare) adj.* hurtful: guilty. — *n.* one who is hurtful or guilty. — *adv.* **nō'cently.** [L. *nocēns, -entis,* pr.p. of *nocēre,* to hurt.]

nochel. See **notchel.**

nociceptive *nō-si-sep'tiv, adj.* sensitive to pain: causing pain. [L. *nocēre,* to hurt, and re*ceptive.*]

nock *nok, n.* a notch, or a part carrying a notch, esp. on an arrow or a bow: the forward upper end of a sail that sets with a boom. — *v.t.* to notch: to fit (an arrow) on the string. [Origin obscure — poss. connected with Sw. *nock,* tip; appar. not the same as **notch**.]

nocket. See **nacket.**

noct- *nokt-,* **nocti-** *nok-ti-,* in composition, night. [L. *nox, noct-.*]

noctambulation *nok-tam-bū-lā'shən, n.* sleep-walking. — *ns.* **noctam'bulism; noctam'bulist.** [L. *nox, noctis,* night, *ambulāre, -ātum,* to walk.]

Noctilio *nok-til'i-ō, n.* a South American genus, the hare-lipped bat. [L. *nox, noctis,* night, and the ending of *vespertiliō,* bat.]

Noctiluca *nok-ti-lōō'ka, -lū', n.* a genus of phosphorescent marine flagellate infusorians, abundant around the British coasts: (without *cap.*) a member of the genus. — *n.* **noctilu'cence.** — *adjs.* **noctilu'cent** (-*sənt*), **noctilu'-cous** (-*kəs*) phosphorescent: shining in the dark. [L. *noctilūca,* the moon, a lantern — *nox, noctis,* night, *lūcēre,* to shine.]

noctivagant *nok-tiv'ə-gənt, adj.* wandering in the night. — *n.* **noctivagā'tion.** — *adj.* **noctiv'agous.** [L. *nox, noctis,* night, *vagārī,* to wander.]

Noctua *nok'tū-ə, n.* a generic name sometimes used (without *cap.*) as a general name for any member of the **Noctū'idae,** a large family (or group of families) of mostly nocturnal, strong-bodied moths, the owlet-moths. — *n.* **noc'tuid.** [L. *noctua,* an owl — *nox,* night.]

noctuary *nok'tū-ə-ri, n.* a record of the events or thoughts of night. [L. *nox, noctis,* night, on the analogy of **diary.**]

noctule *nok'tūl, n.* the great bat, the largest British species. [Fr., — It. *nottola,* L. *nox, noctis,* night.]

nocturn *nok'tûrn, n.* any one of the three sections of the office of Matins: a daily portion of the psalter used at nocturns (*obs.*). — *adj.* **nocturn'al** belonging to night: happening, done, or active by night. — *n.* an astronomical instrument for finding the hour by night: a person, animal, or spirit active by night. — *adv.* **nocturn'ally.** — *n.* **nocturne** (*nok'tûrn* or -*tûrn'*) a dreamy or pensive piece, generally for the piano, esp. associated with the name of its inventor John Field (1782–1837) and Chopin, who developed it: a moonlight or night scene (*paint.*). [L. *nocturnus* — *nox,* night.]

nocuous *nok'ū-əs, (rare) adj.* hurtful. — *adv.* **noc'uously.** — *n.* **noc'uousness.** [L. *nocuus* — *nocēre,* to hurt.]

nod *nod, v.i.* to give a quick forward motion of the head, esp. in assent, salutation, or command: to let the head drop in weariness: to lean over as if about to fall: to bend or curve downward, or hang from a curved support: to dance or bob up and down: to make a careless slip. — *v.t.* to incline: to signify or direct by a nod: — *pr.p.* **nodd'ing;** *pa.t.* and *pa.p.* **nodd'ed.** — *n.* a quick bending forward of the head: a slight bow: a movement of the head as a gesture of assent or command. — *n.* **nodd'er.** — *n.* and *adj.* **nodd'ing.** — *v.t.* and *v.i.* **nodd'le** to nod slightly: to keep nodding. — *n.* **nodd'y** an inverted pendulum with a spring, used to test oscillation. — **nodding acquaintance** slight acquaintance: someone with whom one is only slightly acquainted: superficial, incomplete knowledge or understanding; **nodding duck** see **duck**[3]. — **Land of Nod** sleep (in punning allusion to the biblical land, Gen. iv. 16); **nod off** (*coll.*) to fall asleep; **nod through** in parliament, to allow to vote by proxy: to pass without discussion, a vote, etc.; **on the nod** (*slang*) on tick: by general assent, i.e. without the formality of voting, without adequate scrutiny, etc. [M.E. *nodde*, not known in O.E.]

nodal, etc. See **node**.

noddle *nod'l, n.* the back of the head (*obs.*): the nape of the neck (*dial.*): now jocular, the head. [Origin obscure.]

noddy[1] *nod'i, n* a simpleton, noodle: an oceanic bird (*Anous*) akin to the terns, unaccustomed to man and therefore easily taken and deemed stupid: an old game like cribbage: the knave in this and other games: an old form of cab with a door at the back. [Origin obscure: connection among meanings doubtful.]

noddy[2]. See **nod**.

node *nōd, n.* a knot: a knob or lump: a swelling: a place, often swollen, where a leaf is attached to a stem: a point of intersection of two great circles of the celestial sphere, esp. the orbit of a planet or the moon and the ecliptic: a point at which a curve cuts itself, and through which more than one tangent to the curve can be drawn (*geom.*): a similar point on a surface, where there is more than one tangent-plane (*geom.*): a point of minimum displacement in a system of stationary waves: a meeting-place of lines, roads, or parts: a complication in a story (*fig.*). — *adj.* **nō'dal** of or like a node or nodes. — *v.t.* **nōd'alise, -ize** to make nodal. — *n.* **nōdal'ity** knottedness: state of being nodal. — *adj.* **nōd'āted** knotted. — *n.* **nōdā'tion** knottiness: a knotty place. — *adjs.* **nodical** (*nōd'* or *nod'*) pertaining to the nodes of a celestial body: from a node round to the same node again; **nodose** (*nōd-ōs', nōd'ōs*) having nodes, knots or swellings: knotty. — *n.* **nodosity** (*nō-dos'i-ti*) knottiness: a knotty swelling. — *adjs.* **nōd'ous** knotty; **nodular** (*nod'ū-lər*) of or like a nodule: in the form of nodules: having nodules or little knots; **nōd'ulāted** having nodules. — *ns.* **nōd'ule** a little rounded lump: a swelling on a root inhabited by symbiotic bacteria. — *adjs.* **nōd'ūled; nōd'ūlose, nōd'ūlous.** — *n.* **nōd'us** (L.) a knotty point, difficulty, complication: a swelling at the junction of nervures in an insect's wing: — *pl.* **nōd'i** (-*ī*). [L. *nōdus;* dim. *nōdulus*.]

noël *nō-el,* (Fr.) *n.* a Christmas carol. **Noël.** See **Nowel(l).**

noesis *nō-ē'sis, n.* the activity of the intellect. — *adj.* **noemat'ical.** — *adv.* **noemat'ically.** — *adj.* **noetic** (*nō-et'-ik*) purely intellectual. [Gr. *noēsis* — *noeein*, to perceive, think.]

Noetian *nō-ē'shən, n.* a Patripassian or follower of *Noëtus* of Smyrna (3rd cent.). — Also *adj.* — *n.* **Noe'tianism.**

nog[1] *nog, n.* Norwich strong ale (*obs.*): egg-nog or similar drink. [Origin unknown.]

nog[2] *nog, n.* a stump or snag: a wooden peg, pin, or cog: a brick-sized piece of wood inserted in a wall to receive nails. — *n.* **nogg'ing** a brick filling between timbers in a partition. [Origin unknown.]

nogaku. See **no**[4].

noggin *nog'in, n.* a small mug or wooden cup: its contents, a dram of about a gill: a drink (of beer, spirits, etc.) (*coll.*): the head (*coll.*). [Origin unknown; Ir. *noigín,* Gael. *noigean,* are believed to be from English.]

noh. See **no**[4].

nohow *nō'how, adv.* not in any way, not at all: in no definable way. — *adj.* (*coll.*; also **no'howish**) out of sorts.

noils *noilz, n.pl.* short pieces of wool or other fibre separated from the longer fibres e.g. by combing. — Also *n.sing.* **noil** the wool or other fibre so separated. [Origin unknown.]

noint, 'noint. An aphetic form of **anoint**.

noise *noiz, n.* sound of any kind: an unmusical sound: an over-loud or disturbing sound: din: frequent or public talk: rumour (*obs.*): report (*Shak.*): a band of musicians (*obs.*): interference in the transference of heat, in an electrical current, etc.: meaningless extra bits or words removed from data, or ignored, at the time of use (*comput.*): interference in a communication channel, as detected by hearing or (**visual noise** — e.g. snow on a television screen) sight. — *Spens.* **noyes.** — *v.t.* (usu. with *about, abroad*) to spread by rumour. — *v.i.* to talk or call out loud (*rare*). — *adjs.* **noise'ful; noise'less.** — *adv.* **noise'lessly.** — *n.* **noise'lessness.** — *adv.* **nois'ily.** — *n.* **nois'iness.** — *adj.* **nois'y** making a loud noise or sound: attended with noise: clamorous: turbulent. — **a big, top noise** a person of great importance; **make a noise in the world** to achieve great notoriety. [Fr. *noise,* noise; perh. from L. *nausea,* disgust, possibly influenced by L. *noxia,* in its (albeit disputed) meaning, disturbance, strife.]

noisette[1] *nwa-zet', n.* a hybrid between China rose and musk-rose. [From Philippe *Noisette,* its first grower.]

noisette[2] *nwa-zet', n.* a small piece of meat (usu. lamb) cut off the bone and rolled: a nutlike or nut-flavoured sweet. [Fr., hazelnut.]

noisome *noi'səm, adj.* injurious to health: disgusting to sight or smell. — *adv.* **noi'somely.** — *n.* **noi'someness.** [**noy.**]

nole (*Shak.*). See **noll.**

nolens volens *nō'lenz vō'lenz, nō'lāns vō', wō'lāns,* (L.) willynilly.

noli-me-tangere *nō-li-mē-tan'jə-ri* (**noli me tangere** *nō-lē mā tang'ge-rā;* Vulgate, John xx. 17) *n.* a warning against touching: lupus, etc., of the face (*arch.*): a species of balsam, *Impatiens noli-(me-)tangere,* that ejects its ripe seeds at a light touch. — *adj.* warning off. [L. *nōlī* (imper. of *nōlle*) be unwilling, do not, *mē,* me, *tangĕre,* to touch.]

nolition *nō-lish'ən, n.* unwillingness: absence of willingness: a will not to do. [L. *nōlle,* to be unwilling.]

noll, noul, nowl (*Spens.* **noule,** *Shak.* **nole**) *nōl, n.* the top of the head. [O.E. *hnoll.*]

nolle prosequi *no'le pros'ə-kwī,* (L.; *law*) (an entry on a record to the effect that) the plaintiff or prosecutor will proceed no further with (part of) the suit.

nolo contendere *nō'lō kon-ten'də-ri,* (L.) I do not wish to contend (*lit.*) — a legal plea by which the accused does not admit guilt, but accepts conviction (e.g. when wishing to avoid lengthy legal proceedings) — the charges can be denied if referred to in a separate case.

nolo episcopari *nō'lō e-pis-ko-pär'ī,* (L.) I do not wish to be a bishop (*lit.*): refusal of responsible position.

nom *nɔ̃,* (Fr.) *n.* name. — **nom de guerre** (*də ger*) an assumed name: pseudonym (**nom de plume** (see separate entry) is not French).

noma *nō'mə, n.* a destructive ulceration of the cheek, esp. that affecting debilitated children. [L. *nomē,* ulcer — Gr. *nomē,* ulcer, feeding — *nemein,* to feed, consume.]

nomad, nomade *nōm'ad,* -*əd,* also *nom', n.* one of a wandering pastoral community: a rover. — Also *adj.* — *nomadic* (*nōm-* or *nom-ad'ik*). — *adv.* **nomad'ically.** — *n.* **nomadisā'tion, -z-.** — *v.i.* **nom'adise, -ize** to lead a nomadic or vagabond life. — *v.t.* to make nomadic. — *ns.* **nom'adism; nom'ady** living as or like a nomad. [Gr. *nomas, nomados* — *nemein,* to drive to pasture.]

nomarch, nomarchy. See **nome.**

nombril *nom'bril,* (*her.*) *n.* a point a little below the centre of a shield. [Fr., navel.]

nom de plume *nɔ̃ də plüm', ploom',* or *nom,* a pen-name, pseudonym. [Would-be Fr. — Fr. *nom*, name, *de*, of, *plume*, pen.]

nome *nōm*, *n.* a province or department, esp. in ancient Egypt or modern Greece. — *ns.* **nomarch** (*nom'ärk*) the governor of a nome; **nom'archy** a nome of modern Greece; **nom'os** (Gr.) a nome. [Gr. *nomos.*]

nomen *nō'men*, (L.) *n.* a name, *esp.* of the gens or clan, a Roman's second name as Gaius *Julius* Caesar: — *pl.* **nō'mina.** — **nomen nudum** (*nū'dəm, noo'doom*) in biology, a mere name published without a description.

nomenclator *nō'mən-klā-tər, n.* one who bestows names, or draws up a classified scheme of names: one who announces or tells the names of persons, esp. (*hist.*) in canvassing for a Roman election: a book containing a list of words, a vocabulary (*obs.*). — *adjs.* **no'menclātive, nomenclatorial** (*nō-men-klə-tō'ri-əl, -tō'*), **nomenclā'tural.** — *n.* **nō'menclāture** (or *nō-men'klə-chər*) a system of names: terminology: a list of names: a vocabulary (*obs.*): mode of naming: (now considered *loose*) a name. [L. *nōmenclātor* — *nōmen*, a name, *calāre* to call.]

nomic *nom'ik, adj.* customary: conventional, esp. of spelling. [Gr. *nomikos* — *nomos*, custom.]

-nomic. See **-nomy.**

nominal *nom'in-əl, adj.* pertaining to, or of the nature of, a name or noun: of names: by name: only in name: so-called, but not in reality: inconsiderable, hardly more than a matter of form: nominalistic (*rare*): according to plan (*space flight*). — *n.* a noun or phrase, etc. standing as a noun (*gram.*). — *ns.* **nom'inalism** the doctrine that general terms have no corresponding reality either in or out of the mind, being mere words; **nom'inalist.** — *adj.* **nominalist'ic.** — *adv.* **nom'inally** by name: as a noun: in name only. — **nominal par, nominal value** see **par¹**. [L. *nōminālis* — *nōmen, -inis*, a name.]

nominate *nom'in-āt, v.t.* to name: to mention by name: to appoint: to propose formally for election. — *adj.* (chiefly *Scots law*) nominated: elect. — *adj.* **nom'inable** namable: fit to be named. — *adv.* **nom'inately** by name. — *n.* **nominā'tion** the act or power of nominating: state of being nominated: naming: in horse breeding, the arranged mating of a mare with a stallion. — *adj.* **nominatival** (*nom-in-ə-tī'vl*, or *nom-nə-*). — *adv.* **nominatī'vally.** — *adj.* **nominative** (*nom'in-ə-tiv, nom'nə-tiv; gram.*) naming the subject: in the case in which the subject is expressed: (also *nom'in-ā-tiv*) nominated, appointed by nomination. — *n.* the nominative case: a word in the nominative case. — *adv.* **nom'inatively.** — *n.* **nom'inātor** one who nominates. — **nominative absolute** a nominative combined with a participle, but not connected with a finite verb or governed by any other word. [L. *nōmināre, -ātum*, to name — *nōmen.*]

nominee *nom-in-ē', n.* one who is nominated by another: one on whose life an annuity or lease depends: one to whom the holder of a copyhold estate surrenders his interest. [L. *nōmināre, -ātum*, to nominate, with *-ee* as if from Fr.]

nomism *nōm'izm, nom'izm, n.* religious legalism: the view that moral conduct consists in the observance of a law. — *adj.* **nomist'ic** (*nom-*) based on law, or on a sacred book. [Gr. *nomisma*, established custom, *nomos*, a law.]

nomocracy *nom-ok'rə-si*, or *nōm-, n.* government according to a code of laws. [Gr. *nomos*, law, *kratos*, power.]

nomogeny *nom-* or *nōm-oj'ə-ni, n.* the origination of life according to natural law, not miracle — opp. to *thaumatogeny*. [Gr. *nomos*, law, and the root *gen-*, as in *genesis*, origination.]

nomography *nom-* or *nōm-og'rə-fi, n.* the art of drawing up laws. — *ns.* **nomog'rapher; nom'ogram** a chart or diagram of scaled lines or curves used to help in calculations, comprising three scales in which a line joining values on two determines a third. — Also called **nom'ograph**, isopleth. — *adjs.* **nomograph'ic, nomograph'ical.** [Gr. *nomos*, law, *graphein*, to write.]

nomology *nom-* or *nōm-ol'ə-ji, n.* the science of law: the

science of the laws of the mind. — *adj.* **nomological** (*-ə-loj'*). — *n.* **nomol'ogist.** [Gr. *nomos*, law, *logos*, discourse.]

nomos. See **nome.**

nomothete *nom'ō-thēt*, or (Gr.) **nomothetes** (*nom-oth'i-tēz*), *ns.* a lawgiver: a legislator: in ancient Athens, one of a body charged with revision of the laws. — *adjs.* **nomothetic** (*-thet'ik*), **nomothet'ical.** [Gr. *nomothetēs* — *nomos*, law, and the root *the-*, as in *tithenai*, to set.]

-nomy *-nə-mi*, in composition, a science or field of knowledge, or the discipline of the study of these. — **-nōm'ic** adjective combining form. [Gr. *-nomia*, administration, regulation.]

non¹ *non*, a Latin word used as a prefix, not: sometimes used of someone or something with pretensions who, which, is ludicrously unworthy of the name mentioned, e.g. **non-hero, non-event;** the words given below include the most common words with *non-* but the prefix is living and many other words using it may be formed. — *ns.* **non-abil'ity** incapacity: inability: **non= accept'ance** want of acceptance: refusal to accept; **non-ac'cess** (*law*) want of opportunity for sexual intercourse; **non-admiss'ion** refusal of admission: failure to be admitted; **non-aggress'ion** abstention from aggression (also *adj.*). — *adjs.* **non-alcohol'ic** not alcoholic: not containing alcohol; **non-aligned'** not aligned: not taking sides in international politics, esp. not supporting either of the main international blocs, i.e. the Warsaw Pact countries or the USA and the western European democracies. — *ns.* **non-align'ment; non= appear'ance** failure or neglect to appear, esp. in a court of law; **non-arri'val** failure to arrive; **non-attend'ance** a failure to attend: absence; **non-atten'tion** inattention; **non-Chris'tian** one who is other than Christian (also *adj.*); **non'-claim** a failure to make claim within the time limited by law. — *adjs.* **non-cog'nisable** of an offence, that cannot be judicially investigated; **non= collē'giate** not belonging to a college (also *n.*). — *ns.* **non-com'** (*coll.*) a non-commissioned officer; **non-com'-batant** any one connected with an army who is there for some purpose other than that of fighting, as a surgeon, a chaplain: a civilian in time of war. — *adjs.* **non-commiss'ioned** not having a commission, as an officer in the army below the rank of commissioned officer or warrant officer; **non-committ'al** not committing one, or refraining from committing oneself, to any particular opinion or course of conduct: free from any declared preference or pledge: implying nothing, one way or the other. — *adv.* **non-committ'ally.** — *n.* a non-committal state or utterance. — *ns.* **non-commun'-icant** one who does not take communion on any particular occasion or in general, esp. formerly according to the rites of the Church of England: one who has not yet communicated; **non-commun'ion; non-com-pear'ance** (*Scots law*) failure to appear in a court of law; **non-compli'ance** neglect or failure of compliance. — *adj.* **non-comply'ing.** — *ns.* **non-compound'er** one who does not compound or make composition: a Jacobite who would restore James II unconditionally (*hist.*); **non-con'** (*coll.*) a Nonconformist (also *adj.*); **non-concurr'ence** refusal to concur. — *adjs.* **non-con-curr'ent; non-conduct'ing** not readily conducting, esp. heat or electricity. — *n.* **non-conduct'or** a substance or object that does not readily conduct heat or electricity. — *adj.* **nonconform'ing** not conforming, esp. to an established church. — *ns.* **nonconform'ist** one who does not conform: esp. one who refused to conform or subscribe to the Act of Uniformity in 1662: usu. applied in England (*cap.*) to a Protestant separated from the Church of England (also *adj.*); **nonconform'ity** want of conformity, esp. to the established church; **non'-content** one not content: in House of Lords, one giving a negative vote. — *adjs.* **non-conten'tious** not subject to contention; **non-contrib'utory** not based on contributions. — *ns.* **non-co-operā'tion** failure or refusal to co-operate, esp. (in India before 1947) with the government; **non-deliv'ery** failure or neglect to

deliver: the fact of not having been delivered. — *adjs.*
non-denominā'tional not exclusively belonging to or
according to the beliefs of any single denomination of
the Christian church; **non-destruc'tive** having no destructive effect, esp. in tests on products, substances
or organisms. — *n.* **nondisjunc'tion** (*biol.*) the failure
of paired chromosomes to separate during meiosis. —
adjs. **non-drip'** (of paint) thixotropic, of such a consistency that it does not drip when being applied; **non=
effect'ive** having no effect: not efficient or serviceable:
unfitted or unavailable for service: relating to those so
unfitted or unavailable. — *n.* a member of a force who
is unfitted or unavailable for active service. — *adj.*
non-effi'cient not up to the standard required for
service. — *n.* a soldier who has not yet undergone the
full number of drills. — *n.* **non-e'go** in metaphysics,
the not-I, the object as opposed to the subject, whatever is not the conscious self. — *adj.* **non-elect'** not
elect. — *n.* **non-elec'tion** state of not being elect: fact
of not having elected or been elected. — *adjs.* **non=
elec'tive** not chosen by election; **non-elec'tric** (*obs.*)
conducting electricity. — *n.* (*obs.*) a conductor. — *ns.*
non-elec'trolyte a substance, such as sugar, that gives
a non-conducting solution; **non-en'try** (*Scots law, hist.*)
a vassal's heir's failure to renew investiture: a casualty
that was due to the superior on such failure. — *adj.*
non-essen'tial not essential: not absolutely required. —
n. something that is not essential, or is not of extreme
importance. — *adj.* **non-Euclid'ean** not according to
Euclid's axioms and postulates. — *n.* **non-event'** see
above at **non.** — *adj.* **non-exec'utive** (of e.g. directors)
not employed by a company full-time, but brought in
for advisory purposes (also *n.*). — *n.* **non-exist'ence** the
condition of not being: a thing that has no existence.
— *adj.* **non-exist'ent.** — *n.* **non-feasance** see separate
article. — *adjs.* **non-ferr'ous** containing no iron: other
than iron: relating to metals other than iron; **non=
fic'tion** of a literary work, without any deliberately
fictitious element (**non-fiction novel** one whose material
is entirely drawn from people and events in real life);
non-fic'tional; non-flamm'able not easily set on fire: not
flammable; **non-for'feiting** of a life insurance policy,
not forfeited by reason of non-payment. — *ns.* **non=
fulfil'ment** the fact of not fulfilling or not being fulfilled;
non-gre'mial a non-resident member, esp. of Cambridge University. — *adj.* applied to the examinations
afterwards called *local.* — *adj.* **nonharmon'ic.** — *ns.*
non-interven'tion a policy of systematic abstention
from interference in the affairs of other nations;
non-intru'sion in Scottish Church history, the principle
that a patron should not force an unacceptable minister on an unwilling congregation; **non-intru'sionist;
non-involve'ment** the fact of not involving or not being
involved. — *adj.* **non-iss'uable** not capable of being
issued: not admitting of issue being taken on it. — *n.*
non-join'der omission to join all the parties to an action
or suit. — *adj.* **non-judg(e)men'tal** relating to or having
an open attitude without implicit judgment, esp.
moral. — *adv.* **non-judg(e)men'tally.** — *adj.* **nonjur'ing**
not swearing allegiance. — *n.* **nonjur'or** one who
refuses to swear allegiance, esp. (with *cap.*) one of the
clergy in England and Scotland who would not swear
allegiance to William and Mary in 1689, holding
themselves still bound by the oath they had taken to
the deposed king, James II. — *adjs.* **non-lin'ear** not
linear; **non-marr'ying** not readily disposed to marry.
— *ns.* **non'-mem'ber** one who is not a member; **non'=
met'al** an element that is not a metal. — *adjs.* **non=
metall'ic** not metallic: not of metal or like metal;
non-mor'al unconcerned with morality: involving no
moral considerations; **non-nat'ural** not natural: forced
or strained. — *n.* in old medicine (usu. in *pl.*) anything
not considered of the essence of man, but necessary
to his well-being, as air, food, sleep, rest, etc. — *adjs.*
non-nu'cleated not nucleated; **non-objec'tive** (*paint.*)
non-representational. — *n.* **non-observ'ance** neglect or
failure to observe: disregard. — *adjs.* **non-opera'tional**

not operational; **nonpar'ous** not having given birth;
non-partic'ipating not taking part: (of shares, etc.) not
giving the right to a share in profits; **non-partisan'** (or
-pärt') not partisan: impartial; **non-par'ty** independent
of party politics. — *ns.* **non-pay'ment; non-perform'-
ance** neglect or failure to perform; **non'-per'son** one
previously of political, etc., eminence, now out of
favour: a complete nonentity. — *adjs.* **non-play'ing** (of
e.g. the captain of a team) not taking active part in
the game(s); **nonpo'lar** without any permanent electric
dipole moment; **non-prior'ity** without privilege of priority. — *n.* **non-produc'tion.** — *adjs.* **non-produc'tive;
non-profess'ional** not professional or of a profession:
not done in a professional capacity. — *n.* **non-profi'-
cient** one who has made no progress in the art or study
in which he is engaged. — *adjs.* **non-prof'it-making** not
organised or engaged in with the purpose of making
a profit. — *n.* **non-prolifera'tion** lack of proliferation,
esp. a limit imposed on the proliferation of (usu.
nuclear) weapons. — *adjs.* **non-provi'ded** (of an elementary school or education in England and Wales)
maintained but not provided by the local education
authority, and managed by a committee in which the
trustees form the majority; **non-quo'ta** not included in
a quota. — *n.* **non-regard'ance** (*Shak.*) want of due
regard. — *adj.* **non-representā'tional** not aiming at the
depicting of objects. — *n.* **non-res'idence** the fact of
not residing at a place, esp. where one's official or
social duties require one to reside or where one is
entitled to reside. — *adj.* and *n.* **non-res'ident.** — *n.*
non-resist'ance the principle of not resisting violence
by force, or of not resisting authority: passive submission. — *adjs.* **non-resist'ant, non-resist'ing; non-restric'-
tive** (*gram.*) used of a relative clause that does not
restrict its antecedent; **non-return'able** of a bottle, jar
or other container, on which a returnable deposit has
not been paid; **non-rig'id** of airships, having a balloon
or gasbag with no internal framework to brace it, and
no rigid keel; **non-sched'uled** not according to a schedule: of an airline, operating between specified points
but not to a specific schedule of flights; **non-skid',
non-slip'** designed to reduce chance of slipping to a
minimum. — *n.* **non-smo'ker** one who does not smoke:
a railway compartment in which smoking is supposed
to be forbidden. — *adjs.* **non-smok'ing; non-soci'ety**
not belonging to a society, esp. not a member of a
trade union: employing men who are not members of
a trade union; **non-spec'ialist** not devoting oneself to
one particular subject, task, etc. — Also *n.* — *adj.*
non-specif'ic not specific: of a disease, not caused by
any specific agent. — *n.* **non-start'er** a horse which,
though entered for a race, does not run: a person, idea,
etc., with no chance at all of success. — *adj.* **non-stick'**
of e.g. a pan, treated so that food or other substance
will not stick to it. — *adj.* and *adv.* **non'-stop'** uninter-
rupted(ly): without any stop or halt. — *ns.* **non'-term**
(*obs.*) a vacation between terms: a time of inactivity;
non-thing' something which does not exist: something
trivial. — *adjs.* **non-U** see **U; non-u'nion** not attached
to a trade union: employing, or produced by, non-
union workers. — *ns.* **non-u'nionist; non-u'sager** a
Nonjuror who rejected the usages; **non-u'ser** (*law*)
omission to take advantage of a right. — *adj.* **non=
util'ity** not of the special kind made or sold for utility's
sake. — *n.* **non-vi'olence** (the ideal or practice of)
refraining from violence on grounds of principle. —
adjs. **non-vi'olent; non-vo'ting** not voting: of shares,
etc., not giving the right to vote on company decisions.
— *n.* **non-white'** (a member of) a race other than the
white race (also *adj.*). [L. *nōn,* not.]
non[2] *non, nōn,* (L.) not. — **non obstante** (*ob-stan'tē,
ob-stan'te*) not hindering: notwithstanding.
nonage *non'ij, nōn'ij, n.* legal infancy, minority: time of
immaturity generally. — *adj.* **non'aged.** [O.Fr.
nonage — pfx. *non-* (L. *nōn*) and *age,* age.]
nonagenarian *nōn-* or *non-ə-ji-nā'ri-ən, n.* one who is
ninety years old or between ninety and a hundred. —

adj. of that age. [L. *nōnāgēnārius,* relating to ninety — *nōnāgintā,* ninety.]

nonagesimal *nōn-* or *non-ə-jes'i-məl, adj.* ninetieth. — *n.* point of the ecliptic 90° from its intersection by the horizon. [L. *nōnāgēsimus,* ninetieth.]

nonagon *non'ə-gon, n.* an enneagon. [L. *nōnus,* ninth, Gr. *gōniā,* angle.]

nonane *nōn'ān, n.* a hydrocarbon (C_9H_{20}), ninth in the methane series. — **nonanoic acid** same as **pelargonic acid.** [L. *nōnus,* ninth.]

nonary *nōn'ə-ri, adj.* based on nine. [L. *nōnārius.*]

nonce[1] *nons, n.* (almost confined to the phrase *for the nonce,* which in M.E. is sometimes a mere tag for rhyme's sake) the particular or express purpose (*Shak.*): the occasion: the moment, time being. — *adj.* occrring, adopted or coined for a particular occasion only, as **nonce'-word.** [From *for the nones,* i.e. *for then ones,* for the once, *then* being the dative (O.E. *tham*) of **the** and *ones* the genitivc (O.E. *ānes*) of **one** substituted for the dative.]

nonce[2] *nons,* (*prison slang*) *n.* a sexual offender, esp. one who assaults children. [Ety. uncertain.]

nonchalance *non'shə-ləns, n.* unconcern: coolness: indifference. — *adj.* **non'chalant.** — *adv.* **non'chalantly.** [Fr., — *non,* not, *chaloir,* to matter, interest — L. *calēre,* to be warm.]

non-come *non-kum', -kom',* (*Shak.*) *n.* one of Dogberry's blundering words, perh. a confusion of *nonplus* and *non compos mentis.*

nonconformist, -ity. See **non**[1].

nondescript *non'di-skript, adj.* not described (*obs.*): not easily classified: not distinctive enough to be described: neither one thing nor another. — *n.* a person or thing not yet, or not easily, described or classed. [L. *nōn,* not, *dēscrībĕre, -scrīptum,* to describe.]

none *nun, pron.* (*pl.* or *sing.*) not one: no person or persons: not the thing in question: not any: no portion or amount. — *adj.* (separated from the noun; otherwise *arch.*; formerly esp. before a vowel or *h*) no. — *adv.* in no degree: by no means: not at all. — **none'-so= prett'y,** Nan'cy-prett'y London Pride (*Saxifraga umbrosa*). — *adj.* **none'-spar'ing** (*Shak.*) all-destroying. — *adv.* **none'-the-less'** (or **none the less**) nevertheless. — **none other** (often with *than*) no other person; **none the** (followed by *compar.* adjective) in no way, to no degree; **none too** (*coll.*) not very. [O.E. *nān — ne,* not, *ān,* one.]

nonentity *non-en'ti-ti, n.* the state of not bcing: a thing not existing: a person or thing of no importance. [L. *nōn,* not, *entitās* (see **entity**).]

Nones *nōnz, n.pl.* in the Roman calendar, the ninth day before the Ides (both days included) — the 7th of March, May, July, and October, and the 5th of the other months: (without *cap.*) a church office originally for the ninth hour, or three o'clock, afterwards earlier. [L. *nōnae — nōnus,* ninth.]

non(e)such *non', nun'such, n.* a unique, unparalleled, or extraordinary thing: black medick. [**none, such.**]

nonet, nonette *nō-net',* (*mus.*) *n.* a composition for nine performers. — Also **nonet'to:** — *pl.* **nonet'tos, -ti** (*-tē*). [It. *nonetto.*]

non-feasance *non-fē'zəns, n.* omission of something which ought to be done. [Pfx. *non-,* not, O.Fr. *faisance,* doing — *faire* — L. *facĕre,* to do.]

nong *nong,* (*Austr. slang*) *n.* a fool, idiot. [Origin uncertain.]

nonillion *nō-nil'yən, n.* a million raised to the ninth power: one thousand raised to the tenth power (*U.S.*). — *adj.* **nonill'ionth.** [L. *nōnus,* ninth, in imitation of **million, billion.**]

nonjuring, etc. See **non**[1].

nonny *non'i, n.* a meaningless word in old ballad refrain, etc., usually 'hey, nonny', 'hey nonny nonny', or 'hey nonny no' — once a cover for obscenity.

nonpareil *non-pə-rel', -rāl', non', n.* a person or thing without equal: a fine variety of apple: a kind of comfit: an old type size, approximately, and still used syn-

onymously for, six-point (*print.*). — *adj.* unequalled: matchless. [Fr. *non,* not, *pareil,* from a L.L. dim. of L. *pār,* equal.]

nonplus *nonplus', n.* a state in which no more can be done or said: great difficulty: perplexity. — *v.t.* to perplex completely, make uncertain what to say or do: — *pr.p.* **nonpluss'ing;** *pa.t.* and *pa.p.* **nonplussed'.** [L. *nōn,* not, *plūs,* more.]

nonsense *non'səns, n.* that which has no sense: language without meaning: absurdity: trifling: foolery: humbug: trivial things: that which is manifestly false: absurd, illogical, or unintelligible statement or action. — Also *interj.* — *adj.* **nonsensical** (*-sens'*) without sense: absurd. — *ns.* **nonsensicality** (*non-sens-i-kal'i-ti*), **nonsens'icalness.** — *adv.* **nonsens'ically.** — **nonsense verse** verse deliberately written to convey an absurd meaning, or without obvious meaning at all. — **no-nonsense** see **no**[2]. [Pfx. *non-,* not, and **sense.**]

non-sequitur *non-sek'wi-tər, n.* (the drawing of) a conclusion that does not follow logically from the premises: (*loosely*) a remark, action, that has no rclation to what has gone before. — Also **non sequitur.** [L. *nōn,* not, and *sequitur,* follows, 3rd sing. pres. ind. of *sequi,* to follow.]

nonsuch. See **non(e)such.**

nonsuit *non'sūt, -sōot, n.* in England, the stopping of a suit by voluntary withdrawal of the plaintiff, or by the judge when the plaintiff has failed to make out cause of action or to bring evidence. — *v.t.* to subject to a nonsuit. [A.Fr. *no(u)nsute,* does not pursue.]

nonuple *non'ū-pl, adj.* ninefold: having nine parts. — *n.* **non'uplet** a group of nine: esp. a group of nine notes played in the time of six or eight. [L. *nōnus,* ninth; *nonuplus,* not in L., formed on the analogy of *duplus, quadruplus,* etc.]

noodle[1] *nōōd'l, n.* a simpleton: a blockhead. — *n.* **nood'le-dom.** [Cf. **noddy**[1].]

noodle[2] *nōōd'l, n.* a flat, usu. ribbon-shaped, pasta, usu. made with eggs. [Ger. *Nudel.*]

noodle[3] *nōōd'l, v.i.* to improvise on a musical instrument in a casual or desultory way, esp. in jazz. [Ety. uncertain.]

nook *nōōk, n.* a corner: a narrow place formed by an angle: a recess: a secluded retreat. — *adj.* **nook'y.** — *adj.* **nook'-shott'en** (*arch.*) shot out into nooks and corneis. [M.E. *nok, noke;* prob. Scand.; Gael. and Ir. *niuc* is prob. from the Northern form **ncuk.**]

nooky[1]. See **nook.**

nooky[2], **nookie** *nōō'ki,* (*slang*) *n.* sexual intercourse. [Ety. uncertain.]

noology *nō-ol'ə-ji, n.* the science of the intellect. — *ns.* **nöogen'esis** evolution of mind; **nöom'etry** mind-measurement; **nö'osphere** (*Teilhard de Chardin*) the sphcre of the mind, the collective memory and intelligence of the human race. [Gr. *noos,* the mind, *logos,* discourse, *metron,* measure, *sphaira,* sphere.]

noon *nōōn, n.* the ninth hour of the day in Roman and ecclesiastical reckoning, three o'clock p.m.: afterwards (when the church service called *Nones* was shifted to midday) midday: middle: greatest height. — *adj.* belonging to midday: meridional. — *v.i.* to rest at noon. — *n.* **noon'ing** (esp. *U.S. dial.*) a repast or rest about noon. — **noon'day** midday: the time of greatest prosperity. — *adj.* pertaining to midday: meridional. — **noon'tide** the time of noon, midday. — *adj.* pertaining to noon: meridional. [O.E. *nōn* — L. *nōna* (*hōra*), the ninth (hour).]

no-one. See **no**[2].

noop *nōōp,* (*Scott*) *n.* a knob, tip (of the elbow). [Cf. **knop.**]

noose *nōōs,* also *nōōz, n.* a loop with running knot which ties the firmer the closer it is drawn: a snare or bond generally, esp. hanging or marriage. — *v.t.* to tie or catch in a noose. — **put one's head in a noose** to put oneself into a dangerous or vulnerable situation. [Perh. O.Fr. *nous,* pl. of *nou* (Fr. *nœud*) — L. *nōdus,* knot.]

nopal *nō'pəl, -päl, n.* a Central American cactus of the genus **Nopalea**, used for rearing cochineal insects. [Sp. *nopal* — Mex. *nopalli*.]

nope *nōp, adv.* an emphatic, originally American, form of **no**[1], pronounced with a snap of the mouth.

nor[1] *nör, conj.* and not: neither — used esp. in introducing the second part of a negative proposition — correlative to *neither*. [App. from *nother*, a form of **neither**.]

nor[2] *nör, (Scot.* and *dial.) conj.* than. [Origin obscure.]

NOR *nör, (comput.) n.* a logic circuit that has two or more inputs and one output, the output signal being 1 if all its inputs are 0, and 0 if any of its inputs is 1. [*not or*.]

nor' *nör,* a shortened form of **north.**

noradrenalin *nör-ə-dren'ə-lin,* **noradrenaline** *-lin, -lēn, ns.* a neurotransmitter hormone related to adrenalin, produced by the adrenal glands. — Also (esp. *U.S.*) **norepinephrine** *(nör-ep-i-nef'rin, -rēn).*

Norbertine *nör'bərt-īn, -in, n.* and *adj.* Premonstratensian. [From *Norbert,* the founder (1119).]

Nordic *nör'dik, adj.* of a tall, blond, dolichocephalic type of (generally Germanic) peoples in N.W. Europe: loosely used by Nazis. — Also *n.* — **Nordic skiing** competitive skiing involving cross-country and jumping events. [Fr. *nord,* north.]

norepinephrine. See **noradrenalin.**

norethisterone *nör-ə-thist'ə-rōn, n.* an oral progestogen.

Norfolk *nör'fək, adj.* belonging to the English county of *Norfolk.* — **Norfolk capon** a red herring; **Norfolk dumpling** or **turkey** a native or inhabitant of Norfolk; **Norfolk jacket** a loose pleated coat with a waistband. — **Norfolk Island pine** a lofty Araucaria of Norfolk Island (in the Pacific, named after the ducal family of *Norfolk*). [O.E. *northfolc,* north folk.]

nori *nō'ri* or *nō'ri, n.* a seaweed of the genus *Porphyra* used as a foodstuff in Japan in the form of dried sheets or as paste. [Jap.]

noria *nō'ri-ə, nō', n.* an endless chain of buckets on a wheel for water-raising. [Sp. *noria* — Ar. *nā'ūrah.*]

norimon *nor'i-mon, n.* a Japanese palanquin. [Jap. *nori,* to ride, *mono,* thing.]

norite *nō'rīt, n.* a gabbro with a rhombic pyroxene. [*Norway.*]

nork *nörk, (Austr. slang) n.* a woman's breast. [Perh. fr. Norco Co-operative Ltd, NSW butter manufacturers.]

norland, norlan' *nör'lən(d) (Scot.* and *poet.) n.* the north country. — *adj.* belonging to or coming from the north. [**north, land**[1].]

norm *nörm, n.* a rule: a pattern: an authoritative standard: a type: the ordinary or most frequent value or state: an accepted standard of behaviour within a society. — *n.* **nor'ma** a rule: a standard: a square for measuring right angles. — *adj.* **nor'mal** according to rule: not deviating from the standard: ordinary: well-adjusted: functioning regularly: having an unbranched chain of carbon atoms (*chem.*): (of a solution) having one gramme-equivalent of dissolved substance to a litre: perpendicular (*geom.*). — *n.* a perpendicular: a normal instance or specimen. — *ns.* **nor'malcy** (an ill-formed word) normality, often of political, economic, etc., conditions; **normalisā'tion, -z-.** — *v.t.* **nor'malise, -ize** to make normal: to bring within or cause to conform to normal standards, limits, etc.: to heat (steel) in order to refine the crystal structure and to relieve internal stress. — *v.i.* to become normal, regular. — *n.* **normal'ity.** — *adv.* **nor'mally** in a normal manner: usually: typically. — *adj.* **nor'mative** of, or pertaining to, a norm: establishing a standard: prescriptive. — **normal distribution** (*statistics*) a frequency distribution represented by a symmetrical, bell-shaped curve; **normal school** a training-college for teachers; **normal solution** see above and also **standard solution; norm'-ref'erencing** (*education*) comparing a pupil's abilities with those of his peers. — *adj.* **norm'-referenced.** [L. *norma,* a rule.]

Norma *nör'mə, n.* the Rule, a small southern constel-

lation. [L. *norma,* a rule.]

normal, etc. See **norm.**

Norman *nör'mən, n.* a native or inhabitant of Normandy: one of that Scandinavian people which settled in northern France about the beginning of the 10th century, founded the Duchy of Normandy, and conquered England in 1066: the Norman-French dialect: — *pl.* **Nor'mans.** — *adj.* pertaining to the Normans or to Normandy. — *v.t.* **Nor'manise, -ize** to give a Norman character to. — *n.* **Nor'manism.** — **Norman architecture** a massive Romanesque style, prevalent in Normandy (10th–11th cent.) and England (11th–12th), the churches with semicircular apse and a great tower, deeply recessed doorways, small, round-headed windows and arches, zigzag, billet, nail-head, and other characteristic ornaments; **Norman Conquest** the conquest of England by Duke William of Normandy (1066); **Norman cross** an elaborate memorial cross like a Gothic turret with pinnacles and with niches for figures. — *n.* and *adj.* **Nor'man-French'** French as spoken by the Normans. [O.Fr. *Normanz, Normans,* nom. and accus. pl. of *Normant,* Northman, from Scand.]

norman *nör'mən, (naut.) n.* a bar inserted in a windlass on which to fasten or veer a rope or cable.

normative. See **norm.**

Norn[1] *nörn, (Scand. myth.) n.* one of the three Fates — Urd, Verdande, and Skuld. — Also (Latinised) **Norn'a.** [O.N. *norn.*]

Norn[2] *nörn, n.* the old Norse dialect of Orkney and Shetland. — Also *adj.* [O.N. *norræna.*]

Norroy *nor'oi, (her.) n.* an English king-of-arms whose jurisdiction lies north of the Trent. — Since 1943, **Norroy and Ulster.** [O.Fr. *nord,* north, *roy,* king.]

Norse *nörs, adj.* Norwegian: ancient Scandinavian. — *n.* the Norwegian language: the language of the ancient Scandinavians — also **Old Norse.** — *n.* **Norse'man** a Scandinavian or Northman. [Perh. Du. *noor(d)sch;* cf. Icel. *Norskr;* Norw. *Norsk.*]

norsel *nörs'l, (rare) n.* a short piece of line for fastening fishing nets and hooks. — *v.t.* and *v.i.* (*obs.*) to fit with or fit norsels. — *n.* (*obs.*) **nors'eller.** [O.E. *nostel, nostle, nosle,* a fillet or band.]

north *nörth, adv.* in the direction of that point of the horizon or that pole of the earth or heavens which at equinox is opposite the sun at noon in Europe or elsewhere on the same side of the equator, or towards the sun in the other hemisphere: in the slightly different direction (*magnetic north*) in which a magnetic needle points. — *n.* the point of the horizon in that direction: the region lying in that direction: the part placed relatively in that direction: the north wind. — *adj.* lying towards the north: forming the part, or that one of two, that is towards the north: blowing from the north: (of a pole of a magnet, usually) north-seeking. — *v.i.* (*arch.*) to turn or move towards the north. — *n.* **norther** (*nörth'ər*) a wind or gale from the north, esp. applied to a cold wind that blows in winter over Texas and the Gulf of Mexico. — *v.i.* (*nördh'ər; arch.*) to shift or veer to north. — *n.* **north'erliness** (*-dh-*). — *adj.* **north'erly** (*-dh-*) being toward the north: blowing from the north. — *adv.* toward or from the north. — *n.* a north wind. — *adj.* **north'ern** (*-dh-*) pertaining to the north: being in the north or in the direction toward it: proceeding from the north. — *n.* a native of the north. — *n.* **north'erner** (*-dh-*) a native of, or resident in, the north, esp. of the northern United States. — *v.t.* **north'ernise, -ize** (*-dh-*) to give a northern character to. — *n.* **north'ernism** (*-dh-*) northern idiom. — *adjs.* **north'ermost** (*-dh-; obs.*), **north'ernmost** (*-dh-*), **north'most** (*-th-*) most northerly. — *n.* **north'ing** (*-th-*) motion, distance, or tendency northward: distance of a heavenly body from the equator northward: difference of latitude made by a ship in sailing: deviation towards the north. — *adjs., advs.,* and *ns.* **north'ward, nor'ward, norward** (*nörth'wərd, nör'wərd, nor'əd*). — *adj.* and *adv.* **north'wardly.** — *adv.* **north'wards.** — *adjs.* **north'-bound**

bound for the north: travelling northwards; **north'=country** belonging to the northern part of the country, esp. of England. — **north-coun'tryman.** — *adjs.* and *advs.* **north-east', nor'-east'** (also *nörth', nör'*) midway between north and east. — *ns.* the direction midway between north and east: the region lying in that direction: the wind blowing from that direction. — **north-east'er, nor'-east'er** a strong wind from the north-east. — *adj.* and *adv.* **north-east'erly** towards or from the north-east. — *adj.* **north'-east'ern** belonging to the north-east: being in the north-east, or in that direction. — *adj.* and *adv.* **north-east'ward** toward the north-east. — *n.* the region to the north-east. — *adj.* and *adv.* **north-east'wardly.** — *adv.* **north-east'wards.** — **northern fern** the hard fern (Lomaria); **northern lights** the aurora borealis; **north'land** (also *adj.*) land, or lands, of the north; **North'man** an ancient Scandinavian. — *ns., adjs.,* and *advs.* **north-north-east'; north-north-west'** (in) a direction midway between north and north-east or north-west. — *adj.* **north polar.** — **north pole** the end of the earth's axis in the Arctic regions: its projection on the celestial sphere: (usually) that pole of a magnet which when free points to the earth's north magnetic pole (logically the other end). — *adj.* **north'=seeking** turning towards the earth's magnetic north pole. — **North Star** a star very near the north pole of the heavens, the Pole Star; **north water** the space of open sea left by the winter pack of ice moving southward. — *adjs.* and *advs.* **north-west', nor'-west'** (also *nörth', nör'*) midway between north and west. — *ns.* the direction midway between north and west: the region lying in that direction: the wind blowing from that direction. — **north-, nor'-west'er** a strong north-west wind. — *adjs.* and *advs.* **north'-west'erly** toward or from the north-west; **north'-west'ern** belonging to the north-west: being in the north-west or in that direction. — *adj., adv.,* and *n.* **north-west'ward.** — *adj.* and *adv.* **north-west'wardly.** — *adv.* **north-west'wards.** — **North Atlantic Treaty Organisation** a political alliance linking the United States and Canada to a group of European States, established by the **North Atlantic Treaty,** 4th April 1949 (abbrev. **Nato); North=east Passage** a passage for ships along the north coasts of Europe and Asia to the Pacific, first made by Baron Nordenskjöld in 1878–79; **North-west Passage** a seaway from the Atlantic into the Pacific north of North America, first made (partly on the ice) by Sir Robert McClure, 1850–54. [O.E. *north*; cf. Ger. *Nord.*]

Northumbrian *nör-thum'bri-ən, n.* a native of the modern *Northumberland,* or of the old kingdom of *Northumbria* (O.E. *Northhymbre, Northhymbraland*) stretching from the Humber to the Forth: the dialect of Old English spoken in Northumbria, later Northern English (including Scots). — *adj.* of Northumberland or Northumbria.

Norueyses (*Spens.*). See **Norway.**

norward, etc. Same as **northward,** etc.

Norway *nör'wā, adj.* Norwegian. — *n.* (*obs.*) a Norwegian: — *pl.* (*Spens.*) **Norueyses.** — **Norway haddock** the rose-fish or bergylt; **Norway lobster** see **lobster; Norway pine** the red pine, *Pinus resinosa:* its wood; **Norway rat** the brown rat; **Norway spruce** *Picea excelsa:* its wood.

Norwegian *nör-wē'j(y)ən, adj.* of Norway, its people, or its language. — *n.* a native or citizen of Norway: the language of Norway: a kind of fishing-boat on the Great Lakes of America. — *adj.* (*Shak.*) **Norweyan** (*-wā'ən*) Norwegian. — **Norwegian oven, nest** a haybox. [L.L. *Norvegia,* Norway — O.N. *Norvegr* (O.E. *Northweg*) — O.N. *northr,* north, *vegr,* way.]

nose *nōz, n.* the projecting part of the face used in breathing, smelling, and to some extent in speaking: the power of smelling: flair, a faculty for tracking out, detecting, or recognising (*fig.*): scent, aroma, esp. the bouquet of wine: a projecting fore-part of anything: a projection: a beak: a nozzle: the projecting edge of a step, a moulding, or a mullion: the withered remains of the flower on a gooseberry, apple, etc., opposite the stalk: the connecting part of a pair of spectacles: an informer (*slang*). — *v.t.* to smell: to examine by smelling or as if by smelling: to track out, detect, or recognise (often with **out**): to touch, press, or rub with the nose: to thrust the nose into: to make (way) by feeling or pushing with the nose: to come or be face to face with (*arch.*): to oppose rudely face to face (*arch.*): to furnish with a nose (*arch.*): to remove the nose from (a gooseberry, etc.): to sound through the nose. — *v.i.* to sniff (*arch.*): to pry: to nuzzle: to move nose-first: to taper away in a noselike form. — *adjs.* **nosed** having a nose — esp. in composition, as *bottle-nosed, long-nosed,* etc.; **nose'less.** — *n.* **nos'er** a blow on the nose: a bloody nose: a severe rebuff: a strong head-wind: a prying person. — *adj.* **nos'ey, nos'y** long-nosed: large-nosed: prying: ill-smelling: fragrant: sensitive to smells: nasal in sound. — *n.* a nickname for a nosey person. — *adv.* **nos'ily.** — *ns.* **nos'iness** a tendency to pry; **nos'ing** the act of nosing: the projecting rounded edge of the step of a stair, sill, moulding, etc. — **nose'bag** a bag for food, hung on a horse's head: a picnicker's bag; **nose'-band** the part of the bridle coming over the nose, attached to the cheek-straps; **nose'-bleed** a bleeding at the nose: yarrow or other plant (*obs.* or *U.S.*); **nose'-bleeding; nose'-cone** the front, usu. conical, part of a spacecraft, etc.; **nose'-dive** a headlong plunge. — *v.i.* to plunge nose-first. — **nose'-flute** a flute blown by the nose; **nose'-herb** (*Shak.*) a herb valued for its smell; **nose'-leaf** a membranous appendage on some bats' snouts. — *adj.* **nose'-led** led by the nose, ruled and befooled completely. — *n.pl.* **nose'-nippers** pince-nez. — **nose'-painting** colouring of the nose by drinking; **nose'-piece** a nozzle: the end of a microscope tube carrying the objective: a nose-band: the nasal in armour; **nose'-rag** (*slang*) a handkerchief; **nose'-ring** an ornament worn in the septum of the nose or in either of its wings: a ring in the septum of the nose for controlling a bull, swine, etc.; **nose'-wheel** the single wheel at the front of a vehicle, etc., esp. an aircraft; **Nosey Parker** (*coll.*; also without *caps.*) a prying person. — **cut off one's nose to spite one's face** to injure or disadvantage oneself through an act of revenge or anger towards another; **follow one's nose** to go straight forward; **get up someone's nose** (*coll.*) to annoy, irritate someone; **keep one's nose clean** (*coll.*) to keep out of trouble, i.e. not to behave badly or dishonestly; **lead by the nose** see **lead¹; look down one's nose at** to look at in a supercilious way; **make a long nose, thumb one's nose** see **long³, thumb; nose out** to move forward slowly into traffic (in a vehicle); **nose to tail** closely following one another; **nose to the grindstone** see **grind; nose up** to direct or turn an aircraft nose upwards; **not see beyond, further than, (the end of) one's nose** to see only what is immediately in front of one, i.e. not to see the long-term consequences of one's actions, etc.; **on the nose** (in horse-race betting) to win only (not to come second or third): unsavoury, offensive (*Austr. coll.*); **put someone's nose out of joint** see **join; rub someone's nose in it** (*coll.*) to remind someone continually of something he has done wrong; **snap off someone's nose** to speak snappily; **through the nose** exorbitantly; **thrust, poke, stick one's nose into** to meddle officiously with; **turn up one's nose at** to refuse or receive contemptuously; **under one's (very) nose** in full view: close at hand; **with one's nose in the air** in a haughty, superior manner. [O.E. *nosu*; Ger. *Nase,* L. *nāsus.*]

nosean *nōz'i-ən, n.* a cubic mineral, aluminium sodium silicate and sulphate. — Also **nos'elite.** [Named after the German mineralogist K. W. *Nose* (d. 1835).]

nosegay *nōz'gā, n.* a bunch of fragrant flowers: a posy or bouquet. [nose, gay.]

noselite. See **nosean.**

nosh *nosh,* (*slang*) *v.i.* to nibble, eat between meals: to eat. — *n.* food. — **nosh'-up** (*slang*) a (large) meal. [Yiddish.]

nosocomial *nos-ō-kō'mi-ǝl, adj.* relating to a hospital. [Gr. *nosokomeion,* hospital — *nosos,* sickness, *komeein,* to tend.]

nosography *nos-og'rǝ-fi, n.* the description of diseases. — *n.* **nosog'rapher.** — *adj.* **nosographic** (*nos-ǝ-graf'ik*). [Gr. *nosos,* disease, *graphein,* to write.]

nosology *nos-ol'ǝ-ji, n.* the science of diseases: the branch of medicine which treats of the classification of diseases. — *adj.* **nosological** (*-ǝ-loj'*). — *n.* **nosol'ogist.** [Gr. *nosos,* disease, *logos,* discourse.]

nosophobia *nos-ǝ-fō'bi-ǝ, n.* morbid dread of disease. [Gr. *nosos,* a disease, *phobos,* fear.]

nostalgia *nos-tal'ji-ǝ, n.* home-sickness: sentimental longing for past times. — *adj.* **nostal'gic.** — *adv.* **nostal'gically.** [Gr. *nostos,* a return, *algos,* pain.]

nostalgie de la boue *nos-tal-zhē dǝ la boo,* (Fr.) nostalgia for mud, craving for a debased physical life without civilised refinements or fastidiousness.

Nostoc *nos'tok, n.* a genus of blue-green Algae, beaded filaments forming gelatinous colonies on damp earth, etc., once thought derived from stars: (without *cap.*) an alga of this genus. [Appar. coined by Paracelsus.]

nostology *nos-tol'ǝ-ji, n.* the study of senility or return to childish characteristics. — *adjs.* **nostologic** (*-ǝ-loj'*), **-al.** [Gr. *nostos,* return, *logos,* discourse.]

nostomania *nos-tō-mā'ni-ǝ, n.* an abnormal desire to go back to familiar places. [Gr. *nostos,* return, **mania.**]

nostopathy *nos-top'ǝ-thi, n.* an abnormal fear of going back to familiar places. [Gr. *nostos,* return, *pathos,* suffering.]

nostos *nos'tos,* (Gr.) *n.* a poem describing a return or a return journey.

Nostradamus *nos-trǝ-dā'mǝs, n.* one who professes to foretell the future. — *adj.* **nostradamic** (*-dam'ik*). [From the French astrologer (1503–1566).]

nostril *nos'tril, n.* one of the openings of the nose. [M.E. *nosethirl* — O.E. *nosthyr(e)l* — *nosu,* nose, *thyrel,* opening; cf. **drill**[1] and **thrill.**]

nostrum *nos'trǝm, n.* any secret, quack, or patent medicine: any favourite remedy or scheme. [L. *nostrum* (neut.), our own — *nōs,* we.]

nosy. See **nose.**

not[1] *not, adv.* a word expressing denial, negation, or refusal: —enclitic form **-n't.** — **not'-being** the state or fact of not existing; **not'-I** that which is not the conscious ego. — *adj.* and *adv.* **not-out'** (*cricket*) still in: at the end of the innings without having been put out. — **not on** (*coll.*) not possible: not morally, socially, etc. acceptable. [Same as **naught, nought.**]

NOT *not,* (*comput.*) *n.* a logic circuit that has one input and one output, the output signal being 1 if its input is 0, and 0 if its input is 1. [**not.**]

not[2], **nott** *not, adj.* with close-cut hair: polled. — *adjs.* **not'-head'ed; not'-pat'ed** (*Shak.*). [O.E. *hnot.*]

nota bene *nō'tǝ ben'i, bēn', no'tä ben'e,* (L.) mark well, take notice — often abbrev. **N.B.**

notabilia. See **notable.**

notable *nō'tǝ-bl, adj.* worthy of being known or noted: remarkable: memorable: distinguished: noticeable: considerable: (*arch.*; sometimes with old pronunciation *not'*) housewifely: capable, clever, industrious (*arch.*). — *n.* a person or thing worthy of note, esp. in *pl.* for persons of distinction and political importance in France in pre-Revolution times. — *n.pl.* **notabil'ia** (L.) things worthy of notice: noteworthy sayings. — *ns.* **notabil'ity** the fact of being notable: a notable person or thing; **no'tableness.** — *adv.* **no'tably.** [L. *notābilis* — *notāre,* to mark.]

notaeum *nō-tē'ǝm, n.* the upper surface of a bird's trunk — opp. to *gastraeum.* [Latinised from Gr. *nōtaion* (neut.), adj. — *nōtos* or *nōton,* the back.]

notal. See **note**[1], **notum.**

notandum *nō-tan'dǝm, n.* something to be specially noted or observed: — *pl.* **notan'da.** [L., ger. of *notāre,* to note.]

notaphily *nō-taf'i-li, n.* the collecting of bank-notes, cheques, etc. as a hobby. — *adj.* **notaph'ilic.** — *ns.*

notaph'ilism; notaph'ilist. [Cf. **note**[1], **phil-.**]

notary *nō'tǝ-ri, n.* an officer authorised to certify deeds, contracts, copies of documents, affidavits, etc. (generally **notary public**): anciently, one who took notes or memoranda of others' acts. — *adj.* **notā'rial.** — *adv.* **notā'rially.** — *v.t.* **no'tarise, -ize** to attest to, authenticate (a document, etc.) as a notary. — **apostolical notary** the official who dispatches the orders of the pope; **ecclesiastical notary** in the early church, a secretary who recorded the proceedings of councils, etc. [L. *notārius.*]

notation *nō-tā'shǝn, n.* a system of signs or symbols: annotation (*rare*): the act of notating or writing down. — *v.t.* **notate'** to write (music, etc.) in notation. — *adj.* **notā'tional.** [L. *notātiō, -ōnis* — *notāre, -ātum,* to mark.]

notch *noch, n.* a nick: an indentation: a narrow pass. — *v.t.* to make a nick in: to cut unevenly, as hair (*obs.*): to form, fix, or remove by nicking: to fit arrow to bowstring (also **nock**): to record by a notch: (often with *up*) to score, achieve. — *adj.* **notched** nicked. — *n.* **notch'ing** a method of joining timbers, by fitting into a groove or grooves. — *adj.* **notch'y** having notches: (of a manual gearbox) not operating smoothly or easily. — **notch'back** a car whose rear does not slope continuously from the roof to the bumper, but juts out from the bottom of the rear window (also *adj.*); **notch'-board** a board that receives the ends of the steps of a staircase. [Supposed to be from Fr. *oche* (now *hoche*) with *n* from the indefinite article; not conn. with **nock.**]

notchel, nochel *noch'l, n.* (*coll.*) notice that one will not be responsible for another's debts. — *v.t.* to repudiate the debts of (someone). [Origin unknown.]

note[1] *nōt, n.* a significant or distinguishing mark: a characteristic: that by which a person or thing is known: a mark or sign calling attention: a written or printed symbol other than a letter: a stigma or mark of censure: an observation or remark: a comment attached to a text, explanatory, illustrative, critical, or recording textual variants: a jotting set down provisionally for use afterwards: an impression: a short statement or record: a bill or account (*obs.*): a memorandum: a short informal letter: a diplomatic paper: a small size of paper used for writing: a mark representing a sound (**whole note,** a semibreve) (*mus.*): a key of a piano or other instrument: the sound or tone represented by the printed or written note: the song, cry, or utterance of a bird or other animal: a tune (*obs.*): music (*poet.*): a paper acknowledging a debt and promising payment, as a bank-note, a note of hand or promissory note: a voucher or receipt (*obs.*): notice: attention: cognisance: distinction: reputation: eminence: importance: consequence: notability: intimation (*Shak.*). — *v.t.* to make a note of: to notice: to attend to: to indicate: to mark: to stigmatise (*obs.*): to mention: to record in writing or in musical notation: to add musical notation to: to set to music: to annotate: to denote. — *adjs.* **nōt'al; nōt'ed** marked: well known: celebrated: eminent: notorious. — *adv.* **not'edly.** — *n.* **nōt'edness.** — *adj.* **note'less** not attracting notice: unmusical. — *ns.* **note'let** a short annotation or letter: a folded sheet of notepaper, usu. with printed decoration, for short letters; **nōt'er** one who notes or observes: one who makes notes, an annotator. — **note'book** a book for keeping notes or memoranda: a billbook; **note'-case** a pocket-book for bank-notes; **note'-pad** a pad of paper for writing notes on; **note'-paper** writing-paper intended for letters; **note row** tone row; **note'-shav'er** (*U.S.*) one who discounts bills at an exorbitant rate: a usurer; **note'worthiness.** — *adj.* **note'worthy** worthy of note or of notice. — **note a bill** to record a refusal of acceptance, as a ground of protest; **note of hand** promissory note; **of note** well-known, distinguished: significant, worthy of attention; **strike the right (a false) note** to act or speak appropriately (inappropriately); **take note** to observe carefully,

closely (often with *of*). [Fr., — L. *nota*, a mark.]
note², **n'ote**, **no'te** *nōt*, (*Spens.*) *v.t.* wot not: (wrongly) could not. [O.E. *nāt*, for *ne wāt*; see **ne, wot.**]
nothing *nuth'ing*, *n.* no thing: the non-existent: zero number or quantity: the figure representing it, a nought: a thing or person of no significance or value: an empty or trivial utterance: a low condition: a trifle: no difficulty or trouble. — *adv.* in no degree: not at all. — *ns.* **nothingā'rian** one who has no particular belief, esp. in religion; **nothingā'rianism; noth'ingism** nothingness: triviality; **noth'ingness** non-existence: the state of being nothing: worthlessness: insignificance: vacuity: a thing of no value. — **noth'ing-gift** (*Shak.*) a gift of no value. — **be nothing** to not to be important to or concern (someone); **come to nothing** to have little or no result: to turn out a failure; **for nothing** in vain: free of charge; **make nothing of** see **make; next to nothing** almost nothing; **nothing but** only; **nothing doing** an emphatic refusal: an expression of failure; **nothing for it but** no alternative but; **nothing if not** primarily, above all: at the very least; **nothing on** (*slang*) no claim to superiority over: no information about (used esp. by police of criminals): no engagement; **nothing to it** having nothing in it worth while: easy; **nothing less than, short of** at least: downright; **stop, stick at nothing** to be ruthless, unscrupulous; **sweet nothings** (esp. whispered) words of affection and endearment; **to say nothing of** not to mention (see **mention**); **think nothing of** to regard as easy or unremarkable: to have a low opinion of. [**no², thing.**]
Nothofagus *noth-ō-fā'gəs*, *n.* a genus of timber-trees of the southern hemisphere, closely allied to beech. [Gr. *nothos*, spurious, L. *fāgus*, beech.]
notice *nō'tis*, *n.* intimation: announcement: information: warning: a writing, placard, board, etc., conveying an intimation or warning: time allowed for preparation: cognisance: observation: heed: mention: a short book, dramatic or artistic review: civility or respectful treatment: a notion (*obs.*). — *v.t.* to mark or observe: to regard or attend to: to mention: to make observations upon: to write or publish a notice of: to show sign of recognition of: to treat with civility. — *adj.* **no'ticeable** that can be noticed: worthy of notice: likely to be noticed. — *adv.* **no'ticeably.** — **no'tice-board** a board for fixing a notice on. — **at short notice** with notification only a little in advance; **give notice** to warn beforehand: to inform: to intimate, esp. the termination of an agreement. [Fr. *notice* — L. *nōtitia* — *nōscĕre*, *nōtum*, to get to know.]
notify *nō'ti-fī*, *v.t.* to make known: to declare: to give notice or information of: — *pr.p.* **no'tifying;** *pa.t.* and *pa.p.* **no'tified.** — *adj.* **no'tifiable** that must be made known: (of diseases) that must be reported to public health authorities. — *ns.* **notification** (*-fi-kā'shən*) the act of notifying: the notice given: the paper containing the notice; **not'ifier.** [Fr. *notifier* — L. *nōtificāre*, *-ātum* — *nōtus*, known, *facĕre*, to make.]
notion *nō'shən*, *n.* a concept in the mind of the various marks or qualities of an object: an idea: an opinion, esp. one not very well founded: a caprice or whim: a liking or fancy: (*Shak.*, *Milton*) a mind: any small article ingeniously devised or invented, usually in *pl.* —*adj.* **no'tional** of the nature of a notion: having a full meaning of its own, not merely contributing to the meaning of a phrase: theoretical: ideal: fanciful: imaginary, unreal. — *n.* **no'tionalist** a theorist. — *adv.* **no'tionally** in notion or mental apprehension: in idea, not in reality. — *n.* **no'tionist** one who holds ungrounded opinions. [Fr., — L. *notiō, -ōnis* — *nōscĕre*, *nōtum*, to get to know.]
notitia *nō-tish'i-ə*, *n.* a roll, list, register: a catalogue of public functionaries, with their districts: a list of episcopal sees. [L. *nōtitia*; cf. **notice.**]
notochord *nō'tō-körd*, *n.* a simple cellular rod, foreshadowing the spinal column, persisting throughout life in many lower vertebrates, as the Amphioxus, etc. — *adj.* **notochord'al.** [Gr. *nōtos*, back, *chordē*, a string.]

Notodonta *nō-tō-dont'ə*, *n.* a genus of moths whose larvae have toothlike humps, giving name to the family **Notodont'idae.** — *n.* **notodont'id** a member of the family. [Gr. *nōtos*, back, *odous, odontos*, tooth.]
Notogaea *nō-tō-jē'ə*, *n.* a zoological realm including Australia, the islands north of it, New Zealand, and Polynesia. — *adjs.* **Notogae'an, Notogae'ic.** [Gr. *notos*, south, *gaia*, land.]
notonectal *nō-tō-nek'təl*, *adj.* swimming on the back, as certain insects: of the water-boatman genus (**Notonec'-ta**) or family (**Notonec'tidae**) of hemipterous insects. [Gr. *nōtos*, back, *nēktēs*, a swimmer.]
notorious *nō-tō'ri-əs, -tō'*, *adj.* publicly known (now only in a bad sense): infamous. — *n.* **notori'ety** the state of being notorious: publicity: public exposure. — *adv.* **noto'riously.** — *n.* **noto'riousness.** [L.L. *nōtōrius* — *nōtus*, known.]
Notornis *no-tör'nis*, *n.* a genus of flightless rails, long thought extinct, but found surviving in New Zealand in 1948: (without *cap.*) a bird of this genus. [Gr. *notos*, south, *ornis*, a bird.]
Notoryctes *nō-tō-rik'tēz*, *n.* a blind burrowing marsupial of South Australia, the marsupial mole. [Gr. *notos*, south, *oryktēs*, digger.]
Nototherium *nō-tō-thē'ri-əm*, *n.* a genus of Tertiary Australian fossil marsupials. [Gr. *notos*, south, *thērion*, a wild beast.]
Nototrema *nō-tō-trē'mə*, *n.* the pouch-toad, a South American genus of tree frogs, with a brood-pouch on the female's back. [Gr. *nōtos*, the back, *trēma*, a hole.]
notoungulate, notungulate *nōt(-ō)-ung'ū-lāt*, *n.* any one of an extinct group of herbivorous, hoofed mammals common in South America between the Palaeocene and Pleistocene eras. — Also *adj.* [Gr. *nōtos* back, L. *ungulatus*, hoofed.]
notour *nō'tər*, (*Scot.*; now only *legal*) *adj.* well known, notorious. [L.L. *nōtōrius*.]
Notre-Dame *not-r'- däm*, (Fr.) *n.* Our Lady.
no-trump(s). See **no².**
nott. Same as **not².**
notum *nō'təm*, *n.* the dorsal aspect of the thorax in insects. — *adj.* **nō'tal** of or pertaining to the back (of an insect). [Latinised from Gr. *nōton*, back.]
notungulate. See **notoungulate.**
Notus *nō'təs*, *n.* the south or south-west wind. [L. *nōtus* — Gr. *nōtos*.]
notwithstanding *not-with-stand'ing*, or *-widh-*, *prep.* in spite of. — *conj.* in spite of the fact that, although. — *adv.* nevertheless, however, yet. [Orig. a participial phrase in nominative absolute = L. *non obstante*.]
nougat *nōō'gä*, *nug'ət*, *n.* a confection made of a sweet paste filled with chopped almonds or pistachio nuts. [Fr. (cf. Sp. *nogado*, an almond-cake), — L. *nux, nucis*, a nut.]
nought *nöt*, *n.* not anything: nothing: the figure 0. — *adv.* in no degree. — *adj.* same as **naught.** — **noughts and crosses** a game in which one seeks to make three noughts, the other three crosses, in a row in the spaces of crossed parallel lines; **set at nought** to despise, disregard, flout. [Same as **naught.**]
noul, (*Spens.*) **noule** *nōl*, *n.* Same as **noll.**
nould, noulde, n'ould (*Spens.*) *pa.t.* of **nill.**
noumenon *nōō'* or *now'mi-non*, *n.* an unknown and unknowable substance or thing as it is in itself: — *pl.* **nou'mena.** — *adj.* **nou'menal.** [Gr. *nooumenon* (contraction for *noeomenon*), neuter of pr.p. pass. of *noeein*, to think — *noos* (*nous*), the mind.]
noun *nown*, (*gram.*) *n.* a word used as a name: formerly including the adjective. — *adjs.* **noun'al; noun'y** having many nouns: having the nature or function of a noun. — **noun clause** a clause equivalent to a noun. [A.Fr. *noun* (O.Fr. *non*; Fr. *nom*) — L. *nōmen, nōminis*, a name.]
nouns *nownz*, (*obs.*) *n.pl.* used as a minced oath, in full *odds nouns*, for **God's wounds.**
noup *nōōp, nöp*, (*obs.* Shetland; *Scott*) *n.* a crag: a steep

headland.   [O.N. *gnūpr*.]

nourice *nur'is*, (*obs.*) *n.* a nurse. — **nour'ice-fee'** payment for a nurse.   [O.Fr. *nurice*; see **nurse**.]

nourish *nur'ish*, *v.t.* to suckle (*obs.*): to feed: to furnish with food: to support: to help forward the growth of in any way: to allow to grow: to bring up: to cherish (*fig.*): to educate. — *adj.* **nour'ishable.** — *n.* **nour'isher.** — *adj.* **nour'ishing** affording nourishment or much nourishment. — *n.* **nour'ishment** the act of nourishing: the state of being nourished: that which nourishes: nutriment.   [O.Fr. *norir, nourir, -iss-* (Fr. *nourrir*) — L. *nūtrīre*, to feed.]

nouriture, nourriture *nur'i-chər*, *n.* nourishment: food: bringing up, nurture (*obs.*).   [See **nurture**.]

noursle *nûrs'l*, (*Spens.*) *v.t.* to bring up: to foster. — Also **nousle, nousell, nuzzle²**.   [A form of **nuzzle** influenced by **nurse**.]

nous *noōs, nows, n.* intellect: talent: common sense (*slang*; *nows*).   [Gr. *nous*, contracted from *noos*.]

nousell, nousle. See **noursle.**

nousle. See **nuzzle¹**.

nout. See **nowt¹**.

nouveau *noō-vō*, fem. **nouvelle** *-vel*, (Fr.) *adj.* new. — *n.* **nouvelle** a long short-story. — **nouveau riche** (*rēsh*) one who has only lately acquired wealth, but who has not acquired good taste or manners: an upstart: — *pl.* **nouveaux riches; nouveau roman** (*rō-mä*) the anti-novel (q.v.); **nouvelle cuisine** (*kwē-zēn*) a style of simple French cooking excluding rich creamy sauces, etc. in favour of fresh vegetables and light sauces; **Nouvelle Vague** (*väg*) a movement in the French cinema (beginning just before 1960) aiming at imaginative quality in films in preference to size, expense, box-office appeal. — As *adj.* applied to movements in other arts. — **art nouveau** see **art.**

nova *nō'və*, *n.* a star that suddenly increases in brightness for a number of days or years: — *pl.* **no'vae** (*-vē*), **no'vas.**   [L. *nŏva* (*stella*), new (star); fem. of *novus*, new.]

novaculite *nō-vak'ū-līt*, *n.* a hone-stone, a very hard fine-grained siliceous rock, sometimes containing minute garnets.   [L. *novācula*, razor.]

novalia *nō-vā'li-ə*, (*Scots law*) *n.pl.* waste lands newly reclaimed.   [L. *novālia*.]

Novatian *nō-vā'sh*(*y*)*ən*, *adj.* of or pertaining to the antipope *Novatianus* (251), or his party or sect, who favoured severity against the lapsed. — *ns.* **Novā'-tianism; Novā'tianist.**

novation *nō-vā'shən*, *n.* the substitution of a new obligation for the one existing: innovation.   [L. *novātiō, -ōnis — novus*, new.]

novel *nov'l*, *adj.* new (*obs.*): new and strange: of a new kind: felt to be new. — *n.* that which is new (earlier *no-vel'*; *obs.*): a piece of news (*obs.*): a new constitution or decree of Justinian or other Roman emperor, supplementary to the Codex: a fictitious prose narrative or tale presenting a picture of real life, esp. of the emotional crises in the life-history of the men and women portrayed. — *ns.* **nov'eldom** the world of fiction; **novelese** (*-ēz'*; *derog.*) the hackneyed style typical of poor novels; **novelette'** a short novel, esp. one that is feeble, trite, and sentimental: Schumann's name for a short piano piece in free form. — *adj.* **novelett'ish.** — *n.* **novelett'ist.** — *n.* **novelisātion, -z-.** — *v.t.* **nov'elise, -ize** to make new or novel: to turn into a novel or novels. — *v.i.* to innovate: to write as a novelist. — *n.* **nov'eliser, -z-.** — *adj.* **nov'elish** savouring of a novel. — *ns.* **nov'elism** innovation, novelty (*obs.*): favouring of innovation: novel-writing; **nov'elist** an innovator (*obs.*): a news-monger or news-writer (*obs.*): a novel-writer. — *adj.* **novelist'ic.** — *ns.* **novella** (*-el'a*; L.) a Roman Emperor's decree (*pl.* **novellae** *-ē*): (*-el'la*; It.) a tale, short story (*pl.* **novelle** *-lā*): (*-e'lə*) in recent times, a short novel (*pl.* **novelle, novellas** *-lā, -əs*); **nov'elty** newness: unusual appearance: anything new, strange, or different from what was known or usual before: a small, usually cheap, manufactured article of unusual or gimmicky design: — *pl.* **nov'elties.**

[Partly through O.Fr. *novelle* (Fr. *nouvelle*), partly through It. *novella*, partly direct, from L. *novellus*, fem. *novella — novus*, new.]

November *nō-vem'bər*, *n.* the eleventh month, ninth of the most ancient Roman year.   [L. *November — novem*, nine.]

novena *nō-vē'nə*, *n.* a devotion lasting nine days, to obtain a particular request, through the intercession of the Virgin or some saint.   [L. *novēnus*, nine each, *novem*, nine.]

novenary *nov'ə-nə-ri* (or *-ē'nər-i*), *adj.* pertaining to the number nine. — *n.* a set of nine things.   [L. *novēnārius — novem*, nine.]

novennial *nō-ven'yəl*, *adj.* recurring every ninth year.   [L. *novennis — novem*, nine, *annus*, a year.]

novercal *nō-vûr'kl*, *adj.* pertaining to or befitting a step-mother.   [L. *novercālis — noverca*, a stepmother.]

noverint *nōv'e-rint*, *n.* a writ — beginning with the words *noverint universi*, let all men know.   [L. *nōverint*, 3rd pers. pl. perf. subj. of *nōscĕre*, to get to know.]

Novial *nō'vi-əl, nō-vi-äl'*, *n.* an artificial language devised by Otto Jespersen (1860–1943).   [L. *novus*, new, and the initials of *i*nternational *a*uxiliary *l*anguage.]

novice *nov'is*, *n.* one new in anything: a beginner: a new convert or church member: an inmate of a religious house who has not yet taken the vows: a competitor that has not yet won a recognised prize. — *ns.* **nov'-icehood; nov'iceship; noviciate, novitiate** (*-ish'i-āt*) the state of being a novice: the period of being a novice: the novices' quarters in a religious house: a novice.   [Fr., — L. *novīcius — novus*, new.]

novity *nov'i-ti*, (*obs.*) *n.* innovation: newness.   [L. *novitās, -ātis — novus*, new.]

Novocain(e)® *nō'və-kān*, *n.* a proprietary name for pro-caine (q.v.)

novocentenary *nō-vō-sen-tē'nər-i*, *n.* a nine-hundredth anniversary.   [L. *novem*, nine, **centenary**.]

novodamus *nō-vō-dā'məs*, (*Scots law*) *n.* a charter or similar document containing a clause by which certain rights, privileges, etc. are granted anew: the clause itself.   [L. (*de*) *novo damus*, we grant anew.]

novum *nō'vəm*, (*Shak.*) *n.* a game at dice in which the chief throws were nine and five.   [Poss. L. *novem*, nine.]

novus homo *nōv'əs hō'mō, nov'ōos ho'mō*, (L.) a Roman magistrate whose ancestors had never held office: a new man.

now *now*, *adv.* at the present time, or the time in question, or a very little before or after: as things are: used meaninglessly, or with the feeling of time lost or nearly lost, in remonstrance, admonition, or taking up a new point. — *adj.* present. — *n.* the present time or the time in question. — *conj.* at this time when and because it is the fact: since at this time. — *interj.* expressing admonition, warning or (when repeated) reassurance. — *n.* **now'ness** the quality of constantly being in or taking place at the present moment: a lively and up-to-date quality. — **now and then**, or **again**, sometimes: from time to time; **now ... now** at one time ... at another time; **now of late** (*arch.*) lately; **now then!** interjection expressing admonition or rebuke; **the now** (*Scot.*) at present: presently: very lately.   [O.E. *nū*; Ger. *nun*, L. *nunc*, Gr. *nȳn*.]

nowadays *now'ə-dāz*, *adv.* in these times. — Also *adj.* —*Spens.* **now a** (or **of**) **dayes.**   [**now** and **days**, O.E. *dæges*, gen. of *dæg*, day, to which the prep. **a** (O.E. *on*, which governed the dative) was later added.]

noway, noways, nowise. See **no²**.

nowed *nowd*, (*her.*) *adj.* knotted.   [Fr. *noué*.]

Nowel(l), Noël *nō-el'*, (*obs.* except in Christmas carols) *n.* Christmas.   [O.Fr. (Fr. *noël*; cf. Sp. *natal*, It. *natale*). — L. *nātālis*, belonging to a birthday.]

nowhere *nō'(h)wār*, *adv.* in or to no place: out of the running. — *n.* a non-existent place. — *advs.* **no'whence** from no place; **no'whither** to no place: in no direction. — **nowhere near** not nearly.   [**no²**, **where**, **whence**, **whither**.]

nowl *nōl*, (*Shak.*) *n.* Same as **noll.**

nown *nōn*, (*obs.*) *adj.* own. [Orig. by wrong division of mine own, thine own.]

nowt[1], nout *nowt*, (*Scot.*) *n.* cattle. — **nowt′-herd.** [O.N. *naut*; cognate with **neat**[1], O.E. *nēat.*]

nowt[2] *nowt*, (*dial.*) *n.* nothing. [**naught.**]

nowy *nō′i*, *now′i*, (*her.*) *adj.* having a convex curvature near the middle. [O.Fr. *noé* (Fr. *noué*) — L. *nōdātus*, knotted.]

noxious *nok′shəs*, *adj.* hurtful. — *adj.* **noxal** (*noks′l*) relating to wrongful injury by an object or animal belonging to another. — *adv.* **nox′iously.** — *n.* **nox′- iousness.** [L. *noxius* — *noxa*, hurt — *nocēre*, to hurt.]

noy *noi*, *v.t.* (*Spens.*) to vex, hurt, annoy. — *n.* (*obs.* or *dial.*) vexation, hurt, trouble. — *ns.* **noy′ance** (*Spens.*, *Shak.*) annoyance; **noyes** (*noiz*; *Spens.*) noise (see **noise**). — *adjs.* **noy′ous** (*Spens.*) vexatious: grievous: injurious; **noy′some** (*obs.*) noisome: hurtful. [Aphetic forms of **annoy**, etc.; see also **noisome.**]

noyade *nwä-yäd′*, *n.* wholesale drowning, as by Carrier at Nantes, 1793–94. [Fr., — *noyer*, to drown.]

noyau *nwä-yō′*, *n.* a liqueur flavoured with bitter almonds or peach-kernels. [Fr., fruit-stone — L. *nucālis*, nutlike — *nux, nucis*, a nut.]

nozzle *noz′l*, *n.* a little nose: the snout: a projection: an outlet tube, or spout: an open end of a tube. [Dim. of **nose.**]

-n′t. Shortened (enclitic) form of **not**[1].

nth. See **N.**

nu *nū, nü*, *n.* the thirteenth letter (N, ν) of the Greek alphabet, answering to N: as a numeral ν′ = 50, ‚ν = 50 000. [Gr. *nȳ.*]

nuance *nü-äs, nwäs, nū-äns′, nū′əns, nū′ans*, *n.* a delicate degree or shade of difference. — *v.t.* to give nuances to. — *adj.* **nuanced.** [Fr., — L. *nūbēs, nūbis*, a cloud.]

nub[1]. See **knub.**

nub[2] *nub*, (*obs. slang*) *n.* the gallows. — *v.t.* to hang. — **nubb′ing-cheat** the gallows; **nubb′ing-cove** a hangman. [Origin unknown.]

nub[3] *nub*, *n.* the point or gist. [Prob. from **knub.**]

nubbin *nub′in*, (*U.S.*) *n.* a small or underdeveloped ear of corn, fruit, etc. [Dim. of **nub**[1].]

nubble[1], **nubbly**, **nubby.** See **knub.**

nubble[2]. See **knubble.**

nubecula *nū-bek′ū-lə*, *n.* a cloudiness: — *pl.* **nūbec′ulae** (*-lē*) the Magellanic Clouds. [L. *nūbēcula*, dim. of *nūbēs*, cloud.]

nubia, **nubiferous**, etc. See **nubilous.**

nubile *nū′bīl, -bil*, *adj.* (esp. of a woman) marriageable: sexually mature: sexually attractive. — *n.* **nubility** (*-bil′i-ti*). [L. *nūbilis* — *nūbēre*, to veil oneself, hence to marry.]

nubilous *nū′bi-ləs*, *adj.* cloudy. — *n.* **nu′bia** a fleecy head-wrap formerly worn by women. — *adjs.* **nubif′- erous** cloud-bringing; **nu′biform** cloudlike; **nubigenous** (*-bij′i-nəs*) cloud-born. [L. *nūbēs*, a cloud.]

nucellus *nū-sel′əs*, *n.* the mass of tissue within the integuments of the ovule, containing the embryo-sac. — *adj.* **nucell′ar.** [A modern dim. from L. *nux, nucis*, a nut; L. has dim. *nucella*, a little nut.]

nucha *nū′kə*, *n.* the nape of the neck. — *adj.* **nū′chal.** [L.L. *nucha* — Ar. *nukhā′*, spinal marrow.]

nuciferous *nū-sif′ər-əs*, *adj.* nut-bearing. [L. *nux, nucis*, nut, *ferre*, to bear.]

nucivorous *nū-siv′ə-rəs*, *adj.* nut-eating. [L. *nux, nucis*, nut, *vorāre*, to devour.]

nucleal, **nuclear**, etc. See **nucleus.**

nucleus *nū′kli-əs*, *n.* a central mass or kernel: that around which something may grow: a core of flint from which pieces have been flaked off: the densest part of a comet's head or a nebula: a nut kernel (*obs.*): a nucellus (*obs.*): a rounded body in the protoplasm of a cell, the centre of its life (*biol.*): the massive part of an atom, distinguished from the outlying electrons (*phys.*): a stable group of atoms to which other atoms may be attached so as to form series of compounds (*phys.*). — *pl.* **nuclei** (*nū′kli-ī*). — *adjs.* **nū′cleal** (*-kli-əl; rare*),

nu′clear (*-kli-ər*) of, or of the nature of, a nucleus (also nu′cleary): pertaining to the nucleus of an atom, nuclei of atoms: pertaining to, powered by, or derived from, fission or fusion of atomic nuclei. — *v.t.* nu′clearise, -ize to make nuclear: to supply or fit with nuclear weapons. — *ns.* **nuclearīsā′tion, -z-; nu′cleāse** any of a number of enzymes inducing hydrolysis in nucleic acids. — *v.t.* and *v.i.* **nu′cleate** (*-kli-āt*) to form into, or group around, a nucleus. — *v.t.* to act, in a process of formation, as a nucleus for (e.g. *to nucleate crystals*). — *adjs.* **nu′cleate, -d** having a nucleus. — *ns.* **nucleā′tion** the action or process of nucleating: seeding clouds to control rainfall and fog formation; **nu′clein** (*-kli-in*) a colourless amorphous substance of varying composition, got from cell nuclei. — *adjs.* **nuclē′olar** of, or of the nature of, a nucleolus; **nu′cleolate, -d** having a nucleus or a nucleolus: (of a spore) containing one or more conspicuous oil-drops. — *ns.* **nu′cleole** a nucleolus; **nuclē′olus** a body (sometimes two bodies) observed within a cell nucleus, indispensable to growth: — *pl.* **nuclē′oli** (*-lī*); **nu′cleon** a general name for a neutron or a proton. — *n.sing.* **nucleon′ics** nuclear physics, esp. its practical applications. — *ns.* **nu′cleo= pro′tein** any of a group of compounds containing a protein molecule combined with a nuclein — important constituents of the nuclei of living cells; **nu′cleoside** a compound consisting of a purine or pyramidine base bound to a sugar (usu. ribose or deoxyribose); **nucleo- syn′thesis** the process in which atomic nuclei bind together to form chemical elements (e.g in stars); **nuc′leotide** a compound of a nucleoside and phosphoric acid, which forms the principal constituent of nucleic acid; **nuclide** (*nū′klīd, -klid*) a species of atom of any element distinguished by the number of neutrons and protons in its nucleus, and its energy state: — also sometimes **nucleide.** — **nuclear energy** a more exact term for *atomic energy*, energy released or absorbed during reactions taking place in atomic nuclei; **nuclear family** the basic family unit consisting of the mother and father with their children; **nuclear fission** spontaneous or induced splitting of atomic nucleus; **nuclear** (or **atomic**) **fuel** material, as uranium or plutonium, consumed to produce atomic energy; **nuclear fusion** the creation of a new nucleus by merging two lighter ones, with release of energy; **nuclear medicine** diagnosis and treatment of disease using radiation-detecting instruments or radioactive materials; **nuclear physics** the science of forces and transformations within the nucleus of the atom; **nuclear power** power obtained from a controlled nuclear reaction (*adj.* **nuclear-powered**); **nuclear reaction** a process in which an atomic nucleus interacts with another nucleus or particle, producing changes in energy and nuclear structure; **nuclear reactor** an assembly of uranium, with moderator, in which a nuclear chain reaction can develop; **nuclear sexing** testing a person's sex by examining cells from inside the cheek which, in females, have a material near the nucleus that can be stained blue; **nuclear warfare; nuclear warhead; nuclear weapon; nuclear winter** conditions of severe cold and lack of sunlight predicted by scientists as the aftermath of nuclear war; **nucleic acid** any of the complex acid components of nucleo-proteins. — **nuclear-free zone** an area in which the transport, storage, manufacture and deployment of nuclear weapons, and the transport of nuclear waste, are officially prohibited; **nuclear magnetic resonance** resonance which can be produced in nuclei of most isotopes of the elements and from which a clue can be obtained to the particular atoms involved. [L. *nucleus* — *nux, nucis*, a nut.]

nucule *nūk′ūl*, *n.* a nutlet. [L. *nucula*, dim. of *nux, nucis*, a nut.]

nude *nūd*, *adj.* naked: bare: undraped: without consideration (*law*). — *n.* a nude figure or figures: undraped condition. — *n.* **nudā′tion** the act of making bare. — *adv.* **nude′ly.** — *n.* **nude′ness.** — *adjs.* **nu′dibranch** (*-brangk*) having naked gills (also *n.*): belonging to the

Nudibranchiā'ta, shell-less marine gasteropods with gills exposed on the back and sides of the body; **nudibranch'iate; nudicau'date** having a hairless tail, as a rat; **nu'dicaul, -ous** having a leafless stem; **nu'die** (*coll.*) naked or featuring nudity, esp. of films, shows, magazines, etc. — Also *n.* — *ns.* **nu'dism** the practice of going naked: (esp. *U.S.*) naturism; **nu'dist** one who goes naked, or approves of going naked: (esp. *U.S.*) a naturist. — Also *adj.* — *n.* **nu'dity** the state of being nude: a nude figure: — *pl.* **nu'dities** naked parts usually covered. [L. *nūdus*, naked.]

nudge *nuj, n.* a gentle poke or push, as with the elbow. — *v.t.* to poke or push gently, esp. to draw someone's attention to something. — **nudge, nudge, (wink, wink)** (*coll.*) imputing some disreputable practice or indicating a sexual innuendo. — Also **nudge'-nudge'.** [Origin obscure; perh. connected with Norw. *nugge*, to rub, or with **knock, knuckle.**]

nuée ardente *nü-ā är-dāt,* a cloud of hot gas, ash, etc., from a volcano, spreading horizontally. [Fr., burning cloud.]

nugae *nü'gē, -jē, nōō'gī,* (L.) *n.pl.* trifles.

nugatory *nü'gə-tə-ri, adj.* trifling: worthless: inoperative: unavailing: futile. — *n.* **nu'gatoriness.** [L. *nūgātōrius* — *nūgae,* trifles, trumpery.]

nuggar *nug'ər, n.* a large boat used to carry cargo on the Nile. [Ar. *nuqqār.*]

nugget *nug'it, n.* a lump, esp. of gold: anything small but valuable (*fig.*). — *adj.* **nugg'ety** (*Austr.*) stocky, thickset. [Origin unknown; there is a Sw. dialect word *nug,* a lump, block.]

nuisance *nü'səns, n.* hurt or injury (*obs.*): that which annoys or hurts, esp. if there be some legal remedy: that which is offensive to the senses: a person or thing that is troublesome or obtrusive in some way. — *n.* **nui'sancer.** [Fr., — L. *nocēre,* to hurt.]

nuke *nük,* (*slang*) *n.* a nuclear weapon. — *v.t.* to attack using nuclear weapons. [Contr. of **nuclear.**]

null[1] *nul, adj.* of no legal force: void: invalid: empty of significance: amounting to nothing. — *n.* something of no value or meaning, a cipher or nought (*obs.*). — *v.t.* to annul, nullify: to wipe out (*obs.*). — *ns.* **null'ity** the state of being null or void: nothingness: want of existence, force, or efficacy; **null'ness.** — **decree of nullity** a decree that a marriage has never existed. [L. *nūllus,* not any, from *ne,* not, *ūllus,* any.]

null[2] *nul, n.* a knurl: a kink. — *v.i.* to kink. — *n.* **null'ing** knurling. [**knurl.**]

nulla(h), nala, nalla(h) *nul'ə, n.* a ravine: a water-course, not necessarily a dry one. [Hind. *nālā.*]

nulla-nulla *nul'ə-nul'ə, n.* an Australian aborigine's hardwood club. — Also **null'a.** [Aboriginal.]

nullifidian *nul-i-fid'i-ən, adj.* having no faith, esp. religious. — *n.* one who has no faith. [L. *nūllus,* none, *fidēs,* faith.]

nullify *nul'i-fī, v.t.* to make null: to annul: to render void or of no force: — *pr.p.* **null'ifying;** *pa.t.* and *pa.p.* **null'ified.** — *ns.* **nullification** (-*fi-kā'shən*) a rendering void or of none effect, esp. (*U.S.*) of a contract by one of the parties, or of a law by one legislature which has been passed by another; **null'ifier** (-*fī-ər*). [Late L. *nūllificāre* — *nūllus,* none, *facēre,* to make.]

nullipara *nul-ip'ə-rə, n.* a woman who has never given birth to a child, esp. if not a virgin. — *adj.* **nullip'arous.** — *n.* **nulliparity** (-*i-par'i-ti*). [L. *nūllus,* none, *parēre,* to bring forth.]

nullipore *nul'i-pōr, -pör, n.* a coralline seaweed. [L. *nūllus,* none, *porus,* a passage, pore.]

nulli secundus *nul'ī si-kund'əs, nōōl'ē se-kōōn'dōōs,* (L.) second to none.

nullity, nullness. See **null**[1].

numb *num, adj.* having diminished power of sensation or motion: powerless to feel or act: stupefied: causing (*Shak.*) or of the nature of (*Milt.*) numbness. — *v.t.* to make numb: to deaden: — *pr.p.* **numbing** (*num'ing*); *pa.t.* and *pa.p.* **numbed** (*numd*). — **numbskull** see **numskull.** [O.E. *numen,* pa.p. of *niman,* to take.]

numbat *num'bat, n.* a small Australian marsupial (*Myrmecobius fasciatus*) which feeds on termites. [Aboriginal.]

number *num'bər, n.* that by which single things are counted or reckoned: quantity reckoned in units: a particular value or sum of single things or units: a representation in arithmetical symbols of such a value or sum: a full complement: a specified or recognised set, class, or group: the multitude (*obs.*): some or many of the persons or things in question (often in *pl.*): more than one: numerousness: (in *pl.*) numerical superiority: numerability: a numerical indication of a thing's place in a series, or one assigned to it for reference, as in a catalogue: a label or other object bearing such an indication: a person or thing marked or designated in such a way: an item: an issue of a periodical or serial publication: an integral portion of an opera or other composition: arithmetical faculty: (in *pl.*) rhythm, verses, music: the property in words of expressing singular, dual, trial, etc. and plural (*gram.*): a single item in a programme, esp. of popular music and/or variety turns: an item of merchandise on show, usu. of clothing (*coll.*): a girl (*slang*): (with *cap.,* in *pl.*) fourth book of the Old Testament, in which an account of a census is given. — *v.t.* to count: to count out in payment (*Milt.*): to apportion: to have lived through: to reckon as one: to mark with a number or assign a number to: to amount to. — *v.i.* to be reckoned in the number: to be of like number. — *n.* **num'berer.** — *adj.* **num'berless** without number: more than can be counted. — **number cruncher** (*slang*) a computer designed to carry out large quantities of complex numerical calculations; **number crunching; number eight** (*Rugby*) the forward whose position is at the back of the scrum; **number nine** a purgative pill; **number one** chief, most important: he or that whose number is one, the first in the numbered series: self, oneself (*slang*): lieutenant, first officer (under the rank of commander; *naut. slang*); **number plate** the plaque on a motor vehicle showing its registration number; **number system** (*math.*) any set of elements which has two binary operations called addition and multiplication, each of which is commutative and associative, and which is such that multiplication is distributive with respect to addition; **number ten** (*coll.*) 10 Downing St., official residence of the Prime Minister; **number two** second-in-command. — **any number of** many; beyond, without **number** too many to be counted; **by numbers** (of a procedure, etc.) performed in simple stages, each stage being identified by a number; **have,** or **get someone's number** to size someone up; **his number is up** he is doomed, has not long to live; **in numbers** in large numbers; **number of the beast** see **Apocalypse; one's (its) days are numbered** one's (its) end is imminent. [Fr. *nombre* — L. *numerus.*]

numbles, numble-pie. See **umbles, humble-pie.**

numdah *num'dä, n.* an embroidered felt rug made in India. [Cf. **numnah.**]

numen. See **numinous.**

numerable *nü'mər-ə-bl, adj.* that may be numbered or counted. — *n.* **numerabil'ity.** — *adv.* **nu'merably.** — *ns.* **nu'meracy** the state of being numerate; **numeraire** (*nü'mə-rer;* also (Fr.) **numéraire** *nü-mā-*) a standard for currency exchange rates, etc. — *adj.* **nu'meral** pertaining to, consisting of, or expressing number. — *n.* a figure or mark used to express a number, as 1, 2, I, V, α', β', etc.: a word used to denote a number (*gram.*): (in *pl.*) a badge indicating regiment, year of curriculum, etc. — *adv.* (*rare*) **nu'merally** according to number. — *adj.* **nu'merary** belonging to a certain number: contained within or counting as one of a body or a number — opp. to **supernumerary.** — *v.t.* **nu'merate** to read off as numbers (from figures): orig. to enumerate, to number. — *adj.* having some understanding of mathematics and science: able to solve arithmetical problems: (see also **innumerate**). — Also *n.* — *ns.* **numerā'tion** the act of numbering: the art of reading figures and expressing the value in numbers; **nu′merātor** one who numbers: the upper number of a vulgar fraction, which expresses the number of fractional parts taken. — *adjs.* **numeric** (*-mer′ik*), **-al** belonging to, expressed in, or consisting in, number: in number independently of sign: identical (*obs.*; often with *same*). — *adv.* **numer′ically.** — *ns.* **numerol′ogy** the study of numbers as supposed to show future events; **numeros′ity** numerousness: condition in respect of number: harmonious flow. — *adj.* **nu′merous** great in number or quantity: many: consisting of or pertaining to a large number: rhythmical. — *adv.* **nu′merously.** — *n.* **nu′merousness.** — **numerical analysis** the study of methods of approximation and their accuracy, etc.; **numerical control** automatic control of operation of machine tools by means of numerical data stored on magnetic or punched tape or on punched cards. [L. *numerus*, number.]

numerus clausus *nū′mə-rəs klö′zəs, nōō′me-rōōs klow′sōōs* a quota restricting the number of students (esp. those of a particular race or creed) entering an academic institution. [L., lit. closed or restricted number.]

numinous *nū′min-əs, adj.* pertaining to a divinity: suffused with feeling of a divinity. — *ns.* **numen** (*nū′men*) a presiding deity: — *pl.* **nu′mina** (*-min-ə*); **nu′minousness.** [L. *nūmen, -inis,* divinity.]

numismatic *nū-miz-mat′ik, adj.* pertaining to money, coins, or medals. — *n.sing.* **numismat′ics** the study or collection of coins and medals. — *ns.* **numis′matist; numismatol′ogist; numismatol′ogy.** [L. *numisma* — Gr. *nomisma,* current coin — *nomizein,* to use commonly — *nomos,* custom.]

nummary *num′ə-ri, adj.* relating to coins or money. — *adjs.* **numm′ular** coin-shaped; **numm′ulary** nummary; **numm′ūlated** coin-shaped. — *n.* **nummūlā′tion** arrangement of blood corpuscles in rouleaux. — *adj.* **numm′ūline** coin-shaped: nummulitic. — *n.* **numm′ūlite** a large coin-shaped fossil foraminifer, forming limestones. — *adj.* **nummūlitic** (*-lit′ik*) pertaining to, composed of, or containing nummulites. [L. *nummus,* a coin.]

numnah *num′nə, n.* a felt or, now usu., sheepskin, cloth or pad placed under a saddle to prevent chafing. [Hind. *namdā.*]

numskull *num′skul, n.* a blockhead. — *adj.* **num′skulled.** — Also **numb′skull.** [**numb, skull.**]

nun[1] *nun, n.* a woman who, under a vow, has secluded herself in a religious house, to give her time to devotion: a kind of pigeon with feathers on its head like a nun's hood: a blue tit: a male smew: a tussock moth (*Psiluria monacha*), a pest in pine-forests. — *ns.* **nun′hood** the condition of a nun; **nunn′ery** a house for nuns: nunship. — *adj.* **nunn′ish.** — *ns.* **nunn′ishness; nun′ship** the condition of a nun. — **nun's-fidd′le** a tromba marina; **nun′s-flesh′** an ascetic temperament; **nun′s-veil′ing** a woollen cloth, soft and thin, used by women for veils and dresses. [O.E. *nunne* — L.L. *nunna, nonna,* a nun, an old maiden lady, orig. mother; cf. Gr. *nannē,* aunt, Sans. *nanā,* a child's word for mother.]

nun[2] *nun,* (*obs.*) *n.* a spinning top. — **nun′-buoy** a buoy that tapers conically each way.

nunatak *nōō′na-tak, n.* a point of rock appearing above the surface of land-ice: — *pl.* **nu′nataks,** or (Sw.) **nu′nataker.** [Eskimo.]

nunc dimittis *nungk di-mit′tis,* the song of Simeon (Luke ii. 29–32) in the R.C. Breviary and the Anglican evening service. [From the opening words, *nunc dīmittis,* now lettest thou depart.]

nuncheon *nun′shən, n.* a light meal: a lunch. [M.E. *noneschenche,* noon-drink — O.E. *nōn,* noon, *scenc,* drink; cf. **noon, skink.**]

nuncio *nun′shi-ō, n.* a messenger: one who brings tidings: an ambassador from the pope to an emperor or a king: — *pl.* **nun′cios.** — *n.* **nun′ciature** a nuncio's office or term of office. [It. (now *nunzio*) — L. *nūntius,* a messenger, conjectured to be a contr. of *noventius*; cf. *novus,* new.]

nuncle *nung′kl,* (*Shak.*) *n.* a contr. of **mine uncle.**

nuncupate *nung′kū-pāt, v.t.* to utter as a vow: to declare orally. — *n.* **nuncūpā′tion.** — *adjs.* **nunc′ūpātive** (of a will) oral: designative; **nunc′ūpatory** (*-pə-tə-ri; obs.*) nuncupative: dedicatory. [L. *nuncupāre,* to call by name — prob. from *nōmen,* name, *capĕre,* to take.]

nundine *nun′dīn, -din, n.* the ancient Roman market-day, every eighth day (ninth by Roman reckoning, counting both days). — *adj.* **nun′dinal** (*-din-*) pertaining to a fair or market. [L. *nūndinae,* market-day — *novem,* nine, *diēs,* a day.]

nunnation *nun-ā′shən, n.* the addition of a final *n* in the declension of nouns. [As if L. *nunnātiō* — Ar. *nūn,* the letter n.]

nunnery. See **nun**[1].

nuoc mam *nwok mäm,* a spicy sauce made from raw fish. [Viet.]

Nuphar *nū′fär, n.* the yellow water-lily genus. [Pers. *nūfar,* reduced form of *nīnūfar*; see **Nenuphar.**]

nuptial *nup′shəl, adj.* pertaining to marriage: pertaining to mating (*zool.*). — *n.* (usu. in *pl.*) marriage: wedding ceremony. — *n.* **nuptiality** (*-shi-ul′i-ti*) nuptial character or quality: marriage-rate: (in *pl.*) wedding ceremonies and festivities. [L. *nuptiālis* — *nuptiae,* marriage — *nubĕre, nuptum,* to marry.]

nur, nurr. See **knur.**

nuraghe *nōō-rä′gä,* **nurhag** *nōō-räg′, ns.* a broch-like Sardinian round tower, probably of the Bronze Age: — *pls.* **nuraghi** (*-gē*), **nurhags.** — *adj.* **nuragh′ic** relating to, found in, etc., nuraghi. [Sardinian dialect.]

nurd. See **nerd.**

nurl. See **knurl.**

nurse[1] *nûrs, n.* one who suckles a child: one who tends a child: one who has the care of the sick, feeble, or injured, or who is trained for the purpose: one set apart to guide an incompetent officer or other: a worker bee, ant, etc., that tends the young: a budding form in tunicates: one who or that which feeds, rears, tends, saves, fosters, or develops anything, or preserves it in any desired condition: a shrub or tree that protects a young plant (*hort.*): the state of being nursed (in the phrases *at nurse, out to nurse*). — *v.t.* to suckle: to tend, as an infant or a sick person: to bring up: to cherish: to manage with care and economy: to play skilfully, manipulate carefully, keep watchfully in touch with, in order to obtain or preserve the desired condition: to hold or carry as a nurse does a child. — *adj.* **nurse′like.** — *ns.* **nurs(e)′ling** that which is nursed or fostered: an infant; **nurs′er; nurs′ery** nursing (*Shak.*): a place for nursing: an apartment for children: a place where young animals are reared, or where the growth of anything is promoted: a piece of ground where plants are reared for sale or transplanting: a race for two-year-old horses (also **nursery stakes**). — *adj.* pertaining to a nursery, or to early training. — **nurse′-child** a child in the care of a nurse: a foster child; **nurse′maid** a maid servant who takes care of children; **nursery cannon** (*billiards*) a cannon (esp. one of a series) with the three balls close together and being moved as little as possible; **nurs′ery-gov′erness** a governess for children who still require a nurse's care; **nurs′erymaid** a maid employed in keeping a nursery: a nursemaid; **nurs′eryman** a man who owns or works a nursery: one who is employed in cultivating plants, etc., for sale; **nursery rhyme** a traditional rhyme known to children; **nursery school** a school for very young children (aged two to five). — *n.pl.* **nursery slopes** slopes set apart for skiing novices. — *v.t.* and *v.i.* **nurse′-tend** to attend as a sick-nurse. — **nurse′-tender; nurse′-tending; nur′sing-chair** a low chair without arms, used when feeding a baby; **nurs′ing-fa′ther** (*B.*) a foster-father; **nursing home** a private hospital; **nursing officer** any of several grades of nurses having administrative duties. — **put (out) to nurse** to commit to a nurse, usu. away from home: to put (an estate) under trustees. [O.Fr. *norrice* (Fr. *nourrice*) — L. *nūtrīx, -īcis* — *nūtrīre,* to nourish.]

nurse[2] *nûrs, n.* a shark: a dogfish. — **nurse′-hound** a European dogfish (*Scylliorhinus caniculus*); **nurse shark**

any shark of the family *Orectolobidae*. [Earlier *nuss*, perh. for (*an*) *huss*, *husk*, a dogfish.]

nursle *nûrs'l*, a mistaken form of **nousle**, **nuzzle**.

nurture *nûr'chər*, *n.* upbringing: rearing: training: whatever is derived from the individual's experience, training, environment, distinguished from *nature*, or what is inherited: food. — *v.t.* to nourish: to bring up: to educate. — *adjs.* **nur'tural**; **nur'turant**. — *n.* **nur'turer**. [O.Fr. *noriture* (Fr. *nourriture*) — L.L. *nūtritūra* — L. *nūtrīre*, to nourish.]

nut *nut*, *n.* popularly, any fruit with seed in a hard shell: a hard dry indehiscent fruit formed from a syncarpous gynaeceum (*bot.*): often the hazel-nut, sometimes the walnut: the head (*slang*): a hard-headed person, one difficult to deal with, a tough: a young blood (*slang*; also **knut** *nut*): a crazy person (also **nut'-case**, **nut'case**; *slang*): a small block, usu. of metal, for screwing on the end of a bolt: an en (*print.*): the ridge at the top of the fingerboard on a fiddle, etc. (*mus.*): the mechanism for tightening or slackening a bow (*mus.*): a small lump of coal: a small biscuit or round cake: a coconut-shell drinking-cup: a source of joy (in *pl.*; *slang*): the testicles (in *pl.*; *slang*). — *v.i.* to look for and gather nuts: to butt with the head (*slang*). — *pr.p.* **nutt'ing**; *pa.t.* and *pa.p.* **nutt'ed**. — *ns.* **nutā'rian** one who thinks nuts the best kind of food; **nut'let** a one-seeded portion of a fruit that divides as it matures, as in labiates: the stone of a drupe. — *adj.* **nuts** crazy (*slang*). — Also *interj.* expressing defiance, contempt, disappointment, etc. — *ns.* **nutt'er** one who gathers nuts: nut-butter: a crazy person (*slang*); **nutt'ery** an area of nut-trees: a lunatic asylum (*slang*); **nutt'iness**; **nutt'ing** the gathering of nuts. — *adj.* **nutt'y** abounding in nuts: having the flavour of nuts: foolishly amorous (*slang*): mentally unhinged (*slang*). — *adj.* **nut'-brown** brown, like a ripe hazel-nut. — **nut'-butt'er** a butter-substitute made from nuts; **nut'cracker** a bird (*Nucifraga*) of the crow family: (usu. in *pl.*) an instrument for cracking nuts. — *adj.* like a pair of nutcrackers, as toothless jaws. — **nutcracker man** a type of early man found in Tanzania in 1959, by some distinguished as a separate species *Zinjanthropus*; **nut'-gall** a nut-like gall, produced by a gall-wasp, chiefly on the oak; **nut'-grass** American sedges of various kinds, esp. one with edible tuberous root; **nut'hatch** a bird (*Sitta*) that hacks nuts and seeks insects on trees like a creeper — also **nut'jobber**, **nut'pecker**; **nut'-hook** a stick with a hook for pulling down nut-bearing boughs: a bailiff: a thief who uses a hook; **nut'house** (*slang*) a mental asylum: a place where people's behaviour is crazy (*fig.*); **nut'meal** meal made from nuts; **nut'-oil** an oil got from walnuts or other nuts; **nut'-pine** the stone-pine or other species with large edible seeds; **nut'shell** the hard covering of a nut; **nut'-tree** any tree bearing nuts, esp. the hazel; **nut'-wee'vil** a weevil (*Balaninus*) whose larvae live on hazelnuts; **nut'-wrench** an instrument for turning nuts on screws. — **a (hard) nut to crack** a difficult problem; **be nuts on**, **about** (*slang*) to be very fond of; **do one's nut** (*slang*) to become extremely angry, to rage; **in a nutshell** in very small space: briefly, concisely; **not for nuts** (*coll.*) not very well, incompetently; **nuts and bolts** the basic facts, the essential, practical details; **off one's nut** (*slang*) mentally unhinged, crazy. [O.E. *hnutu*; O.N. *hnot*, Du. *noot*, Ger. *Nuss*.]

nutant *nū'tənt*, *adj.* nodding: drooping. — *v.i.* **nutate'** to nod: to droop: to perform a nutation. — *n.* **nutā'tion** a nodding: a fluctuation in the precessional movement of the earth's pole about the pole of the ecliptic (*astron.*): the sweeping out of a curve by the tip of a growing axis (*bot.*). — *adj.* **nutā'tional**. [L. *nūtāre*, to nod.]

nutmeg *nut'meg*, *n.* the aromatic kernel of an East Indian tree (*Myristica*), much used as a seasoning in cookery. — *adjs.* **nut'megged**; **nut'meggy**. [M.E. *notemuge* — *nut* and inferred O.Fr. *mugue*, musk — L. *muscus*, musk.]

nutria *nū'tri-ə*, *n.* the coypu: its fur. [Sp. *nutria*, otter — L. *lutra*.]

nutrient *nū'tri-ənt*, *adj.* feeding: nourishing. — *n.* any nourishing substance. — *n.* **nu'triment** that which nourishes: food. — *adj.* **nutrimental** (-*ment'l*). — *n.* **nutri'tion** the act or process of nourishing: food. — *adj.* **nutri'tional**. — *n.* **nutri'tionist** an expert in foods and their nutritional values. — *adj.* **nutri'tious** nourishing. — *adv.* **nutri'tiously**. — *n.* **nutri'tiousness**. — *adj.* **nu'tritive** nourishing: concerned in nutrition. — *adv.* **nu'tritively**. [L. *nūtrīre*, to nourish.]

nux vomica *nuks vom'ik-ə*, a seed that yields strychnine: the East Indian tree (*Strychnos nux-vomica*; family Loganiaceae) that produces it. [L. *nux*, a nut, *vomēre*, to vomit.]

nuzzer *nuz'ər*, *n.* a present to a superior. [Hind. *nazr*, gift.]

nuzzle[1], **nousle** *nuz'l*, *v.t.* and *v.i.* to poke, press, burrow, root, rub, sniff, caress, or investigate with the nose. — *v.t.* to thrust in (the nose or head). — *v.i.* to snuggle: to go with the nose toward the ground. [Freq. vb. from **nose**.]

nuzzle[2] *nuz'l*, *v.t.* to train: to bring up: to foster. [Origin obscure; confused with **nurse**; see **nousle**.]

ny. An obs. spelling of **nigh**.

nyaff *nyaf*, (*Scot.*) *n.* a small or worthless person or thing. — *v.i.* to yelp, yap: to talk frivolously or argue snappishly. [Perh. imit. of a small dog's bark.]

nyala (*ə*)*n-yä'lə*, *n.* a large South African antelope. [Bantu (*i*)*nyala*.]

nyanza *nyan'zə*, also *ni*- or *nī-an'zə*, *n.* a lake (esp. in African proper names). [Bantu.]

nyas *nī'əs*, *n.* an old form of **eyas** (q.v.).

nychthemeron *nik-thē'mə-ron*, *n.* a complete day of 24 hours, a night and a day. — *adj.* **nychthē'meral**. [Gr. *nychthēmeron* — *nyx*, *nyktos*, night, *hēmerā*, day.]

Nyctaginaceae *nik-tə-jin-ā'si-ē*, *n.pl.* a family of plants, mainly tropical American, akin to the goosefoots and the pinks, including the marvel of Peru. — *adj.* **nyctaginā'ceous**. [Gr. *nyx*, *nyktos*, night.]

nyctalopia *nik-tə-lō'pi-ə*, *n.* properly, night-blindness, abnormal difficulty in seeing in a faint light: by confusion sometimes, day-blindness. — *adj.* **nyctalōp'ic**. — *n.* **nyc'talops** (-*lops*) one affected with nyctalopia: — *pl.* **nyctalō'pes**. [Gr. *nyktalōps*, night-blind, day-blind — *nyx*, *nyktos*, night, *alaos*, blind, *ōps*, eye, face.]

nyctinasty *nik'ti-nas-ti*, *n.* sleep-movement in plants, joint effect of changes in light and temperature. — *adj.* **nyctinas'tic**. [Gr. *nyx*, *nyktos*, night, *nastos*, pressed.]

nyctitropism *nik-tit'ro-pizm*, *n.* the assumption by plants of certain positions at night. — *adj.* **nyctitropic** (-*trop'*). [Gr. *nyx*, *nyktos*, night, *tropos*, turning.]

nyctophobia *nik-tō-fō'bi-ə*, *n.* morbid fear of the night or of darkness. [Gr. *nyx*, *nyktos*, night, and **phobia**.]

nye[1]. An obs. spelling of **nigh**.

nye[2] *nī*, *n.* a variant of **nid**, **nide**.

nying (*obs.*) *pr.p.* of **nie**, **ny**, **nye**[1].

nylghau, **nilgau**. See **nilgai**.

nylon *nī'lən*, -*lon*, *n.* any of numerous polymeric amides that can be formed into fibres, bristles, or sheets: any material made from nylon filaments or fibres: a stocking made of nylon. [Formerly a trademark.]

nymph *nimf*, *n.* one of the divinities who lived in mountains, rivers, trees, etc. (*myth.*): a young and beautiful maiden (often ironical): an insect pupa (*obs.*): an immature insect, similar to the adult but with wings and sex-organs undeveloped. — *n.pl.* **nymphae** (-*ē*) the labia minora. — *ns.* **Nymphaea** (-*ē'ə*) the white water-lily genus, giving name to a family of dicotyledons **Nymphaeā'ceae**, akin to the buttercup family; **nymphae'um** a temple, sanctuary, or grotto of the nymphs. — *adj.* **nymph'al**. — *n.* **nymph'alid** a butterfly of the **Nymphal'idae**, a brush-footed family with useless, reduced fore-legs. — *adj.* **nymphē'an**. — *n.* **nymph'et** a young nymph: a very young girl with strong sex-attraction. — *adjs.* **nymph'ic**, -**al**; **nymph'ish**; **nymph'-like**; **nymph'ly**. — *ns.* **nymph'o** a nymphomaniac: — *pl.* **nym'phos; nymph'olepsy** a species of ecstasy or frenzy said to have seized those who had been a nymph: a yearning for the unattainable; **nymph'olept** a person so affected. — *adj.* **nympholept'ic.** — *n.* **nymphomā'nia** morbid and uncontrollable sexual desire in women. — *n.* and *adj.* **nymphomā'niac.** [L.

nympha — Gr. *nymphē*, a bride, a nymph.]
nys *nis, niz, (Spens.)* is not.   [**ne, is.**]
nystagmus *nis-tag'məs, n.* a spasmodic, lateral oscillatory movement of the eyes, found in miners, etc. — *adjs.* **nystag'mic; nystag'moid.**   [Latinised from Gr. *nystagmos — nystazein,* to nap.]

For other sounds see detailed chart of pronunciation.

O

O¹, o ō, *n.* the fifteenth letter of our alphabet, derived
from Greek omicron, chief sounds in English being
those in *note, not, for, work, son, do*: anything round
or nearly so: a spangle: in telephone, etc., jargon,
nought or nothing: — *pl.* **Oes, O's, oes, o's** (ōz): as a
mediaeval Roman numeral, **O** = 11, **Ō** = 11 000:
prefixed *o*- stands for *ortho*- (*chem.*). — **O grade,
Ordinary grade** in Scotland, (a pass in) an examination
generally taken at the end of the 4th year of secondary
education. — Also *adjs.* (often with *hyphen*); **O level,
Ordinary level** esp. in England and Wales, (a pass in)
an examination generally taken at the end of the 5th
year of secondary education. — Also *adjs.* (often with
hyphen).
O², oh ō, *interj.* used in addressing or apostrophising,
marking the occurrence of a thought, reception of
information, or expressing wonder, admiration, disapprobation, surprise, protest, pain, or other emotion.
The form O is chiefly used in verse (*O for, O that*). —
Fifteen O's fifteen meditations on Christ's Passion,
each beginning with O, composed by St Bridget; **O's
of Advent** seven anthems each beginning with O, sung
on the days before Christmas Eve.
o', o ō, ə, a worn-down form of **of** and of **on**.
O' ō, *prefix*, in Irish patronymics, descendant of. [Ir.
ó, ua — O.Ir. *an*, descendant.]
oaf ōf, *n.* a changeling: a dolt: an idiot: a lout: — *pl.* **oafs,**
(rarely) **oaves.** — *adj.* **oaf'ish** idiotic, doltish: lubberly:
loutish. [O.N. *ālfr*, elf; cf. **elf, ouphe.**]
oak ōk, *n.* a genus (*Quercus*) of trees of the beech family:
its timber, valued in shipbuilding, etc.: extended to
various other trees, as **poison-oak, she-oak** (qq.v.). —
adj. of oak. — *adj.* **oak'en** of oak. — *n.* **oak'ling** a
young oak. — *adj.* **oak'y** like oak, firm: abounding in
oaks. — **oak'-apple** a gall caused by an insect on an
oak twig; **oak'-egg'er** an egger moth whose caterpillars
feed on oak; **oak'enshaw** a little oak-wood; **oak'-fern**
a fern (*Thelypteris dryopteris*) of the polypody family
(translation of Gr. *dryopteris*, name perh. given to
ferns growing on oak-trees, transferred by Linnaeus
to this species); **oak'-gall** a gall produced on the oak;
oak'-leather a fungus mycelium in the fissures of old
oaks; **oak'-lump** the lichen lungwort; **oak'-mast** acorns
collectively; **oak'-nut** a gall on the oak; **oak'-tree; oak
wilt** a serious fungal disease of oak trees, causing
wilting and discoloration of foliage; **oak'-wood.** —
Oak-apple Day the 29th of May, the anniversary of
the Restoration in 1660, when country boys used to
wear oak-apples in commemoration of Charles II
hiding in the branches of an oak (the **Royal Oak**) from
Cromwell's troopers after the Battle of Worcester;
sport one's oak (*university slang*) to keep one's outer
door shut when one does not want visitors; **The Oaks**
a great English race (founded 1779) for three-year-old
fillies — so named from an estate near Epsom. [O.E.
āc; O.N. *eik*, Ger. *Eiche*.]
oaker (*Spens.*). Same as **ochre.**
oakum ōk'əm, *n.* old (usu. tarred) ropes untwisted and
teased out for caulking the seams of ships. [O.E.
ācumba (*æcumbe*) from *ā*-, away from, and the root of
cemban, to comb.]
oar ōr, ör, *n.* a light bladed pole for propelling a boat: a
stirring-pole: a swimming organ: an oarsman. — *v.t.*
to impel as by rowing. — *v.i.* to row. — *n.* **oar'age** oars
collectively: rowing movement. — *adjs.* **oared** furnished with oars; **oar'less; oar'y** having the form or
use of oars. — **oar'-fish** a ribbon-fish (*Regalecus*). —
adj. **oar'-footed** having swimming feet. — **oar'-lap** a
rabbit with its ears standing out at right angles to the

head; **oar'-lock** (*rare*) a rowlock; **oars'man, oars'woman**
a rower: one skilled in rowing; **oars'manship** skill in
rowing; **oar'weed** same as **oreweed.** — **lie** or **rest on
one's oars** to abstain from rowing without removing
the oars from the rowlocks: to rest, take things easily:
to cease from work; **put one's oar in** to interpose when
not asked. [O.E. *ār*.]
oasis ō-ā'sis, sometimes ō'ə-sis, *n.* a fertile spot or tract
in a sandy desert: any place of rest or pleasure in the
midst of toil and gloom: (with *cap.*; ®) a block of soft
permeable material used to hold cut flowers, etc. in
place in a flower arrangement: — *pl.* **oases** (-sēz).
[Gr. *oasis*, an Egyptian word; cf. Coptic *ouahe*.]
oast ōst, *n.* a kiln to dry hops or malt. — *n.* **oast'-house.**
[O.E. *āst*.]
oat ōt (oftener in *pl.* **oats** ōts), *n.* a well-known genus
(*Avena*) of grasses, esp. *A. sativa*, whose seeds are
much used as food: its seeds: a musical pipe of
oat-straw: a shepherd's pipe: pastoral song generally.
— *adj.* **oat'en** consisting of an oat stem or straw: made
of oatmeal. — **oat'cake** a thin hard dry cake made
with oatmeal. — **oat'-grass** a grass of Avena or kindred
genus used more as fodder than for the seed; **oat'meal'**
meal made of oats. — *adj.* of the colour of oatmeal.
— **feel one's oats** to be frisky or assertive; **get one's
oats** (*slang*) to have sexual intercourse; **off one's oats**
without appetite, off one's food (*coll.*); **sow one's wild
oats** to indulge in youthful dissipation or excesses; **wild
oats** a wild species of oat (*A. fatua*). [O.E. *āte*, pl.
ātan.]
oath ōth, *n.* a solemn appeal to a god or something holy
or reverenced as witness or sanction of the truth of a
statement: the form of words used: a more or less
similar expression used lightly, exclamatorily, deco-
ratively, or in imprecation: a swear-word: a curse: —
pl. **oaths** (ōdhz). — *adj.* **oath'able** (*Shak.*) capable of
taking an oath. — **oath'-breaking** (*Shak.*) perjury. —
on, under, upon oath sworn to speak the truth: attested
by oath; **take an oath** to have an oath administered to
one. [O.E. *āth*; Ger. *Eid*, O.N. *eithr*.]
oats; oaves. See **oat; oaf.**
ob ob, *n.* an objection (in the phrase *ob and sol*, objection
and solution). — **ob-and-soll'er** a disputant. [From
the marginal note *ob* in old books of controversial
divinity.]
obang ō'bang, *n.* an old Japanese oblong gold coin.
[Jap. *ōban*.]
obbligato ob-(b)li-gä'tō, *adj.* that cannot be done without.
— *n.* a musical accompaniment of independent importance, esp. that of a single instrument to a vocal piece:
— *pl.* **obbliga'tos, -ti** (-tē). [It.]
obcompressed ob'kəm-prest, (*bot.*) *adj.* flattened from
front to back. [L. pfx. *ob-*, towards; in mod. L., in
the opposite direction, reversed.]
obconic, -al ob-kon'ik, -əl, (*bot.*) *adjs.* conical and attached
by the point. [L. pfx. *ob-*, as in **obcompressed.**]
obcordate ob-kör'dāt, (*bot.*) *adj.* inversely heart-shaped,
as a leaf. [L. pfx. *ob-*, as in **obcompressed.**]
obdiplostemonous ob-dip-lō-stē'mən-əs, (*bot.*) *adj.* having
two whorls of stamens, the outer being situated opposite the petals. [L. pfx. *ob-*, as in **obcompressed.**]
obdurate ob'dū-rāt, sometimes (as *Shak., Milt.*) -dū', *adj.*
hardened in heart or in feelings: difficult to influence,
esp. in a moral sense: stubborn: hard. — *v.t.* and *v.i.*
to make or become obdurate. — *n.* **ob'dūracy** (or
ob-dū'rə-si) state of being obdurate: invincible hardness of heart. — *adv.* **ob'dūrately** (or *-dū'*). — *ns.*
ob'dūrateness (or *-dū'*), **obdūrā'tion.** — *v.t.* and *v.i.*
obdūre' to obdurate. [L. *obdūrāre, -ātum* — *ob-*,

fāte; fär; hûr; mīne; mōte; för; mūte; mōōn; fŏŏt; dhen (then); *el'ə-mənt* (element)

intens., against, *dūrāre*, to harden — *dūrus*, hard.]

obeah. See **obi**[1].

obeche *ō-bē'chē, n.* a large West African tree or its whitish wood. [Nigerian name.]

obedience *ō-bē'dyəns, -di-əns, n.* the act of doing what one is told: the state of being obedient: willingness to obey commands: dutifulness: the collective body of persons subject to any particular authority: a written instruction from the superior of an order to those under him: any official position under an abbot's jurisdiction: an obeisance (*arch.*). — *adjs.* **obě'dient** obeying: ready to obey; **obediential** (*ō-bē-di-en'shl*) pertaining to, of the nature of, obedience. — *n.* **obēdientiary** (*-en'sha-ri*) one subject to obedience: one charged with an obedience in a monastery. — *adv.* **obě'diently.** — **canonical obedience** the obedience, as regulated by the canons, of an ecclesiastic to another of higher rank; **passive obedience** unresisting and unquestioning obedience to authority, like that taught by some Anglican divines as due even to faithless and worthless kings like Charles II and James II. [L. *obēdientia*; see **obey.**]

obeisance *ō-bā'səns, n.* obedience (*obs.*): a bow or act of reverence: an expression of respect. — *adj.* **obei'sant.** [Fr. *obéissance* — *obéir* — L. root as **obey.**]

obelus *ob'i-ləs, n.* a sign (– or ÷) used in ancient manuscripts to mark suspected, corrupt, or spurious words and passages: a dagger-sign (†) used esp. in referring to footnotes (**double obelus** ‡; *print.*): — *pl.* **ob'eli** (*-lī*). — *n.* **obelion** (*ō-bē'li-on*) a point in the sagittal suture of the skull between the two parietal foramina. — *adjs.* **obelisc'al** of, or of the nature of, an obelisk; **obelisc'oid** of the form of an obelisk: obeliscal. — *v.t.* **ob'elise, -ize** to mark with an obelus: to condemn as spurious, doubtful, corrupt, etc. — *n.* **ob'elisk** a tall, four-sided, tapering pillar, usually of one stone, topped with a pyramid: an obelus. [L. *obelus* — Gr. *obelos* (dim. *obeliskos*), a spit.]

Oberon *ō'bə-ron, n.* king of the fairies, husband of Titania. [O.Fr. *Auberon*; prob. Frankish.]

obese *ō-bēs', adj.* abnormally fat. — *ns.* **obese'ness, obesity** (*-bēs', -bes'*). [L. *obēsus* — *ob-*, completely, *edĕre, ēsum*, to eat.]

obey *ō-bā', v.i.* to render obedience: to do what one is told: to be governed or controlled. — *v.t.* to do as told by: to comply with: to be controlled by. — *n.* **obey'er.** [Fr. *obéir* — L. *obēdīre* — *oboedīre* — *ob-*, towards, *audīre*, to hear.]

obfuscate *ob-fus'kāt, v.t.* to darken: to obscure. — *adj.* **obfuscat'ed** (*coll.*) drunk. — *n.* **obfuscā'tion.** [L. *obfuscāre, -ātum* — *ob-*, intens., *fuscus*, dark.]

obi[1] *ō'bi,* **obeah** (*obs.* **obia**) *ō'bi-ə, ns.* witchcraft and poisoning practised by Negroes of the West Indies, Guyana, etc.: a fetish or charm. — *v.t.* to bewitch. — *ns.* **o'beahism, o'beism, o'biism.** — **o'bi-man; o'bi-woman.** [Of W. African origin.]

obi[2] *ō'bi, n.* a broad sash worn with a kimono by the Japanese. [Jap. *obi* — *obiru*, to wear.]

obiit *ob'i-it, ō'bi-it,* (L.) *pa.t.* died. — **obiit sine prole** (*sīn'ē prō'lē, sin'e prō'le*) died without issue.

obit *ob'it,* or *ō'bit, n.* death (*obs.*): date of death: funeral ceremonies: office for a dead person: a death anniversary: an anniversary or other commemoration of a death: short for **obituary.** — *adjs.* **ob'ital, obit'ūal** pertaining to obits. — *n.* **obit'ūarist** a writer of obituaries. — *adj.* **obit'ūary** relating to or recording the death of a person or persons. — *n.* a register of deaths, orig. in a monastery: an account of a deceased person, or a notice of his death: a collection of death-notices in a newspaper often extended to include notices of births and marriages, etc. [L.L. *obitus* — *obīre, -ītum,* to go to meet, travel over, die — *ob,* in the way of, *īre,* to go.]

obiter *ob', ōb'it-ər, ob'it-er,* (L.) *adv.* by the way, cursorily. — **obiter dictum** (*dik'təm, -tōōm*) something said by the way, a cursory remark: — *pl.* **obiter dicta** (*dik'ta*).

object *ob'jikt, n.* a thing presented or capable of being presented to the senses (opposed to *eject*): a thing observed: a material thing: that which is thought of, regarded as being outside, different from, or independent of, the mind (opposed to *subject*): that upon which attention, interest, or some emotion is fixed: an oddity or deplorable spectacle: that towards which action or desire is directed, an end: part of a sentence denoting that upon which the action of a transitive verb is directed, or standing in an analogous relation to a preposition (*gram.*): interposition (*obs.*): presentation to view or to the mind (*Shak.*). — *v.t.* **object** (*əb-jekt', ob-*) to put in front or in the way of anything or anybody (*arch.*): to present to sense or mind (*arch.*): to present, bring forward, or adduce (*arch.*): to offer in opposition: to bring as an accusation: to impute (*obs.*). — *v.i.* to be opposed, feel or express disapproval (with *to, that, against*): to refuse assent. — *adj.* (*obs.*) opposed, interposed, exposed. — *n.* **objectificā'tion** (*-jekt-*). — *v.t.* **object'ify** to make objective. — *n.* **objec'tion** act of objecting: anything said or done in opposition: argument or reason against (with *to, against*): inclination to object, dislike, unwillingness. — *adj.* **objec'tionable** that may be objected to: requiring to be disapproved of: distasteful. — *adv.* **objec'tionably.** — *v.t.* **object'ivate** to render objective. — *n.* **objectivā'tion.** — *adj.* **object'ive** (also *ob'*) relating to or constituting an object: existing or considered only in relation to mind, subjective (*scholastic philos., obs.*): of the nature of, or belonging to, that which is presented to consciousness (opposed to *subjective*), exterior to the mind, self-existent, regarding or setting forth what is external, actual, practical, uncoloured by one's own sensations or emotions (*mod. philos.*): denoting the object (*gram.*): in the relation of object to a verb or preposition: objecting: (of lenses) nearest the object. — *n.* (*-jekt'*) the case of the grammatical object: a word in that case: an object-glass: the point to which the operations (esp. of an army) are directed: a goal, aim. — *adv.* **object'ively.** — *n.* **object'iveness.** — *v.t.* **object'ivise, -ize** to objectify. — *ns.* **object'ivism** a tendency to lay stress on what is objective: a theory that gives priority to the objective; **object'ivist.** — *adj.* **objectivist'ic.** — *n.* **objectiv'ity.** — *adj.* **ob'jectless** having no object: purposeless. — *n.* **object'or.** — **ob'ject=ball** (*billiards,* etc.) a ball that a player aims at striking with his own ball; **ob'ject-finder** a device in microscopes for locating an object in the field before examination by a higher power; **ob'ject-glass** in an optical instrument, the lens or combination of lenses at the end next to the object; **object language** a language that is being investigated or described by another language; **ob'ject=less'on** a lesson in which a material object is before the class: a warning or instructive experience; **ob'ject-soul** a vital principle attributed by the primitive mind to inanimate objects. — **money,** etc., **no object** money, etc., not being a thing aimed at; **distance,** etc., **no object** distance, etc., not being reckoned worth consideration (perh. by confusion with the foregoing); **object of virtu** an article valued for its antiquity or as an example of craftsmanship, etc. [L. *objectus,* pa.p. of *ob(j)icĕre,* or partly the noun *objectus, -ūs* (found in the abl.), or the freq. vb. *objectāre* — *ob,* in the way of, *jacĕre,* to throw.]

objet *ob-zhā,* (Fr.) *n.* an object. — **objet d'art** (*där*) an article with artistic value; **objet de vertu** (*də ver-tü*) a Gallicised (by the English) version of object of virtu (q.v.); **objet trouvé** (*trōō-vā*; same as **found object**): — *pls.* **objets** (*-zhā*) **d'art, de vertu, trouvés** (*-vā*).

objure *ob-jōōr', v.i.* to swear. — *v.t.* to bind by oath: to charge or entreat solemnly. — *n.* **objurā'tion** act of binding by oath: a solemn charge. [L. *objūrāre,* to bind by oath — *ob-,* down, *jūrāre,* to swear.]

objurgate *ob'jər-gāt,* or *-jûr', v.t.* and *v.i.* to chide. — *n.* **objurgā'tion.** — *adjs.* **objur'gative, objur'gatory.** [L. *objurgāre, -ātum,* to rebuke — *ob-,* intens., *jurgāre,* to chide.]

oblanceolate *ob-län'si-ō-lāt,* (*bot.*) *adj.* like a lance-head reversed, as a leaf — about three times as long as broad, tapering more gently towards base than apex. [Pfx. *ob-*, as in **obcompressed.**]

oblast *ob'last*, *n.* a province or district.   [Russ.]

oblate[1] *ob'lāt, ob-lāt'*, *adj.* dedicated: offered up. — *n.* a dedicated person, esp. one dedicated to monastic life but not professed, or to a religious life. — *n.* **oblā'tion** act of offering: a sacrifice: anything offered in worship, esp. a eucharistic offering: an offering generally. — *adjs.* **oblā'tional; oblatory** (*ob'lǝ-tǝ-ri*).   [L. *oblātus*, offered up, used as pa.p. of *offerre*, to offer; see **offer.**]

oblate[2] *ob'lāt, ob-lāt', ō-blāt', adj.* flattened at opposite sides or poles, as a spheroid — shaped like an orange (opp. to *prolate*). — *n.* **oblateness.**   [On analogy of **prolate;** L. pfx. *ob-*, against, or (mod. L.) in the opposite direction.]

oblige *ǝ-blīj', ō-blīj',* formerly *-blēj', v.t.* to bind morally or legally: to constrain: to bind by some favour rendered; hence to do a favour to. — *v.i.* (*coll.*) to do something as a favour. — *n.* **obligant** (*ob'li-gǝnt; Scots law*) one who binds himself to another to pay or to perform something. — *v.t.* **ob'ligate** (*-li-gāt*) to constrain (*U.S.* and *arch.*): to bind by contract or duty: to bind by gratitude (*arch.* or *coll.*). — *adj.* (*bot.*) by necessity, without option. — *n.* **obligation** (*ob-li-gā'shǝn*) act of obliging: a moral or legal bond, tie, or binding power: that to which one is bound: a debt of gratitude: a favour: a bond containing a penalty in case of failure (*law*). — *adv.* **obligatorily** (*o-blig'-ǝ-tǝr-i-li* or *ob'lig-, ǝb-*). — *n.* **oblig'atoriness** (or *ob'lig-, ǝb-*). — *adj.* **oblig'atory** (or *ob'lig-, ǝb-*) binding: imposing duty: imposed as an obligation: obligate. — *ns.* **obligee** (*ob-li-jē'*) the person to whom another is bound by obligation (*law*): one who is under an obligation for a favour; **oblige'ment** a favour conferred. — *adj.* **oblīg'ing** disposed to confer favours: ready to do a good turn: courteous. — *adv.* **oblīg'ingly.** — *ns.* **oblīg'ingness; obligor** (*ob'li-gör; law*) the person who binds himself to another.   [Fr. *obliger* — L. *obligāre, -ātum* — *ob-*, down, *ligāre*, to bind.]

oblique *ō-blēk', ǝ-blēk', adj.* slanting: neither perpendicular nor parallel: not at right angles: not parallel to an axis: not straightforward: indirect: underhand: not a right angle (*geom.*): having the axis not perpendicular to the plane of the base: skew: asymmetrical about the midrib (*bot.*): monoclinic (*crystal.*). — *n.* an oblique line, figure, muscle, etc.: an oblique movement or advance, esp. one about 45° from the original direction. — *v.i.* to deviate from a direct line or from the perpendicular, to slant: to advance obliquely by facing half right or left and then advancing. — *v.t.* to turn aslant. — *ns.* **obliquation** (*ob-li-kwā'shǝn*), **obliqueness** (*-blēk'*), **obliquity** (*ob-lik'wi-ti*) state of being oblique: a slanting direction: crookedness of outlook, thinking, or conduct, or an instance of it: irregularity (*obs.*). — *adv.* **oblique'ly.** — *adjs.* **obliquid** (*ob-lik'wid; Spens.*) oblique; **obliq'uitous.** — **oblique case** any case other than nominative and vocative (see **case); oblique motion** (*mus.*) upward or downward motion of one part while another remains stationary; **oblique narration** or **speech** indirect speech (see **indirect). — obliquity of the ecliptic** the angle between the plane of the earth's orbit and that of the earth's equator.   [L. *oblīquus — ob-*, intens., and the root of *līquis*, slanting.]

obliterate *ō-blit'ǝ-rāt, v.t.* to blot out, so as not to be readily or clearly readable: to efface: to close up and do away with (as a tubular element; *med.* and *biol.*). — *adj.* **oblit'erāted** effaced: without defined margins. — *n.* **oblitera'tion.** — *adj.* **oblit'erative.** — *adj.* **oblit-terāre, -ātum — *ob-*, over, *littera* (*lītera*), a letter.]

oblivion *ǝb-liv'i-ǝn, ob-, n.* forgetfulness: a state of having forgotten: amnesty: a state of being forgotten. — *adj.* **obliv'ious** forgetful: prone to forget: causing, or associated with, forgetfulness (*poet.*): raptly or absent-mindedly unaware (with *of, to*): forgotten (*obs.*). — *adv.* **obliv'iously.** — *ns.* **obliv'iousness; obliviscence** (*ob-li-vis'ǝns*) forgetfulness: forgetting.   [L. *oblīviō, -ōnis*, from the root of *oblīvīscī*, to forget.]

oblong *ob'long, adj.* long in one way: longer than broad: nearly elliptical, with sides nearly parallel, ends blunted, two to four times as long as broad (*bot.*). — *n.* a rectangle longer than broad: any oblong figure, whether angular or rounded.   [L. *oblongus — ob-* (force obscure), and *longus*, long.]

obloquy *ob'lǝ-kwi, n.* reproachful language: censure: calumny: disgrace.   [L. *obloquium — ob*, against, *loquī*, to speak.]

obmutescent *ob-mū-tes'ǝnt, adj.* speechless: persistently silent. — *n.* **obmutesc'ence.**   [L. *obmūtēscēns, -entis*, pr.p. of *obmūtēscěre*, to become dumb — *ob-*, intens., *mūtus*, dumb.]

obnoxious *ob-nok'shǝs, ǝb-, adj.* liable (to hurt, punishment, or censure; *obs.*): subject to the authority (*obs.*): exposed (*rare*): objectionable: offensive: noxious, hurtful (*erron.*). — *adv.* **obnox'iously.** — *n.* **obnox'iousness.**   [L. *obnoxius — ob*, exposed to, *noxa*, hurt.]

obnubilation *ob-nū-bi-lā'shǝn, n.* clouding, darkening. — *v.t.* **obnū'bilate.**   [L. *obnūbilāre*, to cloud over — L. *ob-*, over, *nūbilus*, cloudy.]

oboe *ō'bō,* (*arch.*) *ō'boi, n.* a double-reed treble woodwind instrument: an organ stop of similar tone. — *n.* **o'bōist** a player on the oboe. — **oboe d'amore** (*ō'bō dä-mō'rä;* It., oboe of love) an old oboe a minor third lower; **oboe di caccia** (*dē kat'cha;* of the chase) an obsolete alto or tenor oboe.   [It. *oboe* — Fr. *hautbois*; see **hautboy.**]

obol *ob'ol, n.* in ancient Greece, the sixth part of a drachma in weight, or in money (about 1½d.). — *adj.* **ob'olary** extremely poor. — *n.* **ob'olus** (L.) an obol: in the Middle Ages applied to various small coins, as the English halfpenny: — *pl.* **ob'oli** (*-ī*).   [Gr. *obolos*.]

obovate *ob-ō'vāt,* (*bot.*) *adj.* egg-shaped in outline, with the narrow end next to the base. — *adv.* **obō'vātely.** — *adj.* **obō'void** solidly obovate.   [Pfx. *ob-*, as in **obcompressed.**]

obreption *ob-rep'shǝn, n.* surprising by stealth (*obs.*): obtaining or seeking to obtain a gift, etc., by false statement — different both in sense and in etymology from *subreption* (*law*). — *adj.* **obreptitious** (*-tish'ǝs*).   [L. *obreptiō, -ōnis — ob*, in the way of, *rēpěre*, to creep.]

obscene *ob-sēn', adj.* filthy: offensive to the senses or the sensibility, disgusting: indecent esp. in a sexual sense: (less strongly) offending against an accepted standard of morals or taste: (of publications, etc.) tending to deprave or corrupt (*law*): ill-omened (*obs.*). — *adv.* **obscene'ly.** — *ns.* **obscene'ness, obscenity** (*-sen'* or *-sēn'*).   [L. *obscēnus*.]

obscure *ob-skūr', adj.* dark: not distinct: not easily understood: not clear, legible, or perspicuous: unknown: hidden: inconspicuous: lowly: unknown to fame: living or enveloped in darkness. — *n.* darkness: an obscure place: indistinctness. — *v.t.* to darken: to dim: to hide: to make less plain: to render doubtful. — *v.i.* to hide: to darken. — *ns.* **ob'scūrant** (*-ant*, or *ob-skūr'ǝnt*) one who labours to prevent enlightenment or reform; **obscūrant'ism** (or *-skūr'*) opposition to inquiry, reform or new knowledge; **obscūrant'ist** (or *-skūr'*) an obscurant. — *adj.* pertaining to obscurantism. — *n.* **obscūrā'tion** the act of obscuring or state of being obscured. — *adv.* **obscūre'ly.** — *ns.* **obscūre'ment; obscūre'ness; obscūr'er; obscūr'ity** state or quality of being obscure: darkness: an obscure place, point, or condition.   [Fr. *obscur* — L. *obscūrus — ob-*, over, and the root seen in L. *scūtum*, shield, Gr. *skeuē*, covering.]

obsecrate *ob'si-krāt, v.t.* to beseech: to implore. — *n.* **obsecrā'tion** supplication: one of the clauses in the Litany beginning with *by*.   [L. *obsecrāre, -ātum*, to entreat; *ob*, before, *sacrāre — sacer*, sacred.]

obsequent *ob'si-kwǝnt, adj.* flowing in a contrary direction to the original slope of the land, parallel to the *consequent* and perpendicular to the *subsequent* streams.   [L. *ob*, face to face with, *sequēns, -entis,* pr.p. of *sequī*, to follow.]

obsequies *ob'si-kwiz, n.pl.* funeral rites and solemnities: — *sing.* (*rare*) **ob'sequy** (*Milt.* **obsequie**). — *adjs.* **obse-**

quial (*-sē'kwi-əl*), **obsē'quious** (*Shak.*; see also next word). [L.L. *obsequiae*, a confusion of L. *exsequiae*, funeral rites, and *obsequium*; see next word.]

obsequious *ob-sē'kwi-əs, adj.* orig., compliant, obedient, dutiful: now, compliant to excess: fawning. — *adv.* **obsē'quiously.** — *n.* **obsē'quiousness.** [L. *obsequiōsus*, compliant, *obsequium*, compliance — *ob-*, towards, *sequī*, to follow.]

observe *ob-zûrv', v.t.* to keep in view: to watch: to subject to systematic watching: to regard attentively: to direct watchful and critical attention to with a view to ascertaining a fact: to ascertain by such attention: to notice: to attend to: to remark in words: to comply with: to act according to: to heed and to carry out in practice: to keep with ceremony: to celebrate: to keep (as silence): to be deferential to, to humour (*Shak.*). — *v.i.* to take observations: to make remarks. — *n.* (*Scot.*) a remark. — *adj.* **observ'able** discernible, perceptible: worthy of note: notable: to be observed. — *n.* something that can be observed by the senses, with or without the help of instrument(s). — *n.* **observ'ableness.** — *adv.* **observ'ably.** — *ns.* **observ'ance** the keeping of, or acting according to, a law, duty, custom, ceremony: the keeping with ceremony or according to custom: a custom observed or to be observed: a rule of religious life: an order or company accepting it (esp. the Observants), or their house: a deferential act or treatment: watchful heed (*Shak.*): now rarely, observation; **observ'ancy** observance: observation: a house of Observants. — *adj.* **observ'ant** observing: having powers of observing and noting: taking notice: keeping an observance: carefully attentive. — *n.* an obsequious attendant (*Shak.*): one strict to comply with a custom, etc. — *ns.* **Observ'ant** or **Observ'antine** (*-ən-tin, -tēn*) a Franciscan friar of stricter rule. — *adv.* **observ'antly.** — *n.* **observā'tion** act of observing: habit, practice, or faculty of seeing and noting: attention: the act of recognising and noting phenomena as they occur in nature, as distinguished from *experiment*: a reading of an instrument: the result of such observing: watching: now rarely, observance: that which is observed: a remark: the fact of being observed. — *adj.* **observā'tional** consisting of, or containing, observations or remarks: derived from observation, as distinguished from *experiment*. — *adv.* **observā'tionally.** — *adj.* **observ'ative** observant: observational. — *ns.* **ob'servātor** (now *rare* or *obs.*) one who observes in any sense: a remarker; **observ'atory** a building or station for making astronomical and physical observations: a viewpoint: a spying-place; **observ'er** one who observes in any sense: one whose function it is to take observations: formerly, an airman who accompanied a pilot to observe, now, **flying officer** (q.v.): a member of the Royal Observer Corps, a uniformed civilian organisation affiliated to the Royal Air Force: one deputed to watch proceedings. — *adj.* **observ'ing** habitually taking notice: attentive. — *adv.* **observ'ingly.** — **observation car** a railway carriage designed to allow passengers to view scenery; **observation post** a position (esp. military) from which observations are made (and from which artillery fire is directed). [Fr. *observer* — L. *observāre, -ātum — ob*, towards, *servāre*, to keep.]

obsess *ob-ses', v.t.* to besiege (*obs.*): to beset (*arch.*): to occupy the thoughts of obstinately and persistently. — *n.* **obsession** (*-sesh'ən*) a siege (*obs.*): persistent attack, esp. of an evil spirit (*arch.*): the state of being so molested from without — opp. to *possession*, or control by an evil spirit from within (*arch.*): morbid persistence of an idea in the mind, against one's will: a fixed idea. — *adj.* **obsess'ional.** — *n.* **obsess'ionist** one who is obsessed by a fixed idea. — *adj.* **obsess'ive** relating to obsession: obsessing. [L. *obsidēre, obsessum*, to besiege.]

obsidian *ob-sid'i-ən, n.* a vitreous acid volcanic rock resembling bottle-glass. [From *obsidiānus*, a false reading of L. *obsiānus* (*lapis*), a stone found by one

Obsius (wrongly *Obsidius*) in Ethiopia, according to Pliny.]

obsidional *ob-sid'i-ən-əl, adj.* pertaining to a siege. — Also **obsid'ionary.** [L. *obsidiō, -ōnis*, a siege; see **obsess.**]

obsign *ob-sīn', obsignate* *ob-sig'nāt, vs.t.* to seal, confirm. — *n.* **obsignā'tion** (*-sig-*). — *adj.* **obsig'natory.** [L. *obsīgnāre*, to seal up — *ob-*, over, *sīgnāre*, to mark, seal.]

obsolescent *ob-sə-les'ənt, adj.* going out of use: in course of disappearance: tending to become obsolete. — *v.i.* **obsolesce** (*-les'*) to be in process of going out of use. — *n.* **obsolesc'ence.** — *adj.* **ob'solete** (*-lēt*) gone out of use: antiquated: no longer functional or fully developed. — *adv.* **ob'soletely.** — *ns.* **ob'soleteness; obsolē'- tion** (*rare*); **ob'solētism.** — **planned obsolescence** the deterioration or the going out of date of a product according to a prearranged plan. [L. *obsolēscĕre, obsolētum*, perh. from pfx. *obs-* (*ob-*, completeness) and the root of *alĕre*, to nourish.]

obstacle *ob'stə-kl, n.* anything that stands in the way of or hinders advance. — *adj.* (*Shak.*) stubborn. — **obstacle race** a race in which obstacles have to be passed, gone through, etc. [Fr., — L. *obstāculum — ob*, in the way of, *stāre*, to stand.]

obstetric, -al *ob-stet'rik, -əl, adjs.* pertaining to midwifery. — *n.* **obstetrician** (*ob-sti-trish'ən*) a man or woman skilled in practising, or qualified to practise, obstetrics. — *n.sing.* **obstet'rics** the science of midwifery. [L. *obstetrīcius* (the *-īc-* confused with the suffix *-ic*) — *obstetrīx, -īcis*, a midwife — *ob*, before, *stāre*, to stand.]

obstinate *ob'sti-nit, adj.* blindly or excessively firm: unyielding: stubborn: not easily subdued or remedied. — *ns.* **ob'stinacy** (*-nə-si*), **ob'stinateness.** — *adv.* **ob'sti-nately.** [L. *obstināre, -ātum — ob*, in the way of, *stanāre* (found in compounds), a form of *stāre*, to stand.]

obstipation *ob-sti-pā'shən, n.* extreme constipation. [L. *ob*, against, *stīpāre, -ātum*, to press.]

obstreperous *ob-strep'ə-rəs, adj.* making a loud noise: clamorous: noisy: unruly. — *v.t.* **obstrep'erate** (*Sterne*). — *adv.* **obstrep'erously.** — *n.* **obstrep'erousness.** [L. *obstreperus — ob*, before, against, *strepĕre*, to make a noise.]

obstriction *ob-strik'shən, n.* obligation. [L. *obstringĕre, obstrictum*, to bind up.]

obstropalous, obstropulous *ob-strop'ə-ləs, -ū-ləs*, illit. forms of **obstreperous.**

obstruct *ob-strukt', əb-, v.t.* to block up: to hinder from passing or progressing: to shut off: to hamper. — *v.i.* to be an obstruction: to practise obstruction. — *ns.* **obstruc'ter** (*rare*); **obstruc'tion** act of obstructing: a state of being obstructed: that which hinders progress or action: an obstacle: opposition by dilatory tactics, as in a legislative assembly; **obstruc'tionist** a politician who practises obstruction. — *adj.* **obstruct'ive** tending to obstruct: hindering. — *n.* a hindrance: a hinderer of progress. — *adv.* **obstruct'ively.** — *n.* **obstruct'or.** — *adj.* **obstruent** (*ob'strōō-ənt*) obstructing: blocking up. — *n.* anything that obstructs, esp. in the passages of the body: an astringent drug: a stop or a fricative (*phon.*). [L. *obstruĕre, obstructum — ob*, in the way of, *struĕre, structum*, to pile up, build.]

obtain *ob-tān', əb-, v.t.* to get: to procure by effort: to gain: to reach (*arch.*): to hold, occupy (*obs.*). — *v.i.* to be established: to continue in use: to hold good: to prevail, to succeed (*arch.*): to attain (*obs.*). — *adj.* **obtain'able.** — *ns.* **obtain'er; obtain'ment; obtention** (*-ten'shən*) getting. [Fr. *obtenir* — L. *obtinēre*, to occupy — *ob*, against, *tenēre*, to hold.]

obtect, obtected *ob-tekt', -id, adjs.* having wings and legs immovably pressed against the body in a hard chitinous case, as many insect pupae. [L. *obtegĕre, obtectum*, to cover over — *ob-*, over, *tegĕre*, to cover.]

obtemper *ob-tem'pər, v.t.* to yield obedience to. — Also *v.i.* (with *to, unto*). — Also **obtem'perate.** [L. *obtemperāre, -ātum — ob*, before, *temperāre*, to restrain oneself.]

obtend *ob-tend'*, *(obs.)* *v.t.* to hold out in opposition: to put forward, allege. [L. *obtendĕre*, to stretch before — *ob*, in front of, *tendĕre*, to stretch.]

obtest *ob-test'*, *v.t.* to call to witness: to adjure. — *v.i.* to protest. — *n.* **obtestā'tion.** [L. *obtestārī*, to call as a witness — *ob*, before, *testis*, a witness.]

obtrude *ob-trōōd'*, *əb-*, *v.t.* to thrust forward, or upon one, unduly or unwelcomely. — *v.i.* to thrust oneself forward. — *ns.* **obtrud'er; obtrud'ing; obtrusion** (*-trōō'zhən*) an unwanted thrusting in or forward, or upon one. — *adj.* **obtrusive** (*-trōō'siv*) disposed to thrust oneself in or forward: unduly prominent or projecting. — *adv.* **obtru'sively.** — *n.* **obtru'siveness.** [L. *obtrūdĕre* — *ob*, against, *trūdĕre*, *trūsum*, to thrust.]

obtruncate *ob-trung'kāt*, *v.t.* to cut or lop off the head of. [L. *obtruncāre*, *-ātum*, to cut in pieces, mutilate — *ob-*, intens., *truncāre*, cut off.]

obtund *ob-tund'*, *v.t.* to blunt or dull: to deaden. — *adj.* **obtund'ent** dulling. — *n.* an application to deaden irritation. [L. *obtundĕre*, to strike upon — *ob*, against, *tundĕre*, to thump.]

obturate *ob'tū-rāt*, *v.t.* to stop up. — *ns.* **obturā'tion** stopping up: in gunnery, stopping of a hole to prevent the escape of gas; **ob'turātor** a structure or device that closes a cavity: the structures closing a large opening in the hip-bone (*anat.*). [L. *obtūrāre*, *-ātum*, to stop up; etymology obscure.]

obtuse *ob-tūs'*, *əb-*, *adj.* blunt: not pointed: blunt or rounded at the tip (*bot.*): greater than a right angle (*geom.*): dull: dull-witted: insensitive. — *adv.* **obtuse'ly.** — *ns.* **obtuse'ness, obtus'ity.** — *adjs.* **obtuse'-ang'led, -ang'ular** having an angle greater than a right angle. [L. *obtūsus* — pa.p. of *obtundĕre*; cf. **obtund.**]

obumbrate *ob-um'brāt*, *v.t.* to overshadow. — *n.* **obumbrā'tion.** [L. *obumbrāre*, *-ātum* — *ob*, in the way of, *umbra*, shadow.]

obvention *ob-ven'shən*, *(obs.)* *n.* any incidental occurrence, or advantage, esp. a fee. [L. *obvenīre*, *-ventum*, to come to meet, come by chance — *ob*, face to face with, *venīre*, to come.]

obverse *ob'vûrs*, *ob-vûrs'*, *adj.* turned towards one: complemental, constituting the opposite aspect of the same fact: having the base narrower than the apex (*bot.*): got by obversion (*log.*). — *n.* **obverse** (*ob'vûrs*) the side of a coin containing the head, or principal symbol: the face or side of anything normally presented to view: a counterpart or opposite aspect: a proposition obtained from another by obversion (*log.*). — *adv.* **obverse'ly.** — *n.* **obver'sion** the act of turning a thing toward one: a species of immediate inference where the contradictory of the original predicate is predicated of the original subject, the quality of the proposition being changed — e.g. to infer from All A is B that No A is not B — also called *permutation* and *equipollence* (*log.*). — *v.t.* **obvert'** to turn in the direction of, or face to face with, something: to infer the obverse of. [L. *obversus*, turned against, or towards — *ob-*, towards, *vertĕre*, to turn.]

obviate *ob'vi-āt*, *v.t.* to meet on the way (*obs.*): to prevent or dispose of in advance: to forestall. — *n.* **obviā'tion.** [L. *obviāre*, *-ātum* — *ob*, in the way of, *viāre*, *viātum*, to go — *via*, a way.]

obvious *ob'vi-əs*, *adj.* meeting one in the way (*obs.*): easily discovered or understood: clearly or plainly evident. — *adv.* **ob'viously.** — *n.* **ob'viousness.** [L. *obvius* — *ob*, *via*; see foregoing.]

obvolute, -d *ob'və-lūt*, *-lōōt*, or *-vo-*, *-id*, *(bot.)* *adjs.* arranged so that each leaf of a pair is conduplicate and enfolds one-half of the other. — *adj.* **obvolvent** (*-vol'vənt*) enwrapping: curved downward or inward (*entom.*). [L. *obvolūtus*, pa.p., and *obvolvēns*, *-entis*, pr.p., of *obvolvĕre*, to enwrap — *ob*, over, *volvĕre*, *volūtum*, to roll.]

oca *ō'kə*, *n.* a South American wood-sorrel with edible tubers. [Sp. from Quechua.]

ocarina *ok-ə-rē'nə*, *n.* a fluty-toned musical toy, orig. of terracotta. [It., dim. of *oca*, a goose.]

Occamism, Ockhamism *ok'əm-izm*, *n.* the doctrine of the nominalist schoolman, William of *Occam* or *Ockham* (who died about 1349). — *n.* **Occ'amist, Ockhamist.** —**Occam's, Ockham's razor** the principle that entities are not to be multiplied beyond necessity.

occamy *ok'ə-mi*, *n.* a silvery alloy. [**alchemy.**]

occasion *ə-kā'zhən*, *n.* a case, instance, time of something happening: events, course of events (*Shak.*): a suitable juncture: a special time or season: a chance of bringing about something desired: opportunity: an event which, although not the cause, determines the time at which another happens: a reason, pretext, or excuse: requirement: need: (usu. in *pl.*) business: (in *pl.*) necessary bodily functions (*obs.*): a special ceremony, celebration, or event: communion service (*Scot.* formerly): doing, occasioning, matter of responsibility (*Shak.*). — *v.t.* to give occasion or rise to: to cause: to accustom (*obs.*). — *adj.* **occā'sional** happening, occurring infrequently, irregularly, now and then: resulting from accident (*obs.*): produced on or for some special event or for special occasions: constituting the occasion. — *ns.* **occā'sionalism** the Cartesian explanation of the apparent interaction of mind and matter by the direct intervention of God on the occasion of certain changes occurring in one or the other; **occā'sionalist; occāsional'ity.** — *adv.* **occā'sionally** casually (*obs.*): on or for an occasion: now and then. — *n.* **occā'sioner.** — **occasional cause** the event which in the Cartesian philosophy is only the occasion, not the true cause: that by which the efficient cause comes into operation; **occasional conformist** (*hist.*) a Dissenter who qualified for office by conforming to the Church of England upon occasion; **occasional table** a small portable ornamental table. — **occasioned by** (which was) a consequence of (*obs.*): caused by: necessitated by; **on occasion** in case of need: as opportunity offers: from time to time; **rise to the occasion** see **rise; take occasion** to take advantage of an opportunity (to). [L. *occāsiō*, *-ōnis*, opportunity — *ob*, in the way of, *cadĕre*, *cāsum*, to fall.]

Occident, occident *ok'si-dənt*, *n.* the quarter of the sky where the heavenly bodies set: the west — opp. to *Orient.* — *adj.* **Occidental, occidental** (*-dent'l*) western: characteristic of the West (esp. Europe, America, the Western United States): relatively less precious, as a gem (because the best stones were presumed to come from the East). — *n.* a westerner: a language invented by Edgar de Wahl (1922). — *v.t.* **occiden'talise, -ize** to cause to conform to western ideas or customs. — *ns.* **Occiden'talism** the culture and ways of Occidental peoples; **Occiden'talist** a student of Occidental languages: an Oriental who favours western ideas, customs, etc. — *adv.* **occiden'tally.** — **occidental topaz** a semi-precious yellow quartz; **occidental turquoise** odontolite. [L. *occidēns*, *-entis*, setting, pr.p. of *occidĕre* — *ob*, towards, down, *cadĕre*, to fall.]

occiput *ok'si-put*, *n.* the back of the head or skull. — *adj.* **occip'ital** pertaining to the back of the head. — *n.* the occipital bone, the bone at the back of the skull. — *adv.* **occip'itally.** [L. *occiput* — *ob*, over against, *caput*, head.]

occlude *o-klōōd'*, *ə-*, *v.t.* to shut in or out: to cut or shut off: to stop (as a passage, cavity, or opening): to bring together (as the teeth or eyelids): to absorb or retain (as a gas by a metal or other solid). — *v.i.* to bite or close together (as the teeth). — *adj.* **occlu'dent** serving to occlude: occluding. — *n.* that which occludes. — *adj.* **occlu'sal** (*-səl*) pertaining to occlusion of teeth. — *n.* **occlu'sion** (*-zhən*) a closing of an opening, passage, or cavity: the act of occluding or absorbing: the bite or mode of meeting of the teeth: the formation, or condition, of an occluded front. — *adj.* **occlu'sive** (*-siv*) serving to close: characterised by occlusion. — *n.* (*phon.*) a sound produced by closing the breath passage. — *n.* **occlu'sor** that which closes, esp. a muscle for closing an opening. — **occluded front** an advancing cold front into which a mass of warm air has been driven obliquely, forming a bulge which narrows as the warm air is lifted up and the cold air flows in beneath. [L. *occlūdĕre, -clūsum* — *ob*, in the way of, *claudĕre*, to shut.]

occult *ok-ult', ok'ult, adj.* hidden: of a line, faint, or dotted, or to be rubbed out later (*rare*): secret: esoteric: unknown: not discovered without test or experiment (*obs.*): beyond the range of sense: transcending the bounds of natural knowledge: mysterious: magical: supernatural. — *v.t.* **occult** (*ok-ult'*) to hide: to hide by interposing. — *v.i.* to become temporarily invisible (esp., of a heavenly body, by occultation). — *n.* **occultā'tion** a concealing, esp. of one of the heavenly bodies by another: the state of being hidden. — *adjs.* **occult'ed; occult'ing** (of a lighthouse, beacon, etc. light) becoming temporarily invisible at regular intervals. — *ns.* **occ'ultism** the doctrine or study of things hidden or mysterious — theosophy, etc.; **occ'ultist** one who believes in occult things. — *adv.* **occultly.** — *n.* **occultness.** — **occult sciences** alchemy, astrology, magic, palmistry, etc. [L. *occultus*, pa.p. of *occulĕre*, to hide — *ob-*, over, and the root of *celāre*, to hide.]

occupance, etc., **occupation,** etc. See **occupy.**

occupy *ok'ū-pī, v.t.* to take possession of: to capture: to hold: to keep possession of by being present in: to fill (a post, office): to take up, as a space, time, etc.: to tenant: to busy: to lay out in trade (*B.*): to cohabit with (*obs.*). — *v.i.* to hold possession (*obs.*): to trade (*obs.*): to cohabit (*obs.*): — *pr.p.* **occ'upying;** *pa.t.* and *pa.p.* **occ'upied.** — *ns.* **occ'upance** (*rare*), **occ'upancy** the act or fact of occupying, or of taking or holding possession (esp. of that which previously had no owner): possession: the time during which one occupies; **occ'upant** one who takes or has possession. — *v.t.* **occ'upāte** (*obs.*) to occupy. — *adj.* (*obs.*) occupied. — *n.* **occūpā'tion** the act of occupying: possession: the state of being employed or occupied: the time during which a country, etc., is occupied by enemy forces: that which occupies or takes up one's attention: one's habitual employment, profession, craft, or trade. — *adj.* occupational. — *adjs.* **occūpā'tional** connected with habitual occupation; **occ'upātive** held by tenure based on occupation. — *n.* **occ'upier** (*-pī-ər*) one who occupies: an occupant: one who practises (*obs.*): a dealer (*obs.*). — **occupational ailment, disease, hazard** a disease, injury, etc., common among workers engaged in a particular occupation because encouraged by the conditions of that occupation; **occupational therapy** the treatment of a disease (incl. a mental disease) or an injury by a regulated course of suitable work; **occupation level** in an archaeological site, any of several distinct layers of debris left by successive occupations, from which the site can be dated. — **army of occupation** troops stationed in the territory of a defeated enemy or subject country to keep order, to ensure compliance with the terms of a peace treaty, to prop up a weak or unpopular government, etc. [Fr. *occuper* — L. *occupāre, -ātum* — *ob-*, to, on, *capĕre*, to take; the *-y* is unexplained.]

occur *o-kûr', v.i.* to meet (*obs.*): to come into the mind of (with *to*): to be, be found: to happen: (of festivals) to fall on the same day: — *pr.p.* **occurr'ing;** *pa.t.* and *pa.p.* **occurred'.** — *n.* **occurrence** (*-kur'*) the act or fact of occurring: anything that happens: an event, esp. one unlooked for or unplanned. — *adj.* **occurr'ent** occurring: happening: turning up: to be found: incidental. — *n.* one who or that which meets or comes in contact (*obs.*): an occurrence, an item of news (*arch.*). [L. *occurrĕre* — *ob*, in the way of, *currĕre*, to run.]

ocean *ō'shən, n.* the vast expanse of salt water that covers the greater part of the surface of the globe: any one of its great divisions (Atlantic, Pacific, Indian, Arctic, Antarctic; also Southern — i.e. the belt of water round the earth between 40° and 66½° south — and German — i.e. the North Sea): any immense expanse or vast quantity (*fig.*). — *adj.* pertaining to the great sea. —

ns. **oceanarium** (*ō-shən-ār'i-əm*) an enclosed part of the sea (also called **seaquarium**), or a large salt-water pond, in which dolphins, porpoises, etc., are kept and tamed; **oceanaut** (*ō'shə-nöt*) one who lives, observes, explores, under the sea. — *adjs.* **Oceanian** (*ō-shi-ā'ni-ən*) pertaining to *Oceania*, which includes Polynesia, Micronesia, Melanesia, with or without Australasia; **oceanic** (*ō-shi-an'ik*) pertaining to the ocean: found or formed in the ocean or high seas, pelagic: wide like the ocean. — *ns.* **oceanid** (*ō-sē'ən-id*) a daughter of Oceanus (with *cap.*): an ocean nymph: — *pl.* **ocē'anids** or **oceanides** (*ō-sē-an'id-ēz*); **oceanographer** (*ō-shi-ən-og'rə-fər*, or *ō-shən-*, or *ō-si-ən-*). — *adjs.* **oceanographic** (*ō-shi-an-ō-graf'ik*, or *ō-shən-*, or *ō-si-an-*), **-al.** — *ns.* **oceanog'raphy** the scientific study and description of the ocean. — *adj.* **oceanolog'ical.** — *ns.* **oceanol'ogist; oceanol'ogy** oceanography. — **o'cean-bā'sin** the depression in which the waters of an ocean are contained. — *adj.* **o'cean-going** sailing, or suitable for sailing, across the ocean. — **o'cean-grey'hound** a very fast steamer; **oceanic islands** islands far from the mainland; **ocean perch** a scorpion-fish, *Sebastes marinus*, also known as the *bergylt, redfish,* or *rosefish;* **o'cean=stream'** (*Milt.*) the river Oceanus (Okeanos), supposed to encircle the land of the world. [O.Fr. *occean* — L. *Ōcĕānus* — Gr. *Ōkĕănos*, the river, or its god.]

ocellus *ō-sel'əs, n.* a simple eye or eye-spot, distinguished from a compound eye, in insects and other lower animals: an eyelike or ringed spot of colour: — *pl.* **ocell'ī.** — *adjs.* **ocell'ar** of, or of the nature of, an ocellus or ocelli; **ocell'ate, -d** (or *os'əl-āt, -id*) eyelike and ringed: having an eyelike spot or spots. — *n.* **ocellation** (*os-ə-lā'shən*). [L. *ŏcellus*, dim. of *oculus*, an eye.]

ocelot *o'- or ō'si-lot, n.* an American cat (*Felis pardalis*), like a small leopard: its fur. — *adj.* **o'celoid.** [Mex. *ocelotl,* jaguar.]

och *ohh, interj.* expressing impatience, or contemptuous dismissal — pshaw, tut (*Scot.*): in Ireland and part of Scotland, expressing regret.

oche *ok'i,* (*darts*) *n.* the line, groove or ridge behind which a player must stand to throw. — Also **hockey (line).** [Ety. uncertain; a connection with O.E. *oche,* to lop (— O.Fr. *ocher,* to nick, cut a groove in), has been suggested.]

ocher, ocherous, etc. See **ochre.**

ochidore *ok'i-dōr, -dör, n.* Kingsley's name (not otherwise known) for a shore-crab.

ochlocracy *ok-lok'rə-si, n.* mob-rule. — *n.* **och'locrat** (*-lō-krat*). — *adjs.* **ochlocrat'ic, -al.** — *adv.* **ochlocrat'ically.** — *n.* **ochlophobia** (*ok-lə-fō'bi-ə;* Gr. *phobos,* fear); fear of crowds. — *n.* **ochlopho'biac.** — *adj.* **ochlophō'bic.** [Gr. *ochlokratiā* — *ochlos,* a crowd, *kratos,* power.]

ochone. See **ohone.**

Ochotona *ok-ō-tō'nə, n.* the pika genus. [Mongol *ochodona.*]

ochre (*U.S.* **ocher**) *ō'kər, n.* a native pigment composed of fine clay and an iron oxide (limonite in yellow ochre, haematite in red): a paint manufactured from it, used for colouring walls, etc.: an earthy metallic oxide of various kinds: money, esp. gold (*slang*). — *v.t.* to mark or colour with ochre. — *adjs.* **ochrā'ceous, ochreous** (*ō'kri-əs*), **o'chroid, o'chrous** (sometimes **o'cherous**), **o'chry** (also **o'chrey, o'chery**) consisting of, containing, or resembling, ochre; **ochroleu'cous** (Gr. *leukos,* white) yellowish white. [Fr. *ocre* — L. *ōchra* — Gr. *ōchrā* — *ōchros,* pale yellow.]

ochrea. See **ocrea.**

ochrous, ochry, etc. See **ochre.**

ocker *ok'ər,* (*Austr. coll.*) *n.* an oafish uncultured Australian. — *adj.* boorish, uncultured: Australian. — Also with *cap.* — *n.* **ock'erism, Ock'erism** boorishness in Australians. [After a character in a television programme; a form of *Oscar.*]

Ockhamism, Ockham's razor. See **Occamism.**

o'clock. See **clock.**

ocotillo *ō-kō-tē'yō, n.* a shrub, *Fouquieria splendens,* of

Mexico and the south-western part of the United States, with spines and clusters of red flowers: — *pl.* **-os.** [Amer. Sp., dim. of *ocote*, a type of tree — Nahuatl *ocotl*.]

ocrea (*commonly* **ochrea**) *ok'ri-ə*, (*bot.*) *n.* a sheath formed of two stipules united round a stem: — *pl.* **oc(h)'reae** (*-ē*). — *adj.* **oc(h)'reāte.** [L. *ocrea*, a legging.]

oct(a)- *okt*(*-a, -ə*)-, also **octo-** (q.v.), in composition, eight. — *n.* **octachord** (*ok'tə-körd*; Gr. *chordē*, a gut string) an eight-stringed instrument: a diatonic series of eight tones. — *adj.* **octachord'al.** — *n.* **octagon** (*ok'tə-gon*; Gr. *gōniā*, an angle) a plane figure of eight sides and eight angles. — Also *adj.* — *adj.* **octagonal** (*-tag'ən-əl*). — *adv.* **octag'onally.** — *n.* **octahedron** (*ok-tə-hē'dron*; Gr. *hedrā*, a base) a solid bounded by eight plane faces: — *pl.* **octahē'drons, octahē'dra.** — *adj.* **octahē'dral.** — *n.* **octahē'drite** anatase, crystallising in square bipyramids. — *adj.* **octamerous** (*ok-tam'*; Gr. *meros*, a part) having parts in eights. — *n.* **octameter** (*ok-tam'i-tər*; Gr. *metron*, a measure) a line of eight feet or measures. — *n.pl.* **Octan'dria** (Gr. *anēr, andros*, a man) a Linnaean class of plants with eight stamens. — *adjs.* **octan'drian; octandrous** (*ok-tan'drəs; bot.*) having eight stamens; **octangular** (*ok-tang'gū-lər*) having eight angles. — *n.* **octapody** (*ok-tap'ə-di*; Gr. *pous, podos*, foot; *pros.*) a line of eight feet. — *adj.* **octapodic** (*ok-tə-pod'ik*). — *n.* **octastich** (*ok'tə-stik*; Gr. *stichos*, row, line; *pros.*) a strophe of eight lines — also **octastichon** (*ok-tas'ti-kon*). — *adjs.* **octas'tichous** (*bot.*) in eight rows; **octastroph'ic** (Gr. *strophē*, strophe; *pros.*) consisting of eight strophes; **octastyle** (*ok'tə-stīl*; Gr. *stŷlos*, a column; *archit.*) having eight columns at the end. — *n.* a building or portico so designed. — Also **oc'tostyle.** [Gr. *okta-*, combining form of *oktō*, eight.]

octad *ok'tad*, *n.* a set of eight things. — *adj.* **octad'ic.** [Gr. *oktas, -ados*.]

octagon ... to ... **octahedrite.** See **oct(a)-.**

octal *ok'təl*, *adj.* pertaining to, or based on, the number eight. [Gr. *oktō*, eight.]

octamerous ... to ... **octandrian.** See **oct(a)-.**

octane *ok'tān*, *n.* any of a group of eighteen isomeric hydrocarbons (C_8H_{18}), eighth in the methane series. — **octane number, rating** the percentage by volume of so-called iso-octane in a mixture with normal heptane which has the same knocking characteristics as the motor fuel under test. [Gr. *oktō*, eight, suff. *-ane*, as in methane.]

Octans *ok'tanz*, *n.* a southern constellation containing the south celestial pole. [L. *octāns*, an eighth part.]

octant *ok'tənt*, *n.* an arc of one-eighth of the circumference of a circle: a sector of one-eighth of a circle: an angle-measuring instrument with such an arc: a division of space or of a solid figure or body divided into eight by three planes, usu. at right angles: a position 45° distant from another position, esp. of the moon from conjunction or opposition (*astron.*). — *adj.* **octantal** (*-tant'əl*). [L. *octāns, -antis*, an eighth.]

octapla *ok'tə-plə*, *n. sing.* a book of eight (esp. Biblical) parallel texts. [Gr. *oktaplā* (contracted pl.), eightfold.]

octaploid *ok'tə-ploid*, *adj.* eightfold: having eight times the basic number of chromosomes (*biol.*). — *n.* a cell, organism, or form with eight sets of chromosomes. — *n.* **oc'taploidy** the condition of being octaploid. — Also **oc'toploid**, etc. [Gr. *oktaploos*, eightfold, *eidos*, form.]

octapody, octapodic. See **oct(a)-.**

octaroon. See **octoroon.**

octastich ... to ... **octastyle.** See **oct(a)-.**

octave *ok'tiv, -tāv*, *n.* a set of eight: the last day of eight beginning with a church festival: the eight days from a festival to its octave: an interval, or an interval of twelve semitones (*mus.*): a note or sound an eighth above (or below) another (*mus.*): the range of notes or keys from any one to its octave (*mus.*): an organ stop sounding an octave higher than the keys indicate: a cask containing the eighth part of a pipe of wine: an

eight-lined stanza: the first eight lines of a sonnet. — *adj.* consisting of eight (esp. lines): in octaves: sounding an octave higher. — *adj.* **octāv'al** pertaining to an octave: based on the number eight. — **oc'tave-flute'** the piccolo, an octave above the ordinary flute. — **great octave** the bass octave, conventionally represented by capital letters, from C, on the second line below the bass stave, up; **law of octaves** the relationship which arranges the elements in order of atomic weight and in groups of eight, with recurring similarity of properties; **small octave** the tenor octave, from the second space in the bass. [Fr., — L. *octāvus*, eighth.]

octavo *ok-tā'vō*, *adj.* having eight leaves to the sheet: (*conventionally*) of a size so obtained, whether so folded or not. — *n.* a book printed on sheets so folded: (*conventionally*) a book of such a size: contracted **8vo** — usually meaning a medium octavo $5\frac{3}{4} \times 9$ inches (146 × 228mm): — *pl.* **octā'vōs.** [L. *in octāvō*, in the eighth — *octāvus*, eighth.]

octennial *ok-ten'yəl, -i-əl*, *adj.* happening every eighth year: lasting eight years. — *adv.* **octenn'ially.** [L. *octennium*, eight years — *annus*, year.]

octet, octett, octette *ok-tet'*, *n.* a group of eight (lines of verse, electrons, musicians, etc.): a composition for eight musicians. [On analogy of **duet**, as It. *ottetto*, Ger. *Oktett*.]

octillion *ok-til'yən*, *n.* a million raised to the eighth power, expressed by a unit with forty-eight ciphers: in U.S., one thousand raised to the ninth power, i.e. a unit with twenty-seven ciphers. — *n.* and *adj.* **octill'ionth.** [Modelled on **million** — L. *octō*, eight.]

octingenary *ok'tin-jē'nə-ri*, *n.* an eight-hundredth anniversary. — Also **octingentenary** (*-jen-tē'*). [L. *octingēnārius*, 800 each.]

octo- *ok-tō-, -to-*, also **oct(a)-** (q.v.), in composition, eight. — *n.* **octocentenary** (*ok-tō-sin-tēn'ə-ri* or *-sin-ten'* or *-sen'tin-*) an eight-hundredth anniversary. — *adjs.* **octofid** (*ok'tō-fid*; root of L. *findĕre*, to cleave; *bot.*) cleft into eight segments; **octogynous** (*ok-toj'i-nəs*; Gr. *gynē*, wife; *bot.*) having eight pistils or styles. — *n.pl.* **Octogyn'ia** in various Linnaean classes, an order with eight pistils. — *n.* **octohe'dron** an octahedron. — *adjs.* **octopetalous** (*ok-tō-pet'ə-ləs*) having eight petals; **octopod** (*ok'tō-pod*; Gr. *pous, podos*, foot) eight-footed or eight-armed. — *n.* an octopus or other member of the **Octopoda** (*-top'*), an order of dibranchiate cephalopods. — *adj.* **octop'odous.** — *ns.* **octopus** (*ok'tō-pəs*, formerly, *ok-tō'*) a genus (*Octopus*) of eight-armed cephalopods: any eight-armed cephalopod: (*fig.*) a person, organisation, with widespread influence: — *pls.* **oc'topuses**, (*arch.*) **octop'odēs** (or *-top'*), (**oc'topī** is wrong). — *adjs.* **octosepalous** (*ok-tō-sep'ə-ləs*) having eight sepals; **octos'tichous** octastichous. — *n.* and *adj.* **oc'tostyle** octastyle. — *adj.* **octosyllabic** (*ok'tō-sil-ab'ik*) consisting of eight syllables. — *n.* a line of eight syllables. — *n.* **octosyllable** (*-sil'ə-bl*) a word of eight syllables. [Gr. *oktō*, and L. *octō*.]

October *ok-tō'bər*, *n.* the tenth month, eighth in the most ancient Roman calendar: strong ale brewed in that month. — *n.* **Octo'brist** a member of a Russian moderate liberal party who made the tsar's manifesto of October 1905 their basis. [L. *octōber* — *octō*.]

octodecimo *ok-tō-des'i-mō*, *adj.* having eighteen leaves to the sheet: contracted **18mo**, often read eighteenmo. — *n.* a book with sheets so folded: — *pl.* **-mos.** [L. *octōdecim*, eighteen; cf. **octavo**.]

octofid. See **octo-.**

octogenarian *ok-tō-ji-nā'ri-ən*, *n.* one who is eighty years old, or between eighty and ninety. — Also *adj.* — *adj.* **octogenary** (*ok-tō-jē'nə-ri, ok-toj'i-nə-ri*). [L. *octō-gēnārius*, pertaining to eighty.]

octogynous ... to ... **octohedron.** See **octo-.**

octonary *ok'tə-nə-ri*, *adj.* based on the number eight. — *n.* a set of eight: an eight-line stanza. — *adj.* **octonarian** (*ok-tō-nā'ri-ən*) having eight feet. — *n.* a line of eight feet. — *n.* **octonā'rius** an octonarian: — *pl.* **octonā'riī.** [L. *octōnārius*.]

octonocular *ok-tō-nok'ū-lər, adj.* having eight eyes. [L. *octōnī*, eight at a time, *oculus*, eye.]

octoploid. Same as octaploid.

octopod, etc., octopus, etc. See octo-.

octoroon, octaroon *ok-tə-rōōn', n.* the offspring of a quadroon and a person of European descent: one who has one-eighth Negro blood. [Modelled on quadroon — L. *octō*, eight.]

octosepalous ... to ... octosyllable. See octo-.

octroi *ok'trwä* or *ok-trwa', n.* formerly, and still in some European countries, a commercial privilege, as of exclusive trade: a toll or tax levied at the gates of a city on articles brought in: the place where, or officials to whom, it is paid: payment for passage of car on a road. [Fr., — *octroyer*, to grant, from some such L.L. form as *auctōrizāre*, to authorise — L. *auctor*, author.]

octuor *ok'tū-ör, n.* an octet. [L. *octo*, eight; modelled on *quattuor*, four.]

octuple *ok'tū-pl, adj.* eightfold. — *v.t.* or *v.i.* to multiply by eight. — *n.* oc'tuplet a group of eight notes to be played in the time of six (*mus.*): one of eight born at a birth. — *adj.* octūp'licate eightfold: multiplied by eight. — Also *n.* [L. *octuplus*; cf. duple, double.]

ocular *ok'ū-lər, adj.* pertaining to the eye or to vision: formed in, addressed to, or known by, the eye: received by actual sight: eyelike. — *ns.* an eyepiece: an eye (*facet.*); oc'ularist (Fr. *oculariste*) a person who makes artificial eyes. — *adv.* oc'ularly. — *adjs.* oc'ulate, -d having eyes, or spots like eyes. — *n.* oc'ulist a specialist in diseases and defects of the eye, an ophthalmologist. — oculo- (*ok'ū-lō-, -lo'-*) in composition, of or pertaining to the eye or eyes. — *adj.* oc'ulomō'tor pertaining to or causing movements of the eye. — *n.* oculus (*ok'ū-ləs*) a round window: — *pl.* -lī. [L. *oculus*, the eye.]

od¹ *od* or *ōd, n.* Reichenbach's arbitrary name for a force supposed by him to manifest itself in light, magnetism, chemical action, hypnotism, etc. — *adj.* o'dic. — o'dism belief in od; od'yl(e) (Gr. *hȳlē*, matter) od; od'ylism. — od'-force od.

od², odd *od, n.* and *interj.* a minced form of god. — od's-bobs' God's body; od's-bod'ikins God's body; od's-life' God's life; od's-nouns (*-nownz'*) God's wounds; od's-pit'ikins (*Shak.*) God's pity; odzooks' same as gadzooks. — These are often written without an apostrophe.

OD *o'dē', (slang) n.* an overdose (of drugs). — also *v.i.:* — *pr.p.* OD'ing; *pa.t.* and *pa.p.* OD'd.

oda *ō'də, n.* a room in a harem. [Turk.; cf. odalisque.]

odal, odaller. Same as udal, udaller.

odalisque, odalisk *ō'də-lisk,* odalique *-lik, ns.* a female slave in a harem. [Fr., — Turk. *ōdaliq* — *ōdah,* a chamber.]

odd¹ *od, adj.* unpaired: not matching (*Spens.*): left over: additional: extra: not one of a complete set: one in excess of half the number: left over after a round number has been taken: with something additional in lower denominations or lower powers of ten: not exactly divisible by two (opp. to *even*): strange: queer: casual: out-of-the-way: standing apart: at variance (*Shak.*). — *adv.* (*Shak.*) oddly. — *n.* one stroke above the like (*golf*): a stroke allowed in handicap (*golf*): one trick above book (*whist*): —in *pl.* odds (*odz,* sometimes treated as *sing.*) inequality: difference in favour of one against another: more than an even wager: the amount or proportion by which the bet of one exceeds that of another: the chances or probability: advantage: dispute: scraps: miscellaneous pieces, as in the phrase odds and ends (perh. orig. meaning points and ends; cf. odds and sods below). — *adj.* odd'ish. — *n.* odd'ity the state of being odd or singular: strangeness: a singular person or thing. — *adj.* odd'= like (*Scot.*) odd: odd-looking. — *adv.* odd'ly. — *ns.* odd'ment something remaining over: one of a broken set — often in *pl.*; odd'ness. — odd'ball an eccentric person, nonconformist in some respect. — Also *adj.*

(of e.g. a thing, plan, circumstance). — odd'-come= short a short remnant: (in *pl.*) odds and ends; odd'= come-short'ly an early day, any time. — *adj.* or *n.* odd-e'ven (*Shak.*) apparently, neither one thing nor another, as the time about midnight. — Odd'fellow a member of a secret benevolent society called Oddfellows. — *adj.* odd'-job. — odd jobs see job; odd-jobb'er, odd-job'man. — *adj.* odd'-look'ing. — odd lot a block of less that one hundred shares; odd-lott'er one who deals in odd lots; odd'-man odd-jobman: an umpire: one who has a casting vote; odd man, one, out the singling out or elimination of one from a number for any purpose: a person who is left out when numbers are made up: a person set apart, willingly or unwillingly, by difference of interests, etc., from a group in which he finds himself; odds'man (*Scot.*) an umpire or arbiter. — *adj.* odds'-on' of a chance, better than even. — at odds at variance (with); long odds, short odds see long³, short; make no odds to make no significant difference; odds and sods (*coll.*) miscellaneous people, things, etc.; over the odds more than expected, normal, necessary, etc.; shout the odds (*slang*) to talk overmuch or too loudly; what's the odds? what difference does it make? [O.N. *oddi,* point, a triangle, odd number; cf. O.N. *oddr,* O.E. *ord,* point.]

odd². See od².

ode *ōd, n.* orig., a poem intended to be sung: an elaborate lyric, often of some length, generally addressed to somebody or something. — *adj.* o'dic. — *n.* o'dist a writer of odes. [Fr. *ode* — Gr. *ōidē,* contr. from *aoidē* — *aeidein,* to sing.]

odea. See odeon.

Odelsting, Odelsthing *ō'dəls-ting, n.* the lower house of the Norwegian parliament. [Norw. *odel,* allodium, *ting* (thing), court, parliament.]

odeon *ō'di-ən, -dyən, -dē'-, n.* in ancient Greece, a theatre for musical contests, etc.: a concert-hall. — Also ō'deum a Roman odeon: — *pl.* ō'deums, ō'dea. [Gr. *ōideion,* L. *ōdēum.*]

odic¹. See od¹.

odic². See ode.

Odin *ō'din, n.* the Scandinavian equivalent of Woden. — *ns.* O'dinism the ancient worship of Odin: a modern revival of this; O'dinist. [O.N. *Ōthenn.*]

odism; odist. See od¹; ode.

odium *ō'di-əm, n.* hatred: offensiveness: blame: reproach attaching to (with *of*): the quality of provoking hate. — *adj.* o'dious hateful: offensive: repulsive: causing hatred. — *adv.* o'diously. — *n.* o'diousness. [L. *ōdium.*]

odium theologicum *ōd'i-əm thē-o-lo'ji-kəm, od'i-ōōm the-o-lo'gi-kōōm,* (L.) the hatred of theologians for each other's errors (or persons).

odograph *od'ō-gräf, n.* a device for plotting automatically a course travelled: an odometer: a pedometer. [Gr. *hodos,* a way, *graphein,* to write.]

odometer, odometry. See hodometer.

Odonata *ō-don-ā'tə, (zool.) n.pl.* the dragonfly order. — *ns.* odon'atist, odonatol'ogist one who studies, or is an expert on, dragonflies; odonatol'ogy. [Ionic Gr. *odōn,* a tooth.]

odont(o)- *od-ont(o)-,* in composition, tooth. — *ns.* odon-talgia (*-al'ji-ə;* Gr. *algos,* pain), odontal'gy toothache. — *adjs.* odontal'gic; odon'tic dental. — *ns.* odont'ist (*facet.*) a dentist; odont'oblast (Gr. *blastos,* a shoot) a dentine-forming cell; odon'tocete (*-sēt;* Gr. *kētos,* whale) a toothed whale. — *adj.* odontogenic (*-jen'ik*). — *ns.* odontogeny (*-oj'i-ni*) the origin and development of teeth; Odontogloss'um (Gr. *glōssa,* tongue) a tropical American genus of orchids: (without *cap.*) a plant of this genus; odont'ograph an instrument for obtaining approximate curves for gear-teeth; odontog'raphy description of teeth. — *adj.* odont'oid toothlike (odontoid peg, process a projection from the second vertebra of the neck) — *n.* odont'olite (Gr. *lithos,* stone) bone turquoise or occidental turquoise, a fossil bone or tooth coloured blue with phosphate of iron. — *adjs.*

odontolog'ic, -al. — *ns.* odontol'ogist; odontol'ogy the science of the teeth; odontō'ma a tumour arising in connection with the teeth: — *pl.* -mas, -mata. — *adjs.* odontō'matous pertaining to odontoma; odontophoral (-tof'ə-rəl; Gr. *phoros,* bearing), odontoph'oran. — *n.* odon'tophore (-*to-fōr, -fōr*) the rasping apparatus in molluscs — the radula, its support, or the whole apparatus. — *adj.* odontoph'orous. — *n.* Odontoph'orus a genus of American quails. — *n.pl.* odontornithes (-*ör-nī'thēz,* or -*ör'ni-thēz;* Gr. *ornis, ornīthos,* bird) fossil birds with teeth (not a natural class). — *adj.* odontostom'atous (Gr. *stoma, -atos,* mouth) having biting or toothed jaws. [Gr. *odous, odontos,* a tooth.]

odour, *U.S.* odor, *ō'dər, n.* smell: savour (*fig.*): repute (*fig.*). — *adjs.* o'dorant, o'dorate, odorif'erous emitting a (usually pleasant) smell. — *adv.* odorif'erously. — *n.* odorif'erousness. — *adj.* odorous (*ō'də-rəs;* sometimes formerly *ōd-ō'rəs*) emitting an odour or scent: sweet-smelling: fragrant: bad-smelling (*coll.*). — *adv.* o'dorously. — *n.* o'dorousness. — *adjs.* o'doured; o'dourless. — in bad odour in bad repute or standing (with): (similarly, but less commonly) in good odour; the odour of sanctity a fragrance after death alleged to be evidence of saintship: facetiously applied to the living who have denied themselves the sensual indulgence of washing: a sanctimonious manner. [A.Fr. *odour* — L. *odor, -ōris.*]

odso od'sō, *interj.* expressing surprise: — *pl.* od'sos. [For gadso.]

odyl(e), odylism. See od[1].

Odyssey od'is-i, *n.* a Greek epic poem, ascribed to Homer, describing the ten years' wanderings of *Odysseus* (Ulysses) on his way home from the Trojan war to Ithaca: (also without *cap.*) a long wandering, or a tale of wandering. — *adj.* Odyssē'an. [Gr. *Odysseia.*]

odzooks. See od[2].

oe. Same as oy.

oecist ē'sist, oikist oi'kist, (*hist.*) *ns.* the founder of a colony. [Gr. *oikistēs — oikos,* a house.]

oecology, etc., oecumenic(al), etc. See ecology, ecumenic (and council).

oedema ē-dē'mə, *n.* dropsy: pathological accumulation of fluid in tissue spaces: an unhealthy mass of swollen parenchyma (*bot.*). — *adjs.* oede'matose; oede'matous. — Also edē'ma, etc. [Gr. *oidēma, -atos,* swelling.]

Oedipus ē'di-pəs, *n.* a king of Thebes who solved the Sphinx's riddle and unwittingly killed his father and married his mother. — *adjs.* Oe'dipal; (*irreg.*) Oedipē'an. — Oedipus complex (*psych.*) the attachment of a son to his mother with unconscious rivalry and hostility towards his father. [Gr. *Oidipous,* lit. Swellfoot.]

œil-de-bœuf œ'ē-də-bœf, *n.* a little round window: an octagonal vestibule at the court of Versailles, hence one elsewhere: — *pl.* œils-de-bœuf (*œ'ē-*). [Fr., ox-eye.]

œillade œ-yäd', formerly āl'yad, il'yad, il'i-ad (*Shak.* illiad, eliad) *n.* a glance or wink (*Shak.*): an ogle. — Formerly also ey(e)liad (ī'li-ad). [Fr. *œillade — œil,* eye.]

oen(o)- ēn(ō)-, in composition, wine. — Also oin(o)-. — *adjs.* oenan'thic (Gr. *anthos,* flower) having or imparting the characteristic odour of wine; oenolog'ical. — *ns.* oenol'ogist; oenol'ogy the science of wines; oe'nomancy divination from the appearance of wine poured out in libations; oenomā'nia dipsomania; oen'omel (Gr. *meli,* honey) wine mixed with honey; oenom'eter a hydrometer for measuring the alcoholic strength of wines; oen'ophil, oenoph'ilist a connoisseur of wine — also (now usu.) oen'ophile (-fīl); oenoph'ily love of, and knowledge of, wines. [Gr. *oinos,* wine.]

Oenothera ē-nō-thē'rə, by some ē-noth'ə-rə, *n.* the evening-primrose genus of Onagraceae. [Gr. *oinothēras,* perh. a wrong reading for *onothēras,* a plant whose roots smelt of wine, perh. oleander.]

o'er ōr, ör (*Scot.* owr) shortened form of over. For compounds, see over-.

o'ercome owr'kum, (*Scot.*) *n.* the burden of a song:

overplus. — o'er'lay a large cravat; o'er'word a refrain: a catchword.

oerlikon ûr'li-kon, *n.* (also with *cap.*) an aircraft or anti-aircraft cannon of Swiss origin. [*Oerlikon,* near Zürich.]

oersted ûr'sted, *n.* the C.G.S. unit of magnetic field strength. [After H.C. *Oersted* (1777–1851), Danish physicist.]

o'erword. See under o'ercome.

oes ōz, a plural of o.

oesophagus, esophagus ē-sof'ə-gəs, *n.* the gullet: — *pl.* -gi (gī). — *adj.* oesophageal (-fə-jē'əl). [Gr. *oisophagos,* gullet; origin unknown; app. connected with *phagein,* to eat.]

oestrus ēs'trəs, *n.* a gadfly or bot: a vehement stimulus or frenzy: (in the following meanings and words, also es- es-) heat or sexual impulse, esp. in female mammals: oestrous cycle. — Also oes'trum. — *adj.* oes'tral. — *ns.* oestradī'ol a natural oestrogen (C$_{18}$H$_{24}$O$_2$), also synthesised for use in cancer treatment and menstrual etc. disorders; oestrogen (ēs'trō-jən) any one of the female sex-hormones: a substance found in plants, or synthesised, that has similar effects. — *adjs.* oestrogenic (-jen'); oes'trous. — oestrous cycle the series of physiological changes from the beginning of one period of oestrus to the beginning of the next. [L. *oestrus* — Gr. *oistros.*]

œuvre œ-vr', (Fr.) *n.* work (of an artist, writer, etc.): — *pl.* œuvres (œ-vr').

of ov, uv, əv, *prep.* from: from among: out from: belonging to: among: proceeding or derived from: made from, having for material: having, or characterised by: in the manner that characterises: with respect to: owing to: with: over: concerning: during: by: on: in: specified as: constituted by: short of, to (in giving the time, e.g. *quarter of five*) (*U.S.*): measuring: aged: owning. [O.E. *of;* Du. *af,* Ger. *ab,* L. *ab,* Gr. *apo.*]

ofay ō'fā, ō-fā' (*U.S. Negro derog. slang*) *n.* a white person. — Also *adj.* [Ety. uncertain; prob. of African origin.]

off of, öf, *adv.* away: in or to a position that is not on something: in motion: out of continuity: out of connection, supply, activity, operation, or validity: to a finish, up: no longer available: in deterioration or diminution: into freedom. — *adj.* most distant: on the opposite or farther side: on the side of a cricket-field: on the side opposite that on which the batsman stands (normally the bowler's left; *cricket*): (of a horse or vehicle) right: out of condition or form: not devoted to the particular or usual activity (as *off-day, off-season*). — *prep.* from: away from: removed from: opening out of: in or to a position or condition that is not on: disengaged from: disinclined to, not wanting: out to sea from: from a dish of: from a ball bowled by (*cricket*): with a handicap of (*golf*): not up to the usual standard of: not eating or drinking: not subject to or following. — *n.* the offside. — *v.t.* to put off: to take off: to kill (*U.S. slang*). — *v.i.* (or *v.t.* with *it*) to go off: to take off (with *with; coll.*). — *interj.* away! depart! — *n.* off'ing the region some distance offshore: a place or time some way off (in the offing in sight, at hand). — *adj.* off'ish aloof in manner. — *adv.* off'-ward(s) off, away from, esp. shore. — *adj. and adv.* off'-and-on' occasional(ly): intermittent(ly). — *adj.* off-beam see off beam below. — *n.* any of the usually unaccented beats in a musical bar. — *adj.* off'beat away from standard: out of the usual: eccentric; off'-board (*commerce*) of or relating to over-the-counter securities transactions. — off'-break (*cricket*) of a ball on pitching, deviation inwards from the offside: spin given to a ball to cause such a deviation: a ball bowled so as to have such a deviation. — *adj.* off'-cen'tre not quite central. — off'-chance, off chance a remote chance (on the off(-)chance (with *that* or *of*) just in case, or in the hope that, (something might happen)). — *adjs.* off'-col'our, -ed unsatisfactory in colour (as a diamond) and so inferior: half-caste, not pure white:

(**off-colour**) not completely healthy: (of jokes, etc.) smutty, blue. — **off′-come** a subterfuge (*Scot.*): a pretext (*Scot.*): the manner of coming off, issue, success; **off′cut** a small piece cut off or left over from a larger piece of some material (e.g. wood); **off′-day** see **off** *adj.* above: a day when one is not at one's best or most brilliant; **off′-drive** (*cricket*) a drive to the off side. — Also *v.i.* and *v.t.* — *adj.* **off′-du′ty** not on duty. — *adv.* **offhand′** extempore: at once: without hesitating. — *adjs.* **off′hand** without study: impromptu: free and easy: ungraciously curt or summary; **off′hand′ed.** — *adv.* **offhand′edly.** — **offhand′edness.** — *adj.* **off′-key′** out of tune (*lit.* and *fig.*): not in keeping. — **off′-li′cence** a licence to sell alcoholic liquors for consumption off the premises only: a shop having such a licence (*coll.*). — *adjs.* **off′-lim′its** prohibited, out of bounds; **off′-line** (*comput.*) not under the direct control of the central processing unit: not connected, switched off. — Also *adv.* — *v.t.* and *v.i.* **off′load** (*orig. S. Afr.*) to unload: to get rid of (something unwanted) by passing to someone else (with *on to*). — *adjs.* **off′peak′** not at time of highest demand; **off′-plan′** pertaining to a home, etc. bought before (completion of) building on the basis of plans seen, or to the buyer of such a property. — **off′print** a reprint of a single article from a periodical; **off′put** (*Scot.*) the act of putting off (in any sense); **off′-putter; off′-putting** an act of putting off. — *adj.* that puts off: disconcerting: causing disinclination or aversion. — **off′-reck′oning** (usu. in *pl.*) a deduction: an account between army officers and governments concerning men's clothes, etc. (*obs.*). — *v.t.* and *v.i.* **off′saddle** to unsaddle. — *n.* **off-sales′** (*S. Afr.*) a shop where alcoholic drinks can be bought for consumption elsewhere. — *n.*, *adj.*, and *adv.* **off′season** (of, at) a time (for e.g. a holiday) other than the most popular and busy. — **off′scouring** (usu. in *pl.*) matter scoured off: refuse: anything vile or despised; **off′scum** scum, refuse; **off′set** a thing set off against another as equivalent or compensation: a lateral shoot that strikes root and forms a new plant: a mountain spur: a side branch of anything: a sudden change of direction in a pipe: a reduction of thickness or the (usually sloping) ledge formed where part of a wall, buttress, bank, etc., is set back from the general face: a hillside terrace (*U.S.*): a smudge on a newly printed sheet from another laid on it: offset printing (see below): in surveying, a perpendicular from the main line to an outlying point. — *v.t.* (*of-set′*, *of′set*) to set off against something as an equivalent or compensation. — *v.i.* to branch off: (*of′set*) to make an effort. — *adj.* **offset′able** (or *of′-*). — *v.t.* **off-shake′** to shake off (*pa.p.* Spens. **off-shakt′**). — **off′shoot** a branch or derivative of anything. — *adv.* **offshore′** and *adj.* **off′shore** from the shore: at a distance from the shore: (placed) abroad. — **off′side** the far side: a horse's or vehicle's right towards the middle of the road: (*cricket*) see **off** *adj.*: (*football*, etc.) the field between the ball and the opponents' goal. — *adj.* and *adv.* (**offside′**) on the offside: between the ball, or the last player who had it, and the opponents' goal. — **offsīd′er** a subordinate or side-kick (*Austr. coll.*). — *adj.* and *adv.* **off(-)site′** (working, happening, etc.) away from a site. — *n.pl.* **off′-sorts** wool set aside in sorting, or unsuitable for a given purpose. — **off′-spin** (*cricket*) (an) off-break; **off′-spinner** (*cricket*) one who bowls off-breaks; **off′spring** a child or children: progeny: issue: ancestry (*obs.*): source (*obs.*). — *advs.* and *adjs.* **off′-stage** not on the stage as visible to the spectators; **off′-stream** of an industrial plant, etc., not in operation or production. — *adj.* **off′-street** of parking, in a car park. — **off′take** the act of taking off in any sense: a take-off: that which is taken off: a channel, passage, or pipe for removing a fluid. — *adjs.* **off-the-peg** see **peg**; **off′-white** not quite white. — *n.* a colour, paint, etc., which is off-white. — **a bit off** (*coll.*) of behaviour, etc., unfair or unacceptable; **badly off** ill off; **be off** to go away quickly (as a command, also **be off with you**); **break off, come off** see **break¹, come; from off** from a

position on; **go off** see **go¹**; **ill off** poor or ill provided; **make off (with)** see **make¹**; **off and on** same as **off-and-on** above; **off beam, off′-beam′** mistaken, wrong, in what one is thinking; **off one's oats, feed, head, rocker, trolley** see **oat, feed¹, head, rock³**; **offset printing** a method of printing lithographs, etc., by firstly taking an impression from a plate on a rubber cylinder and then transferring the impression to paper, or metal, etc.; **offshore purchase** a purchase by one country in another; **off the cuff** see **cuff²**; **off the face, shoulder** (of a woman's hat, dress, etc.) so as to reveal the face, shoulder; **off the peg** see **peg; off the wall** (*U.S. slang*) off the cuff, unofficially, without preparation: unorthodox, strange; **off with** take off at once; **put off, show off, take off** see **put¹, show, take; tell off** to count: to assign, as for a special duty: to chide; **walk off (with)** see **walk; well off** rich, well provided: fortunate. [Same as **of.**]

offal *of′l*, *n.* waste or rejected parts, esp. of a carcase: an edible part cut off in dressing a carcase, esp. entrails, heart, liver, kidney, tongue, etc.: anything worthless or unfit for use: refuse. [**off, fall¹**.]

offbeat ... **to** ... **off-duty.** See **off.**

offend *o-fend′*, *ə-*, *v.t.* to displease: to make angry: to do harm to: to hurt the feelings of: to affront: to cause to stumble or sin (*B.*): to violate (a law). — *v.i.* to sin: to break the law: to cause anger: to be made to stumble or sin (*B.*). — *n.* **offence′** a stumbling (*B.*): any cause of anger or displeasure: an injury: a transgression, an infraction of law: a crime: a sin: affront: assault. — *adjs.* **offence′ful** (*Shak.*) giving offence or displeasure: injurious; **offence′less** (*Milt.*) unoffending: innocent. — *ns.* **offend′er:** — *fem.* (*Shak.*) **offend′ress; offense′** (chiefly *U.S.*) same as **offence.** — *adj.* **offens′ive** causing offence, displeasure, or injury: used in attack: making the first attack. — *n.* the act or course of action of the attacking party: the posture of one who attacks: a great and sustained effort to achieve an end, as *peace offensive.* — *adv.* **offens′ively.** — *n.* **offens′iveness.** **give offence** to cause displeasure; **take offence** to feel displeasure, be offended. [L. *offendĕre, offensum* — *ob*, against, *fendĕre, fēnsum*, to strike (found in compounds); cf. **defend**.]

offer *of′ər*, *v.t.* to present, esp. as an act of devotion, homage, charity, etc.: to express willingness: to hold out for acceptance or rejection: to lay before one: to present to the mind: to attempt: to make a show of attempting, make as if: to propose to give, pay, sell, or perform. — *v.i.* to present itself: to be at hand: to incline: to make an offer: — *pr.p.* **off′ering;** *pa.t.* and *pa.p.* **off′ered.** — *n.* the act of offering: the state of being offered: the first advance: that which is offered: a proposal made: an attempt, essay: a knob on an antler. — *adj.* **off′erable** that may be offered. — *ns.* **offeree′** one to whom something is offered; **off′erer,** (*law*) **off′eror; off′ering** the act of making an offer: that which is offered: a gift: that which is offered on an altar (*B.*): a sacrifice: (in *pl.*) in Church of England, certain dues payable at Easter; **off′ertory** the act of offering: the thing offered: the verses or the anthem said or sung while the offerings of the congregation are being made: the money collected at a religious service: anciently a linen or silken cloth used in various ceremonies connected with the administration of the eucharist. — **offer up** in e.g. joinery, to position on a trial basis, in order to test for size and suitability before fixing; **on offer** being offered for sale, consumption, etc.: for sale as a special offer; **special offer** esp. in a shop, the act of offering something for sale, or that which is offered, usu. for a short time, at a bargain price. [L. *offerre* — *ob*, towards, *ferre*, to bring.]

offhand, etc. See **off.**

office *of′is*, *n.* an act of kindness or attention: a service: (with *ill*, etc.) a disservice: a function or duty: settled duty or employment: a position imposing certain duties or giving a right to exercise an employment: the possession of a post in the government: business: an act of worship: the order or form of a religious service, either public or private: that which a thing is designed or fitted to do: a place where business is carried on: a body or staff occupying such a place: a state department: the building in which it is housed: a doctor's consulting-room (*U.S.*): a cockpit in an aeroplane (*slang*): a lavatory: a hint (*slang*): (*pl.*) the apartments of a house or the subsidiary buildings in which the domestic, etc., work is carried out. — *n.* **off′icer** one who holds an office: a person who performs some public duty: a person holding a commission in an army, navy, or air force: one who holds a similar post in any force or body organised on a similar plan: a policeman: an office-bearer in a society. — *v.t.* to furnish with officers: to command, as officers. — *adj.* **official** (*of-ish′əl*) pertaining to an office: depending on the proper office or authority: done by authority: issued or authorised by a public authority or office: recognised in the pharmacopoeia (cf. **officinal**). — *n.* one who holds an office: a subordinate public officer: the deputy of a bishop, etc. — *ns.* **offic′ialdom** officials as a body: the world of officials: officialism; **officialese′** stilted, wordy, and stereotyped English alleged to be characteristic of official letters and documents; **offic′-ialism** official position: excessive devotion to official routine and detail: the self-importance of a Jack-in-office; **officiality** (*of-ish-i-al′i-ti*), **officialty** (*of-ish′əl-ti; rare*) the charge, office, or jurisdiction of an official: the official headquarters of an ecclesiastical or other deliberative and governing body: officialism. — *adv.* **officially** (*of-ish′ə-li*). — *n.* **officiant** (*of-ish′i-ənt*) one who officiates at a religious service, one who administers a sacrament. — *v.i.* **offic′iate** to perform the duties of an office. — *n.* **offic′iator.** — **off′ice-bearer** one who holds office: one who has an appointed duty to perform in connection with some company, society, church, etc.; **off′ice-block** a large building in which an office or variety of offices is housed; **off′ice-book** a book of forms of service; **off′ice-boy** a boy employed to do minor jobs in an office: — *fem.* **off′ice-girl; off′ice-holder** one who holds a government office: a civil servant, usu. in administration (*U.S.*); **office hours** the time during which an office is open for business, typically 9 a.m. to 5 p.m. Monday to Friday; **off′ice= hunter** a self-seeking candidate for public employment; **off′ice-seeker** a candidate for office. — **last offices** rites for the dead: the preparation of a corpse for burial; **officer of arms** (also with *caps.*) any of the thirteen officers of the College of Arms (q.v.); **official list** a list of the current prices of stocks and shares published daily by the London Stock Exchange; **official receiver** see **receive.** [Fr., — L. *officium*, a favour, duty, service.]

officinal *of-is′in-əl, -i-sīn′, adj.* belonging to, used in, a shop: used in medicine: recognised in the pharmacopoeia (now *official*): sold by druggists. [L.L. *officīnālis* — L. *officīna*, a workshop, later a monastic storeroom — *opus*, work, *facĕre*, to do.]

officious *of-ish′əs, adj.* obliging (*obs.*): dutiful (*Shak.*): too forward in offering unwelcome or unwanted services: intermeddling: in diplomacy, informal, not official. — *adv.* **offic′iously.** — *n.* **offic′iousness.** [L. *officiōsus — officium.*]

offing, offish. See **off.**

offload, offpeak, offprint, offput, offsaddle, offset, offside, offspring, etc. See under **off.**

oflag *of′läg, -lähh, n.* a German prisoner-of-war camp for officers. [Ger., short for *Offizierslager*, officers' camp.]

oft *oft, öft,* **often** *of′n, öf′n, of′ən, of′tən, advs.* frequently: many times. — *adj.* **oft′en** (*B.*) frequent. — *n.* **oft′enness** frequency. — *advs.* **oft′times, oft′entimes** many times: frequently. — **as often as not** in about half of the instances, quite frequently. [O.E. *oft*; Ger. *oft*, Goth. *ufta.*]

ogam, ogham *og′əm, ō′əm, n.* an ancient Celtic alphabet of straight lines meeting or crossing the edge of a stone:

any of its twenty characters. — *adjs.* **og(h)am′ic** (or *og′, ō′*), **og′mic.** [O.Ir. *ogam*, mod. Ir. *ogham.*]

ogdoad *og′dō-ad, n.* a set of eight. [Gr. *ogdoas, -ados — oktō*, eight.]

ogee *ō′jē, ō-jē′, n.* a moulding S-shaped in section: an S-shaped curve. — *adj.* having S-shaped curves. — *adj.* **ogee′d.** [Fr. *ogive*; see **ogive.**]

oggin *og′in* (*naval slang*) *n.* the sea. [Said to be from earlier *hogwash*, the sea.]

ogham, oghamic. See **ogam.**

ogive *ō′jīv, ō-jīv′,* (*archit.*) *n.* a diagonal rib of a vault: a pointed arch or window. — *adj.* **ogī′val.** [Fr.; origin doubtful, poss. — Ar. *auj*, summit.]

ogle *ō′gl, v.t.* to look at fondly, or impertinently, with side glances: to eye greedily. — *v.i.* to cast amorous glances: to stare impertinently. — *ns.* **o′gle; o′gler; o′gling.** [Cf. L.G. *oegeln*, freq. of *oegen*, to look at; Ger. *äugeln*, to leer, *Auge*, eye.]

ogmic. See **ogam.**

Ogpu *og′pōō, og-pōō′, n.* the Russian secret police of 1922–34. [From the initials of *Obedinennoe Gosudarstvennoe Politicheskoe Upravlenie*, Unified State Political Directorate.]

ogre *ō′gər, n.* a man-eating monster or giant of fairy tales: an ugly, cruel or bad-tempered person, or one whose sternness inspires fear: — *fem.* **o′gress.** — *adj.* **o′gr(e)ish.** [Fr. *ogre*, prob. invented by Perrault.]

Ogygian *ō-gij′i-ən, ō-jij′i-ən, adj.* pertaining to the mythical Attic king *Ogȳgēs*: prehistoric, primaeval: very old: of Calypso's island, *Ogȳgiā.* — **Ogygian deluge** a flood said to have occurred during the reign of Ogyges.

oh *ō, interj.* denoting surprise, pain, sorrow, etc. [See **o.**]

ohm *ōm, n.* the unit of electrical resistance in the SI and the M.K.S.A. systems, the resistance in a conductor in which a potential difference of one volt produces a current of one ampere: formerly defined as the resistance of a specified column of mercury under stated conditions. — *adj.* **ohm′ic.** — *n.* **ohmmeter** (*ōm′mēt-ər*) an instrument for measuring electrical resistance. — **Ohm's law** the law that strength of electric current is directly proportional to electromotive force and inversely to resistance. [Georg Simon *Ohm*, German electrician, 1787–1854.]

oho *ō-hō′, interj.* expressing triumphant surprise or gratification: — *pl.* **ohos′.**

-oholic, -oholism. See **-aholic.**

ohone, ochone *ō-hōn′, -hhōn′,* (*Ir.* and *Highland*) *interjs.* of lamentation. [Ir. and Gael. *ochoin.*]

oi *oi, interj.* used to attract attention, etc. [Imit.]

-oid *-oid,* in composition, (something) which resembles or has the shape of, as in *anthropoid, asteroid, deltoid.* — **-oidal** adjective combining form. [Gr. *-eidēs — eidos*, shape, form.]

oidium *ō-id′i-əm, n.* the conidial stage of the vine-mildew and other fungi: — *pl.* **oid′ia** (*-ə*). [Gr. *ōion*, an egg, with dim. suffix *-idion* Latinised.]

oik *oik,* (*coll.*) *n.* a cad: an ignorant, inferior person: a chap, bloke (*slightly derog.*). [Ety. uncertain.]

oikist. See **oecist.**

oil *oil, n.* the juice from the fruit of the olive-tree: any similar liquid got from parts of other plants: any similar (usu. flammable) greasy liquid got from animals, plants, mineral deposits or by artificial means, and used as a lubricant, fuel, foodstuff, etc.: (in *pl.*) oil-paints, or painting: (in *pl.*) oilskins: news, information, esp. in *the good oil* (*Austr.*). — *v.t.* to smear, lubricate, or anoint with oil. — *v.i.* to take oil aboard as fuel. — *adj.* **oiled** smeared, treated, lubricated or impregnated with oil: preserved in oil: tipsy (*slang*). — *ns.* **oil′er** one who, or that which, oils: an oilcan: (in *pl.*) oilskins: a ship driven by oil: a ship that carries oil; **oil′ery** the commodities, business or establishment of an oil-man. — *adv.* **oil′ily.** — *n.* **oil′iness.** — *adj.* **oil′y** consisting of, containing, or having the qualities of, oil: greasy: unctuous. — **oil′-bath** a receptacle containing lubricating oil through which part of a machine passes; **oil'-beetle** a beetle (*Meloe* and kindred) that emits a yellowish oily liquid from the legs when disturbed; **oil'-belt** a belt of country yielding mineral oil; **oil'-bird** the guacharo; **oil'-burner** a ship that uses oil as fuel: a lamp-burner for use with oil; **oil'-cake** a cattle-food made of the residue of oil-seeds when most of the oil has been pressed out; **oil'can** a can for carrying oil or for applying lubricating oil; **oil'cloth** a canvas coated with linseed-oil paint; **oil'-colour** a colouring substance mixed with oil; **oil'-cup** a small cup-like container, usu. attached to machinery, for holding and dispensing lubricating oil; **oil'-drum** a cylindrical metal barrel for oil; **oil'-engine** an internal-combustion engine burning vapour from oil; **oil'-field** an area which produces mineral oil. — *adj.* **oil'-fired** burning oil as fuel. — **oil'-gas** illuminating gas or heating gas made by destructive distillation of oil; **oil'-gauge** an instrument for indicating the level of lubricating oil in an engine, etc.; **oil'-gland** the uropygial gland in birds, forming a secretion used in preening the feathers; **oil length** the ratio of drying oil to resin in e.g. a varnish (*adjs.* **long'-oil** having a high proportion, **short'-oil** a low proportion, of oil); **oil'-man** one who deals in oils: one who owns an oil-well: one involved in the operation of an oil-well, oil-rig, etc.; **oil'-mill** a grinding-mill for expressing oil from seeds, etc.; **oil'nut** the North American butter-nut, the buffalo-nut, or other oil-yielding nut; **oil'-paint** an oil-colour; **oil'-paint'ing** a picture painted in oil-colours: the art of painting in oil-colours; **oil'-palm** a palm (*Elaeis guineensis*) whose fruit-pulp yields palm-oil; **oil'-pan** the sump in an internal-combustion engine; **oil'-paper** paper which has been oiled, e.g. to make it waterproof; **oil platform** a steel and/or concrete structure, either fixed or mobile, used in offshore drilling to support the rig and to keep stores; **oil'-press** a machine for expressing oils from seeds or pulp. — *adj.* **oil'-rich** having much oil. — **oil'-rig** the complete plant (machinery, structures, etc.) required for oil-well drilling: (*loosely*) a mobile oil platform; **oil sand** sand or sandstone occurring naturally impregnated with petroleum: tar sand; **oil'-seed** any seed that yields oil; **oil'-shale** a shale containing diffused hydrocarbons in a state suitable for distillation into mineral oils; **oil'-silk** a transparent silk fabric impregnated with oxidised oil; **oil'skin** cloth made waterproof by means of oil: a garment made of oilskin; **oil slick** a patch of oil forming a film on the surface of water or (*rarely*) a road, etc.; **oil'stone** a whetstone used with oil; **oil'-tanker** a vessel constructed for carrying oil in bulk; **oil'-tree** any of several trees or shrubs from which oil is got, that mentioned in Isa. xii. 19 probably being the oleaster; **oil'-well** a boring made for petroleum. — *adjs.* **long-oil, short-oil** see **oil length** above; **no oil-painting** (*coll.*) not very beautiful; **someone's palm** to bribe a person; **oil the wheels** (*fig.*) to do something in order to make things go more smoothly, successfully, etc.; **strike oil** see **strike**. — See also **tall-oil**. [O.Fr. *oile* (Fr. *huile*) — L. *oleum* — Gr. *elaion* — *elaiā*, olive-tree, olive.]

oillet *oi'lit*, *n.* an obs. form of **eyelet**.

oino- *oi-nō-*, in composition, an occasional variant in words beginning **oeno-**.

ointment *oint'mənt*, *n.* anything used in anointing: any greasy substance applied to diseased or wounded parts (*med.*): an unguent. — *v.t.* **oint** (*Dryden*) to anoint. [Fr. *oint*, pa.p. of *oindre* — L. *unguĕre*, to anoint.]

Oireachtas *er'əhh-thəs*, *n.* the legislature of the Republic of Ireland (President, Seanad, and Dáil). [Ir., assembly.]

oiticica *oi-ti-sē'kə*, *n.* any of several South American trees, esp. *Licania rigida* and *Couepia grandiflora* (both rosaceous), whose nuts yield an oil used for quick-drying paints and varnishes. [Port., — Tupi *oitycica*.]

ojime *ō'ji-mā*, *n.* a carved bead through which pass the two cords attached to an inro and which when slid down the cords serves to keep the inro closed. [Jap.

o, string, *shime*, fastening.]

OK, okay *ō-kā'*, (*coll.*) *adj.* all correct: all right: satisfactory. — *adv.* yes: all right, certainly. — *n.* approval: sanction: endorsement: — *pl.* **OK's, okays.** — *v.t.* to mark or pass as right: to sanction: — *pr.p.* **OK'ing, OKing, okaying;** *pa.t.* and *pa.p.* **OK'd, OKed, okayed.** [Various explanations of the letters have been given; evidence suggests that *OK* originated as an abbreviation of *orl korrekt*, a facetious misspelling of *all correct* current in the US in the 1830s, and was then used as a slogan by Van Buren's party in the 1840 U.S. presidential election (Van Buren was born at Kinderhook, near Albany in New York and was known as Old *Kinderhook*).]

okapi *ō-kä'pē*, *n.* an animal of Central Africa related to the giraffe: — *pl.* **oka'pis.** [Native name.]

okay. See **OK.**

oke[1] *ōk*, *n.* a Turkish weight of about 2⅘ lb. [Turk. *ōqah*, appar. through Gr. from L. *uncia*, ounce.]

oke[2] *ōk*, (*slang*) *adv.* same as **OK.** — *adj.* and *adv.* **okey-dokey** (*ō'ki-dō'ki*; *slang*) OK.

okimono *ō-ki-mō'nō*, *ok-*, *n.* a Japanese ornament or figurine. [Jap. *oku*, to put, *mono*, thing.]

okra *ok'rə*, *ōk'rə*, *n.* a tropical plant, *Hibiscus esculentus*, of the mallow family, with edible pods: the pods themselves: a dish prepared with the pods. — Also known as **gumbo** and **lady's fingers.** [From a W. African name.]

old *ōld*, *adj.* advanced in years: having been long or relatively long in existence, use, or possession: of a specified (or to be specified) age: of long standing: worn or worn out: out of date: superseded or abandoned: former: old-fashioned: antique: ancient: early: belonging to later life: belonging to former times: denoting anyone or anything with whom or with which one was formerly associated, as *old school*, etc.: (of a language) of the earliest, or earliest known, stage: long practised or experienced: having the characteristics of age: familiar, accustomed: in plenty, in excess, or wonderful (esp. in *high old*; *coll.*): a general word of familiar or affectionate approbation or contempt (often *good old* or *little old*; *coll.*): reckoned according to Old Style (see **style**): — *compar.* **old'er, eld'er** (q.v.); *superl.* **old'est, eld'est.** — *adv.* (*Shak.*) of old. — *n.* an old person: olden times, eld. — *v.t.* and *v.i.* **old'en** to age. — *adj.* former, old, past (now usu. only in phrases *in olden days/times*). — *n.* **old'ie, old'y** (*rarely*) (*coll.*) an old person: a film, song, etc. produced, popularised, etc. a considerable time ago. — *adj.* **old'ish** somewhat old. — *ns.* **old'ness; old'ster** a man getting old (*coll.*): a midshipman of four years' standing, a master's mate. — **old age** the later part of life; **old bachelor** somewhat elderly or confirmed bachelor; **Old Bailey** the Central Criminal Court in London; **Old Believer** a Raskolnik; **Old Bill** a soldier with drooping moustache in First World War cartoons by Bruce Bairnsfather; the police (*slang*; sometimes with *the*); **old bird** (*fig.*) an experienced person; **old boy** one's father, husband, etc. (*coll.*): an old or oldish man, esp. one in authority, or one who has some air of youthfulness: a former pupil: an affectionately familiar term of address to a male of any age (*coll.*; also **old bean, old chap, old fellow, old man, old thing**): — *fem.* **old girl; Old Catholic** a member of a body that broke away from the Roman Catholic Church on the question of papal infallibility; **old'-clothes'man** one who buys cast-off garments; **Old Contemptibles** the British Expeditionary Force to France in 1914, from the then Kaiser's probably apocryphal reference to them as a *contemptible* little army; **old country** the mother-country; **old dear** (*slang*) an old lady; **Old Dominion** Virginia; **Old English** see **English:** the form of black-letter used by 16th-century English printers. — *adjs.* **old'-estab'lished** long established; **olde-worlde** (*ō'ldi-wûrld'i*) self-consciously imitative of the past or supposed past. — **old face** the early roman type such as Caslon used. — *adj.* **old'-fash'ioned** in a fashion like one of long ago: out of date: clinging to old things and old styles: with manners like those of a grown-up person (said of a child): knowing. — **old'-fash'ionedness.** — *adjs.* **old'-fog'(e)yish** like an old fogey; **old'-gen'tlemanly** characteristic of an old gentleman. — **old gang, guard** old and conservative element in party, etc.; **Old Glory** the Stars and Stripes; **old gold** a dull gold colour like tarnished gold, used in textile fabrics; **old hand** an experienced performer: an old convict; **Old Harry, Nick, One, Poker, Scratch** the devil. — *adj.* **old hat** out-of-date. — **Old Hundred (Old Hundredth)** a famous tune set in England about the middle of the 16th century to Kethe's version of the 100th Psalm, marked 'Old Hundredth' in Tate and Brady (1696); **old lady** (*coll.*) a person's mother or wife; **Old Light** a member of a relatively less advanced religious school—applied esp. to the party in the Scottish Secession Church who continued to hold unchanged the principle of connection between Church and State; **old maid** a spinster, esp. one who is likely to remain a spinster: a woman, or more often a man, of the character supposed to be common among spinsters — fussy, prim, conventional, over-cautious, methodical: a simple game played by passing and matching cards: also the player left with the odd card; **old'-maid'hood, old'-maid'ism.** — *adj.* **old'-maid'ish** like the conventional old maid, prim. — **old man** unregenerate human nature: an adult male kangaroo: a person's husband, father, or employer (*coll.*): the captain of a merchant ship: a familiar friendly or encouraging term of address: a southernwood. — *adj.* (*Austr.*; also with *hyphen*) of exceptional size, intensity, etc. — **old master** (often *caps.*) any great painter or painting of a period previous to the 19th cent. (esp. of the Renaissance); **old Nick** see **Nick; old Norse** see **Norse; old rose** a deep soft pink; **old salt** an experienced sailor; **old school** those whose ways or thoughts are such as prevailed in the past. — Also *adj.* — **old soldier** an empty bottle: an experienced person who knows how to make himself comfortable; **old song** a mere trifle, a very small price; **old squaw, old'squaw'** (*U.S.*) the hareld; **old story** something one has heard before: something that happened long ago, or has happened often; **Old Style** see **style; old Testament** see **testament.** — *adj.* **old'-time** of or pertaining to times long gone by: of long standing: old-fashioned. — **old'-tim'er** one who has long been where he is: an experienced person, veteran: an old-fashioned person: (esp. as a form of address; *U.S.*) an old person; **Old Tom** a kind of sweetened gin; **old wife** an old woman: one who has the character ascribed to old women: a chimney-cap for curing smoking (*Scot.*): the hareld: a fish of various kinds — sea-bream, file-fish, etc.; **old woman** a person's wife or mother (*coll.*): an old-womanish person. — *adjs.* **old'-wom'anish** like an old woman, esp. fussy; **old'-world** belonging to earlier times: old-fashioned and quaint: (*cap.*) of the Old World. — *n.* **Old World** the Eastern hemisphere. — **an old-fashioned look** a knowing or quizzically critical look; **any old** see **any; come the old soldier over someone** to impose on a person; **of old** long ago: in or of times long past: formerly; **old age pension** a pension for one who has reached old age, esp. under a national system (first instituted in Britain in 1908); **old age pensioner; Old Boy network** (also without *caps.*) the members of a society (usu. upper-class), closely interconnected, who share information, and secure advantages for each other: this form of association; **old man of the sea** a person or burden that one cannot shake off — from the old man in the *Arabian Nights* who, having been carried across a stream by Sinbad the Sailor, refused to get down off his back; **old man's beard** a name for several plants including traveller's joy; **Old Red Sandstone** the lacustrine or continental equivalent of the (marine) Devonian, so called in contradistinction to the New Red Sandstone; **old school tie** a distinctive tie worn by old boys of a school: the emblem of (esp.

upper-class) loyalties shown by such people to each other. [O.E. *ald* (W.S. *eald*); Du. *oud*, Ger. *alt*.]

olden, etc, **oldster.** See **old.**

olé *ō-lā'* (Sp.) *interj.* an exclamation of approval, support, or encouragement, sometimes used in English as an expression of triumph. [Ar. *wa-llāh*, by God.]

Olea *ō'li-ə, n.* the olive genus, giving name to the family **Oleā'ceae,** including ash, privet, and jasmine. — *adj.* **oleā'ceous.** [L. *olea,* olive.]

oleaginous *ō-li-aj'in-əs, adj.* oily. — *n.* **oleag'inousness.** [L. *oleāginus — oleum,* oil.]

oleander *ō-li-an'dər, n.* an evergreen shrub (*Nerium oleander*) of the Apocynaceae, with lance-shaped leathery leaves and beautiful red or white flowers, the rose-bay or rose-laurel. [L.L. *oleander;* derivation from *rhododendron,* influenced by *laurus* and *olea,* has been conjectured.]

Olearia *ō-li-ā'ri-ə, n.* a genus of Australasian evergreen shrubs of the family Compositae, bearing white, yellow or mauve daisy-like flowers: (without *cap.*) a plant of this genus: (without *cap.*) a daisy-tree or bush (*coll.*). [After the German theologian and horticulturalist Johann Gottfried *Olearius* (1635–1711).]

oleaster *ō-li-as'tər, n.* properly the true wild olive: extended to the so-called wild olive, Elaeagnus. [L. *oleāster — olea,* an olive-tree — Gr. *elaiā.*]

oleate *ō'li-āt, n.* a salt of oleic acid. — *adj.* **olefiant** (*ō-li-fī'ənt* or *ō-lē'fi-ənt*) oil-forming (in **olefiant gas** ethylene). — *ns.* **o'lefin, -fine** (*-fin, -fēn*) any hydrocarbon of the ethylene series. — *adjs.* **olē'ic** (or *ō'li-ik*) pertaining to or got from oil (as in **oleic acid** $C_{18}H_{34}O_2$); **oleif'erous** producing oil, as seeds. — *ns.* **olein** (*ō'li-in*) a glycerine ester of oleic acid; **oleo** (*ō'li-ō*) a contraction for oleograph or for oleomargarine: — *pl.* **ō'leos;** **o'leograph** a print in oil-colours to imitate an oil-painting; **oleog'raphy; oleomar'garine** margarine (*U.S.*): a yellow fatty substance got from beef tallow and used in the manufacture of margarine, soap, etc. — *adj.* **oleophil'ic** having affinity for oils: wetted by oil in preference to water. — *n.* **oleum** (*ō'li-əm*) a solution of sulphur trioxide in sulphuric acid (also **fuming sulphuric acid**). — **oleo-res'in** a solution of a resin in an oil. [L. *oleum,* oil.]

olecranon *ō-li-krā'non, n.* a process forming the upper part of the ulna. — *adj.* **olecrā'nal.** [Gr. *ōlekrānon — ōlenē,* elbow, *krānion,* head.]

olefin(e), oleic, olein, etc. See **oleate.**

olent *ō'lənt, adj.* having a smell. [L. *olēns, -entis,* pr.p. of *olēre,* to smell.]

Olenus *ō'len-əs, n.* a typically Upper Cambrian genus of trilobites. — *n.* **Olenell'us** a similar Lower Cambrian genus. [Gr. *Ōlenos,* who was turned to stone.]

oleo. See **oleate.**

oleraceous *ol-ər-ā'shəs, adj.* of the nature of a pot-herb, for kitchen use. [L. (*h)olerāceus — (h)olus, (h)oleris,* a pot-herb, vegetable.]

oleum. See **oleate.**

olfactory *ol-fak'tə-ri, adj.* pertaining to, or used in, smelling. — *v.t.* **olfact'** (*facet.*). — *adj.* **olfact'ible.** — *n.* **olfac'tion.** — *adj.* **olfac'tive.** — *ns.* **olfactol'ogist; olfactol'ogy** the scientific study of smells and the sense of smell. — **olfactronics** (*-tron'iks; electronics*) the precise measurement, analysis and detection of odours using electronic instruments. [L. *olfacěre,* to smell — *olēre,* to smell, *facěre,* to make.]

olibanum *ol-ib'ə-nəm, n.* a gum-resin flowing from incisions in species of *Boswellia,* esp. species in Somaliland and Arabia, frankincense. [L.L., prob. — Gr. *libanos,* frankincense.]

olid *ol'id, adj.* rank-smelling. [L. *olidus — olēre,* to smell.]

olig(o)- *ol-ig-, -i-gō, -i-gə-,* in composition, little, few. — *ns.* **oligaemia** (*ol-i-gē'mi-ə, -jē'mi-ə*) abnormal deficiency of blood; **ol'igarch** (*-ärk;* Gr. *archē,* rule) a member of an oligarchy. — *adjs.* **oligarch'al, oligarch'ic, -ical.** — *ns.* **ol'igarchy** (*-är-ki*) government by a small exclusive class: a state so governed: a small body of men who have the supreme power of a state in their hands; **oligist** (*ol'i-jist*; Fr. *fer oligiste — fer*, iron, Gr. *oligistos*, superl. of *oligos*, little; as containing less iron than magnetite) crystallised haematite. — *adj.* **Oligocene** (*ol'i-gō-sēn*; *geol.*; Gr. *kainos*, new; as having few fossil molluscs of living species) between Eocene and Miocene. — *n.* the Oligocene system, period, or strata. — *n.* **oligochaete** (*ol'i-gō-kēt*; Gr. *chaitē*, bristle) any worm of the **Oligochae'ta**, chaetopods in which the locomotor organs are reduced to bristles — earthworms, etc. — *adj.* **ollgochrome** (*ol'i-gō-krōm*; Gr. *chrōma*, colour) painted in few colours. — Also *n.* — *ns.* **oligoclase** (*ol'i-gō-klās, -klāz*; Gr. *klāsis*, cleavage, because thought to have a less perfect cleavage than albite) a soda-lime triclinic feldspar; **oligocythaemia** (*ol-i-gō-sī-thē'mi-ə*; Gr. *kytos*, a vessel, *haima*, blood) a defect of red cells in the blood. — *adjs.* **oligom'erous** (Gr. *meros*, a part) having few parts: having fewer members than the other whorls of a flower; **oligopolist'ic**. — *ns.* **oligopoly** (*ol-i-gop'o-li*; Gr. *pōleein*, to sell) a situation in which there are few sellers, and a small number of competitive firms control the market — opp. to **oligopsony** (*ol-i-gop'sə-ni*; Gr. *opsōnia*, purchase of food) a situation in which there are few buyers, each competitive buyer influencing the market. — *adjs.* **oligopsonist'ic; oligotrophic** (*-trof'*; Gr. *trophē*, nourishment) (of a lake) having steep, rocky shores and scanty littoral vegetation, lacking in nutrients but rich in oxygen at all levels.   [Gr. *oligos*, little, few.]

olio *ō'li-ō*, *n.* a savoury dish of different sorts of meat and vegetables: a mixture: a medley: a miscellany: a variety entertainment: — *pl.* **o'lios**.   [Sp. *olla* — L. *ōlla*, a pot; cf. **olla**.]

oliphant *ol'i-fənt*, *n.* an obsolete form of **elephant**: an ancient ivory hunting-horn.

olitory *ol'i-tə-ri*, *adj.* pertaining to kitchen vegetables. — *n.* a kitchen-garden: a pot-herb.   [L. (*h*)*olitor*, gardener — (*h*)*olus*, (*h*)*oleris*, a pot-herb, vegetable.]

olive *ol'iv*, *n.* a tree (*Olea europaea*) cultivated round the Mediterranean for its oily fruit: extended to many more or less similar trees: the fruit of the olive-tree: peace, of which the olive was the emblem: a colour like the unripe olive: a person of olive-coloured complexion: an olive-shaped or oval object of various kinds: a gasteropod mollusc (Oliva) of warm seas with olive-shaped shell: a small rolled piece of seasoned meat (usu. in *pl.*), esp. as *beef olives*. — *adjs.* **oliva'-ceous** olive-coloured: olive-green; **ol'ivary** olive-shaped. — *ns.* **olivenite** (*ō-liv'ə-nīt*, or *ol'iv-*) a mineral, hydrated copper arsenate, often olive-coloured; **ol'ivet** an olive-shaped button: an oval mock-pearl used in trade with primitive peoples in Africa; **olivine** (*ol'iv-ēn*) an orthorhombic rock-forming mineral, silicate of iron and magnesium, often olive-green, often altered to serpentine. — **o'live-back** a North American forest thrush (*Hylocichla ustulata*); **olive branch** a symbol of peace: something which shows a desire for peace or reconciliation: a child (Ps. cxxviii. 3; *Pr. Bk.*); **olive drab** the olive green of American uniforms; **olive green** a dull dark yellowish green; **ol'ive-oil** oil pressed from the fruit of the olive; **ol'ive-shell** the shell of the mollusc Oliva; **ol'ive-yard** a piece of ground on which olives are grown; **ol'ivine-rock** dunite.   [Fr., — L. *olīva*.]

Oliver¹ *ol'i-vər*, *n.* the comrade-in-arms of Roland (q.v.).

Oliver². See **Bath**.

oliver *ol'i-vər*, *n.* a forge-hammer worked by foot.   [Origin unknown.]

Oliverian *ol-i-vē'ri-ən*, *n.* an adherent of the Protector, *Oliver* Cromwell (1599–1658).

Olivetan *ol-iv-ē'tən*, *n.* one of an order of Benedictine monks founded in 1313, the original house at Monte *Oliveto*, near Siena.

olla (L.) *ol'a*, *ōl'a*, (Sp.) *ōl'yä*, *n.* jar or urn: an olio. — **olla-podrida** (*ōl'yä-pō-drē'dä*; Sp., rotten pot) a Spanish mixed stew or hash of meat and vegetables: any incongruous mixture or miscellaneous collection.   [L.

ōlla and Sp. *olla*, pot, Sp. *podrida* — L. *putrida* (fem.) — *puter, putris*, rotten.]

ollav, ollamh *ol'äv*, *n.* a doctor or master among the ancient Irish.   [Ir. *ollamh*.]

olm *olm, ōlm, n.* a European, blind, cave-dwelling, eel-like salamander (*Proteus anguinus*).   [Ger.]

-ology. The combining element is properly **-logy** (q.v.). — *n.* **ology** (*ol'ə-ji*) a science whose name ends in -*ology*: any science.

oloroso *ol-ə-rō'sō, -zō, ōl-, n.* a golden-coloured medium-sweet sherry: — *pl.* **oloro'sos**.   [Sp., fragrant.]

olpe *ol'pē*, *n.* a Greek jug.   [Gr. *olpē*.]

olykoek, olycook *ol'i-kōōk*, (*U.S.*) *n.* a kind of doughnut.   [Du. *oliekoek*, lit. oil-cake.]

Olympus *ol-im'pəs*, *n.* the name of several mountains, esp. of one in Thessaly, abode of the greater Greek gods: heaven. — *ns.* **Olym'pia** a district in Elis, also the city of Pisa in it, where the Olympic games in honour of Olympian Zeus were celebrated; **Olym'piad** in ancient Greece, a period of four years, being the interval from one celebration of the Olympic games to another, used in reckoning time (the traditional date of the first Olympiad is 776 B.C.): a celebration of the Olympic games: a celebration of the modern Olympic games: (sometimes without *cap.*) an international contest in bridge or other mental exercise; **Olym'pian** a dweller on Olympus, any of the greater gods, esp. Zeus: a godlike person: a competitor in the Olympic games. — *adj.* of Olympus: godlike: of Olympia (now *rare*). — *adj.* **Olym'pic** of Olympia: of Olympus (now *rare*): of the Olympic games. — *n.pl.* **Olym'pics** the Olympic games, esp. those of modern times: (sometimes without *cap.*) an international contest in some mental exercise such as chess. — **Olympic games** the ancient games celebrated every four years at Olympia: quadrennial international athletic contests held at various centres since 1896; **Olympic torch** since 1936, a lighted torch brought from Olympia, Greece, to kindle the **Olympic flame**, which burns throughout the Olympic games; **Winter Olympics** international contests in skiing, skating, and other winter sports, held in the same years as the Olympics.   [Gr. *Olympos*.]

om *ōm, om, n.* a sacred syllable intoned as part of Hindu devotion and contemplation, symbolising the Vedic scriptures, the three worlds (earth, atmosphere and air), and the Absolute. — Also with *cap*(*s*).   [Sanskrit.]

-oma *-ō-mə, n. suff.* a tumour, abnormal growth, etc., as *carcinoma, angioma, glioma*, etc.: — *pl.* **-ō'mas**, or **-ō'mata**.   [Gr., ending of nouns formed from verbs with infinitive *-oun*.]

omadhaun *om'ə-dön, n.* a fool.   [Ir. *amadan*.]

omasum *ō-mā'səm, n.* a ruminant's third stomach, the psalterium or manyplies: — *pl.* **omā'sa**. — *adj.* **omā'sal**.   [L. *omāsum*, ox tripe; a Gallic word.]

ombre *om'bər, -brä, um'bər, n.* a game played with a pack of forty cards, usually by three persons, one against the others: the solo player.   [Sp. *hombre* — L. *homō, -inis*, a man.]

ombré *om'brä, adj.* (of a fabric, etc.) with colours or tones shading into each other to give a shaded or striped effect.   [Fr., *pa.p.* of *ombrer*, to shade.]

ombrella. See **umbrella**.

ombrometer *om-brom'i-tər, n.* a rain-gauge. — *n.* **om'brophil** (*-fil*), **-phile** (*-fīl*) a plant tolerant of much rain. — *adj.* **ombroph'ilous**. — *n.* **om'brophobe** a plant intolerant of much rain. — *adj.* **ombroph'obous**.   [Gr. *ombros*, a rain-storm, *metron*, measure, *phileein*, to love, *phobeein*, to fear.]

ombú, ombu *om-bōō', n.* a South American tree, a species of Phytolacca, that grows isolated in the pampas: — *pl.* **ombús', ombus'**.   [Sp., — Guaraní *umbú*.]

Ombudsman *om'bōōdz-man, -mən, n.* (also without *cap.*) (orig. in Sweden and Denmark) a 'grievance man', an official who is appointed to investigate complaints against the Administration: in Britain officially 'Parliamentary Commissioner for Administration': (often without *cap*.) any official with a similar function: — *pl*. **-men.** [Sw.]

-ome *-ōm, n. suff.* a mass, as in *rhizome, biome*. [Gr. *-ōma*.]

omega *ō′mig-ə, U.S. -mēg′, n*. the last letter of the Greek alphabet — long o (Ω, ω): the conclusion: as a numeral ω′ = 800, ‚ω = 800000. [Late Gr. *ō mega*, great O; opposed to omicron; the earlier Gr. name of the letter was *ō*.]

omelet, omelette *om′lit, -let, n*. a pancake made of eggs, beaten up, and fried in a pan (with or without cheese, herbs, ham, jam, or other addition). [Fr. *omelette*, earlier *amelette*, apparently by change of suffix and metathesis from *alemelle* (*l'alemelle* for *la lemelle*), a thin plate — L. *lāmella, lāmina*, a thin plate.]

omen *ō′mən, n*. a sign of some future event, either good or evil: threatening or prognosticating character: an event prognosticated (*Shak*.). — *v.t.* to portend. — *adj*. **o′mened** affording or attended by omens, esp. in composition, as *ill-omened*. [L. *ōmen, -inis*.]

omentum *ō-men′təm, n*. a fold of peritoneum proceeding from one of the abdominal viscera to another: — *pl*. **omen′ta.** — *adj*. **omen′tal.** — **great omentum** the epiploön. [L. *ōmentum*.]

omer *ō′mər, n*. a Hebrew dry measure containing about 2¼ litres, 1/10 ephah. [Heb. *'ōmer*.]

omertà, omerta *om-er-ta′, n*. the Mafia code of honour requiring silence about criminal activities and stressing the disgrace of informing: a criminal conspiracy of silence. [It., dial. form of *umiltà*, humility.]

omicron *ō-mī′krən, ōm′i-, om′, n*. the fifteenth letter of the Greek alphabet — short o (O, o): as a numeral o′ = 70, ‚o = 70000. [Late Gr. *o mīcron*, little O; opposed to omega; the earlier Greek name of the letter was *ou*.]

ominous *om′in-əs, adj*. pertaining to, or containing, an omen: portending evil: inauspicious. — *adv*. **om′inously.** — *n*. **om′inousness.** [See omen.]

omit *ō-mit′, v.t.* to leave out: to fail (to): to fail to use, perform: to disregard (*Shak*.): to leave off, let go (*Shak*.): — *pr.p.* **omitt′ing;** *pa.t.* and *pa.p.* **omitt′ed.** — *adj*. **omiss′ible** that may be omitted. — *n*. **omission** (*-mish′n*) the act of omitting: a thing omitted. — *adj*. **omiss′ive** omitting, of the nature of omission. — *ns*. **omitt′ance** (*Shak*.) omission; **omitt′er.** [L. *omittĕre, omissum* — *ob-*, in front, *mittĕre, missum*, to send.]

omlah *om′lä, n*. a staff of officials in India. [Ar. *'umalā*.]

ommateum *om-ə-tē′əm, n*. a compound eye: — *pl*. **ommate′a.** — *ns*. **ommatid′ium** a simple element of a compound eye: — *pl*. **ommatid′ia; ommatophore** (*-at′ō-fōr, -för*) an eye-stalk, as in snails. [Gr. *omma, -atos*, an eye.]

omneity *om-nē′i-ti*, **omniety** *om-nī′i-ti, ns*. allness, the condition of being all. [L. *omnis*, all.]

omni- *om-ni-*, in composition, all. — *n.pl*. **omniana** (*-ä′nə, -ā′nə*) -ana about all sorts of things. — *n*. **omnibenev′olence** universal benevolence. — *adj*. **omnibenev′-olent.** — *n*. **omnicom′petence** competence in all matters. — *adjs*. **omnicom′petent; omnidirec′tional** acting in all directions; **omnifa′rious** of all kinds; **omnif′erous** bearing or producing all kinds; **omnif′ic** all-creating; **om′ni-form** of, or capable of, every form. — *n*. **omniform′ity.** — *v.t.* **om′nify** (*rare*) to make universal. — *adj*. **omnigenous** (*-nij′i-nəs*) of all kinds. — *n*. **omnipar′ity** general equality. — *adjs*. **omnip′arous** producing all things; **omnipā′tient** enduring all things. — *ns*. **omnip′otence, omnip′otency** unlimited power. — *adj*. **omnip′otent** all-powerful. — *adv*. **omnip′otently.** — *n*. **omnipres′ence** the quality of being present everywhere at the same time. — *adj*. **omnipres′ent.** — *n*. **omniscience** (*om-nis′i-əns, -nish′əns, -yəns*) knowledge of all things. — *adj*. **omnisc′ient** all-knowing. — *adv*. **omnisc′iently.** — *ns*. **om′nivore; omniv′ory.** — *adj*. **omniv′orous** all-devouring: feeding on both animal and vegetable food (*zool*.). [L. *omnis*, all.]

omnibus *om′ni-bəs, n*. a large road-vehicle carrying a considerable number of passengers of the general public, or hotel guests (shortened form **bus**): an omnibus box: an omnibus book: a waiter's or waitress's assistant: — *pl*. **om′nibuses.** — *adj*. widely comprehensive: of miscellaneous contents. — **omnibus book** a book containing reprints of several works or items, usually by a single author, or on a single subject, or of the same type; **omnibus box** a theatre box with room for many persons; **omnibus clause** one that covers many different cases; **omnibus edition** (*TV* and *radio*) a programme comprising or edited from all the preceding week's editions of a particular series; **omnibus train** one that stops at every station. [Lit. for all, dative pl. of L. *omnis*.]

omnicompetence . . . omnipotence . . . omniscience. See **omni.**

omnium *om′ni-əm, n*. a Stock Exchange term for the aggregate value of the different stocks in which a loan is funded. — **om′nium-gath′erum** (*coll*.; *sham Latin*) a miscellaneous collection. [L., of all; gen. pl. of *omnis*, all.]

omnivore, omnivorous. See **omni-.**

omohyoid *ō-mō-hī′oid, adj*. pertaining to shoulder-blade and hyoid. — *n*. the muscle joining these. [Gr. *ōmos*, shoulder.]

omophagia *ō-mō-fāj′yə, -i-ə, n*. the eating of raw flesh, esp. as a religious observance. — *ns*. **omophagy** (*ō-mof′ə-ji*). — *adjs*. **omophagic** (*-faj′ik*), **omophagous** (*-mof′ə-gəs*). [Gr. *ōmophagiā* — *ōmos*, raw, *phagein*, to eat.]

omophorion *ō-mō-fō′ri-on, -för′, n*. an Eastern bishop's vestment like the pallium. [Gr. *ōmophŏrion* — *ōmos*, shoulder, *pherein*, to carry.]

omoplate *ō′mō-plāt, n*. the shoulder-blade or scapula. — *n*. **omoplatoscopy** (*-plə-tos′ko-pi*) divination by observing the cracks in a burning shoulder-blade. [Gr. *ōmoplatē* — *ōmos*, shoulder, *platē*, blade, *skopeein*, to look.]

omphacite *om′fə-sīt, n*. a grass-green pyroxene. [Gr. *omphax, -akos*, an unripe grape.]

omphalos *om′fə-los, n*. the navel: a boss: a stone at Delphi held to mark the centre of the world: a centre. — *adjs*. **omphalic** (*-fal′ik*); **om′phaloid** navel-like. — *n*. **om′phalomancy** divination of the number of future children from the knots in the navel-string. [Gr. *omphalos*, navel.]

omrah *om′rä, n*. a Muslim lord. [Hindi *umrā*, orig. pl. of Ar. *amīr*.]

on *on, prep*. in contact with the upper, supporting, outer, or presented surface of: to a position in contact with such a surface of: in or to a position or state of being supported by: having for basis, principle, or condition: subject to: in a condition or process of: towards or to: directed towards: in the direction of: against: applied to: with action applied to: with inclination towards: close to, beside: exactly or very nearly at: at the time, date, or occasion of: very little short of: just after: concerning, about: with respect to: by (in oaths and adjurations): at the risk of: assigned to: in addition to: in (*obs*.): (of gaining, taking) from (*Shak., Milt*.): of (*obs*. or *dial*.): (of marriage) to (*Scot*.): (of waiting) for (*Scot*.): against, as *one on one* (*U.S*.): at the expense of, to the disadvantage of (*coll*.). — *adv*. in or into a position on something: towards something: in advance: on the way to being drunk (*slang*): forward: in continuance: in, or into, or allowing connection, supply, activity, operation, or validity: in progress: on the stage, the table, the fire, the programme, the menu, or anything else: not off. — *interj*. forward!, proceed! — *adj*. on the side on which the batsman stands (normally the bowler's right) (*cricket*): in a condition expressed by the adverb on: agreed upon: willing to participate. — *n*. the on side. — *v.i.* to go on (*coll*.): (with *with*) to put on (*coll*.). — *adjs*. **on′-board′, on′board** in, installed inside or carried aboard a vehicle or craft; **oncome** (*on′kum, -kəm; Scot*.) a coming on: a sudden fall of rain or snow: the beginning of an attack by an insidious disease; **on′coming** an approach. — *adj*. advancing:

approaching. — **on'cost** overhead expenses: an oncost-man. — *adj.* paid by time: causing oncost. — **on'cost-man** a mine-worker paid by the day; **on'ding** (*Scot.*) onset, esp. a sudden fall of rain or snow; **on'-drive** (*cricket*) a drive to the on side. — Also *v.i.* and *v.t.* — **on'fall** an attack, onslaught, esp. (*Scot.*) of illness: a fall of rain or snow (*Scot.*); **on'flow** a flowing on: an onward flow; **on'going** a going on: a course of conduct: an event: (in *pl.*) proceedings, behaviour, esp. misbe-haviour. — *adj.* (**on'-going**) currently in progress: continuing: which will not stop. — *adj.* **on'-job'** com-bined with or in the course of normal work duties and conditions. — *v.t.* **on'-lend** to lend (money which has already been borrowed from another company, etc.). — **on'-licence** a licence to sell alcoholic liquors for consumption on the premises. — *adj.* **on'-line** (*comput.*) attached to, and under the direct control of, the central processing unit: got from or by means of on-line equipment: taking place as part of, or pertaining to, a continuous (esp. production) process. — **on'looker** a looker on, observer. — *adjs.* **on'looking; on'-off'** (of a switch, etc.) which can be set to one of only two positions, either *on* or *off*. — **on'rush** a rushing onward; **on'set** a violent attack: an assault: a storming: the beginning, outset. — *ns.* **on'setter** (*arch.*) an assailant: **on'setting** incitement. — *adj.* **onshore** (*on'shōr, -shör*) towards the land. — *adv.* **on'-shore**. — *adj.* and *adv.* **on'side** not offside. — *n.* (*cricket*) see **on** *adj.* — *adj.* and *adv.* **on'-stage** on a part of the stage visible to the audience. — **onstead** (*on'sted; Scot.*) a farmstead: a farmhouse with its offices: the offices alone. — *adj.* and *adv.* **on'-stream** of an industrial plant, etc., in, or going into, operation or production: passing through or along a pipe, system, etc. (also *fig.*). — *prep.* **onto** see **on to:** to the whole of (*math.*). — *adj.* (*math.*) describing a mapping of one set to a second set, involving every element of the latter. — *adj.* **onward** (*on'wərd*) going on: advancing: advanced. — *adv.* (also **on'wards**) towards a place or time in advance or in front: forward: in continuation of forward movement. — *adv.* **on'-wardly** (*rare*). — **on to** to a place or position on (also **on'to**): forward to: aware of, cognisant of (*coll.*); **on and off** same as **off and on; on and on (and on)** used in phrases containing the particle *on* to emphasise duration, distance, etc.; **on stream** same as **on-stream.** [O.E. *on;* Du. *aan;* O N. *ā;* Ger. *an;* Gr. *ana.*]

on- on-, a dial. form of the prefix **un-**.

onager *on'ə-jər, n.* the wild ass of Central Asia: an ancient military engine for throwing great stones. [L., — Gr. *onagros — onos,* an ass, *agrios,* wild — *agros,* a field.]

Onagra *on'ə-grə,* (*bot.*) *n.* an old name for Oenothera, giving name to the family **Onagrā'ceae.** — *adj.* **onagrā'-ceous.** [Gr. *onagrā,* the plant also known as *oinothēras;* see **Oenothera.**]

onanism *ō'nən-izm, n.* coitus interruptus: masturbation. — *n.* **o'nanist.** — *adj.* **onanist'ic.** [See Gen. xxxviii. 9.]

once *wuns, adv.* a single time: on one occasion: at a former time: at some time in the future (*rare*): firstly (*obs.*): in short (*obs.*): at any time. — *n.* one time. — *adj.* former. — *conj.* when once: as soon as. — *n.* **onc'er** one who goes to church once on Sunday (*eccles. slang*): a £1 note (*slang*). — *adjs.* **once-accent'ed** marked with one accent — applied to the octave beginning with middle C; **once'-errand** see **errand; once'-for-all'** done, etc., once and for all. — *n.* **once-o'ver** a single compre-hensive survey. — **at once** without delay: alike: at the same time; **for once** on one occasion only; **once and again** more than once: now and then; **once (and) for all** once only and not again; **once in a way, while** occasionally: rarely; **once or twice** a few times; **once upon a time** at a certain time in the past — the usual formula for beginning a fairy-tale. [O.E. *ānes,* orig. gen. of *ān,* one, used as adv.]

onchocerciasis *ong-kō-sər-kī'-ə-sis, n.* a disease of man,

also known as river blindness, common in tropical regions of America and Africa, caused by infestation by a filarial worm (*Onchocerca volvulus*) which is transmitted by various species of black fly, and char-acterised by subcutaneous nodules and very often blindness. [Gr. *onkos,* a hook, *kerkos,* a tail.]

Oncidium *on-sid'i-əm, n.* a tropical American genus of orchids: (without *cap.*) an orchid of this genus. [Gr. *onkos,* a hook.]

oncology *ong-kol'ə-ji, n.* the study of tumours. — *ns.* **oncogen** (*-ko-jen'*) an agent causing oncogenesis; **onco-gene** (*-ko-jēn'*) a type of gene involved in the onset and development of cancer; **oncogen'esis** the formation of cancerous tumours; **oncogenet'icist** one who studies oncogenes. — *adj.* **oncogenic** (*-kō-jen'*) causing tu-mours. — *ns.* **oncol'ogist; oncom'eter** an instrument for measuring variations in bulk of bodily organs; **on'cor-navirus** an oncogenic RNA virus; **oncot'omy** incision into a tumour. [Gr. *onkos,* bulk, mass, tumour.]

oncome, oncoming. See **on.**

Oncorhynchus *ong-kō-ringk'əs, n.* a North Pacific genus of salmon. [Gr. *onkos,* hook, *rhynchos,* beak.]

oncost, oncostman. See **on.**

oncus. See **onkus.**

ondatra *on-dat'rə, n.* the musquash. [Huron Indian.]

ondine. Same as **undine.**

onding. See **on.**

on-dit *ō-dē, n.* rumour: hearsay: — *pl.* **on-dits** (*-dē, -dēz*). [Fr.]

one *wun, adj.* single: of unit number: undivided: the same: a certain: a single but not specified: first. — *n.* the number unity: a symbol representing it: an individual thing or person: a thing bearing or distinguished by the number one. — *pron.* somebody: anybody: I (*formal*). — *ns.* **one'ness** singleness: uniqueness: iden-tity: unity: homogeneity, sameness; **oner** (*wun'ər;* all meanings *coll.* or *slang*) a person or thing unique or outstanding in any way: an expert: a single, uninter-rupted action: a heavy blow: a heavy blow: a big lie. — Also **one'-er, wunn'er.** — *pron.* **oneself', one's self** the emphatic and reflexive form of **one.** — **one'=and-thir'ty** an old card-game like vingt-un, in which it was sought to make the pips add up to 31 and no more. — *adjs.* **one'-day'** (of an event, etc.) lasting for one day; **one'-eyed** having but one eye; **one'fold** simple, single-minded; **one'-hand'ed** with, by, or for, one hand; **one'-horse** drawn by a single horse: petty, mean, inferior; **one'-ide'a'd** entirely possessed by one idea; **onc'-legged.** — **one'-lin'er** (*coll.*) a short pithy remark: a wisecrack, quip: a joke delivered in one sentence. — *adj.* **one'-man** of, for, or done by, one man. — *n.* **one-nighter** see **one night stand.** — *adj.* **one'-off'** made, intended, etc. for one occasion only. — Also *n.* — *adjs.* **one'-one'** one-to-one; **one'-piece** made in one piece; **one'-shot** (intended to be) done, used, etc. on only one occasion or for one particular purpose or project: one-off: not part of a serial. — Also *n.* — *adj.* **one'-sid'ed** limited to one side: partial: developed on one side only: turned to one side. — *adv.* **one'-sid'edly.** — **one'-sid'edness; one'-step** a dance of U.S. origin danced to quick march time. — *v.i.* to dance a one-step. — *adjs.* **one'-time** former, erstwhile; **one'-to-one'** cor-responding each one uniquely to one; **one'-track'** incapable of dealing with more than one idea or activity at a time: obsessed with one idea to the exclusion of others. — **one'-two'** (*coll.*) in boxing, etc., a blow with one fist followed by a blow with the other (also *fig.*): in football, a movement in which a player passes the ball to another player then runs forward to receive the ball which is immediately passed back to him. — **one-up'manship** (*facet.; Stephen Potter*) the art of being one up, i.e. scoring or maintaining an advan-tage over someone. — *adj.* **one'-way** proceeding, or permitting, or set apart for traffic, in one direction only. — **a, the, one** a person special or remarkable in some way (*coll.*); **a one for** an enthusiast; **all one** just the same: of no consequence; **at one** of one mind:

reconciled (with); **be made one** (*arch.*) to get married; **be one up on** to score an advantage over (another); **(all) in one** combined: as one unit, object, etc.; **just one of those things** an unfortunate happening that must be accepted; **one and all** everyone without exception; **one another** see **another**; **one-armed bandit** a fruit machine (q.v.); **one by one** singly in order; **one-horse race** (*fig.*) a race, competition, etc., in which one particular competitor or participant is certain to win; **one-man band** a musician who carries and plays many instruments simultaneously: (also **one-man show**) an organisation, activity, etc., run very much by one person who refuses the help of others (*fig.*); **one-man show** a show performed by one man: a one-man band (*fig.*) or the person running it; **one-night stand** (also **one= night'er**) a performance or performances, or anything similar, given on one single evening in one place by one or more people who then travel on to another place: an amorous relationship lasting only one night (*coll.*); **one or two** a few; **one-parent family** a family in which, due to death, divorce, etc., the children are looked after by only one parent; **one-way glass, mirror** glass which can be looked through from one side but which appears from the other side to be a mirror. [O.E. *ān*; O.N. *einn*, Ger. *ein*; L. *ūnus*; Gr. *oinē*, ace.]
oneiric *ō-nī'rik, adj.* belonging to dreams. — *n.* **oneirocrit'ic** an interpreter of dreams. — *adj.* **oneirocrit'ical.** — *ns.* **oneirocrit'icism; oneirodynia** (*-ō-din'i-ə*) troubled sleep: nightmare; **oneirology** (*on-ī-rol'ə-ji*) the study of dreams; **oneir'omancer; oneir'omancy** divination by dreams; **oneiros'copist** an interpreter of dreams; **oneiros'copy.** — Also **oni'ric,** etc. [Gr. *oneiros,* a dream, *kritikos,* judging, *odynē,* pain, *logos,* discourse, *manteiā,* divination, *skopiā,* watching.]
onely. A Spenserian spelling of **only.**
onerous *on'ə-rəs, ō'nər-əs, adj.* burdensome: oppressive. — *adv.* **on'erously.** — *n.* **on'erousness.** [L. *onerōsus* — *onus,* a burden.]
oneyre, oneyer *wun'yər, n.* (1 *Hen. IV* II, i) probably the same as **oner.** [See **one.**]
onfall ... to ... **ongoing.** See **on.**
onion *un'yən, n.* a pungent edible bulb of the lily family: the plant yielding it (*Allium cepa*): applied also to some kindred species: a flaming rocket used against aircraft: the head (*slang*). — *v.t.* to apply an onion to: to produce by means of an onion. — *adj.* **on'iony.** — **onion dome** a bulb-shaped dome having a sharp point, characteristic of Eastern Orthodox, esp. Russian, church architecture. — *adj.* **on'ion-eyed** (*Shak.*) having the eyes full of tears. — **on'ion-skin** a very thin variety of paper. — **know one's onions** to know one's subject or one's job well (*coll.*); **off one's onion** (*slang*) off one's head. [Fr. *oignon* — L. *ūniō, -ōnis,* union, a large pearl, an onion; see **union**[2].]
oniric, etc. See **oneiric.**
Oniscus *on-is'kəs, n.* a genus of woodlice. — *adj.* **onis'coid** of the family of Oniscus: like a woodlouse. [Gr. *oniskos,* dim. of *onos,* an ass.]
onkus, oncus *ong'kəs,* (*Austr. coll.*) *adj.* disordered: bad.
on-lend ... to ... **onlooking.** See under **on.**
only *ōn'li, adj.* single in number: without others of the kind: without others worthy to be counted. — *adv.* not more, other, or otherwise than: alone: merely: barely: just: pre-eminently (*obs.*): singly (*rare*). — *conj.* but: except that. — *prep.* (*dial.*) except. — **if only** (I, he, etc.) wish (wished, etc.) ardently that; **only too** very, extremely. [O.E. *ānlic* (adj.) — *ān,* one, *-līc,* like.]
onocentaur *on-ō-sen'tör, n.* a kind of centaur, half-man, half-ass. [Gr. *onos,* ass.]
onomastic *on-ə-mas'tik, adj.* pertaining to a name, esp. pertaining to the signature to a paper written in another hand. — *n.* **onomas'ticon** a dictionary of proper names. — *n. sing.* **onomas'tics** the study of the history of proper names. [Gr. *onomastikos, -on* — *onoma,* a name.]
onomatopoeia *on-ō-mat-ō-pē'ə, n.* the formation of a word in imitation of the sound of the thing meant: a word

so formed: the use of words whose sounds help to suggest the meaning (*rhet.*). — Also **onomatopoesis** (*-pō-ē'sis*) or **onomatopoiesis** (*-poi-ē'sis*). — *adjs.* **onomatopoeic** (*-pē'ik*), **onomatopoetic** (*-pō-et'ik*). [Gr. *onomatopoiiā, -poiēsis — onoma, -atos,* a name, *poieein,* to make.]
onrush ... to ... **onside.** See under **on.**
onslaught *on'slöt, n.* an attack or onset: assault. [Prob. Du. *aanslag* or Ger. *Anschlag,* refashioned as Eng.]
onst *wunst, adv.* a *dial.* form of **once.**
onstead ... to ... **onto.** See under **on.**
ontogenesis *on-tō-jen'i-sis, n.* the history of the individual development of an organised being, as distinguished from **phylogenesis.** — Also **ontogeny** (*on-toj'i-ni*). — *adjs.* **ontogenet'ic, ontogen'ic.** — *advs.* **ontogenet'ically, -gen'ically.** [Gr. *ōn, ontos,* pr.p. of *einai,* to be, *genesis,* generation.]
ontology *on-tol'ə-ji, n.* the science that treats of the principles of pure being: that part of metaphysics which treats of the nature and essence of things. — *adjs.* **ontologic** (*-tə-loj'ik*), **-al.** — *adv.* **ontolog'ically.** — *n.* **ontol'ogist.** [Gr. *ōn, ontos,* pr.p. of *einai,* to be, *logos,* discourse.]
onus *ō'nəs, n.* burden: responsibility. — **onus probandi** (*ō'nəs prō-ban'dī, o'nŏŏs pro-ban'dē*) the burden of proving. [L. *ŏnus, -eris.*]
onward, etc. See under **on.**
onymous *on'i-məs, adj.* bearing the author's name. [**anonymous.**]
onyx *on'iks, n.* an agate formed of alternate flat layers of chalcedony, white or yellow and black, brown or red, used for making cameos (*min.*): onychite, onyx-marble: a fingernail-like opacity in the cornea of the eye. — *ns.* **onycha** (*on'i-kə*) an ingredient in ancient Jewish incense: the nail-like operculum of a mollusc; **onych'ia** inflammation of the nail-bed; **on'ychite** onyx-marble; **onychī'tis** inflammation of the soft parts about the nail; **onych'ium** a pulvillus in insects; **onychocrypto'sis** ingrowing toenail; **on'ychomancy** divination by the fingernails; **onychophagist** (*-kof'ə-jist*) a nail-biter; **onychoph'agy.** — *n.pl.* **Onychoph'ora** Prototracheata, the class to which Peripatus belongs. — **on'yx-mar'ble** a banded travertine or stalagmite, also called oriental alabaster. [Gr. *onyx, onychos,* nail, claw, onyx.]
oo[1], **oo'** *ōō,* Scots forms of **wool.**
oo[2] *ōō,* a Scots form of **we.** — **oor** our.
oo- *ō'ə-,* in composition, egg. — *n.* **oocyte** (*ō'ə-sīt;* see **cyte**) an ovum before it matures and begins to divide. — *adj.* **oog'amous.** — *ns.* **oogamy** (*ō-og'ə-mi;* Gr. *gamos,* marriage) union of unlike gametes; **oogenesis** (*ō-ə-jen'i-sis;* Gr. *genesis,* formation) the genesis and development of the ovum — also **oogeny** (*ō-oj'i-ni*). — *adj.* **oogenet'ic.** — *n.* **oogonium** (*ō-ə-gō'ni-əm;* Gr. *gonos,* offspring) the female reproductive organ in seaweeds and fungi: — *pl.* **oogo'nia.** — *adj.* **oogo'nial.** — *n.* **oolite** (*ō'ə-līt;* Gr. *lithos,* a stone; *geol.*) a kind of limestone composed of grains like the eggs or roe of a fish: (with *cap.*) stratigraphically the upper part of the Jurassic in Britain, consisting largely of oolites. — *adj.* **oolitic** (*ō-ə-lit'ik*). — *ns.* **ool'ogist; oology** (*ō-ol'ə-ji;* Gr. *logos,* discourse) the science or study of birds' eggs; **o'ophyte** (*ō'ə-fīt;* Gr. *phyton,* plant) in ferns and mosses, the gametophyte; **oosphere** (*ō'ə-sfēr;* Gr. *sphaira,* sphere) an unfertilised ovum; **oospore** (*ō'ə-spōr, -spör;* Gr. *sporos,* seed) a zygote, esp. a resting zygote. [Gr. *oion,* egg.]
oobit. See **woubit.**
oocyte. See **oo-.**
oodles *ōō'dlz, n. sing.* or *pl.* abundance. — Also **ood'lins.** [Perh. **huddle.**]
oof *ōōf,* (*slang*) *n.* money — orig. **oof'tish.** [Yiddish — Ger. *auf (dem) Tische,* on the table.]
oogamous ... to ... **oogonial.** See **oo-.**
ooh *ōō, interj.* expressing pleasure, surprise, etc. — Also *n.* and *v.i.* [Imit.]
ooidal *ō-oi'dl, adj.* egg-shaped. [Gr. *ōioeidēs — ōion* and *eidos,* form.]

oolakan $\overline{oo}'l\partial$-k∂n. Same as **eulachon**.

oolite ... to ... oologist. See **oo-**.

oolong, oulong $\overline{oo}'long$, _n._ a variety of black tea with the flavour of green. [Chin. _wu-lung_, black dragon.]

oom $\overline{oo}m$, (_S. Afr._) _n._ uncle: used as term of respect for an elderly man. [Du.]

oomia(c)k, oomiac. Same as **umiak**.

oompah $\overline{oo}m'p\ddot{a}$, _n._ a conventional representation of the deep sound made by a large brass musical instrument such as a tuba. — Also _v.i._ and _v.t._

oomph $\overline{oo}mf$, $\overline{oo}mf$, (_slang_), _n._ vitality: enthusiasm: sex-appeal: personal magnetism. [Origin obscure.]

oon $\overline{oo}n$, _n._ a Scots form of **oven**.

oons $\overline{oo}nz$, (_arch._) _interj._ a minced oath, for God's _wounds_.

oont $\overline{oo}nt$, _n._ in India, a camel. [Hindi $\tilde{u}\underline{t}$.]

oop. See **oup**.

oophoron $\overline{o}$-of'∂r-on, _n._ (_zool._) an ovary. — _ns._ **oophorec'-tomy** (_surg._) removal of one or both ovaries, or of an ovarian tumour; **oophorec'tomise, -ize; oophori'tis** inflammation of the ovary. [Gr. _ōiophoros, -on_, egg-bearing.]

oophyte. See **oo-**.

oops $\overline{oo}ps$, _interj._ an exclamation drawing attention to, apologising for, etc., a mistake.

oor. See **oo²**.

oorial. Same as **urial**.

oorie. Same as **ourie**.

Oort cloud $\overline{oo}rt$ klowd, a cloud of frozen comet nuclei orbiting the solar system. [After the Dutch astronomer Jan Hendrik _Oort_ (born 1900).]

oose $\overline{oo}s$, **oosy** (both _Scot._). Same as **ooze², oozy**.

oosphere, oospore. See **oo-**.

ooze¹ $\overline{oo}z$, _n._ sap (_obs._): the liquor of a tan vat: gentle flow, as of water through sand or earth: slimy mud: a fine-grained, soft, deep-sea deposit, composed of shells and fragments of foraminifera, diatoms, and other organisms. — _v.i._ to flow gently: to percolate, as a liquid through pores or small openings: to leak. — _v.t._ to exude. — _adv._ **ooz'ily.** — _n._ **ooz'iness.** — _adj._ **ooz'y** resembling ooze: slimy: oozing. [Partly O.E. _wōs_, juice, partly O.E. _wāse_, mud.]

ooze² $\overline{oo}z$, (_Scot._) _n._ fluff: nap. — _adj._ **ooz'y.** [Prob. pl. of oo'.]

op _op._ Short for **operation** and (in **op art**, see below) **optical**: abbrev. for **opus**.

opacity, opacous. See under **opaque**.

opah $\overline{o}'p\partial$, _n._ the kingfish (_Lampris_), a large sea-fish with laterally flattened body, constituting a family of uncertain affinities. [West African origin.]

opal $\overline{o}'pl$, _n._ amorphous silica with some water, usually milky white with fine play of colour, in some varieties precious: opal-glass: the colouring of opal. — _adj._ of opal: like opal. — _adj._ **o'paled.** — _n._ **opalesc'ence** a milky iridescence. — _adj._ **opalesc'ent.** — _adj._ **o'paline** (-ēn, -īn) relating to, like, or of, opal. — _n._ opal-glass: a photographic print fixed on plate-glass. — _adj._ **o'palised, -z-** converted into opal: opalescent. — **o'pal-glass'** white or opalescent glass. [L. _opalus_; Gr. _opallios_, perh. — Sans. _upala_, gem.]

opaque $\overline{o}$-pāk', _adj._ shady: dark: dull: that cannot be seen through: impervious to light or to radiation of some particular kind: obscure, hard to understand (_fig._): impervious to sense: doltish. — _v.t._ to make opaque. — _n._ **opacity** ($\overline{o}$-pas'i-ti) opaqueness. — _adj._ **opacous** ($\overline{o}$-pā'k∂s). — _adv._ **opaque'ly.** — _n._ **opaque'ness** quality of being opaque: want of transparency. [L. _opācus_.]

op art _op ärt_, art using geometrical forms precisely executed and so arranged that movement of the observer's eye, or inability to focus, produces an illusion of movement in the painting. [_optical_.]

ope $\overline{o}p$, _adj._, (_poet._) _v.t._ and _v.i._ a short form of **open**.

opeidoscope _op-ī'd∂-skōp_, _n._ an instrument for illustrating sound by means of light. [Gr. _ops_ (found in the oblique cases), voice, _eidos_, form, _skopeein_, to look at.]

open $\overline{o}'pn$, _adj._ not shut: allowing passage out or in: exposing the interior: unobstructed: free: unenclosed: exposed: uncovered: liable: generally accessible: available: ready to receive or transact business with members of the public: willing to receive or accept (with _to_): public: free to be discussed: obvious: unconcealed: undisguised: unfolded, spread out, expanded: unrestricted: not restricted to any class of persons, as _open championship_: (of a town) without military defences: not finally decided, concluded, settled, or assigned: not dense in distribution or texture: widely spaced: loose: much interrupted by spaces or holes: showing a visible space between (_naut._): clear: unfrozen: not frosty: not hazy: free from trees: frank: unreserved: unstopped (_mus._): without use of valve, crook, or key: (of an organ pipe) not closed at the top: (of a vowel sound) low, with wide aperture for the breath: (of a consonant) without stopping of the breath stream: (of a syllable) ending with a vowel. — _v.t._ to make open: to make as an opening: to make an opening in: to clear: to expose to view: to expound: to declare open: to begin. — _v.i._ to become open: to have an opening, aperture, or passage: to serve as passage: to begin to appear: to begin: to give tongue: to speak out. — _n._ a clear space: public view: open market: an opening. — _adj._ **o'penable.** — _ns._ **o'pener; o'pening** the act of causing to be, or of becoming, open: an open place: an aperture: a gap: a street or road breaking the line of another: a beginning: a first stage: a preliminary statement of a case in court: the initial moves, or mode of beginning, in a game, etc.: an event at which a new exhibition, shop, display, etc., is first opened to the public: the two pages exposed together when a book is opened: an opportunity for action: a vacancy. — Also _adj._ — _adv._ **o'penly.** — _n._ **o'penness.** — **open access** public access to the shelves of a library; **open aestivation** aestivation without overlap or meeting of the edges of the perianth leaves. — _adjs._ **o'pen-air'** outdoor; **o'pen=and-shut'** simple, obvious, easily decided; **o'pen-armed'** cordially welcoming. — **open book** anything that can be read or interpreted without difficulty; **open borstal** a borstal run on the same lines as an open prison (q.v.); **Open Brethren** that section of the Plymouth Brethren whose members are allowed to associate fully with non-members; **open bundle** a vascular bundle with cambium; **o'pen-cast'** in mining, an excavation open overhead. — Also _adj._ and _adv._ — _adj._ **o'pen-chain'** (_chem._) with atoms linked together as a chain with loose ends. — **open circuit** an electrical circuit broken so that current cannot pass: in television, the customary system in which the showing is for general, not restricted, viewing; **open court** a court proceeding in public; **open day** a day on which an institution (esp. a school) is open to the public, usu. with organised exhibitions or events; **open diapason** one of the chief foundation stops of an organ; **open door** free and equal opportunity of trading for all: unrestricted admission or immigration. — _adjs._ **o'pen-door'; o'pen-end'(ed)** not closely defined, general and adaptable to suit various contingencies: (of question, debate, etc.) allowing free unguided answers or expressions of opinion: (of investment trust) offering shares in unlimited numbers, redeemable on demand: (**o'pen-end'ed**) without fixed limits; **o'pen-eyed** watchful (_Shak._): astonished: fully aware of what is involved; **o'pen-field** having the arable land in unenclosed strips held by different cultivators. — **open fire** an exposed fire on a domestic hearth. — _adj._ **o'pen-hand'ed** with an open hand: generous: liberal. — **o'pen-hand'edness; open harmony** chords not in close position. — _adj._ **o'pen-heart'ed** with an open heart: frank: generous. — **o'pen-heart'edness.** — _adj._ **o'pen-hearth** making use of, or having, a shallow hearth of reverberating type. — **open house** hospitality to all comers; **opening time** the time when bars, public houses, etc., can begin selling alcoholic drinks; **open letter** a letter addressed to one person but intended for public reading; **open market** a market in which buyers and sellers compete without restriction; **open marriage** a form of marriage which allows the partners social and sexual independence; **open mind** freedom from prejudice: readiness to receive and consider new ideas. — *adj.* **o′pen-mind′ed**. — **o′pen-mind′edness**. — *adj.* **o′pen-mouthed′** gaping: expectant: greedy: clamorous: surprised, astonished. — **open note** a note produced by an unstopped string, open pipe, or without a crook, etc.: a printed or written note without a solid black head — a semibreve or minim (*U.S.*); **open order** spaced-out formation for drill, etc. — *adj.* **o′pen-plan′** having few, or no, internal walls, partitions, etc. (see also **open-plan house** below). — **open prison** a prison without the usual close security, allowing prisoners considerably more freedom of movement than in conventional prisons; **open question** a matter undecided: a question formed so as to elicit a full response or an opinion rather than a yes or no answer; **open sandwich** one which has no bread, etc., on top; **open score** one with a separate stave for each part; **open sea** unenclosed sea, clear of headlands; **open season** a time of the year when one may kill certain game or fish (also *fig.*); **open secret** a matter known to many but not explicitly divulged; **open sesame** a spell or other means of making barriers fly open — from the story of Ali Baba and the Forty Thieves in the *Arabian Nights*; **open shop** a factory not confined to union labour; **open side** the part of the field between the scrum, etc., and the farther touch-line (*rugby*); **open skies** the open air; reciprocal freedom for aerial inspection of military establishments; **o′pen-stitch** (*Scot.* **o′pen-steek**) a kind of open-work stitching. — *adj.* **o′pen-top′** (*esp.* of a vehicle) without a roof or having an open top; **open town** one without troops or military installations, and hence, according to international law, immune from attack of any kind; **open university** (also with *caps.*) a British university (1971) having no fixed entry qualifications, whose teaching is carried out by correspondence and by radio and television; **open verdict** a verdict that a crime has been committed without specifying the criminal; **o′pen-work** any work showing openings through it. — *adj.* open-cast. — **open fire** to begin to shoot; **open-heart surgery** surgery performed on a heart which has been stopped and opened up while blood circulation is maintained by a heart-lung machine; **open out** to make or become more widely open: to expand: to disclose: to unpack: to develop: to bring into view: to open the throttle, accelerate; **open-plan house** one whose rooms run from front to back with windows on both faces; **open up** to open thoroughly or more thoroughly: to lay open: to disclose: to make available for traffic, colonisation, or the like: to accelerate: to begin firing; **with open arms** cordially. [O.E. *open*; cf. Du. *open*, O.N. *opinn*, Ger. *offen*; prob. related to **up**.]

opera[1] *op′ə-rə*, *n.* musical drama: a company performing opera: an opera-house. — *adj.* used in or for an opera. — *adj.* **operatic** (*-at′ik*) pertaining to or resembling opera: (*loosely*) histrionic. — *adv.* **operat′ically**. — **opera** (Fr. **opéra** *o-pā-ra*) **bouffe** (*bōof*) funny or farcical opera; **opera buffa** (*bōof′ə, op′ā-ra bōof′a*; It.) comic opera, esp. of the 18th century — opp. to *opera seria*; **opéra comique** (*kom-ēk*) (Fr.) opera with some spoken dialogue — in the 18th century, opera having subjects less lofty than those of *grand opéra* (Eng. grand opera), in the 19th century, having no restriction as to subject (either comic or tragic); **opera seria** (*sē′ri-ə, se′rya*; It.) serious opera; **comic opera** opéra comique: opera of an amusing nature: an absurd emotional situation; **grand opera** opera without dialogue, esp. if the subject is very dramatic or emotional; **light opera** a lively and tuneful opera: an operetta (q.v.); **soap opera** see **soap**. — See also **music-drama, musical, musical comedy.** — **op′era-cloak** an elegant cloak for evening wear, esp. in the auditorium of a theatre; **op′era-danc′er** one who dances in ballets introduced into operas; **op′era=glass(es)** a small binocular telescope for use in the theatre; **op′era-hat** a collapsible tall hat; **op′era-house** a theatre for opera; **op′era-sing′er**. [It., — L. *opera*; cf. **operate**.]

opera[2] *op′ə-rə*, *pl.* of **opus**.

operate *op′ə-rāt*, *v.i.* to work: to exert strength: to produce any effect: to exert moral power: to be in activity, act, carry on business: to take effect upon the human system (*med.*): to perform some surgical act upon the body with the hand or an instrument. — *v.t.* to effect, bring about, cause to occur: to work: to conduct, run, carry on. — *adj.* **op′erăble** admitting of a surgical operation: able to be operated: practicable. — *n.* **op′erand** something on which an operation is performed, e.g. a quantity in mathematics. — *adj.* **op′erant** operative: active: effective. — *n.* an operator. — *adj.* **op′erāting**. — *n.* **operā′tion** the act or process of operating: that which is done or carried out: agency: influence: a method of working: an action or series of movements: a surgical performance. — shortened to **op** esp. in military or surgical sense. — *adjs.* **operā′tional** relating to operations: ready for action; **operā′tions** relating to problems affecting operations, esp. military (as in *operations research*); **op′erătive** having the power of operating or acting: exerting force: producing effects: efficacious. — *n.* a workman in a factory: a labourer. — *adv.* **op′eratively**. — *ns.* **op′erativeness**; **op′erātor** one who, or that which, operates: one charged with the operation of a machine, instrument, or apparatus: one employed to connect calls, etc., at a telephone exchange: one who deals in stocks: the owner of a store, business, mine, etc. (*U.S.*): a symbol, signifying an operation to be performed (*math.*): a crooked or calculating person, a shark (*coll. esp. U.S.*). — **operant conditioning** (*psych.*) a learning procedure in which the subject's spontaneous response to a stimulus is reinforced if it is a desired response; **operating system** (*comput.*) a software system which controls a computer's operational processes; **operating table, theatre** one set apart for use in surgical operations; **operational, operations, research** research to discover how a weapon, tactic, or strategy can be altered to give better results: similar research to promote maximum efficiency in industrial spheres; **operative words** the words in a deed legally effecting the transaction (e.g. *devise and bequeath* in a will): (*loosely*; often in *sing.*) the most significant word or words. [L. *operārī, -ātus* — *opera*, work, closely connected with *opus, operis*, work.]

operculum *ō-pûr′kū-ləm, n.* a cover or lid (*bot.*): the plate over the entrance of a shell (*zool.*): the gill-cover of fishes: a coal-hole cover in a pavement: — *pl.* **oper′cula**. — *adjs.* **oper′cular** belonging to the operculum; **oper′-culate, -d** having an operculum. [L. *operculum* — *operīre*, to cover.]

opere citato *op′ə-rē sīt-ā′tō, op′er-e kit-ä′tō*, (L.) in the work cited: —abbrev. **op. cit.**

operetta *op-ə-ret′ə, n.* a short, light, rather trivial, musical drama: often esp. formerly, light opera (see **opera**[1]). — *n.* **operett′ist** a composer of operettas. [It., dim. of *opera*.]

operose *op′ə-rōs, adj.* laborious: tedious. — *adv.* **op′erosely.** — *ns.* **op′eroseness, operosity** (*-os′i-ti*). [L. *operōsus* — *opus, operis*, work.]

ophi(o)- *of-i(-ō)-, -o′-*, in composition, snake. — *ns.* **ophical′cite** a marble containing green serpentine; **oph′-icleide** (*-klīd*; Fr. *ophicléide* — Gr. *kleis, kleidos*, key) a keyed wind-instrument developed from the serpent, a bass or alto keybugle. — *n.pl.* **Ophid′ia** (Gr. *ophidion*, dim.) the snakes as an order or suborder of reptiles. — *n.* and *adj.* **ophid′ian.** — *ns.* **ophidiā′rium** a snake-house; **Ophiogloss′um** (Gr. *glōssa*, tongue) the adder's-tongue genus, giving name to the **Ophioglossā′ceae**, a family of eusporangiate ferns; **ophiol′ater** a snake-worshipper; **ophiol′atry** (Gr. *latreiā*, worship) snake-worship. — *adj.* **ophiol′atrous.** — *n.* **oph′iolite** serpentine (*obs.*): verd-antique. — *adjs.* **ophiolit′ic; ophiolog′ic, -al.** — *ns.* **ophiol′ogist; ophiol′ogy** the study of snakes; **oph′iomorph** (Gr. *morphē*, form) a caecilian amphibian. — *adjs.* **ophiomorph′ic, -ous** snakelike; **ophioph′agous** (Gr. *phagein*, to eat) snake-eating. —

ns. **ophioph′ilist** a snake-lover; **Oph′ism** the creed or religion of the Ophites; **oph′ite** a name given to various rocks mottled with green: at one time, serpentine-rock: later, a kind of diabase: (with *cap.*) one of a Gnostic sect that reverenced snakes. — *adj.* **ophitic** (*of-it′ik*) pertaining to ophite: having pyroxene crystals enclosing feldspar laths: (with *cap.*) of the Ophites. — *ns.* **Oph′itism; Ophiuchus** (*-i-ōōk′əs, -ūk′*) the Serpent-Bearer, a constellation between Aquila and Libra on the celestial equator; **Ophiura** (*-i-ōō′rə, -ū′rə*; Gr. *ourā*, tail) a genus of brittle-stars. — *ns.* and *adjs.* **ophiu′ran; ophiu′rid; ophiu′roid.** — *ns.pl.* **Ophiu′rida, Ophiuroid′ea** the brittle-stars, a class of echinoderms like starfish with long snaky sharply differentiated arms. [Gr. *ophis*, snake.]

ophthalm(o)- *of-thal-m(ō)-, -o′-*, in composition, eye. — *n.* **ophthal′mia** inflammation of the eye, esp. of the conjunctiva. — *adj.* **ophthal′mic** pertaining to the eye. — *ns.* **ophthal′mist** an ophthalmologist; **ophthalmī′tis** ophthalmia. — *adj.* **ophthalmolog′ical.** — *ns.* **ophthalmol′ogist; ophthalmol′ogy** the science of the eye, its structure, functions, and diseases; **ophthalmom′eter** an instrument for eye-measurements; **ophthalmom′etry; ophthalmophō′bia** the fear of being stared at; **ophthalmoplegia** (*-plē′jyə*; Gr. *plēgē*, a stroke) paralysis of one or more of the muscles of the eye; **ophthal′moscope** an instrument for examining the interior of the eye. — *adjs.* **ophthalmoscop′ic, -al.** — *adv.* **ophthalmoscop′ically.** — *n.* **ophthalmos′copy** examination of the interior of the eye with the ophthalmoscope. — **ophthalmic optician** an optician qualified both to prescribe and to dispense spectacles, etc. [Gr. *ophthalmos*, eye.]

opiate *ō′pi-āt, -ət, n.* a drug containing opium to induce sleep: that which dulls sensation, physical or mental. — *adj.* inducing sleep. — *v.t.* (*ō′pi-āt*) to treat with opium: to dull. — *adj.* **o′piated.** — Also **ō′pioid.** [**opium.**]

opificer *op-if′i-sər, n.* an artificer. [L. *opifex, -icis — opus*, work, *facĕre*, to make.]

opine *ō-pīn′, v.t.* to suppose: to form or express as an opinion. — *adj.* **opin′able** capable of being thought. [Fr. *opiner* — L. *opīnārī*, to think.]

opinicus *o-pin′i-kəs,* (*her.*) *n.* a half-lion, half-dragon. [Origin unknown.]

opinion *ō-pin′yən, n.* what seems to one to be probably true: judgment: estimation: favourable estimation: self-confidence (*Shak.*): arrogance (*Shak.*): reputation (*Shak.*). — *adjs.* **opin′ionāted, opin′ionātive, opin′ioned** unduly attached to one's own opinions: stubborn. — *advs.* **opin′ionately** (*obs.*), **opin′ionātively.** — *ns.* **opin′ionātiveness; opin′ionator** one who holds or gives an opinion: an opinionated person. — Also (*rare*) **opin′ionist.** — **opinion poll** see **poll**[1]. — **a matter of opinion** a matter about which opinions differ. [L. *opīniō, -ōnis*.]

opisometer *op-i-som′i-tər, n.* a map-measuring instrument with a wheel that traces a line on the map and then runs backward along a straight scale until the wheel reaches its original position on the screw that holds it. [Gr. *opisō*, backward, *metron*, measure.]

opisth(o)- *o-pisth(-ō, -ə)-, -o′-*, in composition, behind. — *n.* and *adj.* **opisthobranch** (*o-pis′thō-brangk*; Gr. *branchia*, gills). — *n.pl.* **Opisthobranch′ia** an order of gasteropods having the gills behind the heart. — *adj.* **opisthocoelian** (*-sē′li-ən*; Gr. *koilos*, hollow) hollow or concave behind, as a vertebra. — Also **opisthocoe′lous.** — *n.* **opisthodomos** (*op-is-thod′o-mos*) a rear-chamber in a Greek temple. — *adjs.* **opisthogloss′al** (Gr. *glōssa*, tongue) having the tongue attached in front, free behind, as in frogs; **opisthog′nathous** (Gr. *gnathos*, jaw) having retreating jaws. — *n.* **opis′thograph** a manuscript or slab inscribed on the back as well as the front. — *adj.* **opisthograph′ic.** — *n.* **opisthog′raphy.** — **opisthot′onos** extreme arching backwards of the spine and neck as a result of spasm of the muscles in that region. — *adj.* **opisthoton′ic.** [Gr., drawn backwards, — *teinein*, to stretch, pull tight.]

opium *ō′pi-əm, n.* the dried narcotic juice of the white poppy: anything considered to have a stupefying or tranquillising effect on people's minds, emotions, etc. — **opium den** a resort of opium-smokers; **o′pium-eat′er, -smoker** one who makes a habitual use of opium. [L. *ŏpium* — Gr. *opion*, dim. from *opos*, sap.]

opobalsam *op-ō-böl′səm, n.* balm of Gilead. [Gr. *opobalsamon — opos*, juice, *balsamon*, balsam-tree.]

opodeldoc *op-ō-del′dok, n.* a name given by Paracelsus to various local applications: soap-liniment. [Derivation unknown, apparently Gr. *opos*, juice.]

opopanax *ō-pop′ə-naks, n.* a gum-resin formerly used in medicine, got from the roots of a Persian (and S. European) species of parsnip: a perfume got from *Commiphora*. [Gr. *opos*, juice, *panax*, a panacea.]

oporice *ō-por′i-sē, n.* a medicine prepared from quinces, pomegranates, etc. [Gr. *opōrikē — opōrā*, late summer, summer fruits.]

opossum *ō-pos′əm, n.* any member of the American genus *Didelphys*, or family Didelphyidae, small marsupials, often pouchless, mainly arboreal, with prehensile tail: in Australia, a phalanger: opossum-fur. — Also (*Austr.* and *U.S.*) **possum,** (*formerly*) **'possum.** [American Indian.]

opotherapy *op-ō-ther′ə-pi, n.* treatment by administration of extracts of animal organs, especially of ductless glands. [Gr. *opos*, juice, and **therapy.**]

oppidan *op′i-dən, n.* a townsman: in university towns, one who is not a member of the university, or a student not resident in a college: at Eton (formerly elsewhere) a schoolboy who is not a foundationer or colleger. — *adj.* urban. [L. *oppidānus — oppidum*, town.]

oppignorate, oppignerate *op-ig′nə-rāt,* (*obs.*) *v.t.* to pawn. — *n.* **oppignorā′tion.** [L. *oppīgnorāre, oppīgnerāre — ob*, against, *pīgnus, -oris, -eris*, a pledge.]

oppilate *op′il-āt, v.t.* to block up, stop up. — *n.* **oppilā′tion.** — *adj.* **opp′ilātive.** [L. *oppīlāre, -ātum — ob*, in the way, *pīlāre*, to ram down.]

opponent *o-pō′nənt, adj.* opposing: antagonistic (with *to*; formerly with *with*): placed opposite or in front. — *n.* one who opposes a course of action, belief, person, etc. — *n.* **oppo′nency.** [L. *oppōnēns, -entis*, pr.p. of *oppōnĕre — ob*, in the way of, *pōnĕre*, to place.]

opportune *op′ər-tūn,* or *-tūn′* (*Shak. op-ör′tūn*) *adj.* occurring at a fitting time: conveniently presented: timely: convenient: suitable: opportunist. — *adv.* **opportune′ly** (or *op′*). — *ns.* **opportune′ness** (or *op′*); **opportun′ism** (or *op′*) the practice of regulating actions by favourable opportunities rather than consistent principles; **opportun′ist** (or *op′*) one (e.g. a politician) who waits for events before declaring his opinions, or shapes his conduct or policy to circumstances of the moment: a person without settled principles. — Also *adj.* — *n.* **opportun′ity** opportuneness (*rare*): fitness (*obs.*): an occasion offering a possibility: advantageous conditions. — **opportunity cost** (*econ.*) the cost of an investment (of money, resources, time, etc.) in terms of its best alternative use. [Fr. *opportun* — L. *opportūnus — ob*, before, *portus, -ūs*, a harbour.]

oppose *o-pōz′, v.t.* to place in front or in the way (with *to*): to place or apply face to face or front to front: to set in contrast or balance: to set in conflict: to place as an obstacle: to face: to resist: to contend with. — *v.i.* to make objection. — *n.* **opposabil′ity.** — *adjs.* **oppos′able** that may be opposed: capable of being placed with the front surface opposite (to — as a thumb to other fingers); **oppo′sing; oppose′less** (*Shak.*) not to be opposed, irresistible. — *n.* **oppos′er.** [Fr. *opposer* — L. *ob*, against, Fr. *poser*, to place — L. *pausāre*, to rest, stop; see **pose**[1].]

opposite *op′ə-zit, adj.* placed, or being, face to face, or at two extremities of a line: facing on the other side: of leaves, in pairs at each node, with the stem between (*bot.*): of floral parts, on the same radius: directly contrary: diametrically opposed: opposed: corresponding. — *adv.* in or to an opposite position or positions. — *prep.* in a position facing, opposing, contrary to, etc.: as a lead in the same film or play as (another lead) (*theat.*, etc.). — *n.* that which is opposed or contrary: an opponent: opposition (*Milt.*). — *n.* **opp'o** see **opposite number.** — *adv.* **opp'ositely.** — *n.* **opp'ositeness.** — *adj.* **oppositive** (*-poz'*) characterised by opposing: adversative: inclined to oppose. — **opposite number** (*slang*; *abbrev.* oppo) one who has a corresponding place in another set: one who is allotted to another as partner, opponent, etc: living partner: mate. — **be opposite with** (*Shak.*) to be perverse and contradictory in dealing with. [Fr., — L. *oppositus* — *ob*, against, *pōnĕre*, *positum*, to place.]

opposition op-ə-zish'ən, *n.* the act of opposing or of setting opposite: the state of being opposed or placed opposite: opposed or opposite position: an opposite: contrast: contradistinction: resistance: a difference of quantity or quality between two propositions having the same subject and predicate (*logic*): a body of opposers: the party that opposes the ministry or existing administration: the situation of a heavenly body, as seen from the earth, when it is directly opposite to another, esp. the sun (*astron.*). — *adj.* of the parliamentary opposition. — *adj.* **opposi'tional.** — *n.* **opposi'tionist** a member of the opposition. [L. *oppositiō, -ōnis*; cf. **opposite.**]

oppress o-pres', *v.t.* to press against or upon: to crush (*obs.*): to smother (*obs.*): to overwhelm: to take by surprise (*obs.*): to distress: to lie heavy upon: to treat with tyrannical cruelty or injustice: to load with heavy burdens: to ravish (*obs.*). — *n.* **oppression** (*o-presh'ən*) an act of oppressing: tyranny: a feeling of distress or of being weighed down: dullness of spirits: pressure (*Shak.*). — *adj.* **oppress'ive** tending to oppress: overburdensome: tyrannical: heavy: overpowering. — *adv.* **oppress'ively.** — *ns.* **oppress'iveness; oppress'or.** [Fr. *oppresser* — L.L. *oppressāre*, freq. of L. *opprimĕre*, *oppressum* — *ob*, against, *premĕre*, to press.]

opprobrium o-prō'bri-əm, *n.* disgrace, reproach, or imputation of shameful conduct: infamy: anything that brings such reproach. — *adj.* **oppro'brious** reproachful, insulting, abusive: infamous, disgraceful (*arch.*). — *adv.* **oppro'briously.** — *n.* **oppro'briousness.** [L. *opprobrium* — *ob*, against, *probrum*, reproach.]

oppugn o-pūn', *v.t.* to assail, esp. by argument: to oppose: to call in question. — *n.* **oppugnancy** (*o-pug'nən-si*; *Shak.*) antagonism. — *adj.* **oppug'nant** opposing: hostile. — *n.* an opponent. — *n.* **oppugner** (*o-pūn'ər*). [L. *oppugnāre* — *ob*, against, *pugna*, a fight.]

ops. A contraction of **operations.**

opsimath op'si-math, *n.* one who learns late in life. — *n.* **opsim'athy** learning obtained late in life. [Gr. *opsimathēs* — *opse*, late, *mathē*, learning.]

opsiometer op-si-om'i-tər, *n.* an optometer. [Gr. *opsis*, sight, *metron*, measure.]

opsonium op-sō'ni-əm, *n.* anything eaten with bread as a relish, esp. fish. — *ns.* **opsomā'nia** any morbid love for some special kind of food; **opsomā'niac.** — *adj.* **opsonic** (*op-son'ik*) relating to opsonin. — *n.* **op'sonin** a constituent of blood-serum which makes bacteria more readily consumed by phagocytes. [Latinised from Gr. *opsōnion* — *opson*, cooked food, relish.]

opt opt, *v.i.* to make a choice, esp. of nationality when territory is transferred: where there is more than one possibility, to decide (to do), to choose (with *for*). — *n.* **opt'ant** one who opts: one who has exercised a power of choosing, esp. his nationality. — *adj.* **optative** (*opt'ə-tiv*, or *op-tā'tiv*) expressing a desire or wish. — *n.* (*gram.*) a mood of the verb expressing a wish. — *adv.* **op'tatively.** — **opt'-out** (*TV* and *radio*) a programme broadcast by a regional station which has temporarily opted out of the main network transmission. — **opt out (of)** to choose not to take part in). [L. *optāre, -ātum*, to choose, wish.]

optic, -al op'tik, *-əl, adjs.* relating to sight, or to the eye, or to optics: (**optical**) constructed to help the sight: acting by means of light: amplifying radiation: visual. — *n.* **op'tic** an eye (now mainly *facet.*): a lens, telescope,

or microscope (*obs.*). — *adv.* **op'tically.** — *n.* **optician** (*op-tish'ən*) formerly one skilled in optics: one who makes or sells optical instruments. — *n.sing.* **op'tics** the science of light. — *adj.* **optoelectron'ic** relating to optoelectronics: using both optical and electronic devices, etc. — *n.sing.* **optoelectron'ics** the combined use of optical and electronic devices, esp. involving the interchange of visual and electronic signals: the study and development of optoelectronic devices, systems, etc. — *ns.* **optol'ogist** an optician; **optol'ogy; optom'eter** an instrument for testing vision. — *adj.* **optomet'rical; optom'etrist** an ophthalmic optician: a person qualified to practise optometry; **optom'etry** the science of vision and eye-care: the practice of examining the eyes and vision: the prescription and provision of optical appliances, etc. for the improvement of vision; **op'tophone** an instrument that translates printed characters into arbitrary sounds, and so enables the blind to read ordinary type. — **optical character reader** (*comput.*) a light-sensitive device for inputting data directly to a computer by means of optical character recognition; **optical character recognition** the scanning, identification and encoding of printed characters by photoelectric means; **optical fibre** a thin strand of glass through which light waves may be bounced, used e.g. in some communications systems, fibre optics, etc.; **optical maser** laser; **optical microscope, telescope** one which operates by the direct perception of light from the object viewed, as opposed to an electron microscope or radio telescope; **optic axis** the axis of the eye — a line through the middle of the pupil and the centre of the eye: in a doubly refracting crystal, a direction in which no double refraction occurs; **optic lobe** part of the mid-brain concerned with sight. [Gr. *optikos*, optic, *optos*, seen.]

Optic® op'tik, *n.* a device attached to a bottle for measuring liquid poured out (also without *cap.*).

optimal, etc. See **optimism.**

optimate op'ti-māt, *n.* (*rare in sing.*) a member of the aristocracy: — *pl.* (L.) **optimā'tēs.** [L. *optimās, -ātis* — *optimus*, best.]

optime op'ti-mi, *n.* formerly, in the university of Cambridge, one of those in the second or third rank of mathematical honours (*senior* or *junior optime*), next to the wranglers. [L. *optimē* (adv.), very well, best.]

optimism op'ti-mizm, *n.* Leibniz's doctrine that the world is the best of all possible worlds: a belief that everything is ordered for the best: a disposition to take a bright, hopeful view of things: hopefulness. — Opp. to *pessimism.* — *adj.* **op'timal** optimum. — *v.t.* **op'timalise, -ize** to bring to the most desirable or most efficient state. — *n.* **optimalisā'tion, -z-.** — *v.i.* **op'timise, -ize** to take the most hopeful view of anything. — *v.t.* to make the most or best of: to make as efficient as possible, esp. by analysing and planning processes: to prepare or revise (a computer system or programme) so as to achieve greatest possible efficiency. — *n.* **optimisā'tion, -z-.** — *n.* **op'timist** one who believes in optimism: commonly, a sanguine person. — *adj.* **optimist'ic.** — *adv.* **optimist'ically.** [L. *optimus*, best.]

optimum op'ti-məm, *n.* that point at which any condition is most favourable: — *pl.* **op'tima.** — *adj.* (of conditions) best for the achievement of an aim or result: very best. [L., neut. of *optimus*, best.]

option op'shən, *n.* an act of choosing: the power or right of choosing: a thing that may be chosen: an alternative for choice: a power (as of buying or selling at a fixed price) that may be exercised at will within a time-limit: a wish (*obs.*). — *adj.* **op'tional** left to choice: not compulsory: leaving to choice. — *adv.* **op'tionally.** — **local option, soft option** see **local, soft.** — **keep, leave one's options open** to refrain from committing oneself (to a course of action, etc.). [L. *optiō, -ōnis* — *optāre*, to choose.]

optoelectronic, optologist, optometry, etc. See **optic.**

opulent op'ū-lənt, *adj.* wealthy: loaded with wealth: luxuriant: over-enriched. — *n.* **op'ulence** riches: abounding riches. — *adv.* **op'ulently.** [L. *opulentus.*]

opulus *op'ū-ləs, n.* short for *Viburnum opulus*, the guelder-rose. [L. *opulus*, a kind of maple.]

Opuntia *ō-pun'shi-ə, n.* the prickly-pear genus of the cactus family: (without *cap.*) a plant of this genus. [L. *Opūntia* (herba, plant), of *Opūs* (Gr. *Opous*), a town of Locris where Pliny said it grew.]

opus *ō'pəs, op'əs, op'ōōs, n.* a work, esp. a musical composition — esp. one numbered in order of publication, as opus 6 (abbrev. op. 6): used in naming various styles of Roman masonry:— *pl.* **o'puses, opera** (*op'ə-rə*). — **opus Dei** (*dā'ē*), the work of God: liturgical worship: in Benedictine monastic practice, the primary duty of prayer: (with *caps.*) an international R.C. organisation of lay people and priests; **opus latericium** (*la-ter-ish'i-əm, -ik', -ik'i-ōōm*) a form of Greco-Roman brickwork; **opus musivum** (*mū-, mōō-sīv'əm, mōō-sēv'ōōm*) mosaic work; **opus operantis** (*op-ər-an'-tis*) the effect of a sacrament ascribed (as by Protestants) to the spiritual disposition of the recipient; **opus operatum** (*op-ər-ā'təm, op-er-ä'tōōm*) due celebration of a sacrament involving grace flowing from the sacramental act (the R.C. view); **opus reticulatum** (*ri-tik-yə-lā'təm, re-tik-ōō-lä'tōōm*) reticulated work. [L. *ŏpus, -eris*, work.]

opuscule *o-pus'kūl, n.* a little work. — Also **opuscle** (*o-pus'l*), **opus'culum:** — *pl.* **-cula.** [L. dim. of *opus.*]

or[1] *ör, (arch.) conj.* (or *adv.*) and *prep.* before (in time). — **or ever, or e'er,** or (by confusion) **or ere** (*poet.*) before ever, before even. [O.E. (Northumbrian) and O.N. *ār*, early, with the sense of O.E. *ǣr*, ere.]

or[2] *ör, conj.* marking an alternative. [M.E. *other.*]

or[3] *ör, (her.) n.* the tincture gold or yellow, indicated in engraving and chiselling by dots. [Fr., — L. *aurum*, gold.]

-or. Agent suff. from L., corr. to **-er** from O.E. In most words one or other ending is standard but in some both endings occur (**-or** used esp. in legal terms or in terms for a non-personal agent).

OR *ör, (comput.) n.* a logic circuit that has two or more inputs and one output, the output signal being 1 if any of its inputs is 1, and 0 if all of its inputs are 0. [**or**[2].]

orach, orache *or'ich, n.* a genus (*Atriplex*) of the goosefoot family, sometimes used as spinach is. [O.Fr. *arace* (Fr. *arroche*) — L. *atriplex* — Gr. *atraphaxys.*]

oracle *or'ə-kl, n.* a medium or agency of divine revelation: a response by or on behalf of a god: the place where such responses are given: the Jewish sanctuary: the word of God: a person with the repute or air of infallibility or great wisdom: an infallible indication: a wise or seeming-wise or mysterious utterance: (with *cap.*; ®) the teletext (q.v.) service of the Independent Broadcasting Authority. — *v.t.* to utter as an oracle. — *v.i.* to speak as an oracle. — *adj.* **oracular** (*or-ak'ū-lər*) of the nature of an oracle: like an oracle: seeming to claim the authority of an oracle: delivering oracles: equivocal: ambiguous: obscure — also **orac'ulous** (now *rare*). — *ns.* **oracularity** (*-lar'i-ti*), **orac'ularness, orac'-ulousness.** — *advs.* **orac'ularly, orac'ulously.** — **work the oracle** see **work.** [L. *ōrāculum* — *ōrāre*, to speak.]

oracy. See **oral.**

ora et labora *ö'ra, ö'rä et la-bö'ra, -bō'rä, (L.)* pray and work; **ora pro nobis** (*prō nō'bis, -bēs*) pray for us.

oragious *ō-rā'jəs, adj.* stormy. [Fr. *orageux.*]

oral *ō'rəl, ö'rəl, adj.* relating to the mouth: near the mouth: uttered by the mouth: spoken, not written: taken through the mouth: pertaining to the infant stage of development when satisfaction is obtained by sucking. — *n.* an oral examination. — *n.* **o'racy** skill in self-expression and ability to communicate freely with others by word of mouth. — *adv.* **o'rally.** — **oral contraception** inhibition of the normal process of ovulation and conception by taking orally, and according to a specified regimen, any of a number of hormone-containing pills; **oral contraceptive** a pill of this type; **oral history** (the study of) information on events, etc. of the past, obtained by interviewing people

who participated in them. [L. *ōs, ōris,* the mouth.]

orang. See **orang-utan.**

orange *or'inj, n.* a gold-coloured fruit (hesperidium, a specialised type of berry) with tough skin, within which are juicy segments: the tree (*Citrus* genus of family Rutaceae) on which it grows: extended to various unrelated but superficially similar fruits and plants: a colour between red and yellow. — *adj.* pertaining to an orange: orange-coloured. — *ns.* **orangeade** (*or-in-jād'*) a drink made with orange juice; **or'angery** (*-ri, -ər-i*) a building for growing orange-trees in a cool climate. — **or'ange-bloss'om** the white blossom of the orange-tree, worn by brides: that of the mock-orange, similarly used. — *adj.* **or'ange-col'oured.** — **or'ange-flower** orange-blossom (**orange-flower water** a solution of oil of neroli); **or'ange-grass** a small American St John's-wort; **or'ange-lil'y** a garden lily with large orange flowers; **or'ange-peel** the rind of an orange, often candied; **or'ange-root** golden-seal; **orange squash** a highly concentrated orange drink; **or'ange-squeezer** an instrument for squeezing out the juice of oranges; **or'ange-stick** a thin stick, esp. of orange-wood used in manicure and make-up. — *adj. and n.* **or'ange-taw'ny** (*Shak.*). — **or'ange-tip'** a butterfly (*Euchloe* or kindred) with an orange patch near the tip of the forewing; **or'ange-tree; or'ange-wife** (*Shak.*) a woman who sells oranges; **or'ange-wood** wood of the orange-tree. — **bitter, Seville,** or **sour, orange** *Citrus aurantium*; **sweet orange** *Citrus sinensis*, native of China and south-east Asia, or any cultivated fruit derived from it. [Fr. ult. from Ar. *nāranj*; cf. L.L. *arangia, aurantia, narancum*; It. *arancia*, early *narancia*; Sp. *naranja*; the loss of the *n* may be due to confusion with the indef. art. (*una, une*), the vowel changes to confusion with L. *aurum, Fr. or*, gold.]

Orange *or'inj, adj.* relating to the family of the princes of *Orange*, a former principality in southern France from the 11th century, passing by an heiress to the house of Nassau in 1531, the territory ceded to France in 1713: favouring the cause of the Prince of Orange in Holland or in Great Britain and Ireland: of or favouring the Orangemen: extreme Protestant Irish Conservative. — *n.* **Or'angism** (**Or'angeism**). — **Or'angeman** a member of a society revived and organised in Ireland in 1795 to uphold Orange principles.

orang-utan *ō-, ö-rang'-ōō-tan', ö', ö'rang-ōō'tan,* **orang-outang** *ō-, ö-rang'-ōō-tang'* *ns.* an anthropoid ape, found only in the forests of Sumatra and Borneo, reddish-brown, arboreal in habit: erroneously, a chimpanzee. — Also **orang'.** [Malay *ōranghūtan*, man of the woods (said not to be applied by the Malays to the ape) — *ōrang*, man, *hūtan*, wood, wild.]

orant *ō'rənt, ö', n.* a worshipping figure in ancient Greek and early Christian art. [L. *ōrāns, -antis,* pr.p. of *ōrāre*, to pray.]

orarian *ō-, ö-rā'ri-ən, adj.* coastal. — *n.* a coast-dweller. [L. *ōrārius* — *ōra*, shore.]

orarium[1] *ō-, ö-rā'ri-əm, n.* a handkerchief (*ant.*): a stole (*obs.*): a scarf attached to a bishops's staff. — *n.* **ora'rion** a Greek Church deacon's stole. [L. *ōrārium* — *ōs, ōris,* mouth.]

orarium[2] *ō-, ö-rā'ri-əm, n.* a book of private devotions. [L. *ōrāre*, to pray.]

oration *ō-, ö-rā'shən, n.* a formal speech: a harangue. — *v.i.* **orate'** (*facet.*) to harangue, hold forth. [L. *ōrātiō, -ōnis — ōrāre,* to pray.]

orator *or'ə-tər, n.* a spokesman (*obs.*): a petitioner (*obs.*): a public speaker: a man of eloquence:— *fem.* **or'atress, oratrix** (*or-ā'triks,* or *or'ə-triks*). — *adjs.* **oratorial** (*or-ə-tō'ri-əl, -tö'*) of an orator, oratory, or an oratory; **orato'rian** of an oratory. — *n.* a priest of an oratory: (with *cap.*), a member of an Oratory. — *adj.* **oratorical** (*-tor'*) characteristic of an orator: addicted to oratory: rhetorical: relating to or savouring of oratory. — *adv.* **orator'ically.** — *n.* **or'atory** the art of the orator: rhetoric: rhetorical utterances or expression: a place for private prayer: a lectern for praying at: a place of public speaking (*obs.*): (with *cap.*) one of various congregations in the R.C. Church, esp. the Fathers of the Oratory, established by St Philip Neri (1515–95): (*cap.*) a church of the Oratorians. [L. *ōrātor, -ōris* — *ōrāre*, to pray.]

oratorio *or-ə-tō'ri-ō, -tö', n.* a story, usually Biblical, set to music, with soloists, chorus, and full orchestra (scenery, costumes, and acting, however, being dispensed with): the form of such composition: — *pl.* **orato'rios.** — *adj.* **orato'rial.** [It. *oratorio* — L. *ōrātōrium*, an oratory, because they developed out of the singing at devotional meetings in church oratories.]

orb[1] *örb, n.* a circle: a sphere: anything round: a celestial body: an eyeball: the mound or globe of a king's regalia: the space within which the astrological influence of a planet operates: a sphere carrying a planet in its revolution: a cycle of time: an orbit: a world. — *v.t.* to surround: to form into an orb. — *adjs.* **orbed** in the form of an orb: circular; **orbic'ular** approximately circular or spherical: round: having the component minerals crystallised in spheroidal aggregates (*petr.*). — *n.* **orbiculā'ris** a muscle surrounding an opening: — *pl.* **orbiculā'rēs.** — *adv.* **orbic'ularly.** — *adj.* **orb'y** orbed. [L. *orbis*, circle.]

orb[2] *örb*, (*obs.*) *adj.* bereaved, esp. of children. — *n.* (*archit.*; *obs.*) an obscure term generally understood to mean a blind window or blank panel. — *n.* **orb'ity** (*obs.*) bereavement, esp. of children. [L. *orbus*, bereft.]

Orbilius *ör-bil'i-əs, n.* a flogging schoolmaster (from the Latin poet Horace's teacher).

orbis terrarum *ör'bis ter-ä'rəm, ter-ä'rŏŏm*, the circle of lands, the whole world. [L.]

orbit *ör'bit, n.* the path in which a heavenly body moves round another, or an electron round the nucleus of an atom (also **or'bital**), or the like: a path in space round a heavenly body: a regular course or beat, sphere of action: loosely, an orb: the hollow in which the eyeball rests (also **or'bita**): the skin round a bird's eye. — *v.t.* of an aircraft, to circle (a given point): to circle (the earth, etc.) in space: to put into orbit. — *adj.* **or'bital.** — *n.* **or'biter** a spacecraft or satellite which orbits the earth or another planet without landing on it. — **orbital engine** an axial two-stroke engine with curved pistons in a circular cylinder-block which rotates around a fixed shaft; **orbital road, motorway,** etc. one which goes round the outside of a town. [L. *orbita*, a wheel-track — *orbis*, a ring, wheel.]

orc *örk, n.* a fierce sea-monster: a killer-whale: an ogre. — *n.* **Or'ca** the killer-whale genus. [L. *orca*.]

Orcadian *ör-kā'di-ən, adj.* of Orkney. — *n.* an inhabitant or a native of Orkney. [L. *Orcadēs* — Gr. *Orkadēs*, Orkney (Islands).]

orcein. See **orcinol.**

orchard *ör'chərd, n.* an enclosed garden of fruit-trees. — *ns.* **or'charding; or'chardist, or'chardman** one who grows and sells orchard fruits. — **or'chard-grass** (*U.S.*) cock's-foot grass; **or'chard-house** a glass-house for cultivating fruits without artificial heat. [O.E. *ortgeard*, prob. L. *hortus*, garden, and O.E. *geard*; see **yard**[2]. Some connect the first part with O.E. *wyrt*; see **wort**[1].]

orchat *ör'chət, n.* an obsolete form of the word **orchard.** [Partly *dial.*, partly due to confusion with Gr. *orchatos*, a row of trees.]

orchel, orchella. See **archil.**

orchestra *ör'kis-trə,* form. *-kes', n.* in the Greek theatre, the place in front of the stage where the chorus danced: now the part of a theatre or concert-room in which the instrumental musicians are placed: a large company of musicians (strings, woodwinds, brasses, and percussion) playing together under a conductor: loosely applied to a small group, as in a restaurant. — *ns.* **orche'sis** the art of dancing or rhythmical movement of the body; **orchesog'raphy** notation of dancing. — *adj.* **orchestic** (*-kes'tik*) relating to dancing. — *n.sing.* **orches'tics** the art of dancing. — *adj.* **orches-**

tral (*-kes'*) of or for an orchestra. — *n.* **orches'tralist** an orchestral composer. — *v.t.* **or'chestrate** to compose or arrange (music) for performance by an orchestra: to organise so as to achieve the best or greatest overall effect (*fig.*). — Also *v.i.* — *ns.* **orchestrā'tion; or'chestrātor.** — *adj.* **orches'tric** orchestic: orchestral. — *ns.* **orchestrina** (*-trē'nə*), **orches'trion** names given to various keyboard or barrel-organ instruments designed to imitate an orchestra. — **orchestra stalls** theatre seats just behind the orchestra. [Gr. *orchēstrā* — *orcheesthai*, to dance.]

orchid *ör'kid, n.* any plant, or flower, of the **Orchidā'ceae** or **Orchid'eae,** a family of monocotyledons, including many tropical epiphytes, with highly specialised, often showy, flowers, the upper petal (*labellum*; by twisting actually the lower) serving as a landing-place for insects, the one fertile stamen (or two) united with the gynaeceum as a *column*, the pollen in masses. — *adjs.* **orchidā'ceous, orchid'eous.** — *ns.* **or'chidist** a fancier or grower of orchids; **orchidol'ogist; orchidol'ogy** the knowledge of orchids; **orchidomā'nia** a craze for orchids; **orchidomā'niac; Or'chis** a genus of orchids, including several of the best-known British species: loosely applied to other genera: (without *cap.*) a flower of any of these genera. — **or'chid-house** a place for growing orchids. [Gr. *orchis*, -ios or -eōs, a testicle (from the appearance of the root-tubers in Orchis and others); the *d* is a blunder, as if the genitive were *orchidos*.]

orchil, orchilla. See **archil.**

orchitis *ör-kī'tis, n.* inflammation of a testicle. — *adj.* **orchitic** (*-kit'ik*). — *ns.* **orchidec'tomy, orchiec'tomy** (*-ki-ek'*) excision of one or both testicles. [Gr. *orchis*, -ios or -eōs, testicle.]

orcinol *ör'sin-ol, n.* a dihydric phenol got from archil and other lichens. — Also **or'cin, or'cine.** — *n.* **orcein** (*ör'si-in*) a purple dyestuff got from orcinol. [See **archil.**]

ord *örd*, (*obs.*) *n.* a point, e.g. of a weapon: a beginning. [O.E. *ord*; cf. **odd**[1].]

ordain *ör-dān', v.t.* to arrange: to establish: to decree: to destine: to order: to assign, set apart: to appoint: to set apart for an office: to invest with ministerial functions: to admit to holy orders. — *adj.* **ordain'able.** — *ns.* **ordain'er; ordain'ment; ordinee'** one who is being, or has just been, ordained. [O.Fr. *ordener* (Fr. *ordonner*) — L. *ordināre, -ātum* — *ordō, -inis*, order.]

ordeal *ör'dēl*, less justifiably *ör-dēl'* or *ör-dē'əl, n.* an ancient form of referring a disputed question to the judgment of God, by lot, fire, water, etc.: any severe trial or examination. — Latinised as **ordalium** (*ör-dā'li-əm*). — *adj.* **ordā'lian.** — **ordeal bean** the Calabar-bean. [O.E. *ordēl, ordāl* (W.S. would be *ordǽl*) — pfx. *or-,* out, *dǽl*, deal, share; cf. Du. *oordeel*, Ger. *Urteil*.]

order *ör'dər, n.* arrangement: sequence: disposition: due arrangement: due condition: the condition of normal or due functioning: a regular or suitable arrangement: a method: a system: tidiness: a restrained or undisturbed condition: a form of procedure or ceremony: the accepted mode of proceeding at a meeting: a practice: grade, degree, rank, or position, esp. in a hierarchy: the degree of a curve or equation: a command: a written instruction to pay money: a customer's instruction to supply goods or perform work: a pass for admission or other privilege: a class of society: a body of persons of the same rank, profession, etc.: a fraternity, esp. religious or knightly: a body modelled on a knightly order, to which members are admitted as an honour: the insignia thereof: a group above a family but below a class (*biol.*): one of the different ways in which the column and its entablature with their various parts are moulded and related to each other (*archit.*): one of the successively recessed arches of an archway: due action towards some end, esp. in old phrase 'to take order': the position of a weapon with butt on ground, muzzle close to the right side: a portion or helping in a restaurant, etc. (*U.S.*):

(*pl.*) the several degrees or grades of the Christian ministry. — *v.t.* to arrange: to set in order: to put in the position of order (*mil.*): to regulate: to conduct (*Shak.*): to command: to give an order for: to order to be (done, etc.) (*U.S.*). — *v.i.* to give command: to request the supply of something, esp. food. — *interj.* used in calling for order or to order. — *ns.* **or'derer; or'dering** arrangement: management: the act or ceremony of ordaining, as priests or deacons. — *adj.* **or'derless** without order: disorderly. — *n.* **or'derliness.** — *adj.* **or'derly** in good order: regular: well regulated: of good behaviour: quiet: being on duty. — *adv* regularly: methodically. — *n.* a non-commissioned officer who carries official messages for his superior officer, formerly the first sergeant of a company: a hospital attendant: a street cleaner. — **or'der-book** a book for entering the orders of customers, the special orders of a commanding officer, or the motions to be put to the House of Commons: the amount of orders received and awaiting completion; **order form** a printed form on which the details of a customer's order are written; **orderly bin** a street receptacle for refuse; **orderly officer** the officer on duty for the day; **orderly room** a room for regimental, company, etc., business; **order paper** paper showing order of deliberative business. — **call to order** see **call¹; full orders** the priesthood; **holy orders** an institution, in the Roman and Greek Churches a sacrament, by which one is specially set apart for the service of religion: the rank of an ordained minister of religion; **in order** with the purpose (with *to, that*): in accordance with rules of procedure at meetings: appropriate, suitable, likely: (also in **good, working,** etc. **order**) operating, or able to operate, well or correctly: in the correct, desired, etc. order; **in short order** (*U.S.*) promptly; **in, of, the order of** more or less of the size, quantity or proportion stated; **minor orders** in the Roman Catholic Church those of acolyte, exorcist, reader, doorkeeper, in the Eastern Churches, reader; **on order** having been ordered but not yet supplied; **order about, around** to give orders to in a domineering fashion; **order in council** an order by the sovereign with advice of the Privy Council; **order of battle** arrangement of troops or ships in preparation for a fight; **order of magnitude** the approximate size or number of something, usu. measured in a scale from one value to ten times that value: loosely, a rising scale in terms of size, quantity, etc.; **order of the day** business set down for the day: a proclamation by a dictator or military commander: something necessary, normal, prevalent, especially popular, etc. at a given time (*fig.*); **out of order** not in order: (of people, events, behaviour) outside normally acceptable standards, excessive or uncontrolled (*coll.*); **sailing orders** written instructions given to the commander of a vessel before sailing; **sealed orders** instructions not to be opened until a specified time; **standing orders** see under **stand; take order** to take measures or steps (*obs.*); **take orders** to be ordained; **tall, large, order** a very great task or demand; **to order** according to, and in fulfilment of, an order. [Fr. *ordre* — L. *ordō, -inis.*]

ordinaire *ör'din-ār*, (*coll.*) *n.* vin ordinaire: table wine. [Fr.]

ordinal *or'din-əl, adj.* indicating order of sequence: relating to an order. — *n.* an ordinal numeral (first, second, third, etc. — distinguished from *cardinal*): a book of rules (*obs.*): a service-book: a book of forms of consecration and ordination. [L.L. *ordinālis* — L. *ordō, -inis,* order.]

ordinance *ör'din-əns, n.* that which is ordained by authority, fate, etc.: regulation: a bye-law (*U.S.*): artistic arrangement: planning: preparation (*obs.*): equipment (*obs.*): ordnance (*obs.*): a decree: a religious practice enjoined by authority, esp. a sacrament: a social class or order (*Shak.*). — *n.* **or'dinand** a candidate for ordination. — *adj.* **or'dinant** (*rare*) ordaining. — *n.* one who ordains. — *n.* **or'dinate** a straight line parallel to an axis cutting off an abscissa: the *y*-co-ordinate in

analytical geometry. — *v.t.* to ordain: to co-ordinate or order. — *adv.* **ord'inately** in an ordered manner: restrainedly: with moderation. — *n.* **ordinā'tion** the act of ordaining: admission to the Christian ministry by the laying on of hands of a bishop or a presbytery: established order. [L. *ordināre, -ātum — ordō,* order.]

ordinary *örd'(i-)nə-ri, Scot.* **ordinar** *örd'nər, adjs.* according to the common order: usual: of the usual kind: customary: of common rank: plain: undistinguished: commonplace: plain-looking (*coll.*): (of a judge or jurisdiction) by virtue of office, not by deputation: (of a judge in Scotland) of the Outer House of the Court of Session (**Lord Ordinary**). — *n.* a judge of ecclesiastical or other causes who acts in his own right, as a bishop or his deputy: a chaplain who attended those condemned to death, esp. the chaplain of Newgate Prison (*hist.*): something settled or customary: usual fare (*obs.*): a meal provided at a fixed charge: a place where such a meal is provided: the company partaking of it (*obs.*): the common run, mass, or course: an ungeared bicycle with one large and one small wheel, a penny-farthing: one of a class of armorial charges, figures of simple or geometrical form, conventional in character (*her.*): a reference-book of heraldic charges. — *adv.* **or'dinarily.** — **Ordinary grade, level** see **O grade, level** at **O¹; ordinary seaman** a seaman ranking below an able seaman; **ordinary shares** shares which rank last for receiving dividend, but which may receive as large a dividend as the profits make possible (**preferred ordinary shares** have limited priority). — **in ordinary** in regular and customary attendance; **ordinary of the mass** the established sequence or fixed order for saying mass; **out of the ordinary** unusual. [L. *ordinārius — ordō, -inis,* order.]

ordinee. See **ordain.**

ordnance *örd'nəns, n.* orig., any arrangement, disposition, or equipment: munitions: great guns, artillery: a department concerned with supply and maintenance of artillery. — **Ordnance datum** the standard sea-level of the Ordnance Survey, now mean sea-level at Newlyn, Cornwall; **Ordnance Survey** the preparation of maps of Great Britain and N. Ireland by the *Ordnance Survey (Department)* (until 1889 under the Board of Ordnance). [**ordinance.**]

ordonnance *ör'də-nəns, n.* co-ordination, esp. the proper disposition of figures in a picture, parts of a building, etc. [Fr.; cf. **ordinance.**]

Ordovician *ör-dō-vish'(y)ən, adj. and n.* Lapworth's word for Lower Silurian. [L. *Ordovicēs,* a British tribe of N. Wales.]

ordure *örd'yər, n.* dirt: dung: excrement: anything unclean (*fig.*). — *adj.* **or'durous.** [Fr., — O.Fr. *ord,* foul — L. *horridus,* rough.]

ore¹ *ōr, ör, n.* a solid, naturally-occurring mineral aggregate, of economic interest, from which one or more valuable constituents may be recovered by treatment: precious metal (*poet.*). — **ore'-body** a mass or vein of ore. [O.E. *ār,* brass, influenced by *ōra,* unwrought metal; cf. L. *aes, aeris,* bronze.]

ore² *ör* (*local*) *n.* seaweed: tangle (*Laminaria*). — Also **ore'weed, oar'weed.** [O.E. *wār.*]

ore³, o're *ōr, ör,* old spellings of **o'er** for **over.** — For compounds see **over-.** — **ore-wrought, -raught** (*Shak.*) for **over-reached** in the sense of overtook; **ore-rested** (*Shak.*) for **overwrested.**

öre *œ'rə, n.* a coin and money of account in Sweden and (**øre**) Norway and Denmark: — *pl.* **öre, øre.** See **krone.**

oread *ör'i-ad, ō'ri-ad, (myth.) n.* a mountain nymph: — *pl.* **o'reads,** or **orē'adēs.** [L. *ōrēas, -adis* — Gr. *oreias, oreiados — oros,* a mountain.]

orectic. See **orexis.**

oregano *ö-ri-gä'nō, ö-reg'ə-nō, n.* origanum: — *pl.* **oreganos.** [Amer. Sp. *orégano,* wild marjoram — L. *orīganum;* see **Origanum.**]

oreide. See **oroide.**

oreography, oreology, etc. See **orography.**

Oreopithecus *ō-, ö-rē-ō-pi-thēk'əs,* or *-pith'ə-kəs, n.* a hominid of which a complete skeleton was found in a Tuscan lignite mine. [Gr. *oros*, mountain, *pithēkos*, ape.]

orepearch. See **overperch.**

ore rotundo. See Appendix of foreign phrases, and **orotund.**

oreweed. See **ore²**.

orexis *ör-ek'sis, n.* appetite. — *adj.* **orec'tic.** [Gr. *ŏrexis*.]

orf *ŏrf, n.* a zoonotic viral infection characterised by the formation of vesicles and pustules on the skin and mucous membranes, esp. on lips, nose and feet. [Dial. *hurf*; O.N. *hrūfa*, scab.]

orfe *ŏrf, n.* a golden-yellow semi-domesticated variety of id. [Ger. *Orfe* — Gr. *orphōs*, the great sea-perch.]

organ *ör'gən, n.* an instrument or means by which anything is done: a part of a body fitted for carrying on a natural or vital operation: a region of the brain fancied to be concerned with some mental or moral quality: a bump marking its position and development: a means of communicating information or opinions: a musical instrument in general (*obs.*): a keyboard wind instrument consisting of a collection of pipes made to sound by means of compressed air: a system of pipes in such an organ, having an individual keyboard, a partial organ: a musical instrument in some way similar to a pipe-organ, incl. pipeless organ: a barrel-organ. — *n.* **organelle'** a specialised part of a cell serving as an organ. — *adjs.* **organic** (*ör-gan'ik*), **-al** pertaining to, derived from, like, of the nature of, an organ (in any sense): of an organism, organum or organisation: organised: inherent in organisation: structural: formed as if by organic process (*art*): belonging to the etymological structure of a word (*philol.*): instrumental: mechanical: containing or combined with carbon (*chem.*): concerned with carbon compounds: of crops, crop production, etc., produced without, or not involving, the use of fertilisers and pesticides not wholly of plant or animal origin: governed in its formation or development by inherent or natural factors rather than by a predetermined plan. — *adv.* **organ'ically.** — *ns.* **organicism** (*ör-gan'i-sizm*) the conception of nature, life, or society as an organism: the theory that all disease is due to an organic lesion; **organ'icist; organīsabil'ity, -z-.** — *adj.* **organīs'able, -z-.** — *n.* **organīsā'tion, -z-** the act of organising: the state of being organised: the manner in which anything is organised: an organised system, body, or society: a political party machine (*U.S.*): the singing of the organum. — *adj.* **organīsā'tional, -z-.** — *v.t.* **or'ganise, -ize** to supply with organs: to form into an organic whole: to co-ordinate and prepare for activity: to arrange: to obtain (*slang*). — *v.i.* to become organic: to be active in organisation. — *adj.* **or'ganised, -z-** having or consisting of parts acting in co-ordination: having the nature of a unified whole: organic. — *ns.* **or'ganiser, -z-** one who organises: part of an embryo that influences the development of the rest: (also **organiser-bag, purse,** etc.) a container with separate divisions, pockets, etc. in which the contents can be arranged for ease and speed of access; **or'ganism** organic structure, or that which has it: that which acts as a unified whole: a living animal or vegetable. — *adj.* **organis'mal.** — *ns.* **or'ganist** one who plays on an organ; **organis'trum** an early form of hurdy-gurdy; **organity** (*-gan'*) an organised whole; **or'ganon** (Gr.) a method of investigation: — *pl.* **or'gana; or'ganum** (L.) an organon: in mediaeval music, a part in parallel motion to the canto fermo usually a fourth or fifth below or above: — *pl.* **or'gana.** — **or'gan-bird** the Australian magpie or pied butcher-bird; **or'gan-builder** one who constructs organs; **or'gan-gallery** a gallery where an organ is placed; **or'gan-grinder** one who plays a hand-organ by a crank; **or'gan-harmō'nium** a large harmonium; **or'gan-pipe** one of the sounding pipes of a pipe-organ (**organ-pipe coral** a coral, Tubipora, with tubes arranged like organ-pipes); **or'gan-point** a pedal-point; **or'gan-screen** an ornamented stone or wood

screen on which an organ is placed. — **organic chemistry** the chemistry of carbon compounds; **organic disease** a disease accompanied by changes in the structures involved; **organic sensation** sensation from internal organs, as hunger; **organic vein** (*obs.*) the jugular vein. — **organ of Corti** (*kör'ti*) the organ in the cochlea which contains the auditory receptors. [L. *organum* — Gr. *organon* — *ergon*, work.]

organelle. See **organ.**

organdie *ör'gən-di, n.* fine muslin: book muslin. — *n.* **organ'za** material transparently thin but made of silk, rayon or nylon, not cotton. [Fr. *organdi*.]

organ(o)- *ör-gən(ō)-, -ō',* in composition, organ: (also *ör-gan'ō-*) organic, as in organometallic compounds in which carbon atoms are linked directly with metal atoms, such as *organolead, organotin,* or in similar compounds in which the inorganic element is nonmetallic, such as *organochlorine, organophosphorus.* — *ns.* **organogeny** (*ör-gən-oj'i-ni*), **organogen'esis** the development of living organs; **organogram** (*-gan'*) a chart showing graded arrangement of personnel in an organisation; **organog'raphy** a description of the organs of plants or animals. — *adjs.* **organolep'tic** affecting a bodily organ or sense: concerned with testing the effects of a substance on the senses, esp. of taste and smell (Gr. root of *lambanein,* to seize); **organometall'ic** (or *-gan'*) consisting of a metal and an organic radical: relating to compounds of this type. — *n.* **organother'apy** treatment of disease by administration of animal organs or extracts of them, esp. of ductless gland extracts. [L. *organum;* see **organ.**]

organon, organum. See **organ.**

organza. See **organdie.**

organzine *ör'gən-zēn, n.* a silk yarn of two or more threads thrown together with a slight twist. [Fr. *organsin* — It. *organzino,* poss. — *Urgenj,* Turkestan.]

orgasm *ör'gazm, n.* immoderate excitement: culmination of sexual excitement: turgescence of any organ (*obs.*). — *v.i.* to experience an orgasm. — *adjs.* **orgas'mic, orgas'tic.** [Gr. *orgasmos,* swelling.]

orgeat *ör'ji-at, -zhat, or-zhä, n.* a syrup or drink made from almonds, sugar, etc., formerly from barley. [Fr. *orge* — L. *hordeum,* barley.]

orgia, orgiast, etc., **orgic.** See **orgy.**

orgillous. See **orgulous.**

orgone (energy) *ör'gōn* (*en'ər-ji*), according to Wilhelm Reich, a vital force permeating the universe, which, concentrated in a specially made **orgone box,** could cure certain diseases. [*orgasm,* and suff. *-one* indicating chemical derivative.]

orgue *örg,* (*obs.*) *n.* a row of stakes let down like a portcullis: a weapon with several barrels in a row. [Fr., organ.]

orgulous *ör'gū-ləs,* **orgillous** *ör'gi-ləs,* (*Shak.*) *adjs.* haughty. [O.Fr. *orguillus;* cf. Fr. *orgueil,* It. *orgoglio,* pride; prob. of Germanic origin.]

orgy *ör'ji, n.* a secret rite, as in the worship of Bacchus (usu. in *pl.*): esp. a frantic unrestrained celebration: a celebration in general: a riotous, licentious, or drunken revel. — Also (properly *pl.*) **or'gia.** — *n.* **or'giast** one who takes part in orgies. — *adjs.* **orgias'tic, or'gic.** [Fr. *orgies* — L. — Gr. *orgia* (pl.).]

oribi *or'i-bi, n.* a small South African antelope, the palebuck. [Afrik., app. from some native language.]

orichalc *or'i-kalk,* (*Spens.* **oricalche**) *n.* a gold-coloured alloy: brass. — *adj.* **orichalceous** (*-kal'si-əs*). [Gr. *oreichalkos* — *oros,* a mountain, *chalkos,* copper; sense influenced by association with L. *aurum,* gold.]

oriel *ō', ō'ri-əl, n.* a small room or recess with a polygonal window, built out from a wall, resting on the ground or (esp.) supported on brackets or corbels: the window of an oriel (in full **o'riel-win'dow**). — *adj.* **o'rielled.** [O.Fr. *oriol,* porch, recess, gallery.]

orient *ō', ō'ri-ənt, adj.* rising, as the sun: eastern: bright or pure in colour. — *n.* the part where the sun rises: sunrise: purity of lustre in a pearl: an orient pearl: (with *cap.*) the East: (with *cap.*) the countries of the

East. — *v.t.* o'rient (or -*ent'*) to set so as to face the east: to build (lengthwise) east and west: to place in a definite relation to the points of the compass or other fixed or known directions: to determine the position of, relatively to fixed or known directions: to acquaint (someone, oneself) with the present position relative to known point(s), or (*fig.*) with the details of the situation. — *n.* o'riency orient quality. — *adj.* oriental, Oriental (-*ent'əl*) eastern: pertaining to, in, or from the east: orient. — *n.* a native of the east: an Asiatic. — *v.t.* orient'alise, -ize. — *ns.* Orient'alism an eastern expression, custom, etc.: scholarship in eastern languages; Orient'alist one versed in eastern languages: an oriental; orientality (-*al'i-ti*). — *adv.* orient'ally. — *v.t.* o'rientate to orient. — *v.i.* to face the east: to be oriented. — *ns.* orientā'tion the act of orienting or orientating: the state of being oriented: determination or consciousness of relative direction: the assumption of definite direction in response to stimulus; o'rientātor an instrument for orientating. — *adjs.* o'riented (or -*ent'*), o'rientated directed (towards); often used in composition as second element of *adj.*: normally aware of the elements of one's situation — time, place, persons (*psychiatry*; *also fig.*). — *n.* orienteer' a person who takes part in orienteering. — *v.i.* to take part in orienteering. — *n.* orienteer'ing the sport of making one's way quickly across difficult country with the help of map and compass. — oriental alabaster onyx-marble; oriental amethyst, emerald, topaz varieties of corundum resembling amethyst, emerald, topaz; oriental ruby the true ruby, a variety of corundum; Oriental Region Southern Asia and its islands from the Persian Gulf to Wallace's Line; oriental turquoise true turquoise; orientation table an indicator of tabular form for showing the direction of various objects — mountains and the like. [L. *oriēns, -entis,* pr.p. of *orīrī,* to rise.]

orifice *or'i-fis, n.* a mouth-like opening, esp. small. — *n.* or'ifex (*Shak.*) an orifice. — *adj.* orificial (-*fish'əl*). [Fr., — L. *ōrificium — ōs, ōris,* mouth, *facĕre,* to make.]

oriflamme *or'i-flam, n.* a little banner of red silk split into many points, borne on a gilt staff — the ancient royal standard of France. [Fr., — L.L. *auriflamma —* L. *aurum,* gold, and *flamma,* a flame.]

origami *or-i-gäm'i, n.* the orig. Japanese art of folding paper so as to make bird forms, etc. [Jap., paper-folding, — *ori,* folding, *kami,* paper.]

Origanum *or-ig'ə-nəm, n.* the marjoram genus of labiates: (without *cap.*) any of various aromatic herbs, of this or other genus, used in cookery. — *n.* or'igan(e) (-*gan*) marjoram, esp. wild marjoram. — See also oregano. [L. *orīganum —* Gr. *orīganon.*]

Origenist *or'i-jən-ist, n.* a follower of *Origen* (*c.* A.D. 185–254) in his allegorical method of scriptural interpretation, or his theology, esp. his heresies — the subordination though eternal generation of the Logos, pre-existence of all men, and universal restoration, even of the Devil. — *n.* Or'igenism. — *adj.* Origenist'ic.

origin *or'i-jin, n.* the rising or first existence of anything: that from which anything first proceeds: the fixed starting-point or point from which measurement is made (*math.*): the point or place from which a muscle, etc. arises (*anat.*): source: derivation. — *adj.* orig'inal pertaining to the origin or beginning: existing from or at the beginning: being such from the beginning: innate: standing in relation of source: not derived, copied, imitated, or translated from anything else: originative: novel: originating or having the power to originate in oneself: creative: independent in invention: odd in character. — *n.* an origin: that which is not itself, or of which something else is, a copy, imitation, or translation: a real person, place, etc., serving as model for one in fiction: an inhabitant, member, etc., from the beginning: a person of marked individuality or oddity: (in *pl.,* *Milt.*) original elements. — *n.* original'ity. — *adv.* orig'inally. — *v.t.* orig'inate to give origin to: to bring into existence. — *v.i.* to have origin:

to begin. — *n.* originā'tion. — *adj.* orig'inātive having power to originate or bring into existence: originating. — *n.* orig'inātor. — original sin innate depravity and corruption held to be transmitted to Adam's descendants in consequence of his sin; originating summons, application, etc. (*law*) one which originates legal proceedings. [L. *orīgō, -inis — orīrī,* to rise.]

orillion *o-ril'yən, n.* a semicircular projection at the shoulder of a bastion intended to cover the guns and defenders on the flank. [Fr. *orillon — oreille,* an ear - L. *auricula,* dim. of *auris,* ear.]

oriole *ōr'i-ōl, ör', n.* a golden yellow bird (*Oriolus galbula,* the golden oriole, loriot) with black wings, or other member of the genus or of the Old World family Oriol'idae, related to the crows: in America applied to birds of the Icteridae (see Baltimore). [O.Fr. *oriol —* L. *aureolus,* dim. of *aureus,* golden — *aurum,* gold.]

Orion *ə-, o-, ö-rī'ən,* (*astron.*) *n.* a constellation containing seven very bright stars, three of which form Orion's belt. [*Oriōn,* a giant hunter slain by Artemis.]

orison *or'i-zən, n.* a prayer. [O.Fr. *orison* (Fr. *oraison*) — L. *ōrātiō, -ōnis — ōrāre,* to pray.]

Oriya *ō-rē'yə, ö-, n.* the language of Orissa in India, closely akin to Bengali: a member of the people speaking it. — Also *adj.*

orle *örl,* (*her.*) *n.* a border within a shield at a short distance from the edge: a number of small charges set as a border. [O.Fr., border, from a dim. formed from L. *ōra,* border.]

orleans *ör'li-ənz, n.* a fabric of cotton warp and worsted weft. — *n.* Or'leanist a supporter of the family of the Duke of Orleans, brother of Louis XIV, as claimants to the throne of France. — Also *adj.* — *n.* Or'leanism. [*Orléans,* a city in France.]

Orlon® *ör'lon, n.* a type of acrylic fibre or crease-resistant fabric made from it.

orlop (deck) *ör'lop* (*dek*), *n.* the lowest deck in a ship, a covering to the hold. [Du. *overloop,* covering.]

Ormazd. See Ormuzd.

ormer *ör'mər, n.* an ear-shell or sea-ear, esp. the edible *Haliotis tuberculata,* common in the Channel Islands. [Channel Island Fr. *ormer* (Fr. *ormier*) — L. *auris maris,* sea-ear.]

ormolu *ör'mo-lōō, n.* an alloy of copper, zinc, and sometimes tin: gilt or bronzed metallic ware: gold-leaf prepared for gilding bronze, etc. [Fr. *or —* L. *aurum,* gold, and Fr. *moulu,* pa.p. of *moudre,* to grind — L. *molĕre,* to grind.]

Ormuzd, Ormazd *ör'muzd, n.* a later form of the name Ahura Mazda — in early Zoroastrianism, the creator and lord of the universe, later the good principle as opposed to Ahriman, the bad. [Pers. *Ahura Mazdâ,* the Wise Lord, or the Living God or Lord (*ahu,* the living, life, or spirit, root *ah,* to be), the Great Creator (*maz, dâ*).]

ornament *ör'nə-mənt, n.* anything meant to add grace or beauty or to bring credit: additional beauty: a mark of honour: (usu. in *pl.*) articles used in the services of the church (*Pr. Bk.*). — *v.t.* (*ör-nə-ment', ör'nə-ment*) to adorn: to furnish with ornaments. — *adj.* ornament'al serving to adorn: decorative, pleasantly striking in dress and general appearance. — *n.* a plant grown for ornament or beauty. — *adv.* ornament'ally. — *ns.* ornamentā'tion the act or art of ornamenting: ornamental work; ornament'er; ornament'ist. [Fr. *orne-ment —* L. *ornāmentum — ornāre,* to adorn.]

ornate *ör-nāt', ör'nāt, adj.* decorated: much or elaborately ornamented. — *adv.* ornate'ly (or *ör'*). — *n.* ornate'ness (or *ör'*). [L. *ornāre, -ātum,* to adorn.]

ornery *ör'nə-ri,* (*U.S.*) *adj.* commonplace (*dial.*): inferior, poor, worthless (*dial.*): touchy, cantankerous (*coll.*): stubborn (*coll.*): mean, contemptible (*coll.*). [A variant of ordinary.]

ornis *ör'nis, n.* the birds collectively of a region, its avifauna. — *adj.* ornithic (*ör-nith'ik*) relating to birds. — *n.* ornithichnite (*ör-nith-ik'nīt;* Gr. *ichnos,* track) a fossil footprint of a bird. — *n.pl.* Ornithischia (-*this'-*

ki-ə; Gr. *ischion*, hip joint) the order of bird-hipped dinosaurs, herbivorous and often heavily armoured. — *n.* and *adj.* **ornithis'chian**. — *n.pl.* **Ornithodel'phia** (Gr. *delphys*, womb) the Prototheria or Monotremata — from the ornithic character of the urogenital organs. — *adjs.* **ornithodel'phian** (also *n.*), **ornithodel'phic**, **ornithodel'phous**. — *ns.* **Ornithogaea** (-nī-thō-jē'ə; Gr. *gaia*, land) the New Zealand biological region; **Ornithog'alum** (Gr. *ornithogalon*, star-of-Bethlehem) a large genus of herbs of the family Liliaceae: (without *cap.*) a plant of this genus. — *adjs.* **ornithoid** (ör'nith-oid; Gr. *eidos*, form) bird-like; **ornitholog'ical**. — *adv.* **ornitholog'ically**. — *ns.* **ornithol'ogist**; **ornithol'ogy** the study of birds; **ornithomancy** (ör-nī'thō-man-si, ör'nith-ō-; Gr. *manteiā*, divination) divination by means of birds, by observing their flight, etc. — *adj.* **ornithoman'tic**. — *n.* **ornithomorph** (ör-nī'thō-mörf, ör'nith-ō-mörf; Gr. *morphē*, form) a figure or design in the form of a bird. — *adjs.* **ornithomorph'ic**; **ornithoph'ilous** (Gr. *phileein*, to love) bird-pollinated. — *ns.* **ornithoph'ily**; **ornithophō'bia** fear of birds; **or'nithopod** a member of the **Ornithop'oda**, a suborder of bipedal ornithischian dinosaurs; **ornithopter** (*op'tər*; Gr. *pteron*, wing) a flying-machine with flapping wings; **Ornithorhynchus** (-ō-ring'kəs; Gr. *rhynchos*, snout) the duckbill genus: (without *cap.*) the duckbill; **ornithosaur** (ör-nī'thō-sör; Gr. *sauros*, lizard) a pterodactyl; **ornithoscopy** (-os'kə-pi; Gr. *skopeein*, to view) augury by observation of birds; **ornitho'sis** psittacosis. [Gr. *ornis, ornīthos*, a bird.]

Orobanche or-ō-bang'kē, *n.* the broom-rape genus of dicotyledons, giving name to the family **Orobanchā'ceae**, root-parasites without green leaves. — *adj.* **orobanchā'ceous**. [Gr. *orobanchē*, dodder, also broomrape — *orobos*, bitter vetch, *anchein*, to strangle.]

orogenesis or-ō-jen'i-sis, ör-, ör-, *n.* mountain-building, the processes which take place during an orogeny. — *n.* **orogen** (or'-) an orogenic belt. — *adjs.* **orogenet'ic**, **orogen'ic**. — *n.* **orogeny** (or-oj'ə-ni, ör-, ör) a period of mountain-building, during which rocks are severely folded, metamorphosed, and uplifted: orogenesis. — **orogenic belt** a usu. elongated region of the earth's crust which has been subjected to an orogeny. [Gr. *oros*, mountain, *genesis*, production.]

orography or-og'rə-fi, *n.* the description of mountains — also **oreography** (or-i-og'). — *adjs.* **or(e)ographic** (-graf'ik), **-al**. — *ns.* **orol'ogy**, **oreology** (or-i-ol') the scientific study of mountains. — *adjs.* **or(e)olog'ical**. — *ns.* **or(e)ol'ogist**. [Gr. *oros*, -*eos*, mountain, *graphein*, to write, *logos*, discourse.]

oroide ō'rō-īd, ö', *n.* an alloy of copper and zinc or tin, etc., imitating gold. — *n.* **o'rēide** a similar or identical alloy. [Fr. *or* — L. *aurum*, gold, Gr. *eidos*, form.]

orology, etc. See **orography**.

oropesa or-ō-pē'zə, -pä'sə, *n.* a fish-shaped float used in marine mine-sweeping to support the sweeping wire. [From the name of a trawler.]

oropharynx ō-rō-far'ingks, ö-, *n.* the part of the pharynx between the soft palate and the epiglottis. [L. *ōs*, *ōris*, a mouth, and **pharynx**.]

orotund o', ō', ö'rō-tund, *adj.* full and round in utterance: pompously mouthed or mouthing. — Also **o'rorotund**. — *ns.* **o(ro)rotund'ity**. [L. *ōs*, *ōris*, mouth, *rotundus*, round; see **ore rotundo** in Appendices.]

orphan ör'fən, *n.* one bereft of father or mother, or (usually) of both. — Also *adj.* — *v.t.* to make an orphan. — *ns.* **or'phanage** the state of being an orphan: a house for orphans; **or'phanhood**, **or'phanism**. — **or'phan-asy'lum**. [Gr. *orphanos*, akin to L. *orbus*, bereaved.]

orpharion ör-fa-rī'ən, ör-fā'ri-ən, *n.* a large lute-like instrument with six to nine pairs of metal strings. — Also **orpheō'reon**. [*Orpheus*, *Arīon*, mythical musicians.]

Orpheus ör'fūs, -fi-əs, *n.* a mythical Thracian musician and poet who could move inanimate objects by the music of his lyre, founder or interpreter of the ancient mysteries. — *adjs.* **Orphē'an** pertaining to Orpheus; **Or'phic** pertaining to the mysteries associated with Orpheus: esoteric. — *n.* **Or'phism** the system taught in the Orphic mysteries: an early 20th-cent. style of abstract art using brilliant colour — also **Orphic Cubism**. — **Orpheus harmonica** the panharmonicon.

orphrey ör'fri, *n.* gold or other rich embroidery, esp. bordering a vestment. [O.Fr. *orfreis* — L. *auriphrygium*, Phrygian gold.]

orpiment ör'pi-mənt, *n.* a yellow mineral, arsenic trisulphide, used as a pigment. [O.Fr., — L. *auripīgmentum* — *aurum*, gold, *pīgmentum*, paint.]

orpine, orpin ör'pin, *n.* a purple-flowered, broad-leaved stonecrop. [Fr. *orpin*.]

Orpington ör'ping-tən, *n.* a breed of poultry (white, black, or buff). [*Orpington* in W. Kent, where it took rise.]

orra or'a, -ə, (*Scot.*) *adj.* odd: not matched: left over: occasional, casual: supernumerary: worthless. — **orra man** a farm-worker kept to do any odd job that may occur. [Origin unknown.]

orrery or'ər-i, *n.* a clockwork model of the solar system. [From Charles Boyle, fourth Earl of *Orrery* (1676–1731) for whom one was made.]

orris[1] or'is, *n.* the Florentine or other iris: its dried rootstock (**orr'is-root'**) smelling of violets, used in perfumery. [Perh. **iris**.]

orris[2] or'is, *n.* a peculiar kind of gold or silver lace: upholsterers' galloon and gimp. [Perh. O.Fr. *orfreis*; see **orphrey**.]

orseille ör-sāl', same as **archil**, **orchil**. — *adj.* **orsellic** (-sel'). [Fr.]

ort ört, *n.* a fragment, esp. one left from a meal — usually *pl.* [Cf. L. Ger. *ort*, refuse of fodder.]

ortanique ör'tan-ēk, *n.* a cross between the orange and the tangerine, or its fruit. [Portmanteau word: *or*ange, *tan*gerine, and un*ique*.]

orthian örth'i-ən, *adj.* high-pitched. [Gr. *orthios*.]

orthicon örth'i-kon, *n.* a television camera tube more sensitive than the earlier iconoscope: a further development is the **image orthicon**. [**ortho-**, *iconoscope*.]

ortho- ör-thō-, in composition, straight: upright: perpendicular: right: genuine: derived from an acid anhydride by combination with the largest number of water molecules (distinguished from *meta*-; *chem.*): having substituted atoms or groups attached to two adjacent carbon atoms of the benzene ring (distinguished from *meta*- and *para*- — in this sense commonly represented by *o*-; *chem.*). — *n.* and *adj.* **or'tho** a contraction for **orthochromatic (plate)**: — *pl.* **or'thos**. — *ns.* **orthoax'is** (*crystal.*) the orthodiagonal: — *pl.* **-ax'es**; **orthobo'rate** a salt of **orthobo'ric acid** boric acid; **orthocaine** (-kā'in, -kān) a white crystalline substance used as a local anaesthetic; **or'thocentre** the point of intersection of the altitudes of a triangle; **Orthoceras** (ör-thos'ə-ras; Gr. *keras*, horn) a genus of fossil cephalopods with straight shell. — *adj.* **orthochromat'ic** (Gr. *chrōma*, colour) correct in rendering the relation of colours, without the usual photographic modifications. — *ns.* **or'thoclase** (-klās, -klāz; Gr. *klasis*, fracture) common or potash feldspar, monoclinic, with cleavages at right angles; **or'tho-compound**; **or'thocousins** children of two sisters or of two brothers; **orthodiag'onal** in a monoclinic crystal, that lateral axis which is perpendicular to the vertical axis; **orthodontia** (-don'shi-ə; Gr. *odous, odontos*, tooth) rectification of abnormalities in the teeth. Also **orthodont'ics**. — *adj.* **orthodont'ic**. — *n.* **orthodont'ist**. — *adj.* **or'thodox** (Gr. *doxa*, opinion) sound in doctrine: believing, or according to, the received or established doctrines or opinions, esp. in religion: (*cap.*) of the Eastern Church. — *n.* **or'thodoxy**. — *adj.* **orthodrom'ic** (Gr. *dromos*, a course, run). — **orthod'romy** great-circle sailing. — Also **orthodrom'ics**. — *adjs.* **orthoepic** (-ep'ik; Gr. *epos*, a word), **orthoep'ical**. — *ns.* **orthō'epist**; **ortho'epy** (the study of) correct pronunciation; **orthogen'esis** (Gr. *genesis*, generation) the evolution of organisms systematically in definite directions and not accidentally in many directions: determinate variation. — *adjs.* **orthogenet'ic** relating to orthogenesis; **orthogen'ic** orthogenetic: concerning the treatment of mentally and emotionally disturbed children. — *n.sing* **orthogen'ics.** — *adjs.* **orthognath'ic, orthog'nathous** (Gr. *gnathos*, jaw) having a lower jaw that neither protrudes nor recedes. — *n.* **orthog'nathism.** — *adj.* **orthog'onal** (Gr. *gōniā*, angle) right-angled (**orthogonal projection** projection by lines perpendicular to the plane of projection). — *adv.* **orthog'onally.** — *ns.* **or'thograph** a drawing in orthographic projection, esp. of the elevation of a building; **orthog'rapher** one skilled in orthography: a speller. — *adjs.* **orthograph'ic, -al** pertaining or according to spelling: spelt correctly: in perspective projection, having the point of sight at infinity. — *adv.* **orthograph'ically.** — *ns.* **orthog'raphist** an orthographer; **orthog'raphy** (Gr. *orthographiā*, spelling, elevation — *graphein*, to write) the art or practice of spelling words correctly: spelling: orthographic projection: apparently for orthographer (Shak., *Much Ado*). — *adjs.* **orthopae'dic, -al, orthopē'dic, -al.** — *n. sing.* **orthopaedics, orthopēdics** (-*pē'diks*; Gr. *pais, paidos*, a child) the art or process of curing deformities arising from disease or injury of bones, esp. in childhood — also **or'thopaedy, or'thopēdy** — formerly **orthopedī'a** (or -*pēd'*); **orthopae'dist, -pē'dist; orthophos'phate** an ordinary phosphate. — *adj.* **orthophosphor'ic** phosphoric. — *n.* **or'thophyre** (-*fīr*; *ortho*clase por*phyr*y) a fine-grained syenitic rock with orthoclase crystals. — *adj.* **orthophyric** (-*fir'ik*). — *ns.* **orthopin'akoid** in monoclinic crystals, a form consisting of two faces parallel to the orthodiagonal and the vertical axis; **orthopnoea** (-*thop-nē'ə*; Gr. *orthopnoia* — *pneein*, to breathe) a condition in which one can only breathe when upright; **or'thopod** (*med. slang*) an orthopaedic surgeon; **or'thopraxis, -praxy** correct, orthodox practice esp. in religion (see **praxis**); **or'thoprism** in monoclinic crystals, a form parallel to the orthodiagonal; **or'thopsychiatry** the branch of psychiatry concerned with prevention and correction of incipient mental illness. — *n.pl.* **Orthop'tera** (Gr. *pteron*, wing) the cockroach order of insects with firm fore-wings serving as covers to the fan-wise folded hind-wings. — *n.* and *adj.* **orthop'teran.** — *ns.* **orthop'terist, orthopterol'ogist** a student of the Orthoptera; **orthopterol'ogy; orthop'teron** (*pl.* **orthop'tera**) any member of the Orthoptera. — *adjs.* **orthop'teroid; orthop'terous** pertaining to the Orthoptera; **orthop'tic** (Gr. *optikos*, optic) relating to normal vision. — *ns.* **orthop'tics** the treatment of defective eyesight by exercises and visual training; **orthop'tist.** — *adjs.* **orthorhom'bic** (Gr. *rhombos*, rhomb; *crystal.*) referable to three unequal axes at right angles to each other; **orthoscop'ic** (Gr. *skopeein*, to look at) having or giving correct vision, true proportion, or a flat field of view. — *ns.* **orthosil'icate** a salt of **orthosilicic** (-*sil-is'ik*) **acid** H_4SiO_4; **orthō'sis** a device which supports, corrects deformities in, or improves the movement of, the movable parts of the body: — *pl.* **orthō'ses.** — *adjs.* **orthostat'ic** (Gr. *orthostatos* — *statos*, standing) standing erect: connected with the erect posture; **orthos'tichous** (Gr. *stichos*, a row) arranged in vertical rows. — *n.* **orthos'tichy** a straight row, as of leaves vertically over one another on an axis. — *adj.* **orthot'ic** of or relating to orthotics. — *n. sing.* **orthot'ics** the branch of medical science dealing with the rehabilitation of injured or weakened joints or muscles through artificial or mechanical support by orthoses. — *ns.* **or'thotist** one skilled in orthotics; **orthotonē'sis** (Gr. *tonos*, accent) accentuation of a proclitic or enclitic — opp. to *enclisis*. — *adjs.* **orthoton'ic** taking an accent in certain positions but not in others — also **or'thotone; orthotop'ic** (*med.*; Gr. *topos*, place; of tissue grafts, organ replacement, etc.) done, put, occurring, etc. at the normal place; **or'thotrop'ic** (Gr. *tropos*, a turn) manifesting orthotropism: (of a material, as wood) having elastic properties varying in different planes. — *ns.* **orthot'-**

ropism growth in the direct line of stimulus, esp. of gravity; **orthot'ropy** (of a material, as wood) the state of being orthotropic. — *adj.* **orthot'ropous** (of an ovule) straight, having the nucellus in direct continuation of the funicle. [Gr. *orthos*, straight, upright, right.]

orthros ör'thros, *n.* one of the Greek canonical hours, corresponding to the Western lauds. [Gr. *orthros*, dawn.]

ortolan ör'tə-lən, *n.* a kind of bunting, common in Europe, and considered a great table delicacy. [Fr., — It. *ortolano* — L. *hortulānus*, belonging to gardens — *hortulus*, dim. of *hortus*, a garden.]

orval ör'vəl, (*obs.*) *n.* clary. [Cf. Fr. *orvale.*]

Orvieto ör-vyā'tō, *n.* a white wine from *Orvieto* in Italy. — *n.* **Orvietan** (ör-vi-ē'tən) a supposed antidote to poison ascribed to an Orvieto man.

Orwellian ör-wel'i-ən, *adj.* relating to or in the style of the English writer George *Orwell* (1903–50): characteristic of the dehumanised authoritarian society described in his novel *1984.* — *n.* a student of Orwell or his ideas.

oryctology or-ik-tol'ə-ji, (*obs.*) *n.* mineralogy: palaeontology. [Gr. *oryktos*, dug, quarried.]

Oryx or'iks, *n.* an African genus of antelopes: (without *cap.*) an antelope of this genus. [Gr. *oryx, -ygos*, a pick-axe, an oryx antelope.]

Oryza ö-, ö-rī'zə, *n.* a tropical genus of grasses, including rice. [Gr. *oryza.*]

os *os*, (L.) *n.* a bone: — *pl.* **ossa** (*os'ə*).

Osage ō-sāj', ō'sāj, *n.* an Indian of a tribe living in Oklahoma, etc. — *adj.* **Osage.** — **Osage orange** a hedge-tree (*Maclura*) of the mulberry family, first found in the Osage country: its orange-like inedible fruit. [Osage *Wazhazhe.*]

Oscan os'kən, *n.* one of an ancient Italic people in southern Italy: their Indo-European language, generally considered akin to Latin. — Also *adj.*

Oscar os'kər, *n.* a gold-plated statuette awarded by the American Academy of Motion Picture Arts and Sciences to a film writer, actor, director, etc., for the year's best performance in his or her particular line: any similar award. [Name fortuitously given, possibly after an Academy employee's uncle.]

oscheal os'ki-əl, *adj.* pertaining to the scrotum. [Gr. *oscheon*, scrotum.]

oscillate os'il-āt, *v.i.* to swing to and fro like a pendulum: to vibrate: to radiate electromagnetic waves: to vary between certain limits: to fluctuate. — *v.t.* to cause to swing or vibrate. — *adj.* **osc'illating.** — *n.* **oscillā'tion.** — *adj.* **osc'illātive** having a tendency to vibrate: vibratory. — *n.* **osc'illātor** one who oscillates: apparatus for producing oscillations. — *adj.* **oscillatory** (os'il-ə-tə-ri) swinging: moving as a pendulum does: vibratory. — *ns.* **oscill'ogram** a record made by an oscillograph; **oscill'ograph** an apparatus for producing a curve representing a number of electrical and mechanical phenomena which vary cyclically; **oscill'oscope** an instrument which shows on a fluorescent screen the variation with time of the instantaneous values and waveforms of electrical quantities, including voltages translated from sounds or movements. [L. *ōscillāre, -ātum*, to swing.]

Oscines os'i-nēz, *n.pl.* the song-birds, forming the main body of the Passeriformes. — *adj.* **osc'inine** or (faultily formed) **osc'ine.** [L. *oscen, oscinis*, a singing-bird.]

oscitancy os'i-tən-si, *n.* yawning: sleepiness: stupidity. — *adj.* **osc'itant.** — *adv.* **osc'itantly.** — *v.i.* **osc'itate** to yawn. — *n.* **oscitā'tion** yawning: sleepiness. [L. *ōscitāre*, to yawn.]

osculant os'kū-lənt, *adj.* kissing: adhering closely: intermediate between two genera, species, etc., linking (*biol.*). — *adj.* **os'cular** pertaining to the mouth or osculum, or to kissing: osculating. — *v.t.* **os'culāte** to kiss: to have three or more coincident points in common with (*math.*). — *v.i.* to be in close contact: to form a connecting link. — *n.* **osculā'tion.** — *adj.* **os'culatory** of or pertaining to kissing or osculation.

— *n.* a carved tablet kissed by the priest and (now rarely) by the people at mass. — *ns.* **os′cule** a little mouth: a small mouthlike aperture; **os′culum** an exhalant aperture in a sponge: a sucker on a tapeworm's head. [L. *ōsculārī, -ātus — ōsculum,* a little mouth, a kiss, dim. of *ōs,* mouth.]

oshac *ō′shak, n.* the ammoniac plant. [Ar. *ushshaq.*]

osier *ōzh′(y)ər, ōz′i-ər, ōz′yər, n.* any willow whose twigs are used in making baskets, esp. *Salix viminalis.* — *adj.* made of or like osiers. — *adj.* **o′siered** covered or fringed with osiers: twisted like osiers. — *n.* **o′siery** osier-work. — **o′sier-bed** a place where osiers grow. [Fr. *osier* of unknown origin; there is a L.L. *ausāria* or *osāria,* willow bed.]

Osiris *ō-sī′ris, n.* the greatest of Egyptian gods, son of Seb and Nut, or Heaven and Earth, husband of Isis, father of Horus. — *adj.* **Osī′rian.** [Gr. *Osīris.*]

-osis *-ō′sis, n. suff.* denoting (1) a condition or process, (2) a diseased condition. [L. *-osis,* Gr. *-ōsis.*]

Osmanli *os-man′li, adj.* of the dynasty of *Osmān,* who founded the Turkish empire in Asia, and reigned 1288–1326: of the Turkish empire: of the western branch of the Turks or their language. — *n.* a member of the dynasty: a Turk of Turkey. [Cf. **Ottoman.**]

osmate. See **osmium.**

osmeterium *os-mē-tē′ri-əm,* or *oz-, n.* a forked process behind the head of certain caterpillars giving out a foul smell: — *pl.* **osmetē′ria.** [Gr. *osmē,* smell, stink, and suff. *-tērion,* denoting instrument.]

osmiate, osmic. See **osmium.**

osmidrosis *os-mi-drō′sis,* or *oz-, n.* the secretion of ill-smelling sweat. [Gr. *osmē,* smell, *hidrōs,* sweat.]

osmium *oz′, os′mi-əm, n.* a grey-coloured metal (Os; atomic number 76) the heaviest substance known, whose tetroxide has a disagreeable smell. — *ns.* **os′mate, os′miate** a salt of the hypothetical osmic acid. — *adjs.* **os′mic** containing osmium in higher valency; **os′mious, os′mous** containing osmium in lower valency. — *n.* **osmirid′ium** iridosmium. — **osmic acid** strictly, a supposed acid H_2OsO_4: usually, osmium tetroxide, an ill-smelling substance used as a stain for fats in microscope work. [Gr. *osmē,* smell.]

osmosis *os-mō′sis,* or *oz-, n.* diffusion of liquids through a porous septum. — Also **os′mose.** — *v.t.* and *v.i.* **osmose′** to (cause to) undergo osmosis. — *ns.* **osmom′eter** an apparatus for measuring osmotic pressure; **osmom′etry; osmoregulā′tion** the process by which animals regulate the amount of water in their bodies and the concentration of various solutes and ions in their body fluids. — *adj.* **osmotic** (*-mot′ik*). — *adv.* **osmot′ically.** — **osmotic pressure** the pressure exerted by a dissolved substance in virtue of the motion of its molecules, or a measure of this in terms of the pressure which must be applied to a solution in order just to prevent osmosis into the solution. [Gr. *ōsmos = ōthismos,* impulse — *ōtheein,* to push.]

Osmunda *os-mun′də, n.* a genus including the royal fern, giving name to a family **Osmundā′ceae.** — *ns.* **osmun′d(a)** any fern of this genus. [Origin unknown.]

osnaburg *oz′nə-bûrg, n.* a coarse linen, originally brought from *Osnabrück* in Germany: a coarse cotton. — Also *adj.*

osprey *os′pri, -prā, n.* a bird of prey (*Pandion haliaetus*) that feeds on fish: an egret or other plume used in millinery, not from the osprey. [Supposed to be from L. *ossifraga,* misapplied; see **ossifrage.**]

ossa. See **os.**

osseous *os′i-əs, adj.* bony: composed of, or like, bone: of the nature or structure of bone. — *ns.* **ossā′rium** an ossuary; **ossein** (*os′i-in*) the organic basis of bone; **osselet** (*os′ə-let, os′let*) a hard substance growing on the inside of a horse's knee; **oss′icle** a little bone or bone-like plate. — *adjs.* **ossic′ular; ossif′erous** yielding or containing bones; **ossif′ic.** — *n.* **ossificā′tion** the process or state of being changed into a bony substance. — *v.t.* **oss′ify** to make into bone or into a bone-like substance. — *v.i.* to become bone: to become

hardened, inflexible, set in a conventional pattern (*fig.*): — *pr.p.* **oss′ifying;** *pa.t.* and *pa.p.* **oss′ified.** — *adj.* **ossiv′orous** feeding on or consuming bones. [L. *os, ossis,* bone.]

osseter *os-et′ər, n.* a species of sturgeon. [Russ. *osetr.*]

ossia *ō-sē′a,* (It.) *conj.* or (giving an alternative in music).

Ossian *os′, osh′i-ən, n.* a legendary Gaelic poet whose poems James Macpherson professed to translate. — *adjs.* **Ossianesque** (*-esk′*) in the manner of Macpherson's Ossian; **Ossianic** (*-an′ik*) relating to Ossian or to Macpherson's publications. [Gael. *Oisin.*]

ossicle, etc. See **osseous.**

ossifrage *os′i-frāj, n.* the lammergeier: the osprey. — *n.* **ossifraga** (*os-if′rə-gə*) the giant fulmar. [L. *ossifraga,* prob. the lammergeier — *os, ossis,* bone, and the root of *frangĕre,* to break.]

ossify, ossivorous, etc. See **osseous.**

ossuary *os′ū-ə-ri, n.* a place where bones are laid, e.g. a vault or charnel-house: an urn for bones. [L. *ossuārium — os,* bone.]

ostensible *os-tens′i-bl, adj.* that may be shown (*obs.*): outwardly showing or professed. — *n.* **ostensibil′ity.** — *adv.* **ostens′ibly.** — *adj.* **ostens′ive** showing: deictic: ostensible. — *adv.* **ostens′ively.** — *ns.* **osten′sory** a monstrance; **ostent′** appearance (*Shak.*): portent: ostentation; **ostentā′tion** (*-tən*) act of showing: display to draw attention or admiration: boasting. — *adj.* **ostentā′tious** given to show: fond of self-display: showy. — *adv.* **ostentā′tiously.** — *n.* **ostentā′tiousness.** [L. *ostendĕre, ostēnsum* (*tendĕre,* to show, and its freq. *ostentāre* — pfx. *obs-,* in front, *tendĕre,* to stretch.]

oste(o)- *os-ti(ō)-,* in composition, bone. — *adj.* **osteal** (*os′ti-əl*) relating to bone: sounding like bone on percussion. — *ns.* **osteitis** (*os-ti-ī′tis*) inflammation of a bone; **osteo-arthrī′tis** a form of arthritis in which the cartilages of the joint and the bone adjacent are worn away; **osteoarthrō′sis** chronic non-inflammatory disease of bones: osteo-arthritis; **os′teoblast** (Gr. *blastos,* a shoot) a bone-forming cell; **osteoclasis** (*os-ti-ok′lə-sis;* Gr. *klasis,* fracture) fracture of a bone for correction of a deformity: absorption and destruction of bone tissue by osteoclasts; **os′teoclast** a surgical instrument for fracturing bone: a bone-destroying cell; **osteocoll′a** (Gr. *kolla,* glue) a calcareous incrustation on roots, etc., once thought able to unite broken bones; **os′teoderm** (Gr. *derma,* skin) a bony dermal plate. — *adjs.* **osteoderm′al, -derm′atous, osteoderm′ic, -derm′ous.** — *ns.* **osteogen′esis, osteogeny** (*-oj′*) formation of bone. — *adjs.* **osteogenet′ic, osteogen′ic, osteog′enous.** — *n.pl.* **Osteoglossidae** (*-glos′i-dē;* Gr. *glōssa,* tongue) a family of bony fishes, including the arapaima. — *n.* **osteog′raphy** description of bones. — *adj.* **ost′eoid** bone-like. — *n.* **Osteol′epis** (Gr. *lepis,* scale) an Old Red Sandstone fossil fish with bone-like scales. — *adj.* **osteolog′ical.** — *n.* **osteol′ogist; osteol′ogy** the study of bones, part of anatomy; **osteō′ma** a tumour composed of bone or bone-like tissue; **osteomalacia** (*-ma-lā′shi-ə;* Gr. *malakos,* soft) softening of bones by absorption of their calcium salts, attributed to deficiency of vitamin D; **osteomyelitis** (*-mī-ə-lī′tis;* Gr. *myelos,* marrow) inflammation of bone and bone-marrow; **os′teopath** (*-path*), **osteop′athist** (*-ə-thist*) a practitioner of osteopathy. — *adj.* **osteopathic** (*ost-i-ō-path′ik*). — *ns.* **osteop′athy** a system of healing or treatment consisting largely of massage and manipulation; **os′teophyte** (*-fīt;* Gr. *phyton,* plant) an abnormal bony outgrowth. — *adjs.* **osteophytic** (*-fit′ik*); **osteoplast′ic.** — *ns.* **os′teoplasty** a plastic operation by which a loss of bone is remedied; **osteoporō′sis** (root as **pore**[1]) development of a porous structure in bone; **osteosarcoma** an osteogenic sarcoma; **os′teotome** (Gr. *tomos,* cutting; *surg.*) an instrument for cutting bones; **osteot′omy** the surgical cutting of a bone. [Gr. *osteon,* bone.]

ostinato *os-tin-ä′tō,* (*mus.*) *n.* a ground-bass: — *pl.* **ostina′tos.** [It.; root as **obstinate.**]

ostium *os′ti-əm, n.* the mouth of a river: a mouth-like opening: — *pl.* **os′tia.** — *adj.* **os′tial.** — *n.* **os′tiary** a doorkeeper: in the Roman Catholic Church, a member of the lowest of the minor orders: a river-mouth (*obs.*). — *adjs.* **os'tiate** having an ostium or ostia; **os'tiolate** having an opening. — *n.* **os'tiole** a small opening.   [L. *ostium.*]

ostler, (*obs.* and *U.S.*) **hostler** *os'lər,* (*U.S.*) *hos'lər,* *ns.* one who attends to horses at an inn: — *fem.* **ost'leress.** [hosteler.]

Ostmen *ōst'men, n.pl.* the Danish settlers in Ireland. [O.N. *Austmen,* Eastmen.]

-ostomy. The combining element is properly **-stomy** (q.v.).

Ostpolitik *ōst'po-li-tēk, n.* the West German policy of establishing normal trade and diplomatic relations with the East European communist countries: any similar policy.   [Ger., Eastern policy.]

ostrakon, ostracon *os'trə-kon, n.* a potsherd or tile, esp. one used in ostracism in Greece or for writing on in ancient Egypt: — *pl.* **os'traka, -ca.** — *adjs.* **ostracean** (*os-trā'shən*), **ostrā'ceous** of the nature of an oyster. — *n.* **Ostracion** (*os-trā'shi-on*) the coffer-fish genus. — *v.t.* **os'tracise, -ize** (*-sīz*) in ancient Greece, to banish by the vote of the people written on potsherds: to exclude from society, or from one's social group. — *ns.* **os'tracism** (*-sizm*) banishment by ostracising: expulsion from society; **os'tracod** a member of the **Ostracō'da,** a class of minute crustacea with bivalve shells; **os'tracoderm** (Gr. *derma,* skin) any member (as *Cephalaspis*) of a group of Silurian and Old Red Sandstone fishes or fish-like animals, generally cased in bony armour with undeveloped lower jaw, with flippers but not ordinary paired fins.   [Gr. *ostrakon,* a shell, tile, potsherd.]

Ostrea *os'tri-ə, n.* the oyster genus. — *adj.* **ostreā'ceous.** — *ns.* **ostreicul'ture** (*os-trē-i-*) oyster culture; **ostrēicul'turist; os'treophage** (*-fāj;* Gr. *phagein,* to eat) an oyster-eater. — *adj.* **ostreophagous** (*os-tri-of'ə-gəs*) oyster-eating. — *n.* **ostreoph'agy** (*-ə-ji*).   [L. *ostrea* — Gr. *ostreon,* oyster.]

ostreger *os'tri-jər.* Same as **austringer.**

ostreophagous, etc. See **Ostrea.**

ostrich *os'trich, -trij, n.* the largest living bird (*Struthio*), found in Africa, remarkable for its speed in running, and prized for its feathers. — *n.* **os'trichism** (*fig.*) the habit or policy of ignoring and refusing to face unpleasant facts. — *adj. and adv.* **os'trich-like** (usu. in reference to the supposed habit of hiding its head when in danger). — **os'trich-egg'; os'trich-farm'; os'trich-feath'er.**   [O.Fr. *ostruche* (Fr. *autruche*) — L. *avis,* bird, L.L. *struthiō* — Gr. *strouthiōn,* an ostrich, *strouthos,* a bird.]

Ostrogoth *os'trō-goth, n.* an eastern Goth — one of the tribe of east Goths who established their power in Italy in 493, and were overthrown in 555. — *adj.* **Os'trogothic.**

Ostyak, Ostiak *os'ti-ak, n.* a member of a Ugrian people of Siberia: their language. — Also *adj.*

otalgia *ō-tal'ji-ə, n.* earache — also **otal'gy.**   [Gr. *ous, ōtos,* ear, *algē,* pain.]

otary *ō'tə-ri, n.* a sea-lion or sea-bear, a seal with external ears: — *pl.* **o'taries.** — *adj.* **ot'arine.**   [Gr. *ōtaros,* large-eared — *ous, ōtos,* ear.]

other *udh'ər, adj.* orig., one of two: second: alternate: different: different from or not the same as the one in question (often with *than*): not the same: remaining: additional: left (prob., *Spens.*). — *pron.* (or *n.*) other one: another: each other (*arch.* and *Scot.*). — *adv.* otherwise. — *adj.* **oth'erguess** see **othergates.** — *n.* **oth'erness.** — *advs.* **oth'erwhere** elsewhere; **other'while, oth'erwhiles** at other times: sometimes; **oth'erwise** in another way or manner: by other causes: in other respects: under other conditions. — *conj.* else: under other conditions. — *n.* **oth'erworld** a world other than, better than, or beyond this. — Also *adj.* — *adj.* **oth'erworld'ish.** — *n.* **otherworld'liness.** — *adj.* **otherworld'ly** concerned with the world to come, or with the world of the imagination, to the exclusion of practical interests. — **other ranks** members of the armed services not holding commissions. — **every other** each alternate; **rather . . . than otherwise** rather than not; **someone (something) or other** an undefined person or thing; **the other day, etc.,** on an unspecified day, etc., not long past.   [O.E. *ōther;* cf. Ger. *ander,* L. *alter.*]

othergates *udh'ər-gāts,* (*obs.*) *adv.* in another way. — *adj.* of another kind. — Also **oth'erguess** (in *Fielding, Goldsmith,* etc., **anotherguess**). — Also spelt as separate words. — **other gates, other guess.**   [other, and gen. of **gate²**.]

otic *ō'tik, adj.* of or pertaining to the ear. — *ns.* **ot'tis** inflammation of the ear; **otocyst** (*ō'tō-sist*) an auditory or equilibristic vesicle; **ot'olith** (Gr. *lithos,* stone) a calcareous concretion in the ear of various animals, the movement of which helps the animal to maintain equilibrium: an ear-bone; **otol'ogist; otol'ogy** knowledge of the ear; **otorhinolaryngology** (*-rī-nō-lar-ing-gol'ə-ji;* Gr. *rhīs, rhīnos,* nose, *larynx, -yngos,* larynx) knowledge of ear, nose, and larynx and their diseases, often shortened to **otolaryngol'ogy; otorrhoea** (*ō-tō-rē'ə;* Gr. *rhoiā,* flow) a discharge from the ear; **otoscler-o'sis** formation of spongy bone in the capsule of the labyrinth; **o'toscope** an instrument for examining the ear.   [Gr. *ous, ōtos,* ear.]

otiose *ō'shi-ōs, adj.* unoccupied: indolent: functionless: futile: superfluous. — *n.* **otiosity** (*-os'i-ti*) ease, idleness.   [L. *ōtiōsus* — *ōtium,* leisure.]

otocyst . . . otolaryngology . . .otology. See **otic.**

-otomy. The combining element is properly **-tomy** (q.v.).

otorhinolaryngology . . . otoscope. See **otic.**

ottar *ot'ər.* See **attar.**

ottava *öt-tä'vä, ō-tä'və, n.* an octave. — *n.* **ottavino** (*-vē'nō*) the piccolo: — *pl.* **ottavin'os.** — **ottava rima** (*rē'mä*) an Italian stanza consisting of eight hendecasyllabic lines, rhyming *a b a b a b c c.*   [It.; cf. **octave.**]

otter *ot'ər, n.* an aquatic fish-eating carnivore (*Lutra vulgaris*) of the weasel family: its brown short fur: a board travelling edge-up, manipulated on the principle of the kite, to carry the end of a fishing-line (or several hooked and baited lines) in a lake, or to keep open the mouth of a trawl (also **ott'er-board**): a paravane. — *v.t.* or *v.i.* to fish with an otter-board. — **ott'er-hound** a dog of a breed used in otter-hunting; **ott'er-hunting; ott'er-shrew'** a large otter-like aquatic West African insectivore (*Potamogale velox*); **ott'er-trawl'** a trawl with otter-boards; **ott'er-trawl'ing.**   [O.E. *otor,* akin to **water.**]

otto *ot'ō.* See **attar.**

Ottoman *ot'ō-mən, adj.* pertaining to the Turkish Empire, founded by *Othmān* or *Osmān:* Osmanli. — *n.* a Turk of Turkey: (the following meanings without *cap.*) a cushioned seat for several persons sitting with their backs to one another: a low, stuffed seat without a back: a variety of corded silk. — *n.* **Ott'amite, Ott'omite** a Turk.

ottrelite *ot'ri-līt, n.* a mineral like chlorite but harder. — **ott'relite-slate** a clay slate with minute plates of ottrelite.   [*Ottrez* in the Ardennes, and Gr. *lithos,* stone.]

ou, ow *ōō,* (*Scot.*) *interj.* expressing concession. — **ou ay** why yes: O yes.

ouabain, wabain *wä-bä'in, n.* a poisonous alkaloid got from apocynaceous seeds and wood (*Strophanthus,* etc.).   [French spelling — Somali *wabayo,* a tree that yields it.]

ouakari. See **uakari.**

oubit *ōō'bit.* See **woubit.**

oubliette *ōō-bli-et', n.* a dungeon with no opening but at the top: a secret pit in the floor of a dungeon into which a victim could be precipitated.   [Fr., — *oublier,* to forget — L. *oblīvīscī.*]

ouch¹ *owch, n.* a brooch: a clasped ornament: the socket of a precious stone.   [O.Fr. *nouche.*]

ouch² *owch, interj.* expressing pain.   [Ger. *autsch.*]

oucht *ohht,* (*Scot.*) *n.* anything.   [Cf. **aught.**]

Oudenarde $\overline{oo}'d\partial$-*närd, n.* a tapestry representing foliage, etc., once made at *Oudenarde* in Belgium.

oughly. See **ouglie.**

ought[1] *öt, n.* a variant of **aught:** also an illit. corr. of **naught.** — *adv.* (*Scot.*) **oughtlings** (*ohh'linz*) at all.

ought[2] *öt, pa.t.* of **owe:** now *obs.* or *dial.* except as an auxiliary verb (with time expressed by tense of the principal verb) should: is or was proper or necessary. — *n.* **ought'ness** rightness.

ouglie, oughly, old spellings of **ugly.** — *adj.* **ough'ly= headed** (*Milt.*).

Ouija® *wē'j∂, n.* a board with an alphabet, used with a planchette. — Also without *cap.* [Fr. *oui,* Ger. *ja,* yes.]

ouistiti. A French spelling of **wistiti.**

ouk, oulk $\overline{oo}k$, *n.* Scots form of **week.**

oulakan, oulachon $\overline{oo}'l\partial$-*k∂n.* See **eulachon.**

oulong. Same as **oolong.**

ounce[1] *owns, n.* the twelfth part of the (legally obsolete) pound troy = 480 grains: $^{1}/_{16}$ of a pound avoirdupois: a minute quantity (*fig.*). — **fluid ounce** the volume of an avoirdupois ounce of distilled water at 62° Fahr., $^{1}/_{20}$ pint 0·1284 litre): $^{1}/_{16}$ U.S. pint (0·0295 litre). [O.Fr. *unce* — L. *uncia,* the twelfth part; cf. **inch**[1].]

ounce[2] *owns, n.* originally, and still sometimes, a lynx: now generally the snow leopard: the jaguar: the cheetah: sometimes vaguely any moderate-sized wild beast of the cat tribe. [Fr. *once,* perh. for *lonce* (as if *l'once*) — Gr. *lynx.*]

oundy *own'di, adj.* wavy: undé (*her.*). [Fr. *ondé;* cf. **undate.**]

oup, oop $\overline{oo}p$, (*Scot.*) *v.t.* to bind round with thread or cord: to join. [Appar. **whip.**]

ouphe, ouph *owf,* $\overline{oo}f$, (*Shak.*) *n.* Same as **oaf.**

our *owr, pron.* (*gen.*) or *poss. adj.* pertaining or belonging to us — when used absolutely, **ours** (*owrz*), *dial.* **ourn** (*owrn*). — *reflex.* and *emphatic* **ourself'** myself (regally or editorially): — *pl.* **ourselves** (-*selvz'*). [O.E. *ūre,* gen. of *wē,* we.]

ourali $\overline{oo}$-*rä'lē.* See **wourali.**

ourang-outang. Same as **orang-utan.**

ourari $\overline{oo}$-*rä'rē.* See **wourali.**

ourebi. Same as **oribi.**

ourie, oorie, owrie $\overline{oo}'ri$, (*Scot.*) *adj.* dingy: shabby: dreary: drooping: chill: inclined to shiver or shudder.

ouroboros $\overline{oo}$-*rob'or-os,* (*myth.*) *n.* a representation of a serpent with its tail in its mouth, symbolising completion, totality, endlessness, etc. [Gr., lit. 'tail-devouring' — *ourā,* a tail, *boraein,* to eat.]

ourology, ouroscopy, etc. Same as **urology,** etc. at **uro-.**

ousel. See **ouzel.**

oust *owst, v.t.* to eject or expel. — *n.* **oust'er** (*law*) ejection, dispossession. [A.Fr. *ouster* (O.Fr. *oster;* Fr. *ôter*), to remove; of obscure origin.]

oustiti $\overline{oo}$-*sti-tē', n.* a lock-opening tool, outsiders (q.v.). [Fr., marmoset.]

out (see also **out-**) *owt, adv.* (shading into *adj.* predicatively), not within: forth: abroad: to, towards, or at the exterior or a position away from the inside or inner part or from anything thought of as enclosing, hiding, or obscuring: from among others: from the mass: beyond bounds: away from the original or normal position or state: at or towards the far end, or a remote position: seawards: away from home or a building: in or into the open air: in or into a state of exclusion: not in office: not in use or fashion: ruled out, not to be considered: no longer in the game: no longer in as a batsman, dismissed: not batting: out of the contest and unable to resume in time: in the condition of having won: away from the mark: at fault: in error: not in form or good condition: at a loss: in or into a disconcerted, perplexed, or disturbed state: not in harmony or amity: in distribution: in or into the hands of others or the public: on loan: to or at an end: in an exhausted or extinguished state: completely: thoroughly: subjected to loss: in or to the field: in quest of or expressly aiming at something: in rebellion: on strike: in an exposed state: no longer in concealment or obscurity: in or into the open: before the public: in or into society: on domestic service: in existence: at full length: in an expanded state: in bloom: in extension: loudly and clearly: forcibly: unreservedly. — *adj.* external: outlying: remote: played away from home: outwards: not batting: exceeding the usual: in any condition expressed by the adverb *out.* — *n.* one who is out: that which is outside: a projection or outward bend (as in *outs and ins*): an omission in setting type: a paying out, esp. (in *pl.*) rates and taxes, etc. (*dial.*): an outing (*dial.*): a disadvantage, drawback (*U.S.*): permission to go out (*U.S.*): a way out. — *prep.* forth from (now usu. *from out*): outside of (now *rare*): without (*obs.*). — *v.t.* to put out: to knock out. — *v.i.* to go out: (with *with*) to bring out: (with *with*) to say suddenly or unexpectedly. — *interj.* away, begone: you are, he is, out: alas: shame (usu. *out upon; arch.*). — *n.* **out'age** the amount of a commodity lost in transport or storage: the amount of fuel used on a flight: stoppage of a mechanism due to failure of power: a period during which electricity fails or is cut off. *adjs.* **out'ed** ejected; **out'er** (O.E. *ūterra,* comp.) more out or without: external — opp. to *inner* (**outer bar** the junior barristers who plead outside the bar in court, as opposed to King's (Queen's) Counsel and others who plead within the bar). — *n.* the outermost ring of a target, a shot striking it: in an electrical distribution system either of the conductors whose potential is above or below the earth's: an unenclosed area for spectators at a racecourse (*Austr.*). — *adjs.* **out'ermost, out'most** (-*m∂st,* -*mōst;* O.E. *ūtemest,* superl.) most or farthest out: most distant. — *ns.* **out'ing** ejection: distance out: an outdoor excursion or airing; **out'ness** state of being out: externality to the perceiving mind, objectiveness. — *adj., adv., prep., n.* **outside** see separate article. — *adj.* **out'ward** toward the outside: on the outside: outer: external: exterior: appearing externally: apparent: formal: not inherent, adventitious: worldly, carnal (*theol.*): dissolute (*dial.*). — *adv.* toward the exterior: away from port: to a foreign port: superficially. — *n.* external appearance (*Shak.*): the outside. — *adv.* **out'wardly** in an outward manner: externally: in appearance. — *n.* **out'wardness** externality: objectivity. — *adv.* **out'wards** in an outward direction. — *adj.* **out'-and-out** thorough-going: thorough-paced: utter: absolute: unqualified. — *adv.* **out-and-out'** finally and completely: definitely: unreservedly. — *n.* **out-and-out'er** any person or thing that is a complete or extreme type: a thorough-going partisan: a great lie. — *adj.* and *adv.* **out'back** (*Austr.*) in, to, or of, the back-country. — *n.* the back-country. — *adv.* **outback'er** one from the back-country. — *n.pl.* **out'bounds** (*Spens.*) boundaries. — **out'building** a building separate from, but used in connection with, a dwelling-house or a main building: an outhouse. — *adv.* **outby, outbye** (*owt-bī', ōōt-bī'; Scot.*) out of doors: a little way off: outwards: towards the shaft (*mining*). — *adj.* **out'by(e)** outdoor: outlying. — **out'-dweller** one who dwells elsewhere, esp. one who owns land in a parish but lives outside it; **out'edge** the farthermost bound; **outer space** the immeasurable expanse beyond the solar system, or, loosely, at a distance from the earth reached only by rocket; **out'erwear** clothes, as suits, dresses, worn over other clothes; **out'field** arable land continually cropped without being manured — opp. to *infield* (*Scot.*): any open field at a distance from the farmsteading: any undefined district or sphere: at cricket and baseball, the outer part of the field: the players who occupy it; **out'fielder** one such player; **out'guard** a guard at a distance, or at the farthest distance, from the main body; **out'-half** (*Rugby football*) a stand-off half; **out'house** a separate building subsidiary to a main building; **outing flannel** a flannelette; **out'land** a foreign land: land granted to tenants: an outlying land or territory. — *adj.* foreign: outlying. — **out'- lander** a foreigner: an uitlander. — *adj.* **outland'ish**

foreign (*arch.*): queer, bizarre: out-of-the-way. — *adv.*
outland'ishly. — **outland'ishness; out'line** the outer line: the line by which any figure or object as seen is bounded: a sketch showing only the main lines: representation by such lines: a general statement without details: a statement of the main principles: a set-line in fishing. — *v.t.* to draw the exterior line of: to delineate or sketch. — *adj.* **outlinear** (*owt-lin'i-ər*) like an outline. — **out'lodging** a lodging beyond bounds; **out'marriage** exogamy. — *adjs.* **out-of-date'** not abreast of the times: obsolete: no longer valid; **out-of-door(s)'** out-door (see **out-**): outside of parliament. — *n.* **out=of-doors'** the open air. — *adv.* (without hyphens; see below). — *adjs.* **out-of(-the)-bod'y** of or pertaining to an occurrence in which an individual has the experience of being outside his own body; **out-of-the-way'** uncommon: singular: secluded: remote. — *n.pl* and *adj.* **out-of-work'** unemployed (persons). — *adv.* and *prep.* **out-o'ver, out-owre** (*owt-owr', ōōt-owr'; Scot.*) out over: over. — **out'-parish** a parish associated with a town but beyond the boundary: an outlying parish; **out'part** a part remote from the centre; **out'-patient** a hospital patient who is not an inmate; **out'-pension** a pension granted to one who is not resident in an institution. — *v.t.* to grant an out-pension to. — **out'-pensioner** a non-resident pensioner; **out'port** a port out of or remote from the chief port: a port away from the town or customs area: a place of export; **out'-porter** a porter who carries luggage to and from, and not merely in, the place where he is employed; **out'post** a post or station beyond the main body or in the wilds: its occupants: a remote settlement. — *n.pl.* **out'quarters** quarters situated away from headquarters. — **outre-lief'** outdoor relief (see under **out-**); **out'ride** an unaccented syllable or syllables added to a foot, esp. in sprung rhythm; **out'rigger** a projecting spar for extending sails or any part of the rigging: a projecting contrivance ending in a float fixed to the side of a canoe against capsizing: an iron bracket fixed to the outside of a boat carrying a rowlock at its extremity to increase the leverage of the oar: a light racing-boat with projecting rowlocks: a projecting beam for carrying a suspended scaffold in building: a projecting frame to support the controlling planes of an aeroplane: an extension from the splinter-bar of a carriage to take another horse. — *adj.* **out'right** out-and-out: unqualified: unmitigated: downright: direct. — *adv.* **outright'** directly: straight ahead: unreservedly: undisguisedly: at once and completely. — **out'run** an outlying pasture or run; **out'-sentry** a sentry placed at a distance; **out'settlement** an outlying settlement. — *adj.* and *n.* **out'size** (a size, or a garment, etc., that is) exceptionally large. — **out'skirt** (usu. in *pl.*) the border area; **out'sole** the outer sole of a boot or shoe which rests on the ground; **out'station** a subsidiary branch or post, esp. in an outlying area: a place far from the source of services, at which Australian aborigines live in a traditional manner; **out'-take** an unwanted section cut out of a film; **out'-tray** a shallow container for letters, etc., ready to be dispatched; **out'voter** a voter not resident in the constituency; **out'-wall** the outside wall of a building: external appearance (*Shak.*). — *prep.* **outwith** (*owt'with, ōōt'with, -with'; Scot.*) outside of. — *adv.* outwards. — **out'work** a work outside the principal wall or line of fortification: outdoor work, field work: work done away from the shop or factory; **out'worker.** — **at outs** (*U.S.*) at odds; **from out** out from; **murder will out** see **murder; out and about** able

to go out, convalescent: active out of doors; **out and away** by far: beyond competition; **out at elbow** see **elbow; out for** abroad in quest of: aiming at obtaining, achieving: dismissed from batting with a score of; **out from under** out of a difficult situation; **out of** from within: from among: not in: not within: excluded from: from (as source, material, motive, condition, possession, language, etc.): born of: beyond the bounds, range, or scope of: deviating from, in disagreement with: away or distant from: without, destitute or denuded of; **out of course** out of order; **out of doors** in or into the open air; **out of it** excluded from participation: without a chance; **out on one's feet** as good as knocked out: done for, but with a semblance of carrying on; **outs and ins** see **ins and outs** at **in**[1]; **out to** aiming, working resolutely, to; **out to out** in measurement from outside to outside: overall; **out upon** shame on; **out with** away with; not friendly with: see also **out** *v.i.* above; **out'ward-bound'** bound outwards or to a foreign port; **out'ward-saint'ed** appearing outwardly to be a saint. — See also **character, join, place, pocket, print, question, sight**[1]**, sort, temper, time, use**[2]**, wood**[1]**,** etc. [O.E. *ūte, ūt;* Goth. *ut,* Ger. *aus,* Sans. *ud.*]

out- (see also **out**) in composition, (1) meaning 'away from the inside or inner part', *lit.* and *fig.*, and prefixed to, instead of following, verbs (often *poet.*) and related nouns and adjectives, e.g. *to outspread, an outpouring, outgoing;* (2) with prepositional force, meaning 'outside of', e.g. *outboard, outdoor;* (3) meaning 'through, throughout', or 'beyond', or 'completely', e.g. *outwatch, outflank, outweary;* (4) indicating the fact of going beyond a norm, standard of comparison, or limit, 'more than', 'more successfully than', 'farther than', 'longer than', etc., e.g. *outweigh, outmanoeuvre, outstep, outlast, out-Herod* (and other similar constructions). (Words in which **out** has the adjectival senses of 'outside, not within', 'outlying', are given at **out**.) — *vs.t.* **out-ask'** to proclaim the banns of for the last time; **outbal'ance** to outweigh; **outbar'gain** to get the better of in a bargain; **outbid'** to make a higher bid than; **outblust'er** to exceed in blustering: to get the better of by bluster: to deprive (of) by bluster. — *adj.* **out'board** outside of a ship or boat: towards, or nearer, the ship's side: having engines outside the boat. — *adv.* outside of, or towards the outside of. — *adj.* **out'bound** bound for a distant port. — *vs.t.* **outbrag'** to surpass in bragging or boasting: to excel in beauty or splendour (*Shak.*); **outbrave'** to excel in boldness or splendour (*Shak.*): to outface. — *n.* **out'break** a breaking out: a distance. — *v.i.* **outbreak'** to burst forth. — *adjs* **outbreath'd** (*-bretht'; Shak.*) out of breath; **out'bred** resulting from outbreeding. — *v.i.* **outbreed'.** — *ns.* **outbreed'ing** breeding from parents not close akin: exogamy; **out'burst** a bursting out: an eruption or explosion: a sudden violent expression of feeling; **out'cast** one who is cast out of society or home: anything rejected, eliminated, or cast out: a quarrel (*Scot.*); **out'caste** one who is of no caste or has lost caste. — *vs.t.* **outcaste'** to put out of caste; **outclass'** to surpass so far as to seem in a different class. — *adj.* **outclassed'.** — *n.* **out'come** the issue: consequence: result. — *v.t.* **outcraft'y** (*Shak.*) to exceed in craft. — *n.* **out'crop** the cropping out of a rock: a sudden emergence or occurrence. — *v.i.* (*-krop'*) to crop out. — *v.t.* **outcross'** to breed individuals of different strains but the same breed: to outbreed. — *ns.* **out'cross; out'crossing; out'cry** a loud cry of protest, distress, etc.:

For many words beginning **out-**, *see* **out** *or* **out-**.

For other sounds see detailed chart of pronunciation.

a confused noise: a public auction: public bargaining by a group. — *vs.t.* **outdare'** to surpass in daring: to defy; **outdate'** to put out of date. — *adj.* **outdāt'ed.** — *vs.t.* **outdis'tance** to leave far behind: to outstrip; **outdo'** to surpass: to excel: to overcome. — *adj.* **out'door** outside the door or the house: in or for the open air (**outdoor relief,** help formerly given to a pauper not living in the workhouse). — *adv.* **outdoors'** out of the house: abroad. — *n.* the world outside dwellings, the open air. — *adj.* **outdoor'sy** of, characteristic of, suitable for or having a liking for the outdoors. — *vs.t.* **outdure'** to outlast (*obs.*); **outdwell'** to stay beyond (*Shak.*); **outface'** to stare down: to confront boldly: to contradict (*obs.*): to force from (*Shak.*): to maintain boldly or impudently to the face of (that; *obs.*). — *ns.* **outfall** (*owt'föl*) the outlet of a river, drain, etc.: a sortie: a quarrel (*dial.*); **out'fit** the act of fitting out for an enterprise: complete equipment: a set of (esp. selected and matching) clothes: expenses for fitting out: a company travelling, or working, together for any purpose, formerly esp. in charge of cattle (*U.S.*): any set of persons, a gang. — *v.t.* to fit out, equip. — *v.i.* to get an outfit. — *ns.* **out'fitter** one who furnishes outfits. one who deals in clothing, haberdashery, sporting equipment, etc.; **out'fitting.** — *v.t.* **outflank'** to extend beyond or pass round the flank of: to circumvent. — *ns.* **out'fling** a sharp retort or gibe; **out'flow** a flowing out: an outward current: outfall: amount that flows out; **out'flush** a sudden glow. — *vs.t.* **outfoot'** to outstrip: to outsail; **outfox'** to get the better of by cunning: to outwit; **outfrown'** to frown down. — *v.t.* **outgas'.** — *n.* **outgass'ing** loss of, or removal of, occluded or adsorbed gas from a solid under vacuum conditions: also removal of gas from a liquid. — *n.* **out'gate** (*Spens.* and *Northern*) an outlet: an exit. — *v.t.* **outgen'eral** to get the better of by generalship: to prove a better general than. — *n.* **out'giving** a disbursement: an utterance: a declaration of policy. — *vs.t.* **outglare'** to glare more than: to be more glaring than; **outgo'** to outstrip: to surpass: to pass or live through: to overreach (*obs.*). — *v.i.* to go out: to come to an end: — *pa.t.* **outwent'**; *pa.p.* **outgone'.** — *ns.* **out'go** (*pl.* **out'goes**) that which goes out: expenditure — opp. to *income*; **out'going** act or state of going out: extreme limit: expenditure. — *adj.* departing — opp. to *incoming,* as a tenant. — *v.t.* **outgrow'** to surpass in growth: to grow out of, grow too big for: to eliminate or become free from in course of growth. — *ns.* **out'growth** that which grows out from anything: an excrescence: a product. — *v.t.* **outgun'** to defeat by means of superior weapons, forces (*lit.* and *fig.*). — *n.* **out'haul** a rope for hauling out the clew of a sail (also **out'hauler**). — *vs.t.* **out-Her'od** to overact the part of (*Herod*) in violence (*Hamlet* III, ii): to outdo, esp. in what is bad; **outhire'** (*Spens.* **outhyre**) to give out as if on hire. — *v.t.* **outjest'** to overcome by jesting (*Shak.*): to excel in jesting. — *ns.* **out'jet, out'jut** a projection. — *ns.* and *adjs.* **outjett'ing, outjutt'ing.** — *n.* **out'lash** a sudden burst or stroke. — *vs.t.* **outlast'** to last longer than; **outlaunch'** (*Spens.* **outlaunce**) to launch forth. — *n.* **out'lay** that which is laid out: expenditure. — *v.t.* **outlay'** to lay out in view: to expend: to surpass in laying. — *n.* **out'leap** an act of leaping out: an excursion: an outburst. — *v.t.* **outleap'** to leap beyond or over: to surpass in leaping. — *v.i.* to leap out. — *v.t.* **outlearn'** to elicit (*Spens.*): to surpass: to excel in learning: to get beyond the study of. — *n.* **out'let** the place where or means by which anything is let out,

provided or sold: the passage outward, vent. — *v.t.* **outlie'** to surpass in telling lies. — *v.i.* **outlie'** to lie in the open: to camp: to lie stretched out. — *v.t.* to lie beyond. — *n.* **out'lier** one who lies in the open: one who lodges or lies apart from others or from a place with which he is connected: an outsider: a detached portion of anything lying some way off or out: an isolated remnant of rock surrounded by older rocks (*geol.*). — *v.t.* **outlive** (-*liv'*) to live longer than: to survive: to live through: to live down. — *n.* **out'look** a vigilant watch: a place for looking out from: a view, prospect: a prospect for the future: mental point of view. — *v.t.* **outlook'** (*Shak.* owt') to face courageously. — *v.i.* to look out. — *v.t.* **outlus'tre** (*Shak.*) to outshine. — *adj.* **out'lying** lying out or beyond: lodging apart: remote: on the exterior or frontier: detached. — *vs.t.* **outman'** to outdo in manliness: to outnumber in men; **outmanoeu'vre** to surpass in or by manoeuvring; **outman'tle** to excel in dress or ornament; **outmeas'ure** to exceed in extent; **outmode'** to put out of fashion. — *adj.* **outmod'ed.** — *vs.t.* **outmove'** to move faster than: to get the better of by moving; **outname'** to surpass in notoriety; **outnight'** (Shak., *Merch. of Ven.* V, i) to surpass in mentioning nights; **outnum'ber** to exceed in number; **outpace'** to walk faster than: to outstrip; **out-par'amour** (*Shak.*) to exceed in addiction to mistresses; **outpass'ion** to go beyond in passionateness; **outpeer'** (*Shak.*) to surpass or excel; **outperform'** to outdo or surpass in a specific field of activity; **outplay'** to play better than, and so defeat; **outpoint'** to score more points than. — *n.* **out'pouring** a pouring out: a passionate or fluent utterance. — *vs.t.* **outpower'** to surpass in power; **outpray'** to exceed in earnestness or length of prayer: to overcome in or by prayer; **outprice'** to offer a better price, financial return, etc. than; **outprize'** (*Shak.*) to exceed in estimation. — *n.* **out'put** quantity produced or turned out: data in either printed or coded form after processing by a computer: punched tape or printed page by which processed data leave a computer: signal delivered by a telecommunications instrument or system. — *v.t.* (of a computer, etc.) to send out, supply, produce as output (data, etc.). — *vs.t.* **outrank'** to rank above; **outrate'** to offer a better rate of return than; **outreach'** to reach or extend beyond: to overreach: to stretch forth. — *n.* a reaching out: the extent or distance something can reach or stretch out: an organisation's involvement in or contact with the surrounding community, esp. that of a church for purposes of evangelism or that of community welfare organisations taking their services out to, esp. disadvantaged, individuals and groups rather than expecting them to approach the welfare organisations. — *vs.t.* **outred', outredd'en** to surpass in redness; **outreign'** to reign longer than: (*Spens.* **outraigne**) to reign to the end of; **outride'** to ride beyond: to ride faster than: to ride safely through (a storm). — *n.* **out'rider** a man who rides beside a carriage as a guard: one sent ahead as a scout, or to ensure a clear passage. — *v.t.* **outrun'** to go beyond in running: to exceed: to get the better of or to escape by running (**outrun** or **overrun the constable,** to run into debt: to live beyond one's means). — *n.* **out'runner.** — *vs.t.* **outsail'** to leave behind in sailing: to sail beyond; **outscorn'** (*Shak.*) to face out with scorn; **outsell'** to fetch a higher price than: to exceed in value: to surpass in the number or amount of sales. — *ns.* **out'set** a setting out: beginning: an outward current; **out'setting; out'shot** (*Scot.*) a projection in a building, or a recess made in the wall

---

For many words beginning **out-,** *see* **out** *or* **out-.**

---

of a room; **out'sight** power of seeing external things: (*owt'sīt, ōōt'sihht*) outdoor possessions (*Scot.*). — Also *adj.* — *v.t.* **outsit'** to sit beyond the time of: to sit longer than. — *adj.* **out'size** over normal size. — *n.* an exceptionally large size: anything, esp. a garment, of exceptionally large size. — *adj.* **out'sized.** — *vs.t.* **outsleep'** to sleep longer than: to sleep through: to sleep to or beyond the time of; **outsmart'** (*coll.*; *orig. U.S.*) to show more cleverness or cunning than, to outwit; **outspend'** to spend more than. — *adjs.* **outspent'** thoroughly tired out; **outspō'ken** frank or bold of speech: uttered with boldness. — *n.* **outspō'kenness.** — *v.t.* **outsport'** (*Shak.*) to sport beyond the limits of. — *v.t.* and *v.i.* **outspread'** to spread out or over. — *adj.* **out'spread** (or *owt-spred'*) spread out. — *n.* an expanse. — *adj.* **outspread'ing.** — *v.i.* **outspring'** to spring out. — *n.* **out'spring** outcome. — *v.t.* **outstand'** to withstand: to stand or endure through or beyond. — *v.i.* to stand out or project: to stand out (to sea): to stand over, remain. — *adj.* **outstand'ing** prominent: excellent, superior: unsettled: unpaid: still to be attended to or done. — *adv.* **outstand'ingly.** — *vs.t.* **outstare'** to stare down (*Shak.*): to face the stare of unabashed: to gaze at without being blinded; **outstay'** to stay beyond or throughout: to stay longer than: to endure longer than; **outstep'** to step beyond, overstep; **outstrain'** to stretch out; **outstretch'** to stretch out: to reach forth: to spread out: to stretch to the end of: to stretch beyond; **outstrike** (*owt-strīk'*, or *owt'*) to outdo in striking; **outstrip'** to outrun: to leave behind: to surpass; **outstrip'** to outdo in denuding oneself; **outsum'** to outnumber; **outswear'** to exceed in swearing: to overcome by swearing; **outsweet'en** to excel in sweetness; **outswell'** to swell more than (*Shak.*): to overflow. — *ns.* **out'swing** an outward swing or swerve; **out'swinger** a ball bowled to swerve from leg to off (*cricket*): a ball kicked to swerve away from the goal or from the centre of the pitch. — *v.t.* **outtake'** (*obs.*) to take out: to except. — *n.* **out'-take** a sequence of film removed from the final edited version. — *prep.* (*obs.*) **outtake',** (*obs.*; *orig. pa.p.*) **outtak'en** except. — *vs.t.* **outtell'** to tell forth: to tell to the end: to tell or count beyond; **outtongue'** (*Shak.*) to speak louder than; **outtop'** to reach higher than: to excel. — *n.* **out'turn** the amount of anything turned out, produced or achieved. — *vs.t.* **outven'om** (*Shak.*) to exceed in poisonousness; **outvill'ain** (*Shak.*) to exceed in villainy; **outvoice'** (*Shak.*) to exceed in clamour or noise: to drown the voice of; **outvote'** to defeat by a greater number of votes; **outwatch'** to watch longer than: to watch throughout the time of; **outwear'** to wear out: to spend, live through: to outlive, outgrow: to outlast; **outwea'ry** to weary out completely; **outweed'** (*Spens.*) to root out; **outweep'** to weep out, shed wholly: to surpass in weeping; **outweigh'** to exceed in weight or importance. — *v.t.* and *v.i.* **outwell'** to pour or well out. — *v.t.* **outwent'** see outgo. — *v.i.* **outwick'** in curling, to strike the outside of another stone and so send it within a circle. — *vs.t.* **outwin'** (*Spens.*) to get out of; **outwind** (*-wīnd'*) to unwind, extricate; **outwing'** to outstrip in flying: to fly beyond: to outflank; **outwit'** to surpass in wit or ingenuity: to defeat by superior ingenuity: — *pr.p.* **outwitt'ing;** *pa.t.* and *pa.p.* **outwitt'ed; outwork'** (*Shak.*) to surpass in work: to work out or bring to an end: to finish: — *pa.t.* and *pa.p.* **outwrought'.** — *adj.* **outworn'** (or *owt'*) worn out: obsolete. — *vs.t.* **outworth'** (*Shak.*) to exceed in value; **outwrest'** (*Spens.*) to extort.

outdacious *owt-dā'shəs, adj.* an illiterate perversion of **audacious.**

outfangthief *owt'fang-thēf, n.* the right of judging and fining thieves taken outside of one's own jurisdiction. [O.E. *ūtfangene-thēof* — *ūt,* out, the root of *fōn,* to take, *thēof,* thief.]

outher *ow'dhər, ō'dhər,* an old form, now *dial.,* of **either.**

outlaw *owt'lö, n.* one deprived of the protection of the law: (*loosely*) a bandit: an outcast: a wild, dangerous or unmanageable animal (*U.S.*). — *v.t.* to place beyond the law: to deprive of the benefit of the law: to ban. — *n.* **out'lawry** the act of putting a man out of the protection of the law: state of being an outlaw. [O.E. *ūtlaga* — O.N. *ūtlāgi* — *ūt,* out, *lög,* law.]

outler *ōōt'lər,* (*Burns*) *adj.* not housed. — *n.* a beast that is not housed: one who is out of office. [Poss. **outlier.**]

outrage *owt'rij, -rāj, n.* excess, undue divergence from a mean (*Spens.*): violence beyond measure (*Shak.*): clamour (*Spens.*): gross or violent injury: an act of wanton mischief: an atrocious act: gross offence to moral feelings: great anger or indignation: violation: rape. — *v.t.* to treat with excessive abuse: to shock grossly: to injure by violence, esp. to violate, to ravish. — *adj.* **outrageous** (*owt-rā'jəs*) violent: furious: turbulent: atrocious: monstrous: immoderate. — *adv.* **outrā'geously.** — *ns.* **outrā'geousness.** [O.Fr. *ultrage* — *outre,* beyond — L. *ultrā;* the word is not connected with **out** and **rage** but influenced by them.]

outrance *ōō-trãs, n.* the utmost extremity: the bitter end (à **outrance** to the bitter end of a combat — erroneously in Eng. use, à **l'outrance**). [Fr., — *outre,* beyond.]

outré *ōō'trā, adj.* beyond what is customary or proper: extravagant, fantastic. [Fr.]

outrecuidance *ōōt-ər-kwē'dəns, ōōt-r'- kwē'dãs,* (*Scott*) *n.* presumption, overweening. [Fr. *outre,* beyond, O.Fr. *cuider,* think, plume oneself — L. *cōgitāre.*]

outremer *ōō-tr' -mer, n.* the region beyond the sea: overseas. [Fr. *outre,* beyond, *mer,* sea.]

outroop *owt'rōōp,* (*obs.*) *n.* an auction sale. — *n.* **out'-rooper** (*obs.*) an auctioneer: the Common Crier of the City of London. [Du. *uitroepen,* to cry out, proclaim.]

outrope, -er *owt'rōp, -ər.* Same as **outroop, -er.**

outside *owt'sīd, owt'sīd, owt-sīd', n.* the outer side: the farthest limit: the outer surface: the exterior: an outside passenger: the outer part: (in *pl.*) the top and bottom quires of a ream of paper. — *adj.* on or from the outside: carried on the outside: exterior: superficial: external: extreme: beyond the limit: not enjoying membership: (of a criminal activity) carried out by person(s) not having contacts with someone near the victim: at a distance from a major centre of population (*Austr.*): of a position near(er) the edge of the field (*Rugby,* etc.). — *adv.* **outside'** (sometimes *owt'*) on or to the outside: not within: out of prison. — *prep.* **out'side** outside of: except, apart from (*dial.*): (*Rugby,* etc.) in a position nearer the edge of the field than. — *n.* **outsid'er** one who (or that which) is not a member of a particular company, profession, etc., a stranger, a layman: one not considered fit to associate with: one who is not an inmate: one who is not participating: a racehorse, competitor, team, etc. not included among the favourites in the betting: one whose place in a game, at work, etc., is on the outside: (in *pl.*) a pair of nippers for turning a key in a keyhole from the outside. — **outside broadcast** a broadcast not made from within a studio; **out'side-car** an Irish jaunting-car in which the passengers sit back to back; **outside chance** a remote

---

outroar' (*Shak.*) *v.t.* out- (1).	**outshoot'** *v.t.* out- (3), (4).	**outtalk'** *v.t.* out- (4).
outroot' *v.t.* out- (1).	**out'shoot** *n.* out- (1).	**outthink'** *v.t.* out- (4).
outrush' *v.i., n.* out- (1).	**outsoar'** *v.t.* out- (4).	**outtrav'el** *v.t.* out- (3), (4).
outscold' (*Shak.*) *v.t.* out- (4).	**outspeak'** *v.t.* out- (1), (4). —	**outval'ue** *v.t.* out- (4).
outshine' *v.i.* out- (1). —	**outspeak'** *v.i.* out- (1).	**outvie'** *v.t.* out- (4).
outshine' *v.t.* out- (4).	**outstare'** *v.t.* out- (4).	**outwalk'** *v.t.* out- (3), (4).

For many words beginning **out-,** *see* **out** *or* **out-.**

chance; **outside edge** see **edge; outside half** (*Rugby*) a stand-off half; **outside left, right** in some games, a forward player on the extreme left, right; **outside novel** the type of novel which deals with the author's thoughts and his relationship with the world. — **get outside of** (*coll.*) to eat or drink; **outside in** turned so that outside and inside change places: intimately, thoroughly (of knowing anything); **outside of** in or to a position external to: apart from, except (*coll.*, esp. *U.S.*). [**out, side**[1].]

outspan *owt'span*, or *-span'*, *v.t.* and *v.i.* to unyoke or unharness from a vehicle. — *n.* (*owt'*) a stopping-place. [Du. *uitspannen*.]

outspeckle *ōōt-spek'l*, (*obs. Scot.*) *n.* a laughing-stock, spectacle. [Perh. conn. with **kenspeckle.**]

ouvert *ōō'ver, fem.* **ouverte** *-vert*, (Fr.) *adj.* open.

ouvirandra *ōō-vi-ran'drə, n.* the lattice-leaf of Madagascar. [From the Malagasy name.]

ouvrage *ōō-vräzh*, (Fr.) *n.* work.

ouvrier *ōō-vrē-ā, fem.* **ouvrière** *ōō-vrē-er*, (Fr.) *n.* worker, operative.

ouzel, ousel *ōō'zl* (*Shak.* **woo'sel, woo'sell**) *n.* a blackbird (*arch.*): apparently, a dark-complexioned person (*Shak.*). — **ou'zel-cock.** — **ring'-ou'zel** a blackish thrush with a broad white band on the throat; **wa'ter-ou'zel** the dipper. [O.E. *ōsle*; cog. with Ger. *Amsel.*]

ouzo *ōō'zō, n.* an aniseed liqueur: — *pl.* **ou'zos.** [Mod. Gr. *ouzon.*]

ova. See **ovum**, under **ov(i)-**.

oval *ō'vəl, adj.* strictly, egg-shaped, like an egg in the round or in projection, rounded, longer than broad, broadest near one end: loosely, elliptical or ellipsoidal, or nearly: rounded at both ends, about twice as long as broad, broadest in the middle (*bot.*): pertaining to eggs (*obs.*). — *n.* an oval figure or thing, e.g. an oval field. — *adv.* **o'vally.** [L. *ōvum*, egg; *ōvālis* is modern Latin.]

ovalbumin, ovarian, ovary, etc. See **ov(i)-**.

ovate[1] *ov'āt, n.* an Eisteddfodic graduate neither a bard nor a druid. [W. *ofydd*, a philosopher, or lord; fancifully identified with the unrelated Celtic word preserved in Gr. as *ouāteis* (pl.), Gaulish soothsayers.]

ovate[2]. See **ovation.**

ovate[3]. See **ov(i)-**.

ovation *ō-vā'shən, n.* in ancient Rome, a lesser triumph: an outburst of popular applause, an enthusiastic reception: rejoicing (*arch.*). — *v.t.* **ovate** (facetious backformation) to receive with an ovation. — *n.* **ova'tor.** — **standing ovation** see **stand.** [L. *ovātiō, -ōnis* — *ovāre*, to exult.]

oven *uv'n, n.* an arched cavity or closed chamber for baking, heating, or drying: a small furnace. — **o'ven= bird** a name for various birds that build oven-shaped nests, esp. the South American genus *Furnarius*; **oven glove** a type of thick reinforced glove worn when handling hot dishes. — *adj.* **ov'en-ready** of food, prepared beforehand so as to be ready for cooking in the oven immediately after purchase. — **ov'en-tit** the willow-warbler; **ov'enware** dishes, as casseroles, that will stand the heat of an oven; **ov'enwood** brushwood. [O.E. *ofen*; Ger. *Ofen.*]

over *ō'vər, prep.* above in place, rank, power, authority, contention, preference, value, quantity, number, etc.: in excess of: above and from one side of to the other: down from or beyond the edge of: from side to side or end to end of: along: throughout the extent of:

during: until after: across: on or to the other side of: on, on to, about, or across the surface of, or all or much of: in discussion, contemplation, study of, or occupation with: concerning: on account of: recovered from the effects of: in a sunk, submerged, or buried state beyond the level of. — *adv.* on the top: above: across: to or on the other side: from one person, party, condition, etc., to another: into a sleep: outwards so as to overhang, or to fall from: away from an upright position: through, from beginning to end, esp. in a cursory or exploratory way: throughout: into a reversed position: across the margin: again, in repetition: too much: in excess: left remaining: at an end. — *interj.* in telecommunications, indicates that the speaker now expects a reply. — *adj.* (usu. treated as a prefix) upper or superior: surplus: excessive. — *n.* the series of balls (as *six-ball, eight-ball, over*) or the play, between changes in bowling from one end to the other (*cricket*): anything that is over: a surplus copy, etc.: an excess, overplus. — *v.t.* to go, leap, or vault over. — Also, only as *adv.* and *prep.*, **o'er** (now usu. *poet.*), **ore** (*obs.*), **o're** (*obs.*), all pronounced *ōr* or *ōr*, and in Scots **owre, o'er**, pronounced *owr* or *ōr*. — **o'ver-and-un'der** a double-barrelled gun having the barrels one on top of the other rather than side by side (also **un'der-and= o'ver**). — **all over** at an end: everywhere: at his, her, its, most characteristic: covered with, besmeared or bespattered with; **be all over (someone)** to make a fuss of, fawn on (someone); **over again** anew; **over against** opposite; **over and above** in addition to: besides; **over and over (again)** many times: repeatedly; **over head and ears** completely submerged; **over seas** to foreign lands. [O.E. *ofer*; Ger. *über*, L. *super*, Gr. *hyper*; cf. **up.**]

over- in composition, used with certain meanings of **over** *prep., adv.*, or *adj.*, as (1) above, across, across the surface; (2) beyond an understood limit; (3) down, away from the upright position; (4) upper; (5) beyond what is usual or desirable; (6) completely. — *v.i.* **overachieve'** to do better than predicted or expected. — *v.t.* **overact'** to act with exaggeration, to overdo the performance of. — Also *v.i.* — *adj.* **o'ver-age'** above the limiting age: too old. — *adv.* **overall', over-all'** everywhere (*Spens.*): above all: altogether: over the whole. — *adj.* **o'verall** including everything: everything being reckoned: all-round. — *n.* **o'verall** a protective garment worn over ordinary clothes for dirty work or weather: (*pl.*) trousers or leggings or combined shirt and trousers of this kind: cavalryman's trousers. — *adj.* **o'veralled.** — *v.t.* **overarch'** to arch over: to form above into an arch. — *v.i.* to hang over like an arch. — *n.* (*ō'-*) an overhead arch. — *adj.* and *adv.* **o'verarm** with the arm raised above the shoulder. — *vs.t.* **overawe'** to daunt by arousing fear or reverence; **overbal'ance** to exceed in weight, value, or importance: to cause to lose balance. — *v.i.* to lose balance, fall over. — *n.* excess of weight or value. — *v.t.* **overbear'** to bear down, overpower: to overwhelm: to overrule (objections, an objector). — *v.i.* to be too productive. — *adj.* **overbear'ing** inclined to domineer: haughty and dogmatical: imperious. — *adv.* **overbear'ingly.** — *n.* **overbear'ingness.** — *v.t.* **overbid'** to outbid: to make a bid that is greater than or counts above: to bid more than the value of. — Also *v.i.* — *n.* (*ō'-*) a higher bid: an unduly high bid. — *ns.* **overbidd'er; overbidd'ing; o'verbite** (*dentistry*) the (amount of) extension of the upper incisors beyond the lower when the mouth is

---

overabound' *v.i.* over- (5).	**overboil'** *v.t., v.i.* over- (2), (5).	**overcarr'y** *v.t.* over- (1, *obs.*),
overabound'ing *adj.* over- (5).	**overbold'** *adj.* over- (5).	(2), (5).
overabun'dance *n.* over- (5).	**overbold'ly** *adv.* over- (5).	**overcharge'** *v.t.* over- (5).
overac'tive *adj.* over- (5).	**overbound'** *v.t.* over- (1).	**o'vercharge** *n.* over- (5).
overactiv'ity *n.* over- (5).	**o'verbridge** *n.* over- (1).	**overclad'** *adj.* over- (5).
o'ver-anxi'ety *n.* over- (5).	**overbridge'** *v.t.* over- (1).	**overcol'our** *v.t.* over- (1), (5).
o'ver-anx'ious *adj.* over- (5).	**overbrimmed'** (*Scott*) *adj.* over- (5).	**over-con'fidence** *n.* over- (5).
o'ver-anx'iously *adv.* over- (5).	**overbur'densome** *adj.* over- (5).	**over-con'fident** *adj.* over- (5).
overbeat' *v.t., v.i.* over- (3).	**overcapac'ity** *n.* over- (5).	**over-cool'** *v.t.* over- (5).
o'verblanket *n.* over- (1).	**overcare'ful** *adj.* over- (5).	**overcov'er** *v.t.* over- (6).

closed. — *v.i.* **overblow'** to blow over, be past its violence: to blow with too much violence: to produce a harmonic instead of the fundamental tone, by excess of wind-pressure (*mus.*). — *v.t.* to blow away: to blow across: to overturn by blowing: to blow (an instrument) too strongly (*mus.*): to cover with blossoms. — *adj.* **overblown'** blown over or past: burnt by an excessive blast, in the Bessemer steel process: inflated to excess: more than full-blown. — *adv.* **overboard'** over the board or side: from on board: out of a ship (**go overboard about** or **for** (*slang*) to go to extremes of enthusiasm about or for). — *vs.t.* **overbook'** to make more reservations than the number of places (in a plane, ship, hotel, etc.) actually available (also *v.i.*); **overbrow'** to overhang like a brow; **overbuild'** to cover with buildings: to build above: to build in excess: to build too much upon or in; **overbulk'** (*Shak.*) to oppress by bulk, or to dwarf by greater bulk; **overburd'en, overburth'en** to burden overmuch. — *n.* (*ō'vər-*) an excessive burden: alluvial soil, etc., overlying a bed of clay or other substance to be dug, mined, or quarried. — *v.t.* **overburn'** to burn too much. — *v.i.* to be too zealous. — *adj.* **overbus'y** too busy: officious. — *v.t.* to busy too much. — *v.t.* **overbuy'** to buy too dear (*Shak.*): to buy dearer than: to put in the position of having bought too much (*refl.*): to buy too much of. — *v.i.* to buy too much: — *pa.t.* and *pa.p.* **overbought'.** — *adv.* **overby'** a little way over — mainly in Scots forms, **owerby, o'erby** (*owr-bī'*). — *v.t.* **overcall'** (*bridge*) to outbid: to bid above: to bid too high on: to rank as a higher bid than. — *n.* (*ō'-*) a higher bid than the opponent's preceding one. — *v.t.* **overcan'opy** to cover as with a canopy: — *pa.p.* **overcan'opied** (*Shak.* **overcann'oped**). — *n.* **overcapitalisā'tion, -z-.** — *v.t.* **overcap'italise, -ize** to fix the capital to be invested in, or the capital value of, too high; **overcast'** to overthrow: to cast as a covering: to cast a covering over: to shade (*Spens.*): to sew stitches over (a raw edge): to cover with stitches: to recover, get over (*Scot.*): to compute too high, overestimate. — *v.i.* to grow dull or cloudy. — *adj.* clouded over. — *n.* (*ō'-*) a cloudy covering. — *n.* **overcast'ing.** — *vs.t.* **overcatch'** (*obs.* or *dial.*) to overtake (*pa.p.* **overcaught'**). — *n.* **o'vercheck** a large prominent check pattern combined with a smaller: a cloth so checked: a check-rein. — *v.t.* **overcloud'** to cover over with clouds: **to cause gloom or sorrow to.** — Also *v.i.* — *vs.t.* **overcloy'** to surfeit; **over-club'** (*golf*) to hit (a shot) too far through using a club with insufficient loft. — Also *v.i.* — *ns.* **o'vercoat** an outdoor coat worn over all else, a topcoat; **o'vercoating** cloth for overcoats. — *v.t.* **overcome'** to cover, overspread (*arch.*): to come over: to get the better of: to conquer or subdue: to surmount. — *v.i.* to be victorious. — *n.* (*Scot.*) **o'ercome, owrecome** (*owr'kəm*) a crossing over: a surplus, excess: a fit or sudden access of illness: a refrain, byword, or recurring theme. — *v.t.* **overcom'pensate** to allow too much in compensation to: to allow pursuit of compensation to become obsessive and exclusive (*psych.*). — Also *v.i.* (**with** *for*). — *n.* **overcompensā'tion.** — *adj.* **overcompen'satory.** — *v.t.* **overcorrect'** to apply so great a correction to as to deviate in the opposite way: to correct beyond achromatism, so that the red rays come to a focus nearer the lens than the violet (*opt.*). — *n.* **overcorrec'tion.** — *vs.t.* **overcount'** to outnumber: to reckon too high: to over-reach; **o'vercrop** to take too much out of by cultivation;

overcrow', Spens. overcraw', Shak. orecrowe' to crow, triumph, over. — *adjs.* **overdat'ed** out of date; **over= deter'mined** too firmly resolved (to): too resolute, stubborn: having more than the necessary determining data or factors; **overdight** (*-dīt'; Spens.*) dight or covered over: overspread. — *v.t.* **overdo'** to do overmuch: to overact: to exaggerate: to carry too far: to harass, to fatigue: to cook too much: to excel. — *n.* **overdo'er.** — *adj.* **overdone'.** — *ns.* **overdos'age; o'verdose** an excessive dose of drugs, medicine, etc. — *v.t.* and *v.i.* **overdose'.** — *ns.* **o'verdraft** the act of overdrawing: the excess of the amount drawn over the sum against which it is drawn; **o'verdraught** (*-dräft*), in U.S. **o'ver-draft,** a current of air passing over, or coming from above, a fire in a furnace, kiln, etc. — *v.t.* **overdraw'** to exaggerate in drawing: to exaggerate: to draw beyond one's credit. — *v.t.* and *v.i.* **overdress'** to dress too ostentatiously or elaborately. — *v.t.* **overdrive'** to drive too hard: to outdrive. — *n.* **o'verdrive** a gearing device which transmits to the driving shaft a speed greater than engine crankshaft speed. — *adjs.* **over= drowsed'** (*Wordsworth* **o'er-drows'ed**) overcome by drowsiness; **overdue'** (or *ō'vər-*) behind time for arrival: still unpaid after the time it is due. — *adj.* **overearn'est** too earnest: severe in manner (*Shak.*). — *v.t.* **overeat'** (often with *oneself*) to surfeit with eating: perh. to nibble all over, perhaps, to surfeit on (*Shak.*). — *v.i.* to eat too much. — *v.t.* **overexpose'** to expose too much, esp. to light. — *adj.* **over-ex'quisite** excessively exact in imagining details (*Milt.*). — *v.t.* **overeye'** to survey, look upon: to watch. — *n.* **o'verfall** a rippling or race of water: a sudden increase of depth: a place or structure for overflow of surplus waters: a waterfall (*obs.*). — *v.t.* **overfall'** to fall on or over: to assail. — *adv.* **overfar'** too far: to too great an extent (*Shak.*). — *adj.* **overfin'ished** (of cattle and sheep) having too much finish (q.v.). — *n.* **o'verflight** a flight above and over. — *v.t.* **o'verflour'ish** to cover with blossom, or with flourishes or ornament; **overflow'** to flow over the edge of: to flow over the surface of: to flood: to flow over and beyond: to cause to run over: (of e.g. people) to fill and then spread beyond (e.g. a room): — *pa.t.* **overflowed';** *pa.p.* **overflowed',** formerly and still sometimes **overflown'.** — Also *v.i.* — *n.* **o'verflow** a flowing over: that which flows over, *lit.* and *fig.* (**overflow meeting** a supplementary meeting of those unable to find room in the main meeting): a pipe or channel for spare water, etc.: an inundation: a superabundance. — *adj.* **overflow'ing** flowing over: running over: over-full: overabounding: exuberant. — Also *n.* — *adv.* **overflow'ingly.** — *adj.* **overflush'** too flush. — *n.* **o'ver-flush** superfluity. — *v.t.* **overfly'** to outsoar: to fly over. — *n.* **o'verfold** a fold tilted over so that the dip on both sides of the axis is in the same direction. — *v.t.* **overfold'** to fold over: to thrust into an overfold. — *adj.* **overfond'** foolish to excess (*obs.*): too fond: too fond (of). — *v.t.* **overfreight'** to overload: — *pa.p., adj.* **overfraught'.** — *n.* **o'verfreight** an excessive load. — *vs.t.* **overgall'** to blister or inflame all over, or greatly; **overgang'** (*Scot.* **o'ergang,** *owr-gang'*) to dominate: to overspread: to exceed. — *n.* **o'vergarment** a garment worn on top of others. — *vs.t.* **overget'** to overtake (*obs.*): to get over, recover from (*dial.* or *arch.*): to overcome, possess the mind of; **overgive'** (*Spens.*) to give over or up; **overglaze'** to glaze over: to cover speciously. — *n.* **o'verglaze** an additional glaze given

---

overcredu'lity *n.* over- (5).
overcred'ulous *adj.* over- (5).
overcrowd' *v.t., v.i.* over- (5).
overdar'ing *adj.* over- (5).
overdevel'op *v.t., v.i.* over- (5).
overdevel'opment *n.* over- (5).
o'verdress *n.* over- (4).
overdust' *v.t.* over- (1).
overdye' *v.t.* over- (1), (5).
overes'timate *v.t., n.* over- (5).

overestima'tion *n.* over- (5).
over-exact' *adj.* over- (5).
overexcitabil'ity *n.* over- (5).
overexcit'able *adj.* over- (5).
overexcite' *v.t.* over- (5).
overexert' *v.t.* over- (5).
overexer'tion *n.* over- (5).
overexpos'ure *n.* over- (5).
overfall' *v.i.* over- (3).
overfeed' *v.t., v.i.* over- (5).

overfed' *pa.t., pa.p.* over- (5).
overfill' *v.t., v.i.* over- (5).
o'verfine' *adj.* over- (5).
o'verfine'ness *n.* over- (5).
overfire' *v.t.* over- (5).
overfish' *v.t.* over- (5).
overflush' *v.t.* over- (1).
overfond'ly *adv.* over- (5).
overfond'ness *n.* over- (5).
overfor'ward *adj.* over- (5).

to porcelain, etc. — *adj.* applied to, or suitable for painting on, a glazed surface. — *vs.t.* **overgloom'** to cover with gloom: to scowl over; **overgo'** to exceed: to surpass: to overpower: to go over: to pass over, traverse: to spread over: to pass over, forbear to speak of. — *v.i.* to go over: to pass on: — *pa.t.* **overwent'**. — *n.* **overgo'ing** passing over: crossing, traversing: transgression. — *v.t.* and *v.i.* **overgrain'** to grain over (a surface already grained). — *n.* **overgrain'er** a brush for overgraining. — *vs.t.* **overgrass'** to grass over, conceal with grass; **overgreen'** to cover with green or verdure: to conceal (*fig.*, *Shak.*). — *adj.* **overground'** above ground. — *v.t.* **overgrow'** to grow beyond: to grow more than: to grow too great for: to rise above: to cover with growth. — *v.i.* to grow beyond the normal or suitable size. — *adj.* **overgrown** (*ō'vər-grōn*, or *-grōn'*) grown beyond the natural size: covered over with a growth. — *n.* **o'vergrowth** excessive or abnormally great growth: excess or superfluity resulting from growth: that which grows over and covers anything: growth of a crystal around another (*crystal.*). — *v.t.* **overhaile'**, **overhale'** to draw over (*Spens.*): to overtake, overpower (*obs.*): to examine (*obs.*). — *n.* **o'verhair** the long hair overlying the fur of many animals. — *adv.* **overhand'** (or *ō'*) with hand above the object: palm downwards: with hand or arm raised above the shoulders or (in swimming) coming out of the water over the head: from below (*min.*): with stitches passing through in one direction and back round the edges (*needlework*). — *adj.* **o'verhand** done or performed overhand (**overhand knot** the simplest of all knots, tied by passing the end over the standing part and through the bight). — *v.t.* to sew overhand. — *adj.* and *adv.* **overhand'ed** with hand above: with too many hands. — *adj.* **overhand'led** (*Shak.*) handled or discussed too much. — *v.t.* **overhang'** to hang over: to project over: to impend over: to cover with hangings. — *v.i.* to hang over, lean out beyond the vertical. — *n.* **o'verhang** a projecting part: degree of projection. — *v.t.* **overhaul'** to haul or draw over: to turn over for examination: to examine: to overtake or gain upon (*naut.*). — *n.* **o'verhaul** a hauling over: examination, esp. with a view to repair. — *adv.* **overhead'** above one's head: aloft: in the zenith: in complete submergence: now *Scot.*, taking one with another, in the lump, on the average, apiece. — *adj.* **o'verhead** above one's head: well above ground level: all-round, general, average. — *n.* (often in *pl.*; also **overhead costs, charges**) the general expenses of a business — as distinct from the direct cost of producing an article: that which is overhead (**overhead projector** one which, set up on a speaker's desk, projects transparencies on a screen behind him). — *vs.t.* **overhear'** to hear without being meant to hear: to hear by accident: to hear over again or in turn (*Shak.*); **overheat'** to heat to excess. — *v.i.* to become too hot. — *v.t.* and *v.i.* to make or become agitated. — *n.* **o'verheat** too great heat. — *vs.t.* **overhent'** (*Spens.*) to overtake: — *pa.t.* and *pa.p.* **overhent'**; **overhit'** to hit (a ball, etc.) beyond the intended target: to hit a ball, etc. beyond (the intended target): to go beyond the right, fitting, or intended level, point, etc. (*fig.*); **overhold'** (*Shak.*) to overvalue. — *adj.* **overhung'** overhanging: suspended from above: covered over, adorned with hangings. — *v.t.* **overinform'** to give an excessive amount of information to: to animate too much. — *n.* **overinsur'ance**. — *vs.t.* **overinsure'** to insure

for more than the real value; **overiss'ue** to issue in excess, as bank-notes or bills of exchange. — *n.* **o'verissue** excessive issue. — *v.t.* **overjoy'** to fill with great joy: to transport with delight or gladness. — *n.* **o'verjoy** joy to excess, transport. — *vs.t.* **overjump'** to jump (too far) over: to jump farther than: to pass over (*fig.*); **overkest'** (*Spens.*) for **overcast** (*pa.t.* and *pa.p.*). — *ns.* **o'verkill** something, esp. power for destruction, in excess of what is necessary or desirable; **o'verking** a king holding sovereignty over inferior kings. — *adj.* **o'verknee** reaching above the knee. — *vs.t.* **overla'bour** to labour excessively over: to be too nice with: to overwork; **overlade'** to overburden: — *pa.p.* **overla'den**; **overlaid** *pa.p.* of **overlay**; **overlain** *pa.p.* of **overlie**. — *adj.* **o'verland** passing entirely or principally by land. — *adv.* **overland'** (or *ō'*) by or over land. — *v.t.* and *v.i.* (*Austr.*) to drive (flocks or herds) a long distance across country: to journey across country, esp. a long way. — *n.* **o'verlander** (or *-land'*). — *v.t.* **overlap'** to extend over and beyond the edge of: to reach from beyond, across the edge, and partly rest on: to coincide in part with: to ripple over. — *v.i.* (*Soccer, Rugby*, etc.) to advance down the flank as an attacking manoeuvre. — *n.* **o'verlap** an overlapping part or situation: a disposition of strata where the upper beds extend beyond the boundary of the lower beds of the same series (*geol.*). — *vs.t.* **overlard'** to smear over as with lard: to overload with fulsomeness; **overlaunch'** in shipbuilding, to unite by long splices or scarfs; **overlay'** to cover by laying or spreading something over: to span (*Milt.*): to put an overlay or overlays on (*print.*): to cover to excess, encumber: to lay or place as a covering (*rare*): by confusion, to overlie: — *pa.t.* and *pa.p.* **overlaid'**. — *ns.* **o'verlay** a piece of paper pasted on the impression-surface of a printing-press, so as to increase the impression in a place where it is too faint: a covering: anything laid on or over for the purpose of visual alteration: a cravat (*Scot.*); **overlay'ing** a superficial covering: that which overlays: plating. — *adv.* **overleaf'** on the other side of the leaf of a book. — *v.t.* **overleap'** (*Scot.* **owerloup'**) to leap over: to pass over without notice (**overleap oneself,** to leap too far). — *n.* **o'verleather** (*Shak.*) the upper part of a shoe. — *v.i.* **overlend'** to lend too much. — *adj.* **overlent'**. — *v.t.* **overlie'** to lie above or upon: to smother by lying on: — *pr.p.* **overly'ing**; *pa.t.* **overlay'**; *pa.p.* **overlain'**. — *n.* **o'verlier** (or *-lī'*). — *v.t.* **overlive** (*-liv'*) to survive: to outlive: to outlive the appropriate date of, or usefulness of (*refl.*). — *v.i.* to survive: to live too long: to live too fast, or so as prematurely to exhaust the fund of life: to live on too high a standard of luxury. — *v.t.* **overload'** to load or fill overmuch. — *n.* (*ō'*) an excessive load. — *v.t.* **overlook'** to look over: to see from a higher position: to view carefully: to oversee, superintend: to fail to notice or take into account: to pass by without cognisance or punishment: to slight: to bewitch by looking upon with the evil eye. — *ns.* **overlook'er**; **o'verlord** a lord over other lords: a feudal superior: (with *cap.*) operational name for the Anglo-American invasion (1944) of Normandy in World War II. — *v.t.* **overlord'**. — *n.* **o'verlordship**. — *adv.* **o'verly** (*-li*; *coll.*) excessively, too: superciliously (*obs.*): casually (*Scot.*). — *adj.* supercilious, superior (*obs.*): casual (*Scot.*). — *adj.* **overly'ing** lying on the top. — *n.* **o'verman** an overseer in mining, the man in charge of work below ground: superman. — *v.t.* **overman'** to

---

furnish with too many men. — *n.* **o'vermantel** an ornamental structure, often with a mirror, set on a mantel-shelf. — *vs.t.* **overmast'** to furnish with a mast or masts too long or too heavy; **overmas'ter** to gain or have the mastery of: to overpower: to dominate; **overmatch'** to be more than a match for: to defeat, overcome. — *ns.* **o'vermatch** one who is more than a match: an overmatching (*obs.*); **o'vermatter** (*print.*) overset type matter; **overmeas'ure** (or *ō'*) something given over the due measure. — *v.t.* (*-mezh'*) to measure above the true value. — *adj.* **overmerr'y** extremely merry. — *v.t.* **overmount'** to rise above: to excel in mounting. — *v.i.* to mount too high. — *adj.* and *adv.* **o'vermuch** (or *-much'*) too much. — *v.i.* **overmul'tiply** to become too numerous. — *n.* **overmultiplicā'tion.** — *vs.t.* **overmult'itude** (*Milt.*) to outnumber; **overname'** (*Shak.*) to name over; **overnet'** to cover with a net: to overfish with nets. — *adj.* **overnice'** too fastidious. — *adv.* **overnice'ly.** — *n.* **overnice'ness.** — *n.* **o'vernight** (*Shak.*; now chiefly *U.S.*) the evening just past. — *adv.* **overnight'** all night: during the night: in the course of the night: on the evening of the day just past. — *adj.* done or occurring or existing overnight: for the time from afternoon till next morning: (**overnight bag, case** a small case for carrying the clothes, toilet articles, etc., needed for an overnight stay). — *n.* **o'vernighter** an overnight bag. — *v.t.* **overoff'ice** (*Shak.* **o're-office**) apparently, to lord it over by virtue of office, or perhaps to exercise one's office over. — *adv.* **overpage'** overleaf. — *vs.t.* **overpaint'** to put too much paint on: to depict with exaggeration; **overpart'** to assign too difficult a part to; **overpass'** to pass over: to pass by without notice: to exceed. — *v.i.* to pass over: to elapse. — *n.* (*ō'-*) a road bridging another road or railway, canal, etc. — *adj.* **overpast'** over: at an end. — *v.t.* **overpay'** to pay too much: to be more than an ample reward for. — *n.* **overpay'ment.** — *v.i.* **overped'al** to make excessive use of the sustaining pedal of a piano. — *vs.t.* **overpeer'** (partly from **peer**[1], partly **peer**[2]; *Shak.*) to peer over or down upon: to look down on: to tower over: to excel; **overperch'** (*Shak.* **orepearch'**) to fly up and perch on, fly over; **overpersuade'** to persuade against one's inclination; **overpic'ture** to surpass pictorially: to cover with pictures; **overpitch'** to pitch too far, or beyond the best distance. — *adjs.* **overpitched'** steeply pitched, as a roof: (of a cricket ball) bowled so that it pitches too near the stumps; **overplaced'** (*Spens.* **overplast, -pläst'**) placed above. — *v.t.* **overplay'** to overemphasise the importance, value, of: to play better than (an opponent): to try to gain more than one's assets (*lit.* and *fig.*) can be expected to yield (**overplay one's hand;** *fig.*). — *v.t.* and *v.i.* to exaggerate (an emotion, acting rôle, etc.): to hit the ball beyond (the putting green) (*golf*). — *n.* **o'verplay.** — *n.* **o'verplus** that which is more than enough: surplus. — *adj.* surplus. — *vs.t.* **overply'** to ply beyond strength; **overpoise'** to outweigh. — *n.* **o'verpoise** a weight sufficient to weigh another down. — *vs.t.* **overpost'** to hasten over quickly; **overpower'** to overcome, reduce to helplessness, by force: to subdue: to overwhelm: to furnish with too much power. — *adj.* **overpower'ing** excessive in degree or amount: irresistible. — *adv.* **overpower'ingly.** — *v.t.* **overpress'** to oppress: to burden too heavily: to press unduly: to put too much pressure on. — *n.* **overpress'ure** excessive pressure, esp. of work. — *adj.* **overpriced'.** — *v.t.* **overprint'** to print too strongly

or dark: to print too many copies of: to print over already printed matter (esp. a postage stamp). — *n.* **o'verprint** an offprint: that which is printed over an already printed surface, as on a postage stamp. — *v.t.* **overprize'** to value too highly: to surpass in value (*obs.*). — *v.t.* and *v.i.* **overproduce'.** — *n.* **overproduc'tion** excessive production: production in excess of the demand. — *adj.* **overproof'** (or *ō'*) containing more alcohol than does proof-spirit. — *vs.t.* **overrack'** to overstrain; **overrake'** to sweep over. — *adj.* **overrank'** too rank or luxurious. — *v.t.* **overreach'** to reach or extend beyond: to overtake: to outwit or get the better of: (*refl.*) to defeat by one's own oversubtlety or by attempting too much. — *v.i.* to strike the hindfoot against the forefoot, as a horse: — *pa.t.* and *pa.p.* **overreached';** *arch.* **overraught'.** — *n.* **o'verreach** the act of overreaching: the injury thereby done. — *v.t.* **overread** (*-rēd'*) to read over. — *adj.* **overread** (*-red'*) having read too much. — *v.t.* and *v.i.* **overreck'on** to compute too highly. — *vs.t.* **overred'** (*Shak.*) to cover with a red colour; **overren'** an arch. form of **overrun; override'** to injure or exhaust by too much riding: to ride over: to trample down on horseback: to slide or mount on the top or back of: to pass over: to overlap: to set aside: to be valid against: to be more important than, prevail over: to outride, overtake (*obs.*). — *n.* **o'verride** an auxiliary (esp. manual) control capable of temporarily prevailing over the operation of another (esp. automatic) control. — *n.* **o'verrider** an attachment on the bumper of a motor vehicle to prevent another bumper becoming interlocked with it. — *adj.* **overrid'ing** dominant, stronger than anything else. — *v.t.* and *v.i.* **overruff'** to trump with a higher trump. — *n.* **o'verruff** an act of overruffing. — *v.t.* **overrule'** to rule over (*obs.*): to modify or to set aside by greater power: to prevail over the will of, against a previous decision of: to impose an overriding decision upon: to prevail over and set aside: to annul, declare invalid (*law*): to rule against: to disallow. — *v.i.* to prevail. — *n.* **overrul'er.** — *v.t.* **overrun'** to run over, across, through, all about: to run over, crush underfoot or under wheel: to spread over: to flow over: to grow over: to infest, swarm over: to infect widely: to spread over and take possession of: to run beyond: to exceed the limit of: to carry beyond a limit: to carry over into another line or page: to adjust the type of by overrunning: to outdo in running: to escape from by running faster: (*refl.*) to injure or exhaust by too much running. — *v.i.* to run over, overflow: to run beyond a limit: (of a vehicle engine) to slow down in response to a reverse torque transmitted through the gears from the wheels. — *pr.p.* **overrunn'ing;** *pa.t.* **overran';** *pa.p.* **overrun'** (**overrun the constable** see **outrun**). — *ns.* **o'verrun** an act or occasion of overrunning: an overrunning of type (*print.*): the overrunning of a vehicle engine (**overrun brake** a brake fitted to a trailer that prevents it from travelling faster than the towing vehicle when reducing speed or going downhill); **overrunn'er.** — *v.i.* **oversail'** (Fr. *saillir,* to project) to project. — *n.* **o'versail** projection. — *v.t.* **overscore'** to score or draw lines across: to obliterate in this way. — *adjs.* **overscutched** (*-skucht',* *-skuch'id;* *Scott*) worn out (after Shak., *2 Hen. IV* III, ii, where **overschutch** is variously conjectured to mean overworn in service or whipped at the cart's tail); **o'versea,** **o'verseas** across, beyond, or from beyond the sea. — *adv.* **oversea(s)'** in or to lands beyond the sea: abroad.

— *n.* **overseas'** foreign lands. — *v.t.* **oversee'** to see or look over: to superintend: to overlook, disregard: to see without being meant to see. — *adj.* **overseen'** (*obs.*) mistaken, ill-advised: drunk: versed (in). — *n.* **o'verseer** (*-sēr, -sē-ər*) one who oversees: a superintendent: formerly, officer with care of poor, and other duties: the manager of a plantation of slaves: a critic or editor (*obs.*). — *v.t.* and *v.i.* **oversell'** to sell too dear: to sell more of than is available: to exaggerate the merits of: — *p.adj.* **oversold'**. — *v.t.* and *v.i.* **overset'** to oppress, press hard (*obs.*): to upset: to disorder: to set more type or copy than there is space available (*print.*). — *vs.t.* **o'versew** (or *-sō'*) to sew together overhand; **overshade'** to throw a shade or shadow over: to darken; **overshad'ow** to throw a shadow over: to cast into the shade by surpassing, to outshine: to darken: to shelter or protect; **overshine'** (*Shak.*) to shine over or upon, illumine: to outshine. — *n.* **o'vershoe** a shoe, esp. of waterproof, worn over another. — *advs.* **over-shoe'**, **over-shoes'** deep enough to cover the shoes. — *v.t.* **overshoot'** to shoot over or beyond, as a mark: to pass beyond, exceed, fail to stop at: to shoot, dart, or fly across overhead: to surpass in shooting: to injure or exhaust by too much shooting: to shoot with colour over the surface of (**overshoot oneself,** to venture too far, to overreach oneself): — *pa.t.* and *pa.p.* **overshot'**. — Also *v.i.* — *n.* **o'vershoot** a going beyond the mark. — *adj.* **overshot'** shot over: too much shot over: surpassed: overdone: in error by overshooting the mark: drunk (*obs. slang*). — *adj.* **o'vershot** having the upper jaw protruding beyond the lower: fed from above, as a waterwheel. — *v.t.* **overshower'** to shower over. — *adj.* **o'verside** acting or done over the side. — *adv.* **overside'** over the side. — *prep.* (*Spens.* **over side**) over the side of. — *n.* **o'versight** superintendence: a failure to notice: mistake: omission. — *v.t.* **oversize'** to cover with size. — *n.* **o'versize** a large or larger size. — *adj.* **o'versized** (or *-sīzd'*). — *v.t.***overskip'** to skip, leap, or pass over: to overlook: to omit. — *ns.* **overslaugh** (*ō'vər-slö*; Du. *overslaan,* to miss, skip over; *mil.*) exemption from duty in turn when employed on something else: a sand-bar (*U.S.*). — *vs.t.* **overslaugh'** to remit or pass over by overslaugh: to pass over in favour of another (*U.S.*): to hinder; **oversleep'** to indulge in sleeping too long: to sleep beyond. — *v.i.* to sleep too long. — *v.t.* **overslip'** to slip by: to escape the notice of: to slip unnoticed from: to let slip. — *v.i.* to slip by: to make a slip, error, inadvertently. — *ns.* **o'verslip** an inadvertency: a close-fitting under-bodice; **o'versman** an overseer: an umpire (*Scot.*). — **oversold** see **oversell.** — *n.* **o'versoul** the divine principle forming the spiritual unity of all being. — *vs.t.* **oversow'** to sow after something has been already sown: to sow over; **overspend'** to spend beyond: to exhaust or cripple by spending. — *v.i.* to spend too much. — *n.* an instance of overspending: the amount by which an allocated budget, etc., is overspent. — *adj.* **overspent'** excessively fatigued. — *ns.* **o'verspill** that which is spilt over: population leaving a district, or displaced by changes in housing, etc.: (in a public bar) beer, etc. that overflows from a glass as it is being filled; **o'verspin** the spinning of a flying ball in the same direction as if it were rolling on the ground. — *vs.t.* **overstaff'** to provide too many people as staff for; **overstand'** to out-stay; **overstare'** (*Shak.* **ore-stare'**) to outstare; **overstate'** to state too strongly: to exaggerate. — *n.* **overstate'ment.** — *v.i.* **o'versteer** of a motor-car, to exaggerate the degree of turning applied by the steering-wheel. — *n.* the tendency to do this. — *v.t.* **overstep'** to step beyond: to exceed: to transgress. — *n.* **o'verstep** (*geol.*) the transgression of an overlapping stratum

over the edges of underlying unconformable strata. — *v.t.* **overstink'** to stink more than: — *pa.t.* **overstunk'**; *Shak.* **orestunck'.** — *v.t.* and *v.i.* **overstrain'** to strain too much: to strain beyond the elastic limit. — *n.* **o'verstrain** too great strain. — *adj.* **overstrained'** strained to excess: exaggerated. — *vs.t.* **overstretch'** to stretch to excess: to exaggerate; **overstride'** to stride across: to stand astride of; **overstrike'** to strike with a downward blow: — *pa.t.* **overstruck'**; *Spens.* **overstrooke'.** — *adjs.* **overstrung'** too highly strung: (of a piano) having two sets of strings crossing obliquely to save space; **o'verstuffed** covered completely with well-stuffed upholstery. — *v.t.* **oversubscribe'** to subscribe for beyond what is offered. — *n.* **oversubscrip'tion.** — *vs.t.* **oversway'** to overrule: to bear down; **overswear'** to swear anew. — *v.t.* and *v.i.* **overswell'** to overflow. — *vs.t.* **overswim'** to swim across; **overtake'** to come up with: to move past (something or someone travelling in the same direction): to catch up with: to catch: to come upon: to take by surprise. — *adj.* **overta'ken** fuddled. — *vs.t.* **overtalk'** to talk over; **overtask'** to task overmuch: to impose too heavy a task on; **overtax'** to tax overmuch: to require too much of. — *v.i.* **overteem'** to teem, breed, or produce, in excess. — *v.t.* to exhaust or wear out by breeding. — *adj.* **o'ver-the-count'er** (of securities, etc.) not listed on or traded through a stock exchange, but traded directly between buyers and sellers: (of drugs, etc.) able to be bought or sold without a prescription or licence. — *v.t.* **overthrow'** to throw over, overturn, upset: to ruin, subvert: to defeat utterly: to throw too far or too strongly. — *v.i.* (*obs.*) to be overturned: to throw too far. — *ns.* **o'verthrow** act of overthrowing or state of being overthrown: a ball missed at the wicket and returned from the field (*cricket*): a run scored in consequence; **overthrow'er**; **o'verthrust** (**overthrust fault**) a reversed fault or thrust where older rocks are pushed up bodily upon the back of younger. — *v.t.* **overthwart'** to lie athwart: to cross. — *adj.* opposite, transverse: contrary, perverse. — *adv.* crosswise: opposite. — *prep.* across, on the other side of. — *n.* **o'vertime** time employed in working beyond the regular hours: work done in such time: pay for such work. — *adj.* and *adv.*, during, for, or concerning, such time. — *v.t.* (*ō-vər-tīm'*) to time too long (esp. of a photographic exposure). — *adj.* and *adv.* **overtime'ly** (*obs.*) too early, untimely. — *ns.* **o'vertimer** one who works overtime; **o'vertone** a harmonic or upper partial: a subtle meaning, additional to the main meaning, conveyed by a word or statement: implicit quality, or constant association. — *v.t.* **overtop'** to rise over the top of: to be higher than: to surpass: to exceed. — *v.i.* to rise too high. — *v.t.* **overtower'** to tower above. — *v.i.* to soar too high. — *v.i.* **over-trade'** to trade overmuch or beyond capital: to buy in more than can be sold or paid for. — *v.t.* to involve in trade in such a way. — *n.* **over-trad'ing** (one's capital, etc.). — *v.t.* **overtrain'** to train so far as to do harm: to train too high. — *n.* **o'vertrick** (*bridge*) a trick in excess of those contracted for. — *vs.t.* **overtrip'** to trip nimbly over; **overtrump'** to trump with a higher card than one already played; **overturn'** to throw down or over: to upset: to subvert. — *ns.* **o'verturn** an overturning: a turnover; **overturn'er; overvalua'tion; o'vervalue.** — *vs.t.* **overval'ue** to set too high a value on; **overveil'** to veil over or cover. — *ns.* **o'verview** an inspection (*Shak.*): a general survey; **o'verwash** a washing over: material carried by glacier-streams over a frontal moraine (*geol.*). — Also *adj.* — *vs.t.* **overwatch'** to watch over: to watch through: to overcome with long watching; **overwear'** to wear out: to outwear, outlive: — *pa.t.* **overwore'**; *pa.p.* **overworn'** (see below). — *v.t.*

---

overspec'ialise, -ize *v.i.* **over-** (5).	**overstain'** *v.t.* **over-** (1).	**o'verstress** *n.* **over-** (5).
overspecialisā'tion, -z- *n.* **over-** (5).	**overstay'** *v.t.* **over-** (2).	**overstrew'** *v.t.* **over-** (1).
overspread' *v.t.* **over-** (1).	**overstock'** *v.t.* **over-** (5).	**overstrong'** *adj.* **over-** (5).
	o'verstock *n.* **over-** (5).	**overstud'y** *v.t., v.i.* **over-** (5).
	overstress' *v.t.* **over-** (5).	**o'verstudy** *n.* **over-** (5).

overwear'y to overcome with weariness, weary out. — *adj.* excessively weary. — *v.t.* **overweath'er** (*Shak.*) to batter by violence of weather. — *v.i.* **overween'** to expect too much: to be presumptuous or arrogant: to think too highly, esp. of oneself. — *adj.* and *n.* **overween'ing.** — *v.t.* **overweigh'** to be heavier than: to outweigh: to weigh down. — *n.* **o'verweight** weight beyond what is required or what is allowed: preponderance. — *adjs.* **overweight'** above the weight required: above the ideal or desired weight; **over= weight'ed** not fairly balanced in presentation. — *vs.t.* **overweight'** to weigh down: to put too heavy a burden on; **overwent'** see **overgo; overwhelm'** to overspread and crush by something heavy or strong: to flow over: to bear down: to reduce to helplessness: to overpower: to ply overpoweringly: to overhang (*obs.*). — *n.* and *adj.* **overwhel'ming.** — *adv.* **overwhel'mingly.** — *vs.t.* **overwind** (-*wīnd'*) to wind too far: — *pa.t.* and *pa.p.* **overwound; overwing'** to outflank (*obs.*): to fly over. — *v.i.* **overwin'ter** to pass the winter. — *v.t.* and *v.i.* to keep (animals, etc.), or stay, alive through the winter. — *adj.* **overwise'** wise overmuch: affectedly wise: wise in one's own estimation. — *adv.* **overwise'ly.** — *n.* **o'verword, o'erword** (*ōr'*, *ōr'*, *Scot.* owr'; also **owre'- word**) the burden of a song: a habitual saying. — *v.t.* and *v.i.* **overwork'** to work overmuch. — *n.* **o'verwork** additional work: (**o'verwork'**) excess of work. — *adj.* **overworn'** (-*wō'*, -*wö'*) worn out: subdued by toil: spoiled by use: threadbare: trite: exhausted of meaning or freshness by excessive use: out of date: spent or past; **overwound'** *pa.t.* and *pa.p.* of **overwind.** — *vs.t.* **overwrest'** to overstrain; **overwrest'le** (*Spens.*) to overcome by wrestling;**overwrite'** to cover over with writing or other writing: to superscribe: to exhaust by writing too much: to write too much about: to write in a laboured manner. — *v.i.* to write too much or too artificially. — *adj.* **overwrought'** (and *pa.p.* of **over- work**) worked too hard: too highly excited: with highly strained nerves: worked or embellished all over: overdone. — *v.t.* **overyear'** (*obs.*) to keep into a second, or later, year. — *adj.* (*dial.*) kept from one year to the next. — *adv.* (*dial.*) till next year.

overachieve . . . to . . . **overswim.** See **over-.**

overt *ō'vûrt*, *ō-vûrt'*, *adj.* open to view, not concealed: public: evident. — *adv.* **overtly.** — **overt act** something obviously done in execution of a criminal intent. — **market overt** open or public market. [Fr. *ouvert*, *pa.p.* of *ouvrir*, to open.]

overtake . . . to . . . **overtrump.** See **over-.**

overture *o'vər-tūr*, *n.* an opening, aperture (*obs.*): an opening up, disclosure (*Shak.*): an open place (*Spens.*): an opening of negotiations: an offer or proposal: an opening or opportunity: an opening or beginning: an instrumental prelude to an opera, oratorio, etc., or an independent composition in similar form (sonata form): the method in Presbyterian usage of beginning legislation and maturing opinion by sending some proposition from the inferior courts to the General Assembly, and *vice versa*: also the proposal so sent. — *v.t.* to lay a proposal before: to put forward as an overture. [O.Fr. *overture* (Fr. *ouverture*), opening.]

overturn . . . to . . . **overyear.** See **over-.**

ovibos *ōv'i-bos*, *ov'i-bos*, *n.* the musk-ox. — *adj.* **ovibō'- vīne.** [L. *ŏvis*, sheep, *bōs*, *bovis*, ox.]

ovicide *ō'vi-sīd*, (*jocular*) *n.* sheep-killing. [L. *ŏvis*, sheep, *caedĕre*, to kill.]

Ovidian *ō-vid'i-ən*, or *o-*, *adj.* of, like, or relating to, the Latin poet *Ovid* (43 B.C.–A.D. 17).

ov(i)- *ōv-*, *ō-vi-*, in composition, egg: ovum. — *ns.* **oval- bumin** (-*al'bū-min*, -*bū'*) the albumin in egg whites; **ovary** (*ō'və-ri*) the female genital gland: the part of the gynaeceum that contains the ovules (*bot.*). — *adj.* **ovā'rian** of or pertaining to the ovary. — *ns.* **ovā'riōle** one of the egg-tubes forming an insect's ovary; **ovār- iot'omist; ovāriot'omy** (Gr. *tomē*, a cut; *surg.*) the cutting of an ovary: usu. the removal of ovaries because of a tumour. — *adj.* **ovā'rious** (*rare*) consisting of eggs. — *n.* **ovarī'tis** inflammation of the ovary, oophoritis. — *adj.* **ō'vate** egg-shaped: shaped in outline like an egg, broadest below the middle (*bot.*). — *n.* **oviduct** (*ō'vi-dukt*) the tube by which the egg escapes from the ovary (*zool.*; L. *ducĕre*, *ductum*, to convey). — *adjs.* **ovidū'cal, oviduc'tal; oviferous** (*ō-vif'ə-rəs*) egg-carrying (L. *ferre*, *to bear*); **oviform** (*ō'vi-förm*) egg-shaped (L. *fōrma*, form); **ovigerous** (*ōv-ij'ə-rəs*) egg-carrying (L. *gerĕre*, to carry); **oviparous** (*ō-vip'ə- rəs*) egg-laying (L. *parĕre*, to bring forth). — *n.* **ovipar'- ity** (-*par'i-ti*). — *adv.* **ovip'arously.** — *v.i.* **ovipos'it** to deposit eggs with an ovipositor. — *ns.* **oviposition** (-*pə-zish'ən*); **ovipositor** (*ō-vi poz'i tor*) an egg-laying organ (L. *positor* — *pōnĕre*, to place); **ovisac** (*ōv'i-sak*) a brood-pouch: an egg-capsule (L. *saccus*; see **sac**); **ovist** (*ō'vist*) believer in doctrine that ovum contains all future generations in germ. — *adj.* **ovoid** (*ō'void*) egg-shaped and solid in form (sometimes also of a plane figure): egg-shaped and attached by the broad end (*bot.*). — *n.* an egg-shaped figure or body (Gr. *eidos*, form). — *adj.* **ovoid'al** ovoid. — *n.* **ovotest'is** (*pl.* -*tes* -*tēz*) an organ which produces both ova and spermatozoa. — *adj.* **ovoviviparous** (*ō-vō-vi-vip'ə-rəs*, or -*vī-*) producing eggs which are hatched in the body of the parent (L. *vīvus*, living, *parĕre*, to bring forth); **ov'ular** of or pertaining to an ovule. — *v.i.* **ovulate** (*ov'ūl-āt*, *ōv'-*) to release ova from the ovary: to form ova. — *n.* **ovulā'tion.** — *n.* **ovule** (*ōv'ūl*, *ov'*) in flowering plants, the body which on fertilisation becomes the seed, answering to the megasporangium and consisting of the nucellus and its integuments with the embryo-sac (megaspore): an undeveloped seed (from mod. L. dim. of *ovum*). — *adj.* **ōvulif'erous** carrying ovules. — *n.* **ovum** (*ō'vəm*) an egg: the egg-cell, or female gamete (*biol.*): — *pl.* **ō'va.** [L. *ōvum*, egg.]

oviform[1] *ov'i-förm*, *ō'vi-*, *adj.* like a sheep: ovine. — *adj.* **ovine** (*ō'vīn*) of sheep: sheep-like. [L. *ŏvis*, sheep, *fōrma*, form.]

oviform[2] . . . to . . . **ovoidal.** See **ov(i)-.**

ovolo *ō'vō-lō*, *n.* a moulding with the rounded part composed of a quarter of a circle, or of an arc of an ellipse with the curve greatest at the top (*archit.*): — *pl.* **ō'voli** (-*lē*). [It., — L. *ōvum*, an egg.]

ovotestis . . . to . . . **ovum.** See **ov(i)-.**

ow. Same as **ou, ouch[2].**

owche *owch*, *n.* Same as **ouch[1].**

owe *ō*, *v.t.* to own (*obs.* or *dial.*): to be indebted for: to be under an obligation to repay or render: to feel as a debt or as due: to have to thank: to concede or be bound to concede as a handicap. — *v.i.* to be in debt: — *pa.t.* and *pa.p.* **owed.** — The old *pa.t.* **ought** and *pa.p.* **own**, now differently used, are given separately; see also **owing.** [O.E. *āgan*, to own, possess, pres. indic. *āh*, preterite *āhte*, pa.p. *āgen*; O.N. *eiga*, O.H.G. *eigan*, to possess.]

owelty *ō'əl-ti*, (*law*) *n.* equality. [A.Fr. *owelté* — L. *aequālitās*, -*ātis*.]

Owenite *ō'in-īt*, *n.* a disciple of Robert *Owen* (1771–1858), who proposed to establish society on a basis of socialistic co-operation. — *adj.* **Owenian** (*ō-ēn'i-ən*). — *ns.* **Ow'enism; Ow'enist.**

ower Scots form of **over.** For compounds see the forms in **over-.**

owing *ō'ing*, *adj.* due: to be paid: imputable. — **owing to** because of: in consequence of.

---

overstuff' *v.t.* **over-** (5).	**overte'dious** (*Shak.*) *adj.* **over-** (5).	**o'vertrust** *n.* **over-** (5).
oversubt'le *adj.* **over-** (5).		**overuse'** *v.t.* **over-** (5).
oversubt'lety *n.* **over-** (5).	**overtire'** *v.t.* **over-** (5).	**o'veruse** *n.* **over-** (5).
oversupply' *v.t.* **over-** (5).	**overtoil'** *v.t.* **over-** (5).	**overvi'olent** *adj.* **over-** (5).
o'versupply *n.* **over-** (5).	**overtrust'** *v.i.* **over-** (5).	**over-zeal'ous** *adj.* **over-** (5).

owl *owl, n.* any member of the Strigiformes, nocturnal predacious birds with large broad heads, flat faces, large eyes surrounded by discs of feathers, short hooked beaks, silent flight, and howling or hooting cry: one who sits up at night: one who sees badly, or who shuns light: a solemn person: a wiseacre: a dullard: an owl-like breed of pigeon. — *v.i.* to behave like an owl. — *v.t.* (*obs.*) to smuggle (esp. wool or sheep from England to France). — *ns.* **owl'er** (*obs.*) a smuggler (esp. of wool or sheep); **owl'ery** an abode of owls: owlishness (*Carlyle*); **owl'et** an owl: a young owl: a moth of the Noctuidae. — *adj.* **owl'ish** like an owl: solemn: blinking: stupid: dull-looking. — *n.* **owl'-ishness.** — *adj.* **owl'y** owlish. — **owl'-car** (*old U.S.*) a night tram-car. — *adj.* **owl'-eyed** having blinking eyes like an owl. — **Owl'-glass, Owle'-glass, Howle'glass, Owl'spiegle** *Tyll Eulenspiegel*, a mischievous clown hero of a folk-tale popular in Germany from the 16th century or earlier; **owl'-light** dusk; **owl'-moth** a gigantic South American moth of the Noctuidae; **owl'-parr'ot** the kakapo; **owl'-train** (*old U.S.*) a night train. [O.E. *ūle*; Ger. *Eule*, L. *ulula*; imit.]

own¹ *ōn, v.t.* to possess, have belonging to one: to acknowledge as one's own: to claim as one's own (*obs.*): to confess: to allow to be true: to admit, concede: to acknowledge, recognise. — *v.i.* to confess (with *to*). — *n.* **own'er** possessor, proprietor: captain of a warship (*slang*). — *adj.* **own'erless.** — *n.* **own'ership.** — **own'er-dri'ver** one who drives his own car; **own'er-occupa'tion.** — *adj.* **own'er-occ'upied.** — **own'er-occ'u-pier** one who owns the house he lives in. — **own up** to confess freely. [O.E. *āgnian* — *āgen*, one's own; cf. **own²**.]

own² *ōn, adj.* belonging to oneself: often used with reflexive force, *my own, his own,* etc., serving instead of a genitive to *myself, himself,* etc., or transferring the sense of *self* to the subject (e.g. *I bake my own bread* = *I myself bake my bread*): sometimes used as an endearment. — *adj.* **own-brand', own-la'bel** of a commodity, carrying the trademark or label of the store that sells it. — **own goal** in football, a goal scored by mistake for the opposing side: a move that turns out to the disadvantage of the party making it. — **come into one's own** to take possession of one's rights: to have one's talents, merits, realised; **get one's own back** to retaliate, get even; **hold one's own** see **hold¹**; **on one's own** on one's own account: on one's own initiative: by one's own efforts or resources: independently: set up in independence: alone, by oneself. [O.E. *āgen*, pa.p. of *āgan* to possess; cf. **owe**.]

owre¹ Scots form of **over**. For compounds see **over-**.

owre² *owr,* (*Spens.*) *n.* Same as **ore¹**.

owrie. Same as **ourie**.

owsen *ow'sən, n.pl.* Scots form of **oxen**. See **ox**.

owt *owt,* (*dial.*) *n.* anything. [Variant of **aught**.]

ox *oks, n.* a general name for male or female of common domestic cattle (bull and cow), esp. a castrated male of the species: extended to kindred animals: — *pl.* **ox'en** used for both male and female. — *n.* **ox'er** esp. in fox-hunting parlance, an ox-fence: in show-jumping, an obstacle in the form of an ox-fence. — **ox'-ant'elope** any antelope of the hartebeest group; **ox'-bird** the dunlin: the ox-pecker: an African weaver-bird: applied also to various other birds; **ox'blood** a dark reddish-brown colour. — Also *adj.* — **ox'-bot** a warble-fly larva infesting cattle; **ox'-bow** (*-bō*) a collar for a yoked ox: a river-bend returning almost upon itself (forming an *ox-bow lake* when the neck is pierced and the bend cut off); **ox'-eye** a name for various birds, esp. the great titmouse: a wild chrysanthemum, *Chrysanthemum leucanthemum,* with yellow disc and white ray (*ox-eye daisy*): sometimes (*yellow ox-eye*) the corn marigold: an elliptical dormer window. — *adj.* **ox'-eyed** having large, ox-like eyes. — **ox'-fence** a fence for confining cattle: a hedge with a rail and, in many cases, also a ditch; **ox'gang, ox'gate, ox'land** a bovate or one-eighth of a carucate of ploughland, the share attributed to

each ox in a team of eight (averaging about 13 acres); **ox'head** the head of an ox: a blockhead; **ox'-pecker** an African genus (*Buphaga*) of birds akin to starlings, that eat the parasites on cattle — also **beefeater, ox-bird**; **ox'tail** the tail of an ox, esp. as used for soup, stew, etc.; **ox'-tongue** the tongue of an ox, used as food: a yellow-flowered milky-juiced composite (*Picris echioides*); **ox'-war'ble** a swelling on the back of an ox: the fly whose larva produces it. — **have the black ox tread on one's foot** to experience sorrow or misfortune. [O.E. *oxa*, pl. *oxan*; Ger. *Ochse*, Goth. *auhsa*, Sans. *ukṣan*.]

Oxalis *oks'ə-lis, n.* the wood-sorrel genus, giving name to the family **Oxalidā'ceae**, close akin to the Geranium family: (without *cap.*) a plant of this genus. — *adj.* **oxalic** (*-al'ik*) applied to an acid ($C_2H_2O_4$) obtained from wood-sorrel and other plants, used for cleaning metals, and as a bleaching agent. — *n.* **ox'alate** a salt of oxalic acid. [Gr. *oxalis* — *oxys,* sharp, acid.]

oxazine *ok'sə-zēn, n.* any of several isomeric compounds having the formula C_4H_5NO, with the nitrogen, oxygen and carbon atoms arranged in a ring. [**oxy-,** *azine*.]

Oxbridge *oks'brij, n.* and *adj.* (pertaining to) *Ox*ford and Cam*bridge* regarded as typifying an upper-class-oriented kind of education, or as a road to unfair advantages, e.g. in obtaining jobs, or as the home of particular academic attitudes.

Oxford *oks'fərd, adj.* belonging to the city, county, or university of Oxford. — *n.* **Oxfordian** (*-fôrd'i-ən*) a division of the Middle Jurassic. — Also *adj.* — **Oxford bags** very wide trousers; **Oxford blue** a dark blue (see also **blue¹**); **Oxford clay** a dark blue or grey clay of the Oxfordian formation; **Oxford English** a form of standard English in which certain tendencies are (sometimes affectedly) exaggerated, widely believed to be spoken at Oxford; **Oxford groups** informal circles of followers of Dr Frank Buchman, who exchanged religious experiences, and sought divine guidance individually (**the Oxford group** his followers as a body; 1921–1938); **Oxford movement** the Tractarian movement; **Oxford** (*shoe*) a low shoe, usu. laced. [O.E. *Oxnaford,* lit. oxen's ford.]

oxide *oks'īd, n.* a compound of oxygen and some other element or radical. — *ns.* **ox'idant** a substance acting as an oxidiser; **ox'idase** any of a group of enzymes that promote oxidation in plant and animal cells. — *v.t.* **ox'idate** (*-id-āt*) to oxidise. — *n.* **oxidā'tion** oxidising. — *adj.* **oxidis'able, -z-.** — *v.t.* and *v.i.* **ox'idise, -ize** to combine with oxygen: to deprive (an atom or ion) of, or (*v.i.*) to lose, electrons: to make, or become, rusty: to put a protective oxide coating on (a metal surface). — *n.* **oxidīs'er, -z-** an oxidising agent. [Fr. *oxide* (now *oxyde*), formed from *oxygène,* oxygen.]

oxime *oks'ēm,* (*chem.*) *n.* any of a number of compounds obtained by the action of hydroxylamine on aldehydes or ketones. [*Oxygen* and *imide*.]

oximeter *oks-im'i-tər, n.* a photoelectric instrument for measuring oxygen saturation of the blood. [oxi-, older spelling of **oxy-²**, and **-meter**.]

oxlip *oks'lip, n.* originally a hybrid between primrose and cowslip: now, a species of Primula (*P. elatior*) like a large pale cowslip. — Also (*Shak.*) **ox'slip.** [O.E. *oxanslyppe* — *oxan,* gen. of *oxa,* ox, and *slyppe,* slime, a slimy dropping; cf. **cowslip**.]

Oxonian *oks-ō'ni-ən, adj.* of or pertaining to *Ox*ford or to its university. — *n.* an inhabitant, native, student, or graduate of Oxford: a kind of shoe. [L. *Oxonia,* Oxford — O.E. *Oxnaford.*]

oxonium *oks-ō'ni-əm, n.* a univalent basic radical, H_3O, in which oxygen is tetravalent, forming organic derivatives, **oxonium salts.** [*oxygen* and *ammonium*.]

oxslip. See **oxlip**.

oxter *oks'tər,* (*Scot.*) *n.* the armpit. — *v.t.* to take under the arm: to support by taking the arm. [O.E. *oxta*.]

oxy-¹ *oks-i-,* in composition, sharp: pointed: acid.

oxy-² *oks-i,* in composition, oxygen. — *adj.* **ox'y-acet'y-**

lene involving, using, or by means of, a mixture of oxygen and acetylene, esp. in cutting or welding metals at high temperatures. — *ns.* **ox′y-a′cid, ox′y-com′-pound, ox′y-salt,** etc., an acid, compound, salt, etc., containing oxygen: one in which an atom of hydrogen is replaced by a hydroxyl-group; **ox′y-bro′mide, -chlo′-ride, -flu′oride, -hal′ide, -i′odide** a compound of an element or radical with oxygen and a halogen (bromine, etc.); **ox′yhaemoglo′bin** a loose compound of oxygen and haemoglobin. — *adj.* **ox′y-hy′drogen** involving or using a mixture of oxygen and hydrogen. — **ox′y-cal′cium light** limelight. [Gr. *oxys*, sharp.]

oxygen *oks′i-jən, n.* a gas (atomic number 8; symbol O) without taste, colour, or smell, forming part of the air, water, etc., and supporting life and combustion. — *v.t.* **ox′ygenāte** (or *oks-ij′*) to oxidise: to impregnate or treat with oxygen. — *ns.* **oxygenā′tion; ox′ygenator** an apparatus performing functions of heart and lungs during an operation: that which supplies oxygen. — *v.t.* **ox′ygenise, -ize** to oxygenate. — *adj.* **oxyg′enous.** — **oxygen debt** a depletion of the body's store of oxygen occurring during bursts of strenuous exercise, replaced after bodily activity returns to normal levels; **oxygen mask** a masklike breathing apparatus through which oxygen is supplied in rarefied atmospheres to aviators and mountaineers; **oxygen tent** tent-like enclosure in which there is a controllable flow of oxygen, erected round a patient to aid breathing. [Gr. *oxys*, sharp, acid, and the root of *gennaein*, to generate, from the old belief that all acids contained oxygen.]

oxymel *oks′i-mel, n.* a mixture of vinegar and honey. [Gr. *oxymeli* — *oxys*, sour, *meli*, honey.]

oxymoron *oks-i-mō′ron, -mö′, n.* a figure of speech by means of which contradictory terms are combined, so as to form an expressive phrase or epithet, as *cruel kindness, falsely true,* etc. [Gr. neut. of *oxymōros,* lit. pointedly foolish — *oxys*, sharp, *mōros*, foolish.]

oxyrhynchus *oks-i-ring′kəs, n.* an Egyptian fish, sacred to the goddess Hathor, represented on coins and sculptures. [Gr. *oxyrrynchos* — *oxys*, sharp, *rhynchos*, a snout.]

oxytocin *oks-i-tō′sin, n.* a pituitary hormone that stimulates uterine muscle contraction and milk production, also produced synthetically for use in accelerating labour. — *adj., n.* **oxytō′cic** (a drug) stimulating uterine muscle contraction. [Gr. *oxys*, sharp, *tokos*, birth.]

oxytone *oks′i-tōn, adj* having the acute accent on the last syllable (*Gr. gram.*): stressed on the final syllable. — *n.* a word so accented. [Gr. *oxys*, sharp, *tonos*, tone.]

oy, oye, oe *oi, ō-i, ō,* (*Scot.*) *ns.* a grandchild. [Gael. *ogha, odha*.]

oyer *oi′ər, n.* a hearing in a law-court, an assize. — **oyer**

and terminer (*tûr′min-ər*) a royal commission conferring power to hear and determine criminal causes (out of official use 1972). [A.Fr. *oyer* (Fr. *ouïr*) — L. *audīre,* to hear.]

oyez, oyes *ō-yes′, ō′yes, interj.* the call of a public crier, or officer of a law-court, for attention before making a proclamation. — *n.* (*oiz*; *Shak.*) a proclamation. [O.Fr. *oyez,* imper. of *oir* (Fr. *ouïr*), to hear.]

oyster *ois′tər, n.* bivalve shellfish (*Ostrea*) used as food: secretive person: source of advantage: the colour of an oyster, a pale greyish beige or pink. — *adj.* of this colour. — **oys′ter-bank, -bed, -farm, -field, -park** place where oysters breed or are bred; **oys′ter-catcher** the sea pie — a black and white wading bird, with red bill and feet, feeding on limpets and mussels (not oysters); **oys′ter-fish′ery** the business of catching oysters; **oys′-ter-knife** a knife for opening oysters; **oyster mushroom** an edible fungus (*Pleurotus ostreatus* or related species) found esp. in clusters on dead wood; **oys′ter-patt′y** a small pie or pasty made from oysters; **oys′ter-plant** salsify, or a seaside boraginaceous plant, *Mertensia maritima* — both supposed to taste like oysters; **oys′-ter-shell** the shell of an oyster. — *n.pl.* **oys′ter-tongs** a tool for gathering oysters. — **oys′ter-wench, -wife, -woman** (all *obs.*) a woman who sells oysters; **the world is my** (Shak., *Merry Wives* II, ii. 2, **world's mine**), **his,** etc., **oyster** the world lies before me, etc., ready to yield profit or success. [O.Fr. *oistre* (Fr. *huître*) — L. *ostrea* — Gr. *ostreon,* an oyster — *osteon,* a bone.]

oystrige *oi′strij, (Spens.) n.* for **ostrich.**

Oz *oz,* (*Austr. slang*) *n.* Australia. — Also *adj.*

ozaena *ō-zē′nə, n.* a fetid discharge from the nostrils. [Gr. *ozaina,* a fetid polypus of the nose — *ozein,* to smell.]

Ozalid® *oz′əl-id, n.* a method of duplicating printed matter onto chemically treated paper: a reproduction made by this process.

ozeki *ō-zē′ki, n.* a champion sumo wrestler. [Jap. *ōzeki.*]

ozokerite *ō-zō′kər-īt, -kēr′īt,* **ozocerite** *ō-zos′ər-īt, ō-zō-sēr′īt, ns.* a waxy natural paraffin. [Gr. *ozein,* to smell, *kēros,* wax.]

ozone *ō′zōn, n.* an allotropic form (O₃) of oxygen present in the atmosphere, once regarded as health-giving, but harmful in concentration such as may occur in industrial areas: (see also **ozonosphere**). — *ns.* **ozonā′tion, -isā′tion, -z-.** — *adj.* **ozonif′erous** bringing or producing ozone. — *v.t.* **ō′zonise, -ize** to turn into, charge with, or treat with, ozone. — *ns.* **ozonis′er, -z-** apparatus for turning oxygen into ozone; **ozon′osphere, ozone layer** a layer of the upper atmosphere where ozone is formed in quantity, protecting earth from the sun's ultraviolet rays. [Gr. *ozōn,* pr.p. of *ozein,* to smell.]

For other sounds see detailed chart of pronunciation.

P

P, p *pē, n.* the sixteenth letter of our alphabet, and of the Greek (see **pi¹**) representing a voiceless labial stop: in mediaeval Roman notation, P = 400, P̄ = 400000: in chem. *p-* is an abbreviation for para-. — **P-Celt, P-Kelt** see Celt. — *adj.* **p′-type** (i.e. 'positive type') of a semiconductor, having an excess of mobile holes over conduction electrons. — **mind one's p's and q's** see **mind.**

pa¹ *pä, n.* a childish or vulgar word for father. [**papa.**]

pa², pah *pä, n.* a Maori fort or settlement. [Maori.]

pabouche *pə-bōōsh′, n.* a slipper. [See **babouche.**]

pabulum *pab′ū-, -yə-, -ləm, n.* food of any kind, esp. that of lower animals and of plants: provender: fuel: nourishment for the mind. — *adjs.* **pab′ūlar, pab′ūlous.** [L. *pābulum* — *pāscĕre,* to feed.]

paca *pä′kə, n.* the so-called spotted cavy of South America, akin to the agouti. [Sp. and Port., — Tupí *paca.*]

pacable *pāk′ə-bl, pak′, (arch.) adj.* capable of being appeased: willing to forgive. — *n.* **pacation** (*pə-kā′-shən*). [L. *pācāre,* to appease — *pāx, pācis,* peace.]

pace¹ *pās, n.* a stride: a step: the space between the feet in walking, about 30 inches, or (among the Romans) the space between two successive positions of the same foot, over 58 inches: gait: rate of walking, running, etc. (of a man or beast): rate of speed in movement or work, often applied to fast living: a mode of stepping in horses in which the legs on the same side are lifted together: amble: a step of a stair, or the like: a pass or passage (*obs.*). — *v.t.* to traverse with measured steps: to measure by steps (often with *out*): to train to perform paces: to set the pace for: to perform as a pace or paces. — *v.i.* to walk: to walk slowly and with measured tread: to amble. — *adj.* **paced** having a certain pace or gait. — *n.* **pac′er** one who paces: a horse whose usual gait is a pace: a horse trained to pace in harness racing. — *adj.* **pac′(e)y** (*coll.*) fast: lively: smart. — **pace′-bowler** in cricket, a bowler who delivers the ball fast; **pace′-bowling; pace′maker** one who sets the pace as in a race (also *fig.*): a small mass of muscle cells in the heart which control the heart-beat electrically: an electronic device (in later models, with radioactive core) used to correct weak or irregular heart rhythms; **pace′-setter** a pacemaker, except in anatomical and electronic senses. — **go the pace** to go at a great speed: to live a fast life; **keep, hold pace with** to go as fast as: to keep up with; **make, set the pace** to regulate the speed for others by example; **put someone through his paces** to set someone to show what he can do; **show one's paces** to show up with the pace or speed that has been set. [Fr. *pas* — L. *passus,* a step — *pandĕre, passum,* to stretch.]

pace² *pā′sē, prep.* with or by the leave of (expressing disagreement courteously). [L., abl. of *pāx,* peace.]

Pace *pās,* a dial. form of **Pasch.** — **pace egg** an Easter egg, one hard-boiled and dyed; **pace′-egging** begging for eggs, etc., at Easter: rolling pace eggs on the ground.

pacha, pachalic; pachak. See **pasha; putchock.**

pachinko *pə-ching′kō, n.* a form of pin-ball popular in Japan. [Jap. *pachin,* onomatopoeic, representing trigger sound.]

pachisi *pä-chē′sē, -zē, n.* an Indian game like backgammon or ludo. [Hindi *pacīsī,* of twenty-five — the highest throw.]

pachy- *pak′i-,* in combination, thick. — *adjs.* **pachycarp′ous** (Gr. *karpos,* fruit) having a thick pericarp; **pachydac′tyl, -ous** (Gr. *daktylos,* digit) having thick digits. — *n.* **pach′yderm** (Gr. *derma,* skin) strictly, any animal

of the Pachydermata, but usually an elephant, rhinoceros, or hippopotamus: an insensitive person. — *adj.* **pachyderm′al.** — *n.pl.* **Pachyderm′ata** in old classification, those ungulates that do not ruminate — elephant, horse, pig, etc. — *adj.* **pachyder′matous** thick-skinned: of the pachyderms: insensitive. — *n.* **pachyderm′ia** abnormal thickness of skin or mucous membrane. — *adjs.* **pachyderm′ic, pachyderm′ous.** — *n.* **pachym′eter** an instrument for measuring small thicknesses. [Gr. *pachys,* thick.]

pacify *pas′i-fī, v.t.* to appease: to calm: to bring peace to. — *adjs.* **pac′ifiable; pacif′ic** peacemaking: appeasing: inclining towards peace: peaceful: mild: tranquil: (with *cap.*) of, or pertaining to the ocean between Asia and America, so called by Magellan, the first European to sail on it, because he happened to cross it in peaceful weather conditions. — *n.* (with *cap.*) the Pacific Ocean. — *adj.* **pacif′ical** pacific (rare except in phrase *Letters pacifical,* letters recommending the bearer as one in peace and fellowship with the Church — also *Letters of peace, Pacificae*). — *adv.* **pacif′ically.** — *v.t.* **pacif′icate** to give peace to. — *ns.* **pacificā′tion** peacemaking: conciliation: appeasement: a peace treaty; **pacif′icātor** a peacemaker. — *adj.* **pacif′icatory** (*-ə-tə-ri*) tending to make peace. — *ns.* **pacif′icism** (*-sizm*) the beliefs and principles of pacificists; **pacif′icist** (*-sist*) one who is opposed to war, or believes all war to be wrong; **pac′ifier** a person or thing that pacifies: a baby's dummy or teething-ring (*U.S.*); **pac′ifism, pac′ifist** ill-formed, but generally preferred, forms of **pacificism, pacificist.** [Partly through Fr. *pacifier* — L. *pācificus,* pacific — *pācificāre* — *pāx, pācis,* peace, *facĕre,* to make.]

pack¹ *pak, n.* a bundle, esp. orig. one made to be carried on the back by a pedlar or pack-animal: a collection, stock, or store: a bundle of some particular kind or quantity, as of wool, 240 lb. (c. 109 kg.): the quantity packed at a time or in a season: a complete set of playing cards: a number of animals herding together or kept together for hunting: a shepherd's own sheep grazing along with his employer's as part payment (*Scot.*): the forwards in a Rugby football team: a group of Cub Scouts in the Scout movement or of Brownie Guides in the Guide movement: a worthless, disreputable or otherwise objectionable set of persons: a gang, as of thieves: a mass of pack-ice: a sheet for folding round the body to allay inflammation, fever, etc.: the use or application of such a sheet: a built support for a mine-roof: packing material: a cosmetic paste: a number of photographic plates or films exposed together: act of packing or condition of being packed: mode of packing: a person of worthless or bad character (*obs.*): a compact package, esp. of something for sale: a parachute folded in its fabric container: a group of e.g. submarines acting together. — *v.t.* to make into a bundled pack: to place compactly in a box, bag, or the like: to press together closely: to compress: to fill tightly or compactly: to fill with anything: to cram: to crowd: to envelop: to surround closely: to fill the spaces surrounding: to prepare (food) for preservation, transport and marketing: to send away, dismiss (usu. with *off*): to form into a pack: to load with a pack: to carry in packs: to carry, wear (a gun). — *v.i.* to form into a pack: to settle or be driven into a firm mass: to form a scrum: to admit of being put into compact shape: to put one's belongings together in boxes, bags, etc., as for a journey (often with *up*): to travel with a pack: to take oneself off, or depart in haste (usu. with *off*): to plot, intrigue, arrange privately (*Shak.*). — *n.* **pack′age** the act, manner, or privilege of packing: a bundle, packet, or parcel: a case or other receptacle for packing goods in: a composite proposition, scheme, offer, etc. in which various separate elements are all dealt with as essential parts of the whole (see also **package deal**): a computer program in general form, to which the user adds such data as are applicable in a particular case. — *v.t.* to put into a container or wrappings, or into a package. — *adj.* **pack′aged** (*lit.* and *fig.*). — *ns.* **pack′ager** a specialist in the packaging of books, programs, etc.; **pack′aging** anything used to package goods: the total presentation of a product for sale, i.e. its design, wrapping, etc.: the designing and complete production of e.g. illustrated books, programmes for television, etc. for sale to a publisher, broadcasting company, etc.; **pack′er** one who packs: one who packs goods for sending out: an employer or employee in the business of preparing and preserving food: one who transports goods by means of pack-animals (*U.S.*): a machine or device for packing; **pack′et** a small package: a carton: a ship or vessel employed in carrying packets of letters, passengers, etc.: a vessel plying regularly between one port and another (also **pack′et-boat, pack′et-ship,** etc.): a large amount of money (*coll.*): a small group: a cluster of bacteria: used as equivalent to a quantum (*fig.*): a serious injury (*slang*): a block of coded data (*comput.*; see **packet-switching** below). — *v.t.* to parcel up. — *n.* **pack′ing** the act of putting into packs or of tying up for carriage or storing: material for packing: anything used to fill an empty space or to make a joint close. — **package deal** a deal which embraces a number of matters and has to be accepted as a whole, the less favourable items along with the favourable; **package holiday, tour** one whose details are arranged by the organiser before he advertises it and for which he is paid a fixed price which covers all costs (food, travel, etc.); **pack′-an′imal** a beast used to carry goods on its back; **pack′-cinch** (*-sinsh*) a wide girth for a pack-animal; **pack′-cloth** a cloth in which goods are enclosed: packsheet; **pack′-drill** a military punishment of marching about laden with full equipment; **pack′et-note** a size of notepaper 5½ by 9 inches (c. 14 × 23 cm.); **pack′et-switching** (*comput.*) a system of communication in which packets of data are transmitted between computers of varying types and compatibility; **pack′-horse** a horse used to carry goods on its back: a drudge; **pack′-ice** a mass of large pieces of floating ice driven together by winds and currents; **pack′ing-box, -case** a box or framework for packing goods in; **pack′ing-need′le** a strong needle for sewing up packages; **pack′ing-paper** a strong, thick kind of wrapping-paper; **pack′ing-press** a press for squeezing goods into small compass for packing; **pack′ing-sheet, or pack′-sheet,** coarse cloth for packing goods; **pack′-load** the load an animal can carry; **pack′man** a pedlar or a man who carries a pack; **pack′-mule** a mule used for carrying burdens; **pack′-rat** a kind of long-tailed rat, native to the western part of North America; **pack′-saddle** a saddle for pack-horses, pack-mules, etc.; **pack′staff** a staff for supporting a pedlar's pack when he rests (see also **pike**[1]); **pack′-thread** a coarse thread used to sew up packages; **pack′-train** a train of loaded pack-animals; **pack′-twine** thin twine for tying up parcels; **pack′way** a narrow path fit for pack-horses. — **pack a punch** to be capable of giving a powerful blow; **pack it in, up** (*slang*) to stop, give up, doing something; **pack up** (*slang*) to stop: to break down; **send someone packing** to dismiss summarily. [M.E. *packe, pakke,* app. — M. Flem. *pac* or Du. or L. Ger. *pak.*]

pack[2] *pak,* (*obs.*) *n.* a secret or underhand arrangement. — *v.i.* to make such an arrangement (*Shak.*). — *v.t.* (esp. in *pass.*) to bring into a plot as accomplice (*Shak.*): to shuffle (cards) esp. dishonestly (*obs.*): to fill up (a jury, meeting, etc.) with persons of a particular kind for one's own purposes. — **pack cards with**

(*Shak.*, etc.) to make a dishonest arrangement with. [Prob. **pact.**]

pack[3] *pak,* (*Scot.*) *adj.* intimate, confidential.   [Origin unknown.]

package, packet. See **pack**[1].

packfong. An incorrect form of **paktong.**

paco *pä′kō, n.* an alpaca: — *pl.* **pa′cos.**   [Sp., — Quechua *paco.*]

pact *pakt, n.* that which is agreed on: an agreement, esp. informal or not legally enforceable. — *n.* **pac′tion** (chiefly *Scot.*) a pact. — *v.t.* to agree. — *adj.* **pac′tional.** — **Warsaw Pact** a treaty of friendship, assistance and co-operation signed in Warsaw in May 1955 by the USSR and seven other European communist states. [L. *pactum* — *pacīscĕre, pactum,* to contract.]

pactum *pak′tam, -tōōm,* (L.) *n.* a pact. — **pactum illicitum** (*i-lis′i-tam, i-lik′i-tōōm*) an illegal compact; **pactum nudum** (*nū′dam, nōō′dōōm*) a pact without consideration.

pad[1] *pad, n.* a path (*dial.*): a thief on the high-road (usually *footpad*; *arch.*): (contraction of **pad′-horse**) a horse for riding on the road: an easy-paced horse (*arch.* or *dial.*). — *v.i.* to walk on foot: to trudge along: to walk with quiet or dull-sounding tread: to rob on foot (*arch.*): — *pr.p.* **padd′ing**; *pa.t.* and *pa.p.* **padd′ed.** — **padd′ing-ken** (*thieves' slang*) a thieves' or tramps' lodging-house; **pad′-nag** (*arch.* or *dial.*) an ambling nag. — **pad the hoof** (*slang*) to walk, trudge; **stand pad** to beg by the roadside.   [Du. *pad,* a path.]

pad[2] *pad, n.* anything stuffed with a soft material, to prevent friction, pressure, or injury, for inking, for filling out, etc.: a soft saddle: a cushion: a number of sheets of paper or other soft material fastened together in a block: a leg-guard for cricketers, etc.: the fleshy, thick-skinned undersurface of the foot of many animals, as the fox: the foot of a beast, esp. of chase: its footprint: a water-lily leaf (*U.S.*): (usu. in *pl.*) thick watered ribbon for watch-guards: a rocket-launching platform: a bed, room, or home, esp. one's own (*slang*): a device built into a road surface, operated by vehicles passing over it, controlling changes of traffic lights (**vehicle-actuated signals**) so as to give passage for longer time to the greater stream of traffic. — *v.t.* to stuff, cover, or fill out with anything soft: to furnish with padding: to track by footprints: to impregnate, as with a mordant: — *pr.p.* **padd′ing**; *pa.t.* and *pa.p.* **padd′ed.** — *ns.* **padd′er** one who pads, or cushions; **padd′ing** stuffing: matter of less value introduced into a book or article in order to make it of the length desired: the process of mordanting a fabric. — **pad′-cloth** a cloth covering a horse's loins; **padded cell** a room with padded walls in a mental hospital; **pad′-el′ephant** a working elephant wearing a pad but no howdah; **pad′-saddle** a treeless, padded saddle; **pad′-saw** a small saw-blade with detachable handle, used for cutting curves and awkward angles (also **keyhole saw**); **pad′-tree** the wooden or metal frame to which harness-pads are attached.   [Origin obscure; possibly connected with **pod**[1].]

pad[3]. Same as **ped**[1].

padang *pad′ang,* (*Malay*) *n.* a field, esp. a playing-field.

padauk, padouk *pä-dowk′, n.* a Burmese timber tree of the red-sanders genus.   [Burmese.]

paddle[1] *pad′l, v.i.* to wade about or dabble in liquid or semi-liquid: to walk unsteadily or with short steps: to play or toy with the fingers (*arch.*): to trifle (*obs.*): to make (land) bare of grass by constant trampling, etc. (*dial.*). — *v.t.* (*arch.*) to toy with or finger. — *n.* **padd′ler** one who paddles: (in *pl.*) a protective garment worn by children when paddling.   [Cf. **pad**[1], and L. Ger. *paddeln,* to tramp about.]

paddle[2] *pad′l,* **padle** *pä′dl,* **pā′, paidle** *pā′,* (*Scot.*) *ns.* the lumpsucker. — Also **cock′-pad(d)′le, -paid′le** (*masc.*), **hen′-pad(d)′le, -paid′le** (*fem.*).   [Origin unknown.]

paddle[3] *pad′l, n.* a small, long-handled spade: a short, broad, spoon-shaped oar, used for moving canoes: the blade of an oar: one of the boards of a paddle-wheel

or water-wheel: a swimming animal's flipper: a paddle-shaped instrument for stirring, beating, etc.: a small bat, as used in table-tennis (*U.S.*). — *v.i.* to use a paddle, progress by use of paddles: to row gently: to swim about like a duck. — *v.t.* to propel by paddle: to strike or spank with a paddle or the like (esp. *U.S.*). — *ns.* **padd'ler** one who paddles; **padd'ling** the act of paddling: a flock of wild duck on water. — **padd'le=board** one of the boards of a paddle-wheel; **padd'le-boat** a paddle-steamer; **padd'le-box** the covering of a paddle-wheel; **padd'le-shaft** the axle on which paddle-wheels turn; **padd'le-staff** a small spade or paddle; **padd'le-steam'er** a steamer propelled by paddle-wheels; **padd'le-wheel** the wheel of a steam-vessel, which by turning in the water causes the boat to move; **padd'le=wood** the light, strong wood of a Guiana tree (*Aspidosperma*) of the dogbane family. — **paddle one's own canoe** to progress independently. [Origin obscure.]
paddock[1]. See **puddock**.
paddock[2] *pad'ək, n.* an enclosed field under pasture, orig. near a house or stable: a small field in which horses are kept before a race: any enclosed field (*Austr.* and *N.Z.*). [Apparently from earlier *parrock* — O.E. *pearroc*, park.]
paddy *pad'i, n.* growing rice: rice in the husk. — **padd'y=bird** the Java sparrow or rice-bird; **padd'y-field**. [Malay *pādī*, rice in the straw.]
Paddy *pad'i, n.* a familiar name for an Irishman: (without *cap.*) a rage (*coll.*). — *n.* **Padd'yism** a hibernicism. — **Paddy's lantern** the moon; **paddy (train)** (*mining slang*) an underground colliery train for transporting miners from one point to another, pulled by a diesel- or electrically-powered locomotive, or by a rope-haulage system (properly **man'rider** or **manriding train**); **paddy wagon** a black Maria; **padd'y-whack** (*slang*) an Irishman, esp. a big one: a rage: a slap, smack, blow, spanking, beating.
paddymelon. See **pademelon**.
padella *pa-del'ə, n.* a shallow dish of fat with a wick used in illuminations. [It., a frying-pan — L. *patella*.]
pademelon, paddymelon, padymelon *pad'i-mel'ən, n.* any of several small wallabies. [Aboriginal.]
paderero *pad-ə-rā'rō.* Same as **pederero**.
padishah *pä'di-shä, n.* chief ruler: great king, a title of the Shah of Persia, and formerly of the Sultan of Turkey, the Great Mogul, or the (British) Emperor of India. [Pers. *pad*, master, *shāh*, king.]
padle. See **paddle**[2].
padlock *pad'lok, n.* a movable lock with a link turning on a hinge or pivot at one end, catching the bolt at the other. — Also *v.t.* [Origin uncertain, possibly dial. *pad*, a basket, and **lock**[1].]
padma *pud'mə, n.* the sacred lotus. [Sans.]
padouk. Same as **padauk**.
padre *pä'drā, n.* father, a title given to priests: an army chaplain: a parson. — *n.* **padrō'ne** a shipmaster (*arch.*): an innkeeper, café- or restaurant-owner: an employer, esp. among Italian Americans: one who jobs out hand-organs, or who gets children to beg for him (*obs.*): — *pl.* **padrō'ni** (*-nē*). [Port. (also Sp. and It.) *padre*, It. *padrone* — L. *pater*, a father, *patrōnus*, a patron.]
Paduan *pad'ū-ən, adj.* of *Padua*. — *n.* a native of Padua: a counterfeit Roman bronze coin made at Padua in the 16th century: the pavan.
paduasoy *pad'ū-ə-soi, pä'də-soi, n.* a corded silk used in the 18th century: a garment made of it. [Fr. *pou-de-soie* — *pou, pout, poult* (of unknown origin), *de soie*, of silk; apparently influenced by *Padua*.]
padymelon. See **pademelon**.
Paean *pē'ən, n.* the Homeric physician of the gods: later, an epithet of Apollo: (without *cap.*) a lyric to Apollo or Artemis (or some other god): (without *cap.*) a song of thanksgiving or triumph: (without *cap.*) exultation. — Also **pē'an**. — *ns.* **pae'on, paeon'ic** a foot of four syllables, any one long, three short. — *adj.* **paeon'ic**

(*-on'ik*). [L. *Paeān, paeōn* — Gr. *Paiān, -ānos, paiōn, -ōnos.*]
paed(o)-, ped(o)- *pēd-, pē-dō-,* also sometimes **paid(o)-** *pīd-, pī-dō-,* in composition, child, boy. — *adj.* **paeda-gog'ic** see **pedagogic**. — *ns.* **paed'agogue** see **pedagogue**; **paed'erast** (Gr. *erastēs*, lover) one who practises paed-erasty. — *adj.* **paederast'ic.** — *ns.* **paed'erasty** sexual relations of a male with a male, esp. a boy; **paedeut'ic, paideut'ic** (also *n.sing.* **paed-, paideutics**) educational method or theory. — *adj.* **paediat'ric** (Gr. *iātrikos,* medical) relating to the medical treatment of children. — *n.sing.* **paediat'rics** the treatment of children's dis-eases. — *ns.* **paediatrician** (*-ə-trish'ən*), **paedī'atrist; paedī'atry; paedobap'tism** infant baptism; **paedobap'-tist.** — *adj.* **paedodont'ic.** — *n.sing.* **paedodont'ics** the branch of dentistry concerned with care of children's teeth. — *n.* **paedogen'esis** reproduction by an animal in the larval state. — *adj.* **paedolog'ical.** — *ns.* **paedol'-ogist; paedol'ogy** the study of the growth and devel-opment of children. — *adjs.* **paedogenet'ic; paedomor'-phic** of paedomorphism or paedomorphosis. — *ns.* **paedomorph'ism** (Gr. *morphē,* form) retention of juve-nile characters in the mature stage; **paedomor'phosis** a phylogenetic change in which juvenile characteristics are retained in the adult; **paed'ophile** (*-fīl*) one affected with paedophilia; **paedophilia** (*-fil'*) sexual desire whose object is children. — *adjs. and ns.* **paedophil'iac, -phil'ic.** — *ns.* **paed'otribe** (*-trīb*; Gr. *paidotribēs*) in ancient Greece, a gymnastic teacher; **paedot'rophy** (Gr. *tropheiā,* nursing) the art of rearing children. [Gr. *pais, paidos,* boy, child; *paideutēs,* teacher.]
paella *pī-el'ə, pä-el'ya, n.* a stew containing saffron, chicken, rice, vegetables, seafood, etc. [Sp., — L. *patella,* pan.]
paenula *pē'nū-lə, n.* a Roman travelling cloak: a chasuble, esp. in its older form. [L. *paenula.*]
paeon. See **Paean**.
paeony. Same as **peony**.
pagan *pā'gən, n.* a heathen: one who is not a Christian, Jew, or Muslim: more recently, one who has no religion: one who sets a high value on sensual pleas-ures. — Also *adj.* — *v.t.* **pā'ganise, -ize** to render pagan or heathen: to convert to paganism. — *adj.* **pā'ganish** heathenish. — *n.* **pā'ganism** heathenism: the beliefs and practices of the heathen. [L. *pāgānus,* rustic, peasant, also civilian (because the Christians reckoned them-selves soldiers of Christ) — *pāgus,* a district.]
page[1] *pāj, n.* a boy attendant: a boy in buttons employed as a messenger in hotels, clubs, etc.: a messenger, boy or girl, in the U.S. Congress, etc.: a youth training for knighthood, receiving education and performing ser-vices at court or in a nobleman's household (*hist.*): a contrivance for holding up a long skirt in walking (*hist.*). — *v.t.* to attend as a page: to seek or summon by sending a page around: by repeatedly calling aloud for, or by means of a pager. — *ns.* **page'hood** the condition of a page; **pā'ger** an electronic device which pages a person (cf. **bleeper**). — **page'-boy** a page: (also **page-boy hairstyle, haircut**) a hairstyle in which the hair hangs smoothly to approx. shoulder-level and curls under at the ends. [Fr. *page*; of obscure origin.]
page[2] *pāj, n.* one side of a leaf of a book, etc. — 4 pages in a folio sheet, 8 in a quarto, 16 in an octavo, 24 in a duodecimo, 36 in an octodecimo: the type, illus-trations, etc., arranged for printing one side of a leaf: a leaf of a book thought of as a single item: (in *pl.*) rhetorically, writings, literature: an incident, episode, or whatever may be imagined as matter to fill a page: one of the blocks into which a computer memory can be divided for ease of reference. — *v.t.* to number the pages of: to make up into pages (*print.*). — *adj.* **paginal** (*paj'*). — *v.t.* **paginate** (*paj'*) to mark with consecutive numbers, to page. — *ns.* **paginā'tion** the act of paging a book: the figures and marks that indicate the num-bers of pages; **pā'ging** the marking or numbering of the pages of a book. — **page'-proof** a proof of matter made up into pages. — *adj.* **page-three'** shown on, or

appropriate for, **page three**, the page on which, traditionally, certain popular newspapers print nude or semi-nude photographs of female models with well-developed figures. — **page'-turner** an exciting book, a thriller. [Fr., — L. *pāgina*, a page.]

pageant *paj'ənt*, (*arch.*) *pāj'*, *n.* a dramatic performance, scene, or part (*arch.*): a movable stage or carriage for acting on (*obs.*): a stage machine (*obs.*): a spectacle, esp. one carried around in procession: a series of tableaux or dramatic scenes connected with local history or other topical matter, performed either on a fixed spot or in procession: a piece of empty show: display. — *adj.* of the nature of a puppet: specious. — *n.* **page'antry** splendid display: pompous spectacle: a fleeting show. [Origin obscure; Anglo-L. *pāgina* may be the classical word transferred from page to scene in a MS; or *pāgina*, in the sense of slab, may have come to mean boarding, framework.]

paginal, paginate, etc. See **page²**.
pagle. See **paigle**.
pagoda *pə-gō'də*, **pagod** *pag'od*, formerly also *pə-god'*, *ns.* an Eastern temple, esp. in the form of a many-storeyed tapering tower, each storey with a projecting roof: an ornamental building in imitation of this: an idol, a demigod (*obs.*): a former Indian coin, bearing the figure of a pagoda. — **pagoda sleeve** a funnel-shaped outer sleeve turned back to show lining and inner sleeve; **pago'da-tree'** a name for various erect trees of pagoda-like form: a fabulous Indian tree that dropped pagodas (coins) when shaken. [Port. *pagode* — Pers. *but-kadah*, idol-house, or some other Eastern word.]

pagri *pug'rē*, *n.* a turban: a light scarf worn round the hat to keep off the sun. — Also **pugg'aree, pugg'ree, pugg'ery.** [Hindi *pagrī*.]

pagurian *pə-gū'ri-ən*, *n. adj.* (a crustacean) of the hermit-crab genus, *Pagurus*. — Also **pagurid** (or *pag'*). [L. *pagurus* — Gr. *pagouros*, kind of crab.]

pah¹ *pä, interj.* an exclamation of disgust.
pah². See **pa².**
Pahlavi. Same as **Pehlevi.**
pahoehoe *pə-hō'ē-hō-ē n.* a hardened lava with a smooth undulating shiny surface. [Hawaiian.]
paid *pād, pa.t.* and *pa.p.* of **pay¹.** — *adj.* satisfied (*obs.*): drunk (*Shak.*): hired. — *adj.* **paid-up'** paid in full: having fulfilled financial obligations. — **put paid to** to finish: to destroy chances of success in.
paid-. See **paed-.**
paidle. See **paddle².**
paigle, pagle *pā'gl*, (*arch.* and *dial.*) *n.* the cowslip, sometimes also the oxlip. [Origin unknown.]
paik *pāk*, (*Scot.*) *v.t.* to thump, drub. — *n.* a blow: (in *pl.*, with *his*, etc.) a drubbing. [Origin unknown.]
pail *pāl, n.* an open cylindrical or conical vessel with a hooped handle, for holding or carrying liquids (also ice, coal, etc.), a bucket: a pailful. — *n.* **pail'ful** as much as fills a pail. [O.E. *pægel*, a gill measure, apparently combined with or influenced by O.Fr. *paele*, a pan — L. *patella*, a pan, dim. of *patera* — *patēre*, to be open.]
paillasse. Same as **palliasse.**
paillette *pal-yet', pä-, n.* a spangle. — *n.* **paillon** (*pal'yən, pä-yō*) a piece of foil, to show through enamel, etc. [Fr.]

pain *pān, n.* penalty: suffering: bodily suffering: (now only in *pl.*) great care or trouble taken in doing anything: (in *pl.*) the throes of childbirth: a tiresome or annoying person (*coll.*). — *v.t.* to cause suffering to: to put to trouble (*arch.*; esp. *refl.*). — *adjs.* **pained** showing or expressing pain: suffering pain: distressed; **pain'ful** full of pain: causing pain: requiring labour, pain, or care: laborious, painstaking (*arch.*): distressing, irksome. — *adv.* **pain'fully.** — *n.* **pain'fulness.** — *adj.* **pain'less** without pain. — *adv.* **pain'lessly.** — *n.* **pain'lessness.** — **pain'-killer** anything that does away with pain: a nostrum claiming to end pain; **pains'taker** one who takes pains or care: a careful worker. — *adj.* **pains'taking** taking pains or care. — *n.* careful diligence. — **be at pains, take pains (to)** to put oneself to

trouble, be assiduously careful (to); **for one's pains** as reward or result of trouble taken (usu. ironical); **pain in the neck** (*fig.*) a feeling of acute discomfort: an exasperating circumstance: a thoroughly tiresome person; **under** or **on pain of** under liability to the penalty of. [Fr. *peine* — L. *poena*, satisfaction — Gr. *poinē*, penalty.]

painim *pā'nim.* See **paynim.**
paint *pānt, v.t.* to cover over with colouring matter: to represent in a coloured picture: to produce as a coloured picture: to apply with a brush: to apply anything to, with a brush: to describe or present as if in paint (*fig.*): to colour: to apply coloured cosmetics to: to adorn, diversify: to represent speciously or deceptively. — *v.i.* to practise painting: to use coloured cosmetics on the face: to tipple (*slang*). — *n.* a colouring substance spread or for spreading on the surface: a cake of such matter: coloured cosmetics. — *adjs.* **paint'able** suitable for painting; **painted** covered with paint: ornamented with coloured figures: marked with bright colours: feigned. — *n.* **paint'er** one who paints: an artist in painting: one whose occupation is painting: a house-decorator: a vivid describer. — *adj.* **paint'erly** with the qualities of painting, as opposed to drawing, etc. — i.e. with areas of colour, rather than line or drawn detail: as if painted. — *ns.* **paint'iness; paint'ing** the act or employment of laying on colours: the act of representing objects by colours: a painted picture: vivid description in words; **paint'ress** formerly, a woman artist who paints: a woman employed to paint pottery; **paint'ure** (*Dryden*) the art of painting: a picture. — *adj.* **paint'y** overloaded with paint, with the colours too glaringly used: smeared with paint: like paint, in smell, etc. — **paint'-box** a box in which different paints are kept in compartments; **paint'-bridge** a platform used by theatrical scene-painters; **paint'-brush** a brush for putting on paint: the painted cup (see below); **painted cloth** a hanging of cloth painted with figures, a substitute for tapestry, formerly common in taverns; **painted cup** a scrophulariaceous plant (*Castilleja*) with brightly coloured upper leaves; **painted grass** striped canary-grass, gardener's garters; **painted lady** the thistle-butterfly, orange-red spotted with white and black: the painted cup: a parti-coloured pink, sweetpea, gladiolus, etc.; **painted snipe** a genus (*Rhynchaea*) of birds akin to the snipes, the hen brightly coloured; **painter's colic** lead colic; **paint'er-stain'er** a member of the London livery company of painters; **paint roller** roller used in house-painting instead of a brush. — *n.sing.* **paint'works** a paint-making factory. — **fresh as paint** very fresh and bright; **paint the lily** to attempt to beautify that which is already beautiful; **paint the town red** to break out in a boisterous spree. [O.Fr. *peint*, pa.p. of *peindre*, to paint — L. *pingěre*, to paint.]

painter¹ *pānt'ər, n.* a rope for fastening a boat. — **cut the painter** to sever ties; **lazy painter** a small painter for use in fine weather only. [Origin obscure.]
painter² *pānt'ər*, (*U.S.*) *n.* the cougar. [**panther.**]
paiock(e), pajock(e) *pā'ok* ? *pā'jok* ?, *ns.* an obscure word in Shakespeare (*Hamlet* III, ii. 295) conjectured to mean peacock (possibly a misprint for *pacock*; possibly = *pea-jock*).

pair¹ *pār, n.* two things equal, or suited to each other, or growing, grouped or used together: a set of two equal or like things forming one instrument, garment, etc., as a pair of scissors, tongs, trousers: the other of two matching things: a set of like things generally: a pack (of cards; *obs.*): a flight of stairs: a couple: husband and wife: two persons betrothed to or in love with each other: a male and a female animal mated together: two persons or things associated together: a partner: two horses harnessed together: two cards of like designation: (in *pl.* with *sing.vb.*) another name for **Pelmanism:** two voters on opposite sides who have an agreement to abstain from voting: either of such a pair: a duck in both innings (*cricket*): a pair-oar: (in *pl.*) a contest, etc. in which competitors take part in partnerships of two: — *pl.* **pairs, pair** (*coll.*). — *v.t.* to couple: to sort out in pairs. — *v.i.* to be joined in couples: to be a counterpart or counterparts: to mate: of two opposing voters, to arrange to abstain, on a motion or for a period (also *v.t.*, usu. *pass.*). — *adj.* **paired** arranged in pairs: set by twos of a like kind: mated. — *n.* **pair'ing.** — *adv.* **pair'wise** in pairs. — **pair'-bond** a continuing and exclusive relationship between a male and female; **pair'-bonding; pair case** a double casing for a (pocket) watch, usu. consisting of an inner plain casing for the movement and an outer decorative one. — *adj.* **pair'-horse** of a carriage, drawn by a pair of horses. — **pair'ing-time** the time when birds go together in pairs; **pair'-oar** a boat rowed by two. — Also *adj.* — **pair production** (*electronics*) the production of a positron and an electron when a gamma-ray photon passes into the electrical field of an atom; **pair'-roy'al** three cards of the same denomination, esp. in cribbage and in the obs. post and pair: a throw of three dice all falling alike: a set of three (also **pairī'al, prī'al**). — **pair of colours** two flags carried by a regiment, one the national ensign, the other the flag of the regiment: hence an ensigncy; **pair off** to arrange, set against each other, or set aside in pairs: to become associated in pairs. [Fr. *paire*, a couple — L. *paria*, neut. pl. of *pār*, afterwards regarded as a fem. sing., equal.]

pair², **paire** *pār*, obs. aphetic forms of **appair.**

pairial. See **pair².**

pais *pā*, (*arch.*) *n.* the people from whom a jury is drawn. [O.Fr.]

paisa *pī'sä*, *n.* in India and Pakistan, (a coin worth) one one-hundredth of a rupee (in India, for a time, described officially as **naya paisa** (*nə-yä'*) new paisa or pice: — *pl.* **naye paise** (*-yä', -sä*)): in Bangladesh, (a coin worth) one one-hundredth of a taka.

paisano *pī-zä'nō*, *n.* among people of Spanish or American descent in America, a person from the same area or town: hence, a friend: — *pl.* **paisan'os.** [Sp., — Fr. *paysan*, peasant.]

paisley *pāz'li*, *n.* a woollen or other fabric with a pattern resembling Paisley pattern: an article made of this. — **paisley pattern, design** a type of pattern whose most characteristic feature is an ornamental device known as a 'cone' (rather like a tree cone), used in the **Paisley shawl,** a shawl made in *Paisley*, Scotland in the 19th cent. in the style of Kashmir shawls.

paitrick *pā'trik*, *n.* a Scots form of **partridge.**

pajamas. See **pyjamas.**

pajock(e). See **paiock(e).**

pakapoo *pak-ə-pōō'*, (*Austr.* and *N.Z.*) *n.* a Chinese version of lotto, in which betting tickets are filled up with Chinese characters. [Chinese.]

pak-choi cabbage *päk'-choi kab'ij*, same as **Chinese cabbage.**

pakeha *pä'kə-hä, pä'kē-hä*, (*N.Z.*) *n.* a white man: a non-Polynesian citizen. [Maori.]

pakfong. See **pakfong.**

Pakhtu, Pakhto, Pakhtun, Pakhtoon. See **Pushtu.**

Pakistani *pä-kis-tän'i*, *n.* a citizen of Pakistan: an immigrant from, or a person whose parents, etc. are immigrants from, Pakistan. — Also *adj.* — *n.* **Paki** (*pak'i*; *derog. British slang*) a Pakistani. — Also *adj.*

pakka *puk'ə*. Same as **pucka.**

pakora *pə-kō'rə*, *n.* an Indian dish consisting of chopped vegetables, etc. formed into balls, coated with batter and deep-fried. [Hindi.]

paktong *pak'tong*, *n.* nickel-silver. — Also (*erron.*) **pack'-fong, pak'fong.** [Chin. *pak*, white, *t'ung*, copper.]

pal *pal*, (*coll.*) *n.* a partner, mate: chum. — *v.i.* to associate as a pal: — *pr.p.* **pall'ing;** *pa.t.* and *pa.p.* **palled** (*pald*). — *adj.* **pally** (*pal'i*). — *adj.* **pal'sy(-wal'sy)** (*coll.*) over-friendly: ingratiatingly intimate. [Gypsy.]

palabra *pa-lä'brä*, *n.* a word: talk. — **pocas** (*pō'käs*) **palabras** few words. [Sp.]

palace *pal'is*, *n.* the house of a king or a queen: a very large and splendid house: a bishop's official residence: a large public building: a large and usually showy place of entertainment or refreshment. — **pal'ace-car** a sumptuously furnished railway-car; **palace guard** (one of) those responsible for the personal protection of a monarch: the group of intimates and advisers around a head of government, etc.; **palace revolution** a revolution within the seat of authority. — **palace of culture** in the USSR, a cultural and recreational centre; **palais de danse** (*pa-le də däs*; Fr.) a dance-hall. [Fr. *palais* — L. *Palātium*, the Roman emperor's residence on the *Palatine* Hill at Rome.]

paladin *pal'ə-din*, (*hist.*) *n.* one of the twelve peers of Charlemagne's household: a knight-errant, or paragon of knighthood. [Fr., — It. *paladino* — L. *palātīnus*, belonging to the palace; cf. **palatine.**]

palae-, palaeo-, in U.S. also **pale-, paleo-,** *pal-i-, -ō-,* also *pāl-,* in composition, old: of, concerned with, the very distant past. — *adjs.* **Palaearc'tic** of the Old World part of the Holarctic region; **palae(o)anthrop'ic** (Gr. *anthrōpos,* man) of the earliest types of man; **palae(o)anthropolog'ical.** — *ns.* **palae(o)anthropolog'ist; palae(o)anthropol'ogy** the study of the earliest types of man; **Palae(o)an'thropus** (or *-thrō'*) an extinct genus of man, including the Neanderthal and Heidelberg races. — *adjs.* **palaeobiolog'ic, -al.** — *ns.* **palae(o)biol'ogist; palae(o)biol'ogy** the biological study of fossil plants and animals. — *adjs.* **palaeobotan'ic, -al.** — *ns.* **palaeobot'anist; palaeobot'any** the study of fossil plants. — *adj.* **Pal'aeocene** (*geol.*) of or from the oldest epoch of the Tertiary period (also *n.*). — *n.* **palaeoclī'mate** the climate at any stage in the geological development of the earth. — *adjs.* **palaeoclimat'ic; palaeoclimatolog'ic, -al.** — *ns.* **palaeoclimatol'ogist; palaeoclimatol'ogy.** — *adj.* **palaeocrys'tic** (Gr. *krystallos,* ice) consisting of ancient ice. — *adjs.* **palaeoecolog'ic, -al.** — *ns.* **palaeoecol'ogist; palaeoecol'ogy** the ecology of fossil animals and plants; **palaeoenvi'ronment** the environment in earlier ages. — *adjs.* **palaeoenvironment'al; palaeoethnolog'ic, -al.** — *ns.* **palaeoethnol'ogist; palaeoethnol'ogy** the science of early man; **palaeogaea** (*-jē'ə;* Gr. *gaia,* earth) the Old World as a biological region. — *n.* and *adj.* **Palaeogene** (*-jēn;* Gr. *palai(o) genēs,* born long ago) early Tertiary — Eocene and Oligocene. — *n.* **palaeogeog'rapher.** — *adjs.* **palaeogeograph'ic, -al.** — *ns.* **palaeogeog'raphy** the study of the geography of geological periods; **palaeog'rapher** (Gr. *graphein,* to write) one skilled in palaeography. — *adjs.* **palaeograph'ic, -al.** — *ns.* **palaeog'raphist; palaeog'raphy** ancient modes of writing: the study of ancient modes of handwriting. — *adjs.* **palae(o)ichthyolog'ic, -al.** — *ns.* **palae(o)ichthyol'ogist; palae(o)ichthyol'ogy.** — *adj.* **palaeolimnolog'ical.** — *ns.* **palaeolimnol'ogist; palaeolimnol'ogy** the scientific study of lakes of past ages; **pal'aeolith** (Gr. *lithos,* stone) a Palaeolithic artefact. — *adj.* **Palaeolith'ic** of the earlier Stone Age. — *n.* **palaeomag'netism** a study of the magnetism of ancient rocks and fossils, and of bricks, pottery, etc., made in past ages. — *adj.* **palaeontograph'ical.** — *n.* **palaeontog'raphy** the description of fossil remains — descriptive palaeontology. — *adj.* **palaeontolog'ical.** — *ns.* **palaeontol'ogist; palaeontol'ogy** (Gr. *onta,* neut. pl. of pr.p. of *einai,* to be, *logos,* discourse) the study of fossils. — *adjs.* **palaeopatholog'ic, -al.** — *ns.* **palaeopathol'ogist; palaeopathol'ogy** the pathological study of the ancient remains of animals and humans. — *adj.* **palaeopedolog'ical.** — *ns.* **palaeopedol'ogist; palaeopedol'ogy** the study of the soils of past geological ages; **palaeophytol'ogy** palaeobotany; **Palaeothē'rium** (Gr. *thērion,* a wild beast — *thēr,* animal, beast of prey) an odd-toed Eocene fossil ungulate with tapir-like snout; **pal'aeotype** A. J. Ellis's phonetic adaptation of ordinary alphabetical type. — *adjs.* **palaeotypic** (*-tip'ik*); **Palaeozo'ic** (Gr. *zōē,* life) of the division of the fossiliferous rocks, from Cambrian to Permian; **palaeozoolog'ical.** — *ns.* **palaeozool'ogist; palaeozool'ogy** the study of fossil animals. [Gr. *palaios,* old.]

palaestra *pal-ēs'trə, -es', (ant.) n.* a wrestling school: a gymnasium: wrestling: a training-ground. — *adjs.* **palaes'tral, palaes'tric, -al.** [L. *palaestra* — Gr. *palaistrā* — *palaiein*, to wrestle.]
palafitte *pal'ə-fit, n.* a prehistoric lake dwelling. [It. *palafitta* — *palo* (— L. *pālus*), a stake, *fitto*, pa.p. of *figgere* (— L. *figĕre*), to fix.]
palagonite *pal-ag'ə-nīt, n.* an altered basic vitreous lava. — **palag'onite-tuff** a tuff composed of fragments of palagonite. [*Palagonia*, in Sicily.]
palais de danse. See **palace.**
palama *pal'ə-mə, n.* the webbing of a water-bird's foot: — *pl.* **pal'amae** (*-mē*). — *adj.* **pal'amate.** [Latinised from Gr. *palumē*, palm.]
palamino. Same as **palomino.**
palampore, palempore *pal'əm-pōr, -pör, n.* a flowered chintz bedcover common in the East. [From *Palampur*, N. India, place of manufacture.]
palanquin, palankeen *pal-ən-kēn', n.* a light litter for one, a box borne on poles on men's shoulders. [Port. *palanquim*; cf. Hind. *palang*, a bed — Sans. *palyaṅka*, a bed.]
palas *pal-äs', -äsh', n.* the dhak tree. [Hind. *palāś*.]
palate *pal'it, -ət, n.* the roof of the mouth, consisting of the *hard palate* in front and the *soft palate* behind: the prominent part of the lower lip that closes the tube of a personate corolla (*bot.*): sense of taste: relish: mental liking: ability to appreciate the finer qualities of wine, etc. (also *fig.*). — *v.t.* to taste, to relish (*Shak.*). — *adj.* **pal'atable** pleasant to the taste: acceptable to mind or feelings. — *ns.* **palatabil'ity, pal'atableness.** — *adv.* **pal'atably.** — *adj.* **pal'atal** pertaining to the palate: uttered by bringing the tongue to or near the hard palate. — *n.* a sound so produced. — *n.* **palatalisa'tion, -z-.** — *v.t.* **pal'atalise, -ize** to make palatal. — *adj.* **pal'atine** pertaining to the palate. — *n.* a paired bone forming part of the roof of the mouth. — *adj.* **pal'ato= alve'olar** (*phon.*) produced by bringing the tongue to a position at or close to the hard palate and the roots of the upper teeth. — **cleft palate** a congenital defect of the palate, leaving a longitudinal fissure in the roof of the mouth. [L. *palātum*.]
palatial *pə-lā'shl, adj.* of or like a palace. [See **palace.**]
palatine¹ *pal'ə-tīn, adj.* of the Palatine Hill or the palace of emperors there: of a palace: having royal privileges or jurisdiction: of a count or earl palatine (see below). — *n.* an officer of the palace: a noble invested with royal privileges and jurisdiction: a subject of a palatinate: a fur tippet (from the Princess Palatine of 1676): (with *cap.*) one of the seven hills of Rome. — *n.* **palat'inate** (or *pa'lət-*) the office or rank of a palatine: the province of a palatine, esp. an electorate of the ancient German Empire: at Durham University, a light purple blazer. — *adj.* at Durham, light purple or lilac. — **count, earl,** etc., **palatine** a feudal lord with supreme judicial authority over a province; **county palatine** the province of such a lord. [L. *palātīnus*; cf. **palace.**]
palatine². See **palate.**
palaver *pə-lä'vər, n.* a conference, esp. orig. with African or other native tribespeople: a talk or discussion: idle copious talk: talk intended to deceive: a long, boring, complicated and seemingly pointless exercise: a fuss. — *v.i.* to hold a palaver: to prate. — *v.t.* to flatter. — *n.* **palav'erer.** [Port. *palavra*, word — L. *parabola*, a parable, later a word, speech — Gr. *parabolē*; cf. **parable, parabola.**]
palay *pa-lā', pä-lī', -lā', n.* the ivory-tree, a small S. Indian tree (*Wrightia*) of the dogbane family, with hard white wood. [Tamil.]
palazzo *pə-lat'sō, n.* an Italian palace, often one converted into a museum: a house built in this style: — *pl.* **palazz'i** (*-at'sē*). [It., — L. *palātium.*]
pale¹ *pāl, n.* a stake of wood driven into the ground for fencing: any thing that encloses or fences in: a limit: the limit of what can be accepted as decent or tolerable (*fig.*): an enclosure: a marked-off district: a broad

stripe from top to bottom of a shield (*her.*). — *v.t.* to enclose with stakes: to fence: to encircle, crown (*Shak.*). — *adv.* **pale'wise** (*her.*) vertically, like a pale. — *n.* **palifica'tion** (*pal-, pāl-*) the act of strengthening by stakes. — *adj.* **pāl'iform.** — *n.* **pāl'ing** the act of fencing: wood or stakes for fencing: a fence of stakes connected by horizontal pieces: an upright stake or board in a fence. — *adj.* **pāl'y** (*her.*) divided by vertical lines. — **beyond the pale** intolerable: unacceptable; **English Pale** the district in Ireland within which alone the English had power for centuries after the invasion in 1172; **Jewish Pale** that of S.W. Russia in which alone Jews were formerly allowed to live. [Fr. *pal* — L. *pālus*, a stake.]
pale² *pāl, adj.* whitish: not ruddy or fresh: wan: of a faint lustre, dim: wanting in colour. — *v.t.* to make pale. — *v.i.* to turn pale. — *n.* paleness. — *adv.* **pale'ly.** — *n.* **pale'ness.** — *adjs.* **pāl'ish** somewhat pale; **pāl'y** (*arch.*) pale: palish. — **pale ale** a light-coloured pleasant bitter ale; **pale'buck** an antelope, the oribi. — *adjs.* **pale'-dead** (*Shak.*) lustreless; **pale'-eyed** (*Milt.*) dim-eyed. — **pale'-face** (attributed to American Indians) a white person. — *adj.* **pale'-heart'ed** (*Shak.*) dispirited. — *adj.* **pale'=vis'aged** (*Shak.*). [O.Fr. *palle*, pale (Fr. *pâle*) — L. *pallidus*, pale.]
pale³ *pāl, (dial.) n.* a baker's peel: a cheese-scoop. — *v.t.* to test by inserting a cheese-pale. [L. *pāla*, spade.]
pale⁴. See **palea.**
pale-. See **palae-.**
palea *pā'li-ə, n.* the membranous inner bract (*inferior palea*) or bracteole (*superior palea*) of an individual grass-flower, above the glumes: a scale on a fern-leaf or stem: a scale on the receptacle of some composite plants: — *pl.* **pā'leae** (*-ē*). — *n.* **pale** (*pāl*) a grass palea. — *adj.* **paleā'ceous** (*bot.*) chaffy. — *n.* **palet** (*pāl'it*) a palea. [L. *pālea*, chaff.]
palempore. See **palampore.**
paleo-, etc. See **palae-, palaeo-.**
Palestinian *pal-is-tin'i-ən, adj.* pertaining to *Palestine* (Gr. *Palaistīnē*). — *n.* a native or inhabitant of Palestine: a member of a guerrilla movement or political body one of whose aims is to reclaim former Arab lands from Israelis. — **Palestine soup** artichoke soup, by a quibble on *Jerusalem* (see **artichoke**). [Cf. **Philistine.**]
palestra. Same as **palaestra.**
palet. See **palea.**
paletot *pal'tō, n.* a loose overcoat. [Fr.]
palette *pal'it, n.* a little board, usu. with a thumb-hole, on which a painter mixes his colours: the assortment or range of colours used by a particular artist or for any particular picture: a range or selection (*fig.*): a plate against which one leans in working a drill: a small plate covering a joint in armour, esp. at the armpit (*hist.*). — **pal'ette-knife** a thin round-ended knife for mixing colours, cooking ingredients, etc. [Fr., — It. *paletta* — *pala*, spade — L. *pāla*, a spade.]
palfrey *pöl'fri, (arch.* or *poet.) n.* a saddle-horse, esp. for a lady (in *Faerie Queene* applied to Una's ass). — *n.* **palfrenier** (*pal-frə-nēr'*) a groom. — *adj.* **palfreyed** (*pöl'*) riding on, or supplied with, a palfrey. [O.Fr. *palefrei* — L.L. *paraverēdus*, prob. from Gr. *para*, beside, L.L. *verēdus*, a post-horse, app. a Celtic word; confused with L. *frēnum*, a bridle.]
Pali *pä'lē, n.* the sacred language of the Buddhists of India, etc., close akin to Sanskrit. [Sans. *pāli*, canon.]
palification, paliform. See **pale¹.**
palilalia *pal-i-lā'li-ə, n.* a speech abnormality characterised by the increasingly rapid repetition of words or phrases. [Modern L., — Gr. *palin*, again, *lalia*, speech.]
Palilia *pə-lil'i-ə, n.pl.* (or *sing.*) the festival of Pales (L. *Palēs*), Roman goddess of flocks, held on 21st April, traditional date of the founding of Rome.
palillogy *pal-il'ə-ji, n.* a repetition of a word or phrase. [Gr. *palillogiā* — *palin*, again, *logos*, word, speech.]
palimony *pal'i-mən-i, (coll.) n.* alimony or its equivalent demanded by one partner when the couple have been

cohabiting without being married.   [pal, alimony.]

palimpsest *pal'imp-sest, n.* a manuscript in which old writing has been rubbed out to make room for new: a monumental brass turned over for a new inscription. [Gr. *palimpsēston* — *palin*, again, *psāein* (contracted *psēn*), to rub.]

palindrome *pal'in-drōm, n.* a word, verse, or sentence that reads alike backward and forward. — *adjs.* **palindromic** (-*drom'*, -*drōm'*), -**al.** — *n.* **pal'indromist** (or *pə-lin'*) an inventor of palindromes.   [Gr. *palindromos*, running back — *palin*, back, *dromos*, a running.]

paling. See under **pale**[1].

palingenesis *pal-in-jen'i-sis, n.* a new birth: reincarnation: a second creation: regeneration: unmodified inheritance of ancestral characters: the new-formation of a rock by refusion: — *pl.* **palingen'eses** (-*sēz*). — Also **palingenē'sia, palingen'esy.** — *n.* **palingen'esist.** — *adj.* **palingenet'ical.** — *adv.* **palingenet'ically.**   [Gr. *palin*, again, *genesis*, birth.]

palinode *pal'i-nōd, n.* a poem of retraction: a recantation (*rare*). — Also (*obs.*) **pal'inōdy.**   [Gr. *palinōidiā* — *palin*, back, *ōidē*, song.]

palisade *pal-i-sād', n.* a fence of stakes: a stake so used (*mil.*). — *v.t.* to surround or defend with a palisade. — Also **palisā'do:** — *pl.* **palisā'does.** — **palisade tissue** a tissue occurring in leaves, composed of cells placed closely together with their long axes perpendicular to the surface.   [Fr. *palissade* and Sp. *palizada* — L. *pālus*, a stake.]

palisander *pal-i-san'dər, n.* jacaranda or other rosewood. [Fr. *palissandre*, from a name used in Guiana.]

palish. See **pale**[2].

palki, palkee *päl'kē, n.* a palanquin.   [Hind. *pālkī*.]

pall[1] *pöl, n.* a rich cloth (*arch.*): a covering of rich cloth: a corporal: a frontal: a chalice-cover: a cloth spread over a coffin or tomb: a cloak, mantle, outer garment: a pallium: a bearing representing a pallium (*her.*): a curtain, covering, or cloak, as of smoke, darkness (*fig.*). — *v.t.* to cover with, or as with, a pall. — **pall'-bearer** one of the mourners at a funeral who used to hold up the corners of the pall: one of those carrying, or walking beside, a coffin at a funeral.   [O.E. *pæll*, a rich robe — L. *pallium*; see **pallium**.]

pall[2] *pöl, v.i.* to lose strength (*obs.*): to become vapid, insipid, or wearisome: to lose relish. — *v.t.* to daunt (*obs.*): to weaken (*obs.*): to pale (*obs.*): to make vapid: to cloy.   [Prob. from **appal**.]

palla *pal'ə, n.* a Roman woman's mantle: — *pl.* **pall'ae** (-*ē*).   [L. *palla*.]

Palladian[1] *pə-lā'di-ən, adj.* relating to *Pallas*, wisdom, or learning.

Palladian[2] *pə-lā'di-ən, adj.* in the style of architecture introduced by Andrea *Palladio* (1518–80), modelled on Vitruvius. — *n.* **Pallā'dianism.**

Palladium *pə-lā'di-əm, n.* a statue of *Pallas*, on whose preservation the safety of Troy depended: anything of like virtue: a safeguard.   [L., — Gr. *palladion* — *Pallas, Pallados,* Pallas.]

palladium *pə-lā'di-əm, n.* a metallic element (symbol Pd; at. numb. 46) resembling platinum, remarkable for power of occluding hydrogen. — *adjs.* **palladic** (-*lad'*), **pallā'd(i)ous** containing palladium in smaller or greater proportion respectively.   [Named by its discoverer Wollaston (in 1803 or 1804) after the newly discovered minor planet *Pallas*.]

pallah *pal'ə, n.* the impala.   [Tswana *phala*.]

Pallas *pal'as, n.* the Greek goddess Athēnē (also **Pall'as Athē'nē**): a minor planet discovered by Olbers in 1802.

pallescent *pə-les'ənt, adj.* turning pale. — *n.* **pallesc'ence.**   [L. *pallēscēns, -entis,* pr.p. of *pallēscĕre,* to turn pale.]

pallet[1] *pal'it, n.* a palette: a flat wooden tool with a handle, as that used for shaping pottery: a flat brush for spreading gold-leaf: a tool for lettering book-bindings: in a timepiece, the surface or part on which the teeth of the escape wheel act to give impulse to the pendulum or balance: a disc of a chain-pump: a valve of an organ wind-chest, regulated from the keyboard: a board for carrying newly moulded bricks: a piece of wood built into a wall for the nailing on of joiner-work: a platform or tray for lifting and stacking goods, used with the fork-lift truck, and having a double base into which the fork can be thrust. — *adj.* **pall'eted** carried on pallet(s). — *n.* **palletisa'tion, -z-** the adoption of pallets for moving goods: the packing of goods on pallets. — *v.i.* and *v.t.* **pall'etise, -ize.** — *n.* **pall'etiser, -z-.**   [palette.]

pallet[2] *pal'it, n.* a mattress, or couch, properly a mattress of straw: a small or mean bed.   [Dial. Fr. *paillet,* dim. of Fr. *paille,* straw — L. *palea,* chaff.]

pallial, palliament. See **pallium.**

palliard *pal'yärd, (obs.) n.* a professional beggar, a vagabond: a rogue, libertine.   [Fr. *paillard — paille,* straw, from the vagabond's habit of sleeping on straw in barns, etc.]

palliasse *pal-i-as', pal-yas', pal', n.* a straw mattress: an under-mattress. — Also **paillasse.**   [Fr. *paillasse — paille,* straw — L. *palea.*]

palliate *pal'i-āt, v.t.* to cloak (*obs.*): to disguise (*obs.*): to excuse, extenuate: to soften by pleading something in favour: to mitigate: to alleviate. — *adj.* see **pallium.** — *n.* **palliā'tion** the act of palliating. — *adj.* **pall'iative** (-*ə-tiv*) serving to extenuate: mitigating: alleviating. — *n.* that which lessens pain, etc., or gives temporary relief. — *adj.* **pall'iatory.**   [L. *palliāre, -ātum,* to cloak — *pallium,* a cloak.]

pallid *pal'id, adj.* pale, wan. — *ns.* **pallid'ity, pall'idness.** — *adv.* **pall'idly.**   [L. *pallidus,* pale.]

pallium *pal'i-əm, n.* a large, square mantle, worn by learned Romans in imitation of the Greeks — the himation (*hist.*): a white woollen vestment like a double Y, embroidered with crosses, worn by the Pope, and conferred by him upon archbishops: the mantle in molluscs, brachiopods, and birds (*zool.*): — *pl.* **pall'ia.** — *adj.* (*zool.*) **pall'ial.** — *n.* **pall'iament** (*Shak.*) a Roman consular candidate's robe. — *adj.* **pall'iate** having a pallium.   [L. *pallium.*]

pall-mall *pel'-mel', pal'-mal', n.* an old game, in which a ball was driven through an iron ring with a mallet: an alley for the game (hence the street in London (*pal'-mal'*).   [Obs. Fr. *pale-maille — palmaille —* It. *pallamaglio — palla,* ball (cf. O.H.G. *pallâ*), and *maglio* — L. *malleus,* a hammer; cf. **ball**[1]; **pallone.**]

pallone *päl-lō'nā, n.* an Italian game in which a ball is struck with a gauntlet or armguard.   [It., augmentative of *palla,* ball.]

pallor *pal'ər, n.* paleness.   [L. *pallēre,* to be pale.]

pally. See **pal.**

palm[1] *päm, n.* the inner surface of the hand between wrist and fingers: the corresponding part of a forefoot, or of a glove: the sole of the foot (*rare*): a handsbreadth (3 inches, or 4 inches): the length of the hand from wrist to fingertip: a sailmaker's instrument used instead of a thimble: a flat expansion, as of an antler, or the inner surface of an anchor fluke: an act of palming: an old game (also **palm'-play**) in which a ball was struck with the palm. — *v.t.* to touch, or stroke with the palm: to hold or conceal in the palm: to impose, pass off (esp. with *off,* and *on* or *upon*): to bribe. — *adjs.* **palmar** (*pal'mər*) relating to the palm; **palmate** (*pal'*), -**d** hand-shaped: having lobes radiating from one centre (*bot.*): web-footed (*zool.*). — *adv.* **pal'mately.** — *adj.* **palmatifid** (*pal-mat'i-fid; bot.*) shaped like the hand, with the divisions extending about half-way down. — *n.* **palmā'tion** palmate formation: a palmate structure or one of its parts or divisions. — *adjs.* **palmatipart'ite** palmately divided rather more than half-way; **palmatisect** (*pal-mat'i-sekt*) deeply cut in a palmate manner; **palmed** (*pämd*) having a palm: held or concealed in the palm. — *ns.* **palm'ful** as much as the palm will hold; **palmiped** (*pal'mi-ped*), **palmipede** (-*pēd*) a web-footed bird. — *adj.* web-footed. — *ns.* **palmist** (*päm'ist*) one who tells fortune from the lines on the palm; **palm'istry; palmy, -ie** (*päm'i; Scot.*) a stroke of the tawse on the palm.

— **palm'-grease'**, **-oil'** a bribe. — **grease someone's palm** to bribe someone; **in the palm of one's hand** in one's power: at one's command. [L. *palma*; cf. Gr. *palamē*; O.E. *folm*.]

palm² *päm*, *n.* any tree or shrub of the **Palmae** (*pal'mē*), a large tropical and sub-tropical family of monocotyledons, sometimes climbers but usually branchless trees with a crown of pinnate or fan-shaped leaves: a leaf of this tree borne in token of rejoicing or of victory: emblematically, pre-eminence, the prize: a branch of willow or other substitute in symbolic or ceremonial use. — *adjs.* **palmaceous** (*pal-mā'shəs*) of the palm family; **palmarian** (*pal-mā'ri-ən*), **palmary** (*pal'mər-i*) worthy of the ceremonial palm: pre-eminent. — *ns.* **palmette** (*pal-met'*; Fr.) an ancient architectural ornament like a palm-leaf; **palmett'o** (*pal-*) a name for several kinds of palm, notably Sabal and the only European palm Chamaerops: — *pl.* **palmettos, -toes; palmiet** (*pal-mēt'*) a South African aloe-like riverside plant of the rush family (*Prionum palmita*); **palmificā'tion** (*pal-*) artificial fertilisation of dates by hanging a wild male flower-cluster on a cultivated female tree; **palmitate** (*pal'*) a salt of **palmit'ic acid**, a fatty acid ($C_{15}H_{31}$·COOH) got from palm-oil, etc.; **palmitin** (*pal'*) a white fat abundant in palm-oil: a glycerine ester of palmitic acid. — *adj.* **palm'y** bearing palms: flourishing: palmlike. — **pal'ma Christi** castor-oil plant; **palm'= branch'** a palm-leaf; **palm'-butt'er** palm-oil in a solid state; **palm'-cabb'age** the bud of the cabbage-palm; **palm'-cat', palm'-civ'et** the paradoxure. — *adj.* **palm'= court'** suitable to a **palm court**, a large, palm-tree-decorated room or conservatory in a hotel, etc., in which, traditionally, light music is played by a small orchestra, a **palm-court orchestra**. — **palm'-hon'ey** evaporated coquito-palm sap; **palm'house** a glass house for palms and other tropical plants; **palmitic acid** see **palmitate** above; **palm'-ker'nel** the kernel of the oil-palm, yielding **palm-kernel oil**; **palm'-oil** an oil or fat obtained from the pulp of the fruit of palms, esp. of the oil-palm; **palm'-su'gar** jaggery; **Palm Sunday** the Sunday before Easter, in commemoration of the strewing of palm-branches when Christ entered Jerusalem; **palm'-tree; palm'-wine'** fermented palm sap. — **palm= tree justice** justice without litigation and legal processes, from the old Arabic, Jewish, etc. idea of a wise man dispensing justice under a palm tree. [O.E. *palm, pulma, palme*, also directly — L. *palma*, palm-tree, from the shape of its leaves; see preceding.]

palmar, palmate, etc. See **palm¹**.
palmer *pal'mər*, *n.* a pilgrim carrying a palm-leaf in token of having been in the Holy Land: a palmer-worm: a bristly artificial fly. — **palm'er-worm'** a hairy caterpillar of various kinds, originally one of wandering habits. [**palm²**.]
Palmerin *pal'mər-in*, *n.* a knightly champion. [From *Palmerín*, a Spanish (or Portuguese) romance hero found as a child among *palm*-trees.]
palmette, palmiet, palmitin, etc. See **palm²**.
palmipede, palmist, etc. See **palm¹**.
palmy. See **palm¹,²**.
palmyra *pal-mī'rə*, *n.* an African and Asiatic palm (*Borassus flabellifer*) yielding toddy, jaggery, and **palmy'ra= nuts**. — **palmy'ra-wood** properly the wood of the palmyra palm: any palm timber. [Port. *palmeira*, palm-tree, confused with *Palmyra* in Syria.]
palolo *pa-lō'lō*, *n.* an edible sea-worm that burrows in coral-reefs, remarkable for its breeding swarms at a certain phase of the moon, the head remaining behind to regenerate: — *pl.* **palo'los**. — Also **palolo worm**. [Samoan.]
palomino *pal-ə-mē'nō*, *n.* a horse of largely Arab blood, pale tan, yellow, or gold, with white or silver mane and tail: — *pl.* **palomin'os**. [Amer. Sp., — Sp., of a dove.]
palooka *pə-lōō'kə*, (*U.S. slang*) *n.* a stupid or clumsy person, esp. in sports. [Origin unknown.]
palp¹ *palp*, *n.* a jointed sense-organ attached in pairs to

the mouth-parts of insects and crustaceans (also **pal'-pus**: — *pl.* **pal'pī**). — *adj.* **pal'pal**. [L.L. *palpus*, a feeler (L. a stroking) — L. *palpāre*, to stroke.]
palp² *palp*, *v.t.* to feel, examine, or explore by touch: to speak fair (*obs.*). — *n.* **palpabil'ity**. — *adj.* **palp'able** that can be touched or felt: perceptible: easily found out, as lies, etc.: obvious, gross. — *n.* **palp'ableness**. — *adv.* **palp'ably**. — *v.t.* **palp'āte** to examine by touch. — *n.* **palpā'tion** the act of examining by means of touch. — *adj.* **palp'able-gross'** (Shak.). [L. *palpāre, -ātum*, to touch softly, stroke, caress, flatter.]
palpebral *palp'i-brəl*, *adj.* of or pertaining to the eyelid. [L. *palpebra*, the eyelid.]
palpi. See **palp¹**.
palpitate *pal'pi-tāt*, *v.i.* to throb: to beat rapidly: to pulsate: to quiver. — *v.t.* to cause to throb. — *adj.* **pal'pitant** palpitating. — *n.* **palpitā'tion** the act of palpitating: abnormal awareness of heart-beat. [L. *palpitāre, -ātum*, freq. of *palpāre*; cf. **palp¹,²**.]
palpus. See **palp¹**.
palsgrave *pölz'grāv*, *n.* a count palatine: — *fem.* **palsgravine** (*pölz'grə-vēn*). [Du. *paltsgrave* (now *paltsgraaf*); cf. Ger. *Pfalzgraf*; see **palace, Graf**.]
palstave *pöl'stāv*, **palstaff** *-stäf*, *n.* a Bronze Age axe, the flanges of the head joined by a cross ridge to engage the ends of the prongs of the kneed shaft. [Du. *paalstav* — O.N. *pālstafr*.]
palsy *pöl'zi*, *n.* loss of control or of feeling, more or less complete, in the muscles of the body: paralysis. — *v.t.* to affect with palsy: to deprive of action or energy: to paralyse. — *adj.* **pal'sied**. [From **paralysis**.]
palsy(-walsy). See **pal**.
palter *pöl'tər*, *v.i.* to trifle in talk: to use trickery: to haggle: to equivocate. — *n.* **pal'terer**. [Poss. conn. with **paltry**.]
paltry *pöl'tri*, *adj.* mean: trashy: trumpery: not worth considering. — *adv.* **pal'trily**. — *n.* **pal'triness**. [Cf. Dan. *pialter*, rags, L.G. *paltrig* ragged.]
paludal *pal-ū'dl, -ōō'*, also *pal'*, (*rare*) *adj.* pertaining to marshes: marshy: malarial. — *adjs.* **palu'dic** of marshes; **paludic'olous** (L. *colĕre*, to inhabit) marsh-dwelling: growing in marshes; **palu'dinal, pal'udine, palu'dinous** of marshes: marshy. — *n.* **pal'udism** malaria. — *adjs.* **pal'udose, pal'udous** of marshes: marshy: inhabiting marshes: malarial. — *n.* **Pal'-udrine®** proprietary name for *proguanil hydrochloride*, a synthetic anti-malarial drug. — *adjs.* **palustral** (*-us'trəl*), **palus'trian, palus'trine** (*-trīn*) of marshes: inhabiting marshes. [L. *palus, palūdis*, a marsh; *palūster, -tris*, marshy.]
paludament *pə-lū', -lōō', -də-mənt*, *n.* a Roman general's or high military officer's cloak. — Also **paludamen'um**. [L. *palūdāmentum*.]
palustral, etc. See **paludal**.
paly. See under **pale¹,²**.
palynology *pal-i-nol'ə-ji*, *n.* the study of spores and pollen-grains. — *adj.* **palynolog'ical**. — *n.* **palynol'ogist**. [Gr. *palȳnein*, to sprinkle.]
pam *pam*, *n.* the knave of clubs, highest card in loo: a game like nap, in which it is highest card. [Said to be from Fr. *Pamphile* — Gr. *Pamphilos*, lit. beloved of all.]
pampa *pam'pə* (usu. in *pl.* **pampas**, also (*pam'pəs*) used as *sing.*) *n.* a vast treeless plain in southern S. America. — *adj.* **pam'pēan**. — *n.* **pampero** (*pam-pā'rō*) a violent S.W. wind on and from the pampas: — *pl.* **pampe'ros**. — **pampas grass** a tall, ornamental, reed-like grass (*Gynerium*, or *Cortaderia*) with large thick silvery panicles. [Sp., — Quechua *pampa, bamba*, plain.]
pampelmoose, -mouse *pam'pl-mōōs*, *n.* See **pompelmoose**.
pamper *pam'pər*, *v.t.* to feed with fine food (*arch.*): to gratify to the full: to over-indulge. — *ns.* **pam'pered-ness; pam'perer**. [A freq. from (*obs.*) *pamp, pomp*; cf. Ger. dial. *pampen*, to cram.]
pampero. See **pampa**.
pamphlet *pam'flit*, *n.* a small book stitched but not bound: a separately published tractate, usu. controversial, on

some subject of the day. — *n.* **pamphleteer'** a writer of pamphlets. — *v.i.* to write pamphlets. — *n.* and *adj.* **pamphleteer'ing.** [Anglo-L. *panfletus*, possibly from a Latin erotic poem *Pamphilus* (— Gr. *Pamphilos*, beloved of all) very popular in the Middle Ages.]

pan¹ *pan, n.* a broad, shallow vessel for use in the home or in arts or manufactures: anything of like shape, as the upper part of the skull (*brain-pan*), the patella (*knee-pan*): a lavatory bowl: a hollow in the ground, a basin, in which water collects in the rainy season, leaving a salt deposit on evaporation: a salt-pan: a salt-work: the part of a firelock that holds the priming: a hard layer (*hard-pan*) in or under the soil: a small ice-floe: a hollow metal drum as played in a steel band: a panful: the face (*slang*). — *v.t.* to wash in a gold-miner's pan: to obtain by evaporating in a pan: to yield: to obtain: to cook and serve in a pan: to review, criticise, harshly. — *v.i.* to wash earth for gold: to yield gold (usu. with *out*): to result, turn out (with *out*): to come to an end, be exhausted (with *out*): to cake: to enlarge in speech: — *pr.p.* **pann'ing;** *pa.t.* and *pa.p.* **panned.** — *ns.* **pan'ful;** — *pl.* **pan'fuls; pann'ikel** (*obs.*) pannicle; **pann'ikin** a small metal cup: a little pan or saucer: enough to fill a cup; **pann'ing** washing for gold: the gold so got: harsh criticism. — **pan'cake** a thin cake of eggs, flour, sugar, and milk, fried in a pan: see **pancake (make-up)** below: an aeroplane descent or landing with wings nearly horizontal (also *adj.*). — *v.i.* to descend or alight so. — *v.t.* to cause to make a pancake (descent or landing). — **pan drop** (*Scot.*) a hard smooth peppermint sweet made in a revolving pan; **pan'handle** a strip of territory stretching out from the main body like the handle of a pan. — *v.i.* and *v.t.* (*U.S.*) to beg (from someone) esp. on the street. — **pan'handler; pan loaf** (*Scot.*) a loaf of a particular shape, made in a pan. — **flash in the pan** a mere flash in the pan of a flint-lock without discharge: a fitful show of beginning without accomplishing anything; **pancake bell** a churchbell rung on Shrove Tuesday, taken as the signal for pancake-making; **pancake ice** polar sea ice in thin flat slabs, found as winter draws near; **pancake (make-up)** cosmetic in cake form, moist, or moistened before application; **Pancake Tuesday** Shrove Tuesday. [O.E. *panne*; a word common to the West Germanic languages, possibly an early borrowing from L. *patina*.]

pan² *pän*, **pawn** *pön*, *ns.* betel leaf: betel. [Hind. *pān*.]

pan³ *pan, v.t.* to move (a cinema or television camera) about, or as if pivoting about, an axis while taking a picture so as to follow a particular object or to produce a panoramic effect: in broadcasting or recording, to cause (sound) apparently to move by electronic means. — Also *v.i.* — *pr.p.* **pann'ing;** *pa.t.* and *pa.p.* **panned.** [pan(orama).]

Pan *pan, n.* the Greek god of pastures, flocks, and woods, worshipped in Arcadia, and fond of music — with goat's legs and feet, and sometimes horns and ears: later (from association with *pān*, the whole) connected with pantheistic thought. — **Pan'-pipes, Pan's pipes** the syrinx, a musical instrument attributed to Pan, made of reeds of different lengths, fastened in a row. [Gr. *Pān*.]

pan-, pant-, panto- in composition, all. [Gr. *pās, pāsa, pān*, gen. *pantos, pāsēs, pantos*.]

panacea *pan-ə-sē'ə, n.* a universal medicine: a healing plant vaguely indicated (*Spens.* **panachaea, -kē'ə**). — *adj.* **panacē'an.** [Gr. *panakeia* — *akos*, cure.]

panache *pa-näsh', -nash', n.* a plume: knightly splendour: swagger: grand manner, theatricality, sense of style. [Fr., — It. *pennacchio* — *penna*, feather.]

panada *pə-nä'də, n.* a dish made by boiling bread to a pulp in water, and flavouring: a thick binding sauce of breadcrumbs or flour and seasoning. [Sp. *pan* (L. *pānis*), bread.]

Panadol® *pan'ə-dol, n.* a proprietary form of paracetamol.

panaesthesia, in U.S. **panesthesia,** *pan-ēs-thē'zi-ə, -zyə,* or

-es-, n. totality of perception: general awareness. — *n.* **panaesthetism** (*-ēs'* or *-es'thi-tizm*). [Gr. *aisthēsis*, perception.]

Pan-African *pan-af'ri-kən, adj.* including or relating to all Africa, esp. concerning policies of political unity among African states. — *n.* **Pan-Af'ricanism.** [pan- and **African.**]

Panagia. Same as **Panhagia.**

Panama *pan-ə-mä', n.* a republic, town, and isthmus of Central America. — Also *adj.* — *n.* and *adj.* **Panamanian** (*-mä'ni-ən*). — **panama (hat)** a hand-plaited hat made, not in Panama but in Ecuador, of plaited strips of the leaves of a South American cyclanthaceous plant (*Carludovica palmata*): an imitation thereof. [Sp. *Panamá*.]

Pan-American *pan-ə-mer'i-kən, adj.* including all America or Americans, North and South. — *n.* **Pan-Amer'icanism.** [pan- and **American.**]

Pan-Anglican *pan-ang'gli-kən, adj.* representing or including all who hold the doctrines and polity of the Anglican Church. [pan- and **Anglican** (see **Angle**).]

Pan-Arab *pan-ur'əb,* **Pan-Arabic** *-ik, adjs.* of or relating to the policy of political unity between all Arab states. — *n.* **Pan-Ar'abism.** [pan- and **Arab.**]

panaritium *pan-ə-rish'i-əm, n.* a whitlow. [L.L. *panāricium* for *parōnychium* — Gr. *parōnychiā* — *para*, beside, *onyx, -ychos*, nail.]

panarthritis *pan-är-thrī'tis, n.* inflammation involving all the structures of a joint. [pan- and **arthritis.**]

panary *pan'ə-ri, adj.* of or pertaining to bread. — *n.* a bread store. [L. *pānārius* — *pānis*, bread.]

panatella *pan-ə-tel'ə, n.* a long, thin cigar. [American Sp. *panetela*, a long, thin biscuit, — It., small loaf — L. *pānis*.]

Panathenaea *pan-ath-i-nē'ə, n.pl.* the chief national festival of ancient Athens — the lesser held annually, the greater every fourth year. — *adjs.* **Panathenae'an, Panathenā'ic.** [Gr. *Panathēnaia*.]

Panax *pan'aks,* or *pān', n.* a genus of the Aralia family: (without *cap.*) a tree or shrub of the genus *Polyscias*, related to, or included in, the genus Panax. [Gr. *panax*, a name for various healing plants; see **panacea.**]

pancake. See **pan¹.**

pance. See **pansy.**

Panchatantra *pun-chä-tunt'rə, n.* the oldest extant Sanskrit collection of beast-fables, in five books. [Sans., five books.]

panchax *pan'chaks, n.* any of several kinds of brightly coloured fish, genus *Aplocheilus*, native to Africa and S.E. Asia — often stocked in aquariums. [L., former generic name.]

panchayat *pun-chä'yət, n.* a village or town council. [Hindi *pañcāyat* — Sans. *pañca*, five.]

Panchen Lama *pän'chən lä'mə,* Tibetan religious leader second in importance to the Dalai Lama. [Chin. *pan ch'an*.]

pancheon, panchion *pan'shən, n.* a coarse earthenware pan. [App. conn. with **pan¹**; perh. influenced by **puncheon².**]

panchromatic *pan-krō-mat'ik, adj.* equally or suitably sensitive to all colours: rendering all colours in due intensity. — *n.* **panchro'matism.** [Gr. *chrōma, -atos*, colour.]

pancosmism *pan-koz'mizm,* (*philos.*) *n.* the theory that the material universe, within space and time, is all that exists. — *adj.* **pancos'mic.** [cosmism.]

pancratium *pan-krā'shi-əm, n.* a combination of boxing and wrestling. — *adj.* **pancrā'tian.** — *n.* **pancrā'tiast** (*-shi-ast*) a competitor or victor in the pancratium. — *adj.* **pancratic** (*-krat'ik*) of the pancratium: excelling all round in athletics or accomplishments: of a lens, adjustable to different degrees of magnification. — *n.* **pan'cratist.** [Gr. *pankration* — *kratos*, strength.]

pancreas *pan(g)'kri-əs, n.* the sweetbread, a large gland discharging into the duodenum and containing islands of endocrine gland tissue. — *adj.* **pancreat'ic.** — *ns.* **pan'creatin** the pancreatic juice: a medicinal substance to aid the digestion, prepared from extracts of the pancreas of certain animals; **pancreatec'tomy** surgical removal of all or part of the pancreas; **pancreatīt'is** inflammation of the pancreas. — **pancreatic juice** the alkaline secretion from the pancreas into the duodenum to aid the digestive process. [Gr. *kreas, -atos,* flesh.]

pand *pand,* (*Scot.*) *n.* the valance of a bed. [Cf. O.Fr. *pandre,* to hang.]

panda *pan'də, n.* a raccoon-like animal (*Ailurus fulgens*) of the Himalayas (also **common** or **lesser panda**): (also, more correctly, **giant panda**) a larger beast (*Ailuropoda melanoleuca*) of Tibet and China, apparently linking the lesser panda with the bears. — **panda car** a car used by policemen on the beat. [Said to be its name in Nepal.]

Pandaemonium. See **Pandemonium.**

Pandanus *pan-dā'nəs, n.* the screw-pine, the typical genus of the **Pandanā'ceae,** a family of trees and bushes akin to the bulrushes and bur-reeds. — *adj.* **pandanā'ceous.** [Malay *pandan.*]

pandar. See **pander.**

pandation *pan-dā'shən,* (*arch.*) *n.* warping. [L. *pandātiō, -ōnis* — *pandāre, -ātum,* to bend.]

Pandean *pan-dē'ən, adj.* of the god Pan: of Pan-pipes. — **Pandean pipes** Pan-pipes. [Irregularly formed from *Pān.*]

pandect *pan'dekt, n.* a treatise covering the whole of any subject: (in *pl.*; with *cap.*) the digest of Roman law made by command of the Emperor Justinian in the 6th century. — *n.* **pandect'ist.** [L. *pandecta* — Gr. *pandektēs* — *pās, pān,* all, *dechesthai,* to receive.]

pandemic *pan-dem'ik, adj.* incident to a whole people, epidemic over a wide area. — *n.* a pandemic disease. — *n.* **pandemia** (*-dē'mi-ə*) a widespread epidemic. — *adj.* **pandē'mian** vulgar: sensual. [Gr. *pandēmios — dēmos,* people.]

Pandemonium, Pandaemonium *pan-di-mō'ni-əm, n.* the capital of Hell in Milton's *Paradise Lost:* (without *cap.*) any very disorderly or noisy place or assembly: (without *cap.*) tumultuous uproar. — *adjs.* (also without *cap.*) **Pandemō'niac, Pandemonī'acal, Pandemō'-nian, Pandemonic** (*-mon'ik*). [Gr. *pās, pān,* all, *daimōn,* a spirit.]

pander *pan'dər, n.* one who procures for another the means of gratifying his base passions: a pimp. — *v.t.* to play the pander for. — *v.i.* to act as a pander: to minister to the passions: to indulge, gratify (with *to*). — *ns.* **pan'deress** a procuress; **pan'derism** the employment or practices of a pander. — *adjs.* **pan'derly** (*Shak.*) acting as a pander; **pan'derous.** — Also **pan'dar,** etc. [*Pandarus,* in the story of Troilus and Cressida as told by Boccaccio (*Filostrato*), Chaucer, and Shakespeare.]

pandermite *pan-dûr'mīt, n.* a hydrogen calcium borate found massive at *Panderma* (Bandirma) on the Sea of Marmara.

pandiculation *pan-dik-ū-lā'shən, n.* the act of stretching and yawning. [L. *pandiculārī, -ātus,* to stretch oneself.]

Pandion *pan-dī'on, n.* the osprey genus. [Gr. *Pandīōn,* father of Procne and Philomela.]

pandit. Same as **pundit.**

pandoor. See **pandour.**

Pandora *pan-dō', -dō'rə, n.* the first woman, made for Zeus so that he might through her punish man for the theft by Prometheus of heavenly fire, given a box from which escaped and spread all the ills of human life. — **Pandora's box** any source of great and unexpected troubles. [Gr. *pās, pān,* all, *dōron,* a gift.]

pandora *pan-dō', -dō'rə,* **pandore** *pan-dōr', -dōr', ns.* an ancient Eastern musical instrument like a long-necked lute with (commonly) three strings: a bandore. — *n.* **pandū'ra** a pandora: a Neapolitan instrument like a mandoline with eight metal wires, played with a quill. — *adjs.* **pan'dūrate, -d, pandū'riform** (*bot.*) fiddle-shaped. [Gr. *pandoura,* a 3-stringed instrument, fancifully connected with *Pān,* but probably an East-

ern word; cf. **bandore, banjo, mandoline.**]

pandore *pan'dōr, -dōr, n.* an esteemed variety of oysters formerly got at Prestonpans on the Firth of Forth. [Said to be from the *doors* of the salt-*pans,* where they were found.]

pandour *pan'dōōr, n.* an 18th-century Croatian foot-soldier in the Austrian service: a robber. — Also **pan'door.** [Fr., — Serbo-Croat *pàndūr* — L.L. *banderius,* follower of a banner.]

pandowdy *pan-dow'di,* (*U.S.*) *n.* a kind of apple pie or pudding. [Origin unknown.]

pandura, etc. See **pandora.**

pandy[1] *pan'di,* (*coll.*) *n.* a stroke on the palm as a school punishment. — *v.t.* to slap. [L. *pande,* hold out, imper. of *pandēre.*]

pandy[2] *pan'di,* (*coll., obs.*) *n.* an insurgent sepoy in the Indian Mutiny. [Said to be from *Pande,* a common surname.]

pane[1] *pān, n.* a piece of cloth (*obs.*): a piece of cloth pieced together with others, or separated from others by slashing (*arch.*): a rectangular compartment: a panel: a slab of window glass: a flat side or face: a length of wall: the side of a quadrangle: a rectangular piece of ground: a large sheet of stamps issued by the Post Office: half such a sheet separated from the other half by a gutter: a page of a book of stamps. — *v.t.* to insert panes or panels in. — *adj.* **paned** (*pānd*) made of panes or small squares: variegated. [Fr. *pan* — L. *pannus,* a cloth, a rag.]

pane[2]. Same as **pean**[1], **peen.**

panegoism *pan-eg'ō-izm, n.* solipsism. [Gr. *egō,* I.]

panegyric *pan-i-jir'ik* (*U.S.* sometimes *-jīr'*), *n.* a eulogy, esp. public and elaborate (on, upon): laudation. — *adjs.* **panegyr'ic, -al.** — *adv.* **panegyr'ically.** — *n.* **panegyr'icon** in the Greek Church, a collection of sermons for festivals. — *v.t.* **pan'egyrise, -ize** (or *-ej'ər-*) to write or pronounce a panegyric on: to praise highly. — *ns.* **pan'egyrist** (or *-jir',* or *-ej'ər-*); **pan'egyry** a great assembly: a religious festival. [Gr. *panēgyrikos,* fit for a national festival — *pās, pān,* all, *agyris* (*agorā*), an assembly.]

paneity *pa-nē'i-ti, n.* the state of being bread. [L. *pānis,* bread.]

panel *pan'l, n.* a cloth under a saddle (*obs.*): a crude form of saddle: a rectangular piece of any material: rectangular divisions on a page, esp. for the illustrations in children's comics: a compartment: a bordered rectangular area: a thin flat piece sunk below the general surface of a door, shutter, wainscot, or the like, often with a raised border: a board with dials, switches, etc. for monitoring or controlling the operation of an electrical or other apparatus: a compartment or hurdle of a fence: a strip of material inserted in a dress: a slip of parchment: such a slip containing a list of names, esp. of jurors: a jury: prior to the introduction of the national health service, a list of doctors available to treat those who paid into a national health insurance scheme: such a doctor's list of patients: an accused person or persons (in *sing.*; Scots *law*): a thin board on which a picture is painted: a large long photograph: a group of persons chosen for some purpose, as to judge a competition, serve on a brains trust, or be the guessers in radio and television guessing games (**panel games**). — *v.t.* to furnish with a panel or panels: to put on trial (Scots *law*): — *pr.p.* **pan'elling;** *pa.t.* and *pa.p.* **pan'elled.** — *ns.* **pan'elling** panel-work; **pan'ellist** a member of a panel, esp. in panel games. — *pan'el beating** the shaping of metal plates for vehicle body-work, etc.; **panel beater; panel doctor** a doctor who was on the panel or had a panel; **panel heating** indoor heating diffused from floors, walls, or ceilings; **panel pin** a light, narrow-headed nail of small diameter used chiefly for fixing plywood or hardboard to supports; **panel saw** a fine saw for cutting very thin wood; **panel system** a system of office, etc. design, in which partitions are used to create flexible work-areas within an open layout; **panel truck** (*U.S.*) a delivery-van; **panel**

working a method of working a coal-mine by dividing it into compartments. [O.Fr., — L.L. *pannellus* — L. *pannus*, a cloth.]

panentheism *pan-en-thē'izm, n.* the doctrine that the world is a part, though not the whole, of God's being. — *n.* **panenthē'ist.** [pan- and Gr. *en*, in, *theos*, God.]

panettone *pan-e-tōn'ā, n.* a kind of spiced cake, usu. with sultanas, traditionally eaten at Christmas in Italy: — *pl.* **panettōn'i.** [It. *panetto*, a small loaf.]

pang[1] *pang, n.* a violent but not long-continued pain: a painful emotion. — *v.t.* to inflict a pang on. — *adjs.* **pang'ing** (*Shak.*) painful; **pang'less.** [Poss. **prong**; *pronge, prange*, have been found.]

pang[2] *pang, (Scot.) v.t.* to stuff, cram. — *adj.* stuffed, crammed, crowded: tight. — *adj.* **pang'-full', -fu''** filled full. [Origin unknown.]

panga *pang'gə, n.* a broad, heavy African knife used as a tool and as a weapon.

Pangaea, Pangea *pan-jē'ə, n.* the postulated supercontinent that began to break up, forming the present continents of the earth. [**pan-** and Gr. *gē*, the earth.]

pangamy *pan(g)'gə-mi, n.* random mating. — *adj.* **pangamic** (*pan-gam'ik*). [Gr. *gamos*, marriage.]

pangenesis *pan-jen'i-sis, n.* Darwin's theory that every cell of the body contributes gemmules to the germ-cells and so shares in the transmission of inherited characters. — *n.* **pan'gen, -gene** (*-jēn*) a hypothetical unit of living matter. — *adj.* **pangenet'ic.** [Gr. *genesis*, production.]

Pan-German *pan-jûr'mən, adj.* pertaining to or including all Germans. — *n.* **Pan-Ger'manism** a movement for a Greater Germany or union of all German peoples. [**pan-** and **German**.]

Panglossian *pan-glos'i-ən,* **Panglossic** *-ik, adjs.* taking an over-cheerful and optimistic view of the world as did Dr **Pan'gloss** in Voltaire's *Candide.*

pangolin *pang-gō'lin, n.* the scaly ant-eater, an edentate mammal (Manis; order *Pholidota*) of Asia and Africa. [Malay *peng-gōling*, roller, from its habit of rolling up.]

pangrammatist *pan-gram'ə-tist, n.* one who contrives verses or sentences containing all the letters of the alphabet. — *n.* **pan'gram** a sentence containing all the letters of the alphabet, e.g. *the quick fox jumps over the lazy brown dog.* [Gr. *gramma, -atos*, letter.]

Panhagia, Panagia *pan-(h)ä'gi-ə, adj.* all-holy, an epithet of the Virgin in the Eastern Church: a cut loaf elevated in her honour: a medallion of the Virgin worn by bishops. [Gr. *hagios*, holy.]

panhandle. See **pan**[1].

panharmonicon *pan-här-mon'i-kon, n.* a mechanical musical instrument mimicking an orchestra.

panhellenic *pan-hel-ēn'ik,* or *-en', adj.* pertaining to all Greece: including all Greeks: (with *cap.*) of or relating to Panhellenism. — *ns.* **panhellē'nion** or (L.) **panhellē'-nium** a council representing all the sections of the Greeks; **Panhell'enism** (*-ən-izm*) a movement or aspiration for Greek union; **Panhell'enist.** — *adj.* **Panhellenis'tic.** [Gr. *Hellēnikos*, Greek — *Hellas*, Greece.]

panic[1] *pan'ik, n.* frantic or sudden fright: contagious fear: great terror without any visible ground or foundation: a state of terror about investments, impelling men to rush and sell what they possess. — *adj.* relating or due to the god Pan: of the nature of a panic: inspired by panic. — *v.t.* to throw into a panic. — *v.i.* to be struck by panic: — *pr.p.* **pan'icking**; *pa.t.* and *pa.p.* **pan'icked.** — *adj.* **pan'icky** inclined to, affected by, resulting from, or of the nature of, panic. — **pan'ic-bolt'** an easily moved bolt for emergency exits. — *v.i.* and *v.t.* **pan'icbuy'** to buy up stocks of a commodity which threatens to be in short supply (often precipitating a greater shortage than might otherwise have occurred). — **pan'ic-mong'er** one who creates or fosters panics. — *adjs.* **pan'ic-strick'en, -struck** struck with a panic or sudden fear. [Gr. *pānikos*, belonging to Pan; *pānikon* (*deima*), panic (fear), fear associated with the god Pan.]

panic[2] *pan'ik, n.* any grass of the genus Panicum (see below), or of various closely related genera (also **pan'ic-grass'**): the edible grain of some species. — Also **pan'ick, pann'ick.** — *n.* **pan'icle** a raceme whose branches are themselves racemes: loosely, a lax irregular inflorescence. — *adjs.* **pan'icled, panic'ūlate, -d** furnished with, arranged in, or like, panicles. — *adv.* **panic'ūlately.** — *n.* **Pan'icum** a large genus of grasses having the one- or two-flowered spikelets in spikes, racemes or panicles — including several of the millets. [L. *pānicum*, Italian millet.]

panification *pan-i-fi-kā'shən, n.* conversion into bread. [L. *pānis*, bread, *facĕre*, to make.]

panim. A Miltonic spelling of **paynim**.

Panionic *pan-ī-on'ik, adj.* of or including all Ionians. [**pan-** and **Ionic**.]

panisk, panisc *pan'isk, n.* an inferior god, attendant on Pan. [Gr. *Pāniskos*, dim. of *Pān*.]

panislam *pan-iz'läm, n.* the whole Muslim world: pan-islamism. — *adj.* **panislam'ic.** — *ns.* **panis'lamism** an aspiration or movement for the union of all Muslims; **panis'lamist.** [**pan-** and **Islam**.]

Panjabi. Same as **Punjabi**.

panjandrum *pan-jan'drəm, n.* an imaginary figure of great power and importance, a burlesque potentate, from the Grand Panjandrum in a string of nonsense made up by Samuel Foote, 18th cent. English wit, actor and dramatist. — Also **panjan'darum.**

panleucopenia *pan-lū-kō-pē'ni-ə, n.* a viral disease of cats marked by a deficiency of white blood cells and causing fever, diarrhoea, and dehydration. [**pan-** and **leucopenia**.]

panlogism *pan'lə-jizm, n.* the theory that the universe is an outward manifestation of the Logos. [**Logos**.]

panmixia *pan-mik'si-ə,* (*biol.*) *n.* cessation of the influence of natural selection. — Also **panmix'is.** — *adj.* **panmic'tic** of, connected with or exhibiting panmixia. [Gr. *mixis*, mixing.]

pannage *pan'ij,* (*arch.*) *n.* food picked up by swine in the woods, mast: the right to pasture swine in a forest. [O.Fr. *pasnage* — L.L. *pastiōnāticum* — *pascĕre, pastum*, to feed.]

panne *pan, n.* a fabric resembling velvet, with a long nap. [Fr.]

pannelled *pan'ld, v.t.* (*pa.t.*) conjectured to be a misprint for *spanielled*, i.e. followed or fawned on as by a spaniel (Shak., *Ant. and Cleo.* IV, xii. 26).

pannick. See **panic**[2].

pannicle *pan'i-kl,* **panniculus** *pə-nik'ū-ləs, ns.* a thin, sheet-like investment. [L. *panniculus*, dim. of *pannus*, a cloth.]

pannier[1] *pan'yər,* or *pan'i-ər, n.* a provision-basket: a basket carried on the back: one of a pair of baskets slung over a pack-animal's back or over the back of a motor-cycle, etc.: a sculptured basket (*archit.*): a contrivance formerly used for puffing out a woman's dress at the hips: the part so puffed out: a piece of basket-work for protecting archers, or, when filled with gravel or sand, for forming and protecting dikes, embankments, etc.: a covered basket of medicines and surgical instruments (*mil.*): hence (blunderingly) an ambulance (*mil.*). — *adj.* **pann'iered.** [Fr. *panier* — L. *pānārium*, a bread-basket — *pānis*, bread.]

pannier[2] *pan'yər, -i-ər, n.* a coll. name for a robed waiter in the Inns of Court. [Origin unknown.]

pannikel. An *obs.* form of **pannicle**.

pannikell *pan'i-kel,* (*Spens.*) *n.* the skull. [**pannicle**.]

pannikin *pan'i-kin.* See **pan**[1].

pannose *pan'ōs,* (*bot.*) *adj.* like felt. [L. *pannōsus* — *pannus*, cloth.]

pannus *pan'əs, n.* a layer of granulation tissue that forms over the synovial membrane of joints in rheumatoid arthritis, or over the cornea in trachoma. [L. *pannus*, cloth.]

panocha *pä-nō'chə, n.* a Mexican coarse sugar. [Sp.]

panoistic *pan-ō-is'tik,* (*entom.*) *adj.* of an ovary, producing ova only, not yolk-forming cells (opp. to *meroistic*). [Gr. *ōion*, an egg.]

panomphaean *pan-om-fē'ən, adj.* all-oracular, an epithet of Zeus: applied (after Rabelais) to the word 'drink' (which is celebrated by all nations). [Gr. *omphē*, a divine voice.]

panophobia *pan-ō-fō'bi-ə, n.* a form of melancholia marked by groundless fears: erroneously used for **pantophobia**. [Gr. *Pān*, the god who inspired fears, *phobos*, fear.]

panophthalmitis *pan-of-thal-mī'tis, n.* inflammation of the whole eye. — Also **panophthal'mia**. [Gr. *ophthalmos*, eye.]

panoply *pan'ə-pli, n.* complete armour: a full suit of armour: full or brilliant covering or array. — Also *fig.* — *adj.* **pan'oplied** in panoply. [Gr. *panopliā*, full armour of a hoplite — *pās, pān*, all, *hopla* (pl.), arms.]

panoptic *pan-op'tik, adj.* all-embracing: viewing all aspects. — Also **panop'tical**. [Gr. *panoptēs*, all-seeing.]

panopticon *pan-op'ti-kon, n.* a prison in which all prisoners can be watched from one point: an exhibition room. [Gr. *optikon* (neut. adj.), for seeing.]

panorama *pan-ə-rä'mə, n.* a wide or complete view: a picture disposed around the interior of a room, viewed from within in all directions: a picture unrolled and made to pass before the spectator. — *adj.* **panoramic** (-*ram'ik*). — **panorama head** a swivel device fitted to the head of a camera tripod to permit the sideways swinging motion of the camera when taking panning shots; **panoramic camera** one which takes very wide angle views, generally by rotation about an axis and by exposing a roll of film through a vertical slit; **panoramic sight** a gun sight that can be rotated, so enabling the user to fire in any direction. [Gr. *horāma*, a view, from *horaein*, to see.]

panpharmacon *pan-fär'mə-kon, n.* a universal remedy. [Gr. *pharmakon*, a drug.]

Pan-Presbyterian *pan-prez-bi-tē'ri-ən, adj.* of, including, or representing, all Presbyterians. [**pan-** and **Presbyterian** (see **presbyter**).]

panpsychism *pan-sīk'izm, n.* the theory that all nature has a psychic side. — *n.* **panpsych'ist**. — *adj.* **panpsychist'ic**. [**pan-** and **psychism** (see **psyche**).]

pansexualism *pan-seks'ū-əl-izm, n.* the view that all mental activity is derived from sexual instinct. — *adj.* **pansex'ual**. — *n.* **pansex'ualist**. [**pan-** and **sexualism** (see **sex**).]

Pan-Slav *pan-släv', adj.* of, including, or representing, all Slavs. — *adj.* **Pan-Slav'ic**. — *ns.* **Pan-Slav'ism** a movement for the union of all Slav peoples; **Pan-Slav'ist**. — *adj.* **Pan-Slavon'ic**. [**pan-** and **Slav**.]

pansophy *pan'sə-fi, n.* universal knowledge. — *adjs.* **pansophic** (-*sof'ik*), **-al**. — *ns.* **pan'sophism; pan'sophist**. [Gr. *sophiā*, wisdom.]

panspermatism *pan-spûr'mə-tizm*, **panspermism** -*mizm*, **panspermy** -*mi*, **panspermia** -*mi-ə, ns.* the theory that life could be diffused through the universe by means of germs carried by meteorites or that life was brought to earth by this means. — *adjs.* **panspermat'ic, -sper'-mic**. — *ns.* **pansper'matist, -mist**. [Gr. *sperma, -atos*, seed.]

pansy *pan'zi, n.* a name for various species of violet, esp. the heart's-ease (*Viola tricolor*) and garden kinds derived from it, as well as other species with up-turned side petals and large leafy stipules: a soft bluish-purple: an effeminate or namby-pamby man: a male homosexual. — Also (*obs.; Spens.*, etc.) **pance, paunce, pawnce** (*päns, pöns*). — *adj.* bluish-purple: effeminate. — *adj.* **pan'sied**. [A fanciful use of Fr. *pensée*, thought — *penser*, to think — L. *pēnsāre*, to weigh.]

pant¹ *pant, v.i.* to gasp for breath: to run gasping: to throb: to wish ardently, to long, to yearn (with *for*): to bulge and shrink successively, as ships' hulls, etc. — *v.t.* to gasp out. — *n.* **pant** a gasping breath: a throb. — *n.* and *adj.* **pant'ing**. — *adv.* **pant'ingly**. [Apparently related to O.Fr. *pantoisier*, to pant.]

pant² *pänt, (Northern) n.* a public fountain: a puddle by a midden. [Origin obscure.]

pant-. See **pan-**.

pantable *pan'tə-bl*. Same as **pantofle**.

pantagamy *pan-tag'ə-mi, n.* a word that ought to mean universal bachelorhood, applied with unconscious irony to the universal marriage of the Perfectionists, in which every man in the community is the husband of every woman. [Gr. *gamos*, marriage, *agamiā*, bachelorhood.]

pantagraph. See **pantograph**.

Pantagruelism *pan-tə-grōō'əl-izm, -tag'rōō-, n.* the theories and practice of *Pantagruel* as described by Rabelais (d. 1553): burlesque ironical buffoonery as a cover for serious satire. — *adj.* and *n.* **Pantagruelian** (-*el'i-ən*). — *ns.* **Pantagruel'ion** a magic herb, hemp; **Pantagru'-elist** (or -*tag'rōō-*).

pantaleon *pan-tal'i-on, n.* a very large dulcimer invented about 1700 by *Pantaleon* Hebenstreit.

pantalets *pan-tə-lets', n.pl.* long frilled drawers, worn by women and children in the first half of the 19th century: a detachable ruffle for these, or one simulating these: extended to various trouser-like garments worn by women. — Also **pantalettes**. — *adj.* **pantalett'ed**. [Dim. of **pantaloons**.]

Pantaloon *pan-tə-lōōn'*, or *pan', n.* a character in Italian comedy, and afterwards in pantomime, a lean old man (originally a Venetian) more or less a dotard: (without *cap.; Shak.*) a feeble old man: (without *cap.;* in *pl.*) various kinds of trousers worn by or suggesting the stage pantaloon, as wide breeches of the Restoration, later combined breeches and stockings, later 18th-century trousers fastened below the calf or under the shoe, children's trousers resembling these, (usu. **pants**) trousers generally or long woollen underpants. — *n.* **pan'talon** a movement in a quadrille. — *adj.* **pantalooned'**. — *n.* **pantaloon'ery** buffoonery. [Fr. *pantalon* — It. *pantalone*, from St *Pantaleone*, a favourite saint of the Venetians.]

pantechnicon *pan-tek'ni-kon, n.* orig., a building in London intended for the sale of all kinds of artistic work, turned into a furniture-store: a furniture-van (in full **pantech'nicon-van'**): (*loosely*) a receptacle holding a large number of miscellaneous objects. [Gr. *technē*, art.]

panter. See **pantler**.

pantheism *pan'thē-izm, n.* the doctrine that identifies God with the universe: the worship of all gods (*rare*). — *n.* **pan'theist**. — *adjs.* **pantheist'ic, -al**. — *ns.* **pantheol'-ogist; pantheol'ogy** a synthesis of all religions and the knowledge of all gods; **Pantheon** (*pan'thi-on, pan-thē'on*) a temple of all the gods, esp. the rotunda erected by Hadrian at Rome (on the site of Agrippa's of 27 B.C.), now the church of Santa Maria Rotonda, a burial-place of great Italians: a building serving as a general burial-place or memorial of the great dead, as Sainte Geneviève at Paris: an 18th-century place of amusement in London (Oxford Street): all the gods collectively: a complete mythology. [Gr. *theos*, a god, *pantheion*, a Pantheon.]

panthenol *pan'thin-ol, n.* a vitamin of the B-complex, affecting the growth of hair.

pantheologist, etc., **Pantheon**. See **pantheism**.

panther *pan'thər, n.* a leopard, esp. a large one or one in its black phase, formerly believed to be a different species: a puma (*U.S.*): — *fem.* **pan'theress**. — *adjs.* **pan'therine** (-*īn*), **pan'therish**. — **Black Panther** a member of a militant black political movement dedicated to ending domination by whites. [Gr. *panthēr*.]

panties. See **pants**.

pantihose *pan'ti-hōz, n.pl.* tights worn by women or children with ordinary dress, i.e. not theatrical, etc. [**panty, hose**.]

pantile *pan'tīl, n.* a roofing tile whose cross-section forms an ogee curve: a tile concave or convex in cross-section: a flat paving tile (*obs.*). — *adj.* (*obs. slang*) dissenting — chapels being often roofed with these. — *adj.* **pan'tiled**. — *n.* **pan'tiling**. [**pan¹**, **tile**.]

pantine *pan'tēn, (obs.) n.* a pasteboard jumping-jack,

fashionable in the 18th century.   [Fr. *pantine*, afterwards *pantin*.]

pantisocracy *pant-is-ok'rə-si*, or *-īs-*, *n.* a community (planned by Coleridge, Southey, and Lovell) in which all should have equal power. — *n.* **pantis'ocrat**. — *adj.* **pantisocrat'ic**.   [Gr. *pās, pantos*, all, *isos*, equal, *krateein*, to rule.]

pantler *pant'lər*, (*Shak.*) *n.* the officer in a great family who had charge of the bread and other provisions. — Also **pant'er**.   [Fr. *panetier* — L. *pānis*, bread.]

panto. See **pantomime**.

panto-. See **pan-**.

Pantocrator *pan-tok'rə-tər*, *n.* the ruler of the universe, esp. Christ enthroned, as in icons, etc.   [Gr. *kratos*, power.]

pantofle, pantoffle, pantoufle *pan'tof-l, -tof'l, -tŏŏf'l, n.* a slipper: a high chopin (*hist.*): an overshoe (*arch.*). — Also **pantable** (*pan'tə-bl*). — **on one's pantables** on one's dignity, high horse, lofty in manner.   [Fr. *pantoufle*.]

pantograph *pan'tə-gräf, n.* a jointed framework of rods, based on the geometry of a parallelogram, for copying drawings, plans, etc., on the same, or a different, scale: a similar framework for other purposes, as for collecting a current from an overhead wire. — *n.* **pantographer** (*-tog'rə-fər*). — *adjs.* **pantographic** (*-tō-graf'ik*), **-al.** — *n.* **pantog'raphy**. — Also (*faulty*) **pan'tagraph**, etc. — **laser pantography** a technique of tracing a circuit pattern on to a microchip by means of a laser beam.   [Gr. *graphein*, to write.]

pantomime *pan'tə-mīm, n.* a Roman actor in dumb show (*hist.*): a play or an entertainment in dumb show: a theatrical entertainment, usu. about Christmas-time, developed out of this, no longer in dumb show, with showy scenery, topical allusions, songs of the day, buffoonery and dancing strung loosely upon a nursery story, formerly ending with a transformation scene and a harlequinade: dumb show: a situation of fuss, farce or confusion. — *adj.* of pantomime: pantomimic. — *n., adj.* **pan'to** coll. for **pantomime**: — *pl.* **pan'tos**. — *adjs.* **pantomimic** (*-mim'ik*), **-al.** — *adv.* **pantomim'ically**. — *n.* **pan'tomimist** an actor in or writer of pantomime.   [L. *pantomīmus* — Gr. *pantomīmos*, imitator of all — *pās, pantos*, all, *mīmos*, an imitator.]

panton *pan'tən*, (*Scot.*) *n.* a slipper. — **pan'ton-shoe'** a horse-shoe for curing a narrow and hoof-bound heel.   [App. conn. with **pantofle**.]

pantophagy *pan-tof'ə-ji, n.* omnivorousness. — *n.* **pantoph'agist**. — *adj.* **pantoph'agous** (*-gəs*).   [Gr. *phagein*, to eat.]

pantophobia *pan-tə-fō'bi-ə, n.* morbid fear of everything: (by confusion with **panophobia**) causeless fear.   [Gr. *pās, pantos*, all, *phobos*, fear.]

pantopragmatic *pan-tə-prag-mat'ik, adj.* meddling in everybody's business. — *n.* a universal busybody. — *n. sing.* **pantopragmat'ics** the science of universal benevolent interference.   [From Peacock's imaginary society (*Gryll Grange*) — Gr. *pās, pantos*, all, *pragmata* (pl.), business.]

pantoscope *pan'tə-skōp, n.* a panoramic camera: a very wide-angled photographic lens. — *adj.* **pantoscopic** (*-skop'ik*) giving a wide range of vision: bifocal.   [Gr. *skopeein*, to look at.]

pantothenic *pan-to-then'ik, adj.* lit. from all quarters: applied to an acid, a member of the vitamin B complex, so ubiquitous that the effects of its deficiency in man are not known.   [Gr. *pantothen*, from everywhere.]

pantoufle. See **pantofle**.

pantoum *pan-tōōm', properly* **pantun** *pan-tōōn', ns.* a verse-form orig. Malay, quatrains rhyming *ab ab, bc bc*, etc., returning to rhyme *a* at the end.   [Malay.]

pantry *pan'tri, n.* a room or closet for provisions and table furnishings, or where plate, knives, etc., are cleaned. — *ns.* **pan'trymaid; pan'tryman**.   [Fr. *paneterie* — L.L. *pānitāria* — L. *pānis*, bread.]

pants *pants, n.pl.* trousers (esp. *U.S.*): drawers. — *n.pl.* **pant'ies** very short drawers for children and women.

— **pant(s) suit** (esp. *U.S.*) a woman's suit of trousers and jacket. — **fly by the seat of one's pants** to get through a difficult or dangerous situation by resourcefulness; **scare, bore,** etc. **the pants off someone** to scare, bore, etc. someone to a great degree; **(be caught) with one's pants down** (*coll.*) (to be caught) at an embarrassing and unsuitable moment, in a state of unpreparedness.   [**pantaloons**.]

pantun. See **pantoum**.

panty girdle *pan'ti gûr'dl*, a woman's foundation garment consisting of panties made of elasticated material. — **pan'ty-waist** (*U.S.*) an effeminate or cowardly man (from a child's garment of trousers and jacket buttoned together at the waist).   [**panties**.]

panzer *pant'sər*, (Ger.) *n.* armour: a tank. — **panzer division** an armoured division.

paolo *pä'ō-lō, n.* an obsolete papal silver coin: — *pl.* **pa'oli** (*-lē*).   [It. *Paolo*, Paul, i.e. Pope Paul V.]

pap[1] *pap, n.* soft food for infants, as of bread boiled with milk: trivial ideas, entertainment, etc. (*fig.*): mash: pulp. — *v.t.* to feed with pap. — *adj.* **papp'y.** — **pap'-boat** a boat-shaped vessel for pap; **pap'-meat** soft food for infants; **pap'-spoon**.   [Imit.]

pap[2] *pap*, (*dial.*) *n.* a nipple: in place-names, a round conical hill.   [App. Scand.]

papa *pə-pä'* (*U.S.* *pä'pə*), *n.* father (*old-fashioned hypocoristic* or *genteel*): a pope (*pä'pä; obs.*): a priest of the Eastern Orthodox Church (*pä'pä*).   [Partly through Fr. *papa*, partly directly from L.L. *pāpa*, Gr. hypocoristic *papās, pappās*, father.]

papacy *pā'pə-si, n.* the office of pope: a pope's tenure of office: papal government.   [L.L. *pāpātia* — *pāpa*, pope.]

papain *pə-pā'in, n.* a digestive enzyme in the juice of papaw (Carica) fruits and leaves.   [Sp. *papaya*, papaw.]

papal *pā'pl, adj.* of the pope or the papacy. — *adj.* **pap'able** likely to, or qualified to, become pope. — *v.t.* and *v.i.* **pa'palise, -ize** to render or become papal or papalist. — *ns.* **pa'palism** the papal system; **pa'palist** a supporter of the pope and of the papal system. — *adv.* **pa'pally.** — **papal cross** a cross with three cross-bars; **Papal knighthood** a title of nobility conferred by the Pope; **Papal States** States of the Church (see **state**).   [L.L. *pāpālis* — *pāpa*, pope.]

Papanicolaou smear, test *pap-ə-nik'o-low, -nēk', smēr, test*, a smear test for detecting cancer, esp. of the womb, devised by George *Papanicolaou*, 20th cent. U.S. anatomist. — Abbrev. **Pap smear, test**.

papaprelatist *pā-pə-prel'ə-tist*, (*Scott*) *n.* a supporter of popish prelates.

paparazzo *pa-pa-rat'sō, n.* a photographer who specialises in harassing famous people in order to obtain photographs of them in unguarded moments, etc.: — *pl.* **paparazz'i**.   [It.]

Papaver *pə-pā'vər, n.* the poppy genus, giving name to the family **Papaverā'ceae**. — *adj.* **papaveraceous** (*pə-pav-*, or *-pāv-ə-rā'shəs*) of the poppy family. — *n.* **papaverine** (*pə-pav'ə-rēn, -rīn*, or *-pāv'*) an alkaloid got from poppy juice and used medicinally. — *adj.* **papaverous** (*-pav'* or *-pāv'*) resembling or having the qualities of the poppy.   [L. *papāver*, the poppy.]

papaw *pə-pö', pö'pö, n.* the tree *Asimina triloba* (of the custard-apple family) or its fruit, native to the U.S.: the papaya. — Also **paw'paw'**.   [Prob. variant of **papaya**.]

papaya *pə-pä'yə, n.* the tree *Carica papaya*, or its fruit, native to South America but common in the tropics, the trunk, leaves, and fruit yielding papain, the leaves forming a powerful anthelmintic. — Also called **papaw**.   [Sp. *papayo* (tree), *papaya* (fruit) app. from Carib.]

pape *pāp, n.* a Scots form of **pope**[1]. — *adj.* **pāp'ish** popish. — *n.* (*dial.* and *illit.*, by confusion with **papist**) a papist. — *n.* **pāp'isher**.

paper *pā'pər, n.* a material made in thin sheets as an aqueous deposit from linen rags, esparto, wood-pulp, or other form of cellulose, used for writing, printing, wrapping, and other purposes: extended to other materials of similar purpose or appearance, as to papyrus, rice-paper, to the substance of which some wasps build their nests, to cardboard, and even to tinfoil ('silver paper'): a piece of paper: a written or printed document or instrument, note, receipt, bill, bond, deed, etc.: a newspaper: an essay or literary contribution, esp. one read before a society: a set of examination questions: free passes of admission to a theatre, etc., also the persons so admitted: paper-money: paper-hangings for walls: a wrapping of paper: a quantity of anything wrapped in or attached to a paper. — *adj.* consisting or made of paper: papery: on paper. — *v.t.* to cover with paper: to fold in paper: to treat in any way by means of paper, as to sandpaper, etc.: to paste end-papers and fly-leaves to. — *ns.* **pa′perer; pa′pering** the operation of covering with paper: the paper so used. — *adjs.* **pa′perless** using esp. electronic means instead of paper for communication, recording, etc.; **pa′pery** like paper. — **pa′perback** a book with paper cover. — *v.t.* to publish in paperback. — **pa′per-birch′** an American birch with papery bark; **pa′perboard** a type of strong, thick cardboard: pasteboard; **pa′per-boy, -girl** one who delivers newspapers; **pa′per-case** a box for writing materials, etc.; **pa′per-chase** the game of hare and hounds, in which some runners (*hares*) set off across country strewing paper by which others (*hounds*) track them; **pa′per-cigar′** (*obs.*) a cigarette; **pa′per-clip** a clip of bent wire or the like, for holding papers together: a letter-clip; **pa′per-cloth** a fabric prepared in the Pacific islands from the inner bark of the paper-mulberry; **pa′per-coal** a lignite that splits into thin layers; **pa′per-cred′it** credit given to a person because he shows that money is owing to him; **pa′per-cutter** a paper-knife: a machine for cutting paper in sheets, for trimming the edges of books, etc.; **pa′per-day** (*law*) one of certain days in each term for hearing cases down in the paper or roll of business; **pa′per-enam′el** an enamel for cards and fine note-paper; **paper engineering** the technique of making pop-up books, etc. — *adj.* **pa′per-faced** (*Shak.*) having a thin face like a sheet of paper: faced with paper. — **pa′per-fastener** a button with two blades that can be forced through papers and bent back; **pa′per-feeder** an apparatus for delivering sheets of paper to a printing-press, etc.; **pa′per-file** an appliance for filing papers; **pa′per-folder** a folder (2nd sense); **pa′per-gauge** a rule for measuring the type-face of matter to be printed, and the width of the margin; **pa′per-hanger** one who papers walls: a person who makes or deals in forged cheques (*U.S. slang*). — *n.pl.* **pa′per-hangings** paper for covering walls. — **pa′per-knife** a thin, flat blade for cutting open the leaves of books and other folded papers; **pa′per-mâché** papier-mâché; **pa′per-maker** a manufacturer of paper; **pa′per-making; pa′per-mar′-bler** one engaged in marbling paper; **pa′per-mill** a mill where paper is made; **paper money** pieces of paper stamped or marked by government or by a bank, as representing a certain value of money, which pass from hand to hand instead of the coin itself; **pa′per-mul′-berry** a tree (*Broussonetia papyrifera*) of Eastern Asia and Polynesia, of the mulberry family, whose inner bark yields tapa cloth and paper-making material; **pa′per-mus′lin** a glazed muslin; **paper nautilus** the argonaut (see **nautilus**); **pa′per-off′ice** an office where state-papers are kept; **paper profits** the appreciation in value of a bond, share, etc.; **pa′per-pulp** pulpy material for making paper; **pa′per-reed** the papyrus; **pa′per-rul′er** one who, or an instrument which, makes straight lines on paper; **pa′per-sail′or** an argonaut; **pa′per-stain′er** one who prepares paper-hangings: a poor author, scribbler; **paper tape** (*comput.*) a paper data-recording tape, which records information by means of punched holes (**paper tape punch** a machine that perforates paper tape; **paper tape reader** a device that senses and translates the holes punched in a paper tape into machine-processable form); **paper tiger** a person,

organisation, that appears to be powerful but is in fact the reverse; **pa′perware** items made of paper, e.g. books, manuals, packaging, etc.; **pa′per-wash′ing** (*phot.*) water in which prints have been washed; **pa′per-weight** a small weight for keeping loose papers from being displaced; **pa′perwork** clerical work: keeping of records as part of a job. — **on paper** planned, decreed, existing theoretically only: apparently, judging by statistics, but perhaps not in fact; **paper over (the cracks)** to create the impression that there is or has been no dissent, error, or fault; **paper the house** to fill a theatre by issuing free passes. [A.Fr. *papir*, O.Fr. (Fr.) *papier* — L. *papyrus* — Gr. *papyros*, papyrus.]

papeterie *pap-ə-trē′*, *n.* a stationery-case. [Fr., stationery, paper-trade.]

Paphian *pā′fi-ən*, *adj.* pertaining to *Paphos* in Cyprus, sacred to Aphrodite: lascivious. — *n.* a native of Paphos: a votary of Aphrodite: a whore.

Papiamento *pap-i-ə-men′tō*, *n.* a creole language derived from Spanish, spoken in the Dutch Antilles. [Sp. *papia*, talk.]

papier collé *pä-pyā kol-ā*, scraps of paper and odds and ends pasted out as a help to cubist composition. [Fr., glued paper.]

papier-mâché *pap′yā-mä′shā*, *n.* a material consisting of paper-pulp or of sheets of paper pasted together, often treated so as to resemble varnished or lacquered wood or plaster. — *adj.* of papier-mâché. [Would-be French, — Fr. *papier* (see **paper**) *mâché*, chewed — L. *masticātus*.]

Papilio *pə-pil′i-ō*, *n.* the swallow-tailed butterfly genus, giving name to the family **Papilionidae** (*-on′i-dē*), in which all six legs are fully developed in both sexes: (without *cap.*) a butterfly of this genus: — *pl.* **papil′ios.** — *adj.* **papilionā′ceous** of butterflies: butterfly-like: of a form of corolla somewhat butterfly-like, with a large posterior petal (*vexillum*), two side petals or wings (*alae*), and two anterior petals forming a keel (*carina*): of the **Papilionā′ceae**, a family of Leguminosae characterised by such a corolla, including pea, bean, clover, gorse, laburnum, etc. [L. *pāpiliō, -ōnis*, butterfly.]

papilla *pə-pil′ə*, *n.* a small nipple-like protuberance: a minute elevation on the skin, esp. of the finger-tips and upper surface of the tongue, in which a nerve ends: a protuberance at the base of a hair, feather, tooth, etc.: a minute conical protuberance as on the surface of a petal: — *pl.* **papill′ae** (*-ē*). — *adjs.* **papill′ar, papill′ary** like, or of the nature of, or having, papillae; **papill′ate, -d, papillif′erous** (*pap-*) having papillae; **papill′iform** in the form of a papilla. — *ns.* **papilli′tis** inflammation of the head of the optic nerve; **papillō′ma** a tumour formed by hypertrophy of a papilla or papillae, as a wart, etc. — *adjs.* **papillōm′atous; pap′-illōse** full of papillae, warty — also **papill′ous; papill′-ūlate** finely papillose. — *n.* **papill′ūle** a very small papilla. [L., dim. of *papula*.]

papillon *pap-ē-yɔ̃*, *n.* a breed of toy spaniel with erect ears. [Fr., butterfly.]

papillose, papillous. See **papilla.**

papillote *pap′il-ōt*, *n.* a curl-paper: frilled paper used to decorate the bones of chops, etc. (*cook.*): oiled or greased paper in which meat is cooked and served (*cook.*). [Fr., app. — *papillon*, butterfly — L. *pāpiliō, -ōnis*.]

papillule, etc. See **papilla.**

papish. See **pape.**

papist *pā′pist*, *n.* an adherent of the pope: a name slightly given to a Roman Catholic. — *n.* **pā′pism** popery. — *adjs.* **pāpist′ic, -al** pertaining to popery, or to the Church of Rome, its doctrines, etc. — *adv.* **pāpist′ically.** — *n.* **pā′pistry** popery. [L.L. *pāpa*, pope.]

papoose *pə-pōōs′*, *n.* a North American Indian baby or young child. — Also **pappoose′.** [Narraganset *papoos*.]

papovavirus *pə-pō′və-vī′rəs*, *n.* any of a group of DNA-containing oncogenic viruses. [Composite coinage, and **virus**.]

pappadom. See **pop(p)adum.**

pappus *pap'əs, n.* a ring or parachute of fine hair or down, representing the calyx limb, which grows above the seed and helps in wind-dissemination in composites and some other plants (*bot*.): the downy beginnings of a beard. — *adjs.* **papp′ōse** (or *-ōs′*), **papp′ous.** [L. *pappus* — Gr. *pappos*, a grandfather, down, a pappus.]

pappy¹. See **pap¹.**

pappy² *pap′i, (U.S. coll.) n.* father. [**papa**.]

paprika *pap′ri-kə, pa-prēk′ə, n.* Hungarian red pepper, a species of Capsicum. [Hung.]

Papuan *pap′ū-ən, adj.* pertaining to *Papua* or New Guinea. — *n.* a member of the black, dolichocephalic, frizzly-haired race inhabiting Papua, etc. [Malay *papuwa*, frizzled.]

papula *pap′ū-lə*, **papule** *pap′ūl, ns.* a pimple: a papilla: — *pl.* **pap′ūlae** (*-lē*), **pap′ules.** — *adjs.* **pap′ūlar; papūlif′- erous.** — *n.* **papūlā′tion** the development of papules. — *adjs.* **pap′ūlose, pap′ūlous.** [L. *papula*, a pimple.]

papyrus *pə-pī′rəs, n.* the paper-reed (*Cyperus papyrus,* or kindred species), a tall plant of the sedge family, once common in Egypt: its pith cut in thin strips and pressed together as a writing material of the ancients: a manuscript on papyrus: — *pl.* **papy′ri** (*-rī*). — *adj.* **papyraceous** (*pap-i-rā′shəs*) papery. — *ns.* **papyrologist** (*pap-i-rol′ə-jist*); **papyrol′ogy** the study of ancient papyri. [L. *papȳrus* — Gr. *papyros*; probably Egyptian.]

par¹ *pär, n.* state of equality: equal value: norm or standard: state or value of bills, shares, etc., when they sell at exactly the price marked on them — i.e. without *premium* or *discount*: equality of condition: the number of strokes that should be taken for a hole or a round by good play, two putts being allowed on each green (*golf*). — **par contest** (*bridge*) a competition in which points are awarded for the bidding of a prepared hand and for the playing of the hand in a directed contract; **par value** value at par. — **above par** at a premium, or at more than the nominal value; **at par** at exactly the nominal value; **below par** at a discount, or at less than the nominal value: out of sorts (*fig.*); **nominal par** value with which a bill or share is marked, or by which it is known; **no par value** with no stated nominal value; **on a par with** equal to; **par for the course** a normal, average result or (*coll. fig.*) occurrence, state of affairs, etc.; **par of exchange** the value of currency of one country expressed in that of another. [L. *pār*, equal.]

par² *pär, n.* Same as **parr.**

par³ *pär, n.* a colloquial abbreviation of **paragraph.**

para¹ *pär′ə, n.* a small Turkish coin: the 40th part of a piastre: in Yugoslavia the 100th part of a dinar. [Turk. *pārah*.]

para² *par′ə, n.* a colloquial short form of **paratrooper, paragraph.**

Pará *pä-rä′, n.* a city, state, and estuary of Brazil. — **pará grass** piassava; **pará nut** Brazil nut; **pará rubber** that got from *Hevea brasiliensis*.

para-¹ *par′ə-,* in composition, beside: faulty: disordered: abnormal: false: a polymer of: a compound related to: closely resembling, or parallel to (as in *adj*. and *n*. **paramed′ic,** *adj.* **paramed′ical** (a person) helping doctors or supplementing medical work; *adj.* and *n*. **paramilitary** (see separate entry)): in organic chem., having substituted atoms or groups attached to two opposite carbon atoms of the benzene ring — commonly represented by *p-*. — **pa′ra-compound.** [Gr. *para*, beside.]

para-² *par′ə-, pfx.* parachute, as in *ns.* **par′abrake** a parachute used to help brake an aircraft when it has landed; **par′adoctor** a doctor who parachutes to patients; **par′adrop** an air-drop; **par′afoil** a form of steerable parachute, consisting of air-filled nylon cells; **par′aglider** a glider with inflatable wings; **par′agliding** the sport of being towed through the air by plane while fitted with a modified type of parachute, then allowed

to drift to the ground; **par′akiting** the sport of soaring suspended from a parachute which is being towed; **par′amedic(o)** a paradoctor. — *adjs.* **par′amedic(al).**

para-amino-salicylic acid *par-ə-a-mē′nō-sal-i-sil′ik as′id,* a drug used along with streptomycin in the treatment of tuberculosis: —abbrev. **PAS.**

parabaptism *par-ə-bap′tizm, n.* uncanonical baptism. [**para-¹** and **baptism** (see **baptise**).]

parabasis *pə-rab′ə-sis, n.* part of the Old Comedy of Greece in which the chorus came forward and addressed the audience on behalf of the poet. [Gr., a going aside — *para-*, beside, beyond, *basis*, a going.]

parabema *par-ə-bē′mə,* n. in Byzantine architecture, either the chapel of the prothesis or the diaconicon, when walled off from the bema: — *pl.* **parabe′mata.** — *adj.* **parabemat′ic.** [Gr. *para*, beside, beyond, *bēma*, a step.]

parabiosis *par-ə-bī-ō′sis, n.* the union of similar embryos between which a functional connection exists. — *adj.* **parabio′tic.** — **parabiotic twins** Siamese twins. [Gr. *para*, beside, *biōsis*, manner of life.]

parable *par′ə-bl, n.* a similitude: a fable or story of something which might have happened, told to illustrate some doctrine, or to make some duty clear: a proverb (*arch.*): discourse (*arch.*). — *v.t.* to represent by a parable. — *ns.* **parabola** (*pə-rab′ə-lə*) a curve, one of the conic sections, the intersection of a cone and a plane parallel to its side, or the locus of a point equidistant from a fixed point (the *focus*) and a fixed straight line (the *directrix*) — its equation with vertex as origin $y^2 = 4ax$: generalised to include any curve whose equation is $y^n = px^m$: — *pl.* **parab′olas; parab′ole** (*-lē*) in rhetoric, a similitude, simile, or metaphor. — *adjs.* **parabol′ic** (*par-ə-bol′ik*), **-al** of or like a parable or a parabola or a parabole: expressed by a parable: belonging to, or of the form of, a parabola. — *adv.* **parabol′ically.** — *v.t.* **parab′olise, -ize** to set forth by parable: to treat as a parable: to shape like a parabola or paraboloid. — *ns.* **parab′olist; parab′oloid** a surface or solid generated by the rotation of a parabola about its axis. — *adjs.* **parab′oloid, -al.** — **parabolic geometry** Euclidean geometry; **parabolic velocity** (*astron.*) the velocity which a body at a given point would require to describe a parabola about the centre of attraction. [Gr. *parabolē*, a placing alongside, comparison, parabola, etc. — *para*, beside, beyond, *ballein*, to throw.]

parablepsis *par-ə-blep′sis, n.* false vision: oversight. — Also **par′ablepsy.** — *adj.* **parablep′tic.** [Gr., looking askance — *para*, beside, beyond, *blepein*, to see.]

parabola, etc. See **parable.**

parabolanus *par-ə-bō-lā′nəs, n.* in the early Eastern Church, a layman who tended the sick. [Gr. *parabolos*, venturesome, exposing oneself.]

Paracelsian *par-ə-sel′si-ən, adj.* of or relating to the famous German Swiss philosopher and physician, *Paracelsus* (1493–1541), or resembling his theories or practice. The name was coined for himself by Theophrastus Bombastus von Hohenheim, and apparently implied a claim to be greater than Celsus.

paracentesis *par-ə-sen-tē′sis, (surg.) n.* tapping. [Gr. *parakentēsis* — *para*, beside, beyond, *kenteein*, to pierce.]

paracetamol *par-ə-sēt′ə-mol, -set′, n.* a mild analgesic and antipyretic drug, often used instead of aspirin. [Gr. *para*, beside, beyond, *acetam*ide.]

parachronism *par-ak′rən-izm, n.* an error in dating, esp. when anything is represented as later than it really was. [Gr. *para*, beside, beyond, *chronos*, time.]

parachute *par′ə-shoot, n.* an apparatus like an umbrella for descending safely from a height (*coll.* short form **chute**): any structure serving a like purpose, as a pappus, a patagium. — *v.i.* to descend by parachute. — *v.t.* to be taken and dropped by parachute (also *fig.*). — *n.* **par′achutist.** — **parachute troops.** [Fr. *parachute* — It. *para,* imper. of *parare,* to ward — L. *parāre,* to prepare, and Fr. *chute,* fall.]

paraclete *par'ə-klēt, n.* an advocate or legal helper, or intercessor — applied (with *cap.*) to the Holy Ghost (John xiv. 26). [Gr. *paraklētos* — *parakaleein,* to call in, also to comfort — *para,* beside, beyond, *kaleein,* to call.]

paracme *par-ak'mē, n.* the stage of decline or senescence after the culmination of development. [Gr. *para,* beside, beyond, *akmē,* a point.]

paracrostic *par-ə-kros'tik, n.* a poem whose initial letters reproduce its first verse. [**para-**[1] and **acrostic.**]

paracusis *par-ə-kū'sis, n.* disordered hearing. [Gr. *para,* beside, beyond, *akousis,* hearing.]

paracyanogen *par-ə-sī-an'ə-jən, n.* a polymer of cyanogen. [**para-**[1] and **cyanogen.**]

parade *pə-rād', n.* show: display: ostentation: an assembling in order for exercise, inspection, etc.: a procession: ground for parade of troops: a public promenade: a parry (*fencing*). — *v.t.* to show off: to thrust upon notice: to lead about and expose to public attention: to traverse in parade: to marshal in military order. — *v.i.* to march up and down as if for show: to pass in military order: to march in procession: to show off. — **parade'-ground.** [Fr., — Sp. *parada* — *parar,* to halt — L. *parāre, -ātum,* to prepare.]

paradiddle *par'ə-did-l, n.* a drum roll in which the principal beats are struck by the left and right sticks in succession.

paradigm *par'ə-dīm, n.* an example, exemplar: an example of the inflection of a word (*gram.*): a basic theory, a conceptual framework within which scientific theories are constructed. — *adjs.* **paradigmatic** (*-dig-mat'ik*), **-al.** — *adv.* **paradigmat'ically.** [Fr. *paradigme* — Gr. *paradeigma* — *paradeiknynai,* to exhibit side by side — *para,* beside, beyond, *deiknynai,* to show.]

paradise *par'ə-dīs, n.* a park or pleasure-ground esp. in ancient Persia: a park in which foreign animals were kept: the garden of Eden: heaven: the abode (intermediate or final) of the blessed dead: any place of bliss: a parvis: a small private apartment (*arch.*). — *adjs.* **paradisaic** (*par-ə-dis-ā'ik*), **-al, paradisal** (*-dī'səl*), **paradisean** (*-dis'i-ən*), **paradisiac** (*-dis'i-ak, -dis'i-ak*), **paradisiacal** (*-dis-ī'ə-kl*), **paradisial** (*-dis', -diz'*), **paradisic** (*-dis', -diz'*), **paradisic** (*-dis', -diz'*). — **par'adise-fish** a Chinese freshwater fish (*Macropodus*), often kept in aquaria for its beauty of form and colouring. — **bird of paradise** any bird of the family **Paradisē'idae,** inhabitants chiefly of New Guinea, close akin to the crows but extremely gorgeous in plumage; **fool's paradise** see **fool**[1]. [Gr. *paradeisos,* a park — O.Pers. *pairidaēza,* park.]

parados *par'ə-dos, n.* earthworks protecting against a rear attack. [Fr. — L. *parāre,* to prepare, *dorsum,* back.]

paradox *par'ə-doks, n.* that which is contrary to received opinion: that which is apparently absurd but is or may be really true: a self-contradictory statement: paradoxical character. — *adj.* **paradox'al.** — *n.* **par'adoxer.** — *adj.* **paradox'ical.** — *adv.* **paradox'ically.** — *ns.* **paradox'icalness; Paradox'ides** (*-i-dēz*) a typically Middle Cambrian genus of trilobites, some very large (about two feet (60 cm.) long). — *adj.* **paradoxid'ian.** — *ns.* **par'adoxist; paradoxol'ogy** the utterance or maintaining of paradoxes; **par'adoxy** the quality of being paradoxical. — **paradoxical sleep** apparently deep sleep, with actual increased brain activity. [Gr. *paradoxos, -on,* contrary to opinion — *para,* beside, beyond, *doxa,* opinion.]

paradoxure *par-ə-dok'sūr, n.* a civet-like carnivore of Southern Asia and Malaysia, the palm-cat of India. — *adj.* **paradoxū'rine.** [Gr. *paradoxos,* paradoxical — *para,* beside, beyond, and *ourā,* tail.]

paraenesis, parenesis *par-ēn'i-sis,* or *-en', n.* exhortation. — *adjs.* **paraenetic** (*-net'ik*), **-al.** [Gr. *parainesis* — *para,* beside, beyond, *aineein,* to commend.]

paraesthesia, in U.S. **paresthesia,** *par-ēs-thē'si-ə,* or *-es-, n.* abnormal sensation. [Gr. *para,* beyond, *aisthēsis,* sensation.]

paraffin *par'ə-fin, n.* originally, paraffin-wax — so named by its discoverer, Reichenbach, from its having little chemical affinity for other bodies: generalised to mean any saturated hydrocarbon of the methane series, gaseous, liquid, or solid, the general formula being C_nH_{2n+2}: paraffin-oil. — Also **par'affine.** — *v.t.* to treat with paraffin. — *adjs.* **paraffin'ic, par'affinoid, par'affiny.** — **par'affin-oil'** any of the mineral burning oils associated with the manufacture of paraffin, mixtures of liquid paraffin and other hydrocarbons; **par'affin-scale'** unrefined solid paraffin; **paraffin test** a test using paraffin to detect trace elements left on the skin of someone who has been in contact with explosives, etc.; **par'affin-wax'** a white transparent crystalline substance got by distillation of shale, coal, tar, wood, etc., a mixture of solid paraffins. — **liquid paraffin** a liquid form of petrolatum, used as a mild laxative. [L. *parum,* little, *affinis,* having affinity.]

paraffle, parafle *pə-rä'fl,* (*Scot.*) *n.* pretentious display. [Cf. **paraph.**]

parafoil. See **para-**[2].

parage *par'ij, n.* lineage (*obs.*): high birth or rank: equality among persons of whom one does homage for all, the others holding of him (*feudal law*). [Fr.]

paragenesis *par-ə-jen'i-sis,* **paragenesia** *par-ə-jin-ē'zi-ə,* (*geol.*) *ns.* the development of minerals in such close contact that their formation is affected and they become a joined mass. — *adj.* **paragenet'ic.** [**para-**[1], **genesis.**]

paraglider, paragliding. See **para-**[2].

paraglossa *par-ə-glos'ə, n.* either of two appendages of the ligula in insects: — *pl.* **paragloss'ae** (*-ē*). — *adjs.* **paragloss'al; paragloss'ate.** [Gr. *para,* beside, beyond, *glōssa,* tongue.]

paragnathous *pər-ag'nə-thəs, adj.* having equal mandibles. — *n.* **parag'nathism.** [Gr. *para,* beside, beyond, *gnathos,* jaw.]

paragnosis *par-ə-gnō'sis,* (*psych.*) *n.* knowledge of matters not susceptible to investigation by traditional scientific methods. [Gr. *para,* beside, beyond, *gnōsis,* knowing.]

paragoge *par-ə-gō'jē, -gē,* **paragogue** *par'ə-gog, ns.* an addition to the end of a word, as *t* in *against, amidst, amongst, whilst, d* in *drownd* (illiterate for *drown*). — *adjs.* **paragogic** (*-goj'ik, -gog'ik*), **-al.** — **paragogic future** the cohortative tense in Hebrew — a lengthened form of the imperfect or future, usually confined to the first person, giving the sense of 'let me' or 'let us'. [Gr. *paragōgē,* a leading part, addition — *para,* beside, beyond, *agein,* to lead.]

paragon *par'ə-gon, -gən, n.* a model of perfection or supreme excellence: match, equal (*arch.*): mate (*Spens.*): rival (*arch.*): comparison (*Spens.*): emulation, competition (*Spens.*): a diamond of 600 carats or more: a black marble (*obs.*): a camlet used for upholstering and dress (*obs.*): 20-point printing-type intermediate between great-primer and double-pica. — *v.t.* (*arch.* or *rare*) to compare: to match: to surpass (*Shak.*): to hold up as a paragon (*Shak.*). [O.Fr. *paragon* — It. *paragone,* touchstone; origin obscure.]

paragonite *par'ə-gən-īt,* or *pər-ag', n.* a soda-mica, once mistaken for talc. [Gr. *paragōn,* misleading — *para,* beside, beyond, *agein,* to lead.]

paragram *par'ə-gram, n.* a play upon words by change of initial (or other) letter. — *n.* **paragramm'atist** a punster. [Gr. (*skōmmata*) *para gramma,* (jokes) by letter.]

paragraph *par'ə-gräf, n.* a sign (in ancient MSS. a short horizontal line, in the Middle Ages ℭ, now ¶, ℙ) marking off a section of a book, etc.: a distinct part of a discourse or writing marked by such a sign or now usually by indenting: a short passage, or a collection of sentences, with unity of purpose: a musical passage forming a unit: a short separate item of news or comment in a newspaper. — *v.t.* to form into paragraphs: to write or publish paragraphs about. — *ns.* **par'agrapher, par'agraphist** one who writes paragraphs, esp. for newspapers. — *adjs.* **paragraphic**

(-graf'), **-al.** — adv. **paragraph'ically.** [Gr. para-graphos, written alongside — para, beside, beyond, graphein, to write.]
paragraphia par-ə-graf'i-ə, n. writing of wrong words and letters, owing to disease or injury of the brain. — adj. **paragraphic** (-graf'ik). [Gr. para, beside, beyond, graphein, to write.]
Paraguay par-ə-gwī', -gwä', n. a country and river of South America. — **Paraguay tea** maté.
paraheliotropic par-ə-hē-li-ō-trop'ik, (bot.) adj. turning edgewise to the light. — n. **paraheliotropism** (-ot'rə-pizm). [Gr. para, beside, beyond, and hēlios, the sun, and tropos, a turn — trepein, to turn.]
parainfluenza virus par-ə-in-flōō-en'zə vī'rəs, any of a number of viruses causing influenza-like symptoms, esp. in children.
parakeet, parrakeet par'ə-kēt, n. a small long-tailed parrot of various kinds. — Also **paroquet, parroquet** (-ket), **paraquito** (pa-ra-kē'tō; pl. **paraqui'tos**). [Sp. peri-quito, It. parrocchetto, or O.Fr. paroquet (Fr. perro-quet); the origin and relations of these are not determined.]
parakiting. See para-².
paralalia par-ə-la', -lā'li-ə, n. a form of speech disturbance, particularly that in which a different sound or syllable is produced from the one intended. [Gr. para, beside, beyond, lalia, speech.]
paralanguage par-ə-lang'gwij, n. elements of communication other than words, i.e. tone of voice, gesture, facial expression, etc. — adj. **paralinguist'ic.** — n.sing. **paralinguist'ics** the study of paralanguage. [**para-¹**, and **language, linguistic(s).**]
paraldehyde par-al'di-hīd, n. a polymer, $(C_2H_4O)_3$, of acetaldehyde, used to induce sleep. [**para-¹** and **aldehyde.**]
paralegal par-ə-lē'gl, adj. of, concerning or being a person who assists a professional lawyer. — n. (par'ə-lē-gl). [**para-¹** and **legal.**]
paraleipsis, paralipsis par-ə-līp'sis, -lip', ns. a rhet. figure by which one fixes attention on a subject by pretending to neglect it, as 'I will not speak of his generosity', etc. — pls. **paral(e)ip'ses.** — ns. **paral(e)ipom'enon** a thing left out, added in supplement: — pls. **paral(e)ipom'ena,** esp. (in the Septuagint, etc.) the Books of Chronicles. [Gr. paraleipsis, paraleipomenon (neut. pr. part. pass.) — paraleipein, to leave aside — para, beside, beyond, leipein, to leave.]
paralexia par-ə-lek'si-ə, n. a defect in the power of seeing and interpreting written language, with meaningless transposition of words and syllables. [Gr. para, beside, beyond, lexis, a word.]
paralinguistic(s). See paralanguage.
paralipsis, etc. See paraleipsis.
parallax par'ə-laks, n. an apparent change in the position of an object caused by change of position in the observer: in astron., the apparent change (measured angularly) in the position of a heavenly body when viewed from different points — when viewed from opposite points on the earth's surface this change is called the daily or diurnal or geocentric parallax; when viewed from opposite points of the earth's orbit, the annual or heliocentric parallax. — adjs. **parallac'tic, -al.** [Gr. parallaxis — para, beside, beyond, allassein, to change — allos, another.]
parallel par'ə-lel, adj. extended in the same direction and equidistant in all parts: analogous, corresponding: alongside in time: having a constant interval (major and minor being reckoned alike; mus.). — n. a parallel line: a line of latitude: an analogue, or like, or equal: an analogy: a tracing or statement of resemblances: a besieger's trench parallel to the outline of the place besieged: a printer's reference mark of two vertical lines: parallel arrangement. — v.t. to place so as to be parallel: to conform: to represent as parallel: to liken in detail: to find a parallel to: to match: to be or run parallel to. — v.i. to be or run parallel: — pr.p. **par'alleling;** pa.t. and pa.p. **par'alleled.** — v.t. **par'-**

allelise, -ize to furnish a parallel to. — ns. **par'allelism** the state or fact of being parallel: resemblance in corresponding details: a balanced construction of a verse or sentence, where one part repeats the form or meaning of the other: comparison: development along parallel lines: the theory or belief (in full **psychophysical parallelism**) that mind and matter do not interact but correspond; **par'allelist** one who draws a parallel or comparison: a believer in psychophysical parallelism. — adj. **parallelis'tic.** — advs. **par'allelly; par'allelwise.** — ns. pl. **parallel bars** a pair of fixed bars used in gymnastics; **parallel imports** imports brought into a country through other than official channels, thus circumventing regulations, etc. — **parallel importer; parallel motion** a name given to any linkage by which circular motion may be changed into straight-line motion; **parallel processing** (comput.) the processing of several elements of an item of information at the same time; **parallel ruler** or **rulers** rulers joined by two pivoted strips, for ruling parallel lines; **parallel slalom** a slalom race in which two competitors ski down parallel courses. — adj. **par'allel-veined** (bot.) having the main veins running side by side. — **in parallel** of electrical apparatus, so arranged that terminals of like polarity are connected together: simultaneously (fig.). [Gr. parallēlos, as if par' allēloin, beside each other.]
parallelepiped par-ə-lel-ep'i-ped (or -lel'ə-, or -ə-pī'), n. a solid figure bounded by six parallelograms, opposite pairs being identical and parallel. — Also **parallelepip'-edon** (pl. **-da**), improperly **parallelopi'ped, parallelopi'-pedon.** [Gr. parallēlepipedon — parallēlos, epipedon, a plane surface — epi, on, pedon, ground.]
parallelogram par-ə-lel'ō-gram, n. a plane four-sided figure whose opposite sides are parallel. — adjs. **parallelogrammat'ic, -al, parallelogramm'ic, -al.** — **par-allelogram of forces** a figure in which the direction and amount of two component forces are represented by two sides of a parallelogram, those of their resultant by the diagonal. [Gr. parallēlogrammon — grammē, a line.]
paralogia par-ə-loj'i-ə, n. impairment of reasoning power characterised by difficulty in expressing logical ideas in speech. — v.i. **paral'ogise, -ize** to reason falsely. — n. **paral'ogism** false reasoning — also **paral'ogy.** [Gr. paralogismos — para, beside, beyond, logismos — logos, reason.]
paralysis pə-ral'i-sis, n. palsy, a loss of power of motion, or sensation, in any part of the body: deprivation of power of action. — v.t. **paralyse,** in U.S. **paralyze,** (par'ə-līz) to afflict with paralysis: to deprive of power of action. — n. **par'alyser,** in U.S. **-z-.** — adj. **paralytic** (par-ə-lit'ik) of or pertaining to paralysis: afflicted with or inclined to paralysis: helplessly drunk (slang). — n. one who is affected with paralysis. [Gr. paralysis, secret undoing, paralysis — lyein, to loosen.]
paramaecium. See Paramecium.
paramagnetic par-ə-mag-net'ik, adj. magnetic in the ordinary sense — said of bodies that when freely suspended between the poles of a magnet place themselves parallel to the lines of force — opp. to diamagnetic. — n. **paramag'netism.** [**para-¹** and **magnetic** (see magnet).]
paramastoid par-ə-mas'toid, adj. situated near the mastoid, paroccipital. — n. a paramastoid process. [**para-¹** and **mastoid.**]
paramatta, parramatta par-ə-mat'ə, n. a fabric like merino made of worsted and cotton. [App. from Parramatta in New South Wales.]
Paramecium par-ə-mē's(h)i-əm, n. a genus of tiny animals including the slipper animalcule, a slipper-shaped infusorian: (without cap.) an animal of the genus: — pl. **paramē'cia.** — Often misspelled **paramoecium, paramaecium.** [Gr. paramēkēs, long-shaped — para, alongside, mēkos, length.]
paramedic(al). See para-¹, para-².
paramenstruum par-ə-men'strōō-əm, n. the four days be-

fore and the four days after the onset of menstruation. [**para-**[1] and **menstruum**.]

parament *par'ə-mənt*, (*obs.*) *n.* a rich decoration, hanging, or robe. [L. *parāre*, to prepare.]

paramese *pa-ram'i-sē*, (*Gr. mus.*) *n.* the string or tone next above the mese. [Gr. *paramesē*.]

parameter *pə-ram'i-tər*, *n.* a line or quantity which serves to determine a point, line, figure, or quantity in a class of such things (*math.*): a constant quantity in the equation of a curve: in conic sections, a third proportional to any diameter and its conjugate diameter: the latus rectum of a parabola: the intercept upon an axis of a crystal face chosen for purpose of reference (the *parametral plane*): a quantity to which an arbitrary value may be given as a convenience in expressing performance or for use in calculations (*elect.*): variable: a variable which is given a series of arbitrary values in order that a family of curves of two other related variables may be drawn: any constant in learning or growth curves that differs with differing conditions (*psych.*): a boundary or limit (*lit.* and *fig.*). — *adjs.* **param'etral**, **parametric** (*par-ə-met'rik*), **-al**. [Gr. *para*, beside, beyond, *metron*, measure.]

paramilitary *par-ə-mil'i-tər-i*, *adj.* on military lines and intended to supplement the strictly military: organised as a military force. — Also *n.* [**para-**[1] and **military** (see **militant**).]

paramnesia *par-am-nē'zh(y)ə*, *n.* a memory disorder in which words are remembered but not their proper meaning: the condition of believing that one remembers events and circumstances which have not previously occurred. [Gr. *para*, beside, beyond, and the root of *mimnēskein*, to remind.]

paramo *pä'rä-mō*, *n.* a bare wind-swept elevated plain in South America: — *pl.* **par'amos**. [Sp. *páramo*.]

paramoecium. See **Paramecium**.

paramorph *par'ə-mörf*, (*min.*) *n.* a pseudomorph formed by a change in molecular structure without change of chemical composition. — *adj.* **paramorph'ic**. — *n.* **paramorph'ism**. [Gr. *para*, beside, beyond, *morphē*, form.]

paramount *par'ə-mownt*, *adj.* superior to all others: supreme: — opp. to *paravail*. — *n.* a paramount chief: a superior. — *n.* **par'amou(n)t)cy**. — *adv.* **par'amountly**. — **paramount chief** a supreme chief. [O.Fr. *paramont*, *par* (L. *per*) *à mont* (L. *ad montem*); see **amount**.]

paramour *par'ə-mōōr*, *adv.* (*obs.*) by the way of love, as a lover, for love's sake, out of kindness. — *n.* a lover of either sex, formerly in an innocent, now usually in the illicit, sense. [Fr. *par amour*, by or with love — L. *per amōrem*.]

paramyxovirus *par-ə-mik'sō-vī-rəs*, *n.* any of a group of single-stranded ribonucleic acid viruses which includes the mumps and measles viruses. [**para-**[1] and **myxovirus**.]

Paraná *pa-ra-nä'*, *n.* a river and state in Brazil. — **Paraná pine** the tree, *Araucaria brasiliana*, native to S. Brazil, or its wood.

paranephros *par-ə-nef'ros*, *n.* the suprarenal gland, near the kidney. — *adj.* **paraneph'ric**. [Gr. *para*, beside, beyond, *nephros*, kidney.]

paranete *par-a-nē'tē*, (*Gr. mus.*) *n.* the string or tone next below the nete. [Gr. *paranētē*.]

parang *pär'ang*, *n.* a heavy Malay knife. [Malay.]

paranitroaniline *par-ə-nī-trō-an'i-lēn*, *n.* a nitro-derivative of aniline, used in dyeing. [**para-**[1] and **nitroaniline** (see **nitre**).]

paranoia *par-ə-noi'ə*, *n.* a form of mental disorder characterised by fixed delusions, esp. of grandeur, pride, persecution: intense (esp. irrational) fear or suspicion. — Also (*rarely*) **paranoea** (*-nē'ə*). — *adj.* **paranoi'ac** of paranoia. — *n.* a victim of paranoia. — Also **paranoe'ic**, **paranoic** (*-no'ik*). — *adjs.* **par'anoid**, **paranoid'al** resembling paranoia. [Gr. *paranoia* — *para*, beside, beyond, *noos*, mind.]

paranormal *par-ə-nör'məl*, *adj.* abnormal, esp. psychologically: not susceptible to normal explanations. —

n. that which is paranormal. [**para-**[1] and **normal**.]

paranthelion *par-an-thē'li-on*, *n.* a diffuse whitish image of the sun, having the same altitude, at an angular distance of 90° to 140°: — *pl.* **paranthe'lia**. [Gr. *para*, beside, beyond, *anti*, against, *hēlios*, the sun.]

paranthropus *par-an'thra-pəs*, *n.* a hominid ape usu. included in the species *Australopithecus robustus*. [**para-**[1] and Gr. *anthrōpos*, man.]

paranym *par'ə-nim*, *n.* a word whose meaning is altered to conceal an evasion or untruth, e.g. *liberation* used for *conquest*. [**para-**[1] and Gr. *onyma*, *onoma*, name]

paranymph *par'ə-nimf*, (*ant.*; *Milt.*) *n.* a friend who went with the bridegroom to fetch the bride, a groomsman or bridesmaid: one who countenances and supports another. [Gr. *paranymphos* — *para*, beside, beyond, *nymphē*, a bride.]

parapet *par'ə-pit*, *n.* a bank or wall to protect soldiers from the fire of an enemy in front: a low wall along the side of a bridge, edge of a roof, etc. — *adj.* **par'apeted** having a parapet. [It. *parapetto*, from pfx. *para-* (see **parachute**) and It. *petto* — L. *pectus*, the breast.]

paraph *par'af*, *n.* a mark or flourish under one's signature. — *v.t.* to append a paraph to, to sign with initials. [Fr. *paraphe*; cf. **paragraph**.]

paraphasia *par-ə-fā'zh(y)ə*, *n.* a form of aphasia in which one word is substituted for another. — *adj.* **paraphasic** (*-fā'zik*, *-sik*). [**para-**[1] and **aphasia**.]

paraphernalia *par-ə-fər-nāl'yə*, *-i-ə*, *n.pl.* formerly, property other than dower that remained under a married woman's own control, esp. articles of jewellery, dress, personal belongings: (the following all now usu. *n.sing.*) ornaments of dress of any kind: trappings: equipment: miscellaneous accessories. [Late L. *paraphernālia* — *parapherna* — Gr., from *para*, beside, beyond, *phernē*, a dowry — *pherein*, to bring.]

paraphilia *par-ə-fil'i-ə*, *n.* sexual perversion. — *n.* **paraphiliac** (*-fil'i-ak*) one who indulges in abnormal sexual practices. — Also *adj.* [**para-**[1] and Gr. *philia*, fondness, liking for.]

paraphimosis *par-ə-fī-mō'sis*, *n.* strangulation of the glans penis by constriction of the prepuce. [**para-**[1] and **phimosis**.]

paraphonia *par-ə-fō'ni-ə*, *n.* in Byzantine music, a melodic progression by fourths and fifths: a morbid change of voice: an alteration of the voice, as at puberty. — *adj.* **paraphonic** (*-fon'ik*). [Gr. *para*, beside, beyond, *phōnē*, voice.]

paraphrase *par'ə-frāz*, *n.* expression of the same thing in other words: an exercise in such expression: a verse rendering of a biblical passage for church singing, esp. in the Church of Scotland. — *v.t.* to express in other words. — *v.i.* to make a paraphrase. — *ns.* **par'aphraser**, **par'aphrast** (*-frast*) one who paraphrases. — *adjs.* **paraphrast'ic**, **-al**. — *adv.* **paraphrast'ically**. [Gr. *paraphrasis* — *para*, beside, beyond, *phrasis*, a speaking — *phrazein*, to speak.]

paraphraxia, **-phraxis** *par-ə-fraks'i-ə*, *-fraks'is*, *ns.* inability to perform purposive movements properly. [**para-**[1] and Gr. *phraxis*, barricade.]

paraphrenia *par-ə-frē'ni-ə*, *n.* any mental disorder of the paranoid type. [**para-**[1] and Gr. *phrēn*, mind.]

paraphysis *pə-raf'i-sis*, *n.* a sterile filament among spore-bearing structures in lower plants: — *pl.* **paraphyses** (*-sēz*). [Gr., a side-growth — *para*, beside, beyond, *physis*, growth.]

parapineal *par-ə-pin'i-əl*, *adj.* beside the pineal gland — applied to the pineal eye. [**para-**[1] and **pineal**.]

paraplegia *par-ə-plē'j(y)ə*, *n.* paralysis of the lower part of the body. — *adj.* **paraplegic** (*-plēj'* or *-plej'*). — *n.* a person suffering from paraplegia. [Ionic Gr. *paraplēgiē*, a stroke on the side — *para*, beside, beyond, *plēgē*, a blow.]

parapodium *par-ə-pō'di-əm*, *n.* one of the jointless lateral appendages of polychaete worms, etc.: a swimming organ in some molluscs, a lateral expansion of the foot: — *pl.* **parapō'dia**. — *adj.* **parapō'dial**. [Gr. *para*, beside, beyond, *pous, podos*, a foot.]

parapophysis *par-ə-pof'i-sis, n.* a ventral transverse process of a vertebra: — *pl.* **parapoph'yses** (*-sēz*). — *adj.* **parapophysial** (*par-ap-ō-fiz'i-əl*). [**para-**[1] and **apophysis.**]

parapsychism *par-ə-sī'kizm, n.* panpsychistic parallelism. — *adjs.* **parapsy'chic, -al; parapsycholog'ical.** — *ns.* **parapsychol'ogist; parapsychol'ogy** psychical research: the study of phenomena such as telepathy and clairvoyance which seem to suggest that the mind can gain knowledge by means other than the normal perceptual processes; **parapsychō'sis** an abnormal psychosis. [**para-**[1] and **psychism.**]

paraquadrate *par-ə-kwod'rāt, n.* the squamosal. [**para-**[1] and **quadrate.**]

paraquat *par'ə-kwot, n.* a weed-killer very poisonous to human beings. [**para-**[1] and *quat*ernary, part of its formula.]

paraquito *par-ə-kē'tō.* See **parakeet.**

para-red *par'ə-red', n.* an azo-dye for cottons, derived from paranitroaniline. [**para-**[1].]

pararhyme *par'ə-rīm, n.* a form of rhyme in which the consonants, but not the vowel, of the last stressed syllable are identical in sound, as in *hair* and *hour.* [**para-**[1], **rhyme.**]

pararosaniline *par-ə-roz-an'i-lēn, n.* a base entering into various dyestuffs, such as magenta. [**para-**[1] and **rosaniline.**]

pararthria *par-är'thri-ə, n.* disordered articulation of speech. [Gr. *para*, beside, beyond, *arthron*, a joint.]

parasailing *par'ə-sā-ling, n.* a sport similar to paragliding, the participant wearing water-skis and a modified type of parachute, and being towed into the air by motorboat. [**para-**[2], **sailing.**]

parasang *par'ə-sang, n.* an old Persian measure of length, reckoned at 30 stadia, or between 3 and 4 miles. [Gr. *parasangēs*, from O.Pers. (mod. Pers. *farsang*).]

parascending *par'ə-sen-ding, n.* a sport similar to paragliding, the participant being towed into the wind behind a motor vehicle. [**para-**[2], **ascending.**]

parascenium *par-ə-sē'ni-əm, n.* in the Greek theatre, a wing, side-scene: — *pl.* **parascē'nia.** [Gr. *paraskēnion* — *para*, beside, beyond, *skēnē*, tent, stage.]

parasceve *par'ə-sēv, par-ə-sē'vē, n.* preparation (*obs.*): the eve of the Jewish Sabbath, Friday, the day of preparation (*arch.*): Good Friday (*R.C. Church*). [L.L. *parascēvē* — Gr. *paraskeuē*, preparation — *para*, beside, beyond, *skeuē*, equipment.]

parascience *par'ə-sī-əns, n.* the study of phenomena which cannot be investigated by rigorous traditional scientific method. [**para-**[1] and **science.**]

paraselene *par-ə-se-lē'nē, n.* a mock moon: — *pl.* **paraselē'nae** (*-nē*). [Gr. *para*, beside, beyond, *selēnē*, moon.]

parasite *par'ə-sīt, n.* a hanger-on or sycophant who frequents another's table: one who lives at the expense of society or of others and contributes nothing: an organism that lives in or on another organism and derives subsistence from it without rendering it any service in return: in literary but not scientific use extended to an epiphyte. — *n.***parasitaemia** (*-ē'mi-ə;* Gr. *haima*, blood) the presence of parasites in the blood. — *adjs.* **parasitic** (*-sit'ik*), **-al** of, of the nature of, caused by, or like, a parasite. — *adv.* **parasit'ically.** — *ns.* **parasit'icalness; parasiticide** (*-sit'i-sīd*) that which destroys parasites. — *v.t.* **par'asitise, -ize** to be a parasite on (another organism): to infect or infest with parasites. — *n.* **par'asitism** (*-sīt-izm*) the act or practice of being a parasite. — *adj.* **par'asitoid** (*-sīt-*) parasitic in one phase of the life-history, thereafter independent. — Also *n.* — *ns.* **parasitol'ogist; parasitol'ogy; parasītō'sis** infestation with parasites. [Gr. *parasītos* — *para*, beside, and *sītos*, corn, bread, food.]

parasol *par'ə-sol,* or *-sol', n.* a sunshade: an aeroplane with its wings overhead. — **parasol mushroom** a tall white edible mushroom (*Lepiota procera*) resembling a parasol. [Fr., — It. *parasole* — *para*, imper. of

parare, to ward — L. *parāre*, to prepare, and *sole* — L. *sōl, sōlis*, the sun.]

parasphenoid *par-ə-sfē'noid, adj.* alongside the sphenoid bone. — *n.* a bone of the skull, part of the cranial floor. [**para**[1], **sphenoid** (see **sphene**).]

parastatal *par-ə-stā'tl, adj.* indirectly controlled by the state. [**para-**[1] and **statal** (see **state**).]

parastichy *pər-as'ti-ki, (bot.) n.* a secondary spiral joining leaf-bases on an axis, visible where the leaves are crowded together, e.g. the scales of a pine-cone. [Gr. *para*, beside, beyond, *stichos*, a row.]

parasuicide *par-ə-sū'i-sīd, -sōō', n.* a deliberate harmful act against one's own person (such as taking an overdose of drugs) which appears to be an attempt at suicide but which was probably not intended to be successful: a person who performs such an act. [**para-**[1], **suicide.**]

parasympathetic *par-ə-sim-pə-thet'ik.* See **sympathy.**

parasynthesis *par-ə-sin'thi-sis, n.* derivation of words from compounds, as *come-at-able*, where *come* and *at* are first compounded and then the derivative suffix *-able* added. — *adj.* **parasynthetic** (*-thet'ik*). — *n.* **parasyn'theton** a word so formed: — *pl.* **parasyn'theta.** [Gr.]

parataxis *par-ə-tak'sis, (gram.) n.* the arrangement of clauses or propositions without connectives. — *adjs.* **paratac'tic, -al.** — *adv.* **paratac'tically.** [Gr., — *para*, beside, beyond, *taxis*, arrangement.]

paratha *pə-rä'tə, -tä, n.* a thin cake of flour, water and ghee, originating in India. [Hindi.]

parathesis *pə-rath'i-sis, n.* apposition (*gram.*): compounding of words without change, as L. *respublica* from *res* and *publica* (*philol.*). [Gr., placing alongside.]

parathyroid *par-ə-thī'roid, adj.* beside the thyroid. — *n.* any of a number of small ductless glands apparently concerned with calcium metabolism. [**para-**[1] and **thyroid.**]

paratonic *par-ə-ton'ik, (bot.) adj.* induced by external stimulus. [Gr. *para*, beside, beyond, *tonos*, a stretching.]

paratroops *par'ə-trōōps, n.pl.* troops carried by air, to be dropped by parachute. — *n.* **par'atrooper.** [**para-**[2] and **troop.**]

paratyphoid *par-ə-tī'foid, n.* a disease (of various types) resembling typhoid. — Also *adj.* [**para-**[1].]

paravail *par-ə-vāl', adj.* inferior: lowest, said of a feudal tenant: of least account — opp. to **paramount.** [O.Fr. *par aval*, below — L. *per*, through, *ad*, to, *vallem*, accus. of *vallis*, valley.]

paravane *par'ə-vān, n.* a fish-shaped device, with fins or vanes, towed from the bow, for deflecting mines along a wire and severing their moorings — sometimes called an 'otter': an explosive device of similar design for attacking submerged submarines. [**para-**[1] and **vane.**]

paravant, paravaunt *par-ə-vänt', -vönt', (Spens.) adv.* in front, first, beforehand, pre-eminently. [O.Fr. *paravant* — *par*, through, *avant*, before — L. *ab*, from, *ante*, before.]

parawalker *par'ə-wök-ər, n.* a metal structure like an external skeleton worn by a paraplegic to enable him to walk. [**para-**[1] and **walker** (see **walk**).]

Parazoa *par-ə-zō'ə, n.pl.* a division of the animal kingdom, the sponges, co-ordinate with *Protozoa* and *Metazoa* (also without *cap.*). — *n.* and *adj.* **parazō'an.** — *n.* **parazō'on** any member of the group Parazoa: — *pl.* **-zō'a.** [Gr. *para*, beside, beyond, *zōion*, animal.]

parboil *pär'boil, v.t.* orig., to boil thoroughly: (now, by confusion) to boil slightly. [O.Fr. *parboillir* — L.L. *perbullīre*, to boil thoroughly; influenced by confusion with **part.**]

parbreak *pär'brāk, (arch.) n.* a vomit. — *v.t.* and *v.i.* (*pär'* or *-brāk'*) to vomit: — *pa.p.* **parbreaked.** [M.E. *brake*, to vomit; cf. Du. *braken*; the pfx. may be Fr. *par-*.]

parbuckle *pär'buk-l, n.* a purchase made by making fast a rope in the middle and passing the ends under and then over a heavy object to be rolled up or down: a sling made by passing both ends of a rope through its bight. — *v.t.* to hoist or lower by a parbuckle. [Earlier *parbunkel, parbuncle*; origin unknown.]

Parca pär'kə, *n.* a Fate, any one of the Roman goddesses Nona, Decuma, and Morta, identified with the Greek Moirai: — *pl.* **Par'cae** (-sē). [L., prob. conn. with *parĕre*, to produce, not *parcĕre*, to spare.]

parcel pär'sl, *n.* a little part: a portion: a quantity: a group: a set: a pack (depreciatively): a lot: an item (*arch.*): a sum of money lost or won (*coll.*): a package, esp. one wrapped in paper and tied with string: a continuous stretch of land. — *adv.* (*arch.*) partly. — *adj.* (*arch.*) in part. — *v.t.* to divide into portions (esp. with *out*): to make up into parcels or a parcel (esp. with *up*): possibly, to make up into a total, complete, round off, or to add up or detail, item by item (Shak., *Ant. and Cleo.*, V, ii): to cover with tarred canvas (*naut.*): — *pr.p.* **par'celling;** *pa.t.* and *pa.p.* **par'celled.** — *adv.* **par'celwise** by parcels, piecemeal. — **par'cel-bawd** (*Shak.*) one partly a bawd; **parcel bomb** a bomb wrapped in a parcel and designed to detonate when unwrapped. — *adj.* **par'cel-gilt'** partially gilded. — **parcel post** (also, formerly, **parcels post**) a Post Office service forwarding and delivering parcels. [Fr. *parcelle* (It. *particella*) — L. *particula*, dim. of *pars, partis*, a part.]

parcener pär'sən-ər, *n.* a co-heir. — *n.* **par'cenary** (-ə-ri), co-heirship. [A.Fr. *parcener* — L.L. *partōnārius* — *pars*, part.]

parch pärch, *v.t.* to make hot and very dry: to roast slightly: to scorch. — *v.i.* to be scorched: to become very dry. — *adj.* **parched.** — *adv.* **parch'edly.** — *n.* **parch'edness** (or pärcht'). [Origin unknown.]

Parcheesi® pär-chē'zi, *n.* a board game adapted from pachisi (also without *cap.* and with one *e*).

parchment pärch'mənt, *n.* the skin of a sheep, goat, or other animal prepared for writing on, etc.: a piece of this material: a manuscript written on it: a parchment-like membrane or skin. — *adj.* of parchment. — *v.t.* **parch'mentise, -ize** to make like parchment, esp. by treating with sulphuric acid. — *adj.* **parch'menty** like parchment. — **parchment paper** or **vegetable parchment** unsized paper made tough and transparent by dipping in sulphuric acid. — **virgin parchment** a fine kind of parchment made from the skins of new-born lambs or kids. [Fr. *parchemin* — L. *pergamēna* (*charta*), Pergamene (paper) — from Gr. *Pergamos*, Bergama, in Asia Minor.]

parcimony. An arch. spelling of **parsimony.**

parclose pär'klōz, *n.* a screen or railing in a church enclosing an altar or tomb, or separating a chapel or other portion from the main body of the church. [O.Fr. pa.p. (fem.) of *parclore* — L. *per*, through, *claudĕre, clausum*, to close.]

pard¹ pärd, *n.* the leopard. — *ns.* **pard'al** (-əl), **pard'ale** (-əl, -āl; *Spens.*), **pard'alis** a pard: a small pard once supposed a different species. — *adjs.* **pard'ed** spotted; **pard'ine** (-īn). [L. *pardus* (masc.), *pardalis* (fem.) — Gr. *pardos, pardalis*; prob. of Eastern origin.]

pard² pärd, **pard'ner** -nər, (*U.S.*) *ns.* slang forms of **partner.**

pardi, pardie, pardy. See **perdie.**

pardon pär'dn, *v.t.* to forgive: to allow to go unpunished: to excuse: to tolerate: to grant in remission, refrain from exacting or taking: to grant remission of sentence to (even if the condemned has been found innocent). — *v.i.* to forgive: to grant pardon. — *n.* forgiveness, either of an offender or of his offence: remission of a penalty or punishment: forbearance: a warrant declaring a pardon: a papal indulgence: a festival at which indulgences are granted (*obs.*). — *adj.* **par'donable** that may be pardoned: excusable. — *n.* **par'donableness.** — *adv.* **par'donably.** — *n.* **par'doner** one who pardons: a licensed seller of papal indulgences (*hist.*). — *n.* and *adj.* **par'doning.** — *adj.* **par'donless** unpardonable. — **I beg your pardon, pardon?** what did you say?; **pardon me** excuse me — used in apology and to soften a

contradiction. [Fr. *pardonner* — L.L. *perdōnāre* — L. *per*, through, away, *dōnāre*, to give.]

pare pār, *v.t.* to cut or shave off the outer surface or edge of: to trim: to remove by slicing or shaving: to diminish by small amounts. — *ns.* **pār'er; par'ing** the act of trimming or cutting off: that which is pared off: the cutting off of the surface of grassland for tillage. — **paring chisel** a long, thin chisel with bevelled edges. [Fr. *parer* — L. *parāre*, to prepare.]

parecious. See **paroicous.**

paregoric par-i-gor'ik, *adj.* soothing, lessening pain. — *n.* a medicine that soothes pain: an alcoholic solution of opium, benzoic acid, camphor, and oil of anise. [Gr. *parēgorikos* — *parēgoreein*, to exhort, comfort — *para*, beside, beyond, and *agorā*, marketplace.]

pareira pə-rā'rə, *n.* orig., a tropical menispermaceous climbing plant (*Cissampelos pareira*) or its root (now called **false pareira**): a South American plant of the same family (*Chondrodendron tomentosum*, **pareira brava** brä'və, i.e. wild): a tonic diuretic drug derived from its root. — **white pareira** (*Abuta rufescens*) another South American plant of the same family. [Port. *parreira*, wallclimber.]

parella pə-rel'ə, *n.* a crustaceous lichen (*Lecanora parella*) yielding archil: extended to others of like use. — Also **parelle'.** [Fr. *parelle*.]

parencephalon par-en-sef'ə-lon, *n.* a cerebral hemisphere. [Gr. *para*, beside, beyond, *enkephalon*, brain.]

parenchyma pə-reng'ki-mə, *n.* the ordinary soft thin-walled tissue of plants, not differentiated into conducting or mechanical tissue: soft spongy indeterminate tissue in animals. — *adj.* **parenchym'atous.** [Gr. *para*, beside, beyond, *enchyma*, infusion, inpouring.]

parenesis. See **paraenesis.**

parent pā'rənt, *n.* one who begets or brings forth: a father or a mother: one who, or that which, produces: that from which anything springs or branches: an author: a cause: as a Gallicism, a relative. — *adj.* referring to an organisation, etc., which has established (a) branch(es), over which it usu. retains some control. — *v.t.* and *v.i.* to be, act as, a parent (to). — *n.* **pā'rentage** descent from parents: extraction: rank or character derived from one's parents or ancestors: the relation of parents to their children: the state or fact of being a parent: parents collectively, or perh. parent (*Spens.*). — *adj.* **parental** (pə-rent'əl). — *adv.* **parent'ally.** — *ns.* **pā'renthood** the state of being a parent: the duty or feelings of a parent; **pā'renting.** — *adj.* **pā'rentless** without a parent. — **parent company** a company that holds most of the shares of another company; **par'ent= craft** the techniques of nurturing children. [Fr. *parent*, kinsman — L. *parēns, -entis*, old pr.p. of *parēre*, to bring forth.]

parenteral par-en'tər-əl, *adj.* not intestinal: not by way of the alimentary tract (said of the administration of a drug). — *adv.* **paren'terally.** [Gr. *para*, beside, and **enteral.**]

parenthesis pə-ren'thi-sis, *n.* a word or passage of comment or explanation inserted in a sentence which is grammatically complete without it: a figure of speech consisting of the use of such insertion: a digression: an interval, space, interlude: (usu. in *pl.*) a round bracket () used to mark off a parenthesis: — *pl.* **paren'theses** (-sēz). — *v.i.* **parenth'esise, -ize.** — *adjs.* **parenthetic** (*par-ən-thet'ik*), **-al** of the nature of a parenthesis: using or over-using parenthesis. — *adv.* **parenthet'ically.** [Gr., — *para*, beside, beyond, *en*, in, *thesis*, a placing.]

pareo. See **pareu.**

Pareoean par-ē-ē'ən, *adj.* of a race inhabiting South China, Burma, etc. — otherwise called Southern Mongoloid. — Also *n.* [Gr. *para*, beside, *ēōs*, dawn.]

parergon par-ûr'gon, *n.* a by-work, any work subsidiary to another: — *pl.* **parer'ga.** [Gr., — *para*, beside, beyond, *ergon*, work.]

paresis par'i-sis, *n.* a diminished activity of function — a partial form of paralysis. — *adj.* **paretic** (-et'ik). —

general paresis (*med.*) the manifestation of a syphilitic infection of long standing, consisting of progressive dementia and generalised paralysis. [Gr., — *parienai*, to relax.]

paresthesia. See paraesthesia.

pareu *pa-rä'ŏŏ*, **pareo** *pa-rä'ō, ns.* a wraparound skirt worn by men and women in Polynesia. [Tahitian.]

par excellence *pär ek'se-läs, ek'sa-lans,* as an example of excellence: superior to all others of the same sort. [Fr., lit. by excellence.]

parfait *pär-fe', n.* a kind of frozen dessert containing whipped cream and eggs. [Fr., lit. perfect.]

parfleche *pär-flesh', n.* a dried skin, usu. of buffalo: an article made of it. [App. Canadian Fr.]

pargana, pergunnah *par-gun'a, -ä, n.* a division of a zillah in India. [Hind. and Pers. *parganah.*]

pargasite *pär'ga-sīt, n.* a green amphibole. [*Pargas* in Finland.]

parget *pär'jit, v.t.* to plaster over: to cover with ornamental plaster-work: to decorate the surface of: to bedaub: — *pr.p.* **par'geting;** *pa.t.* and *pa.p.* **par'geted.** — *n.* plaster spread over a surface: cow-dung plaster for chimney flues: ornamental work in plaster. surface decoration. — *v.t.* **parge** to plaster. — *ns.* **par'geter; par'geting.** — **parge'-work.** — The irregular forms **par'getting,** etc., are used by some. [App. O.Fr. *parjeter,* to throw all over.]

parhelion *pär-hēl'i-an, n.* a mock sun: — *pl.* **parhē'lia.** — *adjs.* **parhelic** (*-hē'lik, -he'lik*), **parheliacal** (*-hē-lī'a-kl*). [Irregularly — Gr. *parēlion* — *para,* beside, beyond, *hēlios,* sun.]

parhypate *pär-hip'a-tē,* (Gr. *mus.*) *n.* the lowest note but one in a tetrachord — next above the hypate. [Gr. *para,* beside, beyond; see **hypate.**]

pariah *pa-rī'a, par'i-a, pär', n.* a member of a caste in Southern India lower than the four Brahminical castes: one of low or no caste: a social outcast: an ownerless cur of Eastern towns (in full **pariah dog**), a pye-dog. [Tamil *paraiyar.*]

parial. Same as **pairial;** see under **pair[1].**

Parian *pä'ri-an, adj.* of the island of *Paros,* in the Aegean Sea. — *n.* a native or inhabitant of Paros: a fine porcelain like marble. — **Parian marble** a fine white marble found in Paros.

parietal *pa-rī'i-tl, adj.* of a wall or walls: of, attached to, or having connection with, the side, or the inside of the wall, of a cavity, esp. a plant ovary: pertaining to or near the parietal bone: residing, or relating to residence, within the walls of a college (*U.S.*). — *n.* a bone (**parietal bone**), forming with its fellow part of the sides and top of the skull, between the frontal and the occipital. — **parietal cells** cells in the stomach lining that produce hydrochloric acid. [L. *parietālis* — *pariēs, parietis,* a wall.]

pari-mutuel *par-ē-mü-tü-el, n.* a betting-machine which automatically pools stakes and distributes winnings — a totalisator. [Fr., lit. mutual bet.]

pari passu *pä'rī pas'ū, pa'rē pas'ŏŏ,* (L.) with equal pace: together.

paripinnate *par-i-pin'it, -āt,* (*bot.*) *adj.* pinnate without a terminal leaflet. [L. *pär,* equal.]

Paris *par'is, n.* the capital of France. — *adj.* of, originating in, Paris. — *adj.* **Parisian** (*pa-ri'zyan, -zhyan, -zhan*) of or pertaining to Paris. — *n.* a native or resident of Paris: — *Fr. fem.* **Parisienne** (*pa-rē-zē-en, -zyen'*). — **Paris doll** (*obs.*) a small figure dressed in the latest fashions, sent out by Paris modistes; **Paris green** copper arsenite and acetate, a pigment and insecticide. [L. *Parīsiī,* the Gallic tribe of the Paris district.]

parischan(e). See **parochin(e).**

parish *par'ish, n.* a district having its own church and minister or priest of the Established Church: a district assigned by a church to a minister or priest: a division of a county for administrative and local government purposes (not now in Scotland): in Louisiana, a county: the people of a parish: a congregation or a denomination (*U.S.*). — *adj.* belonging or relating to

a parish: employed or supported by the parish: for the use of the parish. — *ns.* **par'ishen** see **parochin; parishioner** (*pa-rish'a-nar*) one who belongs to or is connected with a parish: a member of a parish church. — **parish church** the church of the establishment for a parish; **parish clerk** the clerk or recording officer of a parish: the one who leads the responses in the service of the Church of England; **parish council** a body elected to manage the affairs of a parish; **parish councillor; parish minister, priest** a minister or priest who has charge of a parish; **parish pump** the symbol of petty local interests; **parish register** a book in which the baptisms, marriages, and burials in a parish are recorded; **parish top** a spinning-top formerly kept for the amusement of the parish. — **on the parish** in receipt of poor-relief. [A.Fr. *paroche* (Fr. *paroisse*) — L. *parochia* — Gr. *paroikiā,* an ecclesiastical district — *para,* beside, *oikos,* a dwelling; altered by confusion with Gr. *parochos,* a purveyor.]

parison *par'i-san, n.* a lump of glass before it is moulded into its final shape. [Fr *paraison* — *parer,* to prepare — L. *parāre.*]

parisyllabic *par-i-si-lab'ik, adj.* having the same number of syllables. [L. *pār,* equal.]

paritor *par'i-tar,* (Shak.) *n.* aphetic for **apparitor.**

parity[1] *par'i-ti, n.* equality in status: parallelism: equivalence: a standard equivalence in currency: of numbers, the property of being odd or even (*math.*). — **parity check** (*comput.*) the addition of a redundant bit to a word to make the total number of 1's even or odd in order to detect simple bit errors; **parity law** a law that a symmetry obtains in the natural world with no distinction between right and left, long held as basic, but shown in 1957 not to apply in the field of nuclear physics. [Fr. *parité* — L. *paritās* — *pār,* equal.]

parity[2] *par'i-ti, n.* the condition or fact of having borne children. [L. *parĕre,* to bring forth.]

park *pärk, n.* an enclosed piece of land for beasts of the chase: a tract of land surrounding a mansion, kept as a pleasure-ground: hence often part of the name of a house, street, or district: a piece of ground for public recreation: a football, etc. pitch (*coll.*): a piece of country kept in its natural condition as a nature-reserve or the like: a paddock, grass field (*Scot.*): a field (*Ireland*): a level valley among mountains (*U.S.*): a place occupied by artillery, wagons, etc. (*mil.*): a piece of ground where motor-cars or other vehicles may be left untended: an enclosed basin for oyster-culture. — *v.t.* to enclose in a park: to make a park of: to bring together in a body, as artillery: to place and leave (a vehicle) in a parking-place or elsewhere: to deposit and leave (*coll.*). — *v.i.* to leave a vehicle in a car park, parking-place, or elsewhere. — *ns.* **park'er** a park-keeper (*obs.*): one who parks a vehicle; **park'ing** the action of the verb park: a turf strip, sometimes with trees, along the middle of a street (*U.S.*). — *adjs.* **park'ish; park'like; park'ly.** — *advs.* **park'ward, -s.** — **parking lot** (*U.S.*) a car park; **parking meter** a coin-operated meter that charges for motor-car parking-time; **park'ing-place** a place where one may temporarily stop and leave a vehicle; **park'ing-ticket** a notice of a fine, or summons to appear in court, for a parking offence; **park'-keeper** a park-officer; **park'land, -s** park-like grassland dotted with trees; **park'-off'icer** the keeper of a park; **park'way** a broad road adorned with turf and trees, often connecting the parks of a town. — **science park** see **science.** [O.Fr. *parc,* of Gmc. origin; cf. O.E. *pearruc, pearroc.*]

parka *pärk'a, n.* a fur shirt or coat with a hood, or a similar garment made of a wind-proof material. — Also **parkee, parki** (*pärk'ē*). [Aleutian Eskimo word.]

parkin *pär'kin,* **perkin** *pûr'kin,* (Northern) *ns.* a biscuit or gingerbread of oatmeal and treacle. [Ety. unknown.]

Parkinson's disease *pär'kin-sanz diz-ēz',* shaking palsy, a disease characterised by rigidity of muscles, tremor of

hands, etc.; studied by James *Parkinson* (1755-1824). — Also **Par′kinsonism.**
Parkinson's law *pär′kin-sənz lö*, (*facet.*) any one of the laws propounded by C. Northcote *Parkinson*, esp. the law that in officialdom work expands so as to fill the time available for its completion.
parkleaves *pärk′lēvz, n.* tutsan. [App. **park, leaf.**]
parky *pär′ki*, (*coll.*) *adj.* chilly. [Origin unknown.]
parlance. See under **parle.**
parlando *pär-län′dō* (*mus.*) *adj.* and *adv.* in declamatory style: recitative. [It., speaking; cf. **parle.**]
parlay *pär′lā, v.t.* to bet (orig. stake plus winnings), or lay out (orig. investment plus earnings), in a later venture: to succeed in converting (an asset) into something more valuable. — Also *n.* [Fr. *paroli*; from Neapolitan.]
parle *pärl*, (*arch.*) *v.i.* to talk: to confer: to parley. — *n.* talk: speech: parleying. — *n.* **par′lance** speaking (*arch.*): conversation (*arch.*): diction, phraseology, jargon, mode of speech. — *v.i.* **par′ley** to speak with another: to confer: to treat with an enemy. — *n.* talk: a conference with an enemy: a conference. — *n.* **parley-voo′** (*slang*) French: a Frenchman. — *v.i.* to speak French. [Fr. *parler*, to speak (*parlez-vous?* do you speak?) — L.L. *parlāre* — *parabolāre* — Gr. *parabolē*, a parable, word.]
parley. See under **parle, parliament.**
parliament *pär′lə-mənt, n.* a meeting for deliberation: a legislative body: in France, down to the Revolution, one of certain superior and final courts of judicature, in which also the edicts of the king were registered before becoming law: gingerbread in the form of rectangular biscuits (**par′liament-cake;** *Scot.* **par′ley, par′ly**). — *n.* **parliamentā′rian** an adherent of Parliament in opposition to Charles I: one skilled in the ways of parliament. — *adj.* on the side of parliament. — *adv.* **parliamentarily** (*-ment′ər-i-li*). — *n.* **parliament′-arism** the principles of parliamentary government: the parliamentary system. — *adj.* **parliament′ary** pertaining to parliament: enacted, enjoined, or done by parliament: according to the rules and practices of legislative bodies: (of language) civil, decorous: for Parliament against the Royalists. — *n.* **parliamenting** (*-ment′ing*) acting as member of parliament: debating. — **parliamentary agent** a person employed by private persons or societies for drafting bills or managing business to be brought before parliament; **parliamentary burgh** see **burgh; parliamentary train** a railway train which, by act of parliament (1844), ran daily with sufficient accommodation for passengers at a penny a mile; **par′liament-heel** a slight careening of a ship; **par′liament-hinge′** a hinge allowing a door to be laid back along the wall; **par′liament-house** a building where parliament sits or has sat; **par′liament-man′** a member of parliament: a parliamentarian. — **act of parliament** a statute that has passed through both the House of Commons and the House of Lords, and received the formal royal assent; **(Act of) Parliament clock** a type of wall clock (usu. of mahogany, and with a large uncovered dial; found esp. in taverns) which became popular c. 1797 in response to an act of parliament imposing a tax on all clocks and watches; **Parliamentary Commissioner for Administration** see **Ombudsman.** [Fr. *parlement* — *parler*, to speak.]
parlour *pär′lər, n.* a room where conversation is allowed in a monastery or nunnery: a private room for conversation or conference in a public building, office, etc.: a more or less private room in an inn or tavern: a simple unpretentious drawing-room or dining-room, or a smaller room of similar kind: a family sitting-room or living-room: a shop fitted like a room, or a room attached to a shop, esp. for personal services to customers (*U.S.*). — *adj.* used in or suitable for a parlour. — **par′lour-board′er** a pupil at a boarding-school who enjoys particular privileges; **par′lo(u)r-car** (*U.S.*) a luxuriously fitted railway saloon carriage; **parlour game** an (esp. informal) indoor game; **par′lour-**

maid a maid-servant who waits at table; **parlour pink** a rather tepid Socialist; **parlour tricks** minor social accomplishments: performances intended to impress. — **beauty parlour, funeral parlour** see **beauty, funeral; milking parlour** a special room or building in which cows are milked. [A.Fr. *parlur* (Fr. *parloir*) — *parler*, to speak.]
parlous *pär′ləs, adj.* perilous. — *adv.* (*arch.* and *facet.*) extremely. [A form of **perilous.**]
parly. See under **parliament.**
parmacitie *pär-məs-it′i, n. Shak.* for **spermaceti.**
Parmesan *pär-mi-zan′*, or *pär′, adj.* pertaining to *Parma* in N. Italy. — *n.* Parmesan cheese, a hard dry cheese made from skimmed milk mixed with rennet and saffron. — **Parma violet** Neapolitan violet.
Parnassus *pär-nas′əs, n.* a mountain in Greece, sacred to Apollo and the Muses: a collection of poems. — *adj.* **Parnass′ian** of Parnassus: of the Muses: of a school of French poetry supposed to believe in art for art's sake (from the collections published as *le Parnasse contemporain*, 1866-76). — *n.* a poet: a member of the Parnassian school. — *n.* **Parnass′ianism.** — **grass of Parnassus** a white-flowered plant of wet moors (*Parnassia palustris*) of the saxifrage family.
Parnellism *pär′nəl-izm, n.* the principles and policy of Charles Stewart *Parnell* (1846-91) who sought to promote Home Rule for Ireland. — *n.* **Par′nellite** a follower of Parnell. — Also *adj.*
paroccipital *par-ok-sip′i-tl, adj.* near the occiput. [**para-**[1] and **occiput.**]
parochial *pə-rō′ki-əl, adj.* of or relating to a parish: restricted or confined within narrow limits — of sentiments, tastes, etc.: denominational (*U.S.*). — *v.t.* **parō′chialise, -ize** to make parochial: to form into parishes. — *v.i.* to do parish work. — *ns.* **parō′chialism** a system of local government which makes the parish the unit: provincialism, narrowness of view; **parōchiality** (*-al′*). — *adv.* **parō′chially.** — **parochial board** (formerly, in Scotland) a board charged with poor-relief. [L. *parochiālis* — *parochia*; see **parish.**]
parochin(e), parischan(e), parishen(e) *pä′rish-in*, (*Scot.*) *n.* a parish.
parody *par′ə-di, n.* a burlesque or satirical imitation. — *v.t.* to make a parody of: — *pr.p.* **par′odying;** *pa.t.* and *pa.p.* **par′odied.** — *adjs.* **parod′ic(al).** — *n.* **par′odist.** — *adj.* **parodist′ic.** [Gr. *parōidiā* — *para*, beside, *ōidē*, an ode.]
paroemia *pə-rē′mi-ə, n.* a proverb, adage. — *adj.* **paroe′-miac.** — *n.* (*Gr. pros.*) the anapaestic dimeter catalectic. — *adj.* **paroe′mial.** — *ns.* **paroemiog′rapher** a writer or collector of proverbs; **paroemiog′raphy; paroemiol′ogy** the study of proverbs. [Gr. *paroimiā*, a proverb — *paroimos*, by the road — *oimos*, road.]
paroicous *pə-roi′kəs*, (*bot.*) *adj.* (of certain mosses) having the male and female reproductive organs beside or near each other. — Also **par(o)ecious** (*pə-rē′shəs*). [Gr. *paroikos*, dwelling beside — *para*, beside, *oikos*, a dwelling.]
parol. See **parole.**
parole *pə-rōl′, n.* word of mouth: word of honour (esp. by a prisoner of war, to fulfil certain conditions; *mil.*): the condition of having given one's word of honour, or privilege of having it accepted: conditional release of a prisoner: officers' daily password in a camp or garrison: (usu. *pa-rol′*) language as manifested in the speech of individuals, as opposed to *langue* (*linguistics*). — *adj.* pertaining to parole: (usu. **parol,** usu. *par′*) given by word of mouth — opp. to *documentary*, as *parol* evidence. — *v.t.* **parole′** to put on parole: to release on parole. — *v.i.* to give parole. — *n.* **parolee′** a prisoner who has been conditionally released. [Fr. *parole*, word — L. *parabola*, a parable, saying — Gr.; see **parable.**]
paronomasia *par-on-o-mā′syə*, *-zyə*, *-zh(y)ə, n.* a play upon words — also **paronom′asy** (*-ə-si*, *-ə-zi*). — *adjs.* **paronomastic** (*-mas′tik*), **-al.** — *n.* **paronym** (*par′o-nim*) a word from the same root, or having the same sound,

as another. — *adj.* **paron'ymous.** — *n.* **paron'ymy.** [Gr. *para*, beside, *onoma, onyma*, name.]

paronychia *par-o-nik'i-ə, n.* a whitlow: (with *cap.*) the whitlow-wort genus of plants. — *adj.* **paronych'ial.** [Gr. *para*, beside *onyx, onychos*, nail.]

paroquet. See **parakeet.**

parotid *pə-rot'id, -rōt', adj.* near the ear. — *n.* the parotid gland, a salivary gland in front of the ear — also **parō'tis.** — *adj.* **parōt'ic** near or adjacent to the ear. — *ns.* **parotidī'tis, parotī'tis** inflammation of the parotid gland, as in mumps. [Gr. *parōtis, -idos — para*, beside, *ous, ōtos*, ear.]

parousia *pə-rōō'zi-ə,* or *-row', (theol.) n.* the second coming of Christ. [Gr. *parousiā*, presence, arrival.]

paroxysm *par'oks-izm, n.* a fit of acute pain: a fit of passion, laughter, coughing, etc.: any sudden violent action. — *adj.* **paroxys'mal.** [Gr. *paroxysmos — para*, beyond, *oxys*, sharp.]

paroxytone *par-ok'si-tōn, adj.* in anc. Greek, having the acute accent on the last syllable but one: having a heavy stress on the penultimate syllable. — *n.* a word so accented. [Gr. *paroxytonos — para*, beside, *oxys*, acute, *tonos*, tone.]

parpen *pär'pən, n.* a stone passing through a wall from face to face: a wall of such stones: a partition: a bridge parapet. — Also **par'pane, par'pend, par'pent, par'point, per'pend, per'pent.** — **par'pen-stone; par'pen=wall.** [O.Fr. *parpain*.]

parquet *pär'kā, -kit, pär-kā', -ket', n.* a floor-covering of wooden blocks fitted in a pattern: the stalls of a theatre (*U.S.*; **parquet circle** that part of the floor behind these). — *adj.* of parquetry. — *v.t.* to cover or floor with parquetry: — *pa.p.* **par'queted, parquett'ed.** — *n.* **par'quetry** (*-ki-tri*) flooring in parquet. [Fr. *parquet*, dim. of *parc*, an enclosure.]

parr *pär, n.* a young salmon before it becomes a smolt: the young of several other kinds of fish. [Ety. unknown.]

parrakeet. See **parakeet.**

parral. See **parrel.**

parramatta. See **paramatta.**

parrel, parral *par'əl, n.* a band by which a yard is fastened to a mast. — **parrel truck** a wooden ball strung on a parrel. [Cf. O.Fr. *parail*, rigging.]

parrhesia *pa-rē'syə, -zyə, n.* boldness of speech. [Gr. *parrēsiā — para*, beside, beyond, *rhēsis*, speech.]

parricide *par'i-sīd, n.* the murder of a parent or near relative, or the murder of anyone to whom reverence is considered to be due: one who commits such a crime. — *adj.* **parricīd'al.** [Fr., — L. *parricīdium, pāricīdium* (the offence), *parricīda, pāricīda* (the offender), *caedēre*, to slay; the connection with *pater*, father, is apparently fanciful.]

parritch *pär', par'ich, n.* Scots form of **porridge.**

parrock *par'ək, (dial.) n.* a small field or enclosure, esp. one used for lambs: a paddock. — *v.t.* to confine in a parrock. [O.E. *pearroc*.]

parroquet. See **parakeet.**

parrot *par'ət, n.* one of a family of tropical and subtropical birds with brilliant plumage, hooked bill, and zygodactyl feet, good imitators of human speech: an uncritical repeater of the words of others. — *v.t.* to repeat by rote: to teach to repeat by rote. — *v.i.* to talk like a parrot (also *v.t.* with *it*): — *pa.p.* **parr'oted.** — *ns.* **parr'oter; parr'otry** unintelligent imitation. — *adj.* **parr'oty** like a parrot or parrot-coal. — **parr'ot=beak, -bill, -jaw** the New Zealand glory-pea, from the form of its flowers; **parr'ot-coal** (*Scot.*) cannel coal (possibly from chattering as it burns); **parr'ot-cry'** a catch-phrase senselessly repeated from mouth to mouth; **parr'ot-disease'** psittacosis. — *adv.* **parr'ot=fashion** by rote. — **parr'ot-fish** a name applied to various fishes, esp. of the wrasse family and the kindred Scaridae, from their colours or their powerful jaws; **parrot mouth** a congenital malformation of the jaw that occurs in horses and other grazing animals preventing normal feeding; **parr'ot-wrasse** a parrot-

fish, esp. that of the Mediterranean (*Scarus cretensis*), prized by the ancients. [Possibly Fr. *Perrot*, dim. of *Pierre*, Peter.]

parry *par'i, v.t.* to ward or keep off: to turn aside, block or evade: to avert: — *pr.p.* **parr'ying;** *pa.t.* and *pa.p.* **parr'ied.** — *n.* a turning aside of a blow or a thrust or of an attack of any kind, e.g. an argument or a jibe. [Perh. from Fr. *parez*, imper. of *parer* — L. *parāre*, to prepare, in L.L. to keep off.]

parse *pärz,* also *pärs, (gram.) v.t.* to describe (a word) fully from point of view of classification, inflexion, and syntax: to analyse (a sentence). — *ns.* **pars'er; pars'ing.** [L. *pars (ōrātiōnis)*, a part (of speech).]

parsec *pär'sek* or *pär-sek', n.* the distance (about 19 billion miles) at which half the major axis of the earth's orbit subtends an angle of one second, a unit for measurement of distances of stars. [**parallax, second.**]

Parsee, Parsi *pär'sē,* or *-sē', n.* a descendant of the Zoroastrians who emigrated from Persia to India in the 8th century: a Persian dialect dominant during the time of the Sassanidae. — Also *adj.* — *ns.* **Par'seeism, Par'siism** (or *-sē'*), **Par'sism** the religion of the Parsees. [Pers. *Pārsī — Pārs*, Persia.]

parsimony *pär'si-mən-i, n.* sparingness in the spending of money: praiseworthy economy in use of means to an end: avoidance of excess: frugality: niggardliness. — *adj.* **parsimonious** (*-mō'ni-əs*). — *adv.* **parsimō'niously.** — *n.* **parsimō'niousness.** — **law of parsimony** the principle of Occam's razor (see **Occamism**). [L. *parsimōnia — parcēre, parsus*, to spare.]

parsing. See **parse.**

parsley *pärs'li, n.* a bright green umbelliferous herb (*Carum petroselinum*) with finely divided, strongly scented leaves, used in cookery. — **parsley fern** a fern (*Cryptogramma crispa*) with bright green crisped leaves not unlike parsley. [O.E. *petersilie*, modified by Fr. *persil*, both — L. *petroselīnum* — Gr. *petroselīnon — petros*, a rock, *selīnon*, parsley.]

parsley-piert *pärs'li-pērt,* **parsley-pert** *-pûrt, ns.* a dwarf species of lady's-mantle (*Aphanes arvensis*), a weed of dry waste ground. [Prob. Fr. *perce-pierre*, lit. pierce-stone.]

parsnip, parsnep *pärs'nip, n.* an umbelliferous plant (*Pastinaca sativa* or *Peucedanum sativum*) or its edible carrot-like root. [L. *pastināca — pastinum*, a dibble; prob. affected by **neep.**]

parson *pär'sn, n.* the priest or incumbent of a parish: a rector: any minister of religion: one who is licensed to preach. — *n.* **par'sonage** the residence appropriated to a parson: orig. the house, lands, tithes, etc., set apart for the support of the minister of a parish: tithes (*Scott*). — *adjs.* **parsonic** (*-son'ik*), **-al, par'sonish.** — **par'son-bird** the tui; **parson's nose** the pope's nose (q.v.). [O.Fr. *persone* — L. *persōna*, a person, prob. in legal sense, or a mouthpiece.]

part *pärt, n.* something less than the whole: a portion: that which along with others makes up, has made up, or may at some time make up, a whole: a constituent: a component: a member or organ: an equal quantity: share: region: direction, hand, or side: participation: concern: interest: a rôle or duty: a side or party: a character taken by an actor in a play: the words and actions of a character in a play or in real life: a voice or instrument in concerted music: that which is performed by such a voice or instrument: a copy of the music for it: a constituent melody or succession of notes or harmony: a section of a work in literature (see also **partwork** below), or in music: a separately published portion or number (see also **partwork** below): an inflected form of a verb: a quantity which taken a certain number of times (when unspecified, less than the whole) will equal a larger quantity: (in *pl.*) intellectual qualities, talents, or conduct. — *adj.* in part: partial. — *adv.* in part: partly. — *v.t.* to divide: to separate: to break: to put or keep asunder: to set in different directions: to distribute: to share: to leave, quit (*Shak.*). — *v.i.* to become divided or separated:

to separate: to go different ways: to depart: to come or burst apart: to relinquish (with *with*): to share (*B.*). — *adj.* **part'ed** divided: separated: sundered: departed: assigned a part: endowed with parts or abilities (*Shak.*): deeply cleft, as a leaf (*bot.*). — *n.* **part'er.** — *adj.* **part'ible** that may be parted: separable. — *ns.* **partibil'ity; part'ing** the action of the verb to part: a place of separation or division: a dividing line: a line of skin showing between sections of hair brushed in opposite directions on the head: leave-taking. — *adj.* separating: dividing: departing: leave-taking: of or at leave-taking. — *adv.* **part'ly** in part: in some degree. — **part= exchange'** a transaction in which an article is handed over as part of the payment for another article. — Also *adj.* and *adv.* — **part'ing-cup'** a two-handled drinking-cup; **part'-off** (*West Indies*) a screen used to divide a room into two separate areas; **part'-own'er** a joint owner; **part'-pay'ment** payment in part; **part'= singing; part'-song** a melody with parts in harmony, usu. unaccompanied. — *adj.* and *adv.* **part'-time'** for part of working time only. — *v.i.* to work part-time. — **part'-tim'er; part'work** one of a series of publications (esp. magazines) issued at regular intervals, eventually forming a complete course or book; **part= writing** composition of music in parts. — **for my part** as far as concerns me; **for the most part** commonly; **in bad,** or **ill, part** unfavourably; **in good part** favourably: without taking offence; **in great part** to a great extent; **in part** partly: so far as part is concerned: not wholly but to some extent; **on the part of** so far as concerns: as done or performed by: in the actions of: on the side of; **part and parcel** essentially a part; **part brass rags** (*sea slang*) to quarrel; **part company** to separate; **parting of the ways** a point at which a fateful decision must be made; **part of speech** one of the various classes of words; **take part in** to share or to assist in; **take part with** to take the side of; **take someone's part** to support, side with, someone (in an argument, etc.). [O.E. and Fr. *part* — L. *pars, partis.*]

partake *pär-, pər-tāk'*, *v.i.* to take or have a part or share (usu. with *of* or *in*): to take some, esp. of food or drink: to have something of the nature or properties (of): to make common cause (*Shak.*). — *v.t.* to have a part in: to share: to have a share in the knowledge of: to give a share of (*Shak.*): to inform (*Spens.*): — *pr.p.* **partā'king;** *pa.t.* **partook';** *pa.p.* **partā'ken.** — *ns.* **partā'ker; partā'king.** [Back-formation from **partaker** — **part, taker.**]

partan *pär'tn,* (*Scot.*) *n.* the edible crab. [Gael.]

parterre *pär-ter',* *n.* an arrangement of flower-beds: the pit of a theatre, esp. the part under the galleries. [Fr., — L. *per*, along, *terra*, the ground.]

parthenocarpy *pär-then-ō-kär'pi,* (*bot.*) *n.* the production of a fruit without a preliminary act of fertilisation. — *adj.* **parthenocar'pic.** [Gr. *parthenos*, a virgin, *karpos*, a fruit.]

parthenogenesis *pär-thi-nō-jen'i-sis,* *n.* reproduction by means of an unfertilised ovum. — *adj.* **parthenogenetic** (*-ji-net'ik*). [Gr. *parthenos,* a virgin, *genesis,* production.]

Parthenon *pär'thi-non, n.* the temple of Athēnē *Parthĕnos,* on the Acropolis at Athens. [Gr. *Parthenōn — parthenos,* a virgin.]

Parthian *pär'thi-ən, adj.* of *Parthia.* — *n.* a native of Parthia. — **a Parthian shot** a parting shot, from the Parthian habit of turning round in the saddle to discharge an arrow at a pursuer.

parti *par-tē,* (Fr.) *n.* a group of people: a decision: a marriageable person considered as a match or catch. — **parti pris** (*prē*) bias, preconceived opinion.

partial *pär'shl, adj.* relating to a part only: not total or entire: inclined to favour one person or party: having a preference or fondness (with *to*): of partiality (*Shak.*): component: subordinate (*bot.*). — *n.* a partial tone, one of the single-frequency tones which go together to form a sound actually heard. — *ns.* **par'tialism; par'tialist** one who is biased: one who sees or knows

only part: a particularist (*theol.*); **partiality** (*-shi-al'i-ti*). — *v.t.* **par'tialise, -ize** (*Shak.*) to bias. — *adv.* **par'tially.** — **partial derivative** (*math.*) a derivative obtained by letting only one of several independent variables vary; **partial fraction** one of a number of simple fractions whose sum is a complex fraction; **partial pressure** the pressure exerted by any component in a mixture of gases. — **partial out** (*statistics*) to eliminate (a factor) so as to assess other factors when they are independent of its influence. [Fr., — L.L. *partiālis* — L. *pars,* a part.]

particeps criminis *pär'ti-seps kri'mi-nis, par'ti-keps krē'-mi-nis,* (L.) one who, though not present, helps in any way the commission of a crime or who after the deed aids those who did it.

partible, partibility. See under **part.**

participate *pär-tis'i-pāt, v.i.* to have a share, or take part (in): to have some of the qualities (of). — *v.t.* to receive a part or share of (*arch.*). — *adjs.* **partic'ipable** capable of being participated in or shared; **partic'ipant** participating: sharing. — *n.* a partaker. — *adv.* **partic'ipantly.** — *adj.* **partic'ipating** of insurance, entitling policyholders to a share of the company's additional profits. — *n.* **participā'tion** the act of participating: (as in the phrase **worker participation**) the involvement of employees at all levels in the policy-making decisions of a company, etc. — *adj.* **partic'ipātive** capable of participating: participable. — *n.* **partic'ipator** one who participates: a person who has a share in the capital or income of a company. — *adj.* **participā'tory** participable. [L. *participāre, -ātum* — *pars, partis,* part, *capĕre,* to take.]

participle *pär'ti-sip-l, n.* a word combining the functions of adjective and verb. — **present participle, past** or **perfect participle** referring respectively to an action roughly contemporaneous or past; the present participle is active, the past usually passive. — *adj.* **particip'ial.** — *adv.* **particip'ially.** [O.Fr. (Fr. *participe*), — L. *participium* — *pars, partis,* a part, *capĕre,* to take.]

particle *pär'ti-kl, n.* a little part: a very small portion: a clause of a document: a minute piece of matter: a little hard piece: a material point (*mech.*): a smallest amount: a short, usu. indeclinable word, as a preposition, a conjunction, an interjection: a prefix or suffix: a crumb of consecrated bread or a portion used in the communion of the laity (*R.C. Church*). — *adj.* **particular** (*pər-tik'ū-lər*) relating to a part: predicating of part of the class denoted by the subject (*log.*): pertaining to a single person or thing: individual: special: worthy of special attention: detailed: markedly and discriminatingly or intimately attentive towards a person (*obs.*): noteworthy: definite: concerned with or marking things single or distinct: minutely attentive and careful: fastidious in taste: particularist. — *n.* a distinct or minute part: a single point: a single instance: a detail: an item: personal relation (*Shak.*): a favourite (*coll.*): a favourite drink (esp. *London particular,* a Madeira wine for the London market; hence, from its colour, a London fog; *coll.*). — *n.* **particularīsā'tion, -z-.** — *v.t.* **partic'ularise, -ize** to render particular: to mention the particulars of: to enumerate in detail: to mention as a particular or particulars. — *v.i.* to mention or attend to minute details. — *n.* **partic'ularism** attention to one's own interest or party: a minute description: the doctrine that salvation is offered only to particular individuals, the elect, and not to the race: attention to the interest of a federal state before that of the confederation: the policy of allowing much freedom in this way. — *n.* and *adj.* **partic'ularist.** — *adj.* **particularist'ic.** — *n.* **particularity** (*-lar'i-ti*) the quality of being particular: minuteness of detail: a single instance or case: a detail: peculiarity: marked attention to a person (*obs.*). — *adv.* **partic'ularly** in a particular manner: individually severally: in detail: in the manner of a particular proposition: intimately: notably: in a very high degree. — *n.* **partic'ularness.** — *adj.* **partic'ulate** having form of or relating to particles. — *n.* a partic substance. — **particle accelerator** a device by means of which the speed of atomic particles may be greatly accelerated. — **in particular** especially: in detail: severally, individually (*obs.*).   [L. *particula*, dim. of *pars, partis*, a part.]

parti-coated, parti-coloured. See under **party.**

particular, etc.   See **particle.**

partie carrée *par-tē kar-ā,* (Fr.) a party consisting of two men and two women.

partim *pär'tim,* (L.) *adv.* in part.

partisan[1], **partizan** *pär-ti-zan', pär'ti-zan, n.* an adherent, esp. a blind or unreasoning adherent, of a party or a faction: a light irregular soldier who scours the country and forays: in World War II, an irregular resister within the enemy occupation lines. — Also *adj.* — *n.* **par'tisanship** (or *-zan'*).   [Fr. *partisan,* from a dialect form of It. *partigiano* — *parte* (L. *pars, partis*), part.]

partisan[2] *pär'ti-zan, n.* a kind of halberd or long-handled weapon, common in the Middle Ages: a man armed with one.   [Fr. *partizane* (now *pertuisane*) — It. *partesana,* of doubtful origin.]

partita *pär-tē'tə,* (*mus.*) *n.* (esp. 18th cent.) a suite: a set of variations.   [It.]

partite *pär'tīt, adj.* divided: cut nearly to the base. — *n.* **partition** (*-tish'ən*) the act of dividing: the state of being divided: a separate part: that which divides: a wall between rooms: a barrier, septum or dissepiment: a score (*mus.*). — *v.t.* to divide into shares: to divide into parts by walls, septa, or the like. — *ns.* **parti'tioner** one who partitions property; **parti'tionist** one who favours partition; **parti'tionment.** — *adj.* **par'titive** parting: dividing: distributive: indicating that a part is meant (*gram.*). — *n.* a partitive word. — *adv.* **par'titively.** — *ns.* **Partitur** (*-toor'*; Ger.), **Partitura** (*-too'ra*; It.) a score in music. — **parti'tion-wall'** an internal wall.   [L. *partītus,* pa.p. of *partīrī* or *partīre,* to divide — *pars,* part.]

Partlet *pärt'lit, n.* a proper name for a hen, from Chaucer's *Pertelote* in the Nun's Priest's Tale: sometimes applied to a woman.   [O.Fr. *Pertelote,* a woman's name.]

partlet *pärt'lit,* (*obs.*) *n.* a neck-covering: a ruff: a kind of shirt.   [App. O.Fr. *patelette,* a band.]

partly. See **part.**

partner *pärt'nər, n.* a sharer: an associate: one engaged with another in business: one who plays on the same side with another in a game: one who dances or goes in to dinner with another: a husband or wife: an associate in commensalism or symbiosis: (in *pl.*; *naut.*) a wooden framework round a hole in the deck, supporting a mast, etc. — *v.t.* to join as a partner (*Shak.*): to be the partner of. — *n.* **part'nership** the state of being a partner: a contract between persons engaged in any business.   [Prob. a form of **parcener.**]

parton *pär'ton,* (*phys.*) *n.* a hypothetical particle thought to be a constituent of nucleons.   [**part** and *-on,* formed on the analogy of **neutron, proton,** etc.]

partook *pär-took', pa.t.* of **partake.**

partridge *pär'trij, n.* any member of a genus (*Perdix*) of game-birds of the pheasant family: extended to many other birds, esp. (in North America) the Virginian quail and the ruffed grouse, and (in South America) the tinamou: — *pl.* **partridge(s).** — **par'tridge-berry** a North American trailing plant of the madder family (*Mitchella repens*) or its fruit: applied also to the checker-berry; **par'tridge-wood** a hard variegated tropical American cabinet-maker's wood (*Andira*) of the Papilionaceae: oak or other wood speckled owing to attack by a fungus.   [Fr. *perdrix* — L. *perdīx* — Gr. *perdīx.*]

parture *pärt'yər,* (Spens.) *n.* departure.   [Prob. **part.**]

parturient *pär-tū'ri-ənt, adj.* bringing, or about to bring, forth: of parturition. — *n.* **partūri'tion** the act of bringing forth.   [L. *parturīre,* desiderative from *parĕre,* to bring forth.]

...ty *par'ti, n.* a part (*obs.*): a side in a battle, game, ...wsuit, or other contest: a body of persons united in

favour of a political or other cause: the spirit of factio... a small body of persons associated together in an... occupation or amusement: a detachment: a company. a meeting or entertainment of guests: a game (*obs.*): one concerned in any affair: a person who enters into a contract, e.g. of marriage: a possible match in marriage: a person (*coll.*). — *adj.* pertaining to party: parted or divided (*her.*). — *v.i.* to attend, hold or take part in parties or similar entertainments: to have a good time. — *n.* **par'tyism** devotion to party. — *adjs.* **par'ti-coat'ed, par'ty-coat'ed** having on a coat of various colours; **par'ti-col'oured, par'ty-col'oured** variegated. — **par'ty-call'** a call upon one's host or hostess after a party; **par'ty-cap'ital** advantage or credit to one's party derived from some contingency; **par'ty= gov'ernment** government by the prevailing political party; **par'ty-ju'ry** a jury half of natives and half of aliens; **par'ty-line'** a telephone exchange line shared by two or more subscribers: boundary between properties: the policy rigidly laid down by the party leaders; **party machine** see **machine; par'ty-man'** a partisan; **par'ty-pol'itics** politics viewed from a party standpoint, or arranged to suit the views or interests of a party; **par'ty-spir'it** the unreasonable spirit of a party-man: a festive atmosphere. — *adj.* **par'ty-spir'ited.** — **par'ty= ver'dict** a joint verdict; **par'ty-wall** a wall between two adjoining properties or houses. — **the party's over** a favourable, enjoyable, carefree, etc. situation has ended.   [Fr. *partie,* fem. (and also *parti,* masc.), pa.p. of *partir* — L. *partīre, partīrī,* to divide — *pars,* a part.]

parulis *pə-roo'lis,* (*med.*) *n.* a gumboil.   [Gr. *para,* beside, *oulon,* the gum.]

parure *pa-rür', n.* a set of ornaments, etc.   [Fr.]

parvanimity *pär-və-nim'i-ti, n.* littleness of mind.   [L. *parvus,* little, *animus,* mind.]

parvenu *pär've-nū, -nü, n.* an upstart: one newly risen into wealth, notice, or power, esp. if vulgar or exhibiting an inferiority complex. — Also *adj.* [Fr. pa.p. of *parvenir* — L. *pervenīre,* to arrive.]

parvis, parvise *pär'vis, pär'vēs, ns.* an enclosed space, or sometimes a portico, before a church: a room over a church porch (*erron.*).   [O.Fr. *parevis;* same root as **paradise.**]

parvovirus, Parvo virus *pär'vō-vī-rəs, n.* any of a group of viruses which contain DNA and which are the causes of various animal, including canine, diseases.   [L. *parvus,* little, and **virus.**]

pas *pä, n.* a step: a dance: action: precedence: — *pl.* **pas** (*pä*). — **pas d'armes** (*därm*), a joust, a tilt or a tourney; **pas de bourrée** (*də boo-rā*) a ballet movement in which one foot is swiftly placed behind or in front of the other; **pas de chat** (*də sha*) a ballet leap in which each foot is raised in turn to the opposite knee; **pas de deux, trois, quatre,** etc. (*də də, trwä, kä-tr'*) a dance of two, three, four, or more persons; **pas redoublé** (*rə-doob-lā*) a quickstep; **pas seul** (*sœl*) a dance for one person, a solo dance. — **have the pas of someone** to take precedence of someone.   [Fr., — L. *passus;* cf. **pace.**]

pascal *pas'kal, n.* a unit of pressure, the newton per square metre, a supplementary SI unit. — **Pascal's triangle** a group of numbers arranged to form a triangle in which each number is the sum of the two numbers to its right and left in the line above.   [Blaise *Pascal,* French philosopher and scientist.]

Pasch *pask,* Scot. **Pace** *pās, ns.* the Passover: Easter (*arch.*). — *adj.* **pasch'al.** — **pasch'al-can'dle** a large candle blessed and placed on the altar on the day before Easter; **pasch'al-flow'er** same as **pasque-flower;** **paschal (full) moon** the first full moon on or after the spring equinox, Easter being reckoned in the Roman Catholic church as the first Sunday after the paschal moon; **pasch'al-lamb** the lamb slain and eaten at the Passover; **pasch'-egg** (*Scot.* **pace'-egg**) an Easter-egg. — **Pasch of the Cross** Good Friday.   [L. *pascha* — Gr. *pascha* — Heb. *pesach,* the Passover — *pāsach,* to pass over.]

ascual *pas'kū-əl, adj.* growing on land used for grazing. [L. *pascuum,* pasture.]

pasear *pä-sā-är'* (*U.S. slang* and *dial.*) *v.i.* to take a walk. — *n.* a walk. — *n.* **paseo** (*pä-sā'ō*) a walk: a street or promenade. [Sp.]

pash[1] *pash,* (*Shak.*) *v.t.* to strike, to dash, to crush. — *v.i.* to dash. — *n.* a blow. [Perh. imit.]

pash[2] *pash,* (*Shak.*) *n.* the head. [Origin unknown.]

pash[3] *pash, n.* a slang contraction of **passion.**

pasha *pa'shə, pä-shä', n.* a Turkish title (abolished 1934) given to governors and high military and naval officers. — Also **pacha.** — *n.* **pash'alik, pach'alic** (or *pä-shä'lik*) the jurisdiction of a pasha. [Turk. *paşa*; cf. **bashaw.**]

pashm *push'əm, n.* the fine underfleece of the goats of Northern India, used for making rugs, shawls, etc. — Also **pashim** (*push'ēm*), **pashmina** (*push-mē'nə*). [Pers., wool.]

Pashto, Pashtu, Pashtun. See **Pushtu.**

pasigraphy *pə-sig'rə-fi, n.* a system of ideographic writing. — *adjs.* **pasigraphic** (*pas-i-graf'ik*), **-al.** [Gr. *pāsi* (dat. pl.), to or for all, *graphein,* to write.]

paso doble *pä'sō dō'blä,* (Sp.) a march usu. played at bullfights: a two-step: the music for this dance.

Paspalum *pas'pä-ləm, n.* an American and tropical genus of pasture grasses: (without *cap.*) any plant of this genus, a common example being pampas-grass. [Gr. *paspalos,* millet.]

paspy *päs'pi.* Same as **passepied.**

pasque-flower *päsk'flowr, n.* a species of anemone (*Anemone pulsatilla*): extended to some other species. [Fr. *passefleur,* apparently — *passer,* to surpass, modified after **Pasch,** as flowering about Easter.]

Pasquil *pas'kwil,* **Pasquin** *pas'kwin, ns.* the nickname (perh. after somebody who lived near) of an ancient statue dug up in Rome in 1501, to which it became customary to attach lampoons and satires: an imaginary lampooner or satirist: a lampoon or satire. — *v.t.* and *v.i.* to lampoon or satirise. — *ns.* **pas'quilant, pas'quiler, pasquinä'der** a lampooner; **pasquinäde'** a lampoon. — *v.t.* to lampoon. [It. *Pasquino, Pasquillo.*]

pass *päs, v.i.* to proceed: to go or be transferred from one place to another: to transfer the ball to another player (*football,* etc.): to make one's way: to reach, extend, or have a course: to undergo change from one state to another: to be transmitted: to change ownership: to change: to shade off (*obs.*): to be astir: to circulate: to be accepted or reputed or known: to go by: to go unheeded or neglected: to elapse, to go away: to disappear, come to an end, fade out: to die: to move over, through or onwards: to go or get through an obstacle, difficulty, test, ordeal, examination, etc.: to get through an examination without honours: to be approved: to meet with acceptance: to be sanctioned: to be made law: to be talented: to come through: to be voided: to happen: to be communicated or transacted: to sit or serve (upon a jury): to adjudicate: to be pronounced: to care, reck (with *of* or *for; obs.*): to surpass or beat everything (*obs.*): to exceed bounds: to perform a pass (see noun below): to abstain from making a call or declaration (*cards*). — *v.t.* to go or get by, over, beyond, through, etc.: to undergo, experience: to undergo successfully: to spend (as time): to omit: to disregard: to exceed: to surpass: to cause or allow to pass: to transfer, transmit: to transfer (the ball) to another player (*football,* etc.): to hand: to utter: to circulate: to pledge (as one's word): to emit, discharge: to perform a pass with or upon: to perform as a pass: to esteem (*obs.*): — *pa.t.* and *pa.p.* **passed** (*päst*), rarely **past.** — *n.* a way by which one may pass or cross: a narrow passage, esp. through or over a range of mountains or other difficult region: a narrow defile: an act of passing: the passing of an examination, esp. without honours: currency (*obs.*): reputation (*Shak.*): event, issue, fulfilment, consummation: a state or condition (as in *pretty, sad pass*): a predicament,

critical position: a passport: a written permission to go somewhere or do something: permission to be in a certain area (*S.Afr.*): a free ticket: a thrust (*fencing*): transference of the ball to another team-member (*football,* etc.): transference in a juggling trick: an amorous advance (*coll.*): a movement of the hand over anything, as by a mesmerist: perhaps trick, perhaps conduct (*Shak.,* Meas. for Meas. V.i.375). — *adj.* **pass'able** that may be passed, travelled over, or navigated: that may bear inspection: that may be accepted or allowed to pass: tolerable. — *n.* **pass'ableness.** — *adv.* **pass'ably.** — *ns.* **pass'er; passimeter** (*pas-im'i-tər*) an automatic ticket-issuing machine. — *adj.* **passing** (*päs'ing*) going by, through, or away: transient, fleeting: happening now: incidental: casual: surpassing (*arch.*). — *adv.* (*arch.*) exceedingly: very. — *n.* the action of the verb to pass: a place of passing: a coming to an end: death: gold or silver thread with a silk core. — *adj.* **pass'less** having no pass: impassable. — **pass band** (*elect.*) a frequency band in which there is negligible attenuation; **pass'-book** a book that passes between a trader and his customer, in which credit purchases are entered: a bank-book: a booklet containing permission to be in a certain area, and other documents (*S.Afr.*); **pass'-check** a pass-out ticket; **passed pawn** (*chess*) a pawn having no opposing pawn before it on its own or an adjacent file; **pass'er-by** one who passes by or near: — *pl.* **pass'ers-by; pass'ing-bell** a bell tolled immediately after a death, originally to invite prayers for the soul passing into eternity; **pass'ing-note** (*mus.*) a note or tone effecting a smooth passage, but forming no essential part of the harmony: one forming an unprepared discord in an unaccented place in the measure; **passing shot** (*tennis*) a shot hit past, and beyond the reach of, an opponent; **pass'key** a key enabling one to enter a house: a key for opening several locks. — *n.pl.* **pass laws** (*S.Afr.*) laws restricting the movements of blacks. — **pass'man** one who gains a degree without honours: a prisoner who is permitted to leave his cell in order to carry out certain duties (*slang*). — *adj.* **pass'out** entitling one who goes out to return. — **pass'word** (*mil.*) a secret word by which a friend may pass or enter a camp, etc. — **bring to pass** to bring about, cause to happen; **come to pass** to happen (apparently originally a noun in these expressions); **in passing** while doing, talking about, etc. something else; **make a pass at** to aim a short blow at, especially ineffectually (*coll.*): to make an amorous advance to (*coll.*); **pass as, for** to be mistaken for or accepted as; **pass away** to come to an end, go off: to die: to elapse; **pass by** to move, go beyond or past: to ignore or overlook; **pass off** to impose fraudulently: to palm off: to take its course satisfactorily: to disappear gradually; **pass on** to go forward: to proceed: to die: to transmit, hand on; **pass on, or upon,** to give judgment or sentence upon: to practise artfully, or impose, upon: to palm off; **pass out** to distribute: to die: to faint, become unconscious or dead drunk (*slang*): to go off: to complete military, etc. training; **pass over** to overlook, to ignore: to die; **pass the time of day** to exchange any ordinary greeting of civility; **pass through** to undergo, experience; **pass up** to renounce, to have nothing to do with: to neglect (an opportunity). [Fr. *pas,* step, and *passer,* to pass — L. *passus,* a step.]

passacaglia *pas-a-käl'ya,* (*mus.*) *n.* a slow solemn old Spanish dance-form, slower than the chaconne, in triple time, usually on a ground-bass. [Italianised from Sp. *pasacalle* — *pasar,* to pass, *calle,* street, appar. because often played in the streets.]

passade *pä-säd', n.* the motion of a horse to and fro over the same ground. — *n.* **passado** (*pä-sä'dō; obs.*) in fencing, a thrust with one foot advanced: — *pl.* **passa'do(e)s.** [Fr. *passade,* Sp. *pasada* — L. *passus,* step.]

passage[1] *pas'ij, n.* an act of passing: transit: a crossing: migration: transition: a journey (now only by wate or air, or *fig*.): right of conveyance: possibility of passing: lapse, course: transmission: evacuation of the bowels: the passing of a bill: a means or way of passing: an alley: a corridor or lobby: a navigable channel or route: a crossing-place, ford, ferry, bridge, or mountain-pass: that which passes: traffic (*Shak*.): an occurrence, incident, episode: transaction, interchange of communication or intercourse, dealings together: a continuous but indefinite portion of a book, piece of music, etc., of moderate length: a run, figure, or phrase in music: a stage in the maintenance or controlled development of micro-organisms under analysis, in which they are introduced into the host or culture, allowed to multiply, and extracted (*biol*.): an old dicing game, the object to throw doublets above (passing) ten, with three dice. — *v.i.* to make or perform a passage. — *v.t.* (*biol*.) to submit (a micro-organism) to a passage. — **pass′age-boat** a boat plying regularly for passengers. — *n.pl.* **passage beds** (*geol*.) transitional strata. — **passage grave** a burial chamber situated below ground and connected to the surface by a passage; **pass′age-money** fare; **pass′ageway** a way of access: a corridor: an alley. — **bird of passage** a migratory bird: a transient visitor (*fig*.); **passage of arms** any feat of arms: an encounter, esp. in words. [Fr. *passage* — L. *passus*, step.]

passage² *pas-äzh′, pas′ij, v.i.* to go sideways. — *v.t.* to cause (a horse) to go sideways. [Fr. *passager* — *passéger* — It. *passeggiare*, to walk — L. *passus*, step.]

passament. See **passement.**

passamezzo. See **passy-measure.**

passant *pas′ənt*, (*her*.) *adj.* walking towards the dexter side, with dexter fore-paw raised. [Fr.]

passé, *fem.* **passée**, *pa-sā*, (Fr.) *adj.* past one's best, faded: nearly out of date.

passement, passment *pas′mənt*, **passament** *-ə-mənt, ns.* decorative trimming. — *v.t.* to adorn with passement. — *n.* **passementerie** (*päs-mã-t*(*ə*)*-rē*; Fr.). [Fr.]

passenger *pas′in-jər, n.* one who passes: one who travels in a private or public conveyance (as opposed to one who drives or operates the vehicle, etc.): one carried along by others' efforts (*fig*.). — *adj.* of or for passengers. — **pass′enger-mile** one mile travelled by one passenger, as a measure of volume of traffic; **pass′-enger-pig′eon** an extinct North American pigeon that flew in vast numbers in search of food. [O.Fr. *passagier* (Fr. *passager*), with inserted *n*, as in *messenger, nightingale*.]

passe-partout *päs-pär-tōō′, n.* a means of passing anywhere: a master-key: a card or the like cut as a mount for a picture: a kind of simple picture-frame, usually of pasteboard, the picture being fixed by strips pasted over the edges: adhesive tape or paper. [Fr., a master-key, from *passer*, to pass, *par*, over, *tout*, all.]

passepied *päs-pyā*, *n.* a dance or dance-tune like the minuet, but quicker. [Fr., lit. pass-foot.]

Passeres *pas′ə-rēz, n.pl.* an old order of birds (also called Insessores) comprising more than half of all the birds. — *n.pl.* **Passeriform′ēs** the huge order of perching birds (sparrow-like in form) including amongst others all British songsters. — *adj.* and *n.* **pass′erine** (-*īn*). [L. *passer*, a sparrow.]

passible *pas′i-bl, adj.* susceptible of suffering, or of impressions from external agents. — *ns.* **passibil′ity, pass′ibleness.** — *adv.* **pass′ibly.** [L. *passibilis* — *patī, passus*, to suffer.]

Passiflora *pas-i-flō′rə, -flō′rə, n.* the passion-flower genus, giving name to the family **Passiflorā′ceae** (without *cap*.) a plant of this genus. [L. *passiō*, passion, *flōs, flōris*, flower.]

passim *pas′im*, (L.) *adv.* everywhere: throughout: dispersedly.

passimeter. See **pass.**

passion *pash′n, n.* the sufferings (esp. on the Cross) and death of Christ: martyrdom: suffering: a painful bodily ailment (as *iliac passion*): the fact, condition, or manner of being acted upon: passivity: a passive quality:

strong feeling or agitation of mind, esp. rage, ofte sorrow: a fit of such feeling, esp. rage: an expression. or outburst of such feeling: ardent love: sexual desire: an enthusiastic interest or direction of the mind: the object of such a feeling. — *v.t.* to imbue with passion. — *v.i.* to exhibit passion. — *adj.* **pass′ional.** — *ns.* **pass′ional, pass′ionary** a book of the sufferings of saints and martyrs. — *adj.* **pass′ionate** moved by passion: showing strong and warm feeling: easily moved to passion: intense, fervid: compassionate (*Shak*.): moving to compassion (*Spens*.). — *v.t.* to express with passion: to imbue with passion: to impassion. — *adv.* **pass′ionately.** — *n.* **pass′ionateness.** — *adj.* **pass′ioned** moved by passion: expressing passion: expressed with passion. — *n.* **Pass′ionist** a member of a Roman Catholic congregation devoted to the commemoration of the Passion of Christ by missions, etc. — *adj.* **pass′ionless** free from passion: not easily excited to anger. — **pass′ion-flower** any flower or plant of genus Passiflora, consisting mostly of climbers of tropical and warm temperate America, from a fancied resemblance of parts of the flower to the crown of thorns, nails, and other emblems of Christ's Passion: the plant itself; **pass′ion-fruit** the granadilla: any edible passion-flower fruit; **Pass′ion-mū′sic** music to which words describing the sufferings and death of Christ are set; **Pass′ion-play** a religious drama representing the sufferings and death of Christ; **Pass′ion-Sunday** the fifth Sunday in Lent; **Pass′ion-tide** the two weeks preceding Easter; **Pass′ion-week** Holy week: the week before Holy week. [O.Fr. *passiun* and L. *passiō, -ōnis* — *patī, passus*, to suffer.]

passive *pas′iv, adj.* suffering (*obs*.): acted upon, not acting: inert: lethargic: not reacting: not actively resisting: bearing no interest: under a liability (*Scots law*): (of that voice) which expresses the suffering of an action by the person or thing represented by the subject of the verb (*gram*.). — *n.* the passive voice: a passive verb: a passive person. — *adv.* **pass′ively.** — *ns.* **pass′iveness; pass′ivism** passive resistance; **pass′ivist** a passive resister; **passiv′ity.** — **passive immunity** the short-term immunity acquired either artificially, through the administration of antibodies, or naturally, as in the very young who receive antibodies through the placenta or in colostrum; **passive obedience** absolute submission to the ruling power: obedience to the 'divine right of kings'; **passive resistance** deliberate refusal (from scruples of conscience) to do what law or regulation orders, and submission to the consequent penalties; **passive resister; passive smoking** the involuntary inhalation of tobacco smoke that has been produced by others. [L. *passīvus* — *patī, passus*, to suffer.]

passless to **passman.** See **pass.**

passment. See **passement.**

Passover *päs′ō-vər, n.* annual feast of the Jews, to commemorate the exodus of the Israelites from captivity in Egypt, so named from the destroying angel passing over the houses of the Israelites when he slew the first-born of the Egyptians. — *adj.* pertaining to the Passover.

passport *päs′pōrt, -pört, n.* authorisation to leave a port either to put to sea or to proceed inland: a permit for entering a country: that which gives privilege of entry to anything (*fig*.). [Fr. *passeport*; cf. **pass, port⁴**.]

passus *pas′us, n.* a section, canto, or fytte. [L. *passus*, plur. *-ūs*, a step.]

passy-measure, passemeasure *pas′i-mezh′ər, n.* an old dance, a pavan in quicker time, called also **passamezzo** (*pas-sa-met′sō*; *pl.* **-zōs**), **passy measures pavan** (in *Shak*. app. misprinted *panin*). [It. *passemezzo*.]

past *päst, adj.* bygone: elapsed: ended: in time already passed: expressing action or being in time that has passed, preterite (*gram*.): just before the present: past one's best: having served a term of office. — *n.* time that has passed: things that have already happened: (one's) early life or bygone career, esp. if marked by tragedy or scandal: the past tense: a verb or verbal form in the past tense. — *prep.* after: after the time of: beyond, in place, etc.: beyond the possibility of. — *adv.* by: laid aside in store, for later use (*Scot.*). — *v.t.* and *v.i.* an unusual pa.p. of **pass**. — **past′master** one who has held the office of master (as among freemasons): hence, a thorough proficient (see also **passed master** under **master**); **past participle** see **participle**. — **past it** (*coll.*), **past one's best** having decreased strength, ability, etc. due to advancing age; **past praying for** beyond hope of redemption or recovery; **I**, etc. **would not put it past him** (*coll.*) I, etc. regard him as (esp. morally) capable of (some act).   [An old pa.p. of **pass**.]

pasta *päs′, pas′ta, n.* flour dough in fresh, processed (e.g. spaghetti), and/or cooked form.   [It., paste.]

pastance *pas′təns,* (*arch.*) *n.* a pastime.   [App. Fr. *passetemps,* pastime.]

paste *pāst, n.* a soft plastic mass: dough for piecrust, etc.: a doughy sweetmeat: a smooth preparation of food suitable for spreading on bread: a cement made of flour, water, etc.: material for making pottery: the basis of a man's character (*fig.*): a fine kind of glass for making artificial gems. — *adj.* of paste. — *v.t.* to fasten or cover with paste: to thrash (*slang*). — *ns.* **pāst′er** one who pastes: a slip of gummed paper; **pāst′iness; pāst′ing** (*slang*) a beating. — *adj.* **pāst′y** like paste. — **paste′board** a stiff board made of sheets of paper pasted together: a visiting-card, playing-card, or ticket (*slang*). — *adj.* of pasteboard: sham: trumpery. — **paste′-down** the outer leaf of an endpaper that is pasted down on the inside cover of a book: formerly, a paper used to line the inside cover of a book; **paste′-eel′** a nematoid worm found in paste; **paste′-grain** an imitation of morocco leather, used in binding books and in making fancy goods; **paste′-up** an arrangement of proofs, drawings, etc. pasted on a sheet or board prior to photographing and printing: a collage. — *adj.* **past′y-faced** pale and dull of complexion.   [O.Fr. *paste* (Fr. *pâte*) — L.L. *pasta* — Gr. *pasta,* barley porridge (neut. pl. of *pastos,* sprinkled, salted) — *passein,* to sprinkle.]

pastel *pas′təl, -tel, n.* chalk mixed with other materials and coloured for crayons: a drawing made with pastels: the process or art of drawing with pastels: woad. — *adj.* in pastel: (of colour) soft, quiet. — *n.* **pastellist** (*pas′,* or *-tel′*).   [Fr. *pastel* — It. *pastello* — L. *pasta,* paste.]

pastern *pas′tərn, n.* a hobble for a horse (*obs.*): the part of a horse's foot from the fetlock to the hoof, where the shackle is fastened.   [O.Fr. *pasturon* (Fr. *paturon*) — O.Fr. *pasture,* pasture, a tether for a horse; cf. **pester**.]

Pasteurian *pas-tûr′i-ən, adj.* relating to Louis *Pasteur* (1822–95), French chemist and bacteriologist, or his methods. — *ns.* **Pasteurell′a** a genus of bacteria which cause various serious infectious diseases, including plague: (without *cap.*) a bacterium of this genus: — *pl.* **-as, -ae** (*-ē*); **Pasteurellō′sis** a disease caused by organisms of the genus *Pasteurella:* — *pl.* **-ō′sēs.** **pasteurīsā′tion, -z-** sterilisation of milk, etc., by heating. — *v.t.* **pas′teurise, -ize.** — *ns.* **pasteuris′er, -z-** an apparatus for sterilising milk, etc.; **pas′teurism** Pasteur's method of inoculation with the attenuated virus of certain diseases, esp. hydrophobia.

pastiche *pas-tēsh′, n.* a jumble: a pot-pourri: a composition (in literature, music, or painting) made up of bits of other works or imitations of another's style. — Also **pasticcio** (*pas-tit′chō; pl.* **pasticci, -chē**). — *n.* **pasticheur** (*-ē-shœr′*) one who makes pastiches.   [Fr. (from It.) and It. — It. *pasta,* paste; see **paste**.]

pastil *pas′til, n.* Same as **pastel** or **pastille**.

pastille *pas′til, pas-tēl′, n.* a small cone of charcoal and aromatic substances, burned as incense, or for fumigation, fragrance: a small (often medicated) sweetmeat: a paper tube containing a firework which causes a small wheel to rotate: the same as **pastel** (*art*).   [Fr., — L. *pastillus,* a little loaf.]

pastime *päs′tīm, n.* that which serves to pass away the time: recreation.   [**pass, time.**]

pastis *pas-tēs′, n.* an alcoholic drink similar in flavour to absinthe.   [Fr.]

pastor *päs′tər, n.* one who has care of a flock or of a congregation: a shepherd: a clergyman: in the Catholic Apostolic Church, a minister of the lowest grade: the rose-coloured starling (*Pastor roseus*), from its following sheep for the sake of parasites. — *adj.* **pas′toral** relating to shepherds or to shepherd life: of the nature of pastureland: of or pertaining to the pastor of a church and his obligations to his congregation: addressed to the clergy of a diocese by their bishop. — *n.* a poem, play, romance, opera, piece of music, or picture depicting the life of (usually idealised or conventionalised) shepherds, or rural life in general: such writing as a genre: a pastoral letter: a book on the care of souls: a pastoral staff. — *ns.* **pastorale** (*päs-to-rä′lā;* It.) a pastoral composition in music: a pastoral, rustic, or idyllic opera or cantata; **pas′toralism** pastoral character, fashion, cult, mode of writing; **pas′toralist.** — *adv.* **pas′torally.** — *n.* **pas′torate** the office of a pastor: a pastor's tenure of office: a body of pastors. — *adj.* **pas′torly** becoming a pastor. — *n.* **pas′torship.** — **pastoral address** or **letter** an address or a letter by a pastor to his people, or by a bishop to his clergy; **pastoral charge** position of a pastor: the church, etc., over which a pastor is placed: an address to a newly ordained minister. — *n.pl.* **pastoral epistles** those in the Bible to Timothy and Titus. — **pastoral staff** a crosier, a tall staff forming part of a bishop's insignia, headed like a shepherd's crook; **pastoral theology** that part of theology which treats of the duties of pastors in relation to the cure of souls.   [L. *pāstor* — *pāscĕre, pāstum,* to feed.]

pastourelle *päs-tōō-rel′, n.* a mediaeval poetic genre, esp. Provençal and French, a dialogue between a knight and a shepherdess, or the like: a movement in a quadrille.   [Fr., little shepherdess.]

pastrami *pəs-trä′mi, n.* a smoked, highly seasoned (esp. shoulder) cut of beef.   [Yiddish — Rumanian *pastramă — a păstra,* to serve.]

pastry *päs′tri, n.* articles made of paste or dough collectively: crust of pies, tarts, etc.: a small cake: a place where pastry is made (*Shak.*): the art or practice of making pastry (*obs.*). — **pas′trycook** a maker or seller of pastry.   [**paste.**]

pasture *päs′chər, n.* feeding (*arch.*): food (*Spens.*): grazing: growing grass for grazing: grazing land: a grazing ground, piece of grazing land. — *v.i.* to graze. — *v.t.* to put to graze: to graze on. — *adj.* **past′urable** fit for pasture. — *n.* **past′urage** the business of feeding or grazing cattle: pasture-land: grass for feeding: right of pasture. — *adjs.* **past′ural** of pasture; **past′ureless.** — **past′ure-land** land suitable for pasture.   [O.Fr. *pasture* (Fr. *pâture*) — L. *pāstūra — pāscĕre, pāstum,* to feed.]

pasty[1] *päs′ti, adj.* See under **paste**.

pasty[2] *pas′ti, päs′, n.* a meat-pie baked without a dish.   [O.Fr. *pastée* — L. *pasta;* see **paste**.]

pat[1] *pat, n.* a gentle stroke with a flat surface, as the palm of the hand: such a stroke as a caress or mark of approbation: a sound as of such a stroke: a small lump, esp. of butter, such as might be moulded by patting. — *v.t.* to strike (now only to strike gently) with the palm of the hand or other flat surface: to shape by patting. — *v.i.* to tap: to make the sound of pats, as with the feet: — *pr.p.* **patt′ing;** *pa.t.* and *pa.p.* **patt′ed.** — *adv.* and *adj.* hitting the mark to a nicety: at the right time or place: exactly to the purpose: with or ready for fluent or glib repetition: of a hand in poker, not likely to be improved by drawing (*U.S.*). — *adv.* **pat′ly** (*rare*) fitly, conveniently: glibly, fluently. — *n.* **pat′ness.** — **pat′ball** rounders: gentle hitting in other games. — **pat on the back** a mark of encouragement or approbation; **stand pat** in poker, to decide to play

one's hand as it is: to refuse to change. [Prob. imit.]
pat². See **pit³**.
pat³ *pat*, (*Scot.*) *n.* a pot. — **pat'-lid'**.
Pat *pat*, *n.* a nickname for an Irishman. [**Patrick**.]
pataca *pə-tä'kə*, *n.* the basic unit of currency in the Portuguese colonies of Macao and Timor: a coin of one pataca in value. [Port.]
patagium *pat-ə-jī'əm*, *n.* a bat's wing-membrane: the parachute of a flying-squirrel, etc.: the fold of integument between the upper arm and the forearm of a bird: a paired scale on a moth's pronotum: — *pl.* **patagi'a**. — *adj.* **patagial** (*pə-tā'ji-əl*). [L. *patagīum* — Gr. *patageion*, an edging.]
Patagonian *pat-ə-gō'ni-ən*, *n.* an Indian of Patagonia: a giant. — *adj.* of Patagonia: gigantic. [Sp. *patagón*, big foot: the tallness of the Patagonians was grossly exaggerated by travellers.]
patamar *pat'ə-mär*, *n.* a vessel, on the Bombay coast, with arched keel and great stem and stern rake. [Port., — Konkani *pātamāri*.]
pataphysics, 'pataphysics *pat'ə-fiz-iks*, *n.* 'the science of imaginary solutions' invented by the French dramatist Alfred Jarry (1873–1907), writer of symbolic farce, from which is descended the theatre of the absurd.
Patarin, -ine *pat'ər-in, -ēn*, (*hist.*) *ns.* orig., an adherent of a popular party in Milan opposed to marriage of priests (11th century): later a nickname for Manichaeans, Cathari, and other heretics. [Said to be from *Pattaria*, a district in Milan.]
Patavinity *pat-ə-vin'i-ti*, *n.* the diction of the people of Padua, esp. Livy: the use of dialect, provincialism generally. [L. *patavīnitās* — *Patavium*, Padua.]
patch¹ *pach*, *n.* a piece put on or to be put on to mend a defect: a piece of plaster for a cut or sore: a pad for a hurt eye: a piece of ground, period of time, etc.: an overlay to obtain a stronger impression (*print.*): a small piece of black silk, etc., stuck by ladies on the face, to bring out the complexion by contrast, or as a political party badge — common in the 17th and 18th centuries: a smallish area differing in colour or otherwise from its surroundings: a plot of ground: a scrap or fragment: a scrap pieced together with others: a group of instructions added to a computer program to correct a mistake (*comput.*). — *v.t.* to mend with a patch: to put a patch on: to apply as a patch: to join in patchwork: to mend or construct hastily, clumsily, or temporarily (commonly with *up*): to construct as a patchwork: to mark with patches. — *adjs.* **patch'able; patched**. — *n.* **patch'er**. — *adv.* **patch'ily**. — *n. and adj.* **patch'ing**. — *adj.* **patch'y** covered with patches: diversified in patches: inharmonious, incongruous. — **patch'board** (*telecomm.*, etc.) a panel with multiple electric terminals into which wires may be plugged to form a variety of electric circuits; **patch'-box** a fancy box for holding the patches worn on the face, generally having a mirror inside the lid; **patch'-pocket** a flat, usu. square piece of material attached to the outside of a garment; **patch test** a test for allergy in which allergenic substances are applied to areas of skin which are later examined for signs of irritation; **patch-up'** a provisional repairing; **patch'work** work formed of patches or pieces sewed together: an incongruous combination: work patched up or clumsily executed: a surface diversified in patches. — **hit, strike a bad patch** to experience a difficult time, encounter unfavourable conditions, etc.; **not a patch on** not fit to be compared with. [M.E. *pacche*; origin unknown; poss. conn. with **piece**.]
patch² *pach*, *n.* a fool or jester (*arch.*): a booby (*dial.*): an ill-natured person (*dial.*). — *n.* **patch'ery** (*Shak.*) knavery. — **patch'cocke, patch'ocke** (*Spens.*) perhaps a clown (reading and meaning doubtful; cf. *paiock*). [Perh. from preceding, from the patched coat; nickname of Cardinal Wolsey's fool, Sexton; perh. It. *pazzo*, fool.]
patchouli, patchouly *pach'ōō-lē*, also *pə-chōō'lē*, *n.* a labiate shrub (*Pogostemon patchouly*) of S.E. Asia: a perfume got from its dried branches. [Tamil *pacculi*.]

pate *pāt*, *n.* the crown of the head: the head. — *adj.* **pāt'ed** having a pate. [Origin unknown.]
pâté *pät'-*, *pat'ā*, *n.* orig. a pie, pastry: now usu. a paste made of blended meat, herbs, etc. — **pâté de foie gras** (*də fwä grä*) orig. a pasty of fat goose liver: now usu. the goose liver paste filling. [Fr.]
patella *pə-tel'ə*, *n.* a little pan (*ant.*): the knee-cap (*anat.*): a saucer-like apothecium (*bot.*): (*cap.*) the limpet genus: — *pl.* **patell'as, patell'ae** (*-ē*). — *adjs.* **patell'ar** of the knee-cap; **patell'ate** (or *pat'*) saucer-shaped: limpet-shaped — *n.* **patellec'tomy** the surgical removal of the patella. — *adj.* **patell'iform** patellate. — **patellar reflex** the knee-jerk. [L., dim. of *patina*, a pan.]
paten *pat'ən*, *n.* a plate: a communion plate: a chalice-cover: a metal disc. [O.Fr. *patene* — L. *patena*, *patina*, a plate — Gr. *patanē*.]
patent *pā'tənt*, or (esp. in *letters-patent* and *Patent Office*, and in U.S.) *pat'ənt*, *adj.* lying open: conspicuous, obvious, evident: generally accessible: protected by a patent: spreading (*bot.*): expanding: ingenious (*slang*). — *n.* an official document, open, and having the Great Seal of the government attached to it, conferring an exclusive right or privilege, as a title of nobility, or the sole right for a term of years to the proceeds of an invention: something invented and protected by a patent: a privilege: a certificate. — *v.t.* to secure a patent for. — *n.* **pā'tency** openness: obviousness. — *adj.* **pā'tentable**. — *n.* **pātentee'** one who holds a patent, or to whom a patent is granted. — *adv.* **pā'tently** openly, obviously. — *n.* **pā'tentor** one who grants a patent. — **patent agent** one who obtains patents on behalf of inventors; **patent leather** finely varnished leather; **patent log** a device for recording the speed of a vessel, consisting of a submerged rotator attached by line to a dial on the ship's rail; **patent medicine** (*strictly*) a medicine protected by a patent: (*loosely*) any proprietary medicine, esp. one liable to stamp duty, as made by secret process or for other reason; **Patent Office** an office for the granting of patents for inventions; **patent outside**, or **inside**, a newspaper printed on the outside or inside only, sold to a publisher who fills the other side with his own material, as local news, etc.; **pā'tent-right** the exclusive right reserved by letters-patent. — *n.pl.* **pā'tent-rolls** the register of letters-patent issued in England. — **patent still** a still performing several operations at once, and producing a purer spirit than a pot-still. — **nothing patent** (*slang*) not very good. [L. *patēns*, *-entis*, pr.p. of *patēre*, to lie open.]
pater *pā'tər*, (*slang*) *n.* father. [L. *păter*.]
patera *pat'ə-rə*, *n.* a round flat dish, esp. for receiving a sacrificial libation among the Romans: a round flat ornament in bas-relief in friezes, etc. — often applied loosely to rosettes and other flat ornaments (*archit.*): — *pl.* **pat'erae** (*-rē*). [L., — *patēre*, to lie open.]
patercove *pat'ər-kōv*, *n.* Same as **patrico**.
paterero *pat-ə-rā'rō*, *n.* Same as **pederero**: — *pl.* **patere'roes** (*-rōz*).
paterfamilias *pā-tər-fə-mil'i-as*, or *pat'ər-*, *n.* the father or head of a family or household: — *pl.* strictly **patres-famil'ias** (*-trās-*), sometimes **paterfamil'iases**. [L. *păter*, a father, *familiās*, old gen. of *familia*, a household.]
paternal *pə-tûr'n(ə)l*, *adj.* of a father: on the father's side: derived or inherited from the father: fatherly: showing the disposition or manner of a father. — *n.* **pater'nalism** a system or tendency in which provident fostering care is apt to pass into unwelcome interference. — *adj.* **paternalis'tic**. — *adv.* **pater'nally**. — *n.* **pater'nity** the state or fact of being a father: fatherhood: the relation of a father to his children: origin on the father's side: origination or authorship. — **paternity leave** leave of absence from work granted to a husband so that he can be with his wife and assist her during and after childbirth. [L. *pater* (Gr. *patēr*), a father.]
paternoster *pat-ər-nos'tər*, or *pāt'*, *n.* the Lord's Prayer: a muttered formula or spell: a harangue: a large bead

in a rosary, at which, in telling, the Lord's Prayer is repeated: a rosary: anything strung like a rosary, esp. a fishing-line with hooks at intervals: an ornament shaped like beads, used in astragals, etc. (*archit.*): a lift for goods or passengers, consisting of a series of cars moving on a continuous belt, the floors remaining horizontal at the top and bottom of travel. [L. *Pater noster*, 'Our Father', the first words of the Lord's Prayer.]

pater patriae *pā'tər pā'tri-ē, pa'ter pa'tri-ī,* (L.) the father of his country.

Paterson's curse *pa'tər-sənz kûrs, (Austr.)* any of various naturalised orig. European herbs regarded as harmful to livestock. [Ety. dub.]

pâte-sur-pâte *pät'-sür-pät' n.* a type of decoration used on pottery, in which layers of slip are applied to a low relief. [Fr., paste-upon-paste.]

path *päth, n.* a way trodden out by the feet: a way for pedestrians: a course, route, line along which anything moves: a course of action, conduct: — *pl.* **paths** (*pädhz*). — *v.i.* (*Shak.*) to go. — *adj.* **path'less** without a path: untrodden. — **path'finder** one who explores the route, a pioneer: a radar device used as an aircraft navigational aid: a radar device for guiding missiles into a target area; **path'way** a path: in neurology, the route of a sensory impression to the brain, or of a motor impulse from the brain to the musculature: the sequence of reactions by which one substance is metabolically converted to another (*biochemistry*). [O.E. *pæth*; Ger. *Pfad*.]

Pathan *pə-tan', put-(h)än', n.* an Afghan proper: one of Afghan race settled in India. — Also *adj.* [Afghan *Pakhtun*.]

pathos *pā'thos, n.* the quality that raises pity. — *adj.* **pathetic** (*pə-thet'ik*) relating to or affecting the passions or their expressions (*obs.*): affecting the emotions of pity, grief, sorrow: touching: sadly inadequate: contemptible, derisory (*coll.*): applied to the superior oblique muscle, which turns the eyeball downwards, and to the trochlear nerve connecting with it (*anat.*). — See also **-pathetic** below. — *n.* that which is pathetic: the style or manner fitted to excite emotion: (in *pl.*) attempts at pathetic expression. — *adj.* **pathet'ical.** — *adv.* **pathet'ically.** — *adj.* **pathic** (*path'ik*) passive (and see also **-pathic** below). — *n.* a passive subject: a catamite. — **-path** in composition, a sufferer from a particular disorder: a therapist for a particular disorder; **path'o-** in composition, disease, disorder; **-pathy** in composition, mental or emotional sensitivity or receptiveness: disease, disorder: therapy for a particular disorder; **-pathet'ic, -path'ic** adjective combining forms; **-pathist** noun combining form, a therapist for a particular disorder. — *ns.* **pathogen** (*path'ō-jen*) an organism or substance that causes disease; **pathogen'esis, pathogeny** (*pə-thoj'ə-ni*) (mode of) production or development of disease. — *adjs.* **pathogenetic** (*path-ō-ji-net'ik*), **pathogenic** (*-jen'ik*), **pathog'enous** producing disease. — *n.* **pathogenicity** (*-is'i-ti*) the quality of producing, or the ability to produce, disease. — *adj.* **pathognomon'ic** (*-og-nō-*; Gr. *gnōmōn,* judge, index) indicative of a particular disease. — *ns.* **pathog'nomy; pathog'raphy** a description of, article on, a disease: abnormality. — *adjs.* **patholog'ic, -al** relating to pathology. — *adv.* **patholog'ically.** — *ns.* **pathol'ogist** one skilled in pathology, usu. having as one of his duties the performing of post-mortems; **pathol'ogy** the study of diseases or abnormalities or, more particularly, of the changes in tissues or organs that are associated with disease: a deviation from the normal, healthy state; **pathopho'bia** (Gr. *phobos,* fear) morbid fear of disease; **-pathy** in composition, see above. — **pathetic fallacy** the reading of one's own emotion into external nature. [Gr. *pathos,* experience, feeling, pathos.]

patible *pat'i-bl, adj.* capable of suffering or being acted on: passible. [L. *patibilis — patī,* to suffer.]

patibulary *pə-tib'ū-lə-ri, adj.* of or pertaining to a gibbet or gallows. [L. *patibulum,* a gibbet.]

patience *pā'shəns, n.* the quality of being able calmly to endure suffering, toil, delay, vexation, or the like: sufferance: a card-game of various kinds, generally for one person, the object being to fit the cards, as they turn up, into some scheme: a species of dock (also **pa'tience-dock'**; *Rumex patientia*) used like spinach, or other species of dock: also applied to bistort. — *adj.* **pā'tient** sustaining pain, delay, etc., without repining: not easily provoked: persevering in long-continued or minute work: expecting with calmness: long-suffering: enduring: susceptible (of an interpretation). — *n.* one who bears or suffers: a person under medical or surgical treatment: a physician's client. — *v.t.* (*Shak.*) to make patient. — *adv.* **pā'tiently.** [Fr., — L. *patientia — patī,* to bear.]

patin. Obs. form of **paten.**

patina *pat'i-nə, n.* a shallow Roman pan: a eucharistic paten: a film of basic copper carbonate that forms on exposed surfaces of copper or bronze: a similar film of oxide, etc., on other metals: a film or surface appearance that develops on other substances (wood, flint, etc.) on long exposure or burial: a sheen acquired from constant handling or contact (also *fig.*). — *adj.* **pat'ināted.** — *n.* **patinā'tion.** — *adj.* **pat'ined.** [L. *patina,* a dish.]

patine. Obs. form of **paten.**

patio *pa'ti-ō, -tyō, n.* a courtyard: a paved area usu. adjoining a house, where outdoor meals can be served, etc.: — *pl.* **pat'ios.** [Sp., a courtyard.]

pâtisserie *pa-tēs'rē,* (Fr.) *n.* a pastry shop: pastry.

Patna rice *pat'nə rīs,* a long-grained rice, originally grown at *Patna* in India, served with savoury dishes.

patois *pat'wä, n.* illiterate or provincial dialect: — *pl.* **patois** (*-wäz*). [Fr.: origin disputed, some suggesting corr. of *patrois* — L.L. *patriensis,* a local inhabitant.]

patonce *pə-tons',* (*her.*) *adj.* of a cross, having four arms expanding in curves from the centre, with floriated ends. [Origin unknown.]

patres conscripti *pāt', pat'rēz, -rās, kon-skrip'tī, -tē,* (L.) the conscript fathers, those enrolled as Roman senators.

patresfamilias. See **paterfamilias.**

patria potestas *pā', pa'tria po-tes'täs,* (L.) the authority of a Roman father over his children.

patrial *pā', pa'tri-əl, adj.* pertaining to one's native land: (of a word) denoting a native or inhabitant of the place from whose name the word was formed: pertaining to the legal right to enter and stay in the U.K., or to one who has this right. — *n.* a patrial word: a citizen of the U.K., a British colony or the British Commonwealth, who for certain reasons, e.g. because a parent was born in the U.K., has a legal right to enter and stay in the U.K. — *v.t.* **pa'trialise, -ize.** — *ns.* **patrialisā'tion, -z-; pa'trialism; patrial'ity** the condition of being a patrial. [Obs. Fr. — L. *patria,* fatherland.]

patriarch *pā'tri-ärk, n.* one who governs his family by paternal right: one of the early heads of families from Adam downwards to Abraham, Jacob, and his sons (*B.*): a bishop ranking above primates and metropolitans: the head of certain Eastern Churches: a father or founder: a venerable old man: an oldest inhabitant: an old leader of a flock: the most imposing and greatest of its kind. — *adj.* **patriarch'al** belonging, or subject, to a patriarch: like a patriarch: of the nature of a patriarch. — *ns.* **patriarch'alism** the condition of tribal government by a patriarch; **pa'triarchate** the province, dignity, office, term, or residence of a church patriarch: patriarchy; **pa'triarchism** government by a patriarch; **pa'triarchy** a community of related families under the authority of a patriarch: the patriarchal system. — **patriarchal cross** a cross with two horizontal bars. [Gr. *patriarchēs — patriā,* family — *patēr,* father, *archē,* rule.]

patriation *pā-tri-ā'shən, n.* the transferring of responsibility for the Canadian constitution (as enshrined in the British North America Act of 1867) from the British parliament to the Canadian parliament. — *v.t.*

pāt′riate. [L. *patria*, fatherland.]

patrician *pǝ-trish′ǝn, n.* a member or descendant by blood or adoption of one of the original families of citizens forming the Roman people (opp. to *plebeian*): a nobleman of a new order nominated by the emperor in the later Roman Empire: an imperial Roman provincial administrator in Italy or Africa: a hereditary noble: an aristocrat. — Also *adj.* — *adj.* **patri′cianly.** — *n.* **patriciate** (*pǝ-trish′i-āt*) the position of a patrician: the patrician order. [L. *patrĭcius* — *pater, patris*, a father.]

Patrician. See **patrick.**

patricide *pat′ri-sīd, n.* the murder of one's own father: one who murders his father. — *adj.* **patricī′dal.** [Doubtful L. *patricīda*, as if from *pater, patris*, father, *caedĕre*, to kill; prob. an error for *parricīda*; see **parricide.**]

patrick *pat′rik, n.* a 17th-century Irish halfpenny. — *adj.* **Patrician** (*pǝ-trish′ǝn*) of St. Patrick. — **St Patrick's cabbage** a saxifrage, London pride; **St Patrick's cross** a red saltire on a white ground, representing Ireland. [St. *Patrick* (L. *Patrĭcius*), 5th-century christianiser of Ireland.]

patriclinic, patriclinous, etc. See **patroclinic.**

patrico *pat′ri-kō, (slang) n.* a hedge-priest: — *pl.* **pat′ricoes.** — Also **pat′ercove.** [First part unexplained; see **cove**[2].]

patrifocal *pat′ri-fō-kǝl, (anthrop.,* etc.) *adj.* centred on the father: (of societies, families, etc.) in which authority and responsibility rest with the father. — *n.* **patrifocal′ity.** [L. *pater, patris*, father, *fŏcus*, a hearth.]

patrilineal *pat-ri-lin′i-ǝl*, **patrilinear** *-ǝr, adjs.* reckoned through the father or through males alone. — *n.* **patrilineage** (*-lin′i-ij*). — *adv.* **patrilin′eally.** — *n.* **pat′riliny** patrilineal descent. [L. *pater, patris*, father, *līnea*, line.]

patrilocal *pat-ri-lō′kl, adj.* (of a form of marriage) in which the wife goes to live with the husband's group. [L. *pater, patris*, father, *locālis* — *locus*, place.]

patrimony *pat′ri-mǝn-i, n.* an inheritance from a father or from ancestors: a church estate or revenue. — *adj.* **patrimonial** (*-mō′ni-ǝl*). — *adv.* **patrimō′nially.** [L. *patrimōnium*, a paternal estate — *pater, patris*, father.]

patriot *pā′tri-ǝt,* sometimes *pat′, n.* one who truly, though sometimes injudiciously, loves and serves his fatherland. — *adj.* devoted to one's country. — *adj.* **patriotic** (*pat-ri-ot′ik,* or *pāt-*) like a patriot: actuated by a love of one's country: directed to the public welfare. — *adv.* **patriot′ically.** — *n.* **pā′triotism** (or *pat′*). [Gr. *patriōtēs,* fellow-countrymen — *patrios* — *patēr*, a father.]

Patripassian *pat-ri-pas′i-ǝn, n.* a member of one of the earliest classes of anti-Trinitarian sectaries (2nd cent.), who denied the distinction of three persons in one God, maintaining that the sufferings of the Son could be predicated of the Father. — Also *adj.* — *n.* **Patripass′ianism.** [L. *pater, patris*, father, *patī, passus*, to suffer.]

patristic, -al *pǝ-tris′tik, -ǝl, adjs.* pertaining to the fathers of the Christian Church. — *n.* **patris′ticism** (*-sizm*) the mode of thought, etc., of the fathers. — *n. sing.* **patris′tics** the knowledge of the fathers as a subject of study — sometimes **patrol′ogy.** [Gr. *patēr, pat(e)ros,* a father.]

patroclinic *pat-rō-klin′ik,* **patroclinous** *-klī′nǝs, adjs.* inherited from the father: more like the father than the mother. — *n.* **patroclī′ny.** — Also **patriclinic,** etc. [Gr. *patēr, pat(e)ros,* L. *pater, patris,* father, and *klinein,* to lean.]

patrol *pǝ-trōl′, v.i.* to move systematically round, go the rounds of, an area, for purpose of watching, repressing, protecting, inspecting, etc.: to be on duty on a beat. — *v.t.* to keep (an area) under surveillance by patrolling: to perambulate: — *pr.p.* **patroll′ing;** *pa.t.* and *pa.p.* **patrolled′.** — *n.* the act or service of patrolling: perambulation: a person or group of people

patrolling an area: a body of aircraft, ships, etc. having patrolling duties: a small detachment of soldiers, etc. sent on reconnaissance or to make an attack, etc.: one of the units of eight or so Scouts or Guides forming a troop. — *n.* **patroll′er.** — **patrol car** that used by police to patrol an area; **patrol′man** a policeman on duty on a beat (*U.S.*): a policeman without rank (*U.S.*): (or **patrol**) a man on patrol to help motorists in difficulties:—*fem.* **patrol′woman; patrol′-wagon** (*U.S.*) a prison-van. [O.Fr. *patrouiller,* to patrol, orig. to paddle in the mud.]

patrology. See **patristic.**

patron *pā′trǝn, n.* in ancient Rome, the former master of a freed slave, retaining certain rights: a Roman patrician who gave countenance and legal aid to his client in return for services: formerly, one who accepted a dedication and gave the author a present: a protector: one who countenances or encourages: a customer: a habitual attender: an upholder: a proprietor of a restaurant, etc.: one who has the right to appoint to any office, esp. to a living in the church: a guardian saint: a captain of a Mediterranean vessel: a slave-owner: a pattern (*obs.*): — *fem.* **pā′troness,** (of a restaurant, etc.) **patronne** (Fr.; *pa-tron*). — *n.* **patronage** (*pat′*) support given by a patron: protection (*Spens.*): guardianship of saints: the right of bestowing offices, privileges, or church benefices: habitual commercial dealings. — *v.t.* (*Shak.*) to countenance. — *adj.* **patronal** (*pa-, pǝ-trō′nl, pāt′, pat′rǝn-l*). — *v.t.* **patronise, -ize** (*pat′,* U.S. *pāt′*) to act as a patron toward: to give encouragement to: to assume the condescending air of a patron toward: to give one's custom to, or to frequent, habitually. — *n.* **pat′roniser, -z-.** — *adj.* **pat′ronising, -z-.** — *adv.* **pat′ronisingly, -z-.** — *adj.* **pā′tronless.** — **patron saint** a saint regarded as the protector of a particular group, nation, etc. [L. *patrōnus* — *pater, patris,* a father.]

patronymic *pat-rǝ-nim′ik, adj.* derived from the name of a father or an ancestor. — *n.* a name so derived. [Gr. *patrōnymikos* — *patēr,* a father, *onyma* (*onoma*), a name.]

patroon *pǝ-trōōn′, n.* a captain of a ship: a coxswain of a longboat: a holder of a grant of land under the old Dutch government of New York or New Jersey. — *n.* **patroon′ship.** [Fr. *patron,* Sp. *patrón,* and Du. *patroon*; cf. **patron.**]

patsy *pat′si, (slang) n.* an easy victim, a sucker: a scapegoat, fall guy. [Orig. uncertain.]

patte *pat, pät, n.* a narrow band keeping a belt or sash in its place. [Fr.]

patté, pattée *pa-tā′, pat′i, (her.) adj.* of a cross, spreading towards the ends, or having the ends expanded in three clawlike divisions. [Fr., pawed.]

patten[1] *pat′n, n.* a wooden shoe (*hist.*): a wooden sole mounted on an iron ring to raise the shoe above the mud (*hist.*): the base of a pillar (*archit.*). — *v.i.* (*obs.*) to go on pattens. — *adj.* **patt′ened** with pattens. [O.Fr. *patin,* clog (now skate), perh. — *patte,* paw.]

patten[2]. An old form (*Shak.*) of **paten.**

patter[1] *pat′ǝr, v.i.* to pat or strike often, as hailstones: to make the sound of a succession of light pats: to run with short quick steps. — *n.* the sound of pattering. [Freq. of **pat.**]

patter[2] *pat′ǝr, v.i.* to repeat the Lord's Prayer (*obs.*): to gabble prayers (*obs.*): to talk or sing rapidly and glibly: to talk thus, esp. on the stage, as accompaniment to action or for comic effect. — *v.t.* to repeat hurriedly, to gabble. — *n.* glib talk, chatter: the cant of a class. — *n.* **patt′erer** one who sells articles on the street by speechifying. — **patt′er-song** a comic song in which a great many words are sung or spoken very rapidly. — **patter flash** to talk the jargon of thieves. [**paternoster.**]

pattern *pat′ǝrn, n.* a person or thing to be copied: a model: a design or guide with help of which something is to be made (e.g. a dressmaker's paper pattern): a model of an object to be cast, from which a mould is prepared:

a sample: a typical example: a decorative design: a particular disposition of forms and colours: a design or figure repeated indefinitely: the distribution of shot on a target. — *v.t.* to make or be a pattern for (*Shak.*): to match, parallel (*Shak.*): to take as a pattern: to fashion after a pattern: to make a pattern upon. — **patt'ern-maker** one who makes the patterns for moulders in foundry-work; **pattern race** a race open only to horses in a particular category, e.g. of a certain age or weight; **patt'ern-shop** the place in which patterns for a factory are prepared; **patt'ern-wheel** the countwheel in a clock. [Fr. *patron*, patron, pattern; cf. *patron*.]

pattle *pat'*, *pät'l*, **pettle** *pet'l*, (*Scot.*) *ns.* a small longhandled spade for cleaning a plough. [Origin obscure; cf. **paddle³**.]

patty *pat'i*, *n.* a little pie: a small flat cake of minced beef or other food. — **patt'y-pan** a pan for baking patties. [Fr. *pâté*; cf. **pasty**.]

patulous *pat'ū-ləs*, (esp. *bot.*) *adj.* spreading. — *n.* **pat'ulin** a drug got from the mould *Penicillium patulum*. [L. *patulus* — *patēre*, to lie open.]

patzer *pats'ər*, (*slang*) *n.* a poor chess player. [Ety. obscure.]

paua *pä'wə*, *pow'ə*, *n.* the New Zealand name for the abalone. — Also **paw'a**. [Maori.]

pauciloquent *pö-sil'ə-kwənt*, *adj.* of few words, speaking little. [L. *paucus*, little, *loquī*, to speak.]

paucity *pö'sit-i*, *n.* fewness: smallness of quantity. [L. *paucitās, -ātis* — *paucus*, few.]

paughty *pöhh'ti*, (*Scot.*) *adj.* haughty. [Origin unknown.]

paul¹. Same as **pawl**.

paul² *pöl*, *n.* a paolo. — *ns.* **Paul'ian, Paul'ianist** a follower of Paul of Samosata, a third-century Monarchian Unitarian of Antioch. — Also *adjs.* — *n.* **Paulician** (*-ish'ən*) a member of a seventh-century sect in Armenia and later in Thrace, with Marcionite and Adoptianist affinities (perh. from Paul of Samosata, or the apostle, or one of their founders). — Also *adj.* — *adj.* **Paul'ine** (*-īn*) of the apostle Paul. — *n.* a member of any religious order named after him: a scholar of St Paul's School, London. — *adj.* **Paulinian** (*-in'i-ən*) Pauline. — *ns.* **Paul'inism** the teaching or theology of Paul; **Paul'inist** — *adj.* **Paulinist'ic.** — **Paul Jones** (*jōnz*) a dance in the course of which each man takes a number of partners in succession — perh. from the Scottish-American seaman Paul Jones (1747–92), who excelled in the capture of prizes; **Paul Pry** (*prī*) one who pries into other people's business — from a character in John Poole's play (1825) so named; **Paul's'-man** formerly, a lounger in the middle aisle of St Paul's London. [L. *Paulus, Paullus*, a Roman cognomen, meaning 'little'.]

pauldron *pöl'drən*, **pouldron** *pöl'*, *ns.* a separable shoulderplate in armour. [O.Fr. *espalleron* — *espalle*, the shoulder.]

Paulician, Pauline, etc. See **paul²**.

paulo-post-future *pö'lō-pōst-fū'chər*, *adj.* and *n.* future perfect (*gram.*): future immediately after the present. [L. *paulō*, a little, *post*, after, *futūrum*, future.]

Paulownia *pöl-ō'ni-ə*, *n.* a Chinese and Japanese genus of trees of the figwort family, with showy flowers: (without *cap.*) a tree of this genus. [Named after the Russian princess Anna *Pavlovna*.]

paunce. See **pansy**.

paunch *pönch*, *pönsh*, *n.* the belly: a protuberant belly: the first and largest stomach of a ruminant: a rope mat to prevent chafing (*naut.*). — *v.t.* to eviscerate. — *adj.* **paunch'y** big-bellied. [O.Fr. *panche* (Fr. *panse*) — L. *pantex, panticis*.]

pauper *pö'pər*, *n.* a destitute person: one not required to pay costs in a law suit: one supported by charity or by some public provision: — *fem.* **pau'peress.** — *n.* **pauperisā'tion, -z.** — *v.t.* **pau'perise, -ize** to reduce to pauperism: to accustom to expect or depend on sup-

port from without. — *n.* **pau'perism** the state of being a pauper. [L., poor.]

pause¹ *pöz*, *n.* intermission: a temporary stop: cessation caused by doubt: hesitation: a mark for suspending the voice: a continuance of a note or rest beyond its time, or a mark indicating this (*mus.*). — *v.i.* (*Shak. v.t. refl.*) to make a pause. — *v.t.* to cause to stop. — *adjs.* **paus'al; pause'ful.** — *adv.* **pause'fully.** — *adj.* **pause'less.** — *adv.* **pause'lessly.** — *n.* **paus'er.** — *n.* and *adj.* **paus'ing.** — *adv.* **paus'ingly.** — give pause to cause to hesitate. [Fr., — L. *pausa* — Gr. *pausis*, from *pauein*, to cause to cease.]

pause² *pöz*, (*dial.*) *v.t.* to kick. [Orig. unknown.]

pavage. See **pave**.

pavan *pav'ən*, *n.* a slow dance, once much practised in Spain: music for it, in 4–4 time. — Also **pav'ane** (or, now usu., *pav-än'*), **pav'en, pav'in.** [Fr. *pavane*, or Sp. or It. *pavana*, prob. — L. *pāvō, -ōnis*, peacock.]

pave *pāv*, *v.t.* to cover with slabs or other close-set pieces, so as to form a level surface for walking on: to cover with anything close-set: to be such a covering for. — *n.* (*U.S.*) pavement. — *n.* **pā'vage** a charge, or right to levy a charge, for paving streets. — *adj.* **paved.** — *n.* **pave'ment** a paved surface, or that with which it is paved: a footway by the side of a street (sometimes even when unpaved): paved road (*U.S.*): a floor-like surface: an underlying bed, esp. of fireclay under coal. — *v.t.* to pave: to be a pavement for. — *adj.* **pā'ven** paved. — *n.* and *adj.* **pā'ving.** — *n.* **pā'viour** one who lays pavement or rams sets: a paving-stone. — Also **pā'ver, pā'vior.** — **pavement artist** one who seeks a living by drawing coloured pictures on the pavement; **pavement epithelium** epithelium in the form of a layer of flat cells; **pavement light** a window of glass blocks in the pavement to light a cellar; **pa'ving-stone** a slab of stone or concrete used in a pavement, etc. — **on the pavement** without a lodging; **pave the way for** to prepare the way for: to make easier: to help to bring on. [Fr. *paver*, prob. a back-formation from *pavement* — L. *pavīmentum* — *pavīre*, to beat hard; cog. with Gr. *paiein*, to beat.]

pavé *pa-vā*, (Fr.) *n.* pavement: a setting of jewellery with the stones close together, covering the metal.

pavement, paven. See **pave**.

paven. See **pavan**.

pavid *pav'id*, *adj.* timid. [L. *pavidus*, afraid — *pavēre*, to be frightened.]

pavilion *pə-vil'yən*, *n.* a tent, esp. a large or luxurious one: a tent-like covering: a canopy (*obs.*): a light building for players and spectators of a game: an ornamental or showy building for pleasure purposes: a projecting section of a building, usually with a tent-like roof and much decorated: a hospital block: an exhibition building: an ornamental building often turreted or domed: in gem-cutting, the under-surface of a brilliant, opposite to the crown: the bell of a horn: the outer ear: a flag or ensign (*obs.*). — *v.t.* to furnish with pavilions: to cover, as with a tent. — **pavil'ion-roof** a tent-like roof. — **Chinese pavilion** a set of bells hanging from a frame on a pole. [Fr. *pavillon* — L. *pāpiliō, -ōnis*, a butterfly, a tent.]

pavin. See **pavan**.

pavior, paviour. See **pave**.

pavis, pavise *pav'is*, *n.* a shield for the whole body. [O.Fr. *pavais* — It. *pavese*, prob. from *Pavia* in Italy.]

pavlova *pav-lō'və*, (also with *cap.*) *n.* a type of sweet dish consisting of a meringue base topped with whipped cream and fruit. [Named in honour of the Russian ballerina Anna *Pavlova*.]

Pavlovian *pav-lō'vi-ən*, (*psych.*, *physiol.*) *adj.* relating to the work of the Russian physiologist, Ivan *Pavlov*, on conditioned reflexes: (of reactions, responses, etc.) automatic, unthinking.

Pavo *pā'vō*, *n.* the peacock genus: a southern constellation. — *ns.* **pavonazzo** (*pa-və-nat'sō*) a brightly coloured marble; **pavone** (*pə-vōn'*, *Spens.*) a peacock.

— *adjs.* **pavō′nian, pavonine** (*pav′ən-īn*). [L. *pāvō, -ōnis*, peacock.]

paw[1] *pö, n.* a clawed foot: a hand, or handwriting (*facet.* or *derog.*). — *v.i.* to draw the forefoot along the ground: to strike the ground with the forefoot: to strike out with the paw: to feel about or over anything, esp. offensively. — *v.t.* to scrape, feel, handle, or strike with the forefoot or hand: to handle grossly, coarsely, or clumsily. [O.Fr. *poe, powe*, prob. Gmc.; cf. Du. *poot*, Ger. *Pfote*.]

paw[2] *pö, (obs.) interj.* pah. — *adj.* (also **paw′paw**) foul: obscene.

pawa. See **paua.**

pawaw. See **powwow.**

pawk *pök, (Scot.) n.* a trick. — *adv.* **pawk′ily.** — *n.* **pawk′iness.** — *adj.* **pawk′y** drily or slyly humorous. [Origin unknown.]

pawl *pöl, n.* a catch engaging with the teeth of a ratchet wheel to prevent backward movement. [Origin obscure; poss. conn. with Du. or Fr. *pal*, L. *pālus*, stake.]

pawn[1] *pön, n.* something deposited as security for repayment or performance: the state of being pledged (as *in* or *at pawn*). — *v.t.* to give in pledge: to pledge. — *ns.* **pawnee′** one who takes anything in pawn; **pawn′er** one who gives a pawn or pledge as security for money borrowed. — **pawn′broker** a broker who lends money on pawns; **pawn′broking; pawn′shop** a shop of a pawnbroker; **pawn′ticket** a ticket marked with the name of the article, the amount advanced, etc., delivered to the pawner of anything. [O.Fr. *pan*; cf. Du. *pand*; connection with L. *pannus*, cloth, very doubtful.]

pawn[2] *pön, n.* a small piece in chess of lowest rank and range: a humble tool or lightly valued agent (*fig.*). [O.Fr. *paon*, a foot-soldier — L.L. *pedō, -ōnis* — L. *pēs, pedis*, the foot.]

pawn[3] *pön, n.* a gallery or covered walk. [Cf. Du. *pand*.]

pawn[4], **pown, powin** *pown*, (chiefly *Scot.*) *n.* a peacock. [O.Fr. *poun*, Fr. *paon* — L. *pāvō, -ōnis*.]

pawn[5]. See **pan**[2].

pawnce. See **pansy.**

Pawnee *pö′nē*, or *-nē′, n.* one of a tribe of Indians in Nebraska, etc., afterwards in Oklahoma: their language. — Also *adj.*

pawnee[1] *pö′nē*. See under **brandy.**

pawnee[2]. See under **pawn**[1].

pawpaw. See **paw**[2], **papaw.**

pax[1] *paks, n.* the kiss of peace: an osculatory. — *interj.* truce. — **pax′-board, pax′-brede** (i.e. board) an osculatory. [L. *pāx*, peace.]

pax[2] *paks*, (L.) *n.* peace. — **pax vobiscum** (*vo-bis′kəm, vō-, wō-bēs′koŏom*) peace be with you.

paxiuba *päsh-ē-ōō′bə, n.* a Brazilian palm (*Iriartea exorrhiza*) with stilt-roots. [Port., from Tupí.]

paxwax *paks′waks, n.* the strong tendon in an animal's neck. [Orig. *fax-wax* — O.E. (Anglian) *fæx* (W.S. *feax*), hair, *weaxan*, to grow.]

pay[1] *pā, v.t.* to satisfy, gratify (*obs.*): to give what is due (in satisfaction of a debt, in exchange, in compensation, in remuneration, etc.) to (the person, etc. to whom it is owed): to give (money, etc.) in satisfaction of a debt, in exchange, compensation, remuneration, etc.: to settle, discharge (a claim, bill, debt, etc.): to hand over money, etc., for: (of a sum of money, etc.) to be or yield satisfactory remuneration or compensation for, or enough to discharge: to yield (a certain sum, profit, etc.): to be profitable to, to benefit: to render (attention, heed, court, a visit, etc.): to thrash (*Shak.* and *dial.*): of a rope, to allow or cause to run out (*naut.*). — *v.i.* to hand over money or other equivalent, compensation, etc. (with *for*): to afford, constitute, an equivalent or means of making payment (with *for*): to be worth one's trouble: to be profitable: to suffer or be punished (with *for*): to be the subject of payment: — *pr.p.* **pay′ing;** *pa.t.* and *pa.p.* **paid,** (*obs.* except in the nautical sense) **payed** (*pād*). — *n.* satisfaction (*obs.*): money given for service: salary, wages: receipt of wages, etc., service for wages, etc., hire (esp.

for an evil purpose): payment or time of payment: remunerative yield of mineral. — *adj.* **paid** see separate article. — *adj.* **pay′able** that may or should be paid: due: profitable. — *ns.* **payee′** one to whom money is paid; **pay′er.** — *n.* and *adj.* **pay′ing.** — *n.* **pay′ment** the act of paying: the discharge of a debt by money or its equivalent in value: that which is paid: recompense: reward: punishment. — **pay-as-you-earn** a method of income-tax collection in which the tax is paid by deduction from earnings before they are received: — abbrev. **P.A.Y.E;** **pay bed** a bed, specif. in a National Health Service hospital, available to a patient who pays for its use (**private pay bed** one available to a patient who pays for its use and for his own treatment; cf. **amenity bed**); **pay′-bill, -sheet** a statement of money to be paid to workmen, etc.; **pay′-box, pay′-desk** a box or desk at which a customer pays; **pay′-dirt, -grav′el** gravel or sand containing enough gold to be worth working (**pay-dirt** also *fig.*); **paying guest** a boarder in a private house; **pay′-list, -roll** a list of persons entitled to receive pay, with the amounts due to each: (**payroll**) the money for paying wages; **pay′-load** that part of the cargo of an aeroplane or other conveyance for which revenue is obtained: the part of a rocket's equipment that is to fulfil the purpose of the rocket, as a warhead, or apparatus for obtaining information; **pay′master** the master who pays: one who pays workmen, soldiers, etc.; **Paymaster General** the minister at the head of a department of the Treasury that makes payments on behalf of government departments: in the navy, an officer in charge of the Bureau dealing with payments, clothing, etc. (*U.S.*): formerly also a similar officer in the army (*U.S.*); **pay′-off** (time of) payment — reward or punishment: outcome: an esp. useful or desirable result: dénouement; **pay′-office** the place where payments are made; **pay-out** see **pay out** below; **pay′-packet** envelope containing one's wages: wages; **pay′-phone** a coin-operated public telephone; **pay′roll** see **pay-list; pay′-slip** a note to a worker (giving an analysis) of the sum he has been paid; **pay′-station** (*U.S.*) a telephone call-box. — **in the pay of** receiving payment in return for services, used esp. in a sinister sense; **pay back** to pay in return (a debt): to give tit for tat; **pay cash** to pay for something at the time of the transaction, i.e. not using credit terms; **pay down** to pay (e.g. a first instalment) in cash on the spot; **pay for** to make amends for: to suffer for: to bear the expense of; **pay in** to contribute to a fund: to deposit money in a bank-account; **pay off** to pay in full and discharge: to take revenge upon: to requite: to fall away to leeward (*naut.*): to yield good results, justify itself (see also **pay-off** above); **pay one's** or **its, way** to have, or bring, enough to pay expenses: to compensate adequately for initial outlay; **pay out** to cause to run out, as rope: to disburse (*n.* **pay′-out**): to punish deservedly; **payroll giving** contributions to charity which are deducted from one's wages and paid by one's employer directly to the charity concerned; **pay round** to turn the ship's head; **pay the piper** see **pipe**[1]; **pay through the nose** to pay dearly; **pay up** to pay in full: to pay arrears: to accept the necessity and pay. [Fr. *payer* — L. *pācāre*, to appease; cf. *pāx*, peace.]

pay[2] *pā, v.t.* to smear with tar, etc.: — *pa.t.* and *pa.p.* **payed.** [O.Fr. *peier* — L. *picāre*, to pitch.]

paynim *pā′nim*, (*obs.*) *n.* heathendom: a heathen: a non-christian, esp. a Muslim. — Also *adj.* — Also **pai′nim, pā′nim** (*Milt.*). — *n.* **pay′nimry** heathendom. [O.Fr. *paienisme*, paganism — L. *pāgānismus* — *pāgānus*, a pagan.]

payola *pā-ō′lə, n.* secret payment, a bribe, to secure a favour, esp. the promotion of a commercial product by a disc-jockey. [Facetiously coined from **pay**[1] and Victr*ola*, a make of gramophone, or pian*ola*.]

pays *pā-ē̄*, (Fr.) *n.* country. — **les Pays Bas** (*lā pā-ē̄ bä*) the Low Countries.

paysage *pā-ē̄-zäzh′, n.* a landscape, a landscape painting (*obs.* for a time then reborrowed). — *n.* **paysagist** (*pā'zə-jist*) a landscape-painter. [Fr.]

paysd *pāzd*, (*Spens.*) for **peised, poised.**

paz(z)azz. See **piz(z)azz.**

pea[1] *pē, n.* a new singular formed from **pease** (q.v.) which was mistaken for a plural, with a new plural **peas** — the nutritious seed of the papilionaceous climbing plants *Pisum sativum* (garden pea) and *P. arvense* (field pea): the plant itself (also **pea'-plant**): extended to various similar seeds and plants (esp. of the genus Lathyrus) and to various rounded objects, e.g. roe of salmon and some other fish, very small pieces of coal. — **pea'berry** a small round coffee seed, growing singly; **pea'-crab** a little round crab (*Pinnotheres*) that lives symbiotically in lamellibranch shells. — *n.* and *adj.* **pea'-green** (or **-grēn'**) yellowish-green, the colour of soup made from split peas: bright green like fresh peas. — **pea'-iron** limonite in little round nodules; **pea'nut** monkey-nut or ground-nut (Arachis): (*in pl.*) something very trifling or insignificant, esp. a meagre sum of money, chickenfeed (*coll.*); **peanut butter** a paste made from ground roasted peanuts; **peanut oil** oil expressed from peanuts; **pea'pod'**; **pea'-ri'fle** a rifle throwing a very small bullet; **peas'cod, pea'cod** see **peasecod**; **pea'shooter** a small tube for blowing peas through, used as a toy weapon; **pea'-soup** see **pease=soup**; **pea-soup'er** a fog like pea-soup. — *adj.* **pea-soup'y.** — **pea'-stone** pisolite; **pea'-straw** see **pease=straw**; **pea'-trainer** an erection for pea-plants to climb on; **pea-vin'er** a machine that picks, washes and grades peas. — **Egyptian pea** the chick-pea; **split peas** peas stripped of their membranous covering, dried and halved; **Sturt's desert pea** see under **desert.** [See **pease**[1].]

pea[2] *pē, n.* an obs. term for a **pea'-fowl** — a male or female peacock. — **pea'-chick** a young pea-fowl; **pea'=hen** the female of the peacock. [O.E. *pēa* (*pāwa*) — L. *pāvō*.]

peace *pēs, n.* a state of quiet: freedom from disturbance: freedom from war: cessation of war: a treaty that ends a war: freedom from contention: ease of mind or conscience: tranquillity: quiet: stillness: silence. — *v.i.* (*Shak.*) to be silent — passing in the *imper.* into *interj.* silence: be silent: hist. — *adj.* **peace'able** disposed to peace: peaceful. — *n.* **peace'ableness.** — *adv.* **peace'-ably.** — *adj.* **peace'ful** enjoying peace: tending towards or favouring peace: inclined to peace: belonging to time of peace. consistent with peace: tranquil: calm: serene. — *adv.* **peace'fully.** — *n.* **peace'fulness.** — *adj.* **peace'less.** — *ns.* **peace'lessness; peace'nik** a pacifist, esp. in a depreciatory sense. — **peace'-breaker** one who breaks or disturbs the peace; **Peace Corps** in the U.S., a government agency that sends volunteers to developing countries to help with agricultural, technological and educational schemes; **peace drug, pill** (*coll.*) a hallucinogen (**angel dust**); **peace establishment** the reduced military strength maintained in time of peace; **peace'-keeper.** — *adj.* **peace'-keeping** (**peace-keeping force** a military force sent into an area with the task of preventing fighting between opposing factions). — **peace'maker** one who makes or produces peace: one who reconciles enemies: a revolver (*old facet.*); **peace'-making; peace'-monger** a peacemaker from the point of view of those who think him a sentimental busybody; **peace'-off'ering** among the Jews a thank-offering to God: a gift offered towards reconciliation, propitiation, or deprecation; **peace'-off'icer** an officer whose duty it is to preserve the peace: a police-officer. — *adj.* **peace'-part'ed** (*Shak.*) dismissed from the world in peace. — **peace'-par'ty** a political party advocating the making or the preservation of peace; **peace pill** see **peace drug; peace'-pipe** the calumet; **peace'time** time when there is no war. — *adj.* of peacetime. — **peace'=warrant** a warrant of arrest issued by a Justice of the Peace. — **at peace** in a state of peace: not at war; **breach of the peace** see **breach; hold one's peace** to remain silent; **in peace** in enjoyment of peace; **keep the peace** to refrain from disturbing the public peace: to refrain from, or to prevent, contention; **kiss of peace** see **kiss; letter of peace** see **pacifical** under **pacify; make one's peace with** to reconcile or to be reconciled with; **make peace** to end a war; **peace of God** the protection from acts of private warfare formerly offered by the Church to consecrated persons and places, and on Sundays and holy days; **the king's** or **queen's peace** see **king; swear the peace** to take oath before a magistrate that a certain person ought to be put under bond to keep the peace. [O.Fr. *pais* (Fr. *paix*) — L. *pāx, pācis*, peace.]

peach[1] *pēch, v.t.* (*Shak.*) to accuse, inform against, betray. — *v.i.* (with *on*) to betray one's accomplice: to become informer. — *n.* **peach'er.** [Aphetic form of **appeach.**]

peach[2] *pēch, n.* a sweet, juicy, velvety-skinned stone-fruit: the tree (*Prunus*, or *Amygdalus*, *persica*) bearing it, close akin to the almond: extended to other fruits and fruit-trees, as the quandong: peach-brandy (*U.S.*): anything regarded as a very choice example of its kind, esp. a girl (*slang*; in *U.S.* also **peacherino** *-ə-rē'nō; pl.* **-nos**): a yellow slightly tinged with red. — *adj.* of the peach: of the colour of a peach. — *adj.* **peach'y.** — **peach'-bloom'** the powdery bloom on a peach: a similar appearance on the face, on pottery, etc.: a peach flower (also **peach'-bloss'om**): its pinkish colour: a moth with wings so coloured (*Thyatira batis*); **peach'-blow** a pinkish glaze on porcelain, esp. Chinese porcelain. — Also *adjs.* — **peach'-brand'y** a spirit distilled from the fermented juice of the peach. — *adj.* **peach'-coloured** of the colour of a ripe peach (yellowish, tinged with red) or of peach-blossom (pink). — **peach Melba** a dish named in honour of the Australian soprano Dame Nellie *Melba*, consisting of peach halves served with ice-cream and usu. a raspberry sauce; **peach'-palm** the pupunha, a South American palm (*Bactris* or *Guilielma*) with edible fruit like a peach in appearance; **peach'-stone; peach'-tree; peach'-water** a flavouring extract from peach-leaves; **peach'-wood** the wood of the peach-tree: Nicaragua wood (Caesalpinia); **peach'=yell'ows** a virus disease that turns peach-leaves yellow and kills the tree. [O.Fr. *pesche* (Fr. *pêche*, It. *persica*, *pesca*) — L. *Persicum* (*mālum*), the Persian (apple); its native country is unknown.]

pea-chick. See **pea**[2].

pea-coat. Same as **pea-jacket.**

peacock *pē'kok, n.* a genus (Pavo) of large birds of the pheasant kind, consisting of the common peacock (*P. cristatus*) and the Javan (*P. muticus*), noted for gay plumage, esp., in the former, the deep iridescent greenish blue in the neck and tail-coverts: the male of either species: a vainglorious person: peacock-blue (also *adj.*). — *v.t.* to make like a peacock: to pick the best parts out of (*Austr.*). — *v.i.* to strut about or behave like a peacock: to acquire the choicest pieces of land (i.e. near water) (*Austr.*). — *n.* **peacock'ery** vainglorious ostentation. — *adjs.* **pea'cockish; pea'-cock-like; pea'cocky.** — **pea'cock-blue'** the deep greenish blue of the peacock's neck. — Also *adj.* — **pea'cock=butt'erfly** a butterfly (*Vanessa io*) with spots like those of the peacock's train; **pea'cock-copp'er** copper-pyrites, from the colours of its tarnish; **pea'cock-fish** a variegated Mediterranean wrasse; **pea'cock-flower** a name for various species of Poinciana (flamboyant tree, Barbados pride); **pea'cock-ore'** bornite: copper-pyrites; **pea'cock-pheas'ant** an Asiatic genus (*Polyplectron*) akin to the peacocks and Argus pheasants; **pea'cock-stone'** a jeweller's name for the cartilaginous ligament of some molluscs; **pea'cock-throne'** the throne of the kings of Delhi, carried off to Persia in 1739. [**pea**[2] and **cock,** etc.]

pea-crab. See under **pea**[1].

pea-fowl. See **pea**[2].

peag *pēg*, **peak** *pēk, ns.* North American Indian shell-money. [Massachusetts *piak*.]

pea-hen. See **pea**[2].

pea-jacket *pē'-jak'it, n.* a sailor's coarse thick overcoat.

— Also **pea′-coat**. [Du. *pie* (now *pij*), coat of coarse stuff, and **jacket, coat**.]

peak[1] *pēk, n.* a point: the pointed end or highest point of anything: the top of a mountain, esp. when sharp: a summit: a maximum point in a curve or the corresponding value in anything capable of being represented by a curve, e.g. a point or time of maximum use by the public of a service, etc.: a sharp projection: the projecting front of a cap or (formerly) of a widow's hood: a projecting point of hair on the forehead: a pointed beard: the upper outer corner of a sail extended by a gaff or yard (*naut.*): the upper end of a gaff (*naut.*). — *adj.* maximum: of a maximum. — *v.i.* to rise in a peak: to reach the height of one's powers, popularity, etc.: of prices, etc., to reach a highest point or level (sometimes with *out*). — *v.t.* (*naut.*) to tilt up. — *adjs.* **peaked** having a peak or peaks; **peak′y** having a peak or peaks: like a peak. — **peak′-load** the maximum demand of electricity, or load on a power-station. — **peak (viewing, listening) hours, time** the period in the day when the maximum number of people are watching television (approximately 5.00 p.m.–10.00 p.m.) or listening to the radio. [Found from the 16th cent. (*peked* in the 15th); app. connected with **pike**[1].]

peak[2] *pēk, v.i.* to sneak or slink about (*Shak.*): to mope (*obs.*): to droop, to look thin or sickly. — *adjs.* **peaked**, **peak′ing**, **peak′y** having a pinched or sickly look, sharp-featured. [Origin unknown.]

peak[3]. See **peag**.

peal[1] *pēl, n.* a loud sound: a number of loud sounds one after another: a set of bells tuned to each other: a chime or carillon: the changes rung upon a set of bells. — *v.i.* to resound in peals: to appeal (*Spens.*). — *v.t.* to give forth in peals: to assail with din (*Milt.*). [Apparently aphetic for **appeal**.]

peal[2], **peel** *pēl*, (*local*) *n.* a grilse: a young sea-trout. [Origin unknown.]

pean[1] *pēn, n.* a heraldic fur, differing from ermine only in the ground being sable and the spots or. [Perhaps O.Fr. *pene, panne*.]

pean[2]. Same as **paean**.

pean[3]. Same as **peen**.

peanut. See **pea**[1].

pear *pār, n.* a fruit, a pome tapering towards the stalk and bulged at the end: the tree (*Pyrus communis*) bearing it, of the apple genus: extended to various fruits (**alligator-, anchovy-pear, prickly-pear**, etc.): in gem-cutting, a pear-shaped brilliant. — **pear′-drop** a pear-shaped pendant: a pear-shaped, pear-flavoured sweetmeat; **pear′monger** a seller of pears; **pear′-push, -switch** an electric push-button in a hanging pear-shaped bob. — *adj.* **pear′-shaped** tapering towards one end and bulged at the other: in the shape of a pear: (of a vocal quality) mellow, resonant, non-nasal. — **pear′-tree**. — **go pear-shaped** (*coll.*) to put on weight around the hips, waist or bottom. [O.E. *pere, peru* — L.L. *pira* — L. *pirum* (wrongly *pyrum*), pear.]

pearce, peare. Spenserian spellings of **pierce, peer**.

pearl[1] *pûrl, n.* a concretion of nacre formed in a pearl-oyster, pearl mussel, or other shellfish, around a foreign body or otherwise, prized as a gem: nacre: a paragon or finest example: a lustrous globule: a granule: a tubercle of an antler burr: cataract of the eye: a five-point type (about 15 lines to the inch) (*print.*). — *adj.* of or like pearl: granulated: of an electric light bulb, made from a frosted, rather than clear, glass as a precaution against glare. — *v.t.* to set or adorn with pearls or pearly drops: to make pearly: to make into small round grains. — *v.i.* to take a rounded form: to become like pearls: to fish for pearls. — *adj.* **pearled**. — *ns.* **pearl′er** a pearl-fisher or his boat; **pearl′iness**. — *n.* and *adj.* **pearl′ing**. — *adjs.* **pearl′ised, -ized** treated so as to give a pearly or lustrous surface; **pearl′y** like pearl, nacreous: rich in pearls. — *n.* (in *pl.*) pearl-buttons: (in *pl.*) costermongers' clothes covered with pearl-buttons: a costermonger, or a member of his family, wearing such clothes: — *pl.* **pearl′ies**. — **pearl′-**

ash′ partly purified potassium carbonate; **pearl′-bar′-ley** see **barley**[1]; **pearl′-butt′on** a mother-of-pearl button; **pearl disease** bovine tuberculosis; **pearl′-div′er** one who dives for pearls; **pearl′-essence** a silvery preparation from fish scales used in making artificial pearls; **pearl′-eye** cataract. — *adj.* **pearl′-eyed**. — **pearl′-fisher** one who fishes for pearls; **pearl′-fishery; pearl′-fishing; pearl′-gray′, -grey′** a pale grey. — Also *adj.* **pearl′=mill′et** the bulrush millet or spiked millet (*Pennisetum typhoideum*), a grain much grown in India; **pearl′=muss′el** a freshwater mussel (*Unio margaritifera*) that yields pearls; **pearl′-oys′ter** any oyster that produces pearls, esp. *Avicula* (or *Meleagrina*) *margaritifera*; **pearl′-pow′der** a cosmetic of basic bismuth nitrate or of bismuth oxychloride; **pearl′-sā′go** sago in round granules; **pearl′-shell** mother-of-pearl: pearly or pearl-bearing shell; **pearl′-shell′er; pearl′-shelling; pearl′-spar** a pearly-lustred pale dolomite; **pearl′-stone** perlite; **pearl′-tapiō′ca** tapioca granulated and graded acc. to its size: a potato-starch imitation; **pearl′-white** material made from fish-scales, used in making artificial pearls: basic nitrate of bismuth, used in medicine and as a cosmetic: bismuth trichloride, used as a pigment: lithopone: calcium sulphate; **pearl′-wort** a member of a genus (Sagina) of small plants akin to chickweed; **pearly gates** (Rev. xxi) entrance to heaven; **pearly king** a costermonger whose costume is considered the most splendidly decorated with pearl-buttons:— *fem.* **pearly queen; pearly nautilus** see **nautilus**. — **cultured pearl** a true pearl formed by artificial means, as by planting a piece of mother-of-pearl wrapped in oyster epidermis in the body of an oyster; **false, imitation, simulated pearl** an imitation, as, for instance, a glass bulb coated with pearl essence. [Fr. *perle*, prob. from dim. of L. *perna*, leg, leg-of-mutton-shaped; cf. It. dial. *perna*, pearl, It. *pernocchia*, pearl-oyster.]

pearl[2], **peel** *pûrl, n.* a small loop on the edge of lace, ribbon, etc.: in knitting, purl. — *v.t.* to purl. — *ns.* **pearl′ing, pearl′in** (*Scot.*) lace of silk or of thread: (in *pl.*) edgings of such lace or clothes trimmed with it. — **pearl′-edge** an edging of small loops. [Cf. **purl**[3].]

Pearl Harbour *pûrl här′bər*, (*fig.*) a sudden and devastating attack. — *v.t.* (*rare*) to mount a surprise attack of great force. [*Pearl Harbour*, U.S. naval base near Honolulu, attacked by the Japanese air-force on 7 December 1941.]

pearlite *pûr′līt, n.* a constituent of steel composed of alternate plates of ferrite and cementite. — *adj.* **pearlit′ic**. [**pearl**[1].]

pearmain *pār′mān, n.* a variety of apple. [App. O.Fr. *parmain, permain*.]

pearst. Spenserian spelling of **pierced**.

peart *pērt*, (*dial.*) *adj.* lively: saucy: in good health and spirits. — Also (*obs.*) **piert**. — *adv.* **peart′ly**. [**pert**.]

peasant *pez′ənt, n.* a small farmer: a tiller of the soil: a countryman: a rustic: an ignorant or low fellow (*derog.*). — *adj.* of or relating to peasants, rustic, rural: rude. — *n.* **peas′antry** the body of peasants: the condition or quality of a peasant. — *adj.* **peas′anty** in the style of a peasant. — **peasant proprietor** a peasant who owns and works his own farm; **Peasants' Revolt** Wat Tyler's rising of 1381; **Peasants' War** a popular insurrection in Germany, in 1525. [O.Fr. *paisant* (Fr. *paysan*) — *pays* — assumed L. *pāgēnsis* — *pāgus*, a district.]

pease[1] *pēz, n.* orig., a pea or pea-plant (old *pl.* **peason** *pēz′ən*): now almost wholly superseded by the new singular **pea** (q.v.) and plural **peas** except in a collective sense. — **pease′-bann′ock** a bannock of pease-meal; **pease′-blossom; pease′-brose** brose made of pease-meal; **pease′-cod, peas′cod, pea′cod** the pod of the pea. — *adj.* **pease′cod-bell′ied** of a doublet, peaked downwards in front. — **pease′cod-cuirass′** a cuirass shaped like the peasecod-bellied doublet; **pease′-meal, pease′=porr′idge, pease′-pudd′ing** meal, porridge, or pudding made from pease; **pease′-soup, pea′-soup** soup made from pease: a thick yellow heavy-smelling fog (also pea'-soup'er); **pease'-straw, pea'-straw** the stems and leaves of the pea-plant after the peas have been picked. [M.E. *pēse*, pl. *pēsen* — O.E. *pise*, pl. *pisan* — L.L. *pisa*, L. *pīsum* — Gr. *pīson* or *pīsos*.]

pease². See **peise**.

peaseweep *pēz'wēp*. See **peewit**.

peason. The old *pl.* of **pease¹** (q.v.).

peat¹ *pēt, n.* a shaped block dug from a bog and dried or to be dried for fuel: the generally brown or nearly black altered vegetable matter (chiefly bog-moss) found in bogs, from which such blocks are cut. — *ns.* **peat'ary, peat'ery, pēt'ary, peat'-bank, -bed, -bog, -moor, -moss** a region, bog, moor, etc., covered with peat: a place from which peat is dug. — *adj.* **peat'y** like, of the nature of, abounding in, or composed of, peat. — **peat'-caster** one who digs peats and throws them on the bank to dry; **peat'-casting; peat'-creel** a basket for carrying peats; **peat'-hag, -hagg** a hag in a peat-bog (see **hag³**); **peat'-hole; peat'man** a carter or seller of peats; **peat'-reek'** the smoke of peat, imagined to add a special flavour to whisky: highland whisky; **peat'-reek'er** ornamental apparatus for producing the smell of peat-smoke; **peat'-smoke'; peat'-spade** a spade having a side wing at right angles for cutting peat in rectangular blocks; **peat'-stack'** a stack of peats, drying or stored. [From the 13th cent. in S.E. Scotland in Anglo-Latin as *peta*, a peat; possibly of British origin; cf. **piece**.]

peat² *pēt, (obs.) n.* an endearment applied to a woman or girl or friend or favourite: an advocate favoured by a judge (*Scot.*). — *n.* **peat'ship** (*Scott*). [Origin obscure.]

peau de soie *pō-də-swä', a* type of smooth silk or rayon fabric. [Fr., lit. skin of silk.]

peavey, peavy *pē'vi, (U.S.) n.* a lumberman's spiked and hooked lever. [Joseph *Peavey*, its inventor.]

peaze. See **peise**.

peba *pē'bə, n.* a South American armadillo. [Tupí.]

pebble *peb'l, n.* a small roundish stone, esp. water-worn: transparent and colourless rock-crystal: a lens made of it: a semi-precious agate: a grained appearance on leather, as if pressed by pebbles: a large size of gunpowder. — *adj.* of pebble. — *v.t.* to stone or pelt: to impart pebble to (leather). — *adjs.* **pebb'led; pebb'ly** full of pebbles. — *n.* **pebb'ling.** — **pebble dash** a method of coating exterior walls with small pebbles set into the mortar; **pebb'le-pow'der** gunpowder in large cubical grains; **pebb'le-stone** a pebble; **pebb'le-ware** a fine pottery of mixed coloured clays. [O.E. *papol(-stān)*, a pebble(-stone).]

pébrine *pā-brēn', n.* a destructive protozoan disease of silkworms. [Fr.]

pec *pek, n.* a photoelectric cell. [From the initials.]

pecan *pi-kan', n.* a North American hickory (also **pecan'-tree**): its nut (**pecan'-nut'**). [Indian name; cf. Cree *pakan*.]

peccable *pek'ə-bl, adj.* liable to sin. — *ns.* **peccabil'ity; pecc'ancy** sinfulness: transgression. — *adj.* **pecc'ant** sinning: offending: morbid. — *adv.* **pecc'antly.** [L. *peccāre, -ātum,* to sin.]

peccadillo *pek-ə-dil'ō, n.* a trifling fault, a small misdemeanour: — *pl.* **peccadill'os** (or **peccadill'oes**). [Sp. *pecadillo,* dim. of *pecado* — L. *peccātum,* a sin.]

peccant, etc. See **peccable**.

peccary *pek'ə-ri, n.* either of two species of hog-like South American animals. [Carib *pakira*.]

peccavi *pek-ä'vē, n.* an admission of guilt or sin: — *pl.* **pecca'vis.** [L. *peccavi,* I have sinned.]

pech, pegh *pehh, (Scot.) v.i.* to pant. — *n.* a pant. [Imit.]

Pecht, Peght *pehht, (Scot.) n.* a Pict. [O.E. (Anglian) *Pehtas* (W.S. *Peohtas*), Picts.]

peck¹ *pek, n.* formerly a measure of capacity for dry goods, 2 gallons, or one-fourth of a bushel: a measuring vessel holding this quantity: an indefinitely great amount (as *a peck of troubles*). [M.E. *pekke, pek* — O.Fr. *pek,* generally a horse's feed of oats; origin unknown.]

peck² *pek, v.t.* to strike or pick up with the point of the beak or other sharp instrument: to make (a hole, etc.), render or cause to be (damaged, etc.) by quick movement of the beak, etc.: to eat sparingly or with affectation of daintiness or (*slang*) eat in general: to kiss with dabbing movement. — *v.i.* to strike or feed with the beak or in similar manner: to eat daintily or sparingly (with *at*): to cavil (with *at*): to nag, criticise (with *at*). — *n.* an act of pecking: a hole made by pecking: a kiss: food (*slang*). — *ns.* **peck'er** that which pecks: a woodpecker: a kind of hoe: a part with an up-and-down movement in a telegraph instrument: spirit (as if orig. beak, nose, as in *keep your pecker up; slang*): a penis (*vulg.*); **peck'erwood** (*U.S.*) a woodpecker; **peck'ing.** — *adj.* **peck'ish** somewhat hungry. — *n.* **peck'ishness.** — **pecking order, peck order** a social order among poultry (or other birds) according to which any bird may peck a less important bird but must submit to being pecked by a more important one: order of prestige or power in a human social group: order of importance or prevalence. [App. a form of **pick¹**.]

peck³ *pek, v.t.* (*Shak.* **pecke**) to pitch: to jerk. — *v.i.* to incline: to stumble, esp. of a horse by failing to put the foot down flat. — *n.* **peck'ing** stone-throwing. [A form of **pitch²**, cf. **pick²**.]

Pecksniffian *pek-snif'i-ən, adj.* like, or of, the hypocrite *Pecksniff* in Dickens's *Martin Chuzzlewit*.

Pecora *pek'ə-rə, n.pl.* the Cotylophora, or ruminants other than camels and chevrotains. [L. pl. of *pecus, -oris,* cattle.]

pecten *pek'tən, n.* a comb-like structure of various kinds, e.g. in a bird's or reptile's eye: the pubic bone: a tactile organ in scorpions: (with *cap.*) the scallop genus of molluscs, with ribbed shell: a mollusc of this genus: — *pl.* **pec'tines** (*-tin-ēz*). — *adjs.* **pectinaceous** (*-ā'shəs*) like the scallops; **pec'tinal** of a comb: comb-like: having bones like the teeth of a comb; **pec'tinate, -d** toothed like a comb: having narrow parallel segments or lobes: like the teeth of a comb. — *adv.* **pec'tinately.** — *n.* **pectinā'tion** the state of being pectinated: a comb-like structure. — *adjs.* **pectin'eal** of the pubic bone: comb-like; **pec'tinibranchiate** (*-brangk-i-āt*) having comb-like gills. [L. *pecten, -inis,* a comb.]

pectic *pek'tik, adj.* of, relating to, or derived from, pectin. — *ns.* **pec'tin** a mixture of carbohydrates found in the cell-walls of fruits, important for the setting of jellies; **pectisā'tion, -z-.** — *v.t.* and *v.i.* **pec'tise, -ize** to congeal. — *n.* **pec'tōse** a substance yielding pectin contained in the fleshy pulp of unripe fruit. — **pectic acid** an insoluble substance (of several varieties) formed by hydrolysis of pectins. [Gr. *pēktikos,* congealing — *pēgnynai,* to fix.]

pectinaceous, pectineal, pectines, etc. See **pecten**.

pectolite *pek'tə-līt, n.* a zeolite-like monoclinic acid, calcium sodium silicate. [Gr. *pēktos,* congealed, *lithos,* stone.]

pectoral *pek'tə-rəl, adj.* of, for, on, or near, the breast or chest: coming from the heart or inward feeling (*fig.*). — *n.* armour for the breast of man or horse: an ornament worn on the breast, esp. the breastplate worn by the ancient Jewish high-priest, and the square of gold, embroidery, etc., formerly worn on the breast over the chasuble by bishops during mass: a chest-protector: a medicine for the chest: a pectoral cross: a pectoral fin: either of the two muscles (*pectoralis major, pectoralis minor*) situated on either side of the top half of the chest and responsible for certain arm and shoulder movements. — *adv.* **pec'torally.** — *n.* **pectoril'oquy** (L. *loqui,* to talk) the sound of the patient's voice heard through the stethoscope when applied to the chest in certain morbid conditions of the lungs. — **pectoral cross** a gold cross worn on the breast by bishops, etc.; **pectoral fins** the anterior paired fins of fishes; **pectoral girdle** the shoulder-girdle, consisting of shoulder-blade and collar-bone (and coracoid in vertebrates other than mammals); **pectoral**

theology the theology of those who make much of experience and emotion as guides to a knowledge of divine truth. [L. *pectorālis* — *pectus, pectoris*, the breast.]

pectose. See **pectic**.

peculate *pek'ū-lāt, v.t.* and *v.i.* to appropriate dishonestly to one's own use, pilfer, embezzle. — *ns.* **pecula'tion; pec'ulātor.** [L. *pecūlārī, -ātus* — *pecūlium*, private property, akin to *pecūnia*, money.]

peculiar *pi-kū'lyər, adj.* own: of one's own: belonging exclusively: privately owned: appropriated: preserved: characteristic: special: very particular: odd, strange: having eccentric or individual variations in relation to the general or predicted pattern, as *peculiar motion, velocity (astron.)*: (of a star) having a variable magnetic field. — *n.* private property or right (*obs.*): a parish or church exempt from the jurisdiction of the ordinary or bishop in whose diocese it is placed: anything exempt from ordinary jurisdiction: (usu. with *cap.*) one of the Peculiar People: a type of unusual kind that has to be specially cast (*print.*). — *v.t.* **pecu'liarise, -ize** to set apart. — *n.* **peculiarity** (*-li-ar'i-ti*) quality of being peculiar or singular: that which is found in one and in no other: that which marks anything off from others: individuality: oddity. — *adv.* **pecu'liarly.** — *n.* **pecu'-lium** private property, esp. that given by a father to a son, etc. — **peculiar motion** see **proper motion** under **proper;** **Peculiar People** the Jews, as God's chosen people (N.E. Bible 'special possession', Deut. xxvi. 18, 'a people marked out as his own', Titus ii 14): an Evangelical denomination, founded in 1838, holding inspiration of Holy Scriptures, believers' baptism, Holy Communion, and Divine healing. [L. *pecūlium*, private property.]

pecuniary *pi-kū'nyə-ri, -ni-ə-ri, adj.* relating to money: consisting of money. — *adv.* **pecu'niarily.** — *adj.* **pecu'nious** (*rare*) rich. [L. *pecūnia*, money, from the root that appears in L. *pecudēs* (pl.), cattle, and **fee.**]

ped¹ *ped,* (*dial.*) *n.* a pannier or hamper. — Also **pad.** [Origin unknown.]

ped² *ped, n.* short for **pedestrian.**

ped³ *ped, n.* a naturally-formed unit or mass of soil, such as a crumb, block or aggregate. [Gr. *pedon*, ground.]

ped-¹. See **paed(o)-.**

ped-². See **ped(i)-.**

-ped *-ped,* **-pede** *-pēd,* in composition, foot. — **-pedal** (*-ped'l*) adjective combining form. [L. *pēs, pedis* foot.]

pedagogue *ped'ə-gog, n.* a teacher: a pedant. — *v.t.* to teach. — *adjs.* **pedagogic** (*-gog', -goj'*), **-al.** — *adv.* **pedagog'ically.** — *n.sing.* **pedagog'ics** (*-gog', -goj'*) the science and principles of teaching. — *n.* **ped'agoguery** (*-gog-ə-ri*) a school: schoolmastering: pedagoguish-ness. — *adj.* **ped'agoguish** like a pedagogue. — *ns.* **ped'agoguishness; ped'agog(u)ism** (*-gizm, -jizm*) the spirit or system of pedagogy: teaching; **ped'agogy** (*-gog-i, -goj-i*) the science of teaching: instruction: training. [Partly through Fr. and L. from Gr. *paidagōgos,* a slave who led a boy to school — *pais, paidos,* boy, *agōgos,* leader — *agein,* to lead.]

pedal *ped'l* (*zool.* also *pē'dəl*), *adj.* of the foot: of the feet of perpendiculars: of, with, or pertaining to, a pedal or pedals. — *n.* (*ped'l*) a lever pressed by the foot: the lower and thicker part of a straw: a plait thereof: a pedal-point: a pedal-organ: a pedal-board. — *v.i.* to use a pedal or pedals: to advance by use of the pedals. — *v.t.* to drive by the pedals: — *pr.p.* **ped'alling;** — *pa.t.* and *pa.p.* **ped'alled.** — *ns.* **pedalier** (*-ēr'*) a pedal-board attached to a piano for the bass strings; **ped'aller** one who uses pedals; **ped'alling; pedalo** (*ped'ə-lō*) a pleasure-boat operated by pedal: — *pl.* **ped'alo(e)s.** — **ped'al-ac'tion** the apparatus worked by the pedals of a musical instrument; **ped'al-board, ped'al-clavier'** the keyboards or pedals of an organ or other instrument; **ped'al-bone** a horse's coffin-bone; **pedal cycle; ped'al-organ** the division of an organ played by means of pedals; **ped'al-point** organ point, a tone or tones (usu.

tonic and dominant) sustained normally in the bass, while other parts move independently; **ped'al-pushers** women's knee-length breeches, gathered below the knee. — **pedal steel guitar** an electric steel guitar on a fixed stand and fitted with foot pedals for adjusting pitch, creating glissando effects, etc. [L. *pedālis* — *pēs, pedis,* foot.]

Pedaliaceae *pi-dā-li-ā'si-ē, n.pl.* a family of tubifloral dicotyledons akin to the bignonias. [Gr. *pēdalion,* a rudder, from the keeled fruit.]

pedalier, pedaller, etc. See **pedal.**

pedant *ped'nt, n.* a schoolmaster (*Shak.*): an over-learned person who parades his knowledge: one who attaches too much importance to merely formal matters in scholarship. — *adjs.* **pedantic** (*pid-ant'ik*), **-al** school-masterly: of the character or in the manner of a pedant. — *adv.* **pedant'ically.** — *v.t.* **pedant'icise, -ize** (*-i-sīz*) to make pedantic, give pedantic form to. — *n.* **pedant'-icism** (*-i-sizm*) a pedant's expression. — *v.i.* **ped'antise, -ize** to play the pedant. — *v.t.* to turn into a pedant. — *ns.* **ped'antism** pedantry: pedanticism; **pedantoc'racy** government by pedants; **pedant'ocrat.** — *adj.* **pedantocrat'ic.** — *n.* **ped'antry** the character or manner of a pedant: a pedantic expression: unduly rigorous for-mality. [It. *pedante* (perh. through Fr. *pédant*); connection with **pedagogue** not clear.]

pedate *ped'āt, adj.* footed: foot-like: palmately lobed with the outer lobes deeply cut, or ternately branching with the outer branches forked (*bot.*). — *adv.* **ped'ately.** — *adj.* **pedatifid** (*pi-dat'i-fid*) divided in a pedate manner, but having the divisions connected at the base. [L. *pedātus,* footed — *pēs, pedis,* foot.]

pedder *ped'ər,* **pether** *pedh'ər,* (now *Scot.*) *ns.* a pedlar. — **pedd'er-coffe** (prob. *-kōv; Scott* after *David Lyndsay;* **cove²**). [App. — **ped¹**.]

peddle *ped'l, v.i.* to go about as a pedlar: to trifle. — *v.t.* to sell or offer as a pedlar. — *n.* (esp. *U.S.*) **pedd'ler.** — *adj.* **pedd'ling** unimportant. — *n.* the trade or tricks of a pedlar. [App. partly a back-formation from **pedlar,** partly from **piddle.**]

-pede. See **-ped.**

pederasty, etc. See **paed(o)-.**

pederero *ped-ə-rā'rō, n.* an old gun for discharging stones, pieces of iron, etc., also for firing salutes. — Also **padere'ro, patere'ro, pedre'ro,** etc.: — *pls.* **pedere'ro(e)s,** etc. [Sp. *pedrero* — L. *petra,* stone — Gr. *petrā.*]

pedesis *ped-ē'sis, n.* Brownian movement. — *adj.* **pedetic** (*pi-det'ik*). [Gr. *pēdēsis,* jumping.]

pedestal *ped'is-tl, n.* the support of a column, statue, vase, etc.: the fixed casting which holds the brasses in which a shaft turns, called also *axle-guard* or *pillow-block.* — *v.t.* to place on a pedestal. — *adj.* **ped'estalled.** — **pedestal desk** a desk for which sets of drawers act as the side supports for the writing surface. [Fr. *piédestal* — It. *piedistallo,* for *piè di stallo,* foot of a stall — *piè,* foot (L. *pēs, pedis*), *di,* of (L. *dē*), *stallo,* stall (see **stall.**)]

pedestrian *pi-des'tri-ən, adj.* on foot: of walking: not mounted on Pegasus, hence prosaic, uninspired: flat or commonplace. — *n.* a walker: one who practises feats of walking or running. — *n.* **pedestrianisā'tion, -z-.** — *v.i.* **pedes'trianise, -ize** to walk. — *v.t.* to convert (street) to use by pedestrians only. — *n.* **pedes'trianism** walking, esp. as an exercise or athletic performance: pedestrian quality (*fig.*). — **pedestrian crossing** a part of a roadway (often controlled by traffic lights) marked for the use of pedestrians who wish to cross, and on which they have right of way; **pedestrian precinct** see **precinct.** [L. *pedester, -tris* — *pēs, pedis.*]

pedetentous *ped-i-ten'təs, adj.* proceeding slowly. [L. *pedentim, -temptim* — *pēs, pedis,* foot, *temptāre, -ātum,* to make trial of.]

pedetic. See **pedesis.**

ped(i)- *ped('i)-,* in combination, foot. [L. *pēs, pedis,* foot.]

pediatrics. See **paed(o)-.**

pedicab *ped'i-kab, n.* a light vehicle consisting of a tricycle with the addition of a seat, usu. behind, covered by a half hood, for passenger(s). [L. *pēs, pedis*, the foot, and **cab.**]

pedicel *ped'i-sel, n.* the stalk of a single flower in an inflorescence: the stalk of a sedentary animal: the stalk of an animal organ, e.g. a crab's eye. — *n.* **pedicellā'ria** a stalked (or sessile) bladed snapping forceps on the surface of a starfish or sea-urchin: — *pl.* **pedicellā'riae.** — *adj.* **ped'icellate** (or *-dis'*, or *-sel'*) provided with a pedicel. [Botanists' dim. of L. *pēs, pedis*, the foot.]

pedicle *ped'i-kl, n.* a short stalk or pedicel (*bot.*): a narrow stalk-like structure or short bony process (*zool.*): in deer, a bony protrusion of the skull from which an antler grows. — *adjs.* **ped'icled; pedic'ūlate** stalked: belonging to the **Pediculā'tī**, the angler-fish order, whose pectoral fins have a wrist-like articulation; **pedic'ulated.** [L. *pediculus*, a little foot — *pēs, pedis*, foot.]

Pediculus *pi-dik'ū-ləs, n.* the louse genus: (without *cap.*) a louse. — *adj.* **pedic'ular** of lice: lousy. — *ns.* **Pediculā'-ris** the lousewort genus; **pediculā'tion, pediculō'sis** lousiness. — *adj.* **pedic'ulous** lousy. [L. *pēdiculus*, dim. of *pēdis*, a louse.]

pedicure *ped'i-kūr, n.* the treatment of corns, bunions, or the like: one who treats the feet. — *v.t.* to apply foot-treatment to. — *n.* **ped'icurist.** [L. *pēs, pedis*, foot, *cūra*, care.]

pedigree *ped'i-grē, n.* a line of ancestors: a scheme or record of ancestry: lineage: genealogy: distinguished and ancient lineage: derivation, descent: succession, series, set. — *adj.* of known descent, pure-bred, and of good stock. — *adj.* **ped'igreed** having a pedigree. [App. Fr. *pied de grue*, crane's-foot, from the arrow-head figure in a stemma.]

pediment *ped'i-mənt, (archit.) n.* a triangular structure crowning the front of a Greek building, less steeply sloped than a gable: in later architecture a similar structure, triangular, rounded, etc., over a portico, door, window, or niche. — *adjs.* **pedimental** (*-ment'l*); **ped'imented** furnished with a pediment: like a pediment. [Earlier *periment*, prob. for **pyramid.**]

pedipalp *ped'i-palp, n.* the second paired appendage in Arachnida (also **pedipalp'us**): a whip-scorpion. — *ns.pl.* **Pedipalp'ī, Pedipalp'ida** the whip-scorpions, an order of Arachnida with large pedipalps. [L. *pēs, pedis*, foot, *palpus*, stroking, in L.L. a feeler.]

pedlar *ped'lər, n.* one who goes about with a pack of goods for sale (technically, one who carries it himself — distinguished from a *hawker*, who has a horse and cart, etc.): one who peddles. — *n.* **ped'lary** the wares or occupation of a pedlar. [Prob. from **pedder**, with inserted *l*, as in **tinkler** from **tinker.**]

pedo-. See **paed(o)-.**

pedology *ped-ol'ə-ji, n.* the study of soils. — *adj.* **pedological** (*-ə-loj'*). — *n.* **pedol'ogist.** [Gr. *pedon*, ground, *logos*, discourse.]

pedometer *pid-om'i-tər, n.* an instrument for counting paces and so approximately measuring distance walked. [L. *pēs, pedis*, foot — Gr. *metron*, measure.]

pedrail *ped'rāl, n.* a tractor with foot-like pieces on the circumference of its wheels: one of the pieces so used. [L. *pēs, pedis*, foot, and **rail.**]

pedrero *ped-rā'rō.* See **pederero.**

pedro. See **sancho-pedro.**

peduncle *pi-dung'kl, n.* the stalk of an inflorescence or of a solitary flower: the stalk by which a sedentary animal is attached: a narrow stalk-like connecting part (e.g. between the thorax and abdomen of insects): a tract of white fibres in the brain: a narrow process of tissue linking a tumour to normal tissue. — *adjs.* **pedun'cular, pedun'culate, -d.** [Botanists' L. *pedunculus* — L. *pēs, pedis*, the foot.]

pee[1] *pē, n.* the sixteenth letter of the alphabet (P, p).

pee[2] *pē, (coll.) v.i.* to urinate. — Also *n.* [For **piss.**]

peece. An obsolete spelling of **piece.**

peek *pēk, n.* a sly look, a peep. — *v.i.* to peep. — *n.*

peek'abo(o)' a child's peeping game. [Origin obscure.]

peel[1] *pēl, v.t.* to pill, pillage, plunder (*obs.*): to strip off the skin, bark, or other covering from: to strip off. — *v.i.* to come off as the skin: to lose the skin: to undress (*coll.*). — *n.* rind, esp. that of oranges, lemons, etc., in the natural state or candied. — *adj.* **peeled** pillaged: bald: tonsured: stripped of skin, rind, or bark. — *ns.* **peel'er** one who peels: a plunderer: a plant that impoverishes the soil: an instrument or machine for peeling or decorticating; **peel'ing** the act of stripping: a piece, strip, or shred stripped off: the removing of the layers of a paper overlay, to get a lighter impression (*print.*). — **peel-and-eat'** (*Scot.*) potatoes served in their jackets. — Also *adj.* — **pack and, or, peel** to have dealings (with; *Scott*); **peel off** (*aero.*) to leave a flying formation by a particular manoeuvre: (of ship) to veer away from a convoy. [O.F. *pilian* — L. *pīlāre*, to deprive of hair — *pīlus*, a hair; perh. influenced by Fr. *peler*, to skin; cf. **pill**[2].]

peel[2], **pele** *pēl, n.* a stake (*obs.*): a palisaded enclosure (*hist.*): a peel-house. — **peel'-house, pecl'-tower** (also **pele'-house, -tower;** also with *cap.*) orig. a fortified dwelling-house, usually entered by ladder to the first floor, with vaulted ground floor for cattle, common on the Borders: now loosely used. [A.Fr. *pel* — L. *pālus*, stake.]

peel[3] *pēl, n.* a shovel, esp. a baker's wooden shovel: an instrument for hanging up paper to dry: the blade of an oar (*rare, U.S.; arch.*). [O.Fr. *pele* — L. *pāla*, a spade.]

peel[4] *pēl, (croquet) v.t.* to cause (another player's ball) to go through the next hoop. [After British croquet player Walter *Peel* (fl. 1868).]

peel[5]. Same as **peal**[2].

peeler *pēl'ər, n.* a policeman, from Sir Robert *Peel* who established the Irish police (1812–18) and improved those in Britain (1828–30). — *n.* **Peel'ite** a follower of Peel in the reform of the Corn-laws in 1846.

peelgarlic. See **pilgarlick.**

peelie-wally *pē'li-wal'i, (Scot.) adj.* pale, ill-looking, off-colour. [Thought to be reduplicated form of Scot. *peelie*, thin, emaciated.]

peen, pean, pein, pene *pēn, * **pane** *pān, ns.* the end of a hammer head opposite the hammering face. — *v.t.* to strike or work (metal) with a peen: to fix by hammering into place (as with a rivet) (usu. with *in* or *over*). [Origin uncertain; cf. Norw. *pen*, Ger. *Pinne*, Fr. *panne.*]

peenge *pēnj, pēnzh, (Scot.) v.i.* to whine like a peevish child. [Perh. based on **whinge.**]

peeoy, pioy, pioye *pē-ō'i, (Scot.) n.* a home-made firework, a cone of damp gunpowder.

peep[1] *pēp, v.i.* to cheep like a chicken. — *n.* a high feeble sound. — *n.* **peep'er** a young bird: a tree-frog (*U.S.*). — **not a peep** (*coll.*) no noise, not a sound. [Imit.; cf. **pipe**[1], L. *pīpāre*, Fr. *pépier*, Ger. *piepen, piepsen*, to cheep, Gr. *pīpos*, a young bird.]

peep[2] *pēp, v.i.* to look through a narrow opening: to look out from concealment: to look slyly, surreptitiously, or cautiously: to be just showing: to begin to appear. — *v.t.* to put forth from concealment as if to take a view: to direct as if to view. — *n.* a sly look: a beginning to appear: a speck of light or flame: a glimpse: a slit: an eye (*slang*). — *n.* **peep'er** one that peeps: a prying person: the eye (*slang*): a glass, for various purposes (*slang*). — **peep'-hole** a hole through which one may look without being seen; **peeping Tom** a prying fellow, esp. one who peeps in at windows; **peep'-show** a small entertainment, film or series of pictures, esp. of erotic or pornographic nature, viewed through a small hole, usually fitted with a magnifying glass; **peep'-sight** a back-sight with a small hole. — *adj.* **peep'-through** allowing of being seen through. — **peep'-toe** a shoe cut away so as to show the toe. — **Peep-o'-day Boys** an Ulster Protestant society (1780–95) opposed to the Catholic *Defenders*; **peep of day** the first appearance

of light in the morning. [Origin obscure.]
peep³, peepe *pēp*, (*Shak.*) *n.* earlier forms of **pip³**.
peepul. See **pipal**.
peer¹ *pēr, n.* an equal: a fellow: an antagonist (*Spens.*):
a nobleman of the rank of baron upward: generally,
a nobleman: a member of the House of Lords: one of
Charlemagne's paladins: a member of any similar
body: — *fem.* **peer′ess.** — *v.t.* **peer** to equal: to confer
a peerage on (*coll.*). — *v.i.* to rank as equal. — *adj.*
pertaining to a peer group. — *n.* **peer′age** the rank or
dignity of a peer: the body of peers: a book of the
genealogy, etc., of the different peers. — *adj.* **peer′less**
unequalled: matchless. — *adv.* **peer′lessly.** — *n.* **peer′-
lessness.** — **peer group** a group of people equal in age,
rank, merit, etc.; **peer pressure** compulsion towards
doing or obtaining the same things as others in one's
peer group. — **House of Peers** the House of Lords; **life
peer, peeress** a person invested with a non-hereditary
peerage, entitling them to the title of baron or baroness
and a seat in the House of Lords; **spiritual peer** a bishop
or archbishop qualified to sit in the House of Lords;
temporal peer any other member.   [O.Fr. (Fr. *pair*)
— L. *pār, paris,* equal.]
peer² *pēr, v.i.* to look narrowly or closely: to look with
strain, or with half-closed eyes: to peep: to appear. —
v.t. (*obs.*) to protrude. — *adj.* **peer′y** inclined to peer:
prying: sly. [Origin unknown: perh. partly M.E.
piren (cf. L.G. *pīren*), influenced by *pere,* aphetic form
of **appear,** partly from *pere* itself.]
peerie¹, peery *pēr′i,* (*Scot.*) *n.* a pear- or cone-shaped
wooden peg-top. [App. **pear,** pron. *pēr* in Scots.]
peerie² *pēr′i,* (*Orkney* and *Shetland*) *adj.* small. [Origin
uncertain.]
peesweep *pēz′wēp.* See **peewit.**
peetweet *pēt′wēt,* (*U.S.*) *n.* the spotted sandpiper.
[*Imit.*]
peever *pē′vər,* (*Scot.*) *n.* a tile, slab, or can-lid used in
playing hop-scotch. — *n. sing.* **peev′ers** hop-scotch.
peevish *pēv′ish, adj.* foolish (*obs.*): vexatious (*obs.*): perverse (*Shak.*): wayward: fretful. — *v.t.* **peeve** (back-
formation) to irritate. — *v.i.* to be fretful: to show
fretfulness. — *n.* a fretful mood: a grievance, grouse.
— *adj.* **peeved** (*coll.*) annoyed. — *adv.* **peev′ishly.** — *n.*
peev′ishness. [Origin unknown.]
peewee. See **peewit.**
peewit, pewit *pē′wit,* also *pū′it, n.* the lapwing: its cry. —
(*Scot.*) **pees′weep, pease′weep, pee′wee.** [*Imit.*]
peg *peg, n.* a pin (esp. of wood): a fixture for hanging a
hat or coat on: a pin for tuning a string (*music*): a small
stake for securing tent-ropes, marking a position,
boundary, claim, etc.: a pin for scoring as in cribbage:
a pin in a cup to show how far down one may drink:
hence a drink, esp. of brandy and soda: a degree or
step: a wooden or other pin used in shoemaking: a
turtle harpoon: a clothes-peg: a cricket stump: a piton:
a peg-top: a wooden leg (*coll.*): a leg (*coll.*): a poke or
thrust (*dial.* or *slang*): a theme (*fig.*). — *v.t.* to fasten,
mark, score, furnish, pierce, or strike with a peg or
pegs: to insert or fix like a peg: to score (as at cribbage):
to keep from falling or rising by buying or selling at
a fixed price (*Stock exchange*): to hold (prices, pensions, etc.) at a fixed level, or directly related to the
cost of living: to stabilise: to drive (a coach, etc.) (*obs.
slang*): to throw. — *v.i.* to keep on working assiduously: to make one's way vigorously: — *pr.p.* **pegg′ing;
pa.t.** and *pa.p.* **pegged.** — *adj.* **pegged.** — *n.* **pegg′ing.**
— **peg′board** a board having holes into which pegs are
placed, used for playing and scoring in games or for
display or storage purposes; **peg′-box** part of the head
of a musical instrument in which the pegs are inserted;
peg′-leg a simple wooden leg: a man with a wooden
leg; **peg′-tank′ard** a drinking-vessel having each one's
share marked off by a knob; **peg′-top** a spinning top
with a metal point, spun by winding a string round it
and suddenly throwing it: (in *pl.*) trousers narrowing
at the ankles. — *adj.* shaped like a top. — **a peg too
low** tipsy: depressed; **off the peg** of a garment, (bought)

ready to wear from an already-existing stock: of an
item, (bought) ready to use, not purpose-built: not
adjusted to suit the circumstances, etc. (*fig.*) (*adj.*
off′-the-peg′); **peg away** to work on assiduously; **peg
back** in sport, esp. racing, to gain an advantage over
an opponent; **peg down** to restrict (someone) to an
admission, following a certain course of action; **peg
out** in croquet, to finish by driving the ball against the
peg: in cribbage, to win by pegging the last hole before
show of hands: to mark off with pegs: to become
exhausted, be ruined, or die (*slang*); **round peg in a
square hole** or **square peg in a round hole** one who is
unsuited to the particular position he occupies; **take
down a peg (or two)** to take down, to humble, to snub.
[Cf. L.G. *pigge,* Du. dial. *peg,* Dan. *pig.*]
Pegasus *peg′ə-səs, n.* the winged horse that sprang from
Medusa's blood, by later writers associated with the
Muses: hence, an embodiment of the power that raises
a poet's imagination above the earth: a genus of small
fishes superficially like sea-horses, of the coasts of Asia
and Australia, with large, wing-like, pectoral fins:
(without *cap.*) a fish of this genus: one of the constellations in the northern sky. — *adj.* **Pegasē′an.** [L.
Pēgasus — Gr. *Pēgasos.*]
peggy *peg′i, n.* a small warbler of various kinds — the
white-throat, etc.: a washerwoman's dolly: a size of
roofing slate, 10 by 14 in. (25·4 × 35·6 cm.).
[Hypocoristic from *Margaret.*]
pegh, Peght. See **pech, Pecht.**
pegmatite *peg′mə-tīt, n.* graphic granite: a very coarsely
crystallised granite, as in dikes and veins: any very
coarse-grained igneous rock occurring in like manner.
— *adj.* **pegmatitic** (*-tit′ik*). [Gr. *pēgma,* a bond,
framework, from the root of *pēgnynai,* to fasten.]
Pehlevi *pā′le-vē,* **Pahlavi** *pä′lä-vē, ns.* an ancient West
Iranian idiom of the Sassanide period (3rd–7th cent.
A.D.), largely mixed with Semitic words: the characters
used in writing it. — Also *adj.* [Pers. *Pahlavi,*
Parthian.]
peignoir *pen′wär, n.* a woman's dressing-gown, esp. one
worn when combing the hair: (*loosely*) a morning-
gown. [Fr., — *peigner* — L. *pectināre,* to comb.]
pein. See **peen.**
peinct *pānt.* An obsolete spelling of **paint.**
peine forte et dure *pen fört ā dür,* (Fr.) strong and severe
punishment, a kind of judicial torture involving pressing with weights.
peirastic *pī-ras′tik, adj.* experimental: tentative. — *adv.*
peiras′tically. [Gr. *peirastikos* — *peira,* a trial.]
peise, peize, pease, peaze, peyse *pāz, pēz,* (*obs.*) *n.* weight:
a weight: a balance: a blow (*Spens.*). — *v.t.* to balance
(*Spens., Shak.*): to poise (*Spens.*): to put weights on,
weigh down (*Shak.*). — *v.i.* (*Spens.*) to press or settle
downwards. [O.Fr. *peis,* weight, *peser,* to weigh; cf.
poise.]
peishwa(h). See **peshwa.**
pejorate *pē′jər-āt, pi′, v.t.* to make worse. — *n.* **pejorā′tion**
a making or becoming worse: deterioration. — *adj.*
pejor′ative (or *pē′*) depreciating, disparaging. — *n.* a
depreciating word or suffix. — *adv.* **pejor′atively** (or
pē′). [L. *pējor,* worse.]
pekan *pek′ən, n.* the wood-shock, a large North American
marten. [Canadian Fr. *pékan* — Algonquin *pékané.*]
Pekingese, Pekinese *pē-kin(g)-ēz′, adjs.* of *Peking,* China.
— *n.* a native or inhabitant of Peking: the chief dialect
of Mandarin: a dwarf pug-dog of a breed brought
from Peking (also *coll.* short form **peke**). — **Pekin
(duck)** a large white breed of duck, bred esp. for food;
Peking man a type of fossil man first found (1929)
S.W. of Peking, related to Java man.
pekoe *pēk′ō, pek′ō, n.* a scented black tea. [Chin.
pek-ho, white down.]
pela *pä′lä, n.* white wax from a scale-insect. [Chin.
peh-la, white wax.]
pelage *pel′ij, n.* a beast's coat of hair or wool. [Fr.]
Pelagian *pi-lā′ji-ən, n.* a follower of *Pelagius,* a 5th-cent.

British monk, who denied original sin. — Also *adj.* — *n.* **Pelā'gianism.**

pelagic *pi-laj'ik, adj.* oceanic: of, inhabiting, or carried out in, the deep or open sea: living in the surface waters or middle depths of the sea: deposited under deep-water conditions. — *adj.* **pelagian** (*pi-lā'ji-ən*) pelagic. — *n.* a pelagic animal. [Gr. *pelagos*, sea.]

Pelargonium *pel-ər-gō'ni-əm, n.* a vast genus of the Geraniaceae, having clusters of red, pink or white flowers, often cultivated under the name of geranium: (without *cap.*) any plant of this genus. — **pelargonic acid** an oily fatty acid, obtained esp. from the leaves of plants of the Pelargonium genus — also called **nonanoic acid.** [Gr. *pelargos*, stork, the beaked capsules resembling a stork's head.]

Pelasgic *pe-las'jik, adj.* pertaining to the *Pelasgians* or *Pelasgi,* prehistoric inhabitants of Greece, of unknown affinities. — Also **Pelas'gian.** — **Pelasgian architecture** cyclopean architecture.

Pele *pā'lā, n.* the Hawaiian volcano goddess. — **Pele's hair** volcanic glass drawn out into threads as it flies through the air.

pele¹. See **peel².**

pele². A Spenserian spelling of **peal¹.**

Pelecypoda *pel-e-sip'ə-də, n.pl.* the Lamellibranchs. [Gr. *pelekys,* axe, *pous, podos,* foot.]

pelerine *pel'ə-rin, -rēn, n.* a woman's tippet or cape, esp. one with long ends coming down in front. [Fr. *pèlerine,* tippet, pilgrim (fem.); see **pilgrim.**]

pelf *pelf, n.* riches (in a bad sense): money. [O.Fr. *pelfre,* booty; cf. **pilfer.**]

pelham *pel'əm,* (often with *cap.*) *n.* on a horse's bridle, a type of bit, a combination of the curb and snaffle designs. [Perh. name *Pelham.*]

pelican *pel'i-kən, n.* a large water-fowl, with enormous pouched bill, fabled in the Middle Ages to wound its breast and feed its young with its blood: an alembic with beaks that lead back to the body — used for continuous distillation: a dentist's beaked instrument (*hist.*): an old species of ordnance, or its shot. — **pel'ican-fish** a deep-sea fish (Eurypharynx) with enormous mouth and very little body; **pel'ican-flower** the goose-flower, an Aristolochia with a gigantic flower; **pel'ican's-foot'** a marine gasteropod mollusc (*Aporrhais pes-pelicani*): its shell, with a lip like a webbed foot. — **pelican in her piety** (*her.*) a pelican with wings indorsed, feeding her young with her blood. [L.L. *pelicānus* — Gr. *pelekan, -ānos,* pelican; cf. *pelekās, -āntos,* a woodpecker, and *pelekys,* an axe.]

pelican crossing *pel'i-kən kros'ing,* a pedestrian-operated street crossing, having a set of lights including an amber flashing light which indicates that motorists may proceed only if the crossing is clear. [Adapted from *pe*destrian *li*ght *con*trolled *crossing.*]

pelisse *pe-lēs', n.* orig. a fur-lined or fur garment, esp. a military cloak: a lady's long mantle: (*formerly*) a young child's out-of-door coat. [Fr., — L.L. *pellicea* (*vestis*) — L. *pellis,* a skin.]

pelite *pē'līt, n.* any rock derived from clay or mud. — *adj.* **pēlitic** (*-lit'ik*). — *ns.* **pē'loid** any naturally produced medium used in medical practice as a cataplasm; **pēlol'ogy; pēlother'apy** treatment by mud baths and the like. [Gr. *pēlos,* clay, mud.]

pell *pel,* (*obs.*) *n.* a skin or hide: a roll of parchment. [O.Fr. *pel* (Fr. *peau*) — L. *pellis,* a skin or hide.]

pellach, pellack. See **pellock.**

pellagra *pel-ag'rə, -āg'rə, n.* a deadly deficiency disease marked by shrivelled skin, wasted body, and insanity. — *n.* **pellag'rin** one afflicted with pellagra. — *adj.* **pellag'rous** connected with, like, or afflicted with, pellagra. [Gr. *pella,* skin, *agrā,* seizure; or It. *pelle agra,* rough skin.]

pellet *pel'it, n.* a little ball: a small rounded boss: a small rounded mass of compressed iron ore, waste material, etc.: a small pill: a ball of shot: a mass of undigested refuse thrown up by a hawk or owl. — *v.t.* to form into pellets (*Shak.*): to form (seeds) into a pellet by

surrounding with an inert substance which breaks down with moisture, to make planting easier: to hit or pelt with pellets. — *vs.t.* **pell'etify, pell'etise, -ize** to form (esp. solid waste material, iron ore, etc.) into pellets. — *n.* **pelletīsā'tion, -z-.** [O.Fr. *pelote* — L. *pīla,* a ball.]

pellicle *pel'i-kl, n.* a thin skin or film: a film or scum on liquors. — *adj.* **pellic'ular.** [L. *pellicula,* dim. of *pellis,* skin.]

pellitory¹ *pel'i-tə-ri, n.* a plant (*Parietaria officinalis*) of the nettle family, growing on old walls (called *pellitory of the wall*), or other member of the genus. — cf. **pellitory².** [L. (*herba*) *parietāria* — *parietārius* — *pariēs, parietis,* a wall.]

pellitory² *pel'i-tə-ri, n.* a North African and South European plant (*Anacyclus pyrethrum*), known as *pellitory of Spain,* akin to camomile: extended to various similar plants, as yarrow, feverfew. — cf. **pellitory¹.** [M.E. *peletre* — L. *pyrethrum* — Gr. *pyrethron,* pellitory of Spain; see **pyrethrum.**]

pell-mell *pel'-mel', adv.* confusedly, promiscuously: headlong: helter-skelter: vehemently. — *adj.* confusedly mingled: promiscuous, indiscriminate: headlong. — *n.* disorder: confused mingling: a hand-to-hand fight. [O.Fr. *pesle-mesle* (Fr. *pêle-mêle*), *-mesle* being from O.Fr. *mesler* (Fr. *mêler*), to mix, meddle — L.L. *misculāre* — L. *miscēre*; and *pesle,* a rhyming addition, perh. influenced by Fr. *pelle,* shovel.]

pellock, pellack *pel'ək,* **pellach** *pel'əhh,* (*Scot.*) *ns.* a porpoise. [Origin unknown.]

pellucid *pe-lū'sid, -lōō'sid, adj.* perfectly clear: transparent. — *ns.* **pellucid'ity, pellu'cidness.** — *adv.* **pellu'cidly.** [L. *pellūcidus* — *per,* through, *lūcidus,* clear — *lūcēre,* to shine.]

pelma *pel'mə, n.* the sole of the foot. — *adj.* **pelmatic** (*-mat'ik*). — *n.pl.* **Pelmatozō'a** a division of the Echinodermata, typically stalked, including crinoids and the fossil blastoids and cystoids. [Gr. *pelma, -atos,* sole, stalk.]

Pelmanism *pel'mən-izm, n.* a system of mind training to improve the memory: (usu. without *cap.*) a card game in which the cards are spread out face down and must be turned up in matching pairs. [The *Pelman* Institute, founded 1898, which devised the system.]

pelmet *pel'mit, n.* a fringe, valance, or other device hiding a curtain rod. [Perh. Fr. *palmette.*]

peloid, pelology. See **pelite.**

Pelopid *pel'ō-pid,* a descendant of *Pelops,* son of Tantalus, and grandfather of Agamemnon and Menelaus.

Peloponnesian *pel-ō-pə-nē'sh(y)ən, -zh(y)ən, -zyən, adj.* of the *Peloponnesus* or Peloponnese, the southern peninsula of Greece. — *n.* a native thereof. — **Peloponnesian War** a war between Athens and Sparta, 431–404 B.C. [Gr. *Peloponnēsos,* Peloponnese — *Pelops* (see foregoing), *nēsos,* an island.]

peloria *pi-lō'ri-ə, -lō'ri-ə, n.* regularity in a normally irregular flower. — Also **pelorism** (*pel'ər-izm*), **pel'ory.** — *adjs.* **peloric** (*pi-lor'ik*), **pel'orised, -ized.** [Gr. *pelōr,* a monster.]

pelorus *pel-ōr'əs, -ör', n.* a kind of compass from which bearings can be taken. [Perh. *Pelorus,* Hannibal's pilot.]

pelory. See **peloria.**

pelota *pel-ō'tə, n.* a ball-game, of Basque origin, resembling fives, using a basket catching and throwing device. [Sp. *pelota,* ball.]

pelotherapy. See **pelite.**

pelt¹ *pelt, n.* a raw hide: a hawk's prey when killed, especially when torn. — *n.* **pelt'ry** the skins of animals with the fur on them: furs. — **pelt'monger** a dealer in skins. [App. a back-formation from *peltry* — O.Fr. *pelleterie* — L. *pellis,* a skin.]

pelt² *pelt, v.t.* to assail (formerly with repeated blows, now usu.) with showers of missiles, or of words, reproaches, pamphlets, etc.: to drive by showers of missiles: to shower. — *v.i.* to shower blows or missiles: to beat vigorously, as rain, hail: to speak angrily: to speed. — *n.* a blow: a pelting: a downpour, as of rain: a storm of rage: a rapid pace. — *n.* **pelt′er** one who or that which pelts: a shower of missiles: a sharp storm of rain, of anger, etc. — *v.i.* to go full pelt: to pelt (*dial.*). — *n.* and *adj.* **pelt′ing.** — **(at) full pelt** at full speed. [Origin obscure.]

pelta *pel′tə*, (*ant.*) *n.* a light buckler. — *n.* **peltast** (*pelt′ast*) a light-armed Greek soldier with a pelta. — *adj.* **pelt′ate** (*bot.*) having the stalk attached not to the edge but near the middle of the under-surface. [L., — Gr. *peltē.*]

Peltier effect *pel′ti-ā i-fekt′*, (*phys.*) the generation or absorption of heat at a junction, within an electric circuit, of two metals. [From Jean *Peltier*, 19th-cent. French physicist.]

pelting *pel′ting*, (*Shak.*) *adj.* paltry, contemptible. — *adv.* **pelt′ingly.** [App. conn. with **paltry.**]

Pelton-wheel *pel′tn-*(h)*wēl′, n.* a water-wheel with specially shaped cups around the circumference into which one or more jets of water are aimed at high speed, invented by Lester Allen *Pelton*, American engineer (1829–1908).

peltry. See **pelt**[1].

pelvis *pel′vis, n.* the bony cavity at the lower end of the trunk, of which the part above the plane through the promontory of the sacrum and the pubic symphysis is the *false pelvis*, the part below the *true pelvis*: the bony frame enclosing it: the cavity of the kidney: the basal part of a crinoid cup: — *pl.* **pel′vises, pel′ves** (*-vēz*). — *adjs.* **pel′vic; pel′viform** basin-shaped. — *ns.* **pelvim′eter** an instrument for measuring the pelvis; **pelvim′etry.** — **pelvic fin** a fish's paired fin homologous with a mammal's hindleg; **pelvic girdle** or **arch** the posterior limb-girdle of vertebrates, with which the hind-limbs articulate, consisting of the haunch-bones (ilium, pubis and ischium united), which articulate with the sacrum. [L. *pelvis*, a basin.]

pembroke *pem′brŏok, n.* (in full **pembroke table**) a small four-legged table with hinged flaps. [App. from *Pembroke*, in Wales.]

pemmican, pemican *pem′i-kən, n.* a North American Indian preparation of lean flesh-meat, dried, pounded, and mixed with fat and other ingredients: highly condensed information or reading-matter (*fig.*). [Cree *pimekan.*]

pemoline *pem′ə-lēn, n.* a white crystalline powder, $C_2H_8N_2O_2$, used as a stimulant of the central nervous system, esp. in the treatment of fatigue, depression and memory loss.

pemphigus *pem′fi-gəs, n.* an affection of the skin with watery vesicles. — *adjs.* **pem′phigoid, pem′phigous.** [False Latin — Gr. *pemphix, -īgos*, blister.]

pen[1] *pen, n.* a small enclosure, esp. for animals: a West Indian farm or plantation: a dam or weir: animals kept in, and enough to fill, a pen. — *v.t.* to put or keep in a pen: to confine: to dam: — *pr.p.* **penn′ing;** *pa.t.* and *pa.p.* **penned** or **pent.** — **pen′fold** a fold for penning cattle or sheep: a pound. — **submarine pen** a dock for a submarine, esp. if protected from attack from above by a deep covering of concrete. [O.E. *penn*, pen.]

pen[2] *pen, n.* a large feather: a flight-feather: a quill: a cuttle-bone: an instrument used for writing (with ink or otherwise), formerly made of a quill, but now of other materials: a nib: a nib with a holder: writing: literary style: an author. — *v.t.* to write, to commit to paper: — *pr.p.* **penn′ing;** *pa.t.* and *pa.p.* **penned.** — *n.* **pen′ful** as much ink as a pen can take at a dip: as much as the reservoir of a fountain-pen can hold: what one can write with one dip of ink. — *adj.* **penned** written: quilled. — *n.* **penn′er** (*arch.*) a case for carrying pens. — **pen′-and-ink′** writing materials: a pen drawing. — *adj.* writing: written: executed with pen and ink, as a drawing. — **pen′-case** a receptacle for a pen or pens; **pen′craft** penmanship: the art of composition; **pen′-driver** a clerk; **pen′-feather** a quill feather: pin-feather (*dial.*). — *adj.* **pen′-feathered.** — **pen′-friend, -pal** an otherwise unknown person (usu. abroad) with whom

one corresponds; **pen′-gun** (*Scot.*) a popgun made of a quill; **pen′holder** a rod on which a nib may be fixed; **pen′knife** orig. a knife for making or mending pens: a small pocket-knife; **pen′light** a small pen-shaped electric torch (**penlight battery** a long, thin battery, as used in a penlight); **pen′man** one skilled in handwriting: a writer or author: — *fem.* **pen′woman; pen′manship; pen name** a writer's assumed name; **pen′-nib** a nib for a pen; **pen′-pusher** (*coll.*) a clerk who does boring, routine writing; **pen′-wiper** a piece of cloth, leather, etc., for wiping ink from pens. — **talk like a pen-gun** to chatter volubly. [O.Fr. *penne* — L. *penna*, a feather.]

pen[3]. Slang short form of **penitentiary.**

pen[4] *pen, n.* a female swan. [Origin unknown.]

penal *pē′nl, adj.* pertaining to, liable to, imposing, constituting, or used for, punishment: constituting a penalty: very severe. — *n.* **pēnalīsā′tion, -z-.** — *v.t.* **pē′nalise, -ize** to make punishable: to put under a disadvantage. — *adv.* **pē′nally.** — **penal code** a codified system of law relating to crime and punishment; **penal laws** laws imposing penalties, esp. (*hist.*) in matters of religion; **penal servitude** hard labour in a prison under different conditions from ordinary imprisonment, substituted in 1853 for transportation, abolished 1948; **penal settlement** a settlement peopled by convicts. [L. *poenalis* — Gr. *poinē*, punishment.]

penalty *pen′l-ti, n.* punishment: suffering or loss imposed for breach of a law: a fine or loss agreed upon in case of non-fulfilment of some undertaking: a fine: a disadvantage imposed upon a competitor for breach of a rule of the game, for want of success in attaining what is aimed at, as a handicap, or for any other reason arising out of the rules: a penalty kick, shot or stroke: a loss or suffering brought upon one by one's own actions or condition: a score for an opponent's failure to make his contract or for the bidder's success when the call is doubled (*bridge*). — **penalty area, box** in association football, the area in front of the goal in which a foul by the defending team may result in a penalty kick being awarded against them; **penalty bench, box** in ice-hockey, an area beside the rink in which a player must stay for his allotted penalty period; **penalty corner** in hockey, a free stroke taken on the goal line; **penalty goal** one scored by a penalty kick or shot; **penalty kick** a free kick, or the privilege granted to a player to kick the ball as he pleases, because of some breach of the rules by the opposing side; **penalty line** the boundary of the penalty area; **penalty shot; penalty spot** in association football and men's hockey, a spot in front of the goal from which a penalty kick or shot is taken. — **death penalty** punishment by putting to death; **under** or **on penalty of** with liability in case of infraction to the penalty of. [L.L. *poenalitās*; see foregoing.]

penance *pen′əns, n.* repentance (*obs.*): an act of mortification undertaken voluntarily or imposed by a priest to manifest sorrow for sin: the sacrament by which absolution is conveyed (involving contrition, confession, and satisfaction) (*R.C.* and *Orthodox*): expiation: punishment (*Milt.*): hardship. — *v.t.* to impose penance on. [O.Fr.; cf. **penitence.**]

Penang-lawyer *pi-nang′-lö′yər, n.* a walking stick made from the stem of a prickly dwarf palm (*Licuala acutifida*): misapplied to a Malacca cane. [*Penang*, its place of origin, and **lawyer**, or poss. from Malay *pinang liyar*, wild areca, or *pinang láyor*, fire-dried areca.]

penannular *pen-an′ū-lər*, or *pēn-, adj.* in the form of an almost complete ring. [L. *paene*, almost, *annulāris*, annular.]

penates *pe-nā′tēz, pe-nä′tās, n.pl.* the household gods of a Roman family. [L. *penātēs*, prob. from the root found in *penus*, provisions, storeroom, *penes*, in the house of, *penetrāre*, to penetrate.]

pence *pens, n.* a plural of **penny**: a new penny (*coll.*).

pencel. See **pensil.**

penchant *pã′shä, n.* inclination: decided taste: bias. [Fr., pr.p. of *pencher*, to incline — assumed L.L. *pendicāre* — L. *pendēre*, to hang.]

pencil *pen'sl, n.* a fine paint-brush: a small tuft of hairs: a writing or drawing instrument that leaves a streak of blacklead, chalk, slate, or other solid matter, esp. one of blacklead enclosed in wood and sharpened as required: a small stick of various materials shaped like a lead-pencil, for medical, cosmetic, or other purpose: the art of painting or drawing: a system of straight lines meeting in a point (*geom.*): a set of rays of light diverging from or converging to a point: a narrow beam of light. — *v.t.* to paint, draw, write, or mark with a pencil: (with *in*) to enter provisionally, as in a diary: to note (something) allowing for or expecting later alteration (*fig.*): to apply a pencil to: — *pr.p.* **pen'cilling;** *pa.t.* and *pa.p.* **pen'cilled.** — *adj.* **pen'cilled** painted, drawn, written or marked with a pencil: marked as if with a pencil: showing fine concentric streaking: having pencils of rays: radiated: tufted. — *ns.* **pen'ciller; pen'cilling** the art or act of painting, writing, sketching, or marking with a pencil: marks made with a pencil: fine lines on flowers or feathers: a sketch: the marking of joints in brickwork with white paint. — **pen'cil-case** a case for pencils: metal case receiving a movable piece of blacklead or the like, used as a pencil; **pen'cil-ce'dar** juniper of various kinds suitable for lead-pencils; **pen'cil-com'pass** a compass having a pencil on one of its legs; **pen'cil-lead** graphite for pencils: a stick of it for a metal pencil-case; **pen'cil-ore** radiating botryoidal graphite; **pen'cil-sharpener** an instrument for sharpening lead-pencils by rotation against a blade or blades; **pen'cil-sketch; pencil skirt** a straight, close-fitting skirt; **pen'cil-stone** a pyrophyllite used for making slate-pencils. [O.Fr. *pincel* (Fr. *pinceau*) — L. *pēnicillum*, a painter's brush, dim. of *pēnis*, a tail.]

pencraft. See **pen²**.

pend¹ *pend*, (*Scot.*) *n.* a vaulted passage: a vaulted entrance to a passageway. [L. *pendēre*, to hang.]

pend² *pend, v.i.* to hang, as in a balance, to impend. — *adj.* **pend'ing** hanging: impending: remaining undecided: not terminated. — *prep.* during: until, awaiting. [Fr. *pendre* or L. *pendēre*, to hang; sometimes aphetic for **append** or for **depend**.]

pend³. An old spelling of **penned**, from **pen¹** or **pen²**.

pendant, sometimes **pendent,** *pen'dant, n.* anything hanging, especially for ornament: a hanging ornament worn on the neck: the hanging (esp. decorated) end of a waist-belt: an earring: a lamp hanging from the roof: an ornament of wood or of stone hanging downwards from a roof: a pennant: a pendant-post: anything attached to another thing of the same kind, an appendix: a companion picture, poem, etc. — *n.* **pen'dency** undecided state: droop. — *adj.* **pen'dent,** sometimes **pen'dant,** hanging: dangling: drooping: overhanging: not yet decided: grammatically incomplete, left in suspense. — *n.* **pendentive** (-*dent'*) a spherical triangle formed by a dome springing from a square base (*archit.*): part of a groined vault resting on one pier. — *adv.* **pen'dently.** — *ns.* **pen'dicle** a pendant: a dependency or appendage: something attached to another, as a privilege, or a small piece of ground for cultivation; **pen'dicler** the tenant of a pendicle. — **pen'dant-post** a post placed against a wall, usu. resting on a corbel or capital, with a tie-beam or hammerbeam fixed to its upper end. [Fr. *pendant*, pr.p. of *pendre*, to hang — L. *pendēns, -entis* — pr.p. of *pendēre*, to hang.]

pendente lite *pen-den'tē lī'tē, pen-den'te li'te,* (L.) during the process of litigation.

pendicle. See **pendant.**

pendragon *pen-drag'ən, n.* an ancient British supreme chief. — *n.* **pendrag'onship.** [W. *pen*, head, *dragon*, a dragon, dragon-standard.]

pendulum *pen'dū-ləm, n.* theoretically, a heavy material point suspended by a weightless thread, free to swing without friction (*simple pendulum*): any weight so hung

from a fixed point as to swing freely (*compound pendulum*): the swinging weight which regulates the movement of a clock: anything that swings, passes or is free to swing or be passed to and fro: anything that undergoes obvious and regular shifts or reversals in direction, attitude, opinion, etc.: — *pl.* **pen'dulums.** — *adj.* **pen'dular** relating to a pendulum. — *v.i.* **pen'dulate** to swing, vibrate. — *adj.* **pen'duline** building a pendulous nest. — *n.* **pendulos'ity.** — *adj.* **pen'dulous** hanging loosely: swinging freely: drooping: dangling: overhanging: suspended from the top: floating in air or space. — *adv.* **pen'dulously.** — *n.* **pen'dulousness.** — **compensation pendulum** a pendulum so constructed that its rod is not much altered in length by changes of temperature. [Neut. of L. *pendulus*, hanging — *pendēre*, to hang.]

pene. See **peen.**

Peneian *pē-nē'ən, adj.* relating to the river *Pēnēus* in the famous Vale of Tempe in Thessaly. [Gr. *Pēnēios*, now Salambria.]

penelopise, -ize *pi-nel'ə-pīz, v.i.* to act like *Penelope*, the wife of Ulysses, who undid at night the work she did by day in order to gain time. [Gr. *Pēnelopē.*]

peneplain *pē'ni-plān,* or *-plān', n.* a land surface so worn down by denudation as to be almost a plain. — Also **pe'neplane.** [L. *paene*, almost, and **plain²**.]

penes. See **penis.**

penetrate *pen'i-trāt, v.t.* to thrust or force a way into the inside of: to pierce into or through: to insert the penis into the vagina of: to force entry within a country's borders or through an enemy's front line (*mil.*): to gain access into and influence within (a country, organisation, market, etc.) for political, financial, etc., purposes: to permeate: to reach the mind or feelings of: to pierce with the eye or understanding, see into or through (*fig.*): to understand. — *v.i.* to make way or pass inwards. — *ns.* **penetrability** (-*trə-bil'i-ti*), **pen'etrableness.** — *adj.* **pen'etrable.** — *adv.* **pen'etrably** so as to be penetrated. — *n.pl.* **penetrā'lia** (*pl.* of L. *penetral* or *penetrāle*) the inmost parts of a building: the most holy place in a temple: innermost mysteries. — *adj.* **penetrā'lian.** — *ns.* **pen'etrance** (*genetics*) the frequency, expressed as a percentage, with which a gene exhibits an effect; **pen'etrancy.** — *adj.* **pen'etrant** penetrating. — *n.* (*chem.*) a substance which increases the penetration of a liquid into porous material or between contiguous surfaces, by lowering its surface tension. — *adj.* **pen'etrating** piercing: having keen and deep insight: sharp: keen: discerning. — *adv.* **pen'etratingly.** — *n.* **penetrā'tion** the act or power of penetrating or entering: acuteness: discernment: the space-penetrating power of a telescope: the sexual act of inserting the penis into the vagina: the process and practices of espionage or infiltration within an organisation, country, etc. — *adj.* **pen'etrative** tending or able to penetrate: piercing: having keen and deep insight: reaching and affecting the mind. — *adv.* **pen'etratively.** — *ns.* **pen'etrativeness; pen'etrator.** — **penetration agent** a person employed to penetrate and obtain information within an organisation, country, etc. [L. *penetrāre, -ātum* — *penes*, in the house, possession, or power of; formed on the model of *intrāre*, to enter — *intus*, within; cf. **penates**.]

penfold. See **pen¹**, and cf. **pinfold.**

penguin¹ *peng'gwin, pen', n.* a former name for the great auk: now any bird of the *Sphenisciformes*, flightless sea birds of the Southern Hemisphere, of peculiar structure: a training aeroplane that cannot fly (*slang*): a member of the Women's Royal Air Force, 'flappers who did not fly' (*slang*). — Also **pin'guin.** — *n.* **pen'guinery, pen'guinry** a penguin rookery or breeding-place. [According to some, W. *pen*, head, *gwyn*, white, or the corresponding Breton words, though the great auk had a black head with two white patches: conjectures are *pin-wing*, and L. *pinguis*, fat.]

penguin². Same as **pinguin².**

penholder. See **pen².**

peni. Spenserian spelling of **penny**.

penial. See **penis**.

penicillate *pen-i-sil'it, -āt, pen', adj.* tufted: forming a tuft: brush-shaped. — *adj.* **penicill'iform** paint-brush-shaped. — *ns.* **penicill'in** a group of substances that stop the growth of bacteria, extracted from moulds, esp. *Penicillium notatum*, of the genus of fungi, **Penicill'ium** (Ascomycetes; see **ascus**), which includes also the mould of jam, cheese, etc. (*P. glaucum*); **penicill'-inase** an enzyme, produced by certain bacteria, that inactivates the effect of some penicillins.   [L. *pēnicillus*, paintbrush, dim. of *pēnis*, tail.]

penie. Spenserian spelling of **penny**.

penile. See **penis**.

penillion. Same as **pennillion**.

peninsula *pen-in'sū-lə, n.* a piece of land that is almost an island. — *adj.* **penin'sular**. — *n.* **peninsular'ity**. — *v.t.* **penin'sulate** to form into a peninsula. — **Peninsular War** the war in Spain and Portugal carried on by Great Britain against Napoleon's marshals (1808–14). — **The Peninsula** Spain and Portugal.   [L. *paenīnsula* — *paene*, almost, *īnsula*, an island.]

penis *pē'nis, n.* the external male organ: — *pl.* **pē'nises, pē'nes** (*-nēz*). — *adjs.* **pē'nial, pē'nile**. — **penis envy** (*psych.*) the Freudian concept of a woman's subconscious wish for male characteristics.   [L. *pēnis*, orig. a tail.]

penistone *pen'i-stən, n.* a cloth, a coarse frieze, formerly made at *Penistone* in Yorkshire.

penitent *pen'i-tənt, adj.* suffering pain or sorrow for sin with will to amend: contrite: repentant: expressing sorrow for sin: undergoing penance: appropriate to penance. — *n.* one who sorrows for sin: one who has confessed sin, and is undergoing penance: a member of one of various orders devoted to penitential exercises and work among criminals, etc. — *ns.* **pen'itence; pen'itency** (*rare*). — *adj.* **penitential** (*-ten'shl*) of the nature of, pertaining to, or expressive of, penitence. — *n.* a book of rules relating to penance: a penitent: (in *pl.*) the behaviour or garb of a penitent: black clothes (*coll.*). — *adv.* **peniten'tially**. — *adj.* **penitentiary** (*-ten'shə-ri*) relating to penance: penitential: penal and reformatory. — *n.* a penitent: an officer who deals with cases of penitence and penance: an office (under the *Grand Penitentiary*) at Rome dealing with cases of penance, dispensations, etc.: a book for guidance in imposing penances: a place for the performance of penance (*obs.*): an asylum for prostitutes (*arch.*): a reformatory prison or house of correction: a prison (*U.S.*). — *adv.* **pen'itently**. — **penitent form** a seat for penitents at an evangelistic meeting; **penitential garment** a rough garment worn for penance; **penitential psalms** seven psalms suitable for singing by penitents — the 6th, 32nd, 38th, 51st, 102nd, 130th, 143rd.   [L. *paenitēns, -entis*, pr.p. of *paenitēre*, to cause to repent, to repent.]

penk. Same as **pink**[7].

penknife, penman. See under **pen**[2].

penna *pen'ə, n.* a feather, esp. one of the large feathers of the wings or tail: — *pl.* **penn'ae** (*-ē*). — *adjs.* **pennaceous** (*-ā'shəs*) featherlike; **penn'ate** pinnate: winged, feathered, or like a wing in shape. — *n.* **penne** (*pen*; *Spens.*) a pen: a pinion. — *adjs.* **penned** feathered: quilled: winged; **penn'iform** feather-shaped.   [L. *penna*, feather.]

pennal *pen'əl, pen-äl', n.* formerly, a name for a freshman at a German university. — *n.* **penn'alism** a system of fagging once in vogue at German universities.   [Ger. *Pennal* — L. *pennāle*, pen-case.]

pennant[1] *pen'ənt*, (*naut.*) *pen'ən, n.* a dangling line with a block (*naut.*): a long narrow flag: a signalling flag: a pennon: a flag awarded for victory in a game, championship, etc. (esp. in baseball) (*U.S.*). — **broad pennant** a long swallow-tailed flag flown by a commodore. [A combination of **pendant** and **pennon**.]

pennant[2] *pen'ənt, n.* and *adj.* lit. brook-head, a Welsh place name. — **pennant flag** a Welsh or West Country

stone used for paving (also **pennant grit, rock, stone**). [W. *pen*, head, *nant*, brook.]

pennate. See **penna**.

Pennatula *pen-at'ū-lə, n.* the typical genus of sea-pens: (without *cap.*) a member of the genus: — *pl.* **pennat'-ūlae** (*-ē*), **-as**. — *adj.* **pennatulā'ceous**.   [Fem. of L. *pennātulus*, winged — *penna*.]

penne (*Spens.*). See **penna**.

penneeck, penneech *pen-ēk', (Scott) n.* an old card game with a new trump for every trick.

penniform. See **penna**.

penniless. See **penny**.

pennill *pen'il*, W. *pen'ihl, n.* lit. a verse or stanza: — *pl.* **pennill'ion**. — **pennill'ion-singing** a form of Welsh verse-singing in which the singer improvises an independent melody and verse arrangement against an accompaniment (usu. on the harp) consisting of a traditonal Welsh melody repeated: a modern, modified form of pennillion-singing involving one or more singers and allowing advance preparation.   [Welsh.]

pennine *pen'īn, n.* a mineral of the chlorite group found in the *Pennine* Alps, a hydrous silicate of aluminium, magnesium, and iron. — Also **penn'inite** (*-in-īt*).

Pennisetum *pen-i-sē'təm, n.* a genus, mainly African, of grasses with bristles around the spikelets, including bulrush millet or pearl millet.   [L. *penna*, feather, *saeta*, bristle.]

pennon *pen'ən, n.* a mediaeval knight-bachelor's ensign: a flag or streamer attached to a lance: a flag: a long narrow flag or streamer: a pinion or wing (*Milt.*). — *n.* **penn'oncelle, pen'oncelle, penn'oncel, pen'oncel** a small flag like a pennon. — *adj.* **penn'oned** bearing a pennon.   [O.Fr. *penon*, streamer, arrow-feather, prob. — L. *penna*, feather.]

penn'orth. See **penny**.

penny *pen'i, n.* a coin, originally silver, later copper, bronze from 1860, formerly worth 1/12 of a shilling, or 1/240 of a pound, now (**new penny**) equal to a hundredth part of £1: its value: applied to various more or less similar coins: a cent (*U.S.*): a small sum: money in general: a denarius (*N.T.*): pound, in *fourpenny*, *sixpenny*, *tenpenny nails*, four, six, ten *pound* weight to the thousand: (*pl.* **pennies** *pen'iz*, as material objects; **pence** *pens*, as units of value). — *adj.* sold for a penny: costing a penny. — *adjs.* **penn'ied** possessed of a penny; **penn'iless** without a penny: without money: poor. — *n.* **penn'ilessness**. — *n.* and *v.i.* **penny-a-line'**. — **penny-a-lin'er** a hack writer of the worst, or worst-paid, kind; **penny-a-lin'erism** a hack writer's expression; **penny arcade** an amusement arcade with slot machines orig. operated by a penny; **penn'y-bank** a savings-bank that takes pennies; **penny black** the first adhesive postage stamp, issued by Britain, 1840; **penn'ycress** a cruciferous plant of the genus *Thlaspi*, with round flat pods; **penn'y-dog'** the tope or miller's dog, a kind of shark; **penny dreadful** see **dread**; **penn'y-far'thing** a penny and a farthing: an 'ordinary', an old-fashioned bicycle with a big wheel and a little one; **penn'y-fee** wages in money: (without *hyphen*) a small wage (*Scot.*); **penny gaff** (*slang*) a low-class theatre. — *adj.* **penny'-in-the-slot'** worked by putting a penny in a slot. — **penn'yland** (*hist.*) land valued at a penny a year; **penny mail** (*Scot.*) rent in money, not in kind: a small sum paid to the superior of land; **penn'y-piece** a penny; **penn'y-pig** (*Scot.*) a money-box, properly of earthenware (pig). — *v.i.* **penn'y-pinch'**. — *adjs.* **penn'y-pinch'ing** miserly, too concerned with saving money; **penn'y-plain'** plain, straightforward, unpretentious (from 19th cent. children's paper cut-out figures for toy theatres, costing one penny if plain, twopence if coloured; hence, **penny-plain, twopence-coloured** used of any two basically similar articles, one having a more attractive appearance). — **penn'y-post'** a means of, or organisation for, carrying a letter for a penny; **penn'y-rent'** rent in money: income; **penny share** (*stock exchange*) a share that has fallen to a very low price; **penn'y-stone, -stane** (*Scot.*) a round flat stone used as a quoit; **penn'ystone-**

cast' a stone's throw for such a stone; **penn'y-wedd'ing** a wedding at which the guests contribute money to set up the bride and bridegroom; **penn'yweight** twenty-four grains of troy weight (the weight of a silver penny); **penn'y-whist'le** a tin whistle or flageolet; **penn'y-wis'dom** prudence in petty matters. — *adj.* **penn'y-wise** saving small sums at the risk of larger: niggardly on improper occasions. — **penn'y-wort** a name given to various plants with round leaves, esp. *Hydrocotyle* (an umbelliferous marsh-plant) and navelwort (Cotyledon); **penn'yworth** a penny's worth of anything: the amount that can be got for a penny: a good bargain — also **penn'orth** (*pen'ǝrth; coll.*). — **a penny for your thoughts** (*coll.*) what are you thinking so deeply about?; **a pretty penny** a considerable sum of money; **in penny numbers** a very few, or a very little, at a time; **not a penny the worse** never a whit the worse; **pennies from heaven** money obtained without effort and unexpectedly; **Peter's pence** Rome-scot, a tax or tribute of a silver penny paid to the Pope — in England perhaps from the time of Offa of Mercia, in land from Henry II, abolished under Henry VIII: a similar tax elsewhere: a voluntary contribution to the Pope in modern times; **spend a penny** (*euph.*) to urinate; **the penny drops** now I (etc.) understand; **turn an honest penny** to earn some money honestly; **two a penny** in abundant supply and of little value. [O.E. *penig*, oldest form *pending*; cf. Ger. *Pfennig*; Du. *penning*; O.N. *penningr*.]

pennyroyal *pen-i-roi'ǝl, n.* a species of mint (*Mentha pulegium*) once esteemed in medicine: a related plant, *Hedeoma pulegioides* (*U.S.*). [M.E. *puliol real* — A.Fr. *puliol real* — L. *pūleium, pūlegium*, pennyroyal, and *regālis, -e*, royal.]

pennywinkle. Same as **periwinkle**².

penology, poenology *pē-nol'ǝ-ji, n.* the study of punishment in its relation to crime: the management of prisons. — *adj.* **penological** (*-nǝ-loj'*). — *n.* **penologist** (*-nol'ǝ-jist*). [Gr. *poinē*, punishment, *logos*, discourse.]

penoncel(le). See **pennon**.

pensée *pā-sā*, (Fr.) *n.* thought.

pensel. See **pensil**.

pensieroso *pen-sye-rō'sō*, (It.) *adj.* melancholy: thoughtful.

pensil, pensel, pencel *pen'sl, n.* a small pennon. [A.Fr. *pencel*, dim. of *penon*, pennon.]

pensile *pen'sīl, -sil, adj.* hanging: suspended: overhanging: of birds, building a hanging nest. — *ns.* **pen'sileness, pensility** (*-sil'i-ti*). [L. *pēnsilis* — *pendēre*, to hang.]

pension *pen'shǝn, n.* a periodical payment, as tribute, wages, etc. (*obs.*): an allowance of money as a bribe for future services, as a mark of favour, or in reward of one's own or another's merit: an allowance to one who has retired or has been disabled or reached old age or has been widowed or orphaned, etc.: (now pronounced as Fr., *pā-syɔ̃*) a continental boarding-house: board. — *v.t.* to grant a pension to. — *adjs.* **pen'sionable** entitled, or entitling, to a pension; **pen'sionary** receiving a pension: of the nature of a pension. — *n.* one who receives a pension: one whose interest is bought by a pension: the syndic or legal adviser of a Dutch town (*hist.*). — *n.* **pen'sioner** one who receives a pension: a dependent: a gentleman-at-arms (*obs.*): one who pays out of his own income for his commons, chambers, etc., at Cambridge University = an Oxford *commoner*: a boarder, esp. in a religious house (*obs.*). — **Grand Pensionary** (*hist.*) the president of the States-general of Holland; **pension off** to dismiss, or allow to retire, with a pension. [Fr., — L. *pēnsiō, -ōnis* — *pendēre, pēnsum*, to weigh, pay.]

pensionnat *pā-syo-na*, (Fr.) *n.* a boarding-school.

pensive *pen'siv, adj.* meditative: expressing thoughtfulness with sadness. — *adj.* **pen'siv'd** (*Shak.*) made pensive. — *adv.* **pen'sively.** — *n.* **pen'siveness.** [Fr. *pensif, -ive* — *penser*, to think — L. *pēnsāre*, to weigh — *pendēre*, to weigh.]

Penstemon. See **Pentstemon**.

penstock *pen'stok, n.* a sluice. [**pen**¹, **stock**¹.]

pensum *pen'sǝm, n.* a task: a school imposition (*U.S.*). [L. *pēnsum.*]

pent¹ *pa.t.* and *pa.p.* of **pen**¹, to shut up. — *adj.* **pent'-up'** held in: repressed.

pent² *pent, n.* a penthouse: a sloping or overhanging covering. — **pent'roof** a roof that slopes one way only. [From **penthouse**, app. influenced by Fr. *pente*, slope.]

pent-, penta- in composition, five. — *ns.* **pentachlorophē'nol** a widely used fungicidal and bactericidal compound, used esp. as a wood preservative; **pentachord** (*pen'tǝ-körd*; Gr. *chordē*, string) a musical instrument with five strings: a diatonic series of five notes; **pentacle** (*pent'ǝ-kl*; L.L. *pentaculum*, app. — Gr. *pente*; according to some, O.Fr. *pentacol* — *pendre*, to hang, *à*, on, *col*, the neck) a pentagram or similar figure (sometimes a hexagram) or amulet used as a defence against demons; **Pentacrinus** (*-ak'rin-ǝs*; Gr. *krinon*, lily) a genus of fossil crinoids, in the form of a feathery five-rayed star on a long pentagonal stalk. — *adj.* **pentac'rinoid** like, or akin to, Pentacrinus. — *n.* a young form of some crinoids that resembles Pentacrinus. — *adj.* **pent'act** (Gr. *aktīs, aktīnos*, ray) five-rayed. — *n.* a five-rayed sponge spicule. — *adjs.* **pentactinal** (*-ak'tin-ǝl*, or *-ak-tī'nǝl*); **pentacy'clic** (Gr. *kyklos*, wheel) having five whorls. — *n.* **pent'ad** (Gr. *pentas, -ados*) a set of five things: a period of five years or five days: an atom, element or radical with a combining power of five. — Also *adj.* — *adjs.* **pentad'ic; pentadac'tyl, pentadac'tyle** (*-til*; Gr. *daktylos*, finger, toe) having five digits. — *n.* a person with five fingers and five toes. — *adjs.* **pentadactyl'ic, pentadac'tylous.** — *ns.* **pentadac'tylism; pentadac'tyly.** — *adj.* **pentadel'phous** (Gr. *adelphos*, brother) having five bundles of stamens: united in five bundles. — *n.* **pentagon** (*pen'tǝ-gon*; Gr. *pentagōnon* — *gōniā*, angle) a rectilineal plane figure having five angles and five sides (*geom.*): a fort with five bastions: (with *cap.*) the headquarters of the U.S. armed forces at Washington — from the shape of the building. — *adj.* **pentagonal** (*pen-tag'ǝn-ǝl*). — *adv.* **pentag'onally.** — *ns.* **pen'tagram** (Gr. *pentagrammon* — *gramma*, a letter) a stellate pentagon or five-pointed star: a magic figure of that form; **pen'tagraph** a wrong form of **pantograph**. — *n.pl.* **Pentagynia** (*-jin'i-ǝ*; Gr. *gynē*, a woman, in the sense of female; *obs.*) a Linnaean order of plants (in various classes) with five pistils. — *adjs.* **pentagyn'ian, pentagynous** (*-aj'*). — *n.* **pentahē'dron** (Gr. *hedrā*, seat) a five-faced solid figure: — *pl.* **pentahē'drons, -dra.** — *adj.* **pentahē'dral.** — *ns.* **pental'ogy** a pentad, esp. of published works: a series of five related books; **pental'pha** (Gr. *alpha*, the letter alpha) a pentacle; **Pentam'eron** (It. *Pentamerone* — Gr. *pente, hēmerā*, day) a famous collection of folk-tales in Neapolitan dialect by Giambattista Basile (*d.* 1632) supposed to be told during five days; **pentam'erism** (Gr. *meros*, part) the condition of being pentamerous. — *adj.* **pentam'erous** having five parts or members: having parts in fives. — *ns.* **pentam'ery; pentam'eter** (Gr. *pentametros* — *metron*, a measure) a verse of five measures or feet (**elegiac pentameter** a verse of two penthemimers, the first admitting spondees instead of dactyls, the second dactyls only; **iambic pentameter** a somewhat unsuitable name for the line used in the English heroic couplet and blank verse). — Also *adj.* — *n.pl.* **Pentan'dria** (*obs.*; Gr. *anēr, andros*, a man, a male) in Linnaeus's classification a class of plants with five stamens. — *adjs.* **pentan'drian, pentan'drous.** — *ns.* **pentane** (*pent'ān*) a hydrocarbon (C_5H_{12}), fifth member of the methane series; **pent'angle** a pentacle: a pentagon. — *adjs.* **pentang'ular; pentaploid** (*pent'ǝ-ploid*; Gr. *pentaploos*, fivefold, *eidos*, form) fivefold: having five times the haploid number of chromosomes (*biol.*). — *n.* a cell, organism, or form with five sets of chromosomes. — *n.* **pent'aploidy** the condition of having five sets of chromosomes. — *adj.* **pentapodic** (*pent-ǝ-pod'ik*). — *ns.* **pentapody** (*pen-tap'ǝ-di*; Gr. *pous, podos*, foot) a measure of five feet; **pentap'olis**

(Gr. *polis*, a city) a group of five cities, esp. those of Cyrenaica — Cyrene, Berenice, Arsinoe, Ptolemais, and Apollonia. — *adj.* **pentapolitan** (*pent-ə-pol'i-tən*). — *n.* **pent'aprism** a five-sided prism that corrects lateral inversion by turning light through an angle of 90°, used on reflex cameras to allow eye-level viewing. — *adj.* **pentarch** (*pent'ärk*; Gr. *archē*, beginning) (of roots) having five vascular strands. — *ns.* **pent'arch** (Gr. *archē*, rule) a ruler or governor in a pentarchy; **pentarchy** (*pent'ärk-i*) government by five persons: a group of five kings, rulers, states, or governments; **pentastich** (*pent'ə-stik*; Gr. *stichos*, row, line) a group of five lines of verse: — *pl.* **pentastichs** (*-stiks*). — *adjs.* **pentastichous** (*pen-tas'ti-kəs*) five-ranked; **pen'tastyle** (Gr. *stȳlos*, a pillar) having five columns in front. — *n.* a building or portico with five columns. — *adj.* **pentasyllab'ic** five-syllabled. — *n.* **Pentateuch** (*pen-tə-tūk*; Gr. *pentateuchos*, five-volumed — *teuchos*, a tool; later, a book) the first five books of the Old Testament. — *adj.* **pentateuch'al.** — *ns.* **pentath'lete** a competitor in the pentathlon; **pentath'lon** (Gr. *pentathlon* — *athlon*, contest) a contest in five exercises — wrestling, disc-throwing, spear-throwing, leaping, running. a five-event contest at the modern Olympic games from 1906-1924: a five-event Olympic games contest for women: **(modern pentathlon)** an Olympic games contest consisting of swimming, cross-country riding and running, fencing and revolver-shooting — also (Latin) **pentath'lum.** — *adjs.* **pentatomic** (*pent-ə-tom'ik*; Gr. *atomos*, atom) having five atoms, esp. five atoms of replaceable hydrogen: pentavalent; **pentatonic** (*pent-ə-ton'ik*; Gr. *tonos*, tone) consisting of five tones or notes — applied esp. to a scale, a major scale with the fourth and seventh omitted; **pentavalent** (*pen-tə-vā'-lənt, pen-tav'ə-lənt*) having a valency of five. — *n.* **pentazocine** (*pen-tā'zə-sēn*) a pain-killing drug believed to be non-addictive. [Gr. *pente*, five.]

penteconter *pen-ti-kon'tər, n.* an ancient Greek ship with fifty oars. [Gr. *pentēkontērēs* — *pentēkonta*, fifty.]

Pentecost *pent'i-kost, n.* a Jewish festival held on the fiftieth day after the second day of the Passover, also called the **Feast of Weeks**, and **Shabuoth** or **Shavuot**: the festival of Whitsuntide, seven weeks after Easter. — *adj.* **Pentecost'al** of or relating to Pentecost: of or relating to any of several fundamentalist Christian groups placing great emphasis on the spiritual powers of the Holy Spirit. — *n.* a Pentecostalist: (in *pl.*) offerings formerly made to the parish priest at Whitsuntide. — *n.* **Pentecost'alist** a member of a Pentecostal church. [Gr. *pentēkostē* (*hēmerā*), fiftieth (day).]

Pentel® *pen'tel, n.* (also without *cap.*) a type of felt-tip pen.

Pentelic, -an *pen-tel'ik, -ən, adjs.* of Mount *Pentelicus* near Athens, famous for the marble found there.

pentene. See **pentylene.**

penteteric *pen-ti-ter'ik, adj.* occurring every fourth (by the old mode of reckoning, fifth) year. [Gr. *pentetērikos* — *etos*, a year.]

penthemimer *pen-thi-mim'ər, n.* a metrical group of 2½ feet. — *adj.* **penthemim'eral.** [Gr. *pente*, five, *hēmi-*, half, *meros*, a part.]

penthia *pen'thi-ə, n.* according to Spenser another name for the unidentified plant Astrophel.

penthouse *pent'hows, n.* a shed or lean-to projecting from or adjoining a main building: a separate room or dwelling on a roof: a roofed corridor surrounding the court in real tennis: a (small) select top flat: a protection from the weather over a door or a window: anything of similar form, as an eyebrow: — *pl.* **pent'-houses** (*-how-ziz*). — *v.t.* to provide or cover with, or as with, a penthouse. [For **pentice** — Fr. *appentis* — L.L. *appendicium*, an appendage.]

pentice, pentise *pen'tis.* Same as **penthouse.**

pentimento *pen-ti-men'tō, n.* something painted out of a picture which later becomes visible again: — *pl.* **-ti** *-tē.* [It. — *pentirsi*, to repent.]

pentlandite *pent'lənd-īt, n.* a native sulphide of iron and nickel. [Joseph Barclay *Pentland* (1797-1873), traveller in South America.]

pentobarbitone *pen-tə-bär'bit-ōn, n.* a barbiturate drug, $C_{11}H_{17}N_2O_3$, with hypnotic, sedative, and anticonvulsant effects. — Also (*U.S.*) **pentobarbital.**

pentomic *pen-tom'ik, adj.* of an army division, formed into five units, esp. when using atomic weapons. [Gr. *pente*, five, and **atomic.**]

pentode *pent'ōd, n.* a thermionic tube with five electrodes. [Gr. *pente*, five, *hodos*, way.]

pentose *pent'ōs, n.* a sugar (of various kinds) with five oxygen atoms. — *ns.* **pent'osan** (*-san*), **pent'osane** (*-sān*) a carbohydrate that yields pentose on hydrolysis. [Gr. *pente*, five.]

Pentothal® *pen'tō-thal, n.* registered trademark for thiopentone sodium (in U.S. thiopental sodium), an intravenous anaesthetic, a sodium thiobarbiturate compound. — Also **Pentothal sodium.**

pentoxide *pent-ok'sīd,* (*chem.*) *n.* a compound having 5 atoms of oxygen combined with another element or radical. [Gr. *pente*, five, and **oxide.**]

pentroof. See **pent²**.

Pentstemon *pen(t)-stē'mən, n.* a mainly North American showy-flowered genus of Scrophulariaceae, with a sterile fifth stamen: (without *cap.*) a plant of this genus. — Also, and now more usu., **Penstē'mon.** [Gr. *pente*, five, *stēmōn*, warp, as if stamen.]

pentylene *pent'i-lēn, n.* an unsaturated hydrocarbon (C_5H_{10}) of the olefine series (in several isomers) — amylene. — Also **pent'ene.** [Gr. *pente*, five, *hȳlē*, matter.]

penuche, penuchi. Same as **panocha.**

penuchle. See **pinochle.**

penult *pi-nult', also pē'nult,* **penult'ima** *-imə, ns.* the syllable last but one. — *adj.* **penult'imate** last but one. — *n.* the penult: the last but one. [L. *paenultima* (*syllaba*, etc.) — *paene*, almost, *ultimus*, last.]

penumbra *pen-um'brə, n.* a partial or lighter shadow round the perfect or darker shadow of an eclipse: the less dark border of a sun-spot or any similar spot: the part of a picture where the light and shade blend into each other. — *adjs.* **penum'bral, penum'brous.** [L. *paene*, almost, *umbra*, shade.]

penury *pen'ū-ri, n.* want: great poverty. — *adj.* **penū'rious** in want (*obs.*): scanty (*obs.*): niggardly: miserly. — *adv.* **penū'riously.** — *n.* **penū'riousness.** [L. *pēnūria.*]

peon *pē'on, n.* a day-labourer, esp. formerly in Spanish-speaking America, one working off a debt by bondage: in India (*pūn*), a foot-soldier (*hist.*), a policeman (*hist.*), a messenger: in S.E. Asia, a minor office worker. — *ns.* **pē'onage, pē'onism** agricultural servitude of the above kind. [Sp. *peón* and Port. *peão* — L.L. *pedō, -ōnis*, a foot-soldier — L. *pēs, pedis*, a foot.]

peony, paeony *pē'ə-ni, n.* any plant of the genus *Paeonia*, of the buttercup family, with large showy crimson or white globular flowers: its flower. — Also obs. forms **pī'on(e)y.** [O.E. *peonie* and O.Fr. (Northern) *pione* (Fr. *pivoine*) — L. *paeōnia* — Gr. *paiōniā* — *Paiōn, Paiān*, physician of the gods (see **Paean**) from its use in medicine.]

people *pē'pl, n.* a nation: a community: a body of persons held together by belief in common origin, speech, culture, political union, or other bond: a set of persons: transferred to a set of animals as if forming a nation — in these senses used as *sing.* with a *pl.* **peo'ples** (*B.* **peo'ple**): a body of persons linked by common leadership, headship, etc.: subjects: retainers: followers: employees: servants: congregation: attendants: near kindred: members of one's household: parents: ancestors and descendants: inhabitants of a place: transferred to animal inhabitants: the persons associated with any business: laity: the mass of the nation: general population: populace: the citizens: voters: (approaching a *pron.*) they, one, folks — in these senses used as *pl.* — *v.t.* to stock with people or inhabitants: to inhabit: to occupy as if inhabiting. — **people mover** a car, carriage, etc., used to transport people at airports, etc., usually running on a fixed rail or track; **people's democracy** a form of government in which the proletariat, represented by the Communist Party, holds power — seen ideologically as a transitional state on the way to full socialism; **people's front** same as **popular front; People's Party** see **populist** under **popular; People's Republic** a name adopted by some socialist or communist states. [O.Fr. *poeple* — L. *pŏpulus*.]

pep *pep*, (*coll.*) *n.* vigour, go, spirit. — *v.t.* to put pep into (usu. with *up*). — *adjs.* **pep'ful, pepp'y.** — **pep pill** a pill containing a stimulant drug; **pep talk** a strongly-worded talk designed to arouse enthusiasm for a cause or course of action. [**pepper.**]

peperino *pep-ə-rē'nō, n.* a dark tuff with many crystals and rock-fragments, found in the Alban Hills. [It. *peperino* — L. *piper*, pepper.]

Peperomia *pep-ər-ō'mi-ə, n.* a large genus of subtropical herbaceous plants of the family Piperaceae, many grown as house plants for their ornamental foliage: (without *cap.*) a plant of this genus. [Gr. *peperi*, pepper, *homoios*, like, similar.]

peplos *pep'los*, **peplus** *pep'ləs, ns.* a draped outer robe worn usu. by women in ancient Greece. — *n.* **pep'lum** a peplos: an overskirt supposed to be like the peplos: a short skirt-like section attached to the waist-line of a dress, blouse or jacket. [Gr. *peplos.*]

pepo *pē'pō, n.* the type of fruit found in the melon and cucumber family, a large many-seeded berry formed from an inferior ovary, usually with hard epicarp: — *pl.* **pē'pos.** [L. *pĕpō, -ŏnis* — Gr. (*sikyos*) *pepōn*, (a melon eaten) ripe, distinguished from a cucumber eaten unripe.]

pepper *pep'ər, n.* a pungent aromatic condiment consisting of the dried berries of the pepper plant, entire or powdered (*black pepper*), or with the outer parts removed (*white pepper*): any plant of the genus Piper, esp. *P. nigrum*, or of the family Piperaceae: a plant of the solanaceous genus Capsicum or one of its pods (*red, yellow* or *green pepper*; also called **sweet pepper**): cayenne (also **cayenne pepper**): extended to various similar condiments and the plants producing them. — *v.t.* to sprinkle or flavour with pepper: to sprinkle: to pelt with shot, etc.: to pelt thoroughly: to do for. — *v.i.* to pelt: to shower: to discharge shot, etc., in showers. — *ns.* **pepp'erer** a grocer (*obs.*): one who or that which peppers; **pepp'eriness; pepp'ering.** — *adj.* **pepp'ery** having the qualities of pepper: pungent: hot, choleric, irritable. — *adj.* **pepper-and-salt'** mingled black and white: of hair, flecked with grey. — **pepp'er= box** a pepper-pot: a turret or other object of similar shape; **pepp'er-cake** a kind of spiced cake or ginger-bread; **pepp'er-caster, -castor** a pepper-pot; **pepp'-ercorn** the dried berry of the pepper plant: something of little value. — *adj.* like a peppercorn, as the small tight knots in which certain African peoples wear their hair: trivial, nominal, as *peppercorn rent.* — *adj.* **pepp'ercorny.** — **pepp'er-gin'gerbread** (*Shak.*) hot-spiced gingerbread; **pepp'er-grass** any cress of the genus *Lepidium*: pillwort (*Pilularia*); **pepp'ermill** a small handmill in which peppercorns are ground; **pepp'ermint** an aromatic and pungent species of mint (*Mentha piperita*): a liquor distilled from it: a lozenge flavoured with it; **peppermint cream** a sweet creamy peppermint-flavoured substance: a sweet made of this; **pepp'ermint-drop** a peppermint-flavoured, usu. hard, sweet; **pepp'er-pot** a pot or bottle with a perforated top for sprinkling pepper: a West Indian dish of cassareep, flesh or dried fish, and vegetables, esp. green okra and chillies; **pepper tree** an evergreen tree of the genus *Schinus*, chiefly native to tropical America, often grown for its ornamental appearance; **pepp'erwort** a cress of the genus *Lepidium*, esp. dittander (L. *lati-folium*). — **Jamaica pepper** allspice; **long pepper** the fruit of *Piper longum*; **Negro pepper** the produce of Xylopia (fam. Anonaceae), also called **Ethiopian pepper.** [O.E. *pipor* — L. *piper* — Gr. *peperi* — Sans. *pippali*.]

pepperoni, peperoni *pep-ə-rō'ni n.* a hard, spicy beef and pork sausage. [It. *peperoni*, pl. of *peperone*, chilli, pepper — L. *piper*, pepper.]

Pepper's ghost *pep'ərz gōst*, a phantom produced on the stage by a sheet of glass reflecting an actor on an understage. [John H. *Pepper* (1821–1900) improver and exhibitor of H. Dircks's invention.]

peppy. See **pep.**

pepsin, pepsine *pep'sin, n.* any of a group of closely allied proteins, digestive enzymes of the gastric juice of vertebrates: a preparation containing pepsin from a pig's or other stomach (*med.*). — *v.t.* **pep'sinate** to treat with pepsin: to mix or combine with pepsin. — *n.* **pep'sinogen** a zymogen found in granular form in the stomach mucosa which converts into pepsin in a slightly acid medium. — *adj.* **pep'tic** relating to or promoting digestion: having a good digestion: of or relating to pepsin or the digestive juices. — *n.* **pepticity** (*-tis'i-ti*) eupepsia. — *n.pl.* **pep'tics** (*jocular*) the digestive organs. — *ns.* **pep'tide** any of a number of substances formed from amino-acids in which the amino-group of one is joined to the carboxyl group of another; **peptīsā'tion, -z-.** — *v.t.* **pept'ise, -ize** to bring into colloidal solution: to form into a sol from a gel. — *ns.* **pep'tōne** a product of the action of enzymes on albuminous matter; **peptonīsā'tion, -z-.** — *v.t.* **pep'-tonise, -ize** to convert into peptones. — **peptic ulcer** an ulcer of the stomach or duodenum, etc. [Gr. *pepsis*, digestion — *peptein*, to digest.]

Pepysian *pēp'si-ən, adj.* pertaining to Samuel *Pepys* (1633–1703), his inimitable diary, or the collections he bequeathed to Magdalene College, Cambridge.

per¹ *pûr, pər, prep.* for each, a: (chiefly commercial) by: in the manner or direction of (*her.*). — **as per usual** (*coll.* or *illit.*) as usual. [L. and O.Fr. *per*.]

per² *pûr, per,* (L.) through, by means of, according to. — **per annum (diem, mensem)** (*an'əm, -ŏŏm, dī'əm, dē'em, men'səm, men'sem*) yearly (daily, monthly); **per ardua ad astra** (*är'dū-ə ad as'trə, är'dŏŏ-ä ad as'trä*) by steep and toilsome ways to the stars — Air Force motto; **per capita** (*kap'i-tə, kap'i-tä*), **per caput** (*kap'ŏŏt*) (counting) by heads: all sharing alike; **per contra** (*kon'trə, kon'trä*) on the contrary: as a set-off; **per fas et nefas** (*fas et nē'fas, fäs et ne'fäs*) through right and wrong; **per impossibile** (*im-po-si'bi-lē, im-po-si'bi-le*) by an impossibility: if it were so, which it is not; **per incuriam** (*in-kū'ri-am, in-kŏŏ'ri-am; legal*) through want of care, a phrase designating a court decision that is mistaken and therefore not binding as a precedent; **per minas** (*mī', mē'näs; legal*) by means of threats, by menaces; **per procurationem** (*prok-ū-rā-shi-ō'nem, prō-kŏŏ-rä-ti-ō'nem*) by the agency of another, by proxy; **per saltum** (*sal'təm, sal'tŏŏm*) at a single leap: all at once; **per se** (*sē, sā*) by himself, etc.: essentially: in itself; **per stirpes** (*stûr'pēz, stir'pās*) by stocks: in inheritance, the children of each descendant dividing only the share that would have been their parent's (distinguished from *per capita*).

per- *pûr-, pər-*, in composition (1) in chemistry, indicating the highest degree of combination with oxygen or other element or radical; (2) in words from Latin, through, beyond, or thoroughly, or indicating destruction.

peracute *pûr-ə-kūt', adj.* very sharp or violent. [L. *peracūtus* — *per-*, thoroughly, *acūtus*, sharp.]

peradventure *pûr-əd-ven'chər, adv.* by adventure: by chance: perhaps. — *n.* uncertainty: question. [O.Fr. *per* (or *par*) *aventure*, by chance.]

peraeon, peraeopod. See **pereion.**

perai *pē-rī'.* See **piranha.**

perambulate *pər-am'bū-lāt, v.t.* to walk through, about, around, up and down, or over: to pass through for the purpose of surveying: to beat the bounds of: to patrol: to wheel in a perambulator. — *v.i.* to walk about. — *ns.* **perambulā'tion** the act of perambulating: a survey or inspection by travelling through: beating the bounds: the district within which a person has the right of inspection; **peram'bulātor** one who perambulates: a wheel for measuring distances on roads: a light carriage for a child (now usu. **pram**). — *adj.* **peram'bulatory.** [L. *perambulāre, -ātum* — *per*, through, *ambulāre*, to walk.]

Perca. See **perch**[1].

percale *per-käl', pər-kāl', n.* a closely woven French cambric. — *n.* **percaline** (*pûr-kə-lēn'*, or *pûr'-*) a glossy cotton cloth. [Fr.; cf. Pers. *purgālah*, rag.]

percase *pər-kās', (obs.) adv.* perchance: perhaps. [L. *per*, through, by, *casus*, a chance, a fall.]

perce *pûrs, (Spens.)* same as **pierce.** — Also (*infin.*) **percen.** — *adjs.* (*Spens.*) **perce'able** pierceable; **perce'ant** (*Keats*) piercing.

perceive *pər-sēv', v.t.* to become or be aware of through the senses: to get knowledge of by the mind: to see: to understand: to discern. — *adj.* **perceiv'able.** — *adv.* **perceiv'ably** perceptibly. — *n.* **perceiv'er.** — *n.* and *adj.* **perceiv'ing.** — **perceived noise decibel** a unit used to measure the amount of annoyance caused to people by noise. [O.Fr. *percever* — L. *percipĕre, perceptum* — pfx. *per-*, thoroughly, *capĕre*, to take.]

per cent (usu. written or printed with a point after it as if an abbreviation for *per centum*, but pronounced as a complete word, *pər-sent'*) in the hundred: for each hundred or hundred pounds. — *n.* a percentage: (in *pl.*, in composition) securities yielding a specified percentage (as *three-percents*). — *n.* **percent'age** rate per hundred: an allowance of so much for every hundred: a proportional part: commission (*coll.*): profit, advantage (*coll.*). — *adjs.* **percent'al, percen'tile.** — *n.* **percen'tile** the value below which falls a specified percentage (as 25, 50, 75) of a large number of statistical units (e.g. scores in an examination): percentile rank. — **percentile rank** grading according to percentile group. — **play the percentages** in sport, gambling, etc., to play, operate or proceed by means of unspectacular safe shots, moves, etc. as opposed to spectacular but risky ones whch may not succeed, on the assumption that this is more likely to lead to success in the long run. [L. *per centum.*]

percept *pûr'sept, n.* an object perceived by the senses: the mental result of perceiving. — *n.* **perceptibil'ity.** — *adj.* **percep'tible** that can be perceived: that may be known by the senses: discernible. — *adv.* **percep'tibly.** — *n.* **percep'tion** the act or power of perceiving: discernment: apprehension of any modification of consciousness: the combining of sensations into a recognition of an object: direct recognition: a percept: reception of a stimulus (*bot.*). — *adjs.* **percep'tional; percep'tive** able or quick to perceive: discerning: active or instrumental in perceiving. — *ns.* **percep'tiveness; perceptiv'ity.** — *adj.* **percep'tūal** of the nature of, or relating to, perception. [L. *percipĕre, perceptum*; see **perceive.**]

perch[1] *pûrch, n.* a spiny-finned freshwater fish of the genus **Perca** (*pûr'kə*): extended to various fishes of the same or kindred family, or other. — *n.pl.* **Percidae** (*pûr'si-dē*) the perch family. — *adjs.* **per'ciform, per'cine** (*-sīn*), **per'coid** (*-koid*). [L. *perca* (partly through Fr. *perche*) — Gr. *perkē*, a perch, perh. conn. with *perknos*, dusky.]

perch[2] *pûrch, n.* a pole (*obs.* or *dial.* except in special uses): a pole serving as a navigation mark: a pole joining the fore and hind gear of some vehicles: a bar or frame for stretching cloth for examination: a bar for fixing leather for softening treatment: a peg or bar for hanging things on (*obs.*): a rod for a bird to alight, sit, or roost on: anything serving that purpose for a bird, a person, or anything else: a high seat: a rod or pole, a measure of 5½ yards (5·03 metres) or (*square perch*) 30¼ square yards (25·3 sq. metres): a measure of stonework, 24¾ or 25 cubic feet (0·7 cu. metres). — *v.i.* to alight, sit or roost on a perch: to be set on high: to be balanced on a high or narrow footing: to settle. — *v.t.* to place, as on a perch: to stretch, examine, or treat on a perch. — *adj.* **perch'ed** (*Milt.*) having perches. — *ns.* **perch'er** a bird with feet adapted for

perching; **perch'ing** examination of cloth on a perch: a process of leather-softening. — *adj.* with feet adapted for perching: insessorial. — **perched block** a block of rock transported by land-ice and left aloft, often in an unstable position, when the ice retires; **perching birds** the Passeriformes. [Fr. *perche* — L. *pertica*, a rod.]

perchance *pər-chäns', adv.* by chance: as it may happen: perhaps. [A.Fr. *par chance.*]

percheron *per'shə-rŏ, pûr'shə-ron, n.* a draught-horse of a breed originating in La *Perche* in Southern Normandy. — Also *adj.* [Fr.]

perchloric *pər-klō-rik, -klö'rik, adj.* containing more oxygen than chloric acid — applied to an oily explosive acid, $HClO_4$. — *n.* **perchlō'rate** a salt of perchloric acid. [**per-** (1).]

Percidae, perciform, percine. See **perch**[1].

percipient *pər-sip'i-ənt, adj.* perceiving: having the faculty of perception. — *n.* one who perceives or can perceive: one who receives impressions telepathically or otherwise supersensibly. — *ns.* **percip'ience,** (*rare*) **percip'iency.** [L. *percipiēns, -entis*, pr.p. of *percipĕre*; cf. **perceive, percept.**]

percoct *pər-kokt', adj.* well-cooked: overdone: hackneyed. [L. *percoctus* — *percoquĕre*, to cook thoroughly.]

percoid *pûr'koid.* See **perch**[1].

percolate *pûr'kə-lāt, v.t.* and *v.i.* to pass through pores, small openings, etc.: to filter. — *n.* a filtered liquid. — *ns.* **percolation** (*pûr-kō-lā'shən*); **per'colātor** an apparatus for percolating, esp. for making coffee. [L. *percōlāre, -ātum* — *per*, through, *cōlāre*, to strain.]

percolin *pûr'kə-lin, n.* a small bird, a cross between a partridge and a quail.

percurrent *pər-kur'ənt, adj.* running through the whole length. — *adj.* **percursory** (*-kūr'*) cursory. [L. *percurrĕre*, to run through, *percursor*, one who runs through.]

percuss *pər-kus', v.t.* to strike so as to shake: to tap for purposes of diagnosis. — *adj.* **percuss'ant** (*her.*) bent round and striking the side, as a lion's tail — also **percussed'.** — *n.* **percussion** (*-kush'ən*) striking: impact: tapping directly or indirectly upon the body to find the condition of an organ by the sound (*med.*): massage by tapping: the striking or sounding of a discord, etc., as distinguished from preparation and resolution (*mus.*): collectively, instruments played by striking — drum, cymbals, triangle, etc. (*mus.*): a device for making an organ-pipe speak promptly by striking the reed (*mus.*). — *adj.* **percuss'ional.** — *n.* **percuss'ionist** a musician who plays percussion instruments. — *adj.* **percussive** (*-kus'*). — *adv.* **percuss'ively.** — *n.* **percuss'or** a percussion hammer. — *adj.* **percutient** (*-kū'shyent*) striking or having power to strike. — *n.* that which strikes or has power to strike. — **percuss'ion-bull'et** a bullet that explodes on striking; **percuss'ion-cap** a metal case containing a fulminating substance which explodes when struck, formerly used for firing rifles, etc.: a small paper case of the same type, used to make children's toy guns sound realistic (usu. **cap**); **percuss'ion-fuse** a fuse in a projectile that acts on striking; **percuss'ion-hamm'er** a small hammer for percussion in diagnosis; **percuss'ion-lock** a gun lock in which a hammer strikes a percussion-cap; **percuss'ion-pow'der** powder that explodes on being struck — fulminating powder. — **bulb of percussion** see **bulb.** [L. *percussiō, -ōnis* — *percutĕre, percussum* — pfx. *per-*, thoroughly, *quatĕre*, to shake.]

percutaneous *pər-kū-tā'ni-əs, adj.* done or applied through the skin. — *adv.* **percutā'neously.** [**per-** (2), L. *cutis*, the skin.]

percutient. See **percuss.**

perdendo *per-den'dō, (mus.) adj.* and *adv.* dying away in volume of tone and in speed. — Also **perden'dosi** (*-sē*). [It.]

perdie, perdy *pər-dē', sometimes pûr'dē, (Spens., Shak.) adv.* assuredly. — Also **pardi(e)', pardy'.** [O.Fr. *par dé*, by God.]

perdition pər-dish'ən, n. loss (arch.): ruin (arch.): utter loss or ruin (arch.): the utter loss of happiness in a future state: hell. — adj. **perdi'tionable.** [L. perditiō, -ōnis — perdĕre, perditum — pfx. per-, entirely, dăre, to give, give up.]

perdu, perdue pər-dū', adj. lost to view: concealed: in a post of extreme danger (obs.): on a forlorn hope or on a desperate enterprise (obs.): reckless. — n. an outlying sentinel (Shak.): one lying in concealment or ambush: one on a forlorn hope (obs.). — **lie perdu(e)** (mil.) to lie in ambush, concealed and on the watch. [Fr., pa.p. of perdre, to lose — L. perdĕre, to destroy; see preceding.]

perduellion pər-dū-el'yən, (arch.) n. treason. [L. perduelliō, -ōnis.]

perdurable pər-dūr'ə-bl (rare; Shak. pûr'), adj. very durable, long continued: everlasting. — n. **perdūrabil'ity.** — adv. **perdūr'ably** (Shak. pûr') very durably: everlastingly. — ns. **perdūr'ance; perdūrā'tion.** — v.i. **perdūre'** to endure. [L. perdūrāre — per, through, dūrāre, to last.]

perdy. See perdie.

père per, (Fr.) n. father. — **Père David's** (dā'vidz, dä'vēdz, -vēdz') deer a breed of large grey deer discovered in China by Father A. David, 19th-cent. French missionary, and now surviving only in captivity.

peregal per'i-gl, (obs.) adj. fully equal. — n. equal. [O.Fr. paregal — L. pfx. per-, thoroughly, aequālis, equal.]

peregrine per'i-grin, adj. foreign (arch.): outlandish (arch.): making a pilgrimage or journey (arch.): applied to a species of falcon (Falco peregrinus), so named because taken not from the (inaccessible) nest (as an eyas is) but while in flight from it. — n. (arch.) an alien resident: a pilgrim or traveller in a foreign land: a peregrine falcon. — v.i. **per'egrinate** to travel about: to live in a foreign country: to go on pilgrimage. — v.t. to traverse. — adj. foreign-looking. — ns. **peregrinā'tion** travelling about: wandering: pilgrimage: a complete and systematic course or round: a sojourn abroad; **per'egrinātor** one who travels about. — adj. **per'egrinatory** of or pertaining to a peregrinator: wandering. — n. **peregrin'ity** foreignness: outlandishness. [L. peregrīnus, foreign — peregre, abroad — per, through, ager, field.]

pereion pə-rī'on, -rē', n. the thorax in Crustacea: — pl. **perei'a.** — n. **perei'opod** a crustacean's thoracic walking-leg. — Also in corrected form, **peraeon, peraeopod.** (-rē'). [Faultily formed from Gr. peraioein, to transport, to carry across.]

pereira pə-rē'rə, n. a Brazilian apocynaceous tree, the bark of which is used medicinally: the bark itself. — Both also **pereira bark.** [From Jonathan Pereira, 19th-cent. English pharmacologist.]

peremptory pər-em(p)'tə-ri, or per'əm(p)-, adj. precluding debate or dispute (Rom. law): final: admitting no refusal or denial: definitely fixed (law): utter (obs.): dogmatic: imperious: arrogantly commanding. — adv. **peremp'torily** (or per'). — n. **peremp'toriness** (or per'). [L. peremptōrius — perimĕre, peremptum, to destroy, prevent — pfx. per-, entirely, and emĕre, to take, to buy.]

perennial pər-en'yəl, adj. lasting through the year: perpetual: never failing: growing constantly: lasting more than two years (bot.): of insects, living more than one year. — n. a plant that lives more than two years. — v.i. **perenn'ate** to live perennially: to survive from season to season, esp. through a period of inactivity. — n. **perennā'tion** (per-). — adv. **perenn'ially.** — n. **perennial'ity** the quality of being perennial — also **perenn'ity** (arch.). [L. perennis — per, through, annus, a year.]

perennibranchiate pər-en-i-brang'ki-it, -āt, adj. retaining the gills throughout life. — adj. and n. **perenn'ibranch** (-brangk). [L. perennis, lasting through the years, branchiae, gills.]

perestroika pyi-ryi-stroy'kə, (Russ.) n. reconstruction,

restructuring (of society, the state, etc.)

perfay pər-fā', (arch.) interj. by my faith. [O.Fr. par fei.]

perfect pûr'fekt, -fikt, adj. done thoroughly or completely: completed: mature: complete: having all organs in a functional condition: having androecium and gynaeceum in the same flower: completely skilled or versed: thoroughly known or acquired: exact: exactly conforming to definition or theory: flawless: having every moral excellence: sheer, utter: completely contented (Shak.): certain, convinced (Shak.): of the simpler kind of consonance (mus.): triple (old music; applied to time). — n. the perfect tense: a verb in the perfect tense. — v.t. **perfect** (pər-fekt', or pûr') to make perfect: to finish: to teach fully, to make fully skilled in anything: to print the second side of. — ns. **perfectā'tion** (rare); **perfect'er** (or pûr'). — n.pl. **perfect'i** (-ī) a body of Catharists in the 12th and 13th centuries, of very strict lives. — ns. **perfectibil'ian** a believer in the perfectibility of mankind; **perfect'ibilism** the belief that man is capable of becoming perfect or of progressing indefinitely towards perfection; **perfect'ibilist; perfectibil'ity** capability of becoming perfect: perfectibilism. — adj. **perfect'ible** capable of becoming perfect. — ns. **perfec'tion** state of being perfect: a quality in perfect degree: the highest state or degree: an embodiment of the perfect: loosely, a degree of excellence approaching the perfect. — v.t. **perfec'tionate** to bring to perfection. — ns. **perfec'tionism; perfec'tionist** one who claims to be perfect: one who aims at or calls for nothing short of perfection: one who holds some doctrine concerning perfection: one who thinks that moral perfection can be attained in this life: (with cap.) one of the Bible Communists or Free-lovers, a small American sect founded by J. H. Noyes (1811–86), which settled at Oneida in 1848, holding that the gospel if accepted secures freedom from sin. — adjs. **perfectionist'ic** seeking to attain perfection: being a perfectionist; **perfect'ive** tending to make perfect: of a verb aspect, denoting completed action (gram.). — advs. **perfect'ively; per'fectly.** — ns. **per'fectness** the state or quality of being perfect: completeness; **perfect'o** (Sp., perfect; pl. **perfect'os**) a large tapering cigar; **perfect'or** one who perfects: a machine for printing both sides at once. — **perfect binding** an unsewn bookbinding in which the backs of the gathered sections are sheared off and the leaves held in place by glue; **perfect cadence** one passing from the chord of the dominant to that of the tonic; **perfect competition** (econ.) free competition for the sale of a commodity; **perfect fifth** the interval between two sounds whose vibration frequencies are as 2 to 3; **perfect fluid** an ideal fluid, incompressible, of uniform density, offering no resistance to distorting forces; **perfect fourth** the interval between sounds whose vibration frequencies are as 3 to 4; **perfect gas** same as **ideal gas; perfect insect** the imago or completely developed form of an insect; **perfect interval** the fourth, fifth, or octave; **perfect metals** noble metals; **perfect number** a number equal to the sum of its aliquot parts, as $6 = 1 + 2 + 3$, $28 = 1 + 2 + 4 + 7 + 14$; **perfect pitch** (mus.) a term often used for absolute pitch; **perfect tense** a tense signifying action completed in the past (e.g. I have said) or at the time spoken of (**past perfect, pluperfect** e.g. I had said; **future perfect** e.g. I shall have left by then); **perfect year** see year. — **to perfection** perfectly. [M.E. parfit — O.Fr. parfit; assimilated to L. perfectus, pa.p. of perficĕre — pfx. per-, thoroughly, facĕre, to do.]

perfecta pər-fek'tə, (orig. U.S.) n. a form of bet in which the punter has to select, and place in the correct order, the two horses, dogs, etc. which will come first and second in a race. [Amer. Sp. (quiniela) perfecta, perfect (quiniela); cf. **quinella** and **trifecta.**]

perfervid pər-fûr'vid, (poet.) adj. very fervid: ardent: eager. — ns. **perfervidity** (pûr-fər-vid'i-ti); **perfer'vidness; perfer'vour, -or.** [L. perfervidus — prae, before, fervidus, fervid.]

perfet *pûr'fet, adj.* an older form (used by Milton) of **perfect.**

perficient *pər-fish'ənt, adj.* effectual: actually achieving a result. [L. *perficiēns, -entis,* pr.p. of *perficere,* to complete — pfx. *per-,* thoroughly, *facere,* to do, make.]

perfidious *pər-fid'i-əs, adj.* faithless: unfaithful: basely violating faith. — *adv.* **perfid'iously.** — *ns.* **perfid'iousness, perfidy** (*pûr'fid-i*). [L. *perfidiōsus — perfidia,* faithlessness — pfx. *per-,* implying destruction, *fidēs,* faith.]

perfoliate *pər-fō'li-āt, adj.* (of a leaf) having the base joined around the stem, so as to appear pierced by the stem — orig. said of the stem passing through the leaf, or of the plant. — *n.* **perfolia'tion.** [per- (2), L. *folium,* a leaf.]

perforate *pûr'fə-rāt, v.t.* to bore through or into: to pierce or to make a hole through: to penetrate: to pass through by a hole. — *adj.* pierced by a hole or holes: having an aperture: dotted with pellucid dots (*bot.*): pierced by rows of small holes for easy separation (as postage-stamps) (more usually **per'forated**). — *adj.* **per'forable.** — *n.* **per'forans** the long flexor muscle of the toes, or the deep flexor muscle of the fingers, whose tendons pass through those of the perforatus. — *adj.* **per'forant** perforating. — *n.* **perforation** (*pûr-fə-rā'shən*) the act of making a hole: the formation of a hole or aperture: the condition of being perforated: a hole through or into anything: a series, or one of a series, of small holes, as for ease in tearing paper. — *adj.* **per'forative** having the power to pierce. — *ns.* **per'forator** one who bores: a boring instrument or organ; **perforatus** (*pûr-fə-rā'təs*) the short flexor of the toes or the superficial flexor of the fingers. [L. *perforāre, -ātum — per,* through, *forāre,* to bore.]

perforce *pər-fōrs', -fōrs', adv.* by force: of necessity. [O.Fr. *par force.*]

perform *pər-förm', v.t.* not do: to carry out duly: to act in fulfilment of: to carry into effect: to fulfil: to bring about: to render: to execute: to go through duly: to act: to play in due form. — *v.i.* to do what is to be done: to execute a function: to act, behave: to act a part: to play or sing: to do feats, tricks, or other acts for exhibition: to lose one's temper (*Austr. coll.*). — *adj.* **perform'able** capable of being performed: practicable. — *n.* **perform'ance** the act of performing: a carrying out of something: something done: a piece of work: manner or success in working: execution, esp. as an exhibition or entertainment: an act or action: the power or capability of a machine (esp. a motor vehicle) to perform: an instance of awkward, aggressive, embarrassing, etc., behaviour (*coll.*). — *adj.* **perform'ative** of a statement or verb, that itself constitutes the action described, e.g. *I confess my ignorance.* — *n.* such a statement (opp. of **constative**). — *n.* **perform'er** one who performs: one who does or fulfils what is required of him: an executant: one who takes part in a performance or performances: one who does feats or tricks, esp. in exhibition. — *adj.* **perfor'ming** that performs: trained to perform tricks. — *n.* **performance.** — **performance art** a theatrical presentation in which several art forms, such as acting, music, photography, etc., are combined; **performance test** (*psych.*) a test, usu. to assess a person's intelligence, done by observing his ability to manipulate e.g. blocks of different colours or shapes; **performing arts** those in which an audience is present, as drama, ballet, etc.; **performing right** the right to give a public performance of a piece of music or play. [A.Fr. *parfourmer,* app. an altered form of *parfourner* — O.Fr. *parfournir, par* — L. *per,* through, *fournir,* to furnish.]

perfume *pûr'fūm,* formerly and still sometimes *pər-fūm', n.* sweet-smelling smoke or fumes from burning: any substance made or used for the sake of its pleasant smell: fragrance. — *v.t.* **perfume** (*pər-fūm',* sometimes *pûr'fūm*) to scent. — *adjs.* **per'fumed** (or *pər-fūmd'*); **per'fumeless** (or *-fūm'*). — *ns.* **perfu'mer** one who fumigates: a maker or seller of perfumes; **perfu'mery**

perfumes in general: the art of preparing perfumes: the shop or place in a shop where perfumes are sold. — *adj.* **per'fumy.** [Fr. *parfum* — L. *per,* through, *fūmus,* smoke.]

perfunctory *pər-fungk'tə-ri, adj.* done merely as a duty to be got through: done for form's sake, or in mere routine: acting without zeal or interest: merely formal: hasty and superficial. — *adv.* **perfunc'torily.** — *n.* **perfunc'toriness.** [L. *perfunctōrius — perfunctus,* pa.p. of *perfungī,* to execute — pfx. *per-,* thoroughly, *fungī,* to do.]

perfuse *pər-fūz', v.t.* to pour or diffuse through or over: to force, as a liquid, through an organ or tissue. — *ns.* **perfusate** (*-fūz'āt*) that which is perfused; **perfusion** (*-fū'zhən*) the pouring on or diffusion through. — *adj.* **perfusive** (*-fū'siv*). [L. *perfūsus,* poured over — *per,* through, *fundere, fūsus,* to pour.]

pergameneous *pûr-gə-mē'ni-əs, adj.* parchment-like. — *adj.* **pergamentaceous** (*-mən-tā'shəs*) parchment-like. [L. *pergamēna;* see **parchment.**]

pergola *pûr'gə-lə, n.* a structure with climbing plants along a walk. [It., — L. *pergula,* a shed.]

pergunnah. See **pargana.**

perhaps *pər-haps', adv.* it may be: possibly: as it may happen. [From the pl. of **hap**[1], after the model of **peradventure, percase, perchance.**]

peri *pē'ri, n.* in Persian mythology, a beautiful but malevolent being with supernatural powers: a beautiful fairy. [Pers. *parī* or *perī,* a fairy.]

peri- *per'i-, pə-ri'-,* in composition, (1) around; (2) esp. in astron., near. [Gr. *peri,* around.]

periagua *per-i-ä'gwə.* See **piragua.**

periaktos *per-i-ak'tos, n.* in the ancient Greek theatre, a tall revolving prism at the side of the stage, giving change of scene. [Gr., revolving.]

perianth *per'i-anth,* (*bot.*) *n.* calyx and corolla together, esp. when not clearly distinguishable. — Also *adj.* [**peri-** (1), Gr. *anthos,* flower.]

periapt *per'i-apt,* (*Shak.*) *n.* an amulet. [Gr. *periapton,* something hung round — *peri, haptein,* to fasten.]

periastron *per-i-as'tron,* (*astron.*) *n.* that stage in the orbit of a comet, one component of a binary star, etc. when it is closest to the star around which it revolves. [**peri-** (2), Gr. *astron,* star.]

periblast *per'i-blast, n.* the outer layer of protoplasm surrounding the nucleus of a cell or ovum: cytoplasm. [**peri-** (1), Gr. *blastos,* a sprout.]

periblem *per'i-blem,* (*bot.*) *n.* the layer of primary meristem from which the cortex is formed, covering the plerome. [Gr. *periblēma,* garment, mantle — *peri, ballein,* to throw.]

peribolos *per-ib'o-los, n.* a precinct: its enclosing wall: — *pl.* **perib'oloi.** — Also (Latinised) **perib'olus:** *pl.* **perib'oli.** [Gr., — *peri, ballein,* to throw.]

pericardium *per-i-kär'di-əm,* (*anat.*) *n.* the sac round the heart. — *adjs.* **pericar'diac, pericar'dial, pericar'dian.** — *n.* **pericardī'tis** inflammation of the pericardium. [Latinised from Gr. *perikardion — peri, kardiā,* heart.]

pericarp *per'i-kärp,* (*bot.*) *n.* the wall of a fruit, derived from that of the ovary. — *adj.* **pericar'pial.** [Gr. *perikarpion — peri, karpos,* fruit.]

pericentral *per-i-sen'trəl, adj.* surrounding a centre or central body. — *adj.* **pericen'tric.** [**peri-** (1), Gr. *kentron,* point, centre.]

perichaetium *per-i-kē'shyəm, n.* a sheath or cluster of leaves around the archegonia (or the antheridia) in mosses and liverworts. — *adj.* **perichae'tial** (*-shl*). [**peri-** (1), Gr. *chaitē,* flowing hair.]

perichondrium *per-i-kon'dri-əm, n.* the fibrous investment of cartilage. — *adj.* **perichon'drial.** [**peri-** (1), Gr. *chondros,* cartilage.]

perichoresis *per-i-kor-ē'sis,* (*theol.*) *n.* circumincession. [Gr., rotation — *perichorein,* to rotate — *peri, chorein,* to make room.]

perichylous *per-i-kī'ləs,* (*bot.*) *adj.* having water-storing tissue outside the green tissue. [**peri-** (1), Gr. *chylos,* juice.]

periclase *per'i-klāz, -klās, n.* native magnesia. [Gr. pfx. *peri-*, very, *klasis*, fracture (from its perfect cleavage).]

Periclean *per-i-klē'ən, adj.* of Pericles (*d.* 429 B.C.) or the golden age of art and letters at Athens.

periclinal *per-i-klī'nəl, adj.* quaquaversal (*geol.*): parallel to the outer surface (*bot.*). — *n.* **per'icline** a variety of albite feldspar of oblique appearance. [Gr. *periklīnēs*, sloping on all sides — *peri, klīnein*, to slope.]

periclitate *pər-ik'li-tāt, (arch.) v.t.* to endanger. [L. *perīclitārī, -ātus.*]

pericon *per-i-kōn', n.* an Argentinian folk-dance performed by couples dancing in a ring: — *pl.* **pericones** (-kō'nāz). [Amer. Sp.]

pericope *pər-ik'o-pē, n.* an extract, passage, esp. one selected for reading in church. [Gr. *perikopē* — *peri, koptein,* to cut.]

pericranium *per-i-krā'ni-əm, n.* the membrane that surrounds the cranium: (*loosely*) skull or brain. — *adj.* **pericrā'nial.** — *n.* **per'icrāny** (*obs.*) pericranium. [Latinised from Gr. *perikrānion* — *peri, krānion,* skull.]

periculous *pər-ik'ū-ləs, (obs.) adj.* dangerous. [L. *perīculum,* danger.]

pericycle *per'i-sī-kl, (bot.) n.* the outermost layer or layers of the central cylinder. — *adj.* **pericy'clic.** [Gr. *perikyklos,* all round — *peri, kyklos,* a circle.]

pericynthion *per-i-sin'thi-ən, n.* Same as **perilune.** [**peri-** (2), *Cynthia,* a name of the goddess of the moon.]

periderm *per'i-dûrm, n.* the horny cuticular covering of a hydroid colony: the cork-cambium with the cork and other tissues derived from it, forming a protective outer covering in plants. — *adj.* **periderm'al.** [**peri-** (1), Gr. *derma,* skin.]

peridesmium *per-i-des'mi-əm, (anat.) n.* the areolar tissue round a ligament. [**peri-** (1), Gr. *desmos,* a band.]

peridial. See **peridium.**

peridinian *per-i-din'i-ən, n.* a dinoflagellate. — *n.* **Peridin'ium** a genus of dinoflagellates: (without *cap.*) a member of the genus: — *pl.* **peridin'iums, -ia.** [Gr. *peridinein,* to whirl around.]

peridium *pər-id'i-əm, n.* the outer coat of a fungus fruit-body. — *adj.* **perid'ial.** [Latinised from Gr. *pēridion,* dim. of *pērā,* a wallet.]

peridot *per'i-dot,* **peridote** *-dōt, ns.* olivine: a green olivine used in jewellery. — *adj.* **peridŏt'ic.** — *n.* **peridotite** (-dō'tīt) a coarse-grained igneous rock mainly composed of olivine, usually with other ferro-magnesian minerals but little or no feldspar. [Fr. *péridot;* origin unknown.]

peridrome *per'i-drōm, n.* the space between cell and surrounding pillars in an ancient temple. [Gr. *peridromos,* running round — *peri, dromos,* a run.]

periegesis *per-i-ē-jē'sis, n.* a description in manner of a tour: a progress or journey through. [Gr. *periēgēsis* — *peri, hēgeesthai,* to lead.]

perigastric *per-i-gas'trik, adj.* surrounding the alimentary canal. — *n.* **perigastrī'tis** inflammation of the outer surface of the stomach. [**peri-** (1), Gr. *gastēr,* belly.]

perigee *per'i-jē, (astron.) n.* the point of the moon's, or any artificial satellite's, orbit at which it is nearest the earth — opp. to *apogee.* — *adjs.* **perigē'al, perigē'an.** [Gr. *perigeion,* neut. of *perigeios,* round or near the earth — *peri, gē,* earth.]

perigenesis *per-i-jen'i-sis, n.* reproduction (according to Haeckel's theory) by transmission not only of chemical material but of vibrations of plastidules. [**peri-** (1), Gr. *genesis,* generation.]

periglacial *per-i-glā'si-əl, -glās'yəl, -glā'shəl, adj.* bordering a glacier: of, like or pertaining to a region bordering a glacier. [**peri-** (1), L. *glaciālis,* icy — *glaciēs,* ice.]

perigon *per'i-gən, n.* an angle of 360° — also called a **round angle.** [**peri-** (1), Gr. *gōniā,* angle.]

perigone *per'i-gōn, (bot.) n.* an undifferentiated perianth: a covering of the seed in sedges. — *adj.* **perigō'nial.** — *n.* **perigō'nium** a cluster of leaves round moss antheridia. [**peri-** (1), Gr. *gonē,* generative organ.]

Perigordian *per-i-gör'di-ən, adj.* pertaining to the Palaeolithic epoch to which the Lascaux Cave paintings and other examples of primitive art belong. [*Périgord,* region in S.W. France.]

perigynous *pər-ij'i-nəs, (bot.) adj.* having the receptacle developed as a disc or open cup, with sepals, petals, and stamens borne on its margin, the carpels not embedded in it: of sepals, petals, or stamens, inserted on the receptacle in such a way — distinguished from *epigynous* and *hypogynous.* — *n.* **perig'yny.** [**peri-** (1), Gr. *gynē,* woman (used for female).]

perihelion *per-i-hē'li-ən, n.* the point of the orbit of a planet or a comet at which it is nearest to the sun — opp. to *aphelion:* culmination (*fig.*). — Also *adj.* [**peri-** (2), Gr. *hēlios,* the sun.]

perihepatic *per-i-hi-pat'ik, adj.* surrounding the liver. — *n.* **perihepatitis** (-hep-ə-tī'tis) inflammation of the peritoneum covering the liver. [**peri-** (1), Gr. *hēpar, hēpatos,* liver.]

perikaryon *per-i-kar'i-on, n.* that part of a nerve cell which contains the nucleus: — *pl.* **-kar'ya.** [**peri-** (1), Gr. *karyon,* kernel.]

peril *per'il, n.* danger. — *v.t.* to expose to danger: — *pr.p.* **per'illing;** *pa.t.* and *pa.p.* **per'illed.** — *adj.* **per'ilous** dangerous. — *adv.* **per'ilously.** — *n.* **per'ilousness.** [Fr. *péril* — L. *perīculum.*]

perilune *per'i-lūn, -lōōn, n.* the point in a spacecraft's orbit round the moon where it is closest to it — also **pericynthion.** [**peri-** (2), Fr. *lune* — L. *luna,* moon.]

perilymph *per'i-limf, n.* the fluid surrounding the membranous labyrinth of the ear. [**peri-** (1), and **lymph.**]

perimeter *pər-im'i-tər, n.* the circuit or boundary of any plane figure, or the sum of all its sides (*geom.*): an instrument for measuring the field of vision (*med.*): the boundary of a camp or fortified position: the outer edge of any area. — *adj.* **perimetric** (*per-i-met'rik;* also **perimet'rical**). — *n.* **perim'etry.** [Gr. *perimetros* — *peri, metron,* measure.]

perimorph *per'i-mörf, n.* a mineral enclosing another. — *adjs.* **perimorph'ic, perimorph'ous.** [**peri-** (1), Gr. *morphē,* form.]

perimysium *per-i-miz'i-əm, n.* the connective tissue which surrounds and binds together muscle fibres. [**peri-** (1), *-mysium* — Gr. *mus,* muscle.]

perinaeum, perineum *per-i-nē'əm, n.* the lower part of the body between the genital organs and the anus. — *adj.* **perinae'al, perinē'al.** [Latinised from Gr. *perinaion.*]

perinatal *per-i-nā'tl, adj.* pertaining to the period between the seventh month of pregnancy and the first week of life. [**peri-** (1), and **natal².**]

perinephrium *per-i-nef'ri-əm, n.* the fatty tissue surrounding the kidney. — *adj.* **perineph'ric.** — *n.* **perinephrī'tis** inflammation of the perinephrium. [**peri-** (1), Gr. *nephros,* kidney.]

perineum. See **perinaeum.**

perineurium *per-i-nū'ri-əm, n.* the sheath of connective tissue about a bundle of nerve fibres. — *adj.* **perineu'ral.** — *n.* **perineurī'tis** inflammation of the perineurium. [**peri-** (1), Gr. *neuron,* nerve.]

period *pē'ri-əd, n.* the time in which anything runs its course: an interval of time at the end of which events recur in the same order: the time required for a complete oscillation — reciprocal of the frequency: the time of a complete revolution of a heavenly body about its primary: the difference between two successive values of a variable for which a function has the same value: the recurring part of a circulating decimal: a set of figures (usu. three) in a large number marked off e.g. by commas: a series of chemical elements represented in a horizontal row of the periodic table: a stretch of time: a long stretch, an age: one of the main divisions of geological time: a stage or phase in history, in a man's life and development, in a disease, or in any course of events: a time: a division of the school day, the time of one lesson: the end of a course: a recurring time: (the time of) menstrual discharge: an end (*rare*): a goal (*arch.*): a complete sentence, esp. one of elaborate construction: in music, a division analogous to a sentence: (in *pl.*) rounded rolling rhetoric: a mark (.) at the end of a sentence — a full stop (the word is inserted at the end of a sentence to emphasise the finality of the statement): a rhythmical division in Greek verse. — *adj.* (of e.g. architecture, furniture, a play) characteristic, representative, imitative of, belonging to, or dealing with, a past period. — *v.t.* (*Shak.*) to put an end to. — *adjs.* **periodic** (*pēr-i-od'ik*) relating to a period or periods: of revolution in an orbit: having a period: recurring regularly in the same order: (*loosely*) occurring from time to time: characterised by or constructed in periods: pertaining to periodicals (*rare*); **period'ical** periodic: published in numbers at more or less regular intervals: of, for, or in such publications. — *n.* a magazine or other publication that appears at stated intervals (not usually including newspapers). — *n.* **period'icalist** one who writes in a periodical. — *adv.* **period'ically** at regular intervals: in a periodic manner: in a periodical publication: (*loosely*) from time to time. — *ns.* **periodicity** (*-dis'*) the fact or character of being periodic: frequency; **periodisā'tion, -īzā'tion** division into periods. — **periodic function** (*math.*) one whose values recur in a cycle as the variable increases; **periodic law** that the properties of atoms are periodic functions of their atomic numbers; **periodic sentence** a sentence so constructed that it is not until the final clause that the requirements of sense and grammar are met; **periodic system** the classification of chemical elements according to this law; **periodic table** a table of chemical elements in order of atomic number arranged in horizontal series and vertical groups, showing how similar properties recur at regular intervals; **periodic wind** a wind which blows at or for a certain period — e.g. a trade-wind, a monsoon, a land-breeze, a sea-breeze; **period piece** an object belonging to a past age esp. with charm or value: a person ludicrously behind the times: a play, novel, etc., set in a past time. — **period of grace** a specific time allowed to both parties within a contract to fulfil any obligations arising from that contract; **the period** the current age, or age in question. [Fr. *période* — L. *periodus* — Gr. *periodos* — *peri, hodos,* a way.]

periodate *pər-ī'ō-dāt, n.* a salt or ester of periodic acid. — **periodic acid** (*per-ī-od'ik*) an acid (H₅IO₆) containing more oxygen than iodic acid. [**per-** (1), and **iodine.**]

periodontal *per-i-ō-dont'əl, adj.* (pertaining to tissues or regions) round about a tooth. — *ns.* **periodon'tia** (*-shi-ə*), **periodon'tics** (*n. sing.*), **periodontol'ogy** the branch of dentistry concerned with periodontal diseases; **periodon'tist; periodontī'tis** the inflammation of the tissues surrounding the teeth. [**peri-** (1), *odous, odontos,* tooth.]

perionychium *per-i-o-nik'i-əm, n.* the skin surrounding a fingernail or toenail. [**peri-** (1), Gr. *onux,* a nail.]

Periophthalmus *per-i-of-thal'məs, n.* a genus of fishes, allied to gobies, with protruding mobile eyes and pectoral fins used as legs. [Latinised from Gr. *peri, ophthalmos,* eye.]

periosteum *per-i-os'ti-əm, n.* a tough fibrous membrane covering the surface of bones. — Also **per'iost.** — *adjs.* **perios'teal; periostit'ic.** — *n.* **periostī'tis** inflammation of the periosteum. [Gr. *periosteon* (neut. adj.) — *peri, osteon,* a bone.]

periostracum *per-i-os'trə-kəm, n.* the horny outer layer of a mollusc's shell. [Latinised from Gr. *peri, ostrakon,* shell.]

periotic *per-i-ō'tik, -ot'ik, adj.* around the inner ear. — *n.* a periotic bone. [**peri-** (1), Gr. *ous, ōtos,* the ear.]

peripatetic *per-i-pə-tet'ik, adj.* walking about: Aristotelian: of e.g. a teacher, itinerant. — *n.* a pedestrian: an itinerant: an Aristotelian. — *adj.* **peripatet'ical.** — *n.* **peripatet'icism** (*-i-sizm*) the philosophy of Aristotle. [Gr. *peripatētikos* — *peripatos,* a walk — *peri, pateein,* to walk; Aristotle is said to have taught in the walks of the Lyceum at Athens.]

Peripatus *pər-ip'ə-təs, n.* a genus of arthropods of the Onychophora, showing affinities with worms: (without *cap.*) a member of the genus. [Gr. *peripatos,* a walking about; cf. **peripatetic.**]

peripet(e)ia *per-i-pe-tī'ə, n.* a sudden change of fortune, esp. in drama. — Also **perip'ety.** — *adj.* **peripet(e)i'an.** [Gr. *peripeteia* — *peri,* and *pet-* the root of *piptein,* to fall.]

periphery *pər-if'ə-ri, n.* bounding line or surface: the outside of anything: a surrounding region. — *adj.* **periph'eral** of or relating to a periphery: not of the most important: incidental: minor. — *n.* a peripheral unit. — *adjs.* **peripheric** (*per-i-fer'ik*), **-al** (*arch.*). — **peripheral units, devices** in a computer system, the input (e.g. card reader), output (e.g. magnetic tape), and storage devices, which are connected to or controlled by the central processing unit; **periphery camera** same as **all-round camera.** [Gr. *periphereia* — *peri, pherein,* to carry.]

periphonic *per-i-fon'ik, adj.* or or pertaining to a sound system with many speakers. [**peri-** (1), Gr. *phōnē,* voice.]

periphrasis *pər-if'rə-sis, n.* round-about expression: — *pl.* **periph'rases** (*-sēz*). — *n.* **perIphrase** (*per'i-frāz*) periphrasis: — *pl.* **periphrās'es.** — *v.t.* to say with circumlocution. — *v.i.* to use circumlocution. — *adjs.* **periphrastic** (*per-i-fras'tik*), **-al** using periphrasis: using at least two words instead of a single inflected form, esp. of a verb tense involving an auxiliary. — *adv.* **periphras'tically.** [Gr. *periphrasis* — *peri, phrasis,* speech.]

periphyton *pər-if'i-ton, per-i-fī'ton, n.* aquatic organisms which are attached to, or cling to, stems and leaves of rooted plants, rocks, etc. [**peri-** (1), Gr. *phutos — phutein,* to grow.]

periplast *per'i-pläst, (zool.) n.* intercellular substance: the ectoplasm of flagellates: cuticle covering the ectoplasm. [**peri-** (1), Gr. *plastos,* moulded.]

periplus *per'i-plus, n.* a circumnavigation: a narrative of a coasting voyage. [Gr. *periploos,* contr. *-plous — peri, ploos, plous,* a voyage.]

periproct *per'i-prokt, (zool.) n.* the region about the anus, esp. in a sea-urchin. [**peri-** (1), Gr. *prōktos,* anus.]

peripteral *pər-ip'tə-rəl, (archit.) adj.* having one row of columns all round. — *n.* **perip'tery** a peripteral building: the turbulent air immediately adjacent to a flying or falling object. [Gr. *peripteros — peri,* and *pteron,* a wing.]

perique *pə-rēk', n.* a strongly-flavoured tobacco from Louisiana. [Perh. *Périque,* nickname of a grower.]

perisarc *per'i-särk, (zool.) n.* in some Hydrozoans, the chitinous layer covering the polyps, etc. [**peri-** (1), Gr. *sarx, sarkos,* flesh.]

periselenium *per-i-si-lē'ni-əm, n.* in an elliptical orbit about the moon, that point which is closest to the moon. [**peri-** (2), Gr. *selēnē,* moon.]

periscian *pər-ish'i-ən, n.* a dweller within the polar circle, whose shadow moves round in a complete circle on those days on which the sun does not set. — Also *adj.* [**peri-** (1), Gr. *skiā,* a shadow.]

periscope *per'i-skōp, n.* a tube with mirrors by which an observer in a trench, a submarine, etc., can see what is going on above. — *adj.* **periscopic** (*-skop'ik*). [Gr. *periskopeein,* to look around.]

perish *per'ish, v.i.* to pass away completely: to waste away: to decay: to lose life: to be destroyed: to be ruined or lost. — *v.t.* to destroy: to ruin: to cause to decay: to distress with cold, hunger, etc. — *n.* **perishabil'ity.** — *adj.* **per'ishable** that may perish: subject to speedy decay. — *n.* that which is perishable: (in *pl.*) food or other stuff liable to rapid deterioration. — *n.* **per'-ishableness.** — *adv.* **per'ishably.** — *adj.* **per'ished** distressed by cold, hunger, etc. (*coll.* or *dial.*): of materials such as rubber, weakened or injured by age or exposure. — *n.* **per'isher** (*slang*) a reprehensible and annoying person. — *adj.* **per'ishing** (*coll.* or *dial.*) freezing cold: vaguely used as a pejorative. — Also *adv.* — *adv.* **per'ishingly.** — **do a perish** (*Austr. coll.*) almost to die of lack of food or drink. [O.Fr. *perir*, pr.p. *perissant* — L. *perīre*, *perītum*, to perish — pfx. *per-*, *īre*, to go.]

perisperm *per'i-spûrm*, (*bot.*) *n.* nutritive tissue in a seed derived from the nucellus. — *adjs.* **perispermal, perisper'mic.** [peri- (1), Gr. *sperma*, seed.]

perispomenon *per-i-spō'mən-on*, *adj.* having a circumflex accent on the last syllable. — *n.* a word so accented. [Gr., drawn round, circumflexed — *peri*, *spaein*, to pull, pluck.]

perissodactyl *pər-is-ō-dak'til*, *adj.* having an odd number of toes. — *n.* an animal of the **Perissodac'tyla**, a division of ungulates with an odd number of toes — horse, tapir, rhinoceros, and extinct kinds (distinguished from the *Artiodactyla*). — *adjs.* **perissodac'tylate, perissodactyl'ic, perissodac'tylous.** [Gr. *perissos*, odd, *daktylos*, a finger, toe.]

perissology *per-is-ol'ə-ji*, *n.* verbiage: pleonasm. [Gr. *perissologiā* — *perissos*, excessive, *logos*, speech.]

perissosyllabic *pər-is-ō-sil-ab'ik*, *adj.* having an additional syllable. [Gr. *perissosyllabos* — *perissos*, excessive, *syllabē*, syllable.]

peristalith *pər-is'tə-lith*, *n.* a stone circle. [Irregularly formed from Gr. *peri*, *histanai*, to set up, *lithos*, a stone.]

peristaltic *per-i-stalt'ik*, *adj.* forcing onward by waves of contraction, as the alimentary canal and other organs do their contents. — *n.* **peristal'sis.** — *adj.* **peristalt'ically.** [Gr. *peristaltikos* — *peristellein*, to wrap round — *peri*, *stellein*, to place.]

peristerite *per-is'tər-īt*, *n.* an albite feldspar with pigeon-like play of colour. [Gr. *peristerā*, pigeon.]

peristeronic *pər-is-tər-on'ik*, *adj.* of pigeons: pigeon-fancying. [Gr. *peristerōn*, *-ōnos*, pigeon-house.]

peristome *per'i-stōm*, *n.* the area, or a structure, surrounding a mouth: the fringe of teeth around the mouth of a moss-capsule: the margin of a gasteropod shell. — *adjs.* **peristom'al, peristomat'ic, peristōm'ial.** [peri- (1), Gr. *stoma*, *-atos*, mouth.]

peristrephic *per-i-stref'ik*, *adj.* moving round, revolving, rotatory. [Irregularly — Gr. *peristrephein*, to whirl — *peri*, *strephein*, to turn.]

peristyle *per'i-stīl*, *n.* a range of columns round a building or round a square: a court, square, etc., with columns all round. — *adj.* **peristy'lar.** [L. *peristÿl(i)um* — Gr. *peristÿlon* — *peri*, *stÿlos*, a column.]

peritectic *per-i-tek'tik*, *adj.* in the state between solid and liquid: melting. [**peri-** (1), Gr. *tektikos*, able to melt.]

perithecium *per-i-thē'si-əm*, *-shi-əm*, *n.* a flask-shaped fruit-body in fungi: — *pl.* **-ia.** — *adj.* **perithe'cial.** [peri- (1), Gr *thēkē*, case.]

peritoneum, peritonaeum *per-i-tən-ē'əm*, *n.* a serous membrane enclosing the viscera in the abdominal and pelvic cavities. — *adj.* **peritonē'al, peritonae'al.** — *n.* **peritonēos'copy** the visual examination of the peritoneal cavities by means of an endoscope inserted through an incision in the abdomen. — *adj.* **peritonitic** (*-it'ik*) of peritonitis: suffering from peritonitis. — *n.* **peritonī'tis** inflammation of the peritoneum. [Gr. *peritonaion* — *peri*, *teinein*, to stretch.]

peritrich *per-it'rik*, *n.* a bacterium bearing a ring of cilia around the body: — *pl.* **perit'richa** (*-kə*). — *adj.* **perit'richous** of or pertaining to peritricha: bearing a ring of cilia around the body. [**peri-** (2), Gr. *thrix*, *trichos*, hair.]

peritus *pe-rē'tōōs*, *n.* a theological expert acting as a consultant within the Roman Catholic Church: — *pl.* **periti** (*-tē*). [L.L. — L. skilled.]

perityphlitis *per-i-tif-lī'tis*, *n.* inflammation of some part near the blind-gut. [peri- (1), Gr. *typhlos*, blind.]

periwig *per'i-wig*, (*hist.*) *n.* a wig. — *v.t.* to dress with, or as with, a wig: — *pr.p.* **per'iwigging**; *pa.t.* and *pa.p.* **per'iwigged.** — *adj.* **per'iwig-pā'ted** wearing a periwig. [Earlier *perwyke*, *perwig*, *perywig*, etc. — Fr. *perruque*; see **peruke, wig¹**.]

periwinkle¹ *per'i-wingk-l*, *n.* a creeping evergreen plant, growing in woods (*Vinca minor* and *V. major*; fam. Apocynaceae): the light blue colour of some of its flowers. — *adj.* of this colour. [M.E. *peruenke* — O.E. *peruince*, from L. *pervinca*.]

periwinkle² *per'i-wingk-l*, *n.* an edible gasteropod (*Littorina littorea*) abundant between tide-marks, or other member of the genus: extended to other kinds. — Also **pennywinkle.** [O.E. (pl.) *pinewinclan* (or perh. *winewinclan*) — *wincle*, a whelk.]

perjink *pər-jingk'*, (*Scot.*) *adj.* prim: finical. — Also **perjink'ety.** — *n.* **perjink'ity** a nicety. [Origin unknown.]

perjure *pûr'jər*, *v.t.* to forswear oneself (*refl.*): to cause to swear falsely. — *v.i.* to swear falsely. — *n.* (*Shak.*) a perjured person. — *adj.* **per'jured** having sworn falsely: being sworn falsely, as an oath. — *n.* **per'jurer.** — *adjs.* **perjurious** (*-jōō'ri-əs*), **per'jurous** (*arch.*) guilty of or involving perjury. — *n.* **per'jury** false swearing: the breaking of an oath: the crime committed by one who, when giving evidence on oath or affirmation as a witness in a court of justice, gives evidence which he knows to be false (*law.*). [O.Fr. *parjurer* — L. *perjūrāre* — *per-*, *jūrāre*, to swear.]

perk¹ *pûrk*, (*arch.*) *v.i.* to bear oneself with self-confidence or self-assertion: to cock up: to stick out: to thrust forward (also *v.t.* with *it*): to move with pert briskness: to sit upright: to cock or toss or hold up the head: to prank oneself up. — *adj.* brisk: self-confident in manner. — *adv.* **perk'ily.** — *n.* **perk'iness.** — *adj.* **perk'y** self-assertive: cocky: pert: in good spirits. — **perk up** to recover spirits or energy, esp. in sickness: to jerk up, cock up: to decorate so as to look newer, more interesting, etc., to smarten up. [Origin uncertain.]

perk² *pûrk*, a northern and East Anglian form of **perch².**

perk³ *pûrk*, (*coll.*) *n.* Short for **perquisite.**

perk⁴ *pûrk*, *v.t.* and *n.* Short for **percolate, percolator** (of coffee).

perkin. See **parkin.**

perky. See **perk¹.**

perlite *pûrl'īt*, *n.* any acid volcanic glass with perlitic structure: pearlite. — *adj.* **perlitic** (*-it'ik*) showing little concentric spheroidal or spiral cracks between rectilineal ones. [Fr. *perle*, Ger. *Perle*, pearl.]

perlocution *pûr-lə-kū'shən*, (*philos.*) *n.* an act that is the effect of an utterance, as frightening, persuading, comforting, etc. (cf. **illocution**). — *adj.* **perlocū'tionary.** [**per-** (2) and **locution**.]

perlous *pûr'ləs*, (*Spens.*) *adj.* Same as **perilous.**

perlustrate *pər-lus'trāt*, (*arch.*) *v.t.* to traverse and inspect. — *n.* **perlustrā'tion.** [L. *perlustrāre*, *-ātum*.]

perm¹ *pûrm*, (*coll.*) *n.* short for of **permutation.** — *v.t.* permute: to arrange a forecast according to some defined system of combination or permutation.

perm² *pûrm*, (*coll.*) *n.* short for of **permanent wave.** — *v.t.* (*coll.*) to impart a permanent wave to.

permafrost *pûr'mə-frost*, *n.* permanently frozen subsoil. [*permanent*, *frost*.]

permalloy *pûrm'a-loi*, *n.* any of various alloys of iron and nickel, often containing other elements, e.g. copper, molybdenum, chromium, which has high magnetic permeability. [*permeable alloy*.]

permanent *pûr'mə-nənt*, *adj.* remaining, or intended to remain, indefinitely. — *ns.* **per'manence** the fact or state of being permanent; **per'manency** permanence: a thing that is permanent. — *adv.* **per'manently.** — **permanent magnet** see **magnet**; **permanent press** a process by which clothes can be made to retain pleats, trouser-creases, etc.; **permanent set** (*engineering*) the distortion or extension of a structure, etc., which remains after the elastic limit has been exceeded by stress, load, etc; **permanent teeth** the adult teeth, which come after the milk-teeth lost in childhood; **permanent wave** a long-lasting artificial wave in hair — familiarly contracted **perm**; **permanent way** the finished road of a railway. [L. *permanēns*, *-entis*, pr.p. of *permanēre* — *per*, through, *manēre*, to continue.]

permanganic *pûr-mang-gan'ik*, *adj.* applied to an acid ($HMnO_4$) and its anhydride (Mn_2O_7) containing more oxygen than manganic acid and anhydride. — *n.*

permanganate (*pər-mang'gə-nāt*) a salt of permanganic acid, esp. **potassium permanganate** (KMnO₄) which is used as an oxidising and bleaching agent and as a disinfectant.   [**per-** (1), and **manganese**.]

permeate *pûr'mi-āt, v.t.* to pass through the pores of: to penetrate and fill the pores of: to pervade: to saturate. — *v.i.* to diffuse. — *n.* **permeabil'ity.** — *adj.* **per'meable.** — *adv.* **per'meably.** — *ns.* **permeam'eter** an instrument for measuring permeability, esp. of magnetising force and flux; **per'meance** the act of permeating: the reciprocal of the reluctance of a magnetic circuit; **per'mease** any enzyme which acts to assist the entry of certain sugars into cells; **permea'tion.** — *adj.* **per'meative** having power to permeate. — **magnetic permeability** the ratio of flux density to magnetising force.   [L. *permeāre* — *per*, through, *meāre*, to pass.]

Permian *pûr'mi-ən, (geol.) n.* the uppermost Palaeozoic system. — *adj.* of that system. — *n. and adj.* **Permo-Carbonif'erous** Upper Carboniferous and Lower Permian.   [*Perm*, in Russia, where it is widely developed.]

permis de séjour *per-mē də sā-zhōōr,* (Fr.) permission to reside in a foreign country, given by the police of that country.

permissible, etc. See **permit**.

permit *pər-mit', v.t.* to allow: (*refl.*) to indulge (in) (*arch.*): to leave, refer, submit (to) (*obs.*). — *v.i.* to allow: — *pr.p.* **permitt'ing;** *pa.t. and pa.p.* **permitt'ed.** — *n.* (*pûr'*) permission, esp. in writing. — *n.* **permissibil'ity.** — *adj.* **permiss'ible** that may be permitted: allowable. — *adv.* **permiss'ibly.** — *n.* **permission** (*-mish'ən*) an act of permitting: leave. — *adj.* **permiss'ive** granting permission or liberty: permitted, optional: lenient, indulgent: allowing much freedom in social conduct (as in the **permissive society** — from c. 1960). — *adv.* **permiss'ively.** — *ns.* **permiss'iveness; permitt'ance** (*rare*) permission; **permitt'er; permittiv'ity** (*absolute permittivity*) the ratio of the electric displacement in a medium to the electric field intensity producing it: (*relative permittivity*) the ratio of the electric displacement in a medium to that which would be produced in free space by the same field.   [L. *permittĕre, -missum,* to let pass through — *per, mittĕre,* to send.]

Permo-. See **Permian**.

permute *pər-mūt', v.t.* to interchange: to transmute: to subject to permutation. — *n.* **permutabil'ity.** — *adj.* **permūt'able** interchangeable. — *v.t.* **per'mutate** to subject to permutation. — *n.* **permutā'tion** barter (*obs.*): transmutation: the arrangement of a set of things in every possible order (*math.*): any one possible order of arrangement of a given number of things taken from a given number: immediate inference by obversion (*logic*): esp. in football pools, a forecast of a specified number of results from a larger number of matches based on some defined system of combination or permutation (often shortened to **perm**): any such system.   [L. *permūtāre,* to change thoroughly — pfx. *per-, mūtāre,* to change.]

pern *pûrn, n.* a honey-buzzard (*Pernis*).   [Cuvier's mistake for Gr. *pternis,* a kind of hawk.]

pernancy *pûr'nən-si, (law) n.* receiving.   [A.Fr. *pernance* (O.Fr. *prenance*).]

Pernettya *pər-net'i-ə, n.* a genus (family *Ericaceae*) of evergreen shrubs with bright berries.   [A. J. *Pernetty,* explorer.]

pernicious¹ *pər-nish'əs, adj.* destructive: highly injurious: malevolent. — *adv.* **perni'ciously.** — *n.* **perni'ciousness.** — **pernicious anaemia** see **anaemia**.   [L. *perniciōsus* — pfx. *per-, nex, necis,* death by violence.]

pernicious² *pər-nish'əs,* (Milt.) *adj.* swift, ready, prompt.   [L. *pernīx, -īcis,* nimble.]

pernickety *pər-nik'i-ti, adj.* finical: exacting minute care. — *n.* **pernick'etiness.**   [Scots; origin unknown.]

pernoctation *pûr-nok-tā'shən, n.* passing the night: a watch, vigil.   [**per-** (2), L. *nox, noctis,* night.]

Pernod® *per'nō, n.* an alcoholic drink made in France, flavoured with aniseed.

perone *per'o-nē, n.* the fibula. — *adj.* **peronē'al.** — *n.* **peronē'us** one of several fibular muscles.   [Gr. *peronē.*]

Peronism *pe'ron-izm, pə-rō'nizm, n.* the political beliefs of Juan *Peron* (1895–1974), former president of Argentina. — *ns.* **Peronis'mo** (Sp.) Peronism; **Peronist; Peronist'a** (Sp.).

peroration *per-ə-rā'shən, -ō-, -ö-, n.* the conclusion of a speech: a rhetorical performance. — *v.i.* **per'orate** to make a peroration: to harangue (*coll.*).   [L. *perōrātiō, -ōnis* — *per,* through, *ōrāre,* to speak — *ōs, ōris,* the mouth.]

peroxide *pər-oks'īd, n.* an oxide with the highest proportion of oxygen: one that yields hydrogen peroxide on treatment with an acid: colloquially, the bleach hydrogen peroxide, H₂O₂. — *v.t.* to treat or bleach with hydrogen peroxide. — *ns.* **perox'īdase** an enzyme, found in many plants, bacteria and leucocytes, which acts as a catalyst in the oxidation of various substances by peroxides; **peroxīdā'tion.** — *v.t. and v.i.* **perox'idise, -ize.**   [**per-** (1), and **oxide**.]

perpend¹ *pər-pend', v.t.* to weigh in the mind, to consider carefully.   [L. *perpendĕre* — pfx. *per-, pendĕre,* to weigh.]

perpend² *pûr'pənd,* **perpent** *-pənt.* Same as **parpen**.

perpendicular *pûr-pən-dik'ū-lər, adj.* erect: vertical: upright: in the direction of gravity or at right angles to the plane of the horizon: at right angles (to a given line or surface; *geom.*): in the Perpendicular style of architecture. — *n.* an instrument for determining the vertical line: a straight line or plane perpendicular to another line or surface: verticality or erectness: in a ship, a vertical line from each end of the water-line: a meal or entertainment at which the guests do not sit (*slang*). — *n.* **perpendicularity** (*-lar'i-ti*) the state of being perpendicular. — *adv.* **perpendic'ularly.** — **Perpendicular style** a late English style of Gothic architecture (late 14th- to mid-16th cent.) marked by vertical window-tracery, depressed or four-centre arch, fan-tracery vaulting, and panelled walls.   [L. *perpendiculāris* — *perpendiculum,* a plumb-line — pfx. *per-, pendĕre,* to hang.]

perpent. See **perpend²**.

perpetrate *pûr'pi-trāt, v.t.* to execute or commit (esp. an offence, a poem, or a pun). — *adj.* **per'petrable.** — *ns.* **perpetrā'tion, per'petrātor.**   [L. *perpetrāre, -ātum* — pfx. *per-, patrāre,* to achieve.]

perpetual *pər-pet'ū-əl, adj.* never ceasing: everlasting: not temporary: incessant: uninterrupting: continuously blooming: perennial. — *adv.* **perpetually.** — *n.* a perennial: a continuously blooming hybrid rose. — *ns.* **perpet'ualism; perpet'ualist** one who advocates the perpetual continuation of anything; **perpetuality** (*-al'i-ti*). — *adv.* **perpet'ually.** — **perpetual calendar** a calendar by means of which it may be ascertained on which day of the week any given day has fallen or will fall; **perpetual check** in chess, a situation in which one player's king is continually placed in check by the other player who may thereby claim a draw; **perpetual curate** formerly, in the Church of England, an incumbent of a parish who had no endowment of tithes — since 1868 called vicar; **perpetual motion** a machine, or motion of a machine, that should do work indefinitely without receiving new energy from without; **perpetual-mo'tionist** a believer in the possibility of perpetual motion; **perpetual screw** an endless screw.   [L. *perpetuālis* — *perpetuus,* continuous.]

perpetuate *pər-pet'ū-āt, v.t.* to cause to last for ever or for a very long time: to preserve from extinction or oblivion: to pass on, cause to continue to be believed, known, etc. — *adj.* (*arch.*) perpetuated. — *adj.* **perpet'uable.** — *ns.* **perpet'ūance** perpetuation; **perpetuā'tion** continuation or preservation for ever, or for a very long time: preservation from extinction or oblivion; **perpet'ūātor.**   [L. *perpetuāre, -ātum* — *perpetuus,* perpetual.]

perpetuity *pûr-pi-tū'i-ti, n.* the state of being perpetual:

endless time: duration for an indefinite period: something lasting for ever: the sum paid for a perpetual annuity: the annuity itself: an arrangement whereby property is tied up, or rendered inalienable, for all time or for a very long time.   [L. *perpetuitās, -ātis* — *perpetuus,* perpetual.]

perpetuum mobile *pər-pet'ū-əm mō'bil-i, per-pet'ōō-ōom mō-bil-e,* (L.) perpetual motion (lit. movable).

perplex *pər-pleks', v.t.* to embarrass or puzzle with difficulties or intricacies: to bewilder: to tease with suspense or doubt: to complicate: to interweave: to tangle. — *n. (obs.)* a difficulty. — *adv.* **perplex'edly.** — *n.* **perplex'edness.** — *adj.* **perplex'ing.** — *adv.* **perplex'ingly.** — *n.* **perplex'ity** the state of being perplexed: confusion of mind arising from doubt, etc.: embarrassment: doubt: intricacy: tangle.   [L. *perplexus,* entangled — pfx. *per-, plexus,* involved, pa.p. of *plectĕre.*]

perquisite *pûr'kwi-zit, n.* property acquired otherwise than by inheritance (*law; obs.*): a casual profit: anything left over that a servant or other has by custom a right to keep: a tip expected upon some occasions: emoluments: something regarded as falling to one by right: —often shortened (*coll.*) to **perk.** — *ns.* **perquisition** (*-zish'ən*) a strict search: diligent inquiry; **perquis'itor** the first purchaser of an estate.   [L. *perquīsītum,* from *perquīrĕre,* to seek diligently — pfx. *per-, quaerĕre,* to ask.]

perradius *pər-rā'di-əs, n.* any one of the primary radii of a coelenterate: — *pl.* **perradii** (*-ī*). — *adj.* **perra'dial.** [**per-** (2), and **radius.**]

perrier *per'i-ər, (obs.) n.* a machine or gun for discharging stones.   [O.Fr.]

perron *per'ən, peron-ō', n.* a raised platform or terrace at an entrance door: an external flight of steps leading up to it.   [Fr., — L. *petra,* stone.]

perruque, perruquier. See **peruke.**

perry *per'i, n.* a drink made from fermented pear juice. [O.Fr. *peré* — L.L. *pēra* (L. *pirum*), pear.]

persant, persaunt (*Spens.*). Same as **perceant.**

perscrutation *pûr-skrōō-tā'shən, n.* a thorough search. [**per-** (2), L. *scrūtārī,* to search carefully.]

perse¹ *pûrs, adj.* dark blue, bluish-grey. — *n.* a dark-blue colour: a cloth of such colour.   [O.Fr. *pers.*]

perse² *pûrs,* a Spenserian form of **pierce:** — *pa.p.* and *pa.t.* **perst.**

persecute *pûr'si-kūt, v.t.* to harass, afflict, hunt down, or put to death, esp. for religious or political opinions. — *n.* **persecu'tion.** — *adj.* **per'secutive.** — *n.* **per'secutor.** — *adj.* **per'secutory.** — **persecution complex** (*psych.*) a morbid fear that one is being plotted against by other people.   [L. *persequī, persecūtus* — pfx. *per-, sequī,* to follow.]

Perseid. See **Perseus.**

perseity *pər-sē'i-ti, n.* an independent existence.   [L. *per sē,* in itself.]

perseline *pûr'si-lēn, n.* a Spenserian form of **purslane.**

Perseus *pûr'sūs, -si-əs, n.* a fabled Greek hero who slew the Gorgon Medusa, and rescued Andromeda from a sea-monster: a constellation in the northern sky. — *n.* **Per'seid** (*-si-id*) a meteor of a swarm whose radiant is in the constellation Perseus.   [Gr. *Perseus.*]

persevere *pûr-si-vēr',* formerly (*Shak.*) *pər-sev'ər, v.i.* to continue (*obs.*): to continue steadfastly: to keep on striving. — *n.* **perseve'rance** (formerly *pər-sev'ər-əns*) the act or state of persevering: continued application to anything which one has begun: a going on till success is met with. — *adj.* **persev'erant** steadfast. — *v.i.* **persev'erate** to recur or tend to recur (*psych.*): to repeat the same actions or thoughts. — *ns.* **perseveration** (*pûr-sev-ər-ā'shən*) meaningless repetition of an action, utterance, thought, etc.: the tendency to experience difficulty in leaving one activity for another; **persev'erator.** — *adj.* **perseve'ring.** — *adv.* **perseve'ringly.** — **perseverance of saints** the Calvinistic doctrine that those who are effectually called by God cannot fall away so as to be finally lost.   [Fr. *persévérer* — L.

perseverāre — *persevērus,* very strict — pfx. *per-, sevērus,* strict.]

Persian *pûr'shən, -shyən, -zhən, -zhyən, adj.* of, from, or relating to *Persia* (now Iran), its inhabitants, or language. — *n.* a native or citizen of Persia: the language of Persia: a male figure serving as a column (*archit.*): a Persian cat. — *v.t.* and *v.i.* **Per'sianise, -ize.** — *adj.* **Persic** (*pûr'sik*) Persian. — *n.* the Persian language. — *v.t.* and *v.i.* **Per'sicise, -ize** (*-sīz*) to turn Persian: to assimilate to what is Persian. — *ns.* **Per'sism** a Persian idiom; **Per'sist** one who has a scholarly knowledge of Persian and things Persian. — **Persian berry** the fruit of several buckthorns; **Persian blinds** persiennes; **Persian carpet** a rich, soft carpet of the kind woven in Persia; **Persian cat** a kind of cat with long, silky hair and bushy tail; **Persian lamb** a lamb of the Karakul or Bukhara breed: its black, curly fur used to make coats, hats, etc.; **Persian powder** an insect-powder made from Pyrethrum; **Persian wheel** a large undershot wheel for raising water.

persicaria *pûr-si-kā'ri-ə, n.* a species of knotgrass with black-blotched leaves: extended to other species of Polygonum, by some made a separate genus.   [L.L. *persicāria,* peach-tree, from the similarity in leaves.]

persico, persicot *pûr'si-kō, n.* a cordial flavoured with kernels of peaches and apricots.   [Fr. *persico* (now *persicot*) — It. *persico* — L. *persicum,* a peach.]

persienne *per-si-en', n.* an Eastern cambric or muslin with coloured printed pattern: (in *pl.*) Persian blinds, outside shutters of thin movable slats in a frame.   [Fr., Persian (fem.).]

persiflage *pûr-si-fläzh', pûr', n.* banter: flippancy. — *n.* **persifleur** (*-flûr'*) a banterer.   [Fr., — *persifler,* to banter — L. *per,* through, Fr. *siffler* — L. *sībilāre,* to whistle, to hiss.]

persimmon *pər-sim'ən, n.* a date-plum or date-plum tree. [From an Amer.-Indian word.]

Persism, Persist. See **Persian.**

persist *pər-sist', v.i.* to continue steadfastly or obstinately, esp. against opposition (often with *in*): to persevere: to insist: to continue to be, to remain (*Milt.*): to continue to exist: to remain in the mind after the external cause is removed. — *v.t.* to assert or repeat insistently. — *ns.* **persis'tence, persis'tency** the quality of being persistent: perseverance: obstinacy: duration, esp. of an effect after the exciting cause has been removed. — *adj.* **persis'tent** persisting: pushing on, esp. against opposition: tenacious: fixed: constant or constantly repeated: remaining after the usual time of falling off, withering, or disappearing (*zool., bot.*): continuing to grow beyond the usual time. — Also *n.* — *advs.* **persis'tently; persis'tingly.** — *adj.* **persis'tive** (*Shak.*) persistent. — **persistent cruelty** (*law*) in matrimonial proceedings, behaviour likely to cause danger to the life or health of a spouse.   [L. *persistĕre* — *per, sistĕre,* to cause to stand, to stand — *stāre,* to stand.]

person *pûr'sn, n.* a character represented, as on the stage: a capacity in which one is acting: a living soul or self-conscious being: a personality: a human being, sometimes used slightingly or patronisingly: an individual of a compound or colonial animal: the outward appearance, etc.: bodily form: human figure (often including clothes): bodily presence or action: a personage (*obs.*): a hypostasis of the Godhead (*theol.*): a human being (*natural person*), or a corporation (*artificial person*) regarded as having rights and duties under the law: a form of inflexion or use of a word according as it, or its subject, represents the person, persons, thing, or things speaking (*first person*), spoken to (*second person*), or spoken about (*third person*) (*gram.*): — *pl.* in the sense of an individual human being, usu. **people** (*pē'pl*): in formal, technical, etc. use, **per'sons.** — **-person** (*-pûr-sn*) in composition, used instead of **-man** to avoid illegal or unnecessary discrimination on grounds of sex, e.g. *barperson, chairperson, postperson.* — *n.* **persona** (*pər-sōn'ə*) Jung's term for a person's system of adaptation to, or manner assumed when dealing with, the world — the outermost part of the consciousness, the expression of the personality, masking one's inner thoughts, feelings, etc.: a Roman actor's mask: a character in fiction, esp. in drama: a speaker in a poem: social façade or public image: — *pls.* **-ae** (-*ē, -ī*), **-s**. — *adj.* **per'sonable** having a well-formed body or person: of good appearance. — *ns.* **per'sonableness; per'sonage** bodily frame or appearance: a person: an exalted or august person: a character in a play or story: recognised or imagined character or personality (*Spens.*, etc.). — *adj.* **per'sonal** of the nature of a person: of or relating to a person or personality: relating, referring, or pointing to a particular person or persons: aiming offensively at a particular person or persons: belonging or peculiar to a person: own: one's own: of private concern: relating to private concerns: bodily: in bodily presence: (of telephone call) made to a particular person (timed only from the moment the named person is contacted, but subject to an initial fixed charge): by one's own action: indicating person (*gram.*): tailored to the needs of a particular person: done in person: opposed to *real, orig.* not recoverable by a *real action* (for the restitution of the specific thing), but such as compensation might be claimed for (*English law*): hence (now) passing at death not to the heir (as real property) but to the executor. — *n.pl.* **personalia** (-*ā'li-ə*) notes, anecdotes, or particulars relating to persons. — *n.* **personalisā'-tion, -z-**. — *v.t.* **per'sonalise, -ize** to personify: to apply to, or take as referring to, a definite person: to mark with a person's name, initials, monogram, etc.: to tailor to, or cater for, the desires of a particular person: to give a mark or character to (something) so that it is identifiable as belonging to a certain person (*coll.*). — *ns.* **per'sonalism** the character of being personal: a theory or doctrine that attributes personality, or spiritual freedom and responsibility, as distinct from mere individuality, to human beings, esp. that enunciated by Emmanuel Mounier in 1936; **per'sonalist** one who writes personal notes: a believer in, or follower of, personalism; **personal'ity** the fact or state of being a person or of being personal: existence as a person: individuality: distinctive or well-marked character: a person: direct reference to, or an utterance aimed at, a particular person or persons, esp. of a derogatory nature: personalty (*law, rare*): the integrated organisation of all the psychological, intellectual, emotional, and physical characteristics of an individual, especially as they are presented to other people (*psych.*). — *adv.* **per'sonally** in a personal or direct manner: in person: individually: for my part (*coll.*). — *n.* **per'sonalty** (*law*) all the property which, when a man dies, goes to his executor or administrator, as distinguished from the realty, which goes to his heir-at-law. — *v.t.* **per'sonate** to assume the likeness or character of: to play the part of: to mimic: to pass oneself off as: to represent in the form of a person: to symbolise. — *adj.* feigned (*arch.*): mask-like: of a lipped corolla, closed by an upward bulge of the lower lip (*bot.*). — *adj.* **per'sonāted** feigned. — *ns.* **per'sonāting; personā'tion**. — *adj.* **per'sonātive** dramatic: presenting or presented through persons. — *n.* **per'sonātor**. — *v.t.* **per'sonise, -ize** to personify. — *n.* **personnel'** the persons employed in any service: (*loosely*) people in general: an office or department that deals with employees' appointments, records, welfare, etc. — **personal chair** a university chair created for the period of tenure of a particular person; **personal column** a newpaper column containing personal messages, advertisements, etc.; **personal computer** a single-user microcomputer; **personal effects** those belongings worn or carried about one's person: private or intimate possessions; **personal equation** see under **equal; personal estate, property** the things legally belonging to one, excluding land; **personal exception** (*Scots law*) a ground of objection which applies to an individual and prevents him from doing something which, but for his

conduct or situation, he might do; **personal identity** the continued sameness of the individual person, through all changes, as testified by consciousness; **personality cult** excessive adulation of the individual, orig. in Communist usage; **personality disorder** (*psych.*) any of various types of mental illness in which one tends to behave in ways which are harmful to oneself or others; **personal pronoun** (*gram.*) a pronoun which stands for a definite person or thing; **personal rights** rights which belong to a person as a living, reasonable being; **personal security** security or pledge given by a person, as distinguished from the delivery of some object of value as security; **personal service** delivery of a message or an order into a person's hands, as distinguished from delivery in any other indirect way: attention or service of the proprietor of a concern, rather than one of his employees or assistants; **personal stereo** a small lightweight cassette-player designed to be carried around (e.g. in one's pocket or attached to one's belt) and listened to through earphones; **personal transaction** something done by a person's own effort, not through the agency of another; **Person Friday** a Man or Girl Friday (see **man, girl**); **per'sonpower** manpower, applying to either sex. — *adj.* **per'son-to= per'son** (of telephone call) personal: involving meeting or contact. — Also *adv.* — **in person** in actual bodily presence: by one's own act, not by an agent or representative. [L. *persōna*, a player's mask, perh. from Etruscan *phersu*, masked figures, commonly associated (in spite of difference of quantity) with *persōnāre, -ātum — per, sōnāre,* to sound; cf. **parson**.]

persona[1]. See **person**.

persona[2] *pər-sōn'ə, -a,* (L.) person. — **persona grata** (*grā', grā'tə, -a*) a person who is acceptable, liked, or favoured, esp. one who is diplomatically acceptable to a foreign government (also used as *adj.*); **persona muta** (*mū'tə, mōo'ta*) a character in an opera who neither speaks nor sings. — **dramatis personae** see **drama; in propria persona** (L.L.: *in prō'pri-ə, pro'pri-a*) in person; **persona non grata** opp. of **persona grata**.

personage...to...personnel. See **person**.

personify *pər-son'i-fī, v.t.* to represent as a person: to ascribe personality to: to be the embodiment of: to personate (*rare*): — *pr.p.* **person'ifying;** *pa.t.* and *pa.p.* **person'ified.** — *ns.* **personificā'tion; person'ifier.** [L. *persōna*, a person, *facĕre*, to make: see foregoing.]

personnel. See **person**.

perspective *pər-spek'tiv,* formerly *pûr', n.* optics (*obs.*): a telescope, microscope, or other optical instrument (also **perspective glass**; *obs.*): the art or science of drawing objects on a surface, so as to give the picture the same appearance to the eye as the objects themselves: appearance, or representation of appearance, of objects in space, with effect of distance, solidity, etc.: just proportion in all the parts: a picture in perspective: a picture or model that seems confused except when viewed in the right direction, or in some other way gives a fantastic effect (*Shak.*): a peep-show (*obs.*): a vista: a prospect of the future: inspection (*obs.*). — *adj.* optical (*obs.*): pertaining or according to perspective. — *adj.* **perspectī'val.** — *adv.* **perspec'-tively.** — *n.* **perspec'tivism** the theory that things can only be known from an individual point of view at a particular time (*philos.*): the use of subjective points of view in literature and art. — **perspec'tivist** an artist whose work emphasises the effects of perspective: one who studies the rules of perspective; **perspective plane** the surface on which the picture of the objects to be represented in perspective is drawn. — **in, out of, perspective** according to, against, the laws of perspective: in just, unjust, proportion: in, out of, prospect (*obs.*). [L. (*ars*) *perspectīva*, perspective (art) — *perspicĕre, perspectum — per, specĕre,* to look.]

Perspex® *pûr'speks, n.* a proprietary thermoplastic resin of exceptional transparency and freedom from colour, used for windscreens, etc.

perspicacious *pûr-spi-kā'shəs, adj.* clear-sighted (*arch.*):

clear-minded. — *adv.* **perspicā′ciously.** — *n.* **perspicacity** (*-kas′i-ti*). [L. *perspicāx, -ācis*; see **perspective.**]
perspicuous *pər-spik′ū-əs, adj.* lucid. — *n.* **perspicū′ity.** — *adv.* **perspic′ūously.** — *n.* **perspic′ūousness.** [L. *perspicuus*; see preceding.]
perspire *pər-spīr′, v.i.* to exude: to sweat. — *v.t.* to exhale. — *adj.* **perspīr′able** capable of being perspired or of perspiring. — *v.i.* **perspirate** (*pûr′spir-āt; rare*) to sweat. — *n.* **perspiration** (*-spir-ā′shən*) the act of perspiring: sweat. — *adj.* **perspīr′atory.** [L. *perspīrāre, -ātum — per, spīrāre,* to breathe.]
perst. See **perse[2].**
perstringe *pər-strinj′*, (*obs.*) *v.t.* to constrain: to touch on: to dull: to censure. [L. *perstringĕre* — pfx. *per-,* thoroughly, and *stringĕre,* to bind.]
persuade *pər-swād′, v.t.* to induce by argument, advice, etc.: to bring to any particular opinion: to cause to believe: to convince: to seek to induce (*obs.*): to urge (*Shak.*). — *v.i.* to plead (*obs.*): to prevail (*obs.*): to use persuasive methods. — Also **perswade′** (*obs.*). — *adj.* **persuād′able.** — *ns.* **persuād′er** one who, or that which, persuades: a gun (*slang*): a device used to fit metal type into a chase (*print.*); **persuasibility** (*-swās-i-bil′i-ti*). — *adj.* **persuās′ible** capable of being persuaded. — *n.* **persuasion** (*-swā′zhən*) the act, process, method, art, or power of persuading: an inducement: the state of being persuaded: settled opinion: a creed: a party adhering to a creed: a kind (*facet.*). — *adj.* **persuasive** (*-swās′*) having the power to persuade: influencing the mind or passions. — *n.* that which persuades or wins over. — *adv.* **persuā′sively.** — *n.* **persuā′siveness.** — *adj.* **persuās′ory** persuasive. [L. *persuādēre, -suāsum* — pfx. *per-, suādēre,* to advise.]
persue[1] *pûrs′ū,* (*Spens.*) *n.* a track of blood. [Fr. *percée,* act of piercing, confused with **pursue.**]
persue[2]. An obsolete spelling of **pursue.**
persulphate *pər-sul′fāt, n.* that sulphate of a metal which contains the relatively greater quantity of oxygen or of the acid radical: a salt of **persulphuric** (*-fū′rik*) **acid** ($H_2S_2O_8$). [**per-** (1) and **sulphate.**]
perswade. Obs. spelling of **persuade.**
pert *pûrt, adj.* open (*obs.*): unconcealed: brisk: perky (*Shak.*): flourishing: adroit (*obs.*): forward: saucy: impertinent: presumingly free in speech: objectionable (*obs.*). — *n.* an impudent person. — *adv.* **pert′ly.** — *n.* **pert′ness.** [Aphetic for **apert;** see **peart.**]
pertain *pər-, pûr-tān′, v.i.* to belong: to relate (with *to*). — *ns.* **per′tinence, per′tinency** (*pûr′*) the state of being pertinent: an appurtenance (*obs.*). — *adj.* **per′tinent** pertaining or related: to the point: fitted for the matter on hand: fitting or appropriate: suitable: apposite. — *n.* (chiefly *Scot.*) anything that goes along with an estate. — *adv.* **per′tinently.** [O.Fr. *partenir* — L. *pertinēre* — pfx. *per-, tenēre,* to hold.]
pertake. An old spelling (*Spens., Shak.*) of **partake.**
perthite *pûrth′īt, n.* a parallel intergrowth of orthoclase and albite. — *adj.* **perthitic** (*-it′ik*). [*Perth,* Ontario, where it was found.]
pertinacious *pûr-ti-nā′shəs, adj.* thoroughly tenacious: holding obstinately to an opinion or a purpose: obstinate: unyielding. — *adv.* **pertinā′ciously.** — *ns.* **pertinā′ciousness; pertinacity** (*-nas′i-ti*) the quality of being pertinacious or unyielding: obstinacy: resoluteness. [L. *pertināx, -ācis,* holding fast — pfx. *per-, tenāx,* tenacious — *tenēre,* to hold.]
pertinence, pertinent, etc. See **pertain.**
perttaunt like an obscure phrase in Shakespeare (*Love's Labour's Lost,* V, ii), possibly meaning like a *pair taunt* or *purtaunt′,* a double pair-royal. [**pair[1],** and Fr. *tant,* so much, i.e. counting as much again as a pair-royal in post and pair.]
perturb *pər-tûrb′, v.t.* to disturb greatly: to agitate — also **per′turbate** (*pûr′tər-bāt*). — *adj.* **pertur′bable.** — *ns.* **pertur′bance** perturbation; **perturb′ant** anything that perturbs. — *adj.* **perturbing.** — *n.* **perturbā′tion** the act of perturbing or state of being perturbed: disquiet of mind: irregularity: the disturbance produced in the

simple elliptic motion of one heavenly body about another by the action of a third body, or by the non-sphericity of the principal body (*astron.*): a perturbing agent. — *adjs.* **perturbā′tional; pertur′bative.** — *n.* **per′turbātor.** — *adj.* and *n.* **pertur′batory.** — *adj.* **perturbed′.** — *adv.* **perturb′edly.** — *n.* **pertur′ber.** — **perturbation theory** (*phys.*) a mathematical method of determining the effect of small local changes on the behaviour of a system. [L. *perturbāre, -ātum* — pfx. *per-, turbāre,* to disturb — *turba,* a crowd.]
pertuse *pər-tūs′, adj.* punched: pierced: slit. — Also **pertūs′ate** (or *pûr′*), **pertused** (*-tūst′*). — *n.* **pertusion** (*-tū′zhən*). [L. *pertundĕre, -tūsum — per, tundĕre,* to strike.]
pertussis *pər-tus′is, n.* whooping-cough. — *adj.* **pertuss′al.** [**per-** (2), L. *tussis,* cough.]
Peru *pə-rōō′, n.* a country of S. America. — *adj.* **Peru′vian** of Peru. — *n.* a native, or inhabitant, of Peru. — **Peruvian bark** cinchona bark. — **balsam of Peru, Peru balsam** a fragrant acrid black viscid liquid, containing esters of benzoic and cinnamic acids, got from a tropical American papilionaceous tree, *Myroxylon pereirae;* **marvel of Peru** see **marvel.** [Sp. *Perú.*]
peruke *pər-ōōk′,* formerly *per′, n.* a wig. — Also **perruque** (Fr. *per-ük*). — *adj.* **peruk′ed** wearing a peruke. — *n.* **perru′quier** (*-ōōk′yər,* Fr. *-ük-yā*) a wigmaker. [Fr. *perruque* — It. *parrucca* (Sp. *peluca*); connection with L. *pĭlus,* hair, very doubtful.]
peruse *pər-ōōz′, v.t.* orig. to use up, wear out: to pass in scrutiny, one by one or piece by piece (*Shak.*): to examine in detail: to revise: to read attentively or critically: (*loosely*) to read. — *ns.* **perus′al** the act of perusing: careful examination: scrutiny: study: reading; **perus′er.** [L. pfx. *per-,* thoroughly, *ūtī, ūsus,* to use.]
Peruvian. See **Peru.**
perv *pûrv,* (*coll.*) *n.* a (sexual) pervert: an act of perving (*Austr.*): one who pervs (*Austr.*). — *v.i.* (with *at* or *on*) to look at lustfully or for sexual pleasure (*Austr.*). — Also **perve.** [**pervert.**]
pervade *pər-vād′, v.t.* to pass through (*rare*): to diffuse or extend through the whole of. — *n.* **pervasion** (*-vā′zhən*). — *adj.* **pervasive** (*-vā′siv*) tending or having power to pervade. — *adv.* **perva′sively.** — *n.* **perva′siveness.** [L. *pervādĕre — per,* through, *vādĕre,* to go.]
perverse *pər-vûrs′, adj.* turned aside from right or truth: obstinate in the wrong: capricious and unreasonable in opposition: froward: wrong-headed: wayward: against the evidence or judge's direction on point of law: adverse (*Milt.*). — *adv.* **perverse′ly.** — *ns.* **perverse′ness; perversion** (*-vûr′shən*) the act of perverting: the condition of being perverted: the product of the process of perverting: a diverting from the true object: a turning from right or true: a distortion: a misapplication: a pathological deviation of sexual instinct: the formation of a mirror-image (*math.*): the mirror-image itself; **pervers′ity** the state or quality of being perverse. — *adj.* **pervers′ive** tending to pervert. — *v.t.* **pervert′** to turn wrong or from the right course: to wrest from the true meaning: to corrupt: to turn from truth or virtue: to divert, turn (*Shak.*): to form a mirror-image of (*math.*). — *v.i.* to go wrong or out of the right course. — *ns.* **pervert** (*pûr′vûrt*) one who has abandoned the doctrine assumed to be true: one whose sexual instinct is perverted; **pervert′er.** — *adj.* **pervert′ible.** [Partly through Fr. — L. *pervertĕre, perversum* — pfx. *per-,* wrongly, *vertĕre,* to turn.]
perviate. See **pervious.**
pervicacious *pûr-vi-kā′shəs, adj.* very obstinate. — *ns.* **pervicā′ciousness, pervicacity** (*-kas′i-ti*), **pervicacy** (*pûr′vi-kə-si; obs.*). [L. *pervicāx, -ācis* — pfx. *per-, vincĕre,* to prevail.]
pervious *pûr′vi-əs, adj.* permeable: passable: penetrable: open. — *v.t.* **per′viate,** to make a way through. — *adv.* **per′viously.** — *n.* **per′viousness.** [L. *pervius — per,* through, *via,* a way.]

Pesach, Pesah *pā'sahh, n.* the festival of Passover. [Heb.]

pesade *pə-zäd, -säd', -zäd', n.* dressage manoeuvre in which a horse rears up on its hindlegs without forward movement. [Fr.; from It.]

pesant, pesaunt, old spellings of **peasant**.

pesante *pes-an'tā,* (*mus.*) *adj.* heavy: weighty. — Also *adv.* [It.]

peseta *pe-sā'ta, -ə, n.* the standard monetary unit of Spain. [Sp., dim. of *pesa,* weight.]

pesewa *pə-sōō'a, -sā'wa, -ə, n.* a Ghanaian unit of currency: — *pl.* **-a, -as.** — See **cedi**.

Peshito, Peshitto *pe-shē(t)'tō,* **Peshitta** *-tə, ns.* a Syriac translation of the Bible. — Also *adj.* [Syriac *p'shī(t)tô, -tâ,* the simple.]

peshwa *pāsh'wa, n.* the chief minister of the Mahrattas, later the real sovereign. — Also **peish'wa(h).** [Pers. *pēshwā,* chief.]

pesky *pes'ki,* (*coll.*) *adj.* annoying. — *adv.* **pes'kily.** [Perh. **pest**.]

peso *pā'sō, n.* a Spanish five-peseta piece: a Mexican dollar: in S. and Central America and the Philippines, a coin of various values: — *pl.* **pe'sos.** [Sp., — L. *pēnsum,* weight.]

pessary *pes'ə-ri, n.* a surgical plug, or medicated device, esp. one worn in the vagina. [Fr. *pessaire* — L.L. *pessārium* — Gr. *pessos,* a pebble, pessary.]

pessimism *pes'i-mizm, n.* the worst state (*obs.*): the doctrine that the world is bad rather than good (*philos.*): a temper of mind that looks on the dark side of things: a depressing view of life: (*loosely*) despondency, hopelessness. — *n.* **pess'imist** one who believes that everything is tending to the worst: one who looks too much on the dark side of things — opp. to *optimist.* — *adjs.* **pessimis'tic, -al.** — *adv.* **pessimis'tically.** [L. *pessimus,* worst.]

pest *pest, n.* any deadly epidemic disease: plague: anything destructive: any insect, fungus, etc., destructive of cultivated plants: troublesome person or thing. — *adjs.* **pest'ful** pestilential; **pesticid'al** pertaining to a pesticide. — *n.* **pesticide** (*pes'ti-sīd*) a substance for killing pests. — *adj.* **pestif'erous** bringing plague or pestilence: pestilential: noxious: pestilent: annoying: plague-stricken. — *adv.* **pestif'erously.** — *n.* **pest'ilence** any deadly epidemic disease: bubonic plague: anything that is hurtful to the morals. — *adjs.* **pest'ilent** deadly: producing pestilence: hurtful to health and life: pernicious: mischievous: vexatious; **pestilential** (*-len'shl*) of the nature of pestilence: producing or infested with pestilence: destructive: baneful: detestable: pestering. — *advs.* **pestilen'tially, pest'ilently.** — *adj.* **pestolog'ical.** — *ns.* **pestol'ogist; pestol'ogy** the study of agricultural pests and methods of combating them. — **pest'house** (*hist.*) a hospital for plague or other infectious or contagious disease. — *adj.* **pest'ilence-stricken.** [Fr. *peste* and *pestilence* — L. *pestis, pestilentia.*]

Pestalozzian, *pes-ta-lot'si-ən, adj.* pertaining to Johann Heinrich *Pestalozzi* (1746-1827) or his programme of educational reform. — *n.* a follower of Pestalozzi.

pester, *pes'tər, v.t.* to clog (*obs.*): to huddle (*Milt.*): to infest (*arch.*): to annoy persistently. — *n.* an annoyance. — *n.* **pes'terer.** — *adv.* **pes'teringly.** — *n.* **pes'terment.** — *adj.* **pest'erous.** [App. from O.Fr. *empestrer* (Fr. *empêtrer*), to entangle — L. *in,* in, L.L. *pāstōrium,* a foot-shackle — L. *pāstus,* pa.p. of *pāscĕre,* to feed; cf. **pastern;** influenced by **pest**.]

pesticide, pestiferous, pestilence, etc. See **pest**.

pestle *pes'l,* also *pest'l, n.* an instrument for pounding: a leg, esp. as food (now *dial.*). — *v.t.* to pound. — *v.i.* to use a pestle. [O.Fr. *pestel* — L. *pistillum,* a pounder — *pīnsĕre, pistum,* to pound.]

pesto *pes'tō, n.* an Italian sauce made chiefly of basil and cheese, with nuts, olive oil, etc., originating in Liguria. [It.]

pestology. See **pest**.

pet¹ *pet, n.* a cherished tame animal: an indulged favourite: used as an endearment. — *adj.* kept as a pet:

indulged: cherished: favourite. — *v.t.* to treat as a pet: to fondle: to pamper: to indulge. — *v.i.* (*coll.*) to indulge in amorous caressing: — *pr.p.* **pett'ing;** *pa.t.* and *pa.p.* **pett'ed.** — *adj.* **pett'ed.** — *ns.* **pett'er; pett'ing.** — **pet aversion,** familiar a chief object of dislike; **pet name** a name used in familiar affection; **petting party** (*coll.*) a gathering for the purpose of amorous caressing as an organised sport. [Origin unknown; not from Gael.]

pet² *pet, n.* a slighted and offended feeling: a slight, or childish, fit of aggrieved or resentful sulkiness: the sulks, huff. — *v.i.* to be peevish, to sulk. — *adj.* **pett'ed** in a pet: apt to be in a pet. — *adv.* **pett'edly.** — *n.* **pett'edness.** — *adj.* **pett'ish** peevish: sulky: inclined to sulk: of the nature of or expressive of sulkiness. — *adv.* **pett'ishly.** — *n.* **pett'ishness.** [Origin unknown.]

peta- *pe'tə-,* in composition, one thousand million million, 10^{15}, as in *petajoule, petametre.* [Origin uncertain; prob Gr. **penta-**.]

petal *pet'l, n.* a corolla leaf. — *adjs.* **petalif'erous, pet'alous** having petals; **pet'aline** (*-īn*) of or like a petal. — *n.* **pet'alism** a method of ostracism practised in ancient Syracuse, the name being written on an olive-leaf. — *adj.* **pet'alled** having petals: also used in composition, as *white-petalled.* — *n.* **pet'alody** (Gr. *eidos,* form) transformation, esp. of stamens, into petals. — *adj.* **pet'aloid** having the appearance of a petal. — *n.* **petaloma'nia** abnormal increase in number of petals. — *adj.* **petalous** see above. [Gr. *petalon,* a leaf.]

pétanque *pā-täk', n.* a French (Provençal) game in which steel bowls are rolled or hurled towards a wooden marker ball.

petar. See **petard**.

petara *pi-tä'rə, n.* a travelling box or basket for clothes. — Also **pita'ra(h).** [Hind. *pitārāh, petārāh.*]

petard *pe-tär(d)', n.* a case containing an explosive, used for blowing in doors, etc. (*Shak.* **petar'**): a moving firework. — **hoist with his own petard** see **hoise**. [O.Fr. — *péter,* to crack or explode — L. *pēdĕre,* to break wind.]

petary *pē'tər-i, n.* a peat-bog. [Mediaeval L. *petāria* — root of **peat¹**.]

petasus *pet'ə-səs, n.* a low broad hat worn by the Greeks in antiquity: either the broad petasus that Hermes is represented as wearing in early Greek art or, by association, the winged hat he wears in later art. [Latinised from Gr. *petasos.*]

petaurist *pe-tö'rist, n.* a flying-phalanger. — *adj.* **petaur'ine.** [Gr. *petauristēs,* an acrobat.]

petchary *pech'ə-ri, n.* the grey king-bird. [Imit.]

petcock *pet'kok, n.* a small tap or valve for draining condensed steam from steam-engine cylinders, or for testing the water-level in a boiler. [Poss. obs. *pet,* to fart, or *petty,* and *cock,* a tap.]

petechia *pe-tē'ki-ə, n.* a small red or purple spot on the skin: — *pl.* **pete'chiae** (*-ē*). — *adj.* **petech'ial.** [Latinised from It. *petecchia.*]

peter¹ *pē'tər, v.i.* to dwindle away to nothing, be dissipated or exhausted (with *out*). [Origin unknown; orig. U.S. mining slang.]

peter² *pē'tər, n.* the Blue Peter (flag): in whist, a call for trumps: a high card followed by a low card, so played as a signal to one's partner (*bridge*). — *v.i.* in whist, to signal that one has a short suit: to play a high card followed by a low card (*bridge*). — **pe'ter-boat** a kind of fishing-boat: a dredger's boat that goes equally well forward or astern; **pe'ter-man** a fisherman (in allusion to the apostle); **Peter-see-me'** a Spanish wine (from a grape introduced by Pedro *Ximenes*); **Peter's pence** see **penny**.

peter³ *pē'tər,* (*slang*) *n.* a safe: a prison cell: a till (*Austr.*): the witness box (*Austr.*). — **pe'terman** a safe-blower.

Peterloo *pē-tər-lōō', n.* a popular term for the incident at St Peter's Fields, Manchester, in 1819, in which a peaceable demonstration for reform was charged by cavalry, leaving 11 dead and 400 to 500 injured. [St

Peter's Fields and Water*loo*.]

peter(-)man. See **peter²,³**.

Peter Pan a character in J. M. Barrie's play of that name (1904), the type of the person who never grows up. — **Peter Pan collar** a flat collar with rounded ends.

Peter principle *pē'tər prin'si-pl*, the (*facet.*) theory that members of an organisation, etc., are generally promoted to posts one stage above their level of competence. [Advanced by Laurence Peter and Raymond Hull in their book, *The Peter Principle* (1969).]

petersham *pē'tər-shəm, n.* a heavy greatcoat designed by Lord *Petersham*: rough-napped cloth generally dark blue of which it was made: a heavy corded ribbon used for belts, hat-bands, etc.

pether. See **pedder**.

pethidine *peth'ə-dēn, n.* a synthetic analgesic and hypnotic, having action similar to that of morphine. — Also **meperidine**. [Perh. mixture of *piperidine, ethyl*.]

pétillant *pā-tē-yã,* (Fr.) *adj.* of wine, slightly sparkling.

petiole *pet'i-ōl, n.* a leaf-stalk (*bot.*): a stalk-like structure, esp. that of the abdomen in wasps, etc. (*zool.*). — *adjs.* **pet'iolar** of, or of the nature of, a petiole; **pet'iolāte, -d, pet'ioled** stalked. — *n.* **pet'iolule** (*-ol-ūl*) the stalk of a leaflet in a compound leaf. [L. *petiolus,* a little foot, a petiole.]

petit formerly *pet'it,* now *pet'i, pə-tē',* or as Fr. *pə-tē, adj.* a form of **petty** (q.v.) — in sense of insignificant, *obs.* except in legal and other French phrases: — *fem.* **petite** (*pə-tēt'*) applied to a woman, small-made (with a suggestion of neatness): a variant spelling of **petit,** applied to either sex (*obs.*). — In phrases, the earlier borrowings tend to be the more highly anglicised. — **petit battement** (*bat-mã* ; *ballet*) a light tapping or beating with the foot; **petit bourgeois** (*bōōr-zhwä*) a member of the lower middle class; **petite bourgeoisie** (*bōōr-zhwä-zē*) the lower middle class; **petit déjeuner** (*dā-zhœ-nā*) breakfast; **petit four** (*fōr, för, fōōr*) a small very fancy biscuit; **petit grain** (*grã*) dried unripe bitter oranges, or an oil distilled from them or their leaves and twigs; **petit jury** (*legal*) a 12-man jury, in Britain now the only form of jury (also **petty jury;** see **grand jury**); **petit maître** (*me-tr'*) a fop; **petit mal** (*mal*) a mild form of epilepsy without convulsions; **petit pain** (*pẽ*) a breadroll; **petit point** (*point, pwẽ*) work in tent stitch; **petits pois** (*pə-tē pwa*) small green peas. [Fr. *petit, -e*.]

petition *pə-tish'ən, n.* a supplication: a prayer: a formal request to an authority: a written supplication signed by a number of persons: a written application to a court of law: the thing asked for: a parliamentary bill (*obs.*): an axiom or postulate (*obs.*). — *v.t.* to address a petition to: to ask for. — *adj.* **peti'tionary.** — *ns.* **peti'tioner** one who petitions: (with *cap.*) one of the party that petitioned Charles II in 1680 to summon Parliament — opp. to *Abhorrer* (*hist.*); **petit'ioning;** **peti'tionist.** — *adj.* **petitory** (*pet'i-tə-ri*) petitioning. — **Petition of Right** a parliamentary declaration, in the form of a petition of the rights of the people, assented to by Charles I in 1628. [L. *petītiō, -ōnis* — *petĕre,* to ask.]

petitio principii *pe-tish'i-ō prin-sip'i-ī, pe-tē'ti-ō prēn-kip'i-ē,* (*log.*) a begging of the question. [L. *petītiō prīncipiī*.]

petitory. See **petition**.

Petrarchan *pe-trär'kən,* **Petrarchian** *-ki-ən, adjs.* pertaining to, imitating, the Italian poet Francesco *Petrarca* or *Petrarch* (1304–74). — *ns.* a follower or imitator of Petrarch. — *adj.* **Petrarch'al.** — *ns.* **Petrarch'ianism;** **Petrarch'ianist.** — *v.i.* **Petrarchise, -ize** (*pe'trärk-īz, -trärk'*) to write in Petrarch's manner, imitate Petrarch. — *ns.* **Petrarchism** (*pe'trärk-izm,* or *pe-trärk'-izm*); **Pe'trarchist** (or *-trärk'*). — The older pronunciation of Petrarch, *pē'trärk,* gives alternative pronunciations for the above words. — **Petrarch(i)an sonnet** see **sonnet**.

petrary *pet'rə-ri, n.* an engine for hurling stones. [L.L. *petrāria* — L. *petra* — Gr. *petrā,* rock.]

petre *pē'tər,* (*coll.*) *n.* short for **saltpetre**.

petrel *pet'rəl, n.* any bird of the genus Procellaria akin to the albatrosses and fulmars, esp. the **storm** (popularly **stormy**) **petrel** or Mother Carey's chicken, a dusky sea-bird, rarely landing except to lay its eggs, the smallest web-footed bird known. [L. *Petrus,* Peter, from its seeming to walk on the water; see Matt. xiv. 29.]

Petri, or **petri, dish** *pē'tri, pā'tri, pet'ri dish,* a shallow glass dish with an overlapping cover used for cultures of bacteria. — Also **Petri plate.** [R. J. *Petri,* German bacteriologist.]

petrify *pet'ri-fī, v.t.* to turn into stone: to fossilise by molecular replacement, preserving minute structure (*geol.*): loosely, to encrust with stony matter: to make hard like a stone: to fix in amazement, horror, etc. — *v.i.* to become stone, or hard like stone: — *pr.p.* **pet'rifying;** *pa.t.* and *pa.p.* **pet'rified.** — *n.* **petrifac'tion** turning or being turned into stone: a petrified object: a fossil. — *adjs.* **petrifac'tive, petrif'ic** petrifying. — *n.* **petrificā'tion** petrifaction. [L. *petra* — Gr. *petrā,* rock, L. *facĕre, factum,* to make.]

Petrine *pē'trīn, adj.* pertaining to, or written by, the Apostle *Peter.* — *n.* **Pē'trinism** (*-trin-izm*) the Tübingen theory of F. C. Baur (1792–1860) and his school, of a doctrinal trend in primitive Christianity towards Judaism, ascribed to Peter and his party in opposition to *Paulinism.* [L. *Petrinus* — *Petrus,* Gr. *Petros,* Peter.]

petrissage *pā-trēs-äzh', n.* massage by longitudinal rubbing and lateral squeezing. [Fr., — *pétrir,* to knead.]

petro-¹ *pet'rō-,* in composition, petroleum. — *n.* and *adj.* **petrochem'ical** (of or relating to) any chemical obtained from petroleum. — *ns.* **pet'rocurr'ency, pet'romoney, pet'rodollars, pet'ropounds** currency, etc., acquired by the oil-producing countries as profit from the sale of their oil to the consumer countries. [*petroleum*.]

petro-² *pet-rō-, pi-tro'-,* in composition, rock. — *ns.* **pet'rodrome** (Gr. *dromos,* a running) an African elephant shrew of the genus **Petrodromus; petrogen'esis** (the study of) the origin, formation, etc., of rocks. — *adj.* **petrogenet'ic.** — *n.* **pet'roglyph** (Gr. *glyphein,* to carve) a rock-carving, esp. prehistoric. — *adj.* **petroglyph'ic.** — *ns.* **pet'roglyphy; pet'rogram** (Gr. *gramma,* a drawing) a picture upon stone; **petrog'raphy** (Gr. *graphein,* to write) the systematic description and classification of rocks; **petrog'rapher.** — *adjs.* **petrograph'ic(al).** - *adv.* **petrograph'ically.** — *n.* **petrol'ogy** (Gr. *logos,* discourse) the science of the origin, chemical and mineral composition and structure, and alteration of rocks. — *adj.* **petrolog'ical.** — *adv.* **petrolog'ically.** — *ns.* **petrol'ogist; petrophys'ics** (Gr. *physikos,* natural) that branch of physics pertaining to the physical properties of rocks. — *adj.* **petrophys'ical.** — *n.* **petrophys'icist.** [Gr. *petrā,* rock.]

petrol *pet'rol, -rəl, n.* formerly, petroleum: now a mixture of light volatile hydrocarbons got by fractional distillation or cracking of petroleum, used for driving motor-cars, aeroplanes, etc. (U.S. **gasoline**). — *v.t.* to supply with petrol: — *pr.p.* **pet'rolling;** *pa.t.* and *pa.p.* **pet'rolled.** — *ns.* **pet'rolage** treatment with petrol to stamp out mosquitoes; **petrolatum** (*-ā'təm*) petroleum jelly. — *adj.* **petroleous** (*pi-trō'li-əs*) containing, or rich in, petroleum. — *ns.* **petroleum** (*pi-trō'li-əm*) a (usu. liquid) mineral oil containing a mixture of hydrocarbons got from oil-wells, and used to make petrol, paraffin, lubricating oil, fuel oil, etc.; **pétroleur** (*pā-trol-œr; masc.*), **pétroleuse** (*-øz; fem.*) (Fr.) an incendiary who uses petroleum, as in Paris in 1871. — *adjs.* **petrolic** (*pi-trol'ik*) of petrol or petroleum; **petrolif'erous** (*pet-*) yielding petroleum. — **petrol blue** a vibrant blue colour; **petrol bomb** a petrol-filled Molotov cocktail or the like; **petroleum coke** almost pure carbon, the final by-product of the distillation of crude oil, used in refining, electrodes, as fuel, etc.; **petroleum ether** a volatile mixture of hydrocarbons distilled from petroleum and used as a solvent; **petroleum jelly** soft paraffin (*paraffinum molle*), a mixture of petroleum hydrocarbons used in emollients, as a lubricant, etc. (see also **liquid paraffin** at **liquid**); **petrol lighter** a cigarette-lighter in which the striking of a spark ignites a petrol-soaked wick; **petrol pump** a machine for transferring measured amounts of petrol to motor vehicles; **petrol station** a garage which sells petrol. [L. *petra*, rock, *oleum*, oil.]

petrology. See **petro-**[2].

petronel *pet'rə-nel*, *n.* a large horse pistol. [Fr. *petrinal* — L. *pectus, pectoris*, the chest, whence fired, or L. *petra*, stone, i.e. gun-flint.]

petronella *pet-rən-el'ə*, *n.* a Scottish country-dance.

petrous *pet'rəs*, *adj.* stony: petrosal. — *adj.* **petrosal** (*pi-trōs'əl*) relating to the stony part of the temporal bone about the ear. — Also *n.* [L. *petrōsus* — *petra* — Gr. *petrā*, rock.]

pe-tsai cabbage *pā-tsī' kab'ij*. Same as **Chinese cabbage**.

petted, etc. See **pet**[1,2].

Petter engine *pet'ər en'jin*, a kind of oil-engine. [Makers' name.]

pettichaps, petty-chaps *pet'i-chaps*, *n.* the garden or other warbler. [N. of England; app. **petty** and **chap**[3].]

petticoat *pet'i-kōt*, *n.* orig., a short or small coat: a skirt, esp. an under-skirt, or a garment of which it forms part: any garment or drapery of similar form: a bell-shaped structure, as in telegraph insulators, etc.: a woman (*coll.*). — *adj.* feminine: female: of women. — *adj.* **pett'icoated**. — **pett'icoat-breeches** loose short breeches worn by men in the 17th century; **pett'icoat-tails'** small cakes of shortbread; **petticoat government** domination by women. [**petty, coat**[1].]

pettifogger *pet'i-fog-ər*, *n.* a paltry cavilling lawyer. — *v.i.* **pett'ifog** to play the pettifogger. — *n.* **pett'ifoggery**. — *n.* and *adj.* **pett'ifogging** paltry, trivial, cavilling (behaviour). [**petty**; origin of second part obscure.]

pettish. See **pet**[2].

pettitoes *pet'i-tōz*, *n.pl.* pig's feet as food (formerly app. also other parts and of other animals): human feet (*Shak.*). [Origin obscure, but early associated with **petty** and **toe**.]

pettle[1] *pet'l*, (*Scot.*) *v.t.* to indulge, pet. [Freq. of **pet**[1].]

pettle[2] *pet'l*. Same as **pattle**.

petty *pet'i*, *adj.* small: of less importance: minor: trifling: lower in rank, power, etc.: inconsiderable, insignificant: contemptible: small-minded. — *n.* a junior schoolboy. — *adv.* **pett'ily**. — *n.* **pett'iness**. — **Petty Bag** a former office of the Court of Chancery: a clerk of that office; **petty bourgeois, bourgeoisie** variants of **petit bourgeois, petite bourgeoisie**; **petty cash** miscellaneous small sums of money received or paid: a sum of money kept for minor expenses which usu. do not need to be referred to a higher authority; **petty-chaps** see **pettichaps**; **petty jury** see **petit jury**; **petty larceny** see **larceny**; **petty officer** a naval officer ranking with a non-commissioned officer in the army; **Petty Sessions** a court in which magistrates try trivial cases and refer others to a higher court; **petty whin** a low spiny papilionaceous shrub (*Genista anglica*) like a small whin. [Fr. *petit*.]

petulant *pet'ū-lənt*, *adj.* orig. wanton, lascivious: showing peevish impatience, irritation, or caprice: forward, impudent in manner. — *ns.* **pet'ulance, pet'ulancy**. — *adv.* **pet'ulantly**. [L. *petulāns, -antis* — assumed *petulāre*, dim. of *petĕre*, to seek.]

Petunia *pe-tū'nyə, -ni-ə*, *n.* South American genus of ornamental plants near akin to tobacco: (without *cap.*) a plant of this genus. [Tupi *petun*, tobacco.]

petuntse *pe-tōont'si*, *n.* a feldspathic rock used in making Chinese porcelain. — Also **petuntze**. [Chin. *pai-tun-tse*, little white brick.]

pew *pū*, *n.* an enclosed compartment or fixed bench in a church: formerly, a place for a preacher or reader: a box or stall in another building: a seat (*slang*). — **pew'-chair** an additional seat hinged to the end of a pew; **pew'-fellow** occupant of the same pew: compan-

ion; **pew'-holder** one who rents a pew; **pew'-opener** an attendant who showed people to pews; **pew'-rent** rent paid for the use of a pew. [O.Fr. *puie*, raised place, balcony — L. *podia*, pl. of *podium* — Gr. *podion*, dim. of *pous, podos*, foot.]

pewee. See **peewee**.

pewit *pē'wit, pū'it*. Same as **peewit**.

pewter *pū'tər*, *n.* formerly, an alloy of three to nine parts of tin and one of lead: now tin with a little copper, antimony, and/or bismuth: a vessel made of pewter, esp. a beer-tankard: the bluish-grey colour of pewter: prize-money (*slang*). — *adj.* made of pewter. — *n.* **pew'terer** one who works in pewter. — **pew'ter-mill** a lapidary's pewter polishing-wheel for amethyst, agate, etc. [O.Fr. *peutre*; cf. It. *peltro*, L.G. *spialter*, Eng. **spelter**.]

peyote *pā-yō'tā*, *n.* a Mexican intoxicant made from cactus tops — also called **mescal**. — *ns.* **peyo'tism** the taking of peyote, esp. as part of a religious ceremony: the N. American Indian religion in which peyote is taken sacramentally, a form of Christianity; **peyo'tist**. [Nahuatl *peyotl*.]

peyse. See **peise**.

pezant. An old spelling of **peasant**.

Peziza *pe-zī'zə*, *n.* a genus of discomycete fungi with cup-like apothecia. — *adj.* **pezi'zoid**. [Gr. *pezis*, a puff-ball.]

pfennig *pfen'ig, -ihh*, *n.* a German coin, the hundredth part of a mark. — Also (*obs.*) **pfenn'ing**.

pH (value) *pē-āch' (val'ū)*, *n.* a number used to express degrees of acidity or alkalinity in solutions — formerly, the logarithm to base 10 of the reciprocal of the concentration of hydrogen ions; now, related by formula to a standard solution of potassium hydrogen phthalate, which has value 4 at 15°C.

phacoid *fak' or fāk'oid*, **phacoidal** *fə-koi'dl*, *adjs.* lentil-shaped, lens-shaped. — *ns.* **phacolite** (*fak'ə-līt*) a zeolite often lenticular in shape; **phac'olith** a small lenticular igneous intrusion, shaped by folding in an anticline. [Gr. *phakos*, a lentil, *eidos*, form, *lithos*, stone.]

Phaedra complex *fēd'rə kom'pleks*, (*psych.*) the difficult relationship which can arise between a new step-parent and the (usu. teenage) son or daughter of the original marriage. [Greek story of *Phaedra* who fell in love with her stepson and committed suicide after being repulsed by him.]

phaeic *fē'ik, adj.* dusky. — *n.* **phae'ism** duskiness, incomplete melanism (in butterflies). [Gr. *phaios*, dusky.]

phaelonion. See **phelonion**.

phaen(ō)- *fē-n(ō)-*. Now usu. **phen(o)-**.

phaenogam *fē'nō-gam*, *n.* a spermatophyte or phanerogam. — *n.pl.* **Phaenogamae** (*fē-nog'ə-mē*). — *adjs.* **phaenogamic** (*-nō-gam'ik*), **phaenogamous** (*-nog'ə-məs*). — Also **phe'nogam**, etc. [Gr. *phainein*, to show, *gamos*, marriage.]

phaenology, phaenomenon, phaenotype. Same as **phenology, phenomenon, phenotype**.

phaeo- *fē-ō-*, in composition, dusky, as in **phaeomelanin** (*fē-ō-mel'ə-nin*), a reddish-brown pigment in animals, incl. birds. [Gr. *phaios*.]

Phaeophyceae *fē-ō-fish'i-ē*, *n.pl.* the brown seaweeds, one of the main divisions of algae, in which the chlorophyll is masked by a brown pigment. [Gr. *phaios*, dusky, *phȳkos*, seaweed.]

Phaethon *fā'i-thon*, *n.* the son of Helios, the Greek sun-god, who came to grief in driving his father's chariot: the tropic-bird genus (as seeking to keep to the sun's course). — *adj.* **Phaethon'tic**. [Gr. *Phaethōn, -ontos*, lit. shining; cf. *phaos, phōs*, light.]

phaeton *fā'(i-)tən*, *n.* an open four-wheeled carriage for one or two horses. [From the foregoing.]

phag-, -phaga. See **phag(o)-**.

phage. Short for **bacteriophage**.

-phage. See **phag(o)-**.

phag(o)- *fag(-ō)-*, in composition, used to denote 'feeding', 'eating', as in *phagocyte*. — **-phaga** in zoological names, 'eaters'; **-phage** (*-fāj, -fäzh*) eater, or destroyer;

-phagous (*-fəg-əs*) feeding on; **-phagus** (*-fəg-əs*) one feeding in a particular way, or on a particular thing; **-phagy** (*-fə-ji*) eating of a specified nature. [Gr. *phagein*, to eat.]

phagedaena, phagedena *faj-* or *fag-i-dē'nə*, *n.* rapidly spreading destructive ulceration, once common in hospitals — hospital gangrene. — *adj.* **phagedae'nic, phagedē'nic.** [Gr. *phagedaina — phagein*, to eat.]

phagocyte *fag'ō-sīt*, *n.* a white blood-corpuscle that engulfs bacteria and other harmful particles. — *adjs.* **phagocytic** (*-sit'*), **-al.** — *n.* **phag'ocytism** (*-sīt-*) the nature or function of a phagocyte. — *v.t.* **phag'ocytose** (*-sīt-ōs*) to subject to phagocytic action. — *n.* **phagocytō'sis** destruction by phagocytes. [Gr. *phagein*, to eat, *kytos*, a vessel.]

-phagous, -phagus, -phagy. See **phag(o)-.**

phalange, etc. See **phalanx.**

phalanger *fal-an'jər*, *n.* any one of a group of small arboreal Australasian marsupials. [Gr. *phalangion*, spider's web, from their webbed toes.]

phalanstery *fal'ən-stə-ri*, *n.* the dwelling of the phalange in the ideal social system of Fourier (1772–1837), a vast structure in the midst of a square league of cultivated land. — *adj.* **phalansterian** (*-stē'ri-ən*). — *ns.* **phalanstē'rianism; phal'ansterism; phal'ansterist.** [Fr. *phalanstère*, formed from Gr. *phalanx* on the model of *monastère*, monastery.]

phalanx *fal'angks* (or *fāl'*), *n.* a solid formation of ancient Greek heavy-armed infantry: a solid body of men, etc.: a solid body of supporters or partisans: a Fourierist community: a bone of a digit: the part of a finger or toe answering to it: a joint of an insect's leg: a bundle of stamens: — *pl.* **phal'anxes** or (*biol.*) **phalanges** (*fal-an'jēz*). — *adj.* **phalangal** (*fal-ang'gl*) phalangeal. — *n.* **phalange** (*fal'anj*) a phalanx (in biological senses): (also *fal-ãzh*) a socialistic community in Fourier's scheme, consisting of 1800 persons living in a phalanstery: the Falange, Primo de Rivera's Spanish fascist party: the Christian right-wing group in Lebanon, modelled on the Spanish Falange: — *pl.* **phal'anges.** — *adj.* **phalan'geal.** — *ns.* **phalangid** (*fal-an'jid*) a long-legged arachnid, a harvestman; **phalan'gist** a Spanish falangist: a member of the Lebanese phalange. [Gr. *phalanx, -angos*, a roller, phalanx, phalange, spider.]

phalarope *fal'ə-rōp*, *n.* a wading bird (*Phalaropus*) with coot-like feet. [Gr. *phalaris*, a coot, *pous*, a foot.]

phallus *fal'əs*, *n.* the penis: the symbol of generation in primitive religion: (with *cap.*) the stinkhorn genus of fungi: -- *pl.* **phall'ī, phall'uses.** — *adj.* **phall'ic.** — *ns.* **phall'icism** (*-sizm*), **phall'ism** worship of the generative power of nature; **phall'in, phalloid'in** two of the poisons occurring in the fungus *Amanita phalloides*. — *adj.* **phall'oid** like a phallus. [L., — Gr. *phallos*.]

Phanariot *fa-nar'i-ot*, *n.* one of the Greeks inhabiting the *Fanar* quarter of Constantinople, or of a Greek official class — in Turkish history mostly diplomatists, administrators, and bankers, also hospodars of Wallachia and Moldavia. — *adj.* **Phanar'iot.** — Also **Fan-.** [Gr. *phanarion*, lighthouse, from that on the Golden Horn.]

phanerogam *fan'ər-ō-gam*, *n.* a spermatophyte. — *ns.pl.* **Phanerogamae** (*-og'ə-mē*), **Phanerogamia** (*-ō-gam'i-ə*) a division of plants comprising all spermatophytes. — *adjs.* **phanerogam'ic, phanerog'amous.** [Gr. *phaneros*, visible, *gamos*, marriage.]

phanerophyte *fan'ə-rə-fīt, fə-ner'ə-fīt*, *n.* a tree or shrub with the perennating buds borne more than 25 cm above soil level. [Gr. *phaneros*, visible, *phyton*, plant.]

Phanerozoic *fan-ər-ə-zō'ik*, (*geol.*) *adj.* denoting the geological period of time from the Cambrian period to the present. — Also *n.* [Gr. *phaneros*, visible, *zōion*, an animal.]

phang. An old spelling (*Shak.*) of **fang.**

phansigar *pän'sē-gär, fän'-*, *n.* formerly in India, a thug. [Hind. *phāsī*, a noose, and Pers. agent suffix *-gār*.]

phantasm *fan'tazm*, *n.* a vain, airy appearance: a fancied vision: an apparition: a spectre: a counterfeit: an impostor (*obs.*). — Also **phantas'ma:** — *pl.* **phan'tasms, phantas'mata.** — *n.* **phan'tasim(e)** (*Shak.*) a fantastic person. — *adjs.* **phantas'mal; phantasmā'lian** (*rare*). — *n.* **phantasmal'ity.** — *adv.* **phantas'mally.** — *adjs.* **phantas'mic, -al; phantasmogenet'ic** begetting phantasms. — *adv.* **phantasmogenet'ically.** [Gr. *phantasma — phantazein*, to make visible — *phainein*, to bring to light — *phaein*, to shine.]

phantasmagoria *fan-taz-mə-gō'ri-ə, -gō'*, *n.* a fantastic series of illusive images or of real forms. — *adjs.* **phantasmago'rial** pertaining to or resembling a phantasmagoria; **phantasmagŏr'ic, -al.** [A name given to a show of optical illusions in 1802, from Fr. *phantasmagorie* — Gr. *phantasma;* an appearance, and perh. *agorā*, an assembly.]

phantasy, phantastic, phantastry. Same as **fantasy,** etc. — *n.* **phantā'siast** one of those Docetae who believed Christ's body to have been a mere phantom.

phantom *fan'təm*, (*Spens.*) **phantosme** *fan-tōm'*) *n.* a deceitful appearance: an immaterial form: a visionary experience: a show without reality. — *adj.* illusive: unreal: spectral: imaginary: ghostly-looking: transparent and hardly visible. — *adjs.* (*arch.*) **phantomat'ic, phan'tomish, phan'tomy** relating to a phantom. — **phantom circuit** (as in telecommunications) an additional circuit which does not in fact exist, the extra performance being obtained by suitable arrangements of real circuits; **phantom limb** the sensation experienced by an amputee of the amputated limb still being attached to the body; **phantom pain** a sensation of pain in a phantom limb. [O.Fr. *fantosme* — Gr. *phantasma.*]

Pharaoh *fā'rō*, *n.* a title of the kings of ancient Egypt: faro (*obs.*). — *adj.* **pharaonic** (*fā-rā-on'ik*). — **Pharaoh('s) ant** a tiny yellow-brown tropical ant which has spread through many countries and infests heated buildings, e.g. hospitals, restaurants, blocks of flats; **Pharaoh's serpent** the coiled ash of burning mercuric thiocyanate; **Pharaonic circumcision** the ancient practice of female circumcision by the removal of the clitoris and labia majora and minora. [L. and Gr. *pharaō* — Heb. *par'ōh* — Egypt. *pr-'o*, great house.]

phare *fār*, *n.* a lighthouse. [Fr.; see **pharos.**]

Pharisee *far'i-sē*, *n.* one of a lay democratic party among the Jews, marked by its legalistic interpretation of the Mosaic law, which by the time of Jesus had degenerated into an obsessive concern with the mass of rules covering the details of everyday life: anyone more careful of the outward forms than of the spirit of religion, a formalist: a very self-righteous or hypocritical person. — *adjs.* **pharisā'ic, -al** pertaining to, or like, the Pharisees: hypocritical. — *adv.* **pharisā'ically.** — *ns.* **pharisā'icalness; phar'isāism** (also **phar'iseeism**). [O.E. *phariseus* — L.L. *pharisaeus* — Gr. *pharisaios* — Heb. *pārūsh*, separated.]

pharmaceutic, -al *fär-mə-sū'tik* (or *-kū'tik*), *-əl*, *adjs.* pertaining to the knowledge or art of preparing medicines. — *n.* **pharmaceu'tical** a chemical used in medicine. — *adv.* **pharmaceu'tically.** — *n.sing.* **pharmaceu'tics** the science of preparing medicines. — *n.* **pharmaceu'tist.** [Gr. *pharmakeutikos.*]

pharmacognosy, pharmacology, etc. See **pharmacy.**

pharmacopoeia *fär-mə-kə-pē'(y)ə*, *n.* a book or list of drugs with directions for their preparation: a collection of drugs. — *adjs.* **pharmacopoe'ial, pharmacopoe'ian.** [Gr. *pharmakopoiiā — pharmakon*, a drug, *poieein*, to make.]

pharmacy *fär'mə-si*, *n.* a department of the medical art which consists in the collecting, preparing, preserving, and dispensing of medicines: the art of preparing and mixing medicines: a druggist's shop: a dispensary. — *ns.* **phar'macist** (*-sist*) a druggist, one skilled in pharmacy: one legally qualified to sell drugs and poisons. — *n.sing.* **pharmacodynam'ics** the science of the action of drugs on the body. — *ns.* **pharmacog'nosy** the study of drugs of plant and animal origin; **pharmacog'nosist.** — *adjs.* **pharmacognos'tic; pharmacokinet'ic.** — *n.* **pharmacokinet'icist.** — *n.sing.* **pharmacokinet'ics** the study of the way the body deals with drugs. — *ns.* **pharmacol'ogist; pharmacol'ogy** the science of drugs; **pharmacop'olist** (Gr. *pōleein*, to sell) a dealer in drugs. [Gr. *pharmakeiā*, use of drugs, *pharmakon*, a drug.]

pharos *fā'ros, n.* a lighthouse or beacon. [From the famous lighthouse on the island of *Pharos* in the Bay of Alexandria.]

pharynx *far'ingks, n.* the cleft or cavity forming the upper part of the gullet, lying behind the nose, mouth, and larynx: — *pl.* **phar'ynges** (*-in-jēz*), **phar'ynxes.** — *adjs.* **pharyngal** (*fa-ring'gl*), **pharyngeal** (*fa-rin'ji-əl* or *-jē'əl*); **pharyngitic** (*far-in-jit'ik*) pertaining to pharyngitis. — *n.* **pharyngitis** (*far-in-jī'tis*) inflammation of the mucous membrane of the pharynx. — *ns.* **pharyngol'ogy** the study of the pharynx and its diseases; **pharyngoscope** (*fa-ring'gə-skōp*) and instrument for inspecting the pharynx; **pharyngoscopy** (*far-ing-gos'kə-pi*); **pharyngot'omy** the operation of making an incision into the pharynx. [Gr. *pharynx, -ygos*, later *-yngos*.]

phase[1] *fāz, n.* the appearance at a given time of the illuminated surface exhibited by the moon or a planet — also **phasis** (*fā'sis*): the aspect or appearance of anything at any stage: the stage of advancement in a periodic change, measured from some standard point: a stage in growth or development (*lit.* and *fig.*): the sum of all those portions of a material system which are identical in chemical composition and physical state (*chem.*): a morph (*zool.*): one of the circuits in an electrical system in which there are two or more alternating currents out of phase with each other by equal amounts (*elect.*): — *pl.* **phases** (*fā'ziz, -sēz*). — *v.t.* to do by phases or stages. — *adjs.* **phased** adjusted to be in the same phase at the same time: by stages; **phase'less** unchanging; **pha'sic** (or *-sik*). — **phase= contrast, phase-difference, microscope** one in which the clear detail is obtained by means of a device that alters the speed of some of the rays of light, so that staining is unnecessary. — **in, out of, phase** in the same phase together, or in different phases; **phase in, out** to begin, cease, gradually to use, make, etc.; **primary phase** crude technical raw material. [Gr. *phasis* — *phaein*, to shine.]

phase[2]. See **feeze.**

phasic, phasis. See **phase**[1].

phasis. See **phatic.**

Phasma *faz'mə, n.* the spectre-insect (stick-insect, leaf-insect) genus. — *n.* **phas'mid** a member of the **Phas'midae** or **Phasmat'idae,** the family to which the genus Phasma belongs, or of the (sub)order **Phasmatō'dea.** [Gr. *phasma*, a spectre.]

phatic *fat'ik, adj.* using speech for social reasons, to communicate feelings rather than ideas. — *n.* **phasis** (*fā'sis*). [Gr. *phasis*, utterance.]

pheasant *fez'nt, n.* a richly-coloured gallinaceous bird (*Phasianus colchicus*), a half-wild game-bird in Britain: extended to others of the same or kindred genus (as *golden, silver, Argus, Amherst's* pheasant) and to other birds: the tufted grouse (*U.S.*): a francolin (*S.Afr.*): the lyre-bird (*Austr.*): also the coucal (*swamp pheasant*): the flesh of the bird as food: — *pl.* **pheasant(s).** — *n.* **pheas'antry** an enclosure for rearing pheasants. — **pheas'ant's-eye** a ranunculaceous plant (Adonis) with deep-red dark-centred flowers. [A.Fr. *fesant* — L. *phāsiānus* — Gr. *phāsiānos* (*ornis*), (bird) from the river Phasis, in Colchis.]

pheazar *fē'zər,* (*Shak.*) *n.* perh. one who feezes, perh. for vizier.

pheer, pheere. Same as **fere**[1].

pheeze, pheese. Same as **feeze.**

phellem *fel'əm,* (*bot.*) *n.* cork. — *ns.* **phell'oderm** (Gr. *derma*, skin) a layer of secondary cortex formed by the phellogen on its inner side; **phellogen** (*fel'ō-jen*) a layer of meristem that forms cork without, otherwise cork-cambium. — *adjs.* **phellogenetic** (*-ji-net'ik*); **phell'-**

oid cork-like and formed like cork, but not, or very slightly, suberised. — *n.* **phelloplas'tic** a model in cork. — *n.sing.* **phelloplas'tics** the making of models in cork. [Gr. *phellos,* cork.]

phelonion, phaelonion *fi-lō'ni-on, n.* an Eastern vestment like a chasuble. [Late Gr. *phailŏnion, phĕlŏnion,* dim. of *phailŏnēs, phelŏnēs,* for *phainolēs* — L. *paenula,* a cloak.]

phen-, pheno- *fēn-, fen-ō-,* in composition, showing: visible: related to benzene (**phene**). [Gr. *phainein,* to show.]

phenacetin *fin-as'i-tin, n.* an antipyretic drug, $C_{10}H_{13}NO_2$. [**acetic** and **phene.**]

phenacite *fen'ə-sīt,* **phenakite** *-kīt, ns.* a mineral, beryllium silicate, sometimes deceptively like quartz. — *ns.* **phen'akism** deceit; **phenakist'oscope** an instrument in which figures on a disc seen successively through a slit give the impression of motion. [Gr. *phenax* and *phenākistēs,* a deceiver, *skopeein,* to look at.]

phencyclidine *fen-sī'kli-dēn, n.* an analgesic and anaesthetic drug, $C_{17}H_{25}N \cdot HCl$, also used as a hallucinogen. [*phen*, *cyclo*-, and piperi*dine*.]

phene *fēn, n.* an old name for benzene. — *n.* **phen'ate** a phenolate. — *adj.* **phēn'ic** (or *fen'*) of benzene or of phenyl. [Gr. *phainein,* to show, because obtained in the manufacture of illuminating gas.]

phenetics *fi-net'iks,* (*biol.*) *n.sing.* a system of classification of organisms based on observable similarities and differences irrespective of the relatedness or unrelatedness of the organisms. — *adj.* **phenet'ic** [*pheno*type and **genetics.**]

phengite *fen'jīt, n.* a transparent stone used by the ancients for windows, prob. selenite: sometimes applied to kinds of mica. — Also **phengites** (*fen-jī'tēz*). [Gr. *phengītēs — phengos,* light.]

Phenician. Same as **Phoenician.**

pheno-. See **phen-.**

phenobarbitone *fē-nō-bär'bi-tōn, n.* a sedative and hypnotic drug.

phenocryst *fē'nō-krist, n.* a larger crystal in a porphyritic rock. [Gr. *phainein,* to show, and **crystal.**]

phenogam, etc. See **phaenogam.**

phenol *fē'nol, n.* carbolic acid, a weak acid, C_6H_5OH, got as hygroscopic needles from coal-tar, a powerful disinfectant: extended to the class of aromatic compounds with one or more hydroxyl groups directly attached to the benzene nucleus, weak acids with reactions of alcohols. — *n.* **phēn'olate** a salt of a phenol. — *adj.* **phenol'ic.** — *n.* **phenolphthalein** (*fē-nol-fthal'i-in,* or *-thal'*) a substance ($C_{20}H_{14}O_4$) got from phenol and phthalic anhydride, brilliant red in alkalis, colourless in acids, used as an indicator. — **phenolic resins** a group of plastics made from a phenol and an aldehyde. [See **phene; -ol** from **alcohol.**]

phenology, phaenology *fē-nol'ə-ji, n.* the study of organisms as affected by climate, esp. dates of seasonal phenomena, as opening of flowers, arrival of migrants. — *adj.* **phenological** (*-ə-loj'*). — *n.* **phenol'ogist.** [Gr. *phainein,* to show, *logos,* discourse.]

phenomenon, now rarely **phaenomenon,** *fi-nom'i-nən* or *-non, n.* anything directly apprehended by the senses or one of them: an event that may be observed: the appearance which anything makes to our consciousness, as distinguished from what it is in itself: (*loosely*) a remarkable or unusual person, thing, or appearance, a prodigy: — *pl.* **phenom'ena** (sometimes used *erron.* for *n. sing.*). — *adj.* **phenom'enal** pertaining to a phenomenon: of the nature of a phenomenon: very or unexpectedly large, good, etc. (*coll.*). — *v.t.* **phenom'enalise, -ize** to represent as a phenomenon. — *ns.* **phenom'enalism** the philosophical doctrine that phenomena are the only realities, or that knowledge can only comprehend phenomena — also *externalism*; **phenom'enalist.** — *adj.* **phenomenalist'ic.** — *n.* **phenomenality** (*-al'i-ti*) the character of being phenomenal. — *adv.* **phenom'enally.** — *v.t.* **phenom'enise, -ize** to bring into the world of experience. — *ns.* **phenom'enism**

phenomenalism; **phenom'enist**. — *adj.* **phenomenolog'-ical**. — *ns.* **phenomenol'ogist; phenomenol'ogy** the science, or a description, of phenomena: the philosophy of Edmund Husserl (1859–1938) — opposed to positivism, and concerned with the experiences of the self. [Gr. *phainomenon*, pl. *-a*, neut. pr.p. pass. of *phainein*, to show.]

phenothiazine *fē-nō-thī'ə-zēn, fen-, n.* a toxic, heterocyclic compound, $C_{12}H_9NS$, used as a veterinary anthelmintic: any of a number of derivatives of this, used as tranquillisers. [**pheno-, thio-, azo-** and *-ine*.]

phenotype *fēn'ō-tīp, n.* the observable characteristics of an organism produced by the interaction of genes and environment: a group of individuals having the same characteristics of this kind. — *v.t.* to categorise by phenotype. — *adjs.* **phenotypic(al)** (*-tip'*). [Gr. *phainein*, to show, and **type**.]

phenyl *fē'nil, n.* an organic radical, C_6H_5, found in benzene, phenol, etc. — *adj.* **phenyl'ic**. — *ns.* **phenylal'-anin(e)** an amino-acid present in most food proteins; **phenylbutazone** (*-būt'ə-zōn*) an analgesic and antipyretic used in the treatment of rheumatic disorders and also, illegally, in horse-doping; **phenylketonuria** (*-kē-tō-nū'ri-ə*) an inherited metabolic disorder in infants in which there is an inability to break down phenylalanine, commonly later resulting in mental defect, unless a phenylalanine-free diet is given; **phenylketonū'ric** one who suffers from phenylketonuria. — Also *adj.* [**phene**, and Gr. *hylē*, material.]

pheon *fē'on, (her.) n.* the barbed head of a dart or arrow, esp. as a heraldic bearing. [Ety. dub.]

Pherecratic *fer-e-krat'ik*, **Pherecrataean** *-krə-tē'ən, adjs.* of the Greek poet *Pherecratēs*. — *n.* a metre used by him, spondee, dactyl, spondee, with variations.

pheromone *fer'ə-mōn, n.* a chemical substance secreted by an animal which influences the behaviour of others of its species, e.g. queen bee substance. [Gr. *pherein*, to bear, and **hormone**.]

phese. See **feeze**.

phew *fū, interj.* an exclamation of petty vexation, unexpected difficulty, impatience, relief, contempt, etc. [A half-formed whistle.]

phi *fī, fē, n.* the twenty-first letter (Φ, φ) of the Greek alphabet, orig. as aspirated *p* (as in *upheave*), now pronounced as *f* and transliterated *ph*: as a Greek numeral φ' = 500, ͺφ = 500 000. [Gr. *phei*.]

phial *fī'əl, n.* a vessel for liquids, esp. now a small medicine-bottle. — *v.t.* to put or keep in a phial: — *pr.p.* **phi'alling**; *pa.t.* and *pa.p.* **phi'alled.** — *adj.* **phi'aliform** saucer-shaped. [L. *phiala* — Gr. *phialē*, a broad shallow bowl.]

Phi Beta Kappa *fī' or fē', bē' or bā'tə kap'ə,* the oldest of the American college Greek letter societies. [Gr. Φ.Β.Κ., the initial letters of its motto — *Philosophiā biou kybernētēs*, Philosophy is the guide of life.]

phil- *fil-,* **philo-** *fil-ō-,* in composition, used to denote loving: lover. — **-phil** *-fil,* **-phile** *-fīl,* lover of: loving; **-philia, -phily** love of; **-philic** (also, as *n.* suffix, lover of), **-philous** loving; **-philus** in zoological names, lover of (usu. a specified food). [Gr. *philos*, friend — *phileein*, to love.]

philabeg. See **filibeg**.

Philadelphian *fil-ə-del'fi-ən, adj.* of the Pergamene city of Philadelphia or Philadelpheia (Ala-shehr): of Philadelphia, Pennsylvania: of a mystic sect emphasising brotherly love, founded in London in 1652 under the influence of Boehme. — *n.* a native or inhabitant of Philadelphia: a member of the Philadelphian sect. — **Philadelphia lawyer** a very able, shrewd, or sharp lawyer. [**phil-**, Gr. *adelphos*, a brother, *adelphē*, a sister.]

Philadelphus *fil-ə-del'fəs, n.* a genus of tall deciduous shrubs with showy flowers (fam. **Philadelphā'ceae**): (without *cap.*) any shrub of this genus, esp. the mock-orange. [Mod. L., — Gr. *philadelphon*, loving one's brother.]

philamot. See **filemot**.

philander *fil-an'dər, n.* (with *cap.*) a conventional proper name for a lover: a lover: a dangler after women: a male flirt: a philandering. — *v.i.* to make love: to flirt or coquet. — *n.* **philan'derer.** [Gr. *philandros*, fond of men or of a husband — *anēr, andros,* a man, husband; misapplied as if meaning a loving man.]

philanthropy *fil-an'thrə-pi, n.* love of mankind esp. as shown in services to general welfare. — *ns.* **philanthrope** (*fil'ən-thrōp*), **philan'thropist** one who tries to benefit mankind. — *adjs.* **philanthropic** (*-throp'ik*), **-al** doing good to others, benevolent. — *adv.* **philanthrop'-ically.** [Gr. *philanthrōpiā* — *anthrōpos,* a man.]

philately *fil-at'i-li, n.* the study and collection of postage and revenue stamps and labels. — *adj.* **philatelic** (*fil-ə-tel'ik*). — *n.* **philat'elist.** [Fr. *philatélie,* invented in 1864 — Gr. *atelēs,* tax-free — *a-,* priv., *telos,* tax.]

-phile. See **phil-**.

philharmonic *fil-är-mon'ik,* also *-här-, ͺər-, adj.* loving music. — **philharmonic pitch** a musical pitch slightly higher than French pitch (439 vibrations a second for A). [**phil-,** Gr. *harmoniā,* harmony.]

philhellenic *fil-hel-ēn'ik,* or *-en'ik, adj.* loving Greece, esp. Greek culture: favouring the Greeks. — *ns.* **philhellene** (*-hel'ēn*), **philhellenist** (*-hel'in-ist*) a supporter of Greece, esp. in 1821–32; **philhell'enism.** [**phil-,** Gr. *Hellēn,* a Greek.]

p(h)ilhorse *fil'hörs, pil'hörs, (Shak.) ns.* Same as **fill-horse** or **thill-horse.** [See **fill²**, **thill¹**.]

-philia. See **phil-**.

philibeg. Same as **filibeg**.

Philippian *fil-ip'i-ən, n.* a native of *Philippi* in Macedonia. — Also *adj.*

Philippic *fil-ip'ik, n.* one of the three orations of Demosthenes against Philip of Macedon: (without *cap.*) any discourse full of invective. — *v.i.* **Phil'ippise, -ize** to side with Philip: to utter an oracle inspired by Philip, or by bribery of the prevailing power. [Gr. *philippikos, philippizein* — *Philippos,* Philip.]

philippina, philippine. Same as **philopoena**.

Philistine *fil'is-tīn* (U.S. *fil-is'tīn*), *n.* one of the ancient inhabitants of south-west Palestine, enemies of the Israelites: a name applied by German students to persons not connected with the university (also **Philis'ter;** *Ger.*): (also without *cap.*) a person of material outlook, indifferent or hostile to culture: (without *cap.*) an enemy (*slang*): (without *cap.*) a bailiff (*slang*). — *adjs.* **Philistē'an, Philis'tian** (both *Milt.*), **Phil'istine** (sometimes without *cap.*). — *v.t.* **Phil'istinise, -ize** (*-tin-*). — *n.* **Phil'istinism** (sometimes without *cap.*). [Gr. *Philistīnos, Palaistīnos* — Heb. *P'lıshtım.*]

phillabeg, phillibeg. Same as **filibeg**.

phillipsite *fil'ips-īt, n.* a zeolite, hydrated silicate of potassium, calcium, and aluminium, often cross-shaped by twinning. [J. W. *Phillips,* mineralogist.]

phillumeny *fil-ōō'mən-i, n.* a fantastic word for collecting matchbox labels. — *n.* **phillu'menist.** [L. *lūmen, -inis,* light.]

Phillyrea *fil-ir'i-ə, n.* the mock privet genus, Mediterranean shrubs akin to olive and privet. [Gr. *phillyreā.*]

philo-. See **phil-**.

Philodendron *fil-ō-den'dron, n.* a genus of tropical American climbing plants: (without *cap.*) a plant of this genus. [Gr. *philodendros,* fond of trees.]

philogyny *fil-oj'i-ni, n.* love of women. — *adj.* **philog'-ynous.** — *n.* **philog'ynist.** [Gr. *philogyniā* — *gynē,* a woman.]

philology *fil-ol'ə-ji, n.* the science of language: the study of etymology, grammar, rhetoric, and literary criticism: the study of literary and non-literary texts: the study of culture through texts: orig., the knowledge which enabled men to study and explain the languages of Greece and Rome. — *ns.* **philol'oger, philologian** (*-ə-lō'*), **philol'ogist, phil'ologue** (*-log*) one versed in philology. — *adjs.* **philologic** (*-ə-loj'ik*), **-al.** — *adv.* **philolog'ically.** — **comparative philology** the study of languages by comparing their history, forms, and relationships with each other. [Gr. *philologiā* — **phil-** (q.v.), *logos*, word.]

philomath *fil'ə-math*, *n.* a lover of learning. — *adjs.* **philomath'ic, -al.** — *n.* **philomathy** (*-om'ə-thi*) love of learning. [Gr. *philomathēs*, fond of learning — *math-*, root of *manthanein*, to learn.]

Philomel *fil'ō-mel*, **Philomela** *-mē'lə*, *ns.* the nightingale personified. — Also (*obs.*) **Phil'omene** (*-mēn*). [Gr. *Philomēla*, daughter of Pandion, changed into a nightingale or swallow.]

philomot *fil'ə-mot*, (*Addison*) *n.* Same as **filemot**.

philop(o)ena, philippina *fil-ip-ē'nə*, **philippine** *fil'ip-ēn*, *ns.* a game in which each of two persons eats a twin kernel of a nut, and one pays a forfeit to the other on certain conditions: the nut itself: the gift made as a forfeit. [Apparently from the Ger. formula of claiming the gift, *Guten Morgen, Vielliebchen*, Good morning, well-beloved, confused with Gr. *philos*, friend, *poinē*, penalty, and with Ger. *Philippchen*, little Philip.]

philoprogenitive *fil-ō-prō-jen'i-tiv*, *adj.* having or relating to instinctive love of offspring: inclined to produce offspring. — *n.* **philoprogen'itiveness.** [**philo-**, L. *progeniēs*, progeny.]

philosopher *fi-los'ə-fər*, *n.* a lover of wisdom: one versed in or devoted to philosophy: formerly, a student of natural science or of the occult: now mainly a metaphysician: one who acts calmly and rationally in the affairs and changes of life. — *ns.* **philosophas'ter** (see **-aster**) a superficial philosopher: one who poses as a philosopher; **phil'osophe** (*-sof, -zof,* or *-zof'*) a philosopher: a thinker of the type of the French Encyclopaedists; **philos'opheress, philos'ophess** (both *rare*). — *adjs.* **philosophic** (*-sof'* or *-zof'*), **-al** pertaining to or according to philosophy: skilled in or given to philosophy: befitting a philosopher: rational: calm. — *adv.* **philosoph'ically.** — *v.i.* **philos'ophise, -ize** to reason like a philosopher: to form philosophical theories. — *ns.* **philos'ophiser, -z-** a would-be philosopher; **philos'ophism** would-be philosophy; **philos'ophist.** — *adjs.* **philosophist'ic, -al.** — *n.* **philos'ophy** orig., pursuit of wisdom and knowledge: investigation of the nature of being: knowledge of the causes and laws of all things: the principles underlying any department of knowledge: reasoning: a particular philosophical system: calmness of temper. — **philosopher's stone** an imaginary stone or mineral compound, long sought after by alchemists as a means of transforming other metals into gold; **philosophical pitch** a pitch used in acoustical calculations based on 512 vibrations for treble C. — **moral, natural, philosophy** see **moral, natural.** [Gr. *philosophos* — *sophiā*, wisdom.]

-philous. See **phil-**.

philoxenia *fil-ok-sē'ni-ə*, *n.* hospitality. [Gr. — *xenos*, guest, stranger.]

philtre, philter *fil'tər*, *n.* a drink, or (rarely) a spell, to excite love. [Fr. *philtre* — L. *philtrum* — Gr. *philtron* — *phileein*, to love, *-tron*, agent-suffix.]

-phily. See **phil-**.

phimosis *fi-mō'sis*, *n.* narrowing of the preputial orifice. [Gr. *phimōsis*, muzzling — *phīmos*, a muzzle.]

phinnock. Same as **finnock**.

phisnomy *fiz'nə-mi*, *n.* an old form of **physiognomy**, the face.

phiz *fiz*, **phizog** *fiz-og'*, (*slang*) *ns.* the face. [**physiognomy.**]

phlebitis *fli-bī'tis*, *n.* inflammation of a vein. — *n.* **phlebolite** (*fleb'ə-līt*; Gr. *lithos*, stone) a calcareous concretion found in a vein. — *v.t.* **phlebot'omise, -ize** (Gr. *tomē*, a cut) to bleed. — *ns.* **phlebot'omist** a bloodletter; **phlebot'omy** blood-letting. [Gr. *phleps, phlebos*, a vein.]

Phlegethontic *fleg-i-thon'tik*, *adj.* of or like the *Phlegethon*, a fiery river of Hades. [Gr. *phlegethōn, -ontos*, pr.p. of *phlegethein* — *phlegein*, to burn.]

phlegm *flem*, *n.* the thick, slimy matter secreted in the throat, and discharged by coughing, regarded in old physiology as one (cold and moist) of the four hu-

mours or bodily fluids: the temperament supposed to be due to its predominance, sluggish indifference: calmness: one of the principles of old chemistry, a watery distilled liquid. — Following words pron. *fleg-* unless indicated otherwise. — *adj.* **phlegmagogic** (*-goj'-ik, -gog'ik*). — *ns.* **phleg'magogue** (*-gog*) a medicine expelling phlegm; **phlegmā'sia** inflammation, esp. *Phlegmasia alba dolens*, white-leg. — *adjs.* **phlegmat'ic, -al** abounding in or generating phlegm: cold and sluggish: not easily excited. — *adv.* **phlegmat'ically.** — *n.* **phleg'mon** purulent inflammation. — *adjs.* **phlegmon'ic, phleg'monoid, phleg'monous; phlegmy** (*flem'i*). [By later return to Greek spelling, from M.E. *fleem, fleme, flemme* — O.Fr. *flemme, fleume* — L. *phlegma* — Gr. *phlegma, -atos*, flame, inflammation, phlegm (regarded as produced by heat), *phlegmasiā, phlegmonē*, inflammation — *phlegein*, to burn.]

Phleum *flē'əm*, *n.* a small genus of grasses, timothy-grass. [Gr. *phleōs*, plume-grass.]

phloem *flō'əm*, *n.* the bast or sieve-tube portion of a vascular bundle, by which elaborated food materials are transported in a plant. [Gr. *phloos*, bark.]

phlogiston *flo-jis'ton, -gis'ton,* or *-tən*, *n.* an imaginary element, believed in the 18th century to separate from every combustible body in burning. — *adj.* **phlogis'tic** of, like, or containing phlogiston (*chem.*): combustible (*arch.*): inflammatory (*med.*): fiery. — *v.t.* **phlogis'ticate** to combine with phlogiston. [Gr. neut. of vbl. adj. *phlogistos*, burnt, inflammable — *phlogizein*, to set on fire.]

phlogopite *flog'ə-pīt*, *n.* a magnesia mica, yellow or brown. [Gr. *phlogōpos*, fiery-looking — *phlox*, flame, *ōps*, face.]

Phlomis *flō'mis*, *n.* a genus of labiate herbs and shrubs with whorls of white, yellow or purple flowers and wrinkled, often woolly, leaves: (wthout *cap.*) a plant of this genus. [Gr. *phlomis*, mullein.]

Phlox *floks*, *n.* a Siberian and American genus of Polemoniaceae, well-known garden plants: (without *cap.*) a plant of this genus: — *pl.* **phlox** or **phlox'es**. [Gr. *phlox*, flame, wallflower — *phlegein*, to burn.]

phlyctaena, -tena *flik-tē'nə*, (*med.*) *n.* a small blister or vesicle: — *pl.* **-nae** (*-nē*). [Gr. *phlyktaina*, a blister — *phlyein*, to swell.]

pho. Same as **foh**.

phobia *fō'bi-ə*, **phobism** *fō'bizm*, *ns.* a fear, aversion, or hatred, esp. morbid and irrational. — **-phobe** in composition, one who has a (specified) phobia. — **-phobia** in composition, fear or hatred of (a specified object, condition, etc.). — *adj.* **phō'bic** like or pertaining to a phobia. — *n.* **phō'bist**. [Gr. *phobos*, fear.]

Phoca *fō'kə*, *n.* the common seal genus: (without *cap.*) a seal: (without *cap.*) a scaly sea-monster (*Spens.*): — *pl.* **pho'cas, pho'cae** (*-sē*). — *n.pl.* **Phocidae** (*fō'si-dē*) the true seals, with backward-turned hind-flippers and no external ear. — *adj.* **pho'cine** (*fō'sīn*) relating to seals: seal-like. [L. *phōca* — Gr. *phōkē*, a seal.]

Phocaena *fō-sē'nə*, *n.* the porpoise genus. [Gr. *phōkaina*.]

phocomelia *fō-kō-mēl'i-ə, -mel'*, or *-yə*, *n.* the condition of having one or more limbs like a seal's flippers, shortened and close to the body. [Gr. *phōkē*, seal, *melos*, limb.]

phoebe *fē'bi*, *n.* a N. American flycatcher of the genus *Sayornis*. [Imit.]

Phoebus *fē'bəs*, *n.* Apollo, the Greek sun-god: the sun. — *n.* **Phoebe** (*fē'bē*) his sister Artemis, the moon-goddess: the moon. — *adj.* **Phoebe'an.** [Latinised — Gr. *Phoibos, Phoibē; phoibos, -ē*, bright, *phaein*, to shine.]

Phoenician *fi-nish'ən, -yən*, *adj.* of *Phoenicia*, on the coast of Syria, its people, colonies (including Carthage), language, and arts. — *n.* one of the people of Phoenicia: their Semitic language. [Gr. *Phoinix, -īkos*.]

phoenix *fē'niks*, *n.* a fabulous Arabian bird, worshipped in ancient Egypt, the only individual of its kind, that burned itself every 500 years or so and rose rejuvenated from its ashes: hence anything that rises from its own or its predecessor's ashes: a paragon: a southern constellation. [O.E. *fenix*, later assimilated to L. *phoenix* — Gr. *phoinix*.]

phoh. Same as **foh.**

Pholas *fō'ləs*, *n.* the piddock genus of rock-boring molluscs: (without *cap.*) a mollusc of this genus: — *pl.* **pholades** (*fō'lə-dēz*). [Gr. *phōlas, -ados,* (adj.) lurking in a hole, (n.) the date-shell.]

pholidosis *fol-id-ō'sis*, *n.* arrangement of scales, as in fishes and reptiles. [Gr. *pholis, -idos,* scale.]

phon *fon*, *n.* a unit of loudness level on a logarithmic (decibel) scale. — In composition **phon-, phono-** (*fon-, fō'nō-, fo-nō-*) sound, voice. — *adj.* **phonal** (*fōn'l*) vocal. — *v.i.* **phōnate'** to produce vocal sound, to utter voice. — *n.* **phōnā'tion** production of vocal sound. — *adj.* **phōn'atory** (or *fō-nā'tər-i*). — *ns.* **phonasthenia** (*fō-nas-thē'ni-ə*; Gr. *astheneia,* weakness) weakness of voice: difficulty in speaking; **phonautograph** (*fōn-ö'tə-gräf*) an instrument for recording sound vibrations. — *adj.* **phonautographic** (*-graf'ik*). — *adv.* **phonautograph'ically.** — *n.* **phone** (*fōn*) an elementary speech sound: a telephone receiver: (also **'phone;** *coll.*) a telephone. — *v.t., v.i.* (also **'phone;** *coll.*) to telephone. — **-phone** *adj.* and noun combining form, speaking, or one who speaks (a given language), as in *Francophone.* — *adj.* **phonemat'ic** phonemic. — *adv.* **phonemat'ically.** — *n.* **phoneme** (*fōn'ēm*; Gr. *phōnēma,* a sound) a group or family of speech sounds felt in any one language to be merely variants of one sound. — *adj.* **phonemic** (*-nēm'* or *-nem'*). — *adv.* **phonēm'ically.** — *n.* **phonemicisā'-tion, -z-.** — *v.t.* **phonēm'icise, -ize** to analyse into phonemes: to treat as a phoneme. — *n.* **phonēm'icist.** — *n.sing.* **phonēm'ics** the science of phonemic groups and contrasts. — *n.* **phonend'oscope** (Gr. *endō,* within, *skopeein,* to view) a device which amplifies small sounds (esp. in the human body). — *adj.* **phonetic** (*fō-net'ik, fə-*) of, concerning, according to, or representing the sounds of spoken language. — Also **phonet'ical.** — *adv.* **phonet'ically** according to pronunciation. — *ns.* **phonetician** (*fō-ni-tish'ən*) one versed in phonetics; **phoneticisā'tion, -z-.** — *v.t.* **phonet'icise, -ize** to make phonetic: to represent phonetically. — *ns.* **phonet'icism** phonetic character or representation; **phonet'icist** one who advocates phonetic spelling. — *n. sing.* **phonet'ics** that branch of linguistic science that deals with pronunciation, speech production, etc. — *n.pl.* **phonetic representations.** — *ns.* **pho'netism** phonetic writing; **pho'netist** a phonetician: an advocate or user of phonetic spelling. — *adj.* **phōn'ic** (or *fon'ik*) of sound, esp. vocal sound: voiced. — *n. sing.* **phōn'ics** (or *fon'iks*) the science of sound, or of spoken sounds. — *n.* **phon'meter** same as **phonometer** (see below). — *adj.* **phonocamptic** (*fō-nə-kamp'tik*; Gr. *kamptein,* to bend; *arch.*) reflecting sound, echoing: relating to echoes. — *n. sing.* **phonocamp'tics** the acoustics of echoes. — *ns.* **phō'nofiddle** a one-stringed musical instrument which sounds through a metal amplifying horn; **phonogram** (*fō'nə-gram*) a character representing a sound: a phonographic record; **phonograph** (*fō'nə-gräf*; Gr. *graphein,* to write) a character used to represent a sound: Edison's instrument for recording sounds on a cylinder and reproducing them: the ordinary word for any gramophone (*U.S.*); **phonographer** (*fō-nog'rə-fər*), **phonog'raphist** a writer of phonographic shorthand. — *adj.* **phonographic** (*fō-nə-graf'ik*) phonetic: of phonography: of or by means of the phonograph. — *adv.* **phonograph'ically.** — *ns.* **phonog'raphy** (*fō-nog'rə-fi*) the art of representing each spoken sound by a distinct character: Pitman's phonetic shorthand: the use of the phonograph; **phonolite** (*fō'nə-līt*; Gr. *lithos,* a stone) clinkstone, a fine-grained intermediate igneous rock that rings under the hammer, composed of nepheline (or leucite), sanidine, and other minerals. — *adj.* **phonolitic** (*-lit'ik*). — *n.* **phonology** (*fō-nol'ə-ji*; Gr. *logos,* discourse) phonetics: now generally (the study of) the system of sounds in a language,

and sometimes the history of their changes. — *adj.* **phonolog'ical.** — *ns.* **phonol'ogist; phonom'eter** (Gr. *metron,* measure) apparatus for estimating the loudness level of a sound in phons by subjective comparison; **phon'on** a quantum of thermal energy in a crystal lattice made to vibrate by sound waves or heat; **phonopho'bia** a morbid fear of noise, or of speaking aloud; **phonophore** (*fō'nə-fōr, -för*), **phonopore** (*fō'nō-pōr, -pör;* Gr. *phoros,* carrying, *poros,* passage) a sound-conducting apparatus, of various kinds: a device for telephoning and telegraphing simultaneously by the same wire. — *n.sing.* **phonotac'tics** (Gr., — *tassein,* to arrange) (the study of) the ways in which the sounds of a language can appear in the words of that language; **phonotype** (*fō'nə-tīp;* Gr. *typos,* impression) phonetic type. — *v.t.* to print phonetically. — *adjs.* **phonotyp'ic** (*-tip'ik*), **-al.** — *ns.* **phō'notypist** (or *-tip'ist*); **phō'notypy** (*-tip-i*). — **phone'-call; phone'card** a card, purchasable from newsagents, tobacconists, post offices, etc., which can be used instead of cash to pay for phone-calls from certain public telephone kiosks (also *adj.*); **phone freak, phreak** (*slang*) one who misuses the telephone, by telephoning obscene messages to strangers, by trying to make free calls, etc.; **phone freaking, phreaking; phone'-in** a radio programme which consists mainly of telephone calls from listeners on selected topics; **pho'ner-in'; phonetic alphabet** a system (used in voice communications) in which letters of the alphabet are identified by means of code words: a list of symbols used in phonetic transcriptions; **phonetic spelling** the writing of a language by means of a separate symbol for every sound: often applied to a compromise, or a departure from conventional spelling more or less adapted as a guide to pronunciation; **phonic method** a method of teaching reading through the phonetic value of letters and groups of letters. [Gr. *phōnē,* voice, sound.]

phonal, phonasthenia, phonate, etc., **phonautograph,** etc., **phone, phonematic,** etc., **phonemic,** etc., **phonetic,** etc., See **phon.**

phoney, phony *fō'ni,* (*slang*), *n.* and *adj.* counterfeit: unreal. — *v.t.* to fake, counterfeit, achieve by faking. — *n.* **phon'eyness, phon'iness.** [Origin uncertain; perh. — Ir. *fáinne,* a ring, from the old practice of tricking people into buying gilt rings which they believed to be genuine gold.]

phono-. For words beginning thus, see **phon.**

phony. See **phoney.**

phooey *fōō'i, interj.* an exclamation of contempt, scorn, disbelief, etc. [Perh. conn. with **phew,** or a similar exclamation, or perh. from Yiddish *fooy,* Ger. *pfui.*]

-phor *-för,* in composition used to denote 'carrier', as *semaphore, chromatophore.* — **-phoresis** noun combining form denoting a transmission, migration, as *electrophoresis.* [Gr. *phoros,* bearing — *pherein.*]

phorminx *för'mingks, n.* a kind of cithara: — *pl.* **phormin'ges** (*-jēz*). [Gr.]

Phormium *för'mi-əm, n.* a New Zealand genus of the lily family — New Zealand flax or flax-lily: (without *cap.*) a plant of this genus. [Latinised — Gr. *phormion,* mat, faggot, kind of sage.]

phosgene *fos'jēn, n.* a poisonous gas, carbonyl chloride ($COCl_2$) prepared from carbon monoxide and chlorine in sunlight. [Gr. *phōs,* light, and the root of *gignesthai,* to be produced.]

phosphate, etc., **phosphatide, phosphaturia.** See **Phosphorus.**

phosphene *fos'fēn, n.* light seen when the eyeball is pressed: a luminous pattern seen when the brain is stimulated electrically. [Gr. *phōs,* light, *phainein,* to show.]

Phosphorus *fos'fər-əs, n.* the morning-star: (without *cap.*) a non-metallic element (symbol P; at. numb. 15), a waxy, poisonous, and inflammable element giving out light in the dark. — *n.* **phosphate** (*fos'fāt*) a salt of phosphoric acid. — *v.t.* to treat or coat with a phosphate as a means of preventing corrosion. — *adj.*

phosphatic (*fos-fat'ik*) of the nature of, or containing, a phosphate. — *n.* **phos'phatide** a phospholipid. — *v.t.* **phos'phatise, -ize** to phosphate. — *ns.* **phosphaturia** (*fos-fat-ū'ri-ə*) excess of phosphates in the urine; **phos'phide** (*-fīd*) a compound of phosphorus and another element; **phos'phine** (*-fēn, -fīn*) phosphuretted hydrogen gas (PH₃): extended to substances analogous to amines with phosphorus instead of nitrogen; **phos'phite** a salt of phosphorous acid; **phospholip'id** a lipid which contains a phosphate group and usu. also a nitrogenous group, a component of cell membranes; **phosphon'ium** the radical PH₄, analogous to ammonium; **phosphopro'tein** any of a number of compounds formed by a protein with a substance containing phosphorus, other than a nucleic acid or lecithin; **Phos'phor** the morning-star: (without *cap.*) phosphorus: (without *cap.*) a phosphorescent or fluorescent substance generally. — *v.t.* **phos'phorate** to combine with or impregnate with phosphorus: to make phosphorescent. — *v.i.* **phosphoresce'** to shine in the dark like phosphorus. — *n.* **phosphoresc'ence.** — *adj.* **phosphoresc'ent.** — *n.* **phos'phoret** (or *-et '; obs.*) a phosphide. — *adjs.* **phos'phoretted** (or *-et'*) see **phosphuretted; phosphoric** (*fos-for'ik*) of or like phosphorus: phosphorescent: containing phosphorus in higher valency (*chem.*) (**phosphoric acid** any of the following acids — orthophosphoric, H₃PO₄, metaphosphoric, HPO₃, pyrophosphoric H₄P₂O₇; **phosphoric anhydride** P₂O₅). — *v.t.* **phos'phorise, -ize** to combine or impregnate with phosphorus: to make phosphorescent. — *ns.* **phos'phorism** (*obs.*) phosphorescence: poisoning by phosphorus; **phos'phorite** impure massive apatite. — *adj.* **phos'phorous** phosphorescent: containing phosphorus in lower valency (*chem.*) (**phosphorous acid** H₃PO₃; **phosphorous anhydride** P₂O₃). — *ns.* **phosphor'ylase** an enzyme playing a part in phosphorylation. — *v.t.* **phosphor'ylate.** — *n.* **phosphoryla'tion** the act or process of converting a sugar into a compound of phosphorus and of splitting the latter to yield energy for vital processes; **phosphuret** (*fos'fūr-et* or *-et'; obs.*) a phosphide. — *adj.* **phos'phuretted** (or *-et'*) combined with phosphorus (**phosphuretted** or **phosphoretted hydrogen** phosphine). — *ns.* **phos'phor-bronze'** an alloy of copper, tin and phosphorus; **phossy jaw** necrosis of the jawbone with fatty degeneration of the kidney, common among matchmakers when yellow phosphorus was used. [L. *phōsphorus* — Gr. *phōsphoros,* light-bearer — *phōs,* light, *phoros,* bearing, from *pherein,* to bear.]

phot *fot, fōt, n.* the CGS unit of illumination, 1 lumen per cm². — *adj.* **photic** (*fōt'ik*) of light: light-giving: sensitive to light: accessible to light (as e.g. the uppermost layer of sea). — *n. sing.* **phŏt'ics** optics. — *ns.* **phŏt'ism** sensation of light accompanying another sensation or thought; **photon** (*fō'ton*) a quantum of light or other radiation. — *n.sing.* **photon'ics** the study of the applications of photons, e.g. in communication technology. [Gr. *phōs, phōtos,* light.]

phot- *fōt-,* **photo-** *fō'tō-,* in composition, light. — *adj.* **photoac'tive** affected physically or chemically by light or other radiation. — *ns.* **photobiol'ogist; photobiol'ogy** branch of biology dealing with the effects of light and other forms of radiant energy on organisms; **pho'tocall** a session in which prominent people are photographed for publicity purposes; **pho'tocell** a photoelectric cell. — *adj.* **photochem'ical.** — *ns.* **photochem'ist; photochem'istry** the part of chemistry dealing with changes brought about by light, or other radiation, and with the production of radiation by chemical change. — *adj.* **photochromic** (*-krōm'*) changing colour, and hence changing the amount of light transmitted when the incident light increases, or decreases. — *n.* a photochromic material. — *n. sing.* **photochrom'ics** the science and technology of photochromic materials. — *n.pl.* photochromic materials. — *ns.* **photochrom'ism; pho'tochromy** a former process of colour photography. — *adjs.* **photoconduct'ing, -ive** pertaining to, or show-

ing, photoconductivity. — *ns.* **photoconductivity** (*-kon-duk-tiv'i-ti*) the property of varying conductivity under influence of light; **photodi'ode** a two-electrode semiconductor device, used as an optical sensor. — *adj.* **photoelas'tic** relating to or exhibiting photoelasticity. — *ns.* **photoelastic'ity** the property of certain solids of exhibiting optical changes due to compression or other stresses; **photoelectric'ity** electricity or a change of electric condition, produced by light or other electromagnetic radiation. — *adj.* **photoelectric** (*-i-lek'*) pertaining to photoelectricity, to photoelectrons, or to electric light (**photoelectric cell** any device in which incidence of light of suitable frequency causes an alteration in electrical state, esp. by photo-emission). — *ns.* **photoelec'trode** an electrode which is activated by light; **photoelec'tron** an electron ejected from a body by the incidence of ultra-violet rays or X-rays upon it. — *n.sing.* **photoelectron'ics** the science dealing with the interactions of electricity and electromagnetic radiations, esp. those that involve free electrons. — *ns.* **photo-emiss'ion** emission of electrons from the surface of a body on which light falls; **photofiss'ion** nuclear fission induced by gamma rays; **pho'toflood** (**lamp**) an incandescent tungsten lamp in which excess voltage produces very strong light, but reduces life for the lamp; **photogen** (*fō'tō-jən;* Gr. root of *gignesthai,* to be produced) a light-producing organ in animals: a light paraffin oil (also **photogene**); **pho'togene** (*-jēn*) an after-image: a sensitive emulsion: a photograph (*obs.*). — *adj.* **photogenic** (*-jen'* or *-jēn'*) producing light: produced by light: photographic (*obs.*): having the quality of photographing well: (*loosely*) attractive, striking. — *ns.* **photogeny** (*fō-toj'i-ni; obs.*) photography; **photokinesis** (*-ki-,-kī-nē'sis;* Gr. *kīnēsis,* movement) movement occurring in response to variations in light intensity. — *v.i.* **photoluminesce'** to produce photoluminescence. — *n.* **photoluminesc'ence** luminescence produced by exposure to visible light or infrared or ultraviolet radiation. — *adj.* **photoluminesc'ent.** — *v.t.* **pho'tolyse** to cause photolysis in. — *v.i.* to undergo photolysis. — *n.* **photolysis** (*fō-tol'i-sis;* Gr. *lysis,* loosing — *lyein,* to loose) decomposition or dissociation under the influence of radiation (*chem.*): the grouping of chloroplasts in relation to illumination (*bot.*). — *adj.* **photolytic** (*fō-tō-lit'ik*). — *n.* **photom'eter** an instrument for measuring luminous intensity, usu. by comparing two sources of light. — *adj.* **photomet'ric.** — *ns.* **photom'etry** (the branch of physics dealing with) the measurement of luminous intensity; **photonasty** (*fō'tə-nas-ti;* Gr. *nastos,* close-pressed; *biol.*) response to the stimulus of changed intensity of light without regard to direction. — *adj.* **photonas'tic.** — *n.* **photoperiod** (*fō-tō-pē'ri-əd*) the optimum length of day, as it affects the amount of light received by a plant, for that particular plant's normal growth and development. — *adj.* **photoperiod'ic.** — *ns.* **photoperiodic'ity, photope'riodism** the response of a plant to the relative lengths of day and night. — *adj.* **pho'tophil** (Gr. *phileein,* to love) light-loving: turning towards the light. — *n.* an organism that seeks the light. — *adjs.* **photophil'ic, photophilous** (*-tof'*). — *ns.* **photoph'ily; photophobia** (*fō-tō-fō'bi-ə;* Gr. *phobos,* fear) a shrinking from light. — *n.* and *adj.* **phŏ'tophobe.** — *adj.* **photophobic** (*-fōb'ik*). — *n.* **photophone** (*fō'tō-fōn;* Gr. *phōnē,* voice) an apparatus for transmitting articulate speech to a distance along a beam of light. — *adj.* **photophonic** (*-fon'ik*). — *ns.* **photophony** (*-tof'ə-ni*); **photophore** (*fō'tō-fōr, -för;* Gr. *phoros,* bearing; *zool.*) a luminiferous organ; **photophoresis** (*fō-tō-for-ē'sis;* Gr. *phorēsis,* transference) migration of suspended particles under the influence of light; **photop'ia** vision in a bright light. — *adj.* **photŏp'ic.** — *ns.* **photopsia, photopsy** (*fō-top'si-ə,-top'si;* Gr. *opsis,* appearance) the appearance of flashes of light, owing to irritation of the retina; **photo-recep'tor** a nerve-ending receiving light stimuli. — *adj.* **photoresist'** of an organic material) that polymerises on exposure to ultraviolet light and photo-   1095   phratry

in that form resists attack by acids and solvents. — Also *n*. — *v.t.* **photosens'itise, -ize** to make photosensitive by chemical or other means. — *n.* **photosens'- itiser, -z-.** — *adj.* **photosens'itive** affected by light, visible or invisible. — *ns.* **photosensitiv'ity; photosphere** (*fō'tō-sfēr*) the luminous envelope of the sun's globe, the source of light. — *adj.* **photospheric** (*-sfer'ik*). — *n.* **photosynthesis** (*fō-tō-sin'thi-sis*; *bot.*) the building up of complex compounds by the chlorophyll apparatus of plants by means of the energy of light. — *adj.* **photosynthet'ic.** — *n.* **phototaxis** (*fō-tō-taks'is*; Gr. *taxis,* arrangement; *biol.*) a change of place under stimulus of light.— *adj.* **photoac'tic.** — *ns.* **phototeleg'- raphy** telegraphy by means of light (see also under **photo-**[2]); **phototherapy** (*fō-tō-ther'ɔ-pi*), **phototherapeutics** (*n.sing.*; *-pū'tiks*; Gr. *therapeuein,* to tend) treatment of disease by light. — *adj.* **phototherapeut'ic.** — *ns.* **phototropism** (*fōt-ot'rɔp-lzm*; Gr. *tropos,* turning) orientation in response to the stimulus of light (*bot.*): reversible colour change on exposure to light (*chem.*); **phototrope** (*fō'tō-trōp*) a substance that changes thus. — *adj.* **phototropic** (*fō-tō-trop'ik*). — *n.* **phototor'ropy** change of colour due to wavelength of incident light. — *adj.* **photovoltaic** (*fō-tō-vol-tā'ik*) producing an electromotive force across the junction between dissimilar materials when it is exposed to light or ultraviolet radiation, e.g. in a **photovoltaic cell.** — *n.sing.* **photovolta'ics** the science and technology of photovoltaic devices and substances. [Gr. *phōs, phōtos,* light.]

photo-[1]. For some words beginning thus, see **phot-** (above); for others, see next entry.

photo-[2] *fō'tō-,* in composition, photographic: made by, or by the aid of, photographic means. — *n., v.t., adj.* **photo** a coll. shortening of **photograph(ic, -al)**: — *pl.* **pho'tos.** — *ns.* **pho'to-call** an arranged opportunity for press photographers to take publicity photographs of e.g. a celebrity; **pho'tocomposition** (*print.*) setting of copy by projecting images of letters successively on a sensitive material from which printing plates are made; **pho'tocopier** a machine which makes photocopies; **photocopy** (*fō'tō-ko-pi*) a photographic reproduction of written matter. — *v.t.* to make a photocopy. — *ns.* **pho'tocopying; pho'to-engraving, -etching** any process of engraving by aid of photography, esp. from relief plates; **pho'to-finish** a race finish in which a special type of photography is used to show the winner, etc.: a neck and neck finish of any contest; **Pho'to-fit**® (also without *cap.* and without *hyphen*) a method of making identification pictures, an alternative to identikit (q.v.); **photogeology** (*fō-tō-jē-ol'ɔ-ji*) (the study of) geology by means of air photographs; **photoglyph** (*fō'tō-glif*; Gr. *glyphē,* carving) a photographic engraving: a photogravure. — *adj.* **photoglyph'ic.** — *ns.* **photoglyphy** (*fō-tog'li-fi*); **pho'togram** a photograph: a type of picture produced by placing an object on or near photographic paper which is then exposed to light. — *adj.* **photogrammet'ric.** — *ns.* **photogramm'etrist; photogramm'etry** the making of maps by using air photographs; **photogravure** (*fō-tō-grɔ-vūr'*; Fr. *gravure,* engraving) a method of photo-engraving in which the design etched on the metal surface is intaglio not relief: a picture produced by this method; **photojour'nalism** journalism in which written material is subordinate to photographs; **photojour'nalist; photolithography** (*fō-tō-li-thog'rɔ-fi*) a process of lithographic printing from a photographically produced plate. — *n. and v.t.* **photolith'ograph** (*-o-gräf*). — *n.* **photolithog'rapher.** — *adj.* **photolithographic** (*-graf'ik*). — *n.* **photomac'rograph** a photograph of an object that is unmagnified or only slightly magnified. — *adj.* **photomacrograph'ic.** — *n.* **photomacrog'raphy.** — *adj.* **pho'to-mechan'ical** pertaining to mechanical printing from a photographically prepared plate. — *adv.* **pho'to-mechan'ically.** — *ns.* **photomicrograph** (*fō-tō-mī'krō-gräf*; Gr. *mikros,* little, *graphein,* to write) an enlarged photograph of a microscopic object taken through a microscope; **photomicrographer** (*-krog'rɔ-fɔr*). — *adj.* **photomicro-**

graphic (*-krō-graf'ik*). — *ns.* **photomicrog'raphy; photomon'tage** (*-täzh*) (the art of making) a picture made by cutting up photographs, etc., and arranging the parts so as to convey, without explicitly showing, a definite meaning; **photo opportunity** an opportunity for press photographers to get good or interesting pictures of a celebrity, either arranged by the celebrity (esp. for publicity purposes) or arising more or less by chance during some event the celebrity is participating in; **pho'to-process** any process by which a matrix for printing is got by photographic means; **pho'to-relief** a plate or image in relief got by photographic means; **pho'tosetting** photocomposition; **Photostat**® (*fō'tō-stat*; Gr. *statos,* set, placed) a photographic apparatus for making facsimiles of MSS., drawings, etc., directly: a facsimile so made. — *v.t. and v.i.* to photograph by Photostat. — *ns.* **phototelegraph** (*fō'tō-tel'i-gräf*) an instrument for transmitting drawings, photographs, etc., by telegraphy; **phototeleg'raphy** (see also under **phot-**); **prototype** (*fō'tō-tīp*; Gr. *typos,* impression) a printing block on which the material is produced photographically: a print made from such a block: the process of making such a block. — *v.t.* to reproduce by phototype. — *adj.* **phototypic** (*-tip'ik*). — *ns.* **phototypy** (*fō'tō-tī-pi* or *fō-tot'i-pi*); **photoxylography** (*fō-tō-zī-log'rɔ-fi*; Gr. *xylon,* wood, *graphein,* to write) wood-engraving after a photographic impression on a wood-block; **photozincography** (*fō-tō-zing-kog'rɔ-fi*) the process of engraving on zinc by taking an impression by photography and etching with acids; **photozinc'ograph** a picture so produced. [**photograph.**]

photography *fō-tog'rɔ-fi, n.* the art or process of producing permanent and visible images by the action of light, or other radiant energy, on chemically prepared surfaces. — *n.* **photograph** (*fō'tɔ-gräf*) an image so produced. — *v.t.* to make a picture of by means of photography.— *v.i.* to take photographs: to be capable of being photographed. — *n.* **photog'rapher.** — *adjs.* **photographic** (*-graf'ik*), **-al.** — *adv.* **photograph'ically.** — *n.* **photog'raphist.** [Gr. *phōs, phōtos,* light, *graphein,* to draw.]

photon. See **phot.**

phrase *frāz, n.* manner of expression in language: an expression: a group of words (sometimes as in *Shak.* a single word) generally not forming a clause but felt as expressing a single idea or constituting a single element in the sentence: a pithy expression: a catchword: an empty or high-sounding expression: fussy talk about one's feelings (*Scot.*): a short group of notes felt to form a unit (*mus.*). — *v.t.* to express in words: to style: to flatter, wheedle (*Scot.*): to mark, bring out, or give effect to the phrases of (*mus.*). — *adjs.* **phrās'al** consisting of, of the nature of, a phrase; **phrase'less** incapable of being described. — *ns.* **phraseogram** (*frā'- zi-ō-gram*) a single sign, written without lifting the pen, for a whole phrase (esp. in shorthand); **phra'seograph** a phrase that is so written. — *adjs.* **phraseolog'ic, -al.** — *adv.* **phraseolog'ically.** — *ns.* **phraseol'ogist** a maker or a collector of phrases; **phraseol'ogy** style or manner of expression or arrangement of phrases: peculiarities of diction: a collection of phrases in a language; **phra'ser** a mere maker or repeater of empty phrases; **phra'sing** the wording of a speech or passage: the grouping and accentuation of the sounds in performing a melody (*mus.*). — *adj.* using phrases, esp. (*Scot.*) airing one's views or feelings or making flowery speeches. — *adj.* **phra'sy** inclining to emptiness and verbosity of phrase. — **phrasal verb** a phrase, consisting of a verb and one or more additional words, having the function of a verb; **phrase'-book** a book containing or explaining phrases of a language; **phrase'man, phrase'maker** and (*disparagingly*) **phrase'monger** a user or maker of wordy or fine-sounding phrases. — **turn of phrase** an expression: one's manner of expression. [Gr. *phrăsis* — *phrazein,* to speak.]

phratry *frā'tri, n.* a social division of a people, often exogamous. [Gr. *phrātriā*; cf. L. *frāter,* Eng. **brother.**]

phreatic *frē-at'ik, adj.* pertaining to underground water supplying, or probably able to supply, wells or springs, or to the soil or rocks containing it, or to wells: (of underground gases, etc.) present in, or causing, volcanic eruptions. — *n.* **phreat'ophyte** a deep-rooted plant drawing its water from the water table or just above it. — *adj.* **phreatophyt'ic.** [Gr. *phrear,* well, *phreātia,* cistern.]

phrenesiac *fri-nē'zi-ak, (Scott) adj.* hypochondriac. — *n.* **phrenesis** (*fri-nē'sis*) phrenitis: delirium: frenzy. — For *adj., n.* **phrenetic,** *adj.* **phrenetical,** *adv.* **phrenetically,** see **frenetic.** — *adj.* **phrenic** (*fren'ik*) of or near the midriff: mental (*obs.*). — *n.* **phren'ism** a supposed 'mind-force' perceived by E. D. Cope as active in nature and evolution. — *adj.* **phrenit'ic** of or affected with phrenitis. — *n.* **phreni'tis** inflammation of the brain: brain-fever. — *adjs.* **phrenolog'ic** (*fren-*), **-al.** — *adv.* **phrenolog'ically.** — *v.t.* **phrenol'ogise, -ize** to examine phrenologically. — *ns.* **phrenol'ogist; phrenol'ogy** a would-be science of mental faculties supposed to be located in various parts of the skull and investigable by feeling the bumps on the outside of the head. — *adjs.* and *n.* **phrensical, phrensy, phrentick** old forms of **frenzical, frenzy, frantic** (or **phrenetic).** [Gr. *phrēn, phrenos,* midriff, supposed seat of passions, mind, will.]

phrontistery *fron'tis-tə-ri, n.* a thinking-place. [Gr. *phrontistērion* — *phrontistēs,* a thinker — *phroneein,* to think; applied by Aristophanes to the school of Socrates.]

Phrygian *frij'i-ən, adj.* pertaining to *Phrygia* in Asia Minor, or to its people. — *n.* a native of Phrygia: a Montanist: the language of the ancient Phrygians. — **Phrygian cap** a conical cap with the top turned forward; **Phrygian mode** in ancient Greek music, a mode of two tetrachords with a semitone in the middle of each and a whole tone between the tetrachords (as: *d e f g; a b c d*; but reckoned downwards by the Greeks): in old Church music, an authentic mode extending from *e* to *e,* with *e* as its final.

phthalic (*f*)*thal'ik, adj.* applied to three acids, $C_6H_4(COOH)_2$, and an anhydride, derived from naphthalene. — *ns.* **phthal'ate** a salt or ester of phthalic acid; **phthal'ein** (*-i-in*) any one of a very important class of dye-yielding materials formed by the union of phenols with phthalic anhydride; **phthal'in** a colourless crystalline compound obtained by reducing a phthalein; **phthalocy'anin, -cy'anine** any of a group of green and blue organic colouring matters of great fastness and brilliance. [**naphthalene.**]

phthiriasis (*f*)*thī-rī'ə-sis, n.* infestation with lice. [Gr. *phtheiriāsis* — *phtheir,* a louse.]

phthisis *thī'sis,* also *fthī', tī', n.* wasting disease: tuberculosis, esp. of the lungs. — *n.* **phthisic** (*tiz'ik,* sometimes *thī'sik, fthī'sik, tī'sik*) phthisis: vaguely, a lung or throat disease. — *adjs.* **phthisical** (*tiz'*), **phthis'icky.** [Gr. *phthisis* — *phthi(n)ein,* to waste away.]

phut *fut, n.* a dull sound esp. of collapse, deflation, etc. — Also *adv.,* as in **go phut** to break, become unserviceable: to come to nothing. [Hind. *phatnā,* to split.]

pH value. See **pH.**

phyco- *fī-kō-,* in composition, seaweed. — *ns.* **phycocyan, phycocyanin** (*-sī'an, -ə-nin*; Gr. *kyanos,* dark blue) a blue pigment in algae; **phycoerythrin** (*-e-rith'rin*; Gr. *erythros,* red) a red pigment in algae. — *adj.* **phycolog'ical.** — *ns.* **phycologist** (*-kol'ə-jist*); **phycol'ogy** the study of algae. — *n.pl.* **Phycomycetes** (*-mī-sē'tēz;* Gr. *mykētēs,* pl. of *mykēs,* a fungus) a class of fungi showing affinities with the green seaweeds. — *ns.* **phycomy'cete** a fungus of this class; **phycophaein** (*-fē'in;* Gr. *phaios,* grey) a brown pigment in seaweeds; **phycoxan'thin** (Gr. *xanthos,* yellow) a yellow pigment in diatoms, brown seaweeds, etc. [Gr. *phȳkos,* seaweed.]

phyla. See **phylum.**

phylactery *fi-lak'tə-ri, n.* a charm or amulet: among the Jews, a slip of parchment inscribed with certain passages of Scripture, worn in a box on the left arm or forehead: a reminder: ostentatious display of religious forms: a case for relics: in mediaeval art, a scroll at the mouth of a figure in a picture bearing the words he is supposed to speak. — *adjs.* **phylacteric** (*-ter'ik*), **-al.** [Gr. *phylaktērion* — *phylax,* a guard.]

phyle *fī'lē, n.* a tribe or division of the people of a state in ancient Greece, at first on a kinship, later on a local, basis. — *ns.* **phylarch** (*fī'lärk*) the chief officer of a tribe: in Athens, the commander of the cavalry of a tribe; **phy'larchy** the office of phylarch. [Gr. *phȳlē.*]

phyletic *fī-let'ik, adj.* pertaining to a phylum: according to descent. [Gr. *phȳletikos* — *phȳlē.*]

phyllary *fil'ə-ri,* (*bot.*) *n.* an involucral bract. [Gr. *phyllarion,* dim. of *phyllon,* leaf.]

phyllite *fil'īt, n.* a rock intermediate between clay-slate and mica-schist. [Gr. *phyllon,* a leaf.]

phyllo *fil'ō, n.* a type of pastry of Greece and surrounding regions, made in thin sheets. [Gr. *phyllon,* a leaf.]

phylloclade *fil'ō-klād, n.* a branch with the form and functions of a leaf. [Gr. *phyllon,* leaf, *klados,* shoot.]

phyllode *fil'ōd, n.* a petiole with the appearance and function of a leaf-blade. — *n.* **phyll'ody** (*-ō-di*) transformation of flower parts into leaves. — *adj.* **phyll'oid** leaf-like. [Gr. *phyllon,* leaf, *eidos,* form.]

phyllomania *fil-ō-mā'ni-ə, n.* excessive production of leaves, at the expense of flower or fruit production. [Gr. *phyllon,* leaf, *maniā,* madness.]

phyllome *fil'ōm, n.* any leaf or homologue of a leaf. [Gr. *phyllōma,* foliage.]

phyllophagous *fi-lof'ə-gəs, adj.* leaf-eating. [Gr. *phyllon,* leaf, *phagein,* to eat.]

phyllopod *fil'ō-pod, n.* a crustacean of the order **Phyllopoda** (*-op'ə-də*), entomostracans with foliaceous legs. [Gr. *phyllon,* leaf, *pous, podos,* foot.]

phylloquinone *fil-ō-kwin'ōn,* or *-ōn', n.* vitamin K_1. [Gr. *phyllon,* leaf, and **quinone.**]

phyllotaxis *fil-ō-tak'sis, n.* the disposition of leaves on the stem. — Also **phyll'otaxy.** — *adjs.* **phyllotact'ic, -al.** [Gr. *phyllon,* a leaf, *taxis,* arrangement.]

Phyllotria. See **Elodea.**

Phylloxera *fil-ok-sē'rə, n.* a genus of insects of a family akin to green-fly, very destructive to vines: (without *cap.*) an insect of this genus. [Gr. *phyllon,* a leaf, *xēros,* dry.]

phylogeny *fī-loj'i-ni, n.* evolutionary pedigree or genealogical history — also **phylogenesis** (*fī-lō-jen'i-sis*). — *adj.* **phylogenet'ic.** — *adv.* **phylogenet'ically.** [Gr. *phȳlon,* race, *genesis,* origin.]

phylum *fī'ləm, n.* a main division of the animal or the vegetable kingdom: — *pl.* **phy'la.** [Mod. L. — Gr. *phȳlon,* race, stock.]

Physalia *fī-sā'li-ə, n.* a genus of large oceanic colonial hydrozoans with a floating bladder — including the Portuguese man-of-war: (without *cap.*) a member of the genus. — *ns.* **Physalis** (*fis'* or *fīs'ə-lis*) the Cape gooseberry genus of Solanaceae, with persistent bladdery calyx: (without *cap.*) any plant of this genus; **Physeter** (*fī-sē'tər*) a sperm whale. [Gr. *phȳsallis,* a bladder, *phȳsētēr,* a blower, a whale, bellows — *phȳsaein,* to blow.]

physharmonica *fis-här-mon'i-kə, n.* an early form of harmonium. [Gr. *phȳsa,* bellows, and **harmonica.**]

physic *fiz'ik, n.* orig. natural philosophy, physics (*obs.*): the science, art, or practice of medicine (*obs.*): a medicine (*rare*): anything healing or wholesome (*fig.*). — *adj.* (*obs.*) physical, natural: medicinal. — *v.t.* (*obs.*) to give medicine to: to heal: — *pr.p.* **phys'icking;** *pa.t.* and *pa.p.* **phys'icked.** — *adj.* **phys'ical** pertaining to the world of matter and energy, or its study, natural philosophy: material: materialistic (*obs.*): bodily: requiring bodily effort: involving bodily contact: medical (*rare*): medicinal (*obs.*): wholesome (*Shak.*). — *n.* a physical examination of the body, e.g. to ascertain fitness. — *ns.* **phys'icalism** the theory that all phenomena are explicable in spatiotemporal terms and that all statements are either analytic or reducible to empirically verifiable assertions; **phys'icalist; physical'ity**

preoccupation with the bodily. — *adv.* **phys′ically.** — *ns.* **physician** (*fi-zish′n*) one skilled in the use of physic or the art of healing: one legally qualified to practice medicine: one who makes use of medicines and treatment, distinguished from a surgeon who practices manual operations: a doctor: a healer or healing influence (*fig.*); **physic′iancy** (*-zish′*) the post or office of physician; **physic′ianer** (*rare*) a physician; **physic′ianship**; **phys′icism** (*-sizm*) belief in the material or physical as opposed to the spiritual; **phys′icist** (*-sist*) a student of nature: one versed in physics: one who believes the phenomena of life are purely physical. — *adjs.* **phys′icky** like medicine; **physicochem′ical** relating to or involving both physics and chemistry: pertaining to physical chemistry (see below). — *n. sing.* **phys′ics** orig. natural science in general: now, the science of the properties (other than chemical) of matter and energy. — **physical astronomy** the study of the physical condition and chemical composition of the heavenly bodies; **physical chemistry** the study of the dependence of physical properties on chemical composition, and of the physical changes accompanying chemical reactions; **physical force** force applied outwardly to the body, as distinguished from persuasion, etc.; **physical geography** the study of the earth's natural features — its mountain-chains, ocean-currents, etc.; **physical jerks** (*coll.*) bodily exercises; **physic garden** orig. a garden of medicinal plants: a botanic garden; **physic nut** the purgative seed of the tropical American *Jatropha curcas*, a tree of the spurge family. [Gr. *physikos*, natural — *physis*, nature.]

physi(o)- *fiz-i-(ō-)* in composition, nature. — *ns.* **phys′io** short for **physiotherapist**: — *pl.* **phys′ios**; **physiocracy** (*-ok′rə-si*; Gr. *krateein*, to rule) government, according to François Quesnay (1694–1774) and his followers, by a natural order inherent in society, land and its products being the only true source of wealth, direct taxation of land being the only proper source of revenue; **phys′iocrat** (*-ō-krat*) one who maintains these opinions. — *adj.* **physiocrat′ic.** — *ns.* **physiography** (*-og′rə-fi*; Gr. *graphein*, to describe) description of nature, descriptive science: physical geography; **physiog′rapher.** — *adjs.* **physiographic** (*-ō-graf′ik*), **-al.** — *ns.* **physiolatry** (*-ol′ə-tri*; Gr. *latreiā*, worship) nature-worship; **physiol′ater** a nature-worshipper; **physiology** (*-ol′ə-ji*; Gr. *logos*, discourse) the science of the processes of life in animals and plants. — *adjs.* **physiologic** (*-ə-loj′ik*), **-al.** *adv.* **physiolog′ically.** — *ns.* **physiol′ogist**; **physiol′ogus** a bestiary; **physiotherapy** (*-ō-ther′ə-pi*; Gr. *therapeiā*, treatment) treatment of disease by remedies such as massage, fresh air, electricity, rather than by drugs. — Also *n. sing.* **physiotherapeutics** (*-pūt′iks*). — *adj.* **physiotherapeut′ic.** — *ns.* **physiother′apist**; **physitheism** (*fiz′i-thē-ism*; Gr. *theos*, god) the ascription of physical form and attributes to deity: deification of powers of nature. — *adj.* **physitheis′tic.** [Gr. *physis*, nature.]

physiognomy *fiz-i-on′ə-mi* or *-og′nə-mi*, *n.* the art of judging character from appearance, esp. from the face: the face as an index of the mind: the face (*coll.*): the general appearance of anything: character, aspect. — *adj.* **physiognomic** (*-nom′*), **-al.** — *adv.* **physiognom′ically.** — *n.* **physiogn′omist.** [Gr. *physiognōmiā*, a shortened form of *physiognōmoniā* — *physis*, nature, *gnōmōn, -onos*, an interpreter.]

physitheism, physitheistic. See **physi(o)-**.

physique *fiz-ēk′*, *n.* bodily type, build, or constitution. [Fr.]

phyto- *fī-tō-, -to-*, in composition, plant. — **-phyte** in composition, used to indicate a plant belonging to a particular habitat, or of a particular type. — **-phytic** (*-fit-ik*) adjective combining form. — *ns.* **phytoalex′in** (Gr. *alexein*, to ward off) any substance produced by a plant as a defence against disease; **phytobenthos** (*-ben′thos*; Gr. *benthos*, depth) plants living at the bottom of water collectively; **phytochem′ical** a chemical got from a plant. — *adj.* of chemicals in plants. —

ns. **phy′tochrome** a plant pigment which absorbs red or infra-red rays and acts as an enzyme controlling growth, flowering, germination, etc; **phytogen′esis**, **phytogeny** (*-toj′i-ni*) evolution of plants. — *adjs.* **phytogenet′ic, -al** relating to phytogenesis; **phytogenic** (*-jen′ik*) of vegetable origin. — *n.* **phytogeog′rapher.** — *adj.* **phytogeograph′ic.** — *ns.* **phytogeog′raphy** the geography of plant distribution; **phytog′rapher** a descriptive botanist. — *adj.* **phytograph′ic.** — *ns.* **phytog′raphy** descriptive botany; **phytohor′mone** a plant hormone, regulating growth, etc.; **Phytolacc′a** the pokeweed genus, giving name to the family **Phytolaccā′ceae**, allied to the pinks and the goosefoots. — *adj.* **phytolog′ical.** — *ns.* **phytol′ogist** a botanist; **phytol′ogy** botany; **phy′ton** the smallest part of a plant that when cut off may grow into a new plant; **phytonadione** (*fī-tō-nə-dī′ōn*) phylloquinone, vitamin K₁. — *adj.* **phytopathol′og′ical.** — *ns.* **phytopathol′ogist**; **phytopathology** (Gr. *pathos*, suffering) the study of plant diseases. — *adjs.* **phytophagic** (*-faj′ik*), **phytophagous** (*-tof′ə-gəs*; Gr. *phagein*, to eat) plant-eating. — *ns.* **phytoplank′ton** (Gr. *plankton*, neut., wandering) vegetable plankton; **phyto′sis** the presence of vegetable parasites or disease caused by them; **phytosterol** (*-tos′tə-rol*; formed on the model of *cholesterol*) a substance very like cholesterol got from plants; **phytot′omist**; **phytotomy** (*-tot′ə-mi*; Gr. *tomē*, a cut) plant anatomy. — *adj.* **phytotox′ic** poisonous to plants: pertaining to a phytotoxin. — *ns.* **phytotoxic′ity** harmfulness to plants; **phytotox′in** a toxin produced by a plant; **phytotron** (*fī′tō-tron*) an apparatus that produces climates artificially for the study of plant growth. [Gr. *phyton*, plant.]

pi¹ *pī, pē*, *n.* the sixteenth letter (Π, π) of the Greek alphabet, answering to the Roman P: as a numeral π′ stands for 80, ͵π for 80 000: a symbol for the ratio of the circumference of a circle to the diameter, approx. 3·14159 (*math.*). — **pi-** (or **π-**) **meson** the source of the nuclear force holding protons and neutrons together (*phys.*). — Also called **pion.** [Gr. *pei, pī*.]

pi² (*print.*). Same as **pie³**.

pi³ *pī*, (*slang*) *adj.* an abbreviation of **pious**: religious: sanctimonious. — *n.* a pious, religious, or sanctimonious person or talk. — **pi′-jaw** sermonising: an admonition.

pia¹ *pē′ə*, *n.* a tropical monocotyledonous plant (*Tacca*; fam. *Taccaceae*) with a rhizome yielding E. India or Madagascar arrowroot. [Polynesian name.]

pia² *pī′ə, pē′a*, (L.) *adj.* pious. — **pia desideria** (*dez-i-dēr′i-ə, dā-sēd-er′i-a*) pious regrets; **pia fraus** (*frōz, frows*) pious fraud.

piacevole *pyə-chā′vo-lā*, (*mus.*) *adj.* pleasant, playful. [It.]

piacular *pī-ak′ū-lər*, *adj.* expiatory: requiring expiation: atrociously bad. — *n.* **piacularity** (*-lar′i-ti*). [L. *piāculum*, sacrifice — *piāre*, to expiate — *pius*, pious.]

piaffe *pi-af′, pyaf*, *v.i.* in horsemanship, to advance at a piaffer. — *n.* **piaff′er** a gait in which the feet are lifted in the same succession as a trot, but more slowly. — Also *Spanish-walk*. [Fr. *piaffer*.]

pia mater *pī′ə mā′tər*, the vascular membrane investing the brain: the brain (*Shak.*). [L. *pīa māter*, tender mother, a mediaeval translation of Ar. *umm raqīqah*, thin mother.]

pianoforte *pyä′nō-för-ti, pē-a′, pyä′, pē-ä′*, shortened to **piano** (*pya′, pē-a′*, or *-ä′*), *n.* a musical instrument with wires struck by hammers moved by keys: — *pl.* **pia′nofortes, pian′os.** — *ns.* **pianette** (*pē-ə-net′*) a small upright piano: — *pl.* **piani′nos**; **pianino** (*pya-nē′nō, pē-ə-nē′nō*) orig. an upright piano: a small upright piano; **pi′anism** the technique of the pianoforte. — *adj.* and *adv.* **pianissimo** (*pya-nēs′si-mō, pē-ə-nis′i-mō*) very soft. — *n.* **pianist** (*pē′ə-nist, pyan′*; also *pē-an′ist*) one who plays the pianoforte, esp. expertly — also (Fr.) **pianiste** (*pē-a-nēst′*) sometimes used as *fem.* — *adj.* **pianist′ic** of or relating to pianism or a pianist. — *adv.* **pianist′ically.** — *adj.* and *adv.* **piano** (*pyä′nō, pē-ä′nō*) soft, softly. — *n.* a soft passage. — *n.* **Pianola®** (*pyan-ō′lə, pē-ə-*) a pneumatic contrivance for playing the piano by means of a perforated roll (a **piano roll**). — **pia′no-accord′ion** an elaborate accordion with a keyboard like a piano; **pia′no-or′gan** a piano like a barrel-organ, played by mechanical means; **pian′o= play′er** a mechanical contrivance for playing the piano: a pianist; **piano roll** see at **Pianola®** above; **pian′o-school** a school where piano-playing is taught: a method or book of instruction for the piano; **pian′o-stool** a stool usually adjustable in height for a pianist; **pian′o-wire** wire used for piano strings, and for deep-sea soundings, etc. — **player piano** a piano with a piano-player. [It. — *piano*, soft — L. *plānus*, level, and *forte*, loud — L. *fortis*, strong.]

piano nobile *pjä′nō nō′bi-lā*, (*archit.*) the main floor of a large house or villa, usu. on the first floor. [It., noble storey.]

piarist *pī′ə-rist, n.* one of a religious congregation for the education of the poor, founded in Rome in 1597 by Joseph Calasanza. [L. *patrēs scholārum piārum*, fathers of pious schools.]

piassava *pē-əs-ä′və*, **piassaba** *-bə, ns.* a coarse stiff fibre used for making brooms, etc., got from Brazilian palms, *Attalea* (coquilla) and *Leopoldinia* (chiquichiqui): the tree yielding it. [Port. from Tupí.]

piastre *pi-as′tər, n.* a unit of currency in current or former use in several N. African and Middle Eastern countries, equal to 1/100 of a (Sudanese, Egyptian, etc.) pound: a coin of this value: a piece of eight. [Fr., — It. *piastra*, a leaf of metal; see **plaster**.]

piazza *pē-ät′sə*, also *pē-ad′zə, pē-az′ə, n.* a place or square surrounded by buildings: (*erroneously*) a walk under a roof supported by pillars: a veranda (*U.S.*). — *adj.* **piazz′ian.** [It., — L. *platea* — Gr. *plateia*, a street (fem. of *platys*, broad).]

pibroch *pē′brohh, n.* the classical music of the bagpipe, free in rhythm and consisting of theme and variations. [Gael. *piobaireachd*, pipe-music — *piobair*, a piper — *piob*, from Eng. **pipe¹**.]

pic *pik, n.* a coll. short form of **picture:** — *pl.* **pics, pix.**

pica *pī′kə*, (*print.*) *n.* an old type size, approximately, and still used synonymously for, 12-point, giving about 6 lines to the inch, much used in typewriters. — **small pica** 11-point. [Possibly used for printing *pies*; see **pie²**.]

Pica *pī′kə, n.* the magpie genus: (without *cap.*) a craving for unsuitable food. [L. *pīca*, magpie.]

picador *pik-ə-dōr′, -dör′*, now usu. *pik′ə-dör, n.* a mounted bull-fighter with a lance. [Sp., — *pica*, a pike.]

picamar *pik′ə-mär, n.* a bitter oily liquid got from tar. [L. *pix, picis*, pitch, *amārus*, bitter.]

picaresque. See **picaroon.**

picarian *pik-ā′ri-ən, adj.* belonging to an obsolete order (**Pica′riae**) of birds including the woodpeckers. — *n.* any member of the order. [L. *pīcus*, woodpecker.]

picaroon *pik-ə-rōōn′, n.* one who lives by his wits: a cheat: a pirate. — *adj.* **picaresque** (*-resk′*). — **picaresque novels** the tales of Spanish rogue and vagabond life, much in vogue in the 17th century: novels of like type. [Sp. *picarón*, augmentative of *picaro*, rogue.]

picayune *pik-ə-ūn′, n.* a small coin worth 6¼ cents, current in United States before 1857: a five-cent piece, or other small coin: anything of little or no value (*U.S. coll.*). — *adj.* (*U.S. coll.*) petty. — *adj.* **picayun′ish.** [Prov. *picaïoun*, an old Piedmontese copper coin.]

piccadill *pik′ə-dil*, **pikadell** *-del*, **piccadillo** *-dil′ō*, **piccadilly** *-i*, (*obs.*) *ns.* a cut or vandyked edging, esp. to a woman's collar: a wide high collar of the early 17th century: a stiff support for a collar or ruff: (in the form **piccadilly**) a man's standing-up collar with the points turned over, first worn about 1870: — *pl.* **picc′adills, -dill′oes**, etc. [Cf. Sp. *picadillo*, a kind of hash.]

piccalilli *pik-ə-lil′i, n.* a pickle of various vegetable substances with mustard and spices. [Ety. dub.]

piccaninny, pickaninny *pik-ə-nin′i, n.* a little child: a Negro child: an Aborigine child (*Austr.*). — *adj.* very little.

— *n.* **picc′anin** (*S. Afr.*) a piccaniny. [Port. *pequenino*, dim. of *pequeno*, little, or possibly Sp. *pequeño niño*, little child.]

piccolo *pik′ə-lō, n.* a small flute, an octave higher than the ordinary flute: an organ stop of similar tone: — *pl.* **picc′olos.** [It., little.]

pice *pīs, n.sing.* and *pl.* a money of account and coin, ¼ anna. — **new pice** 1/100 rupee. [Hind. *paisā.*]

Picea *pis′i-ə, pīs′i-ə, n.* the spruce genus of conifers. [L. *picea*, pitch-pine — *pix*, pitch.]

piceous *pis′i-əs, pish′(i-)əs, adj.* like pitch: inflammable: black: reddish black. — *n.* **picene** (*pī′sēn*) a hydrocarbon ($C_{22}H_{14}$) got from tar. [L. *piceus — pix, picis*, pitch.]

pichiciago *pich-i-si-ä′gō*, or *-ā′gō, n.* a small burrowing South American armadillo: — *pl.* **pichicia′gos.** [Amer. Indian.]

pichurim *pich′ŏŏ-rim, n.* a S. American tree (*Nectandra puchury*) of the laurel family: its aromatic kernel (also **pichurim bean).** [Port. *pichurim* — Tupí *puchury*.]

picine. See **Picus.**

pick¹ *pik, n.* a tool for breaking ground, rock, etc., with head pointed at one end or both, and handle fitted to the middle: a pointed hammer: an instrument of various kinds for picking: an act, opportunity, or right of choice: a portion picked: the best or choicest: dirt on a printing type: a diamond in cards, also a spade (*Northern dial.*). — *v.t.* to break up, dress, or remove with a pick: to make with a pick or by plucking: to poke or pluck at, as with a sharp instrument or the nails: to clear, to remove, or to gather, by single small acts: to detach, extract, or take separately and lift or remove: to pluck: to pull apart: to cull: to choose: to select, esp. one by one or bit by bit: to peck, bite, or nibble: to eat in small quantities or delicately: to open (as a lock) by a sharp instrument or other unapproved means: to rifle by stealth: to seek and find a pretext for (as a quarrel). — *v.i.* to use a pick: to eat by morsels: to pilfer. — *adj.* **picked** (*pikt*) selected, hence the choicest or best: plucked, as flowers or fruit: exquisite, refined, punctilious (*Shak.*): having spines or prickles, sharp-pointed. — *ns.* **pick′edness; pick′er** one who picks or gathers up: a tool or machine for picking: one who removes defects from and finishes electrotype plates: a pilferer; **pick′ery** (*Scots law*) pilfering; **pick′ing** the action of the verb to pick: the quantity picked: that which is left to be picked: dabbing in stoneworking: the final finishing of woven fabrics by removing burs, etc.: removing defects from electrotype plates: (in *pl.*) odd gains or perquisites. — *adj.* **pick′y** (*coll.*) fussy or choosy, esp. excessively so: able to pick out or pick over dexterously. — **pick′-cheese** the blue or the great titmouse: the fruit of the mallow; **pick′er-up′; pick′lock** an instrument for picking or opening locks: one who picks locks; **pick′-me-up** a stimulating drink: a medicinal tonic; **pick′-pocket** one who picks or steals from other people's pockets; **pick′-purse** one who steals the purse or from the purse of another; **pick′-thank** one who seeks to ingratiate himself by officious favours, or by tale-bearing; **pick′-tooth** a toothpick; **pick′-up** an act of picking up: reception: a stop to collect something or someone: a recovery: a thing picked up: accelerating power: a device for picking up an electric current: (also **pick-up head)** a transducer, activated by a sapphire or diamond stylus following the groove on a gramophone record, which transforms the mechanical into electrical impulses: a light motor vehicle with front part like a private car and rear in form of truck: a man's chance, informal acquaintance with a woman, usu. implying a sexual relationship: the woman in such a relationship: a game, or a team, for which the captains pick their men alternately. — *adj.* for picking up: picked up. — **pick a hole in someone's coat, pick holes in someone** to find fault with someone; **pick at** to find fault with; **pick oakum** to make oakum by untwisting old ropes; **pick off** to select from a number and shoot: to detach and remove; **pick on** to single out, esp. for anything unpleasant: to nag at: to carp at; **pick one's way** to choose carefully where to put one's feet, as on dirty ground; **pick out** to make out, distinguish: to pluck out: to select from a number: to mark with spots of colour, etc.; **pick over** to go over and select; **pick someone's brains** to make use of another's brains or ideas for one's own ends; **pick to pieces** to pull asunder: to criticise adversely in detail; **pick up** to lift from the ground, floor etc.: to improve gradually: to gain strength bit by bit: to take into a vehicle, or into one's company: to scrape acquaintance informally with, esp. of a man with a woman: to acquire as occasion offers: to gain: to come upon, make out, distinguish (as a signal, a track, a comet, etc.); **pick up the pieces** to restore (esp. emotional) matters to their former equilibrium after they have been brought to disarray or collapse. [Ety. obscure; cf. **peck²**, **pike¹**, **pitch²**.]

pick² *pik*, a Northern form of **pitch¹**: also of **pitch²** esp. *v.i.* to throw the shuttle across the loom, and *n.* a throw of the shuttle, or a weft thread: also a form of **pique¹**. — **pick'-and-pick'** (*weaving*) a term indicating alternate picks of yarns of two different colours or kinds.

pickaback *pik'ə-bak*, *adv.* and *adj.* on the back like a pack: of a vehicle or plane, conveyed on top of another. — *n.* a ride on one's back. — Also **pick'back**, **pick'apack**, **pigg'yback**. [Connection with **pick** (pitch), **pack** and **back** obscure.]

pickaninny. See **piccaninny**.

pickaxe *pik'aks*, *n.* a picking tool, with a point at one end of the head and a cutting blade at the other, used in digging. [M.E. *pikois* — O.Fr. *picois*, a mattock, *piquer*, to pierce, *pic*, a pick.]

pickeer *pi-kēr'*, *v.i.* to forage (*obs.*): to skirmish: to scout: to flirt (*obs.*). — *n.* **pickeer'er.** [Ety. dub.]

pickelhaube *pik-l-how'bə*, *pik'*, *n.* a German spiked helmet. [Ger.]

pickerel *pik'ər-əl*, *n.* a young pike: a pike, esp. of smaller species (*U.S.*). — **pick'erel-weed** pondweed: Pontederia (*U.S.*). [**pike**.]

picket *pik'it*, *n.* a pointed stake or peg driven into the ground for fortification, tethering, military punishment, surveying, or other purpose: a surveyor's mark: a small outpost, patrol, or body of men set apart for some special duty: picket-duty: a person or group set to watch and dissuade those who go to work during a strike: the old military punishment of standing on one foot on a pointed stake. — *v.t.* to tether to a stake: to strengthen or surround with pickets: to peg down: to subject to the picket: to post as a picket: to deal with as a picket or by means of pickets: to place pickets at or near. — *v.i.* to act as picket: — *pr.p.* **pick'eting**; *pa.t.* and *pa.p.* **pick'eted.** — Also **piquet**, **picquet.** — *n.* **pick'eter** one who pickets in a labour dispute. — **pick'et-duty**; **pick'et-fence** (*U.S*) a fence of pales; **pick'et-guard** a guard kept in readiness in case of alarm; **pick'et-line** a line of people acting as pickets in a labour dispute. — **picket out** in a labour dispute, to close or bring to a standstill by picketing. [Fr. *piquet*, dim. of *pic*, a pickaxe.]

pickle¹ *pik'l*, *n.* a liquid, esp. brine or vinegar, in which food is preserved: an article of food preserved in such liquid: (in *pl.*) preserved onions, cucumber, etc., as a condiment: acid or other liquid used for cleansing or treatment in manufacture: a plight (*coll.*): a troublesome child (*coll.*). — *v.t.* to preserve with salt, vinegar, etc.: to rub with salt or salt and vinegar, as an old naval punishment: to clean or treat with acid or other chemical. — *adj.* **pick'led** treated with a pickle: drunk (*slang*). — *n.* **pick'ler** one who pickles: a vessel for pickling: an article suitable, or grown, for pickling. — **pick'le-herring** a pickled herring: a merry-andrew (*obs.*). — **have a rod in pickle** to have a punishment ready. [M.E. *pekille*, *pykyl*, *pekkyll*, *pykulle*; cf. Du. *pekel*; Ger. *Pökel*.]

pickle² *pik'l*, (*Scot.*) *n.* a small quantity: a grain of corn. [Origin unknown.]

pickle³ *pik'l*, *v.t.* and *v.i.* to peck: to pick: to eat sparingly:

to pilfer. [Dim. or freq. of **pick¹**.]

pickmaw *pik'mö*, (*Scot.*) *n.* the black-headed gull. [Perh. **pick** (pitch), **maw** (mew).]

Pickwickian *pik-wik'i-ən*, *adj.* relating to or resembling Mr *Pickwick*, the hero of Dickens's *Pickwick Papers.* — *n.* a member of the Pickwick Club. — **in a Pickwickian sense** in a recondite or merely imaginary sense — a phrase by which a member of the Pickwick Club explained away unparliamentary language.

picnic *pik'nik*, *n.* orig. a fashionable social entertainment, towards which each person contributed a share of the food: an open-air repast of a number of persons on a country excursion: an undertaking that is mere child's play, often ironically. — *adj.* of or for a picnic: picnicking. — *v.i.* to have a picnic — *pr.p.* **pic'nicking**; *pa.t.* and *pa.p.* **pic'nicked.** — *n.* **pic'nicker.** — *adj.* **pic'nicky.** [Fr. *pique-nique*.]

pico- *pē-kō-*, *pī-kō-*, in composition, a millionth of a millionth part, a million millionth, as in **picocurie**, **picosecond**, etc. [Sp. *pico*, a small quantity.]

picornavirus *pi-kör'nə-vī-rəs*, *n.* any of a group of viruses including the enteroviruses and rhinoviruses. [**pico-**, **RNA**, and **virus**.]

picot *pē'kō*, *n.* a loop in an ornamental edging: a raised knot in embroidery. — *v.t.* to ornament with picots. — *adj.* **picoté** (*pē-kō-tā*). [Fr. *picot*, point, prick.]

picotee *pik-ə-tē'*, *n.* a florists' variety of carnation, orig. speckled, now edged with a different colour. [Fr. *picoté*, prickled.]

picotite *pik'ō-tīt*, *n.* a dark spinel containing iron, magnesium, and chromium. [From *Picot*, Baron de la Pérouse, who described it.]

picquet. See **picket**.

picra *pik'rə*, *n.* short for hiera-picra. — *n.* **pic'rate** a salt (highly explosive) of picric acid. — *adj.* **pic'ric** (**picric acid** $C_6H_2(NO_2)_3$.OH, trinitrophenol, used as a yellow dye-stuff and as the basis of high explosives). — *ns.* **pic'rite** a coarse-grained igneous rock composed mainly of olivine with ferromagnesian minerals and usually some plagioclase; **picrocar'mine** a stain for microscope work made from carmine, ammonia, water and picric acid; **picrotox'in** a bitter poisonous principle in the seeds of *Cocculus indicus.* [Gr. *pikros*, bitter.]

Pict *pikt*, *n.* one of an ancient people of obscure affinities, in Britain, esp. north-eastern Scotland: in Scottish folklore, one of a dwarfish race of underground dwellers, to whom (with the Romans, the Druids and Cromwell) ancient monuments are generally attributed: Steele's term for a painted woman. — *adj.* **Pict'ish.** — *n.* the (enigmatical) language of the Picts. — **Picts' house** an earth-house. [L. *Pictī*, Picts: possibly the same as *pictī*, *pa.p.* of *pingĕre*, to paint; cf. **Pecht**.]

pictarnie *pik-tär'ni*, (*Scott*) *n.* a tern. [Origin unknown.]

pictograph *pik'tə-gräf*, *n.* a picture used as a symbol in picture-writing. — *n.* **pic'togram** a pictograph: a graphic representation. — *adj.* **pictographic** (*-graf'ik*). — *adv.* **pictograph'ically.** — *n.* **pictography** (*pik-tog'rə-fi*) picture-writing. [L. *pictus*, painted; Gr. *graphein*, to write, *gramma*, a letter, figure.]

pictorial *pik-tō'ri-əl*, *-tö'*, *adj.* of a painter: of or relating to painting or drawing: of, by means of, like, or of the nature of, a picture, or pictures. — *n.* a periodical in which pictures are prominent. — *adv.* **picto'rially.** — *adj.* **pictorical** (*-tor'i-kl*). — *adv.* **pictor'ically** in the manner of a painter. [L. *pictor*, *-ōris*, painter — *pingĕre*, *pictum*, to paint.]

picture *pik'chər*, *n.* the art or act of painting: an imitative representation of an object on a surface: (*loosely*) a photograph: a portrait: a tableau: a visible or visual image: a mental image: (an image on) a television screen: a person as like another as his own portrait: an impressive or attractive sight, like a painting or worthy of being painted: a visible embodiment: a vivid verbal description: a cinema film: (in *pl.*) a cinema show, or the building in which it is given. — *v.t.* to depict, represent in a picture: to form a likeness of in the mind: to describe vividly in words. — *adj.* **pic′tural** relating to, illustrated by, or consisting of pictures. — *n.* (*Spens.*) a picture. — **pic′ture-book** a book of pictures; **pic′ture-card** a court card; **pic′ture-cord** cord for hanging pictures; **pic′ture-frame** a frame for surrounding a picture; **pic′ture-gallery** a gallery, hall, or building where pictures are exhibited; **pic′ture-goer** one who goes much to the cinema; **pic′ture-hat** a lady's wide-brimmed hat, such as those that appear in portraits by Gainsborough; **pic′ture-house, -palace** a building for cinema shows; **Pic′turephone**® a device which allows speakers on the telephone to see each other; **pic′ture-play′** a story told in motion pictures; **picture postcard** a postcard bearing a picture, commonly a local view; **picture ratio** see **aspect ratio**; **pic′ture= restorer** one who cleans and restores and sometimes ruins old pictures; **pic′ture-rod, -rail, -mould′ing** a rod, moulding, from which pictures may be hung; **pic′ture= win′dow** a usu. large window designed to act as a frame to an attractive view; **pic′ture-wire** wire for hanging pictures; **pic′ture-writ′ing** the use of pictures to express ideas or relate events. — **get the picture** (*coll.*) to understand the situation; **in the picture** having a share of attention: adequately briefed; **put me** (etc.) **in the picture** give me (etc.) all the relevant information.   [L. *pictūra* — *pingĕre, pictum,* to paint.]

picturesque *pik-chə-resk′, adj.* like a picture: such as would make a striking picture, implying some measure of beauty with much quaintness or immediate effectiveness: of language, vivid and colourful, or (*facet.*) vulgar: having taste or feeling for the picturesque. — *adv.* **picturesque′ly.** — *n.* **picturesque′ness.**   [It. *pittoresco* — *pittura,* a picture — L. *pictūra.*]

picul *pik′ul, n.* a Chinese weight, about 60 kg.   [Malay *pikul,* a man's load.]

Picus *pī′kəs, n.* an ancient Italian god, a son of Saturn, turned into a woodpecker by Circe: the woodpecker genus. — *adj.* **pī′cine** (*-sīn*).   [L. *Pīcus.*]

piddle *pid′l, v.i.* to deal in trifles: to trifle: to eat with little relish: to urinate (*coll.*). — *n.* (*coll.*) urine: an act of urination. — *n.* **pidd′ler** a trifler. — *adj.* **pidd′ling** trifling, paltry.   [Origin obscure.]

piddock *pid′ək, n.* the pholas.   [Origin unknown.]

pidgin *pij′in, n.* a Chinese corruption of **business** (also **pidg′eon, pig′eon**): affair, concern (*coll.*; also **pidg′eon, pig′eon**): any combination and distortion of two languages as a means of communication. — *n.* **pidginīsā′- tion, -z-.** — **pidgin English** a jargon, mainly English in vocabulary with Chinese arrangement, used in communication between Chinese and foreigners: any jargon consisting of English and another language.

pi-dog, pie-dog. See **pye-dog.**

pie[1] *pī, n.* a magpie: a chatterer.   [Fr., — L. *pīca.*]

pie[2]**, pye** *pī, n.* a book of rules for determining the Church office for the day. — **by cock and pie** (*Shak.*) a minced oath, app. by God and the pie.   [L.L. *pīca,* possibly the same as L. *pīca,* magpie (from the black and white appearance of the page).]

pie[3]**, pi** *pī, n.* type confusedly mixed: a mixed state: confusion. — *v.t.* to reduce to pie: — *pr.p.* **pie′ing, pye′ing;** *pa.t.* and *pa.p.* **pied.**   [Origin obscure; perh. conn. with **pie**[4], or **pie**[2].]

pie[4] *pī, n.* a quantity of meat, fruit, or other food baked within or under a crust of prepared flour: an easy thing (*slang*): a welcome luxury, prize, or spoil (*coll.*). — *ns.* **pie′-counter** a counter at which pies are sold: the source of patronage, bribes, spoils of office (*U.S.; arch.*); **pie chart, diagram, graph** a circle divided into sections by radii so as to show relative numbers or quantities; **pie′crust** the paste covering or enclosing a pie; **piecrust table** a Chippendale table with carved raised edge; **pie′dish** a deep dish in which pies are made. — *adj.* **pie′-eyed** (*coll.*) drunk. — **pie′man** one who sells pies, esp. in the street; **pie′-plant** (*U.S. dial.*) rhubarb; **pie′= shop.** — **have a finger in the pie** see **finger;** **Périgord pie** a pie of partridge flavoured with truffles (*Périgord,* now contained in the departments of Dordogne and

Lot-et-Garonne); **pie in the sky** some improbable future good promised without guarantee (from early 20th-cent. song).   [Origin unknown; possibly from **pie**[1], as a miscellaneous collector; the Gael. *pighe* is from English.]

pie[5] *pī, n.* a small Indian coin, withdrawn after 1957, equal to 1/3 of a pice, or 1/12 of an anna.   [Marathi *pā′ī,* a fourth.]

piebald *pī′böld, adj.* black and white in patches: (*loosely*) of other colours in patches: motley: heterogeneous. — *n.* a piebald horse or other animal. — Also **pyebald.**   [**pie**[1]**, bald.**]

piece *pēs, n.* a part or portion of anything, esp. detached: a separate lump, mass, body, of any material, considered as an object (in Scots without *of* following): a distance: a span of time: a single article: a definite quantity, as of cloth or paper: a literary, dramatic, musical, or artistic composition: a production, specimen of work: an example: an exemplification or embodiment: a sandwich or a little bread, buttered or not, esp. as a lunch (*Scot.*): a gun: a portion (*obs.*); a wine-cup (*obs*): a coin: a man in chess, draughts, or other game (in chess sometimes excluding pawns): a person — now usually (often disrespectfully) a woman. — *v.t.* to enlarge by adding a piece: to patch: to combine. — **-piece** in composition, consisting of a given number of separate parts, pieces, members, etc., as in *three-piece suite.* — *adj.* **piece′less** not made of pieces. — *adv.* **piece′meal** (**meal**[1] in sense of 'measure') in pieces: to pieces: bit by bit. — *adj.* done bit by bit: fragmentary. — *n.* a small piece: bit by bit proceeding. — *v.t.* to dismember. — *v.t.* **piec′en** (*dial.*) to join (esp. broken threads in spinning). — *ns.* **piec′ener, piec′er** one who is employed in a spinning-factory to join broken threads. — **piece′-goods** textile fabrics made in standard lengths; **piece′-rate** a fixed rate paid according to the amount of work done; **piece′-work** work paid for by the piece or quantity, not by time. — **(all) to pieces** into a state of disintegration or collapse: through and through, thoroughly (*U.S.*); **a piece** each; **a piece of** an instance of: a bit of, something of; **a piece of one's mind** a frank outspoken rating; **go to pieces** to break up entirely (*lit.* and *fig.*): to lose completely ability to cope with the situation; **in pieces** in, or to, a broken-up state; **of a piece** as if of the same piece, the same in nature: homogeneous, uniform: in keeping, consistent (with *with*); **piece of cake** see **cake; piece of goods** (*dial.; derog.*) a woman; **piece of work** a task: a fuss, ado: person (usually with **nasty,** etc.); **piece out** to eke out; **piece together** to put together bit by bit; **piece up** to patch up: perh. to incorporate in one's own share (*Shak.*); **the piece** (*Scot.*) apiece; **to pieces** see **all to pieces.**   [O.Fr. *piece* — L.L. *pecia, petium,* a fragment, a piece of land — thought to be of Celtic (Brythonic) origin; cf. **patch**[1]**, peat**[2]**, petty,** and **Pit-** in place names.]

pièce *pyes,* (Fr.) *n.* a piece, item: (a barrel of) about 220 litres (of wine). — **pièce de résistance** (*də rā-zē-stās*) the substantial course at dinner, the joint: the best item; **pièce d'occasion** (*do-ka-zyõ*) something, usu. a literary or musical work, composed, prepared, or used for a special occasion.

piecen(er), piecer. See **piece.**

pied *pīd, adj.* variegated like a magpie: of various colours. — *n.* **pied′ness.**   [**pie**[1].]

pied-à-terre *pyā-da-ter,* (Fr.) *n.* a dwelling kept for temporary, secondary, or occasional lodging: — *pl.* **pieds= à-terre.**

piedmont *pēd′mənt,* (*U.S.*) *n.* a mountain-foot region. — Also *adj.* — *n.* **pied′montite** a dark red mineral, a hydrous silicate of calcium, aluminium, manganese and iron.   [*Piedmont* in Italy, lit. mountain-foot.]

pied noir *pyā nwär,* (Fr.) a North African (esp. Algerian) person of French descent: — *pl.* **pieds noirs.**

piel′d *pēld,* (*Shak.*) *adj.* tonsured.   [See **peel**[1].]

piend *pēnd, n.* a salient angle.   [Origin unknown.]

piepowder *pī′pow-dər,* (*obs.*) *n.* a wayfarer, itinerant. —

Court of Piepowder(s) an ancient court held in fairs and markets to administer justice in a rough-and-ready way to all comers — also *Court of Dusty Feet*.   [O.Fr. *piedpoudreux* — *pied* (L. *pēs, pedis*), foot, *poudre* (L. *pulvis*), dust.]

pier *pēr, n.* the mass of stonework between the openings in the wall of a building: the support of an arch, bridge, etc.: a masonry support for a telescope or the like: a buttress: a gate pillar: a mass of stone, ironwork, or woodwork projecting into the sea or other water, as a breakwater, landing-stage, or promenade: a jetty or a wharf. — *n.* **pier'age** toll paid for using a pier. — **pier'-glass** orig., a mirror hung between windows: a tall mirror; **pier'-head** the seaward end of a pier; **pier'-table** a table fitted for the space between windows.   [M.E. *pēr*, L.L. *pēra*; origin doubtful.]

pierce *pērs, v.t.* to thrust or make a hole through: to enter, or force a way into: to touch or move deeply: to penetrate: to perforate: to make by perforating or penetrating. — *v.i.* to penetrate. — *n.* a perforation: a stab: a prick. — *adj.* **pierce'able** capable of being pierced. — *adj.* **pier'ced** perforated: penetrated. — *n.* **pierc'er** one who or that which pierces: any sharp instrument used for piercing: a sting: a keen eye (*arch.*). — *adj.* **pierc'ing** penetrating: very acute: keen. — *adv.* **pierc'ingly.** — *n.* **pierc'ingness.**   [O.Fr. *percer*; of doubtful origin.]

Pierian *pī-ē'ri-ən, adj.* of *Pieria*, in Thessaly, the country of the Muses: of the Muses. — *n.* **pierid** (*pī'ə-rid*) any butterfly of the Pieridae. — *n.pl.* **Pierides** (*pī-er'i-dēz*) the nine Muses: — *sing.* **Pī'eris.** — *n.* **Pī'eris** the cabbage butterfly genus, typical of the family **Pier'idae** (*-dē*). — *adj.* **pieridine** (*pī-er'i-dīn*) of the Pieridae.   [Gr. *Pīeriā.*]

Pierrot *pē'ə-rō, pyer-ō, n.* a white-faced buffoon with loose long-sleeved garb: (without *cap*; formerly) a member of a group of entertainers in similar dress at seaside resorts, etc.: an 18th-century women's low-cut basque, with sleeves: — *fem.* **Pierrette'**.   [Fr., dim of *Pierre*, Peter.]

pierst. Spens. for **pierced** (*pa.t.* and *pa.p.*).

piert. Same as **peart;** see also **parsley-piert.**

piet. Same as **pyot.**

pietà *pyā-tä', n.* a representation of the Virgin with the dead Christ across her knees.   [It., — L. *pietās, -ātis*, pity.]

pietra-dura *pyā'trə-dōō'rə, n.* inlaid work with hard stones — jasper, agate, etc.   [It., hard stone.]

piety *pī'i-ti, n.* pity (*obs.*): the quality of being pious: dutifulness: devoutness: sense of duty towards parents, benefactors, etc.: dutiful conduct. — *ns.* **pi'etism;** **pi'etist** one marked by strong devotional feeling: a name first applied to a sect of German religious reformers of deep devotional feeling (end of 17th century). — *adjs.* **pietist'ic, -al.**   [O.Fr. *piete* — L. *pietās, -ātis.*]

piezo- *pī'i-zō-, pī-ē'zō-*, in composition, pressure. — *adj.* **piezo** short for **piezoelectric.** — *n.* **piezochem'istry** the chemistry of substances under high pressure. — *adj.* **piezoelec'tric.** — *n.* **piezoelectri'city** electricity developed in certain crystals by mechanical strain, and the effect of an electric field in producing expansion and contraction along different axes. — *adj.* **piezomagnet'ic.** — *ns.* **piezomag'netism** magnetism developed in a similar way to piezoelectricity, using a magnetic instead of an electric field; **piezometer** (*-om'i-tər*) an instrument for measuring pressure or compressibility.   [Gr. *piēzein*, to press.]

piffero *pif'ə-rō, n.* a fife: an Italian bagpipe: a crude oboe: — *pl.* **piff'eros.** — *n.* **pifferaro** (*-ä'rō*) a piffero-player: — *pl.* **pifferari** (*-rē*).   [It., — O.H.G. *pfīfari*, piper.]

piffle *pif'l, n.* nonsense: worthless talk. — *v.i.* to trifle: to act ineffectually. — *adj.* **piff'ling** trivial, petty. — *n.* **piff'ler.**   [Origin unknown.]

pig[1] *pig, n.* any mammal of the family Suidae, omnivorous ungulates with thick, bristly skin, esp. the domesticated *Sus scrofa*, a farm animal bred as food

for humans: a swine: a young swine: swine's flesh as food, esp. that of the young animal: one who is like a pig, dirty, greedy, gluttonous, or cantankerous (also used mildly in reproach): an oblong mass of unforged metal, as first extracted from the ore: the mould into which it is run, esp. one of the branches, the main channel being the *sow*: a device that is propelled through a pipeline or duct by pneumatic, hydraulic or gas pressure, for clearing, cleaning, tracking or scanning purposes, etc. (*tech.*) (see also **intelligent pig** below): a feast (*slang*): a policeman (*slang; derog.*): a segment of an orange (*slang*): something very difficult (*slang*). — *v.i.* to bring forth pigs: to live, herd, huddle, sleep, or feed like pigs: to eat (*slang*): — *pr.p.* **pigg'ing;** *pa.t.* and *pa.p.* **pigged.** — *ns.* **pigg'ery** a place where pigs are kept: piggishness; **pigg'ing** (*tech.*) operating a pig (q.v.) or running a pig along a pipeline. — *adj.* (*slang*) expressing aversion, of something troublesome, unpleasant or difficult. — *adj.* **pigg'ish** like a pig: greedy: dirty: cantankerous. — *adv.* **pigg'ishly.** — *ns.* **pigg'ishness; pigg'ie, pigg'y, pig'let, pig'ling** a little pig. — *n.pl.* **pigg'ies** a child's word for toes. — *adj.* **pigg'y** like a pig. — **pig'-bed** a pig's sleeping place: a mould of sand in which a pig of iron is cast; **pig'boat** (*U.S. naval slang*) a submarine; **pig'-deer** the babiroussa. — *adjs.* **pig'-eyed** having small dull eyes with heavy lids; **pig'-faced.** — **pig'feed** food for pigs; **pig'-fish** (*U.S.*) a name for various kinds of grunt (*Haemulon*, etc.): in Australia, a name for various wrasses; **piggyback** see separate entry; **pigg'y-bank** a child's money-box, shaped like a pig: sometimes a child's money-box of any design. — *adj.* **pig'head'ed** having a pig-like head: stupidly obstinate. — *adv.* **pig'head'edly.** — **pig'head'edness; pig'-herd.** — *adj.* **pig'-ig'norant** (*coll.; derog.*) very ignorant. — **pig'(gy)-in-the-midd'le** a children's game in which a person standing between two others tries to intercept a ball, etc., passing back and forth between them: one caught between opposing viewpoints, strategies, etc. (*fig.*); **pig'-iron** iron in pigs or rough bars. — *v.i.* **pig'-jump** (*Austr.*; of a horse) to jump from all four legs without bringing them together. — **pig Latin** a secret language or jargon made up by children; **pig'-lead** lead in pigs; **pig'-lily** (*S. Afr.*) the lily of the Nile; **pig'meat** bacon, ham or pork; **pig'-nut** the earth-nut (*Conopodium*); **pig'pen** a pigsty; **pig'-rat** the bandicoot rat; **pig'sconce** a pigheaded fellow: a blockhead; **pig'skin** the skin of a pig prepared as a strong leather: a saddle (*slang*); **pig'-sticker;** **pig'-sticking** boar-hunting with spears; **pig'sty** a pen for keeping pigs; **pig's'-wash, pig'wash** swill; **pig's whisper** a low whisper (*dial.*): a very short space of time; **pig swill, pig'swill** kitchen, etc. waste fed to pigs; **pig'tail** the tail of a pig: the hair of the head plaited behind in a queue or queues: a roll of twisted tobacco; **pig'weed** goosefoot, amaranth, cow-parsnip, or other plant eaten by pigs; **pig'-woman** a woman who roasted pigs at fairs. — **a pig in a poke** see **poke[1]; make a pig of oneself** (*coll.*) to overindulge in food or drink; **make a pig's ear of (something)** (*coll.*) to make a mess of something, to do something badly or clumsily; **pig it** (*coll.*) to live in dirty surroundings; **when pigs fly** (*coll.*) never.   [M.E. *pigge*; cf. Du. *bigge, big.*]

pig[2] *pig,* (*Scot.*) *n.* an earthenware crock, hot-water bottle, or other vessel: earthenware: a potsherd. — **pig'-man, -woman** a dealer in pigs. — **pigs and whistles** wrack and ruin.   [Origin unknown.]

pigeon[1] *pij'ən, -in, n.* orig., a young dove: a dove: any bird of the dove family: extended to various other birds (e.g. the *Cape pigeon*): a girl (*obs.*): one who is fleeced (*slang*): abbrev. for **stool pigeon** (see **stool**). — *v.t.* to gull. — *n.* **pig'eonry** a place for keeping pigeons. — **pig'eon-berry** (*U.S.*) pokeweed or its fruit. — *adj.* **pig'eon-breast'ed, -chested** having a narrow chest with breast-bone thrown forward. — **pig'eon-fancier** one who keeps and breeds pigeons for racing or exhibiting; **pig'eon-fancying; pig'eon-flier, -flyer** one who sends forth homing pigeons; **pig'eon-flying.** — *adj.* **pig'eon=**

heart'ed timid. — **pig'eon-hole, pig'eonhole** a niche for a pigeon's nest: a hole of similar appearance: a compartment for storing and classifying papers, etc.: a compartment of the mind or memory: (in *pl.*) the stocks: (in *pl.*) an old outdoor game like bagatelle. — *v.t.* to furnish with or make into pigeon-holes: to put into a pigeon-hole: to classify methodically, or too rigidly: to lay aside and delay action on, or treat with neglect. — **pig'eon-house** a dovecot. — *adj.* **pig'eon= liv'ered** mild. — **pig'eon-pair** boy and girl twins or a boy and girl as sole children in a family; **pig'eon-pea** dal; **pig'eon-post** transmission of letters by pigeons; **pig'eon's-blood** a dark red colour, ruby; **pigeon's milk** partly digested food regurgitated by pigeons to feed their young: an imaginary liquid for which children are sent, as on 1st April. — *adj.* **pig'eon-toed** in-toed: (of birds) having all toes at one level. — **pig'eon-wing** a caper in dancing. — **clay pigeon** see **clay.** [O.Fr. *pijon* — L. *pīpiō, -ōnis* — *pīpīre*, to cheep.]

pigeon². Same as **pidgin.**

piggin *pig'in, n.* a small pail or bowl of staves and hoops, one stave usually prolonged as a handle: a vessel of various other kinds. [Poss. from **pig²**; the Celtic words seem to be from English.]

piggy. See **pig¹.**

piggyback *pig'i-bak, adv., adj.,* and *n.* a variant of **pickaback.** — *adj.* of a method of heart transplant surgery in which the patient's own heart is not removed and continues to function in tandem with that of the donor.

pight *pīt,* an old *pa.t.* and *pa.p.* (*Spens.*) of **pitch²,** pitched, set: also false archaism for present tense. — *adj.* well-knit (*Spens.*): resolved (*Shak.*).

pigmean. See **pygmy.**

pightle *pī'tl, n.* a small enclosure: a croft. [Ety. dub.]

pigment *pig'mənt, n.* paint: any substance used for colouring: that which gives colour to animal and vegetable tissues: piment (*Scott*). — *adjs.* **pigmental** (*-men'tl*), **pig'mentary, pig'mented.** — *n.* **pigmentā'tion** coloration or discoloration by pigments in the tissues. [L. *pīgmentum* — *pingĕre*, to paint.]

pigmy. Same as **pygmy.**

pignorate, pignerate *pig'nər-āt,* (*arch.*) *v.t.* to give or take in pledge or pawn. — *n.* **pignorā'tion.** [L. *pignus, -eris* or *-oris,* a pledge.]

pigsney, pigsny, pigsnie *pigz'ni, n.* a term of endearment (sometimes contempt), esp. to a woman (*arch.* or *dial.*): an eye (playfully; *obs.*). [**pig's eye,** with prosthetic *n* (from *an eye, mine eye*).]

pi-jaw. See **pi³.**

pika *pī'kə, n.* the tailless hare (Ochotona), a small mammal of the order Rodentia, or, in some classifications, Lagomorpha, found in mountain regions. [Tungus *piika.*]

pikadell. See **piccadill.**

pike¹ *pīk, n.* a sharp point: a weapon with a long shaft and a sharp head like a spear, formerly used by foot-soldiers: a spiked staff: a sharp-pointed hill or summit: a voracious freshwater fish (*Esox lucius*) with pointed snout; extended to various other fishes: a pick (*dial.*). — *v.t.* to kill or pierce with a pike: to pick (*dial.*). — *adj.* **piked** (*pīkt, pīk'id*) spiked: ending in a point. — *n.* **pīk'er** one who picks (*dial.*): a pilferer (*dial.*): one who bets, gambles, speculates, or does anything else in a very small way. — **pike'-head** the head of a pike or spear; **pike'man** a man armed with a pike: one who wields a pick; **pike'-perch** a percoid fish with pike-like jaws; **pike'staff** the staff or shaft of a pike: a staff with a pike at the end. — **plain as a pikestaff** (orig. **packstaff**), perfectly plain or clear. [O.E. *pīc,* pick, spike; but also partly from Fr. *pic* with the same meaning, and *pique* the weapon, and prob. partly from Scand.]

pike² *pīk, v.i.* to speed. — *v.t.* to betake quickly. [Perh. orig. *get oneself a pikestaff* (a pilgrim's spiked staff); perh. Fr. *piquer,* to spur.]

pike³ *pīk, n.* a turnpike: a toll: a main road (*U.S.*). — *n.* **pī'ker** a tramp. — **pike'-keeper, pike'man** a man in charge of a turnpike. [Short for **turnpike.**]

pikelet *pīk'lit, n.* a kind of tea-cake, or crumpet, or muffin (*dial.*): a drop-scone (*Austr.* and *N.Z.*). [W. *bara pyglyd,* pitchy bread.]

pikul. Same as **picul.**

pila. See **pilum.**

pilaff. See **pilau.**

pilaster *pi-las'tər, n.* a square column, partly built into, partly projecting from, a wall. — *adj.* **pilas'tered.** [Fr. *pilastre* — It. *pilastro* — L. *pīla,* a pillar.]

pilau *pi-low', n.* a highly spiced Eastern dish of rice with a fowl, meat, or the like, boiled together or separately. — Also **pillau', pilaw', pilaff'** (or *pil'*), **pilow'.** [Pers. *pilāw,* Turk. *pilāw, pilāf.*]

pilch *pilch,* (*arch.*) *n.* an outer garment, orig. a fur cloak, later a coarse leather or woollen cloak: a rug for a saddle: a light saddle: a flannel cloth for wrapping a child. — *n.* **pilch'er** a scabbard (*Shak.*). [O.E. *pyl(e)ce* — L.L. *pellicea* — L. *pellis,* skin.]

pilchard *pil'chərd, n.* a sea-fish like the herring, but smaller, thicker, and rounder, common off Cornwall. Earlier (*Shak.*) **pil'cher.** [Origin unknown; poss. Scand. (cf. Norw. *pilk,* artificial bait); Ir. *pilseir* is prob. from English.]

pilcorn *pil'körn, n.* the naked oat, a variety in which the glume does not adhere to the grain. [For **pilled corn.**]

pilcrow *pil'krō, n.* a paragraph-mark. [Origin obscure.]

pile¹ *pīl, n.* a set of things fitted or resting one over another, or in a more or less regular figure: a heap of combustibles for cremating a dead body, or for the burnt-offering, or for burning to death: a set of weights fitting one within another: a stack of arms: a heap of shot: a set of wrought-iron bars placed together for welding and rolling into one: a series of alternate plates of two metals for generating an electric current: a set of coins placed vertically one upon another: a great amount of money, a fortune (*slang*): a large supply (*coll.*): a tall building: a nuclear reactor, orig. the graphite blocks forming the moderator for the reactor: the under iron for striking coins (*obs.*): the reverse of a coin (*obs.*). — *v.t.* to lay in a pile or heap: to collect in a mass: to heap up: to load with heaps: to accumulate. — *v.i.* to come into piles: to accumulate: to go in crowds: to get in or out (with *in* or *out*). — *n.* **pī'ler.** — **pile'-cap** the top of a nuclear reactor: see also under **pile²; pile'-up** a collision involving several motor vehicles, players in Rugby, etc. — **pile arms** to prop three muskets, orig. with fixed bayonets, so that the butts remain firm, the muzzles close together pointing obliquely — also **stack arms; pile it on** (*coll.*) to overdo, exaggerate (something); **pile on, up, the agony** (*coll.*) to overdo painful effects by accumulation, etc.; **pile up** to run ashore: to form a disorderly mass or heap: to become involved in a pile-up (q.v.): to accumulate. [Fr., — L. *pīla,* a pillar.]

pile² *pīl, n.* an arrow-head: a Roman javelin: a large stake or cylinder driven into the earth to support foundations: an inverted pyramidal figure (*her.*). — *v.t.* to drive piles into: to support with or build on piles. — **pile'-cap** (*civil engineering*) a reinforced concrete block cast around a set of piles to create a unified support: see also under **pile¹; pile'-driver** an engine for driving in piles: in games, a very heavy stroke, kick, etc.; **pile'-dwelling** a dwelling built on piles, esp. a lake-dwelling; **pile shoe** the iron or steel point fitted to the foot of a pile to give it strength to pierce the earth and so assist driving; **pile'work** work or foundations made of piles; **pile'-worm** a ship-worm. [O.E. *pīl* — L. *pīlum,* a javelin.]

pile³ *pīl, n.* a covering of hair, esp. soft, fine, or short hair: down: human body-hair: a single hair: the raised or fluffy surface of a fabric, carpet, etc.: (as distinguished from *nap*) the raised surface of a fabric made not in finishing but in weaving, either by leaving loops (which may be cut) or by weaving two cloths face to face and cutting them apart. — *adj.* **pil'eous** (*rare*) relating to or consisting of hair; **pilif'erous** bearing hairs: ending in a hair-like point; **pīl′iform** hair-like. [L. *pĭlus*, a hair.]

pile⁴ *pīl*, *n*. (usu. in *pl*.) a haemorrhoid. — *n*. **pile′wort** the lesser celandine (*Ranunculus ficaria*), once thought a remedy for piles. [L. *pĭla*, a ball.]

pileate. See **pileum.**

pileorhiza *pī-li-ō-rī′zə*, (*bot*.) *n*. a root-cap. [L. *pīleus*, *-um* (see next word), Gr. *rhiza*, root.]

pileous. See **pile³.**

pileum *pī′li-əm*, *n*. the top of a bird's head: — *pl*. **pil′ea.** — *n*. **pi′leus** a Roman felt cap: the expanded cap of a mushroom or toadstool, or other fungus: — *pl*. **pilei** (*pī′li-i*). — *adjs*. **pi′leate, -d** cap-shaped: capped: crested. [L. *pĭleum, pĭleus*, for *pilleum, pilleus*, a felt cap; cf. Gr. *pīlos*, felt, a felt cap.]

pilfer *pil′fər*, *v.i.* and *v.t.* to steal in small quantities. — *ns*. **pil′ferage, pil′fering, pil′fery** petty theft; **pil′ferer.** — *adv.* **pil′feringly.** [Prob. connected with **pelf.**]

pilgarlick, peelgarlic *pil-, pēl-gär′lik*, *ns*. a baldpate (*obs*.): a poor wretch: in whimsical self-pity, oneself. — *adj*. **pilgar′licky.** [**pill²**, **peel¹**, and **garlic**, as like a pilled or peeled head of garlic.]

pilgrim *pil′grim*, *n*. a wanderer, wayfarer (*arch*. and *poet*.): one who travels to a distance to visit a holy place: allegorically or spiritually, one journeying through life as a stranger in this world: a Pilgrim Father: an original settler: newcomer. — *adj*. of or pertaining to a pilgrim: like a pilgrim: consisting of pilgrims. — *n*. **pil′grimage** the journeying of a pilgrim: a journey to a shrine or other holy place or place venerated for its associations: the journey of life: a lifetime. — *adj*. visited by pilgrims. — *v.i.* to go on pilgrimage: to wander. — *ns*. **pil′-grimager** (*contemptuously*) one who goes on pilgrimage; **pil′grimer** one who goes on pilgrimage. — *v.i.* (or *v.t.* with *it*) **pil′grimise, -ize** to play the pilgrim. — **pil′grim-bott′le** a flat bottle with ears at the neck for a cord; **Pilgrim Fathers** the Puritans who sailed for America in the *Mayflower*, and founded Plymouth, Massachusetts, in 1620; **pilgrim's shell** a scallop-shell (called a cockle) used as a sign that one had visited the shrine of St James of Compostela; **pilgrim's sign** a badge, often a leaden brooch, obtained at the shrine and worn on the hat by a pilgrim. [Assumed O.Fr. *pelegrin* (Fr. *pèlerin*) — L. *peregrīnus*, foreigner, stranger; see **peregrine**.]

pilhorse *pil′hörs*, or **philhorse** *fil′* (*Shak*.). Same as **fill=horse** or **thill-horse.**

pili¹ *pē-lē′*, *n*. the nut (also **pili′-nut′**) of trees of the burseraceous genus *Canarium*. [Tagálog.]

pili². See **pilus.**

piliferous, pilliform. See **plle³.**

Pilipino *pil-i-pē′nō n*. the official language of the Philippines, based on Tagálog. [Pilipino — Sp. *Filipino*, Philippine.]

pill¹ *pil*, *n*. a little ball of medicine: a ball, e.g. a cannonball, tennis-ball, or (in *pl*.) billiards (*facet*.): anything disagreeable that must be accepted: a tiresome person: a doctor (*slang*; also in *pl*.). — *v.t.* to dose with pills: to blackball (*slang*). — **pill′-box** a box for holding pills: a kind of one-horse carriage (*arch*.): a small blockhouse (*mil. slang*): a small round brimless hat; **pill′-bug** a wood-louse that rolls itself into a ball; **pill′head, pill′popper** (*slang*) a regular, usu. addicted, taker of sedative and/or stimulant pills, e.g. barbiturates and amphetamines; **pill′worm** a millipede that curls up; **pill′wort** a water-fern (*Pilularia*) of lake-margins, with pill-like sporocarps. — **the pill** any of various contraceptive pills (see **oral contraception**); **on the pill** taking contraceptive pills regularly. [L. *pĭla*, perh. through O.Fr. *pile*, or from a syncopated form of the dim. *pĭlŭla*.]

pill² *pil*, *v.t.* and *v.i.* to plunder (*arch*.): to peel (*dial*.): to make or become hairless (*obs*.). — *n*. (*Spens*.) husk, integument. — *n*. **pill′age** the act of plundering: plunder. — *v.t.* and *v.i.* to plunder. — *n*. **pill′ager.** [O.E. *pylian* and O.Fr. *peler*, both — L. *pilāre*, to deprive of hair; cf. **peel.**]

pillar *pil′ər*, *n*. a detached support, not necessarily cylindrical or of classical proportions (*archit*.): a structure of like form erected as a monument, ornament, object of worship, etc.: a tall upright rock: a mass of coal or rock left in a mine to support the roof: anything in the form of a column: a supporting post: the post supporting a bicycle saddle: a cylinder holding the plates of a watch or clock in position: a pillar-box: one who, or anything that, sustains. — *ns*. **pill′arist, pill′ar-saint** an ascetic living on the top of a pillar, a stylite. — **pill′ar-box** a short hollow pillar for posting letters in (**pillar-box red** the bright red colour of most British pillar-boxes); **pill′ar-root** a supporting root descending from a branch. — **from pillar to post** from one state of difficulty to another: hither and thither; **Pillars of Islam** the five major Islamic duties — the statement of faith, prayer, fasting, almsgiving, and pilgrimage to Mecca. [O.Fr. *piler* (Fr. *pilier*) — L.L. *pīlāre* — L. *pīla*, a pillar.]

pillau. See **pilau.**

pillicock *pil′i-kok*, *n*. the penis (allusively in *Shak*.): a term of endearment to a boy. [Cf. Norw. dial. *pill*.]

pillion *pil′yən*, *n*. a pad or light saddle for a woman: a cushion behind a horseman for a second rider (usu. a woman) or for a bag: the passenger-seat of a motorcycle, or a baggage-carrier, usable as an extra seat. — *adv.* on a pillion. — *v.t.* to seat on or furnish with a pillion. — *ns*. **pill′ionist, pill′ion-rider** one who rides pillion; **pill′ion-seat.** [Prob. Ir. *pillín*, Gael. *pillin*, *pillean*, a pad, a pack-saddle — *peall*, a skin or mat, L. *pellis*, skin.]

pilliwinks *pil′i-wingks*, *n.pl.* an instrument of torture for crushing the fingers. [Origin unknown.]

pillock *pil′ək*, (*slang*) *n*. a stupid or foolish person. [**Pillicock** and dial. forms *pillick, pilluck*.]

pillory *pil′ə-ri*, *n*. a wooden frame, supported by an upright pillar or post, with holes through which the head and hands were put as a punishment, abolished in England in 1837. — *v.t.* to set in the pillory: to hold up to ridicule: — *pr.p.* **pill′orying**; *pa.t.* and *pa.p.* **pill′oried.** — Also **pill′orise, -ize.** [O.Fr. *pilori*; Prov. *espilori*; of uncertain origin.]

pillow *pil′ō*, *n*. a cushion for a sleeper's head: any object used for the purpose: a cushion for lace-making: a support for part of a structure. — *v.t.* to lay or rest for support: to serve as pillow for: to furnish or prop with pillows. — *v.i.* (*arch*.) to rest the head. — *adjs*. **pill′owed** supported by, or provided with, a pillow; **pill′owy** like a pillow: round and swelling: soft. — **pill′ow-bere** (*arch*.), **-beer** (*arch*.), **-case, -slip** a cover for a pillow, **pillow-block** see **pedestal**; **pill′ow-cup** a last cup before going to bed; **pill′ow-fight; pill′ow-fighting** the sport of thumping one another with pillows; **pill′ow-lace** lace worked with bobbins on a pillow; **pill′ow-lava** lava showing pillow-structure; **pill′ow=structure** in lavas, separation into pillow-shaped blocks; **pillow talk** talk between lovers in bed. [O.E. *pyle*, also *pylu* — L. *pulvīnus*.]

pillworm, pillwort. See **pill¹.**

pilniewinks. See **pinnywinkle.**

Pilocarpus *pī-lō-kär′pəs*, *n*. a genus of S. American rutaceous shrubs, including jaborandi. — *n*. **pilocar′pin(e)** (*-pēn*) an alkaloid ($C_{11}H_{16}O_2N_2$) got from jaborandi leaves. [Gr. *pīlos*, felt, a felt cap, *karpos*, fruit.]

pilose *pī′lōs*, *adj*. hairy: having scattered soft or moderately stiff hairs. — *adj*. **pī′lous** hairy. — *n*. **pilosity** (*-los′i-ti*). [L. *pĭlōsus* — *pĭlus*, hair.]

pilot *pī′lət*, *n*. a steersman (*arch*.): one who conducts ships in and out of a harbour, along a dangerous coast, etc.: one who actually operates the controls of an aircraft, hovercraft, spacecraft, etc.: one who is qualified to act as pilot: a guide: a cowcatcher (*U.S.*): a pilot film or broadcast. — *adj*. pertaining to pilot(s): acting as guide or control: trial (of e.g. a model on a smaller scale) serving to test the qualities or future possibilities of a machine, plant, etc., or (of a film or broadcast) to test the popularity of a projected radio or television series.

— *v.t.* to act as pilot to. — *n.* **pi′lotage** piloting: a pilot's fee. — *adj.* **pi′lotless** without a pilot: not requiring a pilot, as an automatic aeroplane. — **pi′lot-balloon′** a small balloon sent up to find how the wind blows; **pi′lot-boat** a boat used by pilots on duty; **pilot burner, jet, light** (see also below) a small gas-burner kept alight to light another; **pilot cloth** a coarse, stout cloth for overcoats; **pilot engine** a locomotive sent before a train to clear its way, as a pilot; **pi′lot-fish** a carangoid fish that accompanies ships and sharks; **pi′lot-flag, -jack** the flag hoisted at the fore by a vessel needing a pilot; **pi′lot-house** a shelter for steering-gear and pilot — also *wheel-house*; **pi′lot-jacket** a pea-jacket; **pilot lamp, light** a small electric light to show when current is on, or for other purpose; **pilot officer** in the Air Force, an officer ranking with an army second-lieutenant; **pi′lot-plant** prototype machinery set up to begin a new process; **pilot scheme** a scheme serving as a guide on a small scale to a full-scale scheme; **pi′lot-whale** the ca'ing-whale. [Fr. *pilote* — It. *pilota*, app. for earlier *pedota*, which may be — Gr. *pēdon*, oar, in pl. rudder.]

pilous. See **pilose.**

pilow. See **pilau.**

pils(e)ner *pilz′, pils′nər,* (also with *cap.*) *n.* a light beer. [Ger., from *Pilsen*, a city in Czechoslovakia.]

Piltdown man *pilt′down man′,* Eoanthropus (q.v.).

pilule *pil′ūl, n.* a little pill. — Also **pil′ula.** — *adj.* **pil′ular.** [L. *pilŭla,* dim. of *pīla,* ball.]

pilum *pī′ləm, n.* the heavy javelin used by Roman foot-soldiers: — *pl.* **pī′la.** [L. *pīlum.*]

pilus *pī′ləs, n.* a hair: — *pl.* **pī′lī.** [L. *pīlus.*]

piment *pi-ment′,* (*obs.*) *n.* spiced sweetened wine. — Also (*Scott*) **pigment** (*pig′mənt*). — *n.* **pimento** (*pi-ment′ō*) formerly Cayenne pepper: now allspice or Jamaica pepper, the dried unripe fruits of a W. Indian tree (*Pimenta officinalis*) of the myrtle family: the tree itself: its wood: — *pl.* **pimen′tos.** — *n.* **pimiento** (*pi-mē-en′tō*) the sweet, red, or green, pepper, capsicum: — *pl.* **pimien′tos.** [O.Fr. *piment*, Sp. *pimiento* — L. *pīgmentum*, paint.]

pimp *pimp, n.* one who procures gratifications for the lust of others, a pander: a man who lives with, and sometimes solicits for, a prostitute and lives off her earnings, or one who solicits for a prostitute or brothel and is paid for his services. — *v.i.* to pander. [Origin obscure, perh. related to Fr. *pimpant*, well-dressed, smart — O.Fr. *pimper*, to dress smartly.]

pimpernel *pim′pər-nel, n.* burnet (*obs.*): burnet saxifrage (Pimpinella) (*obs.*): now, the poor man's weather-glass (*Anagallis arvensis*), a plant of the primrose family, with scarlet (or blue, etc.) flowers. — *n.* **Pimpinell′a** the anise and burnet saxifrage genus of umbelliferous plants. — **bastard pimpernel** a small plant (*Centunculus minimus*) akin to the scarlet pimpernel; **bog pimpernel** *Anagallis tenella*; **water pimpernel** brookweed; **yellow pimpernel** the wood loosestrife (*Lysimachia nemorum*). [O.Fr. *pimpernelle,* mod. Fr. *pimprenelle,* and It. *pimpinella,* burnet; origin doubtful.]

Pimpinella. See **pimpernel.**

pimping *pimp′ing, adj.* petty: puny: paltry: sickly. [Origin obscure.]

pimple *pim′pl, n.* a pustule: a small swelling, protuberance, or hill. — *adjs.* **pim′pled, pim′ply** having pimples. [Origin unknown.]

pin *pin, n.* a piece of wood or of metal used for fastening things together: a peg or nail: a sharp-pointed piece of wire with a rounded head for fastening clothes, etc.: an ornamental elaboration of this: a cylindrical part inserted into something, as the stem of a key, or part of a lock that a hollow-stemmed key fits: the projecting part of a dovetail joint: a peg aimed at in quoits: a peg in the centre of an archery target: the rod of a golf flag: a skittle or ninepin: a chess piece (*obs.*): a tuning peg in a stringed instrument: a measuring peg in a drinking-cup: a degree, stage, pitch: a leg (*coll.*): a peak: the projecting bone of the hip: a hard spot or excrescence: a cask of 4½ gallons: short for clothes-pin,

rolling-pin, tirling-pin, etc.: an act of pinning or state of being pinned: anything of little value. — *v.t.* to fasten with a pin: to fix, to fasten, to enclose, to hold down (*fig.*): to make a small hole in: to insert chips of stone between the stones of: to cause an opponent's piece to be unable to move without checking its own king (*chess*): — *pr.p.* **pinn′ing;** *pa.t.* and *pa.p.* **pinned.** — *ns.* **pinn′er,** one who pins: a pin-maker: a pinafore: a head-dress with lappets flying loose: one of these lappets; **pinn′ing** a fastening: a chip of stone, etc., inserted in a joint of masonry. — **pin′ball** a form of bagatelle: a scoring game, played on a slot-machine, in which a ball runs down a sloping board set with pins or other targets; **pin′-butt′ock** (*Shak.*) a sharp, pointed buttock; **pin′case** (*obs.*); **pin curl** a lock of hair made to curl by winding it around one's finger, etc., and securing it with a hairpin; **pin′-cushion** a cushion for holding pins; **pin′-dust,** brass filings, a product of pin-making. — *adj.* **pin′-eyed** long-styled, with the stigma like a pinhead in the throat of the corolla (esp. of a *Primula*). — **pin′-feather** a young, unexpanded feather. — *adjs.* **pin′-feathered; pin′-fire** discharged by a pin driven into the fulminate. — **pin′fish** a spiny fish of various kinds; **pin′head,** the head of a pin: a stupid person (*slang*); **pin′hole** a hole for or made by a pin, or such as a pin might make; **pinhole camera; pinhole photography** the taking of photographs by the use of a pinhole instead of a lens; **pin′-leg′** (*Scot.*) a wooden leg; **pin′-maker; pin′-making; pin′-man** a seller of pins: a matchstick drawing, in which the limbs and body are represented by single lines; **pin′-money** orig., money allotted by a man to his wife or female dependants for private expenses: extra money earned by a man or woman to spend on incidental or luxury items: a trifling amount of money; **pin′-point** the point of a pin: anything very sharp or minute. — *v.t.* to place, define, very exactly. — **pin′-prick** the prick of a pin: (an act of) petty irritation; **pin′-stripe** a very narrow stripe in cloth: cloth with such stripes. — *adj.* **pin′-striped** (of fabric or garments) having pin-stripes: (of a person) wearing a pin-striped suit (*coll.*). — **pin′table** a pinball machine; **pin′tail** a duck, *Anas acuta*, with a pointed tail: a sand-grouse. — *adj.* **pin′tailed** having a long, narrow tail. — **pin′-tuck** a very narrow ornamental tuck. — *adj.* **pin′-up** such as might have her portrait pinned up on a wall for admiration. — *n.* a girl of such a kind: a portrait so pinned up. — **pin′-wheel** a wheel with pins at right angles to its plane, to lift the hammer of a striking clock: a paper toy windmill: a revolving firework. — **a merry pin** (*arch.*) a merry mood; **on pins and needles** in agitated expectancy; **pin and web** (*Shak.*) a disease of the eye, apparently cataract, characterised by a small excrescence like a pin-head, and a film (also **web and pin**); **pin it on (to) (someone)** to prove, or seem to prove, that he did it; **pin one's faith on** to put entire trust in; **pin one's hopes on** to place one's entire hopes on; **pin on one's sleeve** (*obs.*) to make entirely dependent on oneself, or at one's disposal; **pins and needles** a tingling feeling in arm, hand, leg, foot, due to impeded circulation (see also above); **pin someone down** to get someone to commit himself (to), to make someone express a definite opinion. [O.E. *pinn,* prob. — L. *pinna,* a feather, a pinnacle.]

piña *pē′nyə, n.* the pineapple (*obs.*): a fine cloth of pineapple leaf fibre (**pi′ña-cloth**). [Sp., pine-cone, pineapple.]

piña colada *pē′nə kəl-ä′də* (Sp. *pē′nyə*), a drink made from pineapple juice, rum and coconut. [Sp., strained pineapple.]

pinacoid. See **pinakoid.**

pinacotheca *pin-ə-kō-thē′kə, n.* a picture-gallery. — Also **pinakoth′ek** (Ger., from Gr.). [Latinised from Gr. *pinakothēkē* — *pinax, -akos,* a tablet, picture, *thēkē,* repository.]

pinafore *pin′ə-fōr, -för, n.* a loose covering over a dress, esp. a child's. — *adj.* **pin′afored.** — **pinafore dress, skirt** a skirt hung from the shoulders, or combined with a sleeveless bodice. [**pin, afore.**]

pinakoid, pinacoid *pin'ə-koid, n.* a crystal face, or a crystallographic form consisting of a pair of faces, parallel to two axes. — *adj.* **pinakoid'al, pinacoid'al.** [Gr. *pinax, -ăkos,* slab, *eidos,* form.]

pinaster *pī-* or *pi-nas'tər, n.* the cluster-pine. [L. *pīnāster* — *pīnus,* pine.]

pinball, pincase. See **pin.**

pince-nez *pĕs'-nā, n.* a pair of eye-glasses with a spring for catching the nose: — *pl.* **pince'-nez** (*-nāz, -nā*). — *adj.* **pince'-nezed** (*-nād*). [Fr., pinch nose.]

pincer *pin'sər, n.* a grasping claw or forceps-like organ: (in *pl.*) a gripping tool with jaws and handles on a pivot, used for drawing out nails, squeezing, etc.: (in *pl.*) a twofold advance that threatens to isolate part of an enemy's force (*fig.*). — *v.t.* to pinch with pincers. — **pin'cer-movement.** [(O.)Fr. *pincer,* to pinch.]

pinch *pinch, pinsh, v.t.* to compress a small part of between fingers and thumb or between any two surfaces, to nip: to squeeze: to crush: to nip off: to bite (*obs.*): to bring or render by squeezing or nipping: to affect painfully or injuriously, as cold or hunger: to cause to show the effects of such pain or injury: to harass: to hamper: to restrict: to stint: to find fault with (*obs.*): to purloin (*slang*): to arrest (*slang*): to over-urge (*horse-racing*): to move along with a lever. — *v.i.* to nip or squeeze: to be painfully tight: to encroach: to carp: to live sparingly: to narrow, taper off (*mining*). — *n.* an act or experience of pinching: a critical time of difficulty or hardship: an emergency: a pleat (*obs.*): an upward curl of a hat-brim (*obs.*): a place of narrowing, folding, difficulty, or steepness: a quantity taken up between the finger and thumb: an iron bar used as a lever. — *adj.* **pinched** having the appearance of being tightly squeezed: hard pressed by want or cold: (of the face, or general appearance) haggard with cold, tiredness, hunger, etc.: narrowed: straightened. — *n.* **pinch'er** one who, or that which, pinches: (in *pl.*) pincers (*dial.*). — *n.* and *adj.* **pinch'ing.** — *adv.* **pinch'ingly.** — **pinch'cock** a clamp that stops the flow of liquid by pinching a tube; **pinch'commons** a niggard of food; **pinch'fist, pinch'gut, pinch'penny** a niggard. — *v i.* **pinch'-hit** (*baseball*) to bat in place of another in an emergency (also *fig.*). — **pinch'-hitter.** — **at a pinch** in a case of necessity; **feel the pinch** (*coll.*) to be in financial difficulties, to find life, work, etc. difficult because of lack of money; **know where the shoe pinches** to know by direct experience what the trouble or difficulty is; **take with a pinch of salt** see **salt¹.** [O.Fr. *pincier;* prob. Gmc.]

pinchbeck *pinch', pinsh'bek, n.* a yellow alloy of copper with much less zinc than ordinary brass, simulating gold, invented by Christopher *Pinchbeck* (*c.* 1670–1732), watchmaker. — *adj.* sham: in bad taste.

pin-cushion. See **pin.**

pindari, pindaree *pin-dä're, n.* a mercenary freebooter troublesome in India till 1817. [Hind. *pindārī.*]

Pindaric *pin-dar'ik, adj.* after the manner or supposed manner of the Greek lyric poet *Pindar.* — *n.* a Pindaric ode: an irregular ode, according to the 17th-century conception of Pindar. — *v.t.* and *v.i.* **Pin'darise, -ize** (*-dər-īz*). — *ns.* **Pin'darism** manner or supposed manner of Pindar: 'intoxication of style' (*Matthew Arnold*); **Pin'darist.** [Gr. *pindarikos* — *Pindaros.*]

pinder *pin'dər, n.* one who impounds cattle. — Also **pinn'er.** [O.E. *pyndan,* to shut up — *pund;* cf. **poind, pound².**]

pine¹ *pīn, n.* any tree of the north temperate coniferous genus Pinus, with pairs or bundles of needle-leaves on short shoots and scale-leaves only on long shoots, represented in Britain by the **Scots pine** (*P. sylvestris;* often called *Scots fir*): extended to various more or less nearly allied trees and to some plants only superficially like: the timber of the pine: a pineapple plant or its fruit. — *adj.* of pines or pine-wood. — *ns.* **pī'nery** a pine-house: a pine-forest; **pīne'tum** a plantation of pine-trees: a collection of pine-trees for botanical or

ornamental purposes: — *pl.* **pīnē'ta.** — *adj.* **pī'ny** (wrongly **pī'ney**) of, like, or abounding in pine-trees. — **pine'apple** a pine-cone (*obs.*): a large South American multiple fruit shaped like a pine-cone: the bromeliaceous plant (Ananas) bearing it: a finial shaped like a pine-cone or a pineapple: a bomb (*slang*): a hand-grenade (*slang*); **pineapple weed** the rayless mayweed (*Matricaria suaveolens*) — from its smell; **pine'-barr'en** a level sandy tract growing pine-trees; **pine'-beau'ty, -car'pet** kinds of moths whose larvae feed on pine-trees; **pine'-beet'le** any beetle that attacks pine-trees, esp. the **pine'-chã'fer** (*Hylurgus piniperda*) which bores up through the leader; **pine'-cone** the cone or strobilus of a pine-tree; **pine'-finch** an American finch like the goldfinch: a large grosbeak of pine-forests; **pine'-house** a house in which pineapples are grown; **pine'-ker'nel** the edible seed of a pine-tree of various species; **pine'-mar'ten** a British species of marten, *Mustela martes,* now rare, dark brown, with yellowish throat, and partly arboreal in habit; **pine'-need'le** the acicular leaf of the pine-tree; **pine tar** a dark, oily substance obtained from pine-wood, used in paints, etc., and medicines; **pine'-tree; pine'-wood** a wood of pine-trees: pine timber; **pine'-wool** a fibrous substance prepared from the leaves of the pine. — **pine-tree money** a silver money coined at Boston in the 17th century, bearing the figure of a pine-tree. [O.E. *pīn* — L. *pīnus.*]

pine² *pīn, n.* punishment, torture (*obs.*): suffering (*arch.*): want, starvation (*Spens.*). — *v.t.* to torment (*obs.*): to consume, cause to wear away: to starve: to grieve for (*Milt.*). — *v.i.* to waste away, esp. under pain or mental distress: to languish with longing: to long: to repine. [O.E. *pīnian,* to torment — L. *poena,* punishment.]

pineal *pin'i-əl* or *pīn', adj.* shaped like a pine-cone: connected with the pineal body. — **pinealec'tomy** surgical removal of the pineal body. — **pineal body** or **gland** a small body at the end of an upgrowth from the optic thalami of the brain; **pineal eye** a vestigial third eye in front of the pineal body, best developed in the tuatara. [L. *pīnea,* a pine-cone — *pīnus,* pine.]

pineapple, pinery, pinetum, piney. See **pine¹.**

pinfold *pin'fōld, n.* a pound or enclosure for cattle. — *v.t.* to impound. [O.E. *pundfald,* affected by *pyndan;* see **pound², fold², pinder.**]

ping *ping, n.* a sharp ringing or whistling sound as of a bullet. — *v.i.* to make such a sound. — *v.t.* to cause to make such a sound. — *n.* **ping'er** an acoustic transmitter for the study of ocean currents: (Ⓡ, with *cap.*) a domestic clockwork device set to give a warning signal at a chosen time: any of various devices sending out an acoustic signal for directional, timing, etc. purposes. — **Ping'-Pong'**® a trademark for table tennis. — *adj.* (without *cap.*) moving backwards and forwards, to and fro (*fig.*). [Imit.]

pingle *ping'(g)l,* (*Scot.* and *dial.*) *v.i.* to strive: to struggle with difficulties, exert oneself strongly: to work ineffectually: to trifle or dally, esp. with food. — *v.t.* to contend strongly with: to harass, worry: to eat with feeble appetite. — *n.* a strenuous contest or exertion. — *n.* **ping'ler.** — *adj.* **ping'ling.** [Cf. Sw. *pyngla,* to be busy in small matters, to work in a trifling way.]

pingo *ping'gō, n.* a large cone-shaped mound having a core of ice formed by the upward expansion of freezing water surrounded by permafrost: — *pl.* **ping'os, ping'oes.** [Eskimo.]

pinguid *ping'gwid, adj.* fat. — *v.t.* and *v.i.* **ping'uefy** (*-gwi-fī*) to fatten: to make or become greasy. — *ns.* **Pinguic'ula** the butterwort genus; **pinguid'ity, ping'-uitude** fatness. [L. *pinguis,* fat.]

pinguin¹. Same as **penguin¹.**

pinguin² *ping'gwin, n.* a West Indian plant, *Bromelia pinguin:* its fruit. — Also **peng'uin.** [Perh. L. *pinguis,* fat; confused with **penguin¹.**]

pinhead, pinhole. See **pin.**

pinion¹ *pin'yən, n.* a wing: the last joint of a wing: a flight feather, esp. the outermost. — *v.t.* to cut a pinion of: to confine the wings of: to confine by holding or binding the arms. [O.Fr. *pignon* — L. *pinna* (*penna*), wing.]

pinion² *pin'yən*, *n.* a small wheel with teeth or 'leaves'. [Fr. *pignon*, pinion, in O.Fr. battlement — L. *pinna*, *pinnacle*.]

pinite *pin'īt*, *pīn'*, *n.* a greyish-green or brown hydrous silicate of aluminium and potassium, usu. amorphous. [Ger. *Pinit*, from the *Pini* mine in Saxony.]

pink¹ *pingk*, *n.* a small sailing-ship, usu. with a narrow stern. — Also **pink'ie**, **pink'y**. [M.Du. *pin(c)ke*; Ger. *Pinke*.]

pink² *pingk*, *v.t.* to stab or pierce, esp. with a sword or rapier: to decorate by cutting small holes or scallops: to make a serrated edge on. — *n.* a stab: an eyelet. — *adj.* **pinked** pierced or worked with small holes. — **pink'ing-ī'ron** (*arch.*) a tool for pinking or scalloping; **pink'ing-shears** scissors with serrated cutting edges. [Cf. L.G. *pinken*, to peck.]

pink³ *pingk*, *n.* any plant or flower of the caryophyllaceous genus Dianthus, including carnation and sweetwilliam: extended to some other plants, as **sea'-pink** (thrift), **Carolina pink** (see **Carolina**, **pinkroot** below), **Indian pink** (see **pinkroot** below): the colour of a wild pink, a light red: a scarlet hunting-coat or its colour: the person wearing it: one who is something of a socialist but hardly a red (also **pink'ō**: — *pl.* **pink'o(e)s**): the fine flower of excellence: the most perfect condition: the highest point, the extreme: an exquisite (*obs.*). — *adj.* of the colour pink: slightly socialistic. — *v.t.* and *v.i.* to make or become pink. — *ns.* **pink'iness**; **pink'ing** the reddening of gem-stones by heat. — *adj.* **pink'ish** somewhat pink. — *ns.* **pink'ishness**; **pink'ness**. — *adj.* **pink'y** inclining to pink. — **pink'-eye** acute contagious conjunctivitis: an acute contagious infection in horses due to a filterable virus, the eye sometimes becoming somewhat red: a red discoloration in salt fish, etc. — *adj.* **pink'-eyed** having pink eyes (see also **pink⁵**). — **pink elephants** see **elephant**; **pink gin** gin with angostura bitters; **pink'root** Indian pink, Carolina pink, or other species of Spigelia: its root, a vermifuge. — **in the pink** in perfect health or condition; **pink of perfection** the acme of perfection. [Etymology doubtful.]

pink⁴ *pingk*, *n.* a yellow lake. — **Dutch pink** a yellow lake obtained from quercitron bark: blood (*slang*). [Prob. different word from the preceding.]

pink⁵ *pingk*, *v.i.* to wink: to blink: to peer: to peep. — *adj.* (*Shak.*) blinking. — *adj.* **pink'-eyed** having small or half-shut eyes (see also **pink³**); **pink'y** winking. [Du. *pinken*, to wink.]

pink⁶ *pingk*, *adj.* (*Shak.*) small. — *n.* (*Scot.*) anything small, as a peep of light. — *adj.* **pink'ie**, **pink'y** (*Scot.*) small. — *n.* (*Scot.*, *U.S.*) the little finger. [Du. *pink*, the little finger.]

pink⁷ *pingk*, **penk** *pengk*, *n.* a minnow: a samlet. [Cf. Ger. dial. *Pinke*.]

pink⁸ *pingk*, *n.* a tinkling sound: a chaffinch's note: a chaffinch: a type of sea bird (*obs.*). — *v.i.* (of an engine) to detonate or knock. [Imit.]

Pinkerton *ping'kər-tən*, *n.* a private detective. — Also without *cap.* [Allan *Pinkerton*, 1819–84, American detective.]

pinkie, **pinky**. See **pink**[1,3,5,6].

pinko. See **pink³**.

Pinkster *pingk'stər*, (*arch. U.S.*) *n.* Whitsuntide. — Also **Pinxter**. [Du. *pinkster(en)*, M.Du. *pinxter*, ult. — Gr. *pentēkostē*, pentecost.]

pinna *pin'ə*, *n.* a leaflet of a pinnate leaf, or similar expansion: a wing, fin, feather, or similar expansion: the outer ear, esp. the upper part: — *pl.* **pinn'ae** (-ē). — *adjs.* **pinn'ate**, **-d** shaped like a feather: having a row of leaflets on each side of the rachis, or other expansions arranged in like manner: (usu. **pennate**) having wings, fins, or wing-like tufts. — *adv.* **pinn'ately**. — *adjs.* **pinnatifid** (*pin-at'i-fid*) pinnately cut nearly or about halfway down; **pinnatipart'ite** pinnately cut rather more than halfway; **pinn'atiped** of birds, with

lobate feet; **pinnat'isect** pinnately cut nearly to the midrib. — *n.* **pinn'iped** (-*i-ped*), **pinn'ipede** (-*pēd*; L. *pēs*, *pedis*, foot) a member of the **Pinnipe'dia**, or paddle-footed Carnivora, seals, sea-lions, and walruses. — *adjs.* **pinn'ūlate**, **-d**. — *n.* **pinn'ūle** a lobe of a leaflet of a pinnate leaf: a branchlet of a crinoid arm. — Also **pinn'ūla**. [L. *pinna*, a feather, dim. *pinnula*.]

Pinna *pin'ə*, *n.* a genus of molluscs akin to the mussels with triangular shell. [Gr.]

pinnace *pin'is*, -*əs*, *n.* a small vessel with oars and sails: a boat with eight oars: a man-of-war's tender boat: (*vaguely*) a small boat: a whore (*fig.*; *obs.*). [Fr. *pinasse*.]

pinnacle *pin'ə-kl*, *n.* a slender turret or spiry structure in architecture: a high pointed rock or mountain like a spire: the highest point. — *v.t.* to be the pinnacle of: to set on a pinnacle: to raise as a pinnacle: to furnish with pinnacles. — *adj.* **pinn'acled**. [Fr. *pinacle* — L.L. *pinnāculum*, dim. from L. *pinna*, a feather.]

pinnate, etc. See **pinna**.

pinner *pin'ər*. See **pin**, **pinder**.

pinnet *pin'it*, *n.* a pinnacle (*Scott*): a streamer (*Scot.*). [Perh. **pennant**, associated with L. *pinna*, pinnacle.]

pinnie *pin'i*, *n.* short for **pinafore**.

pinniewinkle. See **pinnywinkle**.

pinniped(e). See **pinna**.

pinnock *pin'ək*, (*dial.*) *n.* the hedge-sparrow: the blue tit. [M.E. *pynnuc*.]

pinnoed *pin'ōd*, (*Spens.*) *pa.p.* pinioned. [Perh. a misprint.]

pinnule, etc. See **pinna**.

pinny *pin'i*, *n.* short for **pinafore**.

pinnywinkle, **pinniewinkle**, *pin'i-wingk-l*, **pilniewinks** *pil'ni-wingks*, mistaken forms of **pilliwinks**.

pinochle, **pinocle**, **penuchle** *pin'*, *pēn'ək-l*, *ns.* a game like bezique: a declaration of queen of spades and knave of diamonds. [Origin unknown.]

pinole *pē-nō'lā*, *n.* parched Indian corn or other seeds ground and eaten with milk: a mixture of vanilla and aromatic substances in chocolate. [Sp., — Aztec *pinolli*.]

piñon *pin'yon*, *pēn'yōn*, (*U.S.*) *n.* an edible pine seed: the tree bearing it. [Sp.]

Pinot *pē'nō*, (also without *cap.*) *n.* a variety of both black and white grape: a wine made from the Pinot grapes, e.g. *Pinot Noir*, *Blanc*, *Gris*, *Chardonnay*. [Fr. *pin*, pine, from the similarity of the grape bunch to a pine-cone in shape.]

pinpoint. See **pin**.

pinscher. See **Doberman pinscher**.

pint *pīnt*, *n.* a measure of capacity = half a quart or 4 gills — in imperial measure (liquid or dry), about 568 cubic centimetres, 0·568 litre, 20 fluid ounces — in U.S. measure (liquid) 473 cm³, 16 U.S. fluid ounces, (dry) 551 cm³: a pint of beer (*coll.*). — *n.* **pint'a** (*coll.*; **pint of**) a drink, esp. a pint, of milk. — **pint'-pot** a pot for holding a pint, esp. a pewter pot for beer; a seller or drinker of beer. — *adj.* **pint'-size(d)** (*coll.*) very small, usu. of a person. — **pint'-stoup** a vessel for holding a Scots pint (about 3 imperial pints). [Fr. *pinte*; origin unknown.]

pinta¹. See **pint**.

pinta² *pin'tə*, *n.* a contagious skin disease occurring in the tropics, characterised by loss of skin pigmentation — also called **mal del pinto** (*mal del pin'to*; Sp., disease of the spotted person). [Sp., — L.L. *pinctus* — L. *pictus*, painted.]

pintable. See **pin**.

pintado *pin-tä'dō*, *n.* a kind of petrel, the Cape pigeon: the guinea-fowl: chintz (*obs.*): — *pl.* **pinta'dos**. [Port., painted.]

pintail. See **pin**.

Pinteresque *pin-tər-esk'*, *adj.* in the style of the characters, situations, etc., of the plays of Harold *Pinter*, 20th-cent. English dramatist, marked esp. by halting dialogue, uncertainty of identity, and air of menace.

pintle *pin'tl*, *n.* the penis (*arch.*): a bolt or pin, esp. one on which something turns: the plunger or needle of the injection valve of an oil engine, opened by oil pressure on an annular face, and closed by a spring. [O.E. *pintel*.]

pinto *pin'tō*, (*U.S.*) *adj.* mottled: piebald. — *n.* a piebald horse: — *pl.* **pin'tos.** — **pinto bean** a kind of bean resembling a kidney bean, mottled in colour. [Sp., painted.]

pinxit *pingk'sit*, (L.) painted (this).

Pinxter. See **Pinkster.**

piny[1]. See **pine**[1].

piny[2] *pī'ni*, (*obs.* or *dial.*) *n.* same as **peony**.

Pinyin *pin'yin'*, *n.* an alphabetic system (using Roman letters) for the transcription of Chinese, esp. Mandarin. [Chin., phonetic, alphabetic (transcription).]

piolet *pyo-lā', pyō-lā', n.* an ice-axe, spiked staff for climbing or (*obs.*) skiing. [Fr., — Piedmontese dialect *piola*.]

pion *pī'on*, *n.* a *pi*-meson (see **pi**[1] and **meson**). — *adj.* **pion'ic.**

pioned *pī'ən-id*, (*Shak.*) *adj.* perh. trenched (cf. **pioneer**): perh. overgrown with wild orchises, said to be called **pionies** (**peonies**) at Stratford.

pioneer *pī-ə-nēr', n.* a military artisan, employed in peace-time in painting and repairing barracks, and such work, in war in preparing the way for an army, and minor engineering works, as trenching: an excavator: a labourer: one who is among the first in new fields of enterprise, exploration, colonisation, research, etc. — *v.t.* to act as pioneer to: to prepare as a pioneer. — *ns.* **pi'oner, py'oner** (*Shak.*) a military pioneer: an excavator; **pī'oning** (*Spens.* **py'onings**) pioneer work: trenching. [O.Fr. *peonier* (Fr. *pionnier*) — *pion*, a foot-soldier — L.L. *pedō, pedōnis* — L. *pēs, pedis*, a foot; cf. **pawn**[2], **peon**.]

pioney, piony *pī'ə-ni, n.* obs. forms of **peony**.

pioted. See **pyot**.

piou-piou *pū-pū, n.* a French private soldier. [Fr. slang; perh. *pion;* see **peon**.]

pious *pī'əs, adj.* dutiful: showing, having, or proceeding from piety: professing to be religious. — *adv.* **pi'ously.** — **pious fraud** a deception practised with a good end in view: a religious humbug (*coll.*); **pious opinion** a belief widely held but not made a matter of faith. [L. *pius*.]

pioy, pioye. Same as **peeoy**.

pip[1] *pip, n.* roup in poultry, etc.: an ailment or distemper vaguely imagined: syphilis (*slang*): spleen, hump, disgust, offence (*coll.*). — **give someone the pip** (*coll.*) to annoy or offend someone. [App. — M.Du. *pippe* — L.L. *pipīta* — L. *pītuīta*, rheum.]

pip[2] *pip, n.* a pippin (*obs.*): a small hard body (seed or fruitlet) in a fleshy fruit. — *adjs.* **pip'less; pipp'y.** [App. from **pippin**.]

pip[3] *pip*, earlier **peep, peepe** (*Shak.*) *pēp, ns.* a spot on dice, cards, dominoes: a star as a mark of rank (*coll.*): a speck: on radar screen, indication, e.g. spot of light, of presence of object: a single blossom or corolla in a cluster. — **a pip** (or **peepe**) **out** two-and-thirty, one in excess of the total of pips aimed at in the old card-game of one-and-thirty, hence, having overshot one's mark: tipsy. [Ety. dub.]

pip[4] *pip, n.* a signal sounding like the word 'pip'.

pip[5] *pip*, (*slang*) *v.t.* to blackball: to pluck, plough, reject, or fail in an examination: to foil, thwart, get the better of: to hit with a bullet or the like: to wound: to kill. — *v.i.* to die (esp. with *out; arch.*): — *pr.p.* **pipp'ing;** *pa.t.* and *pa.p.* **pipped.** — **pipped at the post** defeated at the point when success seemed certain, or at the last moment. [Perh. from **pip**[2].]

pip[6] *pip, v.i.* to chirp, as a young bird. [Cf. **peep**[1].]

Pipa *pē'pə, n.* a genus of S. American toads which carry their young on their back: (without *cap.*) a toad of this genus, the Surinam toad. [Surinam dialect.]

pipage. See **pipe**[1].

pipal, pipul, peepul *pē'pul, -pəl, n.* the bo tree. [Hind. *pīpul*.]

pipe[1] *pīp, n.* a musical wind instrument, or part of an instrument, consisting of or including a tube: any tube, or tubular part or thing, natural or artificial: a pipe-like volcanic vent, mass of ore, etc.: an entrance to a decoy: a tube with a bowl at one end for smoking: a fill of tobacco: the smoking of a fill of tobacco: the note of a bird: a voice, esp. a high voice: (usu. in *pl.*) the windpipe: a stick of e.g. pipeclay for curling hair or a wig (*Sterne*): a boatswain's whistle: (often in *pl.*) a bagpipe. — *v.i.* to play upon a pipe: to whistle, as the wind, or a boatswain: to speak or sing, esp. in a high voice: to peep or sing, as a bird: to weep: to become pipy. — *v.t.* to play on a pipe: to lead, call, by means of a pipe: (with *in*) to accompany in with pipe music: to render, or cause to be, by playing a pipe: to propagate by piping (*hort.*): to ornament with piping: to supply with pipes: to convey by pipe: to transmit (television, radio signals) by electricity along a wire. — *n.* **pīp'age** conveyance or distribution by pipe. — *adj.* **piped** (*pīpt*) tubular or fistulous: transported by means of a pipe: transmitted simultaneously to many outlets from a central control location by means of an audio system, telephone or electricity line, etc. — *n.* **pipe'ful** enough to fill a pipe. — *adjs.* **pipe'less; pipe'like.** — *n.* **pīp'er** a player on a pipe, esp. a bagpipe: a broken-winded horse: a young pigeon or other bird: a kind of gurnard: a pipe-smoker: a decoy dog: a kind of caddis-worm. — *adj.* **pīp'ing** playing a pipe: sounding like a pipe: whistling: thin and high-pitched: characterised by pipe-playing (as opp. to martial music — *the piping times of peace*): hissing hot: very hot. — *n.* the action of the verb pipe in any sense: pipe-playing: a system of pipes: tubing: small cord used as trimming for clothes: strings and twists of sugar ornamenting a cake: a slip or cutting from a joint of a stem: hydraulicking. — *adj.* **pīp'y**, pipelike: having pipes: piping. — **pipe'-case** a case for a tobacco-pipe; **pipe'clay** a fine white, nearly pure, kaolin, free from iron, used for making tobacco-pipes and fine earthenware, and for whitening belts, etc. — *v.t.* to whiten with pipeclay. — **pipe cleaner** a length of wire with tufts of fabric twisted into it, used to clean pipe-stems; **piped music** continuous background music played in a restaurant, or piped from a central studio to other buildings; **pipe'-dream** a futile and unreal hope or fancy such as one has when relaxing while smoking a pipe (orig. an opium-smoker's fantasy); **pipe'-dreamer; pipe'fish** a fish (of several species) of the sea-horse family, a long thin fish covered with hard plates, the jaws forming a long tube; **pipe fitting** any of the wide variety of pipe connecting-pieces used to make turns, junctions, and reductions in piping systems; **pipe'-key** a key with a hollow barrel; **pipe'-layer** one who lays pipes for water, gas, etc.: a political wire-puller (*old U.S. slang*); **pipe'-laying; pipeless organ** a musical instrument, played like an organ, in which sounds, built up from whatever harmonics may be chosen, are produced by a loudspeaker; **pipe'-light, -lighter** a spill for lighting a pipe; **pipe'line, pipe'-line** a long continuous line of piping to carry water from a reservoir, oil from an oil-field, etc.: a line of piping to carry solid materials: any continuous line of communication, or supply, or of progress and development (*fig.*): see also **in the pipeline** below: — *adj.* (of a processor, program, etc.) carrying out two or more instructions simultaneously by performing processes in one sequence (*comput.*); **pipe'lining;** — **pipe major** the chief of a band of bagpipers; **Pipe Office** (*hist.*) an office in the Court of Exchequer in which the Clerk of the Pipe made out the Pipe Roll; **pipe'-opener** (*coll.*) a walk or spell of exercise in the fresh air: a practice-game or trial run; **pipe'-organ** a musical organ with pipes; **pipe'-rack** a rack for tobacco-pipes; **Pipe Roll** (*hist.*) the Great Roll of the Exchequer, containing yearly accounts of sheriffs, etc. (possibly from its pipelike form); **pipe'-stem** the tube of a tobacco-pipe; **pipe′stone** a red argillaceous stone used by North American Indians for making tobacco-pipes; **pipe′-stopp′le, -stapp′le** (*Scot.*) a tobacco-pipe stem: anything very thin and brittle-looking; **pipe′-track** the course of a pipe across country; **pipe′-tree** (*obs.*) mock orange (*white pipe-tree*): the lilac (*blue pipe-tree*); **pipe′-work** a vein of ore in the form of a pipe: piping or pipes collectively, as in an organ; **pipe′wort** a rare rush-like water-plant (*Eriocaulon septangulare*) of Ireland and the Hebrides, only European representative of its family, Eriocaulaceae; **pipe′-wrench** a wrench that grips a pipe when turned one way; **piping crow** an Australian bird (*Gymnorhina*) called a magpie, really akin to the shrikes; **piping hare** a pika. — **boatswain's pipe** see **whistle; drunk as a piper** very drunk; **in the pipeline** waiting to be considered or dealt with: in preparation; **pay the piper** to bear the expense (and so **call the tune**, have control): to have to pay heavily; **pipe and tabor** a small recorder, fingered by the left hand, and a small drum beaten by the same player with his right, formerly in use in rustic jollities; **pipe down** to dismiss from muster, as a ship's company (the final order of the day): to subside into silence: to stop talking or be quiet (*coll.*); **pipe of peace** see **calumet; pipe one's eye, tune one's pipes** to weep; **pipe up** (*coll.*) to interject: to begin to speak; **piping hot** hissing hot, usu. hyperbolically; **put that in your pipe and smoke it!** (*coll.*) there! how do you like that? (of something unpleasant). [O.E. *pīpe* — L. *pīpāre*, to cheep; cf. Du. *pijp*, Ger. *Pfeife*.]

pipe² *pīp, n.* a cask or butt (of wine), of two hogsheads, varying according to the wine, ordinarily about 105 gallons in Britain, 126 U.S. gallons: a Portuguese wooden cask or *pipa*, used for storage and as a measure of (esp. port) wine, holding 500 litres (formerly 429 litres): the measure of a pipe. — **pipe′-wine** (*Shak.*) wine from the cask, not bottled. [O.Fr. *pipe*, cask, tube; cf. preceding.]

pip emma *pip em′ə*, (*mil. slang*) the letters PM: afternoon (*post meridiem.*). [Formerly signallers' names for the letters.]

Piper *pīp′ər, n.* the pepper genus, giving name to a family **Piperā′ceae** of dicotyledons. — *adjs.* **piperaceous** (-*ā′shəs*); **piperic** (*pip-er′ik*) applied to an acid (C₁₂H₁₀O₄) got from piperine. — *ns.* **piper′azine** a crystalline nitrogen compound used in medicine, insecticides and anti-corrosion substances; **piper′idine** a liquid base (C₅H₁₁N) got from piperine; **pip′erine** an alkaloid (C₁₇H₁₉O₃N) found in pepper; **pip′eronal** a phenolic aldehyde of very pleasant odour, used as a perfume and in flavourings, etc. — also called **heliotropin.** [L. *piper*, pepper.]

pipette *pip-et′, n.* a tube for transferring and measuring fluids. — *v.t.* to transfer or measure, using a pipette. [Fr., dim. of *pipe*, pipe.]

pipi *pē′pē, n.* a Brazilian Caesalpinia: its pods used in tanning. [Tupí *pipai*.]

piping. See under **pipe¹.**

pipistrelle *pip-is-trel′, n.* a small reddish-brown bat, the commonest British bat. [Fr., — It. *pipistrello*, a form of *vespertilio* — L. *vespertiliō*, bat — *vesper*, evening.]

pipit *pip′it, n.* any member of a lark-like genus (*Anthus*) of birds akin to wagtails. [Prob. imit.]

pipkin *pip′kin, n.* a small pot, now only of earthenware: a piggin (*U.S. dial.*). [Poss. a dim. of **pipe.**]

pippin *pip′in, n.* a fruit pip (*obs.*): an apple of various varieties: something or someone especially nice, attractive, good (*old slang*). [O.Fr. *pepin*.]

pippy. See **pip².**

pipsqueak *pip′skwēk, (slang) n.* something or someone insignificant, contemptible: a German shell of 1st World War: a two-stroke motor-cycle.

pipul. Same as **pipal.**

pipy. See under **pipe¹.**

piquant *pē′kənt, -änt, adj.* stinging: pleasantly pungent: appetising: kindling keen interest. — *n.* **piq′uancy.** — *adv.* **piq′uantly.** [Fr., pr.p. of *piquer*, to prick.]

pique¹ *pēk, n.* animosity or ill-feeling: offence taken: a feeling of anger or vexation caused by wounded pride: resentment of a slight: dudgeon: point or punctilio (*obs.*). — *v.t.* to wound the pride of: to nettle: to arouse, stir, provoke: (*refl.*) to pride oneself (on, upon, *Boswell*) at). [Fr. *pique*, a pike, pique, *piquer*, to prick; cf. **pike², prick.**]

pique² *pēk, n.* in piquet, the scoring of 30 points in one hand before the other side scores at all. — *v.t.* to score a pique against. — *v.i.* to score a pique. [Fr. *pic*; see **piquet².**]

pique³ *pēk, (Browning) n.* for **peak¹.**

piqué *pē′kā, n.* a stiff corded cotton fabric: inlaid work of gold or silver in point or strip (sometimes with mother-of-pearl) on tortoise-shell or ivory. — Also *adj.* — **piqué work** inlaying in piqué: needlework with raised design made by stitching. [Fr., pa.p. of *piquer*, to prick.]

piquet¹. Same as **picket.**

piquet² *pi-ket′, n.* a game for two with 32 cards, with scoring for declarations and tricks. [Fr.; origin unknown.]

Pir *pēr, (also without cap.) n.* a Muslim title of honour given to a holy man or religious leader. [Pers. *pīr*, old man, chief.]

piracy. See **pirate.**

piragua *pi-ra′gwə, -rä′, n.* a South American dugout canoe, or a craft with a single trunk as foundation, often a schooner-rigged barge. — Also **peria′gua,** or (Fr.) **pirogue** (*pi-rōg′*). [Sp. *piragua* — Carib *piraqua.*]

Pirandellian *pir-an-del′i-ən, adj.* pertaining to, or in the style of, the writings of the Italian dramatist and novelist Luigi *Pirandello* (1867–1936).

piranha, piraña *pē-rän′yə,* **piraya** *pē-rä′yə,* **perai** *pe-rī′,* **pirai** *pē-, ns.* a ferocious South American river-fish (*Serrasalmo* or *Pygocentrus*) of the Characinidae. [Port. from Tupí *piranya, piraya.*]

pirarucu *pē-rä-rōō-kōō′, n.* the arapaima.

pirate *pī′rət, -rit, n.* one who, without authority, attempts to capture ships at sea: a sea-robber: a pirates' ship: one who publishes without authority of the owner of the copyright: a private bus, or its driver, plying on the recognised route of others: one who, in ordinary life, shows the predatory spirit of the sea rovers: a person who runs an unlicensed radio station. — *adj.* operating illegally: (*loosely*) operating, produced, sold, etc., separately and in defiance of the official system. — *v.t.* to rob as a pirate: to publish without permission: to copy recordings without copyright consent: to use, tap, operate, produce, etc. (something) illegally. — *n.* **piracy** (*pī′rə-si, pi′*) the crime of a pirate: robbery on the high seas: unauthorised publication: infringement of copyright. — *adjs.* **piratic** (*pī-rat′ik*), **-al** pertaining to a pirate: practising piracy. — *adv.* **pirat′ically.** [L. *pīrāta* — Gr. *peirātēs* — *peiraein*, to attempt.]

piraya. See **piranha.**

piri-piri¹ *pir′ē-pir′ē, pēr′ē-pēr′ē, n.* a sauce made with red peppers. — Also *adj.* [Ety. uncertain; perh. from Swahili *pilipili*, pepper.]

piri-piri² *pir′ē-pir′ē, pēr′ē-pēr′ē, n.* a New Zealand weed with prickly burrs (*Acaenae sanguisorbae*) used medicinally and as a tea. [Maori.]

pirl. See **purl¹.**

pirlicue, purlicue *pir′, pûr′li-kū, (Scot.) n.* a peroration: a résumé in conclusion. — *v.t.* and *v.i.* to summarise in conclusion. [Origin unknown.]

pirn *pûrn, (Scot.) pirn, n.* a reel, bobbin, or spool. — **wind someone a bonny pirn** to set a fine problem for someone, involve someone in difficulties. [Origin unknown.]

pirnie *pir′ni, (Scot.) adj.* unevenly wrought: striped. — *n.* (*Scot.*) a striped woollen nightcap. — *adj.* **pirn′it** (*Scot.*) interwoven with different colours: striped. [App. conn. with **pirn.**]

pirogue *pi-rōg′.* See **piragua.**

pirouette *pir-ōō-et′, n.* a spinning about on tiptoe. — *v.i.* to spin round on tiptoe. — *n.* **pirouett′er.** [Fr.]

pirozhki *pē-rozh'kē*, **piroshki** *pē-rosh'kē, ns.pl.* small, triangular pastries with meat, fish, vegetable, etc., fillings. [Russ., little pies.]

pis aller *pē-zal-ā, pēz a'lā*, (Fr.) the last or worst shift, a makeshift.

Pisces *pis'ēz, pīs'ēz, pis'kēz, pisk'ās, n.pl.* the class of fishes (*zool.*): the Fishes, the twelfth sign of the zodiac, or the constellation that formerly coincided with it (*astron.*): one born under this sign. — *ns.* **piscary** (*pisk'ə-ri*) the right of fishing: a fishing pond; **piscā'tor** an angler: — *fem.* **piscā'trix.** — *adjs.* **piscatorial** (*pis-kə-tō'ri-əl, -tō'*), **piscatory** (*pis'kə-tə-ri*) relating to fishing: fishing; **piscicolous** (*pis-ik'ə-ləs*) parasitic within fishes; **piscicul'tural.** — *ns.* **pis'ciculture** the rearing of fish by artificial methods; **pis'ciculturist**; **piscifau'na** the assemblage of fishes in a region, formation, etc. — *adjs.* **pis'ciform** having the form of a fish; **piscine** (*pis'īn*) of fishes: of the nature of a fish; **pisciv'orous** feeding on fishes. [L. *piscis*, a fish; pl. *piscēs*; *piscātor*, fisher.]

piscina *pis-ē'nə, pis-ī'nə, n.* a fish-pond: a swimming-pool (as in Roman baths): a basin and drain in old churches, usu. in a niche south of an altar, into which was emptied water used in washing the sacred vessels: — *pl.* **pisci'nas,** or **-ae.** — Also **piscine** (*pis'ēn,* or *-ēn'*). [L. *piscīna* — *piscis,* fish.]

piscine[1], **piscivorous.** See **Pisces.**

piscine[2]. See **piscina.**

pisé *pē'zā, n.* rammed earth or clay for walls or floors. — Also *adj.* [Fr.]

pish *pish, interj.,* of impatience or contempt. — *n.* an utterance of the exclamation. — *v.t.* to pooh-pooh. [Imit.]

pishogue *pi-shōg', (Ir.) n.* sorcery. [Ir. *piseog.*]

pisiform *pī'si-förm, piz'i-förm, adj.* pea-shaped. — *n.* a pea-shaped bone of the carpus. [L. *pisum,* pea, *förma,* shape.]

pisky. See **pixie.**

pismire *pis'mīr, n.* an ant or emmet. [**piss,** from the strong smell of the ant-hill, M.E. *mire* (doubtful O.E. *mīre*), ant.]

pisolite *pī'sō-līt, piz'ō-līt, n.* a coarse oolite. — *adj.* **pisolitic** (*-lit'ik*). [Gr. *pisos,* pease, *lithos,* stone.]

piss *pis, (coll.) v.i.* to discharge urine. — *v.t.* to discharge as urine: to urinate on. — *n.* urine. — *adj.* **pissed** (*slang*) extremely drunk. — *n.* **pissoir** (*pē-swär;* Fr.) a public urinal. — **piss'-a-bed** (*dial.*) the dandelion; **piss'-pot** a chamberpot. — **piss about** or **around** (*slang*) to behave in a foolish or time-wasting way; **piss off** (*interj.; vulg.*) go away; **piss (someone) off** (*slang*) to annoy or upset (someone); **pissed off** (*slang*) annoyed: fed up. [Fr. *pisser.*]

pissasphalt *pis'as-falt, n.* a semi-liquid bitumen. [Gr. *pissa,* pitch, *asphaltos,* asphalt.]

pissoir. See **piss.**

pistachio *pis-ta'chi-ō, -shi-ō, -chyō,* or *pis-tä',* or *pis-tä', n.* the almond-flavoured fruit-kernel of a small western Asiatic tree (*Pistacia vera*) of the same genus of the cashew family as the mastic tree: — *pl.* **pista'chios.** [Sp. *pistacho* and It. *pistacchio* — L.L. *pistāquium* — Gr. *pistákion* — Pers. *pistah.*]

pistareen *pis-tə-rēn', n.* an old Spanish two-real piece formerly current in the United States. [Prob. **peseta.**]

piste *pēst, n.* a beaten track, esp. a ski trail in the snow. [Fr.]

pistil *pis'til, (bot.) n.* the ovary of a flower, with its style and stigma. — *adjs.* **pis'tillary; pis'tillate** having a pistil but no (functional) stamens, female. — *n.* **pis'tillode** an abortive pistil. [L. *pistillum,* a pestle.]

pistol *pis'tl, n.* a small hand-gun, held in one hand when fired. — *v.t.* to shoot with a pistol: — *pr.p.* **pis'tolling;** *pa.t.* and *pa.p.* **pis'tolled.** — *n.* **pistoleer'** (*obs.*) one who carries or uses a pistol. — **pistol grip** a handle (usu. with a trigger mechanism) for a camera, etc., shaped like the butt of a pistol; **pis'tol-shot.** — *v.t.* **pis'tol-whip** to hit (someone) with a pistol. — **hold a pistol to someone's head** (*fig.*) to force someone to act according to one's wishes. [Through Fr. and Ger. from Czech.]

pistole *pis-tōl', n.* an old Spanish gold coin = about 17s. (contemporary value): an old 12-pound piece Scots = £1 English. — *n.* **pis'tolet** a pistol: a pistole: a gold coin of various kinds worth about 6s. [O.Fr. *pistole,* earlier *pistolet.*]

pistoleer. See **pistol.**

piston *pis'tən, n.* a cylindrical piece moving to and fro in a hollow cylinder, as in engines and pumps: a valve mechanism for altering the effective length of tube in brass and musical instruments: a push-key for combining a number of organ stops. — **piston ring** a split ring fitted in a circumferential groove around a piston rim forming a spring-loaded seal against the cylinder wall; **pis'ton-rod** the rod to which the piston is fixed, and which moves up and down with it. [Fr., — It. *pistone — pestare,* to pound — L. *pinsĕre, pistum.*]

pit[1] *pit, n.* a hole in the earth: a mine shaft: a mine, esp. a coal-mine: a place whence minerals are dug: a prison, esp. a castle prison entered from above (*arch.*): a cavity in the ground or in a floor for any purpose, as reception of ashes, inspection of motor-cars, a bottom-sawyer: a place beside the course where cars in a race can be refuelled and repaired: a hole for storing root-crops: a covered heap of potatoes, etc.: a grave, esp. one for many bodies: hell, or its lowest depths: a hole used as a trap for wild beasts: an enclosure in which animals are kept (esp. bears): an enclosure for cockfights or the like: orig., the ground floor of a theatre, or its occupants, or the part of the ground floor behind the stalls, now usu. the area in front of the stage reserved for the orchestra in a theatre (also **orchestra pit**): a bed (*slang*): a very dirty or untidy place (*slang*): part of a corn exchange floor assigned to some particular business, now esp. a securities or commodities trading floor (*U.S.*): a noisy card game mimicking a U.S. corn exchange: any hollow or depression, as the *pit of the stomach* below the breastbone: an indentation left by smallpox: a minute depression in a surface: a hollow made by a raindrop: a thin place in a cell-wall, affording communication with another cell (*bot.*): — *v.t.* to mark with little hollows: to lay in a pit: to set to fight, as cocks in a cockpit: to match (with *against*). — *v.i.* to become marked with pits: to retain an impression for a time after pressing (*med.*): — *pr.p.* **pitt'ing;** *pa.t.* and *pa.p.* **pitt'ed.** — *adj.* **pitt'ed** marked with small pits. — *ns.* **pitt'ing; pitt'ite** one who frequents the pit of a theatre. — **pit'-brow** the top of a shaft; **pit'-coal** coal in the ordinary sense — not *charcoal;* **pit'-dwelling** a primitive home made by roofing over a pit; **pit'fall** a lightly covered hole as a trap: a hidden danger (*fig.*); **pit'head** the ground at the mouth of a pit, and the machinery, etc., on it; **pit'man** a man who works in a coal-pit or a saw-pit, esp. at sinking, repair, and inspection of shafts and at pumping in a mine: a rod connecting a rotary with a reciprocating part (*U.S.*); **pit'-pony** a pony employed for haulage in a coal-mine; **pit'-prop** a, usu. timber, support in the workings of a coal-mine; **pit'-saw** a saw used in a saw-pit; **pit'-saw'yer** a bottom-sawyer; **pit'-stop** a stop a racing-car makes during a motor race when it goes into the pits for repairs; **pit'-vill'age** a group of miners' houses near a pit: a cluster of pit-dwellings; **pit'-vi'per** any member of an American group of snakes, including the rattlesnake, with a pit between eye and nose. — **pit and gallows** a feudal baron's right to drown female and hang male felons; **the pits** (*slang*) the absolute worst place, thing, person, etc. possible. [O.E. *pytt* — L. *puteus,* a well.]

pit[2] *pit, n.* a fruit-stone. — *v.t.* to remove the stone from. [App. Du. *pit.*]

pit[3] *pit, (Scot.) v.t.* to put: — *pa.t.* **pat** (*pät*); *pa.ps.* **putten** (*put'n*), **pitt'en.** [See **put**[1].]

pita[1] *pē'tə, n.* the fibre of various species of Bromelia, Agave, etc. — Also **pi'ta-flax', -hemp'.** [Sp., — Quechua *pita,* fine thread.]

pita[2]. See **pitta.**

Pitaka *pit'ə-kə, n.* any one of the three divisions of the

Buddhist canon. [Sans., basket.]

pitapat *pit'ə-pat*, **pitty-pat**, *pit'i-pat*, **pit-pat** *pit'pat'*, *advs.* with palpitation or pattering. — *adjs.* fluttering: pattering. — *ns.* a light, quick step: a succession of light taps: a patter. — *vs.i.* to step or tread quickly: to patter: to palpitate. [Imit.]

pitara(h). See **petara**.

pitch[1] *pich*, *n.* the black shining residue of distillation of tar, etc.: extended to various bituminous and resinous substances, as *Burgundy pitch*. — *v.t.* to smear, cover, or caulk with pitch. — *n.* **pitch'iness.** — *adj.* **pitch'y** like or characteristic of pitch: smeared with pitch: abounding in pitch: black. — *adj.* **pitch'-black** black as pitch. — **pitch'blende** a black mineral of resinous lustre, fundamentally composed of uranium oxides, a source of uranium and radium. — *adj.* **pitch'-dark'** utterly dark. — **pitch'pine** a name for several American pines that yield pitch and timber (*Pinus palustris, P. rigida*, etc.); **pitch'stone** a volcanic glass of resinous lustre, usu. acid; **pitch'-tree** a tree yielding pitch, turpentine, or resin, esp. silver fir, spruce, kauri pine, Amboina pine. [O.E. *pic* — L. *pix, picis*.]

pitch[2] *pich*, *v.t.* to thrust or fix in the ground: to set up: to establish: to set or plant firmly: to set in position: to lay out for sale: to set, cover, stud, or face: to pave with stones set on end or on edge: to make a foundation of stones for: to set in array (*obs.*): to pit in opposition: to determine or fix (*obs.*): to set in a key, to give this or that musical pitch, emotional tone, or degree of moral exaltation, etc., to: to fling, throw, or toss, esp. in such a manner as to fall flat or in a definite position: to loft so as not to roll much on falling (*golf*): to deliver to the batsman by an overhand or underhand throw (*baseball*). — *v.i.* to settle: to alight: to fix the choice (on): to encamp: to plunge forward: to oscillate about a transverse axis: to slope down: to descend or fall away abruptly: to interlock: — *pa.t.* and *pa.p.* **pitched**, *obs.* **pight** (q.v.). — *n.* the act or manner of pitching: a throw or cast: degree, esp. of elevation or depression: highest point (*fig.; lit., arch.*): height: a descent: slope: ground between the wickets (*cricket*): a place set apart for playing or practising a game: the point where a ball alights: a station taken by a street trader, etc.: a salesman's particular line of persuasive talk: the degree of acuteness of sound: a standard of acuteness for sounds (as **concert pitch, French pitch**): degree of intensity: distance between successive points or things, as the centres of teeth in a wheel or a saw, the threads of a screw: (of a propeller) the angle between the chord of the blade and the plane of rotation: the distance a propeller would advance in one revolution. — *ns.* **pitch'er** one who pitches: a paving-stone or sett: a baseball player who delivers the ball to the batsman: one who pitches a stall: a cutting or stake intended to take root; **pitch'ing** the action of the verb to pitch: a facing of stone: a foundation of stone for a road surface: a cobblestone surface of a road. — **pitch-and= toss'** a game in which coins are thrown at a mark, the player who throws nearest having the right of tossing all, and keeping those that come down heads up; **pitch circle** in a toothed wheel, an imaginary circle along which the tooth pitch is measured and which would put the wheel in contact with another that meshed with it; **pitched battle** a deliberate battle on chosen ground between duly arranged sides (also *fig.*); **pitched roof** a roof having two downward-sloping surfaces meeting in a central ridge. — *adjs.* **pitch'ed roofed, pitch'-roofed.** — **pitch'-far'thing** chuck-farthing; **pitch'fork** a fork for pitching hay, etc.: a tuning-fork. — *v.t.* to lift with a pitchfork: to throw suddenly into any position. — **pitching tool** a blunt-edged chisel, used to knock off superfluous stone; **pitch'man** (also **pitch'person**; *fem.* **pitch'woman**) a street or market trader (*U.S.*): an advertising man, esp. in the media: someone who delivers a strong sales pitch; **pitch'pipe** a small pipe to pitch the voice or tune with; **pitch'-wheel** a toothed wheel which operates with another of the same design.

— **pitch and pay** (*Shak.*) to pay ready money; **pitch in** to set to work briskly: to join in, cooperate; **pitch into** to assail vigorously: to throw oneself into (work, a task, etc.); **pitch (up)on** to let one's choice fall (up)on. [14th cent.; ety. uncertain.]

pitcher[1] *pich'ər*, *n.* a vessel, usu. of earthenware, for holding or pouring liquids: a cylindrical tinned milkcan (*Scot.*): a jug or ewer (*U.S.*): a modified leaf or part of a leaf in the form of a pitcher, serving to catch insects. — *n.* **pitch'erful.** — **pitch'er-plant** an insectivorous plant with pitchers, esp. Nepenthes, also Sarracenia, Darlingtonia, etc. — **(little) pitchers have (long) ears** children tell tales: there may be listeners. [O.Fr. *picher* — L.L. *picārium*, a goblet — Gr. *bīkos*, a wine-vessel.]

pitcher[2]. See **pitch**[2].

pitch-pole *pich'pōl*, *n.* a somersault (*obs.*): a type of harrow (*rare*). — *v.i.* to go head over heels: to somersault: to flip over lengthways: (of a boat) to turn stern over bow. — Also **pitch'-poll**. [**pitch**[2], **poll**[1].]

pitchy. See **pitch**[1].

piteous *pit'i-əs*, *adj.* compassionate (*arch.*): fitted to excite pity: paltry (*Milt.*). — *adv.* **pit'eously.** — *n.* **pit'eousness.** [O.Fr. *pitos, piteus;* cf. **pity**.]

pitfall. See **pit**[1].

pith *pith*, *n.* the soft tissue within the ring of vascular bundles in the stems of dicotyledonous plants: similar material elsewhere, as the white inner skin of an orange: spinal marrow: innermost part: condensed substance, essence: mettle: vigour: significant meaning: importance. — *v.t.* to remove the pith of: to sever, pierce, or destroy the marrow or central nervous system of: to kill (animals) in this way. — *adv.* **pith'ily.** — *n.* **pith'iness.** — *adjs.* **pith'ful; pith'less; pith'like; pith'y** full of pith: forcible: strong: energetic: sententious and masterful. — **pith'ball** a pellet of pith; **pith hat, helmet** a sun-helmet of sola pith; **pith'-tree** a tropical African papilionaceous tree (*Herminiera elaphroxylon*) whose very pithlike wood is used for floats, canoes, etc. [O.E. *pitha*; Du. *pit*, kernel.]

pithead. See **pit**[1].

Pithecanthropus *pith-ə-kan'thro-pəs, pith-ē-kan-thrō'pəs, n.* a fossil hominid discovered by Dr Eugene Dubois in Java in 1891–92, a former genus of primitive man, now included in the genus Homo. [Gr. *pithēkos*, ape, *anthrōpos*, man.]

pithecoid *pith-ē'koid*, *adj.* ape-like. [Gr. *pithēkos*, ape, *eidos*, form.]

pithos *pith'os*, *n.* a large Greek storage-jar. [Gr.]

pitiable, pitiless, etc. See **pity**.

pitman. See **pit**[1].

pit-mirk *pit'mirk*, (*Scot.*) *adj.* pitch-dark.

piton *pē'ton*, Fr. *pē-tɔ̃*, *n.* an iron peg or stanchion to which a rope may be attached, used in mountaineering. [Fr.]

Pitot tube *pē'tō tūb* a tube with openings at one end and one side, placed in a stream of liquid, an airstream, etc., to measure the velocity and pressure of flow, speed of an aircraft, etc. [From its originator, Henri *Pitot*, 18th-cent. French physicist.]

Pitta *pit'ə*, *n.* a genus of birds, the so-called ant-thrushes of the Old World: (without *cap.*) a bird of this genus. [Telugu *pitta*.]

pitta (bread), pita (bread) *pit'ə* (*bred*) a type of slightly leavened bread, originating in the Middle East, in the form of a hollow flat cake. [Mod. Gr., a cake.]

pittance *pit'əns*, *n.* a special additional allowance of food or drink in a religious house, or a bequest to provide it: a dole: a very small portion or quantity: a miserable pay. [O.Fr. *pitance* — L. *pietās*, pity.]

pitten. See **pit**[3].

pitter *pit'ər*, *v.i.* to make a sound like a grasshopper. — *adv.* **pitt'er-patt'er** with light pattering sound. — *v.i.* to make, or move with, such a sound. — Also *n.* [Imit.]

pittie-ward *pit'i-wərd*, *n.* an unexplained word in Shakespeare (*Merry Wives* III, i. 5).

pittite. See **pit**[1].

Pittite *pit'īt, n.* a follower of William *Pitt* (1759–1806), British statesman. — Also *adj.* — *n.* **Pitt'ism.**

pitty-pat. See **pitapat.**

pituita *pit-ū-ī'tə,* **pituite** *pit'ū-īt,* (*arch.*) *n.* phlegm, mucus. — *adj.* **pitū'itary** of or relating to phlegm, mucus (*arch.*): of or relating to the pituitary gland. — *n.* **pitū'itrin** a hormone produced by the pituitary body. — **pituitary gland, body** a ductless endocrine gland at the base of the brain affecting growth, once thought to produce mucus. [L. *pītuīta.*]

pituri *pit'ər-i, n.* an Australian solanaceous shrub, *Duboisia hopwoodii*: the narcotic obtained from its leaves. [Aboriginal.]

pity *pit'i, n.* a feeling for the sufferings and misfortunes of others: a cause or source of pity or grief: an unfortunate chance: a matter for regret. — *v.t.* to feel pity for: to feel grief at: to cause pity in (*obs.*): — *pr.p.* **pit'ying;** *pa.t.* and *pa.p.* **pit'ied.** — *adj.* **pit'iable** to be pitied: miserable, contemptible. — *n.* **pit'iableness.** — *adv.* **pit'iably.** — *n.* **pit'ier.** — *adj.* **pit'iful** feeling pity: compassionate: exciting pity: sad: despicable. — *advs.* **pit'iful** (*Shak.*), **pit'ifully.** — *n.* **pit'ifulness.** — *adj.* **pit'iless,** without pity: cruel. — *adv.* **pit'ilessly.** — *n.* **pit'ilessness.** — *adv.* **pit'yingly.** — **it pitieth me, you, them,** etc. (*Pr. Bk.*) it causes pity in me, you, them, etc. [O.Fr. *pite* (Fr. *pitié,* It. *pietà*) — L. *pietās, pietātis* — *pius,* pious.]

pityriasis *pit-i-rī'i-sis, n.* any of several skin diseases marked by the formation and flaking away of branny scales, esp. *pityriasis versicolor.* — *adj.* **pit'yroid** (*arch.*) bran-like. — *n.* **pityrospor'um** a yeast-like fungus which can cause *pityriasis versicolor.* [Gr. *pityron,* bran.]

più *pyōō, pē'ōō,* (It.) *adv.* more. — **più mosso** (*mō'sō, mo'so*) quicker.

pium *pi-ōōm', n.* a small but very troublesome Brazilian biting fly. [Tupi.]

piupiu *pē'ōō-pē-ōō, n.* a skirt, traditionally made from strips of flax, worn by Maori men and women for dances, celebrations and ceremonial occasions. [Maori.]

pivot *piv'ət, n.* a pin on which anything turns: a soldier upon whom, or position on which, a body wheels: a centre-half in football: that on which anything depends or turns: a man of cardinal importance in an industry: a movement of the body as if on a pivot. — *adj.* of the nature of a pivot: cardinal: serving as a pivot. — *v.t.* to mount on a pivot. — *v.i.* to turn on or as if on a pivot. — *adj.* **piv'otal.** — *adv.* **piv'otally.** — *adj.* **piv'oted.** — *ns.* **piv'oter** one who makes and fits pivots: a golfer who turns his body; **piv'oting** the pivot-work in machines. — **piv'ot-bridge** a swing-bridge moving on a vertical pivot in the middle; **piv'ot-man** a man on whom a body of soldiers turns: a man of cardinal importance in industry, etc. [Fr. *pivot,* perh. related to It. *piva,* pipe, peg, pin.]

pix[1] *piks, n.* Same as **pyx.**

pix[2] *piks,* (*coll.*) *n.pl.* short for **pictures,** usu. in sense of photographs: — *sing.* **pic.**

pixel *pik'səl, n.* one of the minute units which make up the picture on a cathode-ray tube, video display, etc. [**pix**[2], element.]

pixie, pixy *pik'si,* (*dial.*; S.W. England) **pisky** *pis'ki, ns.* a small fairy. — *adj.* **pix'ilated, pix'illated** bemused, bewildered: slightly crazy: intoxicated. — *n.* **pixila'tion, pixilla'tion** (*cinema, theatre, TV*) a technique for making human figures or animals appear to be animated artificially e.g. by the use of stop-frame camera methods, usu. to create a whimsical effect: the product of such a technique. — **pix'ie-hood** a hood with a point. — *adj.* **pix'y-led** bewildered. — **pix'y-ring** a fairy-ring; **pix'y-stool** a toadstool or mushroom. [Origin obscure; cf. Sw. *pysk, pyske,* a small fairy.]

pizazz. See **piz(z)azz.**

pize *pīz, n.* a term of imprecation, pox, pest. [Origin unknown.]

pizza *pēt'sə, n.* an open pie of bread dough with tomatoes, cheese, etc. — *adj.* **pizzaiola** (*pēt-sī-ō'-lə*) having a rich sauce made with tomatoes. — *n.* **pizzeria** (*pēt-sə-rē'ə*) a bakery or restaurant where pizzas are sold and/or made. [It.]

piz(z)azz, paz(z)azz *pə-zaz',* (*coll.*) *n.* a combination of flamboyance, panache and vigour, in behaviour, display or performance. [Origin uncertain.]

pizzicato *pit-si-kä'tō,* (*mus.*) *adj.* played by plucking the string, not with the bow — contradicted by *arco* or *col arco.* — *adv.* by plucking. — *n.* a tone so produced: a passage so played: the manner of playing by plucking: — *pl.* **pizzica'tos.** [It., twitched — *pizzicare,* to twitch.]

pizzle *piz'l, n.* a penis: that of a bull used as instrument of punishment, for flogging. [L.G. *pesel* or Flem. *pezel.*]

placable *plak'* or *plāk'ə-bl, adj.* that may be appeased: relenting: willing to forgive. — *ns.* **placabil'ity, plac'-ableness.** — *adv.* **plac'ably.** — *v.t.* **placate** (*plə-kāt', plā-kāt', plak', plāk'āt*) to conciliate. — *n.* **placā'tion** propitiation. — *adj.* **placatory** (*plak'* or *plāk'ə-tə-ri, plə-kā'*) conciliatory. [L. *plācāre,* to appease, akin to *placēre.*]

placard *plak'ärd, n.* an official permit or proclamation with a thin seal (*obs.*): a written or printed paper stuck upon a wall or otherwise displayed as an intimation: a notice written or printed on wood, cardboard or other stiff material, and carried, hung, etc., in a public place: a placcate or placket (*obs.*). — *v.t.* (sometimes *plə-kärd'*) to publish or notify by placard: to post or set up as a placard: to put placards on or in. [O.Fr. *plackart, placard,* etc. — *plaquier,* to lay flat, plaster — M. Flem. *placken,* to plaster.]

placate, etc. See **placable.**

placcat(e) *plak'āt, n.* See **placket.**

place *plās, n.* an open space in a town, a market-place or square: in street names, vaguely a row or group of houses, often short, secluded, or mean: a portion of space: a portion of the earth's surface, or any surface: a position in space, or on the earth's surface, or in any system, order, or arrangement: a building, room, piece of ground, etc., assigned to some purpose (as *place of business, entertainment, worship*): a particular locality: a town, village, etc.: a dwelling or home: a mansion with its grounds: a battlefield (*obs.*): a fortress, fortified town (*obs.*): a seat or accommodation in a theatre, train, at table, etc.: space occupied: room: the position held by anybody, employment, office, a situation, esp. under government or in domestic service: due or proper position or dignity: that which is incumbent on one: precedence: position in a series: high rank: position attained in a competition or assigned by criticism: position among the first three in a race: stead: passage in a book (*obs.*): (in reading-matter) the point which the reader has reached when he stops or is interrupted: a topic, matter of discourse (*obs.*): pitch reached by a bird of prey (*obs.* except in *pride of place*). — *v.t.* to put in any place: to assign to a place: to find a place, home, job, publisher, etc., for: to lay (before) (*fig.*): to induct: to identify: to invest: to arrange (loan, bet, etc.): to put (trust, etc., in): to assign the finishing positions in a race: to ascribe (to) (*arch.*). — *v.i.* (esp. U.S.) to finish a race or competition (in a specified position): to finish a race in second (if otherwise unspecified) position (*horse-racing*). — *adjs.* **placed** set in place or in a place: having a place: among the first three in a race: inducted to a charge; **place'less** without place or office. — *ns.* **place'ment** placing or setting: assigning to places: assigning to a job: a job so assigned; **plac'er; plac'ing** position, esp. a finishing position in a race or competition. — **place card** a card placed before each setting on the table at a banquet, formal dinner, etc., with the name of the person who is to sit there; **place'-hunter** (*arch.*) one who covets and strives after a public post; **place'-kick** in football, a kick made when the ball has been placed on the ground for that purpose; **place'man** one who has a place or office under a government, esp. if gained by selfishness or ambition: — *pl.* **place'men; place mat** a table-mat set at a person's place setting; **place'-monger** one who traffics in appointments to places; **place name** a geographical proper name; **place setting** each person's set of crockery, cutlery and glassware at a dining table. — **all over the place** scattered: in a muddle or mess, confused (*coll*); **give place (to)** to make room (for): to be superseded (by); **have place** to have existence; **in place** in position: opportune; **in place of** instead of; **in the first place** firstly, originally; **out of place** out of due position: inappropriate, unseasonable; **put someone in his, her place** to humble someone who is arrogant, presumptuous, etc.; **take place** to come to pass: to take precedence; **take someone's place** to act as substitute for, or successor to, someone; **take the place of** to be a substitute for. [Partly O.E. (Northumb.) *plæce*, market-place, but mainly Fr. *place*, both from L. *platea* — Gr. *plateia* (*hodos*), broad (street).]

placebo *plə-sē'bō, n.* vespers for the dead: a sycophant (*obs.*): a medicine given to humour or gratify a patient rather than to exercise any physically curative effect: a pharmacologically inactive substance administered as a drug either in the treatment of psychological illness or in the course of drug trials: — *pl.* **placē'bos.** [From the first words of the first antiphon of the office, *Placēbō Dominō,* I shall please the Lord.]

placenta *plə-sen'tə, n.* the structure that unites the unborn mammal to the womb of its mother and establishes a nutritive connection between them: the part of the carpel that bears the ovules (*bot.*): a structure bearing sporangia: — *pls.* **placen'tae** (*-tē*), **placen'tas.** — *adj.* **placen'tal.** — *n.* a placental mammal. — *n.pl.* **Placentalia** (*plas-ən-tā'li-ə*) the Eutheria or placental mammals. — *n.* **placentā'tion** the arrangement and mode of attachment of placentae or of placenta and fetus. — *adj.* **placent'iform** cake-shaped. — *n.* **placentol'ogy** the scientific study of placentae. [L. *placenta*, a flat cake — Gr. *plakoeis* (contr. *plakous*) from *plax, plakos,* anything flat.]

placer *plas'ər, plās'ər, n.* a superficial deposit from which gold or other mineral can be washed. — **plac'er-gold.** [Sp. *placer,* sandbank — *plaza,* place.]

placet¹ *plā'set, pla'ket, n.* a vote of assent in a governing body: permission given, esp. by a sovereign, to publish and carry out an ecclesiastical order, as a papal bull or edict. [L. *plăcet,* it pleases, 3rd sing. pres. indic. of *placēre,* to please.]

placet². A wrong form of **placit.**

placid *plas'id, adj.* calm. — *ns.* **placid'ity, plac'idness.** — *adv.* **plac'idly.** [L. *placidus* — *placēre,* to please.]

placitum *plas'i-təm, plak'i-tōōm, n.* a decision of a court or an assembly: a plea or pleading: — *pl.* **plac'ita.** — Also **plac'it** (wrongly **plac'et).** — *adj.* **plac'itory** relating to pleas or pleading. [L. pa.p. neut. of *placēre,* to please.]

plack *plak, n.* an old Scottish copper coin worth a third part of an English penny of the same period. — *adj.* **plack'less.** [Prob. Flem. *placke,* an old Flemish coin, orig. a flat disc.]

placket *plak'it, n.* in armour, a breastplate or backplate, or a leather doublet with strips of steel (*obs.* **placc'ate):** an apron (*arch.*): a petticoat (*arch.*): an opening in a skirt, for a pocket, or at the fastening: a piece of material sewn behind this: a pocket, esp. in a skirt: a woman. — *Shak.* also **placc'at.** — **plack'et-hole** (*arch.*) a slit in a skirt. [Origin obscure; cf. **placard.**]

placoderm *plak'ō-dûrm, adj.* covered with bony plates, as some fossil fishes. — *n.* a fish so covered. [Gr. *plax, plakos,* anything flat, *derma,* skin.]

placoid *plak'oid, adj.* plate-like: having placoid scales, irregular plates of hard bone, not imbricated, as sharks. [Gr. *plax, plakos,* anything flat and broad, *eidos,* form.]

plafond *pla-fɔ̃, n.* a ceiling, esp. decorated: a soffit: a game like contract bridge. [Fr., ceiling, score above the

line in bridge — *plat,* flat, *fond,* bottom.]

plagal *plā'gl,* (*mus.*) *adj.* of a Gregorian mode, having the final in the middle of the compass instead of at the bottom — opp. to *authentic.* — **plagal cadence** one in which the subdominant chord precedes the tonic. [Gr. *plagios,* sidewise — *plagos,* a side.]

plage *pläzh, n.* a fashionable beach: a bright, highly disturbed area in the chromosphere, usu. presaging, or associated with, a sunspot. [Fr.]

plagiary *plā'ji-ə-ri, n.* (*arch.*) one who steals the thoughts or writings of others and gives them out as his own: the crime of plagiarism. — *adj.* (*obs.*) practising or got by literary theft. — *v.t.* **pla'giarise, -ize** to steal from the writings or ideas of another. — *ns.* **pla'giarism** the act or practice of plagiarising; **pla'giarist** a person who plagiarises. [L. *plagiārius,* a kidnapper, plagiary — *plăga,* a net.]

plagioclase *plā'ji-ō-klās, -klāz,* or *plaj', n.* a feldspar whose cleavages are not at right angles — albite, anorthite, or any mixture of them. [Gr. *plagios,* oblique, *klasis,* a fracture.]

plagiostome *plā'ji-ō-stōm, n.* a plagiostomous fish, one of the **Plagiostomata** (*-stō'mə-tə*) or **Plagiostomi** (*-os'tə-mī*), the cross-mouthed fishes, sharks and rays, having the mouth as a transverse slit on the underside of the head. — *adjs.* **plagiostom'atous, plagios'tomous.** [Gr. *plagios,* crosswise, *stoma, -atos,* mouth.]

plagiotropism *plā-ji-ot'rə-pizm, n.* orienting at an angle to the direction of stimulus. — *adj.* **plagiotropic** (*-ō-trop'ik*). — *adv.* **plagiotrop'ically.** — *adj.* **plagiotropous** (*-ot'rə-pəs*). [Gr. *plagios,* crosswise, *tropos,* a turning.]

plagium *plā'ji-əm, n.* the crime of kidnapping. [L. *plăgium* — *plăga,* a net.]

plague *plāg, n.* a blow or wound (*obs.*): an affliction regarded as a sign of divine displeasure: a deadly epidemic or pestilence, esp. a fever caused by a bacillus (*B. pestis*) transmitted by rat-fleas from rats to man, characterised by buboes, or swellings of the lymphatic glands, by carbuncles and petechiae: murrain: any troublesome thing or person: trouble (*coll.*). — *v.t.* to infest with disease (*rare*): to pester or annoy. — *adj.* **plague'some** (*coll.*) troublesome, annoying. — *adv.* **pla'guily** confoundedly. — *adj.* **plagu(e)y** (*plā'gi*) of, or of the nature of, plague: vexatious: troublesome: confounded. — *adv.* (*Shak.*) confoundedly. — **plague'-pit** a common grave for plague victims; **plague'-sore** an ulcer due to plague; **plague'-spot** a spot on the skin indicating plague: a place where disease is constantly present: an evil place. — *adj.* **plague'-stricken.** — **plague on** may a curse rest on; **what the** (*Shak.* a) **plague** what the devil. [O.Fr. *plague* — L. *plāga,* a blow; cf. Gr. *plēgē.*]

plaice *plās, n.* a yellow-spotted flatfish of the fam. Pleuronectidae (*Pleuronectes platessa*). — **plaice'-mouth** a mouth placed awry. — *adj.* **wry-mouthed.** [O.Fr. *plaïs* (Fr. *plie*) — L.L. *platessa,* a flatfish — perh. Gr. *platys,* flat.]

plaid *plād* (by the English also *plad*), *n.* a long piece of woollen cloth, worn over the shoulder, usually in tartan as part of Highland dress, or checked as formerly worn by Lowland shepherds: cloth for it: a plaidman. — *adj.* like a plaid in pattern or colours. — *adj.* **plaid'ed** wearing a plaid: made of plaid cloth. — *n.* **plaid'ing** a strong woollen twilled fabric. — **plaid'man** a Highlander; **plaid'-neuk'** (*-nük*) a pocket at the end of a plaid. [Perh. Gael. *plaide,* a blanket; but that may be from the Scots word.]

Plaid Cymru *plīd kum'ri,* (W.) the Welsh Nationalist party.

plain¹ *plān,* (*arch.*), *v.t., v.i.* to complain: to lament. — *n.* a complaint. — *n.* **plain'ant** one who complains: a plaintiff. — *adj.* **plain'ful.** — *n.* **plain'ing** (*Shak.*) complaint. [O.Fr. *plaigner* (Fr. *plaindre*) — L. *plangĕre,* to beat the breast, lament.]

plain² *plān, adj.* flat: level: even: unobstructed: without obscurity: clear: obvious: simple: downright, utter: not

ornate: unembellished: unvariegated: uncoloured: unruled: without pattern, striation, markings, etc.: without gloss: uncurled: not twilled: in knitting, denoting a straightforward stitch with the wool passed round the front of the needle (opp. to *purl*): not elaborate: without addition: not highly seasoned: deficient in beauty: (in meiosis) ugly: without subtlety: candid: outspoken: straightforward: undistinguished: ordinary: other than a court card: other than trumps. — *n.* an extent of level land: the open country, esp. as a field of battle or as a setting for pastoral or romantic literature (*poetic*). — *adv.* clearly: distinctly. — *v.t.* (*Shak.*) to make plain. — *adj.* **plain′ish.** — *adv.* **plain′ly.** — *n.* **plain′ness.** — **plain′-chant** plainsong; **plain chocolate** dark chocolate, made with some sugar added but without milk. — *adj.* **plain′-clothes** wearing ordinary clothes, not uniform, as a policeman on detective work. — *v.i.* **plain′-cook** to cook ordinary dishes (also *n.*). — *v.t.* and *v.i.* **plain′-darn** to darn with the ordinary cross pattern. — *n.* and *adj.* **plain′-deal′er** one who is candid and outspoken. — *n.* and *adj.* **plain′-deal′ing.** — *adj.* **plain′= heart′ed** having a plain or honest heart: sincere. — **plain′-heart′edness; plain Jane** (*coll.*) a plain, dowdy girl. — *adj.* ordinary, unremarkable: plain, esp. of a garment. **plain language** straightforward, understandable language; **plain sailing** sailing in open, unrestricted waters (*naut.*): an easy, straightforward task, affair, etc. (*fig.*): see also **plane²; plains′man** a dweller in a plain, esp. in N. America; **plain′song** unmeasured music sung in unison in ecclesiastical modes from early times, and still in use in R.C. and some Anglican churches: a simple melody: that to which a descant can be added. — *adj.* (*Shak.*) singing a simple theme. — **plain′-speaking** straightforwardness or bluntness of speech. — *adj.* **plain′-spoken** plain, rough, and sincere. — **plain′stanes** (*Scot.*) flagstones, pavement (also **plain′stones**); **plain′work** plain needlework, as distinguished from embroidery. — **plain as a pikestaff** see **pike¹.** [Fr., — L. *plānus*, plain.]
plainant, plainful, plaining. See **plain¹.**
Plains *plānz*, (also without *cap.*; esp. *U.S.*) *adj.* of or from the Great Plains of North America and Canada. — **Plains Indian** a member of any of the North American Indian tribes originally inhabiting the Great Plains.
plaint *plānt, n.* lamentation: complaint (*arch.*): a mournful song: a statement of grievance, esp. the exhibiting of an action in writing by a complainant in a court of law. — *adj.* **plaint′ful** (*arch.*) complaining. — *n.* **plaint′iff** (*Eng. law*) one who commences a suit against another — opp. to *defendant*. — Also *adj.* (*Spens.*). — *adj.* **plaint′ive** mournful. — *adv.* **plaint′ively.** — *n.* **plaint′iveness.** — *adj.* **plaint′less.** [O.Fr. *pleinte* (Fr. *plainte*) — L. *plangĕre, planctum*, to beat the breast, lament.]
plaister *plās′tər, n.* an obsolete or Scots form of **plaster.**
plait *plat, plāt, plēt, n.* a pleat or zigzag fold (usu. **pleat,** and pron. *plēt* even when spelt **plait**): a braid in which strands are passed over one another in turn: material so braided: a braided tress or queue (in these senses usu. *plat*, and sometimes spelt **plat**). — *v.t.* to pleat (usu. *plēt*): to braid or intertwine (usu. *plat*). — *adj.* **plait′ed.** — *ns.* **plait′er; plait′ing.** [O.Fr. *pleit, ploit* (Fr. *pli*) — L. *plicāre, -ītum, -ātum*, to fold.]
plan *plan, n.* a figure or representation of anything projected on a plane or flat surface, esp. that of a building, floor, etc., as disposed on the ground: a large-scale detailed map of a small area: a scheme for accomplishing a purpose: a purposed method: a scheme drawn up beforehand: a scheme of arrangement: in the Methodist churches, a quarterly programme of services with preachers for each church in the circuit. — *v.t.* to make a plan of: to design: to lay plans for: to devise: to purpose. — *v.i.* to make plans: — *pr.p.* **plann′ing;** *pa.t.* and *pa.p.* **planned.** — *adjs.* **planned** intended: in accordance with, or achieved by, a careful plan made beforehand; **plan′less.** — *n.* **plann′er.** — **planned obsolescence** see **obsolescent;**

planning permission permission from a local authority to erect or convert a building or to change the use to which a building or piece of land is put; **plan-position indicator** (*radar*) an apparatus in which the position of reflecting objects is shown on the screen of a cathode-ray tube, as if on a plan: —abbrev. **PPI.** [Fr., — L. *plānus*, flat.]
planar, planation. See **plane².**
planarian *plə-nā′ri-ən, adj.* and *n.* turbellarian. [L. *plānārius*, on level ground (taken as if meaning flat) — *plānus*, flat.]
planch *plansh, n.* a plank (*obs.*): a floor (*dial.*): a slab. — *v.t.* (*obs.*) to floor: to board. — *adj.* **planch′ed** (*Shak.*) boarded. — *ns.* **planchet** (*plan′shit*) a blank to be stamped as a coin; **planchette** (*plä-shet, plan-shet′*) a board mounted on two castors and a pencil-point, used as a medium for automatic writing and supposed spirit-messages. [Fr. *planche* — L. *planca*.]
Planck's constant *plangks kon′stənt*, the constant (*h*), in the expression for the quantum of energy, equal to 6.626×10^{-34} Js (joule second). [Max Karl Ernst Ludwig *Planck*, 1858–1947, German physicist.]
plane¹ *plān, n.* any tree of the genus Platanus (see **platane**) esp. the oriental plane (*P. orientalis*) and the N. Amer. plane or buttonwood (*P. occidentalis*), trees with palmatifid leaves shedding their bark in thin slabs: in Scotland, the great maple (*Acer pseudoplatanus*). — **plane′-tree.** [Fr. *plane* — L. *platanus*; see **platane.**]
plane² *plān, n.* a surface of which it is true that, if any two points on the surface be taken, the straight line joining them will lie entirely on the surface (*geom.*): any flat or level material surface: one of the thin horizontal structures used as wings and tail to sustain or control aeroplanes in flight: short for aeroplane or airplane (also **′plane**): an act of planing or soaring: in mines, a main road for transport of coal or other mineral: any grade of life or of development or level of thought or existence. — *adj.* having the character of a plane: pertaining to, lying in, or confined to a plane: level: smooth. — *v.t.* to make plane or smooth (see also **plane³**). — *v.i.* to travel by aeroplane: to soar: to volplane: of a boat, to skim across the surface of the water. — *adj.* **planar** (*plān′ər*). — *ns.* **planation** (*plə-nā′shən*) making level; **planer** (*plān′ər*) one who levels or makes plane: a smoothing instrument (see also **plane³**): a wooden block beaten with a mallet to level a forme of type; **planigraph** (*plan′i-gräf*) an instrument for reducing or enlarging drawings; **planimeter** (*plən-im′i-tər*) an instrument for measuring the area of a plane figure. — *adjs.* **planimetric** (*plān-, plan-i-met′rik*), **-al.** — *ns.* **planimetry** (*plən-im′i-tri*) the mensuration of plane surfaces; **planisphere** (*plan′*) a sphere projected on a plane: a map of the celestial sphere, which can be adjusted so as to show the area visible at any time. — *adjs.* **planispher′ic; plā′no= con′cave** plane on one side and concave on the other; **plā′no-con′ical** plane on one side and conical on the other; **plā′no-con′vex** plane on one side and convex on the other. — *ns.* **planom′eter** (*plən-*) a plane surface used in machine-making as a gauge for plane surfaces; **Planor′bis** a genus of pond-snails with flat spiral shell. — **planar diode** one with plane parallel electrodes; **plane chart** a chart used in plane sailing, the lines of longitude and latitude being projected onto a plane surface, so being represented parallel. — *adj.* **plane′= pol′arised, -ized** (of light) consisting of vibrations in one plane only. — **plane sailing** the calculation of a ship's place in its course as if the earth were flat instead of spherical: see also **plain sailing** under **plain²; plane′= table** an instrument used in field-mapping, with a sighting-telescope for observing objects, whose angles may be noted on a paper on the table of the instrument: an inclined table on which ore is dressed. — *v.t.* to survey with a plane-table. [L. *plānum*, a flat surface, neut. of *plānus*, flat; cf. **plain²** and next word.]
plane³ *plān, n.* a carpenter's tool for producing a smooth surface by paring off shavings: a tool or machine for

smoothing other things. — *v.t.* to smooth or remove with a plane (see also **plane²**). — *n.* **plā′ner** one who uses a plane: a tool or machine for planing. — **plān′ing-machine′** a machine for planing wood or metals. [Fr. *plane* — L.L. *plāna* — *plānāre*, to smooth.]

planet *plan′it, n.* in old astronomy, a heavenly body whose place among the fixed stars is not fixed (including sun and moon): a body (other than a comet or meteor) that revolves about the sun (including the earth) reflecting the sun's light and generating no heat or light of its own: a satellite of a planet (*secondary planet*): an astrological influence vaguely conceived. — *n.* **planetā′rium** a machine showing the motions and orbits of the planets, often by projecting of their images on to a (domed) ceiling: a hall or building containing such a machine: — *pl.* **planetā′ria.** — *adj.* **plan′etary** pertaining to the planets or a planet, or this planet: consisting of, or produced by, planets: under the influence of a planet: erratic: revolving in an orbit. — *n.* **planetes′imal** in one theory of the origin of the solar system, any of many very small units absorbed into the planets as these formed. — *adjs.* **planetic** (*plan-et′ik*), **-al.** — *n.* **plan′etoid** a minor planet: an artificial body put into orbit. — *adj.* **planetoi′dal.** — *ns.* **planetol′ogy** the science of the planets; **planetol′ogist.** — **planetary nebula** a ring-shaped nebula around a star, consisting of a shell of gas, illuminated by the star's short-wave radiation. — *adjs.* **plan′et-strick′en, plan′et-struck** (*astrol.*) affected by the influence of the planets: blasted. — **inferior planets** those within the earth's orbit (Mercury and Venus); **minor planets** the numerous group of very small planets between the orbits of Mars and Jupiter; **superior planets** those outside the earth's orbit. [Fr. *planète* — Gr. *planētēs*, wanderer — *planaein*, to make to wander.]

plangent *plan′jənt, adj.* resounding: noisy, clangorous: resounding mournfully. — *adv.* **plan′gently.** — *n.* **plan′gency.** [L. *plangēns, -entis*, pr.p. of *plangĕre*, to beat.]

planigraph, planimeter, etc. See **plane².**

planish *plan′ish, v.t.* to polish (metal, etc.): to flatten. — *n.* **plan′isher** a tool for planishing. [Obs. Fr. *planir, -issant* — *plan*, flat.]

planisphere. See **plane².**

plank *plangk, n.* a long piece of timber, thicker than a board: a board on which fish, etc., is cooked and served (*U.S.*): one of the principles or aims that form the platform or programme of a party. — *v.t.* to cover with planks: to pay down or table (with *down*): to cook on a plank (*U.S.*): to put down with a thump or plump (often with *down*; *Scot.* or *dial.*). — *n.* **plank′ing** the act of laying planks: a series of planks: work made up of planks. — **plank′-bed** a prison bed of wood without mattress. — **walk the plank** to walk (compulsorily) along a plank projecting over the ship's side into the sea. [L. *planca*, a board.]

plankton *plangk′tən, n.* the drifting organisms in oceans, lakes or rivers. — *adj.* **planktonic** (*-ton′ik*). [Neut. of Gr. *planktos, -ē, -on*, wandering.]

planoblast *plan′ō-blāst, n.* a free-swimming medusa. — *n.* **planogam′ete** a motile gamete. [Gr. *plănos*, wandering.]

plano-concave, etc., **planometer, Planorbis.** See **plane².**

planogamete. See **planoblast.**

plant *plănt, n.* a vegetable organism, or part of one, ready for planting or lately planted: a slip, cutting, or scion: an offshoot: a young person: a sapling: a cudgel: any member of the vegetable kingdom, esp. (*popularly*) one of the smaller kinds: growth: amount planted: the sole of the foot: mode of planting oneself, stand: something deposited beforehand for a purpose: equipment, machinery, apparatus, for an industrial activity: factory: bedded oyster (*U.S.*): a thief's hoard (*slang*): a spy, detective, picket or cordon of detectives, or police trap (*slang*): a deceptive trick, put-up job (*slang*): a shot in which one pockets, or tries to pocket, a red

ball by causing it to be propelled by another red ball which has been struck by the cue ball or by some other red ball (*snooker*). — *v.t.* to put into the ground for growth: to introduce: to insert: to fix: to place firmly: to set in position: to station, post: to found: to settle: to locate: to place or deliver (as a blow, a dart): to leave in the lurch: to bury (*slang*): to hide (*slang*): to place stolen goods, etc., in another's possession so as to incriminate him: to place as a spy, etc. (*slang*): to instil or implant: to furnish with plants: to colonise: to stock: to furnish or provide (with things disposed around): to salt (as a mine) (*slang*). — *v.i.* to plant trees, colonists, or anything else. — *n.* **plant′a** the sole of the foot. — *adj.* **plant′able.** — *n.* **plant′age** (*Shak.*) plants in general. — *adj.* **plant′ar** of the sole of the foot. — *ns.* **plantā′tion** a place planted, esp. with trees: a colony: an estate used for growing cotton, rubber, tea, sugar, or other product of warm countries: a large estate (*Southern U.S.*): the act or process of introduction: the act of planting (*Milt.*); **plant′er** one who plants or introduces: the owner or manager of a plantation: a pioneer colonist: a settler: an instrument for planting: an ornamental pot or other container for plants. — *adj.* **plant′igrade** walking on the soles of the feet. — *n.* an animal that walks so. — *n.* **plant′ing** the act of setting in the ground for growth: the art of forming plantations of trees: a plantation (*Scot.*). — *adj.* **plant′less.** — *ns.* **plant′let, plant′ling** a little plant; **plantoc′racy** a ruling class of plantation owners and managers: government by plantation owners and managers; **plant′ule** a plant embryo. — **plant′-associa′tion, plant′=forma′tion** an assemblage of plants growing together under like conditions, as in a salt-marsh, a pine-wood, etc.; **plantation song** a Negro song, such as the workers sang on American plantations; **plant′-house** a structure for growing plants of warmer climates; **plant′ie-cruive** (*-krŏōv; Orkney* and *Shetland*) a kitchen garden, enclosure for cabbage. — *adj.* **plant′-like.** — **plant′-lore** folklore of plants; **plant′-louse** an aphis or greenfly: — *pl.* **plant′-lice.** — **plant′-pot** a pot for growing a plant in; **plants′man** one who has great knowledge of and experience in gardening. — **plant out** to transplant to open ground, from pot or frame: to dispose at intervals in planting. [O.E. *plante* (n.) — L. *planta*, shoot, slip, cutting, and O.E. *plantian* (vb.), and partly from or affected by Fr. *plante* and L. *planta*, plant, also (perh. a different word) sole.]

plantain¹ *plan′tin, n.* a roadside plant of genus **Plantā′gō** (e.g. waybread, ribgrass; fam. **Plantaginā′ceae**) that presses its leaves flat on the ground. — *adj.* **plantaginaceous** (*plan-taj-i-nā′shəs*). — **plantain lily** a plant of the Hosta genus. [L. *plantāgō, -inis* — *planta*, the sole of the foot.]

plantain² *plan′tin, n.* a musaceous plant: its fruit, a coarse banana: in India, a banana. — **plan′tain-eater** an African bird (*Musophaga*) of a fam. *Musophagidae*, a touraco. [Origin doubtful.]

plantain³ *plan′tin,* (*obs.*) *n.* a platane or plane-tree. [Obs. Fr. *plantain* — L. *platanus.*]

plantar, plantigrade, plantation, etc. See **plant.**

planula *plan′ū-lə, n.* a free-swimming two-layered, often flattened, larva of coelenterates, etc.: — *pl.* **plan′ulae** (*-lē*). — *adjs.* **plan′ular; plan′uliform; plan′uloid.** [Dim. of L. *plănus*, flat.]

planuria *plan-ū′ri-ə, n.* the discharge of urine through an abnormal passage. — Also **plan′ury.** [Gr. *plănos*, wandering, *ouron*, urine.]

planxty *plangks′ti, n.* an Irish dance or dance-tune, like a jig but slower. [Origin unknown; not native Irish.]

plap *plap, n.* a flatter sound than a plop. — *v.i.* to make, or move with, such a sound. [Imit.]

plaque *pläk, plak, n.* a plate, tablet, or slab hung on, applied to, or inserted in, a surface as an ornament, memorial, etc.: a tablet worn as a badge of honour: a patch, such as a diseased area (*med.*): a film of saliva and bacteria formed on teeth (*dentistry*): an area in a bacterial or tissue culture where the cells have been destroyed by infection with a virus. — *n.* **plaquette**' a small plaque. [Fr.; cf. **plack**.]

plash[1] *plash, v.t.* to interweave by partly cutting through, bending and twining the branches: to bend down: to break down: to make, mend, or treat, by cutting, bending, and interweaving stems and branches. — *n.* a plashed branch: a plashed place. — *n.* **plash**'**ing.** [O.Fr. *plassier* — L. *plectĕre,* to twist; cf. **pleach.**]

plash[2] *plash,* (*Spens.* **plesh, plesh**), *n.* a shallow pool: a puddle. — *n.* **plash**'**et** a puddle. — *adj.* **plash**'**y.** [O.E. *plæsc.*]

plash[3] *plash, n.* a dash of water: a splashing sound: a sudden downpour (esp. *Scot.*). — *v.i.* to dabble in water: to splash. — *v.t.* to splash. — *adj.* **plash**'**y.** [Cf. M.L.G. *plaschen,* early Mod. Du. *plasschen;* perh. conn. with preceding.]

plasm *plazm, n.* a mould or matrix: protoplasm: plasma. — *ns.* **plas**'**ma** plasm: a bright green chalcedony: protoplasm: the liquid part of blood, lymph, or milk: a very hot ionised gas, having approximately equal numbers of positive ions and of electrons, highly conducting; **plasmapherē**'**sis** the process of taking plasma only from a blood-donor — the blood is drawn, the blood cells separated from the plasma by a centrifuge and returned to the donor. — *adjs.* **plasmat**'**ic, -al, plas**'**mic** of, or occurring in, plasma: protoplasmic. — *ns.* **plas**'**mid** a circular piece of DNA which can exist and reproduce autonomously in the cytoplasm of cells; **plas**'**min** fibrinolysin; **plasmodesm** (*plaz*'*mō-dezm*; Gr. *desmos,* bond) a thread of protoplasm connecting cells; **plasmo**'**dium** a naked mass of protoplasm with many nuclei, as in slime-fungi: — *pl.* **plasmo**'**dia; plasmog**'**amy** fusion of cytoplasm only. — *v.t.* **plas**'**molyse, -yze** (*-līz*). — *n.* **plasmolysis** (*-mol*'*i-sis;* Gr. *lysis,* loosening) removal of water from a cell by osmosis, with resultant shrinking. — *adj.* **plasmolytic** (*-mō-lit*'*ik*). — *n.* **plasmosō**'**ma, plas**'**mosome** (Gr. *sōma,* body) a nucleolus. [Gr. *plasma, -atos,* a thing moulded — *plassein,* to mould.]

plast, plaste *plāst,* (*Spens.*) *pa.t.* and *pa.p.* of **place.**

plaster *pläs*'*tər, n.* a fabric coated with an adhesive substance for local application as a remedy, for protection of a cut, etc.: a pasty composition that sets hard, esp. a mixture of slaked lime, sand, and sometimes hair, used for coating walls, etc.: plaster of Paris: calcium sulphate. — *adj.* made of plaster. — *v.t.* to apply plaster, or a plaster, to: to treat with plaster: to bedaub: to smear: to cover excessively, injudiciously, or meretriciously: to stick (on or over): to reduce to plaster or a sticky mass: to damage by a heavy attack: to smooth down: to smooth (over): to treat with gypsum: to attach with plaster. — *adj.* **plas**'**tered** daubed, treated, etc., with plaster: shattered: intoxicated (*slang*). — *ns.* **plas**'**terer** one who plasters, or one who works in plaster; **plas**'**tering.** — *adj.* **plas**'**tery** like plaster. — *n.* **plas**'**teriness.** — *n.* **plas**'**terboard** a building slab of plaster faced with paper or fibre: gypsum plasterboard; **plaster cast** a copy got by pouring a mixture of plaster of Paris and water into a mould formed from the object: an immobilising and protective covering of plaster of Paris for a broken limb, etc.; **plaster saint** a virtuous person: one who pretends hypocritically to virtue; **plas**'**terstone** gypsum; **plas**'**ter= work.** — **plaster of Paris** gypsum (originally found near *Paris*) partially dehydrated by heat, which dries into a hard substance when mixed with water. [O.E. *plaster* (in medical sense) and O.Fr. *plastre* (builder's plaster) both — L.L. *plastrum* — L. *emplastrum* — Gr. *emplastron* for *emplaston* — *en,* on, *plassein,* to mould, apply as a plaster.]

plastic *plas*', *pläs*'*tik, adj.* having power to give form: shaping, formative: mouldable: of or pertaining to moulding or modelling: modifiable: capable of permanent deformation without giving way: capable of, or pertaining to, metabolism and growth: made of plastic. — in composition, growing, forming, as in *neoplastic.* — *n.* a mouldable substance, esp. now any of a large number of polymeric substances, most of them synthetic, mouldable at some stage (see **thermoplastic, thermosetting**) under heat or pressure, used to make domestic articles and many engineering products: a modeller or sculptor (*obs.*): the art of modelling or of sculpture (usu. **plastics**). — *n.* **Plas**'**ticine**® (*-ti-sēn*) a substitute for modelling clay. — *n.sing.* **plas**'**tics** plastic surgery: the art of modelling or sculpture. — *adj.* dealing with plastic materials (as *the plastics industry*). — *v.t.* and *v.i.* **plas**'**ticise, -ize** (*-ti-sīz*) to make or become plastic. — *ns.* **plasticis**'**er, -z-** a substance that induces plasticity; **plasticity** (*-tis*'*i-ti*) the state or quality of being plastic: the quality in a picture of appearing to be three-dimensional. — **plastic art** the art of shaping (in three dimensions), as sculpture, modelling: art which is, or appears to be, three-dimensional; **plastic bomb** a bomb made with a certain explosive chemical that **can** be moulded; **plastic bullet** a four-inch cylinder of **PVC** fired as a baton round (q.v.); **plastic clay** clay from which earthenware and bricks are made; **plastic force** the force or power of growth in animals and plants; **plastic money** (*coll.*) credit cards; **plastic operation** a surgical operation which restores a lost part, or repairs a deformed or disfigured part, of the body; **plastic surgery** the branch of surgery concerned with plastic operations. [Gr. *plastikos* — *plassein,* to mould.]

plastid *plas*', *pläs*'*tid, n.* a living cell (*obs.*): a differentiated granule in protoplasm. — *n.* **plast**'**idule** Haeckel's hypothetical unit of living protoplasm. [Gr. *plastis, -idos,* moddler (fem.).]

plastilina *pläs-ti-lē*'*nə, n.* a mixture of clay with oil, zinc oxide, wax, and sulphur for modelling. [It.]

plastique *plas-tēk*', *n.* graceful poses and movements in dancing. [Fr. — Gr. *plastikos* (see **plastic**).]

plastisol *plas*'*ti-sol, n.* a suspension of powdered resin in liquid plasticiser, convertible by heat into a solid plastic and used in castings and linings. [**plastic** and **sol**[2].]

plastogamy *plast-og*'*ə-mi, n.* plasmogamy. [Gr. *plastos,* moulded, *gamos,* marriage.]

plastron *plas*'*tron, n.* a breastplate worn under the hauberk: a fencer's wadded breast-shield: the under part of the shell of a tortoise or turtle, or other animal: the front of a dress-shirt: a separate ornamental front part of a woman's bodice. — *adj.* **plas**'**tral.** [Fr. *plastron* — It. *piastrone* — *piastra,* breastplate; cf. **piastre, plaster.**]

plat[1]. See **plait.**

plat[2] *plat, n.* a plot of ground (*arch.*): a diagram or a plan (*obs.* or *U.S.*): a scheme (*obs.*). — *v.t.* (now *U.S.*) to make a plan of, plot out. [**plot**[1], infl. by **plat**[3].]

plat[3] *plat, n.* a flat thing (*obs.*): the flat, or flat part, or side (*obs.*): a mould-board (*dial.*): a flat place or region (esp. *U.S.*). [App. Fr. *plat.*]

platane, platan *plat*'*ən, n.* a plane-tree, any tree of the genus **Plat**'**anus** (see **plane**[1]), giving name to the family **Platanā**'**ceae,** akin to the witch-hazel family. — *adj.* **platanā**'**ceous.** [L. *platanus* — Gr. *platanos* — *platys,* broad.]

platanna (frog) *plə-tan*'*ə* (*frog*)*, n.* an African frog, *Xenopus laevis,* used in research, and formerly used in tests for pregnancy. [Afrikaans, — *plat-hander,* flat-handed.]

platband *plat*'*band, n.* a fascia or flat moulding projecting less than its own breadth: a lintel or flat arch: an edging of turf or flowers. [Fr. *platebande,* flat band.]

plat du jour *pla dü zhōor,* a dish on a restaurant menu specially recommended that day. [Fr.]

plate *plāt, n.* a sheet, slab, or lamina of metal or other hard material, usually flat or flattish: metal in the form of sheets: a broad piece of armour: a scute or separate portion of an animal's shell: a broad thin piece of structure or mechanism: a plate-like section of earth's crust, involved in plate tectonics (see bel a piece of metal, wood, etc., bearing or to be inscription to be affixed to anything: an engrave of metal for printing from: an impression printed from it, an engraving: a whole-page separately printed and inserted illustration in a book: a mould from type, etc., for printing from, as an electrotype or stereotype: part of a denture fitting the mouth and carrying the teeth: the whole denture: a device worn in the mouth by some children in order to straighten the teeth: a film-coated sheet of glass or other material to photograph on: a plate-rail: a horizontal supporting timber in building: a five-sided white slab at the home base (*baseball*): a light racing horseshoe: a thermionic valve anode (orig. flat): precious metal, esp. silver (*hist.*; Sp. *plata*, silver): a silver coin (*Shak.*): wrought gold or silver: household utensils in gold or silver: table utensils generally: plated ware: a cup or other prize for a race or other contest: a race or contest for such a prize: a shallow dish: a plateful: a portion served on a plate: a church collection: (in *pl.*) the feet (*slang*; orig. rhyming slang for *plates of meat*). — *v.t.* to overlay with metal: to armour with metal: to cover with a thin film of another metal: to make a printing plate of. — *adj.* **plā′ted** covered with plates of metal: covered with a coating of another metal, esp. gold or silver: armoured with hard scales or bone (*zool.*). — *ns.* **plate′ful** as much as a plate will hold; **plate′let** a minute body in blood, concerned in clotting; **plā′ter** one who, or that which, plates: a moderate horse entered for a minor, prob. a selling, race; **plā′ting**. — *adj.* **plā′ty** plate-like: separating into plates. — **plate′-arm′our** protective armour of metal plates; **plate′-basket** a basket for forks, spoons, etc.; **plate′-fleet** (*hist.*) ships that carried American silver to Spain; **plate′-glass** a fine kind of glass used for mirrors and shop-windows, orig. poured in a molten state on an iron plate. — *adj.* made with, consisting of, plate-glass: of a building, having large plate-glass windows, appearing to be built entirely of plate-glass: hence, of any very modern building or institution, esp. recently-founded British universities. — **plate′-layer** one who lays, fixes, and attends to the rails of a railway; **plate′-leather** a chamois leather for rubbing gold and silver; **plate′man** a man who has the care of silver-plate in a hotel, club, etc.; **plate′mark** a hallmark; **plate′-powder** a polishing powder for silver; **plate′-print′ing** the process of printing from engraved plates; **plate′-proof** a proof taken from a plate; **plate′-rack** a frame for holding plates, etc., when not in use or when draining after washing; **plate′-rail** a flat rail with a flange; **plate′-room** a room where silver-plated goods or printing plates are kept; **plate′-ship** (*hist.*) a ship bringing silver to Spain from America; **plate tectonics** (*geol.*) the theory that the earth's crust consists of a number of rigid plates moving over the material below them: the study of the crust in terms of this theory; **plate′-warmer** an apparatus for warming plates or keeping them warm. — **half′-plate** in photography, a size of plate measuring 4³⁄₄ by 6¹⁄₂ in. (4¹⁄₄ by 5¹⁄₂ in U.S.); **quar′ter-plate** 3¹⁄₄ by 4¹⁄₄ in., **whole′-plate** 6¹⁄₂ by 8¹⁄₂ in.; **hand, give, (someone something) on a plate** (*fig.*) to cause or allow (someone) to achieve or obtain (something) without the least effort; **on one's plate** (*fig.*) in front of one, waiting to be dealt with. [O.Fr. *plate*, fem. (and for the dish *plat*, masc.), flat — Gr. *platys*, broad.]

plateasm *plat′i-azm, n.* pronunciation with a wide mouth-opening, as in Doric Greek. [Gr. *plateiasmos* — *platys*, broad.]

plateau *pla′tō, pla-tō′, n.* a tableland: an ornamented tray, plate, or plaque: a lady's flat-topped hat: a temporary stable state reached in the course of upward progress: the part of a curve representing this: — *pl.* **plateaux** (-*tōz*), also **plateaus**. — *v.t.* to reach a level, even out (sometimes with *out*). [Fr., — O.Fr. *platel*, dim. of *plat*.]

...ten *plat′n, n.* the work-table of a machine-tool: a flat **...art** that in some printing-presses pushes the paper **...ainst** the forme: the roller of a typewriter. [Fr. **...ine** — *plat*, flat.]

plateresque *plat-ə-resk′, (archit.) adj.* applied to a sty**l.** resembling silversmith's work. [Sp. *plateresco* — *platero*, silversmith — *plata*, silver.]

platform *plat′fōrm, n.* a plane figure or surface (*obs.*): a ground-plan (*obs.*): a scheme, device, plan of action (*Shak.*): a scheme of church government or of administrative policy: a party programme: a site: a basis: a raised level surface: a terrace: a plateau: a flooring: a raised floor for speakers, musicians, etc.: those who have seats on the platform at a meeting: public speaking or discussion (*fig.*): a medium for discussion: a deck for temporary or special purpose: a position prepared for mounting a gun: a raised walk in a railway station giving access to trains: a floating installation, usu. moored to the sea-bed, for drilling for oil, marine research, etc.: flooring outside an inner entrance to a bus, tram-car, or sometimes a railway carriage: a platform shoe or boot. — *adj.* on, relating to, admitting to, etc., a platform: of shoes, boots, etc., having a very thick sole (**platform sole**), giving extra height. — *v.t.* to furnish with a platform: to sketch, plan: to place on, or as on, a platform. — *v.i.* (*rare*) to speak or appear on a platform. [Fr. *plateforme*, lit. flat form.]

platforming *plat′fōrm-ing, n.* a process for reforming low-grade into high-grade petrol, using a platinum catalyst. [**plat(inum)** and **form.**]

platinum *plat′in-əm, n.* a noble metal (at. numb. 78; symbol Pt), a steel-grey element, very valuable, malleable and ductile, very heavy and hard to fuse — older name **plat′ina.** — *adj.* made of platinum. — *adjs.* **platinic** (*plə-tin′ik*) of platinum, esp. tetravalent; **platinif′erous** platinum-bearing. — *v.t.* **plat′inise, -ize** to coat with platinum. — *ns.* **plat′inoid** one of the metals with which platinum is always found associated — *palladium, iridium,* etc.: an alloy of copper, zinc, nickel, and tungsten resembling platinum; **plat′inotype** (also with *cap.*) an obs. method of photography by reducing a compound of platinum: a photograph so produced. — *adj.* **plat′inous** of bivalent platinum. — **platinum black** platinum in the form of a velvety black powder; **platinum blonde** a woman with metallic silvery hair; **platinum lamp** an electric lamp with a platinum filament. [Sp. *platina* — *plata*, silver.]

platitude *plat′i-tūd, n.* flatness: a dull commonplace or truism: an empty remark made as if it were important. — *n.* **platitudinā′rian** one who indulges in platitudes. — *v.i.* **plat′itudinise, -ize.** — *adj.* **platitud′inous.** [Fr., — *plat*, flat.]

Platonic *plə-ton′ik, adj.* pertaining to Plato, the Greek philosopher (about 427–347 B.C.), or to his philosophy: (often without *cap.*) of love, between soul and soul, without sensual desire (a Renaissance phrase): relating to or experiencing Platonic love. — *n.* a Platonist: a Platonic lover: (usu. in *pl.*) Platonic love. — *adj.* **Platon′ical** (now *rare*). — *adv.* **Platon′ically.** — *n.* **Platon′icism** the doctrine, practice, or profession of Platonic love: Platonism (*obs.*). — *v.t.* **Platonise, -ize** (*plā′ton-īz*) to render Platonic. — *v.i.* to follow Plato. — *ns.* **Plā′tonism** the philosophy of Plato: Platonicism; **Plā′tonist** a follower of Plato. — **Platonic solid** any of the five regular polyhedrons (tetrahedron, hexahedron, octahedron, dodecahedron, and icosahedron); **Platonic year** see **year.** [Gr. *platōnikos* — *Platōn, -ōnos,* Plato.]

platoon *plə-tōōn′, n.* orig. a small body of soldiers in a hollow square or such a body firing together: a subdivision of a company: a squad: a volley (*arch.*). [Fr. *peloton,* ball, knot of men — L. *pīla,* ball.]

Platt-Deutsch *plät′-doich, n.* and *adj.* Low German. [Ger.]

platted, platting. Same as **plaited, plaiting.**

platteland *plä′tə-länt, (S.Afr.) n.* rural districts. [Afrik.]

platter *plat′ər, n.* a large flat plate or dish: a gramophone record (*slang,* esp. *U.S.*). [A.Fr. *plater* — *plat,* a plate.]

platy. See **plate.**

platy- *plat'i-*, in composition, flat, broad. [Gr. *platys*, broad.]

platycephalous *plat-i-sef'ə-ləs*, *adj.* having the vault of the skull flattened. — Also **platycephalic** (*-si-fal'ik*). [**platy-** and Gr. *kephalē*, head.]

Platyhelminthes *plat-i-hel-min'thēz*, *n.pl.* the flat-worms, a phylum including planarians, tape-worms, and flukes. [**platy-** and Gr. *helmins, -inthos*, intestinal worm.]

platypus *plat'i-pəs, -pōos, n.* an acquatic burrowing and egg-laying Australian monotreme (Ornithorhynchus), with broadly webbed feet and duck-like bill. — *pl.* **plat'ypuses.** [**platy-** and Gr. *pous, podos*, a foot.]

platyrrhine *plat'i-rīn*, **platyrrhinian** *plat-i-rin'i-ən*, *adjs.* broad-nosed: belonging to the division of the monkeys found in South America. — *ns.* a New World monkey: a broad-nosed person. [Gr. *platyrrīs, -īnos* — *rhīs, rhīnos*, nose.]

platysma *plat-iz'mə, n.* a broad sheet of muscle in the neck. [Gr. *platysma*, a flat piece.]

plaudit *plö'dit, n.* (now usu. in *pl.*) an act of applause: also praise bestowed, enthusiastic approval. — *adj.* **plaud'itory.** [Shortened from L. *plaudite*, applaud, an actor's call for applause at the end of a play, pl. imper. of *plaudēre, plausum*, to clap the hands.]

plaudite *plö'dit-i, plow'dit-e*, (L.) applaud: clap your hands.

plausible *plö'zi-bl, adj.* that may be applauded (*obs.*): acceptable (*obs.*): likely, reasonable, seemingly true: seemingly worthy of approval or praise: fair-showing: specious: ingratiating and fair-spoken. — *ns.* **plausibil'ity, plaus'ibleness.** — *adv.* **plaus'ibly** in a plausible manner: with applause, by acclamation (*Shak.*): commendably, pleasantly (*obs.*). — *adj.* **plausive** (*plö'ziv*) plausible (*Shak.*): pleasing (*Shak.*): applauding. [L. *plaudēre*, to clap the hands.]

plaustral *plös'trəl, adj.* (*facet.*) of a wagon. [L. *plaustrum*, a wagon.]

play *plā, v.i.* to operate (*obs.*): to move about irregularly, lightly, or freely: to have some freedom of movement: to flicker, flutter, shimmer, pass through rapid alternations: (usu. with *round*) to appear faintly and fleetingly: to move in, discharge, or direct a succession, stream, or shower (as of water, light, waves, missiles): to engage in pleasurable activity: to perform acts not part of the immediate business of life but in mimicry or rehearsal or in display: to amuse oneself: to sport: to make sport: to trifle: to behave without seriousness: to behave amorously or sexually: to take part in a game: to proceed with the game, perform one's part in turn: to send a ball or the like in the course of a game: to contend with weapons (*arch.*): to wield a weapon: to gamble: to have a holiday (*Shak.*; also *Scot.*): to be off work (*N. of England*): to perform on a musical instrument: to give forth music: to come forth as music: to act a part. — *v.t.* to perform: to ply, wield: to cause or allow to play: to set in opposition, pit: to send, let off, or discharge in succession or in a stream or shower: to give a limited freedom of movement to: hence, to manage: to allow (a fish) to tire itself by its struggles to get away: to engage in (a game or recreative mimicry): to oppose (in a game, sport, etc.): to proceed through (a game, part of a game — as a stroke, trick — or an aggregate of games — as a rubber, set): to stake or risk in play: to gamble on (*coll.*): to bring into operation in a game, as by striking (a ball), throwing on the table (a card), moving (a man): to compete against in a game: to compete on the side of (with *for*): to act (e.g. comedy, a named play): to act the part of, in a play or in real life: to act, perform, in (e.g. a circuit of theatres, halls): to make-believe in sport: to perform music on: to perform on a musical instrument: to lead, bring, send, render, or cause to be by playing: to amuse (*refl.*; *obs.* and *Scot.*): — *pr.p.* **play'ing;** *pa.t.* and *pa.p.* **played.** — *n.* activity: operation: action of wielding: light fluctuating movement or change: limited freedom of movement: scope:

recreative activity: display of animals in courtship: amusement: dalliance: a game (*Shak.*): the playing of a game: manner of playing: procedure or policy in a game: holiday (*Shak.* and *Scot.*): a fair or festival (*dial.*): being off work (*N. of England*): gambling: a drama or dramatic performance: manner of dealing, as *fair play* (*fig.*). — *adj.* **play'able** capable (by nature or by the rules of the game) of being played, or of being played on. — *n.* **play'er** one who plays: an actor: a trifler: an instrumental performer: a professional cricketer: a mechanism for playing a musical instrument. — *adj.* **play'ful** sportive: high-spirited, humorous. — *adv.* **play'fully.** — *ns.* **play'fulness; play'let** a short play. — *adj.* **play'some** playful. — *v.i.* **play'-act.** — **play'-acting** performance of plays: pretence; **play'-actor, -actress** (usu. in contempt) professional actor, actress; **play'back** the act of reproducing a recording of sound or visual material, esp. immediately after it is made (see also **play back** below); **play'bill** a bill announcing a play; **play'book** a printed play or book of plays; **play'-box** a box for toys and other valued possessions, esp. in a boarding-school; **play'boy** a boy-actor (*arch.*): a light-hearted irresponsible person, esp. rich and leisured: — *fem.* **play'girl; play'bus** a bus equipped with facilities for children's play, driven to districts where no adequate playground facilities are available; **play'-day** a holiday; **play'-debt** a debt incurred in gambling. — *adj.* **played'-out'** exhausted: used up: no longer good for anything. — **play'er-pian'o** see **pianoforte; play'fellow** a playmate; **playgirl** see **playboy** above; **play'-gōer** one who habitually attends the theatre; **play'-gōing; play'ground** a place for playing in, esp. one connected with a school: a holiday region; **play'group** an informal, usu. voluntarily-run group having morning or afternoon sessions attended by preschool children and mothers, for creative and co-operative play; **play'house** a theatre: a child's toy house, usu. big enough to enter; **play'ing-card** one of a pack (e.g. of fifty-two cards, divided into four suits) used in playing games; **play'ing-field** a grass-covered space set apart, marked out, and kept in order for games; **play'leader** a person trained to supervise and organise children's play in a playground, etc.; **play'-mare** (*Scot.*) a hobby-horse, as in the old morris-dance; **play'mate** a companion in play, esp. child's play; **play'-off** a game to decide a tie: a game between the winners of other competitions: see also **play off** below; **play'-pen** an enclosure within which a young child may safely play; **play'room** a room for children to play in; **play'school** a nursery school or playgroup; **play'-spell** a time allowed for play; **play'suit** a set of clothes for a child or woman, usu. shorts and a top, for sunbathing, relaxing, etc.; **play'thing** a toy: a person or thing treated as a toy; **play'time** a time for play; **play'-way** the educational use of play; **play'-world** an imaginary world feigned in play; **play'wright, play'-writer** a dramatist. — **bring, come, into play** to bring, come, into exercise, operation, use; **hold in play** (*arch.* **hold play**) to keep occupied, esp. to gain time or detain; **in, out of, play**, in, out of, such a position that it may be played; **make a play for** (*coll.*) to try to get; **make great play with, of** to make a lot of: to treat, talk of, as very important; **make play** to keep things going, push on with the game; **play about** to behave irresponsibly, not seriously; **play along (with)** to cooperate, agree with, usu. temporarily; **play a part (in)** to be instrumental, help in doing: to act a theatrical rôle (in) (also *fig.*); **play around** to play about: to have amorous affairs with men/women other than one's spouse; **play at** to engage in the game of: to make a pretence of: practise without seriousness; **play back** to play a sou video, etc. recording that has just been made; **play** to co-operate; **play it, one's cards, close to the c** be secretive about one's actions or intentio particular matter; **play down** to treat (some not very important or probable, esp. less so **play fair** (sometimes with *with*) to act ho

false (sometimes with *with*) (*arch.*) to act dishonestly (towards), betray; **play fast and loose** to act in a shifty, inconsistent, and reckless fashion; **play fine** at billiards, to strike the object-ball near the edge — opp. to **play full**, to strike it nearer the middle than the edge; **play for safety** to play safe; **play for time** to delay action or decision in the hope or belief that conditions will become more favourable later; **play hard to get** to make a show of unwillingness to co-operate with a view to strengthening one's position; **play havoc, hell with** to upset, disorganise: to damage; **play into the hands of** to act so as to give, usu. unintentionally, an advantage to; **play it** (*coll.*; usu. followed by an *adj.*) to behave in, manage, a particular situation in a stated way, as in *play it cool*; **play it by ear** to improvise a plan of action to meet the situation as it develops; **play off** to manipulate so as to counteract: to play from the tee (*golf*): to have as a handicap (*golf*): to toss off (*Shak.*): to bring off (as a hoax); **play on** to strike the ball on to one's own wicket: to direct one's efforts to the exciting of, work upon; **play out** to play to the end: to wear out, to exhaust; **play safe** to take no risks; **play the field** (*coll.*) to spread one's interests, affections or efforts over a wide range of subjects, people, activities, etc., rather than concentrating on any single one; **play the game** to act strictly honourably; **play up** to strike up, begin the music: to redouble one's efforts, play more vigorously: to show up well in a crisis or emergency: to give (esp. undue) prominence to, or to boost: to fool; **play (up)on** to practise upon, work upon; **play (up)on words** a pun or other manipulation of words depending on their sound; **play up to** to act so as to afford opportunities to (another actor): to flatter; **play with** to play in company of, or as partner or opponent to: to dally with: to stimulate (the genitals of), to masturbate (oneself or someone else). [O.E. *pleg(i)an*, vb., *plega*, n.]

playa plä′yə, *n.* a basin which becomes a shallow lake after heavy rainfall and dries out again in hot weather. [Sp.]

plaza plä′zə, *n.* a public square or open, usu. paved, area in a city or town. [Sp.]

plea plē, *n.* a lawsuit (*Scots law* and *hist.*): a pleading: a prisoner's or defendant's answer to a charge or claim: a claim (*Shak.*): an excuse: a pretext: urgent entreaty. — *v.t.* and *v.i.* to dispute in a law-court. — **plea(′-)bargaining** the (esp. *U.S.*) legal practice of arranging more lenient treatment by the court in exchange for the accused's admitting to the crime, turning State's evidence, etc.; **plea(′-)bargain.** [O.Fr. *plai, plaid, plait* — L.L. *placitum*, a decision — L. *placēre, -ītum*, to please.]

pleach plēch, *v.t.* to intertwine the branches of, as a hedge: to fold, as the arms (*Shak.*): to plash. [From form of O.Fr. *pless(i)er* — L. *plectĕre*; see **plash**[1].]

plead plēd, *v.i.* to carry on a plea or lawsuit: to argue in support of a cause against another: to put forward an allegation or answer in court: to implore. — *v.t.* to maintain by argument: to allege in pleading: to put forward as a plea: to offer in excuse: to sue for (*arch., Scot.*): — *pa.t., pa.p.* **plead′ed** also (*Spens., Scot., U.S.,* and *dial.*) **pled.** — *adj.* **plead′able** capable of being pleaded. — *n.* **plead′er** one who pleads: an advocate. — *adj.* **plead′ing** imploring. — *n.* the act of putting forward or conducting a plea: (in *pl.*) the statements of the two parties in a lawsuit: entreaty. — *adv.* **plead′ingly.** — **pleading diet** in Scots law, a preliminary appearance in court of an accused person before his trial, at which he indicates whether he will plead guilty or not guilty, and lodges any special pleas, as of insanity, etc.; **plead guilty** or **not guilty** to state that ᴖne is guilty, or innocent, of a crime with which one ⌐harged; **special pleading** unfair or one-sided argu-⌐t aiming rather at victory than at truth. [O.Fr. ⌐*ier*; cf. **plea.**]

⌐′ōz, *v.t.* to give pleasure to: to delight: to satisfy: ⌐se, to will (to do). — *v.i.* to give pleasure to:

like, think fit, choose (originally impersonal with dative, e.g. *it pleases* (to) *me*; later *me pleases*; then *I please*). — *n.* **pleasance** (*plez′əns*; *arch.* and *poet.*) pleasure: enjoyment: pleasantness: complaisance, pleasant behaviour (*obs.*): that which gives pleasure: a pleasure-ground or specialised part of a garden. — *adj.* **pleas′ant** pleasing: agreeable: inoffensive: affable: good-humoured: cheerful: gay (*obs.*): tipsy (*facet.*). — *adv.* **pleas′antly.** — *ns.* **pleas′antness; pleas′antry** pleasantness, enjoyment (*obs.*): jocularity: a facetious utterance or trick: — *pl.* **pleas′antries.** — *adj.* **pleased** (*plēzd*) grateful: delighted. — *n.* **pleas′er.** — *adj.* and *n.* **pleas′ing.** — *adv.* **pleas′ingly.** — *n.* **pleas′ingness.** — *adj.* **pleasurable** (*plezh′ər-ə-bl*) able to give pleasure: delightful: gratifying: pleasure-seeking (*obs.*). — *n.* **pleas′urableness.** — *adv.* **pleas′urably.** — *n.* **pleasure** (*plezh′ər*) agreeable emotions: gratification of the senses or of the mind: sensuality: dissipation: a source of gratification: what the will prefers: purpose: command. — *v.t.* (*arch.*) to give pleasure to. — *v.i.* (*arch.*) to take pleasure (in). — *adjs.* **pleas′ureful; pleas′ureless.** — *n.* **pleas′urer** a pleasure-seeker. — **pleaseman** (*plēz′-man, -mən; Shak.*) an officious fellow, a pick-thank; **pleas′ure-boat** a boat used for pleasure or amusement. — *adj.* **pleas′ure-giving** affording pleasure. — **pleas′ure-ground** ground laid out in an ornamental manner for pleasure; **pleas′ure-house** a house to which one retires for recreation or pleasure; **pleas′ure-seeker** one who seeks pleasure: a holiday-maker; **pleas′ure-seeking; pleas′ure-trip** an excursion for pleasure. — **at pleasure** when, if, or as, one pleases; **if you please** if you like: a polite formula of request or acceptance: forsooth (*ironically*); **may it please you, so please you** deferential or polite formulas of address or request; **please,** also (now *rare*) **please to,** a polite formula equivalent to **if you please,** now felt as imperative, perh. orig. from the older **please it you, please it** (sometimes printed **pleaseth** in *Shak.*), **please you** may it please you; **pleased as Punch** delighted; **please yourself** do as you like; **pleasure-pain principle** the principle dominating instinctual life in which activities are directed towards seeking pleasure and avoiding pain. [O.Fr. *plaisir* (Fr. *plaire*) — L. *placēre*, to please.]

pleat plēt, *n.* a fold sewn or pressed into cloth. — *v.t.* to make pleats in. [From **plait.**]

pleb. See **plebeian.**

plebeian pli-bē′ən (in *Shak.* also **plebean** *pleb′i-ən*), *adj.* of the Roman plebs: of the common people: low-born: undistinguished: vulgar-looking: vulgar. — *n.* a member of the plebs of ancient Rome: a commoner: a member of a despised social class. — *n.* **pleb** (*coll.*) a person of unpolished manners which are attributed to his low rank in society. — *adj.* **plebb′y** (*coll.*). — *v.t.* **plebei′anise, -ize.** — *ns.* **plebei′anism; plebificā′tion** (*pleb-i-*) the act of making plebeian. — *v.t.* **pleb′ify.** [L. *plēbēius* — *plēbs, plēbis.*]

plebiscite *pleb′i-sit, -sīt,* n. a law enacted by the plebs assembled in the *Concilia tributa* (*Roman hist.*): a direct vote of the whole nation or of the people of a district on a special point: an ascertainment of general opinion on any matter. — *adj.* **plebisc′itary.** [Partly through Fr. *plébiscite* — L. *plēbiscītum* — *plēbs,* plebs, *scītum,* decree — *scīscere,* to vote for.]

plebs *plebz, n.* one of the two divisions of the Roman people, originally the less privileged politically. — See also **plebeian.** [L. *plēbs, plēbis.*]

Plecoptera *ple-kop′tər-ə, n.pl.* the stonefly order of insects, with hind-wings folded fanwise. — *adj.* **plecop′terous.** [Gr. *plekein,* plait, *pteron,* wing.]

Plectognathi *plek-tog′nə-thī, n.pl.* an order of bony fishes including file-fishes, globe-fishes, coffer-fishes, sunfishes. — *adjs.* **plectognathic** (*-to-gnath′ik*), **plectog′nathous** (*-nə-thəs*). [Gr. *plektos,* plaited, *gnathos,* a jaw.]

Plectoptera *plek-top′tə-rə, n.pl.* the mayfly order of insects, otherwise *Ephemeroptera.*—*adj.* **plectop′terous.** [Gr. *plektos,* twisted, *pteron,* a wing.]

plectrum *plek'trəm, n.* the quill or other form of instrument for plucking the strings of the ancient Greek lyre or other musical instrument: a pointed device held in the fingers or on the thumb, with which the strings of e.g. a guitar are struck. — Also **plec'tre** *(-tər)*, **plec'tron:** — *pl.* **plec'tra,** **plec'trums,** **plec'tres,** **plec'trons.** [L. *plēctrum* — Gr. *plēktron* — *plēssein,* to strike.]

pled *pled.* See **plead.**

pledge *plej, n.* something given as a security: a gage: a token or assuring sign: a child, as a token of love or binding obligation: one who becomes surety for another *(obs.)*: a hostage *(obs.)*: a solemn promise: a friendly sentiment expressed by drinking: a state of being given, or held, as a security. — *v.t.* to give as security: to bind by solemn promise: to vow: to give assurance of: to drink a toast in response to: to drink at the invitation of another: to drink to the health of. — *adj.* **pledge'able.** — *ns.* **pledgee'** the person to whom a thing is pledged; **pledger, pledg(e)or** *(plej'ər).* — **take** or **sign the pledge** to give a written promise to abstain from intoxicating liquor. [O.Fr. *plege* (Fr. *pleige*) — L.L. *plevium, plivium,* prob. Gmc.]

pledget *plej'it, n.* a wad of lint, cotton, etc., as for a wound or sore: an oakum string used in caulking. [Origin unknown.]

pledgor. See **pledge.**

-plegia *-plē-ji-ə,* in composition, paralysis, as in *paraplegia.* — adjective and noun combining form **-plēgic.** [Gr. *plēgē,* stroke — *plēssein,* to strike.]

Pleiad *plī'ad, n.* any one of the seven daughters of Atlas and Pleione, changed into stars (one 'lost' or invisible): a brilliant group of seven, esp. seven Alexandrian tragic poets or (usu. as Fr., **Pléiade** *plā-ē-äd*) the poets Ronsard, Du Bellay, Baïf, Daurat, and others variously selected. — *pl.* **Plei'ads, Pleiades** *(plī'ə-dēz)* a group of six naked-eye and a multitude of telescopic stars in the shoulder of the constellation Taurus. [Gr. *pleias, plēias, -ados,* pl. *-adēs.*]

plein-air *plen'-er', adj.* open-air: attaching importance to painting in the open air. — *n.* **plein-air'ist** a plein-air painter. [Fr. *en plein air,* in the open air.]

pleio-, plio- *plī'ō-, plī-o'-,* **pleo-** *plē'ō-, plē-o'-,* in composition, more. [Gr. *pleiōn* or *pleōn,* compar. of *polys,* many, much.]

Pleiocene. Same as **Pliocene.**

pleiochasium *plī-ō-kā'zi-əm, n.* a cymose inflorescence in which each branch bears more than two lateral branches. [Gr. *chasis,* separation; but cf. **monochasium.**]

pleiomerous *plī-om'ər-əs, adj.* having more than the normal number of parts. — *n.* **pleiom'ery** the condition of having more than the normal number. [Gr. *meros,* part.]

pleiotropic *plī-ō-trop'ik, adj.* (of a gene) having an effect simultaneously on more than one character in the offspring. — *n.* **pleiot'ropism.** [Gr. *tropos,* turn.]

Pleistocene *plīs'tō-sēn, adj.* of the geological period following the Pliocene, having the greatest proportion of fossil molluscs of living species. — *n.* the Pleistocene system, period, or strata. [Gr. *pleistos,* most (numerous), *kainos,* recent — from the proportion of living species of molluscs.]

plenary *plē'nə-ri, adj.* full: entire: complete: passing through all its stages — opp. to *summary* (*law*): having full powers. — *adv.* **plē'narily.** — *n.* **plē'narty** the state of a benefice when occupied. — **plenary indulgence** in the Roman Catholic Church, full or complete remission of temporal penalties to a repentant sinner; **plenary inspiration** inspiration which excludes all mixture of error; **plenary powers** full powers to carry out some business or negotiations. [L.L. *plēnārius* — L. *plēnus,* full — *plēre* to fill.]

plenilune *plen', plēn'i-loōn, -lūn, n.* the full moon: time of full moon. — *adj.* **plenilu'nar.** [L. *plēnilūnium* — *plēnus,* full, *lūna,* moon.]

plenipotence *plin-ip'ō-təns, n.* complete power — Also **plenip'otency.** — *adjs.* **plenip'otent** having full power;

plenipotential *(plen-i-pō-ten'shəl);* **plenipoten'tiary** *(-shə-ri, -shyə-ri)* having full powers. — *n.* a person invested with full powers, esp. a special ambassador or envoy to some foreign court. — Arch. coll. short form **plen'ipo:** — *pl.* **plen'ipos, -poes.** [L. *plēnus,* full, *potentia,* power.]

plenish *plen'ish, (arch.* or *Scot.) v.t.* to supply, stock: to provide, as a house or farm, with necessary furniture, implements, stock, etc. — *n.* **plen'ishing** *(Scot.)* furniture. [O.Fr. *plenir, -iss-* — L. *plēnus,* full.]

plenist. See **plenum.**

plenitude *plen'i-tūd, n.* fullness: completeness: plentifulness: repletion. — *adj.* **plenitud'inous.** [L. *plēnitūdō, -inis* — *plēnus,* full.]

pleno jure *plē'nō joōr'ē, plā'nō yōōr'e,* (L.) with full authority.

plenty *plen'ti, n.* a full supply: all that can be needed: abundance. — *adj.* plentiful *(Shak.):* in abundance. — *adv.* (*coll.*) abundantly. — *adj.* **plenteous** *(plen'tyəs)* fully sufficient: abundant: fruitful: well provided: rich: giving plentifully. — *adv.* **plen'teously.** — *n.* **plen'teousness.** — *adj.* **plen'tiful** copious: abundant: yielding abundance. — *adv.* **plen'tifully.** — *ns.* **plen'tifulness; plen'titude** (a mistake or misprint for **plenitude**). — **horn of plenty** see **cornucopia; in plenty** abundant, as *food in plenty.* [O.Fr. *plente* — L. *plēnitās, -ātis* — *plēnus,* full.]

plenum *plē'nəm, n.* a space completely filled with matter — opposed to *vacuum:* a full assembly. — *n.* **plē'nist** one who believes all space to be a plenum. — **plenum system, ventilation** *(archit.)* an air-conditioning system in which the air propelled into a building is maintained at a higher pressure than the atmosphere. [L. *plēnum* (*spatium*) full (space).]

pleo-. See **pleio-.**

pleochroism *plē-ok'rō-izm, n.* the property in some crystals of transmitting different colours in different directions. — *adj.* **pleochroic** *(plē-ō-krō'ik).* [Gr. *chroā,* colour.]

pleomorphic *plē-ō-mör'fik, adj.* polymorphic. — Also **pleomor'phous.** — *ns.* **pleomorph'ism, plē'omorphy.**

pleon *plē'on, n.* the abdomen of a crustacean, bearing the swimming legs. — *n.* **ple'opod** a swimming leg. [Gr. *plēon,* swimming, pr.p. of *plēein.*]

pleonasm *plē'o-nazm, n.* redundancy, esp. of words: a redundant expression. — *ns.* **plē'onast** one who is given to pleonasm; **ple'onaste** (Fr. *pléonaste*) a dark green to black magnesia-iron spinel (from its multitude of faces). — *adjs.* **pleonas'tic, -al.** — *adv.* **pleonas'tically.** [Gr. *pleonasmos* — *pleōn,* more.]

pleonexia *plē-ō-nek'si-ə, n.* greed, avarice. — *adj.* **pleonec'tic.** [Gr.]

pleopod. See **pleon.**

pleroma *pli-rō'mə, n.* fullness: abundance: in Gnosticism, divine being, including all aeons (q.v.) which emanate from it. — *adj.* **pleromatic** *(-mat'ik).* [Gr. *plērōma* — *plērēs,* full.]

plerome *plē'rōm, (bot.) n.* the central part of the apical meristem. [Gr. *plērōma,* filling.]

plerophory *plē-rof'ə-ri, n.* full conviction. — Also **plerophō'ria.** [Gr. *plērophōriā.*]

plesh *plesh, (Spens.) n.* a plash, a pool. [**plash**[2].]

plesiosaur *plē'si-ō-sör, n.* a great Mesozoic fossil Sauropterygian reptile (**Plesiosaurus** or kindred genus) with long neck, short tail, and four flippers. — *adj.* **plesiosaur'ian.** [Gr. *plēsios,* near, *sauros,* lizard.]

plessor, plessimeter, etc. See **plexor.**

plethora *pleth'ər-ə,* sometimes *pli-thō'rə, -thō', n.* excessive fullness of blood: over-fullness or excess in any wa (*loosely*) a large amount. — *adjs.* **plethoric** *(pli-thor* sometimes *pleth'ər-ik),* **plethor'ical.** — *adv.* **plet** ically. [Gr. *plēthōrā,* fullness — *pleos,* full.]

plethysmograph *ple-thiz'mə-gräf, (med.) n.* an ap for measuring variations in the size of part body, e.g. when varying amounts of bl through them. [Gr. *plēthusmos,* er graphein,* to write.]

For other sounds see detailed chart of pronunciation.

pleugh *plōō, plōōhh, n.* Scots form of **plough.** — Also **pleuch.**

pleura *plōō'rə, n.* a delicate serous membrane that covers the lung and lines the cavity of the chest: a side-piece, esp. pleuron: — *pl.* **pleu'rae** (*-rē*). — *adj.* **pleu'ral.** — *ns.* **pleurapoph'ysis** a lateral process of a vertebra, with the morphological character of a rib: a rib: — *pl.* **pleurapoph'yses; pleurisy** (*plōō'ri-si*) inflammation of the pleura. — *adjs.* **pleurit'ic, -al** of, affected with, or causing pleurisy. — *n.* **(pleuritic)** a sufferer from pleurisy. — *n.* **pleurī'tis** pleurisy. — *adj.* **pleur'odont** (*zool.*) with teeth attached to the inside of the jaw-bone, rather than rooted in it. — *ns.* **pleurodynia** (*plōō-rō-din'i-ə;* Gr. *odynē,* pain) neuralgia of the muscles between the ribs; **pleu'ron** the side-wall of a somite, esp. of an insect's thorax: — *pl.* **pleu'ra; pleurŏt'omy** (*med.*) incision into the pleura. — **pleu'risy-root** an American asclepias (*A. tuberosa*) reputed as a diaphoretic and expectorant. **pleuro-pneumō'nia** pleurisy combined with pneumonia: a contagious disease of cattle, caused by a filterable virus, characterised by pleurisy and pneumonia. [Gr. *pleurā* and *pleuron,* rib, side.]

Pleuronectes *plōō-rō-nek'tēz, n.* the plaice genus, giving name to the family **Pleuronec'tidae.** [Gr. *pleurā,* side, *nēktēs,* a swimmer.]

plexiform. See **plexus.**

plexiglass (® in *U.S.,* with cap.) *plek'si-gläs, n.* a type of light, transparent thermoplastic. [*plastic* fl*exi*ble *glass.*]

plexor *pleks'ər,* **plessor** *ples'ər, ns.* a percussion hammer. — *ns.* **plexim'eter, plessim'eter** a small plate to receive the tap in examination by percussion. — *adjs.* **pleximet'ric, plessimet'ric.** — *ns.* **plexim'etry, plessim'etry.** [Gr. *plēxis,* a stroke, *plēssein,* to strike.]

plexus *pleks'əs, n.* a network: — *pl.* **plex'uses** or **plex'us** (L. *plexūs*). — *adj.* **plex'iform** in the form of a network: complex. — *n.* **plex'ure** an interweaving. [L. *plexus, -ūs,* a weaving.]

pliable *plī'ə-bl, adj.* easily bent or folded: flexible: adaptable: easily persuaded: yielding to influence. — *ns.* **plīabil'ity, plī'ableness.** — *adv.* **plī'ably.** — *ns.* **plī'ancy, plī'antness.** — *adj.* **plī'ant** bending easily: flexible: tractable: easily influenced: perh. suitable, perh. of compliant mood (*Shak.*). — *adv.* **plī'antly.** [See **ply**[1].]

plica *plī'kə, n.* a fold: plica Polonica: — *pl.* **plī'cae** (*-sē*). — *adjs.* **plī'cal; plī'cate** (or *-kāt*), **-d** folded fanwise, plaited. — *v.t.* **plī'cate** (also *plī-kāt', plik-āt'*) to plait. — *adv.* **plī'cately.** — *ns.* **plīcā'tion, plicature** (*plik'*) the act of folding: the state of being folded: a fold. — **plica Polonica** a matted condition of the hair, with an adhesive secretion, a parasitic fungus, and vermin, formerly prevalent in Poland. [L. *plīca,* a fold.]

plié *plē'ā, n.* a movement in ballet, in which the knees are bent while the body remains upright. [Fr., bent.]

plied, plier, pliers, plies. See **ply**[1,2].

plight[1] *plīt, n.* risk (*obs.*): pledge (*arch.*): engagement (*arch.*): promise (*arch.*). — *v.t.* to pledge: — *pa.p.* **plight'ed,** also **plight.** — *n.* **plight'er.** — *adj.* **plight'ful** grievous. [O.E. *pliht,* risk; *plēon,* to risk; cf. Du. *plicht,* Ger. *Pflicht,* an obligation.]

plight[2] *plīt, n.* a fold (*Spens.*): a plait, or mode of plaiting (*arch.*): condition, trim (*arch.*): evil state: good condition (*arch.*): mood (*arch.*): array (*Spens.*). — *v.t.* (*obs.*) to plait, weave, fold, enfold: — *pa.p.* **plight'ed,** also (*Spens.*) **plight.** — *adj.* **plight'ed** plaited: involved (*Shak.*). [Assimilated in spelling to the foregoing, but derived from O.Fr. *plite* — L. *plicāre, plīcitum*; see **plait.**]

'm *plim,* (*dial.*) *v.t.* and *v.i.* to swell. [Perh. conn. with **lump**[2].]

oll, plimsole *plim'səl, -sol, -sōl, n.* a rubber-soled was shoe. — **Plimsoll line** or **mark** (*-səl* or *-sol*) a load-line, or set of load-lines for different waters onditions, required by the Merchant Shipping 76) passed at the instance of Samuel *Plimsoll*).

plink *plingk, n.* a short, relatively high-pitched, sound, as of the string of a musical instrument being plucked. — Also *v.t.* and *v.i.* [Imit.]

plinth *plinth, n.* the square block under the base of a column: a block serving as a pedestal: a flat-faced projecting band at the bottom of a wall: a similar projecting base in furniture. [L. *plinthus,* Gr. *plinthos,* a brick, squared stone, plinth.]

plio-. See **pleio-.**

Pliocene *plī'ō-sēn,* (*geol.*) *adj.* of the Tertiary period following the Miocene, and having a greater proportion of molluscan species now living. — *n.* the Pliocene system, period, or strata. [Gr. *pleiōn,* greater, more numerous, *kainos,* recent.]

Pliohippus *plī-ō-hip'əs, n.* a Miocene and Pliocene genus of fossil horses. [Gr. *hippos,* horse.]

pliskie *plis'ki,* (*Scot.*) *n.* condition or plight: a mischievous trick. [Origin unknown.]

plissé *plē-sā,* (Fr.) *adj.* (of a fabric) chemically treated to produce a shirred effect.

ploat. See **plot**[2].

plod[1] *plod, v.i.* to walk heavily and laboriously: to study or work on steadily and laboriously. — *v.t.* to traverse or make by slow and heavy walking: — *pr.p.* **plodd'ing;** *pa.t.* and *pa.p.* **plodd'ed.** — *n.* a heavy walk: a thud. — *n.* **plodd'er** one who plods on: a dull, heavy, laborious man: one who gets on more by sheer toil than by inspiration. — *adj.* and *n.* **plodd'ing.** — *adv.* **plodd'ingly.** [Prob. imit.]

plod[2] *plod,* (*obs.*) *v.t.* to plot. [**plot**[1], by confusion with foregoing.]

plong, plonge, plongd. Spenserian spellings of **plunge, plunged.**

plonk[1] *plongk, v.t.* to put down, etc., so as to make a hollow or metallic sound, or heavily or emphatically. — *v.i.* to plump. — Also *n., adv., interj.* — *n.* **plonk'er** a large marble (also **plunk'er**): anything large, esp. a smacking kiss (*coll.*): a stupid person (*slang*). — *adj.* **plonk'ing** (*coll.*) used to denote great size, often with *great.* [Imit.]

plonk[2] *plongk, n.* (orig. *Austr.* slang) wine, esp. cheap. [Ety. dub.; prob. — (*vin*) *blanc.*]

plook, plookie. See **plouk.**

plop *plop, n.* the sound of a small object falling vertically into water: the sound of the movement of small bodies of water: the sound of a cork coming out of a bottle, or of a bursting bubble. — *adv.* with a plop: plump. — *v.i.* to make the sound of a plop: to plump into water: (*slightly vulg. coll.*) to defecate. — *v.t.* to set with a plop: — *pr.p.* **plopp'ing;** *pa.t.* and *pa.p.* **plopped.** [Imit.]

plosive *plō'siv, -ziv,* (*phon.*) *adj., n.* explosive. — *n.* **plo'sion** (*phon.*) explosion.

plot[1] *plot, n.* a small piece of ground: a spot or small area on any surface (*obs.*): a ground-plan of a building, plan of a field, etc.: the story or scheme of connected events running through a play, novel, etc.: a secret scheme, usually in combination, to bring about something, often illegal or evil, a conspiracy: a stratagem or secret contrivance. — *v.t.* to lay out in plots, dispose: to make a plan of: to create the plot of (a play, etc.): to represent on or by a graph: to conspire or lay plans for. — *v.i.* to conspire: — *pr.p.* **plott'ing;** *pa.t.* and *pa.p.* **plott'ed.** — *adjs.* **plot'ful; plot'less.** — *n.* **plott'er.** — *n.* and *adj.* **plott'ing.** — *adv.* **plott'ingly.** — *adj.* **plot'-proof** safe from any danger by plots. — **plott'ing-paper** paper ruled in squares for graph-drawing. [O.E. *plot,* a patch of ground; influenced by (or partly from) Fr. *complot,* a conspiracy; cf. **plat**[2].]

plot[2] *plot, plŏt,* **ploat** *plŏt,* (*Scot.* and *Northern*) *v.t.* to dip or steep in very hot water: to burn, scald, scorch: to scald and pluck: to pluck, strip of feathers, hair, etc.: to fleece (*fig.*): to remove fluff, etc., from a garment (not *Scot.*). — *n.* **plott'ie, plott'y** a spiced hot drink, as mulled wine. [Cf. M.Du. and Flem. *ploten,* to pluck, but other roots may be involved.]

plotter¹ *plot'ər.* Same as **plouter.**

plotter². See **plot¹.**

plough, (*U.S.* or *arch.*) **plow,** *plow, n.* an instrument for turning up the soil in ridges and furrows: a joiner's plane for making grooves: agriculture (*fig.*): a plough-team: ploughed land: (with *cap.*) seven stars of the Great Bear. — *v.t.* to turn up with the plough: to make furrows or ridges in: to make with a plough: to put into or render with a plough (also *fig.*): to tear, force, or cut a way through: to furrow: to wrinkle: to reject in an examination (*university slang*): to fail in (a subject) (*university slang*). — *v.i.* to work with a plough: (with *through* or *into*) to crash, force one's way, move, drive, etc., violently or uncontrollably (through or into) (see also **plough (one's way) through** below): to fail (*slang*). — *adj.* **plough'able.** — *ns.* **plough'er; plough'ing.** - - *adv.* and *adj.* **plough'wise** as in ploughing. — **plough'boy** a boy who drives or guides horses in ploughing; **plough'gate** (*Scots hist.*) an undetermined or variable unit of land, by later writers taken as about 50 English acres, but earlier much more: a quantity of land of the extent of 100 Scots acres; **plough'-iron** the coulter, share, or other iron part of a plough; **plough'-jogger** (*facet.*) a ploughman; **plough'-land** land suitable for tillage: as much land as could be tilled with one plough (with a proportionate amount of pasture) — a carucate or eight oxgangs (*hist.*); **plough'man** a man who ploughs: — *pl.* **plough'men; ploughman's lunch** a cold meal of bread, cheese, cold meat, pickle, etc.; **ploughman's spikenard** see **spikenard; Plough Monday** an old ploughmen's festival, the Monday after Twelfth Day, supposed to mark the resumption of work after the holidays; **plough'share** (O.E. *scear*, ploughshare — *scieran*, to shear, cut) the detachable part of a plough that cuts the under surface of the sod from the ground: a bird's pygostyle (also **ploughshare bone**); **plough'-staff** a tool for clearing a plough of earth, etc.; **plough'-stilt** a plough-handle; **plough'-tail** the end of a plough where the handles are: farm-labour (*fig.*); **plough'-team** the team of horses, oxen, etc. (usu. two), that pulls a simple plough; **plough'-tree** a plough-handle; **plough'wright** one who makes and mends ploughs. — **plough a lonely furrow** to be separated from one's former friends and associates and go one's own way; **plough back** (*fig.*) to reinvest (profits of a business) in that business; **plough in** to cover with earth by ploughing; **plough (one's way) through** to work, read, eat, etc., steadily but slowly and laboriously through; **plough the sands** to work in vain or to no purpose; **put one's hand to the plough** to begin an undertaking. [Late O.E. *plōh, plōg,* a ploughland; cf. O.N. *plōgr.*]

plouk, plook *plook*, (*Scot.*) *n.* a small lump or knob: a pimple, spot. — *adj.* **plouk'ie, plook'ie.** [Gael. *pluc.*]

plouter, plowter *plow'tər,* (*Scot.*) *v.i.* to dabble in liquid: to potter. — *n.* a paddling or dabbling. — Also **plott'er.** [Prob. imit.]

plover *pluv'ər, n.* a general name for birds of the family (Charadriidae) to which the lapwing and dotterel belong: extended to some related birds: a dupe (*old slang*): a prostitute (*old slang*). — *adj.* **plov'ery** abounding in plovers. — **plover's egg** a lapwing's egg, or substitute. [Fr. *pluvier* — L. *pluvia*, rain; possibly from their restlessness before rain; cf. Ger. *Regenpfeifer*, lit. rain-piper.]

plow *plow* (chiefly American). Same as **plough.**

plowter. See **plouter.**

ploy *ploi, n.* an employment, doings, affair, frolic, escapade, engagement for amusement: a method or procedure used to achieve a particular result: a manoeuvre in a game, conversation, etc. [Prob. **employ.**]

pluck *pluk, v.t.* to pull off, out, or away: to pull forcibly: to snatch away: to rescue: to bring (down), humble (*arch.*): to pull: to tug: to twitch: to strip, as of feathers: to despoil, fleece: to fail, refuse a pass to, in an examination — from the custom of *plucking* (a piece

of silk at the back of) *the proctor's gown,* in protest (*slang*): to swindle (*slang*). — *v.i.* to make a pulling or snatching movement (at). — *n.* a single act of plucking: the heart, liver, and lungs of an animal — hence heart, courage, spirit. — *adj.* **plucked** subjected to plucking: having pluck. — *n.* **pluck'er.** — *adv.* **pluck'ily.** — *n.* **pluck'iness.** — *adj.* **pluck'y** having courageous spirit and pertinacity. — **pluck off** (*Shak.*) to abate, come down the scale; **pluck up** to pull out by the roots: to summon up, as courage: to gather strength or spirit. [O.E. *pluccian*; akin to Du. *plukken*, Ger. *pflücken.*]

pluff *pluf,* (*Scot.* or *dial.*) *n.* a puff: a mild explosion: a shot: a powder-puff. — *v.t.* to puff: to shoot. — — *v.i.* to go off with a puff: to rise, as a cake. — *adj.* **pluff'y** puffed up: fluffy. [Imit.]

plug *plug, n.* a peg stopping, or for stopping, a hole: a bung: a stopper: a mechanism releasing the flow of water in a water-closet: filling for a tooth: volcanic rock stopping a vent: a fitting for a socket for giving electrical connection: a piece of wood inserted in a wall to take nails: a fire-plug: a sparking-plug: a plug-hat (*slang*): a blow or punch: a compressed cake of tobacco: a piece of it cut for chewing: a worn-out horse: a book that will not sell: a piece of favourable publicity, esp. one incorporated in other material (*coll.*): anything worn-out or useless: a dogged plodding. — *v.t.* to stop with a plug or as a plug: to insert a plug in: to insert as a plug: to shoot (*slang*): to punch with the fist (*slang*): to force into familiarity by persistent repetition, esp. for advertising purposes (*slang*): to din into the ears of the public. — *v.i.* (*slang*) to go on doggedly: — *pr.p.* **plugg'ing;** *pa.t.* and *pa.p.* **plugged.** — *ns.* **plugg'er** one who plugs in any sense: that which plugs, esp. a dentist's instrument; **plugg'ing** the act of stopping with a plug, or punching (*slang*), or promoting (*slang*): material of which a plug is made. — **plug'-hat** (*U.S.*) a top-hat; **plug'-ug'ly** (*U.S.*) a street ruffian: a thug, tough. — **plug in** to complete an electric circuit by inserting a plug (*adj.* **plug'-in**); **pull the plug on** (*coll.*) to end, put a stop to. [App. Du. *plug,* a bung, a peg; cf. Sw. *plugg,* a peg, Ger. *Pflock.*]

plum *plum, n.* a drupe or stone-fruit, or the tree producing it (*Prunus domestica* or kindred species) of the rose family: extended to various fruits and trees more or less similar (as *sapodilla plum, coco-plum, date-plum*): a raisin as a substitute for the true plum: plum-colour: a sugar-plum: a big stone embedded in concrete: something choice that may be extracted (sometimes in reminiscence of Jack Horner) or attained to, as one of the best passages in a book, one of the prizes of a career, or a government office as a reward of services, etc.: (formerly) a sum of £100000: its possessor. — *adj.* plum-colour: choice, cushy. — *adj.* **plumm'y** full of plums: plum-like: desirable, profitable: (of voice) too rich and resonant. — **plum'-bloss'om; plum'-cake** a cake containing raisins, currants, etc. — *n.* and *adj.* **plum'-colour** dark purple. — **plum'cot** Luther Burbank's hybrid between *plum* and *apricot;* **plumdamas** (*-dä'məs; Scot.*) a damson; **plum'-duff** a boiled flour-pudding with raisins; **plum'-porr'idge** an antiquated dish, of porridge with plums, raisins, etc.; **plum=pudd'ing** a national English dish made of flour and suet, with raisins, currants, and various spices; **plum=stone; plum'-tree.** [O.E. *plūme* — L. *prūnum;* cf. Gr. *prou(m)non.*]

plumage *plōōm'ij, n.* a natural covering of feathers: feathers collectively. — *adj.* **plum'aged.** [Fr., — *plume* — L. *plūma,* a feather, down.]

plumassier, plumate. See **plume.**

plumb *plum, n.* a heavy mass, as of lead, hung on a string to show the vertical line, or for other purpose: verticality: a sounding lead, plummet. — *adj.* vertical: level, true (*cricket*): sheer, thorough-going, out-and-out. — *adv.* vertically: precisely: utterly (esp. *U.S.,* now *arch.* or *dial.*). — *v.t.* to test by a plumb-line: to make vertical: to sound as by a plumb-line: to pierce the depth of, fathom, by eye or understanding: to weight with lead: to seal with lead: to do or furnish the plumber-work of. — *v.i.* to hang vertically: to work as a plumber. — *n.* **plumbate** (*plum'bāt*) a salt of plumbic acid. — *adj.* **plumbeous** (*plum'bi-əs*) leaden: lead-coloured: lead-glazed. — *ns.* **plumber** (*plum'ər*) orig. a worker in lead: now one who instals and mends pipes, cisterns, and other fittings for supply of water and gas and for household drainage; **plumb'ery** plumber-work: a plumber's workshop. — *adjs.* **plumbic** (*plum'bik*) due to lead: of quadrivalent lead; **plumbiferous** (-*bif'*) yielding or containing lead. — *ns.* **plumbing** (*plum'ing*) the operation of making plumb: the craft of working in lead: the system of pipes in a building for gas, water and drainage: (the design, style, working, etc., of) lavatories (*euph.*): the work of a plumber; **plum'bism** (-*bizm*) lead poisoning; **plum'bite** (-*bīt*) a salt of the weak acid lead hydroxide. — *adj.* **plumb'less** incapable of being sounded. — *n.* **plumbosol'vency.** — *adjs.* **plumbosol'vent** (better **plumbi-**) able to dissolve lead; **plumbous** (*plum'bəs*) of bivalent lead. — *n.* **plumbum** (*plum'bəm*; *obs.*) lead. — **plumb bob** a weight at the end of a plumb-line; **plumb'er-work; plumbic acid** an acid of which lead dioxide is the anhydride; **plumb'-line** a line to which a bob is attached to show the vertical line: a vertical line: a plummet; **plumb'-rule** a board with plumb-line and bob, for testing the verticality of walls, etc. [Fr. *plomb* and its source L. *plumbum*, lead.]

plumbago¹ *plum-bā'gō, n.* (with *cap.*) a Mediterranean and tropical genus of ornamental plants (some cultivated) giving name to the **Plumbaginaceae** (-*baj-i-nā'si-ē*), a family of salt-steppe and seaside plants including sea-pink and sea-lavender, akin to the primrose family: any plant of this genus: — *pl.* **plumbā'gos.** — *adj.* **plumbaginaceous** (-*baj-i-nā'shəs*). [L. *plumbāgō*, Pliny's translation of the Greek name *molybdaina*, lead, lead ore, the plant *Plumbago* (from its blue flowers).]

plumbago² *plum-bā'gō, n.* graphite: — *pl.* **plumbā'gos.** — *adj.* **plumbaginous** (-*baj'i-nəs*). [L. *plumbāgō, -inis* — *plumbum*, lead.]

plumbate, etc., **plumber,** etc. See under **plumb.**

plumber-block. Same as **plummer-block.**

plume *plōōm, n.* a feather: a large showy feather: the vane of a feather: a bunch or tuft of feathers: a feather, or anything similar, used as an ornament, symbol, crest, etc.: a feather as a token of honour: the plumule of a seed: any feathery structure (*obs.*): anything resembling a feather, as smoke, etc. — *v.t.* to preen: (*refl.*) to pride, take credit to (with *on, upon; fig.*): to adorn with plumes: to set as a plume (*Milt.*): to strip of feathers. — *n.* **plumassier** (*plōō-mä-sēr'*), a worker in feathers: a feather-seller. — *adjs.* **plum'ate, plu'mose, plu'mous** feathered: feathery: plume-like; **plumed** feathered: adorned with a plume: plucked (*obs.*). — *adj.* **plume'less.** — *ns.* **plume'let** a plumule: a little tuft; **plum'ery** plumes collectively. — *adjs.* **plumigerous** (-*ij'ə-rəs*) plumaged; **plu'miped** having feathered feet. — *n.* **plu'mist** a feather-dresser. — *adj.* **plu'my** covered or adorned with down or plume: like a plume. — **plume'-bird** a long-tailed bird of paradise; **plume'-grass** a tall grass (*Erianthus*) akin to sugar-cane, with great silky panicles, grown for ornament; **plume'-moth** any moth of the families Pterophoridae and Orneodidae, with deeply cleft wings. — *adj.* **plume'-pluckt** (*Shak.*) stripped of plumes, humbled. [O.Fr., — L. *plūma*, a small soft feather.]

plummer-block *plum'ər-blok, n.* a metal frame or case for holding the end of a revolving shaft. [Origin unknown.]

plummet *plum'it, n.* leaden or other weight, esp. on a plumb-line, sounding-line, or fishing-line: plumb-rule. — *v.t.* to fathom, sound. — *v.i.* to plunge head-long. [O.Fr. *plomet*, dim. of *plomb*, lead; see **plumb.**]

plump¹ *plump, v.i.* to fall or drop into liquid, esp. vertically, passively, resoundingly, without much disturbance: to flop down: to rain suddenly and heavily (esp.

Scot.): to come suddenly or with a burst: to give all one's votes without distribution: to choose, opt, decisively or abruptly (with *for*). — *v.t.* to plunge, souse: to fling down or let fall flat or heavily: to blurt: to strike or shoot (*slang*). — *n.* the sound or act of plumping: a sudden heavy fall of rain (esp. *Scot.*): a blow (*slang*). — *adj. and adv.* with a plump: in a direct line: downright: in plain language: without hesitation, reserve, or qualification. — *n.* **plump'er** a plump, fall or blow: an undistributed vote that could have been divided: one who gives all his votes to one candidate or option: a downright lie (*slang*): anything very big of its kind, a whacker (*slang*). — *adv.* **plump'ly.** [L.G. *plumpen* or Du. *plompen,* to plump into water; prob. influenced by **plumb** and **plump².**]

plump² *plump, adj.* pleasantly fat and rounded: well filled out. — *v.t.* and *v.i.* to make or grow plump: to swell or round. — *v.i.* (*rare*) **plump'en.** — *n.* **plump'er** a pad kept in the mouth to round the cheeks, used by actors. — *adj.* **plump'ish.** — *adv.* **plump'ly.** — *n.* **plump'ness.** — *adj.* **plump'y, plump'ie** (*Shak.*) plump. [App. the same word as Du. *plomp,* blunt, L.G. *plump.*]

plump³ *plump, (arch.* or *dial.) n.* a cluster: a clump, as of trees, spearmen, waterfowl. [Origin unknown.]

plumula *plōōm'ū-lə, n.* a plumule: — *pl.* **plum'ulae** (-*lē*). — *adjs.* **plumulā'ceous, plum'ular.** — *n.* **Plumulā'ria** a genus of Hydrozoa forming feathery colonies. — *n. and adj.* **plumulā'rian.** — *adj.* **plum'ulate** downy. — *n.* **plum'ule** a little feather or plume: a down feather: the embryo shoot in a seed: a scent-giving scale on the forewing of some male butterflies. — *adj.* **plum'ulose.** [L. *plūmula,* dim. of *plūma,* a feather, downfeather.]

plumy. See **plume.**

plunder *plun'dər, v.t.* to carry off the goods of by force: to pillage: to carry off as booty: to carry off booty from. — *v.i.* to pillage, carry off plunder. — *n.* pillage: booty: personal or household goods (*U.S.*). — *ns.* **plun'derage** the stealing of goods on board ship; **plun'derer.** — *adj.* **plun'derous.** [Ger. *plündern,* to pillage — *Plunder,* household stuff, now trash.]

plunge *plunj, v.t.* to put or thrust with suddenness under the surface of a liquid, or into the midst of, the thick of, or the substance of, anything: to immerse. — *v.i.* to fling oneself or rush impetuously, esp. into water, downhill, or into danger or discourse: to turn suddenly and steeply downward: to fire down upon an enemy from a height: to gamble or squander recklessly: to pitch as a ship: to pitch suddenly forward and throw up the hindlegs. — *n.* act of plunging. — *n.* **plung'er** one who plunges: part of a mechanism with a plunging movement, as the solid piston of a force-pump: a suction instrument for cleaning blockages in pipes: a cavalryman (*obs. mil. slang*): a reckless gambler or squanderer. — *adj. and n.* **plung'ing.** — **plunge bath** a bath large enough to immerse the whole body; **plunging neckline** (in woman's dress) a neckline which is cut low. — **take the plunge** to commit oneself definitely after hesitation. [O.Fr. *plonger* — L. *plumbum,* lead.]

plunk *plungk, v.t.* to twang: to pluck the strings of (a banjo, etc.): to plonk. — *v.i.* to plump. — Also *n., adv., interj.* — *n.* **plunk'er** a large marble (also **plonk'er**). [Imit.]

pluperfect *plōō-pûr'fekt, -fikt,* or *plōō',* (*gram.*) *adj.* denoting that an action happened before some other past action referred to. — *n.* the pluperfect tense: a pluperfect verb or form. [L. *plūs quam perfectum* (*tempus*) more than perfect (tense).]

plural *plōōr'l, adj.* numbering more than one: more than onefold: expressing more than one, or, where dual is recognised, more than two (*gram.*). — *n.* (*gram.*) the plural number: a plural word form. — *n.* **pluralisā'tion, -z-.** — *v.t.* **plur'alise, -ize** to make plural. — *v.i.* to hold two or more benefices or offices simultaneously. — *ns.* **plur'alism** plurality: the holding by one person of more than one office at once, esp. ecclesiastical livings: a system allowing this: a philosophy that recognises more than one principle of being (opp. to *monism*) or more than two (opp. to *monism* and *dualism*): a (condition of) society in which different ethnic, etc., groups preserve their own customs, or hold equal power; **plur′alist** one who holds more than one office at one time: a believer in pluralism. — *adjs.* **plur′alist, pluralist′ic.** — *n.* **plurality** (-*al′i-ti*) the state or fact of being plural: numerousness: a plural number: the greater number, more than half: a majority over any other — distinguished from *majority*, which is used for an absolute majority or majority over all others combined (*U.S.*): the holding of more than one benefice at one time: a living held by a pluralist. — *adv.* **plu′rally.** — **plural society** one in which pluralism is found; **plural vote** power of voting in more than one constituency, or more than once in one. [L. *plūrālis* — *plūs, plūris,* more.]

pluri- *plōōr′i-*, in composition, several: usu. more than two. — *adj.* **plurilit′eral** (*Heb. gram.*) containing more letters than three; **pluriloc′ular** multilocular. — *ns.* **plurip′ara** a multipara; **pluripres′ence** presence in more places than one at the same time. — *adjs.* **plurise′rial, -riate** in several rows. [L. *plūs, plūris,* more.]

plurisie *plōōr′i-si,* (*Shak.*) *n.* superabundance. [L. *plūs, plūris,* more; confused with **pleurisy.**]

plus *plus,* (*math.* and *coll.*) *prep.* with the addition of. — *adj.* positive: additional: having an adverse handicap. — *n.* an addition: a surplus: a positive quality or term: the sign (also **plus sign**) of addition or positivity (+); opposed to *minus* (−): — *pl.* **plus′es, pluss′es.** — *v.t.* and *v.i.* to increase (in value): — *pr.p.* **plus(s)ing;** *pa.t.* and *pa.p.* **plus(s)ed.** — *adv.* (*coll.*) moreover: and more, or more. — **plus′(s)age** an extra amount. — **plus strain** (*bot.*) one of the two strains in heterothallism. [L. *plūs,* more.]

plus-fours *plus′-fōrz′, -fōrz,* *n.pl.* baggy knickerbockers or knickerbocker suit. [**plus, four;** from the four additional inches of cloth required.]

plush *plush, n.* a fabric with a longer and more open pile than velvet: (in *pl.*) footman's breeches. — *adj.* of plush: pretentiously luxurious (also **plush′y**). [Fr. *pluche* for *peluche* — L. *pila,* hair; cf. **pile³.**]

pluteus *plōō′ti-əs, n.* a sea-urchin or brittle-star larva, shaped like a many-legged easel. — *adj.* **plu′teal.** [L. *pluteus,* a shed, boarding, desk.]

Pluto *plōō′tō, n.* the Greek god of the underworld: a planet beyond Neptune, discovered 1930. — *n.* **plu′ton** (*geol.*) a mass of rock which has solidified below the earth's surface. — *adjs.* **Pluto′nian** of Pluto: of the underworld; **Plutonic** (-*ton′ik*) of Pluto: hypogene, deep-seated, relating to, or formed under conditions of, subterranean heat (*geol.*): Plutonist. — *n.* **Plutonism** (*plōō′tən-izm*); **Plu′tonist** (*hist. of geol.*) a Vulcanist; **plutō′nium** the element (Pu) of atomic number 94, named as next after neptunium (93), as the planet Pluto is beyond Neptune. [L. *Plūtō, -ōnis* — Gr. *Ploutōn, -ōnos,* Pluto.]

Plutus *plōō′təs, n.* the Greek god of wealth. — *ns.* **plutocracy** (*plōō-tok′rə-si*) government by the wealthy: a ruling body or class of rich men; **plutocrat** (*plōō′tō-krat*) one who is powerful because of his wealth. — *adj.* **plutocrat′ic.** — *ns.* **pluto-democ′racy** a wealth-dominated democracy; **plutol′atry** (Gr. *latreiā,* worship) worship of wealth; **plutol′ogist, pluton′omist;** **plutol′ogy, pluton′omy** political economy. [L. *Plūtus,* Gr. *Ploutos* (Gr. *ploutos,* wealth).]

pluvial *plōō′vi-əl, adj.* of or by rain: rainy. — *n.* (*lit.* a rain-cloak) a cope or ceremonial mantle (*hist.*): a period of prolonged rainfall (*geol.*). — *n.* **pluviom′eter** a rain-gauge. — *adjs.* **pluviomet′ric, -al.** — *n.* **Pluviôse** (*plü-vē-ōz;* Fr.) the fifth month of the French Revolutionary calendar, about 20th January to 18th February. — *adjs.* **plu′vious, plu′viose** rainy. — **pluvius insurance** insurance cover taken out, e.g. by the organiser of a fête, against loss of takings due to rain. [L. *pluvia,* rain.]

ply¹ *plī, n.* a fold: a layer or thickness: a layer of hard rock or of hard or soft in alternation (*min.*): a bend:

a bend or set: a strand: condition, esp. good condition (*Scot.*): — *pl.* **plies.** — *v.t.* and *v.i.* to bend or fold: — *pr.p.* **ply′ing;** *pa.t.* and *pa.p.* **plied;** *3rd pers. sing.* **plies.** — *n.* **pli′er** one who plies: (in *pl.*) small pincers for bending or cutting wire, etc. — **ply′wood** boarding made of thin layers of wood glued together, the grain of each at right-angles to that of the next. [(O.)Fr. *pli,* a fold, *plier,* to fold — L. *plicāre.*]

ply² *plī, v.t.* to work at steadily: to use or wield diligently or vigorously: to keep supplying or assailing (with): to importune: to row, sail, over habitually. — *v.i.* to work steadily: to make regular journeys over a route: to be in attendance for hire: to beat against the wind: to make one's way, direct one's course: — *pr.p.* **ply′ing;** *pa.t.* and *pa.p.* **plied;** *3rd pers. sing.* **plies.** — *n.* **pli′er** one who plies: a trader (*obs.*): a tout (*obs.*). [Aphetic, from **apply.**]

Plymouth *plim′əth, n.* a port in Devon: a port named after it in Massachusetts, with the supposed landing-place of the Pilgrims (Plymouth Rock). — *ns.* **Plym′outhism; Plym′outhist, Plym′outhite, Plymouth Brother** one of the **Plymouth Brethren,** a religious sect, founded in Dublin *c.* 1825, out of a reaction against High Church principles and against a dead formalism associated with unevangelical doctrine — its first congregation was established at Plymouth in 1831; **Plymouth Rock** an American breed of poultry: a nickname for a Plymouth Brother.

plywood. See **ply¹.**

pneuma *nū′mə, n.* breath: spirit, soul: a neume. — *n.* **pneumathode** (*nū′mə-thōd;* Gr. *hodos,* a way) a respiratory opening in plants. — *adjs.* **pneumatic** (-*mat′ik*) relating to air or gases: containing or inflated with air: worked or driven by compressed air: containing compressed air: with air-cavities (*zool.*): spiritual; **pneumat′ical** (*rare*). — *adv.* **pneumatically.** — *n.* **pneumaticity** (*nū-mə-tis′i-ti*) the condition of having airspaces. — *n. sing.* **pneumat′ics** the science of the properties of gases: pneumatology (also **pneumo-dynam′ics**). — *adj.* **pneumatolog′ical.** — *ns.* **pneumatol′ogist; pneumatol′ogy** the theory of spirits or spiritual beings: psychology (*arch.*): the doctrine of the Holy Spirit (*theol.*): pneumatics (*arch.*); **pneumatol′ysis** (Gr. *lysis,* solution) the destructive action of hot vapours of a magma of igneous rock. — *adj.* **pneumatolyt′ic.** — *ns.* **pneumatom′eter** an instrument for measuring the quantity of air breathed or the force of breathing; **pneu′matophore** (or -*mat′*) an upward-growing respiratory root in swamp plants. — **pneumatic trough** a vessel with a perforated shelf, for filling gas-jars over a liquid. [Gr. *pneuma, -atos,* breath — *pneein.*]

pneum(o)-, pneumon(o)- *nū′m(ō)-, -mon-(ō)-,* in composition, lung. — **pneumococc′us** a bacterium in the respiratory tract which is a causative agent of pneumonia; **pneumoconiosis** (*nū-mō-kō-ni-ō′sis;* Gr. *konia,* dust), **pneumokonio′sis, pneumonokonio′sis** any of various diseases caused by habitually inhaling mineral or metallic dust, as in coal-mining; **pneumoconiöt′ic** a person suffering from pneumoconiosis. — *n. sing.* **pneumodynamics** same as **pneumatics.** — *adj.* **pneumogas′tric** (Gr. *gastēr,* belly) pertaining to the lungs and stomach. — *n.* **vagus.** — *ns.* **pneumonec′tomy** surgical removal of lung tissue; **pneumō′nia** inflammation of the lung. — *adj.* **pneumonic** (-*mon′*) pertaining to the lungs. — *n.* a medicine for lung diseases. — *ns.* **pneumonī′tis** pneumonia; **pneu′monoultramicroscopic-sil′icovolcanoconio′sis** a form of pneumoconiosis caused by very fine silicate or quartz dust; **pneumotho′rax** (*med.*) the existence, or introduction of, air between the lung and chest-wall: lung collapse resulting from the escape of air from the lung into the chest cavity — a potential hazard of working in compressed air, e.g. deep-sea diving. — **pneumonia blouse** a low-necked blouse, once an object of disapproval. [Gr. *pneumōn, -onos,* lung — *pneein,* to breathe.]

Pnyx (*p*)*niks, n.* the meeting-place of the ancien° Athenian assembly. [Gr. *pnyx,* gen. *pyknos,* per°

cog. with *pyknos*, crowded.]

po[1] *pō*, (*coll.*) *n.* a shortening of **chamber pot**: — *pl.* **pos.** [**pot** — prob. from a euph. French pronunciation.]

po[2] *pō* (*coll.*) *adj.* a shortening of **po-faced**.

Poa *pō'ə*, *n.* a large genus of grasses, meadow-grass: (without *cap.*) any plant of this genus. — *adj.* **pōā'ceous.** [Gr. *pŏā*, grass.]

poach[1] *pōch*, *v.t.* to cook slowly in boiling liquid. — *n.* **poach'er** one who poaches eggs: a vessel with hollows for poaching eggs in. — **poached egg flower** Romneya: an annual, *Limnanthes douglasii*, with yellow and white flowers. [App. Fr. *pocher*, to pocket—*poche*, pouch, the white forming a pocket about the yolk.]

poach[2] *pōch*, *v.i.* to intrude on another's preserves in order to pursue or kill game, or upon another's fishing to catch fish (also *fig.*): to encroach upon another's rights, profits, area of influence, etc., or on a partner's place or part in a game: to seek an unfair advantage: (*Shak.*, *potche*) to thrust: to trample in mud: to become trampled and muddy. — *v.t.* to take illegally on another's ground or in another's fishing: to seek or take game or fish illegally on: to take in unfair encroachment: to poke or thrust (*dial.*): to stir up (*dial.*): to trample into holes and mud. — *ns.* **poach'er; poach'iness; poach'ing.** — *adj.* **poach'y** spongy and sodden. [A form of **poke**[3] or from O.Fr. *pocher*, to poke.]

poaka *pō-ä'kə*, (*Maori*) *n.* a N.Z. bird, one of the stilts.

poake. A Shakespearian spelling of **poke**[1].

pocas palabras *pō'käs pal-äb'räs*, (Sp.) few words.

po'chaise. See **pochay**.

pochard, pockard, poker *pōch'*, *poch'*, *pok'ərd*, *pōk'ər*, *ns.* a red-headed diving-duck (*Nyroca* or *Aythya ferina*) esp. the male, the female being the dun-bird. [Origin obscure.]

pochay *pō'shā*, **po'chaise** -*shāz*. See **post-chaise** (under **post**[2]).

pochette *posh-et'*, *n.* a small bag, esp. one carried by women: a pocket note-case or wallet. [Fr., dim. of *poche*, pocket.]

pochoir *posh'wär*, *n.* a form of colour stencilling, by hand, on to a printed illustration. [Fr., stencil.]

pock[1] *pok*, *n.* a small elevation of the skin containing pus, as in smallpox. — *adjs.* **pocked; pock'y** marked with pustules: infected with pox: confounded (*obs.*). — **pock'mark, pock'pit** the mark, pit, or scar left by a pock. — *adjs.* **pock'marked, pock'pitted.** [O.E. *poc*, a pustule; Ger. *Pocke*, Du. *pok*; see **pox**.]

pock[2] *pok*, *n.* a Scots form of **poke**[1]. — **pockman'tie, pockmank'y** corrupt forms of **portmanteau**, influenced by **pock**; **pock-pudding** (*pok'-pud'n*) a bag-pudding: a Scottish contemptuous name for a mere Englishman.

pockard. See **pochard**.

pocket *pok'it*, *n.* a little pouch or bag, esp. one attached to a garment or a billiard-table or the cover of a book: a cavity: a rock cavity filled with ore, veinstone, etc.: a portion of the atmosphere differing in pressure or other condition from its surroundings: a small isolated area or patch, as of military resistance, unemployment, etc.: the innermost compartment of a pound-net: stock of money: a bag of wool, etc., containing about ½ sack. — *adj.* for the pocket: of a small size. — *v.t.* to put in one's pocket or a pocket: to appropriate: to take stealthily: to conceal: to enclose: to hem in: to play into a pocket (*billiards*). — *v.i.* to form a pocket: — *pr.p.* **pock'eting;** *pa.t.* and *pa.p.* **pock'eted.** — *n.* **pock'etful** as much as a pocket will hold: — *pl.* **pock'etfuls.** — *adj.* **pock'etless.** — **pocket battleship** a small battleship, built to specifications limited by treaty, etc.; **pock'et-book** a notebook: a wallet for papers or money carried in the pocket: a small book for the pocket: a handbag see **borough**; **pock'et borough** see **borough**; **pock'et-comb** a hair-comb for the pocket; **pock'et-glass** a small looking-glass for the pocket; **pocket gopher** any American burrowing rodent of the family Geomyidae, with outward-opening cheek-pouches; **pock'et-handk'er-chief** a handkerchief for the pocket; **pock'et-hole** the

opening in a garment giving access to a pocke. **pock'et-knife** a knife with one or more blades folding into the handle for the pocket; **pock'et-money** money carried for occasional expenses: an allowance, esp. to a boy or girl; **pocket mouse** a small rodent of genus *Perognathus*, native to the N. American desert; **pock'et-picking** the act or practice of picking the pocket; **pock'et-piece** a coin carried to bring luck; **pock'et-pis'tol** a pistol for the pocket: a small travelling flask for liquor. — *adj.* **pock'et-sized** small enough for the pocket. — **in one's pocket** (*fig.*) under one's control or influence; **in**, or **out of**, **pocket** with, or without, money: the richer, or the poorer, by a transaction (*adj.* **out'-of-pock'et** of expenses, etc., paid in cash); **line one's pockets** to make or take money dishonestly from business entrusted to one; **pick a person's pocket** to steal from his pocket; **pocket an insult, affront**, etc., to submit to or put up with it without protest; **pocket one's pride** to humble oneself to accept a situation. [A.Fr. *pokete* (Fr. *pochette*, dim. of *poche*, pocket).]

pockmanky, pockmantie. See **pock**[2].

pocky, etc. See **pock**[1].

poco *pō'kō*, (It.) *adj.* little. — *adj.* **pococuran'te** (*-kōō-ran'-tā*, *-kū-ran'ti*; It. *curante*, *pr.p.* of *curare*, to care) uninterested: indifferent: nonchalant. — *n.* a habitually uninterested person. — *ns.* **pococuran'tism** (*-kū-rant'izm*), **pococuranteism** (*-kū-rant'i-ism*); **pococurant'ist.** — **poco a poco** little by little.

poculiform *pok'ū-li-förm*, *adj.* cup-shaped. [L. *pōculum*, cup.]

pod[1] *pod*, *n.* the fruit, or its shell, in peas, beans, and other leguminous plants — the legume: sometimes extended to the siliqua: a silk cocoon: a musk-bag: a paunch: a groove along an auger or bit: the socket into which a bit, etc., fits: a protective housing for (external) engineering equipment, e.g. aircraft engines, nuclear reactor, space or submarine instruments, or for weapons carried externally e.g. on an aircraft: a decompression compartment. — *v.t.* to shell or hull. — *v.i.* to form pods: to fill as pods: — *pr.p.* **podd'ing;** *pa.t.* and *pa.p.* **podd'ed.** — *adj.* **podd'y** corpulent. [Origin unknown.]

pod[2] *pod*, *n.* a school, esp. of whales or seals: sometimes applied to groups of other animals and birds. [Origin unknown.]

podagra *pod-ag'rə*, also *po'*, *n.* gout, properly in the feet. — *adjs.* **podag'ral, podag'ric, -al, podag'rous** gouty. [Gr. *podagrā* — *pous*, *podos*, foot, *agrā*, a catching.]

poddy. See **pod**[1].

pod(o)- *pod(ō)-*, *pŏd(ō)-*, in composition, foot. — *adjs.* **pō'dal, podal'ic** of the feet. — *ns.* **Podargus** (*pō-där'gəs*; Gr. *argos*, inactive — *a-*, neg., *ergon*, work) the typical frogmouth genus of birds; **podiatry** (*pod-ī'ə-tri*; Gr. *iātros*, *iātros*, physician) treatment of disorders of the foot; **podi'atrist; Podocarpus** (*pod-ō-kär'pəs*; Gr. *karpos*, fruit) an eastern and southern genus of trees of the yew family; **Podogona** (*-og'ə-nə*; Gr. *gonos*, reproductive organ; see **Ricinulei**) the Ricinulei; **podol'ogist; podol'ogy** the scientific study of the feet. — *adj.* **podophthalmus** (*-of-thal'məs*; Gr. *ophthalmos*, eye) having eyes on stalks, as many higher crustaceans. — *ns.* **Podophyllum** (*-ō-fil'əm*, *-o'fil-əm*; Gr. *phyllon*, leaf) a genus of the barberry family; **podophyll'in** a cathartic resin got from its rhizome; **Podostemon** (*-ō-stē'mon*; Gr. *stēmōn*, warp — as if stamen — from the stalk on which the stamens stand) the typical genus of a family of dicotyledons, **Podostemaceae** (*-mā'si-ē*), growing in tropical waterfalls, the vegetative parts more like a thallus than an ordinary flowering plant; **Podura** (*-dū'rə*; Gr. *ourā*, tail) a genus of springtails. [Gr. *pous*, *podos*, foot.]

podestà *pod-est-tä'*, (*hist.*) *n.* a governor, chief magistrate, or judge in an Italian town. [It. *podestà* — L. *potestās*, *-ātis*, power.]

podex *pō'deks*, *n.* the rump: the anal region. [L. *pōdex*.]

podge *poj*, **pudge** *puj*, *ns.* a squat, fat, and flabby person or thing. — *ns.* **podg'iness, pudg'iness.** — *adjs.* **podg'y,**

pudg'y. [Origin obscure.]

podiatrist, podiatry. See **pod(o)-.**

podium *pō'di-əm, n.* a continuous pedestal, a stylobate: a platform, dais: a foot or hand (*anat.*): a tube-foot: — *pl.* **pō'dia.** — *adj.* **pō'dial.** — *n.* **podite** (*pod'īt*) a walking leg of a crustacean. [Latinised from Gr. *pŏdion*, dim. of *pous, podos*, foot.]

podley *pod'li*, (*Scot.*) *n.* a young coalfish. [**pollack.**]

podo-. See **pod(o)-.**

Podsnappery *pod-snap'ər-i, n.* British Philistinism as exemplified in Mr *Podsnap* in Dickens's *Our Mutual Friend.*

podsol, podzol *pod-zol', pod'-, n.* any of a group of soils characterised by a greyish-white leached and infertile topsoil and a brown subsoil, typical of regions with a subpolar climate. — *adj.* **podsol'ic.** [Russ., — *pod,* under, *zola*, ash.]

Podunk *pō'dungk* (*U.S.*), *n.* an imaginary, typical, dull, out-dated country town. [From either of two villages, near Worcester, Mass., or Hartford, Connecticut.]

poe-bird, poy-bird *pō'i-bûrd*, (*obs.*) *n.* the New Zealand parson-bird or tui. [Captain Cook's name from Tahitian *poe*, pearl beads, taken by him to mean earrings, on account of the side-tufts of the bird's neck.]

poem *pō'im, -em, n.* a composition in verse: a composition of high beauty of thought or language and artistic form, typically, but not necessarily, in verse: anything supremely harmonious and satisfying (*fig.*). — *adj.* **poemat'ic.** [Fr. *poème* — L. *poēma* — Gr. *poiēma* — *poieein*, to make.]

poenology. Same as **penology.**

poesy *pō'i-zi, n.* poetry collectively or in the abstract: a poem (*obs.*): a motto or posy (*obs.*). — *v.i.* (*Keats*) to utter poetry. [Fr. *poésie* — L. *poēsis* — Gr. *poiēsis* — *poieein*, to make.]

poet *pō'it, -et, n.* the author of a poem or (formerly) of any work of literary art: a verse-writer: one skilled in making poetry: one with a poetical imagination: — *fem.* **pō'etess.** — *ns.* **pōetas'ter** (see **-aster**) a petty poet: a writer of contemptible verses; **pōetas'tering, pōetas't(e)ry.** — *adjs.* **poetic** (*pō-et'ik*), **-al** of the nature or having the character of poetry: pertaining or suitable to a poet or to poetry: expressed in poetry: in the language of poetry: imaginative. — *ns.sing.* **poet'ic(s)** the branch of criticism that relates to poetry. — *adv.* **pōet'ically.** — *v.t.* and *v.i.* **poet'icise, -ize** to make poetic: to write poetry about: to write, speak, or treat, poetically. — *ns.* **poet'icism** a word or phrase that is typically, usually tritely, poetic; **pōet'icule** a petty poet. — *v.i.* **pō'etise, -ize** to write as a poet or like a poet. — *v.t.* to make poetical: to record or celebrate in poetry. — *ns.* **pō'etresse** (*Spens.*) a poetess; **pō'etry** the art of the poet: the essential quality of a poem: poetical composition or writings collectively (rarely in *pl.*): poetical quality; **pō'etship.** — **poetic justice** ideal administration of reward and punishment; **poetic licence** a departing from strict fact or rule by a poet for the sake of effect; **Poet Laureate** see **laureate.** — **poetry in motion** exceedingly beautiful, harmonious, rhythmical, etc., movement. [Fr. *poète* — L. *poēta* — Gr. *poiētēs* — *poieein*, to make.]

po-faced *pō'fāst*, (*coll.*) *adj.* stupidly solemn and narrow-minded: stolid, humourless. — Also shortened to **po.** [Perh. *po-faced* or *poor-faced.*]

poffle *pof'l*, (*Scot.*) *n.* a pendicle. [Origin obscure.]

pogge *pog, n.* the armed bullhead (*Agonus cataphractus*), a bony-plated fish. [Origin unknown.]

pogonotomy *pō-gō-not'ə-mi, n.* shaving. [Gr. *pōgōn, pōgōnos,* beard, *tomē,* a cutting.]

pogo stick *pō'gō stik,* a child's toy consisting of a stick with a crossbar on a strong spring on which one stands in order to bounce along the ground. [*Pogo,* a trademark.]

pogrom *pog'rom, pog-rom', n.* an organised massacre, orig. (late 19th cent.) esp. of Russian Jews. [Russ., destruction, devastation.]

poh *pō, interj.* of impatient contempt. [Cf. **pooh.**]

poi *pō'ē, n.* a Hawaiian dish, a paste of fermented taro root. [Hawaiian.]

poignado, poinado *poi-nä'dō,* obsolete forms of **poniard.**

poignant *poin'(y)ənt, adj.* stinging, pricking: sharp: acutely painful: penetrating: pungent: piquant: touching, pathetic. — *n.* **poign'ancy.** — *adv.* **poign'antly.** [O.Fr. *poignant,* pr.p. of *poindre* — L. *pungĕre,* to sting.]

poikilitic *poi-kil-it'ik, adj.* mottled: having small crystals of one mineral irregularly scattered in larger crystals of another (*petr.*). — *n.* **poi'kilocyte** (*-ō-sīt*) an irregular red blood corpuscle. — *n.* **poi'kilotherm** a cold-blooded animal. — *adjs.* **poikilotherm'al, poikilotherm'ic** having variable blood-temperature — 'cold-blooded'. — *n.* **poikilotherm'y** (or *poi'-*) cold-bloodedness. [Gr. *poikilos,* variegated.]

poilu *pwa-lü,* (Fr.) *n.* a French private solider (nickname; meaning 'hairy').

poinado. See **poignade.**

Poinciana *poin-si-ä'nə, n.* a tropical genus of the Caesalpinia family — flamboyant tree, etc.: (without *cap.*) a tree of this genus. [After De *Poinci,* a French West Indian governor.]

poind *pēnd, pind,* (*Scot.*) *v.t.* to distrain: to impound. — *ns.* **poind'er; poind'ing.** [O.E. *pyndan,* to impound; cf. **pound²**.]

poinsettia *poin-set'i-ə, n.* a spurge, *Euphorbia pulcherrima,* with petal-like bracts, usu. scarlet, and small yellow flowers, orig. from Mexico and Central America. [From Joel Roberts *Poinsett* (1779–1851), American Minister to Mexico.]

point¹ *point, n.* a dot: a small mark used in Semitic alphabets to indicate a vowel, to differentiate a consonant, or for other purpose: a dot separating the integral and fractional parts of a decimal: a mark of punctuation: that which has position but no magnitude (*geom.*): a whit (as in *no point; Shak.*): a place or station, considered in relation to position only: a place or division in a scale, course, or cycle (as *boiling point, dead-point*): a moment of time, without duration: a precise moment: a state: a juncture: a critical moment: the verge: a culmination: a conclusion: resolution (*obs.*): condition, case, plight (as in *in good point; obs.*): any one of nine fixed positions on a shield (*her.*): the entry, or the first notes, of a subject, as in a fugue (formerly marked by a dot; *obs.*): a short strain or phrase of music, a call on an instrument, esp. military, as in a *point of war* (*arch.*): a unit in scoring, judging, or measurement: a character taken into account in judging: a distinctive mark or characteristic: a unit of measurement of type, approximately 1/72 inch: one of thirty-two divisions of the compass (**points of the compass**) or the angle between two successive divisions (⅛ of a right angle): a unit in rationing by coupon: in piquet, the strongest suit held and called, or the score for holding it: a particular: a head, clause, or item: a position forming a main element in the structure of an argument or discourse: a matter in debate, under attention, or to be taken into account: that which is relevant: that upon which one insists or takes a stand: the precise matter: the essential matter: that without which a story, joke, etc., is meaningless or ineffective: a clearly defined aim, object, or reason: a particular imparted as a hint: lace made with a needle (also **point'-lace**): (*loosely*) lace: a piece of point-lace (*obs.*): a sharp end: a tip, or free end: a thing, part, or mark with a sharp end: a piercing weapon or tool: an etching-needle: the sharp end of a sword: (in *pl.*) sword-fighting: a tine: a spike: a tapering piece in electrical apparatus, as the end of a lightning-conductor: a cape or headland: the tip of the chin (*boxing*): a horse's or other animal's extremity: a tagged lace formerly used for fastening clothes: a nib: a movable rail for passing vehicles from one track to another: a tapering division of a backgammon board: a fielder or his position, on the offside straight out from and near the batsman (as if at the point of the bat) (*cricket*): the leading party of an advanced guard: a position at the head of a herd: a socket for making connection with electric wiring: pointedness: pungency: sting: the act or position of pointing: the vertical rising of a hawk, indicating the position of the prey: a feat (*obs.*): pointe: 1/100 part of a carat. — *adj.* (*phon.*) articulated with the tip of the tongue. — *v.t.* to insert points in: to mark with points: to mark off in groups of syllables for singing: to sharpen: to give point to: to prick in or turn over with the point of a spade: to show the position or direction of or draw attention to (now usu. with *out*): to place in a certain direction, direct (with *at*): to indicate: to insert white hairs in (a fur): to rake out old mortar from, and insert new mortar in, the joints of: to ration by points. — *v.i.* to have or take a position in a direction (with *at, to, toward*, etc.: to indicate a direction or position by extending a finger, a stick, etc.: of dogs, to indicate the position of game by an attitude: to hint: to aim. — *adj.* **point'ed** having a sharp point: sharp: Gothic (*archit.*): keen: telling: epigrammatic: precise: explicit: aimed at particular persons: having marked personal application. — *adv.* **point'edly.** — *ns.* **point'edness; point'er** one who points, in any sense: a rod for pointing to a blackboard, map, screen, etc.: an index-hand: a hint, tip, suggestion, indication: a tool for clearing out old mortar from joints: a breed of dogs that point on discovering game: (in *pl.*) two stars of the Great Bear nearly in a straight line with the Pole Star; **point'ing.** — *adj.* **point'less.** — *adv.* **point'lessly.** — *n.* **point'lessness.** — *adj.* **point'y** having points, or pointed in shape. — **point'-duty** the duty of a policeman stationed at a particular point to regulate traffic; **point'ing-stock** a thing to be pointed at, a laughing-stock; **point'-lace** (see above). — *adj.* **point'-of-sale'** of, relating to, or occurring at the place where a sale is made. — **point set** (*math.*) an aggregate; **points'man** one on point-duty: one in charge of rail points; **point'-source'** a source of radiation that is, or is considered as, a mathematical point. — *adj.* **point'-to-point'** from one fixed point to another: across country. — *n.* a cross-country race, a steeplechase. — **at (a) point, points, all points** (*Shak.*, etc.) in readiness: resolved: completely: in all respects: **at the point of** on the verge of; **cardinal points** see **cardinal; carry one's point** to gain what one contends for; **dead-point** see **dead; from point to point** from one detail to another (*obs.*); **give points to** to give odds to: to give an advantageous hint on any subject; **in point** apposite; **in point of** in the matter of; **in point of fact** as a matter of fact; **make a point of** to treat as essential, make a special object of; **not to put too fine a point on it** to speak bluntly; **on the point of** close upon: very near; **point for point** exactly in all particulars; **point of honour** see **honour; point of no return** that point on a flight from which one can only go on, for want of fuel to return (also *fig.*); **point of order** a question raised in a deliberative society, whether proceedings are according to the rules; **point of view** the position from which one looks at anything, literally or figuratively; **point of the compass** (see above); **point out** to point to, show, bring someone's attention to; **point up** to emphasise; **potatoes and point** a feigned Irish dish, potatoes alone, with a herring, etc., to point at; **put upon points** to ration by points; **score points off someone** to advance at the expense of another: to outwit, get the better of someone in an argument or repartee; **stand upon points** to be punctilious; **stretch (or strain) a point** to go further (esp. in concession) than strict rule allows; **to the point** apposite; **to point** (*Spens., Shak.*) to the smallest detail; **up to a point** partly, not wholly.   [Partly Fr. *point*, point, dot, stitch, lace, partly Fr. *pointe*, sharp point, pungency — L. *punctum* and L.L. *puncta*, respectively — L. *pungĕre, punctum*, to prick.]

point² *point, v.t.* to appoint, determine, fix.   [Aphetic for **appoint.**]

point-blank *point'-blangk', adj.* aimed directly at the mark without allowing for the downward curve of the trajectory: permitting such an aim, i.e. at very close range: direct: straightforward: blunt. — *adv.* with point-blank aim: directly: bluntly: flat. — *n.* a point-blank shot or range: reach (of jurisdiction) (*Shak.*). [App. from **point** (vb.) and **blank** (of the target).]

point d'appui *pwɛ̃ da-pwē*, (Fr.) a point of support, prop, fulcrum.

point-device, point-devise *point'-di-vīs', n.* (*obs.*) the point of perfection (in the phrase *at point device*). — *adj.* (*arch.*) fastidiously exact, esp. in dress. — *adv.* with exactitude: down to the smallest detail.   [Lit. to the point arranged, or arranged to the point — O.Fr. *devis*, devised.]

pointe *pwɛ̃t*, (Fr.) *n.* in ballet, the extreme tip of the toe, or the position of standing on it.

pointel *poin'tl, n.* a sharp instrument, esp. a style: a pistil (*obs.*).   [O.Fr.]

pointillism *pwan'til-izm*, Fr. **pointillisme** *pwɛ̃-tē-yēzm, ns.* in painting, the use of separate dots of pure colour instead of mixed pigments. — *adj.* **pointillé** (*pwɛ̃-tē-yā*) ornamented with a pattern of dots made by a pointed tool. — *n.* and *adj.* **poin'tillist**, Fr. **pointilliste** (*-tē-yēst*). [Fr. *pointillisme* — *pointille*, dim. of *point*, point.]

poise¹ *poiz, v.t.* to weigh (*obs.*): to hold so as to get some notion of the weight: to ponder, weigh in the mind (*rare*): to weight, weigh down (*obs.*): to make stable, ballast (*obs.*): to balance: to counterbalance (*obs.*): to carry or hold in equilibrium. — *v.i.* to hang in suspense: to hover. — *n.* weight (*obs.*): balance: equilibrium: a weight, as of a clock (*obs.*): bias: momentum (*Spens.*): impact (*Shak.*): carriage or balance of body: dignity and assurance of manner: suspense. — *adj.* **poised** having or showing poise, composure: balanced. — *n.* **pois'er.**   [O.Fr. *poiser* (Fr. *peser*) — L. *pēnsāre*, freq. of *pendĕre*, to weigh, and O.Fr. *pois* — L. *pēnsum*, weight.]

poise² *pwäz, n.* a CGS unit of viscosity (not an SI unit). [J. L. M. *Poiseuille*, French physician.]

poison *poi'zn, n.* any substance which, taken into or formed in the body, destroys life or impairs health: any malignant influence: a substance that inhibits the activity of a catalyst (*chem.*): a material that absorbs neutrons and so interferes with the working of a nuclear reactor. — *v.t.* to administer poison to: to injure or kill with poison: to put poison on or in: to taint: to mar: to embitter: to corrupt. — *adj.* **poi'sonous.** — *adj.* **poi'sonable.** — *n.* **poi'soner.** — *adj.* **poi'sonous** having the quality or effect of poison: noxious: offensive (*coll.*). — *adv.* **poi'sonously.** — *n.* **poi'sonousness.** — **poi'son-fang** one of two large tubular teeth in the upper jaw of venomous snakes, through which poison passes from glands at their roots when the animal bites; **poi'son-gas** any injurious gas used in warfare; **poi'son-gland** a gland that secretes poison; **poi'son-ivy, poi'son-oak, poi'son-sumac(h)** names for various North American sumacs with ulcerating juice; **poi'son-nut** nux vomica; **poison pen** a writer of malicious anonymous letters; **poison pill** (*coll.*) any of various actions, such as merger, takeover, recapitalisation, taken by a company to prevent or deter a threatened takeover bid: a clause or clauses in a company's articles of association put into effect by an unwanted takeover bid, and making such a takeover less attractive. — **what's your poison?** (*coll.*) what would you like to drink?   [O.Fr. *puison*, poison — L. *pōtiō, -ōnis*, a draught — *pōtāre*, to drink; cf. **potion.**]

poisson *pwa-sɔ̃*, (Fr.) *n.* a fish. — **poisson d'avril** (*dav-rēl*) an April fool.

Poisson's distribution *pwä-sɔ̃z dis-tri-bū'shən*, (*statistics*) a distribution that, as a limiting form of binomial distribution, is characterised by a small probability of a specific event occurring during observations over a continuous interval (e.g. of time or distance); **Poisson's**

ratio (*phys.*) one of the elastic constants of a material, defined as the ratio of the lateral contraction per unit breadth to the longitudinal extension per unit length when a piece of material is stretched.   [After S. Denis *Poisson* (1781–1840), French mathematician.]

poitrel poi′trəl, *n.* armour for a horse's breast.   [O.Fr. *poitral* — L. *pectorāle*, a breastplate — *pectus, -oris,* the breast.]

pokal pō-käl′, *n.* an ornamental drinking-vessel.   [Ger., — It. *boccale* — Gr. *baukălis,* a vessel for cooling wine, etc.]

poke[1] pōk, *n.* (now chiefly *dial.; Scot.* **pock**[2]) a bag: a pouch: a pokeful: a pocket. — *n.* **poke′ful** as much as a poke will hold. — **a pig in a poke** a blind bargain, as of a pig bought without being seen.   [M.E. *poke*; affinities uncertain.]

poke[2] pōk, *n.* a projecting brim or front of a bonnet: a poke-bonnet. — *adj.* **poked.** — **poke′-bonnet** a bonnet with a projecting front formerly worn by women. [Perh. from foregoing, or from following word.]

poke[3] pōk, *v.t.* to thrust or push the end of anything against or into: to prod or jab: to cause to protrude: to thrust forward or endwise: to make, put, render, or achieve by thrusting or groping: to stir up, incite: to dress with a poking-stick (*obs.*): (of a man) to have sexual intercourse with (*slang*): to change a number in the memory of a computer: to seclude or confine in a poky place (*coll.*). — *v.i.* to thrust, make thrusts: to protrude: to feel about, grope: to bat gently and cautiously (*cricket*): to potter: to stoop: to pry about: to live a dull or secluded life. — *n.* an act of poking. — *n.* **pō′ker** one who pokes: a rod for poking or stirring a fire: an instrument for doing poker-work: a stiff person: a mace or mace-bearer (*facet.*): a poking-stick. — *adj.* **pō′kerish** like a poker: stiff. — *adv.* **pō′kerishly.** — *adj.* **pō′king** pottering: petty: confined: stuffy: shabby. — *adj.* **pō′ky** poking (usu. confined). — **pō′ker-work** work done by burning a design into wood with a heated point; **pō′king-stick** a small rod formerly used for adjusting the plaits of ruffs. — **better than a poke in the eye (with a burnt, sharp, stick)** (*coll.*) an expression of pleasure, esp. qualified (*Austr.*): generally, referring to something only moderately desirable; **by the holy poker** a facetious oath of unknown meaning, perhaps belonging to **poker**[1] below; **poke fun at** to banter; **poke one's head** to stoop, hold the head forward; **poke one's nose** to pry; **red-hot poker** Kniphofia or Tritoma.   [M.E. *pōken*; app. of L.G. origin.]

poke[4] pōk, *n.* a name for various American species of Phytolacca (also **poke′weed, poke′berry**): American or white hellebore (**Indian poke**).   [Of American Indian origin.]

poker[1] pō′kər, *n.* a bugbear. — *adj.* **pō′kerish** causing terror: uncanny. — **Old Poker** see **old Harry** under **old.** [Cf. Dan. *pokker,* Sw. *pocker.*]

poker[2] pō′kər, *n.* a round game at cards, first played in America about 1835. — **po′ker-face** an inscrutable face, useful to a poker-player: its possessor. — *adj.* **po′ker-faced.**   [Ety. uncertain; poss. from German.]

poker[3]. See **pochard.**

Polabian pō-lā′bi-ən, *n.* a member of a former West Slavonic people occupying the basin of the lower Elbe: their extinct language. — Also *adj.*   [Slav. *po,* beside, *Labe,* the Elbe.]

polacca po-lak′ə, *n.* a three-masted Mediterranean vessel, with fore and main masts each in one piece (also **polacre** po-lä′kər): a polonaise, or composition in the manner of a polonaise.   [It. *polacca, polacra,* Polish (fem.); Fr. *polacre*: application to the vessel not explained.]

Polack pōl′ak, (*slang*; usu. *derog.*) *n.* a Pole. — *adj.* Polish. [Pol. *Polak*; Ger. *Polack.*]

Poland pō′lənd, *adj.* of Poland, Polish. — *n.* **Po′lander** (*obs.*) a Pole.

polar pō′lər, *adj.* of, or pertaining to, a pole (see **pole**[1]) or poles: belonging to the neighbourhood of a pole: referred to a pole: of the nature of, or analogous to,

---

a pole: axial: having polarity: directly opposed. — *n.* (*geom.*) the locus of the harmonic conjugate of a fixed point or pole with respect to the points in which a transversal through it cuts a circle or other conic. — *n.* **polarim′eter** an instrument for measuring the rotation of the plane of polarisation of light, or the amount of polarisation of light. — *adj.* **polarimetric** (*pō-lar-i-met′rik*). — *ns.* **polarimetry** (*pō-lər-im′i-tri*); **Polaris** (*pō-lä′ris*) the Pole Star; **polarisation, -z-** (*pō-lər-ī-zā′shən*) act of polarising: the state of being polarised: development of poles: *loosely,* polarity: the effect of deposition of products of electrolysis upon electrodes, resulting in an opposing electromotive force: the restriction (according to the wave theory) of the vibrations of light to one plane; **polariscope** (*pō-lar′i-skōp*) an instrument for showing phenomena of polarised light. — *v.t.* **polarise, -ize** (*pō′lər-īz*) to subject to polarisation: to give polarity to: to develop new qualities or meanings in (*fig.*): to split into opposing camps (also *v.i.*). — *v.i.* to acquire polarity. — *adj.* **po′larised, -z-.** — *ns.* **po′lariser, -z-** a device for polarising light; **polarity** (*pō-lar′i-ti*) the state of having two opposite poles: the condition of having properties different or opposite in opposite directions or at opposite ends: the tendency to develop differently in different directions along an axis, as a plant towards base and apex, some animals towards head and tail: particular relation to this or that pole or opposed property rather than the other: directedness (*fig.*): opposedness or doubleness of aspect or tendency; **polarog′raphy** a technique for determining the concentration and nature of the ions in a solution by an electrolytic process in which the current through the cell is measured as a function of the applied voltage. — *adj.* **Po′laroid**® a trademark applied to photographic equipment, light-polarising materials, etc. — *n.* **po′laron** a free electron trapped by polarisation charges on surrounding molecules. — **polar axis** (*astron.*) that diameter of a sphere which passes through the poles: in an equatorial telescope, the axis, parallel to the earth's axis, about which the whole instrument revolves in order to keep a celestial object in the field; **polar bear** a large white bear found in the Arctic regions; **polar body** (*biol.*) one of two small cells detached from the ovum during the maturation divisions; **polar circle** the Arctic or the Antarctic Circle; **polar co-ordinates** co-ordinates defining a point by means of a radius vector and the angle which it makes with a fixed line through the origin; **polar distance** angular distance from the pole; **polar equation** an equation in terms of polar co-ordinates; **polar forces** forces that act in pairs and in different directions, as in magnetism; **polar lights** the aurora borealis or australis.   [L. *polāris* — *polus*; see **pole**[1].]

polder pōl′dər, *n.* a piece of low-lying reclaimed land: the first stage in its reclamation. — Also *v.t.*   [Du.]

pole[1] pōl, *n.* the end of an axis, esp. of the earth, the celestial sphere, or any rotating sphere: of a great or small circle on a sphere, either of the two points in which its axis cuts the surface of the sphere: of a crystal face, the point where the normal from the origin cuts the sphere of projection: the end of an elongated body: a differentiated end: either of the two points of a body in which the attractive or repulsive energy is concentrated, as in a magnet: an electric terminal or electrode: a fixed point (*geom.*): a point from which a pencil of rays radiates: a fixed point defining a polar: an opposite extreme (*fig.*): the heavens (*poet.,* after Greek use). — **Pole Star** Polaris, a star near the N. pole of the heavens: a guide or director. — **poles apart, asunder** widely separated, very different.   [L. *polus* — Gr. *polos,* pivot, axis, firmament.]

pole[2] pōl, *n.* a long rounded shaft, rod, or post, usu. of wood: a small tree: a single shaft to which a pair of horses may be yoked: a measuring rod of definite length: hence a measure of length, 5½ yards, of area, 30¼ square yards: the position next to the inner boundary-fence in a racecourse (now usu. **pole posi-**

---

tion): the tail of certain animals. — *v.t.* to propel, push, strike, or stir with a pole: to furnish or support with poles. — *v.i.* to use a pole. — *ns.* **pō′ler** (*Austr.*) one of a pair of bullocks harnessed to the pole: a shirker; **pō′ling** supplying, propelling, or stirring with a pole or poles: poles collectively. — *adj.* **pole′-clipt** (*Shak.*) hedged in with poles. — **pole position** the most advantageous position in any competition, race, etc. (see also above); **pole′-vault** an athletic event in which the competitor uses a pole to achieve great height in jumping over a cross-bar. — Also *v.i.* — **pole′-vaulter.** — **pole on** (*Austr. slang*) to impose on; **under bare poles** with all sails furled; **up the pole** (*slang*) in a predicament: drunk: crazed: in favour (*mil.*). [O.E. *pāl* (Ger. *Pfahl*) — L. *pālus*, a stake.]

Pole *pōl*, *n.* a native or citizen of Poland: a Polish-speaking inhabitant of Poland.

pole-axe, -ax *pōl′aks*, *n.* a battle-axe, originally short-handled: a long-handled axe or halbert: a sailor's short-handled axe for cutting away rigging: a butcher's axe with a hammer-faced back. — *v.t.* to strike or fell with (or as if with) a pole-axe. [Orig. *pollax*, from **poll**, head, and **axe**, confused with **pole²**.]

polecat *pōl′kat*, *n.* a large relative of the weasel, which emits a stink — called also *fitchet* and *foumart* (*Mustela putorius*): a prostitute (*Shak.*): a skunk (*U.S.*). — **pole′cat-ferret** the hybrid offspring of the ferret and polecat. [M.E. *polcat*; poss. Fr. *poule*, hen, and **cat**.]

polemarch *pol′i-märk*, *n.* a title of several officials in ancient Greek states, orig. a military commander. [Gr. *polemarchos* — *polemos*, war, *archē*, rule.]

polemic *po-lem′ik*, *adj.* given to disputing: controversial. — *n.* a controversialist: a controversy: a controversial writing or argument. — *adj.* **polem′ical.** — *adv.* **polem′-ically.** — *ns.* **polem′icist, pol′emist** one who writes polemics or engages in controversy. — *n. sing.* **polem′-ics** the practice or art of controversy. — *v.t.* **pol′emise, -ize.** [Gr. *polemikos* — *polemos*, war.]

Polemonium *pol-i-mō′ni-əm*, *n.* the Jacob's ladder genus of plants, giving name to the **Polemoniā′ceae**, the phlox family: (without *cap.*) any plant of this genus. — *adj.* **polemoniā′ceous.** [Gr. *polemōnion*, St John's wort, or other plant.]

polenta *po-len′tə*, *n.* an Italian porridge of maize, barley, chestnut, or other meal. [It., — L. *polenta*, peeled barley.]

poley *pō′li*, (*Austr.*) *adj.* hornless. — Also *n.* [**poll¹**.]

poleyn *pō′lān*, *n.* a piece of armour protecting the knee. [M.E., — O.Fr. *polain*.]

polianite *pō′li-ən-īt*, *n.* a steel-grey mineral, manganese dioxide. [Gr. *poliainesthai*, to grow grey — *polios*, hoary.]

Polianthes *pol-i-an′thēz*, *n.* the tuberose genus of the amaryllid family. [Gr. *polios*, hoary, *anthos*, a flower.]

police *pəl-ēs′*, *n.* the system of regulations for the preservation of order and enforcement of law (*arch.*): the internal government of a state (*arch.*): a body of men and women employed to maintain order, etc.: its members collectively. — *adj.* of the police. — *v.t.* to control as police: to furnish with police: to guard or to put or keep in order. — **police burgh** see **burgh; police′-con′stable** a policeman of ordinary rank; **police′-court′** a former name for a borough court; **police′-dog′** a dog trained to help the police; **police′=force** a separately organised body of police; **police′=inspect′or** a superior officer of police who has charge of a department, next in rank to a superintendent; **police′-judge, police′-mag′istrate** one who formerly presided in a police-court; **police′man** a member of a police-force; **police′-manure′** (*Scot.*) street sweepings used as manure; **police′-off′ice, -ice** the headquarters of the police of a district, used also as a temporary place of confinement; **police′-off′icer** an ordinary policeman; **police′-state′** a country in which secret police are employed to detect and stamp out any opposition to the government in power; **police′-trap** a strategic

means whereby the police keep motor traffic under scrutiny and detect offenders against the law: a concealed and concerted timing arrangement to enforce a speed limit; **police′woman** a woman member of a police-force. [Fr., — L. *polītīa* — Gr. *polīteiā* — *polītēs*, a citizen — *polis*, a city.]

policy¹ *pol′i-si*, *n.* a constitution (*obs.*): the art of government: statecraft: a course of action: a system of administration guided more by interest than by principle: dexterity of management: prudence: cunning: in Scotland (sometimes in *pl.*), the pleasure-grounds around a mansion. [O.Fr. *policie* (Fr. *police*) — L. *polītīa* — Gr. *polīteiā* (see **police**); in Scots perh. influenced by L. *polītus*, embellished.]

policy² *pol′i-si*, *n.* a writing containing a contract of insurance: a kind of gambling by betting on the numbers to be drawn in a lottery (*U.S.*). — **pol′icy=holder** one who holds a contract of insurance; **pol′icy=shop** a place where the game of policy is played. [Fr. *police*, policy, app. — L.L. *apodissa*, a receipt — Gr. *apodeixis*, proof.]

poliomyelitis *pōl-i-ō-mī-ə-lī′tis* (or *pol-*), *n.* inflammation of the grey matter of the spinal cord: infantile paralysis. — *n.* **polio** (*pōl′i-ō, pol′*) short for poliomyelitis: a sufferer therefrom: — *pl.* **pol′ios.** — Also *adj.* [Gr. *polios*, grey, *myelos*, marrow.]

poliorcetic *pol-i-ər-set′ik*, *adj.* of or pertaining to the beleaguerment of towns or fortresses. — *n.sing.* **poliorcet′ics** siegecraft. [Gr. *poliorkētikos* — *poliorkein*, to besiege — *polis*, city, *erkos*, an enclosure.]

Polish *pō′lish*, *adj.* of Poland, or its people or its language. — *n.* the Slavonic language of the Poles.

polish *pol′ish*, *v.t.* to make smooth and glossy by rubbing: to bring to a finished state: to impart culture and refinement to. — *v.i.* to take a polish. — *n.* an act of polishing: gloss: refinement of manners: a substance applied to produce a polish. — *adjs.* **pol′ishable; pol′-ished** cultured, refined: accomplished. — *ns.* **pol′isher; pol′ishings** particles removed by polishing; **pol′ishment.** — **pol′ishing-paste; pol′ishing-powder; pol′ishing-slate** a diatomaceous slaty stone used for polishing glass, marble, and metals. — **polish off** (*coll.*) to finish off: to dispose of finally; **polish up (on)** to work at, study in order to improve. [O.Fr. *polir*, *polissant* — L. *polīre*, to polish.]

Politburo, -bureau *po-lit′bū-rō*, or *pol′*, *n.* in Communist countries, the policy-making committee, effectively the most powerful organ of the Communist Party's executive (in Russia from 1952 to 1966, name replaced by *Presidium*). [Russ. *politicheskoe*, political, *byuro*, bureau.]

polite *po-līt′*, *adj.* glossy, polished (*obs.*): refined: of courteous manners. — *adv.* **polite′ly.** — *ns.* **polite′ness; politesse** (*pol-ē-tes′*; Fr.) superficial politeness. — **polite literature** belles-lettres — poetry, essays, standard novels, etc., as distinguished from scientific treatises and the like. [L. *polītus*, pa.p. of *polīre*, to polish.]

politic *pol′i-tik*, *adj.* political (*rare*): constitutional (*obs.*): in accordance with good policy: acting or proceeding from motives of policy: prudent: discreet: astutely contriving or intriguing. — *adj.* **polit′ical** pertaining to policy or government: pertaining to parties differing in their views of government: interested or involved in politics: terrible (*obs.*). — *adv.* **polit′ically.** — *ns.* **politicas′ter** (*Milt.*; see also *-aster*) a petty politician; **politician** (*-tish′ən*) one versed in the science of government: one engaged in political life or statesmanship: one interested in party politics: a politic person: one who makes a profession or a game of politics: an intriguer (*U.S.*; *obs.*). — *adj.* (*Milt.*) politic. — *n.* **politicīsā′tion, -z-.** — *v.t.* **polit′icise, -ize** (*-i-sīz*) to make political. — *v.i.* to play the politician: to discuss politics. — *n.* **pol′iticking** engaging in political activity, as seeking votes. — *v.i.* **pol′itick.** — *adv.* **pol′iticly.** — **politico-** noun and adjective combining form denoting politics or political, as in *politico-economic, politico-industrial.* — *adj.* **polit′ico-econom′ic** of political economy: of politics and economics. — *ns.* **pol′itics** (*sing.*) the art or science of government: (*sing.*) the management of a political party: (*sing.* or *pl.*) political affairs or opinions: (*pl.*) manoeuvring and intriguing: (*pl.*) policy-making, as opposed to administration: (*pl.*) the civil rather than the military aspects of government; **politique** (*pol-ē-tēk;* Fr.) in French history, one of a moderate party between Huguenots and Catholics: a religious indifferentist: a temporiser. — **political animal** in the original Aristotelian sense, a social animal, one which lives in communities: one who is enthusiastic about or involved in politics: one who enjoys politicking; **political economy** the science of the production, distribution, and consumption of wealth; **political geography** that part of geography which deals with the division of the earth for purposes of government, as states, colonies, counties, and the work of man, as towns, canals, etc.; **political prisoner** one imprisoned for his or her political beliefs, activities etc.; **political science** the science or study of government, as to its principles, aims, methods, etc.; **political status** the status of a political prisoner; **political verse** Byzantine and modern Greek accentual verse, esp. iambic verse of fifteen syllables. — [Gr. *polítikos* — *polítēs,* a citizen.]

politico *pō-lit′i-kō,* (*coll.*) *n.* a politician, or a person who is interested in politics (usu. *derog.*): — *pl.* **polit′ico(e)s.** [It. or Sp.]

politique. See **politic.**

polity *pol′i-ti, n.* political organisation: form of political organisation, constitution: a body of people organised under a system of government. [Gr. *políteiā.*]

polka *pōl′kə, pol′, n.* a Bohemian dance or its tune, in 2-4 time with accent on the third quaver, invented about 1830: applied to various things fashionable at the same time, esp. a woman's jacket. — *v.i.* **polk** to dance a polka. — **pol′ka-dot** a pattern of dots. [Perh. Czech *půlka,* half-step; or from Pol. *polka,* a Polish woman.]

poll[1] *pōl, n.* the head: the hair of the head: the head and shoulders of a ling (*obs.*): the blunt end of the head of a hammer, miner's pick, etc.: a head as a unit in numbering, an individual: a number of individuals (*Shak.*): a register, esp. of voters: a voting: an aggregate of votes: the taking of a vote: a taking of public opinion by means of questioning (also **opinion poll**): a polled animal. — *adj.* polled: cut evenly (as in **deed poll,** opp. to **indenture**). — *v.t.* to cut the hair, horns, top (of a tree), edge (of a deed) from: to tax excessively, practise extortion upon (*arch.*): to receive or take the votes of: to receive, take, or cast (a vote): to receive (a stated number of votes): to question (someone) in a poll. — *v.i.* to practise extortion (*arch.*): to vote. — *adj.* **polled** shorn: pollarded: deprived of horns: hornless. — *ns.* **poll′er; poll′ing** (*comput.*) a technique by which each of several terminals connected to the same central computer is periodically interrogated in turn by the computer to determine whether it has a message to transmit; **poll′ster** one who carries out, or puts his faith in, a public opinion poll. — **poll′-axe** a pole-axe (q.v.); **poll′ing-booth** the place, esp. the partially-enclosed cubicle, where a voter records his vote; **poll′-money,** **poll′-tax** a tax of so much a head — i.e. on each person alike. — **at the head of the poll** having the greatest number of votes at an election. [Cf. obs. Du. and L.G. *polle,* top of the head.]

poll[2] *pol,* (*Cambridge*) *n.* the mass of students who do not seek or obtain honours: a pass-degree. — **poll′= degree′; poll′man.** [Said to be from Gr. *hoi polloi,* the many.]

Poll, poll *pol, n.* a parrot. — **poll′-parrot.** — *v.t.* and *v.i.* to parrot. [*Poll,* a common name for a parrot; see **Polly.**]

pollack *pol′ək, n.* a common fish of the cod family, with long narrow jaw and no barbel: extended to the coalfish. — Also **poll′ock.** [Ety. obscure; connection with Gael. *pollag* doubtful.]

pollan *pol′ən, n.* an Irish whitefish, esp. that (*Coregonus*

pollan) found in Lough Neagh. [Perh. Ir. *poll,* lake; cf. **powan.**]

pollard *pol′ərd, n.* a tree having the whole crown cut off, leaving it to send out new branches from the top of the stem: a hornless animal of horned kind: fine bran: flour or meal containing it: a base foreign coin bearing a head (*obs.*). — *adj.* pollarded: awnless: bald. — *v.t.* to make a pollard of. [**poll[1].**]

poll-axe. Same as **pole-axe.**

pollen *pol′ən, n.* the fertilising powder formed in the anthers of flowers. — *v.t.* to cover or fertilise with pollen. — *n.* **pollenos′is** hay fever. — *v.t.* **poll′inate** to convey pollen to. — *ns.* **pollinā′tion; poll′inātor.** — *adjs.* **pollin′ic** of or pertaining to pollen; **pollinif′erous** bearing, producing, pollen. — *n.* **pollin′ium** an agglutinated mass of pollen-grains: — *pl.* **pollin′ia.** — **pollen analysis** use of pollen grains in peat bogs, etc., as a means of determining past vegetation and climates or the age of fossil remains; **poll′en-basket** a hollow in a bee's hindleg in which pollen is carried; **pollen count** the amount of pollen in the atmosphere, estimated from deposits on slides exposed to the air; **poll′en-grain** a grain of pollen, the microspore in flowering plants; **poll′en-sac** a cavity in an anther in which pollen is formed, the microsporangium of flowering plants; **poll′en-tube** an outgrowth from a pollen-grain by which the gametes are conveyed to the ovule. [L. *pollen, -inis,* fine flour.]

pollent *pol′ənt, adj.* strong. [L. *pollēns, -entis,* pr.p. of *pollēre,* to be strong.]

pollex *pol′eks, n.* the thumb or its analogue: — *pl.* **pollices** (*pol′i-sēz*). — *adj.* **poll′ical.** [L. *pollex, -icis.*]

pollice verso *pol′i-sē vûr′sō, pol′i-ke ver′, wer′sō,* (L.) with the thumb turned up or outwards (now often assumed, most prob. wrongly, to mean downwards) — the signal made by the spectators for the death of a Roman gladiator.

pollicie, pollicy (*Spens.*). Same as **policy.**

pollicitation *pol-is-i-tā′shən, n.* a promise: a promise which has not yet been accepted. [L. *pollicitātiō, -ōnis.*]

pollination, pollinic, etc. See **pollen.**

polliwig, -wog. See **pollywog.**

pollock. Same as **pollack.**

pollster. See **poll[1].**

pollusion *po-lōō′zhən, -lū′,* (*Love's Lab. Lost,* IV, iii) *n.* Goodman Dull's blunder for **allusion.**

pollute *po-lōōt′, -lūt′, v.t.* to befoul physically: to contaminate, make (any feature of the environment) offensive or harmful to human, animal, or plant life: to make unclean morally: to defile ceremonially, profane. — *adj.* defiled. — *n.* **pollu′tant** something that pollutes. — *adj.* **pollut′ed.** — *adv.* **pollut′edly.** — *ns.* **pollut′edness; pollut′er; pollution** (*po-lōō′shən, -lū′*). — *adj.* **pollu′tive** causing pollution. [L. *polluĕre, pollūtus* — *pol-,* a form of *prō* or *per, luĕre,* to wash.]

Pollux *pol′uks, n.* the twin brother of Castor (*myth.*): a star in the constellation of the Twins. [L. for Gr. *Polydeukēs.*]

Polly *pol′i, n.* a form of **Molly:** a parrot. [Cf. **Poll.**]

polly *pol′i, n.* slang shortening of **Apollinaris (water).**

pollyanna *pol-i-an′ə, n.* one whose naïve optimism may verge on the insufferable (also with *cap.*). — *adj.* **pollyann′(a)ish.** — *n.* **pollyann′aism** a pollyannaish observation. [From *Pollyanna,* fictional creation of Eleanor Hodgman Porter (1868–1920).]

pollywog, polliwog *pol′i-wog,* **pollywig, polliwig** *-wig, ns.* a tadpole. — Also **porwigg′le.** [M.E. *pollwyggle* — **poll[1], wiggle.**]

polo[1] *pō′lō, n.* a game like hockey on horseback — of Oriental origin: a similar aquatic (*water-polo*), bicycle (*bicycle polo*), or skating (*rink polo*) game: a jersey wit a polo neck: — *pl.* **pō′los.** — *n.* **po′loist.** — **polo neck** a pullover collar fitting the neck closely and doub over, as orig. in a polo jersey. [Balti (Tibetan in Kashmir) *polo,* polo ball; Tibetan *pulu.*]

polo[2] *pō′lō, n.* a Spanish gypsy dance: — *pl.* **pō′los.**

an Andalusian popular song.]
polonaise *pol-ə-nāz'*, *n.* a woman's bodice and skirt in one piece, showing an underskirt: a similar child's garment once worn in Scotland: a Polish national dance or promenade of slow movement in 3-4 time: a musical form in the same rhythm.   [Fr., Polish (fem.).]
Polonia *pol-ō'ni-ə*, *n.* the mediaeval Latin name for Poland. — *adj.* and *n.* **Polo'nian.** — *n.* **Polonisation, -z-** (*pō-lən-ī-zā'shən*). — *v.t.* and *v.i.* **po'lonise, -ize** to make or become Polish. — *ns.* **po'lonism** a Polish idiom or characteristic; **polonium** (*pol-ō'ni-əm*) a radioactive element (at. numb. 84; symbol Po) discovered by Mme Curie (a Pole); **polo'ny, -ie** (*Scot.*) a child's polonaise.
polony[1] *po-lō'ni*, *n.* a dry sausage of partly cooked meat. [Prob. *Bologna*, in Italy; perh. *Polonia*.]
polony[2]. See **Polonia.**
polt *pōlt*, *n.* a hard blow (now *dial.*): a club (*obs.*). — *v.t.* (*dial.*) to beat. — **polt'foot** a club-foot. — *adj.* **club-footed.** — *adj.* **polt'-footed.**   [Origin obscure.]
poltergeist *pōl'*, *pol'tər-gīst*, *n.* a mysterious invisible agency asserted to throw things about: a noisy ghost. [Ger. *poltern*, to make a racket, *Geist*, ghost.]
poltroon *pol-trōōn'* (*Shak.* **poul'troone**) *n.* a dastard. — Also *adj.* — *n.* **poltroon'ery** want of spirit.   [Fr. *poltron* — It. *poltrone* — *poltro*, lazy.]
poluphloisboio(tato)tic. See **polyphloisbic** under **poly-.**
polverine *pol'vər-ēn*, (*obs.*) *n.* glass-makers' potash.   [It. *polverino* — L. *pulvis, pulvĕris*, dust.]
poly *pol'i*, *n.* and *adj.* a coll. shortening of **polytechnic(al)** (see below): — *pl.* **pol'ys.**
poly- *pol'i-, pol-i'-*, in composition, many: several: much: denoting a polymer, as *polyethylene* (see below): affecting more than one part (*med.*). — *adjs.* **polyacid** (*-as'id*) having several replaceable hydrogen atoms: capable of replacing several hydrogen atoms of an acid; **pol'yact** (Gr. *aktīs, -īnos*, ray), **polyactī'nal** (or *-akt'in-əl*), **polyact'ine** many rayed. — *n.pl.* **Polyadel'phia** (Gr. *adelphos*, brother) in Linnaeus's system a class of plants with three or more bundles of stamens. — *adj.* **polyadel'phous** (of stamens) united in several bundles: having the stamens so united. — *n.* **polyam'ide** a polymeric amide, as nylon. — *n.pl.* **Polyan'dria** (Gr. *anēr, andros*, man, male) in Linnaeus's system a class of plants with many stamens inserted in the receptacle. — *adj.* **polyan'drous** having or allowing several husbands or male mates (at a time): having a large and indefinite number of stamens or of antheridia (*bot.*). — *ns.* **pol'yandry** (or *-an'*) the condition or practice of being polyandrous: the social usage of some peoples in certain stages of civilisation in which a woman normally has several husbands; **polyan'thus** (Gr. *anthos*, flower) a many-flowered supposed hybrid between cowslip and primrose: also applied to certain hybrid roses: — *pl.* **polyan'thuses.** — *adj.* **pol'yarch** (*-ärk*; Gr. *archē*, origin) having many xylem strands. — *n.* **pol'yarchy** (*-ärk-i*; Gr. *archein*, to rule) government by many persons. — *adjs.* **polyatom'ic** (*chem.*) having many atoms, or replaceable atoms or groups: multivalent; **polyax'ial** (L. *axis*), **polyax'on** (Gr. *axōn*, axis) having many axes or several axis cylinders. — *n.* a monaxonic sponge spicule. — *adjs.* **polyaxon'ic; polybās'ic** capable of reacting with several equivalents of an acid: of acids, having several replaceable hydrogen atoms. — *n.* **polycar'bonate** any of a range of strong thermoplastics. — *adjs.* **polycarp'ic** (Gr. *karpos*, fruit) fruiting many times, or year after year; **polycarp'ous** polycarpic: having an apocarpous gynaeceum; **polycent'ric** multicentric. — *n.pl.* **Polychaeta** (*-kē'tə*; Gr. *chaitē*, bristle) a class of marine chaetopods with numerous bristles. — *ns.* **pol'ychaete** (*-kēt*) any worm of the Polychaeta; **polychlor'oprene** neoprene; **pol'ychrest** (*-krest*; Gr. *polychrēstos* — *chrēstos*, useful) a thing, esp. a medicine, useful in several ways. — *adj.* **polychroic** (*-krō'ik*) pleochroic. — *n.* **pol'ychroism.** — *adj.* **pol'ychrome** (*-krōm*; Gr. *chrōma*, colour) many-loured. — *n.* a work of art (esp. a statue) in several ours: varied colouring. — *adjs.* **polychromat'ic,**

polychrom'ic. — *ns.* **pol'ychromy** the art of decorat. in many colours; **pol'yclinic** a general clinic or hospita — *adj.* **polycon'ic** pertaining to or composed of many cones. — *adj.* and *n.* **pol'ycotton** (of) a material made from polyester and cotton. — *adjs.* **polycotyle'donous** with more than two cotyledons; **polycrot'ic** (Gr. *krotos*, a beat) of the pulse, having several beats to each heart-beat. — *ns.* **polyc'rotism; pol'ycrystal** an object composed of several or many variously orientated crystals. — *adj.* **polycrys'talline.** — *n.* **pol'yculture** the simultaneous production of several different crops and types of livestock in one region. — *adj.* **polycyclic** (*-sī'klik*; Gr. *kyklos*, wheel) having many circles, rings, whorls, turns, or circuits: containing more than one ring of atoms in the molecule. — *n.* **polycythaemia** (*-sī-thē'mi-ə*; Gr. *kytos*, a vessel, as if cell, *haima*, blood) an excess of red blood corpuscles. — *adj.* **polydac'tyl** having more than the normal number of fingers or toes. — Also *n.* — *ns.* **polydac'tylism, -dac'tyly.** — *adj.* **polydac'tylous.** — *ns.* **polyde'monism, polydae'monism** the belief in and worship of numerous supernatural powers; **polydip'sia** (Gr. *dipsa*, thirst) excessive thirst. — *adjs.* **polyem'bryonate; polyembryonic** (*-on'ik*). — *ns.* **polyembryony** (*-em'bri-ən-i*) formation of more than one embryo from one ovule or from one fertilised ovum; **polyes'ter** any of a range of polymerised esters, some thermoplastic, some thermosetting; **polyeth'-ylene, pol'ythene** a generic name for certain thermo-plastics, polymers of ethylene; **Polygala** (*pol-ig'ə-lə*; Gr. *polygalon*, milkwort — *gala*, milk) the milkwort genus, giving name to the fam. **Polygalā'ceae** (without *cap.*) any plant of this genus. — *adj.* **polygalaceous** (*-lā'shəs*). — *n.pl.* **Polygamia** (*pol-i-gā'mi-ə*; Gr. *gamos*, marriage) in Linnaeus's classification, a class having male, female, and hermaphrodite flowers. — *n.* **pol'ygam** a plant of this class. — *adj.* **polygamic** (*-gam'ik*). — *n.* **polygamist** (*pol-ig'*). — *adj.* **polyg'amous.** — *adv.* **polyg'amously.** — *ns.* **polygamy** (*pol-ig'ə-mi*) the rule, custom, or condition of marriage to more than one person at a time, or (now rarely) in life: sometimes used for polygyny: mating with more than one in the same breeding season (*zool.*): occurrence of male, female, and hermaphrodite flowers on the same or on different plants (*bot.*); **pol'ygene** (*-jēn*) any of a group of genes that control a single continuous character (e.g. height); **polygen'esis** multiple origin, esp. of mankind. — *adjs.* **polygenet'ic** of polygenesis: springing from several sources: of dyes, giving different colours with different mordants; **polygen'ic** polygenetic: forming more than one compound with a univalent element. — *ns.* **polyg'enism** belief in multiple origin, esp. of mankind; **polyg'enist.** — *adj.* **polyg'enous** of multiple origin or composition. — *n.* **polyg'eny** polygenesis. — *adj.* **pol'yglot** (Gr. *polyglōttos* — *glōtta*, tongue) in, of, speaking, or writing, many languages. — *n.* one who speaks or writes many languages: a collection of versions in different languages of the same work, esp. a Bible. — Also **pol'yglott.** — *adjs.* **polyglott'al, polyglott'ic, polyglott'ous.** — *n.* **pol'ygon** (*-gon, -gən*; Gr. *gōniā*, angle) a plane figure bounded by straight lines, esp. more than four: an object in the form of a polygon, esp. in the building of earthworks and fortifications. — *adj.* **polyg'onal** (polygonal numbers figurate numbers). — *adv.* **polyg'onally.** — *ns.* **Polygon'atum** (*polygonăton* — *gony, -atos*, knee) the Solomon's seal genus of the lily family: (without *cap.*) any plant of this genus; **Polyg'onum** (Gr. *polygonon*) the knot-grass genus, with swollen joints and sheathing stipules, of the dock family **Polygonā'ceae**: (without *cap.*) any plant of this genus. — *adj.* **polygonā'ceous.** — *ns.* **polyg'ony** (*Spens.*) bistort; **pol'ygraph** a copying, multiplying, or tracing apparatus: a copy: an instrument which measures very small changes in body temperature, pulse rate, respiration, etc., and which is often used as a lie detector. — *adj.* **polygraph'ic.** — *n.* **polygraphy** (*pol-ig'rə-fi*) voluminous writing: the use of the polygraph as a lie detector. —

n.pl. **Polygynia** (*-jin'*; Gr. *gynē*, woman, female) in various Linnaean classes of plants, an order with more than twelve styles. — *adjs.* **polygyn'ian** of the Polygynia; **polygynous** (*-lij'* or *-lig'i-nəs*) having several wives: mating with several females: having several styles: polygynian. — *ns.* **polygyny** (*-lij'* or *-lig'*) the custom, practice, or condition of having a plurality of wives or styles: the habit of mating with more than one female; **polyhalite** (*-hal'īt*; Gr. *hals*, salt) a triclinic mineral, sulphate of magnesium, potassium, and calcium. — *adjs.* **polyhēd'ral; polyhedric** (*-hēd'*, *-hed'*). — *ns.* **polyhēd'ron** (or *-hed'*; Gr. *hedrā*, seat) a solid figure or body bounded by plane faces (esp. more than six): — *pl.* **-rons, -ra; polyhis'tor** (Gr. *polyistōr — histŏreein*, to inquire, learn) a person of great and varied learning; **polyhistorian** (*-tō'ri-ən, -tö'*). — *adj.* **polyhistoric** (*-tor'-ik*). — *ns.* **polyhis'tory** (*-tər-i*); **polyhy'brid** a cross between parents differing in several heritable characters. — *adj.* **polyhy'dric** having several hydroxyl groups. — *ns.* **Polyhymnia** (*pol-i-him'ni-ə*), **Polymnia** (*pol-im'ni-ə*; Gr. *Polўmnia* for *Polyymnia — hymnos*, hymn, ode) the muse of the sublime lyric; **polyī'soprene** a rubber-like polymer of isoprene; **polylemm'a** (*logic*; Gr. *lēmma*, an assumption) a form of argument in which the maintainer of a certain proposition is committed to accept one of several propositions all of which contradict his original contention; **polymas'tia, polymast'ism, pol'ymasty** (Gr. *mastos*, breast) the presence of supernumerary breasts or nipples. — *adj.* **polymas'tic.** — *n.* **pol'ymath** (Gr. *polymathēs —* the root of *manthanein*, to learn) one who knows many arts and sciences. — *adj.* **polymath'ic.** — *ns.* **polym'athy** much and varied learning; **pol'ymer** (Gr. *meros*, part; *chem.*) one of a series of substances alike in percentage composition, but differing in molecular weight, especially one of those of higher molecular weight as produced by polymerisation; **polymerase** (*pol'i-mər-ās*) an enzyme present in cell nuclei which promotes the polymerisation of DNA. — *adj.* **polymeric** (*-mer'ik*) of, in a relation of, or manifesting, polymerism. — *ns.* **polym'eride** a polymer; **polymerīsā'tion, -z-.** — *v.t.* **polym'erise, -ize** to combine to form a more complex molecule having the same empirical formula as the simpler ones combined: to render polymerous. — *v.i.* to change into a polymer. — *n.* **polym'erism.** — *adj.* **polym'erous** having many parts: having many parts in a whorl (*bot.*). — *ns.* **polym'ery** condition of being polymerous; **Polymnia** see **Polyhymnia** above; **pol'ymorph** (Gr. *polymorphos*, many-formed — *morphē*, form) any one of several forms in which the same thing may occur: an organism occurring in several forms: a substance crystallising in several systems. — *adj.* **polymorph'ic.** — *n.* **polymorph'ism.** — *adj.* **polymorph'ous.** — *n.* **polymyositis** (*-mī-ō-sī'tis*; Gr. *mȳs, mȳos*, muscle) inflammation of several muscles at the same time. — *adj.* **Polynē'sian** (Gr. *nēsos*, an island) of *Polynesia*, its prevailing race of brown people, or their languages (a division of the Austronesian). — *n.* a native of Polynesia: a member of the brown race of Polynesia. — *n.* **polyneuritis** (*-nūr-ī'tis*; Gr. *neuron*, a nerve) simultaneous inflammation of several nerves. — *adj.* and *n.* **polynō'mial** multinomial. — *ns.* **polynō'mialism; polynucleotide** (*pol-i-nū'kli-ə-tīd*) a compound (e.g. nucleic acid) that is made up of a number of nucleotides; **polyomino** (*pol-i-om'in-ō*; on the false analogy of *domino*) a flat, many-sided shape made up of a number of identical squares placed edge to edge: — *pl.* **-nos; polyonym** (*pol'i-ō-nim*; Gr. *onyma*, a form of *onoma*, name) a name consisting of several words. — *adjs.* **polyonym'ic** of more than two words; **polyon'ymous** having many names. — *ns.* **polyon'ymy** multiplicity of names for the same thing; **polyp, polype** (*pol'ip*; L. *polypus, -ī*, adopted, and transformed to 2nd declension, from Gr. *polypous, -podos — pous*, foot; see **polypus**) orig. an octopus or cuttlefish (*obs.*): later extended to other animals with many arms or tentacles, esp. coelenterates and Polyzoa: an individual

of a colonial animal: a pedunculated tumour growing from mucous membrane: — *pl.* **pol'yps, polypes** (*pol'-ips*), **polypi** (*pol'i-pī*); **pol'ypary** the common investing structure of a colony of polyps; **polypep'tide** a peptide in which many amino-acids are linked to form a chain. — *adj.* **polypet'alous** with free petals. — *n.* **polyphagia** (*-fā'ji-ə*; Gr. *phagein* (aorist), to eat) bulimia: the habit of eating many different kinds of food. — *adj.* **polyphagous** (*po-lif'ə-gəs*) eating many different kinds of food: eating much. — *ns.* **polyph'agy** (*-ji*) the character of being polyphagous; **polyphar'macy** (Gr. *pharmakeiā*, use of drugs) the (esp. indiscriminate and excessive) use of many different drugs in treating a disease. — *adjs.* **pol'yphase** having several alternating electric currents of equal frequency with uniformly spaced phase differences; **polyphasic** (*-fāz'ik*) going through several phases of activity followed by rest in any twenty-four hours; **Polyphē'mian, Polyphē'mic.** — *n.* **Polyphē'mus** (Gr. *Polyphēmos*) the Cyclops blinded by Odysseus. — *adjs.* **polyphiloprogenitive** (*pol-i-fil-ō-prō-jen'i-tiv*) of imagination or inventiveness, very fertile; **polyphloisbic** (*pol-i-flois'bik*; Gr. *polyphloisbos — phloisbos*, din), **poluphloisboiotic** (*pol-ōō-flois-boi-ot'ik*), **polyphloesboean** (*pol-i-flēs-bē'ən*, the *oi* and *oe* from the genitive ending in Homer's phrase *polyphloisboio thalassēs*, of the much-roaring sea) loud-roaring; **poluphloisboiotatot'ic** (*Thackeray*; as if from a Gr. superl. in *-otatos*). — *ns.* **pol'yphon(e)** (*-fon, -fōn*; Gr. *phōnē*, a voice) a lute-like musical instrument: a musical box playing tunes from perforated metal discs; **polyphone** (*pol'i-fōn*) a symbol with more than one phonetic value. — *adj.* **polyphonic** (*-fon'ik*) many-voiced: of polyphones: of polyphony. — *ns.* **pol'yphonist** a contrapuntist; **polyph'ony** composition of music in parts each with an independent melody of its own. — *adjs.* **polyphyletic** (*pol-i-fil-et'ik*, or *-fīl-*; Gr. *phyletikos*, pertaining to a tribesman — *phylē*, a tribe) of multiple origin: descended by convergent lines from several ancestral groups; **polyphyllous** (*pol-i-fil'əs*; Gr. *phyllon*, leaf) having the perianth leaves free; **polyphȳ'odont** having more than two successive dentitions. — *ns.* **pol'ypide, pol'ypite** a polyp of a colonial animal; **polyp'idom** a polypary (Gr. *domos*, house). — *adj.* **pol'ypine.** — *n.pl.* **Polyplacoph'ora** (Gr. *plax, plakos*, a plate, slab) an order of molluscs, bilaterally symmetrical, with shell composed of eight transverse dorsal plates — the chitons, etc. — *adj.* **polyploid** (*pol'i-ploid*; on the analogy of *haploid, diploid*) having more than twice the normal haploid number of chromosomes. — *ns.* **pol'yploidy** the polyploid condition; **polypod** (*pol'i-pod*) an animal with many feet: polypody; **Polypodium** (*-pō'di-əm*; Gr. *podion*, dim. of *pous*, a foot) the typical genus of **Polypodiā'ceae**, the family with stalked sporangia and vertical annulus to which most ferns belong — so named from the many-footed appearance of the rhizome; **polypody** (*pol'i-pod-i*) any fern of the genus Polypodium, esp. *P. vulgare.* — *adj.* **pol'ypoid** like a polypus. — *ns.* **Polyporus** (*po-lip'ə-rəs*; Gr. *poros*, a pore) a large genus of pore fungi (q.v.), often forming hoof-like and bracket-like growths on trees; **polypō'sis** the presence or development of polypi. — *adj.* **pol'ypous** of the nature of a polyp. — *ns.* **polyprop'ylene** a polymer of propylene, similar in properties to polyethylene; **polyprō'todont** (Gr. *prōtos*, first, *odous, odontos*, tooth) any member of the **Polyprotodont'ia**, the suborder of marsupials, including opossums, dasyures, etc., with many small incisors; **Polyp'terus** (Gr. *pteron*, a fin) an African genus of Crossopterygian river fishes, with the dorsal fin represented by detached rays; **polyptych** (*pol'ip-tik*; Gr. *ptychos*, a fold) a picture, altarpiece, etc., consisting of four or more panels hinged or folding together. — **polypus** (*pol'i-pəs*; Gr. *polypous*) a pedunculated tumour growing from mucous membrane: — *pl.* **pol'ypī; pol'yrhythm** the simultaneous combination of different rhythms in a piece of music. — *adj.* **polyrhyth'mic.** — *ns.* **polysaccharide** (*-sak'ə-rīd*) a carbohydrate of a class including starch, insulin, etc., that hydrolyses into more than one simple sugar; **polyse'mant** (*-sē'*), **pol'yseme** (*-sēm*) a word with more than one meaning; **pol'ysemy.** — *adj.* **polysep'alous** having the sepals separate from each other. — *ns.* **polysilox'ane** any of a number of polymers which are the basis of silicone chemistry; **pol'ysome** a group of ribosomes linked by a molecule of ribonucleic acid and functioning as a unit in the synthesis of proteins; **pol'ysomy** a condition in which one or more extra chromosomes, esp. sex chromosomes, are present in the cells of the body; **Polys'tichum** (*-kəm*; Gr. *stichos*, a row) a genus of shield-ferns also known by the name Aspidium. — *adjs.* **polysty'lar, pol'ystyle** (Gr. *stylos*, column) having many columns. — *n.* **polysty'rene** a polymer of styrene having good mechanical properties, resistant to moisture and to chemicals. — *adjs.* **polysyllabic** (*-ab'ik*), **-al.** — *adv.* **polysyllab'ically.** — *ns.* **polysyllab'icism, polysyll'abism; polysyll'able** a word of many or of more than three syllables; **polysyll'ogism** a series of syllogisms, the conclusion of one serving as the premiss for the next; **polysyndeton** (*pol-i-sin'di-tən*; Gr. *syndeton*, a conjunction — *syn*, together, *deein*, to bind; *rhet.*) figurative repetition of connectives or conjunctions; **polysynthesis** (*-sin'thi-sis*). — *adjs.* **polysynthet'ic, -al** made up of many separate elements: built up of a number of small crystals in parallel growth (*crystal.*): combining many simple words of a sentence in one, as in the native languages of America — also called *incorporating* (*philol.*). — *adv.* **polysynthet'ically.** — *ns.* **polysynthet'icism** (*-i-sizm*), **polysyn'thetism** the character of being polysynthetic. — *adj.* **polytechnic** (*-tek'nik*; Gr. *technikos* — *technē*, art) of many arts or technical subjects. — *n.* a school where such subjects are taught to an advanced level. — *adjs.* **polytech'nical; polytene** (*pol'i-tēn*; L. *taenia*, band) (of abnormally large chromosomes) composed of many reduplicated strands. — *n.* **polytetrafluor(o)eth'ylene** a plastic with non-adhesive surface properties. — *adj.* **polythalamous** (*-thal'ə-məs*; Gr. *thalamos*, a chamber) having several cells or chambers. — *ns.* **polytheism** (*pol'i-thē-izm*; Gr. *theos*, a god) the doctrine of a plurality of gods; **pol'ytheist.** — *adjs.* **polytheist'ic, -al.** — *adv.* **polytheist'ically.** — *n.* **pol'ythene** see polyethylene. — *adjs.* **polytocous** (*pol-it'ə-kəs*; Gr. *tokos*, birth) producing many or several at a birth or in a clutch; **polyton'al.** — *ns.* **polytonal'ity** use at the same time of two or more musical keys; **Polytrichum** (*pol-it'ri-kəm*; Gr. *thrix, trichos*, hair) a genus of tall hairy-capped mosses. — *adjs.* **polytypic** (*-tip'ik*) having many types and representatives; **polyunsat'urated** (*chem.*) containing more than one carbon-carbon double bond in the molecule (**polyunsaturated fats, oils** glycerides of polyunsaturated fatty acids). — *ns.* **polyur'ethane** any of a range of resins, both thermoplastic and thermosetting, used in production of foamed materials, coatings, etc.; **polyu'ria** (*med.*) excessive secretion of urine. — *adj.* **polyvalent** (*pol-i-vā'lənt, pol-iv'ə-lənt*) multivalent. — *n.* **polyvi'nyl** a vinyl polymer. — Also *adj.* (**polyvinyl chloride** a vinyl plastic used as a rubber substitute for coating electric wires, cables, etc., and as a dress and furnishing fabric; abbrev. **PVC**). — *n.* **pol'ywater** a supposed form of water, said to be a polymer, with properties different from those of ordinary water. — *n.pl.* **Polyzō'a** (Gr. *zōion*, an animal) a phylum of aquatic animals, almost all colonial, with cup-shaped body, U-shaped food-canal, and a wreath of tentacles about the mouth: — *sing.* **polyzo'on.** — *n.* and *adj.* **polyzo'an.** — *adj.* **polyzoarial** (*-ā'ri-əl*). — *ns.* **polyzoā'rium, polyzō'ary** a polyzoan colony, or its supporting skeleton. — *adjs.* **polyzō'ic** having many zooids: pertaining to the Polyzoa; **polyzo'nal** (Gr. *zōnē*, belt) composed of many zones or belts; **polyzō'oid** like, or of the nature of, a polyzoon. [Gr. *polys, poleia, poly*, much.]

polyacid . . . to . . . **Polynesian.** See poly-.
polynia, polynya *pol-in'i-ə, -in'yə, n.* open water among

sea ice, esp. Arctic. [Russ. *polyn'ya*.]
polynomial . . . to . . . **polyzooid.** See poly-.
pom¹ *pom, (coll.) n.* short for Pomeranian dog.
pom², Pom *pom, (Austr. and N.Z.) n.* and *adj.* short for pommy (q.v.).
pomace *pum'is, n.* crushed apples for cider-making, or the residue after pressing: anything crushed to pulp, esp. after oil has been expressed. — **pom'ace-fly** a fruit-fly (Drosophila). [App. L.L. *pōmācium*, cider — L. *pōmum*, apple, etc.]
pomaceous. See pome.
pomade *pom-äd', n.* ointment for the hair — Latinised as **pomā'tum.** — *v.t.* to anoint with pomade. [Fr. *pommade* — It. *pomada, pomata*, lip-salve — L. *pōmum*, an apple.]
Pomak *pō-mäk', n.* a Bulgarian Muslim.
pomander *pom-* or *pōm-an'dər, n.* a ball of perfumes, or a perforated globe or box in which this or a similarly perfumed preparation is kept or carried. [O.Fr. *pomme d'ambre*, apple of amber.]
pomato *pom-ä'tō, -ā'tō, n.* a tomato grafted on a potato: — *pl.* **poma'toes.** [Portmanteau-word.]
pomatum. Same as **pomade.**
pombe *pom'be, n.* any of various Central and East African alcoholic drinks. [Swahili.]
pome *pōm, n.* an apple (*rare*): a fruit constructed like an apple, the enlarged fleshy receptacle enclosing a core formed from the carpels: a king's globe or mound: a priest's hand-warming ball of hot water. — *adj.* **pomaceous** (*-ā'shəs*) relating to, consisting of, or resembling, apples: of the apple family or the apple section of the rose family. — *ns.* **pome'roy, pomroy** (*pom', pum'roi*) an old variety of apple; **pom'iculture** fruit growing: pomology. — *adjs.* **pomif'erous** bearing apples, pomes, or fruit generally; **pomolog'ical.** — *ns.* **pomol'ogist; pomol'ogy** the study of fruit-growing. — **pome'-cit'ron** the citron; **pome'-water, pom'water** (*Shak.*) a sweet juicy apple. [L. *pōmum*, a fruit, an apple.]
pomegranate *pom'i-gran-it, pom'ə-, pom', formerly pom-, pum-gran'it, n.* an Oriental fruit much cultivated in warm countries, with a thick leathery rind and numerous seeds with pulpy edible seed-coats: the tree (*Punica granatum*; fam. Punicaceae) bearing it. [O.Fr. *pome grenate* — L. *pōmum*, an apple, *grānātum*, having many grains.]
pomelo *pum', or pom'il-ō, n.* the shaddock: the grapefruit — cf. **pompelmoose:** — *pl.* **pom'elos.** [Ety. dub.]
Pomeranian *pom-i-rā'ni-ən, adj.* of *Pomerania.* — *n.* a native of Pomerania: a spitz or Pomeranian dog, a cross from the Eskimo dog, with a sharp-pointed face and an abundant white, creamy, or black coat.
pomeroy. See pome.
Pomfret a spelling representing the older pronunciation (*pum'frit*) of **Pontefract** *pon'ti-frakt*, a town in Yorkshire. — **Pomfret-** (*pum', pom'*), **Pon'tefract-cake** a round flat liquorice sweetmeat made there. [A.Fr. *Pontfret*, L. *pōns, pontis*, bridge, *fractus*, broken.]
pomfret *pom'frit, n.* any of several fishes, including an East Indian fish valued as food. [Earlier *pamflet* — Fr. *pample* — Port. *pampo*.]
pomiculture, etc. See pome.
pommel *pum'l, n.* a knob (*obs.*): a ball-shaped finial: a knob on a sword-hilt: the high part of a saddle-bow: a heavy-headed ramming tool: either of two handles on top of a gymnastics horse. — *v.t.* (usu. spelt **pummel,** q.v.). — *adjs.* **pomm'elled** having a pommel — in heraldry also **pommelé** (*pom'*), **pomm'etty.** [O.Fr. *pomel* (Fr. *pommeau*) — L. *pōmum*, an apple.]
pommy *pom'i, (Austr. and N.Z.) n.* an immigrant from the British Isles: a British (esp. English) person in general. — Also *adj.* [Origin obscure; perh. from **pomegranate,** alluding to the colour of the immigrants' cheeks or rhyming slang for *jimmygrant*, immigrant.]
pomoerium *pō-mē'ri-əm, n.* an open space around a town, within and without the walls. [L. *pōmoerium*, app. for *postmoerium* — *post* and *moiros*, old form of *mūrus*, wall.]

pomologist, etc. See **pome**.

Pomona *pō-mō′nə, n.* the Roman goddess of fruits. [L. *Pōmōna* — *pōmum*, fruit, apple.]

pomp *pomp, n.* a procession: great show or display: ceremony: ostentation: vain show: worldly vanity: consequential bearing. — *n.* **pomposity** (*-os′i-ti*) solemn affectation of dignity: a ridiculously pompous action, expression, or person. — *adj.* **pomp′ous** stately (*arch.*): self-important. — *adv.* **pomp′ously.** — *n.* **pomp′ousness.** [Fr. *pompe* — L. *pompa* — Gr. *pompē*, a sending, escort, procession — *pempein*, to send.]

pompadour *pom′pə-dōor, n.* a fashion of dressing women's hair by rolling it back from the forehead over a cushion, a corsage with low square neck: a pattern for silk, with pink, blue, and gold leaves and flowers: a pink colour. — *adj.* in, pertaining to, the style of hairdressing or dress described above, associated with Mme de Pompadour's time. [Marquise de *Pompadour*, 1721–64.]

pompano *pomp′ə-nō, n.* a general name for carangoid fishes, esp. American food-fishes of the genus *Trachynotus:* — *pl.* **pomp′ano(s).** [Sp. *pámpano*, a fish of another family.]

Pompeian *pom-pē′ən, adj.* pertaining to *Pompeii*, a city buried by an eruption of Mount Vesuvius in A.D 79, excavated since 1755. — **Pompei′an-red′** a red colour like that on the walls of Pompeian houses.

pompelmoose *pom′pəl-mōōs, n.* the shaddock, esp. the grapefruit. — Also **pam′pelmoose, -mouse, pom′pelmous(e), pum′ple-nose, pom′pelo** (*pl.* **pom′pelos**), **pom′-elo.** [Du. *pompelmoes*; origin obscure.]

pompey *pom′pi*, (*Dickens*) *v.t.* to pamper (q.v.).

Pompey *pom′pi*, (*slang*) *n.* Portsmouth.

pompholyx *pom′fō-liks, n.* a vesicular eruption chiefly on the palms and soles: impure zinc oxide. — *adj.* **pomphol′ygous.** [Gr. *pompholyx, -ygos*, bubble, slag — *pomphos*, a blister.]

pompier *pom′pi-ər*, or (Fr.) *pɔ̃-pyā, adj.* of art, conventional, traditional, uninspired. [Fr., see next.]

pompier-ladder *pom′pi-ər-lad′ər*, or (Fr.) *pɔ̃-pyā, n.* a fireman's ladder, a pole with cross-bars and hook. [Fr. *pompier*, fireman — *pompe*, pump.]

pompion *pump′i-ən*. See **pumpkin.**

pompom[1] *pom′pom*, (*coll.*) *n.* a machine-gun: a usu. multi-barrelled anti-aircraft gun. [Imit.]

pompom[2] *pom′pom*, **pom′pon**, (*obs.*) **pompoon** *pom-pōōn′, ns.* a jewelled hair ornament on a pin: a fluffy or woolly ball, tuft, or tassel worn on a shoe, hat, etc. [Fr. *pompon.*]

pomposity, pompous. See **pomp.**

pomroy, pomwater. See **pome.**

'pon *pon*, aphetic for **upon.**

ponce *pons, n.* a man who lives on the immoral earnings of a woman: an obnoxious person: an effeminate, posturing man. — *v.i.* to act as or like a pimp. — **ponce about, around** to fool about: to act the ponce or in a showy manner. [Ety. dub.]

ponceau[1] *pɔ̃-sō′, n.* and *adj.* poppy colour. — *n.* a red dye: — *pl.* **ponceaux** (*-sōz′*). [Fr.]

ponceau[2] *pɔ̃-sō′, n.* a small bridge or culvert. [Fr.]

poncho *pon′chō, n.* a South American cloak, a blanket with a hole for the head: a cyclist's waterproof cape of like form: any similar garment. — *pl.* **pon′chos.** [Sp. from Araucanian.]

pond *pond, n.* a small, usually artificial lake: the stretch of water between locks in a canal: (also with *cap.*) the Atlantic (*facet.*). — *v.t.* to make into a pond. — *v.i.* to collect into a pond. — *n.* **pond′age** the capacity of a pond. — **pond′-life′** animal life in ponds; **pond′-lily** a water-lily; **pond′-master** the man in charge of a swimming-pond; **pond′-snail** a pond-dwelling snail, esp. Limnaea; **pond′weed** any plant of the genus Potamogeton (**Canadian pondweed** Anacharis). [M.E. *ponde*; cf. **pound[2].**]

ponder *pon′dər, v.t.* to weigh, now only in the mind: to think over: to consider. — *v.i.* to think (often with *on* and *over*). — *n.* **ponderabil′ity.** — *adjs.* **pon′derable** that may be weighed: having sensible weight; **pon′deral** pertaining to weight: ascertained by weight. — *ns.* **pon′derance, pon′derancy** weight. — *v.t.* and *v.i.* **pon′derate** to weigh: to ponder. — *ns.* **pondera′tion** weighing; **pon′derer.** — *adv.* **pon′deringly.** — *ns.* **pon′derment; ponderosity** (*-os′i-ti*). — *adj.* **pon′derous** heavy: weighty: massive: unwieldy: lumbering: solemnly laboured. — *adv.* **pon′derously.** — *n.* **pon′derousness.** [L. *ponderāre*, and *pondus, pondēris*, a weight.]

pondok(kie) *pon′dok, pon-dok′i*, (*S.Afr.*) *ns.* a crude dwelling, a hut, shack, etc. [Hottentot *pondok*, a hut, or perh. Malay *pondók*, a leaf shelter.]

pone[1] *pōn*, (U.S.) *n.* maize bread: a maize loaf or cake. [Algonquian *pone.*]

pone[2] *pō′ni, pōn*, (*cards*) *n.* the player to the right of the dealer who cuts the cards: sometimes the player to the left. [L. *pōnĕ*, imper. of *pōnĕre*, to place.]

ponent *pō′nənt*, (*Milt.*) *adj.* western. [It. *ponente*, setting (of the sun) — L. *pōnēns, -entis*, pr.p. of *pōnĕre*, to put.]

ponerology *pon-ə-rol′ə-ji*, (*theol.*) *n.* the doctrine of wickedness. [Gr. *ponēros*, bad, *logos*, discourse.]

poney. See **pony.**

pong[1] *pong*, (*slang*) *v.i.* to gag, to extend one's part (*theat.*).

pong[2] *pong, v.i.* to smell bad. — *n.* a bad smell. — *adj.* **pong′y.** [Prob. Romany *pan*, to stink.]

pongee *pun-, pon-jē′, n.* a soft silk, made from cocoons of a wild silkworm: a fine cotton. [Perh. Chin. *pun-chī*, own loom.]

pongo *pong′gō, n.* an anthropoid ape, orig. prob. the gorilla, but transferred to the orang-utan: a monkey: a soldier (*services slang*): an Englishman (*Austr. coll.*): — *pl.* **pong′os**, (*Austr.*) **pong′oes.** — *adj.* and *n.* **pon′gid** (*-jid*). [Congo *mpongi.*]

pongy. See **pong[2].**

ponk *ponk, v.i., n.* a rare variant of **pong[2].**

poniard *pon′yərd, n.* a small dagger. — *v.t.* to stab with a poniard. [Fr. *poignard* — *poing* — L. *pugnus*, fist.]

pons *ponz*, (*anat.*) *n.* a connecting part, esp. the *pons Varolii*, a mass of fibres joining the hemispheres of the brain: — *pl.* **pon′tēs.** — *adjs.* **pon′tal, pon′tic, pon′tile** relating to the pons of the brain. [L. *pōns, pontis*, a bridge.]

pons asinorum *ponz as-i-nōr′əm, -nōr′, pōns as-i-nōr′ōōm*, (L.) the asses' bridge (see **ass**): any severe test of a beginner.

pontage *pont′ij, n.* a toll paid on bridges: a tax for repairing bridges. [L.L. *pontāgium* — L. *pōns, pontis*, a bridge.]

pontal. See **pons.**

Pontederia *pont-e-dē′ri-ə, n.* an American genus of monocotyledonous water- or bog-plants, called pickerelweed, giving name to a family **Pontederiā′ceae.** [After Giulio *Pontedera* (1688–1757), Italian botanist.]

Pontefract. See **Pomfret** (former spelling).

pontes. See **pons.**

pontianac, pontianak *pont-i-ä′nak, n.* jelutong. [*Pontianak*, in Borneo.]

Pontic *pon′tik, adj.* of the ancient kingdom and Roman province of *Pontus*, or of the *Pontus* Euxinus or Black Sea. [Gr. *Pontikos* — *pontos*, sea.]

pontic. See **pons.**

ponticello *pon-ti-chel′ō, n.* the bridge of a stringed instrument: — *pl.* **ponticell′os.** [It., dim. of *ponte*, bridge — L. *pōns, pontis.*]

pontie. See **punty.**

pontifex *pon′ti-feks, n.* in ancient Rome a member of a college of priests that had control of matters of religion, their chief being *Pontifex Maximus*: a pontiff: a bridge-builder: — *pl.* **pontifices** (*-tif′i-sēz, -kās*). — *n.* **pon′tiff** a pontifex: a high-priest: a bishop, esp. the pope or *sovereign pontiff* (R.C.): an oracular person. — *adjs.* **pontif′ic, -al** of or belonging to a pontiff: splendid: pompously dogmatic. — *ns.* **pontif′ical** an office-book for bishops; **pontifical′ity.** — *adv.* **pontif′ically.** — *n. pl.* **pontif′icals** the dress of a priest, bishop, or pope. — *n.* **pontif'icate** the dignity of a pontiff or high-priest: the office and dignity or reign of a pope. — *v.i.* to perform the duties of a pontiff: to play the pontiff. — *n.* **pon'tifice** (*-fis; Milt.*) bridge-work, a bridge. — *v.i.* **pon'tify** to play the pontiff. — **pontifical mass** mass celebrated by a bishop while wearing his full vestments.   [L. *pontifex, pontificis* (partly through Fr. *pontife*), which was supposed to be from *pōns, pontis,* a bridge, *facĕre,* to make, but is possibly from an Oscan and Umbrian word *puntis,* propitiatory offering.]

pontil; pontile. See **punty; pons.**

pontile. See **pons.**

Pont-l'Évêque *pō̃-lā-vek,* (Fr.) *n.* a soft Cheddar cheese originating in *Pont-l'Évêque* in north-west France.

pontlevis *pont-lev'is, pō̃-lǝ-vē, n.* a drawbridge.   [Fr.]

pontoon[1] *pon-tōōn', n.* a flat-bottomed boat, a ferryboat, barge, or lighter: such a boat, or a float, used to support a bridge: a bridge of boats: a low vessel carrying plant, materials, and men for work at sea or on rivers: the floating gate of a dock: a boat-like float of a seaplane: a float. — Also **ponton** (*pon'tǝn, pon-tōōn'*). — *v t.* to cross by pontoon. — *ns.* **pontoneer', pontonier', pontonnier', pontoon'er** a builder of pontoon-bridges. — **pontoon'-bridge** a platform or roadway supported upon pontoons.   [Fr. *ponton —* L. *pontō, -ōnis,* a punt, pontoon — *pōns,* a bridge.]

pontoon[2] *pon-tōōn', n.* a card game of chance.   [*vingt=et-un* (q.v.).]

ponty. See **punty.**

pony, formerly also **poney,** *pō'ni, n.* a small horse — usu. one less than 14·2 hands high: £25 (*slang*): a translation, crib or key (*U.S. slang*): a small glass, esp. of beer. — *v.t.* and *v.i.* to pay or settle (with *up*): to prepare or translate by help of a crib. — **po'ny-carr'iage; po'ny-en'gine** a shunting engine; **pony express** in the U.S., a former method of long-distance postal delivery employing relays of horses and riders; **po'ny-skin** the skin of a foal, esp. from the Kirghiz Steppes, used as a fur; **po'ny-tail** a woman's hair style in which the hair is gathered together at the back and hangs down like a pony's tail; **po'ny-trekking** cross-country pony-riding in groups as a pastime. — **Jerusalem pony** an ass. [Scots **pown(e)y, pownie,** prob. — O.Fr. *poulenet,* dim. of *poulain —* L.L. *pullānus,* a foal — L. *pullus,* a young animal.]

poo *pōō, (slang) n., v.i.* same as **poop**[5]. — **in the poo** (*Austr.*) in an awkward situation.

pooch *pōōch, (slang) n.* a dog, esp. a mongrel.

pood *pōōd, n.* a Russian weight, *c.* 36 lb. avoirdupois.   [Russ. *pud.*]

poodle *pōōd'l, n.* a breed of pet dog which has curly hair (often clipped to a standard pattern): a lackey. — **pood'le-dog** a poodle: an assiduous follower; **pood'le=faker** (*Anglo-Indian slang*) a man who sought women's society.   [Ger. *Pudel;* L.G. *pudeln,* to paddle, splash.]

poof, pouf(fe), puff *pōōf, pōōf, puf, (slang) ns.* a male homosexual. — Also **poof'tah, poof'ter, poufter** (*-tǝ(r)*). — *adj.* **poof'y** effeminate.   [Fr. *pouffe,* puff.]

poogye, poogyee *pōō'gē, n.* an Indian nose-flute.   [Hindi *pūgī.*]

pooh *pōō, pŏō, interj.* of disdain. — *v.t.* **pooh-pooh', poo-poo'** to make light of: to ridicule, dismiss contemptuously.   [Imit.]

Pooh-Bah *pōō'-bä', n.* a person who holds many offices simultaneously: one giving himself airs.   [Character in Gilbert and Sullivan's *The Mikado.*]

pooja, poojah. Same as **puja.**

pook, pouk *pōōk, (Scot.) v.t.* to pluck: to pinch: — *pa.t.* and *pa.p.* **pook'it, pouk'it.**   [Origin unknown.]

pooka *pōō'kǝ, n.* in Irish folklore, a malevolent goblin or spirit, sometimes assuming an animal form, said to haunt bogs and marshes.   [Ir. *púca.*]

pool[1] *pōōl, n.* a small body of still water: a temporary or casual collection of water or other liquid: a puddle: a deep part of a stream: an underground accumulation (in the pores of sedimentary rock) of petroleum or gas.

— *n.* and *adj.* **pool'side.**   [O.E. *pōl;* Du. *poel,* Ger. *Pfuhl;* relation to Ir. and Gael. *poll,* W. *pwll,* undetermined.]

pool[2] *pōōl, n.* the stakes in certain games: the collective stakes of a number of persons who combine in a betting arrangement: an organised arrangement for betting in this way: a group of persons so combining: a game, or a set of players, at quadrille, etc.: a game or contest of various kinds in which the winner receives the pool: any of various games played on a billiard-table, each player trying to pocket a number of (esp. coloured and numbered) balls: a common stock or fund: a combination of interest: a combine: an arrangement for eliminating competition: a group of people who may be called upon as required, e.g., a pool of typists: (in *pl.*) football pools, betting by post on the results of a number of football games. — *v.t.* to put into a common fund or stock. — *v.i.* to form a pool. — **scoop the pool** (*coll.; gambling*) to win a substantial amount of money from collective stakes.   [Fr. *poule,* a hen, also stakes (possibly through an intermediate sense of plunder), but associated in English with **pool**[1].]

poon *pōōn, n.* an Indian tree, *Calophyllum inophyllum,* or other species of the genus (family Guttiferae). — **poon'-oil** an oil expressed from its seeds; **poon'-wood.**   [Sinh. *pūna.*]

poonac *pōō'nak, n.* coconut oil-cake.   [Sinh. *punakku.*]

poontang *pōōn'tang, (U.S. slang) n.* sexual intercourse.   [Fr. *putain,* a prostitute.]

poop[1] *pōōp, n.* the after part of a ship: a high deck at the stern. — *v.t.* to break over the stern of: to ship over the stern. — *adj.* **pooped** having a poop.   [Fr. *poupe —* L. *puppis,* the poop.]

poop[2], **poupe** *pōōp, (obs.) v.t.* to befool: to cozen: to undo: to do for: — *pa.p.* in *Shak.* **poupt.**   [Cf. Du. *poep,* clown.]

poop[3] *pōōp, n.* short for **nincompoop.**

poop[4] *pōōp, v.t.* (*slang*) to make out of breath: to exhaust. — *v.i.* (*slang*) to become winded or exhausted: (often with *out*) to cease.   [Orig. unknown.]

poop[5] *pōōp, (slang) n.* faeces: defecation. — *v.i.* to defecate. — **poop scoop, poop'er-scooper** an implement for lifting and removing faeces (esp. one used by dogs' owners to remove faeces deposited on pavements, in parks, etc.).

poo-poo. See **pooh.**

poor *pōōr, adj.* possessing little or nothing: without means: needy: deficient: lacking: unproductive: scanty: mere: inferior: sorry: spiritless: in sorry condition: (in modest or ironical self-deprecation) humble: unfortunate, to be pitied (esp. of the dead). — *adj.* **poor'ish.** — *adv.* **poor'ly** in a poor manner: badly: inadequately: in a small way: meanly. — *adj.* in ill-health. — *n.* **poor'ness.** — **poor'-box** a money-box for gifts for the poor; **Poor Clare** see **Clare; poor'house** (*Scot.* **poor's'=house, puir's'-house, -hoose**) a house established at the public expense for sheltering the poor — a workhouse; **poor-John'** (*Shak.*) salt hake; **poor'-law** (often in *pl.*) the law or laws relating to the support of the poor. — Also *adj.* — *v.i.* **poor'-mouth** to claim poverty. — *v.t.* to malign. — **poor'-rate** a rate or tax for the support of the poor; **poor relation** any person or thing similar but inferior or subordinate to another; **poor'-relief** money, food, etc. for the poor; **poor's'-box** a poor-box. — *adj.* **poor'-spir'ited** lacking in spirit. — **poor'-spir'it-edness; poor's'-roll** (*Scots law*) the list of poor litigants allowed to sue *in formā pauperis;* **poor white** a member of a class of poor, improvident, and incompetent white people in the Southern States of America, South Africa and elsewhere, called by the Negroes *poor white trash.* — **poor man of mutton** (*Scot.*) cold mutton broiled, esp. the shoulder; **poor man's weather-glass** the pimpernel, reputed to close its flowers before rain.   [O.Fr. *poure, povre* (Fr. *pauvre*) — L. *pauper,* poor.]

poor-oot. See **pour-out.**

poort *pōrt, pōōrt, (S.Afr.) n.* a mountain pass.   [Du., L. *porta,* gate.]

ortith *pōōr'tith*, (*Scot.*) *n.* poverty.   [O.Fr. *pouerteit*, *poverteit* — L. *paupertās*, *-ātis.*]
poorwill *pōōr'wil*, *n.* a Western North American nightjar (*Phalaenoptilus*), smaller than the whippoorwill. [From its note.]
poot. See pout[3].
Pooter *pōō'tər*, *n.* a petit bourgeois, conventional and unimaginative. — *n.* Poo'terism.   [Charles *Pooter* in *Diary of a Nobody*, by G. and W. Grossmith.]
pooter *pōō'tər*, *n.* an entomological collecting bottle into which small arthropods are introduced by suction. [Ety. obscure.]
poove *pōōv*, (*slang*) *n.* same as poof (q.v.). — *n.* poo'very. — *adj.* poo'vy.
pop[1] *pop*, *n.* a mild explosive sound, as of drawing a cork: a shot: a pistol (*slang*): ginger-beer, champagne or other effervescing drink (*slang*): pawn, or an act of pawning (*slang*). — *v.i.* to make a pop: to shoot: to burst with a pop: to protrude: to come, go, slip, or pass, suddenly, unexpectedly, or unobtrusively: to pitch or alight: to propose marriage (*slang*). — *v.t.* to cause to make a pop or to burst with a pop: to shoot: to thrust or put suddenly or quickly: to pawn (*slang*): to inject a drug or swallow it in pill form (*drug-taking slang*): — *pr.p.* popp'ing; *pa.t.* and *pa.p.* popped. — *adv.* with a pop: suddenly. — *n.* popp'er one who pops: anything that makes a pop: a press-stud: a utensil for popping corn: (in *pl.*) amyl nitrate; popp'it, popp'et one of usu. a number of beads each having a small protrusion on one side and a hole on the other, by means of which they can be linked together. — pop'-corn maize burst open and swelled by heating: a kind of maize suitable for this; pop'-eye a prominent or protruding eye. — *adj.* pop'-eyed having prominent or protruding eyes: open-eyed, agog (as from interest, excitement, etc.). — pop-fastener (*-fäs'nər*) a press-stud; pop'-gun a tube for shooting pellets by compressed air: a contemptible gun; pop'over a thin hollow cake or pudding made from batter; popp'ing-crease see crease; pop'-shop (*slang*) a pawnshop. — *adj.* pop'-up (of appliances, books, etc.) having mechanisms, pages, etc., that rise or move quickly upwards. — pop'-visit a visit at an odd time, casual visit; pop'-weed bladderwort. — pop off to make off: to die: to fall asleep; pop the question to make an offer of marriage.   [Imit.]
pop[2] *pop*, (*coll.*) *adj.* popular. — *n.* currently popular music (also pop'-music), esp. the type characterised by a strong rhythmic element and the use of electrical amplification. — pop art art drawing deliberately on commonplace material of modern urbanised life; pop=artist; pop'-concert a concert at which pop-music is played; pop'-festival; pop'-group a (usu. small) group of musicians who play pop-music; pop'-record; pop'=singer; pop'-song. — top of the pops (of a record) currently (among) the most popular in terms of sales: currently very much in favour (*fig.*).
pop[3]. See poppa, poppet, poppycock, popular.
pop(p)adum *pop'ə-dəm*, *n.* a thin strip or circle of dough fried in oil, etc. — Many variant spellings.   [Tamil, Malayalam, *poppatam*.]
pope[1] *pōp*, (often *cap.*) *n.* the bishop of Rome, head of the R.C. Church: formerly applied also to the patriarch of Alexandria and other bishops: any spiritual head: a person wielding, assuming, or thought to assume authority like that of the pope: the ruff (fish). — *ns.* pope'dom the office, dignity, or jurisdiction of the pope: a pope's tenure of office; pope'hood, pope'ship the condition of being pope; pope'ling a little pope; pop'ery a hostile term for Roman Catholicism or whatever seems to savour of it. — *adj.* pop'ish (hostile) relating to the pope or to popery. — *adv.* pop'ishly. — Pope Joan a mythical female pope: an old card-game like newmarket; pope's eye the gland surrounded with fat in the middle of the thigh of an ox or a sheep; pope's head a long-handled brush; pope's knights Roman Catholic priests, formerly called Sir; pope's nose, parson's nose the fleshy part of a (esp. cooked)

bird's tail. — Black Pope see black.   [O.E. *pāpa* — L.L. *pāpa* — Gr. *pappas* (late Gr. *papās*), hypocoristic for father.]
pope[2] *pōp*, *n.* a parish priest in the Greek Orthodox Church.   [Russ. *pop* — Late Gr. *papās*; cf. preceding.]
poperin. See poppering.
Popian *pōp'i-ən*, *adj.* pertaining to Alexander *Pope*, the poet (1688–1744).
popinjay *pop'in-jā*, *n.* a parrot: a figure of a parrot set up to be shot at: a fop or coxcomb.   [O.Fr. *papegai*; cf. L.L. *papagallus*; Late Gr. *papagallos* (also *papagas*), a parrot; prob. Eastern; influenced by jay.]
popish. See pope[1].
popjoy *pop'joi*, *v.i.* to amuse oneself.   [Poss. connected with popinjay.]
poplar *pop'lər*, *n.* a genus (*Populus*) of trees of the willow family, including aspen, white poplar, black poplar (with its variety Lombardy poplar), cottonwood, etc.: the tulip-tree, tulip-poplar (*U.S.*).   [O.Fr. *poplier* — L. *pōpulus*, poplar-tree.]
poplin *pop'lin*, *n.* a corded fabric with silk warp and worsted weft: an imitation in cotton or other material. — *n.* poplinette' an imitation poplin.   [Perh. Fr. *popeline* — It. *papalina*, papal, from the papal town of Avignon, where it was made.]
popliteal *pop-lit'i-əl*, often *pop-lit-ē'əl*, *adj.* of the back of the knee. — Also poplit'ic.   [L. *poples*, *-itis*.]
poppa *pop'ə*, (*coll. U.S.*) *n.* papa. — Short form pop, pops.
poppadum. See popadum.
popper[1]. See pop[1].
popper[2] *pop'ə(r)*, (*U.S.*) a corn popper.
Popperian *pop-ē'ri-ən*, *adj.* of or relating to the theories, teachings, etc. of the British philosopher Sir Karl *Popper*. — *n.* a student or supporter of Popper's philosophy.
poppering *pop'ər-ing*, poperin *-in*, *ns.* a variety of pear. — Also poppering pear (*Shak.* pop'rin).   [*Poperinghe* in Belgium.]
poppet[1] *pop'it*, *n.* a puppet: a doll (*obs.*): a darling (short form pop): a timber support used in launching a ship: a lathe-head: a valve that lifts bodily (also popp'et=valve).   [An earlier form of puppet.]
poppet[2], poppit. See pop[1].
popple *pop'l*, *v.i.* to flow tumblingly: to heave choppily: to bob up and down: to make the sound of rippling or bubbling, or of repeated shots. — *n.* a poppling movement or sound. — *adj.* popp'ly.   [Imit.; or a freq. of pop.]
poppy *pop'i*, *n.* a cornfield plant (of several species) or its large scarlet flowers: any other species of the genus Papaver, as the opium poppy, or of the kindred genera *Glaucium* (horned poppy; see horn), Meconopsis (see below), etc.: extended to various unrelated plants. — *adj.* popp'ied covered or filled with poppies: soporific: affected by opium. — popp'y-head a capsule of the poppy: a finial in wood, esp. at a pew end; popp'y-oil a fixed oil from the seeds of the opium-poppy; popp'y=seed; popp'y water a soporific drink made from poppies. — blue poppy a blue Meconopsis of the northern temperate zone; Flanders poppy an emblem, from 1st World War, of British fallen; Poppy Day orig. Armistice Day (q.v.), later the Saturday nearest Armistice Day, or (later) Remembrance Sunday (q.v.), when artificial poppies are sold for war charity; Welsh poppy Meconopsis cambrica, which has pale-yellow flowers.   [O.E. *popig* — L. *papāver*, poppy.]
poppycock *pop'i-kok*, (*slang*) *n.* balderdash. — Short form pop.   [Du. *pappekak*, lit. soft dung.]
poprin. See poppering.
popsy *pop'si*, *n.* term of endearment for a girl. — Also pop'sy-wop'sy.   [Prob. dim. abbrev. of poppet.]
populace *pop'ū-ləs*, *n.* the common people: those nc distinguished by rank, education, office, etc.   [F — It. *popolazzo* — L. *pōpulus*, people.]
popular *pop'ū-lər*, *adj.* of the people: pleasing to, enjc the favour of, or prevailing among, the people by one's associates: suited to the understandin

means of ordinary people: seeking the favour of the common people (*obs.*): democratic: plebeian (*obs.*): vulgar (*obs.*). — *n.* a popular or moderate-priced concert, newspaper, etc. (short form **pop**; cf. **pop**²). — *n.* **popularīsā'tion, -z-.** — *v.t.* **pop'ularise, -ize** to make popular: to democratise: to present in a manner suited to ordinary people: to spread among the people. — *ns.* **pop'ularīser, -z-; popularity** (-*lar'i-ti*) the fact or state of being popular: seeking to gain favour with the people. — *adv.* **pop'ularly.** — *v.t.* **pop'ulate** to people: to furnish with inhabitants: to devastate (*obs.*). — *v.i.* to multiply by propagation. — *adj.* inhabited, peopled. — *ns.* **populā'tion** the act of populating: the number of the inhabitants: the number of inhabitants of a particular class: the plants or animals in a given area: a group of persons, objects, items, considered statistically. — **pop'ulism; pop'ulist** in U.S. a member of the People's Party, founded in 1891, advocating public ownership of public services, graduated income-tax, etc., or of a similar party elsewhere (*hist.*): one who believes in the right and ability of the common people to play a major part in governing themselves: a supporter, wooer or student of the common people. — *adj.* of a political or social programme, cause, etc., appealing to the mass of the people. — *adj.* **pop'ulous** full of people: numerously inhabited: numerous (*Shak.*): popular (*rare*). — *adv.* **pop'ulously.** — *n.* **pop'ulousness.** — **popular front** an alliance of the more progressive or leftward political parties in the state; **population explosion** see **explode; population inversion** (*phys.*) the reversal of the normal ratio of populations of two different energy states, i.e., that normally fewer and fewer atoms occupy states of successively higher energies. [L. *pŏpulus*, the people.]

poral *pō'rəl, pö'.* See **pore**¹.

porbeagle *pör'bē-gl, n.* a North Atlantic and Mediterranean shark of the genus *Lamna*. [From Cornish dialect; origin unknown.]

porcelain *pörs'lin, pörs', -lən, n.* a fine earthenware, white, thin, transparent or semi-transparent, first made in China: China-ware. — *adj.* of porcelain. — *v.t.* **porcellanise, -ize** (*pör-, pör-sel'ən-īz*) **porc'elainise, -ize** to bake into porcelain or porcellanite. — *n.* **porcell'anite** a jasper-like shale highly indurated by contact metamorphism. — *adj.* **porcell'anous** (or *pör', pör'*) like porcelain — also **porcellā'neous, porc'elainous, porcelaineous** (*pör-, pör-sə-lā'ni-əs*). — **porcelain cement** cement for mending china; **porcelain clay** kaolin. [O.Fr. *porcelaine* — It. *porcellana*, cowrie.]

porch *pörch, pörch, n.* a building forming an enclosure or protection for a doorway: a portico or colonnade: a veranda (*U.S.*): the Stoic school of philosophy, from the Painted Porch in the Agora at Athens where Zeno taught. [O.Fr. *porche* — L. *porticus* — *porta*, a gate.]

porcine *pör'sīn, adj.* of pigs: swinish. [L. *porcīnus* — *porcus*, a swine.]

porcpisce *pör'pis, (Spens.) n.* Same as **porpoise**.

porcupine *pör'kū-pīn, n.* a large spiny rodent of various kinds. — **por'cupine-grass** a coarse, hard, spiny, tussocky grass (*Triodia*) that covers vast areas in Australia, commonly called spinefax; **por'cupine-wood** the wood of the coconut palm, from its spine-like markings. [O.Fr. *porc espin* — L. *porcus*, a pig, *spīna*, a spine.]

pore¹ *pōr, pör, n.* a minute passage or interstice, esp. the opening of a sweat-gland. — *adj.* **por'al** of or pertaining to pores. — *n.* **por'iness.** — *adj.* **poromer'ic** permeable to water vapour, as some synthetic leather. — *n.* **poroscope** (*pör',* or *pör'ō-skōp*) an instrument for investigating porosity or for examining pores or fingerprints. — *adj.* **poroscopic** (-*skop'ik*). — *n.* **poroscopy** (-*os'kə-pi*). — *adj.* **porose'** (or *pör'ōs, pör'ōs*). — *n.* **porosity** (-*os'i-ti*) the quality or state of being porous: he ratio of the volume of pores to the total volume f e.g. a rock): a thing or part that is porous. — *adj.* 'ous having many pores: permeable by fluids, etc. . por'ousness. — *adj.* por'y. — **pore fungus** any

fungus having the spore-bearing surface within sma pores or tubes; **porous alloys** alloys obtained by takin the constituents in powder form and pressing them together; **porous plaster** a plaster for the body, with holes to prevent wrinkling. [Fr., — L. *porus* — Gr. *poros,* a passage.]

pore² *pōr, pör, v.i.* to gaze with close and steady attention (usu. with *over* or *upon*): to ponder. — *n.* **por'er.** [Origin obscure.]

porge *pörj, pörj, v.t.* in Jewish ritual, to cleanse (a slaughtered animal) ceremonially by removing the forbidden fat, sinews, etc. [Ladino (Jewish Spanish) *porgar* (Sp. *purgar*) — L. *pūrgāre*, to purge.]

porgy, porgie *pör'gi, n.* a name given to many fishes, chiefly American species of sea-bream. [Partly Sp. and Port. *pargo*, app. — L. *pargus*, a kind of fish; partly from American Indian names.]

Porifera *por-if'ə-rə, n.pl.* a phylum of animals, the sponges. — *n.* **por'ifer** member of the Porifera. — *adjs.* **porif'eral, porif'eran** of the Porifera; **porif'erous** having pores. [L. *porus,* a pore, *ferre,* to bear.]

porism *pör'izm, pör'izm, n.* in ancient Greek geometry a corollary: also a kind of proposition intermediate between a problem and a theorem, according to some a proposition affirming the possibility of finding such conditions as will render a certain problem capable of innumerable solutions. — *adjs.* **porismat'ic** (*pör-*), **-al; poris'tic, -al.** [Gr. *porisma,* a corollary, porism — *poros,* a way.]

pork *pörk, pörk, n.* a swine (*obs.*): swine's flesh as food: government money to be used for a pork barrel (see below) (*U.S.*). — *ns.* **pork'er** a young hog: a pig fed for pork; **pork'ling** a young pig. — *adj.* **pork'y** pig-like: fat. — **pork barrel** (*U.S.*) (a bill or policy promoting spending of Federal or state money on) projects undertaken because of their appeal to the electorate rather than their meeting a real need: the money itself; **pork'-butch'er** one who kills pigs or sells pork; **pork'= chop'** a slice from a pig's rib; **pork'-pie'** a pie made of minced pork. — **pork-pie hat** a hat with a low flat circular crown, shaped somewhat like a pie. [Fr. *porc* — L. *porcus,* a hog.]

porn(o)- *pörn-(ō-),* in composition, obscene. — *n.* and *adj.* **porn, por'no** coll. shortenings of **pornography** and **pornographic.** — *ns.* **pornocracy** (*pör-nok'rə-si;* Gr. *kratos,* rule) the influence of courtesans — esp. over the papal court in the earlier half of the 10th century; **pornography** (*pör-nog'rə-fi;* Gr. *graphein,* to write) description or portrayal of prostitutes and fornication: obscene writing, painting, and the like; **pornog'-rapher.** — *adj.* **pornographic** (*pör-no-graf'ik*). — *adv.* **pornograph'ically.** — *ns.* **por'nōmag** a pornographic periodical; **pornotō'pia** (by facet. analogy with *Utopia*) the perfect setting for the antics described in pornography. — *adj.* **pornotō'pian.** — **porn shop** a shop selling pornographic literature, etc.; **porn squad** the branch of the police-force that enforces the law as regards obscene publications. [Gr. *pornē,* a whore.]

porogamy *pör-* or *pör-og'ə-mi, n.* the entry of the pollentube through the micropyle — opp. to *chalazogamy.* — *adj.* **porogamic** (-*ō-gam'ik*). [Gr. *poros,* a pore, *gamos,* marriage.]

poromeric, poroscope, etc., **porose, porous,** etc. See **pore**¹.

porosis *pö-rō'sis, pö-, n.* formation of callus, the knitting together of broken bones: — *pl.* **poro'ses.** [Gr. *pörōsis* — *pöros,* callus.]

porpentine *pör'pən-tīn, (Shak.) n.* Same as **porcupine**.

porpess, porpesse. See **porpoise**.

Porphyra *pör'fir-ə, n.* a genus of seaweeds, with flat translucent red or purple fronds, purple laver. [Gr. *porphyrā,* purple (dye).]

porphyria *pör-fī'ri-ə, n.* an inborn error of metabolism resulting in the excretion of an abnormal pigment in the urine and characterised by great pain, abnormal skin pigmentation and photosensitivity. [Gr. *por-phyrā,* purple (dye).]

Porphyrio *pör-fir'i-ō, n.* the purple coot genus: (without *cap.*) any bird of this genus: — *pl.* **porphyr'ios.** [Gr. *porphyriōn*, purple coot.]

Porphyrogenite *pör-fĭr-oj'ən-īt, n.* a Byzantine emperor's son born in the purple or porphyry room assigned to empresses: hence, a prince born after his father's accession: one born in the purple. — *ns.* **Porphyrogenitism** (*-ō-jen'it-izm*) the Byzantine principle of the first son born after his father's accession succeeding to the throne; **Porphyrogen'iture.** [L. *porphyrogenitus* for Gr. *porphyrogennētos* — *porphyros*, purple, *gennētos*, born.]

porphyry *pör'fĭr-i, n.* a very hard, variegated rock, of a purple and white colour, used in sculpture (*porfido rosso antico*): loosely, an igneous rock with large crystals in a fine-grained ground mass (*geol.*). — *n.* **por'phyrite** an old-fashioned name for an altered andesite or fine-grained diorite: porphyry. — *adjs.* **porphyritic** (*-it'ik*) like, or of the nature of, porphyry: having large crystals scattered among small or in a fine-grained or glassy groundmass; **por'phyrous** purple. [Gr. *porphyrītēs* — *porphyros*, purple.]

porpoise *pör'pəs, n.* a short-snouted genus (Phocaena) of the dolphin family, 4 to 8 feet long, gregarious, affording oil and leather: extended to similar forms, esp. (*loosely*) the dolphin. — Formerly also **por'pess(e)** (*obs.*), **porc'pisce** (*Spens.*). — *v.i* to move like a porpoise. [O.Fr. *porpeis* — L. *porcus*, a hog, a pig and *piscis*, a fish.]

porporate *pör'por-āt,* (*Browning*) *adj.* clad in purple. [It. *porporato* — L. *purpurātus.*]

porraceous *por-ā'shəs, adj.* leek-green. [L. *porrāceus* — *porrum*, a leek.]

porrect *por-ekt', v.t.* to stretch forth: to present, hold out for acceptance. — *adj.* extended forward. — *n.* **porrec'tion.** [L. *porrigĕre, porrectum*, to stretch out.]

porrenger. See **porringer.**

porridge *por'ij, n.* a kind of dish usually made by slowly stirring oatmeal in boiling water (in Scotland often treated as a *pl.*): pottage (*obs.*): jail, or a jail sentence, esp. in the phrase **do porridge,** to serve a jail sentence (*slang*). — **porr'idge-stick** a stick for stirring porridge. [pottage altered by influence of obs. or dial. *porray*, vegetable soup. — O.Fr. *porée* — L.L. *porrāta* — L. *porrum*, leek.]

porrigo *por-ī'gō, n.* scalp disease of various kinds: — *pl.* **porri'gos.** — *adj.* **porriginous** (*-ij'*). [L. *porrīgō, -inis*, dandruff.]

porringer, porrenger *por'in-jər, n.* a small dish for soup, porridge, etc.: a head-dress shaped like such a dish (*Shak.*). [See **porridge, pottage;** for inserted *n* cf. **passenger, messenger.**]

port¹ *pōrt, pört, n.* the larboard or left side of a ship. — *adj.* left. — *v.t.* and *v.i.* to turn left. (In helm orders, formerly, **port the helm** meant turn the tiller to port, or the upper part of the wheel to starboard, and so the rudder, and the ship, to starboard; since 1933 **port** means turn the ship to port.) [Ety. doubtful.]

port² *pōrt, pört, n.* an instrumental tune: a bagpipe composition. — **port a beul** (*bē'əl*) mouth music. [Gael.]

port³ *pōrt, pört, n.* bearing: demeanour: carriage of the body: imposing bearing: style of living: a retinue (*obs.*): the position of a ported weapon. — *v.t.* to carry or convey (*obs.*): to hold in a slanting direction upward across the body (*mil.*). — *n.* **portabil'ity.** — *adj.* **port'able** easily or conveniently carried or moved about: endurable (*Shak.*): of a computer program, easily adapted for use on a wide range of computers. — *n.* a portable article. — *ns.* **port'age** an act of carrying: carriage: the price of carriage: a space, track, or journey, over which goods and boats have to be carried or dragged overland: a sailor's private venture in a voyage (*Shak.*); **port'ance** (*Spens.; Shak.*) carriage, bearing. — *adjs.* **port'ate** (*her.*) in a position as if being carried; **port'atile** portable; **port'ative** easily carried. — *n.* (obs.) a portable organ (often *pair of portatives*). — **port(e)'-cray'on** (Fr. *porte-crayon*) a handle for holding

a crayon; **porte-bonheur** (*port'-bon-œr'*; Fr.) a charm carried for luck; **porte'-monnaie'** (*-mon-e'*; Fr.) a purse or pocket-book; **port'-fire** a slow-match or match-cord. [Fr. *port, porter* — L. *portāre*, to carry.]

port⁴ *pōrt, pört, n.* a harbour: a town with a harbour. — **port'-ad'miral** the admiral commanding at a naval port. — *n.pl.* **port'-charges** harbour dues. — **port of call** a port where vessels can call for stores or repairs; **port of entry** a port where merchandise is allowed by law to enter. [O.E. *port* — L. *portus, -ūs*, akin to *porta*, a gate.]

port⁵ *pōrt, pört, n.* a gate or gateway (*obs.*): a town gate, or its former position (now chiefly *Scot.*): an opening in the side of a ship: a porthole or its cover: a passage-way for a ball or curling-stone: an outlet or inlet for a fluid: any socket on a data-processor by means of which electronic information can pass to and from peripheral units (*comput.*): part of a bit curved for the tongue. — *n.* **port'age** (*Shak.*) an opening. [Fr. *porte* (perh. also O.E. *port*) — L. *porta*, gate.]

port⁶ *pōrt, pört, n.* a fortified wine (dark-red or tawny, sometimes white) of the Douro valley, shipped from *Oporto*, Portugal. — Also **port'-wine'.** — *adjs.* **port'= win'y, port'y** of the nature or colour of port.

port⁷ *pōrt, pört,* (*hist.*) *n.* a town with market privileges: a borough. — **port'man** (*hist.*) a burgess, esp. one chosen to administer town affairs; **port'reeve** (O.E. *portgerēfa; hist.*) a mayor or principal magistrate. [Connection with **port⁴** and **port⁵** obscure.]

port⁸ *pōrt, pört,* (*Austr. coll.*) *n.* a bag, suitcase. [Abbrev. of **portmanteau.**]

porta *pōr', pör'tə,* (*zool.*) *n.* a gate-like structure, esp. the transverse fissure of the liver. — *adj.* **por'tal.** — **portal system** the portal vein with its tributaries, etc.; **portal vein** the vein that conveys to the liver the venous blood from intestines, spleen, and stomach. [L. *porta*, gate.]

portage. See **port³,⁵.**

portague. See under **Portuguese.**

Portakabin® *pōr', pör'tə-kab-in, n.* a *porta*ble structure used as a temporary office, etc.

portal¹ *pōrt', pört'əl, n.* a gate or doorway, esp. a great or magnificent one: any entrance: the arch over a gate (*archit.*): the lesser of two gates. [O.Fr. *portal* — L.L. *portāle* — L. *porta*, a gate.]

portal². See **porta.**

Portaloo® *pōr', pör'tə-lōō, n.* a *porta*ble lavatory. [**loo¹.**]

portamento *pōr-ta-men'tō,* (*mus.*) *n.* a continuous glide from one tone to another: sometimes applied to an execution between staccato and legato: — *pl.* **portamen'ti** (*-tē*). — Also *adj.* and *adv.* [It.]

portance. See **port³.**

portas. See **portesse.**

portate, etc., **port-crayon.** See **port³.**

portcullis *pōrt-, pört-kul'is, n.* a grating that can be let down to close a gateway: a lattice (*her.*): one of the pursuivants of the English College of Heralds: an Elizabethan silver halfpenny with a portcullis on the reverse. — *v.t.* to obstruct, as with a portcullis. [O.Fr. *porte coleïce*, sliding gate.]

port de bras *por-də-bra,* (Fr.) the practice or technique of arm movements in ballet: a balletic figure illustrating this technique.

Porte *pōrt, pört,* (*hist.*) *n.* the Turkish imperial government, so called from the Sublime Porte or High Gate, the chief office of the Ottoman government at Constantinople. — **porte-cochère** (*port-kosh-er'*; Fr.) a house entrance admitting a carriage. [Fr. *porte* — L. *porta*, gate.]

porte-bonheur, etc. See **port³.**

portend *pōr-, pör-tend', v.t.* to betoken: to presage. — *n.* **portent** (*pōr', pör'tent*) that which portends or foreshows: a foreshadowing import: an evil omen: a prodigy, marvel. — *adj.* **portentous** (*-tent'*) ominous: prodigious, extraordinary: impressive, solemn. — *adv.* **portent'ously.** — *n.* **portent'ousness.** [L. *portendĕre,* *portentum* — *por-*, equivalent to *prō* or *per*, *tendĕre*, to stretch.]

porteous. See **portesse.**

porter[1] *pōrt′*, *pört′ər*, *n.* a door-keeper or gate-keeper: one who waits at the door to receive messages: — *fem.* **port′eress, port′ress.** — *n.* **port′erage** the office or duty of a porter. — **porter's lodge** a house or an apartment near a gate for the use of the porter. [O.Fr. *portier* — L.L. *portārius* — L. *porta*, a gate.]

porter[2] *pōrt′*, *pört′ər*, *n.* one who carries burdens for hire, or does similar manual labour: a dark-brown malt liquor, prob. because a favourite drink with London porters. — *n.* **port′erage** carriage: the charge made by a porter for carrying goods. — *adv.* **port′erly** like a porter. — *adj.* (*obs.*) of a porter: coarse. — **porter′s house** a house where porter is sold: a chop-house; **port′erhouse(-steak)** a choice cut of beefsteak next to the sirloin. [O.Fr. *porteour* (Fr. *porteur*) — L. *portātor*, *-ōris* — *portāre*, to carry.]

portesse *pōrt′*, *pört′əs*, *-es*, (*Spens.*) *n.* a portable breviary. — Also **port′ess, port′as, port′hors, port′house, port′-ous, port′hos, porteous** (*pōrt′*, *pör′tyəs*) — **porteous roll** (*Scots law*) a list of persons to be tried. [O.Fr. *portehors* (L.L. *porteforium*) — L. *portāre*, to carry, *forīs*, out of doors.]

portfolio *pōrt-*, *pört-fō′li-ō*, *n.* a case or pair of boards for loose papers, drawings, etc.: a collection of such papers: a list of securities held: the office of a cabinet minister with responsibility for a government department: — *pl.* **portfo′lios.** [It. *portafogli(o)* — L. *portāre*, to carry, *folium*, a leaf.]

porthole *pōrt′*, *pört′hōl*, *n.* a hole or opening in a ship's side for light and air, or (formerly) for pointing a gun through. [**port**[5], **hole.**]

porthors, porthos, porthouse. See **portesse.**

portico *pōrt′*, *pör′ti-kō*, *n.* a range of columns along the front or side of a building (*archit.*): a colonnade: the Painted Porch (*philos.*): — *pl.* **por′ticos, por′ticoes.** — *adj.* **por′ticoed** furnished with a portico. [It., — L. *porticus*, a porch.]

portière *por-tyer′*, *n.* a curtain hung over the door or doorway of a room: a portress, concierge. [Fr.]

portigue. See under **Portuguese.**

portion *pōr′*, *pör′shən*, *n.* a part: an allotted part: an amount of food served to one person: destiny: the part of an estate descending to an heir: a dowry. — *v.t.* to divide into portions: to allot as a share: to furnish with a portion. — *adj.* **por′tioned.** — *ns.* **por′tioner** (*Scots law*) the holder of a small feu originally part of a greater: a portionist of a benefice (**heir′-por′tioner** see **heir**); **por′tionist** a postmaster of Merton College: one of two or more incumbents sharing a benefice. — *adj.* **por′tionless** having no portion, dowry, or property. [O.Fr., — L. *portiō, -ōnis*.]

Portland *pōrt′*, *pört′land*, *adj.* belonging to or associated with the Isle of *Portland*, a peninsula of Dorset. — *n.* **Portlandian** (*-land′i-ən*) a group of sands and limestones, the middle group of the Upper or Portland Oolite. — Also *adj.* — **Portland arrowroot, Portland sago** a farina prepared in the Isle of Portland from wake-robin tubers; **Portland cement** a cement made by burning a mixture of clay and chalk of the colour of Portland stone; **Portland sheep** a breed of small, black-faced sheep found in the Isle of Portland; **Portland stone** an oolitic building-stone which is quarried in the Isle of Portland.

portland. See **portlast.**

portlast *pōrt′*, *pört′last*, (*obs. naut.*) *n.* probably the gunwale. — Also **portoise** (*pört′*, *pört′iz*) and wrongly **port′land.** — **yards down a portlast** with yards down on or near the deck. [Origin unknown.]

portly *pōrt′*, *pört′li*, *adj.* having a dignified port or mien (*arch.*): corpulent. — *n.* **port′liness.** [**port**[3].]

portman. See **port**[7].

portmanteau *pōrt-*, *pört-man′tō*, *n.* a large travelling-bag that folds back flat from the middle: a rack for hanging clothes (*rare*): Lewis Carroll's term for a word into which are packed the sense (and sound) of two words (also **portman′teau-word** — e.g. *slithy* for *lithe* and *slimy*). — *pl.* **portman′teaus**, or **portman′teaux** (*-tōz*). — Also (both *obs.*) **portman′tle, portman′tua.** — *adj.* combining or covering two or more things of the same kind. [Fr., — *porter*, to carry, *manteau*, a cloak.]

portoise. See **portlast.**

portolano *pör-tə-lä′nō*, *n.* in the Middle Ages, a navigation manual giving sailing directions and illustrated with charts showing ports, coastal features, etc.: — *pl.* **portola′nos, -ni** (*-nē*). — Also **portolan, portulan (chart)** (*por′tə-lən, -tū-*). [It., navigation manual, harbour-master.]

portous. See **portesse.**

portrait *pör′*, *pör′trit*, *n.* the likeness of a real person: a vivid description in words: portraiture (*rare*). — *adj.* (of something rectangular in format) having the shorter sides at the top and bottom. — *v.t.* (*obs.*) to portray. — *ns.* **por′traitist, por′trait-painter; por′traiture** a likeness: the art or act of making portraits: a collection of pictures. — *v.t.* **portray** (*pör-*, *pör-trā′*) to paint or draw the likeness of: to describe in words: to adorn with portraiture or representations (*obs.*). — *ns.* **portray′al** the act of portraying: a representation; **portray′er.** — **por′trait-bust′; por′trait-gallery; por′trait-painting.** [O.Fr. *po(u)rtrait, po(u)rtraire* — L. *prōtrahĕre, -tractum*; see **protract.**]

portray, portrayal. See **portrait.**

portreeve; portress. See **port**[7]; **porter**[1].

Port Salut *pör sa-lü′*, a mild cheese orig. made at the Trappist monastery Le *Port* du *Salut* in Bayonne, France.

Portugaise *pör-*, *pör-tū-gāz′*, *adj.* Portuguese: in a Portuguese style. — **à la Portugaise** cooked with tomato or having a prevalent flavour of tomato: with a tomato-based sauce, often with onion, garlic and herbs. [Fr.]

Portuguese *pör-*, *pör-tū-gēz′*, or *pör′*, *pör′*, *adj.* of Portugal, its people, and its language. — *n.* a native or citizen of Portugal: the language of Portugal: — *pl.* **Portuguese** (whence the vulgar *sing.* **Portug(u)ee′**). — *n.* **portague, portigue** (*pört′*, *pört′ə-gū*) an old Portuguese gold coin, worth about £4. — **Portuguese man-of-war** any of several hydrozoans of the genus Physalia, having tentacles able to give a painful, even deadly, sting.

Portulaca *pör-*, *pör-tū-lā′kə*, *n.* the purslane genus, giving name to the family **Portulacā′ceae,** mostly succulent herbs of dry places, akin to the Caryophyllaceae: (without *cap.*) a plant of this genus. [L. *portulāca*, purslane.]

portulan. See **portolano.**

port-wine, port-winy, porty. See **port**[6].

porwiggle. Same as **pollywog.**

pory. See **pore**[1].

pos *poz*, (*slang*) *adj.* short for **positive.**

posada *pō-sä′də*, *n.* an inn. [Sp., — *posar*, to lodge.]

posaune *pō-zow′nə*, *n.* the trombone. [Ger.]

pose[1] *pōz*, *n.* an attitude: an assumed attitude: an affectation of a mental attitude: in dominoes, the right to begin the game: a secret hoard (*Scot.*). — *v.i.* to assume or maintain a pose: to attitudinise. — *v.t.* to put in a suitable attitude: to posit: to assert: to claim: to propound. — *adj.* **pose′able.** — *ns.* **pos′er** one who poses; **poseur** (*pōz-œr′*; Fr.) an attitudiniser: — *fem.* **poseuse** (*-œz′*). [Fr. *poser*, to place — L.L. *pausāre*, to cease — L. *pausa*, pause — Gr. *pausis*; between Fr. *poser* and L. *pōnĕre, positum*, there has been confusion, which has influenced the derivatives of both words.]

pose[2] *pōz*, *v.t.* (*arch.*) to puzzle: to perplex by questions: to bring to a stand. — *ns.* **pos′er** one who, or that which, poses: a difficult question; **pos′ing.** — *adv.* **pos′ingly.** [Aphetic, for **oppose**, or **appose**, confused with it.]

posé *pō-zā′*, (*her.*) *adj.* standing still. [Fr., pa.p. of *poser*; see **pose**[1].]

Poseidon *pos-ī′don, -dōn, n.* the Greek sea-god, identified

with Neptune by the Romans. — *adj.* **Poseidōn′ian.** [Gr. *Poseidōn, -ōnos.*]
poser. See **pose**[1,2].
poseur, poseuse. See **pose**[1].
posh[1] *posh, (obs. slang) n.* money, esp. a small amount, a halfpenny: a dandy. [App. — Romany *posh*, half.]
posh[2] *posh, (slang) adj.* spruced up, smart: superb. — *v.t.* and *v.i.* (usu. with *up*) to trim up, to polish. — *adv.* **posh′ly.** — *n.* **posh′ness.** [Pop. supposed to be from *'port outward starboard home'*, the most desirable position of cabins when sailing to and from the East before the days of air-conditioning, but no evidence has been found to support this; poss. linked with **posh**[1].]
poshteen. See **posteen.**
posigrade *poz′i-grād, (aero.* and *space flight) adj.* having or producing positive thrust: of or pertaining to a posigrade rocket. — **posigrade rocket** a small propellant rocket that is fired to give forward acceleration when required, esp. on a multi-stage rocket when jettisoning a redundant stage. [*Posi*tive in contrast to retro*grade*.]
posit *poz′it, v.t.* to set in place, dispose: to postulate, assume as true, definitely or for argument's sake: — *pr.p.* **pos′iting;** *pa.t.* and *pa.p.* **pos′ited.** [L. *pōnĕre, positum,* to lay down.]
position *poz-ish′ən, n.* situation: place occupied: attitude, disposition, arrangement: state of affairs: a proposition or thesis: the ground taken in argument or in a dispute: principle laid down: place in society: high standing: a post or appointment: occurrence in an open or closed syllable: situation of the left hand in playing the violin, etc.: method of finding the value of an unknown quantity by assuming one or more values. — *adj.* of or defining position. — *v.t.* to set in place: to determine the position of, locate. — *adjs.* **posi′tional; posi′tioned** placed. — **position ratio** a ratio determining the position of a point in a range or of a ray in a pencil — that of the distances from two fixed points in the range, or of the sines of the angular distances from two fixed rays. [Fr., — L. *positiō, -ōnis* — *pōnĕre, positum,* to place.]
positive *poz′i-tiv, adj.* definitely, formally, or explicitly laid down: express: beyond possibility of doubt: absolute: expressing a quality simply without comparison (*gram.*): downright, out-and-out: fully convinced: over-confident in opinion: matter-of-fact: concrete: material: actual: characterised by the presence of some quality, not merely absence of its opposite: feeling or expressing agreement to or approval of something: having a good or constructive attitude: having qualities worthy of approval: of a bacteriological test, confirming the presence of the suspected organism, etc.: greater than zero, or conventionally regarded as greater than zero, indicating such a quantity (*math.*): in the direction of increase, actual or conventional: in a direction towards the source of stimulus (*biol.*): having the lights and shades not reversed (*phot., opt.*): having a relatively high potential (*elect.*): of, having, or producing, positive electricity (see below): dextrorotatory (*opt.*): having a greater index of refraction for the extraordinary than for the ordinary ray in double refraction: basic (*chem.*). — *n.* that which is positive: reality: a positive quantity: a positive quality: the positive degree, or an adjective or adverb in it: an image in which lights and shades or colours, or both, are unchanged: a photographic plate with the lights and shades of the original: a positive organ (see below). — *adv.* **pos′itively.** — *ns.* **pos′itiveness** the state or quality of being positive: certainty: confidence; **pos′-itivism** actual or absolute knowledge: certainty: assurance: positive philosophy (see below); **pos′itivist** a believer in positivism. — *adj.* **positivist′ic.** — *n.* **positiv′-ity.** — **positive action** same as **affirmative action; positive angle** one generated by a straight line moving counter-clockwise; **positive discrimination** see under **discriminate; positive electricity** such as is developed in glass by rubbing with silk, arising from deficiency of electrons; **positive organ** a small supplementary church organ, originally portable and placed upon a stand; **positive philosophy** the philosophical system originated by Comte (1798–1857) — its foundation the doctrine that man can have no knowledge of anything but phenomena, and that the knowledge of phenomena is relative, not absolute: also 20th-century developments of this (**logical positivism**) much concerned with determining whether or not statements are meaningful; **positive pole,** of a magnet, that end (or pole) which turns to the north when the magnet swings freely; **positive rays** canal-rays, a stream of positively electrified particles towards the cathode of a vacuum-tube (**positive-ray analysis** the detection of gases, and determination of their molecular weights, by measuring the parabolas produced upon a photographic plate by positive rays deflected in two directions at right angles to each other by a magnetic and an electric field); **positive sign** the sign (+ read *plus*) of addition; **positive vetting** a method of screening individuals to ensure their suitability for highly responsible positions. [L. *positīvus,* fixed by agreement — *pōnĕre, positum,* to place.]
positron *poz′i-tron, n.* a particle differing from the electron in having a positive charge: a positive electron. — Also **pos′iton.** — *n.* **positronium** (*-trōn′i-əm*) a positron and an electron bound together as a short-lived unit, similar to a hydrogen atom.
posnet *pos′nit, n.* a small cooking-pot with feet and handle. [O.Fr. *pocenet.*]
posology *pos-ol′ə-ji, n.* the science of quantity: the science of dosage. — *adj.* **posological** (*-ə-loj′i-kl*). [Gr. *posos,* how much, and *logos,* a word, discourse.]
poss[1] *adj.* a slang shortening of **possible.**
poss[2] *pos, (dial.) v.t.* to agitate (clothes) in washing them, with a stick, etc. — *ns.* (*arch.*) **poss′er, poss′-stick** a wooden stick, usu. with a perforated metal plate on the bottom, for possing clothes in a wash-tub. [Perh. imit. modification of Fr. *pousser,* to push — L. *pulsāre,* to beat.]
posse *pos′i, n.* power: possibility: a force or body (of constables). — **in posse** in potentiality; **posse comitatus** (*kom-i-tā′təs, -tä′tōōs*) force of the county, men called out by the sheriff to aid in enforcing the law. [L. *posse,* to be able, *comitātūs,* of the county.]
possess *poz-es′, v.t.* to inhabit, occupy (*obs.*): to have or hold as owner, or as if owner: to have: to seize: to obtain: to attain (*Spens.*): to maintain: to control: to be master of: to occupy and dominate the mind of: to put in possession (with *of,* formerly *in*): to inform, acquaint: to imbue: to impress with the notion or feeling: to prepossess (*obs.*). — *adj.* **possessed′** in possession: self-possessed: dominated by a spirit that has entered one, or other irresistible influence. — *n.* **possession** (*poz-esh′ən*) the act, state, or fact of possessing or being possessed: a thing possessed: a subject foreign territory. — *adjs.* **possess′ional** pertaining to possession; **possess′ionary; possess′ionate** holding or allowed to hold possessions (opp. to *mendicant*). — *n.* a possessionate monk. — *adjs.* **possess′ioned; possess′-ive** pertaining to or denoting possession: unwilling to share what one has with others: reluctant to allow another person to be independent of oneself, too inclined to dominate: genitive (*gram.*). — *n.* (*gram.*) a possessive adjective or pronoun: the possessive case or a word in it. — *adv.* **possess′ively.** — *ns.* **possess′-iveness** extreme attachment to one's possessions: desire to dominate another emotionally; **possess′or; possess′-orship.** — *adj.* **possess′ory.** — **what possesses him,** etc.? what malign influence causes him, etc., to act so foolishly?; **writ of possession** a process directing a sheriff to put a person in possession of property recovered in ejectment. [O.Fr. *possesser* — L. *possidēre, possessum.*]
posset *pos′it, n.* a dietetic drink, milk curdled with e.g. wine, ale, or vinegar. — *v.t.* (*Shak.*) to curdle. — *v.i.*

to make a posset: (of a baby) to vomit slightly after feeding (*dial.*). — **posset cup** a large cup or covered bowl for posset. [M.E. *poschot, possot*; origin unknown.]

possible *pos'i-bl, adj.* that may be or happen: that may be done: not contrary to the nature of things: contingent: potential: practicable: such as one may tolerate, accept, or get on with. — *n.* a possibility: that which or one who is possible: the highest possible score: one's best (*Gallicism*): (in *pl.*) necessaries (*slang*). — *ns.* **poss'ibilism** the policy of confining efforts to what is immediately possible or practicable; **poss'ibilist**; **possibil'ity** the state of being possible: that which is possible: a contingency: (in *pl.*) potential, promise for the future. — *adv.* **poss'ibly** perhaps: by any possible means. [L. *possibilis* — *posse*, to be able.]

possie, pozzy *poz'i, (Austr. coll.) ns.* a position. [Shortened forms of **position**.]

possum, (formerly also **'possum**) *pos'əm, n.* an (orig. colloquial) aphetic form of **opossum**. — *v.i.* (*Austr.* and *U.S.*) to play possum. — **play possum** to feign death, sleep, illness or ignorance: to dissemble; **stir the possum** (*Austr.*) to liven things up.

post[1] *pōst, n.* a stout, stiff stake or pillar of timber or other material, usually fixed in an upright position: an upright member of a frame: a winning-post, starting-post, etc.: the pin of a lock: a solid thickish stratum: a pillar of coal left in a mine as a support: a tavern doorpost, on which a score was chalked (*Shak.*). — *v.i.* to stick up on a post, hence on a board, door, wall, hoarding, etc.: to announce, advertise, or denounce by placard: to placard as having failed in an examination, or failed to be classed: to announce as overdue: to affix a bill or bills to. — *n.* **post'er** a bill-sticker: a large printed bill or placard for posting. — *v.t.* to stick bills on: to advertise or publish by posters. — **poster colours** matt water-colours for designing posters and other reproduction work; **post'-hole** (*archaeol.*) a hole sunk in the ground to take a fence-post, roof-support, etc.; **post'-mill** a windmill pivoted on a post. — **between you and me and the (bed-, lamp-, gate-,** etc.**) post** in confidence; **first past the post** having reached the winning-post first, having won the race (see also **first-past-the-post** under **first**); **from pillar to post** see **pillar**; **sheriff's post** (*hist.*) a post at a sheriff's door. [O.E. *post* — L. *postis*, a doorpost — *pōnĕre*, to place.]

post[2] *pōst, n.* a fixed place or station, esp. a place where a soldier or body of soldiers is stationed: a fixed place or stage on a road, for forwarding letters and change of horses: a body of men stationed at a post: a trading station: an office, employment, or appointment: a messenger carrying letters by stages or otherwise: a postman (*obs.* or *dial.*): a public letter-carrier: an established system of conveying letters: a posthorse (*Shak.*): a mail-coach: a packet-boat (*obs.*): a despatch, delivery, or batch of letters: a post-office, or post-office letter-box: haste (*Shak.*): a size of writing-paper, double that of common notepaper (originally with watermark, a post-horn): full rank as naval captain (see **post-captain** below): a bugle-call (*first* or *last*) summoning soldiers to their quarters or (*last post*) performed at a military funeral: a name often given to a newspaper: a stake in a game: a good or winning hand, as in the old card-game of **post and pair**, in which the players vied on the goodness of their hands, a pair-royal being best. — *v.t.* to station: to entrust to the post-office for transmission: to shift, transfer to another (as blame; with *over* or *off*) (*Shak.*): to transfer to another book, or enter in a book, or carry to an account (*book-k.*): to supply with necessary information: to appoint to a post: to send or appoint (to a ship) as full captain: to move (personnel, a military unit, etc.) to a new location: to stake. — *v.i.* to travel with posthorses or with speed: to move up and down in the saddle, in time with the horse's movements. — *adv.* with posthorses: with speed. — *n.* **post'age** money paid for conveyance by post: travel with posthorses

(*obs.*). — *adj.* **post'al** of or pertaining to the mail-service. — *n.* (*U.S.*; in full **post'al-card**) a postcard issued by the post-office with printed stamp. — *ns.* **post'er** one who travels post (*Shak.*): a posthorse: one who posts a letter; **post'ie** (*Scot.* and *Austr. coll.*) a postman. — *n.* and *adj.* **post'ing**. — **post'age-stamp** an embossed or printed stamp or an adhesive label to show that the postal charge has been paid: something very tiny in area (*facet.*); **postal ballot** the submission of votes by post; **postal order** an order issued by the postmaster authorising the holder to receive at a post-office payment of the sum printed on it; **postal note** (*Austr.* and *N.Z.*) a postal order; **postal tube** a cylinder for sending rolled-up papers by post; **postal union** an association of the chief countries of the world for international postal purposes; **postal vote** a vote submitted by post rather than placed directly into a ballot-box; **post'-bag** a mail-bag: a term used collectively for letters received; **post'-box** a letter-box; **post boy** a boy who rides posthorses or who carries letters: a postilion; **post'-bus** a small bus used for delivering mail and for conveying passengers, esp. in rural areas; **post'-cap'tain** formerly, a naval officer posted to the rank of captain, a full captain distinguished from a commander (called captain by courtesy); **post'card** a card on which a message may be sent by post: such a card not issued by the post-office (*U.S.*). — *v.t.* to send a postcard to. — **post'-chaise** (popularly **po"chay, po'chay, po"chaise**) a carriage, usually four-wheeled, for two or four passengers with a postilion, used in travelling with posthorses. — *v.i.* to travel by post-chaise. — **post'code, postal code** a short series of letters and numbers denoting a very small area used for sorting mail by machine. — *v.t.* to affix or provide with a postcode. — **post'-day** the day on which the post or mail arrives or departs; **post exchange** (*U.S.*) a shop run for military personnel, subsidised by the government (abbrev. **PX**). — *adj.* and *adv.* **post'-free'** without charge for postage: with postage prepaid. **post'haste'** (from the old direction on letters, *haste, post, haste*) haste in travelling like that of a post. — *adj.* speedy: immediate. — *adv.* with utmost haste or speed. — **post'-horn** a postman's horn: a long straight brass horn blown by a coach guard; **post'horse** a horse kept for posting; **post'house** an inn, orig. where horses were kept for posting: a post-office; **post'-letter** a letter in the custody of the post-office; **post'man** a post or courier: a letter-carrier; **post'mark** the mark stamped upon a letter at a post-office defacing the postage-stamp or showing the date and place of expedition or of arrival; **post'master** the manager or superintendent of a post-office: one who supplies posthorses: a portioner, or scholar on the foundation of Merton College, Oxford; **Post'master-Gen'eral** formerly, the minister at the head of the post-office department; **post'mastership**; **post'mistress**; **post'-office** an office for receiving and transmitting letters by post, and other business: **Post Office** formerly, a department of the government which had charge of the conveyance of letters, converted in 1969 into a public corporation, the **Post Office Corporation**. — *adj.* **post'-paid'** having the postage prepaid. — **post'man** a postman or postwoman; **post'person** a postman or postwoman; **post'-road** a road with stations for posthorses; **post'-time** the time for the despatch or for the delivery of letters; **post'-town, post'-village** a town, village, with a post-office; **post'woman** a female letter-carrier. — **general post** a game in which the players change places simultaneously; **postman's knock** a parlour kissing-game; **post-office box** a box in the post-office into which are put the letters addressed to a particular person or firm; **Post Office savings bank** the older name of the **National Savings Bank**. [Fr. *poste* — It. *posta* and *posto* — L. *pōnĕre, positum*, to place.]

post- *pōst-, pfx.* after — as *post-classical, post-primary, post-Reformation, post-war*, etc.: behind — as *post-nasal, post-ocular*. — *adj.* **post-bell'um** after the war.

— *n.* **post-commun'ion** the part of the eucharistic office after the act of communion. — *adj.* succeeding communion. — *v.t.* **post'date'** to date after the real time: to mark with a date (as for payment) later than the time of signing. — *adj.* **post-dilu'vial** after the Flood: after the diluvial period (*obs.* geol.). — *n.* and *adj.* **post-dilu'vian.** — *adj.* **post'-doc'toral** pertaining to academic work carried out after obtaining a doctorate (*coll. abbrev.* **post'-doc'**; also *n.*). — *n.* **post'-entry** an additional entry or merchandise at a custom-house. — *adjs.* **post'-exil'ian, post'-exil'ic** after the time of the Babylonian captivity of the Jews. — *ns.* **post'-exist'ence** existence in a subsequent life; **post'face** something added by way of a concluding note at the end of a written work (opp. to *preface*; *rare*); **post'fix** a suffix. — *v.t.* **postfix'** to add as a suffix. — *adjs.* **post-glā'cial** after the glacial epoch; **post-grad'uate** belonging to study pursued after graduation. — Also *n.* — *adj.* **post-hypnot'ic** (**post-hypnotic suggestion** a suggestion made to a hypnotised subject but not acted upon till some time after he emerges from his trance). — *n.* **Post-Impress'ionism** a movement in painting that came after Impressionism, aiming at the expression of the spiritual significance of things rather than mere representation. — *n.* and *adj.* **Post-Impress'ionist.** — *n.* **post'lude** a concluding movement or voluntary. — *adj.* **post-merid'ian** coming after the sun has crossed the meridian: in the afternoon. — *n.* **post-millenā'rian** a believer in post-millennialism. — *adj.* **post-millenn'ial.** — *ns.* **post-millenn'ialism** the doctrine that the Second Advent will follow the millennium; **post-mod'ernism** a style (in any of the arts) following upon, and showing movement away from or reaction against, a style, theory, etc. termed 'modernist'. — *adjs.* **post-mod'ern, post-mod'ernist; post'-mor'tem** (L. *mortem*, acc. of *mors, mortis*, death) after death. — *n.* a post-mortem examination, autopsy: an after-the-event discussion, as at the end of a hand of cards. — *adjs.* **post-na'sal** behind the nose; **post-na'tal** after birth. — *n.pl.* **post'-nā'tī** see **antenati.** — *adjs.* **post-Ni'cene** after the Nicene council; **post-nup'tial** after marriage; **post-obit** (*-ob'it, -ōb'it*; L. *obitum*, acc. of *obitus, -ūs*, death) taking effect after someone's death. — *n.* a borrower's bond securing payment on the death of someone from whom he has expectations. — *adjs.* **post-op'erative** relating to the period just after a surgical operation; **post'(-)par'tum** after parturition; **post'-pran'dial** (L. *prandium*, a repast) after-dinner. — *ns.* **postscē'nium** the part of the stage behind the scenery; **post'script** (L. *scrīptum*, written, *pa.p.* of *scrībere*, to write) a part added to a letter after the signature: an addition to a book after it is finished: a talk following, e.g. a news broadcast: additional comment or information provided; **post-synchronisā'tion, -z-** (*cinematography*) the process of recording and adding a sound-track to a film after it has been shot (*coll. short forms* **post-synch', post-synch'ing**). — **post-synch'ronise, -ize.** — *v.t.* **post-ten'sion** to stretch the reinforcing wires or rods (in prestressed concrete) after the concrete is set. — *adjs.* **post-ten'sioned; Post-Ter'tiary** later than Tertiary — Pleistocene and Recent. — Also *n.* — *adj.* **post'-war' (post-war credit** a portion of income-tax credited to an individual for repayment after World War II). — **post-viral syndrome** a condition, following a viral infection, characterised by periodic fatigue, diminished concentration, depression, dizziness, etc. [L. *post*, after, behind.]

postage, postal. See **post²**.

posteen *pos-tēn'*, *n.* an Afghan greatcoat, generally of sheepskin with the fleece on. — Also (*erron.*) **poshteen'**. [Pers. *postī*, leather.]

poster. See **post¹·²**.

poste restante *pōst res-tãt*, a department of a post-office where letters are kept till called for. [Fr., remaining post.]

posterior *pos-tē'ri-ər*, *adj.* coming after: later: hinder: on the side next to the axis (*bot.*). — *n.* (usu. in *pl.*)

descendants, posterity: (formerly in *pl.*) hinder parts, buttocks: (in *pl.*) latter part (*Shak.*). — *n.* **posteriority** (*pos-tē-ri-or'i-ti*). — *adv.* **postē'riorly.** — *n.* **posterity** (*-ter'i-ti*) those coming after: succeeding generations: a race of descendants. [L. *postěrior*, compar. of *posterus*, coming after — *post*, after.]

postern *pōst'ərn*, *n.* a back door or gate: a small private door: a sally-port. — *adj.* back: private. [O.Fr. *posterne, posterle* — L. *posterula*, a dim. from *posterus*, coming after.]

posthorse, posthouse. See **post²**.

posthumous *post'ū-məs*, *adj.* after death: born after the father's death: published after the author's or composer's death. — *adv.* **post'humously.** [L. *posthumus, postumus*, superl. of *posterus*, coming after — *post*, after; the *h* inserted from false association with *humāre*, to bury.]

postiche *pos-tēsh'*, *adj.* superfluously and inappropriately superadded to a finished work: counterfeit or false. — *n.* a superfluous and inappropriate addition: a false hairpiece, wig. [Fr., — It. *posticio* — L. *postīcus*, hinder.]

posticous *pos-tī'kəs*, (*bot.*) *adj.* posterior: outward, extrorse. [L. *postīcus*, hinder — *post*.]

postil *pos'til*, *n.* a marginal note, esp. in the Bible: a commentary: a homily: a book of homilies. — *v.i.* to gloss. — *v.t.* and *v.i.* **pos'tillate.** — *ns.* **postillā'tion; pos'tillātor; pos'tiller.** [O.Fr. *postille* (It. *postilla*) — L.L. *postilla*, possibly — L. *post illa* (*verba*), after those (words).]

postilion *pos-* or *pōs-til'yən*, *n.* a postboy: one who guides posthorses, or horses in any carriage, riding on one of them. — Also **postill'ion.** [Fr. *postillon* — It. *postiglione* — *posta*, post.]

postillate, etc. See **postil.**

postliminary *pōst-lim'in-ə-ri*, *adj.* subsequent: sometimes used in error for **postliminiary** (see next word). — Also **postlim'inous** (erron. **postlimin'ious**). [On the analogy of **preliminary**.]

postliminy *pōst-lim'i-ni*, *n.* the right of a returned exile, prisoner, etc., to resume his former status: the right by which persons or things taken in war are restored to their former status. — *adj.* **postlimin'iary.** [L. *postlīminium*, lit. return behind the threshold — *līmen, -inis*, threshold.]

postlude. See **post-.**

postmaster. See **post²**.

post meridiem *pōst mer-id'i-em, -ēd'*, (L.) after noon.

postpone *pōs(t)-pōn'*, *v.t.* to put off to a future time: to defer: to delay: to subordinate. — *ns.* **postpone'ment, postpōn'ence** (*rare*); **postpōn'er; postposition** (*pōst-poz-ish'ən*) placing, or position, after: a word or particle placed after a word, usu. with the force of a preposition. — *adjs.* **postposi'tional; postpositive** (*-poz'*). — *advs.* **postposi'tionally, postpos'itively.** [L. *postpōněre, -positum* — *post*, after, *pōněre*, to put.]

postscenium, postscript. See **post-.**

postulancy, postulant. See **postulate.**

postulate *pos'tū-lāt*, *v.t.* to claim: to take for granted, assume: to assume as a possible or legitimate operation without preliminary construction (*geom.*): to nominate, subject to sanction of ecclesiastical authority. — *v.i.* to make demands. — *n.* a stipulation: an assumption: a fundamental principle: a position assumed as self-evident: an operation whose possibility is assumed (*geom.*): an axiom (*geom.*): a necessary condition: a person nominated to a benefice by the king, pending the pope's consent (*Scot. hist.*). — *ns.* **pos'tulancy** the state, or period, of being a postulant; **pos'tulant** a petitioner: a candidate, esp. for holy orders, or admission to a religious community; **postulā'tion.** — *adj.* **postulā'tional.** — *adv.* **postulā'tionally.** — *adj.* **pos'tulatory** supplicatory: assuming or assumed as a postulate. — *n.* **postulā'tum** a postulate. [L. *postulāre, -ātum*, to demand — *poscěre*, to ask urgently.]

posture *pos'chər*, *n.* relative disposition of parts, esp. of the body: carriage, attitude, pose: state of affairs:

disposition of mind. — *v.t.* to place in a particular manner. — *v.i.* to assume a posture: to pose: to attitudinise. — *adj.* **pos´tural.** — *ns.* **pos´turer, pos´turist** an acrobat: one who attitudinises. — **pos´ture-maker, pos´ture-master** one who teaches or practises artificial postures of the body: a contortionist. [Fr., — L. *positūra* — *pōnĕre, positum,* to place.]

posy *pō´zi, n.* a motto, as on a ring: a bunch of flowers. [**poesy.**]

pot[1] *pot, n.* a deep or deepish vessel for manufacturing, cooking or preserving purposes, or for growing plants, or holding jam, etc., or holding or pouring liquids: the contents, or capacity, of such a vessel: a chamber-pot: a pocket, or a stroke in which the object ball enters a pocket (*billiards*): earthenware: a cup or other prize (*coll.*): a large sum of money: a heavily backed horse: an important person (usu. *big pot*): a pot-shot: a simple helmet: a wicker trap for lobsters, etc.: a size of paper (also **pott**) about 12 in. by 15 in. (from its original watermark): cannabis, marijuana (*slang*). — *v.t.* to put up in pots for preserving: to put in pots: to cook in a pot: to plant in a pot: to drain, as sugar: to shoot for the pot, by a pot-shot, or generally, to bag, win, secure: to pocket (as a billiard-ball): to epitomise, esp. in travesty. — *v.i.* to tipple (*Shak.*): to have a pot-shot: — *pr.p.* **pott´ing;** *pa.t.* and *pa.p.* **pott´ed.** — **pot´ful** as much as a pot will hold: — *pl.* **pot´fuls.** — *adj.* **pott´ed** condensed, concentrated: abridged: (of music, etc.) recorded for reproduction. — *n.* **pott´y** a chamber-pot (esp. as a child's expression or *facet.*): a similar article especially intended for children too young to use a full-size toilet (**pott´y-chair** a child's chair fitted with a potty; **pott´y-training** teaching (a child) to use a potty). — **pot´-ale** refuse from a grain distillery; **pot´-bank´** a pottery; **pot´-bar´ley** barley whose outer husk has been removed by mill-stones. — *adj.* **pot´-bellied.** — **pot´-bell´y** a protuberant belly; **pot´-boiler** a work in art or literature produced merely to secure the necessaries of life: a producer of such works; **pot´-boiling.** — *adj.* **pot´-bound** having roots compressed in a mass without room for growth. — **pot´-boy** a serving boy in a public-house; **pot´-companion** a comrade in drinking; **pot´gun** a mortar: a pop-gun; **pot´-hanger** a device for hanging a pot or a pothook on; **pot´-hat** a bowler hat: formerly, a top-hat; **pot´-head** a stupid person: one who takes cannabis habitually (*slang*); **pot´-herb** a vegetable (esp.) for flavouring — e.g. parsley; **pot´hole** a hole worn in rock in a stream bed by eddying detritus: a deep hole eroded in limestone: a hole worn in a road surface; **pot´holer; pot´holing** the exploration of limestone potholes; **pot´hook** a hook for hanging a pot over a fire: a hooked stroke in writing; **pot´house** an alehouse; **pot´-hunter** one who hunts to get food: one who shoots for the sake of a bag or competes for the sake of prizes; **pot´-hunting; pot´-lid** the cover of a pot: (*Scot.* **pat´-lid´**) a curling-stone played exactly on the tee; **pot´-liquor** a thin broth in which meat has been boiled; **pot´-luck´** what may happen to be in the pot, or available, for a meal, without special preparation for guests (also *fig.*); **pot´-man** a pot-companion: a pot-boy; **pot´-metal** an alloy of copper and lead: scraps of old iron pots, etc.; **pot´-plant** a plant grown in a pot; **pot´-roast** braised meat. — *v.t.* to braise. — **pot´-shop** a small public-house; **pot´-shot** a shot within easy range: a casual or random shot. — *adj.* **pot´-sick** sickly from growing in a pot. — **pot´-stick** a stick for stirring what is being cooked in a pot; **pot´-still** a still in which heat is applied directly to the pot containing the wash (opp. to *patent still*). — *adj.* made in a pot-still. — **pot´stone** impure talc or steatite, a massive finely felted aggregate of talc, usually with mica and chlorite, such as has been cut into pots; **pott´ing-shed** a garden shed in which plants are grown in pots before being planted out in beds; **potty-chair, potty-training** see **potty** above. — *adjs.* **pot´-val´iant, pot´-val´orous** brave owing to drink. — **pot´-val´our; pot´-wall´oper** see **pot-waller.** — **big pot** important person; **go to pot** to go to ruin: to

go to pieces (orig. in allusion to the cooking-pot, not the melting-pot); **keep the pot (a-)boiling** to procure the necessaries of life: to keep going briskly without stop. [Late O.E. *pott*; cf. Ger. *Pott*; Sw. *potta*; Dan. *potte*; Fr. *pot*; origin unknown.]

pot[2] *pot, n.* shortened form of **potentiometer.**

potable *pō´ta-bl, adj.* fit to drink. — *n.* (*rare*) a beverage. [L. *pōtābilis* — *pōtāre,* to drink.]

potage *po´täzh, n.* thick soup. [Fr.]

potamic *pot-am´ik, adj.* of rivers. — *adj.* **potamological** (*pot-ə-mə-loj´i-kl*). — *ns.* **potamologist** (*-mol´ə-jist*); **potamol´ogy** the scientific study of rivers. [Gr. *potamos,* a river.]

Potamogeton *pot-əm-ō-jē´ton, -gē´ton, n.* the pondweed genus of water-plants with floating and submerged leaves, giving name to a family of monocotyledons, **Potamogetonā´ceae:** (without *cap.*) any plant of this genus. [Gr. *potamogeitōn,* pondweed — *potamos,* river, *geitōn,* neighbour.]

potash *pot´ash, n.* a powerful alkali, potassium carbonate, originally got in a crude state by lixiviating wood *ash* and evaporating in *pots* — hence **pot-ashes, pot-ash:** potassium hydroxide (*caustic potash*): sometimes the monoxide or (vaguely) other compound of potassium: potash-water. — *adj.* containing, or rich in, potassium. — *v.t.* to treat with potash. — *ns.* **potass** (*pot-as´, pot´as*; now *rare*) potash; **potass´a** (now *rare*) potassium monoxide, or sometimes hydroxide. — *adj.* **potass´ic** of potassium. — *n.* **potass´ium** an element (symbol K, for *kalium*; at. numb. 19), an alkali metal discovered by Davy in 1807 in potash. — **pot´ash=wa´ter** an aerated water containing potassium bicarbonate. — Also **potass´-wa´ter.** — **potassium-argon dating** estimating the date of prehistoric mineral formation from the proportion of potassium-40 to argon-40, the latter having developed from the former by radioactive decay and being trapped in the rock. [Eng. **pot, ash,** or the corresponding Du. *pot-asschen* (mod. *potasch*).]

potassium. See under **potash.**

potation *pō-tā´shən, n.* drinking: a draught: liquor. — *adj.* **potā´tory.** [L. *pōtātiō, -ōnis* — *pōtāre, -ātum,* to drink.]

potato *pə-* or *pō-tā´tō, n.* originally the sweet-potato, plant or tuber (see under **sweet**): now usu. a S. American plant, *Solanum tuberosum,* widely grown in temperate regions, or its tuber: — *pl.* **potā´toes.** — **potā´to=app´le** the fruit of the potato; **potā´to-blight** a destructive disease of the potato caused by the parasitic fungus *Phytophthora infestans*; **potā´to-bo´gle** (*Scot.*) a scarecrow; **potā´to-chips´** long pieces of potato fried in fat: potato crisps (*U.S.* and elsewhere); **potato crisps** very thin, crisp, fried slices of potato, widely produced commercially; **potā´to-disease´, -rot** any of several bacterial or fungal diseases of potatoes; **potā´to-fing´er** (*Shak.*) a fat finger; **potā´to-pit** a clamp of potatoes; **potato ring** an 18th-century Irish ceramic or metal (esp. silver) ring for standing a bowl on; **potā´to-spir´it** alcohol made from potatoes; **potā´to-trap´** (*slang*) the mouth. — **hot potato** (*slang*) a controversial issue: a tricky problem or assignment that one would prefer not to touch; **small potatoes** (*U.S.*) anything of no great worth; **the (clean) potato** the right thing. [Sp. *patata* — Haitian *batata,* sweet-potato.]

potatory. See **potation.**

pot-au-feu *pot-ō-fø,* (Fr.) *n.* a casserole-dish: a stew, esp. with boiled beef and vegetables.

potch, potche. Same as **poach**[2] in sense of thrust or trample. — *n.* **potch´er** a machine for breaking and bleaching pulp in paper-making.

pote *pōt, v.t.* and *v.i.* to poke, thrust, esp. with the foot (*obs.* except *dial.*): to crimp with a poting-stick (*obs.*). — **pot´ing-stick** (*obs.*) a poking-stick for ruffs, etc. [O.E. *potian.*]

poteen, potheen *po-tyēn´, -chēn´, -tēn´, n.* Irish whiskey illicitly distilled. [Ir. *poitín,* dim. of *pota,* pot, from Eng. **pot** or Fr. *pot.*]

potent *pō'tənt, adj.* powerful: mighty: strongly influential: cogent: formed of or terminating in crutch-heads (*her.*): (of a male) capable of sexual intercourse. — *n.* a prince, potentate (*Shak.*): a support: a crutch (*obs.*). — *n.* **pō'tence** power: a gibbet (*obs.*): a structure shaped like a gibbet: in watchmaking, a bracket for supporting the lower pivot: a revolving ladder in a dovecot: a right-angled military formation. — *adj.* **pō'tencé** (*-sā*) in heraldry, potent. — *n.* (*her.*) a marking of the shape of T. — *ns.* **pō'tency** power: potentiality: a wielder of power: (of a point with respect to a circle) the rectangle between the segments into which a chord of the circle is divided at the point (*geom.*): in a male, the ability to have sexual intercourse; **pō'tentate** one who possesses power: a prince. — *adj.* **pōtential** (*-ten'shl*) powerful, efficacious: latent: existing in possibility, not in reality: expressing power, possibility, liberty, or obligation (*gram.*). — *n.* anything that may be possible: a possibility: the potential mood, or a verb in it: of a point in a field of force, the work done in bringing a unit (of mass, electricity, etc.) from infinity to that point: powers or resources not yet developed. — *n.* **pōtentiality** (*pō-ten-shi-al'i-ti*). — *adv.* **pōten'tially**. — *n.* **pōtentiary** (*-ten'shi-ə-ri; rare*) a person invested with power or influence. — *v.t.* **pōten'tiate** to give power to: to make (drugs or chemicals) more potent or effective by using (them) in combination. — *ns.* **potentia'tion; pōtentiom'eter** (shortened form **pot**) an instrument for measuring difference of electric potential: a rheostat. — *adj.* **potentiōmet'ric**. — *v.t.* **po'tentise, ize** to make potent. — *adv.* **pō'tently**. — **potential difference** a difference in the electrical states existing at two points, which causes a current to tend to flow between them; **potential energy** the power of doing work possessed by a body in virtue of its position. [L. *potēns, -entis,* pr.p. of *posse,* to be able — *potis,* able, *esse,* to be.]

Potentilla *pō-tən-til'ə, n.* a genus of the rose family, including silverweed and barren strawberry, differing from Fragaria (strawberry) in having a dry receptacle: (without *cap.*) any plant of this genus. [L.L., dim. of L. *potēns,* powerful, from its once esteemed medicinal virtues.]

potentiometer. See potent.

pothecary *poth'i-kə-ri, n.* an aphetic form of **apothecary.** — Also **poticary** (*pot'*).

potheen. See poteen.

pother *podh'ər,* formerly *pudh'ər,* **pudder** *pud'ər, ns.* a choking smoke or dust: fuss: commotion: turmoil. — *v.i.* to fluster, to perplex. — *v.i.* to make a pother. — *adj.* **poth'ery.** [Origin unknown; app. not conn. with **powder.**]

pothole, pothook, pothouse. See pot[1].

poticary. See pothecary.

potiche *po-tēsh', n.* an Oriental vase rounded or polygonal in shape, narrowing at the neck. — *n.* **potichomania** (*-shō-mā'ni-ə*) a craze for imitating Oriental porcelain by lining glass vessels with paper designs, etc. [Fr. *potiche, potichomanie.*]

potin *pot-ɛ̃', n.* an old alloy of copper, zinc, lead, and tin. [Fr.]

potion *pō'shən, n.* a draught: a dose of liquid medicine or poison. [Fr., — L. *pōtiō, -ōnis* — *pōtāre,* to drink.]

potlatch *pot'lach, n.* in north-west U.S., an Indian winter festival, the occasion for emulation in extravagant gift-giving and, in one tribe, even property-destruction: any feast or gift (*coll.*). — Also **pot'lach.** [Chinook.]

potometer *pō-tom'ə-tər, n.* an instrument for measuring the rate at which a plant takes in water. [Gr. *poton,* drink.]

potoroo *pōt-ə-rōō', pot-, n.* a small marsupial akin to the kangaroo, a rat-kangaroo. [Aboriginal.]

pot-pourri *pō-pōō'ri, pō', or -rē', n.* orig. mixed stew, olla-podrida: a mixture of sweet-scented materials, chiefly dried petals: a selection of tunes strung together: a literary production composed of unconnected parts:

a hotch-potch. [Fr. *pot,* pot, *pourri,* rotten. — *pa.p.* of *pourrir* — L. *putrēre,* to rot.]

potsherd *pot'shûrd, n.* a piece of broken pottery. — **pot'-shard** (*obs.*), **pot'-share** (*Spens.*). [**pot, shard**[2].]

potstone. See pot.

pott. Another spelling of **pot** as a paper-size.

pottage *pot'ij, n.* vegetables boiled with or without meat (*arch.*): a thick soup: soup: oatmeal porridge (*obs.*). [Fr. *potage,* food cooked in a pot, later, soup — *pot,* jug, pot.]

potter[1] *pot'ər, n.* one who makes articles of baked clay, esp. earthenware vessels. — *n.* **pott'ery** articles of baked clay collectively, esp. earthenware vessels: a place where such goods are manufactured: the art of the potter. [**pot.**]

potter[2] *pot'ər, v.i.* to busy oneself in a desultory way: to dawdle. — *n.* pottering: diffuse talk. — *n.* **pott'erer.** — *n.* and *adj.* **pott'ering.** — *adv.* **pott'eringly.** [**pote.**]

pottingar *pot'in-gər, n.* an old Scottish form of **apothecary.**

pottinger *pot'in-jər, n.* a maker of *pottage.* [For *n* cf. **messenger, passenger,** etc.]

pottle *pot'l, n.* half a gallon, or thereby (*arch.*): a chip basket for strawberries. — *adjs.* **pott'le-bod'ied** having a body shaped like a pottle; **pott'le-deep** to the bottom of the pottle-pot. — **pott'le-pot** (*Shak.*) a half-gallon drinking-vessel. [O.Fr. *potel,* dim. of *pot,* pot.]

potto *pot'ō, n.* a member of a West African genus (Perodicticus) of lemurs: also applied to the kinkajou: — *pl.* **pott'os.** [Said to be a West African name.]

Pott's disease *pots diz-ēz', a* weakening disease of the spine caused by tuberculous infection, often causing curvature of the back. — **Pott's fracture** a fracture and dislocation of the ankle-joint in which the lower tibia and fibula are damaged. [Named after Sir Percival(l) *Pott,* English surgeon (1714–88), who first described them.]

potty[1] *pot'i,* (*coll.*) *adj.* trifling: petty: crazy: dotty. — *n.* **pott'iness.** [Origin obscure.]

potty[2]. See pot[1].

pot-waller *pot'-wöl'ər, n.* in certain English boroughs, before the Reform Bill of 1832, one who satisfied the test as a voter by boiling his pot on his own fireplace within the borough — sometimes in the open air before witnesses to establish a bogus claim. — Variously altered popularly to **pot'-wabb'ler, -wobb'ler, -wall'-oner, -wall'oper.** — *adj.* **pot'-wall'oping.** [**pot** and O.E. *w(e)allan,* to boil.]

pouch *powch,* (*Scot. pōōch*) *n.* a poke, pocket, or bag: any pocket-like structure, as a kangaroo's marsupium, a monkey's cheek-pouch, etc. — *v.t.* to pocket: to form into a pouch: to tip. — *v.i.* to form a pouch: to be like a pouch. — *adj.* **pouched** having a pouch. — *n.* **pouch'ful:** — *pl.* **pouch'fuls.** — *adj.* **pouch'y** baggy. — **pouched mouse** a small marsupial, *Phascologale:* an American jumping rodent (*Dipodomys*) with cheek-pouches opening outwards; **pouched rat** a pocket gopher. [O.N.Fr. *pouche* (O.Fr. *poche*); cf. **poke**[1].]

pouder, poudre. Obsolete spellings of **powder.**

pouf, pouffe, *pōōf, n.* a puffed mode of hairdressing: a pad worn in the hair by women in the 18th century: in dressmaking, material gathered up into a bunch: a soft ottoman or large hassock. — *adj.* **poufed.** [Fr. *pouf.*]

pouf(fe). Less common spelling of **poof.**

pouftah, poufter. Other spellings of **pooftah, poofter.**

Poujadist *pōō-zhäd'ist, n.* a follower of the French politician Pierre Poujade (b. 1920), antiparliamentarian champion of the small man and of tax reduction. — *n.* **Poujad'ism.** [Fr. *Poujadiste.*]

pouk, poukit. See pook.

pouke. See puck[1].

poulaine *pōō-lān', n.* a long, pointed shoe-toe. [O.Fr. (*à la*) *Poulaine,* (in the fashion of) Poland.]

poulard *pōō-lärd', n.* a fattened or spayed hen. [Fr. *poularde — poule,* hen.]

poulder, pouldre. Obsolete spellings of **powder.**

pouldron *pōl'drən.* Same as **pauldron.**
poule *pōōl, n.* a hen, esp. a chicken for boiling: a promiscuous young woman (*slang,* esp. *U.S.*): a movement in a quadrille. [Fr.]
poulp, poulpe *pōōlp, n.* the octopus. [Fr. *poulpe* — L. *pōlypus* — Doric Gr. *pōlypos* = *polypous*; see **polyp.**]
poult *pōlt, n.* a chicken: the young of the common domestic fowl or of other farmyard or game bird. — *ns.* **poult'er** (*Shak.*), **poult'erer** one who deals in dead fowls and game; **poult'ry** domestic or farmyard fowls collectively. — **poulters' measure** a rhymed couplet in which the first line has twelve, the second fourteen, syllables — from the varying number of eggs formerly sold by poulterers as a dozen; **poult'ry-farm, -yard** a farm, yard, where poultry are confined and bred. [Fr. *poulet,* dim. of *poule* — L.L. *pulla,* hen, fem. of L. *pullus,* young animal.]
poult-foot. Same as **poltfoot** (see **polt**).
poultice *pōl'tis, n.* a usu. hot, soft composition applied on a cloth to the skin, to reduce inflammation. — *v.t.* to put a poultice on. [L. *pultēs,* pl. of *puls, pultis* (Gr. *poltos*), porridge.]
poultroone. See **poltroon.**
pounce[1] *powns, n.* a hawk's (or other) claw, esp. the innermost, or any but the hind-claw: a punch (now *dial.*): a puncture (*obs.*): a sudden spring or swoop with attempt to seize. — *v.t.* to emboss by blows on the other side: to puncture, pink (*obs.*): to ornament with small holes: to seize with the claws. — *v.i.* to make a pounce: to dart: to fix suddenly upon anything. — *adj.* **pounced** furnished with claws. [Derived in some way from L. *punctiō, -ōnis* — *pungĕre, punctum,* to prick; cf. **puncheon**[1].]
pounce[2] *powns, n.* sandarach, cuttle-bone, or other fine powder for preparing a writing surface or absorbing ink: coloured powder shaken through perforations to mark a pattern on a surface beneath. — *v.t.* to prepare with pounce: to trace, transfer, or mark with pounce: to powder or sprinkle (*obs.*). — **pounce'-bag, pounce'-box** a perforated bag, box, for sprinkling pounce. [Fr. *ponce,* pumice — L. *pūmex, pūmicis.*]
pouncet-box *pown'sit-boks, n.* a pomander (also shortened to **poun'cet**; *Shak.*): sometimes used for **pounce-box** (see above). [Prob. for *pounced-box,* i.e. perforated box; see **pounce**[1].]
pouncing (*Spens.*). Same as **punching** (**punch**[3]).
pound[1] *pownd, n.* a unit of weight of varying value, long used in western and central Europe, more or less answering to the Roman *libra,* whose symbol *lb.* is used for pound: in avoirdupois weight, 16 ounces avoirdupois, 7000 grains, or 0·45359237 kilogram: formerly, in troy weight, 12 ounces troy, 5760 grains, or about 373·242 grams: a pound-weight (*Shak.*): the balance (*Spens.*): a unit of money, originally the value of a pound-weight of silver: formerly 20 shillings, now 100 (new) pence (the pound sterling, written £, for *libra*): the Australian (formerly), New Zealand (formerly), and Jamaican pound (written £A, £NZ, £J): the *pound scots* (at Union, 1s. 8d.): the unit of currency in certain other countries, including Israel, Egypt, Syria, Lebanon and Turkey: — *pl.* formerly **pound,** now **pounds** (except *coll.* and in compounds and certain phrases). — *v.t.* (*slang*) to bet on as almost a certainty. — *ns.* **pound'age** a charge or tax made on each pound: a commission, or a share in profits, of so much a pound; **pound'al** the foot-pound-second unit of force; **pound'er** a specimen weighing a pound: in composition, anything weighing, or worth, or carrying, or one who has, receives, or pays, so many pounds. — **pound'-cake** a sweet cake containing proportionally about a pound of each chief ingredient; **pound'-day** a day on which gifts of one pound weight of various goods are invited for charity. — *adj.* **pound'-fool'ish** neglecting the care of large sums in attending to little ones. — **pound force** the gravitational force of 1lb weight and mass: a unit of such force (abbrev. *lbf.*); **pound'-weight'** as much as weighs a pound: a weight

of one pound used in weighing. — **pound of flesh** strict exaction of one's due in fulfilment of a bargain, etc., to the point of making the other party suffer beyond what is reasonable (see Shak., *Merch. of Ven.* I, iii. 150, IV, i. 99 ff., etc.). [O.E. *pund* — L. (*libra*) *pondō,* (pound) by weight, *pondō,* by weight — *pendĕre,* to weigh.]
pound[2] *pownd, n.* an enclosure in which strayed animals are confined, or distrained goods kept: any confined place: a pond (now *Scot.* and *dial.*): a level part of a canal between two locks: the last compartment of a pound-net. — *v.t.* to put in a pound: to enclose, confine. — *n.* **pound'age** a charge for pounding stray cattle. — **pound'-keeper, pound'-master; pound'-net** an arrangement of nets for trapping fish. [O.E. *pund* (in compounds), enclosure.]
pound[3] *pownd, v.t.* to beat into fine pieces: to bruise: to bray with a pestle: to bethump: to lay on, shower (*Spens.*). — *v.i.* to beat: to thump: to beat the ground: to make one's way heavily: to struggle on. — *n.* the act or sound of pounding. — *n.* **pound'er.** [O.E. *pūnian,* to beat; *-d* excrescent, as in **sound**[3], **bound**[4].]
poundal. See **pound**[1].
poupe *pōōp,* **poupt** *pōōpt* (*Shak.; pa.p.*). See **poop**[2].
pour *pōr, pōr, v.t.* to cause or allow to flow in a stream: to send forth or emit in a stream or like a stream: to send downstream (*Spens.*): to spread out (*obs.*): to drain (as cooked potatoes; *Scot.*). — *v.i.* to stream: to rain heavily: to pour out tea, coffee, etc.: (of a vessel) to allow liquid contents to run out duly. — *n.* a pouring: an amount poured at a time. — *adj.* **pour'able** that can be poured. — *ns.* **pour'er; pourie** (*pōōr'i; Scot.*) a vessel with a spout: a cream-jug: an oiling-can. — *n.* and *adj.* **pour'ing.** — **pour'-out, poor'-oot** (*Scot.*) the scattering of coins to children as the bride and bridegroom depart after a wedding. — **it never rains but it pours** things never happen singly; **pouring wet** raining hard; **pour oil on troubled waters** to soothe or calm a person or situation. [M.E. *pouren;* origin obscure.]
pourboire *pōōr-bwär', n.* a tip. [Fr., — *pour,* for, *boire,* to drink.]
pourie. See **pour.**
pourparler *pōōr-pär'lā, n.* (usu. in *pl.*) an informal preliminary conference. [Fr.]
pourpoint *pōōr'point, n.* a mediaeval quilted doublet. [Fr.]
poursew, poursue, poursuit(t). Spens. for **pursue, pursuit.**
pourtray an old-fashioned spelling of **portray:** — *pa.p.* in Spens. **pour'trahed** (3 syllables), **pourtrayd, purtraid, purtrayd.** — *n.* **pour'traict** obs. spelling of **portrait.**
pousowdie. See **powsowdy.**
pousse *pōōs,* (*Spens.*) *n.* pease. [**pulse**[2].]
pousse-café *pōōs-ka-fā, n.* a cordial, liqueur, or combination of several in layers, served after coffee. [Fr., push-coffee.]
poussette *pōōs-et', n.* a figure in country-dancing in which couples hold both hands and move up or down the set, changing places with the next couple. — *v.i.* to perform a poussette. [Fr., dim. of *pousse,* push.]
poussin *pōō-sẽ', n.* a chicken reared for eating at four to six weeks old: a small whole poussin, served as an individual serving, roasted, or split and fried or grilled. [Fr.]
pout[1] *powt, v.i.* to push out the lips, in sullen displeasure or otherwise: to protrude. — *v.t.* to protrude. — *n.* a protrusion, esp. of the lips. — *ns.* **pout'er** one who pouts: a variety of pigeon having its breast inflated; **pout'ing.** — *adv.* **pout'ingly.** — *adj.* **pout'y.** [M.E. *powte,* of doubtful origin.]
pout[2] *powt, n.* a fish of the cod family, the bib — also **whit'ing-pout.** — *n.* **pout'ing** the whiting-pout. — **eel'-pout** see **eel; horn'-pout, horned'-pout** an American catfish (*Amiurus*). [O.E. (*ǽle-*) *pūte,* (eel-) pout — perh. conn. with foregoing with reference to the bib's inflatable membrane on the head.]
pout[3], **poot** *pōōt, n.* a Scots form of **poult.** — *v.i.* to shoot at young partridges or young grouse.

pouther *pōō'dhər*, a Scots form of **powder.**
poverty *pov'ər-ti, n.* the state of being poor: necessity: want: lack: deficiency: a band of pipers (*obs.*). — *adj.* **pov'erty-stricken** suffering from poverty. — **poverty trap** a poor financial state from which there is no escape as any increase in income will result in a diminution or withdrawal of low-income government benefits. [O.Fr. *poverte* (Fr. *pauvreté*) — L. *paupertās, -ātis — pauper*, poor.]
pow¹ *pow*, (*Scot.*) *n.* a head, poll: a head of hair. [**poll¹.**]
pow² *pow*, (*Scot.*) *n.* a slow-moving stream, generally found in carse lands: a small creek at the mouth of a river or in an estuary, affording a landing-place for boats, esp. on the Forth. [Scot. *poll.*]
pow³ *pow*, (esp. *U.S.*) *interj.* imitative of impact, etc.
powan *pow'ən, pō'ən, n.* a species of whitefish (Coregonus) found in Loch Lomond and Loch Eck. [Scots form of **pollan.**]
powder *pow'dər, n.* dust: any solid in fine particles: gunpowder: hair-powder: face-powder: a medicine in the form of powder. — *v.t.* to reduce to powder: to sprinkle, daub, or cover with powder: to salt by sprinkling: to sprinkle. — *v.i.* to crumble into powder: to use powder for the hair or face. — *adjs.* **pow'dered** reduced to powder e.g., of food, through dehydration and crushing: sprinkled, or daubed, or dusted with powder: salted; **pow'dery** of the nature of powder: covered with powder: dusty: friable. — **pow'der-box** box for face-, hair-powder, etc.; **powder compact** see **compact¹**; **pow'der-clos'et, pow'dering-clos'et** a small room in which hair was powdered; **pow'der-down'** a kind of down on some birds that readily disintegrates in powder; **powdered sugar** (*Amer.*) very fine sugar produced by grinding granulated sugar; **pow'der-flask, pow'der-horn** a flask (originally a horn) for carrying gunpowder; **pow'dering-gown** a loose dressing-gown worn while the hair was being powdered; **pow'dering-tub** a vessel in which meat is salted: a tub for treatment of venereal disease by sweating (*obs.*); **pow'der-mag'-azine** a place where gunpowder is stored; **pow'der-met'allurgy** the science and art of preparing metals for use by reducing them, as a stage in the process, to powder form; **pow'der-mill** a mill in which gunpowder is made; **pow'der-monk'ey** a boy carrying powder to the gunners on a ship-of-war; **pow'der-puff** a soft, downy ball, etc. for dusting powder on the skin: an effeminate homosexual (*slang*); **pow'der-room** a ship's powder-magazine: a room for powdering the hair (also **pow'dering-room**): a ladies cloakroom. — **keep one's powder dry** to keep one's energies ready for action, play a waiting game: to observe all practical precautions. [O.Fr. *poudre* — L. *pulvis, pulveris*, dust.]
powellise, -ize *pow'əl-īz, v.t.* (of timber) to season and preserve by boiling in a saccharine solution. [W. *Powell*, the inventor of the process.]
Powellism *pow'əl-izm, n.* the views on immigration and on various economic issues expressed by J. Enoch *Powell*, politician and scholar (b. 1912).
powellite *pow'əl-it, n.* a mineral, calcium molybdate. [After John Wesley *Powell* (1834–1902), American geologist, etc.]
power *pow'ər, powr, n.* ability to do anything — physical, mental, spiritual, legal, etc.: capacity for producing an effect: strength: energy: faculty of the mind: moving force of anything: right to command, authority: rule: influence: control: governing office: permission to act: a paper giving authority to act: potentiality: a wielder of authority, strong influence, or rule: that in which such authority or influence resides: a spiritual agent: a being of the sixth order of the celestial hierarchy: a state influential in international affairs: an armed force (*arch.*): a great deal or great many (now *dial.* or *coll.*): a mark of subjection (1 Cor. xi. 10; N.E.B. 'a sign of authority'): the sound-value of a letter: the rate at which a system absorbs energy from, or passes energy into, another system, esp. the rate of doing mechanical work, measured in watts or other unit of work done

per unit of time (*mech.*, physics, etc.): an instrument serving as means of applying energy (see **mechanical**): the product of a number of equal factors, generalised to include negative and fractional numbers (*math.*): the potency of a point with respect to a circle (*geom.*): magnifying strength, or a lens possessing it (*opt.*). — *adj.* concerned with power: worked, or assisted in working, by mechanical power: involving a high degree of physical strength and skill (esp. *sport*, e.g. *power tennis*). — *v.t.* to equip with mechanical energy. — *v.i.* and *v.t.* (*slang*) to move, or propel, with great force, energy or speed. — *adjs.* **pow'ered; pow'erful** having great power: mighty: forcible: efficacious: intense: impressive, esp. in a disagreeable way: very great (*coll.*). — *adv.* (*coll.*) exceedingly. — *adv.* **pow'erfully.** — *n.* **pow'erfulness.** — *adj.* **pow'erless** without power: weak: impotent: helpless. — *adv.* **pow'erlessly.** — *n.* **pow'erlessness.** — *adj.* **pow'er-assist'ed** helped by, using, mechanical power. — **power block** a politically important and powerful group or body; **pow'erboat** a boat propelled by a motor, a motorboat; **power breakfast, lunch, tea,** (*coll.*) a high-level business discussion held over breakfast, lunch, tea; **power cut** an interruption of, or diminution in, the electrical supply in a particular area; **pow'er-dive** a usu. steep dive of an aeroplane, made faster by use of engine(s). — Also *v.i., v.t.* — **pow'er-diving.** — *adj.* **pow'er-driven** worked by (esp. mechanical or electrical) power. — **power'-house** (also *fig.*), **-station** a place where mechanical power (esp. electric) is generated; **pow'er-drill, -lathe, -loom, -press** a drill, lathe, loom, press, worked by mechanical power, as water, steam, electricity; **power pack** a device for adjusting an electric current to the voltages required by a particular piece of electronic equipment; **pow'er-plant** an industrial plant for generating power: the assemblage of parts generating motive power in a motor-car, aeroplane, etc.; **pow'erplay** strong, attacking play designed to pressure the defense by concentrating players and action in one small area (*team sport*): similarly concentrated pressure applied in e.g. military, political or business tactics; **pow'er-point** a point at which an appliance may be connected to the electrical system; **pow'er-politics** international politics in which the course taken by states depends upon their knowledge that they can back their decisions with force or other compulsive action; **power steering** a type of steering system in a vehicle, in which the rotating force exerted on the steering wheel is supplemented by engine power. — **in one's power** at one's mercy: within the limits of what one can do; **in power** in office: in potentiality (*Spens.*); **the powers that be** the existing ruling authorities (from Rom. xiii. 1). [O.Fr. *poer* (Fr. *pouvoir*) — L.L. *potēre* (for L. *posse*), to be able.]
powin, pown. See **pawn⁴.**
pownd. Spenserian spelling of **pound³.**
powney, pownie, powny *pow'ni.* See ety. of **pony.**
powre. Spenserian spelling of **pour.**
powsowdy *pow-sow'di,* (*Scot.*) *n.* any mixture of heterogeneous kinds of food. — Also **pousow'die.** [Origin unknown.]
powter *pow'tər,* (*Scot.*) *v.i.* to poke: to rummage. — *v.t.* to poke: to get by groping. [Origin obscure.]
powwaw *pow-wö',* (*Shak.*) *interj.* pooh.
powwow *pow'wow,* **pawaw** *pä-wö', ns.* an American Indian shaman: a rite, often with feasting: a conference. — *v.i.* **powwow'** to hold a powwow: to confer. [Algonquian *powwaw, powah.*]
pox *poks, n.* (*pl.* of **pock**) pustules: an eruptive disease, esp. smallpox or syphilis (as *sing.*): sheep-pox. — *v.t.* to infect with pox. — *interj.* plague. — *adj.* **pox'y** suffering from pox: spotty: dirty, diseased, rotten (*slang*): (*loosely*) applied to anything unpleasant or troublesome (*slang*). — **pox'virus** any one of a group of DNA-containing animal virusus, including those which cause smallpox, cowpox, myxomatosis and certain fibromata.

poy-bird. See **poe-bird.**

poynant *poin'ənt*, (*Spens.*, etc.) *adj.* Same as **poignant.**

poynt, poyse, poyson. Old spellings of **point, poise, poison.**

poz, pozz *poz*, *adj.* an old slang shortening of **positive.**

pozzy. See **possie.**

pozzolana *pot-sō-lä'nə*, **pozzuolana** *-swō-*, *ns.* a volcanic dust first found at *Pozzuoli*, near Naples, which forms with mortar a cement that will set in air or water. — *adj.* **pozzola'nic.**

praam. Same as **pram[1].**

prabble *prab'l*, (*Shak.*) *n.* a spelling representing the Welsh pronunciation of **brabble.**

practic (old spellings **practick, practique**) *prak'tik*, *adj.* relating to, or of the nature of, practice or action (*arch.*): practising (*obs.*): in practice (*obs.*): skilled (*Spens.*): cunning (*Spens.*). — *n.* practice as opposed to theory (*arch.*): (esp. in *pl.*) practices, doings: practical experience (*arch.*): legal usage or case-law (esp. *Scots law*): a practical man. — *n.* **practicabil'ity.** — *adj.* **prac'ticable** that may be practised, carried out, accomplished, used, or followed: passable, as a road: (of a stage window, light-switch, etc.) functioning, practical (q.v). - *n.* **prac'ticableness.** — *adv.* **prac'ticably.** — *adj.* **prac'tical** in, relating to, concerned with, well adapted to, or inclining to look to, actual practice, actual conditions, results, or utility: practised: practising, actually engaged in doing something: efficient in action: workable: virtual: (of a piece of stage equipment, esp. electric lights, etc.) that can be operated on stage (*theat.*). — *n.* a practical man: a practical examination. — *ns.* **prac'ticalism** devotion to what is practical; **prac'ticalist; practical'ity** practicalness: a practical matter or feature, aspect, of an affair. — *adv.* **prac'tically** in a practical way: by a practical method: to all intents and purposes: very nearly, as good as. — *ns.* **prac'ticalness; prac'tice** (*-tis*) action, performance: actual doing: proceeding: habitual action: custom: legal procedure: repeated performance as a means of acquiring skill, esp. in playing a musical instrument: form so acquired: the exercise of a profession: a professional man's business, as a field of activity or a property: negotiation (*arch.*): scheming: plotting: trickery: working upon the feelings: a compendious way of multiplying quantities involving several units, by means of aliquot parts (*arith.*); **practician** (*-tish'ən*) a practiser or practitioner: a practical man; **prac'ticum** (*-ti-kəm*; *U.S.*) a course of practical work undertaken to supplement academic studies; **prac'tisant** an agent or fellow in conspiracy. — *v.t.* **practise** (*prak'tis*, formerly *-tīz'*; *U.S.* **practice**) to put into practice: to perform: to carry out: to do habitually: to exercise, as a profession: to exercise oneself in, or on, or in the performance of, in order to acquire or maintain skill: to train by practice: to put to use: to frequent (*obs.*): to compass (*obs.*): to contrive (*Milt.*): to plot (*Shak.*). — *v.i.* to act habitually: to be in practice (esp. medical or legal): to exercise oneself in any art, esp. instrumental music: to proceed, esp. to seek to injure, by underhand means: to tamper, work (with *upon, on*): to scheme: to have dealings: to use artifices: to work by artifice (on the feelings). — *adj.* **prac'tised** skilled through practice. — *n.* **prac'tiser.** — *adj.* **prac'tising** actually engaged, e.g. in professional employment: holding the beliefs, following the practices, demanded by a particular religion, etc. — *n.* **practitioner** (*-tish'ən-ər*; irreg. from *practician*) one who is in practice, esp. in medicine: one who practises. — *adj.* **prac'tive** practical. — **practical joke** a joke that consists in action, not words, usually an annoying trick; **practical politics** proposals or measures that may be carried out at once or in the near future. — **general practitioner** one who practises medicine and surgery without specialising. [Obs. Fr. *practique* — L. *practicus* — Gr. *prāktikos*, fit for action — *prāssein*, to do.]

practolol *prak'tə-lol*, *n.* a drug used to treat cardiac arrhythmia, but suspected of causing side effects including eye-damage.

prad *prad*, (*slang*) *n.* a horse. [Du. *paard* — L.L. *paraverēdus*; see **palfrey.**]

prae-; praecoces, praecocial. See **pre-; precocious.**

praedial, predial *prē'di-əl*, *adj.* pertaining to, connected with, or derived from, the land: landed: rural: agrarian: attached to the land. — *n.* a praedial slave. [L.L. *praediālis* — *praedium*, an estate.]

praefect; praeludium. See **prefect; prelude.**

praemunire *prē-mū-nī'ri*, *prī-*, *-nē'*, *n.* a writ issued under statutes of Richard II, summoning a person accused of suing in a foreign court for matters cognisable by the law of England, used especially against papal claims, and later extended to various offences: an offence that could be so dealt with: the penalty for such an offence: a predicament or scrape. [From the words of the writ, *praemūnīre faciās*, cause to warn, or see that thou warn, the word *praemūnīre*, properly to fortify in front, defend, being confused with *prae-monēre*, to forewarn.]

praenomen *prē-nō'mən, prī-nō'men, n.* the name prefixed to the family name in ancient Rome, as *Gaius* in Gaius Julius Caesar: the generic name of a plant or animal. [L. *praenōmen* — *nōmen*, name.]

praepostor; Praeraphaelite; praeses; praesidium. See **preposition; Pre-Raphaelite; preses; presidial.**

Praesepe *prī-sē'pi, n.* a cluster of stars in the constellation Cancer.

praeter-. See **preter-.**

praetor *prē'tər, -tör, prī'tor, n.* a magistrate of ancient Rome next in rank to the consuls. — *adj.* **praetorian** (*-tō', tō'*). — *n.* a former praetor or man of like rank: a member of the emperor's bodyguard. — *ns.* **praeto'rium** a general's tent: a governor's residence: a court or headquarters; **prae'torship.** — **praetorian gate** the gate of a Roman camp in front of the general's tent, and nearest to the enemy; **praetorian guard** the bodyguard of the Roman Emperor. [L. *praetor*, for *praeitor* — *prae*, in front of, before, and *īre, itum*, to go.]

pragmatic *prag-mat'ik, adj.* relating to affairs of state: relating to, or of the nature of, pragmatism: having concern more for matters of fact than for theories: pragmatical. — *n.* an edict: a man of business: a busybody: an opinionative person. — *adj.* **pragmat'ical** active: practical: matter of fact: interfering with the affairs of others: officious: meddlesome: self-important: opinionative: pragmatic. — *n.* **pragmatical'ity.** — *adv.* **pragmat'ically.** — *n.* **pragmat'icalness.** — *n.sing.* **pragmat'ics** the study of inherent practical usage, and social and behavioural aspects, of language: a study of linguistic sign-systems and their use. — *v.t.* **prag'matise, -ize** to interpret or represent as real: to rationalise. — *ns.* **prag'matiser, -z-; prag'matism** pragmatical quality: matter-of-factness: concern for the practicable rather than for theories and ideals: a treatment of history with an eye to cause and effect and practical lessons: humanism or practicalism, a philosophy, or philosophic method, that makes practical consequences the test of truth (*philos.*); **prag'matist** a pragmatic person: one who advocates the practicable rather than the ideal course: a believer in pragmatism. — **pragmatic sanction** a special decree issued by a sovereign, such as that of the Emperor Charles VI, settling his dominions upon Maria Theresa. [Gr. *prāgma, -atos*, deed — *prāssein*, to do.]

prahu *prä'(h)ōō.* Same as **prau.**

Prairial *pre-ri-äl', pre-ryäl', n.* the ninth month of the French revolutionary calendar, about 20th May to 18th June. [Fr., — *prairie*, meadow.]

prairie *prā'ri, n.* a treeless plain, flat or rolling, naturally grass-covered. — *adj.* **prai'ried.** — **prai'rie-chick'en, -hen** an American genus (*Cupidonia* or *Tympanuchus*) of grouse: the sharp-tailed grouse (*Pedioecetes*) of the western United States; **prai'rie-dog** a gregarious burrowing and barking North American marmot (*Cynomys*); **prai'rie-oy'ster** (*U.S.*) a raw egg with condiments; **prai'rie-schoon'er** an emigrants' long covered wagon;

prai′rie-tur′nip breadroot; **prairie value** the value of land in its natural state before it has been improved by man; **prai′rie-wolf** the coyote. [Fr., — L.L. *prātaria* — L. *prātum*, a meadow.]

praise *prāz, v.t.* to assign a value to, appraise (*Shak.*): to speak highly of: to commend: to extol: to glorify, as in worship. — *n.* commendation: glorifying: the musical part of worship: that for which praise is due: (in ejaculatory expressions) God (*Scot.*). — *adjs.* **praise′-ful; praise′less.** — *n.* **prais′er.** — *n.* and *adj.* **prais′ing.** — *advs.* **prais′ingly; praise′worthily.** — *n.* **praise′worthiness.** — *adj.* **praise′worthy** worthy of praise: commendable. [O.Fr. *preiser* — L.L. *preciāre* for L. *pretiāre*, to prize — *pretium*, price.]

praiseach *prash′ahh, n.* an oatmeal porridge, often with vegetables: a mess (also *fig.*): wild mustard (*Brassica arvensis*). [Ir. — L. *brassica*, cabbage.]

Prakrit *prä′krit, n.* a name for (any of) the Indo-Aryan dialects contemporary with Sanskrit, or for (any of) the later languages derived from them. — *adj.* **Prakrit′ic.** [Sans. *prākṛta*, the natural — *prakṛti*, nature.]

praline *prä′lēn, n.* an almond or nut kernel with a brown coating of sugar, or a similar confection made with crushed nuts. — Also **prawlin** (*prö′lin*). [Fr. *praline*, from Marshal Duplessis-*Praslin*, whose cook invented it.]

Pralltriller *präl′tril-ər, (mus.) n.* an upper or inverted mordent, a grace in which the principal note is preceded in performance by itself and the note above. [Ger.]

pram[1], **praam** *präm, n.* a flat-bottomed Dutch or Baltic lighter: a flat-bottomed dinghy with squared-off bow: a barge fitted as a floating battery. [Du. *praam*.]

pram[2] *pram, n.* a shortening (formerly *coll.*) of **perambulator:** a milkman's hand-cart.

prana *prä′nə, n.* the breath of life: in Hindu religion, esp. yoga, breath as the essential life force. — *n.* **pranaya′ma** (*yoga*) controlled breathing. [Sans.]

prance *präns, v.i.* to bound from the hind legs: to go with a capering or dancing movement: to move with exaggerated action and ostentation: to swagger: to ride a prancing horse. — *v.t.* to cause to prance. — *n.* an act of prancing: swagger. — *n.* **pranc′er.** — *adj.* and *n.* **pranc′ing.** — *adv.* **pranc′ingly.** [M.E. *praunce*; origin unknown.]

pranck, prancke. See **prank**[3].

prandial *pran′di-əl, (esp. facet.) adj.* relating to dinner. [L. *prandium*, a morning or midday meal.]

prang *prang, (slang, orig. airmen's slang) n.* a crash: a bombing-attack. — *v.t.* to crash or smash: to bomb heavily: to crash into (e.g. another car). [App. imit.]

prank[1] *prangk, n.* an evil deed (*obs.*): a malicious or mischievous trick: a trick: a practical joke: a frolic. — *v.i.* to play pranks. — *adjs.* **prank′ful, prank′ish, prank′-some, prank′y.** — *n.* **prank′ster.** [Origin unknown.]

prank[2] *prangk, (arch.) v.t.* to dress or adorn showily: to bespangle: to set in adornment. — *v.i.* (also *v.t.* with *it*) to make great show. — *n.* and *adj.* **prank′ing.** — *adv.* **prank′ingly.** [Akin to Du. *pronken*, Ger. *prunken*, to show off; cf. **prink**.]

prank[3], **pranck, prancke** *prangk, (obs.) v.t.* to pleat, fold: to set in order. [Origin unknown.]

prank[4] *prangk, (rare) n.* prancing. — *v.i.* (and *v.t.* with *it*) to prance. — *v.i.* **prank′le** to prance lightly. [Poss. conn. with **prance**.]

prase *prāz, n.* a leek-green quartz. [Gr. *prason*, leek.]

praseodymium *prāz-ī-ō-dim′i-əm, n.* an element (symbol Pr; at. numb. 59), a metal with green salts, separated from the once-supposed element didymium. [Gr. *prasios*, leek-green — *prason*, leek, and **didymium**.]

prat[1] *prat, (slang) n.* the buttocks. — *v.t.* (*Shak.*, punningly) to beat. — *n.* **prat′fall** (*U.S. slang*) a fall landing on the prat: a humiliating blunder or experience (*fig.*). — Also *v.i.* [Origin unknown.]

prat[2] *prat, (slang) n.* used abusively, a fool, an ineffectual person. [Poss. conn. with **prat**[1].]

prate *prāt, v.i.* to talk foolishly: to talk boastfully or insolently: to tattle: to be loquacious. — *v.t.* to utter pratingly: to blab. — *n.* foolish or superfluous talk. — *n.* **pra′ter.** — *n.* and *adj.* **pra′ting.** — *adv.* **pra′tingly.** [Cf. L.G. *praten*, Dan. *prate*, Du. *praaten*.]

pratie, praty *prā′ti, n.* an Anglo-Irish form of **potato.**

pratincole *prat′ing-kōl, n.* a bird akin to the plovers, with swallow-like wings and tail. [L. *prātum*, meadow, *incola*, an inhabitant.]

pratique *prat′ik, -ēk′, n.* permission to hold intercourse or to trade after quarantine or on showing a clean bill of health. [Fr.]

prattle *prat′l, v.i.* to talk much and idly: to utter child's talk. — *v.t.* to utter in a prattling way. — *n.* empty talk. — *ns.* **pratt′lement** prattle; **pratt′ler** one who prattles: a child. — **pratt′lebox** a prattler. [Dim. and freq. of **prate**.]

praty. See **pratie.**

prau *prä′ōō,* **prow, prahu** *prä′(h)ōō,* **proa** *prō′ə, ns.* a Malay sailing- or rowing-boat, esp. a fast sailing-vessel with both ends alike, and a flat side with an outrigger kept to leeward. [Malay *prāū*.]

praunce. Spenser's form of **prance.**

pravity *prav′i-ti, (rare) n.* wickedness. [L. *prāvitās, -ātis.*]

prawle *pröl, n.* Shakespeare's Welsh form of **brawl.**

prawlin. See **praline.**

prawn *prön, n.* a small edible shrimp-like crustacean (*Palaemon serratus* or kindred species). — *v.i.* to fish for prawns. — **come the raw prawn** (*Austr. slang*) to make an attempt to deceive. [M.E. *prayne, prane*; origin unknown.]

praxinoscope *praks′in-ō-skōp, n.* an optical toy giving effect of motion by reflexion of successive pictures in a rotating box. [Irregularly, from Gr. *prāxis,* doing, *skopeein,* to look.]

praxis *praks′is, n.* practice: an example or a collection of examples for exercise: a model or example. [Gr. *prāxis — prāssein,* to do.]

Praxitelean *praks-it-ə-lē′ən, adj.* pertaining to, reminiscent of or in the style of *Praxiteles,* Greek sculptor (fl. *c.* 350 B.C.).

pray[1] *prā, v.i.* to ask earnestly (often with *for*): to entreat: to express one's desires to, or commune with, a god or some spiritual power. — *v.t.* to ask earnestly and reverently, as in worship: to supplicate: to present as a prayer: to render, get, put, or cause to be, by praying: — *pr.p.* **pray′ing;** *pa.t.* and *pa.p.* **prayed.** — *interj.* (often *iron.*) I ask you, may I ask. — *n.* **pray′er** one who prays: (*prār, prā′ər*) the act of praying: entreaty: a petition to, or communing with, a god or spiritual power: the wish put forward or the words used: a form used or intended for use in praying: public worship: (in *pl.*) (a time set aside for) worship in a family, school, etc.: a petition to a public body, e.g. a legislature: in Parliament, a motion addressed to the Crown asking for the annulment of an order or regulation: the thing prayed for. — *adj.* **prayerful** (*prār′fŏŏl*) given to prayer: in a spirit or mental attitude of prayer. — *adv.* **prayer′fully.** — *n.* **prayer′fulness.** — *adj.* **prayer′less** without or not using prayer. — *adv.* **prayer′lessly.** — *n.* **prayer′lessness.** — *n.* and *adj.* **pray′ing.** — *adv.* **pray′ingly.** — (Position of accent on following compounds depends on whether one says *prār′* or *prā′ər*) **prayer′-bead** one of the beads on a rosary: a jequirity bean; **prayer′-book** a book containing prayers or forms of devotion, esp. the Book of Common Prayer of the Church of England; **prayer′-flag** in Tibetan Buddhism, a flag on which a prayer is inscribed; **prayer′-mat** same as **prayer-rug; prayer′-meeting** a shorter and simpler form of public religious service, in which laymen often take part; **prayer′-monger** one who prays mechanically; **prayer′-rug** a small carpet on which a Muslim kneels at prayer; **prayer′-wheel** a drum wrapped with strips of paper inscribed with prayers deemed by Buddhists of Tibet to be proffered when the drum is turned; **praying insect** the mantis. — **pray against** in Parliament, to address a prayer to the Crown for the annulment of (an order or regulation); **pray in aid** (*law*; *Shak.*) to call in, or call for, help. [O.Fr. *preier* (Fr. *prier*), to pray, and O.Fr. *preiere*, prayer (— L.L. *precāria*) — L. *precārī* — *prex, precis*, a prayer.]

pray², Spenser's usual spelling of **prey**.

pre- (as living prefix), **prae-** (L. spelling more common formerly) *prē, prī-, pfx.* (1) in front, in front of, the anterior part of, as *predentate, premandibular, presternum*; (2) before in time, beforehand, in advance, as *prehistoric, pre-war, prewarn*; (3) surpassingly, to the highest degree, as *pre-eminent, pre-potent.* — used without hyphen as *prep.* (*coll.*) before, prior to. [L. *prae*, in front of.]

preace *prēs* (*Spens.*). Same as **press¹**.

preach *prēch, v.i.* to deliver a sermon: to discourse earnestly: to give advice in an offensive, tedious, or obtrusive manner. — *v.t.* to set forth in religious discourses: to deliver, as a sermon: to proclaim or teach publicly: to render or put by preaching. — *n.* (*coll.*) a sermon. — *ns.* **preach′er** one who discourses publicly on religious matters: a minister or clergyman: an assiduous inculcator or advocate; **preach′ership.** — *v.i.* **preach′ify** to preach tediously: to sermonise: to weary with lengthy advice. — *adv.* **preach′ily.** — *ns.* **preach′-iness; preach′ing; preach′ment** a sermon, in contempt: a sermon-like discourse: sermonising. — *adj.* **preach′y** given to tedious moralising: savouring of preaching. — **preach′ing-cross** a cross in an open place at which monks, etc., preached; **preach′ing-fri′ar** a Dominican; **preach′ing-house** a Methodist church. — **preach down, up** to decry, extol; **preaching with a view** preaching as a candidate in a vacant pastoral charge; **the Preacher** the authors or spokesman of the Book of Ecclesiastes: the book itself. [Fr. *prêcher* — L. *praedicāre, -ātum*, to proclaim.]

pre-Adamite *prē-ad′ə-mīt, n.* one who lived, or a descendant of those who lived, or a believer in the existence of a human race, before *Adam.* — *adjs.* **pre-Ad′amite; pre-adamic** (*-a-dam′ik*), **-al** existing before Adam; **pre= adamit′ic, -al.** [Pfx. **pre-** (2).]

preadmonish *prē-ad-mon′ish, v.t.* to forewarn. — *n.* **pre-admoni′tion.** [Pfx. **pre-** (2).]

preamble *prē-am′bl, n.* preface: introduction, esp. that of an Act of Parliament, giving its reasons and purpose: (*Milt.* **praeamble**) a prelude. — Also *v.t.* and *v.i.* — *adjs.* **pream′bulary, pream′bulatory.** — *v.i.* **pream′-būlate** to go first (*obs.*): to make a preamble. [Fr. *préambule* — L. *prae, ambulāre*, to go.]

preamplifier *prē-amp′li-fī-ər, n.* an electronic device that boosts and clarifies the signal from e.g. a radio, gramophone, microphone, etc. before it reaches the main amplifier. [Pfx. **pre-** (2).]

prease, preasse (*Spens.*). Same as **press¹**.

preaudience *prē-ö′di-əns, n.* right to be heard before another: precedence at the bar among lawyers. [Pfx. **pre-** (2).]

prebend *preb′ənd, n.* the share of the revenues of a cathedral or collegiate church allowed to a clergyman who officiates in it at stated times. — *adj.* **prebendal** (*pri-bend′l*). — *n.* **preb′endary** a resident clergyman who enjoys a prebend, a canon: the honorary holder of a disendowed prebendal stall. [L.L. *praebenda*, an allowance — L. *praebēre*, to allow, grant.]

prebiotic *prē-bī-ot′ik, adj.* relating to the time before the appearance of living things. [Pfx. **pre-** (2).]

Pre-Cambrian *prē-kam′bri-ən,* (*geol.*) *adj.* and *n.* (of or relating to) the earliest geological era: Archaean. [Pfx. **pre-** (2).]

pre-cancel *prē-kan′səl, v.t.* to cancel a postage stamp (e.g.

by applying a postmark) before use. — Also *n.* [Pfx. **pre-** (2).]

pre-cancerous *prē-kan′sər-əs, adj.* that may become cancerous. [Pfx. **pre-** (2).]

precarious *pri-kā′ri-əs, adj.* depending upon the will of another: depending on chance: insecure: uncertain: dangerous, risky: supplicating (*obs.*). — *adv.* **precā′-riously.** — *n.* **precā′riousness.** [L. *precārius* — *precārī*, to pray.]

precast *prē′käst′, adj.* of concrete blocks, etc., cast before putting in position. [Pfx. **pre-** (2).]

precatory *prek′ə-tə-ri, adj.* of the nature of, or expressing, a wish, request, or recommendation. — *adj.* **prec′ative** supplicatory: expressing entreaty (*gram.*). [L. *pre-cārī*, to pray.]

precaution *pri-kö′shən, n.* a caution or care beforehand: a measure taken beforehand. — *v.t.* (*obs.*) to forewarn. — *adjs.* **precau′tional, precau′tionary, precau′tious.** [Pfx. **pre-** (2).]

precede *prē-sēd′, v.t.* to go before in position, time, rank, or importance: to cause to be preceded. — *v.i.* to be before in time or place. — *ns.* **precedence** (*pres′i-dəns*; *prēs′*, also *pri-sē′dəns*) the act of going before in time: the right of going before: priority: the state of being before in rank: the place of honour: the foremost place in ceremony — also **precedency** (*pres′i-, prēs′i-, pri-sē′dən-si*); **precedent** (*pres′i-dənt*; also *prēs′*) that which precedes: the original of a copy (*Shak.*): a token (*Shak.*): a model (*obs.*): a past instance that may serve as an example: a previous judicial decision or proceeding. — *adj.* (*pri-sē′dənt*) preceding. — *adjs.* **precedented** (*pres′*; also *prēs′*) having a precedent: warranted by an example; **precedential** (*pres-i-den′shl*) of the nature of a precedent. — *adv.* **pre′cedently.** — *adj.* **precē′ding** going before in time, rank, etc.: antecedent: previous: foregoing: immediately before. — **take precedence of, over** to precede in ceremonial order. [Fr. *précéder* — L. *praecēdĕre, -cēssum,* — *prae, cēdĕre,* to go.]

preceese *pri-sēz′,* a Scots form of **precise.**

precentor *pri-* or *prē-sen′tər* (Scot. *pri-zen′tər*), *n.* the leader of the singing of a church choir or congregation: in some English cathedrals, a member of the chapter who deputes this duty to a succentor: — *fem.* **pre-cen′tress, precen′trix.** — *n.* **precen′torship.** [L.L. *prae-centor, -ōris* — L. *prae, canĕre,* to sing.]

precepit. See **precipice.**

precept *prē′sept, n.* a rule of action: a commandment: a principle, or maxim: the written warrant of a magistrate (*law*): a mandate: an order to levy money under a rate. — *adjs.* **preceptial** (*pri-sep′shl*; *Shak.*) consisting of precepts; **precep′tive** containing or giving precepts: directing in moral conduct: didactic. — *n.* **precep′tor** one who delivers precepts: a teacher: an instructor: a tutor (*U.S.*): the head of a school: the head of a preceptory of Knights Templars: — *fem.* **precep′tress.** — *adjs.* **precepto′rial** (*prē′*); **precep′tory** (*pri-*) giving precepts. — *n.* a community of Knights Templars (occasionally extended to a commandery of the Hospitallers): its estate or buildings. [L. *praeceptum,* pa.p. neut. of *praecipĕre,* to take beforehand — *prae, capĕre,* to take.]

precession *pri-sesh′ən, n.* the act of going before: a moving forward: the precession of the equinoxes (see below): the analogous phenomenon in spinning-tops and the like, whereby the wobble of the spinning object causes its axis of rotation to become cone-shaped. — *v.i.* **precess** (*-ses′*) of a spinning-top, etc., to wobble. — *adj.* **precess′ional.** — **precession of the equinoxes** a slow westward motion of the equinoctial points along the ecliptic, caused by the greater attraction of the sun

---

---

and moon on the excess of matter at the equator, such that the times at which the sun crosses the equator come at shorter intervals than they would otherwise do. [L.L. *praecessiō, -ōnis* — *praecēdĕre*; see **precede**.]
précieuse *prā-syœz'*, *n.* a woman affecting a fastidious over-refinement. [Fr. — from the literary women of 17th-cent. France who were extremely fastidious in their use of language.]
precinct *prē'singkt*, *n.* a space, esp. an enclosed space, around a building or other object (also in *pl.*): a district or division within certain boundaries: a district of jurisdiction or authority: a division for police or electoral purposes (*U.S.*): (in *pl.*) environs. — **pedestrian precinct** a traffic-free area of a town, esp. a shopping centre; **shopping precinct** a shopping centre, esp. if traffic-free. [L.L. *praecinctum*, pa.p. neut. of *praecingĕre* — *prae, cingĕre* to gird.]
precious *presh'əs*, *adj.* of great price or worth: cherished: very highly esteemed: often used in irony for arrant, worthless, 'fine': affecting an over-refined choiceness. — *adv.* **preciously** (*Shak.*): extremely, confoundedly (*coll.*). — *n.* used as a term of endearment. — *n.* **preciosity** (*presh-i-os'i-ti*, or *pres-*) fastidious over-refinement. — *adv.* **prec'iously.** — *n.* **prec'iousness.** — **precious metals** gold, silver (sometimes mercury, platinum, and others of high price); **precious stone** a stone of value and beauty for ornamentation: a gem or jewel. [O.Fr. *precios* (Fr. *précieux*) — L. *pretiōsus* — *pretium*, price.]
precipice *pres'i-pis*, *n.* a headlong fall (*obs.*): a high vertical or nearly vertical cliff. — *n.* **prec'epit** (*Shak.*) a precipice. — *adj.* **prec'ipiced.** — *n.* **precipitabil'ity** (*pri-*). — *adj.* **precip'itable** (*chem.*) that may be precipitated. — *ns.* **precip'itance, precip'itancy** the quality of being precipitate: a headlong fall: headlong haste or rashness: an impulsively hasty action. — *adj.* **precip'itant** falling headlong: rushing down with too great velocity: impulsively hasty. — *n.* anything that brings down a precipitate. — *adv.* **precip'itantly.** — *v.t.* **precip'itate** to hurl headlong: to force into hasty action: to bring on suddenly or prematurely: to bring down from a state of solution or suspension. — *v.i.* to fall headlong (*Shak.*): to rush in haste: to come out of solution or suspension: to condense and fall, as rain, hail, etc. — *adj.* (*-āt* or *-it*) falling, hurled, or rushing headlong: sudden and hasty: without deliberation: rash. — *n.* (*-āt, -it*) a substance separated from solution or suspension, usually falling to the bottom: moisture deposited as rain, snow, etc. — *adv.* **precip'itately.** — *n.* **precipitā'tion** the act of precipitating: a headlong fall or rush: a sheer drop (*Shak.*): an impulsive action: great hurry: rash haste: impulsiveness: rain, hail, and snow (sometimes also dew): the amount of rainfall, etc.: the formation or coming down of a precipitate: separation of a substance suspended in a solution, as a precipitate. — *adj.* **precip'itātive.** — *ns.* **precip'itātor** one who precipitates: a precipitating agent: an apparatus or tank for precipitation; **precip'itin** an antibody which in contact with an antigen produces a precipitate in the blood. — *adj.* **precip'itous** like a precipice: sheer: precipitate (*rare*). — *adv.* **precip'itously.** — *n.* **precip'itousness.** [L. *praeceps, praecipitis*, headlong, *praecipitium*, precipice, *praecipitāre, -ātum*, to precipitate — *prae, caput, -itis*, head.]
précis *prā'sē*, *n.* an abstract: — *pl.* **précis** (*-sēz*). — *v.t.* to make a précis of: — *pr.p.* **précising** (*prā'sē-ing*); *pa.t.* and *pa.p.* **précised** (*prā'sēd*). [Fr.]
precise *pri-sīs'*, *adj.* definite: exact: accurate: free from vagueness: very, identical: scrupulously exact: scrupu-

lous in religion: puritanical: over-exact: prim: formal. — *adv.* **precise'ly.** — *ns.* **precise'ness; precisian** (*pri-sizh'ən*) an over-precise person: a formalist: formerly, in hostility, a Puritan; **precis'ianism; precis'ianist** a precisian; **preci'sion** the quality of being precise: exactness: minute accuracy: mental separation (partly associated with **prescission;** *Berkeley*): a precise definition (*obs.*). — *adj.* for work of, carried out with, accuracy. — *n.* **precis'ionist** one who insists on precision: a purist. — *adj.* **precisive** (*pri-sī'siv*) cutting off: pertaining to precision. [Fr. *précis, -e* — L. *praecīsus*, pa.p. of *praecīdĕre* — *prae, caedĕre*, to cut.]
preclinical *prē-klin'i-kəl*, (*med.*) *adj.* taking place before, or without yet having gained, practical clinical experience with patients: of, relating to or occurring during the stage before the symptoms of a disease are recognisable: (of a drug) prior to clinical testing. [Pfx. **pre-** (2).]
preclude *pri-klōōd'*, *v.t.* to close beforehand: to shut out beforehand: to hinder by anticipation: to prevent. — *n.* **preclusion** (*pri-klōō'zhən*). — *adj.* **preclusive** (*-klōō'siv*) tending to preclude: hindering beforehand. — *adv.* **preclu'sively.** [L. *praeclūdĕre, -clūsum* — *claudĕre*, to shut.]
precocious *pri-kō'shəs*, *adj.* early in reaching some stage of development, as flowering, fruiting, ripening, mental maturity: precocial: flowering before leaves appear: showing early development. — *n.pl.* **praecoces** (*prē'kō-sēz, prī'ko-kās*) praecocial birds (opp. to *altrices*). — *adj.* **precocial, praecocial** (*-kō'shl, -shyəl*) hatched with complete covering of down, able to leave the nest at once and seek food: premature: forward. — *adv.* **precō'ciously.** — *ns.* **precō'ciousness, precocity** (*pri-kos'i-ti*) the state or quality of being precocious: early development or too early ripeness of the mind. [L. *praecox, -ōcis* — *prae, coquĕre*, to cook, ripen.]
precognition *prē-kog-nish'ən*, *n.* foreknowledge: a preliminary examination of witnesses as to whether there is ground for prosecution (*Scots law*): evidence so obtained: a formally-prepared statement of evidence, etc., submitted in advance to an inquiry or court, usu. read out by the submitter at the inquiry (*Scots law*). — *adj.* **precog'nitive** (*pri-*). — *v.t.* **precognosce** (*prē-kog-nos'*) to take a precognition of. [Pfx. **pre-** (2).]
preconceive *prē-kən-sēv'*, *v.t.* to conceive or form a notion of, before having actual knowledge. — *ns.* **preconceit'** a preconceived notion; **preconcep'tion** the act of preconceiving: a previous opinion formed without actual knowledge. [Pfx. **pre-** (2).]
preconcert *prē-kən-sûrt'*, *v.t.* to settle beforehand. — *n.* **preconcert** (*-kon'*) a previous arrangement. — *adv.* **preconcert'edly.** — *n.* **preconcert'edness.** [Pfx. **pre-** (2).]
precondition *prē-kən-dish'ən*, *n.* a condition that must be satisfied beforehand. — *v.t.* to prepare beforehand. [Pfx. **pre-** (2).]
preconise, -ize *prē'kən-īz*, *v.t.* to proclaim: to summon publicly: (of the pope) to proclaim and ratify the election of as bishop. — *n.* **preconisation, -z-** (*prē-kən-ī-zā'shən*, or *-kon-i-*). [L. *praecō, -ōnis*, a crier, a herald.]
preconscious *prē-kon'shəs*, *adj.* (of material) currently absent from, but which can be readily recalled to, the conscious mind (*psych.*): (of something that occurred, existed, etc.) before consciousness, or the conscious self, developed. — *n.* **precon'sciousness.** [Pfx. **pre-** (2).]
precontract *prē-kən-trakt'*, *v.t.* to contract beforehand: to betroth previously. — *n.* **precontract** (*-kon'*) a previous contract or betrothal. [Pfx. **pre-** (2).]

---

predefini'tion *n.* pre- (2).
predevel'op *v.t., v.i.* pre- (2).
predevel'opment *n.* pre- (2).
predoom' *v.t.* pre- (2).
pre-employ' *v.t.* pre- (2).
pre-engage' *v.t.* pre- (2).

pre-engage'ment *n.* pre- (2).
pre'flight' *adj.* pre- (2).
premix' *v.t.* pre- (2).
prenu'bile *adj.* pre- (2).
prenup'tial *adj.* pre- (2).
prepro'grammed *adj.*

pre- (2).
pre'record' *v.t.* pre- (2).
prerecord'ed *adj.* pre- (2).
preset' *v.t.* pre- (2).
pre'-war' *adj., adv.* pre- (2)
pre'-warm' *v.t.* pre- (2).

For other sounds see detailed chart of pronunciation.

precook *prē-kŏŏk'*, *v.t.* to cook partially or completely beforehand. [Pfx. **pre-** (2).]

precordial, praecordial *prē-kör'di-əl*, *adj.* in front of the heart. [**pre-** (1), L. *cor, cordis*, heart.]

precurrer *prē-kur'ər*, (*Shak.*) *n.* a forerunner. — *n.* **precurse** (*pri-kûrs'*; *Shak.*) a prognostication. — *adj.* **precur'sive**. — *n.* **precur'sor** something that exists or goes in advance of another: a predecessor: an indication of the approach of an event: a compound from which another substance is derived or manufactured (*chem.*). — *adj.* **precur'sory**. [L. *praecurrĕre, -cursum* — *currĕre*, to run.]

predacious, (*irreg.*) **predaceous**, *pri-dā'shəs*, *adj.* living by prey: predatory. — *ns.* **predā'ciousness, predac'ity; predā'tion**. — *adj.* **pred'ative**. — *n.* **pred'ator**. — *adv.* **pred'atorily**. — *n.* **pred'atoriness**. — *adj.* **pred'atory** of, relating to, or characterised by, plundering: living by plunder or on prey: deleterious (*obs.*). [L. *praeda*, booty.]

predate *prē-dāt'*, *v.t.* to date before the true date: to antedate: to be earlier than. [Pfx. **pre-** (2).]

predation, predator, etc. See **predacious**.

predecease *prē-di-sēs'*, *n.* death before another's death, or before some other time. — *v.t.* to die before. — *adj.* **predeceased'** deceased at an earlier time. [Pfx. **pre-** (2).]

predecessor *prē-di-ses'ər, prē'*, U.S. chiefly *pre-*, *n.* one who has been before another: a thing that has been supplanted or succeeded: an ancestor. [L. *praedēcessor* — *dēcessor*, a retiring officer — *dē*, away, *cēdĕre*, to go, depart.]

predella *pri-del'ə*, *n.* the platform or uppermost step on which an altar stands: a retable: a painting or sculpture, on the face of either of these: a painting in a compartment along the bottom of an altarpiece or other picture. [It., prob — O.H.G. *pret*, board.]

predentate *prē-den'tāt*, *adj.* having teeth in the forepart of the jaw only. [Pfx. **pre-** (1).]

predesign *prē-di-zīn'*, *v.t.* to design beforehand. — *v.t.* **predesignate** (*prē-dez'ig-nāt*, or *-des'*) to specify beforehand. — *adj.* designated in advance: having the quantification of the predicate distinctly expressed (*log.*; Sir W. Hamilton). — *n.* **predesignā'tion**. — *adj.* **predes'ignatory**. [Pfx. **pre-** (2).]

predestine *prē-* or *pri-des'tin*, *v.t.* to destine or decree beforehand: to foreordain. — *adj.* **predestinā'rian** believing in, or pertaining to, the doctrine of predestination. — *n.* one who holds the doctrine of predestination. — *n.* **predestinā'rianism**. — *v.t.* **predes'tinate** to determine beforehand: to preordain by an unchangeable purpose. — *adj.* (*-it*) foreordained: fated. — *n.* **predestinā'tion** the act of predestinating: God's decree fixing unalterably from all eternity whatever is to happen, esp. the eternal happiness or misery of men (*theol.*): fixed fate. — *adj.* **predes'tinative**. — *ns.* **predes'tinātor** one who predestinates or foreordains: a predestinarian (*obs.*); **predes'tiny** irrevocably fixed fate. [Pfx. **pre-** (2).]

predetermine *prē-di-tûr'min*, *v.t.* to determine or settle beforehand. — *adjs.* **predeter'minable; predeter'minăte** determined beforehand. — *ns.* **predetermina'tion; predeter'minism** determinism. [Pfx. **pre-** (2).]

predevote *prē-di-vōt'*, *adj.* foreordained. [Pfx. **pre-** (2).]

predial. Same as **praedial**.

predicable *pred'i-kə-bl*, *adj.* that may be predicated or affirmed of something: attributable. — *n.* anything that can be predicated of another, or esp. of many others: one of the five attributes — genus, species, difference, property, and accident (*log.*). — *n.* **predicabil'ity**. [L. *praedicabilis* — *praedicāre*, to proclaim, *-abilis*, able.]

predicament *pri-dik'ə-mənt*, *n.* one of the classes or categories which include all predicables (*log.*): a condition: an unfortunate or trying position. — *adj.* **predicamental** (*-ment'l*). [L.L. *praedicāmentum*, something predicated or asserted.]

predicant *pred'i-kənt*, *adj.* predicating: preaching. — *n.* one who affirms anything: a preacher: a preaching friar or Dominican: a predikant. [L. *praedīcāns, -antis*, pr.p. of *praedicāre*; see next.]

predicate *pred'i-kāt*, *v.t.* to preach (*rare*): to affirm: to assert: to state as a property or attribute of the subject (*log.*): to base on certain grounds (*U.S.*): sometimes used wrongly for **predict**. — *n.* (*-it*) that which is predicated of the subject (*log.*): the word or words by which something is said about something (*gram.*). — *n.* **predica'tion**. — *adj.* **predicative** (*pri-dik'ə-tiv*, or *pred'i-kā-tiv*) expressing predication or affirmation: affirming: asserting. — *adv.* **predicatively**. — *adj.* **pred'icatory** affirmative. — **predicate calculus** see **calculus**. [L. *praedīcāre, -ātum*, to proclaim — *prae*, forth, *dīcāre*, (orig.) to proclaim.]

predict *pri-dikt'*, *v.t.* to foretell. — *adj.* **predic'table** that can be predicted: happening, or prone to act, in a way that can be predicted. — *ns.* **predictabil'ity, predic'tableness**. — *adv.* **predic'tably**. — *n.* **prediction** (*-shən*). — *adj.* **predic'tive** foretelling: prophetic. — *n.* **predic'tor** that which predicts: an anti-aircraft rangefinding and radar device. [L. *praedictus*, pa.p. of *praedīcĕre* — *dīcĕre*, to say.]

predigest *prē-di-jest'* or *-dī-*, *v.t.* to digest artificially before introducing into the body. — *n.* **predigestion** (*-jest'yən*) digestion beforehand: hasty digestion (*obs.*). [Pfx. **pre-** (2).]

predikant *prā-di-känt'*, *n.* a Dutch Reformed preacher, esp. in South Africa. [Du., — L. *praedīcāns, -antis*, see **predicant, preach**.]

predilection *prē-di-lek'shən*, *pred-i-*, *n.* favourable prepossession of mind: preference. — *adjs.* **predilect', -ed** chosen: favoured: preferred. [L. *prae*, *dīligĕre, dīlectum*, to love — *dī-, dis-*, apart, *legĕre*, to choose.]

predispose *prē-dis-pōz'*, *v.t.* to dispose or incline beforehand: to render favourable: to render liable. — *adj.* **predispō'sing**. — *n.* **predisposition** (*-pəz-ish'ən*). — *adj.* **predisposi'tional**. [Pfx. **pre-** (2).]

prednisone *pred'ni-zōn, -sōn*, *n.* a drug similar to cortisone, used e.g. as an anti-inflammatory agent. [Perh. — *pregnant, diene* and cor*tisone*.]

predominate *pri-dom'in-āt*, *v.t.* to prevail over (*Shak.*). — *v.i.* to be dominant: to surpass in strength or authority: to prevail: to be most numerous or abounding: to have a commanding position. — *ns.* **predom'inance, predom'inancy**. — *adj.* **predom'inant** ruling: having superior power: ascendant: preponderating: prevailing: commanding in position or effect. — *adv.* **predom'inantly**. — *adj.* **predom'inăte** (*rare*) predominant. — *n.* **predominā'tion**. [Pfx. **pre-** (3).]

Pre-Dravidian *prē-drə-vid'i-ən*, *adj.* of a dark woolly-haired, broad-nosed race of man, including Sakai, Veddas, and Australian aborigines. — Also *n.* [Pfx. **pre-** (2).]

predy pronunciation unknown, (*obs. naut.*) *adj.* cleared for action. — *v.t.* to make ready. [Origin unknown; poss. from make the ship *ready*.]

pree *prē*, (*Scot.*) *v.t.* to make a trial of, esp. by tasting or by kissing. [**prieve** (see under **prief**).]

pre-eclampsia *prē-i-klamp'si-ə*, *n.* a toxic condition occurring in late pregnancy, characterised by high blood pressure, excessive weight gain, proteins in the urine, oedema, and sometimes severe headaches and visual disturbances. [Pfx. **pre-** (2), and **eclampsia**.]

pre-elect *prē-i-lekt'*, *v.t.* to choose beforehand. — *n.* **pre-elec'tion** preference (*obs.*): election in anticipation. — *adj.* before election. [Pfx. **pre-** (2).]

preemie, premie, premy *prē'mē*, (*U.S. slang*) *n.* short for *premature* baby.

pre-eminent *prē-em'in-ənt*, *adj.* eminent above others: more important or influential than others: surpassing others in good or bad qualities: outstanding: extreme. — *n.* **prē-em'inence**. — *adv.* **prē-em'inently**. [Pfx. **pre-** (3).]

pre-emption *prē-em(p)'shən*, *n.* the act or right of purchasing in preference to others: (also **pre-emption right**) the right of a citizen to purchase a certain amount of public land if certain conditions are fulfilled (*U.S.*): a piece of land so obtained: a belligerent's right to seize neutral contraband at a fixed price: seizure: the act of attacking first to forestall hostile action. — *v.t.* **pre=empt** (*prē-empt'*, *-emt'*) to secure as first-comer: to secure by pre-emption: to take possession of. — *v.i.* (*bridge*) to make a pre-emptive bid. — *adjs.* **prē=empt'ible**; **prē-empt'ive**. — *n.* **prē-empt'or.** — **prē-emptive bid** (*bridge*) an unusually high bid intended to deter others from bidding. [L. *prae, emptiō, -ōnis,* a buying — *emĕre,* to buy.]

preen[1] *prēn, v.t.* (of a bird) to clean and arrange (the feathers), or to clean and arrange the feathers of (a part of the body): to adorn, dress or slick (oneself) (*fig.*): to plume, pride or congratulate (oneself) (with *on*). — **preen gland** the uropygial gland that secretes oil used in preening the feathers. [App. **prune**[2] assimilated to the following word.]

preen[2] *prēn,* (*Scot.*) *n.* a pin. — *v.t.* to pin. [O.E. *prēon,* pin, brooch.]

pre-establish *prē-is-tab'lish, v.t.* to establish beforehand. — **pre-established harmony** see **harmonic.** [Pfx. **pre-** (2).]

preeve *prēv, n.* and *v.t.* obs. or Scot. form of **proof** and **prove.**

pre-exilic *prē-eg-zil'ik, adj.* before the exile — of O.T. writings prior to the Jewish exile (*c.* 586–538 B.C.). — Also **pre-exil'ian.** [Pfx. **pre-** (2).]

pre-exist *prē-ig-zist', v.i.* to exist beforehand, esp. in a former life. — *v.t.* to exist before. — *n.* **prē-exist'ence** previous existence, esp. of the soul, before the generation of the body with which it is united in this world. — *adj.* **prē-exist'ent.** [Pfx. **pre-** (2).]

prefabricate *prē-fab'ri-kāt, v.t.* to make standardised parts of beforehand, for assembling later. — *adj.* **prefab'ricated** composed of such parts. — *ns.* **prefabricā'tion**; **prefab'ricātor**; **pre'fab** (*coll.*) a prefabricated house. [Pfx. **pre-** (2).]

preface *pref'is, n.* something said by way of introduction or preliminary explanation: a statement, usually explanatory, placed at the beginning of a book, not regarded as forming (like the introduction) part of the composition: the ascription of glory, etc., in the liturgy of consecration of the eucharist: anything preliminary or immediately antecedent. — *v.t.* to say by way of preface: to precede: to front. — *v.i.* to make preliminary remarks. — *adjs.* **prefacial** (*pri-fā'shl*; *rare*); **prefatorial** (*pref-ə-tō'ri-əl, -tō'*) serving as a preface or introduction. — *advs.* **prefato'rially, prefatorily** (*pref'ə-tər-i-li*). — *adj.* **pref'atory** pertaining to a preface: serving as an introduction: introductory. [Fr. *préface* — L.L. *prēfātia* for L. *praefātiō — prae, fārī, fātus,* to speak.]

prefade *prē-fād', v.t.* intentionally to give (new jeans, material, etc.) a faded appearance. [Pfx. **pre-** (2).]

prefard *pri-färd',* a Spenserian form of **preferred.**

prefatorial, etc. See **preface.**

prefect *prē'fekt, n.* one placed in authority over others (also **praefect**): a commander or magistrate (*Rom. hist.*; also **praefect**): a school pupil with some measure of authority over others (*rarely* **praefect**): the administrative head of a department in France, of a province in Italy, or of any similar administrative district elsewhere. — *adj.* **prefectorial** (*prē-fek-tō'ri-əl, -tō'*). — *n.* **prē'fectship.** — *adj.* **prefect'ural** (*pri-*). — *n.* **prē'fecture** the office, term of office, or district of a prefect: in Japan, any of 46 administrative districts headed by a governor: the house or office occupied by a prefect. — **prefect of police** the head of the Paris police. [O.Fr. *prefect* (Fr. *préfet*) and L. *praefectus,* pa.p. of *praeficĕre — prae, facĕre,* to make.]

prefer *pri-fûr', v.t.* to set in front (*obs.*): to put forward, offer, submit, present, for acceptance or consideration (*arch.* or *law*): to promote: to advance: to hold in higher estimation: to choose or select before others: to like better (with *to,* or *rather than*; not with *than* alone): — *pr.p.* **preferring** (*pri-fûr'ing*); *pa.t.* and *pa.p.* **pre-**

ferred (*pri-fûrd'*). — *n.* **preferabil'ity** (*pref-*). — *adj.* **pref'erable** (*obs.* **preferrable** *pri-fûr'*) to be preferred: having priority. — *adv.* **pref'erably** by choice: in preference. — *n.* **pref'erence** the act of choosing, favouring, or liking one above another: estimation above another: the state of being preferred: that which is preferred: priority: an advantage given to one over another: a card game resembling auction bridge. — *adj.* **preferential** (*pref-ər-en'shl*) having, giving, or allowing, a preference. — *ns.* **preferen'tialism**; **preferen'tialist** one who favours a preferential tariff. — *adv.* **preferen'tially.** — *ns.* **prefer'ment** advancement: promotion: superior place, esp. in the Church; **preferr'er.** — **preference shares** or **stock** shares or stock on which the dividends must be paid before those on other kinds; **preferential tariff** one by which lower customs duties are imposed on goods from certain countries than on goods from others. [Fr. *préférer* — L. *praeferre — ferre,* to bear.]

prefigure *prē-fig'ər, v.t.* to imagine beforehand: to foreshadow by a type. — *adj.* **prefig'urate** (*-ū-rāt*) prefigured. — *v.t.* to prefigure. — *n.* **prefigurā'tion.** — *adj.* **prefig'urātive.** — *n.* **prefig'urement** (*-ər-mənt*). [Pfx. **pre-** (2).]

prefix *prē-fiks', prē'fiks, v.t.* to put before, or at the beginning: to add as a prefix: to fix beforehand. — *n.* **pre'fix** an affix added at the beginning of a word: a title placed before a name, as *Mr, Sir.* — *ns.* **prefixion** (*-fik'shən*); **prefix'ture.** [L. *praefigĕre, -fixum — figĕre,* to fix.]

prefloration *prē-flō-rā'shən, -flō-,* (*bot.*) *n.* aestivation. [Pfx. **pre-** (2), L. *flōs, flōris,* flower.]

prefoliation *prē-fō-li-ā'shən,* (*bot.*) *n.* vernation. [Pfx. **pre-** (2), L. *folium,* leaf.]

preform *prē-förm', v.t.* to form beforehand (*Shak.*): to determine the shape of beforehand. — *ns.* **prēformā'tion**; **prēformā'tionism**; **prēformā'tionist** a believer in the now exploded theory that the plant or animal (and therefore all its descendants) was already preformed in the germ (the ovum according to the ovists, the sperm according to the animalculists) and had only to be unfolded without formation of any new parts. — *adj.* **prēfor'mative.** [Pfx. **pre-** (2).]

prefrontal *prē-front'l, -frunt'l, adj.* in front of, or in the forepart of, the frontal bone, lobe, scale, etc.: pertaining to such a part. — *n.* a bone or scale so situated. [Pfx. **pre-** (1).]

prefulgent *prē-ful'jənt, adj.* extremely bright. [Pfx. **pre-** (3).]

preggers *preg'ərz,* (*coll.,* esp. upper-class) *adj.* pregnant.

pre-glacial *prē-glā'shl, adj.* earlier than the glacial period. [Pfx. **pre-** (2).]

pregnable *preg'nə-bl, adj.* that may be taken by assault or force: vulnerable. [Fr. *prenable — prendre,* to take; see **impregnable.**]

pregnant *preg'nənt, adj.* with child or young: impregnated: fertile: teeming: fruitful: fruitful in results: momentous: significant: threatening: freighted: swelling: full of thoughts, ready-witted, inventive: full of promise: disposed, ready, apt, ready to act (*Shak.*): full of meaning: pithy and to the purpose: conveying a compressed meaning beyond what the grammatical construction can strictly carry: weighty: cogent: obvious: clear. — *ns.* **preg'nance** (*obs.*), **preg'nancy.** — *adv.* **preg'nantly.** [L. *praegnāns, -antis,* from earlier *praegnās, -ātis,* app. — *prae* and the root of *gnāscī,* to be born; but in some meanings from or confused with O.Fr. *preignant,* pr.p. of *preindre* — L. *premĕre,* to press.]

pregustation *prē-gus-tā'shən, n.* a foretaste. [Pfx. **pre-** (2).]

prehallux *prē-hal'uks, n.* a rudimentary innermost toe. [Pfx. **pre-** (1).]

preheat *prē-hēt', v.t.* to heat before using, before heating further, or before subjecting to some other process or treatment. [Pfx. **pre-** (2).]

preheminence. An obsolete spelling of **pre-eminence.**

prehend *pri-hend'*, *v.t.* to seize (*rare*). — *adjs.* **prehen'sible** (*rare*) capable of being grasped; **prehen'sile** (*-sīl*) capable of grasping — also **prehen'sive**, **prehensō'rial** (*prē-*), **prehen'sory** (*pri-*). — *ns.* **prehensility** (*prē-hensil'i-ti*); **prehension** (*pri-hen'shən*); **prehen'sor** one who seizes. [L. *praehendēre, -hēnsum*, to seize.]

prehistoric, -al *prē-his-tor'ik, -əl*, *adjs.* of a time before extant historical records. — *n.* **prēhistō'rian.** — *adv.* **prēhistor'ically.** — *n.* **prēhis'tory.** [Pfx. **pre-** (2).]

prehnite *prān'īt*, *n.* a zeolite-like mineral, an acid calcium aluminium silicate, usu. a pale green. [Named after Col. van *Prehn*, who brought it from South Africa in the 18th century.]

prehuman *prē-hū'mən*, *adj.* at a stage of development before full humanity has been developed: earlier than the appearance of man. [Pfx. **pre-** (2).]

preif, preife *prēf*, obs. forms of **proof.**

pre-ignition *prē-ig-nish'ən*, *n.* too-early ignition of the charge in an internal-combustion engine. [Pfx. **pre-** (2).]

prejink *pri-jingk'.* Same as **perjink.**

prejudge *prē-juj'*, *v.t.* to judge or decide upon before hearing the whole case: to condemn unheard. — *n.* **prejudg'ment** (also **prejudge'ment**). — *adj.* **prejudicant** (*prē-jōōd'i-kənt*). — *v.t.* **prejud'icate** to judge beforehand. — *v.i.* to form an opinion beforehand. — *n.* **prejudicā'tion.** — *adj.* **prejud'icative.** [L. *praejūdicāre*.]

prejudice *prej'ōō-dis*, *n.* a judgment or opinion formed beforehand or without due examination: a prejudgment (*obs.*): (*Spens.* **prejudize**) prognostication: prepossession in favour of or (usu.) against anything: bias: injury or hurt: disadvantage. — *v.t.* to fill with prejudice: to prepossess: to bias the mind of: to injure or hurt: to prejudge, esp. unfavourably (*obs.*). — *adjs.* **prej'udiced** having prejudice: biased; **prejudicial** (*-dish'l*) injurious: detrimental: prejudiced (*obs.*): (*prē-jōō-*) relating to matters to be decided before a case comes into court. — *adv.* **prejudic'ially.** — **without prejudice** a phrase used to require an understanding that nothing said at this stage is to detract from one's rights, to damage claims arising from future developments, or to constitute an admission of liability. [Fr. *préjudice*, wrong, and L. *praejūdicium* — *jūdicium*, judgment.]

prelapsarian *prē-lap-sā'ri-ən*, *adj.* of or pertaining to the time before the Fall (sometimes *fig.*). [**pre-** (2), L. *lāpsus*, a fall.]

prelate *prel'it*, *n.* an ecclesiastic of high rank: a chief priest: a clergyman: — *fem.* **prel'atess.** — *ns.* **prelacy** (*prel'ə-si*) the office of a prelate: the order of bishops or the bishops collectively: church government by prelates: episcopacy; **prel'ateship.** — *adjs.* **prelatial** (*pri-lā'shəl*) of a prelate; **prelatic** (*pri-lat'ik*), **-al** pertaining to prelates or prelacy: (*in hostility*) episcopal or episcopalian. — *adv.* **prelat'ically.** — *n.* **prelā'tion** preferment: promotion: eminence. — *v.t.* and *v.i.* **prel'atise, -ize** to make or to become prelatical. — *adj.* **prel'atish** (*Milt.*). — *ns.* **prel'atism** (*usu.* hostile) episcopacy or episcopalianism: domination by prelates; **prel'atist** an upholder of prelacy; **prel'ature**, (*Milt.*) **prel'aty** prelacy. [Fr. *prélat* — L. *praelātus* — *prae*, before and *lātus*, borne.]

prelect *pri-lekt'*, *v.i.* to lecture. — *ns.* **prelec'tion; prelec'tor** a public reader or lecturer. [L. *praelegēre, -lectum* — *prae, legēre*, to read.]

prelibation *prē-lī-bā'shən*, *n.* a foretaste: an offering of first-fruits. [L. *praelībātiō, -ōnis* — *prae, lībāre*, to taste.]

preliminary *pri-lim'in-ə-ri*, *adj.* introductory: preparatory: preceding or preparing for the main matter. — *n.* that which precedes: an introduction (often in *pl.*, **prelim'inaries**): a preliminary or entrance examination (in student slang shortened to **prelim'** or **prē'lim**; often in *pl.*): (in *pl.*) preliminary pages — titles, preface, contents, introduction, etc. (in printers' slang **prelims'**

or **prē'lims**). — *adv.* **prelim'inarily.** [L. *prae, līmen, -inis*, threshold.]

prelingual *prē-ling'gwəl*, *adj.* before the use of language. [Pfx. **pre-** (2).]

prelude *prel'ūd*, *n.* a preliminary performance or action: an event preceding and leading up to another of greater importance: a preliminary strain, passage, or flourish, often improvised (*mus.*): an introduction or first movement of a suite: a movement preceding a fugue: an overture: an introductory voluntary: a short independent composition such as might be the introduction to another, or developed out of the prelude in the literal sense. — *v.t.* (*prel'ūd*, formerly and still by some *pri-lūd', -lōōd'*) to precede as a prelude, serve as prelude to: to introduce with a prelude: to perform as a prelude. — *v.i.* to furnish a prelude: to perform a prelude: to serve as a prelude. — Also (*ns.*) **preludio** (*pre-lōō'di-ō*; It.; *pl.* **-di** *-dē*), **praeludium** (*prī-lōō'di-ōōm*; L.; *pl.* **-dia**), **prelu'sion** (*-zhən*). — *adjs.* **preludial** and **preludious** (*pri-lōō'*, or *-lū'*; both *rare*); **prelusive** (*-lōō'* or *-lū'siv*) of the nature of a prelude: introductory. — *advs.* **prelu'sively; prelu'sorily.** — *adj.* **prelu'sory** (*-sə-ri*) introductory. [Fr. *prélude* — L.L. *praelūdium* — L. *lūdēre*, to play.]

premandibular *prē-man-dib'ū-lər*, *adj.* in front of the lower jaw. — *n.* a bone so placed in fishes, etc. [Pfx. **pre-** (1).]

premarital *prē-mar'i-təl*, *adj.* before marriage. [Pfx. **pre-** (2).]

premature *prem'ə-tūr, prēm', or -tūr'*, *adj.* ripe before the time: unduly early: of a human baby, born less than 37 weeks after conception, or (sometimes) having a birth weight of between 2½ and 5½ pounds irrespective of length of gestation. — *adv.* **prematurely.** — *ns.* **prematureness; prematur'ity.** [L. *praemātūrus* — *prae, mātūrus*, ripe.]

premaxilla *prē-maks-il'ə*, *n.* a bone in front of the maxilla: — *pl.* **premaxill'ae** (*-ē*). — *adj.* **premaxill'ary** (or *-maks'*). — *n.* the premaxilla. [Pfx. **pre-** (1).]

premedical *prē-med'i-kl*, *adj.* of or pertaining to a course of study undertaken before medical studies. — *adj.* and *n.* **prē'med** (*coll.*) short for **premedical, premedication.** — *n.* (also **premed'ic**) a premedical student: premedical studies: premedication. — *v.t.* **premed'icate.** — *n.* **premedica'tion** drugs given to sedate and prepare a patient, esp. for the administration of a general anaesthetic. [Pfx. **pre-** (2).]

premeditate *prē-med'i-tāt*, *v.t.* to meditate upon beforehand: to design previously. — *v.i.* to deliberate beforehand. — *adj.* **premed'itated.** — *adv.* **premed'itātedly.** — *n.* **premeditā'tion.** — *adj.* **premed'itātive.** [L. *praemeditārī, -ātus* — *prae, meditārī*, to meditate.]

premenstrual *prē-men'strōō-əl*, *adj.* preceding menstruation. — **premenstrual tension** a state of emotional anxiety, etc. caused by hormonal changes preceding menstruation (abbrev. **PMT**). [Pfx. **pre-** (2).]

premia. See **premium.**

premie. See **preemie.**

premier *prem'i-ər, -yər*, by some *prēm'i-ər*, formerly also *pri-mēr'*, *adj.* prime or first: chief: most ancient (*her.*). — *n.* the first or chief: the prime minister: the Secretary of State (*obs.; U.S.*). — *n.* **première** (*prəm-yer', prem'-yər*; from the Fr. *fem.*) a leading actress, dancer, etc.: the first performance of a play or film — also *adj.* — *v.t.* to give a first performance of. — Also *v.i.* — *n.* **prem'iership.** [Fr., — L. *prīmārius*, of the first rank — *prīmus*, first.]

premier cru *prə-myā krü*, (Fr.) the best of the grands crus.

premillenarian *prē-mil-ən-ā'ri-ən*, *n.* a believer in the premillennial coming of Christ. — Also *adj.* — *n.* **premillena'rianism.** [Pfx. **pre-** (2).]

premillennial *prē-mil-en'yəl*, *adj.* before the millennium. — *ns.* **premillenn'ialism** premillenarianism; **premillenn'ialist.** [Pfx. **pre-** (2).]

premise *prem'is*, *n.* a proposition stated or assumed for after-reasoning, esp. one of the two propositions in a syllogism from which the conclusion is drawn (*log.*;

also **prem′iss**): (usu. in *pl.*) the matter set forth at the beginning of a deed: (in *pl.*) the beginning of a deed setting forth its subject-matter: (in *pl.*) the aforesaid, hence, a building and its adjuncts, esp. a public-house: a presupposition (also **prem′iss**): a condition stipulated beforehand (*Shak.*): (in *pl.*) antecedent happenings or circumstances (*Shak.*). — *v.t.* **premise** (*pri-mīz′*, also *prem′is*) to mention or state first, or by way of introduction: to prefix: to state or assume as a premise: to perform or administer beforehand (*med.*). — *adj.* **premī′sed** (*Shak.*) sent before due time. [Fr. *prémisse* and L. (*sententia*, etc.) *praemissa*, (a sentence, etc.) put before — *mittĕre, missum*, to send.]

premium *prē′mi-əm, n.* a reward: a prize: a bounty: payment made for insurance: a fee for admission as a pupil for a profession: excess over original price or par (opp. to *discount*): anything offered as an incentive: — *pl.* **pre′miums,** (*rare*) **pre′mia.** — **Premium (Savings) Bond** a Government bond, the holder of which gains no interest, but is eligible for a money prize allotted by draw held at stated intervals. — **at a premium** above par: in great demand. [L. *praemium* — *prae,* above, *emĕre,* to buy.]

premolar *prē-mō′lər, adj.* in front of the true molar teeth. — *n.* tooth between the canine and molars (called molar or milk-molar in the milk dentition). [Pfx. **pre-** (1).]

premonish *prē-mon′ish, v.t.* to admonish or warn beforehand. — *n.* **premonition** (*prē-mən-ish′ən,* or *prem-*) a forewarning: a feeling that something is going to happen. — *adjs.* **premonitive** (*pri-mon′*), **premon′itory** giving warning or notice beforehand. — *n.* **premon′itor** one who, or that which, gives warning beforehand. — *adv.* **premon′itorily.** [On the model of **admonish** — L. *praemonēre* — *monēre,* to warn.]

Premonstrant. See **Premonstratensian.**

Premonstratensian *pri-mon-strə-ten′sh(y)ən, -si-ən, adj.* of an order of canons regular, the Norbertines or White Canons, founded by St Norbert, in 1119, at *Prémontré,* near Laon, or of a corresponding order of nuns. — *n.* a member of the order. — Also (*n.* and *adj.*) **Premon′-strant.** [L. *prātum mōnstrātum,* the meadow pointed out, or (*locus*) *praemōnstrātus,* (the place) foreshown (in a vision), i.e. *Prémontré.*]

premorse *pri-mörs′, adj.* ending abruptly, as if bitten off. [L. *praemorsus,* bitten in front — *prae, mordēre, morsum,* to bite.]

premosaic *prē-mō-zā′ik, adj.* before the time of *Moses.* [Pfx. **pre-** (2), **Mosaic.**]

premotion *prē-mō′shən, n.* an (esp. divine) impulse determining the will. — *v.t.* **premove′.** — *n.* **premove′ment.** [Pfx. **pre-** (2).]

premy. See **preemie.**

prenasal *prē-nā′zl, adj.* in front of the nose. — *n.* a bone at the tip of the nose, as in pigs. [Pfx. **pre-** (1).]

prenatal *prē-nā′tl, adj.* before birth. [Pfx. **pre-** (2).]

prenominate *pri-nom′in-āt,* (*Shak.*) *adj.* fore-named. — *v.t.* to name or state beforehand. [Pfx. **pre-** (2).]

prenotion *prē-nō′shən, n.* a preconception. [Pfx. **pre-** (2).]

prent *prent,* (*Scot.*). Same as **print.**

prentice, ′prentice *pren′tis,* aphetic for **apprentice.** — *n.* **pren′ticeship, ′pren′ticeship.**

prenzie app. *adj.* in Shak. (*Meas. for Meas.,* III, i. 92, 95) conjectured to mean primsie: according to others princely: or connected with **prone** (homily): or Fr. *prenez garde:* or a misprint.

preoccupy *prē-ok′ū-pī, v.t.* to occupy, fill, or (*obs.*) wear beforehand or before others: to take or have possession of to the exclusion of others or other things: to fill the mind of: to prejudice. — *ns.* **prēocc′upancy** occupying before others: the condition of being preoccupied; **prēocc′upant** a prior occupant. — *v.t.* **prēocc′upate** to preoccupy: to anticipate. — *n.* **prēoccupā′tion.** — *adj.* **prēocc′upied** already occupied: lost in thought, abstracted: having one's attention wholly taken up by (with *with*): of a genus or species name,

not available for adoption because it has already been applied to another group. [Pfx. **pre-** (2).]

preoption *prē-op′shən, n.* first choice. [Pfx. **pre-** (2).]

preoral *prē-ō′rəl, -ö′, adj.* in front of the mouth. — *adv.* **preo′rally.** [Pfx. **pre-** (1).]

preordain *prē-ör-dān′, v.t.* to ordain, appoint, or determine beforehand. — *n.* **preordain′ment.** — *v.t.* **preor′-der** to arrange or ordain beforehand. — *ns.* **preor′-dinance** a rule previously established: that which is ordained beforehand; **preordinā′tion** preordaining. [Pfx. **pre-** (2).]

prep *prep, adj.* coll. short form of *preparatory.* — *n.* school slang for *preparation* or *preparation:* lessons: a preparatory school (also **prep school**): a pupil in a preparatory school. — Also *v.t.* — *adj.* **prepp′y** (*U.S.*) vaguely denoting the values, mores, dress, etc. of a class of people who (might wish to seem to) have attended a (U.S.) preparatory school (q.v.). — Also *n.*

prepack *prē′pak′, v.t.* to pack (e.g. food) before offering for sale. — *p.adj.* **prē′packed′.** [Pfx. **pre-** (2).]

prepaid. See **prepay.**

prepare *pri-pār′, v.t.* to make ready or fit: to bring into a suitable state: to dispose: to adapt: to train, as for an examination: to get up, learn: to make a preliminary study of (work prescribed for a class): to provide, furnish (*arch.*): to subject to a process for bringing into a required state: to make, produce: to cook and dress: to lead up to. — *v.i.* to make oneself ready: to make preparation. — *n.* preparation (*Shak.*). — *n.* **prepara-tion** (*prep-ə-rā′shən*) the act of preparing: a preliminary arrangement: the process or course of being prepared: the preliminary study of prescribed classwork: readiness: that which is prepared or made up, as a medicine: an anatomical or other specimen prepared for study or preservation: the day before the Sabbath or other Jewish feast-day: devotional exercises introducing an office: the previous introduction, as an integral part of a chord, of a note continued into a succeeding dissonance (*mus.*). — *adj.* **preparative** (*pri-par′ə-tiv*) serving to prepare: preliminary. — *n.* that which prepares the way: preparation. — *adv.* **prepar′atively.** — *n.* **prepar′ator.** — *adv.* **prepar′atorily.** — *adj.* **prepar′-atory** preparing: previous: introductory. — *adv.* preparatorily (with *to*). — *adj.* **prepared** (*pri-pārd′*) made ready, fit, or suitable: ready. — *adv.* **prepā′redly.** — *ns.* **prepā′redness; prepā′rer.** — **preparatory school** one which prepares pupils for a public or other higher school: a private school that prepares young people for college (*U.S.*). — **be prepared to** to be ready, or be willing, to (do something). [Fr. *préparer* — L. *praeparāre* — *prae, parāre,* to make ready.]

prepay *prē′pā′, v.t.* to pay before or in advance: — *pa.t.* and *pa.p.* **prē′paid′.** — *adj.* **pre′paid′.** — *adj.* **pre′pay′-able.** — *n.* **pre′pay′ment.** [Pfx. **pre-** (2).]

prepense *pri-pens′, adj.* premeditated: intentional, chiefly in the phrase 'malice prepense' = malice aforethought or intentional. — *v.t.* (*Spens.*) to consider. — *adv.* **prepense′ly.** — *adj.* **prepens′ive** (*Fielding*). [O.Fr. *purpense.*]

prepollence *pri-pol′əns, n.* predominance. — *n.* **prepoll′-ency.** — *adj.* **prepoll′ent.** [L.L. *praepollentia* — *prae, pollēre,* to be strong.]

prepollex *prē-pol′eks, n.* in some animals, a rudimentary innermost finger. [Pfx. **pre-** (1).]

preponderate[1] *pri-pon′də-rāt, v.i.* to weigh more: to turn the balance: to prevail or exceed in number, quantity, importance, influence, or force (with *over*). — *v.t.* (*lit.* or *fig.*) to outweigh. — *ns.* **prepon′derance, prepon′-derancy.** — *adj.* **prepon′derant.** — *advs.* **prepon′der-antly, prepon′derātingly.** [L. *praeponderāre, -ātum* — *prae, ponderāre, -ātum,* to weigh — *pondus,* a weight.]

preponderate[2] *pri-pon′də-rāt,* (*Fielding*) *v.t.* and *v.i.* to ponder beforehand. [Pfx. **pre-** (2).]

preposition *prep-ə-zish′ən, n.* a word placed usually before a noun or its equivalent to mark some relation: a prefix (*obs.*): (*prē-*) position in front. — *adj.* **preposi′tional** (*prep-*). — *adv.* **preposi′tionally.** — *adj.* **prepositive**

(*pri-poz'i-tiv*) put before: prefixed. — *ns.* **praepost'or, prepos'itor** a school prefect (for L. *praepositus*). [L. *praepositiō, -ōnis* — *praepōnĕre, -positum* — *prae, pōnĕre*, to place.]

prepossess *prē-poz-es'*, *v.t.* to possess beforehand: to take beforehand: to fill beforehand, as the mind with some opinion or feeling: to preoccupy: to bias or prejudice, esp. favourably. — *adjs.* **prepossessed'** biased, prejudiced; **prepossess'ing** tending to prepossess: making a favourable impression. — *adv.* **prepossess'ingly.** — *n.* **prepossession** (*-esh'ən*) previous possession: preoccupation: bias, usually favourable. [Pfx. **pre-** (2).]

preposterous *pri-pos'tə-rəs*, *adj.* lit. inverted, having or putting the last first (*rare*): contrary to the order of nature or reason: utterly absurd. — *adv.* **prepos'terously.** — *n.* **prepos'terousness.** [L. *praeposterus* — *prae*, before, *posterus*, after — *post*, after.]

prepotent *prē-pō'tənt*, *adj.* powerful in a very high degree: prevailing over others or another in taking effect: having power to transmit to offspring more characteristics than the other parent: taking precedence in effect. — *ns.* **prepo'tence, prepo'tency.** [Pfx. **pre-** (3).]

preppy. See **prep.**

pre-print *prē'-print*, *n.* part of a publication printed in advance. [Pfx. **pre-** (2).]

prepuce *prē'pūs*, *n.* the loose skin of the penis, the foreskin: a similar fold of skin over the clitoris. — *adj.* **preputial** (*pri-pū'shyəl, -shəl*). [L. *praepūtium*.]

prepunctual *prē-pungk'tū-əl*, *adj.* more than punctual: coming before time. [Pfx. **pre-** (3).]

pre-qualify *prē-kwol'i-fī*, *v.i.* to qualify beforehand (e.g. for a short list). — *n.* **pre-qualificā'tion.** [Pfx. **pre-** (2).]

prequel *prē'kwəl*, (*coll.*) *n.* a film or book produced after some other film or book has proved a success, based on the same leading characters but depicting events happening before those of the first one. [Pfx. **pre-** (2), and **sequel.**]

Pre-Raphaelite (or, as spelt by D. G. Rossetti) **Praeraphaelite** *prē-raf'ā-əl-īt*, *n.* one who seeks to return to the spirit and manner of painters before the time of *Raphael* (1483–1520): a member of a group (the Pre-Raphaelite Brotherhood, or 'P.R.B.', 1848) of painters and others (D. G. Rossetti, W. Holman Hunt, J. E. Millais, etc.) who practised or advocated a truthful, almost rigid, adherence to natural forms and effects. — Also *adj.* — *ns.* **Pre-Raph'aelism, Pre-Raph'aelitism.** — *adjs.* **Pre-Raphaelist'ic, Pre-Raphaelitist'ic; Pre-Raphaelit'ish.** [Pfx. **pre-** (2), *Raphael*, and suff. **-ite.**]

pre-Reformation *prē-ref-ər-mā'shən*, *adj.* before the Reformation: dating from before the Reformation. [Pfx. **pre-** (2).]

prerelease *prē-ri-lēs'*, *n.* the release of a cinematograph film before the normal date: the exhibition of a film so released. — Also *adj.* [Pfx. **pre-** (2).]

prerequisite *prē-rek'wi-zit*, *n.* a condition or requirement that must previously be satisfied. — *adj.* required as a condition of something else. [Pfx. **pre-** (2).]

prerogative *pri-rog'ə-tiv*, *n.* a peculiar privilege shared by no other: a right arising out of one's rank, position, or nature: the right of voting first (*rare*). — *adj.* arising out of, or held by, prerogative: voting first. — *adj.* **prerog'atived** (*Shak.*) having a prerogative. — *adv.* **prerog'atively.** — **Prerogative Court** formerly, a court having jurisdiction over testamentary matters. — **royal prerogative** the rights which a sovereign has by right of office, which are different in different countries. [L. *praerogātīvus*, asked first for his vote — *prae, rogāre, -ātum*, to ask.]

prerosion *prē-rō'zhən*, *n.* corrosion of a crystal by a solvent forming new faces (*prerosion faces*) on the corners and edges. [L. *praerōdĕre, -rōsum*, to gnaw at the tip — *rōdĕre*, to gnaw.]

prerupt *prē-rupt'*, *adj.* broken off: abrupt. [L. *praeruptus* — *prae, rumpĕre*, to break.]

presa *prä'sä, -sə, -zä*, *n.* a symbol (᛬ᐧ ᛬S᛬ or ᛬S᛬) used to indicate the points at which successive voice or

instrumental parts enter a round, canon, etc.: — *pl.* **pre'se** (*-sā, -zā*). [It., an act of taking up.]

presage *pres'ij*, formerly also *pri-sāj'*, *n.* a prognostic: an omen: an indication of the future: a foreboding: a presentiment. — *v.t.* **presage** (*pri-sāj'*) to portend: to forebode: to warn of as something to come: to forecast: to point out, reveal (*Spens.*): to have a presentiment of. — *v.i.* to have or utter a presage. — *adj.* **presage'ful.** — *ns.* **presage'ment** (*obs.*); **presag'er.** [L. *praesāgium*, a foreboding — *prae, sāgus*, prophetic.]

presanctify *prē-sangk'ti-fī*, *v.t.* to consecrate beforehand. — *n.* **presanctificā'tion.** [Pfx. **pre-** (2).]

presbyopia *prez-bi-ō'pi-ə*, *n.* difficulty in accommodating the eye to near vision, a defect increasing with age — also **pres'byopy.** — *n.* **pres'byope** one so affected. — *adj.* **presbyopic** (*-op'ik*). [Gr. *presbys*, old, *ōps, ōpos*, the eye.]

presbyte *prez'bīt*, *n.* etymologically an old man, but used for one who is presbyopic. [Gr. *presbȳtēs*, an old man.]

presbyter *prez'bi-tər*, *n.* an elder: a minister or priest in rank between a bishop and a deacon: a member of a presbytery: a Presbyterian (*obs.*). — *adj.* **presbyt'eral** of a presbyter or presbyters. — *n.* **presbyt'erate** the office of presbyter: a body of presbyters: the order of presbyters. — *adj.* **presbyterial** (*-tē'ri-əl*) of a presbytery: of church government by elders. — *adv.* **presbytē'rially.** — *adj.* **Presbytē'rian** pertaining to, or maintaining the system of, church government by presbyters: of a church so governed. — *n.* a member of such a church: an upholder of the Presbyterian system. — *v.t.* and *v.i.* **Presbytē'rianise, -ize** to make or become Presbyterian: to move towards Presbyterianism. — *ns.* **Presbytē'rianism** the form of church government by presbyters; **pres'bytership; pres'bytery** a church court ranking next above the kirk-session, consisting of the ministers and one ruling elder from each church within a certain district: the district so represented: the Presbyterian system: part of a church reserved for the officiating priests, the eastern extremity: a priest's house (*R.C.*). — **Reformed Presbyterian Church** the Cameronians; **United Presbyterian Church** a religious body formed by the union of the Secession and Relief Churches in 1847, included in the United Free Church from 1900, and (except a minority) in the Church of Scotland from 1929. [Gr. *presbyteros*, compar. of *presbys*, old.]

preschool *prē'skool'*, *adj.* before school: not yet at school. — *n.* **prē'schooler** a preschool child. [Pfx. **pre-** (2).]

prescience *pre'sh(y)əns, -shi-əns, prē', -si-əns*, *n.* foreknowledge: foresight. — *adj.* **pre'scient.** — *adv.* **pre'sciently.** [L. *praesciēns, -entis*, pr.p. of *praescīre* — *prae, scīre*, to know.]

prescientific *prē-sī-ən-tif'ik*, *adj.* before the scientific age, before knowledge was systematised. [Pfx. **pre-** (2).]

prescind *pri-sind'*, *v.t.* to cut off, cut short, separate: to abstract. — *v.i.* to withdraw the attention (usu. with *from*). — *adj.* **prescind'ent.** — *n.* **prescission** (*pri-sish'-ən*). [L. *praescindĕre*, to cut off in front.]

prescious *pre', prē'shyəs*, *adj.* prescient. [L. *praescius* — *praescīre*; cf. **prescience.**]

prescission. See **prescind.**

prescribe *pri-skrīb'*, *v.t.* to lay down as a rule or direction: to give as an order: to appoint: to give directions for, as a remedy (*med.*): to limit, set bounds to: to claim by prescription. — *v.i.* to lay down rules: to give or make out a prescription (*med.*): to make a claim on account of long possession: to become of no force through time. — *ns.* **prescrib'er; prescript** (*prē'skript*; formerly *-skript'*) an ordinance or rule: a remedy or treatment prescribed. — *adj.* (*prē'* or *-skript'*) prescribed. — *n.* **prescriptibil'ity** (*pri-*). — *adj.* **prescrip'tible** subject to prescription: invalidated by lapse of time. — *n.* **prescrip'tion** the act of prescribing or directing: a written direction for the preparation or dispensing of a medicine (*med.*): the medicine itself: a recipe: enjoyment, possession, use, etc. from time immemorial or for a period of time fixed by law by which a legal right or title is acquired (*law*; also **positive prescription**): any claim based on long use, or an established custom taken as authoritative: limitation of time within which action may be taken (*law*; also **negative prescription**). — *adj.* **prescrip′tive** prescribing, laying down rules: consisting in, or acquired by, custom or long-continued use: customary. — *adv.* **prescrip′tively**. — *n.* **prescrip′tiveness**. [L. *praescrībĕre, -scrīptum*, to write before, lay down in advance, demur to — *prae, scrībĕre*, to write.]

prescutum *prē-skūt′əm, n.* in insects, a tergal plate in front of the scutum. [Pfx. **pre-** (1).]

preselect *prē-si-lekt′, v.t.* to select beforehand. — *ns.* **preselec′tion; preselec′tor** a component of a radio receiver, improving reception. [Pfx. **pre-** (2).]

pre-sell *prē-sel′, v.t.* to sell (something) before it has been produced. [Pfx. **pre-** (2).]

presence *prez′əns, n.* the fact or state of being present (opp. to *absence*): immediate neighbourhood: a presence-chamber (*obs.*) or other place where a great personage is: an assembly, esp. of great persons: a present personality: the impression made by one's bearing, esp. imposing bearing: military or political representation or influence: something felt or imagined to be present. — **pres′ence-chamber** the room in which a great personage receives company. — **presence of mind** the power of keeping one's wits about one: coolness and readiness in emergency, danger, or surprise; **real presence** the true and substantial presence, according to the belief of Roman Catholics, Eastern Orthodox, etc., of the body and blood of Christ in the eucharist. [O.Fr., — L. *praesentia*; see **present**[1,2,3].]

presension. See **presension.**

present[1] *prez′ənt, adj.* in the place in question or implied (opp. to *absent*): at hand: ready: found or existing in the thing in question: before the mind: attentive, watchful, not absent-minded: now under view or consideration: now existing: not past or future: denoting time just now, or making a general statement (*gram.*): in or of the present tense: immediate. — *n.* that which is present: the present time: the present tense: a verb in the present tense: the present business or occasion: the present document or (in *pl.*) writings. — *adj.* **presential** (*pri-zen′shl*) relating to presence: having or implying actual presence: present: as if present: formed from the present tense. — *n.* **presentiality** (*-shi-al′i-ti*). — *advs.* **presen′tially; pres′ently** at present, now (*obs.* or *Scot.* and *U.S.*): for the time being (*obs.*): at once (*obs.*): before long: directly, immediately, necessarily. — *n.* **pres′entness**. — *adj.* **pres′ent-day′** belonging to or found in the present time, contemporary. — **at present** at the present time, now; **for the present** for the moment: now, for the time being. [O.Fr., — L. *praesēns, -sentis*, present.]

present[2] *prez′ənt, n.* a gift. [O.Fr. *present*, orig. presence, hence gift (from the phrase *mettre en present à*, to put into the presence of, hence to offer as a gift to).]

present[3] *pri-zent′, v.t.* to set before (someone), introduce into presence or to notice, cognisance, or acquaintance: to introduce at court: to introduce to the public, as on the stage: to put on the stage: to exhibit to view: to have as a characteristic: to put forward: to proffer: to make a gift of: to appoint to a benefice: to nominate to a foundation: to put forward or bring up for examination, trial, dedication, a degree, consideration, etc.: to deliver: to bestow something upon, endow (with *with*): to represent, depict, or symbolise: to represent the character of, act, personate (*arch.*): to point, direct, aim, turn in some direction: to apply: to offer the greetings of, 'remember' (*obs.*): to hold vertically in front of the body in salute to a superior (*mil.*): (*refl.*) to come into presence, attend, appear: (*refl.*) to offer (oneself): (*refl.*) to offer (itself), occur. — *v.i.* to make presentation to a living: to offer: to be directed, to be in position for coming first (*obstetrics*). — *n.* the position of a weapon in presenting arms or

in aiming. — *n.* **presentabil′ity**. — *adj.* **present′able** capable of being presented: fit to be presented: fit to be seen: passable. — *adv.* **present′ably**. — *ns.* **present′-ableness; presentation** (*prez-ən-tā′shən*) the act of presenting: the mode of presenting: the right of presenting: that which is presented: immediate cognition: a setting forth, as of a truth: representation. — *adj.* that has been presented: of or for presentation. — *adj.* **presentā′tional**. — *ns.* **presentā′tionism** the doctrine of immediate cognition of objects; **presentā′tionist**. — *adj.* **presentative** (*pri-zent′ə-tiv*) subject to the right of presentation: presenting to the mind (esp. that which is not imitative): pertaining to immediate cognition. — *ns.* **presentee** (*prez-ən-tē′*) one who is presented to a benefice; **presenter** (*pri-zent′ər*). — *adj.* **present′ive** presenting a conception to the mind, not a mere relation. — *ns.* **present′iveness; present′ment** the act of presenting: a statement: a jury's statement to a court of matters within its knowledge: a representation: an image, delineation, picture: a presentation to consciousness. — **at present** in the position of presenting arms; **present arms** to bring the weapon to a vertical position in front of the body. [O.Fr. *presenter* — L. *praesentāre* — *praesēns*, present (in place or time).]

presential, etc. See **present**[1].

presentient *prē-sen′sh(y)ənt, adj.* having a presentiment. — *n.* **prēsen′sion**. [Pfx. **pre-** (2).]

presentiment *pri-zent′i-mənt*, sometimes *-sent′, n.* a foreboding, esp. of evil. — *adj.* **presentimental** (*-ment′l*). [Pfx. **pre-** (2).]

presentment. See **present**[3].

preserve *pri-zûrv′, v.t.* to keep safe from harm or loss: to keep alive: to keep in existence: to retain: to maintain, keep up: to guard against shooting or fishing by unauthorised persons: to keep sound: to keep from or guard against decay: to pickle, season, or otherwise treat for keeping. — *v.i.* to preserve game, fish, ground, or water, etc. — *n.* preserved fruit or jam (often in *pl.*): a place or water where shooting or fishing is preserved: anything regarded as closed or forbidden to outsiders: (in *pl.*) spectacles to protect the eyes from dust or strong light. — *n.* **preservabil′ity**. — *adj.* **preserv′able**. — *ns.* **preservā′tion** (*prez-*); **preservā′tionist** one who is interested in preserving traditional and historic things. — *adj.* **preserv′ative** serving to preserve. — *n.* a preserving agent: a safeguard: a prophylactic. — *adj.* and *n.* **preserv′atory**. — *n.* **preserv′er**. — **preservation order** a legally binding directive ordering the preservation of a building deemed to be historically important; **preserv′ing-pan** a large pan usu. with a hooped handle and a lip, in which jams, etc. are made. — **well preserved** (*coll.*; of a person) not showing the signs of ageing one would expect in a person of such an age. [Fr. *préserver* — L. *prae, servāre*, to keep.]

preses, praeses *prē′siz*, (chiefly *Scot.*) *n.* a president or chairman: — *pl.* **prē′ses, prae′ses**. [L. *praeses, -idis* — *praesidēre*; see **preside**.]

pre-shrink *prē′-shringk′, v.t.* to shrink (cloth) before it is made up into garments, etc. [Pfx. **pre-** (2).]

preside *pri-zīd′, v.i.* to be in the chair: to be at the head: to superintend: to be guardian or tutelary god: to be at the organ or piano (orig. as a kind of conductor). — *v.t.* (*rare*) to be at the head of. — *ns.* **presidency** (*prez′i-dən-si*) the office of a president, or his dignity, term of office, jurisdiction, or residence: each of three main divisions of India (*hist.*): a Mormon governing council; **pres′ident** one who is chosen to preside over the meetings of a society, conference, etc.: the elected head of a republic: the head of a board, council, or department of government: the title of the head of certain colleges, universities, and other institutions: a colonial or state governor (*hist.*): the chairman of a company, a bank governor, or head of an organisation generally (*U.S.*). — *adj.* (*Milt.*) presiding, superintending. — *n.* **pres′identess**. — *adj.* **presidential** (*-den′shl*) presiding: of a president or presidency. — *n.* **pres′identship**. — **presiding officer** a person in charge of a polling-place. — **Lord President** the presiding judge of the Court of Session; **Lord President of the Council** a member of the House of Lords who presides over the privy council. [Fr. *présider* — L. *praesidēre* — *prae, sedēre*, to sit.]

president[1] (*Spens., Shak., Milt.*) for **precedent**.

president[2]. See **preside**.

presidial *pri-sid'i-əl, adj.* pertaining to a garrison, a presidio, or a president: provincial (*Fr. hist.*). — *adj.* **presid'iary** garrisoning: of a garrison. — *ns.* **presid'io** (*Sp. Amer.*, etc.) a military post: a penal settlement: — *pl.* **presid'ios; presid'ium** a standing committee in the Soviet system (also **praesidium**): — *pl.* **-diums** or **-dia**. [L. *praesidium*, a garrison — *praesidēre*, to preside.]

presignify *prē-sig'ni-fī, v.t.* to intimate beforehand. — *n.* **prēsignificā'tion**. [Pfx. **pre-** (2).]

press[1] *pres*, also (all *obs.*) **preace, prease, preasse**, etc., *près, vs.t.* to exert a pushing force upon: to squeeze: to compress: to clasp: to thrust onwards or downwards: to squeeze out: to imprint, stamp, print: to flatten, condense, dry, shape, or smooth by weight or other squeezing force: to put to death by application of heavy weights: to bear heavily on: to harass: to beset: to urge strongly: to invite with persistent warmth: to offer urgently or abundantly (with *upon*): to throng, crowd: to present to the mind with earnestness: to lay stress upon: to hurry on with great speed. — *vs.i.* to exert pressure: to push with force: to crowd: to go forward with violence: to be urgent in application, entreaty, or effort: to strive: to strain: to strive to do too much, to the loss of ease and effectiveness (*golf*). — *ns.* an act of pressing: pressure: a crowd: crowding: the thick of a fight: stress: urgency: a cupboard or shelved closet or recess: a bookcase: an apparatus for pressing: a printing-machine: printing: a printing organisation: often extended to a publishing house: printing activities: newspapers and periodicals collectively: the journalistic profession: (with *cap.*) a common name for a newspaper: (favourable or unfavourable) reception by newspapers and periodicals generally (also *fig.*). — *ns.* **press'er; press'ful; press'ing** the action of the verb *press*: an article, articles, esp. gramophone records, made from the same mould or press. — *adj.* urgent: importunate: crowding. — *adv.* **press'ingly**. — *n.* **pression** (*presh'ən; rare*) pressure: impress. — **press'-agent** one who arranges for newspaper advertising and publicity, esp. for an actor or theatre; **press association** an association of newspapers formed to act as a news agency for the members of the association, each supplying local news, etc. to the association: (with *caps.*) a British news agency formed as a press association in 1868; **press'-bed** a bed enclosed in a cupboard, or folding up into it; **press'-book** a book printed at a private press; **press'-box** an erection provided for the use of reporters at sports, shows, etc.; **press'-button** a push-button. — Also *adj.* — **press conference** a meeting of a public personage with the press for making an announcement or to answer questions; **press'-cutt'ing** a paragraph or article cut out of a newspaper or magazine; **pressed'-day** the third day of a three days' visit; **pressed glass** glass given shape and pattern by pressure in a mould; **press'-fastener, press'-stud** a form of button fastening in two parts, one of which can be pushed partly into the other; **press'fat** (*B.*) the vat for collecting the liquor from an olive or wine press; **press'-gall'ery** a reporters' gallery; **press'man** one who works a printing-press: a journalist or reporter; **press'-mark** a mark upon a book to show its place in a library; **press'-proof** the last proof before printing; **press release** an official statement or report supplied to the press; **press'-room** a room where printing-presses are worked: a room for the use of journalists; **press'-up** a gymnastic exercise in which the prone body is kept rigid while being raised and lowered by straightening and bending the arms; **press'-work** the operation of a printing-press: printed matter: journal-

istic work. — **at press, in the press** in course of printing: about to be published; **go to press** to begin to print or to be printed; **liberty, freedom, of the press** right of publishing material without submitting it to a government authority for permission; **press ahead, forward, on** to continue, esp. energetically, often in spite of difficulties or opposition; **press of canvas, sail** as much sail as can be carried; **the press** printed matter generally, esp. newspapers: journalists as a class. [Fr. *presser* — L. *pressāre* — *premĕre, pressum*, to press.]

press[2] *pres, v.t.* to carry off and force into service, esp. in the navy: to requisition: to turn to use in an unsuitable or provisional way. — *n.* impressment: authority for impressing. — **press'-gang** a gang or body of sailors under an officer, empowered to impress men into the navy. — Also *v.t.* (also *fig.*). — **press'-money** earnest-money. [**prest**[2].]

pressor *pres'ər, (physiol.) adj.* causing an increase in blood pressure. [L.L., one who presses — *premĕre, pressum*, to press.]

pressure *presh'ər, n.* the act of pressing or squeezing: the state of being pressed: impression, stamp (*Shak.*): constraining force or influence: that which presses or afflicts: urgency: a strong demand: a force directed towards the thing it acts upon, measured as so much weight upon a unit of area: difference of electric potential. — *v.t.* to apply pressure to: to compel by pressure (with *into*). — *n.* **pressurisā'tion, -z-**. — *v.t.* **press'urise, -ize** (of an aeroplane, etc.) to fit with a device that maintains nearly normal atmospheric pressure: to subject to pressure: to force by pressure (into doing something). — **press'ure-cab'in** a pressurised cabin in an aircraft. — *v.t.* **press'ure-cook'** to cook in a pressure cooker. — **pressure cooker** an autoclave, esp. one for domestic use; **pressure group** a set putting pressure on a government for a particular purpose; **press'ure-hel'met** an airman's helmet for use with a pressure-suit; **pressure point** any of various points on the body on which pressure may be exerted to relieve pain, control bleeding, etc.; **pressure ridge** a ridge formed by lateral pressure in floating ice in polar waters; **press'ure-suit** an automatically inflating suit worn by airmen against pressure-cabin failure at very high altitudes; **press'ure-waist'coat** an airman's waistcoat through which oxygen passes under pressure to the lungs to aid breathing at high altitudes. [L. *pressura* — *premĕre*, to press.]

prest[1] *prest*, (*Spens., Shak.*) *adj.* ready. [O.Fr. *prest* — L. *praestō*, at hand.]

prest[2] *prest*, (*obs.*) *v.t.* to lend: to pay in advance: to engage by paying earnest: to enlist: to impress for service. — *n.* a loan: payment in advance: enlistment-money. — *n.* **prestā'tion** payment or service required by custom or promise. [O.Fr. *prester* — L. *praestāre*, to offer, discharge.]

Prestel® *pres'tel, n.* the viewdata (q.v.) system of British Telecom.

Prester John *pres'tər jon*, the mythical mediaeval Christian priest-king of a vast empire in Central Asia (and later in Ethiopia). [O.Fr. *prestre* (Fr. *prêtre*), priest.]

presternum *prē-stûr'nəm, n.* the anterior part of the sternum. [Pfx. **pre-** (1).]

prestidigitation *pres-ti-dij-i-tā'shən, n.* sleight-of-hand. — *n.* **prestidig'itātor**. [Fr. *prestidigitateur* — *preste*, nimble, L. *digitus*, finger.]

prestige *pres-tēzh', n.* orig. a conjuring trick, illusion: glamour: standing or ascendancy in people's minds owing to associations, station, success, etc. — *adj.* consisting in, or for the sake of, prestige: considered to have or give prestige: superior in quality, style, etc. — *n.* **prestigiator** (*pres-tij'i-ā-tər*) a conjurer. — *adj.* **prestigious** (*-tij'əs*) juggling: having prestige, esteemed: deceitful. [Fr., — L. *praestigium*, delusion — *praestringĕre*, to dazzle, blind; see **prestriction**.]

presto *pres'tō, (mus.) adj.* very quick. — *n.* a presto movement or passage: — *pl.* **pres'tos.** — *adv.* quickly, quicker than *allegro*. — *adv.* or *interj.* (usu. **hey presto**

as in conjuring tricks) at once. — *adv.*, *n.*, and *adj.*
(*superl.*) **prestis′simo**: — *pl.* **prestis′simos.** [It., — L. *praestō*, at hand.]

pre-stressed *prē-strest′*, *adj.* (of concrete) strengthened with stretched wires or rods instead of large steel bars as in reinforced concrete. [Pfx. **pre-** (2).]

prestriction *pri-strik′shən*, *n.* blindness: blindfolding. [L. *praestrictiō*, *-ōnis* — *praestringĕre*, to draw tight, bind, restrain, blind.]

presume *pri-zūm′*, *-zōōm′*, *v.t.* to take as true without examination or proof: to take for granted: to assume provisionally: to take upon oneself, esp. with overboldness. — *v.i.* to venture beyond what one has ground for: to act forwardly or without proper right: to rely, count (with *on*, *upon*), esp. unduly. — *adj.* **presūm′able** that may be presumed or supposed to be true. — *adv.* **presūm′ably.** — *n.* **presūm′er.** — *adj.* **presūm′ing** venturing without permission: unreasonably bold. — *conj.* (often with *that*) making the presumption that. — *adv.* **presūm′ingly.** — *n.* **presumption** (*-zum′shən*, *-zump′shən*) the act of presuming: supposition: strong probability: that which is taken for granted: an assumption or belief based on facts or probable evidence: confidence grounded on something not proved: a ground or reason for presuming: conduct going beyond proper bounds: a presumption of fact or presumption of law (*law*). — *adj.* **presumptive** (*-zump′*, *-zum′tiv*) presuming (*obs.*): grounded on probable evidence: giving grounds for presuming (see **heir** for **heir-presumptive**): pertaining to embryonic tissue which will in the normal course of development be differentiated into a particular organ or tissue (*biol.*). — *adv.* **presump′tively.** — *adj.* **presumptuous** (*-zump′tū-əs*, or *-zum′*) presuming. — *adv.* **presump′tuously.** — *n.* **presump′tuousness.** — **presumption of fact** (*law*) an assumption of a fact from known facts; **presumption of law** (*law*) an assumption made failing proof to the contrary: an inference established as a rule of law, not contradictable by evidence. [L. *praesūmĕre*, *-sūmptum* — *prae*, *sūmĕre*, to take — *sub*, under, *emĕre*, to buy.]

presuppose *prē-sə-pōz′*, *v.t.* to assume or take for granted: to involve as a necessary antecedent. — *n.* **presupposition** (*prē-sup-ə-zish′ən*). [Pfx. **pre-** (2).]

presurmise *prē-sər-mīz′*, (*Shak.*) *n* a surmise previously formed. [Pfx. **pre-** (2).]

prêt-à-porter *pre-ta-por-tā* (Fr.) *n.* and *adj.* ready-to-wear (garments).

pre-tax *prē-taks′*, *adj.* before the deduction of tax. [Pfx. **pre-** (2).]

pre-teen *prē-tēn′*, *n.* (usu. in *pl.*) a child slightly younger than a teenager. — Also *adj.* [Pfx. **pre-** (2).]

pretend *pri-tend′*, *v.t.* to stretch forth, or in front (*Spens.*): to offer (*obs.*): to profess, now only falsely: to feign: to claim (*obs.*): to allege (*obs.*): to allege falsely: to make believe: to purpose (*obs.*): to venture, attempt, undertake: to indicate (*obs.*). — *v.i.* to reach or go forward (*obs.*): to be a claimant (*obs.*): to aspire: to be a suitor: to make a claim: to feign: to make believe. — *n.* **pretence′** (*U.S.* **pretense′**) an act of pretending: something pretended: an allegation: an aim, purpose: the thing aimed at: appearance or show to hide reality: false show: a false allegation: a sham: pretentiousness: a pretext: claim. — *adj.* **pretence′less** without a pretext. — *n.* **preten′dant** (or **-ent**) a claimant: a suitor: a pretender. — *adj.* **preten′ded.** — *adv.* **preten′dedly.** — *ns.* **preten′der** a claimant, esp. to a throne: a candidate: a suitor (*obs.*): one who pretends; **preten′dership.** — *adv.* **preten′dingly.** — *n.* **preten′sion** pretence: show: pretext: claim: aspiration, esp. to marriage: pretentiousness. — *adj.* **preten′tious** (*-shəs*) over-assuming: seeming to claim much, or too much. — *adv.* **preten′tiously.** — *n.* **preten′tiousness.** — **Old Pretender, Young Pretender** the son, grandson, of James II and VII as claimants to the British throne. [L. *praetendĕre* — *prae*, *tendĕre*, *tentum*, *tēnsum*, to stretch.]

pre-tension *prē-ten′shən*, *v.t.* to stretch (the reinforcing

wires or rods in pre-stressed concrete) before the concrete is cast. — *adj.* **pre-ten′sioned.** [Pfx. **pre-** (2).]

pretension, etc. See **pretend.**

preter-, (L. spelling occurring chiefly in obs. words) **praeter-,** *prē′tər-*, in composition, beyond. — *adjs.* **preterhu′man** more than human; **preternat′ural** out of the ordinary course of nature: abnormal: supernatural. — *n.* **preternat′uralism** belief in the preternatural: preternatural character or event. — *adv.* **preternat′urally.** — *n.* **preternat′uralness.** — *adjs.* **preterperfect** (*-pûr′fekt*, *-fikt*; *old gram.*) perfect; **preterpluperfect** (*-plōō-pûr′fekt*, *-fikt*) pluperfect (*gram.*): beyond the more than perfect (*facet.*). [L. *praeter.*]

preterite, preterit *pret′ə-rit*, *adj.* past. — *n.* the past tense: a word in the past tense: a form of the past tense. — *ns.* **pret′erist** one who holds the prophecies of the Apocalypse already fulfilled; **pret′eriteness; preterition** (*prē-tə-rish′ən*) the act of passing over: omission of mention in a will: paraleipsis (*rhet.*): the doctrine that God passes over the non-elect in electing to eternal life. — *adjs.* **preteritive** (*pri-ter′i-tiv*) used only in the preterite; **preter′ito-pres′ent, -presen′tial, pret′erite-pres′ent** pertaining to a verb which has an original preterite still preterite in form but present in meaning. — Also *ns.* [L. *praeteritus* — *īre, ītum*, to go.]

preterm *prē′tûrm′*, *adj.* born prematurely. [Pfx. **pre-** (2).]

pretermit *prē-tər-mit′*, *v.t.* to pass by: to omit: to leave undone: to desist from for a time: — *pr.p.* **pretermitt′-ing;** *pa.t.* and *pa.p.* **pretermitt′ed.** — *n.* **pretermission** (*-mish′ən*). [L. *praetermittĕre, -missum* — *mittĕre*, to send.]

pretext *prē′tekst*, *n.* an ostensible motive or reason, put forward as excuse or to conceal the true one. [L. *praetextus, -ūs*, pretext, outward show, *praetextum*, pretext — *praetexĕre, -textum*, to weave in front, border — *texĕre*, to weave.]

pretty *prit′i*, *adj.* orig., tricky: ingenious: (esp. ironically) fine: commendable: neat: stalwart (*arch.* or *Scot.*): pleasing in a moderate way but not deeply: having some superficial attractiveness but not striking beauty: beautiful without dignity: insipidly graceful: considerable. — *n.* a pretty thing or person: a knick-knack: the fairway of a golf-course: the fluted part of a glass. — *adv.* fairly: prettily (*coll.* or *illit.*). — *n.* **prettificā′tion.** — *v t.* **prett′ify** to trick out in an excessively ornamental or namby-pamby way. — *adv.* **prett′ily** in a pretty manner: pleasingly: elegantly: neatly. — *n.* **prett′iness** the quality of being pretty: an instance of the quality: a prettyism. — *adj.* **prett′yish** somewhat pretty. — *ns.* **prett′yism** trivial daintiness of style or an instance of it; **prett′y-prett′iness; prett′y-prett′y** (*coll.*) a knick-knack. — *adj.* **prett′y-spoken** speaking or spoken prettily. — *adj.* **prett′y-spoken** speaking or spoken prettily. — **a pretty penny** a good large sum; **only pretty Fanny's way** (*T. Parnell*) only what must be expected and accepted of the person; **pretty much** very nearly; **pretty well** almost entirely; **sitting pretty** in an advantageous position. [O.E. *prættig*, tricky — *prætt*, trickery; the origin of the word is unknown.]

pretzel *pret′səl*, *n.* a crisp salted biscuit made in rope shape and twisted into a kind of loose knot. [Ger.]

preux chevalier *prø shə-val-yā*, (Fr.) a valiant knight.

prevail *pri-vāl′*, *v.i.* to gain strength (*obs.*): to gain the victory: to succeed: to have the upper hand: to urge successfully (with *on, upon*): to be usual or most usual: to hold good, be in use, be customary. — *v.t.* (*obs.*) to avail: to persuade. — *adj.* **prevail′ing** having great power: controlling: bringing about results: very general or common: most common. — *adv.* **prevail′ingly.** — *ns.* **prevail′ment** (*Shak.*) the power of overcoming; **prevalence** (*prev′ə-ləns*), **prev′alency** the state of being prevalent or widespread: superior strength or influence: preponderance: effective influence. — *adj.* **prev′-alent** prevailing: having great power: victorious: widespread: most common. — *adv.* **prev′alently.** [L. *praevalēre* — *prae, valēre*, to be powerful.]

For other sounds see detailed chart of pronunciation.

prevaricate *pri-var'i-kāt, v.i.* to deviate (*obs.*): to shift about from side to side: to evade the truth: to quibble: to undertake a thing with the purpose of defeating or destroying it (*obs.*): to betray a client by collusion with his opponent (*law*). — *v.t.* (*obs.*) to pervert, transgress. — *ns.* **prevaricā'tion; prevar'icātor** one who prevaricates: formerly in Cambridge University, a satirical orator at Commencement. [L. *praevāricārī, -ātus,* to walk straddlingly or crookedly, to act collusively — *prae, vāricus,* straddling — *vārus,* bent.]

preve. See **prove.**

prevenancy, prevene, etc. See **prevent.**

prevent *pri-vent', v.t.* to precede (*obs.*): to be, go, or act earlier than (*obs.*): to go faster than (*obs.*): to anticipate, forestall (*obs.*): to satisfy in advance (*obs.*): to meet or provide for in advance (*obs.*): to balk: to preclude: to stop, keep, or hinder effectually: to keep from coming to pass. — *n.* **prevenancy** (*prev'ən-ən-si; rare*) courteous anticipation of others' wishes. — *v.t.* **prevene** (*pri-vēn'*) to precede (*rare*): to anticipate (*obs.*). — *n.* **prevē'nience.** — *adj.* **prevē'nient** antecedent: predisposing: preventive. — *n.* **preventabil'ity.** — *adj.* **preven'table** (also **-ible**). — *ns.* **preven'ter** one who, or that which, prevents or hinders: a supplementary rope or part (*naut.*); **preven'tion** the act of preventing: anticipation or forethought: obstruction. — *adjs.* **preven'tive** (also, irregularly, **preven'tative**) tending to prevent or hinder: prophylactic: concerned with the prevention of smuggling. — *ns.* that which prevents: a prophylactic. — *adv.* **preven'tively.** — *n.* **preven'tiveness.** — **preventive detention** specially prolonged imprisonment for persistent offenders of 30 or over for periods of from 5 to 14 years. [L. *praevenīre, -ventum* — *venīre,* to come.]

preverb *prē'vûrb,* (*linguistics*) *n.* a particle or prefix which precedes a verb or verb-root. — *adj.* **prever'bal** occurring or standing before a verb: pertaining to a time before the development of speech. [Pfx. **pre-** (2).]

pre-vernal *prē-vûr'nl, adj.* flowering before spring: coming early into flower or leaf. [Pfx. **pre-** (2).]

preview *prē'vū, n.* a view of a performance, exhibition, etc., before it is open to the public: an advance showing to the public of excerpts from a film, play, etc. — *v.t.* (*prē-vū'*) to look at beforehand: to foresee: (*prē'vū*) to give a preview of. [Pfx. **pre-** (2).]

previous *prē'vi-əs, adj.* going before in time: already arranged: former: premature (*facet.*). — *adv.* previously (usu. with *to*). — *adv.* **prē'viously.** — *n.* **prē'viousness.** — **previous examination** the little go at Cambridge; **previous question** in parliament, a motion 'that the question be not now put'. If the decision be 'ay', the debate is ended without a vote on the main issue. In public meetings the carrying of the 'previous question' means that the meeting passes on to the next business. [L. *praevius* — *prae, via,* a way.]

previse *prē-vīz', v.t.* to foresee: to forewarn. — *n.* **prevision** (*-vizh'ən*) foresight: foreknowledge. — *v.t.* to endow with prevision. — *adj.* **provisional** (*-vizh'ən-əl*). [L. *praevidēre, -vīsum* — *prae, vidēre,* to see.]

pre-wash *prē'-wosh, n.* a preliminary wash before the main wash, esp. in a washing-machine: an instruction setting for this on an automatic washing-machine. [Pfx. **pre-** (2).]

prewyn. A Shakespearian form of **prune** (fruit).

prex *prex,* (*U.S.*) *n.* in college slang, the president of a college (also **prex'y**).

prey *prā, n.* booty, plunder: that which is preserved from loss in battle, as one's own life (*B.*): an animal that is, or may be, killed and eaten by another: a victim (with *to*): depredation: the act of seizing (*Spens., Shak.*). — *v.i.* (commonly with *on* or *upon*) to make depredations: to take plunder: to seek, kill, and feed: to live (on) as a victim: to waste, eat away, distress. — *v.t.* (*Spens.*) to plunder. — *adj.* **prey'ful** (*Shak.*) bent upon prey. — **beast, bird, of prey** one that devours other animals, esp. higher animals — applied usually to the Carnivora

and Falconiformes. [O.Fr. *preie* (Fr. *proie*) — L. *praeda,* booty.]

prezzie *prez'i,* (*coll.*) *n.* a present or gift.

prial *prī'əl.* Same as **pair-royal.**

Priapus *prī-ā'pəs, n.* an ancient deity personifying male generative power, guardian of gardens, later regarded as the chief god of lasciviousness and sensuality. — *adjs.* **Priapean** (*prī-ə-pē'ən*); **Priapic** (*-ap'ik*) of or relating to Priapus: (without *cap.*) of, relating to, exhibiting, etc. a phallus: (without *cap.*) overly concerned or preoccupied with virility and male sexuality. — *n.* **prī'apism** persistent erection of the penis: licentiousness, lewdness. [Latinised from Gr. *Priāpos.*]

pribble *prib'l, n.* a modification of **prabble,** usu. coupled with it. — Also **pribb'le-prabb'le.**

price *prīs* (also sometimes in Spens. **prise** *prīs, prīz*) *n.* the amount, usually in money, for which a thing is sold or offered: that which one forgoes or suffers for the sake of or in gaining something: money offered for capture or killing of anybody: (the size of) the sum, etc., by which one can be bribed: betting odds: preciousness, worth, value (*arch.*): (also **prize**) valuation (*Spens., Shak.*). — *v.t.* to fix, state, or mark the price of: to ask the price of (*coll.*): to pay the price of (*Spens.*): to prize, value (*Shak.*). — *adjs.* **priced** having a price assigned: valued at such-and-such a price; **price'less** beyond price: invaluable: supremely and delectably absurd. — *adv.* **price'lessly.** — *ns.* **price'lessness; pric'er.** — *adj.* **pric'ey,** sometimes **pric'y,** (*coll.*) expensive: — *compar.* **prī'cier; superl.* **prī'ciest.** — *n.* **prī'ciness.** — **Price Code** a set of regulations used by the British government between 1973 and 1979 to control prices, as a measure against inflation; **Price Commission** a body set up by the British government in 1973 (abolished in 1979) to control prices, as a measure against inflation; **price control** the fixing by a government of maximum, or sometimes minimum, prices chargeable for goods or services; **price'-curr'ent** (often in *pl.,* **pric'es-curr'ent**) a list of prevailing prices at any time: a list of prices paid for any class of goods, etc.; **price'-cutting** lowering of prices to secure custom; **price'-fixing** the establishing of the price of a commodity, etc. by agreement between suppliers or by government price control, rather than by the operation of a free market; **price index** an index number which relates current prices to those of a base period or base date, the latter usu. being assigned the value of 100; **price level** the average of many prices of commodities; **price'-list** a list of prices of goods offered for sale; **price ring** a group of manufacturers who co-operate for the purpose of raising or maintaining the price of a commodity above the level that would be established by a free market; **price'-tag** a tag or the like showing price (also *fig.*); **price war** a form of commercial competition in which firms competing in the same market successively lower their prices in order to secure a larger share of that market. — **above, beyond price** so valuable that no price can or would be enough; **at a price** at a somewhat high price; **in great price** in high estimation; **of price** of great value; **price-earnings ratio** the ratio of the market price of a common stock share to its earnings; **price of money** the rate of discount in lending or borrowing capital; **price oneself out of the market** to charge more than customers or clients are willing to pay; **price on one's head** a reward for one's capture or slaughter; **what price** — ? what about (this or that) now?: what do you think of?; **without price** priceless: without anything to pay. [O.Fr. *pris* (Fr. *prix*) — L. *pretium,* price; cf. **praise, prize³.**]

prick *prik, n.* anything sharp and piercing, as a thorn, spine, goad: the act, experience, or stimulus of piercing or puncturing: a puncture: a mark or wound made by puncturing: a note in written music (*obs.*): a graduation on a dial (*Shak.*): a dot (*obs.*): a point of space or time: an hour-point on a clock (*Shak.*): a point, pitch (*Spens.*): the centre of an archery target: a mark or target: a hare's footprint: a penis (*vulg.*): a term of abuse used of a person one dislikes or thinks a fool (*vulg.*). — *v.t.* to pierce slightly with a fine point: to give a feeling as of pricking: to make by puncturing: to urge with, or as with, a spur or goad: to write out in musical notation (*obs.*): to indicate with a prick or dot, to tick off, hence select: to trace with pricks: to pin: to pick with a point: to insert (e.g. seedlings) in small holes (usu. with *in*, *out*, etc.): to stick, stick over: to erect, cock, stick up (sometimes with *up*): to incite (*fig.*): to deck out: to pain. — *v.i.* to pierce, make punctures: to seek insensitive spots by sticking pins in a suspected witch: to have a sensation of puncture or prickling: to begin to turn sour: to stand erect: to ride with spurs, or quickly. — *ns.* **prick′er** a piercing instrument: a witch-finder: a light-horseman: a priming wire; **prick′ing**; **prickle** (*prik′l*) a little prick: a sharp point growing from the epidermis of a plant or from the skin of an animal. — *v.t.* and *v.i.* to prick slightly. — *v.i.* to have a prickly feeling. — *n.* **prick′liness**. — *n.* and *adj.* **prick′ling**. — *adj.* **prick′ly** full of prickles: tingling as if prickled: easily annoyed. — *adj.* **prick′= eared** having erect or noticeable ears. — **prick′le-back** the stickle-back; **prick′ly-ash′** the toothache-tree (Xanthoxylum); **prick′ly-heat** a skin disease, inflammation of the sweat-glands with intense irritation; **prick′ly= pear** a cactaceous genus (Opuntia) with clusters of prickles: its pear-shaped fruit; **prick′-me-dain′ty** (*Scot.*) an affected person. — *adj.* over-precise. — **prick′-song** (*Shak.*) written music: descant; **prick′-spur** a spur with one point; **prick′-the-gar′ter** fast-and-loose; **prick′= (the-)louse** (*Scot.*) a tailor; **prick′wood** the spindle-tree: the dogwood. — **kick against the pricks** to hurt oneself by resisting someone or something, to no avail (Acts ix. 5); **prick up one's ears** to begin to listen intently. [O.E. *prica*, point; cf. Du. *prik*.]

pricket *prik′it*, *n.* a fallow deer buck in his second year, with straight unbranched antlers: a spike serving as a candlestick: a candlestick with such a spike. [**prick**.]

prickle, etc. See **prick**.

pride *prīd*, *n.* the state or feeling of being proud: too great self-esteem: haughtiness: a proper sense of what is becoming to oneself and scorn of what is unworthy: a feeling of pleasure on account of something worthily done or anything connected with oneself: that of which one is proud: splendour: magnificence: beauty displayed: ostentation: a peacock's attitude of display: exuberance: prime: high spirit, mettle: sexual excitement in a female animal (*Shak.*): a company of lions. — *v.t.* to make proud: (*refl.*) to take pride in (with *on*). — *adj.* **pride′ful.** — *adv.* **pride′fully.** — *n.* **pride′fulness.** — *adj.* **pride′less.** — **pride of place** the culmination of an eagle's or hawk's flight: the distinction of holding the highest position (see **place**); **take (a) pride in** to make (a thing) an object in which one's pride is concerned. [O.E *prȳde*, *prȳte* — *prūd*, *prūt*, proud.]

pridian *prid′i-ən*, *adj.* pertaining to yesterday. [L. *prī-diānus* — *prīdiē* — stem of *prius*, before, *diēs*, day.]

pried, **prier**, **pries**. See **pry**.

prie-dieu *prē′dyø′*, *n.* a praying-desk or chair for praying on. [Fr., pray-God.]

prief, **priefe** *prēf*, (*Spens.* or *Scot.*) *n.* proof. — *v.t.* **prieve** to prove: to test. [See derivations of **proof**, **prove**.]

priest *prēst*, *n.* an official conductor of religious rites: a mediator between a god and worshippers (*fem.* **priest′-ess**): a minister above a deacon and below a bishop: a clergyman: a club or mallet for killing fish. — *v.t.* to ordain as priest. — *v.i.* to act as priest. — *ns.* **priest′craft** priestly policy directed to worldly ends; **priest′hood** the office or character of a priest: the priestly order; **priest′liness**; **priest′ling** a contemptible priest. — *adj.* **priest′ly** pertaining to or like a priest. — *n.* **priest′ship.** — **priest′-king′** a king with priestly functions. — *adjs.* **priest′-like; priest′-rid′, -ridden** dominated by priests. — **priest's hole, priest hole** a secret room for a priest in time of persecution or repression. [O.E. *prēost* — L. *presbyter* — Gr. *presbyteros*, an elder.]

prieve. See **prief.**

prig[1] *prig*, *n.* a tinker (*rogues' cant*; *obs.*): a thief (*slang*; *Shak.*). — *v.t.* to filch. — *ns.* **prigg′er** a thief; **prigg′ing**; **prigg′ism.** [Origin unknown.]

prig[2] *prig*, (*Scot.*) *v.i.* to entreat: to importune: to haggle. — **prig down** to seek to beat down (a price or the seller). [Origin unknown.]

prig[3] *prig*, *n.* a coxcomb (*obs.*): a precisian: a person of precise morals without a sense of proportion. — *n.* **prigg′ery.** — *adj.* **prigg′ish.** — *adv.* **prigg′ishly.** — *ns.* **prigg′ishness**, **prigg′ism.** [Origin unknown.]

prill *pril*, *v.t.* to turn into pellet form, e.g. by melting and letting the drops solidify in falling. — *n.* a pellet, or pelleted material, formed by prilling. [Orig. a Cornish mining term, of uncertain origin.]

prim[1] *prim*, *adj.* exact and precise: stiffly formal. — *v.t.* to deck with great nicety: to form, set or purse into primness. — *v.i.* to look prim: to prim the mouth: — *pr.p.* **primm′ing**; *pa.t.* and *pa.p.* **primmed.** — *adv.* **prim′ly.** — *n.* **prim′ness.** [Late 17th-cent. cant.]

prim[2] *prim*, *n.* med. coll. contraction of **primigravida**, as in **elderly prim** (one of 25 and over).

prima. See **primo.**

primacy *prī′mə-si*, *n.* the position of first: the chief place: the office or dignity of a primate.

primaeval. Same as **primeval.**

prima facie *prī′mə fāsh′ē(-ē)*, *prē′mä fak′i-ā*, (L.) on the first view: at first sight: (of evidence) sufficient to support the bringing of a charge (*law*): (of a case) supported by prima facie evidence (*law*).

primage *prīm′ij*, *n.* a payment, in addition to freight, made by shippers for loading, originally a gratuity to captain and crew, afterwards made to owners. [Anglo-L. *primāgium*.]

primal. See **prime**[1].

primary *prī′mə-ri*, *adj.* first: original: of the first order (e.g. in a system of successive branchings): firstformed: primitive: chief: elementary: fundamental: belonging to the first stages of education, elementary: of a feather, growing on the manus: relating to primaries (*U.S.*): (with *cap.*) Palaeozoic (but orig. applied to rocks supposed to be older than any fossiliferous strata; *geol.*). — *n.* that which is highest in rank or importance, a planet in relation to its satellites: a primary coil: a primary feather: a primary school: a substance obtained directly, by extraction and purification, from natural, or crude technical, raw material — cf. **intermediate**: a meeting of the voters of a political party in an electoral division to nominate candidates, or to elect delegates to a nominating convention representing a larger area (*U.S. politics*): an election (also **primary election**) by local members of a party of candidates to be nominated for election, or of delegates to nominate them (*U.S. politics*). — *adv.* **prī′marily.** — *n.* **prī′mariness.** — **primary assembly** in U.S. politics, a primary; **primary battery, cell** one producing an electric current by irreversible chemical action; **primary coil** one carrying an inducing current; **primary colours** those from which all others can be derived — physiologically red, green, violet, or blue, for pigments red, yellow, blue: also red, orange, yellow, green, blue, indigo, and violet; **primary planet** a planet distinguished from a satellite. [L. *prīmārius* — *prīmus*, first.]

primate *prī′māt*, *-mit*, *n.* one who is first: a bishop or archbishop to whose see was formerly annexed the dignity of vicar of the holy see (*R.C. Church*): an archbishop over a province (*Ch. of Eng.*): a member of the order Primates (*zool.*). — *adj.* **primā′tal.** — *n.pl.* **Primates** (*prī-mā′tēz*) the highest order of mammals, including lemurs, monkeys, anthropoid apes, and man. — *n.* **pri′mateship.** — *adjs.* **primā′tial** (*-shl*), **primatic** (*-mat′ik*), **-al.** — *ns.* **primatol′ogist**; **primatol′ogy** the study of the Primates. [L.L. *prīmās*, *-ātis* — L. *prīmus*, first.]

prime[1] *prīm*, *adj.* first in order of time, rank, or importance: primary: chief: main: of the highest quality: of the time of broadcasting of a radio or television programme, occurring during peak viewing or listening time and (therefore) having the highest advertising rates: original: in sexual excitement (*Shak.*): (of a number other than one) divisible by no whole number except unity and itself (*arith.*): (of two or more numbers) relatively prime (with *to*; *arith.*). — *n.* the first of the lesser hours of the Roman breviary: the time of this office, about six in the morning, or sometimes sunrise: the time from the beginning of the artificial day to terce (about nine): the beginning: the spring: the world's youth: the new moon, or its first appearance (*obs.*): the best part: the height of perfection: full health and strength: a prime number: a first subdivision or symbol marking it (′) (*math.*, etc.): a fundamental tone: an old card-game, probably the same as primero: the first guard against sword-thrusts, also the first and simplest thrust (*fencing*). — *adj.* **prī′mal** first: primitive: original: chief, fundamental. — *n.* **primal′ity.** — *advs.* **prī′mally; prime′ly.** — *n.* **prime′ness.** — *adj.* **prīm′y** (*Shak.*) in one's prime, blooming. — **primal (scream) therapy** rebirthing (q.v.); **prime cost** see **cost**[1]; **prime (lending) rate** the lowest rate of interest charged by a bank at any given time, usu. available only to large concerns with high credit ratings, and forming the base figure on which other rates are calculated; **prime meridian** that chosen as zero for reference; **prime minister** the chief minister of state; **prime mover** in mediaeval astronomy, the primum mobile: a natural source of energy: a machine that transforms energy from such a source into motive power: the main cause or instigator of an action, project, etc. (*fig.*); **prime number** a number, other than one, divisible only by itself or unity. — *adj.* **prime′-time** pertaining to prime time (see **prime** *adj.* above). — **prime vertical** a great celestial circle passing through the east and west points of the horizon, and cutting the meridian at right angles at the zenith. — **relatively prime** (*arith.*) having no common integral factor but unity. [L. *prīmus*, first; partly through O.E. *prīm* — L. *prīma* (*hōra*), first (hour).]

prime[2] *prīm, v.t.* to charge, fill: to supply with powder or other means of igniting the charge (of a firearm, bomb, etc.): to lay a train to: to bring into activity or working order by a preliminary charge (as a man by giving him liquor, a pump by pouring in water, an internal-combustion engine by injecting gas or oil): to post up, coach, cram beforehand with information or instructions: to put on a primer in painting: to make up with cosmetics (*obs.*). — *v.i.* to prime a gun: (of a boiler) to send water with the steam into the cylinder: (of the tides) to recur at progressively shorter intervals. — *ns.* **prī′mer** one who primes: a priming-wire: a detonator: a preparatory first coat of paint, etc.: the particular type of paint used for this; **prī′ming** the action of the verb in any sense: the progressive shortening of the interval between tides as spring tide approaches: a detonating charge that fires a propellant charge: a tube for priming an internal-combustion engine: a priming-wire: a first coat of paint. — **prī′ming-iron, -wire** a wire passed through the touch-hole of a cannon to clear it and pierce the cartridge; **prī′ming-pow′der** detonating powder: a train of powder. [Etymology obscure.]

primer *prī′mər,* or *prim′ər, n.* a small book of hours or prayer book for laymen, used also for teaching reading: a first reading-book: an elementary introduction to any subject: (*prim′ər*) printing type of two obsolete sizes, **long primer** (approx. 10-point) and **great primer** (approx. 18-point). [L. *prīmārius,* primary.]

primero *pri-mā′rō, n.* an old card-game. [Sp. *primera.*]

primeur *prē-mœr,* (Fr.) *n.* novelty: early fruit.

primeval, primaeval *prī-mē′vl, adj.* belonging to the first ages. [L. *prīmaevus* — *prīmus,* first, *aevum,* an age.]

primigenial *prī-mi-jē′ni-əl, adj.* first made: original: primal. — Wrongly, also **primoge′nial.** [L. *prīmigenius* — *prīmus,* first, *genus,* kind.]

primigravida *prī-mi-grav′i-də, n.* a woman pregnant for

the first time: — *pl.* **primigrav′idae** (*-dē*) or **-as.** [L. fem. adjs. *prīma,* first, *gravida,* pregnant.]

primine *prī′min, n.* the outer (rarely the inner or first formed) coat of an ovule. [L. *prīmus,* first.]

primipara *prī-mip′ə-rə, n.* a woman who has given birth for the first time only, or is about to do so: — *pl.* **primip′arae** (*-rē*) or **-as.** — *n.* **primipar′ity.** — *adj.* **primip′arous.** [L. *prīma* (fem.), first, *parĕre,* to bring forth.]

primitiae *prī-mish′i-ē, n.pl.* first-fruits: the first year's revenue of a benefice — also **primi′tias** (*Spens.*). — *adj.* **primitial** (*-mish′l*) of first-fruits: (*loosely*) primeval, original. [L. *prīmitiae* — *prīmus,* first.]

primitive *prim′i-tiv, adj.* belonging to the beginning, or to the first times: original: ancient: antiquated, old-fashioned: crude: not derivative: fundamental: first-formed, of early origin (*biol.*): of the earliest formation (*old geol.*): (of a culture or society) not advanced, lacking a written language and having only fairly simple technical skills. — *n.* that from which other things are derived: a root-word: a Primitive Methodist: a painter or picture of pre-Renaissance date or manner: a 19th- and 20th-century school of painting, characterised by a complete simplicity of approach to subject and technique. — *adv.* **prim′itively.** — *ns.* **prim′itiveness; prim′itivism** approbation of primitive ways, primitive Christianity, primitive art, etc.: Primitive Methodism; **prim′itivist.** — **Primitive Methodist** a member of a religious body (Primitive Methodist Connection) founded in 1810, united with the Wesleyan Methodists and United Methodists in 1932. [L. *prīmitīvus,* an extension of *prīmus.*]

primo *prē′mō, adj.* first: — *fem.* **pri′ma.** — *n.* (*mus.*) the first or principal part in a duet or trio: — *pl.* **pri′mos.** — *adv.* **pri′mo** in the first place. — **prima ballerina (assoluta)** (*bal-ə-rēn′ə,* It. *ba-le-rē′na* (*as-so-lōō′ta*)) the leading ballerina (absolute, without rival): — *pls.* **prima ballerinas, prime** (*-ā*) **ballerine assolute; prima donna (assoluta)** (*don′ə,* It. *don′na*) the leading female singer in an opera company (without rival): (**prima donna**) a person, esp. a woman, who is temperamental, over-sensitive and hard to please: — *pls.* **prima donnas, prime** (*-ā*) **donne assolute.** [It., — L. *prīmus.*]

primogenial. See **primigenial.**

primogenit *prī-mō-jen′it,* (*obs.*) *adj.* and *n.* first-born. — *adjs.* **primogen′ital; primogen′itary; primogen′itive.** — *n.* (*Shak.*) primogeniture. — *ns.* **primogen′itor** an earliest ancestor: a forefather: — *fem.* **primogen′itrix; primogen′iture** the state or fact of being first-born: inheritance by or of the first-born child or (*male primogeniture*) son; **primogen′itureship** (*rare*). [L. *prīmōgenitus* — *prīmō,* first (adv.), *genitus,* born, *genitor,* beget-ter.]

primordial *prī-mör′di-əl, adj.* existing from the beginning: original: rudimentary: first-formed. — *n.* the first principle or element. — *ns.* **primor′dialism; primordiality** (*-al′i-ti*). — *adv.* **primor′dially.** — *n.* **primor′dium** the primitive source: the first discernible rudiment. [L. *prīmordium* — *prīmus,* first, *ordīri,* to begin.]

primp *primp, v.i.* to dress in a fussy or affected manner: to preen, titivate. — Also *v.t.* [Conn. **prim.**]

primrose *prim′rōz, n.* a plant (*Primula vulgaris*), or its flower, common in spring in woods and meadows: extended to others of the genus Primula: formerly some other (and brighter) flower: a conventionalised flower, sometimes four-petalled (*her.*): the choicest (*Spens.*). — *adj.* pale yellow, like a primrose. — *v.i.* to go gathering primroses. — *adjs.* **prim′rosed; prim′rosy.** — **Primrose League** an association for Conservative propaganda formed in 1883 in memory of Lord Beaconsfield, named from his supposed favourite flower; **primrose path, way** (both *Shak.*) the life of pleasure; **primrose peerless** the two-flowered daffodil. — **evening primrose** see **evening.** [O.Fr. *primerose,* as if — L. *prīma rosa*; perh. really through M.E. and O.Fr. *primerole* — L.L. *prīmula* — *prīmus,* first.]

primsie *prim′zi,* (*Scot.*) *adj.* prim, demure. [**prim.**]

Primula *prim'ū-lə, n.* the genus of flowers including the primrose, cowslip, oxlip, etc., giving name to the dicotyledonous family **Primulā'ceae**, including pimpernel, water-violet, cyclamen, etc.: (without *cap.*) a plant of this genus. — *adj.* **primulā'ceous**. — *n.* **prim'-uline** (*-lēn*) a yellow coal-tar dye. [L.L., little first one or firstling, — L. *prīmus*, first.]

primum mobile *prī'məm mōb'* or *mob'i-lē, prē'mōŏm mō'bi-le,* in mediaeval astronomy, the outermost of the revolving spheres of the universe, carrying the others round in 24 hours: any great source of motion. [L.]

primus[1] *prī'məs, prē'mōŏs, n.* a presiding bishop in the Scottish Episcopal Church, without metropolitan authority. — *adj.* (*boys' schools*) senior. [L., first.]

primus[2] *prī'məs, prē'mōŏs,* (L.) first. — **primus inter pares** (*in'tər pār'ēz, pär'ās*) first among equals.

Primus® *prī'məs, n.* a portable cooking stove burning vaporised oil. — Also **Primus stove.**

primy. See under **prime**[1].

prince *prins, n.* one of the highest rank: a king or queen (*obs.* or *arch.*): a sovereign (of some small countries): a male member of a royal or imperial family: a title of nobility, as formerly in Germany (*Fürst*): a chief: anybody or anything that is first in merit or demerit, or most outstanding. — *v.t.* (with *it*) to play the prince. — *ns.* **prince'dom** a principality: the estate, jurisdiction, sovereignty, or rank of a prince; **prince'hood** the rank or quality of a prince; **prince'kin** a little or young prince; **prince'let, prince'ling** a petty prince. — *adj.* **prince'like** like a prince: becoming a prince. — *n.* **prince'liness.** — *adj.* **prince'ly** of a prince or princess: of the rank of prince: princelike: becoming a prince: magnificent: sumptuous: lavish. — Also *adv.* — *n.* **prin'cess** (or *-ses'*) *fem.* of **prince:** a prince's wife (of recognised rank): a size of roofing slate, 24 by 14 inches (610 by 356 mm): a woman's garment with skirt and bodice in one piece — in this sense also (Fr.) **princesse** (*prin', or -ses'*), **princess(e)-dress, -skirt,** etc., the style being known as **princess line.** — *adv.* **prin'cessly** like a princess. — *adj.* **prin'cified** ridiculously dignified. — **prince'-bish'op** a bishop ranking as prince or having the power of prince of his diocese; **prince'-con'sort** a prince who is husband of a reigning queen; **prince'-imper'ial** the eldest son of an emperor; **prince's feather** a tall, showy Amaranthus with spikes of rose-coloured flowers: London pride: any of various other plants; **prince's metal** gold-like alloy of copper and zinc, with more zinc than in brass, attributed to Prince Rupert; **prin'cess-roy'al** a title which may be conferred on the eldest daughter of a sovereign. — **prince of darkness, prince of this world** Satan; **Prince of Peace** Christ: the Messiah; **Prince of Wales** since 1301, a title usu. conferred on the eldest son of the English, and later British, sovereign; **Prince Rupert's drops** see **drop.** [Fr., — L. *prīnceps* — *prīmus,* first, *capĕre,* to take.]

principal *prin'si-pl, adj.* taking the first place: highest in rank, character, or importance: chief: of the nature of principal or a principal. — *n.* a principal person: the head of a college or university, or sometimes of a school: one who takes a leading part: money on which interest is paid: a main beam, rafter, girder, or timber: a roof-truss: the structural framework of a roof: the person who commits a crime, or one who aids and abets him in doing it (*law*): a person for whom another becomes surety (*law*): a person who, being *sui juris,* employs another to do an act which he is competent himself to do (*law*): one who fights a duel: an organstop like the open diapason but an octave higher (*mus.*). — *n.* **principality** (*-pal'i-ti*) the status, dignity, or power of a prince: the condition of being a prince: the territory of a prince or the country that gives him title: a member of one order of angels. — *adv.* **prin'-cipally.** — *ns.* **prin'cipalness** the state of being principal or chief; **prin'cipalship** the position of a principal. — **principal boy** (*theat.*) an actress (now sometimes an actor) who plays the role of the hero in pantomime;

principal clause a clause which could function as an independent sentence; **principal parts** those forms (of a verb) from which all other forms may be deduced. — **the Principality** Wales. [L. *prīncipālis* — *prīnceps, -ipis,* chief.]

principate *prin'si-pāt, n.* princehood: principality: the Roman empire in its earlier form in which something of republican theory survived. [L. *prīncipātus* — the emperor's title *prīnceps* (*cīvitātis*), chief (of the city or state).]

principium *prin-sip'i-əm,* L. *pring-kip'i-ŏŏm, n.* the general's quarters in a Roman camp: a beginning: a first principle: an element: — *pl.* **princip'ia.** — *adj.* **princip'-ial** elementary. [L. *prīncipium.*]

principle *prin'si-pl, n.* a beginning (*obs.*): a source, root, origin: that which is fundamental: essential nature: a theoretical basis: a faculty of the mind: a source of action: a fundamental truth on which others are founded or from which they spring: a law or doctrine from which others are derived: a settled rule of action: consistent regulation of behaviour according to moral law: a component: a constituent part from which some quality is derived (*chem.*): motive power or the source of it (*Milt.*). — *v.t.* to establish in principles: to impress with a doctrine. — *adj.* **prin'cipled** holding certain principles: having, or behaving in accordance with, good principles: invoking or founded on a principle. — **first principles** fundamental principles, not deduced from others; **in principle** so far as general character or theory is concerned without respect to details or particular application; **on principle** on grounds of principle: for the sake of obeying or asserting a principle; **principle of contradiction** the logical principle that a thing cannot both be and not be; **principle of excluded middle** (*log.*) the principle that a thing must be either one thing or its contradictory; **principle of sufficient reason** see **reason.** [L. *prīncipium,* beginning — *prīnceps.*]

princox *prin(g)'koks* (*Shak.*), *n.* a conceited fellow: a coxcomb: a jocular, grotesque, or ironical endearment. — Also **prin'cock** (*-kok*). [Origin obscure.]

prink *pringk, v.t.* and *v.i.* to deck up, smarten. [App. conn. with **prank**[2].]

print *print, n.* an impression: a mould or stamp: a moulded pat of butter: exactitude of plaiting, crimping, or setting (a ruff, hair, etc.) (*arch.*): exactitude (*arch.*): printed state: printed characters or lettering: an edition: a printed copy: a printed picture: an engraving: a newspaper: a positive photograph made from a negative (or negative from positive): a printed cloth, esp. calico stamped with figures: a plaster-cast in low relief (*archit.*): a fingerprint. — *adj.* printed (*obs.*): of printed cotton. — *v.t.* to press in: to impress: to mark by pressure: to impress on paper, etc., by means of types, plates, or blocks: to produce or reproduce by such means: to cause to be so printed: to stamp a pattern on or transfer it to: to produce as a positive picture from a negative, or as a negative from a positive (*phot.*): to write in imitation of type: to express in writing (*Shak.*): to designate in print (*Milt.*). — *v.i.* to practise the art of printing: to publish a book: to yield an impression, or give a positive, etc. — *adj.* **print'able** capable of being printed: fit to print. — *ns.* **print'er** one who, or that which, prints: one who is employed in printing books, etc.: a device for printing, as telegraph messages, photographs, the output from a computer, etc.: a cotton cloth made for printing; **print'ing** the act, art, or business of the printer: the whole number of copies printed at one time, an impression. — *adj.* **print'less** receiving or leaving no impression. — **printed circuit** a wiring circuit, free of loose wiring, formed by printing the design of the wiring on copper foil bonded to a flat base and etching away the unprinted foil (**printed circuit board** the combined circuit and supporting base); **printer's devil** see **devil; printer's ink** printing-ink; **printer's mark** an engraved device used by printers as a trademark; **print'ing-house** a building where printing is carried on: a printing-office; **print'ing-ink** ink used in printing — a usually thickish mixture of pigment (as carbon black) with oil and sometimes varnish; **print'ing-machine** a printing-press worked by power; **print'ing-office** an establishment where books, etc., are printed; **printing paper** a paper suitable for printing purposes; **print'ing-press** a machine by which impressions are taken in ink upon paper from types, plates, etc.; **print'-out** the printed information given out by a computer, etc.; **print'-run** a single printing of a book, etc.; **print'-seller** one who sells prints or engravings; **print'-shop** a print-seller's shop; **print'-through** the degree to which matter printed on one side of paper, etc. is visible from the other side (*printing*): in magnetic tape recordings, the transfer of a recording from one layer to another when the tape is wound on a spool (*comput.*, *video*, etc.); **print'-works** an establishment where cloth is printed. — **in print** in exact order, formally set, crimped, or plaited (*obs.*): existing in printed form: printed and still to be had; **out of print** no longer in print: no longer available from a publisher; **print out** to print: to produce a print-out of. [M.E. *print*, *prente*, etc. — O.Fr. *preinte*, *priente* — *preindre*, *priembre* — L. *preměre*, to press.]

prion *prī'on*, *n.* any petrel of the genus *Pachyptila*, blue-grey above and white below, feeding on the plankton of the southern oceans. [Gr. *prīōn*, a saw.]

prior *prī'ər*, *adj.* previous. — *adv.* previously, before (with *to*). — *n.* the officer next under the abbot in an abbey (*claustral prior*): the head of a priory of monks (*conventual prior*) or of a house of canons regular or of friars: in Italy, formerly, a magistrate: — *fem.* **prī'oress.** — *n.* **prī'orāte** the rank or term of office of a prior or prioress: a priory. — *v.t.* and *v.i.* **prior'itise, -ize** to arrange, deal with, etc. according to priority (importance, urgency, etc.). — *n.* **priority** (*prī-or'i-ti*) the state of being first in time, place, or rank: preference: the privilege of preferential treatment: something that ought to be considered, dealt with, in the earliest stage of proceedings. — *adj.* having, entitling to, or allowed to those who have, priority. — *ns.* **prī'orship; prī'ory** a convent of either sex subject to an abbey. — **grand priory** a province of the Knights of St John, under a **grand prior.** [L. *prīor*, *-ōris*, former.]

prisage *prī'zij*, *n.* the former right of the English kings to two tuns of wine from every ship importing twenty tuns or more. [O.Fr. *prise*, taking.]

Priscianist *prish'(y)ən-ist*, *n.* a grammarian. — **break Priscian's head** to commit false grammar. [*Priscianus*, Latin grammarian (fl. *c.* A.D. 500).]

prise. See **price**, and **prize**[1,2,3,4].

priser. Obs. form of **prizer**; see **prize**[3,4].

prism *prizm*, *n.* a solid whose ends are similar, equal, and parallel polygons, and whose sides are parallelograms (*geom.*): an object of that shape, esp. a triangular prism of glass or the like for resolving light into separate colours: a crystal form of three or more faces parallel to an axis (*crystal.*): (*loosely*) prismatic colours or spectrum. — *adjs.* **prismat'ic, -al** resembling or pertaining to a prism: built up of prisms: separated or formed by a prism. — *adv.* **prismat'ically.** — *n.* **pris'-moid** a figure like a prism, but with similar unequal ends. — *adjs.* **pris'moidal; pris'my** prismatic in colour. — **prismatic colours** the seven colours into which a ray of white light is refracted by a prism — red, orange, yellow, green, blue, indigo, and violet; **prismatic compass** a surveying instrument which by means of a prism enables the compass-reading to be taken as the object is sighted; **prismatic powder** pebble-powder. — **triangular, quadrilateral,** etc., **prism** one whose ends are triangles, quadrilaterals, etc. [Gr. *prīsma*, *-atos*, a piece sawn off, sawdust, a prism — *prīein*, to saw.]

prison *priz'n*, *n.* a building for the confinement of criminals or others: a jail: any place of confinement: confinement. — *v.t.* to shut in prison: to enclose: to restrain. — *ns.* **pris'oner** one under arrest or confined in prison: a captive, esp. in war: anyone involuntarily kept under restraint; **pris'onment** (*Shak.*) imprisonment, confinement. — *adj.* **pris'onous** (*Dickens*). — *n.pl.* **pris'on-bars** bars of a prison window, door, etc.: whatever confines or restrains. — *n.sing.* prisoners'-base. — **pris'on-breaker** one who escapes out of prison; **pris'on-breaking; pris'on-crop** hair cut very short; **pris'on-door'; pris'oners'-** (or **prisoner's-**) **base** a game in which those caught are held as prisoners (app. for *prison-bars*); **pris'on-house** a prison or prison building; **prison officer** the official title of a warder (still so-called unofficially) in prison; **pris'on-ship; pris'on-van** a closed conveyance for carrying prisoners; **pris'on-yard.** — **prisoner of conscience** see conscience; **prisoner of war** a person captured during a war, esp. a member of the armed forces, but also including militia, irregular troops and, under certain conditions, civilians; **take prisoner** to capture. [O.Fr. *prisun* — L. *prēnsiō*, *-ōnis*, for *praehēnsiō*, seizure — *praehenděre*, *-hēnsum*, to seize.]

prissy *pris'i*, *adj.* prim, prudish, fussy: effeminate. [Prob. **prim** and **sissy**.]

pristine *pris'tīn*, *-tēn*, *adj.* original: former: belonging to the earliest time: pure, unspoilt, unchanged. [L. *prīstinus*; cf. *prīscus*, antique, *prior*, former.]

prithee *pridh'ē*, *-i*, *interj.* for (**I**) **pray thee.**

prittle-prattle *prit'l-prat'l*, *n.* empty talk. [**prattle.**]

privacy *priv'ə-si*, or *prīv'*, *n.* seclusion: a place of seclusion: retreat: retirement: avoidance of notice or display: secrecy: a private matter. [**private.**]

privado *pri-vä'dō*, (*obs.*) *n.* a private friend, esp. of a prince: — *pl.* **priva'do(e)s.** [Sp., — L. *prīvātus*, private.]

privat-dozent, -docent *prē-vät'-dō-tsent'*, *n.* in German universities, a recognised teacher not a member of the salaried staff. [Ger., — L. *prīvātus*, private, *docēns*, *-entis*, teaching, *docēre*, to teach.]

private *prī'vit*, *adj.* apart from the state: not in public office: (of member of parliament) not holding government office: (of soldier) not an officer or non-commissioned officer: peculiar to oneself: belonging to, or concerning, an individual person or company: not part of, not receiving treatment under, etc. the National Health Service or any similar state scheme: independent: own: relating to personal affairs: in an unofficial capacity: not public: not open to the public: not made known generally: confidential: retired from observation: alone: privy (*obs.*). — *n.* privacy: a private person (*Shak.*, *Milt.*): (in *pl.*) private parts: a private soldier: a secret message (*Shak.*). — *adv.* **prī'vately.** — *ns.* **prī'vateness** (*rare*); **privatisā'tion, -z-.** — *v.t.* **prī'vatise, -ize** to make private: to denationalise. — **private act, bill** one that deals with the concerns of private persons; **private company** a company, with restrictions on the number of shareholders, whose shares may not be offered to the general public; **private detective** see **detective** under **detect; private enterprise** an economic system in which individual private firms operate and compete freely; **private eye** (*coll.*) a private detective; **private hotel** a term of uncertain meaning, popularly understood to imply that the proprietors do not bind themselves to receive chance travellers; **private income** private means; **private investigator** (esp. *U.S.*) a private detective; **private judgment** freedom to judge for oneself, untrammelled by the interpretation of the church; **private law** that part of law which deals with the rights and duties of persons as individuals in relations with each other; **private means** income from investments, etc. as opposed to salary or fees for work done; **private parts** the external sexual organs; **private school** a school run independently by an individual or a group, especially for profit; **private sector** the part of a country's economy owned, operated, etc., by private individuals and firms (opp. to *public sector*); **private treaty** a method of selling property in which the selling price is negotiated directly by the buyer and seller; **private view** the opening of e.g. an art exhibition to a number of invited guests, usu. before opening it to the general public; **private wrong** an injury done to an individual in his private capacity. — **in private** not in public: away from public view: secretly; **private member's bill** one introduced and sponsored by a private member in parliament. [L. *prīvātus*, pa.p. of *prīvāre*, to deprive, to separate.]

privateer *prī-və-tēr'*, *n.* a private vessel commissioned to seize and plunder an enemy's ships: the commander or one of the crew of a privateer. — *v.i.* to cruise in a privateer. — *ns.* **privateer'ing; privateers'man.** [private.]

privation *prī-vā'shən*, *n.* the state of being deprived of something, esp. of what is necessary for comfort: the absence of any quality (*log.*). — *adj.* **privative** (*priv'ə-tiv*) causing privation: consisting in the absence or removal of something: expressing absence or negation (*gram.*). — *n.* that which is privative or depends on the absence of something else: a term denoting the absence of a quality (*log.*): a privative affix or word (*gram.*). — *adv.* **priv'atively.** [L. *prīvātiō, -ōnis, prīvātivus* — *prīvāre*, to deprive.]

privet *priv'it*, *n.* a half-evergreen European shrub (*Ligustrum vulgare*) of the olive family, used for hedges: also applied to other members of the genus. [Origin unknown.]

privilege *priv'i-lij*, *n.* an advantage, right or favour granted to or enjoyed by an individual, or a few: freedom from burdens borne by others: a happy advantage: a prerogative: a sacred and vital civil right: advantage yielded (*Shak.*): right of sanctuary (*Shak.*). — *v.t.* to grant a privilege to: to exempt: to authorise, license. — *adj.* **priv'ileged** enjoying a privilege or privileges. — **breach of privilege** any interference with or slight done to the rights or privileges of a legislative body; **privilege of parliament, parliamentary privilege** special rights or privileges enjoyed by members of parliament, as freedom of speech (not subject to slander laws), and freedom from arrest except on a criminal charge; **question of privilege** any question arising out of the rights of an assembly or of its members; **writ of privilege** an order for the release of a privileged person from custody. [Fr. *privilège* — L. *prīvilēgium* — *prīvus*, private, *lēx, lēgis*, a law.]

privy *priv'i*, *adj.* familiar, intimate (*obs.*): private: pertaining to one person: for private uses: secret: appropriate to retirement: sharing the knowledge of something secret (with *to*). — *n.* a person having an interest in an action, contract, conveyance, etc. (*law*): a room set apart with container in which to evacuate body waste products (esp. one in an outhouse). — *adv.* **priv'ily** privately: secretly. — *n.* **priv'ity** privacy (*arch.*): secrecy (*arch.*): something kept private: innermost thoughts, private counsels (*Spens.*): knowledge, shared with another, of something private or confidential: knowledge implying concurrence: any legally recognised relation between different interests. — **privy chamber** private apartment in a royal residence; **privy council** (also with *caps.*) originally the private council of a sovereign to advise in the administration of government — its membership now consisting of all present and past members of the Cabinet and other eminent people, but with its functions mainly formal or performed by committees, etc.; **privy councillor,** or **counsellor** (also with *caps.*); **privy purse** (also with *caps.*) an allowance for the private or personal use of the sovereign; **privy seal** see **seal**[1]. — **gentlemen of the privy chamber** officials in the royal household in attendance at court; **Lord Privy Seal** see under **seal**[1]. [Fr. *privé* — L. *prīvātus*, private.]

prix fixe *prē fēks*, (Fr.) fixed price.

prize[1], **prise** *prīz*, *v.t.* to force (esp. up or open) with a lever. [Fr. *prise*, hold, grip; see **prize**[2].]

prize[2] (*Spens., Shak.* **prise**), *prīz*, *n.* seizure (*obs.*): that which is taken by force, or in war, esp. a ship. — *v.t.* to make a prize of. — **prize'-court** a court for judging regarding prizes made on the high seas; **prize'-crew** a

crew put aboard a prize to bring her to port; **prize'-money** share of the money or proceeds from any prizes taken from an enemy. [Fr. *prise*, capture, thing captured — L. *praehēnsa* — *praehendēre*, to seize.]

prize[3] (*Spens., Shak.* **prise**) *prīz*, *n.* a reward or symbol of success offered or won in competition by contest or chance, or granted in recognition of excellence: anything well worth striving for: a highly valued acquisition: privilege or advantage (*Shak.*): esteem (*Spens.*): valuation, appraisal (*Shak.*). — *adj.* awarded, or worthy of, a prize. — *v.t.* to set a price on: to value: to value highly: (*Spens.* **pryse**) to pay for. — *adjs.* **prīz'able** valuable; **prized**. — *n.* **priz'er** (*rare*) an appraiser. — **prize'-list** a list of winners; **prize'-man** a winner of a prize, esp. an academic prize; **prize'-winner.** [A differentiated form of **price** and **praise** — O.Fr. *pris* (n.), *prisier* (vb.) — L. *pretium*, price.]

prize[4] (*Spens.* **prise**), *prīz*, *n.* an athletic contest (*obs.*): a match. — *n.* **priz'er** a contestant in a prize or match. — **prize'-fight** a public boxing-match for money; **prize'-fighter** orig. one who fights in a prize: now, a professional pugilist; **prize'-fighting; prize'-ring** a ring for prize-fighting: the practice itself. — **play one's** (or **a**) **prize** to engage in a match: to sustain one's part. [Possibly from the foregoing.]

pro[1] *prō*, (L.) *prep.* for. — **pro aris et focis** (*ār'ēz et fōs'ēz, är'ēs et fōk'ēs*) for altars and firesides: for faith and home; **pro bono publico** (*bo'nō pub'li-kō, bō'nō pōō'bli-kō*) for the public good; **pro forma** (*för'mə, fōr'mä*) as a matter of form: (also with *hyphen*) of an account, etc., made out to show the market price of specified goods: with goods being paid for before dispatch. — *n.* a pro forma invoice: (*loosely*) an official form or record for completion. — Also **profor'ma. — pro hac vice** (*hak vīs'ē, wēk'e, vēk'e*) for this turn or occasion; **pro indiviso** (*in-di-vī'sō, -zō, in-dē-wē'sō, -vē'*) as undivided: applied in law to rights which two or more persons hold in common; **pro memoria** (*mə-mōr'ē-ə, -mōr', me-mō'ri-ä*) for a memorial; **pro patria** (*pā'tri-ə, pä'tri-ä*) for one's country; **pro rata** (*rā'tə, rä'tä*) in proportion; **pro re nata** (*rē nā'tə, rä nä'tä*) for a special emergency, according to the circumstances; **pro tanto** (*tan'tō*) for so much; **pro tempore** (*tem'pə-rē, tem'po-re*) for the time being.

pro[2] *prō*, *n.* a coll. contraction of **professional** (golfer, cricketer, actor, etc.), or **probationary** (nurse), and of **prostitute:** — *pl.* **pros** (*prōz*). — *adj.* of or pertaining to a pro or pros. — *adj.* **pro'-am'** involving both professionals and amateurs.

pro[3] *prō*, *n.* one who favours or votes for some proposal: a reason or argument in favour: — *pl.* **pros** (*prōz*). — *adv.* **pro and con** (L. *prō et contrā*) for and against. — *v.t.* and *v.i.* to consider or discuss for and against: *pr.p.* **pro'ing and conn'ing, pro-and-conn'ing;** *pa.p.* **pro'd and conned, con'd, pro-and-conned'. — pros and cons** reasons or arguments for and against. [L. *prō*, for.]

pro-[1] *prō*, Gr. *pfx.* before (in time or place): earlier than: in front of: the front part of: primitive: rudimentary. [Gr. prep. *prō*, before; cf. L. *prō*, Eng. **for, fore.**]

pro-[2] *prō*, L. *pfx.* used (*a*) as an etymological element with the senses before (in place or time), forward, forth, publicly; (*b*) as a living pfx. with the sense instead of, in place of, acting on behalf of; (*c*) as a living pfx. (in new formations) with the sense in favour of — as *pro-Boer; pro-German; pro-Negro; pro-slavery.* [L. prep. *prō*, earlier *prōd*, in comp. sometimes *prŏ-*; cf. preceding.]

proa *prō'ə*. See **prau.**

proairesis *prō-ā'ri-sis*, or *-ī'*, *n.* the act of choosing. [Gr. *proairesis.*]

pro-am. See **pro**[2].

probable *prob'ə-bl*, *adj.* orig., that can be proved (now *rare*): having more evidence for than against: giving ground for belief: likely: colourable, plausible. — *n.* probable opinion: one that has a good chance, or is likely to turn out or become the thing in question. — *ns.* **probabil'iorism** the doctrine that in case of doubt one is bound to choose the more probable opinion; **probabil'iorist; prob'abilism** the doctrine, in a disputed or doubtful case of law, one should follow the opinion supported by a recognised Doctor of the Church (*R.C. theol.*): the theoretical premise that knowledge, scientific rules, etc. cannot be absolute but can suffice to represent probability (*philos.*); **prob'abilist.** — *adj.* **probabilis'tic.** — *n.* **probabil'ity** the quality of being probable: the appearance of truth: that which is probable: the chance or likelihood of something happening: — *pl.* **probabil'ities.** — *adv.* **prob'ably.** — **probable error** a quantity assumed as the value of an error, such that the chances of the real error being greater are equal to those of its being less; **probable evidence** evidence not conclusive, but admitting of some degree of force. — **in all probability** quite probably. [Fr., — L. *probābilis* — *probāre, -ātum*, to prove.]

proball *prō'bl*, (*Shak.*) *adj.* supposed to mean plausible. [Apparently a contracted form of **probable**.]

proband *prō'band*, *n.* a person who has some distinctive characteristic (esp. a physical or mental disorder) and who serves as the starting-point for a genetic study of the transmission of this feature through his or her descendants. [Perh. — L. *probāre*, to test.]

probang *prō'bang*, *n.* an instrument for pushing obstructions down the oesophagus. [Called *provang* by its inventor, the Welsh judge, Walter Rumsey (1584–1660); origin unknown; prob. influenced by **probe**.]

probate *prō'bāt, -bit*, *n.* the proof before a competent court that a written paper purporting to be the will of a person who has died is indeed his lawful act: the official copy of a will, with the certificate of its having been proved. — *adj.* relating to the establishment of wills and testaments. — *v.t.* (*U.S.*) to establish the validity of (a will) by probate: to place a probate on: to place a probation sentence on. — *n.* **probation** (*prə-, prō-bā'shən*) testing: proof: a preliminary time or condition appointed to allow fitness or unfitness to appear: noviciate: suspension of sentence, allowing liberty under supervision on condition of good behaviour (esp. to young, or first, offenders): time of trial: moral trial. — *adjs.* **probā'tional** relating to, serving purpose of, probation or trial; **probā'tionary** probational: on probation. — *n.* a probationer. — *ns.* **probā'tioner** one who is on probation or trial: an offender under probation: a novice: one licensed to preach, but not ordained to a pastorate (esp. *Scot.*); **probā'tionership.** — *adjs.* **probative** (*prō'bə-tiv*) testing: affording proof; **prō'batory** testing. — **Probate Court** a court created in 1858 to exercise jurisdiction in matters touching the succession to personal estate in England; **probate duty** (*hist.*) a tax on property passing by will; **probation officer** one appointed to advise and supervise offenders under probation. [L. *probāre, -ātum*, to test, prove.]

probe *prōb*, *n.* an instrument for exploring a wound, locating a bullet, and the like: an act of probing: an exploratory bore: a prod: an investigation: any of various instruments of investigation in space research (as a multi-stage rocket), electronics, etc.: a pipelike device attached to an aircraft for making connection with a tanker aeroplane so as to refuel in flight: a device used in docking two space modules. — *v.t.* to examine with or as with a probe: to examine searchingly. — *v.t.* and *v.i.* to pierce. — *n.pl.* **probe'-sciss'ors** scissors used to open wounds, one blade having a button at the end. [L. *proba*, proof, later examination — *probāre*, to prove.]

probit *prō'bit*, *n.* a unit for measuring probability in relation to an average frequency distribution. [*Prob*ability un*it*.]

probity *prob'i-ti*, or *prōb'*, *n.* uprightness: moral integrity: honesty. [L. *probitās, -ātis* — *probus*, good, honest.]

problem *prob'ləm*, *n.* a matter difficult of settlement or solution: a question or puzzle propounded for solution: the question how to win in so many moves beginning with a hypothetical situation (*chess*): a

proposition in which something is required to be constructed, not merely proved as in a theorem (*geom.*): a source of perplexity. — *adjs.* **problemat'ic, -al** of the nature of a problem: questionable: doubtful. — *adv.* **problemat'ically.** — *n.pl.* **problemat'ics** matters that are problematic or that raise questions. — *n.* **prob'lemist** a person who composes or solves chess, etc. problems. — **problem child** one whose character presents an exceptionally difficult problem to parents, teachers, etc.; **problem novel, play** one presenting or expounding a problem, social, moral, etc. [Gr. *problēma, -atos* — *pro*, before, *ballein*, to throw.]

proboscis *prə-, prō-bos'is*, *n.* a trunk or long snout: a trunk-like process, as the suctorial mouth-parts of some insects: a nose (*facet.*): — *pls.* **probosc'ises, probosc'ides** (*-i-dēz*). — *n.pl.* **Proboscid'ea** the elephant order of mammals. — *adjs.* and *ns.* **proboscid'ean, proboscid'ian.** — **proboscis monkey** a very long-nosed monkey (*Nasalis larvatus*). [L., — Gr. *proboskis*, a trunk — *pro*, expressing motive, *boskein*, to feed.]

probouleutic *prō-boo-lū'tik*, *adj.* for preliminary deliberation. [Gr. *probouleusis*, preliminary deliberation.]

procacity *prə-kas'i-ti*, *n.* petulance. — *adj.* **procacious** (*-kā'shəs*). [L. *prŏcācitās, -ātis* — *prŏcāx*, forward, insolent, shameless — *prŏcāre*, to demand.]

procaine *prō'kān*, *n.* a crystalline substance used as a local anaesthetic. [**pro-²** (*b*), **cocaine**.]

procaryon, etc. See **prokaryon**.

procathedral *prō-kə-thē'drəl*, *n.* a church used temporarily as a cathedral. [Pfx. **pro-²** (*b*).]

proceed *prə-, prō-sēd'*, *v.i.* to go on: to continue: to advance: to pass on: to begin and go on: to act according to a method: to go from point to point: to advance to a higher degree (as *to proceed M.A.*) or more developed state: to prosper: to come forth: to result: to be descended: to take measures or action: to take legal action: to prosecute: to go on, be transacted, happen (*Shak.*). — *v.t.* to say in continuation. — *n.* **prō'ceed** (usu. in *pl.*) outcome: money got from anything. — *adj.* **procedural** (*-sēd'yə-rəl*). — *ns.* **procē'dure** a mode of proceeding: a method of conducting business, esp. in a law case or a meeting: a course of action: a step taken or an act performed; **proceed'er; proceed'ing** a going forward: progress: advancement: a course of conduct: perh. an advantage (*Shak.*): a step: an operation: a transaction: (in *pl.*) a record of the transactions of a society. [Fr. *procéder* — L. *prōcēdere* — *prō*, before, and *cēdere, cēssum*, to go.]

proceleusmatic *pros-e-lūs-mat'ik*, *adj.* inciting, encouraging. — *n.* in ancient prosody, a foot of four short syllables. [Gr. *prokeleusmatikos* — *pro*, before, *keleuein*, to urge, order.]

Procellaria *pros-e-lā'ri-ə*, *n.* the petrel genus. — *adj.* **procella'rian.** [L. *procella*, a storm.]

procephalic *prō-si-fal'ik*, *adj.* of the forepart of the head. [Gr. *pro*, before, *kephalē*, head.]

procerebrum *prō-ser'i-brəm*, *n.* the fore-brain: the prosencephalon. — *adj.* **procer'ebral.** [L. *prō*, before, *cerebrum*, brain.]

procerity *prō-ser'i-ti*, *n.* tallness. [L. *prōcēritās, -ātis* — *prōcērus*, tall.]

process *prō'ses*, sometimes (esp. in U.S.) *pros'* (*Milt. prō-ses'*), *n.* a state of being in progress or being carried on: course: a narrative (*Shak.*): a series of actions or events: a sequence of operations or changes undergone: a photo-process (*print.*): a writ by which a person or matter is brought into court (*law*): an action, suit, or the proceedings in it as a whole: progression: proceeding: an edict (*Shak.*): a projecting part, esp. on a bone (*biol.*). — *v.t.* to serve a summons on: to sue or prosecute: to subject to a special process: to produce or print photo-mechanically: to prepare (e.g. agricultural produce) for marketing, by some special process e.g. canning or bottling: to arrange (documents, etc.) systematically: to examine and analyse: to test the suitability of (a person) for some purpose: (of a computer) to perform operations of adding, subtracting, etc., or other operations on (data supplied): to subject (data) to such operations. — *adj.* **prō′cessed** produced by a special process, as synthetically, photomechanically, etc. — *n.* **prō′cessor** a person or thing that processes something: a device which processes data (*comput.*): a central processing unit (*comput.*). — *adj.* **process′ual** governed by or related to an established process: having a direct function (*U.S.*). — **pro′cess-block** a photo-mechanically made block for printing a picture; **process control** direct automatic control of a physical industrial process by computer; **pro′cess-server** a sheriff's officer. — **data processing** the handling and processing of information by computers. — **in (the) process of** carrying out or on (an activity), or being carried out or on. [Fr. *procès* — L. *prōcessus, -ūs*, advance; cf. **proceed.**]

procession *prǝ-, prō-sesh′ǝn, n.* the act of proceeding: a train of persons, or of boats, shadows, etc. moving forward together as in ceremony, display, demonstration, etc.: the movement of such a train: a litany sung in procession. — *v.i.* to go in procession. — *v.t.* to go through or around in procession: to celebrate by a procession. — *v.i.* **process** (*prō-ses′*; back-formation) to go in procession. — *adj.* **process′ional.** — *n.* a book of litanies, hymns, etc., for processions: a hymn sung in procession. — *n.* **process′ionalist.** — *adj.* **process′ionary.** — *ns.* **process′ioner** (*U.S.*) a county officer who determines boundaries; **process′ioning** going in procession: perambulation of boundaries (*U.S.*). — **processionary moth** a European moth (*Cnethocampa processionea*) whose caterpillars go out seeking food in great processions. — **Procession of the Holy Ghost** (*theol.*) the emanation of the Holy Spirit from the Father (*single procession*), or from the Father and Son (*double procession*). [L. *prōcessiō, -ōnis*; cf. **proceed.**]

processor, processual. See **process.**

procès-verbal *pro-se-ver-bäl,* (Fr.) *n.* a written statement or report: — *pl.* **-verbaux** (*ver-bō*).

prochain (-ein) ami (-y) *pro-shen a-mē,* (*law*) next friend (q.v.).

pro-chancellor *prō-chän′sǝl-ǝr, n.* in certain British universities, the deputy to the vice-chancellor (q.v.). [Pfx. **pro-**²(*b*).]

prochronism *prō′kron-izm, n.* a dating of an event before the right time — opp. to *metachronism.* [Gr. *pro,* before, *chronos,* time.]

procidence *pros′, prōs′i-dǝns, n.* prolapse. — *adj.* **pro′cident.** [L. *prōcidentia* — *prō,* forward, *cadĕre,* to fall.]

procinct *prō-singkt′,* (*Milt.*) *n.* preparedness. [L. *prōcinctus, -ūs* — *prō,* beforehand, *cingĕre, cinctum,* to gird.]

proclaim *prǝ-, prō-klām′, v.t.* to cry aloud: to publish abroad: to announce officially: to denounce: to announce the accession of: to place under restrictions by proclamation. — *n.* **proclaim′** a proclamation: a proclaiming. — *ns.* **proclaim′ant; proclaim′er; proclamation** (*prok-lǝ-mā′shǝn*) the act of proclaiming: that which is proclaimed: official notice given to the public: a proscription. — *adj.* **proclamatory** (*-klam′ǝt-ǝr-i*). [Fr. *proclamer* — L. *prōclāmāre, prōclāmāre* — *prō,* out, *clāmāre,* to cry.]

proclitic *prō-klit′ik, adj.* so closely attached to the following word as to have no accent. — *n.* a proclitic word. — *n.* **pro′clisis** (or *prok′*). [A modern coinage on the analogy of **enclitic** — Gr. *pro,* forward, *klīnein,* to lean.]

proclivity *prǝ-, prō-kliv′i-ti, n.* inclination: propensity. — *adj.* **proclive** (*-klīv′; arch.*) inclined: prone: headlong. [L. *prōclīvis* — *prō,* forward, *clīvus,* a slope.]

procoelous *prō-sē′lǝs, adj.* cupped in front. [Gr. *pro,* before, *koilos,* hollow.]

proconsul *prō-kon′sl, n.* a Roman magistrate with almost consular authority outside the city, orig. one whose consulate had expired, often governor of a province: sometimes applied to a colonial or dominion governor: (with *cap.*) a genus of prehistoric African anthropoid

apes: a member of this genus. — *adj.* **procon′sular** (*-sū-lǝr*). — *ns.* **procon′sulate** (*-sū-lit, -lāt*), **procon′sulship** (*-sl-ship*) the office, or term of office, of a proconsul. [L. *prōcōnsul.*]

procrastinate *prō-kras′ti-nāt, v.t.* (*rare*) to put off till some future time, to defer. — *v.i.* to defer action. — *n.* **procrastinā′tion** the act or habit of putting off, dilatoriness. — *adjs.* **procras′tinātive, procras′tinating, procras′tinātory.** — *ns.* **procras′tinātiveness; procras′tinātor.** [L. *procrāstināre, -ātum* — *prō,* onward, *crāstinus,* of tomorrow — *crās,* tomorrow.]

procreate *prō′kri-āt, v.t.* to engender: to beget: to generate. — *v.i.* to produce offspring. — *n.* **prō′creant** (*-kri-ǝnt*) a generator. — *adj.* generating: connected with or useful in reproduction. — *n.* **prōcreā′tion.** — *adjs.* **procreā′tional; prō′creātive** having the power to procreate: generative: productive. — *ns.* **prō′creativeness; prō′creātor** a parent. [L. *prōcreāre, -ātum* — *prō,* forth, *creāre,* to produce.]

Procrustean *prō-krus′ti-ǝn, adj.* violently making conformable to a standard — from *Procrustes* (Gr. *Prŏkroustēs*) a legendary Greek robber, who stretched or cut his captives' legs to make them fit a bed. — Hence, **Procrustean bed** (*fig.*). [Gr. *prokrouein,* to lengthen out.]

procrypsis *prō-krip′sis,* (*biol.*) *n.* protective coloration. — *adj.* **procryp′tic.** — *adv.* **procryp′tically.** [Gr. *pro,* before, *krypsis,* hiding, *kryptein,* to hide.]

proctal *prok′tl, adj.* anal. — *ns.* **proctalgia** (*-al′ji-ǝ;* Gr. *algos,* pain) neuralgic pain in the rectum; **proctī′tis** inflammation of the rectum. — *adj.* **proctodae′al** (*-tō-dē′ǝl*). — *ns.* **proctodae′um** (Gr. *hodaios,* on the way) the posterior part of the alimentary canal, formed by invagination of ectoderm; **proctol′ogy** the medical study and treatment of the rectum; **proctol′ogist; proc′toscope** an instrument for examining the rectum; **proctos′copy.** [Gr. *prōktos,* anus.]

proctor *prok′tǝr, n.* a procurator or manager for another: an attorney in the spiritual courts: a representative of the clergy in Convocation: an official in the English universities whose functions include enforcement of university regulations. — *n.* **proc′torage.** — *adj.* **procto′rial** (*-tōr′, -tör′i-ǝl*). — *adv.* **procto′rially.** — *v.t.* **proc′torise, -ize** to exercise the power of a proctor against. — *n.* **proc′torship.** — **king's, queen's, proctor** an official who intervenes in divorce cases in England if collusion or fraud is suspected. [**procurator.**]

procumbent *prō-kum′bǝnt, adj.* lying or leaning forward: prone: prostrate: lying on the ground (*bot.*). [L. *prōcumbēns, -entis,* pr.p. of *prōcumbĕre* — *prō,* forward, *cumbĕre,* to lie down.]

procurator *prok′ū-rā-tǝr, n.* a financial agent in a Roman imperial province, sometimes administrator of part of it: one who manages affairs for another: one authorised to act for another: an agent in a law court. — *adj.* **procuratorial** (*-rǝ-tō′ri-ǝl, -tōr′*). — *ns.* **proc′uratorship; proc′uratory** (*-rǝ-tǝr-i*) authorisation to act for another. — **proc′urator-fis′cal** see **fisc.** [L. *prōcūrātor, -ōris;* see next word.]

procure *prǝ-, prō-kūr′, v.t.* to contrive to obtain or bring about: to bring upon someone: to induce: to induce to come, bring (*Shak.*): to urge earnestly (*Spens.*): to obtain for another's immoral purposes. — *v.i.* to pander, pimp. — *adj.* **procur′able** to be had. — *ns.* **procuracy** (*prok′ū-rǝ-si*) the office of a procurator; **procurā′tion** the management of another's affairs: the instrument giving power to do so: a sum paid by incumbents to the bishop or archdeacon on visitations: a procuring; **procure′ment** the act of procuring in any sense; **procur′er** one who procures: a pander: — *fem.* **procur′ess** a bawd. [Fr. *procurer* — L. *prōcūrāre,* to manage — *prō,* for, *cūrāre, -ātum,* to care for.]

procureur *prō-kü-rœr,* (Fr.) *n.* a procurator. — **procureur général** (*zhän-ā-ral*) in France, the public prosecutor-in-chief.

Procyon *prō′si-ǝn, n.* a first-magnitude star in the constellation of the Lesser Dog: the raccoon genus, giving name to the family **Procyon'idae** (raccoons, coatis, etc.). [Gr. *Prŏkўŏn*, the star Procyon, rising before the Dogstar — *pro*, before, *kўŏn*, a dog.]

prod *prod*, *v.t.* to prick: to poke, as with the end of a stick: — *pr.p.* **prodd'ing;** *pa.t.* and *pa.p.* **prodd'ed.** — *n.* an act of prodding: a sharp instrument, as a goad, an awl, a skewer. [Origin unknown; O.E. *prodbor* seems to mean auger.]

Prod *prod*, (*offensive slang*) *n.* (esp. in Ireland) a Protestant.

prodigal *prod'i-gl*, *adj.* wasteful of one's means: squandering: lavish. — *n.* a waster: a spendthrift. — *adv.* (*Shak.*) **prodigally.** — *v.t.* **prod'igalise, -ize** to spend lavishly, waste. — *n.* **prodigality** (*-gal'i-ti*) the state or quality of being prodigal: extravagance: profusion: great liberality. — *adv.* **prod'igally.** [Obs. Fr., — L. *prōdigus* — *prōdigĕre*, to squander — pfx. *prōd-* (early form of *prō-*), away, forth, *agĕre*, to drive.]

prodigy *prod'i-ji*, *n.* a portent (*arch.*): any person or thing that causes great wonder: a wonder: a monster: a child of precocious genius or virtuosity. — *n.* **prodigios'ity.** — *adj.* **prodig'ious** like a prodigy (*arch.*): astonishing: more than usually large in size or degree: monstrous. *adv.* **prodig'iously.** — *n.* **prodig'iousness.** [L. *prōdigium*, a prophetic sign — pfx. *prōd-* (earlier form of *prō-*), in advance, prob. the root of *adagium* (see **adage**).]

proditor *prod'i-tər*, *n.* a traitor. — *adjs.* **prodito'rious** (*-tōr', -tŏr'i-əs*), **prod'itory.** [L. *prōditor, -ōris* — *prōdĕre, -itum*, to betray — *prō*, forth, *dāre*, to give.]

prodnose *prod'nōz*, (*slang*) *n.* a prying, meddlesome person: a detective. — *v.i.* (*rare*) to pry. [**prod** and **nose.**]

prodrome *prod'rōm*, *n.* an introductory treatise: a premonitory event: a sign of approaching disease. — Also **prod'romus** (*prod'rōm-əs; pl.* **prod'romī**). — *adjs.* **prod'-romal, prodrom'ic.** [Latinised from Gr. *prodromos*, forerunner — *pro*, before, *dromos*, a run.]

produce *prə-, prō-dūs', v.t.* to bring forward or out: to extend: to bring into being: to bring forth: to yield: to bring about: to make: to put on the stage: to prepare for exhibition to the public. — *v.i.* to yield: to create value. — *ns.* **produce** (*prod'ūs*) that which is produced: product: proceeds: crops: yield, esp. of fields and gardens; **produce'ment** (*Milt.*) product; **produc'er** one who produces, esp. commodities, or a play or similar exhibition: one who exercises general control over, but does not actually make, a motion picture (cf. **director**): a furnace in which a mixed combustible gas is produced by passing air and steam through incandescent coke; **producibil'ity.** — *adj.* **produc'ible** that may be produced: that may be generated or made: that may be exhibited. — *ns.* **product** (*prod'əkt, -ukt*) a thing produced: a result: a work: offspring: a quantity got by multiplying (*math.*): a substance obtained from another by chemical change (*chem.*); **productibil'ity** (*prə-dukt-*) the capability of being produced. — *adj.* **product'ile** capable of being drawn out in length. — *n.* **produc'tion** the act of producing: that which is produced: fruit: product: a work, esp. of art: a putting upon the stage: a bringing out: the creation of values (*pol. econ.*): extension: in Scots law, a document produced in court. — *adjs.* **produc'tional; produc'tive** having the power to produce: generative: that produces: producing richly: fertile: efficient. — *adv.* **produc'tively.** — *ns.* **produc'tiveness; productiv'ity** (*prod-, prōd-*) the rate or efficiency of work, esp. in industrial production. — **producer gas** gas made in a producer, chiefly a mixture of hydrogen and carbon monoxide diluted with nitrogen. — *n.pl.* **producer(s') goods** goods, such as raw materials and tools, used in the production of consumer(s') goods. — **production line** an assembly line (q.v.); **production platform** an oil platform (q.v.); **productivity deal** an agreement whereby employees receive increased wages or salaries if they agree to improve their efficiency and increase their output. — **make a production (out) of** (*coll.*) to make an unnecessary fuss or commotion about (something). [L.

prōdūcĕre, -ductum — *prō*, forward, *dūcĕre*, to lead.]

proem *prō'em*, *n.* an introduction: a prelude: a preface. — *adj.* **proemial** (*prō-ē'mi-əl*). [Fr. *proème* — L. *prooemium* — Gr. *prooimion* — *pro*, before, *oimē*, a song, *oimos*, a way.]

proembryo *prō-em'bri-ō*, (*bot.*) *n.* a group of cells formed in the dividing zygote, from which part the embryo arises: — *pl.* **proem'bryos.** [Pfx. **pro-**[1].]

proenzyme *prō-en'zīm*, *n.* an enzyme in an inactive form which can be activated — often by another enzyme. [Pfx. **pro-**[1].]

prof *prof*, *n.* a familiar contraction of **professor.**

proface *prō-fās'*, (*Shak.*) *interj.* may it profit you! — a phrase of welcome. [O.Fr. *prou*, profit, *fasse*, 3rd pers. sing. pres. subj. of *faire*, to do.]

profane *prə-, prō-fān', adj.* not sacred: secular: showing contempt of sacred things: uninitiated: unhallowed: ritually unclean or forbidden. — *v.t.* to treat with contempt or insult in spite of the holiness attributed: to desecrate: to violate: to put to an unworthy use. — *n.* **profanation** (*prof-ə-nā'shən*). — *adj.* **profanatory** (*prō-fun'ə-tər-i*). — *adv.* **profane'ly.** — *ns.* **profane'ness; profan'er; profanity** (*-fan'*) irreverence: that which is profane: profane language or conduct. [L. *profānus*, outside the temple, not sacred, unholy — *prō*, before, *fānum*, a temple.]

profectitious *prō-fek-tish'əs, adj.* derived from a parent or ancestor. [L.L. *profectīcius* — L. *prŏfĭcīscī, profectus*, to proceed.]

profess *prə-, prō-fes', v.t.* to make open declaration of: to declare in strong terms: to claim (often insincerely) to have a feeling of: to pretend to: to claim to be expert in: to be professor of: to receive into a religious order by profession (*R.C.*). — *v.i.* to enter publicly into a religious state: to pretend friendship (*Shak.*): to be a professor. — *adj.* **professed'** openly declared: avowed: acknowledged: having made profession. — *adv.* **profess'edly.** — *adj.* **profess'ing** avowed: pretending, soi-disant. — *n.* **profession** (*-fesh'ən*) the act of professing: an open declaration: an avowal: religious belief: a pretence: an employment not mechanical and requiring some degree of learning: a calling, habitual employment: the collective body of persons engaged in any profession: entrance into a religious order: the vow then taken. — *adj.* **profess'ional** pertaining to a profession: engaged in a profession or in the profession in question: competing for money prizes or against those who sometimes do so: undertaken as a means of subsistence, as opp. to *amateur*: showing the skill, artistry, demeanour, or standard of conduct appropriate in a member of a profession or of a particular profession: (of a foul, etc.) deliberate, intended (to prevent the opposition from scoring) (*euph.; sport*). — *n.* one who makes his living by an art, or makes it his career (opp. to *amateur, dilettante*): one who engages in sport for livelihood or gain or against those who do so (with various rules of interpretation for each sport) (opp. to *amateur*): a member of a profession: a person following a career: (in full, *professional examination*) any one of the successive examinations towards a degree in medicine (in Scottish universities). — *n.* **professionalisa'tion, -z-.** — *v.t.* **profess'ionalise, -ize** to give a professional character to: to give over to professionals. — *n.* **profess'ionalism** the status of professional: the competence, or the correct demeanour, of those who are highly trained and disciplined: the outlook, aim, or restriction of the mere professional: the predominance of professionals in sport. — *adv.* **profession'ally.** — *ns.* **professor** (*prə-fes'ər*) one who professes: one who openly declares belief in certain doctrines: a university or sometimes a college teacher of the highest grade, esp. the head of a department (prefixed to the name): in the U.S., a university or college teacher of any grade (prefixed to the name), rising from *assistant professor, associate professor* to full *professor* — see also **associate professor:** a title assumed by charlatans, quacks, dancing-masters, etc.:

—*fem.* (*rare*) **profess'oress; profess'orate** professoriate. — *adj.* **professorial** (*prof-es-ō'ri-ǝl, -ō'ri-ǝl*). — *adv.* **professo'rially.** — *ns.* **professo'riate** the office or chair of a professor: his period of office: body of professors; **profess'orship.** [L. *professus,* perf.p. of *profitērī* — *prō,* publicly, *fatērī,* to confess.]

proffer *prof'ǝr, v.t.* to offer for acceptance, to tender, present: to offer to undertake: — *pr.p.* **proff'ering;** *pa.t.* and *pa.p.* **proff'ered.** — *n.* an offer, tender: an incipient act. — *n.* **proff'erer.** [A.Fr. *proffrir* — L. *prō,* forward, *offerre*; see **offer.**]

proficient *prǝ-, prō-fish'ǝnt, adj.* competent: well-skilled: thoroughly qualified. — *n.* one who is making progress in learning (*Shak.*): an expert: an expert. — *ns.* **profi'cience** (now *rare* or *obs.*); **profi'ciency.** — *adv.* **profi'ciently.** [L. *prōficiēns, -entis,* pr.p. of *prōficĕre,* to make progress.]

profile *prō'fīl, -fēl, -fil, n.* an outline: a head or portrait in a side-view: the side-face: the outline of any object without foreshortening: a drawing of a vertical section of country, an engineering work, etc.: a graph: a short biographical sketch, e.g. in a newspaper or magazine: an outline of the characteristic features of e.g. a particular type of person): an outline of the course of an operation: one's manner, attitude or behaviour considered with regard to the extent to which it attracts attention to oneself and one's activities or reveals one's feelings, intentions, etc., or the extent of one's involvement, etc. (as in *low, high,* etc. *profile*): a public image, esp. one created and controlled by design. — *v.t.* to draw in profile: to make an outline of: to show in profile: to give a profile to: to shape the outline of: to write or give a profile of. — *ns.* **prō'filer; prō'filist** one who draws profiles. [It. *profilo* — L. *prō,* before, *fīlum,* a thread.]

profit *prof'it, n.* gain: the gain resulting from the employment of capital: the excess of selling price over first cost: advantage: addition to good or value: benefit: improvement: — *v.t.* to benefit or to be of advantage to. — *v.i.* to gain advantage: to receive profit: to make progress, to improve (*Shak.*): to be of advantage. — *n.* **profitabil'ity.** — *adj.* **prof'itable** yielding or bringing profit or gain: lucrative: productive. — *n.* **prof'itableness.** — *adv.* **prof'itably.** — *n.* **profiteer'** one who takes advantage of an emergency to make exorbitant profits. — *v.i.* to act as a profiteer. — *ns.* **profiteer'ing; prof'iter; prof'iting.** — *adj.* **prof'itless** without profit. — *adv.* **prof'itlessly.** — *adj.* **prof'it-o'rientated** having profit as chief aim. — **prof'it-sharing** a voluntary agreement under which the employee receives a share, fixed beforehand, in the profits of a business; **prof'it-taking** selling off shares, commodities, etc., in order to profit from a rise in the purchase price. [Fr., — L. *prōfectus,* progress — *prōficĕre, prōfectum,* to make progress.]

profiterole *prǝ-fit'ǝ-rōl, n.* a small puff of choux pastry, usu. filled with cream and covered with a chocolate sauce. [Fr.; perh. — *profiter,* to profit.]

profligate *prof'li-gāt, -gǝt, adj.* overthrown, defeated (*obs.*): abandoned to vice: dissolute: prodigal, rashly extravagant. — *n.* one leading a profligate life: one who is recklessly extravagant or wasteful. — *n.* **prof'ligacy** (*-gǝ-si*) state or quality of being profligate: a vicious course of life. — *adv.* **prof'ligately.** [L. *prōflīgātus,* pa.p. of *prōflīgāre* — *prō,* forward, *flīgĕre,* to dash.]

profluent *prō'floo-ǝnt,* (*Milt.*) *adj.* flowing forth. — *n.* **pro'fluence.** [L. *prō,* forth, *fluĕre,* to flow.]

proforma, pro-forma. See **pro forma** under **pro**[1].

profound *prǝ-, prō-fownd', adj.* deep: deep-seated: far below the surface: intense: abstruse: intellectually deep: penetrating deeply into knowledge. — *n.* the sea or ocean: an abyss, great depth. — *adv.* **profound'ly.** — *ns.* **profound'ness, profundity** (*-fund'*) the state or quality of being profound: depth of place, of knowledge, etc.: that which is profound. [Fr. *profond* — L. *profundus* — *pro,* forward, *fundus,* bottom.]

profulgent *prǝ-, prō-ful'jǝnt, adj.* shining forth, radiant. [L. *prō,* forth, *fulgēns, -entis,* pr.p. of *fulgēre,* to shine.]

profuse *prǝ-, prō-fūs', adj.* liberal to excess: lavish: extravagant: over-abounding. — *adv.* **profuse'ly.** — *ns.* **profuse'ness; profuser** (*-fūz'ǝr; Herrick*) a prodigal, spendthrift; **profusion** (*-fū'zhǝn*) the state of being profuse: extravagance: prodigality. [L. *prōfūsus,* pa.p. of *prōfundĕre* — *prō,* forth, *fundĕre,* to pour.]

prog[1] *prog, v.t.* to pierce: to prick: to poke. — *v.i.* to poke about for anything: to forage for food: to beg. — *n.* a pointed instrument: a thrust: provisions, esp. for a journey. [Origin unknown; perh. several distinct words.]

prog[2] *prog, n.* university slang for **proctor.** — *v.t.* to proctorise. — *n.* **progg'ins** a proctor.

progenitor *prō-jen'i-tǝr, n.* a forefather: an ancestor: a parent: the founder of a family: — *fem.* **progen'itress, progen'itrix.** — Also *fig.* — *adj.* **progenito'rial** (*-tōr', -tör'i-ǝl*). — *ns.* **progen'itorship; progen'iture** a begetting; **progeny** (*proj'ǝ-ni*) offspring: descendants: race: lineage (*Shak.*). — Also *fig.* [L. *prōgenitor, prōgeniēs* — *prōgignĕre* — *prō,* before, *gignĕre, genitum,* beget.]

progeria *prō-jer'i-ǝ, n.* a rare disease causing premature ageing in children. [Gr. *pro,* before, *gēras,* old age.]

progesterone *prō-jes'tǝr-ōn, n.* a female sex hormone that prepares the uterus for the fertilised ovum and maintains pregnancy. — *ns.* **proges'tin** (**pro-**[1], *gest*ation, *-in*) any hormone concerned with changes before pregnancy, esp. **proges'togen,** any of a range of hormones of the progesterone type; several synthetic progestogens are used in oral contraceptives. [*proges*tin, *ster*ol, *-one*.]

proggins. See **prog**[2].

proglottis *prō-glot'is, n.* a detachable tapeworm joint: — *pl.* **proglott'idēs.** [Gr. *pro,* before, *glōttis, -idos,* a pipe mouthpiece.]

prognathous *prog'nǝ-thǝs,* also *prog-* or *prōg-nā'thǝs, adj.* with projecting jaw — also **prognathic** (*prog-, prōgnath'ik*). — *n.* **prog'nathism** (or *-nath', -nāth'*). [Gr. *pro,* forward, *gnathos,* a jaw.]

Progne *prog'nē, n.* a personification of the swallow, sometimes of the nightingale: an American genus of swallows. [Philomela's sister, (usu.) Procne (L. *Prognē* — Gr. *Proknē*) transformed into a swallow, or a nightingale.]

prognosis *prog-nō'sis, n.* a forecasting, or forecast, esp. of the course of a disease: — *pl.* **prognōs'es** (*-ēz*). — *n.* **prognostic** (*prog-, prǝg-nost'ik*) a foretelling: an indication of something to come: a presage: a symptom on which prognosis can be based. — *adj.* indicating what is foreshown by signs or symptoms. of prognosis. — *v.t.* **prognos'ticate** to foretell: to indicate as to come. — *n.* **prognostica'tion.** — *adj.* **prognos'ticative.** — *n.* **prognost'icător** a predictor, esp. a weather prophet. [Gr. *prognōsis* — *pro,* before, *gignōskein,* to know.]

prograde *prō'grād, adj.* (of metamorphism) from a lower to a higher metamorphic level, or caused by a rise in temperature or pressure (*geol.*): (of movement or rotation) in a forward direction, i.e. in the same direction as that of adjacent bodies (*astron.*). — *v.i.* (*geog.*) of a coastline, etc., to advance seawards because of a build-up of sediment. — *n.* **progradā'tion.** [Pfx. **pro-**[2] (*a*) and contrast with retro*grade.*]

programme, (esp. *U.S.,* and usu. also in speaking of computers) **program,** *prō'gram, n.* a public notice (*Scot., obs.*): a paper, booklet, or the like, giving a scheme of proceedings arranged for an entertainment, conference, course of study, etc., with relevant details: the items of such a scheme collectively: a plan of things to be done: a TV or radio presentation produced for broadcast singly or as one of a series: the sequence of actions to be performed by an electronic computer in dealing with data of a certain kind: a course of instruction (by book or teaching machine) in which subject-matter is broken down into logical sequence of short items of information, and a student can check immediately the suitability of his responses. — *v.t.* to provide with, enter in, etc., a programme: to prepare a program(me) for (an electronic computer, etc.): to create a certain pattern of thought, reaction, etc. in the mind of (*fig.*). — *n.* **programmabil'ity** (*comput.*). — *adj.* **programm'able** (*comput.*). — *n.* (*comput.*) a programmable calculator. — *adjs.* **programmatic** (*-grə-mat'ik*) of a programme: of, or of the nature of, programme music; **pro'grammed.** — *ns.* **pro'grammer** (*comput.*); **pro'gramming.** — **programmed learning** learning by programme (see definition of **programme** above); **programme music** music that seeks to depict a scene or tell a story; **programming language** a system of codes, symbols, rules, etc. designed for communicating information to, on or by a computer; **Programming Language 1 (PL/1)** a computer programming language which combines the best qualities of commercial- and scientific-oriented languages. [Gr. *programma*, proclamation — *pro*, forth, *gramma*, a letter.]

progress *prō'gres*, sometimes (esp. in U.S.) *pro'*, *n.* a forward movement: an advance: a continuation: an advance to something better or higher in development: a gain in proficiency: a course: a passage from place to place: a procession: a journey of state: a circuit. — *v.i.* **progress'** (formerly, as *Shak., prō'*) to go forward: to make progress: to go on, continue: to go in progress, travel in state: to go. — *v.t.* (*obs.*) to traverse: to cause (esp. building or manufacturing work) to proceed steadily. — *n.* **progression** (*prə-, prō-gresh'ən*) motion onward: the act or state of moving onward: progress: movement by successive stages: a regular succession of chords (*mus.*): movements of the parts in harmony: a change from term to term according to some law (*math.*): a series of terms so related (see **arithmetic, geometry, harmony**). — *adjs.* **progress'ional; progress'-ionary.** — *ns.* **progress'ionism** sympathy with or advocacy of progress: belief that social or other evolution is towards higher or better things; **progress'ionist** a believer in progressionism: a progressive: one who favours progress or reform; **progress'ism** (or *prō', pro'*) progressionism; **progress'ist** (or *prō', pro'*) one who advocates a progressive policy: progressionist. — *adj.* **progress'ive** moving forward: making progress: of the nature of progress: advancing by successive stages: (of a disease, condition, etc.) increasing steadily in severity or extent: (in games, e.g. **progressive whist)** played by several sets of players, some of whom move round from table to table after each hand according to rule: advancing towards better and better or higher and higher: in favour of progress — applied (usu. with *cap.*) to various parties in municipal and national politics more or less favouring reform: of such a party. — *n.* one who favours progress or reform: (usu. with *cap.*) a member of a party called progressive. — *adv.* **progress'ively.** — *ns.* **progress'iveness; progress'ivism; progress'ivist.** — **in progress** going on: in course of publication. [Fr. *progresse* (now *progrès*) — L. *prōgressus, -ūs* — *prō*, forward, *gradī, gressus*, to step.]

progymnasium *prō-jim-nā'zi-əm*, or (Ger.) *prō-gim-nä'-zi-ŏōm, n.* in Germany, a classical school in which the higher classes are wanting. [Ger.]

prohibit *prə-, prō-hib'it, v.t.* to forbid: to prevent. — *ns.* **prohib'iter, -or; prohibition** (*prō-hi-bi'shən* or *prō-i-*) the act of prohibiting, forbidding, or interdicting: an interdict: the forbidding by law of the manufacture and sale of alcoholic drinks. — *adj.* **prohibi'tionary.** — *ns.* **prohibi'tionism; prohibi'tionist** one who favours prohibition, esp. of the manufacture and sale of alcoholic drinks. — *adj.* **prohibitive** (*-hib'*) tending to make impossible or preclude. — *adv.* **prohib'itively.** — *n.* **prohib'itiveness.** — *adj.* **prohib'itory** that prohibits or forbids: forbidding. [L. *prohibēre, prohibitum* — *prō*, before, *habēre*, to have.]

proign *proin*, obs. form of **prune²; proin, proine** *proin*, obs. forms of **prune¹,²,³.**

project *proj'ekt, n.* a notion (*Shak.*): speculative imagination (*obs.*): a projection: a scheme of something to be done: a proposal for an undertaking: an under-

taking. — *v.t.* **project** (*prə-jekt', prō-jekt'*) to throw out or forward: to speak or sing in such a way as to aim (the voice) at the rear of the auditorium (*theat.*): to throw, propel: to cause to jut out, stretch out: to scheme, plan, devise: to set forth, set before the mind (*Shak.*): to cast (as a light, a shadow, an image) upon a surface or into space: to throw an image of: to show outlined against a background: to predict or expect on the basis of past results or present trends: in geom., to derive a new figure from, so that each point corresponds to a point of the original figure according to some rule, esp. by a system of parallel, converging, or diverging rays through the original points meeting a surface: to externalise: to make objective. — *v.i.* to jut out: to throw powder of projection upon the metal to be transmuted (*alchemy*). — *adj.* **projec'tile** caused by projection: impelling: capable of being thrown or thrust forth. — *n.* **projectile** (*proj'ik-tīl*, or *prə-*, now usu. *prō-jek'tīl*, in U.S. *-til*) a body projected by force: a missile, esp. one discharged by a gun. — *n. and adj.* **projec'ting.** — *n.* **projec'tion** (*-shən*) an act or method of projecting: the fact or state of being projected: planning: that which is projected: a jutting out: that which juts out: the standing out of a figure: a figure got by projecting another (*geom.*): a method of representing geographical detail upon a plane, or the representation so obtained (also **map projection**): a projected image: the reading of one's own emotions and experiences into a particular situation (*psych.*): a person's unconscious attributing to other people of certain attitudes towards himself, usu. as a defence against his own guilt, inferiority, etc. (*psych.*): the throwing in of a powdered philosopher's stone, to effect transmutation, hence transmutation itself in general (*alchemy*). — *adj.* **projec'tional.** — *n.* **projec'-tionist** one who projects, makes projections, esp. in map-making: an operator of a film-projector: an operator of certain television equipment. — *adj.* **projec'-tive** projecting: of projection: derivable by projection: unchanged by projection. — *ns.* **projectivity** (*proj-ək-tiv'i-ti*); **project'ment** (*rare*) design; **projec'tor** one who projects enterprises: a promoter of speculative schemes for money-making: an apparatus for projecting, esp. an image or a beam of light: a straight line joining a point with its projection (*geom.*); **projec'ture** a jutting out. — **projecting powder** (*alchemy*) the philosopher's stone in powder; **projective geometry** a branch of geometry dealing with the properties of figures by two- and three-dimensional projections. [L. *prōjicēre, prōjectum* — *prō*, forth, *jacēre*, to throw.]

projet de loi *pro-zhā də lwa*, (Fr.) a legislative bill.

prokaryon *prō-kar'i-ən*, (*biol.*) *n.* the nucleus of a blue-green alga, bacterium, etc., with no membrane separating the DNA-containing area from the rest of the cell (*cf. eukaryon*). — *n.* **prokar'yot(e)** (*-ōt, -ət*) a cell or organism with such a nucleus or nuclei. — Also *adj.* — *adj.* **prokaryŏt'ic.** — Also **procar'yon**, etc. [**pro-¹**, and Gr. *karyon*, a kernel.]

proke *prōk*, (*dial.*) *v.t.* and *v.i.* to poke. — *n.* **prōk'er** a poker. [Origin obscure.]

prolactin *prō-lak'tin, n.* a hormone produced by the pituitary gland, which stimulates lactation and also acts as a contraceptive.

prolamine *prō'lə-mēn*, also **prolamin** *-lə-min, n.* one of a group of alcohol-soluble proteins.

prolapse *prō-laps'*, or *prō'laps*, (*med.*) *n.* a falling down, or out of place. — Also **prolap'sus.** — *v.i.* **prolapse'** to slip out of place. [L. *prōlābī, prōlāpsus*, to slip forward — *prō*, forward, *lābī*, to slip.]

prolate *prō'lāt*, rarely *prō-lāt'*, *adj.* drawn out along the polar diameter, as a spheroid (opp. to *oblate*): widespread. — *v.t.* **prolate'** (*obs.*) to lengthen out in utterance. — *adv.* **prolately.** — *ns.* **prolateness; pro-lation** (*prō-lā'shən*) utterance: the time-ratio of semibreve to minim (in *great* or *perfect* prolation, three minims to a semibreve; *lesser* or *imperfect*, two) (*mediaeval mus.*). — *adj.* **prolative** (*prō-lā'tiv, prō'lə-tiv*;

gram.) completing the predicate. [L. *prōlātus*, produced — *prō*, forward, *lātus*, used as perf.p. of *ferre*, to carry.]

prole[1] *prōl*, (*coll.*) *n.* and *adj.* proletarian.

prole[2], **proler**. Obs. forms of **prowl**, **prowler**.

proleg *prō'leg*, *n.* an insect larva's abdominal leg, distinguished from a thoracic or 'true' leg. [Pfx. **pro-**[2] (*b*), **leg**.]

prolegomena *prō-leg-om'in-ə*, *n.pl.* an introduction, esp. to a treatise: — *sing.* **prolegom'enon**. — *adjs.* **prolegom'-enary**, **prolegom'enous**. [Gr. *prŏlegomenon*, pl. *-a*, pass. part. neut. of *prolegein* — *pro*, before, *legein*, to say.]

prolepsis *prō-lep'sis*, or *-lēp'*, *n.* anticipation: the rhetorical figure of anticipation, use of a word not literally applicable till a later time: a figure by which objections are anticipated and answered: — *pl.* **prolep'sēs**. — *adjs.* **prolep'tic**, **-al**. — *adv.* **prolep'tically**. [Gr. *prŏlēpsis* — *pro*, before, *lambanein*, to take.]

proletarian *prō-li-tā'ri-ən*, *adj.* of the poorest labouring class: of the proletariat: having little or no property. — *n.* a member of the poorest class: a member of the proletariat: a plant without reserves of food (*bot.*). — *n.* **proletarianisā'tion**, **-z-**. — *v.t.* **proletā'rianise**, **-ize**. — *ns.* **proletā'rianism** the condition of the poorest classes; **proletā'riat** (*-ət*), **-ate** the proletarian class: the wage-earning class, esp. those without capital. — *n.* and *adj.* **pro'letary** (*-ər-i*) proletarian. [L. *prōlētārius*, (in ancient Rome) a citizen of the sixth and lowest class, who served the state not with his property but with his *prōlēs*, offspring.]

prolicide *prō'li-sīd*, *n.* the killing of offspring: the killing off of the human race. — *adj.* **prolici'dal**. [L. *prōlēs*, offspring, *caedĕre*, to kill.]

pro-lifer *prō-lī'fər*, *n.* a person in favour of protecting and promoting the life of unborn children: a campaigner against abortion, experiments on embryos, etc. — *adj.* **pro-life'**. [Pfx. **pro-**[2] (*c*) and **life**.]

proliferate *prō-lif'ə-rāt*, *v.i.* to grow by multiplication of parts (cells, buds, shoots, etc.): to reproduce by proliferation: to reproduce abundantly: to increase in numbers greatly and rapidly. — *v.t.* to produce by proliferation. — *n.* **proliferā'tion** growth and extension by multiplication of cells: production of vegetative shoots from a reproductive structure: repeated production of new parts: production of shoots that may become new plants: production of abnormal or supernumerary parts: a structure formed by proliferating: a great and rapid increase in numbers, as if by proliferation (*fig.*). — *adjs.* **prolif'crative**, **prolif'erous**. — *adv.* **prolif'erously**. [L. *prōlēs*, progeny, *ferre*, to bear.]

prolific *prə-*, *prō-lif'ik*, *adj.* reproductive: fertilising: fertile: producing much offspring (also *fig.* as of an author): fruitful: abounding. — *n.* **prolif'icacy** (*-ə-si*). — *adj.* **prolif'ical** (*rare* or *obs.*). — *adv.* **prolif'ically**. — *ns.* **prolificā'tion** the generation of young: development of a shoot by continued growth of a flower (*bot.*); **prolificity** (*-is'i-ti*), **prolif'icness**. [L. *prōlēs*, offspring, *facĕre*, to make.]

proline *prō'lēn*, *-lin*, *n.* an amino-acid commonly occurring in proteins. [Ger. *Prolin*, contr. from *Pyrrolidin*, pyrroline.]

prolix *prō'liks*, or *-liks'*, *adj.* long and wordy: long-winded: dwelling too long on particulars: long (*obs.* or *rare*). — *adj.* **prolixious** (*prō-lik'shəs*; *Shak.*) dilatory. — *n.* **prolix'ity**. — *adv.* **prolix'ly** (or *prō'*). — *n.* **prolix'ness** (or *prō'*). [L. *prōlixus* — *pro*, forward, *līquī*, to flow.]

proll *prōl*, **proller** *prōl'ər*, obs. forms of **prowl**, **prowler**.

prolocutor *prō-lok'ū-tər*, *n.* a spokesman: a chairman, esp. of the lower house of Convocation: — *fem.* **prōloc'-utrix**. — *ns.* **prolocu'tion** (*prō-* or *pro-*) an introductory speech or saying; **prōloc'utorship**. [L. *prōlocūtor* — *prōloquī*, *-locūtus*, to speak out — *loquī*, to speak.]

prologue *prō'log*, *n.* in a Greek play, the part before the entry of the chorus: an introduction to a poem, etc.: a speech before a play: the speaker of a prologue: an introductory event or action. — *v.t.* to introduce: to preface. — *v.i.* **pro'logise**, **-ize** (*-gīz*, *-jīz*) to speak a prologue — also **pro'loguise**, **-ize**. [Fr., — L. *prologus* — Gr. *prologos* — *logos*, speech.]

prolong *prə-*, *prō-long'*, *v.t.* to lengthen out: to postpone (*Spens.*, *Shak.*). — *v.i.* to lengthen out. — *adj.* **prolongable** (*prō-long'ə-bl*). — *v.t.* **prolongate** (*prō'long-gāt*) to lengthen. — *ns.* **prolongation** (*-long-gā'shən*) lengthening out: a piece added in continuation: continuation; **prolonger** (*-long'ər*). [L. *prōlongāre* — *prō*, forward, *longus*, long.]

prolonge *prō-lonj'*, *n.* a rope for a gun-carriage. [Fr.]

prolusion *prō-lōō'zhən*, *-lū'*, *n.* a preliminary performance, activity, or display: an essay preparatory to a more solid treatise. — *adj.* **prolu'sory** (*-sə-ri*). [L. *prōlūsiō*, *-ōnis* — *prō*, before, *lūdĕre*, *lūsum*, to play.]

prom *prom*, *n.* a contraction of **promenade**: a promenade concert.

promachos *prom'ə-kos*, Gr. *-hhos*, *n.* a champion or defender: a tutelary god. [Gr.]

pro-marketeer *prō-mär-ki-tēr'*, *n.* a person in favour of Britain's entry into, or continued membership of, the European Common Market. [Pfx. **pro-**[2] (*c*).]

promenade *prom-i-näd'* or *-näd'*, *n.* a walk, ride, or drive for pleasure, show, or gentle exercise: a processional dance: a school or college dance (*U.S.*): a place where people walk to and fro: a paved terrace on a sea-front: an esplanade. — *v.i.* to walk, ride, or drive about: to make a promenade. — *v.t.* to lead about and exhibit: to walk, ride or drive about or through. — *n.* **promenader** (*-äd'ər*) one who promenades: a member of the standing portion of the audience at a promenade concert. — **promenade concert** one in which part of the audience stands throughout and can move about; **promenade deck** a deck on which passengers walk about. [Fr., — *promener*, to lead about (*se promener*, to take a walk) — L. *prōmināre*, to drive forwards — *prō*, forward, *mināre*, to threaten.]

prometal *prō'met-l*, *n.* a kind of cast-iron highly resistant to heat.

Promethean *prō-mē'thi-ən*, *-thyən*, *adj.* pertaining to *Prometheus* (*-thūs*), who stole fire from heaven, for which Zeus chained him to a rock, to be tortured by a vulture: daringly innovative. — *n.* a glass tube containing sulphuric acid and an inflammable mixture brought together by pressing — an early kind of match. — *n.* **prome'thium** (formerly **prome'theum**) element 61 (symbol Pm). [Gr. *Promētheus*.]

prominent *prom'i-nənt*, *adj.* standing out: projecting: most easily seen: catching the eye or attention: in the public eye. — *ns.* **prom'inence** state or quality of being prominent: a prominent point or thing: a projection; **prom'inency** a prominence. — *adv.* **prom'inently**. — **solar prominence** a reddish cloud of incandescent gas shooting out from the sun, visible during a total eclipse. [L. *prōminēns*, *-entis*, pr.p. of *prōminēre*, to jut forth — *prō*, forth, *minae*, projections, threats.]

promiscuous *prō-mis'kū-əs*, *adj.* confusedly or indiscriminately mixed: collected together without order: indiscriminate (now usu. referring to one indulging in indiscriminate sexual intercourse): haphazard: belonging to a mixed set: far from choice (*old slang*): casual, accidental (*coll.*). — *n.* **promiscu'ity** (*prom-*) mixture without order or distinction: promiscuous sexual intercourse. — *adv.* **promis'cuously**. [L. *prōmiscuus* — *prō*, intens., *miscēre*, to mix.]

promise *prom'is*, *n.* an engagement to do or keep from doing something: expectation, or that which raises expectation: a ground for hope of future excellence: fulfilment of what is promised (*rare*). — *v.t.* to engage by promise to do, give, etc.: to betroth: to encourage to expect: to afford reason to expect: to assure: to engage to bestow. — *v.i.* to make a promise or promises: to afford hopes or expectations: to stand sponsor (*rare*). — *n.* **promisee'** the person to whom a promise is made. — *adjs.* **prom'iseful**; **prom'iseless**. —

n. **prom′iser.** — *adj.* **prom′ising** affording ground for hope or expectation: likely to turn out well. — *adv.* **prom′isingly.** — *n.* **prom′isor** (*law*) the person making a promise. — *adj.* **promiss′ive** (*prə-*) conveying a promise: of the nature of a promise. — *n.* **promiss′or** (*Rom. law*) the maker of a promise. — *adv.* **prom′issorily.** — *adj.* **prom′issory** containing a promise of some engagement to be fulfilled. — **prom′ise-breach** (*Shak.*) violation of promise; **prom′ise-breaker** (*Shak.*). — *adj.* **prom′ise-crammed** (*Shak.*) fed to repletion with empty promises. — **prom′ise-keeping; promised land** the land promised by God to Abraham and his seed: Canaan: heaven; **promissory note** a written promise to pay a sum of money on some future day or on demand. — **be promised** to have an engagement (*Shak.*); **breach of promise** see **breach; the Promise** the assurance of God to Abraham that his descendants should become the chosen people. [L. *prōmissum*, neut. pa.p. of *promittĕre*, to send forward — *prō*, forward, *mittĕre*, to send.]

prommer *prom′ər*, (*coll.*) *n.* a (regular) attender of promenade concerts, esp. a promenader.

promo *prō′mō*, (*slang*) *n.* a shortening of **promotion**: a promotional video recording. — *pl.* **pro′mos.**

promontory *prom′ən-tər-i, -tri*, *n.* a headland or high cape: a projection, ridge, or eminence (*anat.*). — *adj.* standing out like a promontory. [L.L. *prōmontōrium* (L. *prōmuntūrium*), assimilated to *mons*, mountain.]

promote *prə-, prō-mōt′, v.t.* to help forward: to further: to further the progress of: to raise to a higher grade: to take steps for the passage or formation of: to set in motion (as the office of a judge in a criminal suit): to encourage the sales of by advertising. — *ns.* **promō′ter** one who promotes: one who takes part in the setting up of companies: the organiser of a sporting event, esp. a boxing match: a professional informer (*obs.*): a substance that increases the efficiency of a catalyst (*chem.*): a substance that encourages the formation or growth of tumour cells (*med.*); **promotion** (*-mō′shən*) the act of promoting: advancement in rank or in honour: encouragement: preferment: a venture, esp. in show business: advertising in general, or an effort to publicise and increase the sales of a particular product. — *adj.* **promō′tive.** — *n.* **promō′tor** one who presents candidates for graduation in Scottish universities. — **be on one's promotion** to have right or hope of promotion: to be on good behaviour with a view to promotion. [L. *prōmovēre, -mōtum* — *prō*, forward, *movēre*, to move.]

prompt *prom(p)t, adj.* ready in action: performed at once: paid or due at once: ready for delivery: readily inclined (*Shak.*). — *adv.* promptly, punctually, to the minute. — *v.t.* to incite: to instigate: to move to action: to supply forgotten words to, esp. in a theatrical performance: to help with words or facts when one is at a loss: to suggest to the mind. — *n.* a time limit for payment: an act of prompting: words furnished by the prompter. — *ns.* **prompt′er** one who prompts, esp. actors; **prompt′ing; prompt′itude** promptness: readiness: quickness of decision and action. — *adv.* **prompt′ly.** — *ns.* **prompt′ness; prompt′uary** a repository: a reference book of facts; **prompt′ure** (*Shak.*) suggestion: instigation. — **prompt′-book, -copy** a copy of a play for the prompter's use; **prompt′-box** a box for the prompter in a theatre; **prompt′-note** a note of reminder of time-limit of payment; **prompt side** the side of the stage where the prompter is — usually to the actor's left in Britain, to his right in U.S.A. [L. *prōmptus* — *prōmere*, to bring forward.]

promulgate *prom′əl-gāt* (U.S. *prə-mul′*) *v.t.* to proclaim, publish abroad: to make widely known: to put in execution by proclamation (as a law) —(*arch.*) **promulge** (*prō-mulj′*). — *ns.* **promulgā′tion; prom′ulgātor.** [L. *prōmulgāre, -ātum.*]

promuscis *prō-mus′is, n.* a proboscis, esp. of Hemiptera. — *adj.* **promusc′idate** like or having a promuscis. [L. *promuscis, -idis*, a popular perversion of *proboscis.*]

promycelium *prō-mī-sē′li-əm, n.* a short germ-tube put out by some fungal spores, producing spores of different types. [Pfx. **pro-¹** and **mycelium.**]

pronaos *prō-nā′os, n.* the vestibule in front of a temple: — *pl.* **prona′oi.** [Gr. *prŏnāos* — *pro*, before, *nāos*, a temple.]

prone¹ *prōn, adj.* with the face, ventral surface, or palm of the hand downward: prostrate: directed downward: loosely, lying or laid flat: descending steeply: disposed, inclined, naturally tending: willing: ready, eager (*Shak.*): perhaps passive, or with downcast eyes, or fervent (Shak., *Meas. for Meas.*). — **-prone** in composition, liable to suffer a specified thing, as in *accident-prone.* — *v.t.* **prōn′ate** to turn (the foot) sole inwards: to turn (the hand) palm downward or backward with radius and ulna crossed — opp. to *supinate.* — Also *v.i.* (of a hand or foot). — *ns.* **prōnā′tion** the act of pronating; **prōnā′tor** the muscle of the forearm that pronates the hand. — *adv.* **prone′ly,** — *n.* **prone′ness.** [L. *prōnus*, bent forward.]

prone² *prōn*, (*obs.*) *n.* a place in a church where intimations are given out: hence, a homily. — *n.* **proneur** (*prō-nœr′*) a flatterer. [Fr. *prône.*]

pronephros *prō-nef′ros*, (*zool.*) *n.* in vertebrates, the anterior portion of the kidney, functional in the embryo but functionless and often absent in the adult. — *adj.* **proneph′ric.** [**pro-¹** and *nephros*, kidney.]

prong *prong, n.* a fork of any kind (now chiefly *dial.*): a tine, tooth, or spike of a fork or forked object: a tine, spur, or projection, as on an antler: a fork of a stream or inlet (*U.S.*). — *v.t.* to stab with a prong: to furnish with prongs. — *adj.* **pronged** having prongs. — **prong′-buck** the pronghorn (properly the male); **prong′-hoe** a hoe with prongs; **prong′horn** an American antelope-like ruminant (*Antilocapra americana*), only representative of the family *Antilocapridae*, with deciduous horns pronged in front. — *adj.* **prong′-horned.** [M.E. *prange*; origin obscure.]

pronominal. See **pronoun.**

pronotum *prō-nō′təm, n.* the back of an insect's prothorax: — *pl.* **pronō′ta.** — *adj.* **pronō′tal.** [Pfx. **pro-¹**, Gr. *nōton*, back.]

pronoun *prō′nown, n.* a word used instead of a noun, i.e. to indicate without naming. — *adj.* **pronominal** (*prə-, prō-nom′in-əl*) belonging to, or of the nature of, a pronoun. — *adv.* **pronom′inally.**

pronounce *prə-, prō-nowns′, v.t.* to proclaim: to utter formally: to utter rhetorically: to declare: to utter: to articulate. — *v.i.* to pass judgment: to articulate one's words. — *n.* (*Milt.*) pronouncement. — *adjs.* **pronounce′able** capable of being pronounced; **pronounced′** marked with emphasis: marked. — *adv.* **pronoun′cedly** (*-səd-li*). — *ns.* **pronounce′ment** a confident or authoritative assertion or declaration: the act of pronouncing; **pronoun′cer.** — *n.* and *adj.* **pronoun′cing.** — *n.* **pronunciation** (*prō-nun-si-ā′shən*) mode of pronouncing: articulation. [Fr. *prononcer* — L. *prōnūntiāre* — *prō*, forth, *nūntiāre*, to announce — *nūntius*, a messenger.]

pronto *pron′tō*, (*slang*) *adv.* promptly, quickly. [Sp. *pronto* — L. *prōmptus*, at hand.]

Prontosil® *pron′tō-sil*, (now *rare*) *n.* trademark for some of the sulphonamide drugs.

pronucleus *pro-nū′kli-əs, n.* the nucleus of a germ-cell after it has fully matured and before fertilization. — *adj.* **pronū′clear.** [**pro-¹** and **nucleus.**]

pronunciamento *prō-nun-si-ə-men′tō, n.* a manifesto: a formal proclamation: — *pl.* **pronunciamen′tos** or **-oes.** [Sp. *pronunciamiento.*]

pronunciation. See **pronounce.**

proo, pruh *prōō*, (*Scot.*) *interj.* a call to a cow to come near.

prooemium *prō-ē′mi-əm, n.* same as **proem.** — Also **prooe′mion.**

pro-oestrus *prō-ēs′trəs, n.* in mammals, the coming-on of heat in the oestrus cycle. [**pro-¹** and **oestrus.**]

proof *prōōf, n.* that which proves or establishes the truth of anything: the fact, act, or process of proving or showing to be true: demonstration: evidence that convinces the mind and goes toward determining the decision of a court: an instrument of evidence in documentary form: the taking of evidence by a judge upon an issue framed in pleading (*Scots law*): a trial before a judge without a jury (*Scots law*): a checking operation (*arith.*): a test: experience (*obs.*): issue, outcome, upshot (*obs.*): testing, esp. of guns: ability to stand a test: invulnerability: impenetrability: armour of proof: a standard strength of spirit (alcohol and water of relative density 12/13 at 51°F. — i.e. 49·28 per cent. of alcohol): an impression taken for correction (*print.*): an early impression of an engraving: a coin, intended for display, etc., rather than circulation, struck from polished dies on polished blanks (also **proof coin**): the first print from a negative (*phot.*): — *pl.* **proofs.** — *adj.* impervious: invulnerable: of standard strength (of alcohol). — *v.t.* to make impervious, esp. to water: to take a proof of: to test. — **-proof** in composition, (to make) able to withstand or resist, as in *waterproof, childproof, weatherproof*, etc. — *n.* **proof'ing** the process of making waterproof, gasproof, etc.: material used for the purpose. — *adj.* **proof'less** wanting proof or evidence. — **proof'-charge** a charge used to test the strength of a gun. — *v.t.* **proof'-correct** to correct in proof. — **proof'-correcting; proof'-correction; proof'-house** a house fitted up for proving firearms; **proof'-mark** a mark stamped on a gun to show that it has stood the test; **proof'-puller** one who pulls proofs. — *v.t. and v.i.* **proof'-read** to read and correct in proof. — **proof'-reader** one who reads printed proofs to discover and correct errors; **proof'-reading; proof'-sheet** an impression taken on a slip of paper for correction before printing finally; **proof'-spirit** a standard mixture of alcohol and water; **proof'-text** a passage of the Bible adduced in proof of a doctrine. — **armour of proof** armour that has been tested, or can be confidently relied upon; **artist's proof** a first impression from an engraved plate or block; **burden of proof** see **burden[1]; over, under proof** containing in 100 volumes enough alcohol for so many volumes more, or less, than 100; **proof before letters** one taken before the title is engraved on the plate. [O.Fr. *prove* (Fr. *preuve*); see **prove** for explanation of vowel in *obs.* or *Scot.* forms **preeve, prief(e).**]

prootic *prō-ot'ik, adj.* in front of the ear. — *n.* an anterior bone of the auditory capsule. [Pfx. **pro-[1]**, Gr. *ous, ōtos*, ear.]

prop[1] *prop, n.* a rigid support: a supplementary support: a stay: a strut: a timber supporting a mine-roof: a supporter, upholder: a leg (*slang*): a boxer's extended arm (*slang*): in Rugby football, either of the two forwards at the ends of the front row of the scrum (also **prop'(-)for'ward**): an act of propping in a horse (*Austr.*). — *v.t.* to hold up by means of something placed under or against: to support or to sustain: to keep (a failing enterprise, etc.) going: to hit straight or knock down (*slang*). — *v.i.* (*Austr.*) to stop suddenly (of a horse): — *pr.p.* **propp'ing;** *pa.t. and pa.p.* **propped.** — **prop'(-)for'ward** see above; **prop'-root** a root growing down from a trunk or branch, serving to prop up a tree. [M.E. *proppe*; cf. Du. *proppe*, vine-prop, support.]

prop[2] *prop*, (*slang*) *n.* a tie-pin: a brooch. [Du. *prop.*]

prop[3] *prop, n.* a coll. or slang abbrev. of (aircraft) **propeller,** (theatrical) **property,** (geometrical) **proposition.** — *n.pl.* **props** stage properties. — *n.sing.* a property-man.

propaedeutic *prō-pē-dū'tik, n.* (often in *pl.*) a preliminary study. — *adjs.* **propaedeut'ic, -al.** [Gr. *propaideuein*, to teach beforehand — *pro*, before, *paideuein*, to teach.]

propagate *prop'ə-gāt, v.t.* to increase by natural process: to multiply: to pass on: to transmit: to spread from one to another: to increase (*obs.*). — *v.i.* to multiply: to breed. — *adj.* **prop'agable.** — *n.* **propagan'da** a

congregation of the Roman Catholic Church, founded 1622, charged with the spreading of Catholicism (*dē propāgandā fidē*, 'concerning the faith to be propagated' — not a plural but ablative singular): any association, activity, plan, etc., for the spread of opinions and principles, esp. to effect change or reform: the information, etc., spread by such an association. — *v.t. and v.i.* **propagand'ise, -ize.** — *ns.* **propagand'ism** practice of propagating tenets or principles: zeal in spreading one's opinions: proselytism; **propagand'ist.** — Also *adj.* — *n.* **propagā'tion.** — *adj.* **prop'agative.** — *n.* **prop'agātor** one who, or that which, propagates: a heated, covered box in which plants may be grown from seed or cuttings. — *v.t.* **propage** (*prō-pāj'; Congreve*) to beget, propagate. — *ns.* **prop'agule, prōpag'ulum** a small plant outgrowth, e.g. a bud or a spore, which becomes detached from the parent and grows into a new plant: any part of an organism from which a new individual can be produced: the minimum population of a species from which a new colony can be produced (*ecol.*). — **propaganda machine** all the means employed in the process of spreading opinions: the process itself. [L. *prōpāgāre, -ātum*, conn. with *prōpāgō*, a layer.]

propale *prō-pāl', v.t.* to disclose. — *v.i.* (*Scott*) to make a display. [L.L. *prōpalāre* — *prōpalam*, openly — *prō*, forth, *palam*, openly.]

propane *prō'pān, n.* a hydrocarbon gas (C_3H_8), third member of the methane series. — **propanō'ic acid** same as **propionic acid.** [**propionic.**]

proparoxytone *prō-par-ok'si-tōn, adj.* having the acute accent on the third last syllable: having heavy stress on the third last syllable. — *n.* a word thus accented. [Gr. *proparoxytonos*; see **paroxytone.**]

propel *prə-, prō-pel', v.t.* to drive forward: — *pr.p.* **propell'ing;** *pa.t. and pa.p.* **propelled'.** — *n.* **propell'ant** that which propels: an explosive for propelling projectiles: the fuel used to propel a rocket, etc.: the gas in an aerosol spray. — *adj.* **propell'ent** driving. — *n.* a driving agent: a motive. — *ns.* **propell'er** one who, or that which, propels: driving mechanism: a shaft with spiral blades (*screw-propeller*) for driving a ship, aeroplane, etc.: a screw-steamer: a helical blower (*air-propeller, propeller fan*): a spinning-bait; **propel'ment** propulsion: propelling mechanism. — **propell'er-blade'; propell'er-shaft'** the shaft of a propeller: the driving shaft between gear-box and rear axle in a motor vehicle; **propelling pencil** one having a replaceable lead held within a casing that can be turned to push the lead forward as it is worn down. [L. *prōpellĕre — prō*, forward, *pellĕre*, to drive.]

propend *prə-, prō-pend', (Shak.) v.i.* to incline. — *adjs.* **propend'ent; propense** (*-pens'*) inclined: sometimes used in the sense of prepense. — *adv.* **propense'ly.** — *ns.* **propense'ness, propen'sion** (*Shak.*), **propens'ity** inclination of mind: favourable inclination: tendency to good or evil: disposition: tendency to move in a certain direction. — *adj.* **propen'sive.** [L. *prōpendēre, -pēnsum*, to hang forward — *prō, pendēre.*]

propene. Same as **propylene.**

propense. See **propend.**

proper *prop'ər, adj.* own: appropriate: peculiar: confined to one: in natural colouring (*her.*): strict: strictly applicable: strictly so-called (usu. after *n.*): thorough, out-and-out (now *coll.* or *slang*): actual, real: befitting: decorous, seemly: conforming strictly to convention: goodly: belonging to only one: comely: in liturgics, used only on a particular day or festival. — *n.* a service, psalm, etc., set apart for a particular day or occasion. — *adv.* (*coll.*) very, exceedingly. — *adv.* **prop'erly** in a proper manner: strictly: entirely, extremely (*coll.*). — *n.* **prop'erness.** — **proper chant** (*obs.*) the key of C major. — *adj.* **prop'er-false'** (*Shak.*) handsome and deceitful. — **proper fraction** a fraction that has a numerator of a lower value than the denominator; **proper motion** a star's apparent motion relative to the celestial sphere, due partly to its own movement (peculiar motion), partly to that of the solar system (parallactic motion); **proper noun, name** the name of a particular person, animal, thing, place, etc. — opp. to *common* noun. [Fr. *propre* — L. *prŏprĭus*, own.]

properdin *prō-pûr'din, n.* a natural immunising substance varyingly present in the blood, possibly with bearing on resistance to malignant disease. [L. *prō*, for, *perdĕre*, to destroy.]

properispomenon *prō-per-i-spōm'ə-non, n.* a word with the circumflex accent on the penult. — Also *adj.* [Gr. *prŏperispōmenon*, pass. part. neut. of *properispaein*, to put circumflex on the penult.]

property *prop'ər-ti, n.* that which is proper to any person or thing: a quality that is always present: a characteristic: an essential detail (*Shak.*): any quality: propriety, fitness (*obs.*): that which is one's own: the condition of being one's own: a piece of land owned by somebody: right of possessing, employing, etc.: ownership: an article required on the stage (abbrev. **prop**): a mere tool or cat's-paw: individuality, personal identity (*Shak.*). — *v.t.* (*Shak.*) to treat as a property: to appropriate. — *adj.* of the nature of a stage property. — *adj.* **prop'ertied** imbued with properties (*Shak.*): possessed of property. — **prop'erty-man, -mas'ter** one who has charge of stage properties; **property qualification** a qualification (as for office, voting) depending on possession of so much property; **prop'erty-room** the room in which stage properties are kept; **property tax** a tax levied on property, at the rate of so much per cent. on its value. [O.Fr. *properte*; see **propriety**.]

prophase *prō'fāz, (biol.) n.* a preliminary stage of mitosis, preceding the formation of the equatorial plate: the first stage of meiosis. [Pfx. **pro-**[1].]

prophecy *prof'i-si, n.* inspired or prophetic utterance: prediction: public interpretation of Scripture, or preaching (*obs.*). [O.Fr. *prophecie* — L. *prophētīa* — Gr. *prophēteia* — *prophētēs*, prophet.]

prophesy *prof'i-sī, v.i.* to utter prophecies: to speak prophetically: to expound the Scriptures (*obs.*): to preach (*obs.*): to foretell the future. — *v.t.* to foretell: — *pa.t.* and *pa.p.* **proph'esīed.** — *ns.* **proph'esīer; proph'esying.** [A variant of **prophecy**.]

prophet *prof'it, n.* a spokesman of deity: one who proclaims a divine message: an inspired teacher, preacher, or poet: the spokesman of a group, movement, or doctrine: a minister of the second order of the Catholic Apostolic Church: a foreteller, whether claiming to be inspired or not: a tipster: — *fem.* **proph'etess.** — *ns.* **proph'ethood, proph'etship.** — *adjs.* **prophetic** (*prə-fet'ik*), **-al.** — *adv.* **prophet'ically.** — *n.* **proph'etism.** — **former prophets** Joshua, Judges, Samuel, and Kings; **latter prophets** the prophets properly so called; **major prophets** the prophets whose books come before that of Hosea; **minor prophets** the prophets from Hosea to Malachi; **prophet of doom** a person who continually predicts unfortunate events, disasters, etc.; **school of the prophets** a school among the ancient Jews for training young men as teachers of the people; **the Prophet** Mohammed; **the prophets** one of the three divisions into which the ancient Jews divided their Scriptures — consisting of the *former* and the *latter* prophets (see above). [Fr. *prophète* — L. *prophēta* — Gr. *prophētēs* — pro, for, *phanai*, to speak.]

prophylactic *pro-fi-lak'tik, adj.* guarding against disease. — *n.* a preventive of disease: a condom (usu. *U.S.*). — *n.* **prophylax'is** (not a Greek word) preventive treatment against diseases, etc. [Gr. *prophylaktikos* — pro, before, *phylax*, a guard.]

prophyll *prō'fil, (bot.) n.* a bracteole. [Pfx. **pro-**[1], Gr. *phyllon*, leaf.]

propine *prə-pīn', (chiefly Scot., arch.) v.t.* to pledge in drinking: to present, offer. — *n.* a tip: a gift. [L. *propīnāre* — Gr. *propīnein*, to drink first — pro, before, *pīnein*, to drink.]

propinquity *prə-ping'kwi-ti, n.* nearness. [L. *propinquitās, -ātis* — *propinquus*, near — *prope*, near.]

propionic acid *prō-pi-on'ik as'id* one of the fatty acids,

C_2H_5·COOH; the first of the series that yields derivatives of a fatty character. — *n.* **prō'pionate** any ester or salt of propionic acid. [Pfx. **pro-**[1], *pīōn, -on,* fat.]

propitiate *prə-pish'i-āt, v.t.* to render favourable: to appease. — *adj.* **propi'tiable.** — *n.* **propitiā'tion** act of propitiating: atonement: atoning sacrifice. — *adj.* **propi'tiātive.** — *n.* **propi'tiātor.** — *adv.* **propi'tiatorily** (*-shi-ə-tər-i-li*). — *adj.* **propi'tiatory** propitiating: expiatory. — *n.* the Jewish mercy-seat: a propitiation (*arch.*). — *adj.* **propitious** (*-pish'əs*) favourable: disposed to be gracious: of good omen. — *adv.* **propi'tiously.** — *n.* **propi'tiousness.** [L. *propitiāre, -ātum,* to make favourable — *propitius*, well-disposed.]

prop-jet *prop'-jet,* (*aero.*) *adj.* and *n.* (a jet aeroplane) having a turbine-driven propeller. [**prop**(eller) and **jet**.]

propodeon *prō-pod'i-on, n.* in some Hymenoptera, the first abdominal segment, fused with the thorax and so in front of the waist. — Wrongly Latinised as **propod'eum.** [Pfx. **pro-**[1], Gr. *podeōn, -ōnos,* a wineskin neck.]

propolis *prop'ə-lis, n.* bee-glue, a brown sticky resinous substance gathered by bees from trees and used by them as cement and varnish. [Gr. *propolis*.]

propone *prə-pōn', v.t.* (now *Scot.*) to put forward, propose, propound: to put before a court. — *adj.* **propōn'ent** bringing forward, proposing: bringing an action. — *n.* a propounder or proposer: a favourer, advocate. [L. *prōpōnĕre* — *prō*, forward, *pōnĕre*, to place.]

proportion *prə-pōr'shən, -pör', n.* the relation of one thing to another in magnitude: fitness of parts to each other: due relation: relation of rhythm or of harmony: adjustment in due ratio (*Shak.*): ratio: the identity or equality of ratios (*math.*): the rule of three: equal or just share: relative share, portion, inheritance, contribution, quota, fortune: a part or portion (*coll.*): (in *pl.*) dimensions: form, figure (*obs.*). — *v.t.* to adjust or fashion in due proportion: to regulate the proportions of: to be in due proportion to (*Shak.*): to divide proportionally. — *adj.* **propor'tionable** that may be proportioned: having a due or definite relation. — *n.* **propor'tionableness.** — *adv.* **propor'tionably.** — *adj.* **propor'tional** relating to proportion: in proportion: having the same or a constant ratio (*math.*): proportionate, in suitable proportion. — *n.* (*math.*) a number or quantity in a proportion. — *n.* **proportional'ity.** — *adv.* **propor'tionally.** — *adj.* **propor'tionate** in fit proportion: proportional. — *v.t.* to adjust in proportion. — *adv.* **propor'tionately.** — *n.* **propor'tionateness.** — *adj.* **propor'tioned.** — *n.* **propor'tioning** adjustment of proportions. — *adj.* **propor'tionless** ill-proportioned. — *n.* **propor'tionment.** — **proportional representation** a system intended to give parties in an elected body a representation as nearly as possible proportional to their voting strength: often loosely applied to the system of transferred vote. — **in proportion** (often with *to*) in a (given) ratio: having a correct or harmonious relation (with something): to a degree or extent which seems appropriate to the importance, etc. of the matter in hand; **out of (all) proportion** not in proportion. [L. *prōportiō, -ōnis* — *prō*, in comparison with, *portiō,* part, share.]

propose *prə-pōz', v.t.* to put forward or exhibit (*obs.*): to put before one's own or another's mind: to propound: to face (*Shak.*): to imagine, suppose (*Shak.*): to offer for consideration or acceptance: to formulate as something to be exacted (*Shak.*): to proffer: to offer: to suggest or lay before one as something to be done: to purpose or intend: to move formally: to nominate: to invite the company to drink (a health): to enunciate. — *v.i.* to form or put forward an intention or design: to offer, especially marriage: to converse (*Shak.*). — *n.* a proposal (*obs.*): talk, discourse (*Shak.*). — *adj.* **propōs'able.** — *ns.* **propōs'al** an act of proposing: an offer, esp. of marriage: a tender (*U.S.*): anything proposed: a plan; **propōs'er.** [Fr. *proposer* — pfx. *pro-, poser,* to place; see **pose**[1].]

proposition *prop-ə-zish'ən, n.* an act of propounding or (more rarely) proposing: the thing propounded or proposed: an offer (*Shak.*): a question propounded (*Shak.*): a statement of a judgment: a form of statement in which a predicate is affirmed or denied of a subject (*log.*): a premise, esp. a major premise: a statement of a problem or theorem for (or with) solution or demonstration (*math.*): enunciation of a subject in a fugue (*mus.*): a possibility, suggestion, course of action, etc., to be considered: any situation, thing, or person considered as something to cope with, as an enterprise, job, opponent, etc. (*slang*, orig. *U.S.*): an invitation to sexual intercourse (*coll.*). — *v.t.* to make a proposition to someone, esp. to solicit a woman for sexual relations. — *adj.* **proposi'tional.** — **propositional calculus** see **calculus.** [L. *prōpositiō, -ōnis* — *prō*, before; see **position.**]

propound *prə-pownd'*, *v.t.* to offer for consideration: to set forth as aim or reward: to purpose (*Spens.*): to produce for probate (*law*). — *n.* **propound'er.** [**propone.**]

propraetor *prō-prē'tər, -tör, prō-prī'tor, n.* a magistrate of ancient Rome, who, after acting as praetor in Rome, was appointed to the government of a province. — *adjs.* **propraetorial** (*-tō', -tö'ri-əl*), **propraeto'rian.** [L. *prōpraetor* — *prō praetōre*, for the praetor.]

propranolol *prop-ran'ə-lol, n.* a beta-blocker (q.v.) used esp. in the treatment of cardiac arrhythmia, angina and hypertension.

proprietor *prō-prī'ə-tər, n.* an owner: — *fem.* **propri'etress, propri'etrix** (sham Latin). — *n.* **propri'etary** an owner: a body of owners: ownership: a proprietary or patented drug (*med.*). — *adj.* of the nature of property: legally made only by a person or body of persons having special rights, esp. a patent or trademark: pertaining to or belonging to the legal owner: (of a company, etc.) privately owned and run: owning property. — *adj.* **proprietorial** (*-tō', -tö'ri-əl*). — *adv.* **proprieto'ri-ally.** — *n.* **propri'etorship.** [L.L. *proprietārius* — *proprius*, own; **proprietor** has been formed irregularly; it is not a Latin word.]

propriety *prō-prī'ə-ti, n.* ownership (*obs.*): rightness, as in the use of words: appropriateness: seemliness: decency: conformity with good manners: conformity with convention in language and conduct: a character, quality, or property (*obs.*): particular nature, individuality (*Shak.*). [Fr. *propriété* — L. *proprietās, -ātis* — *proprius*, own.]

proprioceptive *prō-pri-ō-sep'tiv, adj.* of, pertaining to, or made active by, stimuli arising from movement in the tissues. — *n.* **propriocep'tor** a sensory nerve-ending receptive of such stimuli. — **proprioceptive sense** the sense of muscular position. [L. *proprius*, own, after **receptive.**]

proproctor *prō-prok'tər, n.* a proctor's substitute or assistant. [Pfx. **pro-**[2] (*b*).]

proptosis *prop-tō'sis, n.* forward displacement, esp. of the eye. [Gr. *proptōsis* — *pro*, forward, *ptōsis*, fall.]

propugnation *prō-pug-nā'shən,* (*Shak.*) *n.* defence. [L. *prō*, for, *pugnāre*, to fight.]

propulsion *prə-pul'shən, n.* driving forward. — *adjs.* **propul'sive, propul'sory.** [L. *prōpellēre, prōpulsum*, to push forward; see **propel.**]

propyl *prō'pil, n.* the alcohol radical C_3H_7. — *ns.* **pro'-pylamine** an amine of propyl; **pro'pylene, pro'pene** a gaseous hydrocarbon (C_3H_6). — *adj.* **propyl'ic.** [**propionic** and Gr. *hylē*, matter.]

propylaeum *prop-i-lē'əm,* **propylon** *prop'i-lon, ns.* a gateway of architectural importance, leading into a temple, etc.: — *pl.* **propylae'a, prop'yla.** — *ns.* **prop'ylite** an andesite altered by solfataric action, orig. applied to andesites of the beginning (or gateway) of the Tertiary time; **propylitisā'tion, -z-.** — *v.t.* **prop'ylitise, -ize.** [Gr. *propylaion* (used in pl., *-a*) and *propylon* — *pro*, before, *pylē*, a gate.]

pro rata. See **pro**[1].

prorate *prō-rāt', prō'rāt,* (mainly *U.S.*) *v.t.* to distribute

proportionately. — *adj.* **prorā'table.** — *n.* **prorā'tion.** [**pro rata.**]

prore *prōr, prör,* (*poet.*) *n.* a prow: a ship. [Obs. Fr., — L. *prōra*, prow — Gr. *prōirā*.]

prorector *prō-rek'tər, n.* a university or college rector's substitute or assistant. [Pfx. **pro-**[2] (*b*).]

prorogue *prə-, prō-rōg', v.t.* to prolong (*obs.*): to postpone (*Shak.*): perh., to keep from exertion (*Shak.*): to discontinue the meetings of for a time without dissolving. — *v.t.* **prō'rogāte** to prorogue: to extend by agreement, in order to make a particular action competent (*Scots law*). — *n.* **prōrogā'tion.** [L. *prōrogāre, -ātum* — *prō*, forward, *rogāre*, to ask.]

prosaic, -al *prō-zā'ik, -əl, adjs.* like prose: unpoetical: matter-of-fact: commonplace: dull: in or relating to prose (*rare*). — *adv.* **prosā'ically.** — *ns.* **prosā'icalness; prosā'icism** (*-i-sizm*) prosaism; **prosā'icness** quality of being prosaic; **prō'sāism** a prose idiom: a prosaic phrase: prosaic character; **prō'sāist** a writer of prose: a commonplace person; **prosateur** see under **prose.** [L. *prosa*, prose.]

prosauropod *prō-sör'ə-pod, n.* a reptile-like dinosaur of the division *Prosauropoda* which lived in the Triassic period. — Also *adj.*

proscenium *prō-sē'ni-əm, n.* the front part of the stage: the curtain and its framework, esp. the arch that frames the more traditional type of stage (**proscenium arch**). [Latinised from Gr. *proskēnion* — *pro*, before, *skēnē*, stage.]

prosciutto *pro-shōō'tō, n.* finely cured uncooked ham, often smoked: — *pl.* **prosciut'ti, prosciutt'os.** [It., lit. pre-dried.]

proscribe *prō-skrīb', v.t.* to put on the list of those who may be put to death: to outlaw: to ostracise: to prohibit: to denounce. — *ns.* **prōscrib'er; prō'script** one who is proscribed; **prōscrip'tion.** — *adj.* **prōscrip'tive.** — *adv.* **prōscrip'tively.** [L. *prōscrībēre* — *prō-*, before, publicly, *scrībēre, scrīptum*, to write.]

prose *prōz, n.* ordinary spoken and written language with words in direct straightforward arrangement without metrical structure: all writings not in verse: a passage of prose for translation from or, usu., into a foreign language, as an exercise: a composition in prose (*obs.*, except as an exercise in Latin or Greek): a narrative (*obs.*): a piece of prosing: a familiar, gossipy, talk (*coll.*; esp. formerly): (something having) prosaic character: a prosy talker. — *adj.* of or in prose: not poetical: plain: dull. — *v.i.* to write prose: to speak or write tediously. — *v.t.* to compose in prose: to turn into prose. — *ns.* **prosateur** (*prō-za tœr; Fr.*) a prose-writer; **prō'ser.** — *adv.* **prō'sily.** — *ns.* **prō'siness; prō'sing** speaking or writing in a dull or prosy way. — *adj.* **prō'sy** dull, tedious, humdrum: addicted to prosing. — **prose'-man** (*Pope*), **prose'man** a writer of prose; **prose poem** a prose work or passage having some of the characteristics of poetry; **prose'-writer.** [Fr., — L. *prōsa* — *prorsus*, straightforward — *prō*, forward, *vertēre, versum*, to turn.]

prosector *prō-sekt'ər, n.* one who dissects a body for the illustration of anatomical lectures: the official anatomist of a zoological society. — *adj.* **prosecto'rial** (*-ōr', -ör'i-əl*). — *n.* **prosec'torship.** [L.L. *prōsector* — *prōsecāre, -sectum*, to cut up — *prō-*, away, *secāre*, to cut.]

prosecute *pros'i-kūt, v.t.* to follow onwards or pursue, in order to reach or accomplish: to engage in, practise: to follow up: to pursue, chase (*obs.*): to pursue by law: to bring before a court. — *v.i.* to carry on a legal prosecution. — *adj.* **pros'ecūtable.** — *ns.* **prosecū'tion** the act of prosecuting in any sense: the prosecuting party in legal proceedings; **pros'ecūtor** one who prosecutes or pursues any plan or business: one who carries on a civil or criminal suit: — *fem.* **pros'ecūtrix** (modern L.): — *pl.* **pros'ecūtrixes, prosecutrices** (*-kū-trī'sēz, -kū'tri-sēz*). — **director of public prosecutions, public prosecutor** one appointed to conduct criminal prosecutions in the public interest (in U.S., **prosecuting**

attorney, district attorney). [L. *prōsequī, -secūtus* — *prō*, onwards, *sequī*, to follow.]

proselyte *pros'i-līt, n.* one who has come over from one religion or opinion to another: a convert, esp. from paganism to Judaism. — *v.t.* and *v.i.* (*U.S.*) to proselytise. — *v.t.* **pros'elytise, -ize** to convert. — *v.i.* to make proselytes. — *ns.* **pros'elytiser, -izer; pros'elytism** being, becoming, or making a convert: conversion. — **proselyte of the gate** a heathen allowed to live in Palestine on making certain concessions to Judaism. [Gr. *prosēlytos*, a newcomer, resident foreigner — *pros*, to, and the stem *elyth-*, used to form aorists for *erchesthai*, to go.]

prosencephalon *pros-en-sef'ə-lon, n.* the fore-brain, comprising the cerebral hemispheres and olfactory processes. — *adj.* **prosencephalic** (*-si-fal'ik*). [Gr. *pros*, to, used as if for *pro*, before, *enkephalon*, brain — *en*, in, *kephalē*, head.]

prosenchyma *pros-eng'ki-mə, n.* a plant-tissue of long cells with pointed ends — conducting or supporting tissue. — *adj.* **prosenchymatous** (*-kim'ə-təs*). [Gr. *pros*, to, *enchyma*, an infusion, inpouring.]

proseuche, -cha *pros-ū'kē, -kə, ns.* a place of prayer, oratory: — *pl.* **proseu'chae** (*-kē*). [Gr. *proseuchē*, prayer, place of prayer — *pros*, to, *euchē*, prayer.]

prosilient *prō-sil'i-ənt, adj.* outstanding. — *n.* **prosil'iency.** [L. *prōsiliēns, -entis*, pr.p. of *prōsilīre*, to leap forward — *prō-*, forward, *salīre*, to leap.]

prosimian *prō-sim'i-ən, n.* a primate of the suborder **Prosimii**, e.g. the lemur, loris, tarsier. — Also *adj.* [pro-[1], L. *simia*, ape.]

prosing. See **prose.**

prosit *prō'sit, interj.* good luck to you, a salutation in drinking healths customary among German students. [L. *prōsit*, used as 3rd pers. sing. pres. subj. of L. *prōdesse*, to be of use — *prō(d)-*, for, *esse*, to be.]

proslambanomenos *pros-lam-ban-om'e-nos,* (*anc. Gr. mus.*) *n.* an additional note at the bottom of the scale. [Gr., pr.p. pass. of *proslambanein*, to take in addition — pfx. *pros-*, *lambanein*, to take.]

prosody *pros'ə-di, n.* the study of versification. — *adjs.* **prosodial** (*pros-, prəs-ō'di-əl*), **prosodic** (*-od'ik*), **-al.** — *ns.* **prosō'dian, pros'odist** one skilled in prosody. — *adv.* **prosod'ically.** [L. *prosōdia*, Gr. *prosōidiā* — *pros*, to, *ōidē*, a song.]

prosopagnosia *pros-ō-pag-nō'si-ə, n.* inability to recognise faces of persons well-known to the sufferer. [L.L. *prosopagnosia* — Gr. *prosōpon*, face, *a*, without, *gnōsis*, knowledge.]

prosopography *pros-ō-pog'rə-fi, n.* a biographical sketch, description of a person's appearance, character, life, etc.: the compiling or study of such material. — *adj.* **prosopograph'ical.** [Gr. *prosōpon*, face, person, *graphein*, to write.]

prosopon *pros-ō-pon', (theol.) n.* the outer appearance, personification or embodiment of one of the persons of the Trinity. — *ns.* **prosopopoeia, prosopopeia** (*pros-ō-pō-pē'ə,*) personification. — *adj.* **prosopop(o)e'ial.** [Gr. *prosōpopoiiā* — *prosōpon*, face, person, *poieein*, to make.]

prospect *pros'pekt, n.* outlook: direction of facing: a look-out or view-point (*Milt.*): a wide view: view, sight, field of view: a scene: a pictorial representation, view: position for being observed (*Shak.*): a survey or mental view: outlook upon the probable future: expectation: chance of success: a wide street (*Russ. prəs-pyekt'*): a prospect-glass (*obs.*): a probable customer (*U.S.*): a place thought likely to yield a valuable mineral (*mining*): a sample, or a test, or the yield of a test of a sample from such a place: a probable source of profit. — *v.i.* **prospect'** to look around: (*prəs-pekt'; U.S. pros'*) to make a search, esp. for chances of mining: to promise or yield results to the prospector. — *v.t.* (*-pekt'*) to face, view: (*-pekt'; pros'pekt*) to explore, search, survey, or test for profitable minerals. — *ns.* **prospect'ing** (*U.S. pros'*) searching a district for minerals with a view to further operations; **prospec'tion**

looking to the future: foresight. — *adj.* **prospec'tive** probable or expected future: looking forward: yielding distant views: looking to the future. — *n.* prospect. — *adv.* **prospec'tively.** — *ns.* **prospec'tiveness; prospec'tor** (*U.S. pros'*) one who prospects for minerals; **prospec'tus** the outline of any plan submitted for public approval, particularly of a literary work or of a joint-stock concern: an account of the organisation of a school: — *pl.* **prospec'tuses.** — **pros'pect-glass** a telescope or field glass; **prospect'ive-glass** a prospect-glass: a scrying crystal. [L. *prōspectus, -ūs* — *prōspicĕre, prōspectum* — *prō-*, forward, *specĕre*, to look.]

prosper *pros'pər, v.i.* to thrive: to get on: to experience favourable circumstances: to flourish: to turn out well. — *v.t.* to cause to prosper. — *n.* **prosperity** (*-per'i-ti*) the state of being prosperous: success: good fortune. — *adj.* **pros'perous** thriving: successful. — *adv.* **pros'perously.** — *n.* **pros'perousness.** [L. *prosper, prosperus.*]

prostaglandins *pros-tə-gland'inz, n.pl.* a group of chemical substances secreted by various parts of the body into the bloodstream and found to have a wide range of effects on the body processes, e.g. on muscle contraction. [*prostate gland*, a major source of these.]

prostate *pros'tāt, n.* a gland in males at the neck of the bladder. — Also **prostate gland.** — *n.* **prostatec'tomy** surgical removal of (part of) the prostate gland. — *adj.* **prostatic** (*pros-tat'ik*). — *ns.* **pros'tatism** (*-tət-izm*) a morbid condition associated with enlargement of the prostate; **prostatī'tis** inflammation of the prostate gland. [Gr. *prostatēs*, one who stands in front, the prostate — *pro*, before, *sta*, root of *histanai*, to set up.]

prosthesis *pros'thə-sis, pros-thē'sis, n.* addition of a prefix to a word, e.g. for ease of pronunciation (*linguistics*): also **prothesis**, q.v.): the fitting of artificial parts to the body: such an artificial part: — *pl.* **prostheses** (*-sēz*). — *adj.* **prosthetic** (*-thet'ik*) relating to prosthesis: pertaining to a group or radical of different nature, as a non-protein part of a protein molecule. — *n.* an artificial part of the body. — *n. sing.* **prosthet'ics** the surgery or dentistry involved in supplying artificial parts to the body. — *n.* **prosthet'ist.** [Gr. *prosthesis*, adj. *prosthetikos* — *pros*, to, *thesis*, putting.]

prosthodontia *pros-thō-don'shi-ə, n.* provision of false teeth. — Also *n. sing.* **prosthodon'tics.** — *n.* **prosthodon'tist.** [Gr. *prosthesis*, addition — *pros*, to, *thesis*, putting, and *odous, odontos*, tooth.]

prostitute *pros'ti-tūt, v.t.* to devote to, or offer or sell for, evil or base use: to hire out for sexual intercourse: to devote to such intercourse as a religious act: to degrade by publicity or commonness. — *adj.* openly devoted to lewdness: given over (to evil): basely venal: hackneyed, debased by commonness (*obs.*). — *n.* a person (usu. a woman or a homosexual man) who accepts money in return for sexual intercourse: a base hireling. — *ns.* **prostitū'tion** the act or practice of prostituting: devotion to base purposes; **pros'titūtor.** [L. *prōstituĕre, -ūtum*, to set up for sale — *prō*, before, *statuĕre*, to place.]

prostomium *prō-stō'mi-əm, n.* part of worm's head in front of the mouth. — *adj.* **prostō'mial.** [Gr. *pro*, before, *stoma*, mouth.]

prostrate *pros'trāt, adj.* prone: lying or bent with face on the ground: loosely, lying at length: procumbent, trailing (*bot.*): lying at mercy: reduced to helplessness: completely exhausted. — *v.t.* **prostrate'** (or *pros'*) to throw forwards on the ground: to lay flat: to overthrow: to reduce to impotence or exhaustion: to bend in humble reverence (*refl.*). — *n.* **prostrā'tion.** [L. *prōstrātus*, pa.p. of *prōsternĕre* — *prō*, forwards, *sternĕre*, to spread.]

prostyle *prō'stīl, (Gr. archit.) n.* a front portico without antae: a building with such a portico and no other. — *adj.* having a prostyle. [Gr. *prostȳlon* — *pro*, before, *stȳlos*, a column.]

prosy. See **prose.**

prosyllogism *prō-sil'ə-jizm, n.* a syllogism whose conclusion becomes the major premise of another. [Gr. *pro*, before, *syllogismos*, syllogism.]

prot-. See **proto-.**

protactinium *prōt-ak-tin'i-əm, n.* radioactive element (at. numb. 91; symbol Pa) that yields actinium on disintegration. [Gr. *prōtos*, first, and **actinium.**]

protagonist *prō-tag'ən-ist, n.* orig., the chief actor, character, or combatant: now, often applied to any (or in *pl.*, all) of the main personages or participants in a story or event: loosely, a champion, advocate. [Gr. *prōtos*, first, *agōnistēs*, a combatant, actor.]

protamine *prō'tə-mēn, n.* any of the simplest proteins, found esp. in the sperm of certain fish. [**proto-, amine.**]

protandry *prōt-an'dri, n.* in hermaphrodite organisms, ripening and shedding of the male elements before the female is ready to receive them: in flowers, opening of the anthers before the stigmas can receive pollen — opp. to *protogyny. — adj.* **protan'drous.** [Gr. *prōtos*, first, *anēr, andros*, man, male.]

protanopia *prō-tən-op'i-ə, n.* a form of colour-blindness in which red and green are confused because the retina does not respond to red. — *n.* **prō'tanope** a sufferer from protanopia. — *adj.* **prōtanop'ic** colour-blind to red. [Mod. L. *protanopia*.]

pro tanto. See **pro**[1].

protasis *prot'ə-sis, n.* the conditional clause of a conditional sentence — opp. to *apodosis*: the first part of a dramatic composition — opp. to *epitasis*: — *pl.* **prot'asēs.** — *adj.* **protatic** (*prə-tat'ik*). [Gr. *protasis*, proposition, premise, protasis — *pro*, before, *tasis*, a stretching, *teinein*, to stretch.]

Protea *prō'ti-ə, n.* a large South African genus of shrubs or small trees, of the mainly Australian family **Proteā'ceae**, with big cone-shaped heads of flowers: (without *cap.*) a plant of the genus. — *adj.* **proteā'ceous.** [**Proteus**; from the varied character of the family.]

Protean, protean. See **Proteus.**

protease. See **protein.**

protect *prə-, prō-tekt', v.t.* to shield from danger, injury, change, capture, loss: to defend: to strengthen: to seek to foster by import duties: to act as regent for (*Shak.*): to screen off for safety (e.g. machinery). — *adjs.* **protect'ed; protect'ing.** — *adv.* **protect'ingly.** — *ns.* **protec'tion** act of protecting: state of being protected: defence: that which protects: guard: a writing guaranteeing against molestation or interference: a fostering of home produce and manufactures by import duties: patronage: concubinage: control of a country's foreign relations, and sometimes internal affairs, without annexation; **protec'tionism; protec'tionist** one who favours the protection of trade by duties on imports — also *adj.* — *adj.* **protec'tive** affording protection: intended to protect: defensive: sheltering. — *n.* that which protects: a condom. — *adv.* **protec'tively.** — *ns.* **protec'tiveness; protec'tor** one who protects from injury or oppression: a protective device: a means of protection: a guard: a guardian: a regent: the head of the state during the Commonwealth (*Lord Protector*): — *fem.* **protec'tress, protec'trix.** — *adj.* **protec'toral** of a protector or a regent. — *n.* **protec'torāte** the position, office, term of office, or government of a protector: (*cap.*) the Commonwealth period (*hist.*): guardianship: authority over a vassal state: relation assumed by a state over a territory which it administers without annexation and without admitting the inhabitants to citizenship. — *adjs.* **protectorial** (*prō-tek-tōr'i-əl, -tör'i-əl*); **protec'torless.** — *ns.* **protec'torship; protec'tory** an institution for destitute or delinquent children. — **protected state** a state under the protection of another state but less subject to the control of that state than a protectorate; **protection money** money extorted from shopkeepers, businessmen, etc., as a bribe for leaving their property, business, etc., unharmed; **protective coloration** likeness in the colour of animals to their natural surroundings tending to prevent them from

being seen by their enemies; **protective custody** detention of a person for his personal safety or from doubt as to his possible actions; **protective tariff** an import tax designed to protect the home markets rather than raise revenue. [L. *prōtegĕre, -tēctum* — *prō-*, in front, *tegĕre*, to cover.]

protégé *prō', or pro'tə-zhā, n.* one under the protection or patronage of another: a pupil: a ward: — *fem.* **pro'tégée** (*-zhā*). [Fr., — pa.p. of *protéger*, to protect — L. *prōtegĕre*.]

proteiform. See **Proteus.**

protein *prō'tē-in, -tēn, n.* any member of a group of complex nitrogenous substances that play an important part in the bodies of plants and animals, compounds of carbon, hydrogen, oxygen, nitrogen, usually sulphur, often phosphorus, etc., easily hydrolysed into mixtures of amino-acids. — *ns.* **pro'tease** (*-tē-ās, -āz*) any enzyme that splits up proteins; **pro'teid** (*-tē-id*; *arch.*) a former name for protein. — *adjs.* **proteinaceous** (*prō-tēn-ā'shəs*), **proteinic** (*prō-tēn'ik*), **protein'ous.** — *n.* **proteolysis** (*-ol'i-sis*) splitting of proteins by enzymes. — *v.t.* **pro'teolyse, -yze** (*-ō-līz*). — *adj.* **proteolytic** (*-ō-lit'ik*). [Gr. *prōteios*, primary — *prōtos*, first.]

pro tem *prō'tem'*, short for **pro tempore** (q.v. under **pro**[1]).

protend *prō-tend', (arch.) v.t.* to stretch forth: to hold out. — *ns.* **protense'** (*Spens.*) extension in time; **proten'sion** duration; **proten'sity.** — *adj.* **proten'sive.** [L. *prōtendĕre, -tentus* (*-tēnsus*) — *prō-*, forward, *tendĕre*, to stretch.]

proteolysis, etc. See **protein.**

proterandry *prot-ər-an'dri, or prōt-, n.* protandry. — *adj.* **proteran'drous.** [Gr. *proteros*, earlier, *anēr, andros*, man, male.]

proterogyny *prot-, prōt-ər-oj'i-ni, or -og', n.* protogyny. — *adj.* **proterog'ynous.** [Gr. *proteros*, earlier, *gynē*, woman, female.]

Proterozoic *prot-ər-ō-zō'ik, or prōt-, n.* and *adj.* orig., Lower Palaeozoic (Cambrian to Silurian): Pre-Cambrian: Upper Pre-Cambrian. [Gr. *proteros*, earlier, *zōē*, life.]

protervity *prō-tûr'vi-ti, n.* peevishness: perversity: wantonness. [L. *prōtervus, prŏtervus*.]

protest *prə-, prō-test', v.i.* to express or record dissent or objection: to make solemn affirmation, professions, or avowal. — *v.t.* to make a solemn declaration of: to declare: to note, as a bill of exchange, on account of non-acceptance or non-payment: to proclaim (*Shak.*): to vow (*Shak.*): to call to witness (*Milt.*): to make a protest against. — *n.* **prō'test** an affirmation or avowal: a declaration of objection or dissent: the noting by a notary-public of an unpaid or unaccepted bill: a written declaration, usually by the master of a ship, stating the circumstances attending loss or injury of ship or cargo, etc. — *adj.* expressing, in order to express, dissent or objection. — *n.* **Protestant** (*prot'is-tənt*) one of those who, in 1529, protested against an edict of Charles V and the Diet of Spires denouncing the Reformation: a member, adherent, or sharer of the beliefs of one of those churches founded by the Reformers (formerly by some confined to Anglicans or Lutherans, now disavowed by some Anglicans): (without *cap.*) an avowed lover (*Herrick*): (without *cap.*; sometimes *prō-tes'tənt*) one who protests. — *adj.* **Protestant** (*prot'*) of, or pertaining to, Protestants, or more usually, Protestantism: (without *cap.;prot'is-*, or *prō-tes'tənt*) protesting. — *v.t.* **Prot'estantise, -ize.** — *ns.* **Prot'estantism** the Protestant religion: the state of being a Protestant; **protestation** (*prō-tes-tā'shən*) an avowal: an asseveration: a declaration in pleading: a protest (*rare*); **protest'er, -or** one who protests, esp. (*Scot. hist.*) a Remonstrant or opponent of the Resolutioners. — *adv.* **protest'ingly.** — **Protestant work ethic** an attitude to life stressing the virtue of hard work over enjoyment, popularly associated with the Protestant denominations; **under protest** unwillingly, having made a protest. [Fr. *protester* — L. *prōtestārī, -ātus*, to bear witness in public — *prō*, before, *testārī* — *testis*, a witness.]

Proteus *prō'tūs, -ti-əs, n.* an ancient Greek sea-god who assumed many shapes to evade having to foretell the future: a European genus of cave-dwelling tailed amphibians with persistent gills: (without *cap.*) a member of the genus, the olm: (with *cap.*) a genus of rodlike bacteria found in the intestines and in decaying organic matter: (without *cap.*) a member of the genus: — *pl.* **pro'teuses.** — *adjs.* **Protean, protean** (*prō-tē'ən* or *prō'ti-ən*) readily assuming different shapes: variable: inconstant; **proteiform** (*prō-tē'i-förm*). [Gr. *Prōteus*.]

Protevangelium *prōt-ev-an-jel'i-əm, n.* the promise to Eve: a gospel attributed to James the Less: an inferred source of the canonical gospels. [Gr. *prōtos*, first, L. *evangelium* — Gr. *euangelion*, gospel.]

prothalamion *prō-thə-lā'mi-on, n.* a poem celebrating a coming marriage: — *pl.* **prothalā'mia.** — Also **prothalā'mium** (*pl.* -**mia**). [App. coined by Spenser from Gr. *pro*, before, *thalamos*, a bride-chamber.]

prothallus *prō-thal'əs*, **prothallium** -*i-əm, ns.* the gametophyte or sexual generation in ferns and their allies, a small plate of tissue derived from a spore and bearing antheridia and archegonia: the homologous stage in gymnosperms: — *pls.* **prothall'ī, prothall'ia.** — *adjs.* **prothall'ial, prothall'ic, prothall'oid.** [Gr. *pro*, before, *thallos*, a young shoot.]

prothesis *proth'i-sis, n.* in the Greek Church the preliminary oblation of the eucharistic elements before the liturgy: the table used: the chapel or northern apse where it stands: development of an inorganic initial sound (*linguistics*). — *adj.* **prothetic** (*prə-, prō-thet'ik*). [Gr. *prothesis* — *pro*, before, and the root of *tithenai*, to place.]

prothonotary, protonotary *prō-t(h)on'ət-ə-ri, prō-t(h)ō-nō'tə-ri, ns.* a chief notary or clerk: a chief secretary of the chancery at Rome: a chief clerk or registrar of a court. — *adj.* **prot(h)onotā'rial.** — *n.* **prot(h)onotā'riat** the college constituted by the twelve apostolical prothonotaries (bishops and senior members of the curia) in Rome. [L.L. *prōt(h)onotārius* — Gr. *prōtos*, first, L. *notārius*, a clerk.]

prothorax *prō-thō'raks, -thör', n.* the anterior segment of the thorax of insects: — *pl.* **prothor'axes, prothor'aces** (*-ə-sēz*). — *adj.* **prothoracic** (-*ras'*). [Pfx. **pro-**[1].]

prothrombin *prō-throm'bin, n.* a proteinlike substance present in blood plasma. [**pro-**[1], **thrombin**.]

prothyl(e). See **protyle**.

Protista *prō-tis'tə, n.pl.* a large group of unicellular organisms on the border-line between plants and animals: a proposed term for a biological kingdom including Protozoa and Protophyta. — *n.* **pro'tist** any member of the Protista. — *adj.* **protist'ic.** — *ns.* **protistol'ogist; protistol'ogy.** [Gr. *prōtistos*, very first — *prōtos*, first.]

protium *prō'ti-əm, -shi-əm, n.* ordinary hydrogen of atomic weight 1, distinguished from deuterium and tritium. [Gr. *prōtos*, first.]

proto- *prō'tō-*, **prot-** *prōt-*, in composition, first: first of a series: first-formed: primitive: ancestral: denoting a protolanguage. [Gr. *prōtos*, first.]

protoactinium *prō-tō-ak-tin'i-əm, n.* a former variant of **protactinium**.

Protochordata *prō-tō-körd-ā'tə, n.pl.* a division of the Chordata, distinguished by absence of a cranium, vertebral column and specialised anterior sense organs. [**proto-, Chordata**.]

Protococcus *prō-tō-kok'əs, n.* an abandoned genus of rounded unicellular algae, one of which renamed *Pleurococcus vulgaris* forms a green film common on trees, etc. — *adj.* **protococc'al.** — *n.pl.* **Protococcales** (*-ā'lēz*) the order of green algae to which *Pleurococcus vulgaris* belongs. [**proto-**, and Gr. *kokkos*, a berry.]

protocol *prō'tō-kol, n.* an original note, minute, or draft of an instrument or transaction: a draft treaty: an official or formal account or record: a factual record of observations, e.g. in scientific experiments (chiefly

U.S.): a record of transfer of lands (*U.S.*): an official formula: a body of diplomatic etiquette: a set of rules governing the transmission of data between two computers which cannot communicate directly. — *v.i.* to issue, form, protocols. — *v.t.* to make a protocol of: — *pr.p.* **pro'tocolling;** *pa.t.* and *pa.p.* **pro'tocolled.** — Also **prō'tocolise, -ize.** — *n.* **prō'tocolist** a registrar or clerk. [Fr. *protocole* — L.L. *prōtocollum* — Late Gr. *prōtokollon*, a glued-on descriptive first leaf of a MS. — Gr. *prōtos*, first, *kolla*, glue.]

protogalaxy *prō-tō-gal'ək-si, n.* a large cloud of gas supposed to be slowly condensing into stars, an early stage in the formation of a galaxy. [**proto-**.]

protogine *prō'tō-jin, -jēn, n.* a gneissose granite of the Alps with sericite. [Gr. *prōtos*, first, *gīnesthai*, to come into being (as once thought to be the first-formed granite).]

protogyny *prōt-oj'i-ni*, or *-og', n.* in hermaphrodite organisms, ripening of the female germ-cells before stamens. — opp. to *protandry*. — *adj.* **protog'ynous.** [**proto-**, and Gr. *gynē*, woman, female.]

proto-historic *prō-tō-his-tor'ik, adj.* belonging to the earliest age of history, just after the prehistoric and before the development of written records, etc. — *n.* **proto= his'tory.** [**proto-**.]

protohuman *prō-tō-hū'mən, n.* a prehistoric primate, a supposed ancestor of modern man. — Also *adj.* [**proto-**.]

protolanguage *prō'tō-lang-gwij, n.* a hypothetical language (as *Proto-Germanic, Proto-Indo-European*) regarded as the ancestor of other recorded or existing languages, and reconstructed by comparing these. [**proto-**.]

protolithic *prō-tō-lith'ik, adj.* of or pertaining to the earliest Stone Age. [**proto-**, and Gr. *lithos*, stone]

protomartyr *prō'tō-mär-tər, n.* the first martyr in any cause, esp. St Stephen. [Late Gr. *prōtomartyr*.]

protomorphic *prō-tō-mörf'ik, adj.* primordial: primitive. [**proto-, morphic**.]

proton *prō'ton, n.* an elementary particle of positive charge and unit atomic mass — the atom of the lightest isotope of hydrogen without its electron. — *adj.* **protonic** (*-ton'ik*). — **proton beam** a beam of protons produced by a proton accelerator; **proton synchrotron** see **accelerator**. [Gr., neut. of *prōtos*, first.]

protonema *prō-tə-nē'mə, n.* a branched filament produced by germination of a moss spore, giving rise to mossplants from buds: — *pl.* **protonē'mata.** — *adjs.* **protonē'mal, protonematal** (*-nem'ə-təl*). [**proto-**, and Gr. *nēma*, thread.]

protonotary. Same as **prothonotary**.

protopathic *prō-tə-path'ik, adj.* of or relating to a certain type of nerve which is only affected by the coarser stimuli, e.g. pain: of or relating to this kind of reaction. — *n.* **protop'athy.** [**proto-, pathic**.]

Protophyta *prōt-of'i-tə, n.pl.* a group of unicellular plants. — *n.* **protophyte** (*prō'tə-fīt*) one of the Protophyta. — *adj.* **protophytic** (*-fit'ik*). [**proto-**, and Gr. *phyton*, a plant.]

protoplasm *prō'tə-plazm, n.* living matter, the physical basis of life. — *adjs.* **protoplasm'ic, protoplas'mal, protoplasmat'ic.** — *n.* **prō'toplast** he who, or that which, was first formed: an original: the first parent: an energid (*biol.*). — *adj.* **protoplas'tic.** [**proto-**, and Gr. *plasma*, form — *plassein*, to form.]

protospatharius *prō-tə-spä-thā'ri-əs, n.* captain of the guards at Byzantium. — Also (Fr.) **protospat(h)aire** (*-thär', -tār'*). [Gr. *prōtos*, first, *spathārios*, a guardsman — *spathē*, a blade.]

protostar *prō'tō-stär, n.* a condensing mass of gas, a supposed early stage in the formation of a star. [**proto-**.]

protostele *prō'tə-stēl, -stēl-i, (bot.) n.* a stele in which the vascular tissue forms a solid core, with centrally-placed xylem surrounded by phloem. [**proto-, stele**.]

Prototheria *prō-tə-thē'ri-ə, n.pl.* the monotremes. — *adj.* **protothē'rian.** [**proto-**, and Gr. *thēr*, wild beast.]

Prototracheata prō-tə-trak-i-ā'tə, n.pl. a class of primitive tracheate arthropods to which Peripatus belongs. [proto-; see **trachea**.]
prototrophic prō-tō-trof'ik, adj. feeding only on inorganic matter. [proto-, and Gr. trophē, food.]
prototype prō'tə-tīp, n. the first or original type or model from which anything is copied: an exemplar: a pattern: an ancestral form. — v.t. to make, or use, a prototype of. — adjs. **pro'totypal, prototypical** (-tip'). [Fr., — Gr. prōtos, first, typos, a type.]
protoxide prō-tok'sīd, n. that oxide of a series which has the smallest number of oxygen atoms. [proto-.]
protoxylem prō-tə-zī'ləm, (bot.) n. the first part of the xylem to be formed. [proto-.]
Protozoa prō-tū-zō'ə, n.pl. the lowest and simplest of animals, unicellular forms or colonies multiplying by fission. — ns. **protozō'an, protozō'on** one of the Protozoa: — pls. -zō'ans, -zō'a. — adjs. **protozō'an; protozō'ic** pertaining to the Protozoa: containing remains of the earliest life of the globe (variously applied) (obs. geol.); **protozoolog'ical** (-zō-ə-). — ns. **protozool'ogist; protozool'ogy.** [proto-, and Gr. zōion, an animal.]
protract prō-trakt', v.t. to draw out or lengthen in time: to prolong: to put off in time (obs.): to lengthen out: to protrude: to draw to scale. — adj. **protrac'ted** drawn out in time: prolonged: postponed (obs.): lengthened out: drawn to scale. — adv. **protrac'tedly.** — adjs. **protrac'tile** (-tīl, in U.S. -til), **protrac'tible** susceptible of being thrust out. — n. **protrac'tion** (-shən) act of protracting or prolonging: the delaying of the termination of a thing: the plotting or laying down of the dimensions of anything on paper: a plan drawn to scale. — adj. **protrac'tive** drawing out in time: prolonging: delaying. — n. **protrac'tor** one who, or that which, protracts: an instrument for laying down angles on paper: a muscle whose contraction draws a part forward or away from the body. [L. prōtrahĕre, -tractum — prō, forth, trahĕre, to draw.]
protreptic prō-trep'tik, adj. hortative. — n. an exhortation. — adj. **protrep'tical.** [Gr. protreptikos — pro, forward, trepein, to turn, direct.]
protrude prō-trōōd', v.t. to thrust or push out or forward: to obtrude. — v.i. to stick out, project. — adjs. **protrud'able, protrusible** (-trōōs'i-bl), **protru'sile** (-sīl, in U.S. -sil) able to be protruded; **protru'dent.** — n. **protru'sion** (-zhən) the act of protruding: the state of being protruded: that which protrudes. — adj. **protru'sive** thrusting or impelling forward: protruding. — adv. **protru'sively.** — n. **protru'siveness.** [L. prōtrūdĕre, -trūsum — prō, forward, trūdĕre, to thrust.]
protuberance prō-tūb'ər-əns, n. a bulging out: a swelling. — adj. **protū'berant.** — adv. **protū'berantly.** — v.i. **protū'berate** to bulge out. — n. **protūberā'tion.** [L. prōtūberāre, -ātum — prō, forward, tūber, a swelling.]
protyle, prothyle prō't(h)īl, **protyl, prothyl** prō't(h)il, ns. a hypothetical primitive matter from which the chemical elements have been thought to be formed. [Gr. prōtos, first, hȳlē, matter.]
proud prowd, adj. having excessive self-esteem: arrogant: haughty: having a proper sense of self-respect: having an exulting sense of credit due to or reflected upon oneself: having a glowing feeling of gratification (because of; with of): giving reason for pride or boasting: manifesting pride: having an appearance of pride, vigour, boldness, and freedom: stately: mettlesome: swelling: sexually excited (esp. of some female animals): projecting, standing out, as from a plane surface, e.g. a nail-head. — adj. **proud'ish** somewhat proud. — adv. **proud'ly.** — n. **proud'ness** (rare) pride. — **proud flesh** a growth or excrescence of flesh in a wound. — adjs. **proud'-heart'ed** (Shak.) having a proud spirit; **proud'-mind'ed** (Shak.) proud in mind; **proud'=pied** (Shak.) gorgeously variegated; **proud'-stom'ached** (arch.) of haughty spirit, arrogant. — **do someone proud** (coll.) to treat someone sumptuously: to give honour to someone. [O.E. prūd, prūt, proud; perh.

from a L.L. word connected with L. prōdesse, to be of advantage.]
proul, prouler. Earlier forms of **prowl, prowler.**
Proustian prōōs'ti-ən, adj. pertaining to Marcel Proust (1871–1922), French novelist. — n. an admirer of Proust.
proustite prōōs'tīt, n. a red silver ore, sulphide of arsenic and silver. [J. L. Proust (1754–1826), French chemist, who distinguished it from pyrargyrite.]
provand, provend prov'ənd, **proviant** prov'i-ənt, ns. an allowance of food: provender (Shak.): provisions: fodder. — adj. **prov'ant** issued to soldiers, hence inferior. [M.L.G. provande, Du. provande, proviand, Ger. Proviant, app. — L.L. provenda for L. praebenda — praebēre, to allow.]
prove prōōv, v.t. to test, experience, suffer: to test the genuineness of: to ascertain: to establish or ascertain as truth by argument or otherwise: to demonstrate: to check by the opposite operation (arith.): to obtain probate of: to cause or allow (dough) to rise. — v.i. to make trial: to turn out: to be shown afterwards: to become (arch.): to turn out well (obs.): (of dough) to rise: — pa.p. **proved.** — Also (obs.) **preve** with pa.p. **prov'en** surviving as the usu. form in U.S. (prōōv'n) and becoming commoner in Britain; already retained specif. for Scots law (prōv'n); also **pree** (Scot.). — adj. **prov(e)'able.** — adv. **prov(e)'ably.** — n. **prov'er.** — adj. **prov'ing** testing, as in **proving ground** a place for testing scientifically (also fig.), **proving flight** test flight. — **the exception proves the rule** the making of an exception proves that the rule holds good otherwise. [O.Fr. prover — L. probāre — probus, excellent; partly perh. — O.E. prōfian, to assume to be — L. probāre. O.Fr. had two forms of the verb, using respectively the vowel developed orig. in stressed, unstressed (as above), positions from L. o, and M.E. also has two forms, giving **preeve, prieve**, etc., as well as **prove**.]
provection prō-vek'shən, (linguistics) n. the transferring of a letter from the end of one word to the beginning of the next, e.g. a newt from an ewt. [L.L. provectio, — L. pro-, forth, vehĕre, to carry.]
proveditor prō-ved'i-tər, **provedor(e), providor** prov-i-dōr', -dōr', ns. a high official, governor, inspector, commissioner: a purveyor. [It. provveditore, Port. provedor, Sp. proveedor.]
proven prōv'n, prōōv'n. See **prove.** — **not proven** a Scottish legal verdict declaring that guilt has been neither proved nor disproved.
provenance prov'i-nəns, n. source, esp. of a work of art. [Fr., — L. prō-, forth, venīre, to come.]
Provençal prov-ä-säl, adj. of or pertaining to Provence, in France, or to its inhabitants or language. — n. a native or the language of Provence, langue d'oc. — adj. **Provençale** (prov-ä-säl) in cooking, prepared with oil and garlic and usu. tomatoes. [L. prōvinciālis — prōvincia, province.]
Provence-rose pro-väs'-rōz, n. the cabbage rose, Rosa centifolia, orig. cultivated in Provence.
provend. See **provand.**
provender prov'in-dər, -ən-dər, n. food: dry food for beasts, as hay or corn: esp. a mixture of meal and cut straw or hay. — v.t. and v.i. to feed. [O.Fr. provendre for provende — L.L. provenda; see **provand.**]
provenience prō-vē'ni-əns, (chiefly U.S.) n. provenance. [L. prōvenīre; see **provenance.**]
proventriculus prō-ven-trik'ū-ləs, (zool.) n. in birds, the anterior thin-walled part of the stomach, containing the gastric glands: in insects and crustaceans, the muscular thick-walled chamber of the gut. [pro-[1], and L. ventriculus, dim. of venter, belly.]
proverb prov'ərb, n. a short familiar sentence expressing a supposed truth or moral lesson: a byword: a saying that requires explanation (B.): (in pl. with cap.) a book of maxims in the Old Testament: a dramatic composition in which a proverb gives name and character to the plot. — v.t. to speak of proverbially: to make a byword of: to provide with a proverb. — adj. **prover'-**

bial (*prə-vûr'bi-əl*) like or of the nature of a proverb: expressed or mentioned in a proverb: notorious. — *v.t.* **prover'bialise, -ize** to speak in proverbs. — *ns.* **prover'bialism** a saying in the form of, or like, a proverb; **prover'bialist.** — *adv.* **prover'bially.** [Fr. *proverbe* — L. *prōverbium* — *prō-*, publicly, *verbum*, a word.]

proviant. See **provand.**

provide *prə-, prō-vīd'*, *v.t.* to make ready beforehand: to prepare for future use (*rare*): to supply: to appoint or give a right to a benefice, esp. before it is actually vacant: to stipulate. — *v.i.* to procure supplies, means, or whatever may be desirable, make provision: to take measures (for or against). — *adj.* **provi'dable.** — *pa.p.* or *conj.* **provi'ded,** *pres.p.* or *conj.* **provī'ding** (often with *that*) on condition: upon these terms: with the understanding. — *n.* **provī'der.** — **provided school** formerly, in England and Wales, a school maintained by, and under the management of, the local authority. [L. *prōvidēre* — *prō*, before, *vidēre*, to see.]

providence *prov'i-dəns*, *n.* foresight: prudent management and thrift: timely preparation: the foresight and benevolent care of God (*theol.*): God, considered in this relation (usu. with *cap.*; *theol.*): an ordering or intervention by God for this purpose (*theol.*): an occurrence attributed to God's ordering or intervention (*theol.*): a disaster (*U.S.*). — *adjs.* **prov'ident** seeing beforehand, and providing for the future: prudent: thrifty: frugal; **providential** (*-den'shl*) affected by, or proceeding from, divine providence: provident (*rare*). — *advs.* **providen'tially; prov'idently.** — **provident society** same as **friendly society.** [L. *prōvidēns, -entis*, pr.p. of *prōvidēre* — *prō*, before, *vidēre*, to see.]

providor. See **proveditor.**

province *prov'ins*, *n.* a portion of an empire or a state marked off for purposes of government or in some way historically distinct: the district over which an archbishop has jurisdiction: a territorial division of the Jesuits, Templars, and other orders: a faunal or floral area: a region: vaguely, a field of duty, activity, or knowledge: a department: (in *pl.*) all parts of the country but the capital (esp. *theat.* and *journalism*). — *adj.* **provincial** (*prə-vin'shl*) relating to a province: belonging to a province or the provinces: local: showing the habits and manners of a province: unpolished: narrow. — *n.* an inhabitant of a province or country district: an unpolished person: the superintendent of the heads of the religious houses in a province (*R.C.*). — *v.t.* **provin'cialise, -ize** to render provincial. — *ns.* **provin'cialism** a manner, a mode of speech, or a turn of thought peculiar to a province or a country district: a local expression: state or quality of being provincial: ignorance and narrowness of interests shown by one who gives his attention entirely to local affairs; **provin'cialist; provinciality** (*-shi-al'i-ti*). — *adv.* **provin'cially.** [Fr., — L. *prōvincia*, an official charge, hence a province.]

provincial-rose *prə-vin'shl-rōz*, *n.* a rose, variety of *Rosa gallica*, cultivated at *Provins* in Seine-et-Marne, France (also **prov'ince-rose, Prov'ins rose**): a shoe rosette (*Shak.*).

provine *prə-vīn'*, *v.t.* and *v.i.* to propagate by layering. [Fr. *provigner* — O.Fr. *provain* — L. *prōpāgō, -inis*, a slip, layer.]

provirus *prō-vī'rəs*, *n.* the form of a virus when it is integrated into the DNA of a host cell. — *adj.* **provī'ral.** [**pro-²** (*b*).]

provision *prə-vizh'ən*, *n.* act of providing: that which is provided or prepared: measures taken beforehand: a clause in a law or a deed: a stipulation: a rule for guidance: an appointment by the pope to a benefice not yet vacant: preparation: previous agreement: a store or stock: (commonly in *pl.*) store of food: (in *pl.*) food. — *v.t.* to supply with provisions or food. — *adj.* **provi'sional** provided for the occasion: to meet necessity: (of e.g. arrangement) adopted on the understanding that it will probably be changed later: con-

taining a provision. — *n.* **Provi'sional** a member of the Provisional Irish Republican Army, the militant breakaway wing of the Official IRA (coll. shortening **Prō'vō**: — *pl.* **Pro'vos**). — *adv.* **provi'sionally.** — *adj.* **provi'sionary** (*rare*) provisional. — **provisional judgment** a judgment given as far as the available evidence admits, but subject to correction under more light; **provisional order** an order granted by a secretary of state, which, when confirmed by the legislature, has the force of an act of parliament; **provisional remedy** a means of detaining in safety a person or property until a decision upon some point in which they are concerned be come to; **provision merchant** a general dealer in articles of food. [Fr., — L. *prōvīsiō, -ōnis* — *prōvidēre*; see **provide.**]

proviso *prə-, prō-vī'zō*, *n.* a provision or condition in a deed or other writing: the clause containing it: any condition: — *pl.* **provī'sos, provī'soes** (*-zōz*). — *adv.* **provī'sorily** (*-zə-ri-li*). — *adj.* **provī'sory** containing a proviso or condition: conditional: making provision for the time: temporary. [From the L. law phrase *prōvīsō quod*, it being provided that.]

provisor *prə-, prō-vī'zər*, *n.* one who provides: a purveyor: a person to whom the pope has granted the right to the next vacancy in a benefice. — **Statute of Provisors** an act of the English parliament passed in 1351 to prevent the pope from exercising the power of creating provisors. [L. *prōvīsor, -ōris*, provider.]

provitamin *prō-vit'ə-min, -vīt'*, *n.* a substance not a vitamin that is readily transformed into a vitamin within an organism. [L. *prō*, before, and **vitamin.**]

Provo. See **Provisional** under **provision.**

provocable, etc. See **provoke.**

provoke *prə-vōk'*, *v.t.* to call forth, evoke (feelings, desires, etc.): to summon (*arch.*): to call out, challenge (*obs.*): excite or call into action, stimulate: to incite, bring about: to excite with anger or sexual desire: to annoy, exasperate. — *v.i.* (*Dryden*) to appeal. — *adj.* **provocable** (*prov'ək-ə-bl*), **provōk'able.** — *ns.* **prov'ocant; provocateur** (*pro-vo-ka-tœr*; Fr.) one who provokes unrest and dissatisfaction for political ends; **provocā'tion** act of provoking: that which provokes: any cause of danger. — *adj.* **provocative** (*-vok'*) tending, or designed, to provoke or excite. — *n.* anything that provokes. — *adv.* **provoc'atively.** — *ns.* **provoc'ativeness; prov'ocātor.** — *adjs.* **provoc'atory; provōk'able** (older spelling **-vōc'-**). — *ns.* **provoke'ment** (*Spens.*); **provōk'er.** — *adj.* **provōk'ing** irritating. — *adv.* **provōk'ingly.** [L. *prōvocāre, -ātum* — *prō-*, forth, *vocāre*, to call.]

provost *prov'əst*, *n.* the dignitary set over a cathedral or collegiate church: in certain colleges, the head: in Scotland, the chief magistrate of a burgh, answering to mayor in England: an officer who arrests and keeps in custody (*Shak.*). — *ns.* **prov'ostry** the office or authority of a provost; **prov'ostship** the office of a provost. — **provost-mar'shal** (*prə-vō'*; U.S. *prō'*) head of military police, an officer with special powers for enforcing discipline and securing prisoners until trial (*army*): officer (master-at-arms) having charge of prisoners (*navy*); **provost-ser'geant** (*prə-vō'*) sergeant of military police. — **Lord Provost** chief magistrate of Edinburgh, Glasgow, Perth, Aberdeen, or Dundee; **Lady Provost** the wife (or other female relative) of a Lord Provost as supporting him in certain of his official duties. [O.E. *profast* (*prafost*), O.Fr. *provost* (Fr. *prévôt*) — L.L. *prōpositus* — *prō-* for *prae*, at the head, *positus*, set.]

prow¹ *prow*, formerly sometimes *prō*, *n.* the forepart of a ship: the nose of an aeroplane: a projecting front part: a ship (*poet.*). [Fr. *proue*, or Port., Sp., or Genoese *proa* — L. *prōra* — Gr. *prōirā*.]

prow² *prow*, *adj.* (*arch.*) valiant: — *superl.* **prow'est.** — *n.* **prow'ess** bravery: valour: daring: accomplishment. — *adj.* **prow'essed.** [O.Fr. *prou* (Fr. *preux*); conn. with L. *prōd-* in *prōdesse.*]

prowl *prowl*, earlier *prōl*, *v.i.* to keep moving about as if in search of something: to rove in search of prey or plunder. — *n.* the act of prowling: a roving for prey. — *n.* **prowl'er.** — *n.* and *adj.* **prowl'ing.** — *adv.* **prowl'-ingly.** — **prowl car** (chiefly *U.S.*) a police patrol car. — **on the prowl** occupied in prowling.   [M.E. *prollen*; origin unknown.]

proximate *proks'i-mit, -māt, adj.* nearest or next: without anything between, as a cause and its effect: near and immediate. — *adj.* **prox'imal** (*biol.*) at the near, inner, or attached end (opp. to *distal*). — *advs.* **prox'imally; prox'imately.** — *ns.* **proximā'tion, proxim'ity** immediate nearness in time, place, relationship, etc. - *adv.* **prox'imo** next month — often written **prox.** (for L. *proximō mēnse*). — **proximate cause** a cause which immediately precedes the effect; **proximate object** immediate object; **proximity fuse** a device for causing a missile to explode when it comes near the object.   [L. *proximus*, next, superl. from *propior* (compar.) — *prope*, near.]

proxy *prok'si, n.* the agency of one who acts for another: one who acts or votes for another: the writing by which he is authorised to do so: a substitute. — *adj.* **prox'y= wedd'ed** (*Tenn.*) wedded by proxy.   [procuracy.]

proyn, proyne *proin.* Obs. forms of **prune**[1,2,3].

prozymite *proz'i-mīt, n.* one who uses leavened bread in the eucharist — opp. to *azymite*.   [Gr. *prozȳmia*, ferments.]

Pruce *proōs, (obs.) n.* Prussia. — *adj.* Prussian.   [A.Fr. *Prus, Pruz*, etc.]

prude *proōd, n.* a person of priggish or affected modesty: one who pretends extreme propriety. — Also *adj.* (*rare*). — *n.* **pru'dery** manners of a prude. — *adj.* **pru'dish.** — *adv.* **pru'dishly.** — *n.* **pru'dishness.**   [O.Fr. *prode*, fem. of *prou, prod*, excellent; cf. **prow**[2], **proud**.]

prudent *proō'dənt, adj.* cautious and wise in conduct: discreet: characterised by, behaving with, showing, having, or dictated by forethought. — *n.* **pru'dence** quality of being prudent: wisdom applied to practice: attention to self-interest: caution. — *adj.* **prudential** (*-den'shl*) having regard to considerations of prudence: relating to prudence: prudent: concerned with administration (*U.S.*). — *n.* (generally *pl.*) a matter or consideration of prudence: a prudent maxim. — *ns.* **pruden'tialism** a system based on prudence alone; **pruden'tialist; prudentiality** (*-den-shi-al'i-ti*). — *advs.* **pruden'tially; pru'dently.**   [L. *prūdēns, prūdentis*, contr. of *prōvidēns*, pr.p. of *prōvidēre*, to foresee.]

prudery. See **prude.**

prud'homme *prü-dom', (obs.) n.* a discreet man: a skilled workman: in France, a member of a board for settling labour disputes.   [O.Fr. *prud* or *prod* (nom. *pros*), good, *homme*, man.]

prudish, etc. See **prude.**

pruh. See **proo.**

pruina *proō-ī'nə, (bot.) n.* a powdery bloom or waxy secretion. — *adj.* **pruinose** (*proō'i-nōs*) covered with pruina: having a frosted look.   [L. *pruīna*, hoar-frost.]

pruine. A Shakespearian spelling of **prune**[3].

prune[1] *proōn, v.t.* to trim by lopping off superfluous parts: to divest of anything superfluous (*fig.*): to remove by pruning. — Formerly also **proin(e), proyn(e).** — *ns.* **pru'ner; pru'ning** the act of pruning or trimming. — **pru'ning-bill, -hook** a hooked bill for pruning with; **pru'ning-knife** a large knife with a slightly hooked point for pruning. — *n.pl.* **pru'ning-shears** shears for pruning shrubs, etc.   [O.Fr. *proignier*; origin unknown.]

prune[2] *proōn, (arch.) v.t.* to preen. — Formerly also **proin(e), proyn(e), proign.**   [Origin obscure.]

prune[3] *proōn, n.* a plum (*obs.*): a dried plum: a plum suitable for drying (*U.S.*): the dark purple colour of prune juice: a dud pilot (*airmen's slang*): a despised or silly person (*coll.*). — Obs. forms **pruine, prewyn** (*Shak.*), **proin(e), proyn(e).** — *adj.* of the colour of prune juice. — **prunes and prisms** part of a formula for setting the lips, 'serviceable in the formation of a demeanour' (Dickens, *Little Dorrit*).   [Fr., — L.

prūna, pl. of *prūnum* (taken for a *sing.*); cf. Gr. *prou(m)non*, plum.]

prunella[1] *proō-nel'ə, n.* sore throat: quinsy: (*cap.*; also **Brunella**) the self-heal genus of labiate plants, once reputed to cure prunella.   [Latinised from Ger. *Bräune*, quinsy (from the brownness of the tongue), or L.L. *brūnus* — general Germanic *brūn*, brown.]

prunella[2] *proō-nel'ə, n.* a strong silk or woollen stuff, formerly used for academic and clerical gowns and women's shoes — also **prunelle', prunell'o** (*pl.* **prunell'-os**). — *adj.* of prunella.   [App. Fr. *prunelle*, sloe, dim. of *prune*, plum.]

Prunella *proō-nel'ə, n.* the generic name for the hedge-sparrow genus — formerly **Accentor**: (without *cap.*) a member of the genus.   [L. *prunum*, a plum.]

prunello[1] *proō-nel'ō, n.* a little prune: a kind of dried plum: — *pl.* **prunell'os.**   [Obs. It. *prunella*, dim. of *pruna* (now *prugna*), plum.]

prunello[2]. See **prunella**[2].

prunt *prunt, n.* a moulded glass ornament on glass: a tool for making it. — *adj.* **prunt'ed.**   [Origin uncertain.]

prurient *proō'ri-ənt, adj.* itching: uneasily or morbidly interested, curious, or craving: dallying with lascivious thoughts: causing itching (*bot., rare*). — *ns.* **pru'rience, pru'riency.** — *adv.* **pru'riently.**   [L. *prūriēns, -entis*, pr.p. of *prūrīre*, to itch.]

prurigo *proō-rī'gō, n.* an eruption on the skin, causing great itching: — *pl.* **pruri'gos.** — *adjs.* **pruriginous** (*-rij'i-nəs*); **prurit'ic** pertaining to pruritus. — *n.* **prurī'tus** itching.   [L. *prūrigō, -inis, prūrītus, -ūs* — *prūrīre*, to itch.]

Prussian *prush'ən, adj.* of or pertaining to *Prussia*, a former state of N. Central Europe. — *n.* an inhabitant, native, or citizen of Prussia. — *v.t.* and *v.i.* **Pruss'ianise, -ize** to make or become Prussian. — *ns.* **Pruss'ianiser, -z-; Pruss'ianism** spirit of Prussian nationality: often used for arrogant militarism; **prussiate** (*prus'* or *prush'-i-āt*) a cyanide: a ferricyanide: a ferrocyanide. — *adj.* **pruss'ic** (also sometimes *proōs'*), pertaining to Prussian blue. — *n.* **Prussificā'tion.** — *v.t.* **Pruss'ify** to Prussianise, assimilate to the Prussian. — **Prussian** (also without *cap.*) **blue** ferric ferrocyanide, a colour pigment, discovered in Berlin: the very dark blue colour of this; **prussic acid** hydrocyanic acid, a deadly poison, first obtained from Prussian blue. — **Old Prussian** the extinct Baltic language of the former inhabitants of East and West Prussia.

pry[1] *prī, v.i.* to peer or peep into that which is private (also *fig.*): to examine things with impertinent curiosity: — *pr.p.* **prying;** *pa.t.* and *pa.p.* **pried;** *3rd pers. sing. pr.t.* **pries.** — *n.* a prying: one who pries — cf. *Paul Pry*, in John Poole's (1792–1879) comedy so called, first produced in 1825. — *n.* **prī'er** one who pries — also **pry'er.** — *n.* and *adj.* **pry'ing.** — *adv.* **pry'ingly.** — **pry out** to investigate or find out by prying.   [M.E. *prien*; origin unknown.]

pry[2] *prī, v.t.* a form of **prize**[1].

prys, pryse. Old spellings of **price, prize**[3].

pryse *prīz, (Scott) n.* a horn-blast at the taking or killing of a deer.   [O.Fr. *pris*, taken; cf. **prize**[2].]

prytaneum *prit-an-ē'əm, (ant.) n.* the town-hall of an ancient Greek city: — *pl.* **prytanē'a.**   [Latinised from Gr. *prytaneion* — *prytanis*, a presiding magistrate.]

pr'ythee, prythee *pridh'ē.* Same as **prithee.**

Przewalski's horse *pr-zhe-val'skiz hörs,* a wild horse discovered in Central Asia by Nikolai *Przewalski* (1839–88). — Various other spellings exist.

psalm *säm, n.* a devotional song or hymn, esp. one of those included in the Old Testament **Book of Psalms.** — *n.* **psalmist** (*säm'ist*) a composer of psalms, esp. (with *cap.*) David. — *adjs.* **psalmodic** (*sal-mod'ik*), **-al** pertaining to psalmody. — *v.i.* **psalmodise, -ize** (*sal', säm'*) to practise psalmody. — *ns.* **psalmodist** (*sal', sä'mə-dist*) a singer of psalms; **psalmody** (*sal',* or *säm';* Gr. *psalmōidiā*, singing to the harp) the singing of psalms, esp. in public worship: psalms collectively. — **psalm'-book** a book containing psalms for purposes of worship; **psalm'-tune**. [O.E. (*p*)*salm*, (*p*)*sealm* — L.L. *psalmus* — Gr. *psalmos*, music of or to a stringed instrument — *psallein*, to pluck.]

Psalter *söl'tər, n.* the **Book of Psalms**, esp. when separately printed: (without *cap.*) a book of psalms. — *adj.* **psalterian** (*söl-tē'ri-ən*) pertaining to a psalter: like a psaltery. — *ns.* **psal'tery** an ancient and mediaeval stringed instrument like the zither, played by plucking: (*cap.*; *rare*) the Psalter; **psal'tress** a woman who plays upon the psaltery. [O.E. *saltere* — L. *psaltērium* — Gr. *psaltērion*, a psaltery.]

psalterium *söl-tē'ri-əm, n.* the third division of a ruminant's stomach, the omasum or manyplies: — *pl.* **psaltē'ria**. [From the appearance of its lamellae, like a stringed instrument; see the foregoing.]

psammite *sam'īt*, (*rare*) *n.* any rock composed of sandgrains. — *adj.* **psammitic** (*-it'ik*). — *n.* **psamm'ophil(e)** a sand-loving plant. — *adj.* **psammoph'ilous**. — *n.* **psamm'ophyte** (*-ō-fīt*) a plant that grows only on sand. — *adj.* **psammophytic** (*-fit'ik*). [Gr. *psammos*, sand.]

psellism (*p*)*sel'izm, n.* a defect in articulation — also **psellis'mus**. [Gr. *psellismos* — *psellos*, stammering.]

psephism (*p*)*sē'fizm, n.* (*ant.*) a decree of the Athenian assembly (from the voting with pebbles). — *n.* **pse'phite** a rock composed of pebbles, a conglomerate. — *adj.* **psephit'ic**. — *n.* **psēphol'ogy** sociological and statistical study of election results and trends — also **psephoanal'ysis**. — *adj.* **psepholog'ical**. — *n.* **psephol'ogist**. [Gr. *psēphos*, a pebble.]

pseud- *sūd-*, **pseudo-** *sū'dō-*, in U.S. *sōō'dō-*, in composition, sham, false, spurious: deceptively resembling: isomerous with: temporary, provisional. — As a separate word, *adj.* **pseu'do, pseud** (*coll.*) false, sham, pretentious. — *ns.* **pseud** (*coll.*) a pretender, pretentious fraud; **pseu'dery** (*coll.*) falseness. — *adj.* **pseud'ish** pretentious: spurious. — *ns.* **pseudaesthē'sia** imaginary feeling, as in an amputated limb; **pseudax'is** a sympodium; **pseudepig'rapha** (*pl.*) books ascribed to Old Testament characters, but not judged genuine by scholars. — *adjs.* **pseudepigraph'ic, -al, pseudepig'raphous**. — *ns.* **pseudepig'raphy** the ascription to books of false names of authors; **pseudimā'go** a subimago; **pseu'do-ac'id** a compound, not an acid but isomeric with and transformable into an acid. — *adj.* **pseu'do-archā'ic** sham antique: artificially archaistic: blunderingly imitative of the old. — *ns.* **pseudo-ar'chãism; pseu'dobulb** a swollen stem internode in some orchids; **pseu'docarp** a fruit formed from other parts in addition to the gynaeceum; **pseu'do-Christian'ity; pseu'doclass'icism; pseudocyesis** (*-sī-ē'sis*; Gr. *kyēsis* — *kyein*, to be pregnant) a psychosomatic condition marked by many of the symptoms of pregnancy. — *adj. and n.* **pseu'dō-Goth'ic** sham or would-be Gothic. — *ns.* **pseu'dograph** a writing falsely ascribed; **pseudog'raphy** unsatisfactory spelling; **pseudohermaph'roditism** a congenital condition in which a man has external genitalia resembling those of a woman, and vice versa; **pseudol'ogy** the science of lying; **pseu'domar'tyr** a false martyr; **pseu'domem'brane** a false membrane; **pseudomō'nad, pseudomō'nas** a member of the **Pseudomonas** (*-dō-mō'nəs*) a genus of schizomycetes comprising short rodshaped bacteria which are found in soil and in water: — *pls.* **pseudomō'nads, pseudomō'nadēs; pseu'domorph** a portion of a mineral showing the outward form of another which it has replaced by molecular substitution or otherwise. — *adjs.* **pseudomor'phic, pseudomor'phous**. — *ns.* **pseudomor'phism; pseu'donym** a fictitious name assumed, as by an author; **pseudonym'ity**. — *adj.* **pseudon'ymous**. — *adv.* **pseudon'ymously**. — *ns.* **pseu'dopod** a psychic projection: a pseudopodium; **pseudopō'dium** a temporary process sent out by the protoplasm of a unicellular organism or phagocyte, for locomotion or feeding: — *pl.* **pseudopō'dia**. — *adj.* **pseudoran'dom** (*comput.*) referring to a set of numbers generated by a computer and therefore not entirely random, but sufficiently so for most purposes. — *ns.* **pseu'doscope** a kind of stereoscope that interchanges

convex and concave in appearance; **pseu'dosolu'tion** a colloidal suspension; **pseu'dosymm'etry** (*crystal.*) a deceptively near approach to a higher degree of symmetry, as in **pseu'docu'bic** or **pseu'dohexag'onal** crystals, simulating cubic or hexagonal symmetry. [Gr. *pseudēs*, false.]

pshaw *pshö, shö, pshə, interj.* expressing contempt or impatience. — *v.i.* to say 'pshaw'. — *v.t.* to say 'pshaw' at. [Spontaneous expression.]

psi (*p*)*sī,* (*p*)*sē, n.* the twenty-third letter (Ψ, ψ) of the Greek alphabet, equivalent to *ps*: as a Greek numeral ψ' = 700, ,ψ = 700 000. — *adj.* **psiŏn'ic**. — **psi particle** an elementary particle with a very long life, formed by an electron-positron collision; **psi phenomena** the phenomena of parapsychology. [Gr. *psei*.]

psilanthropism (*p*)*sī-lan'thrə-pizm, n.* the doctrine that Christ was a mere man. — *adj.* **psilanthropic** (*-throp'*). — *ns.* **psilan'thropist; psilan'thropy**. [Gr. *psilos*, bare, *anthrōpos*, man.]

psilocybin *sī-lō-sī'bin, n.* a hallucinogenic drug, obtained from the Mexican mushroom *Psilocybe mexicana*. [Gr. *psilos*, bare, *kybē*, head.]

psilomelanc (*p*)*sī-lom'ə-lān,* (*p*)*sī-lō-mel'ān, n.* an oxide of manganese, usually with barium, etc., occurring in smooth black botryoidal masses. [Gr. *psilos*, bare, *melās, -anos*, black.]

Psilophyton (*p*)*sī-lō-fī'ton, n.* a very simple Devonian fossil pteridophyte, giving name to the order **Psilophytales** (*-fī-tā'lēz*), early landplants. [Gr. *psilos*, bare, *phyton*, plant.]

psilosis (*p*)*sī-lō'sis, n.* loss of hair: sprue (from loss of epithelium): deaspiration (*Gr. gram.*). — *adj.* **psilot'ic** pertaining to psilosis. [Gr. *psīlōsis* — *psīlos*, bare.]

Psilotum (*p*)*sī-lō'təm, n.* a genus of rootless pteridophytes giving name to the order **Psilotā'ceae**. [Gr. *psīlōton*, the name of some plant — *psīlos*, bare (because of the almost leafless stem).]

psionic. See **psi**.

Psittacus (*p*)*sit'a-kəs, n.* the grey parrot genus. — *adj.* **psitt'acine** (*-sīn*) of or like parrots. — *n.* **psittacosis** (*-kō'sis*) a contagious disease of birds, strictly of parrots, also used of other birds, communicable to man. [Gr. *psittakos*, parrot.]

psoas (*p*)*sō'əs, n.* a muscle of the loins and pelvis: the tenderloin. [Gr. (*pl.*) *psoai*, the accus. *psoās* being mistaken for a nom. sing.]

Psocoptera (*p*)*sō-kop'tər-ə, n.pl.* an order of insects consisting of the book-lice and their kindred. [*Psocus*, a genus included in the order, Gr. *pteron*, wing.]

psora (*p*)*sō', sō'rə, n.* scabies, itch. — *n.* **psorī'asis** a skin disease in which red scaly papules and patches appear. — *adjs.* **psoriat'ic; pso'ric**. [Gr. *psōrā, psōriāsis*, itch.]

ps(s)t *pst, interj.* drawing someone's attention quietly or surreptitiously. [Imit.]

psyche *sī'kē, n.* the soul, spirit, mind: the principle of mental and emotional life, conscious and unconscious: a butterfly: a cheval-glass: (with *cap.*) in late Greek mythology, the personification of the soul, depicted as a young woman with butterfly wings, the beloved of Eros: (*cap.*) a genus of bombycid moths (the females wingless, sometimes legless): (*cap.*) one of the minor planets. — *v.t.* **psych, psyche** (*sīk; slang*) to subject to psychoanalysis: to work out a problem, the intentions of another person, etc., psychologically (often with *out*): to defeat or intimidate by psychological means (sometimes with *out*): to get (oneself) psychologically prepared for (usu. with *up*): to stimulate (usu. with *up*). — *ns.* **psych'agogue** (*-ə-gog*; Gr. *agōgos*, guide) conductor of souls to the underworld (a title of Hermes): a caller-up of spirits: one who guides the mind: a means of restoring consciousness; **psychasthē'nia** (etymologically *-the-nī'ə*; Gr. *asthēneia*, weakness; *obs.*) a severe functional mental disorder, characterised by fixed ideas, ruminative states, and hypochondriacal conditions; **psychedelia** (*-dēl'i-ə*) the production of, or the culture associated with, psychedelic experiences. — *n.pl.* (objects, etc. associated with) psychedelic experiences. — Also **psychodelia.** — *adj.* **psychedelic** see **psychodelic.** — *n.* **psychī'ater** (*arch.*; Gr. *īatros, īātros,* physician) psychiatrist. — *adj.* **psychīat'ric(al).** — *ns.* **psychī'atrist** one who is medically qualified to treat diseases of the mind; **psychī'atry.** — *adjs.* **psych'ic, -al** pertaining to the psyche, soul, or mind; spiritual: spiritualistic: beyond, or apparently beyond, the physical: sensitive to or in touch with that which has not yet been explained physically. — *n.* **psych'ic** that which is of the mind or psyche: a spiritualistic medium. — *adv.* **psych'ically.** — *ns.* **psy'chicism** (*-kəs-*) psychical research; **psy'chicist.** — *n.sing.* **psy'chics** the science of psychology: psychical research. — *ns.* **psy'chism** the doctrine of a universal soul; **psy'chist** a psychologist: one interested in psychical research (also **psy'chicist**). — **psychical research** investigation of phenomena apparently implying a connection with another world; **psychic bid** (*bridge*) bid of a suit in which one is not strong to deceive opponent,or for other reason; **psychic determinism** the Freudian theory that mental processes are always determined by motivations, conscious or unconscious; **psychic force** a power not physical or mechanical, supposed to cause certain so-called spiritualistic phenomena. [Gr. *psȳchē,* soul, butterfly, *Psȳchē,* Psyche.]

psych(o)- *sīk-*(*-ō-*), in composition, soul, spirit: mind, mental: psychological. — *ns.* **psych'ō** coll. shortening of **psychopath** (*pl.* **psych'os**); **psych'oid** the hypothetical regulative principle directing the behaviour of a developing organism. — *adj.* **psychoac'tive** of a drug, affecting the brain and influencing behaviour (also **psychotrop'ic**). — *v.t.* **psychoan'alyse, -yze** to subject to psychoanalysis. — *ns.* **psychoanal'ysis** a method of investigation and psychotherapy whereby nervous diseases or mental ailments are traced to forgotten hidden concepts in the patient's mind and treated by bringing these to light; **psychoan'alyst** one who practises psychoanalysis. — *adjs.* **psychoanalyt'ic, -al.** — *n.* **psych'-obabble** excessive or needless use of psychologists' jargon: needless or meaningless use of jargon generally. — *adj.* **psychobiograph'ical.** — *ns.* **psychobiog'-raphy** a biography concerned mainly with the psychological development of its subject; **psychobiol'ogy** the study of the relationship between the functions of the body and the mind. — *adj.* **psychobiolog'ical.** — *n.* **psychobiol'ogist.** — *adj.* **psychochem'ical.** — *n.* a substance with psychoactive effect, esp. a chemical intended as a weapon of war, specif. a psychogas. — *ns.* **psychochem'istry** the treatment of mental illness by drugs. — *n.* and *n.pl.* **psychodē'lia** see **psychedelia.** — *adj.* **psychodel'ic** (Gr. *dēlos,* visible, clear; the irregularly formed **psychedelic** (*sī-kə-del'ik, -dēl'ik*) is commoner) pertaining to a state of relaxation and pleasure, with heightened perception and increased mental powers generally: pertaining to drugs which cause, or are believed to cause, the taker to enter such a state: pertaining to visual effects and/or sound effects whose action on the mind is a little like that of psychedelic drugs: dazzling in pattern. — *n.* **psychodram'a** a method of mental treatment in which the patient is led to objectify and understand his difficulty by spontaneously acting it out. — *adjs.* **psychodramat'ic; psycho-dynam'ic** pertaining to mental and emotional forces, their source in past experience, and their effects. — *ns.* **psychodynam'ics; psychogas'** a gas which makes a subject's performance deteriorate very seriously without his being aware of it; **psychogen'esis** (the study of) the origin or development of the mind (also **psycho-genet'ics**): origination in the mind. — *adjs.* **psycho-genet'ic, -al; psychogen'ic** having origin in the mind or in a mental condition; **psychogeriat'ric.** — *n.* **psycho-geriatric'ian.** — *n.sing.* **psychogeriat'rics** the study of the psychological problems of old age. — *ns.* **psychog'-ony** origin or development of the mind or soul; **psych'-ogram** a supposed spirit-writing; **psych'ograph** an instrument by which it is got. — *adjs.* **psychograph'ic, -al.** — *ns.* **psychog'raphy** spirit-writing: psychological

biography or delineation; **psychohistor'ian.** — *adj.* **psychohistor'ical.** — *ns.* **psychohis'tory** history studied from a psychological point of view; **psychokinē'sis** movement by psychic agency. — *adj.* **psychokinět'ic.** — *n.* **psycholing'uist.** — *adj.* **psycholinguis'tic.** — *n.sing.* **psycholinguis'tics** the study of language development, language in relation to the mind, thought, etc. — *adjs.* **psycholog'ic, -al.** — *adv.* **psycholog'ically.** — *v.i.* **psychol'ogise, -ize.** — *ns.* **psychol'ogist** one who has studied and qualified in psychology; **psychol'ogism** doctrine depending on psychological conceptions: view that all natural and social sciences should be based on psychology; **psychol'ogy** science of mind: study of mind and behaviour: attitudes, etc., characteristic of individual, type, etc., or animating specific conduct; **psychom'eter** one who has occult power of psychometry: instrument for measuring reaction-times, etc. — *adjs.* **psychomet'ric, -al.** — *ns.* **psychometrician** (*-trish'-ən*), **psychom'etrist.** — *n.sing.* **psychomet'rics** branch of psychology dealing with measurable factors. — *n.* **psychom'etry** psychometrics: occult power of divining properties of things by mere contact. — *adj.* **psy'-chomōtor** pertaining to such mental action as induces muscular contraction. — *n.* **psychoneurō'sis** mental disease without any apparent anatomical lesion: a functional disorder of the mind in one who is legally sane and shows insight into his condition: — *pl.* **psychoneurō'ses.** — *n.* and *adj.* **psychoneurot'ic.** — *adj.* **psychonom'ic.** — *n.sing.* **psychonom'ics** the study of the individual mind in relation to its environment. — *ns.* **psychopannychism** (*-pan'ik-izm;* Gr. *pannychos,* all night long — *pās, pāsa, pān,* all, *nychios,* nightly) (belief in the) sleep of the soul from death to resurrection; **psychopann'ychist** one who holds this belief; **psy'-chopath** (*-path*) one who shows a pathological degree of specific emotional instability without specific mental disorder: one suffering from a behavioural disorder resulting in inability to form personal relationships and in indifference to or ignorance of his obligations to society, often manifested by anti-social behaviour, as acts of violence, sexual perversion, etc. — *adj.* **psychopath'ic** pertaining to psychopathy (also *n.*). — *ns.* **psychop'athist** a psychopathologist; **psychopathol'-ogist; psychopathol'ogy** the branch of psychology that deals with the abnormal workings of the mind: an abnormal psychological condition; **psychop'athy** derangement of mental functions; **psychopharmacol'ogy** the study of the effects of drugs on the mind. — *adj.* **psychophys'ical.** — *n.* **psychophys'icist.** — *n.sing.* **psy-chophys'ics** the study of the relation or correspondence of the mental and physical. — *ns.* **psychophysiol'ogy** experimental or physiological psychology; **psy'-chopomp** (Gr. *pompos,* guide) a conductor of souls to the other world; **psychoprophylax'is** a method of training for childbirth aimed at making labour painless. — *adj.* **psychosex'ual** of or relating to the psychological aspects of sex, e.g. sexual fantasies. — *n.* **psychō'sis** mental condition: a serious mental disorder characterised by e.g. illusions, delusions, hallucinations, mental confusion and a lack of insight into his condition on the part of the patient: — *pl.* **psychō'ses.** — *adjs.* **psychosō'cial** of or relating to matters both psychological and social; **psychosomat'ic** (Gr. *sōma,* body) of mind and body as a unit: concerned with physical diseases having a psychological origin. — *n. sing.* **psychosomat'ics** study of psychosomatic conditions. — *adj.* **psychosomimet'ic** of a drug, producing symptoms like those of mental illness: referring to (e.g. drug-induced) changes in behaviour and personality resembling those due to psychosis. — *ns.* **psychosur'gery** brain-surgery in the treatment of mental cases; **psy-chotherapeut'ics, -ther'apy** treatment of mental illness by hypnosis, psychoanalysis and similar psychological means; **psychother'apist.** — *adj.* **psychot'ic** pertaining to psychosis. — *n.* one suffering from a psychosis. — *n.* **psychot'icism.** — *adjs.* **psychotrop'ic** same as **psycho-active** (also *n.*); **psychotomimet'ic** psychosomimetic. —

psychological block an inability to think about, remember, etc., a particular subject, event, etc., for psychological reasons; **psychological moment** properly the psychological element or factor, misunderstood by a French translator from German and applied to the moment of time when the mind could best be worked upon: hence now often the very moment, the nick of time; **psychological operation** one carried out in **psychological warfare**, the use of propaganda to influence enemy opinion or morale (contracted to **psyop** (*sī'op*), **psywar** (*sī'wör*)). [Gr. *psȳchē*, soul, butterfly.]

psychrometer *sī-krom'i-tər, n.* originally a thermometer: now a wet-and-dry-bulb hygrometer. — *adjs.* **psychrometric** (*sī-krō-met'rik*), **-al.** — *n.* **psychrom'etry.** [Gr. *psȳchros*, cold, *metron*, a measure.]

psychrophilic *sī-krō-fil'ik*, (*bot.*) *adj.* growing best at low temperatures. [Gr. *psȳchros*, cold, *phileein*, to love.]

psyop, psywar. See **psychological operation, warfare** under **psych(o)-**.

ptarmic (*p*)*tär'mik, n.* a substance that causes sneezing. [Gr. *ptarmos*, a sneeze.]

ptarmigan *tär'mi-gən, n.* a mountain-dwelling grouse, white in winter: extended to other species of *Lagopus*, as willow-grouse. [Gael. *tàrmachan*.]

pter(o)- (*p*)*ter(ō-)-*, in composition, feather, wing. — **-ptera** in zoological names, organism(s) having specified type or number of wings or wing-like parts. — adjective combining form **-pteran, -pterous.** [Gr. *pteron*, wing.]

pteranodon (*p*)*ter-an'ə-don, n.* a toothless flying reptile of the Cretaceous period with a horn-like crest. [Gr. *pteron*, wing, *an-*, without, *odous, odontos*, tooth.]

Pterichthys (*p*)*tər-ik'this, n.* a genus of Old Red Sandstone fish-like creatures, with wing-like appendages. [Gr. *pteron*, a wing, and *ichthys*, a fish.]

pteridology. See **Pteris.**

pteridophyte (*p*)*ter'id-ō-fīt, n.* a vascular cryptogam or a member of the **Pteridophyta** (*-of'i-tə*), one of the main divisions of the vegetable kingdom — ferns, lycopods, horsetails. [Gr. *pteris, -idos*, a fern, *phyton*, a plant.]

pteridosperm (*p*)*ter'id-ō-spûrm, n.* a fossil plant of a group resembling ferns, but having seeds. [Gr. *pteris, -idos*, fern, *sperma*, seed.]

pterin (*p*)*ter'in, n.* any of a group of substances occurring as pigments in butterfly wings, important in biochemistry. — **pteroic** ((*p*) *ter-ō'ik*) **acid** the original folic acid found in spinach; **pteroylglutamic** ((*p*)*ter'ō-il-glōō-tam'ik*) **acid** the folic acid that is therapeutically active in pernicious anaemia. [Gr. *pteron*, a wing.]

pterion (*p*)*ter', or* (*p*)*tēr'i-on, n.* in craniometry, the suture where the frontal, squamosal, and parietal bones meet the wing of the sphenoid. — *pl.* **pter'ia.** [Gr. dim. of *pteron*, wing.]

Pteris (*p*)*ter'is,* (*p*)*tē'ris, n.* a genus of ferns with spore-clusters continuous along the pinnule margin, usually taken to include bracken, which some separate as **Pterid'ium.** — *ns.* **pteridol'ogist; pteridol'ogy** the science of ferns; **pteridomā'nia** a passion for ferns; **pteridoph'ilist** a fern-lover. [Gr. *pteris, -idos*, or *-eōs*, male-fern — *pteron*, a feather.]

pterodactyl, pterodactyle (*p*)*ter-ə-dak'til, n.* a fossil (Jurassic and Cretaceous) flying reptile with large and bird-like skull, long jaws, and a flying-membrane attached to the long fourth digit of the forelimb. [Gr. *pteron*, wing, *daktylos*, finger.]

pteroic acid. See **pterin.**

pteropod (*p*)*ter'ə-pod, n.* any member of the **Pteropoda** (*-op'ə-də*), a group of gasteropods that swim by wing-like expansions of the foot. — **pteropod ooze** a deep-sea deposit composed largely of pteropod shells. [Gr. *pteron*, wing, *pous, podos*, foot.]

pterosaur (*p*)*ter'ə-sör, n.* a member of the **Pterosaur'ia**, an extinct order of flying reptiles, including the pterodactyls. — *n. and adj.* **pterosaur'ian.** [Gr. *pteron*, wing, *sauros*, lizard.]

-pterous. See **pter(-o)-**.

pteroylglutamic acid. See **pterin.**

pterygium (*p*)*tər-ij'i-əm, n.* a vertebrate limb: a wing-like growth: a wing-shaped area of thickened conjunctiva which spreads over part of the cornea and sometimes over the eyeball: — *pl.* **pteryg'ia.** — *adj.* **pteryg'ial.** — *n.* a bone in a fin. [Latinised from Gr. *pterygion*, dim. of *pteryx, -ygos*, wing.]

pterygoid (*p*)*ter'i-goid, adj.* wing-like: of or near the pterygoid. — *n.* (in full, **pterygoid bone, plate, process**) in various vertebrates, a paired bone of the upper jaw behind the palatines, known in human anatomy as the pterygoid plates of the sphenoid bone. [Gr. *pteryx, -ygos*, wing.]

Pterygotus (*p*)*ter-i-gō'təs, n.* a genus of Eurypterids named from the broad swimming paddles. [Latinised from Gr. *pterygōtos*, winged.]

pteryla (*p*)*ter'i-lə, n.* a tract of skin bearing contour feathers in birds: — *pl.* **pter'ylae** (*-lē*). — *adjs.* **pterylograph'ic, -al.** — *adv.* **pterylograph'ically.** — *ns.* **pterylog'raphy; pterylō'sis** arrangement of pterylae. [Gr. *pteron*, feather, *hȳlē*, forest.]

ptilosis *til-ō'sis, n.* plumage or mode of feathering. [Gr. *ptilōsis* — *ptilon*, a down feather.]

ptisan *tiz'n, tiz-an', n.* a medicinal drink made from barley: a decoction. — Also **tisane.** [Gr. *ptisanē*, peeled barley, barley-gruel — *ptissein*, to winnow.]

ptochocracy (*p*)*tō-kok'rə-si, n.* the rule of beggars or paupers — wholesale pauperisation. [Gr. *ptōchos*, a beggar, *kratos*, power.]

Ptolemaic *tol-i-mā'ik, adj.* pertaining to the *Ptolemies*, Greek kings of Egypt (from Alexander's general to Caesar's son), or to *Ptolemy* the astronomer (fl. A.D 150) — also **Ptolemaean** (*-mē'ən*). — *n.* **Ptolemā'ist** a believer in the **Ptolemaic system**, Ptolemy's form of the ancient Greek planetary theory, according to which the heavenly bodies revolved about the earth in motions compounded of eccentric circles and epicycles.

ptomaine *tō'mā-īn, -ēn, -in* (these now rare), *tō'mān, tō-mān'* (these orig. illiterate, now established), *n.* a loosely used name for amino-compounds, some poisonous, formed from putrefying animal tissues — putrescine, cadaverine, neurine, choline, etc. — **ptomaine poisoning** (*arch.*) food poisoning — formerly thought to be caused by ptomaines, few of which are now known to be poisonous if eaten. [It. *ptomaina* — Gr. *ptōma*, a corpse.]

ptosis (*p*)*tō'sis, n.* downward displacement: drooping of the upper eyelid: — *pl.* **ptō'ses** (*-sēz*). [Gr. *ptōsis* — *piptein*, to fall.]

ptyalin (*p*)*tī'ə-lin, n.* a ferment in saliva that turns starch into sugar. — *adj.* **ptyalagogic** (*-ə-goj'ik, -gog'ik*). — *n.* **ptyalagogue** (*-al'ə-gog*) a sialagogue. — *v.t.* **pty'alise, -ize** to induce ptyalism in. — *n.* **pty'alism** excessive flow of saliva. [Gr. *ptyalon*, spittle — *ptyein*, to spit.]

ptyxis (*p*)*tiks'is, n.* the folding of each individual leaf in the bud — distinguished from *vernation*, the arrangement of the whole. [Gr. *ptyxis*.]

pub *pub*, (*slang*) *n.* short for **public house.** — **pub'-crawl** a progression from pub to pub. — Also *v.i.*

puberty *pū'bər-ti, n.* the beginning of sexual maturity. — *adjs.* **pū'beral, pū'bertal; pūberulent** (*-ber'ū-lənt*), **pūber'ūlous** feebly or minutely pubescent. — *ns.* **pū'bes** (*-bēz*) the lower part of the hypogastric region: the hair growing thereon at puberty; **pūbescence** (*-es'əns*) puberty: a soft downy covering, esp. in plants, of addressed hairs. — *adjs.* **pūbes'cent; pū'bic** of the pubes or the pubis. — *n.* **pūbis** (for L. *os pūbis*, bone of the pubes) a bone of the pelvis which in man forms the anterior portion of the *os innominatum*: — *pl.* **pū'bises** (**pū'bes** is a blunder). — As a prefix **pū'biō-** (wrongly **pū'bo-**). [L. *pūber* and *pūbēs, -eris*, grown-up, downy, and *pūbēs, -is*, grown-up youth, the pubes.]

public *pub'lik, adj.* of or belonging to the people: pertaining to a community or a nation: general: common to, shared in by, or open to, all: generally known: in open view, unconcealed, not private: engaged in, or concerning, the affairs of the community: devoted or directed to the general good (now *rare* except in *public spirit*): international: open to members of a university as a whole, not confined to a college: of a public house. — *n.* the people: the general body of mankind: the people, indefinitely: a part of the community regarded from a particular viewpoint, e.g. as an audience or a target for advertising: public view of a public place, society, or the open: a public house, tavern (*arch.*). — *ns.* **pub'lican** the keeper of an inn or public house: a tax-farmer (*Roman hist.*): a tax-collector (*Roman hist.*); **publicā'tion** the act of publishing or making public: a proclamation: the act of sending out for sale, as a book: that which is published as a book, etc. — *v.t.* **pub'licise, -ize** (*-sīz*) to give publicity to: to make known to the general public, to advertise. — *ns.* **pub'licist** (*-sist*) one who writes on or is skilled in public law, or on current political topics (*rare*): one who publicises: an advertising agent; **publicity** (*-lis'i-ti*) state of being open to the knowledge of all: notoriety: acclaim: the process of making something known to the general public: advertising. — *adv.* **pub'licly.** — *n.* **pub'licness** (*rare*). — **public bar** one usu. less well appointed than a lounge bar; **public bill, act** a parliamentary bill, act, of legislation affecting the general public; **public company** one whose shares can be purchased on the stock exchange by members of the public; **public convenience** see **convenient; public corporation** one owned by the government and run on business principles, being for the most part self-ruling; **public defender** (*U.S.*) a defence lawyer engaged at public expense to represent those unable to pay legal fees; **public enemy** someone whose behaviour is considered to be a menace to a community in general; **public expenditure** spending by government, local authorities, etc.; **public funds** government funded debt; **public holiday** a general holiday; **public house** a house open to the public (*obs.*): one chiefly used for selling alcoholic liquors to be consumed on the premises: an inn or tavern; **public image** see **image; public inquiry** an investigation held in public into various aspects (e.g. safety, environmental effect) of a proposed engineering or building project. — *adj.* **public key** (*comput.*) of a system of cryptography in which encoding of messages to a particular recipient is done using a public (communal) key, and decoding is by a different key known only to the recipient. — **public lands** lands belonging to government, esp. such as are open to sale, grant, etc.; **public law** the law governing relations between public authorities, as the state, and the individual: sometimes used for international law which, however, may be either public or private; **public lecture** a lecture open to the general public; **public nuisance** an illegal act harming the general community rather than an individual: an annoying, irritating person (*coll.*); **public opinion** the opinion of the general public on matters which affect the whole community; **public orator** an officer of English universities who is the voice of the Senate upon all public occasions; **public ownership** ownership by the state as of nationalised industry; **public prosecutor** an official whose function is to prosecute persons charged with offences; **public relations** the relations between a person, organisation, etc., and the public: the business of setting up and maintaining favourable relations: a department of government, an industrial firm, etc., dealing with this. — Also *adj.* — **public school** school under the control of a publicly elected body: an endowed classical school for providing a liberal education for such as can afford it — Eton, Harrow, Rugby, Winchester, Westminster, Shrewsbury, Charterhouse, St Paul's, Merchant Taylors', etc. — *adj.* **pub'lic-school'.** — **public sector** government-financed industry, social service, etc.; **public servant** a person employed by the government; **public speaking** the making of formal speeches to a large audience: the art of making such speeches; **public spending** spending by the government. — *adj.* **pub'lic-spir'ited** having a spirit actuated by regard to the public interest: with a regard

to the public interest. — *adv.* **pub'lic-spir'itedly.** — **public transport; public trustee** an official who acts as trustee or executor if required; **public utility** a service or supply provided in a town etc., for the public, as gas, electricity, water, transport: (*U.S.*) a company providing such a service, and usually having a monopoly: (in *pl.*) public utility shares; **public woman** (*arch.*) a prostitute. — **go public** to become a public company; **in public** openly, publicly; **public address system** a system that enables (large) groups of people to be addressed clearly, consisting of some or all of the following — microphones, amplifiers, loud speakers, sound projectors; **public health inspector** designation in England of an official whose duty is to enforce regulations regarding e.g. food-handling in shops, maintenance of a clean water-supply, waste-disposal, and to ascertain the fitness of dwellings for human habitation, formerly known as sanitary inspector; **public lending right** an author's right to payment when his/her books are borrowed from public libraries; **public opinion poll** a taking of public opinion based on the answers of scientifically selected elements in the community to questioning. [L. *pūblicus — pop(u)lus*, the people.]

publican, publication. See under **public.**

publish *pub'lish, v.t.* to make public: to divulge: to announce: to proclaim: to send forth to the public: to put forth and offer for sale orig. any article, now books, newspapers, etc.: to put into circulation: of an author, to get published. — *v.i.* to publish a work, newspaper, etc. — *adj.* **pub'lishable.** — *ns.* **pub'lisher** one who makes public: one who publishes books: one who attends to the issuing and distributing of a newspaper: a newspaper proprietor (*U.S.*); **pub'lishment** publication, esp. (*U.S.*) of banns. [Fr. *publier* — L. *pūblicāre*, with *-ish* on the model of other verbs.]

Puccinia *puk-sin'i-ə, n.* a genus of rust-fungi, including the wheat-rust, parasitic in alternate generations on barberry and wheat or other grass. — *adj.* **puccinia'ceous.** [Named after Tomaso *Puccini*, Italian anatomist.]

puccoon *puk-ōōn', n.* bloodroot: extended to species of gromwell and other American plants yielding pigments. [Virginian Indian name.]

puce *pūs, n.* and *adj.* brownish-purple. [Fr. *puce* — L. *pūlex, -icis,* a flea.]

pucelle *pū-sel', (obs.) n.* a maid, virgin, esp. the Maid of Orleans, Jeanne d'Arc (1412–31): a dirty drab, a slut (also **puzzle**). — *n.* **pū'celage** virginity. [Fr., — L.L. *pūlicella*; origin doubtful.]

puck[1] *puk,* **pouke** *pōōk, ns.* a goblin or mischievous sprite: (*cap.*) Robin Goodfellow, a merry fairy in *Midsummer Night's Dream,* etc. (**Puck-hairy** in Ben Jonson's *Sad Shepherd*). — *adj.* **puck'ish** impish: full of mischief. [O.E. *pūca*; cf. O.N. *pūki,* Ir. *puca,* W. *pwca.*]

puck[2] *puk, n.* a rubber disc used instead of a ball in ice-hockey. [Origin unknown.]

pucka, pukka, pakka *puk'ə, (Anglo-Ind.) adj.* out-and-out good: thorough: complete: solidly built: settled: durable: permanent: full-weight: straightforward: genuine: sure. — **pucka sahib** a gentleman. [Hind. *pakkā,* cooked, ripe.]

pucker *puk'ər, v.t.* to wrinkle: to make gathers in. — Also *v.i.* — *n.* a corrugation or wrinkle: a group of wrinkles, esp. irregular ones: agitation, confusion (*coll.*). — *adj.* **puck'ery** astringent: tending to wrinkle. [Cf. **poke**[1].]

puckfist *puk'fist, -fīst, n.* a puff-ball: a braggart (*arch.*): a niggard (*obs.*). [App. **puck**[1] and the root of O.E. *fisting,* breaking of wind.]

puckish. See **puck**[1].

pud[1] *pud, (coll.) n.* a paw, fist, hand — also **pudd'y.** [Cf. **pad**[2] or Du. *poot,* paw.]

pud[2] *pōōd.* Same as **pood.**

pud[3] *pōōd, (coll.) n.* Short for **pudding.**

pudden, puddening, etc. See **pudding.**

pudder *pud'ər.* Same as **pother.**

pudding *pōōd'ing, n.* a skin or gut filled with seasoned minced meat and other materials (as blood, oatmeal), a kind of sausage: stuffing for a cooked carcase (*Shak.*): (usu. in *pl.*) entrails (*arch.*): meat, fruit, etc., cooked in a casing of flour: a soft kind of cooked dish, usually farinaceous, commonly with sugar, milk, eggs, etc.: the dessert course of a meal: a pad of rope, used as a fender on the bow of a boat or elsewhere (also **pudd'ening**): material gain (*fig.*): a fat, dull, or heavy-witted person (*coll.*). — Also (now *coll.* or *dial.*) **pudden** (*pŏŏd'n, pud'n*). — *adj.* **pudd'ingy** (*-ing-i*). — **pudd'ing-bag** a bag for cooking a pudding in: a piece of good fortune. — *adjs.* **pudd'ing-faced** having a fat, round, smooth face; **pudd'ing-head'ed** (*coll.*) stupid. — **pudd'ing-pie** a pudding with meat baked in it: applied to various kinds of pastry; **pudd'ing-pipe** the long pulpy pod of the purging cassia tree; **pudd'ing-plate** a shallow bowl-like plate, usu. smaller than a soup-plate; **pudd'ing-sleeve** a large loose sleeve gathered in near the wrist; **pudd'ing-stone** conglomerate; **pudd'ing-time** (*obs.*) dinner-time: the right moment. — **in the pudding club** (*slang*) pregnant. [M.E. *poding*; origin unknown; relation to L.G. *pudde-wurst*, black pudding, and Fr. *boudin*, obscure.]

puddle *pud'l, n.* a small muddy pool: a non-porous mixture of clay and sand: a muddle (*coll.*): a muddler (*coll.*). — *v.t.* to make muddy: to work into puddle, to stir and knead: to cover with puddle: to make watertight by means of clay: to convert from pig-iron into wrought-iron by stirring in a molten state. — *v.i.* to make a dirty stir. — *ns.* **pudd'ler; pudd'ling.** — *adj.* **pudd'ly** full of puddles. [App. dim. of O.E. *pudd*, ditch.]

puddock *pud'ək,* **paddock** *pad'ək,* (*arch.* and *Scot.*) *ns.* a toad or frog. — **padd'ock-stool** a toadstool. [Dim. from late O.E. *pade, padde,* toad; O.N. *padda.*]

puddy. See **pud**[1].

pudency *pū'dəns-i, n.* (*Shak.*) shamefacedness, modesty. — *adjs.* **pudendal** (*-den'*) pertaining to the pudenda; **puden'dous** (*obs.*) shameful. — *n.* **puden'dum** and *pl.* **puden'da** the external genital organs, esp. female. — *adjs.* **pu'dent** (*rare*) modest; **pu'dibund** shamefaced: prudish. — *n.* **pudibund'ity.** — *adj.* **pu'dic** modest (*obs.*): pudendal. — *ns.* **pudicity** (*-dis'i-ti; rare*) modesty; **pu'dor** (*obs.*) sense of shame. [L. *pudēre,* to make (or be) ashamed, *pudendum,* something to be ashamed of, *pudīcus, pudibundus.*]

pudge *puj,* **pudgy** *puj'i,* **puds(e)y** *pud'zi.* Same as **podge, podgy.**

pueblo *pweb'lō, .n.* a town or settlement (in Spanish-speaking countries): a communal habitation of the Indians of New Mexico, etc.: an Indian of the pueblos: — *pl.* **pueb'los.** [Sp., town — L. *populus,* a people.]

puer *pūr, n.* and *v.t.* Same as **pure** (in tanning).

puerile *pū'ər-īl,* in U.S. *-il, adj.* pertaining to children (*rare*): childish: trifling: silly. — *ns.* **puerilism** (*pū'ər-il-izm; psych.*) reversion to a childlike state of mind; **pūerility** (*-il'i-ti*) quality of being puerile: that which is puerile: a childish expression: an instance of childishness or foolish triviality. [L. *puerīlis — puer,* a boy.]

puerperal *pū-ûr'pər-əl, adj.* relating to childbirth. — *adv.* **pūer'perally.** — *n.* **pūerpē'rium** the time from onset of labour to return of the womb to its normal state. — **puerperal fever** fever occurring in connection with childbirth: now confined to morbid conditions owing to introduction of organisms into the genital tract; **puerperal psychosis** (*arch. mania*) a mental illness sometimes occurring after childbirth. [L. *puerpera,* a woman in labour — *puer,* a child, *parĕre,* to bear.]

puff *puf, v.i.* to blow in whiffs: to breathe out vehemently or pantingly: to snort scornfully (*obs.*): to emit puffs: to issue in puffs: to make the sound of a puff: to go with puffs: to swell up. — *v.t.* to drive with a puff: to blow: to emit in puffs: to play (as a wind instrument) or smoke (as a pipe) with puffs: to inflate or swell: to elate unduly: to extol, esp. in disingenuous advertisement: to put out of breath. — *n.* a sudden, forcible breath, blast, or emission: a gust or whiff: a cloud or

portion of vapour, dust, air, etc., emitted at once: a sound of puffing: a downy pad for powdering: anything light and porous, or swollen and light: a biscuit or cake of puff-paste or the like: a part of a fabric gathered up so as to be left full in the middle: a quilted bed-cover: ostentation: laudation intended as, or serving as, advertisement: a homosexual (*slang*; see **poof**). — *adj.* **puffed** distended: inflated: gathered up into rounded ridges, as a sleeve: out of breath. — *ns.* **puff'er** one who puffs: a steam-engine: a steamboat: one employed to bid at an auction to incite others and run up prices: a pufferfish; **puff'ery** advertisement disguised as honest praise: puffs collectively. — *adv.* **puff'ily.** — *ns.* **puff'iness; puff'ing.** — *adv.* **puff'ingly.** — *adj.* **puff'y** puffed out with air or any soft matter: tumid: bombastic: coming in puffs: puffing: short-winded. — **puff'-adder** a thick, venomous African snake (*Bitis arietans* or kindred species) that distends its body when irritated; **puff'ball** a gasteromycete fungus (*Lycoperdon,* etc.) with ball-shaped fructification filled when ripe with a snuff-like mass of spores: a tight-waisted full skirt gathered in at the hem to an underskirt, so as to be shaped like a ball; **puff'-bird** any bird of a South American family akin to barbets, with the habit of puffing out the head-feathers; **puff'-box** a box for toilet powder and puff; **puff'er(fish)** a globe-fish; **puff'-paste** a flour paste in thin layers: pastry made thereof (**puff'-pastry**); **puff'-puff** (esp. formerly) a child's word for a railway engine or train. — **puffed out** quite out of breath: inflated, distended, expanded; **puffed up** swollen with pride, presumption, or the like. [O.E. *pyffan,* or kindred form; cf. Ger. *puffen,* etc.]

puffin *puf'in, n.* a sea-bird (Fratercula) of the auk family, with brightly coloured parrot-like beak. [Origin obscure: connection with **puff** is conjectured.]

pug[1] *pug, n.* a goblin, a puck (*obs.*; in Ben Jonson, **Pug,** an inferior devil): a term of endearment: a harlot (*obs.*): an upper servant (*arch. slang*): a monkey: a fox: a pug-dog: a pug-nose: a pug-moth: a pug-engine. — *adjs.* **pugg'ish, pugg'y** like a monkey or a pug-dog: snub-nosed. — *n.* **pugg'y** a term of endearment: a monkey (*Scot.*): a fox. — **pug'-dog** a small short-haired dog with wrinkled face, upturned nose, and short curled tail; **pug'-engine** a shunting engine. — *adj.* **pug'-faced** monkey-faced. — **pug'-moth** a name for the smaller moths of the geometrid fam. *Larentidae*; **pug'-nose** a short, thick nose with the tip turned up. — *adj.* **pug'-nosed.** [Connection with **puck**[1] is conjectured.]

pug[2] *pug, n.* clay ground and worked with water. — *v.t.* to beat: to grind with water and make plastic: to pack with pugging. — *n.* **pugg'ing** beating or punching: working of clay for making bricks, in a pug-mill: clay, sawdust, plaster, etc., put between floors to deaden sound. — **pug'-mill** machine for mixing and tempering clay. [Origin unknown.]

pug[3] *pug,* (*Anglo-Ind.*) *n.* a beast's footprint. — *v.t.* to track. [Hind. *pag.*]

pug[4]. See **pugil**[2].

pug[5]. See **pugging**[1].

puggaree, puggery. Same as **pagri.**

pugging[1] *pug'ing,* (*Shak.*) *adj.* thieving. — *v.t.* and *v.i.* **pug** (*dial.*) to tug. [Origin unknown.]

pugging[2]. See **pug**[2].

puggree. See **pagri.**

puggy. See **pug**[1].

pugh. An old spelling of **pooh.**

pugil[1] *pū'jil, n.* orig. a small handful, now as much as the thumb and two fingers can lift, a pinch. [L. *pugillus.*]

pugil[2] *pū'jil, n.* (*obs.*) a boxer. — *ns.* **pu'gilism** the art or practice of boxing: prize-fighting; **pu'gilist** (abbrev. **pug** *pug; slang*). — *adjs.* **pugilist'ic, -al.** — *adv.* **pugilist'ically.** [L. *pugil,* a boxer.]

pugnacious *pug-nā'shəs, adj.* given to fighting: combative: quarrelsome. — *adv.* **pugnā'ciously.** — *ns.* **pugnā'ciousness, pugnacity** (*-nas'i-ti*) inclination to fight: fondness for fighting: quarrelsomeness. [L. *pugnāx, -ācis* — *pugnāre*, to fight.]

Pugwash (conference) *pug'wosh (kon'fər-əns) n.* a conference held at intervals by scientists from many countries to discuss the dangers and difficulties into which the world is running. [Name of village in Nova Scotia.]

puh. A Shakespearian spelling of **pooh.**

puir *pür, pār, adj.* Scots form of **poor.**

puisne (*Shak.*) *pū'ni, adj.* an obsolete form of **puny,** surviving as applied to certain judges — junior: petty, insignificant (*Shak.*). — *n.* a puisne judge. [O.Fr. (Fr. *puîné*), from *puis* — L. *posteā*, after, *nē* — L. *nātus*, born.]

puissant, puissaunt *pū'is-ənt, pwis', (poet.) pū-is', adj.* powerful. — *n.* **puissance, -aunce** (*-əns, -öns', -äns'*) power (*arch.*): (usu. *pwēs'ăs, -äns*) (a showjumping competition with very high jumps showing) the power of a horse. — *adv.* **puissantly** (*-ənt-li*). [Fr. *puissant*, app. formed as a pr.p. from a vulgar L. substitute for L. *potēns, -entis*; see **potent.**]

puja *pōō'jə, n.* worship: reverential observance: a festival. [Sans. *pūjā*, worship.]

puke¹ *pūk, v.t.* and *v.i.* to vomit. — *v.t.* (*arch.*) to cause to vomit. — *n.* vomit: an emetic (*arch.*): a despicable person (*slang*). — *n.* **pū'ker** an emetic. [Poss. connected with Flem. *spukken*, Ger. *spucken*.]

puke² *pūk, (obs.) n.* a fine woollen cloth: a colour between russet or purple and black. — *adj.* made of puke (*Shak.*): of the colour puke. [M.Du. *puuc*, the best woollen cloth.]

pukka. Same as **pucka.**

pulchritude *pul'kri-tūd, n.* beauty. — *adj.* **pulchritud'inous.** [L. *pulchritūdō, -inis* — *pulcher*, beautiful.]

puldron. Same as **pauldron.**

pule *pūl, v.t.* and *v.i.* to pipe: to whimper or whine. — *n.* **pū'ler.** — *n.* and *adj.* **pū'ling.** — *adv.* **pū'lingly.** — *adj.* **pū'ly** whining: sickly. [Imit.; cf. Fr. *piauler.*]

Pulex *pū'leks, n.* the flea genus, giving name to the family **Pulicidae** (*-lis'i-dē*). — *n.* **pū'licide** (*-sīd*; L. *caedēre*, to kill) a poison or other agent which destroys fleas. [L. *pūlex, -icis*.]

Pulitzer prize *pōō'lit-sər, pū', prīz*, any of various annual prizes for American literature, journalism and music. [J. *Pulitzer* (1847–1911), U.S. newspaper publisher who instituted them.]

pulka *pul'kə, n.* a Laplander's boat-shaped sledge. — Also **pulk, pulk'ha.** [Finnish *pulkka*, Lappish *pulkke, bulkke.*]

pull *pōōl, v.t.* to pluck: to remove by plucking: to extract: to pick by hand: to strip, deprive of feathers, hair, etc.: to draw: to move, or try or tend to move, towards oneself or in the direction so thought of: to render, or bring to be, by pulling: to row: to transport by rowing: to move in a particular direction when driving (usu. with *out, over*, etc.): to stretch: to hold back (as a boxing blow, a racehorse to prevent its winning): to take as an impression or proof, orig. by pulling the bar of a hand-press: to strike to the left (right for left-handed person; *cricket, golf*): to bring down: to take a draught of: to draw or fire (a weapon): to snatch, steal (*slang*): to arrest (*slang*): to raid (*slang*): to attract (e.g. a crowd) (*slang*). — *v.i.* to give a pull: to perform the action of pulling anything: to tear, pluck: to drag, draw: to strain at the bit: to exert oneself: to go with a pulling movement: to move in a particular direction, esp. when in a motor vehicle (usu. with *away, out, over*, etc.): to row: to suck: to strike the ball to the left, etc. — *n.* an act, bout, or spell of pulling: a pulling force: a row: a stiff ascent: a draught of liquor: a proof, single impression (*print.*): advantage: influence: an apparatus for pulling: the quantity pulled at one time: resistance. — *n.* **pull'er.** — **pull'-back** a hindrance: a drawback: a retreat, withdrawal: a device formerly used for making a skirt hang close and straight in front (see also **pull back** below); **pull'-in** a stopping-place (also *adj.*): a transport café (see also **pull in** below). — *adj.* **pull'-on** requiring only to be pulled on, without fas-

tening. — *n.* a pull-on garment of any kind. — *adj.* **pull'-out** a section of a magazine, etc., that can be removed and kept separately (see also **pull out** below). — **pull'over** a jersey, a jumper, a body garment put on over the head; **pull'-through** a cord with rag for cleaning a rifle barrel; **pull'-up** an act of pulling up: a sudden stoppage: a suitable place (esp. for lorry-drivers, etc.) for pulling up: an exercise in which one hangs from a bar by the hands, and pulls oneself up so that the chin is level with the bar. — **pull a bird** (*slang*) to succeed in forming a (sexual) relationship with a girl; **pull about** to distort: to treat roughly; **pull a face** to grimace; **pull a fast one on** (*slang*) to take advantage of by a sudden trick; **pull ahead** to move into the lead; **pull apart, to pieces** to bring asunder by pulling: to criticise harshly; **pull away** to pull ahead: to withdraw; **pull back** to retreat, withdraw (see also *n.* **pull'-back** above); **pull caps** (*arch.*) to scuffle; **pull devil, pull baker** (in an argument, competition, etc.) do your best, both sides; **pull down** to take down or apart: to demolish: to bring down: to reduce in health or vigour; **pull for** to row for: to support; **pull in** to draw in: to make tighter: to draw a motor vehicle into the side of the road, or drive into the car-park of a café, etc., and halt (see also *n.* and *adj.* **pull'-in** above): to arrest: to earn: of a train, to arrive at a station; **pull off** to carry through successfully; **pull oneself together** to regain one's self-control: to collect oneself, preparing to think or to act; **pull one's punches** see under **punch³**; **pull one's weight** to give full effect to one's weight in rowing: to do one's full share of work, co-operate wholeheartedly; **pull out** to draw out: to drive a motor vehicle away from the side of the road or out of a line of traffic: of a train, to leave a station: to abandon a place or situation which has become too difficult to cope with (*coll.*; *n.* **pull'-out**; see also above); **pull over** to draw over to the side of the road, either to stop or to allow other vehicles to pass; **pull rank** see under **rank**; **pull round** to bring, or come, back to good health or condition or to consciousness; **pull someone's leg** see under **leg**; **pull the long bow** to lie or boast beyond measure; **pull through** to bring or get to the end of something difficult or dangerous with some success (see also *n.* **pull'-through** above); **pull together** (*fig.*) to co-operate; **pull up** to pull out of the ground: to tighten the reins: to bring to a stop: to halt: to take to task: to gain ground: to arrest; **pull up stakes** to prepare to leave a place. [O.E. *pullian*, to pluck, draw.]

pullet *pōōl'it, n.* a young hen, esp. from first laying to first moult. — **pull'et-sperm'** (*Shak.*) derisively, eggs (lit. the chalaza, once believed to be the male element in the egg). [Fr. *poulette*, dim. of *poule*, a hen — L.L. *pulla*, a hen, fem. of L. *pullus*, a young animal.]

pulley *pōōl'i, n.* a wheel turning about an axis, and receiving a rope, chain, or band on its rim, used for raising weights, changing direction of pull, transmission of power, etc.: a block: a combination of pulleys or blocks: — *pl.* **pull'eys.** [M.E. *poley, puly* — O.Fr. *polie* (Fr. *poulie*) — L.L. *polegia*, supposed to be from a dim. of Gr. *polos*, axle.]

Pullman *pōōl'mən, n.* a luxuriously-furnished railway saloon or sleeping-car, first made by George M. *Pullman* (1831–97) in America. — In full, **Pullman car.**

pullulate *pul'ū-lāt, v.i.* to sprout: to sprout or breed abundantly: to teem: to increase vegetatively. — *n.* **pullulā'tion.** [L. *pullulāre, -ātum* — *pullulus*, a young animal, sprout — *pullus.*]

pulmo *pul'mō, pōōl', n.* lung: — *pl.* **pulmo'nes** (*-nēz*). — *n.* **pul'mobranch** (*-brangk*) a lung-book. — *adj.* **pulmobranch'iate.** — *n.* **Pulmonaria** (*-mə-nā'ri-ə*) the lungwort genus of the borage family. — *adj.* **pul'monary** (*-mən-ər-i*) of the lungs or respiratory cavity: leading to or from the lungs: of the nature of lungs: having lungs: diseased or weak in the lungs. — *n.pl.* **Pulmonā'ta** an air-breathing order of Gasteropoda. — *n.* **pul'monate** a member of the Pulmonata. — *adj.* having lungs, lung-sacs, or lung-books, or similar organs. —

adj. **pulmonic** (-*mon'ik*) of the lungs. — *n.* (*rare*) a sufferer from, or medication for, lung disease. — *n.* **Pul'motor®** an apparatus for forcing air and/or oxygen into and out of the lungs.   [L. *pulmō*, -*ōnis*, lung.]

pulp *pulp, n.* any soft fleshy part of an animal, e.g. the tissue in the cavity of a tooth: the soft part of plants, esp. of fruits: any soft structureless mass: the soft mass obtained from the breaking and grinding of rags, wood, etc., before it is hardened into paper: crushed ore: nonsense (*fig.*): sentimentality (*fig.*): a cheap magazine printed on wood-pulp paper, or of a paltry and sentimental or sensational character (also **pulp'(-)magazine**): fiction of the type published in such a magazine: a film, etc., of such a type. — *v.t.* to reduce to pulp: to make pulpy: to deprive of pulp. — *v.i.* to become pulp or like pulp. — *n.* **pulp'er** a machine for reducing various materials to pulp. — *v.t.* **pulp'ify.** — *adv.* **pulp'ily.** — *n.* **pulp'iness.** — *adjs.* **pulp'ous; pulp'y.** — **pulp'board** cardboard made directly from a layer of pulp; **pulp'-cav'ity** the hollow of a tooth containing pulp; **pulp'-en'gine** a machine for making pulp for paper; **pulp'mill** a machine or factory for pulping wood, roots, or other material; **pulp novcl; pulp novelist; pulp'stone** a grindstone for pulping wood; **pulp'wood** wood suitable for paper-making: a board of compressed wood-pulp and adhesive.   [L. *pulpa*, flesh, pulp.]

pulpit *pōōl'pit, n.* a raised structure for preaching from (also *fig.*): an auctioneer's desk or the like: preachers or preaching collectively: a platform (*obs.*): a safety railing at the bow or stern of a yacht. — *adj.* belonging to the pulpit. — *adj.* **pul'pited.** — *ns.* **pulpiteer', pul'piter** one who speaks from a pulpit: a preacher; **pul'pitry** sermonising; **pul'pitum** a rood-loft.   [L. *pulpitum*, a stage.]

pulpitum; pulpous, pulpy. See **pulpit; pulp.**

pulque *pōōl'kā, -kē, n.* a fermented drink made in Mexico from agave sap.   [Amer. Sp.]

pulsar. See **pulsate.**

pulsate *pul'sāt,* or -*sāt', v.i.* to beat, throb: to vibrate: to change repeatedly in force or intensity: to thrill with life or emotion. — *ns.* **pul'sar** (for 'pulsating star') any of a number of interstellar sources of regularly pulsed radiation, investigated from 1967, which may be rotating neutron stars; **pulsatance** (*pul'sə-təns, pul-sā'-təns*) the angular frequency of a periodic motion, frequency multiplied by 2π. — *adj.* **pul'satile** (-*sə-tīl,* in U.S. -*til*) capable of pulsating: pulsatory: rhythmical: played by percussion (*mus.*). — *ns.* **Pulsatill'a** pasque-flower (because beaten by the wind); **pulsā'tion** a beating or throbbing: a motion of the heart or pulse: any measured beat: vibration. — *adj.* **pulsative** (*pul'sə-tiv* or -*sāt'*). — *n.* **pulsā'tor** (or *pul'sə-tər*) a machine, or part of a machine, that pulsates or imparts pulsation, as for separating diamonds from earth, for regulating the rhythmical suction of a milking machine, for pumping. — *adj.* **pulsatory** (*pul'sə-tər-i,* or -*sā'*) beating or throbbing. — **pulsating current** an electric current that changes periodically in intensity but not direction.   [L. *pulsāre,* -*ātum,* to beat, freq. of *pellĕre, pulsum,* to drive.]

pulse[1] *puls, n.* a beating or throbbing: a measured beat or throb: a vibration: a single variation, beat or impulse: a signal of very short duration (*radio*): the beating of the heart and the arteries: a thrill (*fig.*). — *v.i.* to beat, as the heart: to throb: to pulsate. — *v.t.* to drive by pulsation: to produce, or cause to be emitted, in the form of pulses. — *adjs.* **pulsed; pulse'-less.** — *ns.* **pulse'lessness; puls'idge** (*Shak.*; Mistress Quickly in 2 *Henry IV*) pulse. — *adj.* **pulsif'ic** producing a single pulse. — *ns.* **pulsim'eter** an instrument for measuring the strength or quickness of the pulse; **pulsom'eter** a pulsimeter: a pump that draws in water by condensation of steam in two chambers alternately. — **pulse'jet, puls'ojet** in jet propulsion, an intermittent jet; **pulse'-rate** the number of beats of a pulse per minute; **pulse'-wave** the expansion of the artery, mov-

ing from point to point, like a wave, as each beat of the heart sends the blood to the extremities. — **feel someone's pulse** to test or measure someone's heartbeat, usu. by holding his wrist: to explore a person's feelings or inclinations in a tentative way; **keep one's finger on the pulse** (*fig.*) to keep in touch with current events, ideas, etc.; **pulse code modulation** a system of transmission in which the audio signals are sampled periodically, coded in digital form, and transmitted (abbrev. **PCM**).   [L. *pulsus* — *pellĕre, pulsum*; partly O.Fr. *pouls, pous,* remodelled on Latin.]

pulse[2] *puls, n.* seeds of leguminous plants as food collectively — beans, pease, lentils, etc.: the plants yielding them. — *adj.* **pultā'ceous** macerated and softened.   [L. *puls, pultis,* porridge; cf. Gr. *poltos,* and **poultice.**]

pulsidge (*Shak.*), **pulsojet,** etc. See **pulse**[1].

pultun, pultan, pulton, pultoon *pul'tun, -tən, -tōōn, ns.* an Indian infantry regiment.   [Hind. *pultan* — Eng. **battalion.**]

pulture. See **puture.**

pulu *pōō'lōō, n.* a silky fibre from the Hawaiian tree-fern leaf-bases.   [Hawaiian.]

pulver *pul'vər, v.t.* (*obs.*) to reduce to powder. — *adj.* **pul'verable** (*rare*). — *ns.* **pulverā'tion** (*rare*) pulverisation; **pul'verine** barilla ash. — *adj.* **pul'verisable, -z-** (or -*īz'*). — *n.* **pulverīsā'tion, -z-.** — *v.t.* **pul'verise, -ize** to reduce to dust or fine powder: to defeat thoroughly, destroy (*fig.*). — *v.i.* to fall into dust or powder. — *n.* **pul'veriser, -z-** one who pulverises: a machine for pulverising or for spraying. — *adj.* **pul'verous** dusty or powdery. — *n.* **pulverulence** (-*vûr'ū-ləns*). — *adj.* **pulver'ūlent** consisting of fine powder: powdery: dusty-looking: readily crumbling. — **Pulver Wednesday, pulvering day** (*obs.*) Ash Wednesday.   [L. *pulvis, pulveris,* powder.]

pulvil *pul'vil, n.* perfumed powder: extended to snuff and other powders. — Also **pulvil'io, pulvill'io** (*pl.* **pulvil(l)'ios**), **pulville'.** — *v.t.* **pul'vil** to powder or scent with pulvil: — *pa.t.* and *pa.p.* **pul'villed.** — *adj.* **pul'vilised, -ized.**   [It. *polviglio* — *polve,* powder — L. *pulvis.*]

pulvillar, etc. See **pulvinus.**

pulvinus *pul-vī'nəs, n.* a cushion-like swelling, esp. one at the base of a leaf or leaflet, by whose changes of turgidity movements are effected: — *pl.* **pulvi'ni** (-*nī*). — *adjs.* **pulvill'ar** of a pulvillus: cushion-like; **pulvill'iform.** — *n.* **pulvill'us** a little cushion or pad: a pad between the claws of an insect's foot: — *pl.* **pulvill'i** (-*ī*). — *adj.* **pulvinar** (-*vī'nər*) cushion-like: of a pulvinus. — *n.* (-*när*) a Roman cushioned seat: a small pillow or pad: a knob on the optic thalamus. — *adjs.* **pul'vinate** (-*vin-āt*), **-d** cushion-like: pillowy: bulging. — *n.* **pul'vinule** the pulvinus of a leaflet.   [L. *pulvīnus,* cushion, pillow; dim. *pulvillus; pulvīnar,* a cushioned couch.]

pulwar *pul'wär, n.* a light keelless boat used on the Ganges.   [Hind. *palwār.*]

puly. See **pule.**

pulza-oil *pōōl'zə-oil, n.* an oil obtained from physic-nut seeds.   [Origin unknown.]

puma *pū'mə, n.* the cougar (*Felis concolor*), a large reddish-brown American cat — also called **mount'ain-li'on:** — *pl.* **pu'mas.**   [Amer. Sp., — Quechua.]

pumelo. Same as **pomelo.**

pumice *pum'is, pū'mis, n.* an acid glassy lava so full of gas-cavities as to float in water: a frothy portion of any lava: a piece of such lava used for smoothing or cleaning. — *v.t.* to smooth or clean with pumice-stone — also **pumicate** (*pū'mi-kāt; rare*). — *adj.* **pumiceous** (-*mish'əs*). — **pum'ice-stone; pum'ie (stone), pum'y (stone)** (*Spens.*) a pebble, stone.   [O.E. *pumic(-stān*), pumice(-stone); reintroduced — O.Fr. *pomis*; both — L. *pūmex, -icis.*]

pummel *pum'l, n.* a less usual spelling of **pommel.** — *v.t.* (the usual spelling) to beat, pound, bethump, esp. with the fists: — *pr.p.* **pumm'elling;** *pa.t.* and *pa.p.* **pumm'elled.**   [**pommel.**]

pump[1] *pump, n.* a machine for raising and moving fluids, orig. esp. bilge-water in ships, or for compressing, rarefying, or transferring gases: a stroke of a pump: an act of pumping. — *v.t.* to raise, force, compress, exhaust, empty, remove, or inflate with a pump: to discharge by persistent effort: to move in the manner of a pump: to subject to, or elicit by, persistent questioning: to pump water on (*obs.*): to put out of breath (esp. in *pass.*; often with *out*; *coll.*). — *v.i.* to work a pump: to work like a pump: to move up and down like a pump-handle: to spurt: to propel, increase the speed of, a sailing-boat by rapidly pulling the sails in and out (*naut.*). — *n.* **pump′er.** — *adj.* **pump′-action** of a repeating rifle or shotgun whose chamber is fed by a pump-like movement. — **pumped storage** in a hydroelectric system, the use of electricity at times of low demand to pump water up to a high storage reservoir, to be used to generate electricity at times of high demand; **pump gun** a pump-action gun; **pump′= hand′le** the lever that works a pump; **pump′-head, -hood** a frame covering the upper wheel of a chain-pump, serving to guide the water into the discharge-spout; **pump priming** starting a pump working efficiently by introducing fluid to drive out the air: investing money in order to stimulate commerce, local support, etc.; **pump′-room** the apartment at a mineral spring in which the waters are drunk; **pump′-water** water from a pump; **pump′-well** a well from which water is got by pumping: the compartment in which a pump works. — **pump iron** (*coll.*) to do exercise with weights, to develop one's muscles. [Ety. dub.]

pump² *pump, n.* a light shoe without fastening, worn esp. for dancing. — *adj.* **pumped** wearing pumps. [Origin unknown.]

pumpernickel *poŏmp′ər-nik-l, pump′, n.* a coarse, dark rye bread, much used in Westphalia. [Ger.; the Ger. word means a rackety goblin, a coarse lout, rye bread (poss. from its giving forth a sound like *pump* when struck).]

pumpkin *pum(p)′kin,* in U.S. often *pung′kin, n.* a plant (*Cucurbita pepo*) of the gourd family, or its fruit. — Also **pomp′ion, pump′ion.** [O.Fr. *pompon* — L. *pepō* — Gr. *pepōn,* ripe; see **pepo.**]

pumple-nose. See **pompelmoose.**

pumy. See **pumice.**

pun¹ *pun, v.t.* to pound (*Shak.*): to ram: to consolidate by ramming: — *pr.p.* **punn′ing;** *pa.t.* and *pa.p.* **punned.** — *n.* **punn′er** a tool for punning, a ram. [See **pound³.**]

pun² *pun, v.i.* to play upon words alike or nearly alike in sound but different in meaning: — *pr.p.* **punn′ing;** *pa.t.* and *pa.p.* **punned.** — *n.* a play upon words. — *ns.* **punn′ing; pun′ster** a maker of puns. [A late-17th-century word; origin unknown; It. *puntiglio,* fine point, has been conjectured.]

puna *poō′n′ə, n.* bleak tableland in the Andes: cold wind there: mountain sickness. [Amer. Sp., — Quechua.]

punalua *poō-nə-loō′ə, n.* a system of group marriage, sisters (by blood or tribal reckoning) having their husbands in common, or brothers their wives, or both. — *adj.* **punalu′an.** [Hawaiian.]

punce *puns, (Austr.) n.* an effeminate man.

Punch *punch, punsh, n.* a hook-nosed hunchback, chief character in the street puppet-show 'Punch and Judy': the chief illustrated English comic paper (1841). [Shortened from **Punchinello.**]

punch¹ *punch, punsh,* (*dial.*) *adj.* short and thick. — *n.* a thick-set short man: a short-legged, round-bodied horse, long bred in Suffolk. — *adj.* **punch′y.** [Poss. shortened from **puncheon¹,** or from **Punchinello,** or a variant of **bunch.**]

punch² *punch, punsh,* (*obs. poōnsh*), *n.* a drink ordinarily of spirit, water, sugar, lemon-juice, and spice (with variations). — **punch′-bowl** a large bowl for making punch in: a large bowl-shaped hollow in the ground; **punch′-ladle** a ladle for filling glasses from a punch-bowl. [Traditionally from the five original ingredients, from Hindi *pãc,* five — Sans. *pañca;* but the vowel presents a difficulty.]

punch³ *punch, punsh, v.t.* to prod: to poke: to drive (cattle) (*U.S.*): to strike with a forward thrust, as of the fist: to thump: to kick (*Northern*): to stamp, pierce, perforate, indent, by a forward thrust of a tool or part of a machine: to make, obtain, or remove by such a thrust (often with *out*): to press in vigorously the keys or button of: to record by pressing a key. — *v.i.* to perform an act of punching: to clock (*in* or *out*). — *n.* a vigorous thrust or forward blow: striking power: effective forcefulness: a tool or machine for punching: a die: a prop for a mine-roof. — *n.* **punch′er** one who punches: an instrument for punching: a cow-puncher, drover (*U.S.*): the driver of a team (*Austr.*). — *adj.* **punch′y** vigorous, powerful: punch-drunk (*coll.*). — **punch′-ball** a suspended ball used for boxing practice; **punch′-card, punched card** a card with perforations representing data, used in the operation of automatic computers. — *adj.* **punch′-drunk** having a form of cerebral concussion from past blows in boxing, with results resembling drunkenness: dazed (*coll.* abbrev. **punch′y**). — **punched tape** (*comput.*) same as **paper tape; punch line** the last line or conclusion of a joke, in which the point lies: the last part of a story, giving it meaning or an unexpected twist; **punch′-prop** in mines, a short piece of wood used as a prop; **punch′-up** a fight with fists. — **pull one's punches** to hold back one's blows (also *fig.*). [**pounce¹;** or from **puncheon¹;** possibly in some senses for **punish.**]

puncheon¹ *pun′chn, -shn, n.* a dagger (*obs.*): a tool for piercing, or for stamping: a short supporting post: a split trunk with one face smoothed for flooring, etc. [O.Fr. *poinson* — L. *pungĕre, punctum,* to prick.]

puncheon² *pun′chn, -shn, n.* a cask: a liquid measure of from 70 to 120 gallons. [O.Fr. *poinson,* a cask; origin obscure.]

Punchinello *punch-, punsh-i-nel′ō, n.* a hook-nosed character in an Italian puppet-show: a buffoon, any grotesque personage: — *pl.* **Punchinell′o(e)s.** [It. *Pulcinella,* a Neapolitan buffoon, of doubtful origin.]

punchy. See **punch¹,³.**

punctate, -d *pungk′tāt, -id, adjs.* dotted: pitted. — *ns.* **punctā′tion; punctā′tor** one who marks with dots — esp. applied to the Massoretes who invented the Hebrew vowel-points. [L. *punctum,* a point, puncture — *pungĕre, punctum,* to prick.]

punctilio *pungk-til′i-ō, -yō, n.* a nice point in behaviour or ceremony: a point about which one is scrupulous: nicety in forms: exact observance of forms: — *pl.* **punctil′ios.** — *adj.* **punctil′ious** attentive to punctilio: scrupulous and exact. — *adv.* **punctil′iously.** — *n.* **punctil′iousness.** [It. *puntiglio* and Sp. *puntillo,* dims. of *punto* — L. *punctum,* a point.]

puncto *pungk′tō,* **puncto banco.** See **punto.**

punctual *pungk′tū-əl, adj.* of the nature of a point: pertaining to a point, or points (*math.*): of punctuation: precise, exact (*obs.*): punctilious: exact in keeping time and appointments: done at the exact time: up to time. — *ns.* **punc′tualist** an authority on or observer of punctilios; **punctuality** (-*al′i-ti*). — *adv.* **punc′tually.** [L.L. *punctuālis* — *punctum,* a point.]

punctuate *pungk′tū-āt, v.t.* to mark with points: to mark off with the usual stops, points of interrogation, and the like: to intersperse: to emphasise. — *ns.* **punctuā′-tion** the act or art of dividing sentences by points or marks; **punctuā′tionist** a believer in punctuated equilibrium. — *adj.* **punc′tuātive.** — *n.* **punc′tuātor.** — **punctuated equilibrium, equilibria** (*biol.*) (a theory which states that evolution happens in) short bursts of major change punctuated by long periods of stability. [L.L. *punctuāre, -ātum,* to prick — L. *punctum* (see **punctum**).]

punctum *pungk′təm, (anat.) n.* a point, dot: a minute aperture: — *pl.* **punc′ta.** — *adjs.* **punc′tulate, -d** minutely dotted or pitted. — *ns.* **punctulā′tion; punc′tule** a minute dot, pit, or aperture. — **punctum caecum** (*sē′kəm; poōngk′toōm kī′koōm,* blind spot) the point of the retina from which the optic nerve fibres radiate.

[L. *punctum* — *pungĕre, punctum,* to prick.]
puncture *pungk'chər, n.* a pricking: a small hole made with a sharp point: perforation of a pneumatic tyre. — *v.t.* to make a puncture: to deflate someone's pride, self-confidence, etc. (*fig.*). — *v.i.* to get a puncture. — *adj.* **punc'tured** perforated: pierced: marked with little holes: consisting of little holes. — *n.* **puncturā'tion.** [L. *punctūra* — *pungĕre,* to prick.]
pundigrion *pun-dig'ri-on,* (*obs.*) *n.* a pun. [Origin unknown; It. *puntiglio* is only a conjecture.]
pundit, pandit *pun'dit, n.* one who is learned in the language, science, laws, and religion of India: any learned man: an authority, now, commonly, one who considers himself or herself an authority. — *n.* **pun'ditry.** [Hindi *paṇḍit* — Sans. *paṇḍita.*]
pundonor *poon-dō-nōr', -nör', n.* point of honour: — *pl.* **pundonor'es** (*-ās*). [Sp., — *punto de honor.*]
pungent *pun'jənt, adj.* sharp: ending in a hard sharp point (*bot.*): pricking or acrid to taste or smell: keenly touching the mind: painful: sarcastic. — *ns.* **pun'gency** (*Crabbe,* **pun'gence**). — *adv.* **pun'gently.** [L. *pungēns, -entis,* pr.p. of *pungĕre,* to prick.]
Punic *pū'nik, adj.* of ancient Carthage: Carthaginian: faithless, treacherous, deceitful (as the Romans alleged the Carthaginians to be): purple (*obs.*). — *n.* the Semitic language of ancient Carthage. — *n.* **Pu'nica** the pomegranate genus, constituting the family **Punicā'ceae** (akin to the myrtle and loosestrife families). — *adj.* **punicā'ceous.** — **Punic apple** (*obs.*) the pomegranate; **Punic faith** treachery. [L. *Pūnicus* — *Poenī,* the Carthaginians.]
Punica fides *pū'ni-kə fī'dēz, poo'ni-kä fi'däs,* (L.) Punic faith (see above).
punily. See **puny.**
punish *pun'ish, v.t.* to cause (someone) to suffer for an offence: to cause someone to suffer for (an offence): to handle, beat, severely (*coll.*): to consume a large quantity of (*coll.*). — *v.i.* to inflict punishment. — *n.* **punishabil'ity.** — *adj.* **pun'ishable.** — *n.* **pun'isher.** — *adj.* **pun'ishing** causing suffering or retribution: severe, testing (*coll.*). — *adv.* **pun'ishingly.** — *n.* **pun'ishment** act or method of punishing: penalty imposed for an offence: severe handling (*coll.*). [Fr. *punir, punissant* — L. *pūnīre,* to punish — *poena,* penalty.]
punition *pū-nish'ən, n.* punishment. — *adjs.* **pu'nitive** (*-ni-tiv*) concerned with, inflicting, or intended to inflict, punishment; **pu'nitory.** [L. *pūnīre,* to punish.]
Punjabi, Punja(u)bee, Panjabi *pun-jä'bē, n.* a native or inhabitant of the *Punjab* in India and Pakistan: the language of the Punjab. — *adj.* of the Punjab. [Hindi *Pañjābī.*]
punk[1] *pungk, n.* a prostitute, strumpet (*arch.*): anything or anyone worthless: balderdash: a foolish person: a homosexual, often a boy (*slang*): a follower of punk rock, often recognisable by the use of cheap, utility articles, e.g. razor blades, plastic rubbish bags, safety-pins, as clothes or decoration. — *adj.* rotten: worthless: miserable. — *n.* **punk'iness.** — **punk poetry** poetry inspired by punk rock; **punk rock** a style of popular music of the late 1970s, rhythmical and aggressive, with violent, often obscene lyrics, inspired by a feeling of despair at the cheapness and ugliness of life — also called **new wave.** [Origin unknown; poss from **punk**[2].]
punk[2] *pungk, n.* touchwood: tinder: a preparation of amadou used as tinder. [Poss. **spunk;** or poss. of American Indian origin.]
punka, punkah *pung'kə, n.* a fan: palm-leaf fan: a large mechanical fan for cooling a room. [Hindi *pākhā,* a fan.]
punner, punning, punster. See **pun**[1,2].
punnet *pun'it, n.* a small shallow chip-basket for fruit, as strawberries. [Origin unknown.]
punt[1] *punt, n.* a flat-bottomed boat with square ends. — *v.t.* to propel by pushing a pole against the bottom: to transport by punt. — *v.i.* to go in a punt: to go shooting in a punt: to pole a punt or boat. — *n.* **punt'er.** — **punt'-fishing** fishing from a punt; **punt'-gun** a heavy

gun of large bore used for shooting water-fowl from a punt; **punt'-pole** a pole for propelling a punt; **punts'-man** a sportsman who uses a punt. [O.E. *punt* — L. *pontō, -ōnis,* punt, pontoon; cf. **pontoon**[1].]
punt[2] *punt, v.i.* to stake against the bank: to back a horse. — *n.* **punt'er** one who punts: a professional gambler: customer (*coll.*): an ordinary person (*coll.*). [Fr. *ponter.*]
punt[3] *punt, n.* the act of kicking a dropped football before it touches the ground. — *v.t.* to kick in this manner: to knock. [Origin obscure.]
punt[4] *poont, n.* the Irish pound.
puntee. See **punty.**
punto *pun'tō,* also **puncto** *pungk'tō,* (*obs.*) *ns.* a moment: a point, punctilio: a pass or thrust in fencing (*Shak.* **punc'to**): — *pls.* **punc'tos, pun'tos.** — **punto banco** (It. *banco,* bank) a gambling game similar to baccarat; **punto dritt'o** a direct or straight hit; **punto rever'so** (It. *riverso*) a back-handed stroke. [Sp. and It. *punto* — L. *punctum,* a point.]
punty, puntee, pontie, ponty *pun'ti,* **pontil** *pon'til, ns.* an iron rod used in holding and manipulating glassware during the process of making. [Prob. Fr. *pontil,* app. — It. *pontello, puntello,* dim. of *punto,* point.]
puny *pū'ni, adj.* **puisne** (*obs.*): inexperienced (*Shak.*): stunted: feeble: — *compar.* **pū'nier;** *superl.* **pū'niest.** — *adv.* **pū'nily.** — *n.* **pū'niness.** [puisne.]
pup *pup, n.* a shortened form of **puppy.** — *v.t.* and *v.i.* to whelp: — *pr.p.* **pupp'ing;** *pa.t.* and *pa.p.* **pupped.** — **pup'fish** either of two varieties of tiny fish of the family Cyprinidae, native to the warmer waters of the Western United States; **pup tent** a small tent, easily carried. — **buy a pup** to be swindled; **in pup** of a bitch, pregnant; **sell a pup** to inveigle someone into a specious bad bargain: to swindle.
pupa *pū'pə, n.* an insect in the usually passive stage between larva and imago: an intermediate stage of development in some other invertebrates: — *pl.* **pupae** (*pū'pē*), **pū'pas.** — *adjs.* **pū'pal** of a pupa; **pūpā'rial.** — *n.* **pūpā'rium** the last larval skin separated but retained as a hard protective covering for the pupa: sometimes, the covering and the pupa: — *pl.* **pūpā'ria.** — *v.i.* **pū'pate** to become a pupa. — *n.* **pūpā'tion.** — *adjs.* **pūpigerous** (*-pij'ə-rəs*) having a puparium; **pūpip'arous** having pupae developed within the body of the mother. — **pu'pa-case** a puparium. [L. *pūpa,* a girl, a doll.]
pupil[1] *pū'pl, -pil, n.* a boy up to the age of 14, or a girl up to 12 (*Rom.* and *Scots law*): a ward (*law*): one who is being taught: one who is being or has been taught by a particular teacher. — *adj.* under age. — *ns.* **pu'pillage** the state of being a pupil or student: the time during which one is a pupil or student (in *Shak.,* etc., sometimes taken as two words, **pupil age**); **pupillar'ity** the state or time of being legally a pupil. — *adj.* **pu'pillary** pertaining to a pupil or ward, or one under academic discipline. (The above words are sometimes spelt with one *l.*) — **pupil teacher** a pupil who does some teaching as part of his training for later entry into the profession. [Fr. *pupille* — L. *pūpillus, pūpilla,* dims. of *pūpus,* boy, *pūpa,* girl.]
pupil[2] *pū'pl, -pil, n.* the apple of the eye: the round opening in the eye through which the light passes: a central spot, esp. within a spot. — *n.* **pupilabil'ity** an intentionally unintelligible word in *Tristram Shandy* (IV, i). — *adjs.* **pu'pillary; pu'pillate** (*zool.*) having a central spot of another colour. (The above words sometimes with one *l.*) [L. *pūpilla,* pupil of the eye, orig. the same as in the preceding, from the small image to be seen in the eye.]
pupiparous. See **pupa.**
puppet *pup'it, n.* a doll or image moved by wires or hands in a show: a marionette: one who acts just as another tells him. — *adj.* behaving like a puppet: actuated by others. — *ns.* **puppeteer'** one who manipulates puppets; **pupp'etry** play of, or with, puppets: puppets collectively: puppet-like action: puppet-shows: anything like or associated with puppets: dress of puppets (*obs.*). —

pupp′et-play a drama performed by puppets; **pupp′et-show** an exhibition of puppets: a puppet-play; **pupp′et-valve** same as **poppet-valve**. [Earlier **poppet**; cf. O.Fr. *poupette*, dim. from L. *pūpa*.]

puppodum *pup′ə-dəm*. Same as **popadum**.

puppy *pup′i, n.* a puppet (*dial*.): a lap-dog, toy dog (*obs*.): a young dog: a whelp: a young seal: a young rat: a conceited young man. — *v.t.* and *v.i.* to pup. — *ns.* **pupp′ydom; pupp′yhood.** — *adj.* **pupp′yish.** — *n.* **pupp′yism** conceit in men. — **pupp′y-dog; pupp′y-fat** temporary fatness in childhood or adolescence. — *adj.* **pupp′y-head′ed** (*Shak*.) having the mind of a puppy. — **puppy love** same as **calf-love; pupp′y-walk′er** a person who looks after hound, guide dog, etc., puppies. [App. Fr. *poupée*, a doll or puppet — L. *pūpa*.]

pupunha *pōō-pōōn′yə, n.* the peach-palm: its fruit. [Port. from Tupí.]

pur[1]. See **purr**.

pur[2] *pûr, (obs.) n.* the knave in the game of post and pair.

pur[3] *pŭr, (Fr.) adj.* pure. — **pur sang** (*sã*) pure blood: thoroughbred: total.

Purana *pōō-rä′nə, n.* any one of a class of sacred books in Sanskrit literature, cosmogonical, legendary, religious, etc. — *adj.* **Puranic** (-*rän′ik*). [Sans. *purāna* — *purā*, of old.]

Purbeck *pûr′bek, adj.* of the Isle (really peninsula) of *Purbeck*, in Dorset. — *n.* and *adj.* **Purbeck′ian** (*geol*.) Jurassic of uppermost stage. — **Purbeck marble, stone** a freshwater shelly limestone quarried in the Isle.

purblind *pûr′blīnd, adj.* orig. apparently wholly blind: nearly blind: dim-sighted, esp. spiritually. — *adv.* **pur′blindly.** — *n.* **pur′blindness.** [**pure** (or perh. O.Fr. intens. pfx. *pur*-), and **blind**.]

purchase *pûr′chəs, v.t.* to seek to bring about (*obs*.): to bring about (*obs*.): to acquire: to get in any way other than by inheritance (*law*): to buy: to obtain by labour, danger, etc.: to be amends for (with *out*) (*Shak*.): to raise or move by a mechanical power. — *v.i.* to strive (*Shak*.): to make purchases: to accumulate possessions (*obs*.). — *n.* act of purchasing: seizure(*obs*.): that which is purchased: acquisition: prize, booty (*arch*.): whatever one can do for oneself by shifts (*obs*.): annual rent: bargain (*obs*.): price (*obs*.): any mechanical advantage in raising or moving bodies or apparatus: advantageous hold, or means of exerting force advantageously. — *adj.* **pur′chasable.** — *n.* **pur′chaser.** — **purchase money** the money paid, or to be paid, for anything; **purchase system** the system by which, before 1871, commissions in the British army could be bought; **purchase tax** formerly, a British form of sales-tax levied on specified goods and at differential rates. — **not worth a day's**, etc., **purchase** not likely to last a day, etc.; **so many years' purchase** value, price, of a house, an estate, etc., equal to the amount of so many years' rent or income. [O.Fr. *porchacier* (Fr. *pourchasser*), to seek eagerly, pursue — *pur* (L. *prō*) for, *chacier*, *chasser*, to chase.]

purdah *pûr′də, n.* a curtain, esp. for screening women's apartments: seclusion of women: seclusion generally (*fig*.). [Urdu and Pers. *pardah*.]

purdonium *pûr-dō′ni-əm, n.* a kind of coal-scuttle introduced by one *Purdon*.

pure *pŭr, adj.* clean: unsoiled: unmixed: not adulterated: free from guilt or defilement: chaste: free from bad taste, meretriciousness, solecism, barbarism: modest: mere: that and that only: utter, sheer: of a study, confined to that which belongs directly to it: nonempirical, involving an exercise of mind alone, without admixture of the results of experience: excellent, fine (*obs*.): homozygous, breeding true (*biol*.): unconditional (*law*): free from ritual uncleanness. — *n.* purity: dog's dung or similar substance used by tanners (also **puer**). — *adv.* purely: without admixture: utterly, thoroughly (*obs*.). — *v.t.* to cleanse, refine: to treat with pure (also **puer**). — *adv.* **pure′ly** chastely: unmixedly: unconditionally: wholly, entirely: wonderfully, very much (*dial*.). — *ns.* **pure′ness; purism** (q.v.).

— *adjs.* **pure′-blood, -ed, pure′-bred** of unmixed race. — **pure culture** (*bot*.) a culture containing a pure stock of one species of micro-organism; **pure mathematics** mathematics treated without application to observed facts of nature or to practical life; **pure reason** reason alone, without any mixture of sensibility; **pure science** science considered apart from practical applications. [Fr. *pur* — L. *pūrus*, pure.]

purée, puree *pŭ′rā, n.* food material reduced to pulp e.g. by being processed in a liquidiser: a soup without solid pieces. — *v.t.* to make a purée of. [Fr.]

Purex *pūr′eks, n.* a process for recovering plutonium and uranium from spent uranium fuel by using tributyl phosphate as a solvent. [*purification* and *extraction*.]

purfle *pûr′fl, v.t.* to ornament the edge of, as with embroidery or inlay. — *n.* a decorated border: a profile (*obs*.). — *n.* **pur′fling** a purfle, esp. around the edges of a fiddle. [O.Fr. *pourfiler* — L. *prō*, before, *fīlum*, a thread.]

purfled *pûr′fld, (Scot.) adj.* short-winded. — *adj.* **pur′fly** (*Carlyle*).

purge *pûrj, v.t.* to purify: to remove impurities from: to clear of undesirable elements or persons: to remove as an impurity: to clarify: to clear from accusation: to expiate: to evacuate, as the bowels: to make (someone) evacuate the bowels: to atone for, wipe out (esp. a contempt of court) (*law*). — *v.i.* to become pure by clarifying: to evacuate the bowels: to have frequent evacuations: to take a purgative. — *n.* act of purging: an expulsion or massacre of those who are not trusted: a purgative. — *n.* **purgation** (-*gā′*) a purging: a clearing away of impurities: the act of clearing from suspicion or imputation of guilt (*law*): a cleansing. — *adj.* **purgative** (*pûrg′ə-tiv*) cleansing: having the power of evacuating the intestines. — *n.* a medicine that evacuates. — *adv.* **pur′gatively.** — *adjs.* **purgato′rial, purgato′rian** pertaining to purgatory; **pur′gatory** purging or cleansing: expiatory. — *n.* a place or state in which souls are after death purified from venial sins (*R.C.*): any kind or state of suffering for a time: intense discomfort (*coll*.): a ravine (*U.S.*): a swamp (*U.S.*). — *n.* **purger** (*pûrj′ər*). — *n.* and *adj.* **purging** (*pûrj′*). — **purging cassia, flax** see **cassia, flax.** [Fr. *purger* — L. *pūrgāre*, -*ātum* — earlier *pūrigāre* — *pūrus*, pure.]

puri *pōō′ri, n.* a small round cake filled with a spicy vegetable mixture and deep-fried in oil. [Hind.]

purify *pū′ri-fī, v.t.* to make pure: to cleanse from foreign or hurtful matter: to free from guilt, from ritual uncleanness or from improprieties or barbarisms in language. — *v.i.* to become pure: — *pr.p.* **pu′rifying;** *pa.t.* and *pa.p.* **pu′rified.** — *n.* **purifica′tion.** — *adj.* **pu′rificative.** — *n.* **pu′rificātor** a cloth used during the celebration of Holy Communion to wipe the vessels and the hands and lips of the celebrant. — *adj.* **pu′rificatory** tending to purify or cleanse. — *n.* **pu′rifier.** — **Purification of the Blessed Virgin Mary** a feast observed in the R.C. Church on 2nd February, in commemoration of the purification of the Virgin Mary according to the Jewish ceremonial (Lev. xii. 1–4) forty days after the birth of Christ. [Fr. *purifier* — L. *pūrificāre* — *pūrus*, pure, *facēre*, to make.]

purim *pū′rim, pōōr-ēm′, n.* the Feast of Lots held about 1st of March, in which the Jews commemorated their deliverance from the plot of Haman, as related in Esther (see esp. iii. 7). [Heb. *pūrīm* (sing. *pūr*), lots; origin unknown.]

purin, purine *pūr′in, -ēn, ns.* a white crystalline substance $C_5H_4N_4$, which with oxygen forms uric acid ($C_5H_4N_4O_3$) and is the nucleus of many other derivatives. [Contracted from L. *pūrum ūricum* (*acidum*), pure uric (acid).]

purism *pūr′izm, n.* fastidious, esp. over-fastidious, insistence upon purity (esp. of language in vocabulary or idiom). — *n.* and *adj.* **pūr′ist.** — *adjs.* **pūris′tic, -al.** [L. *pūrus*, pure.]

Puritan *pūr′i-tən, n.* one who in the time of Elizabeth and the Stuarts wished to carry the reformation of the

Church of England further by purifying it of ceremony: an opponent of the Church of England on account of its retention of much of the ritual and belief of the Roman Catholics: an opponent of the Royalists in the 17th century: (the following meanings also without *cap.*) a person of like views with, or in sympathy with, the historical Puritans: a person strictly moral in conduct: slightingly, one professing a too-strict morality: an advocate of purity in any sense. — *adj.* (also without *cap.*) pertaining to the Puritans. — *adjs.* **pūritanic** (-*tan'ik*), **-al** (usu. *derog.*). — *adv.* **pūritan'ically.** — *v.t.* and *v.i.* **pūr'itanise, -ize.** — *n.* **pūr'itanism.** [L. *pūrus*, pure.]

purity *pūr'i-ti, n.* condition of being pure: freedom from mixture of any kind, sin, defilement, or ritual uncleanness: chastity: sincerity: freedom from foreign or improper idioms or words. [L. *pūritās, -ātis* — *pūrus.*]

purl¹ *pûrl, v.i.* to flow with a murmuring sound: to flow in eddies: to curl or swirl. — *n.* a trickling rill: a movement or murmuring as of a stream among stones: an eddy or ripple (also **pirl**). — *n.* and *adj.* **purl'ing.** [Cf. Norw. *purla,* to babble, Sw. dial. *porla,* to purl, ripple.]

purl² *pûrl, v.i.* to spin round: to capsize: to go head over heels: to fall headlong or heavily. — *v.t.* to throw headlong. — *n.* a heavy or headlong fall: an upset. — *n.* **purl'er** a headlong or heavy fall or throw, esp. in phrases *go, come, a purler.* [Perh. conn. with **purl¹.**]

purl³ *pûrl, v.t.* to embroider or edge with gold or silver thread: to fringe with a waved edging, as lace. — *v.t.* and *v.i.* to knit with a purl stitch. — *n.* twisted gold or silver wire: a loop or twist, esp. on an edge (also **pearl**): a succession of such loops, or a lace or braid having them: a fold, pleat, or frilling: knitting with a purl stitch. — *adj.* (also **pearl**) in knitting, denoting an inverted stitch made with the wool passed behind the needle (opp. to *plain*). [Origin unknown: perh. different words; cf. **pearl².**]

purl⁴ *pûrl, n.* formerly, ale with wormwood: ale warmed and spiced. [Origin unknown.]

purler *pûrl'ər,* (*Austr.*) *n.* something extremely good.

purlicue. Same as **pirlicue.**

purlieu *pûr'lū, n.* orig. a tract wrongly added to a royal forest, but disafforested by a new perambulation: (in *pl.*) borders or outskirts. [A.Fr. *puralee,* land severed by perambulation — O.Fr. *pur* (= L. *prō*), *allee,* going; infl. by Fr. *lieu,* place.]

purlin, purline *pûr'lin, n.* a piece of timber stretching across the principal rafters to support the common or subsidiary rafters. [Origin obscure.]

purloin *pər-loin', pûr', v.t.* to filch, steal. — *v.i.* to practise theft. — *n.* **purloin'er.** [A.Fr. *purloigner,* to remove to a distance — *pur-* (L. *prō*), for, *loin* (L. *longē*), far.]

purpie, purpy *pur'pi,* (*obs. Scot.*) *n.* purslane. — **wa'ter=pur'pie** brooklime. [O.Fr. *parpié* — L.L. *pullī pēs,* colt's foot, purslane.]

purple *pûr'pl, n.* crimson (*hist.*): the Tyrian crimson dye, got in ancient times from various shellfish (Murex, Purpura, Buccinum, etc.; *hist.*): the animal yielding it: a crimson cloth or garment anciently worn by kings and emperors (*hist.*): the dignity of king or emperor: cardinalate (from the red hat (former) and robes): bishops (with **the**): now, any mixture of blue and red: a purple pigment: a purple-red pigment in the rods of the mammalian eye and in parts of other eyes (**visual purple**): a purple flower (see **long-purples**): (in *pl.*) purpura (in *pl.*) swine-fever: (in *pl.*) ear-cockle. — *adj.* of the colour purple, mixed red and blue: blood-red, bloody (*hist.*): of writing, fine or over-ornate. — *v.t.* to make purple. — *v.i.* to become purple. — *adjs.* **pur'plish, pur'ply** somewhat purple. — **purple airway** a reserved course for a royal flight. — *adjs.* **pur'ple-born** porphyrogenite; **pur'ple-coloured.** — **purple emperor** one of the largest of British butterflies and one of the most richly coloured (*Apatura iris*); **purple finch** an American finch with red head and breast in the cock; **purple fish** a shellfish yielding purple dye; **purple heart**

the purple-coloured wood of species of Copaifera (fam. Caesalpiniaceae) (also **purple wood**): a mauve heart-shaped tablet of a stimulant drug of amphetamine type: (with *caps.*) a U.S. decoration for wounds received on active service. — *adjs.* **pur'ple=hued; pur'ple-in-grain** fast dyed in purple. — **purple patch** a passage of fine, or (often) over-ornate, writing. — **born in the purple** born in the purple chamber (see **Porphyrogenite**): hence, of exalted birth; **purple of Cassius** a red or purple pigment discovered by Andreas Cassius (*c.* 1683), made from stannous, stannic, and gold chlorides in solution. [O.E. (Northumb.) *purpl*(*e*), purple (adj.) — *purpur* (n.) — L. *purpura* — Gr. *porphȳrā,* purple-fish.]

purport *pûr'pərt, -pōrt, -pört,* formerly also *pûr-pōrt', -pört', n.* meaning conveyed: substance, gist, tenor: outward appearance, guise, as conveying an impression (*Spens.*): purpose (*rare*). — *v.t.* **purport'** (also *pûr'*) to give out as its meaning: to convey to the mind: to seem, claim, profess (to mean, be, etc.): to purpose (*rare*). — *adv.* **purport'edly.** — *adj.* **pur'portless.** [O.Fr., from *pur* (Fr. *pour*) — L. *prō,* for, *porter* — L. *portāre,* to carry.]

purpose *pûr'pəs, n.* idea or aim kept before the mind as the end of effort: power of seeking the end desired: act or fact of purposing: an end desired: a useful function: a definite intention: intention of going (*Shak.*): purport (*Shak.*): conversation, conversational speech (*Spens.*): (in *pl.*) a sort of conversational game. — *v.t.* to intend. — *v.i.* (*Spens.*) to discourse. — *adjs.* **pur'posed** intentional: intended: purposeful; **pur'poseful** directed towards a purpose: actuated by purpose. — *adv.* **pur'posefully.** — *n.* **pur'posefulness.** — *adj.* **pur'poseless** without purpose: aimless: having no purpose in mind. — *adv.* **pur'poselessly.** — *n.* **pur'poselessness.** — *adj.* **pur'pose-like** (*Scot.*) efficient-looking: purposed. — *adv.* **pur'posely** intentionally. — *adj.* **pur'posive** directed towards an end: showing intention or resolution, purposeful. — *n.* **pur'posiveness.** — *adj.* **pur'pose-built'** specially made or designed to meet particular requirements. — **on** (*arch.* **of**) **purpose, of set purpose** with design, intentionally; **to good** (or **some**) **purpose** with good effect; **to the purpose** to the point, or material to the question. [O.Fr. *pourpos, propos* — L. *prōposi-tum,* a thing intended — *prō,* forward, *pōnĕre, positum,* to place; cf. **propose.**]

purpresture *pûr-pres'chər, n.* encroachment upon public property. [O.Fr. *purpresture* — *pour,* for (L. *pro*), *prendre* — L. *praehendĕre,* to take.]

Purpura *pûr'pū-rə, n.* a genus of marine gasteropods yielding purple dye: (without *cap.*) purples, an eruption of small purple spots, caused by extravasation of blood. — *n.* and *adj.* **pur'pure** purple. — *adjs.* **purpū'real** purple; **purpū'ric** relating to purpura. — *n.* **pur'purin** a purple colouring-matter got from madder. [L. *purpura* — Gr. *porphȳrā.*]

purpy. See **purpie.**

purr, pur *pûr, v.i.* to utter a low, murmuring sound, as a cat when pleased. — *v.t.* to say or utter with or by purring. — *ns.* **purr; purr'ing.** — *adv.* **purr'ingly.** [Imit.]

purse *pûrs, n.* a small bag for carrying money: a sum of money in a purse: a sum given as a present or offered as a prize: funds: a live coal flying out of the fire, as an omen: a woman's handbag (*U.S.*): a purse-like receptacle or cavity. — *v.t.* to put into a purse or one's own purse, to pocket: to contract (one's lips) into a rounded, puckered shape, esp. in order to express displeasure, etc.: to contract or draw into folds or wrinkles. — *v.i.* to pucker: to take purses (*obs.*). — *ns.* **purse'ful** as much as a purse can hold: enough to fill a purse; **purs'er** formerly a naval paymaster: an officer in charge of cabins, stewards, etc.; **purs'ership.** — **purse'-bearer** one who has charge of another's money: a treasurer: one who carries in a bag the Great Seal for the Lord Chancellor, or the royal commission for the Lord High Commissioner; **purse'-net** a bag-shaped net that closes by a drawstring at the neck; **purse'-pride.** — *adj.* **purse'-proud** proud of one's wealth: insolent from wealth. — **purse'-seine** a seine-net that can be drawn into the shape of a bag; **purse'-sein'er** a fishing-vessel equipped with such nets; **purse'-snatcher; purse'-snatching; purse'-strings** the strings fastening a purse (usu. *fig.*); **purse'-tak'ing** robbing. — **privy purse** an allowance for a sovereign's private expenses; **public purse** the nation's finances. [O.E. *purs*, app. — L.L. *bursa* — Gr. *byrsa*, a hide.]

pursew Spenser's usual spelling of **pursue.**

purslane *pûrs'lin*, *n.* a pot and salad herb (*Portulaca oleracea*) of the Portulacaceae: any member of the genus or the family. — **sea purslane** a fleshy seaside sandwort (*Arenaria*, or *Honckenya*, *peploides*): orach of various species; **water purslane** a small-flowered prostrate lythraceous plant of wet places (*Peplis portula*). — Also **purslain.** [O.Fr. *porcelaine* — L. *porcilāca*, *portulāca*; see **Portulaca.**]

pursue *pər-sū'*, *-sōō'*, *v.t.* to harass, persecute, persist in opposing or seeking to injure: to prosecute or sue (*Scots law*): to follow in order to overtake and capture or kill: to chase: to hunt: to follow with haste: to follow up: to follow the course of: to be engaged in: to carry on: to seek to obtain or attain: to proceed in accordance with: to proceed with. — *v.i.* to follow: to go on or continue: to act as a prosecutor at law. — *adj.* **pursu'able.** — *ns.* **pursu'al,** (more often) **pursu'ance** pursuit: act of carrying out or (e.g. *in pursuance of this policy*) following out. — *adj.* **pursu'ant** pursuing: in pursuance (with *to*; approaching an *adv.*). — *adv.* **pursu'antly.** — *n.* **pursu'er** one who pursues: a plaintiff (*Scots law*). — *n.* and *adj.* **pursu'ing.** — *adv.* **pursu'ingly.** [A.Fr. *pursuer*, *pursiwer* — popular L. forms *pro-*, *per-sequĕre*, *-īre*, for L. *prōsequī*, *persequī* — *prō-*, *per-* (the prefixes being confused), and *sequī*, to follow.]

pursuit *pər-sūt'*, *-sōōt'*, *n.* the act of pursuing: endeavour to attain: occupation: employment: that which is pursued: a cycle race in which two riders start at opposite sides of a track and try to overtake each other. — **pursuit plane** a type of military aeroplane used in pursuing enemy aeroplanes. [A.Fr. *purseute*, fem. pa.p., see **pursue.**]

pursuivant *pûr's(w)i-vənt*, *n.* an attendant or follower: a state messenger with power to execute warrants: an officer ranking below a herald. [Fr. *poursuivant*, pr.p. of *poursuivre*, to pursue.]

pursy[1] *pûrs'i*, *adj.* puffy: fat and short: short-winded. — *n.* **purs'iness.** [O.Fr. *poulsif*, broken-winded — *poulser* (Fr. *pousser*) — L. *pulsāre*, to drive.]

pursy[2] *pûrs'i*, *adj.* pursed up: puckered. [**purse.**]

purtenance *pûr'tən-əns*, *n.* that which pertains or belongs: the inwards of an animal (*B.*). [Earlier form of **pertinence.**]

purty *pûr'ti*, (*dial.*) *adj.* pretty.

purtraid, purtrayd. See **pourtray.**

purulent *pū'rū-lənt*, *-rōō-*, *adj.* consisting of, of the nature of, forming, full of, characterised by, or like pus. — *ns.* **pū'rulence, pū'rulency.** — *adv.* **pū'rulently.** [L. *pūrulentus* — *pūs*, *pūris*, pus.]

purvey *pûr-vā'*, *v.t.* to provide, furnish: to supply. — *v.i.* to furnish provisions or meals as one's business. — *ns.* **purvey'ance** the act of purveying: preparation in advance (*Spens.*): furnishings, equipment (*Spens.*): a procuring of victuals: that which is supplied: the former royal prerogative of pre-emption of necessaries; **purvey'or** one whose business is to provide victuals or meals: an officer who formerly exacted provisions for the use of the king's household. [A.Fr. *purveier* (Fr. *pourvoir*) — L. *prōvidēre*; see **provide.**]

purview *pûr'vū*, *n.* the body or enacting part of a statute distinguished from the preamble: enactment: scope: range: field of activity or view: competence. [A.Fr. *purveu*, provided, pa.p. of *purveier*; see **purvey.**]

pus *pus*, *n.* a thick yellowish fluid formed by suppuration, consisting of serum, white blood cells, bacteria, and debris of tissue. [L. *pūs*, *pūris*; cf. Gr. *pyon*.]

Puseyism *pū'zi-izm*, *n.* the High Church and Catholic principles of Dr E. B. *Pusey* (1800–1882), and other Oxford divines, as set forth in 'Tracts for the Times'. — *adjs.* **Pūseyist'ic, -al.** — *n.* **Pū'seyite.**

push[1] *pŏosh*, *v.t.* to thrust or press against: to drive by pressure: to press or drive forward: to urge: to press hard: to put forth: to advance, carry to a further point: to promote, or seek to promote, vigorously and persistently: to make efforts to promote the sale of: to effect by thrusting forward: to peddle (drugs): to come near (an age or number). — *v.i.* to make a thrust: to butt (*B.*): to exert pressure: to make an effort: to press forward: to make one's way by exertion: to reach forth: to be urgent and persistent: to play a push-stroke. — *n.* a thrust: an impulse: pressure: a help to advancement: enterprising or aggressive pertinacity: an effort: an onset: an offensive: a push-stroke: a gang of roughs (*Austr.*): a group of people sharing an interest or background (*Austr.*): a company: dismissal or rejection (*coll.*). — *adj.* **pushed** in a hurry (*coll.*): short of money (*coll.*). — *n.* **push'er** one who pushes: a machine or part that pushes: an airscrew placed behind: an aeroplane so propelled: a child's table implement, or a finger of bread, used for pushing food on to a fork: a self-assertive person: one who assiduously seeks social advancement: a dope pedlar. — *adj.* **push'ful** energetically or aggressively enterprising. — *adv.* **push'fully.** — *n.* **push'fulness.** — *adj.* **push'ing** pressing forward in business: enterprising: self-assertive. — *adv.* **push'ingly.** — *n.* **push'iness.** — *adj.* **push'y** aggressive: self-assertive. — **push'-ball** a game in which an enormous ball is pushed; **push'-bicycle** (*coll.* **-bike**), **-cycle** one propelled by foot; **push'-button** a knob which when pressed puts on or cuts off an electric current, as for bells, etc. (*adj.* operated by, or using, push-button, -buttons); **push'-cart** (*U.S.*) a street vender's barrow; **push'-chair** a folding-chair with wheels, for a child; **push'-off** an act of pushing off a boat: a send-off; **push'-over** an easy thing: a person or side easily overcome; **push'-pin** a children's game in which pins are pushed one across another (*Shak.*): a large-headed drawing-pin, used esp. to mark points on maps (*U.S.*). — *adj.* **push'-pull'** of any piece of apparatus in which two electrical or electronic devices act in opposition to each other, as, e.g., of an amplifier in which two thermionic valves so acting serve to reduce distortion. — **push'rod** in an internal combustion engine, a metal rod that opens and closes the valves. — *v.t.* **push'-start'** to start (a motor-car) by pushing it while it is in gear. — *n.* the act of starting the car thus. — **push'-stroke** a push instead of an ordinary hit or stroke at a ball: in billiards, one in which the cue is still or again in contact with the cue-ball when the cue-ball touches the object-ball; **push'-tug** a tug for pushing, rather than pulling, barges. — **at a push** when circumstances urgently require: if really necessary; **give, get the push** to dismiss, reject, be dismissed, be rejected; **push along** (*coll.*) to depart, to go on one's way; **push around** to bully; **push-button civilisation** one in which the ordinary unskilled person has the benefits of technology at the pressing of a button; **push-button war** one carried on by guided missiles, released by push-button; **push for** to make strenuous efforts to achieve; **push off** of a rower or a boat, to leave the bank, shore, etc.: to depart (*coll.*); **push one's fortune** to busy oneself in seeking a fortune; **push one's luck** see **luck; push out** (of person, boat) to row or be rowed out towards open water; **push-pull train** one which can be pulled or pushed by the same locomotive; **push the boat out** see **boat; push the bottle** to take one's liquor and pass the bottle round; **push through** to compel acceptance of; **push up the daisies** to be dead and buried. [Fr. *pousser* — L. *pulsāre*, freq. of *pellĕre*, *pulsum*, to beat.]

push[2] *pŏosh*, (*Shak.*) *interj.* pish. — *n.* an exclamation of 'push'. [**pish.**]

Pushtu, Pashtu, Pushtoo *push'tōō*, **Pushto, Pashto** *-tō*, **Pakhtu** *puhh'tōō*, **Pakhto** *-tō*, *ns.* the language of the

Afghans proper. — *ns.* **Push′tun, Pash′tun, Pakh′tun, Pakh′toon,** etc. a member of a Pushtu-speaking tribe in Pakistan and Afghanistan. — *ns.pl.* the tribe. — Also *adjs.* [Afghan *Pashtō, Pakhtō*.]

pusillanimous *pū-si-lan′i-məs, adj.* wanting firmness of mind: mean-spirited: cowardly. — *adv.* **pusillan′imously.** — *n.* **pusillanim′ity.** [L. *pusillanimis* — *pusillus*, very little, *animus*, mind.]

pusle. An old spelling of **puzzle**[1,2].

puss[1] *pŏŏs, n.* a familiar name for a cat: a hare, in sportsmen's language: a playfully pejorative name for a child or a girl: a puss-moth. — *n.* **puss′y** a dim. of **puss** (also **puss′y-cat**): anything soft and furry: a willow-catkin: the female genitalia (*slang*): sexual intercourse (*slang*): a woman considered as a sexual object (*slang; derog.*). — **puss′-gen′tleman** (*arch.*) a dandy; **puss′-moth** a thick-bodied hairy notodontid moth (*Dicranura*, or *Cerura, vinula*) whose caterpillar feeds on willow or poplar leaves; **Puss′yfoot** U.S. nickname of William E. Johnson (1862–1945) from his stealthy ways as a revenue officer: (without *cap.*) hence, from his prohibitionist campaigns, a prohibitionist — *v.i.* (without *cap.*) to go stealthily: to act timidly, cautiously or non-committally. — **puss′yfooter; puss′y-will′ow** a common American willow, *Salix discolor* or other species with silky spring catkins. — **puss in the corner** a children's game in which the places are continually being changed, while the player who is out tries to secure one of them. [Cf. Du. *poes*, puss; Ir. and Gael. *pus*, a cat.]

puss[2] *pŏŏs, n.* (*slang*) the face. [Ir. *pus*, a mouth.]

pussel *pus′l, puz′l, (Shak.) n.* a dirty drab. [**pucelle**.]

pustule *pus′tūl, n.* a pimple containing pus: a pimple-like or warty spot or elevation. — *adj.* **pus′tulant** causing pustulation. — Also *n.* — *adjs.* **pus′tular, pus′tulous.** — *v.t.* and *v.i.* **pus′tulate.** — *n.* **pustulā′tion.** [L. *pustula*.]

put[1] *pŏŏt, v.t.* to push or thrust: to cast, throw, hurl (esp. by a thrusting movement of the hand from the shoulder): to drive: to impel: to convey, transport: to force, constrain: to incite: to place, or cause to be, in such and such a position, state, predicament, relation, etc.: to set: to place, lay, deposit: to apply: to append, affix: to connect: to add: to commit: to assign: to assign or suggest a course of action to (with *on*, as a diet, a study, a track; or *to*, as a task): to subject: to reduce: to convert: to render: to express: to assert, have: to propound: to submit to a vote: to impose: to impute: to call upon, oblige, stake, venture, invest: to repose (as trust, confidence). — *v.i.* to thrust (*arch.* or *Northern*): to proceed, make one's way (*naut.*): to set out, esp. hurriedly: to flow (*U.S.*): — *pr.p.* **putting** (*pŏŏt′*); *pa.t.* and *pa.p.* **put.** — *n.* a push or thrust: a cast, throw, esp. of a heavy stone from the shoulder: on the stock exchange, an option of selling within a certain time certain securities or commodities, at a stipulated price (also **put option**). — *ns.* **putter** (*pŏŏt′ər*) one who puts: one who pushes or hauls trams in a coal-mine; **putt′ing** the act or sport of hurling a heavy stone or weight from the hand by a sudden thrust from the shoulder (also **putting the shot**). — **put′-and-take** a gambling game played with a top; **put′-down** a snub: an action intended to assert one's superiority; **put′-in** (*Rugby football*) the act of throwing the ball into a set scrum; **put′-off** an excuse, a makeshift, evasion: a postponement; **put′-on** a hoax; **putt′er-on** (*Shak.*) an instigator; **putt′er-out** (*obs.*) one who deposited money on going abroad, on condition of receiving a larger sum on his return, if he ever returned; **putt′ing-stone** a heavy stone used in putting the stone. — *adj.* **put-up′** speciously preconcerted. — **put about** to change the course, as of a ship: to publish, circulate: to distress (*Scot.*); **put a brake on** see **brake; put across** to carry out successfully, bring off: to perform so as to carry the audience with one; **put an end** or **a stop to** to cause to discontinue; **put away** to renounce: to divorce: to kill, esp. an old or ill animal: to stow away, pack up, set aside: to put

into the proper or desirable place: to imprison: to eat; **put back** to push backward: to delay: to repulse: to turn and sail back for port (*naut.*): to reduce one's finances (*coll.*); **put by** to set aside: to parry: to store up; **put case** see **case**[2]; **put down** to crush, quell: to kill, esp. an old or ill animal: to snub, humiliate: to degrade: to confute (*Shak.*): to enter, write down on paper: to reckon: to attribute: to give up (*rare*): to surpass, outshine: to preserve, put in pickle (*dial.*): of an aeroplane, to land (often with *at*): to pay (a deposit): to put (a baby) to bed (*coll.*): in cricket, to drop (a catch); **put for** to make an attempt to gain; **put forth** to extend: to propose: to publish: to exert: to display: to lend at interest: to set out from port: to produce, extrude; **put forward** to propose: to advance; **put in** to introduce: to insert: to lodge, deposit, hand in: to make a claim or application (*for*): to enter: to enter a harbour: to interpose: to perform towards completing a total: to spend, pass, fill up with some occupation: to appoint; **put in an appearance** see **appear; put in mind** to remind, **put it across someone** to defeat someone by ingenuity; **put it on** to pretend (to be ill, etc.); **put it past someone** to judge it inconsistent with someone's character; **put off** to lay aside: to take off (*arch.*): to lay aside the character of: to palm off: to dismiss (*arch.*): to turn aside with evasions, excuses, or unsatisfying substitutes: to divert, turn aside from a purpose: to postpone: to idle away, spend in vain: to disconcert: to cause aversion or disinclination: to push from shore; **put on** to don, clothe with: to assume, esp. deceptively: to mislead, deceive: to superpose: to impose: to affix, attach, apply: to add (as weight, charges, etc.): to stake: to move forward: to move faster (*obs.*): to set to work: to set in operation: to incite: to turn on the supply of: to score: to stage: clad (as *well put on*, or *putten on*; respectably dressed, *pa.p.*; *Scot.*); **put on to** to make aware of: to connect with by telephone; **put out** to expel: to dismiss from a game and innings: to send forth: to stretch forth: to extinguish: to place at interest: to expand: to publish: to disconcert: to put to inconvenience: to offend: to dislocate: to exert: to produce: to place with others or at a distance: to go out to sea, leave port: to remove bodily or blind (an eye): to render unconscious (*slang*): of a woman, to be willing to grant sexual favours (*U.S. slang*); **put over** to refer (*Shak.*): to carry through successfully: to impress an audience, spectators, the public, favourably with: to impose, pass off; **put through** to bring to an end: to accomplish: to put in telephonic communication: to process (*comput.*); **putting the shot, stone, weight** putting (q.v.); **put to** to apply: to add to: to connect with: to harness: to shut: to set to; **put to death** see **death; put to it** to press hard: to distress; **put to rights** see **rights; put to sea** to begin a voyage; **put to the sword** see **sword; put two and two together** to draw a conclusion from various facts; **put up** to start from cover, as a hare: to stow away, put aside: to parcel up: to sheathe: to compound: to endure tamely (*obs.*): to accommodate with lodging: to take lodgings: to nominate or stand for election: to expose for sale: to present (as a good game, fight, or defence, a prayer): to preconcert; **put-up job** a dishonest scheme prearranged usu. by several people; **put upon** to take undue advantage of: to impose upon; **put up to** to incite to: to make conversant with, supply with useful information or tips about; **put up with** to endure; **stay put** to remain passively in the position assigned. [Late O.E. *putian* (found in the verbal-noun *putung*, instigation); there were also *potian* and *pȳtan*, which may account for some of the dialect forms; cf. Dan. *putte*, Sw. *putta*.]

put[2] *put.* See **putt**[1,2,3].

putamen *pū-tā′mən, n.* a fruit-stone: the membrane within an egg-shell: the lateral part of the lenticular nucleus of the cerebrum: — *pl.* **putamina** (-*tam′in-ə*). [L. *putāmen*, clippings, waste, *putāre*, to prune.]

putative *pū′tə-tiv, adj.* supposed: reputed: commonly supposed to be. — **putative marriage** a marriage supposed invalid by canon law, but entered into in good faith by at least one of the parties. [L. *putātīvus* — *putāre, -ātum,* to suppose.]

putcher *pōoch'ər, n.* a conical wicker trap for catching salmon. [Origin unknown.]

putchock, putchuk, pachak *puch-uk', n.* costus-root (so-called; see **Costus**). [Hind. *pachak;* origin obscure.]

puteal *pū'ti-əl, n.* a well-curb. [L. *pūteal, -ālis* — *puteus,* a well.]

puteli *put'e-lē, n.* a flat-bottomed Ganges craft. [Hindi *paṭelī.*]

putid *pū'tid, adj.* rotten: foul. [L. *pūtidus.*]

putlog *put'log,* **putlock** *-lok, ns.* a cross-piece in a scaffolding, the inner end resting in a hole left in the wall. [Origin obscure; **putlock** seems to be the older form.]

putois *pū-twä', n.* a brush of polecat's hair, or substitute, for painting pottery. [Fr.]

put-put *pŏot'-pŏot', put'-put', n.* the noise of a small motor. — *v.i.* to make such a noise: — *pr.p.* **put'= putt'ing;** *pa.t.* and *pa.p.* **-putt'ed.** [Imit.]

putrefy *pū'tri-fī, v.t.* to cause to rot: to corrupt. — *v.i.* to rot: — *pr.p.* **pu'trefying;** *pa.t.* and *pa.p.* **pu'trefied.** — *adj.* **putrefacient** (*-fā'shənt*) causing putrefaction. — *n.* **putrefaction** (*-fak'shən*) rotting. — *adjs.* **putrefac'tive; putrefi'able.** — *n.* **putrescence** (*-tres'əns*) incipient rottenness. — *adjs.* **putresc'ent; putresc'ible.** — *n.* **putresc'ine** (*-ēn, -in*) a substance, $H_2N(CH_2)_4NH_2$, formed in putrefaction of flesh. — *adj.* **pu'trid** rotten: wretchedly bad (*slang*). — *adv.* **pu'tridly.** — *ns.* **putrid'ity, pu'tridness.** — **putrid fever** typhus. [L. *putrefacĕre, putrēscĕre, putridus* — *puter, putris,* rotten.]

putsch *pŏoch, n.* a sudden revolutionary outbreak. [Swiss Ger. dialect.]

putt¹, also **put,** *put, v.t.* to hurl in putting (as a weight, stone; *Scot.*; see **put**): to strike in making a putt (*golf*). — *v.i.* to make a putt or putts: — *pr.p.* **putting** (*put'*); *pa.p.* and *pa.t.* **putted** (*put'*). — *n.* a throw or cast (*Scot.*; see **put**): a delicate stroke such as is made with a putter on, or sometimes near, a putting-green, with the object of rolling the ball, if possible, into the hole (*golf*). — *ns.* **putter** (*put'ər*) one who putts or can putt: a short stiff golf-club with upright striking-face, used in putting; **putt'ing** the exercise of hurling a heavy weight (*Scot.*; see **put;** also **putting the shot**): the act or art of making a putt: a game played with putters and golf-balls on a small course with several holes. — **putt'ing-cleek** a putter of cleek design, the blade long and narrow, running straight from the shaft; **putt'ing= green** the turf, made firm and smooth for putting, round each of the holes of a golf-course: by the rules all within 20 yards of the hole, hazards excluded: a small golf-course with several holes for practice or for putting as an informal game; **putt'ing-stone** see **put¹.** [A Scottish form of **put¹.**]

putt², **put** *put, n.* an old card-game like nap. [Perh. **put¹.**]

putt³, **put** *put,* (*arch.*) *n.* a greenhorn: a bumpkin. [17th-century slang; origin unknown.]

puttee, puttie *put'ē, -i, n.* a cloth strip wound round the leg from ankle to knee, as a legging. [Hindi. *pattī.*]

putten. See **pit³.**

putter¹ *put'ər,* orig. U.S. form of **potter².**

putter². See **putt¹.**

puttie. See **puttee.**

puttier. See **putty.**

putto *pŏot'ō, n.* very young boy, often winged, in Renaissance or Baroque art: — *pl.* **putti** (*pŏot'ē*). [It.]

puttock *put'ək, n.* a kite (*Shak.*): a buzzard: a kite-like person. [M.E. *puttok,* perh. conn. with O.E. *pyttel,* kite.]

putty *put'i, n.* orig. putty-powder (*polishers'* or *jewellers' putty*): a cement of whiting and linseed oil (*glaziers'* or *painters' putty*): a fine cement of slaked lime and water only (*plasterers' putty*): a yellowish grey colour: a weak-willed, easily manipulated person (*fig.*). — *v.t.* to fix, coat, or fill with putty: — *pr.p.* **putt'ying;** *pa.t.*

and *pa.p.* **putt'ied.** — *n.* **putt'ier** a glazier. — *adjs.* **putt'y-coloured; putt'y-faced** having a putty-coloured face. — **putt'y-knife** a blunt, flexible tool for laying on putty; **putt'y-pow'der** stannic oxide (often with lead oxide) used for polishing glass. [Fr. *potée,* potful, putty-powder — *pot.*]

puture *pū'tyər,* **pulture** *pul',* (*hist.*) *ns.* the claim of foresters, etc., to food for man, horse, and dog within the bounds of a forest. [A.Fr. *puture,* Old Northern Fr. *pulture* — L.L. *pu(l)tūra,* app. — L. *puls, pultis,* porridge.]

putz *pŏots, n.* (*U.S.*) in Pennsylvanian Dutch homes, a representation of the Nativity traditionally placed under a Christmas tree: — *pl.* **putz'es.** [Ger. *putzen,* to decorate.]

puy *pwē, n.* a small volcanic cone, as in Auvergne. [Fr., hill — L. *podium,* a height; cf. **pew, podium.**]

puzel, puzzel. Same as **pucelle, pussel.**

puzzle¹ *puz'l, v.t.* to perplex: to bewilder: to afford difficulty of solution to: to set a problem that gives difficulty to: to entangle, complicate: to solve by systematic or assiduous thinking (with *out*). — *v.i.* to be bewildered: to labour at solution: to search about. — *n.* bewilderment: perplexity: anything that puzzles: a problem: a riddle or a toy designed to try ingenuity. — *ns.* **puzz'ledom** (*rare*) bewilderment; **puzz'lement** the state of being puzzled; **puzz'ler.** — *adj.* **puzz'ling** posing: perplexing. — *adv.* **puzz'lingly.** — **puzz'le-head** one who is puzzle-headed. — *adj.* **puzz'le-head'ed** having the head full of confused notions. — **puzz'le-head'- edness; puzz'le-monkey** monkey-puzzle; **puzz'le-peg** a piece of wood so secured under a dog's jaw as to keep his nose from the ground; **puzzle-prize book** a book containing a puzzle, the successful solver of which is rewarded with a prize. [Origin obscure.]

puzzle². See **pucelle.**

puzzolana *pŏot-sō-lä'nə.* Same as **pozzolana.**

PVC. See **polyvinyl chloride.**

PX *pē eks, n.* a shop selling goods for U.S. servicemen and their families overseas. [Abbrev. of **post** and **exchange.**]

pyaemia *pī-ē'mi-ə, n.* infection of the blood with bacteria from a septic focus, with abscesses in different parts of the body. — Also **pye'mia.** — *adj.* **pyae'mic.** [Gr. *pyon,* pus, *haima,* blood.]

pyat. Same as **pyot.**

pycnic. Same as **pyknic.**

pycnidium *pik-nid'i-əm, n.* in some fungi a receptacle like a perithecium, containing hyphae which produce conidia. — *n.* **pycnid'iospore** a conidium produced in a pycnidium. [Gr. *pyknos,* thick, dense, dim. suff. *-idion* Latinised to *-idium.*]

pycnite *pik'nīt, n.* a columnar variety of topaz. [Gr. *pyknos,* dense.]

pycno-, pykno- *pik'nō-, pik-no'-* in composition, dense, close. — *ns.* **pycnoconid'ium** a pycnidiospore; **pycnog'- onid** (Gr. *gony,* knee) a sea-spider. — *n.pl.* **Pycnogon'- ida** the sea-spiders, a class of marine arthropods with more leg than body. — *adj.* **pycnog'onoid.** — *ns.* **pycnom'eter, pyknom'eter** an instrument for determining specific gravities; **pyc'non** in Greek music, that part of the tetrachord (chromatic or enharmonic) where the smallest intervals fell: in mediaeval music, a semitone; **pyc'nospore** a pycnidiospore. — *adj.* **pycno- style** (Gr. *stȳlos,* column) with close-set columns, $1\frac{1}{2}$ diameters apart. — *n.* a pycnostyle building. [Gr. *pyknos,* dense.]

pye. See **pie².**

pyebald. See **piebald.**

pye-dog *pī'-dog, n.* an ownerless or pariah dog. — Also **pi'-dog, pie'-dog.** [Hind. *pāhī,* outsider.]

pyelitis *pī-ə-lī'tis, n.* inflammation of the pelvis of the kidney. — *adj.* **pyelitic** (*-lit'ik*). — *ns.* **py'elogram** an X-ray picture of the renal pelvis, the kidney and the ureter; **pyelography** (*-log'rə-fi*); **pyelonephritis** (*-nef- rī'tis*) inflammation of the kidney and the renal pelvis.

— *adj.* **pyelonephritic** (-*rit'ik*). [Gr. *pyelos*, a trough.]
pyemia. See **pyaemia.**
pyengadu *pyeng-gä-dōō'*, *n.* the ironwood (Xylia; Mimosaceae) of Burma, etc. [Burmese *pyengkadō*.]
pyet. Same as **pyot.**
pygal *pī'gǝl*, *adj.* belonging to the rump or posteriors of an animal. — *n.* the posterior median plate of a chelonian carapace. [Gr. *pȳgē*, rump.]
pygarg *pī'gärg*, (*B.*) *n.* possibly the addax antelope. — N.E.B. says it is the 'white-rumped deer'. [Gr. *pȳgē*, rump, *argos*, white.]
pygidium *pī-gid'i-ǝm*, or -*jid'*, *n.* in insects, the tergum of the last abdominal somite: the tail-shield of a trilobite. — *adj.* **pygid'ial.** [Latinised from Gr. *pȳgidion*, dim. of *pȳgē*, rump.]
pygmy, pigmy *pig'mi*, *n.* a member of the race of dwarfs said by the ancients to have warred with cranes, or of any of the actual dwarf human races, negritos, negrillos, and others: one of the ancient diminutive dwellers in underground houses, etc., in whom some scholars see the historical origins of the fairies and elves of folklore: an elf: an anthropoid ape (*obs.*): a dwarf: any person, animal or thing relatively diminutive or in some way insignificant. — *adj.* dwarfish: diminutive: of the pygmies. — *adjs.* **pygmaean; pyg-, pigmean** (-*mē'ǝn*); **pyg'moid.** [Gr. *pygmaios*, measuring a *pygmē* (13½ inches, distance from elbow to knuckles).]
pygostyle *pī'gō-stīl*, *n.* the bone of a bird's tail. [Gr. *pȳgē*, rump, *stȳlos*, a column.]
pyjamas *pǝ-*, *pi-*, or *pī-jä'mǝz*, *n.pl.* loose trousers tied round the waist, worn by Indians: (in European use) a sleeping-suit. — Also (*U.S.*) **paja'mas.** — *adj.* **pyja'ma'd, pyja'maed** wearing pyjamas. — **pyja'ma-jacket, -trousers.** [Pers. and Hind. *pāëjāmah* — *pāë*, leg, *jāmah*, clothing.]
pyknic *pik'nik*, *adj.* characterised by short squat stature, small hands and feet, relatively short limbs, domed abdomen, short neck, round face. [Gr. *pyknos*, thick.]
pyknometer. Same as **pycnometer.**
pyknosome *pik'nǝ-sōm*. Same as **amplosome.**
pylon *pī'lon*, *n.* a gateway, gate-tower, gatehouse, or mass of building through which an entrance passes, esp. the gateway of an Egyptian temple (*archit.*): a guiding mark at an aerodrome: a structure for support of power-cables: an artificial leg: an external structure on an aeroplane for attaching an engine, etc.: — *pl.* **py'lons.** [Gr. *pylōn, -ōnos* — *pylē*, a gate.]
pylorus *pī-*, *pi-lō'rǝs*, -*lō'*, *n.* the opening from the stomach to the intestines. — *adj.* **pylor'ic** (-*lor'*). [L., — Gr. *pylōros*, gate-keeper, pylorus — *pylē*, an entrance, *ōrā*, care; cf. *ouros*, a guardian.]
pyne. Same as **pine[2].**
pyogenic *pī-ǝ-jen'ik*, *adj.* pus-forming. — *n.* **pyogen'esis.** — *adj.* **py'oid** purulent. — *n.* **pyorrhoea** (-*rē'ǝ*; Gr. *rhoiā*, flow) discharge of pus: now, suppuration in the sockets of teeth. — *adjs.* **pyorrhoe'al, pyorrhoe'ic.** [Gr. *pyon*, pus.]
pyoner, pyonings. See **pioneer.**
pyorrhoea. See **pyogenic.**
pyot, pyat, pyet, piet *pī'ǝt*, (*Scot.*) *n.* a magpie. — *adj.* pied. — *adj.* **pi'oted.** [pie[1].]
pyracanth *pī'rǝ-kanth*, **pyracantha** -*kan'thǝ*, *ns.* a thorny evergreen shrub of the genus *Pyracantha*, near akin to hawthorn. [Gr. *pȳrakantha* — *pȳr*, fire, *akanthos*, thorn.]
pyral. See **pyre.**
pyralis *pir'ǝ-lis*, *n.* an insect feigned to live or breed in fire (*obs.*): (with *cap.*) a genus of moths, giving name to a heterogeneous family, the **Pyralidae** (*pir-al'i-dē*). — *n.* and *adj.* **pyr'alid** (a member) of this family. [Gr. *pȳrǎlis* — *pȳr*, fire.]
pyramid *pir'ǝ-mid*, *n.* a solid figure on a triangular, square, or polygonal base, with triangular sides meeting in a point: any object or structure of that or similar form, esp. a great Egyptian monument: a crystal form

of three or more faces each cutting three axes (*crystal.*): (in *pl.*) a game played on a billiard-table in which the balls are arranged in pyramid shape: — *pl.* usu. **pyr'amids,** also **pyramides** (*pir-am'i-dēz*), and sometimes (*poet.*) **pyram'id(e)s.** — *v.i.* (chiefly *U.S.*) to increase one's holdings, profits, etc. during a boom period by using paper profits for further purchases. — *adjs.* **pyram'idal, pyramid'ic, -al** having the form of a pyramid. — *advs.* **pyram'idally, pyramid'ically.** — *ns.* **pyramid'ion** the small pyramidal apex of an obelisk; **pyram'idist, pyramidol'ogist** one who studies the Egyptian Pyramids; **pyramidol'ogy; pyr'amis** (*Shak.*, etc.) a pyramid: — *pl.* **pyram'ides, pyr'amises; pyram'idon** an organ-stop with pipes like inverted pyramids. — **pyramid selling** a method of distributing goods by selling batches to agents who then sell batches at increased prices to sub-agents, and so on. [Gr. *pyramis, -idos*.]
pyrargyrite *pīr-*, or *pir-är'jir-īt*, *n.* ruby-silver ore, sulphide of silver and antimony. [Gr. *pȳr*, fire, *argyros*, silver.]
pyre *pīr*, *n.* a pile of combustibles for burning a dead body. — *adj.* **pyr'al.** [L. *pyra* — Gr. *pȳrā* — *pȳr*, fire.]
Pyrenaean. See **Pyrenean.**
pyrene[1] *pī'rēn*, *n.* a fruit-stone. — *ns.* **pyre'nocarp** (Gr. *karpos*, fruit) a perithecium; **pyre'noid** a small round albuminous body concerned in starch-formation, found in the chloroplasts of some algae, etc. — *n.pl.* **Pyrēnomyce'tēs** (Gr. *mykēs*, fungus) a group of Ascomycetes whose characteristic fructification is the perithecium. — *adj.* **pyrenomyce'tous.** [Gr. *pȳrēn, -ēnos*, fruit-stone.]
pyrene[2] *pī'rēn*, *n.* a hydrocarbon ($C_{16}H_{10}$) got by dry distillation of coal. [Gr. *pȳr*, fire.]
Pyrenean, Pyrenaean *pir-ǝ-nē'ǝn*, *adj.* of the *Pyrenees*, the mountains between France and Spain. — *n.* a native of the Pyrenees: (in *pl.*) the Pyrenees (*obs.*). — *n.* **pyrenē'ite** a black garnet. — **Pyrenean mountain dog** a large dog with a dense white coat, bred in the Pyrenees to guard flocks. [L. *Pȳrēnaeus* — Gr. *Pȳrēnaios*.]
pyrenoid, etc. See **pyrene[1].**
Pyrethrum *pī-rēth'rǝm*, *pī-reth'rǝm*, *pir-eth'rǝm*, *n.* a former genus of composite plants now merged in Chrysanthemum, including feverfew: (without *cap.*) still applied to various garden flowers, esp. varieties of *Chrysanthemum coccineum*: (without *cap.*) insect-powder of flower-heads of various species of pyrethrum: (without *cap.*) in pharmacy, the root of pellitory of Spain. — *ns.* **pyrēth'rin** (or -*re'*) either of two insecticidal oily esters prepared from pyrethrum flowers; **pyrēth'roid** (or -*re'*) any of various synthetic compounds related to the pyrethrins, and sharing their insecticidal properties. [L., — Gr. *pȳrĕthron*, pellitory of Spain.]
pyretic *pī-ret'ik*, *pir-et'ik*, *adj.* of, of the nature of, for the cure of, fever. — *ns.* **pyretol'ogy** study of fevers; **pyretother'apy** treatment by inducing high body temperature; **pyrex'ia** fever. — *adjs.* **pyrex'ial, pyrex'ic.** [Gr. *pȳretikos*, feverish — *pȳretos*, fever; and *pȳressein*, to be feverish — *pȳr*, fire.]
Pyrex® *pī'reks*, *n.* a type of glassware containing oxide of boron and so resistant to heat. [Gr. *pȳr*, fire, and L. *rēx*, king.]
pyrexia, etc. See **pyretic.**
pyrheliometer *pir-*, *pīr-hē-li-om'i-tǝr*, *n.* an instrument for measuring the heating effect of the sun's rays. — *adj.* **pyrheliometric** (-*ō-met'rik*). [Gr. *pȳr*, fire, *hēlios*, sun, *metron*, measure.]
pyridine *pir'*, or *pīr'i-dēn*, -*dīn*, *n.* a strong-smelling, colourless, strongly basic liquid, C_5H_5N, got in distillation of bone-oil, coal-tar, etc. — *ns.* **pyridox'in(e)** a pyridine derivative, a member of the vitamin B complex; **pyrim'idine** one of a group of heterocyclic compounds forming an essential part of nucleic acids. [Gr. *pȳr*, fire.]
pyriform *pir'i-förm*, *adj.* pear-shaped. [L. *pyrum*, misspelling of *pirum*, a pear, *förma*, form.]

pyrimethamine *pi-ri-meth'ə-mēn*, or *pī-*, *n.* a powerful anti-malaria drug. [Gr. *pȳr*, fire, *methyl*, and **amine**.]

pyrimidine. See **pyridine.**

pyrites *pīr-, pir-ī'tēz, n.* a brassy yellow mineral, iron disulphide, crystallising in the cubic system, occurring in octahedra, pyritohedra, etc. (also called **pyrite** *pī'rīt*, **iron pyri'tes**): extended to a large class of mineral sulphides and arsenides. — *adjs.* **pyritic** (*pir-, pīr-it'ik*), **-al; pyritif'erous.** — *v.t.* **pyr'itise, -ize** to convert into, or replace by, pyrites. — *adj.* **pyritohē'dral.** — *n.* **pyritohē'dron** a pentagonal dodecahedron: — *pl.* **pyritohē'dra.** — *adj.* **pyr'itous.** — **arsenical pyrites** mispickel; **cockscomb pyrites, spear pyrites** twinned forms of marcasite; **copper pyrites** sulphide of copper and iron, chalcopyrite, a mineral much resembling iron pyrites; **magnetic pyrites** pyrrhotite. [Gr. *pyrītēs*, striking fire — *pȳr*, fire.]

pyrithiamine *pi-ri-thī'ə-mēn, n.* an anti-vitamin causing thiamine (vitamin B₁) deficiency. [Gr. *pȳr*, fire, and **thiamine.**]

pyro- *pī'rō-*, in composition, fire, heat, fever: obtained by heating or as if by heating, or by removing (theoretically) a molecule of water (*chem.*). — *adjs.* **pyroacet'ic, pyrophosphor'ic, pyrosulphu'ric, pyrotartar'ic,** etc., related in this way to acetic, phosphoric, etc., acid. — *ns.* **pyrophos'phate, pyrotar'trate,** etc., a salt of such an acid. — *adj.* **pyrochem'ical** relating to, producing, or produced by chemical changes at high temperatures. — *v.t.* **py'rolyse** (*U.S.* **-lyze**) to decompose by pyrolysis. — *n.* **pyrolysis** (*pi-rol'is-is*; Gr. *lysis*, loosing) decomposition of a substance by heat. — *adj.* **pyrolytic** (*-lit'ik*). [Gr. *pȳr*, in compounds *pȳr-*, fire.]

pyro *pī'rō*, (*photog.*) *n.* a familiar short form of **pyrogallol.**

pyroballogy *pī-rō-bal'ə-ji*, (*Sterne*) *n.* the science of artillery. [Gr. *pȳr*, fire, *ballein*, to throw, *logos*, discourse.]

pyroclastic *pī-rō-klas'tik, adj.* formed of fragments by igneous agency. — *n.pl.* **pyroclas'tics** ash and other debris ejected by a volcano (also **py'roclast** *n.*). [Gr. *pȳr*, fire, *klastos*, broken.]

pyro-electric *pī-rō-i-lek'trik, adj.* becoming positively and negatively electrified at opposite poles on heating or cooling: of pyro-electricity. — *n.* **pyro-electricity** (*-el-ik-tris'i-ti*) the property of being pyro-electric: the study of the phenomena shown by pyro-electric crystals. [Gr. *pȳr*, fire, and **electric.**]

pyrogallol *pī-rō-gal'ol, n.* a phenol got by heating *gallic* acid, used in photographic developing — also called **pyrogall'ic acid.**

pyrogenic *pī-rō-jen'ik*, **pyrogenetic** *-jin-et'ik*, **pyrogenous** *-roj'ə-nəs, adjs.* produced by, or producing, heat or fever. — *n.* **py'rogen** a substance causing heat or fever. [Gr. *pȳr*, fire, root of *gignesthai*, to become.]

pyrognostic *pī-rog-nos'tik, adj.* pertaining to testing of minerals by flame. — *n.pl.* **pyrognos'tics** the properties of a mineral revealed by such testing. [Gr. *pȳr*, fire, *gnōstikos*, discriminating.]

pyrography *pī-rog'rə-fi, n.* poker-work. — *n.* **pyrogravure'.** [Gr. *pȳr*, fire, *graphein*, to write.]

pyrokinesis *pī-rō-kī-nē'sis* or *-ki-, n.* the ability to start fires by thought alone. [Gr. *pȳr*, fire, *kīnēsis*, movement.]

Pyrola *pir'ə-lə, n.* the wintergreen genus, giving name to the family **Pyrolā'ceae,** akin to the heaths. [Dim. of *pyrus*, a misspelling of L. *pirus*, a pear-tree.]

pyrolatry *pī-rol'ə-tri, n.* fire-worship. — *n.* **pyrol'ater** a fire-worshipper. [Gr. *pȳr*, fire, *latreiā*, worship.]

pyroligneous *pī-rō-lig'ni-əs, adj.* got by distillation of wood. — **pyroligneous acid** wood-vinegar, a mixture of acetic acid, methyl alcohol, etc.; **pyroligneous alcohol** wood-spirit, methyl alcohol. [Gr. *pȳr*, and L. *ligneus — lignum*, wood.]

pyrolusite *pī-rō-lū'sīt, -loo', n.* native manganese dioxide. [Gr. *pȳr*, *lousis*, washing, from its use in decolorising molten glass.]

pyrolysis, pyrolytic. See **pyro-.**

pyromancy *pī'rō-man-si, n.* divination by fire. — *adj.*

pyromant'ic. [Gr. *pȳr*, fire, *manteiā*, divination.]

pyromania *pī-rō-mā'ni-ə, n.* an incendiary mania. — *n.* and *adj.* **pyromā'niac.** — *adj.* **pyromaniacal** (*-mə-nī'ə-kl*). [Gr. *pȳr*, fire, and **mania.**]

pyromeride *pī-rom'ər-īd, n.* a nodular rhyolite. [Gr. *pȳr*, fire, *meros*, part, as if meaning only partly fusible.]

pyrometer *pī-rom'i-tər, n.* an instrument for measuring high temperatures. — *adjs.* **pyrometric** (*pī-rō-met'rik*), **-al.** — *n.* **pyrom'etry.** [Gr. *pȳr*, fire, *metron*, measure.]

pyromorphite *pī-rō-mōr'fīt, n.* an ore (chloride and phosphate) of lead, so called because the blowpipe bead crystallises on cooling. [Gr. *pȳr*, fire, *morphē*, form.]

pyrope *pī'rōp, n.* a fiery red gemstone (also *poet.* **pyrō'pus**): a red magnesia-alumina garnet, used in jewellery (*min.*). [Gr. *pyrōpos*, fiery-eyed — *ōps, ōpos*, eye, face.]

pyrophone *pī'rō-fōn, n.* an organ producing interference-tones by pairs of flames in tubes, invented by Eugène Kastner (1852–82). [Gr. *pȳr*, fire, *phōnē*, sound, voice.]

pyrophorus *pī-rof'ə-rəs, n.* anything that takes fire on exposure to air: (*cap.*) a genus of tropical American fireflies (elaterid beetles). — *adjs.* **pyrophoric** (*-rō-for'ik*), **pyroph'orous.** [Gr. *pȳrophoros*, fire-bearer — *pȳr*, fire and *pherein*, to carry.]

pyrophotograph *pī-rō-fō'tə-gräf, n.* a burnt-in photograph, as on glass or porcelain. — *adj.* **pyrophotograph'ic.** — *n.* **pyrophotog'raphy.** [Gr. *pȳr*, fire, and **photograph.**]

pyrophyllite *pī-rō-fil'īt, n.* a clay mineral that exfoliates before the blowpipe. [Gr. *pȳr*, fire, *phyllon*, leaf.]

pyropus. See **pyrope.**

pyroscope *pī'rō-skōp, n.* an instrument for measuring the intensity of radiant heat. [Gr. *pȳr*, fire, *skopeein*, to view.]

pyrosis *pī-rō'sis, n.* water-brash. [Gr. *pȳrōsis — pȳr*, fire.]

Pyrosoma *pī-rō-sō'mə, n.* a genus of compound tunicates, with brilliant phosphorescence. — *n.* **py'rosome.** [Gr. *sōma*, body.]

pyrostat *pī'rō-stat, n.* a type of thermostat for use at high temperatures. — *adj.* **pyrostat'ic.** [Gr. *pȳr*, fire, and *thermostat.*]

pyrotechnics *pī-rō-tek'niks, n.* (*sing.*) the art of making fireworks: (*sing.* or *pl.*) display of fireworks: (*sing.* or *pl.*) showy display in talk, music, etc. — *adjs.* **pyrotech'nic, -al.** — *adv.* **pyrotech'nically.** — *ns.* **pyrotech'nist** a maker of fireworks: one skilled in, or given to, pyrotechnics; **py'rotechny** pyrotechnics. [Gr. *pȳr*, fire, *technikos*, skilled — *technē*, art.]

pyroxene *pī'rok-sēn n.* a general name for a group of minerals distinguished from amphiboles by a cleavage angle about 87°, metasilicates of calcium, magnesium, aluminium, and other metals, usually green or black, very common in igneous rocks — augite, diopside, enstatite, etc. — *adj.* **pyroxenic** (*-sen'ik*). — *n.* **pyrox'enite** (*-ən-īt,* or *-ēn'īt*) a rock compound essentially of pyroxene. [Gr. *pȳr*, fire, *xenos*, stranger (because Haüy thought that pyroxene crystals in lava had only been accidentally caught up).]

pyroxylic *pī-rok-sil'ik*, (*obs.*) *adj.* pyroligneous. — *ns.* **pyroxyle** (*-rok'sil*), **pyrox'ylin, -e** nitrated cotton. [Gr. *pȳr*, fire, *xylon*, wood.]

pyrrhic *pir'ik, n.* an ancient Greek war-dance: a foot of two short syllables. — *adj.* pertaining to the dance or to the foot. — *n.* **pyrrhicist** (*pir'i-sist*) a pyrrhic dancer. [Gr. *pyrrichē* (*orchēsis*), pyrrhic dance, said to be from *Pyrrichos*, the inventor.]

Pyrrhic *pir'ik, adj.* of or pertaining to *Pyrrhus*, king of Epirus (318–272 B.C.). — **Pyrrhic victory** a victory gained at too great a cost, in allusion to Pyrrhus's exclamation after his defeat of the Romans at Heraclea on the Siris (280), 'Another such victory and we are lost'.

Pyrrhonism *pir'ən-izm, n.* the complete scepticism of *Pyrrhō* (Gr. *Pyrrōn*) of Elis (3rd cent. B.C.). — *adj.* and *n.* **Pyrrhonian** (*pir-ō'ni-ən*). — *adj.* **Pyrrhonic** (*-on'ik*). — *n.* **Pyrrh'onist.**

pyrrhotite *pir'ō-tīt, n.* magnetic pyrites, an iron sulphide, often with nickel. — Also **pyrrh'otine** (*-tēn*). [Gr. *pyrrotēs*, redness — *pȳr*, fire.]

pyrrhous *pir'əs, adj.* reddish. [Gr. *pyrros*, flame-coloured — *pȳr*, fire.]

pyrrole *pi'rōl, n.* a colourless toxic liquid found in many naturally-occurring compounds, e.g. porphyrins and chlorophyll. — *n.* **pyrrolidine** (*pi-rol'i-dēn*) a colourless strongly alkaline base, C₄H₉N, both occurring naturally and produced from pyrrole. [Gr. *pyrros*, flame-coloured, L. *oleum*, oil.]

Pyrus *pī'rəs, n.* pear and apple genus of the rose family. [Misspelling of L. *pirus*, pear-tree.]

pyruvate *pī-rōō'vāt,* (*chem.*) *n.* a salt or ester of pyruvic acid. — **pyruvic acid** (*-rōō'vik*) an organic acid, an intermediate in the metabolism of proteins and carbohydrates. [Gr. *pȳr*, fire, L. *ūva*, grape.]

Pythagorean *pi-* or *pī-thag-ər-ē'ən, adj.* pertaining to *Pythagoras* (of Samos; 6th cent. B.C.), the Greek philosopher, or to his philosophy: transformed, as if by transmigration of the soul (taught by Pythagoras): vegetarian. of a diatonic scale perfected by Pythagoras, with its intervals based on mathematical ratios (*mus.*). — *n.* a follower of Pythagoras. — *ns.* **Pythagorē'anism, Pythag'orism** his doctrines. — **Pythagorean letter** or **Samian letter** the Greek letter Ψ which was, for Pythagoras, a symbol of the parting of the ways for vice and virtue; **Pythagorean theorem** that the square on the hypotenuse of a right-angled triangle is equal to the sum of the squares on the other two sides.

Pythia *pith'i-ə, n.* the priestess who delivered the oracles of Pythian Apollo at Delphi. — *adj.* **Pyth'ian** of Delphi, the oracle there, the priestess, or the games held near. — *n.* a native or inhabitant of Delphi: the priestess of Apollo there: Apollo. — *adj.* **Pyth'ic** Pythian: ecstatic. — **Pythian games** one of the four national festivals of ancient Greece, in honour of Apollo, held every four years at Delphi; **Pythian verse** the dactylic hexameter.

[Gr. *Pȳthō*, old name of Delphi; see **python.**]

Pythium *pith'i-əm, n.* a genus of fungi, cause of damping-off of seedlings: (without *cap.*) any fungus of this genus. [Gr. *pȳthein*, to cause to rot.]

pythogenic *pī-thō-jen'ik, adj.* produced by filth. [Gr. *pȳthein*, to rot, root of *gignesthai*, to become.]

Python *pī'thən, n.* the great snake killed by Apollo at Pȳthō (Delphi), according to legend from *pȳthein*, to rot, because it rotted: (without *cap.*) a familiar or possessing spirit: (without *cap.*) one possessed by a spirit: (without *cap.*) an utterer of oracles: (without *cap.*) a large snake that crushes its victims, esp. and properly one of the Old World genus *Python*, akin to the boas. — *n.* **Py'thoness** the priestess of the oracle of Apollo at Delphi: (without *cap.*) a witch. — *adj.* **pythonic** (*-thon'ik*). — *n.* and *adj.* **python'omorph** (*-ō-mörf*; Gr. *morphē*, form) (a member) of the *Pythonomorpha*, in some classifications an extinct suborder of *Squamata*, large marine reptiles of the Cretaceous period, with long, scaly bodies and paddle-shaped limbs.

Pythonesque *pī-thən-esk', adj.* of humour, bizarre and surreal, as in the BBC television comedy programme *Monty Python's Flying Circus.*

pyuria *pī-ū'ri-ə, n.* the presence of pus in the urine. [Gr. *pyon*, pus, *ouron*, urine.]

pyx *piks, n.* a box: a vessel in which the host is kept after consecration, now usu. that in which it is carried to the sick (*R.C.*): a box at the Mint in which sample coins are kept for testing. — *v.t.* to test the weight and fineness of, as the coin deposited in the pyx. — *ns.* **pyxid'ium** (*bot.*) a capsule that opens by a transverse circular split: — *pl.* **pyxid'ia; pyx'is** a little box or casket as for jewels, drugs, toilet materials, etc.: — *pl.* **pyx'ides** (*-id-ēz*). — **trial of the pyx** trial by weight and assay of gold and silver coins by a jury of goldsmiths: periodic official testing of sterling coinage. [L. *pyxis*, a box — Gr. *pyxis, -idos,* dim. *pyxidion* — *pyxos,* box-tree.]

pzazz. Same as **pizazz.**

fāte; fär; hûr; mīne; mōte; för; mūte; mōōn; fŏŏt; dhen (then); *el'ə-mənt* (element)

Q

Q, q $k\bar{u}$, *n.* the seventeenth letter of our alphabet, derived from the abandoned Greek letter koppa (q.v.), and representing in English the same sound as k; always in English followed by *u* (*qu* being sounded as *kw*, except in words from or modelled on French, Spanish, etc.), except sometimes in transliteration of the related Semitic letter qōph (pron. *kōf*) as in *qadi* (more usu. *cadi* or *kadi*): Old English used *cw* instead of *qu*, and mediaeval Scots had *quh* for *hw* (*wh*): as a mediaeval Roman numeral Q = 500, $\bar{Q}$ = 500 000: (also **quad, kwod**) a unit of heat energy equal to one quadrillion British thermal units (10^{18} Btu) (*U.S.*). — **Q'-boat** a naval vessel disguised as a merchant ship or fishing-boat, to deceive and destroy submarines; **Q-Celt, Q-Kelt** see **Celt;** **Q'-fever** an acute disease characterised by fever and muscular pains, transmitted by the rickettsia *Coxiella burnetii.* [L. *cū.*]

qa-, qe-, qi-, qo-, qu-. Arabic and Hebrew words spelt thus are in most cases given at **k-** or **c-.**

Qaddish, qadi, qalamdan. Same as **Kaddish, cadi, kalamdan.**

Qajar *ka-jär'*, *n.* the dynasty that united and ruled Iran from 1779 to 1925. — *adj.* of the dynasty, its time, esp. its art, porcelain, etc.

qanat *kä-nät'*, *n.* an underground tunnel for carrying irrigation water. [Ar. *qanāt,* pipe.]

qat. See **kat**[1].

qibla. Same as **kiblah.**

qigong *chē-gōong, n.* a system of exercises for promoting physical and mental health by deep breathing. [Chin. *qì,* breath, *gong,* skill, exercise.]

qintar *kin-tär'*, *n.* an Albanian unit of currency equal to one hundredth of a lek. [Albanian.]

Qoran. Same as **Koran.**

qua *kwā, kwä, adv.* in the capacity of. [L. *quā,* adverbial abl. fem. of *quī,* who.]

quack[1] *kwak*, *n.* the cry of a duck. — *v.i.* to make the sound of a quack. — *v.i.* **quack'le** to quack. [Imit.]

quack[2] *kwak*, *n.* a shortened form of **quacksalver:** a charlatan. — Also *adj.* — *v.i.* to play the quack. — *v.t.* to puff, vend, or treat in the manner of a quack. — *n.* **quack'ery** the pretensions or practice of a quack, esp. in medicine. — **quack'salver** a boastful pretender to knowledge and skill (esp. in medicine) that he does not possess. — *adj.* **quack'salving.** [Du. *quacksalver* (now *kwakzalver*), perh. one who quacks about his salves.]

quad[1] *kwod, n.* a shortening of **quadrangle, quadraphonics, quadraphony, quadrat, quadruped** (i.e. horse), **quadruplet:** see **Q,q.** — *adj.* short for **quadruple.** — *v.t.* to fill with quadrats.

quad[2]**.** Same as **quod**[2]**.**

quadragenarian *kwod-rə-ji-nā'ri-ən, n.* one who is forty years old, or between forty and fifty. — Also *adj.* [L. *quadrāgēnārius* — *quadrāgēnī,* forty each.]

Quadragesima *kwod-rə-jes'i-mə, n.* the forty days of Lent (*obs.*): the first Sunday in Lent. — *adj.* **quadrages'imal** of the number forty: of Lent. [L. *quadrāgēsimus, -a, -um,* fortieth — *quadrāgintā,* forty — *quattuor,* four.]

quadrangle *kwod-rang'gl,* also *kwod',* *n.* a plane figure with four angles (and therefore four sides): an object or space of that form: a court or open space, usually rectangular, enclosed by a building (as a college): sometimes the enclosing building. — *adj.* **quadrang'ular** (*-gū-lər*). — *adv.* **quadrang'ularly.** — **complete quadrangle** a figure composed of four points joined by six straight lines or sides. [Fr., — L. *quadrangulum* — *quattuor,* four, *angulus,* an angle.]

quadrans *kwod'ranz, kwad'räns, n.* a Roman copper coin,

the fourth part of the as: — *pl.* **quadran'tēs.** — *n.* **quadrant** (*kwod'rənt*) the fourth part of a circle or its circumference, a sector or an arc of 90° (also *adj.*): an area, object, street, of that form: an instrument with an arc of 90° for taking altitudes. — *adj.* **quadrantal** (*-rant'l*). [L. *quadrāns, -antis* a fourth part — *quattuor,* four.]

quadraphonics, quadrophonics *kwod-rə-fon'iks, -ro-, n. sing.* a system of sound transmission using a minimum of four speakers fed by four, or sometimes three, separate channels. — Also **quadrophony** (*-rof'*), **quadraph'ony.** — *adj.* **quadraphon'ic, quadrophon'ic.**

quadraplegia, -plegic. Erron. for **quadriplegia, -plegic.**

quadrat *kwod'rat, n.* a piece of type-metal lower than the letters, used in spacing between words and filling out blank lines (commonly **quad**) — distinguished as *en* (▮), *em* (▮), *two-em* (▮▮), and *three-em* (▮▮▮). — *adj.* **quad'rate** (*-rāt, -rit*) square: rectangular: squarish: squared: square, as a power or root: balanced (*fig.*): conformable. — *n.* a square or quadrate figure or object: the quadrate bone, suspending the lower jaw in vertebrates other than mammals: quartile (*obs.*). — *v.t.* and *v.i.* to square: to conform. — *adj.* **quadratic** (*-rat'ik*) of or like a quadrate: involving the square but no higher power, as a *quadratic equation* (*alg.*): tetragonal (*crystal.*). — *n.* a quadratic equation. — *adj.* **quadrat'ical.** — *ns.* **quadrā'trix** a curve by which a curved figure (as the circle) may be squared; **quad'rature** (*-rə-chər*) squareness: a square space (*Milt.*): squaring: the finding of a square equal to a given figure: an angular distance of 90°: the position of a heavenly body at such an angular distance, or the time of its being there; **quadrā'tus** the name of several quadrangular muscles. — **B quadrā'tum** quadrate B (see **B**); **quadrature of the circle** see **square.** [L. *quadrātus,* pa.p. of *quadrāre,* to square — *quattuor,* four.]

quadrella *kwod-rel'ə,* (*Austr.*) *n.* a group of four (esp. the last four) horseraces at a meeting, for which the punter selects the four winners. [L. *quadr-,* four, *-ella,* dim. suffix.]

quadrennium, etc. See **quadr(i)-.**

quadr(i)- *kwod-r(i)-* in composition, four: square. — *adjs.* **quad'ric** of the second degree; **quadricentennial** (*kwod-ri-sen-ten'i-əl;* modelled on **centennial**) lasting four hundred years: once in four hundred years. — *n.* a four-hundredth anniversary. — *n.* **quadriceps** (*kwod'ri-seps;* L. *caput, -itis,* head) the great thigh muscle that extends the leg (from its four insertions). — *adj.* **quadricipital** (*-sip'i-tl*). — *ns.* **quadricone** (*kwod'ri-kōn*) a quadric cone, or cone having a conic as base; **quadriennium** (*kwod-ri-en'i-əm;* L. *annus,* year) four years: — *pl.* **quadrienn'ia.** — *adj.* **quadrienn'ial** lasting four years: once in four years. — *n.* a quadriennial event. — *adv.* **quadrienn'ially.** — The forms **quadrenn'-ium,** etc., are etymologically incorrect but now usual. — *adjs.* **quadrifarious** (*kwod-ri-fā'ri-əs;* L. poss. from *fāri,* to speak) fourfold: in four rows; **quadrifid** (*kwod'-ri-fid;* L. from the root of *findere,* to cleave) cleft in four; **quadrifoliate** (*kwod-ri-fō'li-āt;* L. *folium,* a leaf) four-leaved; **quadriform** (*kwod'ri-förm;* L. *förma,* form) fourfold: having four forms or aspects. — *n.* **quadriga** (*kwod-rī'gə; kwad-rē'ga;* L., a later singular from *quadrīgae,* a team of four, for *quadrijugae* — *jugum,* yoke) in Greek and Roman times a two-wheeled car drawn by four horses abreast: — *pl.* **quadrī'gae** (*-jē, -gī*). — *adjs.* **quadrigeminal** (*kwod-ri-jem'i-nl;* L. *geminī,* twins) having four similar parts. — Also **quadrigem'inate, quadrigem'inous; quadrilateral** (*kwod-*

ri-lat'ər-l; L. *latus, lateris*, a side) four-sided. — *n.* a plane figure bounded by four straight lines (*geom.*): a group of four fortresses, esp. Mantua, Verona, Peschiera, and Legnaga. — *adjs.* **quadrilingual** (-*ling'*-gwəl; L. *lingua*, tongue) using four languages; **quadriliteral** (*kwod-ri-lit'ər-l*; L. *lītera*, a letter) of four letters. — *n.* a word or a root of four letters. — *n.* **quadrillion** (*kwod-, kwəd-ril'yən*; modelled on **million**) a million raised to the fourth power, represented by a unit and 24 ciphers: in U.S., a thousand to the fifth power, a unit with 15 ciphers. — *n.* and *adj.* **quadrill'ionth.** — *adj.* **quadrilocular** (*kwod-ri-lok'ū-lər*; L. *loculus*, dim. of *locus*, place) having four compartments. — *n.* **quadringenary** (*kwod-rin-jē'nər-i*; L. *quadringēnārius*, of four hundred each) a four-hundredth anniversary or its celebration. — *adjs.* **quadrinomial** (*kwod-ri-nō'mi-əl*; irregularly from L. *nōmen, -inis*, a name; *alg.*) of four terms. — *n.* an expression of four terms. — *adj.* **quadripartite** (*kwod-ri-pär'tīt*; L. *partīrī, -ītum*, to divide) in four parts: having four parties: deeply cleft into four parts, as a leaf (*bot.*): divided, as a vault, into four compartments (*archit.*). — *n.* **quadriparti'tion.** — *n.* **quadriplegia** (*kwod-ri-plēj'(i)ə, -plēj'yə*; Gr. *plēgē*, a blow) paralysis of both arms and both legs. — *n.* and *adj.* **quadripleg'ic.** — *n.* **quadrireme** (*kwod'ri-rēm*; L. *rēmus*, an oar) an ancient ship with four sets of oars. — *v.t.* **quad'risect** to divide into four equal parts. — *ns.* **quadrisection** (*kwod-ri-sek'shən*; L. *sectiō, -onis*, cutting) division into four equal parts; **quadrisyllable** (*kwod'ri-sil'ə-bl*) a tetrasyllable. — *adj.* **quadrisyllab'ic.** — *adj.* **quadrivalent** (*kwod-riv'ə-lənt*, or -*vā'lənt*) having a valency of four. — *ns.* **quadriv'alence** (or -*vā'*); **quadrivium** (*kwod-riv'i-əm*; L., the place where four roads meet — *via*, a way) in mediaeval education, the four branches of mathematics (arithmetic, geometry, astronomy, music). — *adj.* **quadriv'ial.** — **complete quadrilateral** a figure consisting of four straight lines intersecting in six points or vertices. [L. *quadri- quattuor*, four.]

quadriliteral . . . quadrivium. See **quadr(i)-.**

quadrille[1] *kwə-dril'* or *kə-*, *n.* one of four groups of horsemen (or others): a square dance for four couples or more, in five movements: music for such a dance. — *v.i.* to dance quadrilles. — *n.* **quadrill'er.** [Fr., — Sp. *cuadrilla*, a troop, app. — *cuadra* — L. *quadra*, a square.]

quadrille[2] *kwə-dril'* or *kə-*, *n.* a four-handed game with 40 cards, not unlike ombre. — *v.i.* to play quadrille. [Fr., perh. — Sp. *cuatrillo*, the game of quadrille, or *cuartillo*, fourth part.]

quadroon *kwod-rōon'*, *n.* a person of one-quarter Negro descent: extended to refer to any person or animal of similarly mixed ancestry. — Also **quarteroon'.** [Sp. *cuarterón* — *cuarto*, a fourth.]

quadrophonics, -phony. See **quadraphonics.**

quadru- *kwod-rōo-*, a variant of **quadr(i)-.** — *adj.* **quadrumanous** (*kwod-rōo'mən-əs*; L. *manus*, a hand) four-handed: of the obsolete order **Quadru'mana**, the Primates other than man. — *ns.* **quadru'man, -mane** (-*man, -mān*); **quadrumvir** (*kwod-rum'vər*; L. *vir*, a man) a member of a **quadrum'virate**, a group of four men acting together in some capacity; **quadruped** (*kwod'-rōo-ped*; L. *pēs, pedis*, a foot) a four-footed animal, usu. a mammal, esp. a horse. — *adj.* **four-footed.** — *adj.* **quadrupedal** (-*rōo'pi-dəl*).

quadruple *kwod'rōo-pl*, also (esp. in Scotland) -*rōo'*, *adj.* fourfold: having four parts, members, or divisions. — *n.* four times as much: a coin worth four pistoles. — *v.t.* to increase fourfold: to equal four times. — *v.i.* to become four times as much. — *n.* **quad'ruplet** (or -*rōo'*) any combination of four things: a group of four notes performed in the time of three: a cycle for four riders: one of four born at a birth. — *adv.* **quad'ruply** (-*pli*, or -*rōo'pli*) in a fourfold manner. — **Quadruple Alliance** a league formed in 1718 by Britain, France, Austria, and Holland against Spain; **quadruple time** (*mus.*) a time with four beats to the bar. [Fr., — L.

quadruplus, from the root of *plēre*, to fill.]

quadruplex *kwod'rōo-pleks, adj.* fourfold: of a telegraphic system, capable of sending four messages at once, two each way, over one wire. — *n.* an instrument of this kind. — *v.t.* to make quadruplex. — *adj.* **quadru'plicate** fourfold. — *n.* one of four corresponding things: fourfoldness. — *v.t.* to make fourfold. — *ns.* **quadruplica'tion**; **quadruplicity** (-*plis'i-ti*); **quad'ruply** (-*plī*; *Scots law*) a reply to a triply. [L. *quadruplex, -icis*, fourfold — *plicāre, -ātum* to fold.]

quaere *kwē'rē, kwī're*, (L. imper. of *quaerēre, quaesītum*, to inquire) *v.imper.* inquire (suggesting doubt, or desirability of investigation). — *n.* a query, question. — See also **query.** — *v.impers.* **quaeritur** (*kwē-rī'tər, kwī'ri-tōōr*) the question is asked. — *n.* **quaesitum** (*kwē-sī'təm, kwī-sē'tōōm*) something sought for: the true value.

quaestor *kwēs'tōr, -tər, kwīs'tor*, *n.* an ancient Roman magistrate, in early times an investigator, prosecutor, or judge in murder cases, later a treasurer with various other functions: in the Middle Ages an officer (usu. **ques'tor**) who granted indulgences: a treasurer. — *n.* **quaes'tionary** (-*tyən-ə-ri; Scott*) a pardoner. — *adj.* **quaestorial** (-*tō'ri-əl, -tō'*). — *n.* **quaes'torship.** — *adj.* **quaes'tuary** money-making: gain-seeking. — *n.* a gain-seeker: a pardoner. [L. *quaestor, -ōris — quaerēre, quaesītum*, to seek.]

quae vide. See **quod**[1].

quaff[1] *kwäf, kwof, v.t.* to drink or drain in large draughts. — *v.i.* to drink largely. — *n.* a draught. — *n.* **quaff'er.** [Origin obscure.]

quaff[2] *kwäf*, a variant of **quaich.**

quag *kwag, kwog, n.* a boggy place, esp. one that quakes underfoot. — *n.* **quagg'iness.** — *adj.* **quagg'y.** [Cf. **quake.**]

quagga *kwag'ə, n.* an extinct S. African wild ass (*Equus quagga*), less fully striped than the zebras, to which it was related. [Perh. Hottentot *quacha*.]

quagmire *kwag'mīr*, or *kwog'*, *n.* wet, boggy ground that yields or quakes under the feet. — *v.t.* to entangle, as in a quagmire. — *adj.* **quag'miry.** [App. **quag, mire.**]

quahaug, quahaug *kwo'hog, -hög, kwə-hog', -hög', n.* an edible Venus mollusc (*Venus mercenaria*) of the N. American Atlantic coast — also known as round clam: also *Cyprina islandica* (black quahog). — Also **cohog.** [Narraganset Ind. *poquauhock*.]

quaich, quaigh *kwāhh, (Scot.) n.* a drinking-cup, orig. of staves and hoops, now usu. of silver or pewter. [Gael. *cuach*, a cup.]

Quai d'Orsay *kā dör-sā*, the French Foreign Office. [Name of a quay on the Seine faced by the French Ministry of Foreign Affairs.]

quail[1] *kwāl, v.i.* to languish, decline (*arch.*): to flinch: to fail in spirit: to slacken (*Shak.*). — *v.t.* (*obs.*) to subdue: to daunt. — *n.* **quail'ing** (*Shak.*). — [M.E. *quayle*; origin obscure.]

quail[2] *kwāl, n.* a genus (*Coturnix*) of small birds of the partridge family: in America extended to various similar small game-birds, as the California quail (*Lophortyx*) and the bobwhite: a whore (*Shak.*). — **quail'-pipe** a whistle for alluring quails into a net (also **quail'-call**): the throat (*obs.*). [O.Fr. *quaille*; prob. Gmc.]

quaint *kwānt, adj.* skilful, esp. in use of language (*Shak.*): cunning (*obs.*): ingenious (*obs.*): fine (*Spens., Milt.*): affectedly fanciful or elaborate (*obs.*): affectedly nice or prim (*Spens.*): pleasantly odd: whimsical. — *adv.* **quaint'ly.** — *n.* **quaint'ness.** [O.Fr. *cointe* — L. *cognitus*, known; perh. confused with *comptus*, neat.]

quair *kwār*, obs. form of **quire**[1].

quake *kwāk, v.i.* to quiver or vibrate, as the earth or a quagmire: to tremble, esp. with cold or fear. — *v.t.* to cause to tremble (*Shak.*): to shake by earthquake. — *n.* a tremor: an earthquake: a shudder. — *ns.* **quā'kiness; quā'king.** — *adv.* **quā'kingly.** — *adj.* **quā'ky** shaky. — **quaking ash** the aspen; **quā'king-grass** a moorland grass of the genus *Briza*, with pendulous, panicled tremulous spikelets. [O.E. *cwacian*; perh. allied to *quick*.]

Quaker *kwā'kər, n.* one of the Religious Society of Friends, founded by George Fox (1624–91): a dummy cannon (also **Quaker gun**). — *adj.* of Quakers: (*U.S.*) of Philadelphia ('the Quaker city', because founded by William Penn, Quaker). — *ns.* **Quā'kerdom; Quā'keress; Quā'kerism.** — *adjs.* **Quā'kerish, Quā'-kerly** like a Quaker. - - **Quā'ker-bird** the sooty albatross; **Quā'ker-butt'ons** the round seeds of nux vomica; **Quā'ker-colour** drab. [Nickname (not adopted by themselves, and earlier applied to another sect) given them by Justice Bennet at Derby, because Fox bade them *quake* at the word of the Lord.]

qualamdan. Same as **kalamdan.**

quale *kwā'li, kwä'li, -lā, (log.) n.* a quality or property of something: — *pl.* **qua'lia** (*-li-ə*). [L., neut. of adj. *qualis*, of what kind.]

qualify *kwol'i-fī, v.t.* to ascribe a quality to: to characterise: to add a quality to the connotation of: to render capable or suitable: to furnish with legal power: to limit by modifications: to moderate: to mitigate: to appease: to abate: to reduce the strength of: to vary: to prove, confirm (*Scots law*). — *v.i.* to take the necessary steps to fit oneself for a certain position, activity, or practice: to fulfil a requirement: to have the necessary qualities or qualifications: — *pr.p.* **qual'-ifying;** *pa.p.* and *pa.t.* **qual'ified.** — *adj.* **qual'ifiable** (*-fī-ə-bl*). — *n.* **qualification** (*-fi-kā'shən*) qualifying: distinctive quality: modification: restriction: that which qualifies: a quality that fits a person for a place, etc.: an accomplishment (*obs.*): a necessary condition: the attaching of quality, or the distinction of affirmative and negative, to a term (*log.*). — *adj.* and *n.* **qual'ificātive.** — *n.* **qual'ificātor** (*R.C.*) one who prepares ecclesiastical causes for trial. — *adj.* **qual'-ificātory.** — *adj.* **qual'ified** (*-fīd*) fitted: competent: having the necessary qualification: modified: limited. — *adv.* **qual'ifiedly** (*-fīd-li*). — *n.* **qual'ifier** (*-fī-ər*). — *n.* and *adj.* **qual'ifying.** — **qualifying round** a preliminary round in a competition, to limit the number of competitors. [Fr. *qualifier* or L.L. *quālificāre* — L. *quālis*, of what kind, *facĕre*, to make.]

qualis ab incepto *kwā'lis ab in-sep'tō, kwä'lis ab in-kep'tō,* (L.) as from the beginning.

quality *kwol'i-ti, n.* that which makes a thing what it is: nature: character: kind: property: attribute: social status: high social status: persons of the upper class collectively: grade of goodness: excellence: profession, esp. (*Shak.*) the actor's profession: manner (*Shak.*): skill, accomplishment: timbre, that character of a sound that depends on the overtones present, distinguished from loudness and pitch: the character of a proposition as affirmative or negative (*log.*): (usu. in *pl.*) a quality newspaper. — *adj.* of high grade of excellence. — *adj.* **qual'itātive** relating to, or concerned with, quality, esp. opp. to *quantitative.* — *adv.* **qual'-itātively.** — *adj.* **qual'itied** endowed with a quality or qualities. - - **quality control** inspection, testing, etc., of samples of a product to ensure maintenance of high standards; **quality newspaper** one seeking to provide material that will interest educated readers. — **quality of life** non-material standard of living measured by environmental and cultural amenities, etc. [O.Fr. *qualité* — L. *quālitās, -tātis* — *quālis*, of what kind.]

qualm *kwäm, kwöm, n.* an access of faintness or sickness: a sickly feeling: an uneasiness, as of conscience: a misgiving. — *adjs.* **qualm'ing; qualm'ish.** — *adv.* **qualm'-ishly.** — *n.* **qualm'ishness.** — *adjs.* **qualm'less; qualm'y.** [Perh. O.E. *cwealm*, death, murder, torment, pain.]

quamash *kwom'ash, kwə-mash'.* Same as **camass.**

quandang. See **quandong.**

quandary *kwon'də-ri, kwon-dā'ri, n.* a state of perplexity: dilemma: a hard plight (*obs.*). [Origin obscure.]

quand même *kā mem,* (Fr.) nevertheless, whatever the consequences may be.

quandong *kwan'* or *kwon'dong, n.* a small Australian tree

(*Santalum acuminatum*) of the sandalwood family; its edible drupe (*native peach*) or edible kernel (**quan'dong=nut**): an Australian tree (*Elaeocarpus grandis*) (**silver, blue** or **brush quandong**): a disreputable person (*Austr. coll.*). — Also **quan'dang, quan'tong.** [Aboriginal.]

quango *kwang'gō, n.* a board funded by, and with members appointed by, central government, to supervise or develop activity in areas of public interest: — *pl.* **quan'gos.** [*qu*asi-*a*utonomous *n*on-*g*overnmental (sometimes national government) *o*rganisation.]

quannet *kwon'it, n.* a file mounted like a plane. [Origin unknown.]

quant *kwant, n.* a punting or jumping pole, with a flat cap. — *v.t.* to punt. [Cf. **kent**[1]; poss. conn. with L. *contus*, Gr. *kontos*.]

quanta, quantal. See **quantum.**

quantic *kwon'tik, (math.) n.* a rational integral homogeneous function of two or more variables. — *adj.* **quan'tical.** [L. *quantus*, how great.]

quantify *kwon'ti-fī, v.t.* to qualify (a term in a proposition) by stating the quantity (*log.*): to fix or express the quantity of: to express as a quantity. — *adj.* **quan'-tifiable.** — *ns.* **quantification** (*-fi-kā'shən*); **quan'tifier.** — **quantification of the predicate** (*log.*) the attachment of a sign of quantity to the predicate. [L. *quantus*, how great, *facĕre*, to make.]

quantise, -ize. See **quantum.**

quantity *kwon'ti-ti, n.* the amount of anything: bulk: size: a sum: a determinate amount: an amount, portion: a considerable amount: a fragment, scrap (*Shak.*): a large portion: length or shortness of duration of a sound or syllable: extension (*log.*): the character of a proposition as universal or particular: anything which can be increased, divided, or measured: proportion (*Shak.*). — *adj.* **quan'titātive** (less justifiably **quan'-titive**) relating to, or concerned with, quantity, esp. opp. to *qualitative.* — *adv.* **quan'titātively.** — **quantity surveyor** one who estimates quantities required, obtains materials, evaluates work done, etc., for construction work. — **unknown quantity** a quantity whose mathematical value is not known: a factor, person or thing whose importance or influence cannot be foreseen (*fig.*). [O.Fr. *quantité* — L. *quantitās, -tātis* — *quantus*, how much.]

quantivalence *kwon-tiv'ə-ləns, -ti-vā'ləns, n.* valency. — *adj.* **quantiv'alent** (or *-vā'*). [L. *quantus*, how much, *valēns, -entis, valēre,* to be worth.]

quantize. See **quantum.**

quantometer *kwon-tom'i-tər, n.* an instrument that shows by spectrographical analysis the percentages of the various elements present in a metallic sample. [L. *quantus*, how much, **meter**[1].]

quantong. See **quandong.**

quantum *kwon'təm, n.* quantity: amount: a naturally fixed minimum amount of some entity which is such that all other amounts of that entity occurring in physical processes in nature are integral multiples thereof (*phys.*): — *pl.* **quan'ta.** — *adj.* **quan'tal** of, or pertaining to, a quantum (*phys.*): having one of only two possible states or values. — *n.* **quantisā'tion, -z-.** — *v.t.* **quan'tise, -ize** to express in terms of quanta or in accordance with the quantum theory. — **quantum jump, leap** the sudden transition of an electron, atom, etc., from one energy state to another: a sudden spectacular advance (*fig.*); **quantum mechanics** a branch of mechanics based on the quantum theory, used in predicting the behaviour of elementary particles; **quantum number** any of a set of integers or half-integers which together describe the state of a particle or system of particles; the **principal quantum number,** for instance, specifies the shell an electron occupies; **quantum theory** Planck's theory of the emission and absorption of energy not continuously but in finite steps. [L. *quantum*, neut. of *quantus*, how much.]

quantum meruit *kwon'təm mer'ū-it, kwan'tŏŏm mer'ōŏ-it,* (L.; as much as he deserved) a fair reward for services rendered where there is no agreed rate of payment.

quantum sufficit _kwon'tɔm suf'is-it, kwan'tōōm sōō'fik-it,_ (L.) a sufficient quantity.

quaquaversal _kwā-kwɔ-vûr'sl, kwä-kwä-, adj._ dipping outward in all directions from a centre (_geol._): facing or bending all ways. — _adv._ **quaquaver'sally.** [L. _quāquā,_ whithersoever, _vertĕre, versum,_ to turn.]

quarantine¹ _kwor'ɔn-tēn, n._ forty days: a time (orig. for a ship forty days) of compulsory isolation or detention to prevent spread of contagion or infection: isolation or detention for such a purpose: the place where the time is spent: any period of enforced isolation (_fig._). — _v.t._ to subject to quarantine. — **quarantine flag** a yellow flag displayed by a ship in quarantine, with a black spot if there be contagious disease on board. [It. _quarantina — quaranta,_ forty — L. _quadrāgintā._]

quarantine². See **quarrender.**

quare impedit _kwā'rē im'pɔ-dit, kwä'rä im-ped'it,_ (L.; why does he hinder?) a writ issued in cases of disputed presentation to a benefice, requiring the defendant to state his reasons for hindering the presentation.

quarenden, quarender. See **quarrender.**

quark _kwörk, kwärk, n._ any of a triplet of particles, not yet found, suggested as the units out of which all other subatomic particles are formed. [From word coined by James Joyce in _Finnegans Wake._]

quarrel¹ _kwor'ɔl, n._ a square-headed arrow as for a cross-bow (_Spens._). **quar'le**): a diamond pane of glass: a square tile. — **quarr'el-pane.** [O.Fr. _quarrel_ (Fr. _carreau_) — L.L. _quadrellus — quadrus,_ a square.]

quarrel² _kwor'ɔl, n._ a complaint, charge (_obs._): an objection (_obs._): action at law (_obs._): ground of complaint or action: a cause contended for: an unfriendly contention or dispute: a breach of friendship: quarrelsomeness (_Shak._): a quarreller (_Shak._). — _v.i._ to cavil, find fault (with): to dispute violently: to fall out: to disagree violently. — _v.t._ to call in question (_obs._): to object to (_obs._): to chide (now _Scot._): to bring, render, by quarrelling: — _pr.p._ **quarr'elling;** _pa.t._ and _pa.p._ **quarr'elled.** — _n._ **quarr'eller.** — _n._ and _adj._ **quarr'elling.** — _adjs._ **quarr'ellous** (_Shak._) quarrelsome; **quarr'elsome** disposed to quarrel. — _adv._ **quarr'elsomely.** — _n._ **quarr'elsomeness.** — **quarrel with one's bread and butter** to act in a way prejudicial to one's means of subsistence; **take up a quarrel** (_Shak._) to settle a dispute. [O.Fr. _querele_ — L. _querēla — querī, questus,_ to complain.]

quarrender, quarender _kwor'ɔn-dɔr,_ **quarantine, quarenden, quarrington** _-ɔn-tin, -dɔn, -ing-tɔn,_ (_S.W. England_) _ns._ a kind of red apple. [Origin unknown.]

quarry¹ _kwor'i, n._ an open excavation for building-stone, slate, etc.: any source of building-stone, etc.: a great mass of stone or rock (_obs._): a source from which information can be extracted. — _v.t._ to dig from, or as from, a quarry: to cut into or cut away: — _pr.p._ **quarr'ying;** _pa.t._ and _pa.p._ **quarr'ied.** — _adj._ **quarr'iable.** — _n._ **quarr'ier** a quarryman. — **quarr'yman** one who works in a quarry; **quarr'ymaster** the owner of a quarry; **quarr'y-sap, quarr'y-water** the water in the pores of unquarried or newly quarried stone. [L.L. _quareia,_ for _quadrāria_ — L. _quadrāre,_ to square.]

quarry² _kwor'i, n._ a deer's entrails given on a hide, to the dogs (_obs._): a hawk's reward for a kill: a bird flown at by a hawk: a hunted animal: prey: a victim: a hunter's heap of dead game: a heap of corpses (_Shak._): (_Shak., Macbeth,_ I, ii) according to some, slaughter, or spoil; others would read **quarrel.** [O.Fr. _cuiree, curee,_ said to be from _cuir_ — L. _corium,_ hide.]

quarry³ _kwor'i, n._ a quarrel of glass: a square paving-tile or slab. — **quarry tile** a square unglazed floor tile. [A form of **quarrel¹;** or perh. from O.Fr. _quarré_ — L. _quadrātus,_ squared.]

quart¹, quarte _kärt, n._ a sequence of four cards in piquet, etc.: the fourth of eight parrying or attacking positions in fencing (also **caste**). — **quart and tierce** practice between fencers. [Fr. _quarte_ — It. and L. _quarta,_ fourth.]

quart² _kwört, n._ the fourth part of a gallon, or two pints

(1·14 litres): a vessel containing two pints: as much as will fill it: a quarter, region (_Spens._): a fourth (_mus._). — _n._ **quartā'tion** the mixing of gold with three parts of silver as a stage towards purification. — **quart'-pot.** [Fr. _quart, -e_ — L. _quārtus, -a, -um,_ fourth — _quattuor,_ four.]

quartan _kwör'tɔn, adj._ occurring every third (by inclusive reckoning fourth) day, as a fever. — _n._ quartan malaria. [L. _quārtānus,_ of the fourth.]

quarte. See **quart¹.**

quarter _kwör'tɔr, n._ a fourth part: the fourth part of a cwt. = 28 (_U.S._ 25) lb. avoirdupois: 8 bushels (perh. orig. a fourth of a ton of corn): the fourth part of an hour — of the year — of the moon's period (or the moon's position at the end of it) — of the world, etc.: a 25-cent piece, 25 cents, quarter of a dollar (_U.S._): a limb with adjacent parts of the trunk, esp. of the dismembered body of one who has been executed, or of a beast's carcass: a haunch: one of the four parts of a quartered shield (_her._): an ordinary occupying one-fourth of the field (_her._): a quartering: a cardinal point, or any point, of the compass: the region about any point of the compass: hence a region generally, and also figuratively: a town district inhabited by a particular class: a part of an army, camp, etc. (_Shak._): lodging, as for soldiers, esp. in _pl._: an assigned station: terms, relations, treatment, esp. favourable (_Shak._): mercy granted to an antagonist (perh. from sending to quarters): the part of a ship's side abaft the beam: a quarter-mile race. — _v.t._ to divide into four equal parts: to divide into parts or compartments: to station, lodge, or impose in quarters: to bear, place, or divide quarterly (_her._): to beat or range as for game: to search thoroughly. — _v.i._ to be stationed: to lodge: to range for game: to drive with wheels between the ruts, or horse astride of a rut: hence, to drive to the side of the road, or from side to side: of the wind, to blow on to a ship's quarter. — In composition, **quar'ter-,** _adjectivally,_ one-fourth part (of); _adverbially,_ to the extent of one-fourth. — _n._ **quar'terage** a quarterly payment: quarters, lodging. — _adjs._ **quar'tered; quar'tering** sailing nearly before the wind: striking on the quarter of a ship, as a wind. — _n._ assignment of quarters: series of small upright posts for forming partitions, lathed and plastered only, or boarded: also (_archit._): the division of a coat by horizontal and vertical lines (_her._): one of the divisions so formed: the marshalling of coats in these divisions, indicating family alliances: any one of the coats so marshalled. — _adj._ **quar'terly** relating to a quarter, esp. of a year: recurring, or published, once a quarter: divided into or marshalled in quarters (_her._). — _adv._ once a quarter: in quarters or quarterings (_her._). — _n._ a quarterly periodical. — **quart'er-back** in American football, a player between the forwards and the half-backs, who directs the attacking play of his team; **quar'ter-blood** a person of one-quarter Negro descent. — _adj._ **quar'ter-bound** having leather or cloth on the back only, not the corners. — **quar'ter-boy, quar'ter-jack** an automaton that strikes the quarter-hours. — _adj._ **quar'ter-bred** having only one-fourth pure blood, as horses, cattle, etc. — **quar'ter-day** the first or last day of a quarter, on which rent or interest is paid; **quar'ter-deck** the part of the deck of a ship abaft the mainmast — used by cabin passengers and by superior officers (and saluted on warships); **quar'ter-decker** (_coll._) a stickler for naval etiquette; **quar'ter-evil, -ill** black-quarter; **quar'ter-fi'nal** the round before the semi-final in a knockout competition; **quar'ter-gallery** a projecting balcony on a ship's quarter; **quar'ter-guard** a guard of a battalion in camp; **quar'ter-gunner** (_U.S._) a naval petty-officer, under the gunner, a gunner's mate; **quar'ter-horse** (_U.S._) a horse that can run a quarter of a mile or so at great speed; **quarter (of an) hour** a period of fifteen minutes. — _adv._ **quar'ter-hour'ly.** — **quar'ter-jack** a quarter-boy: a quartermaster (_slang_); **quarter light** a small window in a car, beside the front seat, for ventilation;

quar'termaster an officer who finds quarters for soldiers, and attends to supplies: a petty officer who attends to the helm, signals, etc. (*naut.*): — *fem.* **quar'termistress** (or **quartermaster**); **quar'termaster=gen'eral** a staff-officer who deals with questions of transport, marches, quarters, fuel, clothing, etc.; **quar'termaster-ser'geant** a non-commissioned officer who assists the quartermaster; **quar'ter-mil'er** an athlete whose speciality is the quarter-mile race; **quar'ter-note** a crotchet (*U.S.*): a quarter-tone; **quar'ter-plate** see **plate**; **quar'ter-rail** a rail stretching from a ship's gangway to its stern. — *adj.* **quar'ter-repeat'ing** of a repeating watch or clock that strikes the quarter hours. — **quar'ter-road** a road divided into four strips by ruts and horse-track; **quar'ter-round** a moulding whose section is about a quadrant, an *ovolo*; **quar'ter-seal** the seal kept by the director of the Chancery of Scotland — known also as 'the testimonial of the Great Seal'; **quarter section** (*U.S.*) an area of land half a mile square, 160 acres; **quar'ter-sessions** a court held quarterly by justices of the peace (superseded in 1972 by crown courts); **quar'ter-staff** a long wooden pole, an old weapon of defence: play with this weapon; **quar'ter-tone** half a semitone; **quar'ter-wind** a wind blowing on a ship's quarter. — **(a) quarter after, past** (an hour) fifteen minutes after that hour; **(a) quarter to** fifteen minutes before the hour; **at close quarters** in very near proximity: hand-to-hand; **keep a (bad) quarter** (*obs.*) to make a disturbance; **keep good quarter** (*Shak.*) to keep good watch or good order. [O.Fr. *quarter* — L. *quārtārius*, a fourth part — *quārtus*, fourth.]

quartern kwör'tə(r)n, *n.* a quarter, esp. of a peck, a stone, a pound (weight), a pint, or a hundred. — **quar'tern=loaf** a four-pound loaf, as is made from a quarter of a stone of flour. [A.Fr. *quartrun*, O.Fr. *quarteron* — *quart(e)*, fourth part.]

quarteroon. Same as **quadroon.**

quartet, quartette, quartett kwör-tet', *n.* a set of four: a composition for four voices or instruments: a set of performers or instruments for such compositions. — Also (It.) **quartet'to** (kwär-tet'tō; *pl.* **quartet'ti** -tē). [It. *quartetto*, dim. of *quarto* — L. *quārtus*, fourth.]

quartic kwör'tik, (*math.*) *adj.* of the fourth degree. — *n.* a function, curve, or surface of the fourth degree. [L. *quārtus*, fourth.]

quartier kär-tē-ā, (Fr.) *n.* a particular district in a French town or city. — **quartier latin** (la-tē) the 'Latin quarter' of Paris, on the left bank of the Seine, orig. inhabited by writers, artists and students.

quartile kwör'tīl, *n.* an aspect of planets when their longitudes differ by 90° (*astrol.*): in frequency-distribution, a value such that a fourth, a half, or three-quarters of the numbers under consideration fall below it. — Also *adj.* — **quartile deviation** the distance between the values below which the last fourth and above which the highest fourth fall. [L. *quārtus*, fourth.]

quarto kwör'tō, *adj.* having the sheet folded into four leaves or eight pages (often written **4to**). — *n.* a book of sheets so folded, or of such a size: — *pl.* **quar'tos** (demy quarto, 8¾ × 11¼in.; medium quarto, 9 × 11½in.; royal quarto, 10 × 12½in.). — **small quarto** a square octavo: a book having eight leaves to a sheet but the shape of a quarto. [L. (*in*) *quārtō*, (in) one-fourth.]

quartodeciman kwör-tō-des'i-mən, *n.* one who celebrated Easter on the 14th of Nisan without regard to the day of the week. — Also *adj.* [L.L. *quartodecimānus* — L. *quārtus decimus*, fourteenth.]

quartz kwörts, *n.* the commonest rock-forming mineral, composed of silica, occurring in hexagonal crystals (clear and colourless when pure) or crypto-crystalline. — *adj.* of quartz. — *adj.* **quartzif'erous** quartz-bearing. — *n.* **quartz'ite** a metamorphosed sandstone with the grains welded together. — *adjs.* **quartzitic** (-it'ik) of or like quartzite; **quartz'ose** of, like, or rich in quartz; **quartz'y.** — **quartz crystal** a disc or rod cut in certain

directions from a piece of piezoelectric quartz and ground so that it vibrates naturally at a particular frequency; **quartz glass** fused quartz resistant to high temperatures and transparent to ultraviolet radiation; **quartz'-mill** a mill or machine for crushing auriferous quartz; **quartz-por'phyry** an igneous rock with crystals of quartz and feldspar in a compact or finely crystalline ground-mass of the same; **quartz'-rock'** quartzite; **quartz'-schist'** a schistose quartzite with mica. — **quartz-crystal clock, watch** one in which a quartz crystal, energised by a microcircuit, does the work of the pendulum or hairspring of the traditional clock or watch; **quartz-halogen lamp,** (commonly **quartz-iodine lamp,** using iodine) a compact source of light used for high-intensity flooding of large areas, car (fog-)lamps, cine-projectors, etc. [Ger. *Quarz.*]

quasar kwā'sär, -zär, -sər, *n.* a point (star-like) source of radiation (radio waves, etc.) outside our galaxy, usu. with a very large red-shift; quasars are the most distant and most luminous bodies so far known. [*quasi-stellar* object.]

quash kwosh, *v.t.* to crush: to subdue or extinguish suddenly and completely: to annul. [O.Fr. *quasser* (Fr. *casser*) — L. *quassāre*, intens. of *quatĕre*, to shake.]

Quashee, Quashie kwosh'i, *n.* a West African Negro personal name: (without *cap.*) a Negro, esp. in the West Indies. [Ashanti name given to one born on Sunday.]

quasi kwā'sī, kwä'zē, *adv.* as if, as it were. — In composition, **quasi-,** in a certain manner, sense, or degree: in appearance only, as **quasi-historical, quasi-stellar.** [L.]

Quasimodo kwas-i-mō'dō, *n.* the first Sunday after Easter, Low Sunday. [From the first words of the introit for the day, 1 Peter, ii. 2; L. *quasi modo geniti infantes*, as new-born babes, etc.]

quassia kwosh'(y)ə, *n.* a South American tree (*Quassia amara*; fam. Simarubaceae), whose bitter wood and bark are used as a tonic: now generally a West Indian tree of the same family (*Picraena excelsa*). [Named by Linnaeus from a Negro *Quassi*, who discovered its value against fever.]

quat kwot, *n.* a pimple: an insignificant person (*Shak.*). [Origin unknown.]

quatch. See **quich.**

quatch-buttock kwoch'-but'ək, (*Shak.*) *n.* appar. a flat or squat buttock.

quatercentenary kwot-, kwat-ər-sen-tēn'ər-i, -sin-, -ten'-ər-i, -sen'tin-, *n.* a quadringenary or 400th anniversary, or its celebration. [L. *quater*, four times.]

quaternary kwo-tûr'nər-i, *adj.* consisting of four: by fours: in fours: of the fourth order: based on four: with four variables: (*cap.*; *geol.*) Post-Tertiary. — *n.* the number four: a set of four: (*cap.*; *geol.*) the Post-Tertiary era or group of strata (Pleistocene and Recent). — *adj.* **quater'nate** in sets of four. — *n.* **quater'nion** a set or group of four: in mathematics, the operation of changing one vector into another, or the quotient of two vectors, depending on four geometrical elements and expressible by an algebraical quadrinomial: (in *pl.*) a calculus concerned with this, invented by Sir William Rowan Hamilton (1805–65). — *adj.* **quater'nion'd** (*Milt.*) divided into groups of four. — *ns.* **quater'nionist** a student of quaternions; **quatern'ity** fourfoldness: a set of four: a fourfold godhead. [L. *quaternī*, four by four.]

quatorze kə-törz', *n.* the four aces, kings, knaves, or tens in piquet, counting 14. — *n.* **quatorzain** (kat'ər-zān, kät-ör'zān) a stanza or poem of fourteen lines. [Fr. *quatorze, quatorzaine.*]

quatrain kwot'rān, *n.* a stanza of four lines usually rhyming alternately. [Fr.]

quatrefoil kat'ər-foil, or kat'rə-foil, *n.* a four-petalled flower or leaf of four leaflets: an openwork design or ornament divided by cusps into four lobes (*archit.*). — Also **quat'refeuille** (-fœ-ē, -fīl). [O.Fr. *quatre*, four, *foil* (Fr. *feuille*), leaf.]

quattrocento *kwät-rō-chen'tō, n.* the 15th century in Italian art and literature. — *ns.* **quattrocent'ism; quattrocen'tist.** [It., four (for fourteen) hundred.]

quaver *kwā'vər, v.i.* to tremble, quiver: to speak or sing with tremulous uncertainty: to trill. — *v.t.* to utter or sing tremulously. — *n.* a trembling, esp. of the voice: half a crotchet (*mus.*). — *n.* **quā'verer.** — *n. and adj.* **quā'vering.** — *adv.* **quā'veringly.** — *adj.* **quā'very.** [Freq. from obs. or dial. *quave,* M.E. *cwavien,* to shake; akin to **quake, quiver**³.]

quay *kē, n.* a landing-place: a wharf for the loading or unloading of vessels. — *n.* **quay'age** provision of quays: space for, or system of, quays: payment for use of a quay. — *n. and adj.* **quay'side.** — Earlier forms **kay** (*kā*), **key.** [O.Fr. *kay, cay,* perh. Celtic; partly assimilated to mod. Fr. spelling *quai.*]

quayd *kwād,* (*Spens.*) *adj.* or *pa.p.* daunted. [Perh. for **quelled.**]

queach *kwēch,* (*obs.*) *n.* a thicket. — *adj.* **queach'y, queech'y** forming a thicket: boggy: sickly. [Origin obscure.]

quean *kwēn, n.* a saucy girl: a woman of worthless character: a girl (*Scot.*). — In N.E. Scotland **queyn, quine** (*k wīn*), dim. **queyn'ie, quinie,** the ordinary words for a girl. [O.E. *cwene,* woman; cf. **queen** (O.E. *cwēn*).]

queasy, queazy *kwē'zi, adj.* unsettled: hazardous: uneasy: causing nausea: sick, squeamish: inclined to vomit: fastidious: nice. — *adv.* **quea'sily.** — *n.* **quea'siness.** [Poss. O.Fr. *coisier,* to hurt; poss. O.N. *kveisa,* a boil.]

Quebec(k)er *kwi-bek'ər, n.* an inhabitant of *Quebec,* in Canada. — *n.* **Québécois** (*kā-bek-wa;* Fr.) an inhabitant of Quebec, esp. a French-speaking one. — Also *adj.*

quebracho *kā-brä'chō, n.* name of several S. American trees yielding very hard wood (*white quebracho,* Aspidosperma — fam. Apocynaceae; *red quebracho,* Schinopsis — fam. Anacardiaceae): their wood or bark: — *pl.* **quebra'chos.** [Sp., — *quebrar,* to break, *hacha,* axe.]

Quechua *kech'wə,* **Quichua** *kēch'wə, ns.* a Peruvian Indian of the race that was dominant in the Inca empire: the language of the Quechua. — Also *adjs.* — *adjs.* **Quech'uan, Quich'uan.** — Also *n.* [Sp. *Quechua, Quichua.*]

queechy. See **queach.**

queen *kwēn, n.* the consort or wife of a king: female monarch: a presiding goddess: a woman or (*fig.*) anything that is pre-eminent in excellence, beauty, etc.: a sexually functional female social insect: female cat: a male homosexual, esp. if adopting female role (*slang*): a playing-card bearing the figure of a queen, in value next below a king: in chess, a piece that can be moved any distance in any straight line: a size of roofing-slate, 3 feet by 2. — *v.t.* to make a queen of: to substitute a queen (or other piece) for: to rule as queen: to supply with a queen: to play the queen (with *it* (*up*)). — *ns.* **queen'craft** craft or policy on the part of a queen; **queen'dom** queenhood: the realm of a queen; **queen'hood** the state of being a queen; **queen'ing** an apple, of various varieties; **queen'ite** a queen's partisan; **queen'let** a petty queen. — *adj.* **queen'less; queen'-like** like a queen. — *n.* **queen'liness.** — *adj.* **queen'ly** becoming or suitable to a queen: like a queen. — *adv.* in the manner of a queen. — *n.* **queen'ship** the state, condition or dignity of a queen. — **queen'-bee** a fertile female bee: a woman who dominates her associates: a woman in an important business position: a senior female secretary; **queen'-cake** a small, soft, sweet cake with currants; **queen'-con'sort** the wife of a reigning king; **queen'-dow'ager** a king's widow; **queen'-fish** a Californian sciaenoid fish, *Seriphus politus*: a tropical food and game fish of the Carangidae; **queen'-moth'er** a queen-dowager that is mother of the reigning king or queen: a queen or queen-bee that is a mother; **queen'=of-the-mead'ow(s)** the meadow-sweet; **queen'-post** one of two upright posts in a trussed roof, resting upon

the tie-beam, and supporting the principal rafter; **queen'-rē'gent** a queen who reigns as regent; **queen'= reg'nant** a queen reigning as monarch; **queen's'-arm** a musket. — **Queen's Guide** the rank awarded to a (Girl) Guide upon reaching the highest level of proficiency and in recognition of service to the community: a Guide of this rank. — *adj.* **queen'-size** larger than standard size, but smaller than the largest sizes, used of furnishings, etc. — **queen's pudding** queen of puddings (see below); **queen'-stitch** an embroidery pattern of square within square; **queen's ware** cream-coloured Wedgwood ware; **queen's yellow** basic mercuric sulphate. — **Queen Anne's Bounty** a fund for augmenting poor livings of the Church of England, formed (1703) out of first-fruits and tenths; **Queen Anne's dead** that is old news; **Queen Anne style** (*archit.*) the simplified Renaissance manner of the early 18th century, or an imitation of it, plain and simple, with classic cornices and details; **queen-bee substance** a substance secreted by a queen-bee which attracts drones and affects workers; **Queen of Heaven** Ashtoreth: Juno: the Virgin Mary (*R.C.*); **queen of puddings** a pudding made with egg, breadcrumbs, fruit or jam, etc., topped with meringue; **Queen of the May** May Queen; **queen's bounty** see **bounty; Queen's tobacco pipe** a kiln at London Docks for burning contraband goods (till 1891). — For **Queen's Bench, Counsel,** etc., see under **king.** [O.E. *cwēn*; Goth. *qēns*; O.N. *kvæn, kvān*; Gr. *gynē*; cf. **quean.**]

queene-apple *kwēn'-ap'l,* (*Spens.*) *n.* app. a quince. [See **quince.**]

Queensberry Rules *kwēnz'bər-i rōōlz,* rules applied to boxing, originally drawn up in 1867 and named after the Marquess of *Queensberry,* who took a keen interest in sport: (*loosely*) standards of proper behaviour in any fight, physical or verbal.

Queensland nut *kwēnzlənd nut,* the macadamia nut. [Orig. found in *Queensland* and New South Wales.]

queer *kwēr, adj.* odd, singular, quaint: open to suspicion: counterfeit: slightly mad: having a sensation of coming sickness: sick, ill (*dial.*): homosexual (*slang*). — *v.t.* (*slang*) to quiz: to cheat: to spoil. — *n.* (*slang*) a male homosexual. — *n.* **queer'dom** (*slang*) the state of being homosexual: homosexuals collectively. — *adj.* **queer'- ish.** — *n.* **queer'ity.** — *adv.* **queer'ly.** — *n.* **queer'ness.** — **queer'-bash'er; queer'-bash'ing** (*slang*) the practice of making gratuitous verbal or physical attacks on homosexuals; **Queer Street** the feigned abode of persons in debt or other difficulties. — **queer someone's pitch** to spoil someone's chances; **queer the pitch** (*showmen's slang*) to make the place of performance unavailable; **shove the queer** (*slang*) to pass bad money. [Perh. Ger. *quer,* across, cf. **thwart.**]

queest *kwēst.* Same as **cushat.** — Also **quest, quoist, quist.**

queez-maddam *kwēz'mad'əm,* (*Scott*) *n.* a French jargonelle pear. [Fr. *cuisse-madame.*]

queint¹ *kwānt,* (*Spens.*) *adj.* Same as **quaint.**

queint² *kwānt, pa.p.* of **quench.**

quelch *kwel(t)sh, v.i.* and *v.t.* to squelch. [Imit.]

Quelea *kwē'li-ə, n.* a genus of African weaver-birds, very destructive to crops: (*without cap.*) a bird of this genus, esp. *Q. quelea.* [From African name.]

quell *kwel, v.t.* to kill (*obs.*): to extinguish: to crush: to subdue: to disconcert, to abash (*Spens.*). — *v.i.* to die, perish (*Spens.*): to subside, abate (*Spens.*). — *n.* slaying (*Shak.*): power of quelling (*Keats*). — *n.* **quell'er** one who quells or crushes: a slayer. [O.E. *cwellan,* to kill, causal of *cwelan,* to die; cf. **quail** (vb.).]

quelque chose *kel-kə shōz,* (Fr.) something unspecified: an unimportant thing.

queme *kwēm,* (*Spens.*) *v.t.* to please, suit, fit. [O.E. *cwēman*; Ger. *bequem,* fit.]

quena *kā'nə, n.* a type of bamboo flute from the Andes, held vertically for playing. [Amer.Sp. — Quechua.]

quench *kwen(t)sh, v.t.* to put out: to put out the flame, light, or sight of: to stop (a discharge of electrically charged particles): to cool with liquid: to slake: to damp down: to put an end to: to put to silence: to destroy: to extinguish hope, etc., in (*obs.*). — *v.i.* to be extinguished: to die down: to lose zeal: to subside in passion, grow cold (*Shak.*). — *n.* quenching. — *adj.* **quench'able**. — *n.* **quench'er** one who, or that which, quenches: a draught or drink. — *n.* and *adj.* **quench'ing**. — *adj.* **quench'less** not to be extinguished. — *adv.* **quench'lessly**. — **quenched spark** an oscillatory spark discharge extinguished after the first few oscillations. [O.E. *cwencan*, found only in the compound *ācwencan*, to quench, causative of *cwincan* (*ācwincan*); cf. Old Fris. *kwinka*, to go out.]

quenelle *kə-nel'*, *n.* a poached forcemeat dumpling of chicken, veal, or fish. [Fr.]

quep *kwep*, *interj.* erroneously for **gup**[1].

Quercus *kwûr'kəs*, *n.* the oak genus of the beech family. — *ns.* **quercetum** (*kwûr-sē'təm*) a collection of oak-trees; **quer'citron** (*-si-trən*) a North American oak, the dyer's oak or yellow-barked oak: its inner bark, yielding a yellow dye (from **citron**). [L. *quercus*, oak.]

querimony *kwer'i-mən-i*, *n.* complaint. — *adj.* **querimonious** (*-mō'ni-əs*). — *adv.* **querimō'niously**. [L. *querimōnia* — *querī*, to complain.]

querist. See **query**.

quern *kwûrn*, *n.* a stone hand-mill. — **quern'stone**. [O.E. *cweorn*; O.N. *kvern*, Goth. (*asilu-*)*qaírnus*, (ass-)mill.]

querpo. See **en cuerpo**.

quersprung *kver'shprōōng*, *n.* in skiing, a jump-turn at right angles. [Ger.]

querulous *kwer'ū-ləs, -ōō-, -ə-, adj.* complaining: peevish. — *adv.* **quer'ulously**. — *n.* **quer'ulousness**. [L.L. *querulōsus* — *querī*, to complain.]

query, formerly often **quaere**, *kwē'ri, n.* an inquiry: doubt: interrogation mark (?). — *v.t.* to inquire into: to question: to doubt: to mark with a query. — *v.i.* to question: — *pa.t.* and *pa.p.* **que'ried**. — *n.* **que'rist** an inquirer. — *n.* and *adj.* **que'rying**. — *adv.* **que'ryingly**. [L. *quaere*, imper. of *quaerere*, *quaesītum*, to inquire.]

quest[1] *kwest, n.* the act of seeking: search: pursuit: an adventure, expedition, or undertaking with the purpose of achieving or finding some definite object: the object sought for: a searching party: a jury of inquest: inquiry, investigation: a collection of alms or donations (*R.C.*): a searching for game by dogs, or their outcry on finding it. — *v.i.* to go in search: to go begging: of dogs, to search for game: to give tongue. — *v.t.* to go in quest of or after. — *ns.* **quest'ant** (*Shak.*), **quest'er, quest'rist** (*Shak.*) one who goes on a quest. — *n.* and *adj.* **quest'ing**. — *adv.* **quest'ingly**. [O.Fr. *queste* (Fr. *quête*) — L. (*rēs*) *quaesīta*, (a thing) sought — *quaerere, quaesītum*, to seek.]

quest[2]. See **queest**.

question *kwes'chən, n.* an inquiry: an interrogation: the putting of a problem: a demand for an answer: an interrogative sentence or other form of words in which it is put: a unit task in an examination: a problem: a subject of doubt or controversy: discussion, conversation (*Shak.*): a subject of discussion, esp. the particular point actually before the house, meeting, or company: subjection to examination: examination by torture (*hist.*): objection, demur: doubt: the measure to be voted upon: vaguely, a relevant matter. — *v.t.* to put questions to: to call to account: to examine by questions: to inquire: to inquire concerning: to throw doubt upon: to regard as doubtful: to challenge, take exception to. — *v.i.* to ask questions: to inquire: to discuss, converse (*Shak.*). — *adj.* **quest'ionable** that may be questioned: doubtful: uncertain: open to suspicion: possibly dishonest, improper, immoral, etc.: such as questions may be put to, not unwilling to be conversed with (*Shak.*). — *ns.* **quest'ionableness; questionabil'ity**. — *adv.* **quest'ionably**. — *adj.* **quest'ionary** asking questions: in the form of questions. — *n.* an asker of questions: a questionnaire: a quaestionary (see **quaestor**). — *n.* **quest'ioner**. — *n.* and *adj.* **quest'ioning**. — *adv.* **quest'ioningly**. — *n.* **quest'ionist** a questioner,

a doubter: formerly, an undergraduate in his last term before proceeding to a degree. — *adj.* **quest'ionless** unquestioning: beyond question or doubt. — *adv.* certainly. — *n.* **questionnaire** (*kwes-chən-ār', kes-tē-on-er'*) a series of questions: a prepared set of written questions, for purposes of compilation or comparison. — **ques'tion-begg'ing** begging the question (see **beg**[2]). — Also *adj.* — **ques'tion-mark** a point of interrogation (?); **ques'tion-mas'ter** one who presides at a gathering whose purpose is the putting and answering of questions; **question time** in parliament, a period during each day when members can put questions to ministers. — **at question** questionable, open to question; **in question** under consideration: in dispute, open to question; **make question** to demur; **out of question** doubtless; **out of the question** not to be thought of; **question of fact** (*Eng. law*) that part of the issue which is decided by the jury; **question of law** that part decided by the judge. [O.Fr., — L. *quaestiō, -ōnis* — *quaerere, quaesītum*, to ask.]

questor. See **quaestor**.

questrist. See **quest**[1].

quetch. See **quich**.

quethe. See **quoth**.

quetsch *kwech, kvech, n.* a variety of plum, or brandy distilled from it. [Ger. dial. *quetsch(e)*, wild plum.]

quetzal *ket-säl', k(w)et'səl, n.* a golden green Central American bird (the *resplendent trogon*) with very long tail-feathers: the Guatemalan currency unit, or dollar. [Aztec *quetzalli*.]

queue *kū, n.* a pendent braid of hair at the back of the head, a pigtail: a file of persons, etc., awaiting their turn: the tail of a beast (*her.*). — *v.t.* to place or arrange in a queue: to track, dog. — *v.i.* to form, or take one's place in, a queue (usu. with *up*). — *adj.* **queued** (*kūd*) tailed: in a queue. — *n.* **queu'ing, queue'ing**. — *v.i.* **queue'-jump'**. — **queue'-jump'ing** going straight to the head of a queue instead of taking one's proper place in it (*lit.* and *fig.*). [Fr., — L. *cauda*, a tail.]

quey *kwā*, (*Scot.*) *n.* a heifer: a young cow that has not yet had a calf. [O.N. *kvíga*; Dan. *kvie*.]

queyn, queynie. See **quean**.

quh- *hw-*, *obs.* Scots spelling for **wh-**. [O.E. *hw -*.]

quia timet *kwē'ə tim'et*, (*law*) of or denoting an (action to obtain an) injunction to prevent a possible future harmful act. [L., because he/she fears.]

quibble *kwib'l*, *n.* an evasive turning away from the point in question into matters irrelevant, merely verbal, or insignificant: a pun: a petty conceit. — *v.i.* to evade a question by a play upon words: to cavil: to trifle in argument: to pun. — *ns.* **quibb'ler; quibb'lin** (*obs.*) a quibble. — *n.* and *adj.* **quibb'ling**. — *adv.* **quibb'lingly**. [Perh. dim. of obs. *quib*, quibble, which may be — L. *quibus*, dat. or abl. pl. of *quī*, who, a word frequent in legal use; or a variant of **quip**.]

quich *kwich*, (*Spens.*) *v.i.* to stir, to move. — Also (*obs.* or *dial.*) **quatch, quetch, quitch**. [O.E. *cweccan*, to shake, causative of *cwacian*, to quake.]

quiche *kēsh*, *n.* a shell of unsweetened pastry filled with egg custard and cheese, etc. [Fr., — Ger. dial. *küche*, dim. of *Kuche*, cake.]

Quichua *kēch'wə*. Same as **Quechua**.

quick[1] *kwik, adj.* living (*arch.*): alive (*arch.*): lively: swift: speedy: nimble: fresh: ready: sensitive: readily responsive: ready-witted: prompt in perception or learning: hasty: pregnant (*arch.*): at the stage of quickening: quickset: active: mobile: piercing. — *adv.* without delay: rapidly: soon. — *n.* the living (*arch.*): a living thing (*Spens.*): a living plant, esp. hawthorn in a hedge (also collectively): the life (*arch.*): the living flesh (*arch.*): the sensitive parts, esp. under the nails: the tenderest feelings. — *v.t.* **quick'en** to give life to: to stimulate: to impart energy or liveliness to: to invigorate: to revive: to accelerate. — *v.i.* to become alive or lively: to revive: to be stimulated: to reach the stage in pregnancy when the mother becomes conscious of the movement of the child: to move faster. — *n.*

quick'ener. — *n.* and *adj.* **quick'ening.** — *n.* **quick'ie** (*coll.*) something that takes, or is to be done in, a short time, e.g. a film, quiz question, crossword, etc.: an alcoholic drink to be rapidly consumed. — Also *adj.* — *adv.* **quick'ly.** — *n.* **quick'ness.** — *adj.* **quick'-an'swered** (*Shak.*) quick at answering. — **quick assets** readily realisable assets. — *adjs.* **quick'-born** born alive; **quick'-change** quick in making a change, esp. (of a performer) in appearance (**quick-change artist** such a performer: a person who changes rapidly or frequently in mood or opinion); **quick'-conceiv'ing** quick at understanding; **quick'-eyed** having acute sight or lively eyes; **quick'-fire, -firing** designed to allow a quick succession of shots. — **quick'-fire** rapid and continuous gunfire; **quick'-firer; quick'-freeze** very rapid freezing of food so that its natural qualities are unimpaired. — Also *v.t.* and *v.i.* — *adj.* **quick'-frozen.** — **quick'-hedge** a hedge of living plants; **quick'lime** unslaked lime (CaO); **quick'-lunch** a snack served promptly. — Also *adj.* — **quick march** (*mil.*) a march at a fast pace. — *interj.* the command to start such a march. — **quick'-match** cotton thread impregnated with an inflammable mixture; **quick'sand** a loose watery sand ready to swallow those who walk on it, boats, etc.: anything similarly treacherous. — *adjs.* **quick'-sandy; quick'-scent'ed, quick'-scent'ing** having a keen scent; **quick'-selling; quick'set** formed of living plants. — *n.* a living plant, slip, or cutting, esp. of hawthorn, or a series of them, set to grow for a hedge: a quickset hedge. — *adj.* **quick'-sighted** having quick sight or discernment. — **quick'-sight'edness; quick'silver** mercury. — *adj.* of mercury. — *v.t.* to overlay or to treat with quicksilver or amalgam. — *adj.* **quick'silvered.** — **quick'silvering** the mercury on the back of a mirror. — *adjs.* **quick'-silverish, quick'silvery.** — **quick'step** a march step or tune in fast time: a fast foxtrot. — *v.i.* to dance a quickstep. — *adv.* **quick'-stick, -s** without delay. — *adj.* **quick'-tem'pered** irascible. — **quick'thorn** hawthorn; **quick time** (*mil.*) a rate of about 120 steps per minute in marching; **quick'-trick** a card that should win a trick in the first or second round of the suit; **quick'-water** a solution of nitrate of mercury. — *adj.* **quick'-witt'ed** having a ready wit. — **quick'-witt'edness.** — **a quick one** a quick drink; **quick on the draw** swift to draw a gun from its holster: prompt in response or action. [O.E. *cwic*; O.N. *kvikr*, living.]

quick² *kwik*, *n.* couch grass or its rootstocks. — Also **quick'en, quick grass.** [Northern form of **quitch¹**.]

quicken¹ *kwik'ən*, (*Northern*) *n.* the rowan. — Also **quick'beam** (*Southern*), **quick'en-tree, wick'en, wick'y.** [O.E. *cwicbēam, cwictrēow*, aspen.]

quicken². See **quick¹,²**.

quid¹ *kwid*, *n.* that which a thing is, substance. [L., what.]

quid² *kwid*, *n.* something chewed or kept in the mouth, esp. a piece of tobacco. [**cud**.]

quid³ *kwid*, (*slang*) *n.* a pound (£1): formerly, a guinea: — *pl.* **quid:** or in sense of ready money (*obs. slang*) **quids.** — **quids in** (*slang*) in a very favourable or profitable situation. [Origin obscure.]

quidam *kwī'dam, kwē'*, *n.* somebody: a certain person: — *pl.* **quidams.** [L. *quīdam*.]

quiddany *kwid'ə-ni*, *n.* a confection of quince-juice and sugar. [L. *cotōnea*, quince — *cydōnia*; see **quince**.]

quiddity *kwid'i-ti*, *n.* the whatness or essence of anything: any trifling nicety: a cavil: a captious question: quibble. — Also (contracted) **quidd'it.** — *adj.* **quidd'itātive.** [Schoolman's L. *quidditās, -tātis*.]

quiddle *kwid'l*, (*dial.*) *v.i.* to trifle. — *ns.* **quidd'le** a fastidious person; **quidd'ler.**

quidnunc *kwid'nungk*, *n.* a newsmonger: a gossip. [L. *quid nunc?*, what now?]

quid pro quo *kwid prō kwō*, (L.) something for something: something given or taken as equivalent to another, often as retaliation: action or fact of giving or receiving thus.

quiesce *kwī-es', kwi-*, *v.i.* to quiet down: to become silent

(as a Hebrew consonant). — *v.t.* (*comput.*) to stop the operations of, make inactive. — *ns.* **quiesc'ence, quiesc'ency** rest: inactivity: silence of a consonant. — *adj.* **quiesc'ent** resting: not sounded: inactive: still. — *adv.* **quiesc'ently.** [L. *quiēscĕre*, to rest.]

quiet *kwī'ət*, *adj.* at rest: calm: undisturbed: unaccompanied by disturbance: without loudness, gaudiness, ostentation, formality, or obtrusiveness of any kind: still: without bustle or restlessness: without much activity: peaceable: gentle: inoffensive. — *n.* rest: repose: calm: stillness: peace: freedom from noise or disturbance. — *v.t.* and *v.i.* to make or become quiet. — *v.t.* and *v.i.* **qui'eten** to quiet. — *n.* and *adj.* **qui'eting.** — *n.* **qui'eter.** — *n.* and *adj.* **qui'eting.** — *ns.* **qui'etism** mental tranquillity: the doctrine that religious perfection on earth consists in passive and uninterrupted contemplation of the Deity; **qui'etist.** — *adj.* **quietist'ic.** — *n.* and *adj.* **qui'etive** sedative. — *adv.* **qui'etly.** — *n.* **qui'etness.** — *adj.* **qui'etsome** (*Spens.*) undisturbed. — *n.* **qui'etude** quietness. — **on the quiet** (or *slang* **on the Q.T.**) clandestinely: unobtrusively. [L. *quiētus*, quiet, calm.]

quietus *kwī-ē'təs, kwi-ā'tōōs*, *n.* an acquittance: discharge from office: discharge from life: extinction: silencing. [L. *quiētus est*, he is quiet.]

quiff *kwif*, *n.* a lock of hair oiled and brushed down on the forehead or turned up and back from it. [Poss. **coif**.]

quight *kwīt*, (*Spens.*). See **quit, quite²**.

qui-hi, -hye *kwī'-hī'*, *n.* an Englishman in India, esp. in Bengal, in colonial days. [Hind. *koī hai*, the call for a servant, Is anyone there? — *koī*, anyone, *hai*, is.]

quill¹ *kwil*, *n.* a reed, hollow stalk or internode, or the like (*obs.*): a small tube (*obs.*): the hollow basal part of a feather: a large feather: a porcupine's spine: a goose or other feather used as a pen: hence a pen generally, or the profession of letters: a thing made from a quill feather, as a toothpick, an angler's float, a plectrum: a weaver's bobbin of reed or other material: a hollow shaft (*mach.*): a musical pipe made from a reed or the like: hence (Shak., *Mids.N.Dr.*, III, i. 134) throat, or perh. voice: a roll of curled bark, as cinnamon: a cylindrical plait (*obs.*). — *v.t.* to goffer: to wind on a bobbin. — *adj.* **quilled** furnished with, or formed into quills: tubular. — *n.* **quill'ing** a ribbon or strip gathered into flutings. — **quill'-driver** (*used derogatorily*) a clerk: an assiduous writer; **quill'-driving; quill'-feather** a large stiff wing or tail feather; **quill'man** a clerk; **quill'-nib** a quill-pen shortened for use with a holder; **quill'-pen; quill'wort** any plant of the genus Isoëtes (from the quill-like leaves). [Origin obscure; cf. L.G. *quiele*, Ger. *Kiel*.]

quill² *kwil*, (*Shak.*) *n.* a combination (in the phrase **in the quill** in a body, in concert). [Fr. *cueille*.]

quillai *ki-lī'*, *n.* the soap-bark tree. — *n.* **Quillaja, Quillaia** (*ki-lī'ə, -lē'ə*) a genus of S. American rosaceous trees whose bark has soaplike properties: (without *cap.*) a tree of this genus, a quillai. [Amer. Sp.]

quillet *kwil'it*, *n.* a subtlety in argument: a quibble. [Perh. L. *quidlibet*, what you will.]

quillon *kē-yõ*, *n.* either arm of the cross-guard of a sword-handle. [Fr.]

quilt *kwilt*, *n.* a bed-cover of two thicknesses with padding sewn in compartments: any material or piece of material so treated, esp. when worn under or instead of armour: a thick coverlet: a thick covering placed over beehive frames: the inner part of a cricket or hockey ball. — *v.t.* to pad, cover, or line with a quilt: to form into a quilt: to stitch in: to seam like a quilt: to cover with interlaced cord: to thrash. — *adj.* **quilt'ed.** — *ns.* **quilt'er** a person or machine that makes quilting; **quilt'ing** the act of making a quilt: that which is quilted: a cloth for making quilts: a cloth with a pattern like a quilt: a covering of rope-yarn: a thrashing with a rope's end. — **quilt'ing-bee** a gathering of women to help someone in quilting a counterpane, combined with social amusement; **quilt'ing-cott'on** cotton wadding; **quilt'ing-frame** an adjustable frame for holding a fabric for quilting. [O.Fr. *cuilte* (Fr. *couette*) — L. *culcita*, a cushion.]

quim *kwim*, (*vulg. slang*) *n.* the female genitalia. [Origin uncertain; a relationship with **coomb, cwm** has been suggested.]

quin *kwin*, *n.* short for **quintuplet**.

quina, kina, china *kē'nə*, *n.* cinchona bark: any tree yielding it: quinine. — Also **quinaquina, kinakina, chinachina** (*kē-nä-kē'nə*), **quinquina** (*kin-* or *king-kē'nə*, *kwing-kwī'nə*). — *adj.* **quinic** (*kwin'ik*). — **quinic acid** an acid got from cinchona bark. [Sp. *quina*, *quinaquina* — Quechua *kina, kina-kina, kinkina,* bark.]

quinacrine *kwin'ə-krēn*, *n.* another name for **mepacrine**. [*quinine, acridine*.]

quinary *kwī'nər-i*, *adj.* fivefold: by fives: in fives: of the fifth order: based on five: with five variables. — *adj.* **qui'nate** in sets of five: with five leaflets arising at one point. [L. *quīnī*, five by five.]

quince *kwins*, *n.* a golden, globose or pear-shaped, fragrant, acid fruit, good for jellies, marmalade, etc., or the tree or shrub (*Cydonia oblonga*), akin to pear and apple, that bears it: extended to the near-allied *Japanese quince* (see **japonica**) and to the unrelated *Bengal quince,* the bael-fruit. [Orig. pl. of *quine* — O.Fr. *coin* (Fr. *coing*) — L. *cotōneum* — Gr. *kydōnion* — *Kydōniā,* in Crete.]

quincentenary *kwin-sin-tēn'ər-i, -sin-ten'ər-i,* or *-sen'tin-ər-i, n.* and *adj.* quingentenary. [Irreg. formed — L. *quīnque,* five, and **centenary**.]

quinche *kwinsh* (*Spens.*), *v.i.* to stir, move. [Ety. dub.]

quincunx *kwin'kungks, n.* an arrangement of five things at the corners and centre of a square, or of a great number of things (esp. trees) spaced in the same way: an aspect of 150° between two heavenly bodies (*astrol.*). — *adj.* **quincuncial** (*-kun'shl*) of or in a quincunx: of aestivation, having two leaves overlapping at each edge, two underlapping at each edge, and one overlapping and underlapping (*bot.*). — *adv.* **quincun'cially.** [L. *quīncunx* — *quīnque,* five, *uncia,* a twelfth part.]

quine. See **quean**.

quinella *kwi-nel'ə,* (orig. *U.S.,* now esp. *Austr.*) *n.* a form of bet in which the punter has to select the two horses, (dogs, etc.) which will come in first and second but not give their order of placing. [U.S. Sp. *quiniela*.]

quingentenary *kwin-jen-tē'nər-i, -ten'ər-i,* or *-jen'tən-ər-i, n.* a five-hundredth anniversary or its celebration. — Also *adj.* [L. *quīngentī,* five hundred.]

quinic. See **quin**.

quinie. See **quean**.

quinine *kwin-ēn', kwin'ēn,* in U.S. *kwī'nīn, n.* a colourless, inodorous, very bitter alkaloid ($C_{20}H_{24}O_2N_2 \cdot 3H_2O$), got from cinchona bark, or one of its salts, used as an antipyretic and analgesic, formerly widely used to treat malaria. — *n.* **quin'idine** (*-i-dēn*) a crystalline alkaloid drug, isomeric with quinine, used to treat irregularities in the heart rhythm. — **quinine water** a beverage made by flavouring water with quinine, lemon, etc. [See **quina**.]

quink-goose *kwingk'-gōōs, n.* the brent-goose.

quinnat *kwin'ət, n.* the king-salmon. [From an Amer. Ind. name.]

quinoa *kē'nō-ə, n.* a South American goosefoot, used like rice (seeds) or spinach (leaves). [Sp. *quinoa* — Quechua *kinua*.]

quinol *kwin'ol, n.* a reducing agent and photographic developer, $C_6H_4(OH)_2$, got by reduction of quinone. — *ns.* **quin'oline** (*-ō-lēn*) a pungent, colourless liquid (C_9H_7N), first got from quinine; **quinone** (*kwin'ōn, kwin-ōn'*) a golden-yellow crystalline compound ($C_6H_4O_2$) usually prepared by oxidising aniline: a reddish or colourless isomer of this: a general name for a benzene derivative in which two oxygen atoms replace two hydrogen atoms. — Also **kinone** (*kē'nōn*). [**quina**.]

quinqu-, quinque- *kwin-kw(i)-,* in composition, five. — *n.* **quinquagenarian** (*kwin-kwə-ji-nā'ri-ən;* L.

quinquagenarius — *quīnquāgēnī,* fifty each) one who is fifty years old, or between fifty and fifty-nine. — Also *adj.* — *adjs.* **quinquecostate** (*kwin-kwi-kos'tāt;* L. *costa,* rib) five-ribbed; **quinquefarious** (*kwin-kwi-fā'ri-əs;* L. poss. from *fārī,* to speak) fivefold: in five rows; **quinquefoliate** (*kwin-kwi-fō'li-āt;* L. *folium,* leaf) with five leaflets. — *n.* **quinquennium** (*kwin-kwen'i-əm;* L. *annus,* year) a period of five years: — *pl.* **quinquenn'ia.** — Also (*irreg.*) **quinquenn'iad.** — *adj.* **quinquenn'ial** occurring once in five years: lasting five years. — *n.* a fifth anniversary or its celebration. — *adv.* **quinquenn'ially.** — *n.* **quinquereme** (*kwin'kwi-rēm;* L. *rēmus,* an oar) an ancient ship with five sets of oars. — *adj.* **quinquevalent** (*kwin-kwev'ə-lənt* or *-kwi-vā'*) having a valency of five. — *n.* **quinquev'alence** (or *-vā'*). [L. *quīnque,* five.]

Quinquagesima *kwin-kwə-jes'i-mə, n.* Shrove Sunday (also **Quinquagesima Sunday**) — apparently as fifty days before Easter Sunday (both counted). — *adj.* **quinquages'imal** of the number fifty: of fifty days. [L. *quīnquāgēsimus, -a, -um,* fiftieth; cf. **Quadragesima, Sexagesima, Septuagesima**.]

quinque-, quinquennium, etc. See **quinqu-**.

quinquina. See **quina**.

quinsy *kwin'zi, n.* suppurative tonsillitis. — *adj.* **quin'sied** suffering from quinsy. — **quin'sy-berry** the blackcurrant; **quins'y-wort** squinancy-wort. [L.L. *quinancia* — Gr. *kynanchē;* see **cynanche**.]

quint *kwint, n.* a fifth (*mus.*): an organ-stop a fifth above the foundation stops: the E string of a violin: a five-stringed tenor viol (also **quinte**): (*kint;* old-fashioned *kent*) a sequence of five cards in piquet. — **quint'-ma'jor** ace to ten; **quint'-mi'nor** knave to seven. [Fr. *quinte* — L. *quīntus, -a, -um,* fifth.]

quint- *kwint-,* in composition, fifth. [L. *quīntus,* fifth.]

quinta *kin'tə, n.* a country house. [Sp. and Port.]

quintain *kwin'tin, -tən, n.* a post for tilting at, often with a turning cross-piece to strike the unskilful tilter: the sport of tilting at such a post. [O.Fr. *quintaine,* thought to be — L. *quīntāna via,* the road adjoining the fifth maniple in a camp.]

quintal *kwin'tl, n.* formerly, a hundredweight: now, 100 kilograms. [Fr. and Sp. *quintal* — Ar. *qintār* — L. *centum,* a hundred.]

quintan *kwin'tən, adj.* occurring every fourth (by inclusive reckoning fifth) day. [L. *quīntānus,* of the fifth.]

quinte[1] *kēt, n.* the fifth of eight parrying or attacking positions in fencing. [Fr.]

quinte[2]. See **quint**.

quintessence *kwin-tes'əns,* or *kwin', n.* orig. a fifth entity, in addition to the four elements: the pure concentrated essence of anything: the most essential part, form, or embodiment of anything. — *adj.* **quintessential** (*-ti-sen'shl*). — *v.t.* **quintessen'tialise, -ize.** [Fr., — L. *quīnta essentia,* fifth essence.]

quintet, quintette, quintett *kwin-tet', n.* a composition for five voices or instruments: a set of performers or instruments for such compositions: a group of five people or things. — Also (It.) **quintet'to** (*kwēn-tet'tō*): — *pl.* **quintet'ti** (*-tē*). [It. *quintetto,* dim. of *quinto* — L. *quīntus,* fifth.]

quintic *kwin'tik, adj.* of the fifth degree.

quintile *kwin'tīl, n.* any of four values which divide the items of a frequency distribution into five classes: an aspect of 72° between two heavenly bodies (*astrol.*). [L. *quīntus,* fifth.]

quintillion *kwin-til'yən, n.* the fifth power of a million, represented by a unit and thirty ciphers: in U.S., the sixth power of one thousand — a unit with eighteen ciphers. — *n.* and *adj.* **quintill'ionth.** [Modelled on **million**.]

quintroon *kwin-trōōn', n.* the offspring of a person of European descent and an octoroon: one who is fifth (inclusive) in descent from a Negro. [Sp. *quinterón* — L. *quīntus,* fifth.]

quintuple *kwin'tū-pl, -tū'pl, adj.* fivefold: having five parts, members, or divisions. — *n.* five times as much.

— *v.t.* and *v.i.* to increase fivefold. — *n.* **quin'tüplet** (also *-tū'*) a set of five things: a group of five notes played in the time of four: one of five born at a birth. [L. *quīntus*, fifth, on the model of **quadruple**.]

quintuplicate *kwin-tū'pli-kāt, adj.* fivefold. — *n.* one of five corresponding things: fivefoldness. — *v.t.* to make fivefold. — *n.* **quintuplicā'tion**. [L. *quīntuplex, -icis* — *quīntus*, fifth, *plicāre*, to fold.]

quinze *kwinz, n.* a card game, like vingt-et-un, the object being to count as nearly to fifteen as possible without going above it. [Fr., fifteen.]

quip *kwip, n.* a short, clever remark, a repartee: a gibe: a quibble: a fanciful jest or action: a knick-knack. — *v.i.* to utter quips. — *v.t.* to assail with quips. — *adj.* **quipp'ish**. — *n.* **quip'ster** one given to making clever remarks. [Perh. from obs. *quippy*, which may be — L. *quippe*, forsooth.]

quipu *kē'poō, n.* a mnemonic contrivance of knotted cords used by the ancient Peruvians — depending on order, colour, and kind. — Also **quip'o** (*pl.* **quip'os**). [Quechua *quipu*, knot.]

quire[1] *kwīr, n.* formerly, four sheets of paper or parchment folded together in eight leaves: later, the twentieth part of a ream, twenty-four sheets, each having a single fold: a (quire-filling) book or poem (*obs.*; also **quair** *kwār*). — *v.t.* to fold in quires. [O.Fr. *quaier* (Fr. *cahier*), prob. from L.L. *quaternum*, a set of four sheets — L. *quattuor*, four.]

quire[2] *kwīr, n.* obs. spelling of **choir**. — *n.* (*obs.*) **quirister** (*kwir'*) chorister.

Quirinus *kwi-rī'nəs*, L. *kwi-rē'nŏŏs, n.* an Italic god of war, etc., afterwards identified with the deified Romulus — *n.* **Quirinal** (*kwir'in-əl*) one of the hills of Rome: the Italian government, as opposed to the Vatican (from the palace on the hill). — *n.pl.* **Quirinalia** (*kwir-i-nā'li-ə*) a festival held in honour of Quirinus, on 17th February. [L. *Quirīnus*.]

quirister. See **quire[2]**.

Quirites *kwi-rī'tēz, kwi-rē'tās, n.pl.* the citizens of ancient Rome in their civil capacity. [L. *Quirītēs*, orig. the Samnite people of *Cures* (united with the Romans).]

quirk *kwûrk, n.* a trick or peculiarity of action, fashion or behaviour: a sudden turn, twist, jerk, or flourish: an artful evasion: a quibble: a quip: a trick, knack, way (*Shak.*): an acute sharp-edged groove alongside a moulding (*archit.*). — *v.i.* to turn sharply: to utter or execute quips: to move jerkily. — *v.t.* to assail with a quirk: to furnish with a quirk. — *n.* **quirk'iness**. — *adjs.* **quirk'ish; quirk'y**. [Origin unknown.]

quirt *kwûrt, n.* a Spanish-American braided hide riding-whip. — *v.t.* to strike with a quirt. [Mexican-Sp. *cuarta*.]

quisling *kwiz'ling, n.* one who aids the enemy: a native puppet prime minister set up by an occupying foreign power. [Vidkun *Quisling*, who played that part in Norway during German occupation (1940–45).]

quist *kwist*. See **queest**.

quit *kwit*, (*arch.*) **quite** (*Spens.* **quight, quyte**) *kwīt, vs.t.* to pay: to repay: to requite: to release from obligation: to clear off: to discharge: to remit: to free: to clear of blame, etc.: to acquit: to depart from: to cease to occupy: to rid (*obs.* except *refl.*): to let go: to leave off: to behave, acquit (*refl.*): to be worth. — *v.i.* to leave off: to depart: — *pr.p.* **quitt'ing** (*arch.* **quīt'ing**); *pa.t.* and *pa.p.* **quitt'ed, quit** (**quīt'ed**). — *adj.* **quit** set free: clear: quits: acquitted: released from obligation. — *adj.* **quits** even: neither owing nor owed. — *ns.* **quitt'al** (*Shak.*) requital; **quitt'ance** release: discharge: acquittance: requital. — *v.t.* (*obs.*) to repay. — *n.* **quitt'er** a shirker: one who gives up easily. — **quit'= claim** a deed of release. — *v.t.* to relinquish claim or title to: to release, discharge. — **quit'-rent** a rent in money or kind in lieu of services. — **cry quits** (formerly **quittance**) to declare oneself even with another, and so satisfied; **double or quits** see **double**; **quit scores** to balance accounts. [O.Fr. *quiter* (Fr. *quitter*) — L.L.

quiētāre, to pay — L. *quiētāre*, to make quiet — *quiētus*, quiet.]

qui tam *kwī tam, kwē tam*, an action by an informer partly on his own behalf, partly on the state's. [From the first words, L. *quī tam*, who as much (for the king as for himself).]

quitch[1] *kwich, n.* couch grass. — Also **quitch grass**. [O.E. *cwice*; cf. **couch grass, quick[2]**.]

quitch[2]. Same as **quich**.

quite[1]. See **quit**.

quite[2] (*Spens.* **quight**) *kwīt, adv.* completely, wholly, entirely: enough fully to justify the use of the word or phrase qualified: somewhat, fairly: exactly, indeed, yes (*coll.*; often **quite so**). — **quite something** (*coll.*) something remarkable or excellent. [**quit**.]

quittance. See **quit**.

quitter[1], quittor *kwit'ər, n.* pus: a fistulous sore on a horse's hoof. [Poss. O.Fr. *quiture*, cooking — L. *coctūra*.]

quitter[2]. See **quit**.

quiver[1] *kwiv'ər*, (*Shak.*) *adj.* nimble, active. [M.E. *cwiver* — O.E. *cwifer*, found in the adverbial form *cwiferlice*, zealously.]

quiver[2] *kwiv'ər, n.* a case for arrows. — *adj.* **quiv'ered** furnished with a quiver: sheathed, as in a quiver. — *n.* **quiv'erful** (*fig.*) a large family (Psalms cxxvii. 5). [O.Fr. *cuivre*; prob. Gmc. in origin; cf. O.H.G. *kohhar* (Ger. *Kocher*) O.E. *cocer*.]

quiver[3] *kwiv'ər, v.i.* to shake with slight and tremulous motion: to tremble: to shiver. — *v.t.* (of a bird) to cause (the wings) to move rapidly. — *ns.* **quiv'er, quiv'ering**. — *adv.* **quiv'eringly**. — *adjs.* **quiv'erish; quiv'ery**. [Perh. conn. with **quiver[1]**.]

qui vive *kē vēv*, alert (in phrase **on the qui vive**). [From the French sentry's challenge, lit. (long) live who? — *qui*, who, *vive*, 3rd pers. sing. pres. subj. of *vivre*, to live — L. *vīvĕre*.]

quixotic *kwiks-ot'ik, adj.* like Don Quixote, the knight-errant in the great romance of Cervantes (1547–1616), extravagantly romantic in ideals or chivalrous in action: (of ideals, actions) absurdly generous and unselfish. — *adv.* **quixot'ically**. — *ns.* **quix'otism; quix'otry**.

quiz *kwiz, n.* an odd-looking person or (*Jane Austen*) thing: a monocle, often with a handle: a piece of banter or quiet mockery: a mocking look: a hoax: one who practises any of these: an oral examination or short test (*U.S.*): a sportive catechism or general-knowledge test: a bandalore (*q.v.; obs.*): — *pl.* **quizz'es**. — *v.t.* to poke fun at: to eye, often with an air of mockery: to catechise, interrogate. — *v.i.* to practise derisive joking: — *pr.p.* **quizz'ing**; *pa.t.* and *pa.p.* **quizzed**. — *ns.* **quizz'er; quizz'ery**. — *adj.* **quizz'ical**. — *n.* **quizzical'ity**. — *adv.* **quizz'ically**. — *n.* **quizzifica'tion** quizzing. — *v.t.* **quizz'ify** to turn into a quiz. — *ns.* **quizz'iness** oddness; **quizz'ing**. — **quiz'-master** question-master; **quizz'ing-glass** a monocle. [Origin obscure.]

quo' *kə, ko, k(w)ō, v.t.* a Scots form of **quoth**. — **quod** an obsolete form of **quoth**, used esp. at the end of a poem, followed by the poet's name.

quoad *kwō'ad, adv.* as far as: to this extent. — **quoad hoc** (*hōk, hok*) as far as this; **quoad omnia** (*om'ni-ə, -a*) in respect of all things; **quoad sacra** (*sā'krə, sa'kra*) as far as concerns sacred matters (of a parish disjoined for ecclesiastical purposes only). [L. *quō*, whither, *ad*, to.]

quod[1] *kwod*, neut. of L. *quī*, which. — **quod erat demonstrandum** (*er'at dem-ən-stran'dəm, er-at' dēm-ōn-stran'dōom*), (abbrev. QED) which was to be proved or demonstrated; **quod erat faciendum** (*fā-shē-en'dəm, fa-ki-en'dōom*), (abbrev. QEF) which was to be done; **quod** (*pl.* **quae** *kwē, kwī*) **vide** (*vī'dē, vi', wi'de*) which see.

quod[2] *kwod*, (*slang*) *n.* prison. — *v.t.* to imprison. [Origin unknown.]

quod[3]. See **quo'**.

quodlibet *kwod'li-bet, n.* a scholastic argument: a humorous medley of tunes. — *n.* **quodlibetā'rian** one given to quodlibets. — *adjs.* **quodlibet'ic, -al.** [L., what you please — *quod*, what, *libet*, it pleases.]

quodlin *kwod'lin,* an obsolete form of **codlin.**

quoif *koif.* Same as **coif.**

quoin *koin, n.* a wedge, esp. for locking type in a forme, or for raising a gun: a salient angle, esp. of a building: a corner-stone, esp. a dressed corner-stone: a keystone: a voussoir. — *v.t.* to wedge: to secure, or raise by wedging. [See **coin.**]

quoist *kwoist.* See **queest.**

quoit *koit, kwoit, n.* a heavy flat ring for throwing as near as possible to a hob or pin: a dolmen cover: a dolmen: (in *pl., sing.*) the game played with quoits. — *v.i.* to play at quoits. — *v.t.* to throw as a quoit. — *n.* **quoit'er.** [Origin obscure.]

quo jure? *kwō jōō'rē, yōō're,* (L.) by what right?

quokka *kwok'ə, n.* a small marsupial, *Setonix brachyurus,* found in W. Australia. [Aboriginal.]

quoll *kwol, n.* a small Australian marsupial (*Dasyurus macrurus*). [Aboriginal.]

quondam *kwon'dam, adj.* former. [L., formerly.]

quonk *kwongk,* (*coll.*) *n.* any accidental noise made too close to a microphone and thus disrupting a radio or television programme. — *v.i.* to make such a noise. [Imit.]

Quonset hut® *kwon'set hut,* the U.S. equivalent of the Nissen hut.

quooke *kwōōk* (*Spens.*), *pa.t.* of **quake.**

quop *kwop,* (*obs.* or *dial*) *v.i.* to throb. [M.E. *quappe*; imit.]

quorum *kwō', kwö'rəm, n.* orig. a number of specially named justices of the peace of whom some had to be present before any business could be done: loosely, the whole body of justices: a minimum number of persons necessary for transaction of business in any body. — *adj.* **quo'rate** having, being (at least) a quorum. [L. *quōrum,* of whom, from the wording of the commission, of whom we will that you, so-and-so, be one (two, etc.).]

quota *kwō'tə, n.* a proportional share, a part assigned: a regulated quantity of goods allowed by a government to be manufactured, exported, imported, etc.: a prescribed number of immigrants allowed into a country per year, students allowed to enrol for a course, fish allowed to be caught, etc.: — *pl.* **quo'tas.** — **quota immigrant** an immigrant (to the U.S.A.) admitted as one of the yearly quota allowed to his country of origin, as opposed to a **non-quota immigrant** (as child, wife, of resident citizen); **quota system** the imposition of specified quotas by a government or other agency. [L. *quota* (*pars*), the how-manieth (part) — *quotus,* of what number — *quot,* how many.]

quote *kwōt, kōt* (*Shak.* **coat, coate, cote**) *v.t.* orig. to divide into chapters, verses, etc., number the chapters of, or mark with references: to refer to: to cite: to adduce as authority, illustration, or example: to give the actual words of: to examine as if looking up a reference (*Shak.*): to record: to note, set down, mention, in writing or mentally: to set down in the prompter's book as due to be called (*theat.*): to give the current price of: to state the market price of (shares, etc.) on the Stock Exchange list: to enclose within quotation-marks. — *v.i.* to make quotations. — used as *interj.* to indicate that what follows immediately is a quotation. — *n.* a quotation: a quotation-mark. — *adj.* **quō'table** lending itself (or himself) to quotation: fit to quote. — *ns.* **quō'tableness, quōtabil'ity.** — *adv.* **quō'tably.** — *n.* **quōtā'tion** act of quoting: that which is quoted: a short passage of music, written or played, extracted from a longer piece: an estimated price submitted to a prospective purchaser: the current price of shares, etc., on the Stock Exchange list: registration of a company with the Stock Exchange so that shares may be listed: a quadrat for filling blanks in type (orig. those between marginal references). — *adjs.* **quōtā'tious, quō'tative** given to quoting. — *ns.* **quō'tative** a source of quotations; **quō'ter.** — *adj.* **quōte'worthy.** — **quōtā'tion-mark** one of the marks (*print.* **quotes**) used to note the beginning and end of a quotation (see also **inverted commas** under **comma**); **quoted company** one whose shares are quoted on the Stock Exchange. [L.L. *quotāre,* to divide into chapters and verses — L. *quotus,* of what number — *quot,* how many.]

quoth *kwōth,* (*arch.*) *v.t.* (1st and 3rd pers. sing., past tense, of the otherwise obs. vb. **quethe**) said (followed by its subject). — *interj.* **quō'tha** forsooth, indeed (lit. quoth he; see **a, pron.**). [O.E. *cwæth,* pret. of *cwethan,* to say; cf. **bequeath.**]

quotidian *kwot-id'i-ən, adj.* daily: everyday, commonplace: of any activity of a living creature or a living part, that follows a regular recurrent pattern. — *n.* a fever or ague that recurs daily. [L. *quotīdiānus* — *quotīdiē,* daily — *quot,* how many, *diēs,* day.]

quotient *kwō'shənt,* (*math.*) *n.* the number of times one quantity is contained in another: a ratio, usu. multiplied by 100, used in giving a numerical value to ability, etc. (see **achievement, intelligence, quotient**). [L. *quotiēns, quotiēs,* how often — *quot,* how many (with *t* from false appearance of being a participle).]

quotition *kwō-tish'ən, n.* a division regarded as repeated subtraction or measuring. [From L. *quot.*]

quotum *kwō'təm, n.* quota. [L. neut. of *quotus*; see **quota.**]

quo warranto *kwō wo-ran'tō,* a writ calling upon one to show by what warrant he holds or claims a franchise or office. [L. *quō warrantō* (abl.), by what warrant.]

Qurân, Quran, Qur'an *kōō-rän', n.* Same as **Koran.** — *adj.* **Quran'ic, Qur'anic.**

qwerty *kwûr'ti, n.* a standard arrangement of keys on a typewriter keyboard: a keyboard having its keys laid out as on a standard typewriter (also **qwer'ty key'board**). — *adj.* of or having such a keyboard. [From the letters at the top left-hand side of the keyboard.]

For other sounds see detailed chart of pronunciation.

R

R, r *är, n.* the eighteenth letter in our alphabet — the
'dog letter', from the trilling (evanescent in Southern
England) of the tip of the tongue: as a mediaeval
numeral, R = 80; R̄ = 80000: **r** is the abbrev. for
röntgen unit. — **R months** the time when oysters are
in season (from the spelling of the names of the months
from September to April); **the three R's** reading,
writing, and arithmetic. [L. *er.*]
Ra *rä, n.* the Egyptian sun-god.
rabanna *rǝ-banʹǝ, n.* a Madagascan raffia fabric. [Mala-
gasy.]
rabat, rabatte *rǝ-batʹ*, (*geom.*) *v.t.* to rotate into coincidence with another plane. — *ns.* **rabattʹing; rabatʹment,
rabatteʹment.** [Fr. *rabattre*, to lower.]
rabato *rǝ-bäʹtō.* Same as **rebato.** — *n.* **rabatine** (*rabʹǝ-tēn;
Scott*) a low collar.
rabbet *rabʹit, n.* a groove cut to receive an edge. — *v.t.*
to groove: to join by a rabbet: — *pr.p.* **rabbʹeting;** *pa.t.*
and *pa.p.* **rabbʹeted.** — **rabbʹeting-machineʹ, -plane,
-saw; rabbʹet-joint.** [Fr. *rabat* — *rabattre*, to beat
back.]
rabbi (with *cap.* when prefixed) *rabʹī, n.* a Jewish expounder or doctor of the law (also **rabbin** *rabʹin*): the
leader of a Jewish congregation: — *pl.* **rabbʹis** (**rabbʹ-
ins**). — *n.* **rabbʹinate** the dignity or tenure of office of
a rabbi: a body of rabbis. — *adjs.* **rabbinʹic, -al**
pertaining to the rabbis or to their opinions, learning,
and language. — *n.* **Rabbinʹic** late Hebrew. — *adv.*
rabbinʹically. — *ns.* **rabbʹinism** the doctrine or teaching
of the rabbis: a rabbinical peculiarity of expression:
the late Jewish belief which esteemed the oral equally
with the written law; **rabbʹinist, rabbʹinite** one who
adheres to the Talmud and traditions of the rabbis;
rabboni (*rab-ōʹni, -nī*) my great master. [Heb. *rabbi*,
my great one — *rabh*, great, master.]
rabbit¹ *rabʹit, n.* a small burrowing animal of any of
several genera of the family *Leporidae*, related to the
hare: its flesh (as food): but incurably inferior player at lawn-tennis or other game:
a timid person: an unimportant, insignificant person.
— *v.i.* to hunt rabbits: to talk at length and in a
rambling fashion (*coll.*; often with *on*; orig. rhyming
slang *rabbit and pork*, talk). — *ns.* **rabbʹiter** one who
hunts rabbits; **rabbʹitry** a place where rabbits are kept:
the play of a rabbit in games. — *adj.* **rabbʹity.** —
rabbʹit-fish the king of the herrings (*Chimaera*) or other
fish fancied to resemble a rabbit; **rabbʹit-hole** a rabbit's
burrow; **rabbʹit-hutch** a box for housing rabbits;
rabbʹit-punch a blow on the back of the neck; **rabbʹit=
squirrel** a viscacha of the genus *Lagidium*, found in the
mountainous parts of western S. America; **rabbʹit=
sucker** (*Shak.*) a sucking rabbit; **rabbʹit-warren** see
warren. — **Welsh rabbit** melted cheese with or without
ale, etc., on hot toast — now more usually **Welsh
rarebit.** [M.E. *rabet*; poss. from O.N.Fr.]
rabbit² *rabʹit, v.t.* to confound (often in *od rabbit, d'rabbit*,
or *drabbit*, for *God rabbit*). [Perh. a facetious substitution for **rat.**]
rabble¹ *rabʹl, n.* a disorderly assemblage or crowd: a mob:
the lowest class of people: a confused stream of words.
— *adj.* of or like a rabble. — *v.t.* and *v.i.* to gabble.
— *v.t.* to mob. — *ns.* **rabbʹlement** a rabble: tumult;
rabbʹling esp. (*Scot. hist.*) the mobbing and ousting of
the Episcopal 'curates' at the Revolution. — *v.i.*
rabbʹle-rouse. — **rabbʹle-rousʹer** one who stirs up the
common people to discontent and violence, a demagogue; **rabbʹle-rousʹing; rabble rout** (*obs.*) the mob,
rabble. [Cf. Du. *rabbelen*, to gabble, L.G. *rabbeln*.]
rabble² *rabʹl, n.* a device for stirring molten iron, etc. in

a furnace. — *v.t.* to stir with a rabble. — *n.* **rabbʹler.**
[Fr. *râble* — L. *rutābulum*, a poker.]
rabboni. See **rabbi.**
Rabelaisian *rab-ǝ-lāʹzi-ǝn, n.* a follower, admirer, or
student of François *Rabelais* (d. 1553 or 1554). — *adj.*
of or like Rabelais: extravagantly humorous: robustly
outspoken: (*loosely*) coarsely indecent. — *n.* **Rabelaisʹ-
ianism.**
rabi *rubʹē, n.* the spring grain harvest in India, Pakistan,
etc. [Ar. *rabīʹ*, spring.]
rabid *rabʹid, adj.* raging: fanatical: affected with rabies.
— *adj.* **rabʹic** of rabies. — *adv.* **rabʹidly.** — *ns.* **rabidʹity,
rabʹidness; rabies** (*rāʹbēz, -bi-ēz*, or *raʹ*) the disease
called hydrophobia, caused by a virus transmitted by
the bite of an infected animal. [L. *rabidus* (adj.),
rabiēs (n.) — *rabēre*, to rave.]
raca *räʹkǝ*, (*B.*) *adj.* worthless. [Chaldee *rēkā* (a term
of reproach).]
rac(c)ahout *rakʹǝ-hōōt, n.* acorn meal. [Fr., — Ar.
rāqaut.]
raccoon, racoon *rǝ-kōōnʹ, n.* an American animal (*Procyon lotor*, or other species) related to the bears: its
fur. — **raccoonʹ-berry** a member of the Podophyllum;
raccoonʹ-dog a raccoon-like wild dog (*Nyctereutes*) of
Eastern Asia. [From an American Indian name.]
race¹ *rās, n.* the descendants of a common ancestor: esp.
those who inherit a common set of characteristics: such
a set of descendants, narrower than a species: a breed:
a stud or herd (*obs.*): ancestry, lineage, stock: the
condition of belonging by descent to a particular
group: inherited disposition: a class or group, defined
otherwise than by descent: a sex (*obs.*): peculiar
flavour, as of wine, by which its origin may be
recognised: raciness, piquancy. — *adj.* **racial** (*rāʹshl,
-shyǝl, -shi-ǝl*) of, relating to, race. — *ns.* **raʹcialism**
race-hatred, rivalry, or feeling: belief in inherent superiority of some races over others, usu. with implication of a right to rule: discriminative treatment based
on such belief; **raʹcialist.** — *adv.* **raʹcially.** — *n.* **raciāʹ-
tion** formation locally of new distinct biological groups
smaller than species. — *adv.* **racily** (*rāsʹi-li*). — *ns.*
raʹciness quality of being racy; **racʹism** racialism (q.v.);
racʹist. — *adj.* **raʹcy** having a distinctive flavour imparted by the soil, as wine: exciting to the mind by
strongly characteristic thought or language: spirited:
pungent: zestful: risqué. — **raceʹ-haʹtred** animosity
accompanying difference of race; **race memory** folk
memory; **race relations** social relations between members of different races living in the same country or
community; **race riot** a riot caused by perceived discrimination on the grounds of race; **raceʹ-suʹicide**
voluntary cessation of reproduction, leading to the
extinction of the race; **racial unconscious** another name
for collective unconscious (q.v. under **collect**). [Fr.,
— It. *razza*, of doubtful origin.]
race² *rās, n.* a run or onward rush (*arch.* and *Scot.*): a
fixed course, track, or path, over which anything runs:
a channel bringing water to or from a wheel: a groove
in which anything runs (as ball-bearings, a rope): a
regular running over a fixed course, as of the sun: a
rapid current: a competitive trial of speed in progression: (in *pl.*) a meeting for horse-racing: a competition
in getting ahead of others figuratively: a running or
racing place (*rare*). — *v.i.* to run swiftly: to contend
in speed: to run wildly (as an engine, a propeller) when
resistance is removed. — *v.t.* to cause (a horse, etc.)
to race: to rush: to contend in a race with. — *ns.* **raʹcer**
one who or that which races: any of several non-
venomous N. American snakes of the genus *Coluber*;

fāte; fär; hûr; mīne; mōte; för; mūte; mōōn; fŏŏt; dhen (then); elʹǝ-mǝnt (element)

ra′cing. — *adj.* **ra′cy.** — **race′-ball** a ball in connection with a race-meeting; **race′-card** a programme for a race-meeting; **race′-course, -path, -track** a course for running races over; **race′-cup** a piece of plate forming a prize at a race; **race′goer** an attender at race-meetings; **race′going; race′horse** horse bred for racing; **race′= meet′ing** a stated occasion for horse-racing; **race′= walk′er; race′-walk′ing** a form of racing in which the competitors walk as fast as possible, but must not run; **race′way** a mill-race: a track for running races over; **ra′cing-bit** light jointed ringbit; **rac′ing-car; racing certainty** a thing certain to happen.   [O.N. *rās*; O.E. *ræs.*]

race³ *rās*, (*Shak.*) *n.* a rootstock of ginger.   [O.Fr. *rais* — L. *rādīx, -īcis,* a root.]

race⁴ *rās*, also **ratch** *rach, ns.* a white streak down a beast's face.   [Origin unknown.]

race⁵ *rās, v.t.* to scratch: to raze (*Spens.*): to erase (*Spens.*): to slash (*Shak.*). — *n.* a cut, slit, scratch.   [An otherwise obs. form of **raze²** or **rase.**]

race⁶ *rās,* (*Spens.*) *v.t.* to tear away or off, pluck, snatch. — Also **rase** (*Shak.*).   [O.Fr. *arrachier.*]

raceme *ra-, rə-, rā-sēm′, ras′ēm, n.* an indefinite inflorescence in which stalked flowers are borne in acropetal succession on an unbranched main stalk: a similar group of sporangia. — *ns.* **racemate** (*ras′i-māt*) a racemic mixture; **racemation** (*ras-i-mā′shən*) a gleaning or gathering of grapes: a residue: a cluster or bunch of grapes or of anything else. — *adjs.* **racemed′** (or *ras′, rās′*) in or having racemes; **racemic** (*ra-sē′mik, -sem′ik*) applied to an acid obtained from a certain kind of grape, an optically inactive form of tartaric acid: hence applied to similar mixtures of dextrorotatory and laevorotatory enantiomorphs. — *n.* **racemisā′tion, -z-** a changing into a racemic form. — *v.t.* and *v.i.* **rac′emise, -ize.** — *n.* **rac′emism** the quality of being racemic. — *adj.* **racemose** (*ras′i-mōs*) of the nature of or like a raceme: of, in, or having racemes: like a bunch of grapes.   [L. *racēmus,* a bunch of grapes.]

rache, also **rach, ratch,** *rach, n.* a dog that hunts by scent.   [O.E. *racc,* setter; O.N. *rakki.*]

rachis, sometimes **rhachis,** *rā′kis, n.* the spine: an axis, as of a feather, an inflorescence, a pinnate leaf: — *pl.* **r(h)a′chises, r(h)achides** (*rak′, rāk′i-dēz*). — *adjs.* **ra′chial;** less correctly **rachidial** (*rə-kid′*), **rachid′ian.** — *ns.* **rachilla** (*rə-kil′ə*) the axis of a grass spikelet; **rachischisis** (*ra-kis′ki-sis;* Gr. *schisis,* cleavage) a severe form of spina bifida.   [Gr. *rhachis, -ios,* or *-eōs,* spine.]

rachitis *ra-, rə-kī′tis, n.* rickets. — *adj.* **rachitic** (*-kit′ik*).   [Gr. *rhachītis,* inflammation of the spine: adopted by Dr Gleeson in 1650 in the belief that it was the etymon of **rickets.**]

Rachmanism *rak′man-izm, n.* conduct of a landlord who charges extortionate rents for property in which very bad slum conditions prevail.   [From the name of one such landlord exposed in 1963.]

racial, etc., **raciness, racism,** etc. See **race¹.**

rack¹ *rak, n.* an instrument for stretching, esp. an instrument of torture: hence an extreme pain, anxiety, or doubt (*fig.*): stress, esp. of weather: a framework, grating, shelf, or the like, on or in which articles are disposed or set aside: a grating from which beasts may pull down fodder: a bar or framework as for chaining a prisoner (*Spens.*): a bar with teeth to work into those of a wheel, pinion, or endless screw. — *v.t.* to stretch forcibly or excessively: to strain: to wrest, overstrain, distort: to torture: to practice rapacity upon: to extort (*Spens.*): to put in a rack: to move or adjust by rack and pinion. — *adj.* **racked** (also erroneously, **wracked**) tortured, tormented. — in composition, tortured, distressed by, as in *disease-racked,* etc. — *n.* **rack′er.** — *n.* and *adj.* **rack′ing.** — **rack′-rail** a cogged rail; **rack′= rail′way** a mountain railway with a rack in which a cog-wheel on the locomotive works; **rack′-rent** a rent stretched to the utmost annual value of the things rented, exorbitant rent: a rack-renter. — *v.t.* to subject

to such rents. — **rack′-rent′er** one who exacts or pays rack-rent; **rack′work** mechanism with a rack. — (**live at) rack and manger** (to live in) wasteful abundance: waste and destruction (perh. from confusion with *rack and ruin*); **rack and pinion** a means of turning rotatory into linear or linear into rotatory motion by a toothed wheel engaging in a rack; **rack one's brains** to strain one's memory, ingenuity, etc.; **rack up** to accumulate points (in a score).   [Prob. M.Du. *recke* (Du. *rek, rak*) or L.G. *reck, recke, rack;* cf. O.N. *rakkr,* straight, Ger. *Rack,* rail, *recken,* to stretch; Eng. **reach¹.**]

rack² *rak, n.* same as **wrack,** destruction: a crash (*Milt.*). — **rack and ruin** a state of neglect and collapse.   [**wrack¹,** or O.N. *rek,* wreckage.]

rack³ *rak, n.* flying cloud (*Shak.*): driving mist: a track: a shallow ford (*Scot.*). — *v.i.* (*Shak.*) to drift, to drive.   [App. O.N. *rek,* drifting wreckage, or some kindred form; cf. **wrack, wreck, wreak;** O.E. *wrecan,* to drive.]

rack⁴ *rak, v.t.* to draw off from the lees.   [Prov. *arracar* — *raca,* husks, dregs.]

rack⁵ *rak, n.* the neck and spine of a forequarter of a carcass (*dial.*): a vertebra (*obs.*): a horse's bones. — *n.* **rack′abones** (*U.S.*) a very thin horse, man, etc.   [Perh. O.E. *hracca,* occiput.]

rack⁶ *rak,* (now *U.S.*) *n.* a horse's gait at which the legs at the same side move nearly together. — *v.i.* to go in that gait. — *n.* **rack′er.**   [Origin obscure.]

rack⁷ *rak, n.* aphetic for **arrack.** — **rack′-punch.**

rack⁸ *rak, n.* a young rabbit's skin.   [Origin unknown.]

racket¹ *rak′it, n.* a bat with usu. roughly elliptical head, of wood or metal strung with catgut or nylon, for playing tennis, badminton, etc.: a snowshoe of like design: (in *pl.*) a simplified derivative of the old game of tennis, similar to squash, played by two or four people in a four-walled court. — *v.t.* to strike with a racket. — **rack′et-court, -ground; rack′et-press** a press for keeping a racket in shape; **rack′et-tail** a humming-bird with two long racket-shaped feathers. — *adj.* **rack′et-tailed.**   [Fr. *raquette,* poss. — Ar. *rāhat,* coll. form of *rāha,* the palm of the hand.]

racket² *rak′it, n.* din: clamour: hubbub: hurly-burly: fuss: noisy or hustling gaiety: dissipation: a noisy merry-making: a dodge: fraudulent, violent, or otherwise unscrupulous money-making activities: strain of excitement: responsibility: liability for expenses. — *v.i.* to make or engage in racket: to go about noisily (often with *about*): to have a full and exciting social life (*arch.*; often with *about*). — *v.t.* to disturb, stir, affect by racket: — *pr.p.* **rack′eting;** *pa.t.* and *pa.p.* **rack′eted.** — *n.* **racketeer′** one who extorts money or other advantage by threats or illegal interference. — *v.i.* to act as a racketeer. — *ns.* **racketeer′ing; rack′eter** a noisy or dissipated person; **rack′etry.** — *adj.* **rack′ety** noisy: energetic and excitable. — **stand the racket** to endure the strain: to take the consequences or responsibility: to pay expenses.   [Prob. imit.]

racket³, rackett *rak′it, n.* an old instrument like the bassoon.   [Origin uncertain.]

raclette *rak-let′, n.* a dish of melted cheese and jacket potatoes, orig. from the Valais region of Switzerland.   [Fr., a small scraper.]

racloir *rä-klwär,* (Fr.) *n.* a scraper.

racon *rā′kon, n.* a radar beacon.   [ra*dar,* bea*con.*]

raconteur *ra-kon-tûr′, rä-kɔ̃-tœr, n.* a teller of anecdotes: — *fem.* **raconteuse** (*-tœz*). — *n.* **raconteur′ing.**   [Fr.]

racoon. See **raccoon.**

Racovian *rə-kō′vi-ən, n.* a 17th-century Polish Socinian — their seminary being at *Raków.* — Also *adj.*

racquet *rak′it, n.* Same as **racket¹.** — **racq′uet ball** (*U.S.*) a game played by or two or four players in a walled court with rubber balls and short-handled strung rackets.

racy. See **race¹,².**

rad¹ *rad* (*Spens.*), *pa.t.* and *pa.p.* of **read¹,** and *pa.t.* of **ride.**

rad² *rad,* (*Scot.*) *adj.* afraid.   [O.N. *hræddr.*]

rad³ *rad, n.* short for **radical** (in politics).

rad⁴ *rad, n.* a unit of dosage of any radiation, equal to 100 ergs of energy for one gram of mass of the material irradiated. [**rad(iation).**]

radar *rā'där, n.* the use of high-powered radio pulses, reflected or regenerated, for locating objects or determining one's own position: equipment for sending out and receiving such pulses. — **radar altimeter** a high altitude radio altimeter; **radar beacon** a fixed radio transmitter whose signals enable an aircraft, by means of its radar equipment, to determine its position and direction; **ra'dar-gun** a gun-like device used by police which, when pointed at a moving vehicle and 'fired', records (by means of radar) the speed of the vehicle; **ra'darscope** a cathode-ray oscilloscope on which radar signals can be seen; **radar trap** a device using radar which enables the police to identify motorists exceeding the speed limit over a particular section of the road (see also **speed trap**).   [American codeword, from *rad*io *d*etection *a*nd *r*anging, appropriately a palindrome word.]

raddle¹ *rad'l, n.* a flexible rod or strip of wood used to make hurdles, fences, or (with plaster) walls, by weaving between uprights: a hurdle, door, fence, or the like so made: a hedge formed by interweaving the branches of trees: a wooden bar used in weaving. — *v.t.* to interweave: to thrash (*Northern*).   [A.Fr. *reidele*, rail.]

raddle² *rad'l, n.* reddle or ruddle (red ochre). — *v.t.* to colour or mark with red ochre: to rouge coarsely. — *adj.* **radd'led** of a person, aged and worsened by debauchery. — **radd'leman.**   [See **ruddle.**]

raddocke *rad'ək* (*Shak.*).   Same as **ruddock.**

rade *rād.* Northern form of **rode¹.**   [See **ride.**]

radial *rā'di-əl, adj.* pertaining to a ray or radius: along, in the direction of, a radius or radii: having rays, spokes, or parts diverging from a centre: arranged like spokes or radii: near the radius of the arm. — *n.* a radiating part: a radial artery, nerve, engine, plate, tyre, etc. — *ns.* **radiale** (*-ā'li; L. ra-di-ā'le*) a wrist-bone in line with the radius — *pl.* **radia'lia; radialisation, -z-** (*rād-yəl-ī-zā'shən*). — *v.t.* **ra'dialise, -ize** to arrange radially. — *n.* **rādiality** (*-al'*) radial symmetry. — *adv.* **rā'dially** in the manner of radii or of rays. — **radial artery** the smaller branch of the brachial artery at the elbow; **radial engine** one with its cylinders radially arranged; **radial symmetry** symmetry about several planes intersecting in a common axis; **radial tyre** a radial-ply tyre; **radial velocity** the component of velocity along the observer's line of sight. — **radial-ply tyre** tyre in which layers or plies of fabric in the carcass are wrapped in a direction radial to the centre of the wheel.   [L.L. *radiālis* — L. *radius.*]

radian *rā'di-ən, n.* a unit of circular measure, the angle subtended at the centre of a circle by an arc equal to the radius, nearly 57·3°.   [L. *radius.*]

radiant *rā'di-ənt, rā'dyənt, adj.* emitting rays: issuing in rays: transmitted by radiation: glowing: shining: beaming with happy emotion. — *n.* that which emits radiations: a point from which rays emanate: the centre from which meteoric showers seem to proceed: a straight line from a point about which it is conceived to revolve (*geom.*). — *ns.* **rā'diance, rā'diancy** the state of being radiant: a measure of the amount of electromagnetic radiation being transmitted from or to a point (on a surface). — *adv.* **rā'diantly.** — **radiant energy** energy given out as electromagnetic radiation; **radiant heat** heat transmitted by electromagnetic radiation.   [L. *radiāns, -antis,* pr.p. of *radiāre,* to radiate — *radius.*]

radiate *rā'di-āt, v.i.* to emit rays: to shine: to issue in rays: to diverge from a point or points: to transmit wirelessly. — *v.t.* to send out in or by means of rays: to communicate by wireless: to broadcast. — *adj.* (*-it, -ət, -āt*) having rays: having ray-florets: spreading like a ray or rays: radial: radially arranged: of the Radiata. — *n.* an animal of the Radiata. — *n.pl.* **Rādiā'ta** in Cuvier's obsolete classification, the lowest sub-king-

dom of animals, radially symmetrical — echinoderms, coelenterates, polyzoans, etc. — *adj.* **rā'diated.** — *adv.* **rā'diately.** — *n.* **rādiā'tion** act of radiating: the emission and diffusion of rays: that which is radiated: energy transmitted in electromagnetic waves: radial arrangement. — *adjs.* **rā'diātive, rādiā'tory.** — *n.* **rā'diātor** that which radiates: apparatus for radiating heat, as for warming a room, or cooling an engine: a wireless transmitting aerial. — **radiation belts** see **Van Allen radiation belts; radiation oncologist** see **radiologist** under **radio-; radiation sickness** an illness due to excessive absorption of radiation in the body, marked by diarrhoea, vomiting, internal bleeding, decrease in blood cells, loss of teeth and hair, reduction of sperm in the male, etc.   [L. *radiāre,* to shine, *radiātus,* rayed — *radius.*]

radical *rad'i-kl, adj.* pertaining to, constituting, proceeding from or going to the root: fundamental: original: intrinsic: inherent: thorough: primary: primitive: implanted by nature: not derived: proceeding from near the root (*bot.*): of or concerning the root of a word (*linguistics*): of or concerning the roots of numbers (*math.*): favouring thorough-going but constitutional social and political reform, advanced Liberal (*politics*; usu. with *cap.*). — *n.* a root, in any sense: a group of atoms behaving like a single atom and passing unchanged from one compound to another — now usually confined to electrically neutral entities as distinguished from charged ions (*chem.*; sometimes **rad'icle**): (*cap.*) an advocate of radical reform or member of the Radical party. — *n.* **radicalīsā'tion, -z-.** — *v.t.* and *v.i.* **rad'icalise, -ize** to make or become radical. — *ns.* **Rad'icalism** the principles or spirit of a Radical; **radicality** (*-kal'i-ti*). — *adv.* **rad'ically.** — *n.* **rad'icalness.** — *adjs.* **rad'icant** rooting from the stem; **rad'icāte** rooted: deeply rooted: firmly established: fixed. — *v.t.* to root: to plant or fix deeply and firmly. — *adj.* **rad'icāted** rooted, established. — *ns.* **radicā'tion** rooting: implanting: rootedness: general character of the root-system; **rad'icel** (*-sel*) a rootlet. — *adjs.* **rad'icellose; radicicolous** (*-sik'ə-ləs*) inhabiting, or parasitic on, roots; **radiciform** (*rə-dis'*) like a root; **radiciv'orous** root-eating. — *n.* **rad'icle** a little root: the part of a seed that becomes the root: a rhizoid: a radical (*chem.*). — *adj.* **radic'ūlar** pertaining to a radicle, a rootlet, or the root of a tooth, nerve, etc. — *n.* **rad'icūle.** — *adj.* **radic'ulose** having many rootlets or rhizoids. — **radical axis** the locus of a point of equal potency with respect to two circles; **radical mastectomy** see under **mastoid; radical sign** the symbol √, indicating a square root.   [L. *rādīx, -īcis,* a root.]

radices. See **radix.**

radii. See **radius.**

radiesthesia *rā-di-es-thē'zi-ə, -zyə, -zhə, n.* sensitivity to forms of radiation from any source, e.g. detecting water with a dowsing-rod, diagnosing illness with a pendulum, etc., considered an extra-sensory power. — *n.* **radiesthē'sist.**   [L. *radius,* ray. Mod. L. *esthesia,* feeling.]

radio- *rā-di-ō-,* in composition (most terms can be spelt as one word, a hyphenated word, or two words), rays, radiation, radium, radius: radio, wireless: (of product or isotope) radioactive, as **rādio-actin'ium, rādio-tho'rium,** both isotopes of thorium, **rādio-el'ement** (*chem.*). — *n.* **rā'dio** a generic term applied to methods of signalling through space, without connecting wires, by means of electromagnetic waves generated by high-frequency alternating currents: a wireless receiving or transmitting set: a wireless message or broadcast: — *pl.* **rā'dios.** — *adj.* of, for, transmitted or transmitting by, electromagnetic waves. — *v.t.* and *v.i.* to communicate by wireless. — *adj.* **rādioact'ive.** — *ns.* **rādioactiv'ity** spontaneous disintegration, first observed in certain naturally occurring heavy elements (radium, actinium, uranium, thorium) with emission of α-rays, β-rays, and γ-rays: disintegration effected by high-energy bombardment; **radio altimeter** see **al-**

timeter; **radio amateur** a person licensed to send and receive wireless messages privately on certain short-wave bands. — Also **radio ham** (*slang*); **radio astronomy** astronomical study by means of radar; study of radio waves generated in space; **rādioaut′ograph** deprecated term for **autoradiograph**; **ra′dio-beacon** apparatus that transmits signals for direction-finding; **radiobiol′ogy** the study of the effects of radiation on living tissue; **radiocar′bon** a radioactive isotope of carbon, *specif*. carbon-14 (**radiocarbon dating** a method of establishing the age of any organic material, e.g. wood, paper, by measuring content of carbon-14); **rādiochem′istry** the chemistry of radioactive elements and compounds; **radio-communicā′tion** wireless telegraphy or telephony; **radio-com′pass** a radio direction-finding instrument; **rādioel′ement** a radio-isotope: **radio frequency** a frequency suitable for radio transmission, about 3kHz to 300 GHz (**radio-frequency heating** heating, such a dielectric heating, by means of a radio-frequency electric current); **radio galaxy** a galaxy emitting a particularly high level of radio-frequency energy. — *adj*. **rādiogenic** (*-jen′ik*) produced by radioactive disintegration: suitable for broadcasting. — *ns*. **rādiogoniom′eter** a radio direction-finder; **rā′diogram** an X-ray photograph, radiograph: a wireless telegram: (for **rādio-gram′ophone**) a combined wireless receiver and gramophone; **rā′diograph** (*-gräf*) a recorded image, usu. a photograph, produced by X-rays: (formerly) the wireless telegraph; **radiog′rapher** a technician involved in radiology, e.g. in the taking of radiographs or in radiotherapy. — *adj*. **radiographic** (*-graf′ik*). — *ns*. **radiography** (*-og′rə-fi*) photography of interior of body or specimen by radiations other than light, as X-rays, etc.: (*formerly*) radiotelegraphy: study of radioactivity; **ra′dioimmunoass′ay** (or *-ā′*) an immunoassay of a substance which has been labelled (q.v.) with a radioactive substance; **radio-ī′sotope** a radioactive isotope of a stable element. — *adj*. **radiola′belled** labelled (q.v.) with a radioactive substance. — *n*. **radiolocā′tion** position-finding by radio signals: radar. — *adjs*. **radiolog′ic, radiolog′ical.** — *ns*. **radiol′ogist** a doctor specialising in the diagnostic use of X-rays and in other methods of imaging the internal structure of the body, now often called a **radiation oncologist; rādiol′ogy** the study of radioactivity and radiation or their application to medicine, e.g. as X-rays, or as treatment for certain diseases; **radioluminesc′ence** luminous radiation arising from radiation from a radioactive material; **rādiöl′ysis** chemical decomposition induced by ionising radiation; **rādiometeor′ograph** same as **radiosonde; rādiom′eter** any instrument that measures radiant energy. — *adj*. **rādiomet′ric.** — *n.sing*. **radiön′ics** a form of healing at a distance using a form of dowsing for diagnosis. — *ns*. **rādionü′clide** any radioactive nuclide; **rā′diopager** a radio receiver which functions as a pager; **rā′diopaging; rā′diophōne** an instrument for producing sound by radiant energy: a radiotelephone. — *adj*. **rādiophonic** (*-fon′ik*) of music, produced electronically. — *n.sing*. **rādiophon′ics.** — *ns*. **rādiophonist** (*-of′ə-nist*); **radioph′ony; radio pill** a capsule which may be swallowed containing a tiny radio transmitter that will send out information about bodily processes; **rā′dioscope** a machine used in **rādiös′copy**, examination by X-rays, etc. — *v.t*. **rādiosen′sitise, -ize** to make (e.g. cancer cells) more radiosensitive. — *adj*. **rādiosen′sitive** quickly injured or changed by radiation. — *ns*. **ra′diosonde** (Fr. *sonde*, plummet, probe) apparatus for ascertaining atmospheric conditions at great heights, consisting of a hydrogen-filled balloon, radio transmitter(s), etc. — also **rādiometeor′ograph; radio spectrum** the range of radio frequencies; **radio star** a discrete source of radio waves in outer space, generally corresponding with no visual object and known only by radio-astronomy; **radio station** a place where radio transmitters and (if radio-communication is involved) receivers are installed: a broadcasting company, asso-

ciation, etc.; **rā′dio-stron′tium** a radioactive isotope of strontium, esp. strontium-90; **rā′diotel′egram, rā′diotel′egraph, -teleg′raphy, rā′diotel′ephone, -teleph′ony** radio telegraph, telephone etc.; **rādiotelem′eter** see **telemeter; rādiotel′ephone** a device which receives and transmits by means of radio waves (rather than wires) and which functions as a telephone (e.g. in cars and other vehicles); **radio telescope** an apparatus for the reception and analysis and transmission in radio-astronomy of radio waves from and to outer space; **rādiotel′etype** a teleprinter that receives and transmits by radio; **rādiotherapeut′ics, -ther′apy** treatment of disease, esp. cancer, by radiation, as by X-rays, etc.; **rādiotox′ic** or relating to the toxic effects of radiation or radioactive material; **radio wave** an electromagnetic wave of radio frequency. [L. *rădius*, a rod, spoke, radius, ray.]

Radiolaria *rā-di-ō-lā′ri-ə, n.pl*. an order of marine Protozoa with fine radial pseudopodia. — *adj*. **radiola′rian.** — Also *n*. — **radiolarian ooze** a deep-sea deposit in which the siliceous skeletons of Radiolaria predominate. [L.L. *radiolus*, dim. of L. *rădius*, radius.]

radish *rad′ish, n*. a cruciferous plant, *Raphanus sativus* or other member of the genus: its pungent root, eaten as a salad. [Fr. *radis* — Prov. *raditz* or It. *radice* — L. *rādīx, -īcis*, a root.]

radium *rā′di-əm, n*. a radioactive metallic element (Ra; at. numb. 88) discovered by the Curies in 1898, found in pitchblende and other minerals, remarkable for its active spontaneous disintegration. — **radium A, B**, etc., successive products in the disintegration of radon; **radium bomb** an apparatus containing radium, emitting gamma rays for medical treatment (better **teleradium unit**); **radium emanation** radon. [L. *rădius*, a ray.]

radius *rā′di-əs, n*. a straight line from the centre to the circumference of a circle or surface of a sphere (*geom*.): a radiating line: anything placed like a radius, as the spoke of a wheel, the movable arm of a sextant: a radial plane of symmetry in a coelenterate: a line from a fixed point (e.g. the focus of a conic) to a point on a curve: the outer bone (in supine position) of the forearm in man, or its homologue in other animals: a barbule of a feather: the third vein of an insect's wing: a ray-flower or the ray-flowers of a head collectively (*rare*): a distance from a centre, conceived as limiting an area or range: — *pl*. **radii** (*rā′di-ī*; L. *ra′di-ē*), **ra′diuses.** — *adj*. **ra′dial** (q.v.). — **radius vector** (*pl*. **radii vectő′res**) a straight line joining a fixed point and a variable point. [L. *rădius*, a rod, spoke, ray.]

radix *rā′diks, rä′dēks, n*. a root, root-number, root-word (*obs*.): a source: a basis: the quantity on which a system of numeration, or of logarithms, etc., is based: — *pl*. **radices** (*rā′di-sez, rä-dē′kās*). [L. *rādīx, -īcis*, root.]

radome *rā′dōm, n*. a protective covering for micro-wave antennae. [*radar dome*.]

radon *rā′don, n*. a gaseous radioactive element (Rn; at. numb. 86), the first disintegration product of radium — radium emanation, formerly called niton. [**radium**, and **-on**, as in *argon, xenon*, etc.]

radula *rad′ū-lə, n*. a mollusc's tongue or rasping ribbon: — *pl*. **rad′ulae** (*-lē*). — *adjs*. **rad′ular; rad′ulate; rad′üliform** rasp-like. [L. *rădula*, a scraper — *rādēre*.]

Raetia(n). See **Rhaetia.**

Raf *raf*, (*coll*.) *n*. the R.A.F. (Royal Air Force).

rafale *rä-fäl′, n*. a burst of artillery in quick rounds. [Fr., gust of wind.]

raff *raf*, (*arch*.) *n*. a heap, a quantity: riff-raff: one of the riff-raff: a rakish, flashy, or blackguardly fellow. — *adj*. **raffish.** — *adj*. **raff′ish** rakish: flashy. — *adv*. **raff′ishly.** — *n*. **raff′ishness.** [Cf. **riff-raff.**]

raffia *raf′i-ə, n*. the Raphia palm or its leaf-bast. [**Raphia**.]

raffinose *raf′i-nōs, n*. a trisaccharide sugar. — *n*. **raff′inate** liquid left after a desired solute has been extracted. [Fr. *raffiner*, to refine.]

raffish, etc. See **raff.**

raffle[1] *raf'l, n.* an old dicing game, the stakes going to the thrower of a pair-royal: a lottery for an article. — *v.t.* to dispose of by raffle. — *v.i.* to engage in a raffle. — *n.* **raff'ler.** [Fr. *rafle,* a pair-royal.]

raffle[2] *raf'l, n.* a rabble: riff-raff: lumber: rubbish: a jumble: a tangle. [Cf. **raff.**]

raffle[3] *raf'l, v.t.* to notch: to crumple. [Ety. dub.]

Rafflesia *raf-lē'zi-ə, n.* a genus (giving name to the family **Rafflesiā'ceae,** akin to the birthwort family) of parasitic plants in Sumatra, Java, etc., one species having the largest known flowers, a yard across, carrion-scented, the rest of the plant reduced to threads within the tissues of its host-plant. [Named after Sir T. Stamford *Raffles* (1781–1826), British governor in Sumatra (1818), who sent it to Brown, the botanist.]

raft[1] *räft, (U.S.) n.* a large number, a heap: a crowd: a miscellaneous lot. [**raff.**]

raft[2] *räft, n.* a flat floating mass of logs or other material (ice, vegetation, etc.): a flat structure of logs, etc., for support or for conveyance on water: a dense mass of floating waterfowl (*U.S.*): a wide layer of concrete to support a building on soft ground. — *v.t.* to transport on a raft: to form into a raft: to traverse by raft. — *v.i.* to manage a raft: to travel by raft: to form into a raft: to pile up by overriding, as ice. — *n.* **raft'er** a raftsman. — **raft'-bridge** a raft used as a bridge: a bridge supported on rafts; **raft'man** a raftsman; **raft'=port** in ships, a large port for timber; **raft'-rope** a rope for towing blubber; **rafts'man** one who works on a raft. [O.N. *raptr,* rafter.]

raft[3] *räft, obs. pa.t.* and *pa.p.* of **reave:** in Keats *pa.p.* of **rive.**

rafter[1] *räf'tər, n.* an inclined beam supporting a roof. — *v.t.* to furnish with rafters: to plough so that a strip is overturned upon unploughed ground. — *adj.* **raft'ered** having (esp. visible) rafters. — *n.* **raft'ering.** — **raft'er=bird** the spotted flycatcher. [O.E. *ræfter,* a beam.]

rafter[2], **raftsman.** See **raft**[2].

rag[1] *rag, n.* a worn, torn, or waste scrap of cloth: a tatter: a shred, scrap, or smallest portion: a farthing (*old slang*): a jagged projection: contemptuously or playfully, a flag, handkerchief, sail, theatre curtain, garment, newspaper, or paper money: the pithy part of an orange, lemon, etc.: a worthless or beggarly person: a person in a state of exhaustion: (in *pl.*) tattered clothing: ragtime, or a piece of ragtime music. — *adj.* of, for, or dealing in rags. — *v.t.* to tear to rags: to make ragged: to perform in ragtime. — *v.i.* to become ragged, to fray: to dress (with *out* or *up*; *U.S. arch. slang*): — *pr.p.* **ragg'ing;** *pa.p.* and *pa.t.* **ragged** (*ragd*). — *adj.* **ragg'ed** shaggy: rough-edged: jagged: uneven in execution: raguly (*her.*): torn or worn into rags: wearing ragged clothes. — *adv.* **ragg'edly.** — *n.* **ragg'edness.** — *adj.* **ragg'edy** ragged-looking. — *n.* **ragg'ery** rags or the ragged collectively: clothes, esp. women's (*slang*): raggedness. — *adj.* **ragg'y** rough: ragged: of the nature of a rag. — **rag-and-bone'-man** one who collects or traffics in rags, bones, or other rubbish; **rag-ba'by** (*arch.*) a rag-doll; **rag'-bag** a bag for rags and abandoned garments: a random or confused collection (*fig.*): a slattern; **rag'bolt** a bolt with barbs to prevent withdrawal; **rag'-book** a child's book mounted on cloth; **rag'-bush** a bush to which shreds of cloth are tied as offerings to the local spirit, esp. by a well; **rag'-doll'** a doll made of rags: a slattern; **rag'-dust** finely divided rags, used for making flock-paper; **rag'-fair** an old-clothes market: a kit inspection (*mil. slang*); **ragg'ed-la'dy** *Nigella damascena;* **ragg'ed=Rob'in** a campion (*Lychnis flos-cuculi*) with deep-cleft petals; **ragged school** (*hist.*) a voluntary school for destitute children; **ragged staff** (*her.*) a stick with branch stubs; **rag'man** a man who collects or deals in rags: the devil; **rag'-mon'ey** (*slang*) paper money; **rag'=paper** paper made from rags; **rag'-picker** one who collects rags from bins, heaps, etc.; **rag'-tag** the rabble (also **ragg'le-tagg'le**). — Also *adj.* — **rag'time** a form of music of American Negro origin, highly syncopated

in the melody: tune, song, or dance in ragtime; **rag'-timer; rag trade** the trade concerned with designing, making and selling clothes; **rag'weed** ragwort: any species of the composite genus *Ambrosia* (*U.S.*); **rag'-wheel** a toothed wheel: a polishing-wheel made of cloth discs clamped together; **rag'-woman; rag'-wool** shoddy; **rag'worm** a pearly white burrowing marine worm (*Nephthys caeca*), used as bait by fishermen; **rag'wort** a common coarse yellow-headed composite weed (*Senecio jacobaea*) of pastures: any similar species of the genus with long rays (from the cut leaves). — **rag-tag and bobtail** riff-raff. [O.E. *ragg,* inferred from the adj. *raggig,* shaggy; O.N. *rögg,* shagginess, tuft.]

rag[2], **ragg** *rag, n.* a rough hard stone of various kinds, esp. one breaking in slabs: a large rough slate (3 ft. by 2). — **rag'stone; rag'work** undressed masonry in slabs. [Poss. from foregoing.]

rag[3] *rag, v.t.* to rate: to banter: to assail or beset with questions, chaff, horseplay. — *v.i.* to wrangle: to indulge in a rag: — *pr.p.* **ragg'ing;** *pa.t.* and *pa.p.* **ragged** (*ragd*). — *n.* an outburst of organised horseplay, usually in defiance of authority: riotous festivity, esp. and orig. of undergraduates — now, in British universities, associated with the raising of money for charity. — *n.* **ragg'ing.** — *adj.* **ragg'y** (*slang*) irritated. — **rag day, rag week** in British universities the particular day or week during which money-making activities, processions, etc. for charity are organised. — **lose one's rag** (*coll.*) to lose one's temper. [Perh. shortened from **bullyrag;** perh. from **rag**[1] as in *red rag.*]

raga *rä'gə, n.* a traditional Hindu musical form or mode, a rhythmic or melodic pattern used as the basis for improvisation: a piece composed in such a mode. [Sans. *rāga,* colour, tone (in music).]

ragamuffin *rag'ə-muf-in,* or *-muf', n.* a ragged, disreputable boy or man: (*cap.; obs.*) the name of a devil. [Poss. **rag**[1].]

rag'd, ragde *ragd,* (*Shak.*) for **ragged,** shaggy, jagged: perh. unruly: poss. also (*räjd*) for **raged,** irritated (as if *pa.p.* of *v.t.*).

rage *rāj, n.* madness: overmastering passion of any kind, as desire or (esp.) anger: inspired frenzy: ardour: a fit of any of these: a mania or craze (for something): vogue: a thing in vogue: violence, stormy or furious activity: a flood (*Shak.*). — *v.i.* to behave or speak with passion, esp. with furious anger: to be violent: to storm: to be prevalent and violent: to scold (with *at* or *on; Scot.*): to be violently bent on (*Milt.*). — *v.t.* see **rag'd.** — *adj.* **rage'ful.** — *n.* **rä'ger.** — *adj.* **rä'ging.** — *adv.* **rä'gingly.** — **all the rage** quite the fashion. [Fr., — L. *rabiēs* — *rabēre,* to rave.]

ragee. See **ragi.**

ragg. See **rag**[2].

ragged(y), raggery. See **rag**[1].

raggee. See **ragi.**

raggle *rag'l,* (*Scot.*) *n.* a groove in masonry, esp. to receive the edge of a roof. — *v.t.* to make a raggle in. [Origin obscure.]

raggle-taggle. See **rag-tag** under **rag**[1].

raggy. See **rag**[1,3], **ragi.**

ragi, ra(g)gee, raggy *rä'gē, rag'i, n.* a millet (*Eleusine coracana*) much grown in India, Africa, etc. [Hind. (and Sans.) *rāgī.*]

ragini *rä'gi-nē, n.* a modified raga. [Sans. *rāginī,* coloured.]

raglan *rag'lən, n.* an overcoat with sleeve in one piece with the shoulder. — *adj.* of a sleeve, in one piece with the shoulder. [From Lord *Raglan* (1788–1855), commander in the Crimea.]

ragman[1] *rag'mən,* **ragment** *rag'mənt, ns.* a catalogue (*obs.*): a document with pendent seals (*obs.*): a rigmarole (*obs. Scot.*). — **Ragman Rolls** a collection of instruments by which the Scottish nobles, etc., subscribed allegiance to Edward I. [Origin obscure.]

ragman[2]. See **rag**[1].

ragmatical *rag-mat'i-kl,* (*Fielding, Smollett*) *adj.* app.

riotous, disorderly. [Perh. from **rag**[1] after **pragmatical**.]

ragment. See **ragman**[1].

Ragnarök *rag′na-rək*, (*Scand. myth.*) *n.* the coming mutual destruction of the gods and the powers of evil, and the end of this world, to be superseded by a better. [O.N. *ragna rök*, history or judgment of the gods (— *rögn*, *régin*, gods — *rök*, reason, judgment), sophisticated into *ragna rökr*, twilight of the gods (—*rökr*, darkness).]

ragout *ra-gōō′*, *n.* a highly seasoned stew of meat and vegetables: a mixture. — *v.t.* to make a ragout of. [Fr. *ragoût* — *ragoûter*, to restore the appetite.]

ragstone, ragwork. See **rag**[2].

ragtime, ragweed, ragwheel, ragworm, ragwort. See **rag**[1].

raguly *rag′ū-li*, (*her.*) *adj.* with projections like oblique stubs of branches. — Also **rag′üled.** [Origin obscure.]

rah, 'rah *rä, rö, interj., n., v.i.*, short form of **hurrah**.

Rahu *rä′hōō*, (*Hindu myth.*) *n.* the demon that swallows the sun and moon at eclipses.

raid[1] *rād*, *n.* a sudden swift inroad, orig. by horsemen, for assault or seizure: an air attack: an invasion unauthorised by government: an incursion of police: an onset or onslaught for the purpose of obtaining or suppressing something: concerted selling by a group of speculators in order to lower the price of a particular stock. — *v.t.* to make a raid on. — *v.i.* to go on a raid. — *n.* **raid′er** one who raids: a raiding aeroplane. — **raid the market** to derange prices artificially for future gain. [Scots form of **road** (revived by Scott) — O.E. *rād*, riding.]

raid[2]. See **ride**.

raik *rāk*, *n.* course, journey: range: pasture. — *v.i.* to go: to range. [O.N. *reik* (n.), *reika* (vb.) walk; coalescing later with **rake**[4].]

rail[1] *rāl*, *n.* a bar extending horizontally or at a slope between supports or on the ground, often to form a support, a fence, a guard, a track for wheels: the railway as a means of travel or transport: a horizontal member in framing or panelling (as in a door): the capping part of bulwarks: (in *pl.*) a racecourse barrier: (in *pl.*) railway shares. — *v.t.* to enclose or separate with rails: to furnish with rails: to send by railway. — *v.i.* (*arch.*) to travel by railway. — *n.* **rail′ing** fencing: fencing materials: (often in *pl.*) a barrier or ornamental structure, usu. of upright iron rods secured by horizontal connections. — *adj.* **rail′less.** — **rail′bus** a light-weight railway coach powered by a bus-type diesel engine, or otherwise resembling a bus. — *adj.* **rail′-borne** carried by railway. — **rail′-car** (*U.S.*) a railway carriage: a self-propelled railway carriage; **rail′card** any of various cards entitling its holder (e.g. a student, old age pensioner, etc.) to reduced train fares; **rail′-fence** (*U.S.*) a fence of wooden posts and rails; **rail′-head** the furthest point reached by a railway under construction: the end of railway transport; **rail′man** a railway employee; **rail′-mo′tor** a self-propelled railway carriage; **rail′road** (chiefly *U.S.* and *Canada*) a railway. — *v.t.* (*coll.*) to force, push forward unduly, as a person into a particular course of action, a bill through parliament, etc. (orig. *U.S.*): to get rid of, esp. by sending to prison on a false charge. — **railroad car** (*U.S.*) a railway carriage or a railway van or truck; **rail′roader** (*U.S.*) a railway worker or official; **rail′-splitter** (*U.S.*) one who splits logs for fence-rails; **rail′way** a track laid with rails for wheels to run on, esp. for locomotives with passengers and goods wagons: a system of such tracks with equipment and organisation. — Also *adj.* — **rail′way-carr′iage** a railway vehicle for passengers; **rail′way-cross′ing** an intersection of railway lines or of road and railway, esp. without a bridge; **rail′wayman** a railway employee; **rail′way-stitch** a name for various quickly worked stitches. — **off the rails** disorganised: not functioning: mad: morally degenerate. [O.Fr. *reille* — L. *rēgula*, a ruler.]

rail[2] *rāl*, *v.i.* to scoff: to use vigorously or mockingly reproachful language: to banter: to revile (usu. with *at* or *against*). — *v.t.* to bring or render by raillery. — *n.* (*Spens.* **rayle**) reviling. — *n.* **rail′er.** — *adj.* and *n.* **rail′ing.** — *adv.* **rail′ingly.** — *n.* **raillery** (*rāl′ər-i*; old-fashioned *ral′*) railing or mockery: banter: playful satire. [Fr. *railler*.]

rail[3] *rāl*, *n.* any bird of the genus *Rallus*, esp. the water-rail, or other member of the family *Rallidae*, esp. the corncrake or land-rail. [O.Fr. *rasle* (Fr. *râle*).]

rail[4] (*Spens.* **rayle, raile**) *rāl*, (*arch.*) *v.i.* to flow, gush. [Origin obscure.]

rail[5] *rāl*, (*obs.* except in **night-rail**) *n.* a garment: a cloak: a neckerchief. — *n.* **raill′y** (*Scott*) a jacket. [O.E. *hrægl*.]

raiment *rā′mənt*, *n.* (*arch.* or *poet.*) clothing. [**array-ment**.]

rain[1] *rān*, *n.* water from the clouds in drops: a shower: a fall of anything in the manner of rain: (in *pl.*) the rainy season. — *v.i.* to fall as or like rain: to send down rain. — *v.t.* to shower. — *n.* **rain′iness.** — *adjs.* **rain′less; rain′y.** — **rain′band** a dark band in the solar spectrum, due to water vapour in the earth's atmosphere; **rain′-bird** a bird, as the green woodpecker and various kinds of cuckoo, supposed to foretell rain. — *adj.* **rain′-bound** detained by rain. — **rain′bow** the coloured bow caused by refraction and internal reflexion of light in raindrops: any similar array of colours: a much discoloured bruise (*slang*): a rainbow-trout: a S. American humming-bird, the cock with rainbow-coloured head. — *adj.* of, or coloured like, the rainbow. — **rain′bow-chaser** a visionary, one who tries to reach the end of the rainbow (**chase rainbows** to pursue an impossible aim). — *adj.* **rain′bow-coloured.** — **rainbow dressing** a gaudy display of flags on a ship. — *adjs.* **rain′bowed, rain′bow-tint′ed.** — **rain′bow-trout** a finely marked and coloured Californian trout (*Salmo gairdneri*). — *adj.* **rain′bowy.** — **rain′-chamber** a compartment for condensing noxious fumes by spray; **rain′-check** (*U.S.*) a ticket for future use given to spectators when a game or a sports meeting is cancelled or stopped because of bad weather (**take a raincheck (on)** (*coll.*, orig. *U.S.*) to promise to accept an invitation at a later date); **rain′-cloud** nimbus, a dense dark sheet of cloud that may shed rain or snow; **rain′coat** a light overcoat proof against moderate rain; **rain′-doctor** a rain-maker; **rain′drop** a drop of rain. — *adj.* **rained off** of a sport, outdoor activity, etc., cancelled because of rain. — **rain′fall** a shower of rain: the amount (by depth of water) of rain that falls; **rain′-forest** broad-leaved, evergreen tropical forest with very heavy rainfall; **rain′-gauge** an instrument for measuring rainfall; **rain′-maker** one who professes to bring rain; **rain′-making** attempting to cause rainfall by techniques such as seeding clouds; **rain′-plover** the golden plover; **rain′-print** a little pit made by a raindrop in clay, etc., sometimes preserved in rocks. — *adj.* **rain′proof** more or less impervious to rain. — *v.t.* to make rainproof. — *n.* a rainproof overcoat. — **rain′-shadow** an area sheltered by hills from the prevailing winds and having a lighter rainfall than the windward side of the hills; **rain′-stone** a stone used in magic rites aimed at bringing rain; **rain′storm.** — *adj.* **rain′tight** rainproof. — **rain′-tree** a S. American tree (*Pithecolobium saman*) of the mimosa family, under which there is a constant rain of juice ejected by cicadas; **rain′-wash** the washing away of earthy matters by rain: downward creep of superficial deposits soaked in rain: matter so transported; **rain′-water** water that falls or has lately fallen as rain. — **a rainy day** (*fig.*) a possible future time of need; **chase rainbows** see **rainbow-chaser** above; **come rain or shine** whatever the weather or circumstances; **rain in** of rain, to penetrate a roof, tent, badly-fitting window, etc.; **right as rain** perfectly in order; **take a raincheck (on)** see **raincheck** above. [O.E. *regn*; Du. *regen*, Ger. *Regen*; O.N. *regn*.]

rain², **raine** (*Spens.*). Same as **reign**.

raird. See **reird**.

raise¹ *rāz*, *v.t.* to cause to rise: to make higher or greater: to lift: to exalt: to advance: to elevate: to set up or upright: to rouse: to stir up: to elate: to rear, grow, or breed: to produce: to give rise to: to build, erect: to bring into being: to bring to life: to utter: to establish: to institute: to bring forward into consideration or notice: to bring into relief: to intensify: to call up: to cause to rise in view by approaching (*naut.*): to contact by radio: to levy, get together, collect: to cause to swell: to extol: to remove, take off: to produce a nap on. — *n.* a rising road: an increase in wages or salary (*coll.*). — *adjs.* **rais(e)'able**. — *ns.* **rais'er** one who, or that which, raises a building, etc.: the riser of a step; **raising**. — **raised beach** (*geol.*) an old sea-margin above the present water-level; **raised pastry, pie** pastry, pie without support of a dish at the sides; **rais'ing-bee** (*U.S.*) a gathering of neighbours to help in raising the frame of a house, etc. — **raise a hand to** to hit, or generally treat badly; **raise an eyebrow, one's eyebrows** to look surprised (at); **raise a siege** to abandon, or put an end to, a siege; **raise Cain, the roof** (*coll.*) to make a lot of noise; **raise hell, the devil** (*coll.*) to make a lot of trouble; **raise money on** to get money by pawning or selling, esp. privately; **raise one's glass** to drink a health (to); **raise one's hat** to take one's hat off in salutation; **raise the market (upon)** to bring about a rise in prices (to the disadvantage of); **raise the wind** to get together the necessary money by any shift.   [M.E. *reisen* — O.N. *reisa*, causative of *rīsa*, to rise; cf. **rise, rear²**.]

raise² *rāz*, (*N. of England*) *n.* a cairn.   [O.N. *hreysi*.]

raisin *rā'zn*, *n.* a dried grape.   [Fr., grape — L. *racēmus*, a bunch of grapes.]

raison d'être *rā-zɔ̃ detr'*, (Fr.) reason for existence (purpose or cause).

raisonné *rā-zon-ā*, (Fr.) *adj.* logically set out, systematically arranged, and (usu.) provided with notes.

raisonneur *rā-zon-œr'*, *n.* in a play or novel, a character who embodies the author's point of view and expresses his opinions.   [Fr., an arguer.]

rait. Same as **ret**.

raiyat, raiyatwari. Same as **ryot, ryotwari**.

raj *rāj*, *n.* rule, sovereignty: government, esp. (with *cap.*) the British government of India, 1858–1947. — *n.* **ra'ja(h)** an Indian prince or king: a Malay chief. — *ns.* **ra'ja(h)ship; raj'pramukh** (*-mŏok*) head of a state or states union in the Democratic Republic of India; **Rajput, -poot** (*rāj'pŏot*) a member of a race or class claiming descent from the original Hindu military and ruling caste.   [Hind. *rāj, rājā, Rājpūt* — Sans. *rājan*, a king (cog. with L. *rēx*), *putra*, son.]

Rajya Sabha *rāj'yə sub'ə*, the upper house of the Indian parliament.   [Hindi *rajya*, state, *sabha*, assembly.]

rake¹ *rāk*, *n.* a toothed bar on a handle, for scraping, gathering together, smoothing, etc.: a tool for various purposes, toothed, notched, or bladed and with long handle (e.g. croupier's implement for drawing in money): a wheeled field implement with long teeth for gathering hay, scraping up weeds, etc.: an extremely thin person or horse. — *v.t.* to scrape, smooth, clear, break up, draw, gather, remove, cover, uncover, search, ransack, with a rake or as if with a rake: to cover with ashes so as to keep smouldering: to graze, scrape: to pass over violently and swiftly: to enfilade: to afford or take a view all over or quite through. — *v.i.* to work with or as if with a rake: to search minutely. — *n.* **rā'ker** one who rakes: a scavenger: a raking implement: in games, a long, fast, low-flying shot (perh. partly from **rake⁴**). — *n.* and *adj.* **rā'king**. — **rake'-off** pecuniary share, esp. unearned or illicit; **rake'shame** (*obs.*) a base, dissolute wretch. — **rake in** (*coll.*) to acquire rapidly and in quantity; **rake up** to revive from oblivion (usu. something scandalous): to collect together.   [O.E. *raca*; Ger. *Rechen*, rake; O.N. *reka*, shovel.]

rake² *rāk*, *n.* a debauched or dissolute person, esp. a man

of fashion. — *v.i.* to lead a rake's life: to make a practice of lechery. — *n.* **rā'kery** dissoluteness. — *adj.* **rā'kish**. — *adv.* **rā'kishly**. — *n.* **rā'kishness**.   [**rakehell**.]

rake³ *rāk*, *n.* inclination from the vertical or horizontal, e.g. of a ship's funnel(s), a theatre stage: an angle, e.g. between the face of a cutting-tool and the surface on which it is working, or the wings and body of an aircraft. — *v.i.* to incline. — *v.t.* to slope: to cut aslant. — *n.* **rā'ker** a sloping shore, support. — *adj.* **rā'kish** with raking masts: swift-looking: pirate-like: dashing: jaunty. — *adv.* **rā'kishly**.   [Ety. dub.]

rake⁴ *rāk*, (now *dial.*) *v.i.* to proceed, esp. swiftly: to roam, range about: of a hawk, to fly wide: of a dog, to follow the scent wanderingly along the ground. — *n.* **rā'ker** a very fast pace: a plunge in betting. — *adj.* **rā'king** advancing swiftly.   [O.E. *racian*, to go forward, hasten.]

rake⁵ *rāk*, (*Northern*) *n.* a track, esp. up a hill or in a gully or a pasture: a pasture: a journey, esp. in fetching things: the amount carried at one journey, load, gang: an irregular, usu. vertical, vein of ore: a string, as of wagons. — *v.i.* to form into single file, as sheep.   [O.N. *rāk*, stripe; partly coalescing with **raik**.]

rakee. See **raki**.

rakehell *rāk'hel*, *n.* an utterly debauched person. — *adjs.* **rake'hell, -y**. — See also **rake²**.   [Prob. **rake¹** and **Hell**: such as might be found by raking out hell.]

rakery. See **rake²**.

rakeshame. See **rake¹**.

raki *rāk'ē*, *n.* a spirituous liquor used in the Levant and Greece. — Also **rak'ee**.   [Turk. *rāqī*.]

rakish. See **rake²,³**.

rakshas, rakshasa *rāk'shəs, -ə*, (*Hindu myth.*) *ns.* an evil spirit.   [Sans. *rākṣasa*.]

râle, rale *räl*, (*path.*) *n.* a sound from a diseased lung.   [Fr.]

rallentando *ral-ən-tan'dō*, (*mus.*) *adj.* and *adv.* becoming slower. — *n.* a slowing: — *pl.* **rallentan'dos**. — Abbrev. **rall**.   [It., pr.p. of *rallentare*, to slacken.]

rallier. See **rally¹,²**.

Rallus *ral'əs*, *n.* the water-rail genus of birds, giving name to the family **Rall'idae**. — *adj.* **rall'ine** (-*īn*).   [Latinised from Fr. *râle*.]

rally¹ *ral'i*, *v.t.* to reassemble: to gather to one's support: to bring together for united effort: to muster by an effort (as the faculties): to pull together, revive. — *v.i.* to come together, esp. from dispersal, or for renewed effort, or in support of a leader, friend, or cause: to recover: to recover in some degree lost health, power, vigour, value, etc.: — *pr.p.* **rall'ying**; *pa.p.* and *pa.t.* **rall'ied**. — *n.* a reassembly for renewed effort: a gathering for a common purpose: a mass-meeting: a competition to test skill in driving, and ability to follow an unknown route (U.S. also **rall'ye**), or to test quality of motor vehicles (see also under **rely**): a pantomime mêlée: a temporary or partial recovery: a quick exchange of blows in boxing: a series of to and fro strokes in deciding a point, as in tennis. — *ns.* **rall'ier; rall'ying** long-distance motor-racing over public roads; **rall'yist; rall'y-cross** motor-racing round a circuit consisting partly of paved road and partly of rough ground; **rall'ying-cry** a slogan to attract support for a cause, etc.; **rall'ying-point**. — **rally round** to support, help someone in need.   [O.Fr. *rallier* — pfx. *re-* and *allier*; see **ally¹**.]

rally² *ral'i*, *v.t.* and *v.i.* to banter: — *pr.p.* **rall'ying**; *pa.t.* and *pa.p.* **rall'ied**. — *n.* **rall'ier**. — *adv.* **rall'yingly**.   [Fr. *railler*; cf. **rail²**.]

rallye. See **rally¹**.

Ralph *ralf, rāf*, *n.* the imp of mischief in a printing-house.   [Personal name — O.E. *Rædwulf*.]

ram *ram*, *n.* a male sheep, a tup: Aries (*astrol.*): a battering-ram: a ship's beak for striking an enemy ship: a warship with such a beak: a water-ram or hydraulic ram (see **hydraulic**): the monkey of a pile-driver: the striking head of a steam-hammer: a piston applying pressure: a machine with such a piston: a rammer: an act of ramming. — *v.t.* to thrust roughly, cram (also *fig.*): to block up: to beat hard: to drive hard down: to strike, batter, pierce with a ram: to strike, dash into, violently: — *pr.p.* **ramm'ing;** *pa.t.* and *pa.p.* **rammed.** — *n.* **ramm'er** one who or that which rams: esp. a paviour's tool. — *adj.* **ramm'ish** rank in smell or taste: strongly sexual. — **ram'cat** a he-cat; **ram'-jet** (engine) a simple form of aero-engine, consisting of forward air intake, combustion chamber, and rear expansion nozzle, in which thrust is generated by compression due solely to forward motion; **ram'rod** a rod for ramming down a charge or for cleaning a gun-barrel: a stern, inflexible person: a strict disciplinarian. — *adj.* rigid, inflexible: stern; **ram's'-horn** the horn of a ram: a trumpet, snuff-box, or other thing like or made of it. — Also *adj.* — **ram-air turbine** a small turbine driven by air used as an emergency power source for aircraft, etc., or to provide power in guided weapons. [O.E. *ram, rom;* Ger. *Ramm.*]

Rāma *rä'mä, n.* an incarnation of Vishnu. — *n.* **Rāmāyana** (*rä-mä'yä-na*) the Sanskrit epic of *Rāma.*

Ramadan, Ramadhan *ram-ə-dän', n.* the ninth month of the Muslim calendar, the month of fasting by day: the fast. [Ar. *Ramadān.*]

ramakin. See **ramekin.**

ramal, ramate, etc. See **ramus.**

Raman effect *räm'ən i-fekt'*, a change in frequency of light passing through a transparent medium — used in the study of molecules. [From Sir Chandrasekhara *Raman* (1888–1970), Indian physicist.]

Ramapithecus *rä-ma-pith'i-kəs, n.* an early Pliocene genus of primates, possibly an ancestor of modern man, known from fossil remains found in N. India. — *n.* and *adj.* **ramapith'ecine.** [*Rama,* with reference to his birth as a prince of Oudh, and Gr. *pithēkos,* ape.]

Rāmāyana. See **Rāma.**

ramble *ram'bl, v.i.* to go as fancy leads: to wander: to walk for pleasure: to wander in mind or discourse: to be desultory, incoherent, or delirious: to straggle or trail, as a plant. — *n.* a roving about: an irregular excursion: a walk for pleasure: rambling. — *n.* **ram'bler** one who rambles: a trailing climbing plant, esp. a rose with small clustered flowers. — *n.* and *adj.* **ram'bling.** — *adv.* **ram'blingly.** [M.E. *romblen;* app. conn. with **roam.**]

rambunctious *ram-bungk'shəs, adj.* difficult to control, boisterous, exuberant. — *adv.* **rambunc'tiously.** — *n.* **rambunc'tiousness.** [Perh. **rumbustious.**]

rambutan *ram-bōō'tən, n.* a lofty Malayan tree (*Nephelium lappaceum*), akin to the longan: its hairy edible fruit. [Malay *rambūtan* — *rambut,* hair.]

ramcat. See **ram.**

rameal, rameous. See **ramus.**

Ramean. See **Ramism.**

ramee. See **rami.**

ramekin, ramequin, ramakin *ram'ə-kin, n.* a mixture of cheese, eggs, etc., baked in small moulds, or served on toast: a baking dish for one person. [Fr. *ramequin* — obs. Flem. *rammeken.*]

ramentum *ra-ment'əm, n.* a chaffy scale, as on ferns: — *pl.* **rament'a.** [L. *rāmentum,* a scraping — *rādĕre,* to scrape.]

rameous. See **ramus.**

ramequin. See **ramekin.**

ramfeezle *ram-fē'zl, (Scot.) v.t.* to weary out.

ramgunshoch *ram-gun'shohh, (Scot.) adj.* rough.

rami, ramie, ramee *ram'ē, n.* rhea or China grass (*Boehmeria nivea*), a plant of the nettle family, long cultivated in China: its fibre, used for cloth, bank-note paper, gas mantles, etc.: a garment thereof. [Malay *rami.*]

ramify, etc. See under **ramus.**

Ramil(l)ie(s) *ram'i-li(z), ns.* a name for several articles and modes of dress in fashion after Marlborough's victory at *Ramillies* (1706) — esp. a form of cocked hat, and a wig with a long plaited tail. — Also *adj.*

Ramism *rā'mizm, n.* the system of logic of Peter *Ramus*

(1515–72). — *ns.* and *adjs.* **Rā'mean, Rā'mist.**

rammer, rammish. See **ram.**

rammy *ram'i, (Scot.) n.* a row, free-for-all fight. [Perh. from Scots *rammle,* an uproar, noisy drinking spree.]

ramose, ramous. See under **ramus.**

ramp¹ *ramp, v.i.* to climb: to grow rankly: to rear as if climbing: to slope from one level to another: to rage: to range about wildly. — *v.t.* to provide with a ramp: to bend into a ramp: to snatch: to rob: to hustle into paying a fictitious debt: to swindle. — *n.* a romp, tomboy (*arch.*): a disorderly or loose woman (*arch.*): an act of ramping: an inclined plane: a low hump made across a road, e.g. to slow down traffic: the slope of a wall-top or the like between two levels: an upwardly concave bend in a handrail: a swindle: a stunt worked for private profit: a worked-up excitement or craze, esp. for some gain: an exploitation of a special situation to increase prices or the like. — *adj.* **rampā'cious** (*Dickens*) rampageous. — *n.* **rampāge'** (*U.S.* also *ram';* *Scot.* **rampauge** *-pöj'*) turbulently or aggressively excited behaviour or rushing about. — *v.i.* to storm: to rush about wildly. — *adj.* **rampā'geous.** — *ns.* **rampā'-geousness; rampall'ian** (*Shak.*) a term of abuse; **ramp'-ancy.** — *adj.* **ramp'ant** rearing: standing in profile, on the left hindleg (*her.*): high-spirited: fierce: unrestrained: unchecked in growth or prevalence: (of an arch) having springers on different levels. — *adv.* **ramp'antly.** — *n.* **ramp'er** one who ramps: esp. one who makes a disturbance to cover the activities of others: a rampsman. — **ramps'man** (*slang*) one who ramps bookmakers. — **on the rampage** storming about, behaving wildly and violently in anger, exuberance, etc. [Fr. *ramper,* to creep, to clamber.]

ramp² *ramp, n.* a kind of wild onion native to N. America: a ramson. [O.E. *wramsa.*]

rampart *ram'pärt, -pərt, n.* a flat-topped defensive mound: that which defends. — *v.t.* to fortify or surround with ramparts. [Fr. *rempart* — O.Fr. *rempar* — *remparer,* to defend — L. pfx. *re-, ante, parāre,* to prepare.]

rampauge. See **ramp.**

Ramphastos. See **Rhamphastos** under **rhamphoid.**

rampick *ram'pik,* **rampike** *-pīk, (arch.* and *U.S.) ns.* a dead tree, or one decayed at the top, broken off, or partly burned. — *adjs.* **ram'pick, -ed.** [Origin obscure.]

rampion *ramp'yən, -i-ən, n.* a bell-flower (*Campanula rapunculus*) whose root is eaten as a salad: any species of the kindred genus *Phyteuma.* [Cf. It. *raponzolo,* Ger. *Rapunzel,* Fr. *raiponce.*]

rampire *ram'pīr, n.* arch. for **rampart.** — *adj.* **ram'pired.**

ramrod. See **ram.**

ramshackle *ram'shak-l, adj.* tumbledown. [Perh. — *ramshackled,* pa.p. of an obs. form of *ransackle* (see **ransha(c)kle).**]

ramson *ram'zən, n.* (orig. pl. of the now *dial.* **rams;** usu. in double pl. form **ramsons**) wild or broad-leaved garlic. [O.E. *hramsa, hramse, hramsan* (pl.).]

ramstam *ram'stam', (Scot.) adj.* and *adv.* headlong. [Poss. **ram.**]

ramus *rā'məs, n.* a branch of anything, esp. a nerve: a process of a bone: the mandible, or its ascending part: a feather barb: — *pl.* **rā'mī.** — *adjs.* **rā'mal, rā'meal, rā'meous, rā'mous** of a branch; **rā'mate, rā'mous, ramose** (*rə-mōs', rā'mōs*) branched. — *n.* **ramification** (*ram-i-fi-kā'shən*) branching: arrangement of branches: a single branch or part of a complex arrangement, or of a situation or problem, esp., when used *fig.*, a consequence that must be taken into account. — *adj.* **ram'iform** having a branched shape. — *v.t.* and *v.i.* **ram'ify** to divide into branches (also *fig.*): — *pr.p.* **ram'ifying;** *pa.t.* and *pa.p.* **rami'fied.** — *adjs.* **ram'ular** of a branch; **ram'ulose, ram'ulous** having ramuli. — *n.* **ram'ulus** a little branch: — *pl.* **ram'ulī.** [L. *rāmus,* a branch.]

ran *pa.t.* of **run.**

Rana *rā'nə, n.* the typical genus of frogs, giving name to the family **Ranidae** (*ran'i-dē*). — *adj.* **ranarian** (*rə-nā'ri-ən*) froggy. — *n.* **ranā'rium** a place where frogs are reared. — *adjs.* **raniform** (*ran'*) frog-like; **ranine** (*rā'nīn*) of the under side of the tongue (seat of ranula); **ranivorous** (*rə-niv'ər-əs*) frog-eating. — *n.* **ranula** (*ran'ū-lə*) a cyst in the gland under the tongue (poss. from a fancied resemblance to a little frog). [L. *rāna,* dim. *rānula,* a frog, ranula.]

rana *rä'nä, n.* a Rajput prince. [Hind.]

ranarium. See **Rana.**

rance *rans,* (chiefly *Scot.*) *n.* a prop, shore: a bar. — *v.t.* to prop: to bar. [Fr. *ranche.*]

rancel. See **ranzel.**

ranch[1] *rän(t)sh, ran(t)sh, n.* a stock-farm, as in western N. America, with its buildings and persons employed: an establishment for rearing any other commercially-important animal. — *v.i.* to manage or work upon a ranch. — *adj.* **ranched** of a fur coat, made from skins of animals from a ranch. — *ns.* **ranch'er, ranchero** (*ran-chā'rō,* Sp. *rän-che'rō; pl.* **-ros**), **ranch'man** one employed in ranching; **rancheria** (*ran-chä-rē'ə,* Sp. *rän-che-rē'a*) a herdsmen's hut or village: a settlement of Indians; **ranch'ing; rancho** (*ran'chō,* Sp. *rän'*) a rude hut, or group of huts, esp. for travellers, a ranch: — *pl.* **ran'chos.** [From Amer. Sp. — Sp. *rancho,* mess, mess-room.]

ranch[2] *rän(t)sh, ran(t)sh,* (*Dryden*) *v.t.* to tear. [Cf. **race**[5].]

rancid *ran'sid, adj.* rank in smell or taste, as butter or oil that is going bad. — *ns.* **rancid'ity, ran'cidness.** [L. *rancidus.*]

rancour, U.S. **rancor,** *rang'kər, n.* harboured bitterness: deep-seated enmity: spite: virulence: sourness (*Shak.*). — *adj.* **ran'corous.** — *adv.* **ran'corously.** [O.Fr., — L. *rancor, -ōris,* an old grudge — *rancēre,* to be rancid.]

rand[1] *rand, n.* a border, margin: a strip, esp. of flesh or of leather: a ridge overlooking a valley (*S.Afr. ront, rand*): the basic unit of the South African decimal coinage, introduced 1961 as equivalent to ten shillings: — *pl.* **rand(s).** — **the Rand** the Witwatersrand goldfield. [O.E. and Du. *rand,* border.]

rand[2] *rand, v.i.* an old form of **rant.**

randan[1] *ran-dan'* or *ran', n.* a din, uproar: riotous conduct: spree. [Origin obscure.]

randan[2] *ran-dan'* or *ran', n.* a boat rowed by three, the second with two oars. — Also **randan gig.** [Origin obscure.]

randem *ran'dəm, n., adj.,* and *adv.* tandem with three horses.

randie. See **randy.**

randle-balk *ran'dl-bök,* **-perch** *-pûrch,* **-tree** *-trē,* (*Scot.* and *N.England*) *ns.* a bar in a chimney for hanging pots; **randle-tree** (*Scott*) applied to a tall, raw-boned woman. — Also **rann'el(l)-, rann'le-, ran'tle-.** [Cf. Norw. *randa-tre* — *rand,* space above a fireplace.]

random *ran'dəm,* also formerly (*Spens., Shak.*) **randon** *-dən, ns.* a rush, full speed (*obs.*): uncontrolled or unguarded state, freedom (*Spens.*): haphazard (*arch.*): elevation of a gun (*obs.*): irregular masonry. — *adj.* haphazard, chance: fired at an elevation: uncontrolled: irregular. — *v.t.* **ran'domise, -ize** to arrange or set up so as to occur in a random manner. — *ns.* **randomīsā'tion, -z-; ran'domiser, -z-.** — *advs.* **ran'domly, ran'-domwise.** — **random access** (*comput.*) access to any data in a large store of information without affecting other data; **random variable** (*statistics*) one which can take any from a range of values which occur randomly. [O.Fr. *randon* — *randir,* to gallop.]

randy, randie *ran'di, adj.* boisterous (*dial.*): aggressively or coarsely loud-spoken (*Scot.*): lustful. — *n.* a violent beggar, esp. a woman: a coarse virago: a romping girl. [Poss. **rand**[2].]

ranee. See **rani.**

rang *rang,* pa.t. of **ring**[2,3].

range *rānj, v.t.* to set in a row or rows: to assign a place among others to: to classify: to arrange: to straighten, level: to traverse freely or in all directions: to sail along: to bring to bear. — *v.i.* to lie in a direction: to extend: to take or have a position in a line, or alongside: to

take sides: to lie evenly: to move, have freedom of movement, occur, or vary, within limits: to rove at large: to beat about, as for game: to be inconstant: to have a range. — *n.* a row or rank: a system of points in a straight line: anything extending in line, as a chain of mountains, a row of connected buildings: a stretch of open country, esp. one used for grazing: a north and south strip of townships six miles wide (*U.S.*): line of lie: an act of ranging: scope, compass: movement, freedom of movement, or variation between limits: space or distance between limits: area, or distance within which anything moves, can move, occurs, is possible, acts efficiently, or varies: a place for practice in shooting: firing elevation of a gun, etc. : an enclosed kitchen fireplace fitted with appliances of various kinds. — *ns.* **ran'ger** a rover: a dog that beats the ground: a forest or park officer: a member of a body of troops, usu. mounted and employed in policing an area: a soldier specially trained for raiding combat: (with *cap.*) a member of a senior branch of the Girl Guide organisation (also **Ranger Guide**): (with *cap.* in *pl.*) a name sometimes taken by football clubs; **rang'-ership; rang'iness.** — *adj.* **ran'gy** disposed or well able to roam: roomy: long-legged and thin: mountainous (*Austr.*). — **range'finder** an instrument for finding the distance of an object: same as **tacheometer; range'land** (often *pl.*) land suitable for grazing, but too dry for growing crops; **range, ranging, pole, rod** a pole or rod used to mark positions in surveying. — **free-range** see **free.** — **range oneself** to side (with), to take sides: (as a Gallicism) to settle down to reputable ways, esp. on marrying. [Fr. *ranger,* to range — *rang,* a rank.]

rani, ranee *rän'ē, fem.* of **raja.** [Hind. *rānī* — Sans. *rājñī,* queen, fem. of *rājan.*]

Ranidae, raniform, ranine, etc. See **Rana.**

rank[1] *rangk, n.* a row: a row of soldiers standing side by side (opp. to *file*): any row thought of as so placed (e.g. of squares along the player's side of a chessboard): (in *pl.*) soldiers, esp. private soldiers — often (with *the*) private soldiers collectively: (in *pl.*) persons of ordinary grade: a row of cabs awaiting hire: a cabstand: a set of organ pipes: arrangement in line: order, grade, or degree: an official position, esp. *mil.*: station: high standing, esp. social. — *v.t.* to place in a line: to assign to a particular class or grade: to place on the list of claims against a bankrupt: to take rank over (*U.S.*). — *v.i.* to have a place in a rank, grade, scale, or class: to move in rank: to be admitted as a claim against the property of a bankrupt. — *adj.* **ranked** (*Shak.*) app. bordered with rows. — *n.* **rank'er** one who serves or has served as a private soldier: an officer who has risen from the ranks. — *adj.* **rank'ing** with a high military, political, etc., position: prominent. — *n.* a position or grade. — **pull rank** to use one's rank to exert authority, get one's own way; **rank and file** common soldiers: ordinary people: those in an organisation, etc. not involved in its management; **take rank of** to take precedence of. [O.Fr. *renc* (Fr. *rang*), perh. — O.H.G. *hring, hrinc,* ring.]

rank[2] *rangk, adj.* strong, lusty, vigorous (*obs.*): violent (*obs.*): growing high and luxuriantly: coarsely over-grown: swollen (*Shak.*): excessive (*law*): abounding (*Spens.*): dense (*Spens.*): out-and-out, arrant, utter: over-productive: offensively strong-scented or strong-tasted: gross: foul: lustful, in heat (*Shak.*): grossly obvious: deep-cutting. — *adv.* (*Spens.*) violently: utterly. — *adv.* **rank'ly.** — *n.* **rank'ness.** — **rank'-rī'der** a hard rider: a moss-trooper: a highwayman. — *adj.* **rank'-rī'ding.** [O.E. *ranc,* proud, strong.]

ranke *rangk,* (Shak., *As You Like It,* III, ii. 103) *n.* app. a jog-trot (perh. a misprint for **rack**[6]): passage otherwise explained as meaning a repetition of the same rhyme like a file (rank) of so many butterwomen.

Rankine *rang'kin, adj.* pertaining to an absolute scale of temperature on which the units are the same as those on the Fahrenheit scale. [After William J. M. *Rankine* (1820–72), Scottish engineer and scientist.]

rankle *rangk'l, v.i.* to fester (*arch.*): to cause festering (*arch.*): to go on vexing, irritating, or embittering. — *v.t.* to cause to fester: to envenom: to embitter. — *n.* (*arch.*) a continual irritation. [O.Fr. *rancler, raoncler* — *draoncler*, app. — L.L. *dra(cu)nculus*, an ulcer, dim. of L. *dracō* — Gr. *drakōn*, dragon.]

rannel(l)-balk, -perch, etc. **rannle-,** etc. See **randle-balk, -perch** etc.

ransack *ran'sak* (or *-sak'*), *v.t.* to search thoroughly: to plunder: to pillage. — *n.* (*arch.*) eager search. — *n.* **ran'sacker.** [O.N. *rannsaka* — *rann*, house, *sækja*, to seek.]

ransel. See **ranzel.**

ransha(c)kle *ran-shak'l,* (*Scott*) *v.t.* to search, ransack. [Dial. Eng. *ransackle, ram-* — **ransack.**]

ransom *ran'səm, n.* redemption from captivity: price of redemption or reclamation: expiation: an extortionate price. — *v.t.* to pay, demand, or accept ransom for: to redeem: to expiate. — *adj.* **ran'somable.** — *n.* **ran'somer.** — *adj.* **ran'somless.** — **a king's ransom** a very large sum of money; **hold to ransom** to retain until a ransom shall be paid: to hold up to gain a concession; **put to ransom** to offer to release for ransom. [Fr. *rançon* — L. *redemptiō, -ōnis,* redemption.]

rant *rant, v.i.* to declaim bombastically: to storm, scold: to sing, play, or make merry, noisily. — *v.t.* to utter declamatorily. — *n.* empty declamation: bombast: a tirade: a noisy frolic (*Scot.*): a lively tune. — *ns.* **ran'ter** one who rants: an extravagant preacher: a member of a Commonwealth antinomian sect: (as a byname) a Primitive Methodist: a roisterer: a noisy musician (*Scot.*); **ran'terism.** — *adv.* **rant'ingly.** [Obs. Du. *ranten,* to rave; L.G. *randen,* Ger. *ranzen.*]

rantipole *rant'i-pōl, n.* a wild reckless person. — Also *adj.* and *v.i.* [Perh. **rant.**]

rantle-. See **randle-.**

ranula. See **Rana.**

Ranunculus *rə-nung'kū-ləs, n.* the buttercup genus: (without *cap.*) any plant of the genus: — *pl.* **ranun'culī,** **ranun'culuses.** — *adj.* **ranunculā'ceous** of the buttercup family (**Ranunculā'ceae**). [L. *rānunculus,* dim. of *rāna,* a frog.]

ranz-des-vaches *rä(s)-dä-väsh, n.* a French Swiss herdsman's song or alpenhorn melody. [Swiss Fr.; *ranz,* of uncertain meaning, Fr. *des vaches,* of the cows.]

ranzel *ran'zl,* **rancel, -sel** *-sl, ns.* formerly in Orkney and Shetland a search for stolen goods. — **ran'zelman,** etc. (*Scott* **Ran'zellaar**) an official who did this. [O.Scot. *ransell;* O.N. *rannsaka;* **ranshackle.**]

rap¹ *rap, n.* a sharp blow: the sound of a knock: a crime or criminal charge (*slang*). — *v.t.* and *v.i.* to strike or knock sharply: to swear or testify, esp. falsely (*obs. slang*): to communicate by raps. — *v.t.* to censure, reprove: to utter sharply. — *v.i.* to rattle, patter: — *pr.p.* **rapp'ing;** *pa.t.* and *pa.p.* **rapped.** — *n.* **rapp'er** one who raps: a door-knocker: a great lie or oath (*arch.*): a spirit-rapper. — **rap sheet** (*slang*) a criminal record. — **beat the rap** (*U.S. slang*) to be acquitted of a crime: to avoid punishment; **take the rap** (*slang*) to take the blame or punishment, esp. in place of another. [Imit.]

rap² *rap, v.t.* to snatch: to grab: to carry away in spirit or with joy (*Shak.*): — *pr.p.* **rapp'ing;** *pa.p.* **rapped** or **rapt.** [Perh. partly akin to M.L.G. *rappen,* Sw. *rappa,* to snatch; mainly a back-formation from **rapt.**]

rap³ *rap, n.* an 18th-century Irish counterfeit halfpenny: as a type of worthlessness, a whit, esp. in *not worth a rap.* [Origin obscure.]

rap⁴ *rap,* (*coll.*) *n.* an informal talk, discussion, chat, etc.: a rhythmic monologue delivered over a musical background. — *v.i.* to have a talk, discussion, etc.: to get along well, sympathise: to deliver a rhythmic monologue to music. — *n.* **rapp'ing.** — **rap session** an informal discussion. [Perhaps from **rapport.**]

rapacious *rə-pā'shəs, adj.* grasping: greedy of gain: living by prey. — *adv.* **rapā'ciously.** — *ns.* **rapā'ciousness;** **rapacity** (*-pas'*). [L. *rapāx, -ācis* — *rapĕre,* to seize and carry off.]

rape¹ *rāp, n.* rapine, plunder, seizure (*obs.*): unlawful sexual intercourse (usu. by force) with another person without that person's consent: violation, despoliation. — *v.t.* to seize and carry off (*obs.*): to commit rape upon: to ravish or transport, as with delight (*obs.*): to violate, despoil. — *ns.* **rā'per; rā'pist.** — *adj.* **rā'ping** tearing prey (*her.*): ravishing, delighting (*obs.*). [Prob. L. *rapĕre,* to snatch, confused with **rap².**]

rape² *rāp, n.* a division of Sussex. [Origin obscure.]

rape³ *rāp, n.* a plant (*Brassica napus*) near akin to the turnip, cultivated for its herbage and oil-producing seeds: applied to various closely allied species or varieties. — **rape'-cake** refuse of rape-seed after the oil has been expressed; **rape'-oil; rape'-seed.** [L. *rāpa, rāpum,* a turnip.]

rape⁴ *rāp, n.* the refuse left after wine-making. [Fr. *râpe.*]

Raphanus *raf'ə-nəs, n.* the radish genus. — *n.* **raphania** (*rə-fā'ni-ə*) ergotism (attributed by Linnaeus to wild radish seeds). [Gr. *rhaphanis.*]

raphe *rā'fē, n.* a seam-like junction: the ridge on the side of an anatropous ovule continuing the funicle to the chalaza: a broad connecting ridge, e.g. that between the halves of the vertebrate brain. — Also **ra'phé.** [Gr. *rhăphē,* a seam.]

Raphia *rā'fi-ə, raf'i-ə, n.* a genus of handsome pinnately-leaved palms: (without *cap.*) raffia. [Malagasy.]

raphis, rhaphis *rā'fis,* **raphide, rhaphide** *rā'fīd, ns.* a needle-like crystal, usu. of calcium oxalate, occurring in plant cells: — *pl.* **r(h)aphides** (*raf'i-dez, rā'fīdz*). [Gr. *rhăphis, -idos,* a needle — *rhaptein,* to sew.]

rapid *rap'id, adj.* swift: quickly accomplished: steeply-sloping: requiring short exposure (*phot.*). — *n.* a very swift-flowing part of a river with steep descent and often broken water but no actual drop (usu. in *pl.*). — *n.* **rapidity** (*rə-pid'i-ti*). — *adv.* **rap'idly.** — *n.* **rap'idness.** — **rapid fire** the quick firing of guns, asking of questions, etc. — *adj.* **rap'id-fire.** — **rapid eye movement** (abbrev. **REM**) an observed manifestation of a phase of sleep during which dreams are particularly vivid: hence, of, pertaining to, this phase. [L. *rapidus* — *rapĕre,* to seize.]

rapier *rā'pi-ər, n.* a long slender sword, suitable for thrusting. [Fr. *rapière.*]

rapine *rap'īn, -in, n.* plundering: prey: ravishment, transport (*Milt.*). [L. *rapīna* — *rapĕre,* to seize.]

rapist. See **rape¹.**

raploch *rap'lohh,* (*Scot.*) *n.* and *adj.* homespun. [Origin unknown.]

rapparee *rap-ər-ē', n.* a wild Irish plunderer, orig. of the late 17th. cent. [Ir. *rapaire,* half-pike, robber.]

rappee *ra-pē', n.* a coarse, strong-flavoured snuff. [Fr. *râpé,* rasped, grated — *râper,* to rasp.]

rappel *rä-, rə-pel', n.* call to arms by beat of drum: abseiling. — *v.i.* same as **abseil:** — *pr.p.* **rappell'ing;** *pa.t.* and *pa.p.* **rappell'ed** [Fr.]

rapper, rapping. See **rap¹.**

Rappist *rap'ist,* **Rappite** *-īt, ns.* Harmonist, follower of George *Rapp.*

rapport *ra-pör', n.* relation: connection: sympathy: emotional bond: spiritualistic touch. [Fr.]

rapporteur *ra-pör-tœr', n.* one whose task it is to carry out an investigation and/or draw up a report (for a committee, etc.). — *n.* **rapportage** (*ra-pör-täzh'*) the description of real events in writing: flat description, lacking in imagination. [Fr. — *rapporter,* to bring back.]

rapprochement *ra-prosh'mä, n.* a drawing together: establishment or renewal of cordial relations. [Fr.]

rapscallion *rap-skal'yən, n.* See **rascal.**

rapt *rapt, adj.* snatched or carried away (*arch.*): abducted (*arch.*): carried out of this world: transported, enraptured, entranced: wholly engrossed. [L. *raptus,* pa.p. of *rapĕre,* to seize and carry off; but partly also pa.p. of **rap².**]

raptor *rap'tər, n.* a ravisher (*arch.*): a plunderer (*arch.*): a (esp. diurnal) bird of prey, member of the abandoned order **Raptores** (-tō'rēz). — *adjs.* **raptatō'rial, raptō'rial** predatory: adapted to predatory life. [L. *raptor*, -*ōris*, a plunderer — *rapĕre*, to seize.]

rapture *rap'chər, n.* a seizing and carrying away: extreme delight: transport: ecstasy: a paroxysm. — *v.t.* to enrapture. — *adjs.* **rap'tured; rap'tureless.** — *v.i.* **rap'-turise, -ize** to go into raptures. — *n.* **rap'turist.** — *adj.* **rap'turous.** — *adv.* **rap'turously.** — **rapture of the deep, depth** nitrogen narcosis. [**rapt.**]

rara avis *rā'rə ā'vis, rä'ra ä'wis.* See *Quotations from Latin, etc.* in Appendices.

ra-ra skirt *rä-rä skûrt,* a very short gathered or pleated skirt, orig. as worn by cheer-leaders. [Prob. — **hurrah.**]

rare[1] *rār, adj.* thin: not dense: sparse: seldom met with: uncommon: excellent: especially good: extraordinary: used as a mere intensive, esp. in **rare** and (*coll.*). — *n.* **rarefac'tion** (*rār-i-, rar-i-*) rarefying. — *adjs.* **rarefac'-tive, rar'efiable.** — *v.t., v.i.* **rar'efy** to make, become less dense, refine: — *pr.p.* **rar'efying;** *pa.t.* and *pa.p.* **rar'efied.** — *adv.* **rāre'ly** seldom: choicely: remarkably well. — *ns.* **rāre'ness; rarity** (*rār'* or *rar'i-ti*) state of being rare: thinness: something valued for its scarcity: uncommonness. — **rare bird** an exceptional person or thing; **rare'bit** a now more common form of (*Welsh*) *rabbit*; **rare earth** an oxide of a **rare-earth element,** any of a group of metallic elements (some of them rare) closely similar in chemical properties and very difficult to separate: now more usu. a rare-earth element itself; **rare gas** inert gas. [Fr., — L. *rārus.*]

rare[2] *rār, adj.* of eggs, lightly cooked (*obs.* or *dial.*): of meat, underdone. [**rear**[3] influenced by **rare**[1].]

rare[3] *rār,* **rear** *rēr,* (*obs.*) *adjs.* and *advs.* early. — *adv.* **rear'ly.** — *adj.* **rare'-ripe** early ripe. [**rathe.**]

rarebit. See **rare**[1].

raree-show *rār'ē-shō, n.* a show carried about in a box: a spectacle. [App. a foreign pron. of **rare show.**]

raring *rā'ring, adj.* eager (for), full of enthusiasm and sense of urgency, esp. in phrase **raring to go.** [**rear**[2].]

rarity. See **rare**[1].

ras *räs, n.* a headland: an Abyssinian prince. [Ar. *ras, ra's,* head.]

rascaille *räs-kä'i, n.* and *adj.* an arch. form of **rascal, rabble** (*Scott,* etc.).

rascal *räs'kl, n.* the rabble (*obs.*): one of the rabble (*obs.*): a knave, rogue, scamp: (playfully) a fellow: a deer out of condition (*Shak.*). — *adj.* of the rabble: knavish: wretched: out of condition. — *ns.* **ras'caldom** the world or conduct of rascals; **ras'calism; rascality** (-*kal'*) the rabble: character or conduct of rascals; **rascallion** (-*kal'yən*), **rapscall'ion** a rascal: a low, mean wretch. — *adjs.* **ras'cal-like, ras'cally** (*superl., Shak.,* **ras'-calliest**). [O.Fr. *rascaille* (Fr. *racaille*), scum of the people.]

raschel *räsh'əl, n.* a type of light loosely-knitted fabric. [Ger. *Raschelmaschine,* a kind of knitting-machine.]

rase *rāz.* Same as **race**[3], **raze**[2]. See also **race**[5,6] and **rise.**

rash[1] *rash, adj.* over-hasty: wanting in caution: operating suddenly (*Shak.*): calling for haste (*Shak.*). — *adv.* rashly. — *adv.* **rash'ly.** — *n.* **rash'ness.** [Cf. Dan. and Sw. *rask;* Du. and Ger. *rasch,* rapid.]

rash[2] *rash, n.* an eruption on the skin: a large number of instances at the same time or in the same place. [Perh. O.Fr. *rasche* (Fr. *rache*).]

rash[3] *rash,* (*obs.*) *v.t.* to tear, drag. [O.Fr. *arrachier,* to uproot; cf. **race**[6].]

rash[4] *rash,* (*Spens.*) *v.t.* to slash. [Variant of **raze**[2], **rase, race**[5].]

rash[5] *rash, v.i.* to dash, rush (*obs.*). — *v.t.* (*Shak.*) to stick, thrust forcibly. [Origin obscure.]

rash[6] *rash, n.* a Scots form of **rush**[2].

rasher *rash'ər, n.* a thin slice of bacon. [Poss. from **rash**[4].]

Raskolnik *ras-kol'nik, n.* in Russia, a dissenter from the Orthodox Church. [Russ.]

rasorial *ra-, rə-sō', -sö'ri-əl, adj.* scraping the ground for food. — *n.pl.* **Rasō'res** (-*rēz*) an obsolete order, galli-

naceous birds with or without the pigeons. [L. *rāsor,* -*ōris,* scraper.]

rasp[1] *räsp, n.* a coarse file: any similar surface: a mollusc's tongue: an insect's stridulating apparatus: a risp at a door: a grating sound or feeling. — *v.t.* to grate as with a rasp: to grate upon: to risp: to utter gratingly. — *v.i.* to have a grating effect: to scrape, as on a fiddle. — *ns.* **rasp'atory** a surgeon's rasp; **rasp'er** one who, or that which, rasps: in hunting, a difficult fence (*coll.*); **rasp'ing** a filing: (in *pl.*) fine breadcrumbs used as a coating for food before frying, etc. — *adj.* grating, harsh. — *adv.* **rasp'ingly.** — *adj.* **rasp'y** rough. — **rasp'-house** (Du. *rasphuis*) a house of correction, where dye-wood was rasped. [O.Fr. *raspe* (Fr. *râpe*); perh. Gmc.]

rasp[2] *räsp,* (now *coll.* and *Scot.*) *n.* a raspberry. — *n.* **raspberry** (*räz'bər-i*) the fruit of *Rubus idaeus:* the plant producing it: extended to some kindred species: a sign of disapproval, esp. a noise produced by blowing hard with the tongue between the lips (*slang*). — *adj.* of, made with, or like raspberry. — **rasp'berry-bush;** rasp-**berry jam tree** an Australian acacia (from the smell of its wood). [Earlier *raspis;* origin unknown.]

rasse *ras'(ə), n.* a small civet, *Viverricula indica.* [Jav. *rase.*]

rast *räst* or *räst,* a Spenserian *pa.p.* of **race**[5,6] = **raze**[2].

Rastafarian, Ras Tafarian *ras-tə-fär'i-ən, n.* a member of a West Indian, esp. Jamaican, cult, which rejects western culture and ideas and regards Haile Selassie, the former Emperor of Ethiopia, as divine. — Also **Ras'ta, Ras'taman.** — *adjs.* **Rastafā'rian, Rastafari** (-*ä'ri*), **Ras'ta** (all also without *cap.*). [From Haile Selassie's title and name, *Ras Tafari.*]

raster *ras'tər,* (*television*) *n.* a complete set of scanning lines appearing at the receiver as a rectangular patch of light on which the image is reproduced. [Perh. — L. *rāstrum,* as next word.]

rastrum *ras'trəm, n.* a music-pen. [L. *rāstrum,* rake.]

rasure, razure *rā'zhər, n.* the act of scraping or shaving: erasure: obliteration. [L. *rāsūra.*]

rat[1] *rat, n.* a genus (*Rattus*) of animals closely allied to mice, but larger: extended to various kindred or superficially similar animals: a renegade, turn-coat (from the rat's alleged desertion of a doomed ship): a strike-breaker: one who works for less than recognised wages: a miserable or ill-looking specimen: a despicable person. — *v.i.* to hunt or catch rats: to desert or change sides for unworthy motives: (of a workman) to work as a rat: — *pr.p.* **ratt'ing;** *pa.t.* and *pa.p.* **ratt'ed.** — *adj.* **rat'proof.** — *interj.* **rats** (*slang*) expressing contemptuous incredulity, annoyance, etc. — *ns.* **ratt'er** a killer of rats, esp. a dog: one who rats; **ratt'ery** apostasy: a place where rats are kept or abound; **ratt'ing** apostasy: rat-hunting. — Also *adj.* — *adjs.* **ratt'ish** rat-like: rat-infested; **ratt'y** rat-like: rat-infested: wretched: unkempt, untidy: angry, irritable (*slang*). — **rat'bag** (*slang*) a term of abuse: a despicable person; **ratbite fever** a disease caused by infection with bacteria conveyed by the bite of a rat; **rat'-catcher** a professional killer of rats; unconventional hunting garb; **rat'-catching; rat'-flea** a flea that infests rats; **rat'-guard** a metal disc put on a hawser to prevent rats from boarding a ship in port; **rat'-hole; rat'-hunting; rat'-kangaroo'** the potoroo, a marsupial of various species about the size of a rabbit, akin to the kangaroo; **rat'pack** (*slang*) a rowdy gang of young people; **rat'-pit** an enclosure where rats are worried by dogs; **rat'-poison** any poison for rats; **rat race** a continual round of hectic and futile activity: the scramble to get on in the world by fair means or foul; **rats'bane** poison for rats, esp. white arsenic: a name for many poisonous plants; **rat's'-tail, rat'-tail** the tail of a rat: anything like a rat's tail: a thin coherent dangling lock of hair: an excrescence on a horse's leg: (**rat'-tail**) the grenadier fish. — *adj.* **rat's'-tail, rat'-tail, rat'-tailed** having a tail like a rat: like a rat's tail: of a spoon, ridged along the back of the bowl. — **rat'-trap** a trap for catching rats:

a toothed bicycle pedal. — Also *adj.* — **rat on** to inform against: to betray the interests of: to desert. **smell a rat** to have a suspicion that something is afoot. [O.E. *ræt*; cf. Ger. *Ratte*.]

rat² *rat, v.t.* (in imprecations) used for **rot**. [Cf. **drat**.]

rata *rä'tə, n.* a myrtaceous New Zealand tree (*Metrosideros*) with hard wood. [Maori.]

ratable, rateable *rā'tə-bl, adj.* See **rate¹**.

ratafia *rat-ə-fē'ə, n.* a flavouring essence made with the essential oil of almonds: a cordial or liqueur flavoured with fruit-kernels: an almond biscuit or cake. [Fr.; ety. dub.; cf. **tafia**.]

ratan *ra-tan', n.* Same as **rattan¹**.

rataplan *rat-ə-plan', n.* a drumming sound. [Fr.]

rat-a-tat *rat-ə-tat'.* Same as **rat-tat**.

ratatouille *rat-ə-tōō'i, ra-ta-twē', n.* a stew of tomatoes, aubergines, peppers, onions and other vegetables, with olive oil. [Fr., — *touiller*, to stir.]

ratch¹ *rach, n.* a ratchet: a ratchet-wheel. — *n.* **ratch'et** a pawl and/or ratchet-wheel. — **ratch'et-wheel** a wheel with inclined teeth with which a pawl engages. [Cf. Ger. *Ratsche*, Fr. *rochet*.]

ratch². Same as **rache**.

ratch³. Same as **race⁴**.

rate¹ *rāt, n.* estimated amount or value (*Shak.*): estimation (*Shak.*): a fixed quantity (*obs.*): price or cost: amount corresponding: ratio, esp. time-ratio, speed: amount determined according to a rule or basis: a standard: a class or rank, esp. of ships or of seamen: manner, mode: extent, degree: (often *pl.*) an amount levied by a local authority according to the assessed value of property: a clock's gain or loss in unit time. — *v.t.* to allot (*Shak.*): to calculate (*Shak.*): to estimate: to value: to settle the relative rank, scale, or position of: to esteem, regard as: to deserve, be worthy of: to value for purpose of rate-paying: to think highly of (*coll.*). — *v.i.* to be placed in a certain class. — *n.* **rāt(e)abil'ity**. — *adj.* **rāt(e)'able**. — *adv.* **rāt(e)'ably**. — *ns.* **rāt'er** one who makes an estimate: (in composition) a ship, etc., of a given rate (as *second-rater*); **rāt'ing** a fixing of rates: classification according to grade: the class of any member of a crew: a sailor of such a class: the tonnage-class of a racing yacht: the proportion of viewers or listeners who are deemed to watch or listen to a particular programme or network. — **rat(e)able value** a value placed on a property, and used to assess the amount of rates payable to the local authority each year. — *v.t.* **rate'-cap'**. — **rate'-capp'ing** the setting by central government of an upper limit on the rate that can be levied by a local authority; **rate'-cutting** a lowering of charges to obtain traffic; **rate'payer** one who pays a local rate; **rate support grant** money contributed by central government to make up the difference between the rate levied and the amount required for local authority spending. — **at any rate** in any case, anyhow. [O.Fr., — L.L. (*pro*) *ratā* (*parte*), according to a calculated part — *rērī, rătus*, to think, judge.]

rate² *rāt, v.t.* to scold: to chide: to reprove: to drive by scolding. — *v.i.* to scold. — *n.* a reproof to a dog. [M.E. *raten;* origin obscure.]

rate³. Same as **ret**.

Ratel *rā'təl, rä'təl, n.* a badger-like genus (*Mellivora*) of Africa and India, akin to the gluttons (without *cap.*) an animal of this genus. [Afrikaans; origin uncertain.]

ratfink *rat'fingk,* (*derog.*) *n.* a mean, deceitful, despicable person. — Also *adj.* [**rat¹, fink.**]

rath¹ *räth,* **rathe** *rādh,* (*arch.*) *adjs.* quick: eager: early: — *compar.* **rather** (*rädh'ər;* Spens.) earlier; *superl.* **rath'est** (*obs.* or *dial.*) earliest. — *adv.* **rathe** (*rädh; Milt.*) early: — *compar.* **rather** (see below); *superl.* **rath'est**. [O.E. *hræd* (rarely *hræth*), quick, *hræthe, hrathe,* quickly; O.N. *hrathr.*]

rath² *räth, n.* a prehistoric hill-fort. [Ir.]

rathe. See **rath¹**.

rather *rä'dhər, adv.* sooner, more quickly (*Shak.*): more readily: more willingly: in preference: more than otherwise: more properly: somewhat, in some degree: — *irreg. superl.* **ra'therest** (*Shak.*). — *interj.* **ra'ther** (sometimes affectedly *rä-dhûr'*) I should think so: yes, indeed. — *adv.* (*coll.*) **ra'therish**. — **the rather** all the more. [Compar. of **rath¹**; O.E. *hrathor*.]

ratheripe *rādh'rīp,* **rathripe** *räth'rīp,* (*arch.* and *dial.*) *adjs.* early ripe. — *ns.* an early-ripening variety. [**rath(e), ripe¹**.]

ratify *rat'i-fī, v.t.* to approve and sanction, esp. by signature: to give validity or legality to: to confirm the correctness of (*obs.*): — *pr.p.* **rat'ifying;** *pa.t.* and *pa.p.* **rat'ified**. — *ns.* **ratifica'tion; rat'ifier**. [Fr. *ratifier* — L. *rătus,* pa.p. of *rērī* (see **rate¹**), *facĕre,* to make.]

ratine, ratteen *rat-ēn', n.* a rough, open dress-fabric. — Also **rat'iné** (*-i-nā;* Fr. *ratiner,* to frieze, put a nap on). [Fr. *ratine.*]

rating. See **rate¹**.

ratio *rā'shi-ō, rāsh'-yō, n.* the relation of one thing to another of which the quotient is the measure: quotient: proportion: a portion, allowance (*rare*): (also **ratio decidendi;** *law*) the reason or principle on which a decision is based: — *pl.* **rā'tios**. — **compound, inverse, ratio** see **compound¹, inverse**. [L. *rătiō, -ōnis,* reason — *rērī, rătus,* to think.]

ratiocinate *rat-* or *rash-i-os'i-nāt, v.i.* to reason. — *n.* **ratiocinā'tion**. — *adjs.* **ratioc'inative, ratioc'inatory**. [L. *ratiōcinārī, -ātus.*]

ration *ra'shən,* sometimes *rā', n.* a fixed allowance or portion: (in *pl.*) food (*coll.*). — *v.t.* to put on an allowance: to supply with rations: to restrict the supply of to so much for each. — **ra'tion-book, -card** a book, card, of coupons or vouchers for rationed commodities; **ra'tion-money** money in lieu of rations. [Fr., — L. *ratiō, -ōnis.*]

rational¹ *rash'ən-əl, adj.* of the reason: endowed with reason: agreeable to reason: sane: intelligent: judicious: commensurable with natural numbers. — *n.* a rational being or quantity: (in *pl.*) rational dress, i.e. knickerbockers instead of skirts for women (*hist.*). — *ns.* **rationale** (*rash-i-ō-nāl', -yə-nāl', -näl'i*) underlying principle: a rational account: a theoretical explanation or solution; **rationalisation, -z-** (*rash-nəl-ī-zā'shən*). — *v.t.* **rat'ionalise, -ize** to make rational: to free from irrational quantities: to conform to reason: to reorganise scientifically: to interpret rationalistically: to substitute conscious reasoning for unconscious motivation in explaining: to organise (an industry) so as to achieve greater efficiency and economy. — *v.i.* to think, or argue, rationally or rationalistically: to employ reason, rationalism, or rationalisation. — *ns.* **rat'ionalism** a system of belief regulated by reason, not authority: a disposition to apply to religious doctrines the same critical methods as to science and history, and to attribute all phenomena to natural rather than miraculous causes; **rat'ionalist**. — *adj.* **rationalist'ic**. — *adv.* **rationalist'ically**. — *n.* **rationality** (*rash-ən-al'i-ti*) quality of being rational: the possession or due exercise of reason: reasonableness. — *adv.* **rat'ionally**. — **rational horizon** see **horizon; rational number** a number expressed as the ratio of two integers. [L. *ratiōnālis, -e* — *ratiō.*]

rational² *rash'ən-əl, n.* the Jewish high-priest's breastplate: a bishop's vestment like the pallium. [L. *ratiōnāle,* Vulgate translation of Gr. *logion,* oracle.]

ratite *rat'īt, adj.* having a keel-less breastbone: of the **Ratitae** (*rä-tī'tē*), flightless birds — ostrich, rhea, emu, kiwi, etc. [L. *ratis,* raft.]

ratlin, -line, -ling, rattlin, -line, -ling *rat'lin, n.* one of the small lines forming steps of the rigging of ships. [Ety. dub.]

ratoon *rat-, rət-ōōn', n.* a new shoot from the ground after cropping, esp. of sugar-cane or cotton. — *v.i.* to send up ratoons. — *v.t.* to cut down so as to obtain ratoons. — *n.* **ratoon'er** a plant that ratoons. [Sp. *retoño,* shoot.]

rat-rhyme *rat'rīm,* (*Scot.*) *n.* a bit of doggerel: a screed.

rattan[1], **ratan** *ra-tan'*, *n.*, a climbing palm (*Calamus* or other) with very long thin stem: a cane made of it. [Malay *rōtan*.]
rattan[2] *ra-tan'*, *n.* the continuous beat of a drum.
rat-tat *rat'-tat'*, *n.* a knocking sound. [Imit.]
ratteen. Same as **ratine.**
ratten *rat'n*, *v.t.* to practise sabotage against (workman, employer). — *n.* **ratt'ening** (found earlier than verb). [Origin uncertain.]
ratter, rattery, ratting, etc. See **rat**[1].
rattle *rat'l*, *v.i.* to make a quick succession or alternation of short hard sounds: to move along rapidly with a rattle: to chatter briskly and emptily. — *v.t.* to cause to rattle: to assail with rattling (*Shak.*): to utter glibly, as by rote (often with *off*): to perform or push through to completion in a rapid, perfunctory, or noisy manner: to scold loudly (*obs.*): to fluster, disconcert, irritate (*slang*). — *n.* an instrument or toy for rattling: an instrument for making a whirring noise, formerly used by watchmen: a similar device used at merrymaking or other gatherings: a dice-box (*old slang*): a plant whose seeds rattle in the capsule — applied to two scrophulaceous plants, yellow-rattle or cock's-comb (*Rhinanthus crista-galli*) and red-rattle or marsh lousewort (*Pedicularis palustris*): the rings of a rattlesnake's tail: a vivacious prattler: the sound of rattling: the crackling of paper: a sound in the throat of a dying person: racket. — *ns.* **ratt'ler** a rattle: a coach (*old slang*): a rattlesnake (*coll.*): a telling blow (*coll.*): an excellent specimen of the kind (*coll.*); **ratt'ling.** — *adj.* making a rattle: smart, lively: strikingly good (*coll.*). — Also *adv.* — *adj.* **ratt'ly** making a rattling noise. — **ratt'lebag** a rattle or rattling apparatus: one who causes commotion (*Scot.*); **ratt'le-brain, -head, -pate** a shallow, voluble, volatile person. — *adjs.* **ratt'le-brained, -headed, -pated.** — **ratt'lesnake** a venomous American pit-viper (Crotalus) with rattling horny rings on the tail; **ratt'le-trap** a contemptuous name for any apparatus, equipment, finery, bric-à-brac: a rickety vehicle: the mouth (*slang*). [M.E. *ratelen*; cf. Ger. *rasseln*, Du. *ratelen*, to rattle; connection with O.E. plant names *hratele*, *hrætelwyrt* is questioned.]
rattlin(e), rattling. Same as **ratlin.**
ratton *rat'n*, (now *Northern*) *n.* a rat. [Fr. *raton*.]
ratty. See **rat**[1].
ratu *rä'toō*, *n.* a chief or petty prince in Indonesia and Fiji. — Also **Ra'too.**
raucle *rök'l*, (*Scot.*) *adj.* rough: vigorous: hale.
raucous *rö'kəs*, *adj.* hoarse, harsh. — *adv.* **rau'cously.** — *n.* **rau'cousness.** — *adj.* **raucid** (*rö'sid*; *Lamb*) raucous. [L. *raucus*, hoarse.]
raught *röt*, obs. or *arch. pa.t.* and *pa.p.* of **reach**[1,2] and **reck.**
raun (*Scott*). Same as **rawn**[1].
raunch[1] *rönsh*, (*Spens.*) *v.t.* Same as **race**[6].
raunch[2]. See **raunchy.**
raunchy *rön'chi, rän'chi*, (*slang*) *adj.* coarse, earthy: carelessly untidy, shabby. — *ns.* **raunch** coarseness, bawdiness; **raunch'iness.** [Origin unknown.]
raunge *rönj*, an obs. form of **range.**
Rauwolfia *rö-wol'fi-ə*, *n.* a tropical genus of apocynaceous trees and shrubs, of which *R. serpentina* and other species yield valuable drugs. [After the German botanist Leonhard *Rauwolf* (d. 1596).]
ravage *rav'ij*, *v.t.* and *v.i.* to lay waste: to destroy: to pillage. — *n.* devastation: ruin. — *n.* **rav'ager.** [Fr. *ravager* — *ravir*, to carry off by force — L. *rapĕre*.]
rave[1] *rāv*, *v.i.* to rage: to talk as if mad, delirious, or enraptured. — *v.t.* to utter wildly. — *n.* infatuation (*slang*): extravagant praise (*slang*). — *adj.* (*slang*) extravagantly enthusiastic: crazy. — *n.* **rā'ver** a person who raves: a lively, uninhibited person (*slang*). — *n.* and *adj.* **rā'ving.** — *adv.* **rā'vingly.** — **rave'-up** (*slang*) a lively celebration: a wild, uninhibited, thoroughly enjoyable party. — **raving mad** frenzied: very angry (*coll.*). [Perh. O.Fr. *raver*, which may be — L. *rabĕre*, to rave.]

rave[2] *rāv*, *n.* a side piece of a wagon. [Ety. obscure.]
rave[3] *rāv*, (*Scot.*) *pa.t.* of **rive.**
ravel *rav'l*, *v.t.* to entangle: to disentangle, untwist, unweave, unravel (usu. with *out*). — *v.i.* to become entangled: to be untwisted or unwoven: to search (with *into*; *obs.*): — *pr.p.* **rav'elling**; *pa.t.* and *pa.p.* **rav'elled.** — *n.* a tangle: a broken thread. — *ns.* **rav'elling** a ravelled out thread; **rav'elment.** [App. Du. *ravelen*.]
ravel bread *rav'l bred*, (*obs.* or *dial.*) wholemeal bread, intermediate between white and brown. — Also **ravelled bread.** [Orig. unknown.]
ravelin *rav'lin*, *n.* a detached work with two embankments raised before the counterscarp. [Fr.]
ravelment. See **ravel.**
raven[1] *rā'vn*, *n.* a large glossy black species of crow, *Corvus corax.* — *adj.* black as a raven. — **rā'ven('s)-bone** the gristle on the spoon of the brisket, the raven's perquisite in the chase; **rā'ven('s)-duck** fine hempen sail-cloth. [O.E. *hræfn*; O.N. *hrafn.*]
raven[2] *rav'in*, *n.* (same as **ravin** *n.*). — *v.t.* to take away by force (*obs.*): to devour hungrily or greedily. — *v.i.* to prey rapaciously: to be intensely hungry: to hunger intensely (*for*): to roam about hungrily after prey. — *n.* **rav'ener.** — *adjs.* **rav'enous, ravening** plundering: rapacious: voracious: (**ravenous**) intensely hungry. — *adv.* **rav'enously.** — *n.* **rav'enousness.** [O.Fr. *ravine*, plunder — L. *rapīna*, plunder.]
ravin also **raven, ravine** *rav'in*, *n.* rapine: preying: prey (*Spens., Milt*). — *adj.* (*Shak.*) ravening. — *v.t.* and *v.i.* same as **raven** *vb.* — *adj.* **rav'in'd** (*Shak.*) prob. sated, gorged. [Same as **raven**[2].]
ravine[1] *rə-vēn'*, *n.* a deep, narrow gorge. — *adj.* **ravined'** scored with ravines: trenched. [Fr., — L. *rapīna*, rapine, violence.]
ravine[2]. See **ravin.**
ravioli *rav-i-ōl'ē*, *n.* little edible pasta cases with savoury filling. [It., *pl.* of *raviòlo.*]
ravish *rav'ish*, *v.t.* to seize or carry away by violence: to abduct: to snatch away from sight or from the world: to rape: to enrapture. — *n.* **rav'isher.** — *adj.* **rav'ishing** delighting to rapture: transporting. — *adv.* **rav'ishingly.** — *n.* **rav'ishment.** [Fr. *ravir, ravissant* — L. *rapĕre*, to seize and carry off.]
raw *rö*, *adj.* not altered from its natural state: not cooked or dressed: unwrought: not prepared or manufactured: not refined: not corrected: not mixed: having the skin abraded or removed (also *fig.*): showing through the skin (*Spens.*): crude: hard, harsh, cruel: untrained: out of condition (*Spens.*): red and inflamed: immature: inexperienced: chilly and damp: naked: (of statistics, data for a computer, etc.) not yet checked, sorted, corrected, etc. — *n.* (with *the*) a skinned, sore, or sensitive place (usu. with *on*): the raw state: that which is raw. — *adj.* **raw'ish.** — *adv.* **raw'ly.** — *n.* **raw'ness.** — *adjs.* **raw'bone** (*Spens.*), **raw'boned** with little flesh on the bones: gaunt. — **raw'head (-and-blood'y-bones')** a bugbear or pair of bugbears to frighten children. — *adj.* **raw'hide** of untanned leather. — *n.* a rope or whip of untanned leather. — **raw material** material (often in its natural state) that serves as the starting-point of a manufacturing or technical process: that out of which something is made, or makable, or may develop (*fig.*); **raw silk** natural untreated silk threads: fabric made from these. — **a raw deal** harsh, inequitable treatment; **in the raw** in its natural state: naked. [O.E. *hrēaw*; Du. *rauw*, O.N. *hrār*, Ger. *roh.*]
rawing. See **rowen.**
rawn[1], **raun** *rön*, (*Scot.*) *n.* fish-roe: a female fish. [Cf. Dan. *ravn*, roe.]
rawn[2]. See **rowen.**
rax *raks*, (*Scot.*) *v.t.* to stretch: to strain: to reach: to reach out, hand. — *v.i.* to stretch: to reach out. — *n.* a stretch: a strain. [O.E. *raxan.*]
ray[1] *rā*, *n.* array (*obs.*). — *v.t.* to array (*obs.*): to dress (*obs.*): to defile, dirty (*Shak.*). [**array.**]
ray[2] *rā*, *n.* a line along which light or other energy, or a stream of particles, is propagated: a narrow beam: a

gleam of intellectual light: a look or glance: a radiating line or part: the radially extended fringing outer part of an inflorescence: a supporting spine in a fin. — *v.t.* to radiate: to furnish with rays. — *v.i.* to radiate. — *adjs.* **rayed; ray'less.** — *n.* **ray'let** a small ray. — **ray flower, floret** any of the small flowers radiating out from the margin of the flower head of certain composite plants; **ray'-fungus** a bacterium (*Actinomyces*) that forms radiating threads, some species pathogenic. – **ray of sunshine** a happy person, one who cheers up others. [O.Fr. *rais* (accus. *rai*) — L. *radius*, a rod.]
ray³ *rā*, *n.* a skate, thornback, torpedo, or kindred flat-bodied elasmobranch fish. [Fr. *raie* — L. *raia*.]
ray⁴. Same as **re¹.**
rayah *rī'a*, *n.* a non-Muslim subject of Turkey. [Ar. *ra'īyah* — *ra'ā*, to pasture.]
rayle, rayne. Obs. or Spens. spellings of **rail²,⁴, rain², reign.**
Rayleigh disc *rā'lē disk*, a small light disc hung by a fine thread at an angle to a progessive sound-wave — its deflection is used to measure the intensity of the sound. [After J. W. Strutt, Lord *Rayleigh*, (1842–1919), English physicist.]
raylet, etc. See **ray².**
rayon *rā'on*, *n.* a ray (*Spens.*): artificial silk (see **silk**). [Fr. *rayon*, ray.]
raze¹ *rāz*, (*Shak.*) *n.* Same as **race³.**
raze², rase *rāz*, *v.t.* to graze: to scrap: to erase: to slash, cut into ornamental devices: to lay level with the ground. — *adj.* **razed, rased.** [Fr. *raser* — L. *rādēre, rāsum*, to scrape.]
razee *rā-zē'*, *n.* a ship cut down by reducing the number of decks. — *v.t.* to remove the upper deck(s) of. [Fr. *rasé*, cut down.]
razmataz. See **raz(z)mataz(z).**
razor *rā'zor*, *n.* a keen-edged implement for shaving. — *adj.* (*fig.*) sharp, keen, precise. — *adj.* **rā'zorable** (*Shak.*) fit to be shaved. — **rā'zor-back** a sharp ridge: a rorqual: a sharp-backed pig. — *adj.* **sharply ridged.** — **rā'zor-bill** a species of auk, with compressed bill; **rā'zor-cut** a haircut done with a razor. — *v.t.* **rā'zor-cut'.** — **rā'zor-blade; rā'zor-edge** a very fine sharp edge, as that on which a balance swings: a critically balanced situation; **rā'zor-fish, -clam** a lamellibranch mollusc (Solen), with shell like a razor handle; **rā'zor-shell** its shell, or the animal itself; **rā'zor-strop.** — **Occam's razor** see **Occamism.** [O.Fr. *rasour*; see **raze²**.]
razure. Same as **rasure.**
razz *raz*, *n.* raspberry in slang sense. — *v.t.* and *v.i.* to jeer (at).
razzamatazz. See **raz(z)mataz(z).**
razzia *raz'ya*, *n.* a pillaging incursion. [Fr., — Algerian Ar. *ghāzīah*.]
razzle-dazzle *raz'l-daz'l*, (*slang*) *n.* a rowdy frolic or spree: dazzling show, confusion, etc. — Also **razz'le.** — **on the razzle** having a spree. [App. from **dazzle.**]
raz(z)mataz(z) *raz-mə-taz'*, **razzamatazz** *raz-ə-mə-taz'*, *ns. to-do, hullabaloo: razzle-dazzle.
re¹ *rā*, (*mus.*) *n.* the second note of the scale in sol-fa notation — also anglicised in spelling as **ray.** [See **Aretinian.**]
re² *rē*, (*commercial jargon*) *prep.* concerning, with reference to. [L. *in rē* (abl. of *rēs*, thing), in the matter.]
re- *rē-*, *pfx.* again: again and in a different way — used so freely, esp. with verbs, that it is impossible to give a full list. [L.]
're *r*, a shortened form of **are.**
reach¹ *rēch*, *v.t.* to stretch forth, hold out: to hand, pass: to deal, strike (*arch.*): to succeed in touching or getting: to arrive at: to extend to: to attain to (*usu.* with *for* or *after*): to get at: to take, snatch, seize (*obs.*): to stretch, lengthen out (*obs.*). — *v.i.* to stretch out the hand: to extend: to amount: to attain: to succeed in going or coming: — *pa.t.* and *pa.p.* **reached,** (*obs.*) **raught** (*röt*).

— *n.* act or power of reaching: extent of stretch: range, scope: artifice (*obs.*): a stretch or portion between defined limits, as of a stream between bends: the distance traversed between tacks (*naut.*): a bay (*obs.*). — *adj.* **reach'able.** — *n.* **reach'er.** — *p.adj.* **reach'ing.** — *adjs.* **reach'less** unattainable; **reach'-me-down** ready-made. — *n.* (often in *pl.*) ready-made or second-hand attire: trousers. [O.E. *rǣcan* (pa.t. *rǣhte, rāhte*; pa.p. *gerǣht*); Ger. *reichen*, to reach.]
reach² *rēch*. Same as **retch¹.**
react¹ *rē'akt'*, *v.t.* to act a second, etc., time.
react² *ri-akt'*, *v.i.* to return an impulse in the opposite direction: to act in return: to act with mutual effect: to act in resistance: to swing back in the opposite direction: to respond to a stimulus: to undergo chemical change produced by a reagent: loosely, to act, behave: of share prices, to fall sharply after a rise. — *ns.* **reac'tance** (*elect.*) the component of impedance due to inductance or capacitance; **reac'tant** (*chem.*) a substance taking part in a reaction; **reac'tion** action resisting other action: mutual action: an action or change in an opposite direction: backward tendency from revolution, reform, or progress: response to stimulus: the chemical action of a reagent: a physical or mental effect caused by medicines, drugs, etc.: a transformation within the nucleus of an atom: acidity or alkalinity: loosely, feeling or thought aroused by, in response to, a statement, situation, person, etc. — *adj.* **reac'tional.** — *ns.* **reac'tionarism; reac'tionarist.** — *adj.* **reac'tionary** of or favouring reaction esp., against revolution, reform, etc. — *n.* one who attempts to revert to past political conditions. — *n.* and *adj.* **reac'tionist** reactionary. — *adj.* **reac'tive** of, pertaining to, reaction: readily acted upon or responsive to stimulus: produced by emotional stress: pertaining to, or having, a reactance. — *adv.* **reac'tively.** — *ns.* **reac'tiveness, reactiv'ity; reac'tor** one who or that which undergoes a reaction: a device which introduces reactance into an electric circuit: a container in which a chemical reaction takes place: a nuclear reactor (see **nucleus).** — **reaction time** the interval between stimulus and reaction. — **reaction turbine** a turbine in which the fluid expands progressively in passing alternate rows of fixed and moving blades, the kinetic energy continuously developed being absorbed by the latter. [L.L. *reagēre, -actum* — *agĕre*, to do.]
reactivate *rē-ak'ti-vāt, v.t.* to restore to an activated state. — *n.* **reactivā'tion.** [Pfx. **re-.**]
reactive. See under **react.**
read¹ *rēd, v.t.* to advise (*arch.*; see **rede**): to make out: to interpret: to expound: to make known (*Spens.*): to declare: to name (*Spens.*): to solve: to look at and comprehend the meaning of written or printed words in: to understand as by interpretation of signs: to collect the meaning of: to go over progressively with silent understanding of symbols or with utterance aloud of words or performance of notes: to accept or offer as that which the writer intended: to learn from written or printed matter: to find recorded: to observe the indication of: to register, indicate: to teach, lecture on: to study: to impute by inference (as to read a meaning into): to retrieve (data) from a storage device (*comput.*). — *v.i.* to perform the act of reading: to practice much reading: to study: to find mention: to give the reader an impression: to endure the test of reading: to deliver lectures: to have a certain wording: — *pa.t.* and *pa.p.* **read** (*red*). — *n.* **read** (*rēd*) a spell of reading: reading-matter: an opportunity of reading (*Scot.*): counsel, a saying, an interpretation (*Spens.*). — *adj.* **read** (*red*) versed in books: learned. — *ns.* **readabil'ity** (*rēd-*), **read'ableness.** — *adj.* **read'able** legible: easy to read: interesting without being of highest quality. — *adv.* **read'ably.** — *ns.* **read'er** one who reads

---

rēabsorb' *v.t.*   **rēaccus'tom** *v.t.*   **rēacquire'** *v.t.*
rēabsorp'tion *n.*   **rēacquaint'** *v.t.*   **rēac'tuate** *v.t.*
rēacclī'matise, -ize *v.t.* and *v.i.*   **rēacquaint'ance** *n.*   **rēadapt'** *v.t.*

or reads much: one who reads prayers in church: a lecturer, esp. a higher grade of university lecturer: a proof-corrector: one who reads and reports on MSS. for a publisher: a reading-book: a pocket-book (*thieves' cant*): a device which projects a large image of a piece of microfilm on to a screen, for reading: a document reader (*comput.*); **read′ership** the post of reader in a university: the total number of readers (of a newspaper, etc.). — *adj.* **read′ing** addicted to reading. — *n.* the action of the verb *read:* perusal: study of books: public or formal recital, esp. of a bill before Parliament (see **first, second** and **third reading** below): the actual word or words that may be read in a passage of a text: the indication that can be read off from an instrument: matter for reading: lettering: an interpretation: a performer's conception of the meaning, rendering. — **read′-in** input of data to a computer or storage device; **reading age** reading ability calculated as equivalent to the average ability at a certain age; **read′ing-book** a book of exercises in reading; **read′ing-boy** (*print.*; *obs.*) a reader's assistant; **read′ing-desk** a desk for holding a book or paper while it is read: a lectern;**read′ing-lamp** a lamp for reading by; **read′ing-machine** a reader for microfilm: a document reader (*comput.*); **reading matter** printed material, e.g. books, magazines; **read′ing-room** a room for consultation, study, or investigation of books in a library: a room with papers, periodicals, etc., resorted to for reading: a proof-readers' room. — *adj.* **read′-on′ly** referring to a type of storage device whose contents have been built in and cannot be altered by programming. — **read′-out** output unit of a computer: the retrieval of data from a computer: data from a computer, printed, or registered on magnetic tape or punched paper tape, or displayed on a screen: data from a radio transmitter. — **first, second** and **third reading** the three successive formal readings of a bill before parliament, when (in Britain) it is introduced, discussed in general, and reported on by a committee; **read between the lines** to detect a meaning not expressed; **read into** to find in a person's writing, words, behaviour, etc. (meanings which are not overtly stated and may not have been intended); **read off** to take as a reading from an instrument; **read (oneself) in** (Church of England) to enter into possession of a benefice by reading the Thirty-nine Articles; **read out** to read aloud: to retrieve data from a computer, etc.; **read someone's mind** to guess accurately what someone is thinking; **read up** to amass knowledge of by reading; **read-write head** (*comput.*) in a disc drive, a head which can retrieve data and also record it; **read-write memory** (*comput.*) one which allows retrieval and input of data. [O.E. *rǣdan* to discern, read — *rǣd,* counsel.]

read² *rēd, n.* a ruminant's fourth stomach, the abomasum. [O.E. *read.*]

ready *red′i, adj.* prepared: dressed, attired (*obs.*): willing: inclined: liable: dexterous: prompt: quick: handy: at hand: immediately available: direct. — *adv.* readily (now only in *compar.* and *superl.,* **read′ier, read′iest**). — *n.* (usu. with *the*) the position of a firearm ready to be fired: ready money (*slang;* also in *pl.*): time of, or for, making ready (*coll.*). — *v.t.* to make (usu. oneself) ready. — *adv.* **read′ily.** — *n.* **read′iness.** — **ready-, ready-to-** in composition, ready to, as in **read′y-mix, read′y-to-eat′, read′y-to-sew′ read′y-to-wear′,** etc. — *adj.* **read′y-made** made before sale, not made to order. — *n.* a ready-made article, esp. a garment. — **ready money** money ready at hand: cash. — *adjs.* **read′y-money** paying, or for payment, in money on the spot; **read′y-moneyed, -monied** having, or of the nature of, ready money. — **ready reckoner** a book of tables giving the value of so many things at so much each, and

interest on any sum of money from a day upwards. — *adj.* **read′y-witted.** — **at the ready** of a firearm, ready to be fired: prepared for instant action; **make, get, ready** to dress, put on one's clothes (*obs.*): to prepare (esp. a forme for printing); **ready, steady, go!** words used by the starter of a race to the competitors. [O.E. (*ge*)-*rǣde*; cf. Ger. *bereit.*]

reaedify. Same as **re-edify.**

reagent *rē-ā′jənt, n.* a substance with characteristic reactions, used as a chemical test. — *n.* **reā′gency.** [See **react.**]

reak¹, reik *rēk,* (*obs.*) *n.* a prank — usu. in *pl.* **reaks, rex** (*reks*) sometimes with an allusion to L. *rēx,* king. [Origin obscure.]

reak². Obs. spelling of **reck.**

real¹ *rē′əl, ri′, adj.* actually existing: not counterfeit or assumed: true: genuine: sincere: authentic: pertaining to things fixed, as lands or houses (*law*). — *adv.* (*coll., U.S., Scot.*) really, quite, veritably. — *n.* a real thing: that which is real: a realist. — *n. pl.* **realia** (*rē-ā′li-ə;* L.L. neuter *pl.* of *realis,* real) realities: objects etc., used as teaching aids to relate classroom work to real life. — *adj.* **reali′sable, -z-** (or *rē′*). — *n.* **realisā′tion, -z-** (or *-li-*). — *v.t.* **rē′alise, -ize** to make real, or as if real: to bring into being or act: to accomplish: to convert into real property or money: to obtain, as a possession: to feel strongly: to comprehend completely: to bring home to one's own experience: to provide a detailed artistic version of music where the composer has (as he often did in the 17th and 18th centuries) left much to be filled in by the performer: to provide the drawings for an animated cartoon. — *n.* **rē′aliser, -z-.** — *adj.* **rē′alising, -z-.** — *ns.* **rē′alism** the mediaeval doctrine that general terms stand for real existences — opp. to *nominalism:* the doctrine that in external perception the objects immediately known are real existences: the tendency to look to, to accept, or to represent things as they really are (often in their most ignoble aspect): literalness and precision of detail, with the effect of reality: the taking of a practical view in human problems; **rē′alist.** — *adj.* **realist′ic** pertaining to the realists or to realism: life-like. — *adv.* **realist′ically.** — *n.* **reality** (*ri-al′i-ti,* or *rē-*) the state or fact of being real: that which is real and not imaginary: truth: verity: the fixed permanent nature of real property (*law*). — *adv.* **rē′ally** in reality: actually: in truth. — *ns.* **rē′alness; re′altie** (*Milt.*) sincerity, honesty; **Realtor®, rē′altor** (*U.S.,* irregularly formed) an agent for the buying and selling of landed property, esp. one who is a member of the National Association of Real Estate Boards; **rē′alty** (*law*) land, with houses, trees, minerals, etc., thereon: the ownership of, or property in, lands — also **real estate.** — **real ale, beer** beer which continues to ferment and mature in the cask after brewing. — *adj.* **re′al-estate′** concerned with or dealing in property in land. — **real image** see **image; real life** everyday life as lived by ordinary people, opp. to glamorous fictional life; **real number** any rational or irrational number; **real presence** see **presence; real school** (Ger. *Realschule, rā-äl′shŏ̄o′lə*) a German school teaching modern languages, science, and technical subjects, not classics — highest grade being the **real gymnasium** (Ger. *Realgymnasium, rā-äl′gimnä′ziŏ̄om*), opp. to the *gymnasium* proper, or classical school. — *adj.* **real′time** (*comput.*) of or relating to a system in which the processing of data occurs as it is generated. — **for real** (*slang*) in reality: intended to be carried out or put into effect; **the real Mackay, McCoy** the genuine article, esp. good whisky (the expression has been variously explained); **the real thing** the genuine thing, not an imitation or a cheap substitute. [L.L. *reālis* — L. *rēs,* a thing.]

rēadaptā′tion *n.*
rēaddress′ *v.t.*
rēadjust′ *v.t.*
rēadjust′ment *n.*

rēadmiss′ion *n.*
rēadmit′ *v.t.*
rēadmitt′ance *n.*
rēadopt′ *v.t.*

rēadop′tion *n.*
rēadvance′ *n., v.t., v.i.*
rēad′vertise, -ize *v.t.* and *v.i.*
rēadver′tisement, -ze- *n.*

fāte; fär; hûr; mīne; mōte; för; mūte; mōͻn; fŏot; dhen (then); el′ə-mənt (element)

real² *rē'əl*, (*obs.*) *adj.* royal. — *n.* **re'alty** (*obs.*) royalty. — **real tennis** royal tennis, or tennis properly so called, not lawn-tennis (also **court tennis**). [O.Fr., — L. *rēgālis*, royal.]

real³ *rā-äl'*, *rē'əl*, *n.* a quarter of a peseta: a former Spanish coin, one-eighth of a dollar. See also **reis²**. — [Sp., — L. *rēgālis*, royal.]

realgar *ri-al'gär*, *-gər*, *n.* a bright red monoclinic mineral, arsenic monosulphide. [Mediaeval L. — Ar. *rahj-al-ghār*, powder of the mine or cave.]

realia. See **real¹**.

realign *rē-ə-līn'*, *v.t.* to align afresh: to group or divide on a new basis. — *n.* **realign'ment.** [Pfx. **re-**.]

realise, etc. See **real¹**.

really¹ *rē-ə-lī'*, (*obs.*) *v.t.* to rally: (*Spens.* **reallie**) to form anew. [Obs. Fr. *realier* = *rallier*; see **rally¹**.]

really². See **real¹**.

realm *relm*, obs. **reame** *rēm*, *ns.* a kingdom: a domain, province, region: a field of study or sphere of action. — *adj.* **realm'less.** [O.Fr. *realme* — hypothetical L.L. *rēgālimen* — L. *rēgālis*, royal.]

realpolitik *rā-äl'po-lē-tēk'*, *n.* practical politics based on the realities and necessities of life, rather than moral or ethical ideas. [Ger.]

realtie, etc. See **real¹**. **realty**. See **real¹,²**.

ream¹ *rēm*, *n.* 20 quires: (in *pl.*) a large quantity (*coll.*). — **printer's ream** 516 sheets of paper. [Ar. *rizmah*, a bundle.]

ream² *rēm*, (*Scot.*) *n.* cream: froth. — *v.i.* to cream: to froth: to overflow. — *v.t.* to skim. — *adjs.* **ream'ing** (*Scot.*) foaming: brimming; **ream'y** (*Scot.*). [O.E. *rēam*.]

ream³ *rēm*, *v.t.* to enlarge the bore of. — *n.* **ream'er** a rotating instrument for enlarging, shaping, or finishing a bore. — **ream'ing-bit.** [Apparently O.E. *rȳman*, to open up, to make room — *rūm*, room.]

reame *rēm*, (*Spens.*, etc.) *n.* See **realm**.

rean. See **rhine**.

reanimate *rē-an'i-māt*, *v.t.* to restore to life: to infuse new life or spirit into. — *v.i.* to revive. — *n.* **reanimā'tion.** [Pfx. **re-**.]

reanswer *rē-än'sər*, (*Shak.*) *v.t.* to be equivalent to. [Pfx. **re-**.]

reap *rēp*, *v.t.* to cut down, as grain: to clear by cutting a crop: to derive as an advantage or reward. — *n.* **reap'er** one who reaps: a reaping-machine. — **reap'ing-hook** a sickle; **reap'ing-machine** a machine for cutting grain; **reap'-silver** money paid in commutation for service in reaping. — **the grim reaper** death. [O.E. *rīpan* or *ripan*.]

rear¹ *rēr*, *n.* the back or hindmost part or position, especially of an army or fleet: a position behind: the buttocks (*euph.*): a latrine (*slang*). — *adj.* placed behind: hinder. — *v.t.* (*Bunyan*) to attack in the rear. — *adjs.* **rear'most** last of all; **rear'ward, rere'ward** in or toward the rear. — *adv.* backward: at the back. — *n.* (*arch.*) rear: rear-guard (partly from A.Fr. *rerewarde*). — **rear-ad'miral** an officer next below a vice-admiral — orig. one in command of the rear; **rear'-arch, -dvos, -dos, -dorter** see **rere-**; **rear'-guard** (O.Fr. *rereguarde*) the rear of an army: a body of troops protecting it; **rear'-lamp, -light** a light carried at the back of a vehicle; **rear'-rank; rear-view mirror** a mirror that shows what is behind a vehicle. — **bring up the rear** to come last (in a procession, etc.). [Aphetic for **arrear**; also partly from O.Fr. *rere* (Fr. *arrière*).]

rear² *rēr*, *v.t.* to raise, cause or help to rise: to set up: to originate, to bring into being (*Spens.*): to erect: to build up: to lift up or off: to hold up: to take up: to take away (*Spens.*): to bring up: to breed and foster: to rouse: to stir up: to dislodge from covert. — *v.i.* to rise on the hind-legs. — *n.* **rear'er.** — **rear'horse** a praying

insect (from its attitude). [O.E. *rǣran*, to raise, causative of *rīsan*, to rise.]

rear³ *rēr*, *adj.* (now *obs.* or *dial.*; see **rare²**) lightly cooked — orig. applied to eggs. — *adjs.* **rear'-boiled; rear'-roast'ed.** [O.E. *hrēr*.]

rear⁴. Same as **rare³**.

rearmouse. Same as **reremouse**.

reascend *rē-ə-send'*, *v.t.* and *v.i.* to ascend again: to go back up: to climb again. — *ns.* **rēascen'sion, rēascent'.** [Pfx. **re-**.]

reason *rē'zn*, *n.* ground, support, or justification of an act or belief: a premise, esp. when placed after its conclusion: a motive or inducement: an underlying explanatory principle: a cause: the mind's power of drawing conclusions and determining right and truth: the exercise of this power: sanity: conformity to what is fairly to be expected or called for: moderation: fair treatment, e.g. satisfaction by a duel, or doing one's fair share in drinking: a remark, a sententious saying (*Shak.*): proportion (*Spens.*). — *v.i.* to exercise the faculty of reason: to deduce inferences from premises: to argue: to debate: to converse (*Shak.*). — *v.t.* to examine or discuss: to debate: to think out: to set forth logically: to bring by reasoning. — *adj.* **rea'sonable** endowed with reason: rational: acting according to reason: agreeable to reason: just: not excessive: not expensive: moderate. — *adv.* (now *illit.*) reasonably. — *n.* **rea'sonableness.** — *adv.* **rea'sonably.** — *adj.* **rea'soned** argued out. — *ns.* **rea'soner; rea'soning.** — *adj.* **rea'sonless.** — **by reason of** on account of: in consequence of; **do someone reason** (*obs.*) to give someone the satisfaction of a duel: to drink without shirking; **it stands to reason** it is obvious, logical; **listen to reason** listen to, and take heed of, the reasonable explanation, course of action, etc.; **no reason but** (*Shak.*) no reason for it being otherwise, hence, no possible alternative; **principle of sufficient reason** that nothing happens without a sufficient reason why it should be as it is and not otherwise; **pure reason** reason absolutely independent of experience; **(with)in reason** within the bounds of what is possible, sensible, etc. [Fr. *raison* — L. *ratiō, -ōnis* — *rērī, rătus*, to think.]

reassure *rē-ə-shōōr'*, *v.t.* to assure anew: to reinsure: to give confidence to: to confirm. — *ns.* **reassur'ance; reassur'er.** — *adj.* **reassur'ing.** — *adv.* **reassur'ingly.** [Pfx. **re-**.]

reast¹, reest, reist *rēst*, *v.i.* to become rancid (esp. of bacon). — *n.* **reast'iness**, etc. — *adj.* **reast'y**, etc. [ME. *rest, reest*, rancid.]

reast². Same as **reest²**.

reata, riata *rē-ä'tä*, *n.* a lariat. [Sp.]

reate *rēt*, *n.* water-crowfoot. [Origin obscure.]

Réaumur *rā-ō-mür*, *adj.* of a thermometer or thermometer scale, having the freezing-point of water marked 0° and boiling-point 80°. [From the French physicist, R. A. F. de *Réaumur* (1683–1757), who introduced the scale.]

reave, also (*orig. Scot.*) **reive** *rēv*, *v.t.* and *v.i.* to plunder: to rob: — *pa.t.* and *pa.p.* **reft** (*obs.* **raft**). — *n.* **reav'er, reiv'er.** [O.E. *rēafian*, to rob; cf. Ger. *rauben*, to rob.]

reback *rē-bak'*, *v.t.* to put a new back on. [Pfx. **re-**.]

re-bar *rē'bär*, *n.* a steel bar in reinforced concrete. [*re-*inforcing *bar*.]

rebarbative *ri-bärb'ə-tiv*, *adj.* repellent. [Fr. *rébarbatif* — *barbe*, beard.]

rebate¹ *ri-bāt'*, *v.t.* to reduce: to abate: to dull: to blunt: to repay a part of: to diminish by removal of a projection (*her.*). — *n.* (or *rē'*) discount: repayment or drawback. — *ns.* **rebāte'ment** abatement: reduction: discount: a narrowing (*B.*); **re'bater.** [Fr. *rabattre*, to beat back — pfx. *re-* and *abattre*, to abate.]

rebate² *rē'bāt, rab'it*. Same as **rabbet**.

---

rēadvise' *v.t., v.i.*	**rēafforestā'tion** *n.*	**reallot'ment** *n.*
rēaffirm' *v.t.*	**rēall'ocate** *v.t.*	**rē-ally'** *v.t.* and *v.i.*
rēaffirmātion *n.*	**rēallocā'tion** *n.*	**rē-al'ter** *v.t.*
rēaffor'est *v.t.*	**rēallot'** *v.t.*	**rē-alterā'tion** *n.*

For other sounds see detailed chart of pronunciation.

rebato rə-bä'tō, (*Shak.*) *n.* a stiff collar or support for a ruff: — *pl.* **reba'toes.** — Also **reba'ter, raba'to** (*pl.* **raba'toes**). [Fr. *rabat.*]

rebec. See **rebeck.**

Rebecca ri-bek'ə, *n.* a leader of those who demolished toll-gates in the **Rebecca riots** in Wales from 1843. — *ns.* **Rebecc'aism; Rebecc'aite.** [Alluding to Gen. xxiv. 60.]

rebecca-eureka ri-bek'ə-ū-rē'kə, *n.* a secondary-radar system in which the interrogating installation is in an aircraft and the fixed beacon responder on the ground.

rebeck, rebec rē'bek, *n.* a mediaeval instrument of the viol class shaped like a mandoline, usu. with three strings. [O.Fr. *rebec* — Ar. *rebāb, rabāb* (change of ending unexplained); other forms occur in European languages, including, in ME. *ribibe, ribible.*]

rebel reb'(ə)l, *n.* one who rebels: one who resents and resists authority or grievous conditions: one who refuses to conform to the generally accepted modes of behaviour, dress, etc. — *adj.* **rebellious.** — *v.i.* (ri-bel') to renounce the authority of the laws and government, or to take up arms and openly oppose them: to oppose any authority: to revolt: to offer opposition: to feel repugnance: — *pr.p.* **rebell'ing;** *pa.t.* and *pa.p.* **rebelled'.** — *ns.* **reb'eldom; rebell'er** (now *rare*) — *adv.* **reb'el-like** (*Shak*). — *n.* **rebell'ion** (-yən) act of rebelling: revolt. — *adj.* **rebell'ious** engaged in rebellion: characteristic of a rebel or rebellion: inclined to rebel: refractory. — *adv.* **rebell'iously.** — *n.* **rebell'iousness.** [Fr. *rebelle* — L. *rebellis,* insurgent — pfx. *re-, bellum,* war.]

rebellow rē-bel'ō, (*Spens.*) *v.i.* to bellow in return: to echo back a loud noise. [Pfx. **re-**].

rebid rē-bid', *v.t.* and *v.i.* to bid again, esp. (*bridge*) on the same suit as a previous bid. — *n.* a renewed bid, esp. on one's former suit. [Pfx. **re-**.]

rebind rē'bīnd', *v.t.* to give a new binding to: to bind again: — *p. adj.* **rē'bound'.** [Pfx. **re-**.]

rebirth rē-bûrth', *n.* reincarnation: revival of, e.g. an interest: spiritual renewal. — **rebirth'ing** a type of psychotherapy involving the reliving of the experience of being reborn, in order to release anxieties, etc. [Pfx. **re-**.]

rebite rē-bīt', *v.t.* to freshen (a plate) by a new application of acid. [Pfx. **re-**.]

reboant reb'ō-ənt, (*poet.*) *adj.* rebellowing: loudly resounding. — *n.* **reboā'tion.** [L. *reboāns, -antis,* pr.p. of *reboāre* — *re,* again, *boāre,* to cry aloud.]

rebore rē'bōr', -bör', *v.t.* to bore again (the cylinder of a car engine) so as to clear it. — Also *n.* [Pfx. **re-**.]

reborn rē-börn', *p. adj.* born again (q.v.).

rebound[1]. See **rebind.**

rebound[2] ri-bownd', *v.i.* to bound back from collision: to spring back (*lit.* and *fig.*): to re-echo: to recover quickly after a setback. — *v.t.* to throw back: to re-echo. — *n.* (rē') act of rebounding. — **on the rebound** after bouncing: while reacting against a setback, disappointment, etc. [Fr. *rebondir;* see **bound**[3].]

rebuff ri-buf', *n.* a blowing back (*Milt.*): a sudden check: unexpected refusal: snub. — *v.t.* to beat back: to check: to repulse: to snub. [O.Fr. *rebuffe* — It *ribuffo,* a reproof — It. *ri-*(= L. *re-*), back, *buffo,* puff.]

rebuke ri-būk', *v.t.* to check, restrain, beat back (*obs.*): to put to shame (*arch.*): to reprove sternly. — *n.* a check (*obs.*): a putting to shame (*obs.*): a reproach: stern reproof, reprimand. — *adjs.* **rebuk'able; rebuke'-ful.** — *adv.* **rebuke'fully.** — *n.* **rebuk'er.** — *adv.* **rebuk'-ingly.** [A.Fr. *rebuker* (O.Fr. *rebucher*) — pfx. *re-, bucher,* to strike.]

rebus rē'bəs, *n.* an enigmatical representation of a word or name by pictures punningly representing parts of the word, as in a puzzle or a coat of arms: such a puzzle: — *pl.* **re'buses.** [L. *rēbus,* by things, abl. pl. of *rēs,* thing.]

rebut ri-but', *v.t.* to drive back: to repel: to meet in argument or proof: to refute. — *v.i.* to recoil (*Spens.*): to return an answer (*law*): — *pr.p.* **rebutt'ing;** *pa.t.* and *pa.p.* **rebutt'ed.** — *n.* **rebut'ment.** — *adj.* **rebutt'able.** — *ns.* **rebutt'al; rebutt'er** a person, or an argument, that rebuts: a defendant's reply to a plaintiff's surrejoinder (*law*). [O.Fr. *rebo(u)ter, rebuter,* to repulse; see **butt**[1].]

recal. See **recall.**

recalcitrate ri-kal'si-trāt, *v.t.* and *v.i.* to kick back. — *v.i.* to have repugnance: to be refractory. — *n.* **recal'-citrance** repugnance or opposition: refractoriness. — *adj.* **recal'citrant** refractory: obstinate in opposition. — *n.* a recalcitrant person. — *n.* **recalcitrā'tion.** [L. *recalcitrāre,* to kick back — *calx, calcis,* the heel.]

recalesce rē-kal-es', *v.i.* to show anew a state of glowing heat. — *n.* **recales'cence** (*phys.*) the renewed glowing of iron at a certain stage of cooling from white-heat. — *adj.* **recales'cent.** [L. *re-,* again, *calēscĕre,* to grow hot.]

recall (*rarely* **recal**) ri-köl', *v.t.* to call back: to command to return: to bring back as by a summons: to remove from office by vote (*U.S.*): to revoke: to call back to mind. — *n.* act, power, or possibility of recalling or of revoking: a signal or order to return: the calling back of a performer to the stage or platform by applause: a right of electors to dismiss an official by a vote (*U.S.*): remembrance of things learned or experienced, esp. in the phrase **total recall,** (power of) remembering accurately in full detail. — *adj.* **recall'-able** capable of being recalled. — *n.* **recal(l)'ment.** [Pfx. **re-**.]

recant ri-kant', *v.t.* to retract. — *v.i.* to revoke a former declaration: to unsay what has been said, esp. to declare one's renunciation of one's former religious belief. — *ns.* **recantā'tion** (rē-); **recant'er** (ri-). [L. *recantāre,* to revoke — *cantāre,* to sing, to charm.]

recap rē-kap'. Short for **recapitulate** and **recapitulation.**

recapitalise, -ize rē-kap'i-təl-īz, *v.t.* to supply again with capital. — *n.* **rēcapitalisā'tion, -z-.** [Pfx. **re-**.]

recapitulate rē-kə-pit'ū-lāt, *v.t.* to go over again the chief points of: to go through in one's own life-history the stages of. — *n.* **recapitulā'tion** act of recapitulating: summing up: the reproduction, in the developmental stages of an individual embryo, in the evolutionary stages in the life history of the race or type (*biol.*): the final repetition of the subjects in sonata form after development. — *adjs.* **recapit'ulātive; recapit'ulatory** repeating again: of the nature of a recapitulation. [L. *recapitulāre, -ātum* — *re-,* again, *capitulum,* heading, chapter — *caput,* head.]

recaption rē-kap'shən, *n.* reprisal: taking back by peaceable means goods, wife, or children from one who has no right to detain them (*law*). [Pfx. **re-**.]

recapture rē-kap'chər, *v.t.* to capture back, as a prize from a captor: to recover by effort. — *n.* act of retaking: recovery: a thing recaptured. — *ns.* **recap'tor; recap'-turer.** [Pfx. **re-**.]

recast rē-käst', *v.t.* to cast or mould anew: to reconstruct: to compute anew: to reassign parts in a theatrical production: to give (an actor) a different part: — *pa.t.* and *pa.p.* **recast'.** — *n.* (rē'käst, rē-käst') shaping anew: that which has been shaped anew. [Pfx. **re-**.]

recce rek'i, (*mil. slang*) *n.* reconnaissance: — *pl.* **recc'es.** — Also (esp. *airforce*) **recc'ō:** — *pl.* **recc'ōs.** — *v.t.* and *v.i.* (**recce**) to reconnoitre: — *pr.p.* **recc'eing;** *pa.t.* and *pa.p.* **recc'ed** or **recc'eed.**

reccy rek'i, (*mil. slang*) *n.* another spelling of **recce.** — Also *v.t.* and *v.i.:* — *pr.p.* **recc'ying;** *pa.t.* and *pa.p.* **recc'ied.**

rēamend' *v.t.*	**rēappar'el** *v.t.*	**rēapply'** *v.i.*
rēamend'ment *n.*	**rēappear'** *v.i.*	**rēappoint'** *v.t.*
rēannex' *v.t.*	**rēappear'ance** *n.*	**rēappoint'ment** *n.*
rēannexā'tion *n.*	**rēapplicā'tion** *n.*	**rēappor'tion** *v.t.*

recede *ri-sēd'*, *v.i.* to go back, go farther off, become more distant (*lit.* and *fig.*): to go, draw, back (from; *lit.* and *fig.*): to differ (from; *arch.*): to grow less, decline: to bend or slope backward: to give up a claim, renounce a promise, etc. — *adj.* **reced'ing.** [L. *recēdĕre, recēssum* — *re-*, back, *cēdĕre*, to go, yield.]

re-cede, recede *rē'sēd'*, *v.t.* to cede again or back. [Pfx. **re-.**]

receipt *ri-sēt'*, *n.* receiving: place of receiving: capacity (*obs.*): a written acknowledgment of anything received: that which is received: a recipe, esp. in cookery (*arch.*): anything prepared after a recipe (*obs.*). — *v.t.* to mark as paid: to give a receipt for (usu. *U.S.*). [O.Fr. *receite, recete* (Fr. *recette*) — L. *recepta*, fem. pa.p. of *recipĕre*, to receive, with *p* restored after L.]

receive *ri-sēv'*, *v.t.* to take, get, or catch, usu. more or less passively: to have given or delivered to one: to experience: to take in or on: to admit: to accept: to meet or welcome on entrance: to harbour: to await in resistance: to experience, or learn of, and react towards: to accept as authority or as truth: to take into the body: to buy, deal in, (stolen goods): to be acted upon by, and transform, electrical signals. — *v.i.* to be a recipient: to participate in communion: to receive signals: to hold a reception of visitors. — *ns.* **receivabil'ity, receiv'ableness.** — *adj.* **receiv'able.** — *n.* **receiv'al** (*rare*). — *adj.* **received'** generally accepted. — *ns.* **receiv'er** one who receives: an officer who receives taxes: a person appointed by a court to manage property under litigation, receive money, etc.: one who receives stolen goods (*coll.*): a vessel for receiving the products of distillation, or for containing gases (*chem.*): the glass vessel of an air-pump in which the vacuum is formed: an instrument by which electrical signals are transformed into audible or visual form, as a telephone receiver: a receiving-set; **receiv'ership** the state of being in the control of a receiver: the office or function of a receiver. — *n.* and *adj.* **receiv'ing.** — **Received (Standard) English** the English generally spoken by educated British people and considered the standard of the language; **Received Pronunciation** the particular pronunciation of British English which is generally regarded as being least regionally limited, most socially acceptable, and is considered the standard; **receiv'er-gen'eral** an officer who receives revenues; **receiv'ing-house** a depot: a house where letters, etc., are left for transmission; **receiv'ing-office** a branch post-office for receipt of letters, etc.; **receiv'ing-order** an order putting a receiver in temporary possession of a debtor's estate, pending bankruptcy proceedings; **receiv'ing-room** a room where patients, inmates, etc., are received; **receiv'ing-set** apparatus for receiving wireless communications; **receiv'ing-ship** a stationary ship for naval recruits. — **official receiver** an official appointed by the Department of Trade and Industry to manage the estate of a person, company, etc. declared bankrupt, until a trustee has been appointed. [A.Fr. *receivre* (Fr. *recevoir*) — L. *recipĕre, receptum* — *re-*, back, *capĕre*, to take.]

recency. See **recent.**

recense *ri-sens'*, *v.t.* to revise critically. — *n.* **recen'sion** a critical revision of a text: a text established by critical revision: a review. [L. *recēnsiō, -ōnis* — *re-*, again, and *cēnsēre*, to value, to assess.]

recent *rē'sənt*, *adj.* of late origin or occurrence: fresh: modern: (*cap.*) of the present geological period — Post-Glacial. — *n.* **rē'cency.** — *adv.* **rē'cently.** — *n.* **rē'centness.** [L. *recēns, recentis.*]

recept *rē'sept*, *n.* an image or idea formed by repeated similar perceptions. — *n.* **receptacle** (*ri-sep'tə-kl*; also, as *Shak.*, *res'ip-tə-kl*) that in which anything is or may be received or stored: the enlarged end of an axis

bearing the parts of a flower or the crowded flowers of an inflorescence: in flowerless plants a structure bearing reproductive organs, spores, or gemmae. — *adj.* **receptacular** (*res-ip-tak'ū-lər*). — *n.* **receptac'ulum** a receptacle: — *pl.* **receptac'ula.** — *n.* **receptibil'ity** (*ri-*). — *adj.* **recept'ible** capable of receiving. — *ns.* **reception** (*ri-sep'shən*) the act, fact, or manner of receiving or of being received: taking in: act or manner of taking up signals: the quality of received radio or television signals: a formal receiving, as of guests: the part of a hotel, suite of offices, etc., where visitors, guests, etc. are received: a reception room: treatment on coming: capacity for receiving (*Milt.*); **recep'tionist** one employed to receive callers, hotel-guests, patients, customers, or the like, and make arrangements. — *adj.* **recep'tive** capable of receiving: quick to receive or take in esp. (*fig.*) ideas: pertaining to reception or receptors. — *ns.* **recep'tiveness, receptivity** (*res-ep-tiv'i-ti*); **recep'tor** a receiver: an element of the nervous system adapted for reception of stimuli, e.g. a sense-organ or sensory nerve-ending: a chemical grouping on the surface of the cell to which a specific antigen may attach itself: a site in or on a cell to which a drug or hormone can become attached, stimulating a reaction inside the cell. — **reception centre** a building, office, etc., where people are received for immediate assistance before being directed to specific centres of help, treatment, etc., as in the case of drug-addicts, or victims of fire, natural disasters, etc.; **reception class** a class for the new intake of children at a school; **reception order** an order for the reception and detention of a person in a mental hospital; **reception room** a room for formal receptions: any public room in a house. [L. *recipĕre, receptum*, to receive.]

recess *rē-ses'*, *n.* a going back or withdrawing: retirement: seclusion: remission of business: a break, interval during a school day: a holiday period during the academic year: part of a room formed by a receding of the wall: a niche or alcove: an indentation: a retired spot: a nook: a sinus or depression. — *v.t.* to make a recess in: to put into a recess. — *v.i.* to adjourn. — *adj.* **recessed'.** — *ns.* **recession** (*ri-sesh'ən*) act of receding: withdrawal: the state of being set back: a slight temporary decline in trade; **recessional** (*ri-sesh'ən-əl*) hymn sung during recession or retirement of clergy and choir after a service. — *adjs.* **recess'ional; recessive** (*-ses'*) tending to recede: of an ancestral character, apparently suppressed in cross-bred offspring in favour of the alternative character in the other parent, though it may be transmitted to later generations (*genetics*; also *n.*): of accent, tending to move toward the beginning of the word. — *adv.* **recess'ively.** — *n.* **recess'iveness.** — **recessed arch** one arch within another. [See **recede.**]

recession[1] *rē-sesh'ən*, *n.* a ceding again or back. [Pfx. **re-.**]

recession[2]. See **recess.**

Rechabite *rek'ə-bīt*, *n.* a descendant of Jonadab, son of *Rechab*, who did not drink wine or dwell in houses (Jer. xxxv. 6–7): a total abstainer from intoxicating drinks, esp. a member of the order so named: a tent-dweller. — *n.* **Rech'abitism.**

rechate (*Shak.*). See **recheat.**

réchauffé *rā-shō'fā*, *n.* a warmed-up dish: a fresh concoction of old material. [Fr.]

recheat *ri-chēt'*, **rechate** *ri-chāt'*, (*Shak.*) *ns.* a horn-call to assemble hounds. — *v.i.* to sound the recheat. [O.Fr. *racheter, rachater*, to reassemble.]

recherché *rə-sher'shā*, *adj.* carefully chosen: particularly choice: rare or exotic. [Fr.]

rechie. See **reech.**

rechlesse *rech'lis*, (*Spens.*) *adj.* Same as **reckless.**

---

recidivism *ri-sid'i-vizm, n.* the habit of relapsing into crime. — *n.* **recid'ivist.** [Fr. *récidivisme* — L. *recidīvus*, falling back.]

recipe *res'i-pi, n.* directions for making something, esp. a food or drink: a prescription (*arch.*): a method laid down for achieving a desired end: — *pl.* **rec'ipes.** [L. *recipe*, take, imper. of *recipĕre*.]

recipient *ri-sip'i-ənt, adj.* receiving: receptive. — *n.* one who or that which receives. — *ns.* **recip'ience, recip'iency** a reception; receptivity. [L. *recipiēns, -entis,* pr.p. of *recipĕre*, to receive.]

reciprocal *ri-sip'rō-kl, adj.* acting in return: mutual: complementary: inverse: alternating: interchangeable: giving and receiving or given and received: expressing mutuality (*gram.*): reflexive. — *n.* that which is reciprocal: the multiplier that gives unity (*math.*). — *n.* **reciprocality** (*-kal'i-ti*). — *adv.* **recip'rocally.** — *n.* **recip'rocant** a differential invariant. — *v.t.* **recip'rocāte** to give and receive mutually: to requite: to interchange: to alternate. — *v.i.* to move backward and forward: to make a return or interchange (*coll.*). — *n.* **reciprocā'tion.** — *adj.* **recip'rocātive** characterised by or inclined to reciprocation. — *ns.* **recip'rocātor** one who or that which reciprocates: a double-acting steam-engine; **reciprocity** (*res-i-pros'i-ti*) mutual relation: concession of mutual privileges or advantages, esp. mutual tariff concessions. — **recip'rocating-en'gine** an engine in which the piston moves to and fro in a straight line. [L. *reciprocus.*]

recision *ri-sizh'ən, n.* cutting back (*obs.*): rescinding. [L. *recīsiō, -ōnis* — *recīdĕre*, to cut off.]

récit *rā-sē, n.* a narrative, esp. the narrative in a book as opposed to the dialogue: a book consisting largely of narrative: a solo part, for voice or instrument (*mus.*): a principal part in a concerted piece (*mus.*): a swell organ (*mus.*). [Fr.]

recite *ri-sīt', v.t.* to repeat from memory: to declaim: to read aloud (*rare*): to narrate: to give (the details of): to repeat to a teacher, have heard a lesson in (*U.S.*). — *v.i.* to give a recitation: to repeat, or have heard, a lesson (*U.S.*). — *ns.* **recī'tal** act of reciting: setting forth: enumeration: narration: a public performance of music, usu. by one performer, or one composer, or of some particular character: that part of a deed which recites the circumstances (*law*); **recitation** (*res-i-tā'shən*) act of reciting: a piece for declaiming: the repeating or hearing of a prepared lesson (*U.S.*): hence a lesson generally (*U.S.*); **recitā'tionist** a declaimer; **recitative** (*-tə-tēv'*) or **recitativo** (*re-sit-ä-tē'vō* or It. *rä-chē-tä-tē'vō; pl.* **-vos,** It. **-vi** *-vē*) a style of song resembling speech in its succession of tones and freedom from melodic form: a passage to be sung in this manner. — *adj.* in the style of recitative. — *n.* **reciter** (*ri-sīt'ər*). — **recitā'tion-room** (*U.S.*) a classroom; **recit'ing-note** the note on which, in a Gregorian chant, the greater part of a verse is sung. [L. *recitāre* — *citāre, -ātum*, to call.]

reck *rek,* (usu. with a negative) *v.t.* to care, desire (with *infin.; arch.*): to care about, heed: (used *impers.*) to concern. — *v.i.* (usu. with *of*) to care, concern oneself: (used *impers.*) to matter: — *pa.t.* and *pa.p.* **recked,** *obs.* or *arch.* **raught** (*röt*). — *n.* care: heed. — *adj.* **reck'less** careless: heedless of consequences: rash. — *adv.* **reck'-lessly.** — *n.* **reck'lessness.** — **what reck?** (*Scot.*) what does it matter? [O.E. *reccan, rēcan;* cf. O.H.G. *ruoh,* care, Ger. *ruchlos,* regardless.]

reckan *rek'ən,* (Scott, ostensibly Cumberland dial.) *adj.* or *pa.p.* perh. **racked** or **ricked.**

reckling *rek'ling, n.* the weakest, smallest, or youngest of a litter or family. — *adj.* puny. [Origin obscure; poss. from O.N. *reklingr,* an outcast.]

reckon *rek'n, -ən, v.t.* to enumerate (*arch.*): to count: to calculate (often with *up*): to include (in an account): to place or class: to estimate, judge to be: to think, believe, suppose, or expect: to attribute (to; *arch.*): to think much of (*slang*). — *v.i.* to calculate: to judge: to go over or settle accounts (with): to concern oneself (with): to count or rely (on, upon). — *ns.* **reck'oner; reck'oning** counting: calculation, esp. of a ship's position: a tavern bill: settlement of accounts: judgment. [O.E. *gerecenian,* to explain; Ger. *rechnen.*]

reclaim *ri-klām', v.t.* orig. to call back (as a hawk): to win back: to win from evil, wildness, waste, submersion: (*rē-klām'*) to claim back. — *v.i.* (*ri-klām'*) to exclaim in protest (*arch.*): to appeal (*Scots law*). — *n.* recall: possibility of reform. — *adj.* **reclaim'able.** — *adv.* **reclaim'ably.** — *ns.* **reclaim'ant; reclaim'er.** [O.Fr. *reclamer* — L. *reclāmāre.*]

reclamation *rek-lə-mā'shən, n.* act of reclaiming: state of being reclaimed. [L. *reclāmātiō, -ōnis* — *reclāmāre* — *clāmāre,* to cry out.]

réclame *rā-kläm, n.* art or practice by which publicity or notoriety is secured: publicity. [Fr.]

recline *ri-klīn', v.t.* to lay on the back: to incline or bend (properly backwards). — *v.i.* to lean in a recumbent position, on back or side: (of the plane of a sundial) to make an angle with the vertical: to rely (on, upon; *arch.*). — *adj.* or *adv.* (*Milt.*) recumbent. — *adjs.* **reclī'nable; reclinate** (*rek'li-nāt*) bent down or back. — *n.* **reclinā'tion** (*rek-li-*) reclining: bending back: angle of a dial with the vertical. — *adj.* **reclīned'** recumbent: reclinate. — *n.* **reclī'ner** someone or something that reclines, esp. a type of easy chair with a back that can be lowered towards a horizontal position. — *adj.* **reclī'ning.** [L. *reclīnāre, -ātum* — *clīnāre,* to bend.]

recluse *ri-kloōs', adj.* enclosed, as an anchorite: secluded: retired: solitary. — *n.* a religious devotee who lives shut up in a cell: one who lives retired from the world. — *adv.* **recluse'ly.** — *ns.* **recluse'ness** seclusion from society: retirement; **reclusion** (*-kloō'zhən*) religious seclusion: the life of a recluse: seclusion in prison. — *adj.* **reclu'sive** (*-siv*) of, living in, etc., seclusion. — *n.* **reclu'sory** a recluse's cell. [L. *reclūsus,* pa.p. of *reclūdēre,* to open, in later Latin, shut away — *re-,* back, away, *claudēre.*]

recognise, -ize *rek'əg-nīz, v.t.* to know again: to identify as known or experienced before: to show sign of knowing (a person): to see, acknowledge, the fact of: to acknowledge (that): to acknowledge the validity of (a claim): to acknowledge the status or legality of (e.g. a government): to allow someone to speak in court proceedings, formal debate, etc. (*U.S.*): to reward (meritorious conduct). — *adj.* **recognīs'able, -z-** (or *rek'*). — *adv.* **recognīs'ably, -z-** (or *rek'*). — *ns.* **recognisance, -z-** (*ri-kog'ni-zəns*) a recognition: acknowledgment: a token (*arch.*): (or *ri-kon'i-zəns*) a legal obligation entered into before a magistrate to do, or not to do, some particular act: money pledged for the performance of such an obligation; **recogniser, -z-** (*rek'əg-nīz-ər,* or *-nīz'ər*); **recognition** (*rek-əg-nish'ən*) act of recognising: state of being recognised: acknowledgment: acknowledgment of status: a sign, token, or indication of recognising: a return of the feu to the superior (*Scots law*). — *adjs.* **recognitive** (*ri-kog'*), **recog'nitory.** [L. *recognōscēre* and O.Fr. *reconoistre, reconoiss-;* see **cognosce, cognition**.]

recoil *ri-koil'* (*Spens.* **recoyle, recule, recuile**) *v.t.* (*obs.*) to force back. — *v.i.* to retreat, fall back (*arch.*): to revert (*obs.*): to start back: to stagger back: to shrink in horror, etc.: to rebound: to kick, as a gun: to degenerate (*Shak.*). — *n.* retreat (*arch.*): a starting or springing back: rebound: the kick of a gun: change in motion of a particle caused by ejection of another particle, or (*sometimes*) by a collision (*nuc.*). — *n.* **recoil'er.** — *adj.* **recoil'less.** — **recoil escapement** same

---

rearrest' *n.* and *v.t.*
reassem'blage *n.*
reassem'ble *v.t.* and *v.i.*

reassem'bly *n.*
reassert' *v.t.*
reassump'tion, *n.*

reattach' *v.t.* and *v.i.*
reattach'ment *n.*
reattain' *v.t.*

as **anchor escapement**. [Fr. *reculer* — *cul* — L. *cūlus*, the hinder parts.]

recollect[1] *rek-əl-ekt'*, *v.t.* to recall to memory: to remember, esp. by an effort: to absorb in mystical contemplation (*arch.*): to recall to the matter in hand, or to composure or resolution (usu. *refl.*). — *n.* (*rek'*) a Franciscan friar of a reformed branch, aiming at detachment from creatures and recollection in God. — Also (Fr.) **récollet** (*rā-kol-ā*). — *adj.* **recollect'ed**. — *adv.* **recollect'edly**. — *ns.* **recollect'edness**; **recollec'tion** (*rek-*) act or power of recollecting: a memory, reminiscence: a thing remembered: mystical contemplation (*arch.*). — *adj.* **recollec'tive**. — **recollected terms** (*Shak.*) variously explained as known by heart, picked, studied, wanting spontaneity. [L. *recolligĕre*, to gather again or gather up — *colligĕre*; see **collect**.]

recollect[2], **re-collect** *rē'kol-ekt'*, *v.t.* to collect (*obs.*): to gather together again: to summon up: to bring back again (*Milt.*). [Partly **recollect**[1]; partly pfx. **re-** and **collect**.]

recombine *rē-kəm-bīn'*, *v.t.* and *v.i.* to join together again. — *adj.* and *n.* **recombinant** (*ri-kom'bi-nənt*). — *n.* **recombinā'tion**. — **recombinant DNA** genetic material produced by the combining of DNA molecules from different organisms — see also **genetic engineering** under **genetic**. [Pfx. **re-**.]

recomfort *ri-kum'fərt*, (*arch.*) *v.t.* to comfort: to console: to reinvigorate: to refresh. — *adj.* **recom'fortless** (*Spens.*) comfortless. — *n.* **recom'forture** (*Shak.*) consolation. [Pfx. **re-**.]

recommend *rek-ə-mend'*, *v.t.* to commend, commit, or consign (*arch.*): to commend or introduce as suitable for acceptance, favour, appointment, or choice: to make acceptable: to advise: to inform (*Shak.*). — *adj.* **recommend'able**. — *adv.* **recommend'ably**. — *n.* **recommendā'tion**. — *adj.* **recommend'atory**. — *n.* **recommend'er**. [Pfx. **re-**.]

recompense *rek'əm-pens*, *v.t.* to return an equivalent to or for: to repay. — *n.* (formerly **recompence**) return of an equivalent: that which is so returned: requital. [O.Fr. *recompenser* — L. *compēnsāre*, to compensate.]

reconcile *rek'ən-sīl*, *v.t.* to restore or bring back to friendship or union: to bring to agreement or contentment: to pacify: to make, or to prove consistent: to admit or restore to membership of a church: to adjust or compose: to regain, conciliate (*Spens.*): to reconsecrate (a desecrated holy place). — *n.* **rec'oncilability** (or *-sīl'*). — *adj.* **rec'oncilable** (or *-sīl'*). — *n.* **rec'-oncilableness** (or *-sīl'*). — *adv.* **rec'oncilably** (or *-sīl'*). — *ns.* **rec'oncilement** (or *-sīl'*); **rec'onciler**; **reconciliā'tion** (*-sil-*). — *adj.* **reconciliatory** (*-sil'i-ə-tər-i*). [L. *reconciliāre, -ātum* — *conciliāre*, to call together.]

recondite *ri-kon'dīt, rek'ən-dīt*, *adj.* hidden: obscure: abstruse: profound. [L. *recondĕre, -itum*, to put away — *re-*, again, *condĕre*, to establish, store.]

recondition *rē-kən-dish'ən*, *v.t.* to repair and refit: to restore to original or sound condition. [Pfx. **re-**.]

reconnaissance *ri-kon'i-səns*, *n.* reconnoitring: a preliminary survey. — **reconnaissance in force** an attack by a large body to discover the enemy's position and strength. [Fr.]

reconnoitre, in U.S. usu. **reconnoiter** *rek-ə-noi'tər*, *v.t.* to examine with a view to military operations or other purpose: to remember (*obs.*). — *v.i.* to make preliminary examination. — *n.* a reconnaissance. — *n.* **reconnoi'trer**. [Fr. *reconnoître* (now *reconnaître*) — L. *recognōscĕre*, to recognise.]

reconsider *rē-kon-sid'ər*, *v.t.* to consider (a decision, etc.) again, with a view to altering or reversing it. — *n.* **reconsiderā'tion**. [Pfx. **re-**.]

reconstitute *rē-kon'sti-tūt*, *v.t.* to constitute anew: to restore the constitution of (esp. dried foods). — *adj.* **reconstit'uent** (*-kən-*). — *n.* **reconstitū'tion** constituting

afresh: refounding: restoration to original condition: theoretical reconstruction on the spot of the details of a crime. [Pfx. **re-**.]

reconstruct *rē-kən-strukt'*, *v.t.* to construct again: to rebuild: to remodel: to restore in imagination or theory. — *n.* **reconstruc'tion** the act of reconstructing: a thing reconstructed: reorganisation: a model representing a series of sections: a theoretical representation or view of something unknown: the upbuilding of moral and material public well-being after a great upheaval: (with *cap.*) the process of restoring the Seceding States to the rights and privileges of the Union after the Civil War (*U.S.*). — *adjs.* **reconstruc'-tional**; **reconstruc'tionary**. — *n.* **reconstruc'tionist**. — *adj.* **reconstruc'tive**. — *n.* **reconstruc'tor**. [Pfx. **re-**.]

reconvalescence *ri-kon-vəl-es'əns*, (*arch.*) *n.* recovery from illness. [Pfx. **re-**.]

reconvert *rē-kən-vûrt'*, *v.t.* to convert again to a former state, religion, etc. — *n.* **reconver'sion**. [Pfx. **re-**.]

reconvey *rē-kən-vā'*, *v.t.* to transfer again to a former owner, as an estate. — *n.* **reconvey'ance**. [Pfx. **re-**.]

record *ri-körd'*, *v.t.* to get by heart (*obs.*): to go over in one's mind (*Spens.*): to repeat from memory (*Spens.*): to narrate, set forth (*arch.*): to sing in an undertone, practise quietly (esp. of birds; *obs.*): to call to mind (*arch.*): to set down in writing or other permanent form: to register (on an instrument, scale, etc.): to trace a curve or other representation of: to perform before a recording instrument: to make a recording of (music, etc., person speaking, etc.): to mark, indicate: to bear witness to: to put on record (an offence, etc.) without taking further measures against the offender: to register (as a vote or verdict): to celebrate. — *v.i.* to sing, warble, esp. in quiet rehearsal (*obs.*): to make a record. — *n.* **record** (*rek'örd*, formerly *ri-körd'*) a register: a formal writing of any fact or proceeding: a book of such writings: past history: a witness, a memorial: memory, remembrance: anything entered in the rolls of a court, esp. the formal statement or pleadings of parties in a litigation: a curve or other representation of phenomena made by an instrument upon a surface: a disc or cylinder on which sound is registered for reproduction by an instrument such as a gramophone: a performance or occurrence not recorded to have been surpassed: a list of a person's criminal convictions. — *adj.* not surpassed. — *adj.* **record'able** (*ri-*) able to be recorded: worthy of record. — *ns.* **recordā'tion** (in *Shak.*, *rek'*) remembrance: commemoration: recording; **record'er** (*ri-*) one who records or registers, esp. the rolls, etc., of a city: a judge of a city or borough court of quarter-sessions: one who performs before a recording instrument: a recording apparatus: a fipple-flute, once called the 'English flute', much used in the 16th to 18th centuries and again in the 20th century (from the *obs.* meanings of the verb); **record'ership** the office of recorder, or the time of holding it; **record'ing** a record of sound or images made, for later reproduction, e.g. on magnetic tape, film, or gramophone disc. — Also *adj.* — *n.* **record'ist**. — **recorded delivery** a service of the Post Office in which a record is kept of the collection and delivery of a letter, parcel, etc.; **recording angel** an angel supposed to keep a book in which every misdeed is recorded against the doer; **Record Office** a place where public records are kept; **rec'ord-player** a small, portable instrument for playing gramophone records, run on batteries or mains electricity, not spring-driven: a larger, more sophisticated, etc. device for the same purpose; **rec'ord-sleeve** a cardboard case for a gramophone record; — **beat** or **break a, the record** to outdo the highest achievement yet recorded; **close the record** an act of a Scottish judge after each party has said all he wishes to say by way of statement and answer; **for the record** (*coll.*) in order

---

rĕattempt' *v.t.*, *v.i.* and *n.*
rĕawake' *v.t.* and *v.i.*
rĕawak'en *v.t.* and *v.i.*

rĕawak'ening *n.*
rĕbaptise', -ize' *v.t.*
rĕbap'tism *n.*

rĕbloom' *v.i.*
rĕbloss'om *v.i.*
rĕboil' *v.t.* and *v.i.*

For other sounds see detailed chart of pronunciation.

to get the facts straight; **go on record as saying, thinking, etc.** to be publicly known to say, think, etc.; **court of record** a court (as the supreme court, county courts and others) whose acts and proceedings are permanently recorded, and which has the authority to fine or imprison persons for contempt; **off the record** not for publication in the press, etc.; **on record** recorded in a document, etc.: publicly known; **public records** contemporary officially authenticated statements of acts and proceedings in public affairs, preserved in the public interest; **set the record straight** to put right a mistake or false impression; **trial by record** a common law mode of trial when a former decision of the court is disputed and the matter is settled by producing the record. [O.Fr. *recorder* — L. *recordārī*, to call to mind, get by heart — *cor, cordis*, the heart.]

recount[1] *ri-kownt'*, *v.t.* to narrate the particulars of: to detail. — *ns.* **recount'al** (*ri-*); **recount'ment** (*Shak.*) relation in detail. [O.Fr. *reconter* — *conter*, to tell.]

recount[2], **re-count** *rē-kownt' v.t.*, *v.i.*, to count over again. — *n.* (*rē'kownt*) a second or new counting (as of votes). [Pfx. **re-**.]

recoup *ri-kōōp'*, *v.t.* to deduct or keep back (from what is claimed by a counterclaim; *law*): to make good (a loss): to indemnify, compensate. — *n.* **recoup'ment.** [Fr. *recouper*, to cut back — *couper*, to cut.]

recoure, recower *ri-kowr'*, (*Spens.*) *v.t.* a variant of **recover.** See also **recure.**

recourse *ri-kōrs', -körs'*, *n.* flowing back (*arch.*): withdrawal (*arch.*): recurrence (*arch.*): flow (*Shak.*): return (*arch.*): freedom to return: access: resort: a source of aid or protection: right to payment, esp. by the drawer or endorser of a bill of exchange not met by the acceptor. — *v.i.* (*Spens.*) to return, go back, revert, in the mind. — **have recourse to** to go to for help, protection, etc.; **without recourse** a qualified endorsement of a bill or promissory note indicating that the endorser takes no responsibility for non-payment (*law, commerce*). [Fr. *recours* — L. *recursus* — *re-*, back, *currĕre, cursum*, to run.]

re-cover, recover *rē-kuv'ər*, *v.t.* to cover again. [**re-**.]

recover *ri-kuv'ər*, *v.t.* to get or find again: to regain: to reclaim: to extract (a valuable substance) from an ore, etc., or (usable material) from waste: to bring back: to retrieve: to cure (*arch.*): to revive: to restore: to rescue: to succeed in reaching: to attain: to obtain as compensation: to obtain for injury or debt. — *v.i.* to regain health or any former state: to get back into position: to obtain a judgement (*law*). — *n.* recovery (*obs.*): possibility of recovery (*obs.*): return to a former position, as in rowing or exercise with a weapon: the position so resumed. — *n.* **recoverabil'ity.** — *adj.* **recov'erable.** — *ns.* **recov'erableness; recoveree'** one against whom a judgment is obtained in common recovery; **recov'erer** one who recovers; **recov'eror** one who recovers a judgment in common recovery; **recov'ery** the act, fact, process, possibility, or power of recovering, or state of having recovered, in any sense: a verdict giving right to the recovery of debts or costs (*law*). — **common recovery** a former method of transferring an entailed estate by a legal fiction; **recover the wind of** (*Shak.*) to get to windward of (so as to drive a hare into a toil, or take the wind out of someone's sails): to gain an advantage over. [O.Fr. *recover* — L. *recuperāre*; see **recuperate.**]

recower. See **recoure.**

recoyle. See **recoil.**

recreant *rek'ri-ənt*, (*arch.*) *adj.* surrendering: craven: false: apostate. — *n.* one who yields in combat: a craven: a mean-spirited wretch: an apostate: a renegade. — *n.* **rec'reance, rec'reancy.** —*adv.* **rec'reantly.** [O.Fr., pr.p. of *recroire*, to yield in combat — L.L. *recrēdĕre*, to surrender — L. *crēdĕre*, to entrust.]

recreate *rē-krē-āt'*, *v.t.* to create again: (in the following senses *rek'ri-āt*) to reinvigorate: to refresh: to indulge, gratify, or amuse by sport or pastime. — *v.i.* to take recreation. — *n.* **recreation** (*rē-krē-ā'shən*) the act of creating anew: a new creation: (in the following senses *rek-ri-ā'shən*), refreshment after toil, sorrow, etc.: pleasurable occupation of leisure time: an amusement or sport: a source of amusement. — *adjs.* **recrea'tional** (*rek-*), **rēcrea'tive** (and *rek'ri-ā-tiv*). — **recreation ground** (*rek-*) an open area for games, sports, etc. [Pfx. **re-**.]

recrement *rek'ri-mənt*, *n.* waste, dross: a secretion that is reabsorbed. — *adjs.* **recremental** (*-ment'l*), **recremen- titial** (*-mən-tish'l*), **recrementi'tious.** [L. *recrēmentum*, dross — *cernĕre*, to sift.]

recriminate *ri-krim'in-āt*, *v.i.* to charge an accuser. — *n.* **recriminā'tion** act of accusing in return: countercharge. — *adj.* **recrim'inative.** — *n.* **recrim'inator.** — *adj.* **recrim'inatory.** [L. *crīminārī*, to accuse.]

recrudesce *rē-krōō-des'*, *v.i.* to break out afresh. — *ns.* **recrudesc'ence, recrudesc'ency.** — *adj.* **recrudesc'ent.** [L. *recrūdēscĕre* — *crūdus*, raw.]

recruit *ri-krōōt'*, *n.* a reinforcement (*obs.*): a new supply (of men, money, health, etc.; *arch.*): renewal: restoration: a soldier or other newly enlisted. — *v.i.* to obtain fresh supplies: to recover in health, pocket, etc.: to enlist new soldiers. — *v.t.* to reinforce: to replenish: to restore: to reinvigorate: to enlist or raise. — *ns.* **recruit'al** renewed supply: restoration; **recruit'er.** — *adj.* **recruit'ing.** — *n.* **recruit'ment** recruiting: in deafness of neural cause, the distressing exaggeration of loud sounds, while soft sounds may be audible. — **recruit'ing-ground** a place where recruits may be obtained. [Obs. Fr. *recrute*, reinforcement, prob. pa.p. fem. of *recroître* — L. *recrēscĕre*, to grow again.]

recrystallise, -ize *rē-kris'təl-īz*, *v.t.* and *v.i.* to dissolve and reform (a crystalline substance), as when purifying chemical compounds. — *v.i.* in metal, to replace deformed crystals by newly generated ones which absorb them. — *n.* **recrystallīsā'tion, -z-.** [Pfx. **re-**.]

recta, rectal, etc. See **rectum.**

rectangle *rek'tang-gl*, or *-tang'*, *n.* a four-sided plane figure with all its angles right angles. — *adjs.* **rec'tang- led** having a right angle; **rectang'ular** of the form of a rectangle: at right angles: right-angled. — *n.* **rectan- gular'ity.** — *adv.* **rectang'ularly.** — **rectangular hyperbola** one whose asymptotes are at right angles; **rectangular solid** one whose axis is perpendicular to its base. [L.L. *rēct(i)angulum* — L. *angulus*, an angle.]

rect(i)- *rekt(i)-*, in composition, right: straight. — *adjs.* **rectilineal** (*rek-ti-lin'i-əl*), **rectilinear** (*rek-ti-lin'i-ər*; L. *līnea*, a line) in a straight line or lines: straight: bounded by straight lines. — *n.* **rectilinearity** (*-ar'i-ti*). — *adv.* **rectilin'early.** — *ns.* **rectipetality** (*rek-ti-pi-tal'i-ti*), **rec- tipetaly** (*-pet'əl-i*; L. *petĕre*, to seek; *bot.*) tendency to grow in a straight line. — *adjs.* **rectirostral** (*rek-ti- ros'trəl*; L. *rōstrum*, a beak) straight-billed; **rectiserial** (*rek-ti-sēr'i-əl*; L. *seriēs*, a row) in straight rows. [L. *rēctus*, straight, right.]

recti. See **rectus.**

rectify *rek'ti-fī*, *v.t.* to set right: to correct: to redress: to adjust: to purify by distillation (*chem.*): to determine the length of (an arc): to change (an alternating current) to a direct current: — *pr.p.* **rec'tifying;** *pa.t.* and *pa.p.* **rec'tified.** — *adj.* **rec'tifiable.** — *ns.* **rectifica'- tion; rec'tifier** one who rectifies (esp. alcohol): apparatus for rectifying (esp. spirit, an alternating current, or electromagnetic waves). [Fr. *rectifier* — L.L. *rēctificāre* — *facĕre*, to make.]

rectilineal, etc. See **rect(i)-.**

rection *rek'shən*, (*gram.*) *n.* syntactical government. [L. *rēctiō, -ōnis*, government.]

rectipetality . . . to . . . **rectiserial.** See **rect(i)-.**

---

rēbrace' *v.t.*
rēbroad'cast *v.t.* and *n.*
rēbuild' *v.t.*

rēbur'ial *n.*
rēbur'y *v.t.*
rēbutt'on *v.t.*

rēcal'culate *v.t.*
rēcatch' *v.t.* and *v.i.*
rēcen'tre *v.t.*

fāte; fär; hûr; mīne; mōte; för; mūte; mōōn; fŏŏt; dhen (then); *el'ə-mənt* (element)

rectitis, rectitic. See **rectum.**

rectitude *rek'ti-tūd, n.* straightness (*obs.*): rightness: uprightness: integrity. — *adj.* **rectitū'dinous** manifesting moral correctness: over-obviously righteous. [Fr., — L.L. *rēctitūdō* — L. *rēctus,* straight.]

recto *rek'tō, n.* the right-hand page of an open book, the front page of a leaf — opp. to *verso:* —*pl.* **rec'tōs.** [L. *rēctō (foliō),* on the right (leaf).]

recto-. See **rectum.**

rector *rek'tər, n.* a ruler, governor, or controller (*obs.*): in the Church of England, a clergyman of a parish where the tithes are not impropriate: an Episcopal clergyman with charge of a congregation in the United States or (since 1890) Scotland: the head-master of certain schools in Scotland, esp. those called academies: the chief elective officer of many Scottish (*Lord Rector*) and foreign universities: a college head (as at Lincoln and Exeter Colleges, Oxford; Science and Technology, London): an ecclesiastic in charge of a congregation, an important mission, a college, or a religious house, esp. the head of a Jesuit seminary (*R.C.*). — *adj.* **rec'toral** of God as a ruler. — *ns.* **rec'torate** a rector's office or term of office; **rec'toress, rec'tress** a female rector: a rector's wife (*coll.*). — *adj.* **rectorial** (*-tō'ri-əl*) of a rector. — *n.* an election of a Lord Rector. — *ns.* **rec'torship; rec'tory** the province or residence of a rector. — **Rector Magnificus** the head of a German university. — **lay rector** a layman who enjoys the great tithes of a parish. [L. *rēctor, -ōris* — *regĕre, rēctum,* to rule.]

rectrix *rek'triks, n.* a female governor: a long tail-feather, used in steering: — *pl.* **rectrices** (*rek'tri-sēz, rek-trī'sēz*). — *adj.* **rectricial** (*-trish'l*). [L. *rēctrīx, -īcis,* fem. of *rēctor.*]

rectum *rek'təm, n.* the terminal part of the large intestine: — *pl.* **rec'ta, rec'tums.** — *adj.* **rec'tal.** — *adv.* **rec'tally.** — *n.* **rectitis** (*rek-tī'tis*) inflammation of the rectum. — *adj.* **rectitic** (*-tit'ik*). — In composition, **rec'to-.** [L. neut. of *rēctus,* straight.]

rectus *rek'təs, n.* a straight muscle: — *pl.* **rec'tī.** [L.]

recuile, recule *ri-kūl' (Spens.).* Same as **recoil.**

recumbent *ri-kum'bənt, adj.* reclining. — *ns.* **recum'bence, recum'bency.** — *adv.* **recum'bently.** [L. *recumbĕre — cubāre,* to lie down.]

recuperate *ri-kū'pər-āt, v.t.* and *v.i.* to recover. — *adj.* **recu'perable** recoverable. — *n.* **recuperā'tion.** — *adj.* **recu'perative** (*-ə-tiv*). — *n.* **recu'perator** an arrangement by which something lost is regained, as the heat of waste gases in a furnace. — *adj.* **recu'peratory.** [L. *recuperāre,* to recover.]

recur *ri-kûr', v.i.* to revert (*arch.*): to have recourse (*arch.*): to come up or come round again, or at intervals: to come back into one's mind: — *pr.p.* **recurr'ing** (or *-kur'*); *pa.t.* and *pa.p.* **recurred'** (*-kûrd*). — *ns.* **recurr'ence, recurr'ency** (*-kur'*). — *adj.* **recurr'ent** (*-kur'*) returning at intervals: running back in the opposite direction or toward the place of origin. — *adv.* **recurr'ently.** — *n.* **recur'sion** (*-kûr'; rare*) a going back, return. — *adj.* (*math.*; of a formula) enabling a term in a sequence to be computed from one or more of the preceding terms. — *adj.* **recur'sive** (*math.*; of a definition) consisting of rules which allow values or meaning to be determined with certainty. — **recurring decimal** a decimal fraction in which after a certain point one figure (*repeating decimal*) or a group of figures (*circulating*) is repeated to infinity. [L. *recurrĕre — currĕre,* to run.]

recure *ri-kūr', v.t.* to cure, remedy, heal, bring back to a better state (*Spens., Shak., Milt.*): to recover, get back (*Spens.*). — *v.i.* (*obs.*) to recover, get well. — *n.* (*obs.*) cure: recovery. — *adj.* **recure'less** (*obs.*) incurable. [Partly L. *recūrāre,* to cure, partly for **recoure** (q.v.).]

recurve *ri-kûrv', v.t.* and *v.i.* to bend back. — *adj.*

recurved'. — *adj.* **recurviros'tral** with up-bent bill. [L. *recurvāre; rōstrum,* beak.]

recuse *ri-kūz', v.t.* to reject, object to (e.g. a judge) (*arch.*). — *ns.* **recusance** (*rek'ū-zəns* or *ri-kū'zəns; rare*), **recusancy** (*-i*); **recusant** (*rek'* or *ri-kū'*) one (esp. a Roman Catholic) who refused to attend the Church of England when it was legally compulsory: a dissenter: one who refuses, esp. to submit to authority. — Also *adj.* — *n.* **recusā'tion** (*law*) an objection or appeal. [L. *recūsāre — causa,* a cause.]

recycle *rē-sī'kl, v.t.* to pass again through a series of changes or treatment: loosely, to remake into something different: to cause (material) to be broken down by bacteria and then reconstitute it: to direct into a different channel. — *adj.* **recy'clable.** [Pfx. **re-.**]

red[1] *red, adj.* (*compar.* **redd'er;** *superl.* **redd'est**) of a colour like blood: extended traditionally to mean golden, and by custom to other colours more or less near red: having a red face (from shame, heat, embarrassment, etc.; see also **red face** below): revolutionary, or supposedly revolutionary. — *n.* the colour of blood: an object of this colour in a set of similar objects: a red pigment: red clothes: the red traffic-light, meaning 'stop': a revolutionary or one who favours sweeping changes, variously applied to radical, republican, anarchist, socialist, communist, etc.: a former squadron of the British fleet: a red cent. — *v.t.* **redd'en** to make red. — *v.i.* to grow red: to blush. — *adj.* **redd'ish.** — *n.* **redd'ishness.** — *adj.* **redd'y.** — *adv.* **red'ly.** — *n.* **red'ness.** — **red admiral** a common butterfly (*Vanessa atalanta*) with reddish-banded wings; **red alert** a state of readiness for imminent crisis, e.g. war, natural disaster; **red algae** one of the great divisions of seaweeds, the *Rhodophyceae* or Florideae; **red'back** (*Austr.*) a poisonous spider, *Latrodectus hasselti,* having a red strip on its back; **red'-belly** char, or other red-bellied fish: the slider, a terrapin; **red biddy** a drink made of red wine and methylated spirit. — *adj.* **red'-blood'ed** having red blood: abounding in vitality, and usually in crudity. — **red'-book** a book bound in red, esp. a court-guide, peerage, directory of persons in the service of the state, official regulations, or the like; **red'-box** a minister's red-covered box for official papers; **red'breast** the robin; **red brick** a brick, made from clay containing iron compounds which are converted into ferric oxide. — *adj.* **red'brick (redbrick university** a general name given to a later English type of university, usu. one founded in the 19th or first half of the 20th. cent., contrasted with Oxford and Cambridge). — **red'-bud** the Judas-tree; **red cabbage** a purplish cabbage used for pickling; **red'-cap** a goldfinch: a Scottish castle goblin (also **red'-cowl**): military policeman (*slang*): railway porter (*U.S.*); **red card** (*football*) a red-coloured card (no longer used in England except in international matches) that a referee holds up to show that he is sending a player off; **red carpet** a strip of carpet put out for the highly favoured to walk on: treatment as a very important person (*fig.*). — *adj.* **red'-car'pet** (usu. *fig.*). — **red cedar** a name for various species of *Cedrela* and of juniper; **red cent** a cent (formerly made of copper) considered as a very small amount (*coll.,* esp. U.S.): a whit; **red clay** a clayey deposit of oceanic abysses, stained reddish or brown by manganese and iron oxides: cave-earth; **red'coat** (*hist.*) a British soldier; **red cock** a figurative name for an incendiary fire; **red corpuscle** an erythrocyte, a blood cell which carries oxygen in combination with the pigment haemoglobin, and removes carbon dioxide; **Red Crag** a middle division of the English Pliocene; **Red Crescent** the Red Cross Society in Muslim countries; **Red Cross** a red cross on a white ground, the old national flag of England (in Spenser's **Redcross Knight,** representing holiness and the Church of England): the

---

rĕchall'enge *v.t.* and *n.*
rĕcharge' *v.t.*
recharge'ble *adj.*

rĕchart' *v.i.*
rĕchart'er *v.i.*
rĕcir'culate *v.t.* and *v.i.*

rĕclassificā'tion *n.*
rĕclass'ify *v.t.*
rĕclimb' *v.t.*

For other sounds see detailed chart of pronunciation.

Swiss flag with colours reversed, the copyrighted symbol of an organisation (known as **the Red Cross**) for tending sick, wounded in war, etc., enjoying privileges under the Convention of Geneva (1864); **redcurr'ant** the small red berry of a shrub of the Gooseberry genus. — *adj.* **red'currant.** — **red deer** the common stag or hind, reddish-brown in summer; **Red Devils** the Parachute Regiment; **red'-dog** the lowest grade of flour in high milling; **Red Ensign** (*slang* **Red Duster**) red flag with Union Jack in canton, till 1864 flag of Red Squadron, now flown by British merchant ships; **red'eye** the rudd: poor quality whisky (*U.S.*); **red face** a blushing from discomfiture (*adj.* **red'-faced'**). — *adj.* **red'-fig'ured** (of Greek vases) having red (unpainted) figures on a black-glazed ground. — **red'fish** a male salmon when, or just after, spawning: any of various red-fleshed fish, of the genus *Sebastes*; **red flag** a flag used as a signal of danger, defiance, no quarter, or an auction sale: the banner of socialism or of revolution: a socialist's song; **red giant, dwarf** a red star of high, low, luminosity; **Red Guard** a member of a strict Maoist youth movement in China, esp. active in the cultural revolution of the late 1960s; **red'-gum** an eruption of the skin in teething infants: a Eucalyptus (of various kinds) with red gum. — *adj.* **red'-haired.** — **red hand** the bloody hand (see **hand**). — *adj.* and *adv.* **red'hand'ed** in the very act, or immediately after, as if with bloody hands. — **red'-hat** a cardinal: a cardinal's hat (award of this to cardinals was discontinued 1969): a staff officer (*army slang*); **red'-head** a person with red hair. — *adj.* **red'-head'ed** having a red head or red hair: angrily excited (*slang*). — **red'-heat** the temperature at which a thing is red-hot. — *adj.* **red'-heeled'.** — **red herring** a herring cured and dried, of reddish appearance: a subject introduced to divert discussion or attention as a herring drawn across a track would throw hounds out. — *adj.* **red'-hot** heated to redness: extreme: (of information) very recently received (*coll.*): (of a telephone line) very busy with calls (*coll.*): (**red-hot poker** the plant Kniphofia or Tritoma). — **Red Indian** an American Indian, esp. of North America. — *adj.* **red'-latt'ice** (*Shak.*) savouring of the alehouse (whose lattice was conventionally painted red). — **red lead** an oxide of lead (Pb₃O₄) of a fine red colour, used in paint-making — also called **minium; red'leg** in the Caribbean, a derog. term for a poor white person, esp. a descendant of original white settlers. — *adjs.* **red'-legged; red'-letter** marked with red letters, as holidays or saints' days in the old calendars: deserving to be so marked, special. — **red light** a rear-light: a danger-signal: the red traffic-light, meaning 'stop': a brothel (*coll.*). — *adjs.* **red'-light'** (*coll.*) of or relating to brothels, as in *red-light district*; **red'-looked** (*Shak.*) having a red look; **red'-mad'** (*Scot.*) stark mad. — **red'-man, red man** a redskin, an American Indian: prob. red mercuric sulphide (*alchemy*); **red meat** dark-coloured meat, as beef and lamb; **red mullet** see **mullet¹; red mud** a type of industrial waste resulting from alumina processing, consisting of silicone oxide, iron oxide, etc.; **red'neck** (U.S.) a derog. term for a poor white farm labourer in the southwestern states. — *adj.* ignorant, intolerant, narrow-minded: pertaining to, characteristic of, this class of labourers. — **red pepper** see **pepper; red'-plague, -murrain** (*Shak.*) bubonic plague; **red'poll** a name for two birds (*lesser* and *mealy redpoll*) akin to the linnet: a beast of a red breed of polled cattle. — *adj.* **red'-polled** having a red poll: red and polled. — **red rag** the tongue (*slang*): a cause of infuriation (as red is said to be to a bull); **red'-rattle** louse'-wort; **red ribbon, riband** the ribbon of the Order of the Bath; **red'-root** a genus (*Ceanothus*) of the buckthorn family — *New Jersey tea*; **red rot** a disease of oaks, etc., caused by *Polyporus*,

the wood becoming brown and dry; **red salmon** any of various types of salmon with red flesh, esp. the sockeye salmon; **red'-san'ders** a papilionaceous tree (*Pterocarpus santalinus*) of tropical Asia, with heavy dark-red heartwood, used as a dye, etc. (see also **sandalwood**); **red seaweed** any of the red algae, esp. one of the genus *Polysiphonia;* **red'-seed** the food of mackerel, small floating crustaceans, etc.; **red'shank** a sandpiper with red legs: (in derision) a Highlander or an Irishman: (**red shank**) a polygonaceous annual plant with a red stem; **red shift** a shift of lines in the spectrum towards the red, usu. considered to occur because the source of light is receding (see under **dopplerite**); **red'-shirt** a follower of Garibaldi (1807–82), from his garb: a revolutionary or anarchist; **red'skin** (*derog.*) a Red Indian; **red snapper** fish of the *Lutianidae* with reddish colouring, common off the east coast of America; **red snow** snow coloured by a microscopic red alga; **red spider (mite)** a spinning mite that infests leaves; **red squirrel** a squirrel of reddish-brown colour, *Sciurus vulgaris*, native to Europe and Asia, in Britain now rarely found outside the Scottish highlands; **red'start** (O.E. *steort*, tail) a bird (*Ruticilla* or *Phoenicurus*) with a conspicuous chestnut-coloured tail: an American warbler, superficially similar; **red'streak** an apple with streaked skin; **red tape** the tape used in government offices: rigid formality of intricate official routine: bureaucracy. — *adj.* **red'-tape'.** — **red-tap'ism, red= tap'ist; red'top** (*U.S.*) a kind of bent grass (*Agrostis stolonifera*); **red'water** a cattle disease (also **babesiosis, babesiasis** qq.v.) due to a protozoan parasite in the blood, that is transmitted by ticks and destroys the red blood cells, causing red-coloured urine to be passed; **red wine** wine coloured by (red) grape skins during fermentation (cf. **rosé**); **red'wing** a thrush with reddish sides below the wings; **red'wood** a species of Sequoia with reddish wood much used commercially: any wood or tree yielding a red dye. — *adj.* **red-wood', -wud'** (*Scot.*) stark mad. — **in the red** overdrawn at the bank, in debt; **red out** to experience a red hazy field of vision, etc., as a result of aerobatics; **Royal Red Cross** a decoration for nurses, instituted 1883; **see red** to grow furious: to thirst for blood; **see reds under the bed** (*coll.*) to be convinced that every misfortune, set-back, etc., is the result of communist infiltration; **the Red Planet** Mars. [O.E. *rēad;* cf. Ger. *rot*, L. *ruber, rūfus*, Gr. *erythros*, Gael. *ruadh*.]

red². Same as **redd¹ˑ².**

redact *ri-dakt', v.t.* to edit, work into shape: to frame. — *ns.* **redac'tion; redac'tor.** — *adj.* **redactŏ'rial** (*re-, rē-*). [L. *redigĕre, redactum*, to bring back — pfx. *red-, agĕre*, to drive.]

redan *ri-dan', (fort.) n.* a fieldwork of two faces forming a salient. [O.Fr. *redan* — L. *re-, dēns, dentis*, a tooth.]

redargue *ri-där'gū, (obs.* or *Scot.) v.t.* to refute: to confute. [L. *redarguĕre* — *re(d)-*, again, *arguĕre*, argue.]

redd¹, red *red*, (chiefly *Scot.*) *v.t.* to put in order, make tidy: to clear up: to disentangle: to comb: to separate in fighting. — *v.i.* to set things in order, tidy up (usu. with *up*): — *pr.p.* **redd'ing;** *pa.t.* and *pa.p.* **redd, red.** — *n.* an act of redding: refuse, rubbish. — *adj.* (*Scots law*) vacated. — *ns.* **redd'er; redd'ing.** — **redd'ing-up'** setting in order, tidying up; **redd'ing-comb, -kame** a haircomb; **redd'ing-straik** a stroke received in trying to separate fighters. [Partly O.E. *hreddan*, to free, rescue (cf. Ger. *retten*, to rescue); prob. partly from or influenced by O.E. *rǣdan* (see **rede, read¹**); cf. also **rid¹.**]

redd², red *red*, *pa.t.* and *pa.p.* of **read¹** (*Spens.*): same as **rede** (*pres.* tense; *Scot.*).

redd³ *red*, (*Scot.*) *n.* fish or frog spawn: a spawning-place. [Origin obscure.]

redden, etc. See **red¹.**

reddendum *ri-den'dəm*, (*law*) *n.* a reserving clause in a

rēclose' *v.t.* **rēcolonisā'tion, -z-** *n.* **rēcommence'ment** *n.*
rēclothe' *v.t.* **rēcol'onise, -ize** *v.t.* **rēcommiss'ion** *n., v.t.* and *v.i.*
rēcoin'age *n.* **rēcommence'** *v.t.* and *v.i.* **rēcommit'** *v.t.*

fāte; fär; hûr; mīne; mōte; för; mūte; mōōn; fōōt; dhen (then); el'ə-mənt (element)

lease: — *pl.* **redden'da.** — *n.* **redden'do** (*Scots law*) service to be rendered or money to be paid by a vassal, or the clause in a charter specifying it: — *pl.* **redden'dos.** [L., to be rendered, gerundive of *reddere*.]

reddle, reddleman. See **ruddle.**

rede *rēd, v.t.* an old spelling of **read**[1] retained as an archaism in the senses of 'to counsel or advise, expound, relate'. — *n.* (*arch.*) advice: resolution: saying, tale: interpretation (*Browning*). — **rede'craft** (*arch.*) logic. — *adj.* **rede'less** (*arch.*) without counsel or wisdom.

redeem *ri-dēm', v.t.* to buy back: to compound for: to recover or free by payment: to free oneself from, by fulfilment: to ransom: to rescue, deliver, free: to get back: to reclaim: to pay the penalty of: to atone for: to compensate for: to put (time) to the best advantage. — *n.* **redeemabil'ity.** — *adj.* **redeem'able.** — *n.* **redeem'ableness.** — *adv.* **redeem'ably.** — *n.* **redeem'er.** — *adjs.* **redeem'ing; redeem'less** not to be redeemed. — **the Redeemer** the Saviour, Jesus Christ. [L. *redimēre* (perh. through Fr. *rédimer*) — *red-*, back, *emēre*, to buy.]

redeliver *rē-di-liv'ər, v.t.* to restore: to free again: to report the words of (*Shak.*). — *ns.* **redeliv'erance; redeliv'erer; redeliv'ery.** [Pfx. **re-**.]

redemption *ri-dem(p)'shən, n.* act of redeeming: atonement. — *adj.* **redemp'tible** redeemable. — *ns.* **redemp'tioner** an emigrant who bound himself to service until his fare was made up; **Redemp'tionist** a Trinitarian friar. — *adj.* **redemp'tive.** — *n.* **Redemp'torist** a missionary priest of a congregation founded by Alfonso Liguori in 1732 for work among the poor. — *adj.* **redemp'tory.** [L. *redimēre, redemptum*; cf. **redeem.**]

redeploy *rē-di-ploi', v.t.* to transfer (e.g. military forces, supplies, industrial workers) from one area to another. — Also *v.i.* — *n.* **redeploy'ment.** [Pfx. **re-**.]

redia *rē'di-ə, n.* a form in the life-cycle of the trematodes: — *pl.* **rē'diae** (-ē). [Named after Francesco *Redi* (d. prob. 1698), Italian naturalist.]

Rediffusion® *rē-di-fū'zhən, n.* a system by which television or radio programmes are transmitted by electricity along a wire rather than by direct broadcast.

redingote *red'ing-gōt, n.* a long double-breasted (orig. man's, later woman's) overcoat. [Fr., — Eng. **riding-coat.**]

redintegrate *red-in'ti-grāt, v.t.* to restore to wholeness: to re-establish. — *adj.* restored: renewed. — *n.* **redintegrā'tion** restoring to wholeness: the recurrence of a complete mental state when any single element of it recurs, e.g. when a piece of music reminds one of an occasion on which it was played (*psych.*). [L. *redintegrāre, -ātum* — *red-*, again, *integrāre*, to make whole — *integer*.]

redisburse *rē-dis-bûrs', (Spens.) v.t.* to refund. [Pfx. **re-**.]

redivivus *red-i-vī'vəs, re-di-wē'wōōs, adj.* resuscitated: come to life again. [L., — *red-*, again, *vivus*, alive — *vivēre*, to be alive.]

redolent *red'ə-lənt, adj.* fragrant: smelling (of, or with): suggestive (of), imbued (with). — *ns.* **red'olence, red'olency.** — *adv.* **red'olently.** [L. *redolēns, -entis* — *red-*, again, *olēre*, to emit smell.]

redouble *ri-dub'l, v.t.* and *v.i.* to double: to repeat: to re-echo: to increase: (*rē'dub'l*) to double after previous doubling. — *n.* (*rē'dub'l*) an act or fact of redoubling, as in bridge. — *n.* **redoub'lement** (*ri-*). [Pfx. **re-**.]

redoubt[1] *ri-dowt', (fort.) n.* a field-work enclosed on all sides, its ditch not flanked from the parapet: an inner last retreat. [Fr. *redoute* — It. *ridotto* — L.L. *reductus*, refuge — L., retired — *redūcēre*; the *b* from confusion with next word.]

redoubt[2] *ri-dowt', v.t.* to fear (*arch.*). — *adjs.* **redoubt'able** formidable: valiant; **redoubt'ed** redoubtable (*arch.*).

[O.Fr. *redouter*, to fear greatly — L. *re-*, back, *dubitāre*, to doubt.]

redound *ri-downd', v.i.* to overflow (*Spens.*): to be in excess (*Milt.*): to surge (*Spens.*): to be filled (*Spens.*): to flow back: to return: to rebound, be reflected or echoed: to turn, recoil, be reflected, as a consequence (to one's credit, discredit, advantage, etc.): to conduce: to rise one above another in receding series (*Spens.*). — *v.t.* (*fig.*) to cast, reflect. — *n.* the coming back, as an effect or consequence, return. — *n.* and *adj.* **redound'ing.** [Fr. *rédonder* — L. *redundāre* — *red-*, back, *undāre*, to surge — *unda*, a wave.]

redowa *red'ō-va, n.* a Bohemian dance: music for it, usually in quick triple time. [Ger. or Fr., — Czech *rejdovák*.]

redox *rē'doks, adj.* of a type of chemical reaction in which one of the reagents is reduced, while another is oxidised. [*Reduction* and *oxidation*.]

redraft *rē-dräft', n.* a revised draft or copy: a new bill of exchange which the holder of a protested bill draws on the drawer or endorsers, for the amount of the bill, with costs and charges. — *v.t.* to make a revised draft of. [Pfx. **re-**.]

redress *ri-dres', v.t.* to set right: to readjust: to restore (*Spens.*): to remedy: to compensate. — *n.* relief: reparation. — *n.* **redress'er** (*ri-*) one who redresses abuses or injuries. — *adj.* **redress'ive** (*Thomson*) affording redress. [Fr. *redresser* (see **dress**); partly from pfx. **re-** and **dress.**]

re-dress *rē'dres', v.t.* and *v.i.* to dress again: to dress in different clothes. [Pfx. **re-**.]

redruthite *red'rōōth-īt, n.* copper-glance, a mineral found at *Redruth* in Cornwall.

redshort *red'shört, adj.* brittle at red-heat. — Also **red'-sear, -share, -shire.** [Sw. *rödskör* — *röd*, red, *skör*, brittle.]

reduce *ri-dūs', v.t.* to bring back (*arch.*): to restore to an old state (*arch.*): to bring into a new state (*arch.*): to put back into a normal condition or place, as a dislocation or fracture (*surg.*): to change to another form: to express in other terms: to range in order or classification: to adapt, adjust: to translate: to put into (writing, practice; with *to*): to bring into a lower state: to lessen: to diminish in weight or girth: to weaken: to degrade (*mil.*): to impoverish: to subdue: to subject to necessity: to drive into (a condition; with *to*): to break up, separate, disintegrate: to disband (*mil., obs.*): to bring to the metallic state: to remove oxygen from, or combine with hydrogen, or lessen the positive valency of (an atom or ion) by adding electrons: to annul (*Scots law*). — *v.i.* to resolve itself: to slim, or lessen weight or girth. — *p.adj.* **reduced'** in a state of reduction: weakened: impoverished: diminished: simplified in structure. — *ns.* **reduc'er** one who reduces: a means of reducing: a joint-piece for connecting pipes of varying diameter; **reducibil'ity.** — *adj.* **reduc'ible** that may be reduced. — *n.* **reduc'ibleness.** — *adj.* **reduc'ing.** — *ns.* **reduc'tant** a reducing agent; **reduc'tase** an enzyme which brings about the reduction of organic compounds; **reduction** (*-duk'shən*) act of reducing or state of being reduced: diminution: lowering of price: subjugation: changing of numbers or quantities from one denomination to another (*arith.*): a settlement of S. American Indians converted by the Jesuits to Christianity, and governed by them (*hist.*); **reduc'tionism** the belief that complex data and phenomena can be explained in terms of something simpler. — *n.* and *adj.* **reduc'tionist.** — *adj.* **reduc'tive** bringing back (*arch.*): reducing. — *adv.* **reduc'tively.** — *n.* **reduc'tiveness.** — **reducing agent** a substance with a strong affinity for oxygen, or the like, serving to remove it from others; **reducing flame** a hot luminous blowpipe flame in which substances can be reduced; **reduction division** (*biol.*)

rĕcommit'ment *n.*	**rĕcompose'** *v.t.* and *v.i.*	**rĕcompress'ion** *n.*
rĕcommitt'al *n.*	**rĕcomposi'tion** *n.*	**rĕcondensā'tion** *n.*
rĕcompact' *v.t.*	**rĕcompress'** *v.t.*	**rĕcondense'** *v.t.* and *v.i.*

meiosis; **reduction works** smelting works. — **in reduced circumstances** (*euph.*) impoverished; **reduce to the ranks** to degrade, for misconduct, to the condition of a private soldier. [L. *redūcĕre, reductum* — *re-*, back, *dūcĕre*, to lead.]

reductio ad absurdum ri-duk′shi-ō ad ab-sûr′dəm, re-dŏŏk′-ti-ō ad ab-sŏŏr′dŏŏm, reduction to absurdity: the proof of a proposition by proving the falsity of its contradictory: the application of a principle so strictly that it is carried to absurd lengths. [L.]

reduit rā-dwē, *n.* an inner fortified retreat for a garrison. [Fr. *réduit*.]

redundant ri-dun′dənt, *adj.* surging (*Milt.*): overflowing (*obs.*): copious: over-copious: superfluous: of workers, no longer needed and therefore dismissed. — *ns.* **redun′dance, redun′dancy.** — *adv.* **redun′dantly.** [L. *redundāns, -antis,* pr.p. of *redundāre,* to overflow.]

reduplicate ri-dū′pli-kāt, *v.t.* to double: to repeat. — *v.i.* to double: to exhibit reduplication (*gram.*). — *adj.* doubled: showing reduplication (*gram.*): in aestivation, valvate with edges turned outwards (*bot.*). — *n.* **reduplicā′tion** a folding or doubling: the doubling of the initial part, in inflection and word-formation, as in L. *fefellī,* perf. of *fullō,* Gr. *tetypha,* perf. of *typtō* (*gram.*): the combination of two rhyming, alliterative, etc. words (the second sometimes a coinage for the purpose) to form one, as in *hurry-skurry, popsy-wopsy, mishmash.* — *adj.* **redū′plicātive.** [L. *reduplicāre, -ātum* — *duplicāre,* to double.]

ree[1] rē. See **ruff**[2].

ree[2] rē, **reed** rēd, (*Scot.*) *ns.* an enclosure, esp. a (partially-) roofed walled yard, as for coal, for wintering cattle, for confining sheep, etc. [Poss. cog. with Du. *rede,* roadstead.]

reebok rā′bok. *n.* a South African antelope. [Du.]

reech rēch. Same as **reek.** — *adj.* **reech′y** (*Shak.* **rechie, reechie**) smoky, grimy.

re-echo rē-ek′ō, *v.t.* to echo back: to repeat as if an echo. — *v.i.* to give back echoes: to resound. — *n.* re-echoing. [Pfx. **re-**.]

reed[1], **reede** (*Spens.*). Same as **rede.**

reed[2] rēd, *n.* a tall stiff hard-culmed marsh or water grass of various kinds, esp. *Phragmites communis:* a thing made, or formerly made, of a reed or reeds — a pen, an arrow, a measuring rod, a music pipe, the vibrating tongue of an organ-pipe or woodwind instrument (with or without the parts to which it is attached), a weaver's appliance for separating the warp threads and beating up the weft: thatching: a small reedlike moulding: a reed-instrument: the metal reed of an organ pipe used as the plate of a capacitor for electronic amplification: — *adj.* (*Shak.*) reed-like. — *v.t.* to thatch. — *adjs.* **reed′ed** covered with reeds: having reed(s); **reed′en** of reed. — *ns.* **reed′er** a thatcher; **reed′iness; reed′ing** the milling on the edge of a coin: a reed moulding; **reed′ling** the bearded titmouse. — *adj.* **reed′y** abounding with reeds: resembling a reed: sounding as a reed instrument. — **reed′-band** a band of reed-instruments; **reed′-bed; reed′-bird** the bobolink; **reed′-bunting** the blackheaded bunting; **reed′-drawing** the combing out of rough straw by means of a frame; **reed′-grass** a reedlike grass of various kinds (as *Phalaris, Arundo*); **reed′-instrument** a woodwind with reed — as clarinet, oboe, bassoon; **reed′-knife** a tool for organ-tuning; **reed′-mace** cat's-tail (Typha); **reed′= or′gan** a keyboard instrument with free reeds, as the harmonium, the American organ; **reed′-pheas′ant** the bearded titmouse; **reed′-pipe** an organ-pipe whose tone is produced by the vibration of a reed, the pipe acting as resonator; **reed′-rand, -rond** (*East Anglia*) a reed thicket; **reed′-sparr′ow** the reed-bunting: the sedge-warbler; **reed′stop** a set of reed-pipes controlled by a single organ-stop; **reed′-war′bler** a warbler that fre-

quents marshy places and builds its nest on reeds — also called **reed′-wren,** the **reed′-thrush** being a larger species (**greater reed-warbler**). — **broken reed** (*fig.*) a person who is too weak or unreliable to be depended upon; **free reed** a reed vibrating in an opening without touching the sides. [O.E. *hrēod;* cf. Du. *riet* and Ger. *Riet.*]

reed[3]. See **ree**[2].

re-edify rē-ed′i-fī, *v.t.* to rebuild. —(*Spens.*) **reæd′ifye.** — *ns.* **re-edificā′tion; re-ed′ifier.** [L. *aedificāre,* to build.]

reedy. See **reed**[2].

reef[1] rēf, *n.* a chain of rocks at or near the surface of water: a shoal or bank: a gold-bearing lode or vein (orig. *Austr.*): the encasing rock of a diamond-mine, all ground in the mine other than diamondiferous (*S.Afr.*). — **reef′-builder** a coral-animal that forms reefs. [Du. *rif* — O.N. *rif.*]

reef[2] rēf, *n.* a portion of a sail that may be rolled or folded up. — *v.t.* to reduce the exposed surface of, as a sail: to gather up in a similar way. — *ns.* **reef′er** one who reefs: a midshipman (*slang*): a reefing-jacket (also **reef′er-jacket**): a cigarette containing marijuana (*coll.*); **reef′ing.** — **reef′-band** a strengthening strip across a sail; **reef′ing-jack′et** a short thick double-breasted jacket; **reef′-knot** a flat knot used in tying reef-points conssting of two loops passing symetrically through each other; — **reef-point** a short rope on a reefband to secure a reefed sail. [O.N. *rif.*]

reefer[1] rē′fər, (*slang*), *n.* a refrigerated railway car: a refrigerated ship. [**refrigerator.**]

reefer[2]. See **reef**[2].

reek rēk, *n.* smoke: vapour: fume. — *v.i.* to emit smoke, fumes, or (esp. evil) smell: to exhale. — *v.t.* to expose to smoke: to exhale. — *adj.* **reek′ing.** — *adj.* **reek′y** (*Scot.* **reek′ie**) smoky: smoked: reeking: foul (*Shak.*). — **Auld Reekie** Edinburgh. [O.E. *rēc;* O.N. *reykr,* Ger. *Rauch,* Du. *rook,* smoke; a Northern form; cf. **reech.**]

reel rēl, *n.* a cylinder, drum, spool, bobbin, or frame on which thread, fishing-line, wire, cables, photographic film, or the like may be wound: a length of material so wound: a loud rattling, a din (*Scot.*): a whirl, a stagger: a lively dance, esp. Highland or Irish: a tune for it, usu. in 4-4, sometimes in 6-8 time: (in *pl.*) revelry (*Shak.*). — *v.t.* to wind on a reel: to take off by or from a reel: to draw (in) by means of a reel: to cause to whirl or roll (*Spens.*): to stagger along (*Shak.*). — *v.i.* to whirl: to seem to swirl or sway: to totter: to stagger: (of e.g. line of battle) to waver: to rattle (*Scot.*): to dance a reel. — *n.* **reel′er** one who reels: the grasshopper-warbler. — *n.* and *adj.* **reel′ing.** — *adv.* **reel′ingly.** — **reel′man** (*Austr.*) the member of a surf life-saving team who operates the reel on which the line is wound. — **(right) off the reel** in uninterrupted course or succession: without stop or hesitation; **reel off** to utter rapidly and fluently; **Virginia reel** an American country-dance. [O.E. *hrēol,* but possibly partly of other origin; Gael. *righil* (the dance) may be from English.]

reen. See **rhine.**

re-enact rē-in-akt′, *v.t.* to enact over again: to reconstruct in action. — *n.* **re-enact′ment.** [Pfx. **re-**.]

re-enforce rē-in-fōrs′, -förs′, *v.t.* to enforce again: to reinforce (*rare*): to reassemble, rally (*Shak.*). — *n.* **re-enforce′ment** reinforcement. [Pfx. **re-**.]

re-enter rē-en′tər, *v.t.* and *v.i.* to enter again or anew: in engraving, to cut deeper. — *p.adj.* **re-en′tering** entering again: pointing inwards: reflex (*math.*). — *n.* **re-en′-trance** act or achievement of entering again: fact of being re-entrant (in this sense also **re-en′trancy**). — *adj.* **re-en′trant** re-entering (opp. to *salient*): reflex (*math.*): returning upon itself at the ends (*elect.*). — *n.* a re-entering angle: a valley, depression, etc., running

---

rĕconfirm′ *v.t.*   **rĕcon′quest** *n.*   **rĕconsiderā′tion** *n.*
rĕconnect′ *v.t.*   **rĕcon′secrate** *v.t.*   **rĕconsol′idate** *v.t.* and *v.i.*
rĕcon′quer *v.t.*   **rĕconsecrā′tion** *n.*   **rĕconsolidā′tion** *n.*

fāte; fär; hûr; mīne; mōte; för; mūte; mōōn; fŏŏt; dhen (then); *el′ə-mənt* (element)

into a main feature: the concavity between two salients. — *n.* **re-en'try** entering again, esp., of a spacecraft, entering the earth's atmosphere again: resumption of possession: the re-opening of an oil-well for further drilling: a card allowing a hand to take the lead again. [Pfx. **re-**.]

reest[1]. See **reast**[1].

reest[2], **reist**, **reast** *rēst*, (*Scot.*) *v.t.* to dry, cure, with smoke. — *v.i.* to be smoke-dried. [Origin obscure.]

reest[3], **reist** *rēst*, (*Scot.*) *v.i.* of a horse, suddenly to refuse to move, to baulk. — *n.* a sudden fit of stubbornness. — *adj.* **reest'y**. [Perh. **rest**[1] or **arrest**.]

reeve[1] *rēv*, (*hist.*) *n.* a high official, chief magistrate of a district: a bailiff or steward. [O.E. *gerēfa*; cf. **grieve**[2] (*Scot.*).]

reeve[2] *rēv*, *v.t.* to pass the end of a rope through: to pass through any hole: to thread one's way through: to fasten by reeving: — *pa.t.* and *pa.p.* **reeved**, **rove**. [Origin obscure.]

reeve[3] *rev*, see **ruff**[2].

ref *ref*, (*coll.*) *n.* and *v.t.*, *v.i.* short for **referee**: — *pr.p.* **reff'ing**; *pa.t.* and *pa.p.* **reffed**.

refection *ri-fek'shən*, *n.* refreshment or relief (*lit.* and *fig.*): a meal. — *v.t.* **refect** (*-fekt'*; back-formation) to refresh. — *v.i.* to take a repast. — *ns.* **refec'tioner**, **refectorian** (*rē-fek-tō', -tō'ri-ən*) the officer in charge of the refectory and its arrangements; **refectory** (*ri-fek'tər-i*; sometimes *ref'ik-*) a dining-hall, esp. monastic. — **refectory table** a long narrow dining-table supported on two shaped pillars each set in a base; **Refection Sunday** Refreshment Sunday. [L. *reficĕre*, *refectum* — *facĕre*, to make.]

refel *ri-fel'*, (*obs.*) *v.t.* to refute: to disprove: to confute: to repulse: — *pr.p.* **refell'ing**; *pa.t.* and *pa.p.* **refelled'**. [L. *refellĕre* — *fallĕre*, to deceive.]

refer *ri-fûr'*, *v.t.* to reproduce, represent (*obs.*): to assign (to): to impute (to): to attribute (to): to bring into relation (to): to deliver, commit, or submit (to): to hand over for consideration (to): to direct for information, confirmation, testimonials, or whatever is required (to): to direct the attention of (to): to postpone (*obs.*): to recount (*arch.*): to direct to sit an examination again, fail. — *v.i.* (with *to* in all cases) to have relation or application, to relate: to direct the attention: to turn for information, confirmation, etc.: to turn, apply, or have recourse: to make mention or allusion: — *pr.p.* **referr'ing**; *pa.t.* and *pa.p.* **referred'**. — *adj.* **referable** (*ref'ər-ə-bl, ri-fûr'i-bl*; sometimes **referrable** *-fûr'*, or **referrible** *-fer'*) that may be referred or assigned. — *n.* **referee** (*ref-ə-rē'*; coll. shortening **ref**) one to whom anything is referred: an arbitrator, umpire, or judge. — *v.t.* to act as referee for. — *v.i.* to act as referee. — *n.* **ref'erence** the act of referring: a submitting for information or decision: the act of submitting a dispute for investigation or decision (*law*): relation: allusion: loosely, one who is referred to: loosely, a testimonial: a direction to a book or passage: a book or passage used for reference. — *v.t.* to make a reference to: to provide (a book, etc.) with references to other sources. — *ns.* **referendary** (*-end'ə-ri*; *obs.*) a referee; formerly a court official who was the medium of communication with the pope, emperor, etc.; **referen'dum** the principle or practice of submitting a question directly to the vote of the entire electorate (*pl.* **-da**, **-dums**); **ref'erent** the object of reference or discussion: the first term in a proposition. — *adj.* **referential** (*-en'shl*) containing a reference: having reference (to): used for reference. — *adv.* **referen'tially**. — *n.* **referr'al** act or instance of referring or being referred, esp. to another person or organisation for, e.g. consideration, treatment, etc. — **reference book** a book to be consulted on occasion, not for consecutive reading: a pass book (*S.Afr.*); **ref'erence=**

mark a character, as *, †, or a cock-up figure, used to refer to notes; **referred pain** pain felt in a part of the body other than its source. — **terms of reference** a guiding statement defining the scope of an investigation or similar piece of work: loosely, the scope itself. [L. *referre*, to carry back — *ferre*, to carry.]

reffo *ref'ō*, (*Austr. slang*) a refugee: — *pl.* **reff'os**.

refigure *rē-fig'ər*, *v.t.* to represent anew, reproduce (*Shak.*): to restore to form: to calculate anew. [Pfx. **re-**.]

refill *rē-fil'*, *v.t.* to fill again. — *n.* (*rē'* or *-fil'*) a fresh fill: a duplicate for refilling purposes. [Pfx. **re-**.]

refine *ri-fīn'*, *v.t.* to purify: to clarify: (*usu.* with *out*) to get rid of (impurities, etc.) by a purifying process: to free from coarseness, vulgarity, crudity: to make more cultured. — *v.i.* to become more fine, pure, subtle, or cultured: to apply or affect subtlety or nicety: to improve by adding refinement or subtlety (with *on* or *upon*). — *adj.* **refined'**. — *adv.* **refin'edly** in a refined manner: with affected elegance. — *ns.* **refin'edness**; **refine'ment** act or practice of refining: state of being refined: culture in feelings, taste, and manners: an improvement: a subtlety: an excessive nicety; **refin'er**; **refin'ery** a place for refining; **refin'ing**. [L. *re-*, denoting change of state, and **fine**[1].]

refit *rē-fit'*, *v.t.* to fit out afresh and repair. — *v.i.* to undergo refitting. — *ns.* **re'fit**, **refit'ment**, **refitt'ing**. [Pfx. **re-** and **fit**[1].]

reflag *rē-flag'*, *v.t.* to replace the national flag of (a ship) with that of a more powerful nation, so it sails under its protection: — *pr.p.* **reflagg'ing**; *pa.t.* and *pa.p.* **reflagged'**. [Pfx. **re-**.]

reflation *rē-flā'shən*, *n.* increase in the amount of currency, economic activity, etc. after deflation: a general increase, above what would normally be expected, in the spending of money. — *v.t.* (back-formation from *n.*) **rēflate'**. — *adj.* **reflā'tionary**. [Pfx. **re-** and *inflation*.]

reflect *ri-flekt'*, *v.t.* to bend or send back or aside: to throw back after striking: to give an image of in the manner of a mirror: to express, reproduce (*fig.*): to cast, shed (e.g. credit, discredit) (*fig.*): to consider meditatively (that, how, etc.). — *v.i.* to bend or turn back or aside: to be mirrored: to cast a light (*Shak.*): to meditate (on): to cast reproach or censure (on, upon): to bring harmful results. — *n.* **reflect'ance**, **reflecting factor** ratio of reflected radiation to incident radiation. — *adj.* **reflect'ed** cast or thrown back: turned or folded back: mirrored. — *n.* **reflect'er** (*Swift*) one who casts reflections. — *adj.* **reflect'ing**. — *adv.* **reflect'ingly** meditatively: with implication of censure. — *n.* **reflection**, also (now chiefly in scientific use) **reflexion** (*ri-flek'shən*) a turning, bending, or folding aside, back, or downwards: folding upon itself: rebound: change of direction when an electromagnetic wave or sound-wave strikes on a surface and is thrown back: reflected light, colour, heat, etc.: an image in a mirror: (production of) a mirror image of a line or figure (by reflecting it in an axis of symmetry): the conformal transformation in which a figure is reflected in a fixed line: the action of the mind by which it is conscious of its own operations: attentive consideration: contemplation: a thought or utterance resulting from contemplation: censure or reproach. — *adjs.* **reflec'tionless**; **reflect'ive** reflecting: reflected: meditative. — *adv.* **reflect'ively**. — *ns.* **reflect'iveness**; **reflectiv'ity** ability to reflect rays: reflectance; **reflect'or** a reflecting surface, instrument, or body: a reflecting telescope; **reflet** (*rə-fle', -flā'*; Fr.) an irridescent or metallic lustre. — *adj.* **reflex** (*rē'fleks*, formerly *ri-fleks'*) bent or turned back: reflected: reciprocal: of an angle, more than 180°: turned back upon itself: involuntary, produced by or concerned with response from a nerve-centre to a stimulus from

---

For other sounds see detailed chart of pronunciation.

without: illuminated by light from another part of the same picture (*paint.*): using the same valve or valves for high-and low-frequency amplification (*radio*). — *n.* reflection: reflected light: a reflected image: an expression, manifestation, outward representation: a reflex action: a reflex radio receiving set. — *v.t.* (*-fleks'*) to bend back: to project, direct (*Shak.*). — *adj.* **reflexed'** (*bot.*) bent abruptly backward or downward. — *n.* **reflexibil'ity.** — *adj.* **reflex'ible; reflex'ive** (*gram.*) indicating that the action turns back upon the subject. — *advs.* **reflex'ively; reflex'ly** (or *rē'*). — *n.* **reflexol'ogy** (*psych.*) the study of the body's reflexes as a guide to behaviour: a form of therapy for treating particular bodily ailments and general stress, carried out through massage on the soles of the feet, on the principle that specific areas of the feet relate to specific parts and organs of the body. — *adj.* **reflexolog'ical.** — **reflecting factor** see **reflectance** above; **reflecting microscope** one using a system of mirrors instead of lenses; **reflecting telescope** one (as, e.g. the Gregorian or Newtonian) which has a concave mirror instead of an object glass (lens or lenses); **reflex arc** the simplest functional unit of the nervous system, by which an impulse produces a reflex action; **reflex camera** one in which the image is reflected on to a glass screen for composing and focusing; **reflex light** a lens with a reflecting back, returning a beam of red light when the headlight, e.g. of a motor-car, shines on it.   [L. *reflectĕre, reflexum — flectăre*, to bend.]

reflet, reflex, etc. See **reflect.**

reflow *rē-flō', v.i.* to ebb: to flow again. — *ns.* **reflow', reflow'ing** ebb: reflux.   [Pfx. **re-**.]

refluent *ref'lŏō-ənt, (rare) adj.* flowing back: ebbing: tidal. — *ns.* **ref'luence** flowing back: ebb; **reflux** (*rē'fluks*) refluence: the process of boiling a liquid in a flask with a condenser attached so that the vapour condenses and flows back into the flask, avoiding loss by evaporation (*chem.*; also *v.i., v.t.*).   [L. *refluēns, -entis,* pr.p. of *refluĕre — fluĕre, fluxum,* to flow; *fluxus, -ūs,* a flow.]

refocillate *ri-fos'il-āt, (obs.) v.t.* to refresh, cherish. — *n.* **refocillā'tion.**   [L. *refocillāre, -ātum,* to cherish — *focus,* a hearth.]

re-form, also **reform** *rē'förm', v.t.* and *v.i.* to form again or anew. — *n.* **rē(-)formā'tion.** — *adj.* **rē(-)formed'.**   [Pfx. **re-**.]

reform *ri-förm', v.t.* to transform: to restore, rebuild (*Milt.*): to amend: to make better: to remove defects from: to redress: to bring to a better way of life: to chastise (*Spens.*): to prune (*Milt.*): to break up in reorganisation, hence to disband, dismiss (*mil. hist.*). — *v.i.* to abandon evil ways. — *n.* amendment or transformation, esp. of a system or institution: a stricter offshoot or branch of a religious order: an extension or better distribution of parliamentary representation. — *adj.* **reform'able** (*-ri-*). — *ns.* **reformabil'ity; reformation** (*ref-ər-mā'shən*) the act of reforming: amendment: improvement: (*cap.*) the great religious revolution of the 16th century, which gave rise to the various evangelical or Protestant organisations of Christendom; **reformā'tionist.** — *adjs.* **reformative** (*ri-förm'ə-tiv*) tending to produce reform; **reform'atory** reforming: tending to produce reform. — *n.* (in U.K., formerly) an institution for reclaiming young delinquents, or women. — *adj.* **reformed'** changed: amended: improved: (*cap.*) Protestant, esp. Calvinistic, in doctrine or polity. — *ns.* **reform'er** one who reforms: one who advocates political reform: (*cap.*) one of those who took part in the Reformation of the 16th century; **reform'ism; reform'ist** a reformer: an advocate of reform, or of not very thorough-going reform. — **Reform flask** a salt-glazed stoneware flask made in the likeness of one of the figures connected

with the 1832 parliamentary Reform Bill; **Reform Judaism** a form of Judaism, originating in the 19th cent., in which the Jewish Law is adapted so as to be relevant to contemporary life; **Reformed Presbyterian** Cameronian; **reform school** reformatory.   [L. *refōrmāre, -ātum — förmāre,* to shape — *förma,* form.]

reformado *ref-ör-mä'dō, -mä'dō, (hist.) n.* a disbanded or dismissed soldier: an officer whose company has been disbanded or who is for other reason without a command: a volunteer serving as an officer: a reformed person: a reformer: — *pl.* **-do(e)s.** — Also **reformāde'** (*Bunyan*). — Also *adj.*   [Sp. *reformado,* reformed.]

refract *ri-frakt', v.t.* (of a medium) to deflect (rays of light, sound, etc., passing into it from another medium): to produce by refraction (*rare*). — *adj.* (*rare*) refracted. — *adjs.* **refract'able** refrangible; **refrac'ted** deflected on passage into another medium: bent sharply back from the base (*bot.*); **refract'ing.** — *n.* **refrac'tion.** — *adj.* **refrac'tive** refracting: of refraction. — *ns.* **refractivity** (*rē-frak-tiv'i-ti*); **refractom'eter** an instrument for measuring refractive indices; **refrac'tor** (*ri-*) anything that refracts: a refracting telescope. — **refracting telescope** one in which the principal means of focusing the light is an object glass; **refraction correction** (*astron.*) the correction made in the calculation of the altitude of a star, planet, etc., to allow for the refraction of its light by the earth's atmosphere; **refractive index** the ratio of the sine of the angle of incidence to that of the angle of refraction when a ray passes from one medium to another. — **angle of refraction** the angle between a refracted ray and the normal to the bounding surface; **double refraction** the separation of an incident ray of light into two refracted rays, polarised in perpendicular planes.   [L. *refringĕre, refrāctum — frangĕre,* to break.]

refractory (*formerly* **refractary**) *ri-frak'tər-i, adj.* unruly: unmanageable: obstinate: perverse: resistant to ordinary treatment, stimulus, disease, etc.: esp. difficult of fusion: fire-resisting. — *n.* a substance that is able to resist high temperatures, etc., used in lining furnaces, etc. — *adv.* **refrac'torily.** — *n.* **refrac'toriness.**   [L. *refrāctārius,* stubborn.]

refrain¹ *ri-frān', n.* a burden, a line or phrase recurring, esp. at the end of a stanza: the music of such a burden.   [O.Fr. *refrain — refraindre —* L. *refringĕre — frangĕre,* to break.]

refrain² *ri-frān, v.t.* to curb (*arch.*): to restrain (*arch.*): to abstain from (*Shak*): to keep away from (*obs.*). — *v.i.* to keep oneself from action, forbear: to abstain (from; *obs.* with *to*).   [O.Fr. *refrener —* L.L. *refrēnāre — re-,* back, *frēnum,* a bridle.]

refrangible *ri-fran'ji-bl, adj.* that may be refracted. — *ns.* **refrangibil'ity, refran'gibleness.**   [See **refract.**]

refresh *ri-fresh', v.t.* to make fresh again: to freshen up: to give new vigour, life, liveliness, spirit, brightness, fresh appearance, coolness, moistness, etc., to. — *v.i.* to become fresh again: to take refreshment, esp. drink (*coll.*). — *v.t.* **refresh'en** to make fresh again. — *ns.* **refresh'ener; refresh'er** one who, or that which, refreshes: a cool drink (*coll.*): a fee paid to counsel for continuing his attention to a case, esp. when adjourned: a douceur to encourage further exertions (*coll.*): a subsequent course of training or instruction to maintain or reattain one's former standard, study new developments, etc. (also *adj.*). — *adj.* **refresh'ful** full of power to refresh: refreshing. — *adv.* **refresh'fully.** — *adj.* **refresh'ing** pleasantly cooling, inspiriting, reviving, invigorating. — *adv.* **refresh'ingly.** — *ns.* **refresh'ment** the act of refreshing: state of being refreshed: renewed strength or spirit: that which refreshes, as food or rest: (in *pl.*) drink or a light meal. — **refresh'ment-room; Refreshment** or **Refection, Sunday** the fourth Sunday in Lent, when the story of the

---

rēdescribe' *v.t.*   **rēdevel'op(e)** *v.t.*   **rēdip'** *v.t.*
rēdeterminā'tion *n.*   **rēdevel'opment** *n.*   **rēdirect'** *v.t.*
rēdeter'mine *v.t.*   **rē'did'.** See **re-do.**   **rediscount'** *v.t.*

fāte; fär; hûr; mīne; mōte; för; mūte; mŏōn; fŏōt; dhen (then); *el'ə-mənt* (element)

loaves and fishes is read in English and R.C. churches. [O.Fr. *refrescher* — *re-*, *freis* (fem. *fresche*), fresh.]

refrigerant *ri-frij'ə-rənt*, *adj*. cooling: giving a feeling of coolness: refreshing. — *n*. a freezing or cooling agent: that which gives a cool feeling. — *v.t.* **refrig'erāte** to freeze: to make cold: to make to feel cold: to expose to great cold (as food for preservation). — *v.i.* to become cold. — *n*. **refrigerā'tion**. — *adj*. **refrig'erative** (*-rə-tiv*) cooling. — *n*. **refrig'erator** (*-rā-tər*) an apparatus or chamber for producing and maintaining a low temperature (contraction **fridge**, esp. when in domestic use). — *adj*. **refrig'eratory** (*-rə-tər-i*) cooling: refrigerative. — *n*. a refrigerator: a chamber in which ice is formed: a water-filled vessel for condensing in distillation. [L. *refrigerāre*, *-ātum* — *re-*, denoting change of state, *frīgerāre* — *frīgus*, cold.]

refringe *ri-frinj'*, *v.t.* (*obs.*) to refract. — *n*. **refring'ency** refractivity. — *adj*. **refring'ent**. [L. *refringĕre*; see **refract**.]

reft *reft*, *pa.t.* and *pa.p.* of **reave**.

refuge *ref'ūj*, *n*. shelter or protection from danger or trouble: an asylum or retreat: a street island for pedestrians: recourse in difficulty. — *v.t.* and *v.i.* (*arch.*) to shelter. — *ns.* **refugee** (*ref-ū-jē'*) one who flees for refuge to another country, esp. from religious or political persecution: a fugitive; **refugium** (*ri-fū'ji-əm*) a region that has retained earlier geographical, climatic, etc. conditions, and thus becomes a haven for older varieties of flora and fauna: — *pl.* **refū'gia** (*-ji-ə*). — **house of refuge** a shelter for the destitute. [Fr., — L. *refugium* — *fugĕre*, to flee.]

refulgent *ri-ful'jənt*, *adj*. casting a flood of light: radiant: beaming. — *ns.* **reful'gence**, **reful'gency**. [L. *refulgēns*, *-entis*, pr.p. of *refulgēre* — *re-*, intens., *fulgēre*, to shine.]

refund[1] *ri-* or *rē-fund'*, *v.t.* to pour back (now *rare*): to repay. — *v.i.* to restore what was taken. — *ns.* **refund** (*rē'fund* or *ri-fund'*); **refund'er**; **refund'ment** (*ri-*). [L. *refundĕre* — *fundĕre*, to pour.]

refund[2] *rē-fund'*, *v.t.* to fund anew: to replace (an old issue) by a new: to borrow so as to pay off (an old loan). [Pfx. **re-**.]

refuse[1] *ri-fūz'*, *v.t.* to decline to take or accept: to renounce: to decline to give or grant: of a horse, to decline to jump over: to fail to follow suit to (*cards*): to decline to meet in battle: to hold back from the regular alignment in action (*mil.*). — *v.i.* to make refusal. — *adj*. **refus'able** (*ri-*). — *ns.* **refus'al** the act of refusing: the option of taking or refusing: a thing refused; **refus(e)nik** (*ri-fūz'nik*) a dissident Russian citizen, esp. a Russian Jew wishing to emigrate: generally, a dissident (*coll.*); **refus'er**. [Fr. *refuser* — L. *refūsum*, pa.p. of *refundĕre* — *fundĕre*, to pour; cf. **refund**[1].]

refuse[2] *ref'ūs*, *adj*. rejected as worthless. — *n*. that which is rejected or left as worthless. [Fr. *refus*; see foregoing.]

refute *ri-fūt'*, *v.t.* to disprove: loosely, to deny. — *adj*. **refutable** (*ref'ūt-ə-bl*, or *ri-fūt'*). — *adv*. **ref'utably** (or *ri-fūt'*). — *ns.* **refu'tal**, **refutā'tion** (*ref-*) act of refuting: that which disproves; **refu'ter**. [L. *refutāre*, to drive back.]

regain *ri-* or *rē-gān'*, *v.t.* to gain or win back: to get back to. — *n*. recovery. — *adj*. **regain'able**. — *ns.* **regain'er**; **regain'ment**. [Fr. *regaigner* (now *regagner*).]

regal[1] *rē'gl*, *adj*. royal: kingly. — *adj*. **regalian** (*ri-gā'li-ən*; *arch.*) regal. — *ns.* **regalism** (*rē'gəl-izm*) royal supremacy, esp. in Church matters; **re'galist**; **regality** (*ri-gal'i-ti*) state of being regal: royalty: sovereignty: a territorial jurisdiction formerly conferred by the king (*Scot.*). — *adv*. **re'gally**. [L. *rēgālis* — *rēx*, a king — *regĕre*, to rule.]

regal[2] *rē'gl*, *n*. a small portable organ. [Fr. *régale*.]

regale[1] *ri-gāl'*, *v.t.* to feast: to treat to (stories, etc.; with *with*): to give pleasure to. — *v.i.* (*arch.*) to feast. — *n*. (*arch.*) a feast: a choice dish. — *n*. **regale'ment**. [Fr. *régaler* — It. *regalare*, perh. — *gala*, a piece of finery.]

regale[2]. See **regalia**[1].

regalia[1] *ri-gā'li-ə*, *rā-gä'li-a*, *n.pl.* royal privileges or powers, as (*hist.*) that of enjoying the revenues of vacant sees, etc. (*sing.* **regale** *ri-gā'lē*): the insignia of royalty — crown, sceptre, etc.: loosely, insignia or special garb generally, as of the Freemasons. [L. *rēgālis*, royal, neut. sing. *-e*, pl. *-ia*.]

regalia[2] *ri-gā'li-ə*, *n*. a big cigar. [Sp., royal right.]

regalism, **regality**, etc. See **regal**[1].

regar. See **regur**.

regard *ri-gärd'*, *v.t.* to look at: to observe: to heed: to look to: to esteem or consider: to esteem highly: to have kindly feelings for: to respect: to take into account: to have respect or relation to. — *v.i.* to look: to give heed. — *n*. orig., look: a thing seen (*Shak.*): intention (*Shak.*): attention with interest: observation: estimation: esteem: kindly, affectionate, or respectful feeling: care: consideration: a thing to be considered: repute: respect: relation: reference: (in *pl.*) in messages of greeting, respectful good will. — *adjs.* **regard'able** worthy of consideration; **regard'ant** attentive: looking backward (*her.*). — *n*. **regard'er**. — *adj*. **regard'ful** heedful: respectful. — *adv*. **regard'fully**. — *n*. **regard'fulness**. — *prep*. **regard'ing** concerning. — *adj*. **regard'less** heedless: inconsiderate. — *adj*. and *adv*. (*coll.*) without regard to consequences: careless (of). — *adv*. **regard'lessly**. — *n*. **regard'lessness**. — **as regards** with regard to, concerning; **in regard of, to** (*arch.*) in comparison with: in reference to: out of consideration for (*Shak.*); **in this regard** in this respect; **with regard to** concerning: so far as relates to. [Fr. *regarder* — *garder*, to keep, watch.]

regatta *ri-gat'ə*, *n*. a yacht or boat race-meeting. [It. (Venetian) *regata*.]

regelation *rē-ji-lā'shən*, *n*. freezing together again (as of ice melted by pressure when the pressure is released). — *v.t.* and *v.i.* **rē'gelāte**. [Pfx. **re-** and L. *gelāre*, to freeze.]

regency *rē'jən-si*, *n*. the office, term of office, jurisdiction, or dominion of a regent: a body entrusted with vicarious government: specif., in French history, the minority of Louis XV, 1715–1723, when Philip of Orleans was regent: in English history, the years 1810–20, when the Prince of Wales (George IV) was Prince Regent. — *adj*. of, or in the style prevailing during, the French or English regency. — *n*. **rē'gence** (*obs.*) government. — *adj*. **regent** ruling: invested with interim or vicarious sovereign authority. — *n*. a ruler: one invested with interim authority on behalf of another: formerly in Scotland and elsewhere, a professor: a master or doctor who takes part in the regular duties of instruction and government in some universities. — *n*. **rē'gentship**. — **rē'gent-bird** a bower-bird (*Sericulus*) named in honour of the Prince Regent. [L. *regēns*, *-entis*, pr.p. of *regĕre*, to rule.]

regenerate *ri-jen'ər-āt*, *v.t.* to produce anew: to renew spiritually (*theol.*): to put new life or energy into: to reform completely: to reproduce (a part of the body): to magnify the amplitude of an electrical output by relaying part of the power back into the input circuit (*elect.*): to produce again in the original form (*chem.*, *nucleonics*, etc.). — *v.i.* to undergo regeneration, to be regenerated. — *adj*. (*-it*, *-āt*) regenerated, renewed: changed from a natural to a spiritual state. — *adj*. **regen'erable**. — *ns.* **regen'eracy** (*-ə-si*); **regenerā'tion** renewal of lost parts: spiritual rebirth: reformation: recovery of waste heat or other energy that would have been lost: rebuilding, revitalising of an area, e.g. the centre of a city. — *adj*. **regen'erative**. — *adv*. **regen'-**

---

redis'count *n*.	**rēdiscov'ery** *n*.	**rēdistil'** *v.t.*
rēdiscov'er *v.t.*	**rēdissolu'tion** *n*.	**rēdistillā'tion** *n*.
rēdiscov'erer *n*.	**rēdissolve'** *v.t.*	**rēdistrib'ute** *v.t.*

For other sounds see detailed chart of pronunciation.

eratively. — *n.* **regen'erātor** one who, or that which, regenerates: a chamber in which waste heat is, by reversal of draught, alternately stored up and given out to the gas and air entering. — *adj.* **regen'eratory** (-*ə-tər-i*).   [L. *regenerāre, -ātum,* to bring forth again. — *re-*, again, *generāre,* to generate.]

regent. See **regency.**

regest *ri-jest',* (*Milt.*) *n.* a register.   [See **register.**]

reggae *reg'ā, rā'gā, n.* a simple, lively, strongly rhythmic rock music of the West Indies, imported into Britain by immigrants in the mid-1960s.

regicide *rej'i-sīd, n.* the killing or killer of a king. — *adj.* **regicī'dal.**   [L. *rēx, rēgis,* a king, on the analogy of **homicide, parricide,** etc.]

régie *rā-zhē,* (Fr.) *n.* a system of government monopoly, esp. in tobacco: the department concerned: tobacco sold by it.

régime *rā-zhēm', n.* regimen: administration. — Also **regime.**   [Fr., — L. *regimen.*]

regimen *rej'i-men, n.* government: system of government: course of treatment, as diet (*med.*): grammatical government: prevailing system or set of conditions. — *adj.* **regim'inal.**   [L. *regimen, -inis* — *regĕre,* to rule.]

regiment *rej'mənt, rej'i-mənt, n.* government (*arch.*): control (*arch.*): rule (*arch.*): regimen (*arch.*): a region under government (*arch.*): (often *rej'mənt*) a body of soldiers constituting the largest permanent unit, commanded by a colonel: a large number (*fig.*). — *v.t.* (*rej'i-ment, -ment'*) to form into a regiment or regiments: to systematise, classify: to organise: to subject to excessive control. — *adj.* **regimental** (-*i-ment'l*) of a regiment. — *n.* (in *pl.*) the uniform of a regiment. — *n.* **regimentation** (-*i-men-tā'shən*).   [L.L. *regimentum* — L. *regĕre,* to rule.]

regiminal. See **regimen.**

regina *ri-jī'nə, n.* queen: title of a reigning queen, abbrev. to R in signature. — *adj.* **reginal** (-*jī'nl*) of a queen: siding with a queen.   [L. *rēgīna.*]

region *rē'jən, n.* a tract of country: any area or district, esp. one characterised in some way: the larger of the two local government administrative units in Scotland (see also **district**): a realm: a portion or division, as of the body: a portion of space: the atmosphere, or a division of it, esp. the upper air (*Shak., Milt.*): the heavens (*obs.*). — *adj.* (*Shak.*) of the air. — *adj.* **rē'gional.** — *n.* **regionalīsā'tion, -z-** the dividing of England (in 1972) and Scotland (in 1973) into regions for local government administration. — *v.t.* **rē'gionalise, -ize.** — *ns.* **rē'gionalism** regional patriotism or particularism; **rē'gionalist.** — *adv.* **rē'gionally.** — *adj.* **rē'gionary.** — **regional council** a council elected to govern the affairs of a region. — **in the region of** near: about, approximately.   [A.Fr. *regiun* — L. *rēgiō, -ōnis* — *regĕre,* to rule.]

régisseur *rā-zhē-sœr,* (Fr.) *n.* manager: stage manager: in a ballet company, a director.

register *rej'is-tər, n.* a written record or official list regularly kept: the book containing such a record: an entry in it: a recording or indicating apparatus, as a cash register: a registrar (now *rare* or *U.S.*): apparatus for regulating a draught: a register-plate: an organ stop or stop-knob: the set of pipes controlled by an organ stop, or a set of strings in a harpsichord: part of the compass of any instrument having a distinct quality of tone (also *fig.*): the compass of an instrument or voice: the range of tones of a voice produced in a particular manner: the form of language used in certain circumstances, situations, or when dealing with certain subjects — e.g. legal, technical, journalistic: exact adjustment of position, as of colours in a picture, or letterpress on opposite sides of a leaf (*print.*): registration: an entry in a register: a certificate of registration: a device for storing small amounts of data

(*comput.*). — *v.t.* to enter or cause to be entered in a register: to record: to indicate: to put on record: to express: to represent by bodily expression: to adjust in register: to send by registered post. — *v.i.* to enter one's name (esp. as a hotel guest): to correspond in register: to make an impression, reach the consciousness (*coll.*). — *adj.* **reg'istered** recorded, entered, or enrolled (as a voter, a letter requiring special precautions for security, etc.): made with a register-plate; **reg'istrable.** — *ns.* **reg'istrant** one who registers, or has registered (a trademark, etc.); **reg'istrar** (-*trär,* or -*trär'*) one who keeps a register or official record: one who makes an official record of births, deaths, and marriages registered locally: a hospital doctor in one of the intermediate grades (**medical, surgical, registrar**); **reg'istrarship** office of a registrar; **reg'istrary** Cambridge University registrar; **registrā'tion** the act or fact of registering: something registered: the act or art of combining stops in organ-playing; **reg'istry** registration: an office or place where a register is kept: a register: an entry in a register. — **Register House** the building in Edinburgh where Scottish records are kept; **register office** a record-office: an employment office: the less common but strictly correct term for a registry office (see below); **reg'ister-plate** in rope-making, a disc with holes to give each yarn its position: a chimney damper; **Reg'istrar-Gen'eral** an officer having the superintendence of the registration of all births, deaths, and marriages; **registration number** the combination of letters and numbers shown on a motor vehicle's number plates, by which its ownership is registered; **registry office** an office for putting domestic servants in touch with employers: a registrar's office, (strictly, **register office**) where births, etc., are recorded and civil marriages are celebrated. — **gross,** or **net register (tonnage)** gross or net tonnage; **Lord Clerk-Register** an officer of the General Register House with duties concerned with the election of Scottish representative peers, formerly custodian of records and registers; **parish register** a book in which births, deaths, and marriages are inscribed; **Registered General Nurse** (abbrev. **RGN**) one who has passed the examination of the General Nursing Council for Scotland; **ship's register** a document showing the ownership of a vessel.   [O.Fr. *registre* or L.L. *registrum,* for L. pl. *regesta,* things recorded — *re-*, back, *gerĕre,* to carry.]

regius *rē'ji-əs, rā'gi-ōōs, adj.* royal, as **regius professor** one whose chair was founded by Henry VIII, or, in Scotland, by the Crown; **rē'gium dō'num** a former annual grant of public money to nonconformist ministers in England, Scotland, and esp. Ireland.   [L. *rēgius* — *rēx,* king.]

reglet *reg'lit, n.* a flat, narrow moulding (*archit.*): a fillet: a strip for spacing between lines (*print.*).   [Fr. *réglet,* dim. of *règle* — L. *rēgula,* a rule.]

regma *reg'mə, (bot.) n.* a fruit that splits into dehiscent parts: — *pl.* **reg'mata.**   [Gr. *rhēgma, -atos,* a breaking.]

regnal *reg'nl, adj.* of a reign. — *adj.* **reg'nant** reigning (often after the noun, as **queen regnant** a reigning queen, not a *queen consort*): prevalent.   [L. *rēgnālis* — *rēgnum,* a kingdom, *rēgnāns, -antis,* pr.p. of *rēgnāre,* to reign.]

regolith *reg'ə-lith, n.* mantle-rock.   [Gr. *rhēgos,* a blanket, *lithos,* a stone.]

regorge *ri-, rē-görj', v.t.* to disgorge, regurgitate: to swallow again (*rare*): to gorge to repletion (*Milt.*). — *v.i.* to gush back.   [Pfx. **re-** and **gorge;** or Fr. *regorger,* to overflow, abound.]

regrate *ri-grāt', (hist.) v.t.* to buy and sell again in or near the same market, thus raising the price — once a criminal offence in England. — *ns.* **regrā'ter, -tor** one who regrates (*hist.*): a middleman (*S.W. England*);

---

rēdistribu'tion *n.*
rēdivide' *v.t.* and *v.i.*
rēdivis'ion *n.*

rē'do' *v.t.:* — *pa.t.* **rē'did';**
pa.p. **rē'-done'.**
rēdoub'le *v.t.* and *v.i.*

rēdraw' *v.t.* and *v.i.*
rēdrive' *v.t.*
rē-ed'it *v.t.*

regrā'ting. [O.Fr. *regrater*; of doubtful origin.]
regrede *ri-grēd'*, *v.i.* to retrograde (*rare*). — *n.* **regrē'dience**
(*Herrick*). [L. *regredī* — *re-*, *gradī*, to go.]
regreet *ri-grēt'*, *v.t.* to greet in return: to greet again
(*Shak.*): to greet (*Shak.*). — *v.i.* to exchange greetings.
— *n.* a greeting, esp. in return: (in *pl.*) greetings,
salutation (*Shak.*). [Pfx. **re-**.]
regress *rē'gres*, *n.* passage back: return: reversion: backward movement or extension: right or power of returning: re-entry. — *v.i.* (*ri-gres'*) to go back: to recede:
to return to a former place or state: to revert: to move
from east to west (*astron.*). — *n.* **regression** (*ri-gresh'ən*)
act of regressing: reversion: return towards the mean:
return to an earlier stage of development, as in an
adult's or adolescent's behaving like a child. — *adj.*
regressive (*ri-gres'iv*) going back: returning. — *adv.*
regress'ively in a regressive manner: by return. — *ns.*
regress'iveness (*ri-*); **regress'ity** (*rē-*). [L. *regressus*
— *regredī*; see **regrede**.]
regret *ri-gret'*, *v.t.* to remember with sense of loss or
feeling of having done amiss: to wish otherwise: —
pr.p. **regrett'ing**; *pa.t.* and *pa.p.* **regrett'ed**. — *n.*
sorrowful wish that something had been otherwise:
sorrowful feeling of loss: compunction: an intimation
of regret or refusal. — *adj.* **regret'ful** feeling regret. —
adv. **regret'fully**. — *adj.* **regret'able** to be regretted. —
adv. **regrett'ably** in a regrettable way: I'm sorry to say,
unfortunately. [O.Fr. *regreter*, *regrater*; poss. conn.
with **greet²**.]
reguerdon *ri-gûr'dən*, (*Shak.*) *n.* reward. — *v.t.* to reward.
[O.Fr. *reguerdon*.]
regula *reg'ū-lə*, *n.* the rule of a religious order: a fillet,
esp. under the Doric taenia, below each triglyph
(*archit.*): — *pl.* **reg'ulae** (*-lē*). — *adj.* **reg'ular** (*-lər*)
subject to a monastic rule (opp. to *secular*): governed
by or according to rule, law, order, habit, custom,
established practice, mode prescribed, or the ordinary
course of things: placed, arranged, etc. at regular
intervals in space or time: of a marriage, celebrated by
a minister of religion after proclamation of banns:
normal: habitual: constant: steady: uniform: periodical: duly qualified: inflected in the usual way, esp. of
weak verbs (*gram.*): symmetrical, esp. (*bot.*) radially
symmetrical or actinomorphic: having all the sides and
angles equal or all faces equal, equilateral, and equiangular, the same number meeting at every corner
(*geom.*): also (of a pyramid) having a regular polygon
for base and the other faces similar and equal isosceles
triangles: permanent, professional, or standing (*mil.*;
opp. to *militia, volunteer*, and *territorial*): (of a satellite) that keeps or scarcely deviates from a circular
orbit around its planet (*astron.*): thorough, out-and-
out, esp. (*U.S.*) in party politics (*coll.*): of the same
way of thinking as the speaker, hence ready to help
or abet him, loyal, swell (*slang*): veritable (*coll.*). — *n.*
a member of a religious order who has taken the three
ordinary vows: a soldier of the regular army: a regular
customer: a loyal supporter of the party leader (*U.S.
politics*). — *n.* **regularisā'tion**, **-z-**. — *v.t.* **reg'ularise**,
-ize to make regular. — *n.* **regularity** (*-lar'i-ti*) state,
character, or fact of being regular. — *adv.* **reg'ularly**.
— *v.t.* **reg'ulate** to control: to adapt or adjust continuously: to adjust by rule. — *v.i.* to make regulations.
— *n.* **regulā'tion** act of regulating: state of being
regulated: a rule or order prescribed: in the E.E.C., a
proposal from the commission which is approved by
the council and immediately becomes law in all member states. — *adj.* prescribed by regulation. — *adj.*
reg'ulātive tending to regulate. — *n.* **reg'ulātor** one
who, or that which, regulates: a controlling device,
esp: for the speed of a clock or watch. a change in the
taxation rate introduced by the Chancellor of the
Exchequer between budgets to regulate the economy.

— *adj.* **reg'ulatory** (*-lə-tər-i*). [L. *rēgula*, a rule —
regēre, to rule.]
Regulo® *reg'ū-lō*, *n.* a thermostatic control system for gas
ovens: loosely, (with a given numeral) one of the
graded scale of temperatures on a gas oven (also
without *cap.*).
regulus *reg'ū-ləs*, *n.* an impure metal, an intermediate
product in smelting of ores: antimony: (*cap.*) a first-
magnitude white star in Leo: the goldcrest genus of birds.
— *adj.* **reg'uline**. — *v.t.* **reg'ulise**, **-ize** to reduce to
regulus. [L. *rēgulus*, dim. of *rēx*, a king.]
regur, regar *rā'*, *rē'gər*, *n.* the rich black cotton soil of
India, full of organic matter. [Hind. *regar*.]
regurgitate *ri-*, *rē-gûr'ji-tāt*, *v.t.* to cast out again: to pour
back: to bring back into the mouth after swallowing.
— *v.i.* to gush back. — *adj.* **regur'gitant**. — *n.* **regur-
gitā'tion**. [L.L. *regurgitāre*, -*ātum* — *re*, back, *gurges,
gurgitis*, a gulf.]
reh *rā*, *n.* an efflorescence of sodium salts on the soil in
India. [Hindustani.]
rehabilitate *rē-(h)ə-bil'i-tāt*, *v.t.* to reinstate, restore to
former privileges, rights, rank, etc.: to clear the character of: to bring back into good condition, working
order, prosperity: to make fit, after disablement, illness
or imprisonment for earning a living or playing a part
in the world: of buildings or housing areas, to rebuild,
restore to good condition. — *n.* **rehabilitā'tion**. — *adj.*
rehabil'itative tending to rehabilitate. [L.L. *rehabil-
itāre*, -*ātum*; see **habilitate**.]
rehash *rē-hash'*, *n.* something made up of materials
formerly used, esp. a restatement in different words
of ideas already expressed by oneself or somone else.
— Also *v.t.* [Pfx. **re-**, **hash**, n.]
rehear *rē-hēr'*, *v.t.* to hear again: to try over again, as a
lawsuit. — *n.* **rehear'ing**. [Pfx. **re-**.]
rehearse *ri-hûrs'*, *v.t.* to repeat, say over, or read aloud:
to enumerate: to recount, narrate in order: to perform
privately for practice or trial: to practise beforehand:
to train by rehearsal. — *v.i.* to take part in rehearsal.
— *ns.* **rehears'al** the act of rehearsing: repetition:
enumeration: narration: a performance for trial or
practice; **rehears'er**; **rehears'ing**. [O.Fr. *rehercer*, *re-
herser* — *re-*, again, *hercer*, to harrow — *herce* (Fr.
herse) — L. *hirpex*, *-icis*, a rake, a harrow.]
reheat *rē-hēt'*, *v.t.* to heat again. — *n.* (*rē'hēt*; the use of)
a device to inject fuel into the hot exhaust gases of a
turbojet in order to obtain increased thrust. — *n.*
reheat'er a person who reheats: an apparatus for
reheating. [Pfx. **re-**.]
rehoboam *rē-(h)ō-bō'əm*, *n.* a large liquor measure or
vessel (esp. for champagne), the size of six normal
bottles (approx. 156 fluid oz.). [*Rehoboam*, king of
Israel.]
rehouse *rē-howz'*, *v.t.* to provide with a new house or
houses. — *n.* **rehous'ing**. [Pfx. **re-**.]
Reich *rīhh*, *n.* the German state: Germany as an empire
(**First Reich** Holy Roman Empire, 962–1806; **Second
Reich** under Hohenzollern emperors, 1871–1918), and
as a dictatorship (**Third Reich** under Nazi régime,
1933–45). — *ns.* **Reichsbank** (*rīhhs'bängk*) the German
state bank; **Reichsland** (*-länt*) imperial territory, i.e.
Alsace-Lorraine, 1871–1919; **reichsmark** (*-märk*) the
German monetary unit 1924–48 (see **mark²**); **Reichsrat**,
earlier **-rath** (*-rät*) upper house of the parliament of
the former Austrian Empire: a deliberative Council of
the Weimar Republic in Germany (1919–33), representing the States; **Reichstag** (*-tähh*) the lower house
of the parliament of Germany during the Second Reich
and the Weimar Republic. [Ger., O.E. *rīce*, kingdom; cf. **bishopric**.]
Reichian *rīhh'i-ən*, *adj.* of or pertaining to the theory or
practice of Wilhelm *Reich*, Austrian-born psychiatrist
(1897–1957), esp. the concept of a universal, sexually-

---

rē-ed'ucate *v.t.*
rē-educā'tion *n.*
rē-elect' *v.t.*

rē-elec'tion *n.*
rē-el'evate *v.t.*
rē-elevā'tion *n.*

rē-eligibil'ity *n.*
rē-el'igible *adj.*
rē-embark' *v.t.* and *v.i.*

generated life energy termed 'orgone'. — **Reichian therapy** (also without *cap.*) therapy designed to release inhibited or disturbed energies by the use of massage, controlled breathing, etc. — also called **bioenerget′ics.**

reif *rēf*, (*Scot.*) *n.* spoliation. [O.E. *rēaf*; cf. **reave.**]

reify *rē′i-fī*, *v.t.* to think of as a material thing: to convert into a material thing, to materialise. — *n.* **reification** (*-fi-kā′shən*) materialisation, turning into an object: depersonalisation (esp. in Marxist terminology). [L. *rēs*, a thing.]

reign *rān*, *n.* kingdom (*obs.*): realm (*obs.*): domain (*obs.*): rule, actual or nominal, of a monarch: predominance: predominating influence: time of reigning. — *v.i.* to be a monarch: to be predominant: to prevail. [O.Fr. *regne* — L. *rēgnum* — *regĕre*, to rule.]

reik. Same as **reak**[1].

Reil's island. See **insula.**

reimbattell'd *rē-im-bat′ld*, (*Milt.*) *pa.p.* drawn up again in battle array. [Pfx. **re-.**]

reimburse *rē-im-bûrs′*, *v.t.* to repay: to pay an equivalent to for loss or expense. — *adj.* **reimburs′able.** *n.* **reimburse′ment.** [L.L. *imbursāre* — *in*, in, *bursa*, purse.]

reim-kennar *rīm′ken-ər*, *n.* an enchanter, enchantress. [App. invented by Scott — Ger. *Reim*, rhyme, *Kenner*, knower.]

reimplant *rē-im-plänt′*, (*med.*) *v.t.* to replace severed body tissue, esp. an organ or member, in its original site surgically. — *n.* (*-im′-*) a section of the body which has been reimplanted. — *n.* **reimplantā′tion.** [Pfx. **re-.**]

rein[1] *rān*, *n.* the strap of a bridle or either half of it: any means of curbing or governing (*fig.*). — *v.t.* to fasten or tie by the rein (*Shak.*): to furnish with reins: to govern with the rein: to restrain or control: to stop or check (with *in* or *up*). — *v.i.* to answer (*Shak.*): to stop or slow up. — *adj.* **rein′less** without rein or restraint. — **rein′-arm, rein′-hand** normally the left (opp. to *whip-hand*); **reins′man** a skilful driver. — **draw rein** to pull up, stop riding; **give rein** (or **a free rein** or **the reins**) **to** to allow free play to, apply no check to; **keep a tight rein** (on) to control closely; **rein in** to check, stop; **take the reins** to take control. [O.Fr. *rein, resne, rene* (Fr.*rêne*), perh. through (hypothetical) L.L. *retina*, from L. *retinēre*, to hold back.]

rein[2]. See **reindeer, reins.**

reincarnate *rē-in-kär′nāt*, *v.t.* to cause to be born again in another body or form: to embody again in flesh. — *adj.* reborn. — *ns.* **rēincarnā′tion; rēincarnā′tionism** belief in reincarnation of the soul; **rēincarnā′tionist.** [Pfx. **re-.**]

reindeer *rān′dēr*, *n.* a large heavy deer (*Rangifer*), wild and domesticated, of northern regions, antlered in both sexes, the American variety (or species) called the caribou: — *pl.* **rein′deer, rein′deers.** — Also (*rare*) **rein.** — **Reindeer Age** (*archaeol.*) the Magdalenian; **reindeer moss** a lichen (*Cladonia rangiferina*), the winter food of the reindeer. [O.N. *hreinndȳri*, or O.N. *hreinn* (O.E. *hrān*) and **deer.**]

reinette *rā-net′*. Same as **rennet**[2].

re infecta *rē, rā in-fek′tə, -tä*, (L.) without finishing the business.

reinflation *rē-in-flā′shən*, *n.* (excessive) reflation which, rather than stimulating the economy, causes further inflation. [Pfx. **re-.**]

reinforce *rē-in-fōrs′, -förs′*, *v.t.* to enforce again (*rare*): to strengthen with new force or support: to strengthen: to increase by addition: to encourage (the response to a stimulus) by giving or not giving a reward (*psych.*). — *v.i.* (*Shak.*) to get reinforcements. — *n.* something that reinforces: a reinforced part near the rear of a gun. — *n.* **reinforce′ment** act of reinforcing: additional force or assistance, esp. of troops (commonly in *pl.*). — **reinforced concrete** concrete strengthened by em-

bedded steel bars or mesh. [Alt., by 17th cent., of **renforce.**]

reinform *rē-in-förm′*, *v.t.* to inform anew: to give form to again: to reanimate. [Pfx. **re-.**]

reinfund *rē-in-fund′*, (*Swift*) *v.i.* to flow in again. [Pfx. **re-**, L. *infundĕre* — *fundĕre*, to pour.]

reins *rānz*, *n.pl.* (*rare* or *obs.* in *sing.*) the kidneys, esp. as formerly supposed seat of emotion: the loins. [O.Fr. *reins* — L. *rēn*, pl. *rēnēs*.]

reinstall *rē-in-stöl′*, *v.t.* to install again. — *n.* **reinstal′ment.** [Pfx. **re-.**]

reinstate *rē-instāt′*, *v.t.* to instate again: to restore to or re-establish in a former station or condition. — *ns.* **reinstāte′ment; reinstā′tion** (*rare*). [Pfx. **re-.**]

reinsure *rē-in-shoōr′*, *v.t.* to insure against the risk undertaken by underwriting an insurance: to insure again. — *ns.* **reinsur′ance; reinsur′er.** [Pfx. **re-.**]

reintegrate *rē-in′ti-grāt*, *v.t.* to integrate again: to redintegrate. — *n.* **reintegrā′tion.**

reintermediation *rē-in-tər-mē-di-ā′shən*, *n.* the return into the banking system of borrowing previously financed outside it to evade corset (q.v.) controls. [Pfx. **re-.**]

reinvest *rē-in-vest′*, *v.t.* to clothe again: to endow again: to invest again. — *n.* **reinvest′ment.** [Pfx. **re-.**]

reinvigorate *rē-in-vig′ər-āt*, *v.t.* to put new vigour into. — *n.* **reinvigorā′tion.** [Pfx. **re-.**]

reioyndure (*Shak.*). See **rejoin**[2].

reird *rērd*, **raird** *rārd*, (*Scot.*) *ns.* an uproar, clamour, din. [O.E. *reord.*]

reis[1] *rīs*. Same as **rice**[2].

reis[2] *rās*, *n.pl.* (*sing.* **real** *rā-äl′*) an obsolete Portuguese and Brazilian money of account, 1000 reis making a *milreis*. [Port.]

reist. Same as **reast**[1], or as **reest**[2,3].

reistafel. See **rijst(t)afel.**

reiter *rī′tər*, *n.* a German cavalry soldier. [Ger.]

reiterate *rē-it′ər-āt*, *v.t.* to repeat: to repeat again and again. — *n.* **reit′erance.** — *adjs.* **reit′erant** reiterating; **reit′erate, -d.** — *adv.* **reit′eratedly.** — *n.* **reiterā′tion** act of reiterating: the printing of the second side of a sheet. — *adj.* **reit′erative.** — *n.* a word expressing reiteration of utterance or act: a word formed by reduplication, the second element usu. differing from the first (e.g. *helter-skelter*). [Pfx. **re-.**]

reive, reiver. Same as **reave, reaver.**

reject *ri-jekt′*, *v.t.* to throw away: to discard: to refuse to accept, admit, or accede to: to refuse: to renounce: of the body, not to accept tissue, a transplanted organ, etc., from another source (*med.*). — *n.* (usu. *rē′*) one who or that which is rejected: an imperfect article, not accepted for export, normal sale, etc., and often offered for sale at a discount. — *adjs.* **rejec′table** or **-ible.** — *n.pl.* **rejectamen′ta** refuse: excrement. — *n.* **rejec′tion.** — *adj.* **rejec′tionist** (of a policy, attitude, etc.) rejecting or clearly inclined towards rejection of e.g. an offer, proposal or (esp. peace) plan: (*specif.*) refusing to accept peace with Israel. — Also *n.* — *adj.* **rejec′tive** tending to reject. — *n.* **reject′or** (also **-er**). [L. *rejicĕre, rejectum* — *re-*, back, *jacĕre*, to throw.]

rejig, re-jig *rē-jig′*, **rejigger** *-jig′ər*, *vs.t.* to re-equip: to change or rearrange in a new or unexpected way that is sometimes regarded as unethical (*commerce*). — *n.* **re′jig, re′-jig.**

rejoice *ri-jois′*, *v.t.* to make joyful (*arch.*): to gladden: to be joyful because of (*Shak.*). — *v.i.* to feel joy (*arch.*): to exult: to make merry. — *adj.* **rejoice′ful.** — *ns.* **rejoice′ment** rejoicing; **rejoic′er; rejoic′ing** act of being joyful: expression, subject, or experience of joy: (in *pl.*) festivities, celebrations, merry-makings. — *adv.* **rejoic′ingly.** — **rejoice in** to be happy because of: (*facet.*) to have. [O.Fr. *resjoir, resjoiss-* (Fr. *réjouir*) — L. *re-, ex, gaudēre*, to rejoice.]

rejoin[1] *ri-join′*, (*law*) *v.i.* to reply to a charge or pleading,

rē-embarkā′tion *n.*　　　rē-emerge′ *v.i.*　　　rē-encourage *v.t.*
rē-embod′iment *n.*　　　rē-emer′gence *n.*　　　re-endorse′ *v.t.*
rē-embod′y *v.t.*　　　rē-em′phasise, -ize *v.t.*　　　re-endorse′ment *n.*

fāte; fär; hûr; mīne; mōte; för; mūte; moon; foot; dhen (then); *el′ə-mənt* (element)

esp. to a plaintiff's replication. — *v.t.* to say in reply, retort. — *n.* **rejoin'der** (*ri-*) the defendant's answer to a plaintiff's replication (*law*): an answer to a reply: an answer, esp. a sharp or clever one.   [O.Fr. *rejoindre.*]

rejoin[2] *ri -*, *rē-join '*, *v.t.* and *v.i.* to join again. — *n.* **rejoin'dure** (**reioyn'dure** *Shak.*) a joining again.   [Pfx. **re-.**]

rejón *re-hhōn'*, (Sp.) *n.* a lance with a wooden handle, used in bull-fighting: --- *pl.* **rejo'nes.** — *ns.* **rejoneador** (*re-hhōn-ā-ad-ör'*, *-ör*) a mounted bull-fighter who uses rejones: — *pl.* **rejoneador'es:** — *fem.* **rejoneador'a; rejoneo** (*re-hhōn-ā'ō*) the art of bull-fighting on horse-back using rejones.

rejourn *ri-jûrn'*, (*Shak.*) *v.t.* to postpone, defer.   [Cf. **adjourn.**]

rejuvenate *ri-jōō'vi-nāt*, *v.t.* to make young again: to restore to youthful condition or appearance or to activity: to restore (by uplift) to earlier condition of active erosion (*geol.*). — *v.i.* to rejuvenesce. — *ns.* **rejuvenā'tion; reju'venator.** — *v.i.* **rejuvenesce** (*-es'*) to grow young again: to recover youthful character: to undergo change in cell-contents to a different, usu. more active, character (*biol.*): to resume growth. — *v.t.* to rejuvenate. — *n.* **rejuvenesc'ence.** — *adj.* **rejuvenesc'ent.** — *v.t.* **reju'venise, -ize** to rejuvenate.   [Pfx. **re-,** L. *juvenis*, young, *juvenēscĕre*, to become young.]

reke *rēk*, (*Spens.*) *v.i.* to reck.   [O.E. *rēcan.*]

relâche *rə-läsh*, (Fr.) *n.* relaxation: rest: no performance.

relapse *ri-laps'*, *v.i.* to slide, sink, or fall back, esp. into evil or illness: to return to a former state or practice: to backslide: to fall away. — *n.* a falling back into a former bad state: the return of a disease after partial recovery (*med.*). — *adj.* **relapsed'** having relapsed. — *n.* **relap'ser.** — *adj.* **relap'sing.** — **relapsing fever** an infectious disease characterised by recurrent attacks of fever with enlargement of the spleen, caused by a spirochaete transmitted by ticks and lice.   [L. *relābī*, *relāpsus* — *lābī*, to slide.]

relate *ri-lāt'*, *v.t.* to recount, narrate, tell: to give an account of (*Milt.*): to bring back (*Spens.*): to refer, bring into connection or relation. — *v.i.* to date back in application (*law*): to have reference or relation: to connect: to get on well (with) (often with *to*; *coll.*): to discourse (*Shak.*). — *adj.* **relā'ted** narrated: referred (to; *rare*): connected: allied by kindred or marriage (also *fig.*). — *ns.* **relā'tedness; relā'ter** one who relates; **relā'tion** act of relating: state or mode of being related: narrative or recital: statement: an information (*law*): way in which one thing is connected with another: a quality that can be predicated, not of a single thing, but only of two or more together (*philos.*): respect, reference: a relative by birth or marriage: (in *pl.*) mutual dealings: (in *pl.*) sexual intercourse (*euph.*). — *adj.* **relā'tional** pertaining to, expressing, or of the nature of, relation esp. syntactic relation in grammatical structures. — *adv.* **relā'tionally.** — *ns.* **relā'tionism** (*philos.*) the doctrine that relations have an objective existence: the doctrine of relativity of knowledge; **relā'tionist.** — *adj.* **relā'tionless** kinless: unrelated. — *n.* **relā'tionship** state or mode of being related: relations: an emotional or sexual affair. — *adjs.* **relatival** (*rel-ə-tī'vl*) pertaining to relation, esp. grammatical relation; **rel'ative** (*-tiv*) in or having relation: correlative: corresponding: having the same key-signature (*mus.*): relevant: comparative: not absolute or independent: relating, having reference (to): referring to an antecedent (*gram.*). — *n.* that which is relative: a relative word, esp. a relative pronoun: one who is related by blood or marriage. — *adv.* **rel'atively.** — *n.* **rel'ativeness.** — *v.t.* and *v.i.* **rel'ativise, -ize** to make or become relative. — *ns.* **rel'ativism** relationism: a doctrine of relativity: the view that accepted standards of right and good vary with environment and from

person to person; **rel'ativist.** — *adj.* **relativis'tic** pertaining to relativity, or to relativism. — *ns.* **relativ'itist** one who studies or accepts relativity; **relativ'ity** state or fact of being relative: (in *pl.*) related aspects of pay, working conditions, etc., between different jobs or the same job in different areas: a principle which asserts that only relative, not absolute, motion can be detected in the universe (Einstein's **Special Theory of Relativity,** 1905, starts from two fundamental postulates: a. that all motion is relative, b. that the velocity of light is always constant relative to an observer; his **General Theory of Relativity,** 1916, which embraces the Special Theory, deals with varying velocities, or accelerations — whereas the Special Theory dealt with constant relative velocity, or zero acceleration — and it is much concerned with gravitation; in each case Einstein derived important equations and made predictions); **relator** (*ri-lā'tər*) one who relates: a narrator: one who lays an information before the Attorney-General, enabling him to take action (*law*). — **relative aperture** in a camera, the ratio of the diameter of the lens to the focal length — usu. expressed as the *f*-number; **relative density** the weight of any given substance as compared with the weight of an equal bulk or volume of water or other standard substance at the same, or at standard, temperature and pressure; **relative humidity** the ratio of the amount of water vapour in the air to the amount that would saturate it at the same temperature. — **relative atomic mass** the inferred weight of an atom of an element relatively to that of oxygen as 16 or, more recently, carbon-12 taken as 12; **relative molecular mass** weight of a molecule relatively to that of an atom of carbon-12 taken as 12; **relativity of knowledge** the doctrine that the nature and extent of our knowledge is determined not merely by the qualities of the objects known but necessarily by the conditions of our cognitive powers.   [L. *relātus, -a, -um*, used as pa.p. of *referre*, to bring back — *re, ferre.*]

relative, etc. See **relate.**

relax *ri-laks'*, *v.t.* and *v.i.* to loosen: to slacken: to make or become less close, tense, rigid, strict, or severe. — *n.* a relaxing. — *adj.* and *n.* **relax'ant** laxative (*arch.*): (a substance) having the effect of relaxing. — *n.* **relaxā'tion** (*re-, rē-*) act of relaxing: state of being relaxed: partial remission (*law*): release from outlawry (*Scots law*): recreation. — *adj.* **relax'ative.** — *n.* **relax'in** a hormone which has a relaxing effect on the pelvic muscles, and is used to facilitate childbirth. — *adj.* **relax'ing** enervating.   [L. *relaxāre, -ātum* — *laxus*, loose.]

relay[1] *ri-lā'*, also *rē'lā, rē'lā', n.* a fresh set of dogs in hunting: a supply of horses, etc., to relieve others on a journey: a station for either of these: a relieving shift of men: a supplementary store of anything: a relay-race, or one of its stages: an electrically-operated switch employed to effect changes in an independent circuit: any device by which a weak electric current or other small power is used to control a strong one: a relayed programme, or act or fact of relaying it. — *v.t.* to place in, relieve, control, supply, or transmit by relay: to rebroadcast (programme received from another station or source). — *v.i.* to obtain a relay: to operate a relay: — *pa.t.* and *pa.p.* **relayed.** — **re'lay-race** a race between teams, each man running part of the total distance.   [O.Fr. *relais*, relay of horses or dogs; origin obscure.]

relay[2] *rē-lā'*, *v.t.* to lay again: — *pa.t.* and *pa.p.* **rēlaid'.** [Pfx. **re-.**]

release[1] *rē-lēs'*, *v.t.* to grant a new lease of.   [Pfx. **re-**]

release[2] *ri-lēs'*, *v.t.* to let loose: to set free: to let go: to relieve: to slacken: to undo: to remit: to relinquish: to surrender, convey, give up a right to (*law*): to make available, authorise sale, publication, exhibition, etc.,

---

rē-endow' *v.t.*   **rē-engage'ment** *n.*   **rē-enlist'ment** *n.*
rē-endow'ment *n.*   **rē-enlist'** *v.t.* and *v.i.*   **rē-equip'** *v.t.* and *v.i.*
rē-engage' *v.t.* and *v.i.*   **rē-enlist'er** *n.*   **rē-erect'** *v.t.*

For other sounds see detailed chart of pronunciation.

of: to make available for public knowledge. — *n.* a setting free: liberation: discharge or acquittance: remission: mode of releasing: the giving up of a claim, conveyance: a catch for holding and releasing: authorisation to make available on a certain date: a thing so made available: a film, gramophone record or other recording made available for sale by its production company — esp. *new release.* — *adj.* **releas'able.** — *ns.* **releasee'** one to whom an estate is released; **release'ment** release; **releas'er; releas'or** (*law*). [O.Fr. *relaissier* — L. *relaxāre*, to relax.]

relegate *rel'i-gāt, v.t.* to banish: to consign (to a, usu. unimportant, place or position): to remove to a lower class (*football*): to assign (to a class): to refer (to another, others) for decision or action: to refer (a person, for something, to another; *arch.*). — *adj.* **rel'egable.** — *n.* **relega'tion.** [L. *relēgāre, -ātum re-*, away, *lēgāre*, to send.]

relent *ri-lent', v.i.* to melt (*obs.*): to soften, become less severe: to give way (*Spens., Milt.*): to abate, slacken (*Spens.*): to slacken pace (*Spens.*). — *v.t.* to melt (*obs.*): to soften, cause to relent (*Spens., Burns*): to relax, moderate (*Spens.*): to slow down (*Spens.*): to regret, repent (*Spens.*). — *n.* relenting: slowing (*Spens.*). — *n.* and *adj.* **relent'ing.** — *adj.* **relent'less** unrelenting: inexorable: merciless, stern. — *adv.* **relent'lessly.** — *ns.* **relent'lessness; relent'ment** (*rare*). [L. *re-*, back, *lentus*, sticky, sluggish, pliant.]

relevant *rel'i-vənt, adj.* bearing upon, or applying to, the matter in hand, pertinent: related, proportional (to): sufficient legally. — *ns.* **rel'evance, rel'evancy.** — *adv.* **rel'evantly.** [L. *relevāns, -antis,* pr.p. of *relevāre*, to raise up, relieve; from the notion of helping; cf. **relieve.**]

reliable, relier. See **rely.**

relic *rel'ik, n.* that which is left after loss or decay of the rest: a corpse (usu. in *pl.*; *arch.*): any personal memorial of a saint, held in reverence as an incentive to faith and piety (*R.C.*): a souvenir: a memorial of antiquity or object of historic interest: (of, e.g. a custom) a survival from the past. — Also (*obs.*) **rel'ique.** — **rel'ic-monger** one who traffics in or collects relics. [Fr. *relique* — L. *reliquiae*; see **reliquiae.**]

relict *rel'ikt, n.* a relic (*obs.*): a survivor or surviving trace (*arch.*): a widow (*arch.*). — *adj.* (*ri-likt'*) left behind: surviving: formed by removal of surrounding materials (*geol.*). [L. *relictus, -a, -um,* left, pa.p. of *relinquĕre*, to leave.]

relide *ri-līd', (Spens.)* for **relied** *pa.p.* of *v.t.* (*obs.*) **relie** to assemble, collect together. [**rely.**]

relied, relier. See **rely.**

relief *ri-lēf', n.* the lightening or removal of any burden, discomfort, evil, pressure, or stress: release from a post or duty: one who releases another by taking his place: that which relieves or mitigates: aid in danger, esp. deliverance from siege: assistance to the poor: fresh supply of provisions: feeding or seeking food (*hunting; obs.*): a certain fine paid to the overlord by a feudal tenant's heir on coming into possession: release from obligation, or right to reimbursement of expenses thereby incurred (*Scots law*): anything that gives diversity: projection or standing out from the general surface, ground, or level: a sculpture or other work of art executed in relief: appearance of standing out solidly: distinctness by contrast, esp. in outline. — *adj.* providing relief in cases of overloading, distress, danger, difficulty. — *adj.* **relief'less.** — **Relief Church** a body that left the Church of Scotland because of oppressive exercise of patronage, organised in 1761, united with the United Secession Church in 1847 to form the United Presbyterian Church; **relief map** a map in which the form of the country is shown by elevations and depressions of the material used, or by the illusion of such elevations and depressions, or

(loosely) by other means. [O.Fr. *relef* — *relever*; see **relieve,** also **rilievo.**]

relieve *ri-lēv', v.t.* to lift up (*Shak.*): to bring, give, or afford relief to: to release: to release from duty by taking the place of: to ease (e.g. a burden): (*refl.*) to urinate or to defecate: to mitigate: to raise the siege of: to set off by contrast: to break the sameness of: to bring into relief: to feed (*obs.*). — *adj.* **reliev'able.** — *n.* **reliev'er.** — *adj.* **reliev'ing.** — **relieving arch** an arch in a wall to relieve the part below it from a superincumbent weight; **relieving officer** an official formerly appointed to superintend the relief of the poor. — **relieve someone of** to take from someone's possession, with or without someone's approval: to steal from someone: to free someone from (a necessity, restriction, etc.). [O.Fr. *relever* — L. *relevāre*, to lift, relieve — *levāre*, to raise — *levis*, light.]

relievo *ri-lē'vō,* also (from It.) **rilievo** *rē-lyā'vō,* (*art*) *ns.* relief: a work in relief: appearance of relief: — *pls.* **relie'vos, rilie'vi** (*-vē*). [It. *rilievo*.]

religieux *rə-lē-zhyø,* (Fr.) *n.* a monk or friar: — *fem.* **religieuse** (*-zhyœz*) a nun.

religio-. See **religion.**

religio loci *ri-lij'i-ō lō'sī, re-lig'i-ō lok'ē.* See Quotations from Latin, etc., in Appendices.

religion *ri-lij'ən, n.* belief in, recognition of, or an awakened sense of, a higher unseen controlling power or powers, with the emotion and morality connected therewith: rites or worship: any system of such belief or worship: devoted fidelity: monastic life: a monastic order: Protestantism (*obs.*). — **relig'io-** in combination, relating to religion or religious matters. — *adj.* **relig'ionary** (*rare*) religious. — *n.* a member of a religious order: a Protestant (*obs.*). — *n.* **relig'ioner** a member of an order: a Protestant (*obs.*). — *v.t.* **relig'ionise, -ize** to imbue with religion. — *v.i.* to make profession of being religious. — *ns.* **relig'ionism** religiosity: bigotry; **relig'ionist** one attached to a religion: a bigot: one professionally engaged in religion, e.g. an evangelist (*U.S.*). — *adjs.* **relig'ionless; religiose** (*-lij'i-ōs,* or *-ōs'*) morbidly or sentimentally religious. — *n.* **religiosity** (*-i-os'it-i*) spurious or sentimental religion: religious feeling. — *adj.* **relig'ious** (*-əs*) of, concerned with, devoted to, or imbued with, religion: scrupulous: bound to a monastic life (*R.C.*): strict, very exact. — *n.* one bound by monastic vows. — *adv.* **relig'iously.** — *n.* **relig'iousness.** [L. *religiō, -ōnis,* n., *religiōsus,* adj., perh. conn. with *religāre*, to bind.]

religiose, etc. See **religion.**

religioso *rə-lij-i-ō'sō,* (It.) *adj.* and *adv.* in a devotional manner (*mus.*).

reline *rē-līn', v.t.* to mark with new lines: to renew the lining of. [Pfx. **re-.**]

relinquish *ri-ling'kwish, v.t.* to give up: to let go. — *n.* **relin'quishment.** [O.Fr. *relinquir, relinquiss-* — L. *relinquĕre, relictum* — *re-, linquĕre*, to leave.]

relique *rel'ik, ri-lēk', n.* an old form of **relic.** — *ns.* **reliquaire** (*rel-i-kwār'*), **rel'iquary** (*-kwər-i*) a receptacle for relics. — *adj.* **rel'iquary** of relics: residual. [Fr.]

reliquiae *ri-lik'wi-ē, re-lik'wi-ī, n.pl.* remains, esp. fossil remains. [L. — *relinquĕre*, to leave.]

relish[1] *rel'ish, n.* a flavour: characteristic flavour: enough to give a flavour: appetising flavour: zest-giving quality or power: an appetiser, condiment: zestful enjoyment: gusto: pleasureful inclination. — *v.t.* to like the taste of: to be pleased with: to enjoy: to appreciate discriminatingly: to give a relish to: to taste, experience (*obs.*). — *v.i.* to savour, smack: to have an agreeable taste: to give pleasure. — *adj.* **rel'ishable.** [O.Fr. *reles, relais,* remainder — *relaisser*, to leave behind.]

relish[2], **rellish** *rel'ish, n.* a musical ornament. — *v.t.* (*Shak.*) to warble. [Origin obscure.]

---

rĕ-erec'tion *n.*
rĕ-estab'lish *v.t.*
rĕ-estab'lishment *n.*

rĕ-examinā'tion *n.*
rĕ-exam'ine *v.t.*
rĕ-exist' *v.i.*

rĕ-exist'ence *n.*
rĕ-expand' *v.t.* and *v.i.*
rĕ-expan'sion *n.*

relive *rē-liv′*, *v.t.* and *v.i.* to live again: (*rē-līv′*) to revive (*Spens.*).

reliver *ri-liv′ər*, (*Shak.*) *v.t.* to deliver back. [O.Fr. *relivrer*; also pfx. **re-**, *liver*, to deliver, *obs.* and *dial.*]

rellish. See **relish**[2].

relocate *rē-lō-kāt′*, *v.t.* to locate again: to move (a firm, workers, etc.) to a different area or site. — *v.i.* to move one's place of business or residence. — *n.* **relocā′tion.** [Pfx. **re-**.]

relucent *ri-lū′*, *-lōō′sənt*, (*arch.*) *adj.* reflecting: shining. [L. *relūcēns*, *-entis*, pr.p. of *relūcēre*, to shine back.]

reluct *ri-lukt′*, (*arch.*) *v.i.* to be unwilling (with *at*): to hold back. — *ns.* **reluc′tance** opposition, resistance (*Milt.*): unwillingness: magnetomotive force applied to whole or part of a magnetic circuit divided by the flux in it; **reluc′tancy.** *adj.* **reluc′tant** struggling (*Milt.*): unwilling: resisting. — *adv.* **reluc′tantly.** — *v.i.* **reluc′tāte** to be reluctant. — *n.* **reluctā′tion** (*rel-*) repugnance (*arch.*). [L. *reluctārī* — **re-**, against, *luctārī*, to struggle.]

relume *ri-lūm′*, *-lōōm′*, (*arch.*) *v.t.* to light anew: to rekindle: to light up again. — *v.t.* (*arch.*) **relu′mine** (*-in*) to relume. [L. *relūmināre* — *lūmen*, *-inis*, light.]

rely *ri-lī′*, *v.i.* to rally (*obs.*): to rest as on a support (*obs.*): to depend confidently (on, upon): — *pr.p.* **rely′ing**; *pa.t.* and *pa.p.* **relied′.** — *n.* **reliabil′ity.** — *adj.* **reli′able** to be relied on, trustworthy. — *n.* **reli′ableness.** — *adv.* **reli′ably.** (The preceding four words are sometimes condemned as formed neither from a trans. verb nor from a noun.) — *n.* **reli′ance** trust: that in which one trusts. — *adj.* **reli′ant.** — *n.* **reli′er** (*Shak.*). — **reliability test, trial** a public test of the qualities of motor vehicles (now known as a **rally**). [O.Fr. *relier* — L. *religāre*, to bind back.]

rem *rem*, *n.* a unit of radiation dosage, the amount which has the same effect as one rad of X-radiation. [*röntgen equivalent man or mammal.*]

remain *ri-mān′*, *v.i.* to stay or be left behind: to continue in the same place: to dwell, abide (*Shak.*): to be left after or out of a greater number: to continue in one's possession, mind: to continue unchanged: to continue to be: to be still to be dealt with (often without subject *it*): to await (*Spens.*, *Milt.*). — *n.* stay, abode (*Shak.*): a surviving part (*arch.*): in most uses, **remains** (*pl.* in form, but occasionally with sing. verb) as follows: — what is left: relics: a corpse: the literary productions of one dead. — *n.* **remain′der** that which remains or is left behind after the removal of a part or after division: the residue, rest: balance of an account (*Shak.*): an interest in an estate to come into effect after a certain other event happens (*legal*): right of next succession to a post or title: residue of an edition when the sale of a book has fallen off. — *adj.* (*Shak.*) left over. — *v.t.* to sell (book) as a remainder. — **remain′der-man** one to whom a legal remainder is devised. [O.Fr. *remaindre* — L. *manēre* — **re-**, back, *manēre*, to stay.]

remake *rē-māk′*, *v.t.* to make anew. — *adj.* **rēmade′.** — *ns.* **rēmade′**, **rēmake′** a thing (as a gutta golf-ball) made over again from the original materials: (**rē′make**) something made again, esp. (a new version of) a film. [Pfx. **re-**.]

remand *ri-mänd′*, *v.t.* to send back (esp. a prisoner into custody or on bail to await further evidence). — *n.* act of remanding: recommittal. — **remand home, centre** in England, a place of detention for children and young persons on remand or awaiting trial: also for some undergoing punishment. — **on remand** having been remanded. [O.Fr. *remander*, or L.L. *remandāre* — *mandāre*, to order.]

remanent *rem′ən-ənt*, *adj.* remaining. — *n.* a remainder: a remnant. — *ns.* **rem′anence**, **-ency**; **rem′anet** a remainder: a postponed case or parliamentary bill. [L. *remanēns*, *-entis*, pr.p., and *remanet*, 3rd pers. sing. pres. indic. of *remanēre*.]

remanié *rə-mä-nyā*, (*geol.*) *n.* a fossil or other relic of an older rock preserved as a fragment in a later deposit. [Fr. pa.p. of *remanier*, to rehandle.]

remark[1] *ri-märk′*, *v.t.* to mark out (*Milt.*): to notice: to comment (that), or say incidentally (that). — *v.i.* to comment, make an observation (often with *on*, *upon*). — *n.* noteworthiness: observation: comment: (also as Fr., **remarque′**) a marginal drawing or other distinguishing mark on an engraving or etching indicating an early state of the plate: also a plate, print or proof bearing this special remark. — *adj.* **remark′able** noteworthy: unusual, singular, strange, distinguished. — *n.* a remarkable thing. — *n.* **remark′ableness.** — *adv.* **remark′ably.** — *adj.* **remarked′** conspicuous: (also **remarqued′**) bearing a remark, as an etching. — *n.* **remark′er.** [O.Fr. *remarquer* — **re-**, intens., *marquer*, to mark.]

remark[2], **re-mark** *rē-märk′*, *v.t.* to mark again. [**re-**.]

remarque. See **remark**[1].

rematch *rē′mach*, *n.* in sport, a second match or return match. — Also *v.t.* (*rē-mach′*). [Pfx. **re-**.]

remblai *rä-ble*, *n.* earth used to form a rampart, embankment, etc.: stowage in a mine. [Fr.]

remble *rem′(b)l*, (*N.E. England*) *v.t.* to remove, clear. [Origin obscure.]

Rembrandtesque *rem-bran-tesk′*, or *-brən-*, *adj.* like the work of *Rembrandt* (1606–69), esp. in his contrast of high lights and deep shadows. — *adj.* **Rem′brandtish.** — *n.* **Rem′brandtism.**

remead. See **remedy.**

remeasure *rē-mezh′ər*, *v.t.* to measure anew: to retrace (*Spens.*). — *n.* **remeas′urement.** [Pfx. **re-**.]

remedy *rem′i-di*, *obs.* and *Scot.* **remede**, **remeid**, **remead** (*ri-mēd′*), *ns.* any means of curing a disease, redressing, counteracting, or repairing any evil or loss: reparation: redress: range of tolerated variation in the weight of a coin. — *v.t.* to cure (a person, diseased part) (*arch.*): to put right, repair, counteract: — *pr.p.* **rem′edying**; *pa.t.* and *pa.p.* **rem′edied.** — *adj.* **remē′diable.** — *adv.* **remē′diably.** — *adj.* **remē′dial** tending or intended to remedy: of or concerning the teaching of slow-learning children. — *adv.* **remē′dially.** — *adj.* **remē′diate** (*Shak.*). — *n.* **remediā′tion.** — *adj.* **rem′ediless** (formerly *-med′*) without remedy: incurable. — *adv.* **rem′edilessly** (or *-med′*). — *n.* **rem′edilessness** (or *-med′*). — **no remedy** (*Shak.*) of necessity; **what remedy?** how can it be helped or avoided? (*obs.*). [A.Fr. *remedie*, O.Fr. *remede* — L. *remedium.*]

remember *ri-mem′bər*, *v.t.* to keep in or recall to memory or mind: to mention, record (*obs.*): to commemorate (*obs.*): to bear in mind as something to be mentioned (*Shak.*): to bear in mind as one deserving of honour or gratitude, or as one to be rewarded, tipped, or prayed for: to remind (*arch.* or *dial.*): to bethink (*refl.*; *Shak.*): to occur to (*impers.*; *arch.*): to regain one's good manners after a temporary lapse (*refl.*): to recall to the memory of another (often as a greeting). — *v.i.* to have the power or perform the act of memory: to have memory (with *of*; *Shak.*, *Milt.*; now *Scot.* and *U.S.*). — *adj.* **remem′berable.** — *adv.* **remem′berably.** — *ns.* **remem′berer; remem′brance** memory: that which serves to bring to or keep in mind: a reminder: a souvenir: a memorandum: a memorial: the reach of memory: (in *pl.*) a message of friendly greeting; **remem′brancer** one who or that which reminds: a recorder: an officer of exchequer responsible for collecting debts due to the Crown (**King's, Queen's Remembrancer**). — **Remembrance Sunday** the Sunday nearest to 11th November commemorating the fallen of the two World Wars (see **Armistice Day**). — **remember your courtesy** (*obs.*) remember to put your hat on, which you have taken off in courtesy. [O.Fr. *remembrer* — L. **re-**, again, *memor*, mindful.]

For other sounds see detailed chart of pronunciation.

remen *rē'mən, n.* a unit of measurement used by the ancient Egyptians (equivalent to 20.62 in. or 524 cm.) also known as a *royal cubit.* [Anc. Egypt.]

remercy *ri-mûr'si, (obs.) v.t.* to thank: — *pa.t. (Spens.)* **remer'cied.** [(O.) Fr. *remercier.*]

remerge *rē-mûrj', v.t.* to merge again. [Pfx. **re-.**]

remex *rē'meks, n.* one of the large feathers of a bird's wing — primary or secondary: — *pl.* **remiges** *(rem'i-jēz).* — *v.i.* **remigate** *(rem'i-gāt)* to row. — *n.* **remigā'tion.** — *adj.* **remigial** *(ri-mij'i-əl).* [L. *rēmex, -igis,* a rower.]

remigrate *rem'i-grāt, v.i.* to change back: (also *rē-mī-grāt')* to migrate again or back. — *n.* **remigrā'tion** *(rem-i-* or *rē-mī-).* [Pfx. **re-.**]

remind *ri-mīnd', v.t.* to put in mind (of), to cause to remember. — *n.* **remind'er** that which reminds. — *adj.* **remind'ful** mindful: reminiscent, exciting memories. [Pfx. **re-** and **mind** *v.t.*]

remineralise, -ize *rē-min'ər-əl-īz, (med.) v.i.* (of bone) to regain depleted minerals, eg. calcium. — *n.* **remineralisā'tion, -z-.** [Pfx. **re-.**]

reminiscence *rem-i-nis'əns, n.* recollection: an account of something remembered: the recurrence to the mind of the past. — *v.i.* **reminisce** *(-nis';* back-formation) to recount reminiscences. — *adj.* **reminisc'ent** suggestive, remindful: addicted to reminiscences: pertaining to reminiscence. — Also *n.* — *adj.* **reminiscen'tial** *(-sen'-shl)* of, or of the nature of, reminiscence. — *adv.* **reminisc'ently.** [L. *reminīscēns, -entis,* pr.p. of *reminīscī,* to remember.]

remise *ri-mīz', n.* surrender of a claim *(law):* (*rə-mēz')* an effective second thrust after the first has missed *(fencing):* a coach-house: a livery-carriage *(obs.).* — *v.t.* *(ri-mīz')* to surrender. [Fr. *remis, remise* — *remettre* — L. *remittĕre,* to send back, remit, relax.]

remiss *ri-mis', adj.* negligent: slack: lax: wanting in vigour. — *n.* **remissibil'ity.** — *adj.* **remiss'ible** that may be remitted. — *n.* **remission** *(ri-mish'ən)* act of remitting: slackening: abatement: relinquishment of a claim: the lessening of a term of imprisonment: pardon: forgiveness. — *adj.* **remiss'ive** remitting: forgiving. — *adv.* **remiss'ly.** — *n.* **remiss'ness.** — *adj.* **remiss'ory** of remission. [L. *remittĕre, remissum;* see **remit.**]

remit *ri-mit', v.t.* to relax: to pardon *(arch.):* to refrain from exacting or inflicting: to give up: to desist from: to transfer: to transmit, as money, etc.: to put again in custody: to refer to another court, authority, etc.: to refer for information: to send or put back. — *v.i.* to abate: to relax: to desist: — *pr.p.* **remitt'ing;** *pa.t.* and *pa.p.* **remitt'ed.** — *n.* *(rē'mit, ri-mit')* reference of a case or matter to another *(legal):* scope, terms of reference: a matter submitted (to a conference or other body) for consideration *(politics,* esp. *N.Z.).* — *ns.* **remit'ment** remission: remitting: remittance; **remitt'al** remission: reference to another court, etc.; **remitt'ance** the sending of money, etc., to a distance: the sum or thing sent; **remittee** *(-ē')* the person to whom a remittance is sent. — *adj.* **remitt'ent** remitting at intervals. — *adv.* **remitt'ently.** — *n.* **remitt'er, remitt'or** one who makes a remittance. — **remitt'ance-man** one dependent upon remittances from home; **remittent fever** a severe type of malaria in which the temperature falls slightly from time to time. [L. *remittĕre, remissum* — *re-,* back, *mittĕre,* to send.]

remnant *rem'nənt, n.* a fragment or a small number surviving or remaining after destruction, defection, removal, sale, etc., of the greater part: esp. a remaining piece of cloth: a tag or quotation: a surviving trace: trace of a fact *(Scott).* — *adj.* remanent, remainder. [**remanent.**]

remonetise, -ize *rē-mun'ə-tīz, -mon', v.t.* to re-establish as legal tender. — *n.* **remonetīsā'tion, -z-.** [Pfx. **re-.**]

remonstrance *ri-mon'strəns, n.* a strong or formal protest, expostulation. — *adj.* **remon'strant** remonstrating: *(cap.)* Dutch Arminian. — *n.* one who remonstrates: *(cap.)* a Protester *(Scot. hist.):* *(cap.)* a member of the Dutch Arminian party whose divergence from Calvinism was expressed in five articles in the Remonstrance of 1610. — *adv.* **remon'strantly.** — *v.i.* **remon'strāte** (sometimes *rem')* to make a remonstrance. — *v.t.* to say or *(obs.)* state in remonstrance: to demonstrate *(obs.).* — *adv.* **remon'stratingly.** — *n.* **remonstrā'tion** *(rem-ən-).* — *adjs.* **remon'strative, remon'stratory** *(-strə-tər-i)* expostulatory. — *n.* **remon'strator** (or *rem').* — **Grand Remonstrance** a statement of abuses presented to Charles I by the House of Commons in 1641. [L. *re-,* again, *mōnstrāre,* to point out.]

remontant *ri-mon'tənt, adj.* blooming more than once in the same season. — *n.* a remontant plant, esp. a rose. [Fr.]

remora *rem'ə-rə, n.* the sucking-fish, formerly believed to stop ships by attaching its sucker: an obstacle. [L. *rĕmŏra,* delay, hindrance — *mora,* delay.]

remoralise, -ize *rē-mor'əl-īz, v.t.* to restore morality to. — *n.* **remoralisā'tion, -z-.** [Pfx. **re-.**]

remorse *ri-mörs', n.* the gnawing pain of conscience: compunction: pity, compassionate feeling *(Spens., Shak., Milt.):* mitigation *(Shak.):* probably, matter of conscience *(Shak.):* bite *(Spens.).* — *adj.* **remorse'ful** penitent: compassionate *(obs.).* — *adv.* **remorse'fully.** — *n.* **remorse'fulness.** — *adj.* **remorse'less** without remorse: cruel: without respite. — *adv.* **remorse'lessly.** — *n.* **remorse'lessness.** [O.Fr. *remors* (Fr. *remords)* — L.L. *remorsus* — L. *remordēre, remorsum,* to bite again — *re-,* again, *mordēre,* to bite.]

remote *ri-mōt', adj.* far removed in place, time, chain of causation or relation, resemblance or relevance: widely separated: very indirect: located separately from the main processor but having a communication link with it *(comput.).* — *n.* an outside broadcast *(TV* and *radio,* esp. *U.S.).* — *adv.* **remote'ly.** — *ns.* **remote'ness; remō'tion** removal *(Shak.):* remoteness *(rare).* — **remote control** control of a device from a distance by the making or breaking of an electric circuit or by means of radio waves; **remote sensing** a method in which remote sensors are used to collect data for transmission to a central computer: observation and collection of scientific data without direct contact, esp. observation of the earth's surface from the air or from space using electromagnetic radiation. [L. *remōtus,* pa.p. of *removēre;* see **remove.**]

remoud *ri-mōōd', pa.t. (Spens.)* for **removed.**

remoulade, rémoulade *rā-mōō-läd', n.* a sauce made with eggs, herbs, capers, etc., or sometimes with mayonnaise, and served with fish, salad, etc. [Fr. dial. *ramolas,* horseradish, — L. *armoracea.*]

remould *rē'mōld', n.* a used tyre which has had a new tread vulcanised to the casing and the walls coated with rubber. — Also *v.t.* [Pfx. **re-.**]

remount *rē-mownt', v.t.* and *v.i.* to mount again. — *n.* a fresh horse, or supply of horses. [Pfx. **re-.**]

remove *ri-mōōv', v.t.* to put or take away: to transfer: to withdraw: to displace: to make away with: (in *pass.;* *Thackeray)* of a dish on the table, to be succeeded (by). — *v.i.* to go away: to change abode. — *n.* removal: the raising of a siege *(Shak.):* absence *(Shak.):* step or degree of remoteness or indirectness: in some schools, an intermediate class: promotion: a dish removed to make way for another, or taking the place of one so removed. — *n.* **removabil'ity.** — *adj.* **remov'able.** — *adv.* **remov'ably.** — *n.* **remov'al** the act of taking away: displacing: change of place: transference: going away: change of abode: a euphemism for murder. — *adj.* **removed'** remote: distant by degrees, as in descent, relationship. — *ns.* **remov'edness; remov'er** one who or that which removes: one who conveys furniture from

---

refoot' *v.t.*
reform'ulate *v.t.*
refortificā'tion *n.*

refort'ify *v.t.*
refound' *v.t.*
refoundā'tion *n.*

refound'er *n.*
refrac'ture *n.*
reframe' *v.t.*

---

fāte; fär; hûr; mīne; mōte; för; mūte; mōōn; fŏot; dhen (then); *el'ə-mənt* (element)

house to house. — **removal terms** (*Scot.*) 28th May and 28th November, called Whitsunday and Martinmas. [O.Fr. *remouvoir* — L. *removēre, remōtum* — *re-*, away, *movēre*, to move.]

remuage rə-mü-äzh′, -mōō-, *n.* the process of turning or shaking wine bottles so that the sediment collects at the cork end for removal. — *n.* **remueur** (rə-mü-œr′, -mōō-ûr′) in wine-making, the person who turns the bottles. [Fr., — *remuer*, to move or turn.]

remuda ri-mū′də, rā-mōō′dha, *n.* a supply of remounts. [Sp., exchange.]

remuncrate ri-mū′nə-rāt, *v.t.* to recompense: to pay for service rendered. — *adj.* **remū′nerable.** — *n.* **remūnerā′tion** recompense: reward: pay. — *adj.* **remū′nerative** profitable. — *ns.* **remū′nerativeness; remū′nerātor.** — *adj.* **remū′neratory** (-ə-tər-i) giving a recompense. [L. *remunerārī* (late *-āre*), *-ātus* — *mūnus, -ĕris*, a gift.]

remurmur ri-mûr′mər, *v.t.* and *v.i.* to echo, repeat, or resound in murmurs. [Pfx. **re-.**]

ren. See **run.**

renague. See **renegade.**

renaissance ri-nā′səns, ren′i-säns, -säns′, *n.* a new birth: (*cap.*) the revival of arts and letters, the transition from the Middle Ages to the modern world. — *adj.* of the Renaissance. — **Renaissance man** a man who typifies the renaissance ideal of wide-ranging culture and learning. [Fr.; cf. **renascence.**]

renal rē′nl, *adj.* of the kidneys. [L. *rēnālis* — *rēnēs* (sing. *rēn*, is rare), the kidneys.]

renascent ri-nas′ənt, also *-nās′*, *adj.* coming into renewed life or vitality. — *n.* **renasc′ence** being born anew: (*cap.*) Renaissance. [L. *renāscēns, -entis*, pr.p. of *renāscī* — *nāscī*, to be born.]

renay, reney ri-nā′, **reny** ri-nī′, (*obs.*) *vs.t.* to renounce, abjure, forswear: to deny: — *pr.p.* **renay′ing, reny′ing;** *pa.p.* **renayed′, renied′.** [O.Fr. *renaier, renier* — L. *renegāre.*]

rencounter ren-kownt′ər, (Fr.) **rencontre** rä-kɔ̃-tr′, *ns.* a chance meeting: an encounter: a casual combat: a collision: an informal meeting of scientists. — *v.t.* to meet: to encounter. [Fr. *rencontre.*]

rend rend, *v.t.* to tear asunder with force: to split: to tear away. — *v.i.* to become torn: — *pa.t.* and *pa.p.* **rent.** [O.E. *rendan*, to tear.]

render ren′dər, *v.t.* to give up: to give back, return, give in return: to make up: to deliver: to hand over: to give: to surrender: to yield: to tender or submit: to show forth: to represent or reproduce, esp. artistically: to perform: to translate: to perform or pay as a duty or service: to present or betake (with *at; refl.*): to cause to be or become: to melt: to extract, treat, or clarify by melting: to plaster with a first coat. — *n.* an act of rendering: that which is rendered. — *adj.* **ren′derable.** — *ns.* **ren′derer; ren′dering; rendi′tion** surrender: rendering: a performance. [O.Fr. *rendre* — L.L. *rendĕre*, app. formed by influence of *prendĕre*, to take — L. *reddĕre* — *re-*, back, *dăre*, to give.]

rendezvous rä′dā-vōō, ron′di-, *n.* appointed meeting-place: a meeting by appointment: a general resort: an arranged meeting, and usu. docking, of two spacecraft (*space tech.*): — *pl.* **rendezvous** (-vōōz), (*obs.*) **rendezvous′es.** — *v.i.* to assemble at any appointed place: — *pa.t.* and *pa.p.* **rendezvoused** (rä′dā-vōōd, ron′di-). [Fr. *rendez-vous*, render yourselves — *rendre*, to render.]

rendition. See **render.**

rendzina ren-dzē′nə, *n.* a fertile soil-type derived from a calcium-rich bedrock and typical of grass or open woodland in humid to semi-arid climates. [Russ., — Pol. *redzina.*]

renegade ren′i-gād, **renegate** *-gāt, ns.* one faithless to principle or party: an apostate: a turncoat: esp. a Christian turned Muslim — also **renegā′do** (or ä′dō;

arch.): — *pl.* **renega′dos.** — *v.i.* **ren′egade** to turn renegade. — *adjs.* **ren′egade, -ate** apostate. — *n.* **renegā′tion.** — *v.t.* **renegue, renege** (ri-nēg′, or *-nāg′*) to renounce: to apostatise from. — *v.i.* to deny (often with *on*): to refuse (often with *on*): to revoke at cards. — Also **renig** (*-nig′*), **renague** (*-nāg′; Ir.*). — *n.* **reneg′-(u)er.** [L.L. *renegātus* — L. *re-*, intens., *negāre, -ātum*, to deny; partly through Sp. *renegado.*]

renew ri-nū′, *v.t.* to renovate: to transform to new life, revive: to begin again: to repeat: to make again: to invigorate: to substitute new for: to restore: to regenerate: to extend the loan of. — *v.i.* to be made new: to begin again. — *adj.* **renew′able.** — *ns.* **renew′al** renewing: shortened form for **urban renewal** (q.v. at **urban**); **renew′edness; renew′er; renew′ing.** [Pfx. **re-**, and **new,** *adj.*]

reney. See **renay.**

renfierst ren-fērst′, (*Spens.*) *pa.p.* made fierce. [App. modelled on the next.]

renforce ren-fōrs′, *-förs′*, (*obs.*) *v.t.* to reinforce: to force again. — *v.i.* to renew efforts: — (in *Spens. pa.t.* **re′nforst′,** *pa.p.* **renforst′**). [(O.)Fr. *renforcer.*]

renga ren′gə. Same as **linked verse.** See **link**[1].

renied. See **renay.**

reniform ren′i-förm, *adj.* kidney-shaped. [L. *rēnēs* (sing. *rēn*), the kidneys, and *fōrma*, form: see **renal.**]

renig. See **renegue** (under **renegade**).

renin rē′nin, *n.* a protein enzyme secreted by the kidneys into the bloodstream, where it helps to maintain the blood pressure. [L. *rēnēs* (sing. *rēn*), the kidneys.]

renitent ri-nī′tənt, ren′i-tənt, (*rare*) *adj.* resistant: reluctant: recalcitrant. — *n.* **renī′tency** (or *ren′*). [L. *renītēns, -entis*, pr.p. of *renītī* to resist.]

renminbi ren-min-bē, (also with *cap.*) *n.* the currency of the Peoples' Republic of China since 1948: a Chinese monetary unit, also called **yuan,** equal to 100 fen. [Chin. *renmin*, the people, *bi*, money.]

renne ren, (*Spens.*) *v.i.* to run. — Also *pa.p.* — *n.* **renn′ing.** [See **run.**]

rennet[1] ren′it, *n.* any means of curdling milk, esp. a preparation of calf's stomach. — **renn′et-bag** the fourth stomach of a ruminant. [O.E. *rinnan*, to run; cf. **earn**[2], **yearn**[3].]

rennet[2] ren′it, *n.* apple of certain old varieties. [Fr. *reinette, rainette*; origin uncertain.]

rennin ren′in, *n.* an enzyme found in gastric juice, which causes coagulation of milk. [**renn**et.]

renormalisation, -z- rē-norm-əl-īz-ā′shən, (*physics*) *n.* a method of obtaining finite answers to calculations (rather than infinities) by redefining the parameters, esp. of mass and charge. — *v.t.* **renorm′alise, -ize** to subject to or calculate using renormalisation. [Pfx. **re-.**]

renounce ri-nowns′, *v.t.* to disclaim: to disown: to reject publicly and finally: to recant: to abjure. — *v.i.* to fail to follow suit at cards. — *n.* a failure to follow suit. — *ns.* **renounce′ment; renoun′cer.** [O.Fr. *renuncer* — L. *renuntiāre* — *re-*, away, *nuntiāre, -ātum*, to announce.]

renovate ren′ō-vāt, *v.t.* to renew or make new again: to make as if new: to regenerate. — *ns.* **renovā′tion; ren′ovātor.** [L. *re-*, again, *novāre, -ātum*, to make new — *novus*, new.]

renown ri-nown′, *n.* fame. — *v.t.* to make famous: to celebrate. — *adj.* **renowned′** famous. — *n.* **renown′er** one who gives renown. [O.Fr. *renoun* (Fr. *renom*) — L. *re-*, again, *nōmen*, a name.]

rensselaerite ren′səl-ə-rīt, ren-səl-ē′rīt, *n.* a kind of firm-textured talc, used for carved or lathe-turned ornaments. [From Stephen Van *Rensselaer* (1764–1839), American statesman.]

rent[1] rent, *n.* an opening made by rending: a fissure. —

rēfreeze′ *v.t.*   **rēfur′bish** *v.t.*   **rēgath′er** *v.t.* and *v.i.*
rēfū′el *v.t.*   **rēfur′nish** *v.t.* and *v.i.*   **rēgive′** *v.t.*
rēfū′el(l)able *adj.*   **rēfū′sion** *n.*   **rēgrade′** *v.t.*

For other sounds see detailed chart of pronunciation.

v.t. and *v.i.* (*obs.* or *dial.*) to rend. — Also *pa.t.* and *pa.p.* of **rend.** [**rend.**]

rent[2] *rent, n.* periodical payment for use of another's property, esp. houses and lands: revenue. — *v.t.* to hold or occupy by paying rent: to let or hire out for a rent: to charge with rent. — *v.i.* to be let at a rent. — *adj.* **rent'able.** — *ns.* **rent'al** a rent-roll: rent: annual value: something rented or hired (*U.S.*): a kindly (q.v.) tenant's lease (*Scot.*); **rent'aller** (*Scot.*) a kindly tenant; **rent'er** a tenant who pays rent: one who lets out property: a farmer of tolls or taxes (*hist.*): a theatre shareholder (*arch.*): a distributor of commercial films to cinemas. — **rent-a(n)-** (*facet.*; also without hyphens) in composition, (as if) rented or hired, organised for a specific occasion or purpose, instantly or artificially created etc., as in **rent'-a-crowd, rent'-a-mob, rent'-an= army. — rental library** (*U.S.*) a lending-library which takes fees for books borrowed; **rent'-boy** (also without hyphen) a young male homosexual prostitute; **rent'= charge** a periodical payment charged upon rent; **rent'= collector; rent'-day.** — *adj.* and *adv.* **rent'-free** without payment of rent. **rent'-restric'tion** restriction of landlord's right to raise rent; **rent'-roll** a list of property and rents: total income from property. — **for rent** (orig. *U.S.*) to let. [Fr. *rente* — L. *reddita* (*pecūnia*), money paid — *reddĕre*, to pay; cf. **render.**]

rente *rāt,* annual income: (in *pl.*; *rāt*) French or other government securities or income from them. — *n.* **rentier** (*rä-tyā*) a fund-holder: one who has, or who lives on, an income from investments. — Also *adj.* [Fr.]

renunciation *ri-nun-si-ā'shən, n.* act of renouncing: self-resignation. — *adjs.* **renun'ciative** (-shə-tiv, -syə-tiv, -si-ā-tiv), **renun'ciatory** (-shə-tər-i, -si-ə-tər-i). [L. *re-nūntiāre,* proclaim; see **nuncio.**]

renverse *ren-vûrs',* (*arch.*) *v.t.* to reverse: to upset: — *pa.t.* and *pa.p.* **renversed', renverst'** (*Spens.*). — *n.* **renverse-ment** (-*vûrs'mənt; aero.*) specif., a half-roll and a half-loop in a combined manoeuvre: any aerial manoeuvre involving a reverse in direction of travel. [Fr. *ren-verser* — pfx. *re-, enverser,* to overturn.]

renvoi, (esp. formerly) **renvoy** *ren-voi',* Fr. *rä-vwä, n.* sending back by a government of an alien to his own country: a referring or relegation of a legal dispute to another jurisdiction. [Fr.]

reny. See **renay.**

reopen *rē-ō'pn, v.t.* and *v.i.* to open again: to begin again. — **reopening clause** in collective bargaining, a clause enabling any issue in a contract to be reconsidered before the contract expires (also **reopener (clause)**). [Pfx. **re-.**]

reorient *rē-ō', -ō'ri-ənt, adj.* rising again. — *v.t.* (-*ent*) to orient again. — *v.t.* **reō'rientate** to reorient. — *n.* **reōrientā'tion.** [Pfx. **re-.**]

rep[1], **repp** *rep, n.* a corded cloth. — Also **reps** (*reps*). — *adj.* **repped** (*rept*) transversely corded. [Fr. *reps,* perh. — Eng. **ribs.**]

rep[2] *rep, n.* a colloquial or slang abbreviation of **repertory** (*theatrical*), **repetition** (*school*), **reputation** (early 18th cent. and *U.S.*), **representative** (esp. *commerce*) and **reprobate.**

rep[3] *rep, n.* unit of radiation dosage, now superseded by **rad.** [*röntgen equivalent physical.*]

rep[4] *rep, v.i.* (*commercial jargon*) to work or act as a commercial representative: — *pr.p.* **repp'ing;** *pa.t.* and *pa.t.* **repped.** — *n.* **repp'ing.** [**rep**[2] — **represent.**]

repaid *pa.t.* and *pa.p.* of **repay.**

repaint *rē-pānt', v.t.* to paint anew. — *n.* (*rē'pānt*) a repainted golf-ball. — *n.* **repaint'ing.** [Pfx. **re-.**]

repair[1] *ri-pār', v.i.* to betake oneself: to go: to resort: to return (*Shak.*). — *v.t.* (*Spens.*) to restore to its position: to withdraw. — *n.* resort: place of resort: concourse. [O.Fr. *repairer,* to return to a haunt — L.L. *repatriāre,*

to return to one's country — L. *re-,* back, *patria,* native country.]

repair[2] *ri-pār', v.t.* to mend: to make amends for: to make good: to restore, refresh, revivify (*Shak.*). — *n.* restoration after injury or decay: supply of loss: sound condition: condition in respect of soundness: part that has been mended, made sound. — *adj.* **repair'able** capable of being mended (esp. of material things): falling to be repaired. — *ns.* **repair'er; reparability** (*rep-ər-ə-bil'i-ti*). — *adj.* **reparable** (*rep'ər-ə-bl*) capable of being made good or (*rare*) being mended: falling to be repaired. — *adv.* **rep'arably.** — *n.* **reparā'tion** repair: supply of what is wasted: amends: compensation. — *adjs.* **reparative** (*ri-par'ə-tiv*); **repar'atory.** — **repair'-man** one who does repairs, esp. on something mechanical; **repair'-shop.** [O.Fr. *reparer* — L. *reparāre* — *parāre,* to prepare.]

repand *ri-pand',* (*bot., zool.*) *adj.* slightly wavy. [L. *repandus* — *re-,* back, *pandus,* bent.]

reparable, etc. See **repair**[2].

repartee *rep-är-tē', n.* a ready and witty retort: skill in making such retorts. — *v.t.* and *v.i.* to retort with ready wit. [O.Fr. *repartie* — *repartir* — *partir,* to set out — L. *partīrī,* to divide.]

repartition *rep-ər-tish'ən, n.* distribution: (*rē-pär-*) a second partition: a division into smaller parts. — *v.t.* (*rē-pär-*) to partition anew. [Pfx. **re-.**]

repass *rē-päs', v.t.* and *v.i.* to pass again: to pass in the opposite direction. — *n.* **repassage** (*rē-pas'ij*). [Pfx. **re-.**]

repast *ri-päst', n.* a meal: refreshment of sleep (*Spens.*). — *v.t.* and *v.i.* (*Shak.*) to feed. — *n.* **repas'ture** (*Shak.*) food. [O.Fr. *repast* (Fr. *repas*) — L.L. *repastus* — L. *pascĕre, pastum,* to feed.]

repatriate *rē-* or *ri-pāt-ri-āt,* or *-pat', v.t.* to restore or send (someone) back to his own country. — *n.* a repatriated person. — *n.* **repatriā'tion.** [L.L. *repa-triāre, -ātum,* to return to one's country — L. *patria.*]

repay *rē-pā', ri-pā', v.t.* to pay back: to make return for: to recompense: to give or give in return. — *v.i.* to make repayment: — *pr.p.* **repay'ing;** *pa.t.* and *pa.p.* **repaid'.** — *adj.* **repay'able** that is to be repaid: due. — *n.* **repay'ment.** [Pfx. **re-.**]

repeal *ri-pēl', v.t.* to revoke: to annul: to quash, repress, set aside (*Spens., Milt.*): to recall from banishment (*obs.*): to try to have restored to favour (*Shak.*). — *n.* abrogation: (*cap.*) dissolution of the Union between Great Britain and Ireland called for by O'Connell. — *adj.* **repeal'able.** — *n.* **repeal'er** one who repeals: (*cap.*) an advocate of Repeal. [O.Fr. *rapeler* — pfx. *re-, apeler,* to appeal.]

repeat *ri-pēt', v.t.* to say, do, perform, go over, again: to iterate: to quote from memory: to say off: to recount: to celebrate (*Milt.*): to say or do after another: to tell to others, divulge: to cause to recur: to reproduce: to repeat the words or actions of (*refl.*): to seek again (*obs.*): to ask back (*obs.*). — *v.i.* to recur: to make repetition: to strike the last hour, quarter, etc., when required: to fire several shots without reloading: to rise so as to be tasted after swallowing: to vote (illegally) more than once (*U.S.*). — *n.* a repetition: a retracing of one's course: a passage repeated or marked for repetition (*mus.*): dots or other mark directing repetition: a unit of a repeated pattern: an order for more goods of the same kind: a radio or television programme broadcast for the second, third, etc., time. — *adj.* done or occurring as a repetition. — *adjs.* **repeat'able** able to be done again: fit to be told to others; **repeat'ed** done again: reiterated. — *adv.* **re-peat'edly** many times repeated: again and again. — *n.* **repeat'er** one who, or that which, repeats, or does a thing that he or it has done before: a decimal fraction in which the same figure (or sometimes figures) is

rēgrant' *n.* and *v.t.*	**rēgrowth'** *n.*	**rēheel'** *v.t.*
rēgrind' *v.t.*	**rēhand'le** *v.t.*	**rēhȳdrā'tion** *n.*
rēgroup' *v.t.*	**rēhand'ling** *n.*	**rē-ignite'** *v.t.*

repeated to infinity: a watch or clock, or a firearm, that repeats: a ship that repeats an admiral's signals: an instrument for automatically retransmitting a message (*teleg.*): a thermionic amplifier inserted in a telephone circuit (also **repeating coil**) or in a cable. — *n.* and *adj.* **repeat'ing.** — **repeat oneself** to say again what one has said already. [Fr. *répéter* — L. *repetĕre, repitītum* — re-, again, *petĕre,* to seek.]

repechage *rep'ɘ-shäzh,* Fr. *rɘ-pesh-äzh,* (*rowing, fencing,* etc.) *adj.* pertaining to a supplementary competition in which second-bests in earlier eliminating competitions get a second chance to go on to the final. [Fr. *repêchage,* a fishing out again.]

repel *ri-pel', v.t.* to drive off or back: to repulse: to reject: to hold off: to provoke aversion in: to repudiate: — *pr.p.* **repell'ing;** *pa.t.* and *pa.p.* **repelled'.** — *ns.* **repell'ence, repell'ency.** — Also **repell'ance, repell'ancy.** — *adj.* **repell'ent** driving back: able or tending to repel: distasteful. — *n.* that which repels. — *adv.* **repell'ently.** — Also **repell'ant; repell'antly.** — *n.* **repell'er.** — *adj.* **repell'ing.** — *adv.* **repell'ingly.** [L. *repellĕre* — *pellĕre,* to drive.]

repent[1] *ri-pent', v.i.* to regret, sorrow for, or wish to have been otherwise, what one has done or left undone (with *of*): to change from past evil: to feel contrition: to sorrow (*Spens.*). — *v.t.* (*refl.* or *impers.*) to affect with contrition or with regret (*arch.*): to regret, or feel contrition for (an action). — *n.* (*Spens.*) repentance. — *n.* **repent'ance** act of repenting: penitent state of mind. — *adj.* **repent'ant** experiencing or expressing repentance. — *n.* (*rare*) a penitent. — *adv.* **repent'antly.** — *n.* **repent'er.** — *adv.* **repent'ingly.** [O.Fr. *repentir* — L. *paenitēre,* to cause to repent.]

repent[2] *rē'pɘnt,* (*bot.*) *adj.* lying on the ground and rooting. — Also **rep'tant.** [L. *repēns, -entis,* pr.p. of *repĕre,* to creep.]

repercuss *rē-pɘr-kus', v.t.* (*obs.,* or now *coll.*) to drive back, reflect, reverberate, or have consequences. — *n.* **repercussion** (*-kush'ɘn*) driving back: reverberation: echo: reflection: a return stroke, reaction, or consequence. — *adj.* **repercussive** (*-kus'iv*) driving back: reverberating: echoing: repeated. [L. *repercutĕre, -cussum* — re-, per, *quatĕre,* to strike.]

repertory *rep'ɘr-tɘr-i, n.* a storehouse, repository: a stock of pieces that a person or company is prepared to perform. — Also *adj.* — *n.* **repertoire** (*rep'ɘr-twär;* Fr. *répertoire*) performer's or company's repertory: a full set of the codes and instructions which a computer can accept and execute (*comput.*). — **repertory theatre** a theatre with a repertoire of plays and a stock or permanent company of actors, called a **repertory company.** [L.L. *repertōrium* — L. *reperīre,* to find again — *parēre,* to bring forth.]

repetend *rep'i-tend, rep-i-tend', n.* the figure(s) that recur(s) in a recurring decimal number (*math.*): a recurring note, word, refrain, etc.: anything that recurs or is repeated. — *adj.* to be repeated. [L. *repetendum,* that which is to be repeated — L. *repetere,* to repeat.]

répétiteur *rā-pā-tē-tœr', n.* a coach, tutor: one who rehearses opera singers, etc. [Fr.; cf. **repeat.**]

repetition *rep-i-tish'ɘn, n.* act of repeating: recital from memory: a thing repeated: power of repeating a note promptly. — *adjs.* **repeti'tional, repeti'tionary, repetitious** (*-tish'ɘs*) of the nature of, or characterised by, repetition: **repetitive** (*ri-pet'i-tiv*) iterative: overmuch given to repetition. — *advs.* **repeti'tiously, repet'itively.** — *ns.* **repeti'tiousness, repet'itiveness.** [L. *repetĕre;* see **repeat.**]

rephrase *rē-frāz', v.t.* to put in different words, usu. so as to make more understandable, acceptable, etc. [Pfx. re-.]

repine *ri-pīn', v.i.* to fret (with *at* or *against*): to feel discontent: to murmur. — *v.t.* (*obs.*) to lament: to

grudge. — *n.* (*Shak.*) a repining. — *ns.* **repīne'ment; repīn'er.** — *n.* and *adj.* **repīn'ing.** — *adv.* **repīn'ingly.** [App. from **pine**[2].]

repique *ri-pēk', n.* at piquet, the winning of thirty points or more from combinations in one's own hand, before play begins. — *v.t.* to score a repique against. — *v.i.* to score a repique. [Fr. *repic.*]

repla. See **replum.**

replace *ri-* or *rē-plās', v.t.* to put back: to provide a substitute for: to take the place of, supplant. — *adj.* **replace'able.** — *ns.* **replace'ment** act of replacing: a person or thing that takes the place of another: the occurrence of a face or faces in the position where the principal figure would have a corner or edge (*crystal.*): the process by which one mineral gradually forms from another in crystalline form by solution and redeposition (*geol.*); **replac'er** a substitute. — **replaceable hydrogen** hydrogen atoms that can be replaced in an acid by metals to form salts. [Pfx. re-.]

replay *rē-plā', v.t.* to play again (a game, match, record, recording, etc.) — *n.* (*rē'plā*) a game, match, played again: a recording played again, esp. (also **action replay**) of a part of a broadcast game or match, often in slow motion. [Pfx. re-.]

replenish *ri-plen'ish, v.t.* to fill again: to fill completely: to stock abundantly: to people. — *adj.* **replen'ished** (*Shak.*) complete, consummate. — *ns.* **replen'isher** one who replenishes: an apparatus for maintaining an electric charge; **replen'ishment.** [O.Fr. *replenir, -iss-,* from *replein,* full — L. re-, again, *plēnus,* full.]

replete *ri-plēt', adj.* full: completely filled: filled to satiety: abounding (with *with*). — *v.t.* to fill to repletion. — *ns.* **replete'ness, replē'tion** superabundant fullness: surfeit: fullness of blood (*med.*): plethora. [L. *replētus,* pa.p. of *replēre* — *plēre,* to fill.]

replevy *ri-plev'i, v.t.* to bail (*arch.*): to recover, or restore to the owner (goods distrained) upon pledge to try the right at law. — *n.* replevin. — *adjs.* **replev'iable, replev'isable** (*-i-sɘb-l*). — *n.* **replev'in** replevying: a writ or action in such a case. — *v.t.* to recover by replevin (*Swift,* etc.). [O.Fr. *replevir* — *plevir,* to pledge.]

replica *rep'li-kɘ, n.* a duplicate, properly one by the original artist: a facsimile: a repeat (*mus.*). [It., — L. *replicāre,* to repeat.]

replicate *rep'li-kāt, v.t.* to fold back: to repeat: to make a replica of: to reply. — *v.i.* of molecules of living material, to reproduce molecules identical with themselves. — *n.* (*mus.*) a tone one or more octaves from a given tone. — *adj.* folded back. — *n.* **replica'tion** a reply: the plaintiff's answer to the defendant's plea: doubling back: copy, reproduction: reverberation, echo (*Shak.*). [L. *replicāre, -ātum,* to fold back — *plicāre,* to fold.]

replum *rep'lɘm, rē'plɘm, n.* a partition in a fruit formed by ingrowth of the placentas, as in Cruciferae: — *pl.* **rep'la.** [L. *replum,* the upright in the frame of a folding door.]

reply *ri-plī', v.t.* to say in answer. — *v.i.* to answer: to respond in action, as by returning gun-fire: to echo: to answer a defendant's plea: — *pr.p.* **reply'ing;** *pa.t.* and *pa.p.* **replied'.** — *n.* an answer, response: a replication (*Scots law*): the answer in a fugue (*mus.*). — *n.* **replī'er.** [O.Fr. *replier* — L. *replicāre;* see **replicate.**]

repo *rē'pō, n.* slang abbreviation for **repossession:** — *pl.* **rē'pos.**

repoint *rē-poynt', v.t.* to repair (stone or brickwork) by renewing the mortar, etc. [Pfx. re-.]

répondez s'il vous plaît *rā-pɔ̃-dā sēl vōō ple,* or **RSVP** (Fr.) please answer (this invitation).

repone *ri-pōn',* (*Scots law*) *v.t.* to restore to office or status: to rehabilitate. [L. *repōnĕre,* to put back — *pōnĕre,* to put.]

report *ri-pōrt', -pört', v.t.* to convey (*Spens.*): to bring

---

rēillume' *v.t.*	**rēimpose'** *v.t.*	**rēinfuse'** *v.t.*
rēillum'ine *v.t.*	**rēimposi'tion** *n.*	**rēinhab'it** *v.t.*
rēimport' *v.t.*	**rēincrease'** *v.t.*	**rēinsert'** *v.t.*

For other sounds see detailed chart of pronunciation.

back, as an answer, news, or account of anything: to give an account of, esp. a formal, official, or requested account: to state in such an account: to relate: to circulate publicly: to transmit as having been said, done, or observed: to write down or take notes of, esp. for a newspaper or radio or television programme: to lay a charge against: to echo back: (*refl.*) to make personal announcement of the presence and readiness of. — *v.i.* to make a statement: to write an account of occurrences: to make a formal report: to report oneself: to act as a reporter. — *n.* a statement of facts: a formal or official statement, as of results of an investigation or matter referred: a statement on a school pupil's work and behaviour or the like: an account of a matter of news, esp. the words of a speech: reporting, testimony (*Shak.*): general talk: rumour: hearsay: repute (*B.*): explosive noise. — *adj.* **report'able.** — *n.* **report'age** journalistic reporting, style, or manner: gossip: a documentary presented through pictures (in film, photographs) without comment or written or spoken narrative. — *adv.* **report'edly** according to report. — *n.* **report'er** one who reports, esp. for a newspaper or legal proceedings. — *n.* and *adj.* **report'ing.** — *adv.* **report'ingly** (*Shak.*) by common report. — *adj.* **reportō'rial** (*rep-ər-, -ör-*). — **reported speech** indirect speech; **reported verses** (Fr. *vers rapportés*) verses that combine a number of parallel sentences by collocation of corresponding parts, as Sidney's 'Virtue, beauty, and speech did strike, wound, charm, My heart, eyes, ears, with wonder, love, delight'; **report stage** the stage at which a parliamentary bill is amended in committee is reported to the House, before the third reading. [O.Fr. *reporter* — L. *reportāre* — *re-*, back, *portāre*, to carry.]

repose *ri-pōz'*, *v.t.* to lay at rest: to rest (oneself) in confidence (on; *arch.*): to give rest to, refresh by rest: to place, set (as confidence): to place in trust. — *v.i.* to rest: to be still: to rely, place one's trust (with *on, upon*; *arch.*). — *n.* rest: quiet: stillness: calm: ease of manner: serenity: restful feeling or effect: a place of rest (*Milt.*). — *n.* **repōs'al** (*Shak.* **repos'all,** another reading **repōs'ure**) reposing. — *adj.* **repōsed'** calm: settled. — *adv.* **repō'sedly.** — *n.* **repōs'edness.** — *adj.* **repōse'ful.** — *adv.* **repōse'fully.** [Fr. *reposer* — L.L. *repausāre*; confused with the following.]

reposit *ri-poz'it*, *v.t.* to lay away, deposit. — *ns.* **reposition** (*rep-ə-zish'ən*) replacing: reinstatement (*Scot.*): laying up; **repos'itor** an instrument for replacing a displaced organ; **repos'itory** a place or receptacle in which anything is laid up: a collection or museum: a mart, esp. for horses: an abode of souls (*arch.*): a tomb, sepulchre (*arch.*): a storehouse, magazine, as of information: a place of accumulation: a confidant. [L. *repōnĕre, repositum,* to put back, lay aside — *pōnĕre,* to put; confused with foregoing.]

re-position, reposition *rē-pəz-ish'ən, v.t.* to put in a different position. [Pfx. **re-.**]

repossess *rē-pəz-es', v.t.* to regain possession of: to take back (goods acquired on credit or by hire-purchase) because payment has not been made: to put again in possession. — *n.* **repossession** (*-esh'ən*). [Pfx. **re-.**]

repost. Same as **riposte.**

reposure. See **repose.**

repoussé *rə-pōō-sā,* or *-pōō', adj.* raised in relief by hammering from behind or within. — *n.* repoussé work. — *n.* **repoussage** (*-säzh'*). [Fr.]

repp. Same as **rep**[1].

repreeve (*Shak.*). See **reprieve.**

reprehend *rep-ri-hend', v.t.* to find fault with: to reprove. — *n.* **reprehend'er.** — *adj.* **reprehen'sible** blameworthy. — *adv.* **reprehen'sibly.** — *n.* **reprehen'sion** reproof: censure. — *adj.* **reprehen'sive** containing reproof: given in reproof. — *adv.* **reprehen'sively.** — *adj.* **reprehen'-**

sory. [L. *repraehendĕre, -hēnsum* — *re-,* intens., *praehendĕre,* to lay hold of.]

represent *rep-ri-zent', v.t.* to exhibit the image of: to use, or serve, as a symbol for: to stand for: to exhibit, depict, personate, show an image of, by imitative art: to act: to be a substitute, agent, deputy, member of parliament, or the like, for: to correspond or be in some way equivalent or analogous to: to serve as a sample of: to present earnestly to mind: to give out, make to appear, allege (that). — *adj.* **represent'able** (*rep-ri-*). — *ns.* **representā'men** (*psych.*) the product of representation; **represent'ant** a representative; **representation** (*-zən-tā'shən*) act, state, or fact of representing or being represented: that which represents: an image: picture: dramatic performance: a mental image: a presentation of a view of facts or arguments: a petition, remonstrance, expostulation: assumption of succession by an heir: a body of representatives. — *adj.* **representā'tional** (*rep-ri-zən-*) esp. of art which depicts objects in a realistic rather than an abstract form. — *ns.* **representā'tionalism** representational art: the doctrine that in the perception of the external world the immediate object represents another object beyond the sphere of consciousness — also **representā'tionism; representā'tionist.** — *adj.* **representative** (*rep-ri-zent'ə-tiv*) representing: exhibiting a likeness: typical: pertaining to representation. — *n.* a sample: a typical example or embodiment: one who represents another or others, as a deputy, delegate, ambassador, member of parliament, agent, successor, heir: the head of a family (*Jane Austen*): a representative legislative body (*obs.*). — *adv.* **represent'atively.** — *ns.* **represent'ativeness; represent'er; represent'ment.** — **representative peers** Scottish and Irish peers chosen by their fellows to sit in the House of Lords. — **House of Representatives** the lower branch of the United States Congress, consisting of members chosen biennially by the people: also of various State and other legislatures. [L. *repraesentāre, -ātum* — *praesentāre,* to place before.]

re-present *rē'pri-zent', v.t.* to present again. — *ns.* **re'(-)presentā'tion, rē'(-)present'ment.** [Pfx. **re-.**]

repress *ri-pres', v.t.* to restrain: to keep under: to put down: to banish to the unconscious. — *adj.* **repress'ible.** — *adv.* **repress'ibly.** — *n.* **repression** (*-presh'ən*). — *adj.* **repress'ive.** — *adv.* **repress'ively.** — *n.* **repress'or.** [L. *reprimĕre, repressum* — *premĕre,* to press.]

re-press *rē'pres', v.t.* to press again. [Pfx. **re-.**]

repriefe *ri-prēf', (Spens.) n.* reproach, insult, shame, reproof. — *v.t.* **reprieve** (*-prēv'*) to reprove. [Same root as **reproof;** for vowel, see **prove.**]

reprieve *ri-prēv' (Shak.* **repreeve'**; *Spens.* **reprive, repryve** *-prīv') v.t.* to delay the execution of: to give a respite to: to rescue, redeem. — *n.* a suspension of a criminal sentence, esp. a death sentence: interval of ease or relief. — *n.* **repriev'al.** [Supposed to be from A.Fr. *repris,* pa.p. of *reprendre,* to take back (see **reprise**); the *v* app. by confusion, perh. with **reprieve,** reprove.]

reprimand *rep'ri-mänd, -mand, n.* a severe reproof. — *v.t.* (also *-mänd', -mand'*) to reprove severely, esp. publicly or officially. [Fr. *réprimande* — L. *reprimĕre, repressum,* to press back — *premĕre,* to press.]

reprime *ri-prīm', (rare) v.t.* to repress. [See **repress.**]

reprint *rē-print', v.t.* to print again: to print a new impression of, esp. with little or no change. — *v.i.* to be reprinted. — *n.* **rē'print** a later impression: printed matter used as copy.

reprise (*Spens.* **reprize**) *ri-prīz', v.t.* to gain anew (*obs.*): to recapture (*obs.*): to renew, repeat, reissue. — *n.* a yearly charge or deduction: reprisal (*Dryden*): a renewed or alternating spell of action: (*-prēz'*) resumption of an earlier subject (*mus.*; also *v.t.*). — *n.* **reprīs'al** seizure in retaliation: a prize (*Shak.*): an act of retaliation: recapture: compensation. [Fr. *reprise* —

rĕinser'tion *n.*   rĕinspire' *v.t.*   rĕinter'ment *n.*
rĕinspect' *v.t.*   rĕinspir'it *v.t.*   rĕinter'pret *v.t.*
rĕinspec'tion *n.*   rĕinter' *v.t.*   rĕinterpretā'tion *n.*

fāte; fär; hûr; mīne; mōte; för; mūte; mōōn; fŏŏt; dhen (then); el'ə-mənt (element)

reprendre — L. *repraehendĕre*.]
reprive (*Spens.*). See **reprieve.**
repro *rē'prō, rep'rō, n.* and *adj.* short for **reproduction,** esp. of modern copies of period styles of furniture. — *n.* (*rē'prō*) short for **reproduction proof:** — *pl.* **re'pros.**
reproach *ri-prōch', v.t.* to cast (something) in someone's teeth (with *to, against,* also *on; Dryden,* etc.): to upbraid: to blame (oneself, etc., for, with): to reprove gently: to bring into discredit. — *n.* upbraiding: reproof: censure: disgrace: a source or matter of disgrace or shame. — *adj.* **reproach'able.** — *n.* **reproach'er.** — *adj.* **reproach'ful** reproving: deserving of reproach, disgraceful (*obs.*). — *adv.* **reproach'fully.** — *n.* **reproach'fulness.** — *adj.* **reproach'less** irreproachable. — **above, beyond, reproach** excellent, too good to be criticised; **the Reproaches** antiphons chanted in R.C. churches on Good Friday, in which Christ reproaches the Jewish people. [Fr. *reprocher,* perh. from L. *prope,* near; cf. **approach;** or from *reprobāre;* see **reprobate.**]
reprobate *rep'rō-bāt, adj.* failing to pass a test (esp. of silver) (*arch.*): base: rejected by God: given over to sin: depraved: unprincipled: condemnatory. — *n.* one rejected by God: an abandoned or profligate person: one lost to shame: (often playfully) a scamp. — *v.t.* to reject: to disapprove of: to censure: to disown (*obs.*). — *ns.* **rep'robacy** (*-bə-si*) state of being a reprobate; **rep'robance** (*Shak.*) reprobation; **rep'robāter; reprobā'tion** the act of reprobating: rejection: foreordination to eternal perdition: utter abandonment: severe censure or condemnation. — *adjs.* **rep'robātive, rep'robatory** condemnatory. — *n.* **rep'robātor** (*Scots law*) an action to prove a witness perjured or biased. [L. *reprobāre, -ātum,* to reprove, contrary of *approbāre* — *probāre,* to prove.]
reprocess *rē-prō'ses, v.t.* to process again, esp. to remake used material into a new material or article. [Pfx. **re-.**]
reproduce *rē-prō-dūs', v.t.* to produce a copy of: to form anew: to propagate: to reconstruct in imagination. — *v.i.* to produce offspring: to prove suitable for copying in some way: to turn out (well, badly, etc.) when copied. — *n.* **reprodū'cer.** — *adj.* **reprodū'cible.** — *n.* **reproduction** (*-duk'shən*) the act of reproducing: the act of producing new organisms — the whole process whereby life is continued from generation to generation: regeneration: a copy, facsimile: a representation. — Also *adj.* (of furniture, etc.). — *adj.* **reproduc'tive.** — *adv.* **reproduc'tively.** — *ns.* **reproduc'tiveness, reproductiv'ity.** — **reproduction proof** (*printing*) a high-quality proof made from strips of typeset copy and photographed to produce a plate for printing from (commonly abbrev. as **repro proof, repro**). [Pfx. **re-.**]
reprography *ri-prog'rə-fi, n.* the reproduction of graphic or typeset material, as by photocopying. — *n.* **reprog'rapher.** — *adj.* **reprograph'ic.** [Fr. *reprographie.*]
reproof *ri-prōōf', n.* a reproving: rebuke: censure: reprehension: shame, disgrace (*Shak.*): disproof (*obs.*): (*rē-*) a second or new proof. — *v.t.* (*rē-*) to make waterproof again. — *n.* **reproval** (*ri-prōō'vl*) reproof. — *v.t.* **reprove'** to rebuke: to censure, condemn: to disprove or refute (*obs.*): to accuse or convict (of; *B.,* A.V.). — *ns.* **repro'ver; repro'ving.** — *adv.* **repro'vingly.** [O.Fr. *reprover* (Fr. *réprouver*) — L. *reprobāre;* see **reprobate.**]
repryve. See **reprieve.**
reps *reps.* See **rep[1].**
reptant. See **repent[2], reptation.**
reptation *rep-tā'shən, n.* squirming along, or up, a smooth-walled narrow passage. — *adj.* **rep'tant** (*biol.*) creeping. [L. *reptāre,* to creep.]
reptile *rep'tīl, adj.* creeping: like a reptile in nature. — *n.* any animal of the class **Reptilia** (*-til'i-ə*), vertebrates with scaly integument, cold blood, right and left aortic

arch, partially divided heart, single occipital condyle, pulmonary respiration, and pentadactyl limbs (sometimes wanting): a creeping thing: a base, malignant, abject, or treacherous person. — *adjs.* **reptilian** (*-til'i-ən*), **rep'tiloid; reptilif'erous** bearing fossil reptiles; **reptil'ious** like a reptile. [L.L. *reptilis, -e* — *repĕre,* to creep.]
republic *ri-pub'lik, n.* the state (*arch.*): a form of government without a monarch, in which the supreme power is vested in the people and their elected representatives: a state or country so governed. — *adj.* **repub'lican** of or favouring a republic: (*cap.*) of the Republican party. — *n.* one who advocates a republican form of government: (*cap.*) in U.S., orig. an Anti-Federal — now a member of the political party opposed to the *Democrats,* and favouring an extension of the powers of the national government. — *v.t.* **repub'licanise, -ize.** — *n.* **repub'licanism.** — **Republican era** the era adopted by the French after the downfall of the monarchy, beginning with 22nd September 1792. — **republic of letters** the world of books and authors. [L. *rēspublica,* commonwealth — *rēs,* affair, *publica* (fem.), public.]
repudiate *ri-pū'di-āt, v.t.* (of a husband) to divorce: to cast off, disown: to refuse, or cease, to acknowledge (debt, authority, claim): to deny as unfounded (a charge, etc.). — *adj.* **repū'diable.** — *ns.* **repūdiā'tion; repūdiā'tionist** one who favours repudiation of public debt. — *adj.* **repū'diative.** — *n.* **repū'diātor.** [L. *repudiāre, -ātum* — *repudium,* divorce — *re-,* away, and the root of *pudēre,* to be ashamed.]
repugn *ri-pūn', v.t.* to fight against, to oppose (*Shak.*): to be repugnant to (*arch.*). — *v.i.* (*arch.*) to be repugnant. — *ns.* **repugnance** (*-ri-pug'*) inconsistency: aversion; **repug'nancy** repugnance: opposition (*Shak.*). — *adj.* **repug'nant** inconsistent with (with *to*): (of things) incompatible: distasteful: disgusting: resisting, unwilling (*arch.*). [L. *repugnāre* — *re-,* against, *pugnāre,* to fight.]
repulse *ri-puls', v.t.* to drive back: to beat off: to rebuff. — *n.* a driving back: a beating off: a check: a refusal: a rebuff. — *n.* **repulsion** (*-pul'shən*) driving off: a repelling force, action, or influence. — *adj.* **repul'sive** that repulses or drives off: repelling: cold, reserved, forbidding: causing aversion and disgust. — *adv.* **repul'sively.** — *n.* **repul'siveness.** [L. *repulsus,* pa.p. of *repellēre* — *re-,* back, *pellēre,* to drive.]
repurify *rē-pūr'i-fī,* **repure** *ri-pūr', vs.t.* to purify again: to refine thoroughly. [Pfx. **re-.**]
repute *ri-pūt', v.t.* to account, deem. — Also (*arch.*) *v.i.* with *of.* — *n.* general opinion or impression: attributed character: widespread or high estimation: fame. — *adj.* **reputable** (*rep'ūt-ə-bl*) in good repute: respectable: honourable: consistent with reputation. — *adv.* **rep'ūtably.** — *n.* **repūtā'tion** (*rep-*) repute: estimation: character generally ascribed: good report: fame: good name. — *adj.* **rep'ūtātive** reputed: putative. — *adv.* **rep'ūtātively** by repute. — *adj.* **reputed** (*ri-pūt'id*) supposed, reckoned to be such: of repute. — *adv.* **repūt'edly** in common repute or estimation. — *adj.* **repute'less** (*Shak.*) without good repute. — *n.* **reput'ing** (*Shak.*) pluming oneself. — **reputed owner** a person who has to all appearance the title to the property; **reputed pint, quart** what is commonly called a pint, quart though not necessarily of legal standard (sometimes as little as half the legal amount). [L. *reputāre, -ātum* — *putāre,* to reckon.]
requere *ri-kwēr', (Spens.) v.t.* to require.
request *ri-kwest', n.* the asking of a favour: a petition: a favour asked for: the state of being sought after. — *v.t.* to ask as a favour: to ask politely: to ask for. — *n.* **request'er.** — **request note** an application for a permit to remove excisable goods; **request stop** a bus stop at

---

rĕinter'pretative *adj.*	**rĕintroduce'** *v.t.*	**rĕiss'uable** *adj.*
rĕinterr'ogate *v.t.*	**rĕintroduc'tion** *n.*	**rĕiss'ue** *v.t.* and *n.*
rĕinterrogā'tion *n.*	**rĕinvolve'** *v.t.*	**rĕjudge'** *v.t.*

For other sounds see detailed chart of pronunciation.

which a bus will stop only if signalled to do so. —
Court of Requests a former English court of equity,
abolished 1641: a local small debt court, superseded
by the County Court — called also *Court of Conscience;* **on request** if, or when, requested. [O.Fr.
requeste (Fr. *requête*) — L. *requīsītum,* pa.p. of *requīrĕre* — *re-,* away, *quaerĕre,* to seek.]
requicken *rē-kwik'n, (Shak.) v.t.* to give new life to.
[Pfx. **re-.**]
requiem *rek'wi-əm, rē'kwi-əm, n.* a mass for the rest of
the soul of the dead: music for it: any music of similar
character: rest (*obs.*). [L., accus. of *requiēs* (*re-,*
intens., *quiēs,* rest); first word of the introit.]
requiescat *re-kwi-es'kat, n.* a prayer for the rest of the
soul of the dead. — **requiescat in pace** (*in pā'sē, pā'chā,
pä'ke*) abbrev. **RIP,** may he (or she) rest in peace. [L.,
third pers. sing. subj. of *requiescĕre.*]
requight a Spenserian spelling of **requite.**
require *ri-kwīr', v.t.* to ask (someone) a question (*obs.*):
to ask for (*obs.*): to demand, exact: to direct (a person
to do something): to request (*arch.*): to call for,
necessitate. — *v.i.* to ask. — *adj.* **requir'able.** — *adj.*
required' compulsory as part of a curriculum. — *ns.*
require'ment a need: a thing needed: a necessary condition: a demand; **requir'er; requir'ing.** [L. *requīrĕre;*
partly through O.Fr. *requerre,* later assimilated to L.]
requisite *rek'wi-zit, adj.* required: needful: indispensable.
— *n.* that which is required, necessary, or indispensable. — *ns.* **req'uisiteness; requisi'tion** the act of requiring: a formal demand or request: a formal call for the
doing of something that is due: a demand for the
supply of anything for military purposes: a written
order for the supply of materials: the state of being in
use or service. — *v.t.* to demand a requisition from:
to demand or take by requisition: to seize: to call in:
to press into service. — *adj.* **requisi'tionary.** — *ns.*
requisi'tionist, requis'itor one who makes a requisition.
— *adj.* **requis'itory.** [L. *requīsītus,* pa.p. of *requīrĕre;*
see **require.**]
requite *ri-kwīt', v.t.* to repay (an action): to avenge: to
repay (a person, for): to retaliate on: to counterbalance, compensate for (*obs.*): — *pa.t.* **requit'ed** (*Spens.*
requit'); *pa.p.* **requit'ed** (*Shak.* **requit', requitt'ed**). —
Also (*Spens.*) **requight** (*-kwīt'*). — *n.* **requite'** requital.
— *v.t.* **requit** (*-kwit';* *obs.*) to requite (*pa.p., Shak.,*
requitt'ed). — *n. (Burns)* requital. — *adj.* **requī'table.**
— *n.* **requī'tal** the act of requiting: payment in return:
recompense: reward. — *adjs.* **requite'ful; requite'less**
without requital, free. — *ns.* **requite'ment; requī'ter.**
[Pfx. **re-,** and **quit.**]
requoyle a Shakespearian spelling of **recoil.**
reradiate *rē-rā'di-āt, v.t.* to radiate again, esp. as a result
of having absorbed an amount of radiation previously.
— *n.* **reradiā'tion.** [Pfx. **re-.**]
rerail *rē-rāl', v.t.* to replace on the rails. [Pfx. **re-.**]
rere- *rēr-,* in composition the same as **rear**[1]. — *ns.*
rere'-arch, rear'-arch an arch supporting the inner part
of a wall's thickness, as in a splayed window; **rere'brace**
(*-brās;* Fr. *bras,* arm) armour for the arm from shoulder to elbow; **rere'dorse, -dosse, -dos** (L. *dorsum,* Fr.
dos, back) a screen or panelling behind an altar or seat:
a choir-screen: the back of a fireplace; **rere'dorter** a
privy behind a monastic dormitory; **rere'-supper** a late
meal, after supper; **rere'ward** rearward.
reread *rē-rēd', v.t.* to read again: — *pa.t.* and *pa.p.* **re'read'**
(*-red*). [Pfx. **re-.**]
reremouse, rearmouse *rēr'mows, n.* a bat: — *pl.* **rere'-,
rear'mice.** [O.E. *hrēremūs,* app. — *hrēran,* to move,
mūs, a mouse.]
rerun *rē'run', v.t.* to run (a race, etc.) again: to broadcast
(a radio, television series) again (also *fig.*). — Also *n.*
(*rē'run*). [Pfx. **re-.**]
resale *rē'sāl, rē-sāl', n.* the selling again of an article. —

resale price maintenance (abbrev. **RPM**) the setting of
a fixed minimum price on an article by the manufacturer. [Pfx. **re-.**]
resalgar *res-al'gər, obs.* variant of **realgar.**
re-scale, rescale *rē-skāl', v.t.* to plan, form, on a new (usu.
reduced) scale. [Pfx. **re-.**]
reschedule *rē-shed'ūl, -sked'ūl, v.t.* to schedule again: to
arrange a new time or timetable for: to rearrange (a
country's debt repayment programme) usu. to alleviate liquidity problems (*econ.*). — *n.* **resched'uling.**
[Pfx. **re-.**]
rescind *ri-sind', v.t.* to cut away: to annul, abrogate. —
n. **rescission** (*-sizh'ən*) abrogation: cutting off (*obs.*). —
adj. **rescissory** (*-sis'ər-i*) annulling. [L. *rescindĕre,*
rescissum — *rē,* back, *scindĕre,* to cut.]
rescore *rē'skōr', -skör', v.t.* to rewrite a musical score for
different instruments, voices, etc. [Pfx. **re-.**]
rescript *rē'skript, n.* the official answer of a pope or an
emperor to any legal question: an edict or decree: a
rewriting. — Also *v.t.* [L. *rescrīptum* — *re-, scrībĕre,*
scrīptum, to write.]
rescue *res'kū, v.t.* to free from danger, captivity, or evil
plight: to deliver forcibly from legal custody: to recover
by force: — *pr.p.* **res'cuing;** *pa.t.* and *pa.p.* **res'cued.** —
n. the act of rescuing: deliverance from danger or evil:
forcible recovery: forcible release from arrest or imprisonment: relief of a besieged place: a beach-rescue:
a rescuer or rescuing party (*arch.*): a person or thing
rescued: a bid **(rescue bid)** to bring one's partner out
of a dangerous situation (*bridge*). — *adj.* **res'cuable.**
— *n.* **res'cuer.** [O.Fr. *rescourre* — L. *re-, excutĕre* —
ex, out, *quatĕre,* to shake.]
rescue-grass *res'kū-gräs, n.* a S. American brome-grass,
Bromus catharticus. [Origin unknown.]
research *ri-sûrch', n.* a careful search: investigation:
systematic investigation towards increasing the sum
of knowledge. — *v.i.* and *v.t.* to make researches (into
or concerning); **re-search** (*rē'*) to search again. — *n.*
research'er. — *adj.* **research'ful.** [Obs. Fr. *recerche*
(mod. Fr. *recherche*); see **search.**]
réseau *rā-zō', n.* a fine meshed ground for lacework: a
network of lines for reference in star-photographs: —
pl. **réseaux** (*rā-zō', -zōz'*), **réseaus.** [Fr., network.]
resect *ri-sekt', v.t.* to cut away part of, esp. the end of a
bone. — *n.* **resection** (*-sek'shən*) cutting away, esp. bone
(*surg.*): a positional fix of a point by sighting it from
two or more known stations (*surveying*). [L. *rese-
cāre, -sectum,* to cut off — *secāre,* to cut.]
Reseda *re'si-də, ri-sē'də, n.* the mignonette genus, giving
name to the family **Resedā'ceae:** (without *cap.;* *re'*) a
pale green colour (often as Fr. **réséda** *rā-zā-dä*). —
Also *adj.* [L. *resēda,* said to be from *resēdā morbīs,*
assuage diseases, first words of a charm used in
applying it as a poultice.]
reseize *rē-sēz', (Spens.) v.t.* to reinstate. [Pfx. **re-** and
seise.]
resemble *ri-zem'bl, v.t.* to be like: to compare (*arch.*): to
depict (*obs.*). — *v.i.* to be like each other: to be like
(with *to; arch.*). — *n.* **resem'blance** likeness: appearance: an image. — *adj.* **resem'blant.** — *n.* **resem'bler.**
— *adj.* **resem'bling.** [O.Fr. *resembler* (Fr. *ressembler*)
— *re-,* again, *sembler,* to seem — L. *simulāre,* to make
like — *similis,* like.]
resent *ri-zent', v.t.* to take in, consider as an injury or
affront: to feel joy or sorrow because of (*obs.*): to
receive (a person), well or ill (*obs.*). — *v.i.* (*obs.*) to
savour (of). — *n.* **resent'er.** — *adj.* **resent'ful.** — *advs.*
resent'fully; resent'ingly. — *adj.* **resent'ive.** — *n.* **resent'-
ment.** [O.Fr. *ressentir* — L. *re-,* in return, *sentīre,* to
feel.]
reserpine *ri-zûr'pin, -pēn, n.* a drug got from *Rauwolfia
serpentina* used against high blood pressure, and as a
tranquilliser.

---

rēkin'dle *v.t.* and *v.i.*
relet' *v.t.:* — *pa.t* and *pa.p.* **relet'.**
ēlight' *v.t.* and *v.i.*

reload' *v.t.* and *v.i.*
rēman' *v.t.*
rēmarr'iage *n.*

rēmarr'y *v.t.* and *v.i.*
rēmod'el *v.t.*
rēmod'ify *v.t.*

reserve *ri-zûrv'*, *v.t.* to hold back: to save up, esp. for a future occasion or special purpose: to keep, retain: to preserve: to spare: to set apart: to book, engage. — *n.* the keeping of something reserved: state of being reserved: that which is reserved: a reservation: a reserved store or stock: a reserve price: a tract of land reserved for a special purpose: a substitute kept in readiness (*sport*): (esp. in *pl.*) a military force kept out of action until occasion serves: (esp. in *pl.*) a force not usually serving but liable to be called up when required: (often *pl.*) resources of physical or spiritual nature available in abnormal circumstances: part of assets kept readily available for ordinary demands: (usu. in *pl.*) an unexploited quantity of a mineral (esp. oil, gas or coal) calculated to exist in a given area: (in *pl.*) amounts of gold and foreign currencies held by a country: artistic restraint: restrained manner: reticence: aloofness: a secret information withheld (*arch.*): limitation, restriction: a mental reservation. — *adj.* kept in reserve: of the reserves. — *adj.* **reserv'able**. — *ns.* **reservā'tion** (*rez-*) the act of reserving or keeping back, or keeping for oneself: an expressed, or tacit, proviso, limiting condition, or exception: something withheld: a tract of public land reserved for some special purpose, as for Indians, schools, game, etc.: the pope's retention to himself of the right to nominate to a benefice: a limitation: the booking of a seat, room, passage, etc.: a booked seat, room, etc.: the strip of grass, etc. between the two roads of a dual carriageway: a clause of a deed by which a person reserves for himself a right, interest, etc. in a property he is granting, as that of ordinary rent (*legal*); **reservatory** (*ri-zûrv'ə-tər-i*; *obs.*) a receptacle: a reservoir. — *adj.* **reserved'** reticent: uncommunicative: aloof in manner: booked: having the original colour of the surface or background (*ceramics*). — *adv.* **reserv'edly**. — *ns.* **reservedness** (*ri-zûrvd'nis*); **reserv'ist** a member of a reserve force. — **reserve bank** one of the U.S. Federal Reserve banks: a central bank holding reserves for other banks (esp. *Austr.* and *N.Z.*); **reserve currency** one ranking with gold in world banking transactions; **reserved list** a list of retired officers in the armed services who may be recalled for active service in the event of war; **reserved occupation** employment of national importance that exempts from service in the armed forces; **reserve price** the minimum price acceptable to the vendor of an article for sale or auction. — **judgment reserved** see under **judge; mental reservation** a reservation made mentally but not openly expressed; **reservation of the sacrament** the practice of reserving part of the consecrated bread of the eucharist for the communion of the sick; **without reserve** frankly, not holding back any information: fully, without reservation: without restrictions or stipulations regarding sale: without a reserve price.   [O.Fr. *reserver* — L. *reservāre* — *re-*, back, *servāre*, to save.]

reservoir *rez'ər-vwär*, *-vwŏr*, *n.* a receptacle: a store: a receptacle for fluids, esp. a large basin, artificial lake, or tank for storing water. — *v.t.* to store. — **reservoir rock** porous rock containing producible oil and/or gas. [Fr.]

reset[1] *ri-set'*, (*Scot.*) *v.t.* to harbour (*arch.*): to receive, knowing to be stolen. — Also *v.i.* — *n.* (*rē'*) harbouring of a proscribed person (*arch.*): receiving of stolen goods. — *n.* **resett'er**.   [O.Fr. *recet(t)er* — L. *receptāre* — *recipĕre*, to receive.]

reset[2] *rē-set'*, *v.t.* to set again.   [Pfx. **re-**.]

res gestae *rēz jes'tē*, *rās ges'tī*, (L.) exploits: facts relevant to the case and admissible in evidence (*law*).

reshuffle *rē-shuf'l*, *v.t.* to shuffle again: to rearrange, esp. cabinet or government offices. — Also *n.*   [Pfx. **re-**.]

resiant *rez'i-ənt*, *-ant*, (*obs.* or *arch.*) *adj.* and *n.* resident.

— *n.* (*obs.* or *arch.*) **res'iance**.   [O.Fr. *reseant*, pr.p. of *reseoir* — L. *residēre*.]

reside *ri-zīd'*, *v.i.* to dwell permanently: to be in residence: to abide: to be vested: to inhere. — *ns.* **residence** (*rez'i-dəns*) act or duration of dwelling in a place: the act of living in the place required by regulations or performance of functions: a stay in a place: a dwelling-place: a dwelling-house, esp. one of some pretensions: that in which anything permanently inheres or has its seat; **res'idency** a residence: the official abode of a resident or governor of a protected state: an administrative district under a resident: a resident's post at a hospital, or the period during which it is held. - *adj.* **res'ident** dwelling in a place for some time: residing on one's own estate, or the place of one's duties, or the place required by certain conditions: not migratory: not moving (*obs.*): inherent. — *n.* one who resides: an animal that does not migrate: a doctor who works in, and usu. resides at, a hospital to gain experience in a particular field: a registered guest at a hotel: a representative at a foreign court of lower rank than an ambassador (*hist.*): a representative of a governor in a protected state: the governor of a residency or administrative district (esp. in the former Dutch East Indies). — *n.* **res'identer** (*Scot. -dent'*) an inhabitant. — *adjs.* **residential** (*-den'shl*) of, for, or connected with, residence: suitable for or occupied by houses, esp. of a better kind; **residentiary** (*-den'shə-ri*) resident: officially bound to reside: pertaining to or involving official residence. — *n.* an inhabitant: one bound to reside, as a canon. — *ns.* **residen'tiaryship; res'identship; resī'der**.   [L. *residēre* — *re-*, back, *sedēre*, to sit.]

residue *rez'i-dū*, in U.S. also *-dōō*, *n.* that which is left, remainder: what is left of an estate after payment of debts, charges, and legacies. — *adj.* **resid'ual** remaining as residue or difference: formed by accumulations of rock waste where the rock has disintegrated (*geol.*). — *n.* that which remains as a residue or as a difference. — *adjs.* **resid'uary** of, or of the nature of, a residue, esp. of an estate; **resid'uous** (*rare*) residual. — *n.* **residuum** (*rə-zij'ōō-əm*, *-wəm*, *rez-id'ū-əm*) a residue: — *pl.* **-ua**.   [L. *residuum* — *residēre*, to remain behind.]

resign *ri-zīn'*, *v.t.* to yield up: to submit calmly: to relinquish (often with *from*): to entrust. — *v.t.* to give up office, employment, etc.: to submit (*rare*). — *n.* **resignation** (*rez-ig-nā'shən*) act of giving up: state of being resigned or quietly submissive: the form by which a vassal returns the feu into the hands of a superior (*Scots law*). — *adj.* **resigned** (*ri-zīnd'*) calmly submissive. — *adv.* **resignedly** (*ri-zīn'id-li*). — *ns.* **resign'edness; resign'er; resign'ment**.   [O.Fr. *resigner* — L. *resignāre*, *-ātum*, to unseal, annul — *signāre*, to seal — *signum*, a mark.]

re-sign *rē-sīn'*, *v.t.* to sign again.   [Pfx. **re-**.]

resile *ri-zīl'*, *v.i.* to recoil: to rebound: to recover form and position elastically: to draw back from a statement, agreement, course: to back out (esp. *Scot.*). — *ns.* **resilience** (*ri-zil'i-əns*) recoil: elasticity, physical or mental; **resil'iency**. — *adj.* **resil'ient** elastic, physically or in spirits.   [L. *resilīre*, to leap back — *salīre*, to leap.]

resin *rez'in*, *n.* any of a number of substances, products obtained from the sap of certain plants and trees (*natural resins*), used in plastics, etc.: any of a large number of substances made by polymerisation or condensation (*synthetic resins*) which, though not related chemically to natural resins, have some of their physical properties, very important in the plastics industry, etc. — *v.t.* to treat with resin: to remove resin from: to rosin. — *ns.* **res'ināte** a salt of any of the acids occurring in natural resins; **res'iner** a resin gatherer. — *adj.* **resinif'erous** yielding resin. — *n.* **resinificā'tion**. — *v.t.* and *v.i.* **res'inify** to make or become a resin or

remort'gage *v.t.* and *n.*   rēnegō'tiate *v.t.*   rēoccupā'tion *n.*
rēname' *v.t.*   rēnegōtiā'tion *n.*   rēocc'upy *v.t.*
rēnegō'tiable *adj.*   rēnum'ber *v.t.*   rēoffend' *v.i.*

For other sounds see detailed chart of pronunciation.

resinous. — *v.t.* **res'inise, -ize** to treat with resin. — *adj.* and *n.* **res'inoid** (a substance) of, like or containing resin. — *n.* **resinō'sis** abnormal flow of resin. — *adj.* **res'inous** of, like, containing, of the nature of, resin: of the lustre of resin: negative (as produced by rubbing a resin; *elect., obs.*). — *adv.* **res'inously.** [Fr. *résine* — L. *rēsīna*.]

resinata *rez-i-nā'tə, n.* Greek white wine with resinous flavour. [L. *rēsīnāta* (fem.), resined.]

resipiscence *res-i-pis'əns, n.* recognition of error, change to a better frame of mind. — Also **resipisc'ency.** — *adj.* **resipisc'ent.** [L. *resipīscentia* — *resipīscĕre* — *re-*, again, *sapĕre*, to be wise.]

res ipsa loquitur *rēz ip'sə lok'wi-tər,* (L.). *rās ip'sə lok'-wi-tŏŏr,* (*law*) the thing speaks for itself — applied in cases in which the mere fact that an accident has happened is deemed to be evidence of negligence unless the defendant proves otherwise.

resist *ri-zist', v.t.* to strive against, oppose: to withstand: to refuse: to hinder the action of: to be little affected by: to be distasteful to (*Shak.*). — *v.i.* to make opposition. — *n.* a protective coating, esp. one on parts of a textile to protect the blank areas of the design that is being printed, an acid-proof coating on parts of a metal plate or a light-sensitive coating on a silicon wafer. — Also *adj.* — *ns.* **resis'tance** act or power of resisting: opposition: the body's ability to resist disease: (with *cap.*) an organisation of (armed) opposition to an occupying enemy force, esp. that of the French in World War II (also **resistance movement**): the opposition of a body to the motion of another: that property of a substance in virtue of which the passage of an electric current through it is accompanied with a dissipation of energy: an electrical resistor; **resis'tant** one who, or that which, resists. — *adj.* **resis'tant** (less usu. **resis'tent**) making resistance: withstanding adverse conditions, as parasites, germs, antibiotics, corrosion. — *n.* one who, or that which, resists. — *n.* **resistibil'ity.** — *adj.* **resis'tible.** — *advs.* **resis'tibly; resis'tingly.** — *adj.* **resis'tive.** — *adv.* **resis'tively.** — *n.* **resistiv'ity** (*rez-*) capacity for resisting: (also **specific resistance**) a property of a conducting material expressed as resistance multiplied by cross-sectional area over length. — *adj.* **resist'less** (*arch.*) irresistible: unable to resist. — *adv.* **resist'lessly.** — *ns.* **resist'lessness; resist'or** anything that resists: a piece of apparatus used to offer electric resistance. — **resis'tance-box** a box containing resistors; **resis'tance-coil** a coil of wire used to offer resistance to the passage of electricity; **resis'tance movement** see above; **resistance pyrometer, thermometer** a device for measuring high temperatures by means of the variation in the electrical resistance of a wire as the temperature changes; **resistance thermometry** temperature measurement of this kind; **resis'tance welding** see **weld**[2]. — **consumer, market, resistance** unwillingness of consumers to buy marketed products (also **sales resistance**); **line of least resistance** the easiest course of action. [L. *resistĕre* — *re-*, against, *sistĕre*, to make to stand.]

resit *rē-sit', v.i.* and *v.t.* to sit (an examination) again after failing. — *n.* (*rē'*) an opportunity or act of resitting. [*Pfx.* re-.]

res judicata *rēz jōō-di-kā'tə, rās yōō-di-kä'ta,* (L.) a case or suit already decided.

reskew, reskue (*Spens.*). Same as **rescue.**

resnatron *rez'nə-tron, n.* a high-power, high-frequency tetrode. [*resona*tor, **-tron.**]

resoluble *rez'əl-ū-bl, adj.* that may be resolved, dissolved, analysed. — *adj.* **resolute** (*rez'əl-ōōt, -ūt*) having a fixed purpose: constant in pursuing a purpose: determined. — *n.* (*Shak.*) a determined person. — *adv.* **res'olutely.** — *ns.* **res'oluteness; resolution** (*rez-əl-ōō'shən, -ū-shən*) act of resolving: analysis: separation of components:

melting: solution: the separation of an optically inactive mixture or compound into its optically active components (*chem.*): the definition of a picture in TV or facsimile (measured by the number of lines used to scan the image of the picture): the smallest measurable difference, or separation, or time interval (*phys.*, electronics, nucleonics): resolving power (q.v.): state of being resolved: fixed determination: that which is resolved: removal of or freedom from doubt: progression from discord to concord (*mus.*): a formal proposal put before a meeting, or its formal determination thereon: substitution of two short syllables for a long: the making visible of detail: the disappearance or dispersion of a tumour or inflammation; **re-solu'tion** (*rē-sol-*) renewed or repeated solution; **resolu'tioner** (*rez-əl-*) one who joins in or accepts a resolution: **Resolutioner** (*Scot. hist.*) one who approved of the resolutions of 1650 admitting to civil and military office all persons except those excommunicate and hostile to the Covenant — opposed to *Protester.* — *adj.* **res'olutive.** — *n.* **resolvabil'ity.** — *adj.* **resolvable** (*ri-zolv'*). — *v.t.* **resolve'** to separate into components: to make visible the details of: to analyse: to break up: to melt: to transform: to relax: to solve: to dissipate: to free from doubt or difficulty: to convince (of; *obs.*): to assure (*obs.*): to inform (*obs.*): to answer (a question; *obs.*): to dispel (fears; *Shak.*): to pass as a resolution: to determine: to disperse, as a tumour: to make (a discord) pass into a concord (*mus.*). — *v.i.* to undergo resolution: to come to a determination (often with *on* to indicate the course chosen): to decide to go to a place (with *on*; *Shak.*): to take counsel (*Spens.*): to lapse (*law*). — *obs.* senses also used reflexively. — *n.* **resolution:** fixed purpose: firmness of purpose: solution (*obs.*). — *adj.* **resolved'** fixed in purpose. — *adv.* **resolvedly** (*ri-zol'vid-li*) resolutely. — *n.* **resol'vedness.** — *adj.* **resol'vent** having power to resolve. — *n.* that which causes or helps solution or resolution. — *n.* **resol'ver.** — **resolving power** the ability of telescope, microscope, etc., to distinguish very close, or very small, objects: the ability of a photographic emulsion to produce finely-detailed images. [L. *resolvĕre*, *resolūtum* — *re-*, intens., *solvĕre*, to loose.]

resolve, etc. See **resoluble.**

resonance *rez'ən-əns, n.* resounding: sonority: the sound heard in auscultation: sympathetic vibration: the ringing quality of the human voice when produced in such a way that sympathetic vibration is caused in the air-spaces in the head, chest and throat: (the state of a system in which) a large vibration (is) produced by a small stimulus of approx. the same frequency as that of the system (*phys.*, *elect.*): increased probability of a nuclear reaction when the energy of an incident particle or photon is around a certain value appropriate to the energy level of the compound nucleus: a property of certain compounds, in which the most stable state of the molecule is a combination of theoretically possible bond arrangements or distributions of electrons (*chem.*): the complex of bodily responses to an emotional state, or of emotional responses to a situation. — *adj.* **res'onant** resounding, ringing: giving its characteristic vibration in sympathy with another body's vibration. — *adv.* **res'onantly.** — *v.i.* **res'onate** to resound: to vibrate sympathetically. — *n.* **res'onator** a resonating body or device, as for increasing sonority or for analysing sound. — **res'onance-box** a chamber in a musical instrument for increasing its sonority by vibration in sympathy with the strings. [L. *resonāre, -ātum* — *re-*, back, *sonāre*, to sound.]

resorb *ri-sörb', v.t.* to absorb back. — *adj.* **resorb'ent.** [L. *resorbēre*, to suck back.]

resorcin *ri-zör'sin, n.* a colourless phenol, $C_6H_4(OH)_2$,

---

rēordain' *v.t.*	**rēorganisā'tion, -z-** *n.*	**rēpā'per** *v.t.*
rēor'der *v.t.*	**rēor'ganise, -ize** *v.t.*	**rēpeo'ple** *v.t.*
rēordinā'tion *n.*	**repack'** *v.t.* and *v.i.*	**rēperus'al** *n.*

fāte; fär; hûr; mīne; mōte; för; mūte; mōōn; fŏŏt; dhen (then); *el'ə-mənt* (element)

used in dyeing, photography, and medicine. — Also **resor'cinol.** [resin and orcin.]

resorption ri-sörp'shən, n. resorbing, esp. of a mineral by rock magma. the breaking-down and assimilation of a substance (med.). — adj. **resorp'tive.** [See **resorb.**]

resort¹ ri-zört', v.i. to revert (obs.): to go (to): to betake oneself: to have recourse: to apply: to go or be habitually. — n. act of resorting: a place much frequented: a haunt: that which one has or may have recourse to: concourse: thronging: repair. — n. **resort'er** a frequenter. — **in the last resort** orig. (a Gallicism, en dernier ressort), without appeal: hence, as a last expedient. [O.Fr. resortir (Fr. ressortir), to rebound, retire — sortir, to go out; origin obscure.]

resort² rē-sört', v.t. to sort anew. [Pfx. **re-.**]

resound ri-zownd', v.t. to echo: to sound with reverberation: to sound or spread (the praises of a person or thing). — v.i. to echo: to re-echo, reverberate: to sound sonorously. — adj. **resound'ing** echoing: thorough, decisive (resounding victory). — adv. **resound'ingly.** [Pfx. **re-.**]

resource ri-sōrs', -sörs', -z-, n. source or possibility of help: an expedient: (pl.) money or means of raising money: means of support: means of occupying or amusing oneself: resourcefulness. — v.t. to provide the (esp. financial) resources for. — adj. **resource'ful** fertile in expedients: clever, ingenious: rich in resources. — n. **resource'fulness.** — adj. **resource'less.** [O.Fr. ressource — resourdre — L. resurgēre, to rise again.]

respeak rē-spēk', (Shak.) v.t. to echo. [Pfx. **re-.**]

respect ri-spekt', v.t. to look to, regard, consider, take into account: to heed: to refer to, relate to, have reference to (arch.): to treat with consideration, refrain from violating: to feel or show esteem, deference, or honour to: to value (a thing; Shak.): to face, look at (obs. and her.). — Also v.i. — n. heed (Spens.): an aspect (obs.): a particular: a relation: reference: regard: consideration: partiality or favour towards (with of): deferential esteem: (often in pl.) a greeting or message of esteem. — n. **respectabil'ity.** — adj. **respec'table** worthy of respect: considerable: passable: mediocre: of good social standing (obs.): fairly well-to-do: decent and well-behaved: reputable: seemly: presentable: timidly or priggishly conventional. — n. **respec'tableness.** — adv. **respec'tably.** — adj. **respec'tant** facing each other (her.): looking back. — n. **respec'ter** one who respects, esp. in respecter of persons, one who, something that, singles out individual(s) for unduly favourable treatment (usu. in neg.). — adj. **respect'ful** showing or feeling respect. — adv. **respect'fully.** — n. **respect'fulness. respect'ing** concerning: considering. — adj. **respec'tive** having respect: regardful, considerate (Shak.): heedful: discriminating: respectful (obs.): worthy of respect (Shak.): relative: particular or several, relating to each distributively. — adv. **respec'tively.** — adj. **respect'less** regardless. — **respect of persons** undue favour, as for wealth, etc.; **in respect of** in the matter of: because of (obs.): in comparison with (obs.); **with respect to** with regard to. [L. respicĕre, respectum — re-, back, specĕre, to look.]

respire ri-spīr', v.i. to breathe: to take breath. — v.t. to breathe: to exhale. — adj. **respirable** (res'pər-ə-bl, ri-spīr'ə-bl) fit for breathing. — ns. **respiration** (res-pər-ā'shən) breathing: the taking in of oxygen and giving out of carbon dioxide, with associated physiological processes: a breath: a breathing-space; **res'pirator** an appliance worn on the mouth or nose to filter or warm the air breathed: a gas-mask. — adj. **respiratory** (res'pər-ə-tər-i, ri-spī'rə-tər-i) of or for, pertaining to, or serving for, respiration. — n. **respirom'eter** an apparatus for measuring breathing. [L. respīrāre, -ātum — spīrāre, to breathe.]

respite res'pīt, -pit, n. temporary cessation of something that is tiring or painful: postponement requested or granted: temporary suspension of the execution of a criminal (law): delay in action (obs.): leisure (obs.). — v.t. to grant a respite to: to relieve by a pause (obs.): to delay, put off: to grant postponement to: to prolong (Shak.): to give up, cease from (obs.). — v.i. to rest (from) (obs.). [M.E. respit — O.Fr. (Fr. répit) — L. respectus, respicĕre; see **respect.**]

resplend ri-splend', v.i. to shine brilliantly. — ns. **resplend'ence, resplend'ency.** — adj. **resplend'ent** shining, brilliant, and splendid. — adv. **resplend'ently.** [L. resplendēre — re-, intens., and splendēre, to shine.]

respond ri-spond', v.i. to answer: to utter liturgical responses: to act in answer: to react. — n. a response to a versicle in liturgy: a half-pillar or half-pier attached to a wall to support an arch (answering to one at the other end of an arcade, etc.). — ns. **respond'ence** response (Spens.): correspondence, agreement; **respond'ency** correspondence. — adj. **respond'ent** answering: corresponding: responsive. — n. one who answers: one who refutes objections: a defendant, esp. in a divorce suit. — ns. **respondentia** (res-pon-den'shə) a loan on a ship's cargo, payable only on safe arrival; **respond'er, respons'er, respons'or** (ris-) one who, or that which, responds: the part of a transponder which replies automatically to the correct interrogation signal. — n.pl. **Respon'sa** a branch of rabbinical literature consisting of written decisions from authorities in reply to questions, problems, etc., submitted to them (n. **respon'sum** one of these decisions). — n. **response'** an answer: an oracular answer: an answer made by the congregation to the priest during divine service: a responsory: a reaction, esp. sympathetic: the ratio of the output to the input level of a transmission system at any particular frequency (electronics). — adj. **response'less.** — n. **responsibil'ity** state of being responsible: a trust or charge for which one is responsible. — adj. **respon'sible** liable to be called to account as being in charge or control: answerable (to person, etc., for something): deserving the blame or credit of (with for): governed by a sense of responsibility: being a free moral agent: morally accountable for one's actions: trustworthy: able to pay: respectable-looking: involving responsibility: correspondent (obs.). — adv. **respon'sibly.** — n.pl. **respon'sions** (-shənz) formerly, the first of three examinations for the B.A. degree at Oxford, 'smalls'. — adj. **respon'sive** ready to respond: answering: correspondent: with responses. — adv. **respon'sively.** — n. **respon'siveness.** — adj. **responsorial** (ri-, rē-spon-sō'ri-əl, -sö'ri-əl) responsive. — n. an office-book containing the responsories. — adj. **respon'sory** making answer. — n. an anthem sung after a lesson: a liturgical response. [L. respondēre, respōnsum — re-, back, spondēre, to promise.]

ressaldar. Same as **risaldar.**

rest¹ rest, n. repose, refreshing inactivity: intermission of, or freedom from, motion or disturbance: tranquillity: repose of death: invigoration by resting (Shak.): a place for resting: a prop or support (e.g. for a musket, a billiard cue, a violinist's chin): motionlessness: a pause in speaking or reading: an interval of silence in music, or a mark indicating it. — v.i. to repose: to be at ease: to be still: to be supported (on): to lean (on): to put trust in (with on): to have foundation in (with on): to settle, alight: to remain: to be unemployed (slang, esp. theatrical). — v.t. to give rest to: to place or hold in support (on): to lean (on): to base (on): (refl.) to give (oneself) rest, or (obs.) to rely (upon). — n. **rest'er.** — adj. **rest'ful** at rest: rest-giving: tranquil. — adv. **rest'fully.** — n. **rest'fulness.** — n. and adj. **rest'ing.** — adj. **rest'less** unresting, not resting, sleeping, or relaxing: never still: uneasily active: impatient (of) (Pope): impatient of inactivity or of remaining still: never-ceas-

---

rēperuse' v.t.
rēplan' v.t. and v.i.
rēplant' v.t.

rēplantā'tion n.
rēpop'ulate v.t.
rēpot' v.t.

rēpott'ing n.
rēpublicā'tion n.
rēpub'lish v.t.

For other sounds see detailed chart of pronunciation.

ing: unrestful, giving or allowing no rest. — *adv.* **rest′lessly.** — *n.* **rest′lessness.** — **rest′-centre** a place of shelter for numbers of people driven from their homes by an emergency; **rest′-cure** treatment consisting of inactivity and quiet; **rest′-day** a day of rest: the first day of a three days' visit; **rest′-home** an establishment for those who need special care and attention, e.g. invalids, old people, etc.; **rest′-house** a house of rest for travellers; **rest′ing-place** a place of rest: a stair-landing: (**one's last resting-place** one's grave); **rest′ing-spore** a spore that can germinate after a period of dormancy; **rest′ing-stage** a state of suspended activity; **rest mass** (*phys.*) the mass of an object when it is at rest; **rest′-room** a room in a building other than a private house with lavatory (lavatories), etc., adjoining; **rest stop** (*U.S.*) a lay-by. — **at rest** stationary: in repose: free from disquiet; **lay to rest** to give burial to. [O.E. *rest*, *ræst*; Ger. *Rast*, Du. *rust*; converging and merging in meaning with the following words.]

rest[2] *rest, n.* remainder: all others: reserve fund: a rapid continuous series of returns (*tennis*, etc.): a stake whose loss ends the game (*primero*). — *v.i.* to remain (see also preceding word). — **for the rest** as regards other matters; **set up one's rest** (*arch.*) to make one's final stake: hence, to take a resolution: to take up abode. [Fr. *reste* — L. *restāre*, to remain — *re-*, back, *stāre*, to stand.]

rest[3] *rest*, (*hist.*) *n.* a contrivance on a breastplate to prevent the spear from being driven back. — *v.t.* (*Shak.*) to arrest. [Aphetic for **arrest**.]

restaurant *rest′(ə-)-rä, -rong, -ront, -rənt, n.* a place where meals may be had. — *n.* **restaurateur** (*res-tər-ə-tûr′, -tær′*) the keeper of a restaurant. — **res′taurant-car** a dining-car. [Fr., — *restaurer*, to restore.]

restem *rē-stem′,* (*Shak.*) *v.t.* to force (a way) back against the current. [Pfx. **re-**.]

rest-harrow *rest′-har-ō, n.* a papilionaceous plant (*Ononis*) with long, tough, woody roots. [**rest**[3], and **harrow**[1].]

restiff *res′tif*, an obsolete form of **restive**.

restiform *res′ti-förm, adj.* cord-like. [L. *restis*, a cord, *förma*, form.]

restitute *res′ti-tūt,* (*arch.*) *v.t.* to restore. — *v.i.* (*arch.*) to make restitution. — *ns.* **restitū′tion** a restoring, return: compensation: (also **restitū′tionism**) restorationism; **restitū′tionist.** — *adj.* **restitūtive** (*ri-stit′*, or *res′tit-*). — *n.* **res′titūtor.** — *adj.* **restit′ūtory.** [L. *restituĕre, -ūtum* — *re-*, *statuĕre*, to make to stand.]

restive *res′tiv, adj.* inert (*obs.*): unwilling to go forward: obstinate, refractory: uneasy, as if ready to break from control. — *adv.* **res′tively.** — *n.* **res′tiveness.** [O.Fr. *restif* — L. *restāre*, to rest.]

restore *ri-stōr′, -stör′, v.t.* to repair: to bring, put, or give back: to make good: to reinstate: to bring back to a (supposed) former state, or to a normal state: to reconstruct mentally, by inference or conjecture. — *n.* (*Spens.*) restitution. — *adj.* **restor′able.** — *ns.* **restor′ableness; restoration** (*res-tō-rā′shən,* or *-tö-, -tə-, -to-*) act or process of restoring: a reinstatement of or in kingship (as the Restoration of the Stuarts, the Bourbons; *usu.* with *cap.*): renovations and reconstruction (sometimes little differing from destruction) of a building, painting, etc.: a reconstructed thing or representation. — *adj.* (with *cap.*) of the time of the Restoration of Charles II. — *ns.* **restorā′tionism** (*theol.*) receiving of a sinner to divine favour: the final recovery of all men; **restorā′tionist** one who holds the belief that after a purgation all wicked men and angels will be restored to the favour of God, a universalist. — *adj.* **restorative** (*ris-tor′ə-tiv, -tör′*) tending to restore, esp. to strength and vigour. — *n.* a medicine that restores. — *adv.* **restor′atively.** — *n.* **restor′er.** [O.Fr. *restorer* — L. *restaurāre, -ātum.*]

restrain *ri-strān′, v.t.* to hold back: to control: to subject to forcible repression: to tighten (*Shak.*): to forbid (*Milt.*). — *v.i.* (*rare*) to refrain. — *adjs.* **restrain′able; restrained′** controlled: self-controlled: showing restraint: forbidden (*Shak.*). — *adv.* **restrain′edly.** — *ns.* **restrain′edness; restrain′er** one who or that which restrains: an ingredient of a photographic developer which checks the development and reduces the tendency to fog. — *n.* and *adj.* **restrain′ing.** — *ns.* **restraint′** act of restraining: state of being restrained: a restraining influence: restriction: forcible control: artistic control or reticence: want of liberty: reserve. — **restraint of princes** embargo; **restraint of trade** interference with free play of economic forces, as by monopolies. [O.Fr. *restraindre, restrai(g)n-* — L. *restringĕre, restrictum* — *re-*, back, *stringĕre*, to draw tightly.]

restrict *ri-strikt′, v.t.* to limit. — *adj.* **restrict′ed.** — *adv.* **restrict′edly.** — *ns.* **restric′tion; restric′tionist** one who favours restriction. — Also *adj.* — *adj.* **restric′tive** restricting: tending to restrict: expressing restriction, as in relative clauses, phrases, etc., that limit the application of the verb to the subject, e.g. *people who like historic buildings should visit Edinburgh.* — *adv.* **restric′tively.** — *v.t.* **restringe** (*ri-strinj′*) to restrict. — *n.* and *adj.* **restrin′gent** astringent. — **restricted area** one from which the general public is excluded: one within which there is a speed limit; **restriction enzyme** an enzyme which can be used to divide genes into segments which can be combined with those of other species; **restrictive practice** a trade practice that is against the public interest, as e.g. an agreement to sell only to certain buyers, or to keep up resale prices: used also of certain trade union practices, as the closed shop, demarcation, working to rule. [L. *restringĕre, restrictum.*]

restringe. See **restrict.**

resty *rest′i, adj.* restive: sluggish (*Shak.*): inoperative, ineffectual (*Spens.*). [**restive** or partly **rest**[1].]

result *ri-zult′, v.i.* to issue (with *in*): to follow as a consequence: to rebound (*obs.*): to be the outcome: to revert (*law*). — *n.* consequence: outcome: outcome aimed at: quantity obtained by calculation: decision, resolution, as of a council (*obs.* and *U.S.*): in games, the (usu. final) score. — *adj.* **result′ant** resulting: resulting from combination (as of tones sounded together). — *n.* a force compounded of two or more forces: a sum of vector quantities: a resultant tone: a result of combination. — *adjs.* **result′ative** expressing result; **result′ful; result′ing; result′less.** — *n.* **result′lessness.** [L. *resultāre*, to leap back — *saltāre*, to leap.]

resume *ri-zūm′, -zōōm′, v.t.* to take back: to summarise, make a résumé of (*arch.*): to assume again: to take up again: to begin again. — *v.i.* to take possession again: to begin again in continuation. — *adj.* **resum′able.** — *ns.* **résumé** (*rā-zü-mā, rez′ū-mā;* Fr. *pa.p.*) a summary: a curriculum vitae (*U.S.*); **resumption** (*ri-zump′shən,* or *-zum′*) act of resuming. — *adj.* **resumptive** (*-zump′, -zum′*). — *adv.* **resump′tively.** [L. *resūmĕre, -sūmptum* — *re-*, *sūmĕre*, to take.]

resupinate *ri-sōō′pin-āt, -sū′, adj.* upside down by twisting (*bot.*). — *n.* **resupinā′tion.** — *adj.* **resupine** (*rē-sū-pīn′,* or *-sōō-*) lying on the back. [L. *resupīnāre, -ātum,* and *resupīnus* — *re-*, back, *supīnus*, bent backward.]

resurge *ri-sûrj′,* (*rare*) *v.i.* to rise again. — *n.* **resur′gence.** — *adj.* **resur′gent.** — *v.t.* **resurrect** (*rez-ər-ekt′;* back-formation) to restore to life: to revive: to disinter. — *v.i.* to come to life again. — *n.* **resurrection** (*-ek′shən*) a rising from the dead esp. (with *cap.*) that of Christ: resuscitation: revival: a thing resurrected: body-snatching. — *adjs.* **resurrec′tional; resurrec′tionary.** — *v.t.* **resurrec′tionise, -ize.** — *ns.* **resurrec′tionism; resurrec′tionist, resurrec′tion-man** one who stole bodies

---

rēpub′lisher *n.*
rēpulp′ *v.t.*
rēpur′chase *v.t.* and *n.*

rēquote′ *v.t.* and *v.i.*
rēreg′ister *v.t.* and *v.i.*
rēreg′ulate *v.t.*

reregulā′tion *n.*
rē′revise *v.t.* and *n.*
rēroute′ *v.t.*

fāte; fär; hûr; mīne; mōte; för; mūte; mōōn; fŏŏt; dhen (then); el′ə-mənt (element)

from the grave for dissection. — *adj.* **resurrect′ive.** — *n.* **resurrect′or.** — **resurrec′tion-pie** a dish compounded of remnants of former meals; **resurrection plant** a plant that curls in a ball in drought and spreads again in moisture, as rose of Jericho, some selaginellas. [L. *resurgĕre, resurrēctum* — *re-, surgĕre,* to rise.]

resuscitate *ri-sus′i-tāt, v.t.* and *v.i.* to bring back to life or consciousness: to revive. — *adjs.* **resusc′itable; resusc′itant.** — *n.* one who, or that which, resuscitates. — *n.* **resuscitā′tion.** — *adj.* **resusc′itātive** tending to resuscitate: reviving: revivifying: reanimating. — *n.* **resusc′itātor** one who, or that which, resuscitates: an oxygen-administering apparatus used to induce breathing after asphyxiation. [L. *resuscitāre, -ātum* — *re-, sus-, sub-,* from beneath, *citāre,* to put into quick motion — *ciēre,* to make to go.]

ret *ret,* **rate, rait** *rāt, vs.t.* to expose to moisture. — *v.t.* and *v.i.* to soak: to soften, spoil, or rot by soaking or exposure to moisture: to rot: — *pr.p.* **rett′ing, rāt′ing, rait′ing;** *pa.t.* and *pa.p.* **rett′ed, rāt′ed, rait′ed.** — *n.* **rett′ery** a place where flax is retted. [App. akin to **rot.**]

retable *ri-tā′bl, n.* a shelf or ornamental setting for panels, etc. behind an altar. [Fr. *rétable* — L.L. *retrōtabulum.*]

retail *rē′tāl,* formerly (still by some) *ri-, rē-tāl′, n.* sale to consumer, or in small quantities. — *adj.* in, of, engaged in, concerned with, such sale. — *adv.* by retail. — *v.t.* (*ri-, rē-tāl′*) to sell by retail: to repeat in detail: to put about, hand on by report. — *ns.* **retail′er; retail′ment.** [O.Fr. *retail,* piece cut off — *tailler,* to cut.]

retain *ri-tān′, v.t.* to keep: to hold back: to continue to hold: to keep up: to employ or keep engaged, as by a fee paid: to keep in mind. — *adj.* **retain′able.** — *ns.* **retain′er** one who or that which retains: a dependent of a person of rank, owing some service to him (*hist.*): a family servant of long standing: an authorisation: a retaining fee (in legal usage, **general** to secure a priority of claim on a counsel's services; **special** for a particular case); **retain′ership; retain′ment.** — **retaining fee** the advance fee paid to a lawyer to defend a cause; **retaining wall** a wall to hold back solid material, as earth, or (loosely) water (also **revetment**). [Fr. *retenir* — L. *retinēre* — *re-,* back, *tenēre,* to hold.]

retake *rē-tāk′, v.t.* to take again: to take back, recapture: — *pa.t.* **retook′;** *pa.p.* **retā′ken.** — *n.* (*rē′*) a second or repeated photographing or photograph, esp. for a motion picture. — *ns.* **retāk′er; retāk′ing.** [Pfx. **re-.**]

retaliate *ri-tal′i-āt, v.t.* to repay in kind (now usu. an injury; sometimes *upon* a person). — *v.i.* to return like for like (esp. in hostility). — *ns.* **retaliā′tion** return of like for like: imposition of a tariff against countries that impose a tariff; **retaliā′tionist.** — *adj.* **retal′iātive.** — *n.* **retal′iātor.** — *adj.* **retal′iatory** (*-āt-ər-i, -ət-ər-i*). [L. *retaliāre, -ātum* — *re-, tāliō, -ōnis,* like for like — *tālis,* such.]

retama *re-tä′mə, n.* a name for various desert switchplants — papilionaceous and caesalpiniaceous — including Spanish broom. [Sp., — Ar. *retām* (pl.).]

retard *ri-tärd′, v.t.* to slow: to keep back development or progress of: to delay: to postpone (*rare*): to delay the timing of (an ignition spark). — *v.i.* to slow down: to delay. — *n.* delay: lag. — *adj.* **retar′dant** serving to delay or slow down a chemical reaction, as rusting. — Also *n.* — *ns.* **retar′date** (*psych.*) a person who is mentally retarded or backward; **retardā′tion** (*rē-*), **retard′ment** slowing: delay: lag. — *adjs.* **retardative** (*ri-tard′ə-tiv*); **retar′datory; retar′ded** delayed or slowed down: slow in development, esp. mental, or having made less than normal progress in learning. — *ns.* **retar′der** retardant: a substance that delays or prevents setting of cement; **retard′ment** see **retardation** above. [L. *retardāre, -ātum* — *re-, tardāre,* to slow.]

retch[1] *rēch,* also *rech, v.i.* to strain as if to vomit. — *n.* an act of retching. [O.E. *hræcan* — *hrāca,* a hawking.]

retch[2] *rech,* **retch′less,** etc. Obs. forms of **reck,** etc.

rete *rē′tē, n.* a network, as of blood-vessels or nerves. — *adj.* **retial** (*rē′shi-əl*). [L. *rēte,* net.]

retene *rē′tēn, ret′ēn, n.* a hydrocarbon ($C_{18}H_{18}$) got from tar. — *ns.* **retinalite** (*ret′,* or *ri-tin′*) a resinous-lustred serpentine; **retinis′pora, retinos′pora** a cypress or kindred conifer in a perpetuated juvenile form, once placed in a separate genus; **ret′inite** pitchstone (*obs.*): a fossil resin; **ret′inol** an oil distilled from resin: vitamin A. [Gr. *rhētinē,* pine resin.]

retention *ri-ten′shən, n.* act or power of retaining: memory: custody: inability to void (*med.*). — *n.* **reten′tionist** a person who advocates the retaining of a policy, etc., esp. that of capital punishment. — *adj.* **reten′tive** retaining: tenacious: retaining moisture. — *adv.* **reten′tively.** — *ns.* **reten′tiveness, retentiv′ity** (*rē-*). [L. *retentiō, -ōnis;* O.Fr. *retentif;* see **retain.**]

retexture[1] *rē-teks′chər, n.* weaving anew. [L. *retexĕre,* to weave anew, earlier to unweave.]

retexture[2] *rē-teks′chər, v.t.* to treat (a material) so as to restore firmness lost through the action of spirit in process of dry-cleaning. [Pfx. **re-, texture** to give a texture to.]

rethink *rē-thingk′, v.t.* to consider again and come to a different decision about. — Also *n.* [Pfx. **re-.**]

retial. See **rete.**

retiarius *rē-shi-ā′ri-əs, rā-ti-ä′ri-ōos, n.* a gladiator armed with a net. — *adj.* **retiary** (*rē′shi-ər-i*) of nets: using a net as a weapon, as a gladiator or a spider. [L. *rētiārius* — *rēte,* net.]

reticent *ret′i-sənt, adj.* reserved or sparing in communication. — *ns.* **ret′icence, ret′icency.** [L. *reticēns, -ēntis,* pr.p. of *reticēre* — *re-, tacēre,* to be silent.]

reticle *ret′i-kl, n.* an attachment to an optical instrument consisting of a network of lines of reference. — *adj.* **reticular** (*ri-tik′ū-lər*) netted: netlike: reticulated: of the reticulum. — *adv.* **retic′ularly.** — *adj.* **retic′ulary.** — *v.t.* **retic′ulate** to form into or mark with a network: to distribute (e.g. water, electricity) by a network. — *v.i.* to form a network. — *adj.* netted: marked with network: net-veined. — *adj.* **retic′ulated** reticulate: (of masonry) of lozenge-shaped stones, or of squares placed diamond-wise: of rusticated work with ridges of uniform width between irregular sinkings. — *adv.* **retic′ulately.** — *ns.* **reticulā′tion** network: netlike structure; **reticule** (*ret′i-kūl*) a reticle: a small bag, orig. and properly of network, carried by ladies; **retic′ulum** a network: the second stomach of a ruminant: (with *cap.*) a southern constellation, also called the Net, between Hydrus and Dorado. [L. *rēticulum,* dim. of *rēte,* net.]

retiform *rē′ti-förm, adj.* having the form of a net. [L. *rēte,* net, *fōrma,* form.]

retina *ret′i-nə, n.* the sensitive layer of the eye: — *pl.* **ret′inas, ret′inae** (*-nē*). — *adj.* **ret′inal.** — *ns.* **retinī′tis** inflammation of the retina; **retinos′copist; retinos′copy** examination of the eye by observing a shadow on the retina; **retinula** (*ri-tin′ū-lə*) a cell playing the part of retina to an ommatidium: — *pl.* **retin′ulae** (*-lē*). — *adj.* **retin′ular.** — **retina camera** an instrument that photographs the minute blood-vessels at the back of the eye in full colour; **retinitis pigmentosa** (*pig-mən-tō′sə*) a familial and hereditary disease in which chronic and progressive degeneration of the choroid in both eyes causes progressive loss of vision. [L.L. *rētina,* app. — L. *rēte,* net.]

retinaculum *ret-i-nak′ū-ləm, n.* a connecting band: a means of retention: the apparatus that holds an insect's forewing and hindwing together: the sticky attachment of a pollen-mass, as in orchids: — *pl.* **retinac′ula.** —

---

rēsalute′ *v.t.* **rēsaid′.**
rēseal′ *v.t.*
rēseat′ *v.t.*

rēselect′ *v.t.*
rēselect′ion *n.*
rēsell′ *v.t.:*—

pa.t. and *pa.p.* **rēsold′.**
rēsent′ence *v.t.*
rēsett′le *v.t.* and *v.i.*

For other sounds see detailed chart of pronunciation.

adj. **retinac'ular.** [L. *retināculum*, a holdfast — *retinēre*; see **retain, retention.**]

retinal. See **retina.**

retinalite, retinite, retinol, etc. See under **retene.**

retinoscopy. See **retina.**

retinue *ret'i-nū*, formerly *ri-tin'ū, n.* a body of retainers: a suite or train. [Fr. *retenue*, fem. pa.p. of *retenir*; see **retain.**]

retinula, etc. See **retina.**

retire *ri-tīr', v.i.* to withdraw: to retreat: to recede: to withdraw from society, office, public or active life, business, profession, etc.: to go into seclusion or to bed: to return (*obs.*). — *v.t.* to withdraw: to draw back: to withdraw from currency: to cause to retire. — *n.* (now *rare*) retirement: retreat (*obs.*): a place of retirement (*obs.*): return (*obs.*): a signal to retreat. — *ns.* **reti'racy** (*U.S.*) seclusion: enough to retire on; **reti'ral** giving up of office, business, etc.: withdrawal. — *adj.* **retired'** withdrawn: reserved in manner: secluded, sequestered: withdrawn from business or profession: recondite (*obs.*). — *adv.* **retired'ly** (or *ri-tī'rid-li*). — *ns.* **retired'ness** (or *ri-tī'rid-nis*); **reti'ree** a person who retires from work; **retire'ment** act of retiring: state of being or having retired: solitude: privacy: a time or place of seclusion; **reti'rer.** — *adj.* **reti'ring** reserved: unobtrusive: retreating: modest: given to one who retires from a public office or service. — *adv.* **reti'ringly.** — *n.* **reti'ringness.** — **retired list** a list of officers who are relieved from active service but receive a certain amount of pay (**retired pay**). [Fr. *retirer* — *re-*, back, *tirer*, to draw.]

retook. See **retake.**

retool *rē-tōōl', v.t.* to re-equip with new tools (in a factory, etc.; also *v.i.*): to remake, refashion (chiefly *U.S.*). [Pfx. **re-.**]

retorsion. See **retort.**

retort *ri-tört', v.t.* to throw back: to return upon an assailant or opponent: to answer in retaliation: to answer sharply or wittily: to reject (*Shak.*): to purify or treat in a retort. — *v.i.* to make a sharp reply. — *n.* retaliation: a ready and sharp or witty answer: the art or act of retorting: a vessel in which substances are placed for distillation, typically a flask with long bent-back neck. — *adj.* **retor'ted** bent back: thrown back: turned back. — *ns.* **retor'ter; retortion** (*-tör'shən*; also **retor'sion**) retorting: bending, turning, or casting back: retaliation. — *adj.* **retor'tive.** [L. *retorquēre, retortum* — *re-*, back, *torquēre*, to twist.]

retouch *rē-tuch', v.t.* to touch again: to touch up, seek to improve by new touches. — *n.* an act of touching up, esp. of a photograph by pencil-work on the negative. — *n.* **retouch'er.** [Pfx. **re-.**]

retour *ri-tōōr', n.* a return: an extract from chancery of the service of an heir to his ancestor (*Scots law*). — *v.t.* to return as heir; to return to chancery. [O.Fr. *retour*, return.]

retrace *ri-,* or *rē-trās', v.t.* to trace back: to go back upon: to run over with the eye or in the memory: (*rē-*) to trace again: (*rē-*) to renew the outline of. — *adj.* **retrace'able** (*ri-*). [Fr. *retracer*.]

retract *ri-trakt', v.t.* to draw back: to withdraw: to revoke: to unsay: to undo (the previous move) (*chess*): to pronounce with tongue drawn back. — *v.i.* to take back, or draw back from, what has been said or granted. — *adj.* **retrac'table** able to be retracted: that can be drawn up into the body or wings (*aero.*): that can be drawn up towards the body of a vehicle. — *n.* **retractā'tion** (*rē-*) revoking: recantation. — *adj.* **retrac'ted** drawn in: turned back: cancelled: revoked: pronounced with tongue drawn in. — *adj.* **retrac'tile** (*-tīl*) that may be drawn back, as a cat's claws. — *ns.* **retractility** (*rē-trak-til'i-ti*); **retraction** (*ri-trak'shən*) drawing back: retractation. — *adj.* **retrac'tive** tending

to retract: involving the reversal of the previous move (*chess*). — *adv.* **retrac'tively.** — *n.* **retrac'tor** a device or instrument for holding parts back, esp. a surgical instrument for this purpose: a muscle that pulls in a part: a chess-problem that involves the reversal of the previous move. [Mainly from L. *retrahēre, retractum*; partly from *retractāre, retractātum* — *re-*, back, *trahēre*, to draw.]

retraict, retrait, retraite *ri-trāt',* obs. forms of **retreat.**

retraitt. See **retrate**[2].

retral *rē'trəl, ret'rəl,* (*biol.*) *adj.* at or towards the rear. — *adv.* **re'trally.** [L. *retro*, backwards.]

retranslate *rē-trans-lāt', -trəns-, -träns-, -z-, v.t.* to translate anew: to translate back into the original language: to transfer back. — *n.* **retranslā'tion.** [Pfx. **re-.**]

retransmit *rē-träns-mit', v.t.* to transmit again: to transmit back: to transmit a stage further. — *n.* **retransmiss'ion.** [Pfx. **re-.**]

retrate[1] *ri-trāt',* (*Spens.*) *n.* and *v.i.* Same as **retreat.**

retrate[2], **retraitt** *ri-trāt',* (*Spens.*) *n.* a portrait, portraiture. [It. *ritratto*.]

retread *rē-tred', v.t.* to tread again: — *pa.t.* **retrod'**; *pa.p.* **retrodd'en:** to remould (a tyre): — *pa.t.* and *pa.p.* **retread'ed.** — *n.* (*rē'tred*) a used tyre which has been given a new tread (also *fig.*): a soldier who fought in the first and second World Wars (*Austr.* and *U.S.*). [Pfx. **re-.**]

re-treat, retreat *rē-trēt', v.t.* to treat again. [Pfx. **re-.**]

retreat *ri-trēt', n.* a withdrawal: an orderly withdrawal before an enemy, or from a position of danger or difficulty: a signal (by bugle or drum) for withdrawal or for retirement to quarters: recall of pursuers (*Shak.*): retirement: seclusion: retirement for a time for religious meditation: a time of such retirement: a place of privacy, seclusion, refuge, or quiet: an institution for treatment of the insane, drunkards, or others. — *v.i.* to draw back: to relinquish a position: to retire: to recede. — *v.t.* (*rare*) to withdraw. — *n.* **retreat'ant** one taking part in a religious, etc. retreat. [O.Fr. *retret, -e*, pa.p. of *retraire* — L. *retrahēre*, to draw back.]

retree *ri-trē', n.* slightly damaged paper. [Perh. Fr. *retret, retrait*; see preceding.]

retrench *ri-trench', -trensh', v.t.* to cut off, out, or down: to protect by a retrenchment. — *v.i.* to cut down expenses. — *n.* **retrench'ment** an act or instance of retrenching: economy: a work within another for prolonging defence (*fort.*). [O.Fr. *retrencher* (Fr. *retrancher*) — *re-*, off, *trencher*; see **trench.**]

retrial. See **retry.**

retribute *ri-trib'ūt, ret'ri-būt, v.t.* to give in return: to give in return for. — *v.i.* to make requital. — *n.* **retribution** (*ret-ri-bū'shən*) requital (now esp. of evil). — *adj.* **retrib'ūtive** (*ri-*) repaying: rewarding or punishing suitably. — *adv.* **retrib'ūtively.** — *n.* **retrib'ūtor.** — *adj.* **retrib'ūtory.** [L. *retribuĕre, -ūtum*, to give back — *re-*, back, *tribuĕre*, to give.]

retrieve *ri-trēv', v.t.* to search for and fetch, as a dog does game: to recover, repossess: to rescue (from, out of): to save (time): to restore (honour, fortune): to make good (a loss, error): to return successfully (in tennis), or to get possession of (in football), (a shot, pass, etc. which is difficult to reach). — *v.i.* to find and fetch in game. — *n.* retrieving. — *adj.* **retriev'able.** — *n.* **retriev'ableness.** — *adv.* **retriev'ably.** — *ns.* **retriev'al** retrieving: the extraction of data from a file (*comput.*); **retrieve'ment** (*rare*); **retriev'er** a dog (of a breed that can be) trained to find and fetch game that has been shot: one who retrieves. — *n.* and *adj.* **retriev'ing.** [O.Fr. *retroev-, retreuv-,* stressed stem of *retrover* (Fr. *retrouver*) — *re-*, again, *trouver*, to find.]

retro *ret'rō* (*slang*) *adj.* old-fashioned: of or relating to the past. — *n.* (*coll.*) a retro-rocket. — *pl.* **ret'ros.**

---

resett'lement *n.*
reshape' *v.t.*
reship' *v.t.* and *v.i.*

reship'ment *n.*
re-site' *v.t.*
resole' *v.t.*

respell' *v.t.*
respray' *v.t.* and *n.*
restaff' *v.t.*

retro- *ret-rō-, rē-trō-, pfx.* backwards: behind. [L. *retrō.*]

retroact *rē-trō-akt',* or *ret'rō-, v.i.* to act backward, or apply to the past (*law*): to react. — *n.* **retroac'tion.** — *adj.* **retroac'tive** applying to, affecting, things past: operating backward. — *adv.* **retroac'tively.** — *n.* **retroactiv'ity.** [L. *retroagĕre, -actum — agĕre,* to do.]

retrobulbar *rē-trō-bul'bər,* or *ret-rō-, adj.* behind the eyeball. [**retro-,** and L. *bulbus,* onion.]

retrocede *ret-rō-, rē-trō-sēd', v.i.* to move back or (*med.*) inwards. — *v.t.* to cede back, grant back. — *adj.* **retrocē'dent.** — *n.* **retrocession** (*-sesh'ən*). — *adj.* **retrocess'ive.** [L. *retrōcēdĕre, -cēssum — cēdĕre,* to go, yield; partly from **retro-** and **cede,** or Fr. *céder.*]

retrochoir *rē'trō-kwīr,* or *ret'rō-,* (*archit.*) *n.* an extension of a church behind the position of the high altar. [Pfx. **retro-.**]

retrocognition *ret'rō-kog-ni'shən, n.* extrasensory knowledge of past events. [Pfx. **retro-.**]

retrod, retrodden. See **retread.**

retrofit *ret'rō-fit, v.t.* to modify (a house, aircraft, etc.) some time after construction by incorporating or substituting more up-to-date parts, etc.: — *pr.p.* **ret'rofitting;** *pa.t.* and *pa.p.* **ret'rofitted.** — *ns.* **ret'rofit; ret'rofitting.** [Pfx. **retro-.**]

retroflex *ret'rō-fleks,* or *rē'trō-, adj.* bent back (also **retroflect'ed, ret'roflexed**): cacuminal (*phon.*; also **ret'roflexed**). — *n.* **retroflexion, retroflection** (*-flek'-shən*). [L.L. *retroflexus* — L. *retro-,* back — L. *flectĕre, flexum,* to bend.]

retrograde *ret'rō-grād* (or *rē'trō-), adj.* moving or directed backward or (*astron.*) from east to west, relatively to the fixed stars: inverse: habitually walking or swimming backwards: degenerating: reverting: contrary (*Shak.*). — *n.* one who goes back or degenerates: backward movement. — *v.i.* to go back or backwards: to have a retrograde movement (*astron.*). — *v.t.* to cause to go back. — *ns.* **retrogradation** (*-grə-dā'shən*) **retrogression** (esp. *astron.*); **ret'rogress** (*-gres*) backward movement: degeneration. — *v.i.* **retrogress'** to retrograde. — *n.* **retrogression** (*-gresh'ən*) a going backward: a decline in quality or merit: retrograde movement (*astron.*). — *adjs.* **retrogress'ional, retrogress'ive.** — *adv.* **retrogress'ively.** [L. *retrōgradus,* going backward, *retrōgressus,* retrogression — *retrō-,* backward, *gradī, gressus,* to go.]

retroject *ret'rō-jekt, v.t.* to throw backwards (opp. to *project*). — *n.* **retrojec'tion.** [Pfx. **retro-** and **project.**]

retrolental *ret-rō-len'təl, adj.* behind the or a lens, esp. that of the eye. [Pfx. **retro-** and L. *lēns, lentis* (see **lens**).]

retromingent *ret-rō-, rē-trō-min'jənt, adj.* urinating backward. — *n.* a retromingent animal. — *n.* **retromin'gency.** [Pfx. **retro-,** and L. *mingĕre,* to urinate.]

retro-operative *ret-rō-, rē-trō-op'ər-ə-tiv, adj.* retrospective in effect. [Pfx. **retro-.**]

retropulsion *ret-rō-, rē-trō-pul'shən, n.* pushing backwards: a tendency in the paralysed to walk backwards. — *adj.* **retropul'sive.** [Pfx. **retro-,** *pulsion* (rare) — L. *pulsiō, -ōnis.*]

retro-rocket *ret'rō-rok'it, rēt', n.* a rocket whose function is to slow down, fired in a direction opposite to that in which a body, e.g. a spacecraft, an artificial satellite, is travelling. [Pfx. **retro-.**]

retrorse *ri-trōrs', adj.* turned back or downward. — *adv.* **retrorse'ly.** [L. *retrōrsus — retrōversus.*]

retrospect *ret'rō-spekt* (or *rē'trō-), n.* reference, regard: a backward view: a view or a looking back: a contemplation of the past. — *v.i.* to look back. — *v.t.* to look back on. — *n.* **retrospec'tion.** — *adj.* **retrospec'tive** looking back: pertaining to or of the nature of a retrospective: retroactive. — *n.* an exhibition, etc. presenting the life's work of an artist, musician, etc.,

or a representative selection thereof: an exhibition, etc. which looks back over the history, development or earlier examples (of something). — *adv.* **retrospec'tively.** [L. *retrōspicĕre* — L. *specĕre, spectum,* to look.]

retroussé *rə-trōōs'ā, rə-trōōs'ā, adj.* turned up (esp. of the nose). — *n.* **retroussage** (*-äzh'*) wiping aside of ink on an engraved plate to soften tones. [Fr. *retrousser* (pa.p. *retroussé*), to turn up.]

retrovert *ret-rō-, rē-trō-vûrt', rē'trō-vûrt, v.t.* to turn back. — *n.* **retrover'sion** a turning or falling back: backward displacement. [L. *retrōvertĕre, -versum — vertĕre,* to turn.]

retrovirus *ret'rō-vī-rəs, n.* any of a group of eukaryotic viruses whose genetic material is encoded in the form of RNA rather than DNA and which are known to cause a number of diseases. [*reverse* transcriptase (the active enzyme in these viruses), and **virus.**]

retry *rē-trī', v.t.* to try again (judicially): — *pr.p.* **retry'ing;** *pa.t.* and *pa.p.* **retried'.** — *n.* **retrī'al.** [Pfx. **re-.**]

retsina *ret-sēn'ə, n.* a Greek resin-flavoured wine. [Gr.]

retted, rettery, retting. See **ret.**

retund *ri-tund', v.t.* to blunt. [L. *retundĕre,* to blunt.]

return *ri-tûrn', v.i.* to come or go back: to revert: to recur: to turn away (*B.*): to continue with change of direction (*archit.*). — *v.t.* to turn round (*Shak.*): to make a turn at an angle (*archit.*): to turn back (*Spens.*): to give, put, cast, bring, or send back: to answer: to retort: to report officially: to report as appointed or elected: hence, to elect to parliament: to give in return: (in games) to lead back or hit back: to requite: to repay: to respond to with the like: to render: to yield: to come back over (*Shak.*). — *n.* the act of returning: a recurrence: reversion: continuation, or a continuing stretch, at an angle, esp. a right angle (*archit.,* etc.): that which comes in exchange: proceeds, profit, yield: recompense: requital: an answer: an answering performance: a thing returned, esp. an unsold newspaper: (in *pl.*) a light-coloured mild tobacco (orig. refuse): the rendering back of a writ by the sheriff, with his report (*law*): an official report or statement, e.g. of one's taxable income (*tax return*) or (esp. in *pl.*) of the votes cast in an election: hence, election to parliament: a return ticket. — *adj.* returning: for return: in return: at right angles. — *adj.* **return'able.** — *n.* **returnee'** one who returns. — *adj.* **return'less.** — **return crease** see **crease**[1]; **returning officer** the officer who presides at an election; **return match** a second match played at a different venue by the same teams of players; **return shock** an electric shock due to induction sometimes felt after a lightning-flash; **return ticket** a ticket entitling a passenger to travel to a place and back to his starting-point. — **by return (of post)** by the next post leaving in the opposite direction; **many happy returns (of the day)** a conventional expression of good wishes said to a person on his or her birthday. [Fr. *retourner — re-,* back, *tourner,* to turn.]

re-turn *rē'tûrn', v.t.* and *v.i.* to turn again or back. [Pfx. **re-.**]

retuse *ri-tūs', adj.* with the tip blunt and broadly notched. [L. *retūsus — retundĕre,* to blunt.]

reunion *rē-ūn'yən, n.* a union, or a meeting, after separation: a social gathering of friends or persons with something in common. — *ns.* **reun'ionism; reun'ionist** one who wishes to have the Anglican and Roman Catholic Churches reunited. — Also *adj.* — *adj.* **reunionis'tic.** [Fr. *réunion — re-,* again, *union,* union.]

reunite *rē-ū-nīt', v.t.* and *v.i.* to join after separation. [Pfx. **re-.**]

rev *rev, n.* a revolution in an internal-combustion engine. — *v.t.* to increase the speed of revolution in (often with *up*). — *v.i.* to revolve: to increase in speed of revolution: — *pr.p.* **revv'ing;** *pa.t.* and *pa.p.* **revved.** [**revolution.**]

---

rĕstage' *v.t.* **rĕstate'** *v.t.* **rĕstring'** *v.t.*
rĕstart' *n.* and *v.i.* **rĕstate'ment** *n.* **rĕstruc'ture** *v.t.*
rĕstart'er *n.* **rĕstock'** *v.t.* **rĕstyle'** *v.t.*

revalenta *rev-ə-len'tə, n.* lentil-meal. — Earlier **ervalen'ta.** [*Ervum lens,* Linnaean name of the lentil — L. *ervum,* bitter vetch, *lēns, lentis,* lentil.]

revalorise, -ize *rē-val'ər-īz, v.t.* to give a new value to, esp. to restore the value of (currency). — *ns.* **rēvalorīsā'tion, -z-; rēvalūā'tion.** — *v.t.* **rēval'ue** to make a new valuation of: to give a new value to. [Pfx. **re-.**]

revamp *rē-vamp', v.t.* to renovate, revise, give a new appearance to. — Also *n.* [Pfx. **re-.**]

revanche *ri-vänch', n.* revenge: policy directed towards recovery of territory lost to an enemy. — *ns.* **revanch'ism, revanch'ist.** — Also *adj.* [Fr.; conn. with **revenge** (q.v.).]

reveal[1] *ri-vēl', v.t.* to make known, as by divine agency or inspiration: to disclose: to divulge: to make visible: to allow to be seen. — *adj.* **reveal'able.** — *n.* **reveal'er.** — *n.* and *adj.* **reveal'ing.** — *n.* **reveal'ment** revelation. [O.Fr. *reveler* (Fr. *révéler*) — L. *revēlāre* — *re-*, back, *vēlāre,* to veil — *vēlum,* a veil.]

reveal[2] *ri-vēl', n.* the side surface of a recess, or of the opening for a doorway or window between the frame and the outer surface of the wall. [O.Fr. *revaler,* to lower.]

reveille *ri-val'i, ri-vel'i, ri-vāl'yi,* (*U.S.*) *rev'ə-lē, n.* the sound of the drum or bugle at daybreak to awaken soldiers: a summons to awake, get up, or begin. [Fr. *réveillez,* awake, imper. of *réveiller* — L. *re-, vigilāre,* to watch.]

revel *rev'l, v.i.* to feast or make merry in a riotous or noisy manner: to take intense delight, to luxuriate (with *in*). — *v.t.* to spend in revelry: — *pr.p.* **rev'elling;** *pa.t.* and *pa.p.* **rev'elled.** — *n.* a riotous feast: merrymaking: a festival or (often in *pl.*) occasion of merrymaking, dancing, masking, etc. — *ns.* **rev'eller; rev'elling; rev'elry** revelling. — **rev'el-rout'** boisterous revelry: a crowd of revellers. — **Master of the Revels** an official organiser of entertainments, esp. at court or in the Inns of Court. [O.Fr. *reveler* → L. *rebellāre,* to rebel.]

revelation *rev-i-lā'shən, n.* the act or experience of revealing: that which is revealed: a disclosure: an enlightening experience: divine or supernatural communication: **Revelation (of St John)** or, popularly, **Revelations** (*n.sing.*), the Apocalypse or last book of the New Testament. — *adj.* **revelā'tional.** — *n.* **revelā'tionist** a believer in divine revelation: one who makes a revelation: the author of the Apocalypse or an apocalyptic book. — *adj.* **rev'elātive.** — *n.* **rev'elātor.** — *adj.* **rev'elatory.** [L. *revēlāre, -ātum;* see **reveal**[1].]

revenant *rev-nä', rev'ə-nənt, n.* one who returns after a long absence, esp. from the dead: a ghost. [Fr., pr.p. of *revenir,* to come back.]

revendicate *rē-vend'i-kāt, v.t.* to make formal claim to, or recover by such claim (e.g. lost territory): to endeavour to have unpaid-for and undamaged goods restored when buyer is bankrupt. — *n.* **revendicā'tion.** [Variant, through Fr., of **vindicate.**]

revenge *ri-venj', v.t.* to inflict injury in retribution for: (esp. *refl.*) to avenge. — *v.i.* to take vengence: — *n.* (the act of inflicting) malicious injury in return for injury received: the desire for retaliation of evil (also in *pl.; Shak.*): avenging (*Shak.*): in games, opportunity of retaliation in a return game: punishment (*obs.*). — *adj.* **revenge'ful** ready to seek revenge. — *adv.* **revenge'fully.** — *n.* **revenge'fulness.** — *adj.* **revenge'less.** — *ns.* **revenge'ment** (now *rare*); **reveng'er.** — *n.* and *adj.* **reveng'ing.** — *adv.* **reveng'ingly.** — *adj.* **reveng'ive** (*Shak.*). [O.Fr. *revenger, revencher* (Fr. *revancher*) — L. *re-, vindicāre,* to lay claim to.]

revenue *rev'in-ū* (formerly also *ri-ven'ū*), *n.* receipts or return from any source: income: the income of a state: a government department concerned with it. — *adj.* **rev'enued.** — **rev'enue-cutt'er** an armed vessel em-

ployed in preventing smuggling. — **Inland Revenue** revenue from excise, income-tax, etc.: the department of the civil service which collects this. [Fr. *revenue,* pa.p. (fem.) of *revenir,* to return — L. *revenīre* — *re-*, back, *venīre,* to come.]

reverberate *ri-vûr'bər-āt, v.t.* to beat or send back: to reflect: to echo: to heat in a reverberatory furnace. — *v.i.* to recoil, rebound: to be reflected: to re-echo: to resound. — *adj.* reverberated: reverberating (*Shak.*). — *v.t.* **reverb'** (after *Shak.*). — *adj.* **rever'berant** reverberating. — *n.* **reverberā'tion.** — *adj.* **rever'berātive** (or *-ət-*). — *n.* **rever'berātor.** — *adj.* **rever'beratory** (*-ət-ər-i,* or *-āt-*). — **reverberatory furnace** a furnace in which the flame is turned back over the substance to be heated. [L. *reverberāre, -ātum* — *re-*, back, *verberāre,* to beat — *verber,* a lash.]

revere *ri-vēr', v.t.* to regard with high respect: to venerate. — *adj.* **revēr'able.** — *n.* **reverence** (*rev'ər-əns*) high respect: respectful awe: veneration: the state of being held in high respect: a gesture or observance of respect. - *v.t.* to venerate. — *n.* **rev'erencer.** — *adj.* **rev'erend** worthy of reverence: clerical (*cap.;* usu. written **Rev.**) a title prefixed to a clergyman's name. — *n.* a clergyman. — *adjs.* **rev'erent** feeling or showing reverence; **reverential** (*-en'shl*) proceeding from reverence: respectful: submissive. — *advs.* **reveren'tially; rev'erently.** — *n.* **reverer** (*ri-vēr'ər*). — **His, Your, Reverence** (now *Ir.* or playful) a mode of referring to or addressing a clergyman; **Most Reverend** is used of an archbishop, **Right Reverend,** a bishop, or Moderator of the Church of Scotland, **Very Reverend,** a dean, a former Moderator, or (if a clergyman) a Scottish University principal; **Reverend Mother,** a Mother Superior of a convent; **save** or **saving (your) reverence** (*obs.* contr. to **sir= reverence**) with all due respect to you — an apology for introducing an unseemly word or subject. [O.Fr. *reverer* (Fr. *révérer*) — L. *reverērī* — *re-*, intens., *verērī,* feel awe.]

reverie, revery *rev'ə-ri, n.* an undirected train of thoughts or fancies in meditation: a fanciful notion (*arch.*): mental abstraction: a piece of music expressing such a state of mind. — *n.* **rev'erist.** [Fr. *rêverie* — *rêver,* to dream.]

revers *ri-vēr', U.S. -vûr', rə-ver', n.* any part of a garment that is turned back, as a lapel: — *pl.* **revers** (pronounced as *sing., -vērz', -vûrz'*). [Fr. — L. *reversus.*]

reverse *ri-vûrs', v.t.* to bring back (*Spens.*): to turn aside (*Spens.*): to turn the other way about, as upside down, outside in, etc.: to invert: to set moving backwards: to annul. — *v.i.* to move backwards or in the opposite direction: to set an engine, etc. moving backwards: to return (*Spens.*). — *n.* the contrary, opposite: the back, esp. of a coin or medal (opp. to *obverse*): a set-back, misfortune, defeat: a back-handed sword-stroke: an act of reversing: a backwards direction: a direction or order opposite to normal: reverse gear. — *adj.* contrary, opposite: turned about: acting in the contrary direction: reversing: back-handed (*obs.*): of the rear (*mil.*). — *n.* **rever'sal** act of reversing. — *adj.* **reversed'.** — *adv.* **rever'sedly.** — *adj.* **reverse'less** unalterable. — *adv.* **reverse'ly.** — *ns.* **rever'ser** one who, or that which, reverses: a reversing device: a borrower on wadset (*Scots law*); **rever'si** (*-sē*) a game in which a captured man is not removed from the board but turned upside down to show the captor's colour: reversis; **reversibil'ity.** — *adj.* **rever'sible** able to be reversed (in any sense): allowing of restoration (of tissues, etc.) to a normal state (*med.*). — *n.* and *adj.* **rever'sing.** — *n.* **rever'sion** (*-shən*) the act or fact of reverting or of returning: that which reverts or returns: the return, or the future possession, of any property after some particular event: the right to succeed to possession or office: a

---

rēsubmit' *v.t.*
rēsurvey' *v.t.*
rēsur'vey *n.*

resynchronisā'tion, -z- *v.t.*
resyn'chronise, -ize *v.t.*
rētell' *v.t.:* — *pa.p.* **rētold'.**

rētell'er *n.*
rētie' *v.t.*
retile' *v.t.*

sum payable upon death: that which is left over, remains: return to ancestral type (*biol.*). — *adj.* **rever'-sional.** — *adv.* **rever'sionally.** — *adj.* **rever'sionary** relating to reversion: of reversion: of the nature of a reversion. — *n.* one who has a reversion. — *ns.* **rever'sioner** a reversionary; **rever'sis** an old card-game in which the taker of fewest tricks wins; **rever'so** a verso: a back-handed sword-stroke: — *pl.* **rever'sos.** — **reverse engineering** the taking apart of a competitor's product to see how it works, e.g. with a view to copying it or improving on it; **reverse gear** a gear combination which causes an engine, etc. to go in reverse; **reverse pass** in football, a pass made when a player runs in one direction and passes in the other direction; **reverse transcriptase** the enzyme in a retrovirus which makes a DNA copy of an RNA genome; **reverse yield gap** (*commerce*) the amount by which the average yield on the shares making up the Financial Times ordinary index, or the return on any particular stocks, falls short of the return on 2½% consolidated annuities; **reversing layer** a layer of the sun's chromosphere that reverses bright lines of the spectrum to dark absorption lines; **reversing light** a light on the back of a motor vehicle which comes on when the vehicle is put into reverse gear, reversed, providing illumination for the driver, a warning to other road-users, etc. — **go into reverse** to engage reverse gear: to move backwards; **reverse the charges** to charge a telephone call to the one who receives it instead of to the caller. [L. *reversāre*, to turn round; partly through Fr.]

revert *ri-vûrt'*, *v.t.* to turn back: to reverse. — *v.i.* to return: to fall back to a former state: to recur to a former subject: to return to the original owner or his heirs. — *adjs.* **rever'ted** reversed: turned backwards; **rever'tible; revert'ive** (*Thomson*). [L. *re-*, *vertĕre*, to turn.]

revery. Same as **reverie.**

revest *ri-vest'*, *v.t.* to clothe again (*Spens.*): to vest again. — *v.i.* to vest again. — *ns.* **revest'iary, revest'ry** a vestry. [O.Fr. *revestir*, or *re-*, *vestir* — L. *revestīre*, *vestīre*, to clothe again, to clothe.]

revet *ri-vet'*, *v.t.* to face with masonry, etc: — *pr.p.* **revett'ing;** *pa.t.* and *pa.p.* **revett'ed.** — *n.* **revet'ment** a retaining wall, facing. [Fr. *revêtir*, to reclothe.]

rêveur *re-vœr*, fem. **rêveuse** *re-vœz*, (Fr.) *ns.* a daydreamer.

revie *re-vī'*, *v.t.* to stake more than an opponent has proposed on (e.g. the taking of a trick): to bandy (words) in emulation (*obs.*). — *v.i.* to stake higher (*obs.*): — *pr.p.* **rēvy'ing;** *pa.t.* and *pa.p.* **rēvied'.** — Also *n.* (*obs.*). [Fr. *renvier* — L. *re-*, *invitāre*, to invite.]

review *ri-vū'*, *n.* a viewing again (also **re-view** *rē'vū'*): a looking back, retrospect: a reconsideration: a survey: a revision: a critical examination: a critique: a periodical with critiques of books, etc.: a display and inspection of troops or ships: the judicial revision of a higher court (*law*). — *v.t.* to see, view, or examine again (also **rē-view'**): to look back on or over: to survey: to examine critically: to write a critique on: to inspect, as troops: to revise. — *v.i.* to write reviews. — *adj.* **review'able** capable of being reviewed. — *ns.* **review'al** a review of a book: reviewing; **review'er** a writer of critiques: a writer in a review. — **review body** a committee set up to review (salaries, etc.); **review copy** a copy of a book sent by the publisher to a periodical for review. [Partly pfx. **re-** and **view;** partly Fr. *revue*, pa.p. (fem.) of *revoir* — L. *revidēre* — *vidēre*, to see.]

revile *ri-vīl'*, *v.t.* to assail with bitter abuse. — *v.i.* to rail, use abusive language. — *n.* **revilement** (*obs.*). — *ns.* **revile'ment** the act of reviling: a reviling speech; **revil'er.** — *n.* and *adj.* **revil'ing.** — *adv.* **revil'ingly.** [O.Fr. *reviler* — L. *re-*, *vīlis*, worthless.]

revindicate *ri-vin'di-kāt*, *v.t.* to claim and get back: to

vindicate anew. — *n.* **revindicā'tion.** [Pfx. **re-**.]

revise *ri-vīz'*, *v.t.* to examine and correct: to make a new, improved version of: to study anew: to look at again (*obs.*). — Also *v.i.* — *n.* the act of revising or being revised: review: a further proof-sheet in which previous corrections have been given effect to. — *adj.* **revīs'able** liable to revision. — *ns.* **revī'sal** revision; **revī'ser** (also **-or**); **revision** (*-vizh'ən*) the act or product of revising. — *adjs.* **revi'sional, revi'sionary** pertaining to revision. — *ns.* **revi'sionism; revi'sionist** an advocate of revision (e.g. of a treaty, of established doctrines, etc.): a Communist favouring modification of stricter orthodox Communism and evolution, rather than revolution, as a means of achieving world domination: opprobriously, a Communist who does not hold to what some other Communist considers to be orthodox Communism (also *loosely* and *fig.*): a reviser of the Bible. — *adj.* **revī'sory.** — **Revised Version** an English translation of the Bible issued 1881–85 (Apocrypha 1895); **revising barrister** till 1918, a barrister appointed to revise the parliamentary voters' roll. [Fr. *reviser* and L. *revīsĕre* — *re-*, back, *vīsĕre*, intens. of *vidēre*, to see.]

revive *ri-vīv'*, *v.t.* and *v.i.* to bring back or come back to life, vigour, being, activity, consciousness, memory, good spirits, freshness, vogue, notice, currency, use, the stage, or natural metallic form. — *n.* **revīvabil'ity.** — *adj.* **revī'vable.** — *adv.* **revī'vably.** — *ns.* **revī'val** the act or fact of reviving: the state of being revived: recovery from languor, neglect, depression, etc.: renewed performance, as of a play: renewed interest or attention: a time of extraordinary religious awakening or sometimes worked-up excitement: a series of meetings to encourage this: quickening: renewal: awakening; **revī'valism; revī'valist** one who promotes religious, architectural, or other revival: an itinerant preacher. — *adj.* **revivalist'ic.** — *ns.* **revive'ment** (*rare*); **revī'ver** one who, or that which, revives: a renovating preparation: a stimulant (*slang*). — *n.* and *adj.* **revī'ving.** — *adv.* **revī'vingly.** — *n.* **revī'vor** (*law*) the revival of a suit which was abated by the death of a party or other cause. — **Gothic Revival** the resuscitation of Gothic architecture in (and before) the 19th century; **Romantic Revival** see **romantic; Revival of Learning** the Renaissance. [L. *revīvĕre*, to live again — *vīvĕre*, to live.]

revivescent. See **reviviscent.**

revivify *ri-viv'i-fī*, *v.t.* to restore to life: to put new life into: to reactivate. — *v.t.* and *v.i.* (*chem.*) to revive, restore (e.g. metal) to its uncombined state: — *pr.p.* **reviv'ifying;** *pa.t.* and *pa.p.* **reviv'ified.** — *n.* **revivificā'tion.** [L.L. *revīvificāre* — *re-*, *vīvus*, alive, *facĕre*, to make.]

reviviscent *rev-i-vis'ənt*, *rē-vī-*, **reviviscent** *-ves'ənt*, *adjs.* reviving. — *ns.* **revivisc'ence, revivisc'ency** (also **-esc-**). [L. *revīvīscĕre*, *-ēscĕre*.]

revoke *ri-vōk'*, *v.t.* to recall, call back (now *rare*): to withdraw (*Spens.*): to check (*Spens.*): to annul: to retract. — *v.i.* to make revocations: to neglect to follow suit at cards. — *n.* revocation, recall: the act of revoking at cards. — *adj.* **revocable** (*rev'ō-kə-bl*). — *ns.* **rev'ocableness, revocabil'ity.** — *adv.* **rev'ocably.** — *n.* **revocā'tion** recall: the act of revoking. — *adj.* **rev'ocatory.** — *n.* **revoke'ment** (*Shak.*) revocation. [L. *revocāre* — *vocāre*, to call.]

revolt *ri-vōlt'*, *v.i.* to renounce allegiance: to rise in opposition: to turn or rise in disgust, loathing, or repugnance. — *v.t.* to turn back (*Spens.*): to cause to rise in revolt (*obs.*): to inspire revulsion or repugnance in. — *n.* a rebellion: insurrection: secession: revulsion (*Shak.*): a rebel (*Shak.*). — *adj.* **revolt'ed** insurgent: shocked, outraged. — *n.* **revolt'er.** — *adj.* **revolt'ing.** — *adv.* **revolt'ingly.** [Fr. *révolter* — L. *re-*, *volūtāre*,

---

reti'tle *v.t.*	rētrans'fer *n.*	rē'tune *n.*
rētrain' *v.t.* and *v.i.*	rētrim' *v.t.*	rēturf' *v.t.*
rētransfer' *v.t.*	rētune' *v.t.*	rē-type' *v.t.*

freq. of *volvĕre, volūtum*, to turn.]
revolute. See **revolve.**
revolution *rev-ǝl-ōō'shǝn*, or *-ū'*, *n.* the act or condition
of revolving: movement in an orbit, as distinguished
from rotation: less commonly, rotation: a complete
turn by an object or figure, through four right angles,
about an axis: a cycle of phenomena or of time:
recurrence in cycles: turning over in the mind (*arch.*):
mutation (*Shak.*): a great upheaval: a complete change,
e.g. in outlook, social habits or circumstances: a
radical change in government: a time of intensified
change in the earth's features (*geol.*). — *adjs.* **revolu'-
tional** of revolution in movement; **revolu'tionary** of,
favouring, or of the nature of, revolution, esp. in
government or conditions. — *n.* one who takes part
in, or favours, a revolution. — *n.* **revolu'tioner** (*hist.*)
a supporter of a revolution, esp. that of 1688. — *v.t.*
revolu'tionise, -ize to cause radical change, or a revolution, in: to make revolutionary. — *ns.* **revolu'tionism;
revolu'tionist** one who favours revolution. — **Revolutionary Calendar** the calendar used in France from
1793 to 1805 (see **Vendémiaire, Brumaire, Frimaire,
Nivôse, Pluviôse, Ventôse, Germinal, Floréal, Prairial,
Messidor, Thermidor, Fructidor**). — **the American
Revolution** the change from the condition of British
colonies to national independence effected by the
thirteen states of the American Union in 1776; **the
French Revolution** the overthrow of the old French
monarchy and absolutism (1789); **the Revolution** the
expulsion of James II from the British throne
(1688–89), and the establishment of a really constitutional government under William III and Mary.
[L.L. *revolūtiō, -ōnis*.]
revolve *ri-volv'*, *v.t.* and *v.i.* to roll back, return (*obs.*): to
ponder: to move about a centre: to rotate. — *n.*
turning, revolution: a part of the stage which can be
revolved by hand or electrical means, providing one
method of scene-changing (*theat.*). — *adj.* **revolute**
(*rev'ǝl-ūt, -ōōt*; *bot.*) rolled backward and usu. downward. — *ns.* **revol'vency** revolution: a tendency to
revolve; **revol'ver** a revolving device of various kinds:
a pistol with a rotating magazine. — *n.* and *adj.*
revol'ving. — **revolving credit** credit which is automatically renewed as the sum previously borrowed is paid
back, so allowing the borrower to make repeated use
of the credit so long as the agreed maximum sum is
not exceeded; **revolving door** a door consisting of usu.
four leaves fixed around a central axis and standing
within a cylindrical structure open at opposite sides
to allow entrance and egress. [L. *revolvĕre, revolūtum*
— *volvĕre*, to roll.]
revue *ri-vū'*, *n.* a loosely constructed theatrical show,
more or less topical and musical. [Fr., review.]
revulsion *ri-vul'shǝn*, *n.* diversion to another part, esp. by
counter-irritation (*med.*): withdrawal: disgust: a sudden change or reversal, esp. of feeling. — *adjs.* **revul'-
sionary; revul'sive** (*-siv*). [L. *revellĕre, revulsum*, to
pluck back — *vellĕre*, to pluck.]
revved, etc. See **rev.**
revying. See **revie.**
rew *rōō* (*Spens.*). Same as **rue**[1,2] and **row**[1].
reward *ri-wörd'*, *n.* that which is given in return for good
(sometimes evil), or in recognition of merit, or for
performance of a service. — *v.t.* to give or be a reward
to or for: to give as a reward (*B.*). — *adj.* **reward'able**
capable or worthy of being rewarded. — *ns.* **reward'-
ableness; reward'er.** — *adjs.* **reward'ful** yielding reward;
reward'ing profitable: yielding a result well worth
while; **reward'less** unrewarded. [O.Fr. *rewarder, regarder* — *re-*, again, *warder, garder*, to guard; see
regard, guard, ward.]
rewarewa *rē'wǝ-rē'wǝ, rā'wǝ-rā'wǝ, n.* a New Zealand tree,
Knightia excelsa, whose wood is used in furniture-

making — also known as **honeysuckle.** [Maori]
reword *rē-wûrd'*, *v.t.* to repeat, re-echo (*Shak.*): to put
into different words. [Pfx. **re-.**]
rewth *rōōth* (*Spens.*). Same as **ruth.**
rex. See **reak**[1].
Rex *reks, n.* king: the title used by a reigning king, abbrev.
to R in signature. — **Rex (cat)** a type of cat (of two
varieties, Devon Rex and Cornish Rex) with curly but
thin coat. — **Rex (rabbit)** a type of domestic rabbit in
which the hair that would normally form the outer
coat is shorter than that of the under coat, one variety
of Rex (**Astrex;** *As*trakhan) having curly or wavy fur.
Reye's syndrome *rīz sin'drōm,* a rare, acute and often fatal
disease of children, affecting the brain and the liver.
[R.D.K. *Reye* (1912–78), Australian paediatrician.]
Reynard, reynard *rān'* or *ren'ärd, -ǝrd, n.* a fox, from the
name given to the fox in the famous beast epic of
L.Ger. origin, *Reynard the Fox.* — in Spens. **Reyn'old.**
[M.Du. *Reynaerd* — O.H.G. *Reginhart,* lit. strong in
counsel.]
Reynolds number *ren'ǝldz num'bǝr,* (*mech.*) a number
designating type of flow of a fluid in a system, obtained
from the product of the fluid's density, velocity and
dimension at a particular point, divided by its viscosity. [Osborne *Reynolds* (1842–1912), British physicist.]
rhabdus *rab'dǝs, n.* a rodlike sponge spicule. — *adj.*
rhab'doid rodlike. — *n.* a rodlike body. — *ns.* **rhab'-
dolith** (Gr. *lithos,* stone) a calcareous rod in some
Protozoa; **rhab'dom** (Gr. *rhabdōma,* bundle of rods) a
fourfold rod in the compound eye of an arthropod;
rhab'domancy (Gr. *manteiā,* divination) divination by
rod, esp. divining for water or ore; **rhab'domantist;
rhabdomyō'ma** a tumour of striped muscle. — *n.pl.*
Rhabdoph'ora the graptolites. — *n.* **rhab'dosphere** an
aggregation of rhabdoliths in oceanic ooze. [Latin-
ised from Gr. *rhabdos,* rod.]
rhachis, rhachitis. Same as **rachis, rachitis.**
Rhadamanthine *rad-ǝ-man'thīn, adj.* rigorously just and
severe, like *Rhadamanthus* (Gr. *-os*), a judge of the
lower world.
Rhaetia, Raetia *rē'sh(y)ǝ, n.* a province of the Roman
Empire, roughly Grisons and Tirol, to which Vindeli-
cia was added. — *adj.* and *n.* **R(h)ae'tian.** — *n.* **Rhaetic**
(*rē'tik; geol.*) uppermost Trias (also **Keuper**) or (acc.
to others) lowest Jurassic: Rhaeto-Romanic. — Also
adj. — **Rhae'to-Roman'ic** a general name for a group
of Romance dialects spoken from south-eastern
Switzerland to Friuli (Romansch, Ladin, Friulian). —
Also **Rhae'tic, Rhae'to-Romance'.** — Also *adjs.*
Rhamnus *ram'nǝs, n.* the buckthorn genus, giving name
to the family **Rhamnā'ceae.** — *adj.* **rhamnā'ceous.**
[Latinised from Gr. *rhamnos.*]
rhamphoid *ram'foid, adj.* hook-beak-shaped. — *ns.*
Rhamphast'os, now us. **Ramphast'os,** the typical
genus of toucans; **Rhamphorhynchus** (*ram-fō-ring'kǝs;*
Gr. *rhynchos,* snout) a genus of pterodactyls; **rhampho-
thē'ca** (Gr. *thēkē,* case) the horny sheath of a bird's
bill. [Gr. *rhamphos,* a hooked beak.]
rhaphe, rhaphide, rhaphis. Same as **raphe, raphide, raphis.**
rhapontic *ra-pon'tik, n.* ordinary kitchen-garden rhubarb.
[L.L. *rhā ponticum,* Pontic rhubarb; see **rhubarb.**]
rhapsody *raps'ǝ-di, n.* an epic or instalment of an epic
recited at one sitting (*Gr. hist.*): a patching or stringing
together of poems (*obs.*): an orderless, unconnected
composition, or collection of things said, beliefs, etc.
(*obs.*): an ecstatic utterance of feeling: an irregular
emotional piece of music. — *n.* **rhapsode** (*raps'ōd*) a
reciter of Homeric or other epics. — *adjs.* **rhapsodic**
(*-od'ik*) of rhapsodes or rhapsodies: of the nature of
rhapsody; **rhapsod'ical** unrestrainedly enthusiastic, rapt. — *adv.* **rhapsod'ically.** — *v.t.* **rhaps'-
odise, -ize** (*-ǝ-dīz*) to piece together (*obs.*): to recite in

rēū'nify *v.t.*   **rēurge'** *v.t.*   **rēuse'** (*-ūs'*), *n.*
rēūnificā'tion *n.*   **rēus'able** *adj.*   **rēutt'er** *v.t.*
rēuphol'ster *v.t.*   **rēuse'** (*-ūz'*), *v.t.*   **rēvac'cinate** *v.t.*

fāte; fär; hûr; mīne; mōte; för; mūte; mōōn; fōōt; dhen (then); *el'ǝ-mǝnt* (element)

rhapsodies. — *v.i.* to write or utter rhapsodies. — *n.* **rhaps'odist** a rhapsode: one who rhapsodises. [Gr. *rhapsōidiā*, an epic, a rigmarole — *rhaptein*, to sew, *ōidē*, a song.]

rhatany *rat'ə-ni, n.* either of two South American caesalpiniaceous plants (species of *Krameria*): the astringent root of either plant. [Sp. *ratania* — Quechua *rataña*.]

rhea *rē'ə, n.* rami. [Assamese *rihā*.]

Rhea *rē'ə, n.* the daughter of Uranus and Ge, wife and sister of Kronos: the fifth satellite of Saturn: (without *cap.*) the South American ostrich (*Rhea*). [Gr. *Rhēā*.]

Rheinberry. See **Rhine.**

rhematic *rē-mat'ik, adj.* of words or verbs: word-making. [Gr. *rhēma, -atos,* word, verb.]

Rhemish *rē'mish, adj.* of *Rheims* (*Reims*) in north-eastern France. — **Rhemish version** the English translation of the New Testament by Roman Catholics of the English college there (1582). — *n.* **Rhē'mist** a translator of the Rhemish version.

Rhenish *ren'ish, rēn', adj.* of the river *Rhine.* — *n.* Rhine wine. — *n.* **rhenium** (*rē'ni-əm*) a chemical element (symbol Re; at. numb. 75) discovered by X-ray spectroscopy in Germany in 1925. [L. *Rhēnus,* the Rhine.]

rheo- *rē'ō-, rē-ō'-,* in composition, current, flow. — *n.* **rhē'ochord, rhē'ocord** a wire rheostat. — *adjs.* **rheolog'ic, -al.** — *ns.* **rheol'ogist; rheol'ogy** the science of the deformation and flow of matter; **rheom'eter** an instrument for measuring a current of fluid: a galvanometer (*obs.*). — *adj.* **rheomet'rical.** — *ns.* **rhē'ostat** an instrument for varying an electric resistance; **rheotax'is** rheotropism; **rhē'otome** (*elect.*) an interrupter; **rhē'otrope** a commutator for reversing an electric current. — *adj.* **rheotrop'ic.** — *n.* **rheot'ropism** (*biol.*) response to the stimulus of flowing water. [Gr. *rheos,* flow.]

rhesus *rē'səs, n.* a macaque, the bandar (*Macacus rhesus,* or *Macaca mulatta*), an Indian monkey. — Also **rhesus monkey.** — **Rhesus factor, Rh(-factor)** any of a group of weakly antigenic agglutinogens usu. found in human red blood cells and in those of rhesus monkeys, inherited according to Mendelian laws, **Rh-positive** persons being those who have the factor and **Rh-negative** those (a very much smaller number) who do not — a difference important in blood transfusion and as explaining haemolytic disease of the newborn. [Gr. *Rhēsos,* a king of Thrace, arbitrarily applied.]

rhetor *rē'tōr, n.* (*Gr. hist.*) a teacher of rhetoric or professional orator. — *n.* **rhetoric** (*ret'ər-ik*) the theory and practice of eloquence, whether spoken or written, the whole art of using language so as to persuade others: the art of literary expression, esp. in prose: false, showy, artificial, or declamatory expression. — *adjs.* **rhetoric** (*ri-tor'ik*); **rhetor'ical** pertaining to rhetoric: oratorical: inflated, over-decorated, or insincere in style. — *adv.* **rhetor'ically.** — *n.* **rhetorician** (*ret-ər-ish'ən*) one who teaches the art of rhetoric: an orator: a user of rhetorical language. — *v.i.* **rhetorise, -ize** (*re'*) to play the orator. — *v.t.* to address rhetorically. — **rhetorical question** a question in form, for rhetorical effect, not calling for an answer. [Gr. *rhētōr.*]

rheum *rōōm, n.* a mucous discharge, esp. from the nose: tears (*poet.*): a cold in the head (*obs.*): rheumatic pains (in *pl.*; *rare*): ill humour (*obs.*). — *adj.* **rheumatic** (*rōō-mat'ik*; *Shak. rōō'*) of the nature of, pertaining to, apt to cause, or affected with, rheumatism or (*obs.*) rheum. — *n.* one who suffers from rheumatism: (in *pl.*) rheumatic pains (*coll.*). — *adj.* **rheumat'ical.** — *adv.* **rheumat'ically.** — *adj.* **rheumat'icky.** — *n.* **rheumatism** (*rōō'mə-tizm*) a condition characterised by pain and stiffness in muscles and joints (*dial.* **rheu'matiz, -tize,**

-tise, -teese). — *adjs.* **rheumatis'mal; rheum'atoid** resembling rheumatism; **rheumatolog'ical.** — *ns.* **rheumatol'ogist; rheumatol'ogy** the study of rheumatism. — *adjs.* **rheumed; rheum'y** of or like rheum: esp. of air, cold and damp. — **rheumatic fever** an acute disease characterised by fever, multiple arthritis, and liability of the heart to be inflamed, caused by a streptococcal infection; **rheumatoid arthritis** a disease or diseases characterised by inflammation and swelling of joints, often leading to their complete stiffening. [Gr. *rheuma, -atos,* flow — *rheein,* to flow.]

Rheum *rē'əm, n.* the rhubarb genus. [Latinised from Gr. *rhēon.*]

rhexis *reks'is, n.* rupture, esp. of a blood-vessel. [Gr. *rhēxis,* breach.]

Rh(-factor). See **rhesus.**

rhime. An obs. spelling of **rhyme, rime**[1].

rhin-, rīn-, rhino- *rīn-ō-* in composition, nose. — *adj.* **rhī'nal** of the nose. — *n.* **rhinencephalon** (*rīn-en-sef'ə-lon*; Gr. *enkephalon,* brain) the olfactory lobe of the brain. — *adj.* **rhinencephalic** (*-al'ik*). — *ns.* **rhini'tis** inflammation of the mucous membrane of the nose; **rhinolalia** (*-lā'li-ə*; Gr. *laliā,* talk) nasal speech; **rhī'nolith** (Gr. *lithos,* stone) a concretion in the nose. — *adj.* **rhinolog'ical.** — *ns.* **rhinol'ogist** a nose specialist; **rhinol'ogy** the study of the nose: nasal pathology; **rhinopharyngitis** (*rī-nō-far-in-jī'tis*) inflammation of the nose and pharynx; **rhinophyma** (*-fī'*; Gr. *phȳma,* growth, tumour) overgrowth of skin and subcutaneous tissue of the nose. — *adj.* **rhinoplas'tic.** — *ns.* **rhī'noplasty** plastic surgery of the nose; **rhinorrhagia** (*rī-nō-rā'jyə*; Ger. *rhēgnynai,* to break) excessive nosebleeding; **rhinorrhoea** (*-rē'ə*; Gr. *rhoiā,* flow) excessive mucous discharge from the nose. — *adj.* **rhinorrhoe'al.** — *ns.* **rhinoscleroma** (*-sklē-rō'mə*) a disease with hard swelling in the nose, etc.; **rhī'noscope** an instrument for examining the nose. — *adj.* **rhinoscop'ic.** — *ns.* **rhinos'copy; rhinothē'ca** (Gr. *thēkē,* case) the sheath of a bird's upper mandible; **rhī'novirus** a virus belonging to a subgroup picornaviruses thought responsible for the common cold and other repiratory diseases. [Gr. *rhīs, rhīnos,* nose.]

Rhine *rīn, n.* a river of Europe. — **Rhine'berry, Rhein'-berry** the buckthorn berry: the buckthorn; **Rhine'grave** a count with possessions on the Rhine: — *fem.* **Rhine'-gravine** (*-ēn*; Du. *Rijngrave,* now -*graaf*; fem. *Rijn-gravin*); **Rhine'stone** (also without *cap.*) a rock-crystal: a paste diamond; **Rhine'-wine** wine made from grapes grown in the Rhine valley. [Ger. *Rhein*; Du. *Rijn.*]

rhine *rēn,* (*Somerset,* etc.) *n.* a ditch or watercourse. Also spelt **reen, rean, rhyne.**

rhinencephalic, rhinencephalon. See **rhin-.**

Rhineodon *rī-nē'ō-don,* **Rhinodon** *rī'nō-don, ns.* a gigantic shark of the Indian Ocean. [Gr. *rhīnē,* a file, a shagreen shark, *odous, odontos,* tooth.]

rhinitis. See **rhin-.**

rhino[1] *rī'nō,* a contraction of **rhinoceros:** — *pl.* **rhī'nos.**

rhino[2] *rī'nō,* (*slang*) *n.* money. — *adj.* **rhinocerical** (*-ser'i-kl; old slang*) rich. [Connection with **rhino, rhinoceros** obscure.]

rhinoceros *rī-nos'ər-əs, ri-,* (*obs.*) **rhinoc'erot** *-ot, -ote -ōt, ns.* a large ungulate of several species in Africa and southern Asia, constituting a family (**Rhinocerot'idae**) characterised by one or two horns on the nose: — *pl.* **rhinoc'eroses,** *obs.* **rhinocerotes** (*-ō'tēz*). — *adj.* **rhinocerot'ic.** — **rhinoc'eros-beetle** a very large beetle (of various genera) with a large up-curved horn on the head; **rhinoc'eros-bird** an ox-pecker that alights on the rhinoceros: a hornbill. [Gr. *rhīnokerōs* — *rhīs, rhīnos,* nose, *keras,* horn.]

Rhinodon. See **Rhineodon.**

rhinolalia . . . rhinotheca. See **rhin-.**

rhipidate *rip'i-dāt, adj.* fan-shaped. — *ns.* **rhipid'ion** in the

---

rēvaccinā'tion *n.*
rēval'idate *v.t.*
rēvictual (*rē-vit'l*), *v.t.* and *v.i.*: —

pr.p. revict'ualling;
pa.t. and **pa.p. revict'ualled.**
rēvis'it *v.t.* and *n.*

rēvis'itant *n.*
rēvisitā'tion *n.*
rēvīt'alise, -ize *v.t.*

For other sounds see detailed chart of pronunciation.

Greek Church, the eucharistic fan or flabellum; **rhipid′-ium** a fan-shaped cymose inflorescence. — *ns.pl.* **Rhipip′tera, Rhipidop′tera** the Strepsiptera. [Gr. *rhīpis, rhīpidos,* a fan.]

rhiz- *rīz,* **rhizo-** *rī-zō* -in composition, root. — *adjs.* **rhīzan′thous** seeming to flower from the root; **rhī′zic** of the root of an equation. — *ns.* **rhī′zine** (*-zin*) a lichen rhizoid; **Rhizō′bium** a genus of bacteria important in nitrogen fixation by leguminous plants: (sometimes without *cap.*) a bacterium of this genus: — *pl.* **rhizō′bia; rhī′zocarp** (Gr. *karpos,* fruit) a water-fern or heterosporous fern: a plant with sporangia on rootlike processes: a perennial herb: a plant fruiting underground. — *adjs.* **rhīzocar′pic, rhīzocar′pous.** — *n.* **rhī′zocaul** (Gr. *kaulos,* stalk) the rootlike stalk of a hydrozoan colony. — *n.pl.* **Rhīzoceph′ala** (Gr. *kephalē,* head) an order of Cirripedes parasitic on crabs. — *adjs.* **rhīzogen′ic, rhīzogenet′ic, rhīzog′enous** producing roots. — *n.* **rhī′zoid** a short hairlike organ in the lower plants, serving as a root. — *adjs.* **rhīzoi′dal; rhīzō′matous.** — *ns.* **rhī′zome** (Gr. *rhizōma,* a root-mass) a rootstock, an underground stem producing roots and leafy shoots; **rhī′zomorph** (Gr. *morphē,* form) a rootlike mass of fungal hyphae. — *adjs.* **rhīzomorph′ous** having the form of a root; **rhīzoph′agous** root-eating; **rhīzoph′ilous** growing on roots. — *ns.* **Rhīzoph′ora** the mangrove genus, with great development of aerial roots, giving name to the family **Rhizophorā′ceae; rhī′zophore** a root-bearing structure, esp. in Selaginella; **rhī′zoplane** the surface of a root together with the soil adhering to it; **rhī′zopod** any member of the **Rhīzop′oda,** protozoa with rootlike pseudopodia; **Rhī′zopus** a genus of moulds: (without *cap.*) a mould of this genus; **rhī′zosphere** the region in the soil surrounding a plant's root system, affected by its excretions and characterised by considerable microbiological activity. [Gr. *rhiza,* root.]

Rh-negative. See **rhesus.**

rho *rō, n.* the seventeenth letter (P, ρ) of the Greek alphabet, answering to R: as a numeral ρ′ = 100, ͵ρ = 100 000: — *pl.* **rhos.** [Gr. *rhō.*]

rhod- *rōd-,* **rhodo-** *rō-dō* in composition, rose: rose-coloured. — *ns.* **rhō′damine** (*-mēn;* see **amine**) a dye-stuff, usually red, akin to fluorescein; **rhō′danate** in dyeing, a thiocyanate. — *adj.* **rhōdan′ic** thiocyanic. — *v.t.* **rhō′danise, -ize** to electroplate with rhodium. — *adj.* **rhō′dic** of rhodium in higher valency. — *ns.* **Rhodites** (*rō-dī′tēz*) a gall-fly that forms bedeguars on the wild-rose; **rhō′dium** a metallic element (Rh; at. numb. 45) of the platinum group, forming rose-coloured salts; **rhodochro′site** (*-krō′sīt;* Gr. *rhodochrōs,* rose-coloured) manganese spar, a pink rhombohedral mineral, manganese carbonate; **rhōdodaph′ne** (or *rod-;* Spens.; Gr. *daphnē,* laurel) oleander; **Rhōdoden′dron** (or *rod-;* Gr. *dendron,* tree) a genus of trees and shrubs of the heath family, with leathery leaves and large showy slightly zygomorphic flowers, some species being called Alpine rose: (without *cap.*) a member of the genus; **rhō′dolite** a pink or purple garnet (gemstone); **rhō′donite** a rose-red anorthic pyroxene, manganese silicate; **rhō′dophane** (Gr. *phainein,* to show) a red pigment in the retinal cones of birds, etc. — *n.pl.* **Rhōdophyceae** (*-fish′i-ē;* Gr. *phȳkos,* seaweed) the red seaweeds (including some forms that are neither red nor found in the sea), one of the main divisions of the algae, in which the chlorophyll is usually masked by a red pigment. — *n.* **rhōdop′sin** (Gr. *opsis,* sight) visual purple. — *adj.* **rhō′dous** of rhodium in lower valency. — *n.* **Rhodymenia** (*rō-di-mē′ni-ə;* Gr. *hymēn,* a membrane) the dulse genus of red seaweeds. — **rhō′dium= wood** the scented wood of Canary Island convolvulus, yielding **oil of rhodium.** [Gr. *rhodon,* rose.]

Rhode Island *rōd ī′lənd,* an island of the United States,

named from a supposed resemblance to the island o͞ *Rhodes:* the state of which it forms part. — **Rhode Island red** an American breed of domestic fowl.

Rhodes *rōdz, n.* an island and ancient city-state of the Aegean. — *n.* and *adj.* **Rhō′dian.** — **Rhodian laws** the earliest system of marine law; **Rhodian school** a school of Hellenistic sculpture, of which the Laocoön is the greatest product. [Gr. *Rhodos.*]

Rhodesia *rō-dē′zhyə, -zhi-ə, -z-, -s-, -sh-, n.* the former name of a region of southern Africa, named after Cecil John *Rhodes,* consisting of Zambia (formerly *Northern Rhodesia*) and Zimbabwe (formerly *Southern Rhodesia,* later simply *Rhodesia*). — *adj.* and *n.* **Rhodē′sian.** — **Rhodesian man** an extinct type of man represented by a skull found at Broken Hill, in Northern Rhodesia, in 1921; **Rhodesian ridgeback** (*rij′bak*) a hunting dog with a ridge of hair along the back.

rhodic . . . **rhododendron.** See **rhod-.**

rhodomontade. Same as **rodomontade.**

rhodonite . . . **rhodopsin.** See **rhod-.**

rhodora *rō-dō′rə, -dō′, n.* a handsome N. American species of Rhododendron, or separate kindred genus. [L. *rhodōra,* meadow-sweet, said to be a Gallic plant-name.]

rhodous, Rhodymenia. See **rhod-.**

Rhoeadales *rē-ə-dā′lēz, n.pl.* an order of dicotyledons including poppies, Cruciferae, etc. — *n.* **rhoe′adine** (*-dēn*) an alkaloid found in poppies. [Gr. *rhoias, -ados,* corn-poppy.]

rhomb *rom(b), n.* an equilateral parallelogram (usu. excluding the square): a lozenge-shaped object: anything that whirls, as (*Milt.*): the wheel of day and night (*obs.*): a magic wheel: a rhombohedron (*crystal.*). — *ns.* **rhombencephalon** (*rom-ben-sef′ə-lon;* Gr. *enkephalon,* brain) the hind-brain; **rhombenporphyr** (*rom-ben-pör′fēr;* from Ger.), **rhomb′(en)por′phyry** an intermediate, moderately fine-grained igneous rock with feldspar phenocrysts rhombic in section. — *adjs.* **rhombic** (*rom′bik*) shaped like a rhombus: orthorhombic (*crystal.*); **rhombohē′dral** of a rhombohedron: trigonal (*crystal.*). — *n.* **rhombohē′dron** (Gr. *hedrā,* seat) a crystal form of six rhombi, in the trigonal or hexagonal system, a hemihedral form of the hexagonal pyramid: — *pl.* **rhombohē′dra, -hē′drons.** — *adj.* **rhomb′-boid** like a rhombus: nearly square, with the petiole at one of the acute angles (*bot.*). — *n.* a figure approaching a rhombus, a parallelogram, usu. one that is not a rhombus nor a rectangle. — *adj.* **rhomboid′al** more or less like a rhomboid. — *ns.* **rhomboi′dēs** (*crystal.* or *obs.*) a rhomboid; **rhom′bos** a bull-roarer: — *pl.* **rhom′-boi; rhom′bus** a rhomb (*geom.*): an object shaped like a rhomb: — *pl.* **rhom′bī, rhom′buses.** [Gr. *rhombos,* bull-roarer, magic wheel, rhombus.]

rhonchus *rong′kəs, n.* a bronchial sound, heard in auscultation: — *pl.* **rhonch′ī.** — *adjs.* **rhonch′al, rhonch′ial** of rhonchus: of snoring. [Latinised from Gr. *rhonchos,* wheezing.]

rhone. Same as **rone.**

rhopalic *rō-pal′ik, adj.* of a verse, having each word a syllable longer than the one before. — *n.* **rhō′palism.** [Gr. *rhopalikos,* club-like, *rhopalon,* a club.]

Rhopalocera *rō-pəl-os′ə-rə, n.pl.* butterflies, distinguished from moths. — *adjs.* **rhopaloc′eral, rhopaloc′erous.** [Gr. *rhopalon,* a club, *keras,* a horn.]

rhotacise, -ize *rō′tə-sīz, v.t.* and *v.i.* to change to an r-sound (esp. from *z*). — *n.* **rhō′tacism** excessive, exceptional, or exceptionable sounding of *r:* burring: a change or tendency to change to *r.* [Gr. *rhōtakizein* — *rhō,* the Greek R.]

rhotic *rō′tik,* (*phon.*) *adj.* r -pronouncing, i.e. denoting a dialect or accent, or speaking a dialect or with an accent, in which *r* is pronounced when it occurs before

---

rēweigh′ *v.t.*   rēwire′ *v.t.*   rēwrite′ *v.t.:* — *pa.t.* rēwrote′;
rēwind′ *v.t.:* — *pa.t.* and *pa.p.*   rēwork′ *v.t.*   *pa.p.* rēwritt′en.
rēwound′.   rēwrap′ *v.t.*   rē′write *n.*

fāte; fär; hûr; mīne; mōte; för; mūte; mōōn; fo͝ot; dhen (then); el′ə-mənt (element)

a consonant or before a pause. [Gr. *rhō*, the Greek R.]

Rh-positive. See rhesus.

rhubarb *rōō'bärb, -bərb, n.* any species of the genus *Rheum*, of the dock family: the root-stock, or a cathartic got from it (chiefly from *R. officinale*): the leaf-stalks (chiefly of *R. rhaponticum*) cooked and used as if fruit: a squabble, row, rumpus (*slang*): a word muttered repeatedly to give the impression of conversation inaudible to the audience (*theat.*): nonsense. — *adj.* **rhu'barby.** — **monk's rhubarb** patience dock. [O.Fr. *reubarbe* — L.L. *rheubarbarum*, for *rhābarbarum* — Gr. *rhā*, rhubarb — *Rhā*, the Volga, and L. *barbarum* (neut.) — Gr. *barbaron*, foreign; influenced by *rhēum*, Gr. *rhēon*.]

rhumb *rum, n.* a loxodromic curve: any point of the compass. — **rhumb'-line, -course, -sailing.** [Fr. *rumb*, or Sp. or Port. *rumbo* — L. *rhombus*; see **rhomb.**]

rhumba. Same as **rumba.**

Rhus *rus, n.* the sumach genus of the cashew-nut family: (without *cap.*) a plant of this genus. [L., — Gr. *rhous.*]

rhy (*Spens.*) for **rye**[1].

rhyme, rime *rīm, n.* in two (or more) words, identity of sound from the last stressed vowel to the end, the consonant or consonant group preceding not being the same in both (all) cases: extended to other correspondences in sound, as *head-rhyme* or alliteration, to inexact correspondences, as *eye-rhyme*, and to variations such as French, *rich rhyme*, or *rime riche* (where the consonants immediately preceding the stressed vowel are alike), *identical rhyme* (where like-sounding words of different meaning are used): a word or group of words agreeing in this way with another: versification, verses, a poem or a short piece of verse, in which this correspondence occurs at the ends of lines (or within the lines, in *internal rhyme*): a jingle. — *v.i.* to be in rhyme: to correspond in sound: to make or find a rhyme or rhymes: to harmonise: to chime: to make rhymes or verses. — *v.t.* to put into rhyme: to compose in rhyme: to use or treat as a rhyme. — *adjs.* **rhymed, rimed** (*rīmd*) in rhyme; **rhyme'less.** — *ns.* **rhy'mer, ri'mer** a user of rhyme: a poet: an inferior poet: a minstrel; **rhyme'ster** a poetaster: a would-be poet; **rhym'ist** a versifier. — **rhyme'-letter** the alliterating letter; **rhyme'-roy'al** (app. a commendatory name) a seven-line stanza borrowed by Chaucer from the French — its formula, *ababbcc*; **rhyme'-scheme** the pattern of rhymes in a stanza, etc.; **rhyme'-word** a word used as a rhyme; **rhyming slang** a form of slang in which a word is replaced by another word, or part or all of a phrase, which rhymes with it. — **identical rhyme, rich rhyme** see **rhyme** above; **without rhyme or reason** without reasonable or sensible purpose or explanation (also in similar phrases, such as **neither rhyme nor reason**); **rhyme to death** to kill by incantations (as rats were supposed to be killed in Ireland): to pester with rhymes. [O.Fr. *rime* — L. *rhythmus* — Gr. *rhythmos*; see **rhythm**[2]; associated and confused with O.E. *rīm*, number.]

rhynch- *ringk-*, **rhyncho-** *ringk-ō*, in composition, snout. — *ns.pl.* **Rhynchobdell'ida** (Gr. *bdella*, leech) an order of leeches with proboscis but no jaw; **Rhynchocephalia** (*-si-fā'li-ə*; Gr. *kephalē*, head) a primitive order of reptiles extinct except for the New Zealand tuatara. — *n.* **rhynch'ocoel** (*-sēl*; Gr. *koilos*, hollow) the cavity in which the proboscis of a nemertine lies. — *adj.* **rhynch'odont** (Gr. *odous, odontos*, tooth) with toothed beak. — *n.* **Rhynchonell'a** a genus of hinged brachiopods with prominent beak. — *n.pl.* **Rhynchoph'ora** (Gr. *pherein*, to bear) a group of beetles with snouts — the weevils. — *adj.* **rhynchoph'orous** of the Rhynchophora: snouted. — *n.pl.* **Rhynchō'ta** the Hemiptera. [Gr. *rhynchos*, a snout.]

rhyne. See rhine.

Rhyniaceae *rī-ni-ā'si-ē, n.pl.* a family of very simple land plants (Psilophytales) found as Old Red Sandstone

fossils at *Rhynie* in Grampian Region, Scotland.

rhyolite *rī'ō-līt, n.* an acid igneous rock with a glassy or cryptocrystalline groundmass and generally phenocrysts of quartz and alkali-feldspar — called also *liparite*. — *adj.* **rhyolitic** (*-lit'ik*). [Irregularly — Gr. *rhyax, -ākos*, a (lava) stream, *lithos*, a stone.]

rhyparography *rip-ə-rog'rə-fi, n.* genre or still-life pictures, esp. of sordid subjects. — *n.* **rhyparog'rapher.** — *adj.* **rhyparographic** (*-graf'ik*). [Gr. *rhyparos*, dirty, *graphein*, to write.]

rhythm[1] *rīm,* an obs. spelling of **rhyme.**

rhythm[2] *ridhm,* or *rithm, n.* regular recurrence, esp. of stress or of long and short sounds: a pattern of recurrence: an ability to sing, move, etc. rhythmically. — *adjs.* **rhyth'mal; rhythmed** (*ridhmd, rithmd*), **rhyth'-mic, -al.** — *n.* **rhyth'mic** (also **rhyth'mics** *n.sing.*) the science or theory of rhythm. — *adv.* **rhyth'mically.** — *n.* **rhythmic'ity.** — *v.t.* **rhyth'mise, -ize** to subject to rhythm. — *v.i.* to act in or observe rhythm. — *n.* **rhyth'mist** one skilled in rhythm. — *adj.* **rhythm'less.** — *ns.* **rhythmom'eter** a kind of metronome; **rhyth-mopoeia** (*-ō-pē'yə*; Gr. *poieein*, to make) the art of composing rhythmically; **rhyth'mus** rhythm. — **rhythm method** a method of birth control requiring the avoidance of sexual intercourse during the period in which conception is most likely to occur; **rhythm section** in a band, those instruments whose main function is to supply the rhythm (usu. percussion, guitar, double-bass and piano): the players of such instruments. — **rhythm and blues** a type of music combining the styles of rock and roll and the blues. [L. *rhythmus* — Gr. *rhythmos* — *rheein*, to flow; cf. **rhyme.**]

rhytidectomy *rī-ti-dek'tə-mi, n.* an operation for smoothing the skin of the face by removing wrinkles, a face-lift. [Gr. *rhytis*, a wrinkle, *ektomē*, cutting out.]

Rhytina *ri-tī'nə, n.* a recently extinct genus of Sirenia — Steller's sea-cow: (without *cap.*) an aquatic mammal of this genus. [Gr. *rhytis*, a wrinkle.]

Rhytisma *rit-iz'mə, n.* a genus of fungi that cause black spots on maple leaves. [Gr. *rhytisma*, a patch or darn.]

rhyton *rī'ton, n.* a drinking-cup or pottery horn (Greek, etc.) with a hole in the point to drink by: — *pl.* **rhy'ta.** [Gr. *rhyton*, neut. of *rhytos*, flowing.]

ria *rē'ə*, (*geol.*) *n.* a normal drowned valley. [Sp. *ría*, river-mouth.]

rial[1] *rī'əl.* Same as **ryal.**

rial[2] *rē'əl, rī'əl, rē-äl', n.* the unit of currency in Iran, Oman and (also **riyal**, q.v.) Saudi Arabia and the Yemen Arab Republic. [Pers. *rial*, Ar. *riyal*; see **riyal.**]

Rialto *rē-al'tō, n.* a district and island of Venice, with a famous bridge over the Grand Canal. [It., contracted from *rivo alto*, deep channel, or possibly *rialzato*, raised.]

riant *rī'ənt, adj.* laughing: gay. — *n.* **ri'ancy.** [Fr., pr.p. of *rire* — L. *rīdēre*, to laugh.]

riata. See reata.

rib[1] *rib, n.* one of the bones that curve round and forward from the backbone: a wife (from Gen. ii. 21–23; *facet.*): a piece of meat containing one or more ribs: a curved member of the side of a ship running from keel to deck: a strengthening bar: a rodlike structure supporting or strengthening a membrane, as one of the greater veins of a leaf, a nervure in an insect's wing, a member supporting the fabric of an aeroplane wing or of an umbrella: a bar of a grate (*Scot.*): the shaft of a feather: one of the parallel supports of a bridge: the side of a guitar, violin, etc: a framing timber: a purlin: a raised band: a prominence running in a line: a ridge: a ridge raised in knitting, by alternating plain and purl stitches, or a similar ridge raised in weaving: the pattern of ribs so formed (also **ribbing**): a moulding or projecting band on a ceiling. — *v.t.* to furnish, form, cover, or enclose with ribs: to plough with spaces between the furrows (**rib'-plough**): — *pr.p.* **ribb'ing;** *pa.t.* and *pa.p.* **ribbed.** — *adj.* **ribbed** having ribs: ridged. — *n.* **ribb'ing**

an arrangement of ribs. — *adjs.* **rib′y**; **rib′less**. — *n.* **rib′let** a small or narrow or shallow rib. — *adj.* **rib′like**. — **rib′-bone** a rib; **rib′cage** the enclosing wall of the chest formed by the ribs, etc.; **rib′-grass** the ribwort plantain. — *v.t.* **rib′-roast** (*obs.*) to beat soundly. — **rib′-roaster** (*arch.*) a severe blow on the ribs; **rib= roast′ing** (*arch.*). — *adj.* **rib′-tickling** very funny, inclining one to laugh uproariously. — **rib′-vaulting**; **rib′work**; **rib′wort** (or **ribwort plantain**) a common weed (*Plantago lanceolata*) with narrow strongly ribbed leaves and short brown heads. — **false rib** one joined indirectly to the breast-bone or (**floating rib**) not at all; **true rib** one joined directly by its cartilage. [O.E. *ribb*, rib, *ribbe*, ribwort; Ger. *Rippe*, rib.]

rib² *rib*, (*slang*) *v.t.* to tease, ridicule, make fun of. [Perh. **rib**¹ — the tickling of one's ribs causing laughter.]

ribald *rib′əld*, *n.* a menial of the lowest grade (*obs.*): a loose, low character (*obs.*): an obscene speaker or writer. — *adj.* low, base, mean: licentious: foulmouthed or coarse: sometimes loosely, jeering, floutingly derisive. — Also **rib′aud**, **ryb′auld** (*Spens.*). — *n.* **rib′aldry** obscenity: coarse jesting. — Also **rib′audry** (*obs.*), **rybaudrye** (*Spens.*) (*-ŏd-ri*). — *adj.* **rib′audred** (*Shak.*, *Ant. and Cleo.*) an obscure word, perh. for *ribaud-rid*, ridden by a ribald, or for *ribaldried*, composed of ribaldry. [O.Fr. *ribald, ribaut* (Fr. *ribaud*); origin uncertain.]

riband, ribband *rib′ən*(*d*), spellings of **ribbon**, used also in derivatives and compounds (e.g. **blue riband**, q.v.), now rare except in heraldic and sporting use.

ribattuta *rē-bät-tōō′tä*, (*mus.*) *n.* the slow beginning of a trill. [It.]

ribaud, ribaudred. See **ribald**.

ribband. Same as **riband**, **ribbon**.

ribble-rabble *rib′l-rab′l*, *n.* a mob: gabble. [**rabble**.]

ribbon *rib′ən*, *n.* material woven in narrow bands or strips: a strip of such or other material: anything resembling such a strip, as a road, a stripe of colour: a torn strip, tatter, shred: a watch-spring: an endless saw: a mollusc's radula: a strip of inking cloth, as for a typewriter: a diminutive of the bend, one-eighth of its width (*her.*): (in *pl.*) driving reins. — *adj.* made of ribbon: like a ribbon: having bands of different colours. — *v.t.* to adorn with ribbons: to stripe: to streak. — *n.* **Ribb′-onism** an Irish secret society movement, at its height about 1835–55, opp. to the Orangemen, named from its badge, a green ribbon. — *adj.* **ribb′ony.** — *n.* **ribb′onry** ribbons collectively. — **ribb′on-building, -development** unplanned building, growth of towns, in long strips along the main roads; **ribb′on-fish** a long, slender, laterally compressed fish of the family Trachypteridae, esp. the oarfish; **ribb′on-grass** gardener's garters, a striped canary-grass; **Ribb′on-man** a member of the Ribbonism movement; **ribbon microphone** a microphone in which the sound is picked up by a thin metallic strip; **ribb′on-seal** a banded North Pacific seal; **ribb′on-weed** sugar-wrack; **ribb′on-worm** a nemertine. [O.Fr. *riban*; origin obscure.]

Ribes *rī′bēz*, *n.* the black and red currant genus of the saxifrage family (generally including gooseberry), in some classifications giving name to a separate family **Ribēsiā′ceae**. [L.L. *ribes* — Ar. *rībās*, sorrel.]

ribibe *rib′ib*, *rib-īb′*, (*obs.*) *n.* a rebeck: an old crone. — *n.* **ribible** (*ri-bib′l*, *ri-bī′bl*) a rebeck. [See **rebeck**.]

ribose *rī′bōs*, *n.* a pentose, $C_5H_{10}O_5$. — *ns.* **riboflavin** (*rī-bō-flā′vin*; L. *flāvus*, yellow) a member of vitamin B complex, in yellowish-brown crystals, promoting growth in children; **ribonuclease** (*rī-bō-nū′kli-ās, -āz*) an enzyme in the pancreas, etc., the first enzyme to be synthesised (1969); **ribonū′cleotide** a nucleotide containing ribose. — *adj.* **ribosō′mal.** — *n.* **ribosome** (*rī′bō-sōm*) one of numerous particles in a cell on which proteins are assembled. — **ribonucleic acids** (*rī′bō-nū-klē′ik*) nucleic acids containing ribose, present in living cells, where they play an important part in the development of proteins. — abbrev. **RNA.** [From **arabinose**, by transposition of letters.]

ribston(e) *rib′stən*, *n.* (in full **Ribston pippin**) a variety of winter apple brought from Normandy to *Ribston Hall* in Yorkshire.

Ricardian *ri-kär′di-ən*, *adj.* pertaining to David *Ricardo* (1772–1823), or his economic teaching. — *n.* a follower of Ricardo.

Riccia *rik′si-ə*, *n.* a genus of liverworts. [From the Italian botanist P. Francisco *Ricci*.]

rice¹ *rīs*, *n.* a grass (*Oryza sativa*) grown in warm climates: its grain, a valuable food. — *v.t.* (esp. *U.S.*) to form soft food, esp. cooked potatoes, into strands by passing through a ricer, sieve, etc. — *n.* **rīc′er** (esp. *U.S.*) a kitchen utensil used for ricing food. — *adj.* **rice′y, ri′cy.** — **rice′-beer** a fermented drink made from rice; **rice′-bird** the bobolink (as a feeder on true rice or so-called wild rice): the paddy bird or Java sparrow; **rice′-bis′cuit** a sweet biscuit made of flour mixed with rice; **rice′-field**; **rice′-flour**; **rice′-glue** a cement made by boiling rice-flour in soft water; **rice′-grain** a marking like a grain of rice on the sun's photosphere: a decoration in pottery made by pressing rice or other seeds into the clay before firing; **rice′-grass** cord-grass; **rice′-milk** milk boiled and thickened with rice; **rice= paper** sliced and flattened pith of an Asiatic tree of the Araliaceae: a similar material made from other plants, or from linen trimmings; **rice′-pol′ishings** the parts rubbed off in milling rice; **rice′-pudd′ing**; **rice′-soup**; **rice′-wa′ter** an invalid's drink of water in which rice has been boiled: a cholera patient's evacuation, of similar appearance. — **Canada, Indian, water,** or **wild rice** *Zizania*. [O.Fr. *ris* — L. *oryza* — Gr. *oryza*, a word of Eastern origin.]

rice² *rīs*, (*obs.* except *dial.*) *n.* twigs or small branches collectively, brushwood: a twig or small branch. — Also **reis.** [O.E. *hrīs*; Ger. *Reis*.]

ricercar *rē-chər-kär′*, **ricercare** *-kä′rā*, **ricercata** *-kä′tä* (*mus.*) *ns.* a contrapuntal forerunner of the fugue: later, a very elaborate form of fugue. [It., — *ricercare*, to seek again with effort.]

rich *rich*, *adj.* abounding in possessions: wealthy: fortunate in having any good thing: abundantly furnished: having any ingredient or quality in great abundance: productive: fertile: deep in colour: full-toned: fullflavoured: abounding in fat, sugar, fruit, or seasonings: full: splendid and costly: sumptuous: elaborately decorated: ample: pregnant with matter for laughter. — *v.t.* (*Shak.*) to enrich. — *v.i.* (*obs.*) to grow rich. — **-rich** in composition, abundantly furnished with a specified thing, as *oil-rich*. — *v.t.* and *v.i.* **rich′en** to make or become richer. — *adv.* **rich′ly.** — *n.* **rich′ness.** — *adj.* **rich′-left** (*Shak.*) left heir to much wealth. [O.E. *rīce*, great, powerful; Ger. *reich*, Du. *rijk*, Goth. *reiks*; perh. reinforced by Fr. *riche*, rich.]

Richardia *ri-chär′di-ə*, *n.* an older name for *Zantedeschia*. [From the French botanists L. C. M. *Richard* (1754–1821) and his son.]

riches *rich′iz*, *n.* (now usu. treated as *pl.*) wealth — (*Spens.*) **rich′esse.** [O.Fr. *richesse* — *riche*, rich.]

richt *rihht*, Scots form of **right**.

Richter scale *rihht′ər skäl*, a seismological scale of measurement. [From its inventor, Dr Charles F. *Richter* (born 1900).]

ricin *rī′sin*, *ris′*, *n.* a highly toxic albumin found in the beans of the castor-oil plant. [See **Ricinus**.]

Ricinulei *ris-i-nū′li-ī*, *n.pl.* the Podogona, a rare order of blind arachnids with male organs on the third leg. [L. *rīcīnus*, a tick.]

Ricinus *ris′i-nəs*, *n.* a genus of one species (*Ricinus communis*, castor-oil plant) of the spurge family. — *adj.* **ricinole′ic** (or *-ŏ′lē-ik*) pertaining to castor-oil, as **ricinoleic acid** ($C_{18}H_{34}O_3$), an oily acid got from castoroil. [L. *ricinus*, the castor-oil plant.]

rick¹ *rik*, *n.* a stack: a heap. — *v.t.* to stack. — *n.* **rick′er** an implement for shocking hay. — **rick′-barton** a stack-yard; **rick′burner** an incendiary who fired stacks; **rick′-lifter**; **rick′stand** a flooring for a stack; **rick′stick** a toothed stick for combing thatch on a stack; **rick′-**

yard. [O.E. *hrēac*; O.N. *hraukr*.]
rick² *rik*, *v.t.* to sprain or strain. — *n.* a sprain or strain. [App. a variant of **wrick**.]
ricker *rik'ər, n.* a spar or young tree-trunk. [Perh. Ger. *Rick*, pole.]
rickets *rik'its, n.sing.* a disease of children, characterised by softness of the bones caused by deficiency of vitamin D. — *adv.* **rick'etily** shakily. — *n.* **rick'etiness** unsteadiness. — *adj.* **rick'ety** (formerly, and still by some, **rick'etty**) affected with rickets: feeble, unstable: tottery, threatening to collapse. [First recorded in S.W. England in the 17th cent., perh. M.E. *wrikken*, to twist; or Gr. *rhachitis* (see **rachitis**).]
Rickettsia *rik-et'si-ə, n.* a genus of micro-organisms found in lice and ticks and, when transferred to man by a bite, causing typhus and other serious diseases (fam. **Rickettsia'ceae** (*-ā'si-ē*); order **Rickettsia'les** (*-ā'lēz*)): (without *cap.*) a member of the genus Rickettsia or the family Rickettsiaceae (also **Rickettsia body**): — *pl.* **rickett'siae** (*-ē*), **-as.** — *adj.* **rickett'sial.** [After Howard Taylor *Ricketts* (1871–1910), American pathologist.]
rickle *rik'l, (Scot.) n.* a loose heap: a rickety or ramshackle structure or collection. — *adj.* **rick'ly.** [Poss. Scand.; connection with **rick¹** very doubtful.]
rick-rack, ric-rac *rik'rak, n.* a decorative braid in even zigzag form, or openwork made with it. [**rack¹**.]
ricksha, rickshaw *rik'shä, -shö, ns.* a small two-wheeled, hooded carriage drawn by a man or men, or powered by a man on a bicycle (also **bicycle ricksha(w)**) or motor-bicycle (also **auto ricksha(w)**). — Also **jinrick'sha, jinrick'shaw, jinrik'isha.** [Jap. *jin*, man, *riki*, power, *sha*, carriage.]
ricochet *rik-ō-shā', -shet',* or *rik', n.* a glancing rebound or skip, as of a projectile flying low. — *v.i.* to glance: to skip along the ground: — *pr.p.* **ricocheting** (*-shā'ing, rik'*), **ricochetting** (*-shet'ing, rik'*); *pa.t.* and *pa.p.* **ricocheted** (*-shād', rik'*), **ricochetted** (*-shet'id, rik'*). [Fr.]
ricotta *ri-kot'ə, n.* a type of soft Italian cottage cheese, often used in ravioli, lasagne, etc. [It. — L. *recocta*, fem. *pa.p.* of *recoquĕre*, to cook again.]
ric-rac. See **rick-rack.**
rictus *rik'təs, n.* the gape, esp. of a bird: the chink or aperture of a lipped corolla: unnatural gaping of the mouth, e.g. in horror. — *adj.* **ric'tal** of the gape: at the corners of the mouth. [L. *rictus, -ūs*.]
rid¹ *rid, v.t.* to free: to deliver: to clear: to disencumber: to expel: to remove, as by banishment, or by murder, make away with (*obs.*): — *pr.p.* **ridd'ing**; *pa.t.* and *pa.p.* **rid** or **ridd'ed.** — *ns.* **ridd'ance** clearance: removal: disencumberment: deliverance: a thing that one is well rid of: — **a good riddance** a welcome relief; **get rid of** to disencumber oneself of; **rid way** (*Shak.*) to cover ground, make progress. [O.N. *rythja*, to clear; with senses converging upon **redd¹**.]
rid², **ridden.** See **ride.**
riddle¹ *rid'l, n.* an obscure description of something which the hearer is asked to name: a puzzling question: anything puzzling. — *v.t.* to solve: to puzzle. — *v.i.* to make riddles: to speak obscurely. — *ns.* **ridd'ler; ridd'ling** propounding of riddles: speaking in riddles. — *adj.* enigmatic, obscure, puzzling: speaking in riddles: explaining riddles. — *adv.* **ridd'lingly.** — *adj.* and *adv.* **riddl'e-like** (*Shak.*). — **ridd'le-me-ree'** a fanciful modification of *riddle me a riddle*, or *riddle my riddle*, hence, *n.* a rigmarole. [O.E. *rǣdelse* — *rǣdan*, to guess, to read — *rǣd*, counsel; cog. with Du. *raad*, Ger. *Rat*.]
riddle² *rid'l, n.* a large coarse sieve. — *v.t.* to separate with a riddle: to make full of holes like a riddle, as with shot. — *v.i.* to use a riddle: to sift. — *ns.* **ridd'ler; ridd'ling.** — *n.pl.* **ridd'lings** the less desirable part, whether finer or coarser, separated by riddling and usu. rejected: refuse. [O.E. *hriddel*, earlier *hridder*.]
ride *rīd, v.i.* to travel or be borne on the back of an animal, on a bicycle, or in a public vehicle, sometimes, and commonly in U.S., in any vehicle or (*U.S.*) boat, also

on a broomstick, the waves, the whirlwind, etc.: to float or seem to float buoyantly: to go on horseback on a raid, in procession, across a ford: to serve as a cavalryman: to lie at anchor: to sit or move as if on horseback: to turn, rest, or grate upon something: to work up out of position: to admit of riding: to weigh when mounted: to copulate (*vulg.*). — *v.t.* to traverse, trace, ford, or perform on horseback, on a bicycle, etc.: to sit on: to bestride: to sit on and control: to travel on: to control at will, or oppressively: to oppress, domineer over, badger, annoy: to improvise on (a theme) (*jazz*): to rest or turn on: to overlap: to mount upon: to sustain, come through, esp. while riding at anchor (also *fig.*): to give a ride to, or cause to ride: to convey by vehicle (*U.S.*): to copulate with (esp. of a male; *vulg.*): — *pa.t.* **rōde,** *arch.* **rid,** *Scot.* **raid, rade;** *pa.p.* **ridd'en,** *arch.* **rid, rode.** — *n.* a journey on horseback, on a bicycle, or in a vehicle: a spell of riding: an act of riding with particular regard to the rider's, driver's, etc. degree of comfort or discomfort, etc.: a road for horse-riding, esp. one through a wood: an excise officer's district: an act of copulation (*vulg.*): a partner (esp. female) in copulation (*vulg.*). — *n.* **ridabil'ity** fitness for riding or driving, or for riding or driving along or across. — *adj.* **rī'dable, ride'able.** — **-ridden** in composition, oppressed by the dominance or prevalence of a specified thing (e.g. **hag-ridden, cliché-ridden**). — *n.* **rī'der** one who rides or can ride: a commercial traveller (*obs.*): a moss-trooper: an object that rests on or astride of another, as a piece of wire on a balance for fine weighing: an added clause or corollary: a proposition that a pupil or candidate is asked to deduce from another: a gold coin bearing a mounted figure (Du. and Flem. *rijder*). — *adjs.* **rī'dered; rī'derless.** — *n.* **rī'ding** the action of the verb ride: a track, esp. a woodland track, for riding on: an excise-officer's district: anchorage. — Also *adj.* — **rī'ding-boot** a high boot worn in riding. — *n.pl.* **rī'ding-breeches** breeches for riding, with loose-fitting thighs and tight-fitting legs. — **rī'ding-cloak; rī'ding-clothes; rī'ding-coat** a coat of a style worn by riders; **rī'ding-committ'ee** a committee of ministers sent by the General Assembly to carry out an ordination or induction, where the local presbytery refused to act, under the 18th-cent. Moderate domination in Scotland; **rī'ding-crop; rī'ding-glove; rī'ding-habit** a woman's dress for riding, esp. one with a long skirt for riding side-saddle; **rī'ding-hood** a hood formerly worn by women when riding; **rī'ding-horse; rī'ding-in'terest** (*Scots law*) an interest depending on other interests; **rī'ding-light** a light hung out in the rigging at night when a vessel is riding at anchor; **rī'ding-master** a teacher of riding; **rī'ding-rhyme** the heroic couplet, perh. from Chaucer's use of it in the *Canterbury Tales*; **rī'ding-robe** a riding-habit; **rī'ding-rod** a light cane for equestrians; **rī'ding-school; rī'ding-skirt; rī'ding-suit; rī'ding-whip.** — **let (something) ride** to let (something) alone, not try to stop it; **ride a hobby** see **hobby¹**; **ride and tie** to ride and go on foot alternately, each tying up the horse, or leaving the bicycle by the roadside, and walking on — also *n., adv., v.i.* **ride'-and-tie'**; **ride down** to overtake by riding: to charge and overthrow or trample; **ride for a fall** to court disaster; **ride herd on** (*orig. U.S.*) to guard (a herd of cattle, etc.) by riding on its perimeter: to control, keep watch on (*fig.*); **ride out** to keep afloat throughout (a storm): to cut out from a herd by riding: to survive, get safely through or past (a period of difficulty, etc.); **ride to hounds** to take part in fox-hunting; **ride up** to work up out of position; **riding the fair** the ceremony of opening a fair by a procession; **take for a ride** to give (someone) a lift in a car with the object of murdering him in some remote place: to play a trick on, dupe. [O.E. *rīdan*; Du. *rijden*, Ger. *reiten*.]
rident *rī'dənt, adj.* laughing or beamingly smiling. [L. *rīdens, -entis*, pr.p. of *rīdēre*, to laugh.]
ridge *rij, n.* the back (*obs.*): the earth thrown up by the

plough between the furrows: a strip of arable land, usu. between furrows: a rib on a stocking, etc.: a long narrow top or crest: the horizontal line of a roof-top: a narrow elevation: a hill-range. — *v.t.* and *v.i.* to form into ridges: to wrinkle. — *adj.* **ridged** having ridges. — *n.* **ridg'ing** the forming of ridges: covering with ridge-tiles. — *adj.* **ridg'y** having ridges. — **ridge'back** Rhodesian ridgeback (q.v.); **ridge'-bone** the spine; **ridge'piece**, **ridge'-pole** the timber forming the ridge of a roof; **ridge'-rope** the central rope of an awning; **ridge'tile** a tile that bestrides the ridge of a roof; **ridge'way** a track along a hill-crest. [O.E. *hrycg*; O.N. *hryggr*, Ger. *Rücken*, back.]

ridgel, **ridgil** *rij'əl*, *n.* a male animal with but one testicle in position or remaining. — Also **ridgling** (*rij'ling*), **rig** (*rig*). — Northern forms **rigg'ald**, **rig'ling**, **rig'lin** (*rig'*). [App. from preceding, from the undescended testicle near the back.]

ridicule[1] *rid'i-kūl*, *n.* absurdity (*rare*): derision: mockery. — *v.t.* to laugh at: to expose to merriment: to deride: to mock. — *n.* **rid'iculer**. — *adj.* **ridic'ulous** deserving or exciting ridicule: absurd. — *adv.* **ridic'ulously**. — *n.* **ridic'ulousness**. [L. *rīdiculus* — *rīdēre*, to laugh.]

ridicule[2] *rid'i-kūl*, *n.* for **reticule**.

Riding *rī'ding*, *n.* one of the three former divisions of Yorkshire: extended to divisions elsewhere. [For *thriding* — O.N. *thrithi*, third.]

riding. See **ride**.

ridotto *ri-dot'ō*, *n.* a public dancing-party: — *pl.* **ridott'os**. [It.]

riebeckite *rē'bek-īt*, *n.* a monoclinic amphibole, silicate of sodium and iron. [Named after the German traveller Emil *Riebeck* (1853–85).]

riel *rē'əl*, *n.* the basic monetary unit of Kampuchea.

riem *rēm*, *n.* a raw-hide thong. — *n.* **riempie** (*rēm'pē*; dim. of *riem*) a long riem about the width of a shoe-lace, used as string, for the weaving of chair-backs and seats, etc. [Afrik.]

Riemannian *rē-man'i-ən*, *adj.* pertaining to the German mathematician Georg Friedrich Bernhard *Riemann* (1826–66), or to his work or concepts, especially to **Riemannian geometry**, the geometry of **Riemannian space**. (With certain nouns the adjective used is **Riemann**, as **Riemann surface**, **Riemann integral**.)

riempie. See **riem**.

Riesling *rēz'ling*, *n.* a dry white table wine, named from a type of grape. [Ger.]

rieve, **riever**. Same as **reave**, **reaver**.

rifacimento *rē-fä-chi-men'tō*, *n.* a recasting of a literary or musical work: — *pl.* **-ti** (*-tē*). [It.]

rife *rīf*, *adj.* prevalent: abounding: current. — Also *adv.* — *adv.* **rife'ly**. — *n.* **rife'ness**. [O.E. *rȳfe*, *rīfe*; Du. *rijf*. O.N. *rīfr*.]

riff *rif*, (*jazz*) *n.* a phrase or figure played repeatedly. [Perh. *refrain*.]

riffle[1] *rif'l*, *n.* a shallow section in a river where the water flows swiftly (*U.S.*). — *v.t.* to form a riffle: to turn or stir lightly and rapidly (as the pages of a book), often in cursory search for something: to treat thus the pages of (a book) (with *through*): to shuffle by allowing the corner of a card from one part of the pack to fall alternately with that of a card in the other. — Also *v.i.* [Cf. **ripple**[1].]

riffle[2] *rif'l*, *n.* (e.g. in gold-washing) a groove or slat in a sluice to catch free particles of ore. [Cf. **rifle**[2].]

riffler *rif'lər*, *n.* a small file with curved ends used by sculptors, wood- or metal-workers, etc., for intricate work. [Fr. *rifloir*, from *rifler*, to scrape, file.]

riff-raff *rif'-raf*, *n.* the scum of the people: rubbish. — *adj.* rubbishy. [M.E. *rif and raf* — O.Fr. *rif et raf*.]

rifle[1] *rī'fl*, *v.t.* to plunder: to ransack: to disarray: (of a hawk) to seize only the feathers of: to injure. — *n.* **rī'fler**. [O.Fr. *rifler*.]

rifle[2] *rī'fl*, *v.t.* to groove spirally: (also *v.i.*) to shoot with a rifle. — *n.* a firearm with a spirally grooved barrel. — *n.* **rī'fling** the spiral grooving of a gun-bore. — **ri'fle-bird**, **ri'fleman-bird** an Australian bird of par-

adise: a New Zealand bushwren; **ri'fle-corps** a body of soldiers armed with rifles; **ri'fle-green** a dark green, the colour of a rifleman's uniform (also *adj.*); **ri'fle=grenade'** a grenade or bomb fired from a rifle; **ri'fleman** a soldier armed with a rifle: a rifle-bird; **ri'fle-pit** a pit to shelter riflemen; **ri'fle-range** the range of a rifle: a place for rifle practice; **ri'fle-shot**. [O.Fr. *rifler*, to scratch; cf. Ger. *riefeln*, and preceding word.]

rift[1] *rift*, *n.* a cleft: a fissure: a chink: a riven fragment (*Spens.*). — *v.t.* and *v.i.* to cleave, split. — *adjs.* **rift'less**; **rift'y**. — **rift valley** a valley formed by subsidence of a portion of the earth's crust between two faults. — **Rift Valley fever** an infectious disease of cattle and sheep in Africa, to which man is also susceptible, characterised by high fever and hepatitis, and caused by a virus probably transmitted by mosquitoes. [Cf. Dan. and Norw. *rift*, a cleft.]

rift[2] *rift*, (*Scot.*) *v.i.* to belch. — Also *n.* [O.N *ryfta*.]

rifte *rift*, (*Spens.*) *pa.p.* of **rive**.

rig[1] *rig*, *v.t.* to fit with sails and tackling (*naut.*): to fit up or fit out: to equip: to set up, set in working order: to dress, clothe (now *coll.*): — *pr.p.* **rigg'ing**; *pa.t.* and *pa.p.* **rigged**. — *n.* the form and arrangement of masts, sails, and tackling: an outfit: garb: general appearance: a driving turnout (*U.S.*): an articulated lorry (*coll.*): a well-boring plant, an oil-rig. — **-rigged** with masts and sails arranged in the manner indicated. — *n.* **rigg'er** one who rigs ships: one who puts together and attends to the rigging of aircraft: one who puts up and looks after the scaffolding, lifting apparatus, etc., that is used for building operations: outrigger: in machinery, a narrow drum. — **-rigger** in composition, a ship rigged in manner indicated. — *n.* **rigg'ing** tackle: the system of cordage which supports a ship's masts and extends the sails: the system of wires and cords in an aircraft. — **rigg'ing-loft** a long workshop where rigging is fitted: the place in a theatre from which the scenery is manipulated; **rig'-out** an outfit. — **rig out** to furnish with complete dress, etc; **rig up** to dress or equip: to put up quickly from available, rather inadequate, materials. [Origin obscure; perh. conn. with Norw. *rigga*, to bind.]

rig[2] *rig*, *n.* the Northern form of **ridge**. — *ns.* **rigg'ing** the roof; **rigg'ing-tree** a roof-tree.

rig[3] *rig*, *n.* a frolic, prank, trick. — *v.t.* to manipulate unscrupulously or dishonestly: to set up fraudulently. — *n.* **rigg'ing** manipulating unscrupulously or dishonestly, as in **price-rigging**. — **run a rig** to play a prank. [Origin obscure.]

rig[4] *rig*, *n.* a wanton. — *v.i.* to wanton: to romp. — *adj.* **rigg'ish** (*Shak.*) wanton. [Origin obscure.]

rig[5]. See **ridgel**.

rigadoon *rig-ə-dōōn'*, *n.* a lively jig-like dance for one couple, or its music. [Fr. *rigaudon*.]

Rigel *rī'gəl*, *-jəl*, *n.* a first-magnitude star in the foot of Orion. [Ar. *rijl*, foot.]

rigg *rig*, *n.* the dogfish. [Ety. unknown.]

riggald. See **ridgel**.

right[1] *rīt*, *adj.* straight: direct: perpendicular: forming one-fourth of a revolution: with axis perpendicular to base: true: genuine: veritable: characteristic: truly judged or judging: appropriate: in accordance, or identical, with what is true and fitting: not mistaken: accurate: fit: sound: intended to be exposed (as a side, e.g. of cloth): morally justifiable or incumbent: just: in accordance with what should be: equitable: justly to be preferred or commended: at or towards that side at which in a majority of people is the better-developed hand (of a river, as referred to one going downstream: on the stage, from the point of view of an actor looking at the audience): for a part of the body, etc. on the right side: sitting at the president's right hand (in Continental assemblies): hence, conservative or inclined towards conservatism, right-wing. — *adv.* straight: straightway: quite: just, exactly: in a right manner: justly: correctly: very (*arch.* and *dial.* or in special phrases): to or on the right side. — *n.* that which is right or correct: rightness: fair treatment: equity: truth: justice: just or legal claim: what one has a just claim to: due: (in *pl.*) a stag's brow, bez, and trez antlers (*arch.*): territory (*Spens.*): the right hand: the right side: a glove, shoe, etc., for the right hand, foot, etc.: the region on the right side: the right wing: the conservatives. — *v.t.* to set right: to set in order: to rectify: to redress: to vindicate: to do justice to: to avenge: to set right side up or erect. — *v.i.* to recover an erect position. — *interj.* expressing agreement, acquiescence, or readiness. — *adj.* **right'able** capable of being righted. — *v.t.* **right'en** to set right. — *n.* **right'er** one who sets right or redresses wrong. — *adj.* **right'ful** having a just claim: according to justice: belonging by right. — *adv.* **right'fully.** — *ns.* **right'fulness** righteousness: justice; **right'ing; right'ist** an adherent of the political right (conservatives). — Also *adj.* — *adj.* **right'less** without rights. — *adv.* **right'ly.** — *n.* **right'ness.** — *interj.* **righto'** (*pl.* **rightos'**), **right-oh'** (*coll.*) expressing acquiescence. — *adj.* and *adv.* **right'-ward** towards the right: more right-wing. — Also *n.* (*rare*). — *adv.* **right'wards.** — **right'-about'** the directly opposite quarter (in drill or dismissal; also **right-about face**). — *adv.* to the right-about (face). — *v.i.* to turn right-about (face). — *adj.* **right'-and-left'** having a right and a left side, part, etc.: bilaterally symmetrical: on both sides: from both barrels. — *n.* a shot or a blow from each barrel or hand. — *adv.* on both sides: on all hands: towards one side, then the other: in all directions. — *adj.* **right-ang'led** having a **right angle**, one equal to a fourth of a revolution. — **right ascension** see **ascension.** — *adj.* **right'-bank** on the right bank. — *adj.* and *adv.* **right'-down** out-and-out. — *adjs.* **right'-drawn** (*Shak.*) drawn in a just cause; **right'-hand** at the right side: towards the right: performed with the right hand: with thread or strands turning to the right: chiefly relied on (as *one's right-hand man*); **right'-hand'ed** using the right hand more easily than the left: with or for the right hand: with rotation towards the right, or clockwise. — *adv.* towards the right. — **right'-hand'edness; right'-hand'er** a blow with the right hand: a right-handed person. — *n.* and *adj.* **Right Honourable** a title of distinction given to peers below the rank of marquis, to privy councillors, to present and past cabinet ministers, to certain Lord Mayors and Lord Provosts, etc. — *adjs.* **right'-lined** rectilinear; **right'-mind'ed** having a mind disposed towards what is right, just, or according to good sense: sane. — **right'-mind'edness; right'-of-way'** a track over which there is a **right of way** (see below): the strip of land occupied by a railway track, a road, etc. (*U.S.*): — *pl.* **right'-of-ways'** or **rights'-of-way'.** — *n.* and *adj.* **Right Reverend** see **reverend.** — **rights issue** (*commerce*) an issue of new shares which shareholders of a company may buy, usu. below the market price, in proportion to their current holdings. — *adj.* **right'-think'ing** of approved opinions. — **right whale** a whale of the typical genus Balaena, esp. the Greenland whale; **right wing** the political right: the wing on the right side of an army, football pitch, etc. — *adj.* **right'-wing** of or on the right wing: pertaining to the political right: (having opinions which are) conservative, opposed to socialism, etc. — **right'-wing'er** a player on the right wing: a person with right-wing views or who supports the right wing of a party, etc. — **all right** see **all; bill of rights** (often *caps.*) an accepted statement of the rights and privileges of the people or of individuals, which the government or state must not infringe (e.g. that embodied in the Bill of Rights, 1689, or in the U.S. Constitution); **by rights** (formerly **right**) rightfully: if all were right; **civil rights** see **civil; do someone right** to do someone justice: to keep pace with someone in drinking: to drink someone's health; **have a right, no right** to be entitled or not entitled: to be under a moral obligation, no obligation (*illit.* or *dial.*); **have right** (*arch.*) to be right; **in one's own right** by absolute and personal right, not through another; **in one's right**

mind quite sane; **in right of** by virtue of: by title vested in; **in the right** right: maintaining a justifiable position; **put, set, to rights** to set in order; **right as a trivet, as rain** see **trivet, rain**[1]; **right away** straightway: without delay; **right down** plainly; **right, left and centre** same as **left, right and centre; right of common** (*law*) a right to take something from, or pasture animals on, the land of another; **right of entry** a legal right to enter a place; **right off** without delay; **right of way** the right of the public to pass over a piece of ground (see also **right-of-way** above); **right on** (*U.S.*) an exclamation expressing enthusiastic agreement or approval; **right out** (*Shak.*) outright; **right the helm** to put it amidships, in a line with the keel; **send**, etc., **to the right-about** (*coll.*) to dismiss summarily, or force to retreat; **she'll be right** (*Austr.*) an expression of assurance or confidence. [O.E. *riht* (n. and adj.), *rihte* (adv.), *rihten* (vb.); cf. Ger. *recht* and L. *rēctus*, straight, right.]

right² (*Shak.*, Milt.) for **rite.**

righteous *rī'chəs, adj.* just, upright. — *adv.* **right'eously.** — *n.* **right'eousness** rectitude: a righteous act. [O.E. *rihtwīs* — *riht*, right, *wīs*, wise, prudent, or *wīse*, wise, manner.]

rigid *rij'id, adj.* stiff: unbending: unyielding: rigorous: strict: of an airship, having a rigid structure to maintain shape: of a truck or lorry, not articulated. — *n.* a rigid person or airship. — *v.t.* and *v.i.* **rigid'ify** to make or become rigid: — *pr.p.* **rigid'ifying;** *pa.t.* and *pa.p.* **rigid'ified.** — *v.t.* **rig'idise, -ize** to rigidify. — *n.* **rigid'ity.** — *adv.* **rig'idly.** — *n.* **rig'idness.** [L. *rigidus* — *rigēre*, to be stiff.]

Rigil *rī'gəl, -jəl, rij'il, n.* a first-magnitude double star in the foot of the Centaur, usu. known as Alpha Centauri. [Cf. **Rigel.**]

riglin, rigling. See **ridgel.**

rigmarole *rig'mə-rōl, n.* a long rambling discourse: a long, complicated series of actions, instructions, etc., often rather pointless, boring or irritating. — *adj.* prolix and incoherent. [**Ragman Roll.**]

rigol, rigoll *rig'əl, n.* a gutter or water-channel: a groove, esp. an encircling groove: a circlet (*Shak.*). [Fr. *rigole*, gutter, groove.]

rigor *rī'gör, rig'ör, n.* a sense of chilliness with contraction of the skin, a preliminary symptom of many diseases (*med.*): failure to react to stimulus, under unfavourable conditions (*bot.*); a rigid irresponsive state caused by a sudden shock, as when an animal is said to sham dead (*zool.*): (*rig'ər*) another, chiefly American, spelling of **rigour.** — *ns.* **rigorism** (*rig'ər-izm*) extreme strictness: the doctrine that in doubtful cases the strict course should be followed; **rig'orist.** — *adj.* **rig'orous** rigidly strict or scrupulous: exact: unsparing: severe: harsh, violent (*Spens.*). — *adv.* **rig'orously.** — *ns.* **rig'orousness; rigour** (*rig'ər*) stiffness: hardness: rigor: severity: unswerving enforcement of law, rule, or principle: strict exactitude: austerity: extreme strictness: severity of weather or climate. — **rigor mortis** (*mör'tis, mor'*) (L.) stiffening of the body after death. [L. *rigor* — *rigēre*, to be stiff.]

Rigsdag *rigz'däg, rēgz'däg, n.* the former parliament of Denmark, replaced in 1953 by the Folketing. [Dan., — *rige*, a kingdom, and *dag*, a day, diet.]

Rigveda *rig-vä'də, -vē', n.* the first of the four Vedas. [Sans. *ric*, a hymn, *veda*, knowledge.]

rigwiddie, rigwoodie *rig-wid'i, -wûd'i, -wud'i,* or *rig',* (*Scot.*) *ns.* a cart-horse's back-band. — *adj.* lean and tough: stubborn: a vague word of reproach, with a suggestion of the *widdy*, or halter. [**rig², widdy** = **withy.**]

rijst(t)afel, reistafel *rīs'tä-fəl, n.* an Indonesian rice dish served with a variety of foods. [Du. *rijst*, rice, *tafel*, table.]

Riksdag *riks'dag, n.* the parliament of Sweden. [Sw. — *rike*, a kingdom, and *dag*, a day, diet.]

rile *rīl, v.t.* a form of **roil**, now the usual form of the verb when used meaning to annoy or irritate. — *adj.* **riley** (*rī'li*) a form of **roily.**

Riley *rī'li*: the life of **Riley** see **life**.
rilievo. See **relievo**.
rill *ril, n.* a very small brook: a runnel: a small trench: a narrow furrow on the moon or Mars (also **rille** from Ger. *Rille*). — *v.i.* to flow in a rill or rills. — *n.* **rill'et** a little rill. — **rill'mark** (*geol.*) a marking produced by water trickling down a beach or bank. [Cf. Du. *ril*, Ger. (orig. L.G.) *Rille*, channel, furrow.]
rillettes *ri-yet', n.pl.* a French type of potted meat made by simmering shreds of lean and fat pork, etc. till crisp, and pounding them to form a paste. [Fr.]
rim[1] *rim, n.* the outermost circular part of a wheel, not including the tire: an edge, border, brim, or margin, esp. when raised or more or less circular: an encircling band, mark, or line. — *v.t.* to form or furnish a rim to: — *pr.p.* **rimm'ing**; *pa.t.* and *pa.p.* **rimmed**. — *adjs.* **rim'less**; **rimmed**. — **rim'-brake** a brake acting on the rim of a wheel. [O.E. *rima* (found in compounds).]
rim[2] *rim, n.* a membrane: the peritoneum. [O.E. *rēoma*; cf. **riem**.]
rima *rī'mə, rē'mə, n.* a chink: *esp.* the gap between vocal cords and arytaenoid cartilages: — *pl.* **rimae** (*rī'mē, rē'mī*). — *n.* **rime** (*rīm; obs.*) chink, fissure. — *adjs.* **rī'mose** (or *-mos'*), **rī'mous** full of chinks: covered with cracks. [L. *rīma*.]
rime[1] *rīm, n.* hoar-frost or frozen dew: ice deposited by freezing of supercooled fog (*meteor.*). — *v.t.* to cover with rime. — *adj.* **rī'my**. [O.E. *hrīm*; Du. *rijm*, Ger. *Reif*.]
rime[2], **rimer**, etc. Same as **ream**[3], **reamer**, **rhyme**, **rhymer**, etc.
rime riche *rēm rēsh*, (Fr.) lit. rich rhyme (q.v. at **rhyme**); **rime suffisante** (*sü-fē-zãt*) lit. sufficient rhyme, corresponding to ordinary rhyme in English.
rimu *rē'mōō, n.* a coniferous tree of New Zealand, *Dacrydium cupressinum*. [Maori.]
rin *rin*, a Scots form of **run**.
rind[1] *rīnd, n.* bark: peel: crust: outside. — *v.t.* to bark. — *adjs.* **rīnd'ed**; **rīnd'less**; **rīnd'y**. [O.E. *rinde*; Du. *rinde*, Ger. *Rinde*.]
rind[2], **rynd** *rīnd, n.* a fitting that supports an upper millstone, cross-shaped with expanded ends. [Cf. M.Du. *rijn*, M.L.G. *rîn*.]
rinderpest *rin'dər-pest, n.* a malignant and contagious disease of cattle. [Ger., cattle-plague.]
rine *rīn*, (*Spens.*, etc.) *n.* Same as **rind**[1].
rinforzando *rin-för-tsan'dō*, (*mus.*) *adj.* with sudden accent. [It., reinforcing.]
ring[1] *ring, n.* a circlet or small hoop, esp. one of metal, worn on the finger, in the ear, nose, or elsewhere: any object, mark, arrangement, group, or course of like form: an encircling band: a rim: a short cylinder for holding a table-napkin: a link of chain-mail: an encircling cut in bark: a zone of wood added in a season's growth, as seen in sections: a mark of fungus growth in turf (**fairy ring**): a flat crowd of very small satellites encircling Saturn: an annulus: a segment of a worm, caterpillar, etc.: a closed chain of atoms: a system of elements in which addition is associative and commutative and multiplication is associative and distributive with respect to addition (*math.*): a circular ripple: a circular earthwork or rampart: an arena: a space set apart for boxing, wrestling, circus performance, riding display of animals, or the like: an enclosure for bookmakers: pugilism: prize-fighters or bookmakers with their associates collectively: a combination or clique, esp. organised to control the market or for other self-seeking purpose: a system operated by some antique dealers who refrain from bidding against each other at an auction, so that one of their number may buy cheaply, and then share the profit made by subsequent resale: a computer system suitable for local-network use, with several microcomputers or peripheral devices connected by cable in a ring. — *v.t.* to encircle: to put a ring on or in: to put on in the manner of a ring: to cut a ring in the bark of: to cut into rings: to go in rings round: to excel, be the quickest

sheep-shearer in (*Austr.*). — *v.i.* to move in rings: to gather or be in a ring: — *pa.t.* and *pa.p.* **ringed;** formerly sometimes, and still in sheep-shearing competitions, **rung**. — *adj.* **ringed** surrounded by, or marked with, a ring or rings: ring-shaped: composed of rings: of a car, put together from parts of other cars (*slang*). — *n.* **ringer** (*ring'ər*) one who rings: a throw of a quoit that encircles the pin: a quoit so thrown: a person or thing of the highest excellence: the quickest, most expert of a group of shearers (*Austr.*). — *n.* and *adj.* **ring'ing**. — *adj.* **ring'less**. — *n.* **ring'let** a little ring: a fairy ring: a fairy dance in a ring: a long curl of hair. — *adj.* **ring'leted**. — *n.* **ring'ster** a member of a ring, esp. in a political or price-fixing sense. — *adv.* **ring'wise**. — **ring'-ar'mature** one with a ring-shaped core. — *v.t.* **ring'-bark** to strip a ring of bark from. — **ring'bit** a horse's bit with rings at the ends; **ring'-bolt** a bolt with a ring through a hole at one end; **ring'bone** a bony callus on a horse's pastern-bone: the condition caused by this; **ring'-canal** a circular canal within the rim of a jellyfish: a circular vessel of the water-vascular system of echinoderms; **ring'-carrier** (*Shak.*) a go-between; **ring circuit** (*elect.*) an electrical supply system in which a number of power-points are connected to the main supply by a series of wires, forming a closed circuit; **ring'-compound** a chemical compound with a closed chain; **ring'-cross** a circle with crossed diameters; **ring'-dance** a round dance; **ring'-dial** a portable sundial; **ring'-dott'erel** the ringed plover; **ring'-dove** the wood-pigeon, from the broken white ring or line on its neck; **ring'-dropping** a sharper's trick of pretending to find a dropped ring and selling it; **ring'-dyke** (*geol.*) a dyke with more or less circular outcrop; **ring'-fence** a fence continuously encircling an estate: a complete barrier: the compulsory separation, for tax purposes, of a company's business interests in North Sea oil from their other business interests, to prevent them from paying less tax on their oil profits by setting against these profits any losses made in other businesses. — *v.t.* to shut off completely. — **ring'-finger** the third finger, esp. of the left hand, on which the wedding-ring is worn; **ring fort** (*archaeol.*) a type of defended dwelling-site of the Iron Age and later, enclosed within a strong circular wall; **ring'-gauge** a gauge in the form of a ring: either a collection of graded rings or a graduated stick for measuring ring- or finger-size; **ring'leader** one who takes the lead in mischief; **ring main** (*elect.*) an electrical supply system in which the power-points and the mains are connected in a ring circuit; **ring'man** the third finger of the hand (*obs.* or *dial.*): a bookmaker; **ring'-master** one who has charge of performances in a circus-ring; **ring'-money** money in the form of rings. — *adj.* **ring'-necked** (*-nekt*) having the neck marked with a ring. — **ring'-ou'zel, -ou'sel** see **ouzel**; **ring'-plov'er** a ring-necked plover of various kinds. — *adj.* **ring'-porous** having annual rings marked by large pores. — **ring pull** the tongue of metal and the ring attached to it, which one pulls from the top of a can of beer, lemonade, etc. to open it; **ring'-road** a road or boulevard encircling a town or its inner part; **ring roller** a type of roller consisting of a number of closely packed wheels on an axle, the rims of the wheels narrowing to form a wedge shape (also **Cambridge roller**); **ring rot** a disease of potatoes caused by the bacterium *Corynebacterium sepedonicum*, characterised by the browning and decay of the ring of vascular bundles in the tubers; **ring'-shake** a defect in timber, separation along the annual rings; **ring'side** the side of the prize-ring; **ring'sider** one who attends prize-fights. — *adj.* **ring'-small** small enough to pass through a ring of standard size. — *n.* stones of such a size. — **ring'-snake** a common English snake, the grass-snake (also **ringed snake**): a harmless American snake with yellow collar; **ring'stand** a stand for chemical vessels, with rings clamped to a vertical rod: a stand for finger-rings; **ring'-stopper** a rope for securing an anchor-ring to the cat-head. — *adjs.* **ring'-straked**

(B.), **-streaked** streaked in rings. — **ring'-tail** a studding-sail set upon the gaff of a fore-and-aft sail (*naut.*): a light sail set abaft and beyond the spanker (*naut.*): the female or young male of the hen-harrier, from a rust-coloured ring on the tail-feathers: (without *hyphen*) a ringtailed cat (see **cacomistle**). — *adjs.* **ring'-tail, -tailed** (*-tāld*) having the tail marked with bars or rings of colour, as a lemur: having a prehensile tail curled at the end, as certain species of opossum. — **ring'-taw** a game of marbles, with rings marked on the ground; **ring'-time** (*Shak.*) time for giving rings; **ring'-walk** an encircling walk; **ring'-wall** an enclosing wall; **ring'way** a ring-road; **ring'-winding** winding that threads a ring. — **ring'work** work executed in rings; **ring'worm** a skin disease characterised by ring-shaped patches, caused by fungi. — **a ringside seat, view** (*fig.*) (a position which allows one to have) a very clear view; **hold, keep, the ring** to watch a fight and keep others from interfering; **ride, or tilt, at the ring** to practise the sport of riding rapidly and catching a hanging ring on a spear; **ring the shed** (*Austr.*) to win a sheep-shearing competition; **make, run, rings round** to be markedly superior to; **throw one's hat into the ring** (*coll.*) to offer oneself as a candidate or challenger: to issue a challenge, institute an attack.   [O.E. *hring*; O.N. *hringr*; Ger. *Ring*, Dan. and Sw. *ring*.]

ring² *ring, v.i.* to give a metallic or bell-like sound: to sound aloud and clearly: to give a characteristic or particular sound: to resound, re-echo: to be filled with sound, or a sensation like sound, or report, or renown: to cause a bell or bells to sound, esp. as a summons or signal. — *v.t.* to cause to give a metallic or bell-like sound: to sound in the manner of a bell: to summon, usher, announce by a bell or bells: to call on the telephone: to re-echo, resound, proclaim: — *pa.t.* **rang,** now rarely **rung,** *obs.* **rong;** *pa.p.* **rung.** — *n.* a sounding of a bell: the characteristic sound or tone, as of a bell or a metal, or of a voice: a ringing sound: a set of bells. — *n.* **ring'er** one who, or that which, rings: a horse raced under the name of another horse, or an athlete or other contestant competing under a false name or otherwise disguised (esp. *U.S.*): an outsider, an impostor (*U.S. slang*): (also **dead ringer**) a person or thing (almost) identical to some other person or thing (with *for*; *coll.*). — *n.* and *adj.* **ring'ing.** — *adv.* **ring'ingly.** — **ring a bell** to begin to arouse a memory; **ring back** to telephone (a previous caller) in response to his call: to follow up a telephone call with a second one; **ring down or up (the curtain)** to give the signal for lowering or raising it; **ring in** to ring more rapidly before stopping, as a final intimation to lingering church-goers; **ring in, out** to usher in, out (esp. the year) with bell-ringing; **ring off** to put an end to a telephone conversation by replacing the receiver; **ring out** to sound loudly, clearly, and suddenly; **ring the bell** to achieve a great success (from the bell of a shooting-gallery bull's-eye); **ring the bells backward** to reverse the order of chimes; **ring true** to sound genuine (like a tested coin); **ring up** to summon by bell, esp. to the telephone.   [O.E. *hringan*; O.N. *hringja*; Ger. *ringen*; Dan. *ringe*.]

ring³ *ring, n.* and *v.i.* an obs. Scots form of **reign:** — *pa.t.* **rang.**

Ringelmann chart *ring'l-man chärt,* a chart giving a scale of shades of grey against which density of smoke may be gauged.   [After the deviser.]

ringent *rin'jənt, adj.* gaping.   [L. *ringēns, -entis,* pr.p. of *ringī.*]

ringgit *ring'git, n.* the unit of currency of Malaysia, comprising 100 sen.   [Malay.]

ringhals *ring'hals,* **rinkhals** *ringk'(h)als, ns.* a Southern African snake, *Haemachatus haemachatus,* which spits or sprays its venom at its victims.   [Afrik. *ring,* a ring, *hals,* a neck.]

rink *ringk, n.* a course for tilting or racing: a portion of a bowling-green, curling-pond, etc., allotted to one set of players: a division of a side playing on such a portion: a piece of ice prepared for skating: a building or floor for roller-skating or ice-skating. — *v.i.* to skate on a rink.   [Orig. Scots; origin obscure.]

rinky-dink *ring-'ki-dingk,* (*U.S. slang*) *n.* something oldfashioned: something old and run down or worn out: something trite or trivial. — Also *adj.*

rinse *rins, v.t.* to wash lightly by pouring, shaking, or dipping: to wash in clean water to remove soap traces. — *n.* an act of rinsing: liquid used for rinsing: a solution used in hair-dressing, esp. one to tint the hair slightly and impermanently. — *adj.* **rins'able, rins'ible.** — *ns.* **rins'er; rins'ing.** — *n.pl.* **rins'ings** liquid in which something has been rinsed.   [O.Fr. *rinser* (Fr. *rincer*).]

rinthereout *rin'dhə-rōōt,* (*Scot.*) *n.* and *adj.* vagrant: vagabond.   [**run thereout.**]

Rioja *rē-ō'hhä, n.* a red or white Spanish table wine.   [From La *Rioja,* a region in northern Spain.]

riot *rī'ət, n.* wild revelry: debauchery: loose living: unrestrained squandering or indulgence: tumult: a great, usu. boisterous, success: a disturbance of the peace by a crowd (legally three or more): of colour, a striking display. — *v.i.* to take part or indulge in riot: to revel. — *ns.* **rī'oter; rī'oting; rī'otise** (*-is, -ēz, -īz*), **-ize** (*-īz*) (*obs.*) riot, extravagance. — *adj.* **rī'otous.** — *adv.* **rī'otously.** — *ns.* **rī'otousness; rī'otry.** — **Riot Act** a statute designed to prevent riotous assemblies: a form of words read as a warning to rioters to disperse; **riot agent** a chemical substance such as tear-gas used to control or disperse rioters; **riot police** police specially equipped with shields, tear-gas grenades, etc. for dealing with rioting crowds. — **read the riot act** (*fig.*) to give vehement warning that something must cease; **run riot** to act or grow without restraint.   [O.Fr. *riot, riotte.*]

rip¹ *rip, v.t.* to slash or tear open, apart, off, or out: to make by such an action: to reopen (with *up*): to cleave or saw with the grain: to strip (as a roof): to utter explosively (with *out*). — *v.i.* to part in rents: to break out violently: to rush, go forward unrestrainedly: — *pr.p.* **ripp'ing;** *pa.t.* and *pa.p.* **ripped,** or (*arch.*) **ript.** — *n.* a rent: an unchecked rush. — **ripp'er** one who rips: a tool for ripping: a person or thing especially admirable (*slang*). — *adj.* **ripp'ing** (*slang*) excellent. — Also *adv.* — *adv.* **ripp'ingly.** — **rip'-cord** a cord for opening a balloon's gas-bag or enabling a parachute to open; **rip'-off** (*slang*) (financial) exploitation: a theft, stealing, cheating, etc.: a film, etc. that exploits the success of another by imitating it; **ripp'ing-saw, rip'-saw** a saw for cutting along the grain. — *adj.* **rip'-roaring** wild and noisy. — **rip'snorter** (*slang*) a fast and furious affair, or person: a gale. — *adj.* **rip'snorting.** — **let rip** to express oneself, or to act, violently or with abandon: to increase speed in greatly: (**let it rip**) to refrain from trying to check an action or process; **rip off** (*slang*) to steal: to steal from: to exploit, cheat, overcharge, etc.   [Uncertain; cf. Fris. *rippe,* Flem. *rippen,* Norw. *rippa.*]

rip² *rip,* (*dial.*) *n.* a wicker basket: a coop. — *ns.* **ripp'er, ripp'ier** (*obs.*) one who carries fish inland to sell.   [O.N. *hrip,* basket.]

rip³ *rip, n.* an inferior horse: a disreputable person.   [Poss. **reprobate.**]

rip⁴ *rip, n.* stretch of broken water: disturbed state of the sea. — *n.* **rip'tide** tidal rip.   [Perh. **rip¹.**]

rip⁵, ripp *rip,* (*Scot.*) *n.* a handful, esp. a plucked handful, of grass or corn.   [Poss. **rip¹;** connection with **reap** involves difficulty.]

riparian *rī-pā'ri-ən, adj.* of or inhabiting a river-bank. — *n.* an owner of land bordering a river. — *adj.* **ripā'rial.**   [L. *rīpārius* — *rīpa,* a river-bank.]

ripe¹ *rīp, adj.* ready for harvest: arrived at perfection: fit for use: fully developed: finished: ready for a particular purpose or action: resembling ripe fruit: mature: (of cheese) mature, strong-smelling: (of language, etc.) somewhat indecent or over-colourfully expressive: rich and strong in quality. — *v.t.* and *v.i.* to ripen. — *adv.* **ripe'ly.** — *v.t.* and *v.i.* **rī'pen** to make or grow ripe or riper. — *n.* **ripe'ness.**   [O.E. *rīpe,* ripe, *rīpian,* to ripen;

conn. with *rīp*, harvest, and perh. **reap;** cf. Du. *rijp*, Ger. *reif*.]

ripe² *rīp*, (*Scot.*) *v.t.* and *v.i.* to grope, search, ransack. — *n.* **rī'per.** [O.E. *rȳpan*, to rob.]

ripeck. See **ryepeck.**

ripidolite *rip-id'ō-līt*, or *rīp-, n.* clinochlore. [Gr. *rhīpis, -idos*, fan.]

ripieno *ri-pyā'nō*, (*mus.*) *adj.* supplementary. — *n.* a supplementary instrument or performer: — *pl.* **ripie'-nos, ripie'ni** (*-nē*). — *n.* **ripie'nist** a supplementary instrumentalist. [It.]

riposte *ri-post', -pōst', n.* a quick return thrust after a parry: a repartee. — *v.t.* and *v.i.* to answer with a riposte. [Fr., — It. *risposta*, reply.]

ripp, ripper, rippier, ripping. See **rip** (various).

ripple¹ *rip'l, n.* light fretting of the surface of a liquid: a little wave: a similar appearance in anything: small periodic variations in a steady current or voltage (*electronics*): a sound as of rippling water: (in *pl.*) repercussions, reverberations. — *v.t.* to ruffle the surface of: to mark with ripples. — *v.i.* to move or run in ripples: to sound like ripples. — *n.* **ripp'let** a small ripple. — *n.* and *adj.* **ripp'ling.** — *adv.* **ripp'lingly.** — *adj.* **ripp'ly.** — **ripp'le-mark** an undulatory ridging produced in sediments by waves, currents, and wind, often preserved in sedimentary rocks. — *adj.* **ripp'le-marked.** [Origin obscure.]

ripple² *rip'l, n.* a toothed implement for removing seeds, etc., from flax or hemp. — *v.t.* to clear of seeds by drawing through a ripple: to remove by a ripple. — *n.* **ripp'ler.** [Cf. L.G. and Du. *repel*, a ripple, hoe, Ger. *Riffel*.]

Rippon *rip'ən*, (*obs.*; in full **Rippon spur**) *n.* a spur made at *Ripon*, once famous for the manufacture.

rip-rap, riprap *rip'rap, n.* loose broken stones, used to form a foundation on soft ground or under water, or in the construction of revetments and embankments: a foundation formed of these. [From an obs. word imit. of the sound of repeated blows.]

Ripstone pippin (*Dickens*) for **Ribstone pippin.**

ript. Same as **ripped** (see **rip¹**).

Ripuarian *rip-ū-ā'ri-ən, adj.* applied to the Franks on the lower Rhine and their laws. — *n.* a Ripuarian Frank. [Generally said to be from L. *rīpa*, a river-bank.]

Rip Van Winkle *rip van wing'kl*, one very much behind the times, as was a character of that name in a story by Washington Irving; according to the story he returned home after having slept in the mountains for twenty years.

risaldar *ris-äl-där', n.* the commander of a troop of Indian cavalry. [Hind. *risāldār*.]

rise *rīz, v.i.* to get up: to become erect, stand up: to come back to life: to become hostile: to revolt (often with *up*): to close a session: to break up camp: to raise a siege: to move upward: to come up to the surface: to fly up from the ground: to come above the horizon: to grow upward: to advance in rank, fortune, etc.: to swell: to increase: to increase in price: to become more acute in pitch: to be excited: to be cheered: to come into view, notice, or consciousness: to spring up: to take origin: to have source: to come into being: to extend upward: to tower: to slope up: to come to hand, chance to come: to respond as to provocation, or to a situation calling forth one's powers: to excavate upward: to feel nausea (also *fig.*). — *v.t.* to cause to rise: to surmount (*U.S.*): to raise, view better by nearing (*naut.*): — *pa.t.* **rose** (*rōz*), Scot. **raise, rase** (*rāz*), *U.S. dial.* **riz;** *pa.p.* **risen** (*riz'n*), *U.S. dial.* **riz.** — *n.* rising: ascent: a coming up to the surface, as of a fish: the sport of making a butt of someone by deception: increase in height: vertical difference or amount of elevation or rising: increase of salary, price, etc.: an upward slope: a sharpening of pitch: origin: occasion: the riser of a step: a shaft excavated from below. — *ns.* **rīs'er** one who rises, esp. from bed: that which rises: the upright portion of a step; a vertical pipe, e.g. in a building or an oil-rig: **rīs'ing** the action

or process of the verb in any sense: a revolt: a prominence: a swelling: a hill. — *adj.* and *pr.p.* ascending: increasing: coming above the horizon: advancing: growing up: approaching the age of: quite as much as (*U.S.*). — **give rise to** to cause, bring about; **on the rise** in process of rising, esp. in price; **rise and shine** a facetiously cheerful invitation or instruction to get out of bed briskly, esp. in the morning; **rise from the ranks** to work one's way up from private soldier to commissioned officer: to become a self-made man; **rise to it, the bait** (*fig.*, from fishing) to take the lure; **rise to the occasion** to prove equal to an emergency; **take a rise out of** to lure into reacting to provocation, or loosely, to make sport of; **take rise** to originate; **the rise of** (*U.S.*) more than. [O.E. *rīsan;* O.N. *rīsa*, Goth. *reisan*, Ger. *reisen*.]

rishi *rish'i, n.* a sage or poet. [Sans.]

risible *riz'i-bl, adj.* able or inclined to laugh: of laughter: ludicrous. — *n.* **risibil'ity** laughter: inclination to laugh: faculty of laughter. [L. *rīsibilis* — *rīdēre, rīsum*, to laugh.]

risk, *also* (*obs.*) **risque,** *risk, n.* hazard, danger, chance of loss or injury: the degree of probability of loss: a person, thing, or factor likely to cause loss or danger. — *v.t.* to expose to hazard: to incur the chance of unfortunate consequences by (doing something). — *n.* **risk'er.** — *adj.* **risk'ful.** — *adv.* **risk'ily.** — *n.* **risk'iness.** — *adjs.* **risk'y** dangerous, liable to mischance: risqué (a Gallicism); **risqué** (*rēs'kā;* from the Fr. *pa.p.*) audaciously bordering on the unseemly. — **risk capital** see **venture capital** under **venture; risk'-money** allowance to a cashier to compensate for ordinary errors. — **at risk** in a situation or circumstances where loss, injury, physical abuse, etc., are possible; **run a risk** to be in, get into, a risky situation; **run a, the, risk of** to risk (failing, etc.). [Fr. *risque* — It. *risco;* origin uncertain.]

risoluto *rē-zō-lōō'tō, adj.* and *adv.* with resolution. [It.]

risorgimento *ri-sōr-ji-men'tō, n.* a revival, rebirth: (with *cap.*) the Renaissance: the liberation and unification of Italy in the 19th century: — *pl.* **risorgimen'tos.** [It., — L. *resurgĕre*, to rise again.]

risotto *ri-zot'ō, n.* a dish of rice cooked in stock with meat, onions and other vegetables, and cheese: — *pl.* **risott'os.** [It., — *riso*, rice.]

risp *risp*, (*Scot.*) *v.t.* to rasp: to grate. — *v.i.* to make a grating sound: to tirl. — *n.* a rasp or coarse file: a baker's grater: a roughened bar, on which a ring is grated, used instead of a knocker or door-bell: a grating sound. — *n.pl.* **risp'ings** portions risped off. [O.N. *rispa*, to scratch.]

rispetto *rēs-pet'ō, n.* a type of Italian folk-song with eight-line stanzas, or a piece of music written in the same style: — *pl.* **rispet'ti** (*-tē*). [It.]

risque, risqué. See **risk.**

Riss *ris, n.* the third stage of glaciation in the Alps. — *adjs.* **Riss, Riss'ian.** [From a tributary of the Danube in Württemberg.]

rissole *ris'ōl, rēs-ōl', n.* a fried ball or cake of minced food. [Fr.]

risus *rī'səs, rē'sŏŏs, n.* a laugh: a grin. — **risus sardonicus** (*sär-don'ik-əs, -ŏōs*) a sardonic grin, or drawing back of the corners of the mouth by spasm of the muscles, as in tetanus. [L. *rīsus, -ūs,* laugh.]

rit, ritt *rit*, (*Scot.*) *v.t.* to score: to scratch: to slit. — *n.* a scratch: a slit. [M.E. *ritten;* cf. Ger. *ritzen*.]

ritardando *rē-tär-dan'dō, adj.* and *adv.* with diminishing speed. — *n.* a ritardando passage: a slowing down: — *pl.* **ritardan'dos.** [It.]

rite *rīt, n.* a ceremonial form or observance, esp. religious: a liturgy. — *adj.* **rite'less.** — **rite of passage, passage rite, rite de passage** (*rēt də pas-äzh;* Fr.; *pl.* **rites de passage**) a term, first used by the French anthropologist Arnold van Gennep, for any of the ceremonies — such as those associated with birth, puberty, marriage, or death — which mark or ensure a person's transition from one status to another within his society. [L. *rītus*.]

ritenuto *rit-ə-nū'tō*, (*mus.*) *adj.* restrained — indicating a sudden slowing-down of tempo. — *n.* a ritenuto passage: — *pl.* **ritenū'tos.** [It., *pa.p.* of *ritenere*, to restrain, hold back.]

ritornello *rit-ör-nel'ō*, *n.* a short instrumental passage in a vocal work, e.g. a prelude or refrain: a passage for the whole orchestra in a concerto: — *pl.* **ritornel'li** (*-lē*), **ritornell'os.** — Also **ritornel'**, **-nell'**, **-nelle'**, **ritournelle'**. [It.]

ritt. See **rit.**

ritter *rit'ər*, *n.* a knight. — *n.* **ritt'-mas'ter** a captain of cavalry. [Ger. *Ritter*, *Rittmeister*.]

ritual *rit'ū-əl*, *adj.* relating to, or of the nature of, rites. — *n.* the manner of performing divine service, or a book containing it: a body or code of ceremonies: an often repeated series of actions: the performance of rites: ceremonial. — *n.* **ritualisā'tion, -z-.** — *v.i.* **rit'-ualise, -ize** to practise or turn to ritualism. — *v.t.* to make ritualistic. — *ns.* **rit'ualism** attachment of importance to ritual, esp. with the implication of undue importance; **rit'ualist** one skilled in or devoted to a ritual: one of the High Church party in the Church of England. — *adj.* **ritualist'ic.** — *adv.* **ritualist'ically.** — *adv.* **rit'ually.** — **ritual choir** part of a church used as a choir; **ritual murder** the killing of a human being as part of a tribal religious ceremony. [L. *rituālis* — *rītus*; see **rite**.]

ritzy *rit'zi*, (*slang*) *adj.* stylish, elegant, ostentatiously rich. [The *Ritz* hotels.]

riva *riv'ə*, *rēv'ə*, (*Shetland*) *n.* a cleft in rock. [O.N. *rīfa*.]

rivage *riv'ij*, *rīv'ij*, (*poet.*) *n.* a bank, shore. [Fr., — L. *rīpa*, a bank.]

rival *rī'vl*, *n.* one pursuing an object in competition with another: one who strives to equal or excel another: one for whom, or that for which, a claim to equality might be made: a partner, fellow (*Shak.*). — *adj.* standing in competition: of like pretensions or comparable claims. — *v.t.* to stand in competition with: to try to gain the same object against: to try to equal or excel: to be worthy of comparison with: — *pr.p.* **rī'valling;** *pa.t.* and *pa.p.* **rī'valled.** — *n.* **rī'valess** a female rival. — *v.i.* **rī'valise, -ize** to enter into rivalry. — *n.* **rī'vality** (*-val'i-ti*) rivalry: equality (*Shak.*). — *adj.* **rī'valless.** — *ns.* **rī'valry** the state of being a rival: competition: emulation: the feeling of a rival; **rī'valship** emulation. — *adj.* **ri'val-hating** (*Shak.*). [L. *rīvālis*, said to be from *rīvus*, river, as one who draws water from the same river.]

rive *rīv*, *v.t.* to tear asunder: to tear: to rend: to split: to discharge as if with rending (*Shak.*): to pierce (*obs.*): to plough up (*Scot.*). — *v.i.* to tug, tear: to split: — *pa.t.* **rīved** — *Scot.* **rave** (*rāv*); *pa.p.* **riven** (*riv'n*), **rived** (*rīvd*) — *Spens.* **rive** (*riv*) — *Keats* **raft.** [O.N. *rīfa*.]

rivel *riv'l*, *v.t.* and *v.i.* to wrinkle. — *adj.* **riv'elled.** [O.E. *rifelede*, rivelled.]

river *riv'ər*, *n.* a large stream of water flowing over the land: sometimes extended to a strait or inlet: a place for hawking (*arch.*): a stream in general. — *adj.* of a river or rivers: dwelling or found in or near a river or rivers. — *adj.* **riv'erain** (*-ān*) of a river or its neighbourhood. — *n.* a riverside dweller. — *adj.* **riv'ered** watered by rivers. — *n.* **riv'eret** (*arch.*) a small river. — *adjs.* **riv'erine** (*-īn, -ēn*) of, on, or dwelling in or near a river; **riv'erless; riv'erlike; riv'ery** of or like a river: well rivered. — **riv'er-bank; riv'er-basin** the whole region drained by a river with its affluents; **riv'er-bed** the channel in which a river flows; **river blindness** a West African disease, onchocerciasis (q.v.); **riv'er-boat** a boat with a flat bottom or shallow draft, for use on rivers; **riv'er-bottom** (*U.S.*) alluvial land along the margin of a river; **riv'er-craft** small vessels that ply on rivers; **riv'er-dragon** Pharaoh (*Milt.*, with ref. to Ezek. xxix. 3): a crocodile; **riv'er-drift** old alluvia of rivers; **riv'er-driver** (*U.S.*) one who conducts logs downstream; **riv'er-flat** a piece of alluvial land by a river;

riv'er-front land, quays, buildings, etc., facing a river; **riv'er-god** the tutelary deity of a river; **riv'er-head** the source of a river; **riv'er-hog** the capybara: an African wild pig; **riv'er-horse** the hippopotamus: the kelpie: a pole bestridden in a primitive method of crossing rivers (*S. Afr.*); **riv'er-jack** (or **river-jack viper**) a West African viper; **riv'erman** one who makes his livelihood on or along a river; **riv'er-mouth; riv'er-mussel** a freshwater mussel; **river novel** see **roman fleuve; riv'er-rat** a thief who prowls about a river; **riv'er-sand** sand from a river-bed; **riv'erscape** a picture of river scenery; **riv'erside** the bank or neighbourhood of a river. — *adj.* beside a river. — **riv'er-terr'ace** a terrace formed when a river eats away its old alluvium deposited when its flood-level was higher; **riv'er-tide** the current of a river: the tide from the sea rising or ebbing in a river; **riv'er-wall** a wall confining a river within bounds; **riv'er-water; riv'erway** a river as a waterway; **riv'erweed** Podostemon. [O.Fr. *rivere* (Fr. *rivière*) — L. *ripārius*, *adj.* — *rīpa*, bank; cf. It. *riviera*.]

rivet[1] *riv'it*, *n.* bearded wheat. [Origin obscure.]

rivet[2] *riv'it*, *n.* a bolt fastened by hammering the end. — *v.t.* to fasten with rivets: to fix immovably: to clinch or hammer out the end of: — *pr.p.* **riv'eting;** *pa.t.* and *pa.p.* **riv'eted** (formerly often **riv'etting, riv'etted**). — *ns.* **riv'eter** one who rivets: a machine for riveting; **riv'eting.** — **riv'et-head; riv'et-hearth** a forge for heating rivets; **riv'et-hole** a hole to receive a rivet. [O.Fr. *rivet* — *river*, to clinch; origin obscure.]

riviera *riv-i-ā'rə*, *n.* a warm coastal district reminiscent of the Riviera in France and Italy on the Mediterranean Sea.

rivière *rē-vyer*, *riv-i-er'*, *n.* a necklace of diamonds or other precious stones, usu. in several strings. [Fr., river.]

rivlin *riv'lin*, (*Scot.*) *n.* a shoe moulded from untanned hide, worn with the hair to the outside: (in *pl.*) tatters, rags. [O.E. *rifling*, O.N. *hriflinger*, hide shoe.]

rivo *rē'vō*, *rī'vō*, (*Shak.*) *interj.* a drinking-cry: — *pl.* **ri'vos.**

rivulet *riv'ū-lit*, *n.* a small river. [L. *rīvulus*, dim. of *rīvus*, a stream, perh. through It. *rivoletto* — *rivolo* — *rivo.*]

rix-dollar *riks'-dol-ər*, *n.* a silver coin, once current in various countries. [Obs. Du. *rijcksdaler* (Du. *rijks-daalder*) — Du. *rijk*, kingdom (O.E. *rīce*), *daler*, dollar.]

riyal *ri-yäl'*, *n.* the unit of currency in Dubai and Qatar, and (also spelt **rial**, q.v.) in Saudi Arabia and the Yemen Arab Republic. [Ar. — Sp. *real*; see **real**[3].]

riz *riz*, (*U.S. dial.*) *pa.t.* and *pa.p.* of **rise.**

rizard. See **rizzer**[2].

rizzer[1], **rizzar, rizzor** *riz'ər*, (*Scot.*) *v.t.* to dry, esp. in the sun. — *n.* a rizzered haddock. [Cf. obs. Fr. *ressorer*, to dry.]

rizzer[2], **rizzar, rizard, rizzart** *riz'ər(d)*, *-ərt*, (*Scot.*) *ns.* a red currant. [Earlier *razour*; origin unknown.]

roach[1] *rōch*, *n.* a silvery freshwater fish of the carp family, with pale red ventral and tail fins: applied to various American fishes. — **as sound as a roach** perfectly sound. [O.Fr. *roche*.]

roach[2] *rōch*, *n.* a concave curve in the foot of a square sail. — *v.t.* to arch: to cut short (as a horse's mane): to cut, or cut the hair or mane of, in an upright ridge. [Origin uncertain.]

roach[3] *rōch*, *n.* a cockroach (*U.S.*): (the butt of) a marijuana cigarette (*slang*; esp. *U.S.*).

road (*Shak., Spens.*, etc., **rode**) *rōd*, *n.* a ride, horseback journey (*Shak.*): a raid, incursion (*Shak., Spens.*): a track suitable for wheeled traffic, esp. for throug' communication (often in street-names): a highway' roadway: a way of approach: course: a mine-pass; (often in *pl.*) a roadstead: a railway (*U.S.*): journe' wayfaring, tour: dismissal (*coll.*): a prostitute (*S* — *n.* **road'ie** (*slang*) a member of the cre' transport, set up and dismantle equipment f' cians, esp. a pop group, on tour. — *adj.* **roa** *n.* **road'ster** a horse, cycle or car, suitable fo' use on the road: a coach-driver or other traveller by road. — **road′-agent** (*U.S.*) a highwayman; **road′-bed** the foundation of a railway track: the material laid down to form a road; **road′block** an obstruction set up across a road, e.g. to prevent the escape of a fugitive; **road′-book** a guide-book to the roads of a district. — *adj.* **road′-borne** carried by road. — **road′-bridge** a bridge carrying a road; **road′-craft** knowledge and skill useful to wayfarers and drivers; **road′-end** the place where a road branches off from another; **road′-hog** a swinishly selfish or boorishly reckless motorist or other user of the road. — Also *v.i.* — *adj.* **road′-hoggish.** — **road′holding** the extent to which a motor vehicle holds the road when in motion; **road′house** a roadside public-house, refreshment-room, or inn, catering for motorists, cyclists, etc.; **road hump** one of a series of low ridges built into a road surface to slow traffic down, a sleeping policeman; **road′-maker; road′-making; road′man** one who keeps a road in repair: one who uses the roads, an itinerant; **road′-map; road′-mender; road′-mending; road′-metal** broken stones for roads; **road′-metalling; road′-roller** a heavy roller used on roads; **road′-runner** the chaparral cock; **road′-scraper** an implement for clearing roads of loose material; **road′-sense** aptitude for doing the right thing in driving or road-using in general; **road′show** a touring group of theatrical or musical performers: (a live broadcast from one of a series of venues, presented by) a touring disc jockey and his retinue: a promotional tour undertaken by any body or organisation seeking publicity for its policies or products; their performances; **road′-side** the border of a road: wayside. — *adj.* by the side of a road. — **road sign** a sign along a road, motorway, etc. giving information on routes, speed limits, etc. to travellers; **roads′man** a driver: a roadman; **road′stead** a place near a shore where ships may ride at anchor; **road′-survey′or** one who supervises roads; **road′-train** in Australia, a number of linked trailers towed by a truck, for transporting cattle, etc.; **road′way** the way or part of a road or street used by horses and vehicles. — *n.pl.* **road works** the building or repairing of a road, or work involving the digging up, etc. of part of a road. — **road′worthiness.** — *adj.* **road′worthy** fit for the road. — **in, out of, the** (or **one's**) **road** (chiefly *Scot.*) in, out of, the way; **one for the road** a last alcoholic drink before setting off; **on the road** travelling, esp. as a commercial traveller or a tramp: on the way to some place; **road fund licence** a round certificate, usu. stuck on a vehicle's windscreen, showing that the vehicle excise duty (or *road fund licence fee*) payable on that vehicle has been paid; **road up** road surface being repaired; **rule of the road** see **rule**; **take the road** to set off, depart; **take to the road** to become a highwayman (*arch.*), or a tramp: to set off for, travel to, somewhere. [O.E. *rād*, a riding, raid; cf. **raid, ride.**]

roading. See **rode³**.

roadster, roadstead. See **road.**

roam *rōm, v.i.* to rove about: to ramble. — *v.t.* to wander over: to range. — *n.* a wandering: a ramble. — *n.* **roam′er.** [M.E. *romen*; origin obscure.]

roan¹ *rōn, adj.* bay or dark, with spots of grey and white: of a mixed colour, with a decided shade of red. — *n.* a roan colour: a roan animal, esp. a horse. [O.Fr. *roan* (Fr. *rouan*).]

roan² *rōn, n.* grained sheepskin leather. — *adj.* of roan. [Poss. *Roan*, early form of *Rouen*.]

roan³. Same as **rone.**

roar *rōr, rör, v.i.* to make a full, loud, hoarse, low-pitched sound, as a lion, fire, wind, the sea, cannon: to bellow: to bawl: to guffaw: to take in breath with a loud noise, as a diseased horse: to behave in a riotous, bullying, noisy manner (*obs.*): to rush forward with loud noise □m the engine. — *v.t.* to utter vociferously: to shout □ouragement, abuse, etc.): to encourage by shout-□esp. with *on*). — *n.* a sound of roaring. — *ns.* □r one who roars: a horse that roars as a result □se: a roaring boy (*obs.*); **roar′ing** the action of

the verb in any sense: a disease of horses marked by roaring. — *adj.* uttering or emitting roars: riotous: proceeding with very great activity or success. — *adv.* **roar′ingly.** — *adj.* **roary, -ie** (*Scot.*) noisy: garish, too bright. — **roaring boy** (*obs.*) a boisterous bullying reveller, swaggerer, or brawler; **roaring drunk** very drunk; **roaring forties** see **forty; the roaring game** curling. [O.E. *rārian*; but partly from M.Du. *roer*, stir, disturbance.]

roast *rōst, v.t.* to cook before a fire: to bake: to parch by heat: to heat strongly: to dissipate the volatile parts of (esp. sulphur) by heat: to criticise excessively, even sarcastically: to banter (*slang*). — *v.i.* to undergo roasting. — *adj.* roasted. — *n.* a joint, esp. of beef, roasted or to be roasted: an operation of roasting: banter (*slang*). — *n.* **roas′ter** apparatus for roasting: a pig, etc., suitable for roasting: a very hot day. — *n.* and *adj.* **roast′ing.** — **roast′-beef; roas′ting-jack** an apparatus for turning a joint in roasting; **roast′-meat.** — **cry roast-meat** to publish one's good luck foolishly; **roast-beef plant** the fetid iris (from its smell); **rule the roast** (mistakenly **roost**) to lord it, predominate. [O.Fr. *rostir* (Fr. *rôtir*), of Gmc. origin.]

roate. An old spelling (*Shak.*) of **rote¹**.

rob¹ *rob, v.t.* to deprive wrongfully and forcibly: to steal from: to plunder: to deprive: to take as plunder: to carry off. — *v.i.* to commit robbery: — *pr.p.* **robb′ing;** *pa.t.* and *pa.p.* **robbed.** — *ns.* **robb′er** one who robs; **robb′ery** theft from the person, aggravated by violence or intimidation: plundering. — **robb′er-crab** a large coconut-eating land-crab of the Indian Ocean: a hermit-crab; **robb′er-fly** any fly of the Asilidae, large, bristly, insect-eating flies. — **daylight robbery** glaring extortion; **Robber Council** or **Synod** a council held at Ephesus in 449, afterwards repudiated, which reinstated Eutyches (from the violence of its proceedings); **rob Peter to pay Paul** to deprive one person in order to satisfy another. [O.Fr. *rober*, of Gmc. origin; cf. **reave,** O.H.G. *roubōn*, Ger. *rauben.*]

rob² *rob, n.* a fruit syrup. [Ar. *robb.*]

robalo *rob′ə-lō, n.* an American pike-like fish (*Centropomus*), of a family akin to the sea-perches: — *pl.* **rob′alos.** [Sp. *róbalo*, bass.]

robe¹ *rōb, n.* a gown or loose outer garment: a gown or dress of office, dignity, or state: a rich dress: a woman's dress: a dressing-gown: (in *pl.*) clothes, garb: a dressed bison hide, or the like. — *v.t.* to dress: to invest in robes. — *v.i.* to assume official vestments. — *n.* **rob′ing** the putting on of robes or clothes: apparel: a trimming on a robe. — **robe-de-chambre** (*rob-də-shā-br′*; *Fr.*) a dressing-gown: — *pl.* **robes-de-chambre** (same pron.); **robe′-maker** a maker of official robes; **rob′ing-room** a room in which official robes may be put on. — **Mistress of the robes** the head of a department in a queen's household; **the robe** or **the long robe** the legal profession. [Fr. *robe*, orig. booty; cf. **rob¹, reave,** O.H.G. *raup* (Ger. *Raub*), booty.]

robe², 'robe *rōb, n.* short for **wardrobe.**

roberdsman *rob′ərdz-man,* (*obs.*) *n.* a stout robber. — Also **rob′ertsman.** [App. from *Robert*; allusion unknown.]

robin¹ *rob′in, n.* the redbreast or **robin redbreast** (*Erithacus rubecula*), a widely-spread singing bird with reddish-orange breast: extended to other birds as a red-breasted thrush of N. America (**American robin**). — **Robin Goodfellow** a tricky English domestic spirit or brownie — Puck; **Robin Hood** a legendary mediaeval English outlaw who robbed the rich to give to the poor; **Rob′in-run′-(in-)the-hedge′** cleavers or goosegrass: ground-ivy: also various other hedgeside plants. [A form of *Robert*; cf. *Jack*daw, *Mag*pie.]

robin² *rō′bin,* (*obs.*) *n.* trimming on a gown. [**robing.**]

Robinia *ro-bin′i-ə, n.* the locust or false acacia genus of Papilionaceae: (without *cap.*) a plant of this genus. [From its introducer to cultivation, the Paris gardener Jean *Robin* (1550–1629).]

roble *rō′blā, n.* a name for various species of oak, *Nothofagus,* and other trees. [Sp., — L. *rōbur*, oak.]

roborant rob'ər-ənt, *n.* a strengthening drug or tonic. — Also *adj.* [L. *rōborāns, -antis*, pr.p. of *rōborāre*, to strengthen, invigorate.]

robot rō'bot, *n.* a mechanical man: a more than humanly efficient automaton: esp. in S. Africa, an automatic traffic signal. — *adj.* **robot'ic.** — *n.sing.* **robot'ics** the branch of technology dealing with the design, construction and use of robots. — *v.t.* **rō'botise, -ize** to cause (a job, etc.) to be done by, or (a house, etc.) to be looked after by, a robot or robots. [Czech *robota*, statute labour; from Karel Čapek's play *R.U.R.* (1920).]

roburite rō'bər-īt, *n.* a flameless explosive, chlorinated dinitro-benzene with ammonium nitrate. [L. *rōbur*, strength.]

robust rō-bust', *adj.* stout, strong, and sturdy: constitutionally healthy: vigorous: thick-set: over-hearty. — *adj.* **robust'ious** (-yəs) robust: violent (*Shak.*): strong or rough (*Milt.*). — *adv.* **robust'iously.** — *n.* **robust'iousness.** — *adv.* **robust'ly.** — *n.* **robust'ness.** [L. *rōbustus* — *rōbur*, strength, oak.]

robusta rō-bus'tə, *n.* coffee produced from the shrub *Coffea robusta*, grown esp. in E. Africa.

roc rok, *n.* a fabulous bird, able to carry off an elephant — also **rok, ruc, rukh** (*rook*). [Pers. *rukh*.]

rocaille rō-kä'ē, *n.* artificial rockwork or similar ornament: scroll ornament: rococo. [Fr.]

rocambole rok'əm-bōl, *n.* a plant close akin to garlic. [Fr.]

Roccella rok-sel'ə, *n.* a genus of lichens, yielding archil and litmus. [It. *orcella*, remodelled on *rocca*, rock; see **archil**.]

roch. See **rotch.**

Rochelle rō-shel', properly **La Rochelle**, a town of France. — **Rochelle'-pow'der** seidlitz powder; **Rochelle'-salt** sodium potassium tartrate, discovered in 1672 by Seignette, a *Rochelle* apothecary.

roche moutonnée rosh' moo-to-nā', *n.* a smooth, rounded hummocky rock-surface due to glaciation: — *pl.* **roches moutonnées** (same pron., or *-nāz*). [Fr. *roche*, a rock, *moutonnée*, a kind of wig; applied by De Saussure.]

rochet roch'it, *n.* a mantle (*obs.*): a close-fitting surplice-like vestment proper to bishops and abbots. [O.Fr., of Gmc. origin; cf. Ger. *Rock*, O.E. *rocc*.]

rock[1] rok, *n.* a large outstanding natural mass of stone: a natural mass of one or more minerals consolidated or loose (*geol.*): any variety or species of such an aggregate: a diamond or other precious stone (*slang*): a stone, pebble, lump of rock (*U.S.*): a hard sweetmeat made in sticks: a sure foundation or support, anything immovable: a danger or obstacle (*fig.*): for rock-fish, rock-pigeon, Plymouth Rock fowl: a coin (*U.S. slang*). — *adj.* of rock: found on, in, or among rocks. — *v.t.* to stone (*U.S. slang*): to clear of calcareous deposit. — *ns.* **rock'er, rock'ier** the rock-dove; **rock'ery** a heap of soil and rock fragments in a garden, for growing rock-plants; **rock'iness; rock'ling** a small fish of the cod family with barbels on both jaws. — *adj.* **rock'y** full of rocks: like rocks. — **rock'-al'um** prepared from alunite; **rock'-badger** the Cape hyrax; **rock'-basin** a lacustrine hollow in rock, excavated by glacier-ice; **rock'-bird** a puffin or other bird that nests or lives on rocks; **rock'-borer** any mollusc or other animal that bores into rocks; **rock'-bottom** bedrock: the very bottom, esp. of poverty or despair. — *adj.* the lowest possible: to, at, the lowest possible level. — *adj.* **rock'-bound** hemmed in by rock: rocky. — **rock'-brake** parsley-fern; **rock'-breaker** a machine for breaking stones; **rock'-butt'er** a butter-like exudation from rocks, containing alum; **rock'-cake** a small hard bun with irregular top; **rock candy** (*U.S.*) the sweetmeat rock; **rock'-climber; rock'-climbing** mountaineering on rocky faces; **rock'-cod** a cod found on rocky sea-bottoms: a name for various Australian and other fishes, mostly of the sea-bass family; **rock'-cook** the small-mouthed wrasse; **rock'-cork** mountain-cork; **rock'cress** a cruciferous plant of the genus Arabis;

rock'-crys'tal colourless quartz, esp. when well crystallised; **rock'-dove** a pigeon that nests on rocks, source of the domestic varieties; **rock'-drill** a tool for boring rock; **rock'-elm** an elm of North America with a corky bark; **rock'-fall** a fall of rock: a mass of fallen rock; **rock'-fish** any fish that haunts rocks or rocky bottoms: applied as a name to several such fishes, as wrasse, striped bass, black goby; **rock'-flour** finely divided rock material, such as is found under glaciers. — *adj.* **rock'-forming** occurring as a dominant constituent of rocks. — **rock'-garden** a rockery; **rock'-gua'no** a rock phosphatised by percolations from guano. — *adj.* **rock'-hewn** hewn out of rock. — **rock'-hopper** a crested penguin; **rock'-lark** the rock-pipit; **rock'-leather** mountain-leather; **rock'-lizard** see **rock-scorpion; rock lobster** see **lobster; rock'-melon** (*Austr.*) the cantaloupe; **rock'-oil** petroleum; **rock'-perch** a scorpion-fish; **rock'-pigeon** the rock-dove; **rock'-pipit** a pipit inhabiting rocky coasts; **rock'-plant** a plant adapted to growing on or among rocks; **rock'-rabb'it** a hyrax. — *adj.* **rock'-ribbed** (*U.S.*) unyielding. — **rock'-rose** a plant of either of the genera *Cistus* and *Helianthemum* of the family Cistaceae; **rock'-salm'on, rock'-tur'bot** dogfish or wolf-fish disguised for the market; **rock'-salt** salt as a mineral, halite; **rock'-scor'pion** a person born in Gibraltar (also **rock'-liz'ard**); **rock'-snake** a python: a krait. — *adj.* **rock'-sol'id** steady: dependable: firm: unwavering: unbeatable. — **rock'-sparrow** a genus (*Petronia*) akin to the true sparrow. — *adj.* **rock-stead'y** absolutely steady. — **rock'-tar'** petroleum; **rock'-temple** a temple hewn out of the solid rock; **rock'-tripe** an edible arctic lichen of various kinds; **rock'-vi'olet** a violet-scented alga growing on mountain rocks; **rock'water** water issuing from a rock; **rock'weed** bladderwrack or kindred seaweed growing on rocks; **rock'-wood'** a wood-like asbestos; **rock wool** mineral wool; **rock'work** masonry in imitation of rock (*archit.*): rocks in rockery: rock-climbing. — **on the rocks** penniless: (of whisky, etc.) on ice; **Rock English** the Gibraltar dialect; **Rock fever** undulant fever (from Gibraltar): **Rocky Mountain goat** a white N. American animal intermediate between goat and antelope; **the Rock** Gibraltar; **the Rockies** the Rocky Mountains. [O.Fr. *roke* — L.L. *rocca*.]

rock[2] rok, *n.* a distaff. — *n.* **rock'ing** (*Scot.*) an evening party, orig. for spinning. [M.E. *roc*; cf. M.Du. *rocke*; O.N. *rokkr*; Ger. *Rocken*.]

rock[3] rok, *v.t.* and *v.i.* to sway to and fro, tilt from side to side: to startle, stagger (*coll.*). — *n.* a rocking movement: (also **rock music**) a form of music with a strong beat, which developed from rock-and-roll but which is more varied and often more complex in style, and less influenced by blues and country-and-western music: rock-and-roll. — *adj.* pertaining to rock music or rock-and-roll. — *n.* **rock'er** one who rocks: an apparatus that rocks: a curved support on which anything rocks: a rocking-horse: a rocking-chair: (*cap.*) a member of a teenage faction of the 1960s who wore leather jackets, rode motor bicycles, and were at enmity with the Mods: a mining cradle: a skate with curved blade: a 180°-turn in skating, so that the skater continues backwards in the same direction: a mezzo-tint engraver's tool for preparing a surface. — *adv.* **rock'ily.** — *n.* **rock'iness.** — *n.* and *adj.* **rock'ing.** — *adj.* **rock'y** disposed to rock: shaky: tipsy: unpleasant, unsatisfactory (*slang*). — **rock'abilly** a form of rock-and-roll with elements of hillbilly music; **rock-and-roll** see **rock-'n'-roll; rocker panel** the part of a vehicle's bodywork below the door-sills of the passenger compartment; **rocker switch** an electric light, etc. switch on a central pivot, the bottom being pushed back to switch on, the top to switch off; **rock'ing-chair** a chair mounted on rockers; **rock'ing-horse** the figure of a horse mounted on rockers or on some other supports which allow the horse to rock; **rock'ing-stone** a logan, or finely poised boulder that can be made to rock; **rock'ing-tool** an engraver's tool for roughing a plate;

rock'-'n'-roll', rock'-and-roll' (also without hyphens) a simple form of music deriving from jazz, country-and-western and blues music, with a strongly accented, two-beat rhythm: dancing thereto; **rock'-shaft** in engines, a shaft that oscillates instead of revolving; **rock'steady** a 1960s dance music of Jamaica, slow in tempo with a heavily stressed off-beat. — **off one's rocker** out of one's right mind; **rock the boat** to make things difficult for one's colleagues, create trouble. [O.E. *roccian*.]

rockaway *rok'ə-wä*, *n.* an American four-wheeled pleasure carriage, formerly made at *Rockaway*, New Jersey.

rocket¹ *rok'it*, *n.* a simple device, a cylinder full of inflammable material, projected through the air for signalling, carrying a line to a ship in distress, or for firework display: a missile projected by a rocket system: a system, or a vehicle, obtaining its thrust from a backward jet of hot gases, all the material for producing which is carried within the rocket: a severe reprimand (*slang*). — *v.i.* to move like a rocket: to fly straight up rapidly when flushed: of e.g. prices, to become higher very rapidly (*fig.*): to come to an important position with remarkable speed (*fig.*). — *v.t* to attack with rockets. — *ns.* **rocketeer'** a rocket technician or pilot of rockets: a specialist in rocketry, especially a designer of rockets; **rock'eter** a game bird which rockets; **rock'etry** the scientific study of rockets. — **rock'et-motor** a jet motor which uses an internally stored oxidiser instead of atmospheric oxygen, for combustion; **rock'et-plane** an aeroplane driven by rocket-motor; **rock'et-range** a place for experimentation with rocket projectiles. [It. *rocchetta*, of Gmc. origin.]

rocket² *rok'it*, *n.* a cruciferous salad plant (*Eruca sativa*) of Mediterranean countries: extended to dame's violet (Hesperis) and other plants of the same family (**sea'-rocket** *Cakile*; **wall'-rocket** *Diplotaxis*; **yell'ow-rocket** winter-cress, *Barbarea*) or of other families (**blue'-rocket** monk's hood: larkspur; **dy'er's-rocket** weld). [O.Fr. *roquette* — L. *ērūca*.]

rocklay. See **rokelay.**

rococo *rō-kō'kō, rō-kō-kō'*, *n.* a debased style of architecture, decoration, and furniture-making prevailing in Louis XV's time, marked by endless multiplication of ornamental details unrelated to structure, with rockwork, shells, scrolls, and unsymmetrical and broken curves, a lighter, freer, frivolous development of the baroque: any art showing the same spirit: — *pl.* **rococos.** — *adj.* in the style of rococo: florid and tasteless: grotesque: old-fashioned and odd (*obs.*). [Fr., prob. — *rocaille* rockwork.]

rocquet *rok'it*, *n.* a rochet. [O.Fr., a Northern form of *rochet.*]

rod *rod*, *n.* a long straight shoot: a slender stick: a slender bar of metal or other matter: such a metal bar forming part of the framework under a railway carriage (see also **ride the rods** below): a sceptre or similar emblem of authority: a stick or bunch of twigs as emblem or instrument of punishment: a stick or wand for magic, divination: a riding-crop: a slender pole or structure carrying a fishing-line: a fisherman using this: a measuring stick: a pole or perch (5½ yards, or 16½ feet): a square pole (272¼ sq. ft): (of brickwork) 272 sq. ft of standard thickness of 1½ bricks or 306 cubic ft: race or tribe (*B.*): a rod-shaped body of the retina sensitive to light: a revolver, a pistol (*U.S. slang*): a penis (*slang*). — *v.t.* to push a rod through (a drain, etc.) so as to clear it: — *pr.p.* **rodd'ing;** *pa.t.* and *pa.p.* **rodd'ed.** — *n.* **rodd'ing.** — *adjs.* **rod'less; rod'like.** — *n.* **rod'ster** an angler. — **rod'fisher; rod'fishing; rod'man, rods'man** one who holds, carries or uses a rod, esp. an angler; **rod puppet** a glove puppet held on one hand, its arms being manipulated by rods held in the other hand. — **a rod in pickle** punishment in reserve; **kiss the rod** to accept punishment with submission; **make a rod for one's own back** to create trouble for oneself; **Napier's rods** see **Napierian; ride the rods** (*U.S.*) to travel

illegitimately on the railway, supporting oneself on the rods (q.v.) of railway carriages. [O.E. *rodd*; cf. O.N. *rudda*, club.]

rode¹ *rōd*, *pa.t.* of **ride.**

rode² *rōd*, (*Spens., Shak.*) *n.* an old spelling of **road.** — *n.* (*Shak.*) **rode'way.**

rode³ *rōd*, *v.i.* to perform a regular evening flight, esp. of woodcock. — *n.* **rōd'ing, road'ing** a woodcock's evening flight. [Origin obscure.]

rodent *rō'dənt, adj.* gnawing: of the Rodentia. — *n.* a member of the Rodentia. — *n.pl.* **Rodentia** (*-den'shə, -shyə*) an order of mammals with prominent incisor teeth and no canines, as squirrels, beavers, rats. — *n.* **roden'ticide** a substance that kills rodents. — **rodent officer** an official rat-catcher. [L. *rōdēns, -entis,* pr.p. of *rōdĕre,* to gnaw.]

rodeo *rō'di-ō, rō-dā'ō*, *n.* a place where cattle are assembled: a round-up of cattle: an exhibition of cowboy skill: a contest suggestive of a cowboy rodeo involving, e.g. motor-bicycles: — *pl.* **ro'deos.** [Sp., — *rodear,* to go round — L. *rotāre,* to wheel.]

rodomontade *rod-ō-mon-tād'*, *n.* extravagant boasting, like that of *Rodomonte* in Ariosto's *Orlando Furioso.* — *v.i.* to bluster or brag. — *n.* **rodomontā'der.**

roe¹ *rō*, *n.* a mass of fish-eggs (also **hard roe**): the testis of a male fish containing mature sperm (also **soft roe**). — *adj.* **roed** containing roe. — *n.* **roe'stone** oolite. [M.E. *rowe*; cf. O.N. *hrogn,* M.H.G. *roge,* Ger. *Rogen.*]

roe² *rō*, *n.* a small species of deer: sometimes applied to the female red deer. — **roe'buck** the male roe; **roe'buck= berry, roe'-blackberry** the stone-bramble; **roe'-deer** a roe. [O.E. *rā, rāha*; Ger. *Reh,* Du. *ree.*]

Roe (Richard). See **Doe (John).**

roemer *rōō'mər*, *n.* a rummer. [Du.]

roentgen. See **röntgen.**

rogation *rō-gā'shən*, *n.* an asking: supplication. — *adj.* **rogatory** (*rog'ə-tə-ri*; **letters rogatory** see **letter**). — **Rogation Days** the three days before Ascension Day, when supplications were recited in procession; **Rogation flower** the milkwort, which was carried in Rogation Day processions; **Rogation Sunday** that before Ascension Day; **Rogation Week** the week in which the Rogation Days occur. [L. *rogātiō, -ōnis* — *rogāre,* to ask.]

Roger *roj'ər*, *n.* a man's personal name: a goose (*cant*): a penis (*vulg.*): a word used in signalling and radio-communication for R, in the sense of received (and understood). — *v.t.* and *v.i.* (*vulg.*) to copulate (with). — *n.* **rog'ering.** — **Jolly Roger** the pirates' skull-and-crossbones flag; (**Sir**) **Roger de Coverley** (*də-kuv'ər-li*) an English country-dance (whence the name of the *Spectator* character). [Fr., of Gmc. origin, equivalent to O.E. *Hrōthgār.*]

Rogerian *roj-ēr'i-ən, adj.* denoting a type of psychological therapy developed by Carl *Rogers* in the 1940s, in which the therapist tries to discover his patients' needs by involving himself in a positive and understanding relationship with them, by means of one-to-one counselling or group discussion.

rogue *rōg*, *n.* a vagrant: a rascal: a wag: a mischievous person (often playfully or affectionately): a plant that falls short of a standard, or is of a different type from the rest of the crop: a sport, or variation from type: a horse that shirks: a savage elephant or other animal cast out or withdrawn from its herd. — *adj.* mischievous: disruptive: diverging from type. — *v.i.* to play the rogue. — *v.t.* to cheat: to eliminate rogues from. — *ns.* **roguery** (*rōg'ər-i*) rascally tricks: fraud: mischievousness: waggery; **rogue'ship;** *adjs.* **roguing** (*rōg'ing*) roaming, or behaving like a rogue; **roguish** (*rōg'ish*) rascally: mischievous: waggish: villainous: confounded. — *adv.* **rog'uishly.** — *n.* **rog'uishness.** — *adj.* **rog'uy** (*obs.*). — **rogue'-el'ephant; rogue'-money** a former assessment in Scotland for the expense of catching, prosecuting and maintaining rogues; **rogues' gallery** a police collection of photographs of criminals; **rogues' Latin** cant; **rogues' march** derisive music played

at a drumming-out. [Cant; origin unknown.]
roi fainéant *rwä fā-nä-ã,* (Fr.) a king without royal power (see **fainéant**).
roil *roil* (also **rile** *rīl*), *v.t.* to make turbid or turbulent: to annoy, irritate (now usu. **rile**). — *adj.* **roil′y** turbid. [Origin doubtful.]
roin, roinish. Same as **royne**[1], **roynish**.
roister, royster *rois′tər, n.* a blusterer: a noisy reveller. — *v.i.* to bluster, swagger: to revel noisily. — *v.i.* **roist, royst** (back-formation from the n.) to roister. — *n.* **rois′terer, roys′terer.** — *adj.* **rois′terous, roys′terous.** — *adj.* **rois′ting, roys′ting** blustering, boisterous: rousingly defiant (*Shak.*). [O.Fr. *rustre,* a rough, rude fellow — O.Fr. *ruste* — L. *rusticus,* rustic.]
rok. Same as **roc**.
roke *rōk, n.* a vapour: steam: mist: small rain: smoke. — *v.t.* and *v.i.* to steam: to smoke. — *adj.* **rōk′y.** [Perh. Scand.]
rokelay, rocklay *rok′(ə)-lā, (Scot.) ns.* a woman's short cloak, worn in the 18th century. [Fr. *roquelaire*; see **roquelaure**.]
roker *rōk′ər, n.* any ray other than skate, esp. the thornback. [Perh. Dan. *rokke,* Sw. *rocka,* ray.]
roky. See **roke**.
rolag *rō′lag, n.* a roll of combed sheep's wool ready for spinning. [Gael. *ròlag,* dim. of *rola,* a roll.]
Roland *rō′lənd, n.* a hero of the Charlemagne legend: hence a hero: a worthy match (with allusion to a drawn contest between Roland and his comrade-in-arms, Oliver). — **a Roland for an Oliver** tit for tat: as good as one got.
role, rôle *rōl, n.* a part played by an actor: a function, part played in life or in any event. — **role′-play, role′-playing** the performing of imaginary roles, esp., as a method of instruction, training or therapy, the acting-out of real-life situations in which the subject might find himself. — *v.t.* and *v.i.* **role′-play.** [Fr.]
Rolfing *rolf′ing, n.* a therapeutic technique for correcting postural faults and improving physical well-being through manipulation of the muscles and connective tissue, so that the body is realigned symmetrically and the best use of gravity made in maintaining balance. [Dr Ida *Rolf,* 1897–1979, originator of the technique.]
roll *rōl, n.* a scroll: a sheet of paper, parchment, cloth, or other material bent spirally upon itself into a nearly cylindrical form: a document in such form: a register: a list, esp. of names: a spirally wound cake, or one of dough turned over to enclose other material: a small, individually-baked portion of bread formed into any of various shapes, that can be cut open and filled with other foods, preserves, etc.: a revolving cylinder: a roller: a more or less cylindrical package, mass, or pad: a cylindrical moulding: a volute: a bookbinder's tool with a small wheel for impressing designs: a part turned over in a curve: an act of rolling: a swaying about an axis in the direction of motion: a full rotation about an axis in the direction of motion: an aeronautical manoeuvre: a continuous reverberatory or trilling sound: an undulation: a wavelike flow. — *v.i.* to move like a ball, a wheel, a wheeled vehicle, or a passenger in one: to perform revolutions: to sway on an axis in the direction of motion: to turn over or from side to side: to swagger: to wallow: to go with a roll: to move in, on, or like waves: to flow: to undulate: to wander: to sound with a roll: to use a roller: to curl: to start: to get under way: to start operating: to make progress. — *v.t.* to cause to roll: to turn on an axis: to move with a circular sweep (as the eyes): to wrap round on itself: to enwrap: to curl: to wind: to drive forward: to move upon wheels: to press, flatten, spread out, thin, or smooth with a roller or between rollers: to round by attrition: to beat rapidly, as a drum: to rumble: to peal: to trill: to pour in waves: (of a clock) to wind (*Scot.*): to attack and rob (*slang*): to rob (someone who is helpless, esp. drunk, asleep, etc.) (*slang*). — *adjs.* **roll′able; rolled.** — *n.* **roll′er** one who or that which rolls: a revolving or rolling cylinder: a contrivance including a heavy cylinder or cylinders for flattening roads or turf: a long, coiled-up bandage (**roll′er-band′age**): a strap buckled round a horse to keep its blanket in place: a long heavy wave: a small solid wheel: a cylinder on which hair is wound to curl it: a kind of tumbler pigeon: a bird (Coracias) of a family akin to the kingfishers, with a habit of flight like a tumbler pigeon (Ger. *Roller*): a kind of canary with a soft trilling song. — *adj.* pertaining to, performed or carried out on, roller-skates. — *n.* **roll′ing.** — *adj.* (of landscape) characterised by a gentle undulation: extremely rich (*slang*): staggering with drunkenness (*slang*): (of a contract, etc.) subject to periodic review: occurring in different places in succession: (of planned events, etc.) organised to take place successively, on a relay or rota system, with a steadily maintained or escalating effect. — *adj.* **roll′-about** podgy. — **roll′-bar** a metal bar that strengthens the frame of a vehicle, lessening the danger to the vehicle's occupants if the vehicle overturns; **roll′-call** the calling of a list of names, to ascertain attendance; **roll′collar** a collar of a garment turned back in a curve; **rolled gold** metal coated with gold rolled very thin; **roll′er-bearing** a bearing consisting of two races between which a number of parallel or tapered rollers are located, usu. in a cage, suitable for heavier loads than ball-bearings; **roll′er-coast′er** a type of switchback railway popular at carnivals, etc., along which people ride in open cars at great speed; **roll′er-skate** a skate with wheels instead of a blade. — Also *v.i.* — **roll′er-skat′er; roll′er-skat′ing; roll′er-tow′el** a continuous towel on a roller; **roll′ing-mill** factory or machine for rolling metal into various shapes between rolls; **roll′ing-pin** a cylinder for rolling dough; **roll′ing-stock** the stock or store of engines and vehicles that run upon a railway; **rolling stone** see phrases below. — *adjs.* **roll′-neck** of a jersey, etc., having a high neck which is made to be folded over loosely on itself; **roll′-on** of a deodorant, etc., contained in a bottle which has a rotating ball in its neck, by means of which the deodorant is applied: of a boat, etc., roll-on-roll-off. — *n.* a roll-on deodorant, etc.: a corset that fits on by stretching. — *adj., n.* **roll-on′-roll-off′** (a ferry-boat or cargo boat, or ferry or cargo service) designed to allow goods vehicles to embark and disembark without unloading and passenger traffic to drive straight on and off. — **roll′-out** bringing out a prototype of an aeroplane to show it to the public: that part of an aeroplane's landing during which it slows down after touch-down. — *adjs.* **roll′-top** having a flexible cover of slats that rolls up; **roll′-up** suitable for rolling up. — *n.* an accumulator bet: a hand-rolled cigarette (*coll.*): assembling in large numbers, a meeting (*Austr.*). — **a rolling stone gathers no moss** a rover does not grow rich; **be rolling in** to have large amounts of (e.g. money); **Master of the Rolls** the head of the Record Office; **heads will roll** severe punishments will be meted out, esp. loss of status or office; **roll along** to arrive by chance, or with a casual air; **rolled into one** combined in one person or thing; **roll in** to arrive in quantity; **roll on!** may (a specified event) come quickly!; **roll over** to defer demand for repayment of (a loan or debt) for a further term (*n.* and *adj.* **roll′-over**); **roll up** (*coll.*) to assemble, arrive. [O.Fr. *rolle* (n.), *roller* (vb.) — L. *rotula,* dim. of *rota,* a wheel.]
rollick[1] *rol′ik, v.i.* to behave in a careless, swaggering, frolicsome manner. — *adj.* **roll′icking.** [Origin unknown.]
rollick[2] *rol′ik,* (*slang*) *v.t.* to rebuke severely. — *n.* a severe scolding. — *n.* **roll′icking** (also **roll′ocking**). [Perh. alteration of **bollock**.]
rollmop *rōl′mop, n.* a fillet of herring rolled up, usu. enclosing a slice of onion, and pickled in spiced vinegar. [Ger. *Rollmops* — *rollen,* to roll, *Mops* a pug-dog.]
rollock. See **rowlock**.
rollocking. See **rollick**[2].

Rolls-Royce® *rōlz-rois'*, *n.* a superior make of car, produced by *Rolls-Royce* Ltd. (also *coll.* **Rolls**): anything thought of as being of superior quality (*fig.*: also *adj.*).

roly-poly *rōl'i-pōl'i*, *n.* a pudding made of a sheet of dough, covered with jam or fruit, rolled up, and baked or steamed (also **roly-poly pudding**): a round, podgy person: an old game in which balls are bowled into holes or thrown into hats placed on the ground: any of several bushy plants, esp. *Salsola kali*, that break off and roll in the wind (*Austr.*). — *adj.* round, podgy. [Prob. **roll**.]

ROM *rom*, (*comput.*) *n.* acronymic abbreviation of read-only memory, a storage device whose contents cannot be altered by a programmer.

rom *rom*, *n.* a gypsy man: — *pl.* **rom'a(s)**. [Romany, man, husband.]

romage *rum'ij*, (*Shak.*) *n.* tumult. [**rummage**.]

Romaic *rō-mā'ik*, *n.* and *adj.* modern Greek. — *n.* **romā'ika** a modern Greek dance. [Mod. Gr. *Rhōmaikos*, Roman (i.e. of the Eastern Roman Empire) — *Rhōmē*, Rome.]

romal *rō-mäl'*, **rumal** *rōō-mäl'*, *ns.* a handkerchief: a head-cloth. [Pers. *rūmāl*.]

Roman *rō'mən*, *adj.* pertaining to Rome, esp. ancient Rome, its people, or the empire founded by them: pertaining to the Roman Catholic religion, papal: (without *cap.*) (of type) of the ordinary upright kind, as opp. to *italic*: (of numerals; see Roman Numerals in Appendices) written in letters (as IV, iv), opp. to *Arabic*: (of handwriting) round and bold: (of a nose) high-bridged. — *n.* a native or citizen of Rome: a Roman Catholic: (without *cap.*) roman letter or type. — *adj.* **Romanic** (*rō-man'ik*) of Roman or Latin origin: Romance. — *n.* the Romance language or languages collectively. — *n.* **Romanisation, -z-** (*rō-mə-nī-zā'shən*). — *v.t.* **Ro'manise, -ize** to make Roman or Roman Catholic: to bring under Roman or Roman Catholic influence: to represent by the Roman alphabet. — *v.i.* to accept Roman or Roman Catholic ways, laws, doctrines, etc.: to become Roman Catholic. — *n.* **Ro'maniser, -z-**. — *adj.* **Ro'manish** (in hostility) Roman Catholic: savouring of Roman Catholicism. — *ns.* **Ro'manism** Roman Catholicism; **Ro'manist** a Roman Catholic: one versed in Romance philology or Roman law or antiquities. — *adj.* Roman Catholic. — *adj.* **Romanist'ic**. — in composition, **Romano-** (*rō-mā'nō-*) Roman: Romanised: Roman and (as **Roma'no-Brit'ish**). — **Roman candle** a firework discharging a succession of white or coloured stars: a bad landing by aeroplane: a landing by parachute when the parachute fails to open. — *v.i.* to make such a landing. — *adj.* **Roman Catholic** recognising the spiritual supremacy of the Pope or Bishop of Rome. — *n.* a member of the Roman Catholic Church. — **Roman Catholicism** the doctrines and polity of the Roman Catholic Church collectively; **Roman cement** a hydraulic cement made from calcareous nodules from the London Clay; **Roman Empire** the ancient empire of Rome, divided in the 4th century into the Eastern and Western Empires (see also under **Holy**); **Roman law** the system of law developed by the ancient Romans — civil law; **Roman nettle** a nettle, rare in Britain, with female flowers in heads, traditionally introduced by the Romans; **Roman numerals** see **Roman** above; **Roman snail** the edible snail (*Helix pomatia*) much valued by the Romans. [L. *Rōmānus* — *Rōma*, Rome.]

roman *ro-mã'*, *n.* a mediaeval romance, tale of chivalry: a novel. — **roman à clef(s), clé(s)** (*nä klā'*; lit. *key novel*) a novel about real people under disguised names; **roman à thèse** (*nä tez'*) a novel that sets out to demonstrate a thesis or proposition; **roman fleuve** (*flœv'*; lit. *river novel*) a novel in a series of self-contained narratives telling the story of a family or other social group over successive generations (also **saga novel**). [Fr.]

Romance *rō-mans'*, *n.* a general name for the vernaculars

that developed out of popular Latin — French, Provençal, Italian, Spanish, Portuguese, Romanian, Romansch, with their various dialects. — Also *adj.* — *n.* **romance'** a tale of chivalry, orig. one in verse, written in one of these vernaculars: any fictitious and wonderful tale: a fictitious narrative in prose or verse which passes beyond the limits of ordinary life: a Spanish historical ballad: romantic fiction as a literary genre: a romantic occurrence or series of occurrences: a love affair: romantic atmosphere or feeling: a leaning towards the romantic: an imaginative lie: romanticism: a composition of romantic character (*mus.*). — *v.i.* to write or tell romances: to talk extravagantly or with an infusion of fiction: to lie: to build castles in the air. — *n.* **roman'cer**. — *adj.* **roman'cical** (*Lamb*) dealing with romance. — *n.* and *adj.* **roman'cing**. [O.Fr. *romanz* — (hypothetical) L.L. *rōmānicē* (adv.), in (popular) Roman language.]

Romanes. See **Romany**.

Romanesque *rō-mən-esk'*, *adj.* of the transition from Roman to Gothic architecture, characterised by round arches and vaults. — *n.* the Romanesque style, art, or architecture. [Fr.]

Romani. See **Romany**.

Romanian *rō-mā'ni-ən*, **Rumanian**, **Roumanian** *rōō-*, **Ruman, Rouman** *rōō'mən*, *adjs.* pertaining to *Romania* or its language. — *n.* a native or citizen of Romania, or member of the same people: the (Romance) language of Romania. [Romanian *România* — L. *Rōmānus*, Roman.]

Romanise, Romanism, etc. See **Roman**.

Romansch, Romansh, R(o)umansch, Rumonsch *rō-*, *rōō-mansh'*, *-mänsh'*, *-monsh'*, *ns.* and *adjs.* Rhaeto-Romanic: sometimes confined to the Upper Rhine dialects. [Romansch.]

romantic *rō-man'tik*, *adj.* pertaining to, of the nature of, inclining towards, or savouring of, romance: fictitious: extravagant, wild: fantastic. — *n.* a romanticist. — *adj.* **roman'tical**. — *n.* **romantical'ity**. — *adv.* **roman'tically**. — *n.* **romanticīsā'tion, -z-**. — *v.t.* **roman'ticise, -ize** (*-ti-sīz*) to make seem romantic. — *v.i.* to have or express romantic ideas. — *ns.* **roman'ticism** (*-sizm*) romantic quality, feeling, tendency, principles, or spirit; **roman'ticist**. — **Romantic Revival** the late 18th-century and early 19th-century revolt against classicism or neo-classicism to a more picturesque, original, free, and imaginative style in literature and art. [Fr. *romantique* — O.Fr. *romant*, romance.]

Romany, Romani *rom'ə-ni*, *rōm'*, **Rommany** *rom'ə-ni*, *ns.* a gypsy: (also **Romanes** *rom'ə-nes*) the Indic language of the gypsies (in pure form not now common in Britain). — *adj.* gypsy. — **Romany rye** (*rī*) a gentleman who affects the society of gypsies. [Gypsy, — *rom*, man.]

romaunt *rō-mönt'*, (*arch.*) *n.* a romance. [O.Fr. *romant*; see **Romance**.]

Rome *rōm*, formerly *rōōm*, *n.* the capital of the Roman Empire, now of Italy: often used for the Roman Catholic Church or Roman Catholicism. — *adj.* and *adv.* **Rome'ward**. — *adv.* **Rome'wards**. — *n.* **Rōm'ic** a phonetic notation devised by Henry Sweet, based upon the original Roman values of the letters. — *adj.* **Rōm'ish** Roman Catholic (*hostile*): Roman (*obs.*). — **Rome'-penny, -scot** (*obs.*) Peter's penny; **Rome'-runner** (*obs.*) a self-seeking cleric who had much resort to Rome. [L. *Rōma*.]

Romeo *rō'mi-ō*, *n.* a young man very much in love: a Don Juan in the making: — *pl.* **Rō'meos**. [Shakespearean character.]

Rommany. See **Romany**.

Romneya *rom'ni-ə*, *n.* a genus of papaveraceous shrubs, with large white poppy-like flowers with yellow centres: (without *cap.*) a plant of this genus. [Thomas *Romney* Robinson (1792–1882), British astronomer and physicist.]

romp *romp*, *v.i.* to frolic actively: to move along easily and quickly, esp. in winning a race. — *n.* one, esp. a girl, who romps: a tomboy: a vigorous frolic: a swift easy run. — *n.* romp'er one who romps: (usu. in *pl.*) a child's garb for play (also romp'er-suit'). — *adv.* romp'ingly. — *adj.* romp'ish. — *adv.* romp'ishly. — *n.* romp'ishness. — romp home to win easily; romp through to do (something) quickly and easily. [ramp.]

roncador *rong-kə-dōr', -dör', n.* a name for various American fishes, esp. of the maigre family, from the sounds they emit. [Sp., snorer.]

rondache *run-dash', -däsh, n.* a buckler. [Fr.]

rondavel *ron-dav'əl, ron', n.* in S. Africa, a round hut, usu. with grass roof: a more sophisticated building of similar shape, used e.g. as guest house. [Afrik. *rondawel.*]

ronde *rond, n.* a script printing-type. [Fr., round (*fem.*).]

rondeau *ron'do, rō-dō, n.* a form of poem characterised by closely-knit rhymes and a refrain, and, as defined in the 17th century, consisting of thirteen lines, divided into three unequal strophes, not including the burden (repeating the first few words) after the eighth and thirteenth lines — brought into vogue by Swinburne: a rondo (*mus.*): — *pl.* ron'deaux (-*dōz*). — *ns.* ron'del a verse-form of thirteen or fourteen lines on two rhymes, the seventh and thirteenth being identical with the first, and the eighth and (if present) the fourteenth with the second: a circular part or ornament in jewellery: a circular badge; rondino (-*dē'nō*; from It. dim.) a short rondo: — *pl.* rondi'nos; ron'do (orig. It., from Fr.) a musical composition whose principal subject recurs in the same key in alternation with other subjects, often the last movement of a sonata: — *pl.* ron'dos; rondolet'to a short rondo: — *pl.* rondolet'tos. [Fr. *rondeau,* earlier *rondel — rond,* round.]

rondure *rond'yər,* a Shakespearian form of roundure.

rone, roan, rhone *rōn, (Scot.) n.* a roof-gutter. [Origin unknown.]

Roneo® *rō'ni-ō, n.* a duplicating machine: — *pl.* Rō'neos. — *v.t.* rō'neo to produce copies of by duplicating machine.

rong *rong (obs.) pa.t.* of ring².

ronggeng *rong'geng, n.* a Malaysian dancing-girl: a kind of dancing, often with singing, in Malaysia. [Malay *rŏnggeng.*]

ronne, ronning (*Spens.*). Same as run (*infin.* and *pa.p.*), running.

ront, ronte (*Spens.*). Same as runt.

röntgen, roentgen *rənt'yən, rent', ront', runt',* also *-gən,* (sometimes *cap.*), *adj.* of the German physicist Wilhelm Conrad *Röntgen* (1845–1923), discoverer of the röntgen rays or X-rays (see X). — *n.* the international unit of dose of X-rays or gamma rays, defined in terms of the ionisation it produces in air under stated conditions. — *v.t.* rönt'genise, -ize to treat by röntgen rays. — *ns.* rönt'genogram a photograph made with these rays; röntgenog'raphy photography by these rays; röntgenol'ogy the study of the rays; röntgenos'copy observation by means of them; röntgenother'apy treatment of disease by means of them.

ronyon, runnion *run'yən, (Shak.) n.* a term of reproach to a woman. [Some connect with Fr. *rogne,* mange.]

roo *rōō, (Austr. coll.) n.* short form of kangaroo.

rood *rōōd, n.* Christ's cross: a cross or crucifix, esp. at the entrance to a church chancel: a rod, pole, or perch, linear or square (with variations in value; *locally*): the fourth part of an acre, or forty square poles. — rood'-beam a beam for supporting the rood; Rood Day (Holyrood Day, Rood'mas Day) the feast of the Exaltation (14th September) or of the Invention (3rd May) of the Cross; rood'-loft a gallery over the rood-screen; rood'-screen an ornamental partition separating choir from nave; rood'-steeple, -tower that over the crossing of a church; rood'-tree (*obs.*) Christ's cross. [O.E. *rōd,* gallows, cross.]

roof *rōōf, n.* the top covering of a building or vehicle: a ceiling: the overhead surface, structure, or stratum of a vault, arch, cave, excavation, etc.: the upper covering of the mouth (the palate) or of any cavity: a dwelling:

a culmination: a high or highest plateau (as *the roof of the world,* the Pamir): an upper limit: an aeroplane's ceiling or limiting height: — *pl.* roofs. — *v.t.* to cover with a roof: to shelter. — *adj.* roofed. — *ns.* roof'er one who makes or mends roofs: a roof-board: a letter of thanks for hospitality (*coll.*); roof'ing covering with a roof: materials for a roof: the roof itself: shelter. — *adj.* for roofing. — *adjs.* roof'less; roof'-like; roof'y having a roof or roofs. — roof'-board a board lying under slates or tiles; roof'-garden a garden on a flat roof; roof'-guard a device to prevent snow from sliding off a roof; roof'-plate a wall-plate that receives the lower ends of the rafters of a roof; roof'-rack a rack which may be fitted to the roof of a car, etc. to carry luggage, etc.; roof'-top the outside of a roof; roof'-tree the ridge-pole: the roof. — have a roof over one's head to have somewhere to live; hit, go through the roof to become very angry; raise the roof to make a great noise or commotion. [O.E. *hrōf*; Du. *roef.*]

rooinek *rō'i-nek, n.* an Afrikaans nickname for an Englishman. [Afrikaans, red neck — Du. *rood, nek,* from his complexion.]

rook¹ *rōōk, n.* a gregarious species of crow: a sharper: a simpleton (*obs.*). — *v.t.* to fleece. — *n.* rook'ery a breeding-place of rooks in a group of trees: a breeding-place of penguins, or seals, etc.: a crowded cluster of mean tenements: an evil resort: a disturbance (*slang* or *dial.*). — *adjs.* rook'ish; rook'y (*Shak.*) abounding in rooks: or poss. black, murky (see roky under roke). [O.E. *hrōc.*]

rook² *rōōk, n.* a chessman whose move is in a vertical or horizontal line, its shape usu. being that of a tower with battlements. [O.Fr. *roc* — Pers. *rukh.*]

rook³ *rōōk (Shak.).* Same as ruck².

rookie, rooky *rōōk'i, (slang) n.* a raw beginner: a callow recruit. [App. from recruit.]

room *rōōm, rōōm, n.* space: necessary or available space: space unoccupied: opportunity, scope, or occasion: stead: a particular place: an assigned place, as in a theatre (*obs.*): a seat (*B.*): appointment, office: a holding of land (*obs.*): a compartment: a chamber: a cottage sitting-room: company in a room. — *v.t.* and *v.i.* (chiefly *U.S.*) to lodge: to share a room or rooms (with with). — *adj.* roomed having rooms. — *ns.* room'er (*U.S.*) a lodger, usu. taking meals elsewhere; roomette' (*U.S.*) a sleeping compartment in a train; room'ful as much or as many as a room will hold: — *pl.* room'fuls. — *adv.* room'ily. — *n.* room'iness. — *adjs.* room'some roomy; room'y having ample room: wide: spacious. — room'-divid'er a low wall or piece of furniture serving as one, dividing a room into two separate sections; room'-fellow one who shares a room; room'ing-house (*U.S.*) a house with furnished rooms to let; room'-mate a fellow-lodger (*U.S.*): one who shares a room. — *adj.* room'-ridden confined to one's room. — room service the serving of food, etc. to people in their room(s) in a hotel, etc.; room temperature the average temperature of a living-room, taken to be be about 20°C. — leave the room esp. of children in school, to go to the toilet. [O.E. *rūm*; Ger. *Raum,* Du. *ruim*].

roon *rōōn,* rund *run(d), rōōn(d), rən(d), (Scot.) ns.* a list or selvage: a strip or thread of cloth. — Also (*Galt*) royne (*roin*). [Origin obscure.]

roop¹ *rōōp, v.i. (Scot.)* to make a hoarse sound. — *n.* a hoarse sound: hoarseness. — *adjs.* roop'it, roop'y (*Scot.*) hoarse. [Variant of roup².]

roop². See stoop⁴.

roosa. See rusa.

roose *rōōz, (Scot.) rüz, (dial.) v.t.* to praise. [M.E. *rosen* — O.N. *hrōsa,* to praise.]

roost¹ *rōōst, n.* a perch or place for a sleeping bird: a henhouse: a sleeping-place: bed: a set of fowls resting together: a loft or garret or its roof (*Scot.*). — *v.i.* to settle or sleep on a roost or perch: to perch: to go to rest for the night. — *n.* roost'er a domestic cock. — come home to roost to recoil upon oneself (the chickens have come home to roost one's actions have had unpleasant consequences): to return to a place (usu. after travel) in order to settle down; **rule the roost** see **roast**. [O.E. *hrōst*; Du. *roest*.]

roost² *rōost*, (*Orkney and Shetland*) *n.* a tidal race. [O.N. *röst*.]

root¹ *rōot*, *n.* ordinarily and popularly, the underground part of a plant, esp. when edible: that part of a higher plant which never bears leaves or reproductive organs, ordinarily underground and descending, and serving to absorb salts in solution, but often above-ground, often arising from other parts, often serving other functions, through morphologically comparable (*bot.*): the source, cause, basis, foundation, occasion of anything, as an ancestor, an element from which words are derived: an embedded or basal part, as of a tooth, a hair, a dam: a growing plant with its root: the factor of a quantity which, taken so many times, produces that quantity (*math.*): any value of the unknown quantity for which an equation is true (*math.*): the fundamental note on which a chord is built (*mus.*): (in *pl.*) one's ancestry, family origins: (in *pl.*) a feeling of belonging in a town, community, etc. — *v.i.* to fix the root: to be firmly established: to develop a root. — *v.t.* to plant in the earth: to implant deeply: to fix by the root: to uproot (usu. with *up*): to remove entirely by uprooting, clear away, eradicate, extirpate (usu. with *out*). — *n.* **root′age** the act of striking root: the state of being rooted: roothold: a root-system. — *adj.* **root′ed** having roots: fixed by roots or as by roots: firmly established. — *adv.* **root′edly.** — *ns.* **root′edness; root′er.** — *adj.* **root′less** having no roots: belonging nowhere, having no home and so constantly shifting about. — *n.* **root′let.** — *adjs.* **root′like; root′y** abounding in, consisting of, or like roots: rank. — *adj.* and *adv.* **root′-and-branch′** without leaving any part: thorough(ly), complete(ly). — **root′-ball** the spherical mass formed by the roots of a plant, with the surrounding soil; **root′-beer** a drink made from roots of dandelion, sassafras, etc. — *adj.* **root′-bound** rooted to the ground (*Milt.*): pot-bound. — **root canal** the narrow passage through which nerves and blood vessels enter the pulp-cavity of a tooth; **root′-cap** a sheath of cells at the tip of a root; **root′-cause** fundamental cause; **root′-climber** a plant that climbs by means of roots, as ivy; **root′-crop** a crop of esculent roots; **root′-eater.** — *adjs.* **root′-fallen** fallen, by roots giving way; **root′-fast** firmly rooted. — **root′-hair** a fine tubular outgrowth from a cell by which a young root absorbs water; **root′hold** maintenance of position by roots: a footing; **root′-house** a summer-house built of roots: a storehouse for potatoes, etc.; **root′-knot** an enlargement of a root caused by a nematode; **root module** (*bot.*) the swelling on the root of a leguminous plant containing nitrogen-fixing bacteria; **root′-par′asite** a plant parasitic on a root; **root′-pressure** an upward forcing of sap, shown by the bleeding of plants. — *v.t.* **root′-prune** to prune the roots of. — **root′-pruning; root′-rubber** rubber got from the roots of certain African apocynaceous plants; **root′-sheath** the sheath of the root of an orchid, a hair, a feather, etc.; **root′stock** rhizome, esp. if short, thick, and more or less erect (*bot.*): a source, ancestral form; **root′-sys′tem; root′-tu′bercle** a swelling on a root, inhabited by symbiotic bacteria; **root vegetable** a vegetable which has an esculent root: the root itself. — **root mean square** the square root of the sum of the squares of a set of quantities divided by the total number of quantities; **strike, take, root** to root, to become established. [Late O.E. *rōt* — O.N. *rōt*; Dan. *rod*; Goth. *waurts*, O.E. *wyrt*.]

root², earlier **wroot**, *rōot*, *v.t.* to turn up with the snout. — *v.i.* to grub: to poke about. — *n.* **root′er.** — *n.* and *adj.* **root′ing.** — *v.t.* and *v.i.* **root′le** to grub. [O.E. *wrōtan* — *wrōt*, a snout; see also **rout³**.]

root³ *rōot*, (orig. *U.S.*) *v.i.* to shout, to applaud, to support or encourage (a contestant, etc.) (with *for*). — *n.* **root′er.** [Prob. from **rout⁴**.]

rooty¹ *rōot′i*, (*mil. slang*) *n.* bread. [Urdu *roti*, loaf.]

rooty². See **root¹.**

rope *rōp*, *n.* a stout twist of fibre, wire, etc., technically over 1 in. round: a string of pearls, onions, etc.: a glutinous stringy formation: a local lineal measure, 20 feet: a climbing party roped together. — *v.t.* to fasten, bind, enclose, mark off, or (*U.S.* and *Austr.*) catch with a rope: to hold back to avoid winning (*horse-racing*). — *v.i.* to form into a rope. — *adjs.* **rop(e)′able** (*Austr.*) of cattle or horses, wild, unmanageable: very angry; **roped** (*rōpt*). — *ns.* **rō′per** a rope-maker: one who ropes a horse: a decoy (also **rō′per-in′**); **rōp′ery** ropework: knavery. — *adv.* **rōp′ily.** — *n.* **rōp′iness.** — *n.* and *adj.* **rōp′ing.** — *adj.* **rō′py, rō′pey** stringy: glutinous: wrinkled like loops of rope: bad of its kind (*slang*). — **rope′-dance** a tight-rope performance; **rope′-dancer; rope′-drilling** boring by a drill alternately raised by a rope and then dropped; **rope′-house** a storehouse for ropes: a house where salt is crystallised from brine trickling along ropes; **rope′-ladder** a ladder of ropes; **rope′-machine; rope′-maker; rope′-making.** — *adj.* **rope′-ripe** deserving to be hanged. — *v.t.* **rope′s-end′** to beat with a rope's end. — *adj.* **rope′-soled** having a sole of rope. — **rope′-stitch** work in stitches laid diagonally side by side; **rope′-trick** a disappearing trick with a rope: poss. a rhetorical figure, or, acc. to some, a trick deserving the gallows (*Shak.*); **rope′-walk** a long narrow shed or alley for rope-spinning; **rope′-walker** a tight-rope performer; **rope′way** a means of transmission by ropes; **rope′work** a rope-walk or rope factory (also *n.sing.* **rope′works**): a system of ropes; **rope′-yarn** yarn for making ropes, or got by untwisting ropes; **rop′ing-down′** abseiling. — **give someone (enough) rope (to hang himself)** to allow a person full scope to defeat his own ends; **know the ropes** see **know; on the high ropes** elated: arrogant; **on the ropes** driven back against the ropes of a boxing ring: nearing defeat, desperate; **rope in** to bring in, enlist (esp. one who has some reluctance); **rope's end** the end of a rope used for flogging; **ropes of sand** a bond with no cohesion; **the rope** capital punishment by hanging. [O.E. *rāp*; O.N. *reip*, Ger. *Reif*.]

roque. See **roquet.**

Roquefort *rok′för*, *n.* a cheese orig. made (of ewe's milk) at *Roquefort* in France.

roquelaure *rok′ə-lōr, -lör*, *n.* a man's knee-length cloak worn in the 18th and early 19th century. [Fr., after the Duc de *Roquelaure* (1656–1738).]

roquet *rō′kā*, *n.* in croquet, a stroke by which the player's ball strikes an opponent's. — *v.t.* to strike by a roquet. — *v.i.* to play a roquet. — *n.* **roque** (*rōk*) an American game, a modification of croquet. [Prob. formed from **croquet**.]

roquette *rō-ket′*, *n.* another form of **rocket²**.

roral. See **roric.**

rore *rōr, rör*, an obs. spelling (*Shak.*) of **roar** (tumult).

roric *rō′rik, rö′, **rorid** *rō′rid, rö′, **roral** *rō′rəl, rö′, *adjs.* dewy. [L. *rōs, rōris*, dew.]

ro-ro *rō′rō, adj., n.* short for roll-on-roll-off (q.v. under **roll**): — *pl.* **ro′-ros.**

rorqual *rör′kwəl, n.* any whale of the genus Balaenoptera (finback). [Fr., — Norw. *røyrkval* — O.N., lit. red whale.]

Rorschach test *rör′shak test*, a test, designed to show intelligence, personality, and mental state, in which the subject interprets ink-blots of standard type. [Hermann *Rorschach* (1884–1922), Swiss psychiatrist.]

rorty *rör′ti*, (*slang*) *adj.* gay: rowdy. — *ns.* **rort** (*Austr.*) a racket; **ror′ter** (*Austr.*) a spiv. [Ety. dub.]

rory, rorie. Same as **roary.**

Rosa *rōz′ə, roz′ə, n.* the rose genus, giving name to the family **Rosā′ceae.** — *ns.* **rosace** (*rō-zäs′, -zäs′*; from Fr.; *archit.*) a rosette: a rose-window; **rosacea** (*rō-zā′shi-ə; med.*; also **acne rosacea**) a chronic disease of the skin of the nose, cheeks and forehead, characterised by flushing and redness of the skin, pimples and pustules. — *adj.* **rosaceous** (*rō-zā′shəs*) of the rose family: roselike. — *ns.* **rosā'rian** a rose-fancier; **rosā'rium** a rose-garden; **rosary** (*rō'zər-i*) a rose-garden or rose-bed (also **rō'sery**): a chaplet (*obs.*): a series of prayers: a string of beads used by Roman Catholics as a guide to devotions. [L. *rŏsa*, rose; *rosārium*, rose-garden; *rosāceus, roseus,* rosy.]

rosaker *ros-ā'kər*. Obs. variant of **realgar**.

rosalia *rō-zä'lyä,* (*mus.*) *n.* a series of repetitions of the same passage, each a tone higher. [Said to be from an Italian folksong, *Rosalia cara mia.*]

rosaniline *rō-zan'i-lin, -lēn, -līn, n.* a base derived from aniline, with red salts used in dyeing. [**rose**[2], **aniline**.]

rosarian, rosary. See **Rosa**.

rosa-solis *rō-zä-sō'lis,* (*obs.*) *n.* the sundew: a cordial, orig. flavoured with sundew juice, afterwards with various spices. [Orig. L. *rōs sōlis,* dew of the sun, altered to *rŏsa,* rose.]

roscid *ros'id, adj.* dewy. [L. *rōscidus* — *rōs,* dew.]

Roscius *rosh'i-əs, rōs'ki-ōos, n.* a famous Roman actor (d. 62 B.C.): hence, a great actor. — *adj.* **Rosc'ian.** [L. *Rōscius.*]

rose[1], *pa.t.* of **rise**.

rose[2] *rōz, n.* the flower of any species of the genus Rosa — national emblem of England: a shrub bearing it, mostly prickly, with white, yellow, pink, orange, or red flowers, numerous stamens and carpels, achenes enclosed in the receptacle: extended to various flowers or plants, some little like the true rose (see, e.g., under **Christmas, guelder-rose, rock**[1]): a paragon: a rosette, esp. on a shoe: a rose-cut stone: a rose-window: a perforated nozzle: a circular moulding from which e.g. a door-handle projects: a circular fitting in a ceiling from which an electric light flex hangs: the typical colour of the rose — pink or light crimson: the pink glow of the cheeks in health: erysipelas. — *adj.* of, for, or like the rose or roses: rose-coloured. — *v.t.* to make like a rose, in colour or scent. — *adjs.* **roseal** (*rō'zi-əl*) roselike; **rō'seate** (*-zi-it, -zi-āt*) rosy: rose-scented: of roses: unduly favourable or sanguine; **rosed** flushed (*Shak.*): having a rose or roses; **rose'less; rose'like.** — *ns.* **rō'sery** a rose-garden (cf. **rosary**); **rosier** (*rō'zhər, Spens.* **rosiere** *rō-zi-ār', -ēr'; Fr. rosier*) a rose tree or bush. — *adv.* **rō'sily.** — *n.* **rōsiness.** — *adj.* **rō'sy** of or abounding in roses: roselike: rose-red: blooming: blushing: bright: hopeful: promising. — *n.* (*old slang*) wine. — *v.t.* and *v.i.* to redden. — **rose'-apple** an E. Indian tree of the clove genus: its edible fruit; **rose'-bay** the oleander (**rose-bay laurel, rose-laurel**): any rhododendron: a willow-herb (**rose-bay willow-herb**) common where woods have been felled or land cleared by fire (also **fireweed** *q.v.*); **rose'-beetle** the rose-chafer: the rose-bug; **rose'-bowl** an ornamental bowl for cut flowers; **rose'-bud; rose'-bug** an American beetle that eats roses; **rose'-bush; rose'-camp'ion** a garden species of campion (*Lychnis coronaria*); **rose'-chafer** a beetle (*Cetonia aurata*) that eats roses. — *adj.* **rose'-cheeked.** — **rose'-colour** pink. — *adj.* **rose'-col'oured** pink: seeing or representing things in too favourable a light. — **rose'-comb** a fowl's low tubercled comb. — *adj.* **rose'=combed.** — **rose'-cross** a cross within a circle: a Rosicrucian. — *adj.* **rose'-cut** cut in nearly hemispherical form, with flat base and many small facets rising to a low point above. — **rose'-di'amond** a rose-cut diamond; **rose'-drop** a rose-flavoured sweet: a red eruption on the nose; **rose'-el'der** the guelder-rose; **rose'= en'gine** an apparatus for engine-turning; **rose'fish** the bergylt; **rose'-garden; rose geranium** a pelargonium (*P. graveolens*) with small pink flowers and fragrant leaves; **rose'-hip** the fruit of the rose. — *adj.* **rose'-hued.** — **rose'-knot** a rosette of ribbon or the like; **rose'-lau'rel** oleander; **rose'-leaf** the leaf of a rose: usu. a rose-petal. — *adj.* **rose'-lipped** having red lips. — **rose'-mall'ow** hollyhock: hibiscus; **rose'-no'ble** an old English gold coin with the figure of a rose. — *adj.* **rose'-pink** rose-coloured: sentimental. — *n.* a pink colour: a pink pigment. — **rose'-quartz** a rose-coloured quartz; **rose'= rash** roseola. — *adj.* **rose'-red** red as a rose. — **rose'-root**

a stonecrop (*Sedum rosea*) with rose-scented root. — *adj.* **rose'-tint'ed** rose-coloured (*lit.* and *fig.*). — **rose'= tō'paz** a topaz coloured pink by heat; **rose'-tree** a standard rose; **rose'-wa'ter** water distilled from rose-leaves. — *adj.* sentimental: superfine. — **rose'-win'dow** a round window with tracery of radiating compartments; **rose'wood** a valuable heavy dark-coloured wood of many trees, notably Brazilian and Indian species of Dalbergia (Papilionaceae), said to smell of roses when fresh-cut; **rose'wood-oil** oil of rhodium. — *adjs.* **ro'sy-bos'omed; ro'sy-cheeked; ro'sy-col'oured.** — **rosy cross** the emblem of the Rosicrucians; **ro'sy-drop** rose-drop. — *adjs.* **ro'sy-fing'ered** Homer's favourite epithet (*rhododáktylos*) of the dawn; **ro'sy-foot'ed.** — **all roses see roses all the way; bed of roses** see **bed**[1]; **look,** or **see, through rose-coloured** or **rose-tinted** or **rosy, spectacles** or **glasses** to view matters over-optimistically; **rose of Jericho** a cruciferous plant (*Anastatica hierochuntica*) of N. Africa and Syria, that curls in a ball in drought; **rose of Sharon** (*Song of Solomon*) probably a narcissus: now applied to a species of hibiscus, and to a species of Hypericum; **roses all the way,** **all roses** pleasant, happy: without difficulties, problems etc.; **under the rose** in confidence; **Wars of the Roses** a disastrous dynastic struggle in England (1455–85) between the Houses of Lancaster and York, from their emblems, the red and the white rose. [O.E. *rōse* — L. *rŏsa,* prob. — Gr. *rhŏdeā,* a rose-bush, *rhodon,* rose.]

rosé *rō'zā, n.* a pinkish table wine in making which grape skins are removed early in fermentation (cf. **red wine**). [Fr. lit., pink.]

roseal, roseate, etc. See **rose**[2].

rosella *rō-zel'ə, n.* a handsome Australian parakeet, first observed at Rose Hill near Sydney. [For *rosehiller.*]

roselle, rozelle *rō-zel', n.* an East Indian hibiscus.

rosemary *rōz'mə-ri, n.* a small fragrant pungent Mediterranean labiate shrub (*Rosmarinus*). [L. *rōs marīnus,* sea dew.]

roseola *rō-zē'ə-lə, n.* rose-coloured rash: German measles (also **rubella**). [Dim. from L. *roseus,* rosy.]

rosery. See **Rosa, rose**[2].

roset, rosit, rozet, rozit *roz'it,* (*Scot.*) *n.* a rosin. — *v.t.* to rosin. — *adj.* **ros'ety** (sometimes **ros'etty**), etc. [**rosin**.]

Rosetta stone *rō-zet'ə stōn,* a tablet, found near Rosetta in Egypt in 1799, which carried the same inscription in hieroglyphics and demotic script and also in Greek and thus enabled a beginning to be made in deciphering hieroglyphics: any comparable first clue.

rosette *rō-zet', n.* a knot of radiating loops of ribbon or the like in concentric arrangement, esp. worn as a badge showing affiliation, or awarded as a prize: a close radiating group of leaves, usu. pressed to the ground: a rose-shaped ornament (*archit.*): any structure, arrangement, or figure of similar shape: a curve whose polar equation is $r = a \sin m\theta$: a disc, esp. of copper, formed by throwing water on molten metal: any of several diseases of plants (also **rosette disease**). — *adj.* **rosett'ed.** [Fr., dim. of *rose.*]

Rosh Hashanah *rosh hə-shä'nə,* the Jewish festival of New Year. [Heb., lit. head of the year.]

Rosicrucian *roz'* or *rōz'i-krōō'sh(y)ən, n.* a member of an alleged secret society whose members made great pretensions to knowledge of the secrets of Nature, transmutation of metals, elemental spirits, magical signatures, etc. — affirmed to have been founded (1459) by Christian *Rosenkreuz*: a member of one or other of various modern fraternities. — Also *adj.* — *n.* **Rosicru'cianism.** [Prob. a Latinisation of *Rosenkreuz,* rose cross, L. *rŏsa,* rose, *crux,* cross.]

rosier, rosily, rosiness. See **rose**[2].

rosin *roz'in, n.* a resin obtained, e.g. when turpentine is prepared from dead pine wood — also called **colophony.** — *v.t.* to rub with rosin: to add rosin to. — *adj.* **ros'ined.** — *ns.* **ros'inate** a resinate; **ros'in-oil** an oil distilled from rosin; **ros'in-plant, -weed** *Silphium.* — *adj.* **ros'iny.** [**resin**.]

Rosinante, Rozinante *roz-in-an'ti, n.* Don Quixote's horse: a sorry nag. [Sp. *Roucinante*, explained as *rocin antes*, formerly a rouncy.]

rosit. See **roset.**

rosmarine[1] *roz'mǝ-rīn*, (*Spens.*) *n.* a walrus, or a sea-monster supposed to lick dew off the rocks. [Dan. *rosmar*, walrus; influenced by the following word.]

rosmarine[2] *roz'mǝ-rīn, -rēn, n.* rosemary (*Spens.*): sea dew (*Jonson*). [See **rosemary.**]

Rosminian *ros-min'i-ǝn, adj.* of Antonio *Rosmini*-Serbati (1797–1855), his philosophy, or the Institute of Charity founded by him. — Also *n.* — *n.* **Rosmin'ianism.**

rosolio, rosoglio *rō-zō'lyō, n.* a sweet cordial made with raisins (formerly, it is said, with sundew). [It. *rosolio* — L. *rōs sōlis*, dew of the sun.]

rosser. Variant spelling of **rozzer.**

rost. An old spelling of **roast.**

rostellum *ros-tel'ǝm, n.* a little beak: a beaklike outgrowth from an orchid column: the forepart of a tapeworm's head. — *adjs.* **rostell'ar, rostell'ate.** [L. *rōstellum*, dim. of *rōstrum*, beak.]

roster *rōs'tǝr* (or *ros'*), *n.* a list of employees, army personnel, etc. with assigned (turns of) duties: any roll of names (*coll.*). — *v.t.* to put in a roster. — *n.* **ros'tering.** [Du. *rooster*, orig. gridiron (from the ruled lines) — *roosten*, to roast.]

rostrum *ros'trǝm, rōs'trŏŏm, n.* a beak: (properly in *pl.*, **ros'tra**) a platform for public speaking, etc. (from the *Rostra* in the Roman forum, adorned with the beaks of captured ships): a part resembling a beak (*biol.*): a raised platform on a stage (*theat.*): platform carrying a camera (*cinema, TV*). — *adjs.* **ros'tral** of or like a rostrum; **ros'trāte, -d** beaked; **rostrocarinate** (*ros-trō-kar'in-āt*; L. *carīna*, keel) beaked and keeled. — *n. a* supposed flint implement with beak and keel. [L. *rōstrum*, beak — *rōdĕre, rōsum*, to gnaw.]

rosula *roz'ū-lǝ, n.* a leaf-rosette. — *adj.* **ros'ūlate** in a rosette. [L.L. dim. of L. *rōsa*, rose.]

rosy. See **rose**[2].

rot *rot, v.i.* to putrefy: to decay: to become corrupt: to suffer from wasting disease, esp. in prison, or sheep-rot: to talk nonsense, to chaff (*slang*). — *v.t.* to cause to rot, to ret: to chaff (*slang*): — *pr.p.* **rott'ing;** *pa.t.* and *pa.p.* **rott'ed.** — *n.* decay: putrefaction: corruption: collapse, disintegration (often *fig.*): applied to various diseases of sheep, timber, etc.: worthless or rotten stuff (*slang*): bosh (*slang*). — *interj.* expressing contemptuous disagreement. — *n.* **rott'er** a thoroughly depraved or worthless person. — **rot'grass** soft grass, butterwort, pennywort, or other plant reputed to cause sheep-rot; **rot'gut** bad liquor; **rot'-stone** rottenstone. [O.E. *rotian*, pa.p. *rotod; cf.* **rotten**[1].]

rota *rō'tǝ, n.* a roster: a course, round, routine, cycle, of duty, etc.: (with *cap.*) the Roman Catholic supreme ecclesiastical tribunal: a round, a canon, a rondo, or other composition with much repetition. — *adj.* **rō'tal.** — *ns.* **Rō'tameter**® a device for measuring the rate of flow of a fluid in which a tapered float moves vertically in a transparent tube in accordance with the speed of flow; **rō'taplane** rotor-plane; **Rōtarian** (*-tā'ri-ǝn*) a member of a Rotary club. — Also *adj.* — *n.* **Rōtā'rianism.** — *adj.* **rotary** (*rō'tǝr-i*) turning like a wheel: of the nature of rotation: working by rotation of a part: (with *cap.*) of an international system of clubs, formed to encourage service to and within the community, with a wheel as a badge, each member being of a different occupation. — *n.* a rotary apparatus: (with *cap.*) a Rotary club: (with *cap.*) Rotarianism: a traffic roundabout (*U.S.*). — *adj.* **rōtāt'able.** — *v.t.* and *v.i.* **rōtāte'** to turn like a wheel: to put, take, go, or succeed in rotation. — *adj.* **rō'tate** wheel-shaped — with united petals in a plane with almost no tube. — *n.* **rotā'tion** a turning round like a wheel: succession in definite order, as of crops: recurrent order: the conformal transformation (q.v.) in which a particular arrangement is rotated about a fixed point (*math.*, etc.). — *adjs.* **rotā'tional; rotative** (*rō'tǝ-tiv*). — *n.*

rotā'tor one who, or that which, rotates: a muscle which rotates a part of the body on its axis (*anat.*). — *adj.* **rotatory** (*rō'tǝ-tǝr-i; rō-tāt'ǝr-i*) rotary. — *vs.t.* **rō'tavate, rō'tovate** (*back-formation*) to till by means of a rotavator. — *ns.* **Rō'tavator**®, **Rō'tovator**® (*rotary* cultivator; also without *cap.*) a motor-powered, hand-operated soil-tilling machine; **rō'tavirus** a wheel-shaped virus causing gastroenteritis. [L. *rŏta*, a wheel, *rotāre, -ātum*, to run.]

rotch, rotche, roch *roch, n.* the little auk. — Also **rotch'ie.** [Cf. Du. *rotje*, petrel; Fris. *rotgies*, pl. of *rotgoes*, brent-goose.]

rote[1] *rōt, n.* mechanical memory, repetition, or performance without regard to the meaning. — *v.t.* (*Shak.* **roate**) to fix by rote (according to others, to root): to discourse by rote. [Origin obscure; L. *rŏta*, a wheel, and O.Fr. *rote*, road, have been conjectured.]

rote[2] *rōt, n.* a mediaeval stringed instrument. [O.Fr. *rote*, a fiddle, prob. through Gmc. from Celt.; W. *crwth*, Gael. *cruit*.]

rote[3] *rōt, (now *U.S.*) *n.* the roar of surf. [Ety. obscure.]

rotenone *rō'ti-nōn, n.* an insecticide and fish poison prepared from derris and other plants. [Origin unknown.]

rother *rodh'ǝr,* (*Shak., emendation*) *n.* an ox, cow. — **roth'er-beast.** [O.E. *hrȳther,* an ox, a cow; cf. Ger. pl. *Rinder,* horned cattle.]

roti *rō'tē, n.* in Indian and Caribbean cooking, a cake of unleavened bread. [See **rooty.**]

rotifer *rōt'if-ǝr, n.* a wheel-animalcule, or member of the **Rotif'era,** minute aquatic animals whose rings of waving cilia suggest a rotating wheel. — *adjs.* **rotif'eral, rotif'erous.** [L. *rŏta,* a wheel, *ferre,* to carry.]

rotisserie, rôtisserie *rō-tis'ǝ-ri, rō-tēs-rē, n.* a cooking apparatus incorporating a spit: a shop or restaurant in which meats are cooked by direct heat. [Fr., cookshop — *rôtir,* to roast.]

rotl *rot'l, n.* a variable Levantine weight: — *pl.* **rot'ls, ar'tal.** [Ar. *ratl.*]

rotograph *rō'tǝ-gräf, n.* a photograph as of a manuscript, made directly by throwing a reversed image on a roll of sensitive paper. — *v.t.* to photograph by this method. [L. *rŏta,* a wheel, Gr. *graphein,* to write.]

rotogravure *rō-tō-grǝ-vūr', n.* a photogravure process using a rotary press: a print so produced. [L. *rŏta,* a wheel, Fr. *gravure,* engraving.]

rotolo *rō'tō-lō,* an Italian form of **rotl:** — *pl.* **ro'tolos.**

rotor *rō'tǝr, n.* a rotating part, esp. of a dynamo, motor, or turbine: a revolving cylinder for propulsion of a ship: a revolving aerofoil. — **ro'tor-plane** a helicopter or autogyro; **ro'tor-ship; ro'tor-station** an aerodrome designed specially for helicopters. [For **rotator.**]

rotovator. See **rota.**

rottan. See **rotten**[2].

rotten[1] *rot'n, adj.* putrefied: decaying: affected by rot: corrupt: unsound: disintegrating: deplorably bad (*slang*): miserably out of sorts (*slang*). — *adv.* **rott'enly.** — *n.* **rott'enness.** — **rotten apple** a corrupt person; **rotten borough** a borough that still (till 1832) sent members to parliament though it had few or no inhabitants; **rott'enstone** a decomposed silicious limestone that has lost most of its calcareous matter, used for polishing metals. — *v.t.* to polish with rottenstone. [O.N. *rotinn; cf.* **rot.**]

rotten[2], **rottan** *rot'n.* Same as **ratton.**

rotter, rotting, etc. See **rot.**

Rottweiler *rot'vīl-ǝr, n.* a large black German dog with smooth coat, used by drovers. [*Rottweil,* in S.W. Germany.]

rotula *rot'ū-lǝ, n.* the knee-pan: a radial piece of Aristotle's lantern in sea-urchins. [L. *rotula,* dim. of *rŏta,* a wheel.]

rotund *rō-tund', adj.* round: rounded: nearly spherical: convexly protuberant: plump. — *v.t.* to round. — *n.* **rotund'a** a round (esp. domed) building or hall. — *adj.* **rotund'ate** rounded off: orbicular. — *n.* **rotund'ity** roundness: a round mass. — *adv.* **rotund'ly.** [L.

rotundus — *rŏta*, a wheel.]

roturier *ro-tü-ryā*, *n.* a plebeian. [Fr., prob. — L.L. *ruptūra*, ground broken by the plough — L. *rumpĕre*, *ruptum*, to break.]

rouble, ruble *roo'bl*, *n.* the Russian monetary unit, 100 kopecks. [Russ. *rubl'*, perh. — *rubit'*, to cut; or Pers. *rūpīya*, a rupee.]

roucou *roo-koo'*, *n.* annatto. [Fr., — Tupí *urucú*.]

roué *roo'ā*, *n.* a profligate, rake, debauchee. [A name given by Philippe, Duke of Orléans, Regent of France 1715–23, to his dissolute companions — Fr. *roué*, broken on the wheel — pa.p. of *rouer* — *roue* — L. *rŏta*, a wheel.]

Rouen cross *roo-ā kros*, a cross in fretwork as a brooch or pendant. [*Rouen* in France.]

rouge[1] *roozh*, *n.* a mixture of safflower and talc, or other powder used to redden the face: a polishing powder of hydrated ferric oxide (also **jeweller's rouge**): French red wine (for *vin rouge*). — *v.t.* to colour with rouge. — *v.i.* to use rouge: to blush. — **Rouge Croix** (*krwä*), **Rouge Dragon** two of the pursuivants of the Heralds' College; **rouge-et-noir** (*roozh-ā-nwär*) a gambling card-game played on a table with two red and two black diamond marks on which stakes are laid. — Also *trente-et-quarante*. [Fr. *rouge* — L. *rubeus*, red.]

rouge[2] *rooj*, (*Eton*) *n.* a scrimmage: a touch-down in football. [Origin unknown.]

rough *ruf*, *adj.* uneven: rugged: unshorn: unshaven: unpolished: harsh: crude: unelaborated: without attention to minute correctness: unbroken (as a horse): coarse: rude: unrefined: ungentle: turbulent: aspirate: astringent: feeling unwell, tired or hung over (*coll.*). — *adv.* roughly: with roughness or risk of discomfort. — *n.* rough state: that which is rough: rough ground, esp. uncut grass, etc., beside a golf fairway: a piece inserted in a horse's shoe to keep him from slipping: a hooligan, a rowdy: a crude preliminary sketch, etc. — *v.t.* to make rough: to ruffle: to roughen the shoes of: to shape roughly: to treat roughly (usu. with *up*). — *n.* **rough'age** refuse of grain or crops: bran, fibre, etc., in food: coarse food that promotes intestinal movement. — *v.t.* **rough'en** to make rough. — *v.i.* to become rough. — *ns.* **rough'er** one who performs preliminary operations; **rough'ie** a dry bough, esp. one used as a torch (*Scott*): a rough or rowdy person (*slang*). — *adj.* **rough'ish.** — *adv.* **rough'ly.** — *ns.* **rough'ness** the quality of being rough: a rough place: roughage (*U.S. dial.*); **rough'y** same as **roughie.** — *adjs.* **rough'-and-read'y** ready to hand or easily improvised, and serving the purpose well enough: willing and moderately efficient; **rough'-and-tumb'le** haphazard and scrambling. — Also *adv.* — *n.* a scuffle: haphazard struggling. — **rough breathing** in ancient Greek, the sound *h*. — *v.t.* **rough'cast** to shape roughly: to cover with roughcast. — *n.* plaster mixed with small stones, used to coat walls. — *adj.* coated with roughcast. — *adj.* **rough'-coat'ed.** — **rough diamond** see **diamond.** — *vs.t.* **rough'-draft, -draw** to draft roughly; **rough'-dry** to dry without smoothing. — *adjs.* **rough'-foot'ed** with feathered feet; **rough'-grained** coarse-grained. — **rough grazing** uncultivated ground, used for pasture. — *vs.t.* **rough'-grind'** to grind roughly; **rough'-hew** (*Shak.*) to hew to the first appearance of form. — **rough'-hew'er.** — *adj.* **rough'-hewn.** — **rough'-hound** a small species of dogfish; **rough'-house** (orig. *U.S.*; also **rough house**) a disturbance: a brawl. — *v.i.* to brawl: to make a disturbance. — *v.t.* to maltreat. — **rough justice** approximate justice, hastily assessed and carried out: a verdict or sentence that is appropriate, though formed without careful attention to the forms and processes of a legal code. — *adj.* **rough'-legged** with feathered or hairy legs. — **rough'neck** an unmannerly lout (*U.S. slang*): a hooligan or tough (*U.S. slang*): a member of an oil-rig crew employed to deal with equipment on the rig floor; **rough passage** a stormy sea voyage: a difficult, trying time. — *adj.* **rough'-per'fect** nearly perfect in the memorising of a part. — **rough'-rider** a

rider of untrained horses: a horse-breaker: an army riding-master's assistant: an irregular cavalryman. — *adj.* **rough'-shod** provided with roughened horse-shoes. — **rough shooting** shooting over moorland (mainly grouse). — *adj.* **rough'-spoken** rough in speech. — **rough'-string** an intermediate support for the steps of a wooden stairway; **rough'-stuff** coarse paint laid on after the priming, and before the finish: violent behaviour; **rough trade** (*slang*) casual sexual partner(s), esp. homosexual: violent or sadistic male prostitute(s). — *adj.* **rough'-wrought** shaped out or done roughly, or in a preliminary way. — **cut up rough** see **cut; ride rough-shod over** to set at nought, domineer over without consideration; **rough in** to sketch in roughly; **rough it** to take whatever hardships come; **rough on** hard luck for: pressing hard upon; **rough out** to shape out roughly; **sleep rough** to sleep out-of-doors. [O.E. *rūh*, rough; Ger. *rauch, rauh*, Du. *ruig*.]

rought *röt*, an obs. *pa.t.* of **reck.**

roul, roule. Obs. forms of **roll.**

roulade *roo-läd'*, *n.* melodic embellishment (*mus.*): a run, turn, etc., sung to one syllable (*mus.*): in cooking, a rolled slice, usu. of meat, usu. with a filling. [Fr.]

rouleau *roo-lō'*, *n.* a roll or coil, often of ribbon: a cylindrical pile or column of coins, blood corpuscles, or other discs: — *pl.* **rouleaus, rouleaux** (*-lōz'*). [Fr.]

roulette *rool-et'*, *n.* a little roller: a game of chance in which a ball rolls from a rotating disc into one or other of a set of compartments answering to those on which the players place their stakes: a tool with a toothed disc for engraving rows of dots, for perforating paper, etc.: a cylinder for curling hair or wigs: the locus of a point carried by a curve rolling upon a fixed curve (*geom.*). [Fr.]

roum *room*, an old spelling of **room.** — *n.* **roum'ing** (see **souming and rouming,** under **soum**).

Rouman, Roumanian. Same as **Romanian.**

Roumansch. Same as **Romansch.**

rounce *rowns*, *n.* in a hand printing-press, the apparatus, or its handle, for moving the carriage. [Du. *ronse*.]

rounceval *rown'si-vl*, *n.* a giant (*obs.*): a great bouncing woman (*obs.*): a marrow-fat pea. — *adj.* gigantic. [Poss. *Roncesvalles*, in the Pyrenees.]

rouncy *rown'si*, (*arch.*) *n.* a riding-horse: a nag. [O.Fr. *ronci*.]

round[1] *rownd*, (*arch.*) *v.t.* to whisper: to whisper to. — *v.i.* to whisper. [O.E. *rūnian*, to whisper; cf. **rune.**]

round[2] *rownd*, *adj.* having a curved outline or surface: approaching a circular, globular, or cylindrical form: in a course returning upon itself: enveloping: with horizontal swing: plump: pronounced with lips contracted to a circle: smooth and full-sounding: sonorous: well finished off: periodic, as a sentence: approximate, without regarding minor denominations: of a number, without fractions: full: not inconsiderable in amount: plain-spoken: candid: honest: unsparing: without mincing: vigorous: unqualified. — *adv.* about: on all sides: every way: in a ring: in a curve: in rotation: from one to another successively: indirectly: circuitously: towards the opposite quarter: roundly (*Shak.*): in the neighbourhood. — *prep.* about: around: on every side of: all over: to every side of in succession: past, beyond. — *n.* a round thing or part: a ring, circumference, circle, or globe, esp. the earth or the sky: a ladder rung or similar rounded connecting part: a whole slice of bread or toast: a sandwich made with two complete slices of bread: a cut of beef acro~~ the thigh-bone: a brewer's vessel for beer dur~~ fermentation: a projecting corner-turret (not nece~~ ily round in shape): a carving in the round: a ~ bend: a circuit: a course returning upon itself: ~ in a ring, or its tune: a canon sung in uniso~ or recurring series of events or doings: ~ revolution or rotation: an accustomed ~ scribed circuit: a patrol: a series of calls (~ postman): a complete series of holes ~ routine: a volley, as of firearms or a~

nition of one shot: a successive or simultaneous action of each member of a company or player in a game: a portion dealt around to each: a set of drinks bought at one time for all the members of a group: a subdivision of a bout, as in boxing: a defined stage in a competition: roundness: the condition of being visible from all sides, not merely in relief (*sculp.*). — *v.t.* to make round: to surround: to go round: to turn round: to finish off: to give finish to. — *v.i.* to become round: to go round: to go the rounds. — *adj.* **round'ed** (of a sound) round: finished, complete, developed to perfection. — *ns.* **round'edness; round'er** one who or that which rounds: a thing that is round (see also **roundure**): one who goes the round: a complete circuit in rounders: (in *pl.*) a bat-and-ball game in which players run from station to station. — *adj.* **round'ing.** — *n.* the process of raising (*up*) or lowering (*down*) a number to an approximation which has fewer decimal places (*comput.*). — *adj.* **round'ish.** — *adv.* **round'ly.** — *n.* **round'ness.** — *adj.* **round'about** circuitous: indirect: cut evenly, without tails or train: plump. — *n.* a circular revolving platform with handles, seats, etc., at playgrounds, etc.: a merry-go-round: a place where traffic circulates in one direction: a devious way: a round earthwork: a round dance: a short jacket (*U.S.*). — *v.i.* to go round and round. — *ns.* (*facet.*) **roundaboutā'tion, roundaboutil'ity.** — *advs.* **roundabout'edly, round'aboutly.** — *n.* **round'aboutness.** — **round angle** same as **perigon.** — *adjs.* **round'arch, -ed** having semicircular arches; **round'-arm** with nearly horizontal swing of the arm. — *n.* a throw made in this way. — *adj.* **round'-backed.** — **round dance** a dance in a ring: a dance in which couples revolve about each other; **round'-down** an instance or rounding down (q.v. above under **rounding** *n.*). — *adjs.* **round'-eared; round'-eyed; round'-faced.** — **round'-fish** any fish other than a flat fish: the carp: an American whitefish; **round game** a game, esp. a card-game, in which each plays for his own hand; **round'hand** a style of penmanship in which the letters are well rounded and free; **Round'head** a Puritan (from the close-cut hair). — *adj.* **round'-head'ed** puritanical: having a round head, top or end: brachycephalic. — **round'-house** a lock-up (*obs.*): a cabin on the after part of the quarter-deck: an engine-house with a turntable (*U.S.*): (a boxing style using) a wild swinging punch (orig. *U.S.*); **rounding error** (*comput.*) an error in a computation caused by repeated rounding. — *adj.* **round'-leaved.** — **round'-mouth** a cyclostome. — *adjs.* **round'-mouthed; round'-nosed.** — **round robin (Robin)** a paper with signatures in a circle, that no one may seem to be a ringleader: any letter, petition, etc., signed by many people: in sports, a tournament in which each player plays every other player. — *adj.* **round'-shoul'dered** with shoulders bending forward from the back. — **rounds'man** one who goes round esp. one sent by a shopkeeper to take orders and deliver goods: a policeman who acts as inspector (*U.S.*). — *adjs.* **round'-ta'ble** meeting on equal terms, like the inner circle of King Arthur's knights, who sat at a round table; **round'-the-clock'** lasting through the day and night, twenty-four-hour (also *adv.*, without hyphens). — **round'-top** a mast-head platform; **round tower** a tall tapering tower of circular section, of early Christian origin, common in Ireland; **round'-trip** a trip to a place and back again: an instance of round-tripping (*coll.*). — *adj.* (*U.S.*) return. — **round'-tripp'ing** (*coll.*) the financial practice of a company re-lending money at a rate higher than that at which they themselves have ̶orrowed it; **round'-up** a driving together or assem-̶ng, as of all the cattle on a ranch, a set of persons ̶̶ed by the police, a collection of facts or informa-̶tc.: an instance of rounding up (q.v. above under ̶̶ *n.*). — *adj.* **round'-winged.** — **round'-worm** a ̶rm or nematode, a member of the Nematoda, ̶̶ed animals with long rounded body, mostly ̶̶ **bring, come, round** see **bring, come; get** ̶ave the time or inclination to do (some-

thing) after delay; **go, make, the rounds** to go or be passed from place to place or person to person: to circulate: to patrol; **in round numbers, figures** to the nearest convenient large number, i.e. ten, hundred, thousand, etc.: roughly, approximately; **in the round** capable of being viewed from all sides, not merely in relief: taking everything into consideration: with all features, etc., fully displayed; **round about** an emphatic form of round: the other way about: approximately; **round down** to lower (a number) to the nearest convenient figure, usu. ten, hundred, etc.; **round off** to finish off neatly; **round on** to turn on, assail in speech; **round out** to fill out to roundness; **round the bend, twist** see **bend¹, twist; round the clock** see **round-the-clock** above; **round to** to turn the head of a ship to the wind; **round up** to ride round and collect: to gather in (wanted persons, facts, etc.): to raise (a number) to the nearest convenient figure, usu. ten, hundred, etc. [O.Fr. *rund* (Fr. *rond*) — L. *rotundus* — *rŏta*, a wheel.]

roundel *rown'dl, n.* anything circular: a circle: a disc: a ladder rung: a ring-dance, a rondel: a round turret: a circular device (*her.*). — *ns.* **roun'delay** a song with a refrain: a dance in a ring; **roun'dle** a roundel; **round'let** (*-lit*) a little circle or disc; **rown'dell** (*Spens.*) a bubble. [O.Fr. *rondel, -le, rondelet,* dims. of *rond,* round.]

roundure *rownd'yər* (*Shak.* **round'er, rond'ure**) *n.* roundness: a round form or space: a circle, circuit: a globe. [Fr. *rondeur* — *rond,* round.]

roup¹ *rowp,* (*Scot.*) *n.* sale by auction. — *v.t.* to sell by auction. — **rouping'-wife** a woman who conducts or buys at auctions. [Scand.]

roup² *ro͞op, n.* an infectious disease of the respiratory passages of poultry: hoarseness (*Scot.*). — *adjs.* **roup'it** (*Scot.*); **roup'y.** [Perh. imit.]

roup³. See **stoop⁴.**

rousant. See **rouse¹.**

rouse¹ *rowz, v.t.* to shake the feathers of (orig. *refl.*; *obs.*): to ruffle, set up (*obs.*): to start, as from cover or lair: to stir up: to awaken: to disturb (*rare*): to excite: to put in action: to haul in (as a cable). — *v.i.* to shake oneself (*obs.*): to rise from cover (*rare*): to stand erect (of hair; *Shak.*): to awake: to be excited to action. — *n.* a shake of the feathers, body, etc. (*obs.*): reveille. — *adj.* **rous'ant** (*her.*) rising as a bird. — *ns.* **rouse'about** (*Austr.*) an odd-job man on a sheep station; **rouse'ment** (*U.S.*) religious excitement; **rous'er** one who, or that which, rouses: anything astonishing. — *adj.* **rous'ing** awakening: stirring: vigorously active: great: violent. — *adv.* **rous'ingly.** — *v.t.* **roust** to stir up: to rout out. — *v.i.* to move energetically. — *ns.* **roust'about** a wharf labourer (*U.S.*): one who does odd jobs (*U.S.*): a rouseabout (*U.S. and Austr.*): a general labourer employed in the maintenance of an oil-rig; **roust'er** a roustabout. — **rouse on** (*Austr.*) to reprove. [Origin obscure.]

rouse² *rowz,* (*arch.*) *n.* a carousal: a bumper. [Prob. from **carouse**; poss. Scand. *rus,* drunkenness.]

roussette *ro͞o-set', n.* a fruit-bat: a dogfish. [Fr.]

roust, roustabout, rouster. See **rouse¹.**

rout¹ *rowt, n.* a tumultuous crowd: a rabble: a pack, herd, or flock: a large party (*arch.*): a fashionable evening assembly (*arch.*): a defeated body: an utter defeat: disorderly flight: a gathering of three or more people for the purpose of committing an unlawful act (*legal*): disturbance: brawl: riot: clamour: a fuss. — *v.i.* to behave riotously. — *v.t.* to defeat utterly: to put to disorderly flight. — *n.* (*arch.*) **rout'ing** going to receptions. — *adj.* (*arch.*) **rout'ous.** — *adv.* (*arch.*) **rout'ously.** — **rout'-cake** (*arch*) a rich sweet cake for receptions; **rout'-seat** (*arch.*) a bench hired out for routs. [O.Fr. *route,* from the pa.p. of L. *rumpĕre, ruptum,* to break.]

rout² *rowt, v.i.* to snore. [O.E. *hrūtan.*]

rout³ *rowt, v.t.* to grub up, as a pig: to scoop out: to turn up: to turn out, fetch out: to rummage out: to bring to light. — *v.i.* to grub: to poke about. — *n.* **rout'er** a person or thing that routs: a tool of various styles for hollowing out, grooving, etc. [An irreg. variant of **root**[2].]

rout[4] *rowt*, *(dial.)* *v.i.* and *v.t.* to roar. [O.N. *rauta*.]

route *rōōt* (formerly, and still in the army, *rowt*), *n.* a way, course that is or may be traversed: marching orders: a regular series of calls (*U.S.*). — *v.t.* to fix the route of: to send by a particular route: — *pr.p.* **rout(e)'ing;** *pa.t.* and *pa.p.* **rout'ed.** — **route'man** (*U.S.*) a shopkeeper's roundsman; **route'-march** a long march of troops in training; **route'-step** an order of march in which soldiers are not required to keep step. — **route-proving flight** a flight of aeroplanes sent out to test the possibilities and advantages of variants of a new service. [Fr., — L. *rupta* (*via*), broken (way); see **rout**[1].]

routh, rowth *rowth*, (*Scot.*) *n.* abundance. — *adj.* plentiful. — *adj.* **routh'ie.** [Origin obscure.]

routine *rōō-tēn'*, *n.* regular, unvarying, or mechanical course of action or round: the set series of movements gone through in a dancing, skating, or other performance: a comedian's, singer's, etc., act (*coll.*): a part of a program performing a specific and separate function (*comput.*). — *adj.* keeping an unvarying round: forming part of a routine. — *n.* **routineer'.** — *adv.* **routine'ly.** — *v.t.* **routinise', -ize'** to render mechanical or uniform: to remove interest from. — *ns.* **routi'nism; routi'nist.** [Fr.]

routous. See **rout**[1].

roux *rōō*, *n.* a thickening made of equal quantities of butter and flour cooked together: — *pl.* **roux** (*rōō*, *rōōz*). [Fr. (*beurre*) *roux*, brown (butter).]

rove[1] *rōv*, *v.t.* to wander over or through: to discharge at random. — *v.i.* to practise piracy: to aim, as in archery, at some casual mark: to wander about: to ramble: to change about inconstantly: to troll with live bait. — *n.* wandering: a mode of incomplete ploughing. — *n.* **rō'ver** a pirate: a robber: a random or distant mark: an arrow for shooting at rovers: a wanderer: an inconstant person: a croquet ball or player ready to peg out: (*formerly*) a member of a senior branch of the (Boy) Scout organisation (also **rover scout**). — *adj.* **rō'ving** wandering: not confined to a particular place, as *roving ambassador, commission.* — Also *n.* — *adv.* **rō'vingly.** — *adj.* **rove'-over** (of a kind of verse in sprung rhythm) having an extra syllable at the end of one line, which forms a foot with the beginning of the next line. — **at rovers** (*arch.*) at a distant mark: at random: conjecturally. [Partly at least from Du. *rooven*, to rob, *roofer*, robber — *roof*, plunder; perh. partly from a Midland form of obs. Northern English *rave*, to wander.]

rove[2] *rōv*, *v.t.* to twist slightly in preparation for spinning. — *n.* a roved sliver. — *ns.* **rō'ver** a machine for roving: one who attends it; **rō'ving** the process of giving the first twist to yarn: rove. [Origin obscure.]

rove[3] *rōv*, *pa.t.* and *pa.p.* of **reeve**[2].

rove[4] *rōv*, *n.* a metal plate or ring through which a rivet is put and clenched over. [O.N. *ró*.]

rove-beetle *rōv'-bē'tl*, *n.* the devil's coach-horse, or other beetle of the family Staphylinidae. [Cf. Du. *roof-kever*, lit. reif chafer — *roof*, robbery.]

row[1] *rō*, *n.* a line or rank of persons or things, as seats, houses, turnips: a series in line, or in ordered succession: often in street-names, of a single or double line of houses. — *v.t.* (*rare*) to set in or with a row or rows. — **row house** (*U.S.*) a terraced house. — **a hard row to hoe** a destiny fraught with hardship; **in a row** in unbroken sequence; **twelve-tone, -note, row** see **twelve, serial.** [O.E. *rāw*; Ger. *Reihe*, Du. *rij*.]

row[2] *rō*, *v.t.* to propel with an oar: to transport by rowing: to achieve, render, perform, effect, compete in, by use of oars: to use, as an oar. — *v.i.* to work with the oar: to be moved by oars. — *n.* an act or spell of rowing: a journey in a rowing-boat. — *adj.* **row'able** capable of being rowed or rowed on. — *n.* **row'er.** — **row'=barge; row'boat** (*U.S.*); **row'ing-boat; row'-port** a small square hole for an oar in a vessel's side. [O.E. *rōwan*.]

row[3] *row*, *n.* a noisy squabble: a brawl: a din, hubbub: a chiding or rating. — *v.t.* (*obs.*) to rag: to rate. — *v.i.* to make a disturbance. [A late 18th-century word, poss. a back-formation from **rouse**[2].]

row[4] *row*, *n.* and *vb.* a Scots form of **roll.**

row[5] *row*, an obs. or dial. form of **rough.**

rowan[1] *row'ən*, also *rō'ən*, *n.* the mountain-ash (*Sorbus*, or *Pyrus*, *aucuparia*), a tree of the rose family with pinnate leaves: its small red berry-like fruit. — **row'an=berry; row'an-tree.** [Cf. Norw. *raun*, Sw. *rönn*.]

rowan[2]. See **rowen.**

row-dow(-dow) *row'-dow'(-dow')*, *n.* the sound of a drum. — *n.* **rowdedow', rowdydow'** hubbub. — *adj.* **row'dy=dow'dy** uproarious. [Echoic.]

rowdy[1] *row'di*, *n.* orig. a lawless American backwoodsman: a noisy, turbulent person. — Also *adj.* — *adv.* **row'dily.** — *n.* **row'diness.** — *adj.* **row'dyish.** — *n.* **row'dyism.** [Origin unknown.]

rowdy[2] *row'di*, (*obs. slang*) *n.* money.

rowdy-dow, rowdy-dowdy. See **row-dow(-dow).**

rowel *row'əl*, *n.* a little spiked wheel on a spur: the rowel-head: a knob, ring, or disc on a horse's bit: a disc used as a seton for animals. — *v.t.* to prick with the rowel: — *pr.p.* **row'elling;** *pa.t.* and *pa.p.* **row'elled.** — **row'el-head** the axis of a rowel; **row'el-spur** a spur with a rowel. [Fr. *rouelle* — L.L. *rotella*, dim. of L. *rōta*, a wheel.]

rowen *row'ən*, *n.* aftermath. — Also **row'an, row'ing, raw'ing, rawn** (*rön*). [From a Northern form of O.Fr. *regain*.]

rowlock *rol'ək*, *rul'*, *rōl'*, *n.* a contrivance serving as fulcrum for an oar. — Also **roll'ock, rull'ock.** [Prob. for **oar-lock** — O.E. *ārloc*.]

rowme *rowm*, (*Spens.*) *n.* room: station. [**room.**]

rownd an obs. spelling of **round**[1,2].

rowndell. See **roundel.**

rowt. Same as **rout**[3].

rowth. Same as **routh.**

Roxburghe *roks'bər-ə*, *n.* a style of binding for books, with cloth or paper sides, plain leather back, gilt top, other edges untrimmed, named from the Duke of *Roxburghe* (1740–1804), book-collector.

royal *roi'əl*, *adj.* of a king or queen: kingly: being a king or queen: of a reigning family: founded, chartered, or patronised by a king or queen: magnificent: of more than common size or excellence: of writing-paper, 19 by 24 in., of printing-paper, 20 by 25 (**royal octavo** a book size $6\frac{1}{4}$ by 10 in.). — *n.* a royal person (*coll.*): a gold coin of various kinds: a sail immediately above the topgallant sail: formerly a stag's second tine, now the third: a stag of twelve points. — *n.* **roy'alet** a petty king. — *v.t.* **roy'alise, -ize** (*Shak.*) to make royal or (*Milt.*) royalist: to fill with royal presence. — *v.i.* to play the king. — *ns.* **roy'alism** attachment to monarchy; **roy'alist** an adherent of royalism: a cavalier during the English civil war: in American history, an adherent of the British government: in French history, a supporter of the Bourbons. — Also *adj.* — *adv.* **roy'ally.** — *n.* **roy'alty** kingship: the character, state, or office of a king: kingliness: the person of the sovereign: members of royal families collectively or (*coll.*) one such member: a queen-bee, queen-termite, etc.: kingdom: royal authority: a right or prerogative granted by a king or queen, esp. a right over minerals: a payment made by oil companies, etc., to the owners of the mineral rights in the area in which they operate: payment to an author, composer, etc., for every copy sold or every public performance: the area of a royal domain: a royal burgh. — **Royal Academy** an academy of fine arts in London, founded in 1768, to whi members and associates are elected (in very lim number): a teaching, degree-giving academy of r in London; **royal assent** see **assent**; **royal blue** a b deep-coloured blue; **royal commission** (also wit a body of persons nominated by the Crown to into and report on some matter; **royal fern** (*regalis*) the most striking of British ferns;

'fish' that is the king's perquisite when cast ashore or caught near the land (whale, sturgeon, porpoise); **royal flush** see **flush**[4]; **royal icing** a kind of hard icing made with white of egg, used esp. on rich fruit cakes; **royal jelly** a secretion produced by worker bees, the food of young larvae and of a developing queen-bee; **royal marriage** in bezique, king and queen of trumps; **royal mast** the fourth and highest part of the mast, commonly made in one piece with the top-gallant mast; **royal palm** a palm (*Oreodoxa regalis*) of the cabbage-palm genus; **Royal Peculiar** an ecclesiastical peculiar whose superior is the sovereign; **royal road** a short and easy way of circumventing difficulties; **royal standard** a banner bearing the British royal arms, flown wherever the monarch is present; **royal tennis** the earlier form of the game of tennis, distinguished from lawn tennis, and played in a wall court (also **real** or **court tennis**); **royal warrant** an official authorisation to supply goods to a royal household; **Royal We** (also without *caps.*) a monarch's use of the first person plural when speaking of himself or herself. — **the Royals** formerly the first regiment of foot in the British Army (the Royal Scots). [Fr., — L. *rēgālis, regal*.]

royne[1] *roin,* (*Spens.*) *v.i.* to mutter, growl, roar. [Prob. conn. with **groin**[3].]

royne[2]. See **roon**.

roynish *roin'ish,* (*Shak.*) *adj.* scurvy, mangy: mean. [O.Fr. *roigne,* mange.]

royster, etc. Same as **roister**, etc.

rozelle. Same as **roselle**.

rozet, rozit. See **roset**.

Rozinante. See **Rosinante**.

rozzer *roz'ǝr,* (*slang*) *n.* a policeman. [Orig. obscure.]

rub[1] *rub, v.t.* to apply friction to: to move something with pressure along the surface of: to move with pressure along the surface of something: to clean, polish, or smooth by friction: to remove, erase, or obliterate by friction (usu. with *away, off, out*): to grind, sharpen, chafe, treat, by friction: to cause to pass by friction (with *in, through,* etc.): to impede (*Shak.*): to irritate, fret: to take a rubbing of. — *v.i.* to apply, or move with, friction: to meet an impediment (esp. of a bowl): to chafe: to grate: to fret: to make shift to get along somehow: to admit of being rubbed: — *pr.p.* **rubb'ing;** *pa.t.* and *pa.p.* **rubbed.** — *n.* process or act of rubbing: an impediment, or a meeting with an impediment (*bowls*): an inequality or uneven place: a difficulty: a hitch: an irritating experience. — *n.* **rubb'er** one who, or that which, rubs or massages: an eraser: a thing for rubbing with, as a hard brush, a file, a whetstone, emery-cloth, a coarse towel, a polishing-pad: a rubbing part of a machine: a soft brick that can be cut and smoothed: an uneven place: a rub or impediment in bowls: a rebuff or irritating experience: caoutchouc, india-rubber, or a substitute: a piece of india-rubber, esp. for erasing, or as part of a brake: (in *pl.*) plimsolls: india-rubber overshoe (*U.S.*): rubber-neck (*U.S.*): condom: (in *pl.*) sheep disease with heat, itchiness. — *adj.* of, yielding, or concerned with, india-rubber. — *v.t.* to coat, cover, or furnish with india-rubber. — *v.i.* (*U.S.*) to rubber-neck. — *v.t.* **rubb'erise, -ize** to treat or coat with rubber. — *adj.* **rubb'ery** resembling rubber in some quality. — *n.* **rubb'ing** application of friction: experience of rubs (*Shak.*): an impression of an inscribed surface produced by rubbing heel-ball or plumbago upon paper laid over it. — **rubber band** a thin loop of rubber used to hold things together; **rubber cement** an adhesive made of rubber dissolved in a solvent; **rubber cheque** (*facet.*) a cheque that bounces. — *adj.* **rubb'er-cored** of a golf-ball, having a tightly wound band of rubber enclosed in a guttapercha cover. — **rubber goods** (*euph.*) condoms; **rubb'er-neck** one who cranes twists his neck in curiosity: a sightseer. — *v.i.* (*slang*) ehave as a rubber-neck. — *v.t.* (*slang*) to stare at. **rubber plant** any of various plants from whose sap ▪ is made, esp. *Ficus elastica*, often grown as an ▪ntal pot-plant; **rubb'er-solu'tion** a solution of

rubber in naphtha or carbon disulphide, for repairing pneumatic tyres; **rubb'er-stamp** stamp of rubber for making inked impressions: one unquestioningly devoted to routine or officialdom: an automatic or unthinking agreement or authorisation: person(s) making such agreement, etc. — *v.t.* to imprint with a rubber-stamp: to approve without exercise of judgment. — Also *adj.* — **rubber tree** a tropical tree, *Hevea brasiliensis*, grown for its latex, a source of rubber; **rubb'ing-post** one for cattle to rub against; **rubb'ing-stone** a stone for smoothing; **rub'down** an act or experience of rubbing down; **rub'stone** a whetstone. — **rub along** to get along, to manage somehow: (*coll.*) to be on more or less friendly terms (with); **rub down** to rub from head to foot: to remove (a surface) by rubbing in order to repaint, etc.: to search by passing the hands over the body; **rub in** to force into the pores by friction: to be unpleasantly insistent in emphasising; **rub off on** (**to**) (*fig.*) to pass to (someone, something, else) by close contact, association, etc.; **rub one's hands** to rub one's palms together, esp. as a sign of satisfaction; **rub on** (or **of**) **the green** (*golf*) a chance outside interference with the ball (also *fig.*); **rub out** to erase: to murder (*slang*); **rub shoulders** to come into social contact (with); **rub someone's nose in it** (*coll.*) to remind someone insistently of a mistake, fault, misdeed, etc.; **rub (up) the wrong way** to irritate by tactless handling; **rub up** to polish: to freshen one's memory of. [Cf. L.G. *rubben*.]

rub[2]. See **rubber**[2].

rub[3] *rub,* a Scots form of **rob**[1]: — *pa.t.* **rubb'it, rubb'et**.

rub-a-dub(-dub) *rub'ǝ-dub(-dub'), n.* the sound of a drum. [Echoic.]

rubaiyat *rōō'bä-yat, n.* a Persian verse form consisting of four-line stanzas, esp. those written in Persia by Omar Khayyam in the late 11th or early 12th cent., and translated by Edward Fitzgerald in 1859. [Arabic *rubā'īyāt*, pl. of *rubā'īyah,* quatrain.]

rubato *rōō-bä'tō,* (*mus.*) *adj., adv.* and *n.* (in) modified or distorted rhythm: — *pl.* **ruba'ti** (*-tē*), **ruba'tos**. [It., *pa.p.* of *rubare,* to steal.]

rubber[1], **rubberise**, etc. See under **rub**[1].

rubber[2] *rub'ǝr, n.* formerly in bowls (also **rubbers,** *sing.* or *pl.*), now chiefly in bridge and whist, the winning of, or play for, the best of three games (sometimes five): vaguely, a spell of card-playing: used generally of a series of games in various sports, as cricket, tennis, etc.: a rub (*bowls;* see **rub**[1]). — Also **rub.** [Origin obscure.]

rubbet. See **rub**[3].

rubbish *rub'ish, n.* fragments of ruinous buildings: waste matter: litter: trash: trumpery: nonsense: worthless or despicable person(s). — Also *adj.* — *v.t.* to criticise, think of or talk about as rubbish. — *adjs.* **rubb'ishing; rubb'ishly** (*rare*); **rubb'ishy** worthless: paltry: trashy. — **rubb'ish-heap.** [Origin obscure; app. conn. with **rubble.**]

rubbit. See **rub**[3].

rubble *rub'l, n.* loose fragments of rock or ruined buildings: undressed irregular stones used in rough masonry and in filling in: masonry of such a kind. — *adj.* of rubble. — *adj.* **rubb'ly.** — **rubb'le-stone; rubb'le-work** coarse masonry. [Origin obscure; cf. **rubbish.**]

rube *rōōb,* (*U.S. slang*) *n.* a country bumpkin: an uncouth, unsophisticated person. [*Reuben.*]

rubefy *rōō'bi-fī, v.t.* to redden. — *adj.* **rubefacient** (*-fā'shǝnt*) reddening. — *n.* an external application that reddens the skin. — *n.* **rubefaction** (*-fak'shǝn*) reddening. [L. *rubefacēre* — *rubeus,* red, *facēre,* to make.]

rubella *rōō-bel'ǝ, n.* German measles, an infectious disease with pink rash, like measles but milder. — *ns.* **rubell'an** (or *rōō'*) an altered biotite; **rubell'ite** a red tourmaline. [Dim. from L. *rubeus,* red.]

rubeola *rōō-bē'ǝ-lǝ, n.* measles. [Dim. from L. *rubeus,* red.]

rubescent *rōō-bes'ǝnt,* (*lit.*) *adj.* growing red: blushing. [L. *rubescere,* to grow red.]

Rubia *rōō′bi-ə, n.* the madder genus, giving name to the **Rubiā′ceae,** a family of sympetalous dicotyledons akin to the Caprifoliaceae. — *adj.* **rubiā′ceous.** [L. *rubia,* madder — *rubeus,* reddish.]

rubicelle *rōō′bi-sel, n.* an orange-coloured spinel. [Fr., prob. — *rubis,* ruby.]

Rubicon *rōō′bi-kon, -kən, n.* a stream of Central Italy (perhaps the Fiumicino, separating Caesar's province of Gallia Cisalpina from Italia proper — its crossing by Caesar (49 B.C.) being thus a virtual declaration of war against the republic: (without *cap.*) in piquet, the winning of a game before one's opponent scores 100. — *v.t.* (without *cap.*) to defeat in this way. — **cross the Rubicon** to take a decisive, irrevocable step. [L. *Rubicō, -ōnis.*]

rubicund *rōō′bi-kund, -kənd, adj.* ruddy. — *n.* **rubicund′ity.** [L. *rubicundus — rubēre,* to be red.]

rubidium *rōō-bid′i-əm, n.* a soft silvery-white metallic element (Rb; at. numb. 37). [L. *rubidus,* red (so called from two red lines in its spectrum).]

rubify. A less commendable spelling of **rubefy.**

rubiginous *rōō-bij′i-nəs, adj.* rusty-coloured. — Also **rubig′inose** (*-nōs*). [L. *rūbīgō* or *rōbīgō, -inis,* rust.]

Rubik's Cube® *rōō′biks kūb,* a cube-shaped puzzle composed of 26 small pieces (cubes or partial cubes) with faces coloured in any of six colours, fixed to a central spindle that allows them to be rotated on three axes, the solved puzzle presenting a uniform colour on each face. [Developed by Ernö *Rubik,* Hungarian designer, in 1974.]

rubin, rubious, etc. See **ruby.**

ruble. See **rouble.**

rubric *rōō′brik, n.* red ochre (*obs.*): a heading, guiding rule, entry, liturgical direction, orig. one in red: a flourish after a signature: a thing definitely settled. — *adj.* in red: ruddy: inscribed with book titles (*obs.*). — *adj.* **ru′brical.** — *adv.* **ru′brically.** — *v.t.* **ru′bricate** to mark with red: to write or print in red: to make a red-letter saint: to furnish with rubrics: to regulate by rubric. — *ns.* **rubricā′tion; ru′bricātor; rubrician** (*-brish′ən*) one who follows, or is versed in, liturgical rubrics. [L. *rubrīca,* red ochre — *ruber,* red.]

Rubus *rōō′bəs, n.* the raspberry and bramble genus of the rose family. [L. *rubus,* a bramble-bush.]

ruby *rōō′bi, n.* a highly-prized stone, a pure transparent red corundum: extended to other stones, as varieties of spinel and garnet: redness: applied to various red things (lip, pimple, wine, glass, blood): a type smaller than nonpareil and larger than pearl (5½ points; *print.*). — *adj.* red as a ruby. — *v.t.* to redden: — *pr.p.* **ru′bying;** *pa.t.* and *pa.p.* **ru′bied.** — *adj.* **ru′bied** red as a ruby. — *n.* **ru′bin, ru′bine** (*-bin; Spens.*) a ruby. — *adjs.* **rubin′eous; ru′bious** ruby, red, ruddy. — *adjs.* **ru′by-coloured; ru′by-red′.** — **ru′by-sil′ver** proustite: pyrargyrite; **ru′by-spinel′** a ruby-red spinel (also *spinel-ruby*); **ru′by-tail** a gold-wasp, or cuckoo-fly; **ru′by-throat** a hummingbird with a ruby gorget. — *adj.* **ru′by-throated.** — **ruby wedding** a fortieth wedding anniversary. [O.Fr. *rubi* and *rubin* — L. *rubeus — ruber,* red.]

ruc. Same as **roc.**

ruche *rōōsh, n.* a pleated frilling. — *v.t.* to trim with ruche. — *n.* **ruch′ing.** [Fr.; prob. Celt.]

ruck¹ *ruk, n.* a wrinkle, fold, or crease. — *v.t.* and *v.i.* to wrinkle (often with *up*). — *n.* **ruck′le** a pucker, crease. — *v.t.* and *v.i.* to pucker, crease. [O.N. *hrukka,* a wrinkle.]

ruck² *ruk, v.i.* to squat: to crouch down: to cower: to huddle. — *v.t.* (*Shak.* **rook** *rōōk, refl.*) to set squatting. [Prob. Scand.; cf. Norw. dial. *ruka,* to crouch.]

ruck³ *ruk, n.* a heap, stack, or rick, as of fuel, hay, etc.: a multitude: the common run: in Rugby, a gathering of players around the ball when it is on the ground: in Australian rules football, the three players who do not have fixed positions but follow the ball about the field. — *v.t.* to heap. — *v.i.* in Rugby, to form a ruck. [Prob. Scand.]

ruck⁴ *ruk,* (*prison slang*) *n.* a fight. [**ruckus.**]

ruckle¹ *ruk′l,* (*Scot.*) *n.* a rattle in the throat: a gurgle. — *v.i.* to rattle: to gurgle. [Cf. Norw. dial. *rukl.*]

ruckle². See **ruck¹.**

rucksack *rŏŏk′, ruk′sak, -zak, n.* a bag carried on the back by hikers, campers, etc. [Ger. dial. *ruck* (Ger. *Rücken*), back, and Ger. *Sack,* bag.]

ruckus *ruk′əs,* (*U.S.*) *n.* a disturbance. [Perh. a combination of **ruction** and **rumpus.**]

ructation *ruk-tā′shən,* (*obs.*) *n.* eructation. [L. *ructāre,* to belch.]

ruction *ruk′shən,* (*slang*) *n.* a disturbance: a rumpus. [Poss. for **insurrection.**]

rud *rud, n.* redness: flush: complexion: ruddle (*dial.*). — *v.t.* (*Spens.*) to redden: — *pa.p.* **rudd′ed.** [O.E. *rudu,* redness, *rēodan,* to redden.]

rudas *rōō′dəs,* (*Scot.*) *n.* a foul-mouthed old woman: a randy, a hag. — *adj.* coarse. [Origin obscure.]

Rudbeckia *rud-* or *rŏŏd-bek′i-ə, n.* a N. American genus of composites, of the sunflower subfamily: (without *cap.*) a plant of this genus. [Named by Linnaeus in honour of Swedish botanist(s) *Rudbeck,* father and/or son.]

rudd *rud, n.* the red-eye, a fish close akin to the roach. [Prob. O.E. *rudu,* redness.]

rudder *rud′ər, n.* a steering apparatus: a flat structure hinged to the stern of a ship or boat for steering: a vertical control surface for steering an aeroplane to right or left: anything that steers, as an aquatic animal's tail: (*fig.*) something, as a principle, that guides a person in life. — *adj.* **rudd′erless.** — **rudd′er-fish** the pilot-fish, or other fish that accompanies ships. [O.E. *rōthor,* oar; Ger. *Ruder,* oar.]

ruddle *rud′l, n.* red ochre. — *v.t.* to mark with ruddle: to rouge coarsely. — Also **radd′le, redd′le.** — **rudd′leman** one who digs or deals in ruddle. — Also **radd′leman, redd′leman.** [Cf. **rud.**]

ruddock *rud′ək, n.* the redbreast: a gold coin: a kind of apple. [O.E. *rudduc;* cf. **rud.**]

ruddy *rud′i, adj.* red: reddish: of the colour of the skin in high health: rosy, glowing, bright: (euphemistically) bloody: — *compar.* **rudd′ier,** *superl.* **rudd′iest.** — *v.t.* to make red: — *pr.p.* **rudd′ying;** *pa.t.* and *pa.p.* **rudd′ied.** — *adv.* **rudd′ily.** — *n.* **rudd′iness.** [O.E. *rudig;* cf. **rud, red¹.**]

rude *rōōd, adj.* uncultured: unskilled: discourteously unmannerly: ungentle: harsh: crude: undeveloped: unwrought: coarse: rugged: rough: roughly or unskilfully fashioned: violent: robust. — *adv.* (*rare*) rudely. — *adv.* **rude′ly.** — *ns.* **rude′ness; rud′ery** (*coll.*); **rudesby** (*rōōdz′bi; Shak.*) an uncivil fellow. — *adj.* **rud′ish.** [L. *rudis,* rough.]

ruderal *rōō′dər-əl,* (*bot.*) *n.* and *adj.* (a plant) growing in waste places or among rubbish. [L. *rūdus, -eris,* rubbish.]

Rüdesheimer, Rudesheimer *rü′, rōō′dəs-hī-mər, n.* a white Rhine wine — named from *Rüdesheim,* opposite Bingen.

rudiment *rōōd′i-mənt, n.* (usu. in *pl.*) a first principle or element: anything in a rude or first state: an organ in the first discernible stage: often applied to an organ that never develops beyond an early stage. — *adj.* **rudimental** (*-ment′l*) rudimentary. — *adv.* **rudimen′tarily.** — *n.* **rudimen′tariness.** — *adj.* **rudimen′tary** of rudiments: elementary: in an early or arrested stage of development. [L. *rudīmentum — rudis,* rough, raw.]

rue¹ *rōō, n.* a strong-smelling shrubby Mediterranean plant (*Ruta graveolens*), with pinnately divided leaves and greenish-yellow flowers, punningly (see next word) symbolic of repentance, compunction, or compassion: any other member of its genus: extended with qualification to other plants (see **goat's-rue, meadow-rue, wall-rue**). — *adj.* **rue′-leaved.** [Fr. *rue* — L. *rūta* — Peloponnesian Gr. *rhytē.*]

rue² *rōō, n.* (*arch.*) repentance: regret: sorrow: pity. *v.t.* to affect with regret, grieve (*arch.*): to be sorry to repent of: to wish not to have been or hap...

to compassionate. — *v.i.* to feel remorse or regret: to take pity: to change one's mind, contemplate backing out: — *pr.p.* rue′ing, ru′ing; *pa.t.* and *pa.p.* rued. — *adj.* rue′ful sorrowful: piteous: deplorable: mournful: melancholy. — *adv.* rue′fully. — *ns.* rue′fulness; ru(e)′-ing repentance. — rue′-bargain a forfeit for withdrawing from a bargain. — take the rue (*Scot.*) to change one's mind, esp. about an intended marriage. [O.E. *hrēow*, n., *hrēowan* vb.; cf. Ger. *Reue*, O.H.G. *hriuwa*, mourning.]

ruelle *rü-el′*, *n.* the space between a bed and the wall: a bed-chamber where great French ladies held receptions in the morning in the 17th and 18th centuries: a morning reception: a narrow lane. [Fr., dim. of *rue*, street.]

Ruellia *roo-el′i-ə*, *n.* a genus of the acanthus family: (without *cap.*) a plant of this genus. [Named after the French botanist Jean *Ruel* (1479–1537).]

rufescent *roo-fes′ənt*, *adj.* inclining to redness. [L. *rūfescens, -entis*, pr.p. of *rūfescere*, to turn reddish — *rūfus*, reddish.]

ruff¹ *ruf*, *n.* a frill, usu. starched and pleated, worn round the neck, esp. in the reigns of Elizabeth I and James; a beast's or bird's collar of long hair or feathers: a ruffed breed of domestic pigeons. — *v.t.* to furnish with a ruff: to ruffle (*Spens.*): to strike without securing (*falconry*). — *adj.* ruffed (*ruft*) having a ruff. [Cf. ruffle¹.]

ruff² *ruf*, *n.* a kind of sandpiper, the male with an erectile ruff during the breeding season: — *fem.* reeve, ree. [Poss. ruff¹, but the fem. is a difficulty.]

ruff³ *ruf*, *n.* an old card-game, slam, trump (also called ruff and honours): an act of trumping. — *v.t.* and *v.i.* to trump. [Perh. conn. with O.Fr. *roffle*, It. *ronfa*, a card-game.]

ruff⁴ *ruf*, *n.* a low vibrating beat of a drum: applause, esp. with the feet (*Scot.*). — *v.t.* and *v.i.* to beat or be beaten with a ruff: to applaud (*Scot.*). — *ns.* ruff′-a= duff′ drumming; ruff′le a ruff of drums. — *v.i.* to ruff. [Prob. imit.]

ruff⁵ *ruf*, a variant of rough.

ruff⁶, ruffe *ruf*, *n.* the pope, a small freshwater fish of the perch family, with one dorsal fin. — *n.* ruff′in (*Spens.*) the ruff. [Perh. rough.]

ruff⁷, ruffe *ruf*, (*obs.*) *n.* pitch or height of exaltation: elation: excitement. [Cf. Sw. *ruff*, spirit.]

ruffian *ruf′i-ən, -yən*, *n.* a brutal, violent person: a bully. — *adj.* brutal: ruffianly: violent. — *v.i.* to play the ruffian. — *adj.* ruff′ianish. — *n.* ruff′ianism. — *adj.* ruff′ianly. — *adj.* ruff′ian-like. [O.Fr. *ruffian* (Fr. *rufien*); source obscure.]

ruffin. See ruff⁶.

ruffle¹ *ruf′l*, *v.t.* to make uneven, disturb the smoothness of: to set up (as feathers): to wrinkle: to disorder: to agitate: to turn the leaves of hastily: to disturb the equanimity of, to irritate, discompose. — *v.i.* to wrinkle: to grow rough: to flutter. — *n.* a frill, esp. at the wrist or neck: a ruff: a rippled condition: annoyance: a quarrel: agitation. — *adj.* ruff′led having a ruffle. — *n.* ruff′ler an apparatus for making ruffles. — *n.* and *adj.* ruff′ling. [Cf. L.G. *ruffelen*.]

ruffle² *ruf′l*, (*arch.*) *v.i.* to struggle: to bluster: to swagger. — *v.t.* to handle roughly or offensively: to snatch (*Shak.*). — *n.* an encounter, a tumult: bustle (*Shak.*). — *n.* ruff′ler a beggar posing as a maimed soldier (*obs.*): a swaggerer. [Origin obscure.]

ruffle³. See ruff⁴.

ruffler. See ruffle¹,².

rufous *roo′fəs*, *adj.* reddish or brownish-red. [L. *rūfus*, akin to *ruber*, red.]

rug¹ *rug*, *n.* a coarse, rough, woollen fabric (*obs.*): a thick, heavy floor-mat, esp. for the hearth: a thick covering or wrap, as for travelling. — *adj.* made of rug. — *n.* rugg′ing. — rug′-gown a gown of rug: a watchman *obs.*). — *adj.* rug′-head′ed (*Shak.*) shock-headed. — ▪ll the rug (out) from under (*fig.*) by a sudden action, ▪ument, discovery, etc., to leave (a person) without

support, defence, a standpoint, etc. [Cf. Norw. *rugga, rogga*, coarse coverlet, Sw. *rugg*, coarse hair.]

rug² *rug*, (*Scot.*) *v.t.* to pull roughly. — *n.* a tug: a haul, share. — *n.* rugg′ing. [Prob. Scand.]

rug³ *rug*, (*old slang*) *adj.* secure: snug.

rugate. See rugose.

Rugby, rugby *rug′bi*, *n.* a form of football using an oval ball which (unlike *Association*) permits carrying the ball: — (*coll.*) rugg′er. — Rugby (Union) football the original form of the game, with 15 players; Rugby League football a modified form of the game subject to professional rules, with 13 players. [From *Rugby* school.]

rugged *rug′id*, *adj.* rough: uneven: uncouth: toilsome: sturdy and rough: massively irregular: robust, vigorous: stormy (now *U.S.*). — *v.t.* rugg′edise, -ize to render rugged: to make so as to withstand rough handling. — *adv.* rugg′edly. — *n.* rugg′edness. — *adj.* rugg′y rough: uneven. [Prob. related to rug¹.]

rugger. See Rugby.

rugose *roo′gōs, -gōs′*, *adj.* wrinkled: covered with sunken lines. — Also ru′gate (*-gāt, -gət*), ru′gate, to wrinkle), ru′gous. — *adv.* ru′gosely (or *-gōs′*). — *n.* rugosity (*-gos′i-ti*). — *adj.* ru′gulose finely rugose. [L. *rūgōsus* — *rūga*, a wrinkle.]

ruin *roo′in, roo′in*, *n.* downfall: collapse: overthrow: complete destruction: wreck: loss of fortune or means: bankruptcy: undoing: seduction or departure from chastity of life: downfallen, collapsed, wrecked, or irretrievably damaged state (often in *pl.*): cause of ruin: broken-down remains, esp. of a building (often in *pl.*): devastation: bad gin (as *blue ruin*; *slang*). — *v.t.* to reduce or bring to ruin. — *v.i.* (*arch.*) to fall headlong: to go to ruin. — *adj.* ru′inable. — *v.t.* ru′inate to ruin, to destroy (*Shak.*): to demolish (*arch.*): to reduce to poverty (*arch.*): to fling headlong (*Spens.*; *refl.*). — *adj.* (*arch.*) in ruins: ruined. — *n.* ruinā′tion act of ruining: state of being ruined. — *adj.* ru′ined. — *n.* ru′iner. — *n.* and *adj.* ru′ining. — *adj.* ru′inous fallen to ruins: decayed: bringing ruin: as of crashing (*Milt.*). — *adv.* ru′inously. — *n.* ru′inousness the state or quality of being ruinous: mischievousness. — ruin agate, marble one with markings like ruins. [L. *ruina* — *ruĕre*, to tumble down.]

ruing. See rue².

rukh. Same as roc.

rule *rool*, *n.* a straight-edged strip used as a guide in drawing straight lines or as a measuring-rod, or means of mechanical calculation: a type-high strip of metal for printing straight lines: a straight line printed or drawn on paper, etc.: a dash: a straight-edge used for securing a flat surface in plaster or cement: a straight shaft of light (*Milt.*): government: control: prevalence: that which is normal or usual: conformity to good or established usage: well-regulated condition: conduct (*obs.*): misrule (*obs.*): a principle: a standard: a code of regulations, as of a religious order: a regulation, whether imposed by authority or voluntarily adopted: an order of a court: a guiding principle: a method or process of achieving a result: a regulation that must not be transgressed: a maxim or formula that it is generally best, but not compulsory, to follow: (in *pl.*) an area around a prison in which privileged prisoners were allowed to live (*hist.*): the privilege of living there (*hist.*): (in *pl.*) Australian football (see Australian rules). — *v.t.* to draw with a ruler: to mark with (esp. parallel) straight lines: to govern: to control: to manage: to prevail upon: to determine or declare authoritatively to be: to determine, decree. — *v.i.* to exercise power (with *over*): to decide: to be prevalent: to stand or range in price. — *adjs.* ru′lable governable: allowable (*U.S.*); rule′less (*Spens.* ru′lesse) unruly, lawless: without rules. — *n.* ru′ler a strip or roller for ruling lines: one who rules. — *v.t.* to strike with a ruler. — *n.* ru′lership. — *adj.* ru′ling predominant: prevailing: reigning: exercising authority. — *n.* a determination by a judge, esp. an oral decision: the act of making ruled lines. — *adj.*

ru′ly orderly in behaviour. — *adj.* **rule-of-thumb′** according to rule of thumb (see below). — **as a rule** usually; **be ruled** take advice; **rule of faith** in polemical theology, the authoritative sources of the doctrines of the faith; **rule of the road** the regulations to be observed in traffic by land, water, or air — thus in Britain drivers, riders, and cyclists take the left side in meeting, and the right in overtaking; **rule of three** the method of finding the fourth term of a proportion when three are given; **rule of thumb** any rough-and-ready practical method; **rule(s), OK** (*slang*; orig. a gang slogan, chiefly found in graffiti) to be dominant, have the ascendancy; **rule out** to exclude as a choice or possibility. [O.Fr. *reule* (Fr. *règle*) — L. *rēgula* — *regĕre* to rule.]

rullion *rul′yən*, (*Scot.*) *n.* a raw-hide shoe. [O.E. *rifeling*.]

rullock. See **rowlock.**

ruly. See **rule.**

rum¹ *rum, n.* a spirit distilled from fermented sugar-cane juice or from molasses: intoxicating liquor generally (*U.S.*). — *n.* **rum′bo** rum-punch: — *pl.* **rum′bos.** — *adj.* **rumm′y.** — **rum′-bloss′om, -bud** a pimple on the nose; **rum′-butt′er** a mixture of butter and sugar with rum, etc.; **rum′-punch′** punch made with rum; **rum′-runn′er** one who smuggles rum; **rum′-runn′ing; rum′-shop; rum′-shrub** a liqueur of rum, sugar, lime or lemon juice, etc. — **rum baba** baba au rhum (see **baba**). [Perh. from **rumbullion** or kindred form.]

rum² *rum, adj.* good (*obs. slang*): queer, droll, odd (*slang*). — *n.* (*arch.*) a queer person. — *advs.* **rum′ly; rumm′ily.** — *n.* **rumm′iness.** — *adjs.* **rumm′ish; rumm′y.** [Cant.]

rumal. See **romal.**

Rumanian. See **Romanian.**

Rumansch, Rumonsch. See **Romansch.**

rumba, rhumba *room′ba, rum′ba, n.* a violent Cuban Negro dance or a modification of it. — *v.i.* to dance the rumba. [Sp.]

rumbelow *rum′bi-lō, n.* a meaningless word, occurring as burden in old sea-songs.

rumble¹ *rum′bl, v.i.* to make a low heavy grumbling or rolling noise: to move with such a noise: to be involved in a gang fight (*slang*). — *v.t.* to give forth, or to agitate or move, with such a sound: to inform against, betray to the police (*slang*). — *n.* a sound of rumbling: a seat for servants behind a carriage, or for extra passengers in a two-seater car (also **rumble seat**): a quarrel, disturbance, gang fight (*slang*). — *n.* **rum′bler.** — *n.* and *adj.* **rum′bling.** — *adv.* **rum′blingly.** — *adj.* **rum′bly.** — **rumble strip** one of a set of rough-textured strips set into a road surface to warn drivers (by tyre noise) of a hazard ahead; **rum′ble-tum′ble** a rumble seat: a lumbering vehicle: a tumbling motion. [Cf. Du. *rommelen,* Ger. *rummeln.*]

rumble² *rum′bl,* (*slang*) *v.t.* to grasp: to see through, discover the truth about. [Obscure.]

rumblegumption. See **rumgumption.**

rumbo. See **rum¹.**

rumbullion *rum-bul′yən,* (*obs.*) *n.* an older name for **rum¹.** [Obscure.]

rumbustious *rum-bust′yəs,* (*coll.*) *adj.* boisterous. — Also (*arch.*) **rumbus′tical.** [Prob. **robust.**]

rume a Shakespearian spelling of **rheum.**

rumelgumption. See **rumgumption.**

rumen *roo′men, n.* the paunch or first stomach of a ruminant: — *pl.* **ru′mina.** [L. *rūmen, -inis,* gullet.]

Rumex *roo′meks, n.* the dock and sorrel genus of Polygonaceae. [L. *rūmex, -icis,* a kind of dart, also sorrel (from its hastate leaves).]

rumfustian *rum-fus′chən, n.* a hot drink, a kind of negus. [**rum¹, fustian.**]

rumgumption *rum-gum(p)′shən,* (*Scot.*) *n.* common sense. — Also **rum(m)el-, rum(m)le-, rumblegump′tion** (*rum′l-*).

rumina. See **rumen.**

ruminant *roo′min-ənt, n.* an animal that chews the cud. — *adj.* cud-chewing: meditative. — *n.pl.* **Ruminantia** (*-an′shyə, -shə*) the cud-chewing division of the even-

toed ungulates. — *adv.* **ru′minantly.** — *v.i.* **ru′mināte** to chew the cud: to regurgitate for chewing: to meditate ((up)on). — *v.t.* to chew over again: to muse on. — *adj.* (*bot.*) mottled as if chewed. — *adv.* **ru′minatingly.** — *n.* **ruminā′tion.** — *adj.* **ru′minative.** — *adv.* **ru′minatively.** — *n.* **ru′minātor.** [L. *rūmināre, -ātum* — *rūmen, -inis,* the gullet.]

rumkin¹ *rum′kin,* (*obs.*) *n.* a kind of drinking-vessel.

rumkin² *rum′kin, n.* a tailless fowl. [App. **rump.**]

rumlegumption. See **rumgumption.**

rummage *rum′ij, n.* orig. stowage of casks, etc., in a ship's hold: a thorough search, as by customs officers: an overhauling search: (*Shak.* **romage**) commotion, upheaval. — *v.t.* to arrange, esp. orig. in a ship's hold (*arch.*): to ransack: to overhaul: to search: to stir. — *v.i.* to make a search. — *n.* **rumm′ager.** — **rummage sale** a sale at which buyers are allowed to rummage among the goods: also a sale of odds and ends or undesired goods. [Fr. *arrumage* (now *arrimage*), stowage.]

rummelgumption, rummlegumption. See **rumgumption.**

rummer *rum′ər, n.* a large drinking-glass. [Du. *roemer;* Ger. *Römer.*]

rummy¹. See **rum¹,².**

rummy² *rum′i, n.* a card-game in which cards are drawn from the stock and sequences, triplets, etc., are laid on the table.

Rumonsch. See **Romansch.**

rumour, in U.S. **rumor,** *roo′mər, n.* clamour (*arch.*): general talk, repute: hearsay: flying report: a current story. — *v.t.* to put about by report. — *adj.* **ru′morous** resounding: full of rumours: of the nature of rumours: vaguely heard. — *n.* **ru′mourer.** [O.Fr. — L. *rūmor, -ōris,* a noise.]

rump *rump, n.* the hinder part of an animal's body, the root of the tail with parts adjoining: a cut of beef between the loin and the round: in birds, the uropygium: usu. contemptuously, a remnant. — *v.t.* to turn one's back upon: to clean out of money (*Scot.*). — **Rump′er** a member or supporter of the Rump Parliament; **rum′ple** (*Scot.*) a rump. — *adj.* **rump′less.** — **rump′-bone′** the coccyx; **rump′-end.** — *adj.* **rump′-fed** (*Shak.*) prob. with well-nourished rump. — **rump′le-bane′** rump-bone; **rump′-post** the share bone or pygostyle of a bird; **rump steak** steak cut from the thigh near the rump. — **the Rump** the remnant of the long Parliament, after Pride's expulsion (1648), of about a hundred Presbyterian royalist members. [Scand.; cf. Dan. *rumpe,* Sw. and Norw. *rumpa,* O.N. *rumpr,* Ger. *Rumpf,* Du. *romp.*]

rumple¹ *rum′pl, n.* a fold or wrinkle. — *v.t.* to crush out of shape: to make uneven. [Du. *rompel;* cf. O.E. *hrimpan,* to wrinkle.]

rumple². See **rump.**

rumpus *rum′pəs, n.* an uproar: a disturbance. — **rumpus room** (orig. *U.S.*) a room in which children can play freely.

rumti-iddity, rumpti-iddity *rum(p)-ti-id′i-ti,* **rum-ti-tum** *rum′ti-tum′, interjs.* meaningless refrains.

run *run,* formerly also **ren** *ren;* Scot. **rin** *rin, vs.i.* to proceed by lifting one foot before the other is down: to go swiftly, at more than a walking pace: to hasten: to proceed quickly: to betake oneself: to flee: to progress, esp. smoothly and quickly: to go about freely: to ride at a running pace: to roll: to revolve: to go with a gliding motion: to slip: to go on wheels: to travel, cover a distance: to make a short journey: to swim in shoals: to ascend a river for spawning: to ply: to have a definite sequence, as of notes, words: to proceed through a sequence of operations, work, or go, as a machine: to follow a course: to keep the stage without interruption: to flow: to spread, diffuse: to emit or transmit a flow: to melt: to fuse: to curdle (now *dial.*): to have a course, stretch, or extent: to range: to average: to elapse: tend: to come to be, become, pass (*arch.*): to be current: to be valid: to recur repeatedly or remain persistent (in the mind): to come undone, as by the dropping breaking of a stitch: to compete in a race: to be a candidate (*U.S.*). — *v.t.* to cause to run: to chase, hunt: to drive forward: to thrust: to pierce: to drive: to pass quickly: to range, run about or throughout: to hurry through: to enter, promote, put forward (as a horse, candidate, or protégé): to render, by running or otherwise: to conduct, manage: to follow: to traverse: to cause to extend, form in a line: to sew slightly: to shoot along or down: to perform, achieve, or score by running, or as if by running: to flee or desert from: to incur: to risk and pass the hazard of: to smuggle: to have or keep current or running: to publish (a regular paper, magazine, etc.): to publish (an article, advertisement) in a newspaper or magazine, esp. in successive issues: to show (a film or TV programme): to compete with in a race: to press or put to it, in competition or difficulty: to coagulate: to fuse: to emit, discharge, flow with: to execute (a program) (*comput.*): to control the activities of (esp. a spy): — *pr.p.* **runn′ing;** *pa.t.* **ran;** *pa.p.* **run.** — *n.* an act, spell, or manner of running: a journey, trip: distance, time or quantity run: a circuit of duty, as a delivery round, etc.: a continuous stretch, spell, series, or period: a shoal, migration, or migrating body: a roulade: a spell of being in general demand: a rush for payment, as upon a bank: a unit of scoring in cricket: a batsman's passage from one popping-crease to the other: a circuit in baseball: flow or discharge: course: prevalence: the ordinary or average kind, the generality: a track: a path made by animals: a small stream (*U.S.*): a range of feeding-ground: a tract of land used for raising stock (*Austr.* and *N.Z.*): an enclosure for chickens, etc.: freedom of access to all parts: the playing of a salmon: general direction: a ladder in knitting or knitted fabrics, esp. stockings: the complete execution of a program (*comput.*): (*pl.* with *the*) diarrhoea (*coll.*). — *adj.* having been poured, smuggled, coagulated: having run. — *n.* **run′let** a runnel. — *adj.* **runn′able** of a stag, fit for hunting. — *n.* **runn′er** one who, or that which, runs or can run: a fugitive: a racer: a messenger: an agent: a tout: an intelligencer: a rooting stem that runs along the ground: a rope to increase the power of a tackle: a smuggler: a Bow Street officer (*hist.*): a ring, loop, or the like, through which anything slides or runs: the part on which a sledge, a skate, or a drawer slides: the passage by which metal is poured into a mould: a strip of cloth as a table ornament: a revolving millstone: a slice across a carcase of beef below the breast (*Scot.*): a climbing plant of the kidney-bean genus (*Phaseolus multiflorus;* **runn′er-bean, scarlet-runn′er**): a breed of domestic duck (**runner duck**): a vessel for conveying fish, oysters, etc.: a long narrow strip of carpet used for passages and staircases. — *adj.* **runn′ing** racing: habitually going at a run: current: successive: continuous: flowing: discharging: easy: cursive: itinerant: done at or with a run: hasty. — *n.* action of the verb: the pace. — *adv.* **runn′ingly.** — *adj.* **runn′y** inclined to run or liquefy. — **run′about** a gadabout: a vagabond: a small light car, boat or aeroplane; **run′around** a runabout (car): see also **get, give the runaround** (below); **run′away** a fugitive: a horse that bolts: a flight. — *adj.* fleeing: done by or in flight: uncontrolled: overwhelming. — *adj.* **run′-down′** in weakened health: (of a building, etc.) dilapidated. — *n.* (usu. **run′down**) a reduction in numbers: a statement bringing together all the main items, a summary (see also **run down** below). — *adj.* **run′flat** (of a tyre) able, after being punctured, to be safely driven on for a considerable distance without sustaining further damage. — **run′-in** an approach: a quarrel, argument (*coll.*; see also **run in** below). — **runn′er-up′** a competitor (orig. a dog) that holds out to the last heat: the competitor next after the winner: one of a number of contestants coming close behind the winner: — *pl.* **runn′ers-up′; runn′ing-banq′uet** a slight or hasty collation; **running** ⋯e a battle between pursuers and pursued: a con- ⋯g skirmish (also *fig.*); **runn′ing-board** a footboard

along the side of a motor-car or (*U.S.*) locomotive, **running commentary** a commentary accompanying a text: a broadcast description of a game or other event in progress; **running dog** (*derog.*) in political jargon, a slavish follower; **running fight** a fight between pursuer and pursued; **running fire** (*mil.*) a rapid succession of firing; **running footman** a servant who ran before or alongside a horseman or carriage; **running gag** (*coll.*) a joke that continually reappears throughout a play, programme, etc.; **runn′ing-gear** the wheels and axles of a vehicle; **runn′ing-hand** a style of rapid writing without lifting the pen; **running head** a running title; **runn′ing-knot** a knot that will form a noose on pulling; **running lights** the lights shown by vessels between sunset and sunrise: small lights at the front and rear of a car which remain on while the engine is running; **running mate** a runner who makes the pace for another: a horse teamed with another, or making the pace for another: in U.S., the candidate for the less important of two associated offices, esp. the candidate for the vice-presidency considered in relation to the presidential candidate; **running ornament** an ornament in which the design is continuous; **running repairs** minor repairs; **running rigging** all the rigging except the shrouds, stays and lower mast-head pendants; **running sore** one which discharges pus: a continual irritation, a long-standing problem; **running stitch** a simple stitch usu. made in a line, in order to gather fabric, etc.; **running title** the title of a book, etc., continued from page to page on the upper margin; **run′-off** a race held to resolve a dead heat or other uncertain result (also *fig.*): rain-water which drains into rivers, rather than being absorbed into the soil: urination (*slang*). — *adj.* **run′-of-the-mill′** constituting an ordinary fair sample, not selected: mediocre. — **run-on′** in verse, carrying the sense on beyond the end of the line (see also **run on** below). — *adj.* **run′-resist′** of stockings, tights, knitted with a stitch which does not ladder readily. — **run′-through** an instance of running through (see **run through** below); **run time** the time needed for the execution of a computer program; **run′-up** an approach (*lit.* and *fig.*; see also **run up** below); **run′way** a trail, track, or passageway: a firm strip of ground for aircraft to take off from and land on. — **give the runaround** (*slang*) to give a vague, indecisive, or deceptive reply to a question or meet a request with evasion; **get the runaround** (*slang*) to be treated thus; **in the long run** in the end or final result; **in, out of, the running** competing with, without, a fair chance of success; **make, take up, the running** to take the lead: to set the pace; **on the run** (*coll.*) pursued, esp. by the police; **run across** to come upon by accident; **run after** to pursue; **run along!** (*coll.*) off you go!; **run a temperature** to be feverish; **run away with** to take away: to win (a prize, etc.) easily; **run down** to pursue to exhaustion or capture: to collide with and knock over or sink: to disparage: to become unwound or exhausted; **run dry** to cease to flow: to come to an end; **run for it** (*coll.*) to attempt to escape, run away from; **run hard, close** to press hard behind; **run in** to go in: to arrest and take to a lock-up: to insert a word, etc., without making a break or new paragraph (*print.*): to bring (new machinery, car) into full working condition by a period of careful operation; **run in the blood, family** to be a hereditary character; **run into** to meet, come across: to extend into; **run into debt** to get into debt; **run it fine** to allow very little margin, as of time; **run itself** of a business enterprise, etc., to need little supervision or active direction; **run low** to run short; **run off** to cause to flow out: to take impressions of, to print: to repeat, recount; **run off one's feet** exhausted by overwork; **run off with** (*coll.*) to take away, steal; **run on** to talk on and on: to continue in the same line, and not in a new paragraph (*print.*); **run one's eyes over** to look at cursorily; **run out** to run short: to terminate, expire: to leak, let out liquid: to put out (a batsman running between the wickets and not yet in his ground): dismissed thus; **run out of** to have no more of; **run out on** (*coll.*) to abandon, desert; **run over** to overflow: to overthrow: to go over cursorily: of a road vehicle, to knock down (a person or animal); **run scared** (*slang*) to be frightened; **run short** to come to be short, lacking, or exhausted; **run through** to exhaust: to transfix: to read or perform quickly or cursorily but completely; **run to** to be sufficient for; **run to earth, ground** see **earth, ground²**; **run together** to mingle or blend; **run to seed** see **seed**; **run up** to make or mend hastily: to build hurriedly: to string up, hang: to send the ball rolling or flying low towards the hole (*golf*): to incur increasingly; **take a running jump** (*slang*) an expression of impatience, contempt, etc. [O.E. *rinnan, irnan, iernan,* to run; causative *rennan,* to curdle; see also **earn²**.]

runagate *run'ə-gāt, n.* a vagabond: a renegade: an apostate: a fugitive. — Also *adj.* [**renegade** influenced by **run, agate²**.]

runch *runsh,* (*Scot.*) *n.* charlock: wild radish. [Origin obscure.]

runcible *run'si-bl, adj.* app. a nonsense-word of Edward Lear's, whose phrase *runcible spoon* has been applied to a sharp-edged, broad-pronged pickle-fork.

runcinate *runs'in-āt,* (*bot.*) *adj.* with backward-pointing lobes. [L. *runcina,* a plane, formerly misunderstood as a saw.]

rund. Same as **roon.**

rundale *run'dāl, n.* a system of holding land in single holdings made up of detached pieces: land or a share of it so held. — Also *adj.* [**run** and the Northern form of **dole¹**.]

rundle *run'dl, n.* a round, a ladder-rung: a ring, circle, disc, or ball. — *adj.* **run'dled.** [**roundel.**]

rundlet *rund'lit,* **runlet** *run'lit,* arch. ns. a liquid measure equal to approx. 15 gallons (U.S. 18 gallons): a small barrel. [Fr. *rondelet.*]

rune *rōōn, n.* a letter of the futhork or ancient Germanic alphabet: a secret, a mystic symbol, sentence, spell, or song: a song, stanza or canto of a Finnish poem, esp. of the *Kalevala* (Finn. *runo,* akin to O.N. *rūn*). — *adjs.* **runed; ru'nic** of, pertaining to, written in, inscribed with runes: Scandinavian: Northern: (wrongly) in the manner of ancient Northumbrian and Celtic interlacing ornament. — **rune'-craft** knowledge of runes; **rune'-singer; rune'-stave** (O.E. *rūnstæf*) a runic letter. [O.E. and O.N. *rūn,* mystery, rune; Goth. and O.H.G. *rūna.*]

rung¹ *rung, n.* a spoke: a cross-bar or rail: a ladder round or step: a ship's floor-timber: a cudgel (*Scot.*). [O.E. *hrung;* Ger. *Runge.*]

rung² *rung.* See **ring¹,².**

rung³ *rung, adj.* having a ring through the nose. [**ring¹.**]

runkle *rung'kl, n.* a wrinkle, crease. — *v.t.* and *v.i.* to wrinkle: to crease. [Prob. Scand.; cf. **ruck¹, ruckle².**]

runlet. See **run, rundlet.**

runnable. See **run.**

runnel *run'l, n.* a little brook. [O.E. *rynel,* dim. of *ryne,* a stream — *rinnan,* to run.]

runner, running. See **run.**

runnet. Dial. variant of **rennet¹.**

runnion. See **ronyon.**

runny. See **run.**

runrig *run'rig,* (*Scot.*) *n.* a form of land-tenure, the same as rundale. — Also *adj.* and *adv.* [**run, rig².**]

runt *runt, n.* a small, stunted, or old ox or cow: a small pig, esp. the smallest of a litter: anything undersized: a large breed of domestic pigeon: a dead tree-stump or trunk: a cabbage-stem: a vague term of reproach, esp. to the old or boorish. — *adjs.* **runt'ed; runt'ish; runt'y.** [Origin uncertain.]

Runyonesque *run-yən-esk', adj.* in the style of the American writer A. Damon *Runyon* (1884–1946), portrayer of gangsters in their milder moments.

rupee *rōō-pē', n.* monetary unit and nickel (orig. silver) coin of India, Pakistan and Bhutan (equal to 100 paisas), Nepal (100 pice), and Sri Lanka, Mauritius, the Seychelles and the Maldive Islands (100 cents).

[Urdu *rūpiyah* — Sans. *rūpya,* wrought silver.]

Rupert's drop *rōō'pərts-drop',* a tailed bulb formed by dropping molten glass in water, bursting when the tail is broken — probably discovered by Prince *Rupert* (1619–82).

rupestrian *rōō-pes'tri-ən, adj.* composed of rock: inscribed on rock. [L. *rūpēs,* rock.]

rupia *rōō'pi-ə, n.* a skin ulcer covered by crusts of dried secretion and dead tissue. [Gr. *rhypos,* filth.]

rupiah *rōō'pi-ə, n.* the standard unit of currency of Indonesia: — *pl.* **ru'piah, ru'piahs.** [Hindi, rupee.]

rupicoline *rōō-pik'ō-līn,* **rupicolous** *-ləs, adjs.* rock-dwelling. [L. *rūpēs,* a rock, *colēre,* to inhabit.]

rupture *rup'chər, n.* a breach, breaking, or bursting: the state of being broken: breach of harmony, relations, or negotiations: hernia, esp. abdominal. — *v.t.* and *v.i.* to break or burst. — **rup'turewort** a caryophyllaceous plant (*Herniaria*), once thought to cure hernia. [L.L. *ruptūra* — L. *rumpĕre, ruptum,* to break.]

rural *rōō'rl, adj.* of the country. — *n.* (*obs.*) a country-dweller. — *n.* **ruralisā'tion, -z-.** — *v.t.* **ru'ralise, -ize** to render rural. — *v.i.* to become rural: to rusticate. — *ns.* **ru'ralism; ru'ralist; rurality** (*-al'i-ti*). — *adv.* **ru'rally.** — *n.* **ru'ralness.** — *adj.* **ruridecanal** (*rōō-ri-di-kā'nl;* sometimes *-dek'ən-l*) of a rural dean(ery). — **rural dean** see **dean².** [L. *rūrālis* — *rūs, rūris,* the country.]

Ruritania *rōōr-i-tān'yə, n.* a fictitious land of historical romance (in S.E. Europe) discovered by Anthony Hope. — *n.* and *adj.* **Ruritān'ian.**

rurp *rûrp,* (orig. *U.S.*) *n.* a very small hook-like piton used in mountaineering. [Acronym of realised ultimate reality *p*iton.]

Rusa *rōō'sə, n.* the genus of deer containing the sambar: (without *cap.*) a sambar. — *adj.* **ru'sine** (*-sīn*). [Malay *rūsa.*]

rusa, roosa *rōō'sə, n.* an Indian grass (**rusa grass**) from which an aromatic oil (**rusa oil**) is distilled. [Hind. *rūsā.*]

rusalka *rōō-sal'kə, n.* a Russian water-nymph. [Russ.]

Ruscus *rus'kəs, n.* a small genus of European evergreen shrubs (family Liliaceae): (without *cap.*) any plant of the genus. [L. *rūscum,* butcher's-broom.]

ruse *rōōz, n.* a trick, stratagem, artifice. — *adj.* **rusé** (*rü-zā;* Fr.) artful, deceitful, cunning. — **ruse contre ruse** (*rüz kõtr' rüz;* Fr.) cunning against cunning; **ruse de guerre** (*də ger;* Fr.) a stratagem of war. [O.Fr. *ruse* — *ruser, reüser,* to get out of the way, double on one's tracks; see **rush¹.**]

rush¹ *rush, v.i.* to move forward with haste, impetuosity, or rashness. — *v.t.* to force out of place: to hasten or hustle forward, or into any action: to move, transport, drive, push, in great haste: to capture, secure, surmount, pass, by a rush: to defraud (*coll.*): to overcharge (*coll.*). — *n.* a swift impetuous forward movement: a sudden simultaneous or general movement (as a *gold rush*): an onset: a stampede: a migratory movement or body: a run upon anything: an unedited print of a motion picture scene or series of scenes for immediate viewing by the film makers: rapidly increased activity: bustling activity: a feeling of euphoria experienced after the taking of a drug, e.g. heroin, amphetamine (*slang*): a sound of rushing: a collective name for a group of pochards. — *adj.* (*coll.*) done or needing to be done quickly. — *n.* **rush'er.** — **rush hour** one of the times during the day of maximum activity or traffic; **rush one's fences** to act precipitately. [A.Fr. *russcher,* O.Fr. *reusser, reüser, ruser* (Fr. *ruser*); see **ruse.**]

rush² *rush, n.* any plant of the grass-like marsh-growi͏͏ genus Juncus: a stalk or round stalk-like leaf of ͏ a plant: extended to various more or less similar ͏ (see **bulrush, club-rush, Dutch** or **scouring-rush rush**): a rushlight, a rush wick: a type of some no value or importance: a rush-ring (*Shak.*). ͏ rush or rushes. — *v.t.* to make or strew ͏͏ — *v.i.* to gather rushes. — *adj.* **rush'en** m͏͏ — *n.* **rush'iness.** — *adjs.* **rush'-like; rus͏͏** abounding in or made of rushes. —

country observance of carrying rushes to strew the church: the day of the festival. — *adj.* **rush'-bottomed** having a seat made with rushes. — **rush'-candle, rush'-light** a candle or night-light having a wick of rush-pith: a small, feeble light. — *adj.* **rush'-grown.** — **rush'-holder** a stand for a rushlight; **rush'-ring** a ring of plaited rush, sometimes formerly used as an improvised wedding-ring. — *adj.* **rush'y-fringed.** [O.E. *risce*; Ger. *Risch*.]

rusine. See **Rusa.**

rusk *rusk, n.* a small cake like a piece of very hard toast. [Sp. *rosca*, a roll; origin unknown.]

rusma *ruz'mə, n.* a depilatory of lime and orpiment. [App. Turk. *khirisma* — Gr. *chrīsma*, ointment.]

russel *rus'l, n.* a ribbed cotton and woollen material. — **russ'el-cord** a kind of rep made of cotton and wool. [Poss. Flem. *Rijssel*, Lille.]

Russellite *rus'əl-īt, n.* a member of the International Bible Students' Association, or Jehovah's Witnesses, a millennialist sect founded by the American Pastor C. T. *Russell* (1852–1916). — Also *adj.*

russet *rus'it, n.* a coarse homespun cloth or dress: a reddish-brown colour: a reddish-brown variety of apple. — *adj.* made of russet: homespun, homely, rustic (*arch.*): reddish-brown: of brown leather. — *v.t.* and *v.i.* to make or become russet in colour. — *n.* **russ'eting** a russet apple. — *adj.* **russ'ety.** [O.Fr. *rousset* — L. *russus*, red.]

Russian *rush'(y)ən, adj.* of *Russia* or its people. — *n.* a native or citizen of Russia: the Slavonic language of most Russians. — *n.* and *adj.* **Russ** (*rus*) Russian. — *adj.* **Russia** (*rush'ə*, *-yə*) Russian. — *ns.* **russ'ia** russia leather; **Russianīsā'tion, -z-.** — *v.t.* **Russ'ianise, -ize** to give Russian characteristics to: to make Russian. — *ns.* **Russ'ianism; Russ'ianist; Russification** (*rus-i-fi-kā'shən*). — *v.t.* **Russ'ify** to Russianise. — *ns.* (*arch.*) **Russ'ky, Russ'ki** (*slang*, usu. *derog.*) Russian; **Russ'ophil(e)** one who favours Russian policy (also *adj.*); **Russoph'ilism; Russoph'ilist; Russ'ophobe** one who dreads or hates the Russians (also *adj.*); **Russoph'-obist; Russophō'bia** the dread of Russian policy. — **russia** (or **Russia**) **leather** a fine brownish-red leather with a characteristic odour; **Russian boots** wide, calf-length leather boots; **Russian dressing** mayonnaise sharpened with chilli sauce, chopped pickles, etc.; **Russian roulette** an act of bravado, specif. that of loading a revolver with one bullet, spinning the cylinder, and firing at one's own head. — *adj.* **Russo-Byzan'tine** Byzantine as developed in Russia.

Russniak *rus'ni-ak, n.* and *adj.* Ruthenian: Ukrainian or Little Russian. [Ruthenian *Rusnjak*.]

rust *rust, n.* the reddish-brown coating on iron exposed to moisture: any similar coating or appearance: a plant disease characterised by a rusty appearance, caused by various fungi of the Uredineae: a fungus causing such disease, notably *Puccinia graminis*, which attacks wheat: corrosion: injurious influence or consequence, esp. of mental inactivity or idleness: the colour of rust. — *v.i.* to become rusty: to affect with rust: to become dull or inefficient by inaction. — *v.t.* to make rusty: to impair by time and inactivity. — *adj.* **rust'ed.** — *adv.* **rust'ily.** — *n.* **rust'iness.** — *n.* and *adj.* **rust'ing.** — *adjs.* **rust'less** free from rust: proof against rust; **rust'y** covered with rust: impaired by inactivity, out of practice: dull: affected with rust-disease: rust-coloured: of a rusty black: time-worn: rough: raucous: obstinate: discoloured. — *adj.* **rust'-coloured** — **rust'-fungus.** — *adjs.* **rust'-proof; rust'-resistant.** — **rust'y-back** the scalefern. — *adj.* **rust'y-coloured.** [O.E. *rūst*; Ger. *Rost*.]

rus'tik, adj. of, or characteristic of, the country or country-dwellers: country-dwelling: like countryfolk [o]r works: simple and plain: awkward: uncouth: [ma]de: roughly made: made of rough branches: of [...] with sunken or chamfered joints, sometimes [rough]ened face. — *n.* a peasant: a clown: a [...]ced brick or stone: rustic masonry: in [...], a fence made of rough branches, etc.

— *adj.* and (*rare*) *n.* **rus'tical.** — *adv.* **rus'tically.** — *v.t.* **rust'icate** to send into the country: to banish for a time from town or college: to build in rustic masonry. — *v.i.* to live in the country: to become rustic. — *adj.* **rust'icated.** — *ns.* **rusticā'tion; rust'icātor.** — *adj.* **rus'ticial** (*-tish'l*; *Scott*, as a false archaism). — *v.t.* and *v.i.* **rus'ticise, -ize** (*-ti-sīz*). — *ns.* **rust'icism** (*-sizm*) a rustic saying or custom; **rusticity** (*-tis'i-ti*) rustic manner: simplicity: rudeness. — **rustic capitals** a type of Roman script using simplified, squared capital letters; **rus'tic-ware** a terracotta of a light brown paste, having a brown glaze; **rus'tic-work** rusticated masonry: summer-houses, etc., of rough branches. [L. *rūsticus* — *rūs*, the country.]

rustle *rus'l, v.i.* to make a soft, whispering sound, as of dry leaves: to go about with such a sound: to stir about, hustle (*U.S.*): to steal cattle (*U.S.*). — *v.t.* to cause to rustle: to get by rustling (*U.S.*). — *n.* a quick succession of small sounds, as that of dry leaves: a rustling: bustle (*U.S.*). — *n.* **rus'tler.** — *n.* and *adj.* **rus'tling.** — *adv.* **rus'tlingly.** — **rustle up** to arrange, gather together. [Imit.; cf. Flem. *ruysselen*.]

rustre *rus'tər,* (*her.*) *n.* a lozenge pierced with a circular opening. — *adj.* **rus'tred.** [Fr.]

rusty. See **rust.** — Also a variant of **reasty** and of **reesty.**

rut¹ *rut, n.* a furrow made by wheels: a fixed course difficult to depart from. — *v.t.* to furrow with ruts: — *pr.p.* **rutt'ing;** *pa.t.* and *pa.p.* **rutt'ed.** — *adj.* **rutt'y.** — **in a rut** following a tedious routine from which it is difficult to escape. [Origin obscure; prob. not Fr. *route*.]

rut² *rut, n.* sexual excitement in male deer: also in other animals. — *v.i.* to be in such a period of sexual excitement. — *v.t.* (*rare*) to copulate with. — *n.* and *adj.* **rutt'ing.** — *adj.* **rutt'ish** lustful. — **rut'-time.** [O.Fr. *ruit, rut* — L. *rugītus* — *rugīre*, to roar.]

Ruta *rōō'tə, n.* the rue genus of dicotyledons, giving name to the family **Rutā'ceae** which is usually made to include the orange, etc. — *adj.* **rutā'ceous.** [L. *rūta*; see **rue¹**.]

rutabaga *rōō-tə-bā'gə,* (*U.S.*) *n.* the Swedish turnip. [Sw. dial. *rotabagge*.]

rutaceous. See **Ruta.**

ruth *rōōth, n.* pity: remorse: sorrow: matter for pity: misfortune, calamity (*obs.*). — *adj.* **ruth'ful** pitiful, sorrowful: piteous, causing pity. — *adv.* **ruth'fully.** — *adj.* **ruth'less** pitiless: unsparing. — *adv.* **ruth'lessly.** — *n.* **ruth'lessness.** [M.E. *ruthe, reuth*; see **rue²**; ending influenced by Scand., as O.N. *hryggth*.]

Ruthene *rōō-thēn', n.* a member of a branch of the Little Russian division of the Slavs on both sides of the Carpathians: the language of the Ruthenes. — *n.* and *adj.* **Ruthēn'ian** Ruthene.

ruthenium *rōō-thē'ni-əm, n.* a metallic element (symbol **Ru**; at. numb. 44) of the platinum group, found in the Ural Mountains. — *adjs.* **ruthē'nic** of or concerning ruthenium, esp. with a high valency; **ruthē'nious** of or concerning ruthenium, esp. with a low valency. [L.L. *Ruthenia*, Russia.]

rutherford *rudh'ər-fərd, n.* a unit of radioactive disintegration, equal to a million disintegrations a second — abbrev. **rd.** — *n.* **rutherford'ium** the name coined in the U.S. for the transuranic element (symbol Rf; at. numb. 104), called by the Russians kurchatovium. [After the physicist Baron *Rutherford* (1871–1937).]

ruthful, ruthless, etc. See **ruth.**

rutilant *rōō'ti-lənt,* (*rare*) *adj.* shining: glowing ruddily. [L. *rutilāns, -antis,* pr.p. of *rutilāre,* to be reddish.]

rutile *rōō'tīl, n.* a reddish-brown mineral of the tetragonal system, titanium oxide. — *adj.* **rutilated** (*rōō'til-āt-id*) enclosing needles of rutile. [L. *rutilus*, reddish.]

rutin *rōō'tin, n.* a drug used against the fragility of small blood-vessels. [Formed from **Ruta**.]

rutter *rut'ər,* (*obs.*) *n.* a mercenary horse-soldier. [M.Du. *rutter* — O.Fr. *routier*.]

rutty, etc. See **rut¹**.

ry- in many words an old spelling of **ri-**.

rya *rē'ə, n.* a type of Scandinavian knotted-pile rug with a distinctive colourful pattern (also **rya rug**): the weave, pattern or style typical of a rya. — Also *adj.* [Sw., conn. with Finn. *ryijy*.]

ryal, rial *rī'əl, (obs.) adj.* and *n.* royal. — esp. *n.* a coin of various kinds — an old English gold coin worth about ten shillings, a Spanish real, and others. [O.Fr. *rial,* royal.]

rybat *rib'ət, n.* a dressed stone at the side of a door, window, etc. [Prob. conn. with **rebate**[2], **rabbet**.]

rybaudrye, rybauld. See **ribald.**

rye[1] *rī, n.* a grass (*Secale*, esp. *S. cereale*) allied to wheat and barley: its grain, used for making bread: rye-grass: rye-whisky. — *adj.* of rye. — **rye'-bread; rye'-coffee** a coffee-substitute made from rye; **rye'-flour; rye'-grass** a pasture and fodder grass (species of Lolium), with flat spikelets appressed edgewise in a two-rowed spike; **rye'-roll'** a dark treacly cookie, understood not to be of rye. — *n.* and *adj.* **rye'-straw.** — **rye'-whis'ky** spirituous beverage made chiefly from rye; **rye'-wolf** (Ger. *Roggenwolf*) an evil creature of German folklore lurking in the rye-fields. [O.E. *ryge*; O.N. *rugr,* Ger. *Roggen* (also *Rocken*).]

rye[2] *rī, n.* a gypsy word for gentleman. [Romany *rei, rai,* lord.]

ryepeck, rypeck, ripeck *rī'pek, (dial.) n.* a pole used for mooring a punt. [Origin obscure.]

ryfe *rīf, (Spens.) adj.* Same as **rife.**

ryke *rīk,* a Scots form of **reach**[1].

rymme an old spelling of **rim**[1,2].

rynd. Same as **rind**[2].

ryokan *rē-ō'kən, n.* a traditional Japanese inn. [Jap.]

ryot, raiyat *rī'ət, n.* an Indian peasant. — *n.* **ry'otwari, raiy'atwari** (*-wä-rē*) a system of land-tenure by which each peasant holds directly of the state. [Hind. *raiyat, raiyatwārī* — Ar. *ra'īyah,* a subject.]

rype *rü'pə, n.* a ptarmigan: — *pl.* **ry'per.** [Dan.]

rypeck. See **ryepeck.**

rythme *rīm,* an old spelling of **rhyme.**

ryve an old spelling of **rive.**

For other sounds see detailed chart of pronunciation.

S

S, s *es, n.* the nineteenth letter in our alphabet, seventeenth in the Roman, a consonant, its usual sound a voiceless alveolar fricative (sibilant), but often voiced, and sometimes a voiceless palato-alveolar fricative (represented usually by *sh*), or voiced (as in *pleasure*): any mark or object of the form of the letter: as a mediaeval Roman numeral, S = 7 or 70; S̄ = 70 000. — **collar of SS** see **ess**.

's *z, s,* a sentence element used to form the possessive of singular nouns (e.g. *John's, the dog's*), some pronouns (e.g. *one's*), and plural nouns not ending in *-s* or a similar sound (e.g. *the children's*): often also to form the plural of numbers or symbols (e.g. 3's): a shortened form of **God's, has, is,** or (*Scot.*) **as, sai¹**: also a shortened form of **us** (pron. *s;* e.g. *let's go*), **his** (e.g., *obs., in's hand*).

sa' *sā, v.t.* an obs. contraction of **save**.

Saam(e), Sabme, Sabmi, Sami *säm(ē), n.* a Lapp: — *pl.* **Saame, Samit.** — *adj.* Lappish. [Lappish.]

Saanen *sä'nən, n.* a Swiss breed of white, short-haired goat: a goat of this breed. [*Saanen,* a town in Switzerland.]

sab¹ *sab,* (*Scot.*) *n.* a form of **sob**.

sab². See **sabot**.

Saba *sä'bä, n.* Sheba, an ancient people of Yemen. — *n.* and *adj.* **Sabaean, Sabean** (*-bē'ən*). — Also applied by confusion to adherents of Sabaism and of Sabianism. [Gr. *Saba* — Ar. *Saba'*; Heb. *Shebā*.]

sabadilla *sab-ə-dil'ə, n.* the seeds of a liliaceous plant, *Schoenocaulon,* yielding veratrine. — Also **cebadill'a, cevadill'a.** [Sp. *cebadilla,* dim. of *cebada,* barley.]

Sabaean. See **Saba**.

Sabahan *səb-ä'hən, n.* a citizen or inhabitant of *Sabah,* a Malaysian state (formerly North Borneo). — *adj.* of, from or pertaining to Sabah.

Sabaism *sä'bā-izm, n.* the worship of the host of heaven. [Heb. *tsābā,* host.]

Sabal *sä'bal, n.* an American genus of palms, the palmettos. [Origin unknown.]

Sabaoth *sa-bā'oth, n.pl.* armies, used only in the Bible phrase, 'Lord of Sabaoth': (*sab'əth*) erroneously for Sabbath (*Spens.*). [Heb. *tsebāōth* (transliterated *sabaōth* in Gr.), pl. of *tsabā,* an army.]

sabaton *sab'ə-ton, n.* armour for the foot, not necessarily broad-toed. [Prov. *sabató;* cf. **sabot**, Sp. *zapata.*]

Sabbath *sab'əth, n.* among the Jews, Saturday, set apart for rest from work: among most Christians, Sunday: sometimes also used for the Muslim day of rest, Friday: a sabbatical year of the Jews: a time of rest: (also **sabb'at**) a witches' midnight meeting. — *adj.* of or appropriate to the Sabbath. — *n.* **Sabbatā'rian** one who observes Saturday as Sabbath: one who believes in or practises observance, or strict observance, of the Sabbath (Saturday or Sunday). — Also *adj.* — *n.* **Sabbatā'rianism.** — *adjs.* **Sabb'athless; sabbatic** (*sab-at'ik*), **-al** pertaining to, or resembling, the Sabbath: enjoying or bringing rest: on, or of, leave from one's work (as *sabbatical leave, sabbatical visit,* etc.). — *n.* **sabbat'ical** a period of leave from one's work, esp. for teachers and lecturers, also esp. to undertake a separate or related project. — *adj.* **sabb'atine** pertaining to Saturday. — *v.t.* **sabb'atise, -ize** to observe as a Sabbath. — *v.i.* to keep a Sabbath. — *n.* **sabb'atism** sabbatical rest: observance of the Sabbath. — **Sabb'ath-breach; Sabb'ath-breaker; Sabb'ath-breaking** (also *adj.*); **Sabb'ath-day** (also *adj.*); **Sabbath-day's journey** 2000 cubits, or about one kilometre, which a Jew was permitted to walk on the Sabbath (Josh. iii. 4); **Sabbath school** (usu. *U.S.*) a Sunday school; **sab-**

batical year every seventh year, in which the Israelites allowed their fields and vineyards to lie fallow: a year off, for study, travel, etc. [Heb. *Shabbāth.*]

Sabean. See **Saba**.

Sabella *sə-bel'ə, n.* a genus of tube-building sea-worms: (without *cap.*) a worm of this genus. [L. *sabulum,* sand.]

Sabellian¹ *sə-bel'i-ən, n.* and *adj.* orig. Sabine: now generally used in a wide sense to include kindred peoples and languages. [L. *Sabellus,* poet. dim. of *Sabīnus.*]

Sabellian² *sə-bel'i-ən, n.* a follower of *Sabellius* (3rd century). — Also *adj.* — *n.* **Sabell'ianism** the teaching of Sabellius, that Father, Son, and Holy Ghost are one and the same person in different aspects.

saber. American spelling of **sabre**.

Sabian *sä'bi-ən,* **Zabian** *zā',* **Tsabian** *tsā', ns.* an adherent of a religion or a group of religions mentioned in the Koran as entitled to toleration, prob. akin to the Mandaeans: Mandaean: by confusion sometimes a Sabaean, sometimes an adherent of Sabaism. — Also *adjs.* — *n.* **Sā'bianism.** [Ar. *Sābi'.*]

sabin *sab'in, sā'bin,* (*phys.*) *n.* a unit of acoustic absorption, equal to the absorption, considered complete, of 1 sq. ft. of a perfectly absorbing surface. [From Wallace C. *Sabine* (1868–1919), U.S. physicist.]

Sabine *sab'īn, n.* one of an ancient people of central Italy, afterwards united with the Romans. — Also *adj.* [L. *Sabīnus.*]

Sabin vaccine *sā'bin vak'sēn, -sin,* a live-virus poliomyelitis vaccine taken by the mouth. [Albert Bruce *Sabin,* American physician (born 1906).]

sable¹ *sā'bl, n.* an arctic and subarctic marten: its lustrous dark brown fur: a paintbrush of its hair. — *adj.* of sable. [O.Fr.; prob. from Slav.]

sable² *sā'bl, n.* and *adj.* black (orig. *her.,* now chiefly *poet.*): dark. — *n.* a sable antelope: (in *pl.*) mourning garments. — *v.t.* to darken. — **sable antelope** a large South African antelope (*Hippotragus niger*), black above, white below. — *adj.* **sa'ble-coloured.** [Fr. *sable;* poss. the same as the foregoing.]

Sabme, Sabmi. See **Saam(e)**.

sabot *sab'ō, n.* a wooden shoe, as worn by the French peasantry: an attachment to guide a projectile through the bore. — *n.* **sabotage** (*-täzh',* now usu. *sab',* also *-tij*) malicious destruction: action taken to prevent the achievement of any aim. — Also *v.t.* and *v.i.* — *ns.* **saboteur** (*-tær'*) one who sabotages (coll. abbrev. **sab**); **sabotier** (*-tyā'*) a wearer of wooden shoes: a Waldensian. [Fr. *sabot.*]

sabra *sä'brə, n.* a native-born Israeli, not an immigrant. [Mod. Hebrew *sābrāh,* type of cactus.]

sabre, in U.S. **saber,** *sā'bər, n.* a curved, cutting, cavalry sword: a light sword used in fencing: a soldier armed with a sabre. — *v.t.* to wound or kill with a sabre. — **sa'bre-cut.** — *v.i.* **sa'bre-ratt'le.** — **sa'bre-rattling** military bluster; **sa'bre-tooth** (in full **sabre-toothed tiger**) a Tertiary fossil carnivore (*Machaerodus*) with extremely long upper canine teeth; **sa'bre-wing** a humming-bird of a group with bent outer primaries in the male. [Fr. *sabre* — Ger. *Sabel* (now *Säbel*); origin unknown.]

sabretache *sab'ər-tash, n.* a flat bag slung from a cavalry officer's sword-belt. [Fr. *sabretache* — Ger. *Säbeltasche* — *Säbel,* sabre, *Tasche,* pocket.]

sabulous *sab'ū-ləs,* **sabulose** *sab'ū-lōs, adjs.* sandy: gritty. [L. *sabulum,* sand.]

saburra *sə-bur'ə, n.* a granular deposit, as in the stomach. — *adj.* **saburr'al.** — *n.* **saburrā'tion** (*med.*) application of hot sand. [L. *saburra,* sand.]

sac[1] *sak*, (*biol.*) *n.* a pouch. — *adjs.* **sacc′ate** pouched: pouch-like: gibbous: enclosed in a sac; **sacciform** (*sak′-si-förm*), **sacc′ular** sac-like; **sacc′ulated** formed in a series of sac-like expansions: enclosed. — *ns.* **saccūlā′-tion; sacc′ule, sacc′ulus** a small sac: — *pl.* **sacc′ules, sacc′ulī.** [L. *saccus*, a bag; see **sack**[1].]

sac[2] *sak*, (*law*) *n.* the privilege of a lord of manor of holding courts. — *adj.* **sac′less** (*Scott*) unchallengeable, not to be molested (see **sack′less** *s.v.*). — See also **soc**. [O.E. *sacu*, strife.]

saccade *sak-äd′, sək-, n.* a short jerky movement, esp. of the eye: a short rapid tug on a horse's reins. — *adj.* **saccad′ic** jerky: consisting of or pertaining to saccades. — *adv.* **saccad′ically.** [Fr. *saccade*, a jerk — O.Fr. *saquer*, to pull.]

Saccharum *sak′ə-rəm, n.* the sugar-cane genus of grasses. — *ns.* **sacch′arase** same as **invertase; sacch′arate** a salt of saccharic acid. — *adjs.* **sacch′arated** sugared, sweetened; **saccharic** (*sak-ar′ik*) of sugar (**saccharic acid** an acid, $H_2C_6H_8O_8$, got by oxidation of sugar). — *n.* **sacch′aride** a carbohydrate: a compound with sugar. — *adj.* **saccharif′erous** sugar-yielding. — *v.t.* **sacchar′-ify** (or *sak′*) to convert into sugar. — *ns.* **saccharim′eter** a polarimeter or other instrument for testing concentration of sugar solutions; **saccharim′etry; sacch′arin, -ine** (*-in, -ēn*) an intensely sweet, white crystalline solid ($C_6H_4COSO_2NH$), prepared from toluene: sickly sweetness (*fig.*). — *adj.* **sacch′arine** (*-īn, -ēn*) of the nature of sugar: of, containing, or yielding sugar: sugary: of sickly sweetness. — *n.* **saccharinity** (*-in′i-ti*). — *adjs.* **sacch′aroid, -oid′al** like loaf-sugar in texture. — *ns.* **saccharom′eter** a hydrometer or other instrument for measuring concentration of sugar solutions; **Saccharomyces** (*-ō-mī′sēz*; Gr. *mykēs*, fungus) the yeast genus of ascomycete fungi; **sacch′arose** (*-ōs*) any carbohydrate, esp. cane sugar. [L. *saccharum* — Gr. *sakcharon*, sugar, a word of Eastern origin; cf. **jaggery, sugar.**]

sacciform. See **sac**[1].

saccos. Same as **sakkos.**

saccular, etc. See **sac**[1].

sacellum *sə-sel′əm, n.* a god's unroofed sanctuary: a little chapel: a tomb or monument in the form of a chapel within a church: — *pl.* **sacell′a.** [L. dim. of *sacrum*, a holy place — *sacer*, consecrated.]

sacerdotal *sas-ər-dō′tl, adj.* priestly: sacerdotalist. — *v.t.* **sacerdō′talise, -ize** to render sacerdotal. — *ns.* **sacerdō′-talism** the spirit of the priesthood: devotion to priestly interests: priestcraft: the belief that the presbyter is a priest in the sense of offering a sacrifice in the eucharist: claim for, or attribution to, a priesthood, of special or supernatural powers: excessive influence of priests over people's thoughts and actions (*derog.*); **sacerdō′talist.** — *adv.* **sacerdō′tally.** [L. *sacerdōs, -ōtis*, a priest — *sacer*, sacred, *dāre*, to give.]

sachem *sä′chəm, n.* a North American Indian chief: a Tammany leader. — *ns.* **sä′chemdom, sä′chemship.** [Algonquian.]

Sachertorte *sähh′ər-tör-tə, zä-, -k-, n.* a kind of sweet spiced chocolate cake made and served at *Sacher's* hotel in Vienna. — Also **Sacher torte.** [See **torte.**]

sachet *sa′shā, n.* a bag of perfume, or a bag for holding handkerchiefs, etc.: a small usu. plastic envelope, containing a liquid, cream, etc., such as shampoo. [Fr.]

sack[1] *sak, n.* a large bag of coarse material: a sackful: a varying measure of capacity: a woman's gown, loose at the back (*hist.*): a train hung from the shoulders of such a gown: a loose coat, hanging at the back: a woman's loose-fitting waistless dress: (with **the**) dismissal (*coll.*): (with **the**) the punishment of death by sewing in a sack and drowning (*arch.*): bed (*slang*). — *v.t.* to put into a sack: to dismiss (*coll.*). — *ns.* **sack′ful** as much as a sack will hold: — *pl.* **sack′fuls; sack′ing** sackcloth. — **sack′cloth** cloth for sacks: coarse cloth, formerly worn in mourning or penance; **sack′-coat** a man's short loose coat. — *adj.* **sack-doudling** (*-dōōd′lin;*

Scott) bagpiping (cf. **doodle**[2] and Ger. *Dudelsack*). — **sack′-race** one in which each runner's legs are encased in a sack; **sack′-tree** the upas (from the use of its inner bark to make sacks). — **hit the sack** to go to bed; **in sackcloth and ashes** showing extreme regret, etc. (*facet.*); **sad sack** one who seems to attract mishap and disaster. [O.E. *sacc* — L. *saccus* — Gr. *sakkos*; prob. Phoenician.]

sack[2] *sak, n.* the plundering or devastation of a town: pillage. — *v.t.* to plunder: to ravage. — *ns.* **sack′age, sack′ing** sack. [Fr. *sac*; according to some the same as the foregoing (putting in a bag).]

sack[3] *sak, n.* the old name of a Spanish wine, the favourite drink of Falstaff. — **sack′-poss′et** posset made with sack. — **burnt sack** mulled sack. [Fr. *sec* — L. *siccus*, dry.]

sackbut *sak′but, n.* an old instrument with a slide like the trombone: a mistranslation of Aramaic *sabbekā*, the sambuca (*B.*). [Fr. *saquebute*, perh. O.Fr. *saquier*, to draw out, and *bouter*, to push.]

sackless *sak′lis*, (*arch.* and *Scot.*) *adj.* innocent: guileless: feeble: dispirited (see also under **sac**). [O.E. *saclēas* — *sacu*; **sac**[2], **sake**[2].]

sacque. A sham-French spelling of **sack**[1] (garment).

sacra. See **sacrum.**

sacral[1] *sā′krəl, adj.* of or relating to sacred rites. — *n.* **sacralisā′tion, -z-** endowing (something) with sacred status or properties: treating (something) as if it were sacred. — *v.t.* **sac′ralise, -ize.** [L. *sacrum*, a sacred object.]

sacral[2]. See **sacrum.**

sacrament *sak′rə-mənt, n.* a religious rite variously regarded as a channel or as a sign of grace — amongst Protestants generally *Baptism* and the *Lord's Supper* — amongst Roman Catholics, also *Confirmation, Penance, Holy Orders, Matrimony*, and *Extreme Unction*: the Lord's Supper specially: the bread or wine in the Lord's Supper: a symbol of something spiritual or secret: a sign, token, or pledge of a covenant: a religious mystery: a Roman soldier's oath on enlistment: a pledge deposited by each party to a suit (*Rom. law*): a solemn oath: an oath of purgation: materials used in a sacrament. — *v.t.* to bind by an oath. — *adj.* **sacramental** (*-ment′l*). — *n.* (*R.C.*) an act or object which may transmit or receive grace. — *ns.* **sacramen′-talism; sacramen′talist** one who attaches importance to the spiritual nature of the sacraments. — *adv.* **sacramen′tally.** — *n.* **sacramentā′rian** one who holds a high or extreme view of the efficacy of the sacraments: a denier of the real presence in the sacrament of the Lord's Supper (*obs.*). — Also *adj.* — *n.* **sacramentā′-rianism.** — *adj.* **sacramen′tary** pertaining to the sacrament or sacraments: sacramentarian. — *n.* a book containing all the prayers and ceremonies used at the celebration of the R.C. sacraments: one who denies the doctrine of the real presence. — **sac′rament-house** an ambry for reservation of the sacrament. — **take the sacrament upon** or **to** to take communion in confirmation of (an oath). [L. *sacrāmentum*, an oath, pledge — *sacrāre*, to consecrate — *sacer*, sacred.]

sacrarium *sā-krā′ri-əm*, L. *sa-krä′ri-ŏŏm, n.* a place where the Penates or other holy things were kept (*Rom. ant.*): the presbytery of a church: — *pl.* **sacra′ria.** [L. *sacrārium* — *sacer*, holy.]

sacred *sā′krid, adj.* consecrated: devoted: set apart or dedicated, esp. to God: holy: proceeding from God: religious: entitled to veneration: not to be violated: accursed. — *adv.* **sa′credly.** — *n.* **sa′credness.** — **sacr** ape the hanuman of India; **sacred beetle** an Egyp′ scarab; **sacred cat** the house cat of Egypt, sacr Pasht or Bast; **Sacred College** the body of car **sacred cow** an institution, custom, etc., so ve that it is above criticism (*coll.*); **sacred fish** ox **Sacred Heart** (*R.C.*) the physical heart adored with special devotion since the 1′ [Pa.p. of obs. *sacre* — O.Fr. *sacrer* — *sacer*, sacred.]

sacrifice *sak'ri-fīs*, in the poets sometimes *-fīz*, *n.* the offering of a slaughtered animal on an altar to a god: any offering to a god: Christ's offering of himself (*theol.*): the Mass (*R.C.*): destruction, surrender, or foregoing of anything valued for the sake of anything else, esp. a higher consideration: loss by selling cheap: a victim offered in sacrifice. — *v.t.* to offer up in sacrifice: to make a sacrifice of: to give up for a higher good or for mere advantage: to make a victim of: to allow to come to destruction or evil. — *v.i.* to offer sacrifice. — *n.* **sac'rificer.** — *adj.* **sacrificial** (*-fish'l*) of or pertaining to sacrifice: (of an object or substance) which protects another from corrosion by its own exposure to and damage by the corrosive (as esp. **sacrificial anode, sacrificial metal**) (*tech.*). — *adv.* **sacrifi'cially.** — *v.t.* and *v.i.* **sac'rify** (*obs.*) to sacrifice: — *pa.p.* (*Spens.*) **sac'rifide.** — **sacrifice hit** in baseball, a hit to enable another player to score or to gain a base. [L. *sacrificium* — *sacer*, sacred, *facĕre*, to make.]

sacrilege *sak'ri-lij*, *n.* a profanation of anything holy: the breaking into a place of worship and stealing therefrom (also *fig.*). — *adj.* **sacrilegious** (*-lij'əs*). — *adv.* **sacrile'giously.** — *ns.* **sacrile'giousness; sacrilē'gist.** [Fr. *sacrilège* — L. *sacrilegium* — *sacer*, sacred, *legĕre*, to gather.]

sacring *sā'kring*, (*arch.*) *n.* consecration. — **sacring bell** in R.C. churches, a small bell rung to call attention to the more solemn parts of the service of the Mass. [See **sacred.**]

sacrist *sak'rist*, *sā'krist*, *n.* a sacristan: a person in a cathedral who copies out music for the choir and takes care of the books. — *ns.* **sacristan** (*sak'*) an officer in a church who has care of the sacred vessels and other movables: a sexton; **sacristy** (*sak'*) an apartment in a church where the sacred utensils, vestments, etc., are kept: vestry. [L.L. *sacrista*, *sacristānus*, a sacristan, *sacristia*, a vestry — L. *sacer*.]

sacro-. See **sacrum.**

sacrosanct *sak'rō-sang(k)t*, *adj.* inviolable. — *n.* **sacrosanc'tity.** [L. *sacrōsanctus* — *sacer*, sacred, *sanctus*, pa.p. of *sancīre*, to hallow.]

sacrum *sā'krəm*, *sak'rəm*, *n.* a triangular bone composed of fused vertebrae wedged between two innominate bones, so as to form the keystone of the pelvic arch: — *pl.* **sa'cra.** — *adj.* **sa'cral.** — **sa'crō-** in composition, sacrum, e.g. *adjs.* **sacrocos'tal** connected with the sacrum and having the character of a rib (also *n.*); **sacrōil'iac** pertaining to the sacrum and ilium. [L. (*os*) *sacrum*, holy (bone), so called for unknown reason.]

sad *sad*, (*compar.* **sadd'er,** *superl.* **sadd'est**) *adj.* orig., sated: steadfast, constant (*Spens.*, *Milt.*): staid (*arch.*): sedate (*arch.*): serious (*arch.*): earnest (*arch.*): grave: sober-minded: sorrowful: deplorable (often playfully): heavy, stiff: doughy: sober, dark-coloured. — *v.t.* **sadd'en** to make sad. — *v.i.* to grow sad. — *adj.* **sadd'ish.** — *adv.* **sad'ly** in a sad manner: unfortunately, sad to relate. — *n.* **sad'ness.** **sad'-coloured;** **sad'-eyed, -faced, -hearted** (all *Shak.*). — **sad'-iron** a flat-iron; **sad sack** see **sack¹.** — **in sober sadness** in serious earnest. [O.E. *sæd*, sated; cf. Du. *zat*, Ger. *satt*; L. *sat*, *satis*.]

saddhu. See **sadhu.**

saddle *sad'l*, *n.* a seat for a rider: a pad for the back of a draught animal: anything of like shape: a col: that part of the back on which the saddle is placed: a mark on that part: a butcher's cut including a part of the backbone with the ribs: the hinder part of a cock's back: a worm's clitellum: in a structure, e.g. a bridge, support having a groove shaped to fit another part. — *v.t.* to put a saddle on: to encumber: to impose as a burden or encumbrance: (of a trainer) to be responsible for preparing and entering (a racehorse) for a race: to bestride or mount (a horse, bicycle, etc.) (*rare*). — *v.i.* to get into the saddle of a horse, bicycle, etc. — *adj.* **saddle'less.** — *ns.* **sadd'ler** a maker or seller of

saddles: a soldier who has charge of cavalry saddles (also **sadd'ler-cor'poral, -ser'geant**): the harp-seal: a saddle-horse (*U.S.*); **sadd'lery** the occupation of a saddler: his shop or stock-in-trade: a saddle-room. — **sadd'leback** a saddle-shaped hill, coping, animal, or object: the great black-backed gull: the hooded crow: the male harp-seal: a breed of goose: a breed of pig: a saddle-roof. — *adj.* (also **sadd'lebacked**) saddle-shaped: with a depression in the middle of the back: marked on the back: of a coping, sloping from the middle to each side. — **sadd'le-bag** a bag carried at, or attached to, the saddle. — *adj.* upholstered in cloth in imitation of camels' saddle-bags. — **sadd'le-bar** a bar for sustaining stained glass in a window; **sadd'le-blanket** a folded blanket used as a saddle-cloth; **sadd'le-bow** (*-bō*) the arched front of a saddle; **sadd'le-cloth** a housing cloth placed under a saddle. — *adj.* **sadd'le-fast** firmly seated in the saddle. — **sadd'le-feather, -hackle** one of the long, slender feathers drooping from a cock's saddle; **sadd'le-girth** a band that holds the saddle in its place; **sadd'le-horse** a riding horse; **sadd'le-lap** the skirt of a saddle. — *adj.* **sadd'le-nosed** with nose sunken at the bridge. — **sadd'le-pillar, -pin** the support of a cycle saddle, which fits a socket in the frame; **sadd'le-roof** a tower roof with two gables; **sadd'le-room** a room where saddles and harness are kept. — *adjs.* **sadd'le-shaped** arched: concave and convex in sections at right angles to each other; **sadd'le-sick, -sore** chafed with riding. — **saddle soap** a kind of soap used for cleaning and treating leather; **sadd'le-spring** a spring supporting a cycle-saddle; **saddle stitch** needlework consisting of long stitches on the top surface and short stitches on the underside of the material: one such stitch: a method of stitching (a booklet, magazine, etc.) together through the back centre fold. — *v.t.* and *v.i.* to sew in saddle stitch. — **sadd'le-tree** the frame of a saddle. — **in the saddle** in control; **put the saddle on the right horse** to impute blame where it is deserved; **saddle up** to saddle a horse: to mount (*S.Afr.*). [O.E. *sadol, sadel*; cf. Du. *zadel*, Ger. *Sattel*.]

Sadducee *sad'ū-sē*, *n.* one of a Jewish priestly and aristocratic party of traditionalists, whose reactionary conservatism resisted the progressive views of the Pharisees, and who rejected, among various other beliefs, that of life after death. — *adjs.* **Sadducae'an, Sadducean** (*-sē'ən*). — *ns.* **Sadd'uceeism, Sadd'ucism** scepticism. [Gr. *Saddoukaios* — Heb. *Tsadūqīm*, from *Zadok* the High Priest, the founder.]

sadhu, saddhu *sä'dōō*, *n.* a Hindu holy man, ascetic and mendicant. [Sans. *sādhu*, — *adj.*, straight, pious.]

sadism *sād'izm*, *n.* pleasure, esp. sexual pleasure, obtained by inflicting pain: love of cruelty. — *n.* **sad'ist.** — *adj.* **sadistic** (*sə-dis'*). — *ns.* **sado-mas'ochism** obtaining pleasure by inflicting pain on oneself or another; **sado-mas'ochist.** — *adj.* **sado-masochist'ic.** [Comte (called Marquis) de *Sade* (1740–1814), who died insane, notoriously depicted this form of pleasure in his novels.]

sae *sā*, *adv.* Scottish form of **so¹.**

saeculum, seculum *sek'ūl-əm*, *n.* an astronomical or geological age. [L., a generation.]

saeter *set'ər*, *sāt'*, *n.* in Norway, an upland meadow which provides summer pasture for cattle, and where butter and cheese are made: a hut on a saeter providing shelter for those looking after the animals. [Norw.]

saeva indignatio *sē'və in-dig-nā'shi-ō, sī'wa, sī'va in-dig-nä'ti-ō*, (L.) fierce indignation (see **ubi** in appendix of quotations).

safari *sə-fä'rē*, *n.* an expedition or caravan, especially for hunting in Africa: a long expedition involving difficulty or danger and/or requiring planning. — *v.i.* to go on safari. — **safari park** an enclosed park where wild animals (mostly non-native) are kept uncaged in the open on view to the public; **safari suit** a suit for men, boys, or women, typically of cotton and consisting of long square-cut **safari jacket** and long or short trousers. [Swahili.]

safe *sāf, adj.* unharmed: free from danger: secure: sound: certain: sure: reliable: cautious. — *n.* a chest or closet, safe against fire, thieves, etc.: a ventilated box or cupboard for meat, etc.: a condom (*U.S. slang*). — *v.t.* to make safe (*obs.*): to bring safely (*Shak.*). — *prep.* (*Spens.*) save. — *adv.* **safe′ly.** — *ns.* **safe′ness; safe′ty** (in Spens. often *sāf′i-ti*) the state or fact of being safe: close custody (*obs.*): a safeguard: a safety-bicycle. — **safe′-blower; safe′-blowing** forcing of safes, using explosives; **safe′-breaker, -cracker; safe′-breaking, -cracking** illegal opening of safes; **safe′-con′duct** a permission to pass or travel with guarantee of freedom from molestation: a convoy. — *v.t.* (*-kon′,* or *-dukt′*) to convoy. — **safe′-deposit, safe′ty-deposit** a safe storage for valuables; **safe′guard** keeping safe, protection: safety: a guard: a contrivance, condition, or provision to secure safety: a safe-conduct: an overskirt for riding (*obs.*). — *v.t.* to protect. — **safe′guarding** protection, especially by import duties; **safe house** (*coll.*) a place unknown to one's pursuers, where one can safely hide; **safe′-keeping** keeping in safety: safe custody; **safe period** that part of the menstrual cycle during which conception is most unlikely; **safe seat** a seat that the specified political party will certainly win in an election; **safe′ty-arch** an arch in the body of a wall to relieve the pressure; **safe′ty-belt** a belt for fastening a workman, etc., to a fixed object while he carries out a dangerous operation: one fastening a passenger to his seat as a precaution against injury in a crash; **safety bicycle** a common low-wheeled bicycle; **safety bolt** the safety lock of a firearm; **safe′ty-cage** a mine-cage with a catch to prevent a fall: in a motor-vehicle chassis, a specially strengthened framework around the seating part to give maximum protection to driver and passengers in a crash (also **safety cell**); **safe′ty-catch** any catch to secure safety, as in a miners' cage or a gun; **safety curtain** a fireproof theatre curtain; **safety factor** the ratio between the ultimate stress in a member, structure, or material, and the safe permissible stress in it; **safety film** photographic or cinematographic film with a non-flammable or slow-burning base of cellulose acetate or polyester; **safety fuse** a slow-burning fuse that can be lighted at a safe distance: a fuse inserted for safety in an electric circuit; **safety glass** a sandwich of plastic between sheets of glass: glass reinforced with wire, or toughened; **safety lamp** a miners' lamp that will not ignite inflammable gases; **safety light** a warning light: a light that will not readily cause a fire; **safety lock** a lock that cannot be picked by ordinary means: in firearms, a device for preventing accidental discharge; **safe′ty-match** a match that can be ignited only on a prepared surface; **safe′ty-net** a net stretched beneath an acrobat, etc., during a rehearsal or performance, in case he or she should fall: any precautionary measure (*fig.*); **safety paper** paper difficult to imitate or tamper with without detection, as for bank-notes; **safe′ty-pin** a pin in the form of a clasp with a guard covering its point: a pin for locking a piece of machinery, a grenade, a mine, etc.; **safe′ty-plug** a plug that melts when the temperature rises too high; **safety razor** a razor with protected blade; **safe′ty-rein** a rein for preventing a horse from running away; **safe′ty-stop** a contrivance for preventing accidents in machinery; **safe′ty-valve** a valve that opens when the pressure becomes too great: any outlet that gives relief (*fig.*); **safe′ty-wear** protective clothing. — **err on the safe side** to choose the safer alternative; **safe and sound** secure and uninjured; **safe as houses** (*coll.*) very safe. [O.Fr. *sauf* — L. *salvus.*]

saffian *saf′i-ən, n.* leather tanned with sumach and dyed in bright colours. [Russ. *saf′yan.*]

safflower *saf′lowr, n.* a thistle-like composite (*Carthamus tinctorius*) cultivated in India: its dried petals, used for making a red dye and rouge. — **safflower oil** an oil produced from this plant and used in cooking, etc. [Cf. Du. *saffloer,* O.Fr. *saffleur.*]

saffron *saf′rən, n.* a species of crocus: its dried stigmas,

used as a dye and flavouring: its colour, orange-yellow. — *adj.* **saff′roned** coloured or flavoured with saffron. — *adj.* **saff′rony** coloured somewhat like saffron. — *n.* **saf′ranin(e)** a coal-tar dye, giving various colours. — **saffron cake** a cake flavoured with saffron. — **bastard saffron** safflower; **meadow saffron** Colchicum; **saffron milk cap** an edible, orange toadstool (*Lactarius deliciosus*). [O.Fr. *safran* — Ar. *za′farān.*]

safrole *saf′rōl, n.* a usu. colourless oily liquid obtained from sassafras and used in perfumes, soaps and insecticides. [*sassa*fras, *-ol.*]

sag *sag, v.i.* to bend, sink, or hang down, esp. in the middle: to yield or give way as from weight or pressure: to hang heavy: to droop: to drag oneself heavily along: to move, drift, to leeward: — *pr.p.* **sagg′ing;** *pa.p.* and *pa.t.* **sagged.** — *n.* a droop. — *adj.* sagging. — *n.* and *adj.* **sagg′ing.** — *adj.* **sagg′y** inclined to sag. — **sag′-bag** a large bag filled with a substance, usu. polystyrene granules, which allows it to be pushed into any shape and used as a chair, cushion, bed, etc. [Cf. Sw. *sacka,* to sink down; L.G. *sacken,* to sink.]

saga¹ *sä′gə, n.* a prose tale of the deeds of Icelandic or Norwegian heroes in the old literature of Iceland: a body of legend about some subject: a long, detailed story (*coll.*). — **sa′gaman** a narrator of sagas; **saga novel** see **roman fleuve.** [O.N. *saga;* cf. **saw³.**]

saga². See **sagum.**

sagacious *sə-gā′shəs, adj.* keen in perception or thought: discerning and judicious: wise. — *adv.* **sagā′ciously.** — *ns.* **sagā′ciousness, sagacity** (*-gas′i-ti*). [L. *sagāx, -ācis.*]

sagaman. See **saga¹.**

sagamore *sag′ə-mōr, n.* an American Indian chief. [Penobscot *sagamo;* cf. **sachem.**]

sagapenum *sag-ə-pē′nəm, n.* a fetid gum-resin, from *Ferula persica.* [Gr. *sagapēnon.*]

sagathy *sag′ə-thi, n.* a woollen stuff. [Origin unknown; cf. Fr. *sagatis,* Sp. *sagatí.*]

sage¹ *sāj, n.* a garden labiate plant (*Salvia officinalis*) used as stuffing for goose, etc.: any plant of the genus, as clary: extended to wood germander (*wood-sage*). — *adj.* **sāg′y.** — **sage′-apple** an edible gall formed on Mediterranean sage; **sage′brush** a plant-formation of shrubby Artemisias, on dry American plains: any of the Artemisias forming it; **sage Derby** a kind of sage-cheese; **sage′-cheese** a cheese flavoured and mottled with sage leaves; **sage′-cock, -grouse** a large North American grouse that feeds on sagebrush; **sage′-green** greyish green, as in sage leaves; **sage′-rabbit** a small hare of the sagebrush; **sage′-tea** an infusion of sage leaves, a domestic tonic; **sage′-thrash′er** the mountain mocking-bird. [O.Fr. *sauge* (It. *salvia*) — L. *salvia* — *salvus,* safe.]

sage² *sāj, adj.* wise. — *n.* a man of great wisdom. — *adv.* **sage′ly.** — *n.* **sage′ness.** — **Seven Sages** see **seven.** [Fr. *sage,* ult. — L. *sapĕre,* to be wise.]

sagene *sə-jēn′, n.* a net. — *n.* **sagenite** (*saj′ən-īt, sə-jē′nīt*) rutile in the form of a network of needles. — *adj.* **sagenitic** (*saj-ən-it′ik*). [Gr. *sagēnē,* drag-net.]

saggar, saggard, sagger, seggar *sag′, seg′ər(d), ns.* a clay box in which pottery is packed for baking. [Perh. **safeguard.**]

sagged, sagging. See **sag.**

sagger. See **saggar.**

saginate *saj′i-nāt, v.t.* to fatten. — *n.* **saginā′tion.** [L. *sagīnāre,* to fatten.]

sagitta *sə-jit′ə, n.* a keystone: a versed sine: the middle stroke of the letter epsilon: (with *cap.*) the Arrow, northern constellation. — *adj.* **sagittal** (*saj′it-l*) arrc shaped: like a sagitta: pertaining or parallel to sagittal suture. — *adv.* **sag′ittally.** — *ns.* **Sagittā′** arrow-head genus; **Sagittā′rius** the Archer, a c lation and a sign of the Zodiac: one born u sign; **sag′ittary** a centaur: an archer. — *adjs.* **sagitt′iform** shaped like an arrow-head wit pointing backwards. — **sagittal suture**

the two parietal bones of the skull. [L. *sagitta*, an arrow.]

sago *sā'gō, n.* a nutritive farinaceous substance produced from the pith of *Metroxylon* and other palms (*Arenga, Caryota, Oreodoxa*), and Cycads (*Cycas*). — **sa'go= palm.** [Malay *sāgū*.]

sago(u)in. See **saguin.**

saguaro *sä-(g)wä'rō, n.* the giant cactus: — *pl.* **sagua'ros.** [From an American Indian language.]

saguin, sagoin, sagouin *sag'win, sag-oin', n.* a titi monkey. [Fr. *sago(u)in* — Port. *saguim* — Tupí *saguin*.]

sagum *sā'gəm,* (L. *sag'ōōm*) *n.* a Roman military cloak: — *pl.* **sa'ga.** [L. *sāgum*; prob. Gaulish.]

Saharan *sə-här'ən, adj.* of, resembling, or characteristic of, the Sahara desert.

Sahelian *sə-hē'li-ən, -hel'i-ən, adj.* of or concerning the countries south of the Sahara desert, including Chad, Niger, Mali, Mauretania, etc., generally between the desert and savanna regions. [Ar. *sāhel*, coastal strip.]

sahib *sä'ib, n.* a term of respect given in India to persons of rank and to Europeans: Sir or Mr: a European: a gentleman: — *fem.* **sah'iba(h).** [Ar. *sāhib*, orig. friend.]

sai *sä'i, n.* the capuchin monkey. [Tupí, monkey.]

saibling *zīp'ling, n.* the char. [Ger. dial.]

saic, saick, saique *sä-ēk', sä'ik, n.* a Levantine vessel like a ketch. [Fr. *saïque* — Turk. *shāïqā*.]

saice. Same as **syce.**

said¹ *sed, pa.t.* and *pa.p.* of **say¹.** — *adj.* before-mentioned. — **saidst, saidest** see **say¹.**

said². See **sayyid.**

saiga *sī'gə, n.* a west Asian antelope. [Russ.]

saikei *sī'kī, n.* a Japanese miniature landscape of bonsai trees, etc., growing on rocks or stones: the art of cultivating saikei. [Jap. *sai*, cultivation, *kei*, scenery.]

saikless *sāk'lis, adj.* a Scots form of **sackless.**

sail¹ *sāl, n.* a sheet of canvas, framework of slats, or other structure, spread to catch the wind, so as to propel a ship, drive a windmill, etc.: a wing, esp. a hawk's: any sail-like organ or object: sails collectively: a ship or ships: a trip in a vessel: an act or distance of sailing: a number sailing or flying together: a condition of having sails set or filled: a submarine's conning-tower. — *v.i.* to progress or travel by sail: to go by water: to set out on a voyage: to make excursions in sailing-craft: to glide or float smoothly along. — *v.t.* to navigate: to cause to sail, as a toy boat: to pass over or along in a ship: to fly through. — *adjs.* **sail'able** navigable; **sailed** having sails. — *ns.* **sail'er** a boat or ship that can sail; **sail'ing** travelling or journey by sails or on water: a ship's departure from port: the act or mode of directing a ship's course. — Also *adj.* — *adj.* **sail'less.** — *ns.* **sail'or** one who is employed in the management of a ship, esp. one who is not an officer: a mariner: a seaman: a navigator: one who is tolerant of the motion of a ship: a sailor-hat (*coll.*); **sail'oring** occupation as a sailor. — *adjs.* **sail'orless; sail'or-like, sail'orly, sail'y.** — **sail arm** one of the arms of a windmill; **sail'board** a small, light, flat-hulled sailing-craft usu. consisting of a surfboard fitted with a single flexible mast, the sail being controlled by a hand-held boom; **sail'boarder** one who sails a sailboard; **sail'boarding** the sport of sailing a sailboard (also called **windsurfing**); **sail'-boat** (esp. *U.S.*) a sailing-boat. — *adjs.* **sail'-borne; sail'= broad** (*Milt.*) broad or spreading like a sail. — **sail'= cloth** a strong cloth for sails; **sail'-fish** a fish that shows a large dorsal fin, esp. the basking shark or a kind of swordfish (Histiophorus); **sail'-fluke** the whiff (from exposing its tail); **sail'-flying** flying in a sailplane; **sail'ing-boat** a boat moved by sails; **sail'ing-master** an officer in charge of navigation, esp. of a yacht (formerly in U.S. navy a warrant officer); **sailing orders** instructions to the captain of a ship at setting forth on a voyage; **sail'ing-ship** a ship driven by sails; **sail'-loft** where sails are made; **sail'-maker; sail'or-hat'** a hat like a man's straw hat: a hat with a wide, brim; **sail'or-man** a seaman; **sail'or-suit** a

child's outfit resembling that of a sailor; **sail'plane** a glider that can rise with an upward current; **sail'-room** a room in a vessel where sails are stowed; **sail'-yard** the yard on which sails are extended. — **full sail** with sails filled with the wind: with all sails set; **good, bad, sailor** a person who is unaffected, made ill, by the motion of a ship; **make sail** to spread more canvas; **put on sail** to set more sails in order to travel more quickly (also *fig.*); **sail close to** (or **near**) **the wind** see **wind; set sail** to spread the sails: to set forth on a voyage (for); **shorten sail** to reduce its extent; **strike sail** to lower the sail or sails: to abate one's pretensions (*Shak.*); **under sail** having the sails spread: moved by sails. [O.E. *segel*; cf. Du. *zeil*, Ger. *Segel*.]

sail² *sāl, v.i.* to project. — *n.* projection. [O.Fr. *saillir*, to jut — L. *salīre*, to leap.]

saim (*Scot.*). See **seam¹.**

saimiri *sī-mē'rē, n.* a squirrel-monkey. [Tupí *sai*, monkey, *miri*, little.]

sain *sān,* (*arch.*) *v.t.* to make the sign of the cross over: (by association with L. *sānāre*) to heal. [O.E. *segnian* — L. *signāre* — *signum*, mark.]

saine *sān,* a Spenserian form of the infin. and the pres. indic. pl. of **say¹:** an editor's reading for **faine** (*Love's Lab. Lost* III, i. 88) taken as a *pa.p.* of **say¹** (*Shak.*).

sainfoin *sān'foin, n.* a leguminous fodder-plant (*Onobrychis viciaefolia*). — Also **saint'foin.** [Fr. *sainfoin*, prob. — *sain*, wholesome, *foin*, hay — L. *sānum fēnum.*]

saint *sānt,* when prefixed to a name *sint, sn*(*t*), *adj.* (or *n.* in apposition) holy. — *n.* a holy person: one eminent for virtue: an Israelite, a Christian, or one of the blessed dead (*B.*): one canonised: an angel (*B., Milt.*): a member of various religious bodies, esp. Puritans, as used of themselves or as a nickname: a sanctimonious person. — *v.i.* (or *v.t.* with *it*) to play the saint. — *v.t.* to make a saint of: to hail as saint. — *n.* **saint'dom.** — *adj.* **saint'ed** made a saint, holy: like a saint: sacred: gone to heaven: canonised. — *ns.* **saint'= ess; saint'hood.** — *adj.* **saint'ish** saintlike. — *n.* **saint'ism** the character or quality of a saint: sanctimoniousness. — *adj.* **saint'like.** — *ns.* **saint'liness; saint'ling.** — *adj.* **saint'ly** of, like, characteristic of, or befitting a saint. — *n.* **saint'ship.** — **saint's day** a day set apart for the commemoration of a particular saint; **St Agnes's Eve** 20th January; **St Agnes's flower** the snowflake; **St Andrew's cross** a cross in the form of the letter X: a white saltire on a blue field, as borne on the banner of Scotland; **St Andrew's Day** 30th November; **St Anthony pig, St Anthony's cross, fire, nut** see **Anthony; St Barbara's cress** yellow-rocket; **St Barnaby's thistle** a knapweed flowering about the saint's day (11th June); **St Bernard's dog** or **(great) St Bernard** a breed of very large dogs, named after the hospice of the Great St Bernard, used, especially formerly, to rescue travellers lost in the snow; **St Crispin's Day** a shoemakers' festival, 25th October; **St Cuthbert's beads, duck** see **Cuthbert; St Dabeoc's heath** a rare Irish heath; **St David's Day** 1st March; **St Elmo's fire** a corposant; **St George's cross** a red cross on a white field; **St George's Day** 23rd April; **St Hubert's disease** hydrophobia; **St Ignatius's bean** the poisonous seed of a plant (*Strychnos ignatii*) akin to nux vomica; **St James's** the British court; **St John's bread** the carob bean; **St John's Day** 27th December; **St Johnston's ribbon** or **tippet** the hangman's rope (**St Johnsto(u)n** = Perth, associated in the 18th cent. with hangings); **St John's wort** any Hypericum; **St Julien** an esteemed red Bordeaux wine from the Médoc region; **St Leger** a horse-race run since 1776 at Doncaster, so called since 1778 from Col. *St Leger*; **St Luke's summer** a spell of pleasant weather about the middle of October; **St Martin's evil** drunkenness; **St Martin's summer** a spell of mild, damp weather in late autumn; **St Nicholas's clerks** thieves; **St Patrick's cabbage** London pride; **St Patrick's Day** 17th March; **St Peter's fish** the dory; **St Peter's wort** square-stalked St John's wort: extended to several plants; **St Stephen's** Houses of Parliament; **St Swithin's Day** 15th July; **(St) Tib(b)'s Eve** never; **St Trinian's** a fictitious girls' school created by the English cartoonist Ronald Searle (b. 1920) and popularised in humorous films. — *adj.* **St Trinian** of, pertaining to or typical of St Trinian's: *coll.* applied to or denoting unruly or riotous behaviour, dress, exploits, etc., usu. of schoolgirls. — *n.* a pupil of St Trinian's. — **St Valentine's Day** 14th February (see **Valentine**); **St Vitus's dance** chorea. [Fr., — L. *sanctus*, holy.]

saintfoin. See **sainfoin**.

Saintpaulia *sānt-pö′li-ə, n.* the genus to which the African violet (q.v.) belongs: (without *cap.*) a plant of this genus. [Baron Walter von *Saint Paul*, who discovered it.]

Saint-Simonism *sən(t)-, sin(t)-sī′mən-izm, n.* the socialistic system of the Comte de *Saint-Simon* (1760–1825). — *ns.* **Saint-Simō′nian** (also *adj.*); **Saint-Simō′nianism**; **Saint-Si′monist.**

saique. See **saic**.

sair *sār,* Scots form of **sore[1], savour, serve**.

saist (*Spens., Milt.*). Same as **sayest** (see **say[1]**).

saith[1] *seth,* (*arch.*) *3rd pers. sing. pres. indic.* of **say[1]**.

saith[2], saithe *sāth,* (*Scot.*) *n.* the coalfish. [O.N. *seithr*.]

Saiva, Shaiva *s(h)ī′və, n.* a votary of Siva. — *ns.* **S(h)ai′vism; S(h)ai′vite.**

sajou *sä-zhōō′, -jōō′, n.* a capuchin monkey. [Fr., — Tupí *sai*, monkey and augmentative *-uassu*.]

Sakai *sä′kī, n.* a group of forest tribes of Malaya: an individual of this group: their language, of the Mon-Khmer group: — *pl.* **Sakai.** — Also *adj.*

sake[1] *sä′ki, sä′kē, n.* a Japanese alcoholic drink made from fermented rice: alcoholic liquor generally. — Also **saké, saki.** [Jap.]

sake[2] *sāk, n.* a cause: account: regard: advantage: behalf: purpose: aim, object. — **for any sake** by all means: I beseech you; **for old sake's sake** for the sake of old times, for auld lang syne; **for the sake of** in order to, for the purpose of. [O.E. *sacu*, strife, a lawsuit; Du. *zaak*, Ger. *Sache*; O.E. *sacan*, to strive, Goth. *sakan*; cf. **sac[2], sackless, seek**.]

saker *sā′kər, n.* a species of falcon (*Falco sacer*) used in hawking, esp. the female: an obsolete small cannon. — *n.* **sa′keret** the male saker. [Fr. *sacre*, prob. — Ar. *saqr*, confounded with L. *sacer*, sacred.]

saki[1] *sä′ki, -kē, n.* a South American monkey of the genus *Pithecia*, with long bushy non-prehensile tail. [Fr., for Tupí *sai*, or *saguin*; cf. **sai, saguin**.]

saki[2]. See **sake[1]**.

sakieh, sakiyeh, sakia *sä′ki-(y)ə, n.* an Eastern waterwheel. [Ar. *sāqiyah*.]

sakkos *sak′os, n.* an Eastern bishop's vestment like an alb or a dalmatic. — Also **sacc′os.** [Gr. *sakkos*, a bag.]

saksaul. Same as **saxaul**.

Sakti, Shakti *s(h)äk′, shuk′tē,* (*Hinduism*) *ns.* the female principle, esp. as personified in the wife of Siva or other god. — *ns.* **S(h)ak′ta** a worshipper of the Sakti; **S(h)ak′tism.** [Sans. *śakti*, divine energy.]

sal[1] *säl,* a Northern form of **shall**.

sal[2]. See **sial**.

sal[3] *säl, n.* a large gregarious tree (*Shorea robusta*; fam. Dipterocarpaceae) of north India with teaklike wood. [Hind. *sāl*.]

sal[4] *sal,* (*chem.* and *pharmacy*) *n.* a salt. — **sal alem′broth** (an alchemists' word of unknown origin) mercury ammonium chloride — also *salt of wisdom*; **sal ammoniac** ammonium chloride; **sal prunella, prunelle** saltpetre cast in cakes; **sal volatile** (*vol-at′i-li*) ammonium carbonate, or a solution of it in alcohol and/or ammonia in water: smelling salts. [L. *sāl*.]

sal Atticum *sal at′i-kəm, säl at′i-koōm,* (L.) Attic salt (see **Attic**).

salaam *sä-läm′, n.* a word and gesture of salutation in the East, chiefly among Muslims: obeisance: greeting. — *v.i.* to perform the salaam. [Ar. *salām*, peace; cf. Heb. *shālōm*.]

salable, salableness, salably. See **sale[1]**.

salacious *sə-lā′shəs, adj.* lustful: lecherous: arousing lustful or lecherous feelings. — *adv.* **salā′ciously.** — *ns.* **salā′ciousness, salacity** (*-las′i-ti*). [L. *salāx, -ācis* — *salīre*, to leap.]

salad *sal′əd,* also (*arch.*) **sallad, sallet** *sal′it, ns.* a cold dish of vegetables or herbs (either raw or pre-cooked), generally mixed, with or without oil and vinegar or other dressing, sometimes including slices of egg, lobster, etc.: a plant grown for or used in salads: something savoury (*fig.*; *Shak.*): a confused mixture. — *n.* **sal′ading** herbs and vegetables for salads. — **salad bowl; salad burnet** the common burnet; **salad cream** a type of bottled mayonnaise; **salad days** the time when one is 'green in judgement, cold in blood' (Shak., *Ant. and Cleo.* I, v. 74) — one's youth, esp. if carefree and showing inexperience; **salad dressing, oil** sauce, olive-oil, used in dressing salads; **salad herb, plant; salad plate; fruit′-salad** see **fruit; word salad** copious but incoherent utterance, sometimes a symptom of schizophrenia. [Fr. *salade* — L. *sāl*, salt.]

salade. Same as **sallet[1]**.

salal, sallal *sal′al, n.* a N.W. American ericaceous shrub (*Gaultheria shallon*). — **sal(l)′al-berry** its edible fruit. [Chinook jargon.]

salamander *sal′ə-man-dər,* or *-man′, n.* a member of a genus (**Salamandra**) of tailed amphibians, closely related to the newts, harmless, but long dreaded as poisonous, once supposed able to live in fire or to put out fire: an elemental spirit believed by Paracelsists to live in fire: one who braves exposure to fire unscathed (physical, military, or amatory): a poker used red-hot for kindling fires: a hot metal plate for browning meat, etc.: a portable stove, used during the construction of a building, in a greenhouse, etc. — *adjs.* **salaman′der= like** (also *adv.*); **salaman′drian; salaman′drine; salaman′droid** (also *n.*). [Fr. *salamandre* — L. *salamandra* — Gr. *salamandrā*; prob. of Eastern origin.]

salami *sə-lä′mi, sə-lä′mē,* (*pl.* of **salame** *-mā*; treated as *sing.*), *n.* a highly seasoned Italian sausage: (as *pl.* thin slices or small amounts (*fig.*). — **salami tactics** a policy of cutting away, one by one, undesirable elements, e.g. particular people from an organisation. — **salami technique** a fraud involving the deduction of almost indiscernable sums of money from numerous and scattered transactions (esp. *comput.*). [It.]

salamon. See **salmon[2]**.

salangane *sal′ang-gān, n.* a swiftlet (*Collocalia*) that builds edible nests. [Tagálog *salangan*.]

salary *sal′ə-ri, n.* salt (*obs.*): a periodical payment (usually at longer intervals than a week) for services other than mechanical. — *v.t.* to pay a salary to. — *n.* **salariat** (*sə-lā′ri-ət*) the salary-drawing class or body. — *adj.* **sal′aried.** [O.Fr. *salarie* (Fr. *salaire*) — L. *salārium*, salt-money, *sāl*, salt.]

salband *säl′band, zäl′bänt,* (*geol.*) *n.* the crust of a dyke or vein. [Ger. *Salband*, selvage — *Selb*, self, *Ende*, end.]

salbutamol *sal-bū′tə-mol, n.* a bronchodilator, used in the treatment of bronchial asthma.

salchow *sal′kō, -kov, n.* in ice-skating, a jump in which the skater takes off from the inside back edge of one skate, spins in the air and lands on the outside back edge of the other skate. [From Ulrich *Salchow*, 20th cent. Swedish skater.]

sale[1] *sāl, n.* act of selling: the exchange of anything for money: power or opportunity of selling: demand: public offer of goods to be sold, esp. at reduced prices or by auction: the state of being offered to buyers. — *adj.* intended for selling: vendible. — *n.* **salabil′ity** (also **saleabil′ity**). — *adj.* **sal(e)′able** that may be sold: in good demand. — *n.* **sal(e)′ableness.** — *adv.* **sal(e)′ably.** — **sale′-cat′alogue; sale′-price** price asked at a special sale; **sale′-room** an auction-room; **sales′-clerk** (*U.S.*) one who sells in a store or shop; **sales′man** a man who sells goods, esp. in a shop: a commercial traveller canvasser (*U.S.*): — *fems.* **sales′woman, sales′**

sales'lady; sales'manship the art of selling: skill in presenting wares in the most attractive light or in persuading purchasers to buy; **sales'person; sales resistance** unwillingness to buy; **sales'-talk** boosting talk to effect a sale; **sales'-tax** a tax on the sale of goods and services, esp. one general in character and flat in rate (cf. **purchase-tax**); **sale'work** work or things (made) for sale: work carelessly done. — **forced sale** a sale compelled by a creditor; **sale of work** a sale of things made by members of a church congregation or association so as to raise money; **sale or, and, return** an arrangement by which a retailer may return to the wholesaler any goods he does not sell. [Late O.E. *sala*, perh. — O.N. *sala*.]

sale² *sāl, n.* sallow: wicker (*Spens.*). — Also **seal.** [Form of **sallow¹** .]

salep *sal'ep, n.* dried Orchis tubers: a food or drug prepared from them. [Turk. *sālep*, from Ar.]

saleratus *sal-ə-rā'təs,* (*U.S.*) *n.* potassium or sodium bicarbonate, used in baking-powders. [L. *sāl aerātus,* aerated salt.]

Salesian *səl-ē'shən, adj.* of St Francis of *Sales* or his order, the Visitants. — *n.* a follower of St Francis: a member of his order.

salet. See **sallet¹.**

salewd (*Spens.*) *pa.t.* of **salue.**

salfern *sal'fərn, n.* gromwell (*Lithospermum arvense*).

Salian¹ *sā'li-ən, adj.* pertaining to a tribe of Franks on the lower Rhine. — *n.* one of this tribe. — *adj.* **Salic** (*sal'ik, sā'lik*), **Salique** (*sal'ik, sa-lēk'*). — **Salic law** a law among the Salian Franks limiting the succession of certain lands to males — held later to apply to the succession to the crown of France. [L. *Saliī,* Salians.]

Salian² *sā'li-ən, adj.* pertaining to the *Saliī,* or priests of Mars in ancient Rome.

saliaunce. See **salient.**

salic *sal'ik, sā'lik, adj.* of minerals, rich in silicon and aluminium. [*s*ilicon, *al*uminium.]

Salic. See **Salian¹.**

Salicaceae *sal-i-kā'si-ē, n.pl.* a family of Archichlamydeae, willows and poplars. — *adj.* **salicā'ceous** (*-shəs*). — *ns.* **sal'icet** (*-set*), **salicional** (*səl-ish'ə-nəl*) organ stops with tones like that of willow pipes; **salicetum** (*-sē'təm*) a thicket or plantation of willows: — *pl.* **salicē'tums, salicē'ta; sal'icin(e)** (*-sin*) a bitter crystalline glucoside ($C_{13}H_{18}O_7$) got from willow-bark, etc.; **salicylate** (*sə-lis'i-lāt*) a salt of salicylic acid. — *v.t.* to treat with salicylic acid. — *adj.* **salicylic** (*sal-i-sil'ik*; Gr. *hȳlē,* matter, material). — **salicylic acid** an acid ($C_7H_6O_3$) originally prepared from salicin. [L. *salix, salicis,* a willow.]

salices. See **Salix.**

Salicornia *sal-i-kör'ni-ə, n.* the glasswort or marsh-samphire genus of the goosefoot family, small cactus-like salt-marsh plants: (without *cap.*) a plant of this genus. [Perh. L. *sāl,* salt, *cornū,* a horn.]

salient *sā'li-ənt, adj.* leaping or springing: projecting outwards, as an angle: outstanding: prominent: striking. — *n.* an outward-pointing angle, esp. of a fortification or line of defences. — *ns.* **sā'lience** the quality or condition of being salient: projection: (*Spens.* **saliaunce**) onset; **sā'liency.** — *n.pl.* **Salientia** (*-en'shyə*) the frog and toad order of Amphibia. — *adv.* **sā'liently.** — **salient point** first rudiment, esp. (formerly) of the heart. [L. *saliēns, -entis,* pr.p. of *salīre,* to leap.]

saliferous *sə-lif'ər-əs, adj.* salt-bearing. [L. *sāl, salis,* salt, *ferre,* to bear.]

salify *sal'i-fī, v.t.* to combine or impregnate with or form into a salt: — *pr.p.* **sal'ifying;** *pa.t.* and *pa.p.* **sal'ified.** — *adj.* **sal'ifiable.** — *n.* **salificā'tion.** [Fr. *salifier* — L. *sāl, salis,* salt, *facĕre,* to make.]

saligot *sal'i-got, n.* the water-chestnut. [Fr.]

salimeter. Same as **salinometer** under **saline.**

salina *sə-lē'nə,* or *-lī', n.* a salt lagoon, lake, marsh, or spring: a salt-pan: a salt-work. [Sp., — L. *salīna* (in pl. only) — *sāl,* salt.]

saline *sā'līn, sa', sə-līn', adj.* salt: salty: of the nature of

a salt: abounding in salt: of the salts of alkali metals and magnesium: adapted to an environment with salt. — *n.* (*sə-līn',* also *sā'līn*) a salina: a salt: crude potash: an effervescent aperient powder: a salt solution used in investigation or treatment of a physiological condition. — *ns.* **salinity** (*sə-lin'i-ti*) saltness; **salinometer** (*sal-i-nom'i-tər*), **salim'eter** a hydrometer for measuring saltness of water. [L. *salīnus,* cf. **salina.**]

Salique. Same as **Salic** (see **Salian**).

saliva *sə-lī'və, n.* spittle, a liquid secreted in the mouth to soften food and begin the process of digestion. — *adjs.* **salī'val** (*rare*); **salivary** (*sal'i-vər-i, sə-lī'*) pertaining to, secreting, or conveying, saliva. — *v.i.* **sal'ivate** to produce or discharge saliva, esp. in excess. — *v.t.* to cause to secrete excess of saliva. — *n.* **salivā'tion** flow of saliva, esp. in excess. [L. *salīva.*]

Salix *sal'iks, sā'liks, n.* the willow genus: (without *cap.*) a plant of this genus: — *pl.* **salices** (*sal'i-sēz, sā'*). [L. *sălix, -icis.*]

Salk vaccine *sö(l)k vak'sēn, -sin,* a vaccine developed by the American Dr Jonas E. *Salk* and others, used against poliomyelitis.

sallad; sallal. See **salad; salal.**

salle *sal,* (Fr.) *n.* hall.

sallee *sal'ē* (*Austr.*) *n.* Acacia of various kinds: a species of Eucalyptus. [From a native word, or **sally³.**]

sallee-man *sal'ē-man, n.* a Moorish pirate: a hydrozoan with sail-like crest. — Also **sall'y-man.** — **sall'ee-rover.** [*Sallee,* on the coast of Morocco.]

sallenders *sal'ən-dərz, n.* a skin disease affecting the hocks of horses. [Cf. Fr. *solandre.*]

sallet¹ *sal'it, n.* a light helmet (esp. 15th century) with neck-guard. — Also **sal'et, salade** (*sä-läd'*). [Fr. *salade*; cf. It. *celata*; perh. — L. *galea caelāta,* engraved helmet.]

sallet². See **salad.**

sallow¹ *sal'ō, n.* a willow, esp. the broader-leaved kinds with comparatively brittle twigs—(*Scot.*) **sauch, saugh** (*söhh*). — *adj.* **sall'owy** abounding in sallows. — **sall'ow-kitten** a small puss-moth whose larva feeds on sallow; **sall'ow-thorn** sea-buckthorn. [O.E. (Anglian) *salh,* late stem *salg-* (W.S. *sealh, sēales*); cf. Ger. *Sal(weide),* L. *salix.*]

sallow² *sal'ō, adj.* esp. of a person's skin, of a pale yellowish colour. — *v.t.* to make sallow. — *adj.* **sall'owish** somewhat sallow. — *n.* **sall'owness.** — *adj.* **sall'owy.** [O.E. *salo, salu*; cf. O.H.G. *salo.*]

sally¹ *sal'i, n.* a leap: a swaying: an outrush: a sudden rushing forth of troops to attack besiegers: a going forth, excursion: outburst of fancy, wit, etc.: a projection: a running from side to side. — *v.i.* (*arch.* or *facet.*; usu. with *forth*) to rush out suddenly: to set forth, issue. — *v.t.* to sway by running from side to side of (a ship): — *pr.p.* **sall'ying;** *pa.t.* and *pa.p.* **sall'ied.** — **sall'yport** a gateway for making a sally from a fortified place: a large port for the escape of the crew from a fire-ship. [Fr. *saillie* — *saillir* (It. *salire*) — L. *salīre,* to leap.]

sally² *sal'i, n.* the raising of a bell by pull of the rope: the woolly grip of a bell rope. — *v.t.* to bring into position of sally. [Perh. from preceding.]

sally³ *sal'i,* a variant of **sallee** and of **sallow¹.**

Sally Army *sal'i ärm'i,* coll. or slang for **Salvation Army.**

Sally Lunn *sal'i lun',* a sweet tea-cake, usu. served hot with butter. [From a girl who sold them in the streets of Bath, *c.* 1797.]

sally-man. See **sallee-man.**

sallyport. See **sally¹.**

salmagundi *sal-mə-gun'di, n.* a dish of minced meat with eggs, anchovies, vinegar, pepper, etc.: a medley, miscellany. — Also **salmagun'dy.** [Fr. *salmigondis*; origin obscure.]

salmanazar *sal-man-ā'zər,* (also with *cap.*) *n.* a large wine bottle, usu. holding the equivalent of 12 standard bottles. — Also **salmana'ser.** [Allusion to Shalmaneser, King of Assyria, II Kings xvii.3.]

salmi, salmis *sal'mē, n.* a ragout, esp. of game: — *pl.*

salmis (*sal'mē*). [Fr.; perh. from preceding, or from It. *salame*, sausage.]

Salmo *sal'mō, n.* the salmon and trout genus of fishes, giving name to the family **Salmonidae** (*sal-mon'i-dē*). — *n.* **sal'monid.** — *n.* and *adj.* **sal'monoid.** [L. *salmō, -ōnis*, salmon.]

salmon¹ *sam'ən, n.* a large, highly esteemed fish (*Salmo salar*), with silvery sides, that ascends rivers to spawn: extended to many closely allied fishes, and to some that resemble it superficially in some respects: the flesh of any of these as food: the colour of salmon flesh, a pinkish orange: — *pl.* **salmon**; or **salmons** of kinds of salmon. — *adj.* salmon-coloured. — *n.* **salm'onet** a samlet. — **salm'on-berry** a salmon-coloured American raspberry; **sal'mon-coble** a salmon-fisher's boat; **salm'-on-colour** an orange-pink. — *adj.* **salm'on-coloured.** — **salm'on-disease** a bacterial disease of salmon formerly attributed to a fungus (*Saprolegnia*); **salm'on-fisher, -fishery, -fishing; salm'on-fly** any artificial fly for taking salmon; **salm'on-fry'; salm'on-ladder** a series of steps to permit a salmon to pass upstream; **salm'on-leap** a waterfall ascended by salmon at a leap; **salm'on-leister, -spear** an instrument for spearing salmon; **salmon pink; salm'on-tackle** rod, line, and fly for taking salmon; **salm'on-trout'** a fish (*Salmo trutta*) like the salmon, but smaller and thicker in proportion: in America applied to various kinds of trout. — **Burnett salmon** the Australian lungfish (from the Burnett River). [O.Fr. *saumon* — L. *salmō, -ōnis*, from *salīre*, to leap.]

salmon² *sam'ən,* **salamon** *sal'ə-mən, (obs.) ns.* supposed to mean the mass, as in the vagrants' inviolable oath *by (the) salmon.* [Origin obscure.]

Salmonella *sal-mə-nel'ə, n.* a large genus of bacteria many of which are associated with poisoning by contaminated food: (without *cap.*) a member of the genus: — *pl.* **-as, -ae** (*-ē*). — *n.* **salmonellos'is** a disease caused by Salmonella bacteria. [Daniel E. *Salmon*, veterinarian.]

salmonet. See **salmon¹.**

salmonid, salmonoid. See **Salmo.**

Salomonic. Same as **Solomonic.**

salon *sal-ô, -on, n.* a drawing-room: a reception-room: a periodic gathering of notable persons in the house of a society queen, literary hostess, etc.: a somewhat elegant shop or business establishment (e.g. *beauty salon*): a room or hall for the exhibiting of paintings, sculptures, etc.: (with *cap.*) a great annual exhibition of works by living artists in Paris. [Fr.]

saloon *sə-lōōn', n.* a spacious hall for receptions, for works of art, etc.: a large public room (for billiards, for dancing, for hairdressing, etc.): a large public cabin or dining-room for passengers: a saloon-carriage: a saloon-car: a drinking-bar (*U.S.*). — *n.* **saloon'ist.** — **saloon'-bar'** a quieter and more comfortably furnished part of a public house than the public bar, usu. separated from it; **saloon'-car'** a motor-car with enclosed body; **saloon'-carr'iage** a railway carriage with interior open from end to end; **saloon'-deck** an upper deck reserved for saloon or first-class passengers; **saloon'-keeper** (*U.S.*) a publican; **saloon'-passenger** a passenger entitled to use the principal cabin: a first-class passenger on board a ship; **saloon'-pistol, saloon'-rifle** one for use in a shooting gallery. [Fr. *salon*.]

saloop *sə-lōōp', n.* salep: a drink made from salep, later from sassafras. [**salep.**]

salop. Same as **salep.** — *adj.* **salop'ian** (*Lamb*).

Salop *sal'əp, n.* Shropshire. — *adj.* **Salopian** (*-ō'pi-ən*) of Shropshire: of Shrewsbury School. — *n.* a native or inhabitant of Shropshire: one educated at Shrewsbury School. [A.Fr. *Sloppesberie* — O.E. *Scrobbesbyrig*.]

salopette *sal'ə-pet, n.* a type of ski suit consisting of usu. quilted trousers extending to the shoulders and held up with shoulder-straps. [Fr.]

salp *salp, n.* a free-swimming tunicate (*Salpa*). — *n.* and *adj.* **salp'ian.** — *adj.* **salp'iform.** [L. *salpa* — Gr. *salpē*, a kind of fish.]

salpicon *sal'pik-on, n.* a mixture of cooked meat or fish,

vegetables, esp. mushrooms or truffles, in a sauce, used in pâtés, or as fillings for pastries, etc. [Fr., — Sp. *salpicar*, to sprinkle with salt.]

salpiglossis *sal-pi-glos'is, n.* any plant of the genus *Salpiglossis*, some of which bear bright, trumpet-shaped flowers. [Gr. *salpinx*, a trumpet, *glōssa*, tongue.]

salpinx *sal'pingks, n.* an ancient Greek trumpet: the Eustachian tube: the Fallopian tube. — *n.* **salpingectomy** (*-pin-jek'tə-mi*) surgical removal of a Fallopian tube. — *adjs.* **salpingian** (*-pin'ji-ən*) of the salpinx; **salpingit'ic** of, of the nature of, salpingitis. — *n.* **salpingitis** (*-jī'tis*) inflammation of a Fallopian tube. [Gr. *salpinx, -ingos*, a trumpet.]

salsa *sal'sə, n.* the name given to a type of rhythmic Latin-American music: a dance performed to this music. — *v.i.* to dance the salsa. [Sp. *salsa*, sauce.]

salse *sals, n.* a mud volcano. [*Salsa*, name of one near Modena.]

salsify, salsafy *sal'si-fi, n.* a purple-flowered species of goat's-beard, cultivated for its root, tasting like oysters or asparagus. — **black salsify** scorzonera. [Fr. *salsifis*, prob. — It. *sassefrica*.]

Salsola *sal'sō-lə, n.* the salt-wort genus of the goosefoot family. — *adj.* **salsolā'ceous.** [Obs. It. dim. of *salso* — L. *salsus*, salt (*adj.*).]

salsuginous *sal-sōō'ji-nəs, adj.* salty: growing in salty soil. [L. *salsūgō, -inis*, saltness.]

salt¹ *sölt, n.* chloride of sodium, occurring naturally as a mineral (rock-salt) and in solution in sea-water, brine-springs, etc.: smack, savour: piquancy: wit and good sense: saving or preserving quality: a salt-marsh or salting: an influx of salt water: a sailor, esp. an old sailor: a salt-cellar: a compound in which metal atoms or electropositive radicals replace one or more of the replaceable hydrogen atoms of an acid — generalised to include the acid itself: (in *pl.*) smelling-salts: Epsom salt or other salt or mixture of salts used in medicine, esp. as a purgative: money collected at montem. — *adj.* containing salt: tasting of salt: seasoned or cured with salt: overflowed with salt water: growing in salt soil: inhabiting salt water: pungent: excessively costly (*coll.*). — *v.t.* to sprinkle, season, cure, impregnate with salt: to immunise (as by inoculation): to season: to acclimatise: to assign an excessive value to or in (*slang*): to add gold, ore, etc., to, in order to give a false appearance of riches (*mining slang*). — *adj.* **salt'ed.** — **salt'er** one who salts, or who makes or deals in salt: a drysalter. — *adv.* **salt'ily.** — *n.* **salt'iness; salt'ing** the act of preserving, seasoning, etc., with salt: the celebration of the Eton montem: a meadow flooded by the tides (suff. *-ing*, indicating a meadow in place-names). — *adj.* **salt'ish.** — *adv.* **salt'ishly.** — *n.* **salt'ishness.** — *adj.* **salt'less.** — *adv.* **salt'ly.** — *n.* **salt'ness.** — *adj.* **salt'y** saltish: piquant, racy, witty. — **salt'-box** a box for holding salt, esp. one with a clapper lid, once used as in burlesque music along with the marrow-bones, tongs, etc.; **salt'-bush** any Australian shrubby plant of the goosefoot family. — *adj.* **salt'-butt'er** (*Shak.*) fed on nothing better than salt butter, gross. — **salt'-cake** crude sodium sulphate; **salt'-cat** a salt mixture given as a digestive to pigeons; **salt'-cellar** (O.Fr. *saliere* — L. *salārium* — *sāl*, salt) a table vessel for holding salt: a depression behind the collar-bone; **salt'-cote** (*obs.*) a building where salt is made; **salt dome, plug** (*geol.*) a diapir formed by a column of rock salt forced up by pressure through upper rock strata, often with cap rock (q.v.) on top; **salt'-fat** (erron. **salt'-foot**) a large salt-cellar marking the class boundary at table: a pickling-tub; **salt flat** a stretch of flat, salt-covered land formed by the evaporation of an area of salt water; **salt'-glaze** a glaze produced on pottery by volatilisation of common salt in the kiln: pottery produced to this glaze; **salt'-glazing; salt'-horse** (*slang*), **salt'-junk** (*sailors' slang*) salt beef; **salt'-lake** an inland lake of saline water; **salt'-lick** a place to which animals resort for salt; **salt'-marsh'** land liable to be flooded with salt water; **salt'-mine** a mine of rock-salt; **salt'= money** an allowance for salt: money collected at montem; **salt'-pan** a large basin for obtaining salt by evaporation: a salt-work: a natural depression in which salt accumulates or has accumulated by evaporation; **salt'-pit** a pit for obtaining salt by evaporation; **salt plug** see **salt dome; salt'-rheum** (also without *hyphen*) a discharge of mucus from the nose (*Shak.*): eczema (*U.S.*); **salt'-spoon** a small spoon for taking salt at table; **salt'-spring** a brine spring. — *adj.* **salt'-water** of salt water. — **salt'-work(s)** a place where salt is made; **salt'-wort** a fleshy, prickly plant (*Salsola kali*) of sandy seashores, of the goosefoot family, or other plant of the genus: sometimes applied to the glasswort (*Salicornia*). — **above, below, the salt** among those of high, or low, social class, the salt-cellar marking the boundary when all dined together; **lay, put, cast salt on someone's tail** to find or catch someone, from the jocularly recommended method of catching a bird; **like a dose of salts** (*coll.*) very quickly; **rub salt in a wound, someone's wounds** to aggravate someone's sorrow, shame, regret, etc.; **salt away** to store away: to hoard; **salt down** to preserve with salt: hence, to lay by, store up; **salt of sorrel** acid potassium oxalate, a solvent for ink-stains; **salt of tartar** a commercial name for purified potassium carbonate; **salt of the earth** the choice few of the highest excellence (Matt. v. 13); **salt of vitriol** sulphate of zinc; **salt of wisdom** sal alembroth; **salt of wormwood** potassium carbonate; **salt out** to obtain as a precipitate by adding a salt; **take with a grain, pinch, of salt** to believe with some reserve; **worth one's salt** valuable, useful — orig. worth the value of the salt one consumes. [O.E. (Anglian) *salt* (W.S. *sealt*); cf. Ger. *Salz*, also L. *sāl*, Gr. *hals*.]

salt² *sölt*, *n.* sexual desire, esp. in bitches. — *adj.* in heat: salacious (*Shak.*). [L. *saltus, -ūs*, leap.]

salt³ *sölt*, *n.* see **sault.**

saltando *säl-tän'dö*, **saltato** -*tä'tö*, *advs.* and *adjs.* arco saltando. [Ger. and pa.p. respectively of It. *saltare*, to jump, skip.]

saltant *sal'tənt*, *söl'tənt*, *adj.* leaping: dancing: salient (*her.*). — *n.* (*biol.*) a changed form developed suddenly. — *v.i.* **sal'tate.** — *n.* **saltā'tion** a leaping or jumping: spurting, pulsation: an abrupt variation or mutation (*biol.*). — *ns.* **saltāt'ionism** the process or concept of saltation, specif. the evolutionary theory that new species come about by saltation; **saltāt'ionist** one who advocates saltationism. — *adjs.* **saltato'rial, saltato'rious; sal'tatory** of or for leaping: dancing: having the power of, or used in, leaping or dancing: changing abruptly. [L. *saltāre, -ātum*, intens. of *salīre*, to leap.]

saltarello *sal-tə-rel'ö*, *n.* a lively dance with skips, for two dancers: its music, in triple time: — *pl.* **saltarell'os.** [It. *saltarello*, Sp. *saltarelo* — L. *saltāre*, to dance.]

saltate, etc. See **saltant.**

saltato. Same as **saltando.**

saltern *sölt'ərn*, *n.* a salt-works. [O.E. *s(e)altern* — *s(e)alt*, salt, *ærn*, house.]

saltier. See **saltire, satyr.**

saltigrade *sal'ti-grād*, *adj.* going by leaps. — *n.* a jumping spider. [L. *saltus, -ūs*, a leap, *gradī*, to go.]

saltimbanco *sal-tim-bangk'ö*, (*obs.*) *n.* a mountebank, a quack: — *pl.* **saltimbanc'os.** [It.]

saltimbocca *sal-tim-bok'ə*, *n.* an Italian dish containing veal and ham, with cheese or other ingredients. [It.]

saltire, saltier *sal'*, *söl'tīr*, (*her.*) *n.* an ordinary in the form of a St Andrew's cross. — *adj.* **sal'tierwise.** [O.Fr. *saultoir, sautoir* — L.L. *saltātōrium*, a stirrup — L. *saltāre*, to leap.]

salto *sal'tö*, *säl'tö*, *n.* a daring leap (also *fig.*): a somersault (*gymnastics*): — *pl.* **sal'tos.** — *v.i.* to perform a salto: — *pa.p.* and *pa.t.* **sal'toed.** [It., a jump, leap; also *salto mortale*, lit. a mortal leap, a somersault.]

saltpetre (*in U.S.* **saltpeter**) *sölt-pē'tər*, *n.* potassium nitrate. — **saltpē'treman** (*hist.*) one authorised to search for saltpetre: one who prepares saltpetre; **saltpe'tre= paper** touch-paper. — **Chile** or **cubic saltpetre** sodium

nitrate; **Norway saltpetre** calcium nitrate. [O.Fr. *salpetre* — L.L. *salpetra*, prob. for L. *sāl petrae*, salt of stone.]

saltus *sal'təs*, (*logic*) *n.* a breach of continuity: a jump to conclusion. [L., a leap, pl. *saltūs*.]

salubrious *sə-loo'bri-əs, -lū'*, *adj.* healthful, health-giving. — *adv.* **salu'briously.** — *ns.* **salu'briousness, salu'brity.** [L. *salūbris* — *salūs, salūtis*, health.]

salue *sal-oō'*, or -*ū'*, or *sal'*, (*obs.*) *v.t.* to salute: — *pa.t.* (*Spens.*) **salewd'** (also **sal'ued**, which may be for **salve'd**, hailed with *salve*, the Latin greeting). [Fr. *saluer* — L. *salūtāre*.]

saluki *sə-loo'kē, -gē*, *n.* a silky-haired Persian or Arabian greyhound. [Ar. *seluqi*.]

salutary *sal'ū-tər-i*, *adj.* promoting health or safety: wholesome. — *adv.* **sal'ūtarily.** — *n.* **sal'ūtariness.** [L. *salūtāris* — *salūs*, health.]

salute *sə-loot', -ūt'*, *v.t.* to greet with words or (now esp.) with a gesture or with a kiss: to greet: to hail: to honour formally by a discharge of cannon, striking of colours, etc.: to affect, act upon (*Shak.*). — *v.i.* to perform the act of saluting, esp. in the military manner. — *n.* the act or position of saluting: a greeting: a kiss: a complimentary discharge of cannon, dipping colours, presenting arms, etc. — *n.* **salutation** (*sal-ū-tā'shən*) the act or words of greeting: a visit of ceremony: the quickening (of the blood), excitement (*Shak.*): the Angelic Salutation (see **ave**). — *adj.* **salūtā'tional.** — *n.* **salutatorian** (*sə-loo-tə-tö'ri-ən, -tö'*) in American colleges, the graduand who pronounces the address of welcome. — *adv.* **salu'tatorily.** — *adj.* **salu'tatory.** — *n.* an audience chamber: an address of welcome, esp. in American colleges. — *n.* **salu'ter** one who salutes: in Spain, one who professed to work miracles in the name of St Catherine (Sp. *saludador*; *hist.*). [L. *salūtāre, -ātum* (vb.), and *salūs, salūtis* (n.), partly through Fr. *salut*.]

salutiferous *sal-ū-tif'ər-əs*, *adj.* conducive to health or well-being. [L. *salūtifer* — *salūs, salūtis*, health, *ferre*, to bring.]

salvable, etc. See **salve¹.**

salvage¹ *sal'vij*, (Spens., Shak., etc.) *n.* and *adj.* Same as **savage.**

salvage² *sal'vij*, *n.* compensation made by the owner to persons, other than the ship's company, for preserving ship or cargo from danger of loss: rescue of property from fire or other peril: the raising of sunken or wrecked ships: saving of waste material for utilisation: anything saved in any of these ways. — *v.t.* to save from danger of loss or destruction: to recover or save as salvage. — *adj.* **sal'vageable.** — **sal'vage-corps** a body of men employed in salvage work. [L.L. *salvāgium* — *salvāre*, to save.]

salvarsan *sal'vər-san, sal'vär'san*, *n.* a compound of arsenic, first used by Paul Ehrlich (1854–1915) as a remedy for syphilis (since superseded by antibiotics). [L. *salvus*, safe, whole, Ger. *Arsen*, arsenic.]

salve¹ *salv*, *v.t.* to explain by hypothesis (*obs.*): to explain, clear up, harmonise (*obs.*): to save (an opinion) from objection (*obs.*): to vindicate (*obs.*): to preserve unhurt (*obs.*): to salvage (also *n.*). — *n.* **salvabil'ity.** — *adj.* **salv'able.** — *ns.* **salvā'tion** the act of saving: the means of preservation from any serious evil: the saving of man from the power and penalty of sin, the conferring of eternal happiness (*theol.*); **Salvā'tionism; Salvā'tionist** a member of the Salvation Army; **sal'vatory** repository. — *adj.* **saving.** — *adjs.* (*obs.*) **salvif'ic(al)** having the purpose or intention of saving. — *adv.* (*obs.*) **salvif'ically.** — **Salvation Army** an organisation for the spread of religion among the masses, founded by William Booth in 1865. [L.L. *salvāre*, to save; partly back-formation from **salvage²**.]

salve² *säv*, also *salv*, *n.* an ointment: a remedy: anything to soothe the feelings or conscience. — *v.t.* to anoint: to smear: to heal: to soothe. — *n.* and *adj.* **salv'ing.** [O.E. *s(e)alf*, ointment; Ger. *Salbe*, Du. *zalf*.]

salve³ *sal'vi*, L. *sal'wā*, *interj.* hail (addressed to one person). — *n.* a greeting: an antiphon beginning *Salve Regina* (*R.C.*). — *interj.* and *n.* **salvē'tē** (L. *sal-wā'tā*) (addressed to more than one person). [L. *salvē*, imper. of *salvēre*, to be well.]

salver[1] *sal'vər, n.* a tray on which anything is presented. — *adjs.* **sal'ver-shaped, sal'verform** of a corolla, having a long tube with limbs spread out flat. [Sp. *salva*, the precautionary tasting of food, as by a prince's taster, hence the tray on which it was presented to the prince — *salvar*, to save — L.L. *salvāre*.]

salver[2]. See **salvor**.

Salvia *sal'vi-ə, n.* the sage genus: (without *cap.*) a plant of this genus. [L. *salvia*, sage.]

salvific, etc. See **salve**[1].

Salvinia *sal-vin'i-ə, n.* a genus of water-ferns, giving name to a family **Salviniā'ceae.** — *adj.* **salviniā'ceous.** [Named after Antonio Maria *Salvini* (1653–1729), Italian Greek scholar.]

salvo[1] *sal'vō, n.* a saving clause: a reservation (*obs.*): a pretext (*obs.*): an expedient for saving appearances, avoiding offence, etc.: — *pl.* **sal'vos.** [L. *salvō*, ablative of *salvus*, safe: (one's right, honour, etc.) being saved.]

salvo[2] *sal'vō, n.* a simultaneous discharge of artillery in salute or otherwise: a simultaneous discharge of bombs, etc.: a round of applause: — *pl.* **sal'vo(e)s.** [It. *salva*, salute — L. *salvē*, hail.]

salvo jure *sal'vō jōō'rē, sal'vō, -wō, yōō're,* (L.) saving the right (the right being saved).

sal volatile. See **sal**[4].

salvor, salver *sal'vər, n.* one who salvages.

sam *sam,* (*Spens.*) *adv.* together. [O.E. *samen.*]

saman *sam-än', n.* the rain-tree. — Also **samaan'.** [Amer. Sp. *samán* — Carib *zamang.*]

samara *sam'ə-rə, sə-mä'rə, n.* a dry indehiscent, usually one-seeded fruit, with a wing. [L. *samara, samera,* elm seed.]

Samaritan *sə-mar'i-tən, adj.* of *Samaria,* in Palestine. — *n.* a native of *Samaria,* an adherent of the religion of Samaria, differing from Judaism in that only the Pentateuch is accepted as holy scripture with Moses the sole prophet of God: the Aramaic dialect of Samaria: one who charitably gives help in need (*good Samaritan;* Luke x. 30–37): a member of a voluntary organisation formed to help people who are distressed or despairing, esp. by talking to them on the telephone. — *n.* **Samar'itanism.** — **Samaritan Pentateuch** a recension of the Hebrew Pentateuch accepted by the Samaritans as alone canonical. [L. *Samarītānus.*]

samarium *sə-mā'ri-əm, n.* a metallic element (Sm; at. numb. 62) observed spectroscopically in samarskite. — *n.* **samarskite** (*sə-mär'skīt*) a mineral containing uranium. [Named in honour of Col. *Samarski,* Russian engineer.]

Samaveda *sä-mä-vä'dä, n.* the name of one of the four Vedas. [Sans. *Sāmaveda.*]

samba *sam'bə, n.* a Brazilian Negro dance in duple time with syncopation: a ballroom development thereof: a tune for it.

sambal *säm'bäl, n.* any of various foods served with curries in Malaya and Indonesia — peppers, pickles, salt fish, coconut, etc. [Malay.]

sambar, sambur *sam'bər, n.* a large Indian deer. [Hindi *sābar.*]

sambo *sam'bō, n.* the offspring of an American Indian or mulatto and a Negro: (with *cap.; derog.*) colloquially used as a proper name for a Negro: — *pl.* **sam'bos.** [Sp. *zambo,* said to be from L. *scambus* — Gr. *skambos,* bow-legged; perh. partly Fulah *sambo,* uncle.]

Sam Browne *sam' brown', a* military officer's belt with shoulder strap. [Invented by General Sir Samuel James *Browne* (1824–1901).]

sambuca *sam-bū'kə, n.* an ancient musical instrument like a harp. [L. *sambūca* — Gr. *sambykē,* prob. an Asiatic word; cf. Aramaic *sabbekā.*]

sambur. Same as **Sambar.**

same *sām, adj.* identical (commonly with *as,* also with

with or a relative): not different: unchanged: unvaried: mentioned before. — *pron.* (*coll.*) the aforesaid, it, them, they, etc. — *n.* (*rare*) an identical thing. — *adj.* **same'ly** unvaried. — *n.* **same'ness** the being the same: tedious monotony. — *adj.* **sā'mey** (*coll.*) (boringly) alike: monotonous. — **all the same** for all that; **at the same time** still, nevertheless; **same here!** (*coll.*) me too!; **the same** the same thing or person: the aforesaid: in the same way. [O.E. *same* (only in phrase *swā same,* likewise); Goth. *sama;* L. *similis,* like, Gr. *homos.*]

samel *sam'l, adj.* underburnt (as a brick). [App. O.E. pfx. *sam-,* half, *æled,* burned.]

samen *sām'ən,* an obs. Scots form of **same.**

samey. See **same.**

samfoo, samfu *sam'fōō, n.* an outfit worn by Chinese women, consisting of a jacket and trousers. [Cantonese.]

Sami. See **Saam(e).**

Samian *sā'mi-ən, adj.* of the Greek island of *Samos.* — *n.* (also **Sā'miot, Sā'miote**) a native of Samos. — **Samian earth** an argillaceous astringent earth; **Samian letter** the Pythagorean letter; **Samian stone** a goldsmiths' polishing stone; **Samian ware** brick-red or black pottery, with lustrous glaze: a later imitation made in Roman Gaul, etc.

samiel *sä'mi-əl, n.* the simoom. [Ar. *samm,* poison, Turk. *yel,* wind.]

Samiot(e). See **Samian.**

samisen *sam'i-sen,* **shamisen** *sham', ns.* a Japanese guitar. [Jap.]

samite *sam'īt, n.* a kind of heavy silk fabric. [O.Fr. *samit* — L.L. *examitum* — Gr. *hexamiton* — *hex,* six, *mitos,* thread.]

samizdat *sam'iz-dat, n.* in the Soviet Union, the secret printing and distribution of government-banned literature. — Also *adj.* [Russ.]

samlet *sam'lit, n.* a young salmon. [**salmon**[1], suff. **-let.**]

samlor *sam'lör, -lōr, n.* a three-wheeled vehicle common in Thailand, usu. motorised and used as a taxi. [Thai.]

Sammy *sam'i, n.* a noodle (*slang*): an American expeditionary soldier (*mil. slang;* from *Uncle Sam*). [**Samuel.**]

Samnite *sam'nīt, n.* a member of an ancient Sabine people of central Italy: their language: a Roman gladiator armed like a Samnite. — Also *adj.* [L. *Samnīs, -ītis.*]

samnitis *sam-nī'tis,* (*Spens.*) *n.* an unknown poisonous plant.

Samoed. See **Samoyed.**

samosa *sa-mō'sə, n.* a small, fried, pastry turnover stuffed with spiced vegetable or meat, an Indian savoury: — *pl.* **samo'sa, samo'sas.** [Hindi.]

samovar *sam'ō-vär, -vär', n.* a Russian water boiler, used for making tea, etc., traditionally heated by charcoal in a tube that passes through it. [Russ. *samovar,* lit. self-boiler.]

Samoyed(e) *sam-ō-yed', or sam', n.* one of a Ugrian people of north-west Siberia: their Ural-Altaic language: (*sa-moi'ed*) a white-coated dog of a breed used by them. — Also *adj.* (*Milt.* **Sam'oed**). — *adj.* **Samoyed'ic.** [Russ. *Samoyed.*]

samp *samp,* (*U.S.*) *n.* a coarsely ground maize: porridge made from it. [From an American Indian word.]

sampan *sam'pan, n.* a Chinese boat. — Also **san'pan.** [Chin. *san,* three, *pan,* board.]

samphire *sam'fīr, sampire -pīr, ns.* an umbelliferous plant (*Crithmum maritimum*) of sea-cliffs, whose fle͞ leaves are used in pickles: extended to other p̵ used in the same way — to *Inula crithmoides,* ͞ related to elecampane (*golden samphire*), to g̵ (*marsh samphire*), to saltwort (*prickly samph͞ (herbe de) Saint Pierre,* Saint Peter('s her̵

sampi *sam'pi, -pē, n.* supposed name of a Gr̵ character, τ, Τ, or ϡ, representing ͞ originally the same as the letter san.

sampire. See **samphire.**

sample *säm'pl, n.* a specimen, a sm̵ the quality of the whole: an ͞

For other sounds see detailed chart of pronunciation.

(*Spens.*, *Shak.*) or (*obs.*) warning. — *adj.* serving as a sample. — *v.t.* to match (*obs.*): to take, try, or offer a sample or samples of. — *ns.* **sam′pler; sam′pling** the taking, testing, etc., of a sample: the examination and analysis of data obtained from a random group in order to deduce information about the population as a whole. [M.E. *essample*; see **example**.]

sampler *säm′plər*, *n.* an exemplar, type, pattern (*obs.*): a test-piece of embroidery formerly expected from a girl, commonly including an alphabet, with figures, often names, etc. — *n.* **sam′plery.** — **sam′pler-work.** [O.Fr. *essemplaire* — L. *exemplar*; see **exemplar**.]

samshoo, samshu *sam′shoo*, *n.* Chinese rice spirit. [Pidgin; origin doubtful.]

Samson *sam′sn*, *n.* an abnormally strong man (from the Hebrew champion of Judges xiii-xvi). — **Samson('s) post** a kind of mousetrap (*obs.*): a strong post in a ship.

samurai *sam′ōō-rī*, *-ū-rī*, (*Jap. hist.*) *n.* a military retainer of a daimio: a member of the military caste: — *pl.* **sam′urai.** [Jap., — *samurau*, to attend (one's lord).]

san¹ *san*, *n.* a discarded letter of the Greek alphabet, Ϲ, perh. originally the same as sampi. [Doric Gr. *san*, sigma.]

san². See **sanatorium.**

sanative *san′ə-tiv*, *adj.* healing. — *n.* **sanatō′rium**, (esp. U.S.) **sanitā′rium**, (imitation Latin) (*coll. abbrev.* **san**) a hospital, esp. for consumptives or convalescents: a health station: — *pl.* **-riums, -ria.** — *adj.* **san′atory** healing: of healing. [L. *sānāre*, *-ātum*, to heal.]

sanbenito *san-be-nē′tō*, *n.* a garment worn by Inquisition victims at public recantation or execution: — *pl.* **sanbeni′tos.** [Sp. *San Benito*, St Benedict, from its resemblance to St Benedict's scapular.]

sancho, sanko *sang′kō*, *n.* a West African guitar: — *pl.* **san′chos, -kos.** [Ashanti *osanku*.]

sancho-pedro *sang′kō-pē′drō*, *n.* a card game — the nine of trumps called **sancho**, the five **pedro.**

sanctify *sang(k)′ti-fī*, *v.t.* to make, declare, regard as, or show to be sacred or holy: to set apart to sacred use: to free from sin or evil: to consecrate: to invest with a sacred character: to make efficient as the means of holiness: to sanction: — *pr.p.* **sanc′tifying;** *pa.t.* and *pa.p.* **sanc′tified.** — *n.* **sanctificā′tion.** — *adj.* **sanc′tified** made holy: sanctimonious. — *adv.* **sanc′tifiedly** (*-fī-id-li*) sanctimoniously. — *n.* **sanc′tifier** (*-fī-ər*) one who sanctifies: (usu. with *cap.*) the Holy Spirit. — *n.* and *adj.* **sanc′tifying.** — *adv.* **sanc′tifyingly.** [Fr. *sanctifier* — L. *sanctificāre* — *sanctus*, holy, *facĕre*, to make.]

sanctimony *sang(k)′ti-mən-i*, *n.* holiness (*obs.*): outward, affected, or simulated holiness. — *adj.* **sanctimonious** (*-mō′ni-əs*) holy (*obs.*): simulating holiness. — *adv.* **sanctimō′niously.** — *n.* **sanctimō′niousness.** [L. *sanctimōnia* — *sanctus*.]

sanction *sang(k)′shən*, *n.* motive for obedience to any moral or religious law (*ethics*): a penalty or reward expressly attached to non-observance or observance of a law or treaty (*law*): a military or economic measure taken by a country in order to persuade another to follow a certain course of action: the act of ratifying, or giving authority: confirmation: support: permission, countenance. — *v.t.* to give validity to: to authorise: to countenance. — **sanc′tions-busting** the breaching of economic sanctions imposed on a country. [L. *sanctiō*, *-ōnis* — *sancīre*, *sanctum*, to ratify.]

[sa]nctitude *sang(k)′ti-tūd*, *n.* saintliness. [L. *sanctitūdō*, *[-]inis*.]

[sanct]ity *sang(k)′ti-ti*, *n.* the quality of being sacred or [holy:] purity: godliness: inviolability: saintship: (in *pl.*) [f]eelings, obligations, or objects. [L. *sanctitās*, [sa]nctity.]

[...] *sang(k)′tū-ər-i*, *n.* a holy place: a place of [...]e most holy part of a temple, church, etc.: [...]: the chancel: a place affording immunity [...]e privilege of refuge therein: a place of [...] retreat: a nature, animal, or plant [...]**′tuarise, -ize** to afford sanctuary to.

Sanctus *sang(k)′təs*, *n.* the hymn *Holy, holy, holy*, from Isa. vi: music for it. — *n.* **sanc′tum** a sacred place: a private room. — **sanc′tum sancto′rum** the Holy of Holies: any specially reserved retreat or room; **sanctus bell** a bell rung at the Sanctus: the sacring bell. [L. *sanctus*, *-a*, *-um*, holy.]

sand *sand*, *n.* a mass of rounded grains of rock, esp. quartz: (in *pl.*) a tract covered with this, as on a sea-beach or desert: a sand-grain (*rare*): (in *pl.*) sandstones: (in *pl.*) moments of time, from use in the hour-glass (*fig.*): firmness of character (*U.S. slang*). — *adj.* of sand. — *v.t.* to sprinkle, cover or mix with sand: to smooth or polish with abrasive material, esp. sandpaper. — *adj.* **sand′ed** yellow (*Shak.*): sprinkled, covered, or mixed with sand: smoothed or polished with sandpaper, etc. — *ns.* **sand′er** a tool (esp. powerdriven) with an abrasive surface, used to sand wood, etc.; **sand′iness** sandy quality, esp. in colour; **sand′ing; sand′ling** the launce. — *adjs.* **sand′y** consisting of, covered with, containing, like, or (*Shak.*) measured by sand: loose: coloured like sand; **sand′yish.** — **sand′bag** a bag of sand or earth: a small bag of sand, etc., used as a cosh: an engraver's leather cushion. — *v.t.* to furnish with sandbags: to assail with a sandbag: — *pa.p.* **sand′bagged.** — **sand′bagger; sand′bank** a bank of sand; **sand′-bar** a long sand-bank in a river or sea; **sand′-bath** a bath in sand: a vessel for heating without direct exposure to the source of heat; **sand′-bed** a layer of sand, esp. one used in founding or moulding: a toper (*fig.*; *Scot.*); **sand′-binder** a plant whose roots or rootstocks fix shifting sands; **sand′-blast** a sand-laden wind: sand driven by a blast of air or steam for glassengraving, finishing metal surfaces, cleaning stone and metal surfaces, etc. — Also *v.t.* — **sand′-blasting.** — *adj.* **sand′-blind** see separate entry. — **sand′-box** a box for sand for sprinkling, for golf-tees, or other purpose: the explosive capsule of a tropical American tree (*Hura*) of the spurge family, formerly used to sprinkle sand on wet ink; **sand′-boy** a boy selling sand, proverbial for jollity; **sand′-break** sandy ground diversifying the country; **sand′-bunker.** — *v.t.* **sand′-cast** to cast in a mould of sand. — **sand′-castle** a model of a castle made by children at play on the sands or in a sand-pit; **sand′-cherry** an American dwarf cherry; **sand′-crack** a crack in a hoof; **sand dab** any of various kinds of small Pacific flatfish often eaten as food; **sand′-dance** a dance performed on a sanded surface; **sand′-dart** a British noctuid moth; **sand′-devil** a small whirlwind; **sand′-dollar** a flat sea-urchin; **sand′-dune** a ridge of loose sand drifted by the wind; **sand′-eel** the launce; **sand′-flag** a fissile sandstone; **sand′-flea** the chigoe or jigger: a sand-hopper; **sand′-fly** a small biting midge (*Simulium*): a small moth-like midge (*Phlebotomus*) that transmits **sand-fly fever,** a fever due to a viral infection; **sand′-glass** a glass instrument for measuring time by the running out of sand; **sand′-grain; sand′-grass** any grass that grows on sand; **sand′groper** a West Australian; **sand′-grouse** any bird of the genera *Pterocles* and *Syrrhaptes*, with long pointed wings, once mistaken for grouse because of their feathered legs but now reckoned as a sub-order (*Pterocletes*) akin to pigeons; **sand′-heap; sand′-hill** a hill of sand; **sand′-hog** (*U.S. slang*) one who works in compressed air; **sand′-hole; sand′-hopper** an amphipod crustacean (*Talitrus*, *Orchestia*, etc.) of the seashore (and also inland regions) that jumps by suddenly straightening its bent body; **sand′-lark** a name applied to various smaller shore birds: a sandpiper; **sand′-launce** the launce; **sand′-lizard** an oviparous lizard (*Lacerta agilis*) of Europe and S. England; **sand′man** a fairy who supposedly throws sand into children's eyes towards bedtime; **sand′-martin** a martin that nests in sandy banks; **sand′-mason** a tube-worm that makes its tube of sand; **sand′-mole** the Cape mole-rat; **sand painting** the making of designs with coloured sand, as in various American Indian ceremonies; **sand′paper** paper or cloth coated with sand. — *v.t.* to smooth or polish with sandpaper. — **sand'-peep** (*U.S.*) any small sandpiper; **sand'-pipe** a tubular hollow in chalk, usually filled with clay, sand, etc., from above; **sand'piper** the name for a large number of birds of the Scotopacidae family of ground- dwelling, wading birds intermediate between plovers and snipe, haunting sandy shores and river banks and uttering a clear piping note; **sand'-pit** a place from which sand is dug: a pit filled with sand for children's play; **sand'-plough** a vehicle like a snow-plough, used for clearing sand from roads, railwaylines, etc.; **sand'-pride** a small river lamprey; **sand'= pump** a pump for raising wet sand or mud; **sand'-saucer** an egg-mass of certain sea-snails; **sand'-screw** a burrowing amphipod (from its wriggling movements); **sand'-shoe** a shoe for walking or playing on the sands, usually with canvas upper and rubber sole; **sand'= skipper** a sand-hopper; **sand'-snake** a short-tailed, boa-like genus (*Eryx*) of Old World snakes; **sand sole** see **lemon²**; **sand'-spout** a moving pillar of sand; **sand'= star** an ophiurid, esp. of the short-armed kind, as *Ophiura*; **sand'stone** a rock formed of compacted and more or less indurated sand (**Old Red Sandstone;** see **old**); **sand'-storm** a storm of wind carrying along clouds of sand; **sand'-sucker** the rough dab; **sand'-table** a tray for moulding sand on or for demonstration of military tactics: an inclined trough for separating heavier particles from a flow of liquid, as in ore-dressing, paper-making (also **sand'-trap**); **sand'-thrower** a tool for throwing sand on newly sized or painted surfaces; **sand'-trap** a bunker: a sand-table; **sand'-wasp** a solitary burrowing insect of several families akin to the true wasps; **sand wedge** a golf club specially designed to hit the ball out of bunkers or sand-traps; **sand'-worm** the lugworm or other worm that lives on the sand; **sand'-wort** any species of Arenaria; **sand'wort-spurr'ey** Spergularia; **sand'-yacht, sand'-yachting** see **yacht**; **sand'y= lav'erock** (*Scot.*) a sand-lark. [O.E. *sand*; Du. *zand*, Ger. *Sand*, O.N. *sandr*.]

sandal¹ *san'dl*, *n.* a sole bound to the foot by straps: an ornate shoe or slipper: a slipper-strap: a slight rubber overshoe. — *adj.* **san'dalled** wearing or fastened with sandals. — **sandal shoon** (*arch.*) sandals. [L. *sandalium* — Gr. *sandalion*, dim. of *sandalon*.]

sandal² *san'dal*, *n.* a long narrow N. African boat. [Turk., Pers., and Ar.]

sandal³ *san'dl*, **sandalwood** -*wŏŏd*, *ns.* a compact and fine-grained very fragrant East Indian wood: the parasitic tree yielding it, *Santalum album* (**white sandalwood**), or other species: extended to other woods, as red-sanders, Barbados pride (*Adenanthera*), both called **red sandalwood**. [L.L. *santalum* — Gr. *sandanon*, — Sans. *candana*, of Dravidian origin.]

sandarach, sandarac *san'dər-ak*, *n.* realgar: the resin (in full **gum sandarach, sandarac resin**) of the Moroccan **sandarach tree** (*Collitris quadrivalvis*; Coniferae) powdered to form pounce and used in making varnish. [L. *sandaraca* — Gr. *sandărăkē*, -*chē*.]

sand-blind *sand'blīnd*, *adj.* half-blind. [Prob. O.E. pfx. *sam-*, half, and **blind**, affected by **sand**.]

Sandemanian *san-di-mā'ni-ən*, *n.* a Glassite, or follower of Robert *Sandeman* (1718–71). — Also *adj.*

sander¹, zander *san'*, *zan'dər*, *n.* a pike-perch. [Ger.]

sander². See **sand**.

sanderling *san'dər-ling*, *n.* a sandpiper without a hind toe. [App. from **sand**.]

sanders *san'*, *sän'dərz*, **sanderswood** -*wŏŏd*, *ns.* sandalwood, esp. red sandalwood (**red-sanders;** see **red**). [O.Fr. *sandre*, variant of *sandal*, *santal*, sandalwood.]

sandhi *sän'dē*, *n.* modification of the sound of a word or affix caused by the context in which it is uttered. [Sans. *saṁdhi*, placing together.]

Sandinista *san-di-nis'tə*, *n.* a member of the left-wing revolutionary movement in Nicaragua which overthrew President Samoza in 1979. — *n.* **Sandinismo** (-*niz'mō*) beliefs and practices of the Sandinistas. [Named after the Nicaraguan rebel general Augusto César *Sandino*, murdered in 1933.]

sandiver *san'di-vər*, *n.* glass-gall.   [O.Fr. *suin de verre*, lit. exudation of glass.]

sandling. See **sand**.

sandwich *san(d)'wich*, -*wij*, *n.* any sort of food between two slices of bread, said to be named from the fourth Earl of *Sandwich* (1718–92), who ate a snack of this kind in order not to have to leave the gaming-table: anything in like arrangement. — *v.t.* to lay or place between two layers: to fit tightly or squeeze between two others or two of another kind: to intercalate. — *adj.* of the nature of a sandwich or sandwich course: relating to or resembling a sandwich or sandwich course. — **sandwich course** an educational course consisting of alternating periods of academic and industrial work; **sand'wich-man** a man who perambulates the streets carrying two advertising boards (**sand'-wich-boards**) hung over his shoulders, so that one is in front, the other behind.

Sandy *san'di*, (*coll.*) *n.* a Scot. [From *Alexander*.]

sane *sān*, *adj.* sound, healthy (*rare*): sound in mind: rational. — *adv.* **sane'ly.** — *n.* **sane'ness.** [L. *sānus*.]

sanei *san'ā*, *n.* a resident of the Americas born of the offspring of Japanese immigrant parents — cf. **issei**, **nisei**. [Jap., third generation.]

Sanforise, -ize *san'fər-īz*, *v.t.* to make (cotton or linen fabrics) proof against shrinking by mechanically compressing the fibres. [After *Sanford* L. Cluett, American inventor of the process.]

sang¹ *sang*, *pa.t.* of **sing**. — *n.* a Scots form of **song¹**.

sang² *sang*, *n.* blood (*Scot.* in oaths; *her. să*): anthrax (*säng; vet.*). — **sang-de-boeuf** (*sä-də-bœf'*) a deep red colour (lit. ox-blood); **sangfroid** (-*frwä'*) coolness, self-possession (lit. cold blood). [Fr., blood.]

sang³ *säng*, *n.* Chinese organ played by mouth.   [Chin. *shêng*.]

sangar, sungar *sung'gər*, *n.* a stone breastwork: a look-out post. [Pushtu *sangar*.]

sangaree *sang-gə-rē'*, *n.* a West Indian drink of wine, diluted, sweetened, spiced, etc. — Also **sangria** (*sang-grē'ə*) a similar Spanish drink. [Sp. *sangria*.]

sangfroid. See **sang²**.

sanglier *sang'li-ər*, (*obs.* and *her.*) *n.* a wild boar.   [Fr., — L. *singulāris*, solitary.]

Sangraal, Sangrail, Sangreal *san(g)-grāl', san(g)'grāl, ns.* the holy grail (see **grail³**).   [saint, grail.]

Sangrado *san(g)-grä'dō*, *n.* a bloodletter, from Dr *Sangrado* in Le Sage's *Gil Blas*: — *pl.* **Sangra'does.** [Sp. *sangrador*, one who lets blood.]

sangria. See **sangaree**.

sangui- *sang-gwi-*, in compounds, blood. — *adj.* **sanguiferous** (-*gwif'ər-əs*; L. *ferre*, to bear) blood-carrying. — *n.* **sanguifica'tion** blood-making. — *v.i.* **sang'uify** (-*fī*) to make blood. — *v.t.* to turn into blood. — *n.* **Sanguinaria** (-*gwi-nā'ri-ə*) the bloodroot genus. — *adv.* **sang'uinarily** (-*gwin-ə-ri-li*). — *n.* **sang'uinariness.** — *adjs.* **sang'uinary** bloody; **sanguine** (*sang'gwin*) of blood (*rare*): blood-red: bloody: of the complexion or temperament in which blood was supposed to predominate over the other humours: hence ardent, confident and inclined to hopefulness: abounding in blood: ruddy: florid: of a full habit. — *n.* a blood-red colour: a red chalk: a drawing in red chalks. — *v.t.* to colour bloodred: to stain with blood. — *adv.* **sang'uinely.** — *n.* **sang'uineness.** — *adj.* **sanguin'eous** of or having blood: blood-red: bloody: sanguine: full-blooded. — *n.* **sanguin'ity** sanguineness. — *adj.* **sanguin'olent** bloody. — *n.* **Sanguisorb'a** the burnet genus (L. *sorbēre*, to absorb, from its supposed styptic properti: — *adj.* **sangu(in)iv'orous** feeding on blood (L. *vor.* to devour). [L. *sanguis*, -*inis*, blood; adjs. *sangu'* *sanguinārius*, *sanguinolentus*; partly through F *guin*.]

Sanhedrim, Sanhedrin *san'i-drim*, -*drin*, -*hed'*, *ns* council or court, esp. the supreme council at Jerusalem (*hist.*): any similar assembl' ment. — *n.* **San'hedrist** a member of th

[Heb. *sanhedrīn* — Gr. *synedrion* — *syn*, together, *hedrā*, a seat.]

sanicle *san'ik-l, n.* a woodland umbelliferous plant (in full **wood'-san'icle**; *Sanicula europaea*) with glossy leaves, head-like umbels, and hooked fruits: any plant of the genus: extended to various other plants. [O.Fr., perh. L. *sānāre*, to heal, from once-supposed power.]

sanidine *san'i-dēn, n.* a clear glassy variety of potash feldspar, usually tabular. [Gr. *sanis, sanidos*, a board.]

sanies *sā'ni-ēz, n.* a thin discharge from wounds or sores. — *adj.* **sa'nious**. [L. *saniēs*.]

sanify *san'i-fī, v.t.* to make healthy. [L. *sānus*, sound, *facēre*, to make.]

sanitary *san'i-tər-i, adj.* pertaining to, or concerned with the promotion of health, esp. connected with drainage and sewage disposal: conducive to health. — *n.* **sanitā'rian** one who favours or studies sanitary measures. — Also *adj.* — *n.* **sanitā'rianism**. — *adv.* **san'itarily**. — *ns.* **san'itarist; sanitā'rium** (sham Latin; esp. *U.S.*) a sanatorium: — *pl.* **-ia, -iums**. — *v.t.* **san'itate** (back-formation) to make sanitary: to furnish with sanitary appliances or ware. — *ns.* **sanitā'tion** measures for the promotion of health and prevention of disease, esp. drainage and sewage disposal; **sanitā'tionist**. — *v.t.* **san'itise, -ize** to make sanitary: to clean up, make more acceptable by removing offensive elements, words, connotations, etc. — *n.* **sanitīsā'tion, -z-**. — **sanitary engineer; sanitary engineering** the branch of civil engineering dealing with provision of pure water supply, disposal of waste, etc.; **sanitary inspector** see **public health inspector; sanitary towel** a pad of absorbent material for wearing during menstruation, etc.; **sanitary ware** coarse-glazed earthenware for sewer pipes: plumbing fixtures such as sinks, baths, lavatories, etc. [Fr. *sanitaire* — L. *sānitās*, health.]

sanity *san'i-ti, n.* health (*arch.*): soundness of mind: rationality. [L. *sānitās* — *sānus*, healthy.]

sanjak *san'jak, n.* formerly, a subdivision of a Turkish vilayet or eyalet. [Turk. *sancak*, flag, sanjak.]

sank *sangk, pa.t.* of **sink.**

Sankhya *sāng'kyə, n.* one of the six great systems of orthodox Hindu philosophy. [Sans. *sāṁkhya*.]

sanko. See **sancho.**

sannup *san'əp, n.* the husband of a squaw: a brave. [Amer. Ind. word.]

sannyasi *sun-yä'si, n.* a Hindu religious hermit who lives by begging. — Also **sannya'sin**. [Hindi, — Sans. *saṁnyāsin*, casting aside.]

sanpan. See **sampan.**

sans *sā, sanz, prep.* without. — **sans-appel** (*sāz-a-pel*) one against whose decision there is no appeal; **sansculotte** (*sā-kü-lot*; Fr. *culotte*, knee-breeches) in the French Revolution, the court party's nickname for a democrat (apparently as wearing long trousers instead of knee-breeches): hence generally (usu. in hostility) a strong republican, democrat, or revolutionary: one whose breeches are wanting or defective. — **sansculotterie** (-*rē* or -*ə-rē*). — *adj.* **sansculott'ic**. — *n.pl.* **sansculottides** (-*ēd'*) a proposed name (in honour of the most ardent revolutionaries) for the supplementary days in the French revolutionary calendar. — **sansculott'ism; sansculott'ist; sanserif** (*san-ser'if*; *print.*) a type without serifs. — Also *adj.* — **sans cérémonie** (*sā-rā-mon-ē*) without ceremony; **sans gêne** (*zhen*) at ease, without constraint or consideration of politeness; **sans nombre** (*nɔ̃br'*; *her.*) repeated often, and covering the field; **sans phrase** (*fräz*) without phrases (of courtesy), without more ado; **sans souci** (*soo-sē*) without care, worry. *r.*]

san'sə. Same as **zanze.**

. See **sans.**

ria san-sev-i-ēr'i-ə, n. the bowstring-hemp genus *y* family: (without *cap.*) any plant of this genus useplant with sword-like leaves, known as *law's tongue.*). [Named after the Neapoli-

tan inventor Raimondo di Sangro, Prince of *San Severo* (1710–71).]

Sanskrit, or (old-fashioned) **Sanscrit**, *sans'krit, n.* the ancient Indo-European literary language of India. — Also *adj.* — *adj.* **Sanskrit'ic**. — *n.* **Sans'kritist** one skilled in Sanskrit. [Sans. *saṁskrta*, put together, perfected — *sam*, together, *karoti*, he makes, cog. with L. *creāre*, to create.]

Santa Claus *san'tə klöz'*, a fat rosy old fellow who brings children Christmas presents (also known as **Father Christmas**): an improbable source of improbable benefits. [Orig. U.S. modification of Du. dial. *Sante Klaas*, St Nicholas.]

santal *san'tal, n.* sandalwood. — *n.pl.* **Santalā'ceae** (-*ā'si-ē*) the sandalwood family. — *adj.* **santalā'ceous**. — *ns.* **san'talin** the colouring matter of red sandalwood; **San'talum** the sandalwood genus. [Gr. *santalon.*]

santir *san-tēr', santur, santour -toor', ns.* an Eastern dulcimer. [Ar. *santīr*, Pers. and Turk. *sāntūr*.]

Santolina *san-tō-lē'nə, n.* a genus of fragrant Mediterranean shrubs related to the camomile, with dissected leaves and clustered flower heads: (without *cap.*) a plant of the genus. [It. *santolina*, — L. *sanctus*, holy, *līnum*, flax.]

santon *san'ton, n.* an Eastern dervish or saint. [Sp. *santón* — *santo*, holy — L. *sanctus*, holy.]

santonica *san-ton'i-kə, n.* the dried unexpanded flower-heads of a species of wormwood. — *n.* **san'tonin** (-*tən*) an anthelmintic extracted from it. [Gr. *santonikon*, as found in the country of the *Santones* in Gaul.]

santour, santur. See **santir.**

saouari. Same as **souari.**

sap[1] *sap, n.* vital juice: juice generally: sapwood: a saphead: a plodding student: a fool (*slang*): any object used as a bludgeon. — *v.i.* to play the part of a ninny: to be studious. — *v.t.* to drain or withdraw the sap from: to drain the energy from, exhaust: to strike with, or as if with, a sap. — *adjs.* **sap'ful** full of sap; **sap'less.** — *ns.* **sap'lessness; sap'ling** a young tree (also *adj.*): a young greyhound; **sapp'iness.** — *adj.* **sapp'y.** — **sap'-green** a green paint made from the juice of buckthorn berries: its colour (also *adj.*); **sap'head** a silly fellow. — *adj.* **sap'headed.** — **sap'-cup** a wooden ale-cup of staves and hoops; **sap'-rot** dry-rot; **sap'wood** alburnum. [O.E. *sæp*; L.G. *sap*, juice, Ger. *Saft*.]

sap[2] *sap, n.* sapping: a trench (usually covered or zigzag) by which approach is made towards a hostile position. — *v.t.* to undermine. — *v.i.* to make a sap: to proceed insidiously: — *pr.p.* **sapp'ing**; *pa.p.* and *pa.t.* **sapped.** — *n.* **sapp'er** one who saps: a private in the Royal Engineers (formerly Royal Sappers and Miners). — **sap'head** the furthest point reached by a sap. [It. *zappa* and Fr. *sappe* (now *sape*); cf. L.L. *sappa*, a pick.]

sapajou *sap'ə-joo, n.* a capuchin monkey: a spider monkey (*obs.*). [Fr. from a Tupí name.]

sapan. Same as **sappan.**

sapego. See **serpigo.**

sapele *sa-pē'lē, n.* a wood resembling mahogany, used for furniture: a tree of the genus *Entandrophragma* giving such wood, esp. *E. cylindricum.* [W. African name.]

saphead. See **sap[1,2].**

sapid *sap'id, adj.* perceptible by taste: having a decided taste: well-tasted: savoury: grateful, relishing, exhilarating. — *n.* **sapid'ity.** — *adj.* **sap'idless** (*Lamb*) insipid. [L. *sapidus* — *sapēre*, to taste.]

sapience *sā'pi-əns, n.* discernment: wisdom (often ironical): judgment. — *adjs.* **sā'pient; sāpiential** (-*en'shl*). — *adv.* **sā'piently.** [L. *sapientia* — *sapēre*, to be wise.]

Sapindus *sə-pin'dəs, n.* the soapberry genus, giving name to the **Sapindā'ceae**, a family akin to the maples and horse-chestnuts. — *adj.* **sapindā'ceous.** [L. *sāpō Indicus*, Indian soap.]

sapi-outan. See **sapi-utan.**

Sapium *sā'pi-əm, n.* the tallow-tree genus of the spurge family.

sapi-utan sä-pi-ōō'tän, n. the wild ox of Celebes. — Also **sapi-ou'tan.** [Malay sāpi, cow, hūtan, wild, wood.]

sapling. See sap[1].

sapodilla sap-ō-dil'ə, n. a large evergreen sapotaceous tree of W. Indies, etc., Achras sapota (naseberry): its edible fruit (**sapodilla plum**): its durable timber. [Sp. zapotilla, dim. of zapota (see **Sapota**).]

saponaceous sap-ō-, or sap-ə-nā'shəs, adj. soapy: soaplike. — ns. **sapogenin** (-jen'in) a compound derived from saponin, often used in synthesising steroid hormones; **Saponā'ria** the soapwort genus. — adj. **saponifiable** (sap-on'i-fī'ə-bl). — n. **saponificā'tion** the turning into or forming of soap: hydrolysis of esters. — v.t. **sapon'ify** to convert into soap. — v.i. to become soap: — pr.p. **sapon'ifying;** pa.t. and pa.p. **sapon'ified.** — ns. **saponin** (sap'ə-nin) a glucoside from soapwort, etc., that gives a soapy froth; **sap'onite** a soapy amorphous silicate of magnesium and aluminium found in cavities in serpentine. [L. sāpō, -ōnis, soap, prob. from Gmc.]

sapor sā'pör, n. taste. — adj. **sā'porous** (-pər-əs). [L. sapor, -ōris.]

Sapota sə-pō'tə, n. a genus (by some included in Achras) giving name to the **Sapotaceae** (sap-ō-tā'si-ē), a tropical family mostly of trees, often abounding in milky juice (gutta-percha): (without cap.) a member of the genus: (without cap.) sapodilla. — adj. **sapotā'ceous** (-shəs). [Sp. zapote — Nahuatl tzapotl.]

sappan, sapan sap'an, -ən, n. brazil-wood (Caesalpinia sappan) — usu. **sap(p)'an-wood.** [Malay sapang.]

sapped, sapper, sapping. See sap[2].

sapperment sap-ər-ment', interj. a German oath. [Ger. Sakrament, sacrament.]

sapphire saf'īr, n. a brilliant precious variety of corundum, generally of a beautiful blue: the blue colour of a sapphire. — adj. of sapphire: deep pure blue. — adj. **sapph'ired** coloured with sapphire blue. — adj. **sapph'irine** (-ir-īn) of, or like, sapphire. — n. a blue mineral, aluminium-magnesium silicate. — **sapph'ire-quartz** a blue quartz; **sapph'ire-wing** a blue-winged humming-bird. [O.Fr. safir — L. sapphīrus — Gr. sappheiros, lapis lazuli.]

Sappho saf'ō, n. a great Greek lyric poetess (c. 600 B.C.) of Lesbos: a kind of humming-bird. — adj. **Sapph'ic.** — n. usu. in pl. (also without cap.) verses in a form said to have been invented by Sappho in stanzas of four lines each, three Lesser Sapphics thus: –◡|–◡|–◡◡|–◡|–◡, followed by an Adonic, viz. –◡◡|–◡. — ns. **Sapph'ism** (also without cap.) lesbianism, of which she was accused; **sapph'ist** a lesbian. [Gr. Sapphō.]

sapples sap'lz, (Scot.) n.pl. soap-suds.

sappy. See sap[1].

sapr(o)- sap-r(ō)-, in composition, rotten, decayed. — n. **sapraemia** (sap-rē'mi-ə; Gr. haima, blood) the presence of products of putrefactive bacteria in the blood. — adj. **sapraе'mic.** — n. **saprobe** (sap'rōb; Gr. bios, life) an organism living in foul water. — adjs. **saprobiotic** (sap-rō-, sap-rə-bī-ot'ik) feeding on dead or decaying plants or animals; **saprogenic, saprogenous** (sap-rō-jen'ik or -rə-, sə-proj'i-nəs; Gr. root of gignesthai, to produce) growing on decaying matter: causing or caused by putrefaction. — ns. **Saprolegnia** (sap-rō-leg'ni-ə or -rə-; Gr. legnon, border) a genus of fungi, one species of which grows on diseased salmon and was formerly thought to be the cause of the disease: (without cap.) any fungus of the genus; **sap'rolite** (Gr. lithos, stone) a soft, partially decomposed rock that has remained in its original site; **sapropel** (sap-rə-pel; Gr. pēlos, clay, mud) slimy sediment laid down in water, largely organic in origin. — adj. **sapropel'ic** pertaining to, living in, or derived from, sapropel. — n. **sapropel'ite** coal formed from sapropel. — adj. **saprophagous** (sap-rof'ə-gəs; Gr. phagein (aor.), to eat) feeding on decaying organic matter. — n. **saprophyte** (sap'rō-fīt or -rə-; Gr. phyton, a plant) a plant that feeds upon decaying organic matter. — adj. **saprophytic** (-fit'ik). — adv. **saprophyt'ically.** — n. **sap'ro-**

phytism. — adj. **saprozō'ic** feeding on dead or decaying organic material. [Gr. sapros, rotten.]

sapsago sap-sā'gō, sap'sə-gō, n. a hard green cheese made from skim milk and melilot: — pl. **sapsagos.** [Ger. Schabziger.]

sapsucker sap'suk-ər, n. a N. American woodpecker (Sphyrapicus) which feeds on the sap from trees. [sap[1], suck.]

sapucaia sap-ōō-kä'yə, n. a Brazilian tree (Lecythis) whose urn-shaped fruit (monkey-pot) contains a number of finely-flavoured oval seeds or nuts. — **sapuca'ia-nut.** [Tupí.]

sar[1] sär. See **Sargus.**

sar[2], sa'r sär, a Scots form of savour (both n. and vb.: — pr.p. **sār'ing;** pa.t. and pa.p. **sared**).

saraband sar'ə-band, n. a slow Spanish dance, or dance-tune: a suite-movement in its rhythm, in 3–4 time strongly accented on the second beat (a dotted crotchet or minim). [Sp. zarabanda.]

Saracen sar'ə-sən, n. a Syrian or Arab nomad: a Muslim: an opponent of the Crusaders: a Moor or Berber: a non-Christian (obs.). — Also adj. — adj. **Saracenic** (-sen'ik), **-al.** — n. **Sar'acenism.** — **Saracenic architecture** a general name for Muslim architecture; **Saracen's-stone** see **sarsen.** [O.E. Saracene (pl.) — L. Saracēnus — late Gr. Sarakēnos.]

sarafan sar-ə-fan', or sar', n. a Russian peasant woman's cloak. [Russ.]

sarangi sä'rung-gē, n. an Indian fiddle. [Hind.]

Sarapis. See **Serapis.**

Saratoga sar-ə-tō'gə, n. (in full **Saratoga trunk;** U.S.) a large travelling trunk. [Saratoga Springs, resort in New York State.]

sarbacane sär'bə-kān, n. a blowpipe (weapon). [Fr.]

sarcasm sär'kazm, n. a bitter sneer: a satirical remark in scorn or contempt, often but not necessarily ironical: a jibe: the quality of such sayings. — adjs. **sarcas'tic, -al** containing or inclined to sarcasm (coll. shortening **sar'ky**). — adv. **sarcas'tically.** [L. sarcasmus — Gr. sarkasmos — sarkazein, to tear flesh like dogs, to speak bitterly — sarx, sarkos, flesh.]

sarcenchyme sär-seng'kīm, n. a soft tissue of sponges with close-packed cells and reticulated gelatinous matrix. — adj. **sarcenchymatous** (-kim'ə-təs). [Gr. sarx, sarkos, flesh, enchyma, an infusion.]

sarcenet. See **sarsenet.**

sarco- sär'kō, -ko'-, in composition, flesh. — ns. **sarcocarp** (sär'kō-kärp; Gr. karpos, fruit; bot.) the fleshy pericarp of a stone fruit; **Sarcocystis** (sär-kō-sis'tis; Gr. kystis, a bladder) a genus of Sporozoa parasitic in muscles of mammals: (without cap.) a member of the genus; **sarcolemma** (sär-kō-lem'ə; Gr. lemma, husk) the sheath of muscle fibre; **sarcol'ogy** (Gr. logos, discourse) the anatomy of the fleshy parts; **sarcomere** (sär'kō-mēr; Gr. meros, part) a unit of myofibril of a muscle tissue; **sar'coplasm** the protoplasmic substance separating the fibrils in muscle fibres. — adj. **sarcoplas'mic.** — n. **Sarcoptes** (sär-kop'tēz; irreg., from Gr. koptein, to cut) the itch-mite genus. — adjs. **sarcop'tic; sarcosaproph'agous** (-sap-rof'ə-gəs; Gr. sapros, rotten, phagein, to eat) feeding on decaying fish; **sarcous** (sär'kəs) of flesh or muscle. [Gr. sarx, sarkos, flesh.]

sarcocolla sär-kō-kol'ə, n. a Persian gum from Astragalus or other plants, reputed to heal wounds. [Gr. sarkokolla — kolla, glue.]

Sarcocystis. See **sarco-.**

sarcode sär'kōd, n. protoplasm, esp. of Protozoa. — n. **Sarcodes** (sär-kōd'ēz) the Californian snow-plant genus. — adj. **sarcodic** (-kod'ik) protoplasmic: flesh-like. — n.pl. **Sarcodina** (-kō-dī'nə) a class of Protozoa with pseudopodia. — adj. **sar'coid** flesh-like. — n. short for sarcoidosis. — n. **sarcoidō'sis** a chronic disease of unknown cause characterised by the formation of nodules in the lymph nodes, lungs, skin, etc. [Gr. sarkōdēs, sarkoeides — eidos, form.]

sarcolemma, sarcology. See **sarco-.**

sarcoma sär-kō'mə, n. a tumour derived from connective

tissue: any fleshy excrescence: a fleshy disc (*bot.*): — *pl.* **sarco′mas, sarcō′mata.** — *n.* **sarcomatō′sis** a condition characterised by the formation of sarcomas in many areas of the body. — *adj.* **sarcō′matous.** [Gr. *sarkōma* — *sarx*, flesh.]

sarcomere. See **sarco-.**

sarconet. See **sarsenet.**

Sarcophaga *sär-kof′ə-gə, n.* a genus of flesh-flies. — *adjs.* **sarcoph′agal** flesh-eating: pertaining to sarcophagi; **sarcoph′agous** feeding on flesh. — *ns.* **sarcoph′agus** a limestone used by the Greeks for coffins, thought to consume the flesh of corpses: a stone coffin, esp. one with carvings: a tomb or cenotaph of similar form: — *pl.* **sarcoph′agi** (-jī, -gī), **sarcoph′aguses; sarcoph′agy** (-ji) flesh-eating. [Latinised from Gr. *sarkophagos* — *phagein* (aor.), to eat.]

sarcoplasm, sarcoplasmic, Sarcoptes, sarcoptic, sarcosaprophagous, sarcous. See **sarco-.**

sard *särd, n.* a deep-red chalcedony. — Also **sard′ius.** [L. *sarda, sardius,* and Gr. *sardion,* also *sardios* (*lithos*), the Sardian (stone) — *Sardeis,* Sardis, in Lydia.]

Sard *särd, n.* and *adj.* Sardinian. [L. *Sardus.*]

sardana *sär-dä′nə, n.* a Catalan dance in a ring formation: the music for this, played esp. on the flute and drum. [Catalan *sardana.*]

sardel *sär-del′,* **sardelle** -*del*(-ə), *ns.* a small fish related to the sardine.

sardine[1] *sär′dēn, sär-dēn′, n.* a young pilchard, commonly tinned in oil: applied at various times and places to other fishes. — **packed like sardines** crowded closely together. [Fr. *sardine* — It. *sardina* — L. *sardīna*; Gr. *sardīnos,* or -*ē*.]

sardine[2] *sär′dīn,* -*din, n.* sard (stone). — Also *adj.* (Rev. iv. 3). — Also **sar′dius.** [Gr. *sardīnos* (*lithos*) — *sardios*; see **sard.**]

Sardinian *sär-din′i-ən,* -*yən, adj.* of the island or former kingdom of *Sardinia* or of the inhabitants. — *n.* a native, citizen, or member of the people of Sardinia: their language or dialect of Italian.

sardius. See **sard, sardine**[2].

sardonic *sär-don′ik, adj.* scornful, heartless, or bitter, said of a forced unmirthful laugh: sneering. — *adjs.* **sardō′nian** (*obs.*); **sardon′ical.** — *adv.* **sardon′ically.** [Fr. *sardonique* — L. *sardonius* — late Gr. *sardonios,* doubtfully referred to *sardonion,* a plant of Sardinia (Gr. *Sardō*) which was said to screw up the face of the eater.]

sardonyx *sär′də-niks, n.* an onyx with layers of cornelian or sard. [Gr. *sardonyx* — *Sardios,* Sardian, *onyx,* a nail.]

saree. See **sari.**

sargasso *sär-gas′ō, n.* gulf-weed (*Sargassum*): a floating mass or expanse of it, as the **Sargasso Sea** in the North Atlantic: — *pl.* **sargass′os.** [Port. *sargaço.*]

sarge. Coll. shortening of **sergeant.**

Sargus *sär′gəs, n.* a genus of sea-breams (without *cap.*; also **sar, sar′gō** (*pl.* **sar′gōs**)) a fish of this genus. [Gr. *sargos.*]

sari *sär′ē, n.* a Hindu woman's chief garment, a long cloth wrapped round the waist and passed over the shoulder and head. — Also **sar′ee.** [Hind. *sārī.*]

sarin *sär′in, n.* a compound of phosphorus ($C_4H_{10}FPO_2$) used as a lethal nerve gas. [Ger.]

sark *särk,* **serk** *serk,* (*Scot.*) *ns.* a shirt or chemise: a surplice. — *ns.* **sark′ful; sark′ing** a lining for a roof: material for shirts. — **sark′-tail′** the tail, skirt, of a shirt or chemise. [O.E. *serc*; O.N. *serkr.*]

sarky. See **sarcasm.**

Sarmatia *sär-mā′shyə,* -*shi-ə, n.* anciently a region reaching from the Vistula and Danube to the Volga and Caucasus: Poland (*poet.*). — *n.* and *adj.* **Sarmā′tian.** — *adj.* **Sarmatic** (-*mat′ik*).

sarment *sär′mənt, n.* a cut twig or cutting (*obs.*): a sarmentum: a long weak twig. — *adjs.* **sarmentaceous** (-ā′shəs), **sar′mentose** (or -*ōs′*), **sarmentous** (-*ment′əs*) having sarmenta or runners: creeping. — *n.* **sarmentum** (-*ment′əm*) a runner: — *pl.* **sarment′a.** [L. *sarmentum,*

a twig — *sarpēre,* to prune.]

sarnie, sarney *sär′ni, n.* a coll. shortening of **sandwich.**

sarod *sa′rod, n.* an Indian instrument like a cello, with strings that are plucked. [Hind.]

sarong *sä′rong, sə-rong′, n.* a Malay skirt-like garment for a man or woman: a cloth for making it. [Malay *sārung.*]

saros *sä′ros, sä′ros, n.* a Babylonian cycle of 3600 years: now (from a misunderstanding) an astronomical cycle of 6585 days and 8 hours, after which relative positions of the sun and moon recur. — *adj.* **saronic** (*sə-ron′ik*). [Gr. *saros* — Babylonian *shāru,* 3600.]

sarpanch *sär′punch, n.* an elected head of a village council in India. [Hind. *sar,* head, *panca,* five.]

Sarracenia *sär-ə-sē′ni-ə, n.* the side-saddle flower, an American genus of insectivorous plants, with pitchers, giving name to the family **Sarraceniā′ceae,** akin to the sundew family: (without *cap.*) a plant of this genus. [After Dr *Sarrazin,* who sent them to Europe from Quebec.]

sarrasin, sarrazin *sär′ə-zin, n.* buckwheat. [Fr. (*blé*) *sarrasin,* Saracen (corn).]

sarrusophone *sə-rus′ō-fōn, n.* a reed instrument of brass, devised by a French bandmaster, *Sarrus.* [Gr. *phōnē,* voice.]

sarsaparilla *sär-sə-pə-ril′ə, n.* any tropical American Smilax: its dried root: a soft drink flavoured with this (*U.S.*): a medicinal preparation from it: extended to various plants or roots of like use. — Shortened to **sar′sa, sar′za.** [Sp. *zarzaparilla* — *zarza,* bramble (from Basque), and a dim. of *parra,* vine.]

sarsen *sär′sn, n.* a grey-wether. — Also **sars′den, sar′senstone, Sar′acen's-stone.** [App. forms of **Saracen.**]

sarsenet, sarcenet, sarconet, sarsnet *särs′nit,* -*net, n.* a thin tissue of fine silk. — *adj.* of sarsenet: mild (*Shak.*). [A.Fr. *sarzinett,* probably *Sarzin,* Saracen.]

sartor *sär′tōr,* (*facet.*) *n.* a tailor. — *adj.* **sartorial** (-*tō′ri-əl,* -*tō′*) of or relating to a tailor, tailoring, dress, or the sartorius. — *adv.* **sarto′rially.** — *adj.* (*rare*) **sarto′rian.** — *n.* **sarto′rius** (orig. mod. L. adj.) a thigh muscle that crosses the leg, as when a tailor sits. [L. *sartor,* a patcher.]

Sartrian *sär′tri-ən, adj.* pertaining to the French philosopher, dramatist and novelist Jean-Paul *Sartre* (1905–1980). — *n.* a follower or admirer of Sartre.

sarus *sä′rəs, sä′rəs, n.* an Indian crane. — Also **sarus crane.** [Hind. *sāras.*]

Sarvodaya *sär-vō′da-ya, n.* in India, the promotion of the welfare of the community. [Sans. *sārva,* all, *udayā,* prosperity.]

sarza. See **sarsaparilla.**

sa sa *sä sä′, interj.* of incitement: a fencer's exclamation on thrusting. [Fr. *ça ça,* there, there.]

sasarara. Same as **siserary.**

sash[1] *sash, n.* (orig. **shash,** *shash*) a turban cloth: a band or scarf, worn round the waist or over the shoulder. — *v.t.* to dress or adorn with a sash. [Ar. *shāsh.*]

sash[2] *sash, n.* a frame, esp. a sliding frame, for window panes. — *v.t.* to furnish with sashes. — **sash′-cord** a cord attaching a weight to the sash in order to balance it at any height; **sash′-door** a door having panes of glass; **sash′-frame** the frame in which the sash of a window is suspended; **sash′-tool** a glazier's brush for removing oil: a house-painter's small brush; **sash′-window** a window with a sash or sashes, opp. to *casement window.* [Fr. *châssis.*]

sashay *sa-shā′, v.i.* to walk, move, in a gliding or ostentatious way. — *n.* an excursion (esp. *fig.*). [Alteration of **chassé.**]

sashimi, *sash′-ə-mi, n.* a Japanese dish of thinly-sliced raw fish. [Jap.]

sasin *sas′in, n.* the common Indian antelope. [Nepalese.]

sasine *sä′sin,* (*Scots law*) *n.* the act of giving legal possession of feudal property, infeftment. [A variant of **seisin,** Law L. *sasina.*]

saskatoon *sas-kə-tōōn′, n.* the shadbush: its fruit. [Cree *misáskwatomin.*]

sasquatch *sas′kwach, -kwoch, n.* a large hairy manlike creature thought by some to inhabit parts of North America. [Indian name.]

sass *sas*, **sassy** *sas′i* (*U.S.*). Same as **sauce**, **saucy**.

sassaby *sə-sā′bi, n.* the bastard hartebeest, a large S. African antelope. [Tswana *tessébe.*]

sassafras *sas′ə-fras, n.* a tree (*Sassafras officinale*) of the laurel family common in N. America: the bark, esp. of its root, a powerful stimulant: an infusion of it: extended to various plants with similar properties. — **sassafras nut** the pichurim bean; **sassafras oil** a volatile aromatic oil distilled from sassafras. [Sp. *sasafrás.*]

Sassanid *sas′ə-nid, n.* one of the **Sassanidae**, the dynasty that ruled Persia from A.D. 226 to 641. — *adj.* **Sassā′-nian.**

sassarara. Same as **siserary**.

sasse *sas*, (*obs.*) *n.* a sluice or lock. [Du. *sas.*]

Sassenach *sas′ə-nahh, n.* a Saxon: an Englishman: a Lowlander (*Scott*, etc.). [Gael. *Sasunnach.*]

sassolite *sas′ə-līt, n.* native boric acid — first found near Sasso (a province of Pisa). — Also **sass′olin.**

sassy. See **sass**.

sastruga. See **zastruga**.

sat *sat, pa.t.* and *pa.p.* of **sit**.

Satan *sā′tən* (old-fashioned *sat′ən*), *n.* the chief fallen angel: the chief evil spirit, adversary of God and tempter of men, the Devil: a devil. — Also **Satanas** (*sat′ən-as*), **Sathan** (*sā′thən*), **Sathanas** (*sath′*). — *adjs.* **satanic** (*sə-tan′ik*), **-al.** — *adv.* **satan′ically.** — *ns.* **satan′icalness; sā′tanism** devilish disposition: Satan-worship: the characteristics of the Satanic school. — *n.* and *adj.* **Sā′tanist.** — *ns.* **satanity** (*sə-tan′*) devilishness; **sātanol′ogy; sātanoph′any** (Gr. *phainein*, to show) an appearance of Satan; **sātanophō′bia** (Gr. *phobos*, fear) fear of the Devil. — **Satanic school** Southey's name for Byron, Shelley, and other unorthodox revolutionaries; **Satan monkey** the black saki. [Gr. and L. *Satān, Satanās* — Heb. *sātān,* enemy — *sātan,* to be adverse.]

satara *sä-tä′rə, sat′ə-rə, n.* a ribbed, hot-pressed and lustred woollen cloth. [*Sátára* in India.]

satchel *sach′l, n.* a small bag, esp. with shoulder strap, as for school-books. — *adj.* **satch′elled.** [O.Fr. *sachel* — L. *saccellus,* dim. of *saccus;* see **sack¹**, **sac¹**.]

sate¹ *sāt, v.t.* to satisfy fully: to glut. — *adjs.* **sāt′ed; sate′less** insatiable. — *n.* **sāt′edness.** [Blend of M.E. *sade* (cf. **sad**) and L. *sat,* enough, or **satiate** shortened.]

sate² *sat,* also (in rhyme) *sāt,* an archaism for **sat**.

sateen *sa-tēn′, n.* a glossy cotton or woollen fabric resembling *satin*.

satellite *sat′ə-līt, n.* an attendant: an obsequious follower: a body revolving about a planet, esp. now a man-made device used for communication, etc. (see **artificial satellite** below): a smaller companion to anything: a subordinate or dependent state, community, etc. — Also *adj.* — *v.t.* to transmit by satellite. — *n.* **satelles** (*sat-el′ēz; obs.*) a satellite: — *pl.* **satell′ites** (*-i-tēz; Pope*). — *adj.* **satellitic** (*-lit′ik*). — **satellite state, country** one which relies on and obeys the dictates of a larger, more powerful state; — **satellite television** the broadcasting of television programmes via artificial satellite; **satellite town** a town, often a garden city, limited in size, built near a great town to check overgrowth. — **artificial, earth, satellite** any man-made body, including spacecraft, launched by rocket into space and put into orbit round the earth. [L. *satelles, satellitis,* an attendant.]

satem languages *sä′təm lang′gwij-əz,* the group of Indo-European languages in which an original palatal consonant developed as a sibilant (as in Avestic *satem,* hundred); cf. **centum languages**.

Sathan(as). See **Satan**.

sati. Same as **suttee**.

satiate *sā′shi-āt, v.t.* to gratify fully: to glut. — *adj.* glutted. — *n.* **sātiabil′ity.** — *adj.* **sā′tiable.** — *ns.*

sātiā′tion; satiety (*sə-tī′ə-ti*) the state of being satiated: surfeit. [L. *satiāre, -ātum* — *satis,* enough.]

satin *sat′in, n.* a closely woven silk with a lustrous and unbroken surface showing much of the warp. — *adj.* of, like, or (*obs.*) clad in satin. — *v.t.* to make satiny. — *n.* **satinet′, satinette′** (*Scott,* **satinett′a**) a thin satin: a modification of satin with a slightly different weave: a cloth with a cotton warp and a woollen weft. — *adj.* **sat′iny** like satin. — **sat′in-bird** or **satin bower-bird** a satiny blue and black bower-bird; **sat′in-fin′ish** a satiny polish; **sat′in-paper** a fine, glossy writing-paper; **sat′in-sheet′ing** a twilled cotton and silk fabric with a satin surface; **sat′in-spar** a satiny fibrous calcite, or aragonite, or gypsum; **sat′in-stitch** an embroidery stitch, repeated in parallel lines, giving a satiny appearance; **sat′in-stone** a fibrous gypsum; **sat′inwood** a beautiful, smooth, satiny ornamental wood from India: the rutaceous tree (*Chloroxylon swietenia*) yielding it: extended to several more or less similar woods and trees. [Fr. *satin,* app. — L.L. *sēta,* silk (L. *saeta,* bristle), or from Ar. *zaytūnī, — Zaitūn,* a town in China where it was produced.]

satire *sat′īr, n.* a literary composition, orig. in verse, essentially a criticism of folly or vice, which it holds up to ridicule or scorn — its chief instruments, irony, sarcasm, invective, wit, and humour: satirical writing as a genre: its spirit: the use of, or inclination to use, its methods: satirical denunciation or ridicule: (from confusion with **satyr**) a satirist (*obs.*). — *adjs.* **satiric** (*sə-tir′ik*), **-al** pertaining to, or conveying, satire: sarcastic: abusive. — *adv.* **satir′ically.** — *n.* **satir′icalness** the state or quality of being satirical. — *v.t.* **satirise, -ize** (*sat′ər-īz*) to make the object of satire: to censure severely. — *v.i.* to write satire. — *n.* **sat′irist** a writer of satire. [L. *satira, satura* (*lanx*), full (dish), or medley.]

satisfy *sat′is-fī, v.t.* to pay in full: to compensate or atone for: to give enough to: to be enough for: to supply fully: to fulfil the conditions of: to meet the requirements of: to content: to free from doubt: to convince. — *v.i.* to give content: to make payment or atonement: — *pr.p.* **sat′isfying;** *pa.t.* and *pa.p.* **sat′isfied.** — *n.* **satisfaction** (*-fak′shən*) the act of satisfying: the state of being satisfied, content: payment: quittance: gratification: comfort: that which satisfies: amends: atonement: reparation: satisfying of honour, as by a duel: conviction. — *adv.* **satisfac′torily.** — *n.* **satisfac′toriness.** — *adjs.* **satisfac′tory** satisfying: giving contentment: such as might be wished: making amends or payment: atoning: convincing; **sat′isfiable; sat′isfied.** — *n.* **sat′isfier.** — *adj.* **sat′isfying.** — *adv.* **sat′isfyingly.** — **satisfaction theory** (of the Atonement) the ordinary theory of Catholic orthodoxy that Christ made satisfaction to Divine justice for the guilt of human sin by suffering as the human representative, and that thus Divine forgiveness was made possible. [O.Fr. *satisfier* — L. *satisfacěre* — *satis,* enough, *facěre,* to make.]

satis verborum *sā′tis vûr-bō′rəm, -bō′, sat′is ver-, wer-bō′rōōm,* (L.) enough of words.

sative *sā′tiv,* (*obs.*) cultivated. [L. *sativus.*]

satori *sa-tō′rē, -tö′, n.* sudden enlightenment — sought in Zen Buddhism. [Jap., — *toshi,* be quick.]

satrap *sat′rap, -rəp, sā′trap, n.* a viceroy or governor of an ancient Persian province: a provincial governor, esp. if powerful or ostentatiously rich: a tyrannical person. — *adjs.* **sat′rapal, satrap′ic, -al.** — *n.* **sat′rapy** a satrap's province, office, or time of office. [Gr. *satrapēs,* from Old Pers. *khshathrapāvan-,* country-protector.]

sat sapienti *sat sap-i-en′tī, -tē,* (L.) enough for the wise, a nod to the wise.

Satsuma *sat′sōō-mə, sat-sōōm′ə, n.* a province of S.W. Japan. — **satsuma (orange)** a thin-skinned seedless type of mandarin orange, or its tree; **Satsuma ware** a yellowish pottery with gilding and enamel made in Satsuma from end of 16th century.

saturate *sat′ū-rāt, sa′chə-rāt, v.t.* to interfuse: to soak: to imbue: to charge to the fullest extent possible: to satisfy all the valencies of: to cover (a target area) completely with bombs dropped simultaneously. — *adj.* saturated: deep in colour, free from white. — *n.* a saturated compound (*chem.*). — *adjs.* **sat'urable; sat'urant** which saturates. — *n.* a saturating substance. — *adj.* **sat'-urated** (of a solution) containing as much of a solute as can be dissolved at a particular temperature and pressure: containing no carbon-carbon double bonds in the molecule and consequently not susceptible to addition reactions (*chem.*). — *n.* **satura'tion.** — Also used as *adj.*, meaning of very great, or greatest possible, intensity (e.g. *saturation bombing*). — *n.* **sat'urātor.** — **saturated fat** an animal fat (usu. solid, e.g. lard, butter) containing a high proportion of saturated fatty acids; **saturation diving** diving to great depths using a special chamber at the same temperature as the water, to which the diver can return frequently for rest spells, etc., thus reducing the frequency of (and hence time spent in) decompression; **saturation point** the point at which saturation is reached: dewpoint: the limit in numbers that can be taken in, provided with a living, used, sold, etc.: the limit of emotional response, endurance, etc. [L. *saturāre, -ātum* — *satur*, full, akin to *satis*, enough.]

Saturday *sat'ər-di, n.* the seventh day of the week, dedicated by the Romans to Saturn, the Jewish Sabbath. [O.E. *Sæter-, Sætern(es)dæg*, Saturn's day.]

Saturn *sat'ərn, n.* the ancient Roman god of agriculture: commonly used for the Greek Kronos, with whom he came to be identified: the second in size and sixth in distance from the sun of the major planets, believed by the astrologers to induce a cold, melancholy, gloomy temperament: the metal lead (*alch.*). — *n.pl.* **Saturnā'lia** the festival of Saturn in mid-December, when slaves and masters exchanged garb and parts: hence (often as *sing.* without capital) an orgy. — *adj.* **saturnā'lian** of the Saturnalia: riotously merry. — *n.* **Satur'nia** (*sat-, sət-*) a genus of very large moths. — *adj.* **Satur'nian** pertaining to Saturn, whose fabulous reign was called the golden age: happy: pure: simple: in the metre in which the oldest Latin poems were written: of the planet Saturn: of the genus Saturnia. — *n.* one born under Saturn, or of saturnine temperament: the son of Saturn (Jupiter or Zeus): a fancied inhabitant of Saturn. — *adjs.* **satur'nic** affected with lead-poisoning; **sat'urnine** grave: gloomy: phlegmatic: caused or poisoned by lead. — *ns.* **sat'urnism** lead-poisoning; **sat'urnist** (*obs.*) a gloomy person. — **Saturn's tree** an arborescent deposit of lead from a solution of a lead salt. [L. *Sāturnus* — *serĕre, sătum*, to sow.]

satyagraha *sut'yə-gru-hə*, or *-grä', n.* orig. Mahatma Gandhi's policy of passive resistance to British rule in India, now any non-violent campaign for reform. [Sans., reliance on truth.]

satyr *sat'ər, n.* a Greek god of the woodlands, with tail and long ears, represented by the Romans as part goat: a desert demon (*B.*): a very lecherous person: an orang-utan: any butterfly of the Satyridae: (formerly, by confusion) a satire or satirist. — Shakespeare's **saltiers** (*Wint. Tale* IV, vi. 353) is perh. meant to mark a rustic confusion of satyr and saultier (jumper): — *fem.* **sat'yra, sat'yress.** — *n.* **sat'yral** (*her.*) a monster compounded of man, lion, and antelope. — *adj.* **satyresque'.** — *n.* **satyrī'asis** morbid, overpowering sexual desire in men, corresponding to nymphomania in women. — *adjs.* **satyric** (*sə-tir'ik*), **-al** of satyrs: having a chorus of satyrs. — *n.* **sat'yrid** any butterfly of the family **Satyridae** (*-tir'i-dē*) (otherwise **Satyrī'nae**, a sub-family of Nymphalidae) including meadow-browns, heaths, marbled whites, etc. — *n.* **sat'yrisk** a little satyr. [L. *satyrus* — Gr. *satyros*.]

sauba *sä-ōō'bə, sö'bə, n.* a S. American leaf-carrying ant. — Also **sau'ba-ant.** [Tupí.]

sauce *sös, n.* a dressing poured over food: anything that gives relish (*fig.*): vegetables eaten with meat (*U.S.*):

stewed fruit (*U.S.*): a solution of salt, etc., used in individual processes: a pert or impudent person (*obs.*): pert or impertinent language or behaviour (*coll.*). — *v.t.* to add or give sauce to: to make piquant or pleasant: to be impertinent to: to rebuke (*Shak.*): to make to pay dear (*Shak.*): to belabour (*obs.*). — *adv.* **sauc'ily.** — *n.* **sauc'iness.** — *adj.* **sauc'y** (*compar.* **sauc'-ier;** *superl.* **sauc'iest**) tasting of sauce: pert: piquantly audacious, esp. arousing sexual desire: smart and trim (as of a ship): disdainful: lascivious (*Shak.*). — **sauce'-alone'** garlic mustard; **sauce'-boat** a vessel for sauce; **sauce'-box** a saucy person; **sauce-crayon** (*sōs krā-yɔ̃*; Fr.) a soft black pastel used for backgrounds; **sauce'-pan** a handled and usu. lidded metal pan for boiling, stewing, etc. — orig. for sauces; **sauce'pan-fish** the king-crab. [Fr. *sauce* — L. *salsa* — *sallēre, salsum*, to salt — *sāl*, salt.]

saucer *sö'sər, n.* orig., a dish for salt or sauce: a shallow dish, esp. one placed under a tea or coffee cup: anything of like shape. — *n.* **sau'cerful:** — *pl.* **sau'-cerfuls.** — **sau'cer-eye** a large round eye. — *adj.* **sau'cer-eyed.** — **flying saucer** see **fly.** [O.Fr. *saussiere* — L.L. *salsārium* — L. *salsa*, sauce.]

sauch, saugh *söhh*, a Scots form of **sallow**[1].

saucisse *sö-sēs', saucisson -ɔ̃, ns.* a tube of powder for firing a mine. [Fr., sausage.]

sauerkraut *sow', zow'ər-krowt, n.* a German dish of cabbage allowed to ferment with salt, etc. — Also **sour'-crout.** [Ger., sour cabbage.]

saufgard *söf-gärd', (Spens.) n.* Same as **safeguard.**

sauger *sö'gər, n.* a small American pike-perch.

saul. A Scots form of **soul.**

saulge *söj, (Spens.) n.* Same as **sage**[1].

saulie *sö'li, (Scot.) n.* a hired mourner. [Origin obscure.]

sault *sölt, n.* a leap (also **salt**) (*obs.*): in N. America (*sōō*) a waterfall or rapid. [Fr. *saut*, 17th-cent. *sault* — L. *saltus, -ūs*, leap.]

sauna *sö'nə, sow'nə, n.* (a building or room equipped for) a Finnish form of steam bath. [Finn.]

saunt *sönt*, a Scots form of **saint.**

saunter *sön'tər, v.i.* to wander about idly: to loiter: to lounge: to stroll: to dawdle (*obs.*). — *n.* a sauntering: a sauntering gait: a leisurely stroll. — *ns.* **saun'terer; saun'tering.** — *adv.* **saun'teringly.** [Origin obscure.]

saurel *sō-rel', sör'əl, n.* the horse-mackerel, scad. [Fr.]

Sauria *sö'ri-ə, n.pl.* in old classifications an order of reptiles, the lizards with (at first) the crocodiles. — *adj.* **sau'rian.** — *n.* a member of the Sauria: a lizard-like fossil reptile. — *adj.* **saurischian** (*-is'ki-ən*; L. *ischium*, hip joint) of or belonging to the **Sauris'chia** (lit. "lizard-hipped"), an order of dinosaurs including the sauropods and theropods. — *n.* any dinosaur of the Saurischia. — *adjs.* **saurog'nathous** having a lizard-like arrangement of the palate-bones (as woodpeckers, **Saurog'nathae;** Gr. *gnathos*, jaw); **saur'oid** lizard-like. — *n.pl.* **Saurop'oda** (Gr. *pous, podos*, foot) a suborder of gigantic quadrupedal herbivorous dinosaurs, one of the two main groups of lizard-hipped dinosaurs (including Apatosaurus (= Brontosaurus), Diplodocus, Brachiosaurus) — *n.* **saur'opod.** — *adj.* **saurop'odous.** — *n.pl.* **Saurop'sida** (Gr. *opsis, -eōs*, appearance) a main division of the Vertebrata — birds and reptiles. — *n.* and *adj.* **saurop'sidan.** — *n.pl.* **Sauropterygia** (*sö-rop-tər-ij'i-ə*; Gr. *pterygion*, a fin) an order of fossil reptiles, aquatic or amphibious, including Plesiosaurus. — *adj.* **sauropteryg'ian.** — *n.pl.* **Saururae** (*-rōō'rē*; Gr. *ourā*, tail) an extinct (Jurassic) subclass of birds, with teeth and jointed tail — Archaeopteryx, etc. [Gr. *saurā, sauros*, a lizard.]

saury *sö'ri, n.* a sharp-beaked fish (*Scombresox saurus*) akin to the garfish. [Perh. Gr. *sauros*, lizard.]

sausage *sos'ij, n.* chopped or minced meat with fat, cereal, etc. seasoned and stuffed into a tube of gut or the like or formed into the shape of a tube: anything of like shape, e.g. an observation balloon. — **saus'age-bassoon'** the rackett; **saus'age-dog** (*coll.*) a dachshund; **saus'age-meat'** meat prepared for making sausages;

saus'age-poi'soning botulism; **saus'age-roll'** minced meat cooked in a roll of pastry: a curl of hair of similar shape; **sau'sage-tree'** tropical tree (*Kigelia africana*) with bell-shaped flowers and sausage-shaped fruits. — **not a sausage** (*coll.*) nothing at all. [Fr. *saucisse* — L.L. *salsīcia* — L. *salsus*, salted.]

saussurite *sö-sū'rīt, n.* a dull opaque mass of zoisite, albite, etc., formed by the alteration of feldspar. — *adjs.* **saussuritic** (*-it'ik*); **saussu'ritised, -ized.** [After the Swiss geologist H. B. de *Saussure* (1740–99).]

saut *söt,* a Scottish form of **salt**[1].

sauté *sö'tā, adj.* fried lightly and quickly. — Also *v.t.* — *n.* a dish of food that has been sautéed. [Fr. *sauter*, to jump.]

Sauterne(s) *sö-tûrn', -tern', n.* esteemed sweet white wine produced at *Sauternes* in the Gironde, France.

sautoir *sö'twär, n.* a long necklace, or pendant on a long chain or ribbon. [Fr., — L.L. *saltātōrium*, a stirrup; cf. **saltire**.]

Sauvignon *sö'vē-nyɔ̃, n.* a variety of grape originally grown in Bordeaux and the Loire valley: wine made from this.

savable, etc. See **save**.

savage *sav'ij,* also (*obs.*) **salvage** *sal'vij, adjs.* in a state of nature: wild: uncivilised: ferocious: furious. — *n.* a wild beast (now *rare*): an enraged horse or other animal: a human being in a wild or primitive state: a brutal, fierce, or cruel person. — *v.t.* to make savage: to assail savagely, esp. with the teeth. — *v.i.* to play the savage. — *n.* **sav'agedom** a savage state: savages collectively. — *adv.* **sav'agely.** — *ns.* **sav'ageness; sav'- agery** (*-ri, -ər-i*) fierceness: ferocity: uncivilised condition: wildness: wild growth of plants; **sav'agism.** [O.Fr. *salvage* — L. *silvāticus*, pertaining to the woods — *silva*, a wood.]

savanna, savannah *sə-van'ə, n.* a tract of level land, covered with low vegetation, treeless, or dotted with trees or patches of wood. — **savanna flower** a West Indian apocynaceous plant (*Echites*); **savann'a-forest** parklands; **savann'a-sparr'ow** a N. American sparrow (*Passerculus*); **savann'a-watt'le** fiddlewood. [Sp. *zavana* (now *sabana*), said to be from Carib: not from *sábana*, sheet.]

savant *sa'vä, sä-vä', n.* a learned man. [Fr. obs. pr.p. of *savoir*, to know.]

savarin *sav'ər-in, n.* a ring-shaped cake made with yeast, containing nuts, fruit, etc., and often flavoured with rum. [Named after Antheline Brillat-*Savarin* (d. 1826), Fr. politician and gourmet.]

savate *sä-vät', n.* boxing with the use of the feet. [Fr.]

save *sāv, v.t.* to bring safe out of evil: to rescue: to bring or keep out of danger: to protect: to preserve: to prevent or avoid the loss, expenditure, or performance of, or the gain of by an opponent: to reserve: to spare: to deliver from the power of sin and from its consequences: to husband: to hoard: to store (data) on a tape or disk: to be in time for: to obviate, to prevent. — *v.i.* to act as a saviour: to be economical. — *prep.* except. — *conj.* were it not that (*Shak.*): unless. — *n.* an act of saving, esp. in games. — *adj.* **sav'able.** — *n.* **sav'ableness.** — *adj.* **saved.** — *n.* **sa'ver.** — *adj.* **sa'ving** protecting: preserving: redeeming: securing salvation (*theol.*): frugal: making a reservation: directed towards the avoidance of loss rather than the making of profit. — *prep.* excepting. — *n.* the action of the verb: that which is saved: (*pl.*) money laid aside for future use. — *adv.* **sa'vingly.** — *n.* **sa'vingness.** — **save'-all** a contrivance intended to save anything from being wasted or damaged: a miser. — *adj.* stingy. — *v.t.* **save'gard** (*Spens.*) to guard, protect. — **saving clause** a legal clause, or a statement, in which a reservation or condition is made; **saving game** a policy or procedure aimed rather at avoiding loss than at making a profit; **saving grace** see **grace**; **savings bank** a bank established to encourage thrift by taking small deposits, investing under regulations for safety, and giving compound interest; **savings certificate** a certifi-

cate of having invested a small sum in government funds. — **save appearances** to make hypothesis accord with observation (*astron., Milt.*): to keep up an appearance of wealth, comfort, consistency, harmony, propriety, etc; **save as you earn** (abbrev. **SAYE**) a government-operated savings scheme in which regular deductions are made from one's earnings; **save one's bacon, face, save the mark** see **bacon, face, mark**; **save up** to accumulate or hold for some purpose by refraining from spending or using; **save you** (*arch.*) a greeting = God keep you. [Fr. *sauver* — L. *salvāre* — *salvus*, safe.]

saveloy *sav'ə-loi, n.* a highly seasoned sausage, orig. of brains. [Fr. *cervelat, cervelas,* a saveloy — It. *cervellata* — *cervello*, brain — L. *cerebellum*, dim. of *cerebrum*, the brain.]

savey. See **savvy**.

savin, savine *sav'in, n.* a species of juniper (*Juniperus sabina*) with very small imbricated leaves: its tops yielding an irritant volatile oil, anthelmintic and abortifacient: extended to Virginian juniper ('red cedar') and other plants. [O.Fr. *sabine* — L. *sabīna* (*herba*), Sabine (herb).]

saviour *sā'vyər, n.* one who saves from evil: **Saviour** a title applied by Christians to Jesus Christ. [M.E. *sauveur* — O.Fr. *sauveour* — L. *salvātor* — *salūs, salūtis*, health, well-being, safety.]

savoir-faire *sav-wär-fer', n.* the faculty of knowing just what to do and how to do it: tact. [Fr.]

savoir-vivre *sav-wär-vē'vr', n.* good breeding: knowledge of polite usages. [Fr.]

savory *sā'vər-i, n.* a labiate flavouring herb (*Satureia*, esp. *S. hortensis*, summer savory, or *S. montana*, winter savory). [App. — L. *saturēia*.]

savour, also (*U.S.*) **savor,** *sā'vər, n.* taste: odour: flavour: relish: repute (*B.*). — *v.i.* to taste or smell in a particular way: to have a flavour (*lit.* or *fig.*): to smack. — *v.t.* to flavour, season: to taste, smell: to be conscious of: to relish: to perceive critically: to taste with conscious direction of the attention. — *adjs.* **sā'vorous** pleasant to the taste; **sā'voured** having a savour. — *adv.* **sā'vourily.** — *n.* **sā'vouriness.** — *adj.* **sā'vourless.** — *adv.* **sā'vourly** (*obs.*) relishingly: feelingly: understandingly. — *adj.* **sā'voury** of good savour or relish: fragrant: having savour or relish: appetising: salty, piquant or spiced (opp. to *sweet*; also *fig.*): savouring of edification or holiness (*arch.*). — *n.* a savoury course or dish or small item of food. [O.Fr. *sav(o)ur* (Fr. *saveur*) — L. *sapor* — *sapēre*, to taste.]

Savoy *sə-voi', n.* a district, formerly of the kingdom of Sardinia, now of S.E. France, giving name to a former palace and sanctuary and to a theatre in London: (without *cap.*) a winter cabbage with a large close head and wrinkled leaves — originally from *Savoy*. — *n.* **Savoyard** (*sav'oi-ärd*) a native or inhabitant of Savoy, or of the Savoy precinct in London: a performer in, or devotee of, the Gilbert and Sullivan operas produced at the Savoy theatre. — Also *adj.* [Fr. *Savoie, Savoyard*.]

savvy, savvey, savey *sav'i,* (*slang*) *v.t.* and *v.i.* to know: to understand. — *n.* general ability: common sense: know-how, skill. — *adj.* knowledgeable, shrewd. [Sp. *sabe* — *saber*, to know — L. *sapēre*, to be wise.]

saw[1] *sö, pa.t.* of **see**[2].

saw[2] *sö, n.* a toothed cutting instrument. — *v.t.* to cut with, or as with, or as, a saw: to play harshly or crudely (as a fiddler). — *v.i.* to use a saw: to make to and fro movements, as if with a saw: — *pa.t.* **sawed;** *pa.p.* **sawed** or (usu.) **sawn.** — *adj.* **sawed.** — *n.* and *adj.* **saw'ing.** — *adj.* **sawn.** — *ns.* **saw'er** (*rare*); **saw'yer** one who saws timber, esp. at a sawpit: a stranded tree that bobs in a river (*U.S.*). — **saw'-bill** a merganser: a motmot; **saw'-blade; saw'-bones** (*slang*) a surgeon; **saw'-buck** (*U.S.*) a saw-horse: a ten-dollar bill (*slang*); **saw'dust** dust or small particles of wood, etc., detached in sawing. — *v.t.* to sprinkle with sawdust. — *adj.* **saw'dusty.** — **saw'-edge.** — *adj.* **saw'-edged** serrated

— **saw´-fish** a ray (*Pristis*) or (sometimes) a shark (*Pristiophorus*; **saw´-shark**) with a flattened bony beak toothed on the edges; **saw´-fly** a hymenopterous insect of various kinds with saw-like ovipositor; **saw´-frame** the frame in which a saw is set; **saw´-gate, -kerf** the gap made by a saw; **saw´-horse** a trestle for supporting wood that is being sawn: a straight-line diagram showing the three-dimensional structure of a molecule; **saw´-mill** a mill for sawing timber. — *adj.* **sawn´-off** (or **sawed off**) shortened by cutting with a saw: short in stature (*slang*). — **saw´pit** a pit in which one sawyer stands while another stands above; **saw´-set** an instrument for turning saw-teeth to right and left; **saw´-tones** harsh notes; **saw´-tooth**. — Also *adj.* — *adj.* **saw´-toothed**. — **saw´-wort** a name for various composites with serrate leaves (*Serratula, Saussurea*, etc.). [O.E. *saga*; Ger. *Säge*.]

saw³ *sö, n.* a saying: a proverb: a decree (*Spens.*). [O.E. *sagu*, from the root of *secgan*, to say, tell.]

saw⁴ *sö*, a Scots form of **sow²** and of **salve²**.

sawah *sa´wa n.* an irrigated paddy-field. [Malay.]

sawder *sö´dər, v.t.* to flatter, blarney. — *n.* (in phrase *soft sawder*) flattery. [Prob. **solder**.]

sawn *sön, pa.p.* of **saw**; also (*Northern*) of **sow²**, (*Shak.*) perh. of **sow²**, perh. of **see²**.

Sawney, Sawny *sö´ni, n.* an old nickname for a Scotsman. [For *Sandy*, from *Alexander*.]

sawney *sö´ni*, (*slang*) *n.* a fool. [Poss. from prec.; poss. from **zany**.]

sawyer. See **saw²**.

sax¹ *saks, n.* a chopper for trimming slates. [O.E. *sæx* (W.S. *seax*), a knife.]

sax² *saks*, a Scottish form of **six**.

sax³ *saks, n.* a coll. shortening of **saxophone**.

saxatile *sak´sə-tīl, -til, adj.* rock-dwelling. [L. *saxātilis* — *saxum*, a rock.]

saxaul, saksaul *sak´söl, n.* a low, thick, grotesquely contorted tree (*Haloxylon*) of the goosefoot family, found on the salt steppes of Asia.

Saxe *saks, adj.* made in, or characteristic of, Saxony (of china, etc): of a deep shade of light blue (**Saxe blue**, also **Saxon** or **Saxony blue**). — *n.* Saxon blue, a dye colour: an albuminised paper (*phot.*). [Fr. *Saxe*, Saxony.]

saxhorn *saks´hörn, n.* a brass wind-instrument having a long winding tube with bell opening, invented by Antoine or Adolphe *Sax* (1814–94).

saxicavous *sak-sik´ə-vəs, adj.* rock-boring. — *n.* **Saxic´ava** a genus of rock-boring lamellibranchs. [L. *saxum*, a rock, *cavāre*, to hollow.]

saxicolous *sak-sik´ə-ləs, adj.* living or growing among rocks. — *n.* **Saxic´ola** the wheatear genus. — *adj.* **saxic´oline**. [L. *saxum*, a rock, *colēre*, to inhabit.]

saxifrage *sak´si-frij, -frāj, n.* any species of the genus Saxifraga, Alpine or rock plants with tufted foliage and small white, yellow or red flowers: extended to other plants (see **burnet saxifrage, golden saxifrage**). — *n.* **Saxifraga** (-*sif´rə-gə*) the London pride genus, giving name to the family **Saxifragā´ceae**. — *adj.* **saxifragā´ceous**. [L. *saxifraga* — *saxum*, a stone, *frangĕre*, to break (from growing in clefts of rock, or, according to Pliny, from supposed efficacy in breaking up a calculus in the bladder).]

saxitoxin *sak-si-tok´sin, n.* a nerve poison found in molluscs feeding on dinoflagellates of the genus *Gonyaulax*. [*Saxi*domus giganteus, the Alaskan butter clam, from which *toxin* has been isolated.]

Saxon *saks´ən, n.* one of a N. German people that conquered most of Britain in the 5th and 6th centuries (including or excluding the Angles and Jutes): the language of that people on the Continent (Old Saxon) or in Britain (Anglo-Saxon, Old English): an Englishman or Lowland Scotsman: one whose native language is English: the English language: a native, inhabitant, or citizen of Saxony in the later German sense (now in S. Germany). — *adj.* pertaining to the Saxons in any sense, their language, country, or architecture. — *n.* **Sax´ondom** the Anglo-Saxon or English-speaking world. — *adj.* **Saxonic** (-*on´ik*). — *v.t.* and *v.i.* **Sax´onise, -ize** to make or become Saxon. — *ns.* **Sax´onism** a Saxon or English idiom: a preference for native English words, institutions, etc.; **Sax´onist** a scholar in Old English; **sax´onite** a hypersthene peridotite; **sax´ony** a soft woollen yarn or cloth. — **Saxon architecture** a style of building in England before the Norman Conquest, marked by the peculiar 'long and short' work of the quoins, the projecting fillets running up the face of the walls and interlacing like woodwork, and the baluster-like shafts between the openings of the upper windows resembling the turned woodwork of the period; **Saxon(y) blue** see **Saxe; Saxon Shore** (L. *Litus Saxonicum*) in Roman times, the coast districts from Brighton to the Wash, peculiarly exposed to the attacks of the Saxons, or perh. already partly settled by them, and so placed under the authority of a special officer, the 'Count of the Saxon Shore'. [L. *Saxōnēs* (pl.); of Ger. origin; cf. O.E. *Seaxe*; Ger. *Sachsen*; perh. conn. O.E. *sæx* (W.S. *seax*), O.H.G. *sahs*, knife, short sword.]

saxophone *sak´sə-fōn, n.* a jazz, military and dance band instrument with reed, (properly) metal tube, and about twenty finger-keys. — *n.* **saxophonist** (-*sof´ən-ist*). [*Sax*, the inventor (see **saxhorn**), Gr. *phōnē*, the voice.]

say¹ *sā, v.t.* to utter or set forth, as words or in words: to speak: to assert, affirm, state, declare: to tell: to go through in recitation or repetition. — *v.i.* to make a statement: to speak: to declare, set forth in answer to a question: — *2nd sing. pr. ind.* **sayst** (*sāst*), **sayest** (*sā´ist*; both *arch.*); *3rd sing.* **says** (*sez, səz*), archaic **saith** (*seth*); *pr.p.* **say´ing**; *pa.p.* and *pa.t.* **said** (*sed*); *2nd sing.* **saidst** (*sedst*), also **said´est** (both *arch.*). — *n.* something said: a remark: a speech: a saw (*obs.*): what one wants to say: opportunity of speech: a voice, part, or influence in a decision. — *adj.* **say´able**. — *ns.* **say´er**; **say´ing** something said: an expression: a maxim. — **say´-so** an authoritative saying: authority: a rumour: hearsay. — **I'll say!** (*coll.*) a response expressing wholehearted agreement; **I say** an exclamation calling attention or expressing surprise, protest, sudden joy, etc.; **it is said** or **they say** it is commonly reputed; **it says (that)** the text runs thus (*coll.*); **nothing to say for oneself** no defence of oneself to offer: no small-talk; **nothing to say to** no dealings with; **not to say** indeed one might go further and say; **say for example**: suppose: I say (*U.S.*): in 18th-cent. verse a common introduction to a rhetorical question; **says I, says you, he**, etc. (in *illit.* or jocular use) ungrammatical substitutes for said I, you, he, etc.; **says you** *interj.* expressing incredulity; **sooth to say** in truth: if the truth must be told; **that is to say** in other words; **to say nothing of** not to mention; **to say the least** at least: without exaggeration; **what do you say to?** how about?: are you inclined towards?; **you, he can say that again** (*coll.*) you are, he is absolutely right, I agree entirely. [O.E. *secgan* (*sægde, gesægd*); O.N. *segja*, Ger. *sagen*.]

say² *sā*, (*obs.*; *Spens., Shak.*) *n., v.t.*, and *v.i.* an aphetic form of **assay**. — *n.* **say´er**. — **say´-master; say´-piece**.

say³ *sā, n.* a woollen stuff like serge. — *adj.* (*Shak.*) of say. — *n.* **say´on** a mediaeval peasant's sleeveless jacket. [O.Fr. *saie* — L. *saga*, pl. of *sagum*, military cloak.]

sayne *sān*, (*Spens.*) *inf.* and *pl.* of *pr.t.* of **say¹**.

sayonara *sä-yo-nä´ra*, (Jap.) *n.* or *interj.* good-bye.

sayyid, sayid, sayed, said *sī´* or *sā´(y)id, sād, ns.* a descendant of Mohammed's daughter Fatima: an honorary title given to some Muslims. [Ar.]

saz *saz, n.* a stringed instrument of Turkey, N. Africa and the Middle East. [Pers. *sāz*, a musical instrument.]

sazerac® *saz´ə-rak, n.* (*U.S.*) a cocktail based on Pernod and whisky.

sazhen *sä-zhen´, n.* a Russian measure, about 2 metres. [Russ.]

sbirro *zbir'rō, n.* an Italian police officer: — *pl.* **sbirri** (*-rē*). [It.]

'sblood *zblud,* **'sbodikins** *zbod'i-kinz,* **'sbuddikins** *zbud',* **'zbud** *zbud, interjs.* obsolete oaths. [**God's blood, body.**]

scab *skab, n.* vaguely, a skin disease, esp. with scales or pustules, and esp. one caused by mites (as in *sheep scab*): a fungous disease of various kinds in potatoes, apples, etc.: a crust formed over a sore, or in any of these diseases: a scoundrel: a black-leg. — *v.i.* to develop a scab: to play the scab, act as a black-leg. — *adj.* **scabbed** (*skabd, skab'id*) affected or covered with scabs: diseased with scab: vile, worthless. — *ns.* **scabb'-edness; scabb'iness.** — *adj.* **scabb'y.** [App. from an O.N. equivalent of O.E. *scæb, sceabb* (see **shabby**) influenced by association with L. *scabiēs.*]

scabbard *skab'ərd, n.* a sheath, esp. for a sword. — *v.t.* to sheathe. — *adj.* **scabb'ardless.** — **scabb'ard-fish** a long narrow fish (*Lepidopus*) of the hairtail family. [M.E. *scauberc,* app. — A.Fr. *escaubers* (pl.), prob. Gmc.]

scabble *skab'l.* Same as **scapple.**

scaberulous. See **scabrous.**

scabies *skā'bi-ēz, -bēz, n.* the itch. [L. *scăbiēs — scabēre,* to scratch.]

scabious *skā'bi-əs, n.* any plant of the genus **Scabio'sa** of the teasel family, as the *Devil's-bit scabious,* long thought efficacious in treating scaly eruptions: a plant (*Jasione montana; sheep's,* or *sheep's-bit scabious*) of the bell-flower family, of similar appearance. [L. *scăbiōsus — scăbiēs,* the itch.]

scabrous *skā'brəs, adj.* rough: rough with projecting points: scurfy: harsh: beset with difficulties: bordering on the indecent. — *adjs.* **scaberulous** (*skə-ber'ū-ləs*), **scā'brid** somewhat scabrous. — *ns.* **scabridity** (*skə-brid'i-ti*), **scā'brousness.** [L. *scăbrōsus, scăbridus — scăber,* rough.]

scad[1] *skad, n.* a carangoid fish (*Caranx,* or *Trachurus, trachurus*) with armoured and keeled lateral line, superficially like a coarse mackerel, also called *horse-mackerel.* [App. Cornish dial.; perh. **shad.**]

scad[2] *skad,* (esp. *U.S.*) *n.* a large amount, a lot (usu. in *pl.*). [Origin unknown.]

scaff *skaf, n.* food (*Scot.*): riff-raff (also **scaff'-raff**). [Perh. Du. or Ger. *schaffen,* to procure food; cf. **scoff**[2].]

scaffie *skaf'i,* (*Scot. coll.*) *n.* short for **scavenger.**

scaffold *skaf'əld, n.* a temporary erection for men at work on a building, and their tools and materials: a raised platform, as for performers, spectators, or executions: a raised framework, as for hunters, or among some primitive peoples for disposal of the dead: a frame-work: capital punishment (*fig.*). — *v.t.* to furnish with a scaffold: to put on a scaffold: to sustain. — *ns.* **scaff'oldage** (*Shak.* **scaff'olage**) a scaffolding: the gallery of a theatre; **scaff'older; scaff'olding** a frame-work for painters, builders, etc., at work: materials for scaffolds: a frame, framework (*fig.*): the action of the verb. [O.Fr. *escadafault* (Fr. *échafaud*), of obscure origin; cf. It. *catafalco.*]

scag *skag, n.* (*U.S. slang*) heroin. [Origin obscure.]

scaglia *skal'yə, n.* an Italian limestone, usu. reddish. — *n.* **scagliō'la** an imitation stone of cement and chips. — Also *adj.* [It. *scaglia,* scale, dim. *scagliuola.*]

scail. Same as **skail.**

scaith. See **scathe.**

scala *skā'lə, skä'lə, n.* a ladder-like structure, as any of the canals of the cochlea: — *pl.* **scā'lae** (*-lē, -lī*). — *ns.* **scalade** (*skə-lād'*), **scalado** (*-lā'dō, -lä'dō; pl. -dos;* It. *scalada*) an escalade. — *adj.* **scalar** (*skā'lər*) ladder-like: numerical: represented by a point in a scale: having magnitude only, not direction. — *n.* a scalar quantity. — *n.* **Scalaria** (*skə-lā'ri-ə*) the wentletrap genus. — *adj.* **scalariform** (*skə-lar'i-förm*) ladder-like. [L. *scāla,* a ladder.]

scal(l)awag. Same as **scallywag.**

scald[1] *sköld, v.t.* to injure with hot liquid: to cook or heat short of boiling: to treat with very hot water: to burn,

scorch (now *dial.*). — *v.i.* to be scalded: to be hot enough to scald. — *n.* a burn caused by hot liquid. — *n.* **scald'er.** — *n.* and *adj.* **scald'ing.** — **scald'ings** a cry of warning to get out of the way, as if of hot water. [O.Fr. *escalder* (Fr. *échauder*) — L.L. *excaldāre,* to bathe in warm water — *ex,* from, *calidus,* warm, hot.]

scald[2], **scaldic.** Same as **skald, skaldic.**

scald[3] *sköld, adj.* scabby: scurfy: paltry. — *n.* scurf on the head: a scurvy fellow. — **scald'-berry** the black-berry (from a belief that it causes scald-head); **scald'-crow** (*Ir.*) the hooded crow; **scald'fish** the smooth sole; **scald'-head** a diseased scalp: scalp disease of various kinds. [For **scalled.**]

scaldino *skal-, skäl-dē'nō, n.* an Italian earthenware brazier: — *pl.* **scaldi'ni** (*-nē*). [It. *scaldare,* to warm.]

scale[1] *skäl.* Same as **skail.**

scale[2] *skäl, n.* a ladder (*obs.*): a scaling-ladder (*Milt.*): a flight of steps (*obs.*): a graduated series or order: a graduated measure: a system of definite tones used in music: a succession of these performed in ascending or descending order of pitch through one octave or more: the compass or range of a voice or instrument: a numeral system: a system or scheme of relative values or correspondences: the ratio of representation to object: relative extent. — *v.t.* to mount, as by a ladder: to climb: to change according to scale (often with *up* or *down*). — *v.i.* to mount. — *adj.* **scal'able.** — *ns.* **scal'er** an instrument incorporating more than one **scaling circuit** (a device that counts very rapid pulses, by recording at the end of each group of specified numbers instead of after individual pulses): a scaling circuit; **scal'ing** climbing: adjustment to or in a scale. — **scale'-stair'(case)** (*Scot.*) stairs in straight flights; **scal'ing-ladder** a ladder for escalade: a fireman's ladder. — **full-scale** see **full; on a large, small, scale** in a great, small, way; **on the scale of** in the ratio of; **scale and platt** (*Scot.*) stairs with straight flights and land-ings; **to scale** in proportion to actual dimensions. [L. *scāla,* a ladder — *scandēre,* to mount.]

scale[3] *skäl, n.* a thin plate on a fish, reptile, etc.: a readily detached flake: a lamina: an overlapping plate in armour: a small, flat, detachable piece of cuticle: a reduced leaf or leaf-base, often membranous, or hard and woody: a small flat structure clothing a butterfly's or moth's wing: the waxy shield secreted by a scale-insect: an encrustation: a film, as on iron being heated for forging: a side piece of a razor or clasp-knife handle. — *v.t.* to clear of scales: to peel off in thin layers. — *v.i.* to come off in thin layers or flakes. — *adjs.* **scaled** having scales: cleared of scales; **scale'less; scale'like.** — *ns.* **scal'er** one who scales fish, boilers, etc.: an instrument for scaling, as for removing tartar from the teeth; **scal'iness; scal'ing** formation, peeling off, shedding, removal, or arrangement of scales or scale: a scaled-off piece. — Also *adj.* — *adj.* **scal'y** covered with scales: like scales: shabby: formed of scales: inclined to scale. — **scale'-arm'our** armour of overlapping scales; **scale'-board** a very thin slip of wood; **scale'-fern** a fern (*Ceterach officinarum*) whose back is densely covered with rusty-coloured scales; **scale'-fish** a dry-cured fish, as haddock, hake, pollack: a fish with scales; **scale'-insect** any insect of the homopterous family Coccidae, in which the sedentary female fixes on a plant and secretes a waxy shield; **scale'-leaf** a scale that is homologically a leaf; **scale'-moss** a liverwort with small leaf-like structures, as *Jungermannia;* **scale'-work** imbricated ornament; **scal'y-bark** hickory: hickory-nut; **scal'y-leg** a disease of legs and feet in poultry, caused by a mite. [M.E. *scăle* — O.Fr. *escale,* husk, chip of stone, of Gmc. origin; cf. **scale**[4], **shale, shell.**]

scale[4] *skäl, n.* a balance pan: (usu. in *pl.*; by Shak. treated as *sing.*) a balance: (in *pl.*) Libra, a constellation and a sign of the zodiac. — *v.t.* to weigh: to weigh up. — *v.i.* to weigh or be weighed, as a jockey (often *scale in*). — **scale'-beam** the beam of a balance. [A North-ern form from O.N. *skäl,* bowl, pan of balance; cf.

O.E. *scealu*, shell, cup, Du. *schaal*, Ger. *Schale*, and preceding word.]

scale⁵ *skāl*, (Shak., *Cor.* I, i. 97) *v.t.* variously explained as, to spread, disseminate (see **skail**), to lay bare, make clear (see **scale³**) or as a misprint for **stale**.

scalene *skāl'ēn, skal-ēn'*, *adj.* (of a triangle) with three unequal sides: (of a cone or cylinder) with axis oblique to the base: denoting the muscles that connect the upper ribs to the cervical vertebrae, being obliquely situated and unequal-sided. — **scalēnohē'dron** (*crystal.*) a hemihedral form bounded in the hexagonal system by twelve, in the tetragonal by eight, faces, each a scalene triangle. [Gr. *skalēnos*, uneven, *hedrā*, seat.]

scall *sköl*, *n.* (*B.*) scabbiness, esp. of the scalp. — *adj.* (*Shak.*) scurvy: mean. — *adj.* **scalled** (see **scald³**). [O.N. *skalli*, bald head.]

scallion *skal'yən*, *n.* the shallot (*dial.*): the leek: an onion with defective bulb: a spring onion. [O.N.Fr. *escalogne* — L. *Ascalōnia* (*cēpa*), Ascalon (onion).]

scallop *skol'əp, skal'əp*, *n.* a bivalve (Pecten) having a sub-circular shell with sinuous radiating ridges and eared hinge-line: a valve of its shell: a dish or other object of like form: a shallow dish in which oysters, etc., are cooked, baked, and browned: hence, the cooked oysters, etc., themselves: a potato slice cooked in batter: one of a series of curves in the edge of anything: a scallop-shell as pilgrim badge: an escalope. — *v.t.* to cut into scallops or curves: to cook in a scallop with sauce and usu. breadcrumbs. — *v.i.* to gather, search for scallops. — *adj.* **scall'oped** having the edge or border cut into scallops or curves. — **scall'op-shell** the shell of a scallop, esp. that of a Mediterranean species, the badge of a pilgrim to the shrine of St James of Compostela. — Also **scollop**. [O.Fr. *escalope*; of Gmc. origin; cf. Du. *schelp*, shell; Ger. *Schelfe*, husk.]

scallywag, scallawag, scalawag *skal'i-wag, -ə-wag*, *ns.* an undersized animal of little value: a good-for-nothing: a rascal, scamp: a Southerner who co-operated with the Republicans in the Reconstruction period (*U.S. hist.*). [Origin obscure; association with *Scalloway* in Shetland, in allusion to its small cattle or ponies, is regarded as a joke.]

scalp¹ *skalp* (*Scot.* **scaup** *sköp*), *ns.* the skull (*obs.*): the outer covering of the skull: the top or hairy part of the head: the skin on which the hair of the head grows: a piece of that skin torn off as a token of victory by the North American Indians: a bare rock or mountain-top: a bed of oysters or mussels. — *v.t.* to cut the scalp from: to buy cheap in order to resell quickly at a profit: of theatre, travel, or other tickets, to buy up and sell at other than official prices (*U.S.*): to destroy the political influence of (*U.S.*). — *n.* **scalp'er.** — *adj.* **scalp'less.** — **scalp'ing-knife** a knife for scalping enemies; **scalp'ing-tuft** a scalp-lock; **scalp'-lock** a long tuft of hair left unshaven as a challenge. [M.E. *scalp*; perh. Scand.; cf. O.N. *skālpr*, sheath; cf. **scallop**.]

scalp² *skalp*, (*rare*) *v.t.* and *v.i.* to scrape: to cut: to engrave. — *n.* **scalp'el** a small knife for dissecting or operating. — *adj.* **scalpell'iform** shaped like a scalpel. — *n.* **scalp'er** a scalprum: an engraver's scauper. — *adj.* **scalp'riform** chisel-shaped. — *n.* **scalp'rum** a surgeon's rasping instrument. [L. *scalpĕre*, to scrape, cut, *scalper, scalprum*, dim. *scalpellum*, a knife.]

scaly. See **scale³**.

scam *skam*, (*slang*) *n.* a confidence trick, swindle. [Origin unknown.]

scamble *skam'bl*, *v.i.* to scramble (for e.g. something scattered; *Shak.*): to get along somehow (*obs.*): to shamble (*dial.*): to sprawl (*dial.*). — *v.t.* to get together with effort (now *dial.*): to remove piecemeal: to scatter as for a scramble (*dial.*): to squander (*dial.*). — *ns.* **scam'bler** (*Scot.*) a mealtime sponger; **scam'bling** (*obs.*) scrambling: a haphazard meal — also *adj.* — *adv.* **scam'blingly** strugglingly. — *n.pl.* **scam'bling-days** (*obs.*) days of makeshift meals in Lent. [Origin obscure; app. related to **shamble** and **scramble**.]

scamel *skam'l*, (*Shak.*) *n.* alleged to be a Norfolk name for the bar-tailed godwit: or a misprint for **staniel**, **stannel**, or for **sea-mell**, an alleged variant of **sea-mew**.

scammony *skam'ən-i*, *n. Convolvulus scammonia*, a twining Asian plant with arrow-shaped leaves: its dried root: a cathartic gum-resin obtained from its root or that of a substitute. [Gr. *skammōniā*.]

scamp¹ *skamp*, *v.i.* to go about idly (*dial.*): to take to the highway (as a robber; *obs.*). — *n.* a highwayman (*obs.*): a rascal: a lively, tricky fellow. — *v.i.* **scamp'er** to decamp (*obs.*): to run or skip about briskly. — *n.* an act of scampering. — *adj.* **scamp'ish.** — *adv.* **scamp'ishly.** — *n.* **scamp'ishness.** [O.Fr. *escamper* or It. *scampare*, to decamp.]

scamp² *skamp*, *v.t.* to do, execute, perfunctorily or without thoroughness. — *ns.* **scamp'er; scamp'ing.** — **scamp'-work.** [Poss. O.N. *skemma*, to shorten; cf. **skimp, scant.**]

scampi *skam'pi*, *n.pl.* crustaceans of the species *Nephrops norvegicus* (called the Norway lobster or Dublin (Bay) prawn), esp. (treated as *sing.*) when cooked and served as a dish. [Pl. of It. *scampo*, a shrimp.]

scan *skan*, *v.t.* to analyse metrically: to utter so as to bring out the metrical structure: to examine critically: to judge (*obs.*): to interpret, read (*Shak.*): to make out: to examine closely: to scrutinise: to examine all parts of in systematic order: (in television) to pass a beam over every part of in turn: to make pictorial records of (part of) the body by various techniques, e.g. ultrasonics (*med.*): loosely, to cast an eye negligently over: (*Spens.*, in *pa.p.* **scand**) to climb, scale: to search out by swinging the beam (*radar*). — *v.i.* to agree with the rules of metre: — *pr.p.* **scann'ing**; *pa.t.* and *pa.p.* **scanned** (*Spens.* **scand**). — *n.* a scanning. — *n.* **scann'er** one who scans or can scan: a perforated disc (also **scann'ing-disc**) used in television: the rotating aerial by which the beam is made to scan (*radar*): an instrument which scans. — *n.* and *adj.* **scann'ing.** — *n.* **scan'sion** act, art, or mode of scanning verse: scanning in television. — **scanning electron microscope** an electron microscope that produces a three-dimensional image. [L. *scandĕre, scānsum*, to climb.]

scand. See **scan**.

scandal *skan'dl*, *n.* a stumbling-block to faith: anything that brings discredit upon religion: injury to reputation: something said which is injurious to reputation: a false imputation: malicious gossip: slander: opprobrious censure: a disgraceful fact, thing, or person: a shocked feeling. — *v.t.* to defame: to disgrace (*obs.*): to shock (*obs.*). — *n.* **scandalīsā'tion, -z-.** — *v.t.* **scan'dalise, -ize** to give scandal or offence to: to shock: to disgrace: to slander. — *v.i.* to talk scandal. — *adjs.* **scan'dalled** disgraceful: slandered; **scan'dalous** giving scandal or offence: calling forth condemnation: openly vile: defamatory. — *adv.* **scan'dalously.** — *n.* **scan'dalousness.** — **scan'dal-bearer** a propagator of malicious gossip; **scan'dalmonger** one who deals in defamatory reports; **scan'dalmongering, -monging.** — **scandal sheet** a newspaper with a reputation for publishing scandal or gossip; **scan'dalum magnā'tum** slandering high personages, abbrev. *scan. mag.* [L. *scandalum* — Gr. *skandalon*, a stumbling-block.]

scandent *skan'dənt*, *adj.* climbing. [L. *scandēns, -entis.*]

Scandinavian *skan-di-nā'vi-ən*, *adj.* of, or characteristic of, *Scandinavia*, the peninsula divided into Norway and Sweden, but, in a historical sense, applying also to Denmark and Iceland: North Germanic (*philol.*). — *n.* a native of Scandinavia: a member of the dominant Nordic race of Scandinavia. — *n.* and *adj.* **Scan'dian.** — *adj.* **Scan'dic.** — *n.* **scan'dium** a rare metallic element (symbol Sc; at. numb. 21) discovered in 1879 in the Scandinavian mineral euxenite. [L. *Scandināvia* (from Gmc. word which did not have *n* before *d*), applied to the southern part of the peninsula, and its shortened form *Scandia*.]

Scandix *skan'diks*, *n.* the Venus's comb genus of umbelliferous plants. [Gr.]

scanner, scansion. See **scan.**

Scansores *skan-sō'rēz, -sö', n.pl.* in old classifications, an order of birds, climbers, with two toes before and two behind. — *adj.* **scansō'rial** climbing: adapted for climbing. [L. *scandĕre, scānsum,* to climb.]

scant *skant, adj.* not full or plentiful: scarcely sufficient: deficient: short, poorly supplied: sparing. — *n.* scarcity. — *adv.* barely: scantily. — *v.t.* to stint: to restrict: to reduce: to dispense sparingly: to treat inadequately: to slight. — *n.pl.* **scant'ies** (*coll.*) underwear, esp. women's brief panties. — *adv.* **scant'ily.** — *ns.* **scant'iness; scant'ity** (*rare*). — *adv.* **scant'ly.** — *n.* **scant'ness.** — *adj.* **scant'y** meagre: deficient: skimped: wanting in fullness: parsimonious. — **scant'-o'-grace** (*Scot.*) a good-for-nothing. [O.N. *skamt,* neut. of *skammr,* short.]

scantle[1] *skan'tl, v.t.* (*obs.*) to stint: to make scant: to shorten (sail). — *v.i.* (*obs.*) to become scant. — *n.* (*Shak.*; various reading for **cantle**) a portion. — *n.* **scant'ling** a small portion. — *adj.* petty. [Prob. **scant,** with senses merging in the following word.]

scantle[2]. See **scantling**[1].

scantling[1] *skant'ling, n.* a measured size: a measurement: an allotted portion (*arch.*): dimensions of a cross-section: a sample or pattern: a gauge (*obs.*): a narrow piece of timber. — *n.* **scan'tle** a gauge for slates. — *v.t.* to adjust to measure. [O.Fr. *escantillon, eschantillon,* of uncertain etymology, senses merging in **scantle.**]

scantling[2]. See **scantle**[1].

scanty. See **scant.**

scapa. Same as **scarper.**

scape[1] *skāp, n.* an escape: an escapade: a transgression: a slip. — *v.t.* and *v.i.* (also **'scape**) to escape. — *adj.* **scape'less** not to be escaped. — *n.* **scape'ment** an escapement. — **scape'gallows** one who deserves hanging; **scape'grace** a graceless, hare-brained fellow; **scape'-wheel** an escape wheel. [**escape.**]

scape[2] *skāp, n.* a peduncle rising from the ground, without foliage leaves (*bot.*): the basal part of an antenna (*entom.*): the shaft or stem of a feather: the shaft of a column (*archit.*). — *adjs.* **scape'less; scapigerous** (*ska-pij'ər-əs*) having a scape. [L. *scāpus,* a shaft.]

scape[3] *skāp, n.* the cry of the snipe when flushed: the snipe itself. [Prob. imit.]

scape[4] *skāp, n.* a landscape or other picture of scenery. — **-scape** noun combining form indicating a type of scene or view, as *seascape, streetscape.* [**landscape.**]

scapegoat *skāp'gōt, n.* a goat on which, once a year, the Jewish high-priest laid symbolically the sins of the people, and which was then allowed to escape into the wilderness (Lev. xvi): any animal used in like manner: one who is made to bear the misdeeds of another. — *v.t.* to make into or treat as a scapegoat. — *n.* **scape'goating** the practice of making (someone) into or using (someone) as a scapegoat, esp. involving harsh or violent treatment: a psychological syndrome of this nature. [**escape** and **goat.**]

scaphocephalus *skaf-ō-sef'ə-ləs, -kef', n.* a boat-shaped head. — *adjs.* **scaphocephal'ic, scaphoceph'alous.** — *n.* **scaphoceph'aly.** [Gr. *skaphē,* a boat, *kephalē,* a head.]

scaphoid *skaf'oid, adj.* boat-shaped. — *n.* **scaph'oid (bone)** a boat-shaped bone on the thumb side of the wrist joint, the navicular bone. [Gr. *skaphē,* a boat, *eidos,* form.]

Scaphopoda *skaf-op'ə-də, n.pl.* the tusk-shell class of molluscs, in which the foot is trilobed or has a terminal disc and the mantle forms a tube enclosed by the tubular univalve shell. — *n.* and *adj.* **scaph'opod.** [Gr. *skaphos,* a spade, *pous, podos,* a foot.]

scapi; scapigerous. See **scapus; scape**[2].

scapolite *skap'ō-līt, n.* a silicate of aluminium, calcium, and sodium with some chlorine, crystallising in the tetragonal system. [Gr. *skāpos,* a rod, *lithos,* a stone.]

scapple *skap'l,* **scabble** *skab'l, vs.t.* to work without finishing, as stone before leaving the quarry. [O.Fr. *escapeler,* to dress timber.]

scapula *skap'ū-lə, n.* the shoulder-blade. — *adj.* **scap'ular**

of the shoulder-blade or shoulder. — *n.* originally an ordinary working garb, now the mark of the monastic orders, a long strip of cloth with an opening for the head, worn hanging before and behind over the habit: two pieces of cloth tied together over the shoulders, worn by members of certain lay confraternities of the Roman Catholic Church: a supporting bandage worn over the shoulder: a shoulder feather. — *adj.* and *n.* **scap'ulary** scapular. — *adj.* **scap'ulated** with noticeable scapular feathers. — *n.* **scap'ulimancy** (Gr. *manteiā,* divination) divination by means of shoulder-blades. — *adj.* **scapūliman'tic.** [L. *scapulae,* the shoulder-blades.]

scapus *skā'pəs* (L. *skä'pōōs*). Same as **scape**[2]: — *pl.* **scapi** (*-pī;* L. *-pē*). [L.]

scar[1] *skär, n.* the mark left by a wound or sore: any mark or blemish: any mark, trace, or result of injury, material, moral or psychological, etc. (*fig.*): a mark at a place of former attachment, as of a leaf or a muscle. — *v.t.* to mark with a scar. — *v.i.* to become scarred: — *pr.p.* **scarr'ing;** *pa.t.* and *pa.p.* **scarred.** — *adjs.* **scar'less** without scars: unwounded; **scarred.** — *n.* and *adj.* **scarr'ing.** — *adj.* **scarr'y.** [O.Fr. *escare* — L. *eschara* — Gr. *escharā,* a hearth, brazier, burn, scar.]

scar[2] *skär, scaur skör, ns.* a precipitous bare place on a hill-face: a cliff: a reef in the sea. — *adj.* **scarr'y.** [App. O.N. *sker, skera,* to cut.]

scar[3] *skär,* **scar'fish** *-fish, ns.* a parrot-wrasse. — *n.* **Scarus** (*skā'rəs*) the parrot-wrasse genus, giving name to the family **Scaridae** (*skar'i-dē*). [L. *scārus* — Gr. *skāros.*]

scar[4], **scarre** *skär,* (*Shak., Milt., Scot.*) a form of **scare:** — *pa.t.* and *pa.p.* **scarred, scarr'd.**

scarab *skar'əb, n.* a dung-beetle, esp. the sacred beetle of the ancient Egyptians (*Scarabaeus,* or *Ateuchus, sacer,* or kindred species): a gem cut in the form of a beetle: a term of abuse (*obs.*). — *ns.* **scarabaeid** (*skar-ə-bē'id*) any beetle of the *Scarabaeidae;* **scarabae'ist** one who studies dung-beetles; **scarabae'oid** a gem more remotely resembling a beetle; **Scarabae'us** the scarab genus, giving name to the **Scarabae'idae,** a large family of lamellicorn beetles, some of them of great size (chafers, dung-beetles): a scarab; **scar'abee** a scarab; **scar'aboid** a scarabaeoid. — *adj.* like a scarab. [L. *scarabaeus;* cf. Gr. *kārabos.*]

scaramouch *skar'ə-mowch, n.* a bragging, cowardly buffoon. [Fr. *Scaramouche* — It. *Scaramuccia,* a stock character in Italian comedy.]

scarce *skärs, adj.* by no means plentiful: not often found: hard to get: short in supply: short (with *of*): sparing (*obs.*). — *adv.* scarcely: with difficulty (*Milt.*): hardly ever. — *adv.* **scarce'ly** only just: not quite: not at all: scantily (*obs.*). — *ns.* **scarce'ness; scarc'ity** the state or fact of being scarce: shortness of supply, esp. of necessaries: dearth: want: deficiency: niggardliness. — **make oneself scarce** to leave quickly, unobtrusively, for reasons of prudence, tact, etc. [O.N.Fr. *escars* (Fr. *échars*), niggardly, from a L.L. substitute for L. *excerptus,* pa.p. of *excerpĕre* — *ex,* out, *carpĕre,* to pick.]

scarcement *skärs'mənt,* (*Scot.*) *n.* a ledge formed by the setting back of a wall, buttress, or bank. [Poss. from **scarce.**]

scare *skār, v.t.* to startle, to affright: to drive or keep off by frightening. — *v.i.* to become frightened. — *n.* a fright: a panic: a baseless public alarm. — *adj.* **scared** frightened. — *n.* **scar'er.** — *adj.* **scar'y, scarey** frightening: timorous: fluttered. — **scare'crow** anything set up to scare birds: anything scraggy or threadbare: a person meanly clad; **scare'-head, -heading, -line** a newspaper heading designed to raise a scare; **scare'monger** an alarmist, one who causes panic by initiating or encouraging rumours of trouble; **scare'mongering.** — **run scared** to panic; **scare the (living) daylights out of, scare the pants off** (both *coll.*) to frighten considerably; **scare up** to beat up (game) (*U.S.* and *dial.*): to hunt out: to produce quickly. [M.E. *skerre* — O.N. *skirra,* to avoid — *skiarr,* shy; vowel history obscure.]

scarf¹ *skärf, n.* a light, usually decorative piece of dress thrown loosely on the shoulders about the neck, or over the head, etc.: a military or official sash: a band worn about the neck with ends hanging in front, formerly the mark of a clergyman of some degree of dignity, esp. a nobleman's chaplain: hence, a chaplaincy: a crape streamer: a veil: a necktie: a muffler: a cravat: a sling: — *pl.* **scarfs, scarves.** — *v.t.* to cover, as if with a scarf: to wrap as a scarf. — *adj.* **scarfed** decorated with pendants. — *adv.* **scarf'-wise.** — **scarf'-pin** an ornamental pin worn in a scarf: a tie-pin; **scarf'-ring** an ornamental ring through which the ends of a scarf are drawn. [Perh. O.N.Fr. *escarpe* (Fr. *écharpe*), sash, sling.]

scarf² *skärf, n.* a joint between pieces placed end to end, cut so as to fit with overlapping like a continuous piece: an end so prepared: a longitudinal cut in a whale's carcase. — *v.t.* to join with a scarf-joint: to make a scarf in. — *n.* **scarf'ing.** — **scarf'-joint.** [Perh. Scand.]

scarfskin *skärf'skin, n.* the surface skin. [Origin doubtful; perh. **scarf¹**; perh. related to **scurf.**]

Scaridae. See **scar³.**

scarify *skar'i-fī, v.t.* to make a number of scratches or slight cuts in: to break up the surface of: to lacerate: to criticise severely: — *pr.p.* **scar'ifying;** *pa.t.* and *pa.p.* **scar'ified.** — *ns.* **scarification** (-*fi-kā'shən*) a surgical instrument for scarifying: a scarifier; **scar'ifier** one who scarifies: an implement for breaking the surface of the soil or of a road. [L.L. *scarificāre, -ātum,* for L. *scarifāre* — Gr. *skarīphasthai* — *skarīphos,* an etching tool.]

scarious *skā'ri-əs, adj.* thin, dry, stiff, and membranous (*bot.*): scaly, scurfy (*zool.*). [Origin unknown.]

scarlatina *skär-lə-tē'nə, n.* scarlet fever, esp. in a mild form. [It. *scarlattina.*]

scarlet *skär'lit, n.* orig. a fine cloth, not always red: a brilliant red: a brilliant red cloth, garment, or garb, or its wearer. — *adj.* of the colour called scarlet: dressed in scarlet. — *v.t.* to redden. — **scar'let-bean** the scarlet-runner; **scarlet fever** an infectious fever, usually marked by a sore throat and a scarlet rash; **scarlet geranium** a scarlet-flowered pelargonium; **scar'let-hat** a cardinal's (former) hat; **scar'let-runn'er** a scarlet-flowered climber (*Phaseolus multiflorus*) of the kidney-bean genus, with edible beans; **scarlet woman** the woman referred to in Rev. xvii. — variously taken as pagan Rome, Papal Rome, or the world in its anti-Christian sense: a whore. [O.Fr. *escarlate* (Fr. *écarlate*), thought to be from Pers. *saqalāt,* scarlet cloth.]

scarmoge *skär'məj,* (*Spens.*) *n.* same as **skirmish.**

scarp¹ *skärp,* (*her.*) *n.* a diminutive of the bend-sinister, half its width. [O.Fr. *escarpe;* cf. **scarf¹.**]

scarp² *skärp, n.* an escarp: an escarpment. — *v.t.* to cut into a scarp. — *adj.* **scarped.** — *n.* **scarp'ing.** [It. *scarpa.*]

scarper *skär'pər,* (*slang*) *v.i.* to run away, escape, leave without notice. [It. *scappare.*]

scarpines *skär'pinz, n.pl.* an instrument of torture for the feet. — *n.* **scarpet'to** a hemp-soled shoe or climbing-boot: — *pl.* **scarpet'ti** (-*tē*). [It. *scarpino, scarpetto,* dims. of *scarpa,* shoe.]

scarre¹ *skär,* (*Shak.*) *n.* word of unknown meaning in *All's Well* (IV, ii. 38), probably a misprint, but never satisfactorily explained.

scarre². See **scar⁴.**

scarred, scarring, scarry. See **scar¹,²,⁴.**

scart¹ *skärt,* (*Scot.*) *v.t.* to scratch: to scrape. — *n.* a scratch: a dash or stroke of a pen. — *adj.* **scart'-free** (*Scot.*). [See **scrat.**]

scart², scarth; Scarus; scarves; scary. See **skart; scar³; scarf; scare.**

scat¹, scatt *skat,* (*hist.*) *n.* tribute: a tax: esp. udaller's land-tax. [O.N. *skattr;* cf. O.E. *sceatt,* money, Du. *schat,* Ger. *Schatz.*]

scat² *skat, interj.* be off! — *v.t.* to scare away.

scat³ *skat,* (*West of England*) *n.* a blow: a spell: a sudden shower. — *adv.* in collapse: to bankruptcy.

scat⁴, skat *skat, n.* an animal dropping. — *adj.* **scatolog'-ical (sk-).** — *n.* **scatol'ogy (sk-)** study of excrement, esp. in order to assess diet: obscene literature: interest in the obscene. — *adj.* **scatoph'agous** (Gr. *phagein* (2nd aorist), to eat) dung-eating. — *n.* **scatoph'agy.** [Gr. *skōr, skatos,* dung.]

scat⁵ *skat, n.* singing a melody to nonsense syllables. — Also *v.t.* and *v.i.* [Perh. imit.]

scatch *skach, n.* a stilt. [O.N.Fr. *escache* (Fr. *échasse*); cf. **skate¹.**]

scathe *skādh* (*Spens.* also **scath** *skath; Scot.* **skaith, scaith** *skāth*), *ns.* hurt: injury: damage. — *v.t.* to injure: to blast, scorch, wither: to scorch with invective. — *adj.* **scathe'ful** hurtful. — *n.* **scathe'fulness.** — *adjs.* **scathe'-less** (*Scot.* **skaith'less, scaith'less**) without injury; **scath'ing.** — *adv.* **scath'ingly.** [O.N. *skathe;* cf. O.E. *sceatha,* an injurer; Ger. *Schade,* injury.]

scatole. Same as **skatole.**

scatological, etc. See **scat⁴.**

scatt. See **scat¹.**

scatter *skat'ər, v.t.* to disperse: to throw loosely about: to strew: to sprinkle: to dispel: to reflect or disperse irregularly (waves or particles). — *v.i.* to disperse: to throw shot loosely. — *n.* a scattering: a sprinkling: dispersion: the extent of scattering. — *adj.* **scatt'ered** dispersed irregularly, widely, in all directions, or here and there: thrown about: casually dropped (*Spens., Shak.*): distracted. — *adv.* **scatt'eredly** (-*ərd-li*). — *ns.* **scatt'erer; scatt'ering** dispersion: radiation afresh of wave-energy when a ray is incident on an obstacle or when it enters an irregularly ionised region (*phys.*): that which is scattered: a small proportion occurring sporadically: the deflection of photons or particles as a result of collisions with other particles (*phys.*). — *adj.* dispersing: sporadic: diversified. — *adv.* **scatt'-eringly.** — *n.* **scatt'erling** (*Spens.*) a vagrant. — *adj.* **scatt'ery** dispersed: sparse: giving an effect of scattering. — **scatt'er-brain** one incapable of sustained attention or thought. — *adj.* **scatter'-brained.** — **scatt'-ergood** a spendthrift; **scatt'er-gun** a shot-gun. — **scatter rugs, cushions** small rugs, cushions which can be placed anywhere in the room. — *adj.* **scatt'ershot** random, indiscriminate, wide-ranging, as shot from a gun. — **elastic, inelastic scattering** see **elastic, inelastic collision** under **collide.** [Origin obscure; *scattered* occurs in the *O.E. Chronicle* (anno 1137); cf. **shatter.**]

scattermouch *skat'ər-mowch,* (*sailors' slang*) *n.* any Latin or Levantine. [**scaramouch** influenced by **scatter.**]

scatty *skat'i,* (*coll.*) *adj.* slightly crazy and unpredictable in conduct. — *n.* **scatt'iness.** [Poss. *scatter*-brain.]

scaturient *skat-ū'ri-ənt, adj.* gushing. [L. *scatūriēns, -entis* — *scatūrīre,* to gush out.]

scaud *sköd,* a Scots form of **scald¹.**

scaup *sköp,* (*Scot.*) *n.* a scalp: a scaup-duck. — **scaup'-duck** (*Scot.*) a pochard that feeds on mussel-scaups. [**scalp¹.**]

scauper *skö'pər, n.* a tool with semicircular face, used by engravers. [**scalper.**]

scaur¹ *skör,* a Scots form of **scare.**

scaur². Same as **scar².**

scaury *skö'ri, skö',* (*Orkney* and *Shetland*) *n.* a young gull. — Also (*Scott*) **scou'rie, scow'rie.** [O.N. *skāri.*]

scavage *skav'ij, n.* a toll formerly levied in boroughs on goods offered for sale by outsiders: street refuse (*obs.*). — *n.* **scav'ager** the officer who collected the toll, later charged with keeping the streets clean. — *v.t.* **scav'enge** (-*inj, -inzh;* back-formation) to cleanse: to remove impurities from (a substance) (*chem.*). — *v.i.* to act as scavenger: to search (for useful items) among refuse. — *n.* the sweeping out of waste gases from an internal-combustion engine. — *n.* **scav'enger** (-*jər*) one who cleans the streets: a person or apparatus that removes waste: an animal that feeds on garbage: one who deals or delights in filth. — *v.i.* to act as scavenger. — *ns.* **scav'engering; scav'engery** street-cleaning; **scav'enging** street-cleansing: scavenge. [A.Fr. *scawage,* inspection; prob. of Gmc. origin; cf. O.E. *scēawian*, to inspect; see **show**.]

scavenger[1] *skav'in-jər, n.* a perversion of the name of *Skevington*, Lieutenant of the Tower under Henry VIII, inventor of an instrument of torture known as the **scavenger's**, or **Skevington's**, or **Skeffington's daughter**.

scavenger[2]. See **scavage**.

scaw. Same as **skaw**.

scazon *skā'zon, n.* a choliamb. — *n.* and *adj.* **scazontic** *(skə-zon'tik)*. [Gr. *skazōn*, limping.]

sceat, sceatt *shat, (hist.) n.* a small silver (or gold) coin of Old English times: — *pl.* **sceatt'as**. [O.E.]

scedule. See **schedule**.

scelerate *sel'ər-āt, -it, (obs.) adj.* wicked. — *n.* (also **scelerat** after Fr. *scélérat*) a villain. [L. *scelerātus* — *scelus*, crime.]

scena *shā'na, n.* an operatic scene: an elaborate dramatic recitative followed by an aria: — *pl.* **scene** *(shā'nā).* — *n.* **scenario** *(si-, se-, shā-nä'ri-ō)* a skeleton of a dramatic work, film, etc., scene by scene: an outline of future development, or of a plan to be followed, which shows the operation of causes and where points of decision or difficulty occur: *loosely*, any imagined, suggested or projected sequence of events, plan of action, situation, etc.: — *pl.* **scena'rios**. — *n.* **scenarisā'tion, -z-**. — *v.t.* **scenarise, -ize** *(si-nä'rīz, -nā')* to make a scenario of. — *ns.* **scena'rist; scenary** *(sē'nər-i; obs.)* disposition of scenes: scenery. [It., — L. *scēna*.]

scenario. See **scena**.

scend, 'scend. See **send**.

scene *sēn, n.* the stage *(orig.)*: a stage performance *(obs.)*: the place of action in a play (hence in a story, an actual occurrence, etc.): its representation on the stage: a painted slide, hanging, or other object, used for this purpose: a curtain, veil, or screen *(arch.)*: a division of a play marked off by the fall of the curtain, by a change of place, or (in Latin, French, and some English plays) by the entry or exit of any important character: an episode: a dramatic or stagy incident, esp. an uncomfortable, untimely, or unseemly display of hot feelings: a landscape, picture of a place or action: a view, spectacle: the activity, publicity, etc., surrounding a particular business or profession, e.g. *the pop music scene (coll.)*: area of interest or activity *(coll.)*: a situation, state of affairs *(slang)*. — *v.t.* to set in a scene. — *n.* **scēn'ery** dramatic action *(obs.)*: theatrical slides, hangings, etc., collectively: views of beautiful, picturesque, or impressive country. — *adjs.* **scenic** *(sē'nik, sen'ik)* pertaining to scenery: having beautiful or remarkable scenery: dramatic: theatrical; **scen'ical**. — *adv.* **scen'ically**. — *adjs.* **scēnograph'ic, -al**. — *adv.* **scēnograph'ically**. — *n.* **scēnog'raphy** perspective drawing: scene-painting. — **scene dock, bay** the space where scenery is stored; **scene'-man** a scene-shifter; **scene-of-crime officer** a police officer responsible for gathering evidence at the scene of a crime; **scene'-painter** one who paints scenery for theatres; **scene'-shifter** one who sets and removes the scenery in a theatre; **scenic railway** a railway on a small scale, running through artificial representations of picturesque scenery. — **behind the scenes** at the back of the visible stage: away from the public view *(lit. and fig.)*: in a position to know what goes on: in private; **come on the scene** to arrive; **set the scene** to describe the background to an event, etc. [L. *scēna* — Gr. *skēnē*, a tent, stage building.]

scéne à faire *sen a fār,* the climactic scene in a play or opera. [Fr., scene of action.]

scent, earlier **sent**, *sent, v.t.* to track, find, or discern by smell, or as if by smell: to perfume. — *v.i.* to give forth a smell: to sniff: to smell. — *n.* odour: sense of smell: a substance used for the sake of its smell: trail by smell: paper strewn by the pursued in hare and hounds. — *adjs.* **scent'ed** having a smell, fragrant: impregnated or sprinkled with perfumery: endowed with a sense of smell; **scent'ful** *(arch.)* odoriferous: quick of scent. — *n.* and *adj.* **scent'ing**. — *adj.* **scent'less** having no smell:

affording, retaining, or carrying no scent. — **scent'-bag** a scent-gland: a sachet: a bag of strong-smelling stuff dragged over the ground for a drag-hunt; **scent'-bottle** a small bottle for holding perfume; **scent'-box; scent'-gland** a gland that secretes a substance of distinctive smell, for recognition, attraction, or defence; **scent'-organ** a scent-gland: a smelling organ; **scent'-scale** on male butterflies' wings, a scale that gives off a scent. — **put, throw someone off the scent** to mislead someone. [Fr. *sentir* — L. *sentīre*, to perceive.]

scepsis, skepsis *skep'sis, n.* philosophical doubt. [Gr.; see next.]

sceptic, sometimes (and in U.S.) **skeptic**, *skep'tik, adj.* pertaining to the philosophical school of Pyrrho and his successors, who asserted nothing positively and doubted the possibility of knowledge: sceptical *(rarely)*. — *n.* a sceptic philosopher: one who withholds from prevailing doctrines, esp. in religion: one who inclines to disbelieve: an inquirer who has not arrived at a conviction. — *adj.* **scep'tical** of or inclined to scepticism: (now often) doubtful, or inclined towards incredulity. — *adv.* **scep'tically**. — *v.i.* **scep'ticise, -ize** to act the sceptic. — *n.* **scep'ticism** that condition in which the mind is before it has arrived at conclusive opinions: doubt: the doctrine that no facts can be certainly known: agnosticism: sceptical attitude towards Christianity: general disposition to doubt. [L. *scepticus* — Gr. *skeptikos*, thoughtful, *skeptesthai*, to consider.]

sceptre *sep'tər, n.* a staff or baton borne as an emblem of kingship. — *adjs.* **scep'tral** regal; **scep'tred** bearing a sceptre: regal; **scep'treless; scep'try** *(Keats)* sceptred. [L. *scēptrum* — Gr. *skēptron*, a staff — *skēptein*, to prop, stay.]

scerne *sûrn, (Spens.) v.t.* to discern. [**discern**, or It. *scernere*.]

sceuophylax *s(k)ū-of'i-laks, (Greek Church) n.* a sacristan. — *n.* **sceuophylacium** *(-lā'si-əm)* a sacristy. [Gr. *skeuos*, a vessel, *phylax,* a watcher.]

schadenfreude *shä'dən-froi-də, n.* pleasure in others' misfortunes. [Ger., — *Schade*, hurt, *Freude*, joy.]

schalstein *shäl'shtīn, n.* a slaty diabase tuff. [Ger., — *Schale*, shell, scale, *Stein*, stone.]

schappe *shap'ə, n.* a fabric of waste silk with gum, etc., partly removed by fermentation. — *v.t.* to subject to this process. [Swiss Ger.]

schapska. See **chapka**.

schechita(h), schechita(h), shehita(h) *she-hēt'a, n.* the slaughtering of animals in accordance with rabbinical law. [Heb. *shĕhītāh*, slaughter.]

schecklaton. See **checklaton**.

schedule *shed'ūl, sked'ūl,* formerly (as *Shak.*) **scedule** *sed'ūl, ns.* a slip or scroll with writing: a list, inventory, or table: a supplementary, explanatory, or appended document: an appendix to a bill or act of parliament: a form for filling in particulars, or such a form filled in: a timetable, plan, programme, or scheme. — *v.t.* to set as in a schedule: to plan, appoint, arrange. — *adj.* **sched'uled** entered in a schedule: planned, appointed, arranged (to happen at a specified time). — **scheduled castes** in India, the former untouchables; **scheduled territories** sterling area. — **behind schedule** not keeping up to an arranged programme: late; **on schedule** on time. [O.Fr. *cedule* (Fr. *cédule*) — L.L. *sc(h)edula*, dim. of *scheda*, a strip of papyrus — Gr. *schedē*.]

scheelite *shē'līt, n.* native calcium tungstate. — **Scheele's** *(shā'ləz)* **green** a poisonous yellowish-green pigment, copper hydrogen arsenite. [From the Sw. chemist K. W. *Scheele* (1742–86), who investigated them.]

schellum. Same as **skellum**.

schelm. Older form of **skelm**.

schema *skē'mə, n.* a scheme, plan: a diagrammatic outline or synopsis: the image of the thing with which the imagination aids the understanding in its procedure: a kind of standard which the mind forms from past experiences, and by which new experiences can be

scheme 1314 schlieren

evaluated to a certain extent: the monastic habit (*Greek Church*): — *pl.* **schē′mata.** — *adjs.* **schematic** (*ski-mat′ik*), **-al** following, or involving, a particular plan or arrangement: representing something by a diagram, plan, etc. — *adv.* **schemat′ically.** — *n.* **schematisā′tion, -z-.** — *v.t.* **schē′matise, -ize** to reduce to or represent by a scheme. — *ns.* **schē′matism** form or outline of a thing: arrangement, disposition in a scheme; **schē′matist** one who frames a scheme: a projector (*obs.*). [Gr. *schēma, -atos*, form, from the reduced grade of the root of *echein*, to have (as in the fut. *schēsein*).]

scheme *skēm, n.* a rhetorical figure (*obs.*): a diagram of positions, esp. (*astrol.*) of planets: a diagram: a table: a system: a plan of purposed action for achieving an end: a plan for building operations of various kinds, or the buildings, etc., constructed, or the area covered (e.g. *housing scheme, irrigation scheme*): a plan pursued secretly, insidiously, by intrigue, or for private ends: a project: a programme of action: an escapade (*obs.*). — *v.t.* to plan: to reduce to a system: to lay schemes for. — *v.i.* to form a plan: to lay schemes: to indulge in an escapade. — *n.* **schē′mer.** — *n.* and *adj.* **schē′ming.** [**schema.**]

schemozzle. See **shemozzle.**

scherzo *sker′tsō, skûr′, n.* a lively busy movement in triple time, usually with a trio, now generally taking the place of the minuet in a sonata or a symphony: — *pl.* **scher′zos, scher′zi** (-*ē*). — *adj.* and *adv.* **scherzan′do** with playfulness. — *n.* a scherzando passage or movement: — *pl.* **scherzan′dos, scherzan′di** (-*ē*). [It., — Gmc.; cf. Ger. *Scherz*, jest.]

schiavone *skyä-vō′nā, n.* a 17th-century basket-hilted broadsword used by the Doge's bodyguard of Slavs. [It. *Schiavoni*, Slavs.]

Schick('s) test *shik(s) test*, a test for susceptibility to diphtheria, made by injecting the skin with a measured amount of diphtheria toxin. [From Bela *Schick* (1877–1967), American doctor.]

schiedam *skē′dam*, or -*dam′, n.* Holland gin, chiefly made at Schiedam (*s′hhē-däm′*), near Rotterdam.

schiller *shil′ər, n.* a peculiar bronze-like lustre in certain minerals, as hypersthene, due to diffraction caused by minute plates of haematite, etc., developed in separation planes. — *n.* **schillerīsā′tion, -z-,** the development of such plates. — *v.t.* **schill′erise, -ize** to impart a schiller to. — **schill′er-spar** schillerised enstatite (bronzite). [Ger.]

schilling *shil′ing, n.* an Austrian coin (in use after 1925) equal to one hundred groschen, the unit of the Austrian monetary system. [Ger.; cf. **shilling.**]

schimmel *shim′l, n.* a roan horse. [Ger., white horse; also Du.]

schindylesis *skin-di-lē′sis, n.* an articulation formed by the fitting of one bone into a groove in another. — *adj.* **schindyletic** (-*let′ik*). [Gr. *schindylēsis*, cleaving.]

schipperke *skip′ər-kə, -ki*, also *ship′*, or (Du.) *s′hhip′, n.* a small tailless breed of dogs, orig. watchdogs on barges. [Du., little boatman.]

schism *sizm, skizm, n.* a breach, esp. in the unity of a church: promotion of such a breach: a body so formed. — *ns.* **schisma** (*skiz′mə*) half the difference between twelve perfect fifths and seven octaves; **schismatic** (*siz-mat′ik, skiz-*) one who favours a schism or belongs to a schismatic body: a Catholic who avoided penalties by occasional conformity (*R.C.*). — *adjs.* **schismat′ic, -al** tending to, favouring, or of the nature of, a schism. — *adv.* **schismat′ically.** — *n.* **schismat′icalness.** — *v.i.* **schis′matise, -ize** to practise schism: to make a schism. — **schism′-house, -shop** contemptuous Anglican terms for a nonconformist church. — **great Eastern,** or **Greek, schism** the separation of the Greek church from the Latin, finally completed in 1054; **(great) Western schism** the division in the Western church from 1378 to 1417, when there were antipopes under French influence at Avignon. [Gr. *schisma*, a split, rent, cleft, partly through O.Fr. (*s*)*cisme*.]

schist *shist, n.* any crystalline foliated metamorphic rock

not coarse and feldspathic enough to be called gneiss, as mica-schist, hornblende-schist: sometimes extended (as in French) to shaly rocks. — *adj.* **schist′ose.** — *n.* **schistosity** (-*os′i-ti*). — *adj.* **schist′ous.** [Fr. *schiste* — Gr. *schistos*, split; pron. due to German influence.]

Schistosoma *shis-tə-sō′mə, skis-, n.* the Bilharzia genus. — *ns.* **schis′tosome** a member of the genus; **schistosomī′asis** the disease bilharzia. [Gr. *schistos*, split.]

schiz- *skiz-, skīz-*, **schizo-** *skit′sō-, skid′zō-, skīz′ō-, skī-zo′,* in composition, cleave, cloven. — *n.* **Schizaea** (-*zē′ə*) a tropical genus of ferns giving name to the fam. **Schizaeā′ceae,** with sporangia splitting longitudinally by an apical annulus. — *adj.* **schizaeā′ceous.** — *n.* **Schizanthus** (-*an′thəs*; Gr. *anthos*, flower) a showy Chilean genus of Solanaceae. — *adj.* **schizo-affect′ive** marked by symptoms of schizophrenia and manic-depressiveness. — *n.* **schi′zocarp** (-*kärp*; Gr. *karpos*, fruit) a dry fruit that splits into several indehiscent one-seeded portions. — *adjs.* **schizocar′pous, schizocar′pic.** — *n.* **schizogenesis** (-*jen′i-sis*; Gr. *genesis*, generation) reproduction by fission. — *adjs.* **schizogen′ic, schizogenetic** (-*ji-net′ik*), **schizogenous** (-*oj′i-nəs*) reproducing, reproduced, or formed by fission or splitting; **schizogonous** (-*og′ən-əs*). — *n.* **schizog′ony** (Gr. *gonē*, generation) reproduction in Protozoa by multiple fission. — *adjs.* **schizognathous** (-*og′nə-thəs*; Gr. *gnathos*, jaw) of some birds, having the bones of the palate separate; **schizoid** (*skit′soid, skid′zoid*; Gr. *eidos*, form) showing qualities of a schizophrenic personality, such as asocial behaviour, introversion, tendency to fantasy, but without definite mental disorder. — *n.* a schizoid person. — *adj.* **schizoid′al.** — *n.pl.* **Schizomycetes** (-*mī-sē′tēz*; Gr. *mȳkēs,* pl. *mykētēs*, a fungus) the bacteria: — *sing.* **schizomycete** (-*sēt′*). — *adjs.* **schizomycēt′ic, schizomycēt′ous.** — *ns.* **schiz′ont** in Protozoa, a mature trophozoite about to reproduce by schizogony; **schiz′ophrene** (-*frēn*; Gr. *phrēn*, mind) one who suffers from schizophrenia; **schizophrenia** (-*frē′ni-ə*) a psychosis marked by introversion, dissociation, inability to distinguish reality from unreality, delusions, etc.; **schizophrenic** (-*fren′ik*) a schizophrene (*coll.* shortening **schizo** *skit′sō*; *pl.* **schiz′os**). — Also *adj* (*coll.* shortening **schiz′o**). — *adjs.* **schizophrenet′ic(al).** — *adv.* **schizophrenet′ically.** — *adjs.* **schizophrenogenic** (-*jen′ik*; Gr. *genos*, a race) causing or tending to cause schizophrenia; **schizophyceous** (-*fī′shəs, -fī′*) of or belonging to the **Schizophyceae** (-*fī′si-ē*), a group of algae, bluish-green in colour, that grow in fresh or salt water, and can be responsible for the pollution of drinking-water. — *n.pl.* **Schizophyta** (-*of′i-tə*; Gr. *phyton*, plant) plants that multiply only by fission — bacteria and blue-green algae. — *n.* **schiz′ophyte** (-*fīt*). — *adjs.* **schizophytic** (-*fit′ik*); **schi′zopod** (-*pod*; Gr. *pous, podos*, foot) having each leg divided into exopodite and endopodite. — *n.* a member of the **Schizopoda** (-*op′*), an order (according to some) of Malacostraca. — *adjs.* **schizop′odal, schizop′odous.** — *n.* **schizothymia** (-*thī′mi-ə*; Gr. *thymos*, mind, temper) manifestation of schizoid traits within normal limits. — *adj.* **schizothy′mic.** [Gr. *schizein*, to cleave.]

schläger *shlä′gər, n.* a German student's duelling-sword. [Ger., — *schlagen*, to beat.]

schlemiel, schlemihl, shlemiel *shlə-mēl′,* (*slang*) *n.* a clumsy person. [Yiddish.]

schlep, shlep *shlep,* (*slang*) *v.t.* to pull, drag (also **schlepp**): — *pr.p.* **schlepp′ing;** *pa.t.* and *pa.p.* **schlepped.** — *n.* a clumsy, stupid, incompetent person. — *adj.* **schlepp′y.** [Yiddish.]

schlich *shlihh, n.* the finer portions of crushed ore, separated by water. [Ger.]

schlieren *shlē′rən, n.pl.* streaks of different colour, structure, or composition in igneous rocks: streaks in a transparent fluid, caused by the differing refractive indices of fluid of varying density. — **schlieren photography** the technique of photographing a flow of air or other gas, the variations in refractive index according to density being made apparent under a special type of illumination — often used in the testing of models in wind tunnels. [Ger.]

schlimazel, shlimazel *shli-mä′zl, (U.S. slang) n.* a persistently unlucky person. [Yiddish; see **shemozzle.**]

schlock, shlok *shlok′, (U.S. slang) adj.* of inferior quality. — *n.* a thing or things of inferior quality. [Yiddish.]

schloss *shlos, n.* a castle, palace, manor house. [Ger.]

schmaltz *shmölts, shmälts, n.* mush: a production in music or other art that is very sentimental, or showy: sentimentality. — *adj.* **schmaltz′y** old-fashioned, old-style, outmoded: sentimental. [Yiddish — Ger. *Schmalz,* cooking fat, grease.]

schmelz *shmelts, n.* glass used in decorative work. [Ger. *Schmelz,* enamel.]

schmo *shmō, (U.S. slang) n.* a stupid or a boring person: — *pl.* **schmoes.** [Yiddish.]

schmock. See **schmuck.**

schmoe. Same as **schmo.**

schmooze, shmooze, shmoose *shmōōz, -s, (U.S. slang) vs.i.* to gossip. [Yiddish.]

schmuck *shmuk,* **schmock** *shmok,* **schnook** *shnŏŏk,* (orig. *U.S. slang) ns.* a stupid person. [Yiddish.]

schmutter *shmut′ər, (slang) n.* clothing: rag. [Yiddish *schmatte,* rag.]

schnapper *shnap′ər.* Same as **snapper** (Australian fish). [Germanised.]

schnapps, schnaps *shnaps, n.* Holland gin, Hollands. [Ger. *Schnapps,* a dram.]

schnauzer *shnowt′sər, n.* a very old German breed of terrier. [Ger. *Schnauze,* snout.]

Schneiderian *shnī-dē′ri-ən, adj.* pertaining to the German anatomist Konrad Victor *Schneider* (1614–1680). — **Schneiderian membrane** the olfactory mucous membrane, studied by him.

schnell *shnel, (Ger.) adj.* quick. — *adv.* quickly.

schnitzel *shnit′sl, n.* a veal cutlet. [Ger.]

schnook. See **schmuck.**

schnorkel *shnör′kl, n.* a retractable tube or tubes containing pipes for discharging gases from, or for taking air into, a submerged submarine: a tube for bringing air to a submerged swimmer. — Anglicised as **snor′kel, snort.** [Ger., *Schnörkel,* a spiral ornament.]

schnorrer *shnō′, shnö′, shno′rər, (U.S. slang) n.* a beggar. — *v.i.* **schnorr** (*shnōr, shnör*) to beg, esp. in such a way as to make the giver feel in some way beholden. [Yiddish.]

schnozzle *shnoz′əl, (slang) n.* nose. [Yiddish.]

schola cantorum *skō′lə kan-tō′rəm,* a choir or choir school attached to a church, cathedral, etc.: the part of a church, etc., in which the choir is placed for services. [L., school of singers.]

scholar *skol′ər, n.* a pupil: a disciple: a student: (in times of less widespread education) one who could read and write, or an educated person: one whose learning (formerly esp. in Latin and Greek) is extensive and exact, or whose approach to learning is scrupulous and critical: generally a holder of a scholarship. — *adj.* **schol′ar-like** like or befitting a scholar. — *n.* **schol′-arliness.** — *adj.* **schol′arly** of, natural to a scholar: having the learning of a scholar. — *adv.* (*Shak.*) as becomes a scholar. — *n.* **schol′arship** scholarly learning: a foundation or grant for the maintenance of a pupil or student: the status and emoluments of such a pupil or student. — **scholar's mate** in chess, a simple mate accomplished in four moves. [O.E. *scōlere,* and (in part) O.Fr. *escoler,* both from L.L. *scholāris* — *schola;* see **school**[1].]

scholarch *skō′lärk, n.* the head of a school, esp. of philosophy. [Gr. *scholarchēs.*]

scholastic *skol-, skəl-as′tik, adj.* pertaining to schools, universities, or to their staffs or teaching, or to schoolmen: subtle: pedantic. — *n.* a schoolman, one who adheres to the method or subtleties of the Mediaeval schools: a Jesuit who has taken first vows only: a university teacher (esp. with implication of pedantry). — *adj.* (*arch.*) **scholas′tical.** — *adv.* **scholas′tically.** — *n.* **scholas′ticism** (*-sizm*) the aims, methods, and prod-

ucts of thought which constituted the main endeavour of the intellectual life of the Middle Ages: the method or subtleties of the schools of philosophy: the collected body of doctrines of the schoolmen. [Gr. *scholastikos* — *scholē;* see **school**[1].]

scholion *skō′li-on,* **scholium** *-əm, ns.* an explanatory note, such as certain ancient grammarians wrote on passages in manuscripts: an observation or note added to a mathematical proposition: often in *pl.* **scho′lia.** — *n.* **scho′liast** a writer of scholia: an annotator: a commentator. — *adj.* **scholias′tic.** [Gr. *schŏlion* (Mod. L. *scholium*), *schŏliastēs* — *scholē;* see **school**[1].]

school[1] *skōōl, n.* a place for instruction: an institution for education, esp. primary or secondary, or for teaching of special subjects: a division of such an institution: a building or room used for that purpose: the work of a school: the time given to it: the body of pupils of a school: the disciples of a particular teacher: those who hold a common doctrine or follow a common tradition: a group of people meeting in order to play card games, usu. for money (*slang*): a method of instruction: an instruction book (now usu. in music): the body of instructors and students in a university, college, faculty, or department: a group of studies in which honours may be taken: (in *pl.*) academic institutions: (in *pl.*) an academic disputation: (in Oxford, in *pl.*) the B.A. examinations: a university building, now (Oxford) the examination hall. — *adj.* of school, schools, or the schools. — *v.t.* to educate in a school: to train, to drill: to instruct: to coach in a part to be played: to teach overbearingly: to admonish (*obs.*): to discipline. — *adj.* **schooled** trained: experienced. — *ns.* **school′ery** (*Spens.*) something taught, precepts; **school′ing** instruction or maintenance at school: tuition: training: discipline: school fees: reproof: reprimand. — *adj.* and *adv.* **school′ward.** — *adv.* **school′wards.** — **school age** the age at which children attend school. — *adj.* **school′-age.** — **school′bag** a bag for carrying school-books; **school′-bell** a bell to announce time for school; **school′-board** formerly, an elected board of school managers for a parish, town, or district; **school′-book** a book used in school; **school′boy** a boy attending school. — Also *adj.* — *adjs.* **school′boyish; school′-bred′.** — **school′-child; school′craft** learning; **school′-dame** mistress of a dame's school; **school′-day** a day on which schools are open: (in *pl.*) time of being a school pupil; **school′-divine′; school′-divin′ity** scholastic or seminary theology; **school′-doc′tor** a schoolman: a schoolteacher (*obs.*): a physician appointed to examine or attend the pupils of a school or schools; **school′fellow** one taught at the same school at the same time; **school′-friend** one who is or has been a friend at school; **school′-friend′ship; school′girl** a girl attending school. — *adj.* **school′girlish.** — *n.* and *adj.* **school′going.** — **school′house** a building used as a school: a house provided for a school-teacher (**school house** a headmaster's or headmistress's boarding-house: its boarders); **school′-inspec′tor** an official appointed to examine schools; **school′-leav′er** one who is leaving school because he has reached the statutory age, or the stage, for doing so. — *n.* and *adj.* **school′-leav′ing.** — **school′-ma'am** a school-marm; **school′maid** a schoolgirl; **school′man** a philosopher or theologian of mediaeval scholasticism: a teacher (*U.S.*); **school′-marm** (*coll.;* a form of **school-ma'am**) a schoolmistress (*U.S.*): a prim pedantic woman (*coll.*). — *adj.* **school′-marmish.** — **school′master** the master or one of the masters of a school: a tutor (*Shak.*). — Also *v.t.* and *v.i.* — *n.* and *adj.* **school′mastering.** — *adjs.* **school′masterish; school′-masterly.** — **school′mastership; school′-mate** a schoolfriend: a schoolfellow; **school′-miss** a raw or affected schoolgirl; **school′mistress; school nurse** a person employed to visit schools and promote children's health through screening procedures, immunisation, etc.; **school phobia** an irrational fear of attending school; **school′-point** a point for scholastic disputation; **school′-room** a school classroom: in a house, a room for receiving or preparing lessons in; **school'-ship** a training-ship. — *adj.* **school'-taught** taught at school or in the schools. — **school'-teach'er** one who teaches in a school; **school'-teach'ing; school'-term** a word or term in use in the schools or among schoolmen: a division of the school year; **school'-tide** school-days; **school= time** the time at which a school opens, or during which it remains open: school-days. — *adj.* **school'-trained** trained at school. — **school'-work; school year** the period of (more or less) continual teaching during the year comprising an academic unit during which a child or student remains in the same basic class, i.e., in Britain, from autumn to early summer. — **old school** see **old; the schoolmaster is abroad** a phrase of Brougham's implying that education and intelligence are now widely spread. [O.E. *scōl* — L. *schŏla* — Gr. *schŏlē*, leisure, a lecture, a school.]

school² *skōōl*, *n.* a shoal of fish, whales, or other swimming animals: a flock, troop, assemblage, esp. of birds. — *v.i.* to gather or go in schools. — *adj.* (or in composition) going in schools. — *n.* and *adj.* **school'- ing.** — **school'master** the leader of a school, esp. of whales. [Du. *school*; cf. **shoal¹**.]

schoole (*Shak., Macb.* I, vii. 6). Same as **shoal²** (*n.*).

schooner *skōōn'ər*, *n.* a sharp-built, swift-sailing vessel, generally two-masted, fore-and-aft rigged, or with top and topgallant sails on the foremast: a covered emigrant-wagon (**prairie schooner**): a large beer glass (esp. *U.S., Austr.*): also a large sherry glass. — *adj.* **schoon'- er-rigged.** [Early 18th-century (Massachusetts) *skooner, scooner*, said to be from a dial. Eng. word *scoon*, to skim.]

schorl *shörl*, *n.* black tourmaline. — *adj.* **schorlā'ceous.** — **schorl'-rock'** a rock compound of schorl and quartz. [Ger. *Schörl.*]

schottische *sho-tēsh', shot'ish*, *n.* a dance, or dance-tune, similar to the polka. [Ger. (*der*) *schottische* (*Tanz*), (the) Scottish (dance); pronunciation sham French.]

schout *skowt*, *n.* a municipal officer. [Du.]

schrecklich *shrek'lihh*, (*Ger.*) *adj.* frightful. — *n.* **Schreck'- lichkeit** (*-kīt*) frightfulness.

schreech-owl. See under **shriek.**

schtick, schtik. See **shtick.**

schtook, schtuck. See **shtook.**

schtoom. See **shtoom.**

schuit, schuyt *skoit*, *n.* a Dutch flat-bottomed river-boat. [Du.]

schul. Same as **shul.**

schuss *shŏŏs*, *n.* in skiing, a straight slope on which it is possible to make a fast run: such a run. — *v.i.* to make such a run. [Ger.]

schutzstaffel (*abbrev.* **S.S.**) *shŏŏts'shtä-fəl*, (Ger.) *n.* Hitler's bodyguard.

schuyt. See **schuit.**

schwa, shwa *shvä, shwä*, *n.* an indistinct vowel sound shown in Hebrew by two dots (:) — transliterated *ĕ*, etc.: in phonetics, a neutral vowel (ə). — Cf. **sheva.** [Ger., — Heb. *schĕwa*.]

Schwann cell *shvan sel*, a large nucleated cell that produces myelin in peripheral nerve fibres. [Theodor *Schwann* (1810–82), German physiologist.]

schwärmerei *shver'mər-ī, n.* sentimental enthusiasm, as of a schoolgirl. [Ger., swarming.]

schwarzlot *shvarts'lōt, n.* a type of black enamel decoration on glass, pottery and porcelain. [Ger., black lead.]

Schwenkfelder *shvengk'fel-dər, n.* a member of a religious sect, founded by Kaspar von *Schwenkfeld* (1490–1561). — Also **Schwenkfeld'ian.**

scia-. For various words see under **skia-.**

Sciaena *sī-ē'nə, n.* the maigre genus of fishes, giving name to the fam. **Sciae'nidae.** — *adjs.* **sciae'nid, sciae'noid.** [Gr. *skiaina*, a kind of fish.]

sciamachy *sī-am'ə-ki*, **skiamachy** *skī-am'ə-ki, ns.* fighting with shadows: imaginary or useless fighting. [Gr. *skiamakhia*.]

sciarid *sī-ar'id, n.* a minute, dark-coloured, two-winged fly of the family **Sciar'idae.** — Also *adj.* [Gr. *skiaros*, shady, dark-coloured — *skia*, shadow.]

sciatic *sī-at'ik, adj.* of, or in the region of, the hip. — Also **sciat'ical.** — *n.* **sciat'ica** neuritis of the great sciatic nerve which passes down the back of the thigh. [L.L. *sciaticus*, fem. *-a* — Gr. *ischion*, hip-joint.]

science *sī'əns, n.* knowledge (*arch.*): knowledge ascertained by observation and experiment, critically tested, systematised and brought under general principles: a department or branch of such knowledge or study: a skilled craft (*obs.*): trained skill, esp. in boxing (now usu. *jocular*). — *adjs.* **sci'enced** (*arch.*) versed, learned; **sci'ent** (*arch.*) having science; **sciential** (*-en'shl*) of, having, or producing, science: scientific; **scientif'ic** (L. *facĕre*, to make) orig. (of a syllogism) demonstrative, producing knowledge: hence of, relating to, based on, devoted to, according to, used in, or versed in, science. — Also (*rare*) **scientif'ical.** — *adv.* **scientif'ically.** — *ns.* **sci'entism** the methods or mental attitudes of men of science: a belief that the methods used in studying natural sciences should be employed also in investigating all aspects of human behaviour and condition, e.g. in philosophy and social sciences: scientific or pseudo-scientific language; **sci'entist** a man of science, esp. natural science. — *adj.* **scientis'tic.** — *ns.* **Scientol'- ogist; Scientol'ogy®** a religious system which, it is claimed, improves the mental and physical well-being of its adherents by scientific means. — *v.t.* **sci'entise,** **-ize** to treat in a scientific way. — **science fiction** fiction dealing with life on the earth in future, with space travel, and with life on other planets, or the like: — *coll. abbrev.* **scī'-fī'; science park** a centre for industrial research, etc., attached to a university, set up for the purpose of co-operation between the academic and the commercial world; **the (noble) science** the art of boxing. [L. *scientia* — *sciēns, -entis*, pr.p. of *scīre*, to know.]

scienter *sī-en'tər,* (*legal*) *adv.* having knowledge, being aware: wilfully. [L.]

sci-fi *sī'-fī',* coll. abbrev. for **science fiction.**

scilicet *sī'li-set, skē'li-ket, adv.* to wit, namely. [L. *scīlicet* — *scīre licet,* it is permitted to know.]

Scilla *sil'ə, n.* the squill genus of the lily family, including some bright blue spring flowers: (without *cap.*) any plant of this genus. [L., — Gr. *skilla,* the officinal squill.]

Scillonian *si-lō'ni-ən, adj.* of, belonging to, concerning, the Scilly Isles, off the south-west coast of Britain. — *n.* an inhabitant of these islands.

scimitar *sim'i-tər, n.* a short, single-edged, curved sword, broadest at the point end, used by the Turks and Persians. [Poss. through Fr. *cimeterre* or It. *scimitarra* — Pers. *shamshīr;* but doubtful.]

scincoid *singk'oid, adj.* like a skink. — Also **scincoid'ian.** [Gr. *skinkos,* a skink, *eidos,* form.]

scintigraphy *sin-tig'rə-fi, n.* a diagnostic technique in which a pictorial record of the pattern of gamma ray emission after injection of isotope into the body gives a picture, of an internal organ. — *n.* **scint'igram** a picture so produced. [*scint*illation.]

scintilla *sin-til'ə, n.* a spark: a hint, trace. — *adj.* **scin'- tillant** sparkling. — *v.i.* **scin'tillate** to sparkle: to talk wittily. — *v.t.* to emit in sparks: to sparkle with. — *ns.* **scintillā'tion** a flash of light produced in a phosphor by an ionising particle, e.g. an alpha particle, or a photon; **scin'tillātor** an instrument for detecting radioactivity; **scintillom'eter** an instrument for detecting and measuring radioactivity; **scintill'oscope** an instrument which shows scintillations on a screen. — **scintillation counter** a scintillometer. [L., a spark.]

scio-. For various words see under **skia-.**

sciolism *sī'ə-lizm, n.* superficial pretensions to knowledge. — *n.* **sci'olist** a pretender to science. — *adjs.* **sciolis'tic;** **sci'olous.** [L. *sciolus,* dim. of *scius,* knowing — *scīre,* to know.]

sciolto *shol'tō,* (*mus.*) *adj.* and *adv.* free. [It.]

scion *sī'ən, n.* a detached piece of a plant capable of propagating, esp. by grafting: a young member of a family: a descendant, offshoot.   [O.Fr. *sion, cion*; origin obscure.]

sciosophy *sī-os'ō-fi, n.* a system of what claims to be knowledge but is without basis in ascertained scientific fact, as astrology.   [Gr. *skiā*, a shadow, *sophiā*, wisdom.]

scire facias *sī'ri fā'shi-as, skē're fa'ki-äs*, a writ requiring a person to appear and show cause why a record should not be enforced or annulled.   [L. *scīre faciās*, make him to know.]

scirocco. See **sirocco.**

Scirpus *sûr'pɔs, n.* the club-rush genus of the sedge family.   [L., a rush.]

scirrhus *skir'ɔs, sir'ɔs, (med.) n.* a hard swelling: a hard cancer. — *adjs.* **scirr'hoid, scirr'hous.** [Latinised from Gr. *skirros, skīros*, a tumour.]

scissel *sis'l, n.* metal clippings: scrap left when blanks have been cut out. — Also **sciss'il.** [O.Fr. *cisaille* — *ciseler* — *cisel*, a chisel; for the spelling cf. **scissors.**]

scissile *sis'īl, adj.* capable of being cut: readily splitting. — *ns.* **scission** (*sish'ɔn, sizh'ɔn*) cutting: division: splitting: schism; **scissiparity** (*sis-i-par'i-ti*; L. *parĕre*, to bring forth) reproduction by fission; **scissure** (*sish'ɔr*) a cleft: a fissure: a rupture: a division: cutting.   [L. *scissilis, scissiō, -ōnis, scissūra* — *scindĕre, scissum*, to cut, to split, cleave.]

scissors *siz'ɔrz, n.pl.* or (*rare*) *n.sing.* a cutting instrument with two blades pivoted to close together and overlap — usu. smaller than shears: a position or movement like that of scissors: movement of the legs suggesting opening and closing of scissors (*gymnastics*): locking the legs round body or head of an opponent (*wrestling*): a style of high jump in which the leg nearest the bar leads throughout: a pass in Rugy football from one running player to another who is crossing his path. — *v.t.* **sciss'or** to cut with scissors. — *n.* **sciss'orer** a scissors-and-paste compiler. — *adv.* **sciss'orwise.** — **sciss'or-bill** a skimmer; **sciss'or-blade; sciss'or-case; sciss'or-cut; sciss'or-leg** the deformity of crossed legs; **sciss'ors-and-paste'** literary or journalistic matter collected from various sources with little or no original writing. — Also *adj.* — **sciss'or-tail** an American fly-catcher; **sciss'or-tooth** a carnassial tooth.   [O.Fr. *cisoires* — L.L. *cīsōrium*, a cutting instrument — *caedĕre, caesum*, to cut; the spelling *sc-* is due to erroneous association with *scindĕre, scissum*; cf. foregoing.]

scissure. See **scissile.**

Scitamineae *sit-ɔ-min'i-ē, n.pl.* an order of monocotyledons including the banana, ginger, Indian shot, and arrowroot families. — *adj.* **scitamin'eous.** — Also **Musales.** [App. — L. *scītāmenta*, delicacies.]

Sciurus *sī-ū'rɔs, n.* the squirrel genus, giving name to the fam. **Sciu'ridae.** — *adjs.* **sciurine** (*-sī-ūr'īn*, or *sī'*); **sciuroid** (*-ū'*). — *n.* **Sciurop'terus** (Gr. *pteron*, wing) a genus of flying squirrels.   [L. *sciūrus* — Gr. *skiouros* — *skiā*, shadow, *ourā*, tail.]

sclaff *sklaf, skläf, n.* a light slap or its sound (*Scot.*): a stroke in which the sole of the club scrapes the ground before striking the ball (*golf*). — *v.t.* and *v.i.* to strike or play with a sclaff.   [Imit.]

sclate *sklāt, slāt,* a Scots form of **slate**[1]. — **sclate'-stane'** a piece of slate (such as money got from the Devil turned into).

sclaunder, sclave, Sclav, Sclavonian, etc., *sklön'dɔr,* etc., obs. forms of **slander, slave, Slav, Slavonian,** etc.

sclera *sklēr'ɔ, n.* the sclerotic. — *adj.* **sclē'ral.** — *ns.* **sclere** (*sklēr*) a skeletal element: a sponge spicule; **sclereid, -eide** (*sklēr'i-id*; *bot.*) a thick-walled cell; **sclerema** (*sklɔr-ē'mɔ*) hardening of (esp. subcutaneous) tissues; **sclerenchyma** (*sklɔr-eng'ki-mɔ*; Gr. *enchyma*, in-filling) plant tissue with thick, lignified cell-walls; hard skeletal tissue, as in corals. — *adj.* **sclerenchymatous** (*sklēr-eng-kim'ɔ-tɔs*). — *ns.* **scleri'asis** hardening of tissue: a hard tumour: an induration; **sclē'rite** a hard skeletal plate or spicule; **scleritis** (*sklɔr-ī'tis*) sclerotitis. — *adj.* **sclerocaulous** (*sklēr-ō-kö'lɔs*). — *ns.* **sclē'rocauly** (Gr.

kaulos, stem) possession of a hard, dry stem; **scleroderm** (*skler', sklēr'*) a hard integument. — *adj.* **scleroder'matous.** — *ns.* **scleroder'm(i)a** hardness and rigidity of skin by substitution of fibrous tissue for subcutaneous fat. — *adjs.* **scleroder'mic, scleroder'mous** hardskinned: pertaining to a scleroderm or to sclerodermia. — *n.* **scleroder'mite** the integument of a segment in arthropods. — *adj.* **sclē'roid** (*bot.* and *zool.*) hard: hardened. — *ns.* **sclerō'ma** hardening: morbid hardening: formation of nodules in the nose, etc.; **sclerom'eter** an instrument for measuring the hardness of minerals; **sclerophyll** (*sklēr'ō-fil*) a hard, stiff leaf. — *adj.* **sclerophyll'ous.** — *ns.* **scleroph'ylly** possession of sclerophylls; **scleroprō'tein** insoluble protein forming the skeletal parts of tissues. — *v.t.* **sclerose** (*sklɔr-ōs'*, or *sklēr'*) to harden: to affect with sclerosis. — *v.i.* to become sclerosed. — *adj.* **sclerosed** (or *sklēr'*). — *n.* **sclerosis** (*sklɔr-ō'sis*) hardening: morbid hardening, as of arteries (*med.*): hardening of tissue by thickening or lignification (*bot.*). — *adj.* **sclerō'tal** sclerotic. — *n.* a bony plate in the sclerotic of some animals. — *adj.* **sclerŏt'ic** hard, firm, applied esp. to the outer membrane of the eye-ball: of sclerosis: sclerosed. — *n.* the outermost membrane of the eye-ball. — *n.* **sclerotī'tis** (*skler-, sklēr-*) inflammation of the sclerotic. — *adjs.* **sclerō'tioid, sclerō'tial.** — *ns.* **sclerotium** (*sklɔ-rō'shi-ɔm*) a hard, tuber-like body, the resting stage of many fungi: — *pl.* **sclerō'tia; sclerot'omy** (*med.*) incision into the sclerotic. — *adj.* **sclē'rous** hard or indurated: ossified or bony. — **disseminated** (or **multiple**) **sclerosis** see **disseminate.** [Gr. *sklēros*, hard.]

scliff, skliff *sklif, (Scot.) n.* a small segment or piece.   [Imit.]

sclim, sklim *sklim,* a Scots form of **climb.**

scoff[1] *skof, n.* mockery: a jibe, jeer: an object of derision. — *v.i.* to jeer (with *at*). — *v.t.* (*Shak.*) to jeer at. — *n.* **scoff'er.** — *n.* and *adj.* **scoff'ing.** — *adv.* **scoff'ingly.** [Cf. obs. Dan. *skof*, jest, mockery, O.Fris. *schof*.]

scoff[2], **skoff** *skof, (dial.* and *slang) v.t.* to devour: to plunder. — *v.i.* to feed quickly or greedily. — *n.* food: a meal.   [App. **scaff,** reinforced from S. Africa by Du. *schoft*, a meal.]

scofflaw *skof'lö, (U.S. coll.) n.* a person who is contemptuous of the law.   [**scoff**[1], **law**[1].]

scog. See **skug**[1].

Scoggin, Scogan *skog'ɔn, n.* a supposed fool of Edward IV, on whom the contents of a 16th-century jest-book were fathered: hence a buffoon.

scoinson *skoin'sɔn.* Same as **scuncheon.**

scold *skōld, n.* a rude clamorous woman or other: a scolding. — *v.i.* to brawl: to vituperate: to find fault vehemently or at some length. — *v.t.* to chide: to rebuke. — *n.* **scold'er.** — *n.* and *adj.* **scold'ing.** — **scold's bridle** see **branks.** [App. O.N. *skāld*, poet (through an intermediate sense, lampooner).]

scolex *skō'leks, n.* a tapeworm head: — *pl.* **scoleces** (*skō-lē'sēz*; erroneously **scō'lices**). — *adjs.* **scō'lecid** (*-lɔ-sid*), **scōleciform** (*-les'i-förm*) like a scolex. — *n.pl.* **Scōleciform'ia** the lugworm order. — *n.* **scō'lecite** (*-sīt*) a member of the zeolite group of minerals. — *adj.* **scōlecoid** (*-lē'koid*) like a scolex. [Gr. *skolēx, -ēkos*, a worm.]

scoliosis *skol-i-ō'sis, n.* lateral spinal curvature. — Also **scoliom'a.** — *adj.* **scoliotic** (*-ot'ik*). [Gr. *skoliōsis*, obliquity.]

scollop. Same as **scallop.**

Scolopax *skol'ɔ-paks, n.* the woodcock genus, giving name to the fam. **Scolopacidae** (*-pas'i-dē*). — *adj.* **scolopaceous** (*-pā'shɔs*). [Gr. *scolopax, -ăkos*, a woodcock.]

Scolopendra *skol-ɔ-pen'drɔ, n.* a genus of centipedes, some a foot long: (without *cap.; Spens.*, etc.) a fabulous fish that voided the hook. — *n.* **scolopen'drid** any centipe of the family *Scolopendridae.* — *adjs.* **scolopen'drifo scolopen'drine.** — *n.* **Scolopen'drium** the hart's-to fern genus (from the appearance of the sori). [Gr. *skolopendra, skolopendrion.*]

Scolytus *skol'i-təs, n.* typical genus of **Scolytidae** (*-it'i-dē*), a family of bark-beetles. — *adj.* **scol'ytoid.** [Gr. *skolyptein*, to strip.]

Scomber *skom'bər, n.* the mackerel genus, giving name to the fam. **Scom'bridae** (*-bri-dē*). — *n.* **Scom'bresox** (L. *esox*, pike) the skipper genus, giving name to the **Scombresocidae** (*-sos'i-dē*). — *adj.* **scom'broid** of or like the mackerel family. [L. *scomber* — Gr. *skombros*, a mackerel.]

scomfish *skum'fish*, (*Scot.*) *v.t.* to stifle: to disgust. [From *discomfish*, a by-form of **discomfit**, from the stem appearing in the Fr. pr.p.]

sconce[1] *skons, n.* a small fort or earthwork: a shelter: a chimney-seat: a slab of floating ice. — *v.t.* to entrench: to screen. — **build a sconce** to run up a debt (e.g. in a tavern) and have to keep away. [Du. *schans*.]

sconce[2] *skons, n.* the head: the crown of the head: brains, wits. [Origin obscure.]

sconce[3] *skons,* (*Oxford*) *n.* a fine (paid in ale or otherwise): a two-handled mug used for the purpose (holding about a quart): a forfeit. — *v.t.* to fine. [Origin obscure.]

sconce[4] *skons, n.* a candlestick or lantern with a handle: a bracket candlestick: a street wall-lamp. [O.Fr. *esconse* — L.L. *absconsa*, a dark lantern — *abscondĕre*, to hide.]

sconcheon. Same as **scuncheon.**

scone *skon*, in the South of England often pronounced *skōn*, (*Scot.*) *n.* a flattish, usually round or quadrant-shaped plain cake of dough without much butter, with or without currants, baked on a girdle or in an oven. [Perh. from Du. *schoon* (*brot*), fine (bread).]

scontion. Same as **scuncheon.**

scoog. See **skug**[1].

scoop *skōōp, n.* a bailing-vessel: a concave shovel or lipped vessel for skimming or shovelling up loose material: an instrument for gouging out apple-cores, samples of cheese, etc.: anything of like shape: an act of scooping: a sweeping stroke: a scooped-out place: anything got by or as by scooping, a haul: the fore-stalling of other newspapers in obtaining a piece of news: an item of news so secured (also *adj.*). — *v.t.* to bail out: to lift, obtain, remove, hollow, or make with, or as if with, a scoop: to secure in advance of or to the exclusion of others. — *adjs.* **scooped.** — *ns.* **scoop'er** one who scoops: an engraver's tool: the avocet; **scoop'-ful;** — *pl.* **scoop'fuls; scoop'ing.** — *adj.* **scooped'-out.** — **scoop neck** a low rounded neckline; **scoop'-net** a long-handled dipping net: a net for scooping along the bottom. — **scoop the pool** see **pool**[2]. [Prob. partly M.L.G. or M.Du. *schôpe*, bailing-vessel, partly M.Du. *schoppe*, shovel.]

scoot[1] *skōōt, v.t.* and *v.i.* (*Scot.*) to squirt. — *v.i.* to slip suddenly (*Scot.*): to make off with celerity (*coll.*): to travel on a scooter (*coll.*). — *n.* a squirt (*Scot.*): an act of scooting. — *n.* **scoot'er** one who scoots: a child's toy, a wheeled footboard with steering handle, pro-pelled by kicking the ground: a development thereof driven by a motor (also *motor-scooter, auto-scooter*): a boat for sailing on ice and water (*U.S.*): a swift motor-boat: a simple form of plough (*U.S.*). [Prob. from O.N., akin to **shoot**[1].]

scoot[2] *skōōt*, (*Scot.*) *n.* an insignificant person.

scopa *skō'pə, n.* a bee's pollen-brush; — *pl.* **sco'pae** (*-pē*). — *adj.* **scō'pate** tufted. — *n.* **scopula** (*skop'ū-lə*) a little tuft of hairs. — *adj.* **scop'ulate.** [L. *scōpae*, twigs, a broom.]

scope[1] *skōp, n.* point aimed at: aim: range: field or opportunity of activity: room for action: spaciousness: length of cable at which a vessel rides at liberty. [It. *scopo* — Gr. *skopos*, watcher, point watched, (*fig.*) aim — *skopeein*, to view.]

⸺ ne[2] *skōp, n.* short for **microscope, telescope, horoscope,** ⸺ c.

⸺ e *-skōp*, in composition, an instrument for viewing, ⸺ mining, or detecting as in *telescope, oscilloscope,* ⸺ oscope. [Gr. *skopeein*, to view.]

Scopelus *skop'ə-ləs, n.* a genus of deep-water fishes with luminous spots, giving name to the fam. **Scopelidae** (*-el'i-dē*). [Gr. *skopelos*, a rock, thought by Cuvier to mean a kind of fish.]

scopolamine *sko-pol'ə-mēn, n.* an alkaloid got from the genus **Scopolia** and other plants of the Solanaceae (see **hyoscine**) with sedative properties, used e.g. to prevent travel sickness and as a truth drug. [Named after *Scopoli* (1723–88), Italian naturalist; **amine**.]

scopophilia *skop-ō-fil'i-ə, n.* the practice of obtaining sexual pleasure from things seen, as e.g. naked bodies. — *n.* **scopophil'iac.** — *adj.* **scopophil'ic.** [Gr. *skopos*, watcher (*skopeein*, to view), *philia*, loving.]

scopophobia *skop-ō-fō'bi-ə, n.* fear of being looked at. [Gr. *skopeein*, to view, *phobos*, fear.]

Scops *skops, n.* a genus of owls. [Gr. *skōps*.]

scoptophilia, etc. Same as **scopophilia,** etc.

scopula, scopulate. See **scopa.**

-scopy *-skə-pi*, in composition, indicating viewing, exam-ining, or observing, as in *autoscopy, poroscopy, or-nithoscopy.* [Gr. *skopeein*, to view.]

scorbutic, -al *skör-bū'tik, -əl, adjs.* of, like, of the nature of, or affected with, scurvy. [L.L. *scorbūticus*, poss. from M.L.G. *schorbuk*.]

scorch[1] *skörch, v.t.* to burn slightly or superficially: to parch: to dry up, wither, or affect painfully or injuri-ously by heat or as if by heat: to wither with scorn, censure, etc. — *v.i.* to be burned on the surface: to be dried up: to cycle or drive furiously (*coll.*). — *n.* an act of scorching: an injury by scorching. — *adj.* **scorched.** — *n.* **scorch'er** one who, that which, scorches: a day of scorching heat (*coll.*): anything stinging. — *n., adj.,* and *adv.* **scorch'ing.** — *adv.* **scorch'ingly.** — *n.* **scorch'ingness.** — **scorched earth** country devastated before evacuation so as to be useless to an advancing enemy; **scorched-earth policy.** [Perh. M.E. *skorken*; cf. O.N. *skorpna*, to shrivel; poss. affected by O.Fr. *escorcher*, to flay.]

scorch[2] *skörch*, (*Shak.; Scott*) *v.t.* to slash (in *Macbeth* Theobald conjecturally read *scotch'd* for *scorch'd*). [Perh. **score**, influenced by **scratch**.]

scordato *skör-dä'tō*, (*mus.*) *adj.* put out of tune. — *n.* **scordatura** (*-tōō'rə*) a temporary departure from nor-mal tuning. [It.]

score *skōr, skör, n.* a notch, gash, or scratch: an incised line: a boldly drawn line, as one marking a deletion: a line marking a boundary, starting-place, or defined position: an arrangement of music on a number of staves (perh. orig. with the bar divisions running continuously through all): a composition so dis-tributed: a notch in a tally: an account of charges incurred (as in a tavern) by tallies or (later) chalk marks or the like: a debt incurred: a reckoning, account, ground: total number, tale (*Spens.*): the total or record of points made in a game: an addition made thereto: a set of twenty (sometimes verging upon numeral *adj.*): applied also to an indefinitely large number: twenty or twenty-one pounds: twenty paces (*Shak.*): a fixed number (20 to 26) of tubs of coal. — *v.t.* to mark with or by scores: to record in or with a score: to make a score through as a mark of deletion (with *out*): to write in score: to distribute among the instruments of the orchestra: to make as a score: to add to a score: to achieve: to enumerate: to record: to rebuke (*U.S.*). — *v.i.* to keep or run up a score (*obs.*): to make a point: to achieve a success: of a man, to achieve sexual intercourse (*slang*): to obtain drugs (*slang*). — *ns.* **scor'er** one who, or that which, scores: one who keeps the marks in a game; **scor'ing.** — **score'-board, scor'ing-board** a board on which the score is exhibited, as at cricket; **score'-card, scor'ing-card, score'-sheet** a card, sheet, for recording the score in a game; **score'-draw** (esp. *football*) a drawn result other than nil all; **score'-line** a score in a match, etc. — **go off at score** to make a spirited start; **know the score** to know the hard facts of the situation; **on that score** as regards that matter; **pay off, settle, old scores** to repay old grudges; **run up**

a **score** to run up a debt; **score an own goal** (*coll.*) to do something unintentionally to one's own disadvantage; **score off, score points off** (*coll.*) to achieve a success against, get the better of.   [Late O.E. *scoru* — O.N. *skor, skora*; cf. O.E. *sceran* (pa.p. *scoren*), to shear.]

scoria *skō′, skö′ri-ə, n.* dross or slag from metal-smelting: a piece of lava with steam-holes: — *pl.* **sco′riae** (*-ri-ē*). — *adjs.* **sco′riac, scoriaceous** (*-ri-ā′shəs*). — *n.* **scorifica′tion** reduction to scoria: assaying by fusing with lead and borax; **sco′rifier** a dish used in assaying. — *v.t.* **sco′rify** to reduce to scoria: to rid metals of (impurities) by forming scoria. — *adj.* **sco′rious.** [L., — Gr. *skōriā* —*skōr,* dung.]

scorn *skörn, n.* hot or extreme contempt, usu. less self-conscious than disdain: an expression of contempt (*arch.*): the object of contempt. — *v.t.* to feel or express scorn for: to refuse with scorn: to make a mock of (*obs.*). — *v.i.* (*obs.*) to scoff. — *n.* **scorn′er.** — *adj.* **scorn′ful.** — *adv.* **scorn′fully.** —*ns.* **scorn′fulness; scorn′ing.** — **think scorn of** (*arch.*) to disdain or think beneath one. [O.Fr. *escarn,* mockery; of Gmc. origin; cf. O.H.G. *skern,* mockery.]

scorodite *skor′ō-dīt, n.* hydrous ferric arsenate. [Gr. *skorodon,* garlic, from the smell under the blowpipe.]

Scorpaena *skör-pē′nə, n.* a genus of large-headed, spiny fishes giving name to the fam. **Scorpae′nidae,** the scorpion-fishes or sea-scorpions. — *adj.* and *n.* **scorpae′noid.** [Gr. *skorpaina,* a kind of fish.]

scorper *skör′pər, n.* a gouging chisel. [For **scauper.**]

scorpioid *skör′pi-oid, adj.* like a scorpion, or a scorpion's curled tail. — **scorpioid cyme** a uniparous cymose inflorescence in which the plane of each daughter axis is at right angles, to right and left alternately, with its parent axis, that of the whole coiled in bud — a cincinnus or cicinnus. [Gr. *skorpios,* scorpion, *eidos,* form.]

scorpion *skör′pi-ən, n.* any member of the **Scorpionid′ea** or **Scorpionida** (*-on′i-də*), an order of Arachnida with head and thorax united, pincers, four pairs of legs, and a segmented abdomen including a tail with a sting: a form of scourge (*B.*): an old engine for hurling missiles: any person of virulent hatred or animosity: a rock-scorpion (*mil. slang;* see **rock**[1]): (*cap.*) the constellation or the sign Scorpio (*astron.*). — *n.* **Scor′pio** (*-pi-ō*) a genus of scorpions: a constellation (also **Scor′pius**): a sign of the zodiac: one born under this sign (also without *cap.*; *pl.* **-os**). — *adj.* **scorpion′ic.** — **scor′pion-fish** any of the Scorpaenidae; **scor′pion-fly** an insect of the Mecoptera (from the male's upturned abdomen); **scor′pion-grass** forget-me-not; **scor′pion= spider** a whip-scorpion. [L. *scorpiō, -ōnis* — Gr. *skorpios.*]

scorse[1] *skōrs, skörs,* (*Spens.*) *v.t.* to chase. [It. *scorsa,* a run — *scorrere* — L. *excurrĕre.*]

scorse[2] *skōrs, skörs,* (*Spens.*) *n.* exchange. — *v.t.* and *v.i.* (*obs.*) to exchange (also **scourse**). — *n.* **scors′er** (*obs.*) one who barters. [Poss. from *horse-scorser* for **horse= courser.**]

scorzonera *skör-zō-nē′rə, n.* a plant like dandelion, with edible root — *black salsify.* [It.]

scot *skot,* (*hist.*) *n.* a payment, esp. a customary tax: a share of a reckoning (also **shot**). — *adj.* **scot′-free′** free from scot: untaxed: entirely free from expense, injury, etc. — **scot and lot** an old legal phrase embracing all parochial assessments for the poor, the church, lighting, cleansing, and watching. [O.E. *scot, sceot;* but prob. partly from O.N. *skot,* and O.Fr. *esco;* see **shot**[2], **escot.**]

Scot *skot, n.* one of a Gaelic-speaking people of Ireland, afterwards also in Argyllshire (now part of Strathclyde) (*hist.*): (now) a Scotsman or Scotswoman of any race or language. — *n.* **Scotland** (*skot′lənd*) Ireland (*hist.*): now, the country forming the northern member of the United Kingdom. — *adv.* **Scot(t)ice** (*skot′i-sē*) in Scots. — *v.t.* **Scott′icise, -ize** to render Scottish or into Scots. — *n.* **Scott′icism** (*obs.* **Scot′icism**) a Scottish

idiom: Scottish feeling. — *v.t.* **Scot(t)′ify** to make Scottish: — *pr.p.* **Scot(t)′ifying;** *pa.t.* and *pa.p.* **Scot(t)′- ified.** — *n.* **Scot(t)ificā′tion.** — *adj.* **Scottish** (*obs.* **Scotish;** *skot′ish;* O.E. *Scottisc,* earlier *Scyttisc*) of Scotland, its people, or its English dialect. — *n.* **Scots** (see separate entry): (as *pl., rare*) the Scots. — *v.t.* to translate into Scots. — *ns.* **Scott′ishman; Scott′ishness; Scott′y, Scott′ie** a nickname for a Scotsman: a Scotch terrier (*coll.*) — **Scotland Yard** earliest or (New Scotland Yard) two more recent headquarters (1890 and 1967) of the Metropolitan Police (said to be from a palace of the kings of Scotland on the orig. site): hence the London Criminal Investigation Department. — **Irish Scot** (*obs.*) a Highlander; **Scottish Certificate of Education** in secondary education in Scotland, a certificate obtainable at Ordinary and Higher grades (see **O level** and **Higher (grade),** for proficiency in one or more subjects. [O.E. *Scottas* (pl.) — L.L. *Scottus;* see also **Scotch, Scotia, Scots.**]

Scotch *skoch, adj.* a form of **Scottish** or **Scots,** in common use even among Scottish dialect speakers, though disliked or resented by many Scotsmen: applied esp. to products or supposed products of Scotland: having the character popularly attributed to a Scotsman — an excessive leaning towards defence of oneself and one's property. — *n.* Scotch whisky, or a glass of it: the Scottish (Northern English) dialect: (as *pl.*) the Scots. — *ns.* **Scotch′ness; Scotch′y** a nickname for a Scotsman. — *adj.* having Scottish characteristics. — **Scotch attorney** (*W. Indies*) a climber (Clusia) that strangles trees; **Scotch barley** pot or hulled barley; **Scotch bluebell** the harebell; **Scotch bonnet** a round flat blue woollen cap with a tuft on the top: the fairy-ring mushroom; **Scotch broth** broth made with pot-barley and plenty of various vegetables chopped small; **Scotch cart** (*S. Afr.; arch.*) a strong, springless, two-wheeled uncovered farm cart with one shaft; **Scotch catch** or **snap** a short accented note followed by a longer — not peculiar to Scottish music; **Scotch collops** minced beef (sometimes called **scotched collops**); **Scotch cuddy** (cuddy = donkey) a Scotch draper; **Scotch curlies** a variety of kale; **Scotch draper** an itinerant dealer differing from a pedlar in not carrying his goods about with him: a credit itinerant draper (also **Scotch cuddy**); **Scotch egg** a hard-boiled egg (often cut in two) enclosed in sausage-meat; **Scotch elm** the wych-elm (*Ulmus montana*): sometimes the common English elm (*U. campestris*); **Scotch fiddle** the itch (from the movements of the fingers it excited); **Scotch fir** Scots pine; **Scotch hand** a wooden bat for manipulating butter. — *adj.* and *n.pl.* (*U.S.*) **Scotch′-Ir′ish** Irish of Scottish descent. — **Scotch kale** a variety of kale; **Scotch′man** a Scotsman: a florin (from a tradition of a Scotsman who benefited from its resemblance to a half-crown; *S. Afr.; obs.*); **Scotch mist** a fine rain; **Scotch pebble** an agate or similar stone; **Scotch pine, fir** see under **Scots;** **Scotch rose** the burnet rose (*Rosa spinosissima*); **Scotch snap** a Scotch catch (see above); **Scotch tape**® a transparent tape, adhering to paper, etc., when pressure is applied; **Scotch terrier** a rough-haired, prick-eared, strongly-built little dog (also **Scottish terrier, Scottie, Scotty**); **Scotch thistle** the cotton thistle, national emblem of Scotland (not native); **Scotch verdict** not proven; **Scotch′woman; Scotch woodcock** egg and anchovies on toast. — **Scotch and English** prisoners' base (q.v.). [From **Scottish.**]

scotch[1] *skoch, v.t.* to gash: to score: (from Theobald's conjecture in *Macbeth;* see **scorch**[2]) to maim, cripple for the time without killing: to frustrate: to quash. — *n.* gash (*Shak.*): a score on the ground (as for hop-scotch). [Origin unknown.]

scotch[2] *skoch, n.* a strut, wedge, block, etc., to prevent turning or slipping, as of a wheel, gate, ladder. — *v.t* to stop or block: to frustrate. [Perh. a form c **scratch.**]

scoter *skō′tər, n.* a duck of the genus *Oedemia* or *Melan* of northern sea-ducks, usu. black or nearly. — *.*

scoter duck. [Origin obscure.]

scotia *sko'ti-ə, -shi-ə, n.* a hollow moulding, esp. at the base of a column. [Gr. *skōtiā* — *skotos*, darkness.]

Scotia *skō'sh(y)ə, n.* (*poet.*) Scotland. — *adjs.* **Sco'tian** (*rare*); **Scotic** (*skot'ik*) of the ancient Scots of Ireland; **Scot'ican** (*eccles.*) of Scotland. — For **Scotice, Scoticism, Scotish** see **Scot.** [L.L. *Scōtia, Scōticus.*]

Scotism *skō'tizm, n.* the metaphysical system of Johannes Duns *Scotus* (*c.* 1265–1308), a native of Maxton in Roxburghshire (not Duns, Berwickshire, Dunstane, Northumberland, or Down, Northern Ireland), the great assailant of the method of Aquinas in seeking in speculation instead of in practice the foundation of Christian theology — his theological descendants were the Franciscans, in opposition to the Dominicans, who followed Aquinas. — *n.* **Scō'tist** a follower of Duns Scotus. — *adj.* **Scotist'ic.**

scoto- *skot-ō-,* in composition, dark. — *ns.* **scotodinia** (*-din'i-ə;* Gr. *dīnos,* whirling) dizziness with headache and impairment of vision; **scotoma** (*-ōm'ə;* Gr. *skotōma,* dizziness) a blind spot due to disease of the retina or optic nerve: — *pl.* **scotō'mata, scotō'mas.** — *adj.* **scotō'matous.** — *ns.* **scot'omy** (*obs.*); **scotōp'ia** vision in a dim light. — *adj.* **scotop'ic** (*-op'*). [Gr. *skotos,* darkness.]

Scots *skots, adj.* Scottish (almost always used of money, measures, law, and preferably of language). — *n.* the dialect of Lowland Scotland, Northern English. — **Scots Greys** a famous regiment of dragoons, established in 1683, amalgamated with the 3rd Carabiniers in 1971; **Scots Guards** a Scottish force which served the kings of France from 1418 to 1759, nominally to 1830: a well-known regiment of Guards in the British army, formerly Scots Fusilier Guards; **Scots'man; Scots pine** (often called **Scots fir**) the only native British pine, *Pinus sylvestris* (also **Scotch**); **Scots'woman;** see also **mile, pint, pound.** [Shortened form of Scots *Scottis,* Scottish.]

Scottish, etc. See **Scot.**

scoug. Same as **skug**[1].

scoundrel *skown'drəl, n.* a low mean blackguard: a man without principle. — *ns.* **scoun'dreldom** the world of scoundrels; **scoun'drelism.** — *adj.* **scoun'drelly.** [Origin unknown.]

scoup, scowp *skowp,* (*Scot.*) *v.i.* to bound: to caper: to scamper. [Origin unknown.]

scour[1] *skowr, v.t.* to clean, polish, remove, or form by hard rubbing: to scrub: to cleanse: to free from grease, dirt, or gum: to flush or cleanse by a current: to purge, esp. drastically: to clear out: to rake with fire: to punish (*fig.*). — *v.i.* to scrub or polish: to be scoured: (of cattle or other livestock) to have diarrhoea. — *n.* the action, place, or means of scouring: diarrhoea in cattle, etc.: a swig of liquor (*Scot.*). — *ns.* **scour'er** one who scours: an instrument or container for scouring: a cathartic; **scour'ing** scrubbing: vigorous cleansing: clearing: erosion: purging: (often in *pl.*) matter removed or accumulated by scouring: off-scouring. — Also *adj.* **scour'ing-rush** Dutch rush; **scour'ing-stick** a rod for scouring a gun. [Prob. M.Du. or M.L.G. *schūren* — O.Fr. *escurer* — L. *ex cūrāre,* take care of.]

scour[2] *skowr, v.i.* to rush or scurry along: to range about, esp. in quest or pursuit: to make off. — *v.t.* to range over or traverse swiftly, vigorously, riotously, or in pursuit: to search thoroughly: to molest as a scourer. — *n.* **scour'er** (*obs.* **scowr'er;** *hist.*) a member of a roistering band that scoured the streets, maltreating watchmen and others. [Poss. O.N. *skūr,* storm, shower; cf. **shower.**]

scourer[1] *skowr'ər, n.* a scout. [Aphetic; see **discover.**]

scourer[2]. See **scour**[1,2].

scourge *skûrj, n.* a whip: an instrument of divine punishment: a cause of widespread affliction. — *v.t.* to whip severely: to afflict. — *n.* **scourg'er.** [A.Fr. *escorge* — L. *excoriāre,* to flay — *corium,* leather (perh. as made f a strip of leather, perh. as a flaying instrument).]

~rie. See **scaury.**

scourse. See **scorse**[2].

scouse *skows,* (*coll.*) *n.* a native of Liverpool: the northern English dialect spoken in and around Liverpool: lobscouse. [Short for **lobscouse.**]

scout[1] *skowt, n.* watch, spying (*arch.*): one (or *obs.,* a party) sent out to bring in information: a spy: a member of the Scout Association (formerly **Boy Scout**): a patrolman on the roads: one who watches or attends at a little distance: a fielder, as in cricket: a person (usually term of approbation; *slang*): a person who seeks out new recruits, sales opportunities, etc.: a ship for reconnoitring: a small light aeroplane orig. intended for reconnaissance: a light armoured car for reconnaissance (now usu. **scout car**): a college servant at Oxford (perh. a different word; cf. Cambridge *gyp,* and Dublin *skip*). — *v.t.* to watch closely. — *v.i.* to act the scout: to reconnoitre (often with *about* or *around*). — *ns.* **scout'er** an adult working with instructors, etc., in the Scout Association; **scout'ing.** — **Scout Association** (formerly, the **Boy Scouts**) a worldwide movement for young people, intended to develop character and a sense of responsibility, founded (for boys) by Lord Baden-Powell in 1908; **scout's pace** alternately walking and running for a set number of paces; **scout car** see **scout** *n.*; **scout'craft** the knowledge and skill proper to a scout; **scout'-law** the code of rules of the Scout Association; **scout'-master** the leader of a band of scouts: formerly, an adult in charge of a troop of Boy Scouts. [O.Fr. *escoute* — *escouter* — L. *auscultāre,* to listen.]

scout[2] *skowt,* (*arch.*) *v.t.* to mock, flout: to dismiss or reject with disdain. [Cf. O.N. *skūta,* a taunt.]

scout[3]. Same as **scoot**[2].

scouth, scowth *skōōth, skowth,* (*Scot.*) *n.* free range: scope: plenty.

scouther, scowther *skow'dhər,* **scowder** *skow'dər,* (*Scot.*) *vs.t.* to scorch, singe: to overheat: to toast slightly: to blight. — *vs.i.* to drizzle: to theaten to rain or snow. — *ns.* a scorch or burn: a slight or flying shower. — *adjs.* **scou'thering, scow'dering** scorching, blighting. — *ns.* a scorching, blighting: a sprinkle of snow. — *adj.* **scou'thery.** [Conn. with **scald**[1].]

scow *skow, n.* a flat-bottomed boat. [Du. *schouw.*]

scowl *skowl, v.i.* to contract the brows in a look of baleful malevolence: to look gloomy and threatening. — *v.t.* (*Milt.*) to give forth with a scowl. — *n.* a scowling look. — *adj.* **scow'ling.** — *adv.* **scow'lingly.** [Cf. Dan. *skule,* to cast down the eyes, look sidelong.]

scowp, scowrer, scowth, scowther. See **scoup, scour**[2], **scouth, scouther.**

scowrie. See **scaury.**

scrab *skrab, v.t.* to scratch: — *pr.p.* **scrabb'ing;** *pa.p.* and *pa.t.* **scrabbed.** — *v.t.* and *v.i.* **scrabb'le** to scratch: to scrape: to scrawl. — *v.i.* to scramble. — *n.* a scrawl: (® with *cap.*) a word-building game. — *n.* **scrabb'ler.** [Du. *schrabben,* to scratch, freq. *schrabbelen;* cf. **scrape.**]

scrae *skrā,* (*Scott*) *n.* Same as **scree.**

scrag[1] *skrag, n.* a sheep's or (*slang*) human neck: the bony part of the neck: a lean person or animal. — *v.t.* to hang: to throttle: to wring the neck of: to tackle by the neck: — *pr.p.* **scragg'ing;** *pa.t.* and *pa.p.* **scragged.** — *adj.* **scragg'ed** (or *skragd*) scraggy. — *n.* **scragg'edness.** — *adv.* **scragg'ily.** — *n.* **scragg'iness.** — *adj.* **scragg'y** lean, skinny, and gaunt. — **scrag'-end'** the scrag of a neck. [Prob. **crag**[2].]

scrag[2] *skrag, n.* a stump: a rough projection. — *adjs.* **scragged, scragg'ling, scragg'ly, scragg'y** irregular, straggling. — *adv.* **scragg'ily.** — *n.* **scragg'iness.** — **scrag'-whale** a whale with knobbed back. [Cf. **scrog.**]

scraich, scraigh *skrāhh,* (*Scot.*) *v.i.* to screech: to make a scratchy sound. — *n.* a screech: a scratchy sound. [Cf. **scraugh, skreigh.**]

scram[1] *skram,* (*slang*) *v.i.* (esp. in the *imper.*) to be off: — *pr.p.* **scramm'ing;** *pa.t.* and *pa.p.* **scrammed.** [Perh. **scramble.**]

scram[2] *skram, adj.* (*S.W. England*) puny: withered. —

v.t. to benumb (*S.W. England*): to paralyse (*S.W. England*): to shut down (an atomic reactor), esp. in an emergency: — *pr.p.* **scramm'ing**; *pa.t.* and *pa.p.* **scrammed.** — *n.* **scram** atomic reactor shut-down. [Cf. **scrimp.**]

scramble *skram'bl, v.i.* to make one's way with disorderly struggling haste: to get along somehow: to clamber: to wriggle irregularly: to sprawl: to dash or struggle for what one can get before others: of an aircraft or its crew, to take off immediately, as in an emergency. — *v.t.* to throw down to be scrambled for: to put, make, get together, scramblingly: to jumble up (a message) so that it can be read only after decoding: to beat (eggs) up and heat to thickness with milk, butter etc.: to make (a radiotelephone conversation) unintelligible by a device that alters frequencies: to order (an aircraft-crew) to take off immediately. — *n.* act of scrambling: a disorderly performance: a dash or struggle for what can be had: an emergency take-off by an aircraft: a form of motor or motor-cycle trial. — *n.* **scram'bler** one who, or that which, scrambles, esp. a telephone device. — *adj.* **scram'bling** confused and irregular. — *n.* the action of the verb scramble: participation in motor-cycle, etc. scrambles. — *adv.* **scram'blingly.** — **scrambled eggs** eggs cooked as described above: the gold braid on a military officer's cap (*slang*). [Cf. the dialect verb *scramb*, to rake together with the hands.]

scramjet *skram'jet, n.* a jet engine in which the fuel burns at a supersonic speed. [*supersonic combustion ramjet.*]

scran *skran, n.* provisions: broken victuals. — **bad scran to you** (*Ir.*) bad fare to you. [Ety. dub.]

scranch *skranch, skransh, v.t.* to crunch. [Prob. imit.; cf. Du. *schransen*, to eat heartily.]

scrannel *skran'l*, (*arch.*) *adj.* thin: meagre: squeaking: grating, scratchy (*Milt.*). — *adj.* **scrann'y** thin, scrawny.

scrap[1] *skrap, n.* a small fragment: a piece of left-over food: a remnant: a punched-out picture, cutting, or the like, intended or suited for preservation in a scrap-book: residue after extraction of oil from blubber, fish, etc.: metal clippings or other waste: anything discarded as worn-out, out of date, or useless. — *adj.* consisting of scrap. — *v.t.* to consign to the scrap-heap: to discard: — *pr.p.* **scrapp'ing**; *pa.p.* and *pa.t.* **scrapped.** — *adv.* **scrapp'ily.** – *n.* **scrapp'iness.** — *adj.* **scrapp'y** fragmentary: disconnected: made up of scraps. — **scrap'-book** a blank book for pasting in scraps, cuttings, etc.; **scrap'-heap** a place where old iron is collected: rubbish-heap; **scrap'-iron, scrap'-metal** scraps of iron or other metal, of use only for remelting; **scrap'-man, scrap'-merchant** one who deals in scrap-metal; **scrap'-yard** a scrap-merchant's premises for the storing of scrap. — **not a scrap** not in the least; **throw on the scrap-heap** to reject as useless. [O.N. *skrap*, scraps; cf. **scrape.**]

scrap[2] *skrap,* (*slang*) *n.* a fight: scrimmage. — Also *v.i.* (*pr.p.* **scrapp'ing**; *pa.t.* and *pa.p.* **scrapped**). — *adj.* **scrapp'y** belligerent.

scrape *skrāp, v.t.* to press a sharp edge over: to move gratingly over: to smooth, clean, clear, reduce in thickness, abrade, remove, form, collect, bring, render, by such an action: to get together, collect by laborious effort (often *scrape together, scrape up*): to erase: contemptuously, to fiddle. — *v.i.* to graze: to scratch: to scratch the ground: to grate: to make a grating sound (as with the feet, in disapprobation): to draw back the foot in making obeisance: to fiddle: to save penuriously: to get with difficulty (with *through, along, home*, etc.). — *n.* an act, process, or spell of scraping: a shave: a stroke of the bow: a grating sound: a stroke (of a pen): a scraped place in the ground: an abrasion: a mass of earth scraped up, as by a rabbit: a backward movement of one foot accompanying a bow: a scraping or thin layer: thin-spread butter: a predicament that threatens disgrace or friction with authority. — *ns.* **scrāp'er** one who scrapes: a fiddler: a barber: a

scraping instrument or machine, esp. for shoe-soles, hides, roads: an engraver's tool: a scratching bird; **scrāp'ie** a virus disease of sheep causing acute itching, the animals rubbing against trees, etc. to relieve it; **scrāp'ing** the action of the verb: its sound: a piece scraped off. — **scrape'-good** (*arch.*) a miser; **scrape'-gut** (*arch.*) a fiddler; **scrape'-penny** (*arch.*) a miser; **scrap'er-board** a clay-surface board on which drawings can be made by scraping tints off as well as applying them: such a drawing: this method. — **bow and scrape** to be over-obsequious; **scrape acquaintance with** to contrive somehow to get on terms of acquaintance with; **scrape the bottom of the barrel** to utilise the very last of one's resources. [O.E. *scrapian* or O.N. *skrapa*.]

scrapie. See under **scrape.**

scrapple *skrap'al,* (*U.S.*) *n.* a type of meat loaf made with scraps of (or minced) meat, usu. pork, cornmeal, seasonings, etc., served sliced and fried. [**scrap[1]**.]

scrat *skrat,* (*obs.* or *dial.*) *v.t.* and *v.i.* to scratch. [M.E. *scratte*; origin doubtful.]

scratch *skrach, v.t.* to draw a sharp point over the surface of: to hurt, mark, render, seek to allay discomfort in, by so doing: to dig or scrape with the claws: to write hurriedly: to erase or delete (usu. with *out*): to strike along a rough surface: to withdraw from a competition. — *v.i.* to use the nails or claws: to scrape: to make a grating or screechy noise: to retire from a contest or engagement: to get (along or through) somehow (*coll.*). — *n.* an act, mark, or sound of scratching: a slight wound: a scrawl: the line up to which boxers are led — hence test, trial, as in *come up to* (*the*) *scratch* (q.v. below): the starting-point for a competitor without handicap: one who starts from scratch: a fluke, esp. in billiards: a scratch-wig: (in *pl.*) a disease in horses with the appearance of scratches on the pastern. — *adj.* improvised: casual: hastily or casually got together: without handicap. — *n.* **scratch'er.** — *adv.* **scratch'ily.** — *n.* **scratch'iness.** — *n.* and *adj.* **scratch'ing.** — *adv.* **scratch'ingly.** — *adjs.* **scratch'less; scratch'y** like scratches: uneven: ready or likely to scratch: grating or screechy: itchy. — **scratch'-back** a backscratcher: a toy that makes a sound of tearing cloth (*hist.*); **scratch'-brush** a wire brush; **scratch'-coat** a first coat of plaster; **scratch pad** a note-pad; **scratch test** (*med.*) a test for allergy to a certain substance, made by introducing it to an area of skin that has been scratched; **scratch'-wig** a wig that covers only part of the head; **scratch'-work** sgraffito in plaster. — **come up to** (**the**) **scratch** (*fig.*) to reach an expected standard: to fulfil an obligation; **start from scratch** (*fig.*) to start at the beginning: to embark on (a task, career, etc.) without any advantages or without any preparatory work having been done; **you scratch my back and I'll scratch yours** (*coll.*) do me a favour and I'll do you one in return. [Poss. M.E. *cracchen*, to scratch, modified by **scrat**.]

Scratch *skrach, n.* the Devil (also **Old Scratch**). [Cf. O.N. *skratte*, goblin, monster.]

scrattle *skrat'l,* (*W. of England*) *v.i.* to keep scratching: to scuttle. [Freq. of **scrat**.]

scraugh, scrauch *skröhh,* (*Scot.*) *n.* a raucous squawk. — *v.i.* to make a scraugh. [Imit.]

scraw *skrö,* (*arch.*) *n.* a thin sod or turf. [Ir. *sgrath*.]

scrawl *skröl, v.t.* and *v.i.* to make or write irregularly or hastily: to scribble. — *n.* irregular, hasty, or bad writing: a letter, etc., written thus: a small crab (*Lincolnshire; Tennyson*). — *n.* **scrawl'er.** — *n.* and *adj.* **scrawl'ing.** — *adv.* **scrawl'ingly.** — *adj.* **scrawl'y.** [Perh. conn. with **crawl[1]** or **sprawl**.]

scrawm *skröm,* (*dial.*) *v.t.* to scratch. [Prob. Du. *schrammen*, to graze.]

scrawny *skröni,* (orig. *U.S.*) *adj.* lean, meagre.

scray, scraye *skrā, n.* the tern. [Cf. W. *ysgräell*.]

screak *skrēk,* (*dial.*) *v.t.* to screech: to creak. — *n.* a screech: a creak. — *adj.* **screak'y.** [Cf. O.N. *skrækja*.]

scream *skrēm, v.t.* and *v.i.* to cry out in a loud shrill voice, as in fear or pain: to laugh shrilly and uncontrolledly:

to shriek. — *v.i.* (of colours) to be acutely inharmonious (*coll.*): to be all too loudly evident (*coll.*): to move with a screaming noise. — *n.* a shrill, sudden cry, as in fear or pain: a shriek: a loud whistling sound: anything or anyone supposed to make one scream with laughter (*coll.*). — *n.* **scream′er** one who screams: a large spur-winged S. American bird (Anhima, *horned screamer*; Chauna, *crested* and *black-necked screamer*) with loud harsh cry: a different S. American bird, the seriema (sometimes known as *crested screamer*): anything likely or intended to thrill with emotion, as a sensational headline (*slang*): an exclamation mark (*slang*). — *adj.* **scream′ing.** — *adv.* **scream′ingly.** — **screaming farce** one highly ludicrous; **screaming habdabs, abdabs** see **habdabs**; **screaming meemies** (U.S. nickname for German shells in World War I), hysterical fear or wild attack of nerves. [Late O.E. *scrǣmen.*]

scree *skrē, n.* a sloping mass of débris at the base of a cliff. [O.N. *skritha*, a landslip — *skrītha*, to slide.]

screech *skrēch, v.i.* to give forth a harsh, shrill, and sudden cry or noise. — *v.t.* to utter in such tones. — *n.* a harsh, shrill, and sudden cry: a strident creak: a screeching or screaming bird (as barn-owl, swift, missel-thrush). — *n.* **screech′er** one who screeches: the swift or other screeching bird. — *adj.* **screech′y** shrill and harsh, like a screech. — **screech′-hawk** the nightjar; **screech′-martin** the swift; **screech′-owl** the barn-owl: a bringer of bad news; **screech′-thrush** the missel-thrush: the fieldfare. [M.E. *scrichen*; cf. **scritch.**]

screed *skrēd, n.* a shred: a strip: a border: a long effusion, spoken or written: a drinking bout (*obs.*): a band of plaster laid on the surface of a wall as a guide to the thickness of a coat of plaster to be applied subsequently (*building*): a layer of mortar finishing off the surface of a floor (also **screed′ing**): a strip of wood or metal temporarily inserted in a road surface to form a guide for the template for forming the final surface of the road (*civil engineering*): a rent, a tear (*Scot.*). — *v.t.* to repeat glibly. — *v.i.* to rend. — *n.* **screed′er** a person whose job is to lay screeds on floors or walls. [O.E. *scrēade*, shred.]

screen *skrēn, n.* a shield against danger, observation, wind, heat, light, or other outside influence: a piece of room furniture in the form of a folding framework or of a panel on a stand: a clothes-horse (*Scot.*): a protection against wind on a vehicle: a large scarf: a sheltering row of trees: a body of troops or formation of ships intended as a cover: a wall masking a building: a partial partition cutting off part of a room, a church choir, or side chapel: a coarse sifting apparatus: a net-ruled plate for half-tone photography: a mosaic of primary colours for colour photography: a white sheet or the like on which images may be projected: hence, the cinematograph: a white erection against which the batsman sees the bowler (*cricket*): a screen grid. — *v.t.* to shelter or conceal: to sift coarsely: to sort out by, or subject to, tests of ability, desirability, etc.: to test for illness, etc.: to protect from stray electrical interference: to prevent from causing outside electrical interference: to project or exhibit on a screen or on the screen: to make a motion-picture of. — *v.i.* to show up on, or be suitable for, the screen. — *ns.* **screen′er; screen′ing.** — *n.pl.* **screen′ings** material eliminated by sifting. — **screen′craft** the technique of making films; **screen grid** an electrode placed between the control grid and anode in a valve, having an invariable potential to eliminate positive feedback and instability; **screen′play** the written text for a film, with dialogue, stage-directions, and descriptions of characters and setting; **screen printing, screen process** see **silk-screen printing; screen test** one to determine whether an actor or actress is suitable for cinema work; **screen′-wiper** a contrivance for wiping the windscreen of a car in rain; **screen′-writer** a writer of screenplays. — **screen off** to hide behind, or separate by, a screen: to separate by sifting; [App. related in some way to

O.Fr. *escran* (Fr. *écran*), which may be — O.H.G. *skirm, skerm* (Ger. *Schirm*).]

screeve *skrēv*, (*slang*) *v.t.* and *v.i.* to write, esp. begging letters: to draw on the pavement. — *n.* piece of writing: begging letter. — *ns.* **screev′er; screev′ing.** [Prob. It. *scrivere* — L. *scrībĕre*, to write.]

screich, screigh. See **skreigh.**

screw *skrōō, n.* a cylinder with a helical groove or (the *thread*) ridge, used as a fastening driven into wood, etc. by rotation (a *male screw*; for *female screw*, see **female**), as a mechanical power, and otherwise: anything of similar form: a screw-propeller or ship driven by one: a thumbscrew: a corkscrew: a twisted cone of paper, or portion of a commodity contained in it: a turn of the screw: pressure (*fig.*): a twist: a spin imparted to a ball: a stingy fellow, an extortioner, a skinflint (*slang*): a prison officer (*slang*): a broken-winded horse: an act of sexual intercourse (*vulg.*): salary, wages (*coll.*). — *v.t.* to fasten, tighten, compress, force, adjust, extort by a screw, a screwing motion, or as if by a screw: to apply a screw to: to twist: to turn in the manner of a screw: to pucker: to summon up (courage, etc.; with *up*): to have sexual intercourse with (*vulg.*): to practise extortion upon: to cheat (*slang*): to disrupt, spoil (often with *up*; *coll.*): to enter by means of a skeleton key (*slang*): to burgle (*slang*). — *v.i.* to admit of screwing: to wind: to worm: to have sexual intercourse (*vulg.*). — *adj.* **screwed** (*slang*) tipsy. — *n.* **screw′er.** — *n.* and *adj.* **screw′ing.** — *adv.* **screw′-wise.** — *adj.* **screwy** exacting: close: worthless: tipsy: eccentric, slightly mad: fishy, not quite normal or honest. — **screw′ball** (*U.S.*) a ball in baseball that breaks contrary to its swerve: a crazy person, an eccentric. — Also *adj.* — **screw′-bolt** a bolt with a screw-thread; **screw′-cap** a lid that screws on to a container. — *adj.* **screw′-down** closed by screwing. — **screw′driver** an instrument for turning and driving screws; **screw eye** a screw formed into a loop for attaching rope, wire, etc.; **screw jack** a jack for lifting heavy weights, operated by a screw; **screw′-nail** a nail made in the form of a screw; **screw′-pile** a pile for sinking into the ground, ending in a screw; **screw′-pine** a plant of the genus Pandanus or its family — from the screw-like arrangement of the leaves; **screw′-plate** a plate of steel with holes for cutting screw-threads; **screw′-press** a press worked by a screw; **screw′-propell′er** a propeller with helical blades; **screw′-steam′er** a steamer driven by screw; **screw′-thread** the ridge of a screw; **screw′top** a bottle with a stopper that screws in or on, esp. a beer-bottle of the kind with its contents; **screw′-worm** a larva which develops under the skin of various animals, often causing death; **screw′-wrench** a tool for gripping screw-heads. — **a screw loose** something defective (esp. mentally); **put on, turn, the screw** to apply pressure progressively: to exact payment; **put the screws on** to coerce; **screw it, them, you,** etc. (*vulg. slang*) an interjection expressing disgust, scorn, frustration, etc. [Earlier *scrue*; app. O.Fr. *escroue*, of obscure origin; prob. conn. with L.G. *schrûve*, Ger. *Schraube*.]

scribable, scribacious, etc. See **scribe.**

scribble[1] *skrib′l, v.t.* to scrawl: to write badly, carelessly, or worthlessly (in handwriting or substance). — *n.* careless writing: a scrawl. — *ns.* **scribb′lement; scribb′ler** a petty author; **scribb′ling.** — *adv.* **scribb′lingly.** — *adj.* **scribb′ly.** — **scribb′ling-book, -pad, -paper.** [A freq. of **scribe**, or L.L. *scrībillāre* — L. *scrībĕre*, to write.]

scribble[2] *skrib′l, v.t.* to card roughly. — *ns.* **scribb′ler** a carding machine: one who tends it; **scribb′ling.** [Prob. from L.G.]

scribe *skrīb, n.* an expounder and teacher of the Mosaic and traditional law (*B.*): a writer: a public or official writer: a clerk, amanuensis, secretary: a copyist: a penman: a pointed instrument to mark lines on wood, metal, etc. — *v.t.* to mark, score with a scribe, etc.: to fit by so marking: to incise: to write. — *v.i.* to play the scribe. — *adjs.* **scrī'bable** capable of being written upon; **scribā'cious** (*arch.*) given to writing. — *n.* (*arch.*) **scribā'ciousness.** — *adj.* **scrī'bal.** — *ns.* **scrī'ber** a scribing tool, a scribe; **scrī'bing; scrī'bism.** [L. *scrība*, a scribe, and *scrībēre*, to write.]

scriech. See **skreigh.**

scriene (*Spens.*). Same as **screen.**

scrieve *skrēv*, (*Scot.*) *v.i.* to glide swiftly along. [Prob. O.N. *skrefa* — *skref*, stride.]

scrieve-board. See **scrive.**

scriggle *skrig'l*, *v.i.* to writhe: to wriggle. — *n.* a wriggling. — *adj.* **scrigg'ly.** [Cf. **struggle.**]

scrike *skrīk*, (*Spens.*) *v.i.* to shriek. — *n.* (*obs.*) a shriek. [Prob. Scand.]

scrim *skrim*, *n.* open fabric used in upholstery, bookbinding, for curtains, etc. [Ety. obscure.]

scrimmage *skrim'ij*, **scrummage** *skrum'ij*, *ns.* a tussle: a scrum. — *v.i.* to take part in a scrimmage. — *ns.* **scrimm'ager, scrumm'ager.** [See **skirmish.**]

scrimp *skrimp*, *adj.* scanty: stinted. — *adv.* (*obs.*) barely. — *v.t.* to stint: to keep short. — *v.i.* to be sparing or niggardly. — *adj.* **scrimped** pinched. — *adv.* **scrimp'ily.** — *n.* **scrimp'iness.** — *adv.* **scrimp'ly** sparingly: scarcely. — *n.* **scrimp'ness.** — *adj.* **scrimp'y** scanty. [Cf. Sw. and Dan. *skrumpen*, shrivelled, O.E. *scrimman*, to shrink.]

scrimshander, scrimshandy. See **scrimshaw.**

scrimshank. Same as **skrimshank.**

scrimshaw *skrim'shö*, *n.* a sailor's spare-time handicraft, as engraving fanciful designs on shells, whales' teeth, etc.: anything so executed. — Also **scrim'shander, scrim'shandy.** — *v.t.* and *v.i.* to work or decorate in this way. — *n.* **scrim'shoner** one who does scrimshaw. [Origin obscure.]

scrimure *skrīm'yər*, (*Shak.*) *n.* a fencer. [Fr. *escrimeur*.]

scrine, scryne *skrīn*, (*Spens.*) *n.* a chest for records: a shrine. [O.Fr. *escrin* — L. *scrīnium*, a chest; cf. **shrine.**]

scrip¹ *skrip*, *n.* a writing: a scrap of paper or of writing: (for *subscription*) a preliminary certificate, as for shares allotted: share certificates, or shares or stock collectively: paper money less than a dollar (*U.S. hist.*): a dollar bill, money (*old U.S. slang*): a paper token issued instead of currency in special e.g. emergency circumstances (*U.S.*). — *n.* **scripoph'ily** the collecting of bond and share certificates, esp. those of historical, etc., interest: the items thus collected. — *ns.* **scrip'ophile, scripoph'ilist.** — **scrip** issue a bonus issue (q.v. at **bonus**). [**script, subscription;** partly perh. **scrap¹.**]

scrip² *skrip*, *n.* a small bag: a satchel: a pilgrim's pouch. — *n.* **scripp'age** (*Shak.*) contents of a scrip. [Cf. O.N. *skreppa*, a bag, and O.Fr. *escrep(p)e*.]

script *skript*, *n.* a writing: an original document (*law*): a list of actors and their parts (*Shak.*): the actors', director's, etc., written copy of the text of a play: a text for broadcasting: handwriting, system or style of handwriting: scenario (*cinema*): handwriting in imitation of type: type in imitation of handwriting: (also **'script**) short for *manuscript* or *typescript*: a set of characters used in writing a language (as *Cyrillic script*). — *v.t.* to write a script for, or make a script from, esp. for broadcasting or the theatre or cinema. — **script'writer.** [L. *scrīptum* — *scrībēre*, to write.]

scriptorium *skrip-tō'ri-əm*, *-tō'ri-əm*, *n.* a writing-room, esp. in a monastery: — *pl.* **scripto'ria.** — *adjs.* **scripto'rial; scrip'tory** (*-tər-i*) by, in, or relating to writing. [L. *scrīptōrium* — *scrībēre*.]

scripture *skrip'chər*, *n.* handwriting: something written: (in *sing.* or *pl.*) sacred writings of a religion, esp. (*cap.*) the Bible: a biblical text (*rare*). — Also *adj.* — *adj.* **scrip'tural** of, in, warranted by Scripture: of writing. — *ns.* **scrip'turalism** literal adherence to the Scriptures; **scrip'turalist** a literalist in obedience to the letter of Scripture: a student of Scripture (*obs.*). — *adv.* **scrip'turally.** — *ns.* **scrip'turism; scrip'turist** one versed in Scripture: one who bases his belief on the Bible and the Bible alone. — **scrip'ture-read'er** one who read the

Bible in cottages, barracks, etc., to those who could not read for themselves. [L. *scrīptūra* — *scrībēre*, to write.]

scritch *skrich*, *n.* a screech. — *v.t.* and *v.i.* to screech. — **scritch'-owl.** [See **screech.**]

scrive *skrīv*, (*arch.*) *v.t.* to describe: to scribe. — **scrive'=board, scrieve'-board** a shipbuilder's drawing-board.

scrivener *skriv'nər*, (*obs.*) *n.* a scribe: a copyist: one who draws up contracts, etc.: one who lays out money at interest for others. — *ns.* **scriv'enership; scriv'ening** writing. — **scrivener's palsy** writer's cramp. [O.Fr. *escrivain* (Fr. *écrivain*) — L.L. *scrībānus* — L. *scrība*, a scribe.]

scrobe *skrōb*, *n.* a groove. — *adj.* **scrobic'ulate** (*skrob-*) pitted. [L. *scrobis*, a ditch.]

scroddled *skrod'ld*, *adj.* (of pottery) made of clay scraps of different colours. [Cf. L.G. *schrodel*, scrap.]

scrofula *skrof'ū-lə*, *n.* tuberculosis, esp. of the lymphatic glands, called also king's evil. — *adj.* **scrof'ulous.** [L. *scrōfulae* — *scrōfa*, a sow (supposed to be liable to it).]

scrog *skrog*, (*Scot.*) *n.* a stunted bush or small tree: a crab-apple, fruit or tree: a bushy place: scrubby wood: a broken branch: a branch (*her.*). — *adj.* **scrogg'ie, scrogg'y** covered with scrogs: stunted. — **scrog'-apple; scrog'-bush (-buss).** [Origin obscure.]

scroll *skrōl*, *n.* a roll of paper, parchment, etc.: a ribbon-like strip, partly coiled or curved, often bearing a motto: a writing in the form of a roll: a rough draft: a schedule: a spiral ornament or part, such as a flourish to a signature representing a seal. — *v.t.* to set in a scroll: to draft. — *v.i.* to curl. — *v.t.* (*comput.*) to move (a text) up or down or from side to side in order to view data that cannot all be seen on a VDU at the same time. — *v.i.* (*comput.*) of a text, to move in such a way. — *adj.* **scrolled** formed into a scroll: ornamented with scrolls. — *ns.* **scroll'ery, scroll'work** ornament in scrolls. — *adv.* **scroll'wise.** — **scroll'-saw** a saw for cutting scrolls. [Earlier **scrowl(e)**, formed (perh. as dim.) from **scrow.**]

scrooge. See **scrouge.**

Scrooge *skrōōj*, *n.* a miser. [From Ebenezer Scrooge in Dickens's *Christmas Carol*.]

scroop *skrōōp*, (*dial.*) *n.* a scraping noise. — *v.i.* to make a scroop. [Imit.]

Scrophularia *skrof-ū-lā'ri-ə*, *n.* the figwort genus, giving name to the **Scrophulariaceae** (*-lar-i-ā'si-ē*), a family of sympetalous dicotyledons with zygomorphic flowers, including foxglove, mullein, speedwell, eyebright: (without *cap.*) a plant of this genus. — *adj.* **scrophulariā'ceous.** [L. *scrōfulae*, as reputedly cure for scrofula (q.v.).]

scrotum *skrō'təm*, *n.* the bag that contains the testicles. — *adj.* **scrō'tal.** [L. *scrōtum*.]

scrouge, scrowdge *skrowj*, **scrooge** *skrōōj*, *vs.t.* and *vs.i.* to squeeze: to crowd. — *n.* **scroug'er** (*U.S. arch.*) a whopper: something large. [Cf. **scruze.**]

scrounge *skrownj*, (*orig. mil. slang*) *v.t.* to purloin: to cadge. — *v.i.* to hunt around: to sponge. — *ns.* **scroung'er; scroung'ing.** [Origin doubtful.]

scrow *skrō*, *n.* a scroll: a writing: a hide clipping. [A.Fr. *escrowe*; see **escroll, escrow, scroll.**]

scrowdge. See **scrouge.**

scrowl, scrowle *skrōl*, old spellings of **scroll.**

scroyle *skroil*, (*Shak.*) *n.* a wretch. [Origin doubtful.]

scrub¹ *skrub*, *v.t.* to rub hard: to wash by hard rubbing with a stiff brush: to purify (*gas-making*): to cancel (*slang*). — *v.i.* to use a scrubbing-brush: to drudge: to make a rapid to-and-fro movement as if with a scrubbing-brush: — *pr.p.* **scrubb'ing;** *pa.t.* and *pa.p.* **scrubbed.** — *n.* an act of scrubbing: a worn or short-bristled brush or broom: a drudge. — *ns.* **scrubb'er** one who scrubs: apparatus for freeing gas from tar, ammonia, and sulphuretted hydrogen: any device that filters out impurities: an unattractive woman or one with loose morals (*slang*); **scrubb'ing.** — **scrubb'ing=board** a washing-board; **scrubb'ing-brush** a brush with short stiff bristles for scrubbing floors, etc. — **scrub**

round (*slang*) to cancel: to ignore intentionally; **scrub up** of a surgeon, to wash the hands and arms thoroughly before performing an operation. [Perh. obs. Du. *schrubben*, or a corresponding lost O.E. word.]

scrub² *skrub*, *n.* a stunted tree: stunted trees and shrubs collectively: brushwood: country covered with bushes or low trees, esp. the Australian evergreen xerophytic dwarf forest or bush of Eucalyptus, Acacia, etc.: hence, a remote place, far from civilisation (*Austr. coll.*): an undersized or inferior animal, esp. one of indefinite breed: a player in a second or inferior team: a team of inferior players, or one with too few players: an insignificant or mean person: anything small or mean. — *adj.* mean: insignificant: undersized: (of a team) improvised, hastily got together for the occasion: (of a player) in a second or inferior team. — *adj.* **scrubb′ed** (*Shak.*) stunted. — *n.* **scrubb′er** (*Austr.*) an animal that has run wild. — *adj.* **scrubb′y** stunted: covered with scrub: mean. — **scrub′-bird** an elusive Australian bird (*Atrichomis*); **scrub′land** an area covered with scrub; **scrub′-rider** one who looks for cattle that stray into the scrub; **scrub′-turkey, -fowl** a mound-bird; **scrub′ty′phus** a typhus-like disease transmitted by a mite. — **the Scrubs** coll. abbrev. for **Wormwood Scrubs**, an English prison. [A variant of **shrub¹**.]

scruff¹ *skruf*, *n.* the nape of the neck.   [See **scuft**.]

scruff² *skruf*, *n.* scurf: an untidy, dirty person (*coll.*). — *n.* **scruff′iness**. — *adj.* **scruff′y** scurvy: untidy, dirty (*coll.*).   [**scurf**.]

scrum *skrum*, *n.* a scrimmage: a closing-in of rival forwards round the ball on the ground, or in readiness for its being inserted (by the scrum-half) between the two compact pushing masses (*Rugby*). — *v.i.* to form a scrum: — *pr.p.* **scrumm′ing**; *pa.t.* and *pa.p.* **scrummed**. — **scrum′-half** (*Rugby*) a half-back whose duty it is to put the ball into the scrum and secure it as soon as it emerges therefrom. [Abbreviation of **scrummage**; see **scrimmage, skirmish**.]

scrummage. See **scrimmage**.

scrummy. See **scrumptious**.

scrump, skrump *skrump*, **skrimp** *skrimp*, (*dial.*) *vs.t.* to shrivel up: to gather windfalls, hence to raid orchards. — *ns.* anything shrivelled, small or undersized, esp. an apple: an undersized person. — *n.* **scrump′y** cider made from small, sweet apples.   [See **scrimp**.]

scrumptious *skrump′shəs*, (*slang*) *adj.* delightful: delicious. — Also **scrumm′y**. — *adv.* **scrump′tiously**. [Origin uncertain.]

scrumpy. See **scrump**.

scrunch *skrunch*, *skrunsh*, variant of **crunch**. — *adj.* **scrunch′y**.

scrunt *skrunt*, (*Scot.*) *n.* anything stunted (as an apple, a tree) or worn: a niggard. — *adj.* **scrunt′y**.

scruple *skrōō′pl*, *n.* a small weight. — in apothecaries' weight, 20 grains: a sexagesimal division, as a minute of time or arc (*obs.*): a very small quantity (*arch.*): a difficulty or consideration, usu. moral, obstructing action, esp. one turning on a fine point or one that is baseless: a doubt, disbelief, or difficulty: protest, demur: scrupulousness. — *v.i.* to hesitate from a scruple. — *v.t.* to cause to feel scruples (*obs.*): to question, doubt (*arch.*): to have scruples about (*arch.* when followed by noun, but current followed by infinitive). — *ns.* **scru′pler; scrupulosity** (-*pū-los′i-ti*). — *adj.* **scru′pulous** directed by scruples: having scruples, doubts, or objections: conscientious: cautious: exact: captious. — *adv.* **scru′pulously**. — *n.* **scru′-pulousness**. — **make no scruple(s), make scruples, about** (formerly **to, at**) to offer (no) moral objections to. [L. *scrūpulus*, dim. of *scrūpus*, a sharp stone, anxiety.]

scrutiny *skrōō′ti-ni*, *n.* a vote by poll: close, careful, or minute investigation or examination: a searching look: official examination of votes: examination of the catechumens (*hist.*). — *adj.* **scru′table** accessible to scrutiny. — *ns.* **scrutā′tor** a close examiner: a scrutineer; **scrutineer′** one who makes a scrutiny, esp. of votes. — *v.t.* and *v.i.* **scru′tinise, -ize** to examine closely.

— *n.* **scru′tiniser, -z-**. — *adj.* **scru′tinising, -z-**. — *adv.* **scru′tinisingly, -z-**. — *adj.* **scru′tinous**. — *adv.* **scru′-tinously**. — **scrutin de liste** (*skrü-tɔ̃̃ də lēst*; Fr.) a method of voting for the French Chamber of Deputies, in which the voter casts his ballot for any combination of the whole number of candidates for the department — opp. to **scrutin d'arrondissement** (*dar-ɔ̃-dēs-mä*), in which method he votes only for his local candidates. [L. *scrūtinium*, and *scrūtāri*, to search even to the rags — *scrūta*, rags, trash.]

scruto *skrōō′tō*, (*theat.*) *n.* a kind of stage trap-door: — *pl.* **scru′tos**.   [Origin obscure.]

scrutoire *skrōō-twär′, -tōr′, -tör′, n.* Same as **escritoire**.

scruze *skrōōz*, (*Spens.*) now *dial.*) *v.t.* to squeeze.   [Perh. **screw** combined with **squeeze**.]

scry *skrī*, *v.t.* to descry (*arch.* and *dial.*). — *v.i.* to practise crystal-gazing: — *pr.p.* **scry′ing**; *pa.t.* and *pa.p.* **scried**, (*Spens.*) **scryde**. — *ns.* **scry′er; scry′ing**.   [Aphetic for **descry**.]

scryne (*Spens.*). Same as **scrine**.

scuba *skōō′bə, skū′, n.* a device used by skin-divers. — Also *adj.* — **scu′ba-diver; scu′ba-diving**.   [self-contained *u*nderwater *b*reathing *a*pparatus.]

scuchin, scuchion. Spenserian forms of **scutcheon**.

scud¹ *skud*, *v.i.* to sweep along easily and swiftly: to drive before the wind. — *v.t.* to traverse swiftly: — *pr.p.* **scudd′ing**; *pa.t.* and *pa.p.* **scudd′ed**. — *n.* act of scudding: driving cloud, shower or spray: a gust: a swift runner (*school slang*). — *n.* **scudd′er**. — *v.t.* **scudd′le** to scuttle.   [Perh. Du. or L.G.]

scud² *skud*, (*Scot.*) *v.t.* to slap, spank: — *pr.p.* **scudd′ing**; *pa.t.* and *pa.p.* **scudd′ed**. — *n.* a slap: (in *pl.*) a spanking.

scud³ *skud*, (*Scot.*) *n.* a state of nudity. — **in the scud** naked, without clothes.   [Origin obscure.]

scuddaler, scudler. Same as **skudler**.

scuddle. See **scud¹**.

scudo *skōō′dō*, *n.* an old Italian silver coin: — *pl.* **scu′di** (-*dē*).   [It., — L. *scūtum*, a shield.]

scuff¹ *skuf*, *n.* a form of **scruff¹** or **scuft**.

scuff² *skuf*, *v.t.* and *v.i.* to shuffle: to brush, graze, touch lightly: to abrade: to make or become shabby by wear. — *v.t.* to cuff. — *n.* (*Scot.*) a glancing touch or blow or its sound. — *adv.* (*arch.*) with a scuff. — *v.i.* **scuff′le** to struggle confusedly: to shuffle. — *v.t.* to hoe, scarify: to shuffle: to poke at, scuff, with the foot (*U.S.*): (of esp. money) to gather, scrape together (with *up* or *up on*; *U.S.*). — *n.* a confused struggle: a thrust-hoe (*U.S.*): an agricultural scuffler. — *n.* **scuff′ler** one who scuffles: an implement for scarifying the soil. — *adj.* **scuff′y** (*Scot.*) shabby: rubbed, abraded: with the sound of a light rubbing.   [Cf. Sw. *skuffa*, to shove; Du. *schoffelen*; **shove, shovel, shuffle**.]

scuft *skuft*, (*dial.*) *n.* the nape of the neck. — Also **scuff, scruff**.   [Poss. O.N. *skopt, skoft*, the hair.]

scug. See **skug¹**.

scul, scull, sculle *skul*, (*Shak., Milt.*) *n. obs.* spellings of **school²**.

sculdudd(e)ry, skulduddery *skul-dud′(ə-)ri*, (*Scot., facet.*) *n.* breach of chastity: bawdy talk or writing. — *adj.* bawdy. — *n.* **sculduggery**, more usu. **skulduggery**, (-*dug′*) (perh. a different word) underhand malpractices.   [Origin obscure.]

sculk. Obs. spelling of **skulk**.

scull¹ *skul*, *n.* a short, light spoon-bladed oar for one hand: an oar used over the stern: a small, light rowing-boat propelled by sculls: an act or spell of sculling: (in *pl.*) a race between small, light rowing-boats rowed by one person. — *v.t.* to propel with sculls, or with one oar worked like a screw over the stern. — *v.i.* to use sculls. — *ns.* **scull′er** one who sculls: a small boat pulled by one man with a pair of sculls; **scull′ing**. — **scull′ing-boat**.   [Origin obscure.]

scull², **skull** *skul*, *n.* a shallow basket for fish, etc.   [Poss. O.N. *skjōla*, pail.]

scull³. Obs. spelling of **skull¹**.

scull⁴, sculle. See **scul**.

scullery *skul′ər-i, n.* a room for rough kitchen work, as cleaning of utensils. — **scull′ery-maid.** [O.Fr. *escuelerie* — L. *scutella*, a tray.]

scullion *skul′yən*, (*arch.*) *n.* a servant for drudgery: a mean, contemptible person. — *adj.* base. [Poss. O.Fr. *escouillon*, a dish-clout — L. *scōpa*, a broom; or from Fr. *souillon*, scullion, influenced by **scullery.**]

sculp *skulp*, *v.t.* and *v.i.* to carve: to engrave: to sculpture. [L. *sculpĕre*; not a back-formation from **sculptor, sculpture.**]

sculpin *skul′pin*, *n.* the dragonet: a marine Cottus or other large-headed, spiny, useless fish (*U.S.*): a good-for-nothing person or animal (*slang*). [Poss. **Scorpaena.**]

sculpsit *skulp′sit*, *skōōlp′sit*, (L.) (he) sculptured (this), sometimes appended to the signature of the sculptor.

sculpt *skulpt*, *v.t.* and *v.i.* to sculpture: to carve. [Fr. *sculpter* — L. *sculpĕre*, to carve; not, as commonly thought, a back-formation from **sculptor, sculpture.**]

sculptor *skulp′tər*, *n.* an artist in carving: a statuary: — *fem.* **sculp′tress.** — *adj.* **sculp′tural** (-*chər-əl*). — *adv.* **sculp′turally.** — *n.* **sculp′ture** the act of carving, esp. in stone: extended to clay-modelling or moulding for casting: work, or a piece of work, in this kind: engraving (*obs.*): shaping in relief: spines, ridges, etc., standing out from the surface (*biol.*). — *v.t.* to carve: to represent in sculpture: to shape in relief: to mark with sculpturings: to mould, or form, so as to have the appearance, or (*fig.*) other quality, of sculpture: to modify the form of (the earth's surface). — *adjs.* **sculp′tured** carved: engraved: (of features) fine and regular: having elevations on the surface (*bot., zool.*); **sculpturesque′** statue-like. — *n.* **sculp′turing.** [L. *sculptor, -ōris, sculptūra* — *sculpĕre, sculptum*, to carve.]

scum *skum*, *n.* foam or froth: matter coming to or floating on the surface: offscourings of the population i.e. worthless people, or person. — *v.t.* to skim. — *v.i.* to form, throw up a scum: — *pr.p.* **scumm′ing;** *pa.t.* and *pa.p.* **scummed.** — *n.* **scumm′er** a skimming instrument. — *n.pl.* **scumm′ings** skimmings. — *adj.* **scumm′y.** **scum′bag** (*slang*) a condom: a general term of abuse. [Cf. Dan. *skum*, Ger. *Schaum*, foam.]

scumber *skum′bər*, (*arch.*) *v.t.* and *v.i.* to defecate (of dog or fox). — *n.* dung. — Also **skumm′er.** [Prob. O.Fr. *descumbrer*, to disencumber.]

scumble *skum′bl*, *v.t.* to soften the effect of by a very thin coat of opaque or semi-opaque colour, or by light rubbing or by applying paint with a dry brush. — *n.* colour so laid: the effect so produced. — *n.* **scum′bling.** [Freq. of **scum.**]

scumfish. Same as **scomfish.**

scuncheon, sconcheon, scontion *skun′, skon′shən, n.* the inner part of a jamb. [O.Fr. *escoinson.*]

scunge *skunj*, (*dial.*) *v.i.* to slink about: to scrounge. — Also *v.t.* — *n.* a scrounger: a dirty, sneaky person: accumulated sticky dirt (*Austr.* and *N.Z.*). — *adj.* **scun′gy** (*Austr.* and *N.Z.*) dirty: unkempt: sordid: mean. [Cf. **scrounge.**]

scunner *skun′ər*, (*Scot.*) *v.i.* to take a loathing. — *v.t.* to excite a loathing in: to disgust, nauseate. — *n.* a loathing: an object, or a manifestation, of loathing. — **take a scunner to** to take a strong dislike to. [Perh. M.E. *scurn*, to shrink; origin unknown.]

scup *skup*, **scuppaug** *skup′ōg*, or *-ŏg′, ns.* the porgy. [Narraganset *mishcuppauog.*]

scupper[1] *skup′ər, n.* a hole to drain a ship's deck. [Origin disputed.]

scupper[2] *skup′ər*, (*slang*) *v.t.* to slaughter: to do for: to ruin: to sink (a ship). [Perh. conn. with above.]

scuppernong *skup′ər-nong, n.* a grape from the *Scuppernong* river, N. Carolina: wine from it.

scur *skûr.* Same as **skirr.**

scurf *skûrf, n.* small flakes or scales of dead skin, esp. on the scalp: a crust of branny scales: an incrustation. — *n.* **scurf′iness.** — *adj.* **scurf′y.** [O.E. *scurf, sceorf.*]

scurrier. See **scurriour.**

scurril(e) *skur′il, adj.* (*arch.*) like or worthy of a vulgar buffoon: indecently opprobrious or jocular. — *n.*

scurril′ity. — *adj.* **scurr′ilous** indecently abusive. — *adv.* **scurr′ilously.** — *n.* **scurr′ilousness.** [L. *scurrīlis* — *scurra*, a buffoon.]

scurriour, scurrier *skur′i-ər*, (*obs.*) *n.* a scout. [See **discoverer.**]

scurry, skurry *skur′i*, *v.i.* to hurry briskly or flutteringly: to scuttle. — *n.* flurried haste: a flurry. [From **hurry-skurry,** reduplication of **hurry;** or back-formation of **scurrier;** or from **scour**[2].]

scurvy *skûr′vi, adj.* scurfy: shabby: vile, contemptible. — *n.* a disease marked by bleeding and sponginess of the gums, due to lack of fresh vegetables and consequently of vitamin C. — *adv.* **scur′vily** in a scurvy manner: meanly, basely. — *n.* **scur′viness.** — **scur′vy-grass** a cruciferous plant (*Cochlearia officinalis*) used by sailors as an anti-scorbutic: ale medicated with it. [**scurf;** the application to the disease helped by similarity of sound; see **scorbutic.**]

scuse, 'scuse *skūs, n.* and *skūz, v.t.* aphetic for **excuse.**

scut *skut, n.* a short erect tail like a hare's: a hare: a contemptuous term for a (small) person (*dial.*). [Origin obscure.]

scuta. See **scute.**

scutage *skū′tij,* (*hist.*) *n.* a tax on a knight's fee, esp. one in lieu of personal service. [L.L. *scūtāgium* — L. *scūtum*, shield.]

scutal, scutate. See **scute.**

scutch[1] *skuch, v.t.* to dress (e.g. flax) by beating: to switch. — *n.* a tool for dressing flax, a swingle: a bricklayer's cutting tool. — *ns.* **scutch′er** a person, tool, or part of a machine that scutches: the striking part of a threshing-mill; **scutch′ing.** — **scutch′-blade.** [Prob. O.Fr. *escousser*, to shake off.]

scutch[2] *skuch*, **scutch grass.** Forms of **quitch**[1], **quitch grass** (see **couch grass.**)

scutcheon *skuch′ən, n.* an aphetic form of **escutcheon.**

scute *skūt, n.* a scutum: an écu: a dermal plate. — *adjs.* **scūt′al; scūt′ate** protected by scutes: shield-shaped; **scūt′iform.** — *ns.* **scūt′iger** (*jocular*) a squire; **scūt′um** the oblong shield of Roman heavy-armed infantry (*hist.*): a scute: the second tergal plate of a segment of an insect's thorax: — *pl.* **scūt′a.** [L. *scūtum*, a shield.]

scutellum *skūt-el′əm, n.* a scale of a bird's foot: the third tergal plate of a segment of an insect's thorax: a structure, supposed to be the cotyledon, by which a grass embryo absorbs the endosperm: — *pl.* **scūtell′a.** — *adjs.* **scūtell′ar** of a scutellum; **scūt′ellate.** — *n.* **scūtellā′tion** scale arrangement. [L. *scutella*, a tray, dim. of *scutra*, a platter, confused in scientific use with *scūtulum*, dim. of *scūtum*, a shield.]

scutiform, scutiger. See **scute.**

scutter *skut′ər, v.i.* to run hastily: to scurry. — *n.* a hasty run. [A variant of **scuttle**[3].]

scuttle[1] *skut′l, n.* a shallow basket: a vessel for holding coal. — *n.* **scutt′leful.** [O.E. *scutel* — L. *scutella*, a tray.]

scuttle[2] *skut′l, n.* an opening in a ship's deck or side: its lid: a shuttered hole in a wall, roof, etc.: its shutter or trap-door. — *v.t.* to make a hole in, esp. in order to sink: to destroy, ruin. — **scutt′le-butt** (in U.S. **scutt′le-butt**) a cask with a hole cut in it for drinking-water (also **scutt′le-cask**): a drinking fountain on a ship (*U.S.*): rumour, gossip (*U.S.*). [O.Fr. *escoutille*, hatchway.]

scuttle[3] *skut′l, v.i.* to dash with haste. — *n.* an act of scuttling. — *n.* **scutt′ler.** [**scuddle.**]

scutum. See **scute.**

scybalum *sib′ə-ləm, n.* a hard fecal mass in the intestine: — *pl.* **scyb′ala.** — *adj.* **scyb′alous.** [Latinised from Gr. *skybalon*, dung.]

scye *sī, n.* an opening for insertion of a sleeve. [Origin obscure.]

Scylla *sil′ə, (myth.) n.* a six-headed monster who sat over a dangerous rock opposite Charybdis. [Gr. *Skylla*.]

scyphus *sīf′əs, n.* a large Greek drinking-cup (*ant.*): a cup-shaped structure: — *pl.* **scyph′ī.** — *adj.* **scyph′iform.** — *n.* **scyphis′toma** the segmenting polyp stage of a jellyfish (Gr. *stoma*, mouth): — *pl.* **scyphis'tomas, -stomae.** — *ns.pl.* **scyphomedū'sae, Scyphozō'a** the jellyfishes as a class. [Gr. *skyphos*, cup.]

scytale *sit'ə-lē, n.* a Spartan secret writing on a strip wound about a stick, unreadable without a stick of like thickness. [Gr. *skytalē*, a staff.]

scythe *sīdh, n.* an instrument with a large curved blade for mowing: a blade attached to a war-chariot wheel. — *v.t.* and *v.i.* to mow with a scythe. — *adj.* **scythed** armed or cut with scythes. — *n.* **scyth'er** one who uses a scythe. — **scythe'man** scyther; **scythe'-stone** a whet for scythes. [O.E. *sīthe*; cf. O.N. *sigthr*, Ger. *Sense*.]

Scythian *sith'i-ən, adj.* of *Scythia*, an ancient country N. and E. of the Black Sea, of its nomadic people or of their language. — *n.* a member of the people: the language of Scythia. — **Scythian lamb** barometz.

sdaine, sdayn. See **sdeigne.**

'sdeath *zdeth, (obs.) interj.* an exclamation of impatience — for *God's death.*

sdeigne, sdein, sdaine, sdayn *zdān, (Spens., Milt.) v.t.* and *v.i.* to disdain. — *adj.* **sdeign'full.** — *adv.* **sdeign'fully.** [It. *sdegnare*, aphetic for *disdegnare*; or Eng. **disdain.**]

sdrucciola *zdrōōt'chō-la, adj.* (of rhyme) triple. [It., slippery.]

sea *sē, n.* the great mass of salt water covering the greater part of the earth's surface: the ocean: any great expanse of water: a great (esp. salt) lake — mainly in proper names: swell or roughness: a great wave: the tide: a wide expanse. — *adj.* **marine.** — *adj.* **sea'-like** like the sea. — *adv.* in the manner of the sea. — *adj., adv.* **sea'ward** towards the (open) sea. — *n.* seaward side, direction or position. — *adj., adv.* **sea'wardly.** — *adv.* **sea'wards.** — **sea'-a'corn** an acorn-shell; **sea'-add'er** a pipefish: a marine stickleback; **sea'-air'** the air at sea or by the sea; **sea'-an'chor** a floating anchor used at sea to slow a boat down, or maintain its direction; **sea'-anem'one** a solitary soft-bodied polyp of the Zoantharia; **sea'-ape** the sea-otter: the thresher shark: a manatee; **sea'-bank** the seashore: an embankment to keep out the sea; **sea'-bass** (*-bas*) a perch-like marine fish of various kinds, especially of the Serranidae and the Sciaenidae; **sea'-bat** a name for various fishes with long or outspread fins; **sea'-ba'ther; sea'-ba'thing; sea'-beach** a strip of sand, gravel, etc., bordering the sea; **sea'-bean'** the cacoon (*Entada*) or other foreign seed cast up by the sea: a mollusc's operculum, worn as an amulet; **sea'-bear** the polar bear: the fur-seal; **sea'-beast.** — *adjs.* **sea'-beat, -en** lashed by the waves. — **sea'bed** the bottom of the sea; **sea'-beet** wild beet; **sea'berry** Haloragis; **sea'-bird** any marine bird; **sea'-bis'cuit** ship-biscuit; **sea'-blite** a salt-marsh plant (*Suaeda maritima*) of the goosefoot family; **sea'-blubb'er** a jellyfish. — *adj.* **sea'-blue** blue like the sea. — **sea'board** the country bordering the sea. — Also *adj.* — **sea'-boat** a craft considered with reference to her behaviour in bad weather; **sea'-boots** long, waterproof boots worn by sailors. — *adjs.* **sea'-born** produced by the sea; **sea'borne** carried on the sea. — **sea'-bottle** a translucent inflated seaweed (*Valonia*): bladderwrack; **sea'-bott'om** the floor of the sea; **sea'-boy** (*Shak.*) a sailor-boy; **sea'-breach** an inroad of the sea; **sea'-bream** any fish of the Sparidae, a family of spiny-finned fishes, with teeth of the character of incisors and molars: any fish of the Bramidae, a family akin to the mackerels; **sea'-breeze** a breeze from the sea, esp. owing to convection in the daytime; **sea'-buck'thorn** a willow-like seaside shrub (*Hippophae rhamnoides*) of the family *Eleagnaceae*; **sea'-bun** a heart-urchin; **sea'-bur'dock** clotbur (Xanthium); **sea'-butt'erfly** a pteropod; **sea cabbage** sea-kale; **sea'-calf** the common seal; **sea'-canā'ry** the white whale; **sea'-cap** (*Shak.*) a cap worn on shipboard; **sea'-captain** the captain of a merchant ship; **sea'-card** a compass card: a sea-chart; **sea'-cat** a catfish: a weever, *Trachinus draco*: a sea-wolf: also other sea creatures; **sea'-change** a change effected by the sea (*Shak.*): a transformation; **sea'-chart** a chart of the sea, its coasts, etc.; **sea'-chest**

a seaman's trunk; **sea'-cliff** a cliff fronting or formed by the sea; **sea'-coal** (*arch.*) coal in the ordinary sense, not charcoal (possibly as first worked where exposed by the sea). — Also *adj.* — **sea'coast** the land adjacent to the sea; **sea'-cob** a seagull; **sea'-cock** a gurnard: a valve communicating with the sea through a vessel's hull: a bold mariner or sea rover (*arch.*); **sea'-cole'wort** sea-kale: wild cabbage; **sea'-cook** a ship's cook (by sailors supposed to disgrace his son); **sea'-cow** the walrus: rhytina (**Steller's sea-cow**) or other sirenian: the hippopotamus (*S.Afr.*; Du. *zeekoe*); **sea'craft** skill in navigation: seamanship: sea-going craft; **sea'-craw'fish, -cray'fish** a spiny lobster; **sea'-crow** a name of many birds, as skua, chough, cormorant; **sea'-cu'cumber** a holothurian (as trepang, bêche-de-mer); **sea'-dace** the bass; **sea'-dev'il** a devil dwelling in the sea: a devil-fish; **sea'-dog** the seal: a dogfish: an old sailor: a pirate: a beast like a talbot with dorsal fin and beaver's tail (*her.*); **sea'-dott'erel** the turnstone; **sea'-dove** the little auk; **sea'-drag'on** the dragonet: the fish Pegasus: an Australian pipefish; **sea'drome** a floating aerodrome; **sea'-duck** any duck of the pochard group; **sea'-dust** dust from distant land falling at sea; **sea'-ea'gle** erne or other *Haliaetus*: the eagle-ray; **sea'-ear** an earshell (Haliotis); **sea'-eel** a conger; **sea'-egg** a sea-urchin; **sea'-el'ephant** the elephant-seal; **sea'-fan** an alcyonarian coral with fan-like skeleton; **sea'-farer** a traveller by sea, usu. a sailor; **sea'faring.** — Also *adj.* — **sea'-feath'er** a feathery alcyonarian, sea-pen; **sea'-fight** a battle between ships at sea; **sea'-fir** a sertularian colony; **sea'-fire** phosphorescence at sea; **sea'-fish** any salt-water or marine fish; **sea'-fish'er; sea'-fish'ing; sea'-floor** the bottom of the sea; **sea'-foam** the froth of the sea; **sea'-fog** fog coming from the sea; **sea'-folk** seafaring people; **sea'food** food got from the sea, esp. shellfish; **sea'-fowl** a sea-bird; **sea'-fox** the thresher, or fox-shark; **sea'-fret** fog coming in off the sea; **sea'-front** the side of the land, of a town, or of a building that looks towards the sea: a promenade with its buildings fronting the sea; **sea'-froth** the foam of the sea; **sea'-fur'below** a brown seaweed (*Saccorhiza*) with a bulb of tentacular outgrowths above the primary holdfast; **sea'-gate** a seaward gate of a tidal basin, etc.: an outlet to the sea; **sea'-gill'iflower, -gill'yflower** thrift; **sea'-gin'ger** millepore coral; **sea'-gir'dle** tangle, esp. *Laminaria digitata.* — *adj.* **sea'-girt** surrounded by sea. — **sea'-god, -godd'ess** a god, goddess, ruling over or dwelling in the sea. — *adj.* **sea'-going** sailing on the deep sea: suitable for deep-sea voyage. — **sea'-goose'berry** a common ctenophore like a gooseberry in shape; **sea'-gown** (*Shak.*) a short-sleeved garment worn at sea; **sea'-grape** any plant of the genus Ephedra, or its fruit: seaside-grape: glasswort: gulfweed: (in *pl.*) cuttlefish eggs in masses; **sea'-grass** a grass or grasslike plant growing by or in the sea — Enteromorpha, thrift, grasswrack, etc., often dried and used to make matting, rope, chair-seats, etc.; **sea'-green** green like the sea. — Also *adj.* (see also **sea-green incorruptible** below). — Also **sea'-water-green** (*Shak.*). — **sea'gull** a gull: a dock-labourer not yet admitted to a union (*N.Z.*); **sea'-haar** a haar (q.v.); **sea'-hare** a tectibranch gasteropod (*Aplysia*) with ear-like tentacles; **sea'-hawk** a skua; **sea'-heath'** a wiry heath-like pink-flowered plant (Frankenia) of salt-marshes and chalk-cliffs; **sea'-hedge'hog** a sea-urchin: a globe-fish; **sea'-hog** a porpoise; **sea'-holl'y** eryngo; **sea'horse** the fabulous hippocampus: Hippocampus or kindred fish: the walrus: the hippopotamus (*obs.*); **sea'-hound** dogfish; **sea'-ice'.** — *adj.* **sea'-island** (of cotton) of the kind grown on the islands off the coast of South Carolina. — **sea'-jell'y** a jellyfish; **sea'-kale** a fleshy glaucous cruciferous seaside plant (*Crambe maritima*) cultivated for its blanched sprouts; **sea-kale beet** chard; **sea'-keeping** the maintenance of navigational control and stability on (rough) seas. — Also *adj.* — **sea'-king** a king of the merfolk: Poseidon or Neptune: a viking chief; **sea'-lane** a navigable passage between islands, ships, ice-floes, etc.; **sea′-lark** a name for various shore-birds, as sandpipers: the rock-pipit; **sea′-lav′ender** a plumbaginaceous genus (*Limonium*) of salt-marsh plants; **sea′-law** maritime law, esp. mediaeval customary law; **sea′-law′yer** a captious sailor: a shark; **sea′-legs** ability to walk on a ship's deck when it is pitching: resistance to seasickness; **sea′-lem′on** shell-less mollusc (fam. Do-rididae) with smooth yellow body; **sea′-len′til** gulf-weed; **sea′-leop′ard** a spotted seal of the southern seas: wolf-fish skin; **sea′-lett′er, -brief** a document of description that used to be given to a ship at the port where she was fitted out: a document issued to a neutral merchant vessel in wartime, allowing it to pass freely (also **sea′-pass**); **sea′-lett′uce** a seaweed (*Ulva*) with flat translucent green fronds — green laver; **sea′-lev′el** the mean level of the surface of the sea. — **sea′-lil′y** a crinoid; **sea′-line** a coastline: a sea-horizon: a line for sounding or fishing in deep water; **sea′-lion** a seal with external ears and with hind flippers turned forward (usu. excluding the sea-bears or fur-seals): a lion with the tail of a fish (*her.*); **sea′-loach** a rockling; **sea′-loch** (*Scot.*) a lakelike arm of the sea; **sea′-long′worm** a long nemertean (*Lineus*); **sea′-lord** a naval member of the Board of Admiralty; **sea′-lungs** a ctenophoran; **sea′-maid** a mermaid (*Shak.*): a sea-nymph; **sea′man** a sailor: a man other than an officer or apprentice, employed aboard ship: a merman. — *adjs.* **sea′manlike** showing good seamanship; **sea′manly** characteristic of a seaman. — **sea′manship** the art of handling ships at sea; **sea′-marge, sea′= mar′gin** the margin of the sea; **sea′mark** a mark of tidal limit: any object serving as a guide to those at sea: a danger-signal; **sea′-mat** hornwrack (*Flustra*), a common polyzoan like a flat horny seaweed; **sea′-maw** (now *Scot.*) a sea-mew; **sea-mell** an alleged variant of **sea-mew**; **sea′-mew** any gull; **sea′-mile** a geographical or nautical mile; **sea′-milk′wort** Glaux; **sea′-mon′ster** any huge marine animal, esp. fabulous; **sea′-moss** carrageen: seaweed: a polyzoan; **sea′-mount, sea′mount** a mountain under the sea of at least 3 000 ft; **sea′-mouse** an elliptical polychaet (*Aphrodite*) covered with iridescent silky hairs; **sea′-nett′le** a jellyfish; **sea′-nymph** a minor sea-goddess; **sea′-on′ion** the officinal squill; **sea′-or′ach(e)** any seaside species of orach; **sea′-or′ange** a large globose orange-coloured holothurian; **sea′= ott′er** a N. Pacific animal (*Enhydris*) akin to the true otters: its silvery brown fur, now very rare; **sea′-owl′** the lumpsucker; **sea′-parr′ot** a puffin; **sea′-pass** see **sea-letter** above; **sea′-pass′age** a journey by sea; **sea′= path′** (*Milt.*) a way that a fish may take; **sea′-pay′** pay for actual service on a ship in commission; **sea′-pen′** a feather-like alcyonarium (Pennatula or kindred form): a squid's internal shell; **sea′-perch** a bass or other fish of the Serranidae; **sea′-pie** a sailor's dish made of salt meat, vegetables, and dumplings baked: the oyster-catcher; **sea′-piece** a picture, poem, piece of music, etc., representing a scene at sea; **sea′-pig′** a porpoise: a dolphin: a dugong; **sea′-pike′** a pike-like marine fish of various kinds — robalo, Belone, hake, etc.; **sea′-pink** thrift; **sea′plane** an aeroplane with floats instead of landing-wheels; **sea′plane-carr′ier** a ship that carries seaplanes; **sea′-poach′er** the pogge; **sea′-por′cupine** the globe-fish (*Diodon*); **sea′port** a port or harbour on the sea: a place with such a harbour; **sea′-power** a nation strong at sea: naval strength; **sea′-purse** a mermaid's purse; **sea′-purs′lane** see **purslane**; **sea′quake** a seismic disturbance at sea; **seaqua′rium** see **oceanarium**; **sea′= ran′ger** in the Girl Guide organisation a ranger who trains specially in seamanship and the like; **sea′rat** a pirate; **sea raven** a species of sculpin; **sea′-reed** marram-grass; **sea′-risk** hazard of injury or loss by sea; **sea′-road** a route followed by ships; **sea′-robb′er** a pirate; **sea′= rob′in** an American fish (esp. *Prionotus*) of the gurnard family, with red or brown colouring; **sea′-rock′et** a fleshy cruciferous seaside plant (*Cakile*); **sea′-room** space to manoeuvre a ship safely; **sea′-rose′mary** sea-lavender; **sea′-ro′ver** a pirate (ship); **sea′-ro′ving** piracy;

sea′-salm′on inaptly, coalfish, pollack; **sea′-salt′** salt got from sea-water. — *adj.* salt as the sea. — **sea′-sand′** sands of the seashore; **sea′satyre** (*Spens.*) sea-monster of some kind; **sea′scape** a picture, photograph, of the sea; **sea′-scor′pion** scorpion-fish: a father-lasher (*Cottus scorpius*); **Sea′-Scout** a member of a marine branch of the Scout Association; **sea′-scout′ing**; **sea′-serp′ent** an enormous marine animal of serpent-like form, frequently seen and described by credulous sailors, imaginative landsmen, and common liars: a sea-snake; **sea′-ser′vice** service on board ship; **sea′-shan′ty** same as **shanty²**; **sea′shell** a marine shell; **sea′shore′** the land immediately adjacent to the sea: the foreshore (*law*). — *adj.* **sea′-should′ring** (*Spens.*) having shoulders that displace the sea. — **sea′-shrub′** a sea-fan. — *adj.* **sea′sick′** sick owing to the rolling of a vessel at sea: travel-worn (*Shak.*). — **seasick′ness**; **sea′side** the neighbourhood of the sea. — Also *adj.* — **sea′side-grape′** the grape-tree (*Coccoloba*) or its fruit; **sea′-sleeve′** a cuttlefish; **sea′-slug** a nudibranch: a holothurian; **sea′= snail** any snail-like marine gasteropod: an unctuous fish (*Liparis*) akin to the lumpsucker; **sea′-snake** a snake that lives in the sea, esp. of the very venomous family Hydrophidae of the Indian and Pacific oceans: the sea-serpent; **sea′-snipe** a sandpiper: the snipe-fish; **sea′-sol′dier** a marine; **sea′-sorr′ow** (*Shak.*) afflictions at sea; **sea′-spi′der** a pycnogonid; **sea′-squill** sea-onion; **sea′-squirt** an ascidian; **sea′-star′** a starfish; **sea′-stick** a herring cured at sea; **sea′-stock** fresh provisions for use at sea; **sea′-storm′**; **sea′-strand′**; **sea′-sur′geon** a tropical genus (*Acanthurus*) of spiny-finned fishes with a lancet-like spine ensheathed on each side of the tail; **sea′-swall′ow** a tern: the storm petrel: a flying-fish. — *adj.* (*Shak.*) **sea′-swall′ow′d.** — **sea′-swine** a porpoise: the ballan-wrasse; **sea′-tang, -tan′gle** any of various kinds of brown seaweed, esp. of genus Laminaria; **sea′-term** a nautical word. — *adj.* **sea(s)′-tost** (*Shak.*). — **sea′-trout** the salmon-trout (*Salmo trutta*), or its variety the bull-trout (var. *eriox*): extended to various other fishes in U.S. and Australia; **sea′-turn** a gale from the sea; **sea′-tur′tle** a marine turtle: a black guillemot; **sea′-ū′nicorn** the narwhal; **sea′-ur′chin** one of the Echinoidea, a class of Echinoderms with globular, ovoid, or heart-shaped, sometimes flattened body and shell of calcareous plates, without arms; **sea′-vam′pire** a giant ray, or devil-fish; **sea′-view′** a view of the sea: a seascape; **sea′-wall′** a wall to keep out the sea. — *adj.* **sea′-walled** walled against or by the sea. — **sea′-ware** seaweed; **sea′-wa′ter** water of or from the sea; **sea′= wave; sea′-way** (often **sea′way**) a way by sea: progress through the waves: a heavy sea: a regular route taken by ocean traffic: an inland waterway on which ocean-going vessels can sail; **sea′weed** marine algae collectively: any marine alga; **sea′-whis′tle** a seaweed (*Ascophyllum nodosum*) whose bladders can be made into whistles; **sea′-wife** a kind of wrasse; **sea′-wind′** a wind from the sea; **sea′-wing** a sail; **sea′-wolf** the wolf-fish: the bass: the sea-elephant (*obs.*): a viking: a pirate; **sea′-woman** a mermaid; **sea′-worm** any marine worm. — *adj.* **sea′-worn** worn by the sea or by seafaring. — **sea′worthiness.** — *adj.* **sea′worthy** fit for sea: able to endure stormy weather. — **sea′-wrack** coarse seaweeds of any kind: grasswrack. — **all at sea** out of one's reckoning: completely at a loss; **at full sea** at full tide; **at sea** away from land: on the ocean: astray; **follow the sea, go to sea** to become a sailor; **heavy sea** a sea in which the waves run high; **molten sea** the great brazen laver of 1 Kings vii. 23–26; **sea-green incorruptible** one honestly and unshakably devoted to an ideal or purpose, esp. in public life (orig. used by Carlyle of Robespierre); **short sea** a sea in which the waves are choppy, irregular, and interrupted; **the four seas** those bounding Great Britain; **Seven Seas** see **seven**. [O.E. *sǣ*; Du. *zee*, Ger. *See*, O.N. *sǣr*, Dan. *sö*.]

Seabee *sē′bē* (the letters *cb* phonetically represented), *n.* a member of a U.S. Navy construction *battalion*.

seacunny *sē′kun-i, n.* a lascar steersman or quartermaster.

[App. Pers. *sukkānī* — Ar. *sukkān*, rudder, confused with **sea** and **con³**.]

seal¹ *sēl, n.* a piece of wax, lead or other material, stamped with a device and attached as a means of authentication or attestation: a wafer, circular mark, or other substitute: a piece of wax, etc., stamped or not, used as a means of keeping closed a letter, door, etc.: the design stamped: an engraved stone or other stamp for impressing a device, or a trinket of like form: an adhesive label, esp. decorative, for a Christmas parcel, etc., sold for charity: a confirming token: that which closes: an obligation to secrecy: an impression: a device to prevent passage of a gas: water in a gas-trap: an otter's (or other) footprint. — *v.t.* to set a seal to: to stamp: to fasten with a seal: to confirm: to ratify: to close up: to enclose: to settle irrevocably: to set apart. — *v.i.* to set one's seal to something. — *n.* **seal'ant** something that seals a place where there is a leak. — *adj.* **sealed.** — *ns.* **seal'er** a person or thing that seals: a substance used to coat a surface for protection, impermeability, etc.; **seal'ing.** — **seal'-cyl'inder** a cylinder-seal. — *adj.* **sealed'-beam** of car headlights, consisting of a complete unit sealed within a vacuum. — **sealed book** something beyond one's knowledge or understanding; **seal'-engrav'ing** the art of engraving seals; **seal'ing-day** (*Shak.*) a day for sealing; **seal'ing-wax** formerly beeswax, now usually a composition of shellac, turpentine, vermilion or other colouring matter, etc., for sealing — also (*obs.*) **seal'-wax; seal'-pipe** a dip-pipe; **seal'-ring** a signet-ring. — **Great Seal** (also without *caps.*) the state seal of the United Kingdom; **Lord Privy Seal** formerly the keeper of the Privy Seal, now the senior cabinet minister without official duties; **Privy Seal** (also without *caps.*) formerly, the seal appended to documents that were to receive, or did not require, authorisation by the Great Seal, in Scotland used esp. to authenticate royal grants of personal rights; **seal off** to make it impossible for any thing, person, to leave or enter (e.g. an area); **set one's seal to, on** to give one's authority or assent to; **the seals** symbolically the office of Lord Chancellor or of Secretary of State; **under seal** authenticated; **under sealed orders** under orders only to be opened at sea. [O.Fr. *seel* — L. *sigillum*, dim. of *signum*, a mark.]

seal² *sēl, n.* a member of the Pinnipedia, usually excluding the walrus and often excluding the otaries: sealskin. — *adj.* of seal or sealskin. — *v.i.* to hunt seals. — *ns.* **seal'er** a seal-fisher; **seal'ery** seal-fishery; **seal'ing.** — **seal'-fish'er** a hunter of seals: a sealing ship; **seal'-fish'ing; seal'-point** a variety of Siamese cat, with dark brown face, paws and tail; **seal'-rook'ery** a seals' breeding-place; **seal'skin** the prepared fur of the fur-seal, or an imitation (as of rabbit-skin, or of mohair): a garment made of this. — Also *adj.* [O.E. *seolh* (gen. *sēoles*); O.N. *selr.*]

seal³. Same as **seel¹.**

seal⁴ *sēl, v.t.* to tie up. — *n.* a rope or chain for tying up an animal. [O.E. *sǽlan* — *sāl*, rope.]

seal⁵. See **sale².**

seal⁶. See **seel².**

sealgh, sealch *selhh,* (*Scot.*) *n.* a seal. [**seal².**]

Sealyham *sēl'i-əm, n.* (also without *cap.*; in full **Sealyham terrier**) a long-bodied, short-legged, hard-coated terrier, first bred at *Sealyham* in Pembrokeshire.

seam¹, seame *sēm, n.* grease (*Shak.*): hog's lard (*Scot.* **saim** *sām*). — *v.t.* to grease. [O.Fr. *saim,* O.E. *seime;* cf. L. *sagīna,* stuffing, feasting.]

seam² *sēm, n.* a line of junction between edges sewn together, or between other edges generally: the turned-up edges of such a line on the wrong side of the cloth: ornamentation of such a junction: a suture: a crack: the mark of a cut: a wrinkle: a stratum, esp. if thin or valuable: a piece of sewing-work: coll. shortening for seam bowling. — *v.t.* to join, furnish, or mark with seams: to pick out the seams of. — *ns.* **seam'er** one who, or that which, seams: a ball delivered by seam bowling (*cricket*); **seam'iness.** — *adj.* **seam'-**

less. — *ns.* **seamster** (*sem'*), **seam'stress** see **sempster; seam'stressy** (*Sterne*) sewing. — *adj.* **seamy** (*sēm'i*) having a seam or seams: showing the disreputable side: sordid. — **seam allowance** in dressmaking, the margin allowed for the seams along the edge of the pieces of a garment; **seam bowler; seam bowling** (*cricket*) bowling in which the seam of the ball is used in delivery to make the ball swerve in flight or first to swerve and then to break in the opposite direction on pitching; **seam'ing-lace** a lace, braid, etc., to insert in or cover seams. — *adj.* **seam'-rent** rent along a seam. — **seam'-set** a tool for flattening seams in metal, etc.; **seam welding** resistance welding of overlapping sheets of metal using wheels or rollers as electrodes: welding two pieces of sheet plastic along a line by dielectric heating; **seam'y-side** (*Shak.*) the wrong side of a garment. — **seamy side** the disreputable or unpleasant side or aspect (of something). [O.E. *sēam* — *sīwian,* to sew; Du. *zoom,* Ger. *Saum.*]

seam³ *sēm,* (*obs.* except *dial.*) *n.* a pack-horse load (e.g. 8 bushels of grain, 9 pecks of apples, 120 lb. of glass): a cartload. [O.E. *sēam,* a burden — L.L. *sauma* — Gr. *sagma,* a pack-saddle.]

sean *sē n.* Same as **seine.**

Seanad (Eireann) *shan'ədh* (*e'rən*), the upper house of the legislature of the Republic of Ireland. [Ir., senate.]

séance *sā' äs, n.* a sitting, esp. of psychical researchers or Spiritualists. [Fr., — L. *sedēre,* to sit.]

seannachie *sen'ə-hhē, n.* Highland or Irish genealogist and transmitter of family lore. — Also **seann'achy, senn'-achie.** [Gael. *seanachaidh.*]

sear¹ *sēr, n.* the catch that holds a gun at cock or half-cock. — **tickle(d) a th' sere** (*Shak.*) ready to go off. [Cf. O.Fr. *serre* — L. *sera,* a bar.]

sear² *sēr, adj.* (usu. **sere**) dry and withered: (*Spens.* **seare**) burning. — *v.i.* (rarely **sere**) to become sere. — *v.t.* to make sere: to dry up: to scorch: to brand: to cauterise: to render callous or insensible. — *n.* a mark of searing. — *adj.* **seared.** — *n.* **seared'ness.** — *n.* and *adj.* **sear'ing.** — *ns.* **sear'ness, sere'ness.** — **sear'ing-iron.** — **the sere, the** (so *Shak.*; not **and**) **yellow leaf** the autumn of life. [O.E. *sēar,* dry, *sēarian,* to dry up; L.G. *soor,* Du. *zoor.*]

searce *sûrs,* **search** *sûrch,* (*obs.*) *vs.t.* to sift. — *ns.* (*obs.*) a sieve. [O.Fr. *saas; r* unexplained.]

search *sûrch, v.t.* to explore all over with a view to finding something: to examine closely: to examine for hidden articles by feeling all over: to ransack: to scrutinise: to probe: to penetrate all parts of (*arch.*): to put to the test: to seek out (usu. with *out*). — *v.i.* to make a search. — *n.* the act or power of searching: thorough examination: quest: a search-party (*Shak.*). — *adj.* **search'-able.** — *n.* **search'er** one who searches: one appointed to search, as a custom-house officer: an inspector of various kinds: a probe. — *adj.* **search'ing** penetrating: thoroughgoing. — *adv.* **search'ingly.** — *n.* **search'-ingness.** — *adj.* **search'less** unsearchable. — **search'-light** a lamp and reflector throwing a strong beam of light for picking out objects by night: the light so projected; **search'-par'ty** a party sent out in search of somebody or something; **search'-warr'ant** a warrant authorising the searching of a house, etc. — **right of search** the right of a belligerent to search neutral ships for contraband of war; **search me** (*slang*) I don't know. [O.Fr. *cerchier* (Fr. *chercher*) — L. *circāre,* to go about — *circus,* a circle.]

seare. See **sear².**

sease. See under **seize.**

season *sē'zn, n.* one of the four divisions of the year: the usual, natural, legal, or appropriate time, or time of year, for anything: any particular time: time, esp. of some continuance, but not long: a season ticket (*coll.*): seasoning (*obs.*). — *v.t.* to mature: to temper: to bring into suitable condition: to inure: to render savoury: to flavour: to imbue: to preserve from decay (*Shak.*): to mature, confirm, imbue with the flavour of (*Shak.*). — *v.i.* to become seasoned. — *adj.* **sea'sonable** in due season: timely. — *n.* **sea'sonableness.** — *adv.* **sea'-**

sonably. — *adj.* **sea′sonal** according to season. — *n.* **seasonal′ity** the quality of being seasonal. — *adv.* **sea′sonally.** — *adj.* **sea′soned.** — *ns.* **sea′soner; sea′- soning** the process or act by which anything is sea- soned: the process of acclimatisation: that which is added to food to give relish: in diamond-cutting, the charging of the laps or wheels with diamond-dust and oil: the coating of dyed leather with liquid albumen. — *adj.* **sea′sonless** without difference of seasons. — **sea′soning-tub** a trough in which dough is set to rise; **season ticket** a ticket valid any number of times within a specified period. — **close season** see **close**[1]; **in season** ripe, fit and ready for use: allowed to be killed: of a bitch, ready to mate: on heat: fit to be eaten; **in season and out of season** at all times; **out of season** inoppor- tune: not in season. [O.Fr. *seson* (Fr. *saison*) — L. *satiō, -ōnis,* a sowing.]

seasure. Sec under **seize.**

seat *sēt, n.* anything used or intended for sitting on: a chair, bench, saddle, etc.: part of a chair on which the body rests: a sitting: a mode of sitting: a place where one may sit, as in a theatre, church, etc.: a right to sit: a constituency: membership: that part of the body or of a garment on which one sits: that on which anything rests: site, situation: a place where anything is located, settled, or established: post of authority: a throne: a capital city: station: abode: mansion: sitting-room. — *v.t.* to place on a seat: to cause to sit down: to place in any situation, site, etc.: to establish: to fix: to assign a seat to: to furnish with a seat or seats: to fit accurately: to make baggy by sitting. — *v.i.* to sit or lie down (*Spens.*): to become baggy by sitting. — *adj.* **seat′ed.** — *ns.* **-sea′ter** (in composition) a vehicle, sofa, etc., seated for so many; **seat′er** one who seats; **seat′ing** the taking, provision, or arrangement of seats: a supporting surface: material for seats. — *adj.* **seat′less.** — **seat′-belt** a belt which can be fastened to hold a person firmly in his seat in car or aircraft, for safety; **seat earth** a bed of clay underlying a coal seam; **seat′-rent** (*hist.*) payment for a church sitting; **seat′= stick** a walking-stick that can be made to serve as a seat. — **by** or **in the seat of one's pants** instinctively, by intuition (*adj.* **seat-of-the-pants** instinctive); **lord of seat** a lord of Session; **lose one's seat** to fail to be re-elected to Parliament; **take a seat** to sit down; **take one's seat** to take up one's seat, esp. in Parliament. [O.N. *sǣti,* seat; cf. O.E. *sǣt,* ambush.]

seaward, seawardly, seawards. See **sea.**

seaze; sebaceous, etc. See **seize; sebum.**

se-baptist *sē-bap′tist, n.* one who baptises himself. [L. *sē,* himself.]

Sebat. See **Shebat.**

sebesten *si-bes′tən, n.* an Oriental boraginaceous tree (*Cordia*): its edible plum-like fruit. [Ar. *sabastān.*]

sebum *sē′bəm, n.* the fatty secretion that lubricates the hair and skin. — *adjs.* **sebaceous** (*si-bā′shəs*) tallowy: of, like, of the nature of, or secreting sebum; **sebacic** (*si-bas′ik*) applied to an acid, (CH$_2$)$_8$(COOH)$_2$, got from fats. — *n.* **sebate** (*sē′bāt*) a salt of sebacic acid. — *adjs.* **sebif′erous** (*si-*) bearing fatty matter; **sebif′ic** producing fatty matter. — *n.* **seborrhoea** (*seb-ə-rē′ə*) excessive discharge from the sebaceous glands. — *adj.* **seborrhoe′ic.** [L. *sēbum,* suet.]

sebundy *si-bun′di, n.* Indian irregular soldiery or soldier. [Urdu *sibandī.*]

sec[1] *sek, adj.* dry, of wines. [Fr.]

sec[2]. See **secant.**

sec[3]. See **second.**

secant *sē′kənt, sek′ənt, adj.* cutting. — *n.* a cutting line: a straight line which cuts a curve in two or more places (*geom.*): orig., a straight line from the centre of a circle through one end of an arc to the tangent from the other end (*trig.*): now, as a function of an angle, the ratio of the hypotenuse to the base of a right-angled triangle formed by dropping a perpendicular from a point on one side of the angle to the other (negative if the base is the side produced) — in trigonometrical

notation written **sec.** [L. *secāns, -antis,* pr.p. of *secāre,* to cut.]

sécateur *sek′ə-tûr, -tûr′, n.* (usu. in *pl.* and without accent) pruning-shears. [Fr.]

secco *sek′kō, adj.* (*mus.*) unaccompanied: plain: of wine, etc., dry. — *n.* painting on dry plaster: — *pl.* **sec′cos.** [It., dry — L. *siccus.*]

secede *si-sēd′, v.i.* to withdraw, esp. from a party, religious body, federation, or the like. — *ns.* **secē′der** one who secedes: one of a body of Presbyterians (**Secession Church;** see **presbyterian**) who seceded from the Church of Scotland about 1733; **secession** (*-sesh′ən*) the act of seceding: a body of seceders. — Also *adj.* — *adj.* **secess′ional.** — *ns.* **secess′ionism; secess′ionist** (*U.S. slang* also **secesh′, secesh′er**) one who favours or joins in secession. — Also *adjs.* — **War of Secession** the American Civil War. [L. *sēcēdĕre, sēcessum, sē-,* apart, *cēdĕre,* to go.]

secern *si-sûrn′, v.t.* to separate: to discriminate: to secrete. — - *n.* and *adj.* **secern′ent.** — *n.* **secern′ment.** [L. *sēcernĕre, sēcrētum,* to separate.]

sech *sesh, n.* a conventional abbreviation of *h*yperbolic *secant.*

seckel *sek′l, n.* a variety of pear. [Owner's name.]

seclude *si-klōōd′, v.i.* to shut off, esp. from association or influence. — *adj.* **seclud′ed** retired: withdrawn from observation or society. — *adv.* **seclud′edly.** — *ns.* **seclusion** (*si-klōō′zhən*) the act of secluding: the state of being secluded: retirement: privacy: solitude; **seclu′- sionist.** — *adj.* **seclu′sive** (*-siv*) tending to or favouring seclusion. [L. *sēclūdĕre, -clūsum,* — *sē-,* apart, *claudĕre,* to shut.]

secodont *sek′ə-dont,* (*zool.*) *adj.* with cutting back teeth. — Also *n.* [L. *secāre,* to cut, Gr. *odous, odontos,* tooth.]

Seconal® *sek′ə-nəl, n.* a hypnotic and soporific barbitu- rate.

second *sek′ənd, adj.* next after or below the first: other, alternate: additional: supplementary: another, as it were: inferior: subordinate: referring to the person or persons addressed (*gram.*): helpful, favouring (*Shak.*). — *adv.* next after the first: in the second place. — *n.* one who, or that which, is second or of the second class: a place in the second class: second gear: one who attends another in a duel or a prize fight: a supporter: the 60th part of a minute of time, or of angular measurement (abbreviated as **sec**): a time interval variously measured (see under **atom, Ephemeris, uni- verse**): a very small amount of time (*coll;* esp. in short form **sec**): a second class university degree (*coll.*): the second person (*gram.*): the interval between successive tones of the diatonic scale (*mus.*): (in *pl.*) goods of a second quality: (in *pl.*) a second helping of food (*coll.*). — *v.t.* to follow: to act as second to: to back: to further: to assist: to encourage: to support after the mover of a nomination or resolution: to sing second to (*mus.*): to follow up with another: to transfer temporarily to some special employment (*si-kond′, -gōond′;* esp. *mil.*). — *adv.* **sec′ondarily.** — *n.* **sec′ondariness.** — *adj.* **sec′- ondary** subordinate: subsidiary: of a second order: of a second stage: derivative: induced: of education, between primary and higher: of a feather, growing in the second joint of the wing (*cap.; geol.*) Mesozoic. — *n.* a subordinate: a delegate or deputy: a satellite: that which is secondary, as a feather, coil, etc. — *ns.* **secondee** (*sek-on-dē′*) a person who is on secondment; **sec′onder** one who seconds a motion, etc.: a supporter: a member of a second group. — *adv.* **sec′ondly** in the second place. — *n.* **second′ment** temporary transfer to another position. — **Second Advent, Coming** a second coming of Christ; **Sec′ond-ad′ventist** one who expects a second coming of Christ; **secondary action** secondary picketing; **secondary alcohol** one containing the group CH·OH; **secondary battery, cell** one on which the chemical action is reversible; **secondary coil** one carry- ing an induced current; **secondary colours** those pro- duced by mixing two primary colours; **secondary elec-**

tron an electron in a beam of secondary emission; **secondary emission** emission of electrons from a surface or particle by bombardment with electrons, etc., from another source; **secondary growth** a cancer somewhere other than at the original site; **secondary modern** formerly, a type of secondary school offering a less academic, more technical education than a grammar school; **secondary picket**; **secondary picketing** the picketing by workers of a firm with which they are not directly in dispute but which has a trading connection with their own firm, in order to maximise the effects of a strike; **secondary (surveillance) radar** radar in which a responder is triggered by received pulses so that it retransmits a signal; **secondary school** a school for secondary education; **secondary smoking** passive smoking; **second ballot** a system of election whereby a second vote is taken, the candidate or candidates who received fewest votes in the first ballot being eliminated; **second banana** a subordinate (*slang*; orig. a vaudeville performer who played a secondary role). — *n.* and *adj.* **sec'ond-best** next to the best (**come off second-best** to get the worst of a contest). — **second chamber** in a legislature of two houses, the house with fewer powers, usu. acting as a check on the other; **second childhood** mental weakness in extreme old age; **second class** the class next to the first. — *adj.* **sec'ond-class** (see also below). — **second cousin** one who has the same pair of great-grandparents, but different grandparents: loosely, a first cousin's child, or a parent's first cousin (properly first cousin once removed); **sec'ond-day'** Monday; **second degree**; **second floor** (see **floor** for British and U.S. senses). — *adj.* **sec'ond-floor'**. — **second growth** a new growth of a forest after cutting, fire, etc.; a second crop of grapes in a season. — *v.t., v.i.* **sec'ond-guess'** (*coll.,* chiefly *U.S.*) to say with hindsight: to predict: to outdo in guessing. — *adj.* **sec'ond-hand'** derived from another: not original: already used by a previous owner: dealing in second-hand goods. — *n.* (*sek'*) a hand on a watch or clock that indicates seconds (see also **seconds-hand** below). — *adv.* indirectly, at second hand: after use by a previous owner. — **second home** a holiday home: a house owned in addition to one's main residence: a place where one feels as at home as in one's own house; **sec'ond-in-command'** the next under the commanding officer or other person in charge; **sec'ond-lieuten'ant** an army officer of lowest commissioned rank — formerly ensign or cornet; **second man** a man assisting the driver of a train (formerly, in steam trains, the fireman); **sec'ond-mark** the character ", used for seconds of arc or time or for inches; **second mortgage** a subsequent mortgage on an already-mortgaged property; **second nature** a deeply ingrained habit. — *adj.* **sec'ond-rate** inferior: mediocre. — **second-rat'er**; **second self** a person with whom one has the closest possible ties, sharing beliefs, attitudes, feelings, ways of behaving; **sec'onds-hand** a hand that marks seconds; **sec'ond-sight** a gift of prophetic vision attributed to certain persons, esp. Highlanders; **sec'-onds-pen'dulum** a pendulum that makes one swing a second; **second storey** the first floor; **second strike** a counterattack (in nuclear warfare) following an initial attack by an enemy. — *adj.* (also with *hyphen*) (of a nuclear weapon) specially designed so as to be ready to be used to strike back after a first attack by an enemy and to withstand such an attack. — **second string** an alternative choice, course of action, etc.; **second thoughts** reconsideration. — *adj.* **second'-to-none'** supreme: unsurpassed. — **second wind** recovery of breath in prolonged exertion. — **at second hand** through an intermediate source, indirectly: by hearsay; **second-class citizen** a member of a group in the community not given the full rights and privileges enjoyed by the community as a whole; **second-class mail, post** mail sent at a cheaper rate either because of its character or because the sender is prepared to accept

slower delivery. [Fr., — L. *secundus — sequī, secūtus,* to follow.]

seconde *si-kond', sə-gɔd,* (*fencing*) *n.* a position in parrying. [Fr.]

secondo *si-kon'dō,* (It.) *n.* the lower part in a duet: — *pl.* **secon'di** (-*ē*).

secret *sē'krit, adj.* kept back from knowledge of others: guarded against discovery or observation: unrevealed: hidden: secluded: recondite, occult: preserving secrecy: admitted to confidence, privy. — *adv.* (*poet.*) secretly. — *n.* a fact, purpose, method, etc., that is kept undivulged: participation in knowledge of such a fact: a nostrum (*obs.*): anything unrevealed or unknown: secrecy: a secret or private place (*obs.*): a piece of armour hidden by clothes: the key or principle that explains or enables: an inaudible prayer, esp. in the Mass: (in *pl.*) external sex organs (*obs.*). — *n.* **secrecy** (*sē'kri-si*) the state or fact of being secret: concealment: seclusion: confidence: power or habit of keeping secrets: the keeping of secrets: a secret. — *n.pl.* **secreta** (*si-krē'tə*) products of secretion. — *n.* **sē'cretage** treatment of furs with mercury before felting. — *v.t.* **secrete** (*si-krēt'*) to hide: to appropriate secretly: to form and separate by the activity of living matter. — *ns.* **secre'tin** a hormone that stimulates the pancreas; **secre'tion** the act of secreting: that which is secreted: a mass of mineral matter formed by inward growth in a cavity. — *adjs.* **secrē'tional; sē'cretive** (also *si-krē'tiv*) given to secrecy: very reticent: indicative of secrecy. — *adv.* **secretively.** — *n.* **secretiveness.** — *adv.* **sē'cretly** in secret: in concealment: inaudibly (of prayers). — *n.* **sē'cretness.** — *adj.* **secrē'tory** secreting. — **secret agent** one employed in secret service; **secret police** a police force which operates in secret, usu. dealing with matters of politics, national security, etc.; **Secret Service** a department of government service whose operations are not disclosed: its activities: (without *cap.*) espionage. — **in secret** with precautions against being known: in confidence, as a secret: secretly; **in the secret** admitted to, participating in, knowledge of the secret; **keep a secret** not to divulge a secret; **of secret** (*Shak.*) of a secret character; **open secret** see **open**; **secret of, secret de** (*sə-krā də*), **Polichinelle** (*po-lē-shē-nel';* Fr. name and character equivalent to **Punchinello**) something known to everyone. [L. *sēcernĕre, sēcrētum — sē-,* apart, *cernĕre,* to separate.]

secretaire See **secretary.**

secretary *sek'ri-tə-ri, n.* one employed to write or transact business for another or for a society, company, etc.: the minister at the head of certain departments of state: an ambassador's or minister's assistant: a secretaire: secretary hand: secretary type. — *n.* **secretaire** (*sek'ri-tār, sək-rə-ter;* from Fr.) a secret repository: a writing desk, escritoire. — *adj.* **secretarial** (-*tār'i-əl*). — *ns.* **secretā'riat(e)** (-*ət*) secretaryship: a secretary's office: the administrative department of a council, organisation, legislative or executive body: a body of secretaries; **sec'retaryship** the office, duties, or art of a secretary. — **sec'retary-bird** a long-legged snake-eating African bird of prey (*Serpentarius*), said to be named from the tufts of feathers at the back of its head like pens stuck behind the ear; **sec'retary-gen'eral** the chief administrator of an organisation, e.g. the United Nations; **secretary hand** an old legal style of handwriting; **secretary type** a type in imitation of secretary hand. — **secretaire à abattant** (*a ab-at-ā*) a writing cabinet with a desk-flap that closes vertically; **Secretary of State** a cabinet minister holding one of the more important folios: in U.S., the foreign secretary. [M.E. *secretarie* — L.L. *sēcrētārius* — L. *sēcrētum;* see **secret.**]

secrete, secretin, etc. See **secret.**

sect[1] *sekt, n.* a body of followers: a school of opinion, esp. in religion or philosophy: a subdivision of one of the main religious divisions of mankind: an organised denomination, used esp. by members of the greater churches to express their disapprobation of the lesser:

a dissenting body: a party: a class of people: a sex (now *illit*.). — *adjs*. **sectā'rial** distinguishing a sect (esp. in India); **sectā'rian** of a sect or sectary: narrow, exclusive: denominational. — *n*. an Independent (*hist*.): one of a sect: one strongly imbued with the characteristics of a sect, esp. if bigoted. — *v.t*. **sectā'rianise, -ize**. — *ns*. **sectā'rianism; sectary** (*sekt'ər-i*) a follower, a votary: one of a sect: a dissenter; **sectā'tor** (*rare*) an adherent of a school or party. [L. *secta*, a school or following - *sequī, secūtus*, to follow, influenced by *secāre*, to cut.]

sect² *sekt, n*. (*Shak*.) a cutting. — *adj*. **sectile** (*sek'tīl*) capable of being cut with a knife without breaking. - - *ns*. **sectility** (*-til'i-ti*); **sec'tion** (*-shən*) the act of cutting: a division: a portion: one of the parts into which anything may be considered as divided or of which it may be built up: the line of intersection of two surfaces: the surface formed when a solid is cut by a plane: an exposure of rock in which the strata are cut across (*geol*.): a plan of anything represented as if cut by a plane or other surface: a thin slice for microscopic examination: in surgery, any process involving cutting: a one-mile square of American public lands: a subdivision of a company, platoon, battery, etc.: a number of men detailed for a special service: a district or region (*U.S*.): a frame for a honeycomb: a section-mark: a building plot (*N.Z*.). — *v.t*. to divide into sections: to make a section of. — *adj*. **sec'tional** of a section: in section: of sectionalism: built up of sections. — *n*. **sectionalisā'tion, -z-**. — *v.t*. **sec'tionalise, -ize** to make sectional: to divide into sections. — *n*. **sec'tionalism** a narrow-minded concern for the interests of a group, area, etc., at the expense of the general or long-term: class spirit. — *adv*. **sec'tionally**. — *v.t*. **sec'tionise, -ize** to section. — *n*. **sec'tor** (*-tər*) a plane figure bounded by two radii and an arc: an object of like shape: an instrument of like shape for measuring angular distance (*astron*.): a length or section of a fortified line or army front: a mathematical instrument consisting of two graduated rules hinged together, originally with a graduated arc: a telescope turning about the centre of a graduated arc: a division, section, of (usu.) a nation's economic operations. — *v.t*. to divide into sectors. — *adjs*. **sec'toral** of a sector; **sectorial** (*-tō'ri-əl, -tö'*) sectoral: adapted for cutting. — *n*. a carnassial tooth: a vein in the wings of insects. — **sec'tion-cutter** an instrument for making sections for microscopic work; **sec'tion-mark** the sign §, used to mark the beginning of a section of a book or as a reference mark. [L. *secāre, sectum*, to cut.]

secular *sek'ū-lər, adj*. pertaining to or coming or observed once in a lifetime, generation, century, age (*Rom. hist*. about 100 to 120 years): appreciable only in the course of ages: age-long: age-old: pertaining to the present world, or to things not spiritual: civil, not ecclesiastical: lay: not concerned with religion: not bound by monastic rules (opp. to *regular*): of the secular clergy: lasting for a long time: occurring in cycles. — *n*. a layman: an ecclesiastic (as a parish priest) not bound by monastic rules. — *n*. **seculārisā'tion, -z-**. — *v.t*. **sec'ularise, -ize** to make secular. — *ns*. **sec'ularism** the belief that the state, morals, education, etc., should be independent of religion: G. J. Holyoake's (1817–1906) system of social ethics. — *n*. and *adj*. **sec'ularist**. — *adj*. **secularist'ic**. — *n*. **secularity** (*-lar'*). — *adv*. **sec'ularly**. — **secular arm** the civil power; **secular games** (*Rom. hist*.) games held at long intervals; **secular hymn** a hymn for the secular games. [L. *saeculāris — saeculum*, a lifetime, generation.]

seculum. See **saeculum**.

secund *sē'kund*, also *sek'und, si-kund', adj*. (*bot*.) all turned to the same side. — *ns*. **sec'undine** (*-in, -īn*) the inner (rarely outer and second formed) coat of an ovule: (in *pl*.) the afterbirth; **secundogeniture** (*-jen'*) inheritance of or by a second child or son. [L. *secundus*, following, second.]

secundum *si-kun'dum, se-kōōn'dŏŏm*, (L.) following, according to. — **secundum artem** (*är'tem*) skilfully: professionally; **secundum ordinem** (*ör'di-nem*) in order; **secundum quid** (*kwid*) in some respects only.

secure *si-kūr', adj*. without care or anxiety: confident: over-confident: free from danger: safe: assured: affording safety: stable: firmly fixed or held: in police, etc., custody. — *adv*. (*poet*.) in security. — *v.t*. to make secure, safe, or certain: to make secure the possession of: to establish in security: to prevent (*obs*.): to seize and guard: to get hold of: to contrive to get: to plight or pledge (*obs*.): to guarantee: to fasten. — *v.i*. to make sure: to be, or make oneself, safe. — *adj*. **secūr'able**. — *n*. **secūr'ance** (*rare*). — *adv*. **secūre'ly**. — *ns*. **secure'ment; secure'ness; secūr'er; secūr'itan** (*obs*.) one who dwells in fancied security; **securitisā'tion, -z-** the procedure, practice or policy of making (loans, mortages, etc.) into negotiable securities. — *v.t*. **secur'itise, -ize** to make (debts) into securities. — **secūr'ity** the state, feeling, or means of being secure: protection from espionage: certainty: carelessness (*arch*.): a pledge: a surety: a guarantee: a right conferred on a creditor to make him sure of recovery: (usu. in *pl*.) a bond or certificate in evidence of debt or property. — *adj*. for securing security. — **secure unit** a government-run institution for the confinement of difficult or mentally disordered persons, juvenile offenders, etc.; **security blanket** a blanket, piece of material, etc., that a child comes to depend upon for a sense of comfort and security: something that (irrationally) makes one feel secure or happy (*fig*.): an official set of measures, a policy, etc., applied to conceal a matter of security; **Security Council** a body of the United Nations consisting of five permanent members (China, France, U.K., U.S.A., U.S.S.R. — each with the right of veto) and six elected two-yearly members, charged with the maintenance of international peace and security; **security risk** a person considered from his political affiliations or leanings to be unsafe for state service: a person in a company, etc., who is considered capable of divulging confidential matters, industrial secrets, etc. [L. *sēcūrus — sē-*, without, *cūra*, care.]

securiform *si-kū'ri-förm, adj*. axe-shaped. [L. *secūris*, axe — *secāre*, to cut, *förma*, form.]

sed, se'd. Miltonic spellings of **said** (*pa.t*. and *pa.p*.).

sedan *si-dan', n*. a covered chair for one, carried on two poles (also **sedan'-chair**; *hist*.): a litter: a palanquin: a large closed motor-car (*U.S*.), a saloon-car. [App. not conn. with *Sedan* in France; poss. It. *sedere*, to sit.]

sedate *si-dāt', adj*. composed: staid. — *v.t*. to calm, quieten, by means of sedatives. — *adv*. **sedāte'ly**. — *ns*. **sedāte'ness; sedā'tion** the act of calming, or state of being calmed, by means of sedatives. — *adj*. **sedative** (*sed'ə-tiv*) calming: composing: allaying excitement or pain. — *n*. a sedative medicine or agent. [L. *sēdātus*, pa.p. of *sēdāre*, to still.]

se defendendo *sē di-fend-end'ō, sā de-fend-end'ō*, (L.) in self-defence.

sedent *sē'dənt, adj*. seated. — *adv*. **sedentarily** (*sed'ən-tər-i-li*). — *n*. **sed'entariness**. — *adj*. **sed'entary** sitting much: requiring much sitting: inactive: stationary: not migratory: lying in wait, as a spider: attached to a substratum (*zool*.). — **sedentary soil** soil remaining where it was formed. [L. *sedēns, -entis* (pr.p.), and *sedentārius — sedēre*, to sit.]

Seder *sā'dər, n*. the ceremonial meal and its rituals on the first night or first two nights of the Passover. [Heb., order.]

sederunt *si-dē'runt, si-dā'rənt, sā-dā'rōōnt, n*. in Scotland a sitting, as of a court: a list of persons present. — **Acts of Sederunt** ordinances of the Court of Session. [L. *sēdērunt*, there sat — *sedēre*, to sit.]

sedes *sē'dēz, sed'ās*, (L.) *n*. seat. — **sedes impedita** (*im-pə-dī'tə, im-ped'i-ta*) a papal or episcopal see where there is a partial cessation by the incumbent of his episcopal duties; **sedes vacans** (*vā'kənz, va', wa'kanz*) also **sede vacante** (*sē'dē və-kan'ti, sed'e va-, wa-kan'te; ablative*) a term of canon law to designate a papal or episcopal see when vacant.

sedge[1] *sej, n.* any species of Carex or other plant of the Cyperaceae, a family distinguished from grasses by its solid triangular stems and leaf-sheaths without a slit: extended to iris and other plants: (also **sedge fly**) any of several mayflies or caddis flies common along rivers: an artificial fly resembling a sedge fly. — *adjs.* **sedged** of sedge: bordered with sedge; **sedg'y** of, like, abounding with sedge. — **sedge'land**; **sedge'-war'bler** (also **sedge'-bird, sedge'-wren**) a common British warbler of watery places. [O.E. *secg*; cf. L.G. *segge*.]

sedge[2] *sej, n.* See **siege**.

sedigitated *sē-dij'i-tā-tid, adj.* six-fingered. [L. *sēdigitus* — *sex*, six, *digitus*, finger.]

sedilia *si-dil'i-ə, n.pl.* seats (usu. three, often in niches) for the officiating clergy, on the south side of the chancel: — *sing.* **sedile** (*si-dī'li,* L. *se-dē'le*). [L. *sedīle*, pl. *sedīlia*, seat.]

sediment *sed'i-mənt, n.* what settles at the bottom of a liquid: dregs: a deposit. — *v.t.* to deposit as sediment: to cause or allow to deposit sediment. — *adj.* **sedimentary** (*-men'tər-i*). — *n.* **sedimentā'tion** deposition of sediment. — *adj.* **sedimentolog'ical.** — *ns.* **sedimentol'ogist**; **sedimentol'ogy** the study of sedimentary rock (*geol.*). — **sedimentary rocks** those formed by accumulation and deposition of fragmentary materials or organic remains. [L. *sedimentum* — *sedēre*, to sit.]

sedition *si-dish'ən, n.* insurrection (*arch.*): public tumult: (vaguely) any offence against the state short of treason. — *n.* **sedi'tionary** an inciter to sedition: inducement to attempt, otherwise than by lawful means, alteration in church or state. — *adj.* **sedi'tious.** — *adv.* **sedi'tiously.** — *n.* **sedi'tiousness.** [O.Fr., — L. *sēditiō, -ōnis* — *sēd-*, away, *īre, ītum,* to go.]

seduce *si-dūs', v.t.* to draw aside from party, belief, allegiance, service, duty, etc.: to lead astray: to entice: to corrupt: to induce to have sexual intercourse. — *ns.* **seduce'ment** the act of seducing or drawing aside: allurement; **sedū'cer.** — *n.* and *adj.* **sedū'cing.** — *adv.* **sedū'cingly.** — *n.* **seduction** (*si-duk'shən*) the act of seducing: allurement. — *adj.* **seduc'tive** alluring. — *adv.* **seduc'tively.** — *ns.* **seduc'tiveness; seduc'tor** (*obs.*) one who leads astray; **seduc'tress.** [L. *sēdūcĕre, sēductum* — *sē-*, aside, *dūcĕre,* to lead.]

sedulous *sed'ū-ləs, adj.* assiduous. — *ns.* **sedulity** (*si-dū'li-ti*); **sed'ulousness.** — *adv.* **sed'ulously.** [L. *sēdulus* — *sē dolō,* without deception, hence in earnest.]

Sedum *sē'dəm, n.* the stonecrop genus of Crassulaceae: (without *cap.*) a plant of the genus. [L. *sĕdum,* house-leek.]

see[1] *sē, n.* a seat, esp. of dignity or authority (*obs.*): a throne, esp. a bishop's (*arch.*): the office of bishop of a particular diocese: (wrongly according to some) a cathedral city, also a diocese. — **Holy See** the papal court. [O.Fr. *se, sied* — L. *sēdēs, -is* — *sedēre,* to sit.]

see[2] *sē, v.t.* to perceive by the sense seated in the eye: to perceive mentally: to apprehend: to recognise: to understand: to learn: to be aware by reading: to look at: to judge, to deem: to refer to: to ascertain: to make sure: to make sure of having: to wait upon, escort: to call on: to receive as a visitor: to meet: to consult: to experience: to meet and accept by staking a similar sum: to spend on seeing (*Shak.*; with *away*). — *v.i.* to have power of vision: to see things well enough: to look or inquire: to be attentive: to consider: — *pa.t.* **saw** (illit. **see, seed, seen**); *pa.p.* **seen.** — *imper.,* passing into *interj.,* see look: behold. — *n.* (*rare*) an act of seeing. — *adj.* **see'able.** — *n.* **see'ing** sight: vision: clear-sightedness: atmospheric conditions for good observation (*astron.*). — *adj.* having sight, or insight: observant: discerning. — *conj.* (also **seeing that**) since: in view of the fact. — *n.* **seer** (*sē'ər*) one who sees: (*sēr*) one who sees into the future: — *fem.* **seer'ess.** — **see'ing stone** a scrying crystal. — *adj.* **see'-through** transparent. — **have seen better days, one's best days** to be now on

the decline; **let me see** a phrase employed to express reflection; **see about** to consider: to do whatever is to be done about: to attend to; **see fit** to think it appropriate (to); **see off** to accompany (someone) at his departure: to reprimand (*slang*): to get rid of (*coll.*); **see one's way clear to** (*coll.*) to feel that one will be able to; **see out** to conduct to the door: to see to the end: to outlast; **see over, round** to look or be conducted all through e.g. premises, property; **see red** see **red**[1]; **see someone right** (*coll.*) to take care of someone, usu. in the sense of giving them a tip or reward; **see the light** to experience a religious conversion: to come round to another's way of thinking, to come to understand and agree with someone (usu. *facet.*); **see things** see **thing**; **see through** to participate in to the end: to back up till difficulties end: to understand the true nature of, esp. when faults or bad intentions are concealed by a good appearance; **see to** to look after: to make sure about; **see what I can do** do what I can; **see you (later), be seeing you** (*coll.*) goodbye for now; **well (ill) seen** well (ill) versed. [O.E. *sēon*; Ger. *sehen,* Du. *zien*.]

see[3] *sē, n.* the third letter of the alphabet (C, c).

seecatch *sē'kach, n.* an adult male Aleutian fur seal: — *pl.* **see'catchie.** [Russ. *sekach,* prob. from Aleutian Indian.]

seed[1] *sēd, n.* that which is sown: a multicellular structure by which flowering plants reproduce, consisting of embryo, stored food, and seed-coat, derived from the fertilised ovule (*bot.*): a small hard fruit or part in a fruit, a pip: a seed-like object or aggregate: semen: spawn: the condition of having or proceeding to form seed: sown land: grass and clover grown from seed: a first principle: germ: a crystal introduced to start crystallisation: offspring, descendants, race: a small bubble in glass: a tournament player who has been seeded (*coll.*). — *v.i.* to produce seed: to run to seed. — *v.t.* to sow: to sprinkle, powder, dust: to remove seeds from: in lawn-tennis tournaments, etc., to so arrange (the draw) so that the best players do not meet in the early rounds: to deal with (good players) in this way: to introduce particles of material (into something, e.g. a chemical solution) to induce crystallisation or precipitation: (*specif.*) to induce rainfall, disperse a storm or freezing fog, etc., by scattering cloud with particles of an appropriate substance (also **cloud seeding**). — *adj.* **seed'ed** cleaned of seeds: having seeds: bearing seed: full-grown: sown: showing seeds or carpels (*her.*): of a tournament player, who has been seeded. — *n.* **seed'er** a seed-drill: an apparatus for removing seeds from fruit: a seed-fish. — *adv.* **seed'ily.** — *n.* **seed'iness.** — *n.* and *adj.* **seed'ing.** — *adjs.* **seed'less; seed'-like.** — *n.* **seed'ling** a plant reared from the seed: a young plant ready for planting out from a seedbed: a seed oyster. — Also *adj.* — *n.* **seed'ness** (*Shak.*) sowing. — *adj.* **seed'y** abounding with seed: having the flavour of seeds: not cleared of seeds: run to seed: worn out: out of sorts: shabby. — **seed'bed** a piece of ground for receiving seed: an environment, etc., that fosters a particular thing (esp. something considered undesirable); **seed'box** a plant capsule; **seed'cake** a cake with caraway seeds; **seed'-coat** the covering derived from the ovule's integuments; **seed'-coral** coral in small irregular pieces; **seed'-corn** grain for sowing: assets likely to bring future profit; **seed'-drill** a machine for sowing seeds in rows; **seed'-field** a field in which seed is sown; **seed'-fish** a fish about to spawn; **seed'-lac** granular residues of lac after trituration; **seed'-leaf** a cotyledon, leaf contained in a seed; **seed'lip** a sower's basket (O.E. *sǣdlēap* — *lēap,* basket); **seed'-lobe** a cotyledon; **seed money** money with which a project or enterprise is set up; **seed'-oil** oil expressed from seeds; **seed'-oyster** a very young oyster; **seed'-pearl** a very small pearl; **seed'-plant** a spermatophyte or flowering plant: a plant grown from or for seed; **seed'-plot** a piece of nursery ground, a hot-bed; **seed'-potato** a potato tuber for planting; **seed'-shop; seeds'-**

man a dealer in seeds: a sower; **seed'-stalk** the funicle; **seed'-time** the season for sowing seeds; **seed'-vessel** a dry fruit: the ovary of a flower; **seed'y-toe** a disease of the horse's foot. — **go**, **run**, **to seed** to grow rapidly and untidily in preparation for seeding, instead of producing the vegetative growth desired by the grower: to disappoint expectation of development: to become exhausted: to go to waste: (usu. **go**) to become unkempt, shabby; **sow the seed(s) of** to initiate. [O.E. *sǣd*; cf. *sāwan*, to sow; O.N. *sǣth*; Ger. *Saat*.]

seed². See **see²**.

seek *sēk*, *v.t.* to look for: to try to find, get, or achieve: to ask for: to aim at: to resort to, betake oneself to: to advance against: to try: to search, examine (*arch.*). — *v.i.* to make search: to resort (*Milt.*): — *pa.t.* and *pa.p.* **sought** (*söt*). — *n.* **seek'er** one who seeks: an inquirer: a dissector's probing instrument: a telescopic finder: (with *cap.*) a member of a 17th-century sect who sought for the true church. — **seek-no-furth'er** a reddish winter apple. — **seek after** to go in quest of; **seek for** to look for; **seek out** to look for and find: to bring out from a hidden place; **sought after** in demand; **to seek** not to be found: wanting: at a loss to know (*arch.*; e.g. *What real good is, I am to seek*): defective (in; *arch.*). [O.E. *sēcan* (pa.t. *sōhte*, pa.p. *gesōht*); cf. Ger. *suchen*.]

seel¹ *sēl*, *v.t.* to sew up the eyelids of, as a hawk: to blindfold: to blind, hoodwink. [O.Fr. *siller*, *ciller* — *cil* — L. *cilium*, eyelid, eyelash.]

seel², **sele**, **seal** (*Scot.* **seil**) *sēl*, (*dial.*) *n.* happiness: good fortune: opportune time: season: time of day. — *adj.* **seel'y** fortunate, happy, good (*obs.*): simple, innocent (*Spens.*): pitiful, wretched, trifling: to be pitied, poor (*obs.*): foolish (see **silly**). — **pass the seel of the day** to greet in passing. [O.E. *sǣl*, time, due time, happiness; see **silly**.]

seel³ *sēl*, (*naut.*; *obs.*) *v.i.* to heel over suddenly. — *n.* a sudden heeling. [Origin obscure.]

seeld *sēld*, **seeling**. Spenserian forms of **seld**, **ceiling**.

seely. See **seel²**.

seem *sēm*, *v.i.* to appear: to appear to oneself: to appear to be: to be fitting (*Spens.*). — *v.t.* (*arch.*) to beseem, befit. — *ns.* **seem'er**; **seem'ing** appearance: semblance: a false appearance: way of thinking. — *adj.* apparent: ostensible. — *adv.* apparently: in appearance only (esp. in composition, as **seem'ing-sim'ple**, **seem'ing-vir'tuous**). — *adv.* **seem'ingly** apparently: as it would appear. — *n.* **seem'ingness**. — *adj.* **seem(e)'less(e)** (*Spens.*) unseemly: indecorous. — *ns.* **seem'lihe(a)d** (*Spens.* **seem'lyhed**) seemliness; **seem'liness**. — *adj.* **seem'ly** (*compar.* **seem'lier**; *superl.* **seem'liest**) becoming: suitable: decent: handsome. — Also *adv.* (*arch.*). — **it seems** it appears: it would seem; **it would seem** it turns out: I have been told; **meseems**, **meseemed**, **himseemed**, etc., (*arch.*) it seems, seemed, to me, etc. [O.N. *sǣma*, to beseem.]

seen. See **see²**.

seep *sēp*, *v.i.* to ooze, percolate. — *n.* **seep'age**. — *adj.* **seep'y**. [Cf. **sipe¹**.]

seer¹ *sēr*, *n.* an Indian weight of widely ranging amount, officially about 2 lb. [Pers. *sīr*.]

seer², **seeress**. See **see²**.

seersucker *sēr'suk-ər*, *n.* a thin crinkly Indian linen (or cotton) striped or checked fabric. [Pers. *shīr o shakkar*, lit. milk and sugar.]

seesaw *sē'sö'*, *sē'sö*, *n.* alternate up-and-down or back-and-forth motion: repeated alternation, as a cross-ruff at cards, sing-song speech: a plank balanced so that its ends may move up and down alternately: the sport of rising and sinking on it. — *adj.* going like a seesaw. — *adv.* in the manner of a seesaw. — *v.i.* to play at seesaw: to move or go like a seesaw. — *v.t.* to make to go up and down. [Prob. a redup. of **saw²**, from a sawyer's jingle — *See saw sack a down*.]

seethe *sēdh*, *v.t.* to boil: to soak to a condition as if boiled. — *v.i.* to boil: to surge (*lit.* or *fig.*): to be agitated (by anger, excitement, etc.): — *pa.t.* **seethed**, (*arch.*) **sod**;

pa.p. **seethed**, (*arch.*) **sodd'en**. — *n.* surge. — *n.* **seeth'er**. — *n.* and *adj.* **seeth'ing**. [O.E. *sēothan* (pa.t. *sēath*, pl. *sudon*; pa.p. *soden*); O.N. *sjōtha*, Ger. *sieden*.]

seewing. A Spenserian spelling of **suing** (see **sue**).

seg¹ *seg*, (*obs.* or *dial.*) *n.* Same as **sedge¹**.

seg² *seg*, *n.* a stud or small metal plate in the sole of a shoe to protect it from wearing down, esp. at the toe or heel. [Poss. from O.N. *sigg*, hard skin, a callous.]

segar *si-gär'*, *n.* a variant of **cigar**.

seggar. Same as **saggar**.

seg(h)ol *se-gōl'*, *n.* a vowel-point in Hebrew with sound of *e* in *pen*, placed under a consonant, thus (˸). — *n.* **seg(h)'ōlate** a disyllabic noun form with tone-long vowel in the first and a short seghol in the second syllable. [Heb.]

segment *seg'mənt*, *n.* a part cut off: a portion: part of a circle, ellipse, etc., cut off by a straight line, or of a sphere, ellipsoid, etc., by a plane: a section: one of a linear series of similar portions, as of a vibrating string between nodes, a somite or metamere of a jointed animal, or a joint of an appendage: a lobe of a leaf-blade not separate enough to be a leaflet. — *v.t.* and *v.i.* (also **-ment'**) to divide into segments. — *adj.* **segmental** (**-ment'l**) of a segment: by segments: forming or formed of a segment, segments, arc, or arcs. — *adv.* **segmen'tally**. — *adjs.* **seg'mentary**, **seg'mentate**. — *n.* **segmentā'tion**. — *adj.* **segment'ed** (or *seg'*). — **segmental arch** an arch forming an arc of a circle whose centre is below the springing. [L. *segmentum* — *secāre*, to cut.]

segno *sā'nyō*, (*mus.*) *n.* a sign to mark the beginning or end of repetitions — 𝄋 — *pl.* **se'gnos**. [It., — L. *signum*, a mark.]

sego *sē'gō*, *n.* a showy liliaceous plant (*Calochortus*) of western U.S.: — *pl.* **sē'gos**. [Ute Indian name.]

segol. See **seg(h)ol**.

segreant *seg'ri-ənt*, (*her.*) *adj.* generally understood to mean with raised wings. [Earlier *sergreant*, origin unknown.]

segregate *seg'ri-gāt*, *v.t.* to set apart: to seclude: to isolate: to group apart. — *v.i.* to separate out in a group or groups or mass. — *adj.* set apart. — *n.* that which is segregated. — *adj.* **seg'regable**. — *n.* **segregā'tion** the act of segregating: the state of being segregated: dispersal (*Shak.*): separation of dominants and recessives in the second generation of a cross (*genetics*): the separation of hereditary factors from one another during spore formation: the separation into patches or undistributed areas of impurities, inclusions, and alloying constituents in metals: a segregated mass or group: separation of one particular class of persons from another, as on grounds of race; **segregā'tionist** a believer in racial or other segregation. — *adj.* **seg'regative**. [L. *sēgregāre*, **-ātum** — *sē-*, apart, *grex*, *gregis*, a flock.]

segue *sā'gwā*, (*mus.*) follows, usu. as a musical direction to proceed immediately with the next song, movement, etc., i.e. without a pause. — *n.* the term or direction to segue: the act or result of segueing: segued music (live or recorded): a compilation, esp. in popular recorded music, in which tracks follow on continuously. — *v.i.* to proceed immediately with the next movement, etc. (also *fig.*): — *pr.p.* **se'gueing**; *pa.t.* and *pa.p.* **se'gued**. [It.]

seguidilla *seg-i-dēl'yä*, *n.* a Spanish dance: a tune for it, in triple time. [Sp.]

sei *sā*, *n.* a kind of rorqual (*Balaenoptera borealis*) — also **sei whale**. [Norw. *sejhval*, sei whale.]

seicento *sā-chen'tō*, *n.* in Italian art, literature, etc., the seventeenth century. [It., abbrev. of *mille seicento*, one thousand six hundred.]

seiche *sāsh*, *sesh*, *n.* a periodic fluctuation from side to side of the surface of lakes. [Swiss Fr.]

Seidlitz *sed'lits*, *adj.* applied to an aperient powder (or rather pair of powders), Rochelle salt and sodium bicarbonate mixed together, and tartaric acid — totally different from the mineral water of *Sedlitz* in Bohemia.

seif *sāf, sīf, n.* a long sand-dune lying parallel to the direction of the wind that forms it. [Ar. *saif*, sword.]

seignior *sā', sē'nyər,* **seigneur** *sen-yær, ns.* a title of address: a feudal lord, lord of a manor. — *ns.* **seign'iorage, seign'orage** lordship: a right, privilege, etc., claimed by an overlord: an overlord's royalty on minerals: a percentage on minted bullion; **seign'ioralty** seignory. — *adjs.* **seignio'rial, seigneu'rial, seignoral** *(sān', sen'),* **signo'rial** *(sin-)* manorial. — *ns.* **seign'iorship; seign'- (i)ory** feudal lordship: the council of an Italian city-state *(hist.):* (also **seigneurie** *sen'yə-rē*) a domain. — **grand** *(grã)* **seigneur** a great lord: a man of aristocratic dignity and authority; **Grand Seignior, Signior** *(hist.)* the Sultan of Turkey. [Fr. *seigneur* — L. *senior, -ōris,* compar. of *senex,* old. In L.L. *senior* is sometimes equivalent to *dominus,* lord.]

seil¹. Same as **sile.**

seil² *(Scot.).* See **seel².**

seine *sān,* or *sēn, n.* a large vertical fishing-net whose ends are brought together and hauled. — *v.t.* and *v.i.* to catch or fish with a seine. — Also **sean.** — *ns.* **sein'er; sein'ing.** — **seine'-boat; seine'-fishing; seine'-net; seine'- shooting.** [O.E. *segne* — L. *sagēna* — Gr. *sagēnē,* a fishing-net.]

seise *sēz, v.t.* an old spelling of **seize,** still used legally in the sense of to put in possession: — *pa.p.* **seis'ed** *(Spens.)* reached, attained. — *n.* **seis'in** possession (now, as freehold): an object handed over as a token of possession: sasine *(Scots law).*

seism *sīzm, n.* an earthquake. — *adjs.* **seis'mal, seis'mic, -al.** — *ns.* **seismicity** *(-mis'i-ti)* liability to or frequency of earthquakes; **seis'mism** earthquake phenomena. — **seismo-** in composition, earthquake. — *ns.* **seis'mo-gram** a seismograph record; **seis'mograph** an instrument for registering earthquakes; **seismog'rapher.** — *adjs.* **seismograph'ic, -al.** — *n.* **seismog'raphy** the study of earthquakes. — *adjs.* **seismolog'ic, -al.** — *ns.* **seis-mol'ogist; seismol'ogy** the science of earthquakes; **seis-mom'eter** an instrument for measuring earth-movements. — *adjs.* **seismomet'ric, -al.** — *n.* **seismom'etry.** — *adj.* **seismonas'tic.** — *ns.* **seismonas'ty** (Gr. *nastros,* pressed; *bot.)* response to mechanical shock; **seis'-moscope** an instrument for detecting earthquakes. — *adj.* **seismoscop'ic.** — **seismic prospecting** investigating the depth and character of subsurface rock formations by noting the travel times of reflected and refracted artificial shock waves. [Gr. *seismos,* a shaking — *seiein,* to shake.]

seity *sē'i-ti, n.* a self: selfhood, personal identity. [L. *sē,* oneself.]

seize, form., and still in legal sense, **seise** *(Spens., Shak., Milt.,* **sease, seaze, ceaze,** etc.) *sēz, v.t.* to put in legal possession: to fix: to take possession of: to grasp suddenly, eagerly, or forcibly: to take by force: to take prisoner: to apprehend: to lash or make fast: to reach, attain *(naut.* and *Spens.).* — *v.i.* to lay hold: to clutch: to penetrate *(Spens.):* to jam or weld partially for want of lubrication. — *adj.* **seiz'able.** — *ns.* **seiz'er; seiz'in** seisin (see **seise**); **seiz'ing** the action of the verb: a cord to seize ropes with; **seizure** *(sē'zhər; obs.* **sea'sure**) the act of seizing: capture: grasp: a thing seized: a sudden fit or attack of illness. — **be seized with** or **by** to have a sudden strong attack of (e.g. remorse, pneumonia); **seize, seise, of** to put in possession of; **seized, seised, of** in (legal) possession of: aware of: in process of considering; **seize up** to jam, seize. [O.Fr. *seisir, saisir* — L.L. *sacīre,* prob. Gmc.; cf. O.H.G. *sazzan,* to set, Ger. *setzen,* Eng. *set.*]

sejant *sē'jənt, (her.) adj.* sitting (upright). — Also **sē'jeant.** [O.Fr. *seiant,* Fr. *séant,* pr.p. of *seoir* — L. *sedēre,* to sit.]

Sejm *sām, n.* the unicameral parliament of the Polish People's Republic. [Pol., assembly.]

sekos *sē'kos, n.* a sacred enclosure. [Gr. *sēkos.*]

Sekt *sekt, n.* German sparkling wine or champagne (also without *cap.*). [Ger.]

sel *sel, (Scot.) n.* self.

selachian *si-lā'ki-ən, n.* any fish of the shark class. — Also *adj.* [Gr. *selachos.*]

seladang *se-lä'dang,* **sladang** *slä'dang, ns.* the gaur. [Malay *seladang, saladang.*]

Selaginella *si-laj-i-nel'ə, n.* a genus of heterosporous club-mosses constituting the family **Selaginellā'ceae:** (without *cap.*) a plant of the genus. [Dim. of L. *selāgō, -inis,* a plant mentioned by Pliny.]

selah *sē'lä, n.* in the psalms, a Hebrew word probably meaning pause.

Selbornian *sel-bör'ni-ən, adj.* of *Selborne* in Hampshire, or of Gilbert White (1720–93), author of *The Natural History and Antiquities of Selborne:* of Gault and Upper Greensand *(geol.).* — *n.* an admirer of Gilbert White: the Gault and Upper Greensand.

selcouth *sel'kōōth, (Spens.) adj.* strange. [O.E. *sel(d)cūth* — *seldan,* seldom, *cūth,* known — *cunnan,* to know.]

seld *seld, adj. (Spens.)* rare, uncommon. — *adv. (obs.)* seldom, rarely. — *adjs.* **seld'seen** *(obs.)* rarely seen; **seld'shown** *(Shak.)* rarely shown. [See **seldom.**]

seldom *sel'dəm, adv.* rarely. — *adj.* infrequent. — *n.* **sel'domness.** — *adv.* **sel'dom-times.** [O.E. *seldum,* altered (on the analogy of *hwīlum,* whilom) from *seldan;* Ger. *selten.*]

sele. Same as **seel².**

select *si-lekt', v.t.* to pick out from a number by preference: to free-select *(Austr.).* — *adj.* picked out: choice: exclusive. — *adj.* **selec'ted.** — *n.* **selec'tion** the act of selecting: a thing or collection of things selected: a pot-pourri *(mus.):* a horse selected as likely to win a race: free-selection: a number or group of things from which to select. — *adj.* pertaining to or consisting of collection. — *adj.* **selec'tive** having or exercising power of selection: able to discriminate, e.g. between different frequencies: choosing, involving, etc., only certain things or people. — *adv.* **selec'tively.** — *ns.* **selectiv'ity** *(sel-)* ability to discriminate; **select'ness; select'or.** — *adj.* **selecto'rial.** — **select committee** a number of members of parliament chosen to report and advise on some matter; **selective weedkiller** a weedkiller that does not destroy garden plants; **select'-man** in New England towns, one of a board of officers chosen to manage local business. [L. *sēligĕre, sēlectum — sē-,* aside, *legĕre,* to choose.]

Selene *se-lē'nē, n.* the Greek moon-goddess — Artemis, Phoebe. — *n.* **selenate** *(sel'i-nāt)* a salt of selenic acid. — *adj.* **selenic** *(si-lē'nik, -len'ik)* of the moon: of selenium in higher valency (**selenic acid** H_2SeO_4). — *n.* **selenide** *(sel'i-nīd)* a compound of selenium with an element or radical. — *adjs.* **sele'nious, sele'nous** of selenium in lower valency (**selenious acid** H_2SeO_3). — *n.* **selenite** *(sel'i-nīt)* a moon-dweller: gypsum, esp. in transparent crystals (anciently supposed to wax and wane with the moon): a salt of selenious acid. — *adj.* **selenitic** *(sel-i-nit'ik).* — *n.* **selenium** *(si-lē')* a non-metallic element (symbol Se: at. numb. 34) discovered by Berzelius in 1817 and named from its resemblance to tellurium. — *adj.* **sele'nodont** (Gr. *odous, odontos,* tooth) having crescentic ridges on the crowns of the molar teeth. — *ns.* **sele'nograph** a delineation of the moon; **selenographer** *(sel-in-og'rə-fər)* a student of selenography. — *adjs.* **selenographic** *(si-lē-nə-graf'ik),* **-al.** — *n.* **selenography** *(sel-i-nog'rə-fi)* the delineation or description of the moon: the study of the moon's physical features. — *adj.* **selēnolog'ical.** — *ns.* **selenol'-ogist** a selenographer; **selenol'ogy** the scientific study of the moon; **selenomorphol'ogy** the study of the surface of the moon. — **selenium cell** a photoelectric cell depending on the fact that light increases the electric conductivity of selenium. [Gr. *selēnē,* moon.]

Seleucid *se-lū'sid, n.* a member of the dynasty (**Seleu'-cidae**) that ruled Syria from 312 to 65 B.C., beginning with Alexander's general, *Seleucus I* (Nicator). — Also *adj.* — *adj.* **Seleu'cidan.**

self *self, pron. (obs., commercial,* or *illit.)* oneself, myself, himself, etc. — *n.* an identical person, personality, ego:

a side of one's personality: identity: personality: what one is: self-interest: a self-coloured plant or animal: a thing (esp. a bow) made in one piece: — *pl.* **selves** (*selvz*); of things in one colour or one piece, **selfs**. — *adj.* very, same, identical (*arch.*): own (*arch.*): uniform in colour: made in one piece: made of the same material. — *v.t.* to fertilise by the same individual (self-fertilise) or by the same strain (inbreed). — *n.* **self'hood** personal identity: existence as a person: personality: selfishness. — *adj.* **self'ish** chiefly or wholly regarding one's own self: void of regard to others. — *adv.* **self'ishly.** — *ns.* **self'ishness; self'ism** concentration upon self: the selfish theory of morals — that man acts from the consideration of what will give him the most pleasure; **self'ist.** — *adj.* **self'less** having no regard to self. — *ns.* **self'lessness; self'ness** egotism: personality. — **one self** (*Shak.*) one and the same, one only; **one's self** see **oneself; second self** see **second.** [O.E. *self*; Du. *zelf*; Ger. *selbe*, Goth. *silba*.]

self- *self-*, in composition, acting upon the agent: by, of, in, in relation to, etc., oneself or itself: automatic. — **self'-aban'donment** disregard of self; **self'-abase'ment; self'-abnega'tion** renunciation of one's own interest: self-denial. — *adj.* **self'-absorbed'** wrapped up in one's own thoughts or affairs. — **self'-absorp'tion** the state of being self-absorbed: self-shielding (*phys.*); **self'-abuse'** self-deception (*Shak.*): revilement of oneself: masturbation; **self'-abus'er; self'-accusā'tion.** — *adjs.* **self'-accus'atory; self'-acknow'ledged; self'-act'ing** automatic. — **self'-ac'tion** spontaneous or independent action; **self'-activ'ity** an inherent power of acting; **self'-actualisā'tion, -z-** (*psych.*) the realisation of one's whole personality and one's understanding and development of all its aspects. — *adjs.* **self'-addressed'** addressed to oneself; **self'-adhē'sive** able to stick to a surface without the use of (additional) glue, etc.; **self'-adjust'ing** requiring no external adjustment; **self'-admin'istered.** — **self'-admirā'tion; self'-admiss'ion** (*Shak.*) admission of self-will alone as motive; **self'-advance'ment; self'-advert'isement; self'-ad'vertiser.** — *n.pl.* **self'-affairs'** (*Shak.*) one's own affairs. — *adj.* **self'-affec'ted** (*Shak.*) affected well towards oneself. — **self'-affirma'tion** assertion of the existence of the self. — *adj.* **self'-affright'ed** (*Shak.*) frightened at oneself. — **self'-aggrand'isement; self'-anal'ysis.** — *adj.* **self'-anneal'ing** of metals such as lead, tin, and zinc, recrystallising at air temperature and so able to be cold-worked with little or no strain-hardening. — **self'-annihilā'tion** the losing of one's sense of individual existence when contemplating the divine: a sense of union with God. — *adj.* **self'-anoin'ted.** — **self'-applause'.** — *adj.* **self'-appoint'ed.** — **self'-appreciā'tion; self'-approbā'tion; self'-appro'val.** — *adjs.* **self'-approv'ing; self'-assert'ing, self'-assert'ive** given to asserting one's opinion or to putting oneself forward. — **self'-asser'tion.** — *adj.* **self'-assumed'** assumed by one's own act. — **self'-assump'tion** conceit; **self'-assū'rance** assured self-confidence. — *adjs.* **self'-assured'; self'-aware'.** — **self'-aware'ness.** — *adjs.* **self'-bal'anced** balanced without outward help: stable; **self'-bast'ing** (*cook.*) not requiring to be basted by hand; **self'-begot', self'-begott'en** being its own parent, as the phoenix. — **self'-betray'al; self'-bind'er** a reaping-machine with automatic binding apparatus: a portfolio that grips loose sheets. — *adjs.* **self'-blind'ed; self'-born'** born of itself, as the phoenix; **self'-borne'** (*Shak.*) perh. carried by and against itself, perh. native-born. — **self'-boun'ty** (*Shak.*) native goodness; **self'-breath'** (*Shak.*) one's own utterances. — *adj.* **self'-build'** built, or to be built, by the purchaser or owner. — **self'-capac'itance** capacitance (see **capacity**). — *adjs.* **self'-cat'ering** of a holiday, accommodation, etc., in which one cooks for oneself; **self'-cen'tred** fixed independently: centred in self: selfish. — **self'-char'ity** (*Shak.*) love of oneself. — *adjs.* **self'-clean'ing; self'-clōs'ing** shutting automatically. — **self'-cock'er** a firearm in which the hammer is raised by pulling the trigger. — *adjs.* **self'-cock'ing;**

self'-collect'ed self-possessed. — **self'-colour** uniform colour: natural colour. — *adj.* **self'-coloured.** — **self'=command'** self-control; **self'-commit'ment; self'-commun'ion** communing with oneself, introspective meditation; **self'-compar'ison** (*Shak.*) something to compare with oneself; **self'-complā'cence** satisfaction with oneself, or with one's own performances. — *adj.* **self'-complā'cent.** — **self'-conceit'** an over-high opinion of oneself, one's own abilities, etc.: vanity. — *adj.* **self'-conceit'ed.** — **self'-conceit'edness; self'-concentrā'tion** concentration of one's thoughts upon oneself; **self'-con'cept** one's concept of oneself; **self'-concern';** **self'-condemna'tion.** — *adjs.* **self'-condemned'** condemned by one's own actions or out of one's own mouth; **self'-condemn'ing; self'-confessed'** admitted, openly acknowledged (by oneself). — **self'-con'fidence** confidence in, or reliance on, one's own powers: self-reliance. — *adj.* **self'-con'fident.** — *adv.* **self'-con'fidently.** — *adj.* **self'-confid'ing** relying on one's own powers. — **self'-congratulā'tion.** — *adjs.* **self'-congrat'-ulatory** congratulating oneself; **self'-con'jugate** conjugate to itself; **self'-con'scious** conscious of one's own mind and its acts and states: conscious of being observed by others. — **self'-con'sciousness; self'-con'-sequence** self-importance. — *adjs.* **self'-con'sequent; self'-consid'ering** considering in one's own mind, deliberating. — **self'-consist'ency** consistency of each part with the rest: consistency with one's principles. — *adjs.* **self'-consis'tent; self'-con'stituted** constituted by oneself; **self'-consūmed'; self'-consūm'ing** consuming oneself, or itself; **self'-contained'** wrapped up in oneself, reserved: of a house, flat, room, etc., not approached by an entrance common to others: complete in itself. — **self'-contempt'; self'-content'** self-complacency; **self'-contradic'tion** the act or fact of contradicting oneself: a statement whose terms are mutually contradictory. — *adj.* **self'-contradic'tory.** — **self'-control'** power of controlling oneself. — *adj.* **self'-convict'ed** convicted by one's own acts or words. — **self'-convic'tion.** — *adjs.* **self'-correct'ing; self'-cov'ered** (*Shak.*) perh. disguised by oneself, perh. clothed in one's native semblance; **self'-creā'ted.** — **self'-creā'tion.** — *adj.* **self'-crit'ical.** — **self'-crit'icism** critical examination and judgment of one's own works and thoughts; **self'-cult'ure** development and education of one's personality by one's own efforts. — *adj.* **self'-damn'ing.** — **self'-dān'ger** (*Shak.*) danger to oneself; **self'-deceit'** self-deception. — *adjs.* **self'-deceit'ful; self'-deceived'.** — **self'-deceiv'er; self'-decep'tion** deceiving oneself. — *adj.* **self'-defeat'ing** that defeats its own purpose. — *ns.* **self'-defence'** defending one's own person, rights, etc. (**art of self-defence** orig. boxing, now used more loosely); **self'-degradā'tion; self'-delight'** delight in one's own being or thoughts; **self'-delu'sion** the delusion of oneself by oneself; **self'-deni'al** forbearing to gratify one's own appetites or desires. — *adj.* **self'-deny'ing.** — *adv.* **self'-deny'ingly.** — **self'-depen'dence.** — *adjs.* **self'-depen'dent; self'-depraved'** depraved by one's own act; **self'-dep'recating; self'-deprec'iating** lowering its (or one's) own value: undervaluing oneself or itself. — **self'-despair'** a despairing view of one's own nature, prospects, etc.; **selfe'-despight'** (*Spens.*) injury to oneself. — *adj.* **self'-destroy'ing.** — *v.i.* **self'=destruct'.** — **self'-destruc'tion** the destruction of anything by itself: suicide. — *adj.* **self'-destruc'tive.** — **self'-determinā'tion** determination without extraneous impulse: direction of the attention or will to an object: the power of a population to decide its own government and political relations or of an individual to live his own life. — *adjs.* **self'-deter'mined; self'-deter'-mining.** — **self'-devel'opment.** — *adjs.* **self'-devel'oping; self'-devō'ted; self'-devō'tion** self-sacrifice. — *adjs.* **self'-direct'ed; self'-direct'ing. — self'-direc'tion; self'=direct'or; self'-dis'cipline.** — *adj.* **self'-disliked'** (*Spens.* **selfe'-dislik'ed**). — **self'-dispar'agement.** — *adj.* **self'=displeased'.** — **self'-dispraise'; self'-distrust'; self'=doubt';** **self'-dramatisā'tion, -izātion** presentation of oneself as if a character in a play: seeing in oneself an exaggerated dignity and intensity. — *adjs.* **self'-draw'-ing** (*Shak.*) of one's, its, own drawing, or drawn from itself; **self'-drive'** of a motor vehicle, to be driven by the hirer; **self'-driv'en** driven by its own power; **self'-ed'ucated** educated by one's own efforts. — **self'-efface'ment** keeping oneself in the background out of sight: withdrawing from notice or rights. — *adjs.* **self'-effac'ing; self'-elect'ed** elected by oneself or itself; **self'-elect'ing, self'-elect'ive** having the right to elect oneself or itself, as by co-option of new members. — **self'-elec'tion.** — *adj.* **self'-employed'** working independently in one's own business. — **self'-employ'ment; self-end'** (*obs.*) a private or selfish end. — *adj.* **self'-endeared', -indeared'** self-loving. — **self'-enjoy'ment** internal satisfaction; **self'-enrich'ment; self'-esteem'** good opinion of oneself: self-respect; **self'-ev'idence.** — *adjs.* **self'-ev'ident** evident without proof; **self'-evolved'.** — **self'-examinā'tion** a scrutiny into one's own state, conduct, etc.; **self'-exam'ple** one's own example. — *adjs.* **self'-excit'ed** (*elect.*); **self-excīt'ing** (*elect.*) itself supplying the exciting current; **self'-ex'-ecuting** (*legal*) automatically coming into effect, not needing legislation to enforce. — **self'-exer'tion.** — *adj.* **self'-ex'iled.** — **self'-exist'ence.** — *adjs.* **self'-exist'ent** existing of or by oneself or itself, independent of any other cause; **self'-explan'atory, self'-explain'ing** obvious, bearing its meaning in its own face. — **self'-explicā'tion** the power of explaining oneself; **self'-express'ion** the giving of expression to one's personality, as in art. — *adjs.* **self'-faced'** undressed or unhewn, esp. of a stone showing a natural cleavage; **self'-fed'** fed by itself or automatically: fed upon itself. — **self'-feed'er** a device for supplying anything automatically, esp. a measured amount of foodstuff for cattle, etc. — *adj.* **self-feed'ing.** — **self'-feel'ing** one's own experience. — *adj.* **self'-fer'tile** fertile by its own pollen or sperm. — **self'-fertilīsā'tion, -īzā'tion; self'-fertil'ity.** — *adj.* **self'-fig'ured** of one's own devising. — **self'-fill'er** a fountain-pen that can be filled without a dropping-tube. — *adjs.* **self'-finan'cing; self'-flatt'-ering.** — **self'-flatt'ery.** — *adjs.* **self'-fo'cusing; self'-forget'ful** unselfishly forgetful of self. — *adv.* **self'-forget'fully.** — *adj.* **self'-fulfill'ing.** — **self'-fulfil'ment.** — *adjs.* **self'-gen'erating; self-giv'ing; self'-glazed'** glazed in one tint. — **self'-glorificā'tion.** — *adjs.* **self'-glō'rious** boastful; **self'-gov'erning.** — **self'-gov'ernment** self-control: autonomy: government without outside interference: democracy. — *adjs.* **self'-gra'cious** gracious towards oneself or spontaneously gracious; **self'-harm'ing.** — **self'-hate', self'-hāt'red; self-heal'** prunella; **self'-heal'ing** spontaneous healing: healing oneself. — Also *adj.* — **self'-help'** doing things for oneself without help of others. — Also *adj.* — *adj.* **self'-het'erodyne** autodyne. — **self'-humiliā'tion; self'-hypnō'sis, self'-hyp'notism; self'-iden'tity** identity of a thing with itself: the conscious realisation of the individual identity; **self'-im'age** one's own idea of oneself; **self'-immolā'tion** offering oneself up in sacrifice: suttee; **self'-import'ance** an absurdly high sense of one's own importance: pomposity. — *adj.* **self'-import'ant.** — *adv.* **self'-import'antly.** — **self'-improve'-ment** improvement, by oneself, of one's status, education, job, etc. — *adj.* **self'-imposed'** taken voluntarily on oneself. — **self'-impregnā'tion** impregnation of a hermaphrodite by its own sperm. — *adjs.* **self'-incompat'ible** having reproductive organs that cannot function together; **self'-induced'** induced by oneself: produced by self-induction (*elect.*). — **self'-induc'tance** the property of an electric circuit whereby self-induction occurs; **self'-induc'tion** the property of an electric circuit by which it resists any change in the current flowing in it; **self'-indul'gence** undue gratification of one's appetites or desires. — *adj.* **self'-indul'gent.** — **self'-infec'tion** infection of the entire organism from a local lesion. — *adj.* **self'-inflict'ed** inflicted by oneself on oneself. — *v.i.* **self'-inject'.** — **self'-injec'tion; self'-insū'rance** laying aside a fund to cover losses; **self'-in'terest** private interest: regard to oneself. — *adjs.* **self'-in'terested; self'-invī'ted** invited by nobody but oneself; **self'-involved'** wrapped up in oneself or one's own thoughts: inwoven into itself. — **self'-judg'ment; self-justificā'tion.** — *adjs.* **self'-jus'tifying** justifying oneself: automatically arranging the length of the lines of type (*print.*); **self'-killed'.** — **self'-kill'er.** — *adj.* **self'-know'ing.** — **self'-knowl'edge** knowledge of one's own nature. — *adjs.* **self'-left'** left to oneself; **self'-lev'elling** automatically adjusting so as to be level. — **self'-life'** self-existence: life only for oneself. — *adjs.* **self'-light'ing** igniting automatically; **self'-like** exactly similar; **self'-lim'ited** (*path.*) running a definite course; **self'-liq'uidating** of a loan, business enterprise, etc., yielding sufficient increase to pay for its own redemption, initial outlay, etc.; **self'-load'ing** of a gun, automatically reloading itself; **self'-lock'ing** locking automatically; **self'-lost'** lost by one's own act. — **self'-love'** the love of oneself: tendency to seek one's own welfare or advantage: desire of happiness. — *adjs.* **self'-lov'ing; self'-lum'lnous** emitting a light of its own; **self'-made'** made by oneself: risen to a high position from poverty or obscurity by one's own exertions. — **self'-man'-agement** self-control: the management of a factory, etc., by its own workers; **self'-mas'tery** self-command: self-control; **self'-mett'le** (*Shak.*) natural spirit. — *adj.* **self'-misused'** spoken ill of by oneself. — **self'-mo'tion** spontaneous motion. — *adjs.* **self'-mo'tivated** naturally enterprising: motivated by inherent energy, enthusiasm, ambition, etc., without external impetus; **self'-moved'** moved spontaneously from within. — **self'-mov'ing; self'-mur'der** suicide; **self'-mur'derer.** — *adj.* **self'-mur'dering.** — **self'-neglect', -ing** (*Shak.*) neglect of oneself; **self'-observā'tion** (*psych.*) the observation of one's own behaviour, personality, mental processes, etc. — *adj.* **self'-occ'upied.** — **self'-offence'** one's own offence: failure in what is due to oneself. — *adjs.* **self-o'pened** opened of its own accord; **self'-op'erating.** — **self'-opin'ion** high, or unduly high, opinion of oneself or of one's own opinion. — *adjs.* **self'-opin'-ionated, -opin'ionātive, -opin'ioned** obstinately adhering to one's own opinion; **self'-ordained'.** — **self'-par'ody** parody of oneself or one's own work. — *adjs.* **self'-perpet'uating; self'-pī'ous** hypocritical. — **self'-pit'y** pity for oneself. — *adjs.* **self'-plant'ed** planted without man's agency; **self'-pleas'ing; self'-poised'** balanced without outside help. — **self'-pollinā'tion** transfer of pollen to the stigma of the same flower (or sometimes the same plant or clone); **self'-pollu'tion** masturbation; **self'-por'trait** a portrait of oneself painted by oneself; **self'-por'traiture.** — *adj.* **self'-possessed'** having self-possession. — **self'-possess'ion** collectedness of mind: calmness; **self'-praise'** the praise of oneself by oneself; **self'-preservā'tion** care, action, or instinct for the preservation of one's own life. — *adjs.* **self'-preser'vative, self'-preser'ving.** — **self'-pride'** self-esteem. — *adjs.* **self'-proclaimed'; self'-produced'; self'-professed'.** — **self'-prof'it** private interest. — *adjs.* **self'-prop'agating** propagating itself when left to itself; **self'-propelled'; self'-propell'ing** carrying its own means of propulsion. — **self'-propul'sion; self'-protec'tion** self-defence. — *adjs.* **self'-protect'ing; self'-protec'tive.** — **self'-prun'ing** natural shedding of twigs; **self'-pub'licist** one who actively creates or seeks publicity for himself; **self'-public'ity; self'-pun'ishment.** — *adjs.* **self'-raised'** raised by oneself: grown without cultivation; **self'-rais'ing** (of flour) already mixed with something that causes it to rise (also **self'-ris'ing**). — **self'-realīsā'tion, -z-** attainment of such development as one's mental and moral nature is capable of. — *adjs.* **self'-record'ing** recording its own readings; **self'-referr'ing** (of e.g. literature) containing references to (other parts of) itself. — **self'-regard'** self-interest: self-respect. — *adjs.* **self'-regard'ing; self'-reg'istering** self-recording; **self'-reg'ulating** regulating itself. — **self'-regulā'tion.** — *adj.* **self'-regulāt'ory** (or *reg'*). — **self'-relī'ance** healthy confidence in one's own abilities. — *adjs.* **self'-reli'ant; self'-rely'ing.** — **self'-renuncia'tion** self-abnegation; **self'-repress'ion** restraint of expression of the self; **self'-reproach'** prickings of conscience; **self'-reproof', self'-reprov'ing** reproof of conscience; **self'-repug'-nance.** — *adj.* **self'-repug'nant** self-contradictory: inconsistent. — **self'-resem'blance** (*Spens.*) appearance of being what one really is; **self'-respect'** respect for oneself or one's own character. — *adjs.* **self'-respect'-ful; self'-respect'ing; self'-restrained'** restrained by one's own will. — **self'-restraint'** a refraining from excess: self-control. — *adj.* **self'-reveal'ing.** — **self=revela'tion; self'-rev'erence** great self-respect. — *adjs.* **self'-rev'erent; self'-right'eous** righteous in one's own estimation: pharisaical. — **self'-right'eousness.** — *adjs.* **self'-right'ing** righting itself when capsized; **self'-rig'-orous** rigorous towards oneself; **self'-ris'ing** see **self=raising** above; **self'-rolled'** (*Milt.* **self'-rowld'**) coiled on itself. — **self'-rule'.** — *adj.* **self'-rul'ing.** — **self'-sac'-rifice** forgoing one's own good for the sake of others. — *adjs.* **self'-sac'rificing; self'-same** the very same. — **self'-same'ness** identity; **self'-satisfac'tion** satisfaction with oneself: complacence. — *adjs.* **self'-sat'isfied; self'-sat'isfying** giving satisfaction to oneself; **self=schooled; self'-seal'ing** of envelopes, etc., that can be sealed by pressing two adhesive surfaces together: of tyres, that seal automatically when punctured. — **self'-seed'er** a plant that propagates itself by growing from its own seeds shed around it; **self'-seek'er** one who looks mainly to his own interests: a device which automatically tunes a radio to required wavelengths by means of a push button control. — *n.* and *adj.* **self'-seek'ing.** — **self'-ser'vice** helping oneself, as in a restaurant, petrol station, etc. — Also *adj.* — *adj.* **self'-ser'ving** taking care of one's own interests above all others. — Also *n.* — *adj.* **self'-severe'** (*Milt.*). — **self'-shield'ing** (*phys.*) in large radioactive sources, the absorption in one part of the radiation arising in another part. — *adj.* **self'-slain'.** — **self'-slaugh'ter** suicide. — *adj.* **self'-slaugh'tered.** — **sclf'-slay'er; self'=sov'ereignty** sovereignty over, or inherent in, oneself. — *adjs.* **self'-sown'** sown naturally without man's agency; **self'-standing** independent, standing or functioning alone, without support. — **self'-star'ter** an automatic contrivance for starting a motor: a car fitted with one: a person with initiative and drive. — *adj.* **self'-ster'ile** unable to fertilise itself. — **self'-steril'ity; self'-stud'y** study on one's own, without a teacher. — *adjs.* **self'-styled'** called by oneself: pretended; **self=subdued'** (*Shak.*) subdued by one's own power; **self=substan'tial** (*Shak.*) composed of one's own substance. — **self'-suffi'ciency.** — *adjs.* **self'-suffi'cient** requiring nothing from without: excessively confident in oneself; **self'-suffic'ing.** — **self'-sugges'tion** autosuggestion; **self'-support'** support or maintenance without outside help: paying one's way. — *adjs.* **self'-support'ed; self'=support'ing.** — **self'-surren'der** a yielding up of oneself or one's will. — *adjs.* **self'-surviv'ing** remaining as a mere ruin of itself; **self'-sustained'** sustained by one's own power; **self'-sustain'ing.** — **self'-sustain'ment; self'=sus'tenance, self'-sustenta'tion.** — *adjs.* **self'-taught; self'-tempt'ed; self'-think'ing** thinking for oneself. — **self'-tor'ment.** — *adj.* **self'-torment'ing.** — **self'-tormen-t'or.** — *adj.* **self'-tor'turable** (*Shak.*). — **self'-tor'ture.** — *adj.* **self'-trained'.** — **self'-transforma'tion; self'=treat'ment; self'-trust'** self-reliance: confidence in one's own faithfulness to oneself (*Shak.*). — *adj.* **self'-una'ble** (*Shak.*) insufficient of one's own ability. — **self'=vi'olence** suicide; **self'-vindica'tion; self'-will'** obstinacy. — *adjs.* **self'-willed'; self'-wind'ing** (of a watch) wound by the wearer's spontaneous movements, or by opening and shutting the case: automatically wound by electricity. — **self'-wor'ship; self'-wrong'** (*Shak.*) wrong done to a person by himself. [O.E. *self*; Du. *zelf*, Ger. *selbe*, Goth. *silba*.]

-**self** -*self*, *pl.* -**selves** -*selvz*, a suff. forming reflexive and emphatic pronouns. — **be oneself, himself,** etc., to be

in full possession of one's powers: to be (once more) at one's best: to be alone (*Scot.*); **by oneself,** etc., alone.

selictar *se-lik'tär, n.* a sword-bearer. [Turk. *silihdār* — Pers. *silahdār* — Ar. *silh*, weapon.]

Seljuk *sel-jook', n.* a member of any of the Turkish dynasties (11th–13th cent.) descended from *Seljūq* (grandfather of Togrul Beg): a Turk subject to the Seljuks. — *adjs.* **Seljuk', Seljuk'ian.**

selkie. See **silkie.**

sell[1], **selle** *sel, n.* a seat (*arch.*): a saddle (*Spens.*). [O.Fr. *selle* — L. *sella* — *sedēre*, to sit.]

sell[2] *sel, v.t.* to give or give up for money or other equivalent: to betray: to impose upon, trick: to promote the sale of: to cry up (*obs.*): to make acceptable: to cause someone to accept (e.g. an idea, plan): to convince of the value of something. — *v.i.* to make sales: to be sold, to be in demand for sale: — *pa.t.* and *pa.p.* **sold.** — *n.* (*slang*) a deception: let-down: an act of selling: a particular quality emphasised in order to sell: stocks to be sold: an order to sell stocks. — *adj.* **sell'able** that can be sold. — *n.* **sell'er** one who sells: that which has a sale: a selling race, plate (*coll.*). — **sellers', seller's market** one in which sellers control the price, demand exceeding supply; **sell'ing-pla'ter** a horse fit only to race in a selling race (also *fig.*); **sell'ing-price** the price at which a thing is sold; **selling race, plate** a race of which the winning horse must be put up for auction at a price previously fixed (coll. **sell'er;** cf. **claiming race**); **sell'-out** a betrayal: a show for which all seats are sold. — **sell someone a bargain** see **bargain; sell down the river** to play false, betray; **sell off** to sell cheaply in order to dispose of (*n.* **sell'-off**); **sell on** to sell (what one has bought) to someone else; **sell one's life dearly** to do great injury to the enemy before one is killed; **sell out** to dispose entirely of: to sell one's commission: to betray; **sell short** to belittle, disparage: to sell (stocks, etc.) before one actually owns them, when intending to buy at a lower price; **sell the pass** to betray a trust; **sell up** to sell the goods of, for debt; **to sell** for sale. [O.E. *sellan*, to give, hand over; O.N. *selja*, Goth. *saljan*.]

sell[3] *sel, n.* a Scots form ot **self:** — *pl.* **sells.**

Sellotape® *sel'ə-tāp*, (also without *cap.*) *n.* a brand of usu. transparent adhesive tape. — *v.t.* to stick with Sellotape.

seltzer *selt'sər, n.* a mineral water from Nieder-*Selters* near Wiesbaden in Germany, or an imitation. — *n.* **selt'zogene** a gazogene.

selva *sel'və, n.* (usu. in *pl.* **selvas**) wet forest in the Amazon basin. [Sp., Port. — L. *silva*, wood.]

selvage, selvedge *sel'vij, n.* a differently finished edging of cloth: a border. — *v.t.* to border. — *n.* **sel'vagee** (or -*jē'*) a marked hank of rope, used as a strap or sling. [self, edge.]

selves *selvz, pl.* of **self.**

semantic *si-man'tik, adj.* relating to meaning, esp. of words. — *n. sing.* **seman'tics** the science of the meaning of words. — *n.pl.* (*loosely*) differences in, and shades of, meaning of words. — *n.* **seman'teme** a unit of meaning, a word or the base of a word, that conveys a definite idea. — *adv.* **seman'tically.** — *ns.* **seman'ticist;** **sememe** (*se'mēm, sē'mēm*) a unit of meaning, usu. specif. the smallest linguistically analysable unit. [Gr. *sēmantikos*, significant.]

semantron *sem-an'tron, n.* a wooden or metal bar used instead of a bell in Orthodox churches and in mosques: — *pl.* **seman'tra.** [Gr. *sēmantron*, sign, signal.]

semaphore *sem'ə-fōr, -för, n.* a signalling apparatus, an upright with arms that can be turned up or down — often the signaller's own body and arms with flags. — *v.t.* and *v.i.* to signal thus. — *adv.* **semaphor'ically.** [Fr. *sémaphore* — Gr. *sēma*, sign, signal, *-phoros*, bearing, bearer.]

semasiology *si-mā-zi-ol'ə-ji*, or *-si-, n.* the science of semantics. [Gr. *sēmāsia*, meaning.]

sematic *si-mat'ik*, (*biol.*) *adj.* serving for recognition, attraction, or warning. [Gr. *sēma*, sign.]

semble[1] *sem'bl, v.i.* (*obs.*) to seem: to be like (to). — *v.t.* (*obs.*) to pretend: to picture, image: to make a picture, image, of. — *adj.* **sem'blable** (*Shak.*) resembling, similar, like. — *n.* (*Shak.*) like, fellow. — *adv.* **sem'blably** (*Shak.*) in like manner. — *n.* **sem'blance** likeness: appearance: outward show: apparition: image. — *adj.* (*arch.*) **sem'blant** resembling: seeming. — *n.* (*Spens.*) semblance: cheer, countenance, entertainment: demeanour. — *adj.* **sem'blative** (*Shak.*) resembling or seeming: simulative. [Fr. *sembler*, to seem, to resemble — L. *simulāre* — *similis*, like.]

semble[2] *sem'bl, v.t.* to bring together, collect, esp. as some female moths do males by scent. — **sem'bling-box** a collector's box enclosing a captive female. [Aphetic from **assemble**.]

semé, semée *sem'ā*, (*her.*) *adj.* strewn or scattered over with small bearings, powdered. [Fr., pa.p. of *semer* — L. *sēmināre*, to sow.]

semeiology *sem-i-*, *sēm-i-ol'ə-ji, n.* the study of symptoms: the study of signs and symbols (now usu. **semiology**). — *n.* **semeion** (*sē-mī'on*) in ancient prosody, the unit of time: one of the two divisions of a foot: a mark of metrical or other division: — *pl* **semei'a.** — *adj.* **semeiot'ic** pertaining to symptoms. — *n.sing.* **semeiot'ics** semeiology: semiotics. [Gr. *sēmeion*, sign.]

sememe. See **semantic.**

semen *sē'men, n.* the liquid that carries spermatozoa. — See also **seminal.** [L. *sēmen, -inis*, seed.]

semester *si-mes'tər, n.* a university half-year course or term. — *adjs.* **semes'tral, semes'trial** half-yearly. [L. *sēmēstris* — *sex*, six, *mēnsis*, a month.]

semi- *sem'i-, pfx.* half: (*loosely*) nearly, partly, incompletely. — *ns.* **sem'i** (coll. shortening) a semi-detached house: a semi-bajan (also **sem'ie**); a semi-finished (q.v.) article of steel, copper, etc.; **sem'iangle** a half-angle. — *adj.* **sem'i-ann'ual** (chiefly *U.S.*) half-yearly. — *adv.* **sem'i-ann'ually.** — *adj.* **sem'i-ann'ular** half-ring-shaped. — *n.* and *adj.* **sem'i-Ā'rian** homoiousian. — *n.* **sem'i-Ā'rianism.** — *adjs.* **sem'i-attached'** partially bound; **sem'i-automat'ic** partly automatic but requiring some tending by hand. — *ns.* **sem'i-ax'is** a half-axis; **sem'i-bā'jan** (*hist., Scot. univ.*) a second-year student. — *n.* and *adj.* **sem'i-barbā'rian.** — *ns.* **sem'i-bar'barism; sem'ibrēve** half a breve (2 minims or 4 crotchets); **sem'ibull** a pope's bull issued between election and coronation; **sem'icar'bazide** a base (H₂N·CO·NH·NH₂) reacting with aldehydes and ketones to form **semicar'-bazones.** — *adj.* **sem'i-centenn'ial** occurring at the completion of fifty years. — *n.* (*U.S.*) a jubilee. — *ns.* **sem'ichōr'us** half, or part of, a chorus: a passage sung by it; **sem'icircle** half a circle, bounded by the diameter and half the circumference. — *adjs.* **sem'icircled; sem'icir'cular** (**semicircular canals** the curved tubes of the inner ear concerned with equilibrium): — *adv.* **sem'icir'cularly.** — *ns.* **sem'icirque** (*poet.*) a semicircular hollow: a semicircle; **sem'icolon** (or *-kō'lon*) the point (;) marking a division greater than the comma; **sem'icō'ma** a condition approaching coma. — *adjs.* **sem'icō'matose; sem'iconduct'ing.** — *ns.* **sem'iconductiv'ity; sem'iconduct'or** formerly, any substance with electrical conductivity between that of metals and of non-conductors: now, any solid, non-conducting at low temperatures or in pure state, which is a conductor at high temperatures or when very slightly impure. — *adj.* **sem'icon'scious.** — *ns.* **sem'icyl'inder** a longitudinal half-cylinder; **sem'idem'isem'iquaver** half a demisemiquaver. — *adj.* **sem'idepō'nent** passive in form in the perfect tenses only. — Also *n.* — *adj.* **sem'i-detached'** partly separated: joined by a party wall to one other house only. — *n.* **sem'i-diam'eter** half the diameter, esp. the angular diameter. — *adjs.* **sem'i-diur'nal** accomplished in twelve hours: pertaining to half the time or half the arc traversed between rising and setting; **sem'i-divine'** half-divine: of, of the nature of, a demigod. — *ns.* **sem'idocument'ary** a cinematograph film with an actual background but an invented plot; **sem'i-dome'** half a dome, esp. as formed by a vertical

section. — *adjs.* **sem'idomes'ticated** partially domesticated: half-tame; **sem'i-doub'le** having only the outermost stamens converted into petals. — *n.* a festival less solemn than a double. — *adj.* **sem'i-dry'ing** of oils, thickening without completely drying on exposure. — *n.* **sem'i-ellipse'** half of an ellipse, bounded by a diameter, esp. the major axis. — *adj.* **sem'i-ellip'tical;** — *n.* **sem'i-ev'ergreen** a plant which is evergreen in its original habitat but not completely so in other places it now grows, dropping leaves in severe weather conditions. — Also *adj.* — *adj.* **sem'i'fi'nal** in competitions, sports contests, etc., of the contest immediately before the final. — *n.* a last round but one. — *n.* **sem'iff'nalist** a competitor in a semifinal. — *adjs.* **sem'i-fin'ished** partially finished, specif. of metal shaped into rods, sheets, etc., in preparation for further processing into finished goods; **sem'iflu'id** nearly solid but able to flow to some extent. — Also *n.* — *adj.* **sem'iglob'ular.** — *n.* **sem'i-grand'** a square piano with curtailed keyboard. — Also *adj.* — *n.* and *adj.* **sem'i-im'becile.** — *adj.* **sem'i-independ'ent** not fully independent. — *ns.* **sem'i-ju'hilee** the twenty-fifth anniversary; **sem'i-latus rectum** half the latus rectum, terminated at the focus. — *adjs.* **sem'i-liq'uid** half-liquid; **sem'ilog(arithmic)** of graph paper, graph, etc., having one scale logarithmic, the other arithmetical; **sem'ilu'cent** half-transparent; **sem'i-lu'nar, -lu'nate** half-moon shaped. — *ns.* **sem'-ilune** (*-lōōn*) a half-moon-shaped object, body, or structure; **sem'imanufac'ture** a manufactured product, material, etc., used to make an end-product. — *adj.* **sem'imen'strual** half-monthly. — *n.* **sem'i-met'al** (*obs.*) a metal that is not malleable. — *adj.* **sem'i-month'ly** (chiefly *U.S.*) half-monthly. — *n.* a half-monthly periodical. — *adj.* **sem'i-mute'** with speech impaired by loss of hearing. — Also *n.* — *adjs.* **sem'i-nūde'** half-naked; **sem'i-occā'sional** (*U.S.*) occurring now and then. — *adv.* **sem'i-occā'sionally.** — *adj.* **sem'i-offic'ial** partly official. — *adv.* **sem'i-offic'ially.** — *n.* **sem'i-ō'pal** a dull variety of opal. — *adj.* **sem'i-opaque'** partly opaque; **sem'iovip'arous** producing imperfectly developed young; **sem'ipal'mate** half-webbed: half web-footed. — *ns.* **sem'ipalmā'tion; sem'ipar'asite** a partial parasite, feeding partly independently. — *adj.* **sem'-iparasit'ic.** — *n.* **sem'iped** in verse, a half-foot. — *n.* and *adj.* **Sem'i-Pelā'gian.** — *n.* **Sem'i-Pelā'gianism** the middle course between Augustinian predestination and Pelagian free-will. — *adj.* **sem'ipellu'cid** imperfectly transparent. — *n.* **sem'iperim'eter** half the perimeter. — *adj.* **sem'i-per'meable** permeable by a solvent but not by the dissolved substance. — *ns.* **sem'iplume** a feather with ordinary shaft but downy web; **sem'ipor'celain** a coarse ware resembling porcelain. — *adj.* **sem'i-prec'ious** valuable, but not valuable enough to be reckoned a gemstone. — *n.* **sem'iquaver** half a quaver. — *adj.* **sem'i-rig'id** of an airship, having a flexible gas-bag and stiffened keel. — *n.* **sem'i-ring** a half-ring. — *adj.* **sem'i-sag'ittate** shaped like half an arrowhead. — *n.* and *adj.* **Sem'i-Sax'on** (*obs.*) Early Middle English (c. 1150–1250). — *adjs.* **sem'i-skilled'; sem'i-soft'** (of cheese) fairly soft; **sem'iterete'** half-cylindrical. — *n.* **sem'itone** half a tone — one of the lesser intervals of the musical scale as from B to C. — *adj.* **sem'iton'ic.** — *n.* **sem'itranspā'rency.** — *adjs.* **sem'itranspā'rent** imperfectly transparent; **sem'i-trop'ical** subtropical; **sem'i-tū'bular** like half of a tube divided longitudinally; **sem'i-un'cial** intermediate between uncial and minuscule. — *n.* a semi-uncial letter. — *n.* **sem'ivowel** a sound partaking of the nature of both a vowel and a consonant: a letter representing it, in English, chiefly *w* and *y*, and sometimes used of the liquid consonants *l* and *r*; **semi-water-gas** see **water.** — *adj.* **sem'i-week'ly** issued or happening twice a week. — Also *n.* and *adv.* [L. *sēmi-*, half-; cf. Gr. *hēmi-*, O.E. *sam-*.]

seminal *sem'in-l, adj.* pertaining to, or of the nature of, seed or of semen: of or relating to the beginnings, first development, of an idea, study, etc.: generative: notably creative or influential in future development (*fig.*). — *n.* **seminal'ity** germinating principle: germ. — *adv.* **sem'inally.** — *v.t.* **sem'ināte** to sow: to propagate. — *n.* **seminā'tion** sowing: seed-dispersal: seeding. — *adj.* **seminif'erous** seed-bearing: producing or conveying semen. [L. *sēmen, -inis,* seed.]

seminar *sem'i-när, n.* (orig. *Ger.*) a group of advanced students working in a specific subject of study under a teacher: a class at which a group of students and a tutor discuss a particular topic: a discussion group on any particular subject. — *adjs.* **seminarial** (*-ā'ri-əl*); **seminā'rian** of a seminary. —*n.* a student in a seminary, esp. of R.C. theology. — *ns.* **sem'inarist** (*-ər-ist*) a student in a seminary or in a seminar: a Roman Catholic priest educated in a foreign seminary: a teacher in a seminary; **sem'inary** (*-ə-ri*) a seed-plot: a breeding-place: a place of origin and fostering, nursery: formerly, a pretentious name for a school (esp. for young ladies): a college, esp. for R.C. (in *U.S.* also other) theology: a seminary priest. — *adj.* **seminal:** of a seminary: of a seminar: of great importance and/or influence, esp. as leading to or indicating new insights, new developments or new trends. [L. *sēminārium,* a seed-plot — *sēmen,* seed.]

Seminole *sem'i-nōl, n.* an American Indian of an offshoot of the Creeks, originally in Florida, now mostly in Oklahoma. [Creek *Simánole,* lit. runaway.]

semiology *sem-i-ol'ə-ji,* (*linguistics*) *n.* the science of signs or signals in general: (*loosely*) semiotics. — Also **semeiology.** — *n.sing.* **semiot'ics** the theory of sign-systems in language. — *adj.* **semiot'ic.** [Gr. *semeion,* sign.]

semis *sē'mis, sā'mis, n.* a bronze coin of the ancient Roman republic, half an as. [L. *sēmis, sēmissis.*]

semitar, semitaur. Obs. spellings of **scimitar.**

Semite *sem'* or *sēm'īt, n.* a member of any of the peoples said (Gen. x) to be descended from Shem, or speaking a Semitic language. — *adj.* **Semitic** (*sem-, sim-, sam-it'ik*). — *n.* any Semitic language. — *n.sing.* **Semit'ics** Semitic studies. — *n.* **Semitīsā'tion, -z-.** — *v.t.* **Sem'-ltlse, -ize** to render Semitic in language, religion, or otherwise. — *ns.* **Sem'itism** a Semitic idiom or characteristic: Semitic ways of thought: the cause of the Semites, esp. the Jews; **Sem'itist** a Semitic scholar. — **Semitic languages** Assyrian, Aramaic, Hebrew, Phoenician, Arabic, Ethiopic, etc. [Gr. *Sēm,* Shem.]

semmit *sem'it,* (*Scot.*) *n.* an undershirt.

Semnopithecus *sem-nō-pith-ē'kəs, n.* the hanuman genus. [Gr. *semnos,* honoured, *pithēkos,* an ape.]

semolina *sem-ə-lē'nə, -lī'nə, n.* the particles of fine, hard wheat that do not pass into flour in milling. [It. *semolino,* dim. of *semola,* bran — L. *simila,* fine flour.]

semper *sem'pər, -per,* (L.) always. — **semper idem** (*ī'dem, id'em, ē'dem*) always the same; **semper paratus** (*pə-rā'-təs, pa-rä'tōōs*) always ready. — *n.* **sempervivum** (*-vī'vəm*) any plant of the Crassulaceae, including the house-leek and various ornamental plants.

sempiternal *sem-pi-tûr'nl, adj.* everlasting. — Also **semp'i-tern.** — *ns.* **sempiter'nity; sempiter'num** (*obs.*) a durable woollen cloth. [L. *sempiternus — semper,* ever.]

semple *sem'pl, adj.* a Scottish form of **simple,** esp. meaning not of gentle birth.

semplice *sem'plē-che,* (*mus.*) *adj.* simple, without embellishments. [It.]

sempre *sem'pre,* (*mus.*) *adv.* always, throughout. [It., — L. *semper,* always.]

sempster, seamster *sem'stər, n.* one who sews — orig. *fem.,* now only *masc.:* — *fem.* **semp'stress, seam'stress.** — *ns.* **semp'stering, semp'stressing, semp'stress-ship.** [O.E. *sēamestre;* see **seam**[2].]

semsem *sem'sem, n.* sesame. [Ar. *simsim.*]

semuncia *si-mun'sh(y)ə, n.* a Roman half-ounce: a bronze coin, an as in its ultimate value. — *adj.* **semun'cial.** [L. *sēmuncia — sēmi-,* half, *uncia,* a twelfth.]

sen[1] *sen, n.* a Japanese monetary unit, the hundredth part of a yen: a former Japanese coin, of the value of this: — *pl.* **sen.** [Jap.]

sen[2] *sen, n.* a monetary unit, one-hundredth of a rupiah, a ringgit, or a riel: a coin of this value. [cent.]

senary *sēn', sen'ər-i, adj.* of, involving, based on, six. — *n.* a set of six: a senarius. — *n.* **senarius** (*se-nā'ri-əs*) a verse of six iambs or equivalents. [L. *sēnārius — sēnī,* six each — *sex,* six.]

senate *sen'it, n.* the governing body of ancient Rome: a legislative or deliberative body, esp. the upper house of a national or state legislature: a body of venerable or distinguished persons: the governing body of certain British universities (in Scotland, **Senā'tus Academ'icus**). — *n.* **senator** (*sen'ə-tər*) a member of a senate **(Senator of the College of Justice** a Lord of Session). — *adj.* **senatorial** (*sen-ə-tō'ri-əl, -tō'ri-əl*). — *adv.* **senato'rially** with senatorial dignity. — *n.* **sen'atorship.** — **sen'ate-house** the meeting-place of a senate. — **senā'tus consult'** (L. *senātūs consultum*) a decree of the senate. [L. *senātus — senex, senis,* an old man.]

senatus populusque Romanus *sə-nā'təs pop'ul-əs-kwē rōm-an'əs, sen-ä'tōōs pop-ōōl-ōōs'kwe rō-mä'nōōs,* (L.) the Roman senate and people: —abbrev. **SPQR.**

send *send, v.t.* to cause, direct, or tell to go: to propel: to cause to be conveyed: to dispatch: to forward: to grant: orig. of jazz, to rouse (someone) to ecstasy. — *v.i.* to dispatch a message or messenger: to pitch into the trough of the sea (*naut.;* sometimes **scend, 'scend):** — *pa.t.* and *pa.p.* **sent;** *naut.* **send'ed.** — *n.* a messenger (*Scot.*): one or more sent to fetch a bride (*Scot.*): a message: an impetus or impulse: a plunge. — *ns.* **send'er** one who sends: a transmitting instrument; **send'ing** dispatching: pitching: transmission: that which is sent (esp. by a wizard). — **send'-off** a demonstration at departing or starting a journey; **send'-up** a process of making fun of someone or something: a play, film, novel, etc., doing this. — **send down** to rusticate or expel; **send in** to submit (an entry) for a competition, etc.; **send for** to require by message to come or be brought; **send off** in football, etc., to order a player to leave the field and take no further part in the game, usu. after an infringement of the rules; **send on** to send in advance: to re-address and re-post (a letter or package); **send up** to make fun of: to sentence to imprisonment; **send word** to send an intimation. [O.E. *sendan;* O.N. *senda,* Goth. *sandjan,* Ger. *senden.*]

sendal *sen'dəl, n.* a thin silk or linen. [O.Fr. *cendal,* prob. — Gr. *sindōn;* see **sindon.**]

Seneca *sen'i kə, n.* an Iroquois Indian of a tribe in New York state, etc. — *adj.* **Sen'ecan.** — **Seneca oil** crude petroleum, used by them.

Senecan *sen'i-kən, adj.* of, in the manner of, Lucius Annaeus *Seneca,* Stoic philosopher and writer of declamatory tragedies (*c.* 4 B.C.–A.D. 65).

Senecio *se-nē's(h)i-ō, n.* the groundsel and ragwort genus of composite plants: (without *cap.*) any plant of this genus: — *pl.* **senē'cios.** [L. *senex,* an old man, from the hoary pappus.]

senega *sen'i-gə, n.* an American milkwort (*Polygala senega;* **senega snakeroot):** its dried root, reputed by the *Seneca* Indians good for snakebites.

senescent *si-nes'ənt, adj.* verging on old age: ageing. — *n.* **senesc'ence.** [L. *senēscēns, -entis,* pr.p. *of senēscĕre,* to grow old — *senex,* old.]

seneschal *sen'i-shl, n.* a steward: a major-domo. — *n.* **sen'eschalship.** [O.Fr. (Fr. *sénéchal*), of Gmc. origin, lit. old servant; cf. Goth. *sineigs,* old, *skalks,* O.E. *scealc,* servant.]

sengreen *sen'grēn, n.* the house-leek. [O.E. *singrēne,* evergreen, house-leek, periwinkle — *pfx. sin-,* one, always (cf. L. *semel,* once), *grēne,* green; cf. Ger. *Sin(n)grüne,* periwinkle.]

Senhor *se-nyōr', -nyör',* **Senhora -a, Senhorita** *-ē'ta, ns.* the Portuguese forms corresponding to the Spanish **Señor, Señora, Señorita.**

senile *sē'nīl, adj.* characteristic of or attendant on old age: showing the decay or imbecility of old age. — *adv.* **sēn'ilely.** — *n.* **senility** (*si-nil'i-ti*) old age: the imbecility of old age. — **senile dementia** mental decay in old age, senility. [L. *senīlis — senex, senis*, old.]

senior *sēn'yər, adj.* elder: older or higher in standing: more advanced: first. — *n.* one who is senior: a fourth-year student (*U.S.*). — *ns.* **seniority** (*sē-ni-or'i-ti*) state or fact of being senior: priority by age, time of service, or standing: a body of seniors or senior fellows. — **senior citizen** an old age pensioner; **senior common room** see under **junior**; **senior optime** see **optime**; **senior service** the navy. [L. *senior, -ōris,* compar. of *senex,* old.]

senna *sen'ə, n.* a shrub (Cassia, of various species): its purgative dried leaflets. — **senna tea** an infusion of senna. — **bladder senna** a papilionaceous shrub (*Colutea*) with similar properties. [Ar. *sanā.*]

sennachie. Same as **seannachie.**

sennet *sen'it,* (*Shak.*) *n.* a trumpet or woodwind announcement of a stage entrance (or exit) in state. [App. a form of **signet.**]

sennight *sen'īt,* (*arch.*) *n.* a week. [**seven, night.**]

sennit *sen'it,* **sinnet** *sin'it, ns.* a flat braid of rope yarn. [Origin uncertain.]

Senonian *si-nō'ni-ən,* (*geol.*) *n.* a Cretaceous stage answering to the English Upper Chalk. — Also *adj.* [L. *Senonēs,* a tribe of central Gaul.]

Señor *se-nyōr', -nyör', n.* a gentleman: in address, sir: prefixed to a name, Mr: — *fem.* **Señora** (*se-nyō'ra, -nyö'*) a lady: madam: as a title, Mrs. — *n.* **Señorita** (*sen-yō-rē'ta, -yö-*) a young lady: Miss. [Sp., — L. *senior,* older.]

Senoussi. See **Senussi.**

sens *sens, adv.* (*Spens.*) since.

sense *sens, n.* faculty of receiving sensation, general or particular: immediate consciousness: inward feeling: impression: opinion: mental attitude: discernment: understanding: appreciation: feeling for what is appropriate: discerning feeling for things of some particular kind: (usu. in *pl.*) one's right wits: soundness of judgment: reasonableness: sensible or reasonable discourse: that which is reasonable: plain matter of fact: the realm of sensation and sensual appetite: a sense-organ (*Shak.*): meaning: interpretation: purport: gist: direction (esp. in *geom.*, after Fr. *sens*). — *adj.* pertaining to a sense or senses. — *v.t.* to have a sensation, feeling, or appreciation of: to appreciate, grasp, comprehend: to become aware (that): of computers, to detect (e.g. a hole, constituting a symbol, in punched card or tape). — *n.* **sensation** (*sen-sā'shən*) awareness of a physical experience, without any element derived from previous experiences: awareness by the senses generally: an effect on the senses: power of sensing: an emotion or general feeling: a thrill: a state, or matter, of general excited interest in the public, audience, etc.: melodramatic quality or method: enough to taste, as of liquor (*slang*). — *adj.* **sensā'-tional.** — *ns.* **sensā'tionalism** the doctrine that our ideas originate solely in sensation: a striving after wild excitement and melodramatic effects; **sensā'tionalist.** — *adj.* **sensātionalist'ic.** — *adv.* **sensā'tionally.** — *ns.* **sensā'tionism; sensā'tionist; sensā'tion-monger** a dealer in the sensational. — *adjs.* **sensed** endued with meaning; **sense'ful** significant: full of good sense; **sense'less** unconscious: deficient in good sense: meaningless. — *adv.* **sense'lessly.** — *ns.* **sense'lessness; sensibil'ity** sensitiveness, sensitivity: capacity of feeling or emotion: readiness and delicacy of emotional response: sentimentality: (often in *pl.*) feelings that can be hurt. — *adj.* **sen'sible** perceptible by sense: perceptible: easily perceived: appreciable: having power of sensation: conscious: sensitive: having sensibility (*obs.*): easily affected: delicate: cognisant: aware: emotionally conscious: having or marked by good sense, judicious. — *n.* an object of sense: that which is sensible. — *n.* **sen'sibleness.** — *adv.* **sen'sibly** in a sensible manner: to a sensible or perceptible degree: so far as the senses show. — *adj.* **sensile** (*sen'sīl*) sentient: capable of affecting the senses. — *n.* **sensill'um** in insects, a small sense organ on the integument: — *pl.* **sensill'a.** — *n.*

and *adj.* **sen'sing.** — *ns.* **sen'sism** sensationalism in philosophy; **sen'sist; sensitisā'tion, -z-.** — *v.t.* **sen'sitise, -ize** to render sensitive, or more sensitive, or sensitive in a high degree. — *adj.* **sen'sitised, -z-.** — *n.* **sen'sitiser, -z-.** — *adj.* **sen'sitive** having power of sensation: feeling readily, acutely, or painfully: capable of receiving stimuli: reacting to outside influence: ready and delicate in reaction: sensitised: susceptible to the action of light (*phot.*): pertaining to, or depending on, sensation: of documents, etc., with secret or controversial contents. — *n.* one who or that which is sensitive, or abnormally or excessively sensitive. — *adv.* **sen'sitively.** — *ns.* **sen'sitiveness, sensitiv'ity** response to stimulation of the senses: heightened awareness of oneself and others within the context of personal and social relationships: abnormal responsiveness as to an allergen: degree of responsiveness to electric current, or radio waves, or to light: (of an instrument) readiness and delicacy in recording changes; **sensitom'eter** an instrument for measuring sensitivity, as of photographic films; **sen'sor** a device that detects a change in a physical stimulus and turns it into a signal which can be measured or recorded, or which operates a control. — **sensori-, senso-** in composition, sensory, as in **sen'sorineu'ral, sen'sorimō'tor, sen'soparal'ysis.** — *adj.* **senso'rial** sensory. — *ns.* **senso'rium** the seat of sensation in the brain: the brain: the mind: the nervous system; **sen'sory** the sensorium. — *adj.* of the sensorium: of sensation. — *adj.* **sen'sual** (*-sū-əl, -shōō-əl*) of the senses, as distinct from the mind: not intellectual or spiritual: carnal: worldly: connected with gratification, esp. undue gratification of bodily sense: voluptuous: lewd. — *n.* **sensualisā'tion, -z-.** — *v.t.* **sen'sualise, -ize** to make sensual: to debase by carnal gratification. — *ns.* **sen'sualism** sensual indulgence: the doctrine that all our knowledge is derived originally from sensation: the regarding of the gratification of the senses as the highest end; **sen'sualist** one given to sensualism or sensual indulgence: a debauchee: a believer in the doctrine of sensualism. — *adj.* **sensualist'ic.** — *n.* **sensual'ity** (*Milt.* **sen'sualty**) indulgence in sensual pleasures: lewdness. — *adv.* **sen'sually.** — *ns.* **sen'-sualness; sen'suism** (*philos.*) sensationalism; **sen'suist; sen'sum** sense-datum: — *pl.* **sen'sa.** — *adj.* **sen'suous** pertaining to sense (without implication of lasciviousness or grossness): connected with sensible objects: easily affected by the medium of the senses. — *adv.* **sen'suously.** — *n.* **sen'suousness.** — **sensa'tion-monger** see **sensationist** above; **sensation novel** one dealing in violent effects and strained emotion; **sense'-datum** what is received immediately through the stimulation of a sense-organ; **sense'-organ** a structure specially adapted for the reception of stimuli, as eye, ear, nose; **sense'-percep'tion** perception by the senses; **sensible horizon** the visible horizon; **sensible note** leading note; **sensitive flame** a flame that rises or falls in response to sound; **sensitive plant** a plant, esp. *Mimosa pudica,* that shows more than usual irritability when touched or shaken, by movements of leaves, etc.; **sensory deprivation** the reduction to a minimum of all external stimulation reaching the body, a situation used in psychological experiments and sometimes as a method of interrogation. — **five senses** the senses of sight, hearing, smell, taste, and touch; **bring someone to his senses** to make someone recognise the facts: to let someone understand he must mend his behaviour; **come to one's senses** to regain consciousness: to start behaving sensibly (again); **common sense** see **common; in a sense** in a sense other than the obvious one: in a way: after a fashion; **in, out of, one's senses** in or out of one's right wits, normal rational condition; **make sense** to be understandable or sensible, rational; **make sense of** to understand: to see the purpose in, or explanation of; **sixth sense** an ability to perceive what lies beyond the powers of the five senses; **take leave of one's senses** to go mad, start behaving unreasonably. [L. *sēnsus — sentīre,* to feel.]

sent[1]. An earlier spelling (*Spens.*, *Shak.*, *Milt.*) of **scent** *n.*, *v.t.*, and *v.i.*, smell; sense.

sent[2] *sent*, *pa.t.* and *pa.p.* of **send**.

sentence *sen'tǝns*, *n.* opinion: a judgment, decision: determination of punishment pronounced by a court or a judge: a maxim: a number of words making a complete grammatical structure, in writing generally begun with a capital letter and ended with a full-stop or its equivalent: an assertion in logic or mathematics: sense, meaning, matter (*obs.*): a group of two or more phrases forming a musical unit. — *v.t.* to pronounce judgment on: to condemn. — *n.* **sen'tencer.** — *adj.* **sentential** (*-ten'shl*). — *adv.* **senten'tially.** — *adj.* **senten'tious** full of meaning: aphoristic, abounding (often superabounding) in maxims. — *adv.* **senten'tiously.** — *n.* **senten'tiousness.** — **Master of the Sentences** Peter Lombard (12th cent.), from his collection of opinions from Augustine, etc.; **open sentence** a sentence which, having an undefined variable is, as it stands, neither true nor false (*math.*). [Fr., — L. *sententia* — *sentīre*, to feel.]

sentient *sen'sh(y)ǝnt*, *adj.* conscious: capable of sensation: aware: responsive to stimulus. — *n.* that which is sentient: a sentient being or mind. — *ns.* **sen'tience, sen'tiency.** [L. *sentiēns, -entis*, pr.p. of *sentīre*, to feel.]

sentiment *sen'ti-mǝnt*, *n.* a thought or body of thought tinged with emotion: opinion: judgment: a thought expressed in words: a maxim: a thought or wish propounded to be ratified by drinking: emotion: feeling bound up with some object or ideal: regard to ideal considerations: sensibility, refined feelings: consciously worked-up or partly insincere feeling: sentimentality. — *adj.* **sentimental** (*-men'tl*) pertaining to, given to, characterised by, expressive of, sentiment: given to, indulging in, expressive of, sentimentality. — *v.i.* **sentimen'talise, -ize** to behave sentimentally: to indulge in sentimentality. — *v.t.* to make sentimental: to treat sentimentally. — *ns.* **sentimen'talism, sentimentality** (*-mǝn-tal'i-ti*) disposition to wallow in sentiment: self-conscious working up of feeling: affectation of fine feeling: sloppiness; **sentimen'talist** one who affects, seeks to work up, or luxuriates in sentiment: one guided by mere sentiment: one who regards sentiment as more important than reason. — *adv.* **sentimen'tally.** [L.L. *sentīmentum* — L. *sentīre*, to feel.]

sentinel *sen'ti-nl*, *n.* one posted on guard, a sentry: guard. — *adj.* acting as a sentinel. — *v.t.* to watch over: to post as a sentinel: to furnish with sentinels. — *v.i.* to keep guard. — **sentinel crab** a crab of the Indian Ocean with long eye-stalks. [Fr. *sentinelle* — It. *sentinella*, watch, sentinel.]

sentry *sen'tri*, *n.* a sentinel: a soldier on guard: watch, guard. — **sen'try-box** a box to shelter a sentry; **sen'try-go** a sentry's beat or duty: a watch-tower (*obs.*). [Etymology obscure.]

Senussi *sen-ōōs'ē*, *n.* a member of a Muslim sect or confraternity, chiefly in N.E. Africa, founded by Sidi Mohammed ben Ali es-Senussi (d. 1860; named from the *Senus* Mountains): — *pl.* **Senussi.** — Also **Senoussi.**

senvy *sen'vi*, (*obs.*) *n.* mustard (plant or seed). [O.Fr. *senevé* — L. *sinapi* — Gr. *sinapi*, mustard.]

senza *sen'tsä*, (*mus.*) *prep.* without. [It.]

sepad *sǝ-päd'*, *v.t.* to suppose: to warrant. [A ghost-word; from J. M. Barrie's mishearing of **I'se** (= I sal) **uphaud**, I shall uphold.]

sepal *sep'l*, also *sēp'l*, *n.* a member of a flower calyx. — *adjs.* **sep'aline** (*-īn*), **sep'aloid, sep'alous.** — *n.* **sep'alödy** (Gr. *eidos*, form) transformation of other members into sepals. [Fr. *sépale*, invented by N. J. de Necker (1790) from Gr. *skepē*, cover.]

separate *sep'ǝ-rät*, *v.t.* to divide: to part: to sunder: to sever: to disconnect: to disunite: to remove: to isolate: to keep apart: to seclude: to set apart for a purpose: to shut off from cohabitation, esp. by judicial decree: to remove cream from by a separator. — *v.i.* to part: to withdraw: to secede: to come out of combination or contact: to become disunited. — *adj.* (*sep'ǝ-rit, -rät,*

sep'rit) separated: divided: apart from another: distinct. — *n.* an off-print: (in *pl.*) items of dress, e.g. blouse, skirt, etc., forming separate parts of an outfit. — *n.* **separability** (*-ǝ-bil'i-ti*). — *adj.* **sep'arable** that may be separated or disjoined. — *n.* **sep'arableness.** — *advs.* **sep'arably; sep'arately.** — *ns.* **sep'arateness; separä'tion** act of separating or disjoining: state of being separate: disunion: chemical analysis: cessation of cohabitation by agreement or judicial decree, without a formal dissolution of the marriage tie; **separä'tionist** one who favours separation, esp. political or ecclesiastical; **sep'aratism** (*-ǝ-tizm*); **sep'aratist** one who withdraws or advocates separation from an established church, federation, organisation, etc.: a dissenter: an Independent (*hist.*): (by Unionists) a Home Ruler: a believer in separate authorship of parts, esp. of the Homeric poems. — *adj.* **sep'arative** (*-ǝ-tiv*) tending to separate. — *ns.* **sep'arätor** one who, or that which, separates: a machine for separating cream from milk by whirling; **separatory** (*sep'ǝr-ǝ-tǝr-i*) an instrument for separating. — *adj.* having the function of separating. — *ns.* **sep'arätrix** a separating line; **separä'tum** a separate off-print. — **separate development** segregation of different racial groups, each supposed to progress in its own way; **separate maintenance** a provision made by a husband for his separated wife; **separation allowance** government allowance to a serviceman's wife and dependents. [L. *sēparāre, -ātum* — *sē-*, aside, *parāre*, to put.]

Sephardim *si-fär'dēm*, *-dim*, *n.pl.* the Spanish and Portuguese Jews. — *adj.* **Sephar'dic.** [Heb.]

sephen *sef'en*, *n.* a sting-ray. [Ar. *safan*, shagreen.]

sepia *sē'pi-ǝ*, *n.* a cuttlefish, esp. of **Sepia** or kindred genus: cuttlefish ink: a pigment made from it, or an artificial imitation: its colour, a fine brown: a sepia drawing. — *adj.* of the colour of sepia: done in sepia. — *ns.* **sē'piolite** (Gr. *lithos*, stone) meerschaum; **sē'piost, sēpiostaire'** (Fr. *sépiostaire* — Gr. *osteon*, bone), **sē'pium** cuttle-bone. [L., — Gr. *sēpiä*, cuttlefish, *sēpion*, cuttle-bone.]

sepiment *sep'i-mǝnt*, *n.* a hedge, a fence. [L. *saepīmentum*, a hedge.]

sepiolite, sepiost, sepium. See **sepia.**

sepoy *sē'poi*, *n.* an Indian soldier in European service (*hist.*): a soldier: a policeman. [Urdu and Pers. *sipāhī*, horseman.]

seppuku *sep-ōō'kōō*, *n.* hara-kiri. [Jap.]

seps *seps*, *n.* a very venomous snake known to the Greeks: (with *cap.*) a genus of almost legless skinks. [Gr. *sēps.*]

sepsis *sep'sis*, *n.* putrefaction: invasion by pathogenic bacteria: — *pl.* **sep'sēs.** [Gr. *sēpsis*, putrefaction.]

sept[1] *sept*, *n.* orig. in Ireland, a division of a tribe. — *adj.* **sept'al.** [Prob. for **sect**[1], influenced by L. *saeptum*; see next.]

sept[2] *sept*, *n.* an enclosure: a fence. — *n.pl.* **sept'a** see **septum** below. — *adjs.* **sept'al** partitional: growing in hedges; **septä'rian.** — *n.* **septä'rium** a nodule with a network of mineral-filled cracks: — *pl.* **septä'ria.** — *adj.* **sept'ate** partitioned. — *n.* **septä'tion** division by partitions. — *adjs.* **septici'dal** (L. *caedĕre*, to cut) with splitting of septa, as when a fruit dehisces by separation of the carpels; **septif'erous** having partitions; **sept'iform** in the form of a partition; **septif'ragal** (root of L. *frangĕre*, to break) with separation of the outer walls of the carpels from the septa. — *n.* **sept'um** (*biol.*) a partition: — *pl.* **sept'a.** [L. *saeptum* (used in pl.), a fence, enclosure — *saepīre*, to fence.]

sept-, septi-, septem- *sept-, -i-, -em-, ǝm-*, in composition, seven. — *adj.* **septemfid** (*sep'tǝm-fid*; root of L. *findĕre*, to cleave) seven-cleft. — *n.* **septemvir** (*sep-tem'vir*; L. *vir*, man) one of a board of seven: — *pl.* **septem'virī, -virs.** — *n.* **septem'virate** the office of a septemvir: a board of septemviri: a group of seven men. — *adj.* **septilateral** (*sep-ti-lat'ǝr-ǝl*; L. *latus, lateris*, a side) seven-sided. — *n.* **septillion** (*sep-til'yǝn*; modelled on **million**) the seventh power of a million: the eighth power of a thousand (*U.S.*). [L. *septem.*]

September *səp-, sep-tem'bər, n.* ninth, earlier seventh, month of the year. — *adj.* **Septem'berish.** — *ns.* **Septembriser** (*sep'təm-brī-zər*) a Septembrist: a partridge-shooter; **Septem'brist** a participator in the September massacres in Paris, 2 — 7 Sept. 1792. [L. *September, -bris.*]

septenarius *sep-ti-nā'ri-əs, n.* a seven-foot verse, esp. a trochaic tetrameter catalectic. — *adj.* **septenary** (*sep-tē'nə-ri,* or *sep'tə-nə-ri*) numbering or based on seven. — *n.* a seven, set of seven (esp. years): a septenarius. [L. *septēnārius,* of seven.]

septennium *sep-ten'i-əm, n.* seven years: — *pl.* **septenn'ia.** — *n.* **septenn'ate** a period of seven years. — *adj.* **septenn'ial.** — *adv.* **septenn'ially.** — **Septennial Act** a statute of 1716, in force till 1911, limiting the length of a parliament to seven years. [L. *septennis — annus,* a year.]

septentrion *sep-ten'tri-ən,* (*obs.*) *n.* the north: — *pl.* **septen'-trions, septentriō'nēs** the seven stars of the Plough: the Great Bear. — *adjs.* **septen'trion** (*Milt.*), **-al** northern. — *adv.* **septen'trionally.** [L. *septentriōnēs,* i.e. *septem triōnēs,* the seven plough-oxen.]

septet, septette, septett *sep-tet', n.* a composition for seven performers: a set of seven (esp. musicians). [Ger. *Septett* — L. *septem.*]

sept-foil *set'foil, n.* tormentil: a figure divided by seven cusps. [Fr. *sept,* seven, O.Fr. *foil* — L. *folium,* a leaf.]

septic *sep'tik, adj.* putrefactive. — *n.* **septicaemia** (*sep-ti-sē'mi-ə;* Gr. *haima,* blood) presence of pathogenic bacteria in the blood. — *adv.* **sep'tically.** — *n.* **septicity** (*-tis'i-ti*). — **septic tank** a tank in which sewage is decomposed by anaerobic bacteria. [Gr. *sēptikos — sēpein,* to putrefy.]

septicidal, septiferous, septillion, etc. See **sept²**, **sept-.**

septimal *sep'ti-ml, adj.* relating to, based on, seven. — *ns.* **septime** (*sep'tēm*) the seventh position in fencing; **sep'timole** (*-mōl*) a group of seven notes to be played in the time of four or six. [L. *septimus,* seventh — *septem,* seven.]

septleva *set'lə-vä, n.* in basset, seven times as much added to the first stake. [Fr. *sept-et-le-va,* seven and the first stake.]

septuagenarian *sep-tū-ə-ji-nā'ri-ən, n.* a person seventy years old, or between seventy and eighty. — *adj.* of that age. — *adj.* **septuagenary** (*-ə-jē'nər-i, -aj'in-ər-i*) consisting of or relating to seventy. — *n.* one seventy years old. [L. *septuāgēnārius — septuāgēnī,* seventy each.]

Septuagesima *sep-tū-ə-jes'i-mə, n.* the third Sunday before Lent (also **Septuagesima Sunday**) — apparently in continuation of the sequence Quadragesima, Quinquagesima, etc. [L. *septuāgēsimus, -a, -um,* seventieth.]

Septuagint *sep'tū-ə-jint, n.* the Greek Old Testament, traditionally attributed to 72 translators at Alexandria in the 3rd century B.C. — usually expressed by LXX. — *adj.* **Septuagin'tal.** [L. *septuāgintā — septem,* seven.]

septum. See **sept².**

septuor *sep'tū-ör, n.* a septette. [Fr., — L. *septem,* after *quattuor.*]

septuple *sep'tū-pl,* also *-tū', -tōō-, -tōō', adj.* sevenfold. — *v.t.* to multiply sevenfold. — *n.* **sep'tūplet** a septimole: one of seven at a birth. [L.L. *septuplus* — L. *septem,* seven; cf. **quadruple.**]

sepulchre *sep'əl-kər, n.* a tomb: a recess, usually in the north chancel wall, or a structure placed in it, to receive the reserved sacrament and the crucifix from Maundy Thursday or Good Friday till Easter (**Easter sepulchre**): burial. — *v.t.* (formerly sometimes *si-pul'kər*) to entomb: to enclose as a tomb. — *adjs.* **sepulchral** (*si-pul'krəl*) of, of the nature of, a sepulchre: funeral: as if of or from a sepulchre: funereal, gloomy, dismal: hollow-toned; **sepul'chrous** (*rare*), **sepul'tural.** — *n.* **sep'ulture** burial: a tomb or burial-place. — *v.t.* to entomb. — **whited sepulchre** see **white.** [L. *sepulcrum,*

sepultūra — sepelīre, sepultum, to bury.]

sequacious *si-kwā'shəs, adj.* ready to follow a leader or authority: compliant: pliant: observing logical sequence or consistency: in long-drawn-out sequence or train. — *ns.* **sequā'ciousness, sequacity** (*si-kwas'i-ti*). [L. *sequāx, sequācis — sequī,* to follow.]

sequel *sē'kwəl, n.* that which follows: followers (*obs.*): successors (*obs.*): consequences: upshot: a resumption of a story already complete in itself: sequence (*Shak.*): an allowance to mill servants in thirlage (*Scots law*). — *n.* **sequela** (*si-kwē'lə*) morbid affection following a disease: the psychological, etc. after-effect of any trauma: — often in *pl.* **sequē'lae** (*-lē*). [L. *sequēla — sequī,* to follow.]

sequence *sē'kwəns, n.* a state or fact of being sequent or consequent: succession: order of succession: a series of things following in order: a succession of quantities each derivable from its predecessor according to a law (*math.*): a set of three or more cards consecutive in value: that which follows: consequence: successive repetition in higher or lower parts of the scale or in higher or lower keys (*mus.*): in cinematography, a division of a film: in liturgics, a hymn in rhythmical prose, sung after the gradual and before the gospel. — *v.t.* to place in sequence: to discover the sequence or order of. — *adj.* **sē'quent** following: consequent: successive: consecutive. — *n.* a follower (*Shak.*): that which follows. — *adj.* **sequential** (*si-kwen'shl*) in, or having, a regular sequence: sequent: of data, stored one after another in a system (*comput.*). — *n.* **sequentiality** (*-shi-al'i-ti*). — *adv.* **sequen'tially.** — **sequence of tenses** the relation of tense in subordinate clauses to that in the principal. [L. *sequēns, -entis,* pr.p. of *sequī,* to follow.]

sequester *si-kwes'tər, v.t.* to set aside: to seclude: to set apart: to confiscate: to remove from someone's possession until a dispute can be settled, creditors satisfied, or the like: to hold the income of for the benefit of the next incumbent: to sequester the estate or benefice of: to remove or render ineffective (a metal ion) by adding a reagent that forms a complex with it (e.g. as a means of preventing or getting rid of precipitation in water). — *v.i.* (*obs.*) to seclude oneself. — *n.* (*sek'wes-tər; Shak.*) seclusion. — *adj.* **seques'tered** retired, secluded. — *n.* **seques'trant** (*chem.*) a substance which removes an ion or renders it ineffective, by forming a complex with the ion. — *v.t.* **sequestrate** (*sek', sēk',* or *si-kwes'*) to sequester: to make bankrupt. — *ns.* **sequestrā'tion** (*sek-, sēk-*) act of sequestering: bankruptcy (*Scots law*): the action of a sequestrant (*chem.*); **seq'uestrātor.** [L.L. *sequestrāre, -ātum* — L. *sequester,* a depositary — *secus,* apart.]

sequin *sē'kwin, n.* an old Italian gold coin: a spangle. [Fr., — It. *zecchino — zecca,* the mint; of Ar. origin.]

Sequoia *si-kwoi'ə, n.* a genus of gigantic conifers, the Californian big tree or mammoth-tree and the redwood — sometimes called Wellingtonia: (without *cap.*) a tree of this genus. [After the Cherokee Indian scholar *Sequoiah.*]

sera. See **serum.**

sérac, serac *sā-rak', sā'rak, n.* one of the cuboidal or pillar-like masses into which a glacier breaks on a steep incline. [Swiss Fr., originally a kind of cheese.]

serafile. See **serried.**

seraglio *sə-, se-rä'li-ō, -lyō, n.* women's quarters in a Muslim house or palace: a harem: a collection of wives or concubines: an enclosure: a Turkish palace, esp. that of the sultans at Constantinople: — *pl.* **sera'glios.** [It. *serraglio* — L. *sera,* a door-bar, confused with Turk. *saray, serāī,* a palace.]

serai *se-rä'i, n.* a khan, caravanserai: erron., a seraglio, harem. [Turk. (orig. Pers.) *saray, serāī.*]

serail *se-räl', n.* a seraglio. [Fr. *sérail.*]

seral. See **sere³.**

serang *se-rang', n.* a lascar boatswain. [Pers. *sarhang,* a commander.]

serape *se-rä'pä, n.* a Mexican riding-blanket. [Sp. *sarape*.]

seraph *ser'əf, n.* a six-winged celestial being (Isa. vi): an angel of the highest of the nine orders: a person of angelic character or mien: — *pl.* **ser'aphs, ser'aphim**, formerly also **ser'aphin, ser'aphins, ser'aphims**, the plurals in *-im* and *-in* also occurring as *obs. sing.* — *adjs.* **seraphic** (*-af'*), **-al.** — *adv.* **seraph'ically.** — *n.* **ser'aphine** (*-ēn*) a keyboard reed instrument, precursor of the harmonium. — **Seraphic Doctor** St Bonaventura: St Teresa; **Seraphic Father** St Francis; **Seraphic Order** the Franciscans. [Heb. *Serāphīm* (pl.).]

Serapis, Sarapis *sə-, se-rä'pis, n.* a god of the Greeks of Egypt, identified with Apis and Osiris. — *n.* **Serapeum** (*ser-ə-pē'əm*) a temple of Serapis. — *adj.* **Ser-, Sarapic** (*-ap'ik*). [Gr. *Sarāpis*, later (also L.) *Serāpis*.]

seraskier *ser-as-kēr', n.* a Turkish commander-in-chief or war minister. — *n.* **seraskier'ate** the office of seraskier. [Turk. pron. of Pers. *ser'asker — ser*, head, Ar. *'asker*, army.]

Serb *sûrb,* **Serbian** *sûr'bi-ən, ns.* a native or citizen of Serbia (formerly a kingdom, now a republic of Yugoslavia): a member of the people principally inhabiting Serbia: the South Slav language of Serbia. — *adj.* of Serbia, its people, or their language. — *ns.* and *adjs.* **Serbo-Cro'at, Serbo-Croatian** (*-krō-ā'shən*) (of) the official language of Yugoslavia. [Serb. *Srb.*]

Serbonian *sər-bō'ni-ən, adj.* like *Sirbōnis, Serbōnis*, a now dry lake in the N.E. corner of Egypt, 'Where armies whole have sunk' (*Paradise Lost*, II, 594).

serdab *sər-däb', n.* an underground chamber: a secret chamber in an Egyptian tomb. [Pers. *sard*, cold, *āb*, water.]

sere[1]. See sear[1,2].

sere[2] *sēr,* (*obs.*) *n.* a claw. [O.Fr. *serre — serrer*, to hold.]

sere[3] *sēr, n.* a series of plant communities following each other. — *adj.* **sēr'al.** — **seral community** a plant community which is not stabilised but represents a stage in a succession. [L. *seriēs*, series.]

serein *sə-rē', n.* fine rain from a cloudless sky. [Fr., — L. *sērum*, evening, *sērus*, late.]

serenade *ser-i-nād', n.* a composition like a symphony, usually slighter and in more movements: a performance in the open air by night, esp. at a lady's window: a piece suitable for such performance. — *v.t.* to entertain with a serenade. — *v.i.* to perform a serenade. — *ns.* **serenā'der; serenata** (*-i-nä'tä*) a (symphonic) serenade: a pastoral cantata; **ser'enate** (*Milt.*) a serenade. [Fr. *sérénade*, and It. *serenata* — L. *serēnus*, bright clear sky; meaning influenced by L. *sērus*, late.]

serendipity *ser-ən-dip'i-ti, n.* the faculty of making happy chance finds. — *n.* **serendip'itist** one who believes in serendipity: one who has this faculty. — *adj.* **serendip'-itous** discovered by luck or chance: pertaining to or having serendipity. — *adv.* **serendipitously.** [*Serendip*, a former name for Sri Lanka. Horace Walpole coined the word (1754) from the title of the fairy-tale 'The Three Princes of Serendip', whose heroes 'were always making discoveries, by accidents and sagacity, of things they were not in quest of'.]

serene[1] *sə-rēn', adj.* calm: unclouded: unruffled: an adjunct to the titles of some princes (translating Ger. *Durchlaucht*). — *n.* calm brightness: serenity: serene sky or sea: pure air. — *v.t.* to tranquillise: to clear. — *adv.* **serene'ly** calmly, coolly. — *ns.* **serene'ness; serenity** (*-ren'i-ti*) — **all serene** (*slang*) everything as it should be: all right; **drop serene** (*Milt.*) amaurosis. [L. *serēnus*, clear.]

serene[2] *ser'ēn, sə-rēn', (obs.) n.* a supposedly unwholesome night-dew: serein. [serein.]

serf *sûrf, n.* a person in modified slavery, esp. one attached to the soil: a villein: — *pl.* **serfs.** — *ns.* **serf'age, serf'dom, serf'hood, serf'ship.** — *adj.* **serf'ish.** [Fr., — L. *servus*, a slave.]

serge[1] *sûrj, n.* a strong twilled fabric, now usually of worsted. — *adj.* of serge. [Fr., — L. *sērica*, silk; see Seric.]

serge[2]. See cerge.

sergeant, serjeant *sär'jənt, n.* orig. a servant: an officer who made arrests (*obs.*): (usu. with *g*) a non-commissioned officer next above a corporal: (with *g*) an officer of police: (usu. with *g*) alone or as a prefix, designating certain officials: (with *j*) formerly, a barrister of highest rank (in full **ser'jeant-at-law'**). — *ns.* **ser'gean(t)cy, ser'jean(t)cy** office or rank of sergeant, serjeant; **ser'geantship, ser'jeantship; ser'jeantry** serjeanty; **ser'jeanty** a condition of tenure by service in person to the king (**grand serjeanty**) or rendering some small object (**petty serjeanty**). — **ser'geant-** (or **ser'jeant-) at-arms'** an officer of a legislative body or the Court of Chancery, for making arrests, etc.; **ser'-geant-drumm'er** drum-major; **ser'geant-fish** a fish with stripes, esp. the cobia (*Rhachicentron*) of S.E. U.S., akin to the mackerels; **ser'geant-mã'jor** formerly, an officer of rank varying from major to major-general: now, the highest non-commissioned officer (**company sergeant-major** the senior warrant-officer in a company; **regimental sergeant-major** a warrant-officer on the staff of a battalion, regiment, etc.). — **Common Serjeant** in London, an assistant to the Recorder. [Fr. *sergent* — L. *serviēns, -entis*, pr.p. of *servīre*, to serve.]

serial, seriate, seriatim. See series.

Seric *ser'ik, adj.* Chinese: (without *cap.*) silken. — *adj.* **sericeous** (*sə-rish'əs*) silky: covered with soft silky appressed hairs: with silky sheen. — *ns.* **sericin** (*ser'i-sin*) the gelatinous substance of silk; **ser'icite** a silky soapy potash mica. — *adj.* **sericitic** (*-sit'ik*). — *ns.* **sericitīsā'tion, -z-** conversion (esp. of orthoclase) into sericite; **ser'iculture** silkworm breeding — also **serici-culture** (*ser'i-si-kul-chər*); **ser(ic)icul'turist; ser'igraph** a print made by silk-screen process; **serig'rapher.** — *adj.* **serigraph'ic.** — *n.* **serig'raphy.** [Gr. *sērikos — Sēr*, a Chinese, a silkworm (pl. *Sērēs*).]

sericon *ser'i-kon, n.* conjectured to be a red (or black) tincture in alchemy.

sericulture. See Seric.

seriema *ser-i-ē'mə, -ā'mə, n.* either of two S. American birds of the family *Cariamidae*, related to the cranes and the rails, somewhat like a small crested crane in form. — Also, now obsolescent, **caria'ma.** [Tupí *çariama*.]

series *sē'rēz, -iz,* rarely *sē'ri-ēz, n.* a set of things in line or in succession, or so thought of: a set of things having something in common, esp. of books in similar form issued by the same publishing house: a set of things differing progressively: the sum where each term of a sequence is added to the previous one (*math.*): a taxonomic group (of various rank): a geological formation: succession: sequence: linear or end-to-end arrangement: in music, a set of notes in a particular order, taken, instead of a traditional scale, as the basis of a composition — the twelve-note row of twelve-tone music is an example: — *pl.* **se'ries.** — *adj.* **se'rial** forming a series: in series: in a row: in instalments: of publication in instalments: using series as the basis of composition (*mus.*): of supernumerary buds, one above another. — *n.* a publication, esp. a story, in instalments: a motion picture, television or radio play appearing in instalments. — *v.t.* **se'rialise, -ize** to arrange in series: to publish serially. — *ns.* **serialisā'-tion, -z-** publication in instalments: the use of notes and/or other elements of music in regular patterns; **se'rialism** serial technique, or use of it (*mus.*); **se'rialist** a writer of serials, or of serial music; **seriality** (*-al'i-ti*). — *adv.* **se'rially.** — *adj.* **se'riate** in rows. — *v.t.* to arrange in a series, or in order. — *adv.* **se'riately.** — *n.* **seriā'tion.** — *adv.* **seriā'tim** one after another. — **serial number** the individual identification number marked on each one of a series of identical products; **serial technique** the technique of music based on series; **serial time** time regarded as an infinite regression of successive times each needed for the description of its predecessor (J. W. Dunne, 1875–1949). — **arithmetical series** a series progressing by constant difference; **geometrical series** a series progressing by constant ratio. [L. *seriēs* — *serēre, sertum*, to join.]

serif *ser'if, n.* the short cross-line at the end of a stroke in a letter. — Also **seriph** and **ceriph**. [Origin obscure; poss. Du. *schreef*, stroke.]

serigraph, serigrapher, etc. See under **Seric.**

serin *ser'in, n.* a smaller species of canary. — *n.* **serinette'** a small barrel-organ for training songbirds. [Fr., canary.]

seringa *sə-ring'gə, n.* a Brazilian rubber-tree (Hevea): mock-orange (*Philadelphus*). [Port.; see **syringa.**]

serious *sē'ri-əs, adj.* grave: staid: earnest: disinclined to lightness: in earnest: not to be taken lightly: approaching the critical or dangerous: concerned with weighty matters: professedly religious. — *adjs.* **se'riocom'ic, -al** partly serious and partly comic. — *adv.* **se'riously.** — *n.* **se'riousness.** [L.L. *sēriōsus* — L. *sērius.*]

seriph. See **serif.**

serjeant. See **sergeant.**

serk. See **sark.**

serkali *ser-käl'ē, n.* the Government: white rulers. [Swahili.]

sermon *sûr'mən, n.* a discourse, esp. one delivered, or intended to be delivered, from the pulpit, on a Biblical text: a harangue. — *v.t.* and *v.i.* to preach: to discourse. — *ns.* **sermoneer', ser'moner** (both *rare*) a preacher: a sermoniser; **sermonet(te)'** a little sermon. — *adjs.* **sermonic** (*-mon'ik*), **-al.** — *n.* **ser'moning.** — *v.i.* **ser'monise, -ize** to compose sermons: to preach. — *v.t.* to preach to. — *n.* **ser'moniser, -z-.** — *adj.* **ser'monish.** [L. *sermō, sermōnis*, speech, prob. ult. from *serēre*, to join.]

sero-, serologist, etc. See **serum.**

seron, seroon *si-rōn', -ron', -rōōn', (arch.) ns.* a crate or hamper: a bale wrapped in hide. [Sp. *serón.*]

serosa *si-rō'zə, (zool.) n.* the chorion: the serous membrane (see **serum**): — *pl.* **serō'sas, -sae** (*-zē*). [Modern L.; fem. of *serōsus* — *serum* (see **serum**).]

serosity, serotherapy, etc. See **serum.**

serotine *ser'ō-tīn, -tin, n.* a small reddish bat. — *adj.* late, in occurrence, development, flowering, etc. — *adj.* **serotinous** (*si-rot'i-nəs*). — *n.* **serotō'nin** a potent vasoconstrictor and neurotransmitter found particularly in brain and intestinal tissue and blood-platelets. [L. *sērōtinus* — *sērus*, late.]

serotype *ser'ə-tīp, n.* a group of bacteria or other microorganisms that have a certain set of antigens in common: the combination of antigens by which such a group is marked. — *v.i.* to classify according to the composition of antigens. — *n.* **ser'otyping.** [L. *serum*, whey, **-type.**]

serous, etc. See **serum.**

serow *ser'ō, n.* a Himalayan goat-antelope. [Lepcha (Tibeto-Burman language) *sa-ro.*]

serpent *sûr'pənt, n.* formerly, any reptile or creeping thing, esp. if venomous: now, a snake: a person treacherous or malicious: an obsolete wooden leather-covered bass wind instrument shaped like a writhing snake: a twisting firework: (*cap.*) a northern constellation. — *adj.* serpentlike: serpent's. — *v.i.* to wind. — *adjs.* **serpentiform** (*-pent'*) snake-shaped; **ser'pentine** (*-tīn*) snakelike: winding: tortuous. — *n.* a winding track: an old kind of cannon: a soft, usually green mineral, a hydrated magnesium silicate, occurring in winding veins and in masses, formed by alteration of olivine, etc.: a rock (in full **ser'pentine-rock**), commonly an altered peridotite, composed mainly of the mineral serpentine. — *v.t.* and *v.i.* to wind: to insinuate. — *adv.* **ser'pentinely.** — *adj.* **serpentinic** (*-tin'ik*). — *n.* and *adj.* **ser'pentining.** — *adv.* **serpentī'ningly.** — *n.* **serpentinisā'tion, -z-** (*-tin-īz-*). — *v.t.* **ser'pentinise, -ize** to convert into serpentine. — *v.i.* to wind. — *adj.* **ser'pentīnous** of serpentine: winding. — *v.i.* **ser'pentise,**

-ize to wind. — *v.t.* to make to wind. — *adj.* and *adv.* **ser'pentlike.** — *n.* **ser'pentry** serpents collectively. — **ser'pent-eater** the secretary-bird: the markhor; **ser'pent-god, -goddess** a deity in the form of a snake: a deified snake; **serpentine verse** a line that begins and ends with the same word (from the figure of a snake with its tail in its mouth, common as a symbol of eternity); **ser'pent-liz'ard** the lizard Seps; **ser'pent-star** a brittle-star; **ser'pent-stone** an ammonite: a snakestone; **ser'pent-wor'ship.** — **the old serpent** Satan. [L. *serpēns, -entis*, pr.p. of *serpere*, to creep; cf. Gr. *herpein.*]

serpigo *sər-pī'gō, n.* (*Shak.* **sapego,** or **suppeago**) any spreading skin disease: — *pl.* **serpigines** (*-pij'in-ēz*); **serpī'goes.** — *adj.* **serpiginous** (*-pij'*). [L.L. *serpīgo* — L. *serpere*, to creep.]

serpula *sûr'pū-lə, n.* a polychaete worm (**Serpula** or kindred genus) with twisted calcareous tube: — *pl.* **ser'pulae** (*-lē*). — *n.* **ser'pulite** a fossil resembling a worm-tube. [L., a snake — *serpere*, to creep.]

serr, serre. See **serried.**

serra *ser'ə, n.* a saw: anything sawlike (L.): a mountain-range (Port.): — *pl.* **serr'ae** (*-ē*; L.); **serr'as.** — *ns.* **serradill'a, serradell'a** (Port.) bird's-foot (Ornithopus); **serr'an** a fish of the genus Serranus, or its family; **Serranus** (*sə-rā'nəs*) the typical genus of **Serranidae** (*-ran'i-dē*), the sea-perch family, akin to the perches. — *ns.* and *adjs.* **serranid** (*ser'ən-id*); **serr'anoid.** — *n.* **Serrasal'mo** (L. *salmō*, salmon) the piranha genus of fishes: (without *cap.*) a fish of this genus: — *pl.* **-sal'mos.** — *adjs.* **serr'āte, serrā'ted** notched like a saw: with sharp forward-pointing teeth (*bot.*). — *v.t.* **serrate'** to notch. — *n.* **serrā'tion** saw-edged condition: (usu. in *pl.*) a sawlike tooth. — *adjs.* **serratiros'tral** (L. *rōstrum*, beak) saw-billed; **serratulate** (*sər-at'ū-lāt*) minutely serrate. — *ns.* **serrature** (*ser'ə-chər*) serration; **serrā'tus** one of several muscles of the thorax. — *adjs.* **serricorn** (*ser'*; L. *cornū*, horn) having serrate antennae; **serr'ulate, -d** finely serrate. — *n.* **serrulā'tion.** [L. and Port. (from L.) *serra*, a saw.]

serrate(d), etc., **serricorn.** See **serra.**

serried *ser'id, adj.* close-set. — *v.t.* **serr, serre** (*sûr*) to press close: to close the ranks of. — *n.* **serrefile, serafile** (*ser'ə-fīl*; see **file[1]**) a file of officers or men detailed to ride in rear of the rear rank of a squadron when in line: a soldier so detailed. — *v.t.* and *v.i.* **serr'y** to close together. [Fr. *serrer* or its pa.p. *serré* — L. *sera*, bar, lock.]

serrulate, etc. See **serra.**

serry. See **serried.**

Sertularia *sûr-tū-lā'ri-ə, n.* a common genus of hydroids with double row of sessile hydrothecae. — *n.* and *adj.* **sertulā'rian.** [L. *serta*, garlands.]

seruewe (i.e. **servewe**). Spenserian spelling of **surview.**

serum *sē'rəm, n.* a watery liquid, esp. that which separates from coagulating blood: blood serum containing antibodies, taken from an animal that has been inoculated with bacteria or their toxins, used to immunise persons or animals: watery part of a plant fluid: — *pl.* **sēr'ums, sēr'a.** — *adj.* **sē'ro-** in composition, serum. — *adj.* **serolog'ical.** — *adv.* **serolog'ically.** — *ns.* **serol'ogist; serol'ogy** the study of serums and their properties; **seros'ity; serotaxon'omy** serological analysis as a source of information for taxonomic classification; **sērother'apy** treatment or prevention of disease by injecting blood-serum containing the appropriate antibodies. — *adj.* **sē'rous** pertaining to, like, of the nature of, serum. — **serous membrane** a thin membrane, moist with serum, lining a cavity and enveloping the viscera within, e.g. the pericardium, the peritoneum; **serum hepatitis** a virus infection of the liver, usu. transmitted by transfusion of infected blood or use of contaminated instruments, esp. needles, consequently often occurring in drug addicts; **sēr'um-ther'apy** serotherapy. [L. *sērum*, whey.]

serval *sûr'vl, n.* a large, long-legged, short-tailed African cat or tiger-cat. [Port. (*lobo*) *cerval*, lit. deer-wolf, transferred from another animal.]

servant *sûr'vənt, n.* one who is hired to perform service, especially personal or domestic service of a menial kind, or farm labour, for another or others: one who is in the service of the state, the public, a company, or other body: one who serves: a ministrant: formerly, a man conventionally accepted by a lady (called his *mistress*) as binding himself to devoted attendance: in formal epistolary use, formerly in greeting and leave-taking, now sometimes in colloquial jocularity, applied in seeming humility to oneself: a slave: (in *pl.*) formerly a designation conceded by a great personage to a company of actors, to evade legal difficulties. — *v.t.* to subject. — *adj.* **ser'vantless.** — *ns.* **ser'vantry** servants collectively; **ser'vantship** position or relation of a servant. — **ser'vant-girl, ser'vant-lass, ser'vant-maid** a female domestic servant; **ser'vant-man** a male servant; **servants' hall** a servants' dining-and sitting-room. — **civil servant** one in the civil service (see **civil**). [Fr., pr.p. of *servir* — L. *servīre*, to serve.]

serve *sûrv, v.t.* to be a servant to: to be in the service of: to worship (*obs.*): to work for: to render service to: to perform service for or under: to perform the duties or do the work connected with: of a male animal, to copulate with: to attend as assistant: to be of use to or for: to avail: to suffice for: to satisfy: to further: to minister to: to attend to the requirements of: to supply: to furnish with materials: to help to food, etc.: to send or bring to table: to deal: to put into action, bring to bear (*Spens.*): to put into play by striking (*tennis*, etc.): to treat, behave towards: to be opportune to: to conform one's conduct to: to undergo, work out, go through: to bind (rope, etc.) with cord, etc.: to deliver or present formally, or give effect to (*law*): to declare (heir) (*Scots law*). — *v.i.* to be a servant: to be in service or servitude: to render service: to be a member, or take part in the activities, of an armed force: to perform functions: to wait at table: to attend to customers: to act as server: to answer a purpose, be of use, do: to be opportune or favourable: to suffice. — *n.* service of a ball. — *ns.* **ser'ver** one who serves, esp. at meals, mass, or tennis: a salver: a fork, spoon, or other instrument for distributing or helping at table; **serv'ery** a room or rooms adjoining a dining-room, from which meals and liquors are served and in which utensils are kept. — *n.* and *adj.* **serv'ing.** — **serv'ing-mall'et** a mallet with grooved head used in serving ropes; **serv'ing-man** (*arch.*) a man-servant. — **serve as** to act as: to take the place of; **serve someone a trick** to play a trick on someone; **serve someone right** (of something unpleasant) to be no more than deserved; **serve one's time** to pass through an apprenticeship or a term of office; **serve out** to deal or distribute: to punish: to retaliate on; **serve the** (or **one's**) **turn** to suffice for one's immediate purpose or need; **serve time** to undergo a term of imprisonment, etc.; **serve up** to bring to table. [Fr. *servir* — L. *servīre*, to serve.]

servewe. A Spens. spelling of **surview.**

Servian[1] (*obs.*). Same as **Serbian.**

Servian[2] *sûr'vi-ən, adj.* of *Servius* Tullius, legendary king of Rome.

service[1] *sûr'vis, n.* the condition or occupation of a servant or of one who serves: work: the act or mode of serving: employ: employment as a soldier, sailor, or airman, or in any public organisation or department: the personnel so employed: the force, organisation, or body employing it (in *pl.* usu. the fighting forces): that which is required of its members: that which is required of a feudal tenant: performance of a duty or function: actual participation in warfare: a warlike operation: a performance of religious worship: a liturgical form or office or a musical setting of it: a good turn, good offices, benefit to another: duty or homage ceremonially offered, as in health-drinking, correspondence, or greeting: use: hard usage: availability: disposal: supply, as of water, railway-trains, etc.: expediting: waiting at table: that which is served,

a course: order of dishes: a set, as of dishes for a particular meal: supplementary activities for the advantage of customers: the checking, and (if necessary) repairing and/or replacing of parts, of machinery, etc. to ensure efficient operation: cost of interest and sinking-fund charges: cord or other material for serving a rope. — *adj.* of the army, navy, or air force: (sometimes in *pl.*) of the army, navy and air force collectively: for the use of servants: providing services rather than manufactured products (see e.g. **service industry** below). — *v.t.* to provide or perform service for (e.g. motor-cars). — *ns.* **serviceabil'ity, ser'viceableness.** — *adj.* **ser'viceable** able or willing to serve: advantageous: useful: capable of rendering long service, durable. — *adv.* **ser'viceably.** — *adj.* **ser'viceless.** — **ser'vice-book** a book of forms of religious service: a prayer-book; **service charge** a charge made for service in a restaurant or hotel, usu. a percentage of the bill; **ser'vice-court** in lawn-tennis, the area outside of which a served ball must not fall; **ser'vice-flat** a flat in which domestic service is provided, its cost being included in rent; **service hatch** one connecting dining room to kitchen, etc., through which dishes, etc., may be passed; **service industry** an industry which provides a service rather than a product, e.g. catering, entertainment, transport; **ser'vice-line** the boundary of the service-court, in lawn tennis 21 feet from the net; **ser'viceman, ser'vicewoman** a member of a fighting service; **ser'vice-pipe, -wire** a branch from a main to a building; **ser'vice-res'ervoir** a reservoir for supplying water to a particular area; **service road** a minor road parallel to a main road and serving local traffic without obstructing the main road; **ser'vice-room** a room in a club or hotel where visitors' requirements are attended to; **service station** an establishment providing general services for motorists. — **active service** service of a soldier, etc., in the field (widely interpreted by the authorities); **at your service** at your disposal: also a mere phrase of civility; **civil service** see **civil**; **have seen service** to have fought in war: to have been put to long or hard use. [Fr., — L. *servitium*.]

service[2] *sûr'vis, n.* a tree (*Sorbus domestica*) very like the rowan — also **sorb.** — **ser'vice-berry** its pear-shaped fruit: shadbush or its fruit (*U.S.*); **ser'vice-tree.** — **wild service** a tree of the same genus (*S. torminalis*) with sharp-lobed leaves. [O.E. *syrfe* — L. *sorbus*.]

servient *sûr'vi-ənt, adj.* subordinate: subject to a servitude or easement. [L. *serviēns, -entis,* pr.p. of *servīre*, to serve.]

serviette *sûr-vi-et', (*in older Scottish use and now general, but not the preferred term) *n.* a table-napkin. [Fr.]

servile *sûr'vīl, adj.* pertaining to slaves or servants: slavish: meanly submissive: cringing: controlled, subject: slavishly or unintelligently imitative: expressing mere grammatical relations. — *n.* a servile person. — *adv.* **ser'vilely.** — *ns.* **ser'vilism** (*-vil-izm*) systematic or habitual servility: servile spirit: a system based on slavery or advocacy of it; **servility** (*-vil'i-ti*) servitude: slavishness of manner or spirit: slavish deference. [L. *servīlis* — *servus*, a slave.]

Servite *sûr'vīt, n.* a member of the mendicant order of Servants of the Virgin, founded at Florence in 1233.

servitor *sûr'vi-tər, n.* one who serves: a servant: a man-servant: one who serves in war (*obs.*): an assistant, apprentice, lawyer's clerk, assistant schoolmaster, or the like (*Scot., obs.*): a follower or adherent: formerly, in Oxford, an undergraduate partly supported by the college, his duty to wait on the fellows and gentlemen commoners at table: in Edinburgh, a classroom janitor: — *fem.* **ser'vitress.** — *adj.* **servito'rial.** — *n.* **ser'vitorship.** [L.L. *servītor, -ōris* — L. *servīre*, to serve.]

servitude *sûr'vi-tūd, n.* a state of being a slave or (now *rare*) servant: slavery: subjection: compulsory labour: subjection to irksome conditions: a burden on property obliging the owner to allow another person or thing an easement (*legal*). [L. *servitūdō.*]

servo *sûr'vō, adj.* of a system in which the main mechanism is set in operation by a subsidiary mechanism and is able to develop a force greater than the force communicated to it. — **ser'vo-control'** a reinforcing mechanism for the pilot's effort, usu. small auxiliary aerofoil; **ser'vo-mech'anism** a closed-cycle control system in which a small input power controls a larger output power in a strictly proportionate manner; **ser'vo-mo'tor** a motor using a servo-mechanism. [L. *servus*, a servant, slave.]

servus servorum Dei *sûr'vəs sûr-vō'rəm, -vō'rəm, dē'ī, ser'vōōs, -wōōs, ser-vō'rōōm, -wō', de'ē,* (L.) a servant of the servants of God (a title adopted by the popes).

sesame *ses'ə-mi, n.* a plant (*Sesamum indicum*) of the Pedaliaceae, yielding gingili-oil. — *adj.* **ses'amoid** shaped like a sesame seed. — *n.* a small rounded bone in the substance of a tendon. — **ses'ame-grass** gamagrass; **sesame seed**. — **open sesame** see **open**. [Gr. *sēsamē*, a dish of sesame (Gr. *sēsamon*).]

sese. See **sessa**.

Seseli *ses'ə-li, n.* a genus of the Umbelliferae: (without *cap.*) a plant of this genus. [Gr. *seseli*, a name for several umbellifers of this and other genera.]

sesey. See **sessa**.

sesqui- *ses'kwi-,* in composition, in the ratio of one and a half to one, or one and an *n*th to one. — *adj.* **sesqualter** (*-al'tər*; L. *alter*, second) as three to two. — *ns.* **sesquial'tera** (*mus.*) a perfect fifth: three notes against two: an organ stop reinforcing harmonics; **sesquicenten'ary, sesquicentenn'ial** a hundred and fiftieth anniversary. — Also *adjs.* — *n.* **sesquiox'ide** an oxide with three atoms of oxygen to two of the other constituent. — *adjs.* **sesquip'edal, sesquipedā'lian** (L. *sēsquipedālis* — *pēs, pedis,* foot; of objects or words) a foot and a half long — of words (after Horace, *Ars Poetica,* line 97), very long and pedantic. — *ns.* **sesquipedā'lianism, sesquipedality** (*-pi-dal'i-ti*). — *adj.* **sesquip'licate** (L. *sēsquiplex, -plicis*) of, or as, the square roots of the cubes. — *ns.* **sesquisul'phide** a compound with three atoms of sulphur to two of the other element or radical; **sesquiter'pene** any of a group of terpene derivatives of the empirical formula $C_{15}H_{24}$; **sesquiter'tia** a perfect fourth: four notes against three. [L. *sēsqui* — *sēmisque* — *sēmis* (for *sēmi-as*), half a unit, *que,* and.]

sess *ses, n.* Same as **cess**.

sessa *ses'ə,* **sesey** *ses'ē,* (*Shak.*) *interj.* or *interjs.* of disputed meaning. — Other readings are **caese, cease; ceas, sese.** [Poss. reduplication of *sa*; poss. Sp. *cesa,* or Fr. *cessez,* cease.]

sessile *ses'īl, -il, adj.* stalkless: sedentary. — *adj.* **sess'ile-eyed.** [L. *sessilis,* low, squat — *sedēre, sessum,* to sit.]

session *sesh'ən, n.* an act of sitting: a seated position: the enthronement of Christ at God's right hand: a sitting, series of sittings, or time of sitting, as of a court or public body: the time between the meeting and prorogation of Parliament: a school year (sometimes a school day): in Scotland, etc., a division of the academic year (**winter session** of two terms, **summer session** of one): the kirk session: formerly, the Court of Session: (in *pl.*) quarter-sessions: a period of time spent engaged in any one activity (*coll.*). — *adj.* **sess'ional.** — *adv.* **sess'ionally.** — **sess'ion-clerk'** the official who records the transactions of a kirk session; **sess'ion-house** a building where sessions are held (also **sess'ions-house):** the room where a kirk session meets; **session singer, musician** a person who provides vocal or instrumental backing on records as an occupation. — **Court of Session** the supreme civil court of Scotland. [Fr., — L. *sessiō, sessiōnis* — *sedēre, sessum,* to sit.]

sesspool. Same as **cesspool**.

sesterce *ses'tərs, n.* a Roman coin, the *sestertius,* worth 2½ asses, later 4 asses. — *n.* **sester'tium** (*-shi-əm*) a money of account equal to 1000 sesterces: — *pl.* **sester'tia.** [L. *sestertius,* two and a half — *sēmis,* half, *tertius,* third; *sestertium,* prob. orig. gen. pl. for *mille sestertium,* a thousand sesterces.]

sestet, sestett, sestette *ses-tet', n.* a group of six: the last six lines of a sonnet: a composition for six performers (also **sestet'to:** — *pl.* **-tos).** [It. *sestetto* — *sesto* — L. *sextus,* sixth.]

sestina *ses-tē'nə, n.* an old verse-form of six six-lined stanzas having the same end-words in different orders, and a triplet introducing all of them. — Also **sestine** (*-tēn'*). [It., — L. *sextus,* sixth.]

seston *ses'ton, n.* a very small plankton organism. [Gr. *seston* — *sethein* to strain, filter.]

set *set, v.t.* to seat: to place: to put: to fix: to put, place, or fix in position or required condition: to adjust to show the correct (or a specified) time, etc.: to apply: to cause to be: to plant: to stake: to put on eggs: to put under a hen: to dispose, array, arrange: to put to catch the wind: to spread, lay, cover (a table) with the food, dishes, etc. for a meal, or (*Scot.* and *dial.*) to cover the table with the food, dishes, etc. for (a meal): to compose, as type: to put in type: to embed: to frame: to mount: to beset or bestow about: to stud, dot, sprinkle, variegate: to form or represent, as in jewels: to imprint (*Shak.*): to cause to become solid, coagulated, rigid, fixed, or motionless: to begin to form (as fruit or seed): to regulate: to appoint: to ordain: to assign: to prescribe: to propound: to present for imitation: to put upon a course, start off: to incite, direct: to escort (*North.*): to put in opposition: to posit: to rate, value: to pitch, as a tune: to compose or fit music to: to sharpen, as a razor: to indicate by crouching: to lease or let to a tenant (*Scot.* and *local*): to become, befit (chiefly *Scot.*): conversely, to appear to advantage in: to arrange (hair) in a particular style when wet, so that it will remain in it when dry: to defeat (a bridge contract), (usu. by a stated number of tricks). — *v.i.* to sit (now *arch.* or *dial.*): to hang in position: to be in session: to go down towards or below the horizon, to decline: to offer a stake: to become rigid, fixed, hard, solid, or permanent: to coagulate: of a bone, to knit: to settle down: to begin to develop, as fruit: to have or take a course or direction: to begin to go: to dance in a facing position: to acquire a set or bend: of dogs, to point out game: to apply or betake oneself: — *pr.p.* **sett'ing;** *pa.t.* and *pa.p.* **set.** — *adj.* in any of the senses of the participle: prescribed: deliberate, intentional: prearranged: formal: settled: fixed: rigid: determined: regular: established: ready: of mature habit of body. — *n.* a group of persons or things, esp. such as associate, occur, or are used together or have something in common: a clique: a coterie: a complete series, collection, or complement: a company performing a dance: a series of dance movements or figures: a complete apparatus, esp. for wireless or television receiving: an act, process, mode, or time of setting: a setting: an inclination: direction of flow: a dog's indication of game: bodily build (now *dial.*): permanent effect of strain: hang of a garment: a set hair-style: a young plant-slip, bulb, or tuber, for planting: the scenery, properties, etc. set up for a scene (*cinematography*): the place where filming takes place (*cinematography*): any collection of objects, called 'elements', defined by specifying the elements (*math.*): habitual or temporary form, posture, carriage, position, or tendency: the items performed by a singer or band at a concert: (for the following senses, **set** or **sett**) the number of a weaver's reed, determining the number of threads to the inch: the texture resulting: a square or a pattern of tartan: a paving-block of stone or wood: a lease or letting (*Scot.*): a mining lease or area worked (*Cornwall,* etc.): a place with fixed fishing-nets: a tool for setting in various senses: a badger's burrow: a group of games in which the winning side wins six, with such additional games as may be required in the case of deuce (*tennis*): the constitution of a burgh. — *ns.* **set'ness; sett'er** one who or that which sets: a dog that sets: a dog of a breed derived from the spaniel and (probably) pointer: one who finds victims for thieves, etc.: a spy; **sett'ing** act of one who sets:

direction of current: fixation: surroundings: environment: a level of power, volume, etc., to which a machine or other device can be set: mounting of jewellery: the period of time in which a play, novel, etc., is set: adaptation to music: music composed for a song, etc.: a system of dividing pupils in mixed-ability classes into ability groups for certain subjects only: the period of play after a game has been set (to two, three or five) (*badminton*). — **set′back** a check, reverse, or relapse; **set′-down′** an unexpected rebuff: a snub: a rating; **set′-line** any of various kinds of fishing-line suspended between buoys, etc., and having shorter baited lines attached to it; **set′-off′** a claim set against another: a cross-claim which partly offsets the original claim: a counterbalance: an ornament: a contrast, foil: a setting forth: an offset (*archit.*, *print.*); **set′-out′** an outfit: preparations: a display of dishes, dress, etc.: a company, clique; **set piece** a piece of theatrical scenery with a supporting framework, distinguished from a side-scene or drop-scene: a picture in fireworks: an elaborately prepared performance: in football, etc., a (carefully planned and executed piece of team-work at a) corner or free kick. — *adj.* **set′-piece′**. — **set′-pot** a fixed copper or boiler; **set′-screw** a screw used to prevent relative motion by exerting pressure with its point; **set speech** a studied oration; **set square** a right-angled triangular drawing instrument. — *adj.* **set′-stitch′d** (*Sterne*) perh. embroidered. — **set terms** deliberately picked, usually outspoken, language; **sett′er-forth′**; **sett′er-off′**; **sett′er-on′**; **sett′er-out′**; **sett′er-up′**; **set′-to** a bout: a hot contest: — *pl.* **set′-tos′, set′-to's′**; **set′-up** bodily carriage and physique: configuration, arrangement, structure, situation (see **set up** below). — **dead set** determined (on): indisputable (*Austr. slang*); **set about** to begin, take in hand: to attack: to spread, as a rumour; **set against** to assail; **set (a)going** to put in motion; **set alight, set light to, set fire to, set on fire** to cause to break into flame and burn; **set apart** to put aside, or out of consideration; **set aside** to put away: to reject: to annul: to lay by; **set at naught** see **naught**; **set back** to check, delay, reverse: to cost (in money; *slang*): to place at some distance behind: to surprise, take aback; **set by** to lay up: to put aside: to value or esteem, to care (*arch.*); **set down** to lay on the ground: to put in writing: to appoint (*Shak.*, a time for): to judge, esteem: to snub: to pitch, encamp (*Shak.*): to attribute, charge: to lay down authoritatively; **set eyes on** to see, catch sight of; **set fair** steadily fair (**set fair to** favourably disposed to: about to); **set fire to** see **set alight** above; **set forth** to exhibit, display: to expound, declare: to praise, recommend: to publish: to start on a journey; **set free** to release, put at liberty; **set hand to** to set to work on; **set in** to begin: to become prevalent: to run landwards; **set in hand** to undertake: to set someone about doing; **set little, much,** etc., **by** to regard, esteem little, much, etc.; **set off** to mark off, lay off: to start off: to send off: to show in relief or to advantage: to counterbalance: to make an offset, mark an opposite page; **set on** to move on: to incite to attack: to instigate: bent upon; **set one's face against** see **face**; **set one's hand to** to sign; **set one's heart on** see **heart**; **set oneself** to bend one's energies; **set oneself against** to discountenance, oppose; **set one's teeth** to clench the teeth, as in strong resolution; **set on fire** see **set alight** above; **set on foot** to set agoing, to start; **set out** to mark off: to equip and send forth: to start, go forth: to begin with an intention: to adorn: to expound: to display; **set sail** see **sail**; **set to** to affix: to apply oneself: to set, as a bone (*Shak.*); **set (a game) to two, three, five** in badminton, to set, in the final stages of a game, a new deciding score of two, three, or five points; **set up** to erect: to put up: to exalt (jeeringly in Scots, **set you, him,** etc., **up**): to arrange: to begin: to enable to begin: to place in view: to put in type: to begin a career: to make pretensions: to arrange matters so that another person is blamed, embarrassed, made to look foolish, etc. (*slang*; *n.* **set′-up**); **set upon** (to) set on.

[O.E. *settan*; cog. with Ger. *setzen*, O.N. *setja*, Goth. *satjan*; *settan* is the weak causative of *sittan*, to sit; the noun is from the verb, but may be partly from O.E. *set*, seat, partly from O.Fr. *sette* — L. *secta*, sect.]

seta *sē′ta, n.* a bristle: a bristle-like structure: the stalk of a moss capsule: — *pl.* **se′tae** (*-tē*). — *adjs.* **setaceous** (*si-tā′shəs*), **setose** (*sē′tōs, -tōs′*). [L. *saeta* (*sēta*), bristle.]

se-tenant *sə-tə-nã,* (*philately*) denoting two or more stamps joined together in an unsevered row or block, (at least) one of which differs (e.g. in design or value) from the other(s). [Fr., holding together.]

seton *sē′tn, n.* a thread or the like passed through the skin as a counter-irritant and means of promoting drainage: an issue so obtained. [L.L. *sētō, -ōnis*, app. — L. *sēta, saeta*, bristle.]

sett. See **set**.

settee[1] *se-tē′, n.* a long seat with a back. [Prob. **settle**.]

settee[2] *se-tē′, n.* a single-decked Mediterranean vessel with long prow and lateen sails. [Prob. It. *saettia*.]

setter[1], **setting.** See under **set**.

setter[2] *set′ər,* (chiefly *Northern*) *v.t.* to treat with a seton of setterwort root. — *n.* an issue so produced in cattle. — **sett′erwort** stinking hellebore. [Perh. from M.L.G.]

settle *set′l, n.* a long high-backed bench: a ledge (*B.*). — *v.t.* to dispose in stability, rest, or comfort: to adjust: to lower: to compact, cause to subside: to regulate: to fix: to establish, set up, or install (e.g. in residence, business, marriage, a parish): to colonise: to make clear: to determine: to decide: to put beyond doubt or dispute: to restore to good order: to quiet: to compose: to secure by gift or legal act: to create successive interests in, use or income going to one person while the corpus of the property remains another's: to make final payment of: to dispose of, put out of action, stun, kill. — *v.i.* to alight: to come to rest: to subside: to sink to the bottom (or form a scum): to dispose oneself: to take up permanent abode: to become stable: to fix one's habits (often with *down*): to grow calm or clear: to come to a decision or agreement: to adjust differences: to settle accounts (often with *up*). — *adj.* **sett′led.** — *ns.* **sett′ledness**; **sett′lement** act of settling: state of being settled: payment: arrangement: placing of a minister: a subsidence or sinking: a settled colony: a local community: an establishment of social workers aiming at benefit to the surrounding population: a settling of property, an instrument by which it is settled, or the property settled, esp. a marriage-settlement: residence in a parish or other claim for poor-relief in case of becoming destitute; **sett′ler** one who settles: a colonist: a decisive blow, argument, etc.; **sett′ling**; **sett′lor** (*law*) one who settles property on another. — **sett′le-bed** a settle adaptable as a bed; **settling day** a date fixed by the stock exchange for completion of transactions. — **settle for** to agree to accept (usu. as a compromise); **settle in** to prepare to remain indoors for the night: to adapt to a new environment; **settle with** to come to an agreement with: to deal with. [O.E. *setl*, seat, *setlan*, to place; the vb. may be partly from, or influenced by, late O.E. *sehtlian*, to reconcile.]

setwall *set′wol, n.* orig. zedoary: now, valerian. — Also **setuale** (*-ū-āl; Spens.*), **cet′ywall**, etc. [O.Fr. *citoual* — L.L. *zedoāria* — Ar. *zedwār*.]

seven *sev′n, n.* the cardinal number next above six: a symbol representing it (7, vii, etc.): a set of that number of persons or things: a shoe or other article of a size denoted by that number: a card with seven pips: a score of seven points, tricks, etc.: the seventh hour after midday or midnight: the age of seven years. — *adj.* of the number seven: seven years old. — *adj.* **sev′enth** last of seven: next after the sixth: equal to one of seven equal parts. — *n.* a seventh part: a person or thing in seventh position: a tone or semitone less than an octave: a note at that interval. — *adv.* **sev′enthly** in the seventh place. — **sev′en-a-side** a speedy form of

Rugby football played by seven men on each side instead of fifteen (also **sev′ens**). — *adj.* **sev′en-day** for seven days. — *adj.* and *adv.* **sev′enfold** in seven divisions: seven times as much. — *adj.* **sev′en-league** taking seven leagues at a stride, as the ogre's boots acquired by Hop-o′-my-Thumb. — **sev′enpence** the value of seven pennies. — *adj.* **sev′enpenny** costing or worth sevenpence. — *n.* a sevenpenny book. — *n.* and *adj.* **sev′en-score**. — **sev′enth-day** Saturday. — *adj.* observing Saturday as Sabbath. — **Seven against Thebes** the war of seven heroes to reinstate Polynices in Thebes against Eteocles; **Seven Champions of Christendom** St George for England, St Andrew for Scotland, St Patrick for Ireland, St David for Wales, St Denis for France, St James for Spain, St Anthony for Italy; **seven deadly sins** pride, covetousness, lust, anger, gluttony, envy, and sloth; **Seven Sages** Solon of Athens, Thales of Miletus, Pittacus of Mitylene, Bias of Priene in Caria, Chilon of Sparta, Cleobulus tyrant of Lindus in Rhodes, and Periander tyrant of Corinth: an Eastern cycle of tales in which seven wise men contend in story-telling against a woman for the life of a belied prince; **Seven Seas** the Arctic, Antarctic, North and South Atlantic, North and South Pacific, and Indian Oceans; **Seven Sleepers** seven Christian youths at Ephesus said to have slept walled up in a cave *c.* A.D 250 to 447; **Seven Stars** the planets known to the ancients: the Plough: the Pleiades; **Seventh-day Adventists** a sect that expect the second coming of Christ and observe Saturday as the Sabbath; **seventh heaven** see **heaven**; **Seven Wonders of the World** the Pyramids, the Hanging Gardens of Babylon, the Temple of Artemis at Ephesus, Phidias's statue of Zeus at Olympia, the Mausoleum at Halicarnassus, the Colossus of Rhodes, and the Pharos of Alexandria; **Seven Years' War** the struggle for Silesia between Frederick the Great and the Empress Maria Theresa (1756–63). [O.E. *seofon*; Du. *zeven*, Ger. *sieben*, Goth. *sibun*, Gr. *hepta*, L. *septem*.]

seventeen *sev-n-tēn′*, or *sev′*, *n.* and *adj.* seven and ten. — *adj.* **sev′enteen-hund′er** (*Burns*) woven with a reed of 1700 divisions, i.e. fine linen. — *adj.* and *n.* **sev′enteenth** (or *-tēnth′*). — *adv.* **seventeenth′ly**. [O.E. *seofontīene* — *seofon*, *tīen*, ten.]

seventy *sev′n-ti*, *n.* and *adj.* seven times ten: — *pl.* **sev′enties** the numbers seventy to seventy-nine: the years so numbered in a life or any century: a range of temperature from seventy to just less than eighty degrees. — *adj.* **sev′entieth** last of seventy: next after the sixty-ninth: equal to one of seventy equal parts. — *n.* a seventieth part: a person or thing in seventieth position. — **sev′enty-eight** a seventy-eight-revolutions-per-minute gramophone record, standard before the introduction of long-playing microgroove records — usu. written 78. — **the Seventy** the Jewish Sanhedrim: the disciples sent out in Luke x: the Septuagint translators — often LXX. [O.E. (*hund*)*seofontig*.]

sever *sev′ər*, *v.t.* and *v.i.* to separate: to divide: to cleave. — *adj.* **sev′erable**. — *n.* **sev′erance**. — **severance pay** an allowance granted to an employee on the termination of his employment. [Fr. *sevrer*, to wean — L. *sēparāre*, to separate.]

several *sev′ər-l*, *adj.* separate: private: belonging or pertaining distributively, not jointly: particular: distinct: different: various: sundry: more than one (usu. more than three), but not very many. — *n.* privately owned land, esp. enclosed pasture: private property: a detail, particular (*Shak.*): an individual person (*Shak.*): a few. — *adj.*, *adv.* **sev′eralfold**. — *adv.* **sev′erally** separately. — *n.* **sev′eralty** separateness: individual ownership. — **in several** separately, individually. [O.Fr., — L. *sēparāre*, to separate.]

severe *si-vēr′*, *adj.* rigorous: very strict: unsparing: pressing hard: hard to endure: austerely restrained or simple. — *adv.* **severe′ly**. — *ns.* **severe′ness; severity** (*si-ver′i-ti*). [L. *sevērus*.]

severy *sev′ə-ri*, *n.* a compartment of vaulting. [O.Fr.

civoire — L. *cibōrium*; see **ciborium**.]

Sèvres *sev′r′*, *adj.* made at *Sèvres*, near Paris. — *n.* Sèvres porcelain.

sew[1] *sō*, *v.t.* to join, attach, enclose, or work upon with a needle and thread or with wire. — *v.i.* to ply the needle: — *pa.t.* **sewed** (*sōd*); *pa.p.* **sewn** (*sōn*) or **sewed**. — *ns.* **sew′er; sew′ing** the act of sewing: that which is being sewn. — **sew′ing-machine**. — **sew up** to enclose or close up by sewing: to complete satisfactorily (*slang*): to tire out, bring to a standstill, nonplus, or make drunk (*slang*). [O.E. *sīwian*, *sēowian*; O.H.G. *siuwen*, Goth. *siujan*.]

sew[2] (*Spens.*). Same as **sue**.

sew[3] *sū*, *v.t.* (*dial.*) to drain. — *v.i.* to ooze (*dial.*): to be aground (*naut.*). — *ns.* **sew′age** refuse carried off by sewers; **sewer** (*sōō′ər*, *sū′ər*, old-fashioned *shōr*, *shōr*) a channel for receiving the discharge from house-drains and streets. — *v.t.* to provide with sewers. — *ns.* **sew′erage** system or provision of sewers: sewage; **sew′ering**. — **sew′age-farm** a place where sewage is treated so as to be used as manure: also a farm on which sewage is used as fertiliser; **sew′age-works** a place where sewage is treated and purified before being discharged; **sew′er-gas** the contaminated air of sewers; **sew′er-rat** the brown rat. [O.Fr. *essever*, to drain off — L. *ex*, out, *aqua*, water.]

sewel. See **shewel**.

sewellel *si-wel′əl*, *n.* an American rodent linking beavers and squirrels. [Chinook *shewallal*, a robe of its skin.]

sewen. See **sewin**.

sewer[1] *sū′ər*, *n.* an officer who superintends the service at table. [O.Fr. *asseour* — *asseoir*, to set down — L. *ad*, to, *sedēre*, to sit. Skeat makes it from M.E. *sew*, to set, serve, *sew*, pottage — O.E. *sēaw*, juice.]

sewer[2]. See **sew**[1].

sewer[3], **sewerage**. See **sew**[3].

sewin, sewen *sū′in*, *n.* a Welsh sea-trout grilse. [Origin unknown.]

sewn. See **sew**[1].

sex *seks*, *n.* that by which an animal or plant is male or female: the quality of being male or female: either of the divisions according to this, or its members collectively: the whole domain connected with this distinction: sexual intercourse: (by confusion) sect. — Also *adj.* — *v.t.* to ascertain the sex of. — *adj.* **sexed** (*sekst*) having sex: being male or female: having sexual characteristics, feelings or desires to a specified degree (as in **over-**, **under-**, **highly-**, etc., **sexed**). — *ns.* **sex′er** one who ascertains the sex of birds, etc.; **sex′iness; sex′ism** discrimination against, stereotyping of, patronising or otherwise offensive behaviour towards, (orig. women, now women or men) on the grounds of sex. — *n.* and *adj.* **sex′ist**. — *adj.* **sex′less** of neither sex: without sex: without sexual feelings. — *n.* **sex′lessness**. — *adj.* **sexolog′ical**. — *ns.* **sexol′ogist; sexol′ogy** the study of (human) sexual behaviour and relationships. — *adj.* **sex′ual** of, by, having, characteristic of, sex, one sex or other, or organs of sex. — *v.t.* **sex′ualise, -ize** to attribute sex to. — *ns.* **sex′ualism** emphasis on sex; **sex′ualist; sexual′ity**. — *adv.* **sex′ually**. — *adj.* **sex′y** over-concerned with sex: of a person, very attractive to the opposite sex: stimulating sexual instincts: involved in sexual activity, esp. sexual intercourse. — **sex′-appeal′** power of attracting, esp. of exciting desire in, the other sex; **sex′-bomb** (*coll.*) a person, esp. female, with a lot of sex-appeal; **sex′-cell** an egg-cell or sperm; **sex′-change** (esp. of humans) a changing of sex. — Also *adj.* — **sex′-chro′mosome** a chromosome that determines sex; **sex′-determinā′tion** the settling of what the sex of a new organism is to be; **sex drive** the natural impulse and appetite for sexual relations; **sex hormones** hormones produced by the gonads; **sex′-in′tergrade** an intersex; **sex′-kitten** a young woman (mischievously) playing up her sex-appeal. — *adjs.* **sex′-lim′ited** developed only in one sex; **sex′-linked′** inherited along with sex, that is, by a factor located in the sex-chromosome. — **sexploitā′tion** the e**x**ploitation of *sex* for commercial gain in literature and the performing arts, esp. films; **sex′pot** (*slang*) a person of very great or obvious physical attraction; **sex′-rever′sal** change from male to female or female to male in the life of the individual; **sex shop** a shop selling items connected with sexual arousal, behaviour, etc. — *adj.* **sex′-starved** suffering from a lack and need of the pleasures and satisfactions of sexual activity. — **sexual athlete** one who peforms sexual intercourse skilfully and/or frequently; **sexual intercourse** the uniting of sexual organs, esp. involving the insertion of the male penis into the female vagina and the release of sperm; **sexual reproduction** the union of gametes or gametic nuclei preceding the formation of a new individual; **sexual selection** the province of natural selection in which preference for mates having certain characters comes into play; **sexual system** the Linnaean system of plant classification according to sexual organisation; **sex(ual) therapist** one who deals with problems relating to sexual intercourse; **sex(ual) therapy.** — **the sex** (*arch.*) the female sex, women.   [L. *sexus, -ūs.*]

sex-, *seks-*, **sexi-** *-i-*, in composition, six. — *adj.* **sex′fid** six-cleft. — *n.* **sex′foil** a window, design, etc., with six lobes or leaves. — *adjs.* **sex(i)vā′lent** (or *-iv′ə-lənt*) of valency six; **sexloc′ūlar** with six compartments; **sexpart′ite** parted in six: involving six participants, groups, etc.   [L. *sex*, six.]

sexagenarian *sek-sə-ji-nā′ri-ən, n.* a person sixty years old, or between sixty and seventy. — *adj.* of that age. — *adj.* **sexagenary** (*sek-sə-jē′nər-i, -saj′in-ər-i*) of, containing, based on, sixty: sexagenarian. — *n.* a sexagesimal fraction: a sexagenarian.   [L. *sexāgēnārius*, pertaining to sixty — *sexāgintā*, sixty.]

Sexagesima *sek-sə-jes′i-mə, n.* the second Sunday before Lent (also **Sexagesima Sunday**) — apparently so named on the false analogy of Quadragesima, etc. — *adj.* **sexages′imal** pertaining to, based on, sixty. — *n.* a sexagesimal fraction. — *adv.* **sexages′imally** by sixtieths.   [L. *sexāgēsimus, -a, -um*, sixtieth.]

sexcentenary *sek-sin-tēn′ər-i, -sin-ten′*, or *-sen′tin-ər-i, n.* a 600th anniversary. — Also *adj.*

sexennial *sek-sen′yəl, adj.* lasting six years: recurring every six years. — *adv.* **sexenn′ially.**   [L. *sex*, six, *annus*, year.]

sext *sekst, n.* the office of the sixth hour, said at midday, afterwards earlier (*eccles.*): a sixth (*mus.*): an organ stop giving the twelfth and the tierce (a sixth apart). — *adj.* **sex′tan** recurring every fifth day (sixth by old reckoning).   [L. *sextus*, sixth — *sex*, six.]

sextans *seks′tanz, n.* a Roman bronze coin worth a sixth of an as. — *n.* **sex′tant** (*-tənt*) the sixth part of a circle or its circumference, a sector or an arc of 60°: an instrument with an arc of a sixth of a circle, for measuring angular distances. — *adj.* **sextantal** (*-tant′l*).   [L. *sextāns, -antis*, a sixth.]

sextet, sextett, sextette *seks-tet′, n.* altered forms (partly through Ger.) of **sestet.**

sextile *seks′tīl, -til, (astrol.) n.* a position 60° apart (also **sextile aspect**).   [L. *sextīlis*, sixth.]

sextillion *seks-til′yən, n.* the sixth power of a million: the seventh power of 1000 (*U.S.*).   [For *sexillion*, after **billion**, etc.]

sextodecimo *seks-tō-des′i-mō, n.* a book or a size of book made by folding each sheet into sixteen leaves: — *pl.* **sextodec′imos.** — Also *adj.*   [L. *(in) sextō decimō* (in) one-sixteenth.]

sextolet *seks′tə-let, n.* a group of six notes performed in the time of four.   [Ger. *Sextole* — L. *sex.*]

sexton *seks′tən, n.* an officer who rings a church bell, attends the clergyman, digs graves, etc.: a buryingbeetle (also **sex′ton-bee′tle**). — *ns.* **sex′toness; sex′-tonship.**   [**sacristan.**]

sextuor *seks′tū-ör, n.* a sextet.   [Fr., — L. *sex*, after *quattuor*, four.]

sextuple *seks′tū-pl, adj.* sixfold. — *n.* six times as much. — *v.t.* and *v.i.* to increase or multiply sixfold. — *n.*

sex′tūplet a sextolet (*mus.*): one of six born at a birth.   [L.L. *sextuplus.*]

sexual, sexy, etc. See **sex.**

sey *sī, (Scot.) n.* part of a carcase of beef including the sirloin.   [Origin obscure.]

seyen, seysure. Shakespearean spellings of **scion, seizure.**

sez. Slang spelling of **says.**

sferics. See **spherics**[1].

'sfoot *sfoot, (Shak.) interj.* for **God's foot.**

sforzando *sför-tsän′dō*, **sforzato** *sför-tsä′tō, (mus.) adjs.* and *advs.* forced, with sudden emphasis. Abbrev. *sf* and *sfz*, or marked >, ∧. — Also *ns.* — Also **forzando, forzato**: — *pls.* (s)**forzan′dos, -di** (*-dē*), (s)**forza′tos, -ti** (*-tē*).   [It., pr.p. and pa.p. of *sforzare*, to force — L. *ex*, out, L.L. *fortia*, force.]

sfumato *sfoo-mä′tō, (paint.) n.* a misty, indistinct effect got by gradually blending together areas of different colour: — *pl.* **sfuma′tos.**   [It., pa.p. of *sfumare*, to shade off, — L. *ex*, out, *fūmāre*, to smoke.]

sgian-dubh *skē′ən-doo′ n.* Same as **skene-dhu.**

sgraffito *zgräf-fē′tō, n.* decorative work in which different colours are got by removal of parts of outer layers of material laid on: pottery with such decoration: — *pl.* **sgraffi′ti** (*-tē*).   [It., — L. *ex-*, and It. *graffito*, q.v.]

sh *sh, interj.* hush: — *pl.* **sh's.**

shabble *shab′l, (Scot.) n.* an old rusty sword.   [Cf. It. *sciabola*, Pol. *szabla*, and **sabre.**]

shabby *shab′i, adj.* dingy, threadbare, or worn, as clothes: having a look of poverty: mean in look or conduct: low: paltry. — *adv.* **shabb′ily.** — *n.* **shabb′iness.** — *adj.* **shabb′y-genteel′** keeping up or affecting an appearance of gentility, though really very shabby. — *n.* **shabb′y=gentil′ity.**   [Obs. or dial. *shab*, scab — O.E. *sceabb.*]

shabrack *shab′rak, n.* a trooper's housing or saddle-cloth.   [Ger. *Schabracke*, prob. — Turk. *çäprāq.*]

Shabuoth, Shavuot(h) *shav-ū′oth, -ot, n.* the Jewish Feast of Weeks, celebrated 7 weeks after the first day of Passover, orig. marking the end of harvest, now generally taken as a commemoration of the giving of the Law to Moses. — Also called **Pentecost.**   [Heb. *shabuot(h)*, weeks.]

shack *shak, n.* a roughly-built hut. — **shack up (with)** (*slang*) to live with someone, esp. though unmarried.   [Amer.; origin obscure.]

shackle *shak′l, n.* a prisoner's or slave's ankle-ring or wrist-ring, or the chain connecting a pair: a hobble: a staple-like link, closed with a pin: the curved movable part of a padlock: a coupling of various kinds: (in *pl.*) fetters, manacles: a hindrance. — *v.t.* to fetter: to couple: to hamper.   **shack′le-bolt** the pin of a shackle; **shack′le-bone** (*Scot.*) the wrist.   [O.E. *sceacul.*]

shad *shad, n.* an anadromous fish akin to the herring: extended to various other fishes. — *adj.* **shad′-bell′ied** flat-bellied — opp. to *pot-bellied*: of a coat, sloping away gradually in front. — **shad′berry** the fruit of the **shad′bush**, the Juneberry (*Amelanchier*), a N. American rosaceous shrub flowering at shad spawning-time.   [O.E. *sceadd.*]

shaddock *shad′ək, n.* an Oriental citrus fruit like a very large orange, esp. the larger pear-shaped variety, distinguished from the finer grapefruit: the tree that bears it.   [Introduced to the W. Indies *c.* 1700 by Captain *Shaddock.*]

shade[1] *shād, n.* partial or relative darkness: interception of light: obscurity: a shadow: a momentary expression of face: a shady place: (in *pl.*) the abode of the dead, Hades: shelter from light or heat: that which casts a shadow: a screen: a window-blind (*U.S.*): a cover to modify or direct light of a lamp: an inverted glass vessel formerly put over a clock or ornament: a projecting cover to protect the eyes from glare: (in *pl.*; *slang*) sunglasses: an awning for a shop-window: a lace head-covering (*obs.*): a variety or degree of colour: a hue mixed with black: the dark part of a picture: a slight difference or amount: the disembodied soul: a ghost. — *v.t.* to screen: to overshadow: to mark with gradations of colour or shadow: to soften down: to darken: to shadow, represent (*Spens.*): to lower very slightly, as a price (orig. *U.S.*). — *v.i.* to pass imperceptibly (*away, into*, etc.). — *adjs.* **shā′ded; shade′less.** — *adv.* **shā′dily.** — *ns.* **shā′diness; shā′ding** making a shade: the marking of shadows or shadow-like appearance: the effect of light and shade: fine gradations: nuances: toning down: modification of sound by anything put on top of an organ-pipe: slight lowering of prices. — *adj.* **shā′dy** having, or in, shade: sheltered from light or heat: not fit to bear the light, disreputable (*coll.*): mysterious, sinister. — **shade′-plant** a plant adapted to light of low intensity; **shade′-tree** a tree planted to give shade. — **in the shade** sheltered from strong light: overlooked, forgotten, in relative obscurity; **on the shady side of** over (a specified age); **put in the shade** to outdo completely; **shades of** (a specified person or thing)! an exclamation greeting something which reminds one in some way of the person or thing. [O.E. *sceadu*; see **shadow**.]

shade² *shād*, (*Scot.*) *v.t.* to part (the hair). [Northern form of **shed¹**.]

shadoof, shaduf *shä-doōf′, n.* a contrivance for raising water by a bucket on a counterpoised pivoted rod. [Egyptian Ar. *shādūf*.]

shadow *shad′ō, n.* shade cast by the interception of light by an object: the dark figure so projected on a surface, mimicking the object: the dark part of a picture: a reflected image: a mere appearance: a ghost, spirit: an unreal thing: a representation: a person or thing wasted away almost to nothing: an inseparable companion: a spy or detective who follows one: shade: protective shade: darkness: gloom: affliction. — *adj.* unreal: feigned: existing only in skeleton: inactive, or only partly active, but ready for the time when opportunity or need arises: denoting, in the main opposition party, a political counterpart to a member or section of the party in power. — *v.t.* to shade: to cloud or darken: to represent as by a shadow: to typify: to hide: to attend like a shadow, follow and watch: to maintain a position close to, follow every movement of: to shadowcast. — *v.i.* to cast a shadow: to darken. — *ns.* **shad′ower; shad′owiness; shad′owing.** — *adjs.* **shad′owless; shad′owy** shady: like a shadow: symbolic: secluded: unsubstantial. — **shadow box** a frame or box-like structure (often with shelves and a clear protective front) used to display articles; **shad′ow-box′ing** sparring practice with an imaginary opponent: making a show of opposition or other action, as a cover for taking no effective steps; **shadow cabinet** a body of opposition leaders meeting from time to time and ready to take office. — *v.t.* **shad′owcast** in microscopy, to cast shadows of projecting parts of (a specimen) by exposing to a stream of vapour of a heavy metal. — **shad′owcasting; shad′ow-fight** a fight between or with shadows or imaginary foes; **shad′ow-fig′ure** a silhouette; **shad′owgraph** an image produced by throwing a shadow on a screen: a radiograph; **shad′ow-mark** the trace of an archaeological site revealed by observation from the air; **shad′ow-pan′tomime, -play** one in which the spectators see only shadows on a screen. — **afraid of one's own shadow** extremely timid; **may your shadow never grow less** may you continue to prosper; **shadow of death** the darkness of death: the threatening approach of death. [O.E. *sceadwe*, gen., dat., and accus. of *sceadu* (**shade** representing the nom.); cf. O.H.G. *scato*, Gr. *skotos*, darkness.]

Shafiite *shaf′i-īt, n.* a member of one of the four principal sects of the Sunnites, or orthodox Muslims. [Ar. *Shāfi′ī*, the name of the founder.]

shaft *shäft, n.* anything long and straight: a stem: an arrow: a missile (esp. *fig.*): the main, upright, straight, or cylindrical part of anything: the part of a cross below the arms: the part of a column between the base and the capital: the rachis of a feather: the thill of a carriage on either side of the horse: a straight handle: a pole: a ray or beam of light: a rotating rod that transmits motion: a well-like excavation or passage:

the penis (*vulg. slang*): a woman's body (purely as a sexual object) (*U.S. vulg. slang*). — *v.t.* to have sexual intercourse with (a woman) (*vulg. slang*): to dupe, swindle, treat unfairly (*U.S. slang*). — *adj.* **shaft′ed.** — *ns.* **shaft′er, shaft′-horse** a horse harnessed between shafts; **shaft′ing** a system of shafts. — *adj.* **shaft′less.** — **make a shaft or a bolt of it** (*Shak.* **on′t**) to venture and take what comes of it — the shaft and the bolt being the arrows of the long-bow and the crossbow respectively. [O.E. *sceaft*; perh. partly Ger. *Schacht*, pit-shaft.]

shag *shag, n.* a ragged mass of hair, or the like: a long coarse nap: a kind of tobacco cut into shreds: the green cormorant (app. from its crest), or other species: an act of sexual intercourse (*vulg. slang*): a partner, usually female, in sexual intercourse (*vulg. slang*). — *adj.* shaggy: shaggy-haired. — *v.t.* to make shaggy. — *v.i.* (*Spens.*) to hang in shaggy clusters. — *v.t. and v.i.* to have sexual intercourse (with) (*vulg. slang*): — *pr.p.* **shagg′ing;** *pa.t.* and *pa.p.* **shagged** (*shagd*) — *adj.* **shagged** (*shagd*) shaggy, rough (also *shag′id*): tired out (often with *out*) (*coll.*): exhausted after sexual intercourse (*vulg. slang*). — *n.* **shagg′edness.** — *adv.* **shagg′ily.** — *n.* **shagg′iness.** — *adj.* **shagg′y** long, rough, and coarse: having long, rough, coarse hair, wool, vegetation, etc.: unkempt: rugged. — **shag′-bark** a kind of hickory tree. — *adj.* **shag′eared** (*Shak.* **shagge-ear′d**). — **shaggy (ink) cap, shaggy mane** an edible fungus (*Coprinus comatus*) having a white, cylindrical, shaggy-scaled cap. — *adj.* **shag′-haired.** — **shaggy dog story** (from the shaggy dog featured in many) a whimsically extravagant story humorous from its length and the inconsequence of its ending. [O.E. *sceacga*; cf. O.N. *skegg*, a beard.]

shagreen *shə-grēn′, n.* a granular leather made from horse's or ass's skin: the skin of shark, ray, etc., covered with small nodules — formerly **chagrin′.** — *adj.* **shagreen(ed)′** of, or covered with, shagreen. [Fr. *chagrin* — Turk. *sagri*, horse's rump, shagreen.]

shagroon *shə-groōn′, n.* an original settler in New Zealand of other than English origin. [Perh. Ir. *seachrán*, wandering.]

shah *shä, n.* the king of Persia (now Iran): also formerly of certain other Eastern countries. [Pers. *shāh*.]

shaikh. Same as **sheikh.**

shairn. Same as **sharn.**

Shaitan *shī-tän′, n.* Satan: (without *cap.*) an evil spirit: a devilish person: a dust storm. [Ar. *shaitān* — Heb. (see **Satan**).]

Shaiva. See **Saiva.**

shake *shāk, v.t.* to move with quick, short, to-and-fro movements: to brandish: to cause to tremble or to totter: to disturb the stability of: to cause to waver: to disturb: to put, send, render, cause to be, by shaking: to scatter or send down by shaking: to split: to get rid of, give up. — *v.i.* to be agitated: to tremble: to shiver: to shake hands: to trill: — *pa.t.* **shook,** *obs.* **shāked, shākt;** *pa.p.* **shāk′en,** *obs.* **shāked, shākt, shook.** — *n.* a shaking: tremulous motion: a damaging or weakening blow: a shaken-up photo: a trillo, rapid alternation of two notes a tone or semitone apart, commonly ending with a turn: a fissure (esp. in rock or in growing timber): a moment (*coll.*). — *adjs.* **shak(e)able; shāk′en.** — *ns.* **shāk′er** one who shakes: a contrivance for shaking (e.g. drinks): a perforated container from which something is shaken: (*cap.*) a name applied to members of various religious bodies, as the Quakers, the Believers in Christ's Second Appearing (founded in Manchester about 1750), the Children of God (founded about 1864); **shāk′erism.** — *adv.* **shāk′ily.** — *n.* **shāk′iness.** — *n. and adj.* **shāk′ing.** — *adj.* **shāk′y** shaking or inclined to shake: loose: tremulous: precarious: uncertain: wavering: unsteady: full of cracks or clefts. — **shake′-bag** a fighting-cock turned out of a bag: a large fighting-cock; **shake′-down** a temporary bed (orig. made by shaking down straw): a trial run, operation, etc. to familiarise personnel with procedures and machinery (chiefly *U.S.*): any action of the phrasal verb 'shake down'; **shake'-out** a drastic reorganisation or upheaval: a recession in a particular commercial or industrial activity, esp. when accompanied by increased unemployment; **shake'-rag** (*obs.*) a disreputable ragged fellow; **shake'-up** a disturbance or reorganisation (*coll.*). — **(no) great shakes** of (no) great account; **shake a leg** (*coll.*) to hurry up; **shake down** (*slang*) to cheat of money at one stroke: to extort protection money from: to search thoroughly: to frisk (a person for weapons, etc.): to go to bed (esp. in a temporary bed): to settle down; **shake hands with** to salute (someone) by grasping his or her hand and (often) moving it up and down; **shake, shiver, in one's shoes** to be extremely afraid, shiver with fear; **shake off** to get rid of, often by shaking: also *fig.*; **shake (off) the dust (of) from one's feet** used *lit.* and symbolically in Mat. x. 14 (*B.*): (*fig.*) to leave hurriedly or gladly; **shake one's head** to turn one's head from side to side in token of reluctance, rejection, denial, disapproval, etc.; **shake one's sides** to laugh uproariously; **shake out** to empty or cause to spread or unfold by shaking; **shake up** to rouse, mix, disturb, loosen by shaking: to reorganise (*coll.*): to upbraid (*Shak.*); **two shakes (of a lamb's tail**, etc.), **a brace of shakes**, etc. (*coll.*) a very short time. [O.E. *sc(e)acan*.]

Shakespearian, Shaksperian, Shakespearean *shāk-spē'-ri-ən, adj.* of or relating to *Shak(e)spe(a)re*, or his works. — *n.* a student of Shakespeare. — *n.* **Shak(e)spe(a)riana** (*-i-ä'nə*) items or lore relating to Shakespeare. — **Shakespearian sonnet** see **sonnet**.

shako *shak'ō, n.* a nearly cylindrical military cap.: — *pl.* **shak'o(e)s.** [Hung. *csákó*.]

Shakta, Shakti(sm). See **Sakti.**

shakudo *shak'ōō-dō* or *-dō', n.* an alloy of copper and a small percentage of gold, used in Japanese decorative art, esp. in sword fittings, to give a blue-black patina. — *adj.* made of or with shakudo. [Jap.]

shakuhachi *shak-ōō-hach'ē, shäk-ōō-häch'ē, n.* a Japanese, end-blown, bamboo flute. [Jap.]

shale[1] *shāl, n.* clay rock splitting readily into thin laminae along the bedding-planes. — *adj.* **shā'ly.** — **shale'-mine; -miner; shale'-oil** oil distilled from oil-shale. [Ger. *Schale*, lamina; or from the following word.]

shale[2] *shāl,* (*Shak.*) *n.* a shell or husk. — *v.t.* to shell. [O.E. *sc(e)alu*; cf. **scale**.]

shall *shal, shəl, v.t.* originally expressing debt or moral obligation, now used with the infinitive of a verb (without *to*) to form (in sense) a future tense, expressing in the first person mere futurity (as **will** in the second and third), in the second and third implying also promise, command, decree, or control on the part of the speaker (rules for use of *shall, will*, are often ignored): must, will have to, is to, etc. (2nd and 3rd persons, and interrogatively 1st): may be expected to, may chance to, may well (all persons): may in future contingency, may come to (all persons): — *inf.* obsolete; no *participles*; *2nd pers. sing.* (*arch.*) **shalt**; *3rd*, **shall**; *pa.t.* **should** (*shŏŏd, shəd*); *2nd pers.* (*arch.*) **shouldest, shouldst.** [O.E. *sculan, pr.t. sceal, scealt, sceal*; *pa.t. sceolde*; cf. Ger. *soll*, Goth. *skal*, O.N. *skal*.]

shalli. See **challis.**

shallon *shal'ən, n.* salal.

shalloon *shə-lōōn', n.* a light woollen stuff for coat-linings, etc. [Perhaps made at *Châlons-sur-Marne*.]

shallop *shal'əp, n.* formerly, a heavy fore-and-aft-rigged boat: a dinghy: a small or light boat. [Fr. *chaloupe*; cf. **sloop**.]

shallot, shalot *shə-lot', eschalot esh-ə-lot',* or *esh', ns.* a garlic-flavoured species (*Allium ascalonicum*) of onion. [O.Fr. *eschalote*, variant of *escalogne*; see **scallion**.]

shallow *shal'ō, adj.* of no great depth, concavity, profundity, penetration: superficial. — *adv.* at or to no great depth. — *n.* a shallow place: (used in plural with **the**) the shallow part. — *v.t.* to make shallow. — *v.i.* to grow shallow. — *n. and adj.* **shall'owing.** — *adv.* **shall'owly** simply, foolishly (*Shak.*): in a shallow man-

ner. — *n.* **shall'owness.** [M.E. *schalowe*, perh. related to **shoal**[2].]

shalm *shä m.* Same as **shawm.**

shalom (aleichem) *shal-ōm' (əl-āhh'əm), shal-om'*, (Heb.) *interj.* peace (be with you) — a greeting or valediction used esp. by Jewish people.

shalot. See **shallot.**

shalt *shalt, 2nd pers. sing.* of **shall.**

shalwar *shul'vär, shal'war, n.* loose-fitting trousers worn (by both sexes) in many parts of S. Asia. — **shal'war= kameez'** a S. Asian outfit (for women) of loose-fitting trousers and a long tunic. [Urdu *shalwār*, Hindi *salvar* — Pers. *shalwar*; Urdu *kamis* — Ar. *qamīs*, shirt.]

shaly. See **shale**[1].

sham *sham, n.* a hoax (*obs.*): a counterfeit. — *adj.* pretended: false. — *v.t.* to pretend: to feign: to impose upon (*obs.*). — *v.i.* to make false pretences: to pretend to be (as *to sham dead, sick*): — *pr.p.* **shamm'ing**; *pa.t.* and *pa.p.* **shammed.** — *n.* **shamm'er.** — **sham Abraham** see **Abraham-man.** [First found as slang, late 17th cent.]

shama *shä'mə, n.* an Indian songbird of the thrush family. [Hindi *śāmā*.]

shaman *shäm'an, -ən, n.* a doctor-priest working by magic, primarily of N. Asia: — *pl.* **sham'ans.** — Also *adj.* — *adj.* **shamanic** (*-an'*). — *ns.* **Sham'anism** (also without *cap.*) the religion of N. Asia, based essentially on magic and sorcery; **sham'anist.** — *adj.* **shamanist'ic.** [Russ., — Tungus.]

shamateur *sham'ə-tœr, -tūr, n.* one rated as an amateur in sport who yet makes gains from playing or competing. — Also *fig.* — *n.* **sham'ateurism.** [**sham, amateur.**]

shamble[1] *sham'bl, v.i.* to walk with an awkward, unsteady gait. — *n.* a shambling gait. — *n. and adj.* **sham'bling.** [Poss. from next word, in allusion to trestle-like legs.]

shamble[2] *sham'bl, n.* a butcher's market stall: in *pl.* (sometimes treated as *sing.*) a flesh-market, hence, a slaughterhouse. — *n.sing.* **sham'bles** a place of carnage (*fig.*): a mess, muddle (*coll.*). — *adj.* **shambol'ic** (*slang*; ill-formed) chaotic. [O.E. *scamel* (Ger. *Schemel*), stool — L.L. *scamellum*, dim. of *scamnum*, a bench.]

shame *shām, n.* the humiliating feeling of having appeared to disadvantage in one's own eyes, or those of others, as by shortcoming, offence, or unseemly exposure, or a like feeling on behalf of anything one associates with oneself: susceptibility to such feeling: fear or scorn of incurring disgrace or dishonour: modesty: bashfulness: disgrace, ignominy: disgraceful wrong: cause or source of disgrace: a thing to be ashamed of: an instance or a case of hard or bad luck (*coll.*): those parts of the body that it is felt to be immodest to expose (*arch.*). — *v.t.* to make ashamed: to cover with reproach: to disgrace: to put to shame by greater excellence: to drive or compel by shame. — *v.i.* to be ashamed. — *adjs.* **shamed** ashamed; **shame'ful** disgraceful. — *adv.* **shame'fully.** — *n.* **shame'fulness.** — *adj.* **shame'less** immodest: done without shame. — *adv.* **shame'lessly.** — *ns.* **shame'lessness; shā'mer** one who or that which makes ashamed. — *adj.* **shame'faced** (orig. **shame'fast,** O.E. *scamf æst*) very modest or bashful: abashed. — *adv.* **shame'facedly** (*-fāst-li* or *fā'sid-li*). — *ns.* **shame'facedness, shame'fastness** modesty. — *adjs.* **shame'-proof** (*Shak.*) insensible to shame; **shame'worthy.** — **for shame** an interjectional phrase, you should be ashamed; **put to shame** to disgrace, esp. by excelling; **shame on (you, them)!,** etc. (you, they, etc.) should be ashamed; **tell the truth and shame the devil** put the devil to disgraceful defeat by boldly telling the truth; **think shame** to be ashamed. [O.E. *sc(e)amu*; Ger. *Scham*.]

shamiana(h) *shä-mē-ä'nə, n.* a large tent or canopy. [Hindi *shāmiyāna*; from Pers.]

shamisen. See **samisen.**

shammy *sham'i, n.* (in full **shamm'y-leath'er**) a soft leather, originally made from chamois-skin, now usually from

sheepskin, by working in oil: a piece of it. — Also *adj.*
— *v.t.* **sham'oy** (or *-moi'*) to prepare thus.   [**chamois.**]
shampoo *sham-pōō'*, *v.t.* to massage: to wash and rub (the
scalp and hair): to clean (a carpet, etc.) by rubbing
with a special preparation: — *pa.t.* and *pa.p.* **sham-
pooed'**, **shampoo'd'** — *n.* an act or process of shampooing: a preparation for the purpose: — *pl.* **sham-
poos'**. — *n.* **shampoo'er**.   [Hindi *cā̆pnā*, to squeeze.]
shamrock *sham'rok, n.* the national emblem of Ireland,
a trifoliate leaf or plant: in living popular tradition the
lesser yellow trefoil: in the English poets often wood-
sorrel: according to some, white clover, hop-trefoil,
black medick, or some other (or any) leaf or plant with
three leaflets.   [Ir. *seamróg*, Gael. *seamrag*, dim. of
seamar, trefoil.]
shamus *shā'məs, shā', (U.S. slang) n.* a detective: — *pl.*
sha'muses.   [Perh. — Yiddish *shames*, a sexton, caretaker, with influence from Ir. *Seamas*, James.]
shan. See **shand.**
Shan *shän, n.* a member of a people akin to the Thais,
in China, Thailand, Burma, and Assam: their language. — Also *adj.*
shanachie *shan'ə-hhē.* Same as **seannachie.**
shand, shan *shan(d), (cant) ns.* a base coin.
Shandean *shan'di-ən, shan-dē'ən, adj.* characteristic of
Tristram *Shandy* or the Shandy family, or their creator
Laurence Sterne. — *n.* a person of Shandean character.
shandry *shan'dri, (N. England) n.* a light cart on springs.
— *n.* **shan'drydan** a shandry: an old-fashioned chaise:
a rickety vehicle.   [Origin unknown.]
shandy *shan'di, n.* a mixture of beer and ginger beer or
lemonade. — Also **shan'dygaff.**   [Origin unknown.]
shanghai[1] *shang-hī', v.t.* to drug or make drunk and ship
as a sailor: to trick into performing an unpleasant task:
— *pr.p.* **shanghai'ing;** *pa.t.* and *pa.p.* **shanghaied',
shanghai'd'** — *n.* **shanghai'er**.   [*Shanghai* in China.]
shanghai[2] *shang-hī', (Austr.* and *N.Z.) n.* a catapult. —
v.t. to shoot with a shanghai.   [Ety. dub.]
Shangri-la *shang'gri-lä, n.* an imaginary pass in the
Himalayas, an earthly paradise, described in James
Hilton's *Lost Horizon* (1933): hence, any remote or
imaginary paradise.
shank *shangk, n.* the leg from knee to foot: the corresponding part in other vertebrates: the lower part of
the foreleg, esp. as a cut of meat: a shaft, stem, straight
or long part: the part of a shoe connecting sole with
heel: the leg of a stocking: a long-handled ladle for
molten metal: an act of shanking a golf-ball: the end,
latter part *(dial.)*. — *v.i.* to be affected with disease of
the footstalk: to take to one's legs (also *v.t.* with *it*).
— *v.t.* to dispatch unceremoniously *(Scot.)*: to strike
with junction of the shaft *(golf)*. — *adj.* **shanked** having
a shank: affected with disease of the shank or footstalk.
— **shank'-bone.** — **on Shanks's mare, nag, pony,** etc.,
on foot.   [O.E. *sc(e)anca*, leg; Du. *schonk*, L.G.
schanke.]
shanny *shan'i, n.* the smooth blenny.   [Origin obscure.]
shan't *(sometimes* **sha'n't**) *shänt, (coll.)* a contraction of
shall not.
shantung *shan-tung', -tōōng', n.* a plain rough cloth of
wild silk: a similar cotton or rayon fabric.   [*Shantung*
province in China.]
shanty[1] *shant'i, n.* a roughly built hut: a ramshackle
dwelling: a low public-house. — **shanty'man** one, esp.
a logger, who lives in a shanty; **shanty town** a town,
or an area of one, where housing is makeshift and
ramshackle.   [Perh. Fr. *chantier*, a timber-yard (in
Canada a woodcutters' headquarters); perh. Ir. *sean
tig*, old house.]
shanty[2] *shan'ti, n.* a song with chorus, sung by sailors
while heaving at the capstan, or the like — also **chanty,
chantie, chanty** *(shan'ti)*. — *n.* **shant'yman** the solo-
singer in shanties.   [Said to be from Fr. *chantez*
(imper.), sing.]
shape *shāp, v.t.* to form: to fashion: to give form to: to
body forth: to embody: to devise: to purpose *(obs.)*:
to direct: to determine. — *v.i.* to take shape: to develop:

to give promising signs: to conduce *(Shak.)*: to become
fit: — *pa.t.* **shaped,** *Spens.* **shope** *(shōp)*; *pa.p.* **shāped,**
arch. **shāp'en.** — *n.* form: figure: disposition in space:
guise: form or condition: that which has form or figure:
an apparition: a pattern: a mould *(cook.)*: a jelly,
pudding, etc., turned out of a mould. — *adjs.* **shāp'able,
shape'able; shaped** having a shape, or a definite, determinate, or adapted shape. — Also in composition, as
L-shaped. — *adj.* **shape'less** of ill-defined or unsatisfactory shape: purposeless *(Shak.)*. — *ns.* **shape'lessness; shape'liness.** — *adjs.* **shape'ly** well-proportioned;
shap'en fashioned: definitely shaped. — *n.* **shap'er.** —
n. and *adj.* **shap'ing.** — **in any shape or form** (often
merely) at all; **in (good) shape** in good condition; **in the
shape of** in the guise of: of the nature of; **out of shape**
deformed, disfigured: in poor physical condition, unfit;
shape one's course to direct one's way; **shape up** to
assume a shape: to develop, to be promising; **take shape**
to assume a definite form or plan: to be embodied or
worked out in practice.   [O.E. *scieppan*, pa.t. *scōp*,
pa.p. *scapen*, to create, form, with new present developed from the pa.p., influenced by the n. *gesceap*,
creation, form; cf. O.N. *skapa*, Ger. *schaffen, schöpfen*.]
shaps *shaps, n.pl.* short for **chaparejos.**
shard[1] *shärd, (Shak.) n.* a piece of cow-dung. — *adj.*
shard'ed *(Shak.)* sheltered under dung. — **shard'-beetle**
a dor-beetle, laying its eggs under cow-dung. — *adj.*
shard'-borne (see separate article).   [Cf. **sharn.**]
shard[2] *shärd, sherd shürd, ns.* a gap (now *dial.*): a boundary water *(Spens.)*: a scrap, broken piece, esp. of
pottery.   [O.E. *sceard*, cleft, potsherd; cf. *sceran*, to
cut; Ger. *Scharte*, notch.]
shard[3] *shärd.* Same as **chard.**
shard[4] *shärd, n.* a beetle's wing-case.   [From a misunderstanding of Shakespeare's **shard-borne.**]
shard[5]**, shar'd** *shärd, (Spens.) pa.t.* and *pa.p.* **share**[1,2].
shard-borne *shärd'börn, -bōrn, (Shak.) adj.* born in dung:
later used as meaning borne on elytra.   [**shard**[1]; cf.
shard[4].]
share[1] *shār, n.* a part allotted, contributed, owned, taken,
or *(Spens.)* cut off: a division, section, portion: a fixed
and indivisible section of the capital of a company. —
v.t. to divide into shares: to apportion: to give or take
a share of: to participate in: to have in common. —
v.i. to have, receive, or give a share. — *ns.* **shar'er;
shar'ing.** — **share bone** the pubis; **share'-cap'ital** money
derived from the sale of shares in a business, and used
for carrying it on; **share'cropper** a tenant farmer who
himself supplies only his labour, receiving seed, tools,
etc., from his landlord and, with adjustment to allow
for what he has already received, a share of the crop.
— *v.i.* **share'crop.** — **share'holder** one who owns a
share, esp. in a company; **share'holding; share'man,
shares'man** a fisherman who shares profits with the
owners; **share'-out** a distribution in shares; **share'-
pusher** one who seeks to sell shares otherwise than
through recognised channels or by dubious advertisement, etc. — **go shares** to divide; **lion's share** see **lion;
share and share alike** in equal shares.   [O.E. *scearu;*
cf. **shear.**]
share[2] *shār, n.* a ploughshare or corresponding part of
another implement. — *v.t.* to cut, cleave: — *pa.t.* and
pa.p. **shared;** *(Spens.)* **shard** *(shärd)*.   [O.E. *scear;* cf.
foregoing word, and **shear.**]
Sharia(t) *shə-rē'ə(t), ns.* same as **Sheria(t).** — Also without *cap.*
shark *shärk, n.* a general name for elasmobranchs other
than skates, rays, and chimaeras — voracious fishes,
with fusiform body, lateral gill-slits, and mouth on the
under side: sometimes confined to the larger kinds,
excluding the dogfishes: an extortioner: a swindler: a
sharper: a sponging parasite: a person dangerous to
sailors. — *v.i.* to play the shark: to sponge. — *v.t.* to
get by sharking: to get together hastily, to pick up
(with *up*). — *ns.* **shark'er; shark'ing.** — **shark'-oil** oil
from shark's liver, used like cod-liver oil; **shark'skin** a
woollen or worsted suiting in twill weave: a heavy

rayon material with dull finish: shagreen. [Origin doubtful; Ger. *Schurke*, scoundrel, Austrian Ger. *Schirk*, sturgeon, Fr. dial. *cherquier*, to seek, L. *carcharus*, dogfish — Gr. *karcharos*, jagged, have been suggested.]

sharn *shärn*, (*dial.*) *n.* cow-dung. — *adj.* **sharn′y.** — **sharny peat** a cake of cow-dung mixed with coal. [O.E. *scearn*; cf. O.N. *skarn*.]

Sharon fruit *shar′ən frōōt*, a persimmon. [From the *Sharon* valley in Israel where it is esp. grown.]

sharp *shärp*, *adj.* cutting: piercing: penetrating: acute: having a thin edge or fine point: affecting the senses as if pointed or cutting: severe: harsh: keen: eager: hungry (*Shak.*): alive to one's own interests: barely honest: of keen or quick perception: alert: fit, able: pungent, sarcastic: brisk: abrupt: having abrupt or acute corners, etc.: sudden in onset: clear-cut: unblurred: well-defined: stylish (*slang*): too dressy (*slang*): high in pitch, or too high: raised a semitone: voiceless (*obs. phon.*). — *adv.* high or too high in pitch: punctually, precisely: sharply. — *n.* a note raised a semitone: the symbol for it: the key producing it: sharpness (*Milt.*): a long slender needle: a small sword or duelling-sword: (in *pl.*) hard parts of wheat, middlings: (in *pl.*) sword-fighting in earnest: a sharper. — *v.t.* and *v.i.* (*obs.* or *dial.*) to sharpen: to shark. — *v.t.* and *v.i.* **sharp′en** to make or become sharp in any sense. — *ns.* **sharp′ener; sharp′er** a cheat; **sharp′ie** a flat-bottomed, two-masted vessel with triangular sails, formerly of the U.S. Atlantic coast: one of a set of stylishly dressed teenagers (*Austr.* and *N.Z.*); *n.* and *adj.* **sharp′ing** cheating. — *adj.* **sharp′ish.** — *adv.* **sharp′ly.** — *n.* **sharp′ness.** — *adjs.* **sharp′-cut** well-defined: clear-cut; **sharp′-edged; sharp′-eyed; sharp′-ground** ground to a sharp edge; **sharp′-looking** (*Shak.*) hungry-looking; **sharp′-nosed** having a pointed nose: keen of scent; **sharp′-pointed.** — **sharp practice** unscrupulous dealing, verging on dishonesty. — *adjs.* **sharp′-set** hungry: keen in appetite for anything, esp. food or sexual indulgence: set with a sharp edge; **sharp′-shod** (of a horse) having spikes in the shoes to prevent slipping. — **sharp′shooter** a good marksman: a soldier set apart for work as a marksman: (*loosely*) someone with a talent for scoring in any sport; **sharp′shooting.** — *adjs.* **sharp′=sight′ed** having acute sight: shrewd; **sharp′-tongued′** critical, sarcastic, harsh in speech; **sharp′-toothed′; sharp′-vis′aged** thin-faced; **sharp′-witt′ed** having an alert intelligence, wit or perception. — **look sharp** be quick: hurry up; **sharp's the word** be brisk; **sharp-tailed grouse** a grouse of western Canada and U.S. whose middle tail-feathers are longer than the rest. [O.E. *scearp*; O.N. *skarpr*, Ger. *scharf*.]

shash¹. See **sash¹.**

shash² *shash*, *n.* in telecommunications, noisy interference (to a sound or picture signal). [Imit.]

shashlik *shash-lik′, shash′-*, *n.* a type of lamb kebab. [Russ. *shashlyk*.]

shaster *shas′tər*, **shastra** *shäs′trä*, *ns.* a holy writing. [Sans. *śāstra* — *śās*, to teach.]

shat. See **shit.**

shatter *shat′ər*, *v.t.* to scatter (*Milt.*): to dash to pieces: to wreck. — *v.i.* to break into fragments. — *n.* a fragment: an impaired state. — *adj.* **shatt′ered** (*coll.*) exhausted: extremely upset; **shatt′ery** brittle. — **shatt′er-brain, shatt′er-pate** a scatter-brain. — *adjs.* **shatt′er-brained; shatt′er-proof** proof against shattering. [Perh. L.G.; cf. **scatter**.]

shauchle *shöhh′l*, (*Scot.*) *v.i.* to shuffle. — *v.t.* to put out of shape or down-at-heel. — *n.* a shuffling gait: a down-at-heel shoe. — *adj.* **shauch′ly.** [Origin obscure.]

shave *shāv*, *v.t.* to scrape or pare off a superficial slice, hair (esp. of the face), or other surface material from: to tonsure: to remove by scraping or paring: to pare closely: to graze the surface of: to plunder, fleece. — *v.i.* to remove hair with a razor: to pass or escape with little margin: — *pa.p.* **shāved** or *arch.* **shāv′en.** — *n.* the

act or process of shaving: a paring: a narrow miss or escape (esp. *close shave*): a paring or slicing tool. — *n.* **shave′ling** a tonsured cleric. — *adj.* **shā′ven** shaved: tonsured: close-cut: smoothed. — *ns.* **shā′ver** one who shaves: an electric razor: a barber: a sharp or extortionate dealer: a chap, a youngster (*coll.*); **shā′vie** (*Scot.*) a trick; **shā′ving** the act of scraping or using a razor: a thin slice, esp. a curled piece of wood planed off. — **shave′-grass** Dutch rush; **shā′ving-brush** a brush for lathering the face; **shā′ving-soap** soap for lathering in preparation for shaving; **shā′ving-stick** a cylindrical piece of shaving-soap. [O.E. *sc(e)afan*; Du. *schaven*, Ger. *schaben*.]

Shavian *shā′vi-ən*, *adj.* pertaining to the dramatist George Bernard *Shaw* (1856–1950). — *n.* a follower or admirer of Shaw.

Shavuot(h). See **Shabuoth.**

shaw¹ *shö*, *n.* a small wood. [O.E. *sc(e)aga*; O.N. *skōgr*, Dan. *skov*.]

shaw² *shö*, *v.t.* and *v.i.* Scots form of **show**. — *n.* show, appearance: the above-ground parts of a potato plant, turnip, etc.

shawl *shöl*, *n.* a loose covering for the shoulders, etc. — *v.t.* to wrap in a shawl. — *n.* **shawl′ing.** — *adj.* **shawl′less.** — **shawl collar** a large rolled collar tapering from the neck to (near) the waistline; **shawl′-patt′ern** a pattern like that of an Eastern shawl such as those woven in Kashmir; **shawl′-waist′coat** a waistcoat with a large prominent pattern like that of an oriental or Paisley shawl. — **Paisley shawl** see **paisley**. [Pers. *shāl*.]

shawm *shöm*, **shalm** *shäm*, *ns.* a musical instrument of the oboe class, having a double reed and a flat circular piece against which the lips are rested. [O.Fr. *chalemie, -mel* — L. *calamus*, reed.]

Shawnee *shö-nē′*, *n.* an Indian of an Algonquin tribe now mostly in Oklahoma. — **shawnee′-wood** a species of Catalpa. [Shawnee *Shawunogi*.]

shay *n.* See **chaise**.

shaya. See **chay²**.

shchi, shtchi *shchē*, *n.* cabbage soup. [Russ.]

she *shē* (or when unemphatic *shi*), *nom.* (irregularly or ungrammatically *accus.* or *dat.*) *fem. pron.* of the 3rd *pers.* the female (or thing spoken of as female) named before, indicated, or understood (*pl.* **they**). — *n.* (*nom.*, *accus.*, and *dat.*) a female (*pl.* **shes**). — *adj.* female (esp. in composition, as **she′-ass′, she′-bear′, she′-dev′il**). [Prob. O.E. *sēo*, fem. of the def. art., which in the 12th cent. came to be used instead of the pron. *hēo*.]

shea *shē, shē′ə, n.* an African tree (**shea′-tree**, *Butyrospermum*) whose seeds (**shea′-nuts**) yield **shea′-butt′er**. [Mungo Park's spelling of Mandingo (W.Afr. language) *si*.]

sheading *shē′ding*, *n.* one of the six divisions or districts of the Isle of Man. [**shedding**.]

sheaf *shēf*, *n.* a bundle of things bound side by side, esp. stalks of corn: a bundle of (usually 24) arrows: — *pl.* **sheaves** (*shēvz*). — *vs.t.* **sheaf, sheave** to bind in sheaves. — *vs.i.* to make sheaves. — *adj.* **sheaf′y.** — *adj.* **sheaved** in sheaves: flared: perh., made of straw (*Shak.*). [O.E. *scēaf*; cf. Ger. *Schaub*, Du. *schoof*.]

sheal¹, sheel, shiel *shēl*, **shill** *shil*, (*Shak.*) *vs.t.* to shell or husk. — **sheal′ing- (sheel′ing-**, etc.**) hill** a hill where grain is winnowed by the wind. [Related to **shell, shale, scale.**]

sheal², shealing. Same as **shiel², shieling.**

shear *shēr*, *v.t.* to cut, or clip, esp. with shears: to cut superfluous nap from: to achieve or make by cutting: to tonsure: to reap with a sickle (*Scot.*): to subject to a shear: to strip, fleece (also *fig.*). — *v.i.* to separate: to cut: to penetrate: to reap with a sickle: — *pa.t.* **sheared**, *arch.* and *poet.* **shore**; *pa.p.* **shorn**, also, less commonly in ordinary senses, but always of deformation and usually of metal-cutting, **sheared**. — *n.* a shearing or clipping: a strain, stress, or deformation in which parallel planes remain parallel, but move parallel to themselves. — *ns.* **shear′er** one who shears sheep: a reaper (*Scot.*); **shear'ing; shear'ling** a sheep that has been shorn for the first time: the fleece of such a sheep. — *n.pl.* **shears** orig. scissors (also *Scot.*): now usu. a larger instrument of similar kind, with pivot or spring: applied by Spenser to wings (**winged sheares**) as instruments for cutting the air: a hoisting apparatus (see **sheers**). — **shear'-hog** a shearling; **shear'-hulk, -leg** see **sheer²**; **shear'man** one who shears superfluous nap from cloth; **shear'-steel** steel suitable for making shears, etc.; **shear'water** one of a genus (*Puffinus*; not the puffins, but akin to the petrels) of oceanic birds that skim the water.   [O.E. *sceran*; O.N. *skera*, to clip, Ger. *scheren*, to shave.]

'sheart *särt*, (*obs.*) *interj.* for **God's heart.**

sheat-fish *shēt'-fish*, **sheath-fish** *shēth'*, *ns.* a gigantic fish (*Silurus glanis*, the European catfish) of European rivers: any kindred fish.   [Ger. *Scheidfisch*.]

sheath *shēth, n.* a case for a sword or blade: a close-fitting (esp. tubular or long) covering: a clasping leaf-base, or similar protective device structure: an insect's wing-case: a contraceptive device for men: — *pl.* **sheaths** (*shēdhz*). — *v.t.* **sheathe** (*shēdh*) to put into or cover with a sheath or casing. — *adj.* **sheathed** (*shēdhd*) having or enclosed in a sheath. — *n.* **sheath'ing** (*-dh-*) that which sheathes: casing: the covering of a ship's bottom. — *adjs.* **sheath'less; sheath'y** (*-th-* or *-dh-*) sheath-like. — **sheath'-bill** either of two Antarctic sea-birds (*Chionis*) having a white plumage and a horny sheath at the base of the bill; **sheath'-knife** a knife encased in a sheath. — *adj.* **sheath'-winged** coleopterous. — **sheathe the sword** to end war.   [O.E. *scēath, scǣth*; Ger. *Scheide*, O.N. *skeithir*.]

sheave¹ *shēv, n.* a shive, slice, slab: a grooved wheel, pulley-wheel: a fragment: a speck, particle of impurity, as in paper.   [Related to **shive**.]

sheave², **sheaves**, etc. See **sheaf**.

Sheba *shē'bə*. Same as **Saba.**

shebang *shi-bang'*, (*slang*, orig. *U.S.*) *n.* a room, house, shop, hut, etc.: a vehicle: affair, matter, etc.   [Of uncertain origin; perh. conn. with **shebeen.**]

Shebat *shē'bät, n.* the fifth (ecclesiastically eleventh) Jewish month, parts of January and February. — Also **Se'bat.**   [Heb. *Sh'bāt.*]

shebeen *shi-bēn', n.* an illicit liquor-shop. — *v.i.* to keep a shebeen. — *ns.* **shebeen'er; shebeen'ing.**   [Anglo-Ir.]

Shechinah *shi-kī'nə, n.* Same as **Shekinah.**

shechita(h). See **schechita(h).**

shecklaton. See **checklaton.**

shed¹ *shed, v.t.* to part, separate: to cast off: to drop: to emit: to pour forth: to cast, throw (as light): to impart: to cause effusion of: to spill (*dial.*): to besprinkle (*Spens.*). — *v.i.* to fall off: to dispense (*Spens.*): — *pr.p.* **shedd'ing;** *pa.t.* and *pa.p.* **shed.** — *n.* (*obs.* or *dial.*) a parting. — *adj.* cast: spilt, emitted. — *ns.* **shedd'er** one who (or that which) sheds: a female salmon or the like after spawning; **shedd'ing.**   [O.E. *scādan, scēadan* (strong vb.), to separate; Ger. *scheiden.*]

shed² *shed, n.* a structure, often open-fronted, for storing or shelter: an outhouse.   [App. a variant of **shade.**]

she'd *shēd,* a contraction of **she had** or **she would.**

sheel, sheeling. See under **sheal¹.**

sheen *shēn, adj.* (*poet.*) beautiful: bright: shining. — *n.* shine: lustre: radiance: glistening attire. — *v.i.* (*obs.* except *Scot.*) to shine: to gleam: to have a lustre. — *adj.* **sheen'y** lustrous: glistening.   [O.E. *scēne* (W.S. *scīene, scȳne*), beautiful; Du. *schoon*, Ger. *schön*; influenced by **shine.**]

sheeny *shēn'i*, (*slang*) *offensive) n.* a Jew. — *adj.* Jewish.   [Origin unknown.]

sheep *shēp, n.* a beardless woolly wild or domestic animal (*Ovis*) of the goat family: sheepskin: a sheepish person: one who is like a sheep, as in being a member of a flock (or congregation), in following an example, in being at the mercy of the wolf or the shearer, in tameness of spirit, etc.: — *pl.* **sheep.** — *adj.* **sheep'ish** like a sheep: embarrassed through having done something foolish or wrong. — *adv.* **sheep'ishly.** — *n.*

sheep'ishness. — *adj.* **sheep'y** (*rare*) sheeplike. — **sheep'-biter** a dog that bites or worries sheep: prob. an oppressive supervisor (*Shak.*). — *adj.* **sheep'-biting** given to biting sheep: (*fig. arch.*) sneaking, thieving. — Also *n.* — **sheep'-cote** an enclosure for sheep; **sheep'-dip** a disinfectant vermin-killing preparation used in washing sheep: a place for dipping sheep, specif. the trough of sheep-dip through which they are driven; **sheep'dog** a dog trained to watch sheep, or of a breed used for that purpose: a chaperon (*slang*). — *adj.* **sheep'-faced** sheepish, bashful. — **sheep'-farmer; sheep'fold; sheep'-hook** a shepherd's crook; **sheep'-ked** a wingless fly (*Melophagus*) that sucks sheep's blood; **sheep'-louse** a louse (*Trichodectes*) that infests sheep: loosely, a sheep-ked: — *pl.* **sheep'-lice; sheep'-master** an owner of sheep; **sheep'meat** the meat of the sheep; **sheep'-pen; sheep'-plant** vegetable sheep; **sheep'-pox** a contagious eruptive disease of sheep, resembling small-pox; **sheep'-rot** liver rot; **sheep'-run** a tract of grazing country for sheep; **sheep's'-bit** (or **sheep's scabious**) a campanulaceous plant (*Jasione*) with blue heads resembling scabious, also **sheep'-scab** a mange in sheep transmitted by mites; **sheep'-scor'ing** the counting of sheep (**sheep-scoring numerals** numerals of Welsh origin, used by shepherds, knitters, and in counting-out rhymes by children); **sheep's'-eye** a wishful amorous look; **sheep's fescue** a temperate tufted pasture grass (*Festuca ovina*); **sheep's'-foot** a printer's claw-hammer; **sheep'shank** a sheep's leg: something of slender importance (*Scot.*): a nautical knot for shortening a rope; **sheep's'-head** the head of a sheep, esp. as food (also *adj.*): a dolt: an American fish allied to the porgie; **sheep'-shearer; sheep'-shearing; sheep'-silver** money paid in commutation of some right connected with sheep; **sheep'skin** the skin of a sheep, with or without the fleece attached: leather or parchment prepared from it. — Also *adj.* — **sheep station** (*Austr.*) a large sheep farm; **sheep'-stealer; sheep'-stealing; sheep'-tick** strictly, a tick (*Ixodes*) that infests sheep: commonly, a sheep-ked; **sheep'-track; sheep'walk** a range of pasture for sheep; **sheep'-wash** a sheep-dip. — *adj.* **sheep'-whis'tling** (*Shak.*) tending sheep. — **black sheep** the disreputable member of a family or group; **separate the sheep from the goats** to identify (esp. by some test) the superior members of any group.   [O.E. *scēap*; Ger. *Schaf.*]

sheer¹ *shēr, adj.* bright, clear (*arch.*): thin: pure: unmingled: mere, downright: plumb: unbroken: vertical or very nearly. — *adv.* clear: quite: plumb: vertically. — *n.* a very thin fabric. — *adv.* **sheer'ly** completely, thoroughly, wholly, etc.   [M.E. *schēre*, perh. from a lost O.E. equivalent of O.N. *skærr*, bright.]

sheer² *shēr, v.i.* to deviate: to swerve. — *v.t.* to cause to deviate. — *n.* a deviation: an oblique position: the fore-and-aft upward curve of a ship's deck or sides. — *n.pl.* **sheers, shears** an apparatus for hoisting heavy weights, having legs or spars spread apart at their lower ends, and hoisting tackle at their joined tops. — **sheer'-hulk, shear'-hulk** an old dismantled ship with a pair of sheers mounted on it: popularly, a mere hulk, as if from **sheer¹; sheer'-leg, shear'-leg** one of the spars of sheers: (in *pl.*) sheers. — **sheer off** to move aside: to take onself off.   [Partly at least another spelling of **shear;** perh. partly from the L.G. or Du. equivalent, *scheren*, to cut, withdraw.]

sheet¹ *shēt, n.* a large wide expanse or thin piece: a large broad piece of cloth, esp. for a bed, a penitent, or a corpse: a piece of paper, esp. large and broad: a section of a book printed upon one piece of paper, a signature: as much copy as will fill a sheet: a pamphlet, broadside, or newspaper: a sail (*poet.*): a sill (**intrusive sheet;** *geol.*): sheet-rubber: one of the separate pieces or planes that make up a surface: aircraft structural material under 0·25 in. (6·35 mm) thick, thinner than 'plate'. — *adj.* in the form of a sheet: printed on a sheet. — *v.t.* to wrap or cover with, or as with, a sheet: to furnish with sheets: to form into sheets. — *v.i.* to form or run in a

sheet. — *adj.* **sheet′ed** wrapped or covered with a sheet, esp. a winding-sheet: with a white band or belt, as a cow: spread as a sheet. — *n.* **sheet′ing** cloth for sheets: protective boarding or metal covering: formation into sheets. — *adj.* **sheet′y.** — **sheet′-copper, -iron, -lead, -metal, -rubber, -tin,** etc., copper, iron, etc., in thin sheets; **sheet′-glass** a kind of crown-glass made in a cylinder and flattened out; **sheet′-light′ning** the diffused appearance of distant lightning; **sheet music** music written or printed on (unbound) sheets. [O.E. *scēte* (W.S. *scīete*), *scēat*; cf. next word.]

sheet² *shēt, n.* a rope attached to the lower corner of a sail: (in *pl.*) the part of a boat between the thwarts and the stern or bow. — **sheet′-bend′** a type of knot used esp. for joining ropes of different sizes. — **a sheet,** or **three sheets, in the wind** half-drunk, or drunk. [O.E. *scēata,* corner; akin to foregoing.]

sheet-anchor *shēt′angk′ər, n.* an anchor for an emergency: chief support: last refuge. [Formerly *shut-, shot-, shoot-anchor,* origin doubtful.]

Sheffield plate *shef′ēld plāt,* a type of metalware developed in Sheffield and produced between the mid-18th and mid-19th century, of copper coated with silver. [*Sheffield,* city in S.Yorkshire and **plate.**]

shehita(h). See **schechita(h).**

sheikh, sheik *shāk, shēk, n.* an Arab chief: a girl's young man or ideal film hero (*old slang*): a Hindu convert to Islam. — *n.* **sheik(h)′dom** a sheik's territory. [Ar. *shaikh — shākha,* to be old.]

sheila *shē′lə, n.* a young girl or a woman (*Austr.*): a white Teddy girl (*S.Afr.*). [From proper name.]

sheiling. Same as **shieling.**

shekel *shek′l, n.* a Jewish weight (about 14 grams) and coin of this weight: the unit of currency of Israel: (in *pl.*) money (*slang*). [Heb. *sheqel — shāqal,* to weigh.]

Shekinah, Shechinah *shi-kī′nə, n.* the divine presence. [Heb. *shekīnāh — shākan,* to dwell.]

shelduck *shel′duk, n.* (*fem.* or generic) a large duck (*Tadorna*) with free hind-toe. — Also **sheld′duck, shell′duck, shiel′duck;** (esp. *masc.*)(**shel′drake, shell′-drake, shiel′drake.** [Prob. dial. *sheld* (cf. Du. *schillede*), variegation, and **duck, drake.**]

shelf *shelf, n.* a board fixed on a wall, in a bookcase, etc., for laying things on: a shelf-ful: a terrace: a ledge: a shoal: a sandbank: — *pl.* **shelves** (*shelvz*). — *v.t.* to shelve. — *n.* **shelf′-ful** enough to fill a shelf: — *pl.* **shelf′-fuls.** — *adj.* **shelf′y.** — **shelf′-cat′alogue** a library catalogue arranged by shelves; **shelf′-life** the length of time a product can be stored without deterioration occurring; **shelf′-mark** an indication on a book of its place in a library; **shelf′room** space or accommodation on shelves; **shelf′talker** a marketing device, e.g. a notice or mini-poster, attached to a shelf in a shop, to promote a specific product. — **on the shelf** shelved: laid aside from employment or prospect of marriage. [O.E. *scylf,* shelf, ledge, pinnacle, or L.G. *schelf*; perh. partly from some other source.]

shell *shel, n.* a hard outer covering, esp. of a shellfish, a tortoise, an egg, or a nut: a husk, pod, or rind: a shelled mollusc: an outer framework: a crust: a hollow sphere or the like: a mere outside, empty case, or lifeless relic: any frail structure: a frail boat: a light coffin: a conch trumpet: a lyre of tortoise-shell: an explosive projectile shot from a cannon: a piece of quicklime: in some schools, an intermediate class (from one that met in an apse at Westminster). — *adj.* of, with, or like shell or shells. — *v.t.* to separate from the shell: to case: to throw, fire, etc. shells at. — *v.i.* to peel, scale: to separate from the shell. — *n.* **shellac, shell-lac** (*shel-ak′*; also *shel′ak*) lac in thin plates, got by melting seed-lac, straining, and dropping. — *v.t.* to coat with shellac (*shel-ak′*) to beat (*U.S.*): to trounce (*U.S.*): — *pr.p.* **shellacking;** *pa.t.* and *pa.p.* **shellacked.** — *n.* **shellacking.** — *adj.* **shelled** having a shell: separated from the shell. — *ns.* **shell′er; shell′ful; shell′iness; shell′ing.** — *adjs.* **shell′-less; shell′y** of or like shell or shells: abounding in shells: having a shell: testaceous. — **shell′back**

an old sailor; **shell′bark** a hickory with peeling bark. — *adj.* **shell′bound** unable to escape from the shell. — **shell′-crater** a hole in the ground made by a bursting shell; **shelldrake, shellduck** see **shelduck; shell′-egg** one in the shell, in its natural state; **shell′fire** bombardment with shells; **shell′fish** a shelled aquatic invertebrate, esp. a mollusc or crustacean, or such animals collectively; **shell′-heap** a heap of shells: a kitchen midden; **shell′-hole** a shell-crater; **shell′-ice** ice no longer supported by water; **shell′-jack′et** a tight, short undress military jacket. — *adj.* **shell′-like.** — **shell′-lime** lime made from seashells; **shell′-lime′stone** a limestone mainly consisting of shells; **shell′-marl** a white, earthy lacustrine deposit; **shell′-mon′ey** wampum; **shell′-mound** a shell-heap; **shell′-or′nament** decoration in which a shell-form is prominent; **shell′-par(r)akeet, -parrot** the budgerigar; **shell′-pink′** a pale yellow-tinged shade of pink. — Also *adj.* — *adj.* **shell′proof** able to resist shells or bombs. — **shell′-sand** sand consisting in great part of calcareous organic remains; **shell′shock** mental disturbance due to war experiences, once thought to be caused by the bursting of shells: mental disturbance due to similar violent, etc. experiences. — *adj.* **shell′shocked.** — **shell′work** work composed of or adorned with shells; **shell′ycoat** (*Scot.*) a water goblin dressed in shells: a sheriff's messenger. — **come out of one's shell** to cease to be shy and reticent; **electron shell** see **electron; shell out** (*slang*) to pay up: to disburse. [O.E. *scell* (W.S. *sciell*); Du. *schil,* O.N. *skel.*]

she'll *shēl,* a contraction of **she shall** or **she will.**

Shelta *shel′tə, n.* a secret jargon used by vagrants in Britain and Ireland. [*Shelrū,* poss. a perversion of O.Irish *béulra,* language.]

shelter *shel′tər, n.* a shielding or screening structure, esp. against weather: (a place of) refuge, retreat, or temporary lodging in distress: asylum: screening: protection. — *v.t.* to screen: to shield: to afford asylum or lodging to: to harbour. — *v.i.* to take shelter. — *adj.* **shel′tered** affording shelter. — *n.* **shel′terer.** — *n.* and *adj.* **shel′tering.** — *adjs.* **shel′terless; shel′tery** affording shelter. — **sheltered housing** housing for the elderly or disabled consisting of separate units with a resident housekeeper or similar person to look after the tenants' well-being. [Origin obscure.]

sheltie, shelty *shel′ti, n.* a Shetland pony or sheepdog. [Perh. O.N. *Hjalti,* Shetlander.]

shelve *shelv, v.t.* to furnish with shelves: to place on a shelf: to put aside, postpone. — *v.i.* to slope, incline. — *n.* a ledge: a shelf. — *n.pl.* **shelves** *pl.* of **shelf** and of **shelve.** — *n.* **shelv′ing** provision of, or material for, shelves: shelves collectively: the act of putting upon a shelf or setting aside: a slope. — *adj.* **shallowing:** sloping. — *adj.* **shel′vy** having sandbanks: overhanging. [See **shelf.**]

Shema *shə-mä′, n.* a Jewish prayer with a long history, recited at morning and evening. [Heb., hear.]

Shemite, etc. Earlier forms of **Semite,** etc.

shemozzle *shi-moz′l, (slang) n.* a mess: a scrape: a rumpus. — Also **shimozz′le, shlemozz′le, schemozz′le.** — *v.i.* to make off. [Yiddish, — Ger. *schlimm,* bad, Heb. *mazzāl,* luck; cf. **schlimazel.**]

shenanigan *shi-nan′i-gən, (slang;* usu. in *pl.) n.* trickery: humbug. [Origin unknown.]

shend *shend, (obs.* or *poet.) v.t.* to put to shame: to disgrace: to reproach: to punish: to discomfit: — *pa.t.* and *pa.p.* **shent.** [O.E. *scendan,* to disgrace.]

she-oak *shē′-ōk, (Austr.) n.* a casuarina tree. [**she,** denoting inferior, and **oak,** from its grain.]

She'ol *shē′ōl, n.* the place of departed spirits. [Heb. *she′ōl.*]

shepherd *shep′ərd, n.* one who tends sheep (*fem.* **shep′-herdess**): a swain: a pastor. — *v.t.* to tend or guide as a shepherd: to watch over, protect the interests of, or one's own interests in. — *v.i.* to tend sheep. — *adj.* **shep′herdless.** — *n.* **shep′herdling** a little shepherd. — **Shepherd kings** the Hyksos; **shepherd(′s) check, plaid, tartan** (cloth with) small black-and-white check; **shep-**

herd's club great mullein; shepherd's cress a small cruciferous plant, *Teesdalia*; shepherd's glass scarlet pimpernel; shepherd's myrtle butcher's-broom; shepherd's needle Venus's comb; shepherd's pie a dish of meat cooked with potatoes on the top; shepherd's purse a cosmopolitan cruciferous weed with flat obcordate pods (*Capsella bursa-pastoris*); shepherd's rod the small teasel. — the Good Shepherd Jesus Christ (John x. 11). [O.E. *scēaphirde*; see sheep, herd.]

sherardise, -ize *sher'ərd-īz*, *v.t.* to coat with zinc by heating with zinc-dust in absence of air.   [From *Sherard* Cowper-Coles, the inventor of the process.]

Sheraton *sher'ə-tən, n.* a kind or style of furniture designed by Thomas *Sheraton* (1751–1806). — Also *adj.*

sherbet *shûr'bət, n.* a fruit-juice drink: an effervescent drink, or powder for making it: a kind of water-ice. [Turk. and Pers. *sherbet*, from Ar.; cf. shrub², syrup.]

sherd *shûrd, n.* See shard².

shere. A Spenserian spelling of sheer¹.

Sheria(t) *shə-rē'ə(t), ns.* the body of Islamic religious law. — Also without *cap.*   [Turk. *sheri'at*, law.]

sherif, shereef *shə-rēf', n.* a descendant of Mohammed through his daughter Fatima: a prince, esp. the Sultan of Morocco: the chief magistrate of Mecca. — *adj.* sherif'ian, shereef'ian.   [Ar. *sharīf*, noble, lofty.]

sheriff *sher'if, n.* the king's representative in a shire, with wide powers judicial and executive (*hist.*): now in England, the chief officer of the crown in the shire, county, with duties chiefly ministerial rather than judicial: in Scotland, the chief judge of the town or region: in the United States, the chief executive officer of the county, his principal duties to maintain peace and order, attend courts, guard prisoners, serve processes and execute judgments. — *ns.* sher'iffalty shrievalty; sher'iffdom the office, term of office, or territory under the jurisdiction of a sheriff; sher'iffship the office of sheriff. — sher'iff-clerk' in Scotland, the registrar of the sheriff's court, who has charge of the records of the court: — *pl.* sher'iff-clerks'; sher'iff= court' the sheriff's court; sher'iff-dep'ute in Scotland, till the abolition of the heritable jurisdictions in 1748, a lawyer who acted as deputy for the sheriff: thereafter sometimes the sheriff himself: — *pl.* sher'iff-dep'utes; sher'iff-prin'cipal in Scotland, a sheriff properly so-called; sher'iff-off'icer in Scotland, an officer connected with the sheriff-court, charged with arrests, serving of processes, etc.; sher'iff's-post (*hist.*) a painted post at a sheriff's door for affixing proclamations; sher'iff-sub'stitute a Scottish acting-sheriff, appointed by the crown, in most cases resident in his judicial district: — *pl.* sher'iffs-sub'stitute. — high sheriff an English sheriff proper: the chief executive officer of a district (*U.S.*); honorary sheriff-substitute one who may act in the absence of the sheriff-substitute; un'der= sheriff an English sheriff's deputy who performs the execution of writs.   [O.E. *scīrgerēfa* — *scīr*, shire, *gerēfa*, reeve; cf. reeve, grieve², Ger. *Graf*, count.]

Sherlock (Holmes) *shûr'lok (hōmz), n.* one who shows highly developed powers of observation and deduction, as did the detective, Sherlock Holmes, in the stories of Conan Doyle (1859–1930) — often used ironically.

Sherpa *shûr'pə, n.* one of an eastern Tibetan people living high on the south side of the Himalayas: — *pl.* Sher'pa, Sher'pas.   [Tibetan *shar*, east, *pa*, inhabitant.]

sherris *sher'is, (Shak.) n.* Same as sherry. — sherr'is-sack' sack imported from *Xeres*.

sherry *sher'i, n.* a fortified wine grown in the neighbourhood of Jerez de la Frontera in Spain: a wine of like type. — sherry-cobb'ler a drink composed of sherry, lemon, sugar, ice, etc.; sherry party a gathering at which sherry is drunk.   [*Xeres*, earlier form of Jerez.]

she's *shēz*, a contraction of she is or she has.

shet *shet*, *obs.* or *dial.* form of shut.

shetland *shet'lənd*, (usu. with *cap.*) *adj.* pertaining to the Shetland Islands off the N. coast of Scotland. — Shetland pony a small, hardy pony with a thick coat,

originating in the Shetland Islands; Shetland sheep a breed of sheep of Shetland and formerly Aberdeenshire; Shetland sheepdog a breed of dog resembling and presumably bred from, the collie, though smaller in size and with a thicker coat; Shetland wool a fine loosely twisted wool obtained from Shetland sheep.

sheuch, sheugh *shōohh, (Scot.) n.* a ditch, drain. — *v.t.* to plant temporarily.   [sough².]

sheva *shə-vä', n.* Hebrew point or sign (simple, or in compound forms) indicating absence of vowel or a neutral vowel. — Cf. schwa.   [Heb. *shewā*.]

shew *shō*, formerly (as *Milt.*) *shōo*. Same as show: — *pa.p.* shewn (*shōn*). — shew'bread the twelve loaves offered weekly in the sanctuary by the Jews.

shewel *shōo'əl, n.* a scarecrow or mark to scare deer. — Also sew'el.   [Connected with shy¹.]

Shia(h) *shē'ə, n.* a Muslim sect, or a member of it, recognising Ali, Mohammed's son-in-law, as his successor. — Shiism (*shē'izm*); Shiite (*shē'īt*) a member of this sect. — Also *adj.* — *adj.* Shiitic (-*it'ik*).   [Ar. *shī'a*, sect.]

shiatsu *shi-at'sōo, n.* a Japanese healing and health-promoting therapy using massage with fingers, palms, etc.   [Jap., lit. finger pressure.]

shibboleth *shib'ə-leth, n.* the Gileadite test-word for an Ephraimite, who could not pronounce *sh* (Judg. xii. 5–6; *B.*): any such test: a peculiarity of speech: the criterion or catchword of a group: a cant phrase. [Heb. *shibbōleth*, an ear of corn, or a stream.]

shibuichi *shi-bōo-i'chē, n.* an alloy of three parts copper to one part silver, widely used in Japanese decorative art to give a silver-grey patina. — *adj.* made of or with shibuichi.   [Jap. *shi*, four, *bu*, part, *ichi*, one.]

shicker *shik'ər, n.* strong drink. — *adj.* shick'ered drunk. [Yiddish.]

shicksa. Same as shiksa.

shidder *shid'ər, (Spens.) n.* a female animal.   [she, deer; cf. hidder.]

shied. See shy¹,².

shiel¹. Same as sheal¹.

shiel², sheal *shēl, (Scot.) n.* a hut: a shelter. — *n.* shiel'ing, sheal'ing a shepherd's summer hut: a summer grazing. [Prob. from a lost O.N. equivalent of O.N. *skāli*, hut.]

shield *shēld, n.* a broad plate carried to ward off weapons, esp. one with a straight top and tapering curved sides: a protective plate, screen, pad, or other guard: a protection: a tubular structure pushed forward in tunnelling: a shield-shaped escutcheon used for displaying arms: a shield-shaped piece of plate as a prize: any shield-shaped design or object: the area of Archaean rocks in the earth's crust: a policeman's badge (*U.S.*). — *v.t.* to protect by shelter: to ward off: to forfend (*Shak.*). — *n.* shiel'der. — *adj.* shield'less. — *n.* shield'ling a protected person. — shield'-bearer; shield'-bug a heteropterous insect with much developed scutellum (fam. *Pentatomidae*); shield'-fern Aspidium; shield'-hand the left hand; shield'-maid, -maiden, -may an Amazon: a Valkyrie. — *adj.* shield= shaped usu., shaped like the conventional shield: sometimes, buckler-shaped: peltate. — shield'wall a defence of interlocked shields. — shield of brawn the thick skin of a pig's side, esp. when stuffed with meat.   [O.E. *sceld* (W.S. *scield*); Ger. *Schild*, O.N. *skjöldr*, protection.]

shieldrake, shieldduck. See shelduck.

shieling. See shiel².

shier, shies; shiest. See shy¹,²; shy¹.

shift *shift, v.i.* to manage, get on, do as one can: to change: to change position: to fluctuate: to change one's clothes (*arch.* or *dial.*): to resort to expedients: to move: to go away: to move quickly (*coll.*): to undergo phonetic change. — *v.t.* to change: to change the clothes of (*dial.*): to change the position of: to remove: to dislodge: to transfer: to evade (*obs.*): to rid: to quit: to swallow (*slang*): to put off. — *n.* an expedient: an artifice: provision of clothes or (*arch.*) other things for use in rotation or substitution: hence, (*arch.*) a smock:

a chemise: a shirt (*dial*.): a loose dress roughly triangular or oblong: a set of persons taking turns (esp. in working) with another set: the time of working of such a set: a change: a change of position: a general or bodily displacement of a series (as of lines in the spectrum, consonant or vowel sounds, faulted strata): displacement of an ordered set of data to the left or right (*comput*.): in violin-playing, any position of the left hand except that nearest the nut: a removal. — *adj.* **shift′ed**. — *n.* **shift′er** one who shifts, esp. a scene-shifter: one who resorts to shifts, tricks, evasions, or sophistry. — *adv.* **shif′tily**. — *ns.* **shift′iness; shift′ing**. — *adj.* moving about: unstable: shifty. — *adj.* **shift′less** without a smock: without resource or expedient: inefficient: feckless. — *adv.* **shift′lessly**. — *n.* **shift′lessness**. — *adj.* **shift′y** full of, or ready with, shifts or expedients: evasive, tricky, suggesting trickery. — **shif′ting-boards** partitioning to prevent shifting of cargo; **shifting register** same as **shift register; shift′-key** a typewriter key used to bring a different set of letters (as capitals) into play; **shift register** (*comput*.) a register (q.v.) which carries out shifts on data (bits or digits); **shift′-work** (a system of) working in shifts; **shift′-worker; shift′-working**. — **make (a) shift** to contrive to do somehow; **shift about** to vacillate: to turn quite round to the opposite point; **shift for oneself** to depend on one's own resources; **shift one's ground** (usu. *fig*.) to change the position one has taken, e.g. in a discussion. [O.E. *sciftan*, to divide, allot; O.N. *skipta*.]

shigella *shig-el′ə, n.* a rod-shaped bacterium of the genus **Shigella,** esp. one of the species which cause dysentery. [After K. *Shiga* (1870–1957), the Japanese bacteriologist who discovered it.]

shih tzu *shēd-zōō′, n.* a small dog of Tibetan and Chinese breed.

Shiism, Shiite, Shiitic. See **Shiah.**

shiitake *shi-it-äk′ā, n.* the variety of mushroom (*Lentinus edodes*) most widely used in Oriental cookery, cultivated on tree logs: — *pl.* **shiitake**. [Jap. *shii*, a type of tree, *take*, mushroom.]

shikar *shi-kär′, n.* hunting, sport. — *ns.* **shikar′ee, shikar′i** a hunter. [Urdu, from Pers. *shikār*.]

shiksa, shikse *shik′sə, n.* a non-Jewish woman. [Yiddish.]

shill¹, shilling. See **sheal¹.**

shill² *shil,* (*slang*; esp. *U.S.*) *n.* an accomplice to a tradesman, etc., who poses as a genuine customer to encourage trade or interest: a gambler's or con man's sidekick: a decoy. — Also *v.i.* [Prob. abbrev. of **shillaber**.]

shillaber *shil′ə-bər,* (*old U.S. slang*) *n.* an enthusiastic or satisfied customer: a shill. [Orig. uncertain.]

shillela(g)h *shi-lā′li, -lə, n.* an Irishman's oak or blackthorn cudgel, or any similar stout club, etc. [*Shillelagh*, an oak-wood in County Wicklow, or *sail*, willow, *éille* (*gen*.) thong.]

shilling *shil′ing, n.* a coin or its value, 12 old pence, 5 (new) pence or (**East Africa shilling;** Kenya, etc.) 100 cents. — *adj.* costing or offered for a shilling: also in compounds, as **two′-shilling, three′-shilling,** etc. — *adj.* **shill′ingless**. — *n.* **shill′ingsworth** as much as can be purchased for a shilling. — **shill′ing-mark** a solidus sign; **shilling shocker** a sensational story, orig. one published at a shilling. — **take the (king's, queen's) shilling** to enlist as a soldier by accepting a recruiting officer's shilling — discontinued in 1879. [O.E. *scilling*, Ger. *Schilling*.]

shilly-shally *shil′i-shal′i, adv.* in silly hesitation. — *n.* vacillation: one who vacillates. — *v.i.* to vacillate. — **shill′y-shall′ier**. [A redup. of **shall I?**]

shilpit *shil′pit,* (*Scot*.) *adj.* sickly-looking: washy: puny: insipid: inferior. [Ety. dub.]

shily. See **shy¹.**

shim *shim, n.* a slip of metal, wood, etc., used to fill in space or to adjust parts. [Ety. dub.]

shimmer *shim′ər, v.i.* to gleam tremulously, to glisten. — *ns.* **shimm′er, shimm′ering** a tremulous gleam. — *adj.*

shimm′ery. [O.E. *scimerian* — *scimian*, to shine; Ger. *schimmern*.]

shimmy *shim′i, n.* a shivering dance (also **shimm′y-shake**): a shaking of the hips: vibration in a motor-car or an aeroplane. — *v.i.* to dance the shimmy, or make similar movements: to vibrate. [App. from **chemise**.]

shimozzle. See **shemozzle.**

shin *shin, n.* the forepart of the leg below the knee: the lower part of a leg of beef. — *v.i.* to swarm, climb by gripping with the hands and legs (usu. with *up*): to use one's legs, hasten along. — *v.t.* to climb by gripping with the hands and legs: to kick on the shins. — **shin′-barker** a cur that barks at one's shins; **shin′-bone** the tibia; **shin′-plas′ter** (*U.S.*) a brown-paper patch for a sore on the shin: paper money of small value. [O.E. *scinu*, the shin; Du. *scheen*; Ger. *Schiene*, a thin plate.]

shindig *shin′dig,* (*slang*) *n.* a lively celebration or party: a row. [Cf. **shindy.**]

shindy *shin′di,* (*slang*) *n.* a row, rumpus. — **kick up a shindy** to make a disturbance. [Perh. **shinty.**]

shine *shīn, v.i.* to give or reflect light: to beam with steady radiance: to glow: to be bright: to appear pre-eminent. — *v.t.* to cause to shine: — *pa.t.* in the sense of polished, **shone** (*shon*) or **shined;** *pa.p.* **shone,** in Biblical usage, and in the sense of polished, **shined**. — *adj.* (*Spens*.) sheen. — *n.* brightness: lustre: sunshine: a dash, brilliant appearance: an act or process of polishing: a tea-party or the like (*slang*): a shindy (*slang*). — *adj.* **shine′less**. — *ns.* **shīn′er** one who or that which shines: a coin, esp. a sovereign (*slang*): a small glittering fish of various kinds: a black eye (*slang*); **shīn′iness**. — *adj.* **shīn′ing**. — *adv.* **shīn′ingly**. — *n.* **shīn′ingness**. — *adj.* **shīn′y** clear, unclouded: glossy. — Also *adv.* (*Spens*.). — **take a shine to** (*coll*.) to fancy, take a liking to; **shine at** to be very good at; **take the shine out of** (*slang*) to outshine, eclipse: to take the brilliance or pleasure-giving quality out of. [O.E. *scīnan;* Ger. *scheinen;* in some senses perh. a different word; cf. **shindy.**]

shiness. See **shy¹.**

shingle¹ *shing′gl, n.* a wooden slab (or substitute) used as a roofing-slate: these slabs collectively: a board: a small signboard or plate (*U.S.*): a mode of hair-cutting showing the form of the head at the back (from the overlap of the hairs). — *v.t.* to cover with shingles: to cut in the manner of a shingle. — *adj.* **shing′led**. — *ns.* **shing′ler; shing′ling**. — *adj.* **shing′le-roofed**. [L.L. *scindula*, a wooden tile — L. *scindĕre*, to split.]

shingle² *shing′gl, n.* coarse gravel: small water-worn pebbles found esp. on beaches: a bank or bed of gravel or stones. — *adj.* **shing′ly**. [Origin obscure.]

shingles *shing′glz, n.pl.* the disease *Herpes zoster,* an eruption usually running along an intercostal nerve with acute inflammation of the nerve ganglia. [L. *cingulum,* a belt — *cingĕre,* to gird.]

shinne *shin,* (*Shak*.) *n.* a form of **chin.**

shinny¹. Same as **shinty.**

shinny² *shin′i,* (*U.S.*) *v.i.* to shin (usu. with *up, down,* etc.). [**shin.**]

Shinto *shin′tō, n.* the Japanese nature and hero cult, the indigenous religion of the country. — *ns.* **Shin′tōism; Shin′tōist**. [Jap., — Chin. *shin tao* — *shin,* god, *tao,* way, doctrine.]

shinty *shin′ti,* **shinny** *shin′i, ns.* a game like hockey, of Scottish origin, played by teams of 12: the slim curved club (the caman, also **shin′ty-stick**) or leather-covered cork ball (or substitute) used therein. [Perh. from Gael. *sinteag,* a bound, pace.]

shiny. See **shine.**

ship *ship, n.* a large vessel, esp. a three-masted square-rigged sailing vessel: a racing-boat: sometimes any floating craft: an aircraft: a ship's crew: a spaceship. — *v.t.* to put, receive, or take on board: to send or convey by ship: to send by land or air: to dispatch, send (off): to engage for service on board: to fix in position. — *v.i.* to embark: to engage for service on shipboard: — *pr.p.* **shipp′ing;** *pa.t.* and *pa.p.* **shipped**. — *n.* **ship′ful**. — *adj.* **ship′less**. — *n.* **ship′ment** the act of putting on board: a consignment orig. by ship, now extended to other forms of transport. — *adj.* **shipped** furnished with a ship or ships (*Shak.*): embarked. — *ns.* **shipp'er** one who sends goods by ship; **shipp'ing** ships collectively: accommodation on board ship: (the act of) putting aboard ship: transport by ship: a voyage (*Shak.*). — **ship'-bis'cuit** hard biscuit for use on shipboard; **ship'board** a ship's side, hence a ship; **ship'-boy** a boy that serves on a ship; **ship'-breaker** one who breaks up old ships; **ship'broker** a broker for sale, insurance, etc., of ships; **ship'builder; ship'building; ship'-canal'** a canal large enough for ships; **ship'=cap'tain** one who commands a ship; **ship('s)'-car'penter** a carpenter employed on board ship or in a shipyard; **ship'-chand'ler** a dealer in supplies for ships; **ship'=chand'lery; ship'-fē'ver** typhus; **ship'-hold'er** a remora; **ship'lap** an arrangement of boards or plates in which the lower edge of one overlaps the upper edge of the next below it. — Also *v.t.* and *v.i.* — **ship'-lett'er** a letter sent by a vessel which does not carry mails; **ship'-load** the actual or possible load of a ship; **ship'man** (*arch.*) a sailor: a skipper: a pilot: — *pl.* **ship'men; ship'-master** the captain of a ship; **ship'mate** a fellow sailor; **ship'-money** a tyrannical tax imposed by the king on seaports, revived without authorisation of parliament by Charles I in 1634–37; **ship'-of-the-line'** before steam navigation, a man-of-war large enough to take a place in a line of battle; **ship'-owner** the owner of, or owner of a share in, a ship or ships; **shipping agent** a person (or company) that manages the administrative business of a ship on behalf of the owner; **shipp'ing-art'icles** articles of agreement between the captain and his crew; **shipping clerk** a person employed to deal with the receiving and dispatching of goods by ship; **ship'pound** in the Baltic ports, twenty lispounds; **ship'-rail'way** a railway for carrying ships overland. — *adjs.* **ship'-rigged** having three masts with square sails and spreading yards; **ship'shape** in a seamanlike condition: trim, neat, proper. — **ship's husband** see **husband; ship's papers** documents that a ship is required to carry; **ship'-tire** (*Shak.*) a shiplike head-dress; **ship'=way** a sliding-way for launching ships: a support for ships under examination or repair: a ship-canal; **ship'=worm** a wormlike lamellibranch mollusc (Teredo, etc.) that makes shell-lined tunnels in wood; **ship'wreck** the wreck or destruction (esp. by accident) of a ship: destruction, ruin, disaster: wreckage (*rare*). — *v.t.* to wreck: to make to suffer wreck. — *v.i.* to suffer wreck. — **ship'wright** a wright or carpenter employed in shipbuilding; **ship'yard** a yard where ships are built or repaired. — **on shipboard** upon or within a ship; **ship a sea, water** to have a wave come aboard; **ship it green** to ship waves, not mere spray; **ship of the desert** the camel; **ship the oars** to put the oars in the rowlocks: to bring the oars into the boat; **ship water** see **ship a sea; take ship** or **shipping** to embark; **when one's ship comes home** (or **in**) when one becomes rich. [O.E. *scip*; Goth. *skip*, O.N. *skip*, Ger. *Schiff*.]

-ship *-ship*, in composition, denoting (1) a condition or state, as *friendship, fellowship*; (2) position, rank, status, as *lordship*; (3) a specified type of skill, as *craftsmanship, scholarship*; (4) the number of people who are (something), as *membership*. [O.E. *-scipe*, conn. with **shape**.]

shippen, shippon *ship'n*, (*dial.*) *n.* a cowhouse, cattle-shed. [O.E. *scypen*; cf. **shop**.]

shippo *ship-ō'*, *n.* Japanese cloisonné ware. [Jap. *shippô*, seven precious things, hence something beautiful.]

shir. See **shirr**.

shiralee *shir'ə-lē*, (*Austr.*) *n.* a swagman's bundle. [Orig. unknown.]

shire *shīr* (in composition *-shir, -shər*), *n.* a county: applied also to certain smaller districts as Richmondshire and Hallamshire: a rural district having its own elected council (*Austr.*). — **shire'-horse** a large, strong draught-horse, once bred chiefly in the Midland shires; **shire'-man** a sheriff; **shire'-moot** (O.E. *scīrgemōt*; *hist.*) the

court of the shire; **shire'-reeve** a sheriff (see ety. at **sheriff**). — **the Shires** (often *shērz*) those English counties whose names end in -shire, esp. (for hunting) Leicestershire, Rutlandshire (later Rutland), Northamptonshire, and part of Lincolnshire. [O.E. *scīr*, office, authority.]

shirk *shûrk, v.t.* to evade: to slink out of facing or shouldering. — *v.i.* to go or act evasively. — *n.* one who shirks. — *n.* **shirk'er.** [Cf. **shark.**]

Shirley poppy *shûr'li pop'i*, a variety of common poppy produced at *Shirley*, Croydon.

shirr, shir *shûr, n.* a puckering or gathering. — *v.t.* to pucker, make gathers in: to bake (eggs broken into a dish). — *adj.* **shirred.** — *n.* **shirr'ing.** [Origin unknown.]

shirra *shir'ə, n.* a Scots form of **sheriff**.

shirt *shûrt, n.* a man's loose sleeved garment for the upper part of the body, typically with fitted collar and cuffs: a woman's blouse of similar form: an undershirt: a nightshirt: a close covering. — *v.t.* to put a shirt on. — *n.* **shirt'ing** cloth for shirts. — *adjs.* **shirt'less; shirt'y** (*slang*) ruffled in temper, annoyed. — **shirt'-band** the neckband of a shirt; **shirt'-butt'on; shirt dress** a straight dress with a shirt-type collar, resembling an elongated shirt: a shirtwaister (*U.S.*); **shirt'-frill'** a frill on the breast of the shirt; **shirt'-front'** the breast of a shirt: a dickey; **shirt'-pin** an ornamental pin fastening a shirt at the neck; **shirt'-sleeve; shirt'-stud; shirt'-tail'** the flap at the back of a shirt; **shirt'waist** (*U.S.*) a woman's blouse; **shirt'waister** a tailored dress with shirtwaist top. — **Black Shirt** a fascist; **boiled shirt** a white shirt (with starched front); **Brown Shirt** a Nazi; **in one's shirt** wearing nothing but a shirt, or nothing over the shirt; **in one's shirt-sleeves** with one's jacket or jersey off; **keep one's shirt on** to keep calm; **lose one's shirt** to lose all one has; **put one's shirt on** to bet all one has on; **Red Shirt** a follower of Garibaldi. [O.E. *scyrte*; cf. **short**.]

shish kebab. See **kebab**.

shit, shite *shit, shīt*, (*vulg.*) *ns.* excrement: a contemptuous term for a person. — *vs.i.* to evacuate the bowels. — *vs.t.* (*fig.* and *refl.*): — *pr.p.* **shit(t)'ing;** *pa.t.* and *pa.p.* **shit, shat.** — *interjs.* expressing annoyance, disappointment, etc. — *adj.* **shitt'y** soiled with or like shit: very bad or unpleasant. — **bull'shit** see **bull[1]**. — **no shit** (*U.S. slang*) no fooling; **shit oneself** (*slang*) to be very scared; **the shits** (*slang*) diarrhoea. [O.E. *scitan*, to defecate.]

shittim *shit'im, n.* in full **shitt'im wood** (*B.*), the wood of the **shitt'ah (tree)**, believed to be an acacia: applied also to various other trees. [Heb. *shittāh*, pl. *shittīm*.]

shiv. See **chiv**.

Shiva. See **Siva**.

shivaree *shiv-ə-rē'*, (*old U.S.*) *n.* a form of **charivari**. — *v.t.* to give a mock serenade to.

shive *shīv, n.* a slice, as a loaf of bread (*Scot.*): a thin wide cork or bung. [M.E. *schive*; cf. O.N. *skīfa*; Du. *schijf*, Ger. *Scheibe*.]

shiver[1] *shiv'ər, n.* a splinter: a chip: a small fragment. — *v.t.* and *v.i.* to shatter. — *adj.* **shiv'ery** brittle. — **shiver my timbers** a stage sailor's oath. [Early M.E. *scifre*; cf. **shive, sheave;** Ger. *Schiefer*.]

shiver[2] *shiv'ər, v.i.* to quiver: to make an involuntary muscular movement as with cold. — *v.t.* to cause to quiver. — *n.* a shivering movement or feeling. — *n.* and *adj.* **shiv'ering.** — *adv.* **shiv'eringly.** — *adj.* **shiv'ery** inclined to shiver or to cause shivers. — **shiver in one's shoes** see **shake; the shivers** (*coll.*) a shivering fit: the ague: a thrill of horror or fear. [M.E. *chivere*.]

shivoo *shə-vōō', n.* a (noisy) party. [From N. Eng. dial. *sheevo*, a shindy; perh. conn. with Fr. *chez vous*, at your house.]

shlemiel. See **schlemiel**.

shlemozzle. See **shemozzle**.

shlep. See **schlep**.

shlimazel. See **schlimazel**.

shlock. See **schlock**.

shmoose, shmooze. See **schmooze**.

shoal[1] *shōl, n.* a multitude of fishes, etc., swimming together: a flock, swarm, great assemblage. — *v.i.* to gather or go in shoals, swarm. — *adv.* **shoal'wise** in shoals. [O.E. *scolu*, troop; cf. **school**[2].]

shoal[2] *shōl, adj.* shallow. — *n.* a shallow. — *v.i.* to grow shallow: to come to shallow water. — *v.t.* to find to be shallowing: to make shallow. — *ns.* **shoal'ing; shoal'ness.** — *adj.* **shoal'y** full of shallows. — **shoal'-mark** an indication of shoal-water; **shoal'-water.** [O.E. *sceald*, shallow.]

shoat, shote, shot(t) *shōt, n.* a young hog. [From M.E.; conn. Flem. *shote.*]

shochet *shohh'ət, n.* a slaughterer qualified to kill cattle or poultry according to prescribed Jewish ritual. — *pl.* **shoch'etim** (*-tim*). [Heb. *shōhēt*, pr.p. of *shāhat*, to slaughter.]

shock[1] *shok, n.* a violent impact, orig. of charging warriors: a dashing together: a shaking or unsettling blow: a sudden shaking or jarring as if by a blow: a blow to the emotions or its cause: outrage at something regarded as improper: a convulsive excitation of nerves, as by electricity: the prostration of voluntary and involuntary functions caused by trauma, a surgical operation, or excessive sudden emotional disturbance: a stroke of paralysis (*coll.*). — *v.t.* to meet or assail with a shock: to shake or impair by a shock: to give a shock to: to harrow or outrage the feelings of: to affect with abashed and horrified indignation. — *v.i.* to outrage feelings: to collide with violence. — *adj.* **shocked.** — *n.* **shock'er** (*coll.*) a very sensational tale: any unpleasant, offensive, etc. person or thing. — *adj.* **shock'ing** giving a shock: revolting to the feelings, esp. to oversensitive modesty: execrable: deplorably bad. — *adv.* (*coll.*) deplorably. — *adv.* **shock'ingly.** — *n.* **shock'ingness.** — **shock'-absorber** a contrivance for damping shock, as in an aeroplane alighting or a car on a bad road. — *adj.* **shock'-proof** protected in some way from giving, or suffering the effects of, shock: unlikely to be upset, or to feel moral outrage; **shock stall** (*aero.*) loss of lift at high speed caused by the formation of shock waves; **shock tactics** orig. tactics of cavalry attacking in masses and depending for their effect on the force of impact: any action that seeks to achieve its object by means of suddenness and force (*fig.*); **shock therapy, treatment** the use of electric shocks in treatment of mental disorders: the use of violent measures to change one's way of thinking (*fig.*); **shock'-troops** troops trained or selected for attacks demanding exceptional physique and bravery; **shock wave** a wave of the same nature as a sound wave but of very great intensity, caused, e.g. by an atomic explosion, or by a body moving with supersonic velocity: the reaction to a sensation or a scandal, thought of as spreading in ever-widening circles. — **shock horror** (*coll.*) an ironic expression denoting boredom, disinterest, etc. (e.g. towards news that lacks impact or novelty), alluding esp. to banner headlines in tabloid newspapers. — Also *adj.* [App. Fr. *choc* (n.), *choquer* (vb.), or perh. directly from a Gmc. source; cf. Du. *schok.*]

shock[2] *shok, n.* a stook, or propped-up group of sheaves, commonly twelve: three score. — *v.t.* to set up in shocks. — *n.* **shock'er.** [M.E. *schokke*; the corresponding word in some Gmc. languages has come to mean sixty.]

shock[3] *shok, n.* a dog with long, shaggy hair: a mass of shaggy hair. — Also *adj.* — **shock'-dog; shock'-head.** — *adjs.* **shock'-head, -ed.** [Cf. **shough.**]

shod. See **shoe.**

shoddy *shod'i, n.* wool from shredded rags: cloth made of it, alone or mixed: anything inferior seeking to pass for better than it is. — *adj.* of shoddy: inferior and pretentious: cheap and nasty: sham. — *adv.* **shodd'ily.** — *n.* **shodd'iness.** [Origin unknown.]

shoder *shōd'ər, n.* a set of skins in which goldleaf is beaten the second time (see **cutch**[2]). [From obs. Fr. *chaucher*, to press; ult. from L. *calx*, heel.]

shoe *shōō, n.* a stiff outer covering for the foot, not coming above the ankle (or in U.S. not much above): a rim of iron nailed to a hoof: anything in form, position, or use like a shoe, as in a metal tip or ferrule, a piece attached where there is friction, a drag for a wheel, the touching part of a brake, the block by which an electric tractor collects current: in gambling, a box-like device for dispensing playing-cards singly: — *pl.* **shoes** (*shōōz*); also, *arch.* and *dial.* **shoon** (*shōōn, Scot. shün, shin*). — *v.t.* to put shoes or a shoe on: — *pr.p.* **shoe'ing;** *pa.t.* and *pa.p.* **shod** (*shod*), **shoed** (*shōōd*). — *adj.* **shod.** — *n.* **shoe'ing.** — *adj.* **shoe'less.** — *n.* **shoer** (*shōō'ər*) a horse-shoer. — **shoe'bill** a large African wading bird (*Balaeniceps rex*) with heavy bill (also **shoebill stork, whale-head, whale-headed stork**); **shoe'black** one who blacks shoes; **shoe'-brush; shoe'-buckle** a buckle for the front of a shoe, as fastening or ornament; **shoe'horn, shoe'ing-horn** an instrument for helping the heel into the shoe: any means of drawing on. — *v.t.* **shoe'horn** (*fig.*) to fit, squeeze or compress into a tight or insufficient space. — **shoe'ing-smith; shoe'-lace** a string passed through eyelet holes to fasten a shoe; **shoe'-latchet** a thong for fastening a shoe, sandal, etc.; **shoe'-leather** leather for shoes: shoes or shoeing generally; **shoe'maker** one who makes (now more often only sells or mends) shoes and boots; **shoe'making; shoe'-nail** a nail for fastening a horseshoe: a nail for a shoe sole; **shoe'-peg** a peg for fastening parts of a shoe together; **shoe'-rose** a rosette on a shoe; **shoe'shine** (the act of) polishing shoes: the shiny appearance of polished shoes; **shoe'-shop; shoe'string** a shoe-lace (*U.S.*): a minimum of capital. — *adj.* operated, produced, etc. on a minimum of capital: petty, paltry (*U.S.*). — **shoestring fungus** any fungus forming long rhizomorphs, esp. one that destroys trees; **shoe'-tie** a shoe-lace, esp. an ornate one; **shoe'-tree** a support, usually of wood or metal, inserted in a shoe when it is not being worn in order to preserve its shape. — **another pair of shoes** (*coll.*) quite a different matter; **be in, step into, someone's** or **a dead man's, shoes** to be in, or succeed to, someone's place; **die in one's shoes** to die by violence, esp. by hanging; **on a shoestring** with an extremely small amount of capital. [O.E. *scōh* (pl. *scōs*); Goth. *shōhs*, Ger. *Schuh.*]

shofar *shō'fär, n.* a kind of trumpet made from a ram's horn, blown in Jewish religious ceremonies and in ancient times as a call to battle, etc.: — *pl.* **shō'fars, shōfroth** (*-frōt'*). — Also **shophar.** [Heb. *shōphār*, ram's horn.]

shog *shog, v.i.* to shake: to sway: to jog: to move on, be gone. — *v.t.* to shake: — *pr.p.* **shogg'ing;** — *pa.t.* and *pa.p.* **shogged.** — *n.* a jog, shock. [M.E. *shogge*, perh. related to **shock**[1] and O.H.G. *scoc*, a swing.]

shoggle *shog'l,* (*dial.*) *v.t.* to shake, rock. — *v.i.* to wobble, shake. — *adj.* **shogg'ly.** [Cf. **shoogle; shog.**]

shogun *shō'gŏŏn, -gōōn, n.* the commander-in-chief and real ruler of feudal Japan. — *adj.* **shō'gunal.** — *n.* **shō'gunate** the office, jurisdiction or state of a shogun. [Jap., — *sho*, to lead, *gun*, army.]

shoji *shō'jē, n.* a screen of paper covering a wooden framework, forming a wall or sliding partition in Japanese homes. [Jap., — *sho*, to separate, *ji*, a piece.]

shola[1] *shō'lə,* (*India*) *n.* a thicket. [Tamil *çolai.*]

shola[2]. Same as **sola**[2].

Shona *shō'nə, n.* a group of African peoples living south of the Zambesi: any member of the group: any language spoken by the group: (**Union Shona**) a literary language designed for use by the whole group.

shone *shon, pa.t.* and *pa.p.* of **shine.**

shoo *shōō, interj.* used to scare away fowls, etc. — *v.i.* to cry 'Shoo!' — *v.t.* to drive away by calling 'Shoo!': to cause or allow (a horse) to win a race (*U.S. slang*): to fix (a race) so that a particular horse wins (*U.S. slang*). — *n.* **shoo'-in** (*U.S. slang*) a horse that is shooed in: any certain winner of a race, competition, etc.: a sure thing. [Instinctive; cf. Ger. *schu*, Gr. *sou*.]

shoogie *shoōg'ē, shoōg'ē*, (*Scot. dial.*) *v.i.* to swing, sway back and forth. — *n.* a swing (as of a pendant): a swaying movement. [Cf. **shoogle; shog.**]

shoogle *shoōg'l*, (*Scot.*) *v.i.* to shake, tremble: to sway, rock back and forth. — *v.t.* to shake, rock. — *n.* a swaying, rocking motion. — *adj.* **shoog'ly.** [Cf. **shog.**]

shoo-in. See **shoo.**

shook[1] *shook, pa.t.* of **shake.**

shook[2] *shook, n.* a bundle of sheaves, a shock, stook: a set of cask staves and heads, or of parts for making a box, etc. [Orig. unknown.]

shool[1] *shool, v.i.* to saunter about, skulk: to beg: to sponge. [Perh. Ir.]

shool[2] *shool, shol*, Scot. *shül, shil, n.* and *v.* a dialect form of **shovel.**

shoon. See **shoe.**

shoot[1] *shoōt, v.t.* to dart: to let fly with force: to discharge: to precipitate, launch forth: to tip out, dump: to cast: to send down a shoot: to kick or hit at goal (*games*): to score, for a hole or the round (*golf*): to thrust forward: to pull (one's shirt cuffs) forward so that they project from the sleeves of one's jacket: to slide along: to slide the bolt of· to put forth in growth: to crystallise: to pass rapidly through, under, or over: to hit, wound, or kill with a shot: to photograph, esp. for motion pictures: to variegate: to produce a play of colour in (usu. in *pa.p.*): to inject (esp. oneself) with (a drug) (*slang*): to play (a round of golf, game of pool, etc.): to detonate. — *v.i.* to dart forth or forward: of a cricket ball, to start forward rapidly near the ground: to send darting pains: to sprout: of vegetables, to bolt: to elongate rapidly: to jut out far or suddenly: to begin, esp. to speak one's mind or to tell what one knows (*coll.*; usu. in *imper.*): to tower: to send forth a missile, etc.: to discharge a shot or weapon: to use a bow or gun in practice, competition, hunting, etc.: to crystallise: — *pa.t.* and *pa.p.* **shot;** see also **shott'en.** — *n.* a shot (*Shak.*): a shooting: a shooting match, party, expedition: a shooting pain: a movement of the shuttle: a weft thread: the shooting of a film: new growth: a sprout: the stem and leaf parts of a plant: a dump: a chute (see **chute**[1]). — *adj.* **shoot'able** that may be shot, or shot over. — *ns.* **shoot'er** a cricket ball that shoots (see above): a gun, etc. (*coll.*); **shoot'ing** the action of the verb in any sense: a twinge of quick pain: the killing of game with firearms over a certain area: the right to do so: the district so limited: the planing of edges that are to be joined. — Also *adj.* — **shoot'ist** (*slang*; now esp. *U.S.*) someone who shoots: a skilled marksman. — **shoot'ing-board** a board for steadying a piece of wood for shooting; **shoot'ing-box, -lodge** a small house in the country for use in the shooting season; **shoot'ing-brake** a motor-car for the carriage both of passengers and of burden, an estate car; **shoot'ing-gall'ery** a long room used for practice or amusement with firearms; **shoot'ing-iron** (*slang*) a firearm, esp. a revolver; **shoot'ing-jack'et** a short coat for shooting in; **shoot'ing-range** a place for shooting at targets; **shoot'ing-star** a meteor; **shoot'ing-stick** a printer's tool for driving quoins: a walking-stick with a head that opens out into a seat; **shooting war** actual war as distinct from cold war; **shoot'-out** a gunfight, esp. to the death or other decisive conclusion (also *fig.*). — **get shot of** (*slang*) to get rid of; **have shot one's bolt** see **bolt**[1]; **shoot a line** (*slang*) to brag, exaggerate (*n.* **line'-shooter**); **shoot down** to kill, or to bring down (an aeroplane) by shooting: to rout in argument; **shoot down in flames** (*slang*) to reprimand severely; **shoot from the hip** (*coll.*) to speak bluntly or hastily, without preparation or without caring about the consequences (*adj.* **shoot'-from-the-hip'**); **shoot home** to hit the target (also *fig.*); **shoot it out** to settle by military action (also *fig.*); **shoot off** to discharge a gun: to begin: to rush away; **shoot one's mouth off** see **mouth**; **shoot the sun** to take the sun's altitude; **shoot the works** (*slang*) at games of chance, to risk (one's all) on one play: hence, to make one's maximum effort; **shoot up** to kill or injure by shooting: to grow very

quickly; **the whole shoot, shooting-match** (*coll.*) the whole lot. [O.E. *scēotan*; Du. *schieten*, Ger. *schiessen*; in some senses merging with Fr. *chute*, fall.]

shoot[2]. Same as **shoat.**

shop *shop, n.* a building or room in which goods are sold: a place where mechanics work, or where any kind of industry is pursued: a place of employment or activity, esp. a theatre: prison (*slang*): talk about one's own business. — *v.i.* to visit shops, esp. for the purpose of buying. — *v.t.* to imprison, or cause to be imprisoned (*slang*): to betray (someone), e.g. to inform against (him) to the police (*slang; n.* **shopp'er**): to give employment to: — *pr.p.* **shopp'ing;** *pa.p.* **shopped.** — *ns.* **shopahol'ic** a compulsive shopper (see **-aholic**); **shop'ful; shopp'er** one who shops: a shopping bag, basket; **shopp'ing** visiting shops to buy or see goods: goods thus bought. — *adj.* for shopping. — *adj.* **shopp'y** commercial: abounding in shops: given to talking shop: concerning one's own pursuit. — **shop'-assist'ant** one who sells goods in a shop; **shop'-bell** a bell that rings at the opening of a shop-door; **shop'board** a counter: a bench on which tailors work; **shop'-boy, -girl** a boy or girl employed in a shop; **shop'breaker** one who breaks into a shop; **shop'breaking; shop'-door; shop-floor'** that part of a factory, etc., housing the production machinery and the main part of the work-force: the people who work on the shop-floor. — *adj.* **shop'-floor.** — **shop'-front; shop'keeper** one who keeps a shop of his own; **shop'keeping; shop'-lift'er; shop'-lift'ing** stealing from a shop; **shop'man** one who serves in a shop: a shopkeeper (*rare*): a workshop man (*U.S.*); **shopping bag, basket** a receptacle for goods bought; **shopping centre** a place where there is a concentration of shops of different kinds; **shopping list** a list of items to be bought: a list of items to be obtained, done, acted upon, considered, etc. (*fig.*); **shopping precinct** see **precinct; shop'-sign** indication of trade and occupier's name over a shop. — *adj.* **shop'-soiled** somewhat tarnished by shop exposure (also *fig.*). — **shop'-stew'ard** a representative of factory or workshop hands elected from their own number; **shop'-walker** one who walks about in a shop to see customers attended to; **shop'-win'dow** a window of a shop in which wares are displayed (also *fig.*); **shop'-woman.** — *adj.* **shop'worn** shop-soiled (also *fig.*). — **all over the shop** dispersed all around; **on the shop floor** among the workers in a factory or workshop; **set up shop** to open a trading establishment: to begin operations generally; **shop around** to compare prices and quality of goods at various shops before making a purchase; **talk shop** to talk about one's own work or business; **the Shop** former Royal Military Academy at Woolwich; **the wrong shop** the wrong place to look for, e.g. sympathy or help. [O.E. *sceoppa*, a treasury.]

shope *shōp, obs. pa.t.* (*Spens.*) of **shape.**

shophar. See **shofar.**

shoran *shör'an, n.* a system of aircraft navigation using the measurement of the time taken for two dispatched radar signals to return from known locations. [*Sho*rt *ran*ge *n*avigation.]

shore[1] *shōr, shōr, n.* the land bordering on the sea or a great sheet of water: the foreshore. — *v.t.* to set on shore. — *adj.* **shore'less** having no shore, unlimited. — *adj.* and *adv.* **shore'ward.** — *adv.* **shore'wards.** — **shore'-boat** a boat plying near or to the shore; **shore'-crab** a crab (*Carcinus maenas*) very common between tidemarks; **shore'-due** (*Scot.*) a harbour-due. — *adj.* **shore'-going** going, or for going, ashore: land-dwelling. — **shore'-leave** leave of absence to go ashore; **shore'line** the line of meeting of land and water: a rope connecting a net with the land; **shore'man** a dweller on the shore: a landsman: (*U.S.* also **shores'man**) one who has a shore-going job connected with fishery; **shore'-side** the neighbourhood of the score. — Also *adj.* — **shore'-weed** a plant (*Litorella lacustris*) of lake-margins of the plantain family. — **on shore** on the land: ashore. [M.E. *schore*; cf. Du. *schoor, schor*.]

shore[2] *shōr, shör, n.* a prop. — *v.t.* to prop (often with *up*). — *ns.* **shor'er; shor'ing** propping: a set of props. [Cf. Du. *schoor*, O.N. *skortha*.]

shore[3] *shōr, shör, (Scot.) v.t.* to warn, threaten: to offer. — *n.* threatening. [Origin obscure.]

shore[4] *shōr, (arch.* and *coll.) n.* a sewer — usu. (as *Shak.*) **common-shore.** [Perh. **sewer;** perh. **shore**[1].]

shore[5] *shōr, shör, pa.t.,* **shorn** *shörn, pa.p.* See **shear.**

short *shört, adj.* of little length, tallness, extent, or duration: in the early future (as *short day, date*): concise: curt: abrupt: snappish: crisp yet readily crumbling: brittle: on the hither side: failing to go far enough or reach the standard: deficient: lacking: scanty, in inadequate supply: in want, ill supplied: in default: unable to meet engagements: pertaining to the sale of what one cannot supply: in accentual verse, loosely, unaccented (*pros.*): undiluted with water, neat (*coll.*): having short wool: of certain fielding positions, relatively near the batsman (*cricket*). — *adv.* briefly: abruptly: without leaving a stump: on this or the near side: see **sell short:** at a disadvantage (e.g. *taken short*). — *n.* that which is short: shortness, abbreviation, summary: a short-circuit: (in *pl.,* formerly) small-clothes, (now) short trousers (i.e. thigh-length, as opposed to ankle-length): (in *pl.*) undershorts (*U.S.*): (in *pl.*) the bran and coarse part of meal, in mixture: (in *pl.*) short-dated securities: a short film subordinate to a main film in a programme: a short alcoholic drink (*coll.*). — *v.t.* to shortchange. — *v.t.* and *v.i.* to shorten (*obs.*): to short-circuit: to fall short of, or perh. make to fail (*Shak.*). — *n.* **short'age** a lack, deficiency. — *v.t.* **short'en** to make shorter: to make to seem short or to fall short: to draw in or back: to check: to make friable (by adding butter, lard, etc.): to put in short-clothes. — *v.i.* to become shorter. — *ns.* **short'ener; short'ening** making or becoming shorter: fat for making pastry short; **short'ie, short'y** (*coll.*) a very short person, garment, etc. — Also *adj.* — *adj.* **short'ish.** — *adv.* **short'ly** soon: briefly: curtly: for a short time (*rare*): a little: with shortness in that which is indicated. — *n.* **short'ness.** — **short'bread** a brittle crumbling cake of flour and butter; **short'cake** shortbread or other friable cake: a light cake, prepared in layers with fruit between, served with cream (*U.S.*). — *v.t.* **short'change'** to give less than the correct change to: to deal dishonestly with (a person). — *adj.* **short'-change'** pertaining to cheating. — **shortchan'ger; short'-cir'cuit** a new path of comparatively low resistance between two points of a circuit (*elect.*): a deviation of current by a path of low resistance. — *v.t.* to establish a short-circuit in: to interconnect where there was obstruction between (*surg.*): to provide with a short-cut (*fig.*). — *v.i.* to cut off current by a short-circuit: to save a roundabout passage. — **short'-clothes, short'-coats** the shortened skirts of a child when the first long clothes are left off. — *v.t.* **short'-coat** to put into short-coats. — **short'-coming** an act of coming or falling short: a neglect of, or failure in, duty: a defect; **short commons** minimum rations; **short covering** (*Stock exchange*) the buying of securities, etc., to cover a short sale: the securities, etc., bought for this purpose. — *adj.* **short'-cut** cut short instead of in long shreds. — *n.* tobacco so cut: (also **short'cut, short cut**) a shorter way than the usual. — *adj.* **short'-dāt'ed** having little time to run from its date, as a bill: of securities, redeemable in under five years. — **short'-divi'sion** division without writing down the working out; **short'fall** the fact or amount of falling short; **short game** in golf, play on and around the green(s); **short'gown** (*Scot.*) a woman's loose jacket; **short'hand** a method of swift writing to keep pace with speaking: writing of such a kind. — Also *adj.* — *adjs.* **short'-hand'ed** short of workers: with short hands: with a small or reduced number on the team, in the crew, etc.; **short'-haul'** involving transportation, etc., over (relatively) short distances. — *v.t.* **short'-head'** (*coll.*) to beat by a short head (see below). — Also *adj.* — **short'-horn** one of a breed of cattle having very short horns — *Durham* or *Teeswater*; **short'-leg** (*cricket*) the fielder or the field near (and in line with) the batsman on the leg side. — *adj.* **short'-life** having a short duration, existence, etc. — **short list** (see also **leet**[1]) a selected list of candidates for an office. — *v.t.* **short'-list** to include (someone) in a short list. — *adj.* **short'-līved** (or *-livd*) living or lasting only for a short time. — **short measure** less than the amount promised or paid for; **short metre** a form of four-line stanza of which the first, second and last lines have six syllables and the third line eight; **short odds** in betting, a nearly even chance, favourable odds in terms of risk, unfavourable in terms of potential gain. — *adjs.* **short-oil** see **oil** length under **oil; short'-priced** having short odds; **short'-range** of or relating to a short distance or period of time. — **short'-rib** a floating rib; **short sale** a sale of something which the seller does not yet own; **short score** a musical score with some of the parts omitted; **short selling** see **short sale** above and **sell short** under **sell; short sheep** short-woolled sheep. — *adj.* **short'-sight'ed** having clear sight only of near objects: lacking foresight. — *adv.* **short'-sight'edly.** — **short'-sight'edness; short'-slip** (*cricket*) the fielder, or the field, near the batsman on the off side behind the wicket. — *adjs.* **short'-spō'ken** curt in speech; **short'-stā'ple** having the fibre short. — **short'-stop** the player at baseball between the second and third base; **short'sword** a sword with a short blade. — *adj.* **short'-tem'pered** easily put into a rage. — **short tennis** a form of tennis for young children, using a smaller court and modified equipment and rules. — *adj.* **short'-term** extending over a short time: concerned with the immediate present and future as distinct from time further ahead. — **short'-term'ism** (a tendency towards) the adopting of only short-term views, solutions to problems, etc.; **short'time'** (the condition of) working fewer than the normal number of hours per week. — *adj.* **short'-time.** — **short track** a shortening for **short track (speed)skating** (see below); **short'-wave** of, or using wavelength 50 metres or less; **short'-wind'ed** soon becoming breathless. — **at short sight** payable soon after being presented; **by a short head** by a distance less than the length of a horse's head: narrowly, barely (*fig.*); **caught, taken short** (*coll.*) having a sudden need to relieve oneself; **cut short** see **cut; fall short** see **fall; for short** as an abbreviation; **in short** in a few words; **in short supply** not available in desired quantity, scarce; **in the short run** over a brief period of time; **make short work of** to settle or dispose of promptly; **run short** see **run; short for** a shortened form of; **short of** less than: without going so far as: (also **short on;** *coll.*) having insufficient supplies of; **short-term memory** a section of the memory with limited capacity capable of storing information for a short time only; **short track (speed)skating** the sport of individual, relay and pursuit speedskating on an indoor ice track over any of several distances between 500m and 5000m; **stop short** come to a sudden standstill; **take (up) short** to take by surprise or at a disadvantage: to interrupt curtly; **the short and the long (of it)** (*Shak.*) same as **the long and the short.** [O.E. *sc(e)ort*; cf. O.H.G. *scurz.*]

shot[1] *shot, pa.t.* and *pa.p.* of **shoot.** — *adj.* hit or killed by shooting: elongated by rapid growth: advanced (in years; *Spens.*): with warp and weft of different colours, as *shot silk*: showing play of colours: rid (with *of*; *coll.*). — *n.* a rejected animal.

shot[2] *shot, n.* act of shooting: a blast: an explosive charge: a photographic exposure, esp. for motion pictures: a unit in film-production: a stroke or the like in a game: an attempt: a spell: a turn: a guess: the casting of a net: a set of nets or length of net cast: an aggressive remark: an injection (*coll.*): a dram (*coll.*): a marksman: a projectile, esp. one that is solid and spherical, without bursting charge: a cannonball: a weight for putting (*athletics*): a bullet: a small pellet of which several are shot together: such pellets collectively: flight of a missile, or its distance: range, reach: a plot of land: (also **scot**) a payment, esp. of a tavern reckoning: a contribution. — *v.t.* to load with shot: — *pr.p.* **shott′ing**; *pa.t.* and *pa.p.* **shott′ed.** — *adj.* **shott′ed.** — **shot′-blasting** the cleaning of metal, etc., by means of a stream of shot; **shot′-clog** (*arch.*) one who is good for nothing but paying the bill; **shot′firer** in blasting, one who fires the charge. — *adj.* **shot′-free** scot-free: safe from shot. — **shot′gun** a smooth-bore gun for small shot, a fowling-piece. — *adj.* pertaining to a shotgun: involving coercion (e.g. *a shotgun merger, marriage*): covering a wide field in random, haphazard fashion with a resultant hit-or-miss effect. — **shot′-hole** a hole made by a shot, or in timber by a boring insect, or in a leaf by a fungus: a hole in a wall for shooting from: a hole bored for a blast; **shot′maker** (*sport*, esp. *tennis* and *golf*) a person who produces winning, attacking or skilful shots or strokes; **shot′making.** — *adj.* **shot′proof** proof against shot. — **shot′-put** in athletics, the event of putting the shot; **shot′-tower** a tower where small shot is made by dropping molten lead into water; **shot′-window** (*obs.*). app. a window with a hinged shutter or a projecting window. — **a shot across the bows** one thus directed so as to warn a ship off rather than damage it (often *fig.*); **a shot in the arm** an injection in the arm (*med.*): a revivifying injection, as of money, new effort, fresh talent (*fig.*); **a shot in the dark** a random guess; **a shot in the locker** something yet in reserve; **big shot** (*coll.*) a person of importance; **like a shot** instantly, quickly: eagerly, willingly; **stand shot** to pay the bill.   [O.E. *sc(e)ot, gesc(e)ot*; cf. **shoot.**]

shote, shot(t). Same as **shoat.**

shotten *shot′n, old* or *dial. pa.p.* of **shoot.** — *adj.* (of a herring, etc.) having ejected the spawn: effete, exhausted: in composition, dislocated, distorted: bursting or shooting out, as something violently dispersed.

shottle. See **shuttle².**

shough (*Shak.* **showghe**) *shog, shok, shuf, n.* a shaggy kind of lapdog.   [Perh. **shock³.**]

should *shōod, pa.t.* of **shall.**   [O.E. *sceolde.*]

shoulder *shōl′dər, n.* the part about the junction of the body with the forelimb: the upper joint of a foreleg cut for the table: part of a garment covering the shoulder: a coat-hanger: a bulge, protuberance, offshoot like the human shoulder: a curve like that between the shoulder and the neck or side: either edge of a road. — *v.t.* to thrust with the shoulder: to take upon the shoulder or in a position of rest against the shoulder: to undertake: to take responsibility for: to set shoulder to shoulder: to fashion with a shoulder or abutment. — *v.i.* to jostle. — *adj.* **shoul′dered** having a shoulder or shoulders (**shouldered arch** a lintel on corbels). — *n.* and *adj.* **shoul′dering.** — **shoul′der-bag** a bag suspended from a strap worn over the shoulder; **shoul′der-belt** a belt that passes across the shoulder; **shoul′der-blade** the broad, flat, blade-like bone forming the back of the shoulder, the scapula; **shoul′der‑bone** shoulder-blade; **shoul′der-clapp′er** (*Shak.*) a bailiff; **shoul′der-gir′dle** the pectoral girdle. — *adv.* **shoul′der-height** as high as the shoulder. — *adj.* and *adv.* **shoul′der-high** as high as the shoulder. — **shoul′der-joint; shoul′der-knot** a knot worn as an ornament on the shoulder; **shoul′der-mark** (*U.S.*) a badge of naval rank worn on the shoulder; **shoul′der-note** a note at the upper outside corner of a page; **shoulder pad** a pad inserted into the shoulder of a garment to raise and square it. — *adj.* **shoul′der-shott′en** (*Shak.*) with dislocated or sprained shoulder. — **shoul′der-slip** a sprain of the shoulder. — *adj.* **shoul′der-slipped.** — **should′er-strap** a strap worn on or over the shoulder esp. on suspending a garment, etc.: a narrow strap of cloth edged with gold lace worn on the shoulder with uniform to indicate rank (*U.S.*). — **cold shoulder** see **cold; put one's shoulder to the wheel** to set to work in earnest, as if to get a coach out of the mire; **shoulder‑of-mutton sail** a triangular sail; **shoulder to shoulder** side by side: in unity; **(straight) from the shoulder**

frank(ly) and forceful(ly).   [O.E. *sculdor*; Ger. *Schulter*, Du. *schouder.*]

shouldest, shouldst. See **shall.**

shouldn't *shōod′ənt*, a contraction of **should not.**

shout *showt, n.* a loud cry: a call: a call for a round of drinks (*slang*): a turn to buy a round of drinks (*slang*). — *v.i.* to utter a shout: to speak in a raised, esp. angry, voice (with *at*): to stand drinks all round (*slang*). — *v.t.* to utter with or as a shout. — *n.* **shout′er.** — *n.* and *adj.* **shout′ing.** — *adv.* **shout′ingly.** — **shouting match** (*coll.*) a quarrel or argument in which both sides loudly insult each other. — **all over bar the shouting** of a happening, contest, etc., as good as over, virtually finished or decided; **shout down** to make (another speaker) inaudible by shouting or talking loudly. [Ety. dub., poss., as **scout²**, conn. with O.N. *skuta*, a taunt.]

shouther *shōō′dhər*, Scots form of **shoulder.**

shove *shuv, v.t.* and *v.i.* to thrust: to push: to jostle. — *n.* a push, thrust. — *n.* **shov′er** one who shoves: punningly, a chauffeur. — **shove′-groat** (also without *hyphen*) shovel-board (also *adj.* as in **shove′-groat shilling** a smooth-worn shilling suitable for playing shovel-board); **shove′-half′penny** a similar game. — **shove off** to push (a boat) from the shore: to go away (*coll.*). [O.E. *scúfan*; Du. *schuiven*, Ger. *schieben.*]

shovel *shuv′l, n.* a broad spade-like tool for scooping, the blade usu. curved forward at the sides: a (part of) a machine having a similar shape or function: a scoop: a shovelful: a shovel-hat. — *v.t.* to move with, or as if with, a shovel: to gather in large quantities. — *v.i.* to use a shovel: — *pr.p.* **shov′elling**; *pa.t.* and *pa.p.* **shov′elled.** — *ns.* **shov′elful** as much as a shovel will hold: — *pl.* **shov′elfuls; shov′eller** one who shovels: a duck (Spatula) with expanded bill (more commonly **shov′eler**) — **shov′el-hat** a hat with a broad brim, turned up at the sides, and projecting in front — affected by Anglican clergy; **shov′el-head** a shark with a flattish head, related to the hammerhead: a shovel-nose; **shov′elnose** a sturgeon of the Mississippi, having a broad snout.   [O.E. *scofl*, from *scúfan*, to shove.]

shovel-board *shuv′l-bōrd, -bŏrd*, **shuffle-board** *shuf′*, *ns.* an old game in which a coin or other disc was driven along a table by the hand: a modern development played in America: a deck game played with wooden discs and cues: a table for the game: a shove-groat shilling (*Shak.*).   [App. **shove** and **board,** confused with **shovel** and **shuffle.**]

show (now rarely **shew**), *shō, v.t.* to present to view: to exhibit: to display: to set forth: to cause or allow to be seen or known: to prove: to manifest: to indicate: to usher or conduct (with *in, out, over, round, up,* etc.). — *v.i.* to appear: to come into sight: to be visible: to arrive, turn up (*slang*): — *pa.t.* **showed,** rarely **shewed** (*shōd*); *pa.p.* **shown, shewn** (*shōn*), or **showed, shewed.** — *n.* act of showing: display: exhibition: a sight or spectacle: an entertainment: parade: a demonstration: appearance: plausibility: pretence: a sign, indication: an indication of the presence of oil or gas in an exploratory well: performance: in childbirth, a small discharge of blood and mucus at the start of labour. — *adj.* of the nature of, or connected with, a show: for show. — *n.* **shower** (*shō′ər*). — *adv.* **show′ily.** — *ns.* **show′iness; show′ing** act of displaying, pointing out, etc.: appearance: a setting forth, representation. — *adj.* **show′y** cutting a dash: making a show: ostentatious: gaudy: flashy. — **show′-bill** a bill announcing a show; **show′-boat** a steamer serving as a travelling theatre; **show′-box** a showman's box out of which he takes his materials; **show′bread** see **shewbread; show business** the entertainment business, esp. the branch of the theatrical profession concerned with variety entertainments — also (*coll.*) **show′biz, show biz** (*adj.* **show′bizzy**); **show′card** a shopkeeper's advertising card: a card of patterns; **show′case** a glass case for a museum, shop, etc.: any setting in which something or someone can be displayed to advantage. — *v.t.* to display, exhibit.

— **show'-down** in poker, putting one's cards face-up on the table: the name of a card-game similar to poker: an open disclosure of plans, means, etc.: an open clash; **show'girl** a girl who takes part in variety entertainments usu. as a dancer or singer; **show'ground** ground where a show is held; **show house** a house, usu. on a new housing estate, opened for public viewing as an example of the builders' work; **show'jumper** a horse or rider in a showjumping competition; **show'jumping** a competition in which riders on horseback have to jump a succession of obstacles (also adj.); **show'man** one who exhibits, or owns, a show: one who is skilled in publicly showing off things (e.g. his own merits). — adj. **show'manly.** — **show'manship** skilful display, or a talent for it; **show'-off** one who behaves in an ostentatious manner in an effort to win admiration; **show'-piece** something considered an especially fine specimen of its type, etc.: an exhibit, something on display, etc.; **show'place** a place visited or shown as a sight: a place where shows are exhibited; **show'room** a room where goods or samples are displayed; **show-stopper** see **stop the show** below; **show trial** one held purely for propaganda, the charges usu. being false, and the confession forcibly extracted; **show'-yard** a yard for cattle-shows. — **for show** for the sake of outward appearances: to attract notice; **give the show away** to let out a secret; **good, bad, show** well, not well, done: fortunate, unfortunate, occurrence or circumstances; **run the show** (coll.) to take, be in charge: to take over, dominate; **show a leg** (coll.) to get out of bed; **show fight** to show a readiness to resist; **show forth** to manifest, proclaim; **show off** to display or behave ostentatiously; **show of hands** a vote indicated by raising hands; **show up** to expose: to appear to advantage or disadvantage: to show clearly by contrast: to be present: to appear, arrive (coll.): to lodge, hand in, as a school exercise; **steal the show** to win the most applause: to attract the most publicity or admiration; **stop the show** to be applauded with so much enthusiasm as to interrupt the show, play, etc. (hence n. **show'-stopper** the act, line, etc., so applauded). — Also fig. [O.E. scēawian, to look; Du. schouwen, Ger. schauen, to behold.]

shower show('ə)r, n. a short fall, or fall of rain: a fall of drops of liquid: a fall, flight, or accession of many things together, as meteors, arrows, blows, volcanic dust or (esp. U.S.) wedding gifts: a party at which gifts are presented (U.S.): a shower-bath: an attack, a pang (obs.): fast particles in number arising from a high-energy particle: a disparaging term for a particular group of people (slang). — v.t. and v.i. to drop in shower or showers: to sprinkle: to water. — v.i. to take a shower-bath. — The position of the accent in the following words depends on whether one says show'ər or showr. — adj. **shower'ful.** — n. **shower'iness.** — n., adj. **shower'ing.** — adjs. **shower'less; shower'y** marked by showers: raining by fits and starts. — **shower'-bath** a bath of water showered from above: the apparatus for the purpose. — adj. **shower'proof** impervious to showers. — v.t. to render showerproof. [O.E. scūr; O.N. skūr, Ger. Schauer.]

showghe. See **shough.**
shraddha. See **sraddha.**
shrank shrangk, pa.t. of **shrink.**
shrapnel shrap'nl, n. a shell filled with musketballs with a bursting-charge, invented by General Shrapnel (1761–1842): pieces scattered by the bursting of a shrapnel or other shell: any later improved version of the orig. shell.
shred shred, n. a scrap, fragment: a paring, esp. a curled paring: a ragged strip. — v.t. to prune (obs.): to cut, cut off: to cut, tear or scrape into shreds. — v.i. to be reduced to shreds: — pr.p. **shredd'ing;** pa.t. and pa.p. **shredd'ed, shred.** — adj. **shredd'ed.** — ns. **shredd'er** a device or machine for shredding, e.g. vegetables, waste paper; **shredd'ing.** — adjs. **shredd'y; shred'less.** — **shred'-pie** mince-pie. [O.E. scrēade; cf. screed; Ger. Schrot.]

shreek, shreik. See **shriek.**
shrew shrōō, n. a small mouselike animal of the Insectivora, formerly thought venomous: an evil being (obs.): a brawling, troublesome person, now only a woman, a scold. — v.t. (Shak.) to beshrew. — adj. **shrewd** evil, hurtful, ill-natured, ill-conditioned, mischievous: (obs. or dial.) severe, hard (obs.): formidable (obs.): uncomfortably near the mark: biting, keen (arch.): shrewish, vixenish (obs.): showing keen practical judgment, astute. — adv. (Shak.) keenly. — adv. **shrewd'ly.** — n. **shrewd'ness.** — adj. **shrew'ish** of the nature of a shrew or scold: ill-natured. — adv. **shrew'-ishly.** — n. **shrew'ishness.** — **shrew'mouse** a shrew (the beast): — pl. **shrew'mice.** — adjs. **shrew'-run, -struck** blasted by a shrew. — **a shrewd turn** an ill turn, disservice. [O.E. scrēawa, a shrewmouse.]
Shri. See **Sri.**
shriche-owl. See under **shriek.**
shriech. See **shriek, shritch.**
shriek shrēk, v.i. to utter a shriek. — v.t. to utter shriekingly. — n. a shrill outcry: a wild piercing scream: an exclamation mark (slang). — Also **shreek** (Shak., Spens.), **shreik** (Milt.), **shriech** (Spens.). — n. **shriek'er.** — n. and adj. **shriek'ing.** — adv. **shriek'ingly.** — **shriek'-owl,** also (Spens.) **shriech-, shriche-,** etc., **schreech-** (Shak.), a screech-owl. [Cf. **screak, screech.**]
shrieval shrē'vl, adj. pertaining to a sheriff. — n. **shriev'-alty** the office, term of office, or area of jurisdiction, of a sheriff. [Shrieve, obs. form of **sheriff.**]
shrieve shrēv. Same as **shrive.**
shrift shrift, n. orig. a prescribed penance: absolution: confession: a confessional (Shak.). — **short shrift** short time for confession before execution: summary treatment of a person or a matter. [O.E. scrift — scrīfan, to shrive.]
shright shrīt, (Spens.) n. a shriek. See also **shritch.** [Perh. a misreading of Chaucer, Troilus IV, 1147.]
shrike[1] shrīk, n. a butcher-bird, a passerine bird, of which some kinds impale small animals on thorns. [App. O.E. scrīc, perh. thrush.]
shrike[2] shrīk, v.i. to shriek (Spens., Shak.): to pipe as a bird. — n. (Spens., Shak.) a shriek. [Cf. **scrike, shriek.**]
shrill shril, adj. high-pitched and piercing: keen: pungent. — adv. shrilly: often in compounds, as **shrill-shrik'ing** (Shak.). — n. a piercing sound. — v.t. and v.i. to sound or cry shrilly. — n. and adj. **shrill'ing.** — n. **shrill'ness.** — adj. **shrill'y** somewhat shrill. — adv. **shril'ly.** — adjs. **shrill'-gorged** (Shak.) shrill in throat; **shrill'-tongued; shrill'-voiced.** [Cf. L.G. schrell, whence prob. Ger. schrill.]
shrimp shrimp, n. a little wizened or dwarfish person: a small edible crustacean, esp. a decapod of Crangon or kindred genus: the colour of a shrimp, a bright pink: a very small person (coll.). — v.i. to fish for shrimps. — n. **shrimp'er.** — n. and adj. **shrimp'ing.** — **shrimp'-girl** a girl who sells shrimps; **shrimp'-net.** [Cf. **scrimp,** and O.E. scrimman, to shrink.]
shrine shrīn, n. orig. a chest or cabinet: a casket for relics or an erection over it: a place hallowed by its associations: app. an image (Shak.). — v.t. to enshrine. — adj. **shrī'nal.** [O.E. scrīn — L. scrīnium, a case for papers — scrībĕre, to write.]
shrink shringk, v.i. to contract: to shrivel: to give way: to draw back: to withdraw: to feel repugnance: to recoil. — v.t. to cause to contract: to withdraw: to fix by allowing to contract: — pa.t. **shrank,** old-fashioned **shrunk;** pa.p. **shrunk.** — n. act of shrinking: contraction: withdrawal or recoil: a psychiatrist, contracted from **head'shrinker** (slang, orig. U.S.). — adj. **shrink'-able.** — ns. **shrink'age** a contraction into a less compass: extent of such diminution: in meat-marketing, the loss of carcase weight during shipping, preparation for sale, etc.: in manufacturing, etc., the loss of goods resulting from pilfering, breakages, etc.; **shrink'er.** — adv. **shrink'ingly.** — adjs. **shrunk, shrunk'en** contracted,

reduced, shrivelled. — **shrink′pack** a shrinkwrapped package. — *adjs.* **shrink′-proof, -resis′tant** that will not shrink on washing. — **shrink′-resis′tance.** — *v.t.* **shrink′wrap** to package (goods) in a clear plastic film that is subsequently shrunk (e.g. by heating) so that it fits tightly. [O.E. *scrincan, scranc, gescruncen.*]

shritch *shrich*, (*obs.* or *dial.*) *v.i.* to shriek, screech (*pa.t.*, *Spens.* **shright** *shrīt*). — *n.* (*Spens.* **shriech**) a shriek. — **shritch′-owl** screech-owl. [Cf. **scritch**.]

shrive *shrīv*, also (after *Spenser*) **shrieve** *shrēv*, *vs.t.* to hear a confession from and give absolution to: to confess: to disburden by confession or otherwise. — *vs.i.* to receive or make confession: — *pa.t.* **shrōve, shrīved, shrieved** (*shrēvd*); *pa.p.* **shriven** (*shriv′ən*), **shrīved, shrieved.** — *ns.* **shrī′ver** one who shrives: a confessor; **shrī′ving** (*Spens.*) shrift. — **shrī′ving-time** (*Shak.*) time for confession. [O.E. *scrīfan*, to write, to prescribe penance — L. *scrībēre.*]

shrivel *shriv′l*, *v.i.* and *v.t.* to contract into wrinkles: — *pr.p.* **shriv′elling;** *pa.t.* and *pa.p.* **shriv′elled.** [Cf. Sw. dial. *skryvla*, to wrinkle.]

shroff *shrof*, *n.* in the East, a banker, money-changer, or money-lender: an expert in detection of bad coin. — *v.t.* to examine with that view. — *v.i.* to practise money-changing. — *n.* **shroff′age** commission for such examination. [Ar. *sarāf.*]

shroud[1] *shrowd*, *n.* a garment, clothes (*obs.*): a winding-sheet: (with *cap.*) a long piece of linen stained with the impression of a crucified body, preserved in Turin, Italy, as the shroud of Jesus: a covering, screen, shelter, or shade: (in *pl.*) a set of ropes from the masthead to a ship's sides to support the mast. — *v.t.* to enclose in a shroud: to cover: to hide: to shelter. — *v.i.* to take shelter. — *adj.* **shroud′ed.** — *n.* and *adj.* **shroud′ing.** — *adjs.* **shroud′less** without a shroud; **shroud′y** giving shelter. — **shroud′-line** any one of the cords of a parachute by which the load is suspended from the canopy. [O.E. *scrūd*; O.N. *skrúth*, clothing.]

shroud[2] *shrowd*, (*dial.*) *n.* a branch: loppings. — *v.t.* to lop. [Prob. same as preceding, with sense from the root meaning of cut.]

shrove *shrōv*, *pa.t.* of **shrive**.

Shrove *shrōv*, *n.* (*obs.*) Shrovetide. — *v.i.* (*obs.*) **shrove** to celebrate Shrovetide (*to go a-shroving*, to go round singing for money at Shrovetide). — **Shrove′tide** the days preceding Ash Wednesday; **Shrove Tuesday** the day before Ash Wednesday. [Related to O.E. *scrīfan*, to shrive.]

shrow *shrō*, **shrowd** *shrōd*, old forms (*Shak.*) of **shrew, shrewd.**

shrub[1] *shrub*, *n.* a low woody plant, a bush, esp. one with little or no trunk: a scrub (*obs.*). — *v.t.* to lop: to cudgel (*obs.*). — *adj.* **shrubb′eried.** — *ns.* **shrubb′ery** a plantation of shrubs; **shrubb′iness.** — *adjs.* **shrubb′y** of, like, having the character of, a shrub: covered with shrubs; **shrub′less.** [O.E. *scrybb*, scrub.]

shrub[2] *shrub*, *n.* a drink of lemon or other juice with spirits, esp. rum, or (*U.S.*) of fruit juice (as raspberry) and vinegar. [Ar. *sharāb*, for *shurb*, drink.]

shrug *shrug*, *v.i.* to shudder, shiver: to hitch: to draw up the shoulders, a gesture expressive of doubt, indifference, etc. — *v.t.* to shrink: to raise in a shrug: — *pr.p.* **shrugg′ing;** *pa.t.* and *pa.p.* **shrugged.** — *n.* a jerk: an expressive drawing up of the shoulders. — **shrug off** to shake off: to show indifference to or unwillingness to tackle (e.g. responsibility, a difficulty). [Origin obscure.]

shrunk, shrunken. See **shrink**.

shtchi. See **shchi**.

shtetl *shtet′əl*, *n.* a Jewish community in an Eastern European town or village. [Yiddish, small town — M.H.G. *stetel*, dim. of *stat*, town.]

shtick, schtick, schtik *shtik*, *n.* a familiar routine, line of chat, etc., adopted by, and associated with, a particular comedian, etc. [Yiddish *shtik*, piece, slice — M.H.G. *stücke.*]

shtook, schtook, s(c)htuck *shtŏŏk*, *n.* trouble, bother. —

in shtook, etc. (*slang*) in trouble. [Origin unknown.]

shtoom, schtoom, shtum(m) *shtŏŏm*, (*slang*) *adj.* silent, quiet. [Yiddish, — Ger. *stumm*, silent.]

shubunkin *shŏŏ-bung′kin, -bŏŏng′, n.* a type of variegated large-finned goldfish. [Jap.]

shuck *shuk*, (*U.S.*) *n.* a husk, shell, or pod. — *v.t.* to remove the shuck from: to strip off, away, to discard (with *off*). — *ns.* **shuck′er; shuck′ing.** — *interj.* **shucks** (*slang*) expressive of disappointment, irritation or embarrassment. [Origin unknown.]

shudder *shud′ər*, *v.i.* to shiver as from cold or horror. — *n.* a tremor as from cold or horror. — *n.* and *adj.* **shudd′ering.** — *adv.* **shudd′eringly.** — *adjs.* **shudd′-ersome; shudd′ery.** [Cf. Ger. (orig. L.G.) *schaudern.*]

shuffle *shuf′l*, *v.t.* to mix at random, as playing-cards: to jumble: to put (*out, in, off*, etc.) surreptitiously, evasively, scramblingly, or in confusion: to manipulate unfairly: to patch up: to shove (the feet) along without lifting clear: to perform with such motions. — *v.i.* to mix cards in a pack: to scramble: to behave shiftily: to shift ground; to evade fair questions: to move by shoving the feet along: to shamble: to hitch about. — *n.* act of shuffling: a shuffling gait or dance: an evasion or artifice. — *n.* **shuff′ler.** — *n.* and *adj.* **shuff′ling.** — *adv.* **shuff′lingly.** — **shuff′le-cap** a game in which money is shaken in a cap. — **shuffle off** to thrust aside, put off, wriggle out of. [Early modern; cf. **scuffle, shove, shovel;** L.G. *schüffeln.*]

shuffle-board. See **shovel-board**.

shufti, shufty *shuf′ti*, (*coll.*) *n.* a look. [Coll. Ar. *shufti*, have you seen? — *shaffa*, to see.]

shul *shŏŏl, shŏŏl, n.* a synagogue. [Yiddish — M.H.G. *schuol*, school.]

shun *shun*, *v.t.* to avoid: — *pr.p.* **shunn′ing;** *pa.t.* and *pa.p.* **shunned.** — *adj.* **shun′less** (*Shak.*) not to be shunned. — **upon the shun** bent on evading notice. [O.E. *scunian.*]

shunamitism *shŏŏ′nə-mit-izm*, *n.* rejuvenation of an old man by means of a young woman. [Abishag the *Shunammite* (I Kings i. 3).]

shunt *shunt*, *v.t.* and *v.i.* to turn or move aside: to move to another track, esp. a side-track. — *v.t.* to by-pass: to side-track: to shelve: to get rid of. — *v.i.* (*coll.*) to be off. — *n.* an act of shunting: a conductor diverting part of an electric current: a switch: a road accident, crash, mishap (orig. *racing motorists′ slang*). — *n.* **shunt′er.** — *n.* and *adj.* **shunt′ing.** [Perh. conn. with **shun**.]

shush *shush*, *v.t.*, *v.i.*, *interj.* (to) hush.

shut *shut*, *v.t.* to shoot, as a bolt (*obs.*): to lock: to fasten: to bar: to stop or cover the opening of: to place so as to stop an opening: to forbid entrance into: to bring together the parts or outer parts of: to confine: to catch or pinch in a fastening. — *v.i.* to become closed: to admit of closing: to close in: — *pr.p.* **shutt′ing;** *pa.t.* and *pa.p.* **shut.** — *adj.* made fast: closed: rid (with *of; coll.*). — *n.* (*Milt.*) time of shutting. — *n.* **shutt′er** one who, or that which, shuts: a close cover for a window: a device for regulating the opening of an aperture, as in photography, cinematography: a removable cover, gate, or piece of shuttering. — *v.t.* to close or fit with a shutter or shutters. — *adj.* **shutt′ered.** — *n.* **shutt′ering** closing and fitting with a shutter: material used as shutters: temporary support for concrete work. — **shut′-down** a temporary closing, as of a factory: the reduction of power in a nuclear reactor to the minimum; **shut′-eye** (*coll.*) sleep. — *adj.* **shut-in′** (or *shut′*) enclosed. — *n.* (-*in′; U.S.*) an invalid or cripple confined to his house. — *adj.* **shut′-out** intended to exclude, as (*bridge*) a bid to deter opponents from bidding. — **shut away** to keep hidden or repressed: to isolate: to confine; **shut down** to close down, or stop the operation of, often temporarily; **shut in** to enclose, to confine: to settle down, or fall (said, e.g., of evening); **shut off** to exclude: to switch off; **shut out** to prevent from entering; **shut up** to close finally or completely: to confine: to cease speaking (*coll.*): to reduce to silence. [O.E.

scyttan, to bar; cf. *scēotan*, to shoot.]

shuttle[1] *shut'l, n.* an instrument used for shooting the thread of the woof between the threads of the warp in weaving or through the loop of thread in a sewing-machine: anything that makes similar movements: rapid movement to and fro between two points: a shuttle service or the vehicle, craft, etc., used for this: a shuttlecock. — *v.t.* and *v.i.* to move shuttlewise: to move regularly between two points. — *adv.* **shutt'lewise** to and fro like a shuttle. — **shutt'lecock** a cork stuck with feathers to be driven to and fro with battledores or badminton rackets: the game played with battledores: something tossed to and fro repeatedly. — *v.t.* and *v.i.* to shuttle. — **shuttle diplomacy** shuttle-like travelling between two heads of states by an intermediary, in order to bring about agreement between them; **shuttle service** a train or other transport service moving constantly between two points. [O.E. *scytel*, dart; *scēotan*, to shoot; Dan. and Sw. *skyttel*.]

shuttle[2] *shut'l,* **shottle** *shot'l,* (esp. *Scot.*) *ns.* a small drawer, esp. in a cabinet or chest. [Perh. **shut**; perh. O.E. *scyttel,* bolt, bar.]

shwa. See **schwa**.

shy[1] *shī, adj.* shrinking from notice or approach: bashful: chary: disposed to avoidance (with *of*; also in composition, as in *workshy*): secluded: warily reluctant: unproductive: scanty: lacking: of doubtful repute: (esp. in poker) short in payment: — *compar.* **shy'er** or **shi'er;** *superl.* **shy'est, shi'est.** — *v.i.* to recoil, to shrink (with *away, off*): to start aside, as a horse from fear. — *v.t.* to shun: — *3rd pers. sing.* **shies;** *pr.p.* **shy'ing;** *pa.t.* and *pa.p.* **shied** (*shīd*). — *n.* a sudden swerving aside: — *pl.* **shies.** — *n.* **shi'er, shy'er** a shying horse. — *adj.* **shy'ish.** — *adv.* **shy'ly, shi'ly.** — *n.* **shy'ness** (*obs.* **shi'ness**). — **shy'-cock** one not easily caught. — **fight shy of** to shrink from. [O.E. *scēoh*, timid; cf. **skeigh**, M.H.G. *schiech.*]

shy[2] *shī, v.t.* and *v.i.* to fling, toss: — *3rd pers. sing.* **shies;** *pr.p.* **shy'ing;** *pa.t.* and *pa.p.* **shied.** — *n.* a throw: a fling: a gibe: an attempt, shot: a point in the wall-game: a thing to shy at: — *pl.* **shies.** — *n.* **shi'er, shy'er.** [Origin obscure.]

Shylock *shī'lok, n.* a ruthless creditor, or a very grasping person. [From Shylock in *The Merchant of Venice*.]

shyster *shī'stər, (slang) n.* an unscrupulous or disreputable lawyer: an unscrupulous practitioner in any profession or business. [App. from **shy**[1] in sense of 'of doubtful repute'.]

SI (units) *es ī (ū'nits),* the modern scientific system of units, used in the measurement of all physical quantities (see Appendices). [Système *I*nternational (d'Unités).]

si *sē, n.* the seventh note of the scale, a later addition to the six Aretinian syllables, but superseded by *ti.* [Perhaps from the initial letters of *Sancte Ioannes,* the last line of the hymn which gave the Aretinian (q.v.) syllables.]

sial *sī'al, -əl, n.* the lighter partial outer shell of the earth, rich in *s*ilica and *a*lumina. — Also **sal** (*sal*). — *adj.* **sial'ic.**

siala- *sī'al-ə-, sī-al'ə-,* **sialo-** *sī-al'ō-, -o'-,* in composition, saliva. — *adjs.* **sial'ic** of, relating to, saliva; **sī'aloid** resembling saliva. — *n.* **sialagogue** (faultily **sialogogue;** *sī-al'ə-gog;* Gr. *agōgos,* leading) anything that stimulates flow of saliva. — Also *adj.* — *adj.* **sialagog'ic.** — *ns.* **sial'ogram** a röntgenogram of the salivary tract; **sialog'raphy; sial'olith** (Gr. *lithos,* a stone) a calculus of a salivary gland; **sialorrhoe'a** (Gr. *rhoiā,* flow) excessive secretion of saliva. [Gr. *sialon,* saliva.]

sialic. See **sial** and **siala-**.

sialon *sī'ə-lon, n.* any of various ceramic materials consisting of silicon, aluminium, oxygen, and nitrogen. [From the chemical symbols of the constituent elements — *Si, Al, O, N*.]

siamang *sē'ə-mang, syä'mang, n.* the largest of the gibbons, found in Sumatra and Malacca. [Malay.]

Siamese *sī-əm-ēz', adj.* of Siam (Thailand). — *n.* a native, or citizen, or the language of Siam: a Siamese cat. —

v.t. **siamese', -eze'** to join (e.g. pipes) in a way suggestive of the union of Siamese twins. — **Siamese cat** a domestic fawn-coloured cat, with blue eyes and small head, prob. descended from the jungle cat of India, Africa, etc.; **Siamese twins** Chinese twins (1811–74), born in Siam, joined from birth by a fleshy ligature: any set of twins thus joined: inseparables (*fig.*).

sib (*Spens.* **sybbe,** *Scott* **sibb**) *sib, n.* kinship (*rare*): kindred (*rare*): a kinsman or kinswoman: a blood relation: a brother or sister: a group descended from one ancestor (*gen.*). — *adj.* akin, related by common descent (*Scot.*): of canaries, inbred. — *n.* **sib'ling** one who has a parent or an ancestor in common with another: one who has both parents in common with another but is not of the same birth: such a one whether or not of the same birth. — Also *adj.* — *n.* **sib'ship** a group of sibs: blood-relationship: clan-relationship. [O.E. *sibb,* relationship, *gesibb,* related; Ger. *Sippe*.]

sibilate *sib'i-lāt, v.t.* and *v.i.* to hiss. — *ns.* **sib'ilance, sib'ilancy.** — *adj.* **sib'ilant** hissing. — *n.* a hissing consonant sound, as of *s* and *z.* — *n.* **sibilā'tion.** — *adjs.* **sib'ilatory** (*-ə-tər-i*), **sib'ilous.** [L. *sībilāre, -ātum,* to hiss.]

sibling. See **sib**.

Sibyl *sib'il, n.* one of several ancient prophetesses (*myth.*): (without *cap.*) a prophetess, sorceress, or witch: an old crone. — *adj.* **Sib'ylline** (*-īn*). — *n.* **Sib'yllist** a believer in the Sibylline prophecies. — **Sibylline Books** prophetic books offered to Tarquinius Superbus by the Cumaean Sibyl, of which he ultimately bought three for the price he had refused to give for nine: a later set got together after their destruction. [Gr. *Sibylla*.]

sic[1] *sik, adj.* a Scots form of **such.** — *adjs.* **sicc'an** (for *sic kin,* such kind) such: in exclamation, what; **sic'like** suchlike. — *adv.* in like manner.

sic[2] *sik, sēk,* (L.) so, thus — printed within brackets in quoted matter to show that the original is being faithfully reproduced even though incorrect or apparently so. — **sic passim** (*pas'im*) so throughout.

sic[3]. Same as **sick**[2].

Sican *sik'ən, n.* one of an aboriginal people in Sicily. — *n.* and *adj.* **Sicanian** (*-ā'ni-ən*). [L. *Sīcānus, Sīcānus* — Gr. *Sīkānos.*]

siccan. See **sic**[1].

siccar. Same as **sicker.**

siccative *sik'ə-tiv, adj.* drying. — *n.* a drying agent. — *n.* **siccity** (*sik'si-ti*) dryness. [L. *siccus,* dry.]

sice[1] *sīs,* **size** *sīz, ns.* the number six at dice. [O.Fr. *sis.*]

sice[2]. Same as **syce.**

Sicel *sis'əl, sik'əl,* **Siceliot** *si-sel'i-ot, -kel'.* Same as **Sikel.**

sich *sich,* (*Spens.*) *adj.* a form of **such.**

Sicilian *si-sil'yən, -sil'i-ən, adj.* of Sicily: of a cloth of cotton and mohair. — *ns.* **siciliana** (*sē-chēl-yä'nä;* It.; *pl.* **-ne**), **-no** (*si-sil-yä'nō; pl.* **-nos**) a Sicilian pastoral dance, dance-tune, or movement, in 6-8 or 12-8 time (also *adj.*); **sicilienne** (*si-si-li-en';* Fr. *sē-sēl-yen*) a ribbed silk fabric: a siciliano. — **Sicilian Vespers** the massacre of the French in Sicily in 1282 — beginning, according to a late tradition, at the first stroke of the vesper-bell.

sick[1] *sik, adj.* unwell, ill: diseased: vomiting or inclined to vomit: pining: mortified: thoroughly wearied: out of condition: sickly: of or for the sick: (of humour, joke, comedy) gruesome, macabre, tending to exploit topics not normally joked about, as illness, death, etc.: disappointed (*coll.*). — *v.i.* (*Shak.*) to grow sick. — *v.t.* (*coll.*) to vomit (with *up*). — *v.t.* **sick'en** to make sick: to disgust: to make weary of anything. — *v.i.* to become sick: to be disgusted: to become disgusting or tedious: to become weakened. — *n.* **sick'ener.** — *n.* and *adj.* **sick'ening.** — *adv.* **sick'eningly.** — *n.* **sick'ie** (*coll.*) a day's sick leave. — *adj.* **sick'ish.** — *adv.* **sick'ishly.** — *n.* **sick'ishness.** — *adj.* **sick'lied.** — *adv.* **sick'lily.** — *n.* **sick'liness.** — *adj.* **sick'ly** inclined to be ailing: feeble: languid: pallid: suggestive of sickness: slightly or insipidly sickening: mawkish: of sickness or the sick. — *adv.* in a sick manner: feebly. — *v.t.* (*obs.*) to make sickly-looking. — *n.* **sick′ness.** — **sick′-bay** a compartment for sick and wounded on a ship (also **sick′-berth**): an infirmary at a boarding-school, etc.; **sick′-bed** a bed on which someone lies sick; **sick′-ben′efit** a benefit paid to one who is out of work by illness. — *adjs.* **sick′-fallen** struck with sickness; **sick′-feath′ered** with immature feathers at moulting. — **sick′-flag** a quarantine flag; **sick′-head′ache** headache with nausea; **sick′-house** a hospital; **sick′-leave** leave of absence owing to sickness; **sick′-list** a list of sick. — *adjs.* **sick′-listed** entered on the sick-list; **sick′-mak′ing** (*coll.*) sickening. — **sick′man** (*Shak.*) one who is ill; **sick′nurse** a nurse who attends the sick; **sick′nurs′ing**; **sick′room** (also **sick′-cham′ber**) a room to which one is confined by sickness; **sick′=ser′vice** (*Shak.*) tending in sickness. — *adjs.* **sick′=thought′ed** (*Shak.*) lovesick; **sick′-tired′** (also **sick and tired**; with *of*) (*coll.*) wearied to the point of disgust (by). — **be sick** to vomit; **sick as a dog** (*coll.*) vomiting profusely and unrestrainedly; **sick as a parrot** (*coll.*) suffering from severe disappointment; **sicken for** to show early symptoms of; **sick of** tired of; **sick at, to, one's stomach** (*U.S.*) about to vomit; **the Sick Man** the Ottoman Empire, or Sultan. [O.F. *sēoc*; Ger. *siech*, Du. *ziek*.]

sick² *sik*, *v.t.* to set upon, chase: to incite (e.g. dog) to make an attack (on). [A variant of **seek**.]

sicker, siccar *sik′ər*, *adj.* (*arch.* and *Scot.*) sure, certain, firm. — *adv.* (*Spens.*) surely, certainly. — *adv.* **sick′erly** (*Scot.*). — *n.* **sick′erness** (*Scot.*). [O.E. *sicor* — L. *sēcūrus*; Ger. *sicher*.]

sickle¹ *sik′l*, *n.* a reaping-hook, an implement with a curved blade and a short handle: a sickle-feather. — *adj.* **sick′led** bearing a sickle. — **sick′le-bill** a bird of paradise, humming-bird, etc., with sickle-shaped bill; **sick′le-feath′er** a cock's tail feather; **sick′leman** a reaper. — *adj.* **sick′le-shaped.** — **sickle-cell(ed) anaemia** a severe anaemia in which sickle-shaped red blood-cells appear in the blood. [O.E. *sicol, sicel*, perh. — L. *secula* — *secāre*, to cut.]

sickle² *sik′l*, (*Shak.*) *n.* a shekel. [O.Fr. *sicle* — Heb. *sheqel*.]

Siculian *si-kū′li-ən*, *adj.* of the *Sīcŭlī* (L.), or Sikels, an ancient people that colonised Sicily from Italy. — Also *n.*

Sida *sī′də*, *n.* the Queensland hemp genus of the mallow family, tropical fibre-yielding herbs: (without *cap.*) a plant of this genus. [Gr. *sidē*, a plant name.]

Sidalcea *si-dal′si-ə, -ki-ə*, *n.* a genus of the mallow family, perennials with white, pink, or purple flowers: (without *cap.*) a plant of this genus. [**Sida** and *Alcea*, related genera.]

siddhi *sid′i*, *n.* in Hinduism, Buddhism and Jainism, the supernatural powers that come with the spiritual perfection attained by meditation, etc. — Also with *cap.* and in *pl.* — *n.* **sidd′ha** one who has attained perfection (also **sid′ha**). [Sans., fulfilment.]

siddur *si′door*, *n.* a Jewish prayer-book: — *pl.* **siddur′im, -im′.** [Heb., order.]

side¹ *sīd*, *n.* a line or surface forming part of a boundary, esp. that which is longer: the part near such a boundary: a surface or part turned in some direction, esp. one more or less upright, or one regarded as right or left, not front or back, top or bottom: the part of the body between armpit and hip: half of a carcase divided along the medial plane: either of the extended surfaces of anything in the form of a sheet: a page: a portion of space lying in this or that direction from a boundary or a point: the father's or mother's part of a genealogy: a department or division, as of a school, a prison: an aspect: a direction: a region: a neighbouring region: a border or bank: the slope of a hill: the wall of a vessel or cavity: any party, team, interest, or opinion opp. to another: part (as *on my side*, for my part): the womb (*Milt.*): a spin given to a billiard ball causing it to swerve and regulating its angle of rebound: a pretentious air (*slang*): a speech in a play. — *adj.* at or toward the side: sidewise: subsidiary. — *v.i.* to take sides (with

with). — *v.t.* to cut into sides: to thrust or set aside: to adjudge or assign to one side or other (*Shak.*): to assign in this way to (*Shak.*): to be on the side next (*Spens.*). — *adj.* **sid′ed** having sides: flattened on one or more sides. — *adj.* and *adv.* **side′ling** sidewise: with a slope. — *adj.* **side′long** oblique: sloping: tilted: sideways. — *adv.* in the direction of the side: obliquely: on the side. — *n.* **sid′er** one who takes a side. — *adj.* and *adv.* **side′ward**. — *adv.* **side′wards**. — *adjs., advs.* **side′way(s), side′wise** toward or on one side. — *n.* **sid′ing** a short track for shunting or lying by. — *n.* and *adj.* taking sides. — *v.i.* **sī′dle** (prob. back-formation from **sideling**) to go or edge along sideways, esp. in a furtive or ingratiating manner. — *v.t.* to turn sideways. — **side′arm** (usu. in *pl.*) a weapon worn at the side; **side′-band** (*wireless*) a band of frequencies not much above or below the carrier frequency; **side′-bar** in South Africa, solicitors, as opp. to barristers (who belong to the bar); **side′board** a side table (*arch.*): a piece of dining-room furniture for holding plates, etc., often with drawers and cupboards: a board at the side, as of a cart: (in *pl.*) side-whiskers. — *n.pl.* **side′-bones** ossifications of the lateral cartilages of a horse's hoof. — **side′-box** a box at the side of a theatre. — *n.pl.* **side′burns** short side-whiskers, a modification of the rather more extensive growth pioneered by General *Burnside* of America. — **side′car** a jaunting-car: a small car attached to the side of a motor-cycle usu. for the carriage of a passenger: a kind of cocktail; **side′-chain** a chain of atoms forming a branch attached to a ring; **side′-comb** a small comb in the hair at the side; **side′-cutt′ing** an excavation along the side of a railway or canal to get material for an embankment; **side′-dish** a supplementary dish; **side′-door** a door at the side of a building or of a main door; **side′-drum** a small double-headed drum with snares, slung from the drummer's side or from a stand; **side′-effect, side effect** a subsidiary effect: an effect, often undesirable, additional to the effect sought; **side′-face** profile; **side′=glance** a sidelong glance: a passing allusion; **side′-issue, side issue** something subordinate, incidental, not important in comparison with main issue; **side′-kick** (*slang*) partner, deputy: a special friend; **side′light** light coming from the side: any incidental illustration: a window, as opposed to a skylight: a window above or at the side of a door: a light carried on the side of a vessel or vehicle; **side′-line** a line attached to the side of anything: a branch route or track: a subsidiary trade or activity: (in *pl.*) (the area just outside) the lines marking the edge of a football pitch, etc., hence, a peripheral area to which spectators or non-participants are confined. — *v.t.* to remove (a player) from a team: to suspend from normal operation or activity. — **side′lock** a lock of hair at the side of the head; **side′-note** a marginal note. — *adj.* and *adv.* **side′-on′** with side presented. — **side′-path** a by-path: a way for foot-passengers alongside a roadway; **side′-post** a doorpost: a post supporting a roof at the side; **side′=road** by-road; **side′-saddle** saddle for riding with both feet on one side (also *adv.*); **side′-saddle-flower′** Sarracenia; **side′-show** an exhibition subordinate to a larger one: any subordinate or incidental doings; **side′-slip** an oblique offshoot: a bastard: a skid: a lateral movement of an aircraft: a side-on downward slide (*skiing*). — *v.i.* to slip sideways. — **sides′man** a deputy church-warden: a partisan (*Milt.*). — *adj.* **side′-splitting** extremely funny, making one laugh till one's sides ache. — **side′-step** a step taken to one side: a step attached to the side. — *v.i.* to step aside. — *v.t.* to avoid, as by a step aside. — **side′street** a minor street, esp. if opening off a main street; **side′-stroke** a stroke given sideways: a stroke performed by a swimmer lying on his side; **side′swipe** a blow dealt from the side, not struck head-on: a criticism made in passing, incidentally to the main topic. — **side′-table** a table used as a sideboard, or placed against the wall, or to the side of the main table; **side′-track** a siding. — *v.t.*

to divert or turn aside: to shelve. — **side'-view** a view on or from one side; **side'walk** (*U.S.*) pavement or foot-walk. — *adj.* **side'-wheel** with paddle wheels at the side. — **side'-wheeler** a side-wheel paddle-steamer; **side'-whiskers** hair grown by a man down either side of the face, in front of the ears; **side'-wind** lateral wind: indirect means; **side'winder** a rattlesnake (*Crotalus cerastes*) of the southern U.S. that progresses by lateral looping motions: the name of an air-to-air missile directed at its target by means of a homing device. — **choose sides** to pick teams; **let the side down** to fail one's colleagues, associates, etc., by falling below their standard; **on the side** in addition to ordinary occupation, income, etc.; **on the short, long, tight**, etc., **side** rather too short, long, etc., than the contrary; **put on one side** to shelve; **put on side** to assume pretentious airs; **right, wrong side** the side intended to be turned outward or inward; **side by side** close together: abreast; **take sides** to range oneself with one party or other; **the other side** the spiritual world, to which one passes after death; **this side (of)** between here and . . . : short of. [O.E. *sīde*; Ger. *Seite*, Du. *zijde*.]

side² *sīd*, (now *dial.*; *Shak.*) *adj.* long. — *adj.* and *adv.* **side'long** (*Spens.*). [O.E. *sīd*, ample.]

sidereal *sī-dē'ri-əl, adj.* of, like, or relative to the stars. — *adj.* **sideral** (*sid'ər-əl*) sent from the stars. — *ns.* **siderā'tion** a blast, blight, or stroke: paralysis: erysipelas; **sid'erostat** a mirror, or telescope with a mirror, for reflecting the rays of a star in a constant direction, on the principle of the coelostat. — **sidereal day, time, year** see **day, time, year**. [L. *sīdus, sīderis*, a star, constellation.]

siderite *sid'ər-īt, n.* a meteorite mainly of iron: chalybite, or ferrous carbonate, one of the ores of iron. — *adj.* **sideritic** (*-it'ik*). — *ns.* **sid'erolite** (Gr. *lithos*, stone) a meteorite, partly stony, partly of iron; **sideropēn'ia** deficiency of iron; **siderō'sis** lung disease caused by breathing in iron or other metal fragments. [Gr. *sidēros*, iron.]

siderostat. See **sidereal**.

sidesman, siding, sidle, etc. See **side¹**.

sidha. See under **siddhi**.

siege *sēj, n.* a seat, esp. of dignity (*arch.*): rank or class (*obs.*): a privy (*obs.*): dung (*Shak.*): a work-bench: investment or beleaguering of a town or fortress: a company of herons (also **sedge**). — *v.t.* to besiege. — *n.* **sieg'er** a besieger. — **siege'-artill'ery, siege'-gun** heavy artillery, gun, designed for use in sieges rather than in the field; **siege'-bas'ket** a gabion; **siege'craft** the art of the besieger; **siege'-piece** a coin, generally of imperfect workmanship, issued in a besieged place: a siege-gun; **siege'-train** a train of artillery for besieging a place; **siege'-works** a besieger's engineering works. — **state of siege** a condition of suspension of civil law or its subordination to military law. [O.Fr. *sege* (Fr. *siège*), seat — L. *sēdēs*, seat.]

sield *sēld*, a Spenserian spelling of **ceiled**.

siemens *sē'menz, n.* unit of electrical conductance (an SI additional unit), the equivalent of mho and reciprocal of ohm.

sien *sī'ən*, (*Shak.*) *n.* Same as **scion**.

Sien(n)ese *sē-e-nēz', adj.* of Siena or its school of painting. — *n.* a native of Siena. — *n.* **sienna** (*sē-en'ə*) a fine pigment made from ferruginous ochreous earth — browny-yellow when *raw*, warm reddish-brown when *burnt* (i.e. roasted): its colour.

sient *sī'ənt*, (*Spens.*) *n.* Same as **scion**.

sierra *si-er'ə, n.* a mountain range. — *adj.* **sierr'an.** [Sp., — L. *serra*, saw.]

siesta *si-es'tə, n.* a midday or afternoon nap. [Sp., — L. *sexta* (*hōra*), sixth (hour).]

sieth. A Shakespearian spelling of **scythe**.

sieve *siv, n.* a vessel with meshed or perforated bottom for sifting — generally finer than a riddle: a refuse-basket (*Shak.*). — *v.t.* and *v.i.* to sift. — **sieve'-plate** a perforated area by which a sieve-tube connects with another; **sieve'-tube** a conducting element in phloem.

— **sieve of Eratosthenes** (*er-ə-tos'then-ēz*) a method of finding prime numbers, namely, starting with the odd numbers in order and crossing out every third number above 3, every fifth above 5, etc.; **have a head, memory, like a sieve** to be very forgetful. [O.E. *sife*; Ger. *Sieb*.]

sievert *sē'vərt, n.* the SI unit of radiation dose equivalent (q.v.), equal to one joule per kilogram (or 100 rems); symbol Sv. [R.M. *Sievert* (1896–1966), Swedish physicist.]

sifaka *sif-ä'kə, n.* a lemur, typically long-tailed and black and white, of the genus *Propithecus*, native to Madagascar. [Malagasy.]

siffle *sif'l, v.i.* to whistle, hiss. [Fr. *siffler* — L. *sībilāre*.]

sift *sift, v.t.* to separate as by passing through a sieve: to sprinkle as from a sieve: to examine closely and discriminatingly. — *v.i.* to use a sieve: to find passage as through a sieve. — *n.* a sifting. — *ns.* **sift'er; sift'ing** putting through a sieve: separating or sprinkling by a sieve: (in *pl.*) material separated by a sieve and rejected. — *adj.* **sift'ing.** — *adv.* **sift'ingly.** [O.E. *siftan* — *sife*, a sieve.]

sigh *sī, v.i.* to heave a sigh: to make a whispering sound. — *v.t.* to utter, regret, while away, bring, or render, with sighs. — *n.* a long, deep, audible respiration expressive of yearning, dejection, relief, etc. — *n.* **sigh'er.** — *adjs.* **sigh'ful; sigh'ing.** — *adv.* **sigh'ingly.** — **sigh for** to yearn for. [Prob. a back-formation from the weak pa.t. of M.E. *siche* — O.E. (strong) *sīcan*; Sw. *sucka*.]

sight¹ *sīt, n.* act, opportunity, or faculty of seeing: view: estimation: a beginning or coming to see: an instrumental observation: visual range: that which is seen: a spectacle: an object of especial interest: an unsightly, odd or ridiculous object: a visor (*Shak.*): a guide to the eye on a gun or optical or other instrument: a sight-hole: a great many or a great deal (*slang*). — *v.t.* to catch sight of: to view: to take a sight of: to adjust the sights of. — *v.i.* to take a sight. — *adj.* **sight'ed** having sight, not blind: equipped with a sight: in composition, having sight of a particular kind, as *long-sighted*. — *n.* **sight'er** a sighting-shot. — *adj.* **sight'less** blind: invisible (*Shak.*): unsightly (*Shak.*). — *adv.* **sight'lessly.** — *ns.* **sight'lessness; sight'liness.** — *adjs.* **sight'ly** pleasing to look at: comely; **sight'worthy** worth looking at. — **sight'-hole** an aperture for looking through; **sight'-line** the line from the eye to the perceived object: (in *pl.*) the view afforded e.g. of the stage in a theatre; **sight'-player, -reader, -singer** one who can read or perform music at first sight of the notes; **sight'-playing, -reading, -singing.** — *v.i., v.t.* **sight'-read.** — *v.i.* **sight'-sing.** — **sight'-screen** a screen placed behind the bowler at cricket. — *v.i.* **sight'see** to go about visiting sights, buildings, etc. of interest. — **sight'seeing; sight'seer** (*-sē-ər*). — **at sight** without previous view or study: as soon as seen: on presentation: payable as soon as presented; **at so many days' sight** (of draft, etc.) payable so many days after it is presented; **catch sight of** to get a glimpse of, begin to see; **keep sight of, keep in sight** to keep within seeing distance of: to remain in touch with; **lose sight of** to cease to see: to get out of touch with; **on sight** as soon as seen, at sight; **out of sight** not in a position to be seen or to see: out of range of vision: beyond comparison (*coll.*); **put out of sight** to remove from view: to eat or drink up (*slang*); **sight for sore eyes** a most welcome sight; **sight unseen** without having seen the object in question. [O.E. *sihth, gesiht*; Ger. *Sicht*.]

sight² *sīt*, an old pa.t. of **sigh**.

sigil *sij'il, n.* a seal: a magical mark. — *n.* **Sigillā'ria** a chiefly carboniferous genus of fossil lycopod trees, forming the family **Sigillāriā'ceae**, with parallel rows of seal-like leaf-scars. — *n.* and *adj.* **sigillā'rian.** — *adjs.* **sig'illary** (*-ə-ri*) pertaining to a seal; **sig'illate** sealed: with seal-like impressions. — *n.* **sigillā'tion.** [L. *sigillum*, dim. of *signum*, sign.]

sigisbeo *sē-jēs-bā'ō, si-jis-, n.* Same as **cicisbeo**: — *pl.* **sigisbe'i** (*-ē*). [It.]

sigla *sig'lə, n.pl.* abbreviations and signs, as in MSS, seals, etc. [L.]

sigma *sig'mə, n.* the eighteenth letter (Σ, early form C; σ, or when final, ς) of the Greek alphabet, answering to S: as a numeral σ′ = 200, ͵σ = 200000. — *adj.* **sig′mate** (*-māt*) shaped like Σ, C, or S. — *v.t.* to add σ or ς to. — *adj.* **sigmatic** (*-mat'ik*) characterised by σ. — *ns.* **sigmā′tion** (*-shən*) the adding of σ or ς at the end of a syllable; **sig′matism** repetition of the *s*-sound; **sig′-matron** a machine consisting of two accelerators (cyclotron and betatron), for the generation of very high-energy X-rays. — *adjs.* **sig′moid, -al** C-shaped: S-shaped. — *adv.* **sigmoid′ally.** — *n.* **sigmoid′oscope** an instrument used for examining the interior of the sigmoid colon. — **sigma particles** three hyperons of medium mass, having respectively positive, neutral and negative charge; **sigmoid flexure** (*zool.*, etc.) a C-shaped or S-shaped bend: (also **sigmoid colon**) the convoluted part of the large intestine, between the descending colon and the rectum. [Gr. *sigma.*]

sign *sīn, n.* a gesture expressing a meaning: a signal: a mark with a meaning: a symbol: an emblem: a token: a portent: a miraculous token: an ensign, banner (in *pl.* insignia; *Spens.*): an indication of positive or negative value, or that indicated: a device marking an inn, etc., formerly also a house, instead of a street number: a board or panel giving a shopkeeper's name or trade, etc.: an effigy (*obs.*): a mere semblance (*obs.*): an indication: an outward evidence of disease, perceptible to an examining doctor, etc.: a trail or track of a wild animal, perceptible to a tracker (*U.S.*): a trace: a twelfth part (30°) of the zodiac, bearing the name of, but not now coincident with, a constellation. — *v.t.* to indicate, convey, communicate, direct, mark, by a sign or signs: to mark: to betoken (*arch.*): to cross, make the sign of the cross over: to make the sign of: to attach a signature to: to write as a signature: to designate by signature: to engage by signature. — *v.i.* to make a sign: to bode, promise (*obs.*): to sign one's name. — *ns.* **signary** (*sig'nə-ri*) a system of symbols, as an alphabet or syllabary; **sign′er**; **signet** (*sig'nit*) a small seal: the impression of such a seal: a signet-ring: one of the royal seals for authenticating grants (for **Writer to the Signet** see under **write**). — *adjs.* **sig′neted** stamped with a signet; **sign′less.** — **sign′board** a board bearing a notice or serving as a shop or inn sign; **sig′net-ring** a ring with a signet; **sign′-man′ual** a signature, esp. a king's; **sign′-painter** one who paints signs for shops, etc.; **sign′post** a post for an inn sign: a finger-post or post supporting road-signs: an indication, clue. — *v.t.* to furnish with a signpost: to point out as a signpost does. — **sign′-writer** an expert in lettering for shop-signs, etc.; **sign′-writing.** — **sign away** to transfer by signing; **sign in, out** to sign one's name on coming in, going out; **sign off** to record departure from work: to stop work, etc.: to discharge from employment: to leave off broadcasting: to signal that one does not intend to bid further (*bridge*); **sign of the cross** a gesture of tracing the form of a cross; **sign on** to engage (*v.t.* or *v.i.*) for a job, etc., by signature (also **sign up**): to record arrival at work; **sign on the dotted line** to give one's consent, thereby binding oneself, to a proposed scheme, contract, etc.; **sign out** see **sign in**; **sign up** see **sign on.** [Fr. *signe* — L. *signum.*]

signal *sig'nl, n.* a token: an intimation, e.g. of warning, conveyed to a distance: a transmitted effect conveying a message: the apparatus used for the purpose: a piece of play intended to give information to one's partner (*cards*): an intimation of, or event taken as marking, the moment for action: an initial impulse. — *v.t.* to intimate, convey, or direct by signals: to signalise. — *v.i.* to make signals: — *pr.p.* **sig′nalling**; *pa.t.* and *pa.p.* **sig′nalled.** — *adj.* remarkable: notable. — *v.t.* **sig′-nalise, -ize** to mark or distinguish signally. — *ns.* **sig′naller; sig′nalling.** — *adv.* **sig′nally** notably. — **sig′nal-box** a railway signalman's cabin; **sig′nalman** one who transmits signals: one who works railway

signals. [Fr. *signal* — L. *signum.*]

signary; signatory. See **sign; signature.**

signature *sig'nə-chər, n.* a signing: a stamp: a signed name: an indication of key, also of time, at the beginning of a line of music, or where a change occurs: a letter or numeral at the foot of a page to indicate sequence of sheets: a sheet so marked: the pages formed by such a sheet when folded and cut: a symbolic indication once believed, according to the **doctrine of signatures**, to show what a plant, etc., was good for, e.g. a kidney-shaped leaf to mark a cure for kidney diseases: a signature-tune: the indication of the presence of e.g. an aeroplane on a radar screen. — *n.* **sig′natory** one who has signed. — Also *adj.* — **sig′nature-tune′** a tune used to introduce, and hence associated with, a particular radio or television programme, group of performers, etc. [L.L. *signātūra* — L. *signāre, -ātum,* to sign.]

signet, signeted. See **sign.**

signeur. A Shakespearean spelling of **senior.** — *ns.* **sign′-eurie** (*Shak.*) seniority; **sign′ieur** (*Shak.*) seigneur.

signify *sig'ni-fī, v.t.* to be a sign for: to mean: to denote: to betoken: to indicate or declare. — *v.i.* to be of consequence: — *pr.p.* **sig′nifying**; *pa.t.* and *pa.p.* **sig′-nified.** — *adj.* **sig′nifiable.** — *n.* **signif′icance** (*-i-kəns*) meaning: import — also **signif′icancy.** — *adj.* **signif′icant** having a meaning: full of meaning: important, worthy of consideration: indicative. — *n.* that which carries a meaning: sign. — *adv.* **signif′icantly.** — *ns.* **signif′icate** a thing signified; **significā′tion** meaning: that which is signified: importance. — *adj.* **signif′icative** (*-kə-tiv*) indicative: significant. — *adv.* **signif′icatively.** — *n.* **signif′icātor** (*astrol.*) a planet ruling a house. — *adj.* **signif′icatory** (*-kə-tər-i*). — *n.sing.* **signif′ics** the science of meaning. — *n.* **sig′nifier.** — **significant figures** (*arith.*) the figures 1 to 9, or ciphers occurring medially (the following numbers are expressed to three significant figures — 3·15, 0·0127, 1·01). [L. *signifi-cāre, -ātum* — *signum,* a sign, *facēre,* to make.]

Signor, anglicised as **Signior,** *sē′nyör,* **Signore** *-nyō′rā, -nyō′, n.* an Italian word of address equivalent to Mr or sir: (without *cap.*) a gentleman. — *ns.* **Signora** (*sē-nyō′rā, -nyō′*) feminine of *Signor,* Mrs, madam: (without *cap.*) a lady; **Signorina** (*sē-nyō-rē′nä, -nyö-*) Miss: (without *cap.*) an unmarried lady; **signoria** (*-rē′ä; hist.*) a seignory, the governing body of an Italian city-state: a seignory: a signoria. — **Grand Signior** see **seignior.** [It. *signor, signore.*]

signorial. See **seignior.**

sika *sē′kə, n.* a Japanese deer, small, spotted white in summer. [Jap. *shika.*]

sike¹, syke *sīk, (Scot.) n.* a rill or small ditch. [Northern, — O.E. *sīc.*]

sike². Spenserian spelling of **sic¹.**

Sikel *sik′əl, n.* and *adj.* Siculian. — *adj.* **Sikelian** (*-el′*). — *n.* **Sikel′iot** an ancient Greek colonist in Sicily. — Also **Sicel, Sicelian,** etc. [Gr. *Sikelos, Sikeliōtēs.*]

Sikh *sēk, sik, n.* one of a North Indian monotheistic sect, founded by Nának (1469–1539), later a military confederacy: a Sikh soldier in the Indian army. — Also *adj.* — *n.* **Sikh′ism.** [Hind., disciple.]

silage *sī′lij, n.* fodder preserved by ensilage in a silo. — *v.t.* to put in silo. [**ensilage,** after **silo.**]

silane. See **silicane** under **silica.**

Silastic® *sil-as′tik, n.* a flexible silicone rubber, used in prostheses, etc. — Also without *cap.*

sild *sild, n.* a young herring. [Norw.]

sile, seil *sīl, (dial.) v.t.* to strain. — *v.i.* to rain heavily. — *n.* a strainer (also **sī′ler**). [Scand.; cf. Sw. and Norw. *sila,* to strain.]

silen. See **silenus.**

silence *sī′ləns, n.* absence of sound: abstention from sounding, speech, mention, or communication: a time of such absence or abstention: taciturnity: of spirits, flavourlessness. — *v.t.* to cause to be silent. — *interj.* be silent. — *adj.* **si′lenced** put to silence: forbidden to preach. — *n.* **si′lencer** one who or that which puts to silence: a device for reducing the sound of escaping gases by gradual expansion, used, e.g. for small-arms and internal combustion engines. — *adj.* **si'lent** noiseless: without sound: unaccompanied by sound: refraining from speech, mention, or divulging: taciturn: not pronounced: of distilled spirit, without flavour or odour: inoperative: of the new moon, not yet visible (*Milt.*). — *n.* (*Shak.*) a time of silence. — *n.* **silentiary** (-*len'shi-ər-i*) one who observes or calls for silence. — *adv.* **si'lently.** — *n.* **si'lentness.** — **silent majority** those, in any country the bulk of the population, who are assumed to have sensible, moderate opinions though they do not trouble to express them publicly. [L. *silēre*, to be silent.]

Silene *sī-lē'ni, n.* a large genus (fam. Caryophyllaceae) with variously coloured, often showy, flowers: (without *cap.*) a plant of the genus. [Prob. L. *Silēnus*; see **silenus.**]

silent, etc. See **silence.**

silentium altum. See **altum silentium.**

silenus *sī-lē'nəs, n.* a woodland god or old satyr: **Silenus** their chief, foster-father of Bacchus, pot-bellied, bald, snub-nosed: the lion-tailed macaque. — Also **si'len** (-*lin*). [L. *Silēnus* — Gr. *Seilēnos.*]

silesia *sī-lē'zhə, n.* a thin, twilled cotton or linen used for lining clothes, etc., orig. made in *Silesia* (now part of Poland.)

silex *sī'leks, n.* silica. [L. *silex, silicis,* flint.]

silhouette *sil-ōō-et', n.* a shadow-outline filled in with black. — *v.t.* to represent or show in silhouette. [Étienne de *Silhouette* (1709–67), French minister of finance in 1759 — reason disputed.]

silica *sil'i-kə, n.* silicon dioxide or silicic anhydride, occurring in nature as quartz, chalcedony, etc., and (amorphous and hydrated) as opal. — *adj.* composed of silica. — *ns.* **sil'icane** a gas, silicon hydride, SiH₄ also called **silane** (*sil'ān*); **sil'icate** a salt of silicic acid. — *v.t.* to combine, coat, or impregnate with silica or silicates. — *adjs.* **siliceous, -ious** (-*ish'əs*) of, containing, silica; **silicic** (-*is'ik*) pertaining to, or obtained from, silica (**silicic acid** a general name for a group of acids, as **orthosilicic**, H₄SiO₄; **metasilicic**, H₂SiO₃). — *n.* **sil'icide** (-*sīd*) a compound of silicon and another element. — *adjs.* **silicicolous** (-*sik'*; L. *colěre,* to cultivate, inhabit) growing on siliceous soil; **silicif'erous** containing silica. — *n.* **silicification** (*si-lis-i-fi-kā'shən*). — *adj.* **silicified** (-*lis'*). — *v.t.* **silic'ify** to render siliceous: to impregnate or cement with or replace by silica. — *v.i.* to become siliceous. — *ns.* **sil'icon** (-*kon, -kən*) a non-metallic element (Si; at. numb. 14), most abundant of all except oxygen, forming grey crystals or brown amorphous powder and having semiconducting properties — originally called **silicium** (-*lis', -lish'*); **sil'icone** any of a number of extremely stable organic derivatives of silicon, used in rubbers, lubricants, polishes, etc.; **silicosis** (-*kō'sis*) a disease caused by inhaling silica dust. — *n.* and *adj.* **silicot'ic.** — **silicon chip** see **chip.** [L. *silex, silicis,* flint.]

silicle, silicula, etc. See **siliqua.**

siliqua *sil'i-kwə, n.* a long pod of two carpels with a replum, characteristic of the Cruciferae. — Also **silique** (-*ēk'*). — *n.* **silicula** (-*ik'ū-lə*) a short pod of the same kind. — Also **sil'icle, sil'icule.** — *adjs.* **silic'ulose; sil'iquose.** [L. *siliqua,* pod, dim. *silicula.*]

silk *silk, n.* a fibre produced by the larva of a silkworm moth, mainly of fibroin coated with sericin, formed by the hardening of a liquid emitted from spinning-glands: a similar fibre from another insect or a spider: an imitation (**artificial silk**) made by forcing a viscous solution of modified cellulose through small holes: a thread, cloth, garment, or attire made from such fibres: the silk gown, or the rank, of a king's or queen's counsel: the styles of maize: silky lustre in the ruby, etc. — *adj.* of or pertaining to silk: silky (*Shak.*). — *v.t.* to cover or clothe with silk. — *adj.* **silk'en** of, like, clad in, silk: glossy: soft and smooth: ingratiating: luxurious. — *v.t.* to make silken. — *adv.* **silk'ily.** — *n.*

silk'iness. — *adj.* **silk'y.** — **silk'-cott'on** the silky seed-covering of *Eriodendron anfractuosum* and other trees of the family Bombacaceae; **silk'-gland** a gland (at a silkworm's mouth, on a spider's abdomen) from which silk is spun; **silk'-grass** a name for various plants with fibrous leaves — Karatus (Bromeliaceae), Yucca, Agave; **silk'grower** a breeder of silkworms for silk; **silk'-hat'** a top-hat; **silk'-man** (*Shak.*) a dealer in silks; **silk'-screen** a print produced by the silk-screen process (see below); **silk'tail** the waxwing; **silk'-thrower, -throwster** one who makes raw silk into thread; **silk'weed** another name for **milk-weed**; **silk'worm** the moth (*Bombyx mori* or other) whose larva produces silk: opprobriously, a wearer of silk (*obs.*): one who haunts draper's shops without buying (*obs.*); **silk'worm-gut** the drawn-out glands of the silkworm. — **silk-screen printing, process** a stencil process in which the colour applied is forced through silk or other fine-mesh cloth; **take silk** to become a KC or QC. [O.E. *seolc* — L. *sēricum*; see **Seric.**]

silkie, silky *sil'ki,* **selkie** *sel'ki,* (*Scot.*) *ns.* a seal. [Old Scottish *selich,* O.E. *seolh.*]

sill, cill *sil, n.* the timber, stone, etc., at the foot of an opening, as for a door, window, embrasure, port, dock-entrance, or the like: the bottom (of a title-page, a plough, a ledge): a bed of rock (*mining*): a sheet of intrusive rock more or less parallel to the bedding (*geol.*). [O.E. *syll*; O.N. *syll*; Ger. *Schwelle.*]

sillabub. Same as **syllabub.**

silladar *sil'ə-där, n.* an irregular cavalryman. [Urdu and Pers. *silāhdār.*]

siller *sil'ər, n.* a Scots form of **silver:** money. — Also *adj.*

Sillery *sil'ə-ri, n.* champagne from *Sillery,* near Rheims.

sillimanite *sil'i-mən-īt, n.* aluminium silicate in the form of orthorhombic crystals, occurring in argillaceous metamorphic rocks. — See also **fibrolite.** [After Benjamin *Silliman* (1779–1864), American man of science.]

sillock *sil'ək, (N.Scot.) n.* a young coalfish. [Cf. O.N. *silungr,* a small salmon.]

silly *sil'i, adj.* (of e.g. sheep) harmless: simple, humble (*arch.*): witless: foolish: to be pitied (*arch.*): defenceless (*arch.*): feeble: feeble-minded: senseless: close-in (*cricket*; e.g. *silly mid-off*). — *n.* a silly person. — *adv.* **sill'ily.** — *n.* **sill'iness.** — **sill'y-bill'y** (*coll.*) a foolish person; **sill'y-how** (O.E. *hūfe,* head-dress) a caul; **silly season** a season, usu. late summer, when newspapers fill up with trivial matter for want of more newsworthy material. [O.E. *sælig*; see **seely.**]

silo *sī'lō, n.* a pit or airtight chamber for storing grain, or for ensilage, or for storing other loose materials: a storage tower above ground, typically tall and cylindrical: an underground chamber housing a guided missile ready to be fired: — *pl.* **si'los.** — *v.t.* to put, keep, in a silo: — *pa.p.* **si'lo'd, si'loed.** [Sp., — L. *sīrus* — Gr. *siros, sīros, seiros,* a pit.]

silphium *sil'fi-əm, n.* a plant (perh. the umbelliferous *Ferula tingitana*) imported from Cyrenaica by the Greeks for food and medicine (*hist.*): (*cap.*) a genus of American composites, compass-plants: — *pl.* **sil'phia, sil'phiums.** [L., — Gr. *silphion.*]

silt *silt, n.* fine sediment. — *v.t.* to choke, block, cover, with silt (with *up*). — *v.i.* to become silted up. — *n.* **silta'tion.** — *adj.* **silt'y.** — **silt'stone** rock formed of hardened silt. [M.E. *sylt*; cf. Dan. and Norw. *sylt,* salt-marsh.]

Silurian *sil-ōō'ri-ən, -ū', adj.* of the *Sil'ūrēs,* a British tribe of S. Wales, etc.: applied by Murchison in 1835 to the geological system preceding the Devonian. — Also *n.* — *n.* **sil'urist** a Silurian, applied to the poet Henry Vaughan (1621 or 22–95).

Silurus *sil-ōō'rəs, -ū', n.* the sheat-fish genus, giving name to the family **Silu'ridae.** — *ns.* and *adjs.* **silu'rid; silu'roid.** [Gr. *silouros.*]

silva *sil'və, n.* the assemblage of trees in a region: — *pl.* **sil'vas** or **sil'vae** (-*vē*). — *adj.* **sil'van** of woods: woodland: wooded. — *n.* a wood-god: a forest-dweller. —

adjs. **silvat'ic, silves'trian** of the woods: woodland: rustic. — *adj.* **silvicul'tural.** — *n.* **silvicul'ture** forestry. — All these words are often found spelt with *y*. [L. *silva* (sometimes *sylva*), a wood.]

silver *sil'vər, n.* a white precious metal (Ag, for L. *argentum*; at. numb. 47): silver money: silver ware: cutlery, sometimes even when not of silver: a silver medal. — *adj.* of or like silver: silver-coloured: clear and ringing in tone. — *v.t.* to cover with silver: to make silvery. — *v.i.* to become silvery. — *ns.* **sil'veriness; sil'vering** coating with, or of, silver or quicksilver. — *v.t.* **silverise, -ize** to coat or treat with silver. — *n.* **sil'verling** (*B.*) a small silver coin. — *adv.* **sil'verly** with the appearance or sound of silver. — *adjs.* **sil'vern** made of silver: silvery; **sil'very** like silver: silver-coloured: light in tone. — **Silver Age** the reign of Zeus, less innocent than the Golden Age of Kronos: in Latin literature the time of Martial, Tacitus and Juvenal; **sil'verback** an old gorilla with grey hair on its back and flanks; **sil'ver-bath** (*phot.*) a solution of a silver salt, or a vessel for it, for sensitising plates; **sil'ver-beater** one who beats silver into foil; **sil'ver-bell'** snowdrop-tree (*Halesia*); **sil'verbill** the name of two species of the genus *Lonchura* of weaver-finches, with a silvery sheen to their bills; **silver birch** a species of birch, *Betula pendula*, with silvery-white peeling bark; **sil'ver-fir'** a fir with two white lines on the underside of the needle; **sil'ver-fish** Lepisma, a bristletail: a whitish goldfish, or other white fish; **sil'ver-foil'** silver-leaf. — *adj.* **sil'ver-foot'ed.** — **sil'ver-fox'** an American fox with white-tipped black fur; **silver gate** see **gate**; **sil'ver-gilt'** gilded silver. — Also *adj.* — **sil'ver-glance'** argentite; **sil'ver-grain'** medullary rays in longitudinal section; **silver iodide** a yellow powder that darkens when exposed to light, is used in photography, is scattered on clouds to cause rainfall, and has various medical uses; **silver jubilee** a twenty-fifth anniversary; **Silver Latin** that written by authors of the Silver Age; **sil'ver-leaf** silver beaten into thin leaves: a disease of plum-trees; **silver medal** in athletics competitions, etc., the medal awarded as second prize. — *adj.* **sil'ver-mount'ed.** — **silver nitrate** a poisonous colourless crystalline salt that turns grey or black in the presence of light or organic matter, and has uses in photography, as an antiseptic, etc.; **sil'ver-pap'er** fine white tissue-paper: silver-foil: (usu.) tinfoil (sometimes with a backing of grease-proof paper); **silver pheasant** a white-tailed Chinese pheasant, reared in Europe, etc.; **sil'ver-plate'** utensils of silver: electroplate. — *adj.* **sil'ver-plā'ted.** — **sil'ver-point** the process or product of drawing with a silver-tipped pencil; **silver salmon** the cohoe; **silver screen** the cinema screen. — *adjs.* **sil'ver-shaft'ed** carrying silver arrows, as Diana; **sil'ver-shedding** (*Shak.*) scattering silver. — **sil'verside** the top of a round of beef; **sil'ver-skin** the fine skin of a coffee bean; **sil'versmith** a worker in silver; **sil'versmithing**; **sil'ver-stick** a palace officer — from his silvered wand. — *adj.* **sil'ver-tongued** plausible, eloquent. — **sil'ver-tree** a silvery-leaved S. African proteaceous tree (*Leucadendron argenteum*). — *adj.* **sil'ver-voiced.** — **silver wedding** the twenty-fifth wedding anniversary; **sil'verweed** a roadside plant (*Potentilla anserina*) with leaves silky underneath. — *adj.* **sil'ver-white.** — **born with a silver spoon in one's mouth** born to affluence; **tree of silver** see **tree**. [O.E. *silfer*, *seolfor*; O.N. *silfr*, Ger. *Silber*.]

silvestrian, silviculture. See **silva**.

sim. See **Simeonite**.

sima *sī'mə, n.* the part of the earth's crust underlying the sial. [From *s*ilicon and *m*agnesium.]

simar, simarre *si-mär'.* Same as **cymar**.

Simaruba *sim-ə-rōō'bə, n.* a genus of tropical American trees, giving name to the family **Simarubā'ceae**, akin to the Rutaceae. [Carib name.]

Simeonite *sim'i-ən-īt, n.* a low-churchman — often shortened to **sim**. [Charles *Simeon* (1759–1836).]

simi *sim'i, n.* in East Africa, a short two-edged sword or large knife. [Swahili *sime*.]

simian *sim'i-ən, adj.* of the apes: apelike. — Also *n.* — *adjs.* (*rare*) **sim'ial, sim'ious.** [L. *sīmia*, ape.]

similar *sim'i-lər, adj.* (with *to*) like: resembling: exactly corresponding in shape, without regard to size (*geom.*). — *n.* **similarity** (*-lar'i-ti*). — *adv.* **sim'ilarly.** [Fr. *similaire* — L. *similis*, like.]

simile *sim'i-li,* (*rhet.*) *n.* (an) explicit likening of one thing to another: — *pl.* **sim'iles.** — *adj.* **sim'ilātive** expressing similarity. — *v.t.* **sim'ilise, -ize** to liken. — *v.i.* to use simile. — *n.* **simil'itude** likeness: semblance: comparison: parable. [L. neut. of *similis*, like.]

simillimum *si-mil'i-mum, n.* in homoeopathy, a remedy chosen because it would produce in a healthy person the same symptoms as those exhibited by the patient. [L., neuter superlative of *similis*, like.]

similor *sim'i-lör, n.* a yellow alloy used for cheap jewellery. [Fr., — L. *similis*, like, *aurum*, gold.]

simious. See **simian**.

simitar. Same as **scimitar**.

simkin, simpkin *sim'kin, n.* an Urdu corruption of **champagne**.

Simmental *zim'ən-täl, n.* a breed of cattle, orig. native to Switzerland, used in many parts of Europe for meat and milk. — Also **Simmenthal, -thaler** (*-täl-ər*). [From the *Simmental* or Simme valley.]

simmer *sim'ər, v.i.* and *v.t.* to boil gently. — *v.i.* to be near boiling or breaking out. — *n.* a simmering state. — **simmer down** to calm down. [Earlier *simper*, origin unknown.]

'simmon *sim'ən, n.* short for **persimmon**.

simnel *sim'nl, n.* a sweet cake usu. covered with marzipan for Christmas, Easter, or Mothering Sunday. — Also **sim'nel-bread', -cake'.** [O.Fr. *simenel* — L. *simila*, fine flour.]

Simon Pure *sī'mən-pūr', the real person (or thing). — *adj.* **sī'mon-pure** real, genuine. [From a character in Mrs Centlivre's comedy, *A Bold Stroke for a Wife*.]

simony *sī'mən-i, sim'ən-i, n.* the buying or selling of a benefice. — *n.* **simō'niac** one guilty of simony. — *adjs.* **simonī'acal, simō'nious** (*obs.*). — *adv.* **simonī'acally.** — *n.* **si'monist** one who practises or defends simony. [*Simon* Magus (Acts viii).]

simoom *si-mōōm', n.* a hot suffocating desert wind. — Also **simoon'.** [Ar. *samûm* — *samm*, to poison.]

simorg. See **simurg(h)**.

simp. See **simpleton** under **simple**.

simpai *sim'pī, n.* the black-crested langur of Sumatra. [Malay.]

simpatico *sim-pat'i-kō, adj.* sympathetic in the sense of congenial. [It.]

simper *sim'pər, v.i.* to smile in a silly, affected manner. — *n.* a silly or affected smile. — *n.* **sim'perer.** — *adj.* **simp'ering.** — *adv.* **simp'eringly.** [Cf. Norw. *semper*, smart.]

simpkin. See **simkin**.

simple *sim'pl, adj.* consisting of one thing or element: not complex or compound: not divided into leaflets (*bot.*): easy: plain: unornate: unpretentious: mean, sorry: mere, sheer: ordinary: unlearned or unskilled: of humble rank or origin: unaffected: artless: guileless: unsuspecting: credulous: weak in intellect: silly. — *n.* a simple person (also collectively) or thing: a medicine of one constituent: hence a medicinal herb. — *v.i.* to gather medicinal plants. — *ns.* **sim'pleness; sim'pler** a gatherer of simples; **sim'plesse** (*Spens.*) simplicity; **sim'pleton** a weak or foolish person, one easily imposed on (*coll.* short form **simp**). — *adv.* **simpliciter** (*-plis'i-tər,* *-plik';* L.) simply, not relatively: naturally: unconditionally. — *ns.* **simplicity** (*-plis'*); **simplificā'tion** the process, or an instance, of making simple or simpler. — *adj.* **sim'plificātive.** — *ns.* **sim'plificātor, sim'plifier** one who simplifies. — *v.t.* **sim'plify** to make simple, simpler, or less difficult: — *pr.p.* **sim'plifying;** *pa.t.* and *pa.p.* **sim'plified.** — *ns.* **sim'pling** gathering simples; **sim'plism** affected simplicity: oversimplification of a problem or situation; **sim'plist** one skilled in simples. — *adj.* **simplis'tic** tending to oversimplify, making no

allowances for problems and complexities: naïve. —
advs. **simplis'tically; sim'ply** in a simple manner: considered by itself: alone: merely: without qualification: veritably: absolutely: really (*coll.*). — **simple fraction** a fraction that has whole numbers as numerator and denominator; **simple fracture** see **fracture**. — *adj.* **sim'ple-heart'ed** guileless: frank, sincere. — **simple interest** interest calculated on the principal only. — *adj.* **simple-minded** lacking intelligence: foolish. — **sim'ple-mind'edness; simple sentence** a sentence with one predicate. [Fr. *simple*, and L. *simplus, simplex*.]
simplex *sim'pleks, n.* a figure with the minimum number of vertices for space of a particular number of dimensions (e.g. a triangle in 2-dimensional space): — *pl.* **sim'plices** (*-pli-sēz*). — *adj.* allowing transmission and reception in one direction only (*comput., teleg.*). [L.]
simpliciter, simplicity, simplify, etc. See **simple.**
simpliste *sĕ-plēst', sim-plēst', sim'plist, adj.* simplistic, naïve. [Fr.]
simulacrum *sim-ū-lā'krəm, n.* an image: a semblance: — *pl.* **simula'cra, -crums.** — Also **sim'ulācre.** [L. *simulācrum*.]
simulate *sim'ū-lāt, v.t.* to feign: to have or assume a false appearance of: to mimic. — *adj.* feigned. — *adj.* **sim'ulant** simulating: mimicking (*biol.*). — *n.* a simulator. — *adj.* **sim'ular** counterfeit: feigned. — *n.* a simulator. — *adj.* **sim'ulated** (of a material, e.g. fur, leather, wood) not of such a material but made (usu. in an inferior material) to look like it: not genuine, feigned. — *n.* **simulā'tion** feigning: mimicry: the making of working replicas or representations of machines or the re-creation of a situation, environment, etc., for demonstration or for analysis of problems. — *adj.* **sim'ulātive.** — *n.* **sim'ulātor** one who or that which simulates: a device used for simulating required conditions, etc., e.g. for training purposes. — *adj.* **sim'ulatory.** — **simulated pearl** a bead resembling a pearl. [L. *simulāre, -ātum*; cf. **similar, simultaneous.**]
simulcast *sim'əl-käst, n.* a programme broadcast simultaneously on radio and television: the transmission of such a programme. — Also *v.t.* [*simul*taneous and broad*cast*.]
Simulium *si-mū'li-əm, n.* a genus of small blood-sucking flies, the black flies: (without *cap.*) a fly of this genus. — *n.pl.* **Simulī'idae** (*-dē*) the family of flies of which the Simulium is the type-genus, some species of which are the vectors of diseases such as onchocerciasis. [L. *simulāre*, to imitate.]
simultaneous *sim-əl-tā'nyəs*, (*U.S.*) *sīm'ul-, adj.* being or happening at the same time: satisfied by the same roots (of equations) (*math.*). — *ns.* **simultaneity** (*-tə-nē'i-ti, -nā'-*), **simultā'neousness.** — *adv.* **simultā'neously.** — **simultaneous translation** at a meeting of people of different nationality, translation of a speaker's words into other languages at the same time as he is speaking. [L. *simul*, at the same time.]
simurg(h) *si-mŏŏrg', -mûrg', simorg -mörg', ns.* a monstrous bird of Persian fable. [Pers. *sīmurgh*.]
sin¹, sin' *sin, prep., conj.,* and *adv.* (*arch.* or *Scot.*) since. — **long sin** (*Spens.*) for a long time in the past. [Shortened from **sithen.**]
sin² *sin, n.* moral offence or shortcoming, esp. from the point of view of religion: condition of so offending: an offence generally: a shame, pity. — *v.i.* to commit sin. — *v.t.* to commit: to burden with sin (as *sin one's soul*): to bring, drive, or render by sin (hence *sin one's mercies*, to be ungrateful): — *pr.p.* **sinn'ing;** *pa.t.* and *pa.p.* **sinned.** — *adj.* **sin'ful** tainted with sin: wicked: involving sin: morally wrong. — *n.* **sin'fulness.** — *adj.* **sin'less.** — *adv.* **sin'lessly.** — *ns.* **sin'lessness; sinn'er.** — *v.t.* (with *it*; *Pope*) to act as a sinner. — **sin bin** in ice-hockey, etc., an enclosure to which a player is sent for a statutory length of time when suspended from a game for unruly behaviour: a room or other place to which disruptive school pupils are sent. — **sin'-eat'er** one who by eating bread and salt at a funeral takes upon himself the dead man's sins. — *adj.* **sin'-eat'ing.**

— **sin'-off'ering** a sacrifice in expiation of sin. — **live in sin** to cohabit in an unmarried state; **original sin** see **origin.** [O.E. *synn*; O.N. *synth*; Ger. *Sünde*, perh. L. *sōns, sontis*, guilty.]
sin³. See **sine¹.**
Sinaean *sin-ē'ən* (*Milt.*), **Sinic** *sin'ik, adjs.* Chinese. — *v.t.* and *v.i.* **sin'icise, -ize** (*-sīz*) to make or become Chinese or of Chinese character. — *n.* **Sin'icism** (*-sizm*) a Chinese custom, idiom, etc. [L.L. *Sīnae*, Gr. *Sīnai*, Chinese (pl.).]
Sinaitic *sī-nā-it'ik, adj.* of Mount *Sinai.*
Sinanthropus *sin-* or *sīn-an'thrō-pəs* or *-thrō', n.* Peking (fossil) man. [Gr. *Sīnai*, (the) Chinese, *anthrōpos*, man.]
sinapism *sin'ə-pizm, n.* a mustard plaster. [Gr. *sināpi*.]
sinarchism *sin'är-kizm*, **sinarquism** *-kizm, -kwizm, ns.* (also with *cap.*) the fascist movement in Mexico prominent around the time of the Second World War. — *ns.* and *adjs.* **sin'archist, sin'arquist.** [Sp. *sinarquismo* — *sin*, without, *anarquismo*, anarchism.]
since *sins, adv.* from that time on: after that time: past: ago. — *prep.* after: from the time of. — *conj.* from the time that: seeing that: because. [M.E. *sins, sithens*; see under **sith¹**.]
sincere *sin-sēr', adj.* pure, unmixed: unadulterated: unfeigned: genuine: free from pretence: the same in reality as in appearance. — *adv.* **sincēre'ly.** — *ns.* **sincēre'ness, sincerity** (*-ser'*). [Fr. *sincère* — L. *sincērus*, clean.]
sinciput *sing'si-put, n.* the forepart of the head or skull. — *adj.* **sincip'ital.** [L., — *sēmi-*, half, *caput*, head.]
sind. See **synd.**
Sindhi, Sindi *sin'dē, n.* a native or inhabitant of *Sind*, in S.E. Pakistan: the Indic language spoken mainly in Sind. — Also *adj.*
sindon *sin'dən*, (*arch.*) *n.* fine (esp. linen) cloth, or a garment, etc., made from it: a shroud, esp. that preserved as Jesus's at Turin, Italy. — *ns.* **sindonol'ogy** the study of this shroud and its history; **sindonol'ogist; sindonoph'any** (Gr. *phainein*, to show) the periodic exhibiting of this shroud to the public. [Gr. *sindōn*, fine cloth, winding sheet.]
sine¹ *sīn*, (*math.*) *n.* orig. the perpendicular from one end of an arc to the diameter through the other: now (as a function of an angle) the ratio of the side opposite it (or its supplement) in a right-angled triangle to the hypotenuse. — *abbrev.* **sin.** — *adj.* **sinical** (*sin'i-kl*). — **sine curve** a curve showing the relationship between the size of an angle and its sine, a sinusoid; **sine wave** any oscillation whose graphical representation is a sine curve. [L. *sinus*, a bay.]
sine². Same as **syne**¹,².
sine³ *sī'nē, si'ne*, (L.) *prep.* without. — **sine die** (*dī'ē, di'ā*) without a day (appointed) — of a meeting or other business, indefinitely adjourned; **sine dubio** (*dū'bi-ō, dŏŏb'i-ō*) without doubt; **sine prole** (*prō'lē, prō'le*) without issue; **sine qua non** (*kwä non, kwä nōn*) an indispensable condition.
sinecure *sī'ni-kūr*, or *sin', n.* a benefice without cure of souls: an office without work. — Also *adj.* — *ns.* **sin'ecurism; sin'ecurist.** [L. *sine*, without, *cūra*, care.]
sinew *sin'ū, n.* that which joins a muscle to a bone, a tendon: strength or that which it depends on (*fig.*). — *v.t.* to bind as by sinews: to strengthen. — *adjs.* **sin'ewed; sin'ewless; sin'ewy.** — **sinews of war** money. [O.E. *sinu*, gen. *sinwe*.]
sinfonia *sin-fō-nē'ə, n.* a symphony: a symphony orchestra. — *n.* **sinfonietta** (*-nē-et'tə*) a simple, or light, little symphony: a small symphony orchestra. — **sinfonia concertante** (*kon-chər-tan'ti*) an orchestral work with parts for more than one solo instrument. [It.]
sing *sing, v.i.* to utter melodious sounds in musical succession in articulating words: to emit more or less songlike sounds: to compose poetry: to give a cantabile or lyrical effect: to ring (as the ears): to be capable of being sung: to confess, to turn informer, to squeal (*slang*, esp. *U.S.*). — *v.t.* to utter, perform by voice, musically: to chant: to celebrate: to proclaim, relate,

in song or verse or in comparable manner: to bring, drive, render, pass, etc., by singing: — *pa.t.* **sang** or (now rarely) **sung**; *pa.p.* **sung.** — *adj.* **sing'able.** — *ns.* **sing'ableness; sing'er** a person, bird, etc., that sings: one who sings as a profession: an informer (*slang*, esp. *U.S.*); **sing'ing.** — *adv.* **sing'ingly.** — **sing'ing-bird** a songbird; **singing flame** a flame that gives a musical note in a tube; **sing'ing-gall'ery** a gallery occupied by singers; **sing'ing-hinn'y** (*Northern*) a currant cake that hisses on the girdle; **sing'ing-man** (*Shak.*) one employed to sing, as in a church choir; **sing'ing-master** a teacher of singing; **singing sand** musical sand; **sing'-sing** in New Guinea, a tribal get-together for singing, dancing and feasting; **sing'song** a ballad: jingly verse: monotonous up-and-down intonation: an informal concert where the company sing: a meeting for community singing. — *adj.* of the nature of singsong. — *v.t.* and *v.i.* to sing, speak, utter, in a singsong way. — **sing along** (orig. *U.S.*) of an audience, to join in the familiar songs with the performer (with *with*; *n.* **sing'along**); **sing another song** or **tune** to change to a humbler tone; **sing out** to call out distinctly, to shout: to inform, peach; **sing small** to assume a humble tone. [O.E. *singan*; Ger. *singen*, Goth. *siggwan*.]

singe *sinj*, *v.t.* to burn on the surface: to scorch: to remove by scorching. — *v.i.* to become scorched: — *pr.p.* **singe'ing**; *pa.t.* and *pa.p.* **singed.** — *n.* a burning on the surface: a slight burn. — **singed cat** a person who is better than he looks. [O.E. *sen(c)gan*.]

Singhalese. Same as **Sinhalese.**

single *sing'gl*, *adj.* consisting of one only or one part: unique: one-fold: uncombined: unmarried: for one: man to man: slight, poor (*Shak.*): of ale, weak, small: undivided: unbroken: of a flower, without development of stamens into petals or of ligulate instead of tubular florets: sincere: (of a travel ticket) valid for the outward journey only, not return. — *adv.* **singly.** — *n.* anything single: (usu. in *pl.*) an unmarried, unattached person: (in *pl.*) in tennis, etc., a game played by one against one: a hit for one run: a talon of a hawk: a gramophone record with usu. only one tune, or other short recording, on each side: a one-pound or one dollar note. — *v.t.* to separate: to pick (out): to pick out challengingly (*Milt.*): to take aside: to thin. — *v.i.* (*Spens.*) to come forth alone. — *ns.* **sing'lehood** the state of beng unmarried; **sing'leness** (*-gl-nis*); **sing'let** (*-glit*) a thing that is single: an undershirt; **sing'leton** (*-gl-tən*) a single card of its suit in a hand: anything single; **sing'ling** (*-gling*). — *adv.* **sing'ly** (*-gli*) one by one: alone: by oneself. — *adjs.* **sing'le=act'ing** acting effectively in one direction only; **sing'le=breast'ed** with one thickness over the breast and one row of buttons; **sing'le-chamb'er** having one legislative house. — **single cream** cream with a low fat-content that will not thicken when beaten; **sing'le-deck'er** a vessel or vehicle, esp. a bus, with only one deck; **sing'le-en(d)'** (*Scot.*) a one-room dwelling; **sing'le=en'try** a system of bookkeeping in which each entry appears only once on one side or other of an account. —*adjs.* **sing'le-eyed** one-eyed: devoted, unselfish; **sing'le-figure.** — **single figures** a score, total, etc., of any number from 1 to 9; **single file** see **file; sing'le-foot** a rack or amble. — *adj., adv.* **sing'le-hand'ed** by oneself: unassisted: with or for one hand. — *adj.* **sing'le=heart'ed** sincere: without duplicity: dedicated, devoted in one's attitude. — *adv.* **sing'le-heart'edly.** — **single house** (*Scot.*) a house one room deep. — *adj.* **sing'le=mind'ed** ingenuous: bent upon one sole purpose. — **sing'le-mind'edness; single parent** a mother or father bringing up children alone (hence **single-parent family**). — *adj.* **sing'le-phase** of an alternating electric current, requiring one outward and one return conductor for transmission. — **singles bar, club** one especially for unmarried or unattached people, where friendships can be formed; **sing'le-seat'er** a car, aeroplane, etc., seated for one; **single soldier** (*Scott*) a private. — *adj.* **sing'le-soled** having one thickness of

sole. — **sing'lestick** (*-gl-stik*) a fighting stick for one hand: a fight or game with singlesticks; **single tax** a tax on ground-rent or land-values to supersede all other taxes; **single ten** (*Shak.*) the ten of a card suit; **sing'le-wicket** cricket with one wicket, and with one batsman at a time. [O.Fr., — L. *singuli*, one by one.]

singletree *sing'gl-trē*, *n.* Same as **swingletree.**

sing-sing, singsong. See **sing.**

singspiel *sing'spēl*, Ger. *zing'shpēl*, *n.* a semi-dramatic representation in dialogue and song. [Gr., — *singen*, to sing, *Spiel*, play.]

singular *sing'gū-lər*, *adj.* single: unique: proper: private: denoting or referring to one: pre-eminent: pre-eminently good or efficacious: extraordinary: peculiar: strange: odd. — *adv.* **singularly.** — *n.* an individual person or thing: the singular number or a word in the singular number. — *n.* **singularīsā'tion, -z-.** — *v.t.* **sing'ularise, -ize** to make singular: to signalise. — *ns.* **sing'ularism** a philosophy that recognises but one principle, opp. to *pluralism*; **sing'ularist** one who affects singularity: an upholder of singularism; **singularity** (*-lar'i-ti*) fact or state of being singular: peculiarity: individuality: oddity: oneness: anything curious or remarkable: a point in space-time at which matter is compressed to an infinitely great density. — *adv.* **sing'ularly** in a singular manner: peculiarly: strangely: singly: pre-eminently (*arch.*). [L. *singulāris*.]

singult *sing'gult*, (*arch.*) *n.* a sob. — *n.* **singult'us** (*med.*) hiccuping. [L. *singultus*, a sob.]

sinh *shīn*, *sīn-āch'*, *n.* a conventional abbreviation of hyperbolic *sine*.

Sinhalese *sin'hə-lēz*, *-lēz'*, **Singhalese, Cingalese** *sing'-gəlēz*, *-lēz'*, also **Sinhala** *sin'hə-lə*, *adjs.* of the most numerous people of Sri Lanka (formerly Ceylon): of or in their language, akin to Pali. — *ns.* a member of the Sinhalese people: their language. [Sans. *Simhala*, Ceylon.]

Sinic, sinicise, Sinicism. See **Sinaean.**

sinical *sin'i-kl.* See **sine[1].**

sinister *sin'is-tər*, formerly also *-is'*, *adj.* left: on the left side (in *her.* from the point of view of the bearer of the shield, not the beholder, and similarly sometimes in description of an illustration, etc.): misleading (*obs.*): underhand: inauspicious: suggestive of threatened evil: unlucky: malign. — *n.* **sinisterity** (*-ter'*) left-handedness (*rare*): sinister quality. — *advs.* **sin'isterly; sin'isterwise.** — *adj.* **sin'istral** turning to the left: of flatfish, lying left side up: of a shell, coiled contrary to the normal way. — *n.* a left-handed person. — *n.* **sinistral'ity.** — *adv.* **sin'istrally.** — *adj.* **sinistrous** (*sin-is'* or *sin'is*-) inauspicious: sinister (*obs.*). — *adv.* **sinistrously.** [L.]

sinistrorse *sin-is-trörs'*, or *sin'*, (*biol.*) *adj.* rising spirally and turning to the right, i.e. crossing an outside observer's field of view from right to left upwards (like an ordinary spiral stair): formerly used in the contrary sense (dextrorse). — Also **sinistrors'al.** — *advs.* **sinistrors'ally; sinistrorse'ly.** [L. *sinistrōrsus, sinistrōversus,* towards the left side — *sinister,* left, *vertĕre, versum,* to turn.]

sink *singk*, *v.i.* to become submerged, wholly or partly: to subside: to fall slowly: to go down passively: to pass to a lower level or state: to penetrate: to be absorbed: to slope away, dip: to diminish: to collapse: to be withdrawn inwards. — *v.t.* to cause or allow to sink: in games, to cause to run into the hole (*coll.*): to suppress: to degrade: to conceal: to appropriate surreptitiously: to excavate: to let in, insert: to abandon: to abolish: to merge: to pay: to lose under the horizon: to invest, esp. unprofitably or beyond easy recovery: to damn or ruin (esp. in imprecation): — *pa.t.* **sank,** now rarely **sunk**; *pa.p.* **sunk,** also **sunk'en,** *obs.* exc. as *adj.* — *n.* a receptacle or drain for filth or dirty water: a cesspool: a kitchen or scullery trough or basin with a drain, for washing dishes, etc.: a place where things are engulfed or where foul things gather: a depression in a surface: an area without surface drainage: a swallow-hole (*geol.*): a shaft: a natural or artificial means of absorbing or discharging heat, fluid, etc. (*phys.*, etc.). — *ns.* **sink′age** act or process of sinking: amount of sinking: a sunk area, depression: shrinkage; **sink′er** one who sinks: a weight for sinking anything, as a fishing-line: a doughnut (*U.S. slang*): a mistletoe root. — *n.* and *adj.* **sink′ing**. — *adj.* **sink′y** yielding underfoot. — **sink′-hole** a hole for filth: a swallow-hole (*U.S.*); **sink′ing-fund** a fund formed by setting aside income to accumulate at interest to pay off debt. — *adj.* **sink′ing-ripe** (*Shak.*) ready to sink. — **sink in** to be absorbed: to be understood; **sink unit** a fitting consisting of sink, draining board, with cupboards, etc., underneath. [O.E. *sincan* (intrans.); Ger. *sinken*, Du. *zinken*.]

sink(e)-a-pace. Same as **cinque-pace.**

sinner, etc. See under **sin².**

sinnet *sin′it*. Same as **sennit.**

Sinn Fein *shin fān*, a political movement and party in Ireland championing a republic and later opposing partition. — *ns.* **Sinn Fein′er; Sinn Fein′ism.** [Ir., we ourselves.]

Sinningia *sin-in′ji-ə*, *n.* a Brazilian genus of Gesneriaceae, grown in greenhouses under the name of Gloxinia. [W. *Sinning*, German gardener.]

Sino- *sin′ō-*, *sī′nō-*, *pfx.* Chinese. — *n.* **Sinologue** (*sin′əlog*, or *sīn′*) one versed in Chinese. — *adj.* **Sinolog′ical** (*-loj′*). — *ns.* **Sinologist** (*-ol′ə-jist*); **Sinol′ogy.** — *ns.* and *adjs.* **Sin′ophil(e)** (*-fil*, *-fīl*) (one who is) friendly to the Chinese or attracted by Chinese culture. — *ns.* **Sinoph′ily, Sinoph′ilism.** — **Sino-American**, etc., (pertaining to) Chinese and American, etc. [Gr. *Sīnai*, Chinese (pl.).]

sino- *sin′ō-*, *sī′nō-*, *pfx.* sinus.

sinoekete. See **synoecete.**

sinopia *sin-ō′pi-ə*, *n.* a reddish-brown pigment used for one of the preparatory drawings of a fresco, obtained from **sin′opite**, an iron ore: the drawing. — Also **sinō′pis.** [L. *sinopis*, sinopite.]

sinsyne *sin-sīn′*, (*Scot.*) *adv.* since that time. [**sin¹**, **syne.**]

sinter *sin′tər*, *n.* a deposit from hot springs. — *v.t.* to heat a mixture of powdered metals, sometimes under pressure, to the melting-point of the metal in the mixture which has the lowest melting-point, the melted metal binding together the harder particles. — *v.i.* to coalesce under heat without liquefaction. — *adj.* **sin′tery.** [Ger. *Sinter*; cf. **cinder.**]

sinus *sī′nəs*, *n.* an indentation: a notch: a cavity: an air-filled cavity in the bones of the skull, connecting with the nose: a narrow cavity through which pus is discharged: — *pl.* **sinuses.** — *adjs.* **sinuate** (*sin′ū-āt*), **-d** (*-id*) wavy-edged: winding. — *adv.* **sin′uately.** — *ns.* **sinuā′tion** winding; **sinuitis** (*-ī′tis*), **sinusī′tis** (*sin-* or *sīn-əs-*) inflammation of a sinus of the skull communicating with the nose. — *n.* **sinuose** (*sin′ū-ōs*) sinuous. — *n.* **sinuos′ity.** — *adj.* **sin′uous** wavy: winding: bending in a supple manner. — *adv.* **sin′uously.** — *n.* **sin′uousness.** — *adjs.* **sinupall′ial, -pall′iate** with indented pallial line. — *n.* **sinusoid** (*sī′nəs-oid*) the curve of sines (*y = a* sin *x*): a blood-space in tissue. — *adj.* **sinusoid′al.** — *adv.* **sīnusoid′ally.** [L. *sinus, -ūs*, a bend, fold, bay.]

Sioux *sōō*, *n.* an American Indian of a tribe now living in the Dakotas, Minnesota, and Montana: — *pl.* **Sioux** (*sōō, sōōz*). — Also *adj.* — *adj.* **Siou′an** pertaining to the Sioux, or to a larger group to which the Sioux belong: pertaining to the languages of this group. — *n.* the group of languages spoken by the Siouan peoples. [Fr. from a native word.]

sip *sip*, *v.t.* and *v.i.* to drink, or drink from, in small quantities by action of the lips: — *pr.p.* **sipp′ing**; *pa.t.* and *pa.p.* **sipped.** — *n.* the act of sipping: the quantity sipped at once. — *n.* **sipp′er.** [Cf. **sup**; O.E. *sypian*; L.G. *sippen.*]

sipe¹ *sīp*, (*dial.*) *v.i.* to soak through: to seep. — Also **sype, seep.** [O.E. *sipian*, to soak.]

sipe² *sīp*, *n.* a tiny groove or slit in the tread of a tyre,

aiding water dispersal and improving the tyre's grip. [From **sipe¹**.]

siphon *sī′fən*, *n.* a bent tube or channel by which a liquid may be drawn off by atmospheric pressure: a tubular organ for intake and output of water, as in lamellibranchs: an aerated-water bottle that discharges by a siphon. — *v.t.* to convey, remove by means of (or as if by means of) a siphon (often with *off*). — *n.* **sī′phonage.** — *adj.* **sī′phonal.** — *n.pl.* **Sīphonap′tera** the flea order of insects. — *adj.* **sī′phonate** having a siphon. — *n.* **sī′phonet** a greenfly's honeydew tube. — *adj.* **sīphonic** (*-fon′*). — *ns.* **sīphon′ogam** a seed-plant; **sīphonog′amy** fertilisation by pollen-tube. — *n.pl.* **Sīphonoph′ora** an order of colonial Hydrozoa. — *ns.* **sī′phonophore** (or *sī-fon′*) a hydrozoan of this order; **sīphonostele** (*-stē′lē*, or *-stēl′*) a hollow cylinder of vascular tissue; **sī′phuncle** a tube connecting the chambers of a nautilus: a siphonet. [Gr. *sīphōn, siphōn*, siphon.]

Siporex® *sip′ər-eks*, *n.* a material used by builders, and also by artists, a form of aerated concrete, which can be sawn, etc.

sippet *sip′it*, *n.* a morsel, esp. of bread with soup. — *v.t.* and *v.i.* **sipp′le** to sip at leisure. [Cf. **sip, sup.**]

Sipunculacea, -loidea *sī-pungk-ū-lā′si-ə, -loi′di-ə*, *ns.* a group of marine worms. — *ns.* and *adjs.* **sipunc′ulid, -uloid** (pertaining to) a worm of this group. [Mod. L. — L. *siphunculus*, a little pipe.]

si quis *sī, sē kwis*, a public intimation. [L. *sī quis*, if anybody (wants, knows, has found, etc.).]

sir *sûr*, *n.* a word of respect (or disapprobation) used in addressing a man: a gentleman: (with *cap.*) prefixed to the Christian name of a knight or baronet (hence, a knight or baronet) and formerly used of a priest (hence, **Sir John**, a priest): (with *cap.*) a word of address to a man in a formal letter: formerly used as a translation of L. *dominus*, bachelor of arts (as distinguished from *magister*, master of arts): in *pl.* used in *Scot.* in addressing persons of either sex, passing into an *interj.* of surprise. — *v.t.* to address as 'sir': — *pr.p.* **sirr′ing**; *pa.t.* and *pa.p.* **sirred.** [O.Fr. *sire*, from L. *senior*, an elder.]

sircar, sirkar, circar *sər-kär′, sûr′, n.* government: the authorities: a province or district: an Indian clerk or factotum. [Urdu *sarkār*, a superintendent — Pers. *sar*, head, *kār*, agent.]

sirdar *sər-där′, sûr ′, n.* a military head: a commander-in-chief. [Urdu *sardār* — Pers. *sar*, head, *dār*, holding.]

sire *sīr*, *n.* a senior, elder: a master, lord (*rare*): a term of address to a king (*arch.*): a father, esp. of a horse or other beast: an ancestor. — *v.t.* to beget, esp. of beasts. [See **sir.**]

Siren *sī′rən*, *n.* one of certain sea-nymphs, part woman, part bird, whose songs lured sailors to death (*Gr. myth.*): (without *cap.*) a fascinating woman, insidious and deceptive: a bewitching singer: a mermaid: an instrument for counting sound vibrations: (formerly **sirene**, still *illit.* *sī-rēn′*; without *cap.*) a signalling or warning instrument that produces sound by the escape of air or steam through a rotating perforated plate: (*cap.*) an American genus of eel-like amphibians without hind legs. — Also *adj.* — *n.pl.* **Sirē′nia** an order of aquatic mammals now represented by the dugong and the manatee. — *n.* and *adj.* **sirē′nian.** — *adj.* **sirenic** (*-ren′*). — **siren suit** a close-fitting trousered overall orig. for use in air-raids. [Gr. *Seirēn.*]

sirgang *sûr′gang*, *n.* a green Asiatic jay-like bird. [Prob. from native name.]

sirih, siri *sē′ri*, *n.* betel. [Malay *sīrih.*]

Sirius *sir′i-əs*, *n.* the Dogstar. — *adj.* **Sir′ian.** — *n.* **sirī′asis** sunstroke. [L. *Sīrius* — Gr. *Seirios.*]

sirkar. Same as **sircar.**

sirloin, surloin *sûr′loin*, *n.* the loin or upper part of a loin of beef. [From a by-form of Fr. *surlonge* — *sur*, over, and *longe* (cf. **loin**).]

sirname. Same as **surname.**

sirocco *si-rok'ō*, **scirocco** *shi-, ns.* in Southern Italy, a hot, dry, dusty and gusty wind from North Africa, becoming moist further north: any oppressive south or south-east wind: a wind from the desert: a drying machine: — *pl.* **-os.** — Also **s(c)iroc** (*si-rok'*, *sī'rok*). [It. *s(c)irocco* — Ar. *sharq*, east wind.]

sirrah *sir'ə*, *n.* sir, used in anger or contempt. — **sirree'** (*sûr-ē'; U.S.*) a form of sir, sirrah, used for emphasis, esp. with *yes* or *no*. [An extension of **sir.**]

sir-reverence *sə-rev'ə-rəns*, (*obs.*) the phrase *save reverence*, used apologetically when anything disgusting has to be mentioned: hence *n.* a piece of excrement.

sirup. See **syrup.**

sirvente *sēr-vät'*, *n.* a troubadour's lay. [Fr.]

sis, siss *sis* (esp. *U.S.*) *n.* a contracted form of **sister** (used in addressing a girl). — *n.* and *adj.* **siss'y** (orig. chiefly *U.S.*) cissy.

-sis *-sis*, *n. suff.* signifying action, process: condition caused by: — *pl.* **-ses** (*-sēz*). [Gr.]

sisal *sī'səl*, *sī'zəl*, *n.* (in full **sis'al-hemp'**, or **-grass'**) agave fibre. [First exported from *Sisal*, in Yucatán.]

siserary, sisserary *sis-ər-ā'ri*, **sas(s)arara** *sas-ər-ā'rə*, *ns.* orig. corruption of **certiorari**: a scolding: a blow. — **with a siserary** suddenly: on the spot.

siskin *sis'kin*, *n.* a yellowish-green finch, *Carduelis spinus.* [Ger. dial. *sisschen*; app. Slav.]

siss, sissy. See **sis.**

sisserary. See **siserary.**

sissoo *sis'ōō*, *n.* a papilionaceous Indian timber tree (*Dalbergia*) or its wood. [Hind. *sīsū.*]

sist *sist*, (*Scots law*) *v.t.* to stop, stay: to cite, summon. — *n.* a stay. [L. *sistĕre*, to make to stand.]

sister *sis'tər*, *n.* a daughter of the same parents: a half-sister: formerly, a sister-in-law: a female fellow: a member of a sisterhood: a nun: a senior nurse, esp. one in charge of a ward. — *adj.* of the same origin: fellow: built on the same model. — *v.t.* to be a sister to: to call sister. — *adjs.* **sis'tering** (*Shak.*) neighbouring; **sis'terless; sis'terly** like or becoming a sister: kind: affectionate. — *ns.* **sis'terliness; sis'terhood** the act or state of being a sister: the relationship of sister: a society, esp. a religious community, of women: a set or class of women. — **sis'ter-hook** one of a pair of hooks that close each other; **sis'ter-in-law** a husband's or wife's sister, or a brother's wife: a husband or wife's brother's wife: — *pl.* **sis'ters-in-law.** — *adj.* **sis'ter-like.** [App. O.N. *systir*; O.E. *sweostor*; Du. *zuster*, Ger. *Schwester.*]

Sistine *sis'tīn, -tēn, -tin, adj.* of Pope *Sixtus*, esp. Sixtus IV (1471–84) or V (1585–90) — also **Six'tine.** — **Sistine Chapel** the Pope's chapel in the Vatican, built by Sixtus IV; **Sistine Madonna** a picture by Raphael of the Madonna with Sixtus II (257–8).

sistrum *sis'trəm*, *n.* an ancient Egyptian wire rattle used in Isis-worship: — *pl.* **sis'tra.** [L. *sīstrum* — Gr. *seistron.*]

Sisyphean *sis-i-fē'ən, adj.* relating to *Sisyphus*, king of Corinth, condemned in Tartarus to roll ceaselessly up a hill a huge stone which would roll back to the foot of the hill again each time he neared the top: endless, laborious and futile (*fig.*).

sit *sit*, *v.i.* to rest on the haunches or (*obs.*) knees: to perch, as birds: to brood: to have a seat, as in parliament: to be in session: to reside: to be a tenant: to be located, have station or (as the wind) direction: to pose, be a model: to undergo an examination, be a candidate: to weigh, bear, press: to be disposed in adjustment, hang, fit: to befit. — *v.t.* to seat: to have a seat on, ride: to undergo or be examined in: (in composition) to stay in or with in order to look after: — *pr.p.* **sitt'ing**; *pa.t.* and *pa.p.* **sat**, (*arch.*) **sate** (*sat, sāt*). — *n.* a mode or spell of sitting. — *ns.* **sitt'er** one who sits: one who sits to an artist or with a medium: a baby-sitter: a sitting bird: an easy shot: an easy dupe (*slang*): anything difficult to fail in: a sitting-room (*slang*); **sitt'ing** the state of being seated or act of taking a seat: brooding on eggs: a clutch: a continuous

meeting of a body: a spell of posing to an artist, etc.: a spell: a seat: a church seat. — *adj.* seated: brooding: in the course of a parliamentary session: befitting. — **sit'down** a spell of sitting. — *adj.* that one sits down to: (of a strike) in which workers down tools but remain in occupation of the plant, workshop, etc. — **sit'fast** a lump in a horse's skin under the saddle; **sitt'er-in** a baby-sitter; **sit'-in** the occupation of a building, etc., as an organised protest against some (supposed) injustice, etc. (also *adj.*); **sitt'ing-room** a room in which members of a family commonly sit: a space for sitting; **sitting target** an easy target or victim; **sitting tenant** the tenant currently occupying a property; **sit'-upon** (*coll.*) the buttocks. — **sit at** to live at the rate of expense of; **sit back** to take no active part, or no further active part; **sit by** to look on without taking any action; **sit down** to take a seat: to pause, rest: to begin a siege; **sit down under** to accept, to submit to; **sit in** to act as a baby-sitter: to be present as a visitor, and (usu.) take part, as at a conference or discussion: to have or take part in a sit-in; **sit on** or **upon** to hold an official inquiry regarding: to repress, check (*slang*); **sit out** to sit apart without participating: to sit to the end of: to outstay; **sit tight** to maintain one's seat: to keep one's position quietly and unobtrusively; **sitting pretty** see **pretty**; **sit under** to be in the habit of hearing the preaching of; **sit up** to rise from a recumbent to a sitting position, or from a relaxed to an erect seat: to become alert or startled: to remain up instead of going to bed: to keep watch during the night. [O.E. *sittan*; Ger. *sitzen*, L. *sedēre.*]

sitar *si-tär'*, *n.* a Hindu plucked-string instrument with a long neck. — Also **sittar'.** [Hind. *sitār.*]

sitatunga, situtunga *si-tə-tōōng'gə, -tung'*, also (second spelling only) *si-tōō-*, *n.* a species of African antelope, *Tragelaphus spekei*, notable for its elongated hooves which allow it to walk on marshy ground. [Swahili.]

sitcom *sit'kom*, (*coll.*) *n.* a situation *comedy.*

site *sīt*, *n.* situation, esp. of a building: ground occupied or set apart for a building, etc.: posture (*obs.*). — *v.t.* to locate. [L. *situs*, set — *sinĕre.*]

sith¹ *sith*, (*Shak.*) *adv., prep., and conj.* since — *obs.* **sith'en**, (*Spens., Shak.*) **sith'ence**, **sith'ens.** [O.E. *siththan*, for *sīth than* (instrumental), after that; cf. **since, syne¹.**]

sith², **sithe, sythe** *sīdh*, (*Spens.*) *n.* time: — *pl.* **sith, sithes, sythes.** [O.E. *sīth*, time.]

sithe¹ *sīdh*, (*Spens., Shak., Milt.*) *n.* and *v.t.* Same as **scythe.**

sithe² *sīdh*, *n.* and *v.i.* an obs. or dial. form of **sigh.**

sithe³. See **sith².**

sithen, sithence, sithens. See **sith¹.**

sitiology, sitiophobia. See **sitology.**

Sitka spruce *sit'kə sprōōs*, a spruce tree with sharp blue-green needles. [*Sitka* in Alaska.]

sitology *sī-tol'ə-ji*, **sitiology** *sit-i-*, *ns.* dietetics. — *n.* **sit(i)ophō'bia** morbid aversion to food. [Gr. *sītos*, dim. *sītion*, grain, food.]

sitrep *sit'rep*, (*coll.*) *n.* a report on the current military position (also *fig.*). [*Situation report.*]

Sitta *sit'ə*, *n.* the nuthatch genus. — *adj.* **sitt'ine.** [Gr. *sittē.*]

sittar. See **sitar.**

sitter, sitting, etc. See **sit.**

sittine. See **Sitta.**

Sittlichkeit *zit'lihh-kīt*, (Ger.) *n.* morals, morality: that which is becoming or suitable.

situate *sit'ū-it, adj.* (now *rare*) situated. — *v.t.* (*-āt*) to set, place, locate: to circumstance. — *adj.* **sit'uated** set, located: circumstanced. — *n.* **situā'tion** location: place: position: momentary state: condition: a set of circumstances, a juncture: a critical point in the action of a play or the development of the plot of a novel: office, employment. — *adj.* **situā'tional.** — **situation comedy** a comedy, now esp. in a television or radio series in which the same characters appear in each episode, which depends for its humour on the behaviour of the characters in particular, sometimes contrived, situations; **situation ethics** see **ethic**. [L.L. *situātus* — L. *situēre*, to place.]

situla *sit'ū-lə*, (*ant.*) *n.* a bucket: — *pl.* **sit'ūlae** (*-ē*). [L.]

situs *sī'təs*, *n.* position: the normal position of an organ in the body: — *pl.* **sī'tus** (*-z*). [L., site, position.]

situtunga. See **sitatunga**.

sitz-bath *sits'-bäth*, *n.* a hip-bath. [Ger. *Sitzbad*.]

sitzkrieg *sits'krēg, zits'krēhh*, *n.* the period (September 1939 to May 1940) of comparative military quiet at the opening of World War II, or any similar period in any war. [Ger. *sitzen*, to sit, *Krieg*, war; cf. **blitzkrieg**.]

Sium *sī'əm*, *n.* the water-parsnip genus. [Gr. *sion*.]

Siva *s(h)ē'və, s(h)i'və*, *n.* the third god of the Hindu triad, destroyer and reproducer. — Also **Shiva** (*shē'və, shi'və*). — *n.* **S(h)i'vaism**. — *adj.* **S(h)ivaist'ic**. — *ns.* **S(h)i'vaite; Sivapithē'cus** (or *-pith'*) an Indian Miocene fossil anthropoid; **Sivathē'rium** a gigantic giraffe-like Indian Pliocene fossil animal. [Sans. *śiva*, friendly, gracious.]

Sivan *sē-vän'*, *n.* the ninth month of the Jewish civil, third of the ecclesiastical, year, part of May and June. [Heb. *sīwān*.]

siver. See **syver**.

siwash *sī'wosh*, (also with *cap.*; *north western U.S. derog. coll.*) *n.* a N.W. American Indian. — Also *adj.* [Chinook, — Fr. *sauvage*, wild.]

six *siks*, *n.* the cardinal numeral next above five: a symbol representing it (6, vi, etc.): a set of that number: an article of size denoted by it: a card with six pips: a score of six points, tricks, etc.: the sixth hour after midnight or after midday: a six-cylinder engine or car: a six-syllable line: a division of a Brownie Guide or Cub Scout pack: the age of six years. — *adj.* of the number six: six years old. — *n.* **six'er** anything counting for six (as a hit at cricket) or indicated by six: the leader of a Brownie Guide or Cub Scout six. — *adj.* and *adv.* **six'fold** in six divisions: six times as much. — *adj.* **sixth** last of six: next after the fifth: equal to one of six equal parts. — *n.* a sixth part: a person or thing in sixth position: an interval of five (conventionally called six) diatonic degrees (*mus.*): a combination of two tones that distance apart (*mus.*). — *adv.* **sixth'ly** in the sixth place. — *adjs.* **six'-day** of or for six days (i.e. usu. excluding Sunday); **six'-foot** measuring six feet. — **six'-foot'er** a person six feet high; **sixth form** (the classes studying in it) the (usu.) two years of post-O-level preparation for A level exmaminations; **six'-gun** a six-shooter; **six'-pack** a pack which comprises six items sold as one unit, esp. a pack of six cans of beer; **six'pence** a coin worth six old pence: its value. — *adj.* **six'penny** costing or worth sixpence: cheap: worthless. — *n.* a sixpenny book. — *n.* and *adj.* **six'score.** — **six'-shooter** a six-chambered revolver. — **at sixes and sevens** in disorder; **hit, knock for six** to overcome completely: to take by surprise; **long, short, sixes** candles weighing six to the pound, about 8 or 4 inches long respectively; **six (of one) and half a dozen (of the other)** equal, attributable to both parties equally: having alternatives which are considered equivalent, equally acceptable, etc.; **sixth form college** a school which provides the sixth form education for the pupils of an area; **the Six Counties** Northern Ireland. [O.E. *siex*; Ger. *sechs*; Gael. *sé*; L. *sex*, Gr. *hex*, Sans. *şaş*.]

sixaine *siks-ān'*, *n.* a stanza of six lines. — *n.* **sixte** (*sikst*) a parry with hand on guard opposite the right breast, sword point a little raised to the right. [Fr.]

sixteen *siks-tēn'*, or *siks'*, *n.* and *adj.* six and ten. — *n.* **sixteen'er** a verse of sixteen syllables. — *n.* (*pl.* **-mos**) *adj.* **sixteen'mo** sextodecimo. — *adj.* **sixteenth** (or *siks'*) last of sixteen: next after the fifteenth: equal to one of sixteen equal parts. — *n.* a sixteenth part: a person or thing in sixteenth position. — *adv.* **sixteenth'ly.** [O.E. *siextēne* (*-tēne*); see **six, ten**.]

sixty *siks'ti*, *adj.* and *n.* six times ten: — *pl.* **six'ties** the numbers sixty to sixty-nine: the years so numbered in a life or century: a range of temperature from sixty to

just less than seventy degrees. — *adj.* **six'tieth** last of sixty: next after the fifty-ninth: equal to one of sixty equal parts. — *n.* a sixtieth part: a person or thing in sixtieth position. — **sixty-four dollar question** (from a U.S. quiz game), the final and most difficult question one has to answer to win sixty-four dollars, having first won one dollar and placed this on oneself to win double on the second question, and so on until sixty-four dollars are at stake: hence, a hard question to answer, the supreme or crucial question. — Also **sixty-four thousand dollar question.** [O.E. *siextig*.]

size[1] *sīz*, *n.* an assize (*obs.*): a portion of food and drink (*obs.*): an allowance (*obs.*): bigness: magnitude. — *v.t.* to arrange according to size: at Cambridge, to buy or score, as rations: to measure. — *v.i.* to draw a size: to assume size. — *adj.* **sī'zable** (or **size'able**) of a fair size. — *ns.* **sī'zar** (also **sī'zer**) at Cambridge and Dublin, a student receiving an allowance from his college towards his expenses; **sī'zarship.** — *adj.* (usu. in composition) **sized** having this or that size. — *ns.* **sī'zer** a measurer: a gauge: a thing of considerable or great size (*slang*); **sī'zing** sorting by size: order for extra food from a college buttery. — **of a size** of the same size; **size up** to take mental measure of; **the size of it** (*coll.*) a description of the situation or state of affairs now obtaining. [**assize**.]

size[2] *sīz*, *n.* a weak glue or gluey material. — *v.t.* to cover or treat with size. — *adj.* **sized**. — *ns.* **sī'zer; sī'ziness; sī'zing** application of size, or material for the purpose. — *adj.* **sī'zy.** [Origin obscure.]

size[3] *sīz*. Same as **sice**[1].

sizel *siz'l*. Same as **scissel**.

sizzle *siz'l*, *v.i.* to make a hissing sound of frying. — *v.t.* and *v.i.* to fry, scorch, sear. — *n.* a hissing sound: extreme heat. — *ns.* **sizz'ler** a sizzling heat or day: a thing strikingly fierce or effective; **sizz'ling** a hissing. — *adj.* very hot: very striking. [Imit.]

sjambok *sham'bok*, *n.* a whip of dried hide. — *v.t.* to flog. [Afrik. — Malay *samboq* — Urdu *chābuk*.]

ska *skä*, *n.* a form of Jamaican music similar to reggae.

skail, scail, scale *skāl*, (*Scot.*) *v.t.* and *v.i.* to disperse: to scatter: to spill. [Ety. dub.; prob. not connected with Gaelic *sgaoil*.]

skaines mate *skānz māt*, (*Shak.*) perh. a companion, a scapegrace.

skaith. See **scathe**.

skald, scald *sköld*, *n.* a poet: a Scandinavian bard. — *adj.* **skald'ic, scald'ic**. [O.N. *skáld*.]

skart, scart *skärt*, **scarth, skarth** *skärth*, (*Scot.*) *ns.* a cormorant. [O.N. *skarfr*.]

skat *skät*, *n.* a three-handed card-game. [O.Fr. *escart*, laying aside.]

skat[2]. Same as **scat**[1].

skat[3]. See **scat**[4].

skate[1] *skāt*, *n.* a sole or sandal mounted on a blade (for moving on ice): the blade itself: a boot with such a blade fixed to it: a roller-skate: a spell of skating. — *v.i.* to go on skates. — *ns.* **skā'ter; skā'ting**. — **skate'-board** a narrow wooden, fibreglass, etc. board mounted on roller-skate wheels, on which one balances to ride; **skate'boarder; skate'boarding; skā'ting-rink**. — **get one's skates on** (*coll.*) to hurry; **skate round** (*fig.*) to avoid discussing or answering; **skate on thin ice** see **ice; skate over** (*fig.*) to hurry over lightly. [Du. *schaats* — O.N.Fr. *escache*, stilt — L.G. *schake*, shank.]

skate[2] *skāt*, *n.* a kind of ray (*Raia batis*, or kindred species). [O.N. *skata*.]

skatole *skat'ōl, skā'tōl*, *n.* a compound (C_9H_9N) found in faeces. [Gr. *skōr, skatos*, dung.]

skatt. Same as **scat**[1].

skaw, scaw *skö*, *n.* a low cape, ness (in place names). [O.N. *skagi*.]

skean. See **skene:** also old spelling of **skein**.

skear, skeary. Dial. forms of **scare, scary**.

skedaddle *ski-dad'l*, (*coll.*) *v.i.* to scamper off. — *n.* a scurrying off. [Ety. unknown.]

skeely *skē′li*, (*Scot.*) *adj.* skilful. [**skill.**]
skeer, skeery. Dial. forms of **scare, scary.**
skeesicks *skē′ziks*, (*U.S.*) *n.* a rascal.
skeet *skēt, n.* a form of clay-pigeon shooting.
skeeter *skēt′ər*, (*U.S.*) *n.* short for **mosquito.**
Skeffington's daughter. See **scavenger**[1].
skeg *skeg*, (*naut.*) *n.* a brace between keel and rudder: a projection from, or in place of, a keel: a stabilising fin projecting from the underside of a surfboard. [Du. *scheg.*]
skegger *skeg′ər, n.* a young salmon. [Origin obscure.]
skeigh *skēhh*, (*Scot.*) *adj.* shy: coy: aloof: skittish. [Cf. O.E. *scēoh*, shy.]
skein *skān, n.* a loosely tied coil or standard length of thread or yarn: a tangle: a web: the nuclear network (*biol.*): a flock of wild geese in flight. [O.Fr. *escaigne.*]
skelder *skel′dər*, *v.i.* to beg: to swindle. [Cant; of obscure origin.]
skeleton *skel′i-tn, n.* the hard parts of an animal: the bones: the veins of a leaf: a framework or outline of anything: a scheme reduced to its essential or indispensable elements: a set of persons reduced to its lowest strength: an emaciated person or animal. — Also *adj.* — *adjs.* **skel′etal; skeletogenous** (*-toj′*) skeleton-forming. — *v.t.* **skel′etonise, -ize** to reduce to a skeleton. — **skeleton key** a key with its serrated edge or the shaped part of its bit filed down, so that it can open many locks; **skel′eton-shrimp′** a ghostly-looking amphipod (Caprella, etc.); **skeleton suit** an early 19th-cent. boy's suit with trousers buttoning over the coat. — **skeleton in the cupboard, closet, house,** etc. a hidden domestic sorrow or shame. [Gr. *skeleton* (*sōma*), dried (body) — *skellein*, to dry.]
skelf *skelf*, (*Northern*) *n.* a splinter of wood, esp. in the finger, etc. [Prob. — obs. Du. *schelf.*]
skellie. See **skelly.**
skelloch *skel′ohh*, (*Scot.*) *v.i.* to yell. — *n.* a yell.
skellum *skel′əm*, (*Scot.*) *n.* a ne'er-do-well: a scamp. [Du. *schelm*, a rogue; cf. **skelm.**]
skelly, skellie *skel′i* (*Scot.*) *n., adj.,* and *v.i.* (to) squint. [Prob. O.N.; cf. O.E. *sceolh*, squint.]
skelm *skelm*, (*S.Afr.*) *n.* a rascal. [Du. *schelm*, Ger. *Schelm.*]
skelp *skelp*, (*Scot.*) *v.t.* to slap. — *v.i.* to move briskly along: to bound along. — *n.* a slap. — *adj.* **skelp′ing** very big or full: smacking: lusty. — *n.* a smacking. [Gael. *sgealp*, a slap with the palm of the hand.]
skelter *skel′tər*, *v.i.* to scurry. — *n.* a scurry.
skene *skēn, skean *skē′ən, n.* an Irish or Highland dagger, knife, or short sword. — **skene′-dhu, skean′-dhu** (*-dōō′*) a dirk, dagger, stuck in the stocking; **skene′-occle** (*-ok′l*) one carried in the sleeve. [Ir. and Gael. *sgian*, knife, *dhu*, black, *achlais*, armpit.]
skeo. Same as **skio.**
skep *skep, n.* a basket: a beehive. — *v.t.* to hive: — *pr.p.* **skepp′ing;** *pa.t.* and *pa.p.* **skepped.** — *n.* **skep′ful.** [O.N. *skeppa.*]
skeptic, skepsis. Same as **sceptic, scepsis.**
sker. Same as **skirr.**
skerrick *sker′ik*, (*dial.*) *n.* (chiefly with negative) a minute quantity, a scrap. [Ety. uncertain.]
skerry *sker′i, n.* a reef of rock. [O.N. *sker.*]
sketch *skech, n.* a drawing, slight, rough, or without detail, esp. as a study towards a more finished work: an outline or short account: a short and slightly constructed play, dramatic scene, musical entertainment, etc.: a short descriptive essay. — *v.t.* to make or give a sketch of: to outline, or give the principal points of. — *v.i.* to practise sketching. — *n.* **sketchabil′ity.** — *adj.* **sketch′able** worth sketching. — *n.* **sketch′er.** — *adv.* **sketch′ily.** — *n.* **sketch′iness.** — *adj.* **sketch′y** like a sketch: incomplete: slight: imperfect, inadequate. — **sketch′-book** a book of or for sketches (in drawing, literature or music). [Du. *schets*, prob. — It. *schizzo* — L. *schedium*, an extempore — Gr. *schedios*, off-hand.]
skeuomorph *skū′ə-mörf, n.* a decoration or decorative

feature in architecture, etc., derived from the nature of the material (originally) used, or the way of working it: a retained but no longer either functional or incidental characteristic of an artefact, e.g. the 'casting seams' knapped on to a flint knife, imitated from those on a cast bronze knife (*archaeol.*), or, modernly, the imitation stitching on plastic upholstery. — *adj.* **skeuomorph′ic.** — *n.* **skeuomorph′ism.** [Gr. *skeuos*, vessel, tool, *morphe*, shape.]
Skevington's daughter. See **scavenger**[1].
skew[1] *skū, adj.* oblique: of statistics or a curve representing them, not symmetrical about the mean. — *adv.* awry. — *n.* obliquity. — *v.t.* and *v.i.* to set, go, or look obliquely. — *adj.* **skewed** distorted: skew. — **skew′= back** (*archit.*) the part or inclined surface on which a segmented arch abuts; **skew′-bridge** a bridge having its arch or arches set obliquely on its abutments. — *adj.* and *adv.* **skew-whiff′** (*coll.*) crooked, awry. [App. O.N.Fr. *eskiu(w)er* — O.Fr. *eschuer*; see **eschew;** or M.Du. *schuwe*, to shun; cf. **shy.**]
skew[2] *skū, n.* the coping or a coping stone of a gable. — **skew′-corbel, -put, -table** the corner-stone supporting the coping of a gable. [O.Fr. *escu* — L. *scūtum*, a shield.]
skewbald *skū′böld, adj.* marked in white and another colour (not black). — *n.* a skewbald horse. [Origin obscure.]
skewer *skū′ər, n.* a long pin of wood or metal, esp. for meat. — *v.t.* to fasten or pierce with a skewer: to transfix. [**skiver.**]
ski *skē*, (formerly also *shē*) *n.* a long narrow runner orig. of wood, now also of metal, etc., fastened to the foot to enable the wearer to slide across snow, etc.: — *pl.* **ski** or **skis.** — *v.i.* to travel on skis: — *pr.p.* **ski′ing;** *pa.t.* and *pa.p.* **skied, ski′d.** — *adj.* **ski′able** (of surface) in condition for skiing on. — *ns.* **ski′er; ski′ing.** — **ski′-bob** a vehicle used for gliding down snow-slopes, consisting of a short front-pivoting ski, turned by handlebars, and a longer fixed rear ski with a seat attached. — Also *v.i.* — **ski′-bobbing; ski′-flying** ski-jumping from a high take-off point, so that a longer time is spent in the air; **ski(-)joring** (*-jör′, -jör′*), Norw. **skikjöring** (*shihh-yūr′ing*) the sport of being towed on skis by a horse or motor vehicle; **ski′-jump′ing; ski′= kiting** water-skiing holding on to a bar on a kite-like device; **ski′-lift, -tow** devices for taking skiers uphill; **ski′-run** a slope for skiing on; **ski-runn′ing; ski′-school; ski′-slope; ski′-stick** one of a pair of sticks, usu. pointed with a disc near the tip, used by skiers for balance or propulsion. — **bird-, dry, water-skiing** see **bird, dry, water.** [Norw. — O.N. *skīth*, snow-shoe, piece of split wood; O.E. *scīd.*]
skia- *skī′ə-, -a′-*, in composition, shadow. — Also **scia-** (*sī-*), **skio-, scio-.** — *ns.* **ski′agram, ski′agraph** an X-ray photograph; **skiamachy** (*-am′ə-ki;* Gr. *machē*, a fight) a sham fight: a fight with shadows; **skias′copy** retinoscopy; **ski′atron** a cathode-ray tube in which an electron beam varies the transparency of a phosphor, which is illuminated from behind so that its image is projected on to a screen. [Gr. *skiā*, a shadow.]
skid *skid, n.* a support on which something rests, is brought to the desired level, or slides: a ship's wooden fender: a shoe or other device to check a wheel on a down-slope: an aeroplane runner: a skidding: a side-slip. — *v.i.* to slide along without revolving: to slip, esp. sideways. — *v.t.* to check with a skid: to make to skid. — **skid′-lid** (*slang*) a crash helmet; **skid pad, pan** a piece of slippery ground on which motorists can learn to control a skidding car; **skid′pan** (*slang*) a drag for a wheel (also *fig.*); **skid road, row** (esp. *U.S.*) a squalid quarter where vagrants, chronic drunks, etc., live. — **put the skids on, under** (*slang*) to cause to hurry: to put a stop to, thwart; **the skids** (*fig.; coll.*) a downward path. [Prob. related to **ski.**]
Ski-doo®, skidoo *ski-dōō′, n.* a motorised sledge, fitted with endless tracks at the rear and steerable skis at the front.

skier[1]. See **ski.**
skier[2], **skiey.** See under **sky.**
skiff[1] *skif, n.* a small light boat. [Akin to **ship.**]
skiff[2] *skif, (Scot.) v.i.* and *v.t.* to skim. — *n.* a skimming or grazing movement or blow: a slight touch: a sketch: a puff.
skiffle *skif'l, n.* a strongly accented jazz type of folk-music played by guitars, drums, and often unconventional instruments, etc., popular about 1957. [Origin obscure.]
ski(-)joring, skikjöring. See **ski.**
skill *skil, n.* reason (*Shak.*): discrimination (*obs.*): expertness: expert knowledge (*arch.*): a craft or accomplishment: (in *pl.*) aptitudes and competencies appropriate for a particular job, e.g. of the secretarial kind. — *v.t.* and *v.i.* (*arch.*) to matter: to make (a difference): to signify. — *adj.* **skil'ful.** — *adv.* **skil'fully.** — *n.* **skil'-fulness.** — *adjs.* **skilled** expert: skilful: (of a job) requiring special training; **skill'-less, skil'less; skill'y, skeel'y** (*Scot.*) skilful. — **Skill'centre** a Government-funded training establishment to assist those who wish to develop new occupational skills. [O.N. *skil,* distinction, *skilja,* to separate.]
skillet *skil'it, n.* a small, long-handled pan: a frying-pan (esp. *U.S.*). [Origin doubtful.]
skilligalee, skilligolee. See **skilly.**
skilling[1] *skil'ing, n.* an obsolete coin of Scandinavian countries, of small value. [Dan.]
skilling[2]. See **skillion.**
skillion *skil'yən, (Austr.) n.* an outhouse or lean-to, esp. one with a sloping roof. — Also **skill'ing.** — **skillion roof** a roof slanting out from the wall of a building. [Eng. dial. *skilling,* an outhouse, lean-to.]
skilly[1] *skil'i, n.* thin gruel. — Also **skilligalee', skilligolee'.** [Ety. dub.]
skilly[2]. See **skill.**
skim *skim, v.t.* to remove floating matter from the surface of: to take off by skimming (often with *off;* also *fig.*): to glide lightly over: to read superficially and skippingly. — *v.i.* to pass over lightly: to glide along near the surface: to become coated over: — *pr.p.* **skimm'ing;** *pa.t.* and *pa.p.* **skimmed.** — *n.* the act of skimming: skim-milk. — *ns.* **skimm'er** one who or that which skims: a utensil for skimming milk: an apparatus for clearing a water-surface of debris, e.g. in a swimming pool: a sea-bird (*Rhyncops*) that skims the water; **skimm'ing.** — *adv.* **skimm'ingly.** — **skim'-milk** milk from which the cream has been skimmed. [App. related to **scum.**]
skimble-skamble *skim'bl-skam'bl, adj.* wild, rambling, incoherent. [A reduplication of **scamble.**]
Skimmia *skim'i-ə, n.* an Asiatic genus of rutaceous shrubs, cultivated for its holly-like leaves and drupes: (without *cap.*) a plant of this genus. [Jap. *shikimi.*]
skimmington *skim'ing-tən, n.* a burlesque procession in ridicule of husband or wife in case of infidelity or other ill-treatment. [Ety. unknown.]
skimp *skimp, v.t.* and *v.i.* to scrimp: to stint. — *adj.* scanty, spare. — *adv.* **skimp'ily.** — *adj.* **skimp'ing.** — *adv.* **skimp'ingly.** — *adj.* **skimp'y.** [Poss. **scamp** combined with **scrimp.**]
skin *skin, n.* the natural outer covering of an animal: a hide: a thin outer layer or covering: an integument: a membrane: a wine vessel made of an animal's skin: short for **skinhead** (q.v. below) (*slang*). — *adj.* of skin. — *v.t.* to cover with a skin: to strip the skin from: to fleece. — *v.i.* to become covered with skin: to slip through or away: — *pr.p.* **skinn'ing;** *pa.t.* and *pa.p.* **skinned.** — *n.* **skin'ful** as much liquor as one can hold. — *adjs.* **skin'less; skinned** (usu. in composition). — *ns.* **skinn'er** one who prepares hides; **skinn'iness.** — *adj.* **skinn'y** of or like skin: emaciated: (of a pullover, etc) tight-fitting. (*coll.*). — *adj.* **skin'-deep** superficial: shallow, not deeply fixed. — **skin'-diver** orig., a naked pearl-diver: one involved in skin-diving; **skin'-diving** diving and swimming under water, with simple equipment, not wearing the traditional diver's helmet and

suit, and not connected with a boat; **skin effect** the tendency, increasing with frequency, for an alternating current to be greater in the surface layer of a conductor; **skin'flick** (*slang*) a film in which some of the characters appear in the nude and which usually includes scenes of sexual intercourse; **skin'flint** a very niggardly person; **skin'food** a cosmetic intended to nourish the skin; **skin'-game** a swindling trick; **skin'-head** a member of certain gangs of young people wearing simple, severe, clothes, the boys having closely cropped hair. — *v.i.* **skinn'y-dip'** (esp. *U.S.*) to bathe naked. — **skinn'y-dipp'er; skinn'y-dipp'ing.** — *v.i.* **skin'-pop** (*slang*) to inject drugs. — **skin'-popping; skin test** a test made by applying a substance to, or introducing a substance beneath, a person's skin, to test for an allergy, immunity from a disease, etc. — *adj.* **skin'-tight** fitting close to the skin. — *n.* (in *pl.*) tights. — **skin'-wool** wool from a dead sheep. — **by** or **with the skin of one's teeth** very narrowly; **get under someone's skin** to annoy someone: to interest someone seriously; **no skin off one's nose** (*coll.*) a matter about which one feels unconcerned or indifferent because it does not harm or inconvenience one, or because it may be to one's benefit; **save one's skin** to save one's life. [O.N. *skinn;* late O.E. *scinn.*]
skink[1] *skingk, v.i.* and *v.t.* to pour out. — *n.* (*Scot.*) liquor. — *n.* **skink'er.** — *adj.* **skink'ing** (*Scot.*) thin, watery. [Perh. L.G. *schenken;* cf. O.E. *scencan;* Ger. *schenken.*]
skink[2] *skingk, n.* an African lizard (*Scincus*) or kindred kind. [L. *scincus* — Gr. *skinkos.*]
skink[3] *skingk, n.* (*Scot.*) shin-bone soup: a shin of beef. [M.Du. *schenke,* L.G. *schinke.*]
skinny. See **skin.**
skint *skint, (slang) adj.* without money, hard up. [skinned.]
skio, skeo *skyō, (Orkney* and *Shetland) n.* a hut: a shed: — *pl.* **skios, skeos.** [Norw. *skjaa.*]
skio-. See **skia-.**
skip[1] *skip, v.i.* to progress by hopping on each foot alternately: to spring or hop lightly: to make jumps over a twirling rope: to pass discontinuously. — *v.t.* to overleap: to omit: to cut, not go to (a class): — *pr.p.* **skipp'ing;** *pa.t.* and *pa.p.* **skipped.** — *n.* an act of skipping: a belt of inaudibility in wireless transmission: a college servant. — *n.* **skipp'er** one who skips: a dancer: a young and thoughtless person (*Shak.*): a hairy-bodied butterfly of the Hesperiidae, with short jerky flight: the saury. — *adj.* **skipp'ing** flighty, giddy. — *n.* the art or activity of jumping over a twirling rope. — *adv.* **skipp'ingly.** — **skip'jack** a pert fop: any of a number of species of fish that jump out of, or swim at the surface of, the water, such as the bonitos, the bluefish, the saurel, and either of two species of tuna (the **skipjack tuna,** *Katsuwonus pelamis,* and the **black skipjack,** *Euthynnus yaito*): a click-beetle: a jumping toy made of a fowl's wishbone; **skip'-kennel** (*obs.*) a lackey; **skipp'ing-rope** a rope for skipping with; **skip zone** an area round a broadcasting station where transmissions cannot be received. — **skip it!** (*coll.*) never mind, forget it! [Cf. O.N. *skopa,* to run.]
skip[2] *skip, n.* a box or truck for raising minerals from a mine: a large container for transporting building materials, etc., theatrical costumes or refuse. [**skep.**]
skip[3] *skip, n.* the captain of a rink in bowls or curling. — *v.t.* and *v.i.* to act as a skip. [**skipper.**]
skipper[1] *skip'ər, n.* a ship captain: the captain of an aeroplane: the captain of a team. — *v.t.* to act as skipper. — **skipper's daughters** white-topped waves. [Du. *schipper.*]
skipper[2] *skip'ər, (old cant) n.* a barn, outhouse, etc., esp. as a sleeping-place for vagrants. — *v.i.* to sleep rough in barns, etc. — *n.* **skipp'ering** (*current slang*) sleeping rough. [Perh. Corn., *sciber* or W. *ysgubor,* barn.]
skippet *skip'it, n.* a flat box for protecting a seal (as of a document). [Origin unknown.]
skirl *skirl, skûrl, (Scot.) v.t.* and *v.i.* to shriek or sing shrilly. — *v.i.* to make the sound of the bagpipes. —

n. a shrill cry: the sound of the bagpipes. — *n.* **skirl'ing** a shrill sound. — **skirl'-in-the-pan'** the noise of frying: a fried dish. [Scand.]

skirmish *skûr'mish, n.* an irregular fight between small parties. — *v.i.* to fight slightly or irregularly. — *ns.* **skir'misher; skir'mishing.** [O.Fr. *escarmouche.*]

skirr, sker, scur, squirr *skûr, v.t.* to scour, search, range over (*Scot.*): to send skimming. — *v.i.* (*Shak.*) to scurry. [Origin doubtful.]

skirret *skir'it, n.* a water-parsnip with edible roots. [M.E. *skirwhit,* as if *skire white,* pure white, but perh. altered from O.Fr. *eschervis.*]

skirt *skûrt, n.* a garment, or part of a garment, generally a woman's, that hangs from the waist: the lower part of a gown, coat, or other garment or anything suggesting this: a saddle-flap: a midriff (of meat): a rim, border, margin: a part of, or attachment to, an object that suggests a skirt, e.g. the flap of material hanging down around the base of a hovercraft to contain the air-cushion, or a similar flap around a racing-car: a woman (*slang*; also **bit of skirt**). — *v.t.* to border: to pass along the edge of: to scour the outskirts of. — *v.i.* to be on or pass along the border: to leave the pack. — *adj.* **skirt'ed** wearing or having a skirt. — *ns.* **skir'ter** a huntsman who dodges his jumps by going round about; **skir'ting** material for skirts: skirting-board: (in *pl.*) dirty wool from the skirts of a fleece. — Also *adj.* — *adj.* **skirt'less.** — **skirt'-danc'ing** dancing with waving of flowing skirts; **skir'ting-board** the narrow board next to the floor round the walls of a room. — **divided skirt** trousers made to look like a skirt. [O.N. *skyrta,* a shirt, kirtle; cf. **shirt.**]

skit *skit, n.* a piece of banter or burlesque, esp. in dramatic or literary form: a humorous hit: a hoax: a sudden slight shower of rain or snow, etc. (*dial.*). — *v.i.* **skite, skyte** (*skīt; Scot.*) to dart or glide obliquely. — *n.* a glancing blow: a spree: a trick: a queer person. [Perh. related to O.N. *skjōta,* to shoot.]

skite *skīt,* (*Austr. slang*) *v.i.* to boast. — *n.* a boaster. [**blatherskite.**]

skitter *skit'ər, v.i.* to skim over the surface of water: to fish by drawing the bait over the surface: to scamper lightly. [Perh. from **skite** (see **skit**).]

skittish *skit'ish, adj.* unsteady: light-headed: frivolous: frisky: lively: volatile: changeable: wanton: coy. — *adv.* **skitt'ishly.** — *n.* **skitt'ishness.** [Perh. conn. with **skit.**]

skittle *skit'l, n.* a pin for the game of **skittles,** a form of ninepins in which a ball or cheese (see **cheese¹**) is used. — *v.t.* to knock down. — **skitt'le-alley, -ball, -ground.** [Prob. alteration of **kail¹,** through intermediate *kittle*; see **kittle-pins.**]

skive¹ *skīv, v.t.* to pare, split. — *ns.* **skī'ver** split sheepskin leather; **skī'ving.** [O.N. *skīfa*; cf. **shive.**]

skive² *skīv,* (*slang*) *v.t.* and *v.i.* (often with *off*) to evade (a duty, work, etc.). — Also *n.* — *n.* **skī'ver.** — *adj.* **skī'vy.** [Origin uncertain.]

skiver *skiv'ər,* (*dial.*) *n.* and *v.t.* same as **skewer.** [Origin unknown.]

skivie *skī'vi,* (*obs. Scot.*) *adj.* deranged: askew. [Cf. O.N. *skeifr.*]

skivvy¹ *skiv'i,* (*slang*) *n.* a disrespectful word for a maid-servant. [Origin uncertain.]

skivvy² *skiv'i, n.* a man's undervest (esp. *U.S. slang*): a knitted cotton polo-necked sweater (*Austr.* and *N.Z.*). [Ety. uncertain.]

sklate *sklāt,* Scottish form of **slate¹.**

sklent *sklent,* Scottish form of **slant.**

skliff. Same as **scliff.**

sklim. Same as **sclim.**

skoal *skōl, interj.* hail!: a friendly exclamation in salutation before drinking, etc. [O.N. *skāl*; Norw. *skaal,* a bowl, Sw. *skå*; cf. **scale³,⁴.**]

skoff. See **scoff².**

skokiaan *skö'ki-än,* (*S. Afr.*) *n.* a strong home-brewed drink made from yeast. [Afrik.]

skol *skol.* Same as **skoal.**

skolion *skö'li-on, n.* a short drinking-song in ancient

Greece, taken up by the guests in irregular succession: — *pl.* **skö'lia.** [Gr. *skŏlion.*]

skolly, skollie *skol'i,* (*S. Afr. derog.*) *n.* a Coloured hooligan, esp. a member of a gang. [*Afrik.,* prob. from Du. *schoelje,* rascal.]

skran. Same as **scran.**

skreaky. Same as **screaky.**

skreen (*Spens.* **skreene**). Same as **screen** (esp. partition of wood or stone).

skreigh, skriech, skriegh, screich, screigh, scriech *skrēhh,* (*Scot.*) *n.* and *vb.* (to) screech, shriek. — **skreigh of day** cock-crow, daybreak. [Imit. improvement upon **screak.**]

skrik *skrik,* (*S.Afr.*) *n.* a fright. [Afrik., from Du. *schrik,* fright.]

skrimmage. Same as **scrimmage.**

skrimp. See **scrump.**

skrimshank, scrimshank *skrim'shangk,* (*mil. slang*) *v.i.* to evade work or duty. — *n.* evasion of work. — *n.* **skrim'shanker.** [Origin obscure.]

skrump. See **scrump.**

skry, skryer. Same as **scry, scryer.**

skua *skū'ə, n.* a genus (*Stercorarius*) of large predatory gulls. — **skū'a-gull.** [O.N. *skūfr.*]

skudler, scuddaler, scudler *skud'lər,* (*Shetland*) *n.* the leader of a band of guisers: the conductor of a festival. [Origin obscure.]

skug¹, scug *skug* (*Scot.* **scoug, scoog** *skōōg,* **scog** *skog*), *n.* orig. shadow: shelter. — *v.t.* and *v.i.* to shelter. [O.N. *skuggi,* shadow.]

skug² *skug,* (*dial.*) *n.* a squirrel.

skulduddery, skulduggery. See **sculdudd(e)ry.**

skulk *skulk, v.i.* to sneak out of the way: to lurk: to malinger. — *ns.* **skulk, skulk'er** one who skulks. — *n.* and *adj.* **skulk'ing.** — *adv.* **skulk'ingly.** — **skulk'ing-place.** [Scand., as Dan. *skulke.*]

skull¹ *skul, n.* the bony case that encloses the brain: the sconce, noddle: a skullcap, esp. of metal: a crust of solidified metal on a ladle, etc. — **skull'cap** a close-fitting cap: a protective cap of metal for the top of the head: the top of the skull: a labiate plant (*Scutellaria*) with helmet-like calyx. — **skull and crossbones** see **crossbones** under **cross.** [M.E. *scolle*; perh. Scand.]

skull². Same as **scull².**

skulpin. Same as **sculpin.**

skummer. See **scumber.**

skunk *skungk, n.* a small American musteline animal that emits an offensive fluid: its fur: a low fellow. — *v.t.* (*U.S.*) to defeat without allowing to score. — **skunk'-bird, -black'bird** the bobolink (from his colouring); **skunk'-cabb'age** an ill-smelling plant (*Symplocarpus*) of the arum family. [Algonkian *segonku.*]

Skupshtina *skōōp'shti-nə, n.* the Yugoslav (*hist.* Serbian and Montenegrin) national assembly. [Serb.]

skurry, skuttle. Same as **scurry, scuttle.**

skutterudite *skōōt'ər-ōō-dīt, n.* a cubic mineral, cobalt arsenide. [*Skutterud* in Norway, a source.]

sky *skī, n.* the apparent canopy over our heads: the heavens: the weather: the upper rows of pictures in a gallery: sky-blue: — *pl.* **skies.** — *v.t.* to raise aloft: to hit high into the air: to hang above the line of sight. — *n.* **sky'er, skī'er** (*cricket*) a hit high into the air. — *adjs.* **sky'ey, skī'ey** (or **skī'ey**) of the weather: of or like the sky; **sky'ish** (*Shak.*) like or approaching the sky, lofty. — *adj.* and *adv.* **sky'ward.** — *adv.* **sky'wards.** — *adj.* **sky'-aspiring** (*Shak.*). — *n.* and *adj.* **sky'-blue** light blue like the sky. — *adjs.* **sky'born** of heavenly birth; **sky'-bred; sky'clad** naked. — **sky'-col'our.** — *adj.* **sky'-col'oured.** — **sky'-diver; sky'-diving, -jumping** jumping by parachute as a sport, using a special steerable parachute, and delaying opening it for a specified time. — *adj.* **sky'-high** very high. — Also *adv.* — *v.t.* **sky'jack** (*coll.*) to hijack (an aeroplane). — *ns.* **sky'jacker; sky'jacking; sky'lab** an orbiting experimental space-station, specif. (with *cap.*) that launched and manned by the U.S., 1973-74; **sky'lark** the common lark. — *v.i.* to frolic boisterously. — *v.t.* to trick.

— **sky'larking** running about the rigging of a ship in sport: frolicking; **sky'light** a window in a roof or ceiling: light from or in the sky: light through the bottom of an empty glass; **sky'line** the horizon: a silhouette or outline against the sky; **sky'man** a paratrooper; **sky marshal** an armed plain-clothes officer on an air-flight, having the job of protecting passengers and dealing with hijacking attempts; **sky'-par'lour** a lofty attic; **sky'-pī'lot** (*slang*) a clergyman, chaplain. — *adj.* **sky'-plant'ed** placed in the sky. — **sky'rock'et** a firework that bursts high in the sky. — *v.i.* to shoot up high: to rise high and fast. — **skysail** (*skī'sl*) a sail above the royal; **sky'scape** a view or a picture of the sky; **sky'scraper** a very lofty building: a triangular skysail: anything very high; **sky'-sign** an elevated advertising sign, as of lights on a high building. — *adj.* **sky'-tinc'tured** of the colour of the sky. — **sky'-troops** paratroopers: airborne troops; **sky wave** a radio wave reflected from the ionosphere; **sky'way** a route for aircraft; **sky'-writing** tracing of words by smoke from an aircraft. — **the sky is the limit** (*coll.*) there are no restrictions on amount or extent (of something); **to the skies** (*coll.*) in a lavish or enthusiastic manner. [O.N. *skȳ*, cloud.]

Skye *skī*, *n.* (in full, **Skye terrier**) a small long-haired Scotch terrier. [From the island of *Skye*.]

skyr *shür*, *skēr*, *n.* curds. [Norw., Sw., and Icel., — O.N.]

skyre *skīr*, (*Scot.*) *v.i.* to shine, be gaudy, flaunt. [Origin obscure.]

skyte. Same as **skite** (see **skit**).

slab¹ *slab*, *n.* a plane-sided plate: a large thick slice of cake, etc.: outer plank sawn from a log: a thin flat piece of stone, etc. — *v.t.* to cut slabs from: to form into slabs: to cover with slabs. — *adj.* **slabbed.** — *adj.* **slab'-sid'ed** (*U.S.*) flat-sided: tall and lank. — **slab'-stone** flagstone. [Origin obscure.]

slab² *slab*, *adj.* semi-liquid, viscous. — *n.* mud. — *n.* **slabb'iness.** — *adj.* **slabb'y** muddy. [Scand.; cf. Norw., Sw. *slabb*, wet filth.]

slabber *slab'ər*, *v.i.* to slaver, to drivel. — *v.t.* to beslaver, beslubber, or beslubber: to gobble sloppily and grossly. — *n.* **slabb'erer.** — *adj.* **slabb'ery.** [Cf. L.G. and Du. *slabberen* and **slobber.**]

slack¹ *slak*, *adj.* lax or loose: not firmly extended or drawn out: not holding fast: remiss: not strict: not eager or diligent, inattentive: not busy: not violent or rapid, slow: pronounced with wide, not tense, tongue (*phon.*). — *adv.* in a slack manner: partially: insufficiently. — *n.* the slack part of a rope, belt, etc.: a time, occasion, or place of relaxed movement or activity: a slack-water haul of a net: (in *pl.*) long, loose trousers. — *vs.i.* **slack, slack'en** to become loose or less tight: to be remiss: to abate: to become slower: to fail or flag: to be inactive or lax. — *vs.t.* to make slack or less tight: to loosen: to slow, retard: to be remiss or dilatory in: to relax: to slake. — *n.* and *adj.* **slack'ening.** — *n.* **slack'er** an idler: one who is reprehensibly inactive: a shirker. — *adv.* **slack'ly.** — *n.* **slack'ness.** — *v.t.* **slack'-bake** to half-bake. — *adj.* **slack'-hand'ed** remiss. — **slack'-jaw** (*slang*) impudent talk; **slack'-rope** a loosely stretched rope for a funambulist; **slack'-water** turn of the tide: a stretch of still or slow-moving water. — *adj.* pertaining to slack-water. — **slack away** to ease off freely; **slack in stays** slow in going about, of a ship; **slack off, slacken off** to ease off; **slack up, slacken up** to ease off: to slow. [O.E. *slæc* (*sleac*); cf. Sw. *slak*, O.N. *slakr*.]

slack² *slak*, *n.* coal-dross. [Cf. Ger. *Schlacke*.]

slack³ *slak*, (*Scot.*) *n.* a cleft between hills: a boggy place. [O.N. *slakki*, dell.]

sladang. Same as **seladang.**

slade¹ *slād*, *n.* a little valley or dell: a piece of low, moist ground. [O.E. *slæd*, dell.]

slade² *slād*, Scots *pa.t.* of **slide.**

slae *slā*, a Scots form of **sloe.**

slag¹ *slag*, *n.* solid scum on melted metal: vitrified cinders: scoriaceous lava: coal-mining waste: a piece of slag.

— *v.t.* and *v.i.* to form into slag. — *adj.* **slagg'y.** — **slag'-wool** fibre made from molten slag. [M.L.G. *slagge*; cf. Ger. *Schlacke*, dross.]

slag² *slag*, (*slang*) *n.* a slovenly or dissolute woman. [**slag¹.**]

slag³ *slag*, (*slang*) *v.t.* to criticise, mock, deride (esp. with *off*). [**slag¹.**]

slag⁴ *slag*, (*Austr. slang*) *n.* spit. — *v.i.* to spit. [Prob. **slag¹.**]

slaid *slād*. Same as **slade².**

slain *slān*, *pa.p.* of **slay.**

slàinte *slän'chə*, (Gael.) *interj.* good health!

slairg *slārg*, (*Scot.*) *v.t.* to spread or smear sloppily. — *v.i.* to eat messily. — *n.* a dollop: a smear. [Cf. Ger. dial. *schlarggen*, to smear.]

slaister *slās'tər*, (*Scot.*) *n.* a slobbery mess: wet slovenly work. — *v.t.* to bedaub. — *v.i.* to do anything in a wet, dirty, slobbery way. — *adj.* **slais'tery.** — *n.* slops: drudgery. [Origin obscure.]

slake¹ *slāk*, *v.t.* to quench: to extinguish: to deaden: to abate, mitigate, allay, reduce, moderate: to moisten: to hydrate (as lime): to refresh with moisture: to slacken. — *v.i.* to become slaked: to subside: to abate: to die down. — *adj.* **slake'less** that cannot be slaked. [O.E. *slacian*, *sleacian*, to grow slack — *slæc*, *sleac*, slack.]

slake² *slāk*, (*Scot.*) *v.t.* and *v.i.* to lick, smear, daub. — *n.* a slabbery daub: a smear. [O.N. *sleikja*, to lick; Ger. *schlecken*, to lick.]

slake³ *slāk*, (*Northern*) *n.* mud: slime: a mud-flat.

slalom *slä'ləm*, *n.* a race in which tactical skill is required, esp. a downhill or zigzag ski-run among posts or trees or an obstacle race in canoes. — *v.i.* and *v.t.* (*fig.*) to move in a zigzag course. [Norw.]

slam¹ *slam*, *v.t.* or *v.i.* to shut or strike with violence and noise: to bang: to censure, criticise (*coll.*): — *pr.p.* **slamm'ing;** *pa.t.* and *pa.p.* **slammed.** — *n.* the act or sound of slamming: a harsh criticism (*coll.*). — *adv.* with a slam (also *fig.*). — *n.* **slamm'er** (*slang*) prison. [Cf. Norw. *slemma*.]

slam² *slam*, *n.* an old card-game, also called ruff or trump: in whist, the winning of every trick: in bridge, the winning of every trick (*grand slam*) or of all but one (*small* or *little slam*). — *v.t.* to inflict a slam upon. [Origin unknown.]

slammakin, slammerkin *slam'ə(r)-kin*, (*obs.*) *ns.* a loose gown: a slovenly-dressed woman: a slattern. — *adj.* slovenly. [Origin obscure.]

slander *slän'*, *slan'dər*, *n.* a false or malicious report: injurious defamation by spoken words or by looks, signs, or gestures (distinct from *libel*; *Eng. law*): defamation whether spoken or written (*Scots law*): calumny. — *v.t.* to defame: to calumniate. — *n.* **slan'derer.** — *adj.* **slan'derous.** — *adv.* **slan'derously.** — *n.* **slan'derousness.** [O.Fr. *esclandre* — L. *scandalum* — Gr. *skandalon*, snare, scandal.]

slane *slān*, *n.* a turf-cutting spade. [Ir. *sleaghan*.]

slang¹ *slang*, *n.* a jargon of thieves and disreputable persons: the jargon of any class, profession, or set: words and usages not accepted for dignified use. — Also *adj.* — *v.t.* to scold, vituperate. — *adv.* **slang'ily.** — *ns.* **slang'iness; slang'ing** a scolding. — Also *adj.* — *adv.* **slang'ingly.** — *adjs.* **slang'ish; slang'ular** (*Dickens*); **slang'y.** — *v.t.* and *v.i.* **slang'-whang** to rail, to rant. — **slang'-whanger.** — **slanging match** a bitter verbal quarrel, usu. involving an exchange of insults. — **back-slang** see **back¹.** [Of cant origin; connection with **sling¹** very doubtful.]

slang² *slang*, (*slang*) *n.* a counterfeit weight or measure: a travelling show, or performance: a hawker's licence. [Cant; origin obscure.]

slang³ *slang*, *n.* a watch-chain: (in *pl.*) leg-irons. [Perh. Du. *slang*, snake.]

slangish, slangular, slangy. See **slang¹.**

slant¹ *slänt*, *slant*, *v.t.* and *v.i.* to slope: to turn, strike, fall, obliquely. — *v.t.* to bias in a certain direction in presentation. — *n.* a slope: obliquity: a sloping surface,

line, ray, or movement: a divergence from a direct line: a glance (*U.S. coll.*): a jibe: a point of view, way of looking at a thing: a chance (*slang*). — *adj.* sloping: oblique: inclined from a direct line. — *adjs.* **slant'ed** biased, prejudiced; **slantendic'ular, slantin(g)dic'ular** oblique (*jocular*; founded on *perpendicular*). — *adj.* **slant'ing.** — *advs.* **slan'tingly, slant'ingways, slant'ly, slant'ways, slant'wise.** — *adj.* **slant'-eyed.** [M.E. *slent*; cf. Norw. *slenta*, Sw. *slinta*, to slope, slip.]
slant² *slänt, slant, n.* a transitory breeze. [Earlier *slent*; Scand.; cf. Norw. *slett*.]
slap¹ *slap, n.* a blow with the hand or anything flat: a snub, rebuke: stage make-up (*theat.*). — *v.t.* to give a slap to: to bring or send with a slap: to rebuke (also with *down*): to apply without much care or attention (usu. with *on*): — *pr.p.* **slapp'ing;** *pa.t.* and *pa.p.* **slapped.** — *adv.* with a slap: suddenly, violently: directly, straight. — *n.* **slapp'er** one who or that which slaps: a whopper, a thing very big of its kind (*slang*). — *adj.* **slapp'ing** (*slang*) whopping. — *adv.* **slap'-bang** violently, all at once. — *adj.* dashing, violent. — *n.* a cheap eating-house: a simple firework that makes a noise when thrown down. — *adv.* **slap'-dash** in a bold, careless way. — *adj.* off-hand, rash. — *n.* roughcast: careless work. — *v.t.* to do in a hasty, imperfect manner: to roughcast. — *adj.* **slap'-happy** (*coll.*) recklessly or boisterously happy: slap-dash, happy-go-lucky: punch-drunk. — **slap'jack** (*U.S.*) a flapjack, griddle-cake: a card game in which players try to win the pack by being the first to slap a hand over the jack, as it is turned over on top of the pile: **slap'stick** a harlequin's double lath that makes a noise like a slap: (also **slapstick comedy**) knockabout low comedy or farce. — *adj.* **slap'-up** (*slang*) superlatively fine. — **slap and tickle** (*coll.*) amorous frolicking, with kissing, petting, etc.; **slap in the face** (*coll.*) an insult or rebuff; **slap on the back** (*coll.*) a mark of congratulations; **slap on the wrist** (*coll.*) a mild reprimand. [Allied to L.G. *slapp*, Ger. *Schlappe*; imit.]
slap² *slap, (Scot.) n.* a gap in a fence, wall, hedge, etc.: a hill pass: a passage in a salmon cruive: hence the weekly close time when the passage is open. — *v.t.* to breach: to pierce. [Du. or L.G. *slop*.]
slash¹ *slash, v.t.* to cut by striking with violence and at random: to make long cuts in: to slit so as to show lining or material underneath: to lash: to criticise very harshly: to crack as a whip: to cut down, reduce drastically or suddenly (*coll.*): to clear by felling trees (*U.S.*). — *v.i.* to strike violently and at random with an edged instrument: to strike right and left. — *n.* a long cut: a cut at random: a cut in cloth to show colours underneath: a stripe on a non-commissioned officer's sleeve: débris of trees (*U.S.*): a forest clearing, esp. cumbered with débris (*U.S.*): an act of urination (*vulg.*). — *adj.* **slashed** cut with slashes: gashed. — *ns.* **slash'er** one who or that which slashes: a machine for sizing warp threads (*weaving*): a circular saw for slicing logs into regular lengths; **slash'ing** a slash or slashes: the felling of trees as a military obstacle: felled trees: a clearing. — *adj.* cutting mercilessly, unsparing: dashing: very big, slapping. [Perh. O.Fr. *esclachier*, to break; or conn. with **lash.**]
slash² *slash, (U.S.) n.* a low-lying, swampy area. [Poss. alteration of **plash**³.]
slash³ *slash, (vulg.) v.i.* to urinate. *n.* an act of urinating. [Cf. Scot. *slash*, a large splash, poss. from O.Fr. *esclache.*]
slat¹ *slat, v.t.* and *v.i.* to strike, beat: to flap. — *n.* a sudden sharp blow. [Poss. O.N. *sletta*, to slap, splash.]
slat² *slat, n.* a slate or roofing slab (*dial.*): a thin strip of wood, etc. — *adj.* **slatt'ed** having, or composed of, slats. [O.Fr. *esclat.*]
slate¹ *slāt, n.* a fine-grained argillaceous rock which by regional metamorphism has developed a cleavage along close-spaced planes independent of the bedding, usu. a dull blue, grey, purple, or green: a slab of this material (or a substitute) for roofing, or for writing

on: a preliminary list of candidates: slate-colour. — *adj.* of slate: slate-coloured, dull dark blue. — *v.t.* to cover with slate: to enter on a slate: to clear of fine hair with a slater: to note down for nomination or appointment (*U.S.*): to propose; to schedule (*U.S.*). — *adj.* **slat'ed** covered with slates. — *ns.* **slat'er** one who covers roofs with slates: a tool with slate blade for removing fine hair from hides: a wood-louse (*dial.*); **slat'iness; slat'ing** covering with slates: a covering of slates: materials for slating. — *adj.* **slat'y** of or like slate. — **slate'-axe** a slater's sax; **slate'-club** a society whose members make weekly contributions towards benefits against misfortune or towards getting Christmas cheer. — *adjs.* **slate'-coloured** dark greenish or bluish grey; **slate'-gray, -grey** of a light slate colour. — **slate'-pencil** a cut or turned stick of soft slate, compressed slate-powder, or pyrophyllite, for writing on slate; **slate'-writer; slate'-writing** mysterious production of writing on a covered slate; **slaty cleavage** fissility like that of slate along planes independent of bedding. — **a slate loose** (*slang*) a slight mental derangement; **clean slate** see **clean; on the slate** (*coll.*) on credit; **wipe the slate clean** to allow a person to make a fresh start in a job, relationship, etc. by ignoring past mistakes, crimes, etc. [O.Fr. *esclate*; cf. **slat**².]
slate² *slāt, v.t.* to abuse: to review unsparingly: to reprimand: to bait with dogs (*dial.*): to set on (*dial.*). — *n.* **slā'ting.** [From the O.N. word answering to O.E. *slǣtan*, to bait.]
slather *sladh'ǝr,* (esp. *U.S.* and *dial.*) *n.* a large quantity. — *v.t.* to slop or smear: to squander. — **open slather** (*Austr.* and *N.Z.*) carte blanche, a free rein: a free-for-all. [Origin uncertain.]
slattern *slat'ǝrn, n.* a slut, a dirty untidy woman. — *v.i.* **slatt'er** (*dial.*) to be untidy or slovenly. — *v.t.* (*dial.*) to spill, splash, slop about. — *n.* **slatt'ernliness.** — *adj.* **slatt'ernly** sluttish. — Also *adv.* — *adj.* **slatt'ery** (*dial.*) sloppy: slovenly. [App. **slat**¹.]
slaughter *slö'tǝr, n.* killing of animals, esp. for food: killing of great numbers: wanton or inexcusable killing, esp. of the helpless: carnage: butchery: bodies of the slain. — *v.t.* to make slaughter of. — *adj.* **slaugh'terable** fit or due for slaughter. — *n.* **slaugh'terer.** — *adj.* **slaugh'terous** given to slaughter: destructive: murderous. — *adv.* **slaugh'terously.** — *n.* **slaugh'tery** (*rare*) slaughter: a slaughterhouse. — **slaugh'terhouse** a place where beasts are killed for the market; **slaugh'terman** a man employed in killing or butchering animals. [O.N. *slātr*, butchers' meat, whence *slātra*, to slaughter (cattle).]
Slav *släv, n.* one whose language is Slavonic, i.e. belongs to that division of the Indo-European tongues that includes Russian, Polish, Wendish, Czech, Slovak, Serbian, Slovenian, and Bulgarian. — *adjs.* **Slav, Slav'ic.** — *n.* **Slav'dom** the Slavs collectively, the Slavonic world. — *v.t.* **Slav'ify** to assimilate to the Slavs. — *ns.* **Sla'vism** a Slavonic idiom used in another language: enthusiasm for Slavic ways or culture: anything characteristic of the Slavs; **Slavonia** (*slǝ-, slä-vō'ni-ǝ*) a region bounded by the Danube, Sava, and Drava. — *adj.* **Slavo'nian** of Slavonia: Slav. — Also *n.* — *adj.* **Slavonic** (*-von'ik*) of the group of languages indicated above, or the peoples speaking them. — *n.* the parent language of the Slavs or any of its descendants. — *v.t.* **Slavon'icise, -ize, Slavonise, -ize** (*slav'-ǝn-īz*) to make Slavonic. — *adj.* **Slav'ophil(e)** favourable or friendly to Slavs. — Also *n.* — *adj.* **Slav'ophobe** hostile to Slavs. — Also *n.* [Mediaeval L. *Sclavus* — Late Gr. *Sklabos*, from the stem of Slav *slovo*, word, *sloviti*, to speak; cf. **Slovene.**]
slave *slāv, n.* a person held as property: an abject: one who is submissive under domination: one who is submissively devoted: one whose will has lost power of resistance: one who works like a slave, a drudge: a mechanism controlled by another mechanism, e.g. in computing, by the central processor: a master-slave manipulator. — Also *adj.* — *v.i.* to work like a slave:

to drudge. — *v.t.* to enslave: to treat as a slave: perh. make subservient to one's own views (*Shak.*; *King Lear* IV, i. 69). — *ns.* **slāv′er** a slave-trader: a ship employed in the slave-trade; **slāv′ery** the state of being a slave: the institution of ownership of slaves: drudgery; **slāv′ey** (*slang*) a domestic drudge, a maid of all work. — *adj.* **slāv′ish** of or belonging to slaves: befitting a slave: servile: abject: servilely following or conforming: laborious. — *adv.* **slāv′ishly.** — *ns.* **slāv′ishness; slāvoc′racy** slave-owners collectively: their power, interests, etc.; **slāv′ocrat.** — **slave′-ant** an ant kept as a worker in a community of another species. — *adj.* **slave′-born** born in slavery. — **slave′-driver** one who superintends slaves at their work: a hard taskmaster; **slave′-fork** a long and heavy forked branch fixed on a slave's neck to prevent escape. — *adj.* **slave′-grown** grown by slave-labour. — **slave′-holder** an owner of slaves; **slave′-holding; slave′-hunt** a hunt after runaway slaves or after persons to enslave; **slave′-labour; slave′-owner, -owning; slave′-ship** a ship used for transporting slaves; **slave states** those states of the American Union which maintained domestic slavery before the Civil War — Delaware, Maryland, Virginia, North and South Carolina, Georgia, Florida, Alabama, Mississippi, Louisiana, Texas, Arkansas, Missouri, Kentucky, and Tennessee; **slave′-trade, -traff′ic** the buying and selling of slaves; **slave′-trader, -traff′icker.** [O.Fr. (Fr.) *esclave*, orig. a Slav.]

slaver[1] *slav′ər* (*Scot.* *slāv′ər*), *n.* spittle running from the mouth. — *v.i.* to let spittle run out of the mouth: to drivel: to fawn. — *v.t.* to beslobber. — *n.* **slav′erer.** — *adj.* **slav′ering.** — *adv.* **slav′eringly.** — *adj.* **slav′ery** slabbery. [Akin to **slabber**.]

salver[2]. See **slave**.

slavocracy, -crat. See **slave**.

Slavonian, Slavonic, etc. See **Slav**.

slaw *slö, n.* cabbage salad. [Du. *sla* — *salade*.]

slay *slā, v.t.* and *v.i.* to kill: — *pa.t.* **slew** (*slōō*); *pa.p.* **slain** (*slān*). — *v.t.* (*coll.*) to amuse very much: to impress very much: — *pa.t.* **slayed,** sometimes **slew;** *pa.p.* **slayed,** rarely **slain.** — *n.* **slay′er.** [O.E. *slēan,* to strike, to kill; O.N. *slā,* Goth. *slahan,* Ger. *schlagen,* to strike.]

sleave *slēv, n.* (*Shak.*) a fine filament that can be separated from a silk fibre. — *v.t.* (*dial.*) to separate, as threads. — *adj.* **sleaved** used in the term **sleaved silk,** floss silk. [O.E. *slæfan,* to divide.]

sleazy *slē′zi, adj.* flimsy: slatternly (*coll.*): squalid (*coll.*). — *n.* **sleaze** (*back-formation*) sleaziness (*coll.*). — *adv.* **sleaz′ily.** — *n.* **slea′ziness.** [Origin doubtful.]

sled *sled, n.* a sledge, esp. a small sledge: a drag or wheelless structure for conveying goods, formerly for taking the condemned to execution. — *v.t.* to convey by sled. — *v.i.* to go on a sled: — *pr.p.* **sledd′ing;** *pa.t.* and *pa.p.* **sledd′ed.** — *adj.* **sledd′ed** (*Shak.*) having sleds. — *n.* **sledd′ing.** [M.Du. or M.L.G. *sledde;* Ger. *Schlitte,* O.N. *slethi;* cf. **sledge**[1], **sleigh, slide**.]

sleded. See **sleided**.

sledge[1] *slej, n.* carriage with runners for sliding on snow: framework without wheels for dragging goods along: iron- or flint-studded board for threshing corn. — *v.t., v.i.* to convey, or to travel, by sledge. — *ns.* **sledg′er; sledg′ing.** — **sledge′-chair** chair on runners for ice. [M.Du. *sleedse;* cf. **sled**.]

sledge[2] *slej, n.* a large heavy hammer. — Also **sledge′-hammer.** — *n.* **sledg′ing** (*cricket slang, esp. Austr.*) the practice of baiting a batsman in order to spoil his concentration. [O.E. *slecg* — *slēan,* to strike, slay.]

slee *slē,* Scots form of **sly**.

sleech *slēch, n.* slimy mud: a mud-flat. — *adj.* **sleech′y.** [Origin uncertain.]

sleek *slēk, adj.* smooth: glossy: having an oily, plastered-down look: insinuating, plausible: slick: prosperous in appearance. — *v.t.* to make smooth or glossy: to calm or soothe. — *v.i.* to glide. — *adv.* smoothly, oilily. — *v.t.* **sleek′en** to sleek. — *ns.* **sleek′er** a slicker; **sleek′ing.** — *adj.* **sleek′it** (*Scot.*) smooth: sly, cunning, fair-spoken. — *adv.* **sleek′ly.** — *n.* **sleek′ness.** — *adj.* **sleek′y** smooth: sly, untrustworthy. — *adj.* **sleek′-headed.** — **sleek′stone** a polishing stone. [A later form of **slick**.]

sleep *slēp, v.i.* to take rest by relaxation of consciousness: to slumber: to be motionless, inactive, or dormant: to appear still or restful: to take or have the nocturnal position (*bot.*): to be dead: to rest in the grave: to be numb: (of a top) to spin steadily without movement of the axis. — *v.t.* to be in the state of (with *sleep,* etc., as cognate object): to render, make, put, by sleep: to outsleep: to afford sleeping accommodation for: — *pa.t.* and *pa.p.* **slept** (*slept*). — *n.* the state of being asleep: a spell of sleeping: dormancy: vertical disposition of leaves at night (*bot.*): mucous matter which collects at the corners of the eyes (*coll.*). — *n.* **sleep′er** one who sleeps: a horizontal beam supporting and spreading a weight: a support for railway rails: a sleeping-car: a compartment or berth in a sleeping-coach: a Communist (or other) agent who spends a long time (often years) establishing himself as an inoffensive citizen preparing for the moment when he will be required to pass on a particular vital piece of information, etc.: a record, film, etc. which becomes popular after an initial period of not being so (*coll.*). — *adj.* (*Scot.*) **sleep′(e)ry** sleepy. — *adv.* **sleep′ily.** — *ns.* **sleep′iness; sleep′ing** sleep: abeyance. — *adj.* in a state of, occupied with, or for, sleeping: dormant. — *adj.* **sleep′less** without sleep: unable to sleep. — *adv.* **sleep′lessly.** — *n.* **sleep′lessness.** — *adj.* **sleep′y** inclined to sleep: drowsy: inducing or suggesting sleep: partially decayed internally, esp. of a pear, soft and lacking juice. — **sleep′ing-bag** a bag for sleeping in, used by travellers, campers, etc.; **sleep′ing-berth; sleep′ing-car, -carr′iage, -coach** a railway-carriage with berths for sleeping in; **sleep′ing-draught** a drink to induce sleep; **sleep′ing-part′ner** one who has money invested in a business but takes no part in management; **sleep′ing-pill** one containing a sleep-inducing drug; **sleeping policeman** a low hump across a road intended to slow down traffic; **sleep′ing-sick′ness** a deadly disease of tropical Africa, characterised by headache, great drowsiness, and exhaustion, caused by a trypanosome introduced by the bite of a tsetse-fly: sometimes erroneously applied to sleepy-sickness; **sleep′-learn′ing** see **hypnopaedia; sleep′-out** (*Austr.* and *N.Z.*) a partitioned-off section of a veranda for use as a sleeping area; **sleep′-walk′er** a somnambulist; **sleep′-walk′ing; sleep′y-head** a lazy, or sleepy-looking person; **Sleepy Hollow** a very quiet place, from *A Legend of Sleepy Hollow,* by Washington Irving; **sleep′y-sick′ness** encephalitis lethargica: formerly applied to sleeping-sickness. — **get to sleep** to manage to fall asleep; **go to sleep** to fall asleep: to become numb; **in one's sleep** while asleep; **on sleep** (*B.*) asleep; **put to sleep** to anaesthetise: to kill (an animal) painlessly; **sleep around** to be sexually promiscuous; **sleep in** to oversleep: to sleep later than usual; **sleep off** to recover from by sleeping; **sleep on** to consider overnight, postpone a decision on; **sleep together** to have sexual relations with each other; **sleep with** to have sexual relations with. [O.E. *slæpan* (vb.), *slæp* (n.); Ger. *Schlaf,* Goth. *slēps.*]

sleet *slēt, n.* rain mingled with snow or hail: a coating of ice formed when rain or sleet freezes on a cold surface. — *v.i.* to hail or snow with rain mingled. — *n.* **sleet′iness.** — *adj.* **sleet′y.** [Prob. an unrecorded O.E. (Anglian) *slēt;* Ger. *Schlosse,* a hail-stone.]

sleeve *slēv, n.* a covering for the arm: a tube into which a rod or other tube is inserted: a tube, esp. of a different metal, fitted inside a metal cylinder or tube, as protection or to decrease the diameter (*engineering*): a thin covering, container for a gramophone record: a windsock: a drogue. — *v.t.* to furnish with sleeves. — *adjs.* **sleeved** with sleeves: (in composition **-sleeved**) with sleeves of a stated type; **sleeve′less** without sleeves: futile, vain (see **errand**). — *n.* **sleev′er** an old esp. Welsh measure for beer, containing about three quarters of a pint: a straight-sided beer-glass; **sleev′ing** tubula...

flexible insulation for threading over bare conductors. **sleeve'-board** a board for ironing sleeves; **sleeve'-button** a button or stud for the wristband or cuff; **sleeve'-dog** a little dog that could be carried in the sleeve; **sleeve'-fish** the squid; **sleeve'hand** (*Shak.*) a wristband; **sleeve'-link** two buttons joined by a link for fastening a shirt-cuff; **sleeve'-notes** the text on a record sleeve; **sleeve'-nut** a double-nut for attaching the joint-ends of rods or tubes; **sleeve(d) waistcoat** a waistcoat with long sleeves, worn by porters, boots, etc. — **hang, pin,** (oneself, belief, etc.) **on a person's sleeve** to rely, or make depend, entirely upon him, her: to attribute to him, her (*Milt.*): see also **pin; laugh in,** or **up, one's sleeve** to laugh privately or unperceived; **up one's sleeve** in secret reserve; **roll up one's sleeves** to get down wholeheartedly to a job, esp. an unattractive manual one; **wear one's heart on one's sleeve** see **heart.** [O.E. (Anglian) *slēfe* (W.S. *sliefe*).]

sleezy. Same as **sleazy.**

sleided, sleded *slēd'id*, (*Shak.*) adj. app. irregular forms of **sleaved.**

sleigh *slā, n.* (esp. in *U.S.* and *Canada*) a sledge. — *v.i.* to travel by sleigh. — *n.* **sleigh'ing.** — **sleigh'-bell** a small bell attached to a sleigh or its harness. [Du. *slee.*]

sleight (*obs.* **slight**) *slīt, n.* cunning: dexterity: an artful trick: a juggling trick: trickery: a design, device, pattern (*Spens.*). — **sleight'-of-hand'** legerdemain. — Also adj. [O.N. *slægth*, cunning, *slægr*, sly.]

slender *slen'dər*, adj. thin or narrow: slim: slight. — *v.t.* and *v.i.* **slen'derise, -ize** to make or become slender. — *adv.* **slen'derly.** — *n.* **slen'derness.** [Origin obscure.]

slept *slept, pa.t.* and *pa.p.* of **sleep.**

sleuth *slooth, n.* a track or trail: a bloodhound: a relentless tracker, a detective. — *v.t.* and *v.i.* to track. — **sleuth'-hound** a bloodhound: a detective. [O.N. *slōth*, track.]

slew[1] *sloo, pa.t.* of **slay.**

slew[2]**, slue** *sloo, v.t.* and *v.i.* to turn about the axis: to swing round. — *n.* a turn, twist, swing round: a position so taken. — *adj.* **slewed, slued** (*slang*) tipsy. [First recorded as a sailor's word: origin unknown.]

slew[3]**, slue** *sloo,* (*U.S. coll.*) *n.* a large number or amount. [Ir. *slua*, a multitude.]

sley *slā, n.* a weaver's reed. [O.E. *slege* — *slēan*, to strike.]

slice *slīs, n.* a thin broad piece: a flat or broad-bladed instrument of various kinds, esp. a broad knife for serving fish: a slash: a sliced stroke (*golf*): a share (*coll.*): a representative section. — *v.t.* to cut into slices: to cut a slice from: to cut as a slice: in golf, to strike or play so as to send the ball curving to the right (left in left-hand play). — *v.i.* to slash: to cut in the manner of slicing: (of a boat) to move through the water in such a manner: to slice a stroke. — *n.* **slī'cer.** — *n.* and *adj.* **slī'cing.** [O.Fr. *esclice* — O.H.G. *slīzan*, to split.]

slick *slik, adj.* sleek: smooth: smooth-tongued: glib: adroit: trim. — *adv.* smoothly: glibly: deftly: quickly: altogether. — *n.* a smooth place or surface: a slicker: a film of spilt oil: a glossy magazine. — *v.t.* to polish, make glossy: to tidy up: to smooth (hair; with *back* or *down*). — *v.t.* **slick'en** to smooth, polish. — *ns.* **slick'er** a smoothing tool: a waterproof, esp. oilskin (*U.S.*): a swindler: shifty person: a sophisticated city-dweller; **slick'ing.** — *adv.* **slick'ly.** — *n.* **slick'ness.** — **slick'enside** (*geol.*) a smooth, polished or striated surface produced by friction. — *adj.* **slick'ensided.** — **slick'stone** a sleek-stone. [M.E. *sliken* — O.E. *slician*, (in composition) to smooth.]

slid, slidden. See **slide.**

'slid *slid,* (*arch.*) *interj.* for **god's lid** (eyelid).

slidder *slid'ər, v.i.* to slip, slide. — *n.* a steep path or trench down a hillside. — *adj.* **slidd'ery** slippery. [O.E. *slidor*, slippery, *sliderian*, to slip.]

slide *slīd, v.i.* to slip or glide: to pass along smoothly: to glide in a standing position (without skates or snow-shoes) over ice or other slippery surface: to lapse: to

pass quietly, smoothly, or gradually: to take its own course: to decamp (*coll.*). — *v.t.* to thrust along glidingly: to slip: — *pa.t.* **slīd,** *obs.* **slīd'ed,** *Scot.* **slāde, slaid;** *pa.p.* **slīd,** *obs.* **slīd'ed,** *rare* **slīdd'en.** — *n.* a slip: a polished slippery track (on ice): a chute or shoot: a slippery sloping surface in a park for children to slide down: a bed, groove, rail, etc., on or in which a thing slides: a sliding part, e.g. of a trombone: a sliding clasp: a slip for mounting objects for the microscope: a case (*dark slide*) for photographic plates or its sliding cover: a picture for projection on a screen: a sliding lid: a sledge: a runner: a sliding seat: a landslip: a gliding from one note to another (*mus.*): a falling in value. — *ns.* **slīd'er** one who, or that which, slides: a sliding part: ice-cream between wafers (*Scot.*): a red-bellied terrapin. — *n.* and *adj.* **slīd'ing.** — *adv.* **slīd'ingly.** — **slide'-rest** an apparatus for carrying the cutting-tool of a lathe, etc.; **slide'-rule** a mechanical calculating device consisting of two logarithmic graduated scales sliding one against the other (also **slid'ing-rule**); **slide trombone** a trombone; **slide'-valve** a valve in which openings are covered and uncovered by a sliding part; **slid'ing-keel** a centreboard; **sliding scale** a scale, e.g. of duties, varying according to variation in something else, e.g. prices: a slide-rule; **sliding seat** a racing-boat seat, moving with the swing of the rower's body. — **let slide** to take no action over. [O.E. *slīdan*, to slide.]

'slife *slīf,* **'slight** *slīt,* (*arch.*) *interjs.* for **God's life, light.**

slight[1] *slīt, adj.* smooth (*obs.*): flimsy: lacking solidity, massiveness, weight, significance: slim: slender: trifling: small: slighting (*obs.*). — *adv.* slightly: slightingly, meanly. — *v.t.* to smooth (*obs.*): to raze, level to the ground (*arch.*): to ignore or overlook disrespectfully: to insult: to toss contemptuously (*Shak.*). — *n.* contemptuous indifference: discourteous disregard: an affront by showing neglect or want of respect. — *adv.* **slight'ingly.** — *adj.* **slight'ish.** — *adv.* **slight'ly.** — *n.* **slight'ness.** — **(not) in the slightest** (not) at all; **slight off** (*Shak.*) to put off, set aside, with contempt; **slight over** to ignore. [Cf. O.E. *eorthslihtes*, close to the ground; O.N. *slēttr*, O.L.G. *slicht*, plain, Du. *slecht*, bad, Ger. *schlecht*, bad.]

slight[2]. Old spelling of **sleight.**

slily *slī'li, adv.* See under **sly.**

slim *slim, adj.* very thin: slender: slight: crafty (reintroduced from Afrik., now again *rare*). — *compar.* **slimm'er,** *superl.* **slimm'est.** — *v.t.* to make thin: to decrease (*fig.*). — *v.i.* to use means to become more slender: — *pr.p.* **slimm'ing;** *pa.t.* and *pa.p.* **slimmed.** — *adv.* **slim'ly.** — *ns.* **slimm'er; slimm'ing.** — *adj.* **slimm'ish.** — *n.* **slim'ness.** — *adjs.* **slim'sy** (*U.S.*) frail, flimsy; **slim'line** slim, or conducive to slimness (also *fig.*). — **slimmers' disease** anorexia nervosa. [Du., L.G., Fris. *slim*, crafty; Dan. *slem*, worthless, Ger. *schlimm*, bad.]

slime *slīm, n.* ooze: very fine, thin, slippery, or gluey mud: bitumen: any viscous organic secretion, as mucus: matter, esp. as forming the human body: moral filth: obsequiousness: (in *pl.*) finely crushed ore in mud form. — *v.t.* to smear or cover with slime: to grind to slime: to clear of slime. — *v.i.* to go slimily. — *adv.* **slim'ily.** — *n.* **slim'iness.** — *adj.* **slim'y** viscous: covered with slime: disgusting: obsequiously servile. — **slime fungus, slime mould** a myxomycete; **slime'-pit** a hole where bitumen is got: a pit for receiving metallic slimes. [O.E. *slīm*; Ger. *Schleim.*]

sling[1] *sling, n.* a strap or pocket with a string attached to each end, for hurling a stone: a catapult: a ballista: a loop for hoisting, lowering, or carrying a weight: a hanging support for an injured arm or foot: an attached strap for carrying: a throw: a sweep or swing. — *v.t.* to throw with a sling: to hang loosely: to move or swing by means of a rope: to hurl, toss, fling (*coll.*): to utter, to pass (*slang*). — *v.i.* to discharge stones from a sling: to bound along with swinging steps: — *pa.t.* and *pa.p.* **slung.** — *n.* **sling'er.** — **sling'-back** a sling-back shoe; **sling'-fruit** a fruit that ejects its seeds by elastic tissue; **sling'shot** (*U.S.*) a catapult; **sling'stone** a stone to be thrown from a sling. — **sling-back(ed) shoe** one from which the back is absent except for a strap representing the top edge; **sling ink** to write for the press; **sling off at** (*Austr.* and *N.Z. coll.*) to jeer at; **sling one's hook** (*slang*) to go away, remove oneself. [Prob. from several sources; cf. O.N. *slyngva*, to fling, O.E. *slingan*, to wind, twist, L.G. *sling*, noose.] **sling²** *sling, n.* an American drink, spirits and water sweetened and flavoured. [Perh. foregoing in sense of toss off; poss. Ger. *schlingen*, to swallow.] **slink** *slingk, v.i.* to go sneakingly: to miscarry. — *v.t.* to slip: to droop: to cast prematurely: — *pa.t.* and *pa.p.* **slunk.** — *n.* a prematurely born calf or other animal: its flesh or hide: a bastard child: a slinking gait. — *adj.* prematurely born: lean, starved: mean. — *n.* **slink'er.** — *adj.* **slink'y** slinking: lean: sinuous: close-fitting. — **slink'-butch'er** a dealer in slink and diseased meat; **slink'skin** the skin of a slink, or leather made from it; **slink'weed** rose-bay willow-herb or other plant believed to cause cows to slink. [O.E. *slincan*; L.G. *slinken.*]

slip¹ *slip, v.i.* to escape: to pass quietly, easily, unobtrusively, or stealthily: to glide: to get out of position accidentally: to slide, esp. accidentally: to lose one's former skill, grip, or control of the situation (*coll.*): to lose one's footing: to make a slight mistake from inadvertence rather than ignorance: to lapse morally. — *v.t.* to cause or allow to slide: to put with a sliding motion: to convey quietly or secretly: to let pass: to let slip: to cast: to disengage: to let loose: to escape from: to elude: to cast prematurely, slink: to dislocate: — *pr.p.* **slipp'ing;** *pa.t.* and *pa.p.* **slipped,** sometimes **slipt.** — *n.* an act of slipping: a mistake from inadvertence: a slight error or transgression: an escape: an inclined plane, sloping down to the water: a slight dislocation: a landslip: a pillow-case: a garment easily slipped on, esp. one worn under a dress, a petticoat: a leash: the difference between the pitch of a propeller and the distance actually travelled: any of three fielders (*first slip, second slip, third slip*) positioned on the off side somewhat behind the wicket-keeper or (often in *pl.*) their position (*cricket*): a sledge-runner: (in *pl.*) the place at the side of the stage for slipping scenery from: the side of a theatre gallery. — *n.* **slipp'age** (the extent of) failure to reach a set target: act, instance or amount of slipping. — *adj.* **slipp'er** (*Spens., Shak.*) slippery. — *n.* a loose shoe easily slipped on: a skid for a wheel: a sledge-runner: one who slips (e.g. greyhounds). — *v.t.* to furnish with slippers: to beat with a slipper. — *adj.* **slipp'ered.** — *adv.* **slipp'erily.** — *ns.* **slipp'eriness, slipp'-iness.** — *adjs.* **slipp'ery, slipp'y** so smooth or slimy as to allow or cause slipping: elusive: evasive: apt to slip: unstable: uncertain. — **slip angle** attitude angle; **slip'-board** a board sliding in grooves; **slip'-carriage, -coach** a railway carriage that can be detached without stopping the train; **slip'-case** a box-like case for a book or set of books, open at one end to leave the spine(s) visible; **slip'-dock** a dock with a slipway; **slip form** (*building*) a form that can be moved slowly as work progresses (*adj.* **slip'form**); **slipform paver** a machine for laying continuously a concrete road surface; **slip'-knot** a knot that slips along a rope: a knot untied by pulling. — *adjs.* **slip'-on, slip'-over** slipped on or over: slipped over the head without unbuttoning. — *ns.* a garment easily slipped on: one slipped over the head. — **slipped disc** see **disc**; **slipper animalcule** Paramecium; **slipper bath** a partially covered bath, shaped like a slipper: one of a number of single baths for hire at public baths; **slipper limpet** an American mollusc (Crepidula) with somewhat slipper-like shell; **slipper satin** fine satin with a dull finish; **slipper socks** thick esp. patterned socks reinforced with a leather, etc. sole, for use as slippers; **slipp'erwort** calceolaria; **slippery elm** a N. American elm: its mucilaginous bark used as a demulcent; **slip'rail** (*Austr.*) a movable rail serving as a gate: a gap so closed; **slip road** a local bypass: a road by which vehicles come off on or on to a motorway. —

adj. **slip'shod** shod with slippers, or with shoes down at the heel: slovenly: careless, carelessly executed. — **slip'-shoe** (*obs.*) a slipper; **slip stitch** a concealed sewing stitch used on hems, facings, etc. in which only a few threads of the material forming the main body of the garment are caught up by the needle for each stitch; **slip stream, slip'stream** the stream of air driven back by an aircraft propeller or the stream of air behind any moving vehicle or other object; **slip'-string** a crack-halter. — Also *adj.* — **slip'-up** (*coll.*) an error or failure; **slip'way** a pier in a dock or shipyard that slopes down into the water. — **give someone the slip** to escape stealthily from someone; **let slip** to reveal accidentally: to miss (an opportunity); **look slippy** (*coll.*, esp. *imper.*) to be quick, hurry; **slip off** to fall off: to take off quickly: go away quietly; **slip of the tongue** or **pen** a word, etc. said, or written, in error when something else was intended; **slip on** to put on loosely or in haste; **slip one's ways** (*Scot.*) to make one's way quietly; **slip the cable** to let it go overboard instead of waiting to weigh the anchor: to die; **slip up** to make a mistake, to fail (*coll.*): to deceive, disappoint (*Austr.*). [Perh. L.G. or Du. *slippen*; but O.E. has *slipor*, slippery, *slỹpescōh*, slipper.]

slip² *slip, (obs.) n.* a counterfeit coin. [Perh. **slip¹.**]

slip³ *slip, n.* a scion, cutting: a scion, descendant: a young or slender person: a young pig (*dial., Austr.*): a small sole (fish): a strip: anything slender or narrow: a small piece of paper, etc., for a memorandum, or for indexing, etc.: a galley-proof: a memorandum giving details of the kind of cover required, to be signed by the underwriters (*insurance*). — *v.t.* to take cuttings from: to tear obliquely (*her.*). [Perh. M.Du. or M.L.G. *slippe*, strip.]

slip⁴ *slip, n.* a creamy paste for coating and decorating pottery. — **slip'ware** pottery decorated with slip. [O.E. *slipa, slypa,* slime, paste.]

slipe *slīp, n.* in mining, a skip or sledge: a runner. [App. L.G. *slīpe.*]

slippage, slipper, slippery, etc. See **slip¹.**

slipslop *slip'slop, n.* sloppy stuff: twaddle: a malapropism (from Mrs *Slipslop* in Fielding's *Joseph Andrews*): one who commits malapropisms: a loose sandal. — *adj.* **slip'sloppy.**

slipt. See **slip¹.**

slish *slish, (Shak.) n.* a cut. [**slash.**]

slit *slit, v.t.* to cut lengthwise: to split: to cut into strips: — *pr.p.* **slitt'ing;** *pa.t.* and *pa.p.* **slit.** — *n.* a long cut: a narrow opening. — *adj.* cut lengthwise: cut open: having a slit. — *n.* **slitt'er.** — **slit'-pocket** an overcoat pocket with a slit to give access to a pocket within; **slit'-trench** (*mil.*) a narrow trench for one or more people. [M.E. *slitten,* app. related to O.E. *slītan;* Ger. *schlitzen.*]

slither *slidh'ər, v.i.* to slide, esp. interruptedly. — *adj.* slippery. — *n.* a scree. — *adj.* **slith'ery** slippery. [slidder.]

slive *slīv, (dial.) v.t.* and *v.i.* to slip: — *pa.t.* **slove, slived;** *pa.p.* **slived, sliven** (*sliv'ən*). [Cf. O.E. *slēfan,* to slip (on).]

sliver *sliv'ər,* or *slī'vər, v.t.* to split, to tear off lengthwise, to slice. — *n.* a piece cut or rent off, a slice, splinter: a continuous strand of loose untwisted wool or other fibre. [O.E. (*tō-*)*slīfan,* to cleave.]

slivovitz *sliv'ə-vits, n.* a dry plum brandy. — Also **sliv'-ovic(a)** (*-vits(-ə*)), **sliv'owitz.** [Serbo-Croatian *šljivovica* — *šljiva,* plum.]

sloan *slōn, (Scot.) n.* a snub: a reproof. [Ety. dub.]

Sloane Ranger *slōn rān'jər,* a young person, typically upper-(middle-)class and female, favouring expensively casual clothing suggestive of rural pursuits, speaking in distinctively clipped tones, evincing certain predictable enthusiasms and prejudices and resident (during the week) in the *Sloane* Square area of London or a comparable part. — Also **Sloane.** [Coined in mid-1970s by P. Yorke, punning on *The Lone Ranger,* a television cowboy hero.]

slob *slob, n.* mud: ooze: mud-flat: a sloven: a boor (*slang*): a person of wealth but no refinement (*slang*). — *adj.* **slobb'y.** — **slob'land** a mud flat: reclaimed alluvial land. [Ir. *slab*.]

slobber *slob'ər, v.t.* and *v.i.* to slabber. — *adj.* **slobb'ery.** [Cf. Du. *slobberen,* to eat or work in a slovenly way; **slabber, slubber.**]

slockdolager, -iger, -oger. See **sockdologer.**

slocken, sloken *slok'n, slōk'n,* (*Scot.*) *vs.t.* to quench: to slake: to moisten: to extinguish. [O.N. *slokna,* to go out.]

sloe *slō, n.* the blackthorn fruit or bush. — *adj.* of blackthorn wood: made with sloes: black. — **sloe'bush.** — *adj.* **sloe'-eyed** dark-eyed, slant-eyed, or both. — **sloe'-gin** a liqueur made from sloes; **sloe'thorn, sloe'-tree.** [O.E. *slā, slāg, slāh;* Du. *slee.*]

slog *slog, v.t.* and *v.i.* to hit hard. — *v.i.* to work or walk doggedly: — *pr.p.* **slogg'ing;** *pa.t.* and *pa.p.* **slogged.** — *n.* a hard blow (generally with little regard to direction): a strenuous spell of work: something which requires strenuous, esp. protracted, effort. — *n.* **slogg'er.** [Origin uncertain.]

slogan *slō'gən, n.* a clan war-cry: a party catchword: an advertising catch-phrase. — *n.* **sloganeer'** an enthusiastic inventor and user of slogans. — *v.i* to invent or make heavy use of slogans. — *n.* **sloganeer'ing.** — *v.i.* **slo'ganise, -ize** to utter or repeat slogans, esp. as a substitute for reasoned discussion. — *n.* **slo'ganising, -z-.** [Earlier **slog(h)orne, sloggorne;** said to be from Gael. *sluagh,* army, *gairm,* cry; see **slughorn(e).**]

sloid. See **sloyd.**

sloken. See **slocken.**

sloom *slōōm,* (*Northern*) *n.* slumber. — *v.i.* to slumber. — *adj.* **sloom'y.** [O.E. *slūma.*]

sloop *slōōp, n.* a light boat: a one-masted cutter-rigged vessel, differing from a cutter in having a fixed bowsprit and proportionally smaller sails: (also **sloop'-of-war**) formerly a vessel, of whatever rig, between a corvette and a gun vessel, under a commander, carrying from ten to eighteen guns. [Du. *sloep;* cf. **shallop.**]

sloot. See **sluit.**

slop[1] *slop, n.* slush: spilled liquid: a puddle: (in *pl.*) liquid refuse: (in *pl.*) weak or insipid liquor or semi-liquid food: (in *pl.*) gush, wishy-washy sentiment. — *v.t.* and *v.i.* to spill: to splash with slops: to slobber. — *v.t.* to wash away. — *v.i.* to walk in slush: — *pr.p.* **slopp'ing;** *pa.t.* and *pa.p.* **slopped.** — *adv.* **slopp'ily.** — *n.* **slopp'iness.** — *adj.* **slopp'y** wet: muddy: wishy-washy, watery: slipshod (of work or language): sentimental: maudlin. — **slop'-basin, -bowl** a basin for slops at table; **slop'-pail** a pail for removing bedroom slops. — **slop out** (of a prisoner) to take away and empty out one's slops: to take slops from (a cell). [O.E. (*cū-*)*sloppe,* (cow-) droppings (cowslip) — *slūpan,* to slip.]

slop[2] *slop, n.* a loose garment — gown, cassock, smock-frock, etc.: (in *pl.*) wide baggy trousers or breeches: the wide part of these: (in *pl.*) ready-made clothing: (in *pl.*) clothes and bedding issued to seamen. — *adj.* **slop'-built** jerry-built. — **slop'-clothing; slop'-pouch; Sloppy Joe** (*slang*) a large, loose sweater: a runny mixture of minced beef and sauce served on a half roll (*U.S.*); **slop'-seller; slop'-shop** a shop for ready-made clothes; **slop'work** the making of slop-clothing: cheap inferior work. [Cf. O.E. *oferslop,* loose outer garment; M.Du. *slop;* O.N. *sloppr.*]

slop[3] *slop, n.* a policeman. [Back-slang.]

slope *slōp, n.* an incline: an inclined surface: an inclined position: an inclination, upward or downward slant. — *adj.* slanting (*poet.*): moving aslope (*Milt.*). — *adv.* aslant. — *v.t.* to form with a slope, or obliquely: to put in a sloping position: to turn downwards, bow. — *v.i.* to have or take a sloping position or direction: to move down a slope: to decamp, disappear (*slang*). — *adv.* **slope'wise** obliquely. — *adj.* **slop'ing.** — *adv.* **slop'ingly.** — *adj.* **slop'y** sloping. — **at the slope** (of a rifle) on the shoulder with the barrel sloping back and up; **slope arms** to place or hold in this position; **slope**

off (*slang*) to go away, esp. suddenly or furtively. [Aphetic from **aslope.**]

sloppy. See **slop[1,2].**

slops. See **slop[1,2].**

slosh *slosh, n.* slush: a watery mess: a heavy blow (*slang*). — *v.i.* to flounder or splash in slush: to loaf around (*U.S.*): to hit (*slang*). — *v.t.* to splash: to smite, beat (*slang*). — *adjs.* **sloshed** (*coll.*) intoxicated; **slosh'y.** [**slush.**]

slot[1] *slot, n.* a bar or bolt: a crosspiece that holds other parts together. [L.G. or Du. *slot,* lock.]

slot[2] *slot, n.* the hollow down the middle of the breast, cleavage (now *Scot.*): a long narrow depression or opening, as one to receive a coin, an armature winding, or part of a mechanism, or opening into the conduit of an electric or cable tramway or railway: a slit: a (usu. regular) place or position in e.g. a radio or television programme: a niche in an organisation. — *v.t.* to make a slot in, furnish with a slot: to pass through a slot: to put into a slot: to fit into a small space (*lit.* or *fig.;* with *in* or *into*). — *v.i.* (with *in* or *into*) to fit into a slot in something: to fit into a story, etc. (*fig.*): — *pr.p.* **slott'ing;** *pa.t.* and *pa.p.* **slott'ed.** — *n.* **slott'er** a person or machine that cuts slots. — **slot'-machine'** one operated by inserting a coin in a slot, as a vending machine or (*U.S.*) a fruit machine; **slott'ing-machine'** machine for cutting slots. — **slot-car racing** racing on a track by tiny model cars powered and controlled electrically. [O.Fr. *esclot.*]

slot[3] *slot, n.* track, esp. a deer's footprints. — *v.t.* to track. [O.Fr. *esclot* — O.N. *slōth;* cf. **sleuth.**]

sloth *slōth,* or *sloth, n.* laziness, sluggishness: a sluggish arboreal tropical American edentate. — *v.t.* and *v.i.* to pass, spend (time) in sloth. — *adj.* **sloth'ful** given to sloth: inactive: lazy. — *adv.* **sloth'fully.** — *n.* **sloth'fulness.** — **sloth'-bear** a black Indian bear, with prolonged snout and lips. [M.E. *slawthe,* altered from O.E. *slǣwth* — *slāw,* slow.]

slouch *slowch, n.* an awkward lubberly clown: an inefficient person (*U.S. slang*): a slouch-hat: a droop: a stoop: a loose, ungainly stooping gait. — *adj.* drooping. — *v.i.* to go or bear oneself slouchingly: to droop. — *v.t.* to turn down the brim of. — *n.* **slouch'er.** — *adjs.* **slouch'ing; slouch'y.** — **slouch'-hat** a soft, broad-brimmed hat. — *adj.* **slouch'-hatt'ed.** [Cf. O.N. *slōkr,* a slouching fellow.]

slough[1] *slow, n.* a hollow filled with mud: a marsh: (*slōō*) a backwater, a marshland creek (*U.S.*). — *adj.* **sloughed** (*slowd*) bogged, swallowed in a slough. — *adj.* **slough'y.** — **the Slough of Despond** (the state of) extreme despondency, great depression. [O.E. *sloh.*]

slough[2] *sluf, n.* a cast skin: a coating: dead tissue in a sore. — *v.i.* to come away as a slough (with *off*): to cast the skin: to develop a slough. — *v.t.* to cast off, as a slough. — *adj.* **slough'y.** [M.E. *sloh;* origin uncertain.]

Slovak *slō'vak, slō-vak', n.* a member of a Slavonic people living E. of the Czechs: their language. — Also *adj.* — *adjs.* **Slovakian** (*-vak', -vāk'*), **Slovak'ish.** [Slovak *Slovák.*]

slove. See **slive.**

sloven *sluv'n, n.* a person, esp. a man, carelessly or dirtily dressed or slipshod in work. — Also *adj.* — *adj.* **slov'enlike.** — *n.* **slov'enliness.** — *adj.* and *adv.* **slov'enly.** — *n.* **slov'enry** (*Shak.*) slovenliness. [Cf. O.Du. *slof,* *sloef,* L.G. *sluf,* slow, indolent.]

Slovene *slō-vēn', slō', n.* a member of a branch of the Southern Slavs found chiefly in Slovenia, the northernmost constituent republic of Yugoslavia, and adjoining areas. — Also *adj.* — *n.* and *adj.* **Slovē'nian.** [O.Slav. *Slovēne.*]

slow *slō, adj.* not swift: late: behind in time: not hasty: not ready: not progressive: dull: for slow-moving traffic: (of business) slack: (of an oven, etc.) heating gently, cooking slowly: which lessens the speed of the ball, players, etc. (*sport*): acting, etc. slowly. — *n.* anything that is slow. — *adv.* slowly (also in compounds). — *v.t.* to delay, retard, slacken the speed of. — *v.i.* to slacken in speed. — *adj.* **slow′ish.** — *n.* **slow′ing** a lessening of speed. — *adv.* **slow′ly.** — *n.* **slow′ness.** — **slow′back** a lazy lubber; **slow burn** a delayed but finally strong response, reaction, etc.; **slow′coach** a laggard: a sluggish person; **slow-down** see **slow down** below. — *adjs.* **slow′-foot, -ed** slow of pace; **slow′= gait′ed** (*Shak.*) accustomed to walk slowly. — **slow handclap** see **hand**; **slow march** a march at a slow pace. — *v.i.* **slow′-march.** — **slow′-match** a slowly burning rope for firing explosives. — *adjs.* **slow′-mo′tion** much slower than normal or (*cinematograph*) actual motion; **slow′-mov′ing; slow′-paced.** — **slow′poke** (esp. *U.S.*) an irritatingly slow person, a slowcoach. — *adjs.* **slow= release′** (of a medicinal capsule, etc.) releasing its active ingredient little by little over a period of time; **slow′= sight′ed; slow′-winged.** — **go slow, go-slow, go slow with** see **go**[1]; **slow down, up** to slow (*n.* **slow′-down**). [O.E. *slāw*; Du. *slee*, O.N. *sljor*.]

slow-hound *slō′hownd, n.* app. a form of **sleuth-hound**, assimilated to **slow.**

slow-worm *slō′wûrm, n.* the blindworm, a harmless snake-like legless lizard. [O.E. *slāwyrm*, prob. from root of *slēan*, to strike, *wyrm*, worm, assimilated to **slow.**]

sloyd, sloid *sloid, n.* a Swedish system of manual training by woodwork. [Sw. *slöjd*, dexterity; cf. **sleight.**]

slub[1], **slubb** *slub, v.t.* to twist after carding to prepare for spinning. — *n.* a roving. — *ns.* **slubb′er; slubb′ing.**

slub[2] *slub, n.* a lump in yarn. — *adj.* lumpy, knobbly in texture. — *adjs.* **slubbed, slubb′y.** [Origin obscure.]

slubb. See **slub**[1].

slubbed. See **slub**[2].

slubber[1] *slub′ər, v.t.* to smear, soil, daub: to perform hurriedly and carelessly, slur over: to gobble. — *v.i.* to wallow. — *n.* **slubberdegull′ion** a sloven. — *n.* and *adj.* **slubb′ering.** — *adv.* **slubb′eringly.** [Du. *slobberen*, to lap, L.G. *slubbern.*]

slubber[2]. See **slub**[1].

slubby. See **slub**[2].

sludge *sluj, n.* soft mud or mire: half-melted snow: a slimy precipitate, as from sewage: a dark yellowish or brownish green. — *adj.* **sludg′y** miry: muddy. [Cf. **slush.**]

slue. Same as **slew**[2,3].

slug[1] *slug, n.* a heavy, lazy fellow: a land-mollusc with shell rudimentary or absent: a sea-slug: anything slow-moving. — *v.i.* to be inert: to go sluggishly: to hunt for slugs. — *v.t.* to make sluggish. — *n.* **slugg′ard** one habitually inactive. — Also *adj.* — *v.t.* **slugg′ardise, -ize** (*Shak.*) to make lazy. — *adj.* **slugg′ish** habitually lazy: slothful: slow: inert. — *adv.* **slugg′ishly.** — *n.* **slugg′ishness.** — **slug′-a-bed, slugg′abed** (*Shak.*) one who lies long abed. [Cf. Norw. dial. *slugg*, a heavy body, *sluggje*, a slow heavy person, Sw. dial. *slogga*, to be sluggish.]

slug[2] *slug, n.* a lump of crude ore (*mining*): a lump of metal, esp. one for firing from a gun: a bullet: a metal token used in a slot machine: a solid line or section of type cast by a composing machine (*print.*): a strip of metal thicker than a lead, for separating type (*print.*): the gravitational unit of mass, approx. 32·174 pounds (= 14·5939 kg) in the **slug-foot-second** system (47·88 kg in slug-metre-second reckoning). [Perh. conn. with foregoing or following.]

slug[3] *slug, v.t.* and *v.i.* to slog: to fling heavily. — Also *n.* — *n.* **slugg′er.** — **slug′fest** (Ger. *Fest*, festival, celebration) a match, struggle, characterised by heavy blows. [Cf. **slog.**]

slug[4] *slug*, (now esp. *U.S.*) *n.* a gulp, a swallow: a dram. [Poss. Gael. *slug*, a gulp.]

sluggard, sluggish, etc. See **slug**[1].

slughorn(e) *slug′hörn, n.* an old form of **slogan**: by Chatterton (followed by Browning) imagined to be a musical instrument not unlike a hautboy, or a kind of clarion.

sluice *sloos, n.* a structure with a gate for stopping or regulating flow of water: a floodgate or water-gate: a regulated outlet or inlet: a drain, channel: a trough for washing gold from sand, etc.: a sluicing. — *v.t.* to let out or drain by a sluice: to wet or drench copiously: to wash in or by a sluice: to flush or swill by flinging water: to dash. — *adj.* **sluic′y** streaming as from a sluice: sluice-like: soaking. — **sluice′-gate.** [O.Fr. *escluse* (Fr. *écluse*) — L.L. *exclūsa* (*aqua*), a sluice, i.e. (water) shut out, pa.p. of L. *exclūdĕre*, to shut out.]

sluit *slü′it, slōōt,* (*S.Afr.*) *n.* a narrow water-channel. — Also **sloot.** [Du. *sloot*, ditch.]

slum[1] *slum, n.* an overcrowded squalid neighbourhood. — *v.i.* to visit slums, esp. for pleasure: (also *v.t.* with *it*) to adopt a lower standard of social behaviour, a less sophisticated level of cultural or intellectual activity, etc. than is or would be normal for oneself. — *ns.* **slumm′er; slumm′ing.** — *adj.* **slumm′y.** — **slum′-dweller.** [Cant.]

slum[2] *slum, n.* the non-lubricating part of crude oil.

slumber *slum′bər, v.i.* to sleep, esp. lightly: to be negligent or inactive. — *v.t.* to pass in slumber. — *n.* light sleep: repose. — *n.* **slum′berer.** — *adj.* **slum′berful.** — *n.* and *adj.* **slum′bering.** — *adv.* **slum′beringly.** — *adjs.* **slum′-berless; slum′b(e)rous** inviting or causing slumber: sleepy. — *adv.* **slum′b(e)rously.** — *adjs.* **slum′bersome; slum′b(e)ry** sleepy, drowsy. — **slum′berland** the state of slumber. [M.E. *slūmeren* — O.E. *slūma*, slumber.]

slummock *slum′ək, v.i.* to move awkwardly.

slummy. See **slum**[1].

slump[1] *slump, v.i.* to fall or sink suddenly into water or mud: to fail or fall through helplessly: (of prices, trade, etc.) to fall suddenly or heavily: to flop, clump: to plump. — *n.* a boggy place: a sinking into slush, etc.: the sound so made: a sudden or serious fall of prices, business, etc. — opp. to *boom.* — *adj.* **slump′y** marshy. — **slumpflā′tion** an economic situation in which there is a marked decline in investment in industry, at the same time as a marked rise in inflation. — *adj.* **slumpflā′tionary.** [Cf. Norw. *slumpe*, to slump, plump, L.G. *schlump*, marshy place.]

slump[2] *slump*, (*Scot.*) *v.t.* to throw into a lump or mass, to lump. — *v.i.* to flow lumpily. — *n.* a gross amount, a lump. — **slump sum** a lump sum. [Cf. L.G. *slump*, Du. *slomp*, mass.]

slung *slung, pa.t.* and *pa.p.* of **sling**[1]. — **slung′-shot** a weight attached to a cord, used as a weapon.

slunk *slungk, pa.t.* and *pa.p.* of **slink.**

slur *slûr, n.* thin mud (*dial.*): an aspersion, stain, imputation of blame: disparagement: discredit to one's reputation: a slight: a gliding movement in dancing (*obs.*): a gliding throw in cheating with dice (*obs.*): a blur: a running together resulting in indistinctness in writing or speech: a smooth or legato effect (*mus.*): a curved line indicating that notes are to be sung to one syllable, played with one bow, or with a smooth gliding effect. — *v.t.* to smear, besmirch (*dial.*): to disparage, asperse: to slip glidingly out of the dice-box (*obs.*): to cheat (*obs.*): to glide over slyly so as to mask or to avert attention: to blur: to sound indistinctly: to sing or play legato: to go through perfunctorily: — *pr.p.* **slurr′ing;** *pa.t.* and *pa.p.* **slurred.** — *adj.* **slurred.** — *n.* **slurr′y** (*slur′i*) a thin paste or semi-fluid mixture, as, for example, a thin liquid cement, liquid waste from farm animals, liquid waste or residue from mining, coal-washing, etc. [Origin obscure, perh. different words that have run together.]

slurb *slûrb, n.* an area combining the appearance and qualities of a *slum* and a *suburb.*

slurp *slûrp, v.t.* to drink (liquid) or eat (semi-liquid food) noisily. — *v.i.* to flow with, or produce, a slurp or slurps. — *n.* the noise produced by, or similar to that produced by, slurping food or drink. [Du. *slurpen, slorpen,* to sip audibly, gulp.]

slurry. See **slur.**

sluse. A Miltonic spelling of **sluice.**

slush *slush, n.* liquid mud: melting snow: a protective coating for metal: worthless sentimental drivel or gush. — *v.t.* to splash or cover with slush: to sluice, wash by throwing water: to fill the joints of with mortar (with *up*). — *v.i.* to splash in slush. — *adj.* **slush′y.** — **slush fund, money** (*slang*, orig. *U.S.*) a fund of money used, usu. corruptly, in political campaigning and propaganda, bribery, undeclared commissions, etc. [Cf. **slosh.**]

slut *slut, n.* a dirty, untidy woman: a wench, a jade: a bitch, female dog: a greased rag used as a candle. — *adj.* **slutt′ish.** — *adv.* **slutt′ishly.** — *ns.* **slutt′ishness, slutt′ery.** [Cf. Ger. dial. *schlutt(e)*.]

sly *slī, adj.* expert (*obs.* or *dial.*): cunningly made (*obs.*): skilful in doing anything so as to be unobserved: cunning: wily: secretive: surreptitious: done with artful dexterity: with hidden meaning: illicit (*Austr.*): — *compar.* **sly′er, sli′er;** *superl.* **sly′est, sli′est.** — *adj.* **sly′ish.** — *adv.* **sly′ly** (or **slī′ly**). — *n.* **sly′ness.** — **sly′boots** a sly or cunning person or animal. — **on the sly** surreptitiously. [O.N. *slægr*; cf. **sleight**; cf. Ger. *schlau*.]

slype *slīp, n.* a passage between walls: esp. a covered passage from a cloister between transept and chapter-house. [Perh. **slip**[3].]

sma *smö, (Scot.) adj.* small.

smack[1] *smak, n.* taste: a distinctive or distinguishable flavour: a trace, tinge: a mere tasting, enough to taste. — *v.i.* to have a taste (of): to savour (of): to have a suggestion or trace (of) (*fig.*). [O.E. *smæc.*]

smack[2] *smak, n.* a small decked or half-decked coaster or fishing-vessel, usu. rigged as cutter, sloop, or yawl: a fishing vessel containing a well in which fish can be kept alive (esp. *U.S.*). [Du. *smak*; Ger. *Schmacke*.]

smack[3] *smak, v.t.* to strike smartly, to slap loudly: to kiss roughly and noisily: to make a sharp noise with, as the lips by separation: to taste with relish or with smacking sound. — *v.i.* to make such a sound. — *n.* a sharp sound: a crack: a slap: a hearty kiss. — *adv.* sharply, straight. — *n.* **smack′er** (*slang*) a £1 (note): a dollar (bill): a kiss. — *n.* and *adj.* **smack′ing.** [Prob. imit.; Du. or L.G. *smakken*, to smite, Ger. *schmatzen*, to smack.]

smack[4] *smak, (slang) n.* heroin. [Perh. Yiddish *schmeck*, with same meaning.]

smacker, smacking. See **smack**[3].

smaik *smāk, (Scot.) n.* a contemptible fellow, rascal.

small *smöl, adj.* slender: narrow: fine in grain, texture, gauge, etc.: slight: little in size, extent, quantity, value, power, importance, or degree: unimposing, humble: ungenerous, petty, ignoble: dilute: short of full standard: operating on no great scale: soft or gentle in sound: minor. — *n.* a small thing, portion or piece: the narrow part (as of the back, the leg): small-coal (in *pl.*) small-clothes: (in *pl.*) underclothes: (in *pl.*) formerly at Oxford, the examination called Responsions (answering to Little go at Cambridge): a size of roofing slate, 12 × 8 inches (305 × 203 mm). — *adv.* in a low tone: gently: in small pieces: on a small scale: but slightly (*Shak.*). — *v.t.* and *v.i.* to make or become small. — *adj.* **small′ish.** — *n.* **small′ness.** — **small ads** classified advertisements; **small′-ale** ale with little malt and unhopped; **small′-and-earl′y** (*coll.*; *Dickens*, etc.) informal evening party; **small′-arm** (commonly in *pl.*) a weapon that can be carried by a man; **small beer** see **beer.** — *adj.* **small′-bore′** (of a firearm) having a barrel with a small bore, of a calibre not more than ·22 inch. — **small capitals** (*coll.* **small caps**) capital letters of the height of lower case; **small chop** (*W. African*) snacks served with drinks; **small′-clothes** knee-breeches, esp. those of the close-fitting 18th-century form; **small′-coal** coal in small pieces; **small′-craft** small vessels generally; **small′-debts** in Scotland, debts up to £20, recoverable in the Sheriff Court; **smallest room** (*euph.*) a lavatory, esp. in a house; **small′-hand** writing such as is ordinarily used in correspondence; **small′holder; small′holding** a holding of land smaller than an ordinary farm: esp. one provided by a local authority: the working of such; **small′-hours** hours immediately after midnight; **small lady** a size of roofing slate, 14 × 12 inches (356 × 305 mm); **small letter** (usu. in *pl.*) a lower-case letter. —

adj. **small′-mind′ed** petty. — **small pica** see **pica; small′-pipes** the Northumberland bagpipe; **small′pox** (orig. *pl.*) a contagious, febrile disease, characterised by pock eruptions; **small screen** television (*adj.* **small′-screen**); **small′-sword** a light thrusting sword for fencing or duelling; **small′-talk** light or trifling conversation. — *adjs.* **small′-time** (*slang*) unimportant; **small′-town** provincial, petty: naïve, unsophisticated. — **small′-wares** small articles such as tape, braid, buttons, hooks: trifles. — **by small and small** (*Shak.*) little by little; **feel small** to feel insignificant; **in a small way** with little capital or stock: unostentatiously; **in small** on a small scale; **in the smallest** (*Shak.*) in the least; **look small** to look silly: to be snubbed; **small-tooth comb** a comb with a row of fine teeth on each side: an arrangement for minute investigation (*fig.*); **the small print** (place where) important information (is) given inconspicuously. [O.E. *smæl*; Ger. *schmal*.]

smallage *smöl′ij, n.* wild celery. [**small,** Fr. *ache* — L. *apium*, parsley.]

smalm. See **smarm.**

smalt *smölt, n.* glass coloured with cobalt oxide: its powder, used as a pigment: its deep blue colour: smalto. — *adj.* deep blue. — *ns.* **smalt′ite** a cubic mineral, cobalt arsenide; **smalto** (*smöl′tō*; It. *zmäl′tō*) coloured glass or enamel for mosaic work: a cube of it: — *pl.* **-tos, -ti** (*-tē*). [It. *smalto* — O.H.G. *smalzjan* (Gcr. *schmelzen*), to melt.]

smaragd *smar′agd, n.* the emerald. — *adj.* **smarag′dine** (*-din, -dēn, -dīn*) emerald green. — *n.* **smarag′dite** a green amphibole. [L. *smaragdus* — Gr. *smaragdos.*]

smarm *smärm,* **smalm** *smäm, vs.t.* and *vs.i.* to smear, daub, plaster: to sleek. — *vs.i.* to fawn ingratiatingly and fulsomely: to be unctuous. — *adv.* **smarm′ily, smalm′ily.** — *n.* **smarm′iness, smalm′iness.** — *adj.* **smarm′y, smalm′y.** [Origin obscure.]

smart *smärt, v.i.* to feel a smart (also *fig.*): to be punished. — *v.t.* to cause to smart. — *n.* prolonged stinging pain: smart-money: a dandy. — *adj.* sharp and stinging: brisk: acute, witty: pert, vivacious: trim, spruce, fine: fashionable: keen, quick, and efficient in business: considerable (esp. *U.S.*): technologically advanced (*comput.*): computer-guided or electronically controlled (*coll.*). — *adv.* smartly. — *v.t.* and *v.i.* **smart′en** to make or become smart, to brighten (with *up.*). — *adv.* **smart′ly.** — *ns.* **smart′ness; smart′y, smart′ie** a would-be smart fellow. — **smart Al′ick, Al′ec(k), alec** a would-be clever person. — Also *adj.* (with *hyphen*). — **smart′ass, smart′arse** (*slang*) a smarty. — Also *adj.* — **smart card** a plastic card like a banker's card fitted with a microprocessor (including a memory) rather than a magnetic strip, used in commercial transactions, telecommunications, etc., its design intended to combat fraud; **smart′-money** money paid by a recruit for his release before being sworn in: money paid for escape from any unpleasant situation or engagement: excessive damages: money allowed to soldiers and sailors for wounds: money staked or invested by experienced gamblers or investors: the people staking or investing the money; **smart′-tick′et** a certificate granted to one entitled to smart-money; **smart′-weed** water-pepper, from its acridity; **smart′ypants, smart′y-boots** (*coll.*; *pl.* the same) a smarty. — **look smart** to be quick. [O.E. *smeortan*; Du. *smarten.*]

smash *smash, v.t.* to shatter violently: to ruin: to strike overhand with great force (*lawn tennis*, etc.): to dash violently. — *v.i.* to fly into pieces: to be ruined, to fail: to dash violently: to smash a tennis ball, etc. — *n.* an act or occasion of smashing, destruction, ruin, bankruptcy: bad money (*slang*). — *adj.* **smashed** (*slang*) drunk. — *ns.* **smash′er** one who smashes: one who passes bad money (*slang*): anything great or extraordinary (*slang*): a person of dazzling charm (*slang*); **smasheroo′** (*slang*) a person or thing of superlative quality, importance, etc., e.g. a smash-hit. — Also *adj.* — **smash′ing.** — *adj.* crushing: dashing: strikingly good (*slang*). — *adj.* and *n.* **smash-and-grab′** (a robbery) effected by smashing a shop-window and grabbing goods. — **smash'-hit'** (*slang*) overwhelming success; **smash'-up** a serious smash. [Imit; cf. Sw. dial. *smaske*, to smack.]

smatch *smach*, *n.* smack, taste: tincture (*Shak.*): touch: smattering. — *v.i.* to smack, have a flavour. — *v.t.* to smack of. [**smack**[1].]

smatter *smat'ər*, *v.i.* to talk superficially: to have a superficial knowledge: to dabble. — *v.t.* to talk or utter smatteringly: to dabble in. — *n.* a smattering. — *ns.* **smatt'erer; smatt'ering** a scrappy, superficial knowledge. — *adv.* **smatt'eringly.** [M.E. *smateren*, to rattle, to chatter; connections doubtful.]

smear *smēr*, *n.* grease (*obs.*): a rub with, mark or patch of, anything sticky or oily: the matter so applied, esp. to a slide for microscopic study: a fine glaze for pottery: a slur. — *v.t.* to anoint: to overspread with anything sticky or oily: to apply as a smear: to rub smearily: to defame. — *adv.* **smear'ily.** — *n.* **smear'iness.** — *adj.* **smear'y** sticky: greasy: ready to smear: showing smears. — **smear campaign** a series of verbal or written attacks intended to defame or discredit; **smear'-dab** see **lemon**[2]; **smear tactics** such as are employed in a smear campaign; **smear test** a test involving the microscopic study of a smear, as for example a cervical smear (q.v.). [O.E. *smeru*, fat, grease; Ger. *Schmer*, grease; O.N. *smjör*, butter.]

smeath. See **smee.**

smectic *smek'tik*, (*chem.*) *adj.* said of a mesomorphic substance whose atoms or molecules are oriented in parallel planes. [L. *smecticus*, cleansing, — Gr. *smektikos*, detergent, (from the soapy consistency of a smectic substance).]

smeddum *smed'əm*, *n.* fine powder: spirit, mettle (*Scot.*). [O.E. *smed(e)ma*, *smeodoma*, fine flour.]

smee *smē*, **smeath, smeeth** *smēth*, *ns.* names for various ducks — smew, pochard, wigeon, pintail.

smeech *smēch* (*S.W. dial.*), **smeek** *smēk* (*Scots.*) forms of **smoke**, *n.*, *v.t.*, *v.i.*

smeeth. See **smee.**

smegma *smeg'mə*, *n.* a sebaceous secretion, esp. that under the prepuce. [Gr. *smēgma*, *-atos*, soap.]

smell *smel*, *n.* the sense by which gases, vapours, substances very finely divided, are perceived, located in the higher animals in the mucous membrane of the nose: the specific sensation excited by such a substance: a pleasant scent or (often) an unpleasant one: the property of exciting it: an act or instance of exercising the sense: a smack, savour, property of suggesting, intimation (*fig.*). — *v.i.* to affect the sense of smell: to have odour (esp. unpleasant), or an odour (of): to have or use the sense of smell: to have a savour, give a suggestion (of something; *fig.*). — *v.t.* to perceive, detect, find, by smell (often with *out*): to take a smell at: to impart a smell to: to emit a smell of: — *pa.t.* and *pa.p.* **smelled** or **smelt.** — *ns.* **smell'er; smell'iness.** — *n.* and *adj.* **smell'ing.** — *adjs.* **smell'-less; smell'y** having a bad smell. — **smell'-feast** a sponger; **smell'ing-bottle** a bottle of smelling-salts or the like; **smell'ing-salts** a preparation of ammonium carbonate with lavender, etc., used as a stimulant in faintness, etc.; **smell'-trap** a drain-trap. — **smell a rat** see **rat**[1]; **smell at** (formerly **to, of**) to sniff at, take a smell at; **smell of** to have the smell of: to savour of; **smell out** to find out by prying: to detect by witchcraft (*S.Afr.*). [Very early M.E. *smel*, prob. O.E. but not recorded.]

smelt[1] *smelt*, *n.* a fish of or akin to the salmon family, with cucumber-like smell. [O.E. *smelt.*]

smelt[2] *smelt*, *v.t.* to melt in order to separate metal from ore. — *ns.* **smel'ter; smel'tery** a place for smelting; **smel'ting.** — **smel'ting-fur'nace, -house, -works.** [Prob. M.L.G. or M.Du. *smelten*; cf. Norw. *smelta*, Sw. *smälta*.]

smelt[3] *smelt*, (*obs. slang*; *Scott*) *n.* a half-guinea. [Origin obscure.]

smeuse *smūs*, *smūz*, *n.* a dial. form of **meuse**[1].

smew *smū*, *n.* a small species of merganser. [Origin uncertain.]

smicker *smik'ər*, (*obs.*) *adj.* beautiful: smirking, wanton. — *v.i.* to look amorously. — *n.* **smick'ering** an amorous inclination. — *adv.* **smick'ly** amorously. [O.E. *smicer*, beautiful.]

smicket *smik'it*, *n.* a smock. [Prob. dim.]

smiddy *smid'i*, Scots form of **smithy.**

smidgen, smidgeon, smidgin *smij'ən*, *-in*, (*coll.*) *n.* a very small amount. [Ety. uncertain.]

smifligate *smif'li-gāt.* Same as **spiflicate.**

smight. A Spenserian spelling of **smite.**

Smilax *smī'laks*, *n.* a genus of the lily family, mostly climbers with net-veined leaves, some yielding sarsaparilla: (*without cap.*) a southern African twining plant of the asparagus family, with bright green foliage, much used by florists as decoration. [Gr. *smīlax.*]

smile *smīl* (*Shak.*, etc., also **smoile, smoyle** *smoil*) *v.i.* to express amusement, slight contempt, favour, pleasure, etc., by a slight drawing up of the corners of the lips: to look joyous: to be favourable: to drink, esp. whisky (*slang*). — *v.t.* to render, drive, express, by smiling: to smile at (*Shak.*): to give (a smile). — *n.* an act of smiling: the expression of the features in smiling: favour: a drink, a treat (*slang*). — *adjs.* **smile'ful; smile'less.** — *ns.* **smil'er; smil'et** (*Shak.*) a little smile. — *n.* and *adj.* **smil'ing.** — *adv.* **smil'ingly.** — *smil'ingness* the state of being smiling. — **smile at** to show amusement at, disregard of; **smile on** to show favour to, be propitious to. [M.E. *smīlen*; poss. from L.G.]

Smilodon *smīl'ə-don*, *n.* an extinct genus of large, short-limbed, sabre-toothed tigers which inhabited the Americas during the Pleistocene period: (*without cap.*) a member of this genus. [L.L. — Gr. *smilē*, a knife, *odous*, *odontos*, a tooth.]

smir. See **smur.**

smirch *smûrch*, *v.t.* to besmear, dirty: to sully. — *n.* a stain. [Earlier *smorch*, supposed to be from O.Fr. *esmorcher*, to hurt, influenced by **smear.**]

smirk *smûrk*, *v.i.* to smile affectedly, smugly, or foolishly: to look affectedly soft. — *n.* an affected, smug, or foolish smile. — *adjs.* **smirk** trim, spruce; **smirk'y** simpering. [O.E. *smercian.*]

smirr. See **smur.**

smit[1] *smit*, (*obs.* or *poet.*) *pa.t.* and *pa.p.* of **smite.**

smit[2] *smit*, (*Northern dial.*) *v.t.* to stain, mark with ruddle, infect. — *n.* a stain (*obs.*): ruddle, a mark on sheep, infection (*Northern dial.*). — *adj.* (*Northern*) **smitt'le** infectious. [O.E. *smittian*, to befoul, infect, intens. of *smītan*, to smear; *smitte*, spot.]

smite *smīt*, *v.t.* to strike: to beat: to kill: to overthrow in battle: to affect with feeling: to afflict. — *v.i.* to strike: to meet forcibly: — *pa.t.* **smōte** (*arch.* or *poet.* **smit**); *pa.p.* **smitt'en** (**smit**). — *n.* **smī'ter.** — **smite off** to cut off. [O.E. *smītan*, to smear.]

smith *smith*, *n.* one who forges with the hammer: a worker in metals: one who makes anything. — *v.t.* to forge: to fashion. — *v.i.* to do smith's work. — *ns.* **smith'ery** a smithy: smith's work, smithing; **smithy** (*smidh'i*, *smith'i*) a smith's workshop. — *v.t.* and *v.i.* to smith. — **smith'craft.** [O.E. *smith*; Ger. *Schmied.*]

smithereens *smidh-ə-rēnz'*, *n.pl.* shivers, small fragments. — Also **smith'ers.** — *v.t.* **smithereen'** to break into tiny pieces: to shatter. — Also *fig.* [Ir. *smidirín*, dim. of *smiodar*, a fragment.]

Smithsonian *smith-sō'ni-ən*, *adj.* pertaining to James Macie *Smithson* (1765–1829), an Englishman, founder of a great scientific and cultural institution at Washington. — *n.* **smith'sonite** (*-sən-īt*) calamine: also electric calamine. — **Smithsonian parity** parity agreed for major currencies at an international conference at the Smithsonian Institution, Washington, in 1971.

smithy. See **smith.**

smitten *smit'n*, *pa.p.* of **smite.**

smittle. See **smit**[2].

smock *smok*, *n.* a woman's shift, chemise (*arch.*): a smock-frock: a loose, protective garment, usu. of coarse cloth, worn by artists, etc.: a wench (*obs.*). — *v.t.* to clothe in a smock or smock-frock: to decorate with smocking. — *n.* **smock′ing** honeycombing, as on the yoke and cuffs of a smock. — *adj.* **smock′-faced** pale-faced. — **smock′-frock** an outer garment of coarse white linen formerly worn by farm-workers in the south of England; **smock mill** a windmill with a fixed tower and revolvable cap above it bearing the sails (also called **tower mill**) **smock′-race** a race for the prize of a smock. [O.E. *smoc*.]

smog *smog, n.* smoky fog. — *adj.* **smogg′y.**

smoile, smoyle *smoil,* old forms of **smile.**

smoke *smōk, n.* the gases, vapours, and fine particles that come off from a burning body: solid particles suspended in a gas: fumes: vapour: fog: a cloud or column of smoke: that which may be smoked — tobacco, a cigarette, or cigar (*coll.*): a spell of smoking: S. African brandy (**Cape smoke**): tear gas (*coll.*). — *v.i.* to exhale or emit smoke, vapour, dust, etc.: to reek: to send smoke in a wrong direction: to move like smoke: to dash along in a cloud of smoke, vapour, spray, or dust: to suffer (orig. at the stake), smart: to take into the mouth and puff out the smoke of tobacco or the like: to lend itself to, admit of, smoking. — *v.t.* to dry, scent, preserve, fumigate, suffocate, blacken, taint, drive, render by smoke: to take in and emit the smoke from: to scent out, suspect, have an inkling of (*arch.*): to observe (*arch.*): to quiz, ridicule (*arch.*): to thrash (*arch.*). — *adjs.* **smok′able** fit to be smoked; **smoked; smoke′less** emitting no smoke: containing little or no smoke. — *adv.* **smoke′lessly.** — *ns.* **smoke′lessness; smok′er** apparatus for emitting smoke: one who smokes tobacco: a smoking-carriage or compartment: one who smoke-dries meat: a smoking-concert. — *adv.* **smok′ily.** — *n.* **smok′iness.** — *n.* and *adj.* **smok′ing.** — *n.* **smok′o** (*pl.* **smok′os**) smoke-ho. — *adj.* **smok′y** giving out smoke: like smoke: coloured like or by smoke: filled, or subject to be filled, with smoke: tarnished or noisome with smoke: suspicious (*arch.*). — *n.* (*Scot.*) a smoked haddock. — **smoke abatement** (measures directed to) reducing amount of smoke in the atmosphere of towns; **smoke′-ball** a shell emitting smoke as a screen or to drive out an enemy; **smoke′-black** lampblack; **smoke′-board** a board suspended before the upper part of a fireplace to prevent the smoke coming out into the room; **smoke′-bomb** a bomb that emits smoke on bursting; **smoke′-box** part of a steam-boiler where the smoke is collected before passing out at the chimney; **smoke′-bush, -tree** a sumach with light feathery or cloudlike panicles; **smoke′-consumer** an apparatus for burning all the smoke from a fire; **smoke′-detector** a device that activates an alarm when it detects smoke in the air. — *adj.* **smoke′-dried.** — *v.t.* **smoke′-dry** to cure or dry by means of smoke. — **smoke′-helmet** a head-covering for firemen or others who work in dense smoke; **smoke′-ho′** (*Austr.*) orig. a break for a smoke during the working day, now a rest, a tea-break; **smoke′-hole** a fumarole: a hole for escape of smoke; **smoke′-house** a building where meat or fish is cured by smoking, or where smoked meats are stored; **smoke′-jack** a contrivance for turning a spit by means of an ascending current of air: a muddled brain; **smokeless fuel** one authorised for use in a smoke control area; **smokeless zone** (*coll.*) a smoke control area. — *adj.* **smoke′proof** impervious to smoke. — **smoke′-room; smoke′-sail** a small sail hoisted to drive off the smoke from the galley; **smoke′-screen** a cloud of smoke raised to conceal movements (also *fig.*); **smoke signal** (often in *pl.*) a signal or message conveyed by means of patterns of smoke (also *fig.*); **smoke′-stack** the funnel of a ship or railway engine: a chimney. — *adj.* **smoke′tight** impervious to smoke. — **smoke-tree** see **smoke-bush; smoke tunnel** a wind tunnel into which smoke is put at certain points in order to make wind effects visible; **smoking cap, jacket** a light ornamental cap or jacket formerly worn by smokers; **smoking**

carriage, compartment, room a railway-carriage, compartment, room, set apart for smokers; **smok′ing-con′cert** a concert at which smoking (euphemistically) is allowed; **smoky quartz** Cairngorm stone. — **end, go up, in smoke** (of e.g. hopes) to vanish: (of e.g. plan) to come to nothing; **like smoke** very quickly; **sell smoke** (L. *fūmum venděre*, to make empty promises) to swindle; **smoke control area** one in which the emission of smoke from chimneys is prohibited; **smoke out** to discover: to drive out of a hiding place by smoke or fire; **smoke-room story** one unsuitable for telling elsewhere; **the (Big) Smoke** (*coll.*; also without *caps.*) a metropolitan area characterised by atmospheric pollution, esp. London: the (nearest) city or major town (orig. a phrase used by the Australian aborigines), now esp. Melbourne or Sydney. [O.E. *smoca* (n.), *smocian* (vb.); Ger. *Schmauch.*]

smoko. See **smoke.**

smolder. American spelling of **smoulder.**

smolt *smōlt, n.* a young river salmon when it is bluish along the upper half of the body and silvery along the sides. [Orig. Scot.; see **smout**[2].]

smooch *smōōch,* (*coll.*), *v.i.* to kiss, pet. [Origin uncertain; poss. related to **smouch**[1].]

smoor. See **smore.**

smoot *smōōt,* (*slang*) *n.* a compositor who does odd jobs in various houses. — *v.i.* to work in this way. [Origin obscure.]

smooth *smōōdh, adj.* having an even surface: without roughness: evenly spread: glossy: hairless: of even consistency: slippery: gently flowing: easy: bland: fair-spoken: classy or elegant (*slang*). — *adv.* **smoothly.** — *v.t.* **smooth,** rarely **smoothe,** to make smooth: to free from obstruction, difficulty, harshness: to reduce from diphthong to simple vowel: to remove by smoothing (often with *away:* often *fig.*): to calm, soothe: to blandish: to make (difficulties or problems) seem less serious or less important (often with *over*). — *v.i.* to become smooth: to flatter, blandish, behave ingratiatingly (also *v.t.* with *it; Shak.*). — *n.* a smooth place or part: an act of smoothing. — *v.t.* **smooth′en** to make smooth. — *ns.* **smooth′er** one who, or that which, smooths: a smoothing tool: a flatterer (*obs.*); **smooth′ie** (*slang*) a plausible or smooth-spoken person: a person elegant or suave in manner or appearance, esp. insincerely or excessively so. — *n.* and *adj.* **smooth′ing.** — *adj.* **smooth′ish.** — *adv.* **smooth′ly.** — *n.* **smooth′ness.** — *adj.* **smooth′-bore** not rifled (also **smooth′-bored**). — *n.* a gun with a smooth-bored barrel. — *adjs.* **smooth′-browed** with unwrinkled brow; **smooth′-chinned** beardless; **smooth′-coated** not shaggy-haired. — **smooth dab** see **lemon**[2]. — *adjs.* **smooth′-ditt′ied** (*Milt.*) set to words that smoothly fit the tune: or, poss., having a smooth ditty, or set of words; **smooth′-faced** having a smooth face or surface: pleasant-looking: beardless: unwrinkled: plausible. — **smoothing iron** a flatiron; **smoothing plane** a small fine plane used for finishing. — *adj.* **smooth′-leaved.** — **smooth muscle** unstriated muscular tissue (e.g. in the walls of the intestines) whose action is slow rhythmic contraction and relaxation, independent of the will. — *adj.* **smooth′-paced** having a regular easy pace. — **smooth′pate.** — *adjs.* **smooth′-shod** having shoes without spikes; **smooth′-spoken, smooth′-tongued** conciliatory, plausible, flattering, or soft in speech. [O.E. *smōth* (usu. *smēthe*).]

smørbrød *smör′broo, smör′, smær′brö,* (Norw.), **smørrebrød** *smær′ə-brædh, smör′ə-bröd,* (Dan.) *ns.* lit., bread and butter: hors d'œuvres served on slices of buttered bread.

smore *smōr, smör,* **smoor** *smōōr,* (*Scot.*) *vs.t.* and *vs.i.* to smother, suffocate: to put out (a fire, light). — *n.* **smoor** smoke. [O.E. *smorian.*]

smörgåsbord *smör′gas-börd,* Sw. *smær′gös-boörd, n.* a Swedish-style table assortment of hors d'œuvres and many other dishes to which one helps oneself. [Sw.]

smørrebrød. See **smørbrød.**

smorzando *smört-san′dō* (It. *zmort-sän′dō*), **smorzato**

-sä'tō, *adjs.* and *advs.* with a gradual fading away: growing slower and softer. [It.; ger. and pa.p. of *smorzare*, to tone down, extinguish.]

smote *smōt, pa.t.* of **smite.**

smother *smudh'ər, v.t.* to suffocate by excluding the air, esp. by a thick covering: to stifle: to envelop closely: to cover up thickly: to suppress: to conceal. — *v.i.* to be suffocated or suppressed: to smoulder. — *n.* smoke: thick floating dust: a smouldering fire or condition: a welter: suffocation. — *adj.* **smoth'ered.** — *ns.* **smoth'-erer; smoth'eriness.** — *n.* and *adj.* **smoth'ering.** — *adv.* **smoth'eringly.** — *adj.* **smoth'ery** tending to smother: stifling. — **smothered mate** (*chess*) checkmate by a knight, the king having been prevented from moving by the positions of his own forces; **smother'-fly** an aphis. [M.E. *smorther* — O.E. *smorian*, to smother; cf. **smore.**]

smouch[1] *smowch,* (*dial.*) *n.* a smack, a hearty kiss. — *v.t.* to kiss, to buss. [Cf. Ger. *Schmutz.*]

smouch[2] *smowch,* **smous(e)** *smowz, ns.* a Jew (*obs. slang*): a pedlar (*S.Afr.*). — *v.i.* (*S.Afr.*) to trade as a pedlar. — *n.* **smous'er** (*S.Afr.*) a pedlar. [Afrik. *smous,* perh. from Heb. *sh'mū'ōth,* news.]

smouch[3] *smowch, v.t.* to filch. — *v.i.* to cheat.

smouch[4] *smowch, n.* a form of **smutch, smudge.**

smoulder *smōl'dər, v.t.* to smother. — *v.i.* to burn slowly or without flame: to linger on in a suppressed or hidden state. — *n.* smother: smouldering fire. — *n.* and *adj.* **smoul'dering.** — *adj.* **smoul'dry** (*Spens.*). [M.E. *smolder;* origin obscure.]

smous(e), smouser. See **smouch**[2].

smout[1] *smowt.* Same as **smoot.**

smout[2], **smowt** *smowt, n.* Scots form of **smolt:** a small person or child.

smoyle. An old form of **smile.**

smudge[1] *smuj, n.* a smear: a blur: a rubbed blot. — *v.t.* to smear: to blur: to soil: to daub. — *n.* **smudg'er.** — *adv.* **smudg'ily.** — *n.* **smudg'iness.** — *adj.* **smudg'y.** [Cf. **smutch.**]

smudge[2] *smuj, n.* a choking smoke: fuel for obtaining smoke. — *v.t.* to fumigate with smoke. — *adj.* **smud'gy** smoky. [Origin obscure.]

smug[1] *smug, adj.* neat, prim, spruce: smooth: sleek: affectedly smart: offensively self-complacent. — *n.* a smug person: an industrious student who does not take part in social activities (*university slang*). — *v.t.* to make trim. — *adv.* **smug'ly.** — *n.* **smug'ness.** — *adj.* **smug'-faced.** [Connection with L.G. *smuk,* trim, presents difficulty.]

smug[2] *smug,* (*slang*) *v.t.* to seize without ceremony: to steal: to hush up. [Origin obscure.]

smuggle[1] *smug'l, v.t.* to import or export illegally or without paying duty: to convey secretly. — *adj.* **smug'g'led.** — *n.* **smugg'ler** one who smuggles: a vessel used in smuggling. — *n.* and *adj.* **smugg'ling.** [L.G. *smuggeln;* Ger. *schmuggeln.*]

smuggle[2] *smug'l, v.t.* to fondle, cuddle. [Origin obscure.]

smur *smūr,* **smir(r)** *smir,* (*Scot.*) *ns.* fine misty rain, — *vs.i.* to drizzle, rain very finely. — *adjs.* **smurr'y, smirr'y.**

smut *smut, n.* soot: worthless or bad coal: a flake or spot or dirt, soot, etc.: a black spot: a disease of plants, esp. cereals, giving an appearance of soot: the fungus causing it: obscene discourse. — *v.t.* to soil, spot, or affect with smut: to become smutty. — *adj.* **smutt'ed.** — *adv.* **smutt'ily** — *n.* **smutt'iness.** — *adj.* **smutt'y** stained with smut: affected with smut: obscene, filthy. — **smut'-fungus** any member of the Ustilaginales, an order of Basidiomycetes, parasitic on plants, causing smut and bunt. [Cf. L.G. *schmutt;* Ger. *Schmutz,* dirt.]

smutch *smutch, v.t.* to smut: to sully. — *n.* a dirty mark: soot: grime: a stain. [Cf. **smudge**[1].]

smytrie *smīt'ri,* (*Scot.*) *n.* a collection of small things. [Cf. Flem. *smite.*]

snab. See **snob.**

snabble. See **snaffle.**

snack *snak, n.* a snap, bite (*dial.*): a share: a mere taste: a light repast. — *v.i.* to snap (*Scot.*): to share (*obs.*): to take a snack. — **snack'-bar, snack'-counter** a place where light meals can be bought. [Cf. M.Du. *snacken,* to snap; **snatch.**]

snaffle *snaf'l, n.* a jointed bit (less severe than the curb). — *v.t.* to put a snaffle on: to control by the snaffle: (the following meanings *slang;* also **snabb'le**) to arrest: to capture: to purloin: to get possession of. — **snaff'le-bit; snaff'le-bridle; snaff'le-rein; snaff'ling-lay** the trade of highwayman. [Ety. dub.; cf. Du. *snavel,* Ger. *Schnabel,* beak, mouth.]

snafu *sna-foo',* (*U.S. slang*) *n.* chaos. — *adj.* chaotic. [situation *n*ormal — all *f*ouled (or *f*ucked) *u*p.]

snag *snag, n.* a stump, as of a branch or tooth: a jag: a short tine: an embedded tree, dangerous for boats: hence a catch, a hidden obstacle or drawback: a caught thread in a stocking: (usu. *pl.*) sausage (*Austr. slang*). — *v.t.* to catch on a snag: to tear on a snag: to hack so as to form snags: to clear of snags: — *pr.p.* **snagg'ing;** *pa.t.* and *pa.p.* **snagged.** — *adjs.* **snagged, snagg'y.** [Cf. O.N. *snagi,* peg.]

snaggle-tooth *snag'l-tōōth, n.* a broken, irregular or projecting tooth: — *pl.* **-teeth.** — *adj.* **snagg'le-toothed.** [App. from **snag,** and **tooth.**]

snail *snāl, n.* any terrestrial or air-breathing gasteropod mollusc with well-developed coiled shell: extended to other shelled gasteropods and (*dial.*) to slugs: a sluggish person or animal: a snail-wheel: medick of various kinds (from its coiled pods). — *v.i.* to crawl, go very slowly (also *v.t.* with *it*). — *n.* **snail'ery** a place where edible snails are bred. — *adj.* and *adv.* **snail'-like.** — *adj.* **snail'y.** — **snail darter** a small American freshwater fish (*Percina tanasi*); **snail'-fish** the fish called sea-snail; **snail'-flower** any flower pollinated by snails. — *adj.* **snail'-paced.** — **snail'-shell.** — *adj.* **snail'-slow'.** — **snail's pace** a very slow speed; **snail'-wheel** a cam that controls the striking of a clock. — **giant African snail** a 10-inch snail, a serious plant pest except in its place of origin, East Africa. [O.E. *snegl, snægl, snæl.*]

'snails *snālz,* (*obs.*) *interj.* for **God's nails.**

snake *snāk, n.* a serpent, or member of the Ophidia, a class of elongated limbless (or all but limbless) scaly carnivorous reptiles, often venomous, with forked tongue, no eyelids or external ears, teeth fused to the bones that bear them: an ungrateful or treacherous person (in allusion to Aesop): a wretch, drudge: anything snakelike in form or movement: apparatus for blasting a passage through a mine-field: the band (narrower than the **tunnel** allowed by the IMF on the world market) within which the relative values of certain EEC currencies are allowed to float. — *v.i.* to wind: to creep. — *v.t.* to drag. — *adj.* **snake'like.** — *advs.* **snake'wise** in the manner of a snake; **snāk'ily.** — *n.* **snāk'iness.** — *adj.* **snāk'ish.** — *n.* **snāk'ishness.** — *adj.* **snāk'y.** — **snake'bird** the darter: the wryneck; **snake'bite** the bite of a venomous snake: the condition or symptoms of a victim of a snakebite: a drink made of beer and cider in equal measures; **snake'-charmer** one who handles snakes and sets them to perform rhythmical movements; **snake'-cult** serpent-worship; **snake'-dance** a religious dance of the Hopi Indians in which snakes are handled; **snake'-eel** an eel without tail-fin; **snake'-fence** (*U.S.*) a worm-fence; **snake'-fly** a neuropterous insect (*Raphidia*) with neck-like prothorax; **snake'-house** a place where snakes are kept; **snake'-oil** any substance or mixture without medicinal value but sold as medicine; **snake'-pit** (*fig.*) a mental hospital: a place, or circumstances, characterised by disordered emotions and relationships; **snake'root** bistort, milkwort, Aristolochia, or other plant whose root has been thought good for snakebites; **snake's'-head** fritillary; **snake'skin** the skin of a snake, esp. when made into leather. — Also *adj.* — **snake'stone** a fossil ammonite: a stone thought to cure snakebite; **snake'weed** bistort; **snake'wood** letterwood. — **snake in the grass** (*fig.*) one who injures furtively: a lurking danger; **snakes and ladders** a board game played with counters and dice in which 'ladders' afford short cuts to the finish, but 'snakes' oblige one to descend to nearer the starting-point. [O.E. *snaca*.]

snap *snap, v.i.* to make a bite (often with *at*): to speak tartly in sudden irritation: to grasp (with *at*): to shut suddenly, as by a spring: to make a sharp noise: to go with a sharp noise: to break suddenly. — *v.t.* to bite suddenly: to seize, secure promptly (usu. with *up*): to answer or interrupt sharply (often with *up*): to shut with a sharp sound: to cause to make a sharp sound: to send or put with a sharp sound: to utter snappishly (sometimes with *out*): to break suddenly: to take an instantaneous photograph of, esp. with a hand-camera: — *pr.p.* **snapp′ing;** *pa.t.* and *pa.p.* **snapped.** — *n.* an act, instance, or noise of snapping: a small catch or lock: an earring (*rare*): (in *pl.*) a kind of handcuffs: a share: a scrap: a whit: a snack: a crack: a gingerbread biscuit: a quick, crisp, incisive, epigrammatic quality in style: lively energy: a brief theatrical engagement (*slang*): an easy and profitable place or task: a sharpner, a cheat: a riveter's or glass-moulder's tool: a snapshot: a sudden cold spell (also **cold snap**): a type of card game in which the first player to shout 'snap' on spotting a matching pair of cards wins the cards. — *adj.* sudden, unexpected: offhand: (of decision, judgment) taking, made, on the spur of the moment without deep consideration of all possibilities: snapping shut. — *adv.* with a snap. — *interj.* used in claiming cards in the game of snap: also, on meeting or discovering two matching items, circumstances, etc. — *n.* **snapp′er** an animal that snaps: one who snaps or snaps up: an attachment at the end of a whiplash to make it crack (*U.S.*): a snapping-turtle: any fish of the family *Lutjanidae*, akin to the basses: (also **schnapper**) any of several highly esteemed food-fish of the family Sparidae, found in Australian and New Zealand waters: a (Christmas or party) cracker (*U.S.*). — *adv.* **snapp′ily.** — *n.* and *adj.* **snapp′ing.** — *adv.* **snapp′ingly.** — *adj.* **snapp′ish** inclined to snap: quick and tart. — *adv.* **snapp′ishly.** — *n.* **snapp′ishness.** — *adj.* **snapp′y** snappish: snapping: having the quality of snap: instantaneous: smart, fashionable, polished (as in **snappy** *dresser*). — *adj.* **snap′-brim** having a brim that turns down springily. — **snap′dragon** a plant (*Antirrhinum*) of the figwort family whose flower when pinched and released snaps like a dragon: a Christmas game of snatching raisins out of burning brandy; **snap′-fastener** a press-fastener, press-stud; **snap′-link** a link with a side opening closed by a spring; **snapp′er-up′** (*Shak.*) one who snaps up; **snapp′ing-tur′tle** a large American fiercely snapping fresh-water tortoise; **snap′shooter; snap′shooting; snap′shot** a hasty shot: a photograph taken quickly and informally, with simple equipment: an instant record of an event, situation, etc. at a particular time, esp. a stage in a process or sequence (*fig.*): a visual record of the placement of stored data at a specific stage in a program run (*comput.*). — **look snappy, make it snappy** (*coll.*) to hurry; **Scotch snap** see **Scotch; snap into it** to get going quickly; **snap someone's head, nose, off** to answer irritably and rudely; **snap out of it** (*coll.*) to give it (e.g. a mood, habit) up at once; **snap up** to take or purchase eagerly and quickly. [Prob. Du. *snappen*, to snap; Ger. *schnappen*.]

snapha(u)nce *snap′häns, -höns,* **snaphaunch** *-hönsh,* (*obs.*) *ns.* a freebooter: a flintlock or a weapon with one: a spring catch or trap. [Cf. Du. *snapshaan* — *snappen*, to snap, *haan*, a cock.]

snapper[1] *snap′ər,* (*Scot.*) *n.* a stumble: a slip in conduct: a scrape. — *v.i.* to stumble. [Cf. Ger. dial. *schnappen*, to stumble.]

snapper[2]. See **snap.**

snar *snär,* (*Spens.*) *v.i.* to snarl. [Cf. Du. and L.G. *snarren*.]

snare *snär, n.* a running noose for trapping: a trap: an

allurement, temptation, entanglement, moral danger: a loop for removing tumours, etc.: a string stretched across the lower head of a side-drum. — *v.t.* to catch, entangle, entrap, in a snare: to remove with a snare. — *ns.* **snar′er; snar′ing.** — *adj.* **snar′y.** — **snare′-drum** a side-drum. [O.E. *sneare* or O.N. *snara*; prob. partly from Du. *snaar* or L.G. *snare*.]

snark *snärk, n.* an imaginary animal created by Lewis Carroll (1876).

snarl[1] *snärl, v.i.* to make a surly resentful noise with show of teeth: to speak in a surly manner. — *v.t.* to utter snarlingly. — *n.* an ill-natured growling sound: a snarling. — *n.* **snarl′er.** — *n.* and *adj.* **snarl′ing.** — *adv.* **snarl′ingly.** — *adj.* **snarl′y.** [**snar.**]

snarl[2] *snärl, n.* a knot: a tangle: a knot in wood. — *v.t.* to ensnare (*dial.*): to tangle: to raise with a snarling-iron. — *v.i.* to tangle. — *adj.* **snarled.** — *ns.* **snarl′er; snarl′ing.** — **snarl′ing-iron, -tool** a curved tool for raised work in hollow metalware. — **snarl up** (used esp. in *pa.p.* and *p.adj.* forms) to make muddled or tangled and thus stop operating, moving, etc. smoothly (*n.* **snarl′-up**). [**snare.**]

snash *snash,* (*Scot.*) *n.* insolence, abusive language. — *v.i.* to talk impudently. [Prob. imit.]

snaste *snāst,* (now *dial.*) *n.* a wick: a candle-snuff. [Origin obscure.]

snatch *snach, v.t.* to seize suddenly: to pluck away quickly: to grab: to take as opportunity occurs. — *v.i.* to make a snap or seizure. — *n.* a snap (*Shak.*): a seizure or attempt to seize: a grab: a short spell: a fragment, as of song, verse: a snack: a catch (of the voice) (*Shak.*): a quibble (*Shak.*): in weight-lifting, a type of lift in which the weight is raised from the floor to an overhead position in one movement. — *n.* **snatch′er.** — *advs.* **snatch′ily, snatch′ingly.** — *adj.* **snatch′y** irregular. — **snatch′-block** a block with a side opening for the bight of a rope; **snatch′-purse, -thief** a thief who snatches; **snatch squad** a group of policemen, etc. who force a sudden quick passage into e.g a disorderly or rioting crowd in order to arrest trouble-makers or ringleaders: a swift, organised sally by a group of people in order to seize something. — **snatch at** to try to snatch or seize. [M.E. *snacchen*; poss. related to **snack.**]

snath *snath,* **snathe** *snädh,* **snead** *snēd,* **sneath** *snēth,* **sned** *sned, ns.* the curved handle or shaft of a scythe. [O.E. *snǽd,* a scythe handle, a slice.]

snazzy *snaz′i,* (*slang*) *adj.* very attractive or fashionable: flashy. [Origin obscure.]

snead. See **snath.**

sneak *snēk, v.i.* to go furtively or meanly, slink, skulk: to cringe: to behave meanly: to tell tales. — *v.t.* to pass furtively: to steal (*slang*). — *n.* a sneaking fellow: one who sneaks away: a sneaking thief: a tell-tale: a ball bowled along the ground (*cricket*). — *n.* **sneak′er** one who, or that which, sneaks: a soft-soled shoe: a sand-shoe. — *adv.* **sneak′ily.** — *n.* **sneak′iness.** — *adj.* **sneak′ing** mean, crouching: secret, underhand, not openly avowed: lurking under other feelings. — *adv.* **sneak′ingly.** — *adj.* **sneak′ish** befitting a sneak. — *adv.* **sneak′ishly.** — *ns.* **sneak′ishness; sneaks′by** a sneak. — *adj.* **sneak′y** sneaking: cunning. — **sneak′-cup** in some editions of Shakespeare (1 *Hen. IV* III, iii. 99), probably a misreading of a blurred **sneakup** (see **sneak-up**) in the first quartos, but by some taken to be a correction and explained as one who balks his cup, or a stealer of cups; **sneak preview** a special private screening or viewing of a film, exhibition, etc., before it is officially released, made available, etc. to the public; **sneak′-raid** a bombing or other raid made under conditions of concealment; **sneak′-thief** a thief who steals through open doors or windows without breaking in; **sneak′-up** a sneak, shirker, skulker. [Connection with O.E. *snīcan,* to crawl, is obscure.]

sneap *snēp, v.t.* to nip, pinch: to put down, repress, snub. — *n.* a snub, check. — *adj.* **sneap′ing** (*Shak.*). [Earlier *snape* — O.N. *sneypa*.]

sneath. See **snath.**

sneb, snebbe. Old forms of **snib**[1], **snub.**

sneck[1] *snek,* (*Scot.* and *Northern*) *n.* a latch: a door-catch. — *v.t.* to fasten with a sneck. — **sneck′-drawer** one who lifts the latch: an insinuating or crafty person. — Also **sneck′-draw.** — **sneck′-drawing.** — Also *adj.* [Cf. **snack, snatch.**]

sneck[2]. See **snick**[1].

sneck up. See **snick-up.**

sned[1] *sned, v.t.* to cut: to lop: to prune. [O.E. *snædan.*]

sned[2]. See **snath.**

snee *snē,* (*obs.*) *v.i.* to cut. — **snick and snee, snick, stick or snee** see **snickersnee.** [Du. *snijden,* to cut.]

sneer *snēr, v.i.* to show cynical contempt by the expression of the face, as by drawing up the lip (sometimes with *at*): to express such contempt in other ways: to grin (*obs.*). — *v.t.* to utter sneeringly: to sneer at (*obs.*): to render, drive, by sneering. — *n.* a sneering expression: an act of sneering. — *n.* **sneer′er.** — *n.* and *adj.* **sneer′ing.** — *adv.* **sneer′ingly.** — *adj.* **sneer′y.** [Perh. related to Fris. *sneere,* to scorn.]

sneesh *snēsh,* (*Scot.*) *n.* a pinch of snuff: snuff. — *ns.* **sneesh′in(g), sneesh′an** snuff: a pinch of snuff. — **snee′shin-mull** a snuff box. [Poss. **sneeze, sneezing;** or imit.; cf. **snush.**]

sneeze *snēz, v.i.* to make a sudden, involuntary and audible expiration through the nose and mouth, due to irritation of the inner nasal membrane. — *n.* an act of sneezing. — *ns.* **sneez′er; sneez′ing.** — *adj.* **sneez′y.** — **sneeze′-box** (*slang*) a snuffbox; **sneeze′weed** an American composite (*Helenium*); **sneeze′wood** a S. African meliaceous timber tree (*Ptaeroxylon*), or its wood, whose sawdust causes sneezing; **sneeze′wort** a species of yarrow (*Achillaea ptarmica*) once used as a substitute for snuff: white hellebore. — **not to be sneezed at** not to be despised. [M.E. *snesen, fnesen* — O.E. *fnēsan,* to sneeze; Du. *niezen.*]

snell[1] *snel,* (*Scot.*) *adj.* keen, sharp, severe. — *adv.* **snel′ly.** [O.E. *snell,* active; Ger. *schnell,* swift.]

snell[2] *snel, n.* a short piece of hair, gut, etc., attaching a hook to a line. — *v.t.* to attach (a hook) to a line. [Origin obscure.]

Snell's law. See **law**[1].

snib[1] *snib,* (*Spens.*; *Scot.*) *n.* and *v.t.* Same as **snub.**

snib[2] *snib,* (*Scot.*) *n.* a small bolt: a catch for a window-sash. — *v.t.* to fasten with a snib. [Cf. L.G. *snibbe,* beak.]

snick[1] *snik* (*Scott* **sneck** *snek*), *v.t.* to cut out, snip, nick: to deflect slightly by a touch of the bat (*cricket*). — *n.* a small cut: a glancing stroke in cricket. — **snick and, or, snee** see **snickersnee.** [Origin doubtful.]

snick[2] *snik, n., v.t.,* and *v.i.* click. [Imit.]

snicker *snik′ər, v.i.* to snigger: to nicker, neigh. — *v.t.* to say gigglingly. — *n.* a giggle. [Imit.; cf. **nicker**[1], **snigger**[1].]

snicker-snack *snik′ər-snak′, n.* a word coined by Lewis Carroll to evoke the sound of a slicing blade. [Imit.; also cf. **snickersnee.**]

snickersnee *snik′ər-snē′, n.* a large knife for fighting: fighting with knives (*obs.*). — *v.i.* (*obs.*) to fight with knives. — Also earlier **snick′-a-snee′, snick and snee, snick** (earlier **stick**) **or snee.** [App. Du. *steken,* to thrust, *snijden,* to cut.]

snicket *snik′it,* (*dial.*) *n.* a narrow passage or back street: a ginnel. [Orig. obscure.]

snick-up, snick up *snik-up′,* (*Shak.*) *v.i.* used in imper., go hang. — Also **sneck up.**

snide *snīd, adj.* sham: counterfeit: base: mean: dishonest: derogatory in an insinuating way: showing malice. — Also *n.* — *adv.* **snide′ly.** — *n.* **snide′ness.** [Ety. dub.]

sniff *snif, v.t.* to draw in with the breath through the nose: to smell: to suspect or detect by smell or as if by smell. — *v.i.* to draw in air sharply and audibly through the nose: to draw up mucus or tears escaping into the nose: to smell tentatively: to express disapprobation with reticence by a slight sound in the nose: to snuffle: to inhale a dangerous or addictive substance (e.g. glue,

aerosols). — *n.* an act or a sound of sniffing: a smell: a small quantity inhaled by the nose. — *n.* **sniff′er.** — *adj.* trained, designed, etc. to seek out or locate (esp. illicit or dangerous substances). — *adv.* **sniff′ily.** — *n.* **sniff′iness.** — *n.* and *adj.* **sniff′ing.** — *adv.* **sniff′ingly.** — *v.i.* **sniff′le** to snuffle slightly, to sniff. — *n.* an act of sniffling: the sound made by sniffling: (often in *pl.* with *the*) a slight cold: (often in *pl.* with *the*) liquid mucus running out of or blocking the nose. — *n.* **sniff′ler** one who sniffles: a slight breeze. — *adj.* **sniff′y** inclined to be disdainful. — *vs.i.* **snift** to sniff, snivel: to blow out steam, etc.; **snift′er** to sniff. — *n.* a sniff: (in *pl.*) stoppage of the nasal passages in catarrh, the sniffles: a dram (*slang*): a strong breeze: a brandy-glass (*U.S.*). — *adj.* **snift′y** (*slang*) having a tempting smell: inclined to sniff in disdain. — **sniffer dog** a dog trained to smell out drugs or explosives; **snift′ing-valve** an air-valve of a cylinder, etc. — **not to be sniffed at** not to be despised. [Imit.; cf. **snuff**[1].]

snig *snig,* (*dial.*) *n.* a river-eel, esp. an immature (olive and yellow) eel. — *v.t.* to drag a load with chains or ropes. — *v.t.* **snigg′er** to catch (salmon) with a weighted hook. — *v.i.* **snigg′le** to fish for eels by thrusting the bait into their hiding places: to fish for salmon, etc., by striking with a hook. — *v.t.* to catch thus. — *n.* a baited hook. — *ns.* **snigg′ler; snigg′ling.** [Origin obscure.]

snigger[1] *snig′ər, v.i.* to laugh in a half-suppressed way, often offensively. — *v.t.* to say with a snigger. — *n.* a half-suppressed laugh. — *n.* **snigg′erer.** — *n.,* *adj.* **snigg′ering.** — *adv.* **snigg′eringly.** [Imit.]

snigger[2]. See **snig.**

snip *snip, v.t.* to cut as with scissors: to snatch, snap (*obs.*): — *pr.p.* **snipp′ing;** *pa.t.* and *pa.p.* **snipped.** — *n.* a small cut, as with scissors: a small shred: a small, slender or despicable person: a small piece: a notch, slit, or slash: the sound of a stroke of scissors: a white or light patch or stripe on a horse, esp. on the nose: a share: a tailor: a certainty: a bargain. — *ns.* **snipp′er; snipp′et** a little piece snipped off: a scrap, as of literature, news; **snipp′etiness.** — *adj.* **snipp′ety** trivial, fragmentary. — *n.* **snipp′ing** a clipping. — *adj.* **snipp′y** fragmentary: stingy: snappish. — *n.pl.* **snips** hand-shears for sheet-metal. — **snip′-snap′** the action or sound of scissors: quick snappy dialogue. — Also *adj., adv., interj., v.i.*; **snipp′er-snapper** a whipper-snapper. — **snipt taffeta fellow** (*Shak.*) one who goes about in slashed silk. [L.G. or Du. *snippen;* Ger. dial. *schnippen.*]

snipe *snip, n.* a bird akin to the woodcock, with a long straight flexible bill, or other of its genus (*Gallinago* or *Capella*) or family (*Scolopacidae*): a fool or contemptible person (*Shak.*): the butt of a cigar or cigarette (*U.S. slang*): a sniping shot: a verbal attack, criticism: — *pl.* usu. **snipe** of the bird, **snipes** of species of the bird, and in other senses. — *v.i.* to shoot snipe, go snipe-shooting: to shoot at single men from cover: to attack, criticise, esp. from a position of security (*fig.*; often with *at*). — *v.t.* to pick off by rifle-fire from (usu. distant) cover. — *ns.* **snip′er; snip′ing.** — *adj.* **snip′y** snipe-like: snipe-beaked: frequented by snipe. — **snipe′-fish** the trumpet-fish. [Prob. Scand.; the O.E. word is *snite.*]

snipper, snippet. See **snip.**

snip-snap-snorum *snip-snap-snō′rəm, -snō′, n.* a childish game of turning up cards. [L.G. *snipp-snapp-snorum.*]

snirt *snirt, snûrt,* (*Scot.*) *n.* a smothered laugh. — *v.i.* **snirt′le** to snicker. [Imit.]

snitch *snich,* (*slang*) *n.* the nose: a fillip on the nose: an informer. — *v.i.* to inform, peach. — *v.t.* (*coll.*) to pilfer. — *n.* **snitch′er** an informer: a handcuff.

snivel *sniv′l, n.* mucus of the nose: a sniff: a hypocritical snuffle: cant. — *v.i.* to run at the nose: to sniff: to snuffle: to whimper: to cry, as a child. — *v.t.* to utter with snivelling: — *pr.p.* **sniv′elling;** *pa.t.* and *pa.p.* **sniv′elled.** — *n.* **sniv′eller.** — *adjs.* **sniv′elling; sniv′elly.** [O.E. *snofl,* mucus.]

snob *snob, n.* a shoemaker, shoemaker's apprentice, cobbler (*coll.*; *Scot.* **snab**): a townsman (*Cambridge slang*): a person of ordinary or low rank (*obs.*): an ostentatious vulgarian (*obs.*): a blackleg (*obs.*): one who makes himself ridiculous or odious by the value he sets on social standing or rank, by his fear of being ranked too low, and by his different behaviour towards different classes. — *n.* **snobb′ery** snobbishness: snobbish behaviour. — *adj.* **snobb′ish.** — *adv.* **snobb′ishly.** — *ns.* **snobb′ishness; snobb′ism.** — *adj.* **snobb′y.** — *ns.* **snob′ling** a little snob; **snoboc′racy** snobs as a powerful class; **snobog′rapher; snobog′raphy** the description of snobs and snobbery. [Orig. slang.]

snod *snod,* (*Scot.*) *adj.* smooth, neat, trim, snug. — *v.t.* to trim, set in order (with *up*): — *pa.t.* and *pa.p.* **snodd′ed, snodd′it.** [Poss. conn. with O.N. *snothinn,* bald.]

snoek. See **snook²**.

snog *snog,* (*slang*) *v.i.* to embrace, kiss, indulge in love-making. — Also *n.* [Origin obscure.]

snoke. See **snook¹**.

snood *snōōd, n.* a fillet for the hair, once in Scotland the badge of virginity: revived in the sense of a conspicuous net supporting the back-hair: the hair-line, gut, etc., by which a fish-hook is fixed to the line. — *v.t.* to bind, dress, fasten, with a snood. — *adj.* **snood′ed.** [O.E. *snōd.*]

snook¹ *snōōk,* **snoke** *snōk,* (*Scot.*) **snowk** *snowk, vs.i.* to snuff or smell about: to lurk, prowl about. [M.E. *snoken,* to lurk — M.L.G. *snoken,* orig. from Scand.]

snook² *snōōk, n.* one of several fishes — the cobia, a robalo, a garfish, or (in S. Africa and now elsewhere also **snoek** *snōōk*) the barracouta (*Thyrsites atun*). [Du. *snoek,* pike.]

snook³ *snōōk, snōōk, n.* the gesture of putting the thumb to the nose, to express derision, defiance, etc. — Also **snooks.** — **cock a snook** to make that gesture (also *fig.*). [Origin obscure.]

snooker *snōōk′ər, n.* a variety of the game of pool, played with 15 red balls, 1 white cue ball and 6 balls of other colours, the object being to pocket the non-white balls in a certain order and gain more points in so doing than one's opponent: a situation in snooker where the path between the cue ball and the ball to be played is blocked, forcing an indirect shot to be played. — *v.t.* to render a direct stroke impossible for: to thwart (a person or his plans) by making it difficult or impossible for him to act as he intended because of an obstacle one has put in his way (*fig.*). [Pop. believed to be a coinage, at the game's inception in India in 1875, from old milit. slang *snooker,* a raw cadet — **snook¹**.]

snool *snōōl,* (*Scot.*) *n.* one who submits tamely to wrong or oppression. — *v.t.* to keep in subjection: to snub. — *v.i.* to be tamely submissive. [Ety. dub.]

snoop *snōōp,* (*slang*) *v.i.* to go about sneakingly, to pry. — Also *n.* — *n.* **snoop′er.** [Du. *snoepen,* to eat, steal.]

snoot *snōōt, n.* a snout (*illit.*): the nose (*U.S. slang*): an expression of contempt. — *v.t.* to regard contemptuously. — Also *v.i.* — *n.* **snoot′ful** enough alcohol to make one drunk. — *adj.* **snoot′y** haughtily supercilious. [Cf. Du. *snuit,* snout, face.]

snooze *snōōz, v.i.* to doze. — *n.* a nap. — *n.* **snooz′er.** [Origin obscure; perh. orig. slang.]

snoozle *snōō′zl, v.i.* to nuzzle: to snooze. — *v.t.* to thrust nuzzlingly. [Cf. **snooze,** **nuzzle¹**.]

snore *snōr, snōr, v.i.* to breathe roughly and hoarsely in sleep with vibration of uvula and soft palate or of the vocal chords: to snort. — *v.t.* to pass in snoring: to render by snoring. — *n.* a noisy breathing of this kind. — *ns.* **snōr′er; snōr′ing.** [Imit.; cf. **snort.**]

snorkel *snōr′kl,* an anglicised form of **schnorkel.** — *n.* **snor′kelling** swimming with a snorkel.

snort *snort, v.i.* to force the air with violence and noise through the nostrils, as horses: to snore (*Shak.*): to inhale a drug through the nose (*slang*). — *v.t.* to express by or utter with a snort: to force out, as by a snort: to inhale (a powdered drug, esp. cocaine) through the

nose (*slang*). — *n.* an act or sound of snorting: a quick drink (*slang*): the snorkel of a submarine. — *n.* **snort′er** one who snorts: anything characterised by extreme force, esp. a gale (*coll.*). — *n.* and *adj.* **snort′ing.** — *adv.* **snort′ingly.** — *adj.* **snort′y** snorting: inclined to snort (*coll.*): contemptuous and ready to take offence. — **snort′-mast** the snort or snorkel of a submarine. [Imit.]

snot *snot, n.* mucus of the nose: a mean fellow. — *v.t.* to blow (the nose). — *v.i.* **snott′er** to breathe through an obstruction in the nostrils: to sob, snuffle, blubber. — *n.* the wattles of a turkey-cock: snot (*Scot.*). — *n.* **snott′ery** snot, filthiness. — *adv.* **snott′ily.** — *n.* **snott′-iness.** — *adj.* **snott′y** like, or foul with, snot: superciliously stand-offish, with nose in air: mean, of no importance. — *n.* (*naval slang*) a midshipman. — *adj.* **snott′y-nosed.** [O.E. *gesnot; snȳtan,* to blow the nose; cf. Du. *snot;* allied to **snout.**]

snotter *snot′ər, n.* the lower support of the sprit. [Origin obscure.]

snout *snowt, n.* the projecting nose of a beast, as of a swine: any similar projection: a cigar or cigarette (*slang*): a police informer (*slang*). — *v.t.* to furnish with a snout. — *adjs.* **snout′ed; snout′y** like a snout: snouted: haughtily supercilious (see **snooty**). [M.E. *snūte,* prob. from unrecorded O.E.; cf. Sw. *snut;* Ger. *Schnauze,* Du. *snuit;* also **snot.**]

snow¹ *snō, n.* atmospheric vapour frozen in crystalline form, whether in single crystals or aggregated in flakes: a snowfall: any similar substance, as carbonic acid snow (frozen carbon dioxide): snowlike specks on the screen caused by electrical interference (*TV*): a mass or expanse of snow: a winter: anything white, as hair (*fig.*): a white-fleshed variety of apple: linen, esp. drying or bleaching (*slang*): cocaine, morphine, heroin (*slang*). — *adj.* of snow. — *v.i.* to shower snow: to fall as snow or like snow. — *v.t.* to shower like snow: to strew as with snow: to whiten, whiten the hair of (*fig.*): (with *up, under*) to bury, block, shut in, overwhelm, with snow or as if with snow. — *adv.* **snow′ily.** — *n.* **snow′iness.** — *adjs.* **snow′ish** resembling snow; **snow′-less; snow′like; snow′y** abounding or covered with snow: white, like snow: pure. — **snow′ball** a ball made of snow pressed hard together: (also **snow′ball-tree**) a sterile *Viburnum opulus* (see **opulus**): a round white pudding, cake, or sweetmeat: (*ironically*) a Negro, chimney-sweep, etc.: something that grows like a snowball rolled in snow, esp. a distribution of begging letters, each recipient being asked to send out so many copies. — *v.t.* to throw snowballs at. — *v.i.* to throw snowballs: to grow greater ever more quickly. — **snow′-berry** the white berry of an American shrub (*Symphoricarpos*) of the honeysuckle family: the shrub itself; **snow′-bird** any finch of the N. American genus Junco, white underneath, familiar in winter: applied to various other birds that appear in winter. — *adj.* **snow′-blind.** — **snow′-blind′ness** amblyopia caused by the reflection of light from snow; **snow′-blink** a reflection from fields of snow, like ice-blink; **snow′-blower** a snow-clearing machine which takes in the snow in front of it and blows it to the side of the road; **snow′-boot** a boot or overshoe for walking in snow. — *adj.* **snow′-bound** shut in, prevented from travelling, by snow. — **snow′-box** a theatrical apparatus for representing a snowfall; **snow′-break** a melting of snow; **snow′-broth** melted or melting snow; **snow′-bunting** a black-and-white (in summer partly tawny) bunting of the Arctic regions, a winter visitor in Britain; **snow′cap** a cap of snow as on the polar regions or a mountain-top. — *adjs.* **snow′-capped, -capt; snow′-cold** as cold as snow. — **snow′drift** a bank of snow drifted together by the wind; **snow′drop** a drooping white flower of early spring, or the plant (*Galanthus nivalis;* fam. Amaryllidaceae) that bears it; **snow′-dropper** (*slang*) a linen thief; **snow′drop-tree** the fringe-tree: the silverbell or calico-wood (*Halesia*), an American tree of the Styrax family, with white bell-shaped flowers;

snow'-eyes an Eskimo contrivance to prevent snow-blindness — a piece of wood with slits; **snow'fall** a quiet fall of snow: the amount falling in a given time. — *adj.* **snow'-fed** begun or increased by melted snow, as a stream. — **snow'-field** a wide range of snow, esp. where permanent; **snow'-finch** an Alpine bird like the snow-bunting; **snow'flake** a feathery clump of snow crystals: a garden-plant (*Leucojum*) or its flower like a big snowdrop: (also **snow'fleck, -flick**) the snow-bunting; **snow'-flea** a springtail; **snow'-fly** a stone-fly or other insect found on snow; **snow'-goggles** goggles to guard against snow-blindness: snow-eyes; **snow'-goose** a white Arctic American goose; **snow'-guard** a board to keep snow from sliding off a roof; **snow'-hole** a hole dug in snow as a temporary shelter; **snow'-ice** ice formed from freezing slush or compacted snow; **snow-in-summ'er** a white-flowered garden mouse-ear chickweed; **snow job** (*U.S. slang*) an attempt to mislead, persuade or convince by means of insincere or flattering words, exaggeration, inaccurate or complex information, etc.; **snow leopard** the ounce (*Panthera uncia*), an animal related to the leopard, found in the mountainous regions of Central Asia; **snow'line** the limit of perpetual snow; **snow'man** a great snowball made in human form: the abominable snowman (see **abominate**); **snow'mobile** a motorised sleigh or a tractor-like vehicle capable of travelling over snow; **snow'-plant** a red Californian saprophyte of the wintergreen family (*Sarcodes*) appearing among snow: the organism of red snow (see **red**); **snow'-plough** an implement for clearing snow from roads and railways: a skiing position in which the skis form a V, with the tips touching. — *v.i.* in skiing, to assume the snow-plough position in order to reduce speed, stop, etc. — **snow'-scape** a snowy landscape; **snow'-shoe** a long broad framework strapped to the foot for walking on snow: a ski (*obs.*). — *v.i.* to travel on snow-shoes. — **snow-shoe rabbit** a hare of Canada and U.S., white in winter, brownish with white feet in summer; **snow'slip** a small avalanche of snow; **snow'-spec'tacles** spectacles worn as a protection against the glare of snow; **snow'storm; snow'-water** water from melted snow. — *adj.* **snow'-white** as white as snow. — **snow'-wreath** a snowdrift; **snowy owl** a great white owl of northern regions. — **not a snowball's chance (in hell, in an oven)** (*coll.*) no chance at all; **snowed under with** overwhelmed with rapid accumulation of; **snowed in, up** blocked or isolated by snow. [O.E. *snāw;* Ger. *Schnee,* L. *nix, nivis.*]

snow² *snō, n.* a vessel like a brig, with a trysail-mast. [Du. *snaauw.*]

snowk. See **snook¹.**

snub *snub, v.t.* to rebuke: to take up, cut short, rebuff, in a humiliating or mortifying manner: to check: to bring to a sudden stop: to cut or break short: to make snub: — *pr.p.* **snubb'ing;** *pa.t.* and *pa.p.* **snubbed.** — *n.* an act of snubbing: a check: a snub nose: (*Spens.* **snubbe**) a stub, snag, knob. — *adj.* (of the nose) flat, broad, and turned up. — *n.* **snubb'er** one who snubs: a device for stopping a rope: a shock-absorber. — *n.* and *adj.* **snubb'ing.** — *adv.* **snubb'ingly.** — *adjs.* **snubb'-ish, snubb'y** inclined to snub or check: somewhat snub. — **snubb'ing-post** a post for passing a rope round, as to stop a boat or horse; **snub nose** a short turned-up nose. — *adj.* **snub'-nosed.** [O.N. *snubba,* to chide, snub.]

snuck *snuk,* a dial. or U.S. coll. *pa.t.* and *pa.p.* of **sneak.**

snudge¹ *snuj,* (*obs.*) *v.i.* to be snug and quiet. [Origin obscure.]

snudge² *snuj, v.i.* to save in a miserly way. — *n.* a mean stingy fellow. [Origin unknown.]

snuff¹ *snuf, v.i.* to draw in air violently and noisily through the nose: to sniff: to smell at anything doubtfully: to take snuff. — *v.t.* to draw into the nose: to smell, to examine, suspect, or detect by smelling. — *n.* a powdered preparation of tobacco or other substance for snuffing: a pinch of snuff or act of snuffing: a sniff:

resentment, huff. — *ns.* **snuff'er** one who snuffs; **snuff'-iness.** — *n.* and *adj.* **snuff'ing.** — *adj.* **snuff'y** like, smelling of, soiled with or showing traces of, snuff: touchy, huffy. — **snuff'box** a box for snuff; **snuffbox bean** the cacoon; **snuff'-colour, -brown** a yellowish or greyish brown, slightly paler than bistre. — *adj.* **snuff'-coloured.** — **snuff'-dipper, snuff'-dipping** see **dip** snuff at **dip;** **snuff'-mill** a factory or a hand-mill for grinding tobacco into snuff: a snuff-mull; **snuff'-mull** a snuffbox (see **mill¹**); **snuff'-paper** (*Scott; contemptuous*) banknotes; **snuff'-spoon** a spoon for taking snuff from a snuffbox; **snuff'-taker; snuff'-taking.** — **take it in snuff** (*Shak.*) to take offence; **up to snuff** alert, knowing, not likely to be taken in: up to scratch, in good order: of a high, or suitable standard. [M.Du. *snuffen;* Ger. *schnaufen,* to snuff.]

snuff² *snuf, n.* a sooty ill-smelling knob on a wick: a worthless or offensive residue: a heel-tap. — *v.t.* to remove the snuff from: to make brighter: to put out as with snuffers (with *out;* also *fig.*). — *n.* **snuff'er** (in later use **snuffers,** or **pair of snuffers**) an instrument like a pair of scissors for removing snuffs from the wicks of candles, or of oil-lamps: one with a cap-shaped part for extinguishing candles: an attendant, esp. in a theatre, who snuffed candles. — **snuff'-dish** a dish or tray for candle snuffs; **snuff film, movie** a pornographic film which has as its climax the real-life murder of the woman performing the sex act(s). — **snuff it, snuff out** (*slang*) to die. [M.E. *snoffe;* connection with foregoing and with L.G. *snuppen,* Ger. *schnappen,* is obscure.]

snuffle *snuf'l, v.i.* to breathe hard or in an obstructed manner through the nose: to sniff: to speak through the nose. — *v.t.* to sniff: to say or utter nasally. — *n.* an act or sound of snuffling: a snuffling tone: cant: (in *pl.*) an obstructed condition of the nose. — *n.* **snuff'ler** (*snuf'lər, snuf'l-ər*). — *n.* and *adj.* **snuffling** (*snuf'ling, snuf'l-ing*). [Freq. of **snuff¹;** cf. **snivel** and Du. *snuffelen,* Ger. *schnüffeln.*]

snug *snug, adj.* lying close and warm: comfortable: sheltered: not exposed to view or notice: in good order: compact: fitting close. — *n.* a snuggery. — *v.i.* to lie close. — *v.t.* to make snug: to stow away snugly: — *pr.p.* **snugg'ing;** *pa.t.* and *pa.p.* **snugged.** — *n.* **snugg'ery** a snug room or place, esp. a bar-parlour or (*dial.*) a separate small compartment in a bar. — *v.i.* **snugg'le** to nestle. — *v.t.* to hug close: to wrap close. — *adv.* **snug'ly.** — *n.* **snug'ness.** [Origin obscure.]

snush *snush,* (*obs.*) *n.* snuff. — *v.t.* and *v.i.* (*obs.*) to snuff. [Poss. imit.; cf. **sneesh,** Dan. and Sw. *snus.*]

snuzzle *snuz'l,* (*dial.*) *v.i.* to grub or root: to rub or poke and sniff: to nuzzle. [Cf. **nuzzle¹, snoozle.**]

so¹ *sō, adv.* merging in *conj.* or *interj.* in this, that, or such manner, degree, or condition: to such an extent: likewise: accordingly: well: therefore: in due course, thereupon, thereafter: as: soever: thus: for like reason: in a high degree: as has been stated: provided: in case: in order that (*coll.*): be it: that will do: very good. — **so'-and-so** this or that person or thing: such-and-such a person or thing: used to replace a descriptive oath (*coll.;* also *adj.*). — *adj.* **so'-called** styled thus — usu. implying doubt or denial of the meaning or implications of the following term, or a wish to disassociate oneself from the implications of the term. — **so many** such-and-such a number of; **so much** such-and-such an amount: in such a degree: to such an extent: such an amount (of): that amount of: an equal amount. — **and so forth, and so on** and more of the same or the like: and the rest of it; **just so** exactly right, impeccable: quite so; **or so** thereabouts; **quite so** just as you have said, exactly; **so as** in such a manner as or that: in order (with *to*) (*coll.*): if only, on condition that; **so far** to that, or to such an, extent, degree, or point; **so long!,** **so long as** see **long; so much as** as much as: even; **so much for** that disposes of: that is the end of: no more of; **so much so** to such an extent (that); **so so** see **so-so; so that** with the purpose that: with the result that: if

only; **so then** thus then it is, therefore; **so to say** or **speak** if one may use that expression; **so what** see **what**. [O.E. *swā*; O.N. *svā*, Goth. *swa*, Ger. *so*.]
so² *sō*. See **sol¹**.
soak *sōk, v.t.* to steep in a liquid: to drench: to saturate: to draw through the pores: to bathe thoroughly (*U.S.*): to beat, pummel (*slang*): to overcharge, tax heavily, etc. (*slang*). — *v.i.* to be steeped in a liquid: to pass through pores: to drink to excess, to guzzle: to soften by heating: — *pa.p.* **soaked**, rarely **soak'en**. — *n.* the process or act of soaking: a drenching: a marshy place: a hard drinker, a carouse. — *ns.* **soak'age** soaking: liquid that has percolated; **soak'er**. — *n.* and *adj.* **soak'ing**. — *adv.* **soak'ingly**. — **soak'away** a depression into which water percolates. [M.E. *soke* — O.E. *socian*, a weak vb. related to *sūcan*, to suck.]
soap *sōp, n.* an alkaline salt of a higher fatty acid: esp. such a compound of sodium (*hard soap*) or potassium (*soft soap*), used in washing: smooth words, flattery (*slang*): money, esp. used for bribery and other secret political purposes (*U.S. slang*): soap opera. — *v.t.* to rub with soap: to flatter. — *n.* **soap'ie** (*Austr.*) a soap opera. — *adv.* **soap'ily.** — *n.* **soap'iness.** — *adjs.* **soap'less; soap'y.** — **soap'-ball** soap made into a ball, often with starch, as an emollient; **soap'-bark** a S. American rosaceous tree (*Quillaja saponaria*), or its bark, used as soap; **soap'berry** the fruit of *Sapindus saponaria*, or other species, used as soap, or the S. American tree yielding it; **soap'-boiler** a maker of soap; **soap'-boiling; soap'box** a box for packing soap: a wayside orator's improvised platform; **soap'-bubb'le** a globe of air enclosed in a film of soap-suds; **soap'-dish; soap flakes; soap opera** a sentimental, melodramatic serial broadcast on radio or television, written around the lives of the members of a family or other small group, and chiefly concerned with the emotional involvement of the characters (also *fig.*; orig. American and often sponsored by soap manufacturers): broadcast drama of this sort; **soap powder; soap'-root** species of Gypsophila, Saponaria, and other plants whose roots can be used as soap; **soap'stone** steatite, or French chalk, a compact kind of talc with soapy feel; **soap'-suds** soapy water, esp. when frothy; **soap'-test** a test for determining hardness of water by amount of standard soap solution required to make a lather; **soap'-tree** the soap-bark tree, the soapberry tree, or other yielding saponin; **soap'-work(s); soap'wort** a tall herb (*Saponaria officinalis*, or other species) of the pink family, whose roots and leaves contain saponin. [O.E. *sāpe*; Du. *zeep*, Ger. *Seife*.]
soar *sōr, sör, v.i.* to mount high in the air: to fly aloft: to rise to a great height: to glide or skim high in the air: to glide in a rising current: to increase rapidly in number or amount. — *v.t.* to reach, traverse, or accomplish in upward flight. — *n.* and *adj.* **soar'ing.** — *adv.* **soar'ingly.** — *adj.* **soar'away** making spectacular progress. [Fr. *essorer*, to expose to air, raise into air — L. *ex*, out, *aura*, air.]
soar(e). See **sore²**.
Soay (sheep) *sō'ā* (*shēp*)*, n.* a breed of small, wild, dark-coloured sheep found esp. on the island of *Soay* in the Outer Hebrides: one of this breed.
sob *sob, v.i.* to catch the breath convulsively in distress or other emotion: to make a similar sound: to weep noisily. — *v.t.* to utter with sobs: to bring by sobbing: — *pr.p.* **sobb'ing;** *pa.t.* and *pa.p.* **sobbed.** — *n.* a convulsive catch of the breath: any similar sound. — *n.* and *adj.* **sobb'ing.** — *adv.* **sobb'ingly.** — **sob'-sister** (*slang*) a woman (rarely, a man) who seeks to draw tears by writing, acting, etc.: a journalist who answers questions in a woman's magazine; **sob'-story** a pitiful tale told to arouse sympathy; **sob'-stuff** cheap and extravagant pathos, to stir tears: maudlin films or scenes. [Imit.]
sobeit *sō-bē'it, conj.* provided. [**so be it.**]
sober *sō'bər, adj.* not drunk: temperate, esp. in use of intoxicants: moderate: restrained: without excess or extravagance: serious: sedate: quiet in colour: sombre: sane, rational (*obs.*): poor, feeble (*Scot.*). — *v.t.* to make sober (often with *up*). — *v.i.* to become sober (often with *up*). — *adj.* **so'bering** making sober: causing to become serious, grave or thoughtful. — *v.t.* **so'berise, -ize** to make sober. — *adv.* **so'berly.** — *ns.* **so'berness; sobriety** (*sō-* or *sə-brī'i-ti*) the state or habit of being sober: calmness: gravity. — *adjs.* **so'ber-blood'ed** staid; **so'ber-mind'ed.** — *ns.* **so'ber-mind'edness** the state of being sober-minded: freedom from inordinate passion: calmness; **so'bersides** a sedate and solemn person: — *pl.* **so'bersides.** — *adj.* **so'ber-suit'ed** dressed in sad-coloured clothes. [Fr. *sobre* — L. *sōbrius* — *sē-*, apart, not, *ēbrius*, drunk.]
sobole *sō'bōl*, **soboles** *sob'ō-lēz*, (*bot.*) *ns.* a creeping underground stem producing roots and buds: — *pl.* **sob'ōlēs.** — *adj.* **sobolif'erous** having soboles. [L. *sobolēs, subolēs*, a shoot — *sub*, under, and the root of *alĕre*, to nourish, sustain.]
Sobranje *sō-brän'ye, n.* the national assembly of Bulgaria. — Also **Sobran'ye.** [Bulg.]
soubriquet *sō'brē-kā, n.* a nickname. — Also **soubriquet** (*sōō'*). [Fr. *sobriquet*, earlier *soubriquet*, a chuck under the chin.]
soc *sok*, (*law*) *n.* the right of holding a local court. — *ns.* **soc'age, socc'age** tenure of lands by service fixed and determinate in quality; **soc'ager, soc'man, sōke'man** a tenant by socage; **soke** (*sōk*) soc: a district under a particular jurisdiction; **soke'manry** tenure by socage; **sōk'en** a district under a particular jurisdiction. [O.E. *sōcn*, inquiry, jurisdiction.]
so-called *sō'köld, adj.* See under **so¹**.
soccer *sok'ər,* (*coll.*) *n.* association football. — *n.pl.* **socceroos'** (*soccer* and *kangaroos*) the Australian national association football team.
socdolager, -iger, -oger. See **sockdologer**.
sociable *sō'shə-bl, adj.* inclined to society: companionable: favourable to social intercourse: friendly, fond of others' company. — *n.* a four-wheeled open carriage with seats facing: a seat, tricycle, aeroplane, etc., for two persons side by side: a social (*U.S.*). — *ns.* **sociabil'ity, so'ciableness.** — *adv.* **so'ciably.** — *adj.* **social** (*sō'shl*) pertaining to life in an organised community: pertaining to welfare in such: growing or living in communities: pertaining to, or characterised by, friendly association: convivial: gregarious, sociable: pertaining to fashionable circles: sympathetic (*obs.*). — *n.* an informal party or gathering of a club, church, etc.: (with *the*) social security (*coll.*). — *n.* **socialīsā'tion, -z-** the act or process of socialising: the process by which infants and young children become aware of society and their relationships with others. — *v.t.* **so'cialise, -ize** to render social: to put on a socialistic footing. — *v.i.* (*coll.*) to behave in a sociable manner, e.g. at parties, etc. — *ns.* **so'cialism** the theory, principle, or scheme of social organisation which places means of production and distribution in the hands of the community; **so'cialist** an adherent of socialism. — Also *adj.* — *adj.* **socialist'ic.** — *adv.* **socialist'ically** in a socialistic manner. — *ns.* **so'cialite** (*coll.*) one who has a place in fashionable society; **sociality** (*sō-shi-al'i-ti*) the quality or fact of being social: social relations, association, or intercourse: sociability: a social function or formality. — *adv.* **so'cially.** — *ns.* **so'cialness; so'ciate** (*-shi-āt, arch.*) an associate. — Also *adj.* — *adj.* **so'ciātive** expressing association; **soci'etal** (*-sī'*) pertaining to society, social. — *adv.* **soci'etally** by society. — *adj.* **societarian** (*sə-sī-i-tā'ri-ən*) of or pertaining to society or fashionable society: Fourieristic: socialist. — Also *n.* — *adj.* **soci'etary** (*-tər-i*). — *n.* **soci'ety** fellowship, companionship: company: association: a community: the body of mankind, the fashionable world generally: a corporate body: any organised association. — *adj.* of fashionable society. — **social anthropologist; social anthropology** the branch of anthropology which deals with the culture, customs and social structure of, esp. primitive, societies; **social**

climber (often *derog.*) a person who tries to become accepted into a social stratum higher than that to which he belongs by a deliberate policy of getting to know and associating with people belonging to that higher stratum; **social contract** the voluntary agreement between individuals upon which an organised society, its rights, functions, and the relationships within it are founded; **social credit** a movement stressing the element of unearned increment in the returns of industry and advocating the achievement of social well-being by the stable adjustment of production and consumption through monetary reform: (with *cap.*) a theory that the government should distribute national dividends in order to spread purchasing power and thus increase consumption (regarded as a benefit); **social democracy** the practices and policies of socialists who believe that socialism can and should be achieved by a gradual and democratic process; **social democrat** a supporter of social democracy: (with *caps.*) a member or supporter of a Social Democratic party. — *adj.* **social democratic.** — **social evil** (*specif.*) prostitution (*arch.*): any factor which has a damaging, unhealthy or negative effect on or with society as a whole; **social insurance** state insurance by compulsory contributions against sickness, unemployment, and old age; **social science** the scientific study of human society and behaviour, including such disciplines (the *social sciences*) as anthropology, sociology, economics, political science and history; **social secretary** one who is responsible for organising the social activities of a person, club, association, etc.; **social security** security against sickness, unemployment, old age, provided by a social insurance scheme: supplementary benefit; **social service** welfare work (also in *pl.*): (in *pl.*) the public bodies carrying out such work; **Social War** the war (90–88 B.C.) of Rome's Italian allies (*Socii*) against Rome for admission to Roman citizenship; **social whale** the ca'ing whale; **social work** any of various forms of welfare work intended to promote the well-being of the poor, the aged, the handicapped, etc.; **social worker; society verse** vers de société. — **socialism of the chair** professorial socialism, the doctrines of a school of political economists (*c.* 1872) in Germany whose aim was mainly to better the condition of the working-classes by factory-acts, savings-banks, insurance against sickness and old age, etc.; **the alternative society** a better, more humane, form of society as envisaged by those who refuse to follow the ways of society as it is today; **the Societies** the Cameronians organised from 1681 for maintenance of Presbyterianism; **the Society of Jesus** see Jesuit. [L. *socius*, a companion.]

société anonyme *so-syā-tā a-no-nēm*, (Fr.) lit. anonymous society: joint-stock company.

society. See **sociable.**

Socinian *sō-sin'i-ən, adj.* pertaining to or following, Laelius (1525–62) and Faustus (1539–1604) *Socinus*, uncle and nephew, Italian Unitarians. — Also *n.* — *v.t.* and *v.i.* **Socin'ianise, -ize.** — *n.* **Socin'ianism.**

socio- *sō'si-ō-, sō'shi-ō-, -si-o'-, -shi-o'-,* in composition, social, or of or pertaining to society, as *sociocultural, socioeconomic, sociopolitical.* — *adj.* **sociobiolog'ical.** — *ns.* **sociobiol'ogist; sociobiol'ogy** a scientific discipline combining biology and the social sciences which attempts to establish that social behaviour and organisation in humans and animals has a genetic basis and is to be explained in terms of evolution and genetics; **so'ciogram** (-*gram*) a chart representing personal interrelationships within a social group; **socioling'uist.** — *adj.* **sociolinguis'tic** of or pertaining to sociolinguistics: pertaining to language as it functions as a social tool. — *n.sing.* **sociolinguis'tics** the study of language as it functions in society and is affected by social and cultural factors. — *adjs.* **sociolog'ic, -al** pertaining to sociology: dealing solely with environmental factors in considering a human problem: social. — *ns.* **sociol'ogism** a concept or explanation taking into consider-

ation social factors only, disregarding others; **sociol'ogist.** — *adj.* **sociologis'tic.** — *n.* **sociol'ogy** the study of the structure and functioning of human society. — *adj.* **sociomet'ric.** — *ns.* **sociom'etry** the measurement of social phenomena: the study of personal interrelationships within a social group; **so'ciopath.** — *adj.* **sociopath'ic.** — *n.* **sociop'athy** any of several personality disorders resulting in asocial or antisocial behaviour. [L. *socius*, a companion.]

sock[1] *sok, n.* a light shoe, worn by Roman actors of comedy (*obs.* except *hist.* and allusively): now, a covering for the foot and part or all of the lower leg. — **sock'-suspender** a strap to support a sock. — **pull up one's socks** to brace oneself for doing better; **put a sock in it** (*slang*; usu. *imper.*) to become silent, stop talking, etc. [O.E. *socc* — L. *soccus.*]

sock[2] *sok, n.* a ploughshare. [O.Fr. *soc* — Celt., Bret. *souc'h*, Gael. *soc.*]

sock[3] *sok,* (*dial.* and *slang*) *v.t.* to thrust hard: to strike hard: to drub. — *n.* a violent blow, esp. with the fist. — *adj.* **sock'ō** (*U.S.* and *theatrical slang*) excellent, successful, knockout: having a strong impact, full of energy. — *n.pl.* **socks** a beating. — **sock it to** (*slang*) to speak, behave, etc. in a vigorous manner towards. [Ety. dub.]

sockdologer *sok-dol'ə-jər,* also **soc-, sog-, slock-, -dolager, -doliger** (*Amer. slang*) *n.* a conclusive argument: a hard or decisive blow: anything very big, a whopper. [Cf. foregoing; perh. reminiscent of **doxology** as the closing act of a service.]

socker. Same as **soccer.**

socket *sok'it, n.* a hollow into which something is inserted, as the receptacle of the eye, of a bone, of a tooth, of the shaft of an iron golf-club: the hollow of a candlestick: a stroke with the socket of a golf-club. — *v.t.* to provide with or place in a socket: to strike with the socket: — *pr.p.* **sock'eting;** *pa.t.* and *pa.p.* **sock'eted.** — *adj.* **sock'eted.** — **socket chisel** a robust chisel with a socketed metal shaft into which the wooden handle is fitted; **socket spanner** a spanner with a socketed head made to fit over a nut or a bolt; **socket wrench** a wrench with a handle to which a variety of socketed heads can be fitted. [O.Fr. *soket*, dim. of *soc*; see **sock**[2].]

sockeye *sok'ī, n.* the blueback salmon. [Amer. Ind. *sukai*, the fish of fishes, the native name on the Fraser River.]

socking *sok'ing,* (*coll.*) *adj.* huge, whacking (usu. followed by *great*). [Prob. **sock**[3].]

socle *sō'kl, sok'l,* (*archit.*) *n.* a plain face or plinth at the foot of a wall, column, etc. [Fr., — It. *zoccolo* — L. *socculus,* dim. of *soccus,* a shoe.]

Socratic, -al *sō-krat'ik, -i-kl, so-, adjs.* pertaining to *Socrates,* the celebrated Greek philosopher (d. 399 B.C.), to his philosophy, or to his method of teaching, by a series of simple questions revealing to his interlocutors their own ignorance. — *n.* **Socrat'ic** a follower of Socrates. — *adv.* **Socrat'ically.** — *v.i.* **Socratise, -ize** (*sok', sōk'rə-tīz*) to practise the Socratic method.

sod[1] *sod, n.* a turf, usu. one cut in rectangular shape: sward. — *adj.* of sod. — *v.t.* to cover with sod. — *adj.* **sodd'y** covered with sod: turfy. [M.L.G. *sode*; Ger. *Sode.*]

sod[2] *sod.* See **seethe.**

sod[3] *sod,* (*vulg.*) *n.* a term of abuse, affection, etc. — *interj.* (*vulg.*) a term expressing annoyance, etc. (sometimes behaving as a verb with *it, him,* etc. as object). — *adj.* **sodd'ing.** — **sod off** (*vulg.*) to go away; **Sod's law** (*facet.*) the law that states that the most inconvenient thing is the most likely to happen, or if there is a possibility that something will go wrong, it will. [Abbrev. of **sodomite.**]

soda *sō'də, n.* sodium oxide (Na₂O): sodium hydroxide (*caustic soda*): sodium carbonate, the soda of commerce (in powder form, anhydrous, *soda-ash*; in crystals, with water of crystallisation, *washing-soda*): sodium bicarbonate (*baking-soda*): soda-water (*coll.*): a drink made of soda-water with flavouring, ice-cream, etc. (*U.S.*). — *adj.* of or containing soda or sodium. — *adj.* **sodaic** (*sō-dā'ik*) containing, pertaining to, soda. — *ns.* **so'dalite** a cubic mineral consisting of sodium aluminium silicate with chlorine; **so'damide** (*-mīd*) a compound (NaNH₂) formed when ammonia gas is passed over hot sodium. — *adj.* **so'dic.** — *n.* **so'dium** a bluish-white alkaline metal (symbol Na; at. numb. 11), the base of soda. — **so'da-fountain** an apparatus for supplying, counter for serving, sodas, ice-cream, etc.; **soda jerk(er)** (*U.S.*) one who serves at a soda-fountain; **so'da-lake'** a lake containing and depositing much sodium salt; **so'da-lime** a mixture of caustic soda and quicklime; **soda pop** (*U.S.*) a carbonated soft drink of any flavour; **so'da-scone'** a scone made with baking-soda; **so'da-siph'on** a siphon which dispenses soda-water; **so'da-wa'ter** water (now commonly without sodium bicarbonate) charged with carbon dioxide; **sodium amytal** (*am'i-tal*; ℞ with *caps.*; also **amytal sodium**) a sodium salt used as a sedative and hypnotic; **sodium ascorbate** a compound usd as a meat preservative, also in the treatment of vitamin C deficiency; **sodium lamp** a street lamp using sodium vapour and giving yellow light. [It. and L.L. *soda*; origin doubtful.]

sodain, sodaine. Obs. spellings of **sudden.**

sodality *sō-dal'i-ti, n.* a fellowship or fraternity. [L. *sodālitās — sodālis,* a comrade.]

sodden *sod'n, pa.p.* of **seethe.** — *adj.* boiled (*rare*): soaked thoroughly: boggy: doughy, not well baked: bloated, saturated with drink. — *v.t.* and *v.i.* to make or become sodden: to soak. — *n.* **sodd'enness.** — *adj.* **sodd'en= witt'ed** (*Shak.*) heavy, stupid.

soddy. See **sod**¹.

sodger. See **soldier.**

sodium. See **soda.**

Sodom *sod'əm, n.* one of the 'cities of the plain' (see Gen. xviii, xix): any place of utter depravity (*fig.*). — *v.t.* **sod'omise, -ize** to practise sodomy upon. — *n.* **Sod'- omite** (*-īt*) an inhabitant of Sodom: (without *cap.*) one who practises sodomy. — *adjs.* **sodomitic** (*-it'ik*), **-al.** — *adv.* **sodomit'ically.** — *n.* **sod'omy** anal intercourse (with a man or woman) or copulation with an animal, imputed to the inhabitants of Sodom. — **apple of Sodom** see **apple.**

soever *sō-ev'ər, adv.* generally used to extend or render indefinite the sense of *who, what, where, how,* etc.

sofa *sō'fə, n.* in the East, a raised portion of the floor forming a bench: a long upholstered seat with back and arms — formerly **sō'pha.** — **sō'fa-bed** a piece of furniture serving as a sofa by day, a bed at night; **so'fa-ta'ble** a narrow table with a flap at each end, used as a writing-table from *c.* 1790. [Ar. *suffah.*]

sofar *sō'fär, n.* a method of calculating the location of an underwater explosion from measurements of the time taken for the sound vibrations to reach three widely separated shore stations (used in searching for survivors, who drop a special bomb into the sea). [*so*und *f*ixing *a*nd *r*anging.]

soffioni *sof-yō'nē, n.pl.* volcanic steam-holes. [It.]

soffit *sof'it, n.* a ceiling, now generally restricted to the ornamented underside of a stair, entablature, archway, etc. [It. *soffitto* — L. *suffixus,* pa.p. of *suffigĕre,* to fasten beneath — *sub,* under, *figĕre,* to fix.]

Sofi, Sofism. See **Sufi, Sufism.**

soft *soft, söft, adj.* easily yielding to pressure: easily cut: easily scratched (*min.*): malleable: yielding: not rigorous enough: not loud: not glaring: diffused: weak in muscle or mind: out of training: smooth: pleasing or soothing to the senses: tender: mild: sympathetic: gentle: effeminate: unable to endure rough treatment or hardship: (relatively) unprotected: gently moving: easy: free from calcium and magnesium salts, as water: bituminous, of coal: of money, paper rather than metallic: unsized, of paper: rainy (*Scot.*): pronounced with a somewhat sibilant sound, not guttural or explosive: voiced or sonant: of silk, freed from natural gum: apt to fall in price: of drugs, not habit-forming

in an obvious degree: (of radiation) having short wavelengths and therefore not highly penetrating. — *n.* a softy, a fool: (in *pl.*) soft commodities. — *adv.* softly: gently: quietly. — *v.t.* (*Spens.*) to soften. — *interj.* (also **soft you**) hold: not so fast. — *v.t.* **soften** (*sof'n*) to make soft or softer: to mitigate: to tone down, make less glaring or smoother. — *v.i.* to grow soft or softer. — *ns.* **softener** (*sof'nər*); **softening** (*sof'ning*); **soft'ie** a softy. — *adj.* **soft'ish** rather soft. — *n.* **soft'ling** a weakling: an effeminate person: a soft object. — *adv.* **soft'ly.** — *adj.* (*Spens.*) soft: slack in enterprise. — *ns.* **soft'ness; soft'y** a silly person, a weak fool: one who is soft-hearted or sentimental. — **soft'back** a paperback. — Also *adj.* — **soft'ball** an American game similar to baseball, played on a smaller diamond with a soft ball. — *adjs.* **soft'-billed; soft'-bod'ied.** — *v.t.* **soft'-boil'.** — *adjs.* **soft'-boiled** boiled not long enough to be quite solid: soft-hearted (*coll.*); **soft'-cen'tred.** — **soft com- modities** foodstuffs, coffee, cotton, etc., as opposed to metals. — *adjs.* **soft'-con'scienc'd** (*Shak.*) having a not very rigorous conscience; **soft'-core** not explicit, blatant or graphic. — **soft currency** one unstable in value in the international money-market through fluctuation in its gold backing; **soft drink** a non-alcoholic drink. — *adjs.* **soft'-finned** without fin-spines; **soft'= foot'ed** softly treading. — **soft furnishings** curtains, coverings, rugs, etc.; **soft'-goods** cloth, and cloth articles, as opp. to *hardware,* etc.; **soft'-grass** a worthless grass (*Holcus mollis* or other species) akin to oats; **soft'head** a simpleton. — *adjs.* **soft'-head'ed; soft'= heart'ed** kind, generous: tender-hearted. — **soft line** a flexible or lenient attitude, policy, etc.; **soft loan** one without conditions attached: a cheap or interest-free loan, usu. to a developing country. — *adjs.* **soft'ly= soft'ly** cautious, careful, delicate; **soft'ly-spright'ed** (*Shak.*) tame-spirited. — **soft mark** see **mark; soft meat** regurgitated food given by pigeons to their young. — *adj.* **soft'-nosed** of a bullet, with a tip that expands on striking. — **soft option** an alternative that is easy to carry out, undergo, etc.; **soft palate** the back part of the palate. — *adj.* **soft'-paste** of porcelain, made of a paste of various kinds requiring less heat in firing than china-clay. — **soft pedal** a pedal for reducing tone in the piano, esp. by causing the hammer to strike only one string (*una corda*). — *v.t.* and *v.i.* **soft'-ped'al** to play with the soft pedal down: to subdue, tone down, avoid emphasising or alluding to (*slang*). — **soft porn(ography)** mild, soft-core pornography; **soft rock** a form of rock music, usu. rhythmically complex, highly melodious and low in volume; **soft'-saw'der** flattery. — *v.t.* to flatter, blarney. — *adj.* **soft'-sect'ored** (*comput.*) of a floppy disk, formatted by means of an electronic control system and software (compare *hard- sectored*). — **soft'-sect'oring; soft sell** selling or sale by preliminary softening up or other indirect method: mild persuasion, or mildly persuasive tactics. — *adjs.* **soft'-sell; soft'-shell, -ed** having a soft shell: moderate in policy or principles. — **soft'-shell** a soft-shell crab, clam, or river-turtle: a moderate. — *adjs.* **soft'-shoe** characteristic of or pertaining to a form of tap-dancing done in soft-soled shoes; **soft'-slow** (*Shak.*) soft and slow. — **soft soap** a kind of soap containing potash: flattery: blarney. — *v.t.* **soft'-soap** to rub or cover with soft soap: to flatter for some end. — *adj.* **soft'-spo'ken** having a mild or gentle voice: affable: suave: plausible in speech. — **soft spot** see **spot; soft thing** an easy task: a snug job; **soft touch** see **touch; soft underbelly** the vulnerable part; **soft'ware** computer programs, esp. general ones for routine operations (compare *hard- ware*): computer program (or analogous) accessories (other than the actual parts of a computer, etc.): material recorded in microform; **soft wheat** a variety of wheat with soft kernels and a high starch content, suitable for making biscuits, pastry, etc.; **soft'wood** timber of a conifer (also *adj.*). — **be** or **go soft on** to be lenient with; **softening of the brain** a softening of brain tissues: marked deterioration of mental faculties (*coll.*); **soften up** to lessen resistance in (*coll.*): to wear down by continuous shelling and bombing. [O.E. *sōfte*, *sēfte*; Du. *zacht*, Ger. *sanft*.]

softa *sof'tǝ*, *n.* a Muslim theological student, attached to a mosque. [Turk. *sŏfta*.]

sog *sog*, *n.* a soft wet place. — *v.t.* and *v.i.* to soak. — *adj.* **sogged.** — *adv.* **sogg'ily.** — *n.* **sogg'iness.** — *n.* and *adj.* **sogg'ing.** — *adj.* **sogg'y** soaked: soft or heavy with moisture: boggy: soppy: sultry: spiritless. [Ety. dub.]

sogdolager, -iger, -oger. See **sockdologer.**

soger. See **soldier.**

sogged, soggy, etc. See **sog.**

soh. See **sol**[1].

so-ho *sō-hō'*, (*Shak.*) *interj.* a form of call from a distance, a sportsman's halloo. [A.Fr.]

soi-disant *swä-dē-zä*, *adj.* self-styled, pretended, would-be. [Fr.]

soigné, *fem.* **soignée** *swa-nyā*, *adj.* well groomed. [Fr.]

soil[1] *soil*, *n.* the ground: the mould in which plants grow: the mixture of disintegrated rock and organic material which nourishes plants: country. — *adj.* having soil. — *adj.* **soil'-bound** attached to the soil. — **soil creep** (*geol.*) the very slow but continuous movement of soil and rock fragments down a slope; **soil mechanics** a branch of civil engineering concerned with the ability of different soils to withstand the use to which they are put; **soil science** the study of the composition and uses of soil. [O.Fr. *soel*, *suel*, *sueil* — L. *solum*, ground.]

soil[2] *soil*, *n.* a wallowing-place (*obs.*): a watery place where a hunted animal takes refuge: dirt: dung: filth: sewage: a spot or stain. — *v.t.* to make dirty: to stain: to manure. — *v.i.* to take a soil: to tarnish. — *adj.* **soiled.** — *n.* **soil'iness** (*rare*) stain: foulness. — *n.* and *adj.* **soil'ing.** — *adj.* **soil'less** destitute of soil. — *n.* **soil'ure** stain: pollution. — *adj.* **soil'y.** — **soil'-pipe** an upright discharge-pipe which receives the general refuse from water-closets, etc., in a building. [O.Fr. *soil, souil* (Fr. *souille*), wallowing-place.]

soil[3] *soil*, *v.t.* to feed on fresh-cut green food: to purge by so doing: to fatten. — *adj.* **soiled** (*Shak.* **soyled**). [O.Fr. *saouler* — *saol, saoul* — L. *satullus* — *satur*, full; or from **soil**[2].]

soirée *swär'ā, swŏr'ā, n* an evening party: an evening social meeting with tea, etc. [Fr., — *soir*, evening — L. *sērus*, late.]

soixante-neuf *swa-sät-nøf*, (Fr.) *n.* a sexual position in which both partners simultaneously orally stimulate each other's genitalia. [Lit. sixty-nine, from the position adopted.]

soja. See **soy.**

sojourn *sō', so', su'jǝrn*, sometimes *-jûrn', v.t.* to stay for a day: to dwell for a time. — *n.* a temporary residence. — *ns.* **so'journer; so'journing, so'journment.** [O.Fr. *sojourner* — L. *sub*, under, *diurnus*, of a day — *diēs*, a day.]

Sōka Gakkai *sō-kǝ gak'ī*, a Japanese Buddhist sect and political party, characterised by militant nationalism. [Jap., value creating society.]

soke, sokeman, soken. See under **soc.**

Sol *sol*, *n.* the sun personified, Helios or Phoebus: gold (*alch.*): the tincture or (*her.*): (without *cap.*; *sŏl*) the Peruvian monetary unit (one-tenth of a libra), and formerly a coin bearing a sun with rays: — *pl.* **soles** (*sō'lās*), **sols** (*sōlz*). — *adj.* **solar**, etc. see under **solar**[1]. [L. *sōl*, sun.]

sol[1] *sol*, *n.* the fifth note of the scale in sol-fa notation. — Also **so, soh** (*sō*). [See **Aretinian.**]

sol[2] *sol*, *n.* a colloidal suspension in a liquid: a solution of a difficulty (see **ob**). — *n.* **solā'tion** liquefaction of a gel. [For **solution.**]

sol[3] *sol*, *n.* an old French coin, one-twentieth of a livre. [O.Fr. *sol* (now *sou*) — L. *solidus*, solid.]

sola[1] *sō-lä', interj.* a cry to a person at a distance.

sola[2] *sō'lǝ, n.* the hat-plant or spongewood, an Indian papilionaceous plant (*Aeschynomene*): its pithlike stems. — *adj.* of sola. — **sola** (often **solar**) **hat, helmet**

a topi of sola. — Also **sō'lah,** (*corr.*) **sōl'ar.** [Hindi *śolā*.]

sola[3]. See **solus.**

solace *sol'is, -ǝs, n.* consolation, comfort in distress: pleasure, amusement: a source of comfort or pleasure. — *v.t.* to comfort in distress: to console: to allay. — *v.i.* to take comfort. — *n.* **sol'acement.** — *adj.* **solacious** (*-ā'shǝs; arch.*) giving solace. [O.Fr. *solas* — L. *sōlātium* — *sōlārī, -ātus,* to comfort in distress.]

solah. See **sola**[2].

solan *sō'lǝn, n.* the gannet. — Also **soland (goose), solan goose.** [O.N. *sūla.*]

solanaceous. See **Solanum.**

solander *sō-lan'dǝr, n.* a box in the form of a book, invented by the Swedish botanist Daniel *Solander* (1736–82).

solanine. See **Solanum.**

solano *sō-lä'nō, n.* a hot south-east wind in Spain: — *pl.* **sola'nos.** [Sp., — L. *sōlānus* (*ventus*), the east wind — *sōl,* the sun.]

Solanum *sō-lā'nǝm, n.* the potato and nightshade genus, giving name to the family **Solanaceae** (*-lǝ-nā'si-ē*): (without *cap.*) any plant of this genus. — *adj.* **solanā'-ceous.** — *n.* **solanine** (*sol'-, sōl'ǝ-nēn*) a glucoside got from potato sprouts, etc. [L. *sōlānum,* nightshade.]

solar[1] *sō'lǝr, adj.* of, from, like, or pertaining to the sun: measured by the sun: influenced by the sun: powered by energy from the sun's rays: with branches radiating like the sun's rays. — *n.* (also **sō'ler** or **sollar, soller** *sol'ǝr;* O.E. *solor,* or O.Fr. *soler; arch.*) an upper room: a garret: a landing between ladders in a mine. — *ns.* **solarimeter** (*-im'it-ǝr*) a device for measuring solar radiation; **sōlarīsā'tion, -z-** the act, process, or effect of solarising: the reversal of an image by over-exposure (*phot.*): the interruption of photosynthesis by long exposure to bright light (*bot.*). — *v.t.* **sō'larise, -ize** to expose to sunlight or affect by such exposure, esp. excessive or injurious exposure. — *v.i.* to be so affected. — *ns.* **sō'larism** excessive use of solar myths in the explanation of mythology; **sō'larist** one addicted to solarism; **solā'rium** a sundial: a place for sunning or sunbathing. — **solar battery** a battery of solar cells; **solar cell** a photoelectric cell converting the energy of sunlight into electric power; **solar day, time, year** see **day, time, year; solar energy** energy got from the sun's rays, esp. when used for home-heating, etc.; **solar flare** a short-lived bright outburst in the sun's chromosphere, generally associated with sun spots and often the cause of radio and magnetic disturbances on earth; **solar furnace** a furnace using sunlight (guided and focused by a system of mirrors) as a heat source; **solar microscope** an apparatus for projecting an enlarged image; **solar myth** a sun-myth, or a myth allegorising the course of the sun; **solar noise** a hissing background noise heard in radio communication, due to radiation from the sun and its atmosphere; **solar panel** a panel of solar cells; **solar plexus** (*anat.*) a network of nerves behind the stomach (so called from its radiating nerves); **solar power** solar energy (*adj.* **sō'lar-powered**); **solar prominences** large prominent or protruding parts of the great volumes of heated gas surrounding the sun; **solar salt** salt got by evaporation of sea-water by the sun; **solar system** the sun with its attendant bodies — major and minor planets, meteors, comets, satellites; **solar wind** charged particles from the sun travelling at about one and a half million kilometres an hour. [L. *sōlāris,* solar, *sōlārium,* a sundial — *sōl,* the sun.]

solar[2] *sō'lǝr.* See **sola**[2].

solation. See **sol**[2].

solatium *sō-lā'shi-ǝm, sō-lā'ti-ōōm, n.* compensation for disappointment, inconvenience, wounded feelings. [L. *sōlātium.*]

sold[1] *sōld, pa.t.* and *pa.p.* of **sell**[2]. — **sold on** extremely enthusiastic or convinced about.

sold[2] *sold, n.* (*Spens.*) pay, remuneration. — Also **solde** (*Meredith*). [Fr. *solde* — L. *solidus,* a piece of money.]

soldado *sōl-dä'dō, n.* a soldier: — *pl.* **solda'dos.** [Sp.]
soldan *sol'dən, (arch.) n.* a sultan, esp. of Egypt. [Fr.; see **sultan.**]
soldatesque *sol-də-tesk', adj.* soldierlike. [Fr., — *soldat,* a soldier.]
solde. See **sold²**.
solder *sōl'dər,* also *sol', sod', sōd', sōd', n.* a fusible alloy for uniting metals. — *v.t.* to make fast with solder: to join: to mend, patch up. — *v.i.* to adhere. — *ns.* **sol'derer; sol'dering.** — **sol'dering-bolt, -iron** a tool with pointed or wedge-shaped copper bit for use in soldering. [O.Fr. *soudre, souldure* — *souder, soulder,* to consolidate — L. *solidāre,* to make solid.]
soldi. See **soldo.**
soldier *sōl'jər, sōld'yər,* formerly *sō'jər,* **soger** (*dial.*) *sō'jər,* **sodger** (*dial.*) *soj', ns.* a person engaged in military service: a person of military skill: a shirker (*naut.*): an ant, or white ant, of a specialised fighting caste: a scarlet, pugnacious, or armoured animal of various kinds (beetle, fish, etc.): a red herring (*slang*): the ribwort plantain (used by children for a game of soldiers): a diligent worker for a cause: a brick set upright in a wall: a narrow strip of bread-and-butter or toast, esp. for a child to eat. — *v.i.* to serve as a soldier: to shirk. — *n.* **sol'diering.** — *adj.* **sol'dier-like** having the appearance of a soldier: soldierly. — *adv.* in the manner of a soldier. — *n.* **sol'dierliness.** — *adj.* **sol'dierly** befitting a soldier: having the qualities of or befitting a soldier. — *ns.* **sol'diership** the state or quality of being a soldier: military qualities: martial skill; **sol'diery** soldiers collectively: a military body or class: soldiership. — **sol'dier-crab** a hermit crab. — **old soldier** see **old; soldier of fortune** one ready to serve anywhere for pay or his own advancement; **soldier on** to continue doggedly in face of difficulty or discouragement; **soldier's heart** heart symptoms (in various diseases) attributable to soldiering or detected in soldiers. [O.Fr. *soldier* — L. *solidus,* a piece of money, the pay of a soldier.]
soldo *sol'dō, n.* a former Italian coin, one-twentieth of a lira: — *pl.* **sol'di** (*-dē*). [It., — L. *solidus.*]
sole¹ *sōl, n.* the underside of the foot: the bottom of a boot or shoe: the under-surface of a golf-club head: the floor of an oven or furnace: a sill (now *dial.*): the bottom, under-structure, floor, or under-surface of various things: a thrust-plane (*geol.*). — *v.t.* to put a sole on. — **sole'-plate** a bed-plate or similar object. [O.E. and O.Fr. *sole* — L. *solea,* sole, sandal — *solum,* bottom.]
sole² *sōl, n.* an elliptical flat fish (*Solea*) with small twisted mouth and teeth on the underside only. — *n.* **solenette** (*sōl-net', sōl-ə-net'*) a small species of sole. — **lemon= sole** see **lemon².** [Fr. *sole* — L. *solea.*]
sole³ *sōl, adj.* alone: only: without husband or wife: without another: solitary: consisting of one person: exclusive: uniform. — *advs.* **sole; sole'ly** alone: only: singly. — *n.* **sole'ness.** [Fr., — L. *sōlus,* alone.]
sole⁴ *sōl* (*Shak.*), *dial.* **sowl, sowle, soole** *sowl, sōl, sōōl, vs.t.* to pull (by the ears). [Origin obscure.]
solecism *sol'i-sizm, n.* a breach of syntax: any absurdity, impropriety, or incongruity. — *v.i.* **sol'ecise, -ize** to commit solecisms. — *n.* **sol'ecist.** — *adjs.* **solecist'ic, -al.** — *adv.* **solecist'ically.** [Gr. *soloikismos,* said to come from the corruption of the Attic dialect among the Athenian colonists (*oikizein,* to colonise) of *Soloi* in Cilicia.]
solein. An old form (*Spens.*) of **sullen.**
solemn *sol'əm, adj.* attended with or marked by special (esp. religious) ceremonies, pomp, or gravity: attended with an appeal to God, as an oath: grave: in serious earnestness: with formal dignity: awed: awe-inspiring: stately: pompous: glum: sombre. — *v.t.* **solemnify** (*sə-lem'ni-fī*) to make solemn. — *n.* **solemnisation, -z-** (*sol-əm-ni-zā'shən*). — *v.t.* **sol'emnise, -ize** (*-nīz*) to perform religiously or solemnly: to celebrate with rites: to make solemn. — *ns.* **sol'emniser, -z-; solemnity** (*-lem'ni-ti*) a solemn ceremony: high seriousness:

affected gravity; **solemnize'** (*Spens.*) solemnisation. — *adv.* **sol'emnly.** — *n.* **sol'emnness** (also **sol'emness**). — **solemn mass** high mass. [O.Fr. *solempne, solemne* (Fr. *solennel*) — L. *sollemnis, sōlennis,* doubtfully referred to *sollus,* all, every, *annus,* a year.]
Solen *sō'lən, n.* the razor-fish genus of lamellibranch molluscs: (without *cap.*) any mollusc of this genus. — *ns.* **solenodon** (*sō-len'ə-don*) either of two shrew-like West Indian mammals with elongated snouts and hairless tails, growing to about two feet in length; **sō'lenoid** a cylindrical coil of wire, acting as a magnet when an electric current passes through it, converting electrical energy to mechanical energy. — *adj.* **solenoid'al.** — *adv.* **solenoid'ally.** [Gr. *sōlēn,* a pipe.]
solenette. See **sole².**
soler. See **solar¹.**
solera *sō-lā'rä, n.* a system of sherry production involving blending wines of various ages from a series of graded casks to achieve uniformity: collectively, the casks used in this process. — Also *adj.* [Sp., — L. *solus,* ground, base.]
soles. See **Sol.**
soleus *sō'li-əs, n.* the flat muscle of the leg beneath the gastrocnemius. [Mod. L., — L. *soles,* sole.]
sol-fa *sol'fä', (mus.) n.* a system of syllables (*do* or *ut, re, mi, fa, sol* or *so, la, si* or *ti*) representing and sung to the notes of the scale. — *adj.* belonging to the system. — *v.t.* and *v.i.* to sing to sol-fa syllables: — *pr.p.* **sol-faing** (*-fä'ing*); *pa.t.* and *pa.p.* **sol-faed, -fa'd** (*-fäd'*). — *ns.* **sol-fa'ism** singing by syllables: solmisation; **sol-fa'ist** a teacher, practiser, or advocate of solmisation; **solfeggio** (*-fed'jō; It.*) an exercise in sol-fa syllables: — *pl.* **solfeggi** (*-fed'jē*). — **tonic sol-fa** see under **tone¹.** [**sol¹; fa.**]
solfatara *sol-fä-tä'rə, n.* a volcanic vent emitting only gases, esp. one emitting acid gases (hydrochloric acid and sulphur dioxide): — *pl.* **solfata'ras.** — *adj.* **solfata'ric.** [From the *Solfatara* (lit. sulphur-mine, sulphur-hole) near Naples — It. *solfo,* sulphur.]
solfeggio. See **sol-fa.**
solferino *sol-fə-rē'nō, n.* the colour of rosaniline — discovered soon after the battle of *Solferino* in Italy (1859): — *pl.* **solferi'nos.**
soli. See **solo.**
solicit *sō-lis'it, v.t.* to disquiet: to incite: to allure: to urge: to petition: to importune: to seek after: to call for, require: to invite to immorality: to extract gently (*obs.*): to conduct, manage. — *v.i.* to petition: to act as solicitor: (of prostitutes) to make advances: (of beggars) to importune for alms. — *n.* (*Shak.*; another reading **solic'ity**) a solicitation. — *ns.* **solic'itant** one who solicits (also *adj.*); **solicitā'tion** a soliciting: an earnest request: an invitation; **solic'iting** any action of the verb, esp. (of prostitutes) the making of advances; **solic'itor** one who asks earnestly: one who is legally qualified to act for another in a court of law (esp. formerly a court of equity): a lawyer who prepares deeds, manages cases, instructs counsel in the superior courts, and acts as an advocate in the inferior courts: a canvasser (*U.S.*); **solic'itorship.** — *adj.* **solic'itous** soliciting or earnestly asking or desiring: very desirous: anxious: careful. — *adv.* **solic'itously.** — *ns.* **solic'i- tousness, solic'itude** the state of being solicitous: anxiety or uneasiness of mind: trouble. — **Solic'itor= Gen'eral** in England, the law-officer of the crown next in rank to the Attorney-General — in Scotland, to the Lord-Advocate. [L. *sōlicitāre, sollicitāre* — *sō-, sollicitus* — *sollus,* whole, *citus,* aroused — *ciēre,* to cite.]
solid *sol'id, adj.* resisting change of shape, having the particles firmly cohering (opp. to *fluid*; distinguished from *liquid* and *gaseous*): hard: compact: full of matter: not hollow: strong: having or pertaining to three dimensions: substantial: worthy of credit: weighty: of uniform undivided substance: financially sound, wealthy: reliable: sensible: unanimous: unbroken: unvaried. — *n.* a substance, body, or figure that is solid: a solid mass or part. — *ns.* **solidare** (*sol'i-där; Shak.*)

a small coin; **sol'idarism** (*-də-rizm*); **sol'idarist** an advocate of solidarity; **solidarity** (*-dar'i-ti*) oneness of interests, aims, etc. — *adj.* **sol'idary** (*-dər-i*) marked by solidarity: jointly responsible: joint and several. — *v.t.* **sol'idate** (*rare*) to consolidate. — *adj.* **solidifiable** (*sə-lid'i-fī-ə-bl*). — *n.* **solidificā'tion.** — *v.t.* **solid'ify** to make solid or compact. — *v.i.* to grow solid: — *pr.p.* **solid'ifying;** *pa.t.* and *pa.p.* **solid'ified.** — *adj.* **sol'idish.** — *ns.* **sol'idism** the doctrine that refers all diseases to alterations of the solid parts of the body; **sol'idist** a believer in solidism; **solid'ity** the state of being solid: fulness of matter: strength or firmness, moral or physical: soundness: volume: a solid thing (*Shak.*). — *adv.* **sol'idly.** — *ns.* **sol'idness; sol'idum** the die of a pedestal (*archit.*): a complete sum (*Scots law*); **sol'idus** a Roman gold coin introduced by Constantine, later called the *bezant:* in the Middle Ages, a silver coin of 12 denarii: a sign (/) denoting the former English shilling, representing old lengthened form of *s* (£ s. d. = *librae, solidi, denarii*, pounds, shillings, pence), used also for other purposes, as in writing fractions: — *pl.* **solidi** (*-dī*). — **solid colour** a colour covering the whole of an object: a uniform colour. — *adj.* **sol'id-hoofed** with uncloven hoofs. — **solid matter** (*print.*) matter set without leads between the lines. — *adj.* **sol'id-state** of, consisting of, or relating to solid substances: of, consisting of or relating to semiconductor materials (and their electrical properties). — **solid of revolution** a solid figure regarded as formed by a plane figure turning round on an axis; **solid-state light** light produced by means of a semiconductor device; **solid-state physics** branch of physics which covers all properties of solid materials, now esp. electrical conduction in crystals of semiconductors, and superconductivity and photoconductivity; **solid with** packed tight with: on a firm footing of understanding with: supporting fully; **the Solid South** (*U.S.*) the southern states traditionally voting for the Democratic party.   [L. *solidus, -a, -um,* solid.]

solidum. See **solid.**

solidungulate *sol-id-ung'gū-lāt, adj.* with uncloven hoofs. — Also **solidung'ulous.**   [L. *solidus,* solid, *ungula,* a hoof.]

solidus. See **solid.**

solifidian *sō-li-fid'i-ən, n.* one who holds that faith alone is necessary for justification. — Also *adj.* — *n.* **solifid'ianism.**   [L. *solus,* only, *fidēs,* faith.]

solifluxion, solifluction *sol-i-fluk'shən, n.* creep of soil down a slope.   [L. *solum,* soil, *fluxiō, -ōnis,* flow.]

Solifugae *sol-i-fū'jē, n.pl.* an order of spider-like arachnids, with head and three-jointed thorax distinct. [See **Solpuga;** modified by popular association with L. *sōl,* the sun, *fugĕre,* to flee.]

soliloquy *so-, sō-, sə-lil'ə-kwi, n.* a talking to oneself: a speech of this nature made by a character in a play, etc. — *v.i.* **solil'oquise, -ize** to speak to oneself: to utter a soliloquy in a play, etc.   [L. *sōliloquium — sōlus,* alone, *loquī,* to speak.]

soliped *sol'i-ped, n.* an animal with uncloven hoofs. — *adjs.* **sol'iped, solip'edous.**   [L. *sōlus,* alone, *pēs, pedis,* a foot.]

solipsism *sol'ip-sizm, n.* the theory that self-existence is the only certainty, absolute egoism — the extreme form of subjective idealism. — *n.* and *adj.* **sol'ipsist.** — *adj.* **solipsis'tic.**   [L. *sōlus,* alone, *ipse,* self.]

solitaire *sol-i-tār', n.* a recluse: a game played by one person with a board and balls, pegs, etc.: patience (the card game) (*U.S.*): a diamond, etc., set by itself: (18th cent.) a large loose silk necktie: a gigantic flightless pigeon (*Pezophaps solitarius*) of Rodriguez, extinct since the 18th cent.: an American or West Indian fly-catching thrush. — **solitaire'-board** a board with cups, holes, etc. for playing solitaire.   [Fr., see next.]

solitary *sol'i-tər-i, adj.* alone: single, separate: living alone, not social or gregarious: without company: remote from society: retired, secluded: lonely: growing single (*bot.*). — *n.* one who lives alone: a hermit:

solitary confinement (*coll.*). — *n.* **solitarian** (*-tā'ri-ən*) a hermit. — *adv.* **sol'itarily.** — *n.* **sol'itariness.** — **solitary confinement** imprisonment in a cell by oneself. [L. *sōlitārius — sōlus,* alone.]

solito *sol'i-tō,* (*mus.*) *adv.* in the usual manner.   [It.]

soliton *sol'it-ən,* (*phys.*) *n.* a solitary wave: a quantum which corresponds to a solitary wave in its transmission.   [**solitary.**]

solitude *sol'i-tūd, n.* solitariness: absence of company: a lonely place or desert. — *n.* **solitūdinā'rian.** — *adj.* **solitūd'inous.**   [L. *sōlitūdō — sōlus.*]

solivagant *sō-liv'ə-gənt, adj.* wandering alone. — Also *n.* [L. *sōlus,* alone, *vagāns, -antis,* wandering.]

solive *so-lēv', n.* a joist or beam of secondary importance. [Fr., — L. *sublevāre,* to support.]

sollar, soller. See **solar¹.**

solleret *sol'ər-et, n.* a jointed steel shoe.   [O.Fr., dim. of *soler,* slipper.]

solmisation, -ization *sol-mi-zā'shən, n.* sol-faing: a recital of the notes of the gamut.   [**sol¹, mi.**]

solo *sō'lō, n.* a piece or passage for one voice or instrument, accompanied or unaccompanied: any performance in which no other person or instrument participates: a single-seater motorcycle or bicycle as opposed to motorcycle with side-car, tandem, etc.: a card game (**solo whist**) based on whist, in which various declarations are made and the declarer may or may not have a partner: — *pl.* **sō'lōs, soli** (*sō'lē*). — *adj.* performed, or for performances, as a solo: performing a solo: for one: single. — *adv.* alone. — *v.i.* to fly solo: to play (a) solo. — *n.* **sō'lōist.** — **solo stop** an organ stop for imitating a solo performance on another instrument.   [It., — L. *sōlus,* alone.]

Solomon *sol'ə-mən, n.* a person of unusual wisdom, from *Solomon,* king of Israel (see 1 Kings iii. 5–15). — *adjs.* **Solomonian** (*-mō'ni-ən*), **Solomonic** (*-mon'ik*). — **Sol'omon's-seal** any species of Polygonatum, a genus of the lily family, with small dangling greenish flowers (perh. from the scars on the rootstock): a symbol formed of two triangles interlaced or superposed, forming a six-pointed star.

Solon *sō'lon, n.* a famous lawgiver of Athens (594 B.C.), one of the Seven Sages: a sage: a wiseacre: a Congressman (*U.S.*). — *adj.* **Solō'nian.**

solonchak *sol-on'chak, n.* a pale or grey soil-type found in arid to subhumid, poorly drained conditions. [Russ., salt marsh — *sol,* salt.]

solonetz, solonets *sol-on-ets', n.* an alkaline soil-type having a hard, dark subsoil under a thin friable topsoil, formed by the leaching of salts from a solonchak. — *adj.* **solonet'zic.** — *n.* **solonisa'tion, -z-** the process by which a solonetz is formed.   [Russ., salt not produced by boiling.]

so-long, so long *sō-long',* (*coll.* or *slang*) *interj.* good-bye. [Prob. **so¹** and **long³;** poss. **salaam.**]

Solpuga *sol-pū'gə, n.* a genus of very venomous Solifugae. [L. *solpūga, salpūga, solipūga, solipugna,* a venomous animal supposedly the same, a word der. from Spain.]

solstice *sol'stis, n.* the time when the sun reaches its maximum distance from the equator (*summer solstice* when it touches the tropic of Cancer, about 21 June; the *winter solstice* when it touches that of Capricorn, about 21 December): the turning-point then reached. — *adj.* **solstitial** (*-stish'l*) pertaining to, or happening at, a solstice, esp. at the summer solstice.   [Fr., — L. *sōlstitium — sōl,* the sun, *sistĕre, stătum,* to make to stand — *stāre.*]

soluble *sol'ū-bl, adj.* capable of being solved, dissolved, or resolved. — *n.* **solubilisā'tion, -z-.** — *v.t.* **sol'ubilise, -ize** to render soluble: to make more soluble. — *ns.* **solūbil'ity** (a measure of) the ability of a substance to dissolve; **sol'ūte** a dissolved substance. — *adj.* (*sol'* or *-ūt'*) loose: free: not adhering: dissolved. — *n.* **solution** (*səl-, sol-ōō'shən, -ū'shən*) the act of solving or dissolving: the condition of being dissolved: the preparation resulting therefrom: the separating of parts: abnormal separation: an explanation: the removal of a doubt:

the solving of a problem: the crisis of a disease: a breach (as of continuity): the payment of a debt, or similar discharge of an obligation: a solution of rubber. — *v.t.* to mend or cement with rubber solution: to apply or treat with a solution (esp. *U.S.*). — *adj.* **solutional** (*-ōō′* or *-ū′*). — *n.* **solu′tionist** a solver (as of puzzles). — *adj.* **sol′ūtive** tending to dissolve: laxative. — **solution of triangles** (*trig.*) finding the values of the remaining sides and angles, some being given. [L. *solvēre, solūtum*, to loosen.]

solum *sō′ləm, n.* ground, soil: a piece of ground. [L. *sŏlum*, the ground.]

solus *sō′ləs, adj.* alone, orig. in dramatic directions — *fem.* form, **sō′la.** [L. *sōlus*, alone.]

Solutrean, Solutrian *sol-ōōt′ri-ən, -ūt′,* or *-trē′, adj.* belonging to an upper Palaeolithic culture which succeeded the Aurignacian and preceded the Magdalenian. [*Solutré*, in Saône-et-Loire, where objects of this culture have been found.]

solve *solv, v.t.* to unbind: to dissolve: to settle: to clear up or explain: to find an answer to or a way out of. — *n.* **solvabil′ity.** — *adj.* **sol′vable** capable of being solved: capable of being paid, dissolved, or resolved (*rare* or *obs.*): solvent (*obs.*). — *n.* **sol′vate** a definite combination of solute and solvent. — *v.t.* and *v.i.* to (cause to) undergo solvation. — *n.* **solvā′tion** the association of the molecules of a solvent with solute ions or molecules; **sol′vency.** — *adj.* **sol′vent** able to solve or dissolve: able to pay all debts. — *n.* a substance that dissolves another: that component of a solution which is present in excess, or whose physical state is the same as that of the solution: something which provides a solution. — *n.* **sol′ver** one who solves. — **solvent abuse** self-intoxication by inhaling the fumes given off by various solvents — adhesives, petrol, etc. [L. *solvēre*, to loosen, prob. from *sē-, sĕ-*, aside, *luĕre*, to loosen.]

soma¹, Soma *sō′mə, n.* a plant (perhaps an asclepiad), or its intoxicating juice, used in ancient Indian religious ceremonies, and personified as a god. [Sans. *soma* (Avestan *haoma*, juice).]

soma² *sō′mə, n.* an imaginary perfect drug described by Aldous Huxley in *Brave New World*: (with *cap.*; ℝ) a drug which relieves pain and is a muscle-relaxant. [**soma¹**.]

soma³ *sō′mə, n.* the body: the body of an animal or plant excluding the germ-cells. — *n.* **somascope** (*sō′mə-skōp*; Gr. *skopeein*, to view) an instrument using ultrasonic waves converted into a television image to show the character of diseased internal tissues of the body. — *adj.* **somatic** (*-mat′ik*). — *adv.* **somat′ically.** — *ns.* **so′matism** (*-mə-tizm*) materialism; **so′matist** (also *adj.*). — *adjs.* **somatogenic** (*sō-mə-tō-jen′ik*) originating in somatic cells; **somatolog′ic, -al.** — *ns.* **somatol′ogy** the science of the properties of matter: the science of the human body; **so′matoplasm** protoplasm of the somatic cells; **so′matopleure** (*-plōōr*; Gr. *pleurā*, side) the outer body-wall or the layer that gives rise to it; **somatostatin** (*sō-mə-tō-stat′in*) a brain hormone which appears to inhibit the secretion of certain other hormones esp. growth hormone; **somatotōn′ia** a pattern of temperament and body type in which alertness and aggression are combined with mesomorphic build. — *adj.* **somatotonic** (*-ton′*). — *adj.* **somatotrop(h)′ic** promoting bodily growth. — **somatotrop(h)′in** growth hormone; **somat′otype** a type consisting of a physical build paired with a particular temperament. — *v.t.* to place with regard to somatotype. — *n.* **so′mite** a body-segment of a vertebrate embryo or of a segmented invertebrate. — *adjs.* **somital** (*sō′mi-tl*), **somit′ic.** [Gr. *sōma*, body.]

sombre *som′bər, adj.* dark and gloomy: melancholy, dismal. — *v.t.* and *v.i.* to make or become sombre. — *adv.* **som′brely.** — *n.* **som′breness.** — *adj.* **som′brous** sombre. [Fr. *sombre* (cf. Sp. *sombra*, shade) — perh. L. *sub*, under, *umbra*, a shade.]

sombrerite *som-brä′rīt, n.* rock-guano. [*Sombrero* in the West Indies.]

sombrero *som-brā′rō, n.* a broad-brimmed hat: — *pl.* **sombre′ros.** [Sp., hat — *sombra*, shade.]

some *sum, indef. pron.* one, one or other (*obs.*): an indefinite part of the whole number or quantity: (a) certain (undetermined) one(s): a great deal (*U.S.*): a good deal more, esp. as *and then some* (*U.S.*). — *adj.* one or other: in an indefinite number or quantity: a little: not a little: considerable: a certain: certain unspecified: several: a few: in approximate number, length, etc., more or less: remarkable, outstanding, of note (*coll.*, esp. *U.S.*; also *ironical*). — *adv.* somewhat, in some degree, rather, a little (*local*): very much (*U.S.*): sometimes (*Shak.*). — *n.* (or *pron.*) **some′body** some person: a person of importance: — *pl.* **some′bodies.** — *advs.* **some′day** at an unspecified time in the future; **some′deal** (*arch.*), **some′dele** (*Spens.*) in some degree, somewhat; **some′gate** (*Scot.*) somewhere, somehow; **some′how** in some way or other. — *n.* (or *pron.*) **some′one** (also **some one**) somebody. — *adv.* **some′place** somewhere. — *n.* (or *pron.*) **some′thing** a thing undefined: a thing of some account: a portion. — *adv.* in some degree. — *adj.* (*Shak.*) that is something. — Also used as substitute for any word (*n., adj., vb.*) or component of any word forgotten or avoided. — *adv.* **some′time** at a time not fixed: at one time or other: formerly. — *adj.* former: late. — *adv.* **some′times** at times: now and then: sometime (*obs.*). — *adj.* (*Shak.*) sometime. - *advs.* **some′way, -ways, -wise** in some way: somehow. — *n.* **some′what** an unfixed quantity or degree: something. — *adv.* in some degree. — *advs.* (all *rare* except **somewhere**) **some′when** some time or other; **some′whence; some′where** in or to some place; **some′while, -s** sometimes; **some′whither; some′why.** — **someone else** some other person; **someone else's** some other person's. [O.E. *sum;* Goth. *sums,* O.N. *sumr.*]

-some¹ *-sum, -səm, suff.* (1) forming adjectives with the meaning full of, e.g. *gladsome, wholesome*: (2) forming nouns denoting a group with a certain number of members, e.g. *twosome, threesome.* [O.E. *-sum;* Ger. *-sam;* cf. **same.**]

-some² *-sōm, suff.* forming nouns denoting a body, e.g. *chromosome.* [Gr. *soma*, body.]

somersault *sum′ər-sölt, n.* a leap or other movement in which one turns heels over head. — *v.i.* to turn a somersault. — Also **som′erset.** [O.Fr. *sombre saut* (Fr. *soubresaut*) — L. *suprā*, over, *saltus, -ūs*, a leap — *salīre*, to leap.]

somital, somite, somitic. See under **soma³.**

sommelier *som′(ə-)lyā, n.* a butler: a wine waiter. [Fr.]

Somnus *som′nəs, n.* the god of sleep (L.; Gr. *Hypnos*). — *n.* **somnambulance** (*som-nam′bū-ləns;* L. *ambulāre*, to walk) sleep-walking. — *adj.* and *n.* **somnam′bulant.** — *adjs.* **somnam′būlar, -y.** — *v.i.* **somnam′būlate** to walk in one's sleep. — *ns.* **somnambūlā′tion; somnam′būlātor; somnam′būle** a sleep-walker. — *adj.* **somnam′būlic.** — *ns.* **somnam′būlism** walking in sleep: a hysterical state of automatism in which acts are performed that are not remembered afterwards; **somnam′būlist.** — *adjs.* **somnambūlis′tic; som′nial** pertaining to dreams; **somnic′ūlous** drowsy; **somnif′erous** (L. *ferre*, to bring), **somnif′ic** (L. *facēre*, to make) sleep-bringing. — *ns.* **somnil′oquence, somnil′oquism, somnil′oquy** (L. *loquī*, to talk) talking in one's sleep. — *v.i.* **somnil′oquise, -ize.** — *ns.* **somnil′oquist; somniv′olent** (L. *velle*, to wish) one who wishes to sleep; **som′nolence, -ency** sleepiness. — *adj.* **som′nolent.** — *adv.* **som′nolently.** — *adj.* **somnolesc′ent** half-asleep. [L. *somnus*, sleep, *somnium*, a dream.]

son *sun, n.* a male child or offspring: formerly extended to a son-in-law: a descendant, or one so regarded or treated: a disciple: a native or inhabitant: the produce of anything: a familiar (sometimes patronising) mode of address to a boy or to a male younger than oneself. — *adj.* **son′less.** — *ns.* **sonn′y** a little son: a familiar mode of address to a boy; **son′ship** the state or character of a son. — **son′-in-law** a daughter's husband: formerly, a stepson: — *pl.* **sons′-in-law.** — **son of a gun**

see **gun; son of man** a man: applied to Jesus Christ or the Messiah; **son of the manse** a minister's son; **the Son** the second person in the Trinity, Jesus Christ. [O.E. *sunu*; Du. *zoon*, Ger. *Sohn*.]

sonant *sō'nənt, adj.* voiced: syllabic. — *n.* a voiced sound: a syllabic consonant. — *ns.* **so'nance** (*Shak.* **son'uance**, prob. a misprint) a sounding; **so'nancy** sonant character. [L. *sonāns, -antis*, pr.p. of *sonāre*, to sound.]

Sonar *sō'när, n.* the American equivalent of Asdic: (without *cap.*) natural equipment that provides echo location in bats and some marine animals: (without *cap.*) echo-sounding equipment in general. — **sonar buoy** same as **sonobuoy**. [*sound navigation and ranging*.]

sonata *sō-, sə-, so-nä'tə, n.* orig., an instrumental composition: a composition usually of three or more movements designed chiefly for a solo instrument. — *n.* **sonatina** (*son-ə-tē'nə*) a short sonata. — **sonata form** the form usual in the first movement of a sonata or symphony. [It., fem. pa.p. of *sonare* — L. *sonāre*, to sound.]

sonce. See **sonse.**

sondage *sɔ̃-däzh, n.* a trial bore or excavation. [Fr.]

sonde *sond, n.* any device for obtaining information about atmospheric and weather conditions at high altitudes. [Fr.]

sondeli *son'de-li, n.* the Indian musk-shrew. [Kanarese *sundili*.]

sone *sōn, n.* a unit of sound on a scale such that the numerical value is proportional to the perceived loudness. [L. *sonus*, sound.]

soneri *son', sōn'ə-rē, n.* cloth of gold. [Hind. *sonā*, gold.]

son et lumière *son ā lüm'yər,* a dramatic spectacle presented after dark, involving lighting effects on natural features of the country or on a chosen building and an appropriate theme illustrated by spoken words and by music. [Fr.]

song[1] *song, n.* that which is sung: a short poem or ballad suitable for singing or set to music: the melody to which it is sung: an instrumental composition of like form and character: singing: the melodious outburst of a bird: any characteristic sound: a poem, or poetry in general: a theme of song: a habitual utterance, manner, or attitude towards anything: a fuss: a mere trifle. — *adj.* **song'ful** abounding in song: melodious: song-like: like singing: ready to break into song. — *adv.* **song'fully.** — *n.* **song'fulness.** — *adjs.* **song'less** without song or power of song; **song'-like.** — *n.* **song'ster** a singer: — *fem.* **song'stress.** — **song'bird** a bird that sings: any one of the Oscines; **song'book** a service-book (*obs.*): a book of songs; **song'craft** the art of making songs; **song'-cycle** a sequence of songs connected in subject; **song'fest** see **-fest; song form** the form of composition usual in songs; **song'-hit** a song that has made a hit, or caught on; **song'man** (*Shak.*) a singer: a choir singer; **song'-school; song'smith** a composer of songs; **song'-sparrow** an American songbird (*Melospiza*); **song'-thrush** the mavis or throstle (see also **thrush**[1]); **song'writer** one who composes music and/or words for (esp. popular) songs. — **make a song (and dance) about** to make overmuch of: to make an unnecessary fuss about; **Song of Songs** or **of Solomon** Canticles, a book of the O.T. long attributed to Solomon. [O.E. *sang* — *singan*, to sing; Goth. *saggws*, O.N. *söngr*.]

song[2] (*Spens.*) *pa.t.* of **sing.**

sonic *son'ik, adj.* pertaining to or using sound-waves: travelling at about the speed of sound. — *n.sing.* **son'ics** the study of the technological application of sounds, esp. supersonic waves. — **sonic bang, boom** (*aero.*) a loud double report caused by shock-waves projected outward and backward from the leading and trailing edges of an aircraft travelling at supersonic speed; **sonic barrier** the sound barrier; **sonic mine** an acoustic mine. [L. *sonus*, sound.]

sonne. An obs. spelling of **son, sun.**

sonnet *son'it, n.* formerly, a short (esp. lyrical) poem: now, always one of fourteen lines of ten or eleven syllables, rhymed according to one or other of certain definite schemes, forming an octave and a sestet, properly expressing two successive phases of one thought. — *v.i.* to write sonnets. — *v.t.* to celebrate in sonnets. — *adj.* **sonn'etary.** — *n.* **sonneteer'** a sonnet-writer: a poetaster (*obs.*). — *vs.i.* **sonneteer', sonn'etise, -ize** to compose sonnets. — *vs.t.* to celebrate in sonnets. — *n.* and *adj.* **sonneteer'ing.** — *ns.* **sonn'eting; sonn'etist** a sonneteer; **sonn'etry.** — **sonn'et-se'quence** a connected series of sonnets. — **Petrarch(i)an sonnet** one rhymed *abbaabba cdcdcd*; **Miltonic** *abbaabba cdecde*; **Shakespearian** *ababcdcd efefgg*. [It. *sonetto*, dim. of *suono* — L. *sonus*, a sound.]

Sonnite. See **Sunna.**

sonny. See **son.**

sono- *son'ō-,* in composition, sonic. — *n.* **sonobuoy** (*son'ō-boi, U.S.* also *-boō-ē*) sonar equipment dropped to float on the sea and pick up underwater noise, e.g. from a submarine, and to transmit bearings of the source to aircraft; **son'ograph** an instrument for scanning and recording sound and its component frequencies; **sonog'rapher; sonog'raphy.**

sonofabitch *sun'əv-ə-bich', (slang; esp. U.S.) n.* son of a bitch, an opprobrious term of address or of description, or vulgar exclamation: — *pl.* **sons of bitches.**

sonorous *sō-, sə-nō'rəs, -nō', son'ə-rəs, adj.* sounding, esp. loudly, deeply, impressively, etc.: full-sounding: sounding or ringing when struck. — *ns.* **son'orant** a frictionless continuant or nasal (*l, r, m, n, ng*) capable of fulfilling a vocalic or consonantal function: the consonants represented by *w, y,* having consonantal or vocalic articulations; **sonority** (*sō-, sə-nor'i-ti*) sonorousness: type, quality, etc., of sound. — *adv.* **sono'rously** (or *son'*). — *n.* **sono'rousness** (or *son'*) sonorous quality or character. — **sonorous** (or **Chladni**) **figures** patterns made in sand by vibrating a metal plate on which it is spread. [L. *sonōrus* — *sonor, -ōris,* a sound — *sonāre,* to sound.]

sonse, sonce *sons, (Scot.) n.* good luck: abundance. — *adj.* **sons'y, sons'ie** (*Scot.*) luck-bringing: comely: comfortable-looking: good-natured: plump, buxom. [Gael. *sonas,* good fortune.]

sontag *son'tag, zōn'tähh, n.* a woman's knitted cape, tied down round the waist. [From the famous German singer Henriette *Sontag* (1806–1854).]

sonties *son'tiz, (Shak.,* in an oath) *n.pl.* prob. for **sanctities.**

sonuance. See **sonant.**

soogee, soogie *sōō'jē, -ji, (naut.) n.* a solution of soap, soda, etc. for cleaning the decks and paintwork of a ship. — Also **soo'jey, su'jee.** — *v.t.* to clean, wash, esp. with soogee. [Perh. conn. with Hind. *suji,* a type of gruel; or poss. — Jap *sōji,* cleaning.]

sook. Same as **souk.**

soole. See **sole**[4].

soom *sōōm,* a Scots form of **swim.**

soon *sōōn, adv.* immediately or in a short time: without delay: early: readily: willingly: — *compar.* **soon'er.** — *adj.* early (*rare*): speedy (*Shak.*). — *superl.* **soon'est.** — *adv.* (*telegraphese* and *milit. jargon*) as soon as possible. — **no sooner . . . than** immediately; **soon at** (*Shak.*) about; **sooner or later** eventually. [O.E. *sōna.*]

soop *sōōp, (Scot.) v.t.* to sweep. — *n.* **soop'ing** (*Scot.*). — *adv.* **soop'stake** (*Shak.*) with a sweep of the stakes (another reading **swoop'-stake-like**). [O.N. *sōpa;* cf. **sweep, swoop.**]

soot[1] *soot, n.* a black deposit from imperfect combustion of carbonaceous matter: a smut. — *v.t.* to cover, smear, dirty, clog, or treat with soot. — *n.* **soot'erkin** a fabulous afterbirth induced by Dutch women sitting huddled over their stoves: a Dutchman: a Negro: a chimney-sweep: anything supplementary, fruitless, or abortive. — *adv.* **soot'ily.** — *n.* **soot'iness.** — *adjs.* **soot'less; soot'y** of, foul with, or like, soot. — **soot'flake** a smut of soot. [O.E. *sōt;* Dan. *sod.*]

soot[2], **soote** *sōōt, adj.* and *n.* (*obs.*) sweet. — *adv.* (*Spens.*) sweetly. [See **sweet.**]

sooterkin. See **soot**[1].
sooth *sōōth, n.* truth, reality: blandishment (*Shak.*): an augury, foretokening (*obs.*; *Spens.* **soothe**). — *adj.* true: truthful: smooth, soft (*Keats*). — *adv.* in truth: indeed. — *adj.* **sooth′fast** truthful, honest, faithful. — *adv.* **sooth′fastly.** — *n.* **sooth′fastness.** — *adj.* **sooth′ful** truthful: faithful. — *advs.* **sooth′ly, sooth′lich** (*Spens.*) truly, indeed. — *v.i.* **sooth′say** to foretell, to divine. — *n.* a prediction: (*Spens.* **soothsay′**) an omen. — **sooth′sayer** (*Spens.* -sā′) one who foretells, a diviner or prognosticator: a truth-teller (*obs.*); **sooth′saying.** [O.E. *sōth*, truth, true; O.N. *sannr*.]
soothe[1] *sōōdh, v.t.* to prove or declare true (*obs.*): to confirm, support, back up (*obs.*): to blandish, cajole, flatter: to gloss over (*obs.*): to calm, comfort, compose, tranquillise: to appease: to allay, soften. — *v.i.* to have a tranquillising effect. — *n.* **sooth′er.** — *v.t.* (*Ir.*) to flatter, blandish. — *n.* and *adj.* **sooth′ing.** — *adv.* **sooth′ingly.** [O.E. (*ge*)*sōthian*, to confirm as true — *sōth*, true.]
soothe[2]. See **sooth**.
sootily, sootiness, sooty. See **soot**[1].
sop *sop, n.* bread or other food dipped or soaked in liquid: a puddle: a soaking: a propitiatory gift or concession (from the drugged sop the Sibyl gave to Cerberus to gain passage for Aeneas to Hades, *Aen.* vi. 420). — *v.t.* to steep in liquor: to take up by absorption (with *up*): to soak. — *v.i.* to soak in, percolate: to be soaked — *pr.p.* **sopp′ing;** *pa.t.* and *pa.p.* **sopped.** — *adv.* **sopp′ily.** — *n.* **sopp′iness.** — *n., adj.,* and *adv.* **sopp′ing.** — *adj.* **sopp′y** drenched: thoroughly wet: sloppily sentimental. — **sops′-in-wine′** the clove pink (*obs.*): a variety of apple. [O.E. *sopp* (n.), *soppian* (vb.); prob. conn. with *sūpan*, to sup.]
soph *sof, n.* a short form of **sophister** and of **sophomore.**
sopha. See **sofa.**
sopherim *sō′fə-rim, n.pl.* the scribes, the expounders of the Jewish oral law. — *adj.* **sopheric** (-fer′ik). [Heb. *sōferīm*.]
Sophi. Same as **Sophy.**
sophia *sof′i-ə, n.* wisdom: divine wisdom (often personified **Sophia, Hagia Sophia, Saint Sophia**). — *adjs.* **soph′ic, -al.** — *adv.* **soph′ically.** — *ns.* **soph′ism** a specious fallacy; **soph′ist** one of a class of public teachers of rhetoric, philosophy, etc., in ancient Greece: a captious or intentionally fallacious reasoner; **soph′ister** a sophist (*Shak.*): a student in his second or third year (*Cambridge*; *hist.*), in his third or fourth (*Dublin*). — *adj.* **sophis′tic** pertaining to, or of the nature of, a sophist or sophistry: fallaciously subtle. — *n.* (also *n. sing.* **sophis′tics**) the art of sophistry. — *adj.* **sophist′ical.** — *adv.* **sophis′tically.** — *v.t.* **sophis′ticāte** to adulterate: to falsify: to make sophistic(al): to give a fashionable air of worldly wisdom to: to make (e.g., a machine) highly complex and efficient. — *v.i.* to practise sophistry. — *adjs.* **sophis′ticāte, sophis′ticāted** adulterated: falsified: worldly-wise: devoid or deprived of natural simplicity, complex: very refined and subtle: with qualities produced by special knowledge and skill: (of a person) accustomed to an elegant, cultured way of life: with the most up-to-date devices. — *ns.* **sophis′ticāte** a sophisticated person; **sophisticā′tion; sophis′ticātor;** **soph′istry** (an instance of) specious but fallacious reasoning: the art of reasoning speciously. [Gr. *sophiā*, wisdom, *sophisma*, skill.]
Sophoclean *sof-ō-klē′ən, adj.* pertaining to *Sophocles*, the Athenian tragic poet (*c.* 496-*c.* 406 B.C.).
sophomore *sof′ə-mōr, -mör,* (esp. *U.S.*) *n.* a second-year student. — Also *adj.* — *adjs.* **sophomoric** (-mor′), **-al** of a sophomore: bombastic. [Prob. from *sophom* (obs. form of *sophism*) and *-or*, as if from *sophos*, wise, *mōros*, foolish.]
Sophy *sō′fi,* (*obs.*) *n.* the shah of Persia. [From the *Çafī* or Safawi dynasty (1502–1736) descended from *Çafi-ud-dīn*.]
sopite *sō-pīt′, v.t.* to dull, lull, put to sleep: to put an end

to. [L. *sōpītus*, pa.p. of *sōpīre*, to put to sleep, calm, settle.]
sopor *sō′pör,* (*path.*) *n.* unnaturally deep sleep. — *adj.* **soporiferous** (*sop-, sōp-ər-if′ər-əs*) inducing sleep. — *adv.* **soporif′erously.** — *n.* **soporif′erousness.** — *adj.* **soporif′ic** inducing sleep. — *n.* a sleep-bringing agent. — *adjs.* **sop′orōse, sop′orous** sleepy. [L. *sopor, -ōris,* deep sleep, *ferre,* to bring, *facēre,* to make.]
sopped, sopping, soppy. See **sop.**
sopra *sō′pra,* (*mus.*) *adv.* above. [It., — L. *suprā,* above.]
soprano *sō-, sə-prä′nō, n.* the highest variety of voice, treble: a singer with such a voice: a part for such a voice: — *pl.* **sopra′nos, sopra′ni** (*nē*). — *adj.* of, or possessing, a treble voice or a part for it: in a group of instruments of the same type but of different sizes, that with the range close to the range of a soprano voice. — *adj.* **sopranino** (*sō-prə-nē′nō*) (of an instrument) higher than the corresponding soprano. — Also *n.:* — *pl.* **soprani′nos, -ni′ni** (*-nē*). — *n.* **sopra′nist** a soprano singer. [It., from *sopra* — L. *supra* or *super,* above.]
sora *sō′rə, sö′, n.* a N. American short-billed rail. — Also **so′ree.** [Indian name.]
sorage. See **sore**[2].
soral. See **sorus.**
sorb[1] *sörb, n.* the service-tree, the wild service-tree, or (sometimes) the rowan-tree: its fruit (also **sorb′-apple**). — *n.* **sor′bate** a salt of sorbic acid. — **sorbic acid** an acid obtained from the rowan-berry, used in food preservation; **sorb′itol** (-*i-tol*) a white crystalline substance ($C_6H_8(OH)_6$) derived from (and used as a substitute for) sugar. [L. *sorbus* (the tree), *sorbum* (the fruit).]
sorb[2] *sörb, v.t.* to absorb or adsorb. — *adj.* **sorbefacient** (-*i-fā′shənt*) promoting absorption. — Also *n.* — *n.* and *adj.* **sor′bent.** [L. *sorbēre,* to suck in, *faciēns, -entis,* pr.p. of *facēre,* to make.]
Sorb *sörb, n.* a Wend. — *ns.* and *adjs.* **Sor′bian, Sor′bish** Wendish. [Ger. *Sorbe;* cf. **Serb.**]
Sorbaria *sörb-ā′ri-ə, n.* a small Asiatic genus of deciduous shrubs of the family Rosaceae, with long pinnate leaves and large clusters of white flowers: (without *cap.*) any shrub of this genus. [L. *sorbus;* see **sorb**[1].]
sorbate. See **sorb**[1].
sorbefacient, sorbent. See **sorb**[2].
sorbet *sör′bət, sör′bā, n.* sherbet: water-ice. [Fr., — It. *sorbetto;* cf. **sherbet.**]
Sorbian. See **Sorb.**
sorbic acid. See **sorb**[1].
Sorbish. See **sorb.**
sorbitol. See **sorb**[1].
sorbo (rubber) *sör′bō (rub′ər), n.* a spongy type of rubber: — *pl.* **sor′bos, sorbo rubbers.** [From *absorb.*]
Sorbonne *sor-bon′, n.* a theological college of the mediaeval university of Paris, founded in 1253 by Robert of *Sorbon,* long dominant in matters of doctrine, suppressed 1792, revived 1808, seat of the faculties of science and letters (arts). — *adj.* **Sorbon′ical, Sorbonn′ical.** — *n.* **Sor′bonist, Sor′bonnist** a doctor or student of the Sorbonne.
Sorbus *sörb′əs, n.* a large genus of deciduous shrubs and trees of the family **Rosaceae** including the service-tree and the rowan: (without *cap.*) any plant of this genus: — *pl.* **sorb′uses.** [L.; see **sorb**[1].]
sorcery *sör′sə-ri, n.* divination by the assistance of evil spirits: enchantment: magic: witchcraft. — *n.* **sor′cerer:** — *fem.* **sor′ceress.** — *adj.* **sor′cerous.** [O.Fr. *sorcerie* — L. *sors, sortis,* lot.]
sord[1] *sörd, sörd,* (*Milt.*) *n.* a form of **sward.**
sord[2] *sörd, sörd, n.* a flock of mallard. [O.Fr. *sordre* — L. *surgēre,* to rise.]
sordamente. See **sordo.**
sordes *sör′dēz, n. sing.* or *pl.* filth: refuse: a foul accumulation: a crust on the teeth and lips in fevers. — *adj.* **sor′did** dirty: squalid: mean: meanly avaricious: mercenary: of low or unworthy ideals: dirt-coloured. — *adv.* **sor′didly.** — *ns.* **sor′didness; sor′dor** dirt: sordid-

ness. [L. *sordēs* (pl.: sing. defective), dirt, *sordidus*, dirty.]

sordid, etc. See **sordes**.

sordo *sör'dō*, (*mus.*) *adj.* muted, damped: — *fem.* **sor'da.** — *adv.* **sordamente** (-*dä-men'tä*) gently, softly. — *n.* **sordino** (-*dē'nō*) a mute or damper to soften or deaden the sound of an instrument: — *pl.* **sordini** (-*nē*). — Also **sordine** (-*dēn'*; Fr. *sourdine*). — **con sordino** with mute; **senza sordino** without mute. [It., — L. *surdus*, deaf, noiseless.]

sordor. See **sordes**.

sore[1] *sōr, sör, n.* a painful or tender injured or diseased spot: an ulcer or boil: grief: an affliction. — *adj.* wounded: tender: readily sensitive to pain: irritable: touchy: painful: afflicted: vexed: irritated: causing pain: painful to contemplate: grievous: aching (*Scot.*): bringing sorrow or regret: aggrieved (*coll.*). — *adv.* painfully: grievously: severely: distressingly: in distress: hard: eagerly: very much. — *v.t.* to make sore: to wound. — *adv.* **sore'ly.** — *n.* **sore'ness.** — **sore'head** (orig. and esp. *U.S.*) one discontented, e.g. with his reward: an irritable or grumpy person. — *adj.* **sore'-head'ed.** — **sore point** a subject about which someone feels touchy, angry or aggrieved. — **a sore thumb** something obtrusive, too painful or too awkward to be ignored; **stick out like a sore thumb** (*coll.*) to be very obvious, noticeable, etc. [O.E. *sār*; Ger. *sehr*, very, O.N. *sārr*, sore.]

sore[2], **soar, soare** *sōr, sör*, (*obs.*) *adj.* sorrel, reddish-brown: of hawks, etc., in reddish-brown plumage of the first year. — *n.* a hawk of the first year (*obs.*): a buck of fourth year (*Shak.*). — *n.* **sor'age** the first year of a hawk: a sore-hawk. — **sore'-, soar'-ea'gle** (*Milt.*), **-fal'con, -hawk'.** [A.Fr. and O.Fr. *sor* (Fr. *saur, saure*), sorrel, reddish; cf. **sorrel**[2].]

soredium *sō-rē'di-əm, sö-, n.* a small vegetative reproductive body in lichens, consisting of a few algal cells enclosed in fungal hyphae: — *pl.* **sorē'dia.** — *adjs.* **sorē'dial, sorē'diate.** [Gr. *sōros*, a heap.]

soree. See **sora**.

sorehon *sōr'hon, sör', n.* an ancient Irish exaction of free accommodation by a lord from a freeholder or tenant. [See **sorn**.]

sorel(l). See **sorrel**[2].

Sorex *sō'reks, sö', n.* the common shrew genus, giving name to the family **Soricidae** (*sō-ris'i-dē, sö-*): (without *cap.*) any shrew of this genus. — *adjs.* **soric'ident** (L. *dēns, dentis*, tooth) having teeth like the shrew; **soricine** (*sor'i-sīn, -sin*) of the shrew: shrewlike; **sor'icoid** (-*koid*) shrewlike. [L. *sōrex, -icis*, shrew; cf. Gr. *hÿrax*.]

Sorghum *sör'gəm, n.* a tropical Old World genus of grasses near akin to sugar-cane, including durra and Kaffir corn: (without *cap.*) any grass of this genus: (without *cap.*) molasses made from its juice (*U.S.*). — *n.* **sor'go, sor'gho** a variety of durra from which sugar is prepared (**sweet sorghum**, or Chinese sugar-cane): — *pl.* **sor'g(h)os.** [It. *sorgo*, prob. from an East Ind. word, or poss. from (unattested) vulg. L. *Syricum* (*grānum*), Syrian (grain).]

sori. See **sorus**.

Soricidae, etc. See **Sorex**.

sorites *sō-rī'tēz, sö-, n.* a string of propositions in which the predicate of one is the subject of the next (or the same in reverse order): a sophistical puzzle on the model of 'How many grains make a heap?'. — *adjs.* **sorit'ic, -al.** [Gr. *sōreitēs* — *sōros*, a heap.]

sorn *sörn*, (*Scot.*) *v.i.* to obtrude oneself as an uninvited guest. — *ns.* **sor'ner; sorn'ing.** [Obs. Ir. *sorthan*, free quarters.]

soroban *sör'ə-bän, n.* a Japanese abacus. [From Jap. — Chin. words meaning 'calculating board'.]

soroche *so-rō'chā, n.* mountain sickness. [Sp. — Quechua *surúcht*, antimony (present in the Andes and formerly believed to cause the sickness).]

Soroptimist *sor-opt'i-mist, adj.* of an international organisation of women's clubs. — *n.* a member of one of these clubs. [L. *soror*, sister, and **optimist**.]

sororal *sor-ō'rəl, -ö', sororial* -*ri-əl, adjs.* sisterly: of, of the nature of, a sister. — *n.* **soro'rate** (or *sor'ər-āt*) a custom that allows or requires marriage with a wife's sister. — *adv.* **soro'rially.** — *n.* **sororicide** (-*or'i-sīd*; L. *caedēre*, to kill) the killing or killer of a sister. — *v.i.* **sororise, -ize** (*sor'ər-īz*) to associate in a sisterly way. — *ns.* **sorority** (*sor-or'i-ti*) a sisterhood: a women's academic society (*U.S.*); **soro'sis** (*U.S.*) a women's club. [L. *soror*, sister.]

sorosis *so-, sö-, sə-, sō-rō'sis, n.* a fleshy fruit formed from a crowd of flowers, as the pineapple. [Gr. *sōros*, a heap.]

sorption *sörp'shən, n.* absorption and/or adsorption.

sorra. See **sorrow**.

sorrel[1] *sor'l, n.* any of the acid-tasting species of the dock genus, Rumex (**common sorrel** *R. acetosa*; **sheep's sorrel** *R. acetosella*; **French** or **Roman sorrel** *R. scutatus*) or the kindred *Oxyria digyna* (**mountain sorrel**): applied also to other plants as roselle and wood-sorrel. — **salts of sorrel** a very poisonous combination of potassium acid oxalate and oxalic acid. [O.Fr. *sorele, surele* (Fr. *surelle*) — *sur*, sour — O.H.G. *sûr* (Ger. *sauer*), sour.]

sorrel[2] *sor'l, adj.* reddish-brown or light chestnut. — *n.* a reddish-brown colour: a sorrel horse: (also **sorel, sorell** *sör'el, sör'; Shak.*) a third-year buck. [O.Fr. *sorel* — *sor* (Fr. *saur, saure*), sorrel; poss. L.G.; cf. **sore**[2].]

sorrow *sor'ō, n.* pain of mind: grief, sadness: affliction: lamentation: one sorrowed for: the devil (in imprecations, as an emphatic negative, and applied as a term of abuse; Irish **sorra**). — *v.t.* and *v.i.* to grieve. — *adj.* **sorr'owed** (*Shak.*) accompanied with sorrow. — *n.* **sorr'ower.** — *adj.* **sorr'owful** full of sorrow: causing, showing, or expressing sorrow: sad: dejected. — *adv.* **sorr'owfully.** — *n.* **sorr'owfulness.** — *n.* and *adj.* **sorr'owing.** — *adj.* **sorr'owless** free from sorrow. [O.E. *sorg, sorh*; Ger. *Sorge*, O.N. *sorg*.]

sorry *sor'i, adj.* regretful: expressing pity, sympathy, etc.: (often merely formally) apologetic: distressing: poor, miserable, wretchedly bad, contemptible, worthless: — *compar.* **sorr'ier; superl. sorr'iest.** — *interj.* of (often slight) apology. — *adv.* **sorr'ily.** — *n.* **sorr'iness.** — *adj.* **sorr'yish.** [O.E. *sārig*, wounded — *sār*, pain; Du. *zeerig*; influenced in meaning by **sorrow**, but not connected in origin.]

sort *sört, n.* a lot (in **sortilege**) (*Shak.*): a company, group, collection, parcel (*obs.*): a class, kind, or species: quality or rank: one, a specimen or instance, of a kind (often ungrammatically in the singular with *these* or *those*, to denote examples of this or that kind): something of the nature but not quite worthy of the name: a letter, stop, or other character in a fount of type: manner: a woman, esp. an attractive one (*slang*, orig. *Austr.*). — *v.t.* to allot, assign (*Shak.*): to dispose (*Shak.*): to befit (*rare*): to separate into lots or classes: to group, classify, arrange: to pick out: to select: to provide (*Scot.*): to procure (*Scot.*): to set in accord: to adjust, put to rights, attend to (*Scot.*): to geld: to castigate, punish: to deal effectively with (esp. in a vague threat) (*coll.*). — *v.i.* to come about, turn out (*obs.*): to fit, accord: to agree (*Scot.*): to consort (*dial.*). — *adj.* **sort'able** capable of being sorted: assorted: suitable, befitting (*rare*). — *n.* **sort'ance** (*Shak.*) suitableness, agreement; **sortā'tion** a sorting out; **sort'er** one who (or that which) separates and arranges, as letters. — *n.pl.* **sort'es** (-*ēz*; L. -*ās*) divination by chance opening of the Bible, Homer, Virgil, etc. — *ns.* **sort'i-lege** (-*i-lij*; L. *sortilegus*, a diviner) divination; **sortil'eger; sortil'egy.** — *n.* and *adj.* **sort'ing.** — *ns.* **sorti'tion** the casting of lots; **sort'ment** a sorting out: an assortment. — **after a sort** to some extent; **a good sort** a decent fellow; **in a sort** in a manner; **in some sort** in a way: as it were; **in sort** in a body (*Shak.*): inasmuch (*Spens.*); **of a sort, of sorts** inferior; **out of sorts** out of order, slightly unwell: with some sorts of type in the fount exhausted (*print.*); **sort of** (*coll.*, used adverbially and parenthetically) as it were: to an extent: rather; **sort out** to classify, separate, arrange, etc.: to deal with, punish, etc.; **that's your sort** that's right: well done: go on. [L. *sors, sortis,* a lot, *sortīrī,* to draw lots; partly through O.Fr.]

sortie *sör'ti, n.* a sally of besieged to attack the besiegers: a raiding excursion. — *v.i.* to sally. [Fr., — *sortir,* to go out, to issue; origin doubtful.]

sortilege, etc. See **sort.**

sorus *sö'rəs, sö', n.* a cluster of sporangia or soredia: — *pl.* **so'rī.** — *adj.* **so'ral.** [Gr. *sōros,* a heap.]

S O S *es-ō-es', n.* an appeal for help or rescue. — *v.i.* to make such an appeal. [Arbitrary code signal.]

so-so (or **so so**) *sö'sö, adj.* neither very good nor very bad: tolerable: indifferent. — Also *adv.* [**so¹**.]

soss *sos, n.* a mess: a dish of sloppy food: a puddle: a heavy fall: a plump. — *v.t.* to dirty: to slobber up: to throw carelessly about. — *v.i.* to plump down: to splash about. — *adv.* plump. — *n.* **soss'ing.** [Imit.]

sostenuto *sos-te-nōō'tō, -nū', (mus.) adj.* sustained. — *adv.* with full time allowed for each note. [It.]

sot¹ *sot, n.* a fool (*obs.*): one stupefied by drinking: a habitual drunkard. — *v.i.* to play the sot. — *adj.* **sott'ed** besotted. — *n.* **sott'ing.** — *adj.* **sott'ish** like a sot: foolish: stupid with drink. — *adv.* **sott'ishly.** — *n.* **sott'ishness.** [O.Fr. *sot.*]

sot² *sot, sut,* (*Scot.*) *adv.* the emphatic correlative of *not,* meaning on the contrary, etc., used to contradict a negative assertion. [Variant of **so¹** influenced by **not.**]

Sotadic *so-tad'ik,* **Sotadean** *sö-* or *so-tə-dē'ən, adjs.* pertaining to *Sōtadēs,* a lascivious and scurrilous Greek poet (fl. 276 B.C.), or his writings, or his metre: coarse and scurrilous: palindromic. — *n.* a satire in his manner: a catalectic tetrameter of ionics *a majore* (see **Ionic**).

soterial *sö-tē'ri-əl, adj.* pertaining to salvation. — *adj.* **sōteriolog'ical.** — *n.* **sōteriol'ogy** the doctrine of salvation. [Gr. *sōtēriā,* salvation — *sōtēr,* a saviour.]

Sothic *sö'thik, adj.* of or pertaining to Sirius. — **Sothic cycle** or **period** a period of 1460 years, after which the beginning of the Egyptian year of 365 days again coincides with the beginning of the **Sothic year,** which was reckoned from the heliacal rising of Sirius. [Egyptian name of Sirius, given in Gr. as *Sōthis.*]

Sotho *sōō'tōō, sö'tō, n.* See **Basuto.**

sotted, etc. See **sot¹.**

sottisier *so-tēz-yā, n.* a collection of jokes, ridiculous remarks, quotes, etc. [Fr. — *sottise,* folly.]

sotto voce *sot'tō vō'che, adv.* in an undertone, aside. [It., below the voice.]

sou *sōō, n.* a French five-centime piece. [Fr., — L. *solidus*; cf. **sold²**, **soldier, soldo.**]

souari, saouari *sow-ä'ri, n.* a tree (*Caryocar*) of Guiana yielding a durable timber and edible butternuts. — **s(a)oua'ri-nut.** [Fr. *saouari,* from Galibi.]

soubise *sōō-bēz', n.* an 18th-cent. cravat: a sauce made from, or a side dish of, puréed onions. [Fr., after the French Marshal Prince de *Soubise* (1715–87).]

soubrette *sōō-bret', n.* a pert, coquettish, intriguing maid-servant in comedy: a singer of light songs of similar character: a maid-servant, lady's maid. [Fr., — Prov. *soubreto* (fem.), coy.]

soubriquet. See **sobriquet.**

souce, souct. Old spellings (*Spens., Shak.*) of **souse²**, **soused.**

souchong *sōō-shong', -chong', n.* a fine sort of black tea. [Chin. *hsiao,* small, *chung,* sort.]

Soudan(ese). See **Sudan.**

souffle *sōō'fl, n.* a murmuring in auscultation. [Fr.]

soufflé *sōō'flä, n.* a light dish, properly one with white of egg whisked into a froth. — *adj.* prepared thus. [Fr., pa.p. of *souffler* — L. *sufflāre,* to blow.]

sough¹ *sow, suf,* or (*Scot.*) *sōōhh, v.i.* to sigh, as the wind. — *v.t.* to whine out: to sigh out: to hum. — *n.* a sighing of the wind: a deep sigh: a vague rumour: a whining tone of voice. — **keep a calm sough** to keep quiet. [O.E. *swōgan,* to rustle.]

sough² *suf, n.* a drain, sewer, adit. — **sough'ing-tile** a drain-tile. [Cf. Flem. dial. *zoeg,* a small ditch.]

sought *söt, pa.t.* and *pa.p.* of **seek.**

souk *sōōk, n.* among Eastern Muslim people, a market-place. — Also **suk(h), suq.** [Ar. *sūq.*]

soul *söl, n.* life (*obs.*): that which thinks, feels, desires, etc.: the ego: a spirit, embodied or disembodied: innermost being or nature: that which one identifies with oneself: moral and emotional nature, power, or sensibility: nobleness of spirit or its sincere expression: a complete embodiment or exemplification: an element: essence: the essential part: an indwelling or animating principle: the moving spirit, inspirer, leader: a person: the lungs of a goose, etc.: a violin sound-post: (also **soul music**) the popular music of American Negroes, typically emotional and earthy, a blend of blues, jazz, gospel and pop elements. — *adj.* of or relating to soul music: of or characteristic of American Negroes or their food, music, culture, etc. — *interj.* by, upon my soul. — *adjs.* **souled** having a soul, esp., in compounds, of this or that kind; **soul'ful** having or expressive of deep or elevated feeling, sincere or affected. *adv.* **soul'fully.** — *n.* **soul'fulness.** — *adj.* **soul'less** without a soul: lacking animation or nobleness of mind: mean, without spirit. — *adv.* **soul'lessly** in a soulless manner. — *n.* **soul'lessness.** — **soul'-bell** a passing bell; **soul brother, sister** a fellow Negro, Negress. — *adj.* **soul'-confirming** (*Shak.*) ratifying the devoting of the soul. — **soul'-cūr'er** (*Shak.*) a parson. — *adjs.* **soul'-destroying** (of a task, situation, etc.) extremely monotonous, unrewarding, etc; **soul'-fear'ing** (*Shak.*) terrifying the soul. — **soul food** (*U.S.*) food such as chitterlings, corn-bread, etc., traditionally eaten by American Negroes; **soul'-force** (a term for) satyagraha. — *adj.* **soul'-killing** (*Shak.*). — **soul mate** a person to whom one is deeply emotionally or spiritually attached; **soul music** see **soul** above; **soul'-search'ing** a critical examination of one's actions, motives, etc. — Also *adj.* — **soul'-shot, -scot, -scat** a payment to the church on behalf of a dead person, a funeral payment. — *adj.* **soul'-sick** morally diseased. — **soul= sleeper** a psychopannychist. — *adj.* **soul'-stirring.** — **by, upon my soul!** an exclamation of surprise, etc. [O.E. *sāwol*; Ger. *Seele.*]

souldan. An old form of **soldan.**

souldier. An old spelling of **soldier.**

soum, sowm *sōōm, (Scot.) n.* the proportion of sheep or cattle suitable for any pasture: pasture for one cow or its equivalent in sheep, etc. — *v.t.* and *v.i.* to determine in terms of soums. — *n.* **soum'ing.** — **souming and rouming** the determination of the number of soums appropriate to a common pasture, and their apportionment (according to ability to supply fodder through winter) to the various roums or holdings. [Form of **sum.**]

sound¹ *sownd, adj.* safe: whole: uninjured, unimpaired: in good condition: healthy: wholesome: deep (as sleep): solid: thorough (as a beating): well-founded: well-grounded: trustworthy: of the right way of thinking: orthodox. — *adv.* soundly, completely fast, as in sleep. — *adv.* **sound'ly.** — *n.* **sound'ness.** — **sound as a bell** see **bell¹.** [O.E. *gesund*; Ger. *gesund.*]

sound² *sownd, n.* a strait: a fish's swimming bladder. [O.E. *sund,* swimming.]

sound³ *sownd, n.* the sensation of hearing: a transmitted disturbance perceived or perceptible by the ear: esp. a tone produced by regular vibrations (opp. to *noise*): mere noise, without meaning or sense or distinguished from sense: a report, rumour: hearing-distance. — *v.i.* to give out a sound: to resound: to be audible: to be sounded: to be famed: to give an impression on hearing: to tend (*obs.*): to call, as by trumpet. — *v.t.* to cause to make a sound: to produce, utter, make, the sound of: to utter audibly: to pronounce: to announce, publish, proclaim, celebrate, signal, direct, by sound: to mean (*obs.*): to examine by percussion and listening: to tease, goad, provoke (*U.S. slang*). —

ns. **sound′er** that which sounds: a telegraph-receiving instrument in which Morse signals are translated into sound signals; **sound′ing** emission of sound: a signal by trumpet, bell or the like, as for the rise of the curtain: examination by percussion. — *adj.* making a sound: sonorous: resounding: having a magnificent sound. — *adv.* **sound′ingly.** — *adj.* **sound′less.** — *adv.* **sound′lessly.** — **sound′-bar** a bass-bar; **sound barrier** (*aero.*) a difficulty met about the speed of sound when power required to increase speed rises steeply; **sound′-board** a thin resonating plate of wood or metal in a musical instrument: in an organ, the apparatus that conveys the air from the windchest to the appropriate pipes: a sounding-board; **sound′-boarding** boards between joists carrying pugging to make a floor soundproof; **sound′-body** a resonance-box; **sound′-bow** the thick edge of a bell, against which the hammer strikes; **sound′-box** a resonance-box: part of a gramophone supporting the diaphragm; **sound broadcasting, radio** broadcasting by radio as opposed to television; **sound effects** sounds other than dialogue or music used in films, radio and television; **sound′-film** a cinematograph film with sychronised sound-track; **sound′-hole** an *f*-shaped hole in the belly of a violin, etc.; **sound′ing-board** a structure for carrying a speaker's voice towards the audience: a sound-board: any person, object or institution used to test the acceptability or effectiveness of an idea, plan, etc.; **sound mixer** the person who controls the tone and volume of sound(s) to be recorded for a motion picture, gramophone record, etc.: the machine used in performing this task; **sound poem** a poem consisting of a series of euphonic syllables; **sound poet; sound′-post** a short post connecting the belly and back of a violin, etc., under the bridge. — *adj.* **sound′proof** impenetrable by sound. — *v.t.* to render soundproof. — **sound′proofing; sound radio** sound broadcasting; **sound′-ranging** the calculation of position by timing the arrival of sound waves from (three or more) known positions; **sound′-shadow** a region of silence behind a barrier to sound; **sound′-shift** a series of regular changes in stop-consonants differentiating Germanic from other Indo-European languages, or (*second shift*) High German from other Germanic; **sound spectrogram** a record produced by a **sound spectrograph,** an electronic instrument which makes a graphic representation of the qualities of a sound as frequency, intensity, etc.; **sound spectrography; sound system** an electronic system, including amplifier, speakers and one or more devices for playing recorded sound: a highly sophisticated or accessorised music system, e.g. a mobile discothèque; **sound′-track** on a cinematograph film, the magnetic tape on which sounds are recorded: a recording of the sound (esp. musical) accompaniment to a film; **sound′-wave** a longitudinal disturbance propagated through air or other medium. — **sound off (about, on)** to speak loudly and freely, esp. in complaint: to boast. [M.E. *soun* — A.Fr. — L. *sonus*; for *d* cf. **pound**[3].]

sound[4] *sownd, v.t.* to measure the depth of: to probe: to try to discover the inclinations, thoughts, etc., of (often with *out*). — *v.i.* to take soundings: to dive deep, as a whale. — *n.* a probe for examining the bladder, etc. — *ns.* **sound′er** one who sounds: apparatus for taking soundings; **sound′ing** the action of that which or one who sounds: an ascertained depth: (in *pl.*) waters in which an ordinary sounding-line will reach the bottom: a test or measurement of depth, esp. of water by means of an echo-sounder or sounding line: penetrating a particular environment to obtain sample readings, e.g. of temperature: (usu in *pl.*; also with *out*) sample testing of opinion, inclination, etc., usu. of an unofficial kind. — **sound′ing-lead** the weight at the end of a sounding-line; **sound′ing-line** a line with a plummet at the end for soundings; **sounding rocket** a rocket devised to gather high-altitude meteorological data and to radio it back to earth; **sound′ing-rod** a rod for measuring water in a ship's hold. [O.E. *sund-* (in

compounds), cf. **sound**[2]; or perh. O.Fr. *sonder,* to sound, which may be from Gmc.]

sound[5] *sownd,* (*obs.*) *n.* and *v.i.* Same as **swound.** See **swoon.**

sounder *sown′dər, n.* a herd of swine: a young boar. [O.Fr. *sundre*; of Gmc. origin; cf. O.E. *sunor.*]

soup *soop, n.* the nutritious liquid obtained by boiling meat or vegetables in stock: (*loosely*), anything resembling soup in consistency, etc.: a photographic developer (*slang*): stolen plate melted down (*slang*): various slang senses, as nitroglycerine, dope for a horse. — *ns.* **soup′er** in Ireland, one who dispenses soup as a means of proselytising: one really or supposedly so converted. — *adj.* **soup′y.** — *adj.* **soup′ed-up** (*slang*) of e.g. an engine, having had the power increased. — **soup′-kitchen** a place for supplying soup to the poor; **soup′-maigre** (or **mea′gre**) a thin fish or vegetable soup, originally for fast-days; **soup′-plate** a large deep plate; **soup′spoon; soup′-ticket** a ticket entitling one to sup at a soup-kitchen; **soup′-tureen.** — **in the soup** in difficulties or trouble; **soup up** (*slang*) to increase the power of; **the ticket for soup** (*slang*) the ticket (q.v.). [O.Fr. *soupe*; cf. **sop.**]

soupçon *soop-sɔ̃, n.* a hardly perceptible quantity. [Fr., suspicion.]

souple[1] *soop′l, adj.* a form of **supple**[1] (*dial.*): of silk, lightly scoured: clever (*Scot.*). — *v.t.* to make supple or souple.

souple[2] *soop′l, n.* a Scots form of **swipple**: a cudgel (*Scott*).

sour *sowr, adj.* having an acid taste or smell: turned, rancid, or fermented: rank: of beasts, heavy, strong: cold and wet: embittered, crabbed, or peevish: disagreeable: inharmonious (*lit., fig.*): bad, unsuccessful: containing sulphur compounds. — *v.t.* to make sour: to treat with dilute acid. — *v.i.* to become sour. — *n.* an acid drink, as a gin or whisky cocktail that contains lemon or lime-juice: an acid solution used in bleaching, curing skins, etc. — *n.* **sour′ing** turning or becoming sour: vinegar: the crab-apple: treatment with dilute acid in bleaching. — *adj.* **sour′ish.** — *advs.* **sour′ishly; sour′ly.** — *n.* **sour′ness.** — *adj.* **sour′-cold** (*Shak.*). — **sour′-crout** see **sauerkraut; sour′dough** leaven: a piece of dough reserved to leaven a new batch: in Canada and Alaska, an old-timer. — *adj.* **sour′-eyed** moroselooking. — **sour′-gourd** the cream of tartar tree: a tropical grass akin to millet: sorrel; **sour mash** (*U.S.*) new mash (q.v.) mixed with old to increase acidity and promote fermentation; **sour′puss** (*slang*) a sour-tempered person; **sour′-sop** a tropical American fruit: the tree (of the custard-apple genus) that bears it. [O.E. *sūr*; Ger. *sauer,* O.N. *sūrr.*]

source *sōrs, sörs, n.* a spring: the head of a stream: an origin: a rise: (*Spens.* **sourse**) perh. a surging: an originating cause: that from which anything rises or originates: a book or document serving as authority for history, or furnishing matter or inspiration for an author: any person, publication, etc., providing information. — *v.t.* (in *pass.*) to come from, originate: to obtain (from a particular source). — *n.* **sourc′ing.** — **source′-book** a book of original documents for historic study. [O.Fr. *sorse* (Fr. *source*), from *sourdre* — L. *surgēre,* to rise.]

sourdeline *soor′də-lēn, n.* a small bagpipe. [Fr.]

sourdine *soor-dēn′,* (*mus.*) *n.* a mute or sordino. [Fr.; cf. **sordino** under **sordo.**]

sourock *soo′rək,* (*Scot.*) *n.* sorrel. [**sour.**]

sourse. See **source.**

sousaphone *soo′zə-fōn, n.* a large tuba-like brass wind instrument invented by the American bandmaster and composer J. P. *Sousa* (1854–1932).

souse[1], **sous** *sows,* (*obs.*) *n.* Same as **sou:** — *pl.* **souse, sous′es.**

souse[2] *sows, n.* pickled meat, esp. pig's feet or ears: an ear (*dial.* or *facet.*): pickling liquid: a plunge in pickling or other liquid: a ducking: a drenching: a wash: a sluicing with water: a getting drunk (*slang*): a drunkard (*U.S.*): a heavy blow or fall: a thump: an impact: a rising from the ground, taking wing (in the falconer's phrase *at souse, at the souse*, when the hawk gets a chance of striking): hence the downward swoop of a bird of prey. — *adv.* with a plunge: with a heavy impact: plump: suddenly. — *v.t.* to pickle: to marinade and cook in spiced wine or vinegar: to plunge, immerse, duck: to drench, soak: to make drunk: to dash: to fling down: to smite: to swoop down upon. — *v.i.* to fall with a plunge: to be drenched: to wash thoroughly: to get drunk: to strike: to impinge: to fall heavily: to swoop as a hawk. — *adj.* **soused** pickled: very wet: drunk (*slang*). — *n.* and *adj.* **sous'ing.** — **souse'-tub; souse'wife.** — Also **souce, sowce, sows(s)e** in old writers. [Partly O.Fr. *sous, souce* — O.H.G. *sulza*, from the root of **salt**[1]; partly imit. (cf. German *Saus*); partly **source** in its old sense of rising.]

souslik. Same as **suslik.**

sout (*Spens.*). Same as **soot**[1].

soutache *sōō-täsh'*, *n.* a narrow braid.   [Fr.]

soutane *sōō-tän'*, *n.* a cassock.   [Fr., — It. *sottana* — L. *subtus*, beneath.]

soutar. See **souter.**

souteneur *sōōt'nœr*, *n.* a prostitute's bully or exploiter. [Fr., supporter, protector; cf. **sustain**.]

souter *sōō'tər*, (*Scot.*) *n.* a shoemaker, a cobbler. — Also **sow'ter, sou'tar.** — *adj.* **sou'terly.** — **souter's clod** (*Scott*) a brown wheaten roll.   [O.F. *sutere* (O.N. *sūtari*) — L. *sūtor* — *suĕre*, to sew.]

souterrain *sōō-te-rē, sōō'tə-rān*, *n.* an underground chamber: an earth-house.   [Fr.]

south *sowth*, *adv.* in the direction contrary to north. — *n.* the point of the horizon, the region, or the part, in that direction: the south wind: (*cap.*; with *the*) the Southern States of the U.S. — *adj.* lying towards the south: forming the part, or that one of two, that is towards the south: blowing from the south: (of a pole of a magnet, usu.) south-seeking. — *v.i.* (*sowdh*) to move or veer towards the south: to cross the meridian. — *n.* **souther** (*sowdh'ər*) a south wind or gale. — *v.i.* (*sudh'ər*) to move or veer towards the south. — *adj.* **southering** (*sudh'*). — *n.* **southerliness** (*sudh'*). — *adj.* and *adv.* **southerly** (*sudh'*) towards or (of wind) from the south. — *adj.* **southern** (*sudh'*) of the south: in the south or in the direction toward it: (of wind) from the south: (with *cap.*) of, from or pertaining to the South. — *n.* a southerner. — *n.* **southerner** (*sudh'*) a native or inhabitant of the south: (with *cap.*) an inhabitant of the U.S. South. — *v.t.* **southernise, -ize** (*sudh'*) to render southern in character. — *n.* **southernism** (*sudh'*) a form of expression peculiar to the south, esp. the Southern States of America. — *adj.* **southernly** (*sudh'*) southerly. — *adv.* towards the south. — *adjs.* (*superl.*) **south'ermost** (*rare*), **southernmost** (*sudh'*). — *n.* **southing** (*sowdh'*) distance, deviation, tendency or motion to the south: meridian passage. — *adj.* (*superl.*) **south'most.** — *adj.* **southron, Southron, Southroun** (*sudh'rən*; *Scot.*) southern, esp. English as distinguished from Scots. — *n.* a southerner: an Englishman: the English of England. — *adj.*, *adv.*, and *n.* **southward** (*sowth'wərd*; *naut. sudh'ərd*). — *adj.* and *adv.* **south'wardly.** — *adv.* **south'wards.** — *adjs.* **south-bound** (*sowth'*) bound for the south; **south'-country.** — *adj.* and *adv.* **south=east'** (or *sowth'*) midway between south and east. — *n.* the direction midway: the region lying in, the wind blowing from, that direction. — **south-east'er** a strong wind from the south-east. — *adj.* and *adv.* **south=east'erly** towards or (of wind) from the south-east. — *adj.* **south-east'ern** belonging to, or being in, the south-east, or in that direction. — *adj.* and *adv.* **south=east'ward** towards the south-east. — *n.* the region to the south-east. — *adj.* and *adv.* **south-east'wardly.** — *adj.* **south-east'wards.** — **Southern Cross** a conspicuous southern constellation with four bright stars placed crosswise; **southernwood** (*sudh'*) an aromatic plant of southern Europe, of the wormwood genus (Artemisia); **southland** (*sowth'*) the south (also *adj.*); **south'lander.** — *adj.* **south'paw** left-handed: in boxing, leading with

the right hand. — *n.* a left-handed person, esp. in sport: a boxer who leads with his right hand. — *adj.* **south'= po'lar.** — **south pole** the end of the earth's axis in Antarctica: its projection on the celestial sphere: (usually) the south-seeking pole of a magnet (logically the north-seeking); **South Sea** the Pacific ocean. — *adj.* **south-seeking** (*sowth'*) turning towards the earth's magnetic south pole. — *ns., adjs.* and *advs.* **south-south= east', south-south-west'** in a direction midway between south and south-east or south-west. — *adj.* and *adv.* **south-west** (*sowth'* or *sow'*, or *-west'*) midway between south and west. — *n.* the direction between south and west: the region lying that way: the wind blowing from that direction. — **south-**, **sou'-west'er** a gale from the south-west: a waterproof hat with flap at the back of the neck. — *adjs.* **south'-west'erly** toward or (of wind) from the south-west; **south'-west'ern** belonging to, or lying in, the south-west or in that direction. — *adj.*, *adv.*, and *n.* **south-west'ward.** — *adj.* and *adv.* **south= west'wardly.** — *adv.* **south-west'wards.** — **south by east, west** one compass point east, west of south.   [O.E. *sūth*; Ger. *süd*, O.N. *suthr*.]

Southcottian *sowth-kot'i-ən*, *n.* a follower of Joanna *Southcott* (1750–1814) who was expected to give birth to a Shiloh or Prince of Peace. — Also *adj.*

Southdown *sowth'down*, *adj.* pertaining to the *South Downs* in Hampshire and Sussex, the famous breed of sheep so named, or their mutton. — *n.* a sheep of this breed, or its mutton.

southerly, southern, etc., **southron.** See **south.**

southsay, etc. Same as **soothsay,** etc.

souvenir *sōō'və-nēr*, or *-nēr'*, *n.* a memento: a keepsake. — *v.t.* (*Austr.* and *N.Z.*; *coll.*) to collect as a 'souvenir', to steal. — *n.* **sov'ena(u)nce** (*Spens.*) remembrance, memory.   [Fr. *souvenir* — L. *subvenīre*, to come up, to come to mind — *sub*, under *venīre*, to come.]

sov. See **sovereign.**

sovena(u)nce. See **souvenir.**

sovereign, or (after *Milt.*) **sovran,** *sov'rin, -rən, n.* a supreme ruler or head: a monarch: an Irish mayor (*obs.*): a gold coin from Henry VII to Charles I worth 22s. 6d. to 10s., from 1817 a pound (*coll.* **sov** *sov*). — *adj.* supreme: excelling all others: having supreme power residing in itself, himself or herself: of sovereignty: (of contempt) utmost: highly efficacious. — *adv.* **sov'ereignly** supremely: as a sovereign. — *n.* **sov'ereignty,** (*poet.*) **sov'ranty** pre-eminence: supreme and independent power: the territory of a sovereign or of a sovereign state.   [O.Fr. *sovrain* and It. *sovrano* — L. *super*, above.]

soviet *sō'vi-ət, so'*, *n.* a council, esp. one of those forming since 1917 the machinery of local and national government in Russia (the Union of Soviet Socialist Republics) — the local councils elected by workers, peasants, and soldiers, the higher councils consisting of deputies from the lower. — *adj.* (*cap.*) of the U.S.S.R. — *adj.* **soviet'ic.** — *v.t.* **so'vietise, -ize** to transform to the soviet model. — *n.* **so'vietism** the principles and practices of a soviet government, specif. communism: a characteristic mannerism indicative of soviet ideology. — *adj.* **Sovietolog'ical.** — *n.* **Sovietol'ogist** one who has made a special study of the theory and practice of government in the U.S.S.R. and of current affairs there. — **the Soviet** the U.S.S.R.   [Russ. *sovet*, council.]

sovran, sovranty. See **sovereign.**

sow[1] *sow*, *n.* a female pig: a female badger, etc.: a term of reproach for a fat, lazy, greedy, or sluttish person, esp. a woman: a main channel for molten iron, leading to *pigs*: metal solidified there: a movable shed for protecting besiegers (*hist.*). — **sow'-bread** a cyclamen, esp. *C. europaeum*, whose tubers are eaten by swine; **sow'-bug** a wood-louse. — *adj.* **sow'-drunk** (*coll.*) beastly drunk. — **sow'-gelder** one who spays sows. — *n.* and *adj.* **sow'-skin.** — **sow'-thistle** a thistle-like genus of plants (*Sonchus*) with milky juice and yellow flowers. [O.E. *sū, sugu*; Ger. *Sau*, O.N. *syr*; L. *sūs*, Gr. *hȳs*.]

sow² *sō, v.t.* to scatter or put in the ground, as seed: to plant by strewing: to scatter seed over: to spread, strew, disseminate. — *v.i.* to scatter seed for growth: — *pa.t.* **sowed** (*sōd*); *pa.p.* **sown** (*sōn*) or **sowed**. — *ns.* **sow'er; sow'ing.** — **sow'ing-machine'** a machine for sowing seed. — **sow the seeds of** to initiate, implant. [O.E. *sāwan*; Ger. *säen*, O.N. *sā*, Goth. *saian*.]

sowans. See **sowens.**

sowar *sō-wär', n.* an Indian trooper, mounted policeman, or attendant. — *n.* **sowarr'y, sowarr'ee** a mounted retinue, cavalcade. [Urdu *sawār*, horseman.]

sowce. See **souse²**.

sowens, sowans *sō'ənz, (Scot.) n.pl.* a dish made from the farina remaining among the husks of oats, flummery. [Supposed to be from Gael. *sùghan*, the liquid of sowens — *sùgh*, juice.]

sowf(f). See **sowth.**

sowl, sowle. See **sole⁴.**

sowm. See **soum.**

sownd¹ *sownd, (Spens.) v.t.* app., to wield.

sownd² *sownd, (Spens.) n.* Same as **swound, swoon.**

sowne *sown, (Spens.) n.* Same as **sound³.**

sowp *sowp, (Scot.) n.* a spoonful, sip, small drink. [O.N. *saup*; cf. **sop, sup.**]

sowse, sowsse *sows, (Spens.; Shak.) vb.* and *n.* Same as **souse².**

sowter. See **souter.**

sowth *sowth,* **sowf, sowff** *sowf, (Scot.) vs.i.* and *vs.t.* to whistle or hum over softly. [Scots forms of obs. *solf* — Fr. *solfier,* to sol-fa.]

sox *soks, n.pl.* a slang spelling of **socks.**

soy *soi,* **soya** *sō'yə, soi'ə,* **soja** *sō'yə, sō'jə, ns.* a thick, dark, salty sauce made from fermented soy beans and wheat flour (also **soy, soya, soja sauce**): the soy bean, rich in oil and protein: the eastern Asiatic papilionaceous plant (*Glycine soja, G. hispida* or *max*) producing it. — *adj.* made from soy beans or soy flour. — **soy bean; soya bean, soja bean; soy, soya, soja flour.** [Jap. *shō-yu,* coll. *soy,* Du. *soya, soja* — Chin. *shi-yu,* salt bean oil.]

soyle *soil, (Spens.) n.* app., body, prey. [Unexplained.]

soyled. See **soil³.**

sozzle *sŏz'l, v.t. (U.S. and dial.)* to splash: to make sloppy: to intoxicate: to perform sluttishly. — *n. (U.S. and dial.)* slops: sluttishness: a slattern. — *adjs.* **sozz'led** (*coll.*) drunk; **sozz'ly** (*U.S. and dial.*) sloppy. [Cf. **soss.**]

spa *spä,* formerly *spö, n.* a mineral spring: a mineral water resort. — *v.i.* to stay at a spa. — *n.* **spa'ing.** — **spa'-well.** [*Spa* in Belgium.]

space *spās, n.* that in which material bodies have extension: a portion of extension: room: intervening distance: an interval: an open or empty place: regions remote from the earth: an interval between lines or words: a type used for making such an interval: an interval between the lines of the stave: a portion, extent, or interval of time: a short time: opportunity, leisure. — *v.t.* to make, arrange, or increase intervals between. — *v.i. (Spens.)* to walk about. — *adjs.* **spaced; space'less.** — *ns.* **spac'er** one who, or that which, spaces: an instrument for reversing a telegraphic current: a space-bar: a space traveller or spacecraft (*science fiction*): a spacer-plate (q.v. below); **spacing** (*spās'ing*) a space or spatial arrangement: the existence or arrangement of spaces, or of objects in spaces. — *adjs.* **spacial** (*spā'shl*) spatial; **spacious** (*spā'shəs*) extensive: ample: roomy: wide. — *adv.* **spa'ciously.** — *n.* **spa'ciousness.** — *adj.* **spac'y, spac'ey** (*slang*) chiefly *U.S.*) dreamy: behaving as if spaced out: eccentric, unconventional. — **space age** the present time when exploration of, and ability to travel in, space up to the limit of and beyond the earth's atmosphere are increasing; **space'-band** a wedge for justifying the line in mechanical type-setting; **space'-bar** a bar for making spaces in typewriting. — *adj.* **space'borne** carried through

space: effected or operated in space. — **space cadet** a trainee spaceman or -woman: a space-travel enthusiast: a person habitually high on drugs; **space'craft** a vehicle, manned or unmanned, designed for putting into space, orbiting the earth, or reaching other planets. — *adj.* **space'faring** concerned with or engaged in space travel. — Also *n.* — **space'-heater** a device which warms the air in a room or similar enclosed area; **space'-heat'ing; Space Invaders®** an electronic game played on a machine with a screen, involving 'shooting' at graphic representations of supposed invaders from outer space; **space'-lattice** an arrangement of points in three-dimensional space at the intersections of equally spaced parallel lines — such as the arrangement of atoms in a crystal disclosed by X-ray spectroscopy; **space'man, -woman** a traveller in space; **space medicine** branch of medicine concerned with effects of conditions in space on the human body; **space'-platform, space'-station** a platform in space planned as an observatory and/or a landing-stage in space travel; **space probe** a spacecraft designed to obtain, and usu. transmit, information about the environment into which it is sent; **spac'er-plate** (*archaeol.*) a flat bead, e.g. of jet or amber, with several parallel holes, for separating the threads of a multi-string necklace; **space'ship** a spacecraft; **space shuttle** a spacecraft designed to transport men and materials to and from space-stations; **space'-suit** a suit devised for use in space-travel; **space'-time'** normal three-dimensional space plus dimension of time, modified by gravity in relativity theory; **space-time continuum** physical space or reality, regarded as having four dimensions (length, breadth, height and time) in which an event can be represented as a point fixed by four co-ordinates; **space'-travel; space'-traveller; space'-travelling; space vehicle** see **vehicle; space walk** an excursion by an astronaut outside his craft while in space. — Also *v.i.* (with *hyphen*). — **space'-writ'er** one paid by space filled; **spacious times** days of expansion (in knowledge, trade, etc.) and scope (for discovery, adventure, and the like), as in the reign of Queen Elizabeth I. — **space out** to set wide apart or wider apart: to lapse into a drugged, dazed, delirious or light-headed state; **spaced out** (*slang*) in a dazed or stupefied state (as if) caused by the taking of drugs. [Fr. *espace* — L. *spatium*; Gr. *spaein,* to draw.]

spadassin *spad'ə-sin, n.* a swordsman, a bravo. [Fr., — It. *spadaccino* — *spada,* a sword.]

spade¹ *spād, n.* a broad-bladed digging tool: a whaler's knife: a spade's depth, spit. — *v.t.* to dig or remove with a spade. — *n.* **spade'ful** as much as a spade will hold: — *pl.* **spade'fuls.** — *n.* **spa'der** one who spades. — **spade'-beard** a spade-shaped beard; **spade'-bone** the scapula; **spade'-foot** a toad with a digging foot; **spade'-guin'ea** a guinea with spade-shaped shield, coined 1787–99; **spade'-hus'bandry** cultivation by digging instead of ploughing; **spade(s)'man** a worker with the spade; **spade'work** preparatory drudgery. — **call a spade a spade** to speak out plainly without euphemism. [O.E. *spadu, spædu*; akin to Gr. *spathē* (see next word).]

spade² *spād, n.* a playing-card with black leaf-shaped (on Spanish cards sword-shaped) pips: (*offensive*) a Negro or other coloured person. — **in spades** (*U.S. slang*) extremely, emphatically: to a great(er) extent. [Sp. *espada,* sword — L. *spatha* — Gr. *spathē,* a broad blade.]

spade³. See **spado.**

spade⁴. See **spayad.**

spadger *spaj'ər, (slang) n.* a sparrow. [Form of **sparrow.**]

spadices, spadiceous, etc. See **spadix.**

spadille *spə-dil', n.* the ace of spades in the games of ombre and quadrille. — Also (*obs.*) **spadill'o, spadill'io.** [Fr., — Sp. *espadilla,* dim. of *espada*; see **spade²**.]

spadix *spā'diks, (bot.) n.* a fleshy spike of flowers: — *pl.* **spādices** (*-dī'sēz*). — *adjs.* **spadiceous** (*spā-dish'əs*) having, like, of the nature of, a spadix: coloured like a date: shaped like a palm-branch; **spadicifloral** (*spā-dī-si-flō'rəl, -flō'*) having flowers in a spathe, as arum,

For other sounds see detailed chart of pronunciation.

spado

palms, and some other monocotyledons. [Gr. *spādix, -īkos*, a torn-off (palm) branch, in L. date-coloured, bay.]

spado *spā'dō, spā'*, *n.* a castrated or impotent person or animal: — *pl.* **spadones** (*spä-dō'nēz, -nās*), **spā'do(e)s.** — Also (*rare*) **spade.** [L. *spădō, -ōnis* — Gr. *spădōn, -ōnos* — *spaein*, to pull, tear.]

spadroon *spə-drōōn'*, (*hist.*) *n.* a cut-and-thrust sword: swordplay with it. [Fr. (Genevan dialect) *espadron*.]

spae *spā*, (*Scot.*) *v.t.* and *v.i.* to foretell, divine. — *n.* **spā'er.** — **spae'man; spae'wife.** [O.N. *spā*.]

spageric. See **spagyric.**

spaghetti *spä-, spə-get'i*, *n.* an edible, cord-like paste intermediate between macaroni and vermicelli. — *adj.* denoting similarity to spaghetti, esp. in terms of numerous intertwining strands, etc. — **spaghetti (alla) bolognese** ((*al-a*) *bol-on-yāz', bol-ən-āz'*) spaghetti served with a meat and tomato sauce; **spaghetti western** an internationally-financed western, typically filmed in Europe by an Italian producer, characterised by a violent and melodramatic content and a baroque style. [It., *pl.* of *spaghetto*, dim. of *spago*, a cord.]

spagyric, -al *spə-jir'ik, -əl*, *adjs.* alchemical. — *ns.* **spagyr'ic, spagyrist** (*spaj'ər-ist*) an alchemist. — Also **spagir'ic, spager'ic,** etc. [Prob. coined by Paracelsus.]

spahi *spä'hē*, *n.* formerly a Turkish, now a French Algerian cavalryman. — Also **spa'hee.** [Turk. (from Pers.) *sipāhi*; cf. **sepoy.**]

spain. Same as **spane.**

spairge. See **sparge.**

spake *spāk.* See **speak.**

spald. See **spauld.**

spale *spāl*, (*Scot.*) *n.* a splinter: a chip. [Cf. next.]

spall¹ *spöl*, *v.t.* and *v.i.* to split, splinter, to chip. — *n.* a chip or splinter, esp. of stone. — *v.t.* and *v.i.* **spalt** to split, splinter. — *adj.* brittle. — *adj.* **spalt'ed.** — *n.* **spallā'tion** a nuclear reaction in which bombardment by high-energy particles produces a large number of disintegration particles not entirely identifiable. [Cf. M.E. *spalden*, to split; Ger. *spalten*.]

spall², spalle. See **spauld.**

spalpeen *spal-pēn'*, *n.* a rascal, a mischievous fellow: a boy. [Ir. *spailpín*, a (migratory) labourer.]

spalt, spalted. See **spall¹.**

Spam® *spam*, *n.* a type of luncheon-meat made from pork, spices, etc. — *adj.* **spammy** tasting of, containing or like spam or luncheon meat — (*loosely*) bland, unexciting, corny (*coll.*) [*Sp*iced h*am*.]

span¹ *span*, *n.* the space from the end of the thumb to the end of the little finger when the fingers are extended: nine inches: the distance from wing-tip to wing-tip in an aeroplane: the distance between abutments, piers, supports, etc., or the portion of a structure (e.g. a bridge) between: the total spread or stretch: a stretch of time, esp. of life. — *v.t.* to measure by spans: to measure: to arch over: to stretch over: to bridge: to encompass: — *pr.p.* **spann'ing;** *pa.t.* and *pa.p.* **spanned.** — *adj.* **span'less** that cannot be spanned or measured. — **span'-counter, span'-farthing** a game in which one tries to throw a counter or coin within a span of one's opponent's. — *adj.* **span'-long** of the length of a span. — **span'-roof** a roof with equal slopes. [O.E. *spann*; cf. Ger. *Spanne*.]

span² *span*, *n.* a pair of horses: a team of oxen. — *v.t.* to yoke: to wind up (*obs.*). [Du. and L.G. *span*.]

span³ *span*, *adj.* fresh, short for **span'-new'** quite new, new as a fresh-cut chip. — **spick and span** see **spick¹.** [O.N. *spān-nȳr* — *spān*, chip (cf. **spoon²**), *nȳr*, new.]

span⁴ *span.* See **spin.**

spanaemia *span-ē'mi-ə*, *n.* deficiency of red corpuscles in the blood. — *adj.* **spanae'mic.** [Gr. *spanos*, lacking, *haima*, blood.]

spancel *span'sl*, *n.* a hobble, esp. for a cow. — *v.t.* to hobble. — *adj.* **span'celled.** [Du. or L.G. *spansel*.]

spandrel, spandril *span'drəl*, *n.* the space between the curve of an arch and the enclosing mouldings, stringcourse, or the like: a self-contained area of surface space (esp. triangular) available for decorative use, e.g. in graphic design or forming part of a structure. [Poss. conn. with **expand.**]

spane, spain, spean *spān*, (*Scot.*) *v.t.* to wean. [M.Du. or M.L.G. *spanen*, or O.Fr. *espanir*; cf. Ger. *spänen*.]

spang¹ *spang*, *n.* a glittering ornament (*obs.*): a clasp (*arch.*). — *v.t.* (*obs.*) to sprinkle with spangs. — *n.* **spangle** (*spang'gl*) a small, thin, glittering plate of metal: a sparkling speck, flake, or spot. — *v.t.* to adorn with spangles. — *v.i.* to glitter. — *adj.* **spang'led.** — *ns.* **spang'ler; spang'let** (*Shelley*). — *n.* and *adj.* **spang'ling.** — *adj.* **spang'ly.** [O.E. *spang*, clasp; cf. Du. *spang*, Ger. *Spange, Spängel*.]

spang² *spang*, (*dial.* esp. *Scot.*) *n.* a bound: a leap: a sudden movement or blow: a bang. — *v.i.* to bound, spring. — *v.t.* to dash: to fling: to throw or cause to spring into the air. — *adv.* (*U.S.*) bang, exactly, absolutely. — **spang'-cockle** the flicking of a marble, etc., from the forefinger with the thumb-nail. — *v.t.* **spang'hew** to fling into the air, esp. in a seesaw game using a plank, orig. from a practice of torturing frogs using a stick. [Origin obscure, perh. connected with **spring¹** and **spank².**]

spangle, etc. See **spang¹.**

Spaniard *span'yərd*, *n.* a native or citizen of *Spain*: a Spanish ship (*arch.*). [M.E. *Spaignarde* — O.Fr. *Espaignart*.]

spaniel *span'yəl*, *n.* a kind of dog, usu. liver-and-white, or black-and-white, with large pendent ears: one who fawns. — *adj.* like a spaniel: fawning, mean. — *v.t.* (*Shak.*) to follow or fawn on like a spaniel. — *v.i.* (or *v.t.* with *it*) to play the spaniel. — *adj.* and *adv.* **span'iel-like.** — **Blenheim spaniel** red-and-white (see **Blenheim**); **Cavalier King Charles spaniel** a larger variety of King Charles spaniel; **clumber spaniel** lemon-and-white (see **clumber**); **field-** or **land-spaniel** hunting breeds (e.g. *cockers, springers*); (**Irish**) **water-spaniel** a (liver-coloured) spaniel for retrieving water-fowl; **King Charles spaniel** black-and-tan, brought into notice by *Charles II*; **Sussex spaniel** golden-liver or brown; **toy spaniel** a lapdog (e.g. *Blenheim, King Charles*). [O.Fr. *espaigneul* (Fr. *épagneul*) — Sp. *Español*, Spanish.]

spaniolate *span'yō-lāt*, **spaniolise, -ize** *-līz*, *vs.t.* to hispanicise. [O.Fr. *Espaignol*, a Spaniard.]

Spanish *span'ish*, *adj.* of or pertaining to *Spain*. — *n.* the language of Spain. — **Spanish bayonet** a yucca with straight sword-shaped leaves; **Spanish broom** a broom-like Mediterranean shrub (*Spartium junceum*) with showy yellow fragrant flowers; **Spanish chalk** soapstone, French chalk; **Spanish chestnut** the true chestnut; **Spanish cress** a species of pepperwort; **Spanish dagger** *Yucca gloriosa*; **Spanish fly** a cantharid: a preparation of cantharides formerly used medicinally to produce blisters or as an aphrodisiac; **Spanish fowl** a breed of domestic hen — also *white-faced black Spanish*; **Spanish grass** esparto; **Spanish influenza** a severe form of influenza, which, first noted in Spain, spread all over the world in 1918; **Spanish juice** extract of liquorice-root; **Spanish Main** (i.e. mainland) the mainland coast of the Caribbean Sea: often popularly the Caribbean Sea itself; **Spanish moss** any of various plants which grow in tropical and sub-tropical areas in long, trailing strands from tree-branches — esp. *Usnea longissima* or *Tillandsia usneoides*; **Spanish needles** an American weed of the bur-marigold genus with hooked fruits; **Spanish onion** a large mild kind of onion; **Spanish sheep** a merino; **Spanish soap** Castile soap; **Spanish walk** the piaffer; **Spanish windlass** a stick used in rope-making to twist and tighten the strands. — **ride the Spanish mare** (*hist.*) to bestride the boom as a punishment; **walk Spanish** to compel or be compelled to walk on tiptoe, lifted by the collar and the seat of the trousers — hence to proceed or act under force. [*Spain*, with vowel-shortening.]

spank¹ *spangk*, *v.t.* and *v.i.* to move or drive with speed or spirit. — *n.* **spank'er** one who walks with long vigorous strides: a fast-going horse: any person or thing particularly striking or dashing: a gold coin (*obs. slang*): a fore-and-aft sail on the aftermost mast. — *adj.* **spank'ing** spirited, going freely: striking, beyond expectation: very large. — *adv.* **spank'ingly.** [Poss. back-formation from **spanking.**]

spank² *spangk, v.t.* to strike with the flat of the hand, to smack. — *n.* a loud slap, esp. on the buttocks. — *n.* **spank'ing.** [Prob. imit.]

spanner *span'ər, n.* an instrument for winding up a spring (*obs.*): a wrench for nuts, screws, etc. — **throw a spanner in the works** to cause confusion or difficulty, upset plans. [Ger. *Spanner* — *spannen,* to stretch; cf. **span**¹.]

spansule *span'sūl, n.* a type of pill, generally a capsule containing grains coated with varying amounts of a soluble substance, so that the medicine is released into the body continually over a period of time. [**span**¹, cap*sule.*]

spar¹ *spär, n.* a rafter: a pole: a bar or rail (chiefly *Scot.*; *Spens.* **sparre**): an undressed tree stem of medium girth: a general term for masts, yards, booms, gaffs, etc. — *v.t.* to fasten with a spar (*Spens.* **sperre**): to fasten: to shut: to fit with spars. — **spar deck** a light upper deck. [O.E. *gesparrian,* to bar; Du. *spar* (n.) *sperren* (vb.); O.N. *sparri*; Ger. *sperren* (vb.).]

spar² *spär, n.* any bright non-metallic mineral, with a good cleavage (esp. in compounds, as *calc-spar, fluor-spar, feldspar*; also *Iceland spar*): a crystal or fragment thereof: an ornament made of it. — *adj.* **sparry** (*spär'i*) of or like spar. [M.L.G. *spar,* related to O.E. *spær-stān,* gypsum.]

spar³ *spär, v.i.* (of game-cocks) to fight with spurs: to box, or make the actions of boxing: to dispute: — *pr.p.* **sparr'ing;** *pa.t.* and *pa.p.* **sparred.** — *n.* a boxing-match or demonstration: a cock-fight: a dispute. — *ns.* **sparr'er; sparr'ing.** — **sparring partner** one with whom a boxer practises: a friend with whom one enjoys lively arguments. [Perh. O.Fr. *esparer* (Fr. *éparer*), to kick out; prob. Gmc.]

sparable *spar'ə-bl, n.* a small headless nail used by shoemakers. [**sparrow-bill.**]

Sparaxis *spar-ak'sis, n.* S. African genus of cormous plants of the family Iridaceae, having colourful star-shaped flowers with lacerated spathes: (without *cap.*) any plant of this genus. [L.L. — Gr. *sparassein* to tear, lacerate.]

spard *spärd.* Spens. for **spared.**

spare¹ *spär, v.t.* to use frugally (*arch.*): to do without: to part with voluntarily: to afford: to allow oneself, concede to oneself (*Milt.*): to abstain from using: to refrain from: to forbear to hurt, injure, punish, kill, end: to treat mercifully: to relieve or save from: to avoid: to avoid incurring: to save, hoard (*obs.*). — *v.i.* (*arch.* or *rare*) to be frugal: to forbear: to be merciful. — *adj.* sparing: frugal: scanty: lean: not in actual use: not required: kept or available for others or for such purposes as may occur. — *adv.* sparely. — *n.* spareness (*Milt.*): sparing: a spare room: a spare man: a spare part: a duplicate kept or carried for emergencies: in skittles or ten-pin bowling, overturning all the pins with the first two balls — i.e. with a ball to spare (a *double spare,* with first ball only): the score for so doing. — *adj.* spare'less unmerciful. — *adv.* spare'ly. — *ns.* spare'ness; spär'er. — *adj.* spär'ing. — *adv.* spär'ingly. — *n.* spär'ingness. — **spare part** a part for a machine ready to replace an identical part if it becomes faulty (**spare-part surgery** surgery involving the replacement of organs, by transplants or artificial devices); **spare rib** a piece of pork consisting of ribs with a little meat adhering to them; **spare room** a bedroom for visitors; **spare time** leisure time (*adj.* spare'-time); **spare tyre** an extra tyre for a motor-vehicle, carried in case of a puncture: a roll of fat around the midriff (*coll.*). — **go spare** (*slang*) to become furious or frenzied; **to spare** over and above what is required. [O.E. *sparian,* to spare, *spær,* sparing; Ger. *sparen.*]

spare² *spär,* (now *Scot.*) *n.* the opening or slit at the top of a skirt, pair of trousers, etc. [Origin obscure.]

Sparganium *spär-gā'ni-əm, n.* the bur-reed genus, constituting a family **Sparganiā'ceae,** akin to the reed-maces: (without *cap.*) a plant of this genus. [Gr. *sparganion.*]

sparge *spärj, v.t.* to sprinkle —(*Scot.*) **spairge** *spärj.* — *n.* **spar'ger** a sprinkler. [L. *spargěre,* to sprinkle.]

spar-hawk *spär'-hök, n.* same as **sparrow-hawk.**

Sparidae *spar'i-dē, n.pl.* the sea-bream family. — *adjs.* and *ns.* **spar'id, spar'oid.** [Gr. *sparos,* the fish sargus.]

spark *spärk, n.* a glowing or glittering particle: anything of like appearance or character, as easily extinguished, ready to cause explosion, burning hot: a flash: an electric discharge across a gap: anything active or vivid: a gay sprightly person: a lover, a beau (*arch.*). — *v.i.* to emit sparks: to sparkle: to play the gallant or lover (*arch.*). — *v.t.* to send forth as sparks: to send sparks through. — *adj.* **spark'ish** gay, jaunty, showy. — *adv.* **spark'ishly.** — *adj.* **spark'less.** — *adv.* **spark'-lessly.** — *n.* **spark'let** a small spark. — *n.sing.* **sparks** a ship's wireless operator (*naut. slang*): an electrician (*slang*). — **spark chamber** a radiation detector, consisting of a chamber containing inert gas and electrically-charged metal plates, in which tracks of particles can be detected and studied by photographing the spark caused by their ionisation of the gas; **spark'-coil** an induction coil: a connection of high-resistance used to prevent sparking in electrical apparatus; **spark'-gap** the space between electrodes across which electric sparks pass: apparatus with such a space; **spark'ing-plug, spark'-plug** in an internal-combustion engine, a plug carrying wires between which an electric spark passes to fire the explosive mixture of gases. — **make sparks fly** to cause anger, irritation; **spark (off)** to cause to begin, kindle, animate; **spark out** (*slang*) to fall asleep: to pass out: to die (*adj.* sparked out). [O.E. *spærca, spearca*; Du. *spark.*]

sparke *spärk,* (*Spens.*) *n.* a weapon of some kind, perh. an error for **sparthe.**

sparkle *spärk'l, n.* a little spark: glitter: scintillation: emission of sparks: appearance of effervescence (as of carbon dioxide in wine): vivacity: spirited animation: coruscation of wit. — *v.i.* to emit sparks: to glitter: to effervesce with glittering bubbles: to be bright, animated, vivacious, or witty. — *v.t.* to cause to sparkle: to throw out as, in, or like sparks. — *n.* **spark'ler** that which sparkles: a diamond or other gem (*slang*): a small firework which can be held in the hand. — *n.* and *adj.* **spark'ling.** — *adv.* **spark'lingly.** — *adj.* **spark'ly** having sparkles: sparkling. — *n.* (*coll.*) something that sparkles: — *pl.* **spark'lies.** [Dim. and freq. of **spark.**]

sparling *spär'ling,* **sperling, spirling** *spûr', spir'ling,* (now *Scot.*) *ns.* the smelt. [Partly O.Fr. *esperlinge* (of Gmc. origin), partly M.L.G. *spirling* or M.Du. *spierling.*]

sparoid. See **Sparidae.**

sparre. See **spar**¹.

sparrer, sparring, etc. See **spar**³.

sparrow *spar'ō, n.* any member of a family of small finch-like birds (*Passer domesticus,* house-sparrow, *P. montanus,* tree-sparrow, or other of the genus): extended to many other, usually brown, birds, as the hedge-sparrow. — **sparr'ow-bill** see **sparable.** — *adj.* **sparr'ow-blasted** (in contempt) dumbfounded. — **sparr'ow-hawk** a genus (*Accipiter*) of long-legged, short-winged falcons, like the goshawks, but smaller. [O.E. *spearwa*; Goth. *sporwa,* O.N. *spörr,* Ger. *Sperling.*]

sparrow-grass *spar'ō-gräs, n.* a corruption of **asparagus.**

sparry. See **spar**².

sparse *spärs, adj.* thinly scattered: scanty. — Also *adv.* — *advs.* **spars'edly** (now *rare*); **sparse'ly.** — *ns.* **sparse'-ness; spars'ity.** [L. *sparsus,* pa.p. of *spargěre,* to scatter; Gr. *speirein,* to sow.]

spart *spärt, n.* esparto: Spanish broom (*obs.*). — *n.* **sparterie** (-ə-rē; Fr.) articles of esparto. [L. *spartum,* Spanish broom, esparto, and Sp. *esparto.*]

Sparta *spär'tə, n.* a city of Greece, capital of ancient Laconia. — *n.* **Spar'tan** a citizen or native of Sparta or Laconia: one displaying Spartan qualities. — *adj.* of Sparta: Laconian: (also without *cap.*) characteristic of Sparta — simple, hardy, rigorous, frugal, laconic, militaristic, despising culture: of a breed of bloodhounds. — *adv.* **Spar′tanly.** [Gr. *Spartē* (Doric *Spartā*).]

Spartacist *spär′tə-sist, n.* a follower of *Spartacus*, leader of the revolted slaves in the Third Slave War against Rome (73–71 B.C.): a German communist of extreme type in the revolution of 1918.

Spartan. See **Sparta.**

sparteine *spar′tē-ēn, -in, n.* an oily alkaloid obtained from the branches of the common broom plant and the seeds of the lupin, sometimes used to treat heart irregularities. [Mod. L. *Spartium*, — Gr. *spartos*, broom.]

sparterie. See **spart.**

sparth(e) *spärth, (arch.) n.* a long battle-axe. [O.N. *spartha.*]

spasm *spaz′m, n.* a violent involuntary muscular contraction: a sudden convulsive action, movement, or emotion: a section of a performance, e.g. a verse (*slang*). — *v.i.* to go into spasm: to experience a spasm or spasms. — *adjs.* **spasmat′ic,-al** (*rare*); **spasm′ic; spasmod′ic, -al** relating to, or consisting in, spasms: convulsive: intermittent. — *adv.* **spasmod′ically.** — *n.* **spas′modist** one whose work is spasmodic. — *adj.* **spas′tic** of the nature of spasm: characterised or affected by spasms: spasmodic: awkward, clumsy, useless (*slang*). — *n.* one affected with spastic paralysis: a useless or stupid person (*derog. slang*). — *adv.* **spas′tically.** — *n.* **spasticity** (-*tis′i-ti*) tendency to spasm. — **Spasmodic School** a group of English poets, P. J. Bailey, Sydney Dobell, Alexander Smith, etc., whose works are marked by over-strained and unnatural sentiment and expression; **spastic paralysis** permanent muscle constriction or involuntary jerky muscle movement caused by injury to the muscle-controlling part of the brain. [Gr. *spasma, -atos*, and *spasmos, -ou*, convulsion; adjs. *spasmōdēs, spastikos — spaein*, to draw, convulse.]

spat¹ *spat, pa.t.* and *pa.p.* of **spit².**

spat² *spat, n.* the spawn of shellfish. — *v.i.* and *v.t.* to spawn. — *n.* **spat′fall** a mass of planktonic shellfish larvae which has settled prior to developing into adults: the location or occurrence of this settlement.

spat³ *spat, n.* a slap (*rare*): a large drop, as of rain: a splash, spattering: a petty quarrel. — *v.t.* (*rare*) to slap, to strike lightly. — *v.i.* to engage in a petty quarrel. [Prob. imit.; cf. Du. *spat*, spot, stain, spatter.]

spat⁴ *spat, n.* a short gaiter: a fairing covering an aircraft wheel. [**spatterdash.**]

Spatangus *spa-, spə-tang′gəs, n.* the typical genus of heart-urchins. — *adj.* and *n.* **spatang′oid.** — *n.pl.* **Spatangoid′ea** the heart-urchins, an order of sea-urchins, more or less heart-shaped, without Aristotle's lantern, with eccentric anus. [Gr. *spatangēs*, a kind of sea-urchin.]

spatchcock *spach′kok, n.* a fowl killed and cooked at once: a fowl slit lengthways, opened out, and cooked (usu. grilled) flat. — *v.t.* to treat in this way: to interpolate. [Prob. **dispatch** and **cock¹;** cf. **spitchcock.**]

spate, speat *spāt, (orig. Scot.) n.* a flood: a sudden rush or increased quantity. — **in spate** (of a river) in a swollen, fast-flowing condition. [Origin doubtful.]

spathe *spādh, (bot.) n.* a sheathing bract, usu. a conspicuous one enclosing a spadix. — *adjs.* **spathaceous** (*spə-thā′shəs*), **spathed** (*spādhd*) having a spathe. [Gr. *spathē*, a broad blade.]

spathic *spath′ik, adj.* of the nature of, or like, spar: lamellar. — *adj.* **spath′ose** (or *-ōs′*) spathic. — **spathic iron** chalybite. [Ger. *Spat(h)*, spar.]

spathulate *spath′ū-lāt.* Same as **spatulate.**

spatial, spacial *spā′shl, adj.* relating to space. — *n.* **spatiality** (*spā-shi-al′i-ti*). — *adv.* **spā′tially.** — *adj.* **spatiotemp′oral** of space-time or space and time together. [L. *spatium*, space.]

Spätlese *shpāt′lā-zə, (Ger.) n.* lit., a late harvest: a sweet white wine made from grapes harvested after the main vintage. —Also without *cap.*

spattee *spat-ē′, n.* a protective outer stocking or long gaiter. [**spat¹** and **puttee.**]

spatter *spat′ər, v.t.* to throw out or scatter upon: to scatter about: to sprinkle, esp. with mud or liquid. — *v.i.* to fly or fall in drops: to let drops fall or fly about. — *n.* a spattering: what is spattered. — **spatt′erdash** a long gaiter or legging; **spatt′er-dock** (*U.S.*) the yellow water-lily; **spatt′er-work** reproduction of designs by covering the surface with the pattern and spattering colour on the parts exposed. [Cf. Du. and L.G. *spatten.*]

spatula *spat′ū-lə, n.* a broad blunt blade or flattened spoon: (*cap.*) a genus of ducks, the shovellers. — *adjs.* **spat′ular; spat′ulate** shaped like a spatula: broad and rounded at the tip and tapering at the base. — *n.* **spat′ule** a spatula. [L. *spatula, spathula*, dim. of *spatha* — Gr. *spathē*, a broad blade.]

spauld *spöld, (now Scot.) n.* the shoulder: a limb. — Also **spald, spall, spaul** and (*Spens.*) **spalle.** — **spauld′-bone** shoulder-blade; **spauld′-ill** quarter-evil. [O.Fr. *espalde* (Fr. *épaule*) — L. *spatula* (see foregoing).]

spavin *spav′in, n.* see **bone-spavin.** — *Scot.* **spavie** (*spā′vē*). — *adj.* **spav′ined** affected with spavin. — **blood′-spavin, bog′-spavin** see **blood, bog.** [O.Fr. *espa(r)vain* (Fr. *éparvin*); connection with **sparrow** obscure.]

spaw *spö,* **spaw′-well,** etc., obs. forms of **spa, spa-well.**

spawl *spöl, n.* spittle, slaver. — *v.i.* to emit spawl.

spawn *spön, n.* a mass of eggs laid in water: fry: brood: contemptuously, offspring: mushroom mycelium. — *v.t.* to produce as spawn: contemptuously, to generate, esp. in mass. — *v.i.* to produce or deposit spawn: to teem: to come forth as or like spawn. — *n.* **spawn′er** one who spawns: a female fish, esp. at spawning-time. — *n.* and *adj.* **spawn′ing.** — **spawn′-brick, -cake** a consolidated cake of horse-dung with mushroom spawn; **spawn′ing-bed, -ground** a bed or place in the bottom of a stream on which fish deposit their spawn. [O.Fr. *espandre*, to shed — L. *expandĕre*, to spread out.]

spay¹. See **spayad.**

spay² *spā, v.t.* to remove or destroy the ovaries of. [A.Fr. *espeier* — *espee* (Fr. *épée*), sword.]

spayad *spā′ad,* **spayd, spade** *spād,* **spay** *spā, (obs.) ns.* a hart in his third year. [Origin obscure.]

speak *spēk, v.i.* to utter words: to talk: to discourse: to make a speech: to sound: to give tongue: to give expression, information, or intimation by any means. — *v.t.* to pronounce: to utter: to express: to declare: to mention: to describe (*arch.*): to hail or communicate with: to use as a language, talk in: to bring or render by speaking: — *pa.t.* **spoke,** or (*arch.*) **spake;** *pa.p.* **spo′ken,** or (*arch.*) **spoke.** — **-speak** (*coll.*) in composition, a particular jargon or style of language, such as *techno-speak, doublespeak,* etc. — *adj.* **speak′able** able or fit to be spoken or expressed in speech: able to speak (*Milt.*). — *ns.* **speak′er** one who speaks: the president (orig. the mouthpiece) of a legislative body, as the House of Commons: a loudspeaker; **speak′ership** the office of speaker; **speak′ing** the act of expressing ideas in words: discourse. — *adj.* uttering or transmitting speech: seeming to speak, lifelike. — *adv.* **speak′ingly.** — **speak′-eas′y** (*U.S.*) during Prohibition, an illicit dram-shop, shebeen; **speak′erphone** a type of telephone using a combined loudspeaker and microphone; **speaking clock** a British telephone service which states the exact time when dialled; **speaking terms** see **term; speak′ing-trum′pet** an instrument for making the voice heard at a distance; **speak′ing-tube** a tube for speaking through to another room; **speak′-ing-voice** the kind of voice used in speaking. — **so to speak** as one might put it, as it were; **speak a ship** to hail and speak to someone on board her; **speak fair** (*arch.*) to address in conciliatory terms; **speak for** to speak on behalf of or in favour of: to be a proof of: to witness to: to bespeak, engage; **speak in tongues** see **tongue; speak one's mind** see **mind; speak out** to speak boldly, freely, unreservedly, or so as to be easily heard; **speak the same language** see **language**; **speak to** to reprove: to attest, testify to: to discuss; **speak up** to speak so as to be easily heard: to state one's opinions boldly; **to speak of** worth mentioning; **to speak to** so as to have conversation with. [Late O.E. *specan* (for *sprecan*); Ger. *sprechen*.]

speakerine *spēk-rēn*, (Fr.) *n*. (*TV* and *radio*) a female announcer or programme hostess. [Fem. form of *speaker*, announcer — Eng. **speaker**.]

speal *spēl*, *n*. See **spule**.

spean. See **spane**.

spear *spēr*, *n*. a long weapon made of a pole with a pointed head: a barbed fork for catching fish: anything sharp or piercing: a spearman: a spire: a spiky shoot or blade: a reed. — *v.t.* to pierce with a spear. — *adjs*. **speared** armed with the spear; **spear'y**. — **spear'fish** a kind of swordfish (*Tetrapturus*); **spear'-grass** a name for many spearlike grasses; **spear gun** an underwater sporting gun which fires spears; **spear'head** the head of a spear: the front of an attack. — Also *v.t.* — **spear'man** a man armed with a spear; **spear'mint** a common garden-mint; **spear'-point**; **spear'-running** a tourney; **spear'-shaft**; **spear'-side** the male side or line of descent (opp. to *spindle-side*, or *distaff-side*); **spear'-this'tle** a common thistle (*Cnicus lanceolatus* or *Cirsium lanceolatum*); **spear'-thrower** a throwing-stick; **spear'-wood** an Acacia or a Eucalyptus (both Australian) whose wood is good for spear-shafts; **spear'wort** a Ranunculus with lance-shaped leaves (*R. lingua*, **greater**, *R. flammula*, **lesser spearwort**). [O.E. *spere*; Ger. *Speer*; with some senses from **spire**[1].]

speat. See **spate**.

spec[1] *spek*, *n*. a coll. shortening of **speculation**. — **on spec** as a gamble, on the chance of achieving something.

spec[2] *spek*, *n*. a coll. shortening of **specification**.

speccy *spek'i*, (*coll*.) *n*. and *adj*. (one who is) bespectacled. [Cf. **specs, spectacle**.]

special *spesh'l*, *adj*. particular: peculiar: distinctive: exceptional: additional to ordinary: detailed: intimate: designed for a particular purpose: confined or mainly applied to a particular subject. — *n*. any special or particular person or thing: any person or thing set apart for a particular duty — a constable, a railway-train, etc.: a particular dish offered in a restaurant, often at a lower price, etc.: a newspaper extra, a dispatch from a special correspondent. — *n*. **specialīsā'tion, -z-**. — *v.t.* **spec'ialise, -ize** to make special or specific: to differentiate: to adapt to conditions: to specify: to narrow and intensify: to become or be a specialist in (with *in*). — *v.i.* to become or be a specialist: to become differentiated: to be adapted to special conditions. — *ns*. **spec'ialiser, -z-**; **spec'ialism** (devotion to) some particular study or pursuit; **spec'ialist** one who devotes himself to a special subject. — *adj*. **specialist'ic**. — *n*. **speciality** (*spesh-i-al'i-ti*), *U.S.* **specialty** (*spesh'əl-ti*) the particular characteristic skill, use, etc., of a person or thing: a special occupation or object of attention. — *adv*. **specially** (*spesh'ə-li*). — *n*. **spec'ialty** something special or distinctive: any special product, article of sale or of manufacture: any special pursuit, department of study, etc.: speciality (*U.S.*): a special contract for the payment of money: a deed under seal (*law*). — **special area** an earlier name for development area; **Special Branch** a British police department which deals with political security; **special constable** see **constable**; **special correspondent** a person employed to send reports to a particular newspaper, agency, etc.; **special delivery** the delivery of mail by special messenger outside normal delivery times; **special licence, offer, pleading, verdict** see **licence**, etc.; **special school** a school designed for the teaching of children with particular needs, esp. the mentally or physically handicapped. — **in special** (*arch*.) in particular: especially; **Special Drawing Rights** (also without *caps*.; abbrev. **SDR(s)**) a reserve of International Monetary Fund assets which members of the fund may

draw on in proportion to their IMF contributions; **Special Theory of Relativity** see **relate**. [L. *speciālis* — *speciēs*, species.]

spécialité de la maison *spās-yal-ē-tā də la mez-ɔ̃*, the dish regarded by a restaurant as its best and most distinctive. [Fr., speciality of the house.]

speciate, -ation. See **species**.

species *spē'shēz, -shiz, -shi-ēz, n*. outward appearance, visible form (*obs*. except *theol*.): a eucharistic element: a visual image (*obs*.): a group of individuals having common characteristics, specialised from others of the same *genus* (*log*.): a group (sometimes rather arbitrarily defined) of closely allied mutually fertile individuals showing constant differences from allied groups, placed under a genus (*biol*.): a kind, sort: — *pl*. **spē'cies**. — *n*. **speciā'tion** formation of new biological species incl. formation of polyploids. — *v.t.* **spē'ciate**. — *ns*. **specie** (*spē'shē, -shi-ē*; orig. the L. abl. as in the phrase *in speciē*, in kind) formerly, payment or requital in the same kind: commodities, kind (*obs*.): now, coined money; **speciesism** (*spē'shēz-izm*) the assumption that man is superior to all other species of animals and that he is therefore justified in exploiting them to his own advantage; **speciocide** (*spē'shē-ə-sīd*) the destruction of a whole animal species. — **spe'cies-monger** a hairsplitter in classification. [L. *speciēs*, pl. *-ēs*, appearance, kind, species — *specere*, to look at.]

specify *spes'i-fī, v.t.* to mention particularly: to make specific: to set down as requisite: — *pr.p.* **spec'ifying**; *pa.t.* and *pa.p.* **spec'ified**. — *adjs*. **spec'ifiable** (or *fī'*); **specific** (*spi-sif'ik*) constituting or determining a species: pertaining to a species: peculiar to a species: of special application or origin: specifying: precise: of a parasite, restricted to one particular host: of a stain, colouring certain structures or tissues only: of a physical constant, being the ratio per unit volume, area, (or especially) mass, etc. — *n*. a remedy or medicine for a particular disease or part of the body: anything that is specific. — *adj*. **specif'ical**. — *adv*. **specif'ically**. — *v.t.* **specif'icate** to specify. — *ns*. **specificā'tion** (*spes-*) making, becoming, or being specific: the act of specifying: any point or particular specified: a detailed description of requirements, etc.: the description of his invention presented by an applicant for a patent; **specificity** (*spes-i-fis'i-ti*). — *adj*. **spec'ified**. — **specific gravity** relative density; **specific heat (capacity)** the number of heat-units necessary to raise the unit of mass of a given substance one degree in temperature; **specific impulse** a measure of the efficiency of a rocket engine, the ratio of the thrust obtained to the fuel consumed, usu. per second; **specific name** in biological nomenclature, the name of the species, i.e. the second name, the first being the generic name. [O.Fr. *specifier* — L.L. *specificāre* — L. *speciēs*, kind, *facere*, to make.]

specimen *spes'i-min, n*. an object or portion serving as a sample, esp. for purposes of study or collection: a remarkable type: derogatorily, a person (*coll*.). [L. *specimen* — *specere*, to look at.]

specious *spē'shəs, adj*. beautiful (*obs*.): showy: looking well at first sight: fair-showing: plausibly deceptive. — *ns*. **speciosity** (*-shi-os'i-ti*), **spe'ciousness**. — *adv*. **spe'ciously**. [L. *speciōsus*, showy — *speciēs*, form — *specere*, to look at.]

speck[1] *spek, n*. a small spot: a particle: a small American fish, a darter. — *v.t.* to spot. — *adjs*. **speck'less; speck'y**. [O.E. *specca*.]

speck[2] *spek, n*. fat: bacon: blubber. — *n*. **specktioneer** (*spek-shən-ēr'*) the chief harpooner in whale-fishing. [Ger. *Speck*, Du. *spek*, fat; cf. O.E. *spic*, fat bacon.]

speckle *spek'l, n*. a little spot, esp. of colour: a grainy pattern on or forming a photographic image, caused by atmospheric interference (*astron*. and *phys*.). — *v.t.* to mark with speckles. — *adj*. **speck'led**. — *n*. **speck'ledness**. — **speckle interferogram** a visual record produced by speckle interferometry; **speckle interferometry** (*astron*. and *phys*.) a method of obtaining infor-

mation, esp. a visual image, of a distant stellar object by processing and analysis of a number of short-exposure speckle photographs. [speck¹.]
specktioneer. See **speck².**
specs, also **specks,** *speks, n.pl.* a colloquial shortening of **spectacles.**
spectacle *spek'tə-kl, n.* a sight: a show, pageant, exhibition: (in *pl.*) a pair of lenses mounted in frames with side-pieces to grip the temples: (in *pl.*) a marking resembling spectacles, as in the cobra and various animals. — *adjs.* **spec'tacled** wearing spectacles: having rings around the eyes (*fig.*); **spectacular** (*-tak'ū-lər*) of the nature of, or marked by, display: sensational, very impressive. — *n.* a theatrical show, esp. on television, or any display, that is large-scale and elaborate. — *n.* **spectacularity** (*-lar'i-ti*). — *adv.* **spectac'ularly.** — **pair of spectacles** (*cricket*) a duck in both innings. [L. *spectāculum* — *spectāre, -ātum,* intens. of *specēre,* to look at.]
spectator *spek-tā'tər, n.* one who looks on: — *fem.* **spectā'tress, spectā'trix.** — *v.i.* **spectate'** (*back-formation*) to look on. — *adj.* **spectatorial** (*-tə-tō'ri-əl, -tō').* — *n.* **spectā'torship** the action, office, or quality of a spectator. — **spectator sport** a sport that has great appeal for spectators. [L. *spectātor* — *spectāre,* to look.]
spectra, spectral, etc. See **spectrum.**
spectre, in U.S. **specter,** *spek'tər, n.* an apparition: a phantom: a ghost: any insect of the Phasmidae (stick-insects, leaf-insects). — *adj.* **spec'tral** relating to, or like, a spectre. — *n.* **spectral'ity** the state of being spectral: a spectral object. — *adv.* **spec'trally.** — *adj.* **spectrolog'ical.** — *adv.* **spectrolog'ically.** — *n.* **spectrol'ogy** the study of ghosts. — **spec'tre-bat** a leaf-nosed bat; **spec'tre-crab'** a glass-crab; **spec'tre-in'sect** a phasmid; **spec'tre-le'mur** the tarsier; **spec'tre-shrimp'** a skeleton-shrimp. [Fr. *spectre* — L. *spectrum* — *specēre,* to look at.]
spectro- *spek'trō, -tro',* in composition, **spectre, spectrum** (qq.v.).
spectrum *spek'trəm, n.* an after-image: the range of colour produced by a prism or diffraction-grating: any analogous range of radiations in order of wavelength: range of frequencies of sound or a sound: range of opinions, activities, etc. (*fig.*): — *pl.* **spec'tra.** — *adj.* **spec'tral** relating to, or like, a spectrum. — *ns.* **spectral'ity; spec'trochemistry** chemical spectroscopy; **spec'trogram** a photograph of a spectrum: a sound spectrogram (q.v.); **spec'trograph** a spectroscope designed for use over a wide range of frequencies (well beyond visible spectrum) and recording the spectrum photographically (see also **mass spectrograph** at **mass¹**). — *adjs.* **spectrograph'ic, -al.** — *ns.* **spectrog'raphy; spectrohē'liogram** a photograph of the sun by monochromatic light; **spectrohē'liograph** an instrument for taking it; **spectrohē'lioscope** a similar instrument with which one can observe an image of the whole solar disc in the light of a single particular wavelength. — *adj.* **spectrolog'ical.** — *adv.* **spectrolog'ically.** — *ns.* **spectrol'ogy** the science of the spectrum or spectrum analysis; **spectrom'eter** an instrument for measuring refractive indices: one used for measurement of wavelength or energy distribution in a heterogeneous beam of radiation (see also **mass spectrometer** at **mass¹**). — *adj.* **spectromet'ric.** — *ns.* **spectrom'etry; spectrophotom'eter** an instrument for measuring intensity of each colour or wavelength present in an optical spectrum; **spectrophotom'etry; spec'troscope** a general term for an instrument (*spectrograph, spectrometer,* etc.) used in spectroscopy, the basic features of which are a slit and collimator for producing a parallel beam of radiation, a prism or grating for 'dispersing' different wavelengths through differing angles of deviation, and a telescope, camera or counter tube for observing the dispersed radiation. — *adjs.* **spectroscop'ic, -al.** — *adv.* **spectroscop'ically.** — *ns.* **spectroscopist** (*spek-tros'kə-pist,* or *spek'trə-skop-ist*); **spectros'copy** (or *spek'*) the

study of spectra. — **spectrum analysis** determination of chemical composition by observing the spectrum of light or X-rays coming from or through the substance. [L. *spectrum,* an appearance — *specēre,* to look at.]
specular *spek'ū-lər, adj.* mirror-like: having a speculum: by reflection: visual: giving a wide view. — **specular iron** a brilliant steely crystallised haematite; **specular stone** a transparent or semitransparent mineral, as mica, selenite, talc. [L. *speculāris* — *speculum,* a mirror, and *specula,* a watch-tower.]
speculate *spek'ū-lāt, v.t.* to look at or into, view, examine (*lit.* or *fig.*; *arch.*): to observe (*arch.*): to view in a mirror (*obs.*): to make conjectures about (*obs.*). — *v.i.* to reflect: to theorise: to make conjectures or guesses: to take risk in hope of gain, esp. in buying and selling. — *ns.* **specula'tion** act of speculating or its result: vision (*obs.*): viewing (*obs.*): reflection: theorising: conjecture: mere guesswork: a more or less risky investment of money for the sake of unusually large profits: a card game in which trumps are bought and sold: an observer (*Shak.*); **spec'ulātist** a speculative philosopher: a speculator. — *adj.* **spec'ulātive** (or *-ət-*) of the nature of, based on, given to, speculation or theory. — *adv.* **spec'ulātively.** — *ns.* **spec'ulātiveness; spec'ulātor** one who speculates in any sense: a watchman, lookout (*arch.*). — *adj.* **spec'ulatory** exercising speculation: adapted for spying or viewing (*arch.*). — *n.* **spec'ulātrix** a female speculator. [L. *speculātus,* pa.p. of *speculārī* — *specula,* a lookout — *specēre,* to look at.]
speculum *spek'ū-ləm, n.* a mirror: a reflector, usu. of polished metal: an instrument with which to view cavities of the body (*med.*): a bright patch on a wing, esp. a duck's: — *pl.* **spec'ula.** — **speculum metal** an alloy of copper and tin, with or without other ingredients, which can be highly polished and used for mirrors, lamp reflectors, etc. [L. *speculum,* a mirror — *specēre,* to look at.]
sped *sped,* pa.t. and pa.p. of **speed.**
speech *spēch, n.* that which is spoken: language: the power of speaking: manner of speaking: a continuous spoken utterance: a discourse, oration: talk: colloquy: mention: a rumour (*obs.*): a saying (*obs.*): parole (q.v.) (*linguistics*): the sounding of a musical instrument. — *v.t.* and *v.i.* (*rare* or *dial.*) to harangue. — *adj.* **speech'ful** loquacious: expressive. — *ns.* **speech'fulness; speechificā'tion** (*coll.*); **speech'ifier.** — *v.i.* **speech'ify** to make speeches, harangue (implying contempt). — *adj.* **speech'less** destitute or deprived of the power of speech. — *adv.* **speech'lessly.** — *n.* **speech'lessness.** — **speech community** a community using based on a common language or dialect; **speech'craft** philology: rhetoric; **speech'-crī'er** (*hist.*) a hawker of broadsides giving hanged criminals' dying speeches; **speech day** the public day at the close of a school year, or on which prizes won during the previous year are presented; **speech'-maker** one accustomed to speak in public; **speech'-making; speech'-reading** lip-reading; **speech'-song** sprechgesang; **speech therapy** treatment of speech and language defects; **speech'-train'ing** training in clear speech. [Late O.E. *spēc, spæc,* O.E. *sprēc, spræc;* Ger. *Sprache.*]
speed *spēd, n.* success, good fortune (*arch.*): a help to success (*arch.*): quickness, swiftness, dispatch: the rate at which a distance is covered: the time taken for a photographic film to accept an image: amphetamine (*slang*). — *v.i.* to succeed, fare (*arch.*): to move quickly: to hurry: to drive at high, or at dangerously, unduly, or illegally high, speed. — *v.t.* to give or bring success to (*arch.*): to further: to send forth with good wishes: to bring to an end or finished state (*arch.*): to bring to a sorry plight, to do for (in *passive; arch.*): to send swiftly: to push forward: to haste: to betake with speed: to urge to high speed: to set or regulate the speed of: — pa.t. and pa.p. **sped** (also **speed'ed**). — *n.* **speed'er** one who, or that which, speeds or promotes speed. — *adj.* **speed'ful.** — *advs.* **speed'fully; speed'ily.** — *ns.* **speed'iness** quickness; **speed'ing** success: promotion, furtherance: progressive increase of speed (often with

up): motoring at excessive speed. — Also *adj.* — *adj.* **speed'less.** — *ns.* **speedom'eter** a device indicating the speed at which a vehicle is travelling (coll. shortening **speed'o,** *pl.* **speed'os**); **speed'ster** a speedboat: a fast (sports) car: one who speeds. — *adj.* **speed'y** swift: prompt: soon achieved. — **speed'ball** a team sport with eleven players a side, combining many elements of soccer, basketball and rugby: a mixture of cocaine and other opiates, esp. heroin or morphine (*slang*); **speed'-balling** injecting or sniffing speedball; **speed'-boat** a very swift motor-boat; **speed'-boating; speed'-cop** (*slang*) a policeman who watches out for motorists who are exceeding a speed-limit; **speed'-limit** the maximum speed at which motor vehicles may be driven legally on certain roads; **speed merchant** one who drives a motor vehicle exceedingly fast (*slang*); **speed reading** a technique of very rapid reading, by which words are taken in in phrases or other groups instead of singly; **speed'skating** a sport in which two ice- or roller-skaters race on a track for a number of separate distances, the winner being the skater who accumulates the least overall time points; **speed trap** a section of road over which the police (often using radar) check the speed of passing vehicles and identify drivers exceeding the limit (see also **radar trap**); **speed'-up** an acceleration, esp. in work; **speed'way** a road for fast traffic: a motor-cycle racing track: the sport of motor-cycle racing; **speed'well** any species of the scrophulariaceous genus Veronica, typically blue-flowered, posterior petals united, posterior sepal wanting; **Speedwriting®** a type of shorthand, in which letters of the alphabet stand for words or sounds, as *u* for you; **speedy cut, cutting** injury to a horse's foreleg by the opposite shoe. — **speed up** to quicken the rate of working. [O.E. *spēd*; Du. *spoed*.]

speel[1] *spēl,* (*Scot.*) *v.t.* and *v.i.* to climb. — *n.* a climb. — **speel'er** an acrobat (*obs.*): a climber: a climbing-iron. [Poss. L.G. *speler,* a performer.]

speel[2] *spēl,* (*N. dial.*) *n.* a splinter, of wood, etc. [Scand., cf. Norw. *spela, spila,* Sw. *spjela, spjele.*]

speir, speer *spēr,* (*Scot.*) *v.t.* and *v.i.* to ask, inquire. — *n.* **speir'ings, speer'ings** news. [O.E. *spyrian,* to inquire after, *spor,* a trace.]

speisade. See lance speisade under **lance prisado.**

speiss *spīs, n.* a mass of arsenides and commonly antimonides, a first product in smelting certain ores. — **speiss-cob'alt** smaltite. [Ger. *Speise.*]

spekboom *spek'bōm, n.* a S. African succulent shrub of the purslane family. [Du., bacon tree.]

spelaean, spelean *spi-lē'ən, adj.* cave-dwelling. — *adj.* **spel(a)eological** (*spē-li-ə-loj'i-kl, spel-*). — *ns.* **spel(a)eol'ogist; spel(a)eol'ogy** the scientific study of caves: exploration of caves. [Gr. *spēlaion,* cave.]

speld *speld,* **spelder** *spel'dər,* (*Scot*) *vs.t.* to spread open or sprawlingly: to slit and lay open. — *ns.* **spel'din(g), speld'rin(g)** a haddock (or other fish) split open and dried. [Cf. M.E. *spalden,* to split; Ger. *spalten.*]

spelean, etc. See **spelaean,** etc.

spelikin. See **spill**[2].

spelk *spelk,* (*N. dial.*) *n.* a splinter, of wood, etc. [O.E. *spelc.*]

spell[1] *spel, n.* speech, discourse, talk, a sermon (*obs.*): a magic formula: a magic influence: enchantment: entrancement. — *v.t.* to utter (*obs.*): to say a spell over: to bind with a spell: to enchant. — *v.i.* (*obs.*) to discourse. — *adj.* **spell'ful** magical. — *v.t.* **spell'bind** (*back-formation*). — **spell'binder** an orator, usu. political or evangelical, who holds his audience spellbound: any person or thing that entrances. — *adjs.* **spell'bound** bound by a spell: entranced; **spell'-stopt** (*arch.*) brought to a standstill by a spell. [O.E. *spell,* narrative, *spellian,* to speak, announce; cf. Goth. *spill,* O.N. *spjall,* tale.]

spell[2] *spel, v.t.* to read laboriously, letter by letter: to make out, unriddle, come to understand: to scan: to name or set down in order the letters of: to constitute or represent orthographically: to import, amount to (*fig.*). — *v.i.* to spell words, esp. correctly: to contemplate (*poet.*): to express or hint a desire: — *pa.t.* and *pa.p.* **spelled, spelt.** — *n.* a mode of spelling. — *adj.* **spell'able.** — *ns.* **spell'er; spell'ing.** — *adv.* **spell'ingly** letter by letter. — **spell'down** (*U.S.*) a spelling competition; **spell'ing-bee** a spelling competition; **spell'ing-book** a book for teaching to spell; **spelling pronunciation** (*linguistics*) a pronunciation of a word that, as a side-effect of literacy, closely represents its spelling, superseding the traditional pronunciation, e.g. *forehead* as *för'hed* (orig. *for'id*). — **spell backward** to spell in reverse order: perversely to mispresent or misconstrue the qualities of; **spell baker** to do something difficult, prob. because *baker* was one of the first disyllables in old spelling-books; **spell (it) out** to be extremely specific in explaining something. [O.Fr. *espeller* (Fr. *épeler*), of Gmc. origin; cf. foregoing.]

spell[3] *spel, v.t.* to take the place of at work: to relieve, give a rest to: to take a turn at. — *v.i.* to take turns: to rest: — *pr.p.* **spell'ing;** *pa.t.* and *pa.p.* **spelled.** — *n.* a shift: a turn at work: a bout, turn: a short time: a stretch of time: a rest: a fit of irritation, illness, etc. [O.E. *spelian,* to act for another: cf. Du. *spelen,* Ger. *spielen,* to play.]

spell[4] *spel,* (*dial.*) *n.* a splinter: a rung: a trap for throwing up the knur in knur and spell. [Perh. **speld;** but cf. Ger. *spellen,* to split.]

spellikin, spellican. See **spill**[2].

spelt[1] *spelt, n.* an inferior species of wheat (*Triticum spelta*), grown in the mountainous parts of Europe. [O.E. *spelt.*]

spelt[2]. See **spell**[2].

spelter *spel'tər, n.* zinc, esp. impure zinc. [Cf. L.G. *spialter.*]

spence *spens, n.* a larder (*dial.*): a pantry (*dial.*): an inner room, parlour (*Scot.*). [O.Fr. *despense,* a buttery — *despendre* — L. *dispendĕre.*]

spencer[1] *spens'ər, n.* a kind of wig: a short double-breasted overcoat: a woman's short undergarment, formerly over-jacket. [After various persons of the name.]

spencer[2] *spens'ər, n.* in ships and barques, a fore-and-aft sail abaft the fore and main masts. [Perh. the name Spencer, as foregoing.]

Spencerian *spen-sē'ri-ən, adj.* pertaining to the synthetic philosophy or evolutionary cosmology of Herbert Spencer (1820–1903). — *n.* a follower of Spencer. — *n.* **Spence'rianism.**

spend *spend, v.t.* to expend: to pay out: to give, bestow, employ, for any purpose: to shed: to consume: to use up: to exhaust: to waste: to pass, as time. — *v.i.* to make expense: — *pa.t.* and *pa.p.* **spent.** — *n.* an act of, or the sum of money available (usu. on a regular basis) for, spending. — *adj.* **spen'dable.** — *ns.* **spen'der; spen'ding.** — *adj.* **spent** used up: exhausted: of fish, exhausted by spawning. — **spend'all** a spendthrift; **spending money** pocket money; **spend'thrift** one who spends the savings of thrift: a prodigal. — *adj.* excessively lavish; **spent force** a person or thing whose former strength, usefulness, etc., is exhausted. — **spend a penny** see **penny.** [O.E. *spendan* — L. *expendĕre* or *dispendĕre,* to weigh out.]

Spenglerian *speng-glēr'i-ən, adj.* of or pertaining to the German historian Oswald *Spengler* (1880-1936) and his work, esp. the theory that all world civilisations are subject to the same inevitable cycle of growth and decline. — *n.* a follower of Spengler.

Spenserian *spen-sē'ri-ən, adj.* pertaining to Edmund *Spenser* (1552–99) or esp. his stanza in *The Faerie Queene,* of eight decasyllabic lines and an Alexandrine, rhymed *ababbcbcc.*

spent *spent.* See **spend.**

speos *spē'os, n.* grotto-temple or tomb: — *pl.* **spe'oses.** [Gr., cave.]

Spergula *spûr'gū-lə, n.* the spurrey genus, akin to chickweed. — *n.* **Spergulā'ria** the allied sandwort-spurrey genus. [L.L.]

sperling *spûr'ling.* Same as **sparling.**

sperm *spûrm, n.* seed or semen: generative substance: a male gamete or germ-cell: eggs, spawn, brood, offspring (*obs.*): the chalaza of a hen's egg (formerly believed to be contributed by the cock) (*obs.*): a sperm-whale: sperm-oil: a sperm-candle: spermaceti. — **-sperm** in composition, seed. — adjective combining forms **-spermal, -spermous.** — For some compounds beginning **sperma-, spermo-** see **spermato-** (*spûr'mə-tō-*) below. — *ns.* **sper'maduct, sper'miduct** a duct conveying spermatozoa; **spermā'rium** (*pl.* **spermā'ria**), **sper'-mary** the male germ-gland; **sperma(to)thē'ca** (Gr. *thēkē*, receptacle) in female insects, etc., a receptacle in which sperms received are stored. — *adjs.* **spermathē'cal; spermat'ic, -al** of, pertaining to, conveying sperm: generative. — *ns.* **spermat'ic** a spermatic vessel; **sper'matid** a cell that develops directly into a spermatozoon; **sper'matist** a believer in the doctrine that the sperm contains all future generations in germ; **spermatium** (*-mā'shəm*) a non-motile male gamete in red seaweeds: a spore-like structure, possibly sexual, in some fungi: — *pl.* **spermā'tia; sper'matoblast** (Gr. *blastos*, a shoot) a spermatid. — *adj.* **spermatoblas'tic.** — *ns.* **sper'matocele** (Gr. *kēlē*, tumour) tumour of the testicle; **sper'matocyte** (Gr. *kytos*, vessel) a sperm mother-cell or its predecessor; **spermatogenesis** (*-jen'*), **spermatogeny** (*-ə-toj'i-ni*) sperm-formation. — *adjs.* **spermatogenet'ic, spermatogen'ic, spermatog'enous.** — *ns.* **spermatogonium** (*-gō'ni-əm*) one of the cells that by repeated division form the spermatocytes; **sper'-matophore** a case enclosing the spermatozoa. — *n.pl.* **Spermatoph'yta** (also **Spermaph'yta, Spermoph'yta;** Gr. *phyton*, plant) the flowering plants as one of the four phyla of the vegetable kingdom. — *n.* **spermat'o-phyte** (**sperm'aphyte,** etc.). — *adj.* **spermatophytic** (*-fit'-ik*; also **sperma-, spermo-**). — *n.* **spermatorrhoe'a** (Gr. *rhoiā*, flow) involuntary seminal discharge. — *adjs.* **spermatozō'al, spermatozō'an, spermatozō'ic.** — *ns.* **spermatozō'id, spermatozō'on** (Gr. *zōion*, animal; *pl.* **-zō'a**) a male germ-cell. — *adj.* **sper'mic** spermatic. — *n.* **sper'micide** any substance which kills spermatozoa. — *adj.* **spermicī'dal.** — For some compounds in **spermo-** see **spermato-** above. — *ns.* **sper'mogone, spermogō'nium** (*pl.* **-ia**) a flask-shaped structure in which spermatia are produced. — *adj.* **sper'mous** spermatic. — **sperm bank** a store of semen for use in artificial insemination; **sperm'-candle** a candle of spermaceti; **sperm'-cell** a male gamete; **sperm'-oil** oil from the sperm-whale; **sperm'-whale** the cachalot, a whale from which spermaceti is obtained. [Gr. *sperma, -atos,* seed, semen — *speirein,* to sow.]

spermaceti *spûr-mə-set'i, n.* a waxy matter obtained mixed with oil from the head of the sperm-whale and others. — Also *adj.* [L. *sperma cētī* (gen. of *cētus,* a whale — Gr. *kētos*), whale's sperm, from a wrong notion of its origin.]

spermarium, spermatic, etc. See **sperm.**

spermophile *spûr'mō-fīl, -fĭl, n.* a ground-squirrel (Spermophilus), a rodent akin to the true squirrels. [Gr. *sperma,* seed, *phileein,* to love.]

sperre *spûr,* (*Spens.*) *v.t.* to bolt, bar. — In Shak., *Troilus and Cressida,* Prol. 19, **stirre** is probably a misprint for **sperre.** [**spar**[1].]

sperrylite *sper'i-līt, n.* an arsenide of platinum, found at Sudbury, Ontario. [After F. L. *Sperry,* with Gr. *lithos,* stone.]

sperse *spûrs,* (*arch.*) *v.t.* and *v.i.* aphetic form of **disperse:** — *pa.t.* and *pa.p.* (*Spens.*) **sperst;** also **spersed.**

sperthe. Same as **sparth.**

spessartite *spes'ärt-īt, n.* a manganese-alumina garnet found at *Spessart* in Bavaria.

spet *spet,* (*Milt.*) *v.t.* and *v.i.* a form of **spit**[2].

spetch *spech, n.* a piece of skin used in making glue. [N. dial. *speck,* a patch of leather or cloth.]

Spetsnaz, Spetznaz *spets'naz, n.* a select force, controlled by Soviet military intelligence, highly-trained for undercover activities, raids, etc. — Also without *cap.* —

adj. (usu. without *cap.*) of or pertaining to the Spetsnaz. [Russ.]

spew, (*old*) **spue,** *spū, v.t.* to vomit. — *v.i.* to vomit: to ooze, run. — *n.* vomited matter: a marshy spot (*dial.*). — *ns.* **spew'er; spew'iness.** — *adj.* **spew'y** (*dial.*) boggy. [O.E. *spīwan, spīowan,* to spit; Du. *spuwen,* Ger. *speien;* also L. *spuěre,* Gr. *ptyein.*]

sphacelus *sfas'ə-ləs, n.* necrosis. — *adjs.* **sphac'elate, -d** necrosed: dark and shrunken (*bot.*). — *n.* **sphacelā'tion.** [Gr. *sphakelos.*]

sphaer(e). Obs. form of **sphere.**

sphaeridium *sfē-rid'i-əm, n.* a minute spheroidal body on the surface of a sea-urchin, perh. a sense-organ: — *pl.* **sphaerid'ia.** — *ns.* **sphae'rite** a hydrous aluminium phosphate; **sphaerocō'baltite** cobalt carbonate, occurring in rounded masses; **sphaerocrys'tal** a rounded crystalline mass; **sphaerosid'erite** concretionary clay-ironstone. [Gr. *sphairā,* a ball.]

Sphagnum *sfag'nəm, n.* a genus of mosses — peat or bog-moss, constituting the family **Sphagnaceae** (*sfag-nā'si-ē*), peat-formers, formerly useful as wound-dressings. — *adj.* **sphagnic'olous** (L. *colěre,* to inhabit) living in peat-moss. — *ns.* **sphagnol'ogist; sphagnol'ogy** the study of the peat-mosses. — *adj.* **sphag'nous.** [Gr. *sphagnos,* a name for various plants.]

sphalerite *sfal'ər-īt, n.* zinc-blende. [Gr. *sphaleros,* deceptive, from its resemblance to galena.]

sphear(e). See **sphere.**

sphendone *sfen'do-nē, n.* an ancient Greek women's headband: an elliptical or semi-elliptical auditorium. [Gr. *sphendonē,* a sling.]

sphene *sfēn, n.* titanite. — *adj.* **sphe'nic** wedge-like. — *n.pl.* **Sphenisciformes** (*sfē-nis-i-för'mēz*) the penguin order of birds. — *ns.* **Sphenis'cus** (*-kəs*) the jackass-penguin genus; **Sphē'nodon** (Gr. *odous, odontos,* a tooth) genus, also known as Hatteria, to which the tuatara (q.v.) belongs: (without *cap.*) an animal of this genus; **sphē'nogram** a cuneiform character. — *adj.* **sphē'noid** wedge-shaped, applied to a set of bones at the base of the skull. — *n.* a sphenoid bone: a wedge-shaped crystal form of four triangular faces. — *adj.* **sphenoid'al.** [Gr. *sphēn, sphēnos,* a wedge.]

sphere (*Shak., Milt.,* **sphear, speare**) *sfēr, n.* a solid figure bounded by a surface of which all points are equidistant from a centre: its bounding surface: the apparent sphere of the heavens, upon which the stars are seen in projection: any one of the concentric spherical shells which were once supposed to carry the planets in their revolutions: a circle of society, orig. of the higher ranks (as if a planetary sphere): domain, scope, range: a field of activity: condition of life: a world, mode of being: a ball: a spherical object, esp. a planet: an orbit (*Spens.*). — *v.t.* to round: to place in a sphere: to encompass: to send about. — *adjs.* **sphēr'al; sphered; sphere'less; spheric** (*sfer'ik*), **-al** of a sphere or spheres: having the form of a sphere. — *n.* **spherical'ity.** — *adv.* **spher'ically.** — *ns.* **spher'icalness, sphericity** (*-is'i-ti*) state or quality of being spherical. — *n. sing.* **spher'ics** the geometry and trigonometry of the sphere. — *ns.* **spheristē'rion** (Gr. *sphairistērion*) a room or court for ball-games; **sphē'roid** a body or figure nearly spherical, but not quite so — a species of ellipsoid (*prolate spheroid,* a slightly lengthened sphere; *oblate spheroid,* a slightly flattened sphere). — *adj.* **sphēroi'dal.** — *ns.* **sphēroidi'city; sphēroidisā'tion, -z-.** — *v.t.* **sphēr'oidise, -ize** to develop spherulitic or granular structure in. — *n.* **sphērom'eter** an instrument for measuring curvature of surfaces. — *adj.* **spherular** (*sfer'*). — *ns.* **spher'ule** a little sphere; **spher'ulite** a radiating spherical group of minute crystalline fibres in rocks. — *adjs.* **spherulitic** (*-lit'ik*); **sphē'ry** spherical, round: belonging to the celestial spheres. — *adjs.* **sphere'-born; sphere'-like.** — **spherical aberration** loss of image definition which occurs when light strikes a lens or mirror with a spherical surface; **spherical triangle** a three-sided figure on the surface of a sphere, bounded by arcs of great circles; **spherical trigonometry** the branch of trigonometry concerned with measurement of these. — **music, harmony, of the spheres** the music, inaudible to mortal ears, produced according to Pythagoras by the motions of the celestial spheres in accordance with the laws of harmony. [Gr. *sphairā*.]

spherics[1], *U.S.* **sferics** *sfe'riks, sfē', n.pl.* shortened form of **atmospherics**.

spherics[2]. . . **spheroid** . . . **spherular**, etc. See **sphere**.

sphincter *sfingk'tər, (anat.) n.* a ring-like muscle whose contraction narrows or shuts an orifice. — — *adjs.* **sphinc'teral, sphincterial** (*-tē'ri-əl*), **sphincteric** (*-ter'ik*). [Gr. *sphinktēr* — *sphingein*, to bind tight.]

Sphinx, sphinx *sfingks, n.* a monster of Greek mythology, with the head of a woman and the body of a lioness, that proposed riddles to travellers, and strangled those who could not solve them: any similar monster or representation of one: an enigmatic or inscrutable person: a hawk-moth: the Guinea baboon: — *pl.* **sphinx'es, sphinges** (*sfin'jēz*). — *n.* and *adj.* **sphingid** (*sfin'jid*). — *n.pl.* **Sphin'gidae** the hawk-moth family. — **sphinx'-moth** (*U.S.*) the hawk-moth. [Gr., — *sphingein*, to draw tight.]

sphragistic *sfrə-jist'ik, adj.* pertaining to seals and signets. — *n. sing.* **sphragist'ics** the study of seals. [Gr. *sphrāgistikos* — *sphrāgis*, a seal.]

sphygmus *sfig'məs, n.* the pulse. — *adj.* **sphyg'mic.** — *ns.* **sphyg'mogram** a sphygmograph record; **sphyg'mograph** an instrument for recording pulse-beat. — *adj.* **sphygmograph'ic.** — *n.* **sphygmog'raphy.** — *adj.* **sphyg'moid** pulse-like. — *ns.* **sphygmol'ogy** the science of the pulse; **sphygmomanom'eter, sphygmom'eter** an instrument for measuring arterial blood-pressure; **sphyg'mophone** an instrument by means of which a pulse-beat makes a sound; **sphyg'moscope** an instrument for making arterial pulsations visible. [Latinised from Gr. *sphygmos*, pulse.]

spial *spī'əl (obs.) n.* espial: a spy, a scout.

spic *spik, (esp. U.S. derog.) n.* a person from a Spanish-speaking American country, or of Mexican, S. American, etc., origin: a member of one of the Mediterranean races. — Also **spi(c)k.** [Origin uncertain.]

Spica *spī'kə, n.* a first-magnitude star in Virgo: (without *cap.*) a spiral bandage with reversed turns suggesting an ear of barley: (without *cap.*) in birds, a spur. — *adjs.* **spī'cate, -d** in, having, or forming a spike: spike-like. — *ns.* **spicilege** (*spi'si-lij*; L. *spīcilegium* — *legĕre*, to gather) a gleaning: an anthology; **spicula** (*spik'ū-lə*) a spicule, prickle, or splinter. — *adjs.* **spic'ular** of the nature of or like a spicule; **spic'ūlate** having spicules. — *ns.* **spic'ūle** a minute needle-like body, crystal, splinter, or process: one of the spike-like forms seen forming and re-forming on the edge of the sun, caused by ejections of hot gas several thousand miles above its surface; **spic'ūlum** a little spine: a spicula: a snail's dart: — *pl.* **spic'ūla.** [L. *spīca*, an ear of corn.]

spiccato *spik-kä'tō, adj.* and *adv.* half staccato. — *n.* spiccato playing or passage: — *pl.* **spicca'tos.** [It.]

spice *spīs, n.* an aromatic and pungent vegetable substance used as a condiment and for seasoning food — pepper, cayenne pepper, pimento, nutmeg, mace, vanilla, ginger, cinnamon, cassia, etc.: such substances collectively or generally: a characteristic smack, flavour: anything that adds piquancy or interest: an aromatic odour: sweetmeats (*dial.*): a touch, tincture (*fig.*). — *v.t.* to season with spice: to tincture, vary, or diversify. — *adj.* **spiced** impregnated with a spicy odour: seasoned with spice: over-scrupulous (*obs.*). — *ns.* **spic'er** (*obs.*) a dealer in spices or drugs; **spic'ery** spices in general: a repository of spices: spiciness. — *adv.* **spic'ily.** — *n.* **spic'iness.** — *adj.* **spic'y** producing or abounding with spices: fragrant: pungent: piquant, pointed: racy: risqué: showy. — **spice'-box** a box, often ornamental, for keeping spices; **spice'-bush** an aromatic American shrub (*Lindera*) of the laurel family; **spice'-cake** a spiced cake. [O.Fr. *espice* (Fr. *épice*) — L.L. *speciēs*, kinds of goods, spices — L. *speciēs*, a kind.]

spicilege. See under **Spica**.

spick[1] *spik, n.* a nail, a spike. — *adj.* tidy, fresh. — **spick and span** trim and speckless, like a spike new cut and a chip new split; **spick and span new** brand-new. [**spike**[2].]

spick[2]. See **spic.**

spicknel. See **spignel.**

spicule, etc. See under **Spica.**

spicy. See **spice.**

spide. Obs. spelling of **spied** (see **spy**).

spider *spī'dər, n.* an arachnid of the order Araneida, the body divided into two distinct parts — an unsegmented cephalothorax with four pairs of legs, and a soft unsegmented abdomen with spinnerets: formerly, a light high-wheeled vehicle: a frying-pan, properly one with feet: any of various spider-like radiating structures, instruments, tools, etc.: a rest for a cue in billiards: an arrangement of elastic straps with hooks attached, used to fasten luggage, etc., on to the roof-rack of a car or on to a motor-bicycle, etc. — *adjs.* **spi'der-like; spi'dery** spider-like: abounding in spiders. — **spi'der-crab** a crab with long thin legs; **spider flower** an annual plant of the genus *Cleome*, bearing clusters of white or pink flowers with long stamens reminiscent of spider's legs; **spi'der-hole** (*mil.*) a hole in the ground to conceal a sniper; **spi'der-leg** a long thin leg. — *adj.* **spi'der-legged.** — **spi'der-line** a thread of silk spun by a spider: any fine thread in an optical instrument, for measurement, position-marking, etc.; **spi'der-man** an erector of steel building structures; **spi'der-monkey** an American monkey (*Ateles*) with long slender legs and tail; **spider plant** any of various plants of the genus *Chlorophytum*, with spiky, variegated leaves, especially one which grows new plantlets on trailing stems: spider-wort; **spi'der-stitch** a stitch in lace or netting in which threads are carried diagonally and parallel to each other; **spi'der-web** the snare spun by a spider; **spi'der-wheel** in embroidery, a circular pattern with radiating lines; **spi'der-work** lace worked by spider-stitch; **spi'der-wort** any plant of the American commelinaceous genus *Tradescantia*, esp. *T. virginica*, with deep-blue or reddish-violet flowers. [O.E. *spīthra* — *spinnan*, to spin; cf. Dan. *spinder*, Ger. *Spinne*.]

spie (*Spens., Milt.*, etc. spelling of **spy**), **spied.** See **spy**.

spiegeleisen *spē'gl-ī-zn, n.* a white cast-iron containing manganese, largely used in the manufacture of steel by the Bessemer process. [Ger., — *Spiegel* — L. *speculum*, a mirror, Ger. *Eisen*, iron.]

spiel *spēl, shpēl, n.* a (esp. plausible) story or line of talk. — *v.i.* to talk glibly, tell the tale. — Also *v.t.* — *n.* **spiel'er** a person with a glib, persuasive line of talk: a swindler: a card sharper: a gambling den. [Ger. *spielen*, to play.]

spies. See **spy.**

spiff *spif, adj.* (*dial.*) smart, spruce. — Also **spiff'y.** — *adj.* **spiff'ing** (*coll.*) excellent. [Origin obscure.]

spiflicate, spifflicate *spif'li-kāt, (slang) v.t.* to do for: to quell: to confound: to handle roughly. — *n.* **spif(f)licā'tion.**

Spigelia *spī-jē'li-ə, n.* the pink-root genus of Loganiaceae. — *adj.* **Spigē'lian** of van der Spiegel or of Spigelia: applied to the *lobulus Spigelii*, one of the lobes of the liver. [From the Belgian Adrian van der *Spiegel* (1578–1625).]

spight *spīt, vb.* and *n.* (*Spens., Shak.*). Same as **spite.**

spignel *spig'nl, n.* baldmoney (*Meum*). — Also (*obs.*) **spick'nel.** [Origin obscure.]

spigot *spig'ət, n.* a vent-peg or peg controlling a faucet: a faucet (*U.S.*). [Prov. *espigot* — L. *spīculum*.]

spik. See **spic.**

spike[1] *spīk, n.* an ear of corn: an inflorescence in which sessile flowers or spikelets are arranged on a long axis (*bot.*): a kind of lavender (**spike'-lav'ender**). — *v.i.* to develop a spike. — *n.* **spike'let** in grasses, etc., a small crowded spike, itself forming part of a greater inflorescence. — **spike'-grass** *Uniola* or other American grass with conspicuous spikelets; **spike'-oil** the oil of spike-lavender; **spike′-rush** a sedge (*Heleocharis*) with a solitary spike. [L. *spīca*, an ear of corn.]

spike² *spīk, n.* a hard thin pointed object: a large nail: a sharp metal projection, e.g. one of those forming a row along the top of a railing, etc.: a sharp-pointed metal rod set upright on a base, on which to impale documents requiring attention, etc.: (in *pl.*) spiked shoes, worn to prevent slipping: a workhouse or its casual ward (*old slang*): an electric impulse, esp. a very brief, potentially damaging surge of power on an electronic circuit. — *v.t.* to fasten, set, pierce or damage with a spike or spikes: to make useless (as a gun), orig. by driving a spike into the vent: to frustrate, put a stop to: to make (a drink) stronger by adding spirits or other alcohol (*coll.*): to reject (a news article, etc.) (*journalism*): to inject with a drug. — *v.i.* to form a spike or peak: to inject oneself with a drug. — *adj.* **spiked.** — *adv.* **spīk′ily.** — *n.* **spīk′iness.** — *adj.* **spīk′y** having, furnished with, spikes: having a sharp point: irritable, acerbic: characterised by irritable, difficult or jarring disagreements or incidents. — **spike′-fish** a kind of sail-fish; **spike heel** a very narrow metal heel on a woman's shoe; **spike′-nail** a large small-headed nail. [O.E. *spīcing*, a spike-nail; poss. from L. *spīca*, an ear of corn.]

spikenard *spīk′närd, n.* an aromatic oil or balsam yielded by an Indian valerianaceous herb (*Nardostachys*) also called **nard**, or a substitute: the plant itself. — **ploughman's spikenard** a European and N. African spikenard with yellow flowers and aromatic roots (*Inula conyza*). [L. *spīca nardi.*]

spile *spīl, n.* a plug: a spigot: a pile for a foundation: a stake, or post for fencing. — *v.t.* to pierce and provide with a spile. — *n.* **spī′ling.** [Cf. L.G. *spile*, Du. *spijl*, Ger. *Speil.*]

spilikin. See **spill²**.

spilite *spī′līt, n.* a very fine-grained basic igneous rock. — *adj.* **spilitic** (*-it′ik*). — *n.* **spī′losite** a spotted slate, formed by contact metamorphism. [Gr. *spilos*, a spot.]

spill¹ *spil, v.t.* to kill (*obs.*): to destroy (*obs.*): to allow to run out of a vessel: to shed: to waste: to throw from a vehicle or the saddle (*coll.*): to empty from the belly of a sail or empty of wind for reefing: to overlay as if by spilling (*Spens.*). — *v.i.* to come to grief or ruin (*obs.*): to overflow: to be allowed to fall, be lost, or wasted: — *pa.t.* and *pa.p.* **spilled, spilt.** — *n.* a fall, a throw: a spilling. — *ns.* **spill′age** the act of spilling: that which is spilt; **spill′er**; **spill′ing**; **spilth** spilling: anything spilt or poured out lavishly: excess. — **spill′ing-line** a rope for spilling the wind out of a square sail; **spill′over** an overflow (also *fig.*); **spill′stream** an overflow channel: a bayou; **spill′way** a passage for overflow-water. — **spill over** to overflow (also *fig.*); **spill the beans** to cause embarrassment by letting out a secret. [O.E. *spillan*; Du. *spillen*, O.N. *spilla*, to destroy.]

spill² *spil, n.* a spile: a thin strip of wood or paper for lighting a candle, a pipe, etc. — *n.* **spill′ikin** a small slip of wood, ivory, etc., to be picked out from a heap without disturbing the others in the game of **spillikins.** — Also **spilikin, spel(l)ikin, spellican.** [Connection with **spile** or with **spell⁴** doubtful.]

spillage, etc. See **spill¹**.

spilosite. See **spilite**.

spilt *spilt, pa.t.* and *pa.p.* of **spill¹**. — Also *adj.*

spilth. See **spill¹**.

spin *spin, v.t.* to draw out and twist into threads: to draw out a thread as spiders do: to form by spinning: to draw out: to make to last (usu. with *out*): to send hurtling: to twirl, set revolving rapidly: to fish with a swivel or spoon-bait: to reject at an examination (*slang*). — *v.i.* to practise the art or trade or perform the act of spinning: to rotate rapidly: to whirl: to hurtle: to go swiftly, esp. on wheels: to spirt: to stream vigorously: to lengthen out, last (usu. with *out*): to fish with rotating bait: — *pr.p.* **spinn′ing**; *pa.t.* **spun**, arch.

span; *pa.p.* **spun.** — *n.* act or result of spinning: a rotatory motion: a cycle ride: a short trip in a motor-car: a spurt at high speed: a spiral descent (*lit.* and *fig.*): of a subatomic particle, quantised angular momentum in the absence of orbital motion: of a nucleus, quantised angular momentum including contributions from the orbital motion of nucleons: confused excitement. — *ns.* **spin′ar** (*astron.*) a rapidly spinning galactic body; **spinn′er** one who spins: a spider (*Shak.*): a spinneret: a spinning-machine: a ball with imparted spin, causing it to swerve or break (*cricket*): a spin-bowler: an artificial fly that revolves in the water (*fishing*): a rotating display stand (e.g. for books) in a shop, etc.; **spinn′eret** a spinning organ in spiders, etc.: a plate with holes from which filaments of plastic material are expressed (also **spinnerette**); **spinn′erule** (*-ə-rōōl, -rūl*) one of the tubules of a spinneret; **spinn′ery** a spinning-mill. — *n.* and *adj.* **spinn′ing.** — **spin′-bowl′ing** in cricket, a style of bowling in which the ball is give a twisting motion by the bowler's wrist or fingers, in order to make its speed and direction, as it rises after striking the ground, unpredictable; **spin′-bowl′er**; **spin′-dri′er, spin′-dry′er** a device that dries washed clothes without wringing, to a point ready for ironing, by forcing the water out of them under pressure of centrifugal force in a rapidly revolving drum. — *v.t.* **spin′-dry′.** — **spinn′ing-house** (*hist.*) a place of correction where lewd and incorrigible women were made to spin; **spinn′ing-jenn′y** a machine by which a number of threads can be spun at once: a crane-fly (*dial.*); **spinn′ing-mill** a factory where thread is spun; **spinning mule** an early form of spinning machine; **spinning top** see **top²**; **spinn′ing-wheel** a machine for spinning yarn, consisting of a wheel driven by the hand or by a treadle, which drives one or two spindles. **spin′-off** a process of transference of business on the U.S. stock-market: a by-product that proves profitable on its own account. — Also *adj.* — **spin′out** a spinning skid that throws a motor-vehicle off the road, track, etc.; **spin stabilisation** the stabilising of the flight of a projected bullet, space rocket, etc., by giving it a spinning motion. — **flat spin** a state of panic; **spin a yarn** to tell a story; **spin out** to prolong, protract. [O.E. *spinnan*; Ger. *spinnen*.]

spina. See **spine**.

spinach *spin′ij, -ich*, **spinage** *-ij, ns.* a plant (*Spinacia oleracea*) of the goosefoot family: its young leaves used as a vegetable: extended to various other plants. — *adj.* **spinaceous** (*spin-ā′shəs*). — **spin′ach-beet** a kind of beet used like spinach. [O.Fr. *espinage, espinache*; of doubtful origin, poss. — L. *spīna*, poss. Ar. *isfināj*.]

spinal, spinate. See **spine.**

spinar. See **spin.**

spindle *spin′dl, n.* the pin by which thread is twisted: a pin on which anything turns: the fusee of a watch: anything very slender: a spindle-shaped structure formed in mitosis (*biol.*). — *v.i.* to grow long and slender. — *n.* **spin′dling** a person or thing too long and slender: a slender shoot. — *adj.* long and slender. — *adj.* **spin′dly** disproportionally long and slender. — *adjs.* **spin′dle-legged, -shanked** having long slender legs, like spindles. — *ns.pl.* **spin′dle-legs, -shanks** long slim legs: hence (as a *sing.*) an overlong and slender person. — **spin′dle-oil** very light and fluid lubricating oil. — *adj.* **spin′dle-shaped** shaped like a spindle, thickest in the middle and tapering to both ends. — **spin′dle-shell** a gasteropod (*Fusus*) with spindle-shaped shell; **spin′dle-side** the female side or line of descent, distaff-side (opp. to *spear-side*); **spin′dle-tree** a shrub (*Euonymus europaeus*) of the *Celastraceae*, whose hard-grained wood was used for making spindles; **spin′dle-whorl** a heavy ring giving momentum to the spindle. [O.E. *spinel — spinnan*, to spin; Ger. *Spindel.*]

spindrift *spin′drift, n.* the spray blown from the crests of waves. [See **spoon¹**.]

spine *spīn, n.* a thorn, esp. one formed by a modified branch or leaf: a long sharp process of a leaf: a thin, pointed spike, esp. in fishes: the spinal column: any ridge extending lengthways: heartwood: the back of a book. — *n.* **spī′na** the spinal column: a quill of a spinet: a lengthwise barrier in the Roman circus (*ant.*). — *adjs.* **spī′nal** of the backbone; **spī′nate, spined** having a spine or spines; **spine′less** having no spine: weak: vacillating: lacking courage, esp. moral courage. — *adv.* **spine′-lessly.** — *ns.* **spine′lessness; spīnesc′ence.** — *adjs.* **spīn-esc′ent** tapering or developing into a spine: tending to become spinous: somewhat spiny; **spīnif′erous** thorn-bearing; **spī′niform** like a thorn; **spīnig′erous** bearing spines; **spī′nigrade** moving by means of spines, as an echinoderm. — *n.* **spī′niness.** — *adjs.* **spī′nose** (or -*nōs′*) full of spines: thorny; **spī′nous** spinose: like a thorn or spine in appearance (*anat.*, etc.). — *ns.* **spīnos′ity** thorniness; **spinūle** (*spin′* or *spīn′*) a minute spine. — *adjs.* **spin′ūlāte, spinūlesc′ent, spinūlif′erous, spin′ūlōse, spin′ūlous; spī′ny** full of spines: thorny: troublesome: perplexed. — **spīna bifida** (*bif′i-də, bī′*) condition in which (a) vertebra(e) fail to unite perfectly at the embryo stage, exposing the spinal cord; **spinal anaes-thesia** injection of an anaesthetic into the spinal canal, producing loss of sensation but not unconsciousness; **spinal canal** a passage running through the spinal column, containing the spinal cord; **spinal column** in vertebrates, the articulated series of vertebrae extend-ing from the skull to the tip of the tail, forming the axis of the skeleton and enclosing the spinal cord; **spinal c(h)ord** the main neural axis in vertebrates; **spine′-chiller** a frightening story, thought, happening. — *adj.* **spine′-chilling.** [L. *spīna*, a thorn.]

spinel *spi-nel′* (or *spin′əl*), *n.* a mineral, magnesium aluminate or other member of a group of aluminates, ferrates, and chromates, crystallising in octahedra. — **spinel ruby** ruby-spinel, a precious variety of typical spinel formerly confounded with ruby. [It. *spinella*.]

spinescence, etc. See **spine.**

spinet(te) *spin′it,* or *spi-net′, n.* an instrument like a small harpsichord. — Also **spinnet.** [It. *spinetta,* poss. from maker G. *Spinetti* (fl. 1500).]

spiniferous. See **spine.**

Spinifex *spin′, spīn′i-feks, n.* properly, a genus of grasses (Australian, etc.) whose spiny heads blow about and disseminate seed: (without *cap.*) a grass of this genus: (without *cap.*) popularly applied in Australia to por-cupine-grass. [L. *spīna,* spine, and the root of *facere,* to make.]

spiniform, spinigerous, etc. See **spine.**

spink¹ *spingk,* (now *dial.*) *n.* a finch, esp. the chaffinch. [Perh. imit.]

spink² *spingk, n.* the lady's-smock. [Ety. dub.]

spinnaker *spin′ə-kər, n.* triangular sail carried on the side opposite to the mainsail by vessels sailing before the wind: large sail carried by racing yachts. [Prob. **spin,** not *Sphinx* (yacht that carried a spinnaker).]

spinner, spinneret, etc. See **spin.**

spinnet. See **spinet(te).**

spinney, spinny *spin′i, n.* a small clump of trees or copse: — *pl.* **spinn′eys, spinn′ies.** [O.Fr. *espinei* — L. *spīn-ētum,* a thorn-hedge, thicket — *spīna,* thorn.]

spino- *spī-nō-,* in composition, spine.

spinode *spī′nōd,* (*geom.*) *n.* a cusp or stationary point of a curve. [L. *spīna,* thorn, *nōdus,* knot.]

spinose, spinous, etc. See **spine.**

Spinozism *spi-nōz′izm, n.* the pantheistic monism of Benedict *Spinoza* (1632–77). — *n.* **Spinō′zist** a follower of Spinoza. — *adj.* **Spinōzis′tic.**

spinster *spin′stər, n.* a spinner (*obs.; Shak.*): an unmarried woman: an old maid: a woman fit for the spinning-house (*obs.*). — *ns.* **spin′sterdom** the world of old maids collectively; **spin′sterhood.** — *adjs.* **spinsterial** (-*stē′ri-əl*), **spinstē′rian, spin′sterish, spin′sterly.** — *ns.* **spin′-stership; spin′stress** a woman who spins: a spinster. [**spin,** and suffix **-ster.**]

spintext *spin′tekst, n.* a long-winded preacher. [**spin** and **text.**]

spinthariscope *spin-thär′i-skōp, n.* an instrument for counting alpha particles by observing the sparks pro-duced by their impact on a fluorescent screen. [Gr. *spintharis,* a spark, *skopeein,* to observe.]

spinule, spiny, etc. See under **spine.**

spiracle *spīr′ə-kl, n.* a breathing-hole: a vent, orifice, passage. — *adjs.* **spīracular** (-*ak′ū-lər*); **spīrac′ulate.** — *n.* **spīrac′ulum:** — *pl.* **spīrac′ula.** [L. *spīrāculum* — *spīrāre,* to breathe.]

Spiraea *spī-rē′ə, n.* the meadow-sweet genus of the rose family: (without *cap.*) a plant or shrub of the genus. — Also **Spirē′a, spirē′a** (esp. *U.S.*). [Gr. *speiraiā,* meadow-sweet, or privet — *speira,* a coil (from its coiled fruits).]

spiral, etc. See **spire¹,².**

spirant *spī′rənt,* (*phon.*) *adj.* fricative, open, produced by narrowing without stopping the air-passage. — *n.* a spirant consonant (including or excluding nasals, liquids, and semi-vowels). — *n.* **spīrā′tion** breathing: the procession of the Holy Ghost (*theol.*). [L. *spīrāre,* to breathe.]

spiraster, spirated. See **spire².**

spire¹ *spīr, n.* a shoot, sprout: a stalk: a long slender stalk: a tapering or conical body, esp. a tree-top: a flower-spike: a reed or reedlike plant (also collectively): a deer's tine: a spike: a cone: a summit, peak: a tall slender architectural structure tapering to a point. — *v.i.* to sprout: to shoot up. — *v.t.* to furnish with, or form into, a spire: to put forth as a shoot or fruit (*Spens.*). — *adj.* **spīr′al** (*rare*) towering and tapering (see also next article). — *n.* **spir′alism** advancement through, or the concept of, a spirally structured career (social, etc.) system; **spir′alist** one engaged in spiralism. — *adv.* **spir′ally** (also next article). — *adjs.* **spired** having a spire: tapering, conical: peaked: spiked: sprouted; **spire′less.** — *adv.* **spire′wise.** — *adj.* **spīr′y** shooting into spires: spire-like: tapering: abounding in spires (see also next article). — **spire′-steeple** a steeple with a spire. [O.E. *spīr,* shoot, sprout.]

spire² *spīr, n.* a coil: a spiral: the spiral part of a shell, excluding the body-whorl. — *v.i.* to wind, mount, or proceed in spirals. — *adj.* **spīr′al** winding like the thread of a screw: with parts arranged in spirals (*bot.*). — *n.* a spiral line, course, or object: a curve (usu. plane), the locus of a point whose distance from a fixed point varies according to some rule as the radius vector revolves (*math.*): a helix (see also previous article): a gradual but continuous rise or fall, as of prices. — *v.i.* to go in a spiral. — *v.t.* to make spiral. — *adj.* **spīr′aliform** in or based on the shape of a spiral. — *n.* **spīrality** (-*al′i-ti*), — *adv.* **spīr′ally.** — *n.* **spīras′ter** (Gr. *astēr,* star) a coiled sponge-spicule with radiating spines. — *adj.* **spīr′āted** spirally twisted. — *n.* **spīr′ēme** in mitosis, the coiled thread formed by nuclear chro-matin. — *adj.* **spīr′ic** like a tore or anchor-ring. — *n.* a curve, the plane section of a tore. — *n.* **Spīr′ifer** (L. *ferre,* to bear) a genus (chiefly Silurian to Carbonifer-ous) of brachiopods, with coiled arm-supports. — *adj.* **spīrill′ar.** — *ns.* **spīrillō′sis** infection with a spirillum; **spīrill′um** a spirally bent bacterium. — *pl.* **spīrill′a; spīr′ochaete** (-*kēt;* Gr. *chaitē,* hair, mane) a spirally coiled bacterium (genus **Spirochae′ta** or **-tē** or kin-dred), cause of syphilis and other diseases; **spirochaetō′sis** infection with a spirochaete, as in syphilis, relapsing fever, etc.; **Spirogyra** (*spī-rō-jī′rə,* or -*gī′;* Gr. *gȳros,* a ring) a genus of freshwater algae with chlorophyll in spiral bands. — *adj.* **spī′roid** with the form of, or like, a spiral. — *n.* **spironolac′tone** (*med.*) a diuretic steroid often used in the treatment of heart and kidney failure. — *adj.* **spīr′y** spirally coiled (see also previous article). — **spiral arm** an arm of a spiral galaxy; **spiral galaxy** (*astron.*) one of a large class of galaxies, with two spiral arms emerging from a bright central ellipsoidal nucleus about which they rotate; **spiral staircase** a staircase in the form of a spiral, with a central column around which the steps are built. [Gr. *speira,* a coil, a tore.]

spirit *spir′it, n.* vital principle: the principle of thought:

the soul: a disembodied soul: a ghost: an incorporeal being: a kidnapper (*obs.*): enthusiasm: actuating emotion, disposition, frame of mind: a leading, independent, or lively person: animation: verve: courage: mettle: real meaning: essence, chief quality: a breath of wind (*arch. poet.*): a breath (*obs.*): a breathing (*Gr. gram.*): (usu. in *pl.*) a formerly supposed subtle substance in the body: (in *pl.*) cheerful or exuberant vivacity: (in *pl.*) state of mind, mood: (in *pl.*) mental powers (*obs.*): (in *pl.*) spirituous liquor: (the following also in *pl.*, sometimes with vb. in *sing.*) a distilled liquid: an aqueous solution of ethyl alcohol: a solution in alcohol. — *v.t.* to give spirit to: to inspirit, encourage, cheer: to convey away secretly, to kidnap (often with *away, off*). — *adj.* **spir'ited** full of spirit, life, or fire: animated: possessed by a spirit. — *adv.* **spir'itedly.** — *n.* **spir'itedness.** — *adj.* **spir'itful.** — *ns.* **spir'iting** the action of one who spirits in any sense: the offices of a spirit or sprite; **spir'itism** spiritualism: animism; **spir'itist.** — *adjs.* **spiritist'ic; spir'itless** without spirit, cheerfulness, or courage: dejected: dead. — *adv.* **spir'itlessly.** — *n.* **spir'itlessness.** — *adj.* and *adv.* **spiritoso** (-ō'sō; It.) with spirit. — *adj.* **spir'itous** of the nature of spirit, pure: ardent, spirituous. — *n.* **spir'itousness.** — *adj.* **spir'itūal** of, of the nature of, relating to, spirit, a spirit, spirits, the mind, the higher faculties, the soul: highly refined in thought and feeling, habitually or naturally looking to things of the spirit: incorporeal: ecclesiastical, religious: as a Gallicism, witty, clever: spirituous (*obs.* or *rare*). — *n.* that which is spiritual: an American Negro religious song. — *n.* **spiritualisā'tion, -z-.** — *v.t.* **spir'itualise, -ize** to make spiritual: to imbue with spirituality: to refine: to free from sensuality: to give a spiritual meaning to. — *ns.* **spir'itualiser, -z-; spir'itualism** a being spiritual: the philosophical doctrine that nothing is real but soul or spirit: the doctrine that spirit has a real existence apart from matter: the interpretation of a varied series of abnormal phenomena as for the most part caused by spiritual beings acting upon specially sensitive persons or mediums (also **spiritism); spir'itualist** one who has a regard only to spiritual things: (with *cap.*) one who holds the doctrine of spiritualism or spiritism. — *adj.* **spiritualist'ic.** — *n.* **spirituality** (-al'i-ti) state of being spiritual: that which is spiritual: property held or revenue received in return for spiritual service (*hist.*): the clergy (*hist.*). — *adv.* **spir'itually.** — *ns.* **spir'itualness** the state or quality of being spiritual; **spir'itualty** (*obs.* or *hist.*) spirituality: the clergy. — *adj.* **spirituel,** also *fem.* (indiscriminately used) **spirituelle,** (Fr. spē-rē-tü-el'; *coll.* spir-it-ū-el') showing refined and witty grace and delicacy. — *n.* **spirituos'ity** spirituous character: immateriality. — *adj.* **spir'ituous** sprightly (*obs.*): spiritual (*obs.*): containing, of the nature of, a volatile principle (*arch.*): alcoholic. — *ns.* **spir'ituousness; spiritus** (spīr', spir'i-təs; L. spē'ri-tōos) spirit: a breathing (*Gr. gram.*; **spiritus asper** the rough, **lenis** the smooth, breathing). — *adj.* **spir'ity** (*dial.* or *coll.*) spirited: spirituous. — **spir'it-blue** aniline blue; **spir'it-duck** the bufflehead, from its rapid diving; **spirit duplicator** one that uses a solution of alcohol in the copying process; **spir'it-gum** a preparation used by actors for attaching false beards, etc.; **spir'it-lamp** lamp burning methylated or other spirit to give heat; **spir'it-leaf** Ruellia; **spir'it-level** a glass tube nearly filled with, usu., alcohol, showing perfect levelness when the bubble is central; **spirit master** the master sheet used in a spirit duplicator; **spirit photography** the taking of photographs of persons in which other shadowy figures appear; **spir'it-rapper** one who claims to receive messages from disembodied spirits by raps or knocks; **spir'it-rapping.** — *adj.* **spir'it-stirring** rousing the spirit. — **spir'itual-mind'edness; spir'it-varnish** shellac or other resin in a volatile solvent, usu. alcohol; **spir'it-world** the world of disembodied spirits. — **animal spirits** a subtle form of matter formerly believed to be sent along the nerves from the brain: hence constitutional liveliness; **(Holy)**

Spirit see **holy; in spirits** cheerfully vivacious; **out of spirits** depressed; **spirit(s) of ammonia** sal volatile; **spirit(s) of salt** hydrochloric acid in water; **spirit(s) of wine** alcohol. [L. *spīritus,* a breath — *spīrāre,* to breathe.]

spirling. See **sparling.**

spirochaete, etc. See **spire²**.

spirograph *spī'rō-gräf, n.* an instrument for recording breathing movements. — *n.* **spīröm'eter** an instrument for measuring lung capacity. — *adj.* **spīromet'ric.** — *ns.* **spīröm'etry; spī'rophore** (Gr. *phoros,* a bringing) an apparatus for inducing artificial respiration by means of an airtight case for the body and an air-pump. [L. *spīrāre,* to breathe.]

Spirogyra, spiroid. See **spire²**.

spirt¹ *spûrt, v.i.* to shoot out forcibly, or in a fine strong jet. — *v.t.* to squirt in a fine strong jet. — *n.* a sudden fine jet. [Origin uncertain; cf. Ger. dial. *spirzen,* to spit; **spurt.**]

spirt² *spûrt,* (*Shak.*) *v.i.* to sprout, shoot up. [O.E. *spryttan;* cf. **sprout.**]

spirtle. Same as **spurtle.**

spiry. See under **spire¹,²**.

spissitude *spis'i-tūd, n.* density. [L. *spissitūdō — spissus,* thick.]

spit¹ *spit, n.* a broach for roasting meat: jocularly, a sword: a long narrow tongue of land or sand running into the sea: a wire or spindle holding a spool in a shuttle. — *v.t.* to transfix: to string on a rod or wire: — *pr.p.* **spitt'ing;** *pa.t.* and *pa.p.* **spitt'ed.** — *adj.* **spitt'ed.** — *ns.* **spitt'er** a young deer with unbranched antlers; **spitt'ing** piercing. [O.E. *spitu;* Du. *spit,* Ger. *Spiess.*]

spit² *spit, v.t.* to throw out from the mouth: to eject with violence: to utter with hate, scorn or violence: to spawn. — *v.i.* to throw out saliva from the mouth: to rain in scattered drops: to make a spitting sound: to sputter: to feel or be furious (*coll*): — *pr.p.* **spitt'ing;** *pa.t.* and *pa.p.* **spat,** *arch.* **spit,** *obs. pa.p.* **spitt'en, spitt'ed** (*B.*). — *n.* saliva, spume: a light fall of rain or snow: an exact replica (*slang;* usu. *dead* or *very spit,* from the phrase *as like him as if he had spit him out of his mouth*). — *ns.* **spitt'er; spitt'ing** the act of ejecting saliva: the ejection of oxygen, with drops of molten metal, when silver or platinum heated in air cools slowly: the resulting surface-appearance. — Also *adj.* — *ns.* **spitt'le** spit, saliva; **spittoon'** a vessel for spitting in. — **spit'-box** spittoon; **spit'-curl** (*coll.*) a curl pressed flat on the temple; **spit'fire** that which emits fire, e.g. a volcano, cannon: (with *cap.*) a type of fighting aeroplane used in World War II: a hot-tempered person; **spitting image** (form of *dial. spitten image* — for *spit and image*) the exact likeness of (see above); **spitt'lebug, spittle insect** a frog-hopper or froth-fly. — **spit and polish** cleaning up of uniform and equipment, esp. to excess; **spit and sawdust** of or referring to a floor left rough and covered with sawdust, wood chippings, etc., or esp. a bar having this type of floor: also, the character, quality, etc., of such a bar; **spit blood** to rage, be furious; **spit (it) out** to speak out, tell (it). [Northern O.E. *spittan,* O.N. *spýta,* Ger. dial., *spitzen, spützen.*]

spit³ *spit, v.t.* and *v.i.* to dig: to plant with a spade. — *n.* a spade's depth: this amount of earth, a spadeful. [O.E. *spittan,* or (M.)Du. and (M.)L.G. *spit.*]

spital. See **spittle²**.

spitchcock *spich'kok, n.* an eel split and broiled. — *v.t.* to split and broil, as an eel. [Orig. unknown; cf. **spatchcock.**]

spitcher *spit'chə,* (*naval slang*) *adj.* done for. [Maltese *spiĉĉa,* pron. *spitch'a,* finished, ended.]

spite *spīt, n.* grudge: lasting ill-will: hatred: a cause of vexation (*arch.*). — *v.t.* to vex: to thwart: to hate. — *adj.* **spite'ful** full of spite: desirous to vex or injure: malignant. — *adv.* **spite'fully.** — *n.* **spite'fulness.** — **in spite of** in opposition to all efforts of, in defiance of, in contempt of: notwithstanding; **spite (of)** despite. [**despite.**]

spitten. Obs. *pa.p.* of **spit**[2].

spitter. See **spit**[1,2].

spittle[1], **spittoon.** See under **spit**[2].

spittle[2], also **spital**, *spit'l*, (*arch.*) *n.* a hospital, esp. for foul diseases, a lazar-house. — **spitt'le-house.** [hospital.]

spitz *spits, n.* a Pomeranian dog: a group of breeds of dog generally having long hair, pointed ears and a tightly curled tail, incl. husky, samoyed, Pomeranian, etc. [Ger.]

spiv *spiv,* (*slang*) *n.* a flashy black-market hawker: one who makes money by dubious means: an idler. — *n.* **spivv'ery** the world or the practices of spivs. — *adj.* **spivv'y.** [Perh. conn. with **spiff.**]

splanchnic *splangk'nik, adj.* visceral, intestinal. — *n.* **splanch'nocele** (*-sēl*; Gr. *koilos*, hollow) a visceral cavity: the posterior part of the coelom. [Gr. *splanchnon*, pl. *splanchna*, entrails.]

splash *splash, v.t.* to spatter, as with water or mud: to throw about brokenly, as liquid: to dash liquid on or over: to effect by or with splashing: to variegate as if by splashing: to display, print very prominently. — *v.i.* to dabble: to dash liquid about: to move, go, with throwing about of broken liquid: to fly about dispersedly: of bullets, to throw about fragments or molten metal on striking. — *n.* the dispersion of liquid suddenly disturbed, as by throwing something into it or by throwing it about: liquid thrown on anything: a spot formed by or as if by throwing liquid: a little soda-water, tonic, etc. (with a spirit): lead thrown about by a bullet on striking: ostentation, publicity, display: a sensation, excitement, dash: a prominently printed slogan or (a story, article, introduced by such a) headline. — *n.* **splash'er** one who, or that which, splashes: a guard against splashing: a board attached to the foot for walking on mud. — *adv.* **splash'ily.** — *n.* and *adj.* **splash'ing.** — *adj.* **splash'y** splashing: with splashing: wet and muddy: full of puddles: ostentatious, showy. — **splash'-back** a piece of glass, plastic, etc., or area of tiles covering the part of a wall behind a wash-basin to protect against splashing; **splash'-board** a mudguard: a dashboard; **splash'down** (the moment of) the landing of a spacecraft on the sea. — *adj.* **splash'proof.** — **splash down** of spacecraft, to land on the sea on completion of mission; **splash out (on)** (*coll.*) to spend a lot of money (on). [**plash.**]

splat[1] *splat, n.* a thin strip forming the upright middle part of a chair-back. [**plat**[3].]

splat[2] *splat, n.* the sound made by a soft, wet object striking a surface. — *v.i.* to strike a surface with a splat: to cause (droplets of molten metal) to strike and spread over a metal surface, driven by shock waves (*metallurgy*). — *adv.* with this sound. — *n.* **splatt'ing.** — **splat cooling, splat quenching** the technical process of cooling metal rapidly by splatting. [Onomatopoeic.]

splatch *splach,* (*Scot.* and *U.S.*) *n.* a splash or clot of dirt or colour: a splotch. — *v.t.* to splotch. [Cf. **splotch.**]

splatter *splat'ər, v.t.* and *v.i.* to spatter: to splash: to sputter. — *n.* a splash: a spattering. [Cf. **spatter.**]

splay *splā, v.t.* and *v.i.* to display (*obs.*): to slope, slant, or bevel (*archit.*): to spread out. — *n.* a slant or bevel, as of the side of a doorway, window, or the like. — *adj.* having a splay: turned outwards. — *adv.* with a splay. — **splay foot** a flat foot turned outward. — *adjs.* **splay'-foot, -ed; splay'-mouthed** wide-mouthed. [**display.**]

spleen *splēn, n.* a soft, pulpy, blood-modifying organ close to the stomach, once thought the seat of anger and melancholy: hence various meanings, mostly in Shak. and more or less obs. — **spite:** boredom: ill-humour: melancholy: mirth: caprice: impulse: high spirit. — *adjs.* **spleen'ful; spleen'ish; spleen'less; spleen'y** (*Shak.*); **splē'native** (*obs.*) hot-tempered. — *n.* **splenec'tomy** (*splin-*; Gr. *ek*, out, *tomē*, a cutting) excision of the spleen. — *adj.* **splenetic** (*splin-et'ik*; formerly *splēn'i-tik*) of the spleen: affected with spleen: peevish: melancholy. — *n.* a splenetic person. — *adj.* **splenet'ical.** — *adv.* **splenet'ically.** — *adj.* **splenic** (*splē'nik, splen'*) of the spleen. — *ns.* **splēnīsā'tion, -z-** conversion (of the lung) into spleen-like substance; **splenī'tis** (*splin-*) inflammation of the spleen; **splēnomeg'aly** (Gr. *megas, megalē, mega,* big) enlargement of the spleen. — **spleen'-stone** (*obs.*) jade; **spleen'-wort** any fern of the genus Asplenium; **splenic fever** anthrax. [L. *splēn* — Gr. *splēn.*]

splendent *splen'dənt,* (*arch.*) *adj.* brightly shining: renowned (*fig.*). — *adjs.* **splen'did** brilliant, resplendent: magnificent: excellent (*coll.*); **splendid'ious** (*obs.*). — *adv.* **splen'didly.** — *n.* **splen'didness.** — *adjs.* **splen'didous** (*obs.*); **splendif'erous** (now only *coll.*); **splen'd(o)rous.** — *n.* **splen'dour**, U.S. **splendor**, (*-dər*) brilliance: magnificence. [L. *splendēre,* to shine, *splendidus, splendor.*]

splenectomy, splenetic, etc. See **spleen.**

splenial *splē'ni-əl, adj.* splint-like: of the splenium or the splenius. — *ns.* **splē'nium** the round pad-like posterior border of the *corpus callosum,* the bundle of fibres uniting the two cerebral hemispheres; **splē'nius** a large thick muscle on the back of the neck. [Gr. *splēnion,* pad, compress.]

splenic, etc., **splenomegaly.** See **spleen.**

splent. See **splint.**

spleuchan *splōōhh'ən,* (*Scot.*) *n.* a tobacco-pouch: a purse. [Gael. *spliuc(h)an.*]

splice *splīs, v.t.* to unite by interweaving the strands: to join together by overlapping: to unite, esp. (*slang*; also *v.i.*) in matrimony. — *n.* the act of splicing: a joint made by splicing: the part of the handle of a cricket-bat or the like that fits into the blade. — **sit on the splice** (*cricket slang*) to bat defensively, with no attempt to gain runs; **splice the mainbrace** (*nautical slang*) to serve out an allowance of spirits: to fall to drinking. [Du. (now dial.) *splissen.*]

spliff *splif,* (*slang,* esp. *Rastafarian,* orig. *West Indian*) *n.* a marijuana cigarette: the act of smoking such a cigarette.

spline *splīn, n.* a key to make wheel and shaft revolve together: a thin strip or slat. — *v.t.* to put splines on. [Orig. E. Anglian.]

splint *splint,* also **splent** *splent, ns.* an overlapping strip in armour: a strip, slip of wood, lath: a splinter: a contrivance for holding a broken bone, or the like, in position: a bony enlargement on a horse's leg between knee and fetlock: splint-coal. — *v.t.* to put in splints. — *n.* **splint'er** a piece of wood, metal, etc., split off, esp. a needle-like piece: a slender strip of wood, esp. one used as a torch: a splint (*obs.*). — *v.t.* and *v.i.* to split into splinters. — *v.t.* (*Shak.*) to put in splints, hence join, piece. — *adj.* **splint'ery** made of, or like, splinters: apt to splinter. — **splint'-arm'our** armour of narrow overlapping plates; **splint'-bone** a small bone alongside the cannon bone in the horse, etc., the second or the fourth metacarpal or metatarsal; **splint'-coal** a hard coal of uneven fracture that does not cake; **splint'er-bar** the cross-bar of a coach, supporting the springs; **splint'er-bone** the fibula; **splinter party, group** a party or group formed by a breakaway from a larger body. — *adj.* **splint'er-proof** proof against the splinters of bursting shells or bombs, or against splintering. — **splintery fracture** (*min.*) the property of breaking with a surface like broken wood; **splint'wood** sapwood. [M.Du. *splinte* (Du. *splint*) or (M.)L.G. *splinte, splente*; Du. and L.G. *splinter,* Ger. *Splenter.*]

split *split, v.t.* to break in pieces, wreck: to rend: to cleave lengthwise: to divide, share: to disunite: to divulge (*coll.*). — *v.i.* to be dashed to pieces (often with *up*): to suffer shipwreck: to divide or part asunder (often with *up*): to divulge secrets (*coll.*): to divide one's votes instead of plumping: to burst with laughter: to go at full speed: to break off relations (with) (*slang*; often with *up*). — *pr.p.* **splitt'ing;** *pa.t.* and *pa.p.* **split** (*Shak.,* etc., **splitt'ed**). — *n.* a crack or rent lengthwise: a schism: a half-bottle of aerated water, etc., a half-glass of spirits: (in *pl.*) the acrobatic feat of going down to the floor with the legs spread out laterally or one forward and one back: a division, share-out (usu. of money, stolen goods, etc.) (*coll.*): a kind of rough suede made from an inner separated layer of hide, so having the same finish on both sides: a sweet dish, usu. of sliced-open fruit and cream, ice-cream, etc.: a piece of wood for kindling (*Canada*): a split-level house or apartment (*U.S.*). — *adj.* having been split: having a split or break. — *n.* **splitt′er** one who, or that which, splits: one who splits hairs in argument, classification, etc.: a splitting headache (*coll.*). — *adj.* **splitt′ing** rending: cleaving: ear-splitting: of a headache, very severe: very rapid. — **split image** a bisected image, produced in a focusing system in which the two halves are displaced if the camera is out of focus (*phot.*): a spitting image (also **splitt′ing image**); **split infinitive** an infinitive with an adverb between 'to' and the verb. — *adj.* **split′-lev′el** on more than one level (see also below). — **split mind** a mental disorder in which the thoughts may become separated from the emotions: (*loosely*) a divided or dual opinion or feeling (about something). — *adj.* **split′-new** (*Scot.*) brand-new. — **split pea** see **pea**[1]; **split personality** dual personality; **split pin** a pin made of a doubled piece of metal formed into a ring at the head to give tension and usu. inserted in a hole in a bolt to hold a nut, etc., firmly; **split ring** a ring formed as if split spirally, as for keeping keys together; **split screen** a cinematic technique of showing different scenes simultaneously on separate parts of the screen, also used in television: a facility whereby separate areas of the screen may be used to display and carry out separate functions simultaneously. — *adj.* **split′-screen.** — **split second** a fraction of a second. — *adj.* **split′-second** timed to a fraction of a second. — **split shift** a work-shift divided into two separate periods during the day. — **full split** at full speed; **split hairs** see **hair**; **split investment trust** see **trust**; **split-level house** a one-storey house with rooms on more than one level; **split on** (*coll.*) to betray, give (a person) away; **split on a rock** to meet some unforeseen and disastrous difficulty, to go to ruin; **split one's sides** to laugh immoderately; **split-seconds hand** a double seconds hand in a chronograph, of which first one and then the other member can be stopped by pressing a button; **split the difference** to divide equally the sum of matter in dispute, to take the mean. [Du. *splitten*, related to *splijten*, Ger. *spleissen*.]

splodge, splodgily etc. See **splotch.**

splore *splōr, splör,* (*Scot.*) *n.* a frolic: a spree: an escapade: a row: a scrape. [Origin obscure.]

splosh *splosh, n., v.i., v.t.* a usu. humorous variant of **splash.**

splotch *sploch,* **splodge** *sploj, ns.* a big or heavy splash, spot, or stain. — *vs.t.* to mark with splotches or splodges. — *vs.i.* to trudge flounderingly or splashily. — *adv.* **splotch′ily, splodg′ily.** — *n.* **splotch′iness, splodg′iness.** — *adjs.* **splotch′y, splodg′y.** [Perh. conn. with O.E. *splott,* spot.]

splurge *splûrj, n.* any boisterous display. — *v.i.* to make such a display: to spend a lot of money (on). — *adj.* **splur′gy.** [Imit.]

splutter *splut′ər, v.i.* to eject drops: to scatter ink upon a paper, as a bad pen: to scatter liquid with spitting noises: to articulate confusedly as in rage. — *v.t.* to utter splutteringly. — *n.* an act or noise of spluttering. — *n.* **splutt′erer.** — *n.* and *adj.* **splutt′ering.** — *adv.* **splutt′eringly.** — *adj.* **splutt′ery.** [Prob. imit.; cf. **sputter.**]

Spode *spōd, n.* (also without *cap.*) a porcelain made with addition of bone-ash by Josiah *Spode* (1754–1827) at Stoke. — Also *adj.*

spode *spōd,* **spodium** *spō′di-əm, ns.* powder got by calcination: bone-black. — *n.* **spodomancy** (*spod′ə-man-si*) divination by means of ashes. — *adj.* **spodoman′tic.** — *n.* **spod′ūmene** a monoclinic pyroxene, silicate of aluminium and lithium. [Gr. *spodos,* dim.

spodion, ashes; *spodoumenos* (contracted participle), burnt to ashes, from its appearance under the blow-pipe.]

spoffish *spof′ish,* (*arch.*) *adj.* fussy, officious — also **spoff′y.** [Origin obscure.]

spoil *spoil, n.* (often in *pl.*) plunder, booty: acquisitions, prizes: spoliation: pillage: a cast or stripped-off skin: remains of an animal body: material cast out in excavation: damage, impairment (*rare*): a thing spoiled in making (*rare*). — *v.t.* to take by force (*arch.*): to plunder: to despoil: to strip: to deprive: to destroy, end (*Shak.*): to corrupt: to mar: to impair: to make useless: to treat over-indulgently: to harm the character by so doing. — *v.i.* to practise spoliation: to go bad: to deteriorate: — *pa.t.* and *pa.p.* **spoiled** or (only in sense of damage) **spoilt.** — *n.* **spoil′age** waste by spoiling: material so wasted. — *adj.* **spoiled.** — *n.* **spoil′er** any thing or person that spoils: an aerodynamic device fitted to the wings of an aircraft to reduce lift and assist descent: a similar device fitted to motor-vehicles, esp. racing cars, to lessen drag and reduce the tendency to become unstable through a lifting effect at high speeds: a third candidate in a two-way political election, whose only effect is to lessen the votes for one of the main candidates (*U.S.*). — *adj.* **spoil′ful** (*Spens.* **spoylefull**) plundering. — **spoil′-bark, -heap** a deposit of spoil; **spoil′-five** a card game drawn or *spoiled* if no player wins three out of five tricks; **spoils′man** one who looks for profit out of politics (*U.S.*); **spoil′-sport** one who stops or interferes with sport or other people's pleasure: a meddler; **spoils system** the system of supplanting civil servants on a change of government, on the principle that 'to the victor belong the spoils'; **spoilt paper** in a ballot, a voting paper marked, esp. deliberately, in such a way as to be invalid. — **spoiling for** (a fight, etc.) more than ripe or ready for: intent on. [O.Fr. *espoille* — L. *spolium,* spoil.]

spoke[1] *spōk, pa.t.* of **speak.**

spoke[2] *spōk, n.* one of the radiating bars of a wheel. — *adv.* **spoke′wise.** — **spoke′shave** a two-handled planing tool for curved work. — **put a spoke in someone's wheel** to thwart someone. [O.E. *spāca;* Du. *speek,* Ger. *Speiche.*]

spoken *spōk′n, pa.p.* of **speak.** — in composition, of speech, speaking, as **fair′-spoken, plain′-spoken.** — **spo′ken for** chosen, reserved.

spokesman *spōks′mən, n.* one who speaks for another, or for others: — *pl.* **spokes′men:** — *fem.* **spokes′woman; spokes′person.** [speak, man[1].]

spolia opima *spō′li-ə ōp′i-mə, spo′li-a, op-ē′ma,* (L.) the richest booty — spoil taken in battle by a leader from a leader.

spoliate *spō′li-āt, v.t.* and *v.i.* to despoil, to plunder. — *n.* **spōliā′tion** serving to take away or diminish. — *n.* **spō′liātor.** — *adj.* **spō′liatory** (*-ə-tər-i*). [L. *spoliāre, -ātum* — *spolium,* spoil.]

spondee *spon′dē, n.* a foot of two long syllables. — *adjs.* **spondaic** (*-dā′ik*), **spondā′ical.** [L. *spondēus* (*pēs*) — Gr. *spondeios* (*pous*), (a foot) used in the slow solemn hymns sung at a *spondē* or drink-offering — *spendein,* to pour out, make a libation.]

spondulicks, spondulix *spon-doo′liks,* (*U.S. slang*) *n.pl.* money. [Origin unknown.]

spondyl *spon′dil, n.* a vertebra: a thorny oyster (*Spondylus*). — *adj.* **spondylit′ic** affected by spondylitis. — *n.* one suffering from spondylitis. — *n.* **spondylī′tis** inflammation of a vertebra. — *ns.* **spondylolisthē′sis** a partial dislocation of the (usu. lower) vertebrae in which a vertebra slips forward over the one below; **spondylol′ysis** disintegration of one or more vertebrae; **spondylō′sis** vertebral ankylosis. — *adj.* **spon′dylous.** [Gr. *sp(h)ondylos,* a vertebra.]

sponge *spunj, n.* any member of the phylum Porifera, sessile aquatic animals with a single cavity in the body, with numerous pores: the fibrous skeleton of such an animal, remarkable for its power of sucking up water:

a piece of such a skeleton, or a substitute, used for washing, obliterating, absorbing, etc.: a swab for a cannon: any sponge-like substance, as leavened dough, a cake or pudding, swampy ground: a bedeguar: a hanger-on or parasite (*coll.*): a drunkard (*coll.*): an application of a sponge: the life or behaviour of a sponger upon others (*coll.*). — *v.t.* to wipe, wipe out, soak up, remove, with a sponge: to drain, as if by squeezing a sponge: to gain by the art of the parasite. — *v.i.* to suck in, as a sponge: to fish for sponges: to live on others parasitically (often with *on* or *off*). — *adjs.* **spon'geable; spongeous** (*spun'jəs*) spongy. — *n.* **spong'er** one who uses a sponge: a sponge-fisher: a sponge-fishing boat: an apparatus for sponging cloth: a sponge or parasite. — *adjs.* **spongicolous** (*spun-, spon-jik'ə-ləs*; L. *colĕre*, to inhabit) living in association with, usually within, a sponge; **spon'giform** like or akin to a sponge. — *adv.* **spon'gily** in a spongy way, or manner. — *ns.* **spongin** (*spun'jin*) a horny substance in the skeletons of various sponges; **spon'giness.** — *adjs.* **spongiose** (*spun'*, or *-ōs'*), **spongious** (*spun'jəs*), **spongoid** (*spong'goid*). — *ns.* **spongologist** (*spong-gol'ə-jist*); **spongol'ogy** the science of sponges. — *adj.* **spongy** (*spun'ji*) absorptive: porous: wet and soft: drunken: (of vehicle suspension, brakes, etc.) lacking firmness. — **sponge'-bag** a waterproof bag for carrying a sponge: (in *pl.*) checked or striped trousers. — *adj.* checked. — **sponge'-bath** an application of water to the body by or from a sponge, as for a sick or bedridden person; **sponge'-cake** a very light sweet cake of flour, eggs, and sugar; **sponge'-cloth** a cotton cloth of open texture; **sponge'-down** see sponge down below; **sponge'-fing'er** a finger-shaped sponge-cake; **sponge'-fisher; sponge'-fishing; sponge'-rubber** rubber processed into sponge-like form; **sponge'wood** sola; **spon'ging-house, spun'-ging-house** (*obs.*) a bailiff's lodging-house for debtors in his custody before their committal to prison; **spongy parenchyma** (*bot.*) a loose tissue in leaves with much intercellular space; **spongy platinum, platinum sponge** platinum in a finely divided state. — **set a sponge** to leaven a small mass of dough for use in leavening a large quantity; **sponge down** to clean or wipe with a sponge (*n.* **sponge'-down**); **throw up the sponge** to acknowledge defeat by throwing into the air the sponge with which a boxer is rubbed down between rounds: to give up any struggle. [O.E. *sponge, spunge*, and O.Fr. *esponge* — L. *spongia* — Gr. *spongiā*.]

sponsal *spon'sl, adj.* spousal. — *n.pl.* **sponsā'lia** espousals. — *n.* **spon'sion** the act of becoming surety for another. — *adj.* **spon'sional.** — *n.* **spon'sor** one who promises solemnly for another: a surety: a godfather or godmother: a promoter: one who pays for radio or television broadcast introducing advertisement: one who promises to pay a specified sum to a person for taking part in a fund-raising event or activity on behalf of a charity, etc. — *v.t.* to act as a sponsor. — *adj.* **sponso'rial.** — *n.* **spon'sorship.** [L. *spondēre, spōnsum*, promise.]

sponsible *spon'si-bl,* (now *dial.*) *adj.* aphetic for **responsible,** respectable.

sponsing. See **sponson.**

sponsion, sponsional. See **sponsal.**

sponson *spon'sn, n.* an outward expansion from a ship's deck: a short projecting length of plane: a wing-section giving extra lift: an air-filled tank on the side of a canoe to give buoyancy: a structure to give a seaplane steadiness on the water. — Also **spon'sing.** [Ety. dub.]

sponsor. See **sponsal.**

spontaneous *spon-tā'nyəs, -ni-əs, adj.* of one's free will: acting by its own impulse or natural law: produced of itself: impulsive: unpremeditated. — *ns.* **spontaneity** (*-tə-nē'i-ti, -nā'i-ti*), **spontā'neousness.** — *adv.* **spontā'-neously.** — **spontaneous abortion** miscarriage; **spontaneous combustion** catching fire by causes at work within, esp. slow oxidation of a mass of matter; **spontaneous generation** the production of living

organisms from dead matter. [L. *spontāneus* — *sponte*, of one's own accord.]

sponte sua *spon'te sōō'ä,* (L.) of one's own accord.

spontoon *spon-tōōn', n.* a small-headed halberd formerly carried by some infantry officers. [Fr. *sponton* — It. *spontone* — *punto* — L. *punctum*, a point.]

spoof *spōōf,* (*slang*) *n.* a hoaxing game invented and named by Arthur Roberts (1852–1933), comedian: a card game: a parody, take-off. — *adj.* bogus. — *v.t.* and *v.i.* to hoax: to parody. — *ns.* **spoof'er; spoof'ery.**

spook *spōōk, n.* a ghost: a spy, an undercover agent (*slang,* orig. *U.S.*). — *v.i.* to play the spook: to take fright: (of a horse) to shy away. — *v.t.* to frighten, startle. — *adj.* ghostly. — *n.* **spook'ery** things that are spooky: matters pertaining to spooks. — *adv.* **spook'ily.** — *n.* **spook'iness.** — *adjs.* **spook'ish, spook'y.** [App. L.G.; cf. Ger. *Spuk,* Du. *spook.*]

spool *spōōl, n.* a cylinder, bobbin, or reel for winding yarn, etc., upon. — *v.t.* and *v.i.* to wind on spools. — *n.* **spool'er.** [L.G. *spôle;* Du. *spoel,* or O.N.Fr. *espole;* Ger. *Spule.*]

spoom, spooming. See **spoon[1].**

spoon[1] *spōōn, v.i.* to scud before the wind. — Also **spoom.** — *adj.* **spoom'ing** (*Keats*) foaming. — *n.* **spoon'drift** light spray borne on a gale. — Also (orig. *Northern*) **spin'drift.** [Origin unknown.]

spoon[2] *spōōn, n.* an instrument with a shallow bowl and a handle: anything of like shape, as an oar: (a stroke with) a wooden-headed golf-club with face slightly hollowed: a spoon-bait: the wooden spoon (*Cambridge;* see under **wood[1]**): a simpleton: a maudlin love-maker: mawkish love-making. — *v.t.* to transfer with, or as if with, a spoon: to shove, scoop, or hit softly up into the air, instead of striking cleanly and definitely: to dally sentimentally with: to catch with a spoon-bait: to pack together like spoons. — *v.i.* to make love sentimentally: to fish with a spoon-bait. — *n.* **spoon'ful** as much as fills a spoon: a small quantity: — *pl.* **spoon'fuls.** — *advs.* **spoon'ily; spoon'ways, -wise** like spoons packed closely together. — *adj.* **spoon'y, spoon'ey** silly: foolishly and demonstratively fond. — *n.* one who is spoony. — **spoon'-bait, -hook** a lure on a swivel, used in trolling for fish; **spoon'bill** any bird of a family (*Plataleidae*) akin to the ibises, with long, flat, broad bill, spoon-shaped at the tip: a shoveller (*Spatula*). — *adj.* **spoon'-fed** fed with a spoon: artificially fostered (*fig.*): taught by doled-out doses of cut-and-dried information. — *v.t.* **spoon'-feed.** — **spoon'-food; spoon'meat** food taken or given with a spoon. — **born with a silver spoon in one's mouth** see **silver; spoons on** silly in manifestation of love for. [O.E. *spōn,* sliver, chip, shaving, Ger. *Span,* chip, O.N. *spánn, spónn,* chip, spoon.]

spoonerism *spōō'nər-izm, n.* a transposition of initial sounds of spoken words — e.g. 'shoving leopard' for 'loving shepherd'. [Rev. W. A. *Spooner* (1844–1930), a noted perpetrator of transpositions of this kind.]

spoor *spōōr, n.* track, esp. of a hunted animal. — *v.t.* and *v.i.* to track. — *n.* **spoor'er.** [Du. *spoor,* a track; cf. O.E. and O.N. *spor,* Ger. *Spur;* also **speir.**]

sporadic *spor-ad'ik, adj.* scattered: occurring here and there or now and then: occurring casually. — Also (*rare*) **sporad'ical.** — *adv.* **sporad'ically.** [Gr. *sporadikos* — *sporas, sporados,* scattered — *speirein,* to sow.]

spore *spōr, spör, n.* a unicellular asexual reproductive body: sometimes extended to other reproductive bodies. — *adj.* **sporangial** (*spor-an'ji-əl*). — *ns.* **sporan'giole, sporan'giolum** (or *-jī';* pl. *-a*) a sporangium containing one or few spores; **sporan'giophore** the part that bears sporangia; **sporan'giospore** a spore developed in a sporangium; **sporan'gium** (*pl.* **sporan'gia**) a spore-case, sac in which spores are produced. — Also **spore'-case; spor'idesm** (Gr. *desmos,* a bond; *bot.*) a multicellular body or group of spores, of which every cell is capable of germinating. — *adj.* **sporid'ial.** — *ns.* **sporid'ium** (*pl. -a*) a spore borne on a promycelium; **spor'ocarp** (Gr.

For other sounds see detailed chart of pronunciation.

karpos, fruit) a structure containing the sori and sporangia in water-ferns; a multicellular structure in which spores are formed; **spor′ocyst** the cyst developed in the process of sporulation. — *adj.* **sporocyst′ic.** — *n.* **sporogen′esis** production of spores. — Also **sporogeny** (-*oj′*). — *adj.* **sporog′enous** spore-bearing. — *ns.* **sporogonium** (-*gō′*) the capsule or asexual generation in mosses; **spor′ophore** a spore-bearing stalk or structure. — *adjs.* **sporophor′ic, sporoph′orous.** — *ns.* **spor′ophyl(l)** (Gr. *phyllon*, leaf) a leaf that bears sporangia; **spor′ophyte** (Gr. *phyton*, plant) the spore-bearing or asexual generation in the life-cycle of a plant. — *adj.* **sporophytic** (-*fit′ik*). — *n.pl.* **Sporozō′a** a parasitic group of Protozoa reproducing by spores, including the causal organisms of malaria and pébrine. — *n.* **sporozō′ite** (Gr. *zōion*, an animal) in Sporozoa, a minute, mobile, pre-adult, usu. infective stage developed within a spore. — *adj.* **spor′ūlar.** — *v.i.* **spor′ūlate** to produce spores. — *ns.* **sporūlā′tion** formation of spores: breaking up into spores; **spor′ule** a small spore. [Gr. *sporā*, a seed — *speirein*, to sow.]

sporran *spor′ən, n.* an ornamental pouch worn in front of the kilt by the Highlanders of Scotland. [Gael. *sporan*.]

sport *spōrt, spört, v.i.* to play (*arch.*): to frolic (also *v.t.* with *it; arch.*): to make merry: to practise field diversions: to trifle: to deviate from the normal. — *v.t.* to amuse (*obs.*): to wear, use, exhibit, set up, publicly or ostentatiously: to wager: to squander (*rare*): to force open (*obs.*). — *n.* recreation: pastime: dalliance, amorous behaviour: play: a game, esp. one involving bodily exercise: mirth: jest: contemptuous mirth: a plaything (esp. *fig.*): a laughing-stock: field diversion: success or gratification in shooting, fishing, or the like: a sportsman: a person of sportsmanlike character, a good fellow: an animal or plant that varies singularly and spontaneously from the normal type: (in *pl.*) a meeting for races and the like. — *adj.* **sports** suitable for sport. — Also (esp. *U.S.*) **sport.** — *n.* **sportabil′ity** sportiveness. — *adj.* **sport′able.** — *ns.* **sport′ance** (*rare*) play; **sport′er** one who sports: a sportsman. — *adj.* **sport′ful** full of sport: merry: full of jesting. — *adv.* **sport′fully.** — *n.* **sport′fulness.** — *adv.* **sport′ily.** — *n.* **sport′iness.** — *adj.* **sport′ing** relating to, engaging in, or fond of sport: willing to take a chance: sportsmanlike: in the U.K., pertaining to one of the two major classes of dogs recognised by the Kennel Club (the other being *non-sporting*), comprising hounds, gun dogs, and terriers: in the U.S., pertaining to one of the six recognised groups of breeds, essentially comprising the gun dogs (as opposed to hounds, terriers, etc.). — *adv.* **sport′ingly.** — *adj.* **sport′ive** inclined to sport: playful: merry: amorous, wanton. — *adv.* **sport′ively.** — *n.* **sport′iveness.** — *adjs.* **sport′less** without sport or mirth: sad; **sport′y** sportsmanlike (*coll.*): (of a person) who enjoys, takes part in or is proficient at sport: (of a car) that looks or handles like a sports car: stylish, lively. — **sporting chance** as good a chance of winning or being successful as of losing or failing; **sport′ing-house** a public house, hotel, etc., patronised by sportsmen or gamblers (*arch.*): a brothel; **sports car** a low car, usu. for two, capable of attaining high speed; **sports′caster** (*TV* and *radio*; orig. *U.S.*) a commentator on a sports programme; **sports jacket** a man's jacket, usu. tweed, for casual wear; **sports′man** one who practises, or is skilled in, sport: one who shows fairness and good humour in sport. — *adj.* **sports′manlike.** — **sports′manship; sports shirt** a man's casual shirt; **sports′wear** clothing designed to be worn for sport: designer clothes, esp. matching separates, for casual wear; **sports′woman.** — **sport one's oak** see **oak.** [Aphetic for *disport*.]

sporular, etc. See **spore.**

sposh *sposh,* (*U.S.*) *n.* slush. — *adj.* **sposh′y.** [Imit.]

spot *spot, n.* a mark made by a drop of wet matter: a blot: a small discoloured or differently coloured place: a locality, place or limited area, precise place: an eruption on the skin: a moral flaw: one of the marked points on a billiard-table, from which balls are played: a relatively dark place on the sun: a small quantity of anything (*coll.*): a spotlight: a white pigeon with a spot on the forehead: a name for various American fishes: a job, piece (of work) (*obs.*): perhaps, a pattern, or piece, of needlework (*Shak.* **spotte**): a place on e.g. a television or radio programme: a turn, performance, esp. a short one: (in *pl.*) a leopard (*coll.*): a spot deal or commodity (*finance*). — *v.t.* to mark with spots: to tarnish, as reputation: to reprehend (*Spens.*): to pick out, detect, locate, identify (*coll.*): to free from spots (often with *out*): to place on a spot, as in billiards. — *v.i.* to become spotted: to rain slightly, with few and intermittent drops (usu. as *spot with rain*) (*coll.*): — *pr.p.* **spott′ing;** *pa.t.* and *pa.p.* **spott′ed.** — *adj.* on the spot, random (see **spot check** below): of monetary or commodity transactions, etc., to be paid (usu. in cash) or delivered immediately (as in *spot market, spot price*, etc.): involving payment in cash only. — *adj.* **spot′less** without a spot: untainted: pure. — *adv.* **spot′lessly.** — *n.* **spot′lessness.** — *adj.* **spott′ed.** — *ns.* **spott′edness; spott′er** one who spots or detects. — *adv.* **spott′ily.** — *ns.* **spott′iness; spott′ing.** — *adj.* **spott′y.** — **-spotting** in composition, noting, identifying, as in *train-spotting*. — **-spot** verb combining form. — **-spotter** noun combining form. — **spot advertising** advertising by means of brief items, usu. in dramatised form, on television or radio. — *adj.* **spot′-barred** under the condition that the spot-stroke may not be played more than twice consecutively. — **spot cash** money down; **spot check** a check on the spot without warning: a check of random samples to serve in place of a general check; **spot dance** a dance after which a prize is given to the couple spotlighted when the music stopped; **spot height** on a map, a number giving the altitude at that point; **spot kick** a penalty kick; **spot′light** (apparatus for projecting) a circle of light on an actor or a small part of a stage (also *fig.*): an adjustable, focused-beam car lamp additional to fixed lights. — *v.t.* to turn the spotlight on: to draw attention to (*fig.*). — *adj.* **spot-on′** (*coll.*) on the target: accurate. — **spot′-stroke** a stroke in billiards by which the player pockets the red ball from the spot, leaving his own ball in position to repeat the stroke; **spotted dick** a pudding or loaf with currants; **spotted dog** a Dalmatian dog: a spotted dick. — **spotted flycatcher** a European songbird (*Muscicapa striata*). — *v.t.* **spot′-weld** to join metal with single circular welds. — *n.* a weld of this kind. — **spot′-welder.** — **in a spot** in a difficult situation; **knock (the) spots off** to surpass easily; **on the spot** at the very place: there and then: straightway: alert, equal to the occasion: in difficulty or danger (e.g. *put on the spot*, orig. to doom to be murdered) (*adj.* **on-the-spot′**); **soft spot** (*coll.*) affectionate feeling; **tight spot** (*coll.*) a dangerous or difficult situation; **weak spot** (*coll.*) weakness: an area in which one is not knowledgeable. [Cf. obs. Du., L.G., *spot*, O.N. *spotti*.]

spouse *spows, spowz, n.* a husband or wife. — *v.t.* to betroth (*Spens.*): to marry (*Milt.*). — *n.* **spous′age** marriage. — *adj.* **spous′al** nuptial: matrimonial. — *n.* usually in *pl.*, nuptials: marriage. — *adj.* **spouse′less.** [O.Fr. *spus, -e, espous, -e* (Fr. *époux*, fem. *épouse*) — L. *spōnsus*, pa.p. of *spondēre*, to promise.]

spout *spowt, v.t.* to throw out in a jet: to declaim: to pawn (*slang*). — *v.i.* to issue in a jet: to blow as a whale: to declaim (*derog.*). — *n.* a projecting lip or tube for discharging liquid from a vessel, a roof, etc.: a gush, discharge, or jet: an undivided waterfall: a waterspout: the blowing, or the blow-hole, of a whale: a shoot: a lift in a pawnshop (*arch.*): hence, a pawnshop (*arch.*). — *ns.* **spout′er** one who, or that which, spouts: a declaimer: a spouting oil-well: a spouting whale: a whaling ship. — *adjs.* **spout′less; spout′y** spirting water when trodden on. — **spout′-hole** a blow-hole. — **up the spout** (*slang*) pawned: failed, gone wrong: pregnant.

[M.E. *spouten*; cf. Du. *spuiten*, to spout, O.N. *spȳta*, to spit.]

spoylefull (*Spens.*). See **spoil.**

sprachgefühl *sprahh'gə-fül, n.* an instinctive feeling and aptitude for a language, its essential character, word patterns, usage, etc. [Ger. *Sprache*, language, *Gefühl*, feeling.]

sprack *sprak,* (*W. Midland* and *S.W.*) *adj.* vigorous, sprightly, alert. — Also (after the pron. of Sir Hugh Evans, *Merry Wives* IV, i. 85) **sprag.** [Origin obscure.]

sprackle *spräk'l*, **spraickle** *sprāk'l*, (*Scot.*) *vs.i.* to clamber. [Origin obscure.]

sprad *sprad*, (*Spens.*) *pa.p.* of **spread.**

sprag[1] *sprag, n.* a mine prop: a bar inserted to stop a wheel: a device to prevent a vehicle from running backwards. — *v.t.* to prop, or to stop, by a sprag: — *pr.p.* **sprag'ging**; *pa.t.* and *pa.p.* **spragged.** [Origin obscure.]

sprag[2]. See **sprack.**

spraickle. See **sprackle.**

spraid. See **spray**[3].

sprain *sprān, v.t.* to overstrain the muscles of. — *n.* a wrenching of a joint with tearing or stretching of ligaments. [Connection with O.Fr. *espreindre*, to squeeze out, is disputed.]

spraint *sprānt, n.* otter's dung. [O.Fr. *espraintes*, lit. pressed out.]

sprang *sprang, pa.t.* of **spring**[1].

sprangle *sprang'gəl*, (now *U.S.* and *dial.*) *v.i.* to sprawl: to straggle: to ramify: to struggle. — *n.* a straggle. [M.E. *spranglen*.]

sprat *sprat, n.* a fish like the herring, but much smaller: a term of contempt (*Shak.*). — **sprat'-weath'er** the dark days of November and December. — **a sprat to catch a mackerel, herring, whale** a small risk taken in order to make a great gain. [O.E. *sprot*; Du. *sprot*, Ger. *Sprotte*.]

sprattle *sprat'l*, (*Scot.*) *v.i.* to scramble. [Cf. Sw. *sprattla*.]

sprauchle *spröhh'l*, (*Scot.*) a later form of **sprackle.**

sprauncy *sprön'si, adj.* smart, dapper. [Orig. obscure, poss. conn. with dial. *sprouncey*, cheerful, jolly.]

sprawl *spröl, v.i.* to toss or kick about the limbs (*arch.*): to lie or crawl with limbs flung about: to straggle. — *v.t.* to spread stragglingly. — *n.* a sprawling posture, movement, or mass. — *n.* **sprawl'er.** — *adjs.* **sprawl'ing, sprawl'y.** [O.E. *sprēawlian*, to move convulsively.]

spray[1] *sprā, n.* a cloud of small flying drops: an application or dispersion of such a cloud: an apparatus or a preparation for so dispersing. — *v.t.* to sprinkle in or with fine mist-like jets. — *n.* **spray'er.** — *adj.* **spray'ey.** — *adj.* **spray'-dried'.** — **spray drift** spray, esp. a chemical pesticide or herbicide, which remains suspended in the air and is blown away from the original site of spraying by the wind; **spray drying** the rapid drying of a liquid by spraying it into a flow of hot gas; **spray'-gun** a device for applying paint, etc., by spraying. — *adj.* **spray'-on'** applied in a spray, usu. by an aerosol. **spray'-paint** paint that is applied in the form of a spray, usu. an aerosol. — *v.t.* to use spray-paint (on something), to apply with spray-paint. — **spray'-painting** [M.Du. *sprayen*.]

spray[2] *sprā, n.* a shoot or twig, esp. one spreading out in branches or flowers: an ornament, casting, etc., of similar form. — *v.i.* to spread or branch in a spray. — *adj.* **spray'ey** branching. [Poss. conn. with **sprig** or with O.E. *spræc*, twig.]

spray[3] *sprā*, **spreathe, spreethe** *sprēdh*, **spreaze, spreeze** *sprēz*, (*S.W. dial.*) *vs.t.* and *vs.i.* to chap, roughen — usu. in *pa.p.* **sprayed, spraid,** etc. [Origin obscure.]

sprayey. See **spray**[1,2].

spread *spred, v.t.* to cause to extend more widely or more thinly: to scatter abroad or in all directions: to stretch: to extend, esp. over a surface: to apply (a soft substance) by smoothing it over a surface: to open out so as to cover a wider surface: to overlay: to set with

provisions, as a table. — *v.i.* to extend or expand: to be extended or stretched: to become bigger or fatter: to open out: to go further apart: to unfold: to admit of spreading: to be propagated or circulated: — *pa.t.* and *pa.p.* **spread.** — *n.* extent: compass: reach: expanse: an expanded surface: the act or degree of spreading: an expansion: the process of becoming bigger or fatter: that which is spread out, a feast: anything for spreading on bread: a cover, esp. a bedcover: a ranch (*U.S.*): a double page, i.e. two facing pages (*print.*): a large property with grounds (*coll.*): the gap between the bid and offer price of shares (*Stock exchange*). — *adj.* extended: flat and shallow (as a gem). — *n.* **spread'er.** — *n.* and *adj.* **spread'ing.** — *adv.* **spread'ingly.** — **spread'-ea'gle** a heraldic eagle with the wings and legs stretched out: a fowl split and spread out for cooking: a man tied for punishment (*naut.*): a skating figure. — *adj.* bombastic, boastful, and frothy, esp. in American patriotism. — *v.t.* to tie up with outstretched limbs: to spread out: to outrun. — *v.i.* to cut, do, or make, spreadeagles: to lie, fall, etc., with outstretched limbs: to talk in spread-eagle strain. — **spread-ea'gleism.** — *adv.* **spread-ea'glewise.** — **spread'-over** an act of spreading out: an elastic distribution of working hours; **spread'sheet (program)** (*comput.*) a program with which data, formatted in rows and columns of cells, can be viewed on a screen and manipulated to make projections, calculations, etc. — **spread one's wings** to try one's powers or capabilities: to increase the area of one's activities. [O.E. *sprǣdan*; Du. *spreiden*, Ger. *spreiten*.]

spreagh *sprähh, sprehh, n.* a prey: a foray. — *n.* **spreagh'ery, sprech'ery** (*sprehh'*) cattle-lifting: petty possessions, esp. plunder. [Gael. *spréidh*, cattle.]

spreathe, spreaze. See **spray**[3].

sprechery. See **spreagh.**

sprechgesang *shprehh'gə-zang*, (*music*) *n.* a style of vocalisation between singing and speaking, originated by Arnold Schoenberg. — *n.* **sprech'stimme** (*-shtim-ə*) music using this form of vocalisation. [Ger., speaking-song, speaking-voice.]

spreckled *sprek'ld*, (now *dial.*) *adj.* speckled. [Cf. obs. Ger. *gespreckelt.*]

spred, spredd, spredde. Obs. spellings of **spread** (*pres., pa.t.* or *pa.p.*). — Also *inf.* **spredd'en.**

spree *sprē, n.* a merry frolic: a drunken bout: a gathering or party at which a prospective bride displays her wedding gifts (*Scot.*). — *v.i.* to carouse. [Orig. slang.]

spreethe, spreeze. See **spray**[3].

sprent *sprent*, (*arch.*) *adj.* sprinkled. [Pa.p. of obs. *sprenge*—O.E. *sprengen, sprengan,* causative of *springan,* to spring.]

sprig *sprig, n.* a small shoot or twig: a scion, a young person: an ornament like a spray: a headless or almost headless nail: a sprig-like object, ornament, or design, esp. embroidered or applied. — *v.t.* to embroider with representations of twigs: to nail with sprigs: — *pr.p.* **sprigg'ing**; *pa.t.* and *pa.p.* **sprigged.** — *adjs.* **sprigged; sprigg'y** of or like sprigs. [Origin obscure.]

spright *sprīt, n.* an unhistorical spelling of **sprite,** obs. (e.g. *Spens., Shak.*) except perhaps in the sense of impish person. — *v.t.* (*Shak.*) to haunt. — *adj.* **spright'ful** (*Shak.*) spirited. — *adv.* **spright'fully** (*Shak.*). — *n.* **spright'fulness** (*obs.*) — *adj.* **spright'less** (*obs.*) spiritless. — *n.* **spright'liness** — *adj.* **spright'ly** vivacious: animated: lively: brisk: ghostly (*Shak.*).

spring[1] *spring, v.i.* to move suddenly, as by elastic force: to bound: to start up suddenly: to break forth: to appear: to issue: to come into being: to take origin: to sprout: to dawn (*B.*): to branch off: to begin to arch: to give way, split, burst, explode, warp, or start. — *v.t.* to cause to spring up: to start: to release the elastic force of: to let off, allow to spring: to cause to explode: to make known suddenly (with *on* or *upon*): to open, as a leak: to crack, as a mast: to bend by force, strain: to start from an abutment, etc. (*archit.*): to leap over: to set together with bevel-joints: to attach or fit with springs: to procure the escape of (a prisoner) from jail (*slang*): — *pa.t.* **sprang**, now rarely **sprung**, *Spens.* **sprong**; *pa.p.* **sprung**, *Spens.* **sprong**. — *n.* a leap: a sudden movement: a recoil or rebound: elasticity: an elastic contrivance usu. for setting in motion or for reducing shocks: a source of action or life: rise: beginning: cause or origin: a source: an outflow of water from the earth: the time of beginning (*Shak.*): the dawn (*B.*): (often with *cap.*) the season when plants spring up and grow — in North temperate regions roughly February or March to April or May, astronomically from the spring equinox to the summer solstice: a shoot (*obs.*): a youth (*Spens.*): copse (*obs.*): undergrowth (*Spens.*): high water: spring tide: a lively dance-tune (now *Scot.*): a Norwegian dance or dance-tune: a flock of teal: the springing of an arch: a split, bend, warp, etc., esp. a crack in a mast. — *adj.* of the season or spring: sown, appearing, or used in spring: having or worked by a spring. — *ns.* **spring'al, spring'ald** an active springy young man, a youth; **spring'er** one who or that which springs: a kind of spaniel, useful in copses: the bottom stone of an arch (*archit.*): a spring chicken (chiefly *U.S.*). — *adv.* **spring'ily**. — *ns.* **spring'iness; spring'ing** the act of leaping, sprouting, starting, rising, or issuing: the beginning of curvature of an arch: a place of branching: providing with springs. — *adj.* leaping: arising: dawning: sprouting: with the freshness of youth: resilient: starting: beginning to curve. — *adj.* **spring'less**. — *n.* **spring'let** a little spring. — *adjs.* **spring'like; spring'y** elastic: resilient: abounding with springs. — See also **sprung**. — **spring'-bal'ance**, *U.S.* **spring scale**, an instrument for weighing by the elasticity of a spiral spring; **spring'-beau'ty** the plant *Claytonia virginica*; **spring'-bed** a spring-mattress; **spring'-bee'tle** a click-beetle. — *adj.* **spring'-blad'ed** of a knife, having a blade that springs out on pressure of a button. — **spring'board** a springy board for jumping or diving from: anything which serves as a starting-point, or from which one can launch ideas, projects, etc.; **spring'bok** (from Du.) a beautiful S. African antelope, larger than a roebuck (also **spring'buck**): (with *cap.*) a S.A. international sportsman (from emblems of sporting teams, orig. 1906 rugby team; shortened to **Bok**): hence also any South African, esp. when overseas; **spring'-box** a box or barrel in which a spring is coiled: the frame of a sofa, etc., in which the springs are set; **spring'-carr'iage**; **spring'-cart** one mounted upon springs; **spring chicken** a young chicken, usu. between two and ten months old, particularly tender when cooked (chiefly *U.S.*; also **spring'er**): a young, lively, sometimes naïve, person. — *v.t.* and *n.* **spring'= clean'**. — **spring'-clean'er; spring'-clean'ing** a thorough house-cleaning, usu. in spring; **spring'-clip** a spring-loaded clip; **spring fever** (*facet.*) spring lassitude; **spring'-gun** a gun set to go off like a trap; **spring'-haas** (-*häs*; *pl.* **-haas, -hase** -*hä'zə*; Du.), same as **spring'-hare**; **spring'halt** a jerking lameness in which a horse suddenly twitches up his leg or legs; **spring'-hare** the jumping hare; **spring'head** a fountain-head, source: a head- or end-piece for a carriage-spring. — *adjs.* **spring'-head'ed** (*Spens.*) having heads springing afresh; **spring'-heeled** having springs on one's heels, as **spring= heeled Jack,** supposed to do great leaps and play pranks or commit robberies. — **spring'-house** (*U.S.*) a larder, dairy, etc., built over a spring or brook; **spring'= keeper** a salamander; **spring'-lig'ament** a ligament of the sole of the foot. — *adj.* **spring'-load'ed** having or operated by a spring. — **spring'-lock** a lock that fastens by a spring: one that opens when a spring is touched; **spring'-matt'ress** a mattress of spiral springs in a frame; **spring onion** a type of onion, its small bulb and long leaves being eaten raw in salads; **spring roll** a deep-fried savoury pancake enclosing a mixture of vegetables, pork, prawns, etc., orig. Chinese; **spring'tail** any member of the Collembola; **spring'tide** springtime; **spring'= tide', spring tide** a tide of maximum amplitude after new and full moon, when sun and moon pull together;

spring'time the season of spring; **spring'-wa'ter** water of or from a spring; **spring'-wheat** wheat sown in the spring, rather than autumn or winter; **spring'wood** secondary wood with larger and thinner-walled elements formed in spring and early summer; **spring'wort** a magical root, perh. mandrake. — **spring a leak** to begin to leak; **spring a mine** to cause it to explode. [O.E. *springan*; Ger. *springen*.]

spring². See **spring¹**.

springal, springald. See **spring¹**.

springe¹ *sprinj*, *n.* a snare with noose and spring: a gin. — Also **spring** (*spring*). — *v.t.* to catch in a springe: — *pr.p.* **spring'ing**; *pa.t.* and *pa.p.* **springed** (*sprinjd*). — *n.* **springle** (*spring'gl*) a snare. [Earlier *sprenge*, from a probable O.E. *sprencg*; cf. **sprent, spring¹**.]

springe² *sprinj*, (*George Eliot*) *adj.* active, nimble. [Ety. unknown.]

sprinkle *spring'kl*, *v.t.* to scatter in small drops or particles: to scatter on: to baptise with a few drops of water: to strew, dot, diversify. — *v.i.* to scatter in drops. — *n.* an aspersorium or utensil for sprinkling. — *ns.* **sprin'kle, sprin'kling** the act of one who sprinkles: a small quantity sprinkled (also *fig.*): in bookbinding, mottling of edges by scattering a few drops of colour; **sprin'kler** any thing or person that sprinkles: any of various devices for scattering water in drops, e.g. over growing plants, as fire-extinguishers, etc. (**sprinkler system** a system of such fire-extinguishers which operate automatically on a sudden rise in temperature). [Freq. from O.E. *sprengan*, the causative of *springan*, to spring; cf. Ger. *sprenkeln*.]

sprint *sprint*, *n.* a short run, row, cycle or race at full speed. — *v.i.* to run at full speed. — *v.t.* to perform a sprint over (a given distance). — *ns.* **sprin'ter; sprint'= ting**. [Cf. O.N. *spretta*, Sw. *spritta*.]

sprit *sprit*, (*naut.*) *n.* a spar set diagonally to extend a fore-and-aft sail. — **spritsail**. (*sprit'sl*) a sail extended by a sprit. [O.E. *sprēot*, pole; Du. *spriet* and Ger. *Spriet*, sprit.]

sprite *sprīt*, *n.* spirit — *obs.* except in the senses of goblin, elf, imp, impish or implike person: in computer graphics, an icon formed of pixels, which can be moved around a screen by means of a software program. — *adjs.* **sprite'ful, sprite'ly** see **sprightful**, etc. under **spright**. [O.Fr. *esprit*; cf. **spirit, spright**.]

spritsail. See **sprit**.

spritzer *sprit'zər*, *n.* a drink of white wine and soda water. [Ger. *spritzen*, to spray, squirt.]

spritzig *shprit'zig*, (*Ger.*) *adj.* sparkling (esp. of wine). — *n.* a slightly sparkling (usu. German) white wine: the tangy quality of such a wine.

sprocket *sprok'it*, *n.* a tooth on the rim of a wheel or capstan for engaging the chain: a toothed cylinder for driving a cinematograph film: a sprocket-wheel: a piece of wood used to build a roof out over eaves. — **sprock'et-wheel** a wheel with sprockets. [Origin unknown.]

sprod *sprod*, (*Northern*) *n.* a second-year salmon. [Origin obscure.]

sprog *sprog*, *n.* a recruit (*R.A.F. slang*): a child, infant (*coll.*). [Poss. a reversed portmanteau form of **frog spawn** or a recruit's confusion of **sprocket** and **cog²**.]

sprong *sprong*, (*Spens.*) *pa.t.* and *pa.p.* of **spring¹**.

sprout *sprowt*, *n.* a new growth: a young shoot: a side bud, as in **Brussels sprouts** (see **Brussels**): a scion, descendant: sprouting condition. — *v.i.* to shoot: to push out new shoots. — *v.t.* to put forth as a sprout or bud: to cause to sprout: to remove sprouts from (*dial.*). — *adj.* **sprout'ed**. — *n.* and *adj.* **sprout'ing**. [O.E. *sprūtan* (found in compounds), Du. *spruiten*, Ger. *spriessen*.]

spruce *sprōōs*, *adj.* smart: neat, dapper: over-fastidious, finical. — *adv.* sprucely. — *v.t.* to smarten. — *v.i.* to become spruce or smart (often with *up*). — *adv.* **spruce'ly**. — *n.* **spruce'ness**. [Prob. from next word, from the vogue of 'spruce leather' (obtained from Pruce or Prussia) in the 16th century.]

Spruce *sproōs, n.* Prussia (*obs.*): (without *cap.*) any conifer of the genus Picea, with long shoots only, four-angled needles, and pendulous cones (also **spruce fir**): (without *cap.*) its wood: (without *cap.*) spruce-beer. — *adj.* brought from Prussia: (without *cap.*) of spruce or its wood. — **spruce′-beer′** a drink made from a fermentation of sugar or treacle and green tops of spruce; **spruce fir** the spruce tree: extended to some other trees; **spruce pine** a name given to various American pine trees: extended to some varieties of spruce. [For **Pruce**.]

sprue[1] *sproō, n.* a passage by which molten metal runs into a mould: the metal that solidifies in it — *dead-head.* [Origin obscure.]

sprue[2] *sproō, n.* infantile thrush (*obs.*): a tropical disease affecting mouth, throat, and digestion. [Du. *spruw.*]

sprue[3] *sproō,* (*London*) *n.* inferior asparagus.

sprug *sprug,* (*Scot.*) *n.* a sparrow.

spruik *sproōk,* (*Austr.* and *N.Z.*) *v.i.* (of a showman, etc.) to harangue people in public. — *n.* **spruik′er.** [Origin uncertain.]

spruit *sprät, sprü′it, sprīt,* (*S.Afr.*) *n.* a small, deepish watercourse, dry except during and after rains. [Du., sprout.]

sprung *sprung, pa.t.* and *pa.p.* of **spring**[1]. — *adj.* strained: split: loosed: furnished with springs: tipsy (*coll.*). — **sprung rhythm** a poetic rhythm close to the natural rhythm of speech, with mixed feet, and frequent single stressed syllables.

sprush *sproōsh, sprush, adj., adv.,* and *v.t.* a Scots form of **spruce**, or (with *cap.*) **Spruce**.

spry *sprī, adj.* nimble: agile: — *compar.* **spry′er;** *superl.* **spry′est.** — *adv.* **spry′ly.** — *n.* **spry′ness.** [Origin doubtful.]

spud *spud, n.* a small narrow digging tool: a stumpy person or thing: a potato (*slang*). — *v.t.* and *v.i.* to dig with a spud: (esp. with *in*) to start drilling (an oil-well). — *ns.* **spudd′ing, spudd′ing-in** the process of starting to drill an oil-well by boring a hole in the seabed. — *adj.* **spudd′y** podgy. — **spud′-bashing** (*slang*) peeling potatoes. [Origin obscure.]

spue. An old-fashioned spelling of **spew**.

spuilzie. See **spulzie**.

spule *spûl, spül,* (*Scot.*) *n.* the shoulder. — Also **speal** (*spēl*). — **spule′bane (-bone), -blade.** [Relation to **spauld** obscure.]

spulzie, spuilzie, spulyc, spulyie *spül′(y)i,* (*Scot.*) *n.* spoliation. — *v.t.* and *v.i.* to plunder. [See **spoil**.]

spume *spūm, n.* foam: scum. — *v.i.* to foam. — *v.t.* to throw up or off as foam or scum. — *n.* **spūmesc′ence.** — *adjs.* **spūmesc′ent** foamy, frothing; **spū′mous, spū′my.** [L. *spūma* — *spuĕre*, to spew.]

spun *spun, pa.t.* and *pa.p.* of **spin**, and *adj.* — *adj.* **spun′-out** unduly lengthened. — **spun silk** a fabric made from waste silk fibres, sometimes mixed with cotton; **spun sugar** sugar spun into fine fluffy threads, as in candy floss; **spun′-yarn** rope-yarn twisted into a cord.

spunge *spunj,* obs. spelling of **sponge**. — **spun′ging-house** see **sponge**.

spunk *spungk, n.* a spark (*dial.*, esp. *Scot.*): a spirited, usu. small or weak, person (*dial.*): spirit, mettle, courage: touchwood, tinder (*obs.*): a fungus from which tinder is made (*dial.*): a match (*dial.*): semen (*vulg.*). — *v.i.* to take fire, flame up (*arch.*): to fire up: to show spirit (usu. with *up*; *U.S.*): to come to light (*Scot.*, with *out*). — *ns.* **spunk′ie** (*Scot.*) a will-o′-the-wisp: a fiery or mettlesome person: whisky (*Burns*); **spunk′iness.** — *adj.* **spunk′y** spirited: fiery-tempered. [Cf. Ir. *sponc,* tinder, sponge — L. *spongia,* a sponge — Gr. *spongiā.*]

spur *spûr, n.* a goading instrument on a rider′s heel: incitement, stimulus: a hard sharp projection: a claw-like projection at the back of a cock′s or other bird′s leg: an artificial substitute for this on a game-cock: a short, usu. flowering or fruit-bearing, branch: a great lateral root: ergot: a tubular pouch at the base of a petal: an expansion of a leaf-base: anything that projects in the shape of a spur, as an extension from an electrical circuit: a lateral branch, as of a hill range: a siding or branch line of a railway: a strut: a structure to deflect the current from a bank. — *v.t.* to apply the spur to: to urge on: to provide with a spur or spurs: to prune into spurs. — *v.i.* to press forward with the spur: to hasten: to kick out: — *pr.p.* **spurr′ing;** *pa.t.* and *pa.p.* **spurred.** — *adjs.* **spur′less; spurred** having or wearing spurs or a spur: in the form of a spur: urged: affected with ergot, as rye. — *ns.* **spurr′er** one who, or that which, spurs; **spurr′ier** a maker of spurs. — *n.* and *adj.* **spurr′ing.** — *adj.* **spurr′y** like, of the nature of, having, a spur. — *v.t.* **spur′-gall** (*Shak.*) to gall or wound with a spur. — **spur′-gear, -gear′ing** a system of spur-wheels. — *adj.* **spur′-heeled** having a long straight hind-claw. — **spur′-leather** a strap for fastening a spur; **spur′-row′el** the rowel of a spur; **spur′-roy′al, -ry′al, -rī′al** a former English fifteen-shilling piece of gold, bearing a star like a spur-rowel; **spur′-way** (*dial.*) a bridle-road; **spur′-whang** (*Scot.*) a spur-leather; **spur′-wheel** a cog-wheel. — *adj.* **spur′-winged** with a horny spur on the pinion of the wing. — **gilt spurs** a mark of knighthood; **on the spur of the moment** without premeditation; **set spurs to** to apply the spur and ride off quickly; **win one′s spurs** to earn knighthood: to gain distinction by achievement. [O.E. *spura, spora;* O.N. *spori,* Ger. *Sporn.*]

spurge *spûrj, n.* any species of Euphorbia, a genus of very varied habit, with milky, generally poisonous, juice, and an inflorescence (cyathium) of flowers so reduced as to simulate a single flower. — **spurge′-lau′rel** a European evergreen shrub (*Daphne laureola*) with yellowish-green flowers, thick leaves, and poisonous berries. [O.Fr. *espurge* (Fr. *épurge*) — L. *expurgāre,* to purge — *ex,* off, *purgāre,* to clear.]

spurious *spūr′i-əs, adj.* bastard: illegitimate: not genuine: false: sham: forged: simulating but essentially different. — *n.pl.* **spūr′iae** (*-i-ē*) feathers of the bastard-wing. — *n.* **spurios′ity.** — *adv.* **spūr′iously.** — *n.* **spūr′iousness.** [L. *spurius,* false.]

spurling *spûr′ling.* Same as **sparling**.

spurn *spûrn, v.t.* to kick (*arch.*): to tread, esp. in contempt: to reject with contempt. — *v.i.* to trip (*obs.*): to kick (often with *at, against; arch.*). — *n.* a kick (*arch.*): kicking: disdainful rejection. — *n.* **spurn′er.** — *n.* and *adj.* **spurn′ing.** [O.E. *spornan, spurnan,* related to **spur**.]

spurne *spûrn,* (*Spens.*) *v.t.* to spur.

spurrey, *sometimes* **spurry,** *spur′i, n.* any plant of the genus Spergula: applied to kindred plants, Spergularia (*sand-wort-spurrey*) and Sagina (knotted pearlwort or *knotted spurrey*). [Du. *spurrie.*]

spurrier, spurry[1]. See **spur**.

spurry[2]. See **spurrey**.

spurt *spûrt, v.t.* to spout, or send out in a sudden stream or jet. — *v.i.* to gush out suddenly in a small stream: to flow out forcibly or at intervals: to make a sudden short intense effort. — *n.* a sudden or violent gush: a jet: a short spell, esp. of intensified effort, speed, etc. [Variant of **spirt**[1].]

spurtle *spûr′tl,* (*Scot.*) *n.* a porridge-stick: a sword (also **spur′tle-blade**). [Origin doubtful.]

sputa. See **sputum**.

sputnik *spoōt′nik, n.* a man-made earth satellite. [After the Russian *Sputnik* (′travelling companion′) 1, the first such satellite, put in orbit in 1957.]

sputter *sput′ər, v.i.* to spit or throw out moisture in scattered drops: to speak rapidly and indistinctly, to jabber: to make a noise of sputtering. — *v.t.* to spit out or throw out in or with small drops: to utter hastily and indistinctly: to remove atoms from a cathode by positive ion bombardment — the unchanged atoms being deposited on a surface, and the process being used for coating glass, plastic, another metal, etc., with a thin film of metal (*n.* **sputt′ering**). — *n.* sputtering: matter sputtered out. — *n.* **sputt′erer.** — *n.* and *adj.* **sputt′ering.** — *adv.* **sputt′eringly.** — *adj.* **sputt′ery.**

[Imit.; cf. Du. *sputteren*, and **spit²**.]

sputum *spū'təm, n.* matter spat out: — *pl.* **spū'ta.** [L. *spūtum* — *spuĕre*, to spit.]

spy *spī, n.* a secret agent employed to watch others or to collect information, esp. of a military nature: a spying: a look: an eye (*fig.*): — *pl.* **spies.** — *v.t.* to watch, observe, investigate, or ascertain secretly (often with *out*): to descry, make out: to discover. — *v.i.* to play the spy: — *pr.p.* **spy'ing;** *pa.t.* and *pa.p.* **spied;** *3rd pers. pres. indic.* **spies.** — *n.* **spy'al** (*Spens.*) a spy (see **spial**). — *n.* and *adj.* **spy'ing.** — **spy'glass** a small hand-telescope; **spy'-hole** a peep-hole; **spy'master** a person who controls and coordinates the activities of undercover agents; **spy'-money** money paid for secret intelligence. [O.Fr. *espie* (n.), *espier* (vb.); see **espy**.]

spyre. Obs. spelling (*Spens.*) of **spire¹**.

squab *skwob, adj.* fat, clumsy: unfledged, newly hatched: shy, coy: curt, abrupt (*obs.*): having a squab. — *n.* a young pigeon or rook: a fledgling: a young chicken (*U.S.*): a short stumpy person: a soft thick cushion: a padded sofa or ottoman: a carriage cushion: the back part of a motor-car seat. — *v.t.* to upholster or stuff thickly and sew through in places. - *v.i.* to fall heavily. — *adv.* plump and squashily. — *adjs.* **squabb'ish** thick, heavy; **squabb'y** squat. — **squab'-pie** a pie made of mutton or pork, onions, and apples. [Poss. Scand.; cf. Sw. dial. *sqvabb*, loose flesh, *sqvabbig*, flabby.]

squabash *skwə-bash', v.t.* to crush, smash. — *n.* a crushing. — *n.* **squabash'er.** [Prob. **squash¹** and **bash**.]

squabbish. See **squab**.

squabble *skwob'l, v.i.* to dispute in a noisy manner: to wrangle. — *n.* a noisy, petty quarrel: a brawl. — *n.* **squabb'ler.** [Cf. Sw. dial. *sqvabbel*.]

squabby. See **squab**.

squacco *skwak'ō, n.* a small crested heron: — *pl.* **squacc'os.** [It. dial. *sguacco*.]

squad *skwod, n.* a small group of soldiers drilled or working together: any working party: a set or group: a team or a set of players trained in readiness for the selection of a team (*sport*). — *n.* **squadd'y** (*mil. coll.*) a private, an ordinary soldier. — **squad car** a police car. — **awkward squad** a body of recruits not yet competent in drill, etc. [Fr. *escouade*; cf. Sp. *escuadra*, It. *squadra*.]

squadron *skwod'rən, n.* a body of soldiers drawn up in a square (*obs.*): a detachment, body, group: a division of a cavalry regiment under a major or captain: a section of a fleet under a flag-officer: a group of aeroplanes forming a unit under one command. — *v.t.* to form into squadrons. — *adjs.* **squad'ronal; squad'roned.** — **squad'ron-lead'er** an air-force officer answering in rank to a lieutenant-commander or major; **squadrone (volante)** (*skwa-drō'nā* (*vō-län'tā*)*;* It., flying squadron) an early 18th-cent. Scottish political party opposed to the Argathelians. [It. *squadrone* — *squadra*, square.]

squail *skwāl, v.i.* to throw sticks (as at birds or fruit). — *v.t.* to pelt with sticks: to hit by throwing a stick. — *n.* a stick for throwing: a counter for playing squails: (in *pl.*) ninepins: (in *pl.*) a parlour-game in which small discs are snapped from the edge of the table to a centre mark. — *ns.* **squail'er** a throwing-stick; **squail'ing.** [Cf. **kail¹** (obs. *skail, skayle*), a ninepin.]

squalid *skwol'id, adj.* filthy, foul: neglected, uncared-for, unkempt: sordid and dingy: poverty-stricken. — *n.* **squalid'ity.** — *adv.* **squal'idly.** — *ns.* **squal'idness; squal'or** the state of being squalid: dirtiness: filthiness. [L. *squālidus*, stiff, rough, dirty, *squālor*, -*ōris*.]

squall *skwöl, v.i.* to cry out violently: to yell: to sing loudly and unmusically: of wind, to blow in a squall. — *v.t.* to sing or utter loudly and unmusically. — *n.* a loud cry or yell: a short violent wind. — *n.* **squall'er.** — *n.* and *adj.* **squall'ing.** — *adj.* **squall'y** abounding or disturbed with squalls or gusts of wind: gusty, blustering: threatening a squall. — **white squall** a tropical whirlwind, coming on without warning other than a small white cloud. [Prob. imit.]

squaloid *skwā'loid, adj.* of or pertaining to sharks of the suborder *Squaloideae*: like a shark. [L. *squālus*, a sea-fish of the shark or dogfish group.]

squalor. See **squalid**.

squama *skwā'mə, skwä'mə, n.* a scale: a scale-like structure: the exopodite of an antenna in Crustacea: — *pl.* **squa'mae** (-*mē*, -*mī*). — *n.pl.* **Squamā'ta** (*skwə-*) an order of reptiles — snakes and lizards. — *adj.* **squā'mate** scaly. — *ns.* **squamā'tion** (*skwə-*) scaliness: the mode of arrangement of scales; **squame** (*skwām*) a scale or squama; **squamell'a** (*skwə-*) a little scale. — *adj.* **squā'miform** like a scale. — *n.* **squamosal** (*skwə-mō'sl*) a paired membrane bone of the vertebrate skull, the squamous portion of the temporal bone. — Also *adj.* — *adjs.* **squā'mose, squā'mous** scaly. — *ns.* **squāmos'ity; squamula** (*skwam'ū-lə*, or *skwām'*), **squam'ule** a little scale. — *adj.* **squam'ulose.** [L. *squāma*, a scale.]

squander *skwon'dər, v.t.* to scatter, disperse (*obs.*): to spend lavishly or wastefully. — *v.i.* to wander, roam, straggle: to scatter. — *n.* a squandering. — *adj.* **squan'dered.** — *n.* **squan'derer.** — *n.* and *adj.* **squan'dering.** - *adv.* **squan'deringly.** — *n.* **squandermā'nia** (*slang*) a spirit of reckless expenditure (in a government). [Origin obscure.]

square *skwär, n.* an equilateral rectangle: an object, piece, space, figure, of approximately that shape, as a window-pane, paving-stone, space on a chessboard: an open space, commonly but not necessarily of that shape, in a town, along with its surrounding buildings: a rectangular block of buildings (*U.S.*): a body of troops drawn up in that form: the product of a quantity multiplied by itself: the yoke of a garment (*Shak.*): a unit of flooring, 100 square feet: an instrument for drawing or testing right angles: a carpenter's measure: a canon, criterion, rule (*obs.*): squareness: quartile aspect (*old astron.*): due proportion: order: honesty, equity, fairness: quarrel, dissension (*obs.*): possibly part, compartment (*Shak., King Lear* I, i): a person of narrow, traditional outlook and opinions, esp. in musical taste or dress (*slang*). — *adj.* having or approaching the form of a square: relatively broad, thick-set: right-angled: in football, etc., in a line, position, etc., across the pitch: equal to a quantity multiplied by itself: measuring an area in two dimensions: exact, suitable, fitting: true, equitable, fair, honest: even, leaving no balance, equal in score: directly opposed: complete, unequivocal: solid, full, satisfying: (of taste in music, dress, etc.), traditional and orthodox (*slang*): bourgeois in attitude (*slang*). — *v.t.* to make square or rectangular, esp. in cross-section: to make nearly cubical: to form into squares: to construct or determine a square equal to: to multiply by itself: to reduce to any given measure or standard, to adjust, regulate: to bring into accord, reconcile: to place at right angles with the mast or keel (*naut.*): to make equal: to pay: to bribe: (with *with*) to get (someone's) agreement, approval or permission for something. — *v.i.* to suit, fit: to accord or agree: to take an attitude of offence and defence, as a boxer (often with *up to* — see below): to swagger (*obs.*): to make the score or account even. — *adv.* at right angles: solidly: directly: evenly: fairly, honestly. — *adj.* **squared.** — *adv.* **square'ly.** — *ns.* **square'ness; squar'er** one who or that which squares: a fighting, quarrelsome person, or perh. a swaggerer (*Shak.*). — *adv.* **square'-wise.** — *n.* and *adj.* **squar'ing.** — *adj.* **squar'ish.** — **square'-bashing** parade-ground drill (*mil. slang*). — *adj.* **square'-built** of a form suggesting squareness: broad in proportion to height. — **square'-dance** a folk-dance done by a group of couples in a square formation; **square'-danc'ing; square deal** (*coll.*) a fair and honest arrangement, transaction, etc.; **square'-face** (*S.Afr.*) gin (from the shape of the bottle); **square foot, inch, mile** an area equal to that of a square whose side measures a foot, etc.; **square'-head** a Scandinavian or German (*slang*); **square knot** a reef-knot; **square'-leg** (*cricket*) a fielder to the left of, and in line with, the batsman; **square meal** a full, satisfying meal; **square=meas'ure** a system of measures for surfaces, its unit the square of the lineal unit; **square mile** see **square foot**: (usu. with *caps.*) the City of London, specif. the area around and including the Bank of England: financial life, activities, etc. in the City of London (*fig.*); **square number** a number the square root of which is an integer. — *adjs.* **square'-pierced** (*her.*) having a square opening so as to show the field; **square'-rigged** having the chief sails square, and extended by yards suspended by the middle at right angles to the masts — opp. to *fore-and-aft.* — **square'-rigg'er** a square-rigged ship; **square root** that quantity which being multiplied into itself produces the quantity in question; **square'-sail** (*-sl*) a four-sided sail extended by yards suspended by the middle generally at right angles to the mast. — *adjs.* **square'-shoul'dered** with broad, straight shoulders; **square'-toed** ending square at the toes. — **square'-toes** (*pl.*) square-toed shoes: (*sing.*) an old-fashioned, punctilious person (*arch.*). — **back to square one** back to the original position with the problem, etc., unchanged; **how squares go** (*obs.*) what is doing: how things are going; **on the square** honestly; **square up** (*coll.*) to settle (a bill, account, etc.); **square up to** face up to and tackle; **squaring the circle (quadrature of the circle)** finding a square of the same area as a circle — for hundreds of years this was attempted by Euclidian means (i.e. with straight-edge and compass) until in 1882 it was proved impossible: any impossible task. [O.Fr. *esquarre* (Fr. *équerre*) — L. *ex* and *quadra*, a square.]

squarrose *skwar'ōs, skwor'ōs, -ōs'*, *adj.* rough with projecting or deflexed scales, bracts, etc.: standing out straight or deflexed. [L. *squarrōsus*, scurfy.]

squarson *skwär'sn, n.* a clergyman who is also a squire or landowner in his parish. — *n.* **squar'sonage** his residence. [*squire* and *parson.*]

squash¹ *skwosh, v.t.* to press into pulp: to crush flat: to squeeze: to put down, suppress: to snub. — *v.i.* to form a soft mass as from a fall: to crowd: to squelch: to become crushed or pulpy. — *n.* an unripe peascod (*Shak.*): anything soft and unripe or easily crushed: a crushed mass: a drink made from fruit juice: a crushed condition: a close crowd: a squeezing: a soft rubber ball for playing squash: a game for two or four players played with a small rubber ball, which is struck with a racket against the walls of an enclosed court (also **squash rackets, racquets**). — *adv.* with a squash. — *adj.* **squash'able.** — *n.* **squash'er.** — *adv.* **squash'ily.** — *n.* **squash'iness.** — *adj.* **squash'y** pulpy: squelching: sopping. — **squash tennis** a game for two players similar to squash rackets (see above) but played with an inflated ball and larger rackets. [O.Fr. *esquacer* (Fr. *écacher*), to crush — L. *ex, quassāre*; see **quash**.]

squash² *skwosh, n.* the gourd of several species of Cucurbita: the plant bearing it. [Narragansett *askutasquash.*]

squat *skwot, v.i.* to sit down upon the hams or heels: to sit close, as an animal: to settle on land or in unoccupied buildings without title or (*Austr.*) with a view to acquiring a title. — *v.t.* to cause to squat: — *pr.p.* **squat'ing;** *pa.t.* and *pa.p.* **squat'ed.** — *adj.* crouching: short and thick, dumpy. — *n.* the act of squatting: a building in which people are squatting (*coll.*). — *ns.* **squat'ness; squatt'er** one who squats: a large landowner (*Austr.*); **squatt'iness.** — *v.t.* and *v.i.* **squatt'le** to squat down. — *n.* **squattoc'racy** (*Austr.*) the powerful squatter class. — *adj.* **squatt'y** short and thick. [O.Fr. *esquatir*, to crush — L. *ex, coactus*, pa.p. of *cōgere*, to drive together.]

squatter¹ *skwot'ər, v.i.* to splash along. — *n.* a fluttering: a splashing, spattering. [Prob. imit.]

squatter² . . . **squattle** . . . **squatty.** See **squat.**

squaw *skwö, n.* an American Indian woman, esp. a wife. — **squaw'man** a white man with an Indian wife. [Massachusett *squa.*]

squawk *skwök, n.* a croaky call or cry: a complaint, protest (*slang*). — *v.i.* to utter a squawk: to complain (*slang*). — *v.t.* to utter with a squawk. — *n.* **squawk'er.** — *n.* and *adj.* **squawk'ing.** — *adj.* **squawk'y.** [Imit.]

squeak *skwēk, v.i.* to give forth a high-pitched nasal-sounding note or cry: to inform or confess (*slang*). — *v.t.* to utter, sing, render, squeakily. — *n.* a squeaky sound: a narrow escape: a bare chance: the slimmest of margins: a tiny amount: a feeble newspaper (*slang*). — *ns.* **squeak'er** one who or that which squeaks: a young bird: an informer: a squeaking toy consisting of a bladder and a tube; **squeak'ery.** — *adv.* **squeak'ily.** — *n.* **squeak'iness.** — *n.* and *adj.* **squeak'ing.** — *adv.* **squeak'ingly.** — *adj.* **squeak'y,** — — *adj.* **squeak'y-clean'** orig., of wet hair, so clean that it squeaks when pulled: spotlessly clean: (often slightly *derog.*) of a person, impeccable, wholesome, virtuous. — **squeak through** to succeed, pass, win, etc. only by a narrow margin. [Imit.; cf. Sw. *sqväka*, to croak, Ger. *quieken*, to squeak.]

squeal *skwēl, v.i.* to utter a high-pitched cry of some duration: to cry out in pain: to complain: to turn informer (*slang*). — *v.t.* to utter, sing, render, express, with squealing. — *n.* a high sustained cry. — *n.* **squeal'er** one who squeals, esp. a bird of various kinds, a young pigeon: an informer (*slang*). — *n.* and *adj.* **squeal'ing.** [Imit.; cf. Sw. dial. *sqväla*, to cry out.]

squeamish *skwēm'ish, adj.* sick: easily nauseated: qualmish: easily shocked, disgusted, or offended: fastidious: coy: reluctant from scruples or compunction. — *adv.* **squeam'ishly.** — *n.* **squeam'ishness.** [M.E. *scoymous* — A.Fr. *escoymous*; ety. dub.]

squeedge *skwēj,* an *illit.* form of **squeeze.**

squeegee *skwē'jē, -jē',* also **squilgee** *skwil'jē, ns.* an implement with edge of rubber, leather, etc., for clearing water or mud from decks, floors, windows, etc.: a photographer's roller or brush for squeezing out moisture. — *v.t.* to clear, press, or smooth with a squeegee. [App. **squeeze.**]

squeeze *skwēz, v.t.* to crush, press hard, compress: to grasp tightly: to embrace: to force by pressing: to effect, render, or put by pressing: to crush the juice or liquid from: to force to discard winning cards: to fleece, extort from: to take a rubbing of. — *v.i.* to press: to crowd: to crush: to force a way: to yield to pressure. — *n.* the act of squeezing: pressure: a restriction or time of restriction (usually financial or commercial): a crowded assembly: an embrace: a close grasp: a portion withheld and appropriated as by an Oriental official: a rubbing: a few drops got by squeezing: play that forces an opponent to discard a potentially winning card (also **squeeze play**) (*bridge*). — *n.* **squeezabil'ity.** — *adj.* **squeez'able.** — *n.* **squeez'er** one who squeezes: an instrument, machine, or part, for squeezing: a playing-card marked in the corner with suit and value. — *n.* and *adj.* **squeez'ing.** — *adj.* **squeez'y** confined, cramped, contracted. — **squeeze'-box** (*slang*) a concertina. — **squeeze home** to win, succeed, etc. with difficulty or narrowly. [Origin obscure.]

squegging *skweg'ing,* (*electronics* and *telecomm.*) *n.* a type of oscillation in which the oscillations build up to a certain value and then stop for a time before resuming. — Also *adj.* — *v.i.* **squeg** (back-formation) to oscillate intermittently or irregularly. — *n.* **squegg'er** a squegging oscillator. [Orig. uncertain, poss. from *self-quenching.*]

squelch *skwelch, skwelsh, n.* the gurgling and sucking sound of walking in wet mud: a heavy blow on, or fall of, a soft body: its sound: a pulpy mass: a disconcerting or quashing retort or rebuff. — *v.i.* to make, or walk with, the sound of a squelch. — *v.t.* to crush under heel: to put down, suppress, snub, crush. — *n.* **squelch'er** one who squelches: an overwhelming blow, retort, etc. — *n.* and *adj.* **squelch'ing.** — *adj.* **squelch'y.** [Imit.; cf. **quelch.**]

squeteague *skwi-tēg', n.* an Atlantic American spiny-finned food-fish (*Cynoscion*), misnamed salmon or trout. [Narragansett *pesukwiteaug*, they make glue.]

squib *skwib, n.* a firework, consisting of a paper tube fitted with explosive powder, which burns noisily and explodes: a petty lampoon: a paltry fellow (*Spens.*). — *v.t.* to aim squibs at: to lampoon. — *v.i.* to write lampoons: to use squibs: to sound or skip about like a squib. — *n.* and *adj.* **squibb'ing.** — **damp squib** see **damp.** [Perh. imit.]

squid *skwid, n.* any ten-armed cephalopod, esp. Loligo: a bait or lure of, or in imitation of, a squid: an anti-submarine mortar: — *pl.* **squid, squids.** — *v.i.* to fish with a squid. [Origin obscure.]

squidge *skwij, v.t.* to squeeze, squash (something soft, moist, pulpy, etc.). — *adj.* **squid'gy** squashy: soft, wet and springy: gooey. [Imit.]

squier. See **squire**[2].

squiffer *skwif'ər, (slang) n.* a concertina.

squiff(y) *skwif('i), (coll.) adjs.* tipsy.

squiggle *skwig'l, v.i.* to squirm, wriggle: to make wriggly lines. — *n.* a twist, wriggle, wriggly line. — *adj.* **squigg'ly.** [Imit., or poss. from *squi*rm and wri*ggle.*]

squilgee. See **squeegee.**

squill *skwil, n.* any plant of the liliaceous genus Scilla: the sea-onion (*Urginea*), formerly included in that genus: (usu. in *pl.*) its dried bulbs used as a diuretic and expectorant: the mantis shrimp (**Squilla**). [L. *squilla, scilla,* sea-onion, shrimp — Gr. *skilla,* sea-onion.]

squinancy *skwin'ən-si, (obs.) n.* quinsy. — *n.* **squin'ancy=wort** a species of woodruff once thought good for quinsy. [L.L. *squinanchia,* a combination of Gr. *synanchē,* sore throat, and *kynanchē* (see **cynanche**).]

squinch *skwinch, skwinsh, n.* an arch or other support across a re-entrant or interior angle. [**scuncheon.**]

squinny *skwin'i,* **squiny** *skwī'ni, (Shak.) vs.i.* to squint, peer.

squint *skwint, adv.* asquint, obliquely. — *adj.* looking obliquely: looking askance: squinting: strabismic: oblique: indirect. — *v.i.* to look obliquely: to have the eyes focusing in different directions, either by purposely crossing them, or by strabismus: to have a side reference or allusion: to hint disapprobation: to glance aside or casually: to glance. — *v.t.* to cause to squint: to direct or divert obliquely. — *n.* the act or habit of squinting: strabismus: an oblique look: a glance: a peep: an oblique reference, hint, tendency, or aim: an oblique opening in a wall, as a hagioscope. — *n.* **squint'er.** — *n.* and *adj.* **squint'ing.** — *adv.* **squint'ingly.** — **squint'-eye(s)** one who squints. — *adj.* **squint'-eyed.** [Aphetic for **asquint.**]

squiny. See **squinny.**

squire[1] *skwīr, n.* an esquire, an aspirant to knighthood attending a knight: one who escorts or attends a lady: an English or Irish landed gentleman, esp. of old family: one who has been a justice of the peace, etc. (*U.S.*): in some parts of Britain, a form of sometimes ironically respectful address. — *v.t.* to escort or attend. — *ns.* **squir(e)'age, squiral'ity, squir'alty** landed gentry collectively; **squir(e)'arch.** — *adjs.* **squir(e)arch'al, squir(e)arch'ical.** — *ns.* **squir(e)'archy** the rule of squires: the body of squires; **squire'dom; squireen'** (Ir. dim. suff. *-ín; Anglo- Ir.*) a petty squire; **squire'hood.** — *adjs.* and *advs.* **squire'-like, squire'ly.** — *ns.* **squire'-ling** a squire of small possessions; **squire'ship; squir'ess** a squire's wife. — **squire of dames** one who devotes himself to the ladies, from a character in Spenser (*Faerie Queene* III, vii. 53). [**esquire.**]

squire[2], **squier** *skwīr, (Spens., Shak.) n.* a carpenter's square or rule: a canon, rule. — **by the squire** precisely. [See **square.**]

squirm *skwûrm, v.i.* to writhe, go writhing. — *n.* a wriggle. — *adj.* **squirm'y.** [Prob. imit.]

squirr. Same as **skirr.**

squirrel *skwir'əl, n.* a nimble, bushy-tailed arboreal rodent (Sciurus or kindred genus): the pelt of such an animal: a person who hoards things (*fig.*). — *adj.* made of the pelt of a squirrel. — *v.t.* to hoard (usu. with *away*). — *adj.* **squirr'el(l)y** like a squirrel: nervous, jumpy. —

squirr'el-cage a cage with a treadwheel for a squirrel: in an induction motor, a rotor whose winding suggests this; **squirr'el-monkey** a small golden-haired South American monkey; **squirr'el-shrew** a tree-shrew; **squirr'el-tail** a grass of the barley genus with long hair-like awns: a broad-tailed lobworm (*Walton*): a cap of squirrel-skins, with a tail hanging down behind. [O.Fr. *escurel* — L.L. *scurellus,* dim. of L. *sciūrus* — Gr. *skiouros* — *skiā,* shade, *ourā,* tail.]

squirt *skwûrt, v.t.* to throw out in a jet. — *v.i.* to spirt. — *n.* an instrument for squirting: a jet: an unimportant and irritatingly pretentious person (*slang*). — *n.* **squirt'er.** — *n.* and *adj.* **squirt'ing.** — **squirting cucumber** a cucurbitaceous plant (*Ecballium elaterium*) that squirts out its ripe seeds. [Cf. L.G. *swirtjen, swürtjen.*]

squish *skwish, v.i.* to make a squelching or squirting sound. — *n.* the sound of squishing: bosh (*slang*): marmalade (*slang*). — *adj.* **squish'y.** — **squish lip system** a type of diesel engine combustion chamber designed to lessen fumes and noise pollution.

squit *skwit, (slang) n.* a contemptible person: nonsense. [Cf. **squirt.**]

squitch *skwich, n.* quitch-grass.

sraddha, shraddha *s(h)rä'dä, ns.* an offering to the manes of an ancestor. [Sans. *śrāddha.*]

Sri, Shri *shrē,* in India a title of great respect given to a man, now generally used as the equivalent of *Mr.* [Sans. *śrī,* majesty, holiness.]

st, 'st *st, interj.* hush: a sound made to attract someone's attention: — *pl.* **st's.**

'st *st,* a shortened form of **hast.**

stab *stab, v.t.* to wound or pierce by driving in a pointed weapon: to give a sharp pain (also *fig.*): to roughen with a pick so as to hold plaster: to pierce near the back edges, for the passage of thread or wire (*bookbinding*). — *v.i.* to thrust or pierce with a pointed weapon: — *pr.p.* **stabb'ing;** *pa.t.* and *pa.p.* **stabbed.** — *n.* an act of stabbing: a wound with a pointed weapon. — *n.* **stabb'er.** — *n.* and *adj.* **stabb'ing.** — *adv.* **stabb'ingly.** — **have a stab at** (*coll.*) to have a go at, attempt; **stab in the back** (*lit.* and *fig.*) to injure in a treacherous manner. [Cf. **stob.**]

Stabat Mater *stä'bat mä'tər, stä'bat mä'ter,* a Latin hymn on the seven dolours of the Virgin: a musical setting of it. [Its opening words, the mother stood.]

stabile, stabilise, etc., stability. See **stable**[1].

stable[1] *stā'bl, adj.* standing firm: firmly established: durable: firm in purpose or character: constant: not ready to change: not radioactive. — *adj.* **stā'bile** (*-bīl, -bil*) stable (*rare*): not moving: not fluctuating: not decomposing readily, e.g. under moderate heat. — *n.* an abstract art construction of metal, wire, wood, differing from a mobile in having no movement. — *ns.* **stabilisation, -z-** (*stab-, stāb-i-lī-zā'shən,* or *-li-*); **sta'bilisātor, -z-.** — *v.t.* **stabilise, -ize** (*stab', stāb'*) to render stable or steady: to fix: to fix the value of: to establish, maintain, or regulate the equilibrium of. — *ns.* **stab'iliser, -z-** anything that stabilises: an additional plane or other device for giving stability to an aircraft: a gyroscope or other means of steadying a ship: a substance that retards chemical action: (in *pl.*) an extra pair of small wheels attatched to a child's bicycle; **stability** (*stəbil'i-ti*) the state of being stable: steadiness: fixity: the power of recovering equilibrium: the fixing by vow of a monk or nun to one convent for life; **stā'bleness.** — *adv.* **stā'bly.** — **stable equilibrium** the condition in which a body will return to its old position after a slight displacement. [Fr., — L. *stabilis* — *stāre,* to stand.]

stable[2] *stā'bl, n.* a building for horses, or sometimes other animals: a set of horses kept together: a horse-keeping establishment, organisation, or staff (as a horse-keeping establishment often *pl.* in form but treated as *sing.*): a number of skilled trained (esp. young) persons who work together under one head or one manager: a group of commercial (esp. publishing) enterprises under the same ownership or management: (in *pl.*) a cavalry soldier's duty in the stable, or the call summoning to it. — *v.t.* to put or keep in a stable. — *v.i.* to dwell in a stable or as in a stable. — *ns.* sta′bler (*Scot., arch.*) a stable-keeper, an inn-keeper; sta′bling the act of putting into a stable: accommodation for horses, cattle, cycles, etc. — sta′ble-boy, -girl, -man one who works at a stable; stable companion one who lodges in the same place or is a member of the same club, etc. (*coll.*); stable lad, lass one whose job is to look after the horses at a racing-stable; sta′blemate a horse from the same stable as another: anything manufactured, originated, produced, etc., in the same place as another (e.g. different models of the same car), or a person from the same club, etc. as another (*fig.*); sta′ble-room accommodation in a stable. — out of the same stable having the same social background, esp. a privileged one. [O.Fr. *estable* (Fr. *étable*) — L. *stabulum* — *stāre*, to stand.]

stablish *stab′lish*, (*B., Shak., Milt., arch.*) *v.t.* old form of establish: to set up: to make stable: to confirm. — *n.* stab′lishment establishment: confirmed possession (*Shak.*).

staccato *stə-kä′tō, stäk-kä′tō,* (*mus.*) *adj.* and *adv.* with each note detached. — *n.* a staccato performance, manner, or passage: — *pl.* stacca′tos. — *adj.* and *adv.* (*superl.*) staccatis′simo. [It., pa.p. of *staccare,* for *distaccare,* to separate.]

stack[1] *stak, n.* a large built-up pile of hay, corn, wood, etc.: a group or cluster of chimneys or flues, or a single tall chimney: the chimney or funnel of a steamer, steam-engine, etc.: an isolated pillar of rock, often rising from the sea: a set of compactly arranged bookcases for storing books not on the open shelves of a library: a temporary storage area for data in a computer memory: a pyramid of three rifles, etc.: an ordered, built-up pile: a standard quantity of gambler's chips bought at one time: aircraft waiting to land and circling at definite heights according to instructions: a large amount (*slang*). — *v.t.* to pile into a stack: to shuffle (cards) for cheating: to arrange (aircraft waiting to land) in a stack (see above). — *adj.* stacked piled in a stack: of shoe-heels, made of horizontal layers of leather: (also well′-stacked′) of a woman, having a large bust (*slang*). — *ns.* stack′er a person who stacks: a machine for stacking (e.g. products in a manufactory); stack′ing. — stack′-room in a library, a room where books are stored in stacks; stack′yard a yard for stacks. — stack against, in favour of to arrange (circumstances) to the disadvantage, advantage, of (have the cards stacked against, in favour of to be faced with circumstances arranged in this way); stack up to pile or load high. [O.N. *stakkr,* a stack of hay.]

stack[2]. See stick[1].

stacket *stak′it,* (*obs. Scot.*) *n.* a palisade. [Du. *staket.*]

stacte *stak′tē, n.* a Jewish spice, liquid myrrh. — *n.* stactom′eter a pipette for counting drops. [Gr. *staktos, -ē, -on,* dropping.]

stadda *stad′ə, n.* a comb-maker's double-bladed handsaw. [Origin unknown.]

staddle *stad′l, n.* a support, esp. for a stack of hay, etc.: the bottom of a stack: a small tree left unfelled: a stump left for coppice. — stadd′le-stone′ a low mushroomshaped arrangement of a conical and flat, circular stone, used as a support for a hay stack. [O.E. *stathol,* foundation; Ger. *Stadel.*]

stade. See stadium.

stadholder. See stadtholder.

stadia[1] *stā′di-ə, n.* a graduated rod used in measuring distances at one observation, by the angle subtended by the distance between two hairs in the telescope (also sta′dia-rod′): the telescope so used (*U.S.*). [Ety. dub.]

stadia[2], stadial. See stadium.

stadium *stā′di-əm, n.* a Greek measure of length, 600 Greek, or 606¾ English feet: a race-course, sportsground: a stage in development (e.g. of a glacier, culture, geological or evolutionary period): — *pl.* stā′dia, stadiums. — *ns.* stade (*stād*) a stadium; stād′ial a substage within a period of glaciation or the life of a glacier during which the temperature drops or the ice advances. — *adj.* of or pertaining to a stage, stadium or stadial. [Latinised from Gr. *stadion.*]

stadtholder *stat′hōl-dər, stät′,* stadholder *stad′, städ′, ns.* a Dutch viceroy or provincial governor: the head of the Dutch republic (*hist.*). [Du. *stadhouder,* lit. steadholder (Ger. *Statthalter,* Fr. *lieutenant*) — *stad,* place (now only town), *houder,* holder; spelling influenced by Ger. *Stadt,* town.]

staff *stäf, n.* a stick carried in the hand: a prop: a long piece of wood: a pole: a flagstaff: a long handle: a stick or ensign of authority: a token authorising an enginedriver to proceed: a set of lines and spaces on which music is written or printed: a stanza: in a watch or clock, the spindle of a balance-wheel (these have *pl.* staffs or staves *stāvz*; see also stave): a body of officers who help a commanding officer, or perform special duties: a body of persons employed in an establishment, usu. on management, administration, clerical, etc., work as distinct from manual: the body of teachers or lecturers in a school, college, university, etc. (these three meanings have *pl.* staffs *stäfs*). — *adj.* (or in composition) belonging or attached to the staff: applied also to officers of a higher grade. — *v.t.* to provide with a staff. — *n.* staff′er a member of the permanent staff of a business, etc., usu. as opposed to temporary or casual employees. — staff′-coll′ege a college that trains officers for staff appointments; staff′-corps a body of officers and men assisting a commanding officer and his staff: formerly a body that supplied officers to the Indian army; staff′-duty the occupation of an officer who serves on a staff, having been detached from his regiment; staff′-notation musical notation in which a staff is used, as opposed to the tonic sol-fa system; staff nurse a nurse immediately below a sister in rank; staff′-off′icer an officer serving on a staff; staff′room a room for the use of the staff, as of a school; staff′-ser′geant a non-commissioned officer serving on a regimental staff; staff′-sur′geon a navy surgeon of senior grade: an army surgeon on the staff of a hospital, not with his regiment; staff′-sys′tem a block-system that uses a staff; staff′-tree an American shrub (*Celastrus*) akin to spindle-tree. — staff of life staple food, esp. bread. [O.E. *stæf,* O.N. *stafr,* Ger. *Stab.*]

staffage *sta-fäzh′, n.* accessories in a picture. [Sham Fr., — Ger. *staffieren,* to garnish.]

stag *stag, n.* a male deer, esp. a red deer over four years old: a male of various kinds (cock, turkey-cock, etc.): a man who goes to dances, etc., unaccompanied by a woman: a stag-party (*U.S.*): (*Scot.* staig *stāg*) a colt or stallion: (*Scot.* staig) an animal castrated in maturity: one who applies for shares in order to sell at once at a profit: an informer (*obs. slang*). — *adj.* male: of or for males. — *v.t.* to follow, dog, shadow. — *v.i.* to deal as a stag (also *v.t.* with *it* or *the market*): to go as a stag. — *n.* stagg′ard a deer, esp. a red deer, in its fourth year. — stag′-beet′le any beetle of the family *Lucanidae,* from the large antler-like mandibles of the males; stag′-dance one of men only; stag′-head dying back of a tree giving antler-like appearance. — *adj.* stag′-head′ed. — stag′horn stag's antler as a material (stag′horn-fern′ Platycerium, a fern with antler-like leaves; staghorn moss common club-moss); stag′hound the buck-hound: the Scottish deer-hound; stag′-hunt; stag′-party a party of men only, esp. one held for a man about to be married. [O.E. *stagga,* stag; cf. O.N. *steggr,* cock-bird, gander, in mod. Icel. he-cat.]

stage *stāj, n.* a tier, shelf, floor, storey: a tiered structure for plants: a scaffold: an elevated platform, esp. for acting on: the theatre: theatrical representation: the theatrical calling: any field of action, scene: a place of rest on a journey or road: the portion of a journey between two such places: in a microscope, etc., the support for an object to be examined: a subdivision of a geological series or formation: a point reached in, or a section of, life, development, or any process: a stagecoach: one of the sections in a step-rocket: one of the elements in a complex piece of electronic equipment. — *adj.* pertaining to the stage: as conventionally represented on the stage (e.g. *a stage rustic*). — *v.t.* to represent or put on the stage: to contrive dramatically, organise and bring off. — *v.i.* (or *v.t.* with *it*) to travel by stages or by stagecoach (*obs.*). — *adj.* **staged** in storeys or tiers: put on the stage. — *ns.* **sta′ger** one who has had much experience in anything, an old hand (*old stager*): a stage-horse: an actor (*arch.*); **sta′gery** theatrical contrivances. — *adv.* **sta′gily.** — *ns.* **stag′iness; sta′ging** scaffolding: stagecoaching: putting on the stage: the jettisoning of any of the stages of a rocket. — *adj.* **sta′gy** (also **sta′gey**) savouring of the stage: artificially histrionic. — **stage′-box** a box over the proscenium; **stage′coach** formerly, a coach that ran regularly with passengers from stage to stage; **stage′-coaching; stage′coachman; stage′-craft** skill in the technicalities of the theatre; **stage′-direc′tion** in a copy of a play, an instruction to the actor to do this or that; **stage′-door** the actors' entrance to a theatre; **stage′=driver** one who drives a stage; **stage′-effect′** theatrical effect; **stage′-fe′ver** a passion to go on the stage; **stage′-flower** a flower exhibited on a tiered stand; **stage′-fright** nervousness before an audience, esp. for the first time (also *fig.*); **stage′-hand** a workman employed about the stage; **stage′-horse** a stagecoach horse. — *v.t.* **stage′-man′age** (back-formation) used *lit.*: also *fig.*, to arrange (an event) effectively as if it were a stage scene. — **stage′-man′ager** one who superintends the production of plays, with general charge behind the curtain; **stage′-name** a name assumed professionally by an actor or actress; **stage′-play** a play played or intended to be played on a stage; **stage′=play′er.** — *n.pl.* **stage rights** legal rights to perform a play. — *adj.* **stage′-struck** sorely smitten with stage-fever. — **stage′-thun′der** apparatus, such as a thunder-sheet, used in a theatre to produce an imitation of the sound of thunder; **stage′-wag′on** a wagon for conveying goods and passengers at fixed times; **stage′-whis′per** an audible utterance conventionally understood by the audience to represent a whisper: a loud whisper meant to be heard by people other than the person addressed; **sta′ging-area, -base** a point for the assembly of troops en route for an operation; **sta′ging-post** a regular point of call on an air-route. — **stage left, right** at the left or right of the stage, facing the audience. [O.Fr. *estage* (Fr. *étage*), a storey of a house — inferred L.L. *staticus* — L. *stāre*, to stand.]

stagflation *stag-flā′shən, n.* an economic situation in which there is a marked decline in industrial output and consumer demand at the same time as a marked rise in inflation. — *adj.* **stagflā′tionary.** [*stag*nant, in*flation*.]

staggard. See **stag.**

stagger *stag′ər, v.i.* to reel: to go reeling or tottering: to waver. — *v.t.* to cause to reel: to give a shock to: to cause to waver: to nonplus, confound: to dispose alternately or variously: to arrange so that one thing or part is ahead of another. — *n.* a staggering: a wavering: a staggered arrangement (e.g. in aircraft, *positive* where the upper plane of a biplane is advanced, *negative* where the lower): (in *pl.*, often treated as *sing.*) giddiness, also any of various kinds of disease causing horses, sheep, etc., to stagger (**grass** or **stomach staggers,** an acute indigestion; **mad** or **sleepy staggers,** an inflammation of the brain). — *adj.* **stagg′ered.** — *n.* **stagg′erer.** — *n.* and *adj.* **stagg′ering.** — *adv.* **stagg′eringly.** [Earlier *stacker* — O.N. *stakra,* freq. of *staka,* to push.]

Stagirite (*misspelt* **Stagyrite**) *staj′i-rīt, n.* a native or inhabitant of *Stagira* (Gr. *Stagīros*) in Macedonia, esp. Aristotle (384–322 B.C.).

stagnant *stag′nənt, adj.* still, standing, without current:

foul, unwholesome, or dull from stillness: inert. — *ı* **stag′nancy.** — *adv.* **stag′nantly.** — *v.i.* **stagnate′** (o *stag′-*) to be stagnant. — *n.* **stagnā′tion.** — **stagnation point** the point at or near the nose of a body in motion in a fluid, where the flow divides. [L. *stagnāre, -ātum* — *stagnum,* pond.]

stagy. See **stage.**

Stagyrite. See **Stagirite.**

Stahlhelm *shtäl′helm, n.* a German old soldiers' conservative nationalist and militaristic organisation after the 1st World War. — *ns.* **Stahl′helmer, Stahl′helmist.** [Ger., steel helmet.]

Stahlian *stäl′i-ən, adj.* pertaining to Georg Ernst *Stahl,* German physician (1660–1734), or his animism. — *ns.* **Stahl′ianism, Stahl′ism.**

staid *stād, adj.* steady: sober: grave: sedate. — *adv.* **staid′ly.** — *n.* **staid′ness.** [**stayed** — *pa.t.* and *pa.p.* of **stay.**]

staig. See **stag.**

stain *stān, v.t.* to deprive of colour (*obs.*): to pale by comparison (*obs.*): to impart a new colour to: to tinge: to dye: to sully: to tarnish: to impregnate with a substance that colours some parts so as to show composition and structure: to bring reproach on. — *v.i.* to take or impart a stain. — *n.* a dye or colouring-matter: discoloration: a spot: taint of guilt: pollution: a cause of reproach: shame. — *adj.* **stained.** — *n.* **stain′er.** — *n.* and *adj.* **stain′ing.** — *adj.* **stain′less** free from stain: not liable to stain, rust, or tarnish. — *adv.* **stain′lessly.** — *n.* **stain′lessness.** — **stained glass** glass painted with certain pigments fused into its surface; **stainless steel** a steel that will not rust, containing 8 to 25 per cent. of chromium. [**distain.**]

stair *stār, n.* a series of steps (in Scotland, the whole series from floor to floor, elsewhere, usu. in *pl.*, a flight from landing to landing): one such step. — *adj.* **staired** having, or arranged like, stairs. — *adv.* **stair′wise** by steps: in the manner of a stair. — **stair′-car′pet** a long carpet for stairs; **stair′case** the structure enclosing a stair: stairs with banisters, etc.; **stair′foot** the level place at the foot of stairs; **stair′head** the level place at the top of stairs; **stair′-rod** a rod for holding a stair-carpet in place; **stair′-tower, -turret** one enclosing a winding stair; **stair′way** a staircase: a passage by stairs; **stair′=well** the well of a staircase; **stair′-work** backstairs intriguing. — **below stairs** in the basement: among the servants. [O.E. *stæger* — *stīgan,* to ascend; Ger. *steigen,* to climb, Norw. *steg,* step.]

staith(e) *stāth, (N. England) n.* a wharf: a structure for shipping coal: an embankment. [O.E. *stæth,* bank, and O.N. *stöth,* landing-stage.]

stake[1] *stāk, n.* a stick or pole pointed at one end: a post: a post to which one condemned to be burned was tied: hence, death or martyrdom by burning: a tinsmith's anvil. — *v.t.* to fasten to or with, to protect, shut, support, furnish, pierce, with a stake or stakes: to mark the bounds of with stakes (often with *off* or *out*). — **stake′-boat** a boat anchored as a marker for a boat-race, or to which other boats may be moored; **stake′=net** a net hung on stakes. — **stake a claim (for, to)** intimate one's right to or desire to possess; **stake out** (*coll.*) to place (a person, etc.) under surveillance (*n.* **stake′-out**). [O.E. *staca,* stake.]

stake[2] *stāk, v.t.* to deposit as a wager: to risk, hazard: to furnish, supply, fit out, whether free or in expectation of return (with *with* or *to*; *U.S.*). — *n.* anything pledged as a wager: a prize: anything to gain or lose: an interest, concern: the condition of being at hazard: a grubstake: (in *pl.*) a race for money staked or contributed. — **at stake** (*Shak.* also **at the stake**) hazarded: in danger: at issue. [Perh. M.Du. *staken,* to place.]

stakhanovite *stə-kan′ō-vīt, n.* a worker who has received recognition for his part in increasing the rate of production in the factory, etc., where he works. — Also *adj.* — *n.* **Stakhan′ovism.** [*Stakhanov,* a Russian worker.]

stalactite *stal′ək-tīt* (also *sta-lak′tīt*), *n.* an icicle-like pendant of calcium carbonate, formed by evaporation of water percolating through limestone, as on a cave roof: the material it is composed of: anything of similar form. — *adjs.* **stalac'tic, -al, stalac'tiform, stalactī'tal, stal'actīted** (also *-ak'*), **stalactitic** (*-tit'ik*; the usual *adj.*), **-al, stalactitiform** (*-tīt'*), **stalactitious** (*-tish'əs*). — *adv.* **stalactit'ically.** — *ns.* **stalag'ma** stalagmite; **stal'-agmite** (also *-ag'*) an upward-growing conical formation on the floor, formed by the drip from the roof or from a stalactite. — *adjs.* **stalagmitic** (*-mit'ik*), **-al.** — *adv.* **stalagmit'ically.** — *ns.* **stalagmom'eter** an instrument for determining surface tension by drops; **stalagmom'etry.** [Gr. *stalaktos, stalagma, stalagmos,* a dropping — *stalassein,* to drip.]

stalag *stal'ag, shtä'lak, shtä'lähh, n.* a German camp for prisoners of war (non-commissioned officers and men). [Ger. *Stamm,* base, *Lager,* camp.]

stalagma, stalagmite. See under **stalactite.**

stal'd *stöld, (Spens.) pa.p.* See **stall[1].**

stale[1] *stāl, adj.* altered (usu. for the worse) by age: of liquor, old, clear, and strong (*obs.*): no longer fresh: past the best: out of condition by over-training or overstudy: impaired by lapse of time: tainted: vapid or tasteless from age. — *v.t.* and *v.i.* to make or become stale, over-familiar, or insipid. — *adv.* **stale'ly.** — *n.* **stale'ness.** [Perh. from the root *sta-,* as in **stand.**]

stale[2] *stāl, n.* a decoy-bird: a thief's decoy (*obs.*): a lure: a low prostitute employed as a decoy, or generally (*Shak.*): a stalking-horse, cover to a real purpose (*Shak.*): a pretext: a lover made a butt of by or for one preferred. [Cf. A.Fr. *estal, -e,* pigeon used to entice a hawk, O.E. *stælhrān,* decoy-reindeer, Ger. *Stellvogel,* decoy-bird; prob. from root of O.E. *stellan,* to place.]

stale[3] *stāl, n.* urine, now esp. of horses. — *v.i.* to urinate. [Cf. Du. *stalle,* Ger. *Stall,* O.Fr. vb. *estaler.*]

stale[4] *stāl, (dial.) n.* a handle, shaft: a stalk. [O.E. *stalu,* app. part of a harp.]

stale[5] *stāl, (now rare or obs.) n.* and *v.t.* stalemate. — **stale'mate** an unsatisfactory draw resulting when a player not actually in check has no possible legal move (*chess*): an inglorious deadlock. — *v.t.* to subject to a stalemate. [Cf. A.Fr. *estale,* perh. — Eng. **stall.**]

stale[6]. See **steal[1].**

Stalinism *stä'lin-izm, n.* the rigorous rule of the Russian Communist dictator Josef *Stalin* (1879-1953), esp. in its concentration of all power and authority in the Communist world in Russia. — *n.* and *adj.* **Sta'linist.**

stalk[1] *stök, n.* the stem of a plant: a slender connecting part: a shaft: a tall chimney. — *v.t.* to remove the stalk from. — *adjs.* **stalked** having a stalk; **stalk'less; stalk'y** running to stalk: like a stalk. — *adj.* **stalk'-eyed** having the eyes on stalks. [Dim. from the root of O.E. *stela, stalu,* stalk.]

stalk[2] *stök, v.i.* to stride stiffly or haughtily: to go after game keeping under cover. — *v.t.* to approach under cover: to stalk over or through (a tract of country, etc.). — *n.* an act of stalking: a stalking gait. — *n.* **stalk'er.** — *n.* and *adj.* **stalk'ing.** — **stalk'ing-horse** a horse or substitute behind which a sportsman hides while stalking game: anything put forward to mask plans or efforts. [O.E. *(bi)stealcian,* freq. of **steal[1].**]

stalko *stö'kō, (Anglo-Ir.) n.* a gentleman without fortune or occupation: — *pl.* **stalk'oes.** [Perh. Ir. *stócach,* idler.]

stall[1] *stöl, n.* a standing-place: a stable, cowshed, or the like: a compartment for one animal: a bench, table, booth, or stand for display or sale of goods, or used as a working-place: a church-seat with arms, usu. one of those lining the choir or chancel on both sides, reserved for cathedral clergy, for choir, for monks, or for knights of an order: an office entitling one to such a seat: a doorless pew: an individual armed seat in a theatre, etc., esp. an orchestra stall: a working place in a mine: a covering for a finger (as in *fingerstall*): an instance of stalling in aircraft or engine: a standstill: (*Scot.* **staw**) a surfeit. — *v.t.* to put or keep in a stall: to induct, install: to bring to a standstill: to cause (an

aeroplane) to fly in such a way that the angle between the aerofoils and the direction of motion is greater than that at which there is maximum lift and so lose control: to stop (an engine) by sudden braking, overloading, etc.: to mire: to snow up (*U.S.*): (esp. in Scots form **staw**) to surfeit (*Spens.* in *pa.p.* **stal'd** *stöld*) to release on payment by instalments. — *v.i.* to dwell (*obs.*): to inhabit a stall: to share a dwelling (*obs.*): to come to a standstill: of aircraft or engine, to be stalled. — *n.* **stallage** (*stöl'ij*) rent for liberty of erecting a stall in a fair or market. — *adjs.* **stalled** kept or fed in a stall: fatted: having a stall or stalls: stuck: sated (*Scot.* **stawed**). — *ns.* **stall'ing** stabling; **stall'inger, stallenger** (*-in-jər; hist.*) a keeper of a stall: one who paid for the privilege of trading in a burgh of which he was not a freeman. — *adj.* **stall'-fed** fed and fattened in a stall. — *v.t.* **stall'-feed.** — **stall'ing-ken'** (*obs. cant*) a house for receiving stolen goods; **stall'man** a keeper of a stall, esp. a bookstall; **stall'-master** (Ger. *Stallmeister*) a master of horse; **stall'-plate** a plate with a knight's arms affixed to his stall; **stall'-reader** one who stands and reads at a bookstall. — **stall starting gate, starting stall** or **gate** a group of stalls into which horses are shut for the start of a race. [O.E. *stall, steall,* O.N. *stallr,* Ger. *Stall.*]

stall[2] *stöl, n.* a ruse, trick: a decoy, esp. one who diverts attention from a criminal action. — *v.t.* to delay or obstruct: to stave off (with *off*). — *v.i.* to hang back, play for time: to be obstructive, evasive or deceptive. [**stale[2].**]

stallage, stallenger, stallinger. See **stall[1].**

stallion[1] *stal'yən, n.* an uncastrated male horse, esp. one kept for breeding. [O.Fr. *estalon* (Fr. *étalon*) — O.H.G. *stal,* stall.]

stallion[2] *stal'yən, (obs.) n.* a courtesan (*Hamlet*; another reading, *scullion*). [Fr. *estalon;* cf. **stale[2].**]

stallion[3] (*Shak.*). Same as **staniel.**

stalwart *stöl'wərt, adj.* stout, strong, sturdy: determined in partisanship. — *n.* a resolute person. — Also (*arch.*) **stal'worth** (*-wərth*). — *adv.* **stal'wartly.** — *n.* **stal'-wartness.** [Orig. Scots form (popularised by *Scott*) of *stalworth* — O.E. *stælwierthe,* serviceable — *stæl,* place (— *stathol,* foundation), *wierthe,* worth.]

stamen *stā'mən, n.* the pollen-producing part of a flower, consisting of anther and filament: — *pl.* **stā'mens,** and see also **stamina** below. — *adj.* **stā'mened** having stamens. — *n.pl.* **stamina** (*stam'*) stamens (*rare*): germinal elements, rudiments (*arch.*): physical constitution, strength (*rare*). — *n.sing.* native or constitutional strength: staying power: mainstay. — *adjs.* **stam'inal** of stamens or stamina; **stam'inate** having stamens but no carpels; **stamineal** (*stə-* or *stā-min'i-əl*), **stamin'eous** (both *rare*); **staminif'erous** (*stam-* or *stām-*) having stamens. — *ns.* **stam'inode, staminō'dium** a sterile stamen; **stam'inody** metamorphosis of other parts into stamens. — *adj.* **stam'inoid** like, or metamorphosed into, a stamen. [L. *stāmen* (pl. *stāmina*), a warp thread (upright in an old loom) — *stāre,* to stand.]

stamina, etc. See **stamen.**

stammel *stam'l, (hist.) n.* a kind of woollen cloth, usu. dyed red: red colour. — *adj.* of stammel: red. [Fr. *estamel,* or independently formed M.E. *stamin* — O.Fr. *estamin,* both from L. *stāmina,* warp threads.]

stammer *stam'ər, v.i.* to falter in speaking: to speak with involuntary hesitations, to stutter. — *v.t.* to utter falteringly or with a stutter. — *n.* involuntary hesitation in speech, a stutter: a faltering mode of utterance. — *n.* **stamm'erer.** — *n.* and *adj.* **stamm'ering.** — *adv.* **stamm'eringly.** [O.E. *stamerian;* Du. *stemeren.*]

stamnos *stam'nos, n.* an ancient Greek short-necked jar: — *pl.* **stam'noi.** [Gr.]

stamp *stamp, v.t.* to bray, pound, crush: to bring the foot forcibly down upon: to trample: to strike flatwise with the sole (or other part) of: to impress, imprint, or cut with a downward blow, as with a die or cutter: to mint, make, shape by such a blow: to fix or mark deeply: to impress with a mark attesting official approval, ratification, payment, etc.: to affix an adhesive stamp to: to attest, declare, prove to be: to characterise. — *v.i.* to bring the foot down forcibly and noisily: to walk with a heavy tread. — *n.* the act of stamping: an impression: a stamped device, mark, imprint: an adhesive paper used as a substitute for stamping: attestation: authorisation: a coin (*Shak.*): pounded maize (*S.Afr.*): cast, form, character: distinguishing mark, imprint, sign, evidence: an instrument or machine for stamping: accumulated national insurance contributions (*coll.*). — *n.* **stamp′er.** — *n.* and *adj.* **stamp′ing.** — **Stamp Act** an act of parliament imposing or regulating stamp duties, esp. that of 1765 imposing them on the American colonies; **stamp′-album** a book for keeping a collection of postage-stamps in; **stamp′-collector** a receiver of stamp duties: one who makes a hobby of collecting postage-stamps; **stamp duty** a tax imposed on the paper on which legal documents are written; **stamp-hinge** see **hinge**; **stamp′ing-ground** an animal's usual resort: a person's habitual place of resort; **stamp′ing-machine** a machine used for stamping coins, in the stamping of brass-work, or in crushing metallic ores; **stamp′-, stamp′ing-mill** a crushing-mill for ores; **stamp′-note** a certificate from a custom-house officer for goods to be loaded as freight of a ship; **stamp′-office** an office where stamp duties are received and stamps issued; **stamp′-paper** paper bearing a government revenue stamp. — **stamp out** to put out by tramping: to extirpate: to make by stamping from a sheet with a cutter. [M.E. *stampen*, from an inferred O.E. *stampian* from the same root as *stempan*; Ger. *stampfen*.]

stampede *stam-pēd′, n.* a sudden rush of a panic-stricken herd: any impulsive action of a multitude. — *v.i.* to rush in a stampede. — *v.t.* to send rushing in a stampede. — Also *n.* and *v.t.* (*obs.*) **stampē′do.** [Sp. *estampida*, crash — *estampar*, to stamp.]

stance *stans, n.* a station, standing-place (*Scot.*): a building-site (*Scot.*): a mode of standing, as in golf: a stanza (*obs.*). [Fr. *stance* (now meaning 'stanza') — It. *stanza*, a stopping-place, station — L. *stāre*, to stand.]

stanch¹, staunch *stänch, stänsh, stönch, stönsh, v.t.* to stop the flowing of, as blood: to quench, allay. — *v.i.* (*B.*) to cease to flow. — *n.* a styptic: a floodgate. — *n.* **stanch′er; stanch′ing.** — *adj.* **stanch′less** that cannot be quenched or stopped. [O.Fr. *estancher* (Fr. *étancher*) — L.L. *stancāre*, to stanch — L. *stagnāre*, to be or make stagnant — *stagnum*, a pond.]

stanch² (*adj.*), etc. See **staunch¹**.

stanchel, -er. See **stanchion**.

stanchion *stän′shən, stan′shən* (*Scot.* **stanchel** *stän′*, *stān′*, **stan′cher**), *n.* an upright iron bar of a window or screen: an upright beam used as a support (*naut.*). — *v.t.* to fasten by means of or to a stanchion. — *adj.* **stan′-chioned.** [O.Fr. *estançon* — *estance*, prop — L. *stāre*, to stand.]

stanck *stangk,* (*Spens.*) *adj.* faint. [It. *stanco.*]

stand *stand, v.i.* to be, become, or remain upright, erect, rigid, or still: to be on, or rise to, one's feet: to be steadfast: to have or take a position: to be or remain: to be set or situated: to be set down: to have a direction: to hold good: to endure, continue to exist: to scruple, demur: to insist punctiliously: to be a representative, representation, or symbol: to be a candidate: to cost. — *v.t.* to withstand: to tolerate: to endure: to sustain: to suffer, undergo: to abide by: to be at the expense of, offer and pay for: to station, cause to stand: to set erect or in position: — *pa.t.* **stood**; *pa.p.* **stood**, *Scot.* **stood′en, studd′en;** *infin., Spens.,* **stand′en.** — *n.* an act, manner, or place of standing: a taking up of a position for resistance: resistance: the partnership of any two batsmen at the wicket, the period of time of the partnership, or the runs made during it (*cricket*): a standing position: a standstill: a stoppage: a loss, a nonplus: a post, station: a place under cover for awaiting game: a place for vehicles awaiting hire: an erection for spectators: a stop on tour to give one or

more performances, or the place where it is made (*theat.*): a platform: a witness-box (*U.S.*): a base or structure for setting things on: a piece of furniture for hanging things from: a company of plovers: a complete set, esp. (*Scot.*) a suit of clothes or armour: a standing growth or crop: a young tree left standing: a tub or vat. — *n.* **stand′er.** — *adj.* **stand′ing** established: settled: permanent: fixed: stagnant: erect: having a base: done as one stands: from a standing position, without preliminary movement (e.g. *standing jump, start*). — *n.* the action of one who or that which stands: duration: continuance: place to stand in: position or grade in a profession, university, in society: a current ranking within a graded scale, esp. in sport: a right or capacity to sue or maintain an action. — *adj.* **stand′-alone′** (*comput.*) of a system, device, etc. that can operate unconnected to and unaided by any other. — *n.* **stand′-by** that which, or one whom, one relies on or readily resorts to: something, someone, available for use in an emergency (see also **on stand-by** below). — *adj.* (of an airline passenger, ticket, fare, etc.) occupying, for, an aircraft seat not booked in advance but taken as available, usu. with some price-reduction, at the time of departure. — **stand′er-by′** (*Shak.*) a bystander: — *pl.* **stand′ers-by′; stand′-in** a substitute; **stand′ing-bed** a high bedstead, not a truckle-bed; **stand′ing-bowl, -cup** one with a foot; **standing committee** one permanently established to deal with a particular matter; **stand′ing-ground** a place, basis, or principle to stand on; **standing joke** a subject that raises a laugh whenever it is mentioned; **standing order** an instruction from a customer to his bank to make regular payments from his account: an order placed with a shopkeeper, etc. for the regular supply of a newspaper or other goods: a military order with long-term application: (in *pl.*) regulations for procedure adopted by a legislative assembly (also **standing rules**); **standing ovation** one from an audience that rises to its feet in its enthusiasm; **stand′ing-place** a place that one may or does stand on; **stand′ing-rigg′ing** the fixed ropes in a ship; **stand′ing-room** room for standing, without a seat; **stand′ing-stone** (*archaeol.*) a great stone set erect in the ground; **standing wave** the pattern of maxima and minima when two sets of oppositely travelling waves of the same frequency interfere with each other (*phys.*): (in *pl.*) a long-lasting layered cloud-formation seen in hilly regions (*meteor.*); **stand′-off** a Rugby half-back who stands away from the scrum as a link between scrum-half and the three-quarters (also **stand-off half**): deadlock (*coll.*): a tie or draw (*U.S.*): any object that stands, projects or holds another a short distance away, e.g. on a ladder, an attachment that holds it away from the surface supporting it. — *adj.* **stand′-off′ish** inclined to hold aloof, keep others at arm's-length. — **stand′-off′ishness; stand′-patt′er** (*U.S.*) one who stands pat: a political die-hard; **stand′-patt′ism; stand′-pipe** an open vertical pipe connected to a pipeline, to ensure that the pressure head at that point cannot exceed the length of the pipe: one used to obtain water for an attached hose; **stand′point** a viewpoint; **stand′still** a complete stop. — *adj.* stationary: unmoving: forbidding or refraining from movement. — **stand′-to** a precautionary parade or taking of posts. — *adj.* **stand′-up** erect: done or taken in a standing position: of a fight, in earnest: delivering, or consisting of, a comic monologue without feed or other support. — *n.* something that stands upright, either independently or with a support to hold it in position: a broken date (between two people) (*coll.*). — **all standing** everything remaining as it stands: without unrigging: fully clad; **it stands to reason** it is only logical to assume; **make a stand** to halt and offer resistance; **one-night stand** see **one**; **on stand-by** in readiness to help in an emergency; **stand against** to resist; **stand by** to support: to adhere to, abide by: to be at hand: to hold oneself in readiness: to prepare to work at; **stand down** to leave the witness box: to go off duty: to withdraw from a contest or from a controlling position (*v.i.* and *v.t.*): — *pa.p.* **stood down; stand fast** to be unmoved; **stand fire** to remain steady under the fire of an enemy — also *fig.*; **stand for** to be a candidate for: to direct the course towards (*naut.*): to be a sponsor for: to represent, symbolise: to champion: to put up with, endure (*coll.*); **stand from** to direct the course from; **stand in** to cost: to become a party: to have an understanding, be in league: to deputise, act as a substitute (for); **stand in with** to support, act together with; **stand low** (*print.*) to fall short of the standard height; **stand off** to keep at a distance: to direct the course from: to forbear compliance or intimacy (*Shak.*): to suspend temporarily from employment: — *pa.p.* **stood off; stand off and on** to sail away from shore and then towards it; **stand on** to continue on the same tack or course: to insist on: to set store by (see **ceremony**): to behove: to found upon; **stand one's ground** to maintain one's position; **stand one's hand, stand sam** (*coll.*), **stand shot, stand treat** to treat the company, esp. to drinks; **stand on one's own feet** to manage one's own affairs without help; **stand out** to project, to be prominent: not to comply, to refuse to yield; **stand over** to keep (someone who is working, etc.) under close supervision: to postpone or be postponed; **stand pat** (*U.S.*) to play one's hand in poker as it was dealt, without drawing any cards: to adhere to an established political principle, resisting all compromise (*fig.*); **stand to** to fall to, set to work: to back up: to uphold: to take up position in readiness for orders; **stand to gain, win,** etc. to be in a position to gain, win, etc.; **stand up** to get to one's feet: to take position for a dance: to be clad (with *in*): to fail to keep an appointment with (*coll.*); **stand up for** to support or attempt to defend; **stand upon** to stand on: to attack (*B.*); **stand up to** to meet (an opponent, etc.) face to face, to show resistance to: to fulfil (an obligation, etc.) fairly: to withstand (hard wear, etc.); **stand well** to be in favour; **stand with** to be consistent. [O.E. *standan*; Goth. *standan*; cf. Ger. *stehen*, Gr. *histanai*, to place, L. *stāre*, to stand.]

standard *stand'ərd, n.* a flag or military symbolic figure on a pole, marking a rallying-point: a rallying-point (also *fig.*): a long tapering flag notched and rounded at the end, bearing heraldic symbols and fixed in the ground (*her.*): a flag generally: a cavalry regimental flag: a standard-bearer: the uppermost petal of a papilionaceous flower: a streaming wing-feather: that which stands or is fixed: an upright post, pillar, stick: a standing shrub or tree not trained on an espalier or a wall: a tree left growing amidst coppice: a structure erected at a conduit (*obs.*): an exemplar or substance chosen to be or afford a unit: a basis of measurement: a criterion: an established or accepted model: an accepted authoritative statement of a church's creed: in schools (formerly) a grade of classification: a definite level of excellence or adequacy required, aimed at, or possible: fineness of gold or silver. — *adj.* serving as or conforming to a standard: of enduring value: growing as a standard: standing upright. — *n.* **standardīsā'tion, -z-.** — *v.t.* **stand'ardise, -ize** to make, or keep, of uniform size, shape, etc. — *n.* **stand'ardiser, -z-.** — **standard atmosphere** 101 325 newtons per sq. metre, or 1 013 250 dynes per sq. centimetre: a standard of measurement of atmospheric conditions used in comparing the performance of aircraft (*aero.*, etc.); **stand'ard-bearer** one who carries a standard or banner: an outstanding leader; **standard bread** bread made with flour containing 80 per cent. of the whole-wheat including germ and semolina; **Stand'ardbred** a breed of horse orig. developed in the U.S. as harness race-horses for trotting or pacing to a standard minimum speed: (also without *cap.*) a horse of this breed. — Also *adj.* — **standard candle** see **candle; standard deviation** the root of the average of the squares of the differences from their mean of a number of observations; **standard English** the form of English taught in schools, etc., and used, esp. in formal situations, by the majority of educated English-speakers; **standard error** standard deviation: standard deviation divided by the root of the number of observations; **standard lamp** a lamp on a tall support; **standard solution** a solution of known concentration, used for purposes of comparison, commonly containing the equivalent, in grammes, of the solute to a litre of solution (*normal solution*) or some simple fraction (as *decinormal,* one-tenth normal); **stand'ard-wing** a bird of paradise of the Moluccas with a pair of erectile white feathers at the bend of the wing. — **(international) standard book number** a number allotted to a book by agreement of (international) publishers which shows area, publisher and individual title. [O.Fr. *estandart*; prob. conn. either with **extend** or **stand,** and in any case influenced by or partly from **stander.**]

standgale *stand'gāl, n.* a corrupt form of **staniel.**

standish *stan'dish,* (*arch.*) *n.* an inkstand. [Poss. for *stand-dish.*]

stane *stān.* Scots form of **stone.**

stang[1] *stang, n.* a stake, pole. — **riding the stang** punishment by being carried astride of a stang. [O.N. *stöng*; cf. O.E. *stæng,* Du. *stang.*]

stang[2] *stang, stöng,* (*Scot.*) *v.i.* to sting. — *n.* a sting. [O.N. *stanga,* to prick.]

stanhope *stan'əp, -hōp, n.* a light open one-seated carriage first made for Fitzroy *Stanhope* (1787–1864). — **Stanhope press** a printing-press invented by the third Earl *Stanhope* (1753–1816).

staniel, stanyel *stan'yəl,* **stannel** *stan'l* (*Shak.* **stallion** *stal'yən*), *ns.* the kestrel. [O.E. *stāngella,* lit. stone yeller.]

Stanislavski method, system *stan-i-släv'ski, -släf',* method acting (q.v.). [K. *Stanislavski* (1863–1938), Russian actor and director.]

stank[1] *stangk, pa.t.* of **stink.**

stank[2] *stangk,* (chiefly *Scot.*) *n.* a ditch, a pool: a dam: a drain in the street. [O.Fr. *estanc,* a pond — L. *stagnum,* a pond.]

stann- stan-, in composition, tin. — *n.* **stann'ary** (-ə-ri) a tin-mining district (esp. the **Stannaries** in Cornwall and Devon). — Also *adj.* — *ns.* **stann'ate** a salt of stannic acid; **stannā'tor** one of the members of the Stannary Parliament. — *adjs.* **stann'ic** of quadrivalent tin; **stannif'erous** tin-bearing. — *ns.* **stann'ite** a mineral composed of tin, copper, iron, and sulphur (*min.*): a salt of stannous hydroxide, Sn(OH)$_2$, acting as a weak acid (*chem.*); **stann'otype** a photo-mechanical process in which an exposed and developed bichromated film is coated with tinfoil and used directly for pressure printing. — *adj.* **stann'ous** of bivalent tin. — **Stannary Courts** courts (abolished 1896) for the tinners of the Stannaries; **Stannary Parliament** the ancient parliament of tinners, comprising twenty-four representatives (stannators) for all Cornwall, reconvened in 1974 after a lapse of more than 200 years; **stannic acid** H$_2$SnO$_3$. [L. *stannum,* tin.]

stannel, stanyel. See **staniel.**

stanza *stan'zə* (*Shak.* **stanze, stan'zo** (*pl.* **stan'zoes, -zos**)), *n.* a group of lines of verse forming a definite pattern: a pattern so composed. — *adj.* **stanzā'ic.** [It. *stanza* — L. *stāre,* to stand.]

stap *stap, v.t.* an obsolete affectation for **stop,** esp. in the sense of choke or obstruct: also (*stap, stäp*) a Scots form, in the senses of stuff, thrust, cram.

stapedectomy, stapedial, -ius. See **stapes.**

Stapelia *stə-pē'li-ə, n.* the carrion-flower genus: (without *cap.*) any plant of this genus. [After the Dutch botanist J. B. van *Stapel* (d. 1636).]

stapes *stā'pēz, n.* the stirrup-shaped innermost ossicle of the ear. — *n.* **stapedectomy** (*stap-i-dek'tə-mi*) the surgical excision of this bone. — *adj.* **stapedial** (*stə-pē'di-əl*). — *n.* **stape'dius** the muscle of the stapes. [L.L. *stapēs, -edis,* a stirrup.]

staph. See **Staphyloccus** under **staphyle.**

staphyle *staf'i-lē, n.* the uvula. — *n.* **Staphylē'a**

bladder-nut genus of shrubs, giving name to the family **Staphyleā′ceae**, akin to Sapindaceae. — *adj.* **staph′-yline** like a bunch of grapes. — *n.pl.* **Staphylin′idae** the rove-beetle family. — *ns.* **staphylī′tis** inflammation of the uvula; **Staphylococc′us** (Gr. *kokkos*, a grain; also without *cap*.) a pus-causing bacterium found in clustered masses (*coll.* shortening **staph**). — *adj.* **staphylococc′al**. — *ns.* **staphylō′ma** protrusion of the sclerotic or of the cornea; **staphylorrh′aphy** (Gr. *rhaphē*, stitching) the operation of uniting a cleft palate. [Gr. *staphylē*, a bunch of grapes, a swollen uvula.]

staple[1] *stā′pl, n.* a settled mart or market: a leading commodity: a main element (as of diet, reading, conversation): unmanufactured wool or other raw material: textile fibre, or its length and quality. — *adj.* constituting a staple: leading, main. — *v.t.* to grade according to staple. — *n.* **stā′pler** a merchant of a staple: one who grades and deals in wool. — **merchant of the staple** a member of a mediaeval association of merchants privileged to trade in a staple commodity, esp. wool, at the **staple town** (or **towns**) appointed by the king. [O.Fr. *estaple* — L.G. *stapel*, heap, mart.]

staple[2] *stā′pl, n.* a U-shaped rod or wire for driving into a wall, post, etc., as a fastening: a similarly-shaped piece of wire that is driven through sheets of paper and compressed, to fasten them together: the curved bar, etc. that passes through the slot of a hasp, receives a bolt, etc.: the metallic tube to which the reed is fastened in the oboe, etc. — *v.t.* to fasten with a staple. — *n.* **stā′pler** an instrument for (dispensing and) inserting staples into papers, etc. — **sta′pling-machine** a machine that stitches paper with wire. [O.E. *stapol*, post, support; cf. foregoing.]

staple[3], **stapple** *stap′l, (Scot.) n.* See **stopple**[2].

star[1] *stär, n.* any of those heavenly bodies visible by night that are really gaseous masses generating heat and light, whose places are relatively fixed (**fixed stars**): more loosely, these and the planets, comets, meteors and even, less commonly, the sun, moon and earth: a planet as a supposed influence, hence (usu. in *pl.*) one's luck: an object or figure with pointed rays, most commonly five: an asterisk: a starfish: a radial meeting of ways: a star-shaped badge of rank or honour: a white mark on a beast's forehead: a pre-eminent or exceptionally brilliant person: a leading performer, or one supposed to draw the public. — *adj.* of stars: marked by a star: leading, pre-eminent, brilliant. — *v.t.* to make a star of: to have (a specified person) as a star performer: to mark with a star: to shatter or crack in a radiating form: to set with stars: to bespangle. — *v.i.* to shine, as a star: to attract attention: to appear as a star performer: — *pr.p.* **starr′ing;** *pa.t.* and *pa.p.* **starred**. — *n.* **star′dom** the state of being, status of, a star performer esp. of stage or screen. — *adj.* **star′less.** — *n.* **star′let** a kind of starfish (*Asterina*): a little star: a young film actress, esp. one hailed as a future star. — *adj.* and *adv.* **star′like.** — *adj.* **starred** adorned or studded with stars: influenced by or having a star: decorated or marked with a star: turned into a star: star-shaped: radially cracked, fissured. — *adv.* **starr′ily.** — *n.* **starr′iness** — *n.*, *adj.* **starr′ing.** — *adj.* **starr′y** abounding or adorned with stars: consisting of, or proceeding from, the stars: like, or shining like, the stars. — **star′-anise** a Chinese evergreen tree (*Illicium*) of the magnolia family, with aromatic oil; **star′-apple** the fruit of the West Indian sapotaceous tree *Chrysophyllum cainito*; **star billing** prominent display of the name of a performer, etc. on posters, etc.; **star′-blast′ing** the noxious influence of the stars. — *adj.* **star′-bright′** bright as a star or with stars. — **star′-cat′alogue** a list of stars, with their places, magnitudes, etc. — *adj.* **star′-crossed, -crost** thwarted by the stars. — **star′-drift** a common proper motion of a number of fixed stars in the same region; **star′-dust** cosmic dust, meteoric matter in fine particles: distant stars seen like dust-grains: a romantic, magical quality or feeling. — *adj.* glittering, romantic, magical. — **star′fish** any

member of the Asteroidea, a class of echinoderms with five arms merging in a disc, and tube-feet on the under surface: sometimes extended to the ophiuroids; **star fruit** fruit of the carambola. — *v.i.* **star′-gaze.** — **star′-gazer** an astrologer: an astronomer: one who gazes at the sky, or in abstraction: a dreamer or wool-gatherer: a fish with upward-looking eyes (Uranoscopus or other); **star′-gazing; star′-grass** a name for many grasslike plants with star-shaped flowers or leaf-arrangement (see also **star**[2]); **star′-jell′y** Nostoc, once thought to be a fallen star. — *adj.* **star′-led** guided by a star. — **star′light** light from the stars: an unknown plant, otherwise called astrophel or penthia (*Spens.*). — *adj.* of or with starlight: lighted by the stars: bright as a star. — *adj.* **star′lit** lighted by the stars. — **star′-man** an astrologer: a first-offender, wearing a star; **star′-map** a map showing the positions of stars; **star′monger** an astrologer; **star′-nose** (or **star-nosed mole**) a North American mole with star-shaped nose-tip. — *adjs.* **star′-pav′d** (*Milt.*) paved with stars; **star′-proof** (*Milt.*) impervious to starlight. — **star′-read′** (*Spens.*) astronomy. — *adj.* **starr′y-eyed** out of touch with reality: innocently idealistic: radiantly happy. — **star ruby, sapphire** an asteriated ruby, sapphire. — *adj.* **star′-shaped** shaped like a conventional star, with pointed rays. — **star′-shell** a shell that explodes high in the air, lighting up the scene; **star′shine** starlight; **star sign** a sign of the zodiac. — *adj.* **star′-spang′led** spangled or studded with stars (**Star-spangled Banner** the Stars and Stripes: an American national hymn). — **star′spot** an area of relative darkness on the surface of a star; **star′-stone** a sapphire, ruby, or other stone showing asterism. — *adj.* **star′-studded** covered with stars: of the cast of a film, play, etc., having a high proportion of famous performers. — **star′-this′tle** a species of Centaurea with radiating spiny bracts; **star′-trap** a stage trap of several wedge-shaped pieces meeting in a centre; **star′-turn** the chief item in an entertainment: a pre-eminent performer; **Star Wars** a colloquial term for the Strategic Defence Initiative (q.v.). — Also *adj.* (often without *caps.*). — **star′-wheel** a spur-wheel with V-shaped teeth; **star′wort** any plant of the genus Aster (not the China aster): stitchwort: a water-plant (**water-starwort** Callitriche). — *adj.* **star′-ypointing** (*stär′-i-point′ing*; *Milt.*; incorrectly formed; see **y-** *pfx.*) pointing to the stars. — **see stars** (*coll.*) to see spots of light, as result e.g. of blow on the head: to be in a dazed condition; **star-of-Bethlehem** a plant (Ornithogalum) of the lily family with starlike flowers; **Star of David** the Jewish religious symbol — Solomon's-seal (see second meaning of this); **star-of-the-earth** buck's-horn plantain; **star-of-the-night** Clusia; **Stars and Stripes** the flag of the United States of America, with thirteen stripes alternately red and white, and a blue field containing as many stars as there are states. [O.E. *steorra*; cf. **stern**[3], Ger. *Stern*, L. *stēlla* (for *sterula*), Gr. *astēr*.]

star[2], **starr** *stär*, (*Scot.*) *n.* Ammophila or other coarse seaside grass, sedge, or rush. — Also **star(r)′-grass** (see also under **star**[1]). [O.N. *stōrr*.]

staragen *star′ə-gən*, (*obs.*) *n.* the tarragon plant. [Cf. Sp. *estragón*, Fr. *estragon, tarragon*.]

starboard *stär′bə(r)d, -bōrd, -börd, n.* the right-hand side of a ship. — *adj.* and *adv.* of, to, towards, or on, the right. — *v.t.* to turn to the right (see note at **port**[1]) — opp. to *port*. [O.E. *stēorbord* — *stēor*, steering, *bord*, board, side of a ship (ancient Gmc. ships being steered by a paddle at the right side).]

starch *stärch, n.* the principal reserve food-material stored in plants, chemically a carbohydrate, $(C_6H_{10}O_5)_x$, used in the laundry as a stiffener: stiffness, formality. — *adj.* of starch: stiff, rigid, formal. — *v.t.* to stiffen or stick with starch. — *adj.* **starched.** — *adv.* **starchedly** (*stärcht-, stärch′id-*). — *ns.* **starched′ness** (or *-id-*); **starch′er.** — *adv.* **starch′ily.** — *n.* **starch′iness.** — *adj.* **starch′y** of or like starch: stiff: precise. — **starch′-grain** in plants, a layered cell-inclusion of starch; **starch′-**

hy'acinth grape-hyacinth, from its smell; **starch'-paper** a test-paper for iodine, coated with starch and potassium iodide. — *adj.* **starch'-reduced** of bread, etc. for the use of slimmers, containing less than the usual amount of starch. [O.E. *stercan*, to stiffen, inferred from *stercedferhth*, stiff-spirited; cf. Ger. *Stärke*, strength, vigour, starch, and **stark**.]

Star Chamber *stär chām'bər,* a court (abolished 1641) with a civil and criminal jurisdiction, which met in the old council chamber at Westminster and was empowered to act without a jury and to use torture: (also without *caps.*) generally, an over-zealous or secret inquiry or investigation: a closed meeting in which important decisions, resolutions, etc. are made, esp. on matters of public concern. [Prob. named from the gilt *stars* on the ceiling, not from the Jewish bonds (*starrs*) kept in it.]

stare[1] *stär, v.i.* to look with a fixed gaze: to glare: to be insistently or obtrusively conspicuous (with indirect obj. as to *stare one in the face*): to look (as *as like as he can stare;* formerly *coll.*): to stand on end. — *v.t.* to render by staring. — *n.* a fixed look. — *n.* **star'er** one who stares: (in *pl.*) a lorgnette. — *n., adj.,* and *adv.* **star'ing.** — *adv.* **star'ingly.** [O.E. *starian,* from root seen in Ger. *starr,* rigid; also in Eng. **stern**[1].]

stare[2] *stär, n.* a starling. [O.E. *stær.*]

staretz, starets *stär'ets, n.* in Russia, a holy man, a religious teacher. [Russ. *starets.*]

stark *stärk, adj.* stiff: strong: stern: harsh: unyielding: sheer: out-and-out: stark-naked (q.v.). — *adv.* stoutly: utterly. — *v.t.* and *v.i.* to stiffen. — *v.t.* and *v.i.* **stark'en** to make or become stark. — *adj.* **starkers** see **stark=na'ked.** — *adv.* **stark'ly.** — *n.* **stark'ness.** [O.E. *stearc,* hard, strong; O.N. *sterkr,* Ger. *stark.*]

stark-naked *stärk'-nā'kid, adj.* utterly naked: quite bare — shortened to **stark** or (*coll.*) **stark'ers.** — Earlier (now *dial.*) **start'-na'ked.** [M.E. *stert-naked* — O.E. *steort,* tail, *nacod,* naked; influenced by foregoing.]

starling[1] *stär'ling, n.* a bird with black, brown-spotted, iridescent plumage, a good mimic: any other member of its genus, Sturnus. [O.E. *stærling,* dim. of *stær,* see **stare**[2].]

starling[2] *stär'ling, n.* piling protecting a bridge pier. [Prob. for *staddling* from **staddle**.]

starn. Same as **stern**[3]; also (*naut.* or *dial.*) for **stern**[2].

starnie. See **stern**[3].

starosta *stär'os-tə, (hist.) n.* a Russian village headman: a Polish noble holding a **star'osty** or domain by grant of life-estate from the crown. [Russ. and Pol. *starosta,* elder.]

starr[1]. See **star**[2].

starr[2] *stär, n.* a Jewish deed or bond, e.g. of acquittance of debt. [Heb. *sh'tār,* a writing.]

starrily, starry, etc. See **star**[1].

start *stärt, v.i.* to shoot, dart, move suddenly forth, or out: to spring up or forward: to strain forward: to break away: to make a sudden involuntary movement as of surprise or becoming aware: to spring open, out of place, or loose: to begin to move: of a car, engine, etc., to work, to fire, combust: to set forth on a journey, race, career. — *v.t.* to begin: to set going: to set on foot: to set up: to drive from lair or hiding-place: to cause or undergo displacement or loosening of: to startle (*obs.*): to pour out or shoot. — *n.* a sudden movement: a sudden involuntary motion of the body: a startled feeling: a spurt: an outburst or fit: a beginning of movement, esp. of a journey, race, or career: a beginning: a setting in motion: a help in or opportunity of beginning: an advantage in being early or ahead: the extent of such an advantage in time or distance: a beginning of building-work on a new house site (esp. as *house* or *housing starts*). — *n.* **start'er** one who starts, esp. in a race: one who gives the signal for starting: a dog that starts game: an apparatus or device for starting a machine, as that (also called **self-starter**) for starting an internal-combustion engine: anything used to begin a process, as a bacterial

culture in making butter or cheese: (also in *pl.*) the first course of a meal (see also **for starters** below): a potentially successful or profitable idea, project, etc. (*commercial jargon*). — *adj.* **start'ful** apt to start. — *n.* and *adj.* **start'ing.** — *adv.* **start'ingly** (*Shak.*) by starts. — *adj.* **start'ish** apt to start, skittish. — **starter home** a small house or flat built, or considered by the seller, to suit and be affordable by a first-time buyer, esp. a young couple; **starting block** (usu. in *pl.*) a device for helping a sprinter make a quick start to a race, consisting of a framework with blocks of wood or metal attached, on which the sprinter braces his feet; **starting gate, stall** see **stall**[1]; **start'ing-hole** a hiding place: an evasive trick; **start'ing-point** the point from which anything starts, or from which motion begins; **start'ing-post** the post or barrier from which the competitors start in a race; **start'ing-price** odds on a horse when the race begins; **start'-up** an upstart (*Shak.*): a rustic half-boot or short legging (*obs.*): the process of setting up a company or business. — Also *adj.* — **for a start** in the first place, as a preliminary consideration; **for starters** (*coll.*) as the first course of a meal: in the first place, for a start; **start in** to begin; **start out** to begin: to begin a journey; **start up** to rise suddenly: to come suddenly into notice or being: to set in motion. [M.E. *sterten;* closely akin to Du. *storten,* to plunge, Ger. *stürzen.*]

startle *stärt'l, v.i.* to start: to undergo a start: to feel sudden alarm. — *v.t.* to surprise as with fright: to cause to undergo a start: to take aback: to awake, excite. — *n.* sudden alarm or surprise. — *adj.* **start'led.** — *n.* **start'ler.** — *n.* and *adj.* **start'ling.** — *adv.* **start'lingly.** — *adjs.* **start'lish, start'ly** apt to start. [M.E. *stertle* — O.E. *steartlian,* to stumble, struggle, kick, or formed afresh from **start**.]

start-naked. See **stark-naked.**

starve *stärv, v.i.* to die, now only of hunger or (chiefly *Scot.* and *Northern*) cold: to suffer extreme hunger (or cold): to be in want: to deteriorate (*obs.*). — *v.t.* to cause to starve: to afflict with hunger (or cold): to deprive of food: to force, subdue, cure, by want of food: to deprive of anything needful. — *n.* **starva'tion** (attributed to Lord Melville, 1775). — *adj.* **starved.** — *n.* **starve'ling** a lean, hungry, weak, or pining person, animal, or plant. — Also *adj.* — *n.* and *adj.* **starv'ing.** [O.E. *steorfan,* to die; Du. *sterven,* Ger. *sterben,* to die.]

stash *stash, (coll.) v.t.* to stow in hiding (often with *away*): to stop, desist, quit (*old*). — *n.* a secret store, or its hiding-place: a hidden store of a drug, or the drug itself (*slang;* esp. *U.S.*). [Origin obscure.]

stashie. See **stooshie.**

stasidion, stasimon, etc. See **stasis.**

stasis (also **-stasis** in composition) *stā'sis, stas'is,* (chiefly *med.*) *n.* stoppage, arrest, esp. of growth, of blood-circulation or bleeding, or of the contents of the bowels: (maintenance of) a state of equilibrium or constant state. — *ns.* **stasid'ion** (Mod. Gr. *dim.*) a stall in a Greek church; **stas'imon** (Gr., stationary) in Greek tragedy, an ode sung after the chorus had taken their places, or without interruption by dialogue: — *pl.* **stas'ima; stas'imorphy** structural modification by arrested development. [Gr. *stasis,* stoppage, stationariness.]

-stat *-stat,* in composition, used to designate a regulating device that causes something to remain constant or stationary, as in *barostat, hygrostat, thermostat.* [Gr. *-statēs,* causing to stand — *histanai,* to cause to stand.]

statant *stā'tənt, (her.) adj.* standing on four feet. [L. *stāre,* to stand.]

state *stāt, n.* condition: a perturbed condition of mind (*coll.*): mode of existence: circumstances at any time: a phase or stage: an impression taken at a stage of progress in engraving or etching or in printing a book: status: station in life: high station: grave import (*Shak.*): pomp, display, ceremonial dignity: a seat of dignity (*Shak.*): a canopy (*Milt.*): an estate, order, or class in society or the body politic: hence (in *pl.*) the legislature (*hist.*): an exalted personage (*Milt.*): public welfare: constitution: a republic (*obs.*): the civil power: the organisation of the body politic, or of one of the constituent members of a federation: the territory of such a state: high politics: an interest in property (*Spens.*): property, estate (*Shak.*): a body of men united by profession: a statement, report (now chiefly *mil.*). — *adj.* of, belonging to, relating to, the state or a federal state: public: ceremonial: pompous: affectedly solemn and mysterious: magnificent. — *adv.* or *adj.* (*Spens.*) explained in old gloss as stoutly (perh. pompous). — *v.t.* to set forth: to express the details of: to set down fully and formally: to assert, affirm: to install, establish, endow, place in a condition (esp. favourable; *arch.*): to set in state: to specify: perh., to determine the value of (*Milt.*): to settle. — *adjs.* **stāt'able** capable of being stated; **stāt'al** of a federal state; **stāt'ed** settled: established: declared: regular: circumstanced (*obs.*). — *adv.* **stāt'edly**. — *n.* **state'hood** the status of a state. — *adj.* **state'less** without nationality: unworthy to be accounted a state: without pomp. — *n.* **state'lessness**. — *adv.* **state'lily**. — *n.* **state'liness**. — *adj.* **state'ly** showing state or dignity: majestic, greatly impressive. — *adv.* majestically: loftily. — *ns.* **state'ment** the act of stating: that which is stated: a formal account, declaration of facts, etc.: a financial record, e.g. one issued regularly by a bank to a customer, stating his personal balance and detailing debits and credits; **stāt'er**. — *adj.* **state'wide**. — *n.* **stāt'ism** (the belief in) state control of economic and social affairs. — *n., adj.* **stāt'ist** (see also separate entry). — *adj.* **state'-aid'ed** receiving contributions from the state. — **state bank** in the U.S., a bank that is awarded its charter by a state government; **state'= cabin** a stateroom on a ship; **state'craft** the art of managing state affairs; **State Department** in the U.S., the government department dealing with foreign affairs; **state'-house** the building in which a state legislature sits; **stately home** a large, fine old house, esp. one open to the public; **state'-monger** one who would be thought a politician; **state'-paper** an official paper or document relating to affairs of state; **state'-pris'on; state'-pris'oner** a prisoner confined for offence against the state; **state religion** a religion recognised by the state as the national religion; **state'room** a room of state: a private cabin or railway compartment; **state school** one controlled by a public authority, and financed by taxation; **States'-Gen'eral** the representative body of the three orders (nobility, clergy, burghers) of the French kingdom (*hist.*): the Dutch parliament. — *adj., adv.* **State'side** (*coll.*; also without *cap.*) of, in, towards or to the U.S. — **states'man** one skilled in government: one who takes an important part in governing the state, esp. with wisdom and broadmindedness: one who farms his own estate, a small landholder (*N. of England*): — *fem.* **states'woman**. — *adjs.* **states'manlike, states'manly** befitting a statesman. — *ns.* **states'manship; state'-tri'al** a trial for an offence against the state. — **Council, House of States** see under **council; lie in state** of a corpse, to be laid out in a place of honour before being buried; **State Enrolled Nurse** (abbrev. **SEN**) a nurse who has passed a particular examination of the General Nursing Council of England and Wales or the General Nursing Council of Scotland (see also **State Registered Nurse** below); **state of affairs, events** a situation, set of circumstances; **state of play** the situation as it currently stands; **state of the art** the level or position at a given time, esp. the present, of generally accepted and available knowledge, technical achievement, etc. in a particular field, etc.: (*recently,* esp. *marketing*) the level of technological development as yet unsurpassed in a particular field (*adj.* **state'-of-the-art'**); **State Registered Nurse** (abbrev. **SRN**) in England and Wales, a nurse who has passed a more advanced examination of the General Nursing Council of England and Wales than a State Enrolled Nurse (for Scotland, see **Registered**

General Nurse under **register**); **States of the Church** (*hist.*) an area of central Italy ruled by the popes as a temporal domain (also **Papal States**); **the States** the United States; **turn State's evidence** see **evidence**. [L. *status, -ūs — stāre, statum,* to stand; partly through O.Fr. (see **estate**).]

stater *stā'tər, n.* an ancient Greek standard coin of various kinds — gold daric, silver tetradrachm, etc. [Gr. *statēr,* orig. a pound weight — *histanai,* to set, establish, weigh.]

static, -al *stat'ik, -əl, adjs.* pertaining to statics: pertaining to bodies, forces, charges, etc., in equilibrium: stationary: stable: resting: acting by mere weight: pertaining to sense of bodily equilibrium. — *n.* **(static)** statics (*obs.*): atmospheric disturbances in wireless reception: white specks or flashes on a television picture: crackling on a long-playing plastic record: static electricity. — *adv.* **stat'ically**. — *n.sing.* **stat'ics** the science of forces in equilibrium. — **static electricity** electrical charges that are stationary, not moving along in a current; **static line** a cord joining a parachute pack to the aircraft so that, when the wearer of the pack jumps, the parachute is automatically opened. [Gr. *statikos,* bringing to a standstill — *histanai,* to cause to stand, to place in the balance, weigh.]

Statice *stat'i-sē, n.* the sea-lavender genus (*Limonium*). [L. thrift — Gr. *statikē,* fem. of *statikos* (see previous entry), in medical usage meaning astringent.]

station *stā'shən, n.* a standing still: a mode of standing: position: a chosen fixed point: a standing-place: a fixed stopping-place, esp. one on a railway with associated buildings and structures: a place set apart and equipped for some particular purpose: a local office, headquarters, or depot: a branch post office (*U.S.*): a habitat: an actual spot where a species has been found: an assigned place or post: an assigned region for naval duty: a place in India where officials and officers reside: a stock-farm (*Austr.* and *N.Z.*): position in life (esp. a high position) or in the scale of nature: a holy place visited as one of a series, esp. one of (usu. fourteen) representations of stages in Christ's way to Calvary, disposed around a church interior or elsewhere (*R.C.*). — *adj.* of a station. — *v.t.* to assign a station to: to set: to appoint to a post, place, or office. — *adj.* **sta'tional**. — *n.* **sta'tionariness**. — *adj.* **sta'tionary** still: unmoving: fixed: settled: permanently located: continuously resident. — Also *n.* — *n.* **sta'tioner** (L. *statiōnārius,* a shopkeeper, in the Middle Ages a university bookseller, distinguished from an itinerant) a bookseller or publisher (*obs.*): a dealer in writing-materials and the like. — *adj.* **sta'tionery** belonging to a stationer. — *n.* the goods sold by a stationer. — **Stationers' Hall** the hall in London of the Company of Stationers, who until the passing of the Copyright Act in 1842 enjoyed an absolute control over printing and publishing; **Stationery Office** an office for providing books, stationery, etc., to government offices and for arranging the printing of public papers; **sta'tion-hand** (*Austr.*) a man employed on a station; **sta'tion-house** a lock-up at a police station: a police station (*U.S.*): a small railway station; **sta'tion= master, -manager** one in charge of railway station; **sta'tion-wagon** a motor vehicle usable by adjustment for either passengers or light hauling. [L. *statiō, -ōnis — stāre,* to stand.]

statism. See **state**.

statist *stā'tist, n.* a statesman: a politician: an advocate of statism (q.v. under **state**): a statistician. — *adj.* **statistic** (*stə-tist'ik*) statistical: political (*obs.*): relating to status. — *n.* a statistician: (in *pl.*) tabulated numerical facts, orig. those relating to a state, or (with *sing.* verb) the classification, tabulation, and study of such facts: one such fact. — *adj.* **statist'ical** of, concerned with, of the nature of, statistics. — *adv.* **statist'ically**. — *n.* **statistician** (*stat-is-tish'ən*) one skilled in statistics: a compiler or student of statistics. [It. *statista* and Ger. *Statistik* — L. *status,* state.]

stative *stā′tiv, adj.* permanent, fixed (now only of a Roman camp): indicating a physical state or reflex action (of certain Hebrew verbs): indicating a state, as opposed to an action, etc. (*linguistics*). [L. *statīvus* — *stāre*, to stand.]

stato- *stat′ō-*, in composition, standing. — *ns.* **statocyst** (*stat′ō-sist*; Gr. *kystis*, bladder) an organ of equilibrial sense in crustaceans and other invertebrates, containing statoliths: a cell with starch-grains by which a plant is supposed to be sensitive to gravity; **stat′olith** (Gr. *lithos*, stone) a starch grain or other free solid body in a statocyst; **stat′oscope** a sensitive barometer for detecting minute differences. [Gr. *statos*, set, placed.]

stator *stā′tər, n.* a stationary part within which a part rotates. [L. *stător*, stander.]

statue *stat′ū, n.* a representation (usu. near or above life-size) of human or animal form in the round. — Also (*obs.*) **stat′ua.** — *adj.* **stat′uary** of or suitable for sculpture: sculptured: statuesque. — *n.* sculpture: a sculptor. — *adjs.* **stat′ued** furnished with statues: sculptured; **statuesque** (*-esk′*) like a statue. — *adv.* **statuesque′ly.** — *ns.* **statuesque′ness; statuette′** a small statue, figurine. [L. *statua* — *statuĕre*, to cause to stand — *stāre*.]

stature *stach′ər, stat′yər, n.* body height: eminence. — *adj.* **stat′ured** having a stature. [L. *statūra*.]

status *stā′təs, n.* state: condition: standing: position, rank, importance, in society or in any group: — *pl.* (*rare*) **status** (*-tūs*). — **status symbol** a possession or a privilege considered to mark a person out as having a high position in his social group. [L. *stătus*.]

status quo *stā′təs, stat′ōōs, kwō,* (L.) the state in which: the existing condition. — **status quo ante** (*-an′te, an′tā*) the state of affairs which existed before.

statute *stat′ūt, n.* a law expressly enacted by the legislature (as distinguished from a customary law or law of use and wont): a written law: the act of a corporation or its founder, intended as a permanent rule or law: a bond or other proceeding based on a statute: a hiring-fair. — *adj.* **stat′utable** prescribed, permitted, recognised by, or according to statute. — *advs.* **stat′utably; stat′utorily.** — *adj.* **stat′utory** enacted by statute: depending on statute for its authority. — **stat′ute-book** a record of statutes or enacted laws; **stat′ute-cap** (*Shak.*) a kind of cap enjoined by statute (1571) to be worn on Sundays by all below a certain rank; **stat′ute-labour** compulsory labour on roads, etc.; **stat′ute-law** law in the form of statutes; **statute mile** see **mile; statutory rape** (*U.S.*) the criminal offence of having sexual intercourse with a girl who is below the age of consent. — **statute of limitations** a statute prescribing the period of time within which proceedings must be taken to enforce a right or bring a legal action; **Statute of Westminster** an act (1931) of the United Kingdom parliament conferring independent sovereign status on the self-governing dominions. [L. *statūtum*, that which is set up — *statuĕre*.]

staunch[1], **stanch** *stönch, stönsh, stänch, stänsh, adj.* watertight: stout and firm: firm in principle, pursuit, or support: trusty, hearty, constant, zealous. — *adv.* **sta(u)nch′ly.** — *n.* **sta(u)nch′ness.** [O.Fr. *estanche*; see **stanch**[1].]

staunch[2] (*v.t.*). See **stanch**[1].

staurolite *stör′ə-līt, n.* a silicate of aluminium with ferrous oxide, magnesia, and water, common as twinned cruciform crystals. — *adj.* **staurolitic** (*-lit′ik*). [Gr. *stauros*, cross, *lithos*, stone.]

stauroscope *stör′ə-skōp, n.* an optical instrument for studying the structure of mineral crystals. [Gr. *stauros*, cross, *skopeein*, to look at.]

stave *stāv, n.* one of the pieces of which a cask or tub is made: a staff, rod, bar, shaft: a staff (*mus.*): a stanza, verse of a song. — *v.t.* to break a stave or the staves of: to break: to burst inward (often with *in*): to drive off, as with a staff: to delay (e.g. the evil day; with *off*): to ward (off), keep back: to put together, or repair, with staves: to sprain, jar violently (fingers,

toes, etc.) (*Scot.*). — *v.i.* to thrust onward (*Scot.*): to break up: — *pa.t.* and *pa.p.* **staved** or **stove.** — **stave and tail** in bear-baiting, to intervene with staves and by grasping the dogs′ tails. [By-form of **staff**.]

stave-church *stāv′-chûrch, n.* an ancient Norwegian wooden church supported on masts, with gabled roofs rising one above another. [Norw. *stav-kirke* — *stav*, staff, stave, *kirke*, church.]

staves *stāvz,* plural of **staff** and of **stave.**

stavesacre *stāvz′ā-kər, n.* a tall larkspur whose seeds were formerly used against lice. [O.Fr. *stavesaigre* — L.L. *staphisagria* — Gr. *staphis*, raisins, *agrios*, wild.]

staw *stö,* a Scots form of **stall**[1] (*n.* and *v.t.*) and **stole** (*pa.t.* of **steal**[1]).

stay *stā, n.* a rope supporting a mast: a guy: a support: a prop: a connecting piece or brace to resist tension: (in *pl.*) a stiff corset (often **pair of stays**): a stopping, bringing or coming to a standstill: a suspension of legal proceeding: delay: an obstacle (*obs.*): a sojourn: duration: staying-power: a permanent state (*obs.*). — *v.t.* to support or incline with a stay or stays: to put in stays or on the other tack: to support: to prop: to sustain: to abide: to endure: to endure to the end: to stop: to detain: to hold, restrain, check the action of: to bring to rest: to discontinue: to allay: to hold back: to await (*arch.*): to remain to participate in, be present at or endure (*old-fashioned*): to stop for, be stopped by (*Spens.*). — *v.i.* to turn to windward in tacking: to rely, to found (*Shak.*): to stop: to remain: to tarry: to wait: to be kept waiting: to sojourn: to dwell (*Scot.*): to hold out, last, endure: in a race, etc., to maintain one′s pace over a long distance: to wait, attend as a servant (*Shak.*): — *pa.t.* and *pa.p.* **stayed** (now rarely **staid**). — *adj.* **stayed** wearing stays: staid (*Spens.*). — *n.* **stay′er** one who, or that which, remains, stops, holds, or supports: a person or animal of good lasting or staying qualities for a race. — *n.* and *adj.* **stay′ing.** — *adj.* **stay′less** not to be stopped: without stop: without stays: unsupported: impermanent. — *adj.* **stay′-at-home** keeping much at home: untravelled. — *n.* a stay-at-home person. — **stay′-bolt** a bolt or rod binding together opposite plates. — *adjs.* **stay′-down** of a mining strike, without leaving the working-place; **stay′-in′** without leaving the working-place (as a strike). — **stay′ing-power** ability to go on long without flagging; **stay′-lace** a lace for fastening a corset; **stay-maker** a maker of corsets; **staysail** (*stā′sl*) a sail extended on a stay; **stay stitching** in dressmaking, a line of stitching in the seam allowance to prevent stretching and fraying of the material; **stay′-tackle** hoisting-tackle hung from a ship′s mainstay; **stay′-tape** a stay-lace: tape for binding edges. — **come to stay** to become permanent or established; **in stays** head to windward in tacking; **miss stays** see **miss**[1]; **stay on** to remain, tarry after the normal time for departing; **stay out** to outstay: to stay to the end of; **stay over** (*coll.*) to remain overnight; **stay put** not to move from the place or position in which one has been put; **stay the course** to endure to the end of the race (*lit.* and *fig.*); **stay the stomach, the pangs of hunger** to allay cravings of hunger for the time. [Partly O.E. *stæg*, stay (rope); partly O.Fr. *estayer*, to prop, from the same Gmc. root; partly O.Fr. *ester* — L. *stāre*, to stand.]

stayne, stayre. Old spellings (*Spens.* etc.) of **stain, stair.**

stead *sted, n.* a place (now chiefly in compounds and idiomatic phrases): esp. the place which another had or might have: a farm: a site: a bedstead: a space of time (*Spens.*): circumstances, case, condition (*Spens.*): service, avail, advantage. — *v.t.* to set (*obs.*): to set in a plight: to avail, help, serve (*arch.*): to fulfil in substitution (*Shak.* **steed up**): — *pa.t.* and *pa.p.* **stead′ed, stead** (*sted*). — *adj.* **stead′fast** firmly fixed or established: firm: constant: resolute: steady. — *adv.* **stead′fastly.** — *n.* **stead′fastness.** — *adv.* **stead′ily.** — *ns.* **stead′iness; stead′ing** farm-buildings with or without the farmhouse. — *adj.* **stead′y** (*compar.* **stead′i**... *superl.* **stead′iest**) firm in standing or in place: fix...

stable: constant: resolute: consistent: regular: uniform: sober, industrious: (with *to*) (of a hound) seldom diverted from the trail of (a deer, hare, etc.): (with *from*) (of a horse or hound) seldom distracted, upset or diverted by (another animal, a noise, etc.). — *v.t.* to make steady: to make or keep firm: — *pr.p.* **stead'ying;** *pa.t.* and *pa.p.* **stead'ied.** — *n.* a rest or support, as for the hand, a tool, or a piece of work: a regular boyfriend or girlfriend (*coll.*). — *interj.* be careful!: keep calm!: hold the present course (*naut.*): see **ready, steady, go!** under **ready.** — *adj.* **stead'y-going** having, showing steady habits or action. — **steady state** (*astron.*) see **continuous creation.** — **go steady** (*coll.*) (esp. of a boy and girl not yet engaged to be married) to have a steady relationship, to go about regularly together; **stand one in good stead** to prove of good service to one; **steady on!** keep calm!: don't be so foolish, hasty, etc. [O.E. *stede*, place; cf. Ger. *Stadt*, town, *Statt*, place, Du. *stad*, town; O.E. *stedefæst*, **steadfast**.]

steak *stāk, n.* any of several cuts of beef graded for frying, braising, stewing, etc.: a slice of meat (esp. hind-quarters of beef) or fish. — **steak'house** a restaurant specialising in fried or grilled beefsteaks. [O.N. *steik*; *steikja,* to roast on a spit.]

steal[1] *stēl, v.t.* to take by theft, esp. secretly: to take, gain or win by address, by contrivance, unexpectedly, insidiously, gradually, or furtively: to snatch: in golf, to hole (a long putt) by a delicate stroke — the opposite of *gobble*: in baseball, of a runner, to gain (a base) without the help of a hit or error: to put surreptitiously, smuggle. — *v.i.* to practise theft: to take feloniously: to pass quietly, unobtrusively, gradually, or surreptitiously: — *pa.t.* **stole** (*obs.* **stale;** *Scot.* **staw, stealed, stealt**); *pa.p.* **stō'len** (*obs.* **stōle;** *Milt.* **stōln;** *Scot.* **stown, stealed, stealt**). — *n.* (*coll.*) an act of stealing, a theft: something acquired by theft: a bargain, a snip: (esp. *U.S.*) the stealing of a base (*baseball*). — *n.* **steal'er.** — *n.* and *adj.* **steal'ing.** — *adv.* **steal'ingly.** — **steal a march on** see **march**[2]; **steal a marriage** to marry secretly; **steal someone's thunder** to make use of another's invention against him (as when John Dennis's stage thunder was used in a rival's play): to rob someone of the opportunity of achieving a sensational effect by forestalling him; **steal the show** see **show.** [O.E. *stelan*; Ger. *stehlen*, Du. *stelen*.]

steal[2], **steale, steel, stele, steil** *stēl*, (*dial.* and *Spens.*) *n.* a handle, shank, shaft. [O.E. *stela*, stalk, cf. Ger. *Stiel*; conn. **stale**[4].]

stealed, stealt. See **steal**[1].

stealth *stelth, n.* a theft (*Spens., Shak.*): a thing stolen (*Milt.*): secret or unobtrusive going or passage (*Shak.*): secret procedure or manner: furtiveness. — *adj.* (*mil. jargon*) of an aircraft, having various features that help it to avoid detection by radar. — *adv.* **stealth'ily.** — *n.* **stealth'iness.** — *adj.* **stealth'y** acted or acting with stealth: furtive. [**steal**[1].]

steam *stēm, n.* water in the form of gas or vapour or of a mist or film of liquid drops: a steamed dish: steam-power: a spell of travel by steam-power: energy, force, spirit (*fig.*). — *adj.* of, for, using, worked by, steam: outdated, old-fashioned, not using the latest technology (*facet.*) — *v.i.* to rise or pass off in steam or vapour: to emit or generate steam, vapour, or smell: (of windows, etc.) to become dimmed with condensed vapour (often with *up*): to move by means of steam-power. — *v.t.* to exhale: to expose to steam: to cook by means of steam: to dim with vapour. — *adj.* **steamed.** — *n.* **steam'er** one who steams: apparatus for steaming: a steamship: a motor-car, a road-locomotive, fire-engine, etc., worked by steam. — *n.* **steam'ie** (*Scot.*) a public laundry. — *adv.* **steam'ily.** — *n.* **steam'iness.** — *n., adj.,* and *adv.* **steam'ing.** — *adj.* **steam'y** of, like, full of, covered with, as if covered with, emitting, steam or vapour. — **steam bath** a steam-filled compartment, e.g. one at a Turkish bath, etc. in which to refresh oneself by sweating, etc., or

one in a laboratory for sterilising equipment; **steam boat, steam'ship, steam'-vessel** a vessel driven by steam, **steam'-boiler** a boiler for generating steam; **steam'-car, -carriage** steam-driven road vehicle; **steam'-chamber, -chest, -dome** a chamber above a steam-boiler serving as a reservoir for steam; **steam'-coal** coal suitable for raising steam; **steam'-crane; steam'-digger.** — *adj.* **steam'-driv'en.** — **steam'-engine** any engine worked by steam; **steamer duck** a large duck of S. America whose swimming action is suggestive of the motion of a steamer with a paddle-wheel on each side; **steam'-gauge** a pressure gauge for steam; **steam'-gov'ernor** the governor of a steam-engine; **steam'-hamm'er** a vertical hammer worked by steam. — *v.t.* and *v.i.* **steam'-haul** to draw (a conveyance for goods, passengers, etc.) along rails by means of chains, etc. attached to a stationary steam-engine. — **steam iron** an electric iron having a compartment in which water is heated to provide steam to damp material; **steam'-jack'et** a hollow casing supplied with steam; **steam'-launch** a large steam-driven boat; **steam'-naviga'tion** the propulsion of vessels by steam; **steam'-navvy, -shovel** an excavator driven by steam; **steam'-pack'et** a steam-vessel plying between certain ports; **steam'-pipe** a pipe for conveying steam; **steam'-plough** a plough or gang of ploughs worked by a steam-engine; **steam'-port** an opening for the passage of steam; **steam'-power** the force or agency of steam when applied to machinery; **steam radio** (*facet.*) sound radio, considered old-fashioned in comparison with television; **steam'-roll'er** a steam-engine with a heavy roller for wheels, used in road-mending, etc.: any weighty crushing force (*fig.*). — *v.t.* (*coll.*) to crush (objections, etc.): to force (e.g. legislation through parliament, etc.). — **steam-shovel** see **steam-navvy** above. — *adj.* **steam'tight** impervious to steam. — **steam'-trap** a contrivance for allowing the passage of water but not of steam; **steam'-tug** a small steam-vessel used in towing ships; **steam'-tur'bine** an engine in which expanding steam acts on blades attached to a drum; **steam'-whis'tle** a whistle sounded by passage of steam; **steam'-yacht.** — **full steam ahead** forward at the greatest speed possible: with maximum effort; **get up steam** to build up steam pressure: to collect one's forces: to become excited; **let off steam** to release steam into the atmosphere: to work off energy: to give vent to anger or annoyance; **steamed up** of windows, etc., dimmed with condensed vapour: indignant (*slang*); **steam open** to open (esp. envelopes) by softening gum by exposure to steam; **under one's own steam** by one's own unaided efforts. [O.E. *stēam*; Du. *stoom.*]

stean[1], **steen** *stēn,* (*dial.; Spens.* **steane**) *n.* a stone or earthenware vessel. [O.E. *stæne.*]

stean[2]. See **steen**[1].

steane. See **stean**[1].

stear, steard, stearage, stearsman. Obs. spellings of **steer**[2], **steered,** etc.

stearsmate. Another spelling of **steersmate.**

stear-, steat- *stē'ər-, -ar', -ət-, -at',* in composition, suet, fat. — *n.* **stearate** (*stē'ər-āt*) a salt of stearic acid. — *adj.* **stearic** (*stē-ar'ik*) of stearin (**stearic acid** a fatty acid $C_{17}H_{35}COOH$). — *n.* **ste'arin** glyceryl ester of stearic acid: a mixture of stearic and palmitic acids (also **ste'arine**): the solid part of a fat. — *adj.* **ste'arine** made of stearin(e), as candles. — *n.* **steatite** (*stē'ə-tīt*) soapstone. — *adj.* **steatitic** (*-tit'ik*). — *ns.* **steat'ocele** (Gr. *kēlē*, tumour) a fatty tumour in the scrotum; **steatō'ma** a fatty encysted tumour. — *adj.* **steatom'atous.** — *n.* **steatopygia** (*stē-ə-tō-pī'ji-ə, -pij'i-ə;* Gr. *pȳgē,* buttock) an accumulation of fat on the buttocks. — *adj.* **steatopygous** (*-tō-pī'gəs, -top'i-gəs*) fat-buttocked. — *ns.* **steatorrh(o)ea** (*stē-ə-tə-rē'ə;* Gr. *rhoia,* a flow) abnormal fattiness of the faeces; **steatō'sis** fatty degeneration. [Gr. *stĕār, stĕátos,* suet.]

steare *stēr,* (*Spens.*). Same as **steer**[1].

steat-. See **stear-.**

sted, stedd, stedde, stede (*Spens.*), **steed** (*Shak.*), forms of stead (n. and v.t.); **stedfast** an obsolescent spelling (*Shak.*, *Milt.*, etc.) of **steadfast; steddy, steedy** old spellings of **steady.**

steed[1] *stēd, n.* a horse, esp. a spirited horse. [O.E. *stēda*, stud-horse, stallion; cf. O.E. *stōd*, stud; Ger. *Stute*, stud-mare, *Gestüt*, stud.]

steed[2], **steedy.** See **sted.**

steek *stēk*, (*Scot.*) *n.* a stitch. — *v.t.* and *v.i.* to stitch. — *v.t.* to pierce: to fasten: to shut: — *pa.t.* and *pa.p.* **steek'it.** [Partly at least O.E. *stice*, stitch, puncture; perh. partly confused with **stick**[1].]

steel[1] *stēl, n.* iron containing a little carbon with or without other things: a cutting tool or weapon, an instrument, object, or part made of steel, as a steel knife-sharpener, a skate: a piece of steel, as for stiffening a corset, striking fire from a flint: a steel-engraving: extreme hardness, staying power, trustworthiness (*fig.*): any chalybeate medicine. — *adj.* of or like steel. — *v.t.* to cover or edge with steel: to harden: to nerve: to make obdurate. — *adj.* **steeled** made of, covered, protected, provided or edged with, steel: hardened: nerved. — *ns.* **steel'iness; steel'ing.** — *adj.* **steel'y** of or like steel. — **steel band** a West Indian band, using steel drums, etc. — *n.* and *adj.* **steel'-blue'** blue like a reflection from steel. — *adj.* **steel'-clad** clad in armour. — **steel drum** a percussion instrument usu. made from the top of an oil drum, hammered out into a bowl-like shape and faceted so as to produce different notes; **steel'-engrav'ing** engraving on steel plates: an impression or print so got; **steel erector** a spider-man. — *n.* and *adj.* **steel'-grey', -gray'** bluish-grey like steel. — *adj.* **steel'-head'ed.** — **steel'-pen** a nib of steel; **steel'-plate** a plate of steel: one on which a design is engraved: a print from it. — *adj.* **steel'-plat'ed** plated with steel. — **steel'-trap'** one with steel jaws and spring; **steel'-ware** articles of steel collectively; **steel'-wool'** steel shavings used for cleaning and polishing; **steel'work** work executed in steel: (often in *pl.* form) a factory where steel is made; **steel'worker.** [O.E. *style*; Ger. *Stahl*.]

steel[2]. See **steal**[2].

steelbow *stēl'bō*, (*Scots law*) *n.* stock and goods received from a landlord with obligation to return a like amount and value when the lease expires: a contract or tenure on these terms. — Also *adj.* [**steel**[1], in the sense of rigidly fixed, and obs. *bow* — O.N. *bū*, stock of cattle.]

steeld. See **stell.**

steeled. See **steel**[1], and **stellar.**

steelyard *stēl'yärd, n.* a weighing machine consisting of a lever with a short arm for the thing weighed and a long graduated arm on which a single weight moves. [Prob. **steel**[1] and **yard**[1], but suggested or fixed in use by the *Steelyard* or *Stâlhof* (L.G.; prop. sample yard, mistranslated steel yard), the Hanse headquarters in London.]

steem *stēm*, (*Spens.*) *v.t.* Same as **esteem;** also same as **steam.**

steen[1], **stean, stein** *stēn, v.t.* to line (a well) with stone. — *n.* such a lining. — *n.* **steen'ing, stean'ing, stein'ing** such a lining or the process of making it. [O.E. *stænan*.]

steen[2]. See **stean**[1].

steenbok *stän', stēn'bok, n.* a small S. African antelope. — See also **steinbock.** [Du., — *steen*, stone, *bok*, buck.]

steenbras *stēn'bras*, (*S. Afr.*) *n.* any of several edible estuarine S. African fish. [Afk., — Du. *steen*, stone, *brasem*, bream.]

steenkirk *stēn'kûrk, n.* a lace cravat loosely worn. [From the battle of *Steenkerke*, 3 August 1692.]

steep[1] *stēp, adj.* lofty (*obs.*): rising or descending with great inclination: precipitous: headlong: difficult: excessive, exorbitant. — *n.* a precipitous place. — *v.t.* (*S.W. England*) to cause to stoop, slope. — *v.i.* to rise or fall precipitously. — *v.t.* and *v.i.* **steep'en** to make or become steeper. — *n.* **steep'iness** (*obs.*). — *adj.* **steep'ish.** — *adv.* **steep'ly.** — *n.* **steep'ness.** — *adj.* **steep'y** (*poet.*) steep. — *adjs.* **steep(e)'-down(e)** (*Shak.*)

precipitous; **steep'-to'** (*naut.*) going down precipitously into the water; **steep(e)'-up** (*Shak.*) precipitous. [O.E. *stēap*; cf. **stoop**[1].]

steep[2] *stēp, v.t.* to soak: to wet thoroughly: to saturate: to imbue. — *v.i.* to undergo soaking or thorough wetting. — *n.* a soaking process: a liquid for steeping anything in: rennet. — *n.* **steep'er** one who steeps: a vessel for steeping in. [M.E. *stepen*; perh. conn. with **stoup**[1].]

steeple *stēp'l, n.* a church or other tower with or without, including or excluding, a spire: a structure surmounted by a spire: the spire alone. — *adj.* **steep'led** having a steeple or steeples or appearance of steeples. — **steep'le-bush** hardhack; **steep'lechase** orig. an impromptu horse-race with some visible church-steeple as goal: a horse-race across-country: one over a course with obstacles to be jumped: a foot-race of like kind. — *v.i.* to ride or run in a steeplechase. — **steep'lechaser; steep'lechasing; steep'le-crown** a high conical hat. — Also *adj.* — *adj.* **steep'le-crowned.** — **steep'le-fair** (*obs.*) a market in church-livings; **steep'le-hat** a steeple-crowned hat; **steep'le-house** (*obs.*) a church-building; **steep'lejack** one who repairs steeples and chimney-stalks. [O.E. *stēpel, stypel, stīpel*, from root of **steep**[1].]

steer[1] *stēr, n.* a young ox, esp. a castrated one from two to four years old. — *n.* **steer'ling** a little or young steer. [O.E. *stēor*; Ger. *Stier*.]

steer[2] *stēr, v.t.* to direct with, or as with, the helm: to guide: to govern. — *v.i.* to direct a ship, cycle, etc., in its course: to be directed, take or follow a course in answer to the helm. — *adj.* **steer'able.** — *ns.* **steer'age** act or practice of steering: the effect of a rudder on the ship: course: government: apparatus for steering: part (in front of the great cabin) from which a ship used to be steered: part of a passenger ship with lowest fares (also *adj.*); **steer'er; steer'ing.** — **steer'age-way** sufficient movement of a vessel to enable it to be controlled by the helm; **steering column** in a motor vehicle the shaft on which the steering-wheel or handlebars are mounted; **steering committee** a group who decide what measures shall be brought forward and when; **steer'ing-gear** the mechanism that transmits motion from the steering-wheel; **steer'ing-wheel** the wheel whereby a ship's rudder is turned, or a motor-car, etc., guided; **steers'man**, (*obs.*) **steers'mate** one who steers, a helmsman. — **steer clear of** to avoid. [O.E. *stēoran, stȳran*, to steer.]

steer[3] *stēr, n., v.t.,* and *v.i.* a Scots form of **stir**[1]. — *n.* **steer'y** (*Scott*) commotion.

steeve[1] *stēv, n.* angular elevation, esp. of a bowsprit. — *v.t.* and *v.i.* to incline to the horizon. [Origin unknown.]

steeve[2], **stieve** *stēv*, (*Scot.*) *adj.* stiff, firm: sturdy. — Also *adv.* — *adv.* **steeve'ly, stieve'ly.** [M.E. *stef*; ety. doubtful.]

steeve[3] *stēv, v.t.* to stuff, pack close. — *n.* **steev'ing.** [Perh. Fr. *estiver* — L. *stīpāre*, to stuff.]

stegano-, **stego-** *steg'(ən-)ə-, -ō'*, in composition, covered, roofed, hidden, watertight. — *ns.* **steganogram** (*steg'-ən-ə-gram*), **-graph** a cryptogram; **steganographer** (*-og'*) one who works with ciphers. — *adj.* **steganograph'ic.** — *ns.* **steganog'raphist; steganog'raphy; steg'anopod** (Gr. *pous, podos*, foot) any bird of the **Steganop'odēs**, the pelican order of birds, with all four toes webbed together. — *adj.* **steganop'odous.** — *n.* **stegno'sis** constriction of the pores and vessels: constipation. — *adjs.* **stegnot'ic; stegocarp'ous** (Gr. *karpos*, fruit) with lidded capsule. — *n.pl.* **Stegocephalia** (*-se-fā'li-ə*; Gr. *kephalē*, head) an extinct order of amphibians (Labyrinthodon, etc.) having the skull protected by bony plates. — *adj.* and *n.* **stegocephā'lian.** — *adj.* **stegocephalous** (*-sef'ə-ləs*). — *ns.* **stegodon(t)** (*steg'ə-don(t)*; Gr. *odons, odontos*, tooth) an extinct mammal with ridged teeth, related to the mastodon and the elephant; **Stegomyia** (*-mī'yə*; Gr. *myia*, fly) an older name for the Aedes genus of mosquitoes: (without *cap.*) a mosquito of this genus; **stegoph'ilist** one who climbs buildings for sport; **steg'osaur** (Gr. *sauros*, lizard) any of several ornithischian, quadrupedal, herbivorous dinosaurs of the Jurassic period, characterised by armour of various sorts. — *adj.* **stegosaur'ian.** — **Stegosaur'us** a member of the class of stegosaurs, having two lines of kite-shaped plates along the backbone. [Gr. *steganos*, covered, watertight, *stegein*, to cover, hold water, protect, hide, *stegnoein*, to make costive, *stegos*, roof.]

steil. See **steal²**.

stein¹ *stēn, stīn, shtīn, n.* a large beer mug, often earthenware and frequently with a hinged lid. [Ger.]

stein², **steining.** See **steen¹**.

Steinberger *stīn'bûr-gər, shtīn'ber-hhər, n.* an esteemed Rhenish white wine, from *Steinberg*, near Wiesbaden.

steinbock *stīn'bok, n.* the Alpine ibex: also used for **steenbok.** [Ger. *Stein*, stone, *Bock*, buck.]

stele¹ *stē'lē, n.* an upright stone slab or tablet (also **stē'la**): (*stē'lē, stēl*) the central cylinder (vascular bundles with pith and pericycle) in stems and roots of the higher plants (*bot.*): — *pl.* **stē'lae.** — *adjs.* **stē'lar, stē'lene.** [Gr. *stēlē* — root of *histanai*, to set, stand.]

stele². See **steal²**.

stelene. See **stele¹**.

stell *stel, v.t.* to set, post (*Scot.*): to delineate (*arch.; Shak., pa.p.* **steeld** *steld*). — *n.* (*Scot.*) an enclosure (usu. a ringwall) for sheltering sheep, etc. — *adj.* **stelled** fixed (see also under **stellar**). [O.E. *stellan*, to fix, put.]

stellar *stel'ər, adj.* of the stars: of the nature of, relating to, belonging to, characteristic of, a star: starry: relating to a star performer or performance. — *ns.* **stell'arator** (*stellar* and gener*ator*) a twisted torus in which plasma can be confined by a magnetic field, used for producing thermonuclear (i.e. stellar) power by nuclear fusion; **Stellā'ria** the chickweed genus of the pink family. — *adjs.* **stell'ate** star-shaped: with branches radiating from a point: with sides that intersect one another, giving a starlike effect, as in the pentagram; **stellā'ted** stellate: starred. — *adv.* **stell'ately.** — *adjs.* **stelled** starred: (*Shak.* **steel'ed**) perh. formed into stars (but prob. fixed; see **stell** above); **stellif'erous** having or bearing stars or starlike marks or forms; **stell'ified; stell'iform** star-shaped. — *v.t.* **stell'ify** to turn into a star: to set among the stars: to set with stars (*obs.*). — *n.* **stell'ifying.** — *adjs.* **stell'ular, stell'ulate** like a little star. [L. *stēlla*, a star.]

Stellenbosch *stel'ən-bosh, (mil. slang) v.t.* to relegate to a post where incompetence matters less: to supersede. [From *Stellenbosch*, Cape of Good Hope, such a dumping-ground.]

stelliferous, etc. See **stellar**.

stellion *stel'yən,* or **stellio lizard** *stel'i-ō liz'ərd, ns.* a Levantine lizard (*Agama stellio*) with starry spots. — *n.* **stell'ionate** a fraud that does not come under any specific head (*law*). [L. *stēlliō, -ōnis*, a star-spotted lizard, a knave — *stēlla*, star.]

stellular, stellulate. See **stellar**.

stem¹ *stem, n.* the leaf-bearing axis of a plant: a stalk: anything stalk-like, as the slender vertical part of a written musical note, of a wine-glass, the winding shaft of a watch: an upright stroke of a letter: the main line (or sometimes a branch) of a family: a race or family: the base of a word, to which inflectional suffixes are added (*philol.*): a curved timber at the prow of a ship: the forepart of a ship. — *v.t.* to provide with a stem: to deprive of stalk or stem: to oppose the stem to: hence, to make way against, breast: to ram. — *v.i.* to grow a stem: to spring, take rise. — *adj.* **stem'less.** — *n.* **stem'let.** — *adj.* **stemmed.** — *n.* **stem'son** a timber behind the apron of a ship. — **stem cell** (*histology*) a generalised parent cell whose progeny specialise; **stem cup** a Chinese porcelain goblet first produced in the Ming Dynasty, having a roomy bowl mounted on a stem that broadens to form the base; **stem'-form** ancestral form; **stem stitch** an overlapping stitch used in embroidery; **stem'winder** (*U.S.*) a keyless watch. — **from stem to stern** from one end of a vessel to the other:

completely, throughout. [O.E. *stefn, stemn*; Ger. *Stamm*; perh. conn. with **stand**.]

stem² *stem, v.t.* to stop, check: to dam: to tamp: to staunch: in skiing, to slow down by pushing the heels apart: — *pr.p.* **stemm'ing**; *pa.t.* and *pa.p.* **stemmed.** — *n.* in skiing, the process of stemming, used in turning. [O.N. *stemma*.]

stembuck *stem'buk*, **stembok** *-bok*, for **steenbok**.

steme *stēm, (Spens.) v.t.* for **steam**, i.e. evaporate.

stemma *stem'ə, n.* a garland: a scroll: a pedigree, family tree: a diagrammatic tree drawn up (using the internal evidence of manuscripts, etc.) to show the descent and relationships of the texts of a literary work: an ocellus: — *pl.* **stemm'ata.** — *adj.* **stemm'atous.** — *v.t.* **stemme** (*stem; Spens.*) to encircle. [Gr. *stemma*, usu. in pl. *stemmata*.]

stempel, stemple *stem'pl, n.* a cross-timber in a shaft, as support or step. [Cf. Ger. *Stempel*.]

stemson. See **stem¹**.

sten. See **stend** and **sten gun**.

stench *stench, -sh, n.* stink. — *v.t.* to cause to stink. — *adj.* **stench'y.** — **stench'-trap** a device to prevent rise of gases in drains. [O.E. *stenc*, smell (good or bad); cf. **stink**; Ger. *Stank*.]

stencil *sten's(i)l, v.t.* and *v.i.* to paint by brushing over a perforated plate: to make a stencil for producing copies of typewriting or writing: — *pr.p.* **sten'cilling**; *pa.t.* and *pa.p.* **sten'cilled.** — *n.* the plate or the colouring-matter so used: the design or lettering so produced: a piece of waxed paper, etc., on which letters are cut by typewriter or stylus so that ink will pass through. — *adj.* **sten'cilled.** — *ns.* **sten'ciller; sten'cilling.** — **sten'cilplate.** [O.Fr. *estinceller*, to spangle — *estincelle* — L. *scintilla*, a spark.]

stend *stend, (Scot.) v.i.* to bound, stride vigorously. — *n.* a bound or great stride: a dart of pain. — Also **sten**. [Poss. L. *extendĕre*.]

stengah *steng'ga*, **stinger** *sting'ər, ns.* a peg of whisky and soda. [Malay *sa tengah*, one half.]

sten (also **Sten**) **gun** *sten gun*, a small automatic gun. [Shepherd and Turpin, the designers, and E*n*field, as in **bren gun**.]

stenlock *sten'lək, (Scot.) n.* a coalfish: an overgrown coalfish. [Origin doubtful.]

steno- *sten-ō-, -ə-*, in composition, contracted. — *ns.* **stenocar'dia** (Gr. *kardia*, heart) another name for the heart disease angina pectoris; **sten'ochrome** (*-krōm*; Gr. *chrōma*, colour) a print by stenochromy; **sten'ochromy** (or *-ok'rə-mi*) printing in several colours at one printing; **sten'ograph** a shorthand character or report: a machine for writing shorthand, operated by keyboard. — *v.t.* to write in shorthand. — *n.* **stenog'rapher.** — *adjs.* **stenograph'ic, -al.** — *adv.* **stenograph'ically.** — *ns.* **stenog'raphist; stenog'raphy** the art, or any method, of writing very quickly: shorthand. — *adjs.* **stenopaeic** (*-pē'ik*; Gr. *opaios*, holed — *opē*, an opening) with a narrow opening (also **stenopā'ic**); **stenosed** (*sti-nōst'*) morbidly contracted. — *n.* **stenō'sis** constriction, narrowing of a tube or passage: constipation. — *adj.* **stenotic** (*sti-not'ik*). — *ns.* **sten'otype** a phonetic typewriter or its use; **sten'otyper, sten'otypist; sten'otypy.** [Gr. *stenos*, narrow.]

stent¹ *stent, n., v.t.,* and *v.i.* Same as **stint¹**, with meanings shading off into those of next word.

stent² *stent, (Scot.) n.* assessment: valuation: tax. — *v.t.* to assess: to tax: to levy. — *ns.* **stent'or, stent'our** stentmaster. — **stent'master** one who determines amount of tax to be paid. [**extent**, or O.Fr. *estente*; see also **stent¹** and **stint¹**.]

Stentor *stent'ör, n.* a very loud-voiced Greek at Troy (*Iliad*), hence (also without *cap.*) a loud-voiced person: a genus of ciliate protozoans. — *adjs.* **stento'rian; stentorophon'ic** (Gr. *phōnē*, voice). — *n.* **stent'orphone** apparatus for intensifying the voice. [Gr. *Stentōr*.]

stentour. See **stent²**.

step *step, n.* a pace: a movement of the leg in walking, running, or dancing: the distance so covered: a footstep: a footfall: a footprint: gait: a small space: a short walk or journey: a degree of a scale: a stage upward or downward: one tread of a stair: a rung of a ladder: a doorstep: something to put the foot on in mounting or dismounting: a stage in discontinuous or stairwise rise or fall: a move towards an end or in a course of proceeding: coincidence in speed and phase: a support for the end of a mast, pivot, or the like: (in *pl.*) walk, direction taken in walking: (in *pl.*) a step-ladder (often a **pair of steps**): (in *pl.*) a flight of stairs. — *v.i.* to advance, retire, mount, or descend by taking a step or steps: to pace: to walk: to walk slowly or gravely: to walk a short distance. — *v.t.* to perform by stepping: to measure by pacing: to arrange or shape stepwise: to set, as a foot (now *U.S.*): to fix, as a mast: — *pr.p.* **stepp'ing;** *pa.t.* and *pa.p.* **stepped** (also **stept**). — *n.* **stepp'er.** — *adv.* **step'wise** in the manner of steps. — *adj.* **step'-cut** of diamonds and other stones, cut in step-like facets. — **step'-dance** a dance involving an effective display of steps by an individual dancer; **step'-dancer; step'-dancing; step'-down** a decrease in rate, quantity, output, etc. — *adj.* reducing voltage: decreasing by stages. — **step'-fault'** (*geol.*) one of a series of parallel faults throwing in the same direction; **step'-in** a garment that is put on by being stepped into, esp. one that needs no fastening. — Also *adj.* — **step'-ladder** a ladder with flat treads and a hinged prop; **stepp'ing-stone** a stone rising above water or mud to afford a passage: a means to gradual progress (*fig.*); **step'-rock'et** one made in sections operating successively and then discarded; **step'-stone** a door-step; **step'-up'** an increase in rate, quantity, output, etc. — *adj.* increasing or changing by steps: raising voltage. — **break step** to change the sequence of right and left foot, so as to get out of step; **keep step** to continue in step; **in step** with simultaneous putting forward of the right (or left) feet in marching, etc.: (*fig.*) in conformity or agreement (with others); **out of step** not in step; **step by step** gradually, little by little; **step down** to withdraw, retire, resign, from a position of authority, etc.: to decrease the voltage of: to reduce the rate of; **step in** to enter easily or unexpectedly (also **step into**): to intervene; **step on it** (*slang*; see **gas, juice**) to hurry; **step out** to go out a little way: to increase the length of the step and so the speed: to have a gay social life; **step out of line** to depart from the usual, or accepted, course of action; **step short** to shorten the length of one's step; **step up** to come forward: to build up into steps: to raise by a step or steps: to increase the voltage of: to increase the rate of, as production; **take steps** to take action. [O.E. (Mercian) *steppe* (W.S. *stæpe*); Du. *step*, Ger. *Stapfe*.]

step- *step-*, *pfx.* indicating affinity by another marriage or mating. — *ns.* **step'bairn** (*Scot.*), **-child, -daughter, -son** a wife's or husband's but not one's own child, daughter, son; **step'dame** (*arch.*), **step'mother** a father's wife not one's own mother: a bird that hatches another's eggs: a cruel, niggardly, or negligent guardian (*fig.*). — *adj.* **step'motherly.** — *ns.* **step'father** a mother's husband not one's own father; **step'-parent; step'-parenting; step'brother, -sister** the son, daughter, of a stepfather or stepmother. [O.E. *stēop-* (as in *stēopmōdor*), orig. meaning orphan; Ger. *stief-*.]

stephane *stef'ə-nē, n.* an ancient Greek head-dress like a diadem. [Gr. *stephanē* — *stephein*, to encircle.]

stephanite *stef'ə-nīt, n.* brittle silver ore, composed of silver, sulphur, and antimony. [After Archduke *Stephan* (1817–67).]

Stephanotis *stef-ə-nō'tis, n.* a genus of asclepiads of Madagascar, etc., cultivated for their scented flowers: (without *cap.*) any plant of this genus. [Gr. *stephanōtis*, fit for a wreath — *stephanos*, a crown, wreath.]

stepney *step'ni, n.* a spare wheel, often *fig.*: a mistress, esp. a white slaver's. [Said to be from the name of a street where the wheels were made.]

steppe *step, n.* a dry, grassy, generally treeless and uncultivated and sometimes salt plain, as in the south-east of Europe and in Asia. [Russ. *step'*.]

stept. See **step.**

steradian *sti-rā'di-ən, n.* a unit of measurement for solid angles, the angle subtended at the centre of a sphere by an area on its surface numerically equal to the square of the radius. [Gr. *stereos*, solid, and **radian.**]

stercoraceous *stûrk-ə-rā'shəs, adj.* of, of the nature of, dung. — *adj.* **sterc'oral** stercoraceous. — *ns.* **sterc'oranism** an esp. former name for the belief that the sacramental bread is digested and evacuated like other food; **sterc'oranist.** — *adjs.* **stercorā'rious, sterc'orary.** — *v.t.* **sterc'orate** to manure. [L. *stercus, -oris*, dung.]

Sterculia *stər-kū'li-ə, n.* the gum tragacanth genus giving name to the **Sterculiā'ceae,** a family of large trees and shrubs akin to the mallows, including kola and cacao: (without *cap.*) any plant of this genus. [L. *Sterculius*, god of manuring — *stercus*, dung, from the stinking flowers.]

stere *stēr, n.* a timber measure, a cubic metre — about 35·315 cubic feet. — Also in compounds, as **decastere** (*dek'ə-*) 10 steres, **decistere** (*des'i-*) a tenth of a stere. [Fr. *stère* — Gr. *stereos*, solid.]

stereo- *stēr'i-ō-, ster'i-ō-,* in composition solid, hard, three-dimensional. — *n.* **ster'eo** stereophonic reproduction of sound: a piece of stereophonic equipment, such as a record-player, tape-recorder, etc.: a unit comprising such pieces: — *pl.* **ster'eos.** — *adj.* **stereophonic.** — *n., adj., v.t.,* and *v.i.* a contr. of **stereotype, stereoscope, stereoscopic.** — *ns.* **stereoacū'ity** the degree to which a person is aware of the separation of objects along the line of sight; **ster'eobate** (root of Gr. *bainein*, to go, walk) a substructure, foundation. — *adj.* **stereobatic** (-*bat'ik*). — *ns.* **stereochem'istry** the study of the spatial arrangement of atoms in molecules; **ster'eochrome** (Gr. *chrōma*, colour); **ster'eochrōmy** mural painting fixed with waterglass; **stereoflu'oroscope** a fluoroscope giving a three-dimensional view; **ster'eogram** a picture or diagram suggestive of solidity: a stereographic double picture: a radiogram for reproducing stereophonic records; **ster'eograph** a stereogram (in picture senses). — *adjs.* **stereograph'ic, -al.** — *ns.* **stereog'raphy; stereo'īsomer** an isomer having the same chemical composition, molecular weight and structure, but differing spatial arrangement of atoms. — *adj.* **stereoīsomer'ic.** — *ns.* **stereoīsom'erism; ster'eome** mechanical tissue in plants; **stereom'eter** an instrument for measuring specific gravity or for measuring solids. — *adjs.* **stereomet'ric, -al.** — *adv.* **stereomet'rically.** — *n.* **stereom'etry.** — *adj.* **stereophon'ic** giving the effect of sound from different directions in three-dimensional space. — *adv.* **stereophon'ically** by stereophony. — *ns.* **stereoph'ony** stereophonic reproduction of sound; **stereops'is** (Gr. *opsis*, vision) binocular stereoscopic vision; **stereopt'icon** a double projecting lantern, by means of which the one picture dissolves into another. — *n.sing.* **stereop'tics** the optics of stereoscopy. — *n.* **ster'eoscope** an instrument by which the images of two pictures differing slightly in point of view are seen one by each eye and so give an effect of solidity. — *adjs.* **stereoscop'ic, -al.** — *adv.* **stereoscop'ically.** — *ns.* **stereos'copist; stereos'copy.** — *adjs.* **stereoson'ic** stereophonic; **stereospecif'ic** relating to, or (of atoms) having, a fixed spatial arrangement. — *adjs.* **stereotac'tic, -al** (Gr. *tassein*, to arrange) of stereotaxis (*biol.*): (also **stereotax'ic**) relating to the precise location of particular brain structures by three-dimensional survey (*med.*). — *ns.* **stereotax'ia** (*med.*) the electrical destruction of a small area of brain tissue, using stereotactic methods, to relieve disorders such as epilepsy and Parkinsonism; **stereotax'is** the reaction of an organism to the stimulus of contact with a solid body (*biol.*): stereotaxia; **stereot'omy** (Gr. *tomē*, a cut) section-cutting of solids: stone-cutting; **stereot'ropism** (Gr. *tropos*, a turn) the tendency to bend or turn in response to contact with a solid object. — *adj.* **stereotrop'ic.** — *n.* **ster'eotype** a solid metallic plate for printing, cast from a mould (made of papier-mâché or other material) of movable types: the art, method, or process of making such plates: a fixed conventionalised representation. — *adj.* pertaining to, or done with, stereotypes. — *v.t.* to make a stereotype of: to print with stereotypes. to characterise or categorise (esp. a person) too readily or simplistically. — *adj.* **ster'eotyped** transferred as letterpress from set-up movable type to a mould, and thence to a metal plate: fixed, unchangeable, as opinions: conventionalised. — *n.* **ster'eotyper.** — *adjs.* **stereotyp'ic, stereotyp'ical.** — *ns.* **ster'eotyping; ster'eotypy** the producing of stereotype plates: the repetition of senseless movements, actions or words in cases of insanity, etc. (*med.*). — *adj.* **steric** (*ster'ik*) relating to spatial arrangement of atoms. [Gr. *stereos*, solid.]

steric. See **stereo-**.

sterigma *ster-ig'mə, n.* the stalk of a spore: — *pl.* **sterig'-mata.** [Gr. *stērigma*, support.]

sterile *ster'īl* (*U.S.* -*il*), *adj.* unfruitful: barren: not producing, or unable to produce, offspring, fruit, seeds, or spores: of a flower, without pistils: of a glume, not subtending a flower: sterilised: destitute of ideas or results. — *n.* **sterilisation, -z-** (*ster-i-lī-zā'shən*). — *v.t.* **ster'ilise, -ize** to cause to be fruitless: to deprive of power of reproduction: to destroy micro-organisms in: to disallow building or other development in (a tract of countryside). — *ns.* **ster'iliser, -z-** one who, or that which sterilises: apparatus for destroying germs; **steril'-ity** the quality of being sterile: unfruitfulness, barrenness, in regard to reproduction. [L. *sterilis*, barren.]

sterlet *stûr'lit, n.* a small sturgeon. [Russ. *sterlyad*.]

sterling[1] *stûr'ling, n.* an old English silver penny (*obs.*): English, Scottish, or British money of standard value. — *adj.* of sterling or standard English money: genuine: of authority: of thoroughly good character: (of silver) of standard quality, i.e. containing at least 92·5 per cent silver (usu. alloyed with copper). — **sterling area** a group of countries with currencies tied to sterling and freely settling transactions among themselves through London. — **sterling effective rate** see under **effect.** [Prob. a coin with a star — O.E. *steorra*, star — some early Norman pennies being so marked.]

sterling[2] *stûr'ling.* Same as **starling**[2].

Sterling *stûr'ling, n.* a submachine-gun that fires bursts or single shots, and does not jam. [From the makers' name.]

stern[1] *stûrn, adj.* severe: austere: rigorous: unrelenting. — Also *adv.* (*Milt.*). — *adv.* **stern'ly.** — *n.* **stern'ness.** [O.E. *styrne*.]

stern[2] *stûrn, n.* the hind-part of a vessel: the rump or tail: steering-gear, helm, the steersman's place (*obs.; Shak.*). — *v.t.* to back, to row backward. — *n.* **stern'age** (*Shak.*) sterns collectively. — *adjs.* **sterned** having a stern (in compounds); **stern'most** farthest astern. — *advs.* **stern'-ward** (also *adj.*), **-s.** — **stern'board** backward motion of a ship: loss of way in tacking; **stern'-chase** a chase in which one ship follows directly in the wake of another; **stern'-chaser** a cannon in the stern of a ship; **stern'-fast** a rope or chain for making fast a ship's stern to a wharf, etc. — *adv.* **stern'-fore'most.** — **stern'-frame** the framework of a ship's stern; **stern'port** a port or opening in the stern of a ship; **stern'-post** the aftermost timber of a ship, supporting the rudder; **stern'-sheet** (usu. in *pl.*) the part of a boat between the stern and the rowers; **stern'son** the hinder extremity of a ship's keelson, to which the stern-post is bolted; **stern'way** the backward motion of a vessel; **stern'-wheel'er** (*U.S.*) a small vessel with one large paddle-wheel at the stern. — *n.pl.* **stern'works** hinder parts. [O.N. *stjörn*, a steering, or lost O.E. equivalent.]

stern[3] *stûrn, stern, starn* (*obs.* and *Scot.*) *ns.* a star. — *n.* (*dim.*) **starn'ie.** [O.N. *stjarna*.]

sternite, etc. See **sternum**.

sternson. See **stern**[2].

sternum *stûr'nəm, n.* the breast-bone: the under part of a somite in arthropods. — *adj.* **ster'nal.** — *n.* **sternal'gia**

(*med.*; Gr. *algos*, pain) pain around the sternum, angina pectoris. — *adj.* **sternal'gic.** — *ns.* **ster'nebra** (modelled on *vertebra*) a segment of the breast-bone; **ster'nite** the ventral plate of a segment in arthropods. — *adjs.* **sternit'ic; ster'notribe** (Gr. *tribē*, a rub) pollinated by touching an insect's under surface. [Latinised from Gr. *sternon*, chest.]

sternutation *stûr-nū-tā'shən, n.* sneezing. — *adjs.* **sternū'-tative, sternū'tatory** that causes sneezing. — *n.* a substance that causes sneezing. — Also **ster'nūtātor.** [L. *sternūtāre,* intens. of *sternuēre,* to sneeze.]

sterol *stēr'ol, ster', n.* a solid higher alcohol such as cholesterol, ergosterol. — *n.* **stēr'oid** (or *ster'*) any of a class of compounds including the sterols, bile acids, adrenal hormones, etc. [See **cholesterol**.]

stertorous *stûr'tər-əs, adj.* with snoring sound. — *adv.* **ster'torously.** — *n.* **ster'torousness.** [L. *stertĕre,* to snore.]

sterve *stûrv, v.t.* and *v.i.* an old form (*Spens.*) of **starve**, to starve, to die.

stet *stet, v.t.* to restore after marking for deletion: — *pr.p.* **stett'ing;** *pa.t.* and *pa.p.* **stett'ed.** [L., let it stand, 3rd sing. pres. subj. of *stāre,* to stand; written on a proof-sheet with dots under the words to be retained.]

stethoscope *steth'ə-skōp, n.* an instrument for auscultation. — *adjs.* **stethoscopic** (*-skop'ik*), **-al.** — *adv.* **stetho-scop'ically.** — *ns.* **stethoscopist** (*-os'kə-pist*); **stethos'-copy.** [Gr. *stēthos,* chest, *skopeein,* to look at, examine.]

Stetson *stet'sn, n.* a man's felt hat with a broad brim and a soft, high crown. [Maker's name.]

stevedore *stēv'ə-dōr, -dör, n.* one who loads and unloads shipping vessels. — *v.t.* and *v.i.* to load and unload (cargo, a ship). [Sp. *estibador,* packer — *estibar,* to stow — L. *stīpāre,* to press.]

steven *stev'n, n.* a voice (now *dial.*): an outcry (*Spens.*). [O.E. *stefn,* voice.]

Stevengraph *stēv'n-gräf, n.* a silk picture woven in colours. [T. *Stevens,* ribbon weaver.]

stew[1] *stū, n.* a boiling pot (*Spens., Shak.*): a room for hot-air baths: a hot bath: an overheated or sweaty state: mental agitation: worry: (usu. in *pl.* form with sing. or collective sense) a brothel, or prostitutes' quarter (*arch.*): a prostitute (*obs.*): one who studies hard, esp. unintelligently (*slang*): a dish of stewed food, esp. meat with vegetables. — *v.t.* to bathe in hot air or water: to bathe in sweat: to keep in a swelter or narrow confinement: to simmer or boil slowly with some moisture: to over-infuse. — *v.i.* to swelter: to undergo stewing: to be in a state of worry or agitation: to study hard (*slang*). — *adj.* **stewed** having been stewed: drunk (*coll.*). — *n.* **stew'er.** — *n.* and *adj.* **stew'ing.** — *adj.* **stew'y** like a stew: sweltering. — **stew'-can** (*naval slang*) a destroyer; **stew'pan, stew'pot** one used for stewing. — **in a stew** in a state of worry, agitation; **let someone stew in his own juice** to leave someone alone and await developments, let someone reap the consequences of his own actions. [O.Fr. *estuve* (Fr. *étuve*), stove; prob. conn. with **stove**[1].]

stew[2] *stū, n.* a fish-pond: a fish-tank: an artificial oyster-bed. — **stew'pond.** [O.Fr. *estui* (Fr. *étui*).]

steward *stū'ərd, n.* one who manages the domestic concerns of a family or institution: one who superintends another's affairs, esp. an estate or farm: the manager of the provision department or attendant on passengers in a ship, aircraft, etc.: a college caterer: one who helps in arrangements, marshalling, etc., at races, a dance, a wedding, an entertainment: an overseer: a foreman: the treasurer of a congregation, guild, society, etc.: — *fem.* **stew'ardess.** — *ns.* **stew'ardship,** management: the individual's function in the practical work of the Christian church involving obligation to give a share of his time and goods to others; **stew'artry** (*Scot.*) a stewardship, or the extent of a stewardship — applied nominally to the county of Kirkcudbright (now part of Dumfries and Galloway). — **Lord High Steward** one of the great officers of state, and anciently the first officer of the crown in England. [O.E. *stig-weard* — *stig*, hall ('sty'), *weard*, ward, keeper.]

stey *stī*, (*Scot.*) *adj.* steep. [Cf. **stile¹**, **stirrup**.]

sthenic *sthen'ik, adj.* strong, robust: morbidly active. [Gr. *sthenos*, strength.]

stibble *stib'l, n.* a Scots form of **stubble**. — *n.* **stibb'ler** a horse turned out to feed on stubble: one who cuts the handfuls left by the reaper: a probationer (*Scott*).

stibium *stib'i-əm, n.* antimony. — *adj.* **stib'ial**. — *ns.* **stib'ialism** antimony poisoning; **stib'ine** (*-ēn, -īn*) antimony hydride, a poisonous gas; **stib'nite** native antimony trisulphide. [L., — Gr. *stibi, stimmi* — Egypt. *stm* (Copt. *stēm*).]

sticcado *stik-ä'dō*, **sticcato** *-tō, ns.* a kind of xylophone: — *pls.* **-do(e)s, -to(e)s**. [Perh. It. *steccato*, palisade.]

stich *stik, n.* a line of verse or section of prose of comparable length. — *ns.* **stichar'ion** (Gr. *stichārion*) a Greek vestment like the Western alb; **stichē'ron** a short hymn. — *adj.* **stich'ic** of or pertaining to stichs. — *ns.* **stichid'ium** a branch producing tetraspores, in red seaweeds: — *pl.* **stichid'ia; stichol'ogy** metrical theory. — *adjs.* **stichomet'ric, -al.** — *adv.* **stichomet'rically.** — *ns.* **stichom'etry** measurement by lines: division into lines: a statement of such measurements; **stichomythia** (*-mith'*; Gr. *stichomȳthiā*) dialogue in alternate lines. — *adj.* **stichomyth'ic.** — *n.* **stich'os** a line of ordinary length in measuring a manuscript: a verse or versicle (*Gr. Ch.*): — *pl.* **stich'oi.** — *-stichous* in composition, having a certain number of lines or rows, e.g. *distichous*. [Gr. *stichos*, a row — *steichein*, to march.]

stick¹ *stik, v.t.* to pierce, transfix: to stab: to spear: to thrust: to fasten by piercing: to insert: to set in position: to set or cover with things fastened on: to cause to adhere: to endure (esp. with *it*) (*coll.*): to function successfully (*coll.*): to bring to a standstill or nonplus: to leave someone (with) (something unpleasant) (*coll.*). — *v.i.* to be fixed by insertion: to jut, protrude: to adhere: to become or remain fixed: to remain: to be detained by an impediment: to jam: to fail to proceed or advance: to scruple: to hold fast, keep resolutely (with *to*): — *pa.t.* **stuck**, *Scot.* **stack**; *pa.p.* **stuck**, *Scot.* **stick'it.** — *n.* a stoppage (*obs.*): a difficulty (*arch.*): a hitch: adhesiveness. — *ns.* **stickabil'ity** (*coll. facet.*) the ability to stick at something, persistence, perseverance; **stick'er** one who kills pigs, etc.: one who or that which sticks: a piercing weapon: a person or thing difficult to get rid of: one who is constant or persistent: a gummed label or poster: a poser: a piano jack: an upright rod that transmits motion from an organ key. — *adv.* **stick'ily** in a gluey, muggy, etc., way. — *n.* **stick'iness.** — *n.* and *adj.* **stick'ing.** — *adj.* **stick'y** adhesive: tenacious: gluey: muggy: difficult (*coll.*): unpleasant (*coll.*). — *v.t.* to make sticky. — **stick'ing-place, -point** the point at which a thing sticks or stays firmly: the point beyond which a thing cannot proceed; **stick'ing-plaster** an adhesive plaster for closing wounds; **stick'-in-the-mud** an old fogy. — Also *adj.* — **stickit minister** (*Scot.*) a licentiate who never gets a pastoral charge; **stick'jaw** a cloggy pudding or sweetmeat; **stick pin** (*U.S.*) a tie-pin; **stick'up** a stand-up collar: a hold-up; **stick'y-back** a gummed photograph; **stick'ybeak** (*Austr.* and *N.Z. coll.*) a Nosey Parker; **sticky end** an unpleasant end, disaster. — *adj.* **stick'y-fing'ered** (*coll.*) prone to pilfering. — **sticky wicket** a difficult situation to cope with. — *adj.* **stuck'-up'** self-importantly aloof. — **get stuck in(to)** to deal with, consume, attack in a vigorous, aggressive, eager, etc. manner; **stick around** (*coll.*) to remain in the vicinity; **stick at** to hesitate or scruple at (often with *nothing*): to persist at; **stick by** to be firm in supporting, to adhere closely to; **stick 'em up** hold up your hands (or be shot); **stick in** (*Scot.*) to persevere assiduously: also (of a dressing, etc.) to adhere to a wound; **stick in one's throat** to be difficult, or against one's conscience, for one to countenance; **stick it into** to overcharge

systematically; **stick one's neck out** see under **neck; stick or snee** see **snickersnee; stick out** to project: to be obvious: to continue to resist; **stick out for** to insist upon; **stick to** to persevere in holding to; **stick together** to be allies: to support each other; **stick up** to stand up: to waylay and plunder, as a mail-coach by bushrangers; **stick up for** to speak or act in defence of; **stick with** to remain with: to force (a person) to cope with (something unpleasant) — often in passive, i.e. **be stuck with; stuck for** unable to proceed because of the lack of; **stuck on** enamoured of. [O.E. *stician*; cf. **stick²**, **stitch**.]

stick² *stik, n.* a rod of wood, esp. for walking with or for beating: a twig: anything shaped like a rod of wood: a timber tree or trunk: a piece of firewood: a tally: an instrument for beating a percussion instrument: an instrument for playing hockey or other game: a bow for a fiddle, or the wooden part of it: a person of stiff manner: one lacking enterprise: a rod: an oblong or cylindrical piece: a control-rod of an aeroplane: a group of bombs, or of paratroops, released at one time from an aeroplane: a piece of furniture (usu. in *pl.*): a ray of a fan: a support for a candle: (in *pl.*) hurdles in steeple-chasing: a printer's composing-stick: a stickful: blame, criticism (*slang*). — *adj.* in the form of a stick: made of sticks. — *v.t.* to furnish or set with sticks: to arrange in a composing-stick: — *pa.t., pa.p.* **sticked.** — *n.* **stick'ful** as much as a composing-stick holds. — **stick'-in'sect** twig-like phasmid insect; **stick'-lac** twigs with attached lac, insects, ova; **stick'leader** the leader of a stick of paratroops; **stick'work** skill in using one's stick in any game played with one. — **beat to sticks** to defeat and surpass utterly; **carrot and stick** see **carrot; big stick** force, coercion; **give someone stick** (*slang*) to censure, punish someone; **in a cleft stick** in a dilemma; **right** or **wrong end of the stick** a true or mistaken understanding of the situation; **the sticks** rural areas, the backwoods. [O.E. *sticca*; O.N. *stika*.]

stickit (*Scot.*). See **stick¹**.

stickle¹ *stik'l, v.i.* to regulate a contest (*obs.*): to mediate (*obs.*): to interpose (*obs.*): to contend, stand up (with *for*): to be scrupulous or obstinately punctilious. — *v.t.* to compose (*obs.*): to stop contention between (*obs.*): to contend (*obs.*): to scruple. — *n.* **stick'ler** a regulator or umpire, a mediator (*obs. exc. dial.*): a second (*obs.*): a backer (*obs.*): a punctilious and pertinacious insister or contender, esp. for something trifling. — *adj.* or *adv.* **stick'ler-like** (*Shak.*). [Prob. M.E. *stightle* — O.E. *stihtan*, to set in order.]

stickle² *stik'l,* (*S.W. dial.*) *adj.* steep: rapid. — *n.* a rapid. [O.E. *sticol*, steep.]

stickleback *stik'l-bak, n.* a small spiny-backed river-fish. [O.E. *sticel*, sting, prick, and **back¹**.]

sticky. See **stick¹**.

stiddie *stid'i.* Same as **stithy.**

stie. An old spelling of **sty²,³**.

stieve. Same as **steeve²**.

stiff *stif, adj.* not easily bent: rigid: wanting in suppleness: moved or moving with difficulty or friction: dead: approaching solidity: thick, viscous, not fluid: dense, difficult to mould or cut: resistant: difficult: toilsome: pertinacious: stubborn: formidable: strong: firm, high, or inclining to rise (in price, etc.): excessive: not natural and easy: constrained: formal: keeping upright (*naut.*): certain (not to run, to win, to lose; *slang*): excessively bored (with a pun on *board*): unlucky (esp. *Austr.*) — *adv.* stiffly: stark: very, extremely (*coll.*). — *n.* (*slang*) one who, that which, is stiff: a corpse: a good-for-nothing: a racehorse that is a notably poor bet: a customer who fails to tip: negotiable paper: forged paper. — *v.t.* (*slang*) to cheat: to rob: to fail to tip: to murder. — *v.t.* and *v.i.* **stiff'en** to make or become stiff or stiffer. — *n.* **stiff'ener** one who, or that which, stiffens: a strong alcoholic drink (*coll.*): a cigarette-card or the like, used to stiffen a package. — *n.* and *adj.* **stiff'ening.** — *adj.* **stiff'ish.** — *adv.* **stiff'ly.** — *n.* **stiff'ness.** — **stiff'-bit** a jointless bit. — *adj.* **stiff=**

hearted (*B.*) obstinate, stubborn. — **stiff'-neck** a drawing down of the head towards the shoulder, often due to cold or draught: torticollis. — *adj.* **stiff'-necked** obstinate: haughty: formal and unnatural. — **stiff'=necked'ness.** — *adj.* **stiff'-rumped, -rumpt** (*arch.*) proud, unbending. — **stiff upper lip** see **lip; stiff with** (*coll.*) full of, crowded with. [O.E. *stíf*, stiff; Du. *stijf*, Ger. *steif.*]

stifle[1] *stī'fl, v.t.* to stop the breath of by foul air or other means: to make breathing difficult for: to suffocate, smother: to choke down: to suppress: to repress: to make stifling. — *v.i.* to suffocate. — *n.* a stifling atmosphere, smell, or condition. — *adj.* **sti'fled.** — *n.* **sti'fler** one who stifles: the gallows. — *n.* and *adj.* **sti'fling** (*-fling*). — *adv.* **sti'flingly.** [Origin obscure.]

stifle[2] *stī'fl, n.* the joint of a horse, dog, etc., answering to the human knee. — **sti'fle-bone** the knee-cap; **sti'fle=joint.** [Connection with **stiff** doubtful.]

stigma *stig'mə, n.* a brand: a mark of infamy: a disgrace or reproach attached to any one: any special mark: a spot: a bleeding spot: a scar: a spot sensitive to light: the part of a carpel that receives pollen (*bot.*): a spiracle: a pore: (in *pl.*) the marks of Christ's wounds or marks resembling them, claimed to have been impressed on the bodies of certain persons, as Francis of Assisi in 1224: — *pl.* **stig'mata** (or, esp. in religion, *-mä'tə*); also (esp. *bot.* or in sense of *disgrace* or *reproach*) **stig'mas.** — *n.* **Stigmā'ria** the pitted underground part of Sigillaria or other fossil tree. — *adjs.* **stigmā'rian** (also *n.*); **stigmatic** (*-mat'ik*) of, pertaining to, of the nature of, a stigma: marked or branded with a stigma: giving infamy or reproach: anastigmatic, or not astigmatic. — *n.* one who has received the stigmata: one who is branded (*Shak. stig'*, with deformity). — *adj.* **stigmat'ical.** — *adv.* **stigmat'ically.** — *adj.* **stigmat-if'erous** (*bot.*) stigma-bearing. — *n.* **stigmatīsā'tion, -z-** act of stigmatising: production of stigmata or of bleeding spots upon the body, as by hypnotism. — *v.t.* **stig'matise, -ize** to mark with a stigma or the stigmata: to brand, denounce, describe condemnatorily (with *as*). — *ns.* **stig'matism** impression of the stigmata: anastigmatism; **stig'matist** one impressed with the stigmata. — *adj.* **stig'matose.** — *n.* **stig'mē** (*Gr. palaeog.*) a dot used as a punctuation mark. [Gr. *stigma, -atos*, tattoo-mark, brand, *stigmē*, a point.]

stilb *stilb, n.* the CGS unit of intrinsic brightness, one candela/cm². — *n.* **stilbene** (*stil'bēn*) a crystalline hydrocarbon, used in dye-manufacture. [Gr. *stilbein*, to shine.]

stilbestrol. See **stilboestrol.**

stilbite *stil'bīt, n.* a pearly zeolite. [Gr. *stilbein*, to shine.]

stilboestrol, U.S. **stilbestrol,** *stil-bēs'trəl, n.* a synthetic oestrogen. [Gr. *stilbos*, glistening and **oestrus.**]

stile[1] *stīl, n.* a step, or set of steps, for climbing over a wall or fence. [O.E. *stigel*; cf. O.E. *stígan*, Ger. *steigen*, to mount.]

stile[2] *stīl, n.* an upright member in framing or panelling. [Perh. Du. *stijl*, pillar, doorpost.]

stile[3]. An older spelling of **style.**

stilet. See **stylet** (under **style**).

stiletto *sti-let'ō, n.* a dagger with a narrow blade: a pointed instrument for making eyelet-holes: a stiletto heel: — *pl.* **stilett'os.** — *v.t.* to stab with a stiletto: — *pr.p.* **stilett'oing;** *pa.t.* and *pa.p.* **stilett'oed.** — **stiletto heel** a high, thin heel on a woman's shoe. — *adj.* **stilett'o-heeled.** [It., dim. of *stilo*, a dagger — L. *stilus*, a style.]

still[1] *stil, adj.* motionless: inactive: silent: calm: quiet: not sparkling or effervescing: continual, constant (*Shak.*). — *v.t.* to quiet: to silence: to appease: to restrain. — *v.i.* to become still. — *adv.* motionlessly: inactively: quietly: always, constantly (*arch.*; so also in many obvious compounds): up to the present time or time in question: as before: yet, even (usu. with a comparative): even so, even then: nevertheless, for all that. — *n.* calm: quiet: an ordinary photograph, one taken from a cinematographic film. — *n.* **still'er** one who, or

that which, stills or quiets, or prevents splashing over. — *n.* and *adj.* **still'ing.** — *n.* **still'ness.** — *adj.* **still'y** (*poet.*) still: quiet: calm. — *adv.* **stil'ly** (*arch.*) silently: gently. — **still'-birth** birth of the already dead or very nearly dead, as in suspended animation: publication not followed by sales: anything born without life. — *adj.* **still'-born** dead, or in suspended animation, when born (also *fig.*). — **still'-hunt, -hunting** (*U.S.*) stalking. — *v.t.* and *v.i.* **still'-hunt** (*U.S.*). — **still'-hunter** (*U.S.*). — **still'-life** the class of pictures representing inanimate objects: a picture of this class: — *pl.* **still'-lifes.** — Also *adj.* — *adj.* **still'-peer'ing** (*Shak.*) perh. a misprint for **still-piecing** (i.e. repairing) or **still-piercing.** — **still'=stand** a standstill (*Shak.*): an armistice (*obs.*). — **still and anon** (*Shak.*), **still and end** (*Shak.*) from time to time; **still and on** (*Scot.*), **still and all** (*coll.*) nevertheless. [O.E. *stille*, quiet, calm, stable: Du. *stil*, Ger. *still.*]

still[2] *stil, v.t.* to exude or cause to fall by drops: to distil. — *v.i.* to fall in drops. — *n.* an apparatus for distillation. — *n.* **still'er** a distiller. — **still'-head** the head of a still; **still'-house** (*U.S.*) a distillery; **still'-room** an apartment where liquors, preserves, and the like are kept, and where tea, etc., is prepared for the table: a housekeeper's pantry; **still'-room-maid.** [Aphetic for **distil.**]

stillage *stil'ij, n.* a frame, stand, or stool for keeping things off the floor: a box-like container for transporting goods: a cask-stand. — *ns.* **still'ing, still'ion** a cask-stand. [Prob. Du. *stellage, stelling* — *stellen*, to place.]

stillatory *stil'ə-tər-i, n.* a still: a distillery. [L.L. *stil-lātōrium* — L. *stillāre*, to drip, *stilla*, a drop.]

stillicide *stil'i-sīd, n.* a drip: eavesdrop: an urban servitude allowing one's eavesdrop to fall on a neighbour's ground (otherwise forbidden; *Roman law*). [L. *stil-licidium* — *stilla*, drop, *cadĕre*, to fall.]

stilling, stillion. See **stillage.**

Still's disease *stilz di-zēz'*, a disease of children causing arthritis leading to ankylosis, possibly a type of rheumatoid arthritis. [First described by Sir G.F. *Still*, English physician, 1868-1941.]

Stillson wrench® *stil'sən rench, rensh*, an adjustable wrench whose grip is tightened by pressure on the handle. [D.C. *Stillson*, 1830-99, Amer. inventor.]

stilly. See **still**[1].

stilpnosiderite *stilp-nō-sid'ər-īt, n.* limonite. [Gr. *stilp-nos*, shining, *sidēros*, iron.]

stilt *stilt, n.* a thin wooden prop with a foot-rest enabling one to walk above the ground: a tall support: a plough-handle (now *dial.*): a very long-legged wading bird (*Himantopus candidus*) or other species) akin to the avocets (also **stilt'-bird, -plov'er**). — *v.t.* to raise on stilts or as if on stilts. — *adj.* **stilt'ed** elevated as if on stilts: stiff and pompous. — *adv.* **stilt'edly.** — *ns.* **stilt'edness; stilt'er; stilt'iness; stilt'ing.** — *adjs.* **stilt'ish, stilt'y.** — **stilted** arch an arch that springs from above the capital; **stilt'-walker.** [M.E. *stilte*; cf. Du. *stelt*, Ger. *Stelze*, Sw. *stylta*.]

Stilton *stil'tən, n.* a rich white, often blue-veined, cheese first sold chiefly at *Stilton* in Cambridgeshire.

stime; stimie, stimy. Same as **styme; stymie.**

stimulus *stim'ū-ləs, n.* a sting or stinging hair (*arch.*): an action, influence, or agency that produces a response in a living organism: anything that rouses to action or increased action: — *pl.* **stim'ulī.** — *adj.* **stim'ulable** responsive to stimulus. — *n.* **stim'ulancy.** — *adj.* **stim'ulant** stimulating: increasing or exciting vital action. — *n.* anything that stimulates or excites: a stimulating drug: alcoholic liquor. — *v.t.* **stim'ulate** to incite: to instigate: to excite: to produce increased action in (*physiol.*). — *v.i.* to act as a stimulant. — *adj.* **stim'ulating.** — *n.* **stimulā'tion.** — *adj.* **stim'ulātive** tending to stimulate. — *n.* that which stimulates or excites. — *n.* **stim'ulātor** one who stimulates: an instrument for applying a stimulus. [L. *stimulus*, a goad.]

stimy. See **styme.**

sting[1] *sting, n.* in some plants and animals a weapon (hair, modified ovipositor, fin-ray, tooth, etc.) that pierces and injects poison: the act of inserting a sting: the pain or the wound caused: any sharp, tingling, or irritating pain or its cause (also *fig.*): the point of an epigram: stinging power: pungency: a goad: an incitement: (a substantial sum of money gained through) a deception, theft, etc. (*slang*): a trap for criminals set up by the police (*slang*). — *v.t.* to pierce, wound, pain, or incite with or as if with a sting: to cause or allow anything to sting: to rob, cheat, or involve in expense (*slang*). — *v.i.* to have or use a power of stinging: to have a stinging feeling. — *pa.t.* and *pa.p.* **stung.** — *adj.* **stinged** having a sting. — *n.* **sting′er** one who, or that which, stings: anything stinging or pungent: see also separate entry below. — *n.* and *adj.* **sting′ing.** — *adv.* **sting′ingly.** — *adjs.* **sting′less; sting′y** (*coll.*). — **sting′-bull, -fish** the weever; **sting′-ray** (*U.S.* and *Austr.* **stingaree** *sting′-gɔ-rē, -ɔ-rē,* or *-rē′*) a ray (Trygon, etc.) with a formidable barbed dorsal spine on its tail. — **take the sting out of** (*coll.*) to soften the pain of (*lit.* and *fig.*). [O.E. *sting,* puncture, *stingan,* to pierce.]

sting[2] *sting, (Scot.) n.* a pole. — **sting and ling** with a rope slung from a pole: by force (*fig.*). [O.E. *steng.*]

stingaree. See **sting**[1].

stinger[1] *sting′ɔr, n.* same as **stengah**: (esp. *U.S.*) a cocktail containing brandy and white crème de menthe. [**stengah,** influenced by **sting**[1].]

stinger[2]. See **sting**[1].

stingo *sting′gō, n.* strong malt liquor: vigour, punch: — *pl.* **stin′gos.** [**sting**[1].]

stingy[1] *stin′ji, adj.* niggardly: ill-tempered (*dial.*). — *adv.* **stin′gily.** — *n.* **stin′giness.** [Prob. **sting**[1].]

stingy[2]. See **sting**[1].

stink *stingk, v.i.* to give out a strong, offensive smell: to be offensive, have a bad reputation, suggest or imply evil or dishonesty (*fig.*). — *v.t.* to impart a bad smell to: to drive by an ill smell: — *pa.t.* **stank, stunk;** *pa.p.* **stunk.** — *n.* an offensive smell: (in *pl.*) chemistry or science, a science master (*slang*). — *ns.* **stink′ard** one who stinks: a base fellow: the **stinking badger** of Java; **stink′er** one who, or that which, stinks: a disagreeable person or thing (*coll.*): a stinkard: a petrel of offensive smell. — *adj.* **stink′ing** which stinks (*lit.* and *fig.*). — *adv.* very, extremely, esp. as in *stinking rich* (*coll.*). — Also *n.* — *adv.* **stink′ingly.** — **stink′-ball, -pot** (*obs.*) a ball or jar filled with a stinking, combustible mixture, used in boarding an enemy's vessel; **stink′-bird** the hoatzin; **stink′-bomb** a usu. small bomb-like container which releases ill-smelling gases when exploded; **stink′= brand** bunt; **stink′horn** a stinking gasteromycete fungus, *Phallus impudicus*; **stink′stone** a limestone that gives a fetid urinous smell when rubbed; **stink′-trap** a stench-trap; **stink′-wood** the ill-smelling wood of various trees, esp. the lauraceous *Ocotea bullata* of S. Africa. — **like stink** (*coll.*) very much, to a great extent: intensely; **raise a stink** to complain: to cause trouble, esp. disagreeable publicity; **stink out** (*coll.*) to drive out by a bad smell: to fill (a room, etc.) with a bad smell. [O.E. *stincan,* to smell (well or ill).]

stint[1] *stint, v.t.* to stop (*obs.*): to restrain (*arch.* or *dial.*): to check (*arch.*): to limit: to apportion (*esp.* pasturage): to allot (*arch.*): to set as a task or as a day's work (*arch.*): to restrict (*obs.*): to keep short: to be niggardly with or towards: to allot stingily: to spare: to serve successfully, get with foal, lamb, etc. — *v.i.* to cease, stop (*obs.*): to be sparing, go short (*dial.*). — *n.* cessation (*obs.*): limit (*obs.*): restraint, restriction: proportion allotted, fixed amount: allowance: a set task: a (conventional) day's work. — *adj.* **stint′ed.** — *adv.* **stint′edly.** — *ns.* **stint′edness; stint′er.** — *n.* and *adj.* **stint′ing.** — *adv.* **stint′ingly.** — *adjs.* **stint′less; stint′y.** [O.E. *styntan,* to dull — *stunt,* stupid; cf. **stent**[1], **stunt**[1].]

stint[2] *stint, n.* the dunlin or other small sandpiper. [Origin obscure.]

stinty. See **stint**[1].

Stipa *stī′pɔ, n.* the feather-grass genus: (without *cap.*) any grass of this genus. [L. *stipa,* tow.]

stipe *stīp, n.* a stalk, esp. of a fungal fruit-body, a fern-leaf, a pappus, or an ovary. — Also **stipes** (*stī′pēz;* L. *stē′pes; pl.* **stipites** *stip′i-tēz;* L. *stē′pi-tās*). — *adj.* **stipitate** (*stip′*). [L. *stīpes, -itis,* post, stock.]

stipel *stī′pl, n.* a stipule-like appendage at the base of a leaflet. — *adj.* **stipellate** (*stī′pɔl-āt, stip-el′āt*) having stipels. [Dim. from **stipule**.]

stipend *stī′pɔnd, n.* a soldier's pay: a salary, esp. a Scottish parish minister's (*Scot.* *stēp′ɔnd*): a periodical allowance. — *adj.* **stipendiary** (*stī-, sti-pen′di-ɔ-ri*) receiving stipend. — *n.* one who performs services for a salary, esp. a paid magistrate. — *v.t.* **stipen′diate** to provide with a salary. [L. *stīpendium* — *stips,* payment, dole, *pendēre,* to weigh.]

stipes, stipites, stipitate. See **stipe**.

stipple *stip′l, v.t.* to engrave, paint, draw, etc., in dots or separate touches. — *n.* painting, engraving, etc., in this way: the effect so produced: a brush for stippling. — *adj.* **stipp′led.** — *ns.* **stipp′ler; stipp′ling.** [Du. *stippelen,* dim. of *stippen,* to dot.]

stipulaceous, stipular, etc. See **stipule**.

stipulate *stip′ū-lāt, v.t.* to set or require as a condition or essential part of an agreement: to guarantee (*rare*). — *v.i.* to make stipulations: to become surety (*obs.*). — *ns.* **stipulā′tion** act of stipulating: a contract: a condition of agreement: a requiring of such a condition; **stip′ulator.** — *adj.* **stip′ulatory** (*-ɔ-tɔr-i*). [L. *stipulārī, -ātus,* prob. — Old L. *stipulus,* firm, conn. *stīpāre,* to press firm.]

stipule *stip′ūl, n.* a paired, usu. leafy, appendage at a leaf-base. — *adjs.* **stipulā′ceous, stip′ular, -y; stip′ulāte, stip′uled.** [L. *stipula,* straw, stalk, dim. of *stīpes;* new meaning assigned by Linnaeus.]

stir[1] *stûr (Scot.* **steer** *stēr, Spens.* **stire, styre** *stīr*) *v.t.* to set in motion: to move around: to move (something, esp. in liquid or powder form) around by continuous or repeated, usu. circular, movements of a spoon or other implement through it, e.g. in order to mix its constituents: to disturb: to rouse: to move to activity: to excite: to moot. — *v.i.* to make a movement: to begin to move: to be able to be stirred: to go about: to be active or excited: (esp. in *pr.p.*) to be out of bed: to go forth: to cause trouble or dissension (*coll.*): — *pr.p.* **stirr′ing;** *pa.t.* and *pa.p.* **stirred.** — *n.* movement: slight movement: activity: commotion: sensation: an act of stirring. — *adjs.* **stir′less** without stir; **stirred.** — *n.* **stirr′er.** — *n.* and *adj.* **stirr′ing.** — *adv.* **stirr′ingly.** — **stir′about** (*Anglo-Ir.*) porridge: a bustling or stirring person. — *adj.* busy, active. — *v.t.* and *v.i.* **stir′-fry′** to fry (food) rapidly while stirring it in the pan. — **stir abroad, forth, out** to go out of doors; **stir up** to excite: to incite: to arouse: to mix by stirring. [O.E. *styrian;* Du. *storen,* Ger. *stören,* to disturb.]

stir[2] *stûr,* **stirra(h)** *stir′ɔ (Scot.), ns.* app. corruptions of **sir, sirrah,** applied to both sexes.

stir[3] *stûr, (slang) n.* prison. — *adj.* **stir-crā′zy** (*U.S.*) unbalanced from confinement esp. in prison. [Perh. O.E. *stēor, stȳr,* punishment, or various Romany words, e.g. *stiraben, steripen.*]

stire *stīr,* a Spens. form of **steer**[2] and **stir**[1].

stirk *stûrk, n.* a yearling or young ox or cow. [O.E. *stirc,* calf.]

Stirling engine *stûr′ling en′jin,* a closed-cycle external-combustion engine using heated air (devised by Dr Robert *Stirling,* d. 1878), or a more sophisticated 20th-cent. version using, e.g. helium under pressure.

stirps *stûrps, n.* family, race: a permanent variety: pedigree: — *pl.* **stirpes** (*stûr′pēz;* L. *stir′pās*). — Also **stirp:** — *pl.* **stirps.** — *n.* **stirp′iculture** selective breeding. [L. *stirps, stirpis.*]

stirra(h). See **stir**[2].

stirre. See **sperre**.

stirrup *stir′ɔp, n.* a support for a rider's foot: a foot-rest, clamp, support, of more or less similar shape: the stirrup-bone: a rope secured to a yard, having a thimble in its lower end for reeving a foot-rope (*naut.*).

— **stirr′up-bone** the stapes; **stirr′up-cup** a cup (not paid for) taken on horseback on departing, or arriving (also **stirr′up-dram):** a vessel in the form of a fox's head from which a stirrup-cup was drunk (*rare*); **stirr′up-iron** the metal part of a stirrup, usu. reckoned the stirrup itself; **stirr′up-leath′er, -strap** the strap of a stirrup; **stirr′up= pump** a portable pump held in position by the foot in a rest. [O.E. *stigrāp* — *stīgan*, to mount, *rāp*, rope.]
stishie. See **stooshie.**
stitch *stich, n.* a sharp pricking pain, now esp. in the intercostal muscles: a complete movement of the needle in sewing, knitting, surgery, or the like: a loop or portion of thread, etc., so used: a mode of stitching: a fastening with thread or wire through all sections (*bookbinding*): the least scrap of clothing, sails, etc.: a ridge of land (*dial.*): a shock of corn (*dial.*). — *v.t.* to join, adorn, or enclose, with stitches. — *v.i.* to sew. — *adj.* **stitched.** — *ns.* **stitch′er; stitch′ery** (*Shak.*) needle-work; **stitch′ing.** — **stitch′craft** the art of needlework; **stitch′work; stitch′wort** any plant of the chickweed genus (*Stellaria*), once thought good for stitches in the side. — **in stitches** in pained helplessness with laughter. **stitch up** (*slang*) to incriminate by informing on: to swindle; [O.E. *stice*, prick; cf. **stick**[1].]
stithy *stidh′i,* **stiddie** *stid′i, ns.* an anvil: a smithy. — *v.t.* to forge on an anvil. [O.N. *stethi;* Sw. *städ,* an anvil.]
stive *stīv,* (*dial.*) *v.t.* and *v.i.* to stifle. — *adjs.* **stived, stived′-up** without fresh air; **stiv′y** stuffy. [Cf. **stew**[1].]
stiver *stī′vər, n.* formerly, a Dutch penny: a very small coin or sum. [Du. *stuiver.*]
stivy. See **stive.**
stoa *stō′ə, n.* a portico or covered colonnade: esp. the Painted Porch (see **porch):** — *pl.* **sto′as, sto′ae, sto′ai** (-*ī*). [Gr. *stōā.*]
stoat *stōt, n.* a small carnivorous mammal of the weasel family with black-tipped tail, called ermine in its white northern winter coat. [M.E. *stote.*]
stob *stob,* (*Scot.*) *n.* a stake, stump, or stub: an awl. [Variant of **stub.**]
stoccado *stok-ä′dō,* **stoccata** -*tə, ns.* a thrust in fencing: — *pls.* **-dos, -tas.** [It. *stoccata,* thrust — *stocco,* rapier — Ger. *Stock,* stick.]
stochastic *stə-kas′tik, adj.* conjectural (*obs.*): random. [Gr. *stochastikos,* skilful in aiming.]
stock[1] *stok, n.* a trunk or main stem: the perennial part of a herbaceous plant: the rooted trunk that receives a graft: a log: a post: a block: a stump: an upright beam: anything fixed, solid and senseless: a stupid person: a part, usually massive, to which others are attached: an intrusive boss (*geol.*): the wooden part of a gun: a handle: stock-gillyflower (see below; **Virginia stock** a Mediterranean, not Virginian, cruciferous garden plant, *Malcolmia*): a stocking (also **neth′er-stock;** the **upp′er-stock** being the upper part of a hose when separate): a stiff band worn as a cravat, often fastened with a buckle at the back: a fireside ledge (*dial.*): (in *pl.*) a device for holding a delinquent by the ankles, and often wrists: (in *pl.*) a framework on which a ship is built: a box or trough: crosspiece of an anchor: the original progenitor: source: race: kindred: family: a fund: capital of a company, divisible into shares: repute, estimation (*fig.*): shares of a public debt: (in *pl.*) public funds: a tally for money paid to the exchequer (*obs.*): supply, store, equipment: a repertoire of plays done by a stock company (see below): the animals kept on a farm: supply of goods for sale: the undealt part of a pack of cards or set of dominoes: raw material, as foundation for soap, etc.: liquor from simmered meat, bones, etc. — *v.t.* to store: to keep for sale: to put in the stocks: to fit with a stock: to supply or furnish with stock (e.g. a river with fish): to keep unmilked before selling: to root up: to stunt. — *adj.* concerned with stock or stocks: kept in stock: conventionally used, standard: hence banal, trite: used for breeding purposes. — *adv.* **stock′ily.** — *n.* **stock′iness.** — *adj.* **stock′ish** resembling a stock, stupid. — *ns.* **stock′ishness; stock′ist** one who keeps a commodity in

stock. — *adjs.* **stock′less; stock′y** thickset, strong-stemmed: solid. — **stock agent** (*Austr.* and *N.Z.*) a dealer in livestock; **stock′-breeder** one who raises livestock; **stock′-breeding; stock′broker** a stock exchange member who buys and sells stocks or shares for clients having been officially superseded in the British Stock Exchange, on 27 October 1986, by the broker/dealer, combining the jobs of stockbroker and stockjobber (**stockbroker belt** the area outside a city, esp. that to the south of London, in which wealthy businessmen live); **stock′broking; stock company** (*U.S.*) a permanent repertory company attached to a theatre; **stock cube** a cube of compressed meat extract used for making stock; **stock′-dove** a dove like a small wood-pigeon — from nesting in stumps or rabbit-holes, or from representing (as wrongly supposed) the ancestor of the domestic breeds; **stock exchange** a building for the buying and selling of stocks and shares: an association of persons transacting such business: (with *caps.*) the institution in London where such business is done; **stock farm** a farm specialising in the rearing of livestock; **stock′-farmer** a farmer who rears livestock; **stock′-feeder** one who fattens livestock; **stock′-gill′y-flower,** now usu. **stock,** a favourite cruciferous garden plant (*Matthiola incana*; from its half-shrubby character); **stock′holder** one who holds stocks in the public funds, or in a company: a person who owns livestock (*Austr.*); **stock′horse** (*Austr.*) a horse trained for working with sheep and cattle; **stock′-in-trade** all the goods a shopkeeper has for sale: standard equipment or devices necessary for a particular trade or profession: a person's basic intellectual and emotional resources (often implying inadequacy or triteness); **stock′-jobber** a stock exchange member who deals only with other members (in some special group of securities), his job having been abolished in the British Stock Exchange on 27 October 1986, with the introduction of the job of broker/ dealer, combining the jobs of stockbroker and stockjobber: a stockbroker (*U.S.*): an unscrupulous speculator; **stock′-jobbery, -jobbing; stock′-list** a list of stocks and current prices regularly issued; **stock′-lock** a lock with wooden case; **stock′man** (esp. *Austr.*) man in charge of farm-stock; **stock′-market** a stock exchange: stock exchange business; **stock′pile** heap of road-metal, ore, etc.: reserve supply. — Also *v.t.* — **stock′piling** accumulating reserves, as of raw materials; **stock′-pot** the pot in which the stock for soup is kept. — *adj.* **stock′-pun′isht** (*Shak.*) put in the stocks. — **stock′-raising** breeding of stock; **stock′-rider** (*Austr.*) a mounted herdsman; **stock′-room** a store-room: a room in a hotel for display of commercial travellers' wares; **stock route** (*Austr.* and *N.Z.*) a right of way for travelling stock; **stock′-saddle** a cowboy's saddle. — *adj.* and *adv.* **stock′-still** utterly still (as a post or stock). — **stock′take** an act of stocktaking; **stock′taking** inventorying and valuation of stock; **stock′-whip** a herdsman's whip with short handle and long lash; **stock′yard** a large yard with pens, stables, etc., where cattle are kept for slaughter, market, etc. — **in, out of, stock** available, not available, for sale; **on the stocks** in preparation; **stockbrokers′ Tudor** (*archit.*) imitation Tudor; **stock-car racing** motor racing in which modified standard models of cars are used, not cars built as racers; **stocks and stones** inanimate idols; **take stock (of)** to make an inventory of goods on hand: to make an estimate of; **take stock in** to trust to, attach importance to. [O.E. *stocc,* a stick; Ger. *Stock.*]
stock[2] *stok,* (*Shak.*) *n.* a stoccado. [It. *stocco,* rapier.]
stockade *stok-ād′, n.* a barrier of stakes. — *v.t.* to defend with a stockade. [Fr. *estacade* — Sp. *estacada;* cf. **stake**[1].]
stock-and-horn *stok′-ənd-hörn, n.* an old Scottish musical instrument made of a cow's horn, a sheep's thigh bone or elder pipe with stops, and an oaten reed. [O.E. (Northumbrian) *stocc,* trumpet.]
stockfish *stok′fish, n.* unsalted dried hake, cod, etc.,

commonly beaten with a stick before cooking.   [Prob. Du. *stokvisch*.]

stocking *stok'ing, n.* a close covering for the foot and lower leg (esp. *Scot.*) or more usu. the whole leg: distinctive colouring or feathering of an animal's leg: a hoard of savings. — *n.* **stockinet'**, **-ette'**, **stockingette'** an elastic knitted fabric for undergarments, etc. — *adj.* **stock'inged** wearing stockings (but usu. not shoes). — *n.* **stock'inger** (*-ing-ər*) a maker of stockings. — *adj.* **stock'ingless.** — **stock'ing-fill'er** a small present for a Christmas stocking; **stock'ing-foot'** the foot of a stocking; **stock'ing-frame** a knitting-machine; **stock'ing-mask'** a nylon stocking pulled over the head to distort and so disguise the features; **stock'ing-sole'; stock'ing-stitch** a style of knitting in which a row of plain stitch alternates with a row of purl. — **in one's stocking-feet, -soles** with stockings but no shoes.   [**stock¹**, in sense of **netherstock**.]

stockwork *stok'wərk, n.* a mass of veins, impregnations, etc., that can be worked as one deposit.   [Anglicised from Ger. *Stockwerk*.]

stodge *stoj, v.t.* to stuff, cram, gorge: to sate (*arch.*): to bog (*arch.*). — *v.i.* (*arch.*) to trudge: to plod. — *n.* cloggy stuff: heavy, often uninteresting, food. — *n.* **stodg'er** a heavy, dull, spiritless, or unenterprising person. — *adv.* **stodg'ily.** — *n.* **stodg'iness.** — *adj.* **stodg'y** heavy and cloggy: solemnly dull.   [Perh. imit.]

stoechiology, stoechiometry, etc. See **stoich(e)iology.**

stoep *stoop, (S.Afr.) n.* a platform along the front, and sometimes the sides, of a house: a verandah. — U.S. **stoop.**   [Du.; cf. **step.**]

stog(e)y, stogie *stō'gi, (U.S.) n.* a long, inexpensive cigar.   [From Cone*stoga*, Pennsylvania.]

Stoic *stō'ik, n.* a disciple of the philosopher Zeno (d. *c.* 261 B.C.), who taught in the *Stoa Poikilē* (Painted Porch) at Athens. — *adjs.* **Stō'ic, -al** pertaining to the Stoics, or to their opinions: (without *cap.*) indifferent to pleasure or pain: (without *cap.*) uncomplaining in suffering. — *adv.* **stō'ically.** — *ns.* **stō'icalness; stō'icism** (*-sizm*) the philosophy of the Stoics: indifference to pleasure or pain: limitation of wants: austere impassivity: uncomplaining fortitude in suffering.   [Gr. *Stōikos* — *stōā*, a porch.]

stoich(e)iology, stoechiology *stoi-kī-ol'ə-ji, n.* the branch of biology that deals with the elements comprising animal tissues. — *adj.* **stoich(e)iolog'ical, stoechiolog'-ical.** — *n.* **stoich(e)iometry, stoechiometry** (*stoi-kī-om'i-tri*) the branch of chemistry that deals with the numerical proportions in which substances react. — *adj.* **stoich(e)iomet'ric, stoechiomet'ric.**   [Gr. *stoicheion*, an element.]

stoit *stoit, (Scot.) v.i.* to stumble, lurch. — *v.i.* **stoit'er** (*Scot.*) to stagger.   [Perh. Du. *stuiten*, to bounce.]

stoke *stōk, v.t.* to feed with fuel. — *v.i.* to act as stoker. — *n.* **stok'er** one who, or that which, feeds a furnace with fuel. — **stoke'hold** a ship's furnace chamber: a stoke-hole; **stoke'-hole** the space about the mouth of a furnace: the space allotted to the stokers: a hole in a reverberatory furnace for introducing a stirring-tool. — **stoke up** to fuel a fire or furnace (also *fig.*): to make a good meal (*fig.*).   [Du. *stoker*, stoker — *stoken*, to stoke.]

stokes *stōks, n.* the CGS unit of kinematic viscosity. — Also (esp. *U.S.*) **stoke:** — *pl.* **stokes.** — **Stokes' law** either of two laws in physics — (1) the frequency of luminescence excited by radiation is usually less than the frequency of the radiation which excites it; (2) the force needed to move a sphere through a viscous fluid is directly proportional to the velocity of the sphere, its radius, and the viscosity of the fluid.   [Sir G. *Stokes* (1819–1903), British physicist.]

STOL *stol, n.* a system by which aircraft land and take off over a short distance: an aircraft operating by this system. — See also **VTOL.** — **STOL'port** an airport for such aircraft.   [*s*hort *t*ake-*o*ff and *l*anding.]

stola. See **stole².**

stole¹ *stōl, pa.t.* and obs. *pa.p.* of **steal¹.**

stole² *stōl, n.* a long robe (also **stō'la;** L. *stol'a*): a narrow vestment worn on the shoulders, hanging down in front: a woman's outer garment of similar form: loosely, a gown, a surplice. — *adj.* **stoled** (*stōld*) wearing a stole.   [O.E. *stole* — L. *stŏla*, a Roman matron's long robe — Gr. *stolē*, equipment, garment — *stellein*, to array.]

stole³. See **stolon, stole.**

stolen *stōl'ən, pa.p.* of **steal¹.** — Also *adj.* — *adv.* (*arch.*) **stol'enwise** by stealth.

stolid *stol'id, adj.* impassive: blockish: unemotional. — *ns.* **stolid'ity, stol'idness.** — *adv.* **stol'idly.**   [L. *stolidus*.]

Stollen *shtol'ən, n.* rich, sweet German bread made with raisins, etc. and coated with icing sugar.   [Ger., a prop, strut, from the shape of the loaf.]

stolon *stō'lən, n.* a shoot from the base of a plant, rooting and budding at the nodes (also **stole**): a stemlike structure or budding outgrowth from a colony (*zool.*). — *adj.* **stōlonif'erous** producing stolons.   [L. *stolō, -ōnis*, twig, sucker.]

STOLport. See **STOL.**

stoma *stō'mə, n.* a mouthlike opening, esp. one (including its guard-cells or not) by which gases pass through the epidermis of green parts of a plant: — *pl.* **stō'mata.** — *adjs.* **stomatal** (*stōm', stom'ə-tl*), **stomat'ic.** — *ns.* **stomati'tis** inflammation of the mucous membrane of the mouth; **stomatodaeum** (*-dē'əm*), **stomod(a)e'um** (Gr. *hodaios*, on the way) in embryology, the invagination that forms the anterior part of the digestive tract. — *adj.* **stomatogas'tric** of, pertaining to, the mouth and stomach, or the upper alimentary tract. — *ns.* **stomatol'ogy** study of the mouth; **stom'atoplasty** plastic surgery of the mouth; **stom'atopod** a crustacean of the order **Stomatop'oda**, the mantis shrimps, with legs mostly near the mouth. — **-stomous** in composition, with a particular kind of mouth.   [Gr. *stŏma, -atos*, mouth.]

stomach *stum'ək, n.* the strong muscular bag into which food passes when swallowed, and where it is principally digested: the cavity in any animal for the digestion of its food: loosely or euphemistically, the belly: appetite, relish for food, inclination generally: disposition, spirit, courage, pride, spleen. — *v.t.* to brook or put up with: to digest: to turn the stomach of (*arch.*): to resent (*arch.*): to find offensive (*arch.*). — *adj.* of the stomach. — *adjs.* **stom'achal; stom'ached.** — *ns.* **stom'acher** (*-chər, -kər*) a covering or ornament for the chest, esp. one worn under the lacing of a bodice; **stom'achful** as much as the stomach will hold (*pl.* **stom'achfuls**). — *adj.* spirited: haughty: obstinate: resentful: angry. — *n.* **stom'achfulness.** — *adj.* **stomachic** (*stəm-ak'ik*) of the stomach: good for the stomach. — *n.* a stomachic medicine. — *adjs.* **stomach'ical; stom'achless; stom'achous** (*Spens.*) resentful: haughty: spirited: courageous; **stom'achy** (*arch.* or *dial.*) haughty: easily offended: spirited: paunchy. — **stom'ach-ache; stom'ach-pump** a syringe with a flexible tube for withdrawing fluids from the stomach, or injecting them into it.   [O.Fr. *estomac*, L. *stomachus*, Gr. *stomachos*, throat, later stomach — *stoma*, a mouth.]

stomatal, stomodaeum, stomato-, etc. See **stoma.**

stomp *stomp, v.i.* to stamp (*coll.*): to dance (*coll.*). — *n.* an early jazz composition with heavily accented rhythm: a lively dance with foot stamping: a stamp (*coll.*). — **stomp'ing-ground** stamping-ground.   [Variant of **stamp.**]

-stomy *-stəm-i,* in composition, used in naming a surgical operation to form a new opening into an organ.   [Gr. *stoma*, a mouth.]

stond *stond, n.* a Spens. form of **stand.**

stone *stōn, n.* a detached piece of rock, usu. small: the matter of which rocks consist: a gem: a mirror (*Shak.*): a tombstone: a printer's table for imposing: a concretion: a diseased state characterised by formation of a concretion in the body: (now *slang*) a testicle: a hard fruit kernel: a hailstone: (with *pl.* usu. **stone**) a standard weight of 14 lb avoirdupois (other stones have been in use, as that of 24 lb for wool, 22 lb for hay, 16 lb for cheese, etc.). — *adj.* of stone: of the colour of stone: of stoneware: of the Stone Age: not castrated. — *v.t.* to pelt with stones: to free from stones: to lay or wall with stones: to rub or sharpen with a stone: to turn to stone (*Shak.*). — *v.i.* to form a stone. — *adjs.* **stoned** having, containing, or freed from, a stone or stones: very drunk, or very high on drugs (*slang*); **stone′less**; **ston′en, ston′ern** (*obs.* or *dial.*) of stone. — *n.* **ston′er** one who stones: one who weighs, or a horse that carries, so many stone. — *adv.* **ston′ily.** — *ns.* **ston′iness**; **ston′ing.** — *adj.* **ston′y** of or like stone: abounding with stones: hard: pitiless: obdurate: rigid: petrifying: stony-broke. — **Stone Age** a stage of culture before the general use of metal, divided into the Old Stone Age (Palaeolithic) and the New (Neolithic); **stone axe** one made of stone: (with *hyphen*) two-edged axe for cutting stone. — *adj.* **stone′-blind** completely blind. — **stone bass** the wreckfish (q.v.); **stone boat** (*U.S.*) low sled for carrying rocks or other heavy objects; **stone′-boiling** boiling water by putting hot stones in it, **stone′-borer, -eater** any boring mollusc; **stone′-bow** a crossbow or catapult for shooting stones; **stone′-bramble** a bramble (*Rubus saxatilis*) of rocky places; **stone′-brash** a soil of finely-broken rock; **stone′-break** saxifrage; **stone′-breaker** one who, or that which, breaks stones: a stone-crushing machine. — *adj.* **stone-broke** see **stony-broke** below. — **stone′-bruise** a bruise caused by a stone, esp. on the sole of the foot; **stone′-canal** a calcified vertical tube in the water-vascular system of echinoderms; **stone′-cast** (or **stone′s cast**) a stone('s) throw; **stone′-cell** (*bot.*) a cell not much longer than broad with thick lignified walls; **stone′chat** a little black, ruddy and white bird of furzy places, with a note like the clicking of two stones (also **stone′-chatter**); **stone circle** a circle of standing-stones; **stone′-coal** mineral coal, as opp. to charcoal: any hard coal: anthracite. — *adjs.* **stone′-cold′** cold as a stone (**stone-cold sober** completely free of (esp. alcohol-induced) excitement or passion, utterly sober). — *n.* and *adj.* **stone′-colour** grey. — *adj.* **stone′-coloured.** — **stone′-crop** any plant of the wall-pepper genus (Sedum); **stone′-cur′lew** a large plover, the thick-knee; **stone′-cutter** one who hews stone: a machine for dressing stone; **stone′-cutting.** — *adjs.* **stone′-dead, stone′-deaf** dead, deaf, as a stone. — **stone′-dresser** one who prepares stones for building; **stone′-fal′con, -hawk** the merlin; **stone′fish** a poisonous tropical fish of the Scorpaenidae, which resembles a stone on the seabed; **stone′-fly** a plecopterous insect (*Perla*) whose larvae live under stones in streams; **stone′-fruit** a fruit with a stone. — *adj.* **stone′ground** of flour, ground between millstones. — **stone′-hammer** a hammer for breaking stones: (without *hyphen*) a hammer with a stone head; **stone′hand** (*print.*) an imposer, one who sets the type in the chase. — *adj.* **stone′-hard** (*Shak.*) as hard as a stone. — **stone′horse** a stallion; **stone′-lil′y** an encrinite; **stone′-mar′ten** a white-breasted marten, the beech-marten: its fur; **stone′-mason** a mason who works with stone; **stone′-mill** a machine for breaking stone; **stone′-oil** petroleum; **stone parsley** an umbelliferous plant (*Sison amomum*) akin to parsley, with aromatic seeds; **stone′-pine** a Mediterranean nut-pine; **stone′-pit** a quarry; **stone′-plov′er** the stone-curlew; **stone′-rag, -raw** (O.E. *ragu*, lichen) a lichen *Parmelia saxatilis*, yielding a dye; **stone saw** a toothless saw for cutting stone; **stone′shot** a stone-throw: stones or a stone used as shot; **stone′-snipe** an American plover; **stone′(s)′-throw** the distance a stone may be thrown. — *adv.* and *adj.* **stone′-still** (*Shak.*) as still as a stone. — **stonewall′** parliamentary obstruction (*Austr.*): defensive play in cricket. — *v.i.* to obstruct: to block: to offer wall-like resistance. — **stonewall′er; stonewall′ing; stone′ware** a coarse kind of potter's ware baked hard and glazed: a high-fired, vitrified, non-porous ceramic material or

objects made of it; **stone′work** work in stone; **stone′wort** any plant of the Characeae (from the limy crust): stone parsley. — *adjs.* **ston′y-broke′** (*slang*) penniless, or nearly so (also **ston′y, stone′-broke′**); **ston′y-heart′ed** hard-hearted. — **leave no stone unturned** to do everything that can be done in order to secure the effect desired; **mark with a white stone** to mark as particularly fortunate; **stone me!, stone the crows!** (*slang*) expressions of astonishment.   [O.E. *stān*; Ger. *Stein*, Du. *steen*.]

stonen, stonern. See **stone.**

stong. Old form of **stung.**

stonied (*Spens.*). See **stony¹.**

stonker *stong′kər* (*slang*), *v.t.* to kill, destroy, overthrow, thwart. — *n.* **stonk** (*stongk; mil. slang*; back-formation) intense bombardment.   [Ety. dub.]

stonn(e). Old form of **stun.**

stony¹ *stōn′i*, (*obs.*) *v.t.* aphetic for **astony** (see **astonish**; *pa.p.*, *Spens.*, **ston′ied**).

stony². See **stone.**

stood *stŏōd*, *pa.t.*, *pa.p.*, **stooden** *-ən*, (*Scot.*) *pa.p.*, of **stand.**

stooge *stŏōj*, (*slang*) *n.* a performer speaking from the auditorium: an actor's feeder: a stage butt: a subordinate or drudge: a scapegoat. — Also *v.i.* — **stooge around** to wander about leisurely, purposelessly, or idly.   [Origin unknown.]

stook *stŏōk*, *n.* a shock of sheaves, set up in the field. — *v.t.* to set up in stooks. — *n.* **stook′er.**   [Cf. L.G. *stuke*, bundle.]

stool *stŏōl*, *n.* a chair, seat of authority or dignity, throne (*obs.*): a seat without a back: a low support for the feet or knees: a seat used in evacuating the bowels: defecation: faeces: a stand: a stump from which sprouts shoot up: a growth of shoots: the wicket in stoolball: a piece of wood to which a bird is fastened as a decoy. — *v.i.* to evacuate the bowels: to put forth shoots: to lure wildfowl with a stool. — *n.* **stoolie** see **stool-pigeon** below. — **stool′ball** an old game resembling cricket; **stool′-pigeon** a decoy-pigeon: a decoy: a police informer (shortened form **stool′ie**; *slang*). — **fall between two stools** to lose both possibilities by hesitating between them, or trying for both; **groom of the stole** (an old form of **stool**) formerly an officer over the lords of the bedchamber; **stool of repentance** a place in church where delinquents, esp. fornicators, were exposed.   [O.E. *stōl*; Ger. *Stuhl*; cf. Ger. *stellen*, to place.]

stoop¹ *stŏōp*, *v.i.* to bend the body forward: to lean forward: to submit: to descend from rank or dignity: to condescend: to lower oneself by unworthy behaviour: to swoop down, as a bird of prey. — *v.t.* to bend, incline, lower, or direct downward. — *n.* a bending of the body: inclination forward: descent: condescension: a swoop. — *adj.* **stooped** having a stoop, bent. — *n.* **stoop′er.** — *adj.* **stoop′ing.** — *adv.* **stoop′ingly.** — **stoop′-gallant** (*obs.*) that which humbles gallants, orig. the sweating-sickness. — Also *adj.* (*Spens.* **stoope-gallaunt**).   [O.E. *stūpian*; O.N. *stūpa*; the vowel preserved by the following *p*.]

stoop². See **stoup¹.**

stoop³. American spelling of **stoep.**

stoop⁴, stoup *stŏōp*, *n.* a post (*dial.*): a prop, supporter, patron (*Scot.*): a massive supporting pillar of coal in a mine (*dial.*). — **stoop and roop, stoup and roup** (*Scot.*) stump and rump, completely.   [O.N. *stolpi*, post.]

stoope. See **stoup¹.**

stoope-gallaunt. See **stoop¹**

stoor¹, stour *stŏōr*, **sture** *stŭr*, **stowre** *stowr*, (*obs.*) *adjs.* great, formidable: stiff, harsh, austere. stubborn, obstinate, surly.   [Partly M.E. *stūr*, harsh (cf. M.L.G. *stūr*), partly O.E. *stōr*, great.]

stoor² *stŏōr*. See **stour².**

stooshie *stŏōsh′i*, (*Scot.*) *n.* fuss, ado, disturbance: frolic. — Also **stash′ie, stish′ie, stush′ie.**   [Poss. from aphet. form of **ecstasy**.]

stop *stop*, *v.t.* to snuff, block, plug, choke, close up (often with *up*): to thrust, cram (*obs.* except as Scots **stap**): to obstruct: to render impassable: to hinder or prevent the passage of: to bring to a standstill: to bring down, hit with a shot: to cause to cease: to counter: to restrain: to withhold: to hinder: to prevent: to cease from, leave off, discontinue: to limit the vibrating length of, esp. by pressure of a finger (*mus.*): to pinch off (*hort.*): to punctuate: to place a pause in, esp. at the end of a line or couplet (*pros.*): to adjust the aperture of, with a diaphragm: to make fast by lashing (*naut.*). — *v.i.* to come to a standstill, halt: to cease: to desist: to come to an end: to stay, tarry, sojourn (*coll.*): — *pr.p.* **stopp'ing**; *pa.t.* and *pa.p.* **stopped**. — *n.* act of stopping: state of being stopped: cessation: a halt: a pause: a halting-place: hindrance: obstacle: interruption: a contrivance that limits motion: a card that interrupts the run of play: a diaphragm: the stopping of an instrument or string: a fret on a lute or guitar: a finger-hole, a key for covering it, or other means of altering pitch or tone: a set of organ pipes of uniform tone quality: a knob operating a lever for bringing them into use: mechanism on a harpsichord for bringing particular strings into play: a sound requiring complete closure of the breath passage, a mute (*phon.*; also **stop'= consonant**): a punctuation mark. — *adj.* **stop'less**. — *n.* **stopp'age** act of stopping: state of being stopped: stopping of work, as for a strike: obstruction: an amount stopped off pay. — *adj.* **stopped**. — *n.* **stopp'er** one who stops: that which stops: a plug: a plug (usu. glass) for a bottle: a short rope for making something fast (*naut.*). — *v.t.* to close or secure with a stopper. — *ns.* **stopp'ing** the action of one who or that which stops in any sense (**double stopping** simultaneous stopping of and playing on two strings): stuffing or filling material, esp. for teeth. — **stop'-bath** a substance in which a photographic negative or print is immersed in order to halt the action of the developer; **stop'-cock** a short pipe opened and stopped by turning a key or handle: loosely, the key or handle; **stop-frame camera** a cine-camera that can be adjusted to take a reduced number of frames, used in creating the effect of pixillation (q.v.); **stop'-gap** a temporary expedient or substitute. — Also *adj.* — *adj.* **stop'-go'** (of policy) alternately discouraging and encouraging forward movement. — *n.* a stop-go economic policy, etc. — **stop(-loss) order** an order to a stockbroker to sell shares when their value drops below a certain level; **stop'-off, stop'-o'ver** a break of journey, **stopp'ing-out** use in places of a protective covering against acids in etching, against light in photography; **stopp'ing-place; stop'= press** late news inserted in a newspaper after printing has begun: a space for it. — Also *adj.* — **stop'-watch** an accurate watch readily started and stopped, used in timing a race, etc. — **pull out all the stops** to express with as much emotion as possible: to act with great energy; **pull out a** (specified) **stop** to emphasise a (specified) emotional element in a situation; **stop down** of a camera lens, to reduce the size of the aperture; **stop the show** see **show**; **stop off, stop over, stop in**, U.S. **stop by**, to break one's journey, pay a visit to (usu. with *at*); **stop the show** see **show**; **stop thief** a cry for help to catch a thief. [O.E. *stoppian*, found in the compound *forstoppian*, to stop up — L. *stuppa*, tow — Gr. *styppē*.]

stope¹ *stōp, n.* a step-like excavation in mining. — *v.t.* to excavate, or extract in this way. — *n.* **stop'ing**. [Perh. conn. with **step**.]

stope². See stoup¹.

stopple¹ *stop'l, n.* a stopper: a plug. — *v.t.* to stopper, plug. [**stop**.]

stopple² *stop'l, n.* a tobacco-pipe stem — *Scot.* **stap(p)'le**. [M.Du. *stapel*, stem.]

storable, storage. See store.

storax *stō'raks, stö', n.* the resin of *Styrax officinalis*, once used in medicine: now that of *Liquidambar orientale* (*liquid storax*). [L. *storax* — Gr. *styrax*.]

store *stōr, stör, n.* a hoard: a stock laid up: sufficiency

or abundance: keeping: a storehouse: a shop: a co-operative shop or one with many departments or branches: an animal fattening for the market: value, esteem: a computer memory unit, in which programme and data are stored: (in *pl.*) supplies of provisions, ammunition, etc., for an army, ship, etc. — *adj.* and *adv.* (*arch.*) in abundance. — *adj.* of a store: sold in a shop, ready-made. — *v.t.* to stock, furnish, supply: to lay up, keep in reserve: to deposit in a repository: to give storage to: to put (data) into a computer memory. — *adj.* **stor'able**. — *ns.* **stor'age** placing, accommodation, reservation, or safe-keeping, in store: reservation in the form of potential energy: the keeping of information in a computer memory unit: charge for keeping goods in store; **stor'er**. — **storage battery** an accumulator; **storage capacity** the maximum amount of information that can be held in a computer store; **storage heater** an electric heater with a large thermal capacity that accumulates and stores heat during the off-peak periods and releases it over a longer period; **store'= cattle** cattle kept for fattening; **store'-farm** (*Scot.*) a stock-farm, a cattle-farm; **store'-farmer; store'front** (*U.S.*) the façade of a shop or store; **store'house** a house for storing goods of any kind: a repository: a treasury; **store'keeper** a man in charge of stores: a shopkeeper (chiefly *U.S.*): an unsaleable article (*U.S.*); **store'man** a storekeeper (*U.S.*): one who looks after stores or a storeroom; **store'room** a room in which stores are kept: space for storing; **store'-ship** a vessel used for carrying naval stores; **store teeth** (*U.S.*) false teeth. — **in store** in hoard for future use, ready for supply: in reserve, awaiting; **set store by** to value greatly. [O.Fr. *estor, estoire* — L. *instaurāre*, to provide.]

storey (also now less frequently **story**) *stō'ri, stö', n.* all that part of a building on the same floor: a tier: — *pl.* **stor'eys**. — *adj.* **stor'eyed (stor'ied)** having storeys. — **first storey** the ground floor; **second storey** the first floor, etc. [Prob. same word orig. as **story¹**.]

storge *stör'gē, -jē, n.* parental affection. [Gr.]

storiated, storiette, storiology, etc. See **story¹**.

storied. See under story¹ and storey.

stork *störk, n.* a large white and black wading bird (*Ciconia alba*) with a great red bill and red legs: the bringer of babies (*facet.*): any member of its genus or of its family (akin to the ibises). — **stork's'-bill** a genus (*Erodium*) of the geranium family, with beaked fruit: also applied to Pelargonium. [O.E. *storc*; Ger. *Storch*.]

storm *störm, n.* a violent commotion of the atmosphere: a tempest: a wind just short of a hurricane: any intense meteorological phenomenon: a fall of snow, long frost (*Scot.*): a violent commotion or outbreak of any kind: a paroxysm: a violent assault (*mil.*): calamity (*fig.*). — *v.i.* to be stormy: to rage: to rush violently or in attack: to upbraid passionately. — *v.t.* to take or try to take by assault: to disturb by a storm. — *adj.* **storm'ful** stormy. — *adv.* **storm'fully.** — *n.* **storm'fulness.** — *adv.* **storm'ily.** — *n.* **storm'iness.** — *n.* and *adj.* **storm'ing.** — *adjs.* **storm'less; storm'y** having many storms: agitated with furious winds: boisterous: violent: passionate. — *adjs.* **storm'-beat, -beat'en** beaten by storms. — **storm'-belt** a belt around the earth of maximum storm frequency; **storm'-bird** a petrel. — *adj.* **storm'bound** delayed, cut off, confined to port by storms. — **storm cellar** an underground shelter against hurricanes, etc.; **storm'-centre** the position of lowest pressure in a cyclonic storm: any focus of controversy or strife; **storm'-cloud; storm'-cock** the missel-thrush; **storm'= cone, -drum** a cone, drum, hoisted as a storm-signal; **storm cuff** an extra elasticated cuff let into the cuff opening of a jacket, etc., to give extra warmth and protection; **storm'-glass** a tube containing a solution supposed to change appearance with the weather; **storm'ing-par'ty** the party sent to lead in storming a fortress; **storm'-lantern** a lantern with flame protected from wind and weather; **storm petrel** or (popularly) **stormy petrel** see **petrel**. — *adj.* **storm'proof** proof against storms or storming. — **storm'-sail** (-sl, -sāl) a small very strong sail for stormy weather; **storm'= shutter** an outside window-shutter; **storm'-signal** a signal hoisted in warning of the approach of a storm; **storm'-stay** a stay on which a storm-sail is set. — *adjs.* **storm'-stayed** hindered from proceeding by storms; **storm'-tossed** tossed about by storms: much agitated by conflicting passions. — **storm'-track** the path of a storm-centre; **storm'-trooper.** — *n.pl.* **storm'-troops** shock-troops: a body formed in Germany by Adolf Hitler, disbanded 1934. — **storm'-warning; storm'= water** surface drainage in excess of the normal in a storm; **storm'-wind** a stormy wind; **storm'-window** a window raised above the roof, slated above and at the sides: an additional outer casement. — **a storm in a teacup** (or other small vessel) a great commotion in a narrow sphere, or about a trifle; **take by storm** to take by assault: to captivate totally and instantly (*fig.*). [O.E. *storm*; O.N. *stormr*; from root of **stir**[1].]

stornello *stör-nel'ō*, *n.* a short (usually three-lined) popular Italian verse-form: — *pl.* **stornell'i** (-ē). [It.]

Storting, Storthing *stör'ting*, *stör'*, *n.* the legislative assembly of Norway, comprising the Lagting and Odelsting. [Norw. *stor*, great, *ting* (O.N. *thing*), assembly.]

story[1] *stō'ri*, *stö'*, *n.* history (*obs.*): legend: a narrative of incidents in their sequence: a fictitious narrative: a tale: an anecdote: the plot of a novel or drama: a theme: an account, report, statement, allegation: a news article: a lie, a fib. — *v.t.* to tell or describe historically, to relate: to adorn with scenes from history. — *v.i.* to relate. — *adjs.* **sto'riated** decorated with elaborate ornamental designs (also **historiated**); **sto'ried** told or celebrated in a story: having a history: interesting from the stories belonging to it: adorned with scenes from history. — *ns.* **storiette', storyette'** a short tale; **storiol'- ogist; storiol'ogy** the scientific study of folk-tales. — *n.* and *adj.* **sto'rying.** — **sto'ry-book** a book of tales true or fictitious. — *adj.* rather luckier or happier than in real life. — **story line** the main plot of a novel, film, television series, etc., or line along which the plot is to develop; **sto'ry-teller** one who relates tales: a liar; **sto'ry-telling.** — **the same old story** an often-repeated event or situation; **the story goes** it is generally said. [A.Fr. *estorie* — L. *historia*.]

story[2]. See **storey**.

stot[1] *stot*, *n.* a young ox, steer. [O.E. *stot*, horse.]

stot[2] *stot*, (*Scot.*) *v.i.* to rebound, bounce: to stagger: to walk bouncily. — *v.t.* to cause to bounce. — *n.* a rebound. — Also **stott'er.** [Origin obscure.]

stotinka *sto-tingk'ə*, *n.* a Bulgarian unit of currency, worth one hundredth of a lev: — *pl.* **stotin'ki.** [Bulgarian.]

stotious *stō'shəs*, (*Ir.*, *Scot.*) *adj.* drunk. [Origin uncertain: poss. from **stot**[2].]

stotter. See **stot**[2].

stoun *stōōn*, (*Spens.*) *v.t.*: — *pa.t.* and *pa.p.* **stound.** Same as **stun.**

stound[1], **stownd** *stownd, stōōnd*, (*Spens.* and *Scot.*) *n.* a time, moment: a time of trouble: a pang: an assault, stroke: a shock: a din. — *v.i.* to shoot like a pang: to experience a pang. [O.E. *stund.*]

stound[2] *stownd, stōōnd*, (*Spens.*) *v.t.* to stun, astound. — *n.* a stunned or astounded condition. [**stoun** or **astound.**]

stoup[1], **stoop** *stōōp* (*Shak.* **stoope; stope** *stōp*), *n.* a bucket (*obs.*): a drinking vessel (*arch.*): a holy-water vessel. [Cf. O.N. *staup* and Du. *stoop*; O.E. *stēap.*]

stoup[2]. See **stoop**[4].

stour[1]. See **stoor**[1].

stour[2], **stowre, stoor** *stowr, stōōr*, *ns.* battle, assault: tumult: turmoil: dust (*Scot.*). — *adj.* **stour'y** (*Scot.*) dusty. [O.Fr. *estour*, tumult.]

stoush *stowsh*, (*Austr.* and *N.Z.*) a fight, a brawl; a war. — *v.t.* and *v.i.* to fight. [Variant of Scot. **stooshie.**]

stout *stowt*, *adj.* fierce (*B.*, *Spens.*): proud (*obs.*): arrogant (*obs.*): unyielding (*obs.* or *dial.*): stubborn (*obs.*): res-

olute: dauntless: vigorous: enduring: robust: strong: thick: fat. — *adv.* stoutly. — *n.* extra-strong porter. — *v.t.* and *v.i.* **stout'en** to make, or grow, stout(er). — *adj.* **stout'ish.** — *adv.* **stout'ly.** — *n.* **stout'ness.** — *adj.* **stout'-heart'ed.** — *adv.* **stout'-heart'edly.** — **stout'= heart'edness.** [O.Fr. *estout*, bold — Du. *stout*; Ger. *stolz*, proud.]

stouth *stōōth*, (*obs. Scot.*) *n.* theft. — *ns.* **stouth'rie, stouth'erie** theft: stolen goods: provision, furniture; **stouth'rief** (*Scots law*) theft with violence (later only in a dwelling-house). — **stouth and routh** plenty, abundance (cf. **stoop and roop** under **stoop**[4]). [O.N. *stuldr*, theft.]

stovaine *stō-vā'in*, or *stō'*, or *-vān'*, *n.* a local anaesthetic, a substitute for cocaine, used for spinal analgesia. [**stove**[1], Eng. trans. of the name of Prof. Furneau, who first prepared it.]

stove[1] *stōv*, *n.* a hot-air bath (*arch.*): a heated room or chamber (*arch.*): a hothouse: a closed heating or cooking apparatus: a fire-grate: a kiln or oven for various manufacturing operations: a drying room. — *v.t.* to put, keep, heat, or dry in a stove: to stew (*Scot.*). — *n.pl.* (*Scot.*) **stov'ies** stewed potatoes: Irish stew. — *n.* **stov'ing** drying a specially prepared paint quickly by application of heat. — **stove enamel** a type of heat-proof enamel produced by heating an enamelled article in a stove; **stove'pipe** a metal pipe for carrying smoke and gases from a stove: a tall silk hat (*U.S.*; in full **stovepipe hat**); **stove'-plant** a hothouse plant. [O.E. *stofa*; Ger. *Stube.*]

stove[2] *stōv*, *pa.t.* and *pa.p.* of **stave.** — Also used as *pres.t.*

stover *stō'vər*, (*arch.*) *n.* fodder. [Aphetic for **estover.**]

stovies. See **stove**[1].

stow[1] *stō*, *v.t.* to place, put, lodge: to put away: to store: to put under hatches: to put down one's throat (*jocularly*): to desist from (*stow it*, stop it; *slang*): to pack: to have room for: to arrange. — *v.i.* (with *away*) to hide as a stowaway. — *ns.* **stow'age** act or manner of stowing: state of being laid up: room for stowing: a place for stowing things: money paid for stowing goods: things stowed; **stow'er; stow'ing.** — **stow'away** one who hides in a ship, etc., to get a passage. — *adj.* travelling as a stowaway: that can be packed up and stored, carried, etc. — **stow'down** the process of stowing down in a ship's hold. [O.E. *stōw*, place.]

stow[2] *stōō*, (*Scot.*) *v.t.* to crop. [O.N. *stūfr*, stump.]

stown *stown*, a Scots form of **stolen.** — *adv.* **stow(n)'lins** (*Scot.*) by stealth.

stownd. See **stound**[1].

stowre. See **stoor**[1] and **stour**[2].

strabism *strā'bizm*, **strabismus** *strə-biz'məs*, *ns.* a muscular defect of the eye, preventing parallel vision: a squint. — *adjs.* **strabis'mal, strabis'mic, -al.** — *ns.* **strabismom'- eter** (*strab-iz-*), **strabom'eter** an instrument for measuring strabismus; **strabot'omy** (Gr. *tomē*, a cut) the surgical operation for the cure of squinting. [Gr. *strabos* and *strabismos*, squinting; cf. *strephein*, to twist.]

stracchino *strä-kē'nō*, *n.* a North Italian soft cheese: — *pl.* **stracchi'ni** (-nē). [It., — *stracco*, weak.]

strack. See **strike.**

strad. See **Stradivarius.**

straddle *strad'l*, *v.i.* to part the legs wide: to sit, stand, or walk with legs far apart: to seem favourable to both sides, to trim. — *v.t.* to bestride: to set far apart: to overshoot and then shoot short of, in order to get the range, to bracket: to cover the area of with bombs. — *n.* act of straddling: an attempt to fill a noncommittal position: a stock transaction in which the buyer obtains the privilege of either a *put* or a *call*: a vertical mine-timber supporting a set: combination of a shot beyond the mark and one short of it: a style of high jump in which the legs straddle the bar while the body is parallel to it. — *adv.* astride. — *adv.* **stradd'leback** stridelegs. — **straddle carrier** a high self-propelled vehicle which can straddle a container and lift, carry, and deposit where required. — *adj.* **stradd'le-legged**

having the legs wide apart.   [Freq. of **stride**.]

stradiot *strad'i-ot,* (*hist.*) *n.* a Venetian light horseman from Albania or Greece.   [It. *stradiotto* — Gr. *stratiōtēs,* soldier.]

Stradivarius *strad-i-vä'ri-əs,* or *-vä',* **Stradivari** *-vä're,* (*coll.*) **strad,** *ns.* a stringed instrument, usu. a violin, made by Antonio *Stradivari* (1644–1737) of Cremona. — Also **Stradūa'rius.**

strae *strä,* *n.* Scots form of **straw**[1]. — **strae death** natural death in bed.

strafe, straff *sträf* (in U.S. *sträf*), (originally war slang of 1914) *v.t.* to punish: to bombard: to assail: to rake with machine-gun fire from low-flying aeroplanes. — *n.* an attack.   [Ger. *strafen,* to punish, used in the phrase *Gott strafe England,* God punish England, a German slogan of World War I.]

straggle *strag'l,* *v.i.* to wander from one's company or course: to be absent without leave but not long enough to be counted a deserter: to stretch dispersedly or sprawlingly: to grow irregularly and untidily. — *n.* a straggling line or group. — *ns.* **strag** (*dial.*) a straggler: a stray: a vagrant; **stragg'ler.** — *n.* and *adj.* **stragg'ling.** — *adv.* **stragg'lingly.** — *adj.* **stragg'ly** straggling: irregularly spread out.   [Origin obscure.]

straicht. See **straucht.**

straight[1] *strāt,* *adj.* uncurved: in a right line: direct: upright: flat, horizontal: in good order: accurate: frank and honourable: respectably conducted: balanced, even, square: settled: downright: normal: conventional in tastes, opinions, etc. (*slang*): heterosexual (*slang*): in sequence (*poker*): (of games, sets won) in succession (*tennis*): of a theatrical part, portraying a normal person, without emphasis on eccentricities of manner, etc.: not comic: undiluted, neat: uninterrupted: consistent in support of one party or policy. — *n.* a straight condition: good behaviour: a straight line, part, course, flight, esp. the last part of a racecourse: a heterosexual person (*slang*). — *adv.* in a straight line: directly: all the way: immediately: upright: outspokenly: honestly. — *v.t.* to straighten. — *v.t.* and *v.i.* **straight'en** to make or become straight. — *n.* **straight'ener** something that straightens: a bribe (*thieves' slang*). — *adv.* **straight'-forth** directly forward: straightway. — *adj.* **straight'ish.** — *adv.* **straight'ly** in a straight line or manner: straightway. — *n.* **straight'ness.** — *adv.* **straight'way** (*arch.*) directly: immediately: without loss of time. — Also **straight'ways.** — **straight angle** a right angle (*obs.*), now, two right angles. — *adjs.* **straight'-arm** of a Rugby tackle, with the arm extended straight; **straight'away** straight forward; **straight'-cut** cut lengthwise of the leaf, of tobacco. — **straight'edge** a strip or stick for testing straightness or drawing straight lines; **straight fight** esp. in politics, a contest in which only two persons or sides take part. — *adj.* **straightfor'ward** going forward in a straight course: without digression: without evasion: honest: frank. — *adv.* straightforwardly. — *adv.* **straightfor'wardly.** — **straightfor'wardness.** — *adj.* **straight'-jet** (of aircraft or engine) driven or driving by jet directly, without a propeller. — **straight man** an actor who acts as stooge to a comedian. — *adj.* **straight'-out** (*U.S.,* esp. in party politics) out-and-out; **straight'-pight** (*Shak.*) straight, erect. — **straight play** one without music: a serious drama as opposed to a comedy; **straight talk** a candid outspoken talk; **straight ticket** see **ticket**; **straight tip** a racing tip that comes straight from the owner: inside information that can be relied on. — **go straight** to give up criminal activities; **keep a straight bat** (*fig.*) to behave honourably; **keep a straight face** to refrain from smiling; **straight away** immediately; **straighten out** to disentangle, resolve; **straight off** straight away, without hesitation (*coll.*); **straight out** frankly, directly; **straight up** honestly, really (*coll.* often *interrog.*); **the straight and narrow (path)** the virtuous way of life.   [O.E. *streht,* pa.p. of *streccan;* see **stretch**.]

straight[2]. See **straucht.**

straight[3]. See **strait.**

straik[1] *strāk,* *n.* and *vb.* a Scots form of **stroke**[1,2]. — *n.* (*Scott*) proportion of malt in brewing.

straik[2]. See **strake**[2].

strain[1] *strān,* *v.t.* to stretch: to draw tight: to draw with force: to exert to the utmost: to injure by overtasking: to force unnaturally, unduly, or amiss: to exalt emotionally: to change in form or bulk by subjecting to a stress: to constrain (*obs.*): to urge, insist upon, press for (*Shak.*): to press to oneself, embrace: to squeeze, press: to grip, grasp tightly: to compress: to restrain: to squeeze out, express: to sing or play: to filter (esp. coarsely). — *v.i.* to make violent efforts: to tug: to retch: to have difficulty in swallowing or accepting (with *at*): to make efforts at evacuation: to percolate, filter. — *n.* the act of straining: a violent effort: an injury by straining, esp. a wrenching of the muscles: any change of form or bulk under stress: pitch, height: a section of a melody: a melody: an outpouring or flow of language: emotional tone, key, manner. — *adj.* **strained** having been strained: tense, forced or unnatural. — *adv.* **strain'edly** (or **strānd'li**). — *n.* **strain'er** one who, or that which, strains: a sieve, colander, etc. — *n.* and *adj.* **strain'ing.** — **strain'ing-beam, -piece** a tie-beam uniting the tops of queen-posts; **strain hardening** a process by which metal is deformed in order to increase its hardness. — **strain a point** to waive a scruple; **strain at** in Matt. xxiii. 24, to remove by straining, strain in the event of finding (not, as often understood, to be unable to swallow); **strain courtesy** (*Shak., Rom. and Jul.*) to treat with scant courtesy, or (*Venus and Adonis*) to be over-punctilious in courtesy.   [O.Fr. *estraindre* — L. *stringĕre,* to stretch tight.]

strain[2] *strān,* *n.* offspring (*arch.*): breed, race, stock, line of descent: natural, esp. inherited, tendency or element in one's character: kind, type (*arch.*).   [App. O.E. *(ge)strēon,* gain, getting, begetting (see **strene**), with altered vowel by confusion with foregoing.]

straint *strānt,* (*Spens.*) *n.* pressure.   [**strain**[1], on the model of **constraint,** etc.]

strait (formerly also, and still erroneously, **straight;** *Spens., Milt.,* **streight**) *strāt, adj.* (*obs.* or *rare*) close: narrow: strict: rigorous: hard-pressed, needy: sparing in giving: tight (*Shak.*). — *n.* a narrow part, place, or passage, esp. (often in *pl.*) by water: (usu. in *pl.*) difficulty, distress, hardship. — *adv.* (*obs.* or *rare*) tightly: closely: narrowly: strictly: rigorously: with hardship.   *v.t.* (*obs.* or *rare*) to tighten: to narrow: to put in a difficulty: to reduce to hardship. — *v.t.* **strait'en** to tighten (*obs.*): to narrow (*arch.*): to confine (*arch.*): to distress: to put into difficulties: to run short. — *v.i.* (*arch.*) to narrow. — *adj.* **strait'ened.** — *adv.* **strait'ly** (*obs.* or *arch.*) tightly: narrowly: closely: strictly. — *n.* **strait'ness** (*rare*). — **strait'-jacket, -waist'-coat** a garment for restraint of the violently insane: anything which inhibits freedom of movement or initiative (*fig.*). — *v.t.* and *v.i.* **strait'-lace.** — *adj.* **strait'-laced** tightlaced: narrow in principles of behaviour: prudish. — **strait'-la'cer; strait'-la'cing.**   [O.Fr. *estreit* (Fr. *étroit*) — L. *strictus,* pa.p. of *stringĕre,* to draw tight.]

strak. See **strike.**

strake[1] *strāk,* obs. *pa.t.* of **strike.**

strake[2], **straik** *strāk,* *n.* a stripe (*Spens.*): a strip: one breadth of plank or plate in a ship, from stem to stern: a section of a cart-wheel rim: a trough for washing ore.   [Akin to **stretch,** coalescing with **streak**[1].]

stramaçon. See **stramazon.**

stramash *strə-mash',* (*Scot.*) *n.* a tumult, disturbance: a broil: wreck. — *v.t.* to wreck, smash.   [Perh. an elaboration of **smash.**]

stramazon, stramaçon *stram'ə-zon, -son,* (*obs.*) *ns.* a downward cut in fencing.   [It. *stramazzone,* and Fr. *estramaçon.*]

stramineous *strə-min'i-əs, adj.* strawy: light, worthless: straw-coloured.   [L. *strāmineus* — *strāmen,* straw.]

strammel *stram'l.* See **strummel.**

stramonium *strə-mō'ni-əm, n.* the thorn-apple: a drug like belladonna got from its seeds and leaves. [Mod. L., poss. from a Tatar word.]

stramp *stramp*, (*Scot.*) *v.t.* and *v.i.* to tread, stamp, or trample. — *n.* a stamp of the foot.

strand[1] *strand, n.* a sea or lake margin (*poet.*): a landing-place (*Milt.*). — *v.t.* and *v.i.* to run aground. — *adj.* **strand'ed** driven on shore: left helpless without further resource. [O.E. *strand*; Ger. *Strand*, O.N. *strönd*, border.]

strand[2] *strand*, (*Scot.*) *n.* a rivulet: a gutter. — **strand'-scouring** searching of gutters. [Origin obscure.]

strand[3] *strand, n.* a yarn, thread, fibre, or wire twisted or plaited with others to form a rope, cord, or the like: a thread, filament: a tress. — *v.t.* to break a strand of (*arch.*): to insert a strand in (*arch.*): to form of strands. — *adj.* **strand'ed** (of a fur garment) made by resewing skins after they have been cut diagonally into strips. [Origin obscure.]

strange *strānj, adj.* foreign (*Shak.*): alien: from elsewhere: not of one's own place, family, or circle: not one's own: not formerly known or experienced: unfamiliar: interestingly unusual: odd: estranged: like a stranger: distant or reserved: unacquainted, unversed: exceedingly great, exceptional (*obs.*). — *adv.* **strange'ly.** — *ns.* **strange'ness** the quality of being strange: a quantum number, equal to a particle's hypercharge minus its baryon number, which represents unexplained delay in strong interactions between certain elementary particles; **strān'ger** a foreigner: one whose home is elsewhere: one unknown or little known: one who is outside of one's familiar circle or kindred: a visitor: a new-born child (*humorous*): a non-member: an outsider: a person not concerned: one without knowledge, experience, or familiarity (with *to*): a thing believed or feigned to foretell the coming of a visitor, as a tea-leaf floating in a cup, a flake of soot in a fireplace. — *v.t.* (*Shak.*) to make a stranger. — **strangeness number** see **strangeness**; **strange particles** K-mesons and hyperons, which have a non-zero strangeness (q.v.) number; **strangers' gallery** a public gallery, esp. in the House of Commons; **strange woman** a whore. — **make it strange** (*Shak.*) to make difficulties, show reluctance. [O.Fr. *estrange* (Fr. *étrange*) — L. *extrāneus* — *extrā*, beyond.]

strangle *strang'gl, v.t.* to kill by compressing the throat: to choke: to kill (*obs.*): to constrict: to choke back, suppress, stifle: to involve and impede. — *ns.* **strang'lement; strang'ler.** — *n.pl.* **strang'les** a contagious disease of horses. — **strang'lehold** a choking hold in wrestling: a strong repressive influence; **strang'le-weed** dodder: broomrape. [O.Fr. *estrangler* (Fr. *étrangler*) — L. *strangulāre*; see next word.]

strangulate *strang'gū-lāt, v.t.* to strangle: to compress so as to suppress or suspend function. — *adj.* **strang'-ulated** strangled: constricted, much narrowed. — *n.* **strangulā'tion.** [L. *strangulāre, -ātum* — Gr. *strangalaein*, to strangle, *strangos*, twisted.]

strangury *strang'gū-ri, n.* painful retention of, or difficulty in discharging, urine. [L. *strangūria* — Gr. *strangouriā* — *stranx*, a drop, trickle, *ouron*, urine.]

strap *strap, n.* a narrow strip, usu. of leather: a thong: a strop (*obs.* or *dial.*): a metal band or plate for holding things in position: a narrow flat projection, as on a strap-hinge: a looped band: a string or long cluster: anything strap-shaped: an application of the strap or tawse in punishment: a barber (*slang*, after Hugh *Strap* in Smollett's *Roderick Random*): a term of abuse to a woman (*Anglo- Ir.*): credit, esp. for liquor (*slang*). — *v.t.* to beat or bind with a strap: to strop: to hang (*Scot.*): to make suffer from scarcity, esp. of money. — *v.i.* to work vigorously: to admit of or suffer strapping: — *pr.p.* **strapp'ing;** *pa.t.* and *pa.p.* **strapped.** — *adj.* **strap'less** without a strap or straps, esp. (of woman's dress) without shoulder-straps. — *ns.* **strapp'er** one who works with straps, esp. a groom: a vigorous worker: a tall robust person: a whopping lie; **strapp'ing** fastening with a strap: materials for straps:

strengthening bands: a thrashing. — *adj.* tall and robust. — *adj.* **strapp'y** having (many) straps (used esp. of clothing and footwear). — **strap'-game** prick-the-garter. — *v.i.* **strap'-hang.** — **strap'-hanger** standing passenger in a train, bus, etc., who holds on to a strap for safety; **strap'-hinge** hinge fastened by a long leaf or flap; **strap'-oil** (*slang*) a thrashing. — *adj.* **strap'-shaped.** — **strap'-work** (*archit.*) ornamentation of crossed and interlaced fillets; **strap'wort** a seaside caryophyllaceous plant (*Corrigiola littoralis*) of S.W. England, etc., with strap-shaped leaves. — **strapped for** (*slang*) short of. [Northern form of **strop**.]

strapontin *stra-pɔ̃-tɛ̃, (Fr.) n.* a folding seat, as in a taxi, theatre, etc.

strappado *strap-ā'dō, -ä'dō, n.* torture by hoisting to a height and letting fall to the length of the rope (*Shak.*): later, a strapping (*erron.*): — *pl.* **strappa'dos.** — *v.t.* to torture or punish by the strappado. [Sham Spanish, from It. *strappata* — *strappare*, to pull.]

strapper, etc. See **strap.**

strass *stras, n.* paste for making false gems. [Josef *Strasser*, its inventor.]

strata *strā'tə, strä', pl.* of **stratum.**

stratagem *strat'ə-jəm, n.* a plan for deceiving an enemy or gaining an advantage: any artifice generally. [Fr. *stratagème* — L. — Gr. *stratēgēma*, a piece of generalship, trick; see next word.]

strategy *strat'i-ji, n.* generalship, or the art of conducting a campaign and manoeuvring an army: artifice or finesse generally. — *adjs.* **strategetic** (*-jet'ik*), **-al** (both *rare*), **strategic** (*strat-ēj'ik*, *arch. -ej'ik*), **-al** pertaining to, dictated by, of value for, strategy. — *n.sing.* **stratē'gics** strategy. — *adv.* **strateg'ically.** — *n.* **strat'-egist** one skilled in strategy. — **Strategic Defence Initiative** a strategic defence system proposed by the U.S. involving laser-equipped satellites deployed in space for destroying enemy missiles; **strategic materials, metals** materials, metals used for military purposes or necessary for carrying on a war; **strategic position** a position that gives its holder a decisive advantage. [Gr. *stratēgia* — *stratēgos*, a general — *stratos*, an army, *agein*, to lead.]

strath *strath, n.* in the Highlands of Scotland, a broad valley. [Gael. *srath*, a valley — L. *strāta*, a street.]

strathspey *strath-spā', n.* a Scottish dance, allied to and danced alternately with the reel: a tune for it, differing from the reel in being slower, and abounding in the jerky motion of dotted notes and semiquavers. [*Strathspey*, the valley of the *Spey*.]

stratify, etc. See under **stratum.**

Stratiotes *strat-i-ō'tēz, n.* the water-soldier genus. [Gr. *stratiōtēs*, a soldier.]

stratocracy *strat-, strat-ok'rə-si, n.* military despotism. — *n.* **stratocrat** (*strat'ō-krat*). — *adjs.* **stratocrat'ic; stratonic** (*-on'ik*) of an army. [Gr. *stratos*, an army.]

stratum *strā'təm, strä', n.* a layer: a bed of sedimentary rock: a layer of cells in living tissue: a region determined by height or depth: a level of society: — *pl.* **stra'ta.** — *n.* **stratificā'tion** (*strat-*). — *adjs.* **strat'ified; strat'iform** layered: forming a layer. — *v.t.* **strat'ify** to deposit, form or arrange in layers: to classify according to a graded scale (*science* and *social science*). — *v.i.* to form, settle, compose into levels or layers: — *pr.p.* **strat'ifying;** *pa.t.* and *pa.p.* **strat'ified.** — *ns.* **stratig'-rapher, stratig'raphist.** — *adjs.* **stratigraph'ic, -al.** — *adv.* **stratigraph'ically.** — *n.* **stratig'raphy** the geological study of strata and their succession: stratigraphical features. — *adj.* **stra'tose** in layers. — *n.* **stratosphere** (*strat'* or *strāt'ō-sfēr*) a region of the atmosphere beginning about 4½ to 10 miles up, in which temperature does not fall as altitude increases. — *adjs.* **stratospheric** (*-sfer'ik*); **stra'tous** of stratus. — *n.* **stra'-tus** a wide-extended horizontal sheet of low cloud. — **strato-cruiser**® (*strat', strāt'*) an aeroplane for the stratosphere; **stra'to-cū'mulus** a cloud in large globular or rolled masses, not rain-bringing; **stra'topause** the transitional layer between the stratosphere and the mesosphere; **strat′otanker** a type of aeroplane which refuels other planes at high altitudes. [L. *strātum, -ī, strātus, -ūs,* something spread, a bedcover, horsecloth — *sternēre, strātum,* to spread.]

straucht, straught *ströhht,* (*Scot.*) *v.t.* a form of **stretch:** esp. to lay out (a corpse). — *adj.* and *adv.* a form of **straight**[1]. — Also (*adj., adv.*) **straicht, straight** (*strehht*).

straunge *strönj,* (*Spens.*) *adj.* Same as **strange:** foreign, borrowed.

stravaig *strǝ-vāg′,* (*Scot.*) *v.i.* to wander about idly. — *n.* **stravaig′er.** [Cf. **stray, extravagant.**]

straw[1] *strö, n.* the stalk of corn: dried stalks, etc., of corn, or of peas or buckwheat, etc. (*collec.*): a tube for sucking up a beverage: a straw hat: a trifle, a whit. — *adj.* of straw: of the colour of straw. — *adjs.* **straw′en** (*Spens.*) of straw; **straw′less; straw′y** of or like straw. — **straw′board** a thick cardboard, made of straw; **straw boss** (*U.S.*) an assistant, temporary, or unofficial, foreman; **straw′-breadth** the breadth of a straw. — *n.* and *adj.* **straw′-colour** delicate yellow. — *adj.* **straw′= coloured.** — **straw′-cutter** an instrument for chopping straw; **straw′-hat′; straw man** a man of straw (see **man**[1]); **straw′-plait** plaited straw for hats; **straw poll** an unofficial vote taken to get some idea of the general trend of opinion; **straw′-rope** a rope of twisted straw; **straw′= stem** the fine stem of a wine-glass pulled out from the material of the bowl, instead of being attached separately: a wine-glass having such a stem; **straw wine** a sweet wine got from grapes dried on straw; **straw′-work** work done in plaited straw; **straw′-worm** a caddisworm; **straw′-yard** a yard strewn with straw for animals. — **catch, clutch, grasp at a straw** (or **at straws**) to resort to an inadequate remedy in desperation: **last straw** see **last**[4]; **man of straw** see **man**[1]; **straw in the wind** a sign of possible future developments. [O.E. *strēaw;* Ger. *Stroh;* cf. **strae, strew.**]

straw[2] *strö, v.t.* an archaic form of **strew:** — *pa.t.* **strawed;** *pa.p.* **strawed, strawn.**

strawberry *strö′bǝ-ri, -bri, n.* the fruit (botanically the enlarged receptacle) of any species of the rosaceous genus Fragaria, close akin to Potentilla: the plant bearing it. — *adj.* of the colour (pinkish-red) or flavour of strawberries. — **strawberry blonde** a woman with reddish-yellow hair; **straw′berry-leaf′** the leaf of the strawberry plant: symbolically (esp. in *pl.*) the rank of duke or duchess, from the ornaments like strawberry leaves on a duke's (also a marquess's or earl's) coronet; **straw′berry-mark** a reddish birthmark; **straw′berry= shrub** Calycanthus; **strawberry roan** a reddish roan; **straw′berry-toma′to** the Cape gooseberry; **straw′berry= tree** Arbutus unedo, a small tree (wild at Killarney) of the heath family, with red berries. — **barren strawberry** a Potentilla distinguished from the wild strawberry by its dry fruit. [O.E. *strēawberige,* possibly from the chaffy appearance of the achenes.]

stray *strā, v.i.* to wander: to wander away, esp. from control, or from the right way: to get lost. — *v.t.* (*Shak.*) to set astray. — *n.* a domestic animal that has strayed or is lost: a straggler: a waif: anything occurring casually, isolatedly, out of place: a body of strays (*Shak.*): a common: (in *pl.*) atmospherics: a straying (*Shak.*). — *adj.* gone astray: casual: isolated. — *adj.* **strayed** wandering, gone astray. — *n.* **stray′er.** — *n.* and *adj.* **stray′ing.** — *n.* **stray′ling** a stray. [O.Fr. *estraier,* to wander — L. *extrā,* beyond, *vagārī,* to wander.]

strawen, strawy. See **straw**[1].

streak[1] *strēk, n.* an irregular stripe: the colour of a mineral in powder, seen in a scratch: a scratch: a strain, vein, interfused or pervading character: a line of bacteria, etc. (*placed*) on a culture medium: the line or course as of a flash of lightning: a rush, swift dash: a course, succession, as of luck. — *v.t.* to mark with streaks. — *v.i.* to become streaked: to rush past (cf. **streek**) to run naked, or in a state of indecent undress, in public (*coll.*). — *adj.* **streaked** streaky, striped: confused (*U.S.*). — *n.* **streak′er.** — *adv.* **streak′ily.** — *ns.* **streak′-**

iness; **streak′ing.** — *adj.* **streak′y** marked with streaks, striped: fat and lean in alternate layers: uneven in quality. — **like a streak** like (a flash of) lightning. [O.E. *strica,* a stroke, line, mark; Ger. *Strich;* cf. **strike.**]

streak[2]. See **streek.**

stream *strēm, n.* a running water: a river or brook, esp. a rivulet: a flow or moving succession of anything: a large number or quantity coming continuously: a division of pupils on the roll of a school consisting of those of roughly equal ability or similar bent, or those following a particular course of study: any similar division of people: a current: a drift: a tendency. — *v.i.* to flow, issue, or stretch, in a stream: to pour out abundantly: to float out, trail: to wash for ore. — *v.t.* to discharge in a stream: to wave, fly: to wash for ore: to divide (pupils, etc.) into streams. — *n.* **stream′er** a pennon, ribbon, plume, or the like streaming or flowing in the wind: a luminous beam or band of light, as of the aurora: one who washes detritus for gold or tin: a headline: a narrow roll of coloured paper. — *adj.* **stream′ered.** — *n.* **stream′iness.** — *n.* and *adj.* **stream′= ing.** — *adv.* **stream′ingly.** — *adj.* **stream′less** not watered by streams: waterless: without a current. — *ns.* **stream′= let, stream′ling** a little stream. — *adj.* **stream′y** abounding in streams: flowing in a stream. — **stream′-anch′or** a small anchor used in warping or for stemming an easy current; **stream′-gold** placer-gold; **stream′-ice** pieces of drift ice swept down in a current; **stream′line** a line followed by a streaming fluid: the natural course of air-streams. — *v.t.* to make streamlined. — *adj.* **stream′lined** having boundaries following streamlines so as to offer minimum resistance: a term of commendation with a variety of meanings, as efficient, without waste of effort, up-to-the-minute, of superior type, graceful, etc. (*slang*). — **stream′-tin** tin-ore found in alluvial ground. — **on stream** see **on; stream of consciousness** the continuous succession of thoughts, emotions, and feelings, both vague and well-defined, that forms an individual's conscious experience. [O.E. *strēam;* Ger. *Strom,* O.N. *straumr.*]

streek, streak *strēk, v.t.* and *v.i.* a Northern form of **stretch,** not confined to Northern use: esp. (*v.t. Scot.*) to lay out for burial: (*v.i.*) to go at full speed.

streel *strēl,* (*Ir.*) *v.i.* to trail: to stream: to wander. [Cf. Ir. *straoillim,* to trail.]

street *strēt, n.* a paved road, esp. Roman (*ant.*): a road lined with houses, broader than a lane, including or excluding the houses and the footways: those who live in a street or are on the street: a passage or gap through or among anything: brokers as a body: (often in *pl.*) prostitution. — *adj.* of or characteristic of the streets, esp. in densely populated cities, or to the people who frequent them, esp. the poor, the homeless, prostitutes, petty criminals, etc. (also in compounds). — *n.* **street′= age** (*U.S.*) a toll for street facilities. — *adj.* **street′ed** having streets. — *n.* **street′ful:** — *pl.* **street′fuls.** — *adv.* and *adj.* **street′ward** (-wǝrd) towards or facing the street. — *adv.* **street′wards.** — *adj.* **street′y** savouring or characteristic of the streets. — **street arab** see **Arab; street′-boy** a boy who lives mainly on the street; **street′-car** (*U.S.*) a tram-car; **street credibility** (often abbreviated as **street cred**) trust, believability, popularity, support or trust from the man in the street; **street cries** the slogans of hawkers; **street′-door** the door that opens on the street; **street furniture** the various accessorial public items sited in the street, e.g. litter bins, parking meters, road signs; **street hockey** (orig. *U.S.*) a type of hockey played on roller skates, orig. in the street; **street′-keeper** an officer formerly employed to keep order in a street or streets; **street′= lamp, street′light.** — *adj.* **street′-level** at ground level: in or pertaining to the urban street environment, esp. street-trading: pertaining to the general population. — Also *n.* — **street′-or′derly** a scavenger; **street′= rail′road, -rail′way** a town tramway. — *adj.* **street′= raking** (*Scott*) ranging the streets. — **street′-room** space enough in the street. — *adj.* **street′-smart** (*U.S.*) street-wise. — **street'-smarts** (*U.S. slang*) the quality of being street-smart; **street'-sweep'er** one who, or that which, sweeps the streets clean; **street value** the cash value of an item when sold directly to the customer in the street, esp. illegally or on the black market; **street'-walker** any one who walks in the streets, esp. a whore. — *n.* and *adj.* **street'-walking.** — **street'-ward** (*-wörd*) an officer who formerly took care of the streets; **street'way** the roadway. — *adj.* **street'wise'** familiar with the ways, needs, etc. of the people who live and work on the city streets, e.g. the poor, the homeless, the petty criminals, etc: experienced in, and able to cope with, the harsher realities of city life: cynical: wily. — **not in the same street as** much inferior to; **on the street** (*slang*) homeless, destitute; **on the streets** (*slang*) practising prostitution; **streets ahead of** far superior to; **streets apart** very different; **up one's street** (*fig.*) in the region in which one's tastes, knowledge, abilities, lie. [O.E. *strǣt* (Du. *straat*, Ger. *Strasse*, It. *strada*) — L. *strāta* (*via*), a paved (way), from *sternĕre, strātum*, to spread.]

Strega® *strā'gə, n.* a sweet, orange-flavoured Italian liqueur.

streight *strīt.* A Spenserian and Miltonian form of **strait, straight**[1].

streigne. An old spelling of **strain**[1].

strelitz *strel'its, n.* a soldier of the Muscovite guards, abolished by Peter the Great: — *pl.* **strel'itzes, strel'itzi.** [Russ. *strelets*, bowman.]

Strelitzia *strel-it'si-ə, n.* a S. African genus of the banana family, with large showy flowers: (without *cap.*) a plant of the genus. [From Queen Charlotte, wife of George III, of the house of Mecklenburg-*Strelitz.*]

strene *strēn,* (*Spens.*) *n.* a form of **strain**[2], race.

strength *strength, n.* the quality, condition, or degree of being strong: the power of action or resistance: the ability to withstand great pressure or force: force: vigour: a strong place, stronghold: a beneficial characteristic: numbers: a military force: the number on the muster-roll, or the normal number: the point, the truth (*Austr.* and *N.Z.*). — *v.t.* **strength'en** to make strong or stronger: to confirm. — *v.i.* to become stronger. — *n.* **strength'ener.** — *n.* and *adj.* **strength'ening.** — *adjs.* **strength'ful; strength'less** without strength. — **get the strength of** (esp. *Austr.* and *N.Z.*) to comprehend; **go from strength to strength** to move successfully forward, through frequent triumphs or achievements; **on the strength** on the muster-roll; **on** or **upon the strength of** in reliance upon: founding upon. [O.E. *strengthu* — *strang,* strong.]

strenuous *stren'ū-əs, adj.* active: vigorous: urgent: zealous: necessitating exertion. — *ns.* **strenuity** (*stri-nū'i-ti*); **strenuosity** (*stren-ū-os'i-ti*) strenuousness: a straining after effect. — *adv.* **stren'uously.** — *n.* **stren'-uousness.** [L. *strēnuus.*]

strep. See **strepto-**.

strepent *strep'ənt,* (*rare*) *adj.* noisy. — *adjs.* **strep'erous** loud: harsh-sounding; **strep'itant** loud: noisy: clamorous. — *n.* **strepitā'tion.** — *adj.* **strepitoso** (*-i-tō'sō; mus.*; It.) noisy, boisterous. — Also *adv.* — *adj.* **strep'itous.** [L. *strepĕre,* to make a noise; freq. *strepitāre.*]

Strephon *stref'on, -ən, n.* a love-sick shepherd in Sir Philip Sidney's *Arcadia:* a love-sick swain.

strephosymbolia *stref-ō-sim-bō'li-ə, n.* a visual disorder in which items are seen in mirror image: a reading problem in which letters, symbols, words etc. are reversed, transposed or confused. [L.L. — Gr. *strephein,* to twist, turn, *symbolon,* a symbol.]

strepitant, etc., **strepitous.** See **strepent.**

Strepsiptera *streps-ip'tə-rə, n.pl.* an order of insects (or group of Coleoptera) parasitic in other insects, the females wormlike, the males with twisted fore-wings. — *adj.* **strepsip'terous.** [Gr. *strepsis,* a twist, *pteron,* a wing.]

strepto- *strep'tō-,* in composition, bent, flexible, twisted. — *adjs.* **streptococcal** (*-kok'l*), **streptococcic** (*-kok'sik*). — *ns.* **Streptococcus** (*-kok'əs;* Gr. *kokkos,* a grain) a

genus of bacteria forming bent chains, certain species of which can cause scarlet fever, pneumonia, etc.: (without *cap.*) any bacterium of this genus (*coll.* shortening **strep**): — *pl.* **streptococ'ci** (*-ksī, -kī*); **streptomycin** (*-mī'sin;* Gr. *mўkēs,* fungus) an antibiotic got from fission fungi. — *n.pl.* **Streptoneura** (*-nū'rə;* Gr. *neuron,* nerve) a subclass of gasteropods with twisted visceral nerve-loop — limpets, whelks, etc. [Gr. *streptos,* twisted, flexible.]

Strepyan *strep'i-ən, adj.* of the oldest known Palaeolithic culture. [*Strépy,* a village near Charleroi, where stone implements of this stage occur.]

stress *stres, n.* hardship, straits (*obs.*): strain: a constraining influence: physical, emotional or mental pressure: force: the system of forces applied to a body: the insistent assigning of weight or importance: emphasis: relative force of utterance: distraint (*law*). — *v.t.* to apply stress to: to lay stress on: to emphasise. — *adjs.* **stressed; stress'ful; stress'less.** — *n.* **stress'or** an agent or factor that causes stress. [Aphetic for **distress;** prob. partly also from O.Fr. *estrece* — L. *strictus* — *stringĕre,* to draw tight.]

stretch *strech, v.t.* to extend (in space or time): to draw out: to expand, make longer or wider by tension: to spread out: to reach out: to exaggerate, strain, or carry further than is right: to lay at full length: to lay out: to place so as to reach from point to point or across a space: to hang (*slang*). — *v.i.* to be drawn out: to reach: to be extensible without breaking: to straighten and extend fully one's body and limbs: to exaggerate: to go swiftly. — *n.* the act of stretching: the state of being stretched: reach: extension: utmost extent: strain: undue straining: exaggeration: extensibility: a single spell: a continuous journey: an area, expanse: a straight part of a course: a term of imprisonment (*slang*). — *adj.* capable of being stretched. — *adj.* **stretched.** — *n.* **stretch'er** one who stretches: anything used for stretching e.g. gloves, hats, etc.: a frame for stretching a painter's canvas: a frame for carrying the sick or wounded: a rower's footboard: a cross-bar or horizontal member: a brick, stone, sod, sandbag, etc., placed with its length in the direction of the wall: an exaggeration or lie. — *v.t.* to transport (a sick or wounded person) by stretcher. — *adjs.* **stretch'less** no longer liable to stretch; **stretch'y** able, apt, or inclined to stretch. — **stretch'er-bearer** one who carries injured from the field; **stretch'er-bond, stretch'ing-bond** a method of building with stretchers only, the joints of one course falling between those above and below; **stretch'ing-course** a course entirely of stretchers; **stretch'ing-frame** a machine for stretching cotton rovings: a frame on which starched fabrics are dried; **stretch'ing-iron** a currier's tool for dressing leather. — *adj.* **stretch'-mouth'd** (*Shak.*) wide-mouthed. — **at a stretch** continuously, without interruption: with difficulty; **stretch a point** see **point**[1]; **stretch one's legs** to take a walk, esp. for exercise. [O.E. *streccan.*]

stretto *stret'ō, n.* part of a fugue in which subject and answer are brought closely together: (also **strett'a:** — *pl.* **strett'e** *-tā*) a passage, esp. a coda, in quicker time: — *pl.* **strett'i** (*-ē*). [It., contracted.]

strew *strōō* (or *strō*), *arch.* **strow** *strō* (or *strōō*), **straw** *strö, vs.t.* to scatter loosely: to bestrew, cover dispersedly: to spread (*rare*): to level (*poet.*): — *pa.t.* **strewed,** *arch.* **strowed, strawed;** *pa.p.* **strewed, strewn,** *arch.* **strowed, strown, strawed, strawn.** — *ns.* an assemblage of things strewn. — *ns.* **strew'age; strew'er, strow'er; strew'ing, strow'ing; strew'ment** (*Shak.*) strewings. [O.E. *strewian, streowian.*]

strewth *strōōth, interj.* a vulg. minced oath (for *God's truth*).

stria *strī'ə, strē'a, n.* a fine streak, furrow, or threadlike line, usu. parallel to others: one of the fillets between the flutes of columns, etc. (*archit.*): — *pl.* **stri'ae** (*strī'ē, strē'ī*). — *v.t.* **strī'ate** to mark with striae. — *adjs.* **strī'ate, -d.** — *ns.* **striā'tion; striā'tum** the *corpus striatum,* the great ganglion of the fore-brain; **strī'ature**

mode of striation. — **striated muscle** a muscle, or muscular tissue, whose fibres are transversely striated and whose action is controlled by the will. [L. *strīa*, a furrow, flute of a column.]

strich *strich*, (*Spens.*) *n.* the screech-owl. [L. *strix*, prob. modified by **scritch.**]

stricken *strik'n*, *pa.p.* of **strike**, and *adj.*, struck, now chiefly poet. in U.K. or in special senses and phrases: wounded in the chase: afflicted: advanced (*stricken in years*, from the sense of go, make one's way): expunged. — **stricken field** a pitched battle, or the scene of it; **stricken hour** an hour as marked by the clock.

strickle *strik'l*, *n.* an instrument for levelling the top of a measure of grain or shaping the surface of a mould: a template: a tool for sharpening scythes. — *v.t.* to level a measure of grain or shape the surface of a mould with a strickle. [O.E. *stricel.*]

strict *strikt*, *adj.* tight (*Shak.*): narrow (*arch.*): stiff and straight (*bot.*): close, intimate (*obs.*): restricted: exact: rigorous: allowing no laxity: austere: observing exact rules, regular: severe: exactly observed: thoroughgoing. — *adj.* **strict'ish.** — *adv.* **strict'ly.** — *ns.* **strict'ness; strict'ure** a binding: a closure: tightness: abnormal narrowing of a passage (*med.*): strictness (*Shak.*): a (now only adverse) remark or criticism. — *adj.* **strict'ured** morbidly narrowed. [L. *strictus*, pa.p. of *stringĕre*, to draw tight.]

strid, stridden, striddle. See **stride.**

stride *strīd*, *v.i.* to walk with long steps: to take a long step: to straddle. — *v.t.* to stride over: to bestride: — *pa.t.* **ströde**, *obs.* **strid;** *pa.p.* **stridd'en** (*strid'n*). — *n.* a long step: a striding gait: the length of a long step: **stride piano** (*jazz*): (in *pl.*) trousers (*slang*, esp. Austr.). — *n.* **strid** (*strid*) a place where a river can be stridden over (from that on the Wharfe). — *v.i.* **striddle** (*strid'l*) to straddle (back-formation from *stridling*). — *advs.* **stride'ways, stridling** (*strid'*; *dial.*) astride. — *advs.* **stride'legs, stride'legged** (*Scot.*) astride. — **stride piano** (*jazz*) a rhythmic style of piano-playing derived from ragtime, popularised in Harlem during the 1920s. — **be into, get into, hit one's stride** to achieve one's normal or expected level of efficiency, degree of success, etc.; **make great strides** to make rapid progress; **take in one's stride** to accomplish without undue effort or difficulty. [O.E. *strīdan*, to stride.]

stridence *strī'dəns*, **-cy** *-dən-si*, *ns.* harshness of tone. — *adj.* **strī'dent** loud and grating. — *adv.* **strī'dently.** — *n.* **strī'dor** a harsh shrill sound: a harsh whistling sound of obstructed breathing (*med.*). — *adj.* **stridūlant** (*strid'*) stridulating: pertaining to stridor. — *adv.* **strid'ulantly.** — *v.i.* **strid'ūlate** to make a chirping or scraping sound, like a grasshopper. — *ns.* **stridūlā'tion** the act of stridulating; **strid'ūlātor** an insect that makes a sound by scraping: the organ it uses. — *adjs.* **strid'ūlatory; strid'ūlous.** [L. *strīdēre* and *strīdĕre*, to creak.]

stridling. See **stride.**

stridulant, stridulate ... stridulous. See **stridence.**

strife *strīf*, *n.* contention: a contest: variance: striving: any sort of trouble, hassle (*Austr.*, *coll.*). — *adjs.* **strife'ful** (*Spens.*) **stryf'ull; strife'less; strife'-torn** severely disrupted, damaged, etc. by conflict. — *n.* **strift** (*strift*; *arch.*) a struggle. [O.Fr. *estrif*; see **strive.**]

strig *strig*, (*Southern*) *n.* a stalk. — *v.t.* to remove the stalk from: — *pr.p.* **strigg'ing.** [Origin obscure.]

striga *strī'gə*, L. *strig'a*, *n.* a stria: a bristle, usu. an appressed bristle: — *pl.* **strigae** (*strī'jē*, L. *strig'ī*). — *adjs.* **strī'gate; strī'gose** (or *-gōs'*). [L. *strīga*, a swath, a furrow, a flute of a column.]

Striges *strī'jēz*, L. *strig'ās*, also **Strigiformes** *strij-i-för'-mēz*, *ns.pl.* in some classifications, the order comprising the owls. — *adjs.* **strig'iform; strī'gine** owl-like: of the owls. [L. *strix, strigis*, an owl.]

strigil *strij'il*, *n.* a flesh-scraper: in bees, a mechanism for cleaning the antennae. [L. *strigilis.*]

strigine. See **Striges.**

Strigops *strī'gops*, **Stringops** *string'gops*, *ns.* the kakapo

or owl-parrot genus. [Gr. *strinx*, or *strix, stringos*, owl, *ōps*, face.]

strigose. See **striga.**

strike *strīk*, *v.t.* to stroke (*obs.*; *B.*): to smooth (*dial.*): to strickle (*dial.*): to draw, describe, give direction to (as a line, path): to delete, cancel: to constitute (orig. by cutting down a list): to mark off: to lower (as a sail, flag, tent): to take down the tents of (*strike camp*): to dismantle: to remove: to leave off or refuse to continue: to deal, deliver, or inflict: to give a blow to or with: to hit, smite: to come into forcible contact with: to impinge on: to bring forcibly into contact: to impel: to put, send, move, render, or produce by a blow or stroke: to render as if by a blow: to sound by percussion or otherwise: to announce by a bell: to dash: to pierce: to stamp: to coin: to print: to impress: to impress favourably: to thrust in or down, cause to penetrate: to broach (*Shak.*): to fight (a battle) (*Shak.*): to blast, bewitch: to visit, afflict: to assail, affect: to affect strongly or suddenly: to arrive at, estimate, compute, fix, settle (as a balance, an average, prices): to make (a compact or agreement), to ratify: to come upon: to reach: to achieve: to occur to: to assume: to hook by a quick turn of the wrist: to make a sudden demand of (as for a loan or subscription; *slang*): to cause to strike. — *v.i.* to make one's way: to set out: to take a direction or course: to dart, shoot, pass quickly: to penetrate: to jerk the line suddenly in order to impale the hook in the mouth of a fish: to put forth roots: to chance, alight, come by chance: to interpose: to deal or aim a blow, perform a stroke: to sound or be sounded or announced by a bell: to hit out: to seize the bait: to strike something, as a rock, sail, flag: to attempt to hook the ball (*Rugby*): to touch: to run aground: to surrender: to admit of striking: to do menial work (for an officer; *U.S.* army): to go on strike: to blast, blight (*Shak.*): — *pa.t.* **struck**, *obs.* **strake, stroke, strook, strooke;** *Scot.* **strak, strack;** *pa.p.* **struck**, *arch.* **strick'en** (q.v.); *obs.* **strook, strooke, strook'en, strok'en, struck'en.** — *n.* a strickle: a proportion of malt (cf. **straik**[1]): a stroke, striking: an attack, esp. by aircraft: a raid: the direction of a horizontal line at right angles to the dip of a bed (*geol.*): a find (as of oil), stroke of luck: a cessation of work, or other obstructive refusal to act normally, as a means of putting pressure on employers, etc.: the part that receives the bolt of a lock: in tenpin bowling, the knocking down of all the pins with the first ball bowled, or the score resulting from this: a ball missed by the batter, or a similar event counting equivalently against him (*baseball*): the position of facing the bowling, licence to receive the next delivery (*cricket*): blackmail, esp. by introducing a bill in the hope of being bought off (*U.S. slang*): the quantity of coins, etc. made at one time. — *ns.* **strik'er** one who, that which, strikes: a footpad (*Shak.*): a batsman (*baseball*): a forward, attacker (*football*): the batsman facing the bowling (*cricket*): the player who receives the service (*tennis*; also **strik'er-out**); **strik'ing.** — *adj.* that strikes or can strike: impressive, arresting, noticeable. — *adv.* **strik'ingly.** — *n.* **strik'ingness.** — *adj.* **strike'-bound** closed or similarly affected because of a strike. — **strike'-breaker** one who works during a strike or who does the work of a striker esp. if brought in with a view to defeating the strike; **strike'-breaking; strike'=fault** (*geol.*) a fault parallel to the strike; **strike force** a force designed and equipped to carry out a strike (*mil.*): a special police unit trained to strike suddenly and forcefully to suppress crime; **strikeout** see **strike out; strike'-pay** an allowance paid by a trade union to members on strike; **strik'ing-circle** (*hockey*) the area in front of goal from within which the ball must be hit in order to score; **strik'ing-price** (*Stock exchange*) a stipulated price at which a holder may exercise his put or call option. — **be struck off** of doctors, lawyers, etc., to have one's name removed from the professional register because of misconduct; **on strike** taking part in a strike: of a batsman, facing the bowling (*cricket*); **strike a match** to light it by friction or a grazing stroke; **strike at** to attempt to strike, aim a blow at; **strike back** to return a blow: to backfire, burn within the burner; **strike bottom, soundings** to reach the bottom with the lead; **strike down** to fell: to make ill or cause to die; **strike hands** to join or slap together hands in confirmation of agreement; **strike home** to strike right to the point aimed at; **strike in** to enter suddenly: to interpose: to agree, fit (*obs.*); **strike into** to enter upon suddenly, to break into; **strike it rich** (*coll.*) to make a sudden large financial gain, e.g. through discovering a mineral deposit, etc.; **strike off** to erase from an account, to deduct: to remove (from a roll, register, etc.): to print: to separate by a blow; **strike oil** to find petroleum when boring for it: to make a lucky hit; **strike out** to efface: to bring into light: to direct one's course boldly outwards: to swim away: to dismiss or be dismissed by means of three strikes (*baseball*; n. **strike'out**): to strike from the shoulder: to form by sudden effort; **strike root** see **root**[1]; **strike through** to delete with a stroke of the pen; **strike up** to begin to beat, sing, or play: to begin (as an acquaintance); **struck in years** (*Shak.*; same as **stricken in years**); **struck on** inclined to be enamoured of; **take strike** (*cricket*) of a batsman, to prepare to face the bowling. [O.E. *strīcan*, to stroke, go, move.]

Strine *strīn*, (*coll.*) n. a jocular name given to Australian English in terms of its vernacular pronunciation (with frequent assimilation, elision, etc.) — *adj.* Australian. [Alleged pron. of *Australian*, coined by Alastair Morrison (pseudonym Afferbeck Lauder), esp. in his book *Let Stalk Strine*.]

string *string*, n. a small cord or a piece of it: cord of any size: a hangman's rope: a piece of anything for tying: anything of like character, as a tendon, nerve, fibre: a leash: a shoelace (*U.S.*): a stretched piece of catgut, silk, wire, or other material in a musical instrument: (in *pl.*) the stringed instruments played by a bow in an orchestra or other combination: (in *pl.*) their players: the cord of an archery bow: the thread of a necklace or the like: anything on which things are threaded: a filing cord: a set of things threaded together or arranged as if threaded: a train, succession, file, or series: a drove, number, of horses, camels, etc.: a long bunch: in billiards, the buttons strung on a wire by which the score is kept: hence the score itself: a sloping joist supporting the steps in wooden stairs: a string-course: a hoax (*slang*): (in *pl.*) awkward conditions or limitations. — *adj.* of, like or for string or strings. — *v.t.* to fit or furnish with a string or strings: to put in tune (*poet.*): to make tense or firm: to tie up: to hang: to extend like a string: to put on or in a string: to take the strings or stringy parts off: to hoax, humbug (*slang*). — *v.i.* to stretch out into a long line: to form into strings: to be hanged (*Scot.*): in billiards, to drive the ball against the end of the table and back, to decide who is to begin: — *pa.t.* and *pa.p.* **strung.** — *adj.* **stringed** (*stringd*) having strings: of stringed instruments. — n. **stringer** (*string'ər*) one who, or that which, strings: a horizontal member in a framework: an inside horizontal plank, supporting beam-ends of a ship (*naut.*): a narrow mineral vein: a journalist employed part-time by a newspaper or news agency to cover a particular (esp. remote) town or area. — *adv.* **string'ily** in a stringy fashion. — *ns.* **string'iness; string'ing.** — *adjs.* **string'less; string'y** consisting of, or abounding in, strings or small threads: fibrous: capable of being drawn into strings: like string or a stringed instrument. — **string'-bag'** a bag made of string, or (*string'-bag*) for holding string; **string'-band** a band of stringed instruments: the strings of an orchestra; **string bass** a double-bass; **string'-bean** (*U.S.*) the French bean; **string'-board** a board facing the well-hole of a staircase, and receiving or covering the ends of the steps; **string'=course** a projecting horizontal course or line of mouldings running quite along the face of a building; **string**

figure a structure of string looped around the fingers in a symmetrical pattern that can be altered by manipulation, as cat's-cradle; **string'-pea** a pea with edible pods; **string'-piece** a long, heavy, usu. horizontal timber: the string of a staircase; **string quartet** a musical ensemble of two violins, a viola and a cello: music for such an ensemble; **string'-tie** a narrow necktie of uniform width; **string vest** a vest made of a net-like fabric; **string'y-bark** one of a class of Australian gum-trees with very fibrous bark. — **highly-strung** see **high; no strings (attached)** with no conditions or limitations; **on a string** under complete control: kept in suspense; **pull (the) strings** to use influence behind the scenes, as if working puppets (n. **string'-pulling**); **string along** (*v.t.*) to string, fool: to give someone false expectations; (*v.i.*) to go along together, co-operate; **string out** to be under the influence of or addicted to a drug (*U.S.*); **string up** to hang; **strung out** (orig. *U.S.*) suffering from drug-withdrawal symptoms: weak, ill or distressed as a result of drug addiction: addicted to a drug; **strung up** nervously tensed; **two strings to one's bow** see **bow**[2]. [O.E. *streng*; cf. Du. *streng*, Ger. *Strang*, O.N. *strengr*.]

stringent *strin'jənt, adj.* tight: binding: rigorous: convincing: astringent: characterised by difficulty in finding money. — n. **strin'gency.** — *adj.* and *adv.* **stringendo** (-*jen'dō*; It.; *mus.*) hastening the time. — *adv.* **strin'gently.** — n. **strin'gentness.** [L. *stringēns, -entis*, pr.p. of *stringĕre*, to draw together.]

stringer. See **string.**

stringhalt *string'hölt*, n. a catching up of a horse's legs, usu. of one or both hind-legs. — Also **spring'halt.** [App. **string** (sinew) and **halt**[2].]

Stringops. See **Strigops.**

stringy. See **string.**

strinkle *string'kl*, (*Scot.*) *v.t.* to sprinkle. — n. **strink'ling.** [Cf. **sprinkle.**]

strip *strip*, *v.t.* to pull, peel, or tear off: to doff: to divest: to undress: to deprive of livery and dismiss: to reduce to the ranks: to deprive of a covering: to skin, to peel, to husk: to lay bare: to expose: to deprive: to clear, empty: to dismantle: to clear of fruit, leaves, stems, midribs, or any other part: to tear off or wear off the screw-thread from: to press out the last milk from, or obtain in this way: to press out the roe or milt from: to handle as if milking a cow: to cut in strips: to put strips on: to outstrip, press (*obs.*): to remove a constituent from a substance by boiling, distillation, etc. (*chem.*): to unload (esp. a container or lorry). — *v.i.* to undress: to perform a strip-tease: to lose the thread, as a screw: to come off: to go swiftly (*obs.*): — *pr.p.* **stripp'ing;** *pa.t.* and *pa.p.* **stripped.** — n. a long narrow piece: a long thin piece of rolled metal, as steel strip: a narrow space in a newspaper in which a story is told in pictures (also **strip cartoon**): light garb for running, football, etc.: a strip-tease: an airstrip: a row of three or more connected stamps. — n. **stripp'er** one who or that which strips: a strip-tease artist. — *n.pl.* **stripp'ings** the last milk drawn at a milking. — **strip cartoon** see **strip** (n.); **strip club** one which regularly features strip-tease artists; **strip'-leaf** tobacco stripped of stalks; **strip lighting** lighting by means of long fluorescent tubes; **strip map** a map showing a long narrow strip of country, used esp. by airmen; **strip mill** a mill where steel is rolled into strips; **strip'-mine** an opencast mine; **stripped atom** an ionised atom from which one or more electrons have been removed; **strip'-po'ker** poker in which losses are paid by removing articles of clothing; **strip search** a search of a person's body (for hidden items, e.g. drugs, contraband) for which their clothes are removed. — Also *v.t.* — **strip'-tease** an act of undressing slowly and seductively, esp. in a place of entertainment. — **strip down** to dismantle, remove parts from; **strip off** to take one's clothes off; **strip out** (*commerce*) to remove (one or more items) from a balance sheet, usu. to give a truer picture of a firm's trading and financial position. [O.E. *strȳpan*; Ger. *streifen*; perh. partly from other sources.]

stripe *strīp, n.* a blow, esp. with a lash: a band of colour: a chevron on a sleeve, indicating non-commissioned rank or good behaviour: a striped cloth or pattern: a strip: a strain: a kind, particular sort (*U.S.*): magnetic sound track(s) on cinematograph film for sound-film reproduction. — *v.t.* to make stripes upon: to mark with stripes: to lash. — *adjs.* **striped** having stripes of different colours: marked with stripes; **stripe′less.** — *n.* **stripes** (*coll.*) a tiger. — *adj.* **strip′ey** stripy. — *ns.* **strip′iness; strip′lng.** — *adj.* **strip′y** stripe-like: having stripes. [Perh. different words; cf. Du. *streep* (earlier *strijpe*), Ger. *Streif*, stripe, O.N. *strīp*, striped fabric, Du. *strippen,* to whip.]

stripling *strip′ling, n.* a youth: one yet growing. [Dim. of **strip.**]

stripper. See **strip.**

stripy. See **stripe.**

strive *strīv, v.i.* to contend: to be in conflict: to struggle: to endeavour earnestly: to make one's way with effort: — *pa.t.* **strove** (*strōv*), Shak. **strīved;** *pa.p.* **striven** (*striv′n*), Shak. **strove,** B. **strīved.** — *n.* **striv′er.** — *n.* and *adj.* **striv′ing.** — *adv.* **striv′ingly.** [O.Fr. *estriver;* poss. Gmc., from the root of **stride,** or of Ger. *streben,* to strive.]

stroam *strōm,* (*dial.*) *v.i.* to wander idly about: to stride. [Perh. **stroll** and **roam.**]

strobic *strob′ik, adj.* like a spinning-top: spinning or seeming to spin. — *n.* **strobe** (*strōb*) the process of viewing vibrations with a stroboscope: a stroboscope. — *n.* **stroboscope** (*strob′, strōb′ǝ-skōp*) an optical toy giving an illusion of motion from a series of pictures seen momentarily in succession: an instrument for studying rotating machinery or other periodic phenomena by means of a flashing lamp which can be synchronised with the frequency of the periodic phenomena so that they appear to be stationary. — *adj.* **stroboscopic** (*strob-, strōb-ǝ-skop′ik*). — **stroboscopic** (more commonly **strobe**) **lighting** periodically flashing light, or the equipment used to produce it. [Gr. *strobos,* a whirling — *strephein,* to twist.]

strobila *stro-bī′lǝ, n.* in the life-cycle of jellyfishes, a chain of segments, cone within cone, that separate to become medusoids: a chain of segments forming the body of a tapeworm: — *pl.* **strobī′lae** (*-lē*). — *adj.* **strobilaceous** (*strob-i-lā′shǝs*) of or like a strobile: bearing strobiles. — *v.i.* **strob′ilate** to undergo strobilation. — *adj.* of the nature of a strobilus. — *ns.* **strobilā′tion, strobilīsā′tion, -īzā′tion** production or reproduction by strobilae; **strobile** (*strob′* or *strōb′īl, -il*) a strobila: a strobilus. — *adjs.* **strobiliform** (*-il′*), **strob′iline, strob′iloid.** — *n.* **strobi′lus** a close group of sporophylls with their sporangia, a cone: a scaly spike of female flowers, as in the hop: — *pl.* **strobī′li** (*-lī*). [Gr. *strobīlē,* a conical plug of lint, *strobīlos,* a spinning-top, whirl, pine-cone — *strobos* (see foregoing).]

stroboscope, etc. See **strobic.**

stroddle *strod′l,* (*obs.* or *dial.*). Same as **straddle.**

strode *strōd, pa.t.* of **stride.**

strodle *strod′l* (*obs.* or *dial.*). Same as **straddle.**

stroganoff *strog′ǝn-of, adj.* of meat, cut thinly and cooked with onions, mushrooms and seasoning in a sour cream sauce (as in esp. *beef stroganoff*). — *n.* a dish cooked in this way. [After Count Paul *Stroganoff,* 19th-cent. Russ. diplomat.]

stroke¹ *strōk, n.* an act or mode of striking: a hit or attempt at hitting: a blow: a striking by lightning: a reverse: an attack of apoplexy or of paralysis: the striking of a clock or its sound: a dash or line: a touch of pen, pencil, brush, etc.: a trait (*obs.*): a beat, pulse: a sudden movement or occurrence: a particular named style or manner of swimming: a single complete movement in a repeated series, as in swimming, rowing, pumping, action of an engine: a stroke-oar: a single action towards an end: an effective action, feat, achievement. — *v.t.* to put a stroke through or on: to cross (commonly with *out*): to row stroke in or for: to row at the rate of. — *v.i.* to row stroke: to make a

stroke, as in swimming. — **stroke′-oar** the aftmost oar in a boat: its rower (also **stroke, strokes′man**), whose stroke leads the rest; **stroke′-play, stroke′play, stroke play** scoring in golf by counting the total number of strokes played (rather than the number of holes won). — **off one's stroke** operating less effectively or successfully than usual; **on the stroke (of)** punctually (at). [O.E. (inferred) *strāc;* cf. Ger. *Streich.*]

stroke² *strōk, v.t.* to rub gently in one direction: to rub gently in kindness or affection: to put by such a movement: to soothe, or flatter (*obs.*): to milk, strip: to tool in small flutings: to whet: to set in close gathers: to strike, move (a ball, etc.) smoothly. — *n.* an act of stroking. — *ns.* **strok′er; strok′ing.** [O.E. *strācian* — *strāc,* stroke (n.); cf. Ger. *streichen,* to rub.]

stroke³ *strōk,* **stroken** *strōk′n,* obs. forms (*Spens., Shak.*) of **struck.** See **strike.**

stroll *strōl, v.i.* to wander as a vagrant or itinerant: to walk leisurely: to saunter. — *n.* a leisurely walk: a stroller (now *U.S.*). — *n.* **stroll′er** one who strolls: a wanderer: a saunterer: a vagrant: an itinerant: a push-chair (*U.S.*). — *n.* and *adj.* **stroll′ing. — strolling player** an itinerant actor. — **stroll on!** an exclamation of surprise, disbelief (often used ironically). [Perh. Ger. *strolchen* (obs. *strollen*) — *Strolch,* vagrant.]

stroma *strō′mǝ, n.* a supporting framework of connective tissue (*zool.*): a dense mass of hyphae in which a fungus fructification may develop (*bot.*): the denser part of a blood-corpuscle, chloroplast, etc.: — *pl.* **strōm′ata.** — *adjs.* **strōmatic** (*-mat′ik*), **strō′matous.** [Gr. *strōma,* a bed, mattress.]

stromb *strom(b), n.* a very large gasteropod akin to the whelk: its shell with short spire and expanded lip. — *adjs.* **strombūlif′erous** bearing spirally coiled organs or parts; **strombū′liform** top-shaped: spirally twisted. — *n.* **Strom′bus** the stromb, or wing-shell, genus: (without *cap.*) any mollusc of this genus: (without *cap.*) a spirally coiled pod. [Gr. *strombos,* a spinning-top, snail, whirlwind.]

strond *strond,* (*Spens., Shak.*) *n.* Same as **strand¹.**

strong *strong, adj.* powerful: forcible: forceful: fast-moving: vigorous: hale: robust: of great staying power: firm: resistant: difficult to overcome: steadfast: excelling: efficient: of great tenacity of will and effective in execution: able: well-skilled or versed: competent: rich in resources or means to power: well provided: numerous: numbering so many: of vigorous growth: stiff, coarse, and abundant, indicating strength: without ambiguity, obscurity, or understatement: intemperate, offensive and unseemly: gross: violent: grievous: having great effect: intense: ardent and convinced: performed with strength: powerfully, or unpleasantly powerfully, affecting the senses: rank: vivid: marked: stressed, emphasised: bold in definition: in high concentration: showing the characteristic properties in high degree: (of prices, markets) steady or tending to rise: of Germanic verbs, showing ablaut variation in conjugation (*gram.*): of Germanic nouns and adjectives, having a stem originally ending in a vowel or a consonant other than *n*: of the strongest type of interaction between nuclear particles, occuring at a range of less than approx. 10^{-15} cm and accounting for the stability of the atomic nucleus (*phys.*): — *compar.* **stronger** (*strong′gǝr*); *superl.* **strong′est** (*-gist*). — *adv.* **strongly** (*rare*): very (*obs.*). — *adj.* **strongish** (*strong′gish*). — *adv.* **strong′ly.** — **strong′arm** one who uses violence. — *adj.* by, having, or using, physical force. — *v.t.* to treat violently, show violence towards. — **strong′-box** a safe or strongly made coffer for valuables; **strong drink, waters** alcoholic liquors; **strong flour, wheat** one rich in gluten, giving bread that rises well; **strong head** power to withstand alcohol or any dizzying influence; **strong′hold** a fastness or fortified refuge: a fortress: a place where anything is in great strength; **strong interaction** one produced by short-range forces, involving baryons or mesons, and completed in about 10^{-23} seconds. — *adj.* **strong′-knit**

firmly jointed or compacted. — **strong language** swearing: plain, emphatic language; **strong'man** one who performs feats of strength: one who wields political, economic, etc. power; **strong meat** solid food, not milk (Heb. v. 12, 14): anything tending to arouse fear, repulsion, etc. — *adj.* **strong'-mind'ed** resolute, determined, having a vigorous mind — formerly applied by disapprovers to emancipated women. — **strong'= mind'edness; strong'point** (*mil.*) a favourably situated and well-fortified defensive position; **strong point** that in which one excels, one's forte; **strong'room** a room constructed for safe-keeping of valuables or prisoners. — **a strong stomach** resistance to nausea; **come it strong** see **come; going strong** see **going²**.   [O.E. *strang, strong*; O.N. *strangr*, Ger. *streng*, tight.]
strongyle *stron'jil, n.* a blunt rhabdus: a parasitic threadworm (*Strongylus* or kindred genera). — *adj.* and *n.* **stron'gyloid.** — *ns.* **strongyloidiasis** (*-dī'ə-sis*) infestation with a type of tropical or subtropical thread-worm of the genus *Strongyloides*, esp. *Strongyloides stercoralis*; **strongylō'sis** infestation with strongyles.   [Gr. *strongylos*, round.]
strontia, strontian, strontianite. See **strontium.**
strontium *stron'sh(i)-əm, stron'ti-əm, n.* an element (symbol Sr; at. numb. 38), a yellow metal found in celestine. — *ns.* **stron'tia** its oxide; **stron'tian** (*-shi-ən*) (*loosely*) strontium, strontia or strontianite. — Also *adj.* — **stron'tianite** its carbonate, an orthorhombic mineral (first found in 1790 near *Strontian* (*stron-tē'ən*) in Argyllshire). — **strontium-90** a radioactive isotope of strontium, an important element in nuclear fall-out.
strook, strooke *strōōk*, obs. *pa.t.* and *pa.p.* (*Spens., Shak., Milt.*, etc.) and **strook'en**, obs. *pa.p.* of **strike.** — *n.* **strooke** (*strōk; Spens.*) stroke.
strop *strop, n.* a strip of leather, etc., for sharpening razors: a rope or band round a dead-eye (*naut.*). — *v.t.* to sharpen on a strop: — *pr.p.* **stropp'ing;** *pa.t.* and *pa.p.* **stropped.**   [Older form of **strap** — O.E. *strop*, prob. — L. *struppus*, a thong.]
Strophanthus *strof-, strōf-an'thəs, n.* an African and Asiatic genus of the periwinkle family, yielding arrow-poison: (without *cap.*) a plant of the genus, or its dried seeds used in medicine. — *n.* **strophan'thin** a very poisonous glucoside in its seeds.   [Gr. *strophos*, twisted band, *anthos*, flower, from the ribbonlike prolongation of the petals, twisted in bud.]
strophe *strof'i, strōf'i, n.* in a Greek play, the song sung by the chorus as it moved towards one side, answered by an exact counterpart, the *antistrophe*, as it returned: part of any ode thus answered: (*loosely*) a stanza. — *adj.* **stroph'ic.**   [Gr. *strŏphē*, a turn.]
strophiole *strof'i-ōl, (bot.) n.* a caruncle. — *adjs.* **stroph'-iolate, -d.**   [Gr. *strophiolon*, a fringe — *strophos*, a twisted band.]
stroppy *strop'i, (slang) adj.* quarrelsome, bad-tempered: rowdy, obstreperous.   [Perh. **obstropalous.**]
strossers *stros'ərz, (Shak.) n.pl.* trousers.   [Cf. **trousers.**]
stroud *strowd, n.* a blanket made for trading with American Indians. — *n.* **stroud'ing** its material, coarse wool.   [Prob. made at *Stroud*, Gloucestershire.]
stroup *strōōp, (Scot.) n.* a spout, nozzle.   [Cf. Sw. *strupe*, throat.]
strout *strowt, v.i.* to bulge, swell: to stand out, protrude: to flaunt: to strut. — *v.t.* to cause to protrude.   [O.E. *strūtian*, to protrude.]
strove *strōv, pa.t.* of **strive.**
strow, strower, strowing. Same as **strew, strewer, strewing:** — *pa.t.* **strowed;** *pa.p.* **strown.**
stroy *stroi, v.t.* (*Shak.*) to destroy. — *n.* (*Bunyan*) destruction.   [**destroy.**]
struck, strucken. See **strike.**
structure *struk'chər, n.* the manner or (*obs.*) act of putting together: construction: the arrangement of parts: the manner of organisation: a thing constructed: an organic form. — *v.t.* to organise, build up: to construct a framework for: to allot to (a linguistic element) its function or syntactical relationship. — *adj.* **struc'tural.**

— *n.* **struc'turalism** the belief in and study of unconscious, underlying patterns in thought, behaviour, social organisation, etc.; **struc'turalist.** — Also *adj.* — *adv.* **struc'turally.** — **structurā'tion** forming (something) into or applying an organised structure to (something), creating a formal structure (*rare*). — *adjs.* **struc'tured** having a certain structure: having a definite structure or organisation; **struc'tureless.** — **structural formula** a chemical formula showing the arrangement of atoms in the molecule and the bonds between them; **structural isomerism** (*chem.*) the property of substances which are isomeric (q.v.) and differ in molecular structure, often having distinct physical and chemical properties (contrast with **stereoisomerism**); **structural linguistics** the study of language in terms of the interrelations of its basic units; **structural psychology** a type of psychology dealing with the nature and arrangement of mental states and processes; **structural steel** a strong mild steel suitable for construction work; **structural unemployment** unemployment due to changes in the structure of society or of a particular industry.   [L. *structūra* — *struĕre, structum* to build.]
strudel *s(h)trōō'dl, n.* very thin pastry enclosing fruit, or cheese, etc.   [Ger., eddy, whirlpool.]
struggle *strug'l, v.i.* to strive vigorously in resistance, contention, or coping with difficulties: to make great efforts or exertions: to contend strenuously: to make way with difficulty: to move convulsively. — *n.* a bout or course of struggling: strife: a hard contest with difficulties: a convulsive movement. — *n.* **strugg'ler.** — *n.* and *adj.* **strugg'ling.** — *adv.* **strugg'lingly.**   [M.E. *strogelen*; origin unknown.]
Struldbrug *struld'brug, n.* one of a class among the Luggnaggians in Swift's *Gulliver's Travels*, endowed with immortality, but doomed to decrepitude after eighty, and most wretched.   [A capricious coinage.]
strum *strum, v.t.* and *v.i.* to play in a haphazard unskilful way: to sound the strings of a guitar, etc. with a sweep of the hand: to play in this way (rather than plucking individual strings): — *pr.p.* **strumm'ing;** *pa.t.* and *pa.p.* **strummed.** — *n.* a strumming.   [Cf. **thrum.**]
struma *strōō'mə, n.* scrofula: a scrofulous tumour: goitre: a cushion-like swelling (*bot.*): — *pl.* **stru'mae** (*-mē, -mī*). — *adjs.* **strumatic** (*strōō-mat'ik*), **strumose** (*strōō'mōs*), **stru'mous.** — *n.* **strumī'tis** inflammation of the thyroid gland.   [L. *strūma*, a scrofulous tumour.]
strummel *strum'l,* **strammel** *stram'l, (obs. slang) ns.* straw: hence, hair.   [Cf. L. *strāmen*, straw.]
strumose, strumous. See **struma.**
strumpet *strum'pit, n.* a whore. — *adj.* like a strumpet: inconstant: false. — *v.t.* to make a strumpet of: to call a strumpet.   [Origin obscure.]
strung *strung, pa.t.* and *pa.p.* of **string.**
strunt¹ *strunt, (Scot.) v.i.* to strut.   [Cf. Norw. *strunta.*]
strunt² *strunt, (Scot.) n.* spirituous liquor.   [Ety. dub.]
strunt³ *strunt, (Scot.;* often in *pl.*) *n.* the huff, the sulks.   [Origin unknown.]
strut¹ *strut, v.i.* to bulge, protrude (*obs.*): to flaunt, glory (*obs.*): to stand stiffly upright (*obs.*): to walk stiffly in vanity or self-importance: to walk in an ostentatious, swaggering manner: — *pr.p.* **strutt'ing;** *pa.t.* and *pa.p.* **strutt'ed.** — *n.* a strutting gait. — *n.* **strutt'er.** — *n.* and *adj.* **strutt'ing.** — *adv.* **strutt'ingly.** — **strut one's stuff** (*U.S. slang*) to dance: to show off one's talent (at a public activity, etc.): to show off generally.   [O.E. *strūtian* or some kindred form; see **strout.**]
strut² *strut, n.* a rod or member that resists pressure: a prop. — *v.t.* to support as, or with, a strut or struts.   [Cf. L.G. *strutt*, rigid, and foregoing.]
Struthio *strōō'thi-ō, n.* the African ostrich genus. — *n.pl.* **Struthio'nes** (*-nēz*) an order of birds including ostriches, rheas, kiwis, emus, and cassowaries. — *adjs.* **stru'thioid, stru'thious.**   [L., — Gr. *strouthiōn*, an ostrich.]
strychnine *strik'nēn, n.* a very poisonous alkaloid ($C_{21}H_{22}N_2O_2$) got from nux vomica seeds. — *v.t.* to poison with strychnine. — *n.* **strych'nia** (now *rare*)

strychnine. — *adj.* **strych'nic.** — *ns.* **strych'ninism, strych'nism** strychnine poisoning. [Gr. *strychnos*, nightshade (of various kinds).]

stryfull. See **strife.**

stub *stub, n.* a stump: (also **stub'-nail**) a short thick nail or worn horse-shoe nail, esp. in *pl.*, old nails used as scrap: a counterfoil: a short piece left after the larger part has been used (as a cigarette, pencil, etc.): something blunt and stunted. — *v.t.* to grub up: to remove stubs from: to wear or cut to a stub: to wound with a stub: to strike as against a stub: to extinguish by pressing the end on something (often with *out*): — *pr.p.* **stubb'ing;** *pa.t.* and *pa.p.* **stubbed.** — *adj.* **stubbed** cut or worn to a stub: cleared of stubs: stumpy: blunt. — *n.* **stubb'iness.** — *adj.* **stubb'y** abounding with stubs: short, thick, and strong. — *n.* (*Austr.*) a small, squat beer bottle or the beer it contains. [O.E. *stubb, stybb.*]

stubble *stub'l, n.* a stump of reaped corn: such stumps collectively: straw: a reaped field: an ill-shaven beard. — *adjs.* **stubb'led** stubbly; **stubb'ly** low or covered with stubble. — *adj.* **stubb'le-fed** fed on the natural grass growing among stubble. — **stubb'le-field; stubb'le= goose** a goose fed on stubble; **stubb'le-rake** a rake with long teeth for raking stubble. [O.Fr. *estuble* — L.L. *stupula* — from L. *stipula*; see **stipule.**]

stubborn *stub'ərn, adj.* obstinate: unreasonably or troublesomely obstinate: pertinacious: refractory: hard to work or treat: rigid. — *v.t.* (*Keats*) to make stubborn. — *adv.* **stubb'ornly.** — *n.* **stubb'ornness.** [Connection with **stub** is obscure.]

stubby. See **stub.**

stucco *stuk'ō, n.* a plaster used for coating walls, making casts, etc.: work done in stucco (*pl.* **stucc'ōs**). — *v.t.* to face or overlay with stucco: to form in stucco: — *pa.t.* and *pa.p.* **stucc'oed, stucc'ō'd.** — *n.* **stucc'ōer** a worker or dealer in stucco. [It. *stucco*; from O.H.G. *stucchi*, crust, coating.]

stuck¹, stuck-up. See **stick¹.**

stuck² *stuk*, (*Shak.*) *n.* a thrust. [**stock².**]

stud¹ *stud, n.* a horse-breeding establishment: the animals kept there: a collection of horses or other animals, or of cars, belonging to the same owner: short for stud-horse: a sexually potent or active man (*slang*). — *adj.* kept for breeding: of a stud. — **stud'-book** a record of horses' (or other animals') pedigrees; **stud'-farm** a horse-breeding farm; **stud'-groom** a groom at a stud, esp. the head-groom; **stud'-horse** a stallion kept for breeding; **stud poker** a variety of the game of poker. — **at stud, out to stud** being used for breeding purposes. [O.E. *stōd;* cf. **steed¹;** Ger. *Stute*, mare, *Gestüt*, stud.]

stud² *stud, n.* a wooden post (*obs.*): a tree-trunk (*Spens.*): a spur, stump, or short branch: an upright scantling as in a timber framework or partition: a cross-piece strengthening a link in a chain: one of several round projections on the soles of certain types of footwear improving the grip: a projecting boss, knob, or pin: a large-headed nail: a stud-bolt: a type of fastener consisting of two interlocking discs: the height of a room (*U.S.*). — *v.t.* to adorn, set, or secure with studs: to set at intervals: — *pr.p.* **studd'ing;** *pa.t.* and *pa.p.* **studd'ed.** — *adj.* **studd'ed.** — *n.* **studd'ing.** — **stud'-bolt** a bolt with a thread on each end, screwed into a fixed part at one end, receiving a nut upon the other; **stud'work** brickwork walls between studs: studded leather. [O.E. *studu*, post.]

studden. See **stand.**

studding-sail *stun'sl, n.* a narrow sail set at the outer edges of a square sail when wind is light. — Also **stun'sail.** [Origin unknown.]

studdle *stud'l, n.* a post: a prop. [O.E. *stodla.*]

student *stū'dənt, n.* one who studies: one devoted to books or to any study: one who is enrolled for a course of instruction in a college or university: an undergraduate: a member of the foundation of Christ Church, Oxford, answering to a fellow elsewhere: the holder of a studentship: a school pupil: one learning a specified profession, etc. (as *student teacher, student nurse*).

— *ns.* **stu'dentry** students collectively; **stu'dentship** an endowment for a student in a college: in Christ Church, Oxford, the equivalent of a fellowship: the condition or time of being a student. — *adj.* **studied** (*stud'id*) well considered: deliberately contrived, designed: over-elaborated with loss of spontaneity: well prepared by study: deep read: versed. — *adv.* **stud'iedly.** — *ns.* **stud'iedness; stud'ier; studio** (*stū'di-ō*) an artist's work-room: a workshop for photography, cinematography, radio or television broadcasting, the making of gramophone records, etc.: — *pl.* **stu'dios.** — *adj.* **studious** (*stū'di-əs*) devoted to or assiduous in study: heedful: intent: solicitous: studied: deliberate. — *adv.* **stu'diously.** — *n.* **stu'diousness.** — *v.t.* **study** (*stud'i*) to apply the mind to in order to acquire knowledge or skill: to make one's object, seek to achieve: to be solicitous about: to consider: to scrutinise: to look contemplatively at: to take into consideration: to consider the wishes, advantage, feelings of: to devise: to elaborate with self-consciousness: to think out: to instruct (*Shak.*). — *v.i.* to apply the mind closely to books, nature, acquisition of learning or of skill: to take an educational course: to rack one's mind: to muse, meditate, reflect: — *pr.p.* **stud'ying;** *pa.t.* and *pa.p.* **stud'ied.** — *n.* inclination: interest: zeal: an object of endeavour, solicitude, or mental application: (in *pl.*) related objects of mental application or departments of knowledge: a state of doubtful consideration: attentive and detailed examination: a scrutiny: a reverie: application of the mind to the acquisition of knowledge or skill: a department of knowledge: a preliminary essay towards a work of art: an exercise in art: a musical composition affording an exercise in technique: a presentation in literature or art of the results of study: the committing to memory, hence a memoriser (*theat.*): a room devoted to study, actually or ostensibly. — **studio couch** a couch, sometimes without a back, that can be converted into a bed; **studio flat** a small flat consisting of one main room, or an open-plan living area; **studio pottery** pottery individually produced by the potter in a studio, rather than factory-made; **study group** a group of people studying a specific subject, who meet informally at regular intervals to discuss their work or some other topic. [L. *studēre* (pr.p. *studēns, -entis*) to be zealous, *studium* (O.Fr. *estudie;* It. *studio*), zeal, study.]

studio, study, etc. See **student.**

stuff *stuf, n.* stuffing, filling (*obs.*): matter: substance: essence: material: a preparation used or commodity dealt in in some particular industry or trade: garden produce: cloth, esp. woollen: a medicinal mixture: goods: luggage: provision: furniture: money: literary or journalistic copy: liquor (**good stuff** often whisky): rubbish: nonsense: indecent matter (*obs.*). — *adj.* woollen. — *v.t.* to garrison (*obs.*): to store, furnish (*Shak.*): to provision (*obs.*): to line: to be a filling for: to fill very full: to thrust in: to crowd: to cram: to obstruct, clog: to cause to bulge out by filling: to fill with seasoning, as a fowl: to fill the skin of, so as to reproduce the living form: to hoax (*slang*): (of a man) to have sexual intercourse with (*vulg.*): to load (a freight container): in electronics manufacturing, etc., to assemble the internal components of a machine in its external casing: to defeat very convincingly (*slang*). — *v.i.* to feed gluttonously: to practise taxidermy. — *adj.* **stuffed** provisioned: well stored: filled: filled out with stuffing: clogged in nose or throat, etc. (often with *up*). — *n.* **stuff'er.** — *adv.* **stuff'ily.** — *ns.* **stuff'- iness; stuff'ing** that which is used to stuff or fill anything — straw, sawdust, feathers, hair, etc.: savoury ingredients put into meat, poultry, etc., in cooking. — *adj.* **stuff'y** badly ventilated, musty: stifling: stout, sturdy (*Scot.*): stodgy (*slang*): strait-laced: sulky (*U.S.*): stuffed up. — **stuffed shirt** a pompous, unbendingly correct person, esp. if of little real importance; **stuff'= gown** a gown of stuff, not silk, esp. that of a junior barrister; **stuff'ing-box** a cavity filled with packing to make a pressure-tight joint. — **and stuff** and that sort of thing or rubbish; **bit of stuff** (*slang*) girl, woman; **do one's stuff** to do what is expected of one; **get stuffed!** (*vulg. slang*) *interj.* expressing anger, derision, contemptuous dismissal, etc.; **hot stuff** (*coll.*) denoting a very attractive, effective, etc. person or thing; **knock the stuffing out of** to reduce (an opponent) to helplessness; **know one's stuff** to have a thorough knowledge of the field in which one is concerned; **stuff it, them, you**, etc. (*vulg. slang*) *interj.* expressing disgust, scorn, frustration, etc.; **that's the stuff!** excellent!; **(a drop of) the hard stuff** (some) strongly alcoholic drink, esp. whisky. [O.Fr. *estoffe*, stuff — L. *stuppa* — Gr. *styppē*, tow.]

stuggy *stug'i*, (*dial.*) *adj.* thick-set, stout.

stull *stul*, (*dial.*) *n.* a horizontal prop in a mine. — *n.* **stulm** (*stulm*) an adit: a small draining-shaft. [Cf. Ger. *Stollen*.]

stultify *stul'ti-fī, v.t.* to allege or prove to be of unsound mind (*law*): to dull the mind: to cause to appear foolish or ridiculous: to destroy the force of, as by self-contradiction: — *pr.p.* **stul'tifying;** *pa.t.* and *pa.p.* **stul'tified.** — *ns.* **stultificā'tion; stul'tifier; stultil'-oquence** (l. *loquī*, to talk), **stultil'oquy** foolish talk or discourse, babbling. — *adj.* **stultil'oquent.** [L. *stultus*, foolish.]

stum *stum, n.* must, grape-juice unfermented: new wine used to revive dead or vapid wine: a mixture used to impart artificial strength, etc., to weak beer or wine: wine revived by the addition of stum or by a second fermentation. — *v.t.* to renew or doctor with stum: to fume, as a cask of liquor, with burning sulphur: — *pr.p.* **stumm'ing;** *pa.t.* and *pa.p.* **stummed.** [Du. *stom*, must — *stom*, mute; Ger. *stumm*, dumb.]

stumble *stum'bl, v.i.* to take a false step, come near to falling in walking: to walk unsteadily: to err: to lapse into wrongdoing: to flounder: to light by chance or error (with *across* or *on*): to boggle. — *v.t.* to disconcert. — *n.* a trip: a false step: a lapse: a blunder. — *n.* **stum'bler.** — *adv.* **stum'blingly.** — *adj.* **stum'bly** apt to stumble or to cause stumbling. — **stum'blebum** (*slang;* orig. and esp. *U.S.*) an awkward, inept, ineffectual person; **stum'bling-block, -stone** an obstacle: a cause of perplexity or error. [M.E. *stomble, stumble;* cf. Norw. *stumla,* and **stammer.**]

stumer *stū'mər,* (*slang*) *n.* a counterfeit coin or note: a forged or worthless cheque: a sham: a dud: a failure, bankruptcy: a horse sure to lose: a stupid mistake, clanger: a stupid person (*Scot.*). [Origin obscure.]

stumm *stoom.* Same as **shtoom.**

stummel *stum'l, n.* the bowl and adjacent part of a pipe. [Ger.]

stump *stump, n.* the part of a felled or fallen tree left in the ground: a tree-stump used as a platform: hence, a campaign of stump-oratory: a short thick remaining basal part, esp. of anything that projects: a short thick branch: a leg (*facet.*): a wooden leg: anything stumpy: a stumping walk or its sound: a pencil of soft material for softening hard lines, blending, etc.: one of the three sticks forming (with the bails) a wicket (*cricket*): a challenge to perform a feat (*U.S.*). — *adj.* reduced to a stump: stumpy. — *v.t.* to reduce to a stump: to remove stumps from: (of the wicket-keeper; sometimes with *out*) to dismiss by breaking the wicket when the striker is out of his ground (*cricket*): to clear out of money (*slang*): to nonplus, foil, defeat: to soften or tone with a stump: to walk over or strike heavily and stiffly: to traverse making stump-speeches: to dare, challenge (*U.S.*). — *v.i.* to walk stiffly and heavily, as if on wooden legs: to make stump-speeches. — *ns.* **stump'age** (*U.S.*) standing timber, its monetary value, or money paid for it; **stump'er.** — *adv.* **stump'ily.** — *n.* **stump'iness.** — *n.sing.* **stumps** (*cricket*) the end of play. — *adj.* **stump'y** short and thick: full of stumps (*U.S.*). — *n.* (*slang*) cash. — **stump'-orator** one who speaks from an improvised platform, usu. with an implication of rant: in U.S. a political public speaker in general;

stump'-oratory; stump'-speech; stump'-work elaborate raised embroidery of the 15th–17th cents. using various materials and raised by stumps of wood or pads of wool. — **draw stumps** (*cricket*) to end play (also *fig.*); **on the stump** engaged in a (political) speech-making tour, campaign; **stir one's stumps** to move, be active; **stump up** to pay up, fork out. [Cf. Du. *stomp,* M.L.G. *stump,* O.N. *stumpr,* Ger. *Stumpf.*]

stun *stun, v.t.* to render unconscious as by a blow: to stupefy, daze, as with din or sudden emotion: to abrade, bruise: — *pr.p.* **stunn'ing;** *pa.t.* and *pa.p.* **stunned.** — *n.* a shock, stupefying blow: stunned condition. — *adj.* of a weapon, designed to stun rather than kill. — *ns.* **stunn'er** one who, or that which, stuns: a person or thing supremely excellent (*slang*): a very attractive person (*slang*); **stunn'ing** stupefaction. — *adj.* stupefying, dazing: supremely excellent (*slang*): very attractive (*slang*). — *adv.* **stunn'ingly.** — **stun grenade, gun,** etc. one designed to stun its target temporarily without causing serious injury. [O.Fr. *estoner* (Fr. *étonner*), to astonish; cf. O.E. *stunian,* to make a din — *stun,* a din.]

Stundist *stoon'dist, n.* a member of a Russian Protestant sect. — *n.* **Stun'dism.** [Ger. *Stunde,* hour, lesson, from their Bible-reading meetings.]

stung *stung, pa.t.* and *pa.p.* of **sting[1].**

stunk *stungk, pa.t.* and *pa.p.* of **stink.**

stunkard *stungk'ərd,* (*Scot.*) *adj.* sulky: sullen. [Origin obscure.]

stunsail *stun'sl.* See **studding-sail.**

stunt[1] *stunt, adj.* dwarfed: stumpy. — *v.t.* to hinder from growth, to dwarf, check. — *n.* a check in growth: a stunted animal. — *adj.* **stunt'ed** dwarfed. — *n.* **stunt'edness.** [O.E. *stunt,* dull, stupid: O.N. *stuttr,* short.]

stunt[2] *stunt, n.* a difficult, often showy, performance, enterprise, or turn (*orig. U.S.* college *slang*): a newspaper craze or campaign. — Also *adj.* — *v.i.* to perform stunts. — **stunt'man** one paid to perform dangerous and showy feats (esp. a stand-in for a film actor). [Perh. a variant of **stint[1], stent[1];** cf. **stunt[1];** or perh. Ger. *Stunde,* hour, lesson.]

stupa *stoo'pə, n.* a tope or Buddhist dome-shaped memorial shrine. [Sans. *stūpa.*]

stupe[1] *stūp, n.* a medicated piece of tow or cloth used in fomentation. — *v.t.* to treat with a stupe. [L. *stūpa* for *stuppa* — Gr. *styppē,* tow.]

stupe[2]. See **stupid.**

stupefy *stū'pi-fī, v.t.* to make stupid or senseless: to stun with amazement, fear, etc. — *v.i.* to become stupid or dull: — *pr.p.* **stū'pefying;** *pa.t.* and *pa.p.* **stū'pefied.** — *adj.* **stupefacient** (-*fā'shənt*) stupefying. — *n.* a stupefying drug. — *n.* **stupefaction** (-*fak'shən*) the act of stupefying: the state of being stupefied: extreme astonishment. — *adjs.* **stupefac'tive** stupefying; **stu'pefied.** — *n.* **stu'pefier.** — *adj.* **stu'pefying.** [L. *stupēre,* to be struck senseless, *facĕre,* to make.]

stupendous *stū-pen'dəs* (formerly, as *Milt.,* **stupendious** -*i-əs*), *adjs.* astounding: astoundingly huge: often used as a coll. term of approbation or admiration. — *adv.* **stupen'dously.** — *n.* **stupen'dousness.** — *adj.* **stu'pent** (*rare*) astounded: dumbfounded. [L. *stupendus,* gerundive, and *stupēns, -entis,* pres. part. of *stupēre,* to be stunned.]

stupid *stū'pid, adj.* stupefied: senseless: insensible: deficient or dull in understanding: showing lack of reason or judgment: foolish: dull: boring. — *n.* (*coll.*) a stupid person (also *coll.* **stupe**). — *ns.* **stupid'ity, stu'pidness.** — *adv.* **stu'pidly.** [L. *stupidus.*]

stupor *stū'pər, n.* torpor: lethargy: stupefaction: wonder. — *adj.* **stu'porous.** [L. *stupor, -ōris* — *stupēre.*]

stuprate *stū'prāt, v.t.* to ravish, violate. — *n.* **stuprā'tion.** [L. *stuprāre, -ātum.*]

sturdy *stûr'di, adj.* orig., giddy: impetuous, violent, rough (*obs.*): refractory: obstinate: resolute: robust: stout. — *n.* gid, a disease of sheep characterised by staggering, due to a bladderworm in the brain: a sturdy person. — *adj.* **stur'died** affected with sturdy. — *adv.* **stur'dily.**

— *n.* **stur'diness.** [O.Fr. *estourdi* (Fr. *étourdi*), stunned, giddy.]

sture. See **stoor**[1].

sturgeon *stûr'jən, n.* any member of a genus (*Acipenser*) of large fishes of the Chondrostei, with cartilaginous skull, long snout, heterocercal tail, and rows of bony shields on the skin, yielding caviar and isinglass. [A.Fr. *sturgeon*, of Gmc. origin (O.H.G. *sturjo*).]

Sturmabteilung *shtŏŏrm'ap-tī-lŏŏng, n.pl.* storm-troops (q.v.), Brownshirts. [Ger. *Sturm*, storm, *Abteilung*, division.]

Sturmer (Pippin) *stûr'mər (pip'in),* (also without *caps.*) *n.* a variety of dessert apple named after *Sturmer*, a village in Essex where it was developed: an apple of this variety.

Sturm und Drang *shtŏŏrm ŏŏnt drang,* a German literary movement of the latter half of the 18th century, characterised by realism, emotionalism and rousing action: storm and stress. [Ger., lit. storm and stress, title of a play by German dramatist F. M. von Klinger (1752–1831).]

Sturnus *stûr'nəs, n.* the starling genus, giving name to the family **Stur'nidae** (*-ni-dē*). — *adjs.* **stur'nine, stur'noid.** [L. *sturnus*, starling.]

sturt *stûrt,* (chiefly *Scot.*) *n.* contention: a disturbance. — *v.t.* to trouble. — *v.i.* to start with fear. [**strut**.]

stutter *stut'ər, v.i.* and *v.t.* to speak, say, or pronounce with spasmodic repetition of (esp. initial) sounds: to stammer. — *n.* a speech impediment characterised by spasmodic repetition of (esp. initial) sounds. — *n.* **stutt'erer.** — *n.* and *adj.* **stutt'ering.** — *adv.* **stutt'-eringly.** [A freq. of *obs. stut*, to stutter, M.E. *stutten*; cf. O.N. *stauta*; Ger. *stossen*.]

sty[1]**, stye** *stī, n.* a small inflamed swelling on the eyelid. [*Obs.* or *dial. stian, styan* — O.E. *stīgend*, from *stīgan*, to rise.]

sty[2] (*Spens., stye, stie*), *stī, (obs.) v.i.* to mount, rise, climb. — *n.* a path: a ladder. [O.E. *stīgan*, to mount, *stīg,* path, and O.N. *stige,* path, O.E. *stīge,* ascent or descent.]

sty[3]**,** rarely **stye**, *stī, n.* a pen for swine: any place extremely filthy: any place of gross debauchery: — *pl.* **sties, styes.** — *n.* and *v.i.* to lodge in a sty: — *pr.p.* **sty'ing;** *pa.t.* and *pa.p.* **stied, styed;** *3rd pers. sing. pres. ind.* **sties.** [O.E. *stig,* pen, hall; Ger. *Steige*.]

stye. See **sty**[1,2,3].

Stygian *stij'i-ən, -yən, adj.* of the **Styx,** one of the rivers of Hades, across which Charon ferries the shades of the departed: hellish, infernal: black as the Styx. — **Stygian oath** an inviolable oath, like that of the gods, by the Styx. [Gr. *Styx;* cf. *stygein,* to hate.]

stylar, stylate. See **style.**

style *stīl, n.* a pointed instrument for writing on wax tablets: a similar instrument or tool of various kinds, as a graver, a blunt probe, a tracing or cutting point: a slender process of various kinds (*biol.*): the slender part of the gynaeceum, bearing the stigma (*bot.*): the gnomon of a dial: a hand, pointer, index: a literary composition (*obs.*): the manner of writing, mode of expressing thought in language or of expression, execution, action or bearing generally: the distinctive manner peculiar to an author or other: the particular custom or form observed, as by a printing-house in optional matters (*style of the house*), or by lawyers in drawing up deeds: designation: manner: form: fashion: an air of fashion or consequence: a kind, type: a method in calico-printing: a mode of reckoning dates — *Old Style,* according to the Julian calendar, as in Britain till 1752, Russia till 1917; *New Style,* according to the Gregorian calendar, adopted in Britain by omitting eleven days, 3rd to 13th September 1752. — *v.t.* to designate: to arrange, dictate, the fashion or style of. — **-style** *adj.* and *adv.* combining form denoting in the style of, resembling. — *adjs.* **sty'lar; sty'late** having a style or a persistent style; **style'less.** — *n.* **sty'let, stī'let** a probe: a wire in a catheter: a bristle-like process: a graving tool: a writing instrument: a piercing

part of an insect's jaws: a stiletto. — *adjs.* **stylif'erous** bearing a style; **sty'liform** like a style or a bristle. — *n.* **stylīsā'tion, -z-.** — *v.t.* **sty'lise, -ize** to conventionalise. — *adj.* **sty'lish** displaying style: fashionable: showy: imposingly smart: pretending to style. — *adv.* **sty'lishly.** — *ns.* **sty'lishness; sty'list** one with a distinctive and fine (esp. literary, etc.) style: one who arranges a style, esp. in hairdressing. — *adj.* **stylist'ic.** — Also *n.* — *adv.* **stylist'ically.** — *n.sing.* **stylis'tics** the science of the variations in language, including the effective values of different words, forms, and sounds, that constitute style in the literary and also the wider sense. — *adj.* **sty'loid** like a style or bristle: forming a slender process. — *n.* a spiny process of the temporal bone. — *n.* **sty'lus** a style: the cutter used in making gramophone records: a gramophone needle: — *pl.* **sty'li** (*-lī*)**, sty'luses.** — **style'-book** a book of forms for deeds, etc., or rules for printers and editors. — **in style** in a grand manner. [L. *stilus,* a writing instrument, literary composition or style, confused with Gr. *stŷlos,* a column; in some senses perh. from the Gr. word.]

stylise, -ize. See **style.**

stylite *stī'līt, n.* an anchorite living on the top of a pillar. [Gr. *stylītēs* — *stŷlos,* a pillar.]

stylo. See **stylography.**

stylobate *stī'lō-bāt, n.* the substructure of a row of columns. [Gr. *stylobatēs* — *stŷlos,* a column, *batēs,* one who treads, from the root of *bainein,* to go.]

stylography *stī-log'rə-fi, n.* a mode of writing with a style. — *n.* **styl'ograph** (*stī'lə-gräf;* short form **sty'lō:** — *pl.* **sty'lōs**) a stylographic pen, a pencil-like pen from which ink is liberated by pressure on a needle-point. — *adj.* **stylographic** (*-graf'ik*)**.** — *adv.* **stylograph'ically.** [Gr. *stŷlos,* a style, *graphein,* to write.]

styloid. See **style.**

stylometry *stī-lom'ə-tri, n.* a method of studying literary style and development by means of statistical analysis. [Gr. *stŷlos,* a style, *metron,* a measure.]

stylopised, -ized *stī'lop-īzd, adj.* infested (as bees) with a strepsipterous parasite of *Stylops* or kindred genus.

stylopodium *stī-lō-pō'di-əm, n.* the disc from which styles rise in Umbelliferae. [Gr. *stŷlos,* pillar (as if style), *podion,* dim. of *pous, podos,* foot.]

stylus. See **style.**

styme, stime *stīm, (Scot.) n.* a glimmer: a glimpse: a minimum of vision (or of other things). — *v.i.* to peer. — *n.* **stymie, stimie, stimy** (*stī'mi*) a purblind person (*Scot.*): a situation on the putting-green in which an opponent's ball blocks the way to the hole (*golf*). — Also *fig.* — *v.t.* to put in such a situation (also **lay someone a stymie**): to frustrate, thwart, prevent, block, stop: — *pa.t.* and *pa.p.,* *adj.* **sty'mied.** [Origin obscure.]

styptic *stip'tik, adj.* drawing together: astringent: checking bleeding. — *n.* a styptic agent. — *n.* **styp'sis** the use, action, etc. of a styptic. — *adj.* **styp'tical.** — *n.* **stypticity** (*-tis'i-ti*)**.** — **styptic pencil** a healing agent for minor cuts. [Gr. *styptikos* — *stŷphein,* to contract.]

Styrax *stī'raks, n.* a genus of plants abounding in resinous and aromatic substances, as benzoin, giving name to the family **Styracā'ceae,** akin to the ebony family: (without *cap.*) any plant of this genus. — *n.* **sty'rene** an unsaturated hydrocarbon obtained from essential oils (as the balsam storax) and coal-tar, forming thermoplastics on polymerisation. [Gr. *stŷrax;* cf. **storax.**]

styre. See **stir**[1].

Styx *stiks.* See **Stygian.**

suable *sū'* or *sŏŏ'ə-bl, adj.* that may be sued. — Also **sue'able.** — *n.* **suabil'ity.** — Also **sueabil'ity.**

suasion *swā'zhən, n.* persuasion. — *adjs.* **sua'sible** (*-si-bl*)**; sua'sive** (*-siv*)**.** — *adv.* **sua'sively.** — *n.* **sua'siveness.** — *adj.* **sua'sory.** [L. *suāsiō, -ōnis* — *suādēre,* to advise.]

suave *swäv* (formerly *swāv*)**,** *adj.* smooth, bland. — *adv.* **suave'ly.** — *n.* **suavity** (*swav'i-ti*)**.** [Fr., — L. *suāvis,* sweet.]

suaveolent *swə-vē'ə-lənt, adj.* fragrant. [L. *suāveolēns,*

-entis — suāvē, sweetly, olēns, smelling.]
sub- sub-, səb-, pfx. (1) under, below; (2) subordinate,
subsidiary; (3) part of, a subdivision of; (4) almost,
nearly, slightly, imperfectly, bordering on; (5) secretly;
(6) (chem.) in smaller proportion. — n. **sub** (coll.) a
subordinate: a subaltern: a subeditor: a sublieutenant:
a subsidiary: a subway: a subscription (also **subs**): a
subscriber: a substitute: a submarine: subsistence
money, hence a loan, an advance payment. — v.i.
(coll.) to act as a sub: to work as a substitute: to work
as a newspaper subeditor. — v.t. (coll.) to subedit: —
pr.p. **subb'ing**; pa.t. and pa.p. **subbed**. — n. **subb'ing**
(coll.) the advancing of part of the wages while the
work is going on. [L. sub, under, near; in composition also in some degree, secretly.]
subact sub-akt', v.t. to work up: to subdue. — n. **subac'-
tion** (-shən). [L. subactus, pa.p. of subigěre — sub,
under, agěre, to drive, do.]
subacute sub-ə-kūt', adj. slightly or moderately acute:
between acute and chronic (med.). [Pfx. **sub-** (4).]
subadar. See **subah**.
subadult sub-ad'ult, sub-ə-dult', adj. (usu. of an animal)
fully or almost fully grown but not yet having developed all the adult characteristics: adolescent. — n. an
individual at subadult stage. [Pfx. **sub-** (4).]
subaerial sub-ā-ē'ri-əl, adj. in the open air: on the land
surface. — adv. **subāē'rially**. [Pfx. **sub-** (1).]
subah sōō'bä, n. a province of the Mogul empire: a
subahdar. — ns. **suba(h)dar'** the governor of a subah:
an Indian captain; **subahdar'y, su'bahship** the office of
subahdar. [Urdu.]
subalpine sub-al'pīn, adj. bordering on the alpine: at the
foot of the Alps. [Pfx. **sub-** (4), (1).]
subaltern sub'əl-tərn (U.S. except in logic usu. sub-öl'tərn),
adj. ranked successively: subordinate: holding or held
of a vassal: (of officers) under the rank of captain:
particular (log.): being at once a genus and a species
of a higher genus (log.). — n. a subordinate: a subaltern
officer: a proposition differing from another in quantity alone (both being affirmative or both negative,
but one universal, the other particular) (log.). — ns.
subalter'nant (log.) a universal in relation to the subaltern particular; **subalter'nate** a particular proposition in relation to the subaltern universal (log.). — adj.
subservient: alternate with a tendency to become
opposite (bot.). — ns. **subalternation** (sub-öl-tər-nā'-
shən) the relation between a universal and particular
of the same quality; **subalter'nity** subordinate position.
[L. subalternus — sub, under, alter, another.]
subapostolic sub-ap-os-tol'ik, adj. of the time just after
the apostles. [Pfx. **sub-** (4).]
subaquatic sub-ə-kwat'ik, adj. under water (also **sub-
ā'queous**): partially aquatic (zool. and bot.). — adj.
suba'qua of underwater sport. [Pfx. **sub-** (1), (4).]
subarcuate sub-är'kū-āt, adj. somewhat arched: with two
or more arches under a main arch. — n. **subarcūā'tion**.
[Pfx. **sub-** (4), (1).]
subarr(h)ation sub-ə-rā'shən, n. an ancient mode of betrothal by bestowal of a ring or gift. [L. subar-
r(h)ātiō, -ōnis — sub, under, arr(h)a, earnest-money.]
subastral sub-as'trəl, adj. beneath the stars, terrestrial.
[Pfx. **sub-** (1).]
subatom sub-at'əm, n. a constituent part of an atom. —
adj. **subatom'ic** relating to particles constituting the
atom and changes within the atom. —n.sing. **subatom'-
ics** the study of these particles and changes. [Pfx.
sub- (3).]
subaudition sub-ö-dish'ən, n. a sense understood, not
expressed. [Pfx. **sub-** (5).]
subbasal sub'bās'əl, adj. near or below the base. — n. the

lowest part of a base (archit.): a division of a military
base. [Pfx. **sub-** (1), (3).]
subcartilaginous sub-kär-ti-laj'in-əs, adj. composed partly
of cartilage: situated under a cartilage. [Pfx. **sub-** (4),
(1).]
subcellular sub-sel'ū-lər, (biol.) adj. occurring within a
cell: smaller than a cell. [Pfx. **sub-** (3), (6).]
subchanter sub'chänt'ər, n. a precentor's deputy. [**sub-**
(2).]
subclavian sub-klā'vi-ən, **subclavicular** -klə-vik'-ū-lər, adjs.
under the clavicle. [Pfx. **sub-** (1), **clavicle**.]
subclinical sub-klin'i-kəl, adj. of a slightness not detectable by usual clinical methods. [Pfx. **sub-** (4).]
subcompact sub-kom'pakt, n. (U.S.) a small car, such as
a sports car. [Pfx. **sub-** (2).]
subconscious sub-kon'shəs, adj. dimly conscious: away
from the focus of attention: not conscious but of like
nature to the conscious. — n. the subconscious mind
or activities. — adv. **subcon'sciously**. — n. **subcon'-
sciousness**. [Pfx. **sub-** (4).]
subcontinent sub-kon'ti-nənt, n. a great portion of a
continent with a character of its own (a term formerly
applied to South Africa, later to India): a land-mass
hardly great enough to be called a continent. — adj.
subcontinent'al almost continental: underlying a continent. — **Indian subcontinent** the area covered by
India, Pakistan, Bangladesh, Sikkim, Bhutan and
Nepal. [Pfx. **sub-** (2), (4), (1).]
subcontract sub-kon'trakt, n. a contract subordinate to
another contract, as for the subletting of work. — v.i.
subcontract' to make a subcontract. — v.t. to make a
subcontract for: to betroth when already married (as
if subleased by the actual husband to another; Shak.).
— n. **subcontract'or**. [Pfx. **sub-** (2).]
subcontrary sub-kon'trə-ri, adj. contrary in an inferior
degree: (of a particular proposition in relation to
another differing only in quality) such that at least one
must be true (log.). — n. a subcontrary proposition.
— n. **subcontrarī'ety**. [Pfx. **sub-** (4).]
subcosta sub-kost'ə, n. the nervure next to the costa in
an insect's wing. — adj. **subcost'al** near or under a rib
or the ribs: behind or near the costa. —n. the subcostal
nervure. [Pfx. **sub-** (1).]
subcritical sub-krit'i-kl, adj. of insufficient mass to sustain
a chain reaction (phys.): below the critical temperature
for hardening metals. [Pfx. **sub-** (1).]
subculture sub'kul'chər, n. a culture (as of bacteria)
derived from a previous one: a social, ethnic or
economic group with a particular character of its own
within a culture or society. — adj. **sub'cul'tural**. [Pfx.
sub- (2), (3).]
subdeacon sub-dē'kən, n. a member of the order (major
in the R.C., minor in the Eastern churches) of the
ministry next below that of deacon, preparing the
vessels, etc., at the eucharist. — ns. **subdea'conry**,
subdea'conship. [Pfx. **sub-** (2).]
subdelirious sub-də-lir'i-əs, adj. mildly or intermittently
delirious. — n. **subdelir'ium**. [Pfx. **sub-** (4).]
subdew. See **subdue**.
subdivide sub'di-vīd', v.t. and v.i. to divide into smaller
divisions: to divide again. — n. **subdivid'er**. — adj.
subdivisible (-viz'). — n. **subdivision** (-vizh'ən). — adjs.
subdivis'ional; subdivī'sive. [Pfx. **sub-** (3).]
sub divo sub dī'vō, sōōb dē'vō, -wō, (L.) adv. under the
sky: in the open air. — Also **sub Jove** (jō've, yō've,
-we) under Jupiter (the sky-god).
subdolous sub'dō-ləs, (rare) adj. crafty. [L. pfx. sub-, in
sense of somewhat, dolus, a wile.]
subdominant sub'dom'i-nənt, n. (mus.) the tone next below
the dominant. — adj. not quite ranking as dominant:

---

subabdom'inal adj. **sub-** (1).
suba'cid adj. **sub-** (4).
subacid'ity n. **sub-** (4).
subacid'ulous adj. **sub-** (4).
subac'rid adj. **sub-** (4).
subā'gency n. **sub-** (2).

subā'gent n. **sub-** (2).
subang'ular adj. **sub-** (4).
subantarc'tic adj. **sub-** (4).
subappear'ance n. **sub-** (2).
subarach'noid adj. **sub-** (1).
subboresc'ent adj. **sub-** (4).

subarc'tic adj. **sub-** (4).
subar'id adj. **sub-** (4).
subaud'ible adj. **sub-** (4).
subax'illary (or -il') adj. **sub-** (1).
subbase'ment n. **sub-** (1).
sub'branch n. **sub-** (2), (3).

---

partially dominant. [Pfx. **sub-** (1), (4).]

subduce *sub-dūs'*, *v.t.* (*obs.*) to withdraw. — *v.t.* **subduct** (*-dukt'*) to withdraw: to abstract secretly: to lift up: to push underneath by subduction. — *v.i.* to take something away. — *n.* **subduc'tion** a withdrawal, subtraction: the action or process of one part of the earth's crust moving underneath another. [L. *sub*, and *dūcĕre*, *ductum*, to lead, take.]

subdue (*Spens.*, **subdew**) *sub-dū'*, *v.t.* to overcome: to overpower: to subject: to make submissive: to bring into cultivation: to allay: to reduce: to quieten: to tone down: to achieve (*Spens.*). — *adj.* **subdu'able.** — *n.* **subdu'al** subjugation: an overcoming. — *adj.* **subdued'** toned down: quiet: passive. — *adv.* **subdued'ly** (or *-dū'id-li*). — *ns.* **subdued'ness; subdue'ment; subdu'er.** [O.Fr. *souduire* — L. *subdūcĕre*; see foregoing.]

subduple *sub-dū'pl*, *sub'dū-pl*, *adj.* in the ratio of one to two. — *adj.* **subdū'plicate** (of a ratio) expressed as the ratio of square roots. [L.L. *subduplus*.]

subedar. Same as **subahdar.**

subedit *sub-ed'it*, *v.t.* to select and dispose matter for (a newspaper): also, to assist in editing. — *n.* **subed'itor.** — *adj.* **subeditorial** (*-tōr'*, *-tör'*). — *n.* **subed'itorship.** [Pfx. **sub-** (2).]

subentire *sub-en-tīr'* (*bot.*), *adj.* with very faintly indented margin. [Pfx. **sub-** (4).]

suber *sū'bər*, (*bot.*) *n.* cork. — *n.* **su'berate** a salt of suberic acid. — *adjs.* **subē'reous, suberic** (*-ber'ik*) of cork (**suberic acid** an acid, HOOC·(CH₂)₆·COOH, got by action of nitric acid on cork). — *ns.* **su'berin** the chemical basis of cork; **suberīsā'tion, -z-.** — *v.t.* **su'berise, -ize** to convert into cork. — *adjs.* **su'berose, su'berous** corky. [L. *sūber*, *-eris*, the cork oak.]

subfamily *sub'fam'i-li*, *n.* a primary division of a family, of one or more genera. [Pfx. **sub-** (3).]

subfeu *sub'fū*, *n.* a feu granted to a vassal. — *v.t.* **subfeu'** to make a subinfeudation of. — *n.* **subfeudā'tion** subinfeudation. — *adj.* **subfeud'atory.** [Pfx. **sub-** (2).]

subfloor *sub'flōr*, *-flör*, *n.* a rough floor forming the foundation for the finished floor. [Pfx. **sub-** (1).]

subfusc, subfusk *sub'fusk*, *sub-fusk'*, *adj.* (*rare* **subfusc'ous**) dusky: sombre. — *n.* formal academic dress at Oxford University. [L. *subfuscus* — *sub*, *fuscus*, tawny.]

subgenus *sub-jē'nəs*, *n.* a primary division of a genus: — *pl.* **subgenera** (*-jen'ə-rə*), **subge'nuses.** — *adj.* **subgener'ic.** — *adv.* **subgener'ically.** [Pfx. **sub-** (3).]

subgrade *sub'grād*, *n.* levelled ground under the foundations of a road or a railway. [Pfx. **sub-** (1).]

subhastation *sub-has-tā'shən*, *n.* sale by public auction. [L. *sub*, under, *hasta*, a lance (set up as a sign by the Romans).]

subhuman *sub-hū'mən*, *adj.* less than human: below but near the human. [Pfx. **sub-** (4).]

subimago *sub-im-ā'gō*, *n.* a stage in the life of a mayfly, already winged but before the last moult: — *pl.* **subimagines** (*-i-mā'jin-ēz*, *-gin-*), **subimā'gōs.** [Pfx. **sub-** (4).]

subincision *sub-in-sizh'ən*, *n.* the formation of an opening into the urethra by incision of the underside of the penis — practised by some savage tribes. — *v.t.* **subincise'** to perform subincision upon. [Pfx. **sub-** (1).]

subindicate *sub-in'di-kāt*, *v.t.* to hint. — *n.* **subindicā'tion.** — *adj.* **subindic'ative.** [Pfx. **sub-** (4).]

subinfeudation *sub-in-fū-dā'shən*, *n.* the granting of land by a vassal to be held of him by his vassal. — *v.t.* **subinfeu'date.** — *adj. and n.* **subinfeud'atory.** [Pfx. **sub-** (2).]

subintellection *sub-in-ti-lek'shən*, *n.* an understood implication. — Also **subintelligence** (*sub-in-tel'i-jəns*), **subin-**

telligitur (*sub-in-tel-i'ji-tər*; L. *sōob-in-tel-i'gi-tŏor*, *lit.* it is more or less understood). — *adj.* **subintelligen'tial.** [Pfx. **sub-** (5).]

subintelligitur. See **subintellection.**

subintrant *sub-in'trənt*, *adj.* with paroxysms succeeding close upon one another. [Pfx. **sub-** (4).]

subintroduce *sub-in-trō-dūs'*, *v.t.* to bring in surreptitiously or subtly. — *v.t.* **subirr'igate.** [Pfx. **sub-** (5).]

subirrigation *sub-ir-i-gā'shən*, *n.* irrigation by underground pipes: irrigation from beneath. — *v.t.* **subirr'igate.** [Pfx. **sub-** (1).]

subitaneous *sub-i-tā'ni-əs*, *adj.* sudden: hasty: hastily made. [L. *subitāneus* — *subitus*, sudden.]

subito *sōo'bi-tō*, (*mus.*) *adv.* suddenly: immediately. [It.]

subjacent *sub-jā'sənt*, *adj.* underlying. [L. *subjacēns*, *-entis* — *sub*, *jacēre*, to lie.]

subject *sub'jikt*, *adj.* (often with *to*) under rule, government, jurisdiction, or control: owing allegiance: under obligation: subordinate: subservient: dependent: liable: exposed: prone, disposed: cognisable: dependent upon condition or contingency: underlying, spread out below (*Spens.*). — *adv.* conditionally (with *to*). — *n.* one who is subject: one who is under, or owes allegiance to, a sovereign, a state, a feudal superior, etc.: a citizen: a body of such persons (*Shak.*): a thing over which a legal right is exercised: a piece of property (*Scot.*): a substance (*obs.*): that in which attributes inhere: a thing existing independently: the mind regarded as the thinking power (opp. to the *object* about which it thinks): that of which something is predicated, or the term denoting it (*log.*): that part of a sentence or clause denoting that of which something is said (*gram.*): a topic: a matter of discourse, thought, or study: a department of study: a theme: that on which any operation is performed: that which is treated or handled: matter for any action or operation: a ground: a sufferer from disease, a patient: a dead body for dissection (*anat.*): a person peculiarly sensitive to hypnotic influence: that which it is the object of the artist to express: a picture representing action and incident: a theme or phrase upon which a movement of music is built. — *v.t.* **subject** (*səb-jekt'*) to make subject: to make liable: to subordinate: to submit: to subdue: to lay open. — *adj.* **subject'ed** made subject; subjacent (*Milt.*). — *v.t.* **subject'ify** to make subjective. — *n.* **subjec'tion.** — *adj.* **subject'ive** (also *sub'*) relating to the subject: derived from, expressive of, existing in, one's own consciousness: nominative (*gram.*): introspective. — *n.* (*gram.*) the subjective case. — *adv.* **subject'ively.** — *ns.* **subject'iveness; subjectivīsā'tion, -z-.** — *v.t.* **subject'ivise, -ize.** — *ns.* **subject'ivism** a philosophical doctrine which refers all knowledge to, and founds it upon, subjective states; **subject'ivist.** — *adj.* **subjectivist'ic.** — *adv.* **subjectivist'ically.** — *n.* **subjectiv'ity.** — *adj.* **subj'jectless.** — *n.* **subj'jectship** the state of being subject. — **sub'ject-cat'alogue** a catalogue of books arranged according to subjects dealt with; **sub'ject-heading; subj'ject-matter** the subject, theme, topic; **subj'ject-obj'ject** the immediate object of cognition, or the thought itself; **subj'ject-super'ior** a superior who is himself the subject of a sovereign. [L. *subjectus*, thrown under — *sub*, under, *jacēre*, to throw.]

subjoin *sub-join'*, *v.t.* to add at the end or afterwards. — *ns.* **subjoin'der** (*Lamb*) a remark following on another; **subjunc'tion** the act or fact of subjoining. [Pfx. **sub-**, in addition, **join.**]

sub Jove. See **sub divo.**

sub judice *sub jōo'di-sē*, *sōob ū'di-ke*, under consideration. [L.]

---

subjugate *sub'jōō-gāt, v.t.* to bring under the yoke: to bring under power or domination: to conquer. — *ns.* **subjugā'tion; sub'jugātor.** [L. *subjugāre, -ātum* — *sub, jugum,* a yoke.]

subjunctive *səb-jungk'tiv, adj.* subjoined: added to something: expressing condition, hypothesis, or contingency (*gram.*). — *n.* the subjunctive mood: a subjunctive form: a verb in the subjunctive mood. — *adv.* **subjunct'ively.** [L. *subjunctīvus* — *sub, jungĕre,* to join.]

subkingdom *sub'king-dəm, n.* a subordinate kingdom: a phylum (*biol.*). [Pfx. **sub-** (2).]

Sublapsarian *sub-lap-sā'ri-ən, n.* a believer in Sublapsarianism. — Also *adj.* — *n.* **Sublapsā'rianism** a doctrine of moderate Calvinists, that God permitted the fall of Adam without preordaining it. [L. *sub, lāpsus,* fall.]

sublate *sub-lāt', v.t.* to remove (*obs.*): to deny (*log.*): to resolve in a higher unity (*philos.*). — *n.* **sublā'tion.** [L. *sublātum,* used as supine of *tollĕre,* to take away — *sub-* in sense of away, *lātum.*]

sublease *sub'lēs, n.* an underlease or lease by a tenant to another. — *v.t.* and *v.i.* **sublease'.** — *ns.* **sublessee'** the holder of a sublease; **subless'or** one who grants a sublease. [Pfx. **sub-** (2).]

sublet *sub-let', v.t.* and *v.i.* to underlet or lease as by one himself a tenant to another: — *pa.t.* and *pa.p.* **sublet'.** — *n.* a subletting. — *ns.* **sublett'er; sublett'ing.** [Pfx. **sub-** (2).]

sublieutenant *sub-lə-ten'ənt, n.* in the navy formerly *mate,* or *passed midshipman,* an officer ranking with an army lieutenant: **(acting-)** an officer entrant to the navy since the discontinuance of midshipmen in 1957: (*-lef-*) a former rank in the army, now second lieutenant. [Pfx. **sub-** (2).]

sublime *səb-līm', adj.* set aloft (passing into *adv.*): lifted on high: exalted: lofty: majestic: elate: blindly supercilious: supreme: of the highest or noblest nature: awakening feelings of awe and veneration: just under the skin (*anat.*). — *n.* that which is sublime: the lofty or grand in thought or style: the supreme degree. — *v.t.* to raise aloft: to exalt: to transmute into something higher: to object to, or obtain by, sublimation: to deposit as a sublimate: to purify as by sublimation. — *v.i.* to undergo sublimation. — *adj.* **sublīm'able.** — *v.t.* **sublimate** (*sub'lim-āt*) to elevate: to sublime: to purify by sublimation: to transmute into something higher: to direct unconsciously the sexual impulse into some non-sexual activity: to direct into a higher channel. — *n.* a product of sublimation, esp. corrosive sublimate. — *adj.* sublimed or sublimated. — *adj.* **sub'limated.** — *n.* **sublimā'tion** the change from solid to vapour without passing through the liquid state — usu. with subsequent change back to solid: a sublimate: purification by this process: elevation: ecstasy: the acme, height: transmutation into something higher: the unconscious diversion towards higher aims of the energy attaching to an instinct (often sexual instinct). — *adj.* **sublimed** (*səb-līmd'*). — *adv.* **sublime'ly.** — *n.* **sublime'ness.** — *n.* and *adj.* **sublīm'ing.** — *v.t.* **sublimise, -ize** (*sub'lim-*) to exalt: to purify: to refine: to make sublime. — *n.* **sublimity** (*səb-lim'*) loftiness: elevation: grandeur: nobleness of nature, thought, execution: the emotion of awe and veneration: that which evokes it: the summit, height, acme. [L. *sublimis,* in a high position, exalted — *sublimāre, -ātum,* to exalt; origin unknown.]

subliminal *sub-lim'in-əl, adj.* beneath the threshold of consciousness, subconscious. — *adv.* **sublim'inally.** — **subliminal advertising** advertising in the cinema, etc., directed to the subconscious, shown too rapidly and briefly to make a conscious impression. [L. *sub, under, līmen, -inis,* threshold.]

sublinear *sub-lin'i-ər, adj.* under the line: nearly linear (*bot.*). — *n.* **sublineā'tion** underlining. [Pfx. **sub-** (1), (4).]

sublittoral *sub-lit'ə-rəl, adj.* growing, living, occurring, near but not on the shore, whether on land or at sea: of or pertaining to the zone between low-water mark and the edge of the continental shelf. — *n.* a sublittoral zone. [Pfx. **sub-** (4).]

sublunar *sub-lōōn'ər, adj.* under the moon: earthly: of this world: directly under the moon, as a point on the earth's surface where the moon is vertically overhead. — *n.* a being or thing of the earth or of this world. — Also *n.* and *adj.* **sublu'nary.** — *adj.* **sublu'nate** approaching the form of a crescent. [Pfx. **sub-** (1), (4).]

submachine-gun *sub-mə-shēn'-gun, n.* a light machine-gun, usu. one fired from the shoulder. [Pfx. **sub-** (4).]

subman *sub'man, n.* an animal not quite a man: a man of lowest type. [Pfx. **sub-** (4).]

submarginal *sub-mär'ji-nəl, adj.* near the margin: of land, that cannot be farmed profitably. [Pfx. **sub-** (4).]

submarine *sub'mə-rēn, adj.* under the sea: under the surface of the sea. — *n.* a submersible vessel, esp. for warfare: a submarine organism or dweller. — *v.t.* to attack by submarine. — *n.* **submarin'er** (or *-mar'in-*) a member of the crew of a submarine. [Pfx. **sub-** (1).]

submaxillary *sub-maks'i-lə-ri,* or *-il'ə-, adj.* of or under the lower jaw. [Pfx. **sub-** (1).]

submediant *sub-mē'di-ənt,* (*mus.*) *n.* the sixth above the tonic. [Pfx. **sub-** (1).]

submental *sub-ment'əl, adj.* below the chin: of the submentum. — *n.* **subment'um** the basal part of the lower lip in insects. [L. *sub,* under, *mentum,* chin.]

submerge *səb-mûrj', v.t.* to put under the surface of liquid: to sink: to cover over with liquid: to overwhelm: to conceal, suppress. — *v.i.* to sink under the surface of liquid. — *adj.* **submerged'** sunk: entirely under the surface of liquid: growing under water, submersed: obscured, concealed: swamped: sunk hopelessly in poverty and misery (*fig.*). — *ns.* **submerge'ment** (*rare*), **submerg'ence** submersion. — *adj.* **submerg'ible** submersible. — *n.* **submergibil'ity.** — *v.t.* **submerse** (*-mûrs'*) to submerge. — *adj.* **submersed'** (*bot.*) growing quite under water. — *n.* **submers'ibility.** — *adj.* **submers'ible** capable of being submerged at will. — *n.* a submersible boat. — *n.* **submer'sion** (*-shən*) the act of submerging: the state or fact of being submerged. [L. *submergĕre, -mersum* — *sub, mergĕre,* to plunge.]

submicron *sub-mī'kron, n.* a particle visible by ultra-microscope but not by the ordinary microscope (50–2000 angstrom units). [Pfx. **sub-** (1).]

submit *sub-mit', v.t.* to yield, resign: to subordinate: to subject: to refer for decision, consideration, sanction, arbitration, etc.: to put forward in respectful contention: to lodge: to lower, lay down (*obs.*). — *v.i.* to yield: to surrender: to be resigned: to consent: — *pr.p.* **submitt'ing;** *pa.t.* and *pa.p.* **submitt'ed.** — *adjs.* **submiss'** (*arch.*) submissive: subdued, low-toned; **submiss'ible.** — *n.* **submission** (*-mish'ən*) an act of submitting: a reference, or agreement to refer, to arbitration: a view submitted: resignedness: submissiveness: a surrender: a confession (*Shak.*). — *adj.* **submiss'ive** willing or ready to submit: yielding. — *adv.* **submiss'ively.** — *n.* **submiss'iveness.** — *adv.* **submiss'ly** (*arch.*). — *n.* **submiss'ness** (*arch.*). — *adj.* **submitt'ed.** — *n.* **submitt'er.** — *n.* and *adj.* **submitt'ing.** [L. *sub,* beneath, and *mittĕre, missum,* to send.]

submontane *sub-mon'tān, adj.* under or at the foot of a mountain range. [Pfx. **sub-** (1).]

---

sub'dean'ery *n.* sub- (2).
subdecā'nal *adj.* sub- (2).
subdīa'conal *adj.* sub- (2).
subdīa'conate *n.* sub- (2).
subdis'trict *n.* sub- (3).
subeconom'ic *adj.* sub- (1).

subē'qual *adj.* sub- (4).
subequato'rial *adj.* sub- (4).
suberect' *adj.* sub- (4).
subfer'tile *adj.* sub- (4).
subfertil'ity *n.* sub- (4).
subglā'cial *adj.* sub- (1).

subglobose' *adj.* sub- (4).
subglob'ular *adj.* sub- (4).
sub'group *n.* sub- (3).
sub-head', -head'ing *ns.* sub- (3).
subinsinuā'tion *n.* sub- (4), (5).
subinspec'tor *n.* sub- (2).

submucosa *sub-mū-kō′sə, n.* the connective tissue lying under a mucous membrane: — *pl.* **-sae** (*-sē*). — *adjs.* **submucō′sal, submū′cous.** [Pfx. **sub-** (1).]

submultiple *sub-mul′ti-pl, n.* an aliquot part. [L.L. *submultiplus.*]

subnascent *sub-nas′ənt, -nās′, adj.* growing beneath (*obs.*): growing up from beneath. [L. *subnāscēns, -entis.*]

subneural *sub-nūr′əl, adj.* beneath a main neural axis or nervous cord. [Pfx. **sub-** (1).]

subniveal *sub-niv′i-əl, adj.* under snow. — Also **subniv′ean.** [Pfx. **sub-** (1), L. *nix, nivis,* snow.]

subnormal *sub-nör′məl, adj.* less than normal, esp. medically, of a person with a low range of intelligence. — *n.* (*geom.*) the projection of the normal on the axis. — *n.* **subnormal′ity.** [Pfx. **sub-** (4), (1).]

subnuclear *sub-nū′kli-ər,* (*phys.*) *adj.* referring to particles within the nucleus of an atom. [Pfx. **sub-** (3).]

suboccipital *sub-ok-sip′it-əl, adj.* below or behind the occiput, or the occipital lobe. [Pfx. **sub-** (1).]

suboctave *sub-ok′tāv, n.* the octave below: (also **suboctave coupler**) an organ coupler that gives an octave below. [Pfx. **sub-** (1).]

suboctuple *sub-ok-tū′pl, sub-ok′tū-pl, adj.* in the ratio of one to eight. [L.L. *suboctuplus.*]

suboperculum *sub-o-pûr′kū-ləm, n.* in fishes, a bone of the gill-cover below and partly behind it. — *adj.* **suboper′cular.** [Pfx. **sub-** (1).]

suborbital *sub-ör′bi-təl, adj.* below the orbit of the eye: of less than a complete orbit. [Pfx. **sub-** (1).]

subordinary *sub-ör′di-nə-ri,* (*her.*) *n.* a less honourable armorial charge. [Pfx. **sub-** (2).]

subordinate *sub-ör′di-nāt, -nit, adj.* lower in order, rank, nature, power, etc.: dependent: under orders of another: submissive (*obs.*): lower in a series of successive divisions: underlying. — *n.* a person or thing that is subordinate or ranked lower: one who works under another. — *v.t.* to place in a lower order: to consider of less value: to subject. — *n.* **subor′dinancy** subordination. — *adv.* **subor′dinately.** — *ns.* **subor′dinateness; subordinā′tion** the arrangement in a series of successive orders: the disposition of successive recessed arches in an archway: the act of subordinating or placing in a lower order: the state of being subordinate: inferiority of rank or position: submission and obedience to authority; **subordinā′tionism** the doctrine of the inferiority of the second and third Persons of the Trinity to the first. — *adj.* **subor′dinative** tending to, or expressing, subordination. — **subordinate clause** (*gram.*) a clause which cannot function as a separate sentence in its own right, but performs an adjectival, adverbial or nominal function; **subordinating conjunction** (*gram.*) a conjunction which introduces a subordinate clause. [L.L. *subordinātus* — *sub-, ordināre,* to ordain.]

suborn *səb-örn′, v.t.* to bribe or procure to commit perjury or other unlawful or wrongful act: to prepare, provide, or achieve by stealthy means. — *ns.* **subornā′tion** (*sub-ör-*); **suborn′er** (*səb-*). [L. *sub-,* in sense of secret, *ornāre,* to equip.]

subpanation *sub-pan-ā′shən, n.* the doctrine that the body and blood of Christ are locally and materially present in the eucharist under the form of bread and wine. [L. *sub,* under, *pānis,* bread.]

subplot *sub′plot, n.* a subordinate plot, as in a play. [Pfx. **sub-** (2).]

sub poena *sub pē′nə,* under a penalty. — *n.* **subpoena** (*sub-* or *sə-pē′nə*) a writ commanding attendance in court under a penalty. — *v.t.* to serve with such a writ: — *pa.t.* and *pa.p.* **subpoe′na'd, -naed.** [L.]

subpopulation *sub-pop-ū-lā′shən, n.* a subdivision of a statistical population. [Pfx. **sub-** (3).]

subreference *sub-ref′ə-rens, n.* an incomplete or surreptitious reference: an appeal by a veiled understanding. [Pfx. **sub-** (5).]

subreption *sub-rep′shən, n.* procuring an advantage (esp., *Scots law,* a gift of escheat) by concealing the truth (distinguished from *obreption*): a false inference from such a concealment. — *adjs.* **subreptitious** (*-tish′əs*) obtained by subreption: surreptitious; **subrep′tive** surreptitious: arising out of obscure and unconscious suggestions of experience (*philos.*). [L. *subreptiō, -ōnis* — *sub-,* secretly, *rapĕre,* to snatch; cf. **surreptitious.**]

subrogate *sub′rō-gāt,* or *-rə-, v.t.* to substitute: to put in place of another, as successor to his rights (*legal*). — *n.* **subrogā′tion.** [See **surrogate.**]

sub rosa *sub rō′zə, sōōb ro′zä,* (L.) under the rose: privately.

subroutine *sub′rōō-tēn′, n.* a part of a computer program, complete in itself, which performs a specific task, e.g. calculation of a square root, and which can be called into use at any time throughout the running of the main program. [Pfx. **sub-** (2).]

subs. See **sub-.**

subsacral *sub-sāk′rəl, adj.* below (in man in front of) the sacrum. [Pfx. **sub-** (1).]

subscapular *sub-skap′ū-lər, adj.* below (in man in front of) the shoulder-blade. — *n.* a subscapular vessel or nerve. [Pfx. **sub-** (1).]

subscribe *səb-skrīb′, v.t.* to write beneath (*arch.*): to sign (*orig.* and esp. at the bottom): to set down, declare, in writing (*Shak.*): to profess to be (by signing): to declare assent to: to make a signed promise of payment for: to contribute: to give up by signing (*Shak.*). — *v.i.* (*usu.* with *to*) to sign one's name: to assent: to submit (*Shak.*): to make acknowledgment: to undertake to answer: to contribute money: to put one's name down as a purchaser or donor: to make periodical payments by arrangement. — *adjs.* **subscrīb′able; subscrībed′.** — *n.* **subscrīb′er.** — *n.* and *adj.* **subscrīb′ing.** — *adj.* and *n.* **subscript** (*sub′skript*) (a character) written beneath, esp. the iota under a Greek long vowel, in α, η, ω. — *n.* **subscrip′tion** an act of subscribing: that which is subscribed: a signature: assent: submission (*Shak.*): a raising of money from subscribers: a method of sale to subscribers: a contribution to a fund, society, etc.: a membership fee: advance ordering, esp. of a book before publication: an advance order, esp. for a book before publication. — *adj.* **subscrip′tive.** — **subscriber trunk dialling** a dialling system in which subscribers in exchanges in many countries of the world can dial each other directly: —abbrev. **S.T.D.** [L. *subscrībĕre* — *sub, scrībĕre,* to write.]

subsea *sub′sē, adj.* occurring, used, etc., under the surface of the sea. [Pfx. **sub-** (1).]

subsecive *sub′si-siv,* (*arch.*) *adj.* remaining over: spare. [L. *subsecīvus* — *sub, secāre,* to cut.]

subsellium *sub-sel′i-əm, n.* a misericord: — *pl.* **subsell′ia.** [L., a low bench — *sub, sella,* seat.]

subsensible *sub-sen′si-bl, adj.* below the range of sense. [Pfx. **sub-** (4).]

subsequence[1]. See **subsequent.**

subsequence[2] *sub′sē′kwəns, n.* one that forms part of another sequence. [Pfx. **sub-** (3).]

subsequent *sub′si-kwənt, adj.* following or coming after: of a stream, flowing approximately at right angles to the original slope of the land — distinguished from *consequent* and *obsequent.* — Also *adv.* (with *to*) after. — *n.* **sub′sequence.** — *adj.* **subsequential** (*-kwen′shl*) subsequent. — *adv.* **sub′sequently.** [L. *subsequēns,*

---

subinspec′torship *n.* sub- (2).	**submicromin′iature** *adj.* sub- (4).	**suboc′ular** *adj.* sub- (1).
sublan′ceolate *adj.* sub- (4).	**submicroscop′ic** *adj.* sub- (4).	**sub′office** *n.* sub- (2), (3).
sublē′thal *adj.* sub- (4).	**submin′iature** *adj.* sub- (4).	**subor′der** *n.* sub- (3).
sublibrā′rian *n.* sub- (2).	**submin′iaturise, -ize** *v.t.* sub- (4).	**subor′dinal** *adj.* sub- (4).
subling′ual *adj.* sub- (1).	**subnat′ural** *adj.* sub- (4).	**subō′vate** *adj.* sub- (4).
subluxā′tion *n.* sub- (4).	**subocean′ic** *adj.* sub- (1).	**subox′ide** *n.* sub- (6).

-*entis*, pr.p. of *subsequī* — *sub*, under, after, *sequī*, to follow.]

subsere *sub'sēr*, *n.* a secondary sere occurring when a sere has been interrupted. [Pfx. **sub-** (3).]

subserve *sub-sûrv'*, *v.t.* to help forward. — *v.i.* to help in a subordinate way: to be subordinate (*Milt.*). — *ns.* **subser'vience**, **subser'viency**. — *adj.* **subser'vient** subserving: serving to promote: subject: slavish: obsequious. — *n.* a subservient person or thing. — *adv.* **subser'viently**. [L. *subservīre* — *sub*, under, *servīre*, to serve.]

subset *sub'set*, (*math.*) *n.* a set contained within a larger set. [Pfx. **sub-** (3).]

subshrub *sub'shrub*, *n.* a low-growing shrub. — *adj.* **subshrubb'y**. [Pfx. **sub-** (4).]

subside *səb-sīd'*, *v.i.* to settle, sink down: to fall into a state of quiet. — *ns.* **subsidence** (*sub'si-dəns*; often *səb-sī'dəns*), rarely **sub'sidency** (or *-sī'*), the process of subsiding, settling, or sinking. [L. *subsīdĕre* — *sub*, down, *sīdĕre*, to settle.]

subsidy *sub'si-di*, *n.* assistance (*obs.*): aid in money: a special parliamentary grant of money to the king (*hist.*): a payment exacted by a king or feudal lord: a grant of public money in aid of some enterprise, industry, etc., or to keep down the price of a commodity, or from one state to another. — *adv.* **subsid'iarily**. — *adj.* **subsid'iary** furnishing a subsidy, help, or additional supplies: aiding: subordinate: relating to or depending on subsidies. — *n.* one who, or that which, aids or supplies: an assistant: a subordinate: a subsidiary company. — *v.t.* **sub'sidise, -ize** to furnish with a subsidy, grant, or regular allowance: to purchase the aid of, to buy over: to pay for as mercenaries. — **subsidiary company** one of which another company holds most of the shares; **subsidiary troops** mercenaries. [L. *subsidium*, orig. troops stationed behind in reserve, aid — *sub*, under, *sīdĕre*, to settle.]

subsist *səb-sist'*, *v.i.* to have existence (often with *in*): to remain, continue: to hold out, stand fast (*Milt.*): to inhere: to have the means of living (often with *on*). — *n.* **subsist'ence** the state of being subsistent: real being: the means of supporting life: livelihood. — *adj.* (used e.g. of allowance, wage) providing the bare necessities of living. — *adjs.* **subsist'ent** subsisting: having real being: inherent; **subsistential** (*sub-sis-ten'shl*). — **subsistence farming** farming in which the land-yield will support the farmer, but leave little or nothing to be sold; **subsistence level** the level of income which will purchase bare necessities only; **subsistence money, allowance** part of wages paid in advance for immediate needs — colloquially known as **sub:** a special allowance for exceptional circumstances; **subsistence wage** one fixed at subsistance level. [L. *subsistĕre*, to stand still — *sub*, under, *sistĕre*, to stand.]

subsizar *sub-sīz'ər*, *n.* a Cambridge undergraduate ranking below a sizar. [Pfx. **sub-** (1).]

subsoil *sub'soil*, *n.* broken-up rock underlying the soil. — *v.t.* to turn up or loosen the subsoil of. — *ns.* **sub'soiler** one who subsoils: a plough for subsoiling; **sub'soiling** ploughing the subsoil: unseen activities (*fig.*). [Pfx. **sub-** (1).]

subsolar *sub-sōl'ər*, *adj.* directly under the sun, as a point on the earth's surface where the sun is vertically overhead. [Pfx. **sub-** (1).]

subsonic *sub-son'ik*, *adj.* having, or (capable of) travelling at, a speed slower than that of sound. [Pfx. **sub-** (4).]

sub specie *sub spē'shi-ē*, *sōōb spek'i-ā*, (L.) under the appearance, or aspect (of). — **sub specie aeternitatis** (*ē-tûr-ni-tāt'is*, *ī-ter-ni-tät'is*), (seen) under the aspect of eternity: hence, as it essentially is — Spinoza.

substage *sub'stāj*, *n.* apparatus under the stage of a microscope: a division of a stage (esp. *geol.*). — Also *adj.* [Pfx. **sub-** (1), (3).]

substance *sub'stəns*, *n.* that in which qualities or attributes exist, the existence to which qualities belong: that which constitutes anything what it is: the principal part: gist: subject-matter: body: matter: kind of matter, esp. one of definite chemical nature: amount (*Shak.*): wealth, property: solidity, body: solid worth: foundation, ground: — *adj.* **substantial** (*səb-stan'shl*) of or having substance: being a substance: essential: in essentials: actually existing: real: corporeal, material: solid and ample: massy and stable: solidly based: durable: enduring: firm, stout, strong: considerable in amount: well-to-do: of sound worth. — *v.t.* **substan'tialise, -ize** to give reality to. — *ns.* **substan'tialism** the theory that there is a real existence or substratum underlying phenomena; **substan'tialist**; **substantiality** (*-shi-al'i-ti*). — *adv.* **substan'tially**. — *n.* **substan'tialness**. — *n.pl.* **substan'tials** essential parts. — *v.t.* **substan'tiate** (*-shi-āt*, *-si-āt*) to make substantial: to embody: to prove or confirm. — *n.* **substantiā'tion**. — *adj.* **substantival** (*sub-stən-tī'vl*) of, of the nature of, a substantive. — *adv.* **substantiv'ally**. — *adj.* **sub'stantive** (*-tiv*) relating to substance: expressing existence: real: of real, independent importance: substantival: (of dyes) taking effect without a mordant: definite and permanent: considerable in amount. — *n.* (*gram.*) a noun. — *adv.* **sub'stantively**. — *n.* **sub'stantiveness**. — *v.t.* **sub'stantivise, -ize** (or *-stan'*) to turn into a noun. — *n.* **substantiv'ity** substantiality: affinity for a dyestuff. — **in substance** in general: in the most important aspects. [L. *substantia*, substance, essence, property — *sub*, under, *stāre*, to stand.]

substation *sub'stā-shən*, *n.* a subordinate station, esp. a switching, transforming, or converting electrical station intermediate between the generating station and the low-tension distribution network. [Pfx. **sub-** (2).]

substellar *sub-stel'ər*, *adj.* directly under a star, as a point on the earth's surface where the star is vertically overhead. [Pfx. **sub-** (1).]

substitute *sub'sti-tūt*, *n.* a deputy: a proxy (*Shak.*): one nominated in remainder: one put in place of another: a thing used instead of another. — *v.t.* to put in place of another: to appoint as deputy: to nominate in remainder: to use instead of something else (often with *for*): to replace, be a substitute for (*erron.*). — *v.i.* (orig. *U.S.*) to act as substitute. — *n.* **substit'uent** something that may be, is, substituted, esp. an atom or group replacing another in a molecule. — Also *adj.* — *adjs.* **substitū'table**; **sub'stituted**. — *n.* **substitū'tion** (*Shak.*) delegation: the act of substituting: the condition of being a substitute: the substituting of one atom or radical for another without breaking up the molecule (*chem.*). — *adjs.* **substitū'tional**, **substitū'tionary**. — *adv.* **substitū'tionally**. — *adj.* **sub'stitutive**. — *adv.* **sub'stitutively**. — **substitution product** a substance got by substitution of so many equivalents for certain atoms or groups. [L. *substituĕre*, *-ūtum* — *sub*, under, *statuĕre*, to set.]

substract *səb-strakt'*, *v.t.* (now illiterate) to subtract. — *ns.* **substrac'tion** (now illiterate); **substrac'tor** (*Shak.*) a detractor. [L.L. *substrahĕre*, *substractum*, for L. *subtrahĕre*, after the model of **abstract**.]

substrata, substrate, etc. See **substratum**.

substratosphere *sub-strat'ō-sfēr*, *n.* the region of the atmosphere below the stratosphere and over 3½ miles above the earth. [Pfx. **sub-** (4).]

substratum *sub-strā'təm*, *-strä'*, *n.* the substance in which qualities inhere: a basis, foundation, ground: the ma-

---

terial in which a plant grows or on which an animal moves or rests: an underlying layer: — *pl.* **substra′ta.** — *adjs.* **substrā′tal, substrā′tive.** — *n.* **sub′strate** a substratum: a base: the substance on which an enzyme acts: the substances used by a plant in respiration (*bot.*). [L. *substernĕre, -strātum* — *sub, sternĕre,* to spread.]

substruct *sub-strukt′, v.t.* to build beneath, lay as a foundation. — *n.* **substruc′tion.** — *adj.* **substruc′tural.** — *n.* **sub′structure** an understructure: a foundation. [Pfx. **sub-** (1).]

substyle *sub′stīl, n.* the straight line on which the style of a dial is erected. — *adj.* **sub′stylar** (or *-stī′*). [Pfx. **sub-** (1).]

subsultive *sub-sult′iv,* **subsultory** *-ər-i, adjs.* moving by starts: twitching. — *adv.* **subsult′orily.** — *n.* **subsult′us** a convulsive movement. [L. *subsultāre,* to jump, hop — *sub,* up, *salīre,* to leap.]

subsume *sub-sūm′, v.t.* to state as minor premiss: to take in under a more general term or proposition: to include in something larger: to take over (*officialese*). — *n.* **subsumption** (*səb-sump′shən*). — *adj.* **subsump′tive.** [L. *sub,* under, *sūmĕre,* to take.]

subtack *sub′tak′, n.* an underlease in Scotland. — *n.* **sub′tacksman** a holder by subtack. [Pfx. **sub-** (2).]

subtangent *sub′tan′jənt,* (*geom.*) *n.* the projection of the tangent on the axis. [Pfx. **sub-** (1).]

subteen *sub′tēn,* (chiefly *U.S.*) *n.* and *adj.* (a child) younger than thirteen years. [Pfx. **sub-** (1).]

subtemperate *sub′tem′pər-it, -āt, adj.* slightly colder than temperate, cold-temperate. [Pfx. **sub-** (4).]

subtend *səb-tend′, v.t.* to be opposite to (*geom.*): to have in the axil (*bot.*). — *n.* **subtense′** a subtending line. — *adj.* placed so as to subtend an angle, as a rod used as base in tacheometry. [L. *sub,* under, *tendĕre, tentum* or *tēnsum,* to stretch.]

subter- *sub′tər-,* in composition, under. — *n.* **subterfuge** (*sub′tər-fūj;* L. *fugĕre,* to take flight) an evasive device, esp. in discussion: a refuge (*obs.*). — *adjs.* **subterhū′man** less than human: below man; **subterjā′cent** subjacent; **subternat′ural** below nature, less than natural. — *n.* **subterposi′tion** a position or placing underneath. — *adj.* **subtersen′suous** below the level of sense. [L. *subter,* under.]

subterranean *sub-tə-rā′ni-ən, adj.* underground: operating underground: hidden, working, etc., in secret. — *n.* a dweller underground: an underground chamber or dwelling. — *adj.* **subterrā′neous** underground. — *adv.* **subterrā′neously.** — *adj.* **subterrene′** underground. — *n.* an underground dwelling: the underworld. — *adj.* and *n.* **subterres′trial** (a person or thing) existing underground. [L. *sub,* under, *terra,* the earth.]

subtext *sub′tekst, n.* an unstated message conveyed through the form of a picture, film, book, etc. [Pfx. **sub-** (1).]

subthreshold *sub-thresh′ōld, adj.* subliminal. [Pfx. **sub-** (1).]

subtil, subtile, etc. See **subtle.**

subtitle *sub′tī-tl, n.* an additional or second title, as to a book: a half-title: a repetition of the title at the head of the text: descriptive reading matter in a cinematograph film, esp. a printed translation at the foot of the screen of dialogue that is in a language foreign to the viewers. — *v.t.* to provide with a subtitle. [Pfx. **sub-** (2).]

subtle, also (slightly *arch.,* and used chiefly in physical senses) **subtil, subtile,** (*Milt.*) **suttle,** all pronounced *sut′l, adj.* fine, delicate, thin: tenuous: rarefied: impalpable: elusive: showing or calling for fine discrimination: nice: overrefined or overrefining: abstruse: cun-

ning: ingenious: crafty: insidious: penetrating: ticklish, tricky (*Shak.*). — *n.* **subtilīsā′tion, -z-** (*sut-*). — *v.t.* **subtilise, -ize** (*sut′*) to rarefy, refine: to make subtle. — *v.i.* to refine, use subtlety. — *ns.* **subt′il(e)ness,** also **subt′il(e)ness, subtlety,** also **subtil(e)ty** (*sut′l-ti; Milt.* **suttletie**), **subtility** (*sub-til′i-ti*), the state or quality of being subtle: a subtle trick or refinement: an ornamental device in sugar (*cook., obs.*); **subt′list, -ilist** one who practises subtleties. — *adv.* **subt′ly,** also **subt′il(e)ly.** — *adj.* **subt′ile-witt′ed** (*Shak.*). [O.Fr. *soutil* and its source L. *subtīlis* — *sub,* under, *tēla,* a web.]

subtonic *sub-ton′ik,* (*mus.*) *n.* the note next below the tonic, the leading note. [Pfx. **sub-** (1).]

subtopia *sub-tō′pi-ə,* (*derog.*) *n.* a region where the city has sprawled into the country. — *adj.* **subto′pian.** [L. *sub,* under, Gr. *topos,* a place; modelled on **Utopia.**]

subtract *səb-trakt′, v.t.* to withdraw, remove: to withhold: to take from another quantity so as to find the difference (*math.*). — *n.* **subtrac′tion** withdrawal, removal: withholding, esp. in violation of a right: the operation of finding the difference between two quantities by taking one from the other (*math.*). — *adj.* **subtract′ive** indicating, tending towards, of the nature of, subtraction: negative. — *ns.* **subtract′or** a light-filter to eliminate a particular colour; **subtrahend** (*sub′trə-hend*) that which is to be subtracted. [L. *sub-,* in sense of away, *trahĕre, tractum,* to draw, gerundive *trahendus,* requiring to be drawn.]

subtriplicate *sub-trip′li-kit, -kāt, adj.* expressed by the cube root. [L.L. *subtriplus,* in the ratio of one to three.]

subtrist *sub-trist′,* (*arch.*) *adj.* somewhat sad. [L. *subtrīstis* — *sub, trīstis,* sad.]

subtrude *sub-trōōd′, v.i.* to push in stealthily. [L. *sub-,* in sense of secretly, *trūdĕre,* to thrust.]

subucula *sub-ū′kū-lə* (L. *sōōb-ōō′kōō-la*), *n.* a Roman man's undergarment or shirt: in the early English Church, a kind of cassock worn under the alb. [L. *subūcula* — *sub,* and the root of *induĕre,* to put on, *exuĕre,* to take off.]

subulate *sū′bū-lāt, adj.* awl-shaped. [L. *sūbula,* an awl.]

subumbrella *sub-um-brel′ə, n.* the under-surface of a jellyfish's umbrella. — *adj.* **subumbrell′ar.** [Pfx. **sub-** (1).]

subungual *sub-ung′gwəl, adj.* under a nail or hoof. — *n.pl.* **Subungulā′ta** animals by some included in the Ungulata though not typical hoofed animals, by others placed near the Ungulata — elephants and hyraxes. — *adj.* and *n.* **subung′ulate.** [Pfx. **sub-** (1), (4).]

suburb *sub′ərb, n.* a district adjoining a town: (in *pl.*) the outskirts of a town, esp. formerly as the prostitutes' quarters: confines, outskirts generally. — *adj.* suburban: characteristic of the suburbs. — *adj.* **suburban** (*səb-ûr′bən*) situated or living in the suburbs: typical of the suburbs: without the good qualities either of town or country: provincial, narrow in outlook. — *n.* one living in a suburb. — *n.* **suburbanisā′tion, -z-.** — *v.t.* **subur′banise, -ize** to make suburban. — *ns.* **subur′banism** the state of being suburban; **subur′banite** one who lives in the suburbs; **suburbanity** (*sub-ər-ban′i-ti*) suburban quality: suburbanism: a suburban place; **subur′bia** the suburban world. — *adj.* **suburbicā′rian** being near the city, esp. of the dioceses and churches of the cardinal bishops in the suburbs of Rome. [L. *suburbium* — *sub,* under, near, *urbs,* a city.]

subvention *səb-ven′shən, n.* a grant of money in aid. — *adj.* **subven′tionary.** [L. *subventiō, -ōnis,* a coming to help — *sub, venīre, ventum,* to come.]

subvert *səb-vûrt′, v.t.* to overthrow: to overturn: to pervert. — *n.* **subver′sal.** — *v.t.* **subverse′** (*obs.*; *pa.p.* and

---

subster′nal *adj.* **sub-** (1).	**sub′tot′al** *n., v.t.* **sub-** (3).	**subtrop′ics** *n.pl.* **sub-** (4).
sub′sur′face *adj.* **sub-** (1).	**sub′treas′urer** *n.* **sub-** (2).	**sub′type** *n.* **sub-** (3).
sub′system *n.* **sub-** (2).	**sub′treas′ury** *n.* **sub-** (2).	**subu′nit** *n.* **sub-** (3).
sub′ten′ancy *n.* **sub-** (2).	**subtriang′ular** *adj.* **sub-** (4).	**subur′sine** *adj.* **sub-** (4).
sub′ten′ant *n.* **sub-** (2).	**sub′tribe** *n.* **sub-** (3).	**subvari′ety** *n.* **sub-** (3).
subter′minal *adj.* **sub-** (4).	**subtrop′ic, -al** *adjs.* **sub-** (4).	**sub′vassal** *n.* **sub-** (2).

For other sounds see detailed chart of pronunciation.

adj. in *Spens.* **subverst'**). — *n.* **subver'sion** overthrow: ruin. — *adjs.* **subver'sionary, subver'sive** tending to overthrow. — *n.* a subversive person, esp. politically. — *n.* **subvert'er**. [L. *sub*, under, *vertĕre, versum*, to turn.]

subviral *sub-vī'rəl, adj.* referring to, caused by, a structural part of a virus. [Pfx. **sub-** (3).]

sub voce *sub vō'sē, sōob vō'ke, wō', (*L.) under that heading.

subway *sub'wā, n.* a tunnel for foot-passengers: an underground passage for water-pipes, gas-pipes, sewers, etc.: (esp. *U.S.*) an underground railway. [Pfx. **sub-** (1).]

subzero *sub-zē'rō, adj.* less than zero, esp. of temperature. [Pfx. **sub-** (1).]

succade *suk-ād', n.* fruit or vegetable candied or in syrup. [A.Fr. *sukade*, perh. — L. *succus*, juice.]

succedaneum *suk-si-dā'ni-əm, n.* a substitute: — *pl.* **-nea** (*-ni-ə*). — *adj.* **succedā'neous** (esp. *med.*) serving as a substitute. [L., neut. of *succēdāneus* — *succēdĕre*, to come after.]

succeed *sək-sēd', v.t.* to come after: to follow up or in order: to follow: to take the place of, esp. in office, title, or possession: to inherit (*Shak.*): to cause to succeed (*obs.*). — *v.i.* to follow in order: to take the place of another (often with *to*): to devolve, pass in succession (*Shak.*): to turn out (*arch.*): to turn out well: to prosper: to obtain one's wish or accomplish what is attempted: to avail, be successful (with *in*): to approach (*Spens.*). — *ns.* **succeed'er** one who is successful: a successor. — *adj.* **succeed'ing**. — *n.* **success** (*sək-ses'*) fortune (good or bad): upshot (*obs.*): prosperous progress, achievement, or termination: prosperity: attainment of wealth, influence or acclaim: a successful person, book, affair, etc.: sequence (*obs.*): succession (*obs.*). — *adv.* **success'antly** (*Shak.*) in succession. — *adj.* **success'ful** resulting in success: achieving, having achieved, or having, the desired effect or termination: prosperous. — *adv.* **success'fully** with success: with promise of success (*Shak.*). — *ns.* **success'fulness; succession** (*-sesh'ən*) a coming after or following: a coming into another's place: a sequence in time or place: law, recognised mode, right, order, or turn, of succeeding one to another: in Roman and Scots law, the taking of property by one person in place of another: rotation of crops: heirs collectively: posterity: a set of strata which represents an unbroken chronological sequence (*geol.*): in an ecological community, the sequence of changes as one set of species succeeds another. — *adj.* **success'ional**. — *adv.* **success'ionally**. — *n.* **success'ionist** a believer in the necessity of Apostolic succession. — *adjs.* **success'ionless; successive** (*sək-ses'iv; Shak. suk'*) coming in succession or in order: hereditary (*obs.*). — *adv.* **success'ively**. — *n.* **success'iveness**. — *adj.* **success'less**. — *adv.* **success'lessly**. — *ns.* **success'lessness; success'or** (*Shak. suk'*) one who, or that which, succeeds or comes after: sometimes, one appointed to succeed; **success'orship**. — **succession duty** a tax imposed on succession to property, varying with the degree of relationship; **succession house** a forcing-house in a graded series, in which plants are moved on from one to the next; **succession states** states resulting from the break-up of previously existing countries, as those established after the break-up of the Austro-Hungarian empire; **success story** (the record of) a person's rise to prosperity, fame, etc. — **in succession** following one another, one after another; **plant succession** a series of vegetation types following one another in the same region. [L. *succēdĕre, -cessum* — *sub-*, in sense of near, next after, *cēdĕre*, to go.]

succentor *sək-sent'ər, n.* a subcantor: bass soloist in a choir. [L. *succentor* — *succinĕre* — *sub*, under, *canĕre*, to sing.]

succès *sük-se,* (Fr.) *n.* success. — **succès d'estime** (*des-tēm*) a success of esteem or approval (if not of profit); **succès fou** (*foo*) success with wild enthusiasm; **succès de scandale** (*də skā-dal*) success of a book, dramatic entertainment, due not to merit but to its connection with or reference to a topical scandal.

success, etc. See **succeed**.

succi. See **succus**.

succinate. See **succinum**.

succinct *sək-, suk-singkt', adj.* girded up (*arch.* and *poet.*): close-fitting (*arch.* and *poet.*): concise. — *adv.* **succinct'ly**. — *ns.* **succinct'ness; succincto'rium, succinct'-ory** a band embroidered with an Agnus Dei, worn hanging from the girdle by the pope on some occasions. [L. *succinctus* — *sub*, up, *cingĕre*, to gird.]

succinum *suk'sin-əm, n.* amber. — *n.* **suc'cinate** a salt of succinic acid. — *adj.* **succin'ic** of, relating to, or got from, amber. — *n.* **suc'cinite** amber, esp. a variety from which succinic acid was first got. — **succinic acid** an acid, $C_4H_6O_4$, got from resins, etc. [L. *succinum*, amber.]

succor (*U.S.*). See **succour**.

succory *suk'ər-i, n.* a variant of **chicory**.

succose. See **succus**.

succotash *suk'ō-tash, n.* a stew of green Indian corn and beans and sometimes pork. [Narragansett *msiquatash*.]

Succoth. See **Sukkoth**.

succour, U.S. succor, *suk'ər, v.t.* to aid in distress: to relieve. — *n.* aid: relief. — *adj.* **succ'ourable**. — *n.* **succ'ourer**. — *adj.* **succ'ourless**. [A.Fr. *socorre* — L. *succurrĕre*, to run to help — *sub*, up, *currĕre*, to run.]

succous. See **succus**.

succubus *suk'ū-bəs,* **succuba** *-bə, ns.* a devil supposed to assume a female body and consort with men in their sleep: a strumpet: — *pl.* **succ'ubuses, succ'ubas, succ'ubī, succ'ubae** (*-bē*). — *adjs.* **succ'ubine** of a succuba; **succ'ubous** (*bot.*) having the lower leaf-margin overlapping the leaf below. [L. *succuba*, a whore — *sub*, under, *cubāre*, to lie.]

succulent *suk'ū-lənt, adj.* juicy: sappy: juicy and fleshy, or (loosely) merely fleshy (*bot.*). — *n.* a succulent plant. — *ns.* **succ'ulence, succ'ulency**. — *adv.* **succ'ulently**. — **succ'ulent-house** a house for succulent plants. [L. *sūculentus* — *sūcus*, juice.]

succumb *sə-kum', v.i.* to lie down under or sink under pressure, difficulty, temptation, etc. (often with *to*): to die. [L. *sub*, under, *cumbĕre*, to lie down.]

succursal *suk-ûr'səl, adj.* subsidiary (usu. *ecclesiastical*): branch. — *n.* a branch of an institution (often as Fr. fem. **succursale** *sü-kür-sal*). [Fr., — L. *succurrĕre*, to succour.]

succus *suk'əs, n.* juice: fluid secretion of a gland: expressed juice: — *pl.* **succi** (*suk'sī*). — *adjs.* **succ'ose, succ'ous**. [L. *sūcus, succus*, juice.]

succuss *suk-us', v.t.* to shake up. — *ns.* **succussā'tion** a shaking up: a horse's trot (*obs.*); **succussion** (*-ush'ən*) a shaking: a shock: a shaking of the thorax to detect pleural effusion. — *adj.* **succuss'ive**. [L. *succutĕre, succussum*, to toss up — *sub, quatĕre*, to shake.]

such *such, adj.* of that kind, the like kind, or the same kind (often followed by *as* or by a clause beginning with *that*): so characterised: of what kind: what (exclamatorily): so great: before-mentioned: some particular but unspecified. — *adv.* so (preceding the indefinite article if any). — *pron.* such a person, persons, thing, or things: the before-mentioned: that. — *adj.* **such'like** of such a kind. — *pron.* suchlike persons or things (or person or thing). — *n.* **such'ness** (*arch.*) quality. — *adv.* **such'wise** in such a manner. — *adj.* **such'-and-such** this or that, some, some or other (before the indefinite article if any). — *pron.* such-and-such a person. — **as such** as it is described: in a particular capacity; **such as** for example; **such as it is** being what

subver'tebral *adj.* **sub-** (1).
subver'tical *adj.* **sub-** (4).

subvit'reous *adj.* **sub-** (4).
sub'war'den *n.* **sub-** (2).

subzōn'al *adj.* **sub-** (1).
sub'zone *n.* **sub-** (3).

fāte; fär; hûr; mīne; mōte; fōr; mūte; mōōn; fōōt; dhen (then); *el'ə-mənt* (element)

it is (and no better); **such that** in such a way, to such an extent, etc., that. [O.E. *swilc*; cog. with Goth. *swaleiks*; cf. **so**[1], **like**[1].]

suck *suk*, *v.t.* to draw in with the mouth: to draw something (esp. milk) from with the mouth: to apply to or hold in the mouth and perform the movements of sucking: to draw by suction: to render by suction: to absorb: to draw in: to extract: to imbibe: to drain. — *v.i.* to draw with the mouth: to draw the breast: to draw by suction: to make a noise of sucking: to draw in air as a dry pump: to draw in. — *n.* act or spell of sucking: milk drawn from the breast: suction: a short drink, esp. a dram of spirits (*slang*). — *adj.* **sucked**. — *n.* **suck′er** one who, or that which, sucks: a sucking-pig, new-born whale, or other unweaned animal: a sucking-fish: an American fish akin to the carps, that feeds by sucking up small animals from the bottom: an adhesive organ: a device that adheres, draws water, etc., by suction, as a pump piston: a toy consisting of a leather disc and a string, for lifting stones, etc.: a haustorium or other sucking organ: a sweet for sucking (*local*): a shoot rising from underground and developing into a new plant: a new shoot: a parasite, toady, sponge: a hard drinker: a gullible person, one taken advantage of (*coll.*): a native of Illinois (*U.S. coll.*). — *v.t.* to strip off superfluous shoots from: to dupe, make a sucker of. — *v.i.* to develop suckers. — *adj.* **suck′ered** having suckers. — *n.* and *adj.* **suck′ing**. — **suck-in′** (*slang*) a disconcerting disappointment; **suck′ing-bottle** a milk bottle for infants; **suck′ing-fish** remora or other fish with an adhesive disc, e.g. a lumpsucker; **sucking louse** a bloodsucking wingless insect of the order Anoplura; **suck′ing-pig** a young milk-fed pig. — **be a sucker for** (*coll.*) to be unable to resist; **suck in** to engulf; **suck off** (*slang*) to perform fellatio or cunnilingus on; **sucks (to you)!** a derisive expression; **suck up to** (*slang*) to toady to. [O.E. *sūcan*, *sūgan*; Ger. *saugen*; cf. L. *sūgĕre*.]

sucken *suk′n*, (*Scots law*) *n.* the district or population thirled to a mill: thirlage: an area of jurisdiction or field of operation. — *n.* **suck′ener** a tenant so bound. [**soken** (see **soc**).]

sucket *suk′it*, an obs. form of **succade**. — **sucket spoon, fork** an old table implement, spoon at one end, fork at the other.

suckle *suk′l*, *v.t.* to give suck to, as a mammal feeding its young: to put out to suck. — *n.* **suck′ler** an animal that suckles: a suckling. — *n.pl.* **suck′lers** heads of clover. — *n.* **suck′ling** an unweaned child or animal: the act of giving suck: clover, also honeysuckle (*dial.*). — *adj.* giving suck: putting to suck: sucking. [**suck**.]

sucre *sōō′krā*, *n.* the monetary unit of Ecuador. [Named after Antonio José de Sucre (1795-1830).]

sucrose *sōō′*, *sū′krōs*, *n.* cane-sugar ($C_{12}H_{22}O_{11}$) from any source. — *ns.* **su′crase** same as **invertase**; **sucrier** (*sü-kri-ā′*; Fr.) a table vessel for sugar, usu. of porcelain, etc. [Fr. *sucre*, sugar.]

suction *suk′shən*, *n.* the act or power of sucking or of drawing or adhesion by reducing pressure of air. — *n.pl.* **Suctoria** (*suk-tō′ri-ə*, *tō′*) a subclass of Ciliata. — *adj.* **sucto′rial** adapted for sucking. — *n.* and *adj.* **sucto′rian** (a member) of the Suctoria. — **suction pump** a pump for raising fluids by suction; **suction(al) stop** a stop consonant in which the contact of the articulating organs is followed by an inrush of air (*phon.*). [L. *sūgĕre*, *suctum*; related to **suck**.]

sucurujú *sōō-kōō-rōō-zhōō′*, *n.* a S. American Indian name for the anaconda.

sud. See suds.

sudamina *sōō-*, *sū-dam′i-nə*, *n.pl.* whitish vesicles due to retention of sweat in the sweat-glands: — *sing.* **sudamen** (*-dā′mən*). — *adj.* **sudam′inal**. [L. *sūdāmen*, pl. *sūdāmina* — *sūdāre*, to sweat.]

Sudan *sōō-dan′*, *n.* a region of Africa, south of the Sahara and Libyan deserts. — *n.* **Sudanese** (*-ēz′* or *sōō′*) a native or inhabitant of the Sudan: — *pl.* **Sudanese**. — *adj.* of or pertaining to the Sudan or its inhabitants. — *n.* **Sudan′ic** a group of languages spoken in the Sudan. — *adj.* of or relating to these languages: (also without *cap.*) of or relating to the Sudan. — **Sudan grass** a Sorghum, *Sorghum vulgare sudanensis*, grown for hay and fodder. — Also **Soudan(ese)**.

sudate *sū′dāt*, *sōō′*, (*rare*) *v.i.* to sweat. — *ns.* **sudā′rium**, **su′dary** (*-də-ri*) a cloth for wiping sweat, esp. the veil or handkerchief of St. Veronica, believed to have retained miraculously the image of Christ's face: a handkerchief: a veronica; **sudā′tion** sweating: sweat: a watery exudation from plants; **sudatorium** (*-də-tō′ri-əm*, *-tō′*) a hot room in a bathhouse which induces sweating; **su′datory** (*-tə-ri*) a sudatorium: a drug which induces sweating. — *adj.* of sweat: inducing sweating. [L. *sūdāre*, *-ātum*, to sweat.]

sudd *sud*, *n.* a mass of floating vegetable matter obstructing the White Nile: a temporary dam. [Ar. *sudd*, obstruction.]

sudden *sud′n*, *adj.* without warning or apparent preparation: unexpected: hasty: abrupt: prompt: swift in action or production: glancing quickly: improvised. — *adv.* suddenly. — *adv.* **sudd′enly**. — *ns.* **sudd′enness**, (*Scot.*) **sudd′enty**. — **sudden death** (*sport*) an extended period to settle a tied contest, play terminating the moment one of the contestants scores. — **(all) of a sudden**, *arch.* **on a** (or **the**) **sudden** all at once; **sudden infant death syndrome** see **cot death**. [A.Fr. *sodain* — L. *subitāneus*, sudden — *subitus*, coming stealthily — *subīre*, *-itum*, to go stealthily — *sub*, *īre*.]

sudder *sud′ər*, (in India) *adj.* chief. — *n.* a supreme court. [Ar. *çadr*, chief.]

sudor *sū′dör*, *sōō′*, *-ər*, (*med.*) *n.* sweat. — *adjs.* **su′doral**; **sudorif′erous** provoking or secreting sweat; **sudorif′ic** causing sweat. — *n.* a diaphoretic. — *adjs.* **sudorip′arous** secreting sweat; **su′dorous** sweaty. [L. *sūdor*, *-ōris*, sweat.]

Sudra *sōō′dra*, *n.* a member of the fourth and lowest of the Hindu castes. [Sans. *śūdra*.]

suds *sudz*, *n.pl.* froth of soapy water (rarely in *sing.* **sud**). — *n.* **sud′ser** (*slang*) a soap opera. — *adj.* **sud′sy**. [Prob. conn. with **seethe**.]

sue *sū*, *sōō*, (*Spens.* **sew**) *v.t.* to follow: to prosecute at law: to petition for, apply for: to court (*arch.*). — *v.i.* to make legal claim: to make application: to entreat: to be a wooer (*Shak.*): to do service (*Spens.*): — *pr.p.* **su′ing**; *pa.t.* and *pa.p.* **sued**. — *n.* **sueabil′ity** see **suability**. — *adj.* **sue′able** see **suable**. — *n.* **su′er**. — *n.* and *adj.* **su′ing**. — **sue out** to petition for and take out. [O.Fr. *suir* (Fr. *suivre*) — L. *sequī*, *secūtus*, to follow.]

suede, suède *swād* (Fr. *süed*), *n.* undressed kid: its colour. — Also *adj.* — *v.t.* to give a suede finish to (leather or cloth). — *n.* **suedette′** a fabric made to resemble suede. [Fr. (*gants de*) *Suède*, (gloves of) Sweden.]

suet *sū′it*, *sōō′*, *n.* a solid fatty tissue, accumulating about the kidneys and omentum of the ox, sheep, etc. — *adj.* **su′ety** (also **su′etty**). — **suet pudding** a boiled pudding, savoury or sweet, made with suet. [O.Fr. *seu* (Fr. *suif*) — L. *sēbum*, fat.]

suffer *suf′ər*, *v.t.* to undergo: to endure: to be affected by: to permit (*arch.*): to inflict pain on (*Shak.*). — *v.i.* to feel pain or punishment: to sustain loss: to be injured: to die: to be executed or martyred: to be the object of an action. — *adj.* **suff′erable**. — *n.* **suff′erableness**. — *adv.* **suff′erably**. — *ns.* **suff′erance** suffering: endurance: forbearance: tacit assent: permission: toleration; **suff′erer**. — *n.* and *adj.* **suff′ering**. — **on sufferance** tolerated, but not encouraged. [L. *sufferre* — *sub*, under, *ferre*, to bear.]

suffete *suf′ēt*, *n.* one of the chief administrative officials of ancient Carthage. [L. *sūfes*, *-etis*, from a Punic word.]

suffice *sə-fīs′*, *v.i.* to be enough: to be competent or adequate. — *v.t.* to satisfy. — *ns.* **suffic′er**; **sufficiency** (*sə-fish′əns*; *rare*), **sufficiency** state of being sufficient: competence: ability (*arch.*): capacity (*arch.*): a sufficient quantity: means enough for a comfortable living, a competency: conceit. — *adj.* **suffic′ient** sufficing: competent (*arch.*): adequate: effective: well-to-do: (not

a satisfactory word for *enough* in quantity). — *n.* (*coll.*) a sufficient quantity, enough. — *adv.* **suffic′iently.** — *adj.* **suffic′ing.** — *ns.* **suffic′ingness; suffisance** (*suf′i-zəns; obs.*) sufficiency: satisfaction: enjoyment. — **suffice it** be it enough. [Through Fr. — L. *sufficĕre*, to suffice — *sub, facĕre*, to make.]
suffigance *suf′i-gans*, (Shak., *Much Ado*) *n.* Dogberry's blunder for **suffisance.**
suffisance. See **suffice.**
suffix *suf′iks, n.* an affix attatched to the end of a root, stem or word: an index placed after and below a symbol, as *n* in x_n (*math.*). — *v.t.* **suffix′** (also *suf′iks*) to add as a suffix: to subjoin. — *adj.* **suff′ixal.** — *n.* **suffixā′tion.** [L. *suffixus — sub*, under, *figĕre*, to fix.]
sufflate *sə-flāt*, (*obs.*) *v.t.* and *v.i.* to inflate. — *n.* **sufflā′tion.** [L. *sufflare.*]
suffocate *suf′ə-kāt, v.t.* and *v.i.* to choke by stopping of the breath: to stifle (also *fig.*). — *adj.* (*Shak.*) suffocated. — *n.* and *adj.* **suff′ocāting.** — *adv.* **suff′ocātingly.** — *n.* **suffocā′tion.** — *adj.* **suff′ocātive** tending to suffocate. [L. *suffōcare — sub*, under, *faucēs*, the throat.]
Suffolk *suf′ək, n.* an English breed of black-faced sheep without horns: a sheep of this breed. — **Suffolk punch** see **punch**[1].
suffragan *suf′rə-gən, n.* an assistant, a coadjutor-bishop: any bishop in relation to his metropolitan. — Also *adj.* — *n.* **suff′raganship.** [L.L. *suffrāgāneus*, assistant, supporting. — L. *suffrāgium*, a vote.]
suffrage *suf′rij, n.* a prayer, esp. for the dead, or in a litany: a vote: a voting paper, pebble, or the like: sanction: supporting opinion: power of voting. — *ns.* **suffragette** (*suf′rə-jet′*; an improperly formed word) a woman seeking by violent methods (or sometimes otherwise) to obtain votes for women; **suff′ragist** a believer in the right (e.g. of women) to vote; **suff′-ragism.** [L. *suffrāgium*, a vote.]
suffruticose *sə-frŏŏt′i-kōs, adj.* herbaceous with a woody persistent stem-base. [L. *sub*, under, *frutex, -icis*, a shrub.]
suffumigate *sə-fū′mi-gāt, v.t.* to fumigate from below. — *n.* **suffumigā′tion.** [L. *sub, fūmigāre.*]
suffuse *sə-fūz′, v.t.* to pour over: to overspread or cover, as with a liquid, a tint. — *adj.* (*sə-fūs′; bot.*) spread out on the substratum. — *n.* **suffū′sion** (*-zhən*). [L. *sub*, underneath, *fundĕre, fūsum*, to pour.]
Sufi *sŏŏ′fē, n.* a pantheistic Muslim mystic: — *pl.* **Su′fis.** — *n.* **Su′f(i)ism.** — *adjs.* **Su′fic, Suf(i)ist′ic.** — Also **Sofi, Sofism.** [Ar. *çūfī*, prob. man of wool — *çuf*, wool.]
sugar *shŏŏg′ər, n.* a sweet substance (*sucrose, cane-sugar*, $C_{12}H_{22}O_{11}$), obtained chiefly from cane and beet: extended to any member of the same class of carbohydrates: a measure (e.g. a lump, teaspoonful) of sugar: money (*slang*): a term of endearment (*coll.*): flattery (*slang*): heroin, or LSD (*slang*). — *adj.* (*Shak.*) sweet: of sugar. — *v.t.* to sprinkle, coat, or mix with sugar. — *adj.* **sug′ared** sweetened or coated with sugar: sugary. — *ns.* **sug′ariness; sug′aring** sweetening with sugar: coating trees with sugar as a method of collecting insects: formation of sugar from maple sap (*sugaring off; U.S.*). — *adjs.* **sug′arless; sug′ary** like sugar in taste or appearance: abounding in sugar: offensively or cloyingly sweet. — **sug′ar-ally** (*-al′i; Scot.*) liquorice; **sug′ar-apple** the sweet-sop; **sug′ar-baker** (*obs.*) a sugar-refiner: also a confectioner; **sugar basin, bowl** a small basin for holding sugar at table; **sug′ar-bean** the Lima bean; **sug′ar-beet** any variety of common beet, esp. variety *Rapa*, grown for sugar; **sugar bird** a S. African bird, *Promerops cafer*, that sucks nectar from flowers; **sug′ar-can′dy** sugar in large crystals; **sug′ar-cane** a woody grass (*Saccharum officinarum*) from which sugar is chiefly obtained. — *adj.* **sug′ar-coat′ed** coated with sugar. — **sug′ar-cube, -lump** a small square block of sugar; **sug′ar-daddy** an elderly man lavishing money on a young woman or young women; **sugar diabetes** diabetes mellitus; **sugar glider** a type of possum with

wing-like flaps of skin enabling it to make long gliding jumps between trees; **sug′ar-grass** sweet sorghum; **sug′-ar-gum** a eucalyptus with sweetish foliage; **sug′ar-house** a sugar factory; **sug′ar-loaf** a loaf or mass of sugar, usu. more or less conical: a hill, hat, or other object of like form; **sug′ar-ma′ple** a N. American maple (*Acer saccharum* or kindred species) from whose sap sugar is made; **sug′ar-mill** a machine for pressing out the juice of the sugar-cane; **sug′ar-mite** a mite infesting unrefined sugar; **sug′ar-palm** a (N. of many kinds) yielding sugar; **sugar pea** see **mangetout; sug′ar-pine** a Western American pine (*Pinus lambertiana*) with sugary heartwood; **sug′ar-plum** a small round boiled sweet: a compliment or other gratification (*fig.*); **sug′ar-refi′ner; sug′ar-refi′nery; sug′ar-refi′ning; sugar sifter** a container for sugar with a perforated top, enabling the sugar to be sprinkled; **sugar soap** an alkaline cleansing or stripping preparation for paint surfaces; **sugar tongs** small tongs for lifting lumps of sugar at table; **sug′ar-wrack** a kind of tangle (*Laminaria saccharina*) from which mannite is got. — **heavy sugar** (*slang*) big money; **sugar of lead** lead acetate, sweet and poisonous, used as a mordant for dyeing and printing textiles, and as a drier for paints and varnishes; **sugar the pill** to compensate somewhat for an unpleasant prospect, unwelcome imposition, etc. [O.Fr. (Fr.) *sucre* — Ar. *sukkar*; the *g* unexplained; cf. **Saccharum.**]
suggest *sə-jest′*, old-fashioned *sug-*, *v.t.* to introduce indirectly to the thoughts: to call up in the mind: to put forward, as a plan, hypothesis, thought, etc.: to give an impression of: to tempt (*Shak.*): to insinuate (*Shak.*): to influence hypnotically. — *v.i.* to make suggestions. — *ns.* **suggest′er; suggestibil′ity.** — *adj.* **suggest′ible** capable of being suggested, or of being influenced by suggestion, esp. hypnotic. — *ns.* **suggest′ion** (*-yən*) process or act of suggesting: hint: proposal: indecent proposal: incitement, temptation: information without oath, not being pleadable (*law*): a false or underhand representation (*obs.*): communication of belief or impulse to a hypnotised person; **suggestionīsā′tion, -z-.** — *v.t.* **suggest′ionise, -ize** to subject to suggestion. — *ns.* **suggest′ionism** treatment by suggestion: the theory that hypnotic effects are entirely due to the action of suggestion; **suggest′ionist.** — *adj.* **suggest′ive** containing a hint: fitted to suggest: awaking the mind: stimulating: pertaining to hypnotic suggestion: tending to awake indecent imaginations (*coll. euphemism*). — *adv.* **suggest′ively.** — *n.* **suggest′iveness.** [L. *suggerĕre, -gestum, sub*, under, *gerĕre*, to carry.]
sui *sōō′ī, sōō′ē, sōō′ē*, (L.) of himself, herself, itself. — **sui generis** (*jen′ər-is, ge′ne-ris*) of its own kind, the only one of its kind. — **sui juris** (*jōōr′is, ūr′*) having full legal capacity to act: (in Roman law) having the rights of a freeman.
suicide *sū′i-sīd, sōō′, n.* one who kills himself intentionally: self-murder: a self-inflicted disaster. — *adj.* **suicī′-dal.** — *adv.* **suicī′dally.** — **suicide pact** an agreement between people to kill themselves together. — **commit suicide** to kill oneself. [L. *suī*, of himself, *caedĕre*, to kill.]
Suidae *sū′i-dē, sōō′, n.pl.* the pig family. — *adjs.* **suid′ian, su′illine.** [L. *sūs, suis*, pig, adj. *suillus, -a, -um.*]
suint *sōō′int, swint, n.* dried perspiration in wool. [Fr.]
suit *sūt, sōōt, n.* pursuit (*Spens.*): process or act of suing: an action at law: courtship: a petition: a series: a suite (*obs.*): a sequence: a set: a set of cards of the same denomination, in the pack or in one hand: a number of things of the same kind or made to be used together, as clothes or armour. — *v.t.* to attire (*obs.*): to provide, furnish: to fall in with the requirements of: to fit: to become, look attractive on: to please. — *v.i.* to agree: to correspond. — *n.* **suitabil′ity.** — *adj.* **suit′able** that suits: fitting: accordant: adequate. — *n.* **suit′ableness.** — *adv.* **suit′ably.** — *adj.* **suit′ed** (*Shak.*) dressed, clothed. — *ns.* **suit′ing** (sometimes in *pl.*) cloth suitable for making suits; **suit′or** one who sues: a petitioner: a

wooer: —*fem.* **suit′ress.** — *v.i.* (*arch.*) to play the suitor. — **suit′-case** an easily portable oblong travelling-bag for carrying suits or clothes. — **follow suit** to play a card of the suit led: to do the same; **strong suit** one's forte; **suit yourself** do what you like. [Fr. *suite*; cf. **sue, suite.**]

suite *swēt, n.* a train of followers or attendants: a set, as of furniture or rooms: a sequence of instrumental movements, usu. dance-tunes, in related keys: a sequel. [Fr., — a L.L. form of L. *secūta,* fem. pa.p. of *sequī,* to follow.]

suitor, suitress. See **suit.**

suivez *swē-vā,* (Fr.) follow (the solo part, in accompanying).

suk(h). See **souk.**

sukiyaki *s(o͞o-)kē-(y)ä′kē, n.* thinly-sliced beef, vegetables, soya sauce, etc., cooked quickly together, often at table. [Jap.]

Sukkoth *suk′ɔth, suk′ɔt, so͞o′kɔs,* **Sukkot** *suk′ɔt, ns.* the Jewish Feast of Tabernacles. — Also **Succoth.** [Heb., huts, tents.]

sulcus *sul′kɔs, n.* a groove, furrow, fissure: a fissure between two convolutions of the brain: — *pl.* **sul′ci** (-*sī*). — *adj.* **sul′cal** (-*kl*) of a sulcus: grooved: furrowed: pronounced with sulcal tongue. — *v.t.* **sul′calise, -ize** to furrow. — *adjs.* **sul′cate, -d** furrowed, grooved: with parallel longitudinal furrows. — *n.* **sulcā′tion.** [L. *sulcus,* a furrow.]

sulfa, sulfate, sulfur, etc. U.S. spellings of **sulpha, sulphate, sulphur,** etc.; adopted by International Union of Pure and Applied Chemistry.

sulk *sulk, v.i.* to be sullen. — *n.* one who sulks: (usu. in *pl.*) a fit of sulking. — *adv.* **sulk′ily.** — *n.* **sulk′iness.** — *adj.* **sulk′y** sullen: inclined to sulk. — *n.* a light two-wheeled, sometimes bodiless, vehicle for one person. [Prob. from the root seen in O.E. *āseolcan,* to slack, be slow, pa.p. *āsolcen.*]

sullage *sul′ij, n.* filth: refuse, sewage: scum: scoria: silt. [Perh. conn. with **sully.**]

sullen *sul′ən, adj.* gloomily angry and silent: malignant, baleful: dark: dull. — *adv.* **sullenly.** — *n.* (usu. in *pl.*) a fit of sullenness, the sulks. — *adv.* **sull′enly.** — *n.* **sull′enness.** [App. through O.Fr. deriv. from L. *sōlus,* alone.]

sully *sul′i, v.t.* to soil: to spot: to tarnish. — *v.i.* to be soiled: — *pr.p.* **sull′ying;** *pa.t.* and *pa.p.* **sull′ied.** — *n.* spot: tarnish. [O.E. *sylian,* to defile — *sol,* mud; or from O.Fr. *souiller,* to soil.]

sulphur *sul′fər,* **sulfur** (q.v.) *n.* brimstone, a yellow non-metallic element (S; at. numb. 16) and mineral, very brittle, fusible, and inflammable: an impression from a plate spread with molten sulphur: the colour of sulphur, a bright yellow. — *adj.* of sulphur. — *v.t.* to treat or fumigate with sulphur. — *adj.* **sul′pha** of a class of synthetic antibacterial drugs, the sulphonamides. — *ns.* **sulphadī′azine** a sulphonamide used against pneumonia, etc.; **sulphaguan′idine** a sulphonamide used against dysentery, etc.; **sulphanil′-amide** a sulphonamide ($C_6H_8N_2O_2S$) used against bacteria; **sulphapy′ridine** one of the sulphonamides known as M & B formerly much used in the treatment of pneumonia, meningitis, etc.; **sul′phatase** any of a set of enzymes found in animal tissue that help to break down sulphuric acid esters; **sul′phate** a salt of sulphuric acid. — *v.t.* to form a deposit of lead sulphate on: to treat or impregnate with sulphur or a sulphate. — *v.i.* to become sulphated. — *n.* **sulphathī′azole** a sulphonamide used against staphylococci. — *adj.* **sulphatic** (-*at′ik*). — *ns.* **sulphā′tion; sul′phide** a compound of an element or radical with sulphur: a salt of hydrosulphuric acid; **sul′phite** a salt of sulphurous acid. — *pfx.* **sul′pho-** sulphur: obs. for **thio-.** — *n.* **sulphon′amide** an amide of a sulphonic acid, any of a group of drugs with antibacterial action. — *v.t.* **sul′-phonate** to treat (esp. an aliphatic or aromatic compound) with sulphuric acid and so convert it into a sulphonic acid or other substance. — *n.* a substance

so formed. — *ns.* **sulphonā′tion; sul′phone** any of a class of substances consisting of two organic radicals combined with SO_2. — *adj.* **sulphon′ic** containing the group $SO_2·OH.$ — *v.t.* **sul′phūrāte** to combine with, or subject to the action of, sulphur. — *ns.* **sulphūrā′tion; sulphūrā′tor.** — *adj.* **sulphū′reous** sulphury: sulphur-yellow. — *adv.* **sulphū′reously.** — *ns.* **sulphū′reousness; sul′phūret** (*obs.*) a sulphide. — *adjs.* **sul′phūretted** combined with sulphur; **sulphū′ric** containing sulphur in higher valency — opp. to *sulphurous.* — *v.t.* **sul′phurise, -ize** to sulphurate. — *adjs.* **sul′phurous** (-*fūr-*, or -*fər-*) pertaining to, resembling, or containing sulphur: hellish: thundery: heated (of language, behaviour, etc.): containing sulphur in lower valency (*chem.*; -*fūr′*); **sulphury** (*sul′fər-i*) like sulphur. — **sulphite pulp** in paper-making, wood chips treated with calcium or magnesium acid sulphite; **sul′phur-bacte′ria** bacteria that liberate sulphur from sulphuretted hydrogen, etc., and ultimately form sulphuric acid; **sul′phur-bottom** the blue whale (from the yellowish spots underneath); **sulphur dioxide** SO_2, a suffocating gas discharged into the atmosphere in waste from industrial processes, used in manufacture of sulphuric acid, and in bleaching, preserving, etc.; **sulphuretted hydrogen** (*arch.*) hydrogen sulphide; **sulphuric acid** oil of vitriol, H_2SO_4; **sulphurous acid** H_2SO_3; **sul′phur-root, sul′phurwort** an umbelliferous plant (*Peucedanum,* various species) akin to parsnip, with yellow flower and juice; **sulphur trioxide** SO_3, the anhydride of sulphuric acid; **sulphur tuft** a poisonous toadstool, *Hypholoma fasciculare,* having a yellowish cap. — *n.* and *adj.* **sul′phur-yell′ow** pale yellow. — **fuming sulphuric acid** see **oleum.** [L. *sulphur, sulfur, sulpur, -uris.*]

sultan *sul′tən, n.* a Muslim ruler, esp. the Ottoman emperor: the purple coot: a small white (orig. Turkish) variety of hen. — *ns.* **sultana** (*sul-* or *səl-tä′nə*) a lady of a sultan's harem: a king's mistress: a magnificent courtesan: a concubine: a fiddle strung with wires in pairs: a small, pale, seedless raisin; **sul′tanate; sul′-taness.** — *adj.* **sultanic** (*sul-tan′ik*). — *n.* **sul′tanship.** — **sweet sultan, yellow sultan** species of *Centaurea.* [Ar. *sultān.*]

sultry *sul′tri, adj.* sweltering: close and oppressive: hot with anger: passionate, voluptuous: (of language) lurid, verging on the indecent. — *adv.* **sul′trily.** — *n.* **sul′triness.** [**swelter.**]

Sulu *so͞o′lo͞o, n.* a member of a Muslim people of the *Sulu* Archipelago in the S.W. Philippines: their Malayan language. — Also *adj.*

sum *sum, n.* total: whole: aggregate: result of addition: amount: a quantity of money: a problem in addition, hence in arithmetic generally: chief points: substance or result: summary: height, culmination, completion. — *v.t.* (often with *up*) to add: to make up the total of: to be an epitome of, exemplify in little: to summarise: to reckon up, form an estimate of: to complete the development of, bring to perfection (*Milt.*). — *v.i.* to amount, turn out on adding: to do sums: — *pr.p.* **summ′ing;** *pa.t.* and *pa.p.* **summed.** — *ns.* **sum′mand** (or -*and′*) an addend: part of a sum; **summation** see **summa.** — *adjs.* **sum′less** not to be summed or counted: incalculable; **summed.** — *n.* **summ′er** one who sums. — *n.* and *adj.* **summ′ing.** — **summ′ing-up′** a recapitulation or review of the leading points, a judge's summary survey of the evidence given to a jury before it withdraws to consider its verdict; **sum total** complete or final sum. — **in sum** in short: to sum up; **sum and substance** the gist: the essence; **sum of things** the public weal: the universe. [O.Fr. *summe* — L. *summa* — *summus,* highest.]

sumac, sumach *so͞o′, sho͞o′, sū′mak, n.* any tree or shrub of the genus Rhus, esp. *R. coriaria:* the leaves and shoots used in dyeing. [Fr. *sumac* or L.L. *sumach* — Ar. *summāq.*]

sumatra *so͞o-mä′trə, n.* a short, violent squall about the Straits of Malacca, coming from *Sumatra.*

Sumerian *so͞o-mēr′i-ən, adj.* of or relating to the ancient civilisation, people, language, etc. of the region of *Sumer* in southern Babylonia. — *n.* a native of Sumer: the language.

summa *sum'ə, n.* a treatise giving a summary of a whole subject: — *pl.* **summ'ae** (*-ē*). — *adj.* **summar** (*sum'ər; Scot.*) summary (**Summar Roll** a list of cases requiring dispatch). — *adv.* **summ'arily.** — *n.* **summ'ariness.** — *v.t.* **summ'arise, -ize** to present in a summary or briefly. — *ns.* **summ'arist** one who summarises. — *adj.* **summ'ary** summed up or condensed: short: brief: compendious: done by a short method: without unnecessary formalities or delay, without further application to the court. — *n.* an abstract, abridgment, or compendium. — *v.t.* **summate'** to add together. — *n.* **summā'tion** process of finding the sum: addition: accumulation: an aggregate: a summing-up, summary. — *adjs.* **summā'tional; summ'ative** additive. — *n.* **summ'ist** a writer of a summa: an epitomist. — **summary offence** (*legal*) one which is tried by a magistrate. [L. *summa*, sum, *summārium* a summary.]

summa cum laude *sum'ə kum lö'dē, sŏŏm'ä kŏŏm low'de,* (L.) with greatest distinction (*laus, laudis,* praise).

summand. See **sum.**

summar. . . summarise, etc. See **summa.**

summat *sum'ət,* a dial. form of **something, somewhat.**

summation, etc. See **summa.**

summer[1] *sum'ər, n.* the warmest season of the year: a spell of warm weather (see **Indian, St Luke's, St Martin's summer**): a year of age or time. — *adj.* of, for, occurring in, summer. — *v.i.* to pass the summer. — *v.t.* to keep through the summer. — *n.* **summ'ering.** — *adjs.* **summ'erlike; summ'erly** warm and bright like summer; **summ'ery** like summer: suitable for summer. — **summ'er-house** a structure in a garden for sitting in: a summer residence; **summer pudding** a pudding made of soft fruit and bread; **summer school** a course of study held during the summer. — *adj.* **summ'er-seeming** (*Shak.*) perh. hot and passing, like summer. — **summer stock** (*U.S.*) a summer season of plays presented by a repertory company; **summ'ertide** the summer season; **summ'er-time** the summer season: **summer time** time adopted (from 1916; but see **British Standard Time**) for daylight-saving purposes — one hour (**double summer time** two hours) in advance of Greenwich time. — *adj.* **summ'er-weight** of clothes, light enough to be worn in summer. — **summ'erwood** wood with smaller and thicker-walled cells than springwood, formed late in the growing season. [O.E. *sumer, sumor;* Du. *zomer,* Ger. *Sommer.*]

summer[2] *sum'ər, n.* a pack-horse, a sumpter (*obs.*): a great horizontal beam or lintel (also **summ'er-tree**). [See **sumpter.**]

summer[3]. See **sum.**

summersault, summerset. Same as **somersault, somerset.**

summist. See **summa.**

summit *sum'it, n.* the highest point or degree: the top: a summit conference. — *n.* **summiteer'** a participant in summit conferences. — *adj.* **summ'itless.** — *n.* **summ'itry** the practice or technique of holding summit conferences. — **summit conference, talks** a conference between heads of states; sometimes extended to mean a conference between heads of lesser organisations; **summ'it-level** the highest level. [O.Fr. *sommette, somet* (Fr. *sommet*), dim. of *som* — L. *summum,* highest.]

summon *sum'ən, v.t.* to call up, forth, or together: to call upon to appear or to do something: to rouse to exertion. — *adj.* **summ'onable.** — *ns.* **summ'oner** one who summons: an officer who serves summonses: an apparitor; **summ'ons** a summoning or an authoritative call: a call to appear, esp. in court: a call to surrender: — *pl.* **summ'onses.** — *v.t.* to serve with a summons. [O.Fr. *somoner* — L. *summonēre* — *sub-,* secretly, *monēre,* to warn: sense partly from O.E. *somnian,* to assemble.]

summum bonum *sum'əm bō'nəm, sŏŏm'ŏŏm bo'nŏŏm,* (L.) the chief good.

sumo *sŏŏ'mō, n.* a traditional Japanese sport, a form of wrestling: — *pl.* **su'mos.** — *n.* **sumotō'ri** a sumo wrestler. [Jap. *sumō.*]

sump *sump, n.* a bog, pool, puddle (now *dial.*): a hole or depression that receives liquid, as for molten metal, for sea-water at a salt-work, drainage-water in a mine, oil in an engine. [Du. *somp;* Ger. *Sumpf.*]

sumph *sumf,* (*Scot.*) *n.* a soft sheepish fellow. — *adj.* **sumph'ish.** — *n.* **sumph'ishness.** [Origin unknown.]

sumpit *sum'pit,* **sumpitan** *-an, ns.* a Malay blowpipe. [Malay.]

sumpsimus *sump'si-məs, n.* a correct expression displacing an incorrect but common one. [L. *sūmpsimus,* see **mumpsimus.**]

sumpter *sum(p)'tər, n.* a pack-horse. — **sump'ter-horse.** [O.Fr. *sommetier,* a pack-horse driver — Gr. *sagma,* a pack-saddle, *sattein,* to pack.]

sumptuary *sum(p)'tū-ər-i, adj.* pertaining to or regulating expense. — *n.* **sumptuos'ity** sumptuousness. — *adj.* **sump'tuous** costly: magnificently luxurious. — *adv.* **sump'tuously.** — *n.* **sump'tuousness.** [L. *sūmptus,* cost — *sūmĕre, sūmptum,* to take.]

sun *sun, n.* the body which is the gravitational centre and source of light and heat to our planetary system (often with *cap.*): the central body of a system: a great luminary: a climate: sunshine: a year (*poet.*): a day (*poet.*): sunrise: sunset. — *v.t.* to expose to the sun's rays. — *v.i.* to bask: — *pr.p.* **sunn'ing;** *pa.t.* and *pa.p.* **sunned.** — *adj.* **sun'less.** — *n.* **sun'lessness.** — *adjs.* **sun'like; sunned** exposed to the sun. — *adv.* **sunn'ily.** — *n.* **sunn'iness.** — *adj.* **sunn'y** of, from, like or lighted, coloured or warmed by the sun: genial: cheerful. — *adj.* and *adv.* **sun'ward** towards the sun. — *advs.* **sun'wards; sun'wise** in the direction of the sun's apparent revolution. — *adj.* **sun'-and-plan'et** geared so that one wheel moves round another. — **sun'-animal'cule** a heliozoan. — *adj.* **sun'-baked** baked or dried by the heat of the sun. — **sun'bath, -bathe** exposure of the body to the sun's rays. — *v.i.* **sun'bathe.** — **sun'bather** (*-bādh-*); **sun'bathing; sun'beam** a shaft of sunlight. — *adjs.* **sun'beamed, -beamy.** — **sun'-bear** the Malayan bear: sometimes the Himalayan bear. — *adjs.* **sun'beat, -en** continually exposed to the sun. — **sun'bed** a sun-lamp in the form of a bed, upon which one lies in order to obtain an artificial suntan; **sun'belt** a region with a warm, sunny climate, a preferred place to live: a favoured area generally: (often *cap.*) the Southern States of the U.S.; **sun'-bird** any of the *Nectariniidae,* a family of small tropical birds akin to honey-eaters, superficially like humming-birds; **sun bittern** a S. American bird (*Eurypyga helias*) with brilliant many-coloured markings; **sun'-blind** an outside shade or awning for a window. — *adj.* blinded by the sun. — **sun'-blink** (*Scot.*) a gleam of sunshine; **sun'block** a sunscreen that completely blocks off the sun from the skin; **sun'-bonnet** a light bonnet projecting beyond the face to protect from the sun; **sun'bow** an iris formed by the sun, esp. in the spray of a cataract. — *adj.* **sun'bright** bright as the sun. — **sun'burn** reddening (often excessive) or browning of the skin by the sun. — *v.t.* to brown or tan by exposure to the sun. — *v.i.* to become so browned. — *adjs.* **sun'burned, sun'burnt.** — **sun'burst** a strong outburst of sunlight: a jewel or ornament resembling the rayed sun. — *adj.* **sun'-clad** clothed in radiant light. — **sun'-crack** a crack formed in clayey ground as it dries in the sun, often preserved in rocks; **sun'-cult** worship of a sun-god or of the sun. — *adj.* **sun'-cured** cured in the sun. — **sun dance** a N. American Indian ceremonial dance, performed in honour of the sun; **sun'-dawn** the light of the rising sun; **sun'-deck** the upper deck of a passenger ship: a balcony or terrace used for sunbathing; **sun'-dew** an insectivorous bog-plant (*Drosera*); **sun'dial** a device for telling the time by a shadow cast by the gnomon on a graduated flat surface; **sun'-disc** the visible disc of the sun: a winged disc, symbol of the sun-god; **sun'-dog** a mock sun or parhelion; **sun'down** sunset: a woman's broad-brimmed hat (*U.S. coll.*); **sun'-downer** in Australia, a loafer who arrives at a station in time for a meal and lodging, but too late for work: a government official who practises a profession after hours (*U.S.*): in India and Africa, a drink after sunset; **sun'-dress** a low-cut dress, leaving the arms, shoulders and back exposed to the sun. — *adj.* **sun'-dried** dried in the sun. — **sun'-drops** an American evening primrose. — *adjs.* **sun'-expelling** (*Shak.*) keeping off the sun; **sun'fast** (*U.S.*) of fabric colour, not fading in the sunlight. — **sun'-fish** a fish of nearly circular profile, as the opah, or any member of the family *Molidae*: the basking shark; **sun'flower** a composite plant (Helianthus) or its large head with yellow rays, fabled to turn toward the sun: applied to various more or less similar kinds; **sun'glass** a burning-glass: (in *pl.*) dark-lensed spectacles used against strong light; **sun'glow** the glow in the sky before sunrise and after sunset; **sun'-god** a god personifying or concerned with the sun; **sun'hat**, (*arch.*) **sun'-helmet** a hat with shady brim; **sun'-lamp** a lamp that gives out ultraviolet rays curatively or to induce artificial suntan: a lamp producing a very bright light, used in film-making; **sun'light** the light of the sun. — *adj.* **sun'lit** lighted up by the sun. — **sun'-lounge,** U.S. **sun'-parlor,** a room with large windows, or a glass wall, to admit the maximum sunlight; **sun'-lounger** an upholstered couch for sunbathing; **sun'-myth** a solar myth; **sunny side** a pleasant or cheerful part or point of view: an age less than one specified, as *on the sunny side of fifty* (see also below); **sun'-parlor** see **sun-lounge;** **sun'-picture, -print** (*arch.*) a photograph. — *adj.* **sun'-proof.** — **sun'ray** (**sunray pleats** tapering knife pleats giving a flared effect to skirts, etc.); **sun'rise, sun'rising** the rising or first appearance of the sun above the horizon: the time or colour-effects of this rising: the east; **sunrise industry** a new and rapidly-growing industry, often based on electronics; **sun'-roof** see **sunshine-roof; sun'screen** a lotion, cream etc,. that prevents, sunburn by screening the skin from ultraviolet rays; **sun'set, sun'setting** the setting or going down of the sun: the time or phenomenon of going down: the west; **sun'-shade** a parasol: an awning; **sun'shine** bright sunlight: brightness: prosperity: geniality: an informal term of address, often ironic or even admonitory. — *adjs.* **sun'shine** sunshiny: fair-weather; **sun'shiny** bright with sunshine: pleasant: bright like the sun: genial. — **sun'shine-recorder** an instrument for recording duration of sunshine; **sun'shine-roof, sun'-roof** a car-roof that can be slid open; **sun'spot** a relatively dark patch on the surface of the sun: a place with a very warm sunny climate; **sun'-spurge** a spurge (*Euphorbia helioscopia*) supposed to turn with the sun, a common weed; **sun'stone** aventurine feldspar; **sun'stroke** a nervous disease caused by great heat. — *adj.* **sun'struck** affected with sunstroke. — **sun'suit** a child's outfit for playing in the sun, leaving most of the body exposed; **sun'tan** a browning of the skin as a result of exposure to the sun. — *adj.* **sun'tanned.** — **sun'trap** a sheltered, sunny place; **sun'-up** sunrise; **sun'-visor; sun'-worship** adoration of the sun; **sun'-worshipper.** — **a place in the sun** a place or opportunity for good living or attaining prosperity; **a touch of the sun** mild sunburn: mild sunstroke; **between** (*Shak.* 'twixt) **sun and sun, from sun to sun** between sunrise and sunset; **catch the sun** to be sunburnt; **have been in the sunshine, have the sun in one's eyes** to be drunk; **sunny side up** (*coll.*) of an egg, fried on one side only, so that the yolk is visible; **take the sun** to ascertain the sun's meridian altitude: to walk or laze in the sun; **under the sun** on earth. [O.E. *sunne*; O.N. *sunna*, O.H.G. *sunnô*.]

sundae *sun'dā, -di, n.* an ice-cream with syrup or crushed fruit: a mixed nougat or confection. [Perh. **Sunday.**]

sundari *sun'də-rē, n.* an East Indian sterculiaceous timber-tree (*Heritiera*). — Also **sun'dra, sun'dri, sun'der.** [Sans. *sundarī.*]

Sunday *sun'di, n.* the first day of the week, anciently dedicated to the sun, now regarded as the Sabbath by most Christians: a newspaper published on Sundays. — *adj.* of, for, occurring on, Sunday. — **Sunday best** one's best clothes; **Sunday driver** one who drives a car at weekends only: an incompetent driver. — *adj.* **Sun'day-go-to-meeting** appropriated to Sunday and church-going. — **Sunday painters** people who paint seriously but in their spare time; **Sunday punch** (*coll.; U.S.*) a powerful punch intended to knock out one's opponent (also *fig.*); **Sunday saint** one whose religion or morality is confined to Sundays; **Sunday school** a school for religious (orig. general) instruction on Sunday. — **a month of Sundays** a long time. [O.E. *sunnan dæg*; Ger. *Sonntag.*]

sunder[1] *sun'dər, v.t.* and *v.i.* (*arch., poet.*) to separate: to part. — *n.* **sun'derance.** — *adj.* **sun'dered.** — *n.* **sun'derer.** — *n.* and *adj.* **sun'dering.** — *n.* **sun'derment.** — **in sunder** (*B.*) asunder. [O.E. *syndrian*, to separate, *sundor*, separate; O.N. *sundr*, asunder.]

sunder[2], **sundra, sundri.** See **sundari.**

sundry *sun'dri, adj.* separate: more than one or two: several: divers: varied (*Shak.*). — *n.pl.* **sun'dries** sundry things: different small things. — **all and sundry** all collectively and individually. [O.E. *syndrig*; cf. **sunder**[1].]

sung *sung.* See **sing.**

Sung *soong, n.* a Chinese dynasty (960–1279). — *adj.* of the dynasty, or its culture, including its pottery.

sungar. See **sangar.**

sunk[1] *sungk,* **sunken** *sungk'n.* See **sink.**

sunk[2] *sungk,* (*Scot.*) *n.* a turf seat: a pad: a bank. — *n.* **sunk'ie** a stool. [Origin unknown.]

sunket *sung'kit,* (*Scot.*) *n.* a dainty. [From *sumquhat,* Scots form of **somewhat.**]

sunn *sun, n.* an Indian Crotalaria grown for fibre. — Also **sunn'-hemp'.** [Hind. *san.*]

Sunna *soon'ə, sun'ə, n.* Muslim traditional teaching. — *ns.* **Sunn'i** (*-ē*) an orthodox Muslim: — also **Sonn'ite, Sunn'ite; Sunn'ism** the teachings and beliefs of orthodox Muslims. [Ar. *sunnah.*]

sunny, sunward(s), sunwise. See **sun.**

Suomi *soo'ə-mi, n.* the Finnish language. — *n.pl.* the Finns. — *adjs.* **Suo'mic, Suo'mish.**

suovetaurilia *sū-ov-i-tö-ril'i-ə,* L. *soo-o-we-tow-rē'li-a, n.pl.* a Roman sacrifice of a sheep, a pig, and an ox. [L. *sūs,* pig, *ovis,* sheep, *taurus,* ox.]

sup *sup, v.t.* to take into the mouth, as a liquid: to eat with a spoon (*Scot.*): to furnish supper for (*Shak.*). — *v.i.* to eat the evening meal (*arch.*): to sip (*B.*): — *pr.p.* **supp'ing;** *pa.t.* and *pa.p.* **supped.** — *n.* a small mouthful, as of a liquid. [O.E. *sūpan*; O.N. *sūpa,* Ger. *saufen,* to drink; partly from O.Fr. *soper, souper* (Fr. *souper*), to take supper.]

supawn. See **suppawn.**

super- *soo', sū'pər,* in composition, above, beyond, in addition, in excess, very. — *n.* **su'per** a colloquial shortening of **supernumerary** (esp. a supernumerary actor, further abbreviated **supe**), and of **superintendent.** — *adj.* coll. shortening of **superfine:** very good or very delightful. — *v.i.* to act as super. — *v.i.* **superabound'** to be more, very, or excessively abundant. — *n.* **superabun'dance.** — *adj.* **superabund'ant.** — *adv.* **superabund'antly.** — *adj.* **superacute'** abnormally or excessively acute. — *v.t.* **superadd'** to add over and above. — *ns.* **superaddi'tion; superall'oy** an alloy that has good stability at 600°C to 1000°C; **superalt'ar** a slab of stone used as a portable altar to be laid on the top of an unconsecrated altar: a structure over an altar. — *v.t.* **supercal'ender** to give a high polish to by calendering. — *adj.* **supercal'endered.** — *n.* **supercar'go** a person in a ship placed in charge of the cargo and superintending all commercial transactions of the voyage: — *pl.* **supercar'goes.** — *n.* **supercar'goship.** — *adj.* **supercelest'ial** above the heavens: more than heavenly. — *v.t.* **supercharge'** to fill to excess: to charge above the normal: to add pressure to: to charge exorbitantly, overcharge: to place as an overcharge (*her.*). — *ns.* **su'percharge** an excessive, exorbitant, or greater than normal charge: a charge borne upon an ordinary or other charge (*her.*); **su′percharger** a device for increasing the pressure in an internal combustion engine; **su′perclass** a biological category between a division and a class; **superclus′ter** (*astron.*) a large cluster of galaxies. — *adjs.* **su′percold** same as **cryogenic**; **supercolum′nar** (*archit.*) above a column or colonnade: with one colonnade above another. — *ns.* **supercolumniā′tion**; **supercompū′ter** a powerful computer which can perform a large number of mathematical calculations very quickly. — *v.i.* **superconduct′** to conduct electricity without resistance. — *n.* **superconductiv′ity** complete loss of electrical resistivity shown by certain pure metals and alloys at temperatures approaching absolute zero and by certain ceramics at higher temperatures. — *adjs.* **superconduc′ting; superconduc′tive.** — *ns.* **superconduc′tor; supercon′- tinent** any of the vast land-masses from which the continents were orig. formed. — *v.t.* **supercool′** to cool below normal freezing-point without freezing. — *adjs.* **supercrit′ical** capable of sustaining a chain reaction such that the rate of reaction increases; **superdaint′y** (*Shak.*) over-dainty; **su′perdense** (*astron.*) extremely dense. — *ns.* **superdom′inant** (*mus.*) the submediant; **super-Dread′nought** a warship excelling the original Dreadnought class. — *adj.* **su′per-du′per** superlatively fine or great (*coll.*). — *ns.* **super-ē′go** (*psych.*) the strong unconscious inhibitory mechanism which criticises the ego and causes it pain and distress when it accepts unworthy impulses from the id; **supereleva′tion** excess in height: the difference in height between the opposite sides of a road or railway on a curve; **superem′inence** eminence in a superior degree: excellence beyond others. — *adj.* **superem′inent.** — *adv.* **superem′inently.** — *adj.* **superessen′tial** transcending mere being and essence. — *v.t.* **superexalt′** to exalt to a superior degree. — *ns.* **superexaltā′tion; superexc′ellence** excellence above others, or in an uncommon degree. — *adj.* **superexc′ellent.** — *n.* **su′perfamily** a group between a suborder and a family. — *adj.* **superfatt′ed** (of soap) having an excess of fat, so that there is no free alkali. — *n.* **superfecundā′tion** same as **superfetation** below. — *adj.* **su′perfine** of specially fine size or quality (short form **super**): over-nice. — *n.* **su′perfineness.** — *adj.* **superflu′id.** — *ns.* **superfluid′ity** a phenomenon observed in a form of helium (*helium II*), obtained below 2·19 K, in which internal friction is negligible; **super-front′al** a covering hanging over the upper edge of an altar frontal. — *v.t.* **superfuse′** to pour over something else (*obs.*): to supercool. — *ns.* **superfu′sion; supergī′ant** a very bright star of enormous size and low density, such as Betelgeuse and Antares. — *adj.* **superglā′cial** occurring or originating on the surface of a glacier. — *ns.* **su′perglue** (*coll.*) a very strong and quick-acting glue; **su′pergrass** (*slang*) a police informer who has given information leading to the arrest of a great number of criminals. — *v.t.* **superheat′** to heat to excess: to heat (steam, etc.) above the temperature of saturation: to heat above normal boiling-point without vaporisation. — *n.* state of being superheated: amount of superheating. — *n.* **superheat′er.** — *adj.* **superheav′y** having an atomic number or weight heavier than the heaviest known. — *n.* a superheavy element. — *adj.* **superhet′erodyne** heterodyne with beats above audible frequency (*coll.* **superhet′**). — *n.* a superheterodyne receiver. — *ns.* **super-high frequency** see **frequency**; **superhigh′way** (*U.S.*) a wide road for fast motor-traffic; **su′perhive** a detachable upper compartment of a beehive. — *adj.* **superhū′man** above man: above the capacity of man: more or higher than human. — *v.t.* **superhū′manise, -ize.** — *n.* **superhū′manity.** — *adv.* **superhū′manly.** — *n.* **superhū′meral** any vestment worn on the shoulders. — *v.t.* **superimpose′** to set on the top of something else: to place one over another: to establish in superaddition. — *adj.* **superimposed′.** — *ns.* **superimposi′tion; superincum′bence.** — *adj.* **superincum′bent** resting on the top: overlying:

overhanging. — *v.t.* **superinduce′** to bring in over and above, or in supersession of, something else: to super-add. — *ns.* **superinduce′ment, superinduc′tion; superinfec′tion** an infection arising during another infection and caused by a different (or a different variety of the same) micro-organism. — *vs.t.* **superinfect′; superin-tend′** to have or exercise oversight or charge of: to control, manage. — *v.i.* to exercise supervision. — *ns.* **superinten′dence** oversight: direction: management; **superinten′dency** office or district of a superintendent. — *adj.* **superinten′dent** superintending. — *n.* one who superintends: an overseer: the head of a Sunday school: in some Protestant churches a clergyman having the oversight of the clergy of a district: a police officer above a chief inspector: a rank in the RSPCA, between commander and chief inspector: the administrator of a local school system (*U.S.*). — *ns.* **superinten′dentship; su′per-jet** a supersonic jet aircraft. — *adjs.* **superlu′nar, superlu′nary** above the moon: not of this world. — *ns.* **su′perman** a being of higher type than man: ideal man: a dominating man; **su′permarket** (orig. *U.S.*) a large, mainly self-service, retail store selling food and other domestic goods (also **su′permart**). — *adjs.* **supermun′- dane** above the world; **supernat′ional** transcending the national. — *n.* **supernat′ionalism.** — *adj.* **supernat′ural** above or beyond nature: not according to the course of nature: miraculous: spiritual. — *n.* that which is supernatural: a supernatural being. — *v.t.* **supernat′u-ralise, -ize** to bring into the supernatural sphere. — *ns.* **supernat′uralism** the belief in the influence of the supernatural in the world; **supernat′uralist** a believer in the supernatural. — *adj.* of or pertaining to the supernatural. — *adj.* **supernaturalist′ic.** — *adv.* **super-nat′urally.** — *ns.* **supernat′uralness; su′pernature** the supernatural. — *adj.* **supernor′mal** beyond what is normal: in greater number, amount, concentration, etc., than the normal. — *ns.* **su′peroctave** an organ-coupler giving an octave higher: an organ-stop two octaves above the principal; **superord′er** a category between an order and a subclass or sometimes class (*biol.*). — *adjs.* **superord′inal** pertaining to a super-order; **superord′inary** above or beyond the ordinary; **superord′inate** superior in rank: in the relation of superordination. — *n.* a superior in rank. — *v.t.* to make superordinate. — *n.* **superordinā′tion** (*log.*) the relation of a universal proposition to a particular proposition in the same terms. — *adj.* **superorgan′ic** above or beyond the organic, psychical: pertaining to a higher organisation, social. — *ns.* **superorg′anism** a highly organised social community perceptible as a single organism (e.g. a colony of bees); **superovulā′tion** the production of a larger number of ova than usual, e.g. under stimulus of injected hormones; **superphos′- phate** an acid phosphate: now usu. a mixture of calcium sulphate and calcium acid phosphate used as a manure. — *adjs.* **superphys′ical** beyond, or of higher order than, the physical; **su′perplastic** of a material, esp. a metal, which when heated to a high temperature becomes very pliable. — Also *n.* — *ns.* **superplastic′ity; su′perplus** (*obs.*) surplus. — *adj.* **superpos′able.** — *v.t.* **superpose′** to bring, or suppose to be brought, into coincidence: to place vertically over or on something else. — *adj.* **superposed′.** — *ns.* **superposi′tion** act of superposing: state of being superposed: that which is above anything; **su′perpower** a very powerful state, often applied to the U.S. and the U.S.S.R. — *v.t.* **superpraise′** (*Shak.*) to praise excessively. — *ns.* **super-re′alism** surrealism; **superre′alist.** — *adj.* **super-roy′al** of paper-size larger than royal. — *n.* **su′persalt** an acid salt. — *v.t.* **supersat′urate** to saturate beyond the normal point. — *n.* **supersaturā′tion.** — *adj.* **super-sens′ible** above the range, or outside the reach, of the senses. — *adv.* **supersen′sibly.** — *adj.* **supersen′sitive** excessively sensitive. — *n.* **supersen′sitiveness.** — *adjs.* **supersen′sory** beyond the ordinarily recognised senses; **supersen′sual** beyond the senses: extremely sensual; **superser′viceable** (*Shak.*) officious. — *ns.* **su′persound**

sound vibrations too rapid to be audible; **su'perstar** an extremely popular and successful star of the cinema, popular music, etc.; **su'perstate** a greater organisation transcending the state; **su'perstore** a large supermarket, which usu. sells many different goods in addition to food; **superstrā'tum** (or *-strā'*) overlying stratum. — *v.t.* **superstruct'** to build on something else as a foundation. — *n.* **superstruc'tion**. — *adjs.* **superstruct'ive**; **superstruct'ural**. — *n.* **su'perstructure** an upper structure or part of a structure. — *adjs.* **supersubstan'tial** transcending substance, esp. material substance; **supersubt'le, -subt'ile** (*Shak.*) over-subtle: extremely subtle. — *ns.* **su'pertanker** an old name for a large tanker (q.v.); **su'pertax** an extra or additional tax on large incomes (term not in official use). — *adjs.* **superterrā'nean** living or situated on the earth's surface; **superterres'trial** supermundane. — *n.* **superton'ic** the tone next above the tonic. — *adj.* **su'pervolute** (*bot.*) convolute. [L. *super*, above; cf. **over**, Gr. *hyper*.]

superable. See **superate**.

superannuate *sōō-, sū-pər-an'ū-āt, v.t.* to antiquate: to set aside or cause to retire on account of age: to pension off. — *adj.* **superannuated.** — *n.* a superannuated person. — *adjs.* **superann'uable; superann'üated.** — *n.* **superannūā'tion** the act or state of superannuating: a pension: a regular contribution paid by an employee towards a pension. [L. *super*, above; *annus*, year.]

superate *sōō', sū'pər-āt,* (*obs.*) *v.t.* to overcome, outdo, or top. — *adj.* **su'perable.** — *adv.* **su'perably.** — *n.* **superā'tion.** [L. *superāre*, to go over, surmount.]

superb *sōō-, sū-pûrb', adj.* proud, haughty (*obs.*): magnificent: gorgeous: triumphantly effective: supremely excellent (*coll.*). — *n.* **superb'ity.** — *adv.* **superb'ly.** — *n.* **superb'ness.** [L. *superbus*, proud.]

supercalender . . . to . . . **supercharger.** See **super-**.

supercherie *sü-per-shə-rē, n.* a taking at disadvantage: fraud. [Fr.]

superciliary *sōō', sū'pər-sil'i-ər-i, adj.* of, on, or near the eyebrow: marked above the eye. — *n.* a superciliary ridge or mark. — *adj.* **supercil'ious** disdainfully superior in manner: overbearing (*obs.*): superciliary (*rare*). — *adv.* **supercil'iously.** — *n.* **supercil'iousness.** [L. *supercilium*, eyebrow, superciliousness — *super*, above, *cilium*, eyelid.]

superclass . . . to . . . **supereminently.** See **super-**.

supererogation *sōō-, sū-pər-er-ō-gā'shən, n.* doing more than is required. — *v.i.* **supererogate.** — *adj.* **supererogatory** (*-ə-rog'ə-tər-i*). — Also (*rare*) **superer'ogant, supererog'ative.** — **works of supererogation** (*R.C.*) works which, not absolutely required of each individual for salvation, may be done for the sake of greater perfection — affording the church a store of surplus merit, to eke out the deficient merit of others. [L. *super*, above, *ērogāre, -ātum*, to pay out.]

superessential. See **super-**.

superette *sōō-, sū-pər-et,* (*Austr.* and *U.S.*) *n.* a small local supermarket. [*super*market, and dim. suff. *-ette*.]

superexalt . . . **superfatted.** See **super-**.

superfetation *sōō-, sū-pər-fē-tā'shən, n.* fertilisation of an ovum in one already for some time pregnant: superabundant production or accumulation. — *v.i.* **superfē'tate.** [L. *superfētāre* — pfx. *super-*, over, *fētus*, a fetus.]

superficies *sōō-, sū-pər-fish'i-ēz, n.* a surface, that which has length and breadth but no thickness (*geom.*): a bounding or outer surface: a surface layer: a surface area: external features, appearance: — *pl.* **superfic'ies.** — *adj.* **superficial** (*-fish'l*) of, on, or near the surface: not going much deeper than the surface (*derog.*). — *n.* that which is, or those who are, superficial: surface characters. — *v.t.* **superfic'ialise, -ize** to make superficial. — *v.i.* to deal superficially. — *n.* **superficiality** (*-fish-i-al'i-ti*). — *adv.* **superfic'ially.** — *n.* **superfic'ialness.** [L. *superficiēs* — *super, faciēs*, face.]

superfine . . . to . . . **superfluidity.** See **super-**.

superfluous *sōō-, sū-pûr'flōō-əs, adj.* above what is enough: redundant: unnecessary. — *n.* **superfluity**

(*-flōō'*) state of being superfluous: a thing that is superfluous: superabundance. — *adv.* **super'fluously.** — *ns.* **super'fluousness** superfluity; **su'perflux** (*Shak.*) superfluity. [L. *superfluus*, overflowing — *super, fluĕre*, to flow.]

superfoetation. Same as **superfetation**.

superfrontal . . . to . . . **superintendentship.** See **super-**.

superior *sōō-, sū-pē'ri-ər, adj.* upper: higher in nature, place, rank, or excellence: better (with *to*): surpassing others: beyond the influence, rising above (with *to*): supercilious or uppish: (often patronisingly) very worthy and highly respectable: of wider application, generic: set above the level of the line (*print.*): of an ovary, inserted on the receptacle above the other parts (*bot.*): of other parts, seeming to take rise above the ovary (*bot.*). — *n.* one superior to others: the head of a religious house, order, etc.: the feudal lord of a vassal: one to whom feu-duty is paid (*Scots law*): — *fem.* **supe'rioress** the head of a nunnery. — *n.* **superiority** (*-or'i-ti*) quality or state of being superior: pre-eminence: advantage: the right which the superior enjoys in the land held by the vassal (*Scots law*). — *adv.* **supe'riorly** in a superior manner or position. — *n.* **supe'riorship.** — **superiority complex** (*psych.*) overvaluation of one's worth, often affected to cover a sense of inferiority; **superior planets** those more distant from the sun than is the earth. [L., compar. of *superus*, on high — *super*, above.]

superjacent *sōō-, sū-pər-jā'sənt, adj.* lying above. [L. *super, jacēns, -entis*, pr.p. of *jacēre*, to lie.]

superlative *sōō-, sū-pûr'lə-tiv, adj.* raised above others or to the highest degree: superior to all others: most eminent: expressing the highest degree (*gram.*). — *n.* the superlative or highest degree (*gram.*): an adjective or adverb in the superlative degree: any word or phrase of exaggeration. — *adv.* **super'latively.** — *n.* **super'lativeness.** [L. *superlātīvus* — *super, lātus*, carried.]

superlunar . . . to . . . **supermundane.** See **super-**.

supernaculum *sōō-, sū'pər-nak'ū-ləm, adv.* to the last drop. — *n.* liquor of the best kind, too good to leave heel-taps: a bumper. — *adj.* **supernac'ular.** [Sham L. *super naculum*, on the nail — L. *super*, Ger. *Nagel*, nail; from the custom of turning the glass up to show that no more is left than will stand on the thumbnail.]

supernal *sōō-, sū-pûr'nl,* (*poet.*) *adj.* on high: celestial: of a higher world: exalted: topmost. — *adv.* **super'nally.** [L. *supernus* — *super*.]

supernatant *sōō-, sū-pər-nā'tənt, adj.* floating or swimming above, esp. of an upper layer of liquid. [L. *supernatāns, -antis* — *super, natāre*, swim, float.]

supernational . . . to . . . **supernormal.** See **super-**.

supernova *sōō-, sū-pər-nō'və, n.* very brilliant nova resulting from an explosion which blows the star's material into space, leaving an expanding cloud of gas: — *pl.* **supernō'vae** (*-vē*), **supernō'vas.** [L. *super-*, above, and **nova**.]

supernumerary *sōō-, sū-pər-nū'mər-ər-i, adj.* over and above the stated, usual, normal, or necessary number. — *n.* a supernumerary person or thing: an actor without speaking parts. [L.L. *supernumerārius* — L. *super, numerus*, number.]

superoctave . . . to . . . **supersaturation.** See **super-**.

superscribe *sōō-, sū-pər-skrīb', v.t.* to write or engrave above, on the top or on the outside of something: to address (as a letter): to sign at the top. — *adj.* **su'perscript** (*-skript*) written above: superior (*print.*). — *n.* the superscription, address (*Shak.*): a superior character (*print.*). — *n.* **superscrip'tion** act of superscribing: that which is superscribed. [L. *super*, above, *scrībĕre, scrīptum*, to write.]

supersede *sōō-, sū-pər-sēd', v.t.* to desist or refrain from (*obs.*): to override (*obs.*): to set aside: to set aside in favour of another: to come or put in the room of, to replace. — *v.i.* (*obs.*) to refrain, desist. — *ns.* **superse'deas** (*-di-as*) a writ to stay proceedings, or to suspend the powers of an officer (from the use of the L. word *2nd pers. sing. pres. subj.*, you are to desist); **superse'-**

dence; **superse′der**; **supersedere** (-si-dē′ri, soō-per-se-dā′re, infin.) a private agreement among creditors, under a trust-deed, to supersede or sist diligence for a certain period (*Scots law*): an order of court granting protection to a debtor; **supersē′dure**; **supersession** (-sesh′ən). [L. *supersedēre*, to sit above, refrain from — *super*, above, *sedēre*, *sessum*, to sit.]

supersensible. . . to . . . **superserviceable**. See **super-**.

supersession. See **supersede**.

supersonic soō-, sū-pər-son′ik, adj. above the audible limit: too high-pitched for human hearing (ultrasonic): (capable of) (travelling) faster than the speed of sound. — n. a supersonic wave: (in *pl.*) the study of such waves. — n. **su′persound** see **super-**. — **supersonic-combustion ramjet** see **ramjet**. [L. *super*, above, *sonus*, sound.]

superstate. See **super-**.

superstition soō-, sū-pər-stish′ən, n. false worship or religion: an ignorant and irrational belief in supernatural agency, omens, divination, sorcery, etc.: a deep-rooted but unfounded general belief: a rite or practice proceeding from superstitious belief or fear (*obs.*). — adj. **superstit′ious**. — adv. **superstit′iously**. — n. **superstit′iousness**. [L. *superstitiō, -ōnis*.]

superstratum. . . to . . . **supertonic**. See **super-**.

supervene soō-, sū-pər-vēn′, v.i. to come in addition, or closely after. — n. **superven′ience**. — adj. **superven′ient** supervening. — n. **supervention** (-ven′shən). [L. *super*, above, *venīre*, *ventum*, to come.]

supervise soō′, sū′pər-vīz, or -vīz′, v.i. to read over (*Shak.*): to superintend. — Also v.t. — n. (*Shak.*) reading over. — ns. **supervī′sal**, **supervision** (-vizh′ən) act of supervising: inspection: control; **supervisee** (-vīz-ē′) a person who is supervised. **supervisor** (-vī′zər; also soō′, sū′) one who supervises: an overseer: an inspector: an elected local government official (*U.S.*): a spectator (*Shak.*); **supervī′sorship**. — adj. **supervī′sory** pertaining to, or having, supervision. [L. *super*, over, *vidēre*, *vīsum*, to see.]

supervolute. See **super-**.

supine soō′, sū′pīn, or -pīn′, adj. lying on the back: leaning backward, inclined, sloping: negligently inert: indolent: passive. — n. a Latin verbal noun in *-tum* (*first supine*, an old accusative) or *-tū* (*second supine*, an old locative), possibly as formed from the stem of the passive participle: the English infinitive with *to*. — v.t. **su′pinate** (-pin-āt) to bring (the hand) palm upward or forward. — ns. **supinā′tion** the placing or holding of the palm of the hand upward or forward; **su′pinator** a muscle that supinates the hand. — adv. **supine′ly**. — n. **supine′ness**. [L. *supīnus*, supine; related to *sub*, under, *super*, over.]

suppawn, **supawn** sə-pön′, n. maize porridge. [Natick *saupáun*, softened.]

suppeago sə-pē′gō. See **serpigo**.

suppedaneum sə-pə-dā′ni-em, n. a support under the foot of a crucified person: — pl. **suppedā′nea** (-ni-ə). [L. footstool, from *neut.* of *suppedaneus*, beneath the foot.]

supper sup′ər, n. a meal taken at the close of the day. — v.t. to furnish with supper. — adj. **supp′erless**. — **supper cloth** a table-cloth, larger than a tea-cloth, on which supper is served; **supp′ertime** the time at which supper is usually taken. [O.Fr. *soper* (Fr. *souper*).]

supping. See **sup**.

supplant sə-plänt′, v.t. to overthrow, to lay low (*Milt.*): to oust: to supersede: to dispossess and take the place of: to uproot (*Shak.*). — ns. **supplantation** (sup-lən-tā′shən); **supplant′er**. [L. *supplantāre*, to trip up — *sub*, under, *planta*, the sole.]

supple[1] sup′l, adj. pliant: lithe: yielding to the humour of others: fawning. — v.t. (*rare*) to make supple: to make soft or compliant. — v.i. (*rare*) to become supple. — n. **supp′leness**. — adv. **supp′ly**. — **supple jack** a woody liane of many kinds: a pliant cane. [Fr. *souple* — L. *supplex*, bending the knees — *sub*, under, *plicāre*, to fold.]

supple[2] soōp′l, a Scots form of **swipple**. See also **souple**[2].

supplement sup′li-mənt, n. that which supplies a deficiency

or fills a need: that which completes or brings closer to completion: any addition by which defects are made good: a special part of a periodical publication accompanying an ordinary part: the quantity by which an angle or an arc falls short of 180° or a semicircle. — v.t. **supplement** (-ment′; also sup′li-mənt) to supply or fill up: to add to. — adjs. **supplement′al**, **supplement′ary** added to supply what is wanting: additional. — Also ns. — advs. **supplement′ally**, **supplement′arily**. — ns. **supplementā′tion**; **supplement′er**; **supplē′tion** a supplement: the adding of a word to supply a missing form of a conjugation, etc., as *went* for the past tense of *to go* (*gram.*). — adjs. **supp′letive**, **supp′letory** supplemental. — **supplementary benefit** in Britain, a state allowance paid each week to those with low incomes in order to bring them up to a certain established level. [L. *supplēmentum*, a filling up, *supplēre*, to fill up.]

supplial. See under **supply**[1].

suppliance. See **suppliant**[1], **supply**[1].

suppliant[1] sup′li-ənt, adj. supplicating: asking earnestly: entreating. — n. a humble petitioner. — n. **supp′liance** supplication. — adv. **supp′liantly**. [Fr. *suppliant*, pr.p. of *supplier* — L. *supplicāre*; see next.]

suppliant[2], **supplier**. See **supply**[1].

supplicant sup′li-kənt, adj. supplicating: asking submissively. — n. one who supplicates or entreats earnestly. — n. **supp′licat** in the English universities, a petition. — v.t. and v.i. **supp′licate** to entreat earnestly: to petition: to pray. — adj. **supp′licating**. — adv. **supp′licatingly**. — n. **supplicā′tion** act of supplicating: an earnest or humble petition: in ancient Rome, a solemn service or day decreed for giving formal thanks to the gods for victory, etc.: earnest prayer or entreaty, esp. in liturgies, a litany petition for some special blessing. — adj. **supp′licatory** containing supplication or entreaty: humble. — n. **supplicā′vit** formerly a writ issued by the King's Bench or Chancery for taking the surety of the peace against a person. [L. *supplicāre, -ātum* — *supplex*; see **supple**[1].]

supply[1] sə-plī′, v.t. to fill up a deficiency in (*obs.*): to supplement (*obs.*): to reinforce, to help (*obs.*): to make good: to satisfy: to provide, furnish: to fill, occupy (as a substitute): to serve instead of: — pr.p. **supply′ing**; pa.t. and pa.p. **supplied′**. — n. act of supplying: that which is supplied or which supplies a want: amount provided or in hand: available amount of a commodity: amount of food or money provided (used generally in *pl.*): a parliamentary grant for expenses of government: a person who takes another's duty temporarily, a substitute, esp. a teacher. — ns. **supplī′al** the act of supplying; **supplī′ance** (*Shak.*) supplying, something to fill up time, pastime, gratification. — adj. **supplī′ant** (*Shak.*) supplementary, reinforcing. — ns. **supplī′er** one who supplies; **supply′ment** (*Shak.*) replenishment, supplementing. — **supply′-sider** an advocate of supply-side economics. — **Commissioners of Supply** a former administrative and rating authority in Scotland, superseded by the County Council; **supply-side economics** (an economic policy based on) the cutting of taxes in order to stimulate production, in the belief that supply creates demand. [O.Fr. *suppleier*, *supplier* (Fr. *suppléer*) — L. *supplēre*, to fill up.]

supply[2]. See **supple**[1].

support sə-pōrt′, -pört′, v.t. to bear the weight of: to hold up: to endure: to sustain: to maintain: to keep going: to corroborate: to make good: to uphold: to back up: to second: to contend for: to represent in acting: to supply with means of living: to nourish: to strengthen. — n. act or fact of supporting or upholding: that which, or one who, supports, sustains, or maintains: maintenance: backing: a prop: an actor playing a subordinate part with a star. — adj. **support′able** capable of being held up, borne, sustained, or maintained. — n. **support′ableness**. — adv. **support′ably**. — ns. **support′ance** (*Shak.*) support; **support′er** one who, or that which, supports: an adherent: a defender: one who attends matches and watches with interest the fortunes of a team: a figure on each side of the escutcheon (*her.*). — *n.* and *adj.* **support'ing.** — *adjs.* **support'ive; support'less.** — *ns.* (all *rare*) **support'ment; support'ress; support'ure.** — **support hose, stockings** elasticated stockings; **supporting film, programme** a film, films, acts, etc., accompanying the main film, or star performance in a variety show; **support level, area** on the stock market, the price-level below which a commodity does not decline, as it then becomes an investment proposition. [L. *supportāre* — *sub*, up, *portāre*, to bear.]

suppose *sə-pōz'*, *v.t.* to place underneath (*obs.*): to believe (*Shak.*): to incline to believe: to conceive, imagine, guess: to assume provisionally or for argument's sake: to imply, presuppose: to pretend: to expect (*Milt.*): (esp. in *pass.*) to expect in accordance with rules or conventions: to substitute fraudulently (*obs.*). — *n.* a supposition: an instance of supposing or saying 'suppose': (*Shak.*) expectation. — *adj.* **suppo'sable.** — *adv.* **suppo'sably.** — *n.* **suppo'sal** supposition: notion (*Shak.*): proposal (*obs.*). — *adj.* **supposed** (*-pōzd'*; also *-pōz-id*) believed to be: assumed: conjectured: feigned (*Shak.*): supposititious (*obs.*): placed below, or having a note below, the fundamental of the chord (*mus.*). — *adv.* **suppo'sedly** according to supposition. — *ns.* **suppo'ser; suppo'sing.** — **suppose** if: what if: (*Scot.*) even if; **supposing** if: what if, how about. [Fr. *supposer* — pfx. *sup-* (*sub-*), *poser*; see **pose**[1], and cf. **compose, dispose,** etc.]

supposes *sə-pōz'iz*, (Shak., *Taming of the Shrew*, V, i. 120) *n.pl.* perh. substitutes, or substitutions, or suppositions. See repeated play on the word in Shakespeare's source, Gascoigne's *Supposes* (and its original, Ariosto's *I Suppositi*).

supposition *sup-ə-zi'shən*, *n.* an act of supposing: that which is supposed: assumption: presumption, opinion. — *adj.* **supposi'tional** hypothetical: conjectural: supposed. — *adv.* **supposi'tionally.** — *adjs.* **supposi'tionary** suppositional; **supposi'tious** (*-zi'shəs*, *rare*) suppositional: usu. a blunder for *supposititious*; **suppositi'tious** (*sə-poz-i-tish'əs*) put by trick in the place of another: spurious: suppositional. — *adv.* **suppositi'tiously.** — *n.* **suppositi'tiousness.** — *adj.* **suppos'itive** (*-i-tiv*) suppositional. — *n.* **suppos'itory** a medicated plug for administration by the rectum or other canal. [L. *suppōnĕre, -positum*, to set under, substitute — *sub, pōnĕre*, to put.]

suppress *sə-pres'*, *v.t.* to crush, put down: to subdue: to hold or press down (*Spens.*): to ravish (*Spens.*): to hold back, esp. from publication, circulation, divulgation, expression, development: to check, stop, restrain: to hold in: to moderate: to leave out. — *n.* **suppress'ant** a substance, as a drug, that suppresses rather than eliminates. — Also *adj.* — *adj.* **suppressed'.** — *adv.* **suppress'edly.** — *adj.* **suppress'ible.** — *n.* **suppress'ion** (*-presh'*) act of suppressing: stoppage: concealment. — *adj.* **suppress'ive** tending to suppress: subduing. — *n.* **suppress'or** one who suppresses anything: a device for suppressing anything, e.g. the echo of one's own voice on a telephone, electrical interference with television reception. — **suppressor grid** a grid between the anode and screen of a pentode valve to repel secondary electrons back to the anode. [L. *supprimĕre, suppressum* — *sub*, under, *premĕre*, to press.]

suppurate *sup'ū-rāt*, *v.i.* to gather pus or matter. — *n.* **suppurā'tion.** — *adj.* **supp'urative** promoting or attended by suppuration. — *n.* a suppurative agent. [L. *sub*, under, *pūs, pūris*, pus.]

supra- *soo'prə-, sū'prə-*, in composition, above. — *adjs.* **supra-ax'illary** arising above an axil; **supraciliary** (*-sil'*) above the eyebrow; **supracost'al** above or on a rib. — *n.* **Supralapsarian** (*-laps-ā'ri-ən*; L. *lāpsus*, fall) one of a class of Calvinists who make the decree of election and predestination to precede the Creation and the Fall — opp. to *Sublapsarian*. — Also *adj.* — *n.* **Supralapsā'rianism.** — *adjs.* **supralu'nar** beyond the moon: very lofty; **supramun'dane** above the world;

supranat'ional overriding national sovereignty: in, belonging to, more than one nation; **supra-or'bital** above the orbit of the eye; **suprarē'nal** above the kidneys (**suprarenal capsules, glands** the adrenal glands; **suprarenal extract** an extract from these used in the treatment of haemorrhage, Addison's disease, etc.); **suprasegmen'tal** (*phon.*) representing or continuing through two or more speech sounds; **suprasens'ible** above the reach of the senses; **supratemp'oral** transcending time: of the upper part of the temples or temporal region. [L. *suprā*, above.]

supreme *sū-, soo-prēm'*, poet. also *sū', soo', adj.* highest: greatest: most excellent. — *n.* the highest point: the highest authority. — *ns.* **suprem'acism** (belief in) the supremacy of one particular group of people; **suprem'acist** a believer in or supporter of supremacism; **supremacy** (*-prem'ə-si*) state of being supreme: supreme position or power; **Suprematism** (*soo-prem'ə-tizm*) an extreme form of cubism using very simple geometrical shapes. — *n.* and *adj.* **Suprem'atist.** — *adv.* **supremely** (*-prēm'*). — *ns.* **supreme'ness, supremity** (*-prem'*). — **supreme sacrifice** the giving up of one's life; **Supreme Soviet** the legislature of the U.S.S.R., consisting of two bodies, the Council of the Union, in which each deputy represents so many of the population, and the Council of Nationalities, in which each deputy represents one of the Republics or other distinct regions within the U.S.S.R. [L. *suprēmus*, superl. of *superus*, high — *super*, above.]

suprême, supreme *sü-prem, sū-, soo-prēm', n.* a rich cream sauce: a dish of meat, esp. breast of chicken, served in this sauce (also **chicken, veal,** etc. **suprême, supreme**). [Fr.]

supremo *sū-, soo-prā'mō*, also *-prē'mo, n.* a supreme head: — *pl.* **supre'mos.** [Sp., — L. *suprēmus*, highest.]

suq. See **souk.**

sur- *sûr-, pfx.* over, above, beyond. [Fr., — L. *super.*]

sur *sür*, (Fr.) *prep.* on, above. — **sur le tapis** (*lə ta-pē*) on the carpet (table-cover): under discussion, subject of talk; **sur place** (*plas*) on the spot.

sura[1]**, surah** *soo'rə, n.* a chapter of the Koran. [Ar. *sūra, sūrah,* step.]

sura[2] *soo'rə, n.* fermented palm-sap. [Sans. *surā.*]

suraddition *sûr-ə-dish'ən,* (*Shak.*) *n.* an additional title or designation. [Pfx. **sur-.**]

surah[1] *sū', soo'rə, n.* a soft twilled silk or artificial fabric. — Also *adj.* [Poss. from *Surat*.]

surah[2]. See **sura**[1].

sural *sū'rl, adj.* pertaining to the calf of the leg. [L. *sūra*, the calf.]

surance *shoor'əns,* (*Shak.*) *n.* assurance.

surat *soo-rat',* or *soo', n.* coarse uncoloured cotton. [*Surat,* in India.]

surbahar *sär-ba-här', n.* an Indian stringed instrument, larger than a sitar. [Bengali.]

surbase *sûr'bās, n.* a cornice or series of mouldings above the base of a pedestal, etc. — *adj.* **surbased** (*-bāst'*) of an arch, lower than half the span. — *n.* **surbase'ment.** [Pfx. **sur-.**]

surbate *sûr-bāt', v.t.* (*Spens. sûr'*) to bruise with walking, make footsore: — *pa.p.* **surbat'ed,** (*Spens.*) **surbet'.** [O.Fr. *surbatu,* excessively beaten, but with the meaning of Fr. *solbatu.*]

surbed *sûr-bed',* (*obs.*) *v.t.* to set on edge, as a stone with reference to the grain. [Pfx. **sur-.**]

surbet. See **surbate.**

surcease *sûr-sēs',* (*arch.*) *v.i.* to cease. — *v.t.* to desist or refrain from: to end, put a stop to. — *n.* cessation. [O.Fr. *sursis,* pa.p. of *surseoir* — L. *supersedēre,* to refrain from; cf. **supersede;** spelling influenced by **cease.**]

surcharge *sûr-chärj', v.t.* to overcharge: to overload: to overburden: to overstock: to saturate: to charge with overwhelming force (*Spens.*): to print over the original printing: to disallow: to exact a surcharge from. — *n.* **sur'charge** (or *-chärj'*) an overcharge: an extra charge: an excessive load: an overloaded condition: an amount not passed by an auditor, which must be refunded: a new valuation or cancel-mark printed on or over a stamp: the earth supported by a retaining wall above the level of its top. — *adj.* **surcharged'**. — *ns.* **surcharge'ment; surcharg'er.** [Pfx. **sur-**.]

surcingle *sûr'sing-gl, n.* a girth or strap for holding a saddle on an animal's back: the girdle of a cassock. — *v.t.* to gird, fasten, or thrash with a surcingle. [O.Fr. *surcengle* — L. *super, cingulum,* a belt.]

surcoat *sûr'kōt, n.* a mediaeval outer garment, usu. sleeveless, often with heraldic devices, worn by men and women over armour or ordinary dress. [O.Fr. *surcote, surcot — sur,* over, *cote,* garment.]

surculus *sûr'kū-ləs, (bot.) n.* a sucker. — *adj.* **sur'culose** having or producing suckers. [L. *sûrculus,* a twig.]

surd *sûrd, adj.* deaf (*obs.*): senseless (*obs.*): that cannot be expressed in rational numbers (*math.*): voiceless (*phon.*). — *n.* an irrational quantity (*math.*): a voiceless consonant (*phon.*). — *n.* **surd'ity** deafness. [L. *surdus,* deaf.]

sure[1] *shōōr, adj.* secure: safe: fit to be depended on: unerring: stable: bound in alliance (esp. by betrothal or marriage; *obs.*): certain: assured; confident beyond doubt: without other possibility. — *interj.* (*coll.*) certainly, undoubtedly, yes. — *advs.* **sure** (now chiefly *Ir.* or *U.S.,* except in comp. and in conventional phrases), **surely** firmly: confidently: safely: certainly: assuredly: as it would seem (often ironically). — *ns.* **sure'ness; sure'ty** certainty: safeguard: legal security against loss: one who becomes bound for another: a sponsor. — *v.t.* (*Shak.*) to be security for. — *n.* **sure'tyship.** — *adjs.* **sure'-enough'** (*U.S.*) genuine, real; **sure'-fire** (*coll.*) infallible; **sure'footed** not liable to stumble. — *adv.* **surefoot'edly.** — *n.* **surefoot'edness.** — **sure thing** a certainty, certain success: (as *interj.*) certainly, beyond doubt. — **be sure** do not omit; **for sure** certainly: of a certainty; **make sure** see **make**[1]; **stand surety for** to act as guarantor for; **sure enough** no doubt: in very fact: accordingly: there's no denying; **to be sure** certainly: I admit. [O.Fr. *sur, seur* (Fr. *sûr*) — L. *sécurus;* see **secure**.]

sure[2]. An old spelling of **sewer** (see **sew**[3]).

Sûreté *sûr-tā,* (Fr.) *n.* the French criminal investigation department.

surety. See **sure**[1].

surf *sûrf, n.* surging water or waves rushing up a sloping beach: sea-foam. — *v.i.* to bathe in or ride on surf. — *ns.* **surf'er; surf'ing** riding breaking waves on a surf-board or in a surf-canoe. — *adj.* **surf'y.** — **surf'-bathing** bathing in surf; **surf'-bather; surf'-bird** an American Pacific shore-bird (*Aphriza*) akin to sandpipers; **surf'-board, surf'ing-board** a board on which a bather allows himself to be carried inshore by the surf; **surf'boarding; surf'-boat** a boat for use in surf; **surf'-canoe** a slalom canoe or a kayak used for surfing; **surf'-duck** the scoter; **surf'-fish** any fish of a Western American viviparous perch-like family, *Embiotocidae;* **surf'man** one skilful in handling boats in surf; **surf'-riding** riding on a surf-board. [Origin obscure.]

surface *sûr'fis, n.* the outer boundary or face of anything: the outside or upper layer: that which has length and breadth but no thickness (*geom.*): area: outer appearance, character or texture: an aerofoil. — *adj.* of, on, or near a surface. — *v.t.* to put a surface, or some kind of surface or finish, upon. — *v.i.* to bring or rise to the surface: to expose, reveal (*U.S. coll.*) to regain consciousness (*coll.*): to get out of bed (*coll.*). — *adj.* **sur'faced** having this or that kind of surface. — *ns.* **sur'facer** one who, or that which smooths or levels a surface; **sur'facing** giving a surface to anything: material for a surface layer: washing surface deposits for gold. — *adj.* **sur'face-ac'tive** able to alter the surface tension of liquids (see also **surfactant**). — **sur'face-craft** a floating, not submersible, craft; **sur'face-mail** mail sent otherwise than by air; **sur'faceman** one who keeps a railway bed in repair; **surface noise** the noise produced by the friction of a stylus on a record; **surface**

structure (*linguistics*) the formal structure of sentences, esp. when analysed into their constituent parts; **surface tension** that property in virtue of which a liquid surface behaves like a stretched elastic membrane; **surface worker** a person engaged in any of the ancillary jobs in a coal-mine not done underground. — *adj.* **sur'face-to-air'** of a missile, etc., travelling from a base on the ground to a target in the air. — Also *adv.* — *adj.* and *adv.* **sur'face-to-sur'face.** — **sur'face-vessel; sur'face-water** drainage-water. [Fr., from *sur* — L. *super,* and *face* — L. *faciēs,* face.]

surfactant *sər-fak'tənt, n.* a substance, e.g. a detergent, which has the effect of altering the interfacial tension of water and other liquids or solids. [*surf*ace-*act*ive *agent.*]

surfeit *sûr'fit, n.* overfulness: gorging: gluttony: excess: an excessive meal: sickness or satiety caused by overeating or overdrinking. — *v.t.* to feed or fill to satiety or disgust. — *v.i.* to indulge to excess, esp. in food and drink (*arch.*): to suffer from excess (*obs.*). — *adj.* **sur'feited.** — *n.* **sur'feiter.** — *n.* and *adj.* **sur'feiting.** [O.Fr. *surfait,* excess — L. *super, above, facēre,* to make.]

surficial *sûr-fish'l,* (*geol.*) *adj.* superficial, subaerial. [*surface,* altered in analogy with *superficial.*]

surge[1]. An old spelling (*Shak.*) of **serge**.

surge[2] *sûrj, n.* an uprush, boiling or tumultuous movement of liquid: a sudden increase of power: a great wave: a swell: a sudden oscillation: a jerk on a rope: of spacecraft, movement in the direction of travel. — *v.i.* to well up: to heave tumultuously: to slip back: to jerk. — *v.t.* to send in surges: to slack suddenly. — *adjs.* **surge'ful; surge'less; sur'gent.** — *n.* and *adj.* **sur'ging.** — *adj.* **sur'gy.** [L. *surgĕre,* to rise.]

surgeon *sûr'jən, n.* one who treats injuries or diseases by manual operations: an army or naval doctor: a ship's doctor: a surgeon-fish. — *ns.* **sur'geoncy, sur'geonship** the office or employment of a surgeon in the army or navy; **sur'gery** the art and practice of a surgeon: a doctor's or dentist's consulting-room: a doctor's or dentist's time of consultation: a set, usu. regular, time when a member of parliament, local councillor, etc., is available to his constituents for consultation. — *adj.* **sur'gical** pertaining to surgery: incisive: precise. — *adv.* **sur'gically.** — **sur'geon-fish** a sea-surgeon; **surgeon general** the senior officer in the medical branch of the service (*mil.*): head of the public health service (*U.S.*); **surgeon's knot** a knot like a reef-knot but with a double turn in the first part (used in ligaturing a cut artery); **surgical boot, shoe** a boot, shoe designed to correct deformities of the foot; **surgical spirit** methylated spirit with small amounts of castor oil and oil of wintergreen. [A.Fr. *surgien;* see **chirurgeon**.]

surgy. See **surge**[2].

suricate *sū', sōō'ri-kāt, n.* a S. African animal of the civet family. [Origin unknown.]

Surinam *sū-, sōō-ri-nam', sū', sōō', n.* a republic, orig. a Dutch colony, in northern S. America. — **Surinam poison** fish poison got from a S. American papilionaceous plant, *Tephrosia;* **Surinam toad** a S. American amphibian that hatches its eggs in pits in its back.

surjection *sûr-jek'shən,* (*math.*) *n.* a mapping function in which all the elements in one set correspond to all the elements in another set. See also **bijection, injection.** [Pfx. **sur-** and L. *jacĕre,* to throw.]

surloin. Same as **sirloin.**

surly (*Spens.* **syrlye**) *sûr'li, adj.* haughty (*Shak.*): morose: gruff and grumpy: rough and gloomy: refractory. — *adv.* (*Shak.*) surlily. — *adv.* **sur'lily.** — *n.* **sur'liness.** [From **sir** and **like**[1]; cf. **lordly**.]

surmaster *sûr'mäs-tər,* (*arch.*) *n.* a second master in a school. [Pfx. **sur-**.]

surmise *sər-mīz', n.* allegation (*obs.*): suspicion: conjecture. — *v.t.* to imagine: to suspect: to conjecture, guess. — *adj.* **surmis'able.** — *ns.* **surmis'al; surmis'er.** — *n.* and *adj.* **surmis'ing.** [O.Fr., — *surmettre,* to accuse — L. *super,* upon, *mittĕre,* to send.]

surmount *sər-mownt'*, *v.t.* to mount above: to be on or go to the top of: to surpass: to get the better of. — *adjs.* **surmount'able; surmount'ed** surpassed: overcome: higher than half the span (*archit.*): having another figure laid over (*her.*). — *n.* **surmount'er.** — *n.* and *adj.* **surmount'ing.** [O.Fr. *surmunter* (Fr. *surmonter*) — L.L. *supermontāre*; see **mount²**.]

surmullet *sər-mul'it*, *n.* a species of red mullet, admired by the Romans for its colour-changes as it died. [Fr. *surmulet*.]

surname *sûr'nām*, *n.* an additional name (*arch.*): a family name. — *v.t.* to name by a surname. — *adj.* **surnom'-inal.** [On the analogy of Fr. *surnom*, from Eng. **name** and L. *nōmen, -inis*.]

surpass *sər-päs'*, *v.t.* to go or be beyond: to exceed: to excel. — *adjs.* **surpass'able; surpass'ing** passing beyond others: excellent in a high degree. — Also (*obs.* or *poet.*) *adv.* — *adv.* **surpass'ingly.** — *n.* **surpass'ingness.** [Fr. *surpasser* — *sur-, passer*, to pass.]

surplice *sûr'plis*, *n.* a white linen vestment worn over the cassock. — *adj.* **sur'pliced** wearing a surplice. [Fr. *surplis* — L.L. *superpellicium*, an overgarment — *pellis*, skin.]

surplus *sûr'pləs*, *n.* that which is left over: remainder: excess over what is required: excess of revenue over expenditure. — Also *adj.* — *n.* **sur'plusage** surplus: superfluity. [Fr., — L.L. *superplūs* — *super, plūs*, more.]

surprise *sər-prīz'*, *n.* a taking unawares: a sudden capture owing to unpreparedness: the emotion caused by anything sudden or contrary to expectation: (*loosely*) astonishment: anything that causes or is intended to cause this emotion. — Also *adj.* — *v.t.* to come upon suddenly or unawares: to capture by an unexpected assault: to seize (*obs.*): to lead or bring unawares, to betray (with *into*): to strike with wonder or astonishment: to confuse. — *v.i.* (*formal*) to cause surprise. — *n.* **surpris'al** act of surprising. — *adj.* **surprised'.** — *adv.* **surpris'edly.** — *n.* **surpris'er.** — *n.* and *adj.* **surpris'ing.** — *adv.* **surpris'ingly.** — *n.* **surpris'ingness.** — **surprise, surprise** ironic exclamation of surprise; **(much, greatly,** etc.) **to one's surprise** causing one great surprise. [O.Fr. (Fr.) fem. pa.p. of *surprendre* — L. *super, prehendĕre*, to catch.]

surquedry *sûr'kwi-dri*, (*Spens.*) *n.* arrogance. — Also (*obs.*) **sur'quedy.** [O.Fr. *surcuiderie* — *surcuidier* — L. *super*, above, and *cōgitāre, -ātum*, to think.]

surra *soo'rə*, *n.* a trypanosome disease of horses, etc., in Eastern Asia. [Marathi *sūra*, wheezing.]

surrealism *sər-ē'ə-lizm*, *n.* a movement in French art and literature, from about 1919 on, that aimed at drawing upon the subconscious and escaping the control of reason or any preconceptions. — *adj.* **surre'al.** — *adj.* and *n.* **surre'alist.** — *adj.* **surrealist'ic.** — *adv.* **surrealist'ically.** [Fr. *surréalisme* — *sur*, above, and *réalisme*, realism.]

surrebut *sur-i-but'*, *v.i.* to reply to a defendant's rebutter. — *ns.* **surrebutt'al** a plaintiff's evidence or presentation of evidence, in response to a defendant's rebuttal; **surrebutt'er** the plaintiff's reply, in common law pleading, to a defendant's rebutter. [Pfx. **sur-**.]

surreined *sûr'ānd*, *adj.* (*Shak.* **sur-reyn'd**) overridden. [App. **sur-** and **rein**¹.]

surrejoin *sur-i-join'*, *v.t.* and *v.i.* to reply to a defendant's rejoinder. — *n.* **surrejoind'er** a plaintiff's reply to a defendant's rejoinder. [Pfx. **sur-**.]

surrender *sə-ren'dər*, *v.t.* to deliver over: to relinquish: to yield up: to resign. — *v.i.* to yield oneself up: to yield. — *n.* act of surrendering. — *ns.* **surrenderee'** one to whom a legal surrender is made; **surren'derer; surren'-deror** (*law*) one who makes a surrender; **surren'dry** (*obs.*) a surrender. — **surrender value** the amount to be paid to an insured person who surrenders his policy. [A.Fr. *surrender*, O.Fr. *surrendre* — *sur-, rendre*; see **render**.]

surreptitious *sur-əp-tish'əs*, *adj.* done by stealth or fraud: stealthy. — *adv.* **surrepti'tiously.** [See **subreption**.]

surrey *sur'i*, (*U.S.*) *n.* a light four-wheeled vehicle for four, usu. with two seats. [Developed from a vehicle used in *Surrey*.]

sur-reyn'd. See **surreined**.

surrogate *sur'ō-gāt*, also *-git*, *n.* a substitute: a deputy, esp. of an ecclesiastical judge: one who grants marriage licences: a judge of probate (*U.S., local*): a person or thing standing, e.g. in a dream, for another person or thing, or a person who fills the role of another in one's emotional life (as *a mother, a father, surrogate*). — *ns.* **surr'ogacy** the state of being a surrogate: use of a surrogate, esp. of a surrogate mother; **surr'ogateship; surroga'tion** subrogation; **surrogā'tum** (*obs.*) a substitute. — **surrogate mother** a woman who bears a baby for another (esp. childless) couple, after either (artificial) insemination by the male or implantation of an embryo from the female; **surrogate motherhood.** [L. *surrogāre, -ātum* — *sub*, in the place of, *rogāre*, to ask.]

surround *sə-rownd'*, *v.t.* to overflow (*obs.*): to go or extend all around: to encompass, environ: to invest: to make a circuit of. — *n.* an act of surrounding (esp. hunted animals): a border, esp. the floor or floor-covering around a carpet. — *adj.* **surround'ing** encompassing: neighbouring. — *n.* an encompassing: (in *pl.*) environment, things round about. — **surround sound** any form of stereophonic sound reproduction using three or more speakers to give an effect of sound coming from all directions. [O.Fr. *suronder* — L. *superundāre*, to overflow — *super, unda*, wave; confused with **round²**.]

surroyal *sə-roi'əl*, *n.* any tine of a stag's horn above the royal. [Pfx. **sur-**.]

surtarbrand. See **surturbrand**.

surtax *sûr'taks*, *n.* an additional tax: tax payable on incomes above a certain high level (term not in official use in this sense). — *v.t.* to tax additionally: to charge surtax. [Pfx. **sur-**.]

surtitle *sûr'tītl*, *n.* a printed translation of the libretto of an opera in a language foreign to the audience, projected above the proscenium arch. [Pfx. **sur-**.]

surtout *sər-too', -toot'*, *n.* an overcoat (*obs.*): a lady's hood (*obs.*): (19th cent.) a close-bodied frock-coat: a raised portion of the parapet of a work at the angles, to protect from enfilade fire (*fort.*). [Fr., — L.L. *supertōtus*, an outer garment — L. *super, tōtus*, all.]

surturbrand, surtarbrand *sûr'tər-brand*, *n.* lignite found interbedded with lavas in Iceland. [Icel. *surtarbrandr* — *Surtar*, gen. of *Surtr*, name of a fire-giant, *brandr*, brand.]

surucucu *soo-roo-koo-koo'*, *n.* a S. American Indian name for the bushmaster.

surveillance *sər-vā'ləns*, or *-lyəns*, *n.* vigilant supervision: spy-like watching: superintendence. — *v.t.* **surveille** (*-vāl'*) (back-formation; *U.S.*) to observe, keep under surveillance. — *n.* **surveill'ant.** [Fr., — *surveiller* — *sur, veiller*, to watch — L. *vigilāre*.]

survew(e). See **survew**.

survey *sər-vā'*, *v.t.* to view comprehensively and extensively: to examine in detail: to examine the structure of a building: to obtain by measurements data for mapping: to perceive, spy (*Shak.*). — *ns.* **sur'vey** (also *-vā'*) a general view, or a statement of its results: an inspection: collection of data for mapping: an organisation or body of men for that purpose: superintendence; **survey'al; survey'ance; survey'ing; survey'or** an overseer: a measurer of land: an inspector (of roads, of weights and measures, of customs duties, etc.); **survey'orship.** [O.Fr. *surveoir* — L. *super*, over, *vidēre*, to see.]

surview *sər-vū'*, *Spens.* **survew(e)**, *v.t.* to survey, look over: to command a view of. [Pfx. **sur-**.]

survive *sər-vīv'*, *v.t.* to live beyond: to outlive. — *v.i.* to remain alive. — *adj.* **survi'vable.** — *ns.* **survivabil'ity; survi'val** a surviving or living after: anything that continues to exist after others of its kind have disappeared, or after the time to which it naturally belongs. — *adj.* (esp. of standard equipment) designed to help one to survive exposure or other dangerous condition.

— *n.* **survi'valist** a person who takes measures to ensure that he survives a catastrophic event, or measures for his own personal protection from attack, robbery, etc. — Also *adj.* — *n.* **survi'vance** survival: succession or right to succeed on surviving the present holder. — *adj.* **survi'ving.** — *ns.* **survi'vor; survi'vorship.** — **survival of the fittest** the longer average life of the fit in the struggle for existence, and the consequent transmission of favourable variations in greater proportion to later generations. [Fr. *survivre* — L. *super*, beyond, *vīvĕre*, to live.]

Surya *sōōr'yə, n.* the Hindu sun-god. [Sans.]

sus *sus*, (*slang*) *n.* suspicious behaviour, loitering with intent. — *v.i.* (*slang*) to arrest for suspicious behaviour: — *pa.t., pa.p.* **sussed.** — Also **suss.** — **sus(s) out** (*slang*) to investigate: to find out, discover. [**suspect, suspicion.**]

susceptible *sə-sep'ti-bl, adj.* (usu. with *to*) capable, admitting: capable of receiving: impressionable: easily affected by emotion (esp. amatory). — *ns.* **suscep'tance** (*phys.*) the imaginary part of the admittance; **susceptibil'ity, suscep'tibleness.** — *adv.* **suscep'tibly.** — *adj.* **suscep'tive** capable of receiving or admitting: readily admitting. — *ns.* **suscep'tiveness; susceptiv'ity** (*sus-*); **suscep'tor** (*obs.*) a sponsor; **suscip'ient** a recipient, esp. of a sacrament. — *adj.* receiving. [L. *suscipĕre, susceptum*, to take up — *sus-* (*subs-*), up, *capĕre*, to take.]

suscipient. See **susceptible.**

suscitate *sus'i-tāt, v.t.* to excite, rouse. — *n.* **suscitā'tion.** [L. *suscitāre, -ātum* — *sus-* (*subs-*), under, *citāre*, to arouse.]

sushi *sōō'shi, n.* a Japanese dish of small cakes of cold rice and fish, vegetables, etc., and a vinegar sauce. [Jap.]

suslik *sus'lik, sōōs'lik, n.* a spermophile, zizel, or ground-squirrel. [Russ.]

suspect *səs-pekt', v.t.* to mistrust: to imagine to be guilty: to doubt: to be ready to believe, but without sufficient evidence: to incline to believe the existence, presence, or agency of: to have an inkling of: to conjecture. — *v.i.* to imagine guilt, to be suspicious. — *n.* suspicion: (*sus'pekt*) a person suspected. — *adj.* suspected. — *adjs.* **suspect'able; suspect'ed.** — *adv.* **suspect'edly.** — *n.* **suspect'edness.** — *adjs.* **suspect'ful** suspicious; **suspect'less** unsuspicious: unsuspected. [L. *suspicĕre, suspectum*, to look at secretly or askance — *su-* (*sub-*), *specĕre*, to look.]

suspend *səs-pend', v.t.* to hang: to make to depend: to sustain from falling: to put or hold in a state of suspense or suspension: to make to stop for a time: to defer: to debar from any privilege, office, emolument, etc., for a time: to sustain into a following chord, producing discord (*mus.*): to hold in an indeterminate state. — *adj.* **suspen'ded.** — *ns.* **suspend'er** one who, or that which, suspends: a strap to support a sock or stocking: (in *pl.*) braces (*U.S.*); **suspense'** intermission: cessation: deferring, as of judgment: tense uncertainty: indecision. — *adj.* in suspense (*Milt.* **suspens'**, **suspence'**) suspended, held back. — *adj.* **suspense'ful.** — *n.* **suspensibil'ity.** — *adj.* **suspen'sible.** — *ns.* **suspen'sion** (*-shən*) act of suspending: interruption: delay: temporary privation of office or privilege: a conditional withholding: holding a note from a chord into the next chord (*mus.*): a discord so produced (*mus.*): a mixture of a fluid with dense particles which are prevented from settling by viscosity and impact of molecules (*chem.*): in a motor vehicle or railway carriage, the system of springs, etc., supporting the chassis on the axles. — *adj.* **suspen'sive.** — *adv.* **suspen'sively.** — *ns.* **suspen'soid** (*chem.*) a colloid dispersed with difficulty, yielding an unstable solution that cannot be reformed after coagulation; **suspen'sor** a chain of cells to which a plant-embryo is fixed (*bot.*): a suspensory bandage. — *adj.* **suspensorial** (*sus-pen-sō'ri-əl, -sō'*). — *n.* **suspenso'rium** that which holds up a part, esp. the arrangement joining the lower jaw to the cranium in vertebrates below mammals. — *adj.* **suspen'sory** suspending: having the power or effect of delaying or staying: of the suspensorium. — *n.* a suspensorium. — **suspended animation** temporary cessation of the outward signs and of some of the functions of life; **suspended sentence** a legal sentence not served unless another crime is committed; **suspen'der-belt** a woman's undergarment with stocking suspenders; **suspense account** an account in which items are entered which cannot at once be placed in an ordinary account; **suspension bridge** a bridge with roadway supported by chains passing over elevated piers; **suspension building** building round a concrete core and from the top downward. — **suspend payment** publicly to stop paying debts from insolvency. [L. *suspendĕre, -pēnsum* — pfx. *sus-* (*subs-*), *pendĕre*, to hang.]

suspercollate *sus-pər-kol'āt*, (*facet.*) *v.t.* to hang. [*Sus. per coll.*, abbrev. for L. *suspendātur per collum*, let him be hanged by the neck.]

suspicion *səs-pish'ən, n.* act of suspecting: state of being suspected: the imagining of something without evidence or on slender evidence: inkling: mistrust: a slight quantity, as of spirits (*coll.*): ground for suspicion (*Shak.*). — *v.t.* (*dial.* and *U.S. dial.*) to suspect. — *adjs.* **suspi'cionless; suspi'cious** full of suspicion: showing suspicion: inclined to suspect: giving ground for suspicion: liable to suspicion, doubtful. — *adv.* **suspi'ciously.** — *n.* **suspi'ciousness.** — **above, beyond suspicion** too honest, virtuous, etc., to be suspected of a crime or fault; **on suspicion (of)** suspected (of); **under suspicion** suspected. [L. *suspīciō, -ōnis*; see **suspect.**]

suspire *səs-pīr', (arch.* or *poet.*) *v.i.* to sigh: to breathe. — *v.t.* to breathe forth. — *n.* **suspiration** (*sus-pə-rā'shən*) sighing. — *adj.* **suspirious** (*səs-pīr'i-əs*) breathing labouredly: sighing. [L. *suspīrāre* — *su-* (*sub-*), *spīrāre*, to breathe.]

suss. See **sus.**

sussarara. Same as **siserary.**

sustain *səs-tān', v.t.* to hold up: to bear: to support: to provide for: to maintain: to sanction: to keep going: to keep up: to support the life of: to prolong. — *n.* (*Milt.*) means of sustenance. — *adj.* **sustain'able.** — *n.* **sustainabil'ity.** — *adj.* **sustained'.** — *adv.* **sustain'edly.** — *n.* **sustain'er** one who, or that which, sustains: the main motor in a rocket, continuing with it throughout its flight — cf. **booster.** — *n.* and *adj.* **sustain'ing.** — *ns.* **sustain'ment** act of sustaining: sustenance; **sustenance** (*sus'ti-nəns*) that which sustains: maintenance: nourishment. — *adj.* **sustentac'ular** supporting. — *n.* **sustentac'ulum** a supporting part. — *v.t.* **sus'tentate** to sustain. — *n.* **sustentā'tion.** — *adj.* **sustentative** (*sus'tən-tā-tiv, səs-ten'tə-tiv*) sustaining. — *ns.* **sus'tentātor** a sustaining part or structure; **susten'tion** the act of sustaining. — *adjs.* **susten'tive; sus'tinent** sustaining. — **sustaining pedal** a pedal on a piano which sustains the note(s) played by allowing the strings to continue vibrating. [L. *sustinēre* — pfx. *sus-* (*subs-*), *tenēre*, to hold; partly through O.Fr. *sustenir* (Fr. *soutenir*).]

Susu *sōō'sōō, n.* a Negroid people of W. Africa, living mainly in Mali, Guinea and Sierra Leone: its language.

sustenance, sustentacular, sustentation, sustinent, etc. See **sustain.**

susurrus *sū-, sōō-sur'əs,* (*poet.*) *n.* a murmuring: a whisper: a rustling. — *adj.* **susurr'ant.** — *v.i.* **su'ssurate.** — *n.* **susurrā'tion.** [L. *susurrus.*]

sutile *sū', sōō'tīl, -til, (rare) adj.* done by stitching. [L. *sūtilis* — *suĕre*, to sew.]

sutler *sut'lər, (hist.*) *n.* one who sells liquor or provisions to soldiers in camp or garrison: a camp-hawker. — *n.* **sut'lery** a sutler's work or stall. — *v.i.* **sutt'le** to trade as a sutler. [Du. *zoetelaar* (earlier *soeteler*).]

sutor *sū', sōō'tor, -tər, (arch.*) *n.* a cobbler. — *adjs.* **suto'rial, suto'rian** relating to cobbling or to sewing. [**souter**; or directly from L. *sūtor, -ōris*, cobbler.]

sutra *sōōt'rə, n.* in Sanskrit literature, an aphoristic rule or book of aphorisms on ritual, grammar, metre, philosophy, etc.: in Buddhist sacred literature, any of a group of writings including the sermons of Buddha and other doctrinal works. [Sans. *sūtra*, thread.]

suttee, sati *sut′ē, sut-ē′, n.* an Indian widow who burned herself on her husband's pyre: the custom of so doing. — *n.* **suttee′ism.** [Sans. *satī*, a true wife.]

suttle[1] *sut′l, adj.* light (esp. of weight when tare is subtracted; *obs.*). [**subtle.**]

suttle[2] *sut′l, (Milt.) adj.* subtle. — *adv.* **sutt′ly.** — *n.* **sutt′letie** subtlety. [**subtle.**]

suttle[3]. See **sutler.**

suture *sū′, sōō′chər, -tūr, n.* a seam: a stitching: the stitching of a wound: a stitch: a junction or meeting of margins, esp. of bones or of carpels: a line of dehiscence: a line of union. — *v.t.* to stitch up. — *adj.* **su′tural.** — *adv.* **su′turally.** — *adj.* **su′tured.** — *n.* **sutura′tion.** [L. *sūtūra*, a seam — *suĕre*, to sew.]

suum cuique *sōō′əm kwī′* or *kī′kwi, sōō′ōom kōō-ē′kwe,* (L.) to each his own.

suversed *sū-vûrst′, (obs.; trig.) adj.* versed of the supplement. [From the contraction *sup. versed.*]

suzerain *sōō′zə-rān,* or *sū′, n.* a feudal lord: supreme or paramount ruler: a state having supremacy over another. — *adj.* **paramount.** — *n.* **su′zerainty** position or power of a suzerain. [Fr., formed in imitation of *souverain* from *sus-*, over — L. *sūsum* (for *sūrsum, subvorsum*).]

svarabhakti *svä-rä-bäk′tē, n.* development of a vowel between consonants. [Sans. *svara,* vowel, *bhakti,* separation.]

Svarga. Same as **Swarga.**

svastika *svas′tik-ə, n.* Same as **swastika.**

svelte *svelt, adj.* lissom, lithe: in art, free, easy, light and bold. [Fr.]

Svengali *sven-gä′lē, n.* a person who exerts total mental control over another, usu. for evil ends. [Name of the evil hypnotist in George du Maurier's novel *Trilby.*]

swab *swob, n.* a mop for cleaning or drying floors or decks: a brush for wetting foundry moulds: a sponge or the like for cleaning the bore of a fire-arm: a bit of cotton-wool or the like for mopping up blood or discharges, applying antiseptics, cleaning a patient's mouth, or taking a specimen of morbid secretion for examination: a specimen so taken: a naval officer's epaulet (*slang*): a lubber or clumsy fellow (*slang*): in an old form of whist, a card entitling its holder to a share of the stakes. — *v.t.* to mop with a swab: — *pr.p.* **swabb′ing;** *pa.t.* and *pa.p.* **swabbed.** — *n.* **swabb′er** one who uses a swab: a mop for cleaning ovens: a swab in whist as formerly played: (in *pl.*) whist so played (also **whisk and swabbers**). [Du. *zwabber,* swabber.]

swack *swak, swäk, (Scot.) adj.* pliant: nimble. [Cf. L. G. *swak,* Du. *zwak;* Ger. *schwach,* weak.]

swad *swod, n.* a country lout: a soldier. — *n.* **swadd′y** a soldier, esp. a militiaman. [Perh. Scand., or from **squad, squaddy.**]

swaddle *swod′l, v.t.* to swathe: to bandage: to bind tight with clothes, as an infant: to thrash (*obs.*). — *n.* **swaddling-clothes:** a bandage. — *n.* **swadd′ler** (*Anglo-Ir.*) a Methodist or Protestant in general. — *swadd′-ling-band, swadd′ling-cloth** a cloth for swaddling an infant: — *pl.* **swadd′ling-clothes** (*B.*). [O.E. *swæthel, swethel,* bandage; cf. **swathe**[1].]

swaddy. See **swad.**

Swadeshi *swä-dā′shē, n.* a pre-Independence Indian nationalist movement, favouring home industries and boycott of foreign goods: a product made in India. — Also *adj.* — *n.* **Swade′shism.** [Bengali, own country.]

swag *swag, v.i.* to sway: to sag: (often with *it*) to travel around carrying a bundle (*Austr. slang*). — *pr.p.* **swagg′ing;** *pa.t.* and *pa.p.* **swagged.** — *n.* a swagging: a festoon: a subsidence, as of ground over a mine: a depression: a bundle of possessions carried by one travelling on foot (esp. *Austr.*): plunder (*slang*). — *v.i.* **swagg′er** to walk with a blustering or overweening air of superiority and self-confidence: to brag noisily or ostentatiously: to bully. — *v.t.* to do, bring, render, by swaggering. — *n.* a swaggering gait, manner, mien,

or behaviour: a swagman (*slang*). — *adj.* (*slang*) ostentatiously fashionable: smart. — *n.* **swagg′erer.** — *n.* and *adj.* **swagg′ering.** — *adv.* **swagg′eringly.** — *n.* **swagg′ie** (*Austr. slang*) a swagman. — *adj.* **swag′-bellied** having a pendulous belly. — **swag′-belly** a pendulous belly: one whose belly swags; **swagg′er-cane, swagg′er-stick** a short military cane; **swagg′er-coat** a coat which hangs loosely from the shoulder; **swag′man** (*Austr.*) one who carries his swag about with him, esp. in a search for work; **swag′shop** (*slang*) a place where cheap and trashy goods are sold; **swags′man** a swagman: a burglar's accomplice who carries the plunder (*slang*). [Related to **sway;** prob. Scand.]

swage[1] *swāj, n.* a grooved or moulded border (*obs.*): any of several tools including a tool in two grooved parts, for shaping metal. — *v.t.* to shape with a swage: to reduce the cross-section of a rod or tube, e.g. by forcing it through a tapered aperture between two grooved dies. — **swage block** a block with various holes, grooves, etc., for use in metal-working. [O.Fr. *souage.*]

swage[2] *swāj, (Milt.) v.t.* to assuage. [A.Fr. *suagier* — L. *suāvis,* mild, or aphetic for **assuage.**]

swagger, swaggie, swagshop, swagsman. See **swag.**

Swahili *swä-hē′li, n.* the people of Zanzibar and the opposite coast: one of them: loosely, their language (*Kiswahili*), a Bantu tongue modified by Arabic, spoken in Kenya, Tanzania and other parts of East Africa. [Ar. *sawāhil,* pl. *sāhil,* coast, with suffix.]

swain *swān, (arch., poet.,* often *ironical) n.* a young man: a peasant: rustic: a lover. — *n.* **swain′ing** love-making. — *adj.* **swain′ish** boorish. — *n.* **swain′ishness** boorishness. [O.N. *sveinn,* young man, servant; O.E. *swān.*]

swale[1] *swāl, n.* a shady spot: shade: a sunken or marshy place. — *adj.* **swāl′y.** [Cf. O.N. *svalr,* cool.]

swale[2] *swāl, v.i.* to sway.

swale[3], **swaling.** See **sweal.**

swallet. See **swallow**[2].

swallow[1] *swol′ō, n.* a long-winged migratory bird (*Hirundo rustica*), often with a forked tail, that catches insects on the wing: any bird of its genus or family: extended to various unrelated birds of similar form or habits. — **swall′ow-dive** a dive during which one's arms are outstretched to the sides. — Also *v.i.* — **swall′ow-tail** a forked tail: a long-tailed dress coat: a butterfly (*Papilio*) with prolongations of the hind wings: a barbed arrow: a pennon: a swallow-tailed bird (humming-bird, kite). — *adj.* **swall′ow-tailed** with forked and pointed tail. — **swall′ow-wort** an asclepiad (*Cynanchum* or *Vincetoxicum*), from the swallow-tailed appearance of its paired pods: hence any asclepiad: greater celandine (q.v.). [O.E. *swalwe, swealwe;* Ger. *Schwalbe.*]

swallow[2] *swol′ō, v.t.* to receive through the gullet into the stomach: to engulf (often with *up*): to take in: to accept, sit down under (as an affront): to believe credulously. — *v.i.* to perform the action of swallowing something. — *n.* an abyss: a swallow-hole: a throat: an act of swallowing: a gulp: a quantity swallowed at once: capacity for swallowing: the aperture in a block, between the sheave and frame, through which the rope runs (*naut.*). — *ns.* **swall′et** a swallow-hole; **swall′ower.** — **swall′ow-hole** a funnel or fissure through which water passes underground esp. in limestone. — **swallow one's pride** to humble oneself. [O.E. *swelgan* (vb.) *geswelg* (n.); cf. Ger. *schwelgen.*]

swam *swam, pa.t.* (and *Shak.,* etc., *pa.p.*) of **swim.**

swami *swä′mē, n.* a Hindu idol: a Hindu religious instructor, esp. as a form of address. [Hindi *svāmī,* lord, master.]

swamp *swomp, n.* a tract of wet, spongy (in U.S. often tree-clad) land: low ground filled with water. — *v.t.* to sink or involve in, or as in, a swamp: to cause to fill with water, as a boat: to overwhelm, inundate. — *v.i.* to become swamped. — *adj.* of, of the nature o swamp: living or growing in swamps. — *n.* **swamp** (*U.S.*) a person who lives or works in the swamps *adj.* **swamp'y.** — **swamp boat** a flat-bottomed boat with a raised aeroplane engine for travelling over swamps; **swamp cypress** Taxodium, a deciduous conifer of swamps in Southern U.S.; **swamp fever** a viral disease of horses — also called **equine infectious anaemia; swamp'land; swamp oak** Casuarina. [Perh. from L.G.; prob. akin to O.E. *swamm*, mushroom, Ger. *Schwamm*, sponge, fungus.]

swan *swon, n.* any species of *Cygnus*, a genus of large, graceful, stately, long-necked birds of the duck family. — *adj.* **swan'like.** — *n.* **swann'ery** a place where swans are kept or bred. — *adj.* **swann'y** swanlike. — **swan'=goose** the China goose: the coscoroba swan (*Coscoroba coscoroba*) of S. America; **swan'herd** one who tends swans; **swan'-hopping** (*erron.*) swan-upping; **swan'=maid'en** in Germanic folklore, a maiden who can become a swan by putting on her feather-garment; **swan'-mark** the notch made on the swan's upper mandible; **swan'-mussel** a large freshwater mussel; **swan'-neck** an S-shaped bend or piece; **swans'-down, swans'down** the under-plumage of a swan: a soft woollen or mixed cloth: a thick cotton with a soft nap on one side; **swan'-shot** a shot of large size, like buck-shot; **swan'-skin** the unplucked skin of a swan: a soft, nappy, fine-twilled fabric; **swan'-song** the fabled song of a swan just before its death: a writer's or musician's last work: last work of any kind: final appearance; **swan'-upp'ing** an annual expedition up the Thames for the marking of young swans belonging to the Dyers' and Vintners' Companies (those belonging to the crown being unmarked) (see *v.t.* **up**). — **swan about, around** (*slang*) to move about aimlessly; **swan in, up** (*coll.*) to arrive, either aimlessly or gracefully. [O.E. *swan*; Ger. *Schwan*, Du. *zwaan*.]

swang *swang,* (*Wordsworth*) a rare *pa.t.* of **swing**. **swanherd.** See **swan**.

swank *swangk, adj.* (*Scot.*) slender, pliant: agile. — *n.* (*slang*) ostentation: pretentiousness: a person who swanks. — *v.i.* (*slang*) to show off: to swot (*arch.*). — *n.* **swank'er.** — *adj.* **swank'ing** strapping: showing off (*slang*): showy (*slang*). — *n.* **swank'y** (*Scot.*) an active fellow: poor thin beer or any sloppy drink, even sweetened water and vinegar. — Also **swank'ey.** — *adj.* (*slang*) ostentatiously smart. — **swank'pot** a swanker (*coll.*) [Cf. O.E. *swancor*, pliant, M.H.G. *swanken*, to sway.]

swap, swop *swop, v.t.* to strike: to reap close: to slam, plump, slap down: to strike (as a bargain): to give in exchange: to barter. — *v.i.* to smite: to flop: to barter: — *pr.p.* **swapp'ing, swopp'ing;** *pa.t.* and *pa.p.* **swapped, swopped, swapt, swopt.** — *n.* a stroke: an exchange. — *adv.* suddenly. — *n.* **swapp'er, swopp'er** one who swaps: a very big thing, whopper. — *n.* and *adj.* **swapp'ing, swopp'ing.** — **swap line** (*econ.*) a lending arrangement between central banks; **swap'-shop** a shop, meeting, etc., where goods are exchanged for other goods or services rather than money. [M.E. *swappen*; perh. imit.; or conn. with **sweep, swoop**.]

swaraj *swä-räj', (Ind.) n.* self-government, independence, home-rule. — *ns.* **swaraj'ism** formerly, the policy of Indian political independence; **swaraj'ist** an advocate of this. [Sans. *svarājya* — *sva*, own, *rājya*, rule.]

sward *swörd,* (usu. *poet.*) *n.* the grassy surface of land: green turf. — Also **swarth.** — *v.t.* to cover with sward. — *adjs.* **sward'ed, sward'y** covered with sward. [O.E. *sweard*, skin, rind; Du. *zwoord*, Ger. *Schwarte*.]

sware *swär, arch. pa.t.* of **swear**.

swarf¹ *swörf,* **swarve** *swärv,* **swerf** *swûrf,* **swerve** *swûrv* (*Scot.*), *vs.i.* to faint. — *n.* **swarf, swerf** a swoon.

swarf² *swörf, n.* grit from an axle, etc.: stone or metal grindings, filings, turnings, etc. [O.N. *svarf*, file-dust.]

Swarga, Svarga *swär'gä, swur'gə, n.* heaven: Indra's paradise — (*Southey*) **Swer'ga.** [Sans. *Svarga*.]

'warm¹ *swörm, n.* a body of bees going off to found a new community: a colony, offshoot: a throng of insects or other small animals: a throng. — *v.i.* to go off in a swarm: to occur or come in swarms: to abound, teem. — *v.t.* to cause to swarm: to throng (chiefly *U.S.* except in *pass.*). — *n.* **swarm'er.** — *n.* and *adj.* **swarm'ing.** — **swarm'-spore, -cell** a free-swimming generally ciliated asexual reproductive body (*bot.*): an active germ produced by sporulation in Protozoa (*zool.*). [O.E. *swearm*; Ger. *Schwarm*.]

swarm² *swörm, v.t.* and *v.i.* to climb by clasping with arms and legs. [Origin unknown.]

swart *swört,* **swarth** *swörth, adjs.* (*arch.* or *dial.*) black: dusky: blackening, hence, malignant, baleful. — *n.* **swarthiness** (*swör'dhi-nis*). — *adj.* **swarthy** (*swör'dhi*) blackish: dark-skinned. — *n.* **swart'ness.** — *adj.* **swart'y.** — **swart'-back** (O.N. *svartbakr*) the great black-backed gull; **swart star** (*Milt.*) app. the Dog-star, because at the time of its appearance the complexion darkens. [O.E. *sweart*; O.N. *svartr*, Ger. *schwarz*, black.]

swarth *swörth.* Same as **sward, swart,** or (*Shak.*) **swath¹.**

swarty. See **swart**.

swarve. See **swarf¹.**

swash¹ *swosh, n.* slush: pig-wash: a splash: a wash of liquid: a dash: a heavy blow: a clashing or dashing sound: a swashbuckler (*arch.*): swaggering (*arch.*). — *v.t.* and *v.i.* to dash: to splash: to clash. — *n.* **swash'er** (*Shak.*) a blusterer. — *n.* and *adj.* **swash'ing** slashing, crushing: blustering. — *adj.* **swash'y** slushy. — **swash'-buckler** one who clashes a sword on a buckler, hence a bully, a blusterer: a dare-devil. — *adj.* **swash'buckling** of, resembling a swashbuckler: adventurous, exciting. [Imit.]

swash² *swosh, n.* a piece of turner's work with mouldings oblique to the axis: a flourish on a letter. — Also *adj.* — **swash letters** italic capitals with top and bottom flourishes; **swash plate** a disc set obliquely on a revolving axis; **swash'work** turner's work cut obliquely. [Origin unknown.]

swastika *swos'ti-kə, swas',* **svastika** *svas', ns.* an ancient and worldwide symbol, a cross with arms bent at a right angle, esp. clockwise (see also **fylfot**), emblematic of the sun, good luck, anti-semitism, or Naziism. — See also **gammadion.** [Sans. *svastika* — *svasti*, well-being — *su*, good, *asti*, he is.]

swat¹ *swot, v.t.* to hit smartly or heavily. — *n.* a sharp or heavy blow: a swatter. — *n.* **swatt'er** an instrument consisting of a flexible shaft with flap-like head, with which to swat flies. [squat.]

swat² *swot, swöt,* (*Scot.* and *Spens.*) *pa.t.* of **sweat**.

swat³. See **swot**.

swatch *swoch, n.* a sample, esp. of cloth. [Origin unknown.]

swath¹ *swöth, swoth, n.* a band of mown ground or of grass or corn cut by the scythe or mowing-machine or ready for these: a broad band: the sweep of a scythe or mowing-machine. — Also **swathe** (*swädh*). — *v.t.* **swathe** (*Canada*) to cut grain and leave (grain) lying in swathes to ripen on the ground. — *adj.* **swathy** (*swöth'i, swädh'i*). [O.E. *swæth* and *swathu*, track; Du.]

swath² *swoth,* (*Shak.*) *n.* Same as **swathe¹.**

swathe¹ *swädh, v.t.* to bind round, envelop: to bandage. — *n.* a bandage: a wrapping. — *n.pl.* **swath'ing-clothes** (*Shak.*; another reading, **swath'ling-, swoth'ling-), -clouts** swaddling-clothes. [O.E. *swathian.*]

swathe². See **swath¹.**

swats *swots,* (*Scot.*) *n.* new ale. [O.E. *swatan* (pl.), beer.]

swatter¹ *swot'ər, swat'ər, (dial.) v.i.* to squatter: to splash or spill about. [Cf. **squatter.**]

swatter². See **swat¹.**

sway *swä, v.t.* to incline about or from side to side: to cause to incline: to divert: to influence by power or moral force: to wield (*arch.*): to govern: to control (*arch.*): to have a preponderating influence upon (*arch.*): to hoist (*naut.*). — *v.i.* to swing: to oscillate: to swerve: to proceed, bend one's course (*Shak.*): to advance in hostility (*Spens.*): to incline to one side: to rule: to have preponderating weight or influence. —

n. rotation (*Shak.*): a sweep: a swing: a swerve: directing force or influence: preponderance: rule: in thatching, a hazel lath laid horizontally to hold down the straw or reed. — *adjs.* **swayed, sway′-back** bent down in the back, as a horse. — *n.* **sway′er.** — *n.* and *adj.* **sway′ing.** — *n.* **sway′back** a nervous disease of lambs causing difficulty in walking or standing (see also above). — **hold sway (over)** to have power, authority (over). [Perh. from a root O.E. word, or the corresponding O.N. *sveigja*, to bend, swing; prob. partly from L.G. *swâjen* (Ger. *schweien*), to swing.]

swayl, swayling. See **sweal**.

Swazi *swä′zē*, *n.* a racially mixed people inhabiting Swaziland and parts of the Eastern Transvaal of South Africa: a member of this people: its language. [*Mswati*, a former king of this people.]

swazzle, swozzle *swozl*, *n.* an instrument consisting of two convex pieces of metal with a tape stretched between them, placed in the mouth to make the voice of Mr. Punch in a Punch and Judy show. [Perh. from Ger. *schwätzeln*, to chatter, tattle.]

sweal, sweel *swēl*, **swale, swayl** *swāl*, (*dial.*) *vs.t.* to scorch: to singe: to roast in the skin: to burn off, as heather and gorse, soot in a chimney: to cause to gutter: to waste away. — *v.i.* to be burning hot: to gutter as a candle. — *ns.* and *adjs.* **sweal′ing, swal′ing, swayl′ing.** [O.E. *swǣlan* (trans.), *swelan* (intrans.), to burn.]

swear *swār*, *v.i.* to take or utter an oath: to utter imprecations: to utter defiant noises (as a cat): to give evidence on oath (*rare*). — *v.t.* to assert, promise, agree to, confirm, or value, on oath: to assert loudly or boldly: to invoke (*Shak.*): to administer an oath to: to put on oath: to bind by oath: to admit to office by an oath: to bring, put, render, by swearing: — *pa.t.* **swōre**, (*swōr, swor*), *arch.* **swāre**; *pa.p.* **swōrn**, (*swōrn, sworn*), *arch.* and *illit.* **swōre**. — *n.* an oath: an expression that is formally an oath or a curse, or bad language generally. — *n.* **swear′er.** — *n.* and *adj.* **swear′ing.** — *adj.* **sworn** attested: bound by oath: having taken an oath: devoted, inveterate, confirmed, as if by oath. — **swear′-word** a word that is considered bad language. — **swear at** to hurl oaths and curses at: to be very incongruous with, esp. in colour; **swear by** to invoke as witness to an oath: to put complete confidence in; **swear in** to inaugurate by oath; **swear off** to renounce, promise to give up; **swear to** to affirm or identify on oath. [O.E. *swerian*; Du. *zweren*, Ger. *schwören*.]

sweard *swērd*, (*Spens.*) *n.* Same as **sword**.

sweat *swet*, *n.* the moisture excreted by the skin: moisture exuding or seeming to exude from anything: a state, fit, or process of exuding sweat: exercise or treatment inducing sweat: sweating sickness: labour: drudgery: fidgety anxiety: a soldier (*slang*). — *v.i.* to give out sweat or moisture: to toil, drudge for poor wages: to suffer penalty, smart: to exude: to become coated with moisture: to worry, be anxious. — *v.t.* to give forth as, or like, sweat: to wet or soil with sweat: to cause to sweat: to squeeze money or extortionate interest from: to exact the utmost from: to wring evidence or confession from (*U.S. slang*): to extract undue gains from, e.g. by removing gold from a coin: to compel to hard work for mean wages: to unite by partial fusion of metal surfaces: — *pa.t.* and *pa.p.* **sweat′ed** (or **sweat**). — *adj.* **sweat′ed.** — *ns.* **sweat′er** one who sweats: a cause of sweating: a diaphoretic: a heavy jersey, orig. one for reducing weight by sweating, now for intervals in exercise, leisure wear, etc.: one who sweats coins or workers: a London street ruffian in Queen Anne's time who prodded passers-by with his sword; **sweat′iness.** — *n.* and *adj.* **sweat′ing.** — *adj.* **sweat′y.** — **sweat band** the leather or similar band inside a man's hat: a similar band worn to absorb perspiration from the forehead: an absorbent wristlet worn by e.g. tennis players to prevent sweat running down to their hands; **sweated labour** hard work obtained by exploitation; **sweat′er-girl** (*coll.*) a woman with a well-developed bust, usually wearing a tight-fitting sweater; **sweat gland** any of the

glands producing sweat; **sweating sickness** an epidemic disorder (usu. fatal) which ravaged Europe and esp. England in the 15th and 16th centuries — a violent inflammatory fever, with a fetid perspiration over the whole body; **sweating system** the practice of working poor people at starvation wages, for long hours, at home or in unhealthy rooms; **sweat′-shirt** a short- or long-sleeved knitted cotton sweater; **sweat shop** a factory or shop where the sweating system operates; **sweat suit** a loose-fitting suit consisting of sweater and trousers, usu. close-fitting at wrist and ankle, worn by athletes, etc. — **in a cold sweat** (*fig.*) in a state of terror or anxiety; **no sweat** words used to signify assent, or indicating that something will present no problems (*U.S.*); **sweat blood** to work or worry extremely hard; **sweat it out** (*slang*) to endure, live through a time of danger, etc. [O.E. *swǣtan* to sweat; cf. Ger. *schweissen*; the O.E. n. was *swāt*.]

sweath-band *swēth′-band*, (*Spens.*) *n.* a swaddling-band. [**swathe**[1].]

Swede *swēd*, *n.* a native or citizen of *Sweden*: (without *cap.*) a Swedish turnip — a buff-flowered, glaucous-leaved kind. — *adj.* **Swed′ish.** — *n.* the Scandinavian language of Sweden: (as *pl.*) the natives or people of Sweden.

Swedenborgian *swē-dn-bör′ji-ən*, *n.* a follower of Emanuel Swedenborg, a Swedish religious teacher (1688–1772), who claimed to be in direct contact with the spiritual world, and whose followers founded the New Jerusalem Church. — Also *adj.* — *n.* **Swedenbor′gianism.**

swee *swē*, (*Scot.*) *n.* a sway: a swing: the horizontal iron bar which could be swung over an old fireplace, on which cooking vessels were hung. — *v.t.* and *v.i.* to sway: to swing. [**sway**.]

sweel. See **sweal**.

sweeney (todd) *swē′ni (tod)* rhyming slang for **flying squad** in the British police force, esp. in London.

sweeny *swē′ni*, *n.* atrophy of the shoulder muscles of a horse. [O.E. *swindan*, to pine away, disappear.]

sweep *swēp*, *v.i.* to pass swiftly or forcibly, esp. with a swinging movement or in a curve: to move with trailing or flowing drapery, hence with pomp, indignation, etc.: to extend in a long curve: to row with sweeps: to range systematically or searchingly. — *v.t.* to pass something brushingly over: to elicit by so doing (*poet.*): to pass brushingly: to wipe, clean, move, or remove with a broom: to carry along or off with a long brushing stroke or force: to wipe out or remove at a stroke (often with *away*, *up*): to perform with a sweeping movement: to trail with a curving movement: to drag as with a net or rope: to describe, generate, or swing through, as a curve, angle, or area: to row with sweeps: — *pa.t.* and *pa.p.* **swept.** — *n.* act of sweeping: a swinging movement, swing: onrush: impetus: a clearance: range, compass: a curved stair: a curved carriageway before a building: sweepings: a sweepstake: a pump-handle: a long oar: a wire drag used in searching for shoals, mines, etc.: a chimney-sweeper: a blackguard (*slang*): sweepback. — *ns.* **sweep′er** a person who, or thing which sweeps: in association football, a player in front of the goal-keeper who assists the defence; **sweep′ing** the action of the verb in any sense: (usu. in *pl.*) things collected by sweeping, rubbish. — *adj.* performing the action of sweeping in any sense: of wide scope, wholesale, indiscriminate. — *adv.* **sweep′ingly.** — *n.* **sweep′ingness.** — *adj.* **sweep′y** swaying, sweeping, curving. — **sweep′back** the angle at which an aeroplane wing is set back relatively to the axis. — *adjs.* **swept′back; swept′wing** of an aircraft, etc., having wings that are swept back. — **sweep′-net, -seine** a long net paid out in a curve and dragged ashore: an insect net with a handle; **sweep′-saw** a turning-saw; **sweep′stake(s)** a method of gambling by which participators' stakes are pooled, numbers, horses, etc., assigned by lot, and prize(s) awarded accordingly on decision of event: such a prize, race, etc. (for *adv.* see soopstake); **sweep'-wash'er** one who recovers gold or silver from the sweepings of refineries. — **make a clean sweep (of)** to clear out completely: to win all the awards, prizes, etc.; **sweep the board** see **board**. [Prob. from a lost O.E. word related to *swāpan*, to sweep, *geswǣpe*, sweepings; cf. **soop**, **swoop**.]

sweer, sweir *swēr*, (*Scot.*) *adj.* slothful: loth. — Also **sweered, sweert, sweirt**. — *n.* **sweir'ness**. [O.E. *swǣr*, *swǣre*, heavy, grievous, sluggish; cf. Ger. *schwer*.]

sweet *swēt*, *adj.* having one of the fundamental varieties of taste, that of sugar, honey, ripe fruits (distinguished from *salt, acid* or *sour, bitter, dry*): sugary: cloying: sickly in taste, smell, etc.: grateful to the taste, senses, or feelings: taking: fragrant: clear and tuneful: smoothly running: easy, free from harshness, benign: fresh, not salt: fresh, not tainted: wholesome: gracious: amiable: mild, soft, gentle: delightful, charming (*coll.*): all right, satisfactory (*Austr. coll.*): dear, beloved (*arch.*): ingratiating, often insipidly: more or less enamoured (with *on*, or *upon*; *coll.*). — *adv.* sweetly. — *n.* that which is sweet: a sweet dish (pudding, fruit, etc.) as a course: a sweetmeat, confection: (in *pl.*) wines and cordials sweetened with syrup: a beloved person. — *v.t.* (now *rare*) to sweeten. — *v.t.* **sweet'en** to make sweet: to mitigate something unpleasant: to pacify, make (a person) agreeable (often with *up*). — *ns.* **sweet'ener** a substance that sweetens, esp. one not containing sugar: one who sweetens: a bribe (*slang*); **sweet'ening; sweet'ing** a sweet apple: a darling (*Shak.*). — *adj.* **sweet'ish**. — *n.* **sweet'ishness**. — *adv.* **sweet'ly**. — *ns.* **sweet'ness; sweet'y, sweet'ie** a sweetmeat, confection: a sweetheart (*coll.*). — *adjs.* **sweet'-and-sour'** cooked with sugar and vinegar or lemon juice: in Oriental cookery, having a seasoning of sugar, vinegar, soy sauce, etc.; **sweet'-and-twen'ty** at once fair and young — after Shakespeare, who perhaps meant only sweet indeed (see **twenty** for intensive use). — **sweet'= bay** the laurel (*Laurus nobilis*): a kind of magnolia (*U.S.*); **sweet'bread** the pancreas, or sometimes the thymus, esp. as food; **sweet'-brier, -briar** a wild rose with fragrant foliage (*Rosa rubiginosa*); **sweet chestnut** see **chestnut**; **sweet'-cic'ely** an aromatic umbelliferous plant, *Myrrhis odorata*; **sweet'-corn** a sweet variety of maize; **sweetfish** see **ayu**; **sweet'-flag** an aromatic araceous pond-plant, *Acorus calamus*; **sweet'-gale** bogmyrtle, a low-growing aromatic shrub found in bogs; **sweet gas** hydrocarbon gas without sulphur compounds; **sweet'heart** a lover or beloved. — *v.t.* and *v.i.* to court. — **sweetheart agreement, contract** an agreement between a trade union and an employer that excessively favours the employer, and is often concluded without the consent of higher-ranking trade union officials; **sweet'ie-pie** (*coll.*) a term of endearment. — *adj.* **sweet'meal** of biscuits, made of whole meal and sweetened. — **sweet'meat** a confection made wholly or chiefly of sugar: any sweet food (*obs.*); **sweet'-oil** olive-oil: rape-oil: any oil of mild pleasant taste; **sweet'pea'** a S. European papilionaceous garden plant (*Lathyrus odoratus*) with bright-coloured fragrant flowers; **sweet pepper** see **pepper**; **sweet'-potā'to** batata, a tropical and sub-tropical twining plant (*Ipomoea batatas*) of the convolvulus family, with large sweetish edible tubers. — *adjs.* **sweet'-sa'voured; sweet'= scent'ed** having a sweet smell. — **sweet'-sop** a tropical American evergreen (*Anona squamosa*): its pulpy fruit; **sweet'-stuff** confectionery; **sweet talk** flattery, persuasion. — *v.t.* **sweet'-talk** (*coll.*) to coax, flatter, persuade. — *adjs.* **sweet'-tem'pered** having a mild, amiable disposition; **sweet'-toothed'** fond of sweet things; **sweet'= water** freshwater. — *n.* a very sweet white grape. — **sweet'-will'iam** *Dianthus barbatus*, a garden pink with bearded petals; **sweet'-will'ow** one of various trees, e.g. bay-leaved sweet-willow, *Salix pentandra*: sweet-gale; **sweet'wood** a name for various S. American and West Indian lauraceous trees; **sweet'-wort** wort before addition of hops. — **a sweet tooth** a fondness for sweet things; **sweetness and light** an appearance of mildness,

reasonableness, etc. [O.E. *swēte*; Ger. *süss*, Gr. *hēdys*, L. *suāvis*, Sans. *svādu*, sweet.]

sweir, sweirt, etc. See **sweer**.

swelchie *swelhh'i*, (*Orkney*) *n.* a whirlpool: a tidal race. [O.N. *svelgr*, cf. **swallow**².]

swell *swel*, *v.i.* to expand: to increase in volume: to be inflated: to bulge out: to grow louder: to rise into waves: to heave: to well up: to rise and fall in loudness: to be bombastic: to be elated or dilated with emotion: to give a feeling of expansion or welling up. — *v.t.* to augment: to expand: to dilate: to fill full: to louden: to elate: — *pa.t.* **swelled**; *pa.p.* **swelled, swollen** (*swōln, swōl'ən*), sometimes **swōln**. — *n.* act, power, habit, or condition of swelling: distension: a heaving: a bulge: an enlargement: a loudening: a device in an organ for varying tone: a crescendo followed by a diminuendo: a rising ground: a dandy, a fashionable or finely dressed person, a member of the governing class, a bigwig, an adept (*slang*). — *adj.* (*slang*) of, of the nature of, befitting a swell, a vague word of commendation. — *n.* **swell'dom** (*slang*) the fashionable world. — *adj.* **swelled**. — *n.* **swell'er**. — *adj.* and *n.* **swell'ing**. — *adv.* **swell'ingly**. — *adjs.* **swell'ish** (*slang*) foppish, dandified; **swollen** (*swōl'ən*). — **swell box** in an organ, a chamber containing a set of pipes or reeds, which is opened or closed by the swell; **swelled head** self-conceit, esp. in one carried away by success. — *adj.* **swelled'-head'ed,** also **swell'-head'ed, swoll'en-headed** conceited. — **swell'-mob** (*arch. slang*) well-dressed pickpockets collectively; **swell'-mobs'man** (*arch. slang*); **swell organ** the pipes enclosed in the swell box. [O.E. *swellan*; Ger. *schwellen*.]

swelt *swelt*, *v.i.* to die (*obs.* or *dial.*): to faint (*Spens., Scot.*): to swelter: to pass like a fever (*Spens.*): — *pa.t.* **swelt'ed,** (*Spens.*) **swelt.** — *v.i.* **swelt'er** to endure great heat: to sweat copiously: to exude. — *v.t.* to overpower, as with heat: to exude. — *n.* a sweltering: a sweating: sweltered venom. — *adj.* **swelt'ered.** — *n.* and *adj.* **swelt'ering.** — *adj.* **swelt'ry** sultry: oppressive or oppressed with heat. [O.E. *sweltan*, to die.]

swept *swept*, *pa.t.* and *pa.p.* of **sweep**.

swerf. See **swarf**¹.

Swerga. See **Swarga**.

swerve¹ *swûrv*, *v.i.* to turn aside: to deviate: to give way, shrink (*Milt.*): to swarm, scramble (*Dryden*). — *v.t.* to deflect: to cause a ball to swerve in the air. — *n.* a turning aside: a deviation: a deflection: a ball that swerves in the air (*cricket*): the act or trick of making it do so (*cricket*). — *adj.* **swerve'less** unswerving. — *n.* **swerv'er**. — *n.* and *adj.* **swerv'ing**. [M.E.; the O.E. *sweorfan*, to rub, file, scour, is not known to have had this sense.]

swerve². See **swarf**¹.

sweven *swev'n*, (*obs.*) *n.* a dream. [O.E. *swefn*.]

swidden *swid'ən*, *n.* an area of land made cultivable by cutting or burning off the vegetative cover. [O.N. *svithin*, *pa.p.* of *svitha*, to burn.]

swift¹ *swift*, *adj.* fleet: rapid: speedy: prompt. — *adv.* **swiftly**. — *n.* a bird (*Apus*, or *Cypselus, apus*) superficially like a swallow but structurally nearer the humming-birds and goatsuckers: any bird of its genus or family: the common newt: a reel for winding yarn: the main cylinder of a carding-machine: a rapid. — *n.* **swift'let** a bird (*Collocalia*) akin to the swift, the builder of edible nests. — *adv.* **swift'ly**. — *n.* **swift'ness**. — *adjs.* **swift'-foot, -ed; swift'-winged**. [O.E. *swift*, from same root as **swoop**.]

swift² *swift*, *v.t.* to tighten with a rope. — *n.* **swift'er** a rope used to tighten or keep a thing in its place. [Prob. Scand. or L.G.]

Swiftian *swift'ti-ən*, *adj.* of, or in the style of, the (esp. satirical) writings of Jonathan *Swift*, 1667–1745, Anglo-Irish writer and cleric.

swig¹ *swig*, *n.* a pulley with ropes not parallel. — *v.t.* to tighten by hauling at right angles: to castrate by ligature. [Prob. conn. with **swag**.]

swig² *swig*, *n.* a deep draught: toast and ale (*arch.*): a wassail (*Oxford*). — *v.t.* to take a swig or swigs of or from. — *v.i.* to drink, take swigs: — *pr.p.* **swigg′ing;** *pa.t.* and *pa.p.* **swigged.** — *n.* **swigg′er.** [Origin unknown.]

swill *swil, v.t.* or *v.i.* to rinse: to dash water over: to wash: to drink greedily or largely. — *n.* a large draught of liquor: hogwash. — *n.* **swill′er.** — *n.* and *adj.* **swill′ing.** — **swill′-tub** a tub for hogwash. [O.E. *swilian,* to wash.]

swim *swim, v.i.* to propel oneself in water (or other liquid): to float: to come to the surface: to travel or be conveyed by water: to be suffused: to be immersed or steeped: to glide smoothly: to be dizzy. — *v.t.* to pass by swimming: to make to swim or float: to test for witchcraft by immersion: — *pr.p.* **swimm′ing;** *pa.t.* **swam** (*swam*), old-fashioned **swum;** *pa.p.* **swum** (*Shak.,* etc., **swam**). — *n.* an act, performance, or spell of swimming: any motion like swimming: a crossing-place for swimmers: a place where many fishes swim: the general movement or current of affairs: air-bladder of a fish. — *adj.* **swimm′able** capable of being swum. — *ns.* **swimm′er; swimm′eret** a crustacean's abdominal appendage used in swimming. — *n.* and *adj.* **swimm′-ing.** — *adv.* **swimm′ingly** in a gliding manner as if swimming: smoothly, successfully (*coll.*). — *n.* **swimm′-ingness** the state of swimming: a melting look, tearfulness. — *adj.* **swimm′y** inclined to dizziness. — **swim′-bladder** a fish's air-bladder; **swimm′ing-bath; swimm′-ing-bell** a medusoid modified as a swimming organ; **swimming costume** swimsuit; **swimm′ing-pond, -pool;** **swim′suit** a garment for bathing in; **swim′wear** in shops, fashion magazines, etc., garments worn for swimming. — **in the swim** in the main current (of affairs, business, etc.); **swim with, against, the stream, tide** to conform to, go against, normal behaviour, opinions, etc. [O.E. *swimman;* Ger. *schwimmen.*]

swindge (*Milt.; Shak.* — also in **swindge-buckler**). Same as **swinge**[1] and **swinge-buckler.**

swindle *swin′dl, v.t.* and *v.i.* to cheat. — *n.* a fraud: anything not really what it appears to be. — *n.* **swin′dler** a cheat. — *n.* and *adj.* **swin′dling.** — **swin′dle= sheet** (*facet.*) an expense account. [Ger. *Schwindler,* a giddy-minded person, swindler — *schwindeln,* to be giddy.]

swine *swīn, n.* a pig: a sensual person (*arch.*): a term of strong abuse: — *pl.* **swine.** — *ns.* **swine′hood** the status of a swine; **swin′ery** a place where pigs are kept: swinishness: swine collectively. — *adj.* **swin′ish** of or like swine: sensual: filthy: voracious: beastly. — *adv.* **swin′ishly.** — *n.* **swin′ishness.** — *adj.* **swine′-drunk** (*Shak.*) bestially drunk. — **swine′-fe′ver** hog-cholera, a highly contagious disease of swine due to a virus; **swine′-fish** the wolf-fish; **swine′herd** one who herds swine; **swine′-keeping; swine′-pox** a form of chicken-pox: a skin disease of swine; **swine′s′-cress** a cruciferous weed of waste places (*Senebiera* or *Coronopus*): applied to various other plants; **swine′s′-succ′ory** a small plant (*Arnoseris*) akin to chicory; **swine′stone** stinkstone; **swine′-sty** a pig-sty. — **swine vesicular disease** a highly contagious viral disease of pigs, causing sores on the skin of the feet, legs and mouth. [O.E. *swīn,* a pig; Ger. *Schwein,* L. (adj.) *suīnus — sūs,* Gr. *hȳs.*]

swing *swing, v.i.* to sway or wave to and fro, as a body hanging freely: to amuse oneself on a swing: to oscil-late: to hang: to be hanged: to sweep, wheel, sway: to swerve: to move forward with swaying gait: to turn round as a ship (e.g. to test the compass): to attract, excite, be perfectly appropriate to place or mood (*slang*): of a person, to be thoroughly responsive (to jazz, any of the arts, any aspect of living) (*slang*): to be lively or up-to-date (*slang*). — *v.t.* to cause to swing: to set swinging: to control: to sway: to hurl, whirl: to brandish: to transport in suspension: to move in a sweep: to sound or send forth by swinging: to indicate by an oscillation: to impart swing to: to perform as swing-music: to fix up so as to hang freely: to influence the result of (e.g. a doubtful election) in favour of an individual or party: to arrange, fix (*slang*): — *pa.t.* **swung,** rarely **swang;** *pa.p.* **swung.** — *n.* act, manner, or spell of swinging: oscillating, waving, sweeping: motion to and fro: the sweep or compass of a swinging body: the sweep of a golf-club, bat, or the like: sway: scope, free indulgence: impetus: vigorous sweeping rhythm: jazz music with impromptu complications as played in the 1930s and 1940s — also **swing-music:** a suspended seat or carriage for the amusement of swinging: a reversal of fortune: the movement of voters from one party to another as compared with the previous election. — *ns.* **swing′er** (*swing′ər*) a person or thing that swings: either of the middle pair in a team of six horses: a Hindu votary who swings from hooks in his flesh: a ball bowled so as to swerve in the air (*cricket*): an ill-centred gramophone record: a lively and up-to-date person (*slang*): a person engaging freely in sexual activity usu. in groups (*slang*); **swinging** (*swing′ing*) the act of moving to and fro in suspension, esp. as a pastime: hanging (*coll.*): hanging by hooks, as by a Hindu devotee. — *adj.* swaying: turning: with a swing: having a free easy motion: with it, fully alive to, and appreciative of, the most recent trends and fashions in living (*coll.*): up-to-date (*coll.*): lively (*coll.*): daring (*coll.*). — *adv.* **swing′ingly.** — *n.* **swingom′eter** a device which shows the direction and extent of the current swing of the counted votes in an election. — **swing′-back** a reaction: a camera back that can be tilted; **swing′boat** a boat-shaped swinging carriage for fairs, etc.; **swing′-bridge** a bridge that may be opened by swinging it to one side; **swing′-by** the passing of a spacecraft near a planet in order to use its gravitational field to change course; **swing′-door′** a door (usu. one of a pair) that opens either way and swings to of itself; **swing′-han′dle** a pivoted (esp. arched) handle; **swing′-ing-boom** the spar that stretches the foot of a lower studding-sail; **swing′ing-post** the post to which a gate is hung; **swing′-music** big-band jazz with strong rhythm and improvisations; **swing′-plough** a plough without a fore-wheel under the beam; **swing′-shelf** a hanging shelf; **swing′-stock** an upright timber, with a blunt upper edge for swingling flax on — also **swing′ing= block; swing′-swang** a complete (to and fro) oscillation; **swing′tree** a whippletree; **swing′-wheel** the wheel that drives a clock pendulum; **swing′-wing′ (aircraft)** vari-able-geometry aircraft. — **in full swing** in mid-career: in fully active operation; **swings and roundabouts** a situation in which advantages and disadvantages can-cel each other out; **swingtail cargo aircraft** an aircraft with tail that swings aside to give access to the full cross-section of the fuselage for rapid loading and unloading of cargo; **swing the lead** see **lead**[2]. [O.E. *swingan;* Ger. *schwingen.*]

Swing *swing, n.* a fictitious captain in whose name rick-burners sent threatening letters to users of thresh-ing-mills about 1830–33; the movement, operations, or methods of the rick-burners. — Also *adj.* — *n.* **swing′ism.**

swinge[1] *swinj, v.t.* (*arch.*) to beat: to chastise: to lash, sway, flourish: — *pr.p.* **swinge′ing.** — *n.* (*arch.*) **swinge′= buckler** a swashbuckler. — *adj.* **swinge′ing** great, huge, thumping. — *adv.* **swinge′ingly.** — *n.* (*arch.*) **swinger** (*swinj′ər*) any person or thing great or astonishing: a bold lie, a whopper. [M.E. *swenge* — O.E. *swengan,* to shake, causative of *swingan,* to swing.]

swinge[2] *swinj,* (*Spens.*) *v.t.* Same as **singe.**

swingism. See **Swing.**

swingle *swing′gl, n.* a scutching tool: the swipple of a flail. — *v.t.* to scutch. — *n.* **swing′ling.** — **swing′le-bar, swing′letree** a whippletree: a swing-stock; **swing′le= hand** a scutching tool; **swing′ling-stock** a swing-stock. [Cf. O.E. *swingell,* stroke, scourge, rod, and M.Du. *swinghel.*]

swingometer. See **swing.**

swinish. See **swine.**

swink *swingk,* (*arch.*) *v.i.* to toil. — *n.* toil. — *adj.* **swinked**

(*Milt.* **swink't**) toil-worn, fatigued.   [O.E. *swinc* (n.), *swincan* (vb.).]

swipe *swīp, n.* a sweeping stroke: a swath (*arch.*). — *v.t.* to strike with a swipe: to gulp (*arch.*): to purloin (*coll.*). — *v.i.* to make a swipe: to sweep for old anchors. — *ns.* **swip'er; swipes** bad or spoilt beer: small beer. — *adj.* **swip'ey** fuddled with malt liquor.   [O.E. *swipian*, to beat.]

swipple *swip'l, n.* a swingle or striking part of a flail. [Cf. **swipe, sweep.**]

swire *swīr, n.* a neck (*obs.*): in place names, a hollow between two hills.   [O.E. *swēora* (Northern *swīra*), neck.]

swirl *swûrl, n.* an eddy: a whirl: a curl. — *v.t.* to whirl: to wind. — *v.i.* to eddy: to whirl: to spin. — *adj.* **swirl'y**. [Orig. Scot.; cf. Norw. dial. *svirla*.]

swish¹ *swish, n.* the sound of twigs sweeping through the air or of fabric rustling along the ground: dashing spray: a cane or birch. — *v.t.* to whisk with a swish: to flog, thrash. — *v.i.* to go with a swish. — *adv.* with a swish. — *n.* **swish'er**. — *n.* and *adj.* **swish'ing**. — *adj.* **swish'y**.   [Imit.]

swish² *swish*, (*slang*) *adj.* smart, stylish.   [Origin unknown.]

Swiss *swis, adj.* of *Switzerland.* — *n.* a native or citizen of Switzerland: the High German dialect spoken by most of the Swiss: — *pl.* **Swiss** (formerly **Swiss'es**). — *n.* **Swit'zer** a Swiss: a Swiss (or other) mercenary or member of a bodyguard. — **Swiss chard** see **chard; Swiss Cheese plant** a tropical climbing plant (*Monstera deliciosa*) with large, thick, perforated leaves, often grown as a house plant. **Swiss Guards** a body of Swiss mercenaries in the French guards from 1616, wiped out in the Revolution: the Pope's bodyguard; **Swiss roll** a thin cake rolled up with jam: a flexible floating pier.   [Fr. *Suisse*, O.H.G. *swīz*.]

swissing *swis'ing, n.* ordinary calendering.   [Origin unknown.]

switch *swich* (*Shak.* **swits** *swits*), *n.* a long flexible twig: a tapering riding-whip: a rod, cane: an application of a switch: a brushing blow: a whisk, jerk: a tool for beating eggs or cream: a tress, usu. false: the tuft of an animal's tail: a movable rail for shunting: a changeover (esp. in cards to another suit, led or called): a device for making, breaking, or changing an electric circuit: a switchboard: a turn of a switch. — *v.t.* to strike with a switch: to drive, as with a switch: to brush against: to whisk, jerk, lash: to beat up, whip (as an egg, cream): to prune: to shunt: to divert: to turn (off, on, or to another circuit): to race (a horse) under the name of another horse. — *v.i.* to use a switch: to turn aside: to change over: to whisk. — *n.* **switch'ing**. — *adj.* **switch'y**. — **switch'back** orig. a zigzag mountain railway on which the train shunted back at each stage: an up-and-down track on which cars rise by the momentum gained in coming down: an up-and-down road (also *fig.*); **switch'blade (knife)** a flick-knife; **switch'board** a board or frame bearing apparatus for making or breaking an electric current or circuit: a board for connecting telephones; **switch'gear** the apparatus that controls the switches in the electric circuits of a power station; **switch'man** a pointsman; **switch'-over** action of the verb: a changeover; **switch'-plant** a plant with long slim green shoots, the leaves reduced or wanting; **switch selling** the practice of arousing the interest of a prospective buyer by offering him a low-priced article, then telling him the shortcomings of the cheap article and trying to sell him a more expensive one. — **switched on** aware of and responsive to all that is most up to date (*coll.*); under the influence of drugs (*coll.*).   [Earlier *swits* (*Shak.*), *switz*; prob. from Du. or L.G.]

switchel *swich'l, n.* treacle-beer, molasses and water, etc.: in Newfoundland, cold tea.   [Origin unknown.]

swith *swith,* (*obs.*) *adv.* quickly: at once. — *interj.* away. [O.E. *swīthe,* very.]

swither *swidh'ər,* (*Scot.*) *v.i.* to be undecided. — *n.*

indecision: flurry.   [Poss. O.E. *swethrian,* to subside.]

swits. See **switch.**

Switzer. See **Swiss.**

swivel *swiv'l, n.* a ring or link that turns round on a pin or neck: a swivel-gun. — *v.t.* and *v.i.* to turn on a pin or pivot: — *pr.p.* **swiv'elling;** *pa.t.* and *pa.p.* **swiv'elled.** — **swiv'elblock** a block on which a swivel is mounted; **swiv'el-chair** a chair with a seat that swivels round; **swiv'el-eye** a squint-eye; **swiv'el-gun** a gun that turns on a pivot; **swiv'el-hook** a hook secured to anything by means of a swivel.   [O.E. *swīfan,* to move quickly, to turn round.]

swivet *swiv'it,* (*dial.*) *n.* a state of nervous agitation. [Origin unknown.]

swiz *swiz,* **swizzle** *swiz'l,* (*slang*) *ns.* fraud: great disappointment.   [Poss. **swindle.**]

swizzle¹ *swiz'l, v.i.* to drink to excess. — *n.* a mixed or compounded drink containing rum or other spirit. — **swizzle'-stick** a stick or whisk used to mix a swizzle. [Origin unknown.]

swizzle². See **swiz.**

swob, swobber, etc. Same as **swab, swabber,** etc.

swollen *swōl'ən, swōln, pa.p.* of **swell,** and *adj.*

swoln. See **swell.**

swoon *swōōn,* also (*arch.* and *poet.*) **sound** *sownd,* **swoun** *swown,* **swound** *swownd* (*Spens.* **swownd, swone**) *ns.* a fainting fit: a sleep (*Spens.*). — *vs.i.* to faint: to be languorous, give a feeling of fainting (*poet.*): to subside (*poet.*). — *adj.* **swooned** in a swoon. — *n.* and *adj.* **swoon'ing.** — *adv.* **swoon'ingly.**   [Prob. from M.E. *iswowen* — O.E. *geswōgen* (pa.p.; other parts unknown), in a swoon, wrongly analysed as *in swoon.*]

swoop *swōōp, v.i.* to sweep along (*obs.*): to come down with a sweeping rush: to rush suddenly. — *v.t.* (*obs.*) to pounce on, to snatch with a sweep, esp. on the wing. — *n.* an act of swooping: a sudden onslaught. — *adv.* **swoop'stake-like** see under **soop.** — **at one fell swoop** (*Shak.,* Macb. IV, iii. 219) by one terrible blow: (also **in, with**) by one complete decisive action: suddenly. [App. O.E. *swāpan,* to sweep; perh. influenced by **soop.**]

swop, swopt. See **swap.**

swoosh *swōōsh, n.* a noise of or resembling a rush of air, water, etc. — *v.i.* to make this noise.   [Prob. imit., or from **swish¹, swoop.**]

sword *sörd, sōrd, n.* a weapon with a long blade, sharp upon one or both edges, for cutting or thrusting: a blade or flat rod resembling a sword: a swordfish's snout: destruction or death by the sword or by war: war: military force: the emblem of vengeance or justice, or of authority and power: (in *pl.*) a suit in the tarot pack. — *v.i.* (*arch.*) to wield a sword. — *n.* **sword'er** (*arch.*) a gladiator: an assassin, a cut-throat: a swordsman. — *adjs.* **sword'less; sword'-like.** — *adj.* **sword'-and-buck'ler** fought or armed with sword and buckler. — **sword'-arm, -hand** the arm, hand, that wields the sword; **sword'-bay'onet** a bayonet shaped somewhat like a sword, and used as one; **sword'-bean** an Indian papilionaceous plant (*Canavalia*) with long sword-shaped edible pods: its seed; **sword'-bearer** a public officer who carries the sword of state; **sword'-belt** a belt from which the sword is hung; **sword'-bill** a S. American humming-bird with a bill longer than its body; **sword'-blade** the blade of a sword; **sword'-break'er** an old weapon for grasping and breaking an adversary's sword; **sword'-cane, -stick** a cane or stick containing a sword; **sword'craft** swordsmanship: military power; **sword'-cut** a cut with the edge of a sword: a wound or scar so produced; **sword'-dance** a dance performed sword in hand or among or over swords; **sword'-doll'ar** a Scottish silver coin of James VI, worth 30s. Scots (2s. 6d. English), with a sword on the reverse; **sword'fish** a large fish (*Xiphias* or other genus of the family Xiphiidae) with upper jaw compressed and prolonged as a stabbing weapon; **sword'-grass** a name for many plants with sword-shaped leaves; **sword'-guard** the part of a sword-hilt that protects the bearer's hand; **sword'-knot** a ribbon tied to the hilt of a sword;

sword'-law government by the sword; **sword'man** a swordsman: a fighting man; **sword'play** fencing; **sword'player.** — *adj.* **sword'proof** capable of resisting the blow or thrust of a sword. — **sword'-rack** a rack for holding swords. — *adj.* **sword'-shaped.** — **swords'-man** a man skilled in the use of a sword; **swords'-manship; sword'-swallower** a performer who seems to swallow swords; **sword'-tail** a small Central American freshwater Cyprinodont fish with sword-like tail-lobe. — **cross swords with** see **cross; put to the sword** (of armies, etc.; *hist.*) to kill (prisoners, etc.) by the sword. [O.E. *sweord*; Ger. *Schwert*.]

swore, sworn. See **swear.**

swot, swat *swot*, (*slang*) *v.t.* and *v.i.* to study hard: — *pr.p.* **swott'ing, swatt'ing;** *pa.t.* and *pa.p.* **swott'ed, swatt'ed.** — *n.* hard study: one who swots. — *ns.* **swott'er, swatter; swott'ing, swatting.** [**sweat.**]

swothling. See **swathe**[1].

swoun, swound *swownd.* See **swoon.** — (*Spens.*) **swoune, swownd, swowne.**

swounds, 'swounds. Same as **zounds.**

swozzle. See **swazzle.**

swum *swum, pa.p.* and old-fashioned *pa.t.* of **swim.**

swung *swung, pa.t.* and *pa.p.* of **swing.**

swy *swī*, (*Austr. slang*) *n.* two-up (— also **swy game, swy'-up**): a two-year prison sentence. [Ger. *zwei*, two.]

sy-. See **syn.**

Syalon® *sī'ə-lon, n.* a hard, strong, light, ceramic material for use in high-temperature environments, e.g. gas turbines and car engines. [*si*licon, *a*lumina, *oxy-nitrides*, its components.]

Sybarite *sib'ə-rīt, n.* an inhabitant of *Sybaris*, a Greek city in ancient Italy, on the Gulf of Tarentum, noted for luxury: one devoted to luxury. — Also *adj.* — *adjs.* **Sybaritic** (*-rit'ik*), **-al, Sybarīt'ish.** — *n.* **Sy'barītism.** — All words also without *cap.*

sybbe. See **sib.**

sybil. Same as **sibyl.**

sybo(w), syboe *sī'bō, -bā,* (*Scot.*) *n.* a cibol: a young or spring onion: — *pl.* **sy'boes, sybows.** [**cibol.**]

sybotic *sī-bot'ik, adj.* pertaining to a swineherd. — *n.* **sybotism** (*sib'ə-tizm*). [Gr. *sybōtēs*, swineherd — *sȳs*, swine, *boskein*, to feed, tend.]

sycamine *sik'ə-mīn*, (*B.*) *n.* the mulberry-tree. [Gr. *sȳkaminos*, of Semitic origin, influenced by *sȳkon*, a fig.]

sycamore *sik'ə-mōr, -mör, n.* a kind of fig-tree (now often **sycamore** or **sycomore fig**): in England, the great maple (*Acer pseudo-platanus*) called in Scotland the plane (formerly **sycomore**): in U.S., any true plane (Platanus). [Gr. *sȳkomoros* — *sȳkon*, a fig, *moron*, black mulberry.]

syce, sice, saice *sīs,* (*India*) *n.* a groom, mounted attendant: a chauffeur. [Ar. *sā'is.*]

sycee *sī-sē', n.* silver ingots used as Chinese money. — Also **sycee silver.** [Chin. *sí sz'*.]

sycomore. See **sycamore.**

syconium *sī-kō'ni-əm, n.* a multiple fruit in which the true fruits (the pips) are enclosed in a hollow fleshy receptacle — the fig. [Gr. *sȳkon*, a fig.]

sycophant *sik'ō-fənt, n.* a common informer (*Gr. hist.*): a servile flatterer. — *n.* **syc'ophancy** the behaviour of a sycophant: mean tale-bearing: obsequious flattery: servility. — *adjs.* **sycophantic** (*-fant'ik*), **-al.** — *adv.* **sycophant'ically.** — *v.i.* **syc'ophantise, -ize** to play the sycophant. — *adj.* **syc'ophantish** (or *-fant'*). — *adv.* **syc'ophantishly.** — *n.* **syc'ophantry** the arts of the sycophant. [Gr. *sȳkophantēs*, an informer, swindler, confidential agent — *sȳkon*, a fig, *phainein*, to show; variously but unsatisfactorily explained.]

sycosis *sī-kō'sis, n.* inflammation of the hair follicles, esp. of the beard. [Gr. *sȳkōsis*, a fig-shaped ulcer — *sȳkon*, a fig.]

sye *sī,* (now *dial.*) *v.t.* to strain. — *n.* a sieve: a milk-strainer. [O.E. *sīon, sēon*, to strain.]

syen. A Shakespearian spelling of **scion.**

syenite *sī'ən-īt, n.* a coarse-grained plutonic rock composed of orthoclase and a ferromagnesian mineral, usu. hornblende. — *adj.* **syenitic** (*-it'ik*) relating to *Syene* in Egypt: pertaining to syenite. [L. *syēnītēs* (*lapis*), a hornblende granite (not syenite) found at Aswan (Gr. *Syēnē*).]

syke. See **sike**[1].

syker *sik'ər,* (*Spens.*) *adv.* surely. [**sicker.**]

syl-. See **syn-.**

syllable *sil'ə-bl, n.* a word or part of a word uttered by a single effort of the voice. — *v.t.* to express by syllables, to utter articulately. — *n.* **syll'abary** a set of characters representing syllables. — Also **syllabā'rium.** — *adjs.* **syllabic** (*sil-ab'ik*), **-al** of or constituting a syllable or syllables: syllable by syllable. — *adv.* **syllab'ically.** — *v.t.* **syllab'icate** to syllabify. — *ns.* **syllabicā'tion** syllab-ification; **syllabicity** (*-is'i-ti*); **syllab'ics** verse patterned not by stresses but by syllables; **syllabificā'tion** pronunciation as a syllable: division into syllables. — *vs.t.* **syllab'ify** to divide into syllables; **syll'abise, -ize** to form or divide into syllables: to sing to syllables. — *n.* **syll'abism** use of a syllabary: division into syllables. — *adj.* **syll'abled** having (in compounds, so-many) syllables. — **syllabic verse, metre** syllabics. — **in words of one syllable** (*coll.*) very simply, bluntly. [L. *syllaba* — Gr. *syllabē* — *syn*, with, *lab-*, root of *lambanein*, to take; *-le* as in principle, participle.]

syllabub, sillabub *sil'ə-bub, n.* a dish of cream curdled (as with wine), flavoured and frothed up: anything frothy or insubstantial. [Origin obscure.]

syllabus *sil'ə-bəs, n.* an abstract or programme, as of a series of lectures or a course of studies: a catalogue of doctrinal positions or practices condemned by the R.C. Church (1864, 1907): — *pl.* **syll'abuses, syll'abi** (*-bī*). [Originally a misprint for L. *sittybas, accus. pl.* of *sittyba*, Gr. *sittubā*, a book-label.]

syllepsis *sil-ep'sis, n.* a figure in rhetoric by which a word does duty in a sentence in the same syntactical relation to two or more words but has a different sense in relation to each: — *pl.* **syllep'ses** (*-sēz*). — *adjs.* **syllep'-tic, -al.** — *adv.* **syllep'tically.** [Gr. *syllēpsis*, a taking together — *syn*, together, and the root of *lambanein*, to take.]

syllogism *sil'ō-jizm, -ə-jizm, n.* a logical argument in three propositions, two premises and a conclusion that follows necessarily from them: deductive reasoning: a clever, subtle or specious argument. — *n.* **syllogisation, -z-** (*-jī-zā'shən*). — *v.i.* **syll'ogise, -ize** to reason by syllogisms. — *v.t.* to deduce syllogistically. — *n.* **syll'ogiser, -z-.** — *adjs.* **syllogistic** (*-jist'ik*), **-al.** — *n.* **syllogist'ic** (often *pl.*) the branch of logic concerned with syllogisms. — *adv.* **syllogist'ically.** [Gr. *syllogis-mos* — *syllogizesthai* — *syn*, together, *logizesthai*, to reckon — *logos*, speech, reason.]

sylph *silf, n.* a spirit of the air: a sylph-like being: a slim person: a kind of humming-bird. — *n.* **sylph'id, sylph'-ide** a little sylph. — Also *adj.* — *adjs.* **sylph'idine, sylph'ine, sylph'ish, sylph'-like.** [Coined by Paracelsus.]

sylva, sylvan, sylviculture, etc. See **silva.**

sylvaner *sil-vä'nər,* (often with *cap.*) *n.* a German grape, used in making white wine: wine made from this grape. [Ger.]

sylvanite *sil'vən-īt, n.* a mineral, telluride of gold and silver. [Tran*sylvania*, where it is found.]

Sylvia *sil'vi-ə, n.* the warbler genus, giving name to a family **Sylvī'idae** or subfamily **Sylvī'nae** of the thrush family: (without *cap.*) any warbler of this genus. — *adj.* **syl'viine.** [L. *silva*, a wood.]

Sylvian *sil'vi-ən, adj.* of *Sylvius*, i.e. either the French anatomist Jacques Dubois (1478–1555), or Franz de la Boë (1614–72), the Dutch-German iatrochemist. — **Sylvian fissure** a deep lateral fissure in the cerebrum, discovered apparently by the latter.

sylvine *sil'vēn,* **sylvite** *sil'vīt, ns.* native potassium chloride, a source of potash. — *n.* **syl'vinite** (*-vin-īt*) a rock composed of sylvine and rock salt. [Formerly called digestive salt of *Sylvius*.]

sym-. See **syn-.**

symar. Same as **cymar.**

symbiosis *sim-bi-ō'sis, n.* a mutually beneficial partnership between organisms of different kinds: esp. such an association where one lives within the other. — *ns.* **sym'bion, sym'biont** (*-bi-ont*) an organism living in symbiosis. — *adj.* **symbiotic** (*-bi-ot'ik*). — *adv.* **symbiot'ically.** [Gr. *syn*, together, *bios*, livelihood.]

symbol *sim'b(ə)l, n.* an emblem: that which by custom or convention represents something else: a type: a creed, compendium of doctrine, or a typical religious rite, as the eucharist (*theol.*): an object or act representing an unconscious or repressed conflict (*psychol.*). — *v.t.* to symbolise. — *adjs.* **symbolic** (*-bol'ik*), **-al.** — *adv.* **symbol'ically.** — *n. symbol'icalness.* — *n.sing.* **symbol'ics** study of creeds. — *n.* **symbolīsā'tion, -z-.** — *v.t.* **sym'bolise, -ize** to be symbolical of: to represent by symbols: to combine (*obs.*): to formulate in a creed. — *v.i.* (*obs.*) to agree. — *ns.* **sym'boliser, -z-; sym'bolism** representation by symbols or signs: a system of symbols: use of symbols: use of symbols in literature or art: (often with *cap.*) a late 19th-cent. movement in art and poetry that treated the actual as an expression of something underlying: symbolics. — *n.* and *adj.* **sym'bolist.** — *adjs.* **symbolist'ic, -al; sym'bolled** symbolised: bearing symbols. — *ns.* **symbolog'raphy** symbolic writing or representation; **symbol'ogy** (for **symbolol'ogy**) the study or use of symbols; **symbolol'atry** (Gr. *latreiā*, worship) undue veneration for symbols. — **symbolic logic** a branch of logic which uses symbols instead of terms, propositions, etc., in order to clarify reasoning. [Gr. *symbolon*, a token — *syn*, together, *ballein*, to throw.]

symbole. An old spelling of **cymbal.**

symitar(e). Obs. spellings of **scimitar.**

symmetry *sim'i-tri, n.* exact correspondence of parts on either side of a straight line or plane, or about a centre or axis: balance or due proportion: beauty of form: disposition of parts. — *adj.* **symm'etral** of symmetry. — *n.* **symmetrian** (*si-met'ri-ən*) one who studies or theorises on the due proportions of things. — *adjs.* **symmet'ric, -al** having symmetry. — *adv.* **symmet'rically.** — *ns.* **symmet'ricalness; symmetrīsā'tion, -z-.** — *v.t.* **symm'etrise, -ize** to make symmetrical. — *n.* **symmetrophō'bia** (Gr. *phŏbos*, fear) fear or dislike of symmetry. [Gr. *symmetriā* — *syn*, together, *metron*, a measure.]

sympathectomy *sim-pəth-ek'tə-mi, n.* excision of part of a sympathetic nerve. [From **sympathetic**, and Gr. *ektomē*, excision.]

sympathin *sim'pə-thin, n.* a substance, secreted by sympathetic nerve-endings, which constricts and dilates blood-vessels. [From **sympathetic**.]

sympathy *sim'pə-thi, n.* community of feeling: power of entering into another's feelings or mind: harmonious understanding: compassion, pity: affinity or correlation whereby one thing responds to the action of another or to action upon another: agreement: (often in *pl.*) a feeling of agreement or support, or an expression of this. — *adjs.* **sympathet'ic, -al** feeling, inclined to, expressing, sympathy: in sympathy: acting or done in sympathy: induced by sympathy (as sounds in a resonating body): congenial: compassionate: of the sympathetic nervous system (see below): (a Gallicism) able to awake sympathy. — *adv.* **sympathet'ically.** — *v.i.* **sym'pathise, -ize** to be in sympathy: to feel with or for another: to be compassionate: to be in accord, correspond. — *v.t.* (*Shak.*) to be in sympathy, accord, or harmony with: to compound harmoniously: to represent or understand sympathetically: perh., to affect all alike. — *n.* **sym'pathiser, -z-.** — *adj.* **sympatholyt'ic** inhibiting the action of the sympathetic nervous system. — *n.* a drug which has this effect. — *adj.* **sympathomimet'ic** mimicking the action of the sympathetic nervous system. — *n.* a drug which does this.

— **sympathetic ink** see **ink; sympathetic magic** magic depending upon a supposed sympathy, e.g. between a person and his name or portrait, between rainfall and libations; **sympathetic nervous system** a system of nerves supplying the involuntary muscles and glands, esp. those originating from the cervical, thoracic, and lumbar regions of the spinal cord; sometimes also including those from the brain and the sacral region (the **parasympathetic nervous system**); **sympathetic, sympathy, strike** a strike in support of other workers, not in furtherance of the strikers' own claims. — **in sympathy (with)** in agreement (with), in support (of). [Gr. *sympatheia* — *syn*, with, *pathos*, suffering.]

sympetalous *sim-pet'ə-ləs, adj.* having the petals united. — *n.pl.* **Sympet'alae** (*-lē*) a main division of dicotyledons, typically having united petals. [Gr. *syn*, together, *petalon*, leaf.]

symphile *sim'fīl, n.* an animal of another kind kept as a guest or domestic animal in an ants' or termites' nest. — *ns.* **sym'philism** (*-fil-izm*), **sym'phily.** — *adj.* **sym'philous.** [Gr. *symphiliā*, mutual friendship — *syn*, *philos*, a friend.]

symphony *sim'fə-ni, n.* an obs. name for various musical instruments — bagpipe, drum, hurdy-gurdy, virginal: harmony, esp. of sound: an orchestral composition on a great scale in sonata form (*mus.*): an instrumental portion of a work primarily vocal (*arch.*): a symphony orchestra. — *adj.* **symphonic** (*sim-fon'ik*). — *n.* **symphō'nion** a combination of piano and harmonium. — *adj.* **symphonious** (*-fō'ni-əs*) agreeing or harmonising in sound: accordant: harmonious. — *n.* **sym'phonist** a composer or performer of symphonies. — **symphonic poem** a large orchestral composition in programme music with the movements run together; **symphony orchestra** a large orchestra comprising strings, woodwind, brass and percussion, capable of performing symphonies. [Gr. *symphōniā*, harmony, orchestra — *syn*, together, *phōnē*, a sound.]

Symphyla *sim'fi-lə, n.* a class or order of arthropods linking the bristle-tails with the centipedes. — *adj.* **sym'phylous.** [Gr. *symphȳlos*, of the same race — *syn*, with, *phȳlē, phȳlon*, a race, clan.]

symphysis *sim'fi-sis, n.* the union or growing together of parts, concrescence: union of bones by fusion, cartilage, or ligament: a place of junction of parts. — *adj.* **symphyseal, -ial** (*sim-fiz'i-əl*). — *n.* **symphyseot'omy, -iot'omy** (Gr. *tomē*, a cut) the operation of cutting through the pubic symphysis. — *adj.* **symphytic** (*-fit'ik*) by fusion. — *n.* **Sym'phytum** the comfrey genus of the borage family, perh. from its supposed virtue of closing wounds or healing fractures. [Gr. *symphysis* — *syn*, with, *phyein*, to grow.]

sympiesometer *sim-pi-i-zom'i-tər, n.* a barometer with a gas instead of a vacuum: an instrument for measuring the pressure of a current. [Gr. *sympiesis*, a pressing together — *syn*, with, *piezein*, to press, *metron*, a measure.]

symploce *sim'plō-sē, (rhet.) n.* the repetition of a word at the beginning and another at the end of successive clauses. [Gr. *symplokē*, an interweaving — *syn*, with, *plekein*, to weave.]

sympodium *sim-pō'di-əm, (bot.) n.* a stem composed of a succession of branches each supplanting and seeming to continue its parent branch: — *pl.* **sympo'dia.** — *adj.* **sympo'dial.** — *adv.* **sympo'dially.** [Gr. *syn*, together, *pous, podos*, foot.]

symposium *sim-pō'zi-əm, n.* a drinking party (*hist.*): a meeting for philosophic conversation: a conference: a collection of views on one topic: — *pl.* **sympo'sia.** — *adjs.* **sympo'siac, sympō'sial.** — *ns.* **sympō'siarch** (*-ärk*; Gr. *archos*, leader) the master of the feast or conference; **sympō'siast** one who takes part in a symposium. [Latinised from Gr. *symposion* — *syn*, together, *posis*, drinking.]

symptom *sim(p)'təm, n.* a subjective indication of a disease, i.e. something perceived by the patient, not outwardly visible: a characteristic sign or indication of the existence of a state. — *adjs.* **symptomat'ic, -al.** — *adv.* **symptomat'ically.** — *v.t.* **symp'tomatise, -ize** to be a symptom of. — *ns.* **symptomatol'ogy** the study of symptoms: the symptoms of a patient or a disease taken as a whole. — *adj.* **symptomolog'ical.** — *n.* **symptō'sis** wasting: emaciation. — *adj.* **symptotic** (*-tot'-ik*). [Gr. *symptōma, symptōsis* — *syn,* with, and root of *piptein,* to fall.]

syn-, sy-, syl-, sym-, sys- *pfxs.* together, with. [Gr. *syn,* with.]

synadelphïte *sin-ə-del'fīt, n.* a manganese aluminium arsenate. [Gr. *syn,* with, *adelphos,* brother, as found along with kindred minerals.]

synaeresis *sin-ē'rə-sis, n.* the running together of two vowels into one or into a diphthong: the spontaneous expulsion of liquid from a gel. [Gr. *syn,* together, *hairesis,* taking — *haireein,* to take.]

synaesthesia *sin-ēs-thē'zi-ə, -zhə, n.* sensation produced at a point different from the point of stimulation: a sensation of another kind suggested by one experienced (e.g. in colour-hearing). — *adj.* **synaesthet'ic.** [Gr. *syn,* together, *aisthēsis,* sensation.]

synagogue *sin'ə-gog, n.* an assembly of Jews for worship: a Jewish place of worship. — *adjs.* **syn'agogal** (*-gō-gl*), **synagog'ical** (*-gog', -goj'i-kl*). [Gr. *synagōgē* — *syn,* together, *agōgē,* a bringing — *agein,* to lead.]

synallagmatic *sin-a-lag-mat'ik, adj.* mutually or reciprocally obligatory. [Gr. *synallagmatikos* — *synallagma,* a covenant — *syn,* together, *allagma,* exchange.]

synaloepha *sin-ə-lē'fə, n.* the melting of a final vowel or diphthong into the initial vowel or diphthong of the next word. [Latinised from Gr. *synaloiphē* — *synaleiphein,* to coalesce, smear together — *syn,* together, *aleiphein,* to anoint.]

synandrium *sin-an'dri-əm, n.* a mass of united stamens. — *adj.* **synan'drous** having united stamens. [Gr. *syn,* together, *anēr,* a man (male).]

synangium *sin-an'ji-əm, n.* an arterial trunk: a group of united sporangia (found in Marattiaceae). [Gr. *syn,* together, *angeion,* a vessel.]

synantherous *sin-an'thər-əs, adj.* syngenesious. [Gr. *syn,* and **anther.**]

synanthesis *sin-an-thē'sis,* (*bot.*) *n.* simultaneous ripening of stamens and stigmas. — *adjs.* **synanthet'ic; synan'thic** showing synanthy; **synan'thous** synanthic: flowering and leafing simultaneously. — *n.* **synan'thy** abnormal fusion of flowers. [Gr. *syn,* together, *anthēsis,* flowering, *anthos,* a flower.]

synaphea, synapheia *sin-ə-fē'ə, n.* metrical continuity between verses in a system, so that they can be scanned as one verse, as in anapaestics, with possibility of elision at the end of a line. [Gr. *synapheia* — *syn,* together, *haph-,* root of *haptein,* to join.]

synaposematism *sin-ap-ō-sē'mə-tizm, n.* warning coloration common to a number of dangerous species in the same region. — *adj.* **synaposematic** (*-mat'ik*). [Gr. *syn,* together, and **aposematism.**]

synapsis *sin-aps'is, n.* the pairing of chromosomes of paternal and maternal origin before the reducing division: a synapse: — *pl.* **synaps'es** (*-ēz*). — *ns.* **synapse'** (also *sin', sīn'*) an interlacing or enveloping connection of a nerve-cell with another; **synapt'ase** emulsin; **synapte** (*sin-ap'tē*) in the Greek Church, a litany. — *adj.* **synapt'ic.** [Gr. *synapsis,* contact, junction — *syn,* together, *haptein,* to fasten; *synaptē* (*euchē,* a prayer), joined together.]

synarchy *sin'ər-ki, n.* joint sovereignty. [Gr. *synarchiā* — *syn,* with *archein,* to rule.]

synarthrosis *sin-ər-thrō'sis, n.* immovable articulation: — *pl.* **-ses** (*-sēz*). — *adj.* **synarthrō'dial.** — *adv.* **synarthrō'-dially.** [Gr. *synarthrōsis* — *syn,* together, *arthron,* a joint; also *arthrōdiā,* a flattish joint.]

synastry *sin-as'tri,* (*astrol.*) *n.* a coincidence of stellar influences: comparison of the horoscopes of two or more people. [Gr. *syn,* together, *astron,* a star.]

synaxis *si-nak'sis, n.* in the early Church, meeting for worship, esp. for the eucharist. — *n.* **synaxā'rion** (*Gr. Ch.*) a lection containing an account of a saint's life. [Gr. *synaxis,* a bringing together — *syn,* together, *agein,* to lead.]

sync. See **synch.**

syncarp *sin'kärp,* (*bot.*) *n.* a compound fruit formed from two or more carpels, of one or more than one flower. — *adj.* **syncarpous** (*sin-kär'pəs*) of or having united carpels. — *n.* **syn'carpy.** [Gr. *syn,* together, *karpos,* a fruit.]

syncategorematic *sin-kat-i-gor-i-mat'ik, adj.* not able to form a term without other words. — *adv.* **syncategoremat'ically.** [Gr. *synkatēgorēmatikos* — *syn,* with, *katēgorēma,* predicate.]

synch, sync *singk, n., v.i., v.t.* short for **synchronisation, synchronise.** — **out of sync(h)** not synchronised: having different and jarring rhythms: (*loosely*), ill-matched (with *with*).

synchondrosis *sing-kon-drō'sis, n.* connection of bones by cartilage: — *pl.* **-ses** (*-sēz*). [Gr. *synchondrōsis* — *syn,* with, *chondros,* a cartilage.]

synchoresis *sing-kō-rē'sis,* (*rhet.*) *n.* a concession, esp. one made for the sake of a more effective retort. [Gr. *synchōrēsis* — *synchōreein,* to agree, yield ground — *syn,* with, *chōros,* space.]

synchrocyclotron *sing-krō-sī'klō-tron.* See **accelerate.**

synchroflash *sing'krō-flash,* (*phot.*) *n.* a mechanism which synchronises the opening of a camera shutter with the peak of brilliance of a flash bulb. [*synchro*nised *flash.*]

synchromesh *sing'krō-mesh, adj.* of a gear in which the speeds of the driving and driven members are automatically synchronised before coupling, so as to avoid shock and noise in gear-changing. — *n.* such a gear. [*synchro*nised *mesh.*]

synchronal *sing'krə-nl, adj.* coinciding in time. — *adjs.* **synchronic** (*-kron'*), **-al** synchronous: concerned with the study of a subject (esp. a language) at a particular period, without considering the past or the future — opp. to *diachronic.* — *adv.* **synchron'ically.** — *ns.* **synchronicity** (*-is'i-ti*); **synchronīsā'tion, -z-.** — *v.i.* **syn'-chronise, -ize** to coincide or agree in time. — *v.t.* to cause to coincide or agree in time: to time together or to a standard: to represent or identify as contemporary: to make (the sound-track of a film) exactly simultaneous with the picture. — *ns.* **synch'roniser, -z-; synch'ronism** coincidence in time: simultaneity: keeping time together: occurrence of like phrases at the same time: exhibition of contemporary history in one scheme: the bringing together in one picture of different parts of a story. — *adjs.* **synchronis'tic, -al.** — *adv.* **synchronis'tically.** — *n.* **synchronol'ogy** chronological arrangement side by side. — *adj.* **synch'ronous** simultaneous: contemporary: keeping time together. — *adv.* **synch'ronously.** — *ns.* **synch'ronousness; synch'rony** simultaneity. — **synchronised swimming** a sport in which a swimmer or group of swimmers performs a sequence of movements in time to music; **synchronous motor** an electric motor whose speed is exactly proportional to the frequency of the supply current; **synchronous orbit** geostationary orbit. [Gr. *syn,* together, *chronos,* time.]

synchrotron *sing'krō-tron, n.* a type of high-energy particle accelerator. — **synchroton radiation** radiation emitted by charged particles passing through magnetic fields, often used for analysing the structure and behaviour of substances. [Gr. *syn,* together, *chronos,* time, and electron.]

synchysis *sing'ki-sis, n.* confusion of meaning due to unusual arrangement (*rhet.*): fluidity of the vitreous humour of the eye. [Gr. *synchysis* — *syn,* together, with, *cheein,* to pour.]

synclastic *sin-klas'tik, adj.* having the same kind of curvature in all directions. [Gr. *syn,* together, *klastos,* broken.]

syncline *sin'klīn,* (*geol.*) *n.* a fold in which the beds dip downwards towards the axis. — *adj.* **synclīn'al.** — *n.*

a syncline. — *n.* **synclinorium** (*-kli-nō'ri-əm, -nö'*) a great synclinal structure carrying minor flexures. [Gr. *syn*, together, *klīnein*, to cause to lean.]

Syncom *sin'kom, n.* one of a series of communication satellites in a synchronous orbit. [*Syn*chronous *com*munications satellite.]

syncope *sing'kə-pi, n.* a cutting short (*rare*): syncopation (*obs.*): the elision of a letter or syllable from the middle of a word: a fainting fit caused by a sudden fall of blood pressure in the brain (*med.*). — *adj.* **sync'opal** of syncope. — *v.t.* **sync'opate** to shorten by cutting out the middle (of a word): to alter the rhythm of temporarily by transferring the accent to a normally unaccented beat (*mus.*). — *adj.* **sync'opated.** — *n.* **syncopa'tion; sync'opātor.** — *adjs.* **syncopic** (*sing-kop'-ik*); **syncopt'ic.** [Gr. *synkopē*, a cutting up, cutting short, syncope — *syn*, together, *koptein*, to cut off.]

syncretism *sing'kri-tizm,* or *sin', n.* reconciliation of, or attempt to reconcile, different systems of belief, esp. of different forms of Christianity by Georg Calixtus: fusion or blending of religions, as by identification of gods, taking over of observances, or selection of whatever seems best in each; illogical compromise in religion: the fusion of orig. distinct inflectional forms of a word. — *adj.* **syncretic** (*sin-krē'tik,* or *sing-*). — *v.t.* and *v.i.* **syncretise, -ize** (*sing'kri-tīz*). — *n.* **syn'cretist.** — *adj.* **syncretis'tic.** [Gr. *synkrētismos,* a confederation (orig. app. of *Cretan* communities).]

syncytium *sin-sish'i-əm,* (*biol.*) *n.* a multinucleate cell: a tissue without distinguishable cell-walls. — *adj.* **syncyt'ial.** [Gr. *syn,* together, *kytos,* a vessel.]

synd, sind *sīnd, v.t.* to rinse: to wash out or down. — *n.* a rinsing: a washing down with liquor. — *n.pl.* **synd'ings, sind'ings.** — Also **syne** (*Burns*). [Origin obscure.]

syndactyl *sin-dak'til, adj.* with fused digits. — *n.* **syndac'tylism.** — *adj.* **syndac'tylous.** — *n.* **syndac'tyly.** [Gr. *syn, daktylos,* finger, toe.]

synderesis. See **synteresis.**

syndesis *sin'di-sis, n.* a binding: synapsis (*biol.*). — *adjs.* **syndetic** (*-det'ik*), **-al** connective: of a construction in which clauses are connected by conjunctions (*gram.*). — *adv.* **syndet'ically.** [Gr. *syndesis* — *syn, deein,* to bind.]

syndesmosis *sin-des-mō'sis, n.* the connection of bones by ligaments: — *pl.* **-es** (*-ēz*). — *adj.* **syndesmotic** (*-mot'ik*). [Gr. *syndesmos* — *syn, desmos,* a bond.]

syndet *sin'det, n. syn*thetic *det*ergent.

syndetic, etc. See **syndesis.**

syndic *sin'dik, n.* in ancient Greece an advocate, delegate, or judge: at various times and places a magistrate or mayor: a member of a committee of the Senate of Cambridge University: one chosen to transact business for others, esp. the accredited legal representative of a corporation, society, or company. — *adj.* **syn'dical** (**syndical chamber** or **union** a French trade-union). — *ns.* **syn'dicalism** a development of trade-unionism which originated in France, aiming at putting the means of production in the hands of unions of workers; **syn'dicalist.** — Also *adj.* — *adj.* **syndicalist'ic.** — *n.* **syn'dicate** a body of syndics: a council: the office of a syndic: a body of men chosen to watch the interests of a company, or to manage a bankrupt's property: a combination of persons for some common purpose or interest: an association of businessmen or companies to undertake a project requiring a large amount of capital: an association of criminals who organise and control illegal operations: a combined group of newspapers. — *v.t.* to judge, censure (*obs.*): to control, effect, or publish by means of a syndicate: to sell (as an article) for simultaneous publication in a number of newspapers or periodicals: to sell radio or TV programmes for broadcasting by many different radio or TV stations: to join in a syndicate. — *v.i.* to join in a syndicate. — *ns.* **syndicā'tion; syn'dicātor.** [Gr. *syndikos* — *syn,* with, *dikē,* justice.]

syndrome *sin'drōm, sin'drə-mi, -mē,* or *sin'drō-mi, -mē, n.*

concurrence, esp. of symptoms: a characteristic pattern or group of symptoms: a pattern or group of actions, feelings, observed happenings, etc., characteristic of a particular problem or condition. — *adj.* **syndromic** (*-drom'ik*). [Gr. *syndromē.*]

syndyasmian *sin-di-az'mi-ən,* (*anthrop.*) *adj.* pairing, applied to a form of family founded on a loose temporary marriage. [Gr. *syndyasmos,* coupling.]

syne[1] *sīn,* (*Scot.*) *adv.* then, next: afterwards, later: ago, since (as in *auld langsyne*). [**sithen.**]

syne[2]. See **synd.**

synecdoche *sin-ek'də-kē, -ki,* (*rhet.*) *n.* the figure of putting part for the whole, or the whole for part. — *adjs.* **synecdochic** (*-dok'*), **-al.** — *adv.* **synecdoch'ically.** — *n.* **synec'dochism** use of synecdoche: use of part for the whole in sympathetic magic. [Gr. *synekdochē* — *syn,* together, *ekdechesthai,* to receive.]

synechia *sin-e-kī'ə, sin-ē'ki-ə, n.* morbid adhesion, esp. of iris and cornea. [Gr. *synecheia,* continuity — *syn,* together, *echein,* to hold.]

synecology *sin-ē-kol'ə-ji, n.* the ecological study of communities of plants or animals. — *adjs.* **synecolog'ic, -al.** — *adv.* **synecolog'ically.** [Gr. *syn,* together, and **ecology.**]

synecphonesis *sin-ek-fō-nē'sis, n.* synizesis. [Gr. *syn,* together, *ekphōnēsis,* pronunciation — *ek,* out, *phōnē,* voice, utterance.]

synectics *sin-ek'tiks, n.sing.* the study of processes leading to invention, with the end aim of solving practical problems, esp. by a **synectics group** a miscellaneous group of people of imagination and ability but varied interests. — *adj.* **synec'tic.** — *adv.* **synec'tically.** [Gr. *synektikos,* fit for holding together.]

synedrion *sin-ed'ri-on, n.* a judicial assembly: a sanhedrin. — Also **syned'rium:** — *pl.* (of both) **syned'ria.** — *adj.* **syned'rial.** [Gr. *syn,* together, *hedrā,* seat.]

syneidesis *sin-ī-dē'sis, n.* conscience as passing judgment on past acts — opp. to *synteresis.* [Gr. *syneidēsis,* conscience — *syn,* with, together, *eidenai,* to know.]

syneresis. Same as **synaeresis.**

synergy *sin'ər-ji, n.* combined or co-ordinated action. — *adjs.* **synergetic** (*-jet'ik*), **syner'gic** working together. — *n.* **syner'gid** (*bot.*) either of the two cells in the embryosac that seem to guide the pollen-tube. — *v.i.* **syn'ergise, -ize** to act as a synergist (with another substance). — *n.* **synergism** (*sin'* or *-ûr'*) the doctrine that the human will and the Divine Spirit are two efficient agents that co-operate in regeneration — ascribed to Melanchthon: increased effect of two substances, as drugs, obtained by using them together; **syn'ergist** (or *-ûr'*) a substance which increases the effect of another (e.g. pesticide): a muscle, etc., that acts with another. — *adj.* **synergist'ic.** — *adv.* **synergist'ically.** [Gr. *synergiā,* co-operation — *syn,* together, *ergon,* work.]

synesis *sin'ə-sis, n.* syntax having regard to meaning rather than grammatical form. [Gr., sense.]

synfuel *sin'fū-əl, n.* any type of fuel synthesised from a fossil fuel. [*syn*thetic and **fuel.**]

syngamy *sing'gə-mi, n.* free interbreeding: union of gametes. — *adjs.* **syngamic** (*sin-gam'ik*), **syngamous** (*sing'-gə-məs*). [Gr. *syn,* together, *gamos,* marriage.]

syngeneic *sin-ji-nē'ik, adj.* genetically identical. [Gr. *syngeneia,* kinship.]

syngenesis *sin-jen'i-sis, n.* reproduction by fusion of male and female elements, the offspring being derived from both parents. — *n.pl.* **Syngenesia** (*sin-ji-nē'si-ə*) in the Linnaean system a class of plants with syngenesious stamens, answering to the Compositae. — *adjs.* **syngene'sious** having the anthers united in a tube about the style, as in Compositae; **syngenetic** (*-net'ik*) of or by syngenesis: of minerals, formed contemporaneously with the enclosing rock. [Gr. *syn,* together, *genesis,* formation, generation.]

syngnathous *sin(g)'gna-thəs,* or *sing'nath-, adj.* of certain fish, having the jaws fused to form a tubular structure. — *n.pl.* **Syngnathidae** (*sin(g)-gnath'i-dē* or *sing-nath'*) the pipefish family. [Gr. *syn,* together, *gnathos,* jaw.]

syngraph *sing'gräf, n.* a writing signed by both or all of the parties thereto. [Gr. *syn*, together, *graphein*, to write.]

synizesis *sin-i-zē'sis, n.* the union into one syllable of two vowels without forming a recognised diphthong: contraction of chromatin towards one side in karyokinesis. [Gr. *synizēsis*, a collapse — *syn*, with, together, and *hizein*, to seat, to sit down.]

synod *sin'əd, n.* a meeting: an ecclesiastical council: a Presbyterian church court intermediate between presbytery and the General Assembly: the supreme court of the former United Presbyterian Church: conjunction (*astron.*; *obs.*). — *adj.* **syn'odal** of, of the nature of, or done in a synod. — *n.* a payment made by a clergyman on the occasion of a synod, or at a visitation. — *adjs.* **synodic** (*-od'ik*), **-al** synodal: pertaining to conjunction (*astron.*): from conjunction to conjunction (see **month**). — *adv.* **synod'ically. — synodic period** (*astron.*) the time between two successive conjunctions of a heavenly body with the sun; **syn'odsman** a lay member of a synod. — **General Synod of the Church of England** governing body set up in 1970 giving the laity more say in the decisions of the Church. [Gr. *synodos*, a meeting, conjunction — *syn*, together, *hodos*, a way.]

synoecete *sin-ē'sēt,* **sinoekete** *-kēt, ns.* a guest tolerated with indifference in an ants' or termites' nest. — *n.* **synoeciosis** (*-si-ō'sis*) the rhetorical figure of coupling opposites. — *adjs.* **synoecious** (*-ē'shəs*), **synoicous** (*-oi'kəs*) having antheridia and archegonia in the same group. — *v.t.* and *v.i.* **syn'oecise, -ize** (*-ē-sīz*) to unite in one community or city-state. — *ns.* **synoe'cism** union of communities or cities; **synoecology** (*-kol'ə-ji*) same as **synecology**. [Gr. *synoikia*, a living together, community, *synoiketēs*, a house-fellow, *synoikizein*, to unite in one community — *syn*, with, *oikeein*, to dwell.]

synonym *sin'ə-nim, n.* a word having the same meaning with another (usu. very nearly the same meaning): a systematic name to which another is preferred as valid (*biol.*). — *adj.* **synonymatic** (*sin-on-i-mat'ik*), **synonym'ic, -al** of synonyms. — *ns.* **synonym'icon** a dictionary of synonyms; **synon'ymist** one who studies synonyms, or the different names of plants and animals; **synonym'ity** the fact or quality of being synonymous. — *adj.* **synon'ymous** having the same meaning. — *adv.* **synon'ymously.** — *ns.* **synon'ymousness; synon'ymy** rhetorical use of synonyms: a setting forth of synonyms: a list of synonyms. [Gr. *synōnymon* — *syn*, with, *onoma*, a name.]

synopsis *sin-op'sis, n.* a general view: a summary: — *pl.* **synop'sēs.** — *v.t.* **synopsise, -ize** to make a synopsis of. — *adjs.* **synop'tic, -al** affording or taking a general view of the whole. — *adv.* **synop'tically.** — *n.* **synop'tist** one of the writers of the Synoptic Gospels. — *adj.* **synoptis'tic. — Synoptic Gospels** those of Matthew, Mark, and Luke, which readily admit of being brought under one combined view. [Gr. *synopsis* — *syn*, with, together, *opsis*, a view.]

synostosis *sin-os-tō'sis, n.* complete union of bones: — *pl.* **-es** (*-ēz*). [Gr. *syn*, *osteon*, bone.]

synovia *sin-ō'vi-ə, n.* an unctuous fluid in the joints. — *adjs.* **syno'vial; synovitic** (*-vit'ik*) pertaining to synovitis. — *n.* **synovi'tis** inflammation of a synovial membrane. — **synovial membrane** a membrane of connective tissue that lines tendon sheaths and capsular ligaments and secretes synovia. [App. an arbitrary coinage of Paracelsus, who applied it more generally.]

synrok *sin'rok, n.* a type of synthetic rock developed especially to fuse with radioactive waste to be buried deep underground. [*synthetic rock*.]

syntactic, syntagma, etc. See **syntax**.

syntan *sin'tan, n.* a synthetic tanning agent.

syntax *sin'taks, n.* grammatical structure in sentences: one of the classes in some R.C. schools. — *adjs.* **syntac'tic, -al.** — *adv.* **syntac'tically.** — *n.* **syntag'ma** a systematic body, system, or group: a word or words constituting a syntactic unit: — *pl.* **syntag'mata.** — *adj.*

syntagmat'ic. — *n.* **syntag'matite** a kind of hornblende. [Gr. *syntaxis* — *syn*, together — *tassein*, to put in order.]

syntectic(al). See **syntexis**.

syntenosis *sin-tə-nō'sis, n.* the connection of bones by tendons: — *pl.* **-oses** (*-ō'sēz*). [Gr. *syn*, with, *tenōn*, a sinew.]

synteresis *sin-ti-rē'sis, n.* conscience as a guide to future action — opp. to *syneidesis*. — Also **synderē'sis** (from the later Gr. pronunciation). [Gr. *syntērēsis*, observation — *syn*, with, *tēreein*, to watch over.]

syntexis *sin-tek'sis, n.* liquefaction: melting: wasting. — *adjs.* **syntec'tic, -al.** [Gr. *syntēxis* — *syn*, with, *tēkein*, to melt.]

synthesis *sin'thi-sis, n.* building up: putting together: making a whole out of parts: the combination of separate elements of thought into a whole: reasoning from principles to a conclusion — opp. to *analysis*: — *pl.* **syn'theses** (*sēz*). — *v.t.* **syn'thesise, -ize** to put together in synthesis: to form by synthesis. — *ns.* **syn'thesīser, -z-** one who, or that which, synthesises: a computerised instrument for generating sounds, often beyond the range of conventional instruments, used esp. in making electronic music. — *n.* **syn'thesist** one who makes a synthesis. — *adjs.* **synthetic** (*-thet'*), **-al** pertaining to, consisting in, or formed by, synthesis: artificially produced but of like nature with, not a mere substitute for, the natural product: not sincere, sham (*coll.*). — *n.* **synthet'ic** a synthetic substance. — *adv.* **synthet'ically.** — *n.* **synthet'icism** the principles of synthesis, a synthetic system. — *v.t.* **syn'thetise, -ize** to synthesise. — *ns.* **syn'thetīser, -z-, syn'thetist.** — **synthetic drug** a drug made in the laboratory — both those occurring naturally and artificial ones; **synthetic languages** those that use inflectional forms instead of word order, prepositions, etc., to express syntactical relationships; **synthetic philosophy** Herbert Spencer's system, a fusion, as he thought, of the different sciences into a whole. [Gr. *synthesis* — *syn*, with, together, *thesis*, a placing.]

synthronus *sin'thrə-nəs, n.* the seat of the bishop and his presbyters, behind the altar. [Gr. *syn*, together, *thronos*, a throne.]

syntony *sin'tən-i, n.* tuning, or agreement in resonance frequency, of wireless apparatus. — *adj.* **syntonic** (*sin-ton'ik*) tuned together: showing a normal emotional response to one's environment (*psychol.*). — *n.* **syn'tonin** a substance akin to fibrin, found in muscle. — *v.t.* **syn'tonise, -ize** to adjust to agree in frequency. — *adj.* **syn'tonous** syntonic. [Gr. *syn*, together, *tonos*, tone.]

sype. Same as **sipe**[1].

syphilis *sif'i-lis, n.* a contagious venereal disease due to infection with a micro-organism *Spirochaeta pallida* (*Treponema pallidum*). — *n.* **syphilisā'tion, -z-.** — *v.t.* **syph'ilise, -ize** to inoculate or to infect with syphilis. — *adj.* **syphilit'ic.** — *n.* a person suffering from syphilis. — *adj.* **syph'iloid** like syphilis. — *ns.* **syphilol'ogist; syphilol'ogy** the study of syphilis; **syphilō'ma** a syphilitic tumour; **syphilophō'bia** a morbid dread of syphilis. [Title of Fracastoro's Latin poem (1530), whose hero *Syphilus* is infected.]

syphon, syren. Same as **siphon, siren**.

Syrah *sīr'ə, n.* a red wine grape: wine made from this. [The ancient Persian City of *Shiraz*, where the grape is supposed to have originated.]

Syriac *sir'i-ak, n.* the ancient Aramaic dialect of *Syria*. — Also *adj.* — *ns.* **Syr'iacism** (*-ə-sizm*), **Syr'ianism, Syr'iasm, Syr'ism** a Syriac idiom. — *adj.* **Syr'ian** relating to Syria. — *n.* native or citizen of Syria. — *ns.* **Syr'iarch** (*ärk*; Gr. *Syriarchēs*) the chief priest in Roman Syria; **Syrophoenicia** (*sī-rō-fi-nish'yə*) a Roman province between Lebanon and the coast. — *n.* and *adj.* **Syrophoeni'cian.**

syringa, syringe, etc. See **syrinx**.

syrinx *sir'ingks, n.* Pan-pipes: the vocal organ of birds: a fistula or fistulous opening: a rock-cut tunnel, as in

Egyptian tombs: — *pl.* **syringes** (*-in'jēz*) or **syr'inxes**. — *ns.* **syringa** (*-ing'gə*) orig. and still popularly the mock-orange: the lilac: (with *cap.*) after Linnaeus, the generic name of the lilac; **syr'inge** (*-inj* or *si-rinj'*) an instrument for injecting or extracting fluids. — *v.t.* and *v.i.* to clean, spray, or inject with a syringe. — *adj.* **syringeal** (*-in'ji-əl*). — *ns.* **syringitis** (*-jī'tis*) inflammation of the Eustachian tube; **syringomyelia** (*si-ring-gō-mī-ēli-ə*; Gr. *myelos*, marrow) a chronic, progressive disease of the spinal cord, causing paralysis and loss of sensitivity to pain and temperature; **syringotomy** (*sir-ing-got'ə-mi*) cutting for fistula. [Gr. *syrinx, -ingos*, Pan-pipes, gallery.]

syrlye. An old form (*Spens.*) of **surly**.

Syrophoenicia(n). See **Syriac**.

Syrphus *sûr'fəs, n.* a genus of wasp-like flies that hover and dart, giving name to the family **Syr'phidae** (*-fi-dē*). — *n.* and *adj.* **syr'phid**. [Gr. *syrphos*, gnat.]

syrtis *sûr'tis,* (*Milt.*) *n.* a quicksand: — *pl.* **syr'tes** (*-tēz*). [L. *Syrtēs*, Gr. *Syrtides* (sing. of each *Syrtis*), name of two sandy bays of N. Africa — Gr. *syrein*, to draw, sweep along.]

syrup *sir'əp, n.* a saturated solution of sugar boiled to prevent fermentation: any thick sweet liquid: a sugar-flavoured liquid medicine: cloying sweetness (*fig.; coll.*). — *v.t.* to make into syrup: to cover, fill, etc., with syrup. — Also (esp. *U.S.*) **sir'up**. — *adj.* **syr'upy**. — **golden syrup** the uncrystallisable part finally separated in manufacture of crystallised sugar. [Fr. *sirop* — Ar. *sharāb*; cf. **shrub**[2], **sherbet**.]

sys-. See **syn-**.

syssarcosis *sis-är-kō'sis, n.* the connection of one bone with another by intervening muscle: — *pl.* **-oses** (*-ō'sēz*). [Gr. *syn*, together, *sarx*, flesh.]

syssitia *si-sit'i-ə*, or *-sish', n.* the ancient Spartan custom of eating the chief meal together in public. [Gr. *syssitiā* — *syn*, together, *sītos*, food.]

systaltic *sis-tal'tik, adj.* alternately contracting and dilating, pulsatory. [Gr. *systaltikos*, depressing; cf. **systole**.]

system *sis'tim, -təm, n.* anything formed of parts placed together or adjusted into a regular and connected whole: a set of things considered as a connected whole: a group of heavenly bodies moving mainly under the influence of their mutual attraction: a set of bodily organs of like composition or concurring in function: the bodily organism: one of the great divisions of the geological strata, subordinate only to the division into Palaeozoic, Mesozoic, and Cainozoic: a group of (Greek) verses: a body of doctrine: a theory of the universe: a full and connected view of some department of knowledge: an explanatory hypothesis: a scheme of classification: a manner of crystallisation: a plan: a method: a method of organisation: method-icalness: a systematic treatise: (with *the*, often with *cap.*) society seen as a soulless and monolithic organisation thwarting individual effort. — *adjs.* **systemat'ic**, **-al** pertaining to, or consisting of, for the purpose of, observing, or according to system: methodical: habitual: intentional. — *adv.* **systemat'ically**. — *n.* **systematician** (*-ə-tish'ən*). — *n.sing.* **systemat'ics** the science of classification: the study of classification of living things in accordance with their natural relationships. — *ns.* **systematīsā'tion, -z-, systemīsā'tion, -z-**. — *vs.t.* **sys'tematise, -ize, sys'temise, -ize** to reduce to a system. — *ns.* **sys'tematiser, -z-; sys'tematism; sys'tematist; systematol'ogy**. — *adjs.* **sys'temed; systemic** (*-tem'ik*) pertaining to the bodily system or to a system of bodily organs: affecting the body as a whole: (of a pesticide, etc.) spreading through all the tissues, without harming the plant but making it toxic to the insect, etc.; (of a herbicide) spreading through all the tissues of a plant and killing it; **sys'temless** without system: not exhibiting organic structure. — **system building** building using standardised factory-produced components. — *adj.* **sys'tem-built'**. — **sys'tem-maker, -monger** one unduly fond of constructing systems; **systems analysis; systems analyst** one who analyses the operation of a scientific, industrial, etc., procedure, usu. with a computer, in order to plan more efficient methods and use of equipment; **systems engineering** a branch of engineering that uses information theory and systems analysis to design integrated systems; **systems flowchart** (*comput.*) a flowchart designed to analyse the operation of a computing system with a view to improving it; **system software** (*comput.*) the software needed to produce a system that is acceptable to the end user. [Gr. *systēma* — *sy-, syn-*, together, and the root of *histanai*, to set.]

systole *sis'to-lē, -tə-lē, n.* rhythmical contraction, esp. of the heart — opp. to *diastole*: collapse of the nucleus in mitosis: the shortening of a long syllable (*gram.*). — *adj.* **systolic** (*-tol'ik*). [Gr. *systolē* — *syn*, together, *stellein*, to place.]

systyle *sis'tīl,* (*archit.*) *adj.* having an intercolumniation of two diameters. — *n.* such an arrangement: a building or part so constructed. [Gr. *systylos* — *sy-, syn-*, together, *stylos*, a column.]

sythe (*Spens.*). See **sith**[2].

syver, siver *sī'vər,* (*Scot.*) *n.* a drain: a grating over a drain. [Perh. a form of **sewer** (see **sew**[3]).]

syzygy *siz'i-ji, n.* conjunction or opposition: the period of new or full moon: a dipody: — *pl.* **syz'ygies**. — *adj.* **syzyg'ial**. [Gr. *syzygiā*, union, coupling — *sy-, syn-*, with, together, and *zygon*, a yoke.]

Szekely *sek'ə-li, n.* a Transylvanian Magyar. — Also **Szekel** (*sekl*), **Szekler** (*sek'lər*). [Hung. *sékel*, to reside.]

T

T, t *tē, n.* the twentieth letter in our alphabet, eighteenth in the Roman, its usual sound a voiceless stop produced with the tip of the tongue in contact with teeth, gums, or palate: an object or mark in the form of the letter (also **tee**): as a mediaeval Roman numeral T = 160, T̄ = 160 000. — **T′-band′age** a bandage composed of two strips fashioned in the shape of the letter T; **T′-bar** a metal bar with cross-section in the shape of the letter T: a type of ski-lift (also **T′-bar lift**); **T′-bone** a bone shaped like a T, esp. in a sirloin steak; **T′-cart** a four-wheeled pleasure-vehicle without top, having a T-shaped body; **T′-cloth** a plain cotton made for the India and China market — stamped with a T; **T′-cross** a tau-cross; **T′-junction** a road junction in the shape of a T; **T′-plate** a T-shaped plate, as for strengthening a joint in a wooden framework; **T′-rail** a rail with T-shaped cross-section. — *adj.* **T′-shaped.** — **T′-shirt** see **tee**[1]; **T′-square** a T-shaped ruler; **T′-strap** a T-shaped strap on a shoe. — **marked with a T** branded as thief; **to a T** with perfect exactness.

't a shortened form of **it**.

t-, t' an obsolete shortened form of **to** before a vowel, as in Spenser **tadvance,** to advance, **tasswage,** to assuage: in N. of England for **the**.

ta *tä, interj.* (hypocoristic or affected) thank you.

taal *täl, (arch.) n.* Afrikaans or Cape Dutch. [Du., speech.]

tab[1] *tab, n.* a small tag, flap, or strap, forming an appendage: a loop for hanging up by: a loop for drawing a stage curtain: hence, a stage curtain: reckoning, tally, check. — *adj.* **tabbed.** — *v.t.* to fix a tab to: — *pr.p.* **tabb′ing;** *pa.t.* and *pa.p.* **tabbed.** — **keep tabs on** see **keep; pick up the tab** (*coll.*) to pay the bill. [Ety. dub.]

tab[2] *tab, n.* short for **tablet.**

tab[3] *tab, n.* short for (typewriter) **tabulator.** — *v.t.* short for **tabulate.**

Tabanus *ta-bā′nas, n.* the gadfly genus. — *n.* **tabanid** (*tab′a-nid*) any member of the genus, or of its family **Tabanidae** (*ta-ban′i-dē*). [L. *tabānus.*]

tabard *tab′ard, n.* a mediaeval peasant's overcoat: a knight's sleeveless or short-sleeved coat: now, a herald's coat: a woman's outer garment, a sleeveless tunic. — *n.* **tab′erdar** a scholar of Queen's College, Oxford. [O.Fr. *tabart.*]

tabaret *tab′a-ret, n.* an upholsterer's silk stuff, with alternate stripes of watered and satin surface. [Orig. tradename, prob. formed from **tabby.**]

Tabasco® *ta-bas′kō, n.* a hot pepper sauce. [*Tabasco* state in Mexico.]

tabasheer, -shir *tab-a-shēr′, n.* a siliceous substance sometimes found in crude form in hollows of bamboos and also prepared by chemical processes. [Hind., Pers., Ar. *tabāshīr.*]

tabbouleh *ta-boo′le, n.* a Mediterranean salad introduced from Lebanon, made with cracked wheat. [Ar. *tabbūla.*]

tabby *tab′i, n.* a coarse waved or watered silk: an artificial stone: a tabby-cat: a gossiping, interfering woman (*coll.*). — *adj.* brindled. — *v.t.* to water or cause to look wavy: — *pr.p.* **tabb′ying;** *pa.t.* and *pa.p.* **tabb′ied.** — *ns.* **tabb′inet, tab′inet** a more delicate kind of tabby resembling damask, used for window-curtains; **tabb′yhood.** — **tabb′y-cat** a brindled cat, esp. a greyish or brownish cat with dark stripes: hence (or from *Tabitha*) a female cat: an old maid: a spiteful gossiping woman. [Fr. *tabis,* app. from '*Attābiy,* a quarter in Baghdad where it was made.]

tabefaction, tabefy. See **tabes.**

tabellion *ta-bel′yan, n.* an official scrivener in the Roman empire and elsewhere. [L.L. *tabelliō, -ōnis* — L. *tabella,* tablet, dim. of *tabula,* a board.]

taberdar. See under **tabard.**

tabernacle *tab′ar-na-kl, n.* a tent or movable hut: the tent carried by the Jews through the desert and used as a temple: the human body as the temporary abode of the soul: a place of worship, esp. temporary or dissenting: a receptacle for the vessel containing the pyx (*R.C.*): a canopied niche or seat: a canopy: a socket for a mast. — *v.i.* to sojourn. — *v.t.* to put or enshrine in a tabernacle. — *adjs.* **tab′ernacled; tabernacular** (*-nak′ū-lar*). — **tab′ernacle-work** ornamental work over niches, stalls, etc., with canopies and pinnacles, or any work in which this forms a characteristic feature. — **Feast of Tabernacles** (also **Feast of Ingathering, Sukkoth**) a Jewish harvest festival, celebrating the sojourn in tents in the wilderness. [L. *tabernāculum,* dim. of *taberna,* a hut.]

tabes *tā′bēz, n.* wasting away. — *n.* **tabefaction** (*tab-i-fak′shan*) wasting away, emaciation. — *v.t.* and *v.i.* **tab′efy.** — *n.* **tabescence** (*tab-es′ans*) wasting: shrivelling. — *adjs.* **tabesc′ent; tabetic** (*-bet′ik*); **tab′id.** — **tabes dorsa′lis** locomotor ataxia. [L. *tābēs, -is.*]

tabinet. Same as **tabbinet** (see **tabby**).

tabla *tab′la, -lä, n.* an Indian percussion instrument, a pair of small drums played with the hands. [Hind.]

tablature *tab′la-char, n.* a tablet: a painting, picture, pictorial representation or work: an old notation for lute music with a line for each string and letters or figures to indicate the stopping, used with modifications for other instruments. [L. *tabula,* a board.]

table *tā′bl, n.* a slab or board: a layer: a flat surface: a board for painting on: a picture: a quadrangular space on the palm of the hand (*Shak.*): a panel: a stringcourse: a slab with or for an inscription: a slab inscribed with laws: hence, in *pl.,* a code of law (as the **Twelve Tables** of ancient Rome): a writing tablet (esp. in the obs. phrase *a pair of tables*): a board for a game, e.g. chess: each half of a folding board: hence, in *pl.* (*obs.*), backgammon: a broad flat surface on a cut gem: a tabular crystal: an article of furniture consisting of a flat top on legs, pillar, or trestles, for use at meals, work, play, for holding things, etc.: supply of food, entertainment: the company at a table: a board or committee: a dispensing of the communion: a projecting part of a scarfed joint: a flat gravestone supported on pillars: a condensed statement: a syllabus or index: a compact scheme of numerical information: hence, in *pl.,* a collection of these for reference. — *adj.* of, for, like, or pertaining to a table, or meals. — *v.t.* to tabulate: to lay on the table: to pay down: to put forward (a bill, order, etc.) for discussion in parliament: to postpone discussion of (a bill, etc.) for some time or indefinitely (*U.S.*): to board. — *v.i.* to board. — *adj.* **tabled** (*tā′bld*) flat-topped: having a smooth sloping surface of dressed stone: having a table or tables. — *n.* **ta′bleful** as many as a table will hold. — *adj.* and *adv.* **ta′blewise** in the form or in the manner of a table: of the communion table, not altarwise. — *n.* **ta′bling** tabulation: backgammon-playing: board: provision of tables: scarfing: a broad hem on the skirt of a sail. — **ta′ble-beer** light beer for common use; **ta′ble-book** a book of writing tablets, memorandum book, or notebook: an ornamental book intended to lie on a table: a book of tables; **ta′ble-cloth** a cloth for covering a table, esp. at meals; **ta′ble-cover** a cloth for covering a table, esp. at other than meal-times. — *adj.* **ta′ble-cut** (of gems) cut with a flat top. — **table-d'hôte**

tableau 1494 **tach-**

(*tä-bl'-dōt*; Fr., host's table) a meal at a fixed price; **table football** a version of football played on a table with small metal, etc. players usu. suspended on rods, that are made to strike the ball; **table game** a board game; **ta'ble-knife** a knife such as one cuts one's own meat, etc., with; **ta'bleland** an extensive region of elevated land with a flat or undulating surface: a plateau; **ta'ble-leaf** an extension to a table-top, hinged, drawn out, or inserted; **table licence** a licence to serve alcoholic drinks with meals only; **ta'ble-lin'en** linen table-cloths, napkins, etc.; **ta'ble-maid** a maid-servant who sets the table and waits; **table manners** social behaviour during meals; **ta'ble-mat** a mat placed under dishes on a table; **ta'ble-mon'ey** an allowance for official entertainment: restaurateur's euphemism for *cover-charge*; **ta'ble-mu'sic** music in parts that can be read by performers at each side of a table; **ta'ble-nap'kin** a cloth used at table to protect the clothes and to wipe fingers and lips; **table salt** fine salt suitable for use at table; **ta'ble-skitt'les** a game in which a suspended ball is swung to knock down pegs set up on a board; **ta'ble-spoon** one of the largest spoons used at table; **ta'ble-spoon'ful** as much as will fill a table-spoon: — *pl.* **ta'ble-spoon'fuls**; **ta'ble-sport** (*Shak.*) the butt of the company at table; **ta'ble-talk** familiar conversation, as at table, during and after meals; **ta'ble-tenn'is** a game like lawn-tennis played on a table using celluloid or similar balls; **ta'ble-top** the top of a table: a flat top. — *adj.* **ta'ble-topped.** — **ta'ble-turn'ing** movements of tables (or other objects) attributed by spiritualists to the agency of spirits — by the sceptical to collective involuntary muscular action; **ta'ble-ware** dishes, spoons, knives, forks, etc., for table use; **ta'ble-wa'ter** a mineral water suitable for the table; **table wine** an unfortified wine usually drunk with a meal; **ta'ble-work** the setting of type for tables, columns of figures, etc. — **at table** at a meal; **fence the tables** see **fence; lay on the table** to table (a bill, etc.; see **table** *v.t.*, above); **the Lord's table** see **lord; turn the tables** to bring about a complete reversal of circumstances, as if the players at backgammon changed sides; **under the table** not above board: hopelessly drunk. [Partly O.E. *tabule*, *tabele*, partly O.Fr. (and Fr.) *table*, both — L. *tabula*, a board.]

tableau *tab'lō*, *n.* a picture or vivid pictorial impression: a suddenly created situation that takes all aback: — *pl.* **tableaux** (*tab'lōz*). — **tableau curtains** theatre curtains drawn back and up, to give a draped effect when opened; **tableau (vivant)** a 'living picture', a motionless representation by living persons in costume: — *pl.* **tableaux (vivants)** (*tä-blō-vē-vä*). [Fr. dim. of *table*.]

tablet *tab'lit*, *n.* a small slab: a slab or stiff sheet for making notes on: a panel, esp. inscribed or for inscription: an inscribed plate hung up in fulfilment of a vow: a brittle confection of sugar and condensed milk, made in slabs (*Scot.*): a small flat cake of any solid material, often medicinal: a device that converts the movement of a specially adapted pen into digital or analog signals, allowing graphic designs to be displayed on a visual display unit. (*comput.*) — *v.t.* to provide with, inscribe on, or make into, a tablet. [O.Fr. *tablete*, dim. of *table*.]

tabloid *tab'loid*, *n.* anything in a concentrated form, a summary: a newspaper of small format, measuring approx. 30 × 40 centimetres (about 12 × 16 inches), usu. rather informal in style and with many photographs. — *adj.* of, in the form of, tabloids: concentrated. [From *Tabloid*, trademark for a medicine in tablet form.]

taboggan. See **toboggan.**

taboo, tabu *tə-bōō'*, *adj.* subject to taboo: forbidden. — *n.* a Polynesian (or other) system of prohibitions connected with things considered holy or unclean: any one of these prohibitions: any recognised or general prohibition, interdict, restraint, ban, exclusion, ostracism: — *pl.* **taboos'**, **tabus'**. — *v.t.* to forbid approach to or use of: to place under taboo: — *pr.p.*

taboo'ing, tabu'ing; *pa.t.* and *pa.p.* **tabooed', tabued'.** [Tongan *tabu* (pron. *tä'bōō*), holy, unclean.]

tabor, tabour *tä'bər*, *n.* a small drum like a tambourine without jingles, usually played with one stick, along with a pipe: a taborer. — *v.i.* and *v.t.* to play on a tabor: to beat, drum. — *ns.* **tä'borer** (*Spens.* **tabrere** *ta-brēr'*) one who beats the tabor; **tabo(u)rin** (*tab'ə-rin*, or *-rēn*) a small drum longer in body than the tabor, used in like manner; **tabouret**, *U.S.* **taboret** (*tab'ə-ret*, *tä-bōō-rä*) a stool, orig. drum-shaped; **tabret** (*tab'rit*) a small tabor. [O.Fr. *tabour*; an Oriental word.]

Taborite *tä'bər-īt*, *n.* a Hussite of Žižka's party, opposed to the Calixtines or Utraquists. — Also *adj.* [*Tabor* in Bohemia, founded by them as headquarters.]

tabour, tabret. See **tabor.**

tabu. See **taboo.**

tabula *tab'ū-lə*, L. *tab'ōō-la*, *n.* a writing-tablet: an altar frontal: a flattened structure: a horizontal partition in corals: — *pl.* **tab'ulae** (*-lē*; L. *-lī*). — *adj.* **tab'ular** of, in the form of, like, according to, a table: laminated: platy: horizontally flattened. — *n.* **tabularīsā'tion, -z-.** — *v.t.* **tab'ularise, -ize** to tabulate. — *adv.* **tab'ularly.** — *v.t.* **tab'ulate** to reduce to the form of a table or synopsis. — *adj.* tabular: having tabulae. — *ns.* **tabulā'tion; tab'ulātor** a person who, or a machine which, tabulates data: a device in a typewriter which sets and then finds automatically the margins needed in tabular work: a machine which prints very rapidly data from punched cards, etc., on to continuous paper (*comput.*). — *adj.* **tab'ulatory** (*-lə-tə-ri*). — **tabula rasa** (*tab'ū-lə rä'zə, tab'ōō-la rä'sa*) a smoothed or blank tablet: a mind not yet influenced by outside impressions and experience; **tabular spar** another name for **wollastonite.** [L. *tabula*, table.]

tabun *tä-bōōn'*, *n.* an organic phosphorus compound, $C_5H_{11}N_2O_2P$, which can be used as a nerve gas. [Ger.]

tacahout *tak'ə-howt*, *n.* a gall on the tamarisk, a source of gallic acid. [From Berber.]

tacamahac *tak'ə-mə-hak*, *n.* a gum-resin yielded by several tropical trees: the balsam poplar, or its resin. [From Nahuatl.]

Tacan *tak'an*, *n.* an electronic system of air navigation which gives an aircraft a direct reading of distance and bearing from a ground-based transmitter. [*tactical air navigation*.]

tac-au-tac *tak'-ō-tak'*, *n.* in fencing, the parry combined with the riposte: also a series of close attacks and parries between fencers of equal skill. [Fr.]

tace[1] *tā'sē, ta'kā, imper.* be silent. — **tacet** (*tā'set, ta'ket; mus.*) is silent. — **tace is Latin for a candle** a phrase understood as requesting or promising silence. [L. *tacē*, imper., *tacet*, 3rd pers. sing. pres. indic., of *tacēre*, to be silent.]

tace[2]. Same as **tasse.**

tach, tache *tach*, (*B.*) *n.* a fastening or clasp. [O.Fr. *tache*, cf. **tack**[1], **attach.**]

tach- *tak-*, **tache-, tachy-** *tak'i-*, in composition, speed, speedy. — *ns.* **tacheom'eter, tachymeter** (*-im'*) a surveying instrument for rapid measurement of distances. — *adjs.* **tacheomet'rical, tachymet'rical.** — *ns.* **tacheom'etry, tachym'etry; tachis'toscope** (Gr. *tachistos, superl.* of *tachys*) an instrument which flashes images, sentences, etc., on a screen for very brief, exactly timed, periods, now used esp. to increase reading speed. — *adj.* **tachistoscop'ic.** — *ns.* **tach'ogram** a record, made by a tachograph; **tach'ograph** a recording tachometer: a tachogram: an instrument fitted to commercial vehicles to record mileage, speed, number and location of stops, etc.; **tachom'eter** a device showing speed of rotation: an instrument for measuring the velocity of machines or currents. — *adj.* **tachomet'rical.** — *ns.* **tachom'etry; tachycar'dia** (Gr. *kardiā*, heart) abnormal rapidity of heart-beat; **tach'ygraph, tachyg'rapher, -phist.** — *adjs.* **tachygraph'ic, -ical.** — *ns.* **tachyg'raphy** shorthand, esp. ancient Greek and Roman; **tach'ylyte** (also **-lite;** Gr. *lytos*, melted, because easily fused before the blowpipe) a black opaque glass occurring as a thin selvage to intrusive basalt. — *adj.* **tachylytic** (*-lit'ik*). — *ns.* **tachymeter,** etc. see **tacheometer** above; **tachyon** (*tak'i-on*) a theoretical particle moving faster than light; **tachypnoea** (*tak-ip-nē'ə*; Gr. *pnoiā,* breathing) excessive frequency in breathing. [Gr. *tachys,* gen. *-eos,* swift, *tachos,* swiftness.]

tache[1] *tash,* (*coll.*) *n.* short for **moustache.**

tache[2]. Same as **tach.**

tachism(e) *tash'izm, n.* a mid-20th-century movement in abstract painting characterised by a clotted laying on of pigment. — *n.* and *adj.* **tach'ist(e).** [Fr. *tache,* blob (of paint).]

tachogram, etc., **tachymeter,** etc. See under **tach-.**

tacit *tas'it, adj.* unspoken: silent. — *adv.* **tac'itly.** — *n.* **tac'itness.** — *adj.* **tac'iturn** disinclined to speak. — *n.* **taciturn'ity.** — *adv.* **tac'iturnly.** [L. *tacitus, taciturnus.*]

tack[1] *tak, n.* a short, sharp nail with a broad head: a long temporary stitch: a fastening strip: a rope or other fastening for the lower windward corner of a sail: the corner itself: an act of tacking: an alternate course in zigzag: course of action: a change of policy, a strategical move: something tacked on: stickiness. — *v.t.* to attach or fasten, esp. in a slight manner, as by tacks or long stitches: to change the course of by a tack. — *v.i.* to change the course or tack of a ship by shifting the position of the sails: to zig-zag: to shift one's position, to veer. — *adj.* **tacked.** — *ns.* **tack'er; tack'et** (*Scot.*) a hobnail. — *adj.* **tack'ety.** — *ns.* **tack'iness; tack'ing** proceeding by tacks: fastening: fastening by tacks: introducing into a bill (esp. a money bill) provisions beyond its natural scope (*politics*). — *adj.* **tack'y** sticky. — *adj.* **tacked'-on'.** — **tack hammer** a light hammer for driving tacks. — **on the right (wrong) tack** following the right (wrong) course of action, train of thought, etc. [O.Fr. *taque,* doublet of *tache.*]

tack[2] *tak,* (*Scot.*) *n.* a tenure: a lease: a leased tenement: a spell: a take or catch. — **tacks'man** (*Scot.*) a lessee: in the Scottish Highlands, one who holds a lease and sublets. [See **tak, take.**]

tack[3] *tak,* (*dial.*) *n.* any distinctive flavour, smack.

tack[4] *tak, n.* food generally, fare, esp. of the bread kind, as *hard tack* (ship's biscuit), *soft tack* (loaves).

tack[5] *tak, n.* the sound of a sharp tap. [Imit.]

tack[6] *tak, n.* riding harness, saddles, bridles, etc. [**tackle.**]

tacker, tacket(y). See **tack**[1].

tackle *tak'l, n.* the ropes, rigging, etc., of a ship (*naut., tāk'l*): tools, gear, weapons, equipment (for sports, etc.): ropes, etc., for raising heavy weights: a pulley: the act of gripping: an act of tackling (*football*). — *v.t.* to harness: to seize or take hold of: to grapple with: to come to grips with: to begin to deal in earnest with: to confront, encounter, challenge. — *v.t.* and *v.i.* (*Rugby football*) to seize and stop or (*association football*) intercept (a player) in an effort to get the ball away from him. — *adj.* **tackled** (*tak'ld*) furnished with harness or tackle: made of ropes (*Shak.*). — *ns.* **tack'ler; tack'ling** furniture or apparatus belonging to the masts, yards, etc., of a ship: harness for drawing a carriage: tackle or instruments: grappling. [Cf. L.G. *takel.*]

tacky[1] *tak'i,* (*slang*) *n.* a poor ill-conditioned horse or person (*U.S.*). — *adj.* (orig. *U.S.*) shabby: sleazy: vulgar. — *n.* **tack'iness.**

tacky[2]. See **tack**[1].

taco *tä'kō, n.* in Mexican cooking, a very thin rolled pancake with a meat filling, usu. fried crisp: — *pl.* **ta'cos.** [Mex. Sp.]

taconite *tak'ə-nīt, n.* a sedimentary rock containing enough iron to make it a low-grade iron ore. [*Taconic* Mountains in N.E. United States.]

tact *takt, n.* adroitness in managing the feelings of persons dealt with: nice perception in seeing and doing exactly what is best in the circumstances: the stroke

in keeping time (*mus.*). — *adj.* **tact'ful.** — *adv.* **tact'fully.** — *adj.* **tact'ile** (*-īl*) perceptible by touch: pertaining to the sense of touch: concerned in perception by touch: suggestive of touch. — *ns.* **tact'ilist** (*-il-ist*) a painter who aims at tactile effects; **tactil'ity; tac'tion** (*rare*) contact. — *adj.* **tact'less.** — *adv.* **tact'lessly.** — *n.* **tact'lessness.** — *adj.* **tact'ual** relating to, or derived from, the sense of touch. — *n.* **tactual'ity** tactual quality. — *adv.* **tact'ually.** [L. *tactus, -ūs* — *tangĕre, tactum,* to touch.]

tactic, -al *tak'tik, -əl, adjs.* relating to taxis or tactism, or to tactics: (**tactical**) skilful, adroit, calculated. — *n.* **tac'tic** a system, or a piece, of tactics. — *adv.* **tac'tically.** — *ns.* **tactician** (*-tish'ən*) one skilled in tactics; **tactic'ity** the stereochemical arrangement of units in the main chain of a polymer (*chem.*). — *n.sing.* **tac'tics** the science or art of manoeuvring in presence of the enemy. — *n.pl.* purposeful procedure. — *n.* **tac'tism** (*biol.*) taxis. — **tactical voting** the practice of voting for a political party one does not support in order to prevent the election of a party one is even more opposed to. [Gr. *taktikos,* fit for arranging, *taktos,* ordered, verbal adj. of *tassein,* to arrange.]

tad *tad,* (*coll.,* esp. *U.S.*) *n.* a little lad: a small amount. [Short for **tadpole.**]

Tadjik. See **Tajik.**

tadpole *tad'pōl, n.* the larva of a toad or frog, rarely of an ascidian. — **Tadpole and Taper** political hacks, from characters in Disraeli's *Coningsby.* [O.E. *tāde,* toad, and **poll** (head).]

Tadzhik. See **Tajik.**

tae *tā,* a Scots form of **toe, to, too** (also); also in phrase *the tae* for *that ae,* the one (adjectivally). [See **tone**[2], **tother.**]

taedium. Now *obs.,* same as **tedium.** — **taedium vitae** (*tē'di-əm vī'tē, tī'di-ōōm vē'tī, wē'tī*; L.) weariness of life.

tae kwon do *tā' kwon' dō'* a Korean martial art, similar to karate. [Korean *tae,* kick, *kwon,* fist, *do,* method.]

tael *tāl, n.* Chinese *liang* or ounce, about 1⅓ oz. avoir. (38 g.): a money of account (not normally a coin) in China, orig. a tael weight of pure silver. — **tael bar** a gold bullion measure used in the Far East (1, 5 or 10 tael weight). [Port., — Malay *taïl,* weight.]

ta'en *tān,* a contraction of **taken.**

taenia *tē'ni-ə, n.* a ribbon or fillet: the fillet above the architrave of the Doric order: a ribbon-like structure: (with *cap.*) the tapeworm genus: a member of the genus: — *pl.* **tae'niae** (*-ni-ē*), **-s.** — *ns.* **taen'iacide** (*-sīd*) a substance that destroys tapeworms; **taen'iasis** infestation with tapeworm. — *adjs.* **tae'niate, tae'nioid** like a ribbon or a tapeworm. [L., — Gr. *tainiā,* a band.]

tafferel, taffrail *taf'ril, n.* the upper part of a ship's stern timbers. [Du. *tafereel,* a panel — *tafel,* a table — L. *tabula,* a table.]

taffeta *taf'i-tə,* also **taffety** *-ti,* **taffetas** *-tas, ns.* a thin glossy silk-stuff: loosely applied to various similar or mixed fabrics. — *adjs.* of taffeta: florid, over-dainty (*Shak.*). [Through Fr. or L.L. from Pers. *tāftah,* woven — *tāftan,* to twist.]

taffrail. See **tafferel.**

taffy *taf'i, n.* toffee (*q.v.*): flattery, blarney (*U.S.*).

Taffy *taf'i,* (*slang*) *n.* a Welshman. [From *Dafydd,* W. form of David.]

tafia *taf'i-ə, n.* a variety of rum. [Perh. a W. Indian name, but cf. Malay *tāfiā.*]

tag[1] *tag, n.* a flap of a slashed garment: a tab: a tie-on label: the point of a lace: any small thing tacked or attached to another: a loose or flapping end: a shred: a stray, matted, or dirty lock: (in *pl.*) a footman's shoulder-knot: the tip of a tail: a trite quotation (esp. Latin): a moral to a story: a refrain: the rabble: anything mean: in baseball, the act of putting out a runner by touching him with the ball or the hand holding the ball. — *v.t.* to put a tag or tags on: to attach as a tag: to tack, fasten, append: to remove tags from: to dog or follow closely: to put out (a runner) in baseball by a tag. — *v.i.* to make tags, to string words or ideas together: to go behind as a follower (with *on* or *along*): — *pr.p.* **tagg'ing**; *pa.t.* and *pa.p.* **tagged.** — *n.* **tagg'er.** — *n.pl.* **tagg'ers** thin sheet-iron. — **tag'-day** (*U.S.*) a flag-day; **tag'-end** the fag-end; **tagged atom** a radioactive isotopic atom of a tracer element; **tag line** (*U.S.*) a punch line: a watchword, slogan; **tag'rag** the rabble: a fluttering rag, a tatter. — Also *adj.* — **tag'-tail** a worm with a tail like a tag. — **tag along (with)** to follow; **tag, rag, and bobtail** rag-tag and bobtail. [Origin obscure.]

tag² *tag, n.* the game of tig. — *v.t.* to tig. [Ety. dub.]

Tagálog *tä-gä'log, n.* a people of the Philippine Islands: their Austronesian language. — Also *adj.*

Tagetes *tä-jē'tēz, n.* a Mexican and S. American genus of composites with yellow and orange flowers: (without *cap.*) a plant of this genus: — *pl.* **tagē'tes.** [L. *Tagēs*, an Etruscan god.]

taghairm *tə-gûrm', n.* in the Scottish Highlands, divination: esp. inspiration sought by lying in a bullock's hide behind a waterfall. [Gael.]

Tagliacotian. See **Taliacotian.**

tagliarini *täl-yə-rē'ni, n.* pasta cut into flat, very thin strips. [It.]

tagliatelle *tä-lya-tel'ā, tal-yə-tel'i, n.* pasta made in long ribbons. [It.]

taglioni *tal-yō'nē, n.* an early 19th-century overcoat. [Named after a family of dancers.]

tagmeme *tag'mēm, n.* any of the positions in the structure of a sentence into which a certain class of grammatical items can fit. — *adj.* **tagmē'mic.** — *n. sing.* **tagmē'mics** the analysis of the grammar of a language based on the arrangement or positions of the elements in utterances. [Gr. *tagma*, order.]

taguan *ta'gwan, tä'gwän, n.* a large East Indian flying squirrel. [Tagálog.]

taha *tä'hä, n.* a S. African weaver-bird. [Zulu *taka*.]

tahina *tə-hē'nə*, **tahini** *-nē, ns.* a paste made of crushed sesame seeds.

tahr, tehr *tär, n.* a beardless Himalayan wild goat (*Hemitragus jemlaicus*) that frequents forest precipices. [App. its name in the W. Himalaya, confused with Nepali *thār*; see **thar.**]

tahsil *tä(hh)-sēl', n.* in India, a division for revenue and certain other purposes. — *n.* **tahsildar'** an officer of a tahsil. [Hindi *taḥsīl* — Ar.]

tai *tī, n.* a Japanese sea-bream.

T'ai. Same as **Thai.**

t'ai chi (ch'uan) *tī'jē' (chwän'),* a Chinese system of exercise and self-defence in which good use of coordination and balance allows effort to be minimised. [Chin., great art of boxing.]

taiga *tī'gə, n.* marshy pine forest. [Russ. *taigá*.]

taigle *tä'gl, (Scot.) v.t.* to entangle, hinder. — *v.i.* to linger: to loiter: to trudge. [Cf. Sw. (Bornholm) *taggla*, to disorder.]

tail¹ *tāl, n.* the posterior extremity of an animal, usually a slender prolongation beyond the anus: a bird's train of feathers: a fish's caudal fin: anything of like appearance, position, etc.: the back, lower, hinder, latter, down-stream, or inferior part or prolongation of anything (often opp. to the *head*): the stem of a note in music: a downward extension of a letter: a retinue, suite: a queue: a train: anything long and trailing or hanging, as a catkin, train of a comet, long curl of hair: (usu. in *pl.*) the reverse of a coin: the end of a shoal sloping into deeper water: (often in *pl.*) the skirts of a garment: in Turkey, a horse-tail, formerly a mark of rank: (in *pl.*) a tail-coat: one who follows another and keeps constant watch on him (*coll.*): the buttocks (*coll.*): female genitalia (*slang*): sexual intercourse (*slang*): a woman (*slang*; also **piece, bit, of tail**). — *v.t.* to furnish with a tail: to be a tail to: to remove the tail or stalk from: to grip by the tail: to join end to end: to herd (*Austr.*): to dog, shadow (also **tail'-up**). — *v.i.* to straggle: to taper (often with *off* or *away*): to lessen or deteriorate slowly (with *off* or *away*): to show the

tail. — *adj.* **tailed.** — *n.* **tail'ing** inner covered end of a projecting brick or stone in a wall: a winter sport in which a tail-like string of luges is drawn along by a horse-sleigh: (in *pl.*) refuse, dregs. — *adj.* **tail'less** having no tail. — **tail'back** a line of traffic stretching back from anything obstructing or slowing down traffic flow; **tail'-board** a movable board at the hinder end of a cart, wagon or lorry; **tail'-boom** a longeron supporting the tail of an aeroplane; **tail'-coat** a man's formal coat, cutaway at the front and with narrow tails at the back; **tail'-end** the fag-end: (*pl.*) inferior corn sorted out from better: something that comes at the end; **tail'-end'er** (*coll.*) one coming at the end; **tail'-feath'er** one of the rectrices or rudder-feathers of a bird's tail: a feather of the back forming a train, as in the peacock; **tail'-fly** (*fishing*) the fly at the end of the leader; **tail'-gate** lower gate of a lock: a tail-board: a door at the back of a car that opens upwards on hinges at the top: a jazz style of playing esp. the trombone. — *v.t.* to drive dangerously close behind (another vehicle; *slang*). — Also *v.i.* — **tail'-gater** a person who tail-gates; **tail'-light** a light carried at the back of a train, a tram, or other vehicle; **tail'piece** a piece at the tail or end: an engraving, design, etc., occupying the bottom of a page, as at the end of a chapter: a strip of ebony, etc., to which the ends of the strings are attached in a fiddle; **tail'-pipe** the suction-pipe in a pump. — *v.t.* to tie a can or the like to the tail of (to annoy a dog — explanation unknown). — **tail'plane** a horizontal aerofoil on the tail of an aircraft; **tail'race** the channel in which water runs away below a mill-wheel; **tail'-rhyme, tailed rhyme** a verseform in which two or more rhymed lines are followed by a shorter line that does not rhyme with the others; **tail'-rope** a rope attached to the hinder part of anything; **tail'skid** a support under the tail of an aeroplane on the ground: in a motor vehicle, a skid starting with the rear wheels; **tail'-spin** a spiral dive of an aeroplane: a state of great agitation and uncertainty how to act (*fig.*); **tail'-stock** a slidable casting mounted on a lathe, aligned with the head-stock, used to support the free end of the workpiece; **tail wind** a wind blowing in the same direction as one is travelling. — **on someone's tail** following someone very closely; **tail-end Charlie** (*coll.*) a tail-ender; **tail off** to become gradually less or fewer; **tail of the eye** the outer corner of the eye: the margin of the field of vision; **the tail wagging the dog** (*coll.*) an instance where something or someone of less importance decisively influences something or someone of more importance; **turn tail** to turn (and run away); **twist the lion's tail** to irritate Britain; **with the tail between the legs** like a beaten cur. [O.E. *tægl*, *tægel*; Goth. *tagl*, hair.]

tail² *tāl, (law) n.* limitation of inheritance to certain heirs. — *adj.* limited. — **tail male** limitation to male heirs. [Fr. *taille*, cutting.]

tailard. See **tailor².**

tailleur *ta-yûr', n.* a woman's tailored suit. [Fr.]

taillie. See **tailzie.**

tailor¹ *tāl'ər, n.* one whose business is to cut out and make outer garments, esp. for men (*fem.* **tail'oress**). — *v.i.* to work as a tailor. — *v.t.* to make clothes for: to fit with clothes: to fashion by tailor's work: to make or adapt so as to fit a special need exactly (*fig.*). — *n.* **tail'oring.** — **tail'or-bird** an Asian warbler (*Orthotomus sutorius* or kindred) that sews leaves together to form a nest. — *adj.* **tail'or-made** made by a tailor, esp. of plain, close-fitting garments for women: exactly adapted (for a purpose). — *n.* a tailor-made garment: a factory-made cigarette, not one rolled by hand (*coll.*). [A.Fr. *taillour* (Fr. *tailleur*) — L.L. *tāliātor, -ōris* — *tāliāre*, to cut.]

tailor² *tā'lər, (Shak.) interj.* variously explained as referring to the backward fall (opp. to *header*), to the tailor-like squatting position that results, or as the obs. **tailard,** a person with a tail.

tailzie, tailye, taillie *tāl'(y)i,* (*law*) *n.* Scots forms of **tail²**: entail.

Taino *tī'nō, n.* a member of an extinct Indian tribe of the W. Indies (*pl.* **Tai'nos** or collectively **Tai'no**): its language. — Also *adj.*

taint *tānt, n.* attaint (*obs.*): a hit in tilting (*obs.*): tint, tinge (*obs.*): a tincture of some evil quality: a stain: a blemish: pollution: infection: a latent or incipient defect or corruption. — *v.t.* to attaint (*obs.*): to touch in tilting (*obs.*): to tint, tinge (*obs.*): to affect or imbue with anything objectionable: to contaminate: to infect: to impart a scent to. — *v.i.* to become infected or corrupted: to go bad: to weaken, wilt, wither. — *adjs.* **taint'ed; taint'less.** — *adv.* **taint'lessly.** — *n.* **taint'ure** defilement. — **taint'-worm** (*Milt.*) some worm supposedly injurious to flocks. [Partly aphetic for **attaint;** partly O.Fr. *taint* (Fr. *teint*) — L. *tinctus, -ūs — tingĕre, tinctum,* to wet, dye.]

'taint *tānt,* slang or illit. contraction of **it is not.**

taipan¹ *tī'pan, n.* a large venomous Australian snake, *Oxyuranus scutellatus.* [Aboriginal name.]

taipan² *tī'pan, n.* a foreigner living in China and controlling his company's business there. [Chin.]

T'ai-p'ing *tī-ping', n.* the dynasty that Hung Hsiu-ch'üan sought to found in China: a participator in his rebellion (1851–65). [Chin. *t'ai p'ing,* great peace.]

taira. See **tayra.**

taisch, taish *tīsh, n.* in the Scottish Highlands, an apparition or voice of one about to die: second-sight. [Gael. *taibhis, taibhse,* apparition.]

tait¹. Same as **tate.**

tait² *tāt, n.* the long-snouted phalanger (Tarsipes). [Native Australian name.]

taiver. See **taver¹,².**

taivert. See **taver².**

taj *täj, n.* a crown: a dervish's tall conical cap. — **Taj Mahal** (*mə-häl'*) the magnificent mausoleum at Agra erected by Shah Jehan for his wife Mumtāz-i-Mahal (d. 1629). [Ar. and Pers. *tāj,* crown.]

Tajik, Tadjik, Tadzhik *taj'ik, n.* a people of Iranian race living in Afghanistan and Turkestan: a member of this people: its dialect, resembling Farsi. — Also *adj.* [Pers., a Persian.]

tak *tak, täk,* a Scots form of **take.**

taka *tä'kə, n.* the standard unit of currency in Bangladesh. [Beng.]

takahe(a) *tä'kə-hē, n.* a notornis (q.v.). [Maori.]

takamaka *tak'ə-mak-ə.* Same as **tacamahac.**

take *tāk, v.t.* to lay hold of: to get into one's possession: to seize: to catch: to capture: to captivate: to receive or come to have willingly or by an act of one's own: to appropriate: to assume, adopt: to accept: to receive: to admit: to submerge (*Scot.*): to have normally assigned to one: to find out, come upon, surprise, detect: to swallow or inhale: to apply to oneself: to obtain: to engage, secure: to seek and receive: to have recourse to: to attend a course in: to visit: to call for, necessitate, use up: to remove: to cause to go: to subtract: to convey: to escort: to detract: to derive: to understand: to apprehend: (with *it*) to assume, suppose: to mistake: to conceive: to accept as true: to tolerate: to ascertain: to observe or measure: to ascertain something from: to execute, perform: to set down: to portray: to photograph: to charge oneself with: to asseverate: to strike: to come upon and affect: to bewitch: to blight: to deliver, give (*obs.*): to betake. — *v.i.* to have the intended effect: to be effective, to work: to please the public: to cast a spell (*Shak.*): to betake oneself, begin: to bite (as a fish): to make a capture or acquisition: to admit of being taken: to become, fall, e.g. ill (*coll.*): to freeze (*U.S., Canada*): — *pa.t.* **took;** *pa.p.* **tā'ken.** — *n.* an act of taking: a capture: quantity taken on one occasion: the amount of money taken, e.g. from a business enterprise, admission charges, etc.: the filming of one scene (*cinematography*): amount of copy set up by a printer at one time. — *adjs.* **take'able** (or **tā'kable**) **; tā'ken.** — *ns.* **tā'ker; tā'king** action of the

verb in any sense: (usu. in *pl.*) that which is taken, receipts: plight (*Spens.*): bewitchment, malignant influence (*Shak.*): agitation, perplexity (*coll.*). — *adj.* captivating: alluring: infectious, catching. — *adv.* **tā'kingly.** — *n.* **tā'kingness.** — *adj.* **tā'ky** attractive. — *adj.* **take'-away** (of cooked food) sold for consumption away from the place of sale: (of a restaurant) selling such food. — *n.* such a restaurant: a take-away meal. — **take'-down** a humiliation; **take'-in'** a deception, fraud, or disappointment of hopes; **take'-leave** leavetaking; **take'-off** a burlesque mimicking: a drawback: place, act, or mode of leaving the ground for a jump, dive, or flight (also *fig.*). — *adj.* **take'-out** take-away (*U.S.*). — *n.* (*bridge*) a conventional bid asking one's partner to bid a different suit. — **take'over** acquirement of control of a business by purchase of a majority of its shares. — Also *adj.* — **take'-up** the fact, or an instance, of taking up (i.e. using, accepting). — Also *adj.* — **tā'king-off'** removal, assassination. — **on the take** engaged in small-scale dishonest profitmaking; **take after** to follow in resemblance; **take against** to take a dislike to: to oppose; **take back** to retract; **take down** to reduce: to lower: to go above in class: to demolish, pull down: to take to pieces: to report or write down to dictation: to escort to the dining-room: (**a peg**) to humiliate in some degree; **take effect** to come off, succeed: to come into force; **take five** (or **ten**) to take a short break of five (or ten) minutes; **take for** to suppose to be, esp. wrongly; **take heed** to be careful; **take-home pay** pay after deduction of tax, etc.; **take in** to enclose: to comprise: to annex: to subdue: to receive: to conduct to the dining-room: to subscribe for: to tighten: to furl: to grasp, realise: to accept as true: to cheat; **take in hand** to undertake; **take into one's head** to be seized with a notion; **take in vain** to use with unbecoming levity; **take it** (*coll.*) to endure punishment or misfortune without giving way; **take it from there** to deal with a situation appropriately, at whatever point it falls to one to do so; **take it or leave it** to accept something with all its disadvantages, or else to do without it; **take it out of** to exact the utmost from: to exhaust the strength and energy of; **take it out on** to make (an innocent person or object) suffer for one's anger or frustration: to vent one's ill-temper, anger, etc., on; **take me with you** (*Shak.*) let me understand what you mean; **take notice** to observe: to show that observation is made; (with *of*) to remark upon; **take off** to remove: to swallow: to mimic: to leave the ground for a jump or flight: to begin a rapid improvement or expansion; **take on** to receive aboard: to undertake: to assume: to take into employment: to grieve (*coll.*): to accept a challenge from: (of ideas, etc.) to gain acceptance; **take someone up on** to accept someone's offer or challenge with respect to: to put a person's statement to the test; **take out** to remove from within: to extract: to go out with: to obtain on application: to receive an equivalent for: to copy (*Shak.*): to kill, destroy or defeat; **take over** to receive by transfer: to convey across: to assume control of; **takeover bid; takeover bidder; take to** to betake oneself: to adapt oneself to: to become fond of; **take to pieces** to separate into component parts; **take to task** to call to account, reprove; **take to wife** to marry; **take up** to lift, to raise: to pick up for use: to absorb: to accept: to interrupt sharply: to arrest: to adopt the practice, study, etc., of, begin to go in for: to begin to patronise, seek to advance: to resume: to settle, compound (a quarrel; *Shak.*): to reprove (*Shak.*): to cope with (*Shak.*): to buy up: to obtain on credit (*Shak.*): to take in hand: to engross, occupy or fill fully: (usu. in passive) to interest, please (with *about* or *with*; *dial.*): to borrow: to secure, fasten; **take upon oneself** to assume: to presume: to take responsibility for: to undertake: to feign, make believe (*Shak.*); **take up with** to begin to associate with, form a connection with. [Late O.E. *tacan* (pa.t. *tōc*) to touch, take — O.N. *taka* (pa.t. *tōk;* pa.p. *tekinn*).]

takin *tä'kin, tä-kēn', n.* a large ungulate (*Budorcas taxi-*

color) akin to the goats and antelopes.   [Tibetan.]

tala *tä'la, n.* a traditional rhythmic pattern in Indian music. [Sans., hand-clapping.]

talak. See **talaq**.

talapoin *tal'ə-poin, n.* a Buddhist monk, esp. of Pegu, in Burma: a small green W. African guenon monkey. [Port. *talapão* — Old Peguan *tala pôi*, my lord.]

talaq, talak *ta-läk', n.* under Islamic law, a form of divorce.   [Ar. *talāq*, divorce.]

talar, talaria. See under **talus**[1].

tala(u)nt. Spenserian forms of **talon**.

talayot *tä-lä'yot, n.* a prehistoric usually unchambered stone monument of the Balearic Islands.   [Balearic Sp. for Sp. *atalaya*, an outlook — Ar. *al talā'i*, the vanguard.]

talbot *täl'bət, n.* a broad-mouthed large-eared hound, usually white, now extinct.   [Poss. from the *Talbot* family.]

talbotype *täl'bə-tīp, n.* calotype, invented by William Henry Fox *Talbot* (1800–77).

talc *talk, n.* a very soft, pliable, greasy, silvery-white, foliated or compact mineral, acid magnesium silicate: commercially, often muscovite mica: talcum powder. — *adjs.* **talck'y, talc'ose, talc'ous.** — *n.* **talc'um** talc. — **talc'-schist'** a schistose rock composed essentially of talc, with accessory minerals; **talcum powder** purified powdered talc, usu. perfumed, applied to the skin to absorb moisture.   [Fr. *talc* or L.L. *talcum* — Ar. *talq* — Pers. *talk*.]

tale *tāl, n.* an act of telling: a narrative, story: a false story: a mere story: (in *pl.*) things told idly or to get others into trouble: number (*arch.*): reckoning (*arch.*). — *adj.* **tale'ful** abounding in stories. — **tale'bearer** one who maliciously tells tales or gives information; **tale'-bearing.** — Also *adj.* — **tale'-teller** a teller of stories, narrator: a talebearer. — **be in a** (or **one**) **tale** to be in full accord; **old wives' tale** a marvellous story for the credulous; **tell one's** (or **its**) **own tale** to speak for oneself or itself; **tell tales** to play the informer; **tell tales out of school** to reveal confidential matters.   [O.E. *talu*, story, number; Ger. *Zahl*, number.]

talegalla *tal-i-gal'ə, n.* the brush-turkey.   [Malagasy *talèva*, the purple coot, and L. *gallus*, a cock.]

talent[1] *tal'ənt, n.* an ancient unit of weight and of money — 60 minas or 6000 drachmas, or about 38 kilograms (Aeginetan talent), 25 (Euboic), 26 (Attic), of gold or silver: hence (from the parable, Matt. xxv. 14–30) faculty: any natural or special gift: special aptitude: eminent ability short of genius: persons of special ability: young girls or young men, esp. attractive, handsome, etc. (*coll.*): disposition: (*Shak.* **tallent**) perh. wealth, abundance, or perh. golden tresses. — *adjs.* **tal'ented** possessing talent or aptitude; **tal'entless.** — **talent scout, spotter** one whose business is to discover and recruit talented people, esp. on behalf of the entertainment industry.   [L. *talentum* — Gr. *talanton*, a balance, a talent.]

talent[2]. An old form (*Shak., Scott,* now *dial.*) of **talon**.

tales *tā'lēz,* (orig. *pl.*) *n.* the filling up, from those who are present, of a deficiency in the number of jurymen. — **talesman** (*tā'lēz-mən* or *tālz'*) a bystander so chosen. — **pray a tales** to plead that the number of jurymen be completed in this way.   [From the phrase '*tālēs* de circumstantibus', such of the bystanders: *tālēs,* pl. of L. *tālis,* such.]

tali. See **talus**[1].

Taliacotian, Tagliacotian *tal-yə-kō'shən, adj.* pertaining to the Italian surgeon Gasparo *Tagliacozzi* or *Taliacotius* (1546–99), or his rhinoplastic operation.

talion *tal'i-ən, n.* like for like: retaliation. — *adj.* **talion'ic.** [L. *tāliō, -ōnis,* like punishment — *tālis,* such.]

talipes *tal'i-pēz, n.* club-foot. — *adj.* **tal'iped** (*-ped*) having a club-foot. — Also *n.*   [L. *tālus,* ankle, *pēs,* foot.]

talipot, talipat *tal'i-pot, -pat, -put, ns.* an E. Asian fan-palm (*Corypha*).   [Sinh. *talapata* — Sans. *tālī,* palmyra palm, *pattra,* leaf.]

talisman *tal'is-mən,* or *-iz-, n.* an object supposed to be induced with magical powers: an amulet, charm: — *pl.* **tal'ismans.** — *adjs.* **talismanic** (*-man'ik*), **-al.**   [Ar. *tilsam* — Gr. *telesma,* payment, certificate, later completion, rite, consecrated object — *teleein,* to complete, fulfil, consecrate.]

talk *tök, v.i.* to speak, esp. informally or idly: to converse. — *v.t.* to utter: to speak about: to speak in: to bring or render by talking. — *n.* conversation: rumour: discussion: gossip: mention of possibility or proposal: a general theme: utterance: a short informal address. — *adj.* **talk'able** easy to converse with: to be talked about. — *n.* **talk'athon** (*coll.,* orig. *U.S.*) a long-drawn-out discussion, debate, talking session. etc. — *adj.* **talk'ative** given to much talking. — *adv.* **talk'atively.** — *ns.* **talk'ativeness; talk'er; talk'ie** (commonly in *pl.*) a talking film, cinematograph picture accompanied by sound. — *n.* and *adj.* **talk'ing.** — **talk'-back** a two-way radio system; **talk'ee-talk'ee, talk'y-talk'y** a corrupt dialect: chatter: a little harangue. — Also *adj.* — **talk'fest** (*coll.*) an informal meeting for discussion; **talk'-in** (a gathering for the purpose of) an informal yet intensive discussion; **talking book** a recording of a reading of a book, esp. for use by the blind; **talking head** a person talking on television, contrasted with programmes with more action; **talk'ing-machine'** a gramophone, phonograph, or the like; **talk'ing-point** a matter of or for talk; **talking shop** (*coll.*) a meeting or a place for discussion, as opposed to decision or action (also **talk shop**); **talk'ing-to** a reproof; **talk-show** see **chat-show** (under **chat**[2]); **talk'-you-down'** an apparatus by means of which instructions are given to the pilot of an aircraft to help him to land. — **look who's talking** (*iron.*) you're a fine one to be saying that; **now you're talking** (*coll.*) now you are saying something important or to the point; **talk against time** to keep on talking merely to fill up time, as often in parliament; **talk at** to address remarks to indirectly: to talk to incessantly, without waiting for a response; **talk back** to reply impudently; **talk big** to talk boastfully; **talk down** to argue down: to talk as to inferiors in intellect or education: to bring (an aircraft) to a landing by radioed instructions from the ground; **talk-down system; talking of** apropos of, now that mention has been made of; **talk into** to persuade; **talk out** to defeat (a parliamentary bill or motion) by going on speaking until it is too late to vote on it: to resolve (a difference of opinion) by thorough discussion; **talk over** to persuade, convince: to discuss, consider together; **talk round** to talk of all sorts of related matters without coming to the point: to bring to one's way of thinking by persuasive talk; **talk shop** see **shop**; **talk tall** to boast; **talk to** to address: to rebuke; **talk turkey** see **turkey**; **talk up** to speak boldly: to praise or boost: to make much of.   [M.E. *talken,* freq. of **tell**.]

tall *töl, adj.* doughty, stout (*obs.*): high in stature: long, esp. in a vertical direction: lofty: (usu. of a person) of a stated height, as *six feet tall*: great, remarkable: grandiloquent: hardly to be believed. — *n.* **tall'ness.** — **tall'boy** a long narrow top for a smoky chimney: a high chest of drawers, one portion superimposed on another or on a dressing-table: a glass with a long stem; **tall copy** a book with ample margins above and below; **tall hat** a top hat; **tall men** loaded dice; **tall order** see **order; tall ship** a square-rigged ship. — **a tall man of his hands** a deft worker: a sturdy fighter; **talk, walk, tall** see **talk, walk.**   [App. O.E. *getæl,* prompt.]

tallage *tal'ij, n.* a tax levied by the Norman and Angevin kings on their demesne lands and towns, or by a feudal lord on his tenants (*hist.*): an aid, toll, or rate. — *v.t.* to lay an impost upon. — *adj.* **tall'iable** subject to tallage. — *v.t.* **tall'iate** to lay a tallage upon.   [O.Fr. *taillage* — *tailler* to cut, to tax.]

tallat, tallet, tallot *tal'ət,* (W. of England) *n.* a loft.   [W. *taflod* — L.L. *tabulāta,* flooring.]

tallent. See **talent**[1].

tallet. See **tallat**.

talliable, talliate. See **tallage.**

tallier. See **tally.**

tallith *tal'ith, n.* the Jewish prayer shawl. [Heb. *tallūth.*]

tall-oil *tǎl'oil, n.* a by-product of chemical wood-pulp, used in manufacture of paints, linoleums, soaps, etc. [Sw. *tallolja* — *tall,* pine, and *olja,* oil.]

tallot. See **tallat.**

tallow *tal'ō, n.* fat, grease: rendered fat, esp. of ox and sheep: any coarse, hard fat. — *adj.* of, for, or like tallow. — *v.t.* to grease with tallow: to produce tallow. — *adjs.* **tall'owish; tall'owy.** — **tall'ow-can'dle** a candle made of tallow; **tall'ow-catch'** (*Shak.*) perh. a receptacle for tallow, or a lump (keech) of tallow; **tall'ow-chand'ler** a dealer in tallow candles, etc.; **tall'ow-dip'** a candle made by dipping a wick in tallow; **tall'ow-face** (*Shak.*) a person with a pasty yellow face. — *adj.* **tall'ow-faced.** — **tall'ow-tree** any of various trees (as Sapium, *Pentadesma,* Aleurites) yielding a thick oil or vegetable tallow, or a substance capable of making candles. [M.E. *talgh*; cf. Ger. *Talg.*]

tally *tal'i, n.* a stick notched to mark numbers or keep accounts: half of such a stick split across the notches, serving as receipt or record: anything that answers to a counterpart: a score or account, esp. one kept by notches or marks: credit, tick: a mark made in scoring an account: a distinguishing mark: a label: a plant-label: a tag: a number taken as a unit in computation: a full number: — *pl.* **tall'ies.** — *adv.* in concubinage. — *v.t.* to notch or mark as a tally: to count by tally: to reckon: to match, adapt. — *v.i.* to correspond, match, agree: to deal on credit: — *pr.p.* **tall'ying**; *pa.t.* and *pa.p.* **tall'ied.** — *n.* **tall'ier.** — **tally clerk** a checker of ship's cargoes against a list; **tall'yman** one who keeps a tallyshop: a salesman for a tallyshop: one who keeps a score or record: one who lives with a woman without marriage: — *fem.* **tall'ywo'man; tall'yshop** a shop where goods are sold to be paid for by instalments, the seller having one account-book which tallies with the buyer's; **tall'y-sys'tem, -trade** mode of dealing on credit for payment by instalments. — **live tally** to cohabit without marriage. [A.Fr. *tallie* — L. *tālea,* a stick.]

tally-ho *tal-i-hō', interj.* the huntsman's cry betokening that a fox has been sighted. — *n.* cry of tally-ho: a four-in-hand coach: — *pl.* **tally-hos'.** — *v.t.* to greet with tally-ho. — *v.i.* to call tally-ho. [Cf. Fr. *taïaut.*]

talma *tal'mə, n.* a loose cloak or cape. [From F. J. *Talma,* the actor (1763–1826).]

Talmud *tal'mŏŏd, -mud, n.* the fundamental code of Jewish civil and canon law, the *Mishnah* and the *Gemara.* — *adjs.* **Talmud'ic, -al.** — *n.* **Tal'mudist** one learned in the Talmud. — *adj.* **Talmudist'ic.** [Heb. *talmūd,* instruction — *lāmad,* to learn.]

talon *tal'ən, n.* a hooked claw or finger: an ogee moulding: the part of the bolt of a lock that the key presses on when it is turned: cards remaining after the deal, the stock. — *adj.* **tal'oned.** [Fr. *talon* — L.L. *tālō, -ōnis* — L. *tālus,* the heel.]

Talpa *tal'pə, n.* the mole genus of the family **Tal'pidae:** (without *cap.*) an encysted tumour on the head, a wen. [L., a mole.]

taluk *tä-lŏŏk', n.* a tract of proprietary land: a subdivision of a district, a collectorate. — *n.* **taluk'dar** holder of a taluk. [Hind. *ta'alluq,* estate.]

talus[1] *tā'ləs, n.* the ankle-bone or astragalus: — *pl.* **tā'lī.** — *n.* **tā'lar** a robe reaching the ankles. — *n.pl.* **talaria** (*tə-lā'ri-ə*) winged sandals, or wings on the ankles, as of Hermes. [L. *tālus,* ankle.]

talus[2] *tā'ləs, n.* a slope (*arch.*): the sloping part of a work (*fort.*): a scree (*geol.*). [Fr., — L.L. *talutium,* a slope.]

talweg. Same as **thalweg.**

tam. See **Tam o' Shanter.**

tamale *tä-mäl'i, n.* a highly seasoned Mexican dish of crushed maize, with meat. — Also (more correctly) **tamal'.** [Sp. *tamal* (pl. *tamales*), — Nahuatl *tamalli.*]

tamandua *tä-män'dū-ä, -dwä', n.* a S. American ant-eater smaller than the ant-bear. — *n.* **tamanoir** (*tä-mä-nwär';* Carib *tamanoa,* same root as *tamanduà*) the great ant-

bear. [Port. *tamanduá* — Sp. *tamándoa* — Tupí *tamanduà.*]

tamanu *täm'ä-nŏŏ, n.* a lofty gamboge tree of the East Indies and Pacific Islands, its trunk yielding tacamahac. [E. Ind.]

tamara *tam'ə-rə, n.* a mixture of cinnamon, cloves, coriander, etc.

tamarack *tam'ə-rak, n.* the American or black larch. [Amer. Ind.]

tamari *ta-mä'ri, n.* a concentrated sauce made of soya beans and salt. [Jap.]

tamarillo *tam-ə-ril'ō, n.* Same as **tree tomato.**

tamarin *tam'ə-rin, n.* a small S. American squirrel-monkey (Midas). [Fr., from Carib.]

tamarind *tam'ə-rind, n.* a large tropical caesalpiniaceous tree (*Tamarindus indica*): its pod, filled with a pleasant, acidulous, sweet, reddish-black pulp. [Ar. *tamr-Hindī,* date of India.]

tamarisk *tam'ər-isk, n.* a genus (**Tam'arix**) giving name to a family (**Tamaricā'ceae**) of xerophytic plants, one species a naturalised shrub of S. English seashores. [L. *tamariscus, tamarix.*]

tamasha *tə-mä'shä,* (*Ind.*) *n.* an entertainment, show: fuss. [Ar. and Pers. *tamāshā.*]

tamber *tam'bər, n.* Anglicised form of **timbre.**

tambour *tam'bŏŏr, n.* a drum: the bass drum: a frame for embroidery: a rich gold and silver embroidery: embroidery done on a tambour: a cylindrical stone: the drum of a recording instrument: a vestibule in a church porch, etc.: palisading to defend a gate, etc.: a flexible top (as of a desk) or front (as of a cabinet) made of narrow strips of wood fixed closely together on canvas, the whole sliding in grooves. — *v.t.* to embroider on a tambour. — *v.i.* to do tambour-work. — *ns.* **tambour'a** an Eastern instrument like a guitar (also **tambura**); **tambourin** (*tä-bŏŏ-rẽ*) a Provençal dance or dance-tune with drone bass; **tambourine** (*tam-bə-rēn'*) a shallow single-headed drum with jingles, played on with the hand — (*Spens.*) **tam'burin.** [Fr. *tambour,* drum; Pers. *tanbūr,* Ar. *tunbūr,* tamboura.]

tambura. See **tambour.**

tame *tām, adj.* having lost native wildness and shyness: cultivated: domesticated: gentle: spiritless: without vigour: dull, flat, uninspiring: wonted, accustomed (*Shak.*). — *v.t.* to reduce to a domestic state: to make gentle: to subdue: to reclaim. — *v.i.* to become tame. — *n.* **tamabil'ity, tameabil'ity.** — *adjs.* **tam'able, tame'able; tame'less.** — *n.* **tame'lessness.** — *adv.* **tame'ly.** — *ns.* **tame'ness; tam'er; tam'ing.** — **tame cat** (*U.S.*) a person who is happy to be completely dominated by another. [O.E. *tam*; Ger. *zahm*; Gr. *damaein,* L. *domāre,* to tame.]

Tamil *tam'il, n.* a Dravidian language of south-east India and north, east, and central Sri Lanka: one of the people speaking it. — *adjs.* **Tam'il, Tamil'ian, Tamil'ic, Tamūl'ic.**

tamin, tamine *tam'in, n.* a thin worsted stuff, highly glazed. [Fr. *étamine*; cf. **stammel.**]

tamis *tam'is, n.* cloth sieve. — *n.* **tamise** (*tä-mēz'*) name for various thin woollen fabrics. [Fr.]

Tammany *tam'ə-ni, n.* a society notorious for its corrupt influence in New York city politics in the 19th cent. — Also *adj.* — *n.* **Tamm'anyism. — Tammany Hall** its building, leased to the Democratic party of New York. [From an Indian chief, *Tammanend,* who is said to have signed the treaty with Penn.]

Tammie Norie *tam'i nō'ri,* (*Scot.*) *n.* the puffin.

Tammuz *tam'ŏŏz, -uz, n.* a Babylonian sun-god, answering to Adonis: the tenth month of the Jewish civil year, fourth of the ecclesiastical.

tammy[1] *tam'i, n.* a strainer: a glazed woollen or mixed stuff. [App. same as **tamis,** or perh. **tamin.**]

tammy[2] *tam'i, n.* a Tam o' Shanter.

Tam o' Shanter *tam-ō-shan'tər, n.* the hero of Burns's poem so entitled: a cap with broad circular flat top — *coll.* **tam, tamm'y.**

tamp *tamp, v.t.* to stop up (a shot hole) with earth, etc., after the explosive has been introduced: to ram down so as to consolidate (as ballast on a railway track): to pack round. — *ns.* **tamp'er** one who, or that which, tamps: an instrument for pressing down tobacco in a pipe: a casting round the core of a nuclear weapon to delay expansion and act as a neutron reflector; **tamp'-ing** the act of filling up a hole for blasting: the material used; **tamp'ion, tomp'ion** a plug: a protective plug placed in the muzzle of a gun when not in use; **tamp'on** a plug of cotton or other material inserted into a wound or orifice to control haemorrhage, etc.: an inking-pad: a two-headed drumstick. — *v.t.* to plug. — *ns.* **tamponade', tamp'onage** surgical use of a tampon. [Fr. *tampon*.]

tamper¹ *tam'pər, v.t.* (*obs.*) to temper (as clay). — *v.i.* (usu. with *with*) to work, machinate, practise: to have secret or corrupt dealings: to interfere unwarrantably or vitiatingly: to meddle. — *ns.* **tam'perer; tam'pering.** [A by-form of **temper**.]

tamper², tampon, etc. See **tamp**.

Tampico *tam-pē'kō, n.* a port in Mexico. — **Tampico fibre** ixtle.

tam-tam *tum'-tum, tam'-tam, n.* a gong, esp. one used in an orchestra: esp. formerly, a tom-tom. [**tom-tom**.]

Tamulic. See **Tamil.**

tan¹ *tan, n.* oak bark or other material used for tanning: spent bark: a tawny brown colour. — *adj.* tawny. — *v.t.* to convert into leather by steeping in vegetable solutions containing tannin, or mineral salts, or synthesised chemicals: to treat with tan or tannin: to make brown or tawny: to beat (*coll.*). — *v.i.* to become tanned: — *pr.p.* **tann'ing;** *pa.t.* and *pa.p.* **tanned.** — *n.* **tan'ling** (*Shak.*) one tanned by the sun. — *adj.* **tann'-able.** — *ns.* **tann'age** tanning: that which is tanned; **tann'ate** a salt of tannic acid. — *adj.* **tanned.** — *ns.* **tann'er; tann'ery** a place for tanning. — *adj.* **tann'ic** (**tannic acid** tannin). — *ns.* **tann'in** a colourless amorphous substance got from gall-nuts, sumach, and many barks, used in tanning and dyeing; **tann'ing** the art or act of tanning or converting skins and hides into leather. — Also *adj.* — **tan'-balls** tanner's spent bark pressed into lumps for fuel; **tan'-bark** any bark good for tanning; **tan'-bed** (*hort.*) a bark bed. — *adj.* **tan'-coloured.** — **tan'-liq'uor, -ooze, -pickle** an aqueous extract of tan-bark; **tan'-pit, -vat** a vat in which hides are steeped with tan; **tan'-ride** a riding track laid with tan; **tan'yard** a tannery, or a part of it. — **flowers of tan** see **flower.** [O.E. *tannian* (found in pa.p. *getanned*), *tannere*, tanner; also O.Fr. *tan* — Bret. *tann,* oak.]

tan² *tan,* (*trig.*) *n.* a conventional abbrev. of **tangent.**

tana¹, tanna(h), thana(h), thanna(h) *tä'nə, n. a military or police station in India.* — *n.* **t(h)a'nadar** its head. [Hind. *thānā, thāna.*]

tana² *tä'nə, n.* a Sumatran and Bornean species of tree-shrew. [Malay (*tūpai*) *tāna,* ground (squirrel).]

tanager *tan'ə-jər, n.* any bird of the S. American family Thraupidae, closely allied to the finches, the males having brightly-coloured plumage. — *n.* **Tan'agra** a genus of this family. — *adj.* **tan'agrine.** [Tupí *tangará.*]

Tanagra *tan'ə-grə, n.* a town of ancient Boeotia: (without *cap.*) a terracotta figurine made there.

tanaiste *tön'ish-tä, n.* the deputy prime minister of the Republic of Ireland. [Ir., second, next, deputy; cf. **tanist.**]

tandem *tan'dəm, adv.* in the position of horses harnessed singly one before the other. — *n.* a team (usu. two) so harnessed: a vehicle with such a team: a bicycle, tricycle, etc., for two, one before the other: generally, an arrangement of two things, one placed before the other. — Also *adj.* — *adv.* **tan'demwise.** — **in tandem** with one behind the other: together or in conjunction. [Punning application of L. *tandem,* at length.]

tandoori *tan-, tun-dōōr'i, n.* a type of Indian cooking in which meat and vegetables are baked in a clay oven. — Also *adj.* [Hind. *tandoor,* a clay oven.]

tane¹, ta'ne. Obs. spellings (*Spens., Shak.,* etc.) of **ta'en (taken).**

tane² *tän,* (*Scot.*) *pron.* one (**the tane** for *that ane,* the one). [See **tae, tone²,** **tother.**]

T'ang, Tang *tang, n.* a Chinese dynasty (A.D. 618–907). — *adj.* of this dynasty, its period, or its poetry and art. [Chin.]

tang¹ *tang, n.* coarse seaweed. [Cf. Norw. and Dan. *tang.*]

tang² *tang, n.* a ringing sound: a twang. — *v.t.* to cause to ring: to utter ringingly (*Shak.*). — *v.i.* to ring. [Imit.; influenced by next word.]

tang³ *tang, n.* a projecting piece or shank: a point, sting, spike: part of a tool that goes into the haft: a prong: a barb: a sea-surgeon: biting, characteristic, or extraneous flavour, after-taste, or smell: a smack, tinge: pungency. — *adjs.* **tanged** (*tangd*) with a tang: barbed; **tangy** (*tang'i*) having a fresh or sharp taste or smell (also *fig.*). [O.N. *tange,* point, tang.]

tanga *tang'gə, n.* a brief string-like bikini.

tangelo *tan'ji-lō, n.* a hybrid between *Tangerine* orange and *pomelo:* — *pl.* **tan'gelos.** [Portmanteau word.]

tangent *tan'jənt, adj.* touching without intersecting. — *n.* a line that touches a curve: the limiting case of a secant when the two points of intersection coincide: (as a function of an angle) the ratio of the side of a right-angled triangle opposite the given angle to the side opposite the other acute angle (*trig.*) (the tangent of an obtuse angle is equal numerically to that of its supplement, but has the negative sign.) — *abbrev.* **tan:** the striking-pin of a clavichord. — *n.* **tan'gency** (-*jən-si*) fact of being tangent: a contact or touching. — *adj.* **tangential** (-*jen'shəl*) of a tangent: in the direction of a tangent: peripheral, irrelevant (*fig.*). — *n.* **tangentiality** (*tan-jen-shi-al'i-ti*). — *adv.* **tangen'tially** in the direction of a tangent. — **at a tangent** in the direction of the tangent: in continuation in the momentary direction instead of following the general course. [L. *tangēns, -entis,* pr.p. of *tangěre,* to touch.]

Tangerine *tan'jə-rēn,* or *-rēn', adj.* of *Tangier* on the Morocco coast: (without *cap.*) tangerine-coloured. — *n.* a native of Tangier: (without *cap.*) a mandarin or *Tangerine* orange — a small, flattish, loose-skinned variety: (without *cap.*) the colour of this fruit, a reddish orange.

tanghin *tang'gin, n.* a Madagascan poison formerly used for the judicial ordeal: the apocynaceous tree yielding it. — *n.* **tangh'inin** its active principle. [Malagasy *tangèna.*]

tangible *tan'ji-bl, adj.* perceptible by the touch: capable of being possessed or realised: material, corporeal. — *n.* (usu. *pl.*) a tangible thing or asset, i.e. physical property as opposed to goodwill. — *ns.* **tangibil'ity; tan'gibleness.** — *adv.* **tan'gibly.** [L. *tangibilis* — *tangěre,* to touch.]

tangie *tang'i, n.* an Orcadian water-spirit, appearing as a seahorse, or man covered with seaweed. [From **tang¹.**]

tangle¹ *tang'gl, v.t.* to form into, involve in, or cover with, a confused interwoven mass: to entangle: to hamper or trap (*coll.*). — *v.i.* to become tangled: to become involved in conflict or argument (with) (*coll.*): (with *with*) to embrace (*coll.*). — *n.* a tangled mass or condition: a perplexity, complication: a naturalist's dredge consisting of bundles of frayed rope or the like: involved relations, conflict, argument. — *adj.* **tang'led.** — *ns.* **tang'lement; tang'ler.** — *adj.* **tang'lesome.** — *n.* and *adj.* **tang'ling.** — *adv.* **tang'lingly.** — *adj.* **tang'ly** tangled: inclined to tangle. — **tang'lefoot** (*U.S.*) whisky, intoxicating liquor. [App. from earlier *tagle;* see **taigle.**]

tangle² *tang'gl, n.* coarse seaweed, esp. the edible Laminaria. — *adj.* **tang'ly.** — **tang'le-picker** the turnstone (q.v. under **turn**). [App. conn. with O.N. *thöngull,* Laminaria stalk — *thang,* bladder-wrack.]

tangle³ *tang'gl,* (*Scot.*) *n.* any tall and limp person or thing: an icicle. — *adj.* long and limp. — *adj.* **tang'ly.** [Origin obscure.]

tango *tang'gō, n.* a ballroom dance or dance-tune in 4-4 time, of Argentinian origin, characterised by long steps and pauses: — *pl.* **tan'gos.** — *v.i.* to dance the tango: — *pa.t.* and *pa.p.* **tang'oed.** — *n.* **tang'oist.** [Sp., a S. American Negro festival or dance.]

tangram *tan'gram, n.* a Chinese toy, a square cut into seven pieces that will fit in various forms. [Origin obscure.]

tangun *tang'gun, n.* the Tibetan piebald pony. [Hindi *tāghan* — Tibetan *rtanān.*]

tangy. See **tang³.**

tanh *tansh, than,* a conventional abbreviation for *hyperbolic tangent.*

tanist *tan'ist, n.* a Celtic chief's heir elect. — *n.* **tan'istry** the system of succession by a previously elected member of the family. [Ir. *tánaiste,* Gael. *tànaiste,* heir, successor.]

tank *tangk, n.* a pool, pond, reservoir (*India*): a pond (*U.S.*): a large basin or cistern: a reservoir of water, oil, etc.: an armoured, enclosed, armed vehicle moving on caterpillar wheels: a receptacle for developing solutions (*phot.*): a prison or prison cell (*U.S. slang*). — *v.t.* to store in a tank: to plunge into a tank: to defeat (*slang*). — *v.i.* to drink heavily (with *up*): to refuel (often with *up*; *coll.*). — *n.* **tank'age** storing in tanks: charge for such storage: the capacity of a tank or tanks: residue from tanks: a fertiliser got from the dried residues of animal carcases. — *adj.* **tanked** (*slang*; often with *up*) drunk. — *ns.* **tank'er** a ship or heavy vehicle that carries liquids, esp. oil in bulk: an aircraft that refuels others; **tank'ful:** — *pl.* **tank'fuls; tank'ing** (*slang*) a defeat. — **tank'-car, -wag'on** a railway wagon for carrying oil or other liquid in a large tank; **tank'-engine** a locomotive that carries its water and coal in itself (without a tender); **tank farm** an area with tanks for storing oil; **tank'-far'mer; tank'-farming** hydroponics; **tank top** a sleeveless pullover, usu. with a low round neckline, worn over a shirt, etc.; **tank'-trap** an obstacle large enough to stop a military tank. [Port. *tanque* — L. *stagnum,* a pool.]

tanka¹ *tang'kə, täng'kä, n.* (also with *cap.*) the boat population of Canton, inhabiting **tank'a-boats.** — Also **tan'kia.** [Chin.]

tanka² *tang'kə, n.* a Japanese poem of five lines, the first and third lines having five syllables and the others seven. [Jap. *tan,* short, *ka,* verse.]

tankard *tangk'ərd, n.* a large mug-like vessel. — *cool-* **tankard** see **cool.** [Cf. M. Du. *tanckaert.*]

tankia. See **tanka².**

tanling. See under **tan¹.**

tanna. See **tana¹.**

tannable, tannage. See under **tan¹.**

tannah. See **tana¹.**

tannate, tanned. See under **tan¹.**

tanner¹ *tan'ər,* (*slang*) *n.* a sixpence.

tanner², tannic, tannin. See under **tan¹.**

Tannoy® *tan'oi, n.* a sound-reproducing and amplifying system.

tanrec. See **tenrec.**

tansy *tan'zi, n.* a bitter, aromatic roadside composite plant (*Tanacetum vulgare*) with small heads of tubular yellow flowers: extended to other plants, as ragwort, silver-weed, yarrow: a pudding or cake flavoured with tansy, eaten at Easter. — **like a tansy** exactly right. [O.Fr. *tanasie,* through L.L. from Gr. *athanasiā,* immortality.]

Tantalus *tan'tə-ləs, n.* a son of Zeus punished in Tartarus for revealing secrets of the gods by having to stand in water that ebbed when he would drink, overhung by grapes that drew back when he reached for them: the wood-ibis genus: (without *cap.*) a case in which decanters are visible but locked up. — *n.* **tan'talate** a salt of tantalic acid. — *adjs.* **Tantalean** (*-tā'*), **Tantā'lian, Tantalic** (*-tal'ik*) of Tantalus; **tantal'ic** of tantalum (**tantalic acid** HTaO₃). — *n.* **tantalīsā'tion, -z-.** — *v.t.*

tan'talise, -ize to torment by presenting something to excite desire but keeping it out of reach: to torture into unnatural form (*obs.*). — *n.* **tan'taliser, -z-.** — *n.* and *adj.* **tan'talising, -z-.** — *adv.* **tan'talisingly, -z-.** — *ns.* **tan'talism** the punishment of Tantalus: a tormenting; **tan'talite** (*min.*) a black mineral, iron tantalate; **tan'-talum** a metallic element (Ta; at. numb. 73) so named from its inability to absorb water. — **tan'talum-lamp** an electric lamp with tantalum filament; **Tan'talus-cup** a philosophical toy, with a siphon within the figure of a man whose chin is on a level with its bend.

tantamount *tan'tə-mownt, adj.* amounting to as much or to the same: equivalent: equal in value or meaning. [A.Fr. *tant amunter,* to amount to as much.]

tantara *tan-tä'rä, n.* a blast of trumpet or horn. — Also **tantara'ra.** [Imit.]

tanti *tan'tī, tan'tē,* (L.) *adj.* worth while.

tantivy *tan-tiv'i, adv.* at full gallop: headlong. — *n.* a hunting cry: a rapid rush: a Tory High Churchman (*hist.*). — *adj.* headlong: High Church Tory (*hist.*). — *interj.* expressive of galloping or (later) expressive of the sound of the hunting-horn. [Imit.]

tant mieux *tä myø,* (Fr.) so much the better.

tanto *tan'tō,* (L.) *adv.* so much.

tantony. See **Anthony.**

tanto uberior *tan'tō ū-bē'ri-ər, ōō-be'ri-or,* (L.) so much the richer.

tant pis *tä pē,* (Fr.) so much the worse.

Tantra, tantra *tan'-, tun'trə, n.* any of a number of Hindu and Buddhist writings giving religious teaching and ritual instructions (including the use of incantations, diagrams, etc.): the teaching of the Tantras. — *adj.* **Tan'tric, tan'tric.** — *ns.* **Tan'trism** the teaching of the Tantras; **Tan'trist.** [Sans. *tantra,* thread, fundamental doctrine.]

tantrum *tan'trəm, n.* a capricious fit of ill-temper without adequate cause. [Origin unknown.]

Tantum ergo *tan'təm ûr'gō,* L. *tan'tōōm er'gō,* the fifth stanza of the hymn 'Pange, lingua, gloriosi corporis mysterium', written for the office of the Festival of Corpus Christi, which St Thomas Aquinas drew up in 1263. [From its opening words.]

taoiseach *tē'shohh, n.* the prime minister of the Republic of Ireland. [Ir., chief, leader.]

Taoism *tä'ō-izm, tow', dow', n.* the philosophical system supposedly founded by the Chinese philosopher Lao-tzu (perh. b. 604 B.C.), set forth in the *Tao Te Ching* and other works: a religious system combining Taoist philosophy with magic and superstition and the worship of many gods. — *n.* and *adj.* **Ta'oist.** — *adj.* **Taoist'ic.** [Chin. *tao,* way, path.]

tap¹ *tap, n.* a gentle knock or its sound: a shoe sole (*dial.*): a protective piece on a shoe heel: a metal piece attached to the sole and heel of a shoe for tap-dancing: tap-dancing: (in *pl.*) a signal for putting lights out (orig. U.S. mil.). — *v.t.* and *v.i.* to knock gently. — *v.t.* to furnish or repair with a tap: — *pr.p.* **tapp'ing;** *pa.t.* and *pa.p.* **tapped.** — *n.* **tapp'er** one who taps: one who soles and heels: an instrument or part that taps: a decoherer. — *n.* and *adj.* **tapp'ing.** — **tap'-dance.** — Also *v.i.* — **tap'-danc'er; tap'-danc'ing** dancing characterised by rhythmical striking of dancer's tapped shoes on the floor; **tap'-shoe** a tapped shoe for tap-dancing. [O.Fr. *taper.*]

tap² *tap, n.* a peg or stopper: a hole or short pipe with a valve for running off a fluid: a taproom: any particular liquor drawn through a tap: a screw for cutting an internal thread: a taproot: a receiver secretly attached to a telephone wire: an instance of tapping a telephone wire: (often in *pl.*) tap stock. — *v.t.* to pierce, so as to let out fluid: to broach: to draw off: to draw upon, esp. for the first time (*fig.*): secretly to attach a receiver to a telephone wire in order to overhear a conversation: to get money from (*slang*): to furnish with a tap, or with a screw-thread. — *v.i.* to act as a tapster: — *pr.p.* **tapp'ing;** *pa.t.* and *pa.p.* **tapped.** — *ns.* **tapp'er** one who taps trees, etc.: a milking-machine; **tapp'ing** the act or art of drawing out or running off a fluid: an operation for removal of liquid from the body; **tap′ster** one who draws liquor, a barman. — **tap′-bolt** a screwed-in bolt; **tap′-cin′der** slag produced during puddling; **tap′-dress′-ing** well-dressing; **tap′-house** a tavern; **tap issue** tap stocks; **tap′lash** poor stale swipes; **tap′room** a room where beer is served from the tap or cask; **tap′root** a strong main root striking down vertically; **tap stock** government bonds, etc., to which the public can subscribe at any time; **tap′-wa′ter** water from a household tap. — **on tap** kept in cask — opp. to *bottled*: continuously and readily available (*fig.*). [O.E. *tæppa*, tap, *tæppestre*, (female) tapster; Du. *tap*, Ger. *Zapfen*, tap.]

tap³ *tap, n.* a Scots form of **top.** — *adj.* **tapp′it** crested. — **tapp′it-hen′** a crested hen: a liquor vessel of capacity variously stated at 1, 3, or 6 imperial quarts; **taps′man** a servant with principal charge: chief of a company of drovers. — **take one's tap in one's lap** (*Scot.*) to bundle up (one's tow for the distaff) and go home.

tap⁴ *tap, n.* an Indian malarial fever. [Pers.]

tapa¹, tappa *tä′pə, n.* paper-mulberry bark. [Polynesian generally.]

tapa *tä′pa,* (Sp.) *n.* a light snack or appetiser: — *pl.* **ta′pas.**

tapaculo *tä-pä-kōō′lō,* **tapacolo** *-kō′, ns.* a small S. American bird with tilted tail: — *pl.* **-os.** [Sp. *tapaculo* — *tapa,* cover (imper.), *culo,* posterior.]

tapadera *tä-pä-dā′rə,* **tapadero** *-rō* (*pl.* **tapade′ros**), *ns.* the guard in front of a Mexican stirrup. [Sp., lid, cover — *tapar,* to cover.]

tape *tāp, n.* material woven in narrow bands: a strip of such material, used for tying up, connecting, etc.: a ribbon of paper printed by a recording instrument, as in telegraphy: a flexible band that guides the sheets (*print.*): a tape-measure: magnetic tape: a tape-recording: liquor (*slang*). — *v.t.* to furnish, fasten, bind, measure with a tape: to get the range or measure of: to deal out, or use, sparingly (*Scot.*): to tape-record. — *adjs.* **tape′less; tä′pen** made of tape. — *ns.* **tä′per** one who works with tapes; **tä′pist** a red-tapist. — **tape deck** a machine for recording sound on tape and replaying it through a separate amplifier: a tape drive; **tape drive, deck, transport** (*comput.*) a mechanism which moves magnetic tape across the recording and playback heads; **tape′-grass** Vallisneria; **tape′line, -meas′ure** a flexible measuring strip of tape, steel, or other material; **tape′-machine** a telegraphic instrument by which messages received are automatically printed on a tape; **tape punch** (*comput.*) a device which encodes data by punching holes in paper tape; **tape reader** a device which senses data recorded on paper or magnetic tape and converts it into a form suitable for computer processing. — *v.t.* **tape′-record′** to record sound using a tape-recorder. — **tape′-recorder** an instrument for recording sound on magnetic tape and subsequently reproducing it; **tape′-recording** a magnetic tape on which sound has been recorded: the sound so recorded; **tape′script** a tape-recorded reading of a complete text. — *adj.* **tape′-tied** tied up with tape: bound with, or by, red tape (see **red¹**). — **tape transport** see **tape drive; tape′worm** a ribbon-shaped segmented parasitic worm, any cestode, but esp. of Taenia or kindred genus. — **breast the tape** in winning a foot-race, to touch or break with the breast the line stretched across the track at the winning-post; **have (something or someone) taped** to have a thorough understanding of; **magnetic tape** see **magnet; red tape** see **red¹.** [O.E. *tæppe,* tape, fillet.]

taper *tā′pər, n.* a wax-candle (*obs.*): a long, thin waxed wick or spill: a feeble light: lengthwise diminution in width: gradual leaving off. — *adj.* tapering. — *v.i.* to become gradually smaller towards one end: to diminish slowly in size, quantity or importance (with *off*). — *v.t.* to make to taper. — *adj.* **tä′pered** tapering: lighted by tapers. — *n.* **tä′perer** one who bears a taper. — *n.* and *adj.* **tä′pering.** — *adv.* **tä′peringly.** — *n.* **tä′perness.** — *adv.* **tä′perwise.** [O.E. *tapor.*]

tapestry *tap′is-tri, n.* an ornamental textile used for the covering of walls and furniture, and for curtains, made by passing coloured threads among fixed warp threads: a machine-made imitation of this. — *adj.* of tapestry (*Milt.* **tap′stry**). — *v.t.* to hang with tapestry: to work or represent in tapestry. — *adj.* **tap′estried.** [Fr. *tapisserie* — *tapis,* a carpet — L.L. *tapētium* — Gr. *tapētion,* dim. of *tapēs, -ētos,* prob. of Iranian origin.]

tapet *tap′it,* (*Spens.*) *n.* a piece of tapestry. [L. *tapēte,* perh. through O.E. *tæppet.*]

tapeti *tap′ə-ti, n.* the Brazilian rabbit. [Tupi.]

tapetum *tə-pē′təm, n.* a layer of cells surrounding spore mother-cells (*bot.*): the pigmentary layer of the retina (*zool.*): — *pl.* **tapē′ta.** — *adj.* **tapē′tal.** [L. *tapētum* — Gr. *tapēs, -ētos,* carpet.]

taphephobia, tapho- *taf-ə-fō′bi-ə, n.* morbid fear of being buried alive. [Gr. *taphē,* burial, *taphos,* grave, *phobos,* fear.]

tapioca *tap-i-ō′kə, n.* a farinaceous substance got by heating cassava: extended to a kind of sago and a preparation of potato starch: a pudding made from tapioca. — **pearl-tapioca** see **pearl¹.** [Tupi-Guaraní *tipyoca.*]

tapir *tā′pər, n.* a large odd-toed ungulate with short flexible proboscis, of which several species are found in S. America, Malaya, etc. — *adj.* **tä′piroid.** [Tupi *tapira.*]

tapis *tä′pē,* also *tap′is,* (*obs.*) *n.* a covering, hanging, etc., of tapestry or the like. — **on the tapis** on the table: under consideration. [Fr.]

tapist. See **tape.**

tapotement *tä-pot-mã, tə-pōt′mənt, n.* percussion in massage. [Fr.]

tappa. See **tapa.**

tappet *tap′it, n.* a projection that transmits motion from one part of a machine to another by tapping, esp. in an internal-combustion engine from the camshaft to the valves. — **tapp′et-loom, -mō′tion, -ring, -rod,** etc. [**tap¹.**]

tappice *tap′is, v.i.* to lie low. — *v.t.* to hide. [Fr. *tapir, tapiss-.*]

tappit, tappit-hen, tapsman. See **tap³.**

tapsalteerie *tap-sl-tē′ri,* **tapsieteerie** *tap-si-, adv., adj., n.,* Scots forms of **topsyturvy.**

tapstry *tap′stri* (*Milt.*). Same as **tapestry.**

tapu *ta′pōō.* Same as **taboo.** [Maori.]

tar¹ (*Shak.* **tarre**) *tär, v.t.* to set on, incite to fight. [Conn. with O.E. *tergan,* to worry.]

tar² *tär, n.* a dark, viscous mixture got by destructive distillation of wood, coal, peat, etc.: a natural bituminous substance of like appearance (*mineral tar*): a sailor (perh. for **tarpaulin**). — *v.t.* to smear, coat, treat, with tar: — *pr.p.* **tarr′ing;** *pa.t.* and *pa.p.* **tarred.** — *n.* **tarriness** (*tär′i-nis*). — *n.* and *adj.* **tarr′ing.** — *adj.* **tarr′y** (*tär′i*) of, like, covered or soiled with, tar. — **tar′-box** a shepherd's box for tar as salve for sheep: shepherd; **tar′-brush** a brush for applying tar; **tar′-heel** North Carolinian; **tarmacad′am** (also **tar′mac, Tarmac®** in *U.S.*) a road surfacing of broken stone covered or mixed with tar: (**tar′mac**) the runways of an aerodrome. — *v.t.* **tar′mac** to surface with tarmacadam: — *pr.p.* **tar′macking;** *pa.t.* and *pa.p.* **tar′macked.** — **tar′-pa′per** heavy paper treated with tar, used as a building material; **tarr′y-breeks** (*Scot.*) a sailor. — *adj.* **tarr′y-fingered** thievish. — **tar′-sand** a deposit of sand or sandstone saturated with bitumen, from which petroleum can be extracted; **tar′-seal′** (*N.Z.*) a tarmacadam surface on a road: a road so surfaced. — *v.t.* to seal the surface of (a road) by covering with tarmacadam. — **tar′-spot** a black spot of Rhytisma; **tar′-water** a cold infusion of tar in water, once reputed as a medicine; **tar′weed** a name for various heavy-scented American composites. — **tar and feather** to smear with tar and then cover with feathers; **tarred with the same brush** or **stick** with the same defects; **touch of the tar-brush** (*derog.*) a certain amount of e.g. Negro blood resulting in darkish skin. [O.E. *teru, teoro;* Ger. *Teer* (from L.G.), and Du. *teer*.]

tara *tä'rə n.* a variety of bracken with edible rhizome. — Also **ta'ra-fern.**

taradiddle. See **tarradiddle.**

tarakihi *ta-ra-kē-(h)ē*, **terakihi** *te-*, *n.* a morwong. [Maori.]

taramasalata *tar-ə-mə-sə-lä'tə,* (*cook.*) *n.* a Greek dish, a pink creamy paste made of grey mullet or smoked cod's roe with olive oil and garlic. [Mod. Gr., — *taramas*, preserved roe, *salata*, salad.]

tarand *tar'ənd,* (*obs.*) *n.* a northern beast fabled to change colour like the chameleon: a reindeer. [Gr. *tarand(r)os*, a reindeer, or (prob.) elk.]

tarantara. See **taratantara.**

tarantas(s) *tä-rän-täs',* *n.* a four-wheeled Russian vehicle mounted on poles. [Russ. *tarantas*.]

tarantella *tar'ən-tel'ə, n.* a lively Neapolitan dance — in triplets for one couple — thought a remedy for tarantism: a tune for it. — *ns.* **tar'antism** an epidemic dancing mania; **tarantula** (*-an'*) a large venomous South European wolf-spider (Lycosa), long supposed to cause tarantism in South Italy: in America applied to large venomous spiders of the bird-catching family (Aviculariidae): in Africa, a biting but not venomous solpugid: in Australia applied to several large harmless laterigrade spiders: (*cap.*) a genus of pedipalps. — **tarantula juice** (*U.S.*) bad whisky. [It. *tarantella, tarantola* — Gr. *Taras, -antos,* Tarentum, Taranto.]

tarantism, tarantula. See **tarantella.**

taratantara *tär-ä-tan'tä-rä,* or *-tan-tä'rä, n.* the sound of a trumpet. — Also *interj., adj., adv., v.t.,* and *v.i.* — Also **taran'tara.** [Imit.]

Taraxacum *tä-raks'ə-kəm, n.* the dandelion genus: (without *cap.*) its root and rootstock, a tonic laxative. [App. from Ar. *tarakhshaqōq* — Pers. *talkh chakōk,* assimilated to Gr. *taraxis,* disturbance.]

tarboggin. See **toboggan.**

tarboosh, tarboush, tarbush *tär-bōōsh', n.* a fez. [Ar. *tarbūsh.*]

tarcel. See **tercel.**

Tardenoisian *tär-di-noi'zi-ən,* (*archaeol.*) *adj.* belonging to a stage of culture represented by finds at *Tardenois,* Aisne, France, transitional between Palaeolithic and Neolithic.

tardigrade *tär'di-grād, adj.* slow-paced: of, or pertaining to, the Tardigrada. — *n.* a member of the Tardigrada. — *n.pl.* **Tardigrä'da** formerly the sloths: now, a class of arthropods, the bear-animalcules. [L. *tardus,* slow, *gradī,* to step.]

tardy *tär'di, adj.* slow: sluggish: behindhand: too long delayed: late: caught at fault (*obs.*). — *v.t.* (*Shak.*) to retard. — *adv.* **tar'dily.** — *n.* **tar'diness.** — *adj.* **tar'dive** (*-div*) late in development. — *adj.* **tar'dy-gaited** slow-paced. [Fr. *tardif* — *tard* — L. *tardus,* slow.]

tare[1] *tär, n.* a vetch of various kinds, esp. of the lentil-like group: a weed, prob. darnel (*B.*). [Origin obscure.]

tare[2] *tär, n.* the weight of a vessel, wrapping, or container, which subtracted from the gross weight gives the net weight: the weight of an empty vehicle, without cargo, passengers, etc. — *v.t.* to ascertain or allow for the tare of. [Fr., — Sp. *tara* — Ar. *tarhah,* thrown away.]

tare[3] *tär, arch. pa.t.* of **tear**[2].

targe[1] *tärj, n.* a shield, esp. a light shield. [O.Fr. *targe* — O.N. *targe,* shield.]

targe[2] *tärj,* (*Scot.*) *v.t.* to cross-examine: to supervise strictly: to reprimand: to thrash. [Origin unknown.]

target *tär'git, n.* a small buckler or round shield: a shield-like or other mark to shoot at for practice or competition: a surface on which electrons impinge: an object aimed at (also *fig.*): a butt: a result to be aimed at: a shooting score: a neck and breast of lamb: a sight on a levelling staff: an American railway signal. — *adj.* chosen as a target, aimed at. — *v.t.* to aim: to aim at. — *adjs.* **tar'getable** which can be aimed, or aimed at; **tar'geted** provided with a shield: selected as a target, aimed at. — *n.* **targeteer'** one armed with a shield, a peltast. — **target area** an area containing a target, or

which is a target, e.g. of missiles; **target language** the language into which a text is to be translated; **target man** in association football, a tall forward player to whom high passes can be made; **target practice** repeated shooting at a target to improve one's aim. — **on target** on the correct course for a target: on schedule. [O.Fr. *targuete*; cf. **targe**[1].]

Targum *tär-gōōm', tär'gəm, n.* any Aramaic version or paraphrase of the Old Testament: — *pl.* **Targums.** — *adj.* **Targumic** (*tär-gōōm'ik, -gūm', -gūm'*). — *n.* **Tar'gum'ist** a writer of a Targum: a student of the Targums. — *adj.* **Targumist'ic.** [Chaldean *targūm,* interpretation.]

tariff *tar'if, n.* a list or set of customs duties: a list of charges. — *v.t.* to set a tariff on. — **tariff-reform'er** one who favoured the early 20th-century movement for **Tariff Reform** or Protection opposed to Free Trade; **tariff wall** a barrier to the flow of imports made by high rates of customs duties. [It. *tariffa* — Ar. *ta'rif,* explanation — *'arafa,* to explain.]

tarlatan *tär'lə-tən, n.* an open, transparent muslin. [Fr. *tarlatane*; origin doubtful.]

tarmac(adam). See **tar**[2].

tarn *tärn, n.* a small mountain lake. [O.N. *tjörn.*]

tarnal *tär'nl,* **tarnation** *tär-nä'shən,* (*U.S. slang*) *adjs.* and *advs.* softened forms of **eternal** and **damnation,** app. influenced by each other.

tarnish *tär'nish, v.t.* to dull, discolour, render iridescent, diminish the lustre of, by exposure to the air, etc.: to sully. — *v.i.* to become dull: to lose lustre. — *n.* loss of lustre: a surface discoloration or iridescence on metal or mineral: a film of oxide, sulphide, etc. — *adjs.* **tar'nishable; tar'nished.** — *n.* **tar'nisher.** [Fr. *ternir, terniss-* — *terne,* dull, wan; poss. Gmc.]

taro *tä'rō, n.* a plant (Colocasia) of the arum family, widely cultivated for its edible rootstock in the islands of the Pacific: — *pl.* **ta'ros.** [Polynesian.]

tarot *tar'ō,* formerly also **taroc, tarok** *tar'ok, ns.* a card of Italian origin with picture, used in card games and also in fortune-telling: (usu. in *pl.*) a game played with tarots together with cards of the ordinary suits. [Fr. *tarot* — It. *tarocco.*]

tarp *tärp,* (*U.S.* and *Austr.*) short for **tarpaulin.**

tarpan *tär'pan, n.* a small extinct wild horse of the steppes of S. European Russia, not identical with Przewalski's horse. [Tatar.]

tarpaulin *tär-pö'lin, n.* strong linen or hempen cloth waterproofed with tar or otherwise: a sheet of it: a sailor's waterproof hat: a sailor (*coll.*): a sea-bred officer (*obs.*). — Also **tarpaul'ing.** — Also *adj.* [App. **tar**[2] and **palling** — **pall**[1].]

Tarpeian *tär-pē'ən, adj.* of *Tarpeia,* according to legend a Roman officer's daughter who betrayed the Capitol at Rome to the Sabines and was buried beneath the **Tarpeian Rock** on the Capitoline Hill, from which criminals were thrown.

tarpon *tär'pən, n.* a gigantic fish (*Tarpon* or *Megalops*) akin to the herring, angled for on the Florida and Gulf coasts. [Origin unknown.]

tar(r)adiddle *tar-ə-did'l, n.* a fib, a lie: nonsense. [App. founded on **diddle**.]

tarragon *tar'ə-gən, n.* an aromatic Artemisia used for flavouring vinegar, sauces, etc. [Ar. *tarkhūn,* perh. — Gr. *drakōn,* a dragon.]

Tarragona *tar-ə-gōn'ə, n.* a port-like Spanish wine. [Province in Catalonia.]

tarras *tar'əs, n.* Spens. for **terrace.** See also **trass.**

tarre. See **tar**[1]. — Also (*Spens.*) for **tar**[2].

tarriance, tarrier, tarrow. See **tarry**[2].

tarrock *tar'ək,* (*local*) *n.* a sea-bird of various kinds. [Origin obscure.]

tarry[1] *tär'i.* See **tar**[2].

tarry[2] *tar'i, v.i.* to linger: to loiter: to delay: to stay behind: to sojourn: to wait. — *v.t.* (*arch.*) to await: — *pr.p.* **tarr'ying;** *pa.t.* and *pa.p.* **tarr'ied.** — *n.* (*arch.*) delay: sojourn, stay. — *ns.* **tarr'iance** (*arch.*) tarrying: delay: waiting: a sojourn; **tarr'ier** one who tarries or delays.

— *v.i.* **tarr'ow** (*tär'ō*; *Scot.*) to hesitate: to reluct. [History obscure; the form agrees with O.E. *tergan*, to irritate, the meaning with O.Fr. *tarier*.]

tarsal¹, tarsel, tarcel *tär'sl*. See **tercel**.

tarsal², tarsalgia. See **tarsus**.

tarsia *tär'si-ə, tär-sē'ä, n.* intarsia (q.v.). — Also **tar'sia=work**. [It.]

tarsier. See under **tarsus**.

tarsus *tär'səs, n.* the part of the foot to which the leg is articulated: in birds, sometimes applied to the tarso-metatarsus: in insects, the five-jointed foot: a plate of connective tissue at the edge of the eyelid: — *pl.* **tar'sī**. — *adj.* **tar'sal** relating to the tarsus or ankle. — *n.* a bone of the tarsus. — *ns.* **tarsalgia** (-*sal'ji-ə*) pain in the instep; **tar'sier** (-*si-ər*) a spectral-looking lemuroid of the East Indies with long tarsal bones. — *adj.* **tar'sioid** like the tarsier: of the tarsier family. — *ns.* **Tar'sipēs** (L. *pēs*, foot) the long-snouted honey-mouse, an Australian honey-sucking phalanger with feet like the tarsier; **Tarsius** the tarsier genus. — *adj.* **tarsometatar'sal**. — *n.* **tarsometatar'sus** a bird's shank-bone, the combined metatarsals and distal tarsals. [Gr. *tarsos*, the flat of the foot.]

tart¹ *tärt, adj.* sharp: biting: acidulous. — *adj.* **tart'ish**. — *adv.* **tart'ly**. — *n.* **tart'ness**. [O.E. *teart*.]

tart² *tärt, n.* a dish of pastry distinguished from a pie either by being uncovered or by containing sweet, not savoury, materials: a girl (*slang*; often disrespectful): a prostitute (*slang*). — *ns.* **tartine** (-*ēn*; Fr.) a slice of bread with butter or jam; **tart'iness; tart'let** a small tart. — *adj.* **tart'y** (*slang*). — **tart up** (*coll.*) to make more showy or striking, esp. in an inartistic way: to smarten up (*adj.* **tart'ed-up'**). [O.Fr. *tarte*.]

Tartan® *tär'tən, n.* a material used to lay tracks for athletic events, usable in all weathers.

tartan¹ *tär'tən, n.* a woollen (or other) checked stuff: a distinctive checked pattern, as of a Highland clan. — *adj.* of tartan: checked in tartan: Scottish, esp. referring to self-consciously Scottish artefacts or attitudes (*derog.*). — *adj.* **tar'taned** clad in tartan. [Poss. from M.Fr. *tiretaine*, linsey-woolsey.]

tartan², tartane *tär'tən, tär-tän', n.* a Mediterranean vessel with lateen sail. [Fr. *tartane*, poss. — Ar. *tarīdah*, a small ship.]

tartana *tär-tä'nə, n.* a little covered wagon. [Sp.]

tartar *tär'tər, n.* recrystallised and partially purified argol, chiefly acid potassium tartrate (with calcium tartrate, etc.): a deposit of calcium phosphate and other matter on the teeth. — *adjs.* **tartareous** (-*tä'ri-əs*) of or like tartar: with rough crumbly surface (*bot.*); **tartaric** (*tär-tar'ik*) of or got from tartar (**tartaric acid**, $C_4H_6O_6$, prepared from argol). — *v.t.* **tar'tarise, -ize** to treat, mix, or combine with tartar. — *ns.* **tar'trate** a salt of tartaric acid; **tar'trazine** (-*zēn*) a yellow dye used in textiles, food and drugs. — **tartar emetic** a compound of potassium, antimony, carbon, hydrogen and oxygen, used in dyeing and in medicine. — **cream of tartar** purified argol. [L.L. *tartarum*, perh. from Ar.]

Tartar¹ *tär'tər, n.* a Tatar: (without *cap.*) a formidable, rough, unmanageable person: (without *cap.*) one who unexpectedly turns the tables on his assailant. — Also *adj.* — *n.* and *adj.* **Tartarian** (-*tä'ri-ən*) Tartar, Tatar. — *adjs.* **Tartaric** (-*tar'ik*) of the Tartars; **Tar'tarly** like a Tartar: (without *cap.*) ferocious. — **Tartarian lamb** barometz. [See **Tatar**.]

Tartar². See **Tartarus**.

tartareous. See **tartar**.

tartar(e) (sauce) *tär'tər, tär-tär' (sös), n.* a mayonnaise dressing with chopped pickles, olives, capers, etc., added, usu. served with fish. [Fr. *sauce tartare*.]

tartaric, tartarise. See **tartar**.

Tartarus *tär'tə-rəs, n.* in Homer, a deep and sunless abyss, as far below Hades as earth is below heaven: hell. — Also (*Spens., Shak.*) **Tar'tar**, (*Spens.*) **Tar'tare, Tar'-tarie, Tar'tary**. — *adj.* **Tartarean** (-*tä'ri-ən*). [L., — Gr. *Tartaros*.]

tartine. See **tart²**.

tartrate, tartrazine. See **tartar**.

Tartuf(f)e *tär-tüf', n.* a hypocritical pretender to religion. — *adjs.* **Tartuf(f)'ian, Tartuf(f)'ish**. — *n.* **Tartuf(f)'ism**. [From the character in Molière's *Tartuffe* (3-act version 1664, 5-act 1669).]

tarwhine *tär'(h)wīn, n.* an Australian sea-bream. [Aboriginal.]

Tarzan *tär'zan, n.* a man of great strength and agility. [From the hero of stories by Edgar Rice Burroughs (d. 1950) about a man brought up by apes.]

tasar *tus'ər.* Same as **tusser**.

taseometer *tas-i-om'i-tər, n.* an instrument for measuring strains in a structure. [Gr. *tasis, -eōs*, a stretching, *metron*, measure.]

tash¹ *täsh, (Scot.) v.t.* to soil: to blemish: to disfigure: to disarray. [Fr. *tacher*.]

tash² *tash, (coll.) n.* short for **moustache**.

tasimeter *ta-sim'i-tər, n.* an instrument for measuring changes in pressure, etc., by variations in electrical conductivity. [Gr. *tasis*, a stretch, *metron*, measure.]

task *täsk, task, n.* a piece or amount of (esp. burdensome, difficult or unpleasant) work set or undertaken. — *v.t.* to tax (*Shak.*): to impose a task on: to burden with severe work: to employ fully. — *ns.* **task'er** one who imposes or performs a task: one who does piece-work; **task'ing** task-work. — **task'-force, task'-group** a group formed by selection from different branches of the armed services to carry out a specific task: a similar group within the police force: a working party (q.v.) for a civilian purpose; **task'master** one who allots tasks esp. involving hard work: — *fem.* **task'mistress; task'=work** work done as a task, or by the job. — **take to task** to rebuke. [O.Fr. *tasque* (Fr. *tâche*) — L.L. *tasca, taxa* — L. *taxāre*, to rate.]

taslet. See **tasse**.

Tasmanian *tas-, taz-mā'ni-ən, adj.* of Tasmania, discovered in 1642 by Abel Janszoon *Tasman*. — *n.* a native or citizen of Tasmania. — **Tasmanian devil** a ferocious Tasmanian dasyure; **Tasmanian myrtle** a Tasmanian and Victorian evergreen beech; **Tasmanian wolf** (or **tiger**) the thylacine, a striped wolf-like dasyure of Tasmania, now virtually extinct.

tass¹ *täs, (dial.) n.* a mow, a heap. [O.Fr. *tas*, poss. from Du.]

tass² *tas, n.* a drinking-cup: a small drink. — *n.* **tass'ie** (*Scot.*) a small cup. [Fr. *tasse* — Ar. *tāss*, cup.]

tasse, tace *tas, n.* in plate armour, one of a series of overlapping pieces forming a kind of skirt. — *ns.* **tas'let, tass'et** a tasse. [O.Fr. *tasse, tasselet, tassete*.]

tassel¹ *tas'l, n.* a clasp or fastening (*Shak.*): an ornamental hanging tuft of threads: an inflorescence of like appearance, esp. of maize: a ribbon book-mark: a gold or silver plate on a vestment. — *v.t.* to furnish with tassels. — *v.i.* to form tassels, flower: — *pr.p.* **tass'-elling;** *pa.t.* and *pa.p.* **tass'elled**. — *adj.* **tass'elled**. — *n.* **tass'elling**. — *adj.* **tass'elly**. [O.Fr. *tassel*; origin doubtful.]

tassel². See **torsel**.

tassel(l), tassell(-gent), tassel-gentle. See **tercel**.

tasset. See **tasse**.

tassie. See **tass²**.

taste *tāst, v.t.* to try, or to perceive, by the sense seated in the tongue and palate: to try by eating a little: to eat a little of: to partake of: to try, test (*obs.*): to relish, enjoy (*arch.*): to experience, perceive: to enjoy carnally (*Shak.*): to give a flavour to (*rare*). — *v.i.* to try or perceive by the mouth: to have a flavour (of): to act as taster: to have experience. — *n.* the act of tasting: the particular sensation caused by a substance on the tongue: the sense by which we perceive the flavour of a thing: the quality or flavour of anything: a small portion: an experience: discernment of, accordance with, what is socially right: the faculty by which the mind perceives the beautiful: nice perception: choice, predilection, liking. — *adjs.* **tāst'able; tāst'ed** having a taste; **taste'ful** full of taste: having a pleasant or a high relish: showing good taste. — *adv.* **taste'fully.** — *n.* **taste'fulness.** — *adj.* **taste'less** without taste: without good taste: insipid. — *adv.* **taste'lessly.** — *ns.* **taste'-lessness;** **tāst'er** one skilful in distinguishing flavours by the taste: one employed to test the innocuousness of food by tasting it before serving it to his master: any implement or device used to obtain samples for tasting: a publisher's reader (*coll.*). — *adv.* **tāst'ily.** — *n.* **tāst'ing.** — *adj.* **tāst'y** savoury: tasteful (*coll.*). — **taste'-bud, -bulb** a group of cells on the tongue sensitive to taste. — **good taste** intuitive feeling for what is aesthetically or socially right; **to one's taste** to one's liking. [O.Fr. *taster* (Fr. *tâter*), as if from a L.L. freq. of L. *taxāre*, to touch, handle, estimate — *tangĕre*, to touch.]

tastevin *tāst', tast'vẽ, n.* a small shallow cup used for tasting wine. [Fr.]

tat¹, tatt *tat, v.t.* to make by tatting. — *v.i.* to make tatting. — *n.* **tatt'ing** knotted lace edging made by hand with a shuttle from sewing thread: the making of it.

tat² *tät, n.* East Indian hempen matting. [Hindi *ṭāṭ.*]

tat³ *tat, n.* See **tattoo³.**

tat⁴ *tat, n.* a tap. — *v.t.* to touch, tap: to flog. [Cf. **tap¹**, and see **tit²**.]

tat⁵. See **tatt¹.**

ta-ta *tä-tä', (childish* and *coll.) interj.* good-bye.

tatami *ta-tä'mi, n.* a type of mat, of a standard size, made from rice stalks, used as a floor-covering in Japanese houses. [Jap.]

Tatar *tä'tər, n.* orig. a member of any of certain Tungusic tribes in Chinese Tartary: extended to any of the Mongol, Turkish, and other warriors who swept over Asia and Europe: loosely, one of the mixed inhabitants of Tartary, Siberia, and the Russian steppes, including Kazan Tartars, Crim Tartars, Kipchaks, Kalmucks, etc.: a speaker of a Turkic language. — Also *adj.* — *adjs.* **Tatarian** (*tä-tä'ri-ən*), **Tataric** (*-tar'ik*) of the Tatars: of the Turkic group of languages. [Turk. and Pers. *Tatar*; association with Gr. *Tartaros*, hell, seems to have suggested the form **Tartar**.]

tate, tait *tāt, (Scot.) n.* a small portion, pinch, tuft.

tater *tä'tər, n.* a colloquial form of **potato.** — Also **tä'tie.**

tath *täth, (dial.) n.* cattle dung: coarse tufted grass that grows where it has fallen. — *v.t.* to manure. — *v.i.* to drop dung. [O.N. *tath.*]

tatler. See **tattle.**

tatou *ta'tōō,* or *-tōō', n.* an armadillo, esp. the giant armadillo. [Tupí *tatú.*]

tatpurusha *tat-pōō'rŏŏ-shə, n.* a class of compound words in which the first element modifies the second by standing to it in various types of relationship, including possession, as *goatskin,* as the object of an action, as *guitar player,* location, as *fieldmouse,* as agent, as *man-made:* a compound of this class. [Sans. *tatpuruṣa,* lit. his servant.]

tatt¹ *tat, n.* a rag, esp. an old one: (often **tat**) pretentious odds and ends of little real value, e.g. in an antique shop: (often **tat**) tawdry or shabby articles. — *v.t.* to touch up. — *adv.* **tatt'ily.** — *n.* **tatt'iness.** — *adj.* **tatt'y** (of clothes or ornament) fussy: precious, and often bogus: cheap, of poor quality: untidy: shabby. [**tatter**.]

tatt². See **tat¹.**

tatter *tat'ər, n.* a torn shred: a loose hanging rag. — *v.t.* to tear to tatters. — *v.i.* to fall into tatters. — *n.* **tatterdemā'lion** (or *-mal'yən*) a ragged fellow. — *adjs.* **tatt'ered; tatt'ery** ragged. — **in tatters** ragged: ruined. [Cf. Icel. *töturr.*]

Tattersall's *tat'ər-sölz, n.* a famous London horse-mart and haunt of racing-men — founded 1766 by Richard *Tattersall* (1724–95): a sweepstake or lottery agency with headquarters at Melbourne, Australia (*coll.* **Tatts**). — **Tattersall (check)** (a fabric with) a pattern of checks (like the horse-blankets orig. used at Tattersall's horse-mart).

tattie *ta'ti, n.* a Scots form of **potato.** — **tatt'ie-bo'gle** a scarecrow; **tatt'ie-claw** potato soup; **tatt'ie-lift'ing,**

-howk'ing potato harvest; **tatt'ie-shaw** the above-ground parts of a potato plant.

tatting. See **tat¹.**

tattle *tat'l, n.* trifling talk: chatter. — *v.i.* to talk idly or triflingly: to tell tales or secrets. — *v.t.* to tell or utter in tattle. — *n.* **tatt'ler** (formerly **tat'ler**) one given to tattling: any (esp. American) bird of the Totaninae, from their giving warning of gunners. — *n.* and *adj.* **tatt'ling** chattering: tale-telling. — *adv.* **tatt'lingly.** — **tatt'le-tale** (chiefly *U.S.*) a tell-tale. [Used by Caxton to translate M.Du. *tatelen;* imit.]

tattoo¹ *tə-tōō', n.* a beat of drum or other signal calling soldiers to quarters: a drumming: a military fête by night. — **the devil's tattoo** drumming with the fingers on a table, etc., in absence of mind or impatience. [Du. *taptoe* — *tap,* tap (of a barrel), *toe,* to, in the sense of shut.]

tattoo² *tə-tōō',* earlier **tatu** *tə-tōō',* **tattow** *-tow', ns.* a design marked on the skin by pricking in colouring matter. — *v.t.* to mark in this way: — *pa.t.* and *pa.p.* **tattooed'.** — *ns.* **tattoo'er, tattoo'ist.** [Tahitian *ta'tau,* Marquesan *ta'tu.*]

tattoo³ *tut'ŏŏ, n.* a native-bred Indian pony. — Abbreviated **tat** (*tat*). [Hind. *tattū.*]

tattow. See **tattoo².**

Tatts. See **Tattersall's.**

tatty¹. See **tatt¹, taut².**

tatty² *tat'i, n.* an Indian mat of bamboo, cuscus-grass roots, etc., esp. one kept wet in a doorway or window to cool the air. [Hind. *ṭaṭṭī.*]

tatu. See **tattoo².**

tau *tow, n.* the nineteenth letter (T, τ) of the Greek alphabet, answering to T: a tau-cross: as a numeral τ' = 300, ,τ = 300000: tau particle. — **tau'-cross** St Anthony's cross, in the form of a T; **tau particle** a lepton of mass 3600 times greater than that of an electron; **tau'-staff** a staff with a cross-piece at the top like a crutch. [Gr. *tau,* of Semitic origin.]

taube *tow'bə, n.* a German monoplane with recurved wings (1914–18 war). [Ger., dove.]

taught¹ *töt, pa.t.* and *pa.p.* of **teach.**

taught². See **taut¹.**

tauld *töld,* a Scots form of **told** (*pa.t.* and *pa.p.*).

taunt *tönt, v.t.* to reproach stingingly: to censure sarcastically. — *v.i.* to jibe. — *n.* a biting jibe: an object of taunts (*B.*). — *n.* **taunt'er.** — *n.* and *adj.* **taunt'ing.** — *adj.* **taunt'ingly.** [Poss. O.Fr *tanter* — L. *tentāre,* to tempt; or Fr. *tant pour tant,* tit for tat.]

taupe *tōp, n.* and *adj.* (of) a brownish-grey colour. [Fr., mole, — L. *talpa.*]

taupie. See **tawpie.**

Taurus *tö'rəs* (or L. *tow'rŏŏs*), *n.* the Bull, a sign of the zodiac and a constellation formerly coinciding with it: a person born under this sign. — *n.* **Tau'rean** (or *-rē'ən*) (a person) born under Taurus. — *adjs.* **tau'rean, tau'ric** of a bull; **tau'riform** having the form of a bull; **tau'rine** (or *-in*) of a bull: bull-like. — *ns.* **taurobō'lium** (Gr. *taurobólion* — *bŏlē,* a throw, stroke) the sacrifice of a bull, as, for example, in the cult of Cybele: an artistic representation thereof; **tauromachy** (*-om'ə-ki;* Gr. *tauromachiā* — *machē,* fight) bull-fighting: a bull-fight. — *adj.* **tauromor'phous** (Gr. *morphē,* form) bull-shaped. [L. *taurus* and Gr. *tauros.*]

taut¹ (*obs.* **taught**) *töt, adj.* tightly drawn: tense: in good condition. — *v.t.* and *v.i.* **taut'en** to tighten. — *adv.* **taut'ly.** — *n.* **taut'ness.** [Prob. conn. with **tow¹, tight¹.**]

taut², tawt *töt, (Scot.) v.t.* and *v.i.* to mat, tangle. — *adjs.* **taut'it; tawt'ie, tatt'y.** [Cf. O.E. *tætteca,* rag.]

taut- *töt,* **tauto-** *töt'ō-, töt'o-* in composition, the same. — *ns.* **taut'ochrone** (*-krōn;* Gr. *chronos,* time) a curve such that a particle travelling along it under gravity reaches a fixed point in the same time, no matter where it starts; **tautoch'ronism.** — *adjs.* **tautoch'ronous; tautologic** (*-loj'*), **-al.** — *adv.* **tautolog'ically.** — *v.i.* **tautol'ogise, -ize** to use tautology. — *ns.* **tautol'ogism; tautol'ogist.** — *adj.* **tautol'ogous** (*-ə-gəs*) tautological. — *ns.* **tautol'ogy** use of words that (esp. needlessly or pointlessly) say the same thing; **taut′omer** (Gr. *meros*, part) a readily interconvertible isomer. — *adj.* **tautomer′ic**. — *n.* **tautom′erism**. — *adjs.* **tautomet′ric, -al** exactly corresponding in arrangement of syllables. — *n.* **taut′onym** a binomial name in which the specific name repeats the generic. — *adjs.* **tauton′ymous; tautophon′- ical**. — *n.* **tautoph′ony** repetition of a sound. [Gr. *tauto*, for *to auto*, the same.]

tautog *tö-tog′, n.* a labroid fish of the North American Atlantic coast. [Narragansett *tautauog*.]

taver[1], **taiver** *tā′vər, (Scot.) n.* a shred. [Cf. Norw. and Dan. *tave*.]

taver[2], **taiver** *tā′vər, (Scot.) v.i.* to wander: to rave. — *adj.* **ta(i)′vert** muddled: fuddled: stupid. [Cf. Norw. *tava*, to toil, fumble.]

tavern *tav′ərn*, (usu. *arch.* or *literary*) *n.* a public-house. — *ns.* **taverna** (*-ûr′nə*) a type of guest-house with bar in Greece, popular as holiday accommodation; **tav′- erner** a publican. [O.Fr. (Fr.) *taverne* — L. *taberna*, shed, stall, tavern, from root of *tabula*, a board.]

taw[1] *tö, n.* a large or choice marble: a game at marbles: the line shot from at marbles. [Origin unknown.]

taw[2] *tö, v.t.* to prepare and dress, esp. skins for white leather. — *n. (obs.)* tawed leather: a thong or whip. — *ns.* **taw′er** a maker of white leather; **taw′ery** a place where skins are dressed. — *adj.* **taw′ie** *(Scot.)* tractable. — *n.* **taw′ing**. [O.E. *tawian*, to prepare; Du. *touwen*, to curry; O.H.G. *zawjan*, to make, prepare.]

tawdry *tö′dri, adj.* showy without taste or worth: gaudily adorned. — *n.* trumpery: a tawdry-lace *(obs.)*. — *adv.* **taw′drily**. — *n.* **taw′driness**. — **taw′dry-lace′** *(obs.)* a woman's silk necktie (in *Spens.* a waist-belt) such as was sold at St Audrey's Fair at Ely (17 October): trumpery adornment. [From *St Audrey* (i.e. Æthel- thrȳth, daughter of Anna, King of East Anglia), who thought a tumour in her throat a punishment for having worn jewelled necklaces.]

tawer, tawery, tawie. See **taw**[2].

tawny, tawney *tö′ni, adj.* and *n.* yellowish brown. — *n.* **taw′niness**. — **tawny eagle** a tawny-coloured eagle of Africa and Asia, *Aquila rapax*; **tawny owl** a tawny- coloured European owl, *Strix aluco*. [Fr. *tanné*, pa.p. of *tanner*, to tan.]

tawpie, taupie *tö′pi, (Scot.) n.* a clumsy, heedless, or inefficient girl. [Cf. Norw. *taap*, a half-wit.]

taws, tawse *töz, (esp. Scot.) n.sing.* or *n.pl.* a leather strap, usu. cut into fingers at the end, for corporal punish- ment. [Poss. pl. of **taw**[2], n.]

tawt, tawtie. See **taut**[2].

tax *taks, v.t.* to lay a tax on: to register or enrol for fiscal purposes (Luke ii. 1–5): to burden: to accuse, censure (usu. with *with*): to assess: to examine (accounts) in order to allow or disallow items. — *n.* a contribution exacted by the state: anything imposed, exacted, or burdensome: a charge, accusation *(obs.)*. — *n.* **taxabil′- ity**. — *adj.* **tax′able**. — *adv.* **tax′ably**. — *n.* **taxā′tion**. — *adjs.* **tax′ative** taxing: of taxing; **taxed**. — *ns.* **tax′er** (also **tax′or**); **tax′ing** imposition of taxes: censure, satire (*obs.*). — *adj.* demanding: onerous. **tax allowance** a sum which is deducted from total income to arrive at taxable income; **tax avoidance** legal evasion of payment of tax; **tax(ed)′-cart** a light spring-cart (orig. paying a lower tax, later none); **tax′-collect′or**. — *adj.* **tax′-deduct′ible** of expenses, etc., able to be deducted from one's income before it is assessed for tax. — **tax disc** a paper disc displayed on a motor vehicle's windscreen to show that it has been duly taxed; **tax evasion** illegal evasion of payment of tax. — *adj.* **tax′-exempt′** not liable to taxation. — **tax exile** a person living abroad so as not to pay high taxes — *adj.* and *adv.* **tax′-free′** without payment of tax. — **tax′-gath′erer; tax haven** a country or state where taxes are low; **tax′ing-mas′ter** an officer of a court of law who examines bills of costs; **tax′man** (*coll.*) a tax- collector: tax-collectors collectively; **tax′-payer** one who pays tax or taxes: one who is liable to taxation: a building put up for the express purpose of earning

money to pay tax on the land (*U.S.*). — *adj.* **tax′- paying**. — **tax point** the date on which value-added tax becomes payable; **tax return** a yearly statement of one's income, from which the amount due in tax is calcu- lated; **tax shelter** a financial arrangement made in order to pay the minimum taxation. — *adj.* **tax′- shel′tered** of or produced by a tax shelter: of or involving investments legally exempt from tax. — **tax threshold** the level of income at which tax starts to be payable. — **tax reserve certificate** a government receipt for money deposited that may later be used, with certain advantages, for payment of tax. [Fr. *taxe*, a tax — L. *taxāre*, to handle, value, charge.]

taxa. See **taxis**.

Taxaceae. See **Taxus**.

taxameter. See **taximeter**.

taxi *tak′si, n.* a taxicab: loosely, any motor-car on hire: — *pl.* **tax′is, tax′ies**. — *v.i.* to travel by taxi: of an aeroplane, to run along the ground, or (seaplane) on the surface of water, at low speed under its own power: — *pr.p.* **tax′ying, tax′iing**; *pa.t.* and *pa.p.* **tax′ied**; *3rd pers. sing. pres. indic.* **tax′ies**. — **tax′icab** a cab (now usu. a motor-cab) furnished with a taximeter; **tax′i- dancer** person, usu. a girl, hirable as a partner, dance by dance, in a dance- hall; **tax′i-driver; tax′iman** a taxi-driver; **tax′i-rank** a cab-rank; **tax′iway** an air- port, a marked track for aircraft from runways to terminals, etc. [Abbrev. of **taximeter**.]

taxiarch. See under **taxis**.

taxidermy *taks′i-dûr-mi, n.* the art of preparing, stuffing, and mounting skins. — *adjs.* **taxider′mal, taxider′mic**. — *v.t.* **tax′idermise, -ize**. — *n.* **tax′idermist**. [Gr. *taxis*, arrangement, *derma*, a skin.]

taximeter *tak′si-mē-tər, tak-sim′i-tər (obs.* **taxameter**), *n.* an instrument attached to a cab for indicating (dis- tance travelled and) fare due. [Fr. *taxe*, price, Gr. *metron*, measure.]

taxis *tak′sis, n.* arrangement: a division of an ancient Greek army (in Athens the contingent from a phyle): return to position of displaced parts by means of manipulation only (*surg.*): movement of a whole or- ganism in response to stimulus (*biol.*): — *pl.* **tax′ēs**. — *ns.* **tax′iarch** (*-i-ärk*) commander of a taxis; **tax′on** a biological category (e.g. *species*) or its name: — *pl.* **tax′a**. — *n.* **taxon′omer** a taxonomist. — *adjs.* **taxo- nom′ic, -al**. — *adv.* **taxonom′ically**. — *ns.* **taxon′omist; taxon′omy** classification or its principles: classification of plants or animals (now including study of means by which formation of species, etc., takes place). [Gr., — *tassein*, to arrange.]

taxor. See **tax**.

Taxus *tak′səs, n.* the yew genus of conifers, giving name to the family **Taxā′ceae** (*-si-ē*). — *n.* **Taxō′dium** (Gr. *eidos*, form) the swamp cypress genus. [L. *taxus*, yew.]

tayberry *tā′bə-ri, n.* a hybrid plant, a blackberry crossed with a raspberry: the fruit of this plant. [*Tay*side in Scotland, where it was first produced.]

tayra, taira *tī′rə, n.* a large South American species of the weasel family. [Tupi *taira*.]

tazza *tat′sə, n.* a shallow cup mounted on a foot: a saucer-shaped bowl: — *pl.* **taz′ze** (*-sā*), **taz′zas**. [It., cup; cf. **tass**[2].]

tch-. For some words see **ch-**.

tchick *chik, ch′, n.* a sound made by pressing the tongue against the roof of the mouth and then drawing back one side, as in urging a horse on. — *v.i.* to make such a sound. [Imit.]

te. See **ti**[1].

tea *tē*, formerly *tā, n.* a tree, *Camellia sinensis*, fam. Theaceae, cultivated in China, Assam, etc.: its dried and prepared leaves, buds, and shoots: an infusion of the leaves in boiling water: extended to various sub- stitutes (see **Labrador, Paraguay**, etc.): any vegetable infusion as a beverage: rarely, a similar preparation of animal origin (as **beeftea**): a cup of tea: an afternoon meal or light refreshment at which tea is generally served: marijuana (*slang*). — *v.i.* (*coll.*) to take tea. — *v.t.* (*coll.*) to provide tea for. — **tea'-bag** a bag containing tea-leaves for infusion; **tea'berry** wintergreen: a wintergreen berry; **tea biscuit** any of various kinds of sweetish biscuits, often eaten with tea; **tea'-board** a tea-tray; **tea'-bread** light spongy bread or buns to be eaten with tea; **tea'-break** a break for tea during the working day; **tea'-caddy, tea'-can'ister** an air-tight box or jar for holding tea; **tea'-cake** a light cake to be eaten with tea; **tea ceremony** in Japan, the ceremonial making and serving of tea; **tea'-chest** a chest or case in which tea is packed; **tea'-clipper** a fast sailing-ship in the tea-trade; **tea'-cloth** a small table-cloth: a cloth used in washing up after tea; **tea'-cosy** a thick cover for a tea-pot to keep the tea hot; **tea'cup** a cup used in drinking tea; **tea'cupful:** — *pl.* **tea'cupfuls; tea dance** a thé dansant; **tea'-dealer** a buyer and seller of tea; **tea'-dish** an old name for a teacup; **tea'-drinker; tea'= eq'uipage** apparatus for making and serving tea with all that accompanies it; **tea'-fight** (*slang*) a tea-party; **tea'-gar'den** a plantation of tea: an open-air restaurant for tea and other refreshments; **ten'-gown** a loose gown for wearing at afternoon tea at home; **tea'-house** a house in China, Japan, or other eastern countries where tea, etc. is served; **tea'-kettle** a kettle for boiling water for tea; **tea'-lady** a woman who makes and serves tea in an office or factory; **tea'-lead** lead with a little tin for lining tea-chests; **tea'-leaf** a leaf of tea: (usu. in *pl.*) a small piece of such a leaf, esp. when it has been used in making tea: (*slang*) a thief; **tea'-meeting** a public social meeting at which tea is drunk; **tea'-party** a social gathering at which tea is served: the persons present; **tea'-plant; tea'-planta'tion; tea'-planter** a cultivator of the tea-plant; **tea'pot** a spouted vessel for pouring out tea; **tea'-room** a room or restaurant where tea and light refreshments are served; **tea'-rose** a rose supposed to smell of tea; **tea'-ser'vice, -set** a set of utensils for a tea-table; **tea'-shop** a shop where tea is sold: a restaurant in which teas are served; **tea'spoon** a small spoon used with the teacup; **tea'spoonful:** — *pl.* **tea'spoonfuls; tea'-strainer** a small strainer to catch tea-leaves when pouring tea; **tea'-table** a table at which tea is drunk: the company at tea; **tea'-taster** an expert who judges tea by tasting it; **tea'-tasting.** — *n.pl.* **tea'-things** the tea-pot, cups, etc. — **tea'(-)time** the hour of the meal called tea. — Also *adj.* — **tea'-towel** a cloth for drying crockery, etc.; **tea'-tray** a tray for carrying tea-things; **tea'-tree** the common tea plant or shrub: a name of Australian myrtaceous plants (*Melaleuca, Leptospermum*) (also called **manuka**) furnishing substitutes for tea: an African solanaceous shrub (*Lycium*) said to have been labelled by mistake; **tea'-trolley** a small tiered table on wheels used for serving afternoon tea, etc.; **tea'-urn** a large closed urn with a tap, often also a heating device, for making tea in quantity. — **another cup of tea** a very different thing; **black tea** that which has been fermented between rolling and firing (heating with charcoal in a sieve); (usu. **not**) **for all the tea in China** (not) for anything whatever; **green tea** that which is fired immediately after rolling; **high tea** an early evening meal with tea and meat, eggs, fish, or the like; **one's cup of tea** (*slang*) what is to one's taste or appeals to one; **Russian tea** tea with lemon and no milk usually served in a glass. [South Chinese *te*, the common form being *ch'a* or *ts'a*.]

teach *tēch, v.t.* to show: to direct: to impart knowledge or art to: to guide the studies of: to exhibit so as to impress upon the mind: to impart the knowledge or art of: to accustom: to counsel. — *v.i.* to practise giving instructions: — *pa.t.* and *pa.p.* **taught** (*töt*). — *n.* **teachabil'ity.** — *adj.* **teach'able** capable of being taught: apt or willing to learn. — *ns.* **teach'ableness; teach'er** one whose profession is, or whose talent is the ability to impart knowledge, practical skill, or understanding; **teach'ership; teach'ing** the act, practice, or profession of giving instruction: doctrine: instruction. — *adj.* occupied with giving instruction: instructive. — *adj.*

teach'less (*arch.*) incapable of being taught. — **teach'-in** a long public debate consisting of a succession of speeches by well-informed persons holding different views on a matter of general importance, usu. with discussion, etc.; **teaching aid** any object or device used by a teacher to help explain, illustrate, etc., a subject; **teaching hospital** a hospital in which medical students are trained; **teaching machine** any mechanical device capable of presenting an instructional programme. — **teach school** (*U.S.*) to be a teacher in a school; **that'll teach you, him,** etc. (*coll.*) that (unpleasant experience) will teach you, him, etc. to behave better, be more careful, etc. next time. [O.E. *tǣcan*, to show, teach; cf. Ger. *zeigen*, to show; Gr. *dieknynai*, to show.]

teachie. Obs. form of **tetchy.**

tead, teade *tēd,* (*Spens.*) *n.* a torch. [L. *taeda*.]

teagle *tē'gl,* (*dial.*) *n.* a hoist or lift: a baited line for catching birds. — *v.t.* to hoist or catch with a teagle. [Prob. a form of **tackle**.]

Teague *tēg, n.* an old nickname for an Irishman. [*Tadhg,* an Irish name, Thady.]

teak *tēk, n.* a verbenaceous tree (*Tectona grandis*) of India, Malaya, etc.: its hard and durable wood. — **African teak** an African euphorbiaceous tree, *Oldfieldia africana*; **bastard teak** dhak; **white teak** Flindersia. [Malayalam *tēkka*.]

teal *tēl, n.* any of several kinds of small freshwater duck, esp. of the genus *Anas*: a dark greenish-blue colour: — *pl.* **teals, teal.** [M.E. *tēle,* prob. from O.E.; cf. Du. *teling, taling*.]

team *tēm, n.* a brood, a litter (*obs.* or *dial.*): a chain, esp. for hauling a plough, etc. (*dial.*): a set of animals harnessed together: a string of flying ducks, geese, etc.: a set of persons working or playing in combination: a side: a stock of animals: a turn-out (*U.S.*). — *v.t.* to yoke: to join in order to make a team or co-operative effort: to match (clothes, etc.). — *v.i.* to drive a team. — *adj.* **teamed** (*Spens.* **tem'ed, teem'ed**) harnessed in a team. — *ns.* **team'er** a teamster; **team'ing** driving a team: work apportioned to a team: transport by team: removal of excavated material from cutting to bank; **team'ster** one who drives a team: a truck-driver (*U.S.*). — *adv.* **team'wise** harnessed together. — **team'-mate** a fellow member of a team; **team'-spirit** the spirit of self-suppression in co-operation; **teamwork** work done by organised division of labour: co-operation, pulling together, regard to success of the whole rather than personal exploits. — **team up with** to join forces with. [O.E. *tēam,* child-bearing, brood, team; in kindred languages a bridle, rope, draught of a net; cf. O.E. *tēon,* to draw.]

Tean. See **Teian.**

teapoy *tē'poi, n.* a small table or tripod: (by confusion with **tea**) a tea-caddy. [Hind. *tīn, tīr-,* three, Pers. *pāi,* foot.]

tear[1] *tēr, n.* a drop of liquid secreted by the lachrymal gland: an exuding drop: a blob, bead, pear-shaped drop: a small flaw or cavity as in glass. — *adj.* **tear'ful** lachrymose: brimming with, ready to shed, or shedding, tears. — *adv.* **tear'fully.** — *n.* **tear'fulness.** — *adjs.* **tear'less** without tears: sorrowless; **tear'y** tearful. — **tear'-bag** the lachrymal gland: the tear-pit; **tear'-bottle** (*archaeol.*) a small bottle once thought to contain mourners' tears; **tear'-drop** a tear; **tear'-duct** the lachrymal duct. — *adj.* **tear'-fall'ing** (*Shak.*) shedding tears. — **tear'-gas** a gas or volatile substance that blinds temporarily by provoking tears. — *v.t.* to use tear-gas on. — **tear'-gland** the lachrymal gland; **tear'-jer'ker** an extravagantly sentimental song, book, film, etc., inviting pity, grief, sorrow. — *adj.* **tear'-jerking.** — **tear'-pit** in deer, a gland below the eye secreting a waxy substance; **tear'-shell** a shell that disperses tear-gas; **tear smoke** a lachrymatory vapour that (as opp. to tear gas) is visible. — *adj.* **tear'-stained** stained with tears. — **in tears** weeping; **without tears** by an easy or painless method. [O.E. *tēar;* Goth. *tagr;* Gr. *dakry*.]

tear[2] *tār, v.t.* to draw asunder or separate with violence:

to rend: to lacerate: to cause pain, bitterness, etc., to: to make or render by tearing. — *v.i.* to move or act with violence: to rush, move very quickly: to rage: to become torn: — *pa.t.* **tore** (*tör, tōr*), *arch.* **tare; pa.p. torn** (*törn, tōrn*). — *n.* tearing: a rent: a rush (*slang*): a spree. — *ns.* **tear′er** one who, or that which, tears: a boisterous person (*slang*). — *adj.* **tear′ing** great, terrible, rushing. — *adj.* **tear′away** impetuous, reckless: pertaining to a tearaway. — *n.* a reckless and (now also) violent young person. — **tear′-sheet** a page that can be torn out for reference; **tear′-strip** a narrow perforated strip on a paper or card wrapper which can be pulled away to facilitate opening; **tear webbing** webbing in which two adhering layers form a fold that will tear apart so as to lessen the violence of a sudden strain. — **tear a (the) cat** (*obs.*) to rant; **tear a strip off** (*slang*) to reprimand; **tear away** to remove by tearing: to remove (oneself) reluctantly; **tear down** to demolish violently; **tear into** to attack, either physically or with criticism, etc.; **tear off** to remove by tearing: to depart hurriedly: to compose hurriedly; **tear one's hair** to pull the hair in a frenzy of grief or rage (also *fig.*); **tear up** to remove from a fixed state by violence: to pull to pieces; **that's torn it** see **torn.** [O.E. *teran*; cf. Ger. *zehren*.]

tease *tēz, v.t.* to open out the fibres of: to comb or card, as wool: to scratch, as cloth: to raise a nap on: to backcomb (the hair): to vex with importunity, jests, etc.: to plague, irritate, esp. playfully or pleasantly: to tantalise: to banter. — *n.* one who teases: an act of teasing. — *n.* **teas′er.** — *n. and adj.* **teas′ing.** — *adv.* **teas′ingly.** [O.E. *tǣsan*, to card.]

teasel *tēz′l, n.* any species of Dipsacus, esp. *D. fullonum*: its head with hooked bracts used in raising a nap on cloth: an artificial substitute for its head. — *v.t.* to raise a nap on with the teasel: — *pr.p.* **teas′el(l)ing;** *pa.t.* and *pa.p.* **teas′el(l)ed.** — *ns.* **teas′el(l)er; teas′-el(l)ing.** — Also **teazel, teazle,** etc. [O.E. *tǣsel* — *tǣsan*; see **tease.**]

teat *tēt, n.* the small protuberance through which the mammalian young suck the milk: a similar protuberance through which milk is sucked from a baby's feeding-bottle: a nipple. — *adj.* **teat′ed** having a teat or teats. [O.E. *titt, tit*; influenced by O.Fr. *tete* (Fr. *tette*).]

teaze. An obs. spelling of **tease; teazel, teazle** see **teasel.**

tebbad *teb′ad, n.* a sandstorm. [Cf. Pers. *tab*, fever, *bād*, wind.]

Tebeth *teb′eth, n.* the tenth month of the Jewish ecclesiastical, and fourth of the secular, year, parts of December and January. [Heb. *Tēbēt.*]

Tebilise® *teb′il-īz, v.t.* of cotton and linen fabrics, to treat by a finishing process that prevents shrinking and creasing.

′tec *tek, n.* a slang abbrev. for **detective.**

tech *tek, n.* coll. contraction for **technical college.**

technetium *tek-nē′shi-əm, n.* the chemical element of atomic number 43 (Tc), the first element to be artificially made. [Gr. *technētos*, artificial — *technē*, art.]

technic *tek′nik, adj.* technical. — *n.* technology: (often in *pl.* form) technicality, technique. — *adj.* **tech′nical** pertaining to art, esp. a useful art or applied science: industrial: belonging to, or in the language of, a particular art, department of knowledge or skill, profession: so called in strict legal or technical language. — *n.* **technical′ity.** — *adv.* **tech′nically.** — *ns.* **tech′-nicalness; technician** (*-nish′ən*) one skilled in a practical art: a person who does the practical work in a laboratory, etc.. — *v.t.* **tech′nicise, -ize** to render technical or technological. — *ns.* **tech′nicism** (too great) emphasis on or concern with practical results or method; **tech′-nicist** a technician; **Tech′nicolor®** a process of colour photography in motion-pictures. — *adj.* **tech′nicolour** (modelled on above) in bright, artificial colours: cheaply romantic. — *n.sing.* **tech′nics** technology: the study of industry. — *n.* **technique** (*tek-nēk′*) method of performance, manipulation, esp. everything con-cerned with the mechanical part of an artistic performance. — **techno-** in composition, craft, art, e.g. *technography*: technical, technological, e.g. *technophobia, technomania.* — *ns.* **technoc′racy** government or management by technical experts: a state, etc., so governed: a body of technical experts in governing position; **tech′nocrat** (Gr. *kratos*, power) a member of a technocracy: a believer in technocracy. — *adj.* **technocrat′ic.** — *ns.* **tech′nofear** (*coll.*) technophobia; **technog′raphy** the description of the arts, crafts and sciences against their historical and geographical background. — *adj.* **technolog′ical.** — *adv.* **technolog′ically.** — *ns.* **technol′ogist; technol′ogy** the practice of any or all of the applied sciences that have practical value and/or industrial use: technical method(s) in a particular field of industry or art: technical nomenclature: technical means and skills characteristic of a particular civilisation, group, or period; **technomā′nia** a mania for technology; **technomā′niac; tech′nophile** one who likes and promotes technology; **tech′nophobe** one who fears and dislikes technology; **technophō′bia; technop′-olis** a society ruled by technology: a geographical area where projects in technological research and development are concentrated. — *n. and adj.* **technopol′itan.** — **tech′nostructure** the people in control of technology in a society. — **technical chemistry** industrial chemistry: a college of further education that specialises in technical subjects, as industrial skills, secretarial work, etc.; **technical foul** in sport, a foul that does not involve physical contact; **technical hitch** a mechanical fault that brings a broadcast, etc., to a temporary halt; **technical knockout** a boxer's defeat on the referee's decision that, though not actually knocked out, he is unable to continue the fight. [Gr. *technē*, art, adj. *technikos.*]

techy. See **tetchy.**

teckel *tek′l, n.* a dachshund. [Ger.]

tectibranch *tekt′i-brangk, n.* any member of the **Tecti-branchiā′ta,** opisthobranch molluscs with gill covered by the mantle. — *n. and adj.* **tectibranch′iate.** [L. *tegēre, tēctum*, to cover, *branchiae*, gills.]

tectiform *tekt′i-förm, adj.* roof-like: roofing. [L. *tēctum*, a roof, *förma*, shape.]

tectonic *tek-ton′ik, adj.* pertaining to building: structural. — *n.sing.* **tecton′ics** building as an art: structural geology: (*n.pl.*) the constructive arts: (*n.pl.*) structural features. — *adv.* **tecton′ically.** [Gr. *tektōn*, a builder.]

tectorial *tek-tō′ri-əl, -tö′ri-əl, adj.* covering. [L. *tēctōrius* — *tegēre, tēctum*, to cover.]

tectrix *tek′triks, n.* a feather covering the quill-bases of a bird's wings and tail (also called **covert**): — *pl.* **tectrices** (*-trī′sēz*). — *adj.* **tectricial** (*-trish′l*). [L. *tēctrīx, -īcis*, fem. of *tēctor, -ōris*, a coverer, plasterer — *tegēre*, to cover.]

ted *ted, v.t.* to spread as new-mown grass, for drying: — *pr.p.* **tedd′ing;** *pa.t.* and *pa.p.* **tedd′ed.** — *n.* **tedd′er** one who teds: an implement for tedding. [Prob. from a lost O.E. *teddan*; cf. Icel. *tethja*, to manure.]

Ted *ted, n.* a Teddy boy. — **Teddy boy** an unruly adolescent, orig. in the 1950s, affecting a dandyish garb reminiscent of Edward VII's time; **Teddy girl** the Teddy boy's female companion and counterpart in conduct; **Teddy suit.** [Edward.]

teddy *ted′i,* **teddy-bear** (*-bār′*) *ns.* a woolly toy bear. [From Theodore (*Teddy*) Roosevelt, a famous hunter and President of U.S.A. (1901–1909).]

tedesco *te-des′kō, adj.* German: — *pl.* **-deschi** (*-kē*); *fem.* **tedes′ca** (*-ka*): — *pl.* **-desche** (*-kā*). [It.]

Te Deum *tē dē′əm,* L. *tā de′ōom, n.* a famous Latin hymn of the Western Church: a musical setting of it. [From its first words, *Tē Deum laudāmus*, thee, God, we praise.]

tedium, (*obs.*) **taedium,** *tē′di-əm, n.* wearisomeness, esp. owing to length: irksomeness: boredom. — *n.* **tedios′-ity.** — *adj.* **te′dious.** — *adv.* **te′diously.** — *n.* **te′diousness.** — *adjs.* (*Scot.*) **te′disome, te′diousome** (*Scott*), **te′dy.** [L. *taedium* — *taedēre*, to weary.]

tee[1] *tē, n.* the twentieth letter of the alphabet (T, t): an object or mark of that shape. — **tee'-shirt** a slip-on shirt usu. with short sleeves, no collar and no buttons; **tee'-square** see **T.** — **to a tee** exactly, to a tittle.

tee[2] *tē, n.* the mark aimed at (*quoits, curling,* etc.): the sand-cone, peg, or other elevation from which the ball is first played at each hole (*golf*): the strip of ground (also **tee'ing-ground**) where this is done. — *v.t.* (often with *up*) and *v.i.* (with *up*) to place (the golf-ball) on the tee: — *pr.p.* **tee'ing;** *pa.t.* and *pa.p.* **teed, tee'd.** — **tee off** to start (play); **tee up** to prepare (oneself or something) (for). [Origin unknown.]

tee[3] *tē, n.* the umbrella-shaped finial of a dagoba. [Burmese *h'ti,* umbrella.]

teehee, tehee *tē'hē', interj.* expressing derision or merriment. — *n.* a laugh. — *v.i.* to titter. [*Imit.*]

teel. See **til.**

teem[1] *tēm, v.t.* (*obs.*) to bring forth. — *v.i.* to bear or be fruitful: to be pregnant: to be full, abound. — *adjs.* **teem'ful; teem'ing; teem'less** barren. [O.E. *tīeman* — *tēam;* see **team.**]

teem[2] *tēm, v.t.* to pour, empty. — *v.i.* to pour: to flow copiously. — *n.* **teem'er.** [O.N. *tœma,* to empty; cf. **toom.**]

teemed (*Spens.*). See **team.**

teen[1]**, teene, tene** *tēn,* (*arch.*) *n.* injury: affliction: grief: anger: pains. [O.E. *tēona,* injury, anger, grief.]

teen[2] *tēn, n.* any number or year of age, etc., from thir*teen* to nine*teen* (usu. in *pl.*). — *adjs.* **teen'age** in the teens: appropriate to one in the teens; **teen'aged.** — *n.* **teen'ager;** **tee'ny-bopper** (*slang*) a young teenager, esp. a girl, who follows enthusiastically the latest trends in pop-music, clothes, etc. [O.E. suffix -*tīene* — *tīen,* ten.]

teend. See **tind.**

teene[1] *tēn,* (*Spens.*) *v.t.* app., to allot.

teene[2]**.** See **teen**[1]**.**

teeny *tē'ni, adj.* a form of tiny. — Also (*dim.,* often *facet.*) **teen'sy, teen'tsy, teen'ty, teen'y-ween'y.**

teepee. See **tepee.**

teer *tēr, v.t.* to plaster: to daub: to spread. [O.Fr. *terer* — *terre,* earth.]

Teeswater *tēz'wöt-ər, n.* a shorthorn, originating chiefly from a breed in the *Tees* valley (*water*).

tee-tee[1] *tee'-tee'* (*coll.*) *adj.* teetotal. — *n.* teetotaller. [The abbrev. **t.t.** written out.]

tee-tee[2]**.** Same as **titi.**

teeter *tē'tər, n.* see-saw. — *v.t., v.i.* to see-saw: to move unsteadily. — **teet'er-board** a see-saw: (also **teet'er-tott'er**) a board which throws a person into the air when another jumps on the opposite end of it. [tit-ter[2].]

teeth *tēth, pl.* of **tooth:** (legislative) power to make a government recommendation effective (*fig.*). — *v.i.* **teethe** (*tēdh*) to develop or cut teeth. — *v.t.* to furnish with teeth. — *n.* and *adj.* **teething** (*tēdh'ing*). — **teething ring** a ring of plastic, bone, etc., for a baby to chew when teething; **teething troubles** pain and irritation caused by the cutting of teeth: mechanical difficulties encountered on first using a new machine or in the early stages of any undertaking. [O.E. pl. *tēth.*]

teetotal *tē-tō'tl, adj.* abstaining totally from intoxicating drinks: out-and-out (*dial.*). — *n.* a total abstainer: the total abstinence principle, movement, or pledge. — *ns.* **teetō'talism; teetō'taller** a total abstainer from intoxicating drinks. — *adv.* **teetō'tally.** [*Teetotally* prob. established first as a facetious or emphatic reduplicative form of *totally*; *teetotal* subsequently used in a speech advocating abstinence by Richard Turner of Preston in 1833.]

teetotum *tē-tō'təm,* (*arch.*) *n.* a small top inscribed with letters, or a gambling game decided by the letter that came uppermost, T standing for L. *tōtum,* all, i.e. take all the stakes: any small top twirled by the fingers: — *pl.* **teetō'tums.**

tef, teff *tef, n.* an Ethiopian cereal grass, *Eragrostis abyssinica.* [Amharic *têf.*]

Teflon® *tef'lon, n.* a trademark for polytetrafluoroethy-lene as used e.g. to coat the inside of cooking pans to render them non-stick.

teg, tegg *teg, n.* a sheep (or *obs.* a doe) in its second year. [Perh. Scand.]

tegmen *teg'mən, n.* a covering: the inner coat of the testa (*bot.*): the leathery fore-wing in Orthoptera: — *pl.* **teg'mina.** — *adj.* **tegmental** (-*ment'əl*). — *ns.* **tegment'um** a bud-scale; **teg'ument** a covering: an integument. — *adjs.* **tegūment'al, tegūment'ary.** [L. *tegmen, tegmentum, tegumentum* — *tegĕre,* to cover.]

teguexin *te-gwek'sin, n.* a large black and yellow South American lizard. [Aztec *tecoixin.*]

tegula *teg'ū-lə, n.* a flat roofing-tile: a scale at the base of the fore-wing in some insects: — *pl.* **teg'ūlae** (-*lē*). — *adj.* **teg'ūlar.** — *adv.* **teg'ūlarly.** — *adj.* **teg'ūlated** composed of plates overlapping like tiles. [L. *tegula,* a tile — *tegĕre,* to cover.]

tegument, etc. See **tegmen.**

tehee. See **teehee.**

tehr *tār.* Same as **tahr.**

Teian, Tean *tē'yən, adj.* of Teos in ancient Ionia, or of Anacreon, a native of Teos. [Gr. *Tēios,* Teian — *Tēōs,* Teos.]

teichopsia *tī-kops'i-ə, n.* temporary partial blindness with optical illusions, accompanying migraine. [Gr. *teichos,* wall, *opsis,* sight.]

te igitur *tē' ij'i-tər,* L. *tā ig'i-tōor,* the first paragraph of the canon of the mass: a service-book on which oaths were taken. [L. *tē igitur,* thee therefore (the first words).]

teil *tēl, n.* the linden or lime tree. — **teil tree** the lime: the terebinth (*B.*). [O.Fr. *teil* — L. *tilia.*]

teind *tēnd, n.* in Scotland, a tithe. — *v.t.* to assess or take a tithe on. [A form of **tenth, tithe.**]

teinoscope *tī'nō-skōp,* (*obs.*) *n.* a magnifying and diminishing combination of prisms correcting chromatic aberration. [Gr. *teinein,* to stretch, *skopeein,* to look.]

teknonymy *tek-non'i-mi, n.* the naming of the parent from the child. — *adj.* **teknon'ymous.** [Gr. *teknon,* a child, *onyma, onoma,* a name.]

tektite *tek'tīt, n.* a type of small glassy stone, of uncertain and perh. extra-terrestrial origin, found in certain areas of the earth, including Australia (**australite**). [Gr. *tēktos,* molten.]

tel. See **tel(l).**

tel-. See **tele-.**

tela *tē'lə,* L. *tā'lä, n.* a web, tissue: — *pl.* **tē'lae** (-*lē; tā'lī*). — *adj.* **tē'lary** web-spinning. [L. *tēla.*]

telaesthesia, U.S. **telesthesia,** *tel-ēs-thē'zi-ə, -zhi-ə, -zhyə,* or -*is-, n.* an abnormal impression as of sense received from a distance. — *adj.* **tel(a)esthetic** (-*thet'ik*). [tele-(1), Gr. *aisthēsiā,* sensation.]

telamon *tel'ə-mən,* (*archit.*) *n.* a man's figure as a pillar: — *pl.* **telamones** (-*mō'nēz*). [Gr. mythological hero, *Telamōn* — *tlēnai,* to endure, bear.]

telangiectasis *tel-an-ji-ek'tə-sis, n.* dilatation of the small arteries or capillaries. — *adj.* **telangiectatic** (-*ek-tat'ik*). [Gr. *telos,* end, *angeion,* a vessel, *ektasis,* extension.]

telary. See **tela.**

Telautograph® *tel-ö'tə-gräf, n.* a telegraph for reproducing the movement of a pen or pencil and so transmitting writings or drawings: one for transmission of images by electric scanning. — *adj.* **telautographic** (-*graf'ik*). — *n.* **telautography** (-*tog'rə-fi*). [tele- (1), Gr. *autos,* self, *graphein,* to write.]

teld *teld,* (*Spens.*) *pa.t.* and *pa.p.* of **tell.** — (*Scot.*) **teld, tell'd,** told.

tele- *tel-i,* (also **tel-**), in composition, (1) far, distant; (2) television; (3) telephone. [Gr. *tēle,* far.]

tele-ad *tel'i-ad, n.* a classified advertisement submitted to a newspaper, etc., by telephone. [**tele-** (3), **advertisement**.]

telearchics *tel-i-är'kiks.* See **telecontrol.** [**tele-** (1), Gr. *archein,* to rule.]

telecamera *tel'-i-kam-ər-ə, n.* a television camera (see **camera**).

telecast *tel'i-käst, n.* a *tele*vision broad*cast.* — Also *v.t.* — *n.* **tel'ecaster.**

telechir *tel'i-kēr, n.* a form of robot controlled by telecommand by an operator who has feedback from electronic sensors, e.g. television cameras. — *adj.* **telechir'ic.** **tele-** (1), and Gr. *cheir,* hand.]

telecine *tel-i-sin'i, n.* transmission of filmed material by television. **[tele-** (2), **cine-.]**

telecom(s) *tel'i-kom(z).* Short for **telecommunication(s).**

telecommand *tel'i-kom-änd, n.* the operation of machinery by remote electronic control. **[tele-** (1), **command.]**

telecommunication *tel-i-kə-mū-ni-kā'shən, n.* communication of information, in verbal, written, coded, or pictorial form, by telephone, telegraph, cable, radio, television: (in *pl.*) the science of such communication. **[tele-** (1), **communication.]**

telecommute *tel-i-ko-mūt', v.i.* to work at home, communicating with the office by telephone, computer link, etc. — *ns.* **telecommū'ter; telecommū'ting. [tele-** (1), **commute.]**

teleconference *tel-i-kon'fər-əns, n.* a meeting between people physically separated but linked by video, audio and/or computer facilities. — *n.* **telecon'ferencing** the practice of holding such conferences, or the technology involved. **[tele-** (1), **conference.]**

telecontrol *tel-i-kon-trōl', n.* control of mechanical devices remotely, either by radio (as ships and aircraft), by sound waves, or by beams of light. — Also *n.sing.* **telearchics** (-*ark').* **[tele-** (1), **control.]**

teledu *tel'ə-dōō, n.* the stinking badger of Java. — Also **stinkard, stinking badger.** [Javanese.]

téléférique *tā-lā-fār-ēk,* (Fr.) *n.* a light aerial cable-car, esp. one electrically propelled.

telefilm *tel'i-film, n.* a regular sound-film made specially for subsequent television transmission. **[tele-** (2), **film.]**

telega *tel-eg'ə, tel-yeg'ə, n.* a springless Russian wagon. [Russ.]

telegenic *tel-i-jen'ik, adj.* visually suitable for television. **[tele-** (2), modelled on **photogenic.]**

telegnosis *tel-i(g)-nō'sis, n.* the knowledge of events taking place far away, not obtained in any normal way. **[tele-** (1), Gr. *gnōsis,* knowing.]

telegony *ti-leg'ə-ni, n.* the (imaginary) transmitted influence of a previous mate on the offspring of a female by a later mate. **[tele-** (1), Gr. *gonos,* begetting.]

telegram *tel'i-gram, n.* a message sent by telegraph. — *adjs.* **telegrammat'ic, telegramm'ic** of or like a telegram. **[tele-** (1), Gr. *gramma,* that which is written — *graphein,* to write.]

telegraph *tel'i-gräf, n.* a combination of apparatus for transmitting information to a distance, now almost exclusively by electrical impulses: a message so sent (*obs.*): a scoring-board (*cricket,* etc.): often taken as the name of a newspaper. — *v.t.* to convey or announce by telegraph: to signal: to give a premature indication of something to come. — *v.i.* to signal: to send a telegram. — *ns.* **telegrapher** (*ti-leg'rə-fər;* now chiefly *U.S.*) a telegraphist; **tel'egraphese'** the jargon or contracted idiom used in telegrams. — *adj.* **telegraphic** (-*graf'ik*). — *adv.* **telegraph'ically.** — *ns.* **teleg'raphist** one who works a telegraph; **teleg'raphy** the science or art of constructing or using telegraphs. — **tel'egraph (-board)** a scoring-board able to be seen at a distance: a board on which the numbers of the horses and names of jockeys are put up (*racing*); **tel'egraph-ca'ble** a cable containing wires for transmitting telegraphic messages; **telegraphic address** a shortened address registered for use in telegraphing; **tel'egraph-plant** an Indian papilionaceous plant (*Desmodium gyrans*) whose leaflets move like semaphore arms; **tel'egraph-pole** a pole supporting telegraph-wires; **tel'egraph-wire** a wire for carrying telegraphic messages. **[tele-** (1), Gr. *graphein,* to write.]

telejournalist *tel-i-jûr'nə-list, n.* a journalist working in television. — *n.* **telejourn'alism.** **[tele-** (2), **journalist.]**

telekinesis *tel-i-ki-nē'sis, -kī-, n.* the production of motion at a distance by means beyond the range of the senses. — *adj.* **telekinetic** (-*net'ik*). **[tele-** (1), Gr. *kīnēsis,* movement.]

telemark *tel'i-märk, n.* a sudden turn on the outer ski, first practised at *Telemark* in Norway. — *v.i.* to execute a telemark.

telemarketing. See **teleselling.**

Telemessage® *tel'i-mes-ij, n.* a message sent by telex or telephone, superseding the telegram. **[tele-** (1).]

telemeter *ti-lem'i-tər, n.* an instrument for measuring distances: a photographer's rangefinder: an instrument for measuring an electrical or other quantity and signalling the measurement to a distant point (also **radiotelemeter**). — *v.t.* to record and signal by telemeter. — *adj.* **telemetric** (*tel-i-met'rik*). — *n.* **telem'etry.** **[tele-** (1), Gr. *metron,* measure.]

teleo- *tel'i-ō, -o',* in composition, perfect, complete. — *ns.* **Teleosaurus** (*tel-i-ō-sö'rəs;* Gr. *sauros,* a lizard) a Jurassic genus of fossil crocodiles; **tel'eosaur.** — *adj.* and *n.* **teleosau'rian.** — *n.pl.* **Teleostei** (-*os'ti-ī;* Gr. *osteon,* bone) the bony fishes with well-developed bones. — *ns.* and *adjs.* **tel'eost, teleos'tean.** — *n.pl.* **Teleostomi** (-*os'tə-mī;* Gr. *stoma,* mouth) fishes with membrane bones in the skull, jaws, etc. — all ordinary fishes except the sharks and rays. — *n.* **tel'eostome** (-*tōm*). — *adj.* **teleos'tomous.** [Gr. *teleios,* perfect, complete.]

teleology *tel-i-ol'ə-ji, n.* the doctrine of the final causes of things: interpretation in terms of purpose. — *adjs.* **teleologic** (-*ə-loj'ik*), **-al.** — *adv.* **teleolog'ically.** — *ns.* **teleol'ogism; teleol'ogist.** [Gr. *telos,* end, purpose, *logos,* a discourse.]

teleonomy. See **telos.**

telepathy *ti-lep'ə-thi, n.* communication between mind and mind otherwise than through the known channels of the senses. — *n.* **telepath** (*tel'i-path*) one who practises telepathy. — *v.t.* and *v.i.* to communicate by telepathy. — *adj.* **telepath'ic.** — *adv.* **telepath'ically.** *v.t.* **telep'athise, -ize** to affect or act upon through telepathy. — *v.i.* to practise telepathy. — *n.* **telep'athist** one who believes in or practises telepathy. **[tele-** (1), Gr. *pathos,* feeling.]

telepheme *tel'i-fēm, n.* a telephone message. **[tele-** (1), Gr. *phēmē,* a saying.]

telephone *tel'i-fōn, n.* an instrument for reproducing sound at a distance, esp. by means of electricity: specif. an instrument with a microphone and a receiver mounted on a handset, for transmitting speech: the system of communication which uses these instruments. — Also *adj.* — *v.t.* and *v.i.* to communicate by telephone. — *n.* **tel'ephoner.** — *adj.* **telephonic** (-*fon'ik*). — *adv.* **telephon'ically.** — *ns.* **telephonist** (*ti-lef'ə-nist*) one who works a telephone; **teleph'ony** telephonic communication. — **telephone book, directory** a book listing the names, addresses and numbers of telephone subscribers; **telephone box, booth, kiosk** a usu. enclosed place with a telephone for public use; **telephone number** a number which identifies a particular telephone and is dialled to make connections with it; **telephone tapping** see **tap²**. **[tele-** (1), Gr. *phōnē,* a sound.]

telephotography *tel-i-fō-tog'rə-fi, n.* a photography of distant objects by means of suitable lenses: wrongly, phototelegraphy. — *n.* **telepho'tograph** (*tel-i-fō'tō-gräf*). — *adj.* **telephotographic** (-*graf'ik*), contraction **telepho'to.** — **telephoto lens** a lens of long focal length for obtaining large images of distant objects. **[tele-** (1), **photography.]**

teleprinter *tel-i-print'ər, n.* a telegraph transmitter with typewriter keyboard. **[tele-** (1), **printer.]**

teleprocessing *tel-i-prō'ses-ing, n.* the use of a computer to process data transmitted from distant points. **[tele-** (1), **process.]**

teleprompter *tel-i-promp'tər, n.* a device by which a television speaker sees a projection of what he is to say, invisible to the audience. **[tele-** (2).]

teleradium unit. See **radium.**

telerecording *tel-i-ri-kör'ding, n.* recording for broadcasting by television: a television transmission from a recording. — *v.t.* **telerecord'.** [tele- (2), **recording.**]

telergy *tel'ər-ji, n.* a physical force assumed to be at work in telepathy. — *adj.* **teler'gic** (*-ûr'jik*) working at a distance, as in telepathy. — *adv.* **teler'gically.** [tele- (1), Gr. *ergon*, work.]

telesale. See **teleselling.**

telescope *tel'i-skōp, n.* an optical instrument for viewing objects at a distance. — *v.t.* to drive or slide one into another like the movable joints of a telescope: to compress, shorten, make smaller, etc. (*lit.* and *fig.*). — *v.i.* to fit, slide, shorten, etc. in such a way. — *adjs.* **telescopic** (*-skop'ik*), **-al** of, performed by, or like a telescope: seen only by a telescope: sliding, or arranged, like the joints of a telescope: capable of retraction and protrusion. — *adv.* **telescop'ically.** — *adj.* **telescop'iform.** — *ns.* **telescopist** (*ti-les'kə-pist*) one who uses the telescope; **Telescōp'ium** (*astron.*) the Telescope, a small southern constellation between the constellations of *Ara* and *Corona Austrinus*; **teles'copy** the art of constructing or of using the telescope. — **telescope, telescopic sight** a telescope on a gun used as a sight. [tele- (1), Gr. *skopeein*, to see.]

telescreen *tel'i-skrēn, n.* a television screen. [tele- (2), **screen.**]

teleselling *tel'i-sel-ing, n.* the selling of goods or services by using the telephone to seek customers (also called **telemark'eting**). — *n.* **tel'esale** a sale made on the telephone. [tele- (3), **selling**].

teleseme *tel'i-sēm, n.* a signalling apparatus with an indicator. [tele- (1), Gr. *sēma*, a sign.]

teleservices *tel'i-sûr-vis-əz, n. pl.* information, etc., services available to users of teletext and viewdata systems. [tele- (1), **service.**]

telesis. See **telos.**

telesm *tel'ezm, n.* a talisman. — *adjs.* **telesmat'ic, -al.** — *adv.* **telesmat'ically.** [Gr. *telesma*; see **talisman.**]

telesoftware *tel-i-soft'wär, (comput.) n.* software which is transmitted to users by means of a teletext or viewdata system. [tele- (1), **software.**]

telesthesia. See **telaesthesia.**

telestic *ti-les'tik, adj.* relating to the mysteries. [Gr. *telestikos* — Gr. *teleein*, to fulfil, consummate, initiate, perform — *telos*, end, rite, etc.]

telestich *tel-es'tik, tel'es-tik, n.* a poem or block of words whose final letters spell a name or word. [Gr. *telos*, end, *stichos*, row.]

teletex *tel-i-teks, n.* a means of transmitting written data, similar in principle to telex (see below), but using more modern, high-speed electronic apparatus. [tele- (1), **text.**]

teletext *tel'i-tekst, n.* written data, such as business news, etc., transmitted by television companies in the form of coded pulses which can be decoded by a special adaptor for viewing on a conventional television. [tele- (2), **text.**]

telethon *tel'ə-thon, (orig. U.S.) n.* a very long television programme, esp. one seeking support for e.g. a political candidate, or a charity. [*tele*vision mara*thon*.]

teletron *tel'i-tron, n.* a cathode-ray tube for synthesis of television images. [tele- (1), suff. -**tron.**]

Teletype® *tel'i-tīp n.* a printing telegraph apparatus. — **Teletype'setter®** a telegraphic machine which delivers its message as a perforated roll that can be used to actuate a type-setting machine; **teletype'writer** (*U.S.*) a teleprinter. [tele- (1), Gr. *typos*; see **type.**]

teleutospore *ti-lū'tō-spōr, -spör, n.* a thick-walled winterspore of the rust-fungi, producing on germination a promycelium. [Gr. *teleutē*, completion, *sporā*, seed.]

televérité *tel-i-ver'i-tā, n.* the televising of scenes of real life in order to convey a heightened realism. — See also **cinéma vérité**. [tele- (2), modelled on **cinéma vérité.**]

television *tel-i-vizh'ən, n.* the viewing of distant objects or events by electrical transmission: the electrical transmission of these: a television set. — Abbrev. **TV.**

— Also *adj.* — *v.t.* and *v.i.* **tel'eview** to view by television. — *n.* **tel'eviewer** a television watcher. — *v.t.* and *v.i.* **tel'evise** (*tel'i-vīz*) to transmit by television. — *adjs.* **televi'sional, televi'sionary** of, relating to, television. — *n.* **televi'sor** a receiver for television. — *adj.* **televi'sual** televisional: telegenic. — **television set** a television receiver; **TV game** an electronic game, e.g. one similar to Space Invaders, played on a television set. [tele- (1), **vision.**]

telewriter *tel-i-rī'tər, n.* telegraph instrument that reproduces writing. [tele- (1), **writer.**]

telex *tel'eks, n.* an international telegraphic service whereby subscribers hire the use of teleprinters: a teleprinter used in this service: a message transferred by this service. — *v.t.* to send (someone) (a message) by telex. [*tele*printer and *ex*change.]

telic. See **telos.**

tel(l) *tel, n.* in Arab lands, a hill, ancient mound. [Ar. *tall.*]

tell *tel, v.t.* to count: to count out: to utter: to narrate: to disclose: to inform: to discern: to explain: to order, direct, instruct: to bid (goodbye; *U.S.*). — *v.i.* to give an account: to have an effect (on): to have weight: to make an effective story: to play the informer: — *pa.t.* and *pa.p.* **tōld,** (*Scot.*) **teld, tell'd, telt.** — *adj.* **tell'able** capable of being told: fit to tell. — *ns.* **tell'er** one who tells or counts: one who counts votes: a clerk whose duty it is to receive and pay money, esp. in a bank; **tell'ership.** — *adj.* **tell'ing** effective. — *n.* numbering: narration: direction, orders. — *adv.* **tell'ingly.** — **tell'-ing-off** a rating, chiding; **tell'-tale, tell'tale** one who tells the private concerns or misdeeds of others: a tattler (bird): anything revealing or betraying: an indicator, esp. of low tunnels, bridges, etc.: a recording clock: a strip of material outside the playing area at the foot of the front wall of a squash court, which makes a distinctive sound when hit. — *adj.* blabbing: revealing, betraying: indicating. — **take a telling** to do as one is bid without having to be told again; **tell me another** you'll have to tell me a more credible story; **tell off** to count off: to detach on some special duty: to rate, chide; **tell on** (*coll.*) to betray, give away secrets about; **you're telling me** (*interj.*; *slang*) I know that only too well. [O.E. *tellan*; O.N. *telja*, Ger. *zählen*, to number.]

tellar, teller. Same as **tiller**[2].

Tellus *tel'əs, n.* the Roman earth-goddess: the earth. — *adj.* **tell'ural** pertaining to the earth. — *n.* **tell'urate** a salt of telluric acid. — *adjs.* **tell'uretted** combined with tellurium; **tellū'rian** terrestrial. — *n.* an inhabitant of the earth: a tellurion. — *adj.* **tellū'ric** of or from the earth: of tellurium in higher valency (**telluric acid** H_2TeO_4). — *ns.* **tell'uride** a compound of tellurium with another element or radical; **tellū'rion, -an** an apparatus representing the earth and sun, demonstrating the occurrence of day, night, the seasons, etc. — *v.t.* **tell'urise, -ize** to combine with tellurium. — *ns.* **tell'urite** native oxide of tellurium (*min.*): a salt of tellurous acid (*chem.*); **tellū'rium** the element (Te) of atomic number 52, app. so named by Klaproth (1798) as the counterpart of his previous discovery of uranium; **tellūrom'eter** an electronic instrument used to measure survey lines by measurement of the time required for a radar signal to echo back. — *adj.* **tell'urous** of tellurium in lower valency (**tellurous acid** H_2TeO_3). [L. *Tellūs, -ūris.*]

telly *tel'i, (slang) n.* television.

telophase *tel'ō-fāz, n.* in mitosis, the stage of reconstruction of nuclei after separation of daughter chromosomes. [Gr. *telos*, completion, *phasis*, phase.]

telos *tel'os, n.* aim, purpose, ultimate end. — *adj.* **teleonom'ic.** — *ns.* **teleon'omy** the characteristic of being governed by an overall purpose; **tel'esis** the using of natural and social processes for a particular purpose. — *adj.* **tel'ic** expressing purpose: purposive. [Gr. *telos*, end, purpose.]

telpher *tel'fər, adj.* pertaining to a system of telpherage.

— *n.* a car or carrier in such a system. — *ns.* **tel'pherage** any system of automatic electric transport: an electric ropeway or cableway system: overhead traction in general. — **tel'pher-line; tel'pherman; tel'pherway.** [Irreg. coined by Fleeming Jenkin — Gr. *tēle*, far, phoros, bearing — *pherein*, to bear.]

telson *tel'sən, n.* the hindermost part of a crustacean or arachnid. [Gr. *telson*, a headland in ploughing; cf. *telos*, end.]

Telstar *tel'stär, n.* a satellite launched on 10 July 1962, used to relay television pictures and telephone conversations across the Atlantic.

telt *telt* (*Scot.*), *pa.t.* and *pa.p.* of **tell**.

Telugu *tel'ōō-gōō, n.* a Dravidian language of south-east India: one of the people speaking it: — *pl.* **Tel'ugus, Tel'ugu.** — Also *adj.*

temblor *tem'blŏr,* (esp. *U.S.*) *n.* an earthquake: — *pl.* **temblor'es** (*-āz*). [Amer. Sp.]

teme. An *obs.* spelling of **team**.

temenos *tem'e-nos, n.* a place dedicated to a god, a precinct. [Gr., shrine — *temnein*, to cut off.]

temerity *ti-mer'i-ti, n.* rashness: unreasonable contempt for danger. — *adj.* **temerarious** (*tem-ə-rā'ri-əs*; now *rare*) rash, reckless. — *adv.* **temerā'riously.** — *adj.* **tem'erous** rash. — *adv.* **tem'erously.** [L. *temeritās, -ātis,* and *temerārius — temere,* by chance, rashly.]

temp *temp,* (*coll.*) *n.* a temporarily-employed secretarial worker. — *v.i.* to work as a temp. [**temporary**.]

Tempe *tem'pē, n.* the valley of the Pēneios (Peneus) in Thessaly, praised by the classic poets for its matchless beauty: hence, any place of choice beauty. [Gr. *Tempē* (*Tempea*).]

temper *tem'pər, v.t.* to mix in due proportion: to modify by blending or mixture: to moderate: to soften: loosely, esp. formerly, to harden (steel) by heating to red heat and quenching: properly, to heat again, less strongly, and cool in air: loosely, to carry out both operations: to adjust: to tune: to attune: to adjust to a temperament (*mus.*): to bring to a favourable state of mind. — *v.i.* to tamper, meddle (*Shak.*): to soften (*Shak.*): to become tempered. — *n.* due mixture or balance of different or contrary qualities: state of a metal as to hardness, etc.: constitution of the body: temperament: disposition: habitual or actual frame of mind: mood: composure: self-control: uncontrolled anger: a fit of ill-humour or rage: lime or other substance used to neutralise the acidity of cane-juice. — *n.* **tem'pera** (*paint.*; orig. It.) a painting medium in which the pigment is mixed with egg yolk: distemper. — *adj.* **tem'perable** capable of being tempered. — *ns.* **temperal'itie** (*Shak.*) Mrs Quickly's elaboration of temper, frame of mind; **tem'perament** proportioned mixture: state with respect to combination or predominance of qualities (*obs.*): climate (*obs.*): internal constitution or state: combination or predominance of humour (*obs. physiol.*): disposition: type of physical and mental organisation — choleric or bilious, sanguine, melancholy, phlegmatic (*obs. physiol.*): high excitability, nervous instability, and sensitiveness (*coll.*): tempering (*arch.*): compromise (*arch.*): a system of compromise in tuning (*mus.*). — *adjs.* **temperament'al; temperament'ful.** — *adv.* **temperament'ally.** — *n.* **tem'perance** moderation, esp. in the indulgence of the natural appetites and passions — in a narrower sense, moderation in the use of alcoholic liquors, and even entire abstinence from them. — *adj.* advocating or consistent with temperance in or abstinence from alcoholic drinks. — *adj.* **tem'perate** moderate: self-restrained, esp. in appetites and passions: abstemious: moderate in temperature. — *v.t.* (*obs.* or *rare*) to temper: to moderate: to restrain. — *adv.* **tem'perately.** — *n.* **tem'perateness.** — *adj.* **tem'perative** having moderating influence. — *n.* **tem'perature** tempering: tempered condition: mixture: constitution: proportion: degree of hotness: condition determining interchange of heat between bodies: a body temperature above normal (*coll.*). — *adj.* **tem'pered** having a certain specified

disposition or temper: brought to a certain temper, as steel: tuned or adjusted to some mean, or to equal, temperament (*mus.*). — *adv.* **tem'peredly.** — *n.* **tem'perer.** — *n.* and *adj.* **tem'pering.** — **temperance hotel** one which professes to supply no alcoholic liquors; **temperate zones** the parts of the earth of moderate temperature between the tropics and the polar circles. — **absolute temperature** see **absolute; bad temper** an angry humour: an inclination to irascibility; **equal temperament** a compromise in tuning by which the octave is divided into twelve equal intervals; **good temper** an unruffled humour: good-nature; **keep one's temper** to restrain oneself from showing, or losing, one's temper; **lose one's temper** to break out in anger; **out of temper** in an irritable mood: angry; **temperature=humidity index** an index measuring temperature and humidity with regard to human discomfort. [L. *temperāre,* to temper, restrain, compound, moderate, partly through O.E. *temprian.*]

tempest *tem'pist, n.* a violent wind storm: a violent commotion or agitation (*fig.*). — *v.t.* (*Milt.*) to stir violently. — *adjs.* **tempestive** (*-pest'*) timely: seasonable; **tempestŭous** (*-pest'*). — *adv.* **tempest'ŭously.** — *n.* **tempest'ŭousness.** — *adjs.* **tem'pest-beaten, tem'pest=tossed, -tost** (*Shak.*) driven about by storms. [O.Fr. *tempeste* — a L.L. form of L. *tempestās,* a season, tempest — *tempus,* time.]

tempi. See **tempo**.

Templar. See **temple**[1].

template, templet *tem'plit, n.* a mould shaped to a required outline from which to execute moulding: a thin plate cut to the shape required, by which a surface of an article being made is marked out: any model from which others form, are produced, etc. [L. *templum,* a small timber.]

temple[1] *tem'pl, n.* a building or place dedicated to, or regarded as the house of, a god: a place of worship: in France, a Protestant church: (*cap.*) the headquarters of the Knights Templars on or near the site of Solomon's temple in Jerusalem: (*cap.*) in London, two inns of court (*Inner* and *Middle Temple*) on the site once occupied by the Knights Templars, with the Knights' church: a synagogue, esp. of Reform or Conservative Judaism (*U.S.*). — *adj.* **tem'plar** of a temple. — *n.* **Tem'plar** a member of a religious and military order (**Knights Templar(s)**) founded in 1119 for the protection of the Holy Sepulchre and pilgrims going thither — extinguished 1307–14: a student or lawyer living in the Temple, London: member of a U.S. order of Freemasons: see also **good**. — *adj.* **tem'pled.** [L. *templum.*]

temple[2] *tem'pl, n.* the flat portion of either side of the head above the cheekbone. [O.Fr., — L. *tempus, -oris.*]

templet. See **template**.

tempo *tem'pō,* (*mus.*) *n.* time: speed and rhythm: — *pl.* **tem'pos, tem'pi** (*-pē*). [It.]

temporal[1] *tem'pər-l, adj.* pertaining to time: pertaining to time in this life or world — opp. to *eternal*: worldly, secular, or civil — opp. to *spiritual, sacred* or *ecclesiastical*: pertaining to tense, or to length of syllable or vowel (*gram.*). — *n.* **temporality** (*-al'i-ti*) state or fact of being temporal: what pertains to temporal welfare: (usu. *pl.*) secular possessions, revenues of an ecclesiastic proceeding from lands, tithes, and the like. — *adv.* **tem'porally.** — *n.* **tem'poralty** the laity: lay peers: (usu. *pl.*) worldly possessions. — *adj.* **tempora'neous** temporal. — *adv.* **tem'porarily.** — *n.* **tem'porariness.** — *adj.* **tem'porary** for a time only: transient. — *n.* a person employed temporarily (see also **temp**). — *n.* **temporīsā'tion, -z-.** — *v.i.* **tem'porise, -ize** to comply with the time or occasion: to yield to circumstances: to behave so as to gain time. — *n.* **tem'poriser, -z-.** — *n.* and *adj.* **tem'porising, -z-.** — *adv.* **tem'porisingly, -z-.** [L. *tempus, -oris,* time.]

temporal[2] *tem'pər-l, adj.* of or at the temple (of the head). — *n.* a bone, muscle, or scale in that position. —

temporal lobe (*anat.*) a lobe at the side of each cerebral hemisphere by the temple, concerned with hearing and speech. [L. *tempus, -oris*; see **temple²**.]

temporaneous, temporary, etc. See **temporal¹**.

tempore *tem'por-ē, tem'por-e*, (L.) in the time of.

temporise, etc. See **temporal¹**.

tempt *tem(p)t, v.t.* to put to trial: to test: to try or tend to persuade, esp. to evil: to entice. — *n.* **temptabil'ity**. — *adj.* **temp'table**; — *ns.* **temp'tableness**; **temptā'tion** act of tempting: state of being tempted: that which tempts: enticement to evil: trial. — *adj.* **temptā'tious** seductive. — *n.* **temp'ter** one who tempts, esp. (with *cap.*) the devil: — *fem.* **temp'tress**. *n.* **temp'ting** action of the verb. — *adj.* attractive, enticing. — *adv.* **temp'-tingly**. — *n.* **temp'tingness**. [O.Fr. *tempter* — L. *tentāre*, an intens. of *tendĕre*, to stretch.]

'tempt, tempt, aphetic for **attempt**.

tempura *tem'poo-rə, n.* a Japanese dish of sea-food or vegetables deep-fried in batter.

temse, tems *tems, temz, n.* a sieve. — *v.t.* to sift. [O.E. *temesian*, to sift; cf. Du. *tems*.]

temulence *tem'ū-ləns, n.* intoxication. — Also **tem'ulency**. — *adj.* **tem'ulent**. — *adv.* **tem'ulently**. [L. *tēmulentus*, drunk.]

ten *ten, n.* the cardinal number next above nine: a symbol representing it (x, etc.): a set of that number of things or persons: used indefinitely, a large number: an article of a size denoted by 10: a card with ten pips: a score of ten points, tricks, etc.: the tenth hour after midday or midnight: the age of ten years. — *adj.* of the number ten: ten years old. — *adj.* and *adv.* **ten'fold** in ten divisions: ten times as much. — *n.* **tenn'er** (*slang*) a ten-pound note: a ten-dollar bill: ten years. — *adj.* **tenth** the last of ten: next after the ninth: equal to one of ten equal parts. — *n.* a tenth part: a tenth part of the annual profit of a church living: a person or thing in tenth position: an octave and a third (*mus.*): a note at that interval (*mus.*). — *adv.* **tenth'ly**. — *adj.* **ten'-foot** measuring ten feet. — **ten'pence** an amount in money equal to ten pennies; **ten-pence, -penny piece** in Britain, a coin worth 10 pence (also **ten'penny-piece'**). — *adj.* **ten'penny** offered for, or sold at, tenpence. — **tenpenny nail** formerly, a nail sold at tenpence a hundred: a large nail; **tenpin bowling, ten'pins** an American game like skittles; **ten'-point'er** a stag of ten points or tines. — *adj.* **ten'-pound** weighing, worth, sold or offered for, ten pounds. — **ten'-pound'er** something weighing or worth ten pounds: one who was a voter in virtue of occupying property worth ten pounds a year. — *adjs.* **ten'-score** two hundred; **tenth'-rate** of very poor quality. — **long ten** the ten of trumps in catch-the-ten; **ten-gallon hat** (*U.S.*) cowboy's broad-brimmed hat; **ten minute rule** a parliamentary procedure by which a member makes a short speech (lasting no more than ten minutes) requesting permission to introduce a bill. [O.E. (Anglian) *tēn, tēne* (W.S. *tīen, tīene*); Ger. *zehn*, W. *deg*, L. *decem*, Gr. *deka*, Sans. *daśa*.]

tenable *ten'ə-bl* (*arch. tēn'*), *adj.* capable of being retained, kept, or defended. — *ns.* **tenabil'ity, ten'ableness**. [Fr. *tenable* — *tenir*, to hold.]

tenace *ten'ās, -is, n.* the combination in one hand of the cards next above and next below the other side's best in the suit. [Sp. *tenaza*, pincers.]

tenacious *ti-nā'shəs, adj.* retaining or holding fast: sticking stiffly: tough: stubborn. — *adv.* **tenā'ciously**. — *ns.* **tenā'ciousness, tenacity** (*-nas'i-ti*). [L. *tenāx, -ācis* — *tenēre*, to hold.]

tenaculum *te-nak'ū-ləm, n.* a surgical hook or forceps for picking up blood-vessels. [L. *tenāculum*, holder, pincers.]

tenaille *te-nāl', (fort.) n.* an outwork in the main ditch in front of the curtain. — *n.* **tenaillon** (*te-nal'yən*) a work to strengthen the side of a small ravelin. — Also **tenail'**. [Fr., — L. *tenāculum*, pincers — *tenēre*, to hold.]

tenant *ten'ənt, n.* one who holds under another: one who has, on certain conditions, temporary possession of any place: an occupant. — *v.t.* to hold as a tenant: to

occupy. — *v.i.* to dwell. — *n.* **ten'ancy** possession by private ownership: a temporary occupation or holding of land or property by a tenant: time of such holding. — *adjs.* **ten'antable** fit to be tenanted: in a state of repair suitable for a tenant; **ten'antless**. — *ns.* **ten'antry** the state or time of being a tenant: a set or body of tenants; **ten'antship**. — **ten'-ant-at-will'** one who holds only so long as the proprietor wills; **tenant farmer** a farmer who rents a farm; **ten'ant-in-chief'** one who holds lands directly from the sovereign; **tenant right** the right of a tenant, esp. that of a customary tenant to sit continuously at a reasonable rent, the right to receive compensation for his interest from the incoming tenant, and for all permanent or unexhausted improvements from the landlord. [Fr. *tenant*, pr.p. of *tenir* — L. *tenēre*, to hold.]

tench *tench, -sh, n.* a freshwater fish (*Tinca tinca*) of the carp family, very tenacious of life. [O.Fr. *tenche* (Fr. *tanche*) — L. *tinca*.]

tend¹ *tend, v.t.* to attend to: to mind: to watch over or stand by and perform services for or connected with: to minister to, wait upon: to escort (*Shak.*). — *v.i.* (*Shak.*) to attend, hearken: to be in waiting or readiness: to wait, attend. — *n.* **ten'dance** tending: expectation (*Spens.*): attendants collectively (*Shak.*). — *adj.* **ten'ded**. — *n.* **ten'der** one who tends: a small craft that attends a larger: a carriage attached to a locomotive to carry fuel and water. — **tend out on** (*U.S.*) to attend or attend to. [Aphetic for **attend**.]

tend² *tend, v.i.* to stretch, aim at, move, or incline in some direction: to be directed to any end or purpose: to be apt: to conduce. — *ns.* **ten'dence, tendenz** (*ten-dents'*; Ger.) tendency (esp. in composition, tendentious); **ten'dency** a trend, drift, inclination: proneness. — *adjs.* **tendential** (*-den'shl*), **tenden'tious, tenden'cious** purposely tending: with an object: biased. — *adv.* **tenden'-tiously**. — *n.* **tenden'tiousness**. [L. *tendĕre* and Fr. *tendre*, to stretch.]

tender¹. See under **tend¹**.

tender² *ten'dər, v.t.* to offer for acceptance, esp. to offer in payment: to proffer. — *v.i.* to make a tender. — *n.* an offer or proposal, esp. of some service: the paper containing it: the thing offered: a formal offer to save the consequences of non-payment or non-performance. — *ns.* **ten'derer; ten'dering**. — **legal tender** see **legal**. [Fr. *tendre*, to stretch, reach out.]

tender³ *ten'dər, adj.* soft, delicate: easily chewed, not tough: of porcelain, soft-paste: easily impressed or injured: not hardy: gentle: scrupulous, chary: sensitive, esp. to pain: requiring gentle handling: easily moved to pity, love, etc.: careful not to hurt: considerate, careful (with *of*): pathetic: expressive, or of the nature, of the softer passions: compassionate, loving, affectionate: beloved (*Shak.*): apt to lean over under sail. — *v.t.* to treat with tenderness (*Shak.*): to feel tenderness for (*Shak.*): to cherish: to value, have respect to: to make tender. — *n.* care, regard, concern (*Shak.*): tender feeling, fondness (now usu. in Fr. form **tendre**, *tädr'*). — *v.t.* **ten'derise, -ize** to break down the connective tissue of (meat) by pounding or by applying a chemical or marinade. — *ns.* **ten'deriser, -z-** a pounding instrument or a substance that tenderises meat; **ten'-derling** one too much coddled, an effeminate fellow: one of the first horns of a deer. — *adv.* **ten'derly**. — *n.* **ten'derness**. — *adj.* **ten'der-dying** (*Shak.*) dying young. — **ten'derfoot** one not yet hardened to life in the prairie, mining-camp, etc.: a newcomer: a greenhorn: a boy scout or girl guide who has passed only the first tests (*obs.*): — *pl.* **ten'derfeet**. — *adj.* **ten'der-heart'ed** full of feeling. — *adv.* **ten'der-heart'edly**. — **ten'der-heart'edness**. — *adj.* **ten'der-heft'ed** (*Shak.*) perh. set in a tender haft or frame. — **ten'der-loin** the tenderest part of the loin of beef, pork, etc., close to the lumbar vertebrae (*U.S.*): a district juicy with bribes to the police (*U.S. slang*). [Fr. *tendre* — L. *tener*.]

tendon *ten'dən, n.* a cord, band, or sheet of fibrous tissue attaching a muscle to a bone or other structure. —

adj. **ten'dinous.** — *ns.* **tendonitis** (*-ī'tis*) inflammation of a tendon; **tenosynovitis** (*ten-ə-sīn-ə-vīt'is*) a painful swelling of a tendon, associated with repetitive movements. [L.L. *tendō, -inis* or *-ōnis*, app. — Gr. *tenōn, -ontos*, sinew, tendon; cf. *teinein*, to stretch; *d* suggested by L. *tendĕre*.]

tendre. See **tender³.**

tendril *ten'dril, n.* a plant's coiling threadlike climbing organ (leaf, leaflet, or shoot). — *adjs.* **ten'drillar, ten'drillous; ten'drilled.** [Ety. dub.; cf. Fr. *tendrillon*, shoot.]

tendron *ten'drən, n.* a shoot, sprout: (in *pl.*) cartilages of the ribs. [Fr.]

tene. See **teen¹.**

tenebrae *ten'i-brē,* L. *ten'e-brī, n.pl.* (*R.C.*; also with *cap.*) matins and lauds in Holy Week with gradual extinction of lights. — *adj.* **tenebrif'ic** (L. *facĕre*, to make) producing darkness. — *n.* **tenebrio** (*tin-eb'ri-ō*) a night-spirit: a night-prowler: (*cap.*) the meal-worm genus of beetles, giving name to the family **Tenebrionidae** (*-on'i-dē*): — *pl.* **teneb'rios.** — *adj.* **teneb'rious** dark — *ns.* **ten'ebrism** the naturalist school of painting of Caravaggio affecting dark colouring; **ten'ebrist; teneb'-rity.** — *adjs.* **ten'ebrose, ten'ebrous** dark. — *n.* **tene-bros'ity.** [L. *tenebrae*, darkness.]

tenement *ten'i-mənt, n.* a holding, by any tenure: anything held, or that may be held, by a tenant: a dwelling or habitation, or part of it, used by one family: one of a set of apartments in one building, each occupied by a separate family: a building divided into dwellings for a number of families (*Scot.*). — *adjs.* **tenemental** (*-ment'l*); **tenement'ary.** [L.L. *tenementum* — L. *tenēre*, to hold.]

tenendum *ti-nen'dəm, n.* that clause in a deed wherein the tenure of the land is defined and limited. [L. neut. of *tenendus*, ger. of *tenēre*, to hold.]

tenesmus *ti-nes'məs, n.* painful and ineffectual straining to relieve the bowels. [Latinised from Gr. *teinesmos* — *teinein*, to strain.]

tenet *ten'et* (also *tē'nit*) *n.* any opinion, principle, or doctrine which a person holds or maintains as true. [L. *tenet,* (he) holds — *tenēre,* to hold.]

tenfold. See **ten.**

tenia, tenioid, etc. Variant spellings of **taenia, taenioid,** etc.

tennantite *ten'ənt-īt, n.* a mineral composed of sulphur, arsenic, and copper, usu. with iron. [Named after Smithson *Tennant* (1761–1815), English chemist.]

tenné *ten'ā,* (*her.*) *n.* an orange-brown tincture. — Also *adj.* [Obs. Fr.; cf. **tawny.**]

tenner. See **ten.**

tennis *ten'is, n.* an ancient game played with ball, rackets (orig. palms of the hands), and net, in a specially constructed building or enclosed court (distinguished from lawn-tennis as **close, court, real,** or **royal** tennis): now usu. lawn-tennis. — **tenn'is-ball; tenn'is-court; tennis elbow** inflammation of the bursa at the elbow, caused by over-exercise; **tenn'is-match; tenn'is-player; tenn'is-racket; tenn'is-shoe.** — **short tennis** a version of tennis for children, played with a foam rubber ball on a small court. [Prob. Fr. *tenez,* (A.Fr. *tenetz*) imper. of *tenir,* to take, receive.]

tenon *ten'ən, n.* a projection at the end of a piece of wood, etc., inserted into the socket or mortise of another, to hold the two together. — *v.t.* to fix or fit with a tenon. — *n.* **ten'oner.** — **ten'on-saw** a thin back-saw for tenons, etc. [Fr. *tenon* — *tenir,* to hold — L. *tenēre.*]

tenor (*obs.* or *old-fashioned* **tenour**) *ten'ər, n.* continuity of state: general run or course: time of currency: purport: an exact transcript: the higher of the two kinds of voices usu. belonging to adult males (app. because the melody was assigned to it): an instrument, e.g. the viola, of corresponding compass: the part next above the bass in a vocal quartet: one who sings tenor. — Also *adj.* — *ns.* **ten'orist; tenoroon'** an obsolete tenor oboe. — **ten'or-clef'** the C clef placed on the fourth line. [L. *tenor* — *tenēre,* to hold.]

tenorite *ten'ər-īt, n.* melaconite, black copper ore (CuO), found on Vesuvius. [Named after G. *Tenore,* President of the Naples Academy, 1841.]

tenosynovitis. See **tendon.**

tenotomy *tən-ot'əm-i, n.* surgical cutting of a tendon. [Gr. *tenōn,* tendon, *tomē,* a cut.]

tenour. See **tenor.**

tenpence, etc. See **ten.**

tenrec *ten'rek,* **tanrec** *tan'rek, ns.* a large Madagascan insectivore (*Centetes*). [Malagasy *t(r)àndraka.*]

tense¹ *tens, n.* time in grammar, the form of a verb to indicate the time of the action. [O.Fr. *tens* (Fr. *temps*) — L. *tempus,* time.]

tense² *tens, adj.* stretched tight: strained: rigid: pronounced with the tongue tightened or narrowed. — *v.t.* and *v.i.* to make or become tense. — *adv.* **tense'ly.** — *ns.* **tense'ness** state of being tense; **tensibil'ity.** — *adjs.* **tens'ible** capable of being stretched; **tens'ile** (*īl;* in U.S. *-il, -əl*) tensible: in relation to stretching. — *ns.* **tensility** (*-il'i-ti*); **tensiom'eter** an instrument for measuring tension, tensile strength, the moisture content of soil; **tensiom'etry** the branch of physics relating to tension, tensile strength, etc.; **tension** (*ten'shən*) stretching: a pulling strain: stretched or strained state: strain generally: formerly, pressure in gases or vapours: electromotive force: a state of barely suppressed emotion, as excitement, suspense, anxiety, or hostility: a feeling of strain with resultant symptoms (*psych.*): strained relations (between persons): opposition (between conflicting ideas or forces); **tens'ity** tenseness. — *adj.* **tens'ive** giving the sensation of tenseness or stiffness. — *n.* **tens'or** a muscle that tightens a part: a mathematical or physical entity represented by components which depend in a special way on the choice of a coordinate system. — **tensile strength** the strength of a material when being stretched, expressed as the greatest stress it can resist before breaking; **ten'sion-rod** a structural member subjected to tensile stress only. [L. *tēnsus,* pa.p. of *tendĕre,* to stretch.]

tenson *ten'sn, n.* a competition in verse between two troubadours before a court of love: a subdivision of the chanson so composed. — Also **ten'zon.** [Fr., — L. *tēnsiō, -ōnis,* a struggle.]

tensor. See **tense².**

tent *tent, n.* a portable lodge or shelter, commonly of canvas stretched on poles: a temporary field pulpit: a common shelter spun by a company of caterpillars. — *v.i.* to camp in a tent. — *v.t.* to canopy: to lodge in tents. — *n.* **tent'age** tents collectively: material for making tents. — *adj.* **ten'ted** covered with tents: formed like a tent: dwelling in tents. — *ns.* **tent'er** one who lives in a tent; **tent'ful** as many as a tent will hold; **tent'ing.** — *adj.* (*Keats*) having the form of a tent. — *adv.* **tent'wise.** — **tent'-bed** a camp-bed, a bed with a canopy hanging from a central point; **tent coat, dress** etc., one shaped like a circular tent, narrow at the shoulders and wide at the hem; **tent'-cloth** cloth suitable for tents; **tent'-fly** a flap forming a door to a tent: a subsidiary outer roof to a tent; **tent'-guy** a stay or guy-rope for a tent; **tent'-maker; tent'-peg, -pin** a strong notched peg driven into the ground to fasten a tent; **tent'-pegging** the sport of riding at full speed and trying to bear off a tent-peg on the point of a lance; **tent'-pole** a pole to support a tent; **tent'-preaching** open-air preaching; **tent'-rope** a rope for securing a tent to a peg. [Fr. *tente* — L. *tendĕre, tentum,* to stretch.]

tent² *tent, n.* a probe (*obs.*): a plug or roll of soft material for dilating a wound or keeping open an orifice. — *v.t.* to probe (*obs.*): to dilate or keep open with a tent. [Fr. *tente* — L. *tentāre,* to try.]

tent³ *tent, n.* a deep-red Spanish wine. [Sp. *tinto* — L. *tinctus,* pa.p. of *tingĕre,* to dye.]

tent⁴ *tent,* (*Scot.*) *n.* heed. — *v.t.* to take heed or notice of, attend to. — *n.* **tent'er** one who tends, esp. to a machine. — *adj.* **tent'ie, tent'y.** [Aphetic for **attent** and **intent.**]

tent⁵ *tent, n.* (*obs.*) an embroidery or tapestry frame. —

tent stitch an embroidery stitch made in parallel series diagonally to the threads: tent-work; **tent'-work** work in tent-stitch. [Origin obscure; cf. M.E. *tent*, to stretch, **tenter**[1], and L. *tendēre, tentum*.]

tentacle *tent'ə-kl*, *n.* a slender flexible organ for feeling, grasping, etc.: a gland-tipped insect-capturing process in sundew. — Also **tentaculum** (*-ak'ū-ləm*; *pl.* **tentac'-ūla**). — *adjs.* **ten'tacled; tentac'ular; tentac'ūlate; ten-tacūlif'erous.** — *n.* **tentac'ūlite** a ringed tapering Silurian and Devonian fossil, app. a pteropod. [L. *tentāre*, to feel.]

tentation *ten-tā'shən*, *n.* an old form of **temptation**: a method of adjusting by a succession of trials. — *adj.* **tentative** (*ten'tə-tiv*) done or made provisionally and experimentally. — *n.* an experimental attempt. — *adv.* **ten'tatively.** [L. *tentāre*, to try.]

tenter[1] *ten'tər*, *n.* a frame for stretching cloth: a tenter-hook: a hook. — *v.t.* to stretch on hooks. — **ten'ter-hook** a sharp, hooked nail as on a tenter: a hook. — **on tenter-hooks** in impatient suspense. [App. conn. with Fr. *tenture*, hangings, and L. *tendēre*, to stretch.]

tenter[2]. See **tent**[1,4].

tenth. See **ten.**

tentie. See **tent**[4].

tentigo *ten-tī'gō*, *n.* priapism: morbid lasciviousness. — *adj.* **tentiginous** (*-tij'i-nəs*). [L. *tentīgō, -inis* — *tendēre*, to stretch.]

tentorium *ten-tō'ri-əm, -tō'*, *n.* a sheet of the dura mater stretched between the cerebrum and the cerebellum: the internal chitinous skeleton of an insect's head. — *adj.* **tento'rial.** [L. *tentōrium*, a tent — *tendēre*, to stretch.]

tenty. See **tent**[4].

tenue *tə-nü*, *n.* bearing, carriage: manner of dress. [Fr.]

tenuis *ten'ū-is*, L. *-ōō-is*, *n.* an unaspirated voiceless stop consonant — *pl.* **ten'ues** (*-ēz, -ās*). — *adj.* **tenuiros'tral** (L. *rōstrum*, bill) slender-billed. — *n.* **tenū'ity** thinness: slenderness: rarity. — *adj.* **tenū'ous** (*rarely* **tenū'ious**) thin: slender: rarefied. — *adv.* **ten'uously.** — *n.* **ten'u-ousness.** [L. *tenuis*, thin; cf. *tendēre*, to stretch.]

tenure[1] *ten'yər*, *n.* holding, occupation: time of holding: the holding of an appointment in a university or college for an assured length of time: conditions on which property is held: a tenant's rights, duties, etc. — *adjs.* **ten'urable** of a university post, giving tenure; **tenūr'ial.** [A.Fr. *tenure* — *tenir*, to hold.]

tenure[2] (*Shak.*) for **tenor.**

tenuto *te-nōō'tō*, (*mus.*) *adj.* sustained. [It., pa.p. of *tenere*, to hold.]

tenzon. See **tenson.**

teocalli *tā, tē-ō-kal'(y)i*, *n.* a Mexican pyramid temple. [Nahuatl, — *teotl*, god, *calli*, house.]

teosinte *tē-ō-sin'ti*, *n.* a tall grass akin to maize, a native of the southern U.S. and Mexico, often used as a fodder crop. [Nahuatl, — *teotl*, god, *centli*, ear of corn.]

tepal *tē'pəl, te'pəl*, (*bot.*) *n.* one of the members of a perianth that is not clearly differentiated into a calyx and a corolla. [Fr. *tépale*, changed from *pétale, petal*, influenced by *sépale*, sepal.]

tepee, teepee *tē'pē, ti-pē'*, *n.* an American Indian tent formed of skins, etc., stretched over a frame of converging poles. [Sioux *tīpī*, dwelling.]

tepefy *tep'i-fī*, *v.t.* and *v.i.* to make or become tepid. [L. *tepefacēre* — *tepēre*, to be tepid, *facēre*, to make.]

tephigram *tē'fi-gram*, *n.* (*meteor.*) a diagram on which is plotted information about vertical variation of atmospheric conditions. [*t*, for temperature, *phi*, former symbol for entropy.]

tephra *tef'ra*, *n.* ash and debris ejected by a volcano. [Gr. *tephrā*, ashes.]

tephrite *tef'rīt*, *n.* a fine-grained basaltic rock containing a feldspathoid as well as feldspar, but no olivine. — *adj.* **tephritic** (*-rit'ik*). — *ns.* **teph'roite** (*-rō-īt*) an ashy-grey or reddish silicate of manganese; **teph'romancy** divination (Gr. *manteiā*) by ashes, esp. of sacrifice. [Gr. *tephrā*, ashes, *tephros*, ash-coloured.]

tepid *tep'id*, *adj.* moderately warm: lukewarm. — *ns.* **tepidā'rium** (L. *-dä'ri-ōōm*) a warm room between the cold and hot rooms of a Roman bath; **tepid'ity** luke-warmness. — *adv.* **tep'idly.** — *n.* **tep'idness.** [L. *tepidus* — *tepēre*, to be warm.]

tequila, tequilla *tə-kē'lə*, *n.* Mexican intoxicating drink made with an agave. [From district of Mexico.]

ter- *tûr-*, in composition, thrice. — *adj.* **tercentenary** (*tûr'sən-tē'nə-ri*, or *-ten'ə-ri*, or *tûr-sen'ti-nə-ri*) of three hundred (usu. years). — *n.* a 300th anniversary. — *adj.* **tercentennial** (*tûr-sen-ten'yəl*) of 300 years. — *n.* a 300th anniversary. — *n.* **tersanctus** (*tûr-sang(k)'təs*) the Sanctus. — *adj.* **tervalent** (*tûr'və-lənt, tər-vā'lənt*) trivalent. [L.]

tera- *ter'ə-*, *pfx.* ten to the twelfth power, formerly **megamega-**, as in *terawatt*.

terai *ter-ī'*, *n.* a wide-brimmed double-crowned ventilated hat, first worn in the *Terai* (Tarái), India.

terakihi. See **tarakihi.**

teraph *ter'əf*, *n.* in ancient Jewish religion and divination, an image of some sort — *pl.* **ter'aphim** (also used as *sing.*). [Heb.]

teras *ter'əs*, (*med.*) *n.* a monstrosity: — *pl.* **ter'ata.** — *n.* **ter'atism** a monster: an abnormal person or animal, esp. as a foetus. — *adj.* **teratogenic** (*ter-ə-tō-jen'ik*) producing monsters: causing abnormal growth (in a foetus). — *ns.* **terat'ogen** an agent that raises the incidence of congenital malformations; **teratogeny** (*-toj'i-ni*) the production of monsters. — *adjs.* **ter'atoid** monstrous; **teratolog'ic, -al.** — *ns.* **teratol'ogist; tera-tol'ogy** the study of malformations or abnormal growths, animal or vegetable: a tale of marvels; **teratō'ma** a tumour, containing tissue from all three germ-layers: — *pl.* **teratō'mata.** — *adj.* **teratō'matous.** [Gr. *teras, -atos*, a monster.]

terbium *tûr'bi-əm*, *n.* a rare metal (symbol Tb; at. numb. 65) found in certain yttrium minerals. — *adj.* **ter'bic.** [From *Ytterby*; see **yttrium**.]

terce *tûrs*, *n.* a widow's right, where she has no conventional provision, to a life-rent of a third of the husband's heritable property (*Scots law*): the office of the third hour (*hist.*). [See **tierce**.]

tercel *tûrs'əl*, **tiercel** *tēr'səl*, **tarcel, tarsal, tarsel** *tärs'əl*, **tassel(l)** *tas'əl*, *ns.* a male hawk. — *ns.* **terc'elet, tierc'-elet** a tercel. — **ter'cel-gent'le** (*Scott*), **tass'el-gent'le** (*Shak.*), **tass'ell-gent'** (*Spens.*) a male peregrine falcon; **ter'cel-jer'kin** a male gerfalcon. [OFr. *tercel* — L. *tertius*, third, perh. as being one-third smaller than the female, or as supposed to hatch from the last egg of three.]

tercentenary, tercentennial. See **ter-.**

tercet *tûr'sit*, *n.* a group of three lines in verse. [It. *terzetto*.]

tercio *tûr'si-ō, -shi-ō* (*Scott* **tertia**), (*hist.*) *n.* an infantry regiment, orig. Spanish: — *pl.* **ter'cios.** [Sp.]

terebene *ter'i-bēn*, *n.* a light-yellow disinfectant liquid, a mixture of hydrocarbons made from oil of turpentine, used as a solvent for paint. — *n.* **ter'ebinth** the turpentine-tree (*Pistacia terebinthus*; family Anacardiaceae). — *adj.* **terebinth'ine** of or relating to the terebinth: of, relating to, resembling turpentine. [Gr. *terebinthos*.]

terebra *ter'i-bra*, *n.* a Roman engine for boring walls: a boring instrument: a piercing ovipositor: (with *cap.*) a genus of gasteropods with auger-shaped shell. — *pl.* **ter'ebras, ter'ebrae** (*-e*). — *adj.* **ter'ebrant** boring: having a piercing ovipositor. — *n.* (*facet.*) a bore. — *v.t.* and *v.i.* **ter'ebrate** to bore. — *adj.* having scattered perforations: having a borer. — *ns.* **terebrā'tion; Ter-ebrat'ūla** the lamp-shell genus of brachiopods, with perforated beak: (without *cap.*) a member of this genus: — *pl.* **terebrat'ūlas, -ae** (*-ē*). [L. *terebra*.]

Teredo *te-rē'dō*, *n.* the ship-worm genus of molluscs: (without *cap.*) a mollusc of the genus: — *pl.* **terē'dos, -dines** (*-din-ēz*). [L. *terēdō, inis* — Gr. *terēdōn, -onos*, a boring worm — root of *teirein*, to wear away.]

terefa(h) *tə-rā-fä', -rä'*, *adj.* not ritually clean, not kosher. [Heb. *tāraph*, to tear.]

terek *ter'ek, n.* a sandpiper (*Xenus cinereus*) found at the river *Terek* (Russia) and elsewhere (also **Terek sandpiper**).

Terentian *ter-en'shən, -shyən, adj.* pertaining to the Roman comic poet *Terence,* P. Terentius Afer (fl. 165 B.C.).

terephthalic acid *ter-ef-thal'ik a'sid,* a chemical widely used in the manufacture of synthetic, esp. polyester, fibres. [*terebene, phthalic.*]

terete *tə-rēt', ter'ēt,* (*biol.*) *adj.* smooth and cylindrical. [L. *terēs, terĕtis,* smooth, *terĕre,* to rub.]

terf, terfe. Milton's spellings of **turf.**

tergum *tûr'gəm, n.* the back: the back or back plate of a somite. — *adj.* **ter'gal.** — *n.* **ter'gite** (*-jīt*) the back plate of a somite. — *v.i.* **ter'giversate** (*-ji-*; L. *versārī,* to turn) to turn one's back: to desert, apostatise: to shuffle, shift, use evasions. — *ns.* **tergiversā'tion; ter'giversātor.** [L. *tergum,* the back.]

teriyaki *ter-i-yäk'i, n.* and *adj.* in Japanese cookery, (a dish of meat or shellfish) marinated in a soy sauce and grilled or broiled. [Jap. *teri,* sunshine, *yaki,* roast, broiled.]

term *tûrm, n.* a limit, boundary (*arch.*): an end: a term-day: the normal time of childbirth: any limited period: the time for which anything lasts: a division of the academic or school year: a period of sittings: (in *pl.*) conditions, stipulations: (in *pl.*) a footing: (in *pl.*) charge, fee: (in *pl.*) respect (*Shak.*): a quantity added to or subtracted from others in an expression (*alg.*): an item in a series: that which may be a subject or predicate of a proposition: a word used in a specially understood or defined sense: an expression generally: a bust in continuity with its pedestal. — *v.t.* to call, designate. — *n.* **term'er** one who came to town in term (*hist.*): a termor (*obs.*). — *adj.* **term'less** endless: inexpressible (*Shak.*): unconditional. — *adj.* and *adv.* **term'ly.** — *n.* a publication appearing once a term. — *n.* **term'or,** (*obs.*) **term'er** one who holds an estate for a term of years or for life. — **term'-day** a day of the year fixed for some purpose, as payment of rent, beginning or end of a tenancy, hiring of servants, household removals; **term'-time.** — **bring to terms** compel to the acceptance of conditions; **come to terms** to come to an agreement: to submit; **come to terms with** (*fig.*) to find a way of living with (some personal trouble or difficulty); **eat one's terms** see **eat; in terms** in so many words, explicitly: engaged in negotiations; **in terms of** having or using as unit: in the language peculiar to; **keep a term** to give the regular attendance during a period of study; **long, short termer** a person serving a long, short prison sentence; **on speaking terms** friendly enough to speak to each other: well enough acquainted to speak; **on terms** in friendly relations: on an equal footing; **stand upon terms** to insist upon conditions; **term of art** a term having a special meaning in a certain art, craft, etc., a technical term; **term of years** an interest or estate in land for a period; **terms of reference** see **refer; terms of trade** relation between export and import prices in national accounts. [Fr. *terme* — L. *terminus,* a boundary.]

termagant *tûr'mə-gənt, n.* a boisterous brawler or bully, esp. a woman. — *adj.* boisterous: brawling. — *n.* **ter'magancy.** — *adv.* **ter'magantly.** [M.E. *Termagan* or *Tervagant,* a supposed Muslim idol, represented in the old plays and moralities as of a violent character.]

termer. See **term.**

Termes *tûr'mēz, n.* a genus of termites. [L. *termes, -itis,* a wood-worm.]

Terminus *tûr'min-əs, n.* the Roman god of boundaries: (the following meanings without *cap.*) a term (bust) of Terminus, or other: a boundary stone: an end-point, esp. of a route, railway or electric circuit: a railway station at such a point: — *pl.* **ter'mini** (*-ī*). — *n.* **terminabil'ity.** — *adj.* **ter'minable** that may come or be brought to an end. — *n.* **ter'minableness.** — *adv.* **ter'minably.** — *adj.* **ter'minal** of, at, forming, or marking, an end, boundary, or terminus: final: on the

terminal market: suffering from a terminal illness: of a term: occurring every term. — *n.* an end: an ending: a rail, air, or other terminus: the storage base and distribution centre at the head of e.g. an oil pipe-line: a free end in an open electric circuit: a device linked to a computer and at a distance from it, by which the computer can be operated (also **terminal unit**). — *n.pl.* **Terminā'lia** an annual Roman festival in honour of Terminus. — *n.sing.* the myrobalan genus of Combretaceae. — *adv.* **ter'minally.** — *v.t.* and *v.i.* (often with *with* or *in*) **ter'minate.** — *n.* **terminā'tion** ending. — *adjs.* **terminā'tional; ter'minative** tending to terminate or determine: expressive of completion: definitive: absolute. — *adv.* **ter'minatively.** — *n.* **ter'minātor** one who or that which, terminates: the boundary between the illuminated and dark portions of the moon or of a planet. — *adj.* **ter'minatory.** — *ns.* **ter'miner** (*law*) the act of determining; **ter'minism** nominalism (*philos.*): the doctrine that there is a time limit for the operation of grace (*theol.*); **ter'minist.** — *adj.* **terminolog'ical.** — *adv.* **terminolog'ically.** — *n.* **terminol'ogy** nomenclature: the set of terms used in any art, science, etc. — **terminal guidance** a system for guiding sub-units of a missile warhead towards multiple targets near the end of the missile's flight; **terminal illness** a fatal disease in its final stages; **terminal market** in finance, the central market in London for dealing in general commodities; **terminal unit** see **terminal** above; **terminal velocity** speed of object on impact with a target: the greatest speed attained by an object falling or fired through a fluid; **terminological inexactitude** (*facet.*) a lie. [L. *Terminus, terminus;* cf. Gr. *terma,* end.]

terminus *tûr'min-əs, ter'min-ōōs* (L.), *n.* the end, limit. — **terminus ad quem** (*ad kwem*) the limit to which: destination; **terminus a quo** (*ä kwō*) the limit from which: starting-point.

termite *tûr'mīt, n.* a so-called white-ant, a pale-coloured insect of the Isoptera, only superficially like an ant. — *ns.* **termitarium** (*tûr-mi-tā'ri-əm*), **ter'mitary** (*-tər-i-*) a nest or mound of termites. [L. *termes, termitis,* a wood-worm.]

termly, termor. See **term.**

tern[1] *tûrn, n.* a long-winged aquatic bird allied to the gulls. [Cf. O.N. *therna;* O.E. *stearn, tearn.*]

tern[2] *tûrn, n.* a three, set of three: a prize for drawing three winning numbers: a three-masted schooner. — *adjs.* **ter'nal** threefold; **ter'nary** in threes: of three components: based on three: of a third order. — *n.* (*obs.*) a triad. — *adj.* **ter'nate** with three leaflets (*bot.*): grouped in threes. — *adv.* **ter'nately.** — *n.* **ter'nion** a triad: a section of paper for a book containing three double leaves or twelve pages. — **ternary form** (*mus.*) a structure in which a first subject is followed by a second and then a repetition of the first. [L. *ternī,* three each — *trēs,* three.]

terne *tûrn, n.* an alloy, chiefly of lead and tin, known as **terne metal:** sheet-iron or steel coated with this alloy (also **terne plate**). — *v.t.* **terne** to cover with terne metal. [Fr. *terne,* dull.]

ternion. See **tern**[2].

Ternstroemiaceae *tûrn-strēm-i-ā'shi-ē, n.pl.* the Theaceae or tea family of plants. [From a genus *Ternstroemia,* named after Christopher *Ternström,* Swedish naturalist.]

terotechnology *ter'ō-tek-nol'ə-ji, n.* the application of managerial, financial, engineering and other skills to extend the operational life of, and increase the efficiency of, equipment and machinery. [Gr. *tereo,* to watch, observe, and **technology.**]

terpene *tûr'pēn, n.* any one of a group of hydrocarbons with a composition $C_{10}H_{16}$. — *ns.* **ter'penoid** any of a group of substances having a structure like that of terpene; **terpin'eol** a terpene alcohol used extensively as a perfume base. [**turpentine.**]

Terpsichore *tərp-sik'ə-rē, n.* the Muse of choral song and dance. — *adj.* **terpsichorē'an** relating to dancing. [Gr.

Terpsichorē — *terpsis*, delight — *terpein*, to enjoy, *choros*, dance.]

terra *ter'ə, n.* the Latin and Italian word for earth: any area of higher land on the moon's surface: — *pl.* **terr'ae** (*-ē*). — *adj.* **terraqueous** (*ter-ā'kwi-əs*; L. *aqua*, water) of land and water. — *n.* **terrā'rium** a vivarium for land animals or, usu. in the form of a large, often sealed, bottle or the like, for plants: — *pl.* **-iums, -ia.** — **terra alba** (*al'bə*; L., white) any of various white, earth-like substances such as gypsum, kaolin, pipeclay, etc.; **terr'acott'a** (It. *cotta* — L. *cocta*, fem., baked) a composition of clay and sand used for statues, etc., and, esp. formerly, as building material for facings, etc.: an object of art made of it: its colour, a brownish red. — Also *adj.* — **terr'a-fir'ma** properly, mainland: (*coll.* and *erroneously*) dry land; **terra ignota, terra incognita** see separate article; **terr'a-japon'ica** pale catechu or gambier; **terr'ama'ra** (*pl.* **-re -rā**; It. dial. for *terra marna*, marl-earth) a dark earthy deposit formed under prehistoric pile-dwellings in Italy; **terra nullius** (L., nobody's land) land that is not part of the sovereign territory of any country; **terr'a-ross'a** (It. *rossa*, fem., red) a ferruginous red earth, the residue of the weathering of limestone; **terra sigillata** (*sij-i-lä'tə*, L. *sig-i-lä'ta*, sealed earth) Lemnian earth.

terrace *ter'is, n.* a raised level bank or walk: a level stretch along the side or top of a slope: ground or a structure that rises stepwise: a gallery open at the side: a balcony: a flat roof-top: a connected row of houses, properly one overlooking a slope: the open areas rising in tiers around a football stadium, where spectators stand: a defective spot in marble. — *v.t.* to form into a terrace. — *adj.* **terr'aced** in terraces. — *n.* **terr'acing.** — **terrace(d) house** one of the houses forming a terrace. [Fr. *terrasse* — It. *terrazza* — L.L. *terrācea*, an earthen mound — L. *terra*, the earth.]

terracotta. See **terra.**

terrae filius *ter'ē fil'i-əs, ter'ī fēl'i-ōos,* (L.) a son of the soil: a person of humble birth.

terrain¹ *ter'ān,* or *-ān', n.* ground, a tract, regarded as a field of view or of operations, or as having some sort of unity or prevailing character. [Fr., from a L.L. form of *terrēnum,* terrene.]

terrain². See **terrane.**

terra incognita *ter'ə, -a, in-kog'ni-tə, -ta,* (L.) an unknown country. — Also **terra ignota.**

terramara. See **terra.**

Terramycin® *ter-ə-mī'sin, n.* an antibiotic effective against a wide range of bacteria and a few Rickettsiae viruses, and protozoan parasites. [L. *terra,* the earth, and Gr. *mykēs,* fungus.]

Terran *ter'ən, n.* a term sometimes used in science fiction for an inhabitant of the planet earth. [L. *terra,* earth.]

terrane *ter'ān* (*geol.*), *n.* a rock formation, or series of connected formations (also **terrain**). [See **terrain¹.**]

terrapin *ter'ə-pin, n.* an American freshwater or brackish-water tortoise of many kinds: extended to European water tortoises. [Of Algonquin origin.]

terraqueous, terrarium. See **terra.**

terras. See **trass.**

terrazzo *te-rat'sō, -raz'ō, n.* a mosaic covering (sometimes precast) for concrete floors consisting of marble or other chips set in cement and then polished: — *pl.* **terrazz'os.** — Also called **Venetian mosaic.** [It., terrace, balcony.]

terreen. An older spelling of **tureen.**

terrella *ter-el'ə, n.* a magnetic model of the earth. [A mod. dim. of L. *terra,* the earth.]

terremotive *ter-i-mō'tiv, adj.* seismic. [L. *terrae motus,* earthquake.]

terrene *ti-rēn', ter'ēn, adj.* of the earth: earthly: mundane: earthy: terrestrial. — *n.* the world: a region, terrain. — *adv.* **terrene'ly.** [L. *terrēnus* — *terra,* the earth.]

terreplein *ter', tār'plān, n.* orig. the talus on the inner side of a rampart: the top of a rampart, or space behind the parapet. [Fr., — L. *terra,* earth, *plēnus,* full.]

terrestrial *ti-res'tri-əl, adj.* of, or existing on, the earth: earthly: living or growing on land or on the ground: representing the earth. — *n.* a dweller on earth: a man of the world, layman (*Shak.*). — *adv.* **terres'trially.** — **terrestrial telescope** a telescope giving an erect image, used for viewing over distances on the earth's surface rather than astronomically. [L. *terrestris* — *terra,* the earth.]

terret, territ *ter'it, n.* a swivel-ring: a ring for fastening a chain to: a ring or loop through which driving reins pass. — Also **torr'et, turr'et.** [O.Fr. *toret,* dim. of *tor, tour,* a round.]

terre verte *ter vert,* green carth (see **green¹**). [Fr.]

terrible *ter'i-bl, adj.* fitted to excite terror or awe: awful: dreadful: very bad: very notable, exceeding (*coll.*). — *n.* a terrible thing. — *ns.* **terribil'ity** (*rare*); **terr'ibleness.** — *adv.* **terr'ibly** in a terrible manner: very (*coll.*). [L. *terribilis* — *terrēre,* to frighten.]

terricolous *ter-ik'ə-ləs, adj.* living in or on the soil. — *n.* **terr'icole** (*-i-kōl*) a land animal or plant: a burrower. — Also *adj.* [L. *terricola,* a dweller upon earth — *terra,* earth, *colĕre,* to inhabit.]

terrier *ter'i-ər, n.* a small dog of various breeds, orig. one that would follow burrowing animals underground: (*punningly*) a territorial soldier: one who hunts after criminals (*fig.*): a register or roll of a landed estate: an inventory. [O.Fr., — L.L. *terrārius* (adj.) — *terra,* land.]

terrify *ter'i-fī, v.t.* to cause terror in: to frighten greatly: — *pr.p.* **terr'ifying;** *pa.t.* and *pa.p.* **terr'ified.** — *adj.* **terrif'ic** creating or causing terror: fitted to terrify: dreadful: prodigious (*coll.*): (*loosely*) very good, enjoyable, attractive, etc. (*coll.*). — *adv.* **terrif'ically.** [L. *terrificāre* — *terrēre,* to terrify, *facĕre,* to make.]

terrigenous *te-rij'i-nəs, adj.* earth-born: derived from the land. [L. *terrigenus* — *terra,* earth, *genĕre* (*gignĕre*), to produce.]

terrine *te-rēn', n.* a casserole, etc., orig. of earthenware: a dish of meat or fish, etc., cooked in it: an earthenware jar sold containing a table delicacy: a tureen. [Fr.; see **tureen.**]

territ. See **terret.**

territory *ter'i-tər-i, n.* possessions in land: the whole, or a portion, of the land belonging to a state: part of a confederation with an organised government but not yet admitted to statehood: a dependency: a region: a jurisdiction: a field of activity (*lit.* and *fig.*): domain: an area that an animal or bird treats as its own. — *adj.* **territo'rial.** — *n.* a soldier in the Territorial Army. — *v.t.* **territo'rialise, -ize** to make a territory of: to make territorial: to put on a territorial basis. — *ns.* **territo'rialism** landlordism: organisation on a territorial basis: the theory of church government according to which the civil power is supreme over the church; **territō'rialist; territorial'ity.** — *adv.* **territo'rially.** — *adj.* **terr'itoried** possessed of territory. — **Territorial Army** the name (1920–67, and from 1980) of the voluntary military force organised on a territorial basis, founded in 1908 as the **Territorial Force,** and known (1967–80) as the **Territorial and Army Volunteer Reserve; territorial imperative** the instinct, in vertebrate animals, to occupy and defend a particular area; **territorial waters** that part of the sea reckoned as part of the adjacent state — orig. within three-mile limit. [L. *territōrium,* domain of a town, perh. not orig. conn. with *terra.*]

terror *ter'ər, n.* extreme fear: a time of, or government by, terrorism: an object of dread: one who makes himself a nuisance (*coll.*). — *n.* **terrorīsā'tion, -z-.** — *v.t.* **terr'orise, -ize** to terrify: to govern by terror. — *ns.* **terr'oriser, -z-; terr'orism** an organised system of intimidation, esp. for political ends; **terr'orist.** — *adjs.* **terrorist'ic; terr'orless.** — **terror novel** a novel full of supernatural horrors. — *adj.* **terr'or-stricken** smitten with terror. — **King of Terrors** death; **Reign of Terror,** or **the Terror,** the period of fever in the first French Revolution when thousands went to the guillotine.

[L. *terror* — *terrēre*, to frighten.]

terry *ter'i, n.* a pile fabric with uncut looped pile: one of the loops. — Also *adj.* [Origin unknown.]

tersanctus. See **ter-**.

terse *tûrs, adj.* smooth, clean-cut (*obs.*): compact or concise. — *adv.* **terse'ly.** — *ns.* **terse'ness; tersion** (*tûr'shən*) wiping. [L. *tersus* — *tergēre, tersum*, to rub clean.]

tertia. See **tercio**.

tertial *tûr'shl, adj.* of the third rank among flight-feathers of a wing. — *n.* a tertiary flight-feather. — *adj.* **ter'tian** (*-shən*) occurring every other day (i.e. on the *third* day, reckoning both first and last days). — *n.* a fever with paroxysms every other day. — *adj.* **ter'tiary** (*-shər-i*) of the third degree, order, or formation: tertial (*ornith.*): (with *cap.*) of the third great division of the geological record and time, including Eocene, Oligocene, Miocene, Pliocene: ranking above secondary (esp. of education). — *n.* the Tertiary period: (without *cap.*) a member of a third order of a monastic order, a layman who may continue to live an ordinary life in the world: a tertiary feather: that which is tertiary. — **tertiary college** a college, esp. one with vocational courses, for the teaching of sixth-form level students. [L. *tertiālis, tertiānus, tertiārius* — *tertius*, third.]

tertium quid (L.) *tûr'sh(y)əm kwid, ter'ti-ōōm,* a third something related to two specific known things: something intermediate between opposites: the third person in the eternal triangle.

tertius *tûr'sh(y)əs, ter'ti-ōōs,* (L.) *adj.* and *n.* third (person). — **tertius gaudens** (*gö'denz, gow'dāns*) or **gaudet** (*gö'det, gow'*) the third person (who) takes advantage from a dispute between others.

terts *tûrts, n.sing.* tetrachlor(o)ethylene.

teru-tero *ter'ōō-ter'ō, n.* the Cayenne lapwing: — *pl.* **ter'u-ter'os.**

tervalent. See **ter-**.

Terylene® *ter'i-lēn, n.* a synthetic fabric of polyester fibres, light, strong and crease-resistant.

terza rima *ter'tsə rē'mə,* an Italian verse-form in triplets, in which the middle line of each triplet rhymes with the first and third lines of the next with an odd line to end off the canto: — *pl.* **terze rime** (*ter'tsā rē'mā*). [It., third rhyme.]

terzetta *ter-tset'ə, n.* a tercet. — *n.* **terzett'o** a trio: — *pl.* **terzett'ōs, terzett'i** (*-ē*). [It.]

teschenite *tesh'ən-īt, n.* a coarse-grained basic igneous rock composed essentially of plagioclase and augite, usu. with much analcime. [Found near *Teschen*.]

tesla *tes'lə, n.* the unit of magnetic flux density, equal to 1 weber per sq. metre. — **tesla coil** (*elect.*) a simple source of high voltage oscillations for rough testing of vacuums and gas (by discharge colour) in vacuum systems. [N. *Tesla*, U.S. inventor.]

tessara-, tessera- *tes'ə-rə-,* in composition, four. — *n.* **tess'eract** (Gr. *aktis*, ray) a figure of a cube within a cube. — *adj.* **tess'araglot** (Gr. *glōtta*, tongue) in four languages. [Gr. *tessares*, four.]

tessella *tes-el'ə, n.* a little tessera: — *pl.* **tessell'ae** (*-ē;* L. *-ī*). — *adj.* **tess'ellar.** — *v.t.* **tessellate** (*tes'i-lāt*) to pave with tesserae: to mark like a mosaic. — *v.i.* (of a number of identical shapes) to fit together exactly, leaving no spaces. — *adj.* **tess'ellated.** — *n.* **tessellā'tion.** [L. *tessella*, dim. of *tessera;* see next.]

tessera *tes'ə-rə, n.* one of the small pieces of which a mosaic is made: a token or ticket: password: — *pl.* **tess'erae** (*-ē;* L. *-ī*). — **tessera-** in composition, **tesser-act**, see **tessara-**. — *adj.* **tess'eral** of tesserae: cubic, isometric (*crystal.*). [L. *tessera*, a die, small cube — Gr. *tessares, tesseres,* four.]

tessitura *tes-i-tōō'rə, n.* the ordinary compass of a voice. [It., texture.]

test¹ *test, n.* a pot or cupel in which metals are tried and refined: any critical trial: a means of trial: anything used to distinguish or detect substances, a reagent (*chem.*): a trial of fitness for an examination: an oath or other evidence of religious belief required as a condition of office or exercise of rights: a test-match: a testa. — *v.t.* to put to proof: to try or examine critically. — *v.i.* to achieve a stated result in a test. — *n.* **test'a** a hard shell: a seed-coat, derived from the ovule integuments. — *adjs.* **test'able; testaceous** (*-ā'shəs*) of or having a hard shell: brick-red. — *ns.* **testee'; test'er.** — *n.pl.* **Testicar'dines** (*-ēz*) a class of brachiopods with hinged shell and arm skeleton. — *n.* and *adj.* **test'ing.** — **Test Acts** acts meant to secure that none but rightly affected persons and members of the established religion shall hold office — esp. English act of 1673; **test ban** the banning, by mutual agreement between nations, of the testing of any or all nuclear weapons; **test'-bed** an iron framework on which a machine is placed for testing: anything with a like purpose (also *fig.*); **test'-case** a law case that may settle similar questions in the future; **test'-drive** a trial drive of a motor-vehicle, usu. with a view to purchasing the vehicle if it is satisfactory. — Also *v.t.* **test'-flight** a trial flight of a new aeroplane. — *vs.t.* **test'-fly; test'-market** to offer for sale in order to test demand for, success of, etc., a product. — **test'-match** an international cricket match forming one of a series; **test'-paper** a bibulous paper saturated with some substance that changes colour when exposed to certain chemicals: a paper or questions to test fitness for a more serious examination; **test pilot** one whose work is testing new aircraft by flying them; **test'-tube** a glass cylinder closed at one end, used in chemistry, bacteriology, etc. — **test-tube baby** esp. formerly, a child born as as the result of artificial insemination, now usu. one born from an ovum implanted in the womb after fertilisation in a laboratory. [O.Fr. *test* and *teste* — L. *testa*, an earthen pot, a potsherd, a shell.]

test² *test, v.t.* to attest legally and date: to authenticate by a testing clause. — *ns.* **test'acy** (*-ə-si*) the state of being testate; **testā'mur** a certificate of having passed an examination. — *adj.* **test'āte** having made and left a will. — *ns.* **testā'tion** a witnessing, a giving by will; **testā'tor** one who leaves a will: — *fem.* **testā'trix; testā'tum** one of the clauses of an English deed, enumerating the operative words of transfer, statement of consideration, money, etc. — **testing clause** in a Scots deed, the last clause which narrates when and where the parties signed the deed, before what witnesses, by whose hand written, etc. [L. *testārī*, to testify, witness, pa.p. (neut.) *testātum;* 1st pers. pl. *testāmur;* partly through O.Fr. *tester*, to bequeath, partly aphetic for **attest.**]

testament *tes'tə-mənt, n.* that which testifies, or in which an attestation is made: the solemn declaration in writing of one's will: a will: a writing or decree appointing an executor, by the testator (**tes'tament-testament'ar**) or by a court (**tes'tament-dā'tive**) (*Scots law*): (with *cap.*) either of the main divisions (**Old** and **New**) of the Bible (a translation of Gr. *diathēkē,* disposition, compact, covenant). — *adjs.* **testamental** (*-ment'*), **testament'ar** (*Scots law*), **testamen'tary** pertaining to a testament or will: bequeathed or done by will. — *adv.* **testamen'tarily.** [L. *testāmentum.*]

testamur, testate, etc. See **test²**.

teste *tes'ti, -te,* (L.) witness (so-and-so).

testee. See **test¹**.

tester¹ *tes'tər, n.* a canopy or its support, or both, esp. over a bed. [O.Fr. *testre,* the vertical part of a bed behind the head, and *testiere,* a head-covering — *teste* (Fr. *tête*), head — L. *testa,* an earthen pot, the skull.]

tester² *tes'tər,* **testern** *tes'tərn,* (*arch.*) *ns.* a sixpence. — *v.t.* **tes'tern** (*Shak.*) to present or reward with a sixpence. [See **teston.**]

tester³, Testicardines. See **test¹**.

testicle *tes'ti-kl, n.* a male reproductive gland. — *adjs.* **testic'ular** of or like a testicle; **testic'ulate, -d** like a testicle. — *n.* **tes'tis** a testicle: a rounded body like it: — *pl.* **tes'tes** (*-ēz*). [L. *testis* and its dim. *testiculus.*]

testify *tes'ti-fī, v.i.* to bear witness: to make a solemn declaration: to protest or declare a charge (with *against*). — *v.t.* to bear witness to: to affirm or declare solemnly or on oath: to proclaim, declare: — *pr.p.* **tes'tifying;** *pa.t.* and *pa.p.* **tes'tified.** — *ns.* **testif'icate** (*Scots law*) a solemn written assertion; **testifica'tion** the act of testifying or of bearing witness; **testif'icātor.** — *adjs.* **testif'icatory; tes'tified.** — *n.* **tes'tifier.** [L. *testificāri* — *testis,* a witness, *facĕre,* to make.]

testimony *tes'ti-mǝn-i, n.* evidence: declaration to prove some fact: proof: the two tables of the law (*B.*): divine law: protestation. — *v.t.* (*Shak.*) to test, prove, or judge by evidence. — *adj.* **testi'mōnial** of, affording, of the nature of, testimony. — *n.* a written attestation: a writing or certificate bearing testimony to one's character or abilities: a gift or memorial as a token of respect. — *v.t.* **testimō'nialise, -ize** to present with a testimonial. [L. *testimōnium* — *testāri,* to witness.]

testis. See **testicle.**

teston *tes'tǝn, n.* a name for various coins, orig. bearing a king's or duke's head: a Henry VIII shilling: later a sixpence. — *n.* **testoon'** a Portuguese or Italian teston. [Obs. Fr. *teston,* Port. *testão,* It. *testone* — It. *testa,* head.]

testosterone *tes-tos'tǝr-ōn, n.* the chief male sex hormone, a steroid secreted by the testes.

testrill (*Shak.*), **testril** *tes'tril, n.* a sixpence. [**tester**[2].]

testudo *tes-tū'dō, n.* a wheeled shelter used by Roman besiegers: a similar shelter made by joining shields: a vaulted roof: an ancient lyre, said to have been first made of a tortoise-shell: (with *cap.*) the genus containing the typical land tortoises: — *pl.* **testū'dōs, testū'dinēs.** — *adjs.* **testū'dinal, testū'dinary, testūdin'eous** like a tortoise, tortoise-shell, or a testudo. [L. *testūdō, -inis,* tortoise.]

testy *tes'ti, adj.* irritable. — *adv.* **tes'tily.** — *n.* **tes'tiness.** [O.Fr. *testif,* headstrong — *teste* (Fr. *tête*), head — L. *testa,* pot.]

tetanus *tet'ǝ-nǝs, n.* a disease due to a bacillus, marked by painful tonic spasms of the muscles of the jaw and other parts: the state of prolonged contraction of a muscle under quickly repeated stimuli. — *adjs.* **tet'-anal, tet'anoid, tetanic** (*ti-tan'ik*). — *n.* **tetanīsā'tion, -z-.** — *v.t.* **tet'anise, -ize** to produce tetanus or tetanic spasms in. — *n.* **tet'any** heightened excitability of the motor nerves with painful muscular cramps. [L., — Gr. *tetanos* — *teinein,* to stretch.]

tetartohedral *te-tärt-ō-hē'drǝl,* (*crystal.*) *adj.* having one-fourth of the number of faces required for full symmetry. [Gr. *tetartos,* fourth, *hedra,* seat.]

tetchy, techy *tech'i, adj.* irritable. — *adv.* **tetch'ily.** — *n.* **tetch'iness.** [Origin unknown.]

tête[1] *tet,* (*obs.*) *n.* an elaborately dressed head of hair: a head-dress. [Fr.]

tête[2] *tet,* (Fr.) *n.* a head. — **tête-à-tête** (*a-tet*) a private confidential interview: a sofa for two face to face: — *pl.* **tête-à-têtes, têtes-à-têtes.** — *adj.* confidential, secret. — *adv.* in private conversation: face to face. — *adv.* **tête-bêche** (*-besh*) head-to-tail. — **tête-de-pont** (*dǝ-põ*) bridgehead; **tête folle** (*fol*) a scatterbrain.

tether *tedh'ǝr, n.* a rope or chain for confining a beast within certain limits. — *v.t.* to confine with a tether: to restrain within certain limits. — **at the end of one's tether** desperate, having no further strength, resources, etc. [App. O.N. *tjōthr.*]

Tethys *tē'this, teth'is, n.* a sea-nymph, wife of Oceanus: a sea that extended in Mesozoic times from Mexico across the middle Atlantic and the Mediterranean into the centre of Asia (*geol.*). [Gr. *Tēthys.*]

tetra[1] *tet'rǝ, n.* any of various species of freshwater fish of the family *Characidae.* [Short form of *Tetragonopterus,* former name of the genus.]

tetra[2] *tet'rǝ, n.* a plant mentioned by Spenser (*The Faerie Queene* II, vii. 52, 4).

tetra- *tet'rǝ-,* **tetr-,** in composition, four. — *adj.* **tetraba'sic** capable of reacting with four equivalents of an acid: (of acids) having four replaceable hydrogen atoms. —

ns.pl. **Tetrabranchia, Tetrabranchiata** (*-brang'ki-ǝ, -ki-ā'tǝ*; Gr. *branchia,* gills) a former order of the nautilus subclass of cephalopods, with four gills. — *adj.* **tetrabranch'iate** four-gilled. — *ns.* **tetrachlō'ride** any compound with four chlorine atoms per molecule; **tetrachlor(o)eth'ylene** C_2Cl_4, a liquid used in dry-cleaning, as a solvent, etc.; **tet'rachord** (*-körd;* Gr. *chordē,* string) a four-stringed instrument: a series of four sounds, forming a scale of two tones and a half. — *adjs.* **tetrachord'al; tetra'cid** having four replaceable hydrogen atoms: capable of replacing four hydrogen atoms of an acid; **tetract** (*tet'rakt;* Gr. *aktīs, -īnos,* ray) four-rayed. — *n.* a four-rayed sponge spicule. — *adjs.* **tetract'inal** (or *-ī'nǝl*), **tetrac'tine.** — *n.pl.* **Tetractinell'ida** an order of sponges in which some of the spicules are four-rayed. — *adj.* **tetracyclic** (*-sī'klik;* Gr. *kyklos,* ring, wheel) of, in, or with four whorls or rings. — *ns.* **tetracy'cline** a crystalline antibiotic used to treat a wide range of infections, esp. of the respiratory and urinary tracts; **tetrad** (*tet'rad*) a group of four: an atom, radical, or element having a combining power of four (*chem.*). — *adjs.* **tet'rad, tetrad'ic; tetradactyl** (*-dak'til;* Gr. *daktylos,* digit) four-fingered: four-toed. — Also *n.* — *adj.* **tetradac'tylous.** — *ns.* **tetradac'tyly** condition of being tetradactylous; **tet'radite** one who attaches mystic properties to the number four: a believer in a godhead of four persons; **tet'radrachm** (*-dram*) an ancient Greek coin worth four drachmas. — *n.pl.* **Tetradynamia** (*-di-nā'mi-ǝ*) in Linnaeus's system, a class answering to the Cruciferae. — *adjs.* **tetradynamous** (*-din'ǝ-mǝs;* Gr. *dynamis,* power) having four long stamens in pairs and two short, as the Cruciferae; **tetraethyl** (*-eth'il*) having four ethyl groups, as **tetraethyl lead** or **lead tetraethyl,** $Pb(C_2H_5)_4$, used in motor spirit as an antiknock agent. — *n.* **tet'ragon** (*-gǝn, -gon;* Gr. *gōniā,* an angle) a plane figure of four angles. — *adj.* **tetragonal** (*-rag'ǝ-nǝl*) having the form of a tetragon; referable to three axes at right angles, two of them equal (*crystal.*); **tetrag'onous** (*bot.*) with four angles and convex faces. — *ns.* **tetragram** (*-gram;* Gr. *gramma,* a letter) a word or inscription of four letters: the tetragrammaton: a (complete) quadrilateral (*geom.*); **tetragramm'aton** the name YaHWeH, JeHoVaH, etc., as written with four Hebrew letters, regarded as a mystic symbol: any other sacred word of four letters, as the Latin *Deus.* — *n.pl.* **Tetragynia** (*-jin'i-ǝ;* Gr. *gynē,* woman (in the sense of female)) in the Linnaean system an order of plants (in various classes) with four pistils. — *adjs.* **tetragyn'ian, tetragynous** (*-raj'i-nǝs*); **tetrahē'dral.** — *ns.* **tetrahē'drite** grey copper ore, sulphide of copper and antimony: a mineral of tetrahedral habit; **tetrahedron** (*-hē'drǝn;* Gr. *hedrā,* seat) a solid figure or body with four plane faces; **tetrahydrocann'abinol** the main intoxicant substance in marijuana; **tetrakishexahē'dron** (Gr. *tetrakis,* four times) a figure got by erecting equal pyramids on all the faces of a cube. — *adj.* **tetram'eral** four-parted. — *n.* **tetram'erism** division into four parts. — *adj.* **tetram'erous** (Gr. *meros,* part) having four parts, or parts in fours. — *n.* **tetrameter** (*te-tram'i-tǝr;* Gr. *metron,* measure) a verse of four measures (dipodies or feet). — Also *adj.* — *n.* **Tet'ramorph** a pictorial representation of the symbolic attributes of the four evangelists combined in a single figure. — *adj.* **tetramorphic** (*-mör'fik,* Gr. *morphē,* form) having four forms. — *n.pl.* **Tetran'dria** in Linnaeus's classification, a class of plants with four stamens. — *adjs.* **tetran'drian; tetrandrous** (*te-tran'drǝs;* Gr. *anēr, andros,* man (in the sense of male)) having four stamens. — *ns.* **tetraplē'gia** quadriplegia; **tetrapod** (*-pod;* Gr. *pous, podos,* foot) a four-footed animal: any vertebrate above the fishes: a reinforced-concrete block laid against a sea-wall to break the force of the waves. — Also *adj.* — *adj.* **tetrapodous** (*-trap'*). — *ns.* **tetrap'ody** a group of four metrical feet; **tetrapolis** (*te-trap'o-lis;* Gr. *polis,* a city) a group of four towns. — *adjs.* **tetrapol'itan (Tetrapolitan Confession** the Confession which the four cities of

Strassburg, Constance, Memmingen, and Lindau presented to the Diet of Augsburg (11th July 1530), and, properly speaking, the first Confession of the Reformed Church); **tetrap′teran, tetrapterous** (*te-trap′tə-rən, -rəs*; Gr. *pteron*, a wing) four-winged. — *ns.* **tetraptote** (*tet′rap-tōt*; Gr. *ptōsis*, a case) a noun with but four cases; **tetrarch** (*tet′rärk*, or *tē′trärk*; Gr. *archē*, rule, origin) under the Romans, the ruler of the fourth part of a province: a subordinate prince: the commander of a subdivision of a Greek phalanx. — *adj.* (*bot.*; also **tetrarch′ical**) having four xylem strands. — *n.* **tet′rarchy** the office, rank, time of office, or jurisdiction of a tetrarch: the fourth part of a province (also **tet′rarchate**): the condition of being tetrarch (*bot.*). — *adj.* **tetrasemic** (*-sē′mik*; Gr. *sēma*, a sign; *pros.*) equivalent to four short syllables, as a dactyl, anapaest, or spondee. — *ns.* **tet′raspore** (*-spōr, -spör*; Gr. *spora*, seed) a spore formed in groups of four in red seaweeds; **tetrasporangium** (*-spor-an′ji-əm*) the sporangium in which they are formed. — *adjs.* **tetrasporic** (*-spor′ik*), **tetrasporous** (*te-tras′pər-əs*, or *tet-rə-spō′rəs, -spö′*). — *n.* **tet′rastich** (*-stik*; Gr. *stichos*, a row) a stanza or set of four lines. — *adjs.* **tetrastichal** (*ti-tras′ti-kl*), **tetrastichic** (*tet-rə-stik′ik*) of, of the nature of, tetrastichs; **tetras′tichous** in four rows. — *n.* **tet′rastyle** (*-stīl*; Gr. *stȳlos*, a column) a building or portico with four columns in front: a group of four pillars. — Also *adj.* — *n.* **tetrasyllable** (*-sil′ə-bl*) a word of four syllables. — *adjs.* **tetrasyllabic** (*-ab′ik*), **-al.** — *ns.* **tet′ratheism** (*-thē-izm*; Gr. *theos*, god) the belief in four elements in the Godhead — the three persons of the Trinity and a divine essence out of which each of these originates; **tetrathlon** (*te-trath′lən*; Gr. *athlon*, contest) a four-event sporting contest. — *adjs.* **tetratom′ic** having, or composed of, four atoms to a molecule; **tetravalent** (*te-trav′ə-lənt, tet-rə-vā′lənt*) quadrivalent. — *ns.* **tetraxon** (*te-traks′on*; Gr. *axōn, -onos*, an axis) a sponge spicule with four axes; **tetrode** (*tet′rōd*; Gr. *hodos*, a way) a thermionic valve with four electrodes; **tetrox′ide** an oxide with four atoms of oxygen in the molecule; **tetryl** (*tet′ril*) a yellow crystalline explosive compound used as a detonator. [Gr. *tetra-, tettares, tessares*, four.]

Tetrabranchia . . . to . . . **tetrachordal.** See **tetra-**.

tetrachotomy *tet-rə-kot′ə-mi*, *n.* division in fours. — *adj.* **tetrachot′omous.** [Gr. *tetracha*, in four parts, *tomē*, a cut — *temnein*, to cut.]

tetracid . . . to . . . **tetrakishexahedron.** See **tetra-**.

tetralogy *te-tral′ə-ji, n.* a group of four dramas, usu. three tragic and one satyric: any series of four related dramatic or operatic works or stories. [Gr. *tetralogia* — *logos*, discourse.]

tetrameral . . . to . . . **tetrandrous.** See **tetra-**.

tetrapla *tet′rə-plə, n.* an edition of four parallel texts, esp. Origen's of the Old Testament. — *adj.* **tetraploid** (*tet′rə-ploid*) having four times the haploid (twice the normal) number of chromosomes. — *n.* **tet′raploidy** the condition of being tetraploid. [Gr. *tetraploos* (*-plous*, neut.pl. *-pla*), fourfold, *eidos*, form.]

tetrapod . . . to . . . **tetrode.** See **tetra-**.

tetrodotoxin *tet-rō-də-tox′in, n.* a nerve-blocking poison found in a newt and in the Japanese puffer-fish. [*Tetrodon*, a genus of tropical fish, and **toxin**.]

tetronal *tet′rən-əl, n.* a hypnotic and sedative drug rarely used because of its high toxicity.

tetroxide, tetryl. See **tetra-**.

tetter *tet′ər*, (*Shak.*) *n.* a skin eruption. — *v.t.* to affect with a tetter. — *adj.* **tett′erous** (*Shak.*). [O.E. *teter.*]

tettix *tet′iks, n.* a cicada: an ornament for the hair of that shape (*Gr. ant.*). [Gr.]

teuch, teugh *tūhh, adj.* a Scots form of **tough.**

teuchat (*Scot.*). See **tewit.**

teuchter *tūhh′tər*, (*Scot.*) *n.* a derog. term used by Lowland Scots for a dull, thick-witted Highlander. [Origin uncertain.]

Teucrian *tū′kri-ən, n.* and *adj.* Trojan. [Gr. *Teukros*, Teucer, first king of Troy.]

Teuton *tū′tən, n.* any speaker of a Germanic language: (*popularly*) a German. — *adj.* **Teutonic** (*-ton′ik*) Germanic — of the linguistic family that includes English, German, Dutch, and the Scandinavian languages: (*popularly*) German in the narrower sense. — *n.* the parent language of the Teutons, primitive Germanic. — *ns.* **Teuton′icism** (*-i-sizm*), **Teu′tonism** a Germanism: belief in, enthusiasm for, the Teutons: the study of Germanic philology and culture; **Teutonīsā′tion, -z-.** — *v.t.* and *v.i.* **Teu′tonise, -ize** to make or become Teutonic, Germanic, or German. — *n.* **Teu′tonist.** — **Teutonic Knights** a military-religious order founded in 1191–98 to tend wounded Christians and to war on unbelievers, operated first in Palestine and later against the Prussians and Lithuanians. [L. *Teutonēs*, from the root of O.E. *thēod*, people, nation; cf. **Dutch**, Ger. *deutsch*.]

tew *tū, v.t.* to work up: to taw. — *v.i.* to toil, hustle. — *n.* worry: excitement. [Cf. **taw**[2].]

tewart. Same as **tuart.**

tewel *tū′əl, n.* the rectum or anus, esp. of a horse (*dial.*): a flue (*obs.*): a tuyère (*dial.*). [O.Fr. *tuel* (Fr. *tuyau*), tube.]

tewit, tewhit *tē′(h)wit* (*Scot.* **teuchat** *tūhh′ət*), (*dial.*) *ns.* a lapwing. [Imit.]

Texas *tek′səs, n.* a state of the U.S.A.: (without *cap.*) an upper structure on a river-steamer. — *adj.* and *n.* **Tex′an** (a native or inhabitant) of Texas. — **Texas fever** a protozoal cattle-disease transmitted by ticks; **Texas tower** a radar tower built offshore as part of an early-warning system.

Texel *tek′səl, n.* a breed of sheep, originating in Holland and first imported in quantity to Britain for breeding purposes in 1974. [*Texel*, one of the Friesian islands of the Netherlands.]

Tex-Mex *teks′-meks′*, (*U.S.*) *adj.* typical of Mexican-American culture or cuisine. [*Texas, Mexico.*]

text *tekst, n.* the actual words of a book, poem, etc., in their original form or any form they have been transmitted in or transmuted into: a book of such words: words set to music: the main body of matter in a book, distinguished from notes, commentary, or other subsidiary matter: the Bible (*Shak.*): matter commented on: a short passage from the Bible taken as the ostensible subject of a sermon, quoted in authority, displayed as a motto, etc.: a theme: a copybook heading: text-hand. — *adj.* **textile** (*-īl*, in U.S. *-il*) woven: capable of being woven. — *n.* a woven fabric. — *adjs.* **texto′rial** (*arch.*) pertaining to weaving; **tex′tual** pertaining to, or contained in, the text: serving for a text. — *ns.* **text′ualism** (too) strict adherence to a text, esp. that of the Bible: textual criticism, esp. of the Bible; **text′ualist** one learned in the text, esp. of the Bible: a literal interpreter: a quoter of texts. — *adv.* **text′ually.** — *n.* **tex′tuary** a textualist. — *adj.* **text′ural** pertaining to, in the matter of, texture. — *adv.* **textur′ally.** — *n.* **text′ure** anything woven, a web: manner of weaving or connecting: disposition of the parts of a body: structural impression resulting from the manner of combining or interrelating the parts of a whole, as in music, art, etc.: the quality conveyed to the touch, esp. by woven fabrics. — *v.t.* to give (specified) texture to, texturise: to weave. — *adjs.* **text′ured; text′ureless.** — *v.t.* **text′urise, -ize** to give a particular texture to. — *adj.* **text′-book, text′book** (of an operation, example, etc.) exactly as planned, in perfect accordance with theory or calculation. — *n.* a book containing the main principles of a subject. — **text′-hand** a large hand in writing, orig. one suitable for the text of a manuscript book; **text′-man** a quoter of texts: a textualist; **textual criticism** critical study directed towards determining the true reading of a text. — **texturised vegetable protein** a vegetable substance, usu. made from soya beans, prepared to resemble meat in appearance and taste. [L. *texĕre, textum*, to weave.]

textile, texture, etc. See **text.**

textus receptus *teks′təs rə-sep′təs, teks′tŏŏs re-kep′tŏŏs,*

(L.) the received text (of the Greek New Testament).

th- (*obs.*), **th'** (*arch.* or *dial.*), forms of **the**, esp. before a vowel, as in Spenser **thelement**, the element, **thelf**, the elf, **thother**, the other.

thack *thak*, *n.* a Scots form of **thatch**. — **under thack and rape** safely secured under thatch and rope, snug generally.

thae *dhā* (*Scot.*) *pl. demons. pron.* and *demons. adj.* those. [O.E. *thā*; see **tho**[1].]

thagi. See under **thug**.

Thai *tī*, *tä'ē*, *adj.* of Thailand. — *n.* a native of (also **Thai'lander**) or the language of Thailand, country of Asia known before 1939 and between 1945 and 1949 as Siam. — **Thai boxing** a form of boxing practised in Thailand, using gloved fists, and feet, knees and elbows.

thaim *dhām.* Scots form of **them**.

thairm *thārm*, (*Scot.*) *n.* an intestine: catgut, a musical string. [O.E. *tharm, thearm.*]

thalamus *thal'ə-məs*, *n.* an inner room, nuptial chamber: the receptacle of a flower: part of the mid-brain where the optic nerve emerges (**optic thalamus**): — *pl.* **thal'-amī**. — *adj.* **thal'amic** (or **thal-am'ik**) of the thalamus. — *n.pl.* **Thalamiflorae** (*-i-flō'rē, -flō'*; L. *flōs, flōris*, flower) in some systems, a subclass of dicotyledons with petals free and stamens hypogynous. — *adj.* **thalamiflo'ral**. [Gr. *thalamos*, an inner room, bedroom.]

thalassian *tha-las'i-ən*, *adj.* marine. — *n.* a sea turtle. — *n.* **thalassaemia, thalassemia** (*thal-ə-sē'mi-ə*) a hereditary disorder of the blood causing anaemia, sometimes fatal in children. — *adjs.* **thalassae'mic, thalassē'mic; thalass'ic** marine: of the narrow seas. — *ns.* **thalassoc'-racy, thalattoc'racy** (Gr. *kratos*, power) sovereignty of the seas; **thalassog'rapher**. — *adj.* **thalassograph'ic**. — *n.* **thalassog'raphy** the science of the sea. [Gr. *thalassa, thalatta*, sea.]

thale-cress *thāl'-kres*, *n.* a cruciferous wall plant with small white flowers (*Sisymbrium thalianum*). [Named after Johann Thal (1542–83), German physician.]

thaler *tä'lər*, *n.* an obsolete German silver coin. [Ger.; cf. **dollar**.]

Thalia *thə-lī'ə*, *n.* the Muse of comedy and pastoral poetry: one of the Graces. — *adj.* **thalī'an**. [Gr. *Thaleia, Thaliā* — *thallein*, to bloom.]

Thalictrum *thä-lik'trəm*, *n.* the meadow-rue genus: (without *cap.*) a plant of this genus. [Gr. *thaliktron* — *thallein*, to bloom.]

thalidomide *thə-lid'ə-mīd, tha-, n.* a non-barbiturate sedative drug, withdrawn in 1961 because found to cause malformation in the foetus if taken during pregnancy. — **thalidomide baby** an infant showing the teratogenic effects of thalidomide.

thallium *thal'i-əm*, *n.* a highly toxic lead-like metal (Tl; at. numb. 81) discovered in 1861. — *adjs.* **thall'ic** of trivalent thallium; **thall'ous** of univalent thallium. [Gr. *thallos*, a young shoot, from the bright green line in its spectrum.]

thallus *thal'əs, n.* a plant body not differentiated into leaf, stem, and root: — *pl.* **thall'uses, thall'ī**. — *adjs.* **thall'iform; thall'ine; thall'oid**. — *n.pl.* **Thallophy'ta** (Gr. *phyton*, plant) the lowest main division of the vegetable kingdom — bacteria, fungi, algae. — *n.* **thall'ophyte** a member of the Thallophyta. [Gr. *thallos*, a young shoot.]

thalweg *täl'vähh, -veg, n.* the longitudinal profile of the bottom of a river-bed. [Ger., — *Thal* (now *Tal*), valley, *Weg*, way.]

Thammuz *tam'ōōz, -uz* (*Milt.*). Same as **Tammuz**.

than[1] *dhan, dhən, conj.* used after a comparative, actual or felt, to introduce that which is in the lower degree. — *prep.* (popularly, and in some authors, e.g. Shelley) in comparison with (esp. with *whom*, as in Milton). [O.E. *thonne, thanne, thænne*, than, orig. then.]

than[2] *dhan, dhən*, an obs. or dial. form of **then**[1].

thana(h), thanadar. See **tana**[1].

thanage. See **thane**.

thanatism *than'ə-tizm, n.* belief that the soul dies with the body. — *n.* **than'atist**. — *adj.* **thanatognomon'ic** indicating death. — *n.* **thanatog'raphy** a narrative of a death. — *adj.* **than'atoid** apparently dead: deathly: deadly. — *ns.* **thanatol'ogy** the scientific study of death: care or psychological therapy for the dying; **thanatophō'bia** a morbid dread of death; **thanatop'sis** a view of, or reflection upon, death; **thanatō'sis** gangrene. [Gr. *thanatos*, death.]

thane *thān, n.* in Old English times a king's companion, one who held by service, hence a noble of lower rank than eorl or ealdorman: a hereditary (not military) tenant of the crown (*Scot. hist.*). — *ns.* **thā'nage, thane'dom, thane'hood, thane'ship**. — See also **thegn**. [O.E. *thegn*, servant, follower, courtier, nobleman; cf. O.N. *thegn*, a man, warrior, Ger. *Degen*, a soldier, servant, Gr. *teknon*, child.]

thank *thangk, n.* (usu. in *pl.*) gratitude: an expression of gratitude. — *v.t.* to express gratitude to: (*ironically*) to blame. — *n.* **thank'er**. — *adj.* **thank'ful** grateful: gladly relieved. — *adv.* **thank'fully** gratefully, with a thankful feeling: one feels thankful (that). — *ns.* **thank'fulness; thank'ing** (usu. in *pl.*; *Shak.*) thanks. — *adj.* **thank'less** unthankful: not expressing thanks for favours: not gaining even thanks. — *adv.* **thank'lessly**. — *n.* **thank'-lessness**. — **thank'-offering** an offering made to express thanks; **thanks'giver; thanks'giving** the act of giving thanks: a public acknowledgment of divine goodness and mercy: (with *cap.*) a day (**Thanksgiving Day**) set apart for this, esp. that in the U.S.A. since the time of the Pilgrim Fathers, now fixed as the fourth Thursday of November, or that in Canada, fixed as the second Monday in October: a form of giving thanks, a grace, that form preceding the last two prayers of morning or evening prayer or of the litany — the *General Thanksgiving*. — Also *adj.* — *adv.* **thank'worthily**. — *n.* **thank'worthiness**. — *adj.* **thank'worthy** worthy of, or deserving, thanks. — **thank'-you-ma'am** (*U.S.*) a ridge or hollow in a road that causes those who drive over it to bob their heads. — **be thankit** (*Scot.*) thank God; **have (only) oneself to thank for** to be the cause of (one's own misfortune); **I'll thank you, him,** etc. **to** used, usu. in anger, to introduce a request or command; **no thanks to** not owing to, implying that gratitude is far from being due; **thanks, thank you** (*old coll.* **thank'ee**) elliptical forms of thanks be to you, I thank you, or the like; **thanks be** thank God; **thanks to** owing to; **thank you for nothing** an expression implying that no gratitude is due at all. [O.E. *thanc, thonc*; cog. with Ger. *Dank*; from the root of **think**.]

thanna(h). See **tana**[1].

thar *t'här, tär, n.* properly the serow: by confusion applied to the tahr. [Nepali (Indic language of Nepal) *thār*.]

tharborough. See **farborough**.

Thargelia *thär-gē'li-ə*, or *-jē'*, *n.pl.* an ancient Athenian festival, in honour of Apollo, in the month of *Thargēlion* (May–June).

that *dhat, demons. pron.* and *demons. adj.* (*pl.* **those**) pointing out a person or thing: the former: the more distant: not this but the other: the one to be indicated or defined: such (*obs.*): often indicating an accompanying snap of the fingers (as *I don't care that, It wants that*). — *rel. pron.* (*sing.* and *pl.*; *dhət, dhat*) who, whom, or which (esp. when defining or limiting, not merely linking on an addition). — *adv.* (*dhat; coll.* or *dial.*) to that extent. — *conj.* (*dhət, dhat*) used to introduce a noun clause, an adverbial clause of purpose, reason, or consequence, or an expression of a wish in the subjunctive: because (*Shak.*). — *adv.* **that'away** (*U.S. dial.*, or *facet.*) in that direction. — *n.* **that'ness** the quality of being a definite thing, that. — **and all that** and all the rest of that sort of thing — a summary way of dismissing what is vaguely thought of; (**and**) **that's that** (and) that is the end of that matter: no more of that; **at that** at that point: moreover: nevertheless; (**just**)

like that straight off. [O.E. *thæt*, neut. demons. pron. cog. with Ger. *das, dass*; Gr. *to*, Sans. *tad*; see **the**.]

thatch *thach, v.t.* to cover, or roof, with straw, reeds, heather, palm-leaves, or the like. — *v.i.* to do thatching. — *n.* a covering or covering material of the kind: thick hair: a condition of grass in which a mat of dead vegetative fibre builds up, inhibiting the penetration of air to, and the growth of, the roots. — *adj.* **thatched** (or **thatcht**). — *ns.* **thatch'er; thatch'ing** the act or art of covering with thatch: materials used for thatching: the development of thatch in grass. — Also *adj.* — *adj.* **thatch'less.** — **thatch'-board** a building-board made of straw. [O.E. *thæc*, covering, thatch, and *theccan*, to cover; cog. with Ger. *decken*, L. *tegĕre*, Gr. *stegein*, to cover.]

Thatcherism *thach'ər-izm, n.* the policies and style of government associated with Margaret *Thatcher*, British prime minister 1979 — .

thauma- *thö'mə-*, **thaumat-** *-mət-*, in composition, wonder, miracle. — *ns.* **thau'masite** a mineral, hydrated silicate, carbonate, and sulphate of calcium; **thau'- matin** a sweetener extracted from a W. African fruit, *Thaumatococcus daniellii*, 2000 to 4000 times sweeter than sucrose; **thaumatogeny** (*-toj'*) the doctrine of the miraculous origination of life; **thaumatog'raphy** description of natural wonders; **thaumatol'atry** (Gr. *latreiā*, worship) wonder-worship; **thau'matrope** (Gr. *tropos*, a turning) an optical toy that combines pictures by persistence of images in the eye; **thaumaturge** (*thö'mə-tûrj*) a wonder-worker. — *adjs.* **thaumatur'gic, -al.** — *n.pl.* **thaumatur'gics** wonderful, esp. magical, performances: feats of legerdemain. — *ns.* **thaumatur'- gism; thaumatur'gist; thaumaturgus** (*-tûr'gəs*) a wonder-worker: a worker of miracles, applied to certain saints. [Gr. *thauma, -atos*, wonder, *thaumasios*, wonderful, *thaumatourgos* (— *ergon*, work), a wonder-worker.]

thaw *thö, v.i.* to melt or grow liquid, as ice: to become so warm as to melt ice: to become less cold, stiff, or reserved in manner (*fig.*). — *v.t.* to cause to melt. — *n.* the melting of ice or snow by heat: the change of weather that causes it. — Also *fig.* — *n.* and *adj.* **thaw'ing.** — *adjs.* **thaw'less; thaw'y** inclined to thaw. — **thaw out** to return from frozen to normal condition. [O.E. *thawian*.]

the¹ *dhē* (emphatic), *dhə* (usu.), *dhi, dhē* (before vowels), demons. *adj.* called the definite article, used to denote a particular person or thing: also to denote a species: used instead of the pfx. *to-*, this (*Scot.*; as **the day** today, **the night** tonight, **the morn** tomorrow, **the morn's morn** tomorrow morning, **the year** this year). [O.E. *the* (supplanting *se*), masc. of *thæt*, that.]

the² *dhə, adv.* (with comparatives) by how much: by so much. [O.E. *thȳ*, by that, by that much, the instrumental case of the def. art.]

Thea *thē'ə, n.* the tea genus of plants (sometimes including Camellia), giving name to the family **Theā'ceae**, akin to the Guttiferae. — *adj.* **theā'ceous.** [From the root of **tea**, but taken as if from Gr. *theā*, goddess.]

theandric *thē-an'drik, adj.* at once divine and human. [Gr. *theos*, a god, *anēr, andros*, man.]

theanthropic *thē-an-throp'ik, adj.* at once divine and human: embodying deity in human forms. — *ns.* **thean'thropism, thean'thropy** the ascribing of human qualities to deity, or divine qualities to man: a doctrine of union of divine and human; **thean'thropist.** [Gr. *theos*, a god, *anthrōpos*, man.]

thearchy *thē'ärk-i, n.* a theocracy: a body of divine rulers. — *adj.* **thear'chic.** [Gr. *theos*, a god, *archein*, to rule.]

Theatine *thē'ə-tīn, n.* a member of a R.C. religious brotherhood founded in 1524 by John Peter Caraffa, bishop of Chieti (L. *Teāte*), afterwards Pope Paul IV, and others, or of a sisterhood modelled on it. — Also *adj.*

theatre (*U.S.* **theater**) *thē'ə-tər, n.* a structure, orig. in the open air, for drama or other spectacle: a cinema (*U.S.*

and *Austr.*): any place backed by a curving hillside or rising by steps like seats of a theatre: a building or room which is adapted for scholastic exercises, anatomical or surgical demonstrations, etc. (see also **operating theatre**): a scene of action, field of operations: (with *the*) the social unit comprising actors, producers, etc., or its characteristic environment and conditions: an audience, house: (with *the*) plays or a specified group of plays, collectively: material or method judged by its suitability for a dramatic presentation. — *adjs.* **the'atral; theatric** (*-at'*), **-al** relating or suitable to, or savouring of, the stage: stagy: histrionic: aiming at or producing dramatic effects. — *v.t.* **theat'ricalise, -ize** to adapt to dramatic representation: to make stagy. — *v.i.* to act: to attend the theatre. — *ns.* **theat'ricalism, theatrical'ity** staginess, artificiality. — *adv.* **theat'rically.** — *n.* **theat'ricalness.** — *n.pl.* **theat'ricals** dramatic performances: theatrical affairs, properties, or persons. — *v.i.* **theat'ricise, -ize** (*-sīz*) to play a part. — *ns.* **theat'ricism** theatricality, affectation, staginess; **theat'rics** the staging of plays, etc., or the art of doing this: histrionics; **theatromā'nia** a craze for play-going; **theat'rophone** a telephone for transmitting stage dialogue from the theatre. — **the'atre-go'er** one who habitually goes to the theatre; **the'atre-in-the-round'** a theatre with central, or arena, stage and audience on all sides: the style of staging plays in such a theatre; **theatre organ** a cinema-organ; **theatre weapons** weapons for use in a theatre of war, applied esp. to nuclear weapons intended for use in Central Europe. — **theatre of cruelty** a branch of drama, based on the theories of Antonin Artaud (1896–1948), intended to induce in the audience a feeling of suffering and an awareness of the presence of evil; **theatre of fact** a branch of drama using material closely based on real happenings; **theatre of the absurd** a branch of drama dealing with fantastic deliberately unreal situations, in reaction against the tragedy and irrationality of life. [Gr. *theātron* — *theaesthai*, to see.]

theave *thēv*, (*dial.*) *n.* a young ewe, esp. of the first year.

Thebes *thēbz, n.* a city of ancient Boeotia (Greece): a city of ancient Egypt. — *adj.* **Thebaic** (*thē-bā'ik*) of Egyptian Thebes: of opium (as an Egyptian product). — *ns.* **Thebaid** (*thē'bā-id*) a poem on the Seven against Thebes (as that by Statius): the district of Thebes (Egyptian or Greek); **thē'baine** (*-bā-ēn, -bə-ēn*) an alkaloid ($C_{19}H_{21}NO_3$) got from opium. — *adj.* **Thē'ban** of Thebes. — *n.* a native of Thebes: a Boeotian. — **Theban year** the Egyptian year of 365¼ days. [Gr. *Thēbai*, Thebes.]

theca *thē'kə, n.* a sheath, case, or sac: a spore-case: a lobe or loculus of an anther: — *pl.* **thē'cae** (*-sē*). — *adjs.* **thē'cal** of a theca; **thē'cate** having a theca. [Latinised from Gr. *thēkē*, case, sheath.]

Thecla *thek'lə, n.* the hair-streak genus of butterflies.

thecodont *thek'ō-dont, n.* an extinct reptile of the Triassic period, having teeth set in sockets. [Gr. *thēkē*, case, *odous, odontis*, a tooth.]

thé dansant *tā dā-sā*, (Fr.) tea with dancing. — *pl.* **thés dansants.**

thee¹ *dhē, pron., dat.* and *accus.* of **thou¹**: also (*dial.*, and formerly by Quakers) *nom.* — *v.t.* to use *thee* in speaking to. — *v.i.* to use *thee.* [O.E. *thē*, the.]

thee² *thē*, (*Spens.*) *v.i.* to prosper, to thrive. [O.E. *thēon*; cf. Ger. *gedeihen*.]

theek *thēk*, a Scots form of **thatch** (*vb.*).

theft *theft, n.* act of thieving: a thing stolen. — *adj.* **theft'uous** thievish. — *adv.* **theft'uously.** — **theft'boot, -bote** illegal compounding of a theft. [O.E. *thēofth, thīefth* — *thēof*, thief.]

thegither *dhə-gidh'ər*, a Scots form of **together**.

thegn *thān*, (*hist.*) *n.* the older form of **thane**.

theine *thē'īn, -in, n.* caffeine. — *ns.* **thē'ic** one who drinks overmuch tea or who suffers from theism; **thē'ism** a morbid state resulting from overmuch tea-drinking. [**Thea.**]

their *dhār, dhər, pron. (gen. pl.)* or *poss. adj.* of or belonging to them. — *pron.* **theirs** (a double genitive) used predicatively or absolutely. [O.N. *theirra*, superseding O.E. *thǣra*, gen. pl. of the def. art.]

theism[1] *thē'izm, n.* belief in the existence of God with or without a belief in a special revelation. — *n.* **thē'ist.** — *adjs.* **thēist'ic, -al.** [Gr. *theos*, God.]

theism[2]. See **theine.**

thelement, thelf. See **th-.**

Thelemite *thel'ə-mīt, n.* a monk of Rabelais's imaginary abbey of *Thélème*, of an order whose rule was 'Do as you like'. — Also *adj.* [Gr. *thelēma*, will.]

thelytoky *thi-lit'ə-ki, n.* parthenogenetic production of female offspring only. — *adj.* **thelyt'okous.** [Gr. *thēlys*, female, *tokos*, birth.]

them *dhem, dhəm, pron., dat.* and *accus.* of **they.** — *demons. adj. (dial.* or *coll.; dhem)* those. — **them and us** (*coll.*) any of various pairs of groups in society, such as management and workforce, considered to be in opposition to each other. [O.N. *theim* or O.E. (Anglian) *thǣm* (dat.).]

theme *thēm, n.* a subject set or proposed for discussion, or spoken or written about: a thesis, a brief essay or exercise: a ground for action: the stem of a word without its inflexions: subject, a short melody developed with variations or otherwise (*mus.*): an administrative division of the Byzantine empire. — *v.t.* to decorate or equip (a pub, restaurant, etc.) in keeping with a certain subject, e.g. seafaring or the Wild West. — *n.* **thē'ma** (or *them'ə*) a theme: — *pl.* **them'ata.** — *adj.* **thematic** (*thi-mat'ik*) of, or relating to a theme; (of philately) concerned with collection of sets showing flowers, or birds, etc. — *adv.* **themat'ically.** — **thematic vowel** a vowel that comes between root and inflexion; **theme park** a large area with displays, fairground, rides, etc., all devoted to or based on one subject; **theme song** a melody that is repeated often in a musical drama, film, or radio or television series, and is associated with a certain character, idea, emotion, etc.: a person's characteristic, often repeated, complaint, etc. [Gr. *thēma, -atos* — root of *tithěnai*, to place, set; partly through O.Fr. *tesme*.]

Themis *them'is, n.* the Greek goddess of law and justice. [Gr. *Themis*.]

themselves *dhəm-selvz', pron., pl.* of **himself, herself, itself.** [**them, self.**]

then[1] *dhen, dhən, adv.* at that time: afterward: immediately: at another time: further, again: on the other hand, at the same time: for that reason, therefore: in that case. — *adj.* being at that time. — *n.* that time. — *adv.* **thenabout(s)** about that time. — **by then** by that time; **then and there** at once and on the spot. [O.E. *thonne, thanne, thænne*.]

then[2] *dhən,* (*Spens.*, etc.) *conj.* Same as **than**[1].

thenar *thē'när, n.* the palm: the ball of the thumb: the sole. — Also *adj.* [Gr. *thěnär, -äros*.]

thence *dhens, adv.* from that place: from those premises: from that time: from that cause. — *advs.* **thence'forth, thencefor'ward** from that time forward: from that place onward. [M.E. *thennes — thenne* (O.E. *thanon*, thence), with adverbial genitive ending; cf. **hence, whence.**]

theo- *thē'ō-, -o-,* or *-o'-,* in composition, god. — *In the following article, strict alphabetical order is not followed; in most cases, the abstract noun in -y precedes adjectives, etc., dependent on it.* — *ns.* **Theobroma** (*-brō'mə;* Gr. *brōma*, food) the chocolate or cocoa genus of Sterculiaceae; **theobrō'mine** (*-mēn, -mīn, -min*) an alkaloid got from the chocolate nut; **theocracy** (*thē-ok'rə-si;* Gr. *theokratiā — krateein,* to rule) that constitution of a state in which God, or a god, is regarded as the sole sovereign, and the laws of the realm as divine commands rather than human ordinances — the priesthood necessarily becoming the officers of the invisible ruler: the state thus governed; **theocrat** (*thē'ō-krat*) a divine or deified ruler. — *adjs.* **theocrat'ic, -al.** — *adv.* **theocrat'ically.** — *ns.* **theocrasy**

(*thē-ok'rə-si,* or *thē'ō-krā'si;* Gr. *krāsis*, a mixing) a mixture of religions: the identification or equating of one god with another or others: a mystic intimacy with deity reached through profound contemplation; **theodicy** (*thē-od'i-si;* Gr. *dikē*, justice) a vindication of the justice of God in establishing a world in which evil exists. — *n.* and *adj.* **theodicē'an.** — *n.* **theogony** (*thē-og'ə-ni;* Gr. *theogoniā — gonē*, birth, generation) the birth and genealogy of the gods. — *adjs.* **theogonic** (*thē-ə-gon'ik*), **-al.** — *ns.* **theog'onist** a writer on theogony; **theology** (*thē-ol'ə-ji;* Gr. *theologiā — logos*, discourse) the study of God, religion and revelation: a system of theological doctrine; **theologaster** (*-gas'tər*) a shallow theologian; **theol'ogate** (*-gāt*) a seminary for R.C. priests; **theol'oger** (*-jər*) a theologian: sometimes *derog.*; **theologian** (*thē-ə-lō'jyən*) one well versed in theology: a divine, a professor of or writer on divinity, esp. in R.C. usage, a theological lecturer attached to a cathedral or collegiate church. — *adjs.* **theologic** (*thē-ə-loj'ik*), **-al.** — *adv.* **theolog'ically.** — *v.t.* **theol'ogise, -ize** to render theological. — *v.i.* to discourse, speculate, etc., on theology. — *ns.* **theol'ogiser, -z-;** **theol'ogist** (*rare*) a theologian; **the'ologue** (*-log*) a theologian (*rare*): a theological student (*U.S.*); **theomachy** (*thē-om'ə-ki;* Gr. *theomachiā — machē*, a battle) war among or against the gods, as by the Titans and giants: opposition to the divine will; **theom'achist; theomancy** (*thē'ō-man-si;* Gr. *theomanteiā*, spirit of prophecy — *manteiā*, divination) divination by means of oracles, or of persons inspired immediately by some divinity. — *adj.* **theoman'tic.** — *ns.* **theomania** (*-mā'ni-ə;* Gr. *maniā*, madness) religious madness: belief that one is a god; **theomā'niac.** — *adj.* **theomorphic** (*-mör'fik;* Gr. *theomorphos*, of divine form — *morphē*, form) having the form of likeness of a god: in the image of God. — *ns.* **theomor'phism; theon'omy** (Gr. *nomos*, law) government or rule by God: the state of being so ruled. — *adj.* **theon'omous.** — *n.* **Theopaschite** (*-pas'kīt;* Gr. *paschein*, to suffer) a Monophysite, as believing that God had suffered and been crucified. — *adj.* **Theopaschitic** (*-kit'ik*). — *ns.* **Theopas'chitism** (*-kit-izm*); **theopathy** (*thē-op'ə-thi;* Gr. *pathos*, experience, emotion) a religious emotion aroused by meditation about God. — *adj.* **theopathet'ic.** — *n.* **theophagy** (*thē-of'ə-ji;* Gr. *phagein*, to eat) the sacramental eating of a god. — *adj.* **theoph'agous** (*-gəs*). — *n.* **theophany** (*thē-of'ə-ni;* Gr. *theophaneiā*, a vision of God, exhibition of gods' statues — *phainein*, to show) a manifestation or appearance of deity to man. — *adj.* **theophanic** (*thē-ō-fan'ik*). — *n.* **theophilanthropy** (*-fil-an'thrə-pi;* Fr. *théophilanthropie*, love to God and man; cf. **philanthropy**) a deistical system of religion drawn up under the French Directory in 1796, and designed to take the place of Christianity. — *adj.* **theophilanthrop'ic.** — *ns.* **theophilan'thropism; theophilan'thropist; theophobia** (*-fō'bi-ə;* Gr. *phobos*, fear) morbid fear of God: hatred of God; **theophobist** (*-of'ə-bist*). — *adjs.* **theophor'ic** derived from or bearing the name of a god; **theopneust, -ic** (*thē'op-nūst;* Gr. *theopneustos — pneustos*, inspired — *pneein*, to breathe) divinely inspired. — *ns.* **theopneust'y** divine inspiration; **theosophy** (*thē-os'ə-fi;* Gr. *theosophos*, wise in things of God — *sophos*, wise) divine wisdom: immediate divine illumination or inspiration claimed to be possessed by specially gifted men, along with abnormal control over natural forces: the system of doctrine expounded by the Theosophical Society; **theosoph** (*thē'ə-sof*), **theos'opher, theos'ophist.** — *adjs.* **theosoph'ic, -al.** — *adv.* **theosoph'ically.** — *v.i.* **theos'ophise, -ize** to practise theosophy. — *n.* **theos'ophism** theosophical tenets. — *adj.* **theosophist'ical** theosophical: sophistical in theology. — *n.* **theotechny** (*-tek'ni;* Gr. *technē*, art) the employment of gods as the machinery of a poem. — *adj.* **theotech'nic.** — *n.* **theotokos** (*thē-ot'ə-kos;* Gr. *theotokos — tokos*, birth) the mother of God, a title of the Virgin Mary repudiated by Nestorius, accepted by the Council of Ephesus. — **Theosophical Society** a religious body founded by Mme. Blavatsky and others in 1875, whose doctrines include belief in karma and reincarnation. [Gr. *theos*, a god.]

Theocritean *thē-ok-ri-tē'ən, adj.* after the manner of *Theocritus* (3rd cent. B.C.), the greatest of Greek pastoral poets: pastoral, idyllic.

theodolite *thē-od'ə-līt, n.* a surveying instrument for measuring horizontal and vertical angles. [Ety. unknown.]

theophylline *thē-ō-fil'ēn, -īn, -in, n.* an isomer of theobromine found in tea. [**Thea**, and Gr. *phyllon*, leaf.]

theorbo *thē-örb'ō, n.* a large double-necked bass lute: — *pl.* **theorb'os.** — *n.* **theorb'ist.** [It. *tiorba*.]

theorem *thē'ə-rəm, n.* a demonstrable or established but not self-evident principle: a proposition to be proved. — *adjs.* **theoremat'ic, -al.** — *adv.* **theoremat'ically.** — *n.* **theorematist** (*-rem'ə-tist*). — *adjs.* **theoret'ic, -al** pertaining, according, or given to theory: not practical: speculative. — *n.* **theoret'ic** (usu. in *pl.*) the speculative parts of a science. — *adv.* **theoret'ically.** — *ns.* **theoretician** (*-et-ish'ən*) one who is concerned chiefly with the theoretical aspect of a subject; **the'oric, the'orique** (*Shak.*) theory, speculation. — *v.i.* **the'orise, -ize** to form a theory: to form opinions solely by theories: to speculate. — *ns.* **the'oriser, -z-; the'orist** a theoriser: one given to theory and speculation: one who is expert in the abstract principles of a subject; **the'ory** an explanation or system of anything: an exposition of the abstract principles of a science or art: speculation as opposed to practice. [Gr. *theōrēma, -atos*, spectacle, speculation, theorem, *theōriā*, view, theory — *theōreein*, to be a spectator, to view.]

theow *thā'ow, (O.E. hist.) n.* a slave. [O.E. *thēow*.]

theralite *ther'ə-līt, n.* a holocrystalline igneous rock composed essentially of plagioclase, nepheline, and augite. [Gr. *thēraein*, to hunt, seek after, *lithos*, stone, because its discovery was expected.]

Therapeutae *ther-ə-pū'tē, L. ther-a-pū'tī, n.pl.* a traditional ascetic sect, allied to the Essenes, living chiefly near Alexandria. — *adj.* **therapeu'tic** pertaining to the healing art: curative. — *adv.* **therapeu'tically.** — *n. sing.* **therapeu'tics** that part of medicine concerned with the treatment and cure of diseases. — *ns.* **therapeu'tist** one versed in therapeutics; **ther'apist; ther'apy** therapeutics: treatment used to combat a disease or an abnormal condition: curative power. [Gr. *therapeutēs*, servant, worshipper, medical attendant — *therapeuein*, to take care of, to heal, *therapeiā*, service, treatment.]

therapsid *thə-rap'sid, n.* a member of the *Therapsida*, an order of extinct reptiles of the Permian and Triassic periods, showing many mammal-like features and thought to be the ancestors of the mammals. — Also *adj.* [Mod. L. — Gr. *theraps*, an attendant.]

Theravada *ther-a-väd'ə, n.* the doctrines of the Hinayana Buddhists. — *adj.* **Theravad'in.** [Pali, doctrine of the elders.]

therblig *thûr'blig, n.* a unit of work into which an industrial operation may be divided. [Anagram of the name of its inventor, F.B. *Gilbreth* (1868-1924), American engineer.]

there *dher, dhār, adv.* in that place: at that point: to that place: with regard to that: (also *dhr*) used without any meaning of its own to allow the subject to follow the predicate, and also in corresponding interrogative sentences, etc.: used without any meaning to draw or attract attention. — *n.* that place. — *interj.* expressing reassurance, finality, accompanying a blow, etc. — *n.* **there'ness** the property of having relative situation or existence. — *advs.* **there'about, -s** (also *-bowts'*) about or near that place: near that number, quantity, degree, or time; **thereaft'er** after or according to that: accordingly; **thereagainst'** against that: **thereamong'** among that or those; **thereanent'** (*Scot.*) concerning that matter; **thereat'** at that place or occurrence: on that account; **there'away** in that direction: thereabout; **therebeside'** beside that; **thereby'** beside that: about that amount: by that means: in consequence of that;

therefor' for that; **therefore** (*dher'for*) for that reason: consequently; **therefrom'** from that; **therein'** in or into that or it: indoors (*Scot.*); **thereinaft'er, thereinbefore'** later, earlier, in the same document; **therein'to** into that place, thing, matter, etc.; **thereof'** of that: from that: **thereon'** on that; **thereout'** out of that: out of doors (*Scot.*); **therethrough'** through that: by that means; **thereto', thereun'to** to that: in addition; **there'tofore** before that time; **thereun'der** under that; **thereupon'** upon that: in consequence of that (*Shak.*): immediately; **therewith'** with that: thereupon; **there'withal** with that: immediately after: in addition; **therewithin'** within that. — **so there** an expression of triumph, defiance, derision, finality, etc.; **there and then** forthwith; **there or thereabouts** somewhere near; **there you are** used to express triumph when something one predicted would occur does occur, or resignation over something that cannot be changed. [O.E. *thǣr*; akin to **the, that,** etc.]

theriac *thē'ri-ak,* **theriaca** *thē-rī'ə-kə, (arch.) ns.* an antidote to venomous bites, etc. — *adj.* **therī'acal.** [Gr. *thēriakē — thērion,* a wild beast.]

therio-, theri-, thero- *thēr', -i-, -ō-,* in composition, beast, mammal. — *adj.* **therianthrop'ic** (Gr. *anthrōpos,* man) combining human and animal forms. — *n.* **therian'thropism** the representation or worship of therianthropic forms or gods. — *n.pl.* **Theriodontia** (*-ō-don'shyə, -ti-ə*; Gr. *odous,* odontos, a tooth) an extinct order of reptiles with teeth like mammals. — *ns.* **theriol'atry** (Gr. *latreiā,* worship) animal-worship; **ther'iomorph** (Gr. *morphē,* form) an animal form in art. — *adj.* **theriomorph'ic** beastlike: of theriomorphism. — *n.* **theriomorph'ism** belief in gods of the form of beasts. — *n.pl.* **Theriomor'pha (Theromor'pha)** an extinct order of reptiles with affinities to the labyrinthodont Amphibia and mammals. — *n.* **theriomorphō'sis** (or *-mör'*) transformation into a beast. — *adjs.* **theriomor'phous** beastlike: mammal-like of the Theriomorpha; **ther'oid** beastlike. — *ns.* **therol'ogy** the study of mammals; **ther'opod** (Gr. *pous, podos* a foot) any dinosaur of the **Therop'oda,** bipedal, carnivorous, saurischian dinosaurs. [Gr. *thēr,* and *thērion,* a wild beast.]

therm *thûrm, n.* hot baths: a bathing establishment (*Gr.* and *Rom. hist.*): 100,000 British thermal units (used as a unit in reckoning payment for gas). — *n.pl.* **thermae** (*-ē*) hot springs or baths. — *adj.* **therm'al** pertaining to heat: warm: of clothes, designed to prevent the loss of body heat. — *n.* an ascending current of warm air. — *v.t.* **therm'alise, -ize** to reduce the kinetic energy and speed of (fast neutrons) in a nuclear reactor. — *n.* **Therm'alite®** a manufactured material for building blocks, of light density and high insulation value. — *adv.* **therm'ally.** — *adjs.* **therm'ic, -al** of or by heat. — *adv.* **therm'ically.** — *n.* **therm'ion** (Gr. *ion* (*neut.*), going) an electrically charged particle emitted by an incandescent body. — *adj.* **thermion'ic** (**thermionic valve** or **tube** a vacuum tube containing a heated cathode from which electrons are emitted, an anode for collecting some or all of these electrons and, generally, additional electrodes for controlling their flow to the anode). — *n.sing.* **thermion'ics** the science of thermions — *ns.* **thermi'stor** (*therm*al *resistor*) a semi-conductor, a mixture of certain oxides with finely divided copper, of which the resistance is very sensitive to change of temperature; **therm'ite (Thermit®)** a mixture of aluminium powder with oxide of metal (esp. iron), which when ignited evolves great heat, used for local heating and welding; **thermobal'ance** a balance for weighing bodies at high temperatures. — *adj.* **thermochem'ical.** — *ns.* **thermochem'ist; thermochem'istry** the study of heat changes accompanying chemical action; **therm'ocline** in lakes, a region of rapidly changing temperature, found between the epilimnion and the hypolimnion; **therm'o-couple** a pair of metals in contact giving a thermo-electric current. — *adjs.* **thermodū'ric** resistant to heat; **thermodynam'ic.** — *n.sing.* **thermodynam'ics** the science of heat as a mechanical agent.

— *adj.* **thermo-elec′tric.** — *ns.* **thermo-electric′ity** electricity developed by the unequal heating of bodies, esp. between a junction of metals and another part of a circuit; **thermogenesis** (-*jen′*) production of heat, esp. in the body by physiological processes. — *adjs.* **thermogenet′ic, thermogen′ic.** — *ns.* **therm′ogram** a thermograph record of temperature; **therm′ograph** a self-registering thermometer: the photographic apparatus used in thermography. — *adj.* **thermograph′ic.** — *n.* **thermog′raphy** any process of writing, photographing, etc. involving the use of heat: the production of a photographic record or an image on a small picture-tube by using an infra-red camera: a pictorial record of heat emission from the patient's body used in medical diagnosis. — *adj.* **thermolā′bile** readily decomposed by heat. — *ns.* **thermol′ogy** the science of heat; **thermoluminesc′ence** release of light by irradiated material upon subsequent heating; **thermol′ysis** (Gr. *lysis,* loosing) dissociation or dissolution by heat: loss of body heat. — *adj.* **thermolyt′ic.** — *n.* **thermometer** (-*om′i-tər*) an instrument for measuring temperature depending on any of several properties of a substance that vary linearly with change of temperature. — *adjs.* **thermometric** (-*ə-met′rik*), **-al.** — *adv.* **thermomet′-rically.** — *ns.* **thermomet′rograph** a self-registering thermometer; **thermom′etry**; **therm′onasty** nastic movement in relation to heat. — *adjs.* **thermonuc′lear** used of the fusion of nuclei as seen in **thermonuclear reaction,** a power reaction produced by the fusion of nuclei at extremely high temperatures, as in the hydrogen bomb: pertaining to the use of such reactions as a source of power or force; **therm′ophil(e)** (-*fil*), **thermophil′ic, thermoph′ilous** requiring, or thriving best in, a high temperature. — *n.* **therm′opīle** (-*pīl*) an apparatus for the direct conversion of heat into electrical energy. — *adj.* **thermoplast′ic** plastic when heated. — *n.* any resin that can be melted and cooled repeatedly without appreciable change in properties. — *ns.* **therm′os** (orig. trademark for) a brand of vacuum or Dewar flask (also **thermos flask**); **therm′oscope** an instrument for detecting changes of temperature. — *adj.* **thermoscop′ic** indicating, or sensitive to, temperature changes. — *adv.* **thermoscop′ically.** — *adj.* **thermosett′ing** setting, after melting and moulding with change of properties. — *n.* **therm′osphere** the region of the earth's atmosphere above the mesosphere, in which the temperature rises steadily with height. — *adj.* **thermosta′ble** not readily decomposed by heating. — *n.* **therm′ostat** a device for keeping temperature steady. — *adj.* **thermostat′ic.** — *adv.* **thermostat′ically.** — *adjs.* **thermotact′ic, thermotax′ic** of or showing thermotaxis. — *n.* **thermotax′is** a taxis towards a position of higher or lower temperature. — *adjs.* **thermot′ic, -al** of or due to heat. — *n.sing.* **thermot′ics** the science of heat. — *adj.* **thermotrop′ic.** — *n.* a thermotrophic substance. — *n.* **thermot′ropism** (Gr. *tropos,* turning) orientation determined by temperature differences. — **thermal barrier** heat barrier; **thermal dissociation** the splitting of certain molecules into simpler molecules by heat, followed by recombination on cooling; **thermal imaging** the visualisation of objects and scenes by detecting and processing the infra-red energy they emit; **thermal reactor** a nuclear reactor in which fission is induced mainly by low-energy neutrons; **thermal shock** stress, often resulting in fracture, resulting when a body is subjected to sudden changes in temperature; **thermal springs** natural springs of hot water; **thermic lance** a cutting instrument consisting of a steel tube containing metal rods which, with the help of oxygen, are raised to an intense heat. [Gr. *thermos,* hot, *thermē,* heat, *thermotēs,* heat.]

Thermidor *thûr-mi-dör′, n.* the eleventh month of the Fr. Revolutionary calendar, 19th July–17th Aug. — *n.* **Thermido′rian** a participator in the fall of Robespierre. [Gr. *thermē,* heat, *dōron,* gift.]

thero-. See **therio-.**

Thersitic *thər-sit′ik, adj.* like *Thersītēs,* a shameless railer

among the Greeks at Troy.

thesaurus *thi-sö′rəs, n.* a treasury: a storehouse of knowledge, esp. of words, quotations, etc., a dictionary: a book with systematically arranged lists of words and their synonyms, antonyms, etc., a word finder. [L., — Gr. *thēsauros.*]

these *dhēz, demons. adj.* and *demons. pron., pl.* of **this.** [O.E. *thǣs,* a by-form of *thās,* pl. of *thēs, thēos, this,* this; cf. **those.**]

thesis *thē′sis, thes′is, n.* lit. a setting down, a down-beat (*Gr. pros.* and *mus.*): hence the strong position in a bar or foot: understood by the Romans as the weak position: used in English in both senses (opp. to *arsis*): a position or that which is set down or advanced for argument: a subject for a scholastic exercise, esp. one presented for a doctorate: an essay on a theme: — *pl.* **theses** (*thē′sēz*). — *adjs.* **thetic** (*thet′ik*), **-al** positively asserting: bearing the thesis. — *adv.* **thet′ically.** — **thesis novel** roman à thèse (see under **roman**). [Gr. *thēsis,* from the root of *tithenai,* to put, set.]

Thesmophoria *thes-mō-phō′, -phō′ri-ə, n.pl.* an ancient Greek married women's festival in honour of Demeter *Thesmophoros* (law-giving). [Gr. *thesmophŏria.*]

thesmothete *thes′mō-thēt, n.* a law-giver, esp. one of the six junior archons in ancient Athens. [Gr. *thesmothetēs* — *thesmos,* law, *thetēs,* a placer, setter.]

Thespian *thes′pi-ən,* (also without *cap.*) *adj.* pertaining to tragedy: tragic. — *n.* a tragic actor: an actor. [Gr. *Thespis,* founder of Greek tragedy.]

theta *thē′tə, thā′tə, n.* the eighth (orig. ninth) letter of the Greek alphabet (Θ, θ) transliterated *th,* its sound an aspirated *t,* but in modern Greek like English *th*: as a Greek numeral θ′ = 9, ,θ = 9000: a mark of condemnation (from the θ for *thanatos,* death, used in balloting). [Gr. *thēta;* Semitic.]

thetch *thech,* (*Spens.*) *v.i.* to thatch. [O.E. *theccan.*]

thete *thēt,* (*Gr. hist.*) *n.* orig. a serf: a poor freeman in Athens under Solon's constitution. [Gr. *thēs, thētos.*]

thether. See **thither.**

thetic. See under **thesis.**

theurgy *thē′ər-ji, n.* magic by the agency of good spirits: miraculous divine action. — *adjs.* **theur′gic, -al.** — *n.* **the′urgist.** [Gr. *theourgiā* — *theos,* a god, *ergon,* work.]

thew *thū,* (used chiefly in *pl.* **thews, thewes**) *n.* custom: trait: manner: moral quality: later, bodily quality, muscle or strength. — *adjs.* **thewed** mannered (*Spens.*): (*later*) muscular; **thew′less** (see also **thowless**); **thew′y** muscular, strong. [O.E. *thēaw,* manner.]

they *dhā, pron., nom. pl.,* used as *pl.* of **he, she, it:** often used as a *sing.* (with *pl. vb.*) of common gender, he or she, people in general, some. — **they′d** a contraction of **they had** or **they would; they′ll** a contraction of **they will** or **they shall; they′re** a contraction of **they are; they′ve** a contraction of **they have.** [M.E. *thei* — O.N. *their,* which supplanted *hi* (O.E. *hīe*).]

thiamine, thiamin *thī′ə-mēn, -min, n.* vitamin B₁. [Gr. *theion,* sulphur, and **amine.**]

thiasus *thī′ə-səs, n.* a company or troop of worshippers, esp. a Bacchic rout. [Gr. *thiasos.*]

thiazide *thī′ə-zīd, n.* any of a group of drugs used as diuretics and to treat hypertension. [*thio-, azo-, oxide.*]

Thibet. See **Tibet.**

thible *thib′l, thīb′l,* **thivel** *thiv′l, thīv′l,* (*Northern*) *ns.* a porridge-stick. [Origin unknown.]

thick[1] *thik, adj.* having a great (or specified) distance in measurement from surface to surface in lesser dimension: deep: dense: viscous: close set or packed: crowded: intimate, in close confidence (*fig.*): abundant: frequent, in quick succession: aboundingly covered or occupied: foggy: opaque: dull: stupid: gross: husky, muffled: indistinctly articulate: excessive, approaching the intolerable (*slang*). — *n.* the thickest part of anything: the midst: a stupid person (*slang*): a thicket (*Spens.*). — *adv.* thickly: closely: frequently: fast: to a great (or specified) depth. — *v.t.* and *v.i.*

(*Spens.*, *Shak.*) to make or become thick. — *v.t.* and *v.i.* **thick'en** to make or become thick or thicker. — *ns.* **thick'ener; thick'ening** a making or becoming thicker: a thickened place: material added to something to thicken it. — Also *adj.* — *n.* **thick'et** (O.E. *thiccet*) a dense mass of trees or shrubs. — *adjs.* **thick'eted; thick'ety; thick'ish** somewhat thick. — *adv.* **thick'ly.** — *ns.* **thick'ness** a quality or degree of being thick: the space between outer surfaces: a layer; **thick'o** (*slang*) a stupid person: — *pl.* **thick'o(e)s.** — *adjs.* **thick'-and-thin'** unwavering in devotion to party or principle; **thick'-com'ing** (*Shak.*) coming close upon one another. — **thick ear** a bruised, swollen ear, usually a result of a blow administered as punishment. — *adjs.* **thick'-eyed** dim-sighted; **thick'-grown** (*Shak.*). — **thick'head** a blockhead: any bird of an Australian family (*Pachycephalidae*) akin to fly-catchers and shrikes. — *adj.* **thick'-head'ed** having a thick head or skull: stupid. — **thick'-knee** the stone-curlew (Oedicnemus), a large plover with thickened knees. — *adj.* **thick'-lipped** (*Shak.*). — **thick'-lips** (*Shak.*) a Negro. — *adjs.* **thick'-pleached** (*Shak.*) closely interwoven; **thick'-ribbed** (*Shak.*); **thick'set** closely set or planted: having a short thick body. — *n.* a thicket: a stout cotton. — *adj.* **thick'-sight'ed** (*Shak.*) dim-sighted. — **thick'skin** a blockhead. — *adj.* **thick'-skinned'** having a thick skin: insensitive: indifferent to criticism or insult. — **thick'-skull** a blockhead. — *adjs.* **thick'-skull'ed** having a thick skull: doltish; **thick'-sown** planted closely: close-set. — **thick''un** (*slang*) a sovereign: a crown. — *adj.* **thick'-witt'ed** doltish. — **a bit thick** more than one can reasonably be expected to put up with; **as thick as a plank, as thick as two short planks** very stupid; **as thick as thieves** very friendly; **lay it on thick** to praise extravagantly: to exaggerate; **through thick and thin** in spite of all obstacles: without any wavering. [O.E. *thicce*; Ger. *dick*.]

thick[2], thicky *dhik, dhik'i.* See **thilk.**

thief *thēf, n.* one who takes unlawfully what is not his own, esp. by stealth: a flaw in a candle-wick that causes guttering: — *pl.* **thieves** (*thēvz*). — *adj.* and *adv.* **thief'-like.** — **thief'-catcher, -taker** one whose business is to arrest thieves: a detective. — **thieves' kitchen** a haunt of thieves and other criminals. [O.E. *thēof:* cf. Ger. *Dieb.*]

thieve *thēv, v.i.* to practise theft: to steal. — *n.* **thiev'ery** the practice of thieving: what is thieved. — *n.* and *adj.* **thiev'ing.** — *adj.* **thiev'ish** infested by thieves (*Shak.*): given to, or like, theft: thief-like: furtive. — *adv.* **thiev'ishly.** — *n.* **thiev'ishness.** [O.E. *thēofian,* to thieve, and *thēof,* thief.]

thig *thig,* (*Scot.*) *v.i.* to beg: to live on alms. — *v.t.* to beg: to get by begging: — *pa.t.* and *pa.p.* **thigg'it.** — *ns.* **thigg'er; thigg'ing.** — **thigging and sorning** extortionate begging and sponging. [O.N. *thiggja;* cf. O.E. *thicgan,* to take.]

thigh *thī, n.* the thick fleshy part of the leg from the knee to the trunk. — **thigh'-bone** the bone of the leg between the hip-joint and the knee, the femur; **thigh boot** a tall boot covering the thigh. [O.E. *thēoh* (Anglian *thēh*); O.N. *thjō;* O.H.G. *dioh.*]

thigmotropism *thig-mot'rə-pizm,* (*biol.*) *n.* response to stimulus of touch. — *adj.* **thigmotropic** (*-mə-trop'ik*). [Gr. *thigma, -atos,* touch, *tropos,* a turning.]

thilk *dhilk,* (*dial.*) *adj.* and *pron.* the same, that same: this. — Also (*S.W. England*) **thick** (*dhik*), **thick'y.** [**the ilk.**]

thill[1] *thil, n.* the shaft of a vehicle. — *n.* **thill'er.** — **thill'-horse** a shaft-horse, or the last of a team. [Poss. O.E. *thille,* board, plank.]

thill[2] *thil,* (*dial.*) *n.* underclay or floor of a coal-seam: a bed of fireclay. [Origin unknown.]

thimble *thim'bl, n.* a cover for the finger, used in sewing: an object of similar form: a metal ring with a grooved or concave outer edge fitted into a rope ring, etc. to prevent chafing (*naut.*). — *v.i.* to use a thimble. — *v.t.* to use a thimble on. — *n.* **thim'bleful** as much as a thimble will hold: a small quantity: — *pl.* **thim'blefuls.** — **thim'ble-case; thim'ble-rig** a sleight-of-hand trick in which the performer conceals, or pretends to conceal, a pea or small ball under one of three thimble-like cups. — *v.i.* to cheat by such means. — *v.t.* to manipulate in this or analogous way. — **thimb'le-rigger; thim'ble-rigging.** [O.E. *thȳmel,* thumb-stall — *thūma,* thumb.]

thin *thin,* (*adj. compar.* **thinn'er;** *superl.* **thinn'est**) having little thickness: slim: lean: freely mobile: watery: dilute: of little density: rarefied: sparse: slight: flimsy: wanting in body or solidity: meagre: poor: tinkling: too much to the left (golf, etc.). — *n.* that which is thin. — *adv.* **thinly.** — *v.t.* to make thin or thinner: to make less close or crowded (with *away, out,* etc.): to hit (a shot, etc.) too far to the left (*golf*). — *v.i.* to grow or become thin or thinner: — *pr.p.* **thinn'ing;** *pa.t.* and *pa.p.* **thinned.** — *adv.* **thin'ly.** — *ns.* **thinn'er** a person or thing that thins, esp. (often in *pl.*, sometimes treated as *n.sing.*) a diluent for paint; **thin'ness; thinn'ing.** — *adj.* **thinn'ish** somewhat thin. — *adjs.* **thin'-belly** (*Shak.*) narrow in the belly; **thin'-faced** (*Shak.*); **thin'-skinned'** having thin skin: sensitive: irritable. — **thin'-skinned'-ness.** — *adjs.* **thin'-sown** sparsely sown; **thin'-spun** drawn out fine. — **thin''un** a half sovereign. — *adj.* **thin'-walled'.** — **a thin time** a time of hardship, misery, etc.; **into, out of, thin air** into, out of, nothing or nothingness; **thin blue line** a line of policemen drawn up to quell crowd violence, etc., coined in imitation of **thin red line; thin on the ground** present in very small, inadequate, quality or numbers; **thin on top** balding; **thin red line** a designation for the British army, orig. used in reports of the Crimean campaign, when uniforms were still red, conveying an image of indomitability against heavy odds. [O.E. *thynne;* Ger. *dünn;* O.N. *thunnr.*]

thine *dhīn, pron., gen.* of **thou[1],** used predicatively or absolutely, belonging to thee: thy people: that which belongs to thee: adjectively, esp. before a vowel or *h,* thy. [O.E. *thīn.*]

thing *thing, n.* an assembly, parliament, court, council (*hist.*): a matter, affair, problem, point: a circumstance: a fact: an event, happening, action: an entity: that which exists or can be thought of: an inanimate object: a living creature (esp. in pity, tolerant affection, kindly reproach): a possession: a piece of writing, composition, etc.: that which is wanted or is appropriate (*coll.*): a slight obsession or phobia (*coll.*): an unaccountable liking or dislike (*coll.*): (in *pl.*) clothes, esp. a woman's additional outdoor garments: (in *pl.*) utensils, esp. for the table: (in *pl.*) personal belongings. — *ns.* **thing'amy, thing'ummy, thing'amybob, thing'amyjig, thing'um-abob, thing'umajig, thing'umbob, thing'ummybob, thing'ummyjig.** (*coll.*) what-d'you-call-him (-her, -it): what's-his-name, etc. — used when one cannot or will not recall the name; **thing'hood** the state or fact of being a thing: substantiality; **thing'iness, thing'liness** reality, objectivity: a materialistic or matter-of-fact turn of mind; **thing'ness** the character or fact of being a thing: reality. — *adj.* **thing'y** real: actual: objective: matter-of-fact. — *n.* **thingumajig.** — **thing'-in-itself** a noumenon, the Ger. *Ding an sich.* — **a good thing** a fortunate circumstance; **and things** and other (similar) things; **a stupid, wise,** etc., **thing to do** a stupid, wise, etc., action; **be all things to all men** to meet each on his, her, own ground, accommodate oneself to his, her, circumstances and outlook (1 Cor. ix. 22): (loosely, in a bad sense) to keep changing one's opinions, etc., so as to suit one's company; **be on to a good thing** (*coll.*) to be in a particularly profitable position, job, etc.; **do one's (own) thing** (*coll.*) to behave as is natural to, characteristic of, oneself: to do something in which one specialises; **do the handsome thing by** to treat generously; **do things to** to affect in some good or bad way; **for one thing . . . for another (thing)** expressions used in enumerating reasons; **have a good thing going** (*slang*) to be established in a particularly profitable position, etc.; **hear things** to hear imaginary noises, voices, etc.; **know a thing or two** to be shrewd; **make a good thing of it** to reap a good advantage from; **make a thing of** to make an issue, point of controversy, of: to fuss about; **no such thing** something very different: no, not at all; **not a thing** nothing; **not quite the thing** not in very good health (see also **the thing**); **one of those things** a happening one cannot account for or do anything to prevent; **see things** to see something that is not really there; **the (done) thing** that which is conventional, fashionable, approved, right, or desirable.   [O.E. and O.N. *thing*, parliament, object, etc.: Norw., Sw., Dan. *ting*, parliament; Ger. *Ding*, thing.]

think[1] *thingk, v.i.* to exercise the mind (often with *about, of,* or arch. *on, upon*): to revolve ideas in the mind: to judge: to be of opinion: to consider: to bethink oneself: to conceive or hit on a thought: to aspire or form designs (with *of* or *about*): — *v.t.* to form, conceive, or revolve in the mind: to have as a thought: to imagine: to judge: to believe or consider: to expect: to purpose, design: to believe to exist (*Milt.*): to bring by thinking: — *pa.t.* and *pa.p.* **thought** (*thöt*). — *n.* (*coll.*) a spell of thinking: a thought. — *adj.* **think'able** capable of being thought: conceivably possible. — *n.* **think'er.** — *n.* and *adj.* **think'ing.** — *adv.* **think'ingly.** — **think'=tank** (*coll.*) a person or a group of people, usu. expert in some field, regarded as a source of ideas and solutions to problems. — **have another think coming** to be wrong in what one thinks (about future events or actions); **I don't think** I disbelieve: a warning that what was said was ironical (*coll.*); **I shouldn't, wouldn't, think of** I would not under any conditions; **just, to think of it** an expression of surprise, disapproval, longing, etc.; **put on one's thinking-cap** to devote some time to thinking about some problem; **think again** to change one's opinion (of necessity); **think aloud** to utter one's thoughts unintentionally; **think back to** to bring to one's mind the memory of (a past event, etc.); **think better of** to change one's mind concerning on reflection; **think for** to expect; **think little of** to have a poor opinion of — opp. to **think much,** or **well, of; think long** to yearn: to weary (from deferred hopes or boredom); **think nothing of** not to consider difficult, exceptional, etc.; **think nothing of it** it does not matter, is not important; **think out** to devise, project completely: to solve by a process of thought; **think over** to reconsider at leisure; **think shame** to be ashamed; **think through** to solve by a process of thought: to project and consider all the possible consequences, problems, etc. relating to (some course of action); **think twice** (often with *about*) to hesitate (before doing something): to decide not to do; **think up** to find by thinking, devise, concoct.   [O.E. *thencan.*]

think[2] *thingk, v.i.* (*impers.,* arch. with *me* or other dat. pron. prefixed; otherwise *obs.*) to seem: — *pa.t.* **thought** (*thöt*).   [O.E. *thyncan,* to seem.]

thio- *thī'ö-,* in composition, sulphur, indicating in chemistry a compound theoretically derived from another by substituting an atom or more of sulphur for oxygen. — *ns.* **thi'o-acid** an acid analogous in constitution to an oxy-acid, sulphur taking the place of oxygen; **thiobarbit'urate** a salt of **thiobarbitu'ric acid** ($C_6H_4N_2O_2S$), similar in effect to a barbiturate; **thiocy'anate** a salt of **thiocyan'ic acid,** HSCN; **thi'ol** (or *-öl*) mercaptan; **thiopent'one,** (*U.S.*) **thiopent'al,** see Pentothal; **thi'o-salt** a salt of a thio-acid; **thiouracil** (*thī-ö-ū'rə-sil*) a derivative of thiourea that interferes with the synthesis of thyroid hormone; **thiourea** (*thī-ö-ū'ri-ə*) urea with its oxygen replaced by sulphur, a bitter crystalline substance that inhibits thyroid activity and is used e.g. in photographic fixing. — **Thiobacillus ferro-oxidans** a rod-shaped bacillus which, in the presence of water, converts copper sulphide ores into copper sulphate (see **bacterial leaching** under leach[1]).   [Gr. *theion,* sulphur.]

thir *dhir,* (*Scot.*) *pl. demons. pron.* and *demons. adj.* these.   [Origin obscure.]

thiram *thīram, n.* a fungicide.   [*thio*urea and carb*am*ic.]

third *thûrd, adj.* the last of three: next after the second: equal to one of three equal parts. — *n.* a third part: a person or thing in third position: an interval of two (conventionally called three) diatonic degrees (*mus.*): a note at that interval: a handicap of a stroke at six holes out of eighteen (*golf*): third gear. — *adv.* in the third place. — *v.t.* to divide by three: to support after the seconder. — *n.* **third'ing** a third part. — *adv.* **third'ly** in the third place. — *adj.* **third'-class.** — *adv.* **third'=class'.** — **third degree** see degree; **third dimension** depth, thickness: the dimension of depth, distinguishing a solid object from a two-dimensional or planar object. — *adj.* **third-dimen'sional.** — **third force** a group following a middle or uncommitted course between contending extremes. — *adj.* **third'-hand'.** — **third man** (*cricket*) a fielder on the offside between point and slip. — *adjs.* **third'-party** of a person other than the principals (as insured and insurer); **third'-programme** highbrow, in allusion to the Third Programme (1946–70) of the B.B.C. — **third rail** a rail carrying electricity to an electrically-powered train. — *adj.* **third'-rate** of the third order: of poor quality. — **thirds'man** a mediator. — *adj.* **third'-stream** of a style of music, having features of both jazz and classical music. — **Third World** the developing countries not aligned politically with the large power blocks. — **Picardy third** tierce de Picardie.   [O.E. *thridda;* cf. Ger. *dritte,* Gr. *tritos,* L. *tertius.*]

thirdborough *thûrd'bər-ə,* (*hist.*) *n.* an under-constable.   [Supposed to be from O.E. *frithborh,* a surety for peace (see under **frith**).]

thirl[1] *thûrl,* (*dial.*) *n.* a hole: an opening: a short passage between two headings in a mine. — *v.t.* to pierce: to thrill. — *v.i.* to vibrate, tingle, thrill.   [O.E. *thyrel,* hole — *thurh,* through; cf. **thrill.**]

thirl[2] *thûrl, n.* a form of **thrall:** thirlage. — *v.t.* to bind or subject: to confine, restrict. — *n.* **thirl'age** a form of servitude by which the grain produced on certain lands had to be ground (or at least paid for) at a certain mill.

thirst *thûrst, n.* the uneasiness caused by want of drink: vehement desire for drink: eager desire for anything. — *v.i.* to feel thirst. — *n.* **thirst'er.** — *adj.* **thirst'ful.** — *adv.* **thirst'ily.** — *n.* **thirst'iness.** — *adjs.* **thirst'less; thirst'y** suffering from thirst: dry: parched: vehemently desiring.   [O.E. *thurst* (n.), *thyrstan* (vb.); cf. Ger. *Durst, dürsten,* Gr. *tersesthai,* L. *torrēre,* to dry.]

thirteen *thûr'tēn,* or *-tēn', adj.* and *n.* three and ten. — *adj.* **thir'teenth** (or *-tēnth'*) last of thirteen: next after the twelfth: equal to one of thirteen equal parts. — *n.* a thirteenth part: a person or thing in thirteenth position. — *adv.* **thirteenth'ly.**   [O.E. *thrēotīene, -tēne* — *thrēo,* three.]

thirty *thûr'ti, adj.* and *n.* three times ten. — *n.pl.* **thir'ties** the numbers from thirty to thirty-nine: the years so numbered in life or any century: a range of temperatures from thirty to just under forty degrees. — *adj.* **thir'tieth** last of thirty: next after the twenty-ninth: equal to one of thirty equal parts. — *n.* a thirtieth part: a person or thing in thirtieth position. — *adj.,* and *adv.* **thir'tyfold.** — *adjs.* **thir'tyish** somewhere about the age of thirty; **thirty-two'mo** (for *tricesimo secundo,* 32mo) in sheets folded to give 32 leaves (64 pages). — *n.* a book so constructed: — *pl.* **-mos.**   [O.E. *thrītig* — *thrēo,* three, *-tig,* suff. denoting ten.]

this *dhis, sing. demons. pron.* or *adj.* denoting a person or thing near, topical, just mentioned, or about to be mentioned: (up to and including) the present moment: the place where the speaker is: sometimes used almost with the force of an *indef. art.:* — *pl.* **these.** — *adv.* (*Shak.*) thus: to this extent (*coll.*). — *n.* **this'ness** the quality of being this, not something else, haecceity. — **this and that** or **this, that and the other** various minor unspecified objects, actions, etc.   [O.E., neut. of *thes, thēos, this* (instrumental *thīs, thȳs;* nom. pl. *thās, thæs*).]

thistle *this'l, n.* a prickly composite plant (*Carduus, Cnicus, Onopordon,* etc.) — the national emblem of

Scotland. — *adj.* **this′tly** like a thistle: overgrown with thistles. — **this′tle-butterfly** the painted lady, *Vanessa cardui*; **this′tle-down** the tufted feathery parachutes of thistle seeds. — **Order of the Thistle** a Scottish order of knighthood. [O.E. *thistel*.]

thither *dhidh′ər* (*Spens.* often **thether**), *adv.* to that place: to that end or result. — *adv.* on the far side. — *advs.* **thith′erward, -s** toward that place. [O.E. *thider*.]

thivel. See **thible.**

thixotropy *thiks-ot′rə-pi*, *n.* the property of showing a temporary reduction in viscosity when shaken or stirred. — *adj.* **thixotropic** (*-trop′ik*) of, or showing, thixotropy: (of paints) non-drip. [Gr. *thixis*, action of touching, *tropos*, a turn.]

thlipsis *thlip′sis*, *n.* constriction: compression. [Gr. *thlīpsis* — *thlībein*, to press.]

tho¹ *dhō*, (*Spens.*) *pl. demons. adj.* those. [O.E. *thā*, pl. of *se, sēo, thæt*, that.]

tho² *dhō*, (*Spens.*) *adv.* then. [O.E. (and O.N.) *thā*.]

tho′. Same as **though.**

thoft *thoft*, (*dial.*) *n.* a rowing-bench. [O.E. *thofte*.]

thole¹ *thōl*, *n.* a pin in the side of a boat to keep the oar in place: a peg. — Also **thowl, thowel.** — **thole′-pin** a peg, thole. [O.E. *thol*; Du. *dol*, O.N. *thollr*.]

thole² *thōl*, (now *Scot.*) *v.t.* and *v.i.* to endure. [O.E. *tholian*, to suffer; Goth. *thulan*, O.N. *thola*; O.H.G. *dolên*, Ger. *Geduld*, patience, *dulden*, to suffer, L. *tollēre*, Gr. *tolmaein*.]

tholus *thō′ləs, n.* a round building, dome, cupola, or tomb: — *pl.* **thō′li** (*-lī*). — Also **tholos** (*thol′os*; *pl.* **thol′oi**). — *n.* **tholobate** (*thol′ō-bāt*; from root of Gr. *bainein*, to go) the substructure of a dome or cupola. [Gr. *thólos*.]

Thomism *tō′mizm, n.* the doctrines of *Thomas* Aquinas (b. prob. 1225; d. 1274). — *n.* and *adj.* **Thō′mist.** — *adjs.* **Thōmist′ic, -al.**

Thompson submachine-gun *tom′sən sub-mə-shēn′gun*, a tommy-gun. — Also **Thompson gun.**

thon *dhon*, **thon′der** *-dər*, unexplained modern Scots forms of **yon, yonder** prob. influenced by *this* and *that*.

thong *thong*, *n.* a strap: a strip: the lash of a whip or crop: a sandal held on by a thong between the toes, a flipflop. — *adj.* **thonged** having a thong or thongs. [O.E. *thwang*.]

Thor *thör, n.* the Scandinavian thunder-god, Old English Thunor. [O.N. *Thōrr*.]

thoraces, thoracic. See **thorax.**

Thorah. See **Torah.**

thorax *thō′raks, thō′, n.* a corslet (*Gr. ant.*): the part of the body between the head and abdomen, in man the chest, in insects the division that bears legs and wings: — *pl.* **tho′raxes, -races** (*-sēz*). — *adj.* **thoracic** (*-ras′*). — **thoracic duct** the main trunk of the vessels conveying lymph in the body. [Gr. *thōrāx -ākos.*]

thorium *thō′ri-əm, thō′, n.* a radioactive metal (Th; at. numb. 90) resembling aluminium. — *ns.* **thō′rite** a mineral, thorium silicate, in which it was first discovered, by Berzelius; **thoron** (*thō′ron, thō′*) the radioactive gas given off by the decomposition of thorium. [*Thor*, the god.]

thorn *thörn, n.* a sharp hard part (leaf, stem, or root) of a plant: an animal spine: anything prickly: a spiny plant: hawthorn: the Old English and Old Norse letter þ (*th*). — *v.t.* to set with thorns: to prick. — *adj.* **thorned.** — *n.* **thorn′iness.** — *adjs.* **thorn′less; thorn′set** set or beset with thorns; **thorn′y** full of thorns: prickly: troublesome: harassing. — **thorn′-apple** a poisonous plant (*Datura stramonium*, or other species) of the potato family, with a prickly capsule: a haw; **thorn′-back** a ray with nail-like crooked spines in its back; **thorn′-bush** any thorny shrub, esp. hawthorn; **thorn′=hedge** a hedge of hawthorn; **thorn′tree** a thorny tree, esp. a hawthorn; **thorny devil** the Australian Moloch lizard. — **thorn in the flesh** any cause of constant irritation, from 2 Cor. xii. 7. [O.E. *thorn*; O.N. *thorn*, Ger. *Dorn*.]

thoron. See **thorium.**

thorough *thur′ə, adj.* passing or carried through, or to the end: complete: entire: out-and-out: assiduous and scrupulous in completing work. — *prep.* (*obs.*) through. — *n.* that which goes through, a passage: the blind and obstinately tyrannical policy of Strafford and Laud in administering civil and ecclesiastical affairs without regard to opposite convictions. — *adv.* **thor′oughly.** — *n.* **thor′oughness.** — **thor′ough-bass** (*mus.*) a bass part all through a piece, usu. with figures to indicate the chords: (*loosely*) harmony: erron. a deep bass; **thor′oughbrace** (*U.S.*) a leather band supporting the body of a vehicle: a stagecoach. — *adj.* **thor′-oughbred** thoroughly or completely bred or trained: bred from a dam and sire of the best blood, as a horse, and having the qualities supposed to depend thereon: pure-bred: (with *cap.*) pertaining to the Thoroughbred breed of horses. — *n.* an animal, esp. a horse, of pure blood: (with *cap.*) a racehorse of a breed descended from any of three Arabian stallions of the early 18th cent., whose ideal gait is the gallop. — **thor′oughfare** a passage or way through: a road open at both ends: a public way or street: right of passing through. — *adjs.* **thor′oughgoing** going through or to the end: going all lengths: complete: out-and-out; **thor′ough-paced** thoroughly or perfectly paced or trained: complete. — **thor′oughwax, thor′ow-wax** the plant hare′s-ear, from the stem seeming to grow (wax) through the leaves. **post-vintage thoroughbred** a car built between 1st January 1931 and 31st December 1941. [The longer form of **through.**]

thorp, thorpe *thörp*, (*arch.*) *n.* a hamlet: a village. [O.E. *thorp, throp*; O.N. *thorp*, Goth. *thaurp*, Ger. *Dorf*.]

those *dhōz*, demons. *pron.* and *adj.*, *pl.* of **that.** [O.E. *thās*, pl. of *thes*, this.]

Thoth *thōth, thoth, tōt, n.* the ancient Egyptian ibis-headed god of art, science, etc. [Gr. *Thōth* — Egypt. *Tehuti*.]

thother. See **th-.**

thou¹ *dhow, pron.* of the second person sing., the person addressed (now generally used only in solemn address). — *v.t.* to apply the pronoun *thou* to: — *pa.t.* and *pa.p.* **thou′d.** [O.E. *thū*; Goth. *thu*, Doric Gr. *ty*, L. *tū*, Sans. *tvam*.]

thou² *thow*, a coll. short form of **thousand(th),** used esp. as a contraction of *one thousandth of an inch.*

though *dhō, conj.* admitting: allowing: even if: notwithstanding that. — *adv.* nevertheless: however. — **as though** as if. [O.N. *thauh, thō*; O.E. *thēah, thēh*, Ger. *doch*.]

thought¹ *thöt.* See under **think¹,².** [O.E. *thōhte*, pa.t., (*ge*)*thōht*, pa.p.]

thought² *thöt, n.* thinking: mind: consciousness: reasoning: deliberation: that which one thinks: notion: idea: fancy: consideration: opinion: meditation: design: care: considerateness: purpose: resolution: intention: grief, anxiety (*obs.*): a very slight amount, a 'suspicion'. — *adjs.* **thought′ed** having thoughts; **thought′en** (*Shak.*) firm in belief, assured; **thought′ful** full of thought: employed in meditation: attentive: considerate: expressive of or favourable to meditation. — *adv.* **thought′fully.** — *n.* **thought′fulness.** — *adj.* **thought′less** unthinking: incapable of thinking: carefree: careless: inattentive: inconsiderate. — *adv.* **thought′lessly.** — *n.* **thought′lessness.** — *adj.* **thought-ex′ecuting** carrying out the wishes of a master: perh. acting with the speed of thought (*Shak.*). — **thought′-pro′cess** train of thought: manner of thinking; **thought′-reader**; **thought′-reading** discerning what is passing in another′s mind by any means other than the ordinary and obvious. — *adj.* **thought′-sick** (*Shak.*) sick with the thought. — **thought′-trans′ference** telepathy; **thought′=wave** a wave-like progress of a thought among a crowd or a public: a sudden accession of thought in the mind: an impulse in some hypothetical medium assumed to explain telepathy. — **on second thoughts** on reconsideration; **take thought** to bethink oneself: to conceive a purpose: to be anxious or grieved (*obs.*); **upon, with, a**

thought (*Shak.*) in a moment: with the speed of thought. [O.E. (*ge*)*thōht*.]

thous *dhowz*, a Northern contracted form of **thou is**, thou art (*Spens.*) and of **thou sal**, thou shalt.

thousand *thow'zənd*, *n.* and *adj.* ten hundred: often used vaguely or hyperbolically. — *adj.*, *adv.*, and *n.* (a) thou'sandfold a thousand times as much. — *adj.* thou'sandth last of a thousand, or in an equivalent position in a greater number: equal to one of a thousand equal parts. — *n.* a thousandth part: a person or thing in thousandth position. — thou'sand-legs a centipede or millipede. — *adjs.* thou'sand-pound' weighing, costing, priced at a thousand pounds; thou'sand-year lasting, or coming once in, a thousand years. — a thousand and one (*coll.*) very many: an overwhelming number; one in (of) a thousand anything exceedingly rare or excellent. [O.E. *thūsend*; Ger. *tausend*, Goth. *thūsundi*.]

thowel, thowl. See thole[1].

thowless *thow'lis*, (*Scot.*) *adj.* pithless: listless: inert. [App. thewless.]

thrae *thrā*, another form of Scots frae.

thrall *thröl*, *n.* a slave, serf: slavery, servitude: a stand for barrels, pans, etc. — *adj.* (*arch.*) enslaved. — *v.t.* to enslave. — *n.* thral'dom (also thrall'dom) slavery: bondage. [O.E. *thrǣl* — O.N. *thrǣll*.]

thrang *thrang*, a Scots form of throng.

thrapple *thrap'l*, a Scots form of thropple.

thrash[1] *thrash*, *v.t.* to thresh: (with *out*) to discuss exhaustively, or arrive at by debate: to beat soundly: to defeat thoroughly. — *v.i.* to lash out, lay about one: to force one's way (*naut.*). — *n.* an act of threshing or thrashing: a party (*coll.*). — *n.* thrash'er a thresher: a thrasher-shark: one who thrashes. — *n.* and *adj.* thrash'ing threshing: beating. — thrash'ing-floor, -machine, -mill same as threshing-floor, etc. (see thresh[1]). [Orig. a dialect form of thresh[1].]

thrash[2] *thrash*, thresh *thresh*, (*Scot.*) *ns.* a rush (plant). [Obscurely conn. with rush[2].]

thrasher[1] *thrash'ər*, thresher *thresh'ər*, *ns.* any of several American birds akin to the mocking-bird. [Perh. Eng. dial. *thresher*, thrush.]

thrasher[2]. See thrash[1].

thrasonic, -al *thrə-*, *thrā-son'ik*, *-l*, *adjs.* like *Thrasōn*, the bragging soldier, a stock character in Greek New Comedy, or *Thrasō* in Terence's *Eunuchus*: boastful, bragging. — *adv.* thrason'ically.

thrave *thrāv*, threave *thrēv*, (*dial.*) *ns.* two stooks of (usu.) twelve sheaves each: two dozen: a good number. [Scand.; cf. Icel. *threfi*, Dan. *trave*.]

thraw *thrö*, a Scots form of throw[1] with some old senses preserved; also of throe, with senses overlapping throw[1]. — *v.t.* to turn: to twist: to wring: to distort: to wrest: to cross, thwart. — *v.i.* to turn: to twist: to writhe: to sway: to go counter: to be perverse: — *pa.t.* threw; *pa.p.* thrawn. — *adj.* twisted: distorted: wry. — *n.* a twist: a fit of perversity: a throe. — *adj.* thrawn twisted: wry: cross-grained, perverse. — dead thraw the agony of death; heads and thraws side by side, the head of the one by the feet of another.

thrawart, thraward *thrö'ərt*, (*Scot.*) *adj.* froward: crooked. [M.E. *fraward*; see froward; perh. influenced by thraw; cf. thrae.]

thread *thred*, *n.* a very thin line of any substance, esp. linen or cotton, twisted or drawn out: a filament: a fibre: (in *pl.*) clothes (*slang*): the prominent spiral part of a screw: a continuous connecting element in a story, argument, etc. — *v.t.* to pass a thread through: to string on a thread: to pass or pierce through, as a narrow way: to furnish with a thread. — *adj.* made of linen or cotton thread. — *adj.* thread'en (*Shak.*) made of thread. — *ns.* thread'er; thread'iness. — *adj.* thread'y like thread: slender: containing or consisting of thread. — *adj.* thread'bare worn to the bare thread: having the nap worn off: hackneyed: used till its novelty or interest is gone. — thread'bareness; thread'-cell in jellyfishes, etc., a stinging cell that throws out a

stinging thread; thread'-lace lace made of linen thread; thread'maker; thread mark a coloured thread incorporated in bank-notes to make counterfeiting difficult; thread'-paper a piece of thin soft paper for wrapping up a skein of thread; thread'-worm any member of the Nematoda, more or less thread-like worms, many parasitic, others free-living: esp. *Oxyuris vermicularis*, parasitic in the human rectum. — thread and thrum all, the good and bad together; thread of life the thread imagined to be spun and cut by the Fates. [O.E. *thrǣd*; cf. throw[1], thraw.]

Threadneedle Street *thred'nēdl strēt*, a street in the city of London. — Old Lady, Woman, of Threadneedle Street the Bank of England.

threap, threep *thrēp*, (*Scot.* and *Northern*) *v.t.* to rebuke: to maintain persistently: to insist: to urge, to press eagerly: to answer back, make objections: to contradict: — *v.i.* to dispute: — *pa.t.* and *pa.p.* threap'it, threep'it. — *n.* stubborn insistence or assertion: accusation: a traditional belief. [O.E. *thrēapian*, to rebuke.]

threave. See thrave.

three *thrē*, *n.* two and one: a set of three: a symbol for three: a card with three pips: a score of three points, strokes, etc.: an article of a size denoted by three: the third hour after midnight or midday: the age of three years. — *adj.* of the number three: three years old. — *ns.* three'ness the state of being three; three'some a company of three persons: a game or dance for three. — *adj.* for three: triple. — three balls the pawnbroker's sign. — *adjs.* three'-bott'le able to drink three bottles of wine at a sitting; three'-card played with three cards (see also three-card trick below); three'-cen'tred of an arch, composed of circular arcs with three different centres. — three cheers three shouts of 'hurrah', to show approbation, etc. (also *fig.*). — *adjs.* three'-cleft cut halfway down into three lobes; three'-colour involving or using three colours as primary; three'-cor'nered triangular in form or section: having three competitors or three members; three'-deck. — three'-deck'er a ship with three decks or guns on three decks: a building or structure with three floors or tiers: a pulpit with three levels: a three-volume novel: a double sandwich, with two layers of filling, three layers of bread. — Also *adj.* — *adjs.* three'-dimen'sional having, or seeming to have, three dimensions: giving the effect of being seen or heard in an environment of three dimensions — usu. 3-D: (of, e.g. a literary work) developed in detail and thus realistic. — three'-dimensional'ity. — *adj.* three-far'thing. — *n.sing.* three-far'things a silver coin of Queen Elizabeth, distinguished from a penny by a rose behind the queen's head. — *adj.* and *adv.* three'fold in three divisions: three times as much. — *n.* three'foldness. — *adjs.* three'-foot measuring or having three feet; three'-four' (*mus.*) with three crotchets to the bar. — three-halfpence (*thrē-hā'pəns*) an old penny and a halfpenny: a coin of that value. — *adj.* three-halfpenny (*thrē-hāp'ni*). — three-halfpennyworth, threeha'porth (*thrē-hāp'ərth*). — *adjs.* three'-hand'ed having three hands: played by three players; three'-leaved (or -leafed) having three leaves or leaflets: having leaves in threes; three'-legged (-*legd*, -*leg'id*) having three legs: of a race, run by pairs of runners, each with a leg tied to his partner's; three'-man (*Shak.*) worked or performed by three men; three'-

mast'ed. — **three'-mast'er** a ship with three masts. — *n.* and *adj.* **three'-month'ly** quarterly. — *adjs.* **three'= nooked** (*Shak.*) three-cornered; **three'-pair (-of-stairs)** on a third floor. — *n.* a room so situated. — *adjs.* **three'-part** composed in three parts or for three voices; **three'-part'ed** consisting of three parts: parted in three: divided into three nearly to the base. — *adv.* **three'= parts** to the extent of three-fourth. — **threepence** (*threp', thrip', thrup'əns*) money, or a coin, of the value of three old pence. — *adj.* **threepenny** (*threp', thrip', thrup'ni* or *-ə-ni*) sold or offered at threepence: of little worth: mean, vulgar. — *n.* a coin of the value of threepence (also **threepenny bit, piece**). — **threepenny-worth** or **threepenn'orth** (*thrē-pen'i-wərth* or *thrē-pen'-ərth*), also (chiefly *Scot.*) **threep'enceworth.** — *n.pl.* **three'-per-cents'** bonds or other securities paying three per cent. interest, esp. a portion of the consolidated debt of Great Britain. — *adjs.* **three'-piece** comprising three parts, three matching pieces, etc.; **three'-pile** having loops of three threads. — *n.* (*Shak.*) the finest kind of velvet. — *adjs.* **three'-piled** three-pile: piled three high; **three'-ply** having three layers or strands; **three'-pound** costing or weighing three pounds. — **three-pound'er** a thing that weighs three pounds: a gun that shoots a three-pound ball; **three'-pricker** (*airmen's slang*) a three-point landing: anything right or perfect. — *adj.* and *adv.* **three-quar'ter** to the amount of three-fourths: (*adj.*) being three quarters of the normal size or length (used of beds, coats, etc.). — *n.* a three-quarter back. — **three quarters** (a part equal to) three fourths of a whole: the greater part of something. — *n.* and *adj.* **three'score** sixty. — *adjs.* **three'-sid'ed** having three sides; **three'-square** equilaterally triangular; **three'-suit'ed** (*Shak.*) allowed three suits of clothes a year as a serving-man; **three'-vol'ume** in three volumes; **three'-way** giving connection in three directions from a centre. — **three-card trick** a card-sharper's ploy in which the victim is invited to wager on which of three cards, turned face-down and deftly manipulated, is the queen (also *find the lady*); **three-colour process** the method of producing colour pictures from three primary originals — yellow, red, blue — prepared by photography; **three-day event, eventer** see **event; three= line whip** see **whip; three-mile limit** by international law, the outer limit of the territorial waters around a state; **three-point landing** (*aero.*) a landing with all three wheels touching the ground at the same moment — a perfect landing; **three-point turn** the process of turning a vehicle round to face in the opposite direction by moving it forward, reversing, then moving forward again, turning the steering-wheel appropriately; **three= quarter back** a player between half-backs and full-back; **three-quarter face** an aspect between full face and profile: — *adj.* **three-quar'ter-length** (of a coat, sleeve, etc.) being three quarters of the full length. — **three-ring circus** a circus with three rings in which simultaneous separate performances are given: a showy or extravagant event (*fig.*): a confusing or bewildering scene or situation; **three-speed gear** a gear-changing contrivance with three possibilities; **three times three** three cheers thrice repeated; **three= went way** (*dial.*) a meeting-place of three roads. [O.E. *thrēo*, fem. and neut. of *thrī*; Goth. *threis*, Ger. *drei*, L. *trēs, trēs, tria*, Gr. *treis, treis, tria*, Sans. *tri*.]

threep. See **threap.**

thremmatology *threm-ə-tol'ə-ji, n.* the science of breeding domestic animals and plants. [Gr. *thremma, -atos*, a nursling, *logos*, discourse.]

threnody *thren', thren'ə-di, n.* an ode or song of lamentation. — Also **threne** (*thrēn; Shak.*), **thren'ode** (*-ōd*), **thren'os** (*Shak.*). — *adjs.* **threnet'ic, -al; threnō'dial, threnodic** (*-od'*). — *n.* **thren'odist.** [Gr. *thrēnōidiā, thrēnos*, a lament, *ōidē*, song.]

threonine *thrē'ə-nīn, n.* an amino-acid essential for bodily growth and health, present in certain proteins. [Gr. *erythro-*, red, by rearrangement, with *-n-* and *-ine*.]

thresh¹ *thresh, v.t.* to beat out, subject to beating out, by trampling, flail, or machinery: to thrash. — *v.i.* to thresh corn: to thrash. — *n.* an act of threshing. — *ns.* **thresh'el** a flail: a flail-like weapon, the morgenstern; **thresh'er** one who threshes: a flail: a threshing-machine or a beating part of it: a fox-shark (also **thresh'er= shark'**). — *n.* and *adj.* **thresh'ing.** — **thresh'er-whale** a grampus; **thresh'ing-floor** a surface on which grain is threshed; **thresh'ing-machine, -mill** one for threshing corn. [O.E. *therscan;* cf. Ger. *derschen*, to thresh; see **thrash¹**.]

thresh². See **thrash².**

thresher. See **thrasher¹, thresh¹**.

threshold *thresh'ōld, -hōld, n.* the sill of a house door: the place or point of entering: the outset: the limit of consciousness: the point at which a stimulus begins to bring a response, as in *threshold of pain*, etc.: the smallest dose of radiation that will produce a specified result: the point, stage, level, etc., at which something will happen, become true, etc.: in a pay agreement, etc., a point in the rise of the cost of living at which a wage-increase is prescribed. — *adj.* at or constituting a threshold. — **threshold lighting, lights** a line of lights across the ends of a runway or landing area to indicate the usable limits; **threshold of audibility, of sound** the minimum intensity or pressure of sound wave which the normal human listener can just detect at any given frequency. [O.E. *therscold, therscwald, threscold*, app. — *therscan*, to thrash, thresh, in its older sense of trample, tread.]

thretty *thret'i*, a dial. form of **thirty**.

threw *thrōō, pa.t.* of **throw¹**.

thrice *thrīs, adv.* three times: three times as much. [M.E. *thriës* — O.E. *thrīwa, thrīga*, thrice — *thrī*, three, with adverbial gen. ending *-es*.]

thrid *thrid*, (*Spens.*) *n.* a thread. — *v.t.* (*obs.*) to thread. [**thread**.]

thridace *thrid'əs, n.* inspissated lettuce juice. [Gr. *thridax*, lettuce.]

thrift *thrift, n.* the state of thriving: frugality: economy: prosperity (*arch.*): increase of wealth (*arch.*): gain (*arch.*): profitable occupation (*dial.*): savings (*arch.*): sea-pink (Armeria), a seaside and alpine plant of the Plumbaginaceae. — *adv.* **thrift'ily.** — *n.* **thrift'iness.** — *adj.* **thrift'less** not thrifty: extravagant: not thriving. — *adv.* **thrift'lessly.** — *n.* **thrift'lessness.** — *adj.* **thrift'y** showing thrift or economy: thriving by frugality: prosperous, in good condition (*U.S.*): — *compar.* **thrift'ier**, *superl.* **thrift'iest.** — **thrift shop** a shop, usu. run on behalf of a charity, which sells second-hand clothes and other articles. [**thrive**.]

thrill *thril, v.t.* to pierce: to affect with a strong glow or tingle of sense or emotion, now esp. a feeling of extreme pleasure. — *v.i.* to pierce, as something sharp: to pass tinglingly: to quiver: to feel a sharp, shivering sensation. — *n.* a tingle: a shivering feeling or emotion. — *adj.* **thrill'ant** (*Spens.*) piercing. — *n.* **thrill'er** a sensational or exciting story, esp. one about crime and detection. — *adj.* **thrill'ing.** — *adv.* **thrill'ingly.** — *n.* **thrill'ingness.** — *adj.* **thrill'y.** [O.E. *thyrlian*, to bore — *thyrel*, a hole; Ger. *drillen*, to drill a hole.]

thrimsa. See **thrymsa**.

Thrips *thrips, n.* a genus of Thysanoptera, mostly minute black insects, common in flowers: (without *cap.*) an insect of the genus, or of any of the genera of the order (*erron.* **thrip**): popularly extended to leaf-hoppers, and to other small insects: — *pl.* **thrips, thrip'ses.** [Gr. *thrīps, thrīpos*, a wood-worm.]

thrissel, thristle *thris'l, thrus'l*, Scots forms of **thistle**. [Poss. influenced by *thrist*, to thrust.]

thrist *thrist, thrist'y -i*, old forms (*Spens.*) of **thirst** (*n.* and *vb.*), **thirsty**.

thrive *thrīv, v.i.* to grow: to grow healthily and vigorously: to get on, do well: to prosper: to increase in goods: to be successful: to flourish: — *pa.t.* **thrōve**, also **thrīved;** *pa.p.* **thriven** (*thriv'n*). — *adjs.* **thrīve'less** thriftless; **thriven** (*thriv'n*) grown, developed: successful. — *n.* **thrī'ver** (*rare*). — *n.* and *adj.* **thrī'ving.** — *adv.* **thrī'vingly**

(rare). — *n.* **thrī′vingness.** [O.N. *thrīfa*, to grasp.]

thro', thro. Same as **through.**

throat *thrōt, n.* the passage from mouth to stomach: the forepart of the neck, in which are the gullet and windpipe: voice: a narrow entrance, aperture or passage: the narrow part, as of a vase, a corolla: a groove under a coping or moulding: the end of a gaff next the mast (*naut.*). — *adj.* **throat′ed** with a throat. — *adv.* **throat′ily.** — *n.* **throat′iness.** — *adj.* **throat′y** sounding as from the throat: hoarse: croaking: deep or full-throated: somewhat sore-throated: full or loose-skinned about the throat: potent in swallowing. — **throat′-band, -strap, -latch** a band about the throat. — *adj.* **throat′-full′** full to the throat. — **throat microphone** one held directly against the speaker's throat and actuated by vibrations of the larynx: **throat′wort** the nettle-leaved bellflower (*Campanula trachelium*) once reputed good for throat ailments: the giant bellflower (*C. latifolium*). — **cut the, one's, throat** usu., to cut the jugular vein: to pursue some course ruinous to one's interests; **give someone the lie in his throat** to accuse someone to his face of a lie; **jump down someone's throat** see **jump**; **sore throat** an inflamed and uncomfortable condition of the tonsils and neighbouring parts; **stick in one's throat** to be more than one can bear, manage; **thrust, ram, down someone's throat** to assert or force upon someone insistently without listening to an answer. [O.E. *throte*; cf. **throttle.**]

throb *throb, v.i.* to beat strongly, as the heart or pulse: — *pr.p.* **throbb′ing;** *pa.t.* and *pa.p.* **throbbed.** — *n.* a beat or strong pulsation. — *n.* and *adj.* **throbb′ing.** — *adv.* **throbb′ingly.** — *adj.* **throb′less.** [M.E. *throbben*; poss. conn. with L. *trepidus*, trembling.]

throe *throe,* earlier (*Shak., Spens.*) **throw(e),** *thrō,* (*Scot.*) **thraw** *thrö, ns.* a spasm: a paroxysm: a pang, esp. a birth-pang. — *vs.t.* to subject to pangs. — *vs.i.* to suffer pangs. — **in the throes** in travail: in the struggle (of), struggling (with): in the thick (of). [M.E. *thrahes, throwes, thrawes;* perh. there have been cross-influences between O.E. *thrawu,* pang, *thrāg,* paroxysm, *thrōwian,* to suffer, *thrāwan,* to twist, throw; see also **thraw.**]

thrombus *throm′bəs, n.* a clot of blood in a living vessel: — *pl.* **throm′bī.** — *ns.* **throm′bin** an enzyme that causes clotting; **throm′bocyte** a platelet; **thrombo-em′bolism** an embolism caused by an embolus carried by the bloodstream from its point of origin causing a blockage elsewhere; **thrombokī′nase** an enzyme active in the clotting of blood: thromboplastin; **thrombo-phlebī′tis** phlebitis with formation of a thrombus; **thrombo-plast′in** a substance, found esp. in platelets, which participates in clotting. — *v.t.* **thrombose** (*-bōs′*) to cause thrombosis in. — *n.* **thrombō′sis** clotting in a vessel during life: — *pl.* **-ō′sēs.** — *adj.* **thrombot′ic.** [Gr. *thrombos,* clot.]

throne *thrōn, n.* a king's, pope's, or bishop's chair of state: kingship: an angel of the third order. — *v.t.* to enthrone: to exalt. — *v.i.* to sit in state, as on a throne. — *adjs.* **throned; throne′less.** — **throne′-room.** [Gr. *thronos,* a seat.]

throng *throng, n.* a crowd: a great multitude: crowding. — *v.t.* and *v.i.* to crowd: to press: to press hard (*Shak.*). — *adj.* (*coll.*) crowded: busy: intimate. — *adjs.* **thronged** packed, crowded: (with *up*) overpowered (*Shak.*); **throng′ful** thronged. — *n.* and *adj.* **throng′ing.** [O.E. *gethrang* — *thringan,* to press.]

thropple *throp′l* (*Scot.* **thrapple** *thrap′l*), *n.* the throat: the windpipe, esp. of an animal. — *v.t.* to throttle: to strangle. [Poss. O.E. *throtbolla,* windpipe, gullet — *throte,* throat, *bolla,* boll.]

throstle *thros′l, n.* the song-thrush (see **thrush**[1]): a machine for drawing, twisting, and winding fibres (from its sound). — **thros′tle-cock** a male song-thrush or (*dial.*) missel-thrush. [O.E. *throstle;* Ger. *Drossel,* L. *turdus,* thrush.]

throttle *throt′l, n.* the throat or windpipe: a throttle-valve: a throttle-lever. — *v.t.* to choke by pressure on the

windpipe: to strangle (also *fig.*): to check the flow of: to cut down the supply of steam, or of gas and air, to or in. — *v.i.* to breathe hard, as when nearly suffocated. — *n.* **thrott′ler.** — *n.* and *adj.* **thrott′ling.** — **thrott′le-lever** a lever that opens and closes a throttle-valve; **thrott′le-pipe** the vertical pipe between the throttle-valve and the dry-pipe of a locomotive; **thrott′le-valve** a valve regulating the supply of steam or of gas and air in an engine. — **at full throttle** at full speed; **throttle down** to slow down by closing the throttle. [App. dim. of **throat.**]

through *thrōō, prep.* from end to end, side to side, or boundary to boundary of, by way of the interior: from place to place within: everywhere within: by way of: along the passage of: clear of: among: from beginning to end of: up to and including, to or until the end of (*U.S.*): by means of: in consequence of. — *adv.* from one end or side to the other: from beginning to end: all the way: clear: into a position of having passed: in connection or communication all the way. — *adj.* passing, or serving for passage, all the way without interruption. — *adv.* **through′ly** same as **thoroughly** (*obs.*): far through (*arch.*). — *prep.* **throughout′** in, into, through, during, the whole of. — *adv.* in every part: everywhere. — **through ball** (*football*) a ball kicked so as to get past the defence; **through′-bolt** a bolt that passes through from side to side of what it fastens; **through′fare** (*Shak.*) same as **thoroughfare.** — *adj.* **through′-ganging** (*Scot.*) thoroughgoing. — **through′-going** (*Scot.* **-gaun** *-gön*) a scolding. — *adj.* passing through: active, energetic. — *adv.* **through′-other** (*Scot.*) in indiscriminate mixture: higgledy-piggledy. — *adj.* (*Scot.*) confusedly mixed: without orderliness. — **through pass** same as **through ball; through′-put** the amount of material, etc., put through a process; **through′-stone** a bonder or bond-stone in building (see also separate entry below); **through′-tick′et** a ticket for the whole of a journey; **through′-traff′ic** the traffic between two centres at a distance from each other: traffic passing straight through an area, as opposed to that travelling within the area; **through′-train** a train that goes the whole length of a long route; **through′way,** (*U.S.*) **thru′way,** an expressway. — **be through** (*Shak.*; now chiefly *Scot.* and *U.S.*) to have done (with): to be at an end: to have no more to do (with); **through and through** through the whole thickness: completely: in every point; **through the day, night** (*Scot.*) in the daytime, night-time. [O.E. *thurh;* Ger. *durch.*]

through-stone, -stane *thrōōh′-, throhh′-stōn, -stān,* (*Scot.*) *ns.* a horizontal tombstone on pillars. — See also **through-stone** under **through.** [O.E. *thrūh,* sarcophagus, and **stone.**]

throve *thrōv, pa.t.* of **thrive.**

throw[1] *thrō, v.t.* to wind or twist together, as yarn: to form on a wheel, as pottery: to turn, with a lathe: to move (a switch) so as to connect, disconnect: to cast, hurl, fling through the air: to project: to emit: to make a cast of dice amounting to: to dislodge from the saddle: to cast down in wrestling: to defeat, get the better of, or discomfit: to give birth to: to produce: to render suddenly: to cause to be in some place or condition, esp. with suddenness: to put: to execute, perform: to lose (a contest) deliberately, esp. in return for a bribe (*coll.*): to bemuse, perplex, disconcert. — *v.i.* to cast or hurl: to cast dice: to lay about one (*Spens.*): — *pa.t.* **threw** (*thrōō*); *pa.p.* **thrown** (*thrōn*). — *n.* a deflection: amplitude of movement: an act of throwing: a cast, esp. of dice or a fishing-line: a blow (*Spens.*): the distance to which anything may be thrown: the vertical displacement of a fault (*geol.*): a small woollen wrap or rug: a turn, article, etc. (*coll.*). — *n.* **throw′er.** — *n.* and *adj.* **thrown** twisted: cast, flung. — *n.* **throw′ster** one who throws silk: a gambler. — **throw′-away** an advertisement brochure or handbill freely distributed to the public (*U.S.*): a contest without serious competition: a line, or a joke, that an actor purposely delivers without emphasis, often for the sake of realism. — *adj.* of manner or technique, casual, without attempt at dramatic effect: ridiculously cheap, as if being thrown away: discarded or not recovered after use. — **throw'=back** a reversion (e.g. to an earlier developmental type): a set-back; **throw'-down** a home-made firework, slapbang; **throw'-in** an act of throwing in: a throw to put the ball back into play (*football, basketball*, etc.); **throw'ing-stick** a stick for throwing a spear: a throwstick; **throw'ing-table** a potter's wheel; **thrown'-silk** organzine; **throw'-out** an act of throwing out: a rejected thing; **throw rug** a throw; **throw'-stick** a weapon thrown whirling from the hand, as the boomerang. — **throw about** (*Spens.*) to cast about or try expedients; **throw a fit** (*coll.*) to have a fit, behave wildly; **throw a party** (*coll.*) to give a party; **throw away** to reject, toss aside: to squander: to fail to take advantage of: to bestow unworthily; **throw back** to retort, to refuse: to revert to some ancestral character; **throw down** to demolish; **throw in** to interject: to throw the ball in: to add as an extra; **throw in the towel, throw in one's hand** to give up, surrender; **throw in one's lot** see **lot**; **throw mud at** see **mud**; **throw off** to divest oneself of: to disengage or release oneself from: to utter or compose offhand; **throw on** to put on hastily; **throw oneself at** to make a determined and obvious attempt to captivate; **throw oneself into** to engage heartily in; **throw oneself on, upon** to assail: to entrust oneself to the power of; **throw open** to cause to swing wide open: to make freely accessible; **throw out** to cast out: to reject: to expel: to emit: to utter: to cause to project: to disconcert: to distance, leave behind; **throw over** to discard or desert; **throw together** to put together in a hurry: to bring into contact by chance; **throw** (**caution**, etc.) **to the winds** see **wind**[1]; **throw up** to erect hastily: to show prominently: to give up, to resign: to vomit; **throw up (something) against someone** to reproach someone with (something); **throw up the sponge** see **sponge**. [O.E. *thrāwan*, to turn, to twist; Ger. *drehen*, to twist; see also **thraw, throe**.]

throw[2] *thrō*, (*Spens.*) *n.* a while. [O.E. *thrāg, thrāh*.]

throw[3], **throwe**. See **throe**.

thru. A U.S. spelling of **through**, alone or in compounds.

thrum[1] *thrum, n.* the end of a weaver's thread: any loose thread or fringe: bits of coarse yarn. — *adj.* made of or having thrums. — *v.t.* to furnish, cover, or fringe with thrums: — *pr.p.* **thrumm'ing**; *pa.t.* and *pa.p.* **thrummed**. — *adj.* **thrumm'y** made of, or like, thrums. — **thrum'-cap** a cap made of thrums or of coarse, shaggy cloth. — *adj.* **thrum'-eyed** short-styled with the stamens in the throat of the corolla (esp. of a Primula: opp. to *pin-eyed*). — **thrummed hat** (*Shak.*) a hat made of, fringed with, or covered with thrums. [O.E. *thrum* (found in composition); Ger. *Trumm*.]

thrum[2] *thrum, v.t.* and *v.i.* to strum: to hum, drone, repeat in sing-song: to drum with the fingers: — *pr.p.* **thrumm'ing**; *pa.t.* and *pa.p.* **thrummed**. — *n.* a strumming: a purring (*dial.*). — *n.* **thrumm'er**. — *n.* and *adj.* **thrumm'ing**. — *adv.* **thrumm'ingly**.

thruppence, -penny. Coll. for **threepence, -penny**.

thrush[1] *thrush, n.* any member of the subfamily *Turdinae* (fam. *Muscicapidae*) of songbirds, esp. those of the genus *Turdus*, particularly those species having a spotted breast, e.g. the song-thrush (*Turdus philomelos*) and missel-thrush (*T. viscivorus*): applied to other birds more or less similar, such as some of the babblers. [O.E. *thrysce*.]

thrush[2] *thrush, n.* an inflammation in a horse's frog: a disease, usu. of infants, chiefly affecting the mouth and throat. [Cf. Dan. *trøske*, Sw. *torsk*, thrush.]

thrust[1] *thrust, v.t.* and *v.i.* to push: to force: to stab, pierce: to intrude: — *pa.t.* and *pa.p.* **thrust**. — *n.* a push: a pushing force: a stab: pertinacity, determination, drive: the chief message, gist, direction, of an argument, etc.: the force that drives an aircraft forward and its measurement: the horizontal force on the abutment of an arch: a thrust-plane. — *n.* **thrust'er**. — *n.* and *adj.*

thrust'ing. — **thrust'-hoe** a hoe worked by pushing; **thrust'-plane** a plane along which a block of rocks has overridden higher rocks almost horizontally — a reversed fault of very low hade; **thrust stage** a stage that extends into the auditorium. [O.N. *thrȳsta*, to press.]

thrust[2] *thrust*, (*Spens.*) *v.i.* to thirst. — *n.* thirst.

thrutch *thruch*, (*dial.*) *v.t.* to thrust, press, shove: to crush, squeeze. — *v.i.* to make one's way by great effort. — Also *n.* [O.E. *thrycc(e)an*.]

thruway. A U.S. spelling of **throughway**.

thrymsa, thrimsa *thrim'za, -sə, n.* an Anglo-Saxon gold coin, or its value. [O.E., *gen. pl.* of *trymes, trimes*, a coin representing the Roman *tremis*, a third of an aureus; influenced by *thri*, three.]

thud *thud, n.* a dull sound as of a heavy body falling soft. — *v.i.* to make a thud. — *v.t.* to beat. [Perh. O.E. *thyddan*, to strike.]

thug *thug*, properly *t'hug, n.* a member of a religious fraternity that murdered stealthily by strangling or poisoning with datura, extirpated 1826–35 (*India*): a cut-throat: a ruffian. — *ns.* **thuggee'** (**thagi'**), **thugg'ism** the practice and superstition of the thugs; **thugg'ery** thuggism: ruffianly or violent behaviour. [Hindi *thag*, cheat.]

Thuja *thōō'jə, -yə, n.* the arbor vitae genus: (without *cap.*) a tree of this genus. [Gr. *thyiā*, a kind of juniper.]

Thule *thū'lē, n.* an island six days N. of Orkney discovered by Pytheas (4th cent. B.C.), variously identified as Shetland, Iceland, Norway, Jutland: hence (usu. *ultima Thule*) the extreme limit. — *ns.* **thu'lia** thulium oxide, separated from erbia by Cleve; **thu'lite** a red zoisite found in Norway; **thu'lium** a metallic element (Tm; at. numb. 69). [L. *Thūlē* — Gr. *Thoulē* (understood by Cleve as Scandinavia).]

thumb *thum, n.* the short, thick digit, consisting of two phalanges, on the radial side of the human hand: the part of a glove that covers it: in other animals the corresponding digit, or that of the hind foot, esp. when opposable: a thumb's breadth, an inch. — *v.t.* to handle awkwardly: to play, spread, press, touch, wear, or smudge with the thumb: to read assiduously: to turn the pages (of a book) rapidly with the thumb: to signal to with the thumb: to hit (in the eye) with the thumb (*boxing*). — *adj.* **thumbed** having thumbs: marked by the thumb, worn. — *n.pl.* **thumb'(i)kins** (*Scot.*) the thumbscrew. — *adj.* **thumb'less**. — *n.* **thumb'ling** a pygmy. — *adj.* **thumb'y** grubby with thumb-marks: like thumbs, clumsy, awkward. — **thumb'-hole** a hole to insert the thumb in; **thumb'-index** one arranged as indentations on the outer margins of the pages of books; **thumb'-knot** an overhand knot; **thumb'-latch** a latch worked by pressure of the thumb; **thumb'-mark** a mark left by the thumb as on a book: a thumbprint. — *adj.* **thumb'-marked**. — **thumb'nail** the nail of the thumb: a sketch (**thumb'nail sketch**) as small as a thumbnail. — *adj.* brief, concise. — **thumb'-piece** a piece that is pressed by the thumb or receives the thumb; **thumb'pot** a very small flower-pot; **thumb'-print** an impression of the markings of the thumb, taken as a means of identification; **thumb'-ring** a ring worn on the thumb (*Shak.*): a ring to protect an archer's thumb; **thumb'screw** an old instrument of torture for compressing the thumb by means of a screw; **thumbs-down, -up** see **thumbs down, up** below; **thumb'-stall** a covering or sheath for the thumb; **thumb'-tack** (*U.S.*) a drawing-pin. — **be all (fingers and) thumbs, one's fingers are all thumbs, have one's fingers all thumbs** to be awkward and fumbling; **bite one's thumb** to make a sign threatening revenge; **keep one's thumb on** to keep secret; **rule of thumb** a rough-and-ready practical manner, found by experience to be convenient; **thumb a lift, ride** (*coll.*) to beg a lift from passing motorists by signalling from the side of the road with the thumb; **thumb one's nose** to cock a snook (*lit.* and *fig.*) (see **snook**[3]); **thumbs down** a sign indicating disapproval, disallowance, failure, etc. (also *fig.*; see also **pollice verso;** — *n.* **thumbs-down'**); **thumbs up** a sign indicating approval, success, hope of, or wishes for, success etc. (also *fig.*; *n.* **thumbs-up'**); **under one's thumb** under one's domination. [O.E. *thūma*; Ger. *Daumen.*]

Thummim *thum'im.* See **Urim.**

thump *thump, n.* a dull heavy blow or its sound. — *v.t.* and *v.i.* to beat with a dull heavy blow: to make such a sound. — *v.t.* to trounce. — *n.* **thump'er** one who, or that which, thumps: anything very big, a big lie, etc. (*coll.*). — *adj.* **thump'ing** (*coll.*) unusually big. [Prob. imit.]

Thunbergia *thən-bûr'ji-ə, -gi-, toōn-, n.* a genus of evergreen climbing plants of the family Acanthaceae: (without *cap.*) a plant of this genus. [After the Swedish botanist Carl *Thunberg,* 1743-1928.]

thunder *thun'dər, n.* the deep rumbling sound after a flash of lightning: any loud noise: a thunderbolt: vehement denunciation. — *v.i.* to make thunder: to sound as thunder: to inveigh or denounce with vehemence. — *v.t.* to give out with noise or violent denunciation: to deal like thunder. — *ns.* **thun'derer** a thunder-god, Zeus, Thor, etc.: a thundering denunciator, inveigher, orator, journalist, or periodical, esp. *The Times* or its leader-writer: a hand who operates stage-thunder: a bull-roarer; **thun'dering.** — *adj.* discharging thunder: unusually big, tremendous (*coll.*). — Also *n.* and *adv.* — *adv.* **thun'deringly.** — *adjs.* **thun'derless; thun'der-like** (*Shak.*); **thun'derous** (**thun'drous**) like, threatening, or suggesting thunder. — *adv.* **thun'derously.** — *adj.* **thun'dery** indicative of thunder, or attended by it. — *adj.* **thun'der-and-light'ning** in glaring colours. — *n.* a glaringly coloured woollen cloth. — **thun'der-bearer** (*Shak.*) Jove; **thun'derbird** a huge mythical bird thought by some tribes of N. American Indians to cause thunder and lightning: a representation of such a bird; **thun'derbolt** a missile of the thunder-god: a popularly imagined material body seen as lightning: a stone identified therewith, as a belemnite, a stone axe: anything sudden and overwhelming: a fulmination: a violent and irresistible destroyer or hero; **thun'der-box** (*slang*) a close-stool: any primitive or portable toilet; **thun'der-clap** a sudden crash of thunder; **thun'der-cloud** a cloud charged with electricity: a black or livid threatening appearance; **thun'der-dart** a thunderbolt; **thun'der-darter, -master** (both *Shak.*) Jove. — *v.t.* **thun'der-drive** (*Spens*) to strike with thunderbolts. — **thun'der-egg** (*Austr.* and *U.S.*) an agate-filled geode, or a fossil, supposed to have been flung to earth by lightning; **thun'der-flash** a container, such as a blank shell, filled with explosive powder, which makes a flash and a loud explosion when detonated; **thun'der-god** a god that wields thunder; **thun'derhead** a distinctively rounded mass of cumulus cloud projecting above the general cloud mass, usu. the precursor of a storm; **thun'der-peal** a resounding noise of thunder; **thun'der-plump** a heavy fall of rain in a thunder-storm; **thun'der-sheet** a large sheet of tin-plate shaken to produce the sound of thunder or similar noises as a theatrical, etc. sound-effect; **thun'der-shower** a shower accompanied with thunder, or a short heavy shower from a thunder-cloud; **thun'der-stone** (*Shak.*) a thunderbolt; **thun'der-storm** continued discharges of electricity from the clouds, producing lightning and thunder, generally with heavy rain. — *v.t.* **thun'der-strike** to strike with, or as with, lightning. — **thun'der-stroke** (*Shak.*) a stroke or blast by lightning. — *adj.* **thun'der-struck** (also **-stricken**) struck by lightning: struck dumb with astonishment. — **steal someone's thunder** see **steal¹.** [O.E. *thunor,* thunder, *Thunor,* the thunder-god, Thor; Ger. *Donner,* L. *tonāre'*; cf. **Thor, Thursday.**]

Thurberesque *thûr-bər-esk', adj.* similar in style, etc. to the work of James *Thurber* (1894–1961), American writer and cartoonist.

thurible *thū'ri-bl, n.* a censer. — *n.* **thū'rifer** an acolyte who carries the thurible. — *adj.* **thurif'erous** incense-bearing. — *n.* **thurificā'tion.** — *v.t.* **thū'rify** to cense.

— *n.* **thus** (*thus, thūs*) frankincense. [L. *t(h)ūs, t(h)ūris,* frankincense — Gr. *thyos,* a sacrifice; cf. **thyme.**]

Thursday *thûrz'di, n.* the fifth day of the week, originally sacred to Thunor, the English thunder-god. [O.E. *Thunres dæg,* Thunor's day; O.N. *Thōrsdagr,* Thor's day; Ger. *Donnerstag.*]

thus¹ *dhus, adv.* in this or that manner: to this degree or extent: accordingly, therefore. — *n.* **thus'ness** (usu. *facet.*) the state of being thus. — *adv.* **thus'wise** in this manner. — **thus far** so far, up till now. [O.E. *thus.*]

thus². See **thurible.**

Thuya a variant of **Thuja.**

thwack *thwak, v.t.* to whack. — *n.* a whack. — *n.* **thwack'er.** — *n.* and *adj.* **thwack'ing.** [Perh. **whack,** or O.E. *thaccian,* to smack.]

thwaite *thwāt, n.* a piece of reclaimed land — common in place names. [O.N. *thveit.*]

thwart *thwört, adv.* crosswise: from side to side. — *adj.* crosswise, transverse: cross, adverse: cross, perverse, cross-grained. — *prep.* across, athwart. — *v.t.* to cross: to cross the path of: to obstruct: to oppose: to frustrate: to balk: to set crosswise: to plough crosswise. — *v.i.* to cross: to conflict. — *n.* frustration: hindrance: a rower's bench. — *adj.* **thwar'ted** frustrated. — *adv.* **thwar'tedly.** — *n.* **thwar'ter.** — *n.* and *adj.* **thwar'ting.** — *advs.* **thwar'tingly** perversely; **thwart'ly; thwart'-ship(s)** across the ship; **thwart'ways; thwart'wise.** — *adjs.* **thwart'ship, thwart'wise.** [O.N. *thvert,* neut. of *thverr,* perverse.]

thy *dhī, poss. pron.* or *adj.* of thee. [**thine.**]

Thyestean *thī-es'ti-ən, -əs-tē'ən, adj.* of *Thyestes* (Gr. *Thyestēs*), who was made to eat his own sons: cannibal.

thyine *thī'in, adj.* of a tree supposed to be sandarach (Rev. xviii. 12). [Gr. *thyïnos* — *thyon, thyā,* thyine tree.]

thylacine *thī'lə-sēn, -sīn, -sin, n.* the so-called Tasmanian wolf (q.v.). [Gr. *thylakos,* pouch.]

thylose, thylosis. See **tylosis.**

thyme *tīm, n.* any member of the labiate genus Thymus, low half-shrubby plants with two-lipped corolla and calyx and four diverging stamens, esp. the fragrant garden thyme (*T. vulgaris*) and wild thyme (*T. serpyllum*). — *n.* **thymol** (*thī'mol*) an antiseptic phenol obtained from oil of thyme by distillation. — *adj.* **thymy** (*tīm'i*) like, smelling of, or abounding in, thyme. — **basil thyme** a kind of calamint; **lemon thyme** a species of thyme (*T. citriodorus*) with a lemony flavour and scent; **oil of thyme** a fragrant essential oil got from garden and other thymes; **water thyme** Canadian pondweed. [Fr. *thym* — L. *thymum* — Gr. *thymon.*]

thymelaeaceous *thim-, thīm-el-i-ā'sh(y)əs, adj.* of the **Thymelaeā'ceae,** the family to which Daphne belongs. [Gr. *thymelaiā,* supposed to be a species of Daphne — *thymos,* thyme, *elaiā,* olive.]

thymus *thī'məs, n.* a ductless gland near the root of the neck, vestigial in adult man — that of veal and lamb called *neck-sweetbread.* — Also *adj.* — *ns.* **thymec'tomy** surgical removal of the thymus; **thy'midine** (*-ēn*) a nucleoside of thymine, found in DNA; **thymine** (*thī'mēn*) one of the four bases in deoxyribonucleic acids, in close association with adenine; **thy'mocyte** a lymphocyte of the thymus. [Gr. *thymos,* thymus gland.]

thymy. See **thyme.**

thyratron *thī'rə-tron, n.* a gas-filled valve with heated cathode, able to carry very high currents — orig. a trademark for one containing mercury vapour. — *n.* **thyristor** (*thī-ris'tər*) a thyratron-like semiconductor device.

thyroid *thī'roid,* more correctly but less commonly **thyreoid** *-i-oid, adjs.* shield-shaped: pertaining to the thyroid gland or the thyroid cartilage. — *n.* the thyroid gland, a ductless gland in the neck whose overactivity may lead to exophthalmic goitre, and defect to cretinism: the principal cartilage of the larynx, forming the Adam's apple. — *ns.* **thyroidi'tis** inflammation of the thyroid gland; **thyrotoxicō'sis** hyperthyroidism:

hyperthyroidism with goitre and exophthalmia, Grave's disease; **thyrotrō'pin, thyrotrō'phin** a hormone, produced in the anterior lobe of the pituitary gland, which stimulates the thyroid gland; **thyrox'in(e)** an iodine compound, the active principle of the thyroid gland. [Gr. *thȳreoeidēs*, shield-shaped, the thyroid cartilage — *thȳreos*, a (door-shaped) shield — *thȳrā* , a door, *eidos*, form.]

Thyrostraca *thīr-os'tra-ka*, *n.pl.* the cirripedes. [Gr. *thȳrā*, door, valve, *ostrakon*, shell.]

thyrsus *thûr'sas*, *n.* the wand of Bacchus, a staff wreathed with ivy: a dense panicle broadest in the middle (*bot.*): esp. one whose lateral branches are cymose: — *pl.* **thyr'si** (*-sī*). — *n.* **thyrse** (*thûrs*) a thyrsus. — *adjs.* **thyr'soid, -al** having the form of a thyrsus. [Gr. *thyrsos*.]

Thysanoptera *this-an-op'ta-ra*, *n.pl.* an order of insects with fringed wings, as Thrips. — *adj.* **thysanop'terous.** — *n.pl.* **Thysanura** (*-ū'ra*) the bristle-tails, an order of small wingless insects with abdominal appendages. — *adj.* **thysanū'rous.** [Gr. *thysanos*, a fringe, tassel, *pteron*, a wing, *ourā*, a tail.]

thyself *dhī-self'*, *pron.* emphatic for, or usually along with, thou or thee: reflexive for thee. [**thee** (altered to **thy**), and **self.**]

ti[1] *tē*, (*mus.*) *n.* in the tonic sol-fa system a substitute for *si*, to avoid the initial sound of *so* (*sol*). — Also, in anglicised spelling, **te.**

ti[2] *tē*, *n.* a small Pacific liliaceous tree (Cordyline): sometimes also applied (wrongly) to the Australian **tea-tree.** [Polynesian.]

tiara *ti-ä'ra*, *n.* the lofty ornamental head-dress of the ancient Persians: the Jewish high-priest's mitre: the pope's triple crown: the papal dignity: a jewelled head-ornament. — *n.* **tiar** (*tī'ar, tīr; poet.*) a tiara. — *adj.* **tia'ra'd, tia'raed** wearing a tiara. [Gr. *tiārā*.]

Tib *tib*, *n.* used as a typical woman's name (*Shak.*): the ace of trumps in gleek (*obs.*; *Scott*). — **Tib'-cat** a she-cat; **Tib(b)'s Eve see saint.** [Isabella.]

Tibert *tib'art, tīb'art*, *n.* the cat in *Reynard the Fox*: in *Shak.* identified with Tibalt.

Tibet, Thibet *ti-bet'*, *n.* an autonomous region in W. China: (**thibet**) a woollen stuff generally printed in colours: a heavy goat's hair fabric used instead of fur — also **Tibet cloth.** — *adj.* **Tibet'an** (or *tib'*) of Tibet. — *n.* the language of Tibet: a native of Tibet. — **Tibetan apso** same as **lhasa apso.**

tibia *tib'i-a*, *n.* the shinbone, the thicker of the two bones of the leg below the knee in humans: the corresponding bone in other vertebrates: the tibiotarsus in birds: the fourth joint of an insect's leg: an ancient flute or pipe: — *pl.* **tib'ias, tib'iae** (*-i-ē*). — *adj.* **tib'ial.** — *n.* **tibiotar'sus** in birds, a bone formed by the fusion of the tibia and some of the tarsals. [L. *tībia*, shinbone, flute.]

Tibouchina *ti-ba-kī-na, -kē'*, *n.* a genus of shrubs and herbs (fam. Melastomaceae) with purple flowers: (without *cap.*) a plant of this genus. [From a native name in Guiana.]

tic *tik*, *n.* a convulsive motion of certain muscles, esp. of the face: an involuntary habitual response (*fig.*). — **tic'-douloureux** (*-dol-a-roo'*, Fr. *tēk doo-loo-ra*) an affection of the fifth cranial nerve with paroxysms of pain in face and forehead. [Fr.; cf. **tick**[5].]

tical *ti-käl', tik'l*, *n.* an obsolete Siamese silver coin, equal to a rupee, now replaced by the baht: a unit of weight. [Port. *tical*.]

ticca *tik'a*, (*Ind.*) *adj.* hired. [Hind. *thīkā*, hire.]

tice *tīs*, *v.t.* (*Shak.*) to entice. — *n.* an enticement (*Shak.*): a yorker (*cricket*). [Aphetic for **entice**, or — Fr. *atiser*.]

tich *tich*, (*coll.*) *n.* a very small person: often used (with *cap.*) as a nickname. — *adj.* **tich'y.** [From the music-hall artist Harry Relph, known as Little *Tich*.]

tichorrhine *tī'kō-rīn*, *adj.* having an ossified nasal septum, as the fossil woolly rhinoceros. [Gr. *teichos*, wall, *rhīs, rhīnos*, nose.]

tick[1] *tik*, *n.* any of the larger blood-sucking acarids:

applied also to the sheep-ked and similar degenerate bloodsucking Diptera: a small and usu. objectionable person (*coll.*). — **tick fever** East Coast fever: Texas fever: Rocky Mountain spotted fever or any similar disease transmitted by ticks. [O.E. *ticia* (perh. for *tīca* or *ticca*); Du. *teek*, Ger. *Zecke*.]

tick[2] *tik*, *n.* the cover of a mattress: ticking. — *ns.* **tick'en, tick'ing** the cloth of which ticks are made. [L. *thēca* — Gr. *thēkē*, a case; see **theca.**]

tick[3] *tik*, *n.* a light tap or pat (*obs.*): the game of tig: the sound of a watch, clock, etc.: a beat: a moment: a speck: a small mark, often an angular line, used to indicate or mark off as checked or dealt with. — *v.i.* to tap, pat (*obs.*; **tick and toy** to dally): to make a sound as of a clock: to beat. — *v.t.* to mark with a tick (sometimes with *off*): to dot: to measure, record, give out, by ticks (sometimes with *out*). — *adj.* **ticked** speckled. — *ns.* **tick'er** anything that ticks, esp. a telegraph instrument that prints signals on a tape, or (*slang*) a watch: the heart (*slang*). — *n.* and *adj.* **tick'ing.** — **tick'er-tape** paper ribbon on which a ticker prints: anything similar, such as a streamer (**ticker-tape welcome**, etc. a welcome, etc. esp. in New York, in which ticker-tape, confetti, etc. is thrown over the car of a celebrity, etc. as he passes by); **ticking-off** a reprimand; **tick'-tack'** ticking as of a clock: bookmakers' telegraphy by arm signals: (see also **trick-track**) — Also *adj.* — *adv.* with recurring ticking. — **tick-tack-toe'** (*U.S.*) noughts and crosses; **tick'-tick'** a ticking: (**tick'-tick**) a child's word for a watch; **tick'-tock'** a ticking, as of a big clock: a tapping: (**tick'-tock**) a child's word for a clock. — **in two ticks** in a moment; **make (someone** or **something) tick** (*coll.*) to cause to operate or function: to be the driving-force behind: to cause to behave, think, etc. in a certain way; **tick away** (of time, life, etc.) to pass away with the regularity of the ticking of a clock; **tick off** (*slang*) to reprimand; **tick over** of an engine, to run gently, disconnected from the transmission (*n.* **tick'-over**): of a person, to lead an inactive, uneventful existence: to function, operate. [M.E. *tek*; cf. Du. *tik*, L.G. *tikk*; prob. imit.]

tick[4] *tik* (*slang*) *n.* credit: trust. — *v.i.* to get or give credit. — **tick'-shop** a shop where goods are given on credit. [ticket.]

tick[5] *tik*, *n.* crib-biting: a whimsy. [tic.]

ticket *tik'it*, *n.* a card, slip, or (*formerly*) placard bearing a notice or serving as a token of any right or debt, as for admission, penalty for some offence (esp. motoring), etc.: a certificate (*slang*): discharge from the army (*slang*): a list of candidates put forward by a party for election (*U.S.*): any or all of the principles associated with a particular political party, esp. as a basis for its election to government: a visiting-card (*obs.*). — *v.t.* to label: to designate: to issue a ticket to. — **ticket agent** an agent who sells tickets on behalf of a theatre, or a railway, etc.; **tick'et-collec'tor; tick'et-day** the day before settling day on the Stock Exchange; **tick'et-holder** a person possessing a ticket, e.g. for a concert; **tick'et-office** a place where tickets are sold; **tick'et-porter** a licensed porter: a railway porter who collects tickets; **tick'et-punch** an instrument for punching holes in tickets; **tick'et-writer** an expert in shop-window card and similar lettering; **tick'et-writing.** — **straight ticket** all the nominees of a political party, and no others; **the ticket** (*slang*) exactly the right thing or the thing to be done; **ticket of leave** (formerly) a licence to be at large before expiry of sentence; **ticket-of-leave man.** [O.Fr. *estiquet(te)* — *estiquer*, to stick — O.L.G. *stekan*; cf. **stick.**]

tickety-boo, tickettyboo *tik'it-i-boo'*, (*coll.*) *adj.* fine, satisfactory. [Ety. uncertain.]

tickey, ticky *tik'i*, (*S.Afr.*) *n.* a former S. Afr. coin, a threepenny-bit: now used of a decimal coin of small denomination. [Origin uncertain.]

tickle *tik'l*, *adj.* unstable, in unstable equilibrium, delicately set, insecure (*Spens., Shak.*): ticklish, nice (*obs.* or *dial.*). — *v.t.* to excite with a pleasant thrill: to affect with a disturbing feeling of a light touch, usually uncomfortable and tending to excite laughter: to amuse: to please: to perplex: to touch lightly: to beat. — *v.i.* to tingle (*Spens.*): to be the seat of a tickling or itching feeling. — *n.* an act or feeling of tickling: a slight touch of the ball with the bat (*cricket*). — *n.* **tick'ler** one who or that which tickles: a feather-brush: a poker: a cane: a device for reminding: a puzzle: a dram of spirits. — *n.* and *adj.* **tick'ling**. — *adj.* **tick'lish** easily tickled: unstable: precarious: easily affected: nice: critical. — *adv.* **tick'lishly**. — *n.* **tick'lishness**. — *adj.* **tick'ly** tickling: ticklish. — **tick'le-brain** (*Shak.*) strong liquor. — *n.pl.* **tick'ly-bend'ers** thin ice that bends underfoot: a game played on it. — **tickle pink, to death** to please or amuse very much. [Perh. a freq. of **tick**³; perh. by metathesis from **kittle**.]

tick-tack-toe. See **tick**³.
ticky. See **tickey**.
tic-tac. Same as **tick-tack** (see **tick**³).
tid *tid*, (*Scot.*) *n.* fit time or condition: a mood.
tidal. See **tide**¹.
tidbit. Same as **titbit**.
tiddle *tid'l*, *v.i.* to potter, trifle.
tiddled. See **tiddly**¹.
tiddler *tid'lər*, *n.* a small fish, e.g. a minnow or a stickleback: anything very small. [Perh. **tittlebat, tiddly**² or **tiddy**².]
tiddley *tid'li*, (*naval coll.*) *adj.* smart and trim. — Also **tidd'ly**. [Perh. **tiddly**² or **tidy**.]
tiddly¹ *tid'li*, (*slang*) *n.* drink. — *adj.* slightly drunk. — Also **tidd'ley**. — *adj.* **tidd'led** (*coll.*) slightly drunk. — **on the tiddly** (*slang*) drunk. [Earlier *titley*.]
tiddly² *tid'li*, (*coll.* or *dial.*) *adj.* small, tiny. — Also **tidd'ley**. [Perhaps a childish form of **little**; cf. **tiddy**².]
tiddlywink *tid'li-wingk*, *n.* an unlicensed pawnshop or beer-house (*slang*): (also **tiddledywink** *tid'l-di-*) any of the discs used in **tiddlywinks**, or **tiddledywinks**, a game in which small discs are flipped into a cup by pressing the edge of the small disc with a bigger one.
tiddy¹ *tid'i*, (*Scott*) *n.* the four of trumps at gleek.
tiddy² *tid'i*, (*dial.*) *adj.* very small. [Origin uncertain.]
tide¹ *tīd*, *n.* a time: season: festival: opportunity: trend: ebb and flow, esp. of the sea twice daily: a time of ebbing, of flowing, of both, or of suitable state for work: sea-water (*poet.*): a flow: river, river-water, or current (*poet.*): flood-tide: a sudden access or flood of feeling, etc. — *v.t.* (esp. *fig.*) to carry as the tide: to effect by means of the tide. — *v.i.* to run like a tide: to make one's way by taking advantage of the tides (also *v.t.* with *it*). — *adjs.* **tīd'al** of, depending on, regulated by, the tide: flowing and ebbing; **tide'less**. — **tidal wave** the tide-wave: a great wave caused by the tide: improperly, a great wave started by an earthquake and running on with its own velocity; **tide'-gate** a gate that admits water at flood-tide and retains it at ebb; **tide'-gauge** an instrument for registering the state of the tide continuously; **tide'-lock** a lock by which ships may pass out or in at all times of the tide; **tide'mark** a line on the shore made by the tide: a mark of the limit of washing; **tide'mill** a mill moved by tide-water; **tide'-race** a swift tidal current; **tide'-rip** disturbed sea due to currents: a tidal wave; **tides'-man** a customs officer who waited the arrival of ships (orig. coming in with the tide); **tide'-table** a table of times of high-tide; **tide'-waiter** a tides-man: one who waits to see how things go before acting; **tide'-waiter-ship; tide'-water** water brought by the tide: river water affected by the tide (*U.S.*): seaboard (*U.S.*); **tide'-wave** the tide regarded as a wave passing round the earth; **tide'-way** a track followed by the tide: a channel through which there is a strong current or tide. — **tide over** to carry over, or surmount, difficulties, for the time at least. [O.E. *tīd*; Du. *tijd*, Ger. *Zeit*.]
tide² *tīd*, (*arch.*) *v.i.* to happen. [O.E. (*ge*)*tīdan*; cf. **betide**.]
tide³ (*Spens.*) for **tied**.
tidings *tī'dingz*, *n.pl.* news. [Late O.E. *tīdung* — O.E.

tīdan, to tide, happen, or — O.N. *tīthindi*, events, tidings.]
tidivate. Same as **titivate**.
tidy *tī'di*, *adj.* seasonable (*obs.*): in good condition or order (*dial.*): plump (*dial.*): comely (*dial.*): shapely (*dial.*): fairly good or big (*coll.*): trim: orderly: neat. — *n.* a cover for a chair-back: a receptacle for odd scraps. — *v.t.* to make tidy: to clear away for the sake of tidiness: — *pr.p.* **tī'dying;** *pa.t.* and *pa.p.* **tī'died**. — *adv.* **tī'dily**. — *n.* **tī'diness**. [**tide**¹; cf. Ger. *zeitig*.]
tie *tī*, *v.t.* to bind: to fasten: to knot: to make as a knot: to restrict, restrain: to unite: to mark with a curved line indicating sustentation not repetition (*mus.*): to perform or mark in this way (*mus.*): to limit: to oblige: to subject to bonds: to confirm (*Shak.*): to ligature: to make (an artificial fly for angling). — *v.i.* to be equal in votes or score: of dogs, to linger on the scent: — *pr.p.* **ty'ing;** *pa.t.* and *pa.p.* **tied** (*tīd*). — *n.* a knot, bow, etc.: a bond: a string, ribbon, etc., for tying: a band of material passed under the collar of a shirt, etc. and tied under the chin, esp. one having one end wider than the other, tied to hang down the shirt front with the wider end overlying the narrower, worn by men, or as part of a uniform: a tie-wig: a shoe (*U.S.*): a member sustaining only a tension: a railway sleeper (*U.S.*): a restraint: an obligation: a mode of tying: an equality in score or votes: a match in any stage of a tournament in which the losers are eliminated: a curved line drawn over notes of the same pitch to be performed as one, sustained not repeated (*mus.*). — *adjs.* **tied** having been tied: having a tie as a result: of a public-house or garage, denoting one whose tenant is bound to get his supplies from one particular brewer or distiller, or oil and petrol producer: of a house, cottage, etc., denoting one whose tenant may occupy the premises only as long as he is employed by the owner; **tie'less**. — *n.* **tī'er** one who ties: a child's apron (*U.S.*). — **tie'-beam** a beam connecting the lower ends of rafters to prevent moving apart; **tie'-break** in tennis, a number of points played at the end of a tied set to decide the winner; **tie'-breaker** a tie-break: any game(s), question(s) or competition(s) intended to break a tie and decide a winner; **tie'-clip** an ornamental clip which attaches one's tie to one's shirt; **tie'-dye'ing** a method of hand-dyeing textiles in which parts of the material are bound or knotted so as to resist the dye. — Also **tie'-and-dye'; tie'-in** a connection: something, esp. a book, which ties in with something else, e.g. a film; **tie'-neck** a collar terminating in two long pieces that can be tied in a bow, etc. under the chin. — *adj.* (of a blouse, etc.) having a tie-neck. — **tie'-pin** an ornamental pin stuck in a necktie; **tie'-rod** a rod serving as a tie; **tie'tac(k)** a tie-clip; **tie'-up** tape for tying a bookbinding or portfolio: an animal tied up for a bait: a standstill: an entanglement: a connection: a business association; **tie'-wig** a wig tied with ribbon at the back. — **tie down** to fix: to bind by conditions, etc.; **tie in, up, with** to agree with: to be closely associated with: to be linked with, as for example a book containing the story of, or a story concerning the characters in, a popular film or TV series; **tie up** to parcel up: to tie so as to remain up: to tether: to moor: to secure against squandering, alienation, etc., restrict the use of, by conditions. [O.E. *tēah*, band, string, *tīgan*, to tie.]
tier *tēr*, *n.* a row, rank, or layer, esp. one of several placed one above another: a row of guns: a mountain range (*Tasmania*). — *v.t.* to pile in tiers. [O.Fr. *tire*, sequence.]
tierce *tērs*, *n.* a third (*obs.*): one-third of a pipe: a cask or vessel of that capacity: (*tûrs*) a sequence of three cards of the same suit: a third (*mus.*): the note two octaves and a third above a given note (*mus.*): a position in fencing: the third hour of the day (ending 9 a.m.): the office of that hour, the terce. — *adj.* **tiercé** (*tēr'si*; Fr., divided into three parts) of a field, divided into three equal parts, each of a different tincture (*her.*). — *n.* in horse-racing, a system of betting by

which the first, second and third horses must be named in the right order, or a race for which this system obtains. — *n.* **tier′ceron** (*archit.*) in vaulting, a subordinate rib springing from the intersection of two other ribs. — **tierce de Picardie** (*tyers də pē-kar-dē*) a major third closing a piece otherwise in a minor key.   [O.Fr. *tiers, tierce* — L. *tertia* (*pars*).]

tiercel, tiercelet. See **tercel.**

tierceron. See **tierce.**

tiers état *tyer-zā-tä,* (Fr.) the third estate, or commons, formerly in France.

tiff[1] *tif, n.* stale, sour, or thin liquor: a sip: a dram. — *v.i.* to sip: to drink: to lunch. — Also (*Scot.* and *dial.*) **tift.** — *n.* **tiff′ing** sipping: lunch, a light repast (*India,* etc., **tiff′in**).   [Perh. orig. slang.]

tiff[2] *tif, (obs.) v.t.* and *v.i.* to dress, trick out.   [O.Fr. *tiffer* (Fr. *atiffer*), to adorn.]

tiff[3] *tif, n.* a display of irritation, a pet, huff: a slight quarrel. — *v.i.* to be in a huff: to squabble. — Also (esp. *Scot.*)(**tift.**   [Prob. imit.]

tiffany *tif′ə-ni, n.* a silk-like gauze. — *adj.* of tiffany: transparent.   [Gr. *theophaneia,* theophany, or *diaphaneia,* transparency.]

Tiffany *tif′ə-ni, adj.* denoting objects designed or produced by C.L. *Tiffany* (1812-1902), founder of the New York jeweller's, Tiffany and Co., or (esp.) his son L.C. Tiffany (1848-1933), Art Nouveau designer. — **Tiffany glass** another name for **favrile** (q.v.); **Tiffany lamp** a lamp with a distinctive umbrella-shaped shade.

tiffin. See **tiff**[1].

tift. See **tiff**[1,3].

tig[1] *tig, n.* a touch: a twitch: a game in which one who is 'it' seeks to touch another. — *v.t.* to touch, esp. in the game of tig.   [Poss. a form of **tick**[3].]

tig[2] *tig, n.* an old drinking-cup with two or more handles.

tige *tēzh, n.* the shaft of a column.   [Fr., — L. *tībia,* a pipe.]

tiger *tī′gər, n.* a fierce striped Asiatic beast, one of the two largest cats (*Felis tigris*): the leopard (*S.Afr.*): the jaguar (*American tiger*) (*U.S.*): the puma (*red tiger*): a boy in livery usually perched behind a vehicle: a ferocious or bloodthirsty person: a flashy vulgarian: a formidable opponent or competitor (*slang*): a yell to supplement a cheer (*U.S.*): a tiger-beetle, tiger-moth, tiger-shark, tiger-lily, etc.: — *fem.* **ti′gress.** — *adj.* **ti′g(e)rish** like a tiger in disposition: flashy. — *n.* **ti′gerism** swagger. — *adjs.* **ti′gerly; ti′gery, ti′grine** (*-grīn*), **ti′groid** like a tiger. — **tiger badge** a proficiency badge awarded by the Himalayan Club to Sherpas; **ti′ger-bee′tle** any beetle of the Cicindelidae; **ti′ger-cat** a general name for a middle-sized striped or spotted wild cat — margay, ocelot, serval, etc.; **tiger country** (*golf*) dense rough; **ti′ger('s)-eye′** a pseudomorph of quartz after crocidolite; **ti′ger-flower** a Mexican iridaceous plant (Tigridia) with streaked flowers. — *adj.* **ti′ger-foot′ed** (*Shak.*) fiercely swift. — **ti′ger-lil′y** a lily with black-spotted orange flowers; **ti′ger-moth** any one of the Arctiidae; **ti′ger-nut** the edible rhizome of *Cyperus esculentus,* a European sedge: (*U.S.*) the chufa; **ti′ger-shark** a voracious striped shark of the Indian Ocean; **ti′ger-snake** the most deadly of Australian snakes (*Notechis scutatus*), brown with black crossbands; **ti′ger-tail** type of fast-growing hybrid worm; **ti′ger-wolf** the spotted hyena: the thylacine; **ti′ger-wood** any of several showy black-striped woods.   [Fr. *tigre* — L. *tigris* — Gr. *tigris,* prob. from Zend.]

tight[1] *tīt, adj.* close: compact: close-fitting: too close-fitting: cramped: allowing little space, time, or opportunity, for deviation from plan: (of situation) difficult or dangerous: (of contest) close: (of style) concise: taut, not slack: (of e.g. control) very firm, strict: precise: under control: firmly fixed: impervious, not leaky, proof: trim: neat: snug: competent: hampered or characterised by want of money: (of money) scarce, hard to obtain: unwilling to part with money: intoxicated: denoting play in set scrums and line-outs (*Rugby football*). — *adv.* tightly: soundly. — *n.* (*Rugby foot-*

ball) tight play. — *v.t.* and *v.i.* **tight′en** (often with *up*) to make or grow tight or tighter. — *n.* **tight′ener** one who, or that which, tightens: a tensor (*anat.*): a heavy meal (*slang*). — *adj.* **tight′ish.** — *adv.* **tight′ishly.** — *adv.* **tight′ly.** — *n.* **tight′ness.** — *n.pl.* **tights** close-fitting breeches: a close-fitting garment covering the lower part of the body and the legs. — *adj.* **tight′-fisted** stingy. — **tight-head prop** (*Rugby football*) the prop forward on the right of his front row of the scrum. — *v.t., v.i.,* and *adj.* **tight′-lace′.** — *adj.* **tight′-laced′** straight-laced. — *ns.* **tight′-lā′cer; tight′-lā′cing** compression of the waist by tight clothes. — *adjs.* **tight′-knit′, tight′ly-knit′** close-knit: closely integrated: tightly organised; **tight′-lipped** uncommunicative. — **tight′-rope** a taut rope on which feats of balancing and acrobatics are performed: a middle course between dangerous or undesirable alternatives (*fig.*); **tight′wad** a skin-flint, miser. — **a tight corner, spot** a difficult situation; **run a tight ship** to be in control of an efficient, well-run organisation or group.   [Earlier *thight,* app. from an older form of O.N. *thēttr,* influenced by various English words of similar meaning; cf. Ger. *dicht.*]

tight[2] *tīt,* (*Spens.*) *pa.t.* and *pa.p.* of **tie.**

tight[3]. See **tite.**

tigon *tī′gon, n.* the offspring of a tiger and a lioness. — Also **tig′lon.**   [*tiger, lion.*]

tigress. See **tiger.**

tika *tē′kə, n.* a red mark on the forehead of Hindu women, formerly of religious significance but now counted as a beauty spot.   [Hind.]

tike. Same as **tyke.**

tiki *tik′ē, n.* an image, often in the form of a small greenstone ornament, representing an ancestor—in some Polynesian cultures, worn as an amulet.   [Maori.]

til *til, tēl, n.* sesame. — Also **teel.** — **til′-oil; til′-seed.**   [Hind. *til* — Sans. *tila.*]

Tilapia *ti-lap′i-ə, -lā′ n.* an African freshwater genus of edible cichlid fishes: (without *cap.*) a fish of this genus.   [Modern L.]

tilbury *til′bər-i, n.* a kind of gig, for two.   [Said to be so named from its first maker.]

tilde *til′dä, -di, -də, tild, n.* the diacritical sign over *n* in Spanish to indicate the sound *ny* — thus *ñ* (as in *cañon*): used in Portuguese over *a* and *o* to indicate nasalisation.   [Sp., — L. *titulus,* a title.]

tile *tīl, n.* a slab of baked clay (or a substitute) for covering roofs, floors, etc.: a tube of baked clay used in drains: a piece for playing mah-jongg: tiling: a hat (*slang*): a top-hat (*Scot.*). — *v.t.* to cover with tiles: to drain by means of tiles: to secure against intrusion by placing a person at the door: to bind to secrecy. — *adj.* **tiled** covered with tiles: imbricated: (of fish) sun-dried (*Scott*). — *ns.* **ti′ler** a maker or layer of tiles: a freemasons' door-keeper — also **tyl′er; til′ery** a place where tiles are made; **til′ing.** — **tile′-hat** (*Scot.*) a top-hat. — *adj.* **tile′-hung** (of a wall) covered with flat roofing tiles as protection against the weather; **tile′-red** a brownish-red, the colour of baked tiles; **tile′-stone** a flat stone used for roofing, esp. a thin-bedded sandstone. — **Dutch tiles** enamelled earthenware tiles, usu. decorated in blue, with scriptural subjects, etc., for chimney-pieces, etc.; **have a tile loose** (*slang*) to be a little mad; **hung tiles** tiles hung vertically, covering a wall; **on the tiles** on the loose.   [O.E. *tigele* — L. *tēgula* — *tegĕre,* to cover.]

tilefish *tīl′fish, n.* an American Atlantic fish noted for the sudden changes in its numbers.   [App. from its generic name, Lopholatilus, and perh. its tile-like spotted pattern.]

tiler, tilery, tiling. See **tile.**

Tilia *til′i-ə, n.* the lime or linden genus, giving name to the family **Tiliā′ceae,** akin to the mallows. — *adj.* **tiliā′ceous** belonging to the family.   [L. *tilia,* lime-tree.]

till[1] *til, n.* a compartment or drawer in a chest, cabinet, etc. (*obs.*): now, a money-drawer or receptacle in or behind a counter. [Cf. M.E. *tillen*, to draw, O.E. *fortyllan*, to draw aside, seduce.]

till² *til, prep.* to the time of: to (*Scot.*): to, with the infinitive (*Scot.*). — *conj.* to the time when. [O.E. (Northumbrian) *til* — O.N. *til*; cf. O.E. *till*, a fixed point, Ger. *Ziel*, end, goal.]

till³ *til, v.t.* to work, cultivate: to set (*obs.* or *dial.*). — *adj.* **till'able** arable. — *ns.* **till'age** the act or practice of tilling: husbandry: a place tilled; **till'er; till'ing**. [O.E. *tilian*, to aim at, till — *till*, limit; see foregoing word.]

till⁴ *til, n.* a stiff impervious clay (orig. *Scot.*): boulder-clay (*geol.*): shale (*mining*). — *n.* **till'ite** indurated till. — *adj.* **till'y**. [Cf. **thill²**.]

Tillandsia *ti-land'zi-ə, n.* a mainly epiphytic tropical American genus of the pineapple family: (without *cap.*) a plant of this genus. [So called from Finno-Swedish botanist, Elias *Tillands* (d. 1693).]

tiller¹ *til'ər, n.* the handle or lever for turning a rudder. — **till'er-chain, -rope** the chain or rope connecting the tiller with the steering-wheel. [M.E. *tillen*, to draw (see **till¹**), or O.Fr. *telier*, cross-bow stock — L.L. *telārium*, a weaver's beam — L. *tēla*, a web.]

tiller² *til'ər*, **teller, tellar** *tel'ər, ns.* a sapling: a shoot from a tree stool: a sucker from the base of a stem: a side-shoot from the base as in corn, etc. — *v.i.* to form tillers. [O.E. *telgor*, shoot, twig.]

tiller³. See **till³**.

tillite, tilly. See **till⁴**.

tilly-vally, -fally *til'i-val'i, -fal'i*, (*Shak.*) *interjs.* of impatience of what has been said. — Also **till'ey-vall'ey**.

tilt¹ *tilt, n.* a cover, awning, for a wagon, boat, etc.: a tent: a hut. — *v.t.* to cover with a tilt. — *adj.* **tilt'ed**. — **tilt'-boat** a large rowing-boat with a tilt. [O.E. *teld*; cf. Ger. *Zelt*.]

tilt² *tilt, v.i.* to pitch, as a ship: to lean, heel over: to slope: to slant, esp. in a vertical plane: to joust, ride and thrust with a spear: to charge, attack (with *at*): to criticise (with *at*): to thrust. — *v.t.* to incline: to tip out: to send by tilting: to forge with a tilt-hammer. — *n.* an act of tilting: a condition of being tilted: a slope: a joust, a course with a lance: an encounter: a duel: a thrust: a tilt-yard. — *adj.* **tilt'able**. — *ns.* **tilt'er; tilt'ing**. — **tilt'-hammer** a heavy pivoted hammer lifted by a cam; **tilt'-yard** a place for tilting. — **full tilt** at full speed in a headlong course. [O.E. *tealt*, tottering.]

tilth *tilth, n.* cultivation: cultivated land: the depth of soil turned up in cultivation. [From **till³**.]

timariot *ti-mä'ri-ot*, (*hist.*) *n.* a Turkish feudal militiaman. [Fr., — Turk. *timār*.]

timbal, tymbal *tim'bl*, (*arch.*) *n.* a kettledrum. — *n.* **timbale** (*tē-bal, tam'bal, tim'bl*) a dish of meat, fish, etc. cooked in a cup-shaped mould or shell: a mould of pastry. [Fr. *timbale*; see **atabal**; app. influenced by L. *tympanum*.]

timber *tim'bər, n.* wood suitable for building or carpentry, whether growing or cut: standing trees of oak, ash, elm, or (locally by custom) other kinds, forming part of an inheritance (*English law*): material generally: a beam, or large piece of wood in a framework, as of a house, ship, etc.: familiarly, a wooden object or part: a wooden leg: wood (*dial.*): woodland, forest-land (*U.S.*). — *adj.* of timber: wooden: wooden in tone, unmusical (*Scot.*). — *v.t.* to build (*obs.*): to furnish with timber or beams. — *interj.* a warning given when a tree being felled is about to fall. — *adj.* **tim'bered** built: constructed: built of wood: furnished with timber: shored up with timber: app. massive (*Spens.*): wooded. — *n.* **tim'bering** timber collectively: work in timber. — **tim'ber-head** the top of a ship's timber rising above the deck and used as a bollard: a bollard placed in a similar position; **tim'ber-hitch** see **hitch**; **tim'ber-line** the upper limit of timber-trees on the mountains, etc.; **tim'ber-man** one responsible for the timbers in a mine; **tim'ber-mare'** see **horse**; **tim'ber-toes** a person with a wooden leg; **tim'ber-tree** a tree suitable for timber; **tim'ber-wolf** an American variety of the com-

mon wolf, the grey wolf; **tim'ber-yard** a yard or place where timber is stored or sold. [O.E. *timber*, building, wood, *timbrian*, to build; Ger. *Zimmer*, room.]

timbó *tim-bō', n.* a South American sapindaceous climber (*Paullinia pinnata*): a fish-poison and insecticide got from its bark: — *pl.* **timbós'**. [Guarani.]

timbre *tēbr', tim'bər, tam'bər, n.* the quality of a sound, tone-colour, distinguished from pitch and loudness. [O.Fr., bell — L. *tympanum*, a drum.]

timbrel *tim'brəl, n.* an ancient Oriental tabor or tambourine. — *adj.* **tim'brel'd** (*Milt.*) sung to the timbrel. [O.Fr. *timbre* — L. *tympanum*, drum.]

timbrology *tim-brol'ə-ji*, **timbromania** (*-brō-mā'ni-ə*), **timbrophily** (*-brof'i-li*), *ns.* outmoded words for stamp-collecting. — *ns.* **timbrol'ogist, timbromā'niac, timbroph'ilist**. [Fr. *timbre*, postage-stamp.]

time *tīm, n.* a concept arising from change experienced and observed: a quantity measured by the angle through which the earth turns on its axis: (with *cap.*) any of the clock-settings used as standard times in the various time zones, as *Pacific Time, Central European Time*, etc.: a moment at which, or stretch of duration in which, things happen: season: the due, appointed, usual time: the hour of death or of parturition: spell: a period: the actual time of being something or somewhere, as of apprenticeship, residence, sentence, student days, life, etc.: the duration of the world: leisure or opportunity long enough for a purpose: a spell of exciting, usually pleasurable, experience: the time, or shortest time, of performance, as a race: rhythm, tempo: rate of speed: a unit of duration in metre, a mora: an occasion: an occasion regarded as one of a recurring series: one of a number of multiplied instances: generalised as an indication of multiplication (*so many times* = multiplied by so much): (the rate of) payment for work by the hour, day, etc.: back-pay (also **back time**): a reckoning of time: an interval: past time: an allotted period, esp. its completion, as in boxing rounds, permitted drinking hours, etc.: the call, bell, whistle, buzzer, or other signal announcing this: (in *pl.*) the contemporary conditions: (in *pl.* with *cap.*) often the name of a newspaper: (*cap.*) a personification of time, a bald-headed old man with a forelock, a beard, a scythe, often an hour-glass. — *v.t.* to arrange, fix, choose, a time for: to mark, adjust, or observe the rhythm or time of: to ascertain the time of: to regulate as to time. *v.i.* to keep or beat time. — *adj.* of time: reckoned by time: timed: for a future time. — *interj.* indicating that time is up, or that action is now permitted. — *adjs.* **timed; time'less** independent of time: unconnected with the passage of time: untimely: premature (*Shak.*): ill-timed: eternal: failing to keep time or rhythm. — Also *adv.* — *adv.* **time'lessly**. — *ns.* **time'lessness; time'liness**. — *adj.* **time'ly** in good time, early: seasonable: well-timed: temporal (*obs.*): of the time of day (*Spens.*): in time, keeping time (*Spens.*). — *adv.* early, soon: in due time or good time. — *adj.* **tim(e)ous** (*tīm'əs; chiefly Scot.*) in good time: seasonable. — *adv.* **tim(e)'ously** in good time. — *ns.* **tim'er** one who or that which times anything: a clock-like device which sets something off or switches something on or off at a given time: (in composition) one who belongs to, works for, etc., such-and-such a time; **tim'ing** fixing, choosing, adjusting, ascertaining, or recording of times: (the co-ordination of) departure and arrival times: co-ordination in time; **tim'ist** a time-server (*obs.*): one who keeps in time: one who times his movements. — **time'-ball** a ball arranged to drop at a particular time; **time'-bargain** a contract to buy or sell at a certain time in the future. — *adjs.* **time'-beguil'ing** making time seem to pass quickly; **time'-bett'ering** (*Shak.*) in which times are growing better; **time'-bewast'ed** (*Shak.*) spent by time. — **time'-bill** a time-table; **time'-bomb** a bomb that explodes by a time-fuse; **time capsule** a capsule containing objects, etc., representative of the present time, buried in the ground or set in the foundations of a building for discovery at a future date; **time'-card** a card for use with a time-clock; **time'-clock** a clock-like apparatus which stamps on cards the time of arrival and departure of e.g. office or factory workers; **time code** a track separate from the main one on a video or audio tape, on which time is recorded digitally, to help editing. — *adj.* **time'-consum'ing** requiring much time: wasting time. — **time deposit** a bank deposit from which withdrawals may be made only after a certain time or with due notice. — *adj.* **time'-expired** having completed a term of enlistment. — **time'-exposure** (*phot.*) an exposure for a time long in comparison with one called instantaneous; **time'-fuse** a fuse contrived to act at a definite time; **time'-gun** a gun fired to indicate a certain hour. — *adj.* **time'-hon'oured** honoured on account of antiquity. — **time'-keeper** a clock, watch, or other instrument that measures time: one who keeps account of workmen's hours: one who beats or observes time; **time'-killer** a person or thing that kills time (see **kill**). — *n.* and *adj.* **time'-killing.** — **time'-lag** the interval of delay between two connected phenomena. — *adj.* **time'-lapse** of or relating to **time-lapse photography**, a method of recording and condensing long or slow processes by taking a large number of photographs at regular intervals, the resulting film being projected at normal speed. — **time'-lim'it** a time within which something has to be done. — *adj.* **time'ly-part'ed** (*Shak.*) having died at a natural time. — **time'-machine** a hypothetical machine by which one may travel through time; **time'-out'** a short break during a sporting contest for rest, discussion of tactics, etc.: any similar short suspension of activity; **time'piece** a piece of machinery for keeping time, esp. one that does not strike but is bigger than a watch; **time'-pleas'er** (*Shak.*) a time-server. — *n.* and *adj.* **time'-saving.** — **time'scale** the time envisaged for the carrying-out of (the stages of) a project: a statement of the times of appearance, completion, etc. of a series of events, stages, etc. — *adj.* **time'-served** having completed one's apprenticeship, fully trained. — **time'-server** one who serves or meanly suits his opinions to the times or those in authority for the time; **time'-service.** — *n.* and *adj.* **time'-serving.** — **time'-share** the time-sharing of property, etc. — Also *adj.* — **time'-sharer**; **time'-sharing** the optimum utilisation of a computer and its peripheral devices whereby the differential processing-time of each machine is allowed for, and is used accordingly: a scheme by which a person buys the right to use a holiday home for the same specified period of time each year for a specified number of years; **time'-sheet** a record of the time worked by a person; **time'-signal** an intimation of the exact time given by wireless or otherwise from an observatory; **time'-signature** (*mus.*) an indication of measure at the beginning of a line or wherever there is a change; **time'-slot** a particular period of time in the day or week allocated to a certain radio or television programme: a particular period assigned to a certain purpose, etc.; **time'-spirit** the genius of the age; **time'-switch** one working automatically at a set time; **time'table** a table of times, as of classes, etc. — *v.t.* to put on a timetable: to plan, divide into sessions, etc., according to a timetable. — **time'-thrust** a thrust made in fencing at the moment the opponent draws breath for his thrust; **time'-trial** an event, esp. in cycling, in which competitors set off one at a time, and attempt to cover a set distance in the shortest time; **time'-unit; time'-warp** in science fiction, etc., a hypothetical distortion in the time-continuum, allowing one to pass from the present to the past or future, or to stand still in the present; **time'-work** work paid for by the hour or the day — opp. to *piece-work.* — *adj.* **time'-worn** worn or decayed by time. — **time zone** one of 24 longitudinal divisions of the globe, each 15° wide, having a standard time throughout its area: a similar zone adapted to a particular country. — **against time** with the aim or necessity of finishing by a certain time; **ahead of time**

earlier than expected; **ahead of one's time** having ideas, etc. too advanced or progressive to be acceptable at the time; **all in good time** in due course: soon enough; **apparent time** time according to the real sun, without regard to the equation of time — sundial time; **astronomical time** till 1925 the time past mean noon, now midnight, reckoned on to twenty-four hours in mean time; **at one time** formerly: simultaneously; **at the same time** simultaneously: notwithstanding; **at the time** at the time stated or under consideration; **at times** at distant intervals: occasionally; **before one's time** ahead of one's time; **behind time** late; **behind the times** not abreast of changes; **between times** in the intervals; **by times** betimes; **common time** time with two beats or a multiple of two beats to a measure (**compound common time** where each beat is of three quavers or crotchets); **do time** to serve a sentence of imprisonment; **for a time** during a time: temporarily; **for the time being** at the present time or the actual time in question; **from time to time** now and then; **gain time** to provide oneself with more time to do something (e.g. by delaying something else); **half the time** as often as not, frequently; **have a good time** to enjoy oneself; **have a time of it** (*coll.*) to experience problems, difficulties, etc.; **have little, no, time for** to have little, no, interest in or patience with (see also **time**); **in good time** quite early enough: with some time to spare: (*ironically; obs.*) indeed; **in one's time** at some past time in one's life, esp. when one was at one's peak; **in one's own (good) time** at a time, rate, etc. of one's own choosing; **in one's own time** in one's spare time, when not at work; **in time** after a lapse of time: early enough: keeping rhythm; **keep time** to run accurately, as a clock (also **keep good time**): to move or perform in the same rhythm: to record times of workmen, etc.; **know the time of day** to know the state of affairs: to know what one is about, or the best way of doing something; **local time** time reckoned from the local meridian; **lose time** to fall behindhand: to let time pass without full advantage; **make good time** to make speedy progress on a journey; **make time** to regain advantage of lost time: to find an opportunity; **mark time** see **mark¹**; **mean solar time** time reckoned not by the actual but the mean position of the sun; **not before time** rather tardily: none too soon; **no time (at all)** a very short time; **on, upon, a time** once: at a time in the past (usu. imaginary); **on time** up to time: punctually; **out of time** not keeping rhythm: too late (*law*); **sidereal time** the portion of a sidereal day that has elapsed since the transit of the first point of Aries; **solar time** time reckoned by the sun, real or mean; **standard time** a system of time adopted for a wide area instead of local time — usually Greenwich mean time or a time differing from it by a whole number of hours; **summer time** see **summer**; **take one's time** (*coll.*) not to hurry, dawdle; **take Time by the forelock** to seize an opportunity before it is too late; **take time off** (*U.S.* out) to find time to do something, for an activity; **the time of one's life** a very enjoyable time; **time after time** repeatedly; **time about** (chiefly *Scot.*) in turns, alternately; **time and again** repeatedly; **time and motion study** an investigation of the motions performed and time taken in industrial, etc., work with a view to increased production; **time of day** the time by the clock: the point of time reached: a greeting, salutation; **time out of mind** during the whole time within human memory, from time immemorial; **time was** there once was a time (when); **time-zone disease, fatigue** jet lag; **triple time** three beats, or three times three beats, to a measure; **up to time** punctual, punctually: not later than the due time; **what time** (*poet.*) when. [O.E. *tīma*; O.N. *tīmi.*]

timenoguy *tim'ən-og-i, n.* a rope stretched from place to place in a ship, esp. one to prevent the fore-sheet fouling (*naut.*): a makeshift: a what's-its-name. [Origin obscure, perh. Fr. *timon* (see **timon**) and **guy¹**.]

timid *tim'id, adj.* inclined to fear: wanting courage: faint-hearted. — *n.* **timid'ity.** — *adv.* **tim'idly.** — *n.* **tim'idness.** — *adj.* **tim'orous** (*-ər-əs*) timid. — *adv.*

tim′orously. — *n.* **tim′orousness.** — *adj.* **tim′orsome** (*dial.*) easily frightened. [L. *timidus*, timid, *timor*, *-ōris*, fear — *timēre*, to fear.]

timing, timist. See **time.**

timocracy tī-mok′rə-si, *n.* a form of government in which property is a qualification for office: one in which ambition or desire of honour is a ruling principle. — *adjs.* **timocratic** (*-ō-krat′ik*), **-al.** [Gr. *tīmokratiā* — *tīmē*, honour, *krateein*, to rule.]

timon tī′mən, (*obs.*) *n.* a helm. — *n.* **timoneer′** a helmsman. [Fr., — L. *tēmō*, *-ōnis*, a beam.]

Timon tī′mən, *n.* a famous Athenian misanthrope (5th cent. B.C.) celebrated by Aristophanes, Lucian, Plutarch, and Shakespeare: hence, a misanthrope. — *v.i.* **Tī′monise, -ize** to play the misanthrope. — *ns.* **Tī′monism; Tī′monist.**

timorous, etc. See **timid.**

timothy tim′ə-thi, *n.* (in full **timothy-grass**) cat's-tail grass (*Phleum pratense*) much valued for feeding cattle. [*Timothy* Hanson, who promoted its cultivation in America about 1720.]

timous. Same as **timcous** (see **time**).

timpano timp′ə-nō, *n.* an orchestral kettledrum: — *pl.* **tim′pani** (*-nē*), often shortened to **timps** (*coll.*). — *n.* **timp′anist.** [It.; see **tympanum.**]

tim-whisk(e)y tim′-(h)wis′ki, *n.* a whisky (gig).

tin tin, *n.* a silvery-white, easily fusible, malleable metal (symbol Sn for L. *stannum*; at. numb. 50): money (*slang*): a vessel of tin or tin-plate, a can, etc.: a tinful: a tell-tale (*squash*). — *adj.* made of tin or tin-plate or (*coll.*) of corrugated iron: paltry (*coll.*). — *v.t.* to coat or overlay with tin or tinfoil: to cover thinly with solder before soldering: to pack in tins: — *pr.p.* **tinn′ing;** *pa.t.* and *pa.p.* **tinned.** — *n.* **tin′ful:** — *pl.* **tin′fuls.** — *adj.* **tinned.** — *ns.* **tinn′er** a tinsmith: a tin-miner: a canner; **tinn′ing.** — *adj.* **tinn′y** like tin, esp. in sound: lucky (*Austr.* and *N.Z., coll.*). — *n.* (also **tinn′ie**) a mug of tin-plate: a can of beer (*Austr.*). — **tin′-can′; tin′foil** tin or (now) tin-lead alloy (or aluminium) in thin sheets, as for wrapping; **tin god** an overbearing, dictatorial person; **tin hat** (*slang*) a military steel helmet; **tin′horn** (orig. and esp. *U.S.*) a flashy, small-time gambler: a cheap, pretentious, second-rate person. — Also *adj.* — **tin lizzie** (*coll.*) an old or decrepit motor-car; **tin′man** one who works in tin: a dresser of tin-ore: a dealer in tinware; **tin′-opener** an instrument for cutting open tins of food, etc.; **tin′-plate** thin sheet-iron or steel coated with tin. — Also *adj.* — **tin′pot** a pot of or for tin or tin-plate. — *adj.* paltry, rubbishy. — **tin′smith** a worker in tin; **tin′snips** a pair of hand-shears for cutting sheet metal, esp. tin plate; **tin′stone** cassiterite; **tin′-stream′er** one who washes tin from alluvial deposits; **tin′-stream′-ing; tin′-tack′** a tack coated with tin; **tin′-terne′** same as **terne; tin′type** a ferrotype; **tin′ware** articles made of tin; **tin whistle** a cheap six-holed metal flageolet. — **put the tin hat, lid, on** to finish off, bring to an end, suppress; **Tin Pan Alley** orig., a nickname for 28th Street, New York, the centre of the song-publishing district: the popular music publishing district of a city: the realm of popular music production. [O.E. *tin*; O.N. *tin*, Ger. *Zinn*.]

tinaja tin-a′hha, *n.* a very large, full-bellied earthenware jar, used (esp. for storing and maturing wine) in Spain. [Sp.]

tinamou tin′ə-mōō, *n.* a South American partridge-like bird (*Tinamus*) of or akin to the Ratitae. [Fr., — Galibi (Indian language of Fr. Guiana) *tinamu*.]

tincal ting′kəl, *n.* crude borax. [Malay *tingkal*.]

tinchel tin′hhyəl, ting′kəl, *n.* a circle of men who close in round a herd of deer. [Gael. *timchioll*, a circuit.]

tinct tingkt, *n.* a tint: a tinge: the alchemist's elixir (*Shak.*). — *adj.* (*Spens.*) tinged. — *v.t.* (*obs.*) to tint, tinge, dye: to imbue: to subject to transmutation. — *adj.* **tinctō′rial** of dyeing. — *n.* **tinct′ure** a tinge or shade of colour: a colouring matter: a metal, colour, or fur (*her.*): a quality or slight taste added to anything: a principle extracted in solution (*old chem.*): the transmuting elixir

or philosopher's stone (*alchemy*): an alcoholic solution of a drug (*med.*). — *v.t.* to tinge: to imbue. [L. *tingĕre*, *tinctum*, to dye; cf. **tint, tinge.**]

tind tind, *adj.* tīnd (now *dial.*), **teend** tēnd (*Herrick*), **tine** tīn (*Milt.*), *vs.t.* and *vs.i.* to kindle: — *pa.t.* and *pa.p.* **tind′ed, tined** (*Spens.* tīnd, tȳnd, tȳnde). [O.E. *tendan*, and prob. a lost collateral form; cf. **tinder.**]

tindal tin′dəl, *n.* a petty-officer of lascars. [Malayalam *tandal*.]

tinder tin′dər, *n.* dry inflammable matter, esp. that used for kindling fire from a spark. — *adjs.* **tin′der-like** (*Shak.*) inflammable as tinder; **tin′dery** irascible. — **tin′der-box** a box for tinder, and usu. flint and steel. [O.E. *tynder*; O.N. *tundr*, Ger. *Zunder*; O.E. *tendan*, Ger. *zünden*, to kindle.]

tine[1] tīn, *n.* a spike as of a fork, harrow, or deer's horn. — *adj.* **tīned.** [O.E. *tind.*]

tine[2], **tyne** tīn, (*Scot.*) *v.t.* to lose. — *v.i.* to be lost: to be painful (*Spens.*): to perish (*Spens.*): — *pa.t.* and *pa.p.* **tint** (*tint*); *Spens.* **tyned.** — *n.* (*Spens.*) teen, affliction. — *n.* **tinsel** (*tin′sl; Scot.*) loss. [O.N. *tȳna*, to destroy, lose, perish; cf. **teen.**]

tine[3] tīn, (*dial.*) *v.t.* to shut: to enclose. [O.E. *tȳnan*, to surround; cf. **town.**]

tine[4] tīn, (*dial.*) *n.* a wild vetch or tare.

tine[5], **tyne** tīn, (*Shak.*) *adj.* tiny (always preceded by little).

tine[6]. See **tind.**

tinea tin′i-ə, *n.* ringworm: any of several skin diseases caused by fungi: (*cap.*) the clothes-moth genus, giving name to the **Tineidae** (*ti-nē′i-dē*), a large family of small moths. — *adj.* **tineid** (*tin-ē′id*) of or pertaining to the family Tineidae or genus Tinea. — *n.* an individual tineid moth. [L. *tinea*, moth, bookworm, etc.]

ting ting, *v.t.* and *v.i.* to ring. — *n.* the sound of a small bell. — *n.* **ting′-a-ling** a tinkling. — Also *adv.* [Imit.]

tinge tinj, *v.t.* to tint or colour: to suffuse: to impart a slight modification to. — *v.i.* to take on a tinge: — *pr.p.* **ting′ing.** — *n.* a slight colouring or modification. [L. *tingĕre*, *tinctum*; conn. with Gr. *tengein*, to wet, to stain.]

tingle[1] ting′gl, *v.i.* to feel or be the seat of a thrilling sensation: to thrill: to throb: to ring: to vibrate. — *v.t.* to cause to tingle: to ring. — *n.* a tingling sensation. — *n.* **ting′ler** a stinging blow. — *n.* and *adj.* **ting′ling.** — *adjs.* **ting′lish** thrilling; **ting′ly** tingling. [M.E. *tinglen*, a variant of *tinklen.*]

tingle[2] ting′gl, *n.* a small tack or nail: a clip of lead: patch over leak in boat's planking. [Cf. Ger. *Zingel.*]

tinguaite ting′gwə-īt, *n.* a fine-grained igneous rock composed essentially of feldspar, nepheline, and aegirine. [*Tingua* Mountains in Brazil.]

tinhorn. See **tin.**

tinier, etc. See **tiny.**

tink tingk, *n.* a clear high-pitched short bell-like sound: a chime of rhyme: a tinker (coll. short form, *Scot.*). — *v.t.* and *v.i.* to sound in this way: to tinker. — *n.* **tink′er** a mender of kettles, pans, etc.: a botcher or bungler: a slight, temporary, or unskilful patching-up. — *v.t.* (*arch.*) to repair, esp. ineffectually. — *v.i.* to do tinker's work: (often with *with*) to botch, potter, patch up, adjust or deal with in trivial ways. — *n.* **tink′ering.** — *v.i.* **tink′le** to make small, sharp sounds: to jingle: to clink repeatedly or continuously: to go with tinkling sounds: to tingle. — *v.t.* to cause to tinkle: to ring: to make empty sounds or mere sound. — *n.* a sound of tinkling. — *n.* **tink′ler** a small bell: a tinker, gypsy, or vagrant (*Scot.*). — *n.* and *adj.* **tink′ling.** *adv.* **tink′-lingly.** — *adj.* **tink′ly.** — **give someone a tinkle** to call someone on the telephone; **not give a tinker's curse, damn** not to care. [M.E. *tinken*, to tink, *tinkere*, tinker (perh. unconnected).]

tinnie, tinny. See **tin.**

tinnitus ti-nī′təs, *n.* a ringing or other noise in the ears. [L. *tinnītus*, *-ūs*, a jingling — *tinnīre*, to ring.]

tinsel[1] tin′sl, *n.* thin glittering metallic sheets or spangles: anything showy, but of little value. — *adj.* of or like tinsel: gaudy. — *v.t.* to adorn with, or as with, tinsel:

to make glittering or gaudy: — *pr.p.* **tin′selling**; *pa.t.* and *pa.p.* **tin′selled.** — *adj.* **tin′selly** like tinsel, gaudy, showy. — *n.* **tin′selry** glittering and tawdry material. — *n.* and *adj.* **tin′sey** (*obs. dial.*) tinsel. — **tin′sel=slipp′er'd** (*Milt.*). [O.Fr. *estincelle* — L. *scintilla*, a spark.]

tinsel². See **tine²**.

tint¹ *tint*, *n.* a slight tinge distinct from the principal colour: a hue mixed with white: a series of parallel lines in engraving, producing a uniform shading. — *v.t.* to colour slightly: to tinge. — *v.i.* to take on a tint. — *ns.* **tint′er** one who, or that which, tints; **tint′iness**; **tint′ing.** — *adjs.* **tint′less**; **tin′ty** inharmoniously tinted. — *n.* **Tintom′eter®** a name for a colorimeter. — **tint′-block** a block for printing a background; **tint′-tool** an implement for producing a tint by parallel lines. [L. *tinctus*; cf. **tinct**, **tinge**.]

tint² *tint*. See **tine²**.

tintinnabulate *tin-tin-ab′ū-lāt*, *v.i.* to ring. — *adjs.* **tintinnab′ulant, tintinnab′ular, tintinnab′ulary.** — *n.* **tintinnabulā′tion** bell-ringing. — *adj.* **tintinnab′ulous.** — *n.* **tintinnab′ulum** a bell: a bell-rattle: — *pl.* **tintinnab′ula.** [L. *tintinnabulum*, a bell — *tintinnāre*, to jingle, reduplicated from *tinnīre*, to jingle.]

tiny *tī′ni*, *adj.* very small: — *compar.* **ti′nier**, *superl.* **ti′niest.** — *n.* **ti′niness.** [Cf. **tine⁵**.]

tip¹ *tip*, *n.* a slender extremity: the furthest part. — *v.t.* to put a tip to: to be the tip of: to remove the tip from: — *pr.p.* **tipp′ing**; *pa.t.* and *pa.p.* **tipped**, or **tipt.** — *adj.* **tipped (tipt).** — *n.* **tipp′ing.** — *adj.* (*slang*) topping, ripping, excellent. — *adj.* **tipp′y** (*slang*) in the height of fashion: smart. — *adj.* **tip′-tilt′ed** (*Tennyson*) turned up at the tip. — **on the tip of one's tongue** almost, but not yet quite, remembered: on the very point of being spoken; **tip of the iceberg** see **ice**. [Cf. O.N. *typpa*, to tip, Du., Norw., Dan. *tip*, Ger. (dim.) *Zipfel*.]

tip² *tip*, *v.t.* to strike lightly but definitely: to hit glancingly: — *pr.p.* **tipp′ing**; *pa.t.* and *pa.p.* **tipped.** — *n.* a tap. — *n.* **tipp′ing** a mode of articulating with the tongue to give staccato effects on the flute, trumpet, etc. — **tip′-and-run′** a kind of cricket in which the batsman must run if he hits at all. — *adj.* denoting a raid in which the raiders make off at once. [Cf. Du. and Ger. *tippen*, Sw. *tippa*, to tip.]

tip³ *tip*, *v.t.* to give, hand, pass, convey: to give a tip to: to indicate. — *v.i.* to give tips: — *pr.p.* **tipp′ing**; *pa.p.* and *pa.t.* **tipped.** — *n.* a gratuity: a hint or piece of special information supposed to be useful in betting, examinations, etc.: a trick or dodge. — *ns.* **tipp′er**; **tipp′ing**; **tip′ster** one whose business it is to furnish tips. — **tip′-off** a hint, warning, secret information (e.g. about a crime). — **tip off** to give a tip-off to; **tip someone the wink** to convey a secret hint. [Orig. rogues' cant.]

tip⁴ *tip*, *v.t.* to cast down: to upset: to tilt: to shoot, dump, empty out, by tilting: to toss off. — *v.i.* to topple over: to tilt: — *pr.p.* **tipp′ing**; *pa.p.* and *pa.t.* **tipped.** — *n.* a tilt: a place for tipping rubbish, coal, etc.: a dump: a staith or shoot: a tram for expeditiously transferring coal. — *ns.* **tipp′er** one who, or that which, tips: a lorry or truck, the main part of which can be tipped up for unloading (also *adj.*); **tipp′ing.** — **tip′-cart** a cart emptied by being canted up; **tip′-cat** a cat or pointed piece of wood: a game in which the cat is struck with a cat-stick and made to spring up; **tip′-cheese** (*Dickens*) app. tip-cat. — *adj.* **tip′-up** constructed so as to allow of being tilted. — **tip off liquor** to turn up the vessel till quite empty; **tip one's hat** to raise, tilt, or touch the brim of, one's hat as a polite greeting, esp. to a woman; **tip the balance** or **scale(s)** to make more, or less, favourable to someone: to be the deciding factor in a result; **tip the scale(s)** to depress one end of the scales: to weigh (with *at*). [M.E. *type*; origin obscure.]

tipi. Same as **tepee.**

tipper *tip′ər*, *n.* a kind of ale — from Thomas *Tipper*, who brewed it in Sussex.

tippet *tip′it*, *n.* a long band of cloth or fur e.g. on a hanging part of a garment (*hist.*): an ecclesiastical scarf: the hangman's rope (*obs.*, *facet.*): a shoulder cape, esp. of fur: an animal's ruff of hair or feathers: a moth's patagium. [Prob. **tip¹**.]

tipple *tip′l*, *v.t.* and *v.i.* to drink constantly in small quantities: to booze. — *n.* liquor tippled. — *n.* **tipp′ler.** — **tipp′ling-house.** [Cf. Norw. dial. *tipla*, to drip slowly.]

tipstaff *tip′stäf*, *n.* a staff tipped with metal: an officer who carries it, a sheriff's officer: — *pl.* **tip′staffs**, **tip′staves** (*-stāvz*). [**tip¹**, **staff.**]

tipster. See **tip³**.

tipsy *tip′si*, *adj.* partially intoxicated. — *v.t.* **tip′sify** to fuddle. — *adv.* **tip′sily.** — *n.* **tip′siness.** — **tip′sy-cake** a cake made of pastry and almonds, with wine; **tip′sy-key** a watch-key in which the head is released if an attempt is made to turn it backward. [Prob. **tip⁴**.]

tipt. See **tip¹**.

tiptoe *tip′tō*, *n.* the end of the toe or toes, more often merely the toes. — *adv.* on tiptoe, literally or figuratively, through excitement, expectation, etc. — *v.i.* to walk on tiptoe, to go lightly and stealthily: — *pr.p.* **tip′toeing**; *pa.t.* and *pa.p.* **tip′toed.** [**tip¹**, **toe.**]

tiptop *tip′top′*, *n.* the extreme top: the height of excellence. — *adj.* of the highest excellence. — Also *adv.* [**tip¹**, **top¹**.]

Tipula *tip′ū-lə*, *n.* the daddy-long-legs genus of flies, giving name to the family **Tipū′lidae:** (without *cap.*) a fly of this genus. [L. *tippula*, a water-spider.]

tirade *ti-rād′*, *tī-rād′*, *tē-rād′*, *n.* a long vehement harangue: a string of invective: a laisse (*pros.*): a run between two notes (*mus.*). [Fr., — It. *tirata* — *tirare*, to pull.]

tirage à part *tē-räzh a pär*, (Fr.) an offprint or article reprinted separately from a periodical — the German *Abdruck*.

tirailleur *tē-rä-yœr′*, *n.* a skirmisher, sharp-shooter. [Fr.]

tirasse *ti-ras′*, *n.* a pedal-coupler in an organ.

tire¹ *tīr*, (*arch.*) *n.* equipment, furniture (*Shak.*): attire, apparel: a head-dress: a pinafore (*U.S.*). — *v.t.* to attire: to dress, as the head. — *n.* **tir′ing.** — **tire′-val′iant** (*Shak.*) a kind of fanciful head-dress; **tire′-woman** a lady's-maid; **tir′ing-glass**; **tir′ing-house**, **-room** a theatre dressing-room; **tir′ing-woman.** [Aphetic for **attire.**]

tire² *tīr*, *n.* a metal hoop to bind a wheel: an *obs.* or *U.S.* spelling of **tyre.** — *v.t.* to put a tire on. — *adj.* **tired**; **tire′less.** — *n.* **tir′ing.** [Prob. same word as the foregoing.]

tire³ *tīr*, (*Spens.*) *n.* a train: a tier of guns. [Variant of **tier.**]

tire⁴ *tīr*, *n.* a volley: a broadside. [Fr. *tir.*]

tire⁵ *tīr*, (*Shak.*) *v.i.* to tear and tug or feed greedily as a bird of prey: to be intent, occupy oneself, feed one's thoughts or desires. — *n.* **tir′ing** in falconry, a bony or tough portion of meat given to a bird to pull at for exercise. [O.Fr. *tirer.*]

tire⁶ *tīr*, *v.i.* to weary: to become fatigued: to have interest or patience exhausted or worn down. — *v.t.* to weary: to fatigue: to bore: to wear out. — *adj.* **tired** fatigued: wearied, bored (with *of*): showing deterioration through time or usage — e.g. limp, grubby, played out. — *n.* **tired′ness.** — *adj.* **tire′less** untiring. — *adv.* **tire′lessly.** — *ns.* **tire′lessness**; **tire′ling** a tired animal. — Also *adj.* (*Spens.*, *tyreling jade*). — *adj.* **tire′some** fatiguing: wearisome: boring: tedious: loosely, irritating, troublesome, irksome. — *adv.* **tire′somely.** — *n.* **tire′someness.** — *adj.* **tir′ing.** — **tire down** to hunt to exhaustion. [App. O.E. *tēorian*, to be tired.]

tirl¹ *tirl*, (*Scot.*) *v.t.* and *v.i.* to turn: to whirl: to rattle. — *n.* a turnstile or the like. — **tirl′ie-wir′lie** a twirl. — *adj.* twirled: intricate. — **tirl′ing-pin** the pin of a door-latch, rattled to seek admission (*obs.*): now usu. taken to mean a risp. [**trill².**]

tirl² *tirl*, (*Scot.*) *v.t.* to strip. [Cf. **tirr.**]

Tir na n-Og *tēr-na-nōg′*, *n.* the Irish Elysium. [Ir., land of the young.]

tiro *tī′rō* (also **tyro**) *n.* a beginner: a novice: — *pl.* **ti′ros**, also **ty'roes, ti'roes, tyrones** (*tī-rō'nēz*). — *n.* **tirocinium** (*-sin'i-əm*) early training: first experience. [L. *tīrō* (L.L. *tȳrō*), *-ōnis*, a recruit, *tīrōcinium*, a first campaign.]

Tironensian *tī-rō-nen'si-ən, n.* a Benedictine of a congregation founded (1109) at *Tiron* (Thiron, near Nogent-le-Rotrou), absorbed in 1627 by that of St Maur. — Also *adj.* — Also **Tyronen'sian.**

Tironian *tī-rō'ni-ən, adj.* of *Tīrō* (*-ōnis*), Cicero's amanuensis, or of shorthand writing (*Tironian notes*) ascribed to him. — **Tironian sign** ampersand.

Tiros *tī'rōs, n.* the name given to one of a series of satellites giving meteorological information from observation of the clouds. [From *television infra-red observation satellite.*]

tirr *tir,* (*Scot.*) *v.t.* and *v.i.* to strip. [M.E. *tirve;* origin unknown.]

tirra-lirra, tirra-lyra *tir-ə-lir'ə, n.* and *interj.* an old refrain, ascribed by Shakespeare to the lark.

tirrit *tir'it,* (*Shak.*) *n.* Mrs Quickly's word for alarm, fright.

tirrivee, tirrivie *tir'i-vi,* or *-vē',* (*Scot.*) *n.* a tantrum or fit of passion: a commotion.

'tis *tiz,* a contraction of **it is.**

tisane *ti-zan', n.* a medicinal decoction. [See **ptisan.**]

Tisha(h) b(e)'Ab *tish'ə bə-ab, n.* in the Jewish calendar, the ninth day of Ab (q.v.), observed as a fast day to commemorate the destruction of the first and second temples in Jerusalem. — Also **Tisha(h) B(e)'Ab, Tisha(h) B(e)'Av, Tisha(h) b'Av.** [Heb., ninth in Ab.]

Tishri *tish'ri.* Same as **Tisri.**

tisick *tiz'ik,* (*Shak.*) *n.* a cough. [**phthisic.**]

Tisiphone *ti-sif'ə-nē, n.* one of the Furies. [Gr. *Tīsiphonē* — *tīsis,* retribution, *phonos,* murder.]

'tisn't *tiz'nt,* a contraction of **it is not.**

Tisri *tiz'ri, n.* the first month of the Jewish civil year, seventh of the ecclesiastical, usually part of September and October.

tissue *tish'ōō, -ū, tis'ū, n.* anything woven, esp. a rich or gauzy fabric: an aggregate of similar cells (*biol.*): a fabric, mass, or agglomeration, as of lies, nonsense: paper coated with gelatine and pigment (*phot.*): tissue-paper: soft, absorbent paper: a handkerchief made of soft, absorbent paper. — *v.t.* to weave or interweave, esp. with gold or silver thread: to clothe, cover, adorn, with tissue: to variegate. — **tissue culture** the growing of detached pieces of tissue, plant or animal, in nutritive fluids: a piece so grown; **tiss'ue-pa'per** a thin, soft, semitransparent paper (said to have been put between folds of tissue); **tiss'ue-typ'ing** the determination of body tissue types, e.g. to ensure compatibility between the donor and the recipient in transplant surgery. [Fr. *tissu,* woven, pa.p. of *tître* (O.Fr. *tistre*) — L. *texĕre,* to weave.]

tiswas, tizwas *tiz'woz,* (*slang*) *n.* a tizzy, flap, state of excitement, commotion. [Ety. unknown; conn. with **tizzy, tizz.**]

tit¹ *tit, n.* a variant of **teat:** (usu. in *pl.*) a female breast (*vulg.*): a contemptible person (*vulg.*).

tit² *tit, n.* (*dial.*) a tap. — **tit for tat** a tip for a tap, retaliation: a hat — usu. shortened to **tit'fer** (*cockney rhyming slang*).

tit³ *tit, n.* a titmouse (q.v.): a small or inferior horse: a nag: (in real or feigned depreciation) a girl, young woman. [Icel. *tittr,* titmouse.]

tit⁴ *tit,* (chiefly *Scot.*) *n.* a twitch: a tug. — *v.t.* and *v.i.* to tug.

tit⁵. See **tite.**

Titan *tī'tən, n.* a son or daughter (**Tī'taness**) or other descendant of Uranus and Gaea: one of the elder gods and goddesses overthrown by Zeus: the name of one of them, Hyperion: Helios, the sun-god: the sun personified: Prometheus: Saturn's greatest satellite (*astron.*): (without *cap.*) anything gigantic: (without *cap.*) a man of great intellect but not the highest inspiration. — Also *adj.* — *n.* **Titania** (*tī-tā'ni-ə, ti-tä'-ni-ə*) the queen of fairyland, wife of Oberon: a satellite

of Uranus. — *adjs.* **Titanesque** (*-esk'*); **Titā'nian; Titanic, titanic** (*tī-* or *ti-tan'ik*). — *ns.* **Ti'tanism** the spirit of revolt against the universe, the established order, authority, convention; **Titanomachy** (*-om'ə-ki;* Gr. *machē,* fight) the war of the Titans against the Olympian gods; **Titanosau'rus** a gigantic Cretaceous dinosaur; **Titanothē'rium** a huge rhinoceros-like American Oligocene fossil ungulate. [Gr. *Tītān.*]

titanium *tī-tā'ni-əm, n.* a metallic element (Ti; at. numb. 22) found in ilmenite, sphene, rutile, etc. — strong, light and corrosion-resistant. — *n.* **titanate** (*tī'tən-āt*) a salt of titanic acid. — *adjs.* **titanic** (*-tan'ik*) of quadrivalent titanium (**titanic acid** H_2TiO_3; **titanic iron** ilmenite); **titanif'erous** containing titanium. — *n.* **ti'tanite** sphene, a brown, green, or yellow monoclinic mineral, calcium silicate and titanate. — *adj.* **ti'tanous** of trivalent titanium. — **titanium dioxide** a pure white powder (TiO₂) of high opacity used esp. as a pigment; **titanium white** titanium dioxide used as pigment. [Gr. *Tītān,* Titan, on the analogy of **uranium.**]

titbit *tit'bit, n.* a choice delicacy or item. — Also, esp. *U.S.,* **tid'bit.**

titch. Another spelling of **tich.**

tite, tyte, tight *tīt,* **tit** *tit,* **titely,** etc., *-li,* (*obs.*) *advs.* promptly: at once. [Cf. O.N. *tītt,* often.]

titer. See under **titrate.**

titfer *tit'fər.* See **tit².**

tithe, tythe *tīdh, adj.* tenth. — *n.* a tenth part, an indefinitely small part: the tenth of the produce of land and stock allotted originally for church purposes: a rent-charge in commutation of this: any levy of one-tenth. — *v.t.* to take a tithe of or from: to pay a tithe on: to decimate (*obs.*). — *adj.* **tith'able** subject to the payment of tithes. — *adj.* **tithed.** — *ns.* **tith'er** one who collects tithes; **tith'ing** a tithe: exaction or payment of tithes: a district containing ten householders, each responsible for the behaviour of the rest (*hist.*). — **tithe'-barn** a barn for storing the parson's tithe in corn. — *adj.* **tithe'-free** exempt from paying tithes. — **tithe'-gatherer.** — *adj.* **tithe'-paying.** — **tithe'-pig** one pig out of ten paid as a tithe; **tithe'-proctor** a collector of tithes; **tith'ing-man** the chief man of a tithing. [O.E. *tēotha,* tenth; cf. **tenth, teind.**]

titi, tee-tee *tē'tē, n.* a small South American monkey (*Callicebus*).

Titian, titian *tish'ən, -yən, n.* a red-yellow colour used by the Venetian painter *Titian* (Tiziano Vecellio, *c.* 1490–1576). — *adj.* (chiefly of hair) of this colour, or (loosely) of other shade of red or reddish-brown. — *adj.* **Titianesque** (*-esk'*) in the manner of Titian, a combination of the richest surface and colour.

titillate *tit'il-lāt, v.t.* to tickle: to stimulate gently. — *ns.* **titillā'tion; tit'illātor.** [L. *titillāre, -ātum.*]

titivate, tittivate *tit'i-vāt, tidivate *tid',* (*slang*) *vs.i.* and *vs.t.* to smarten up, by dress or otherwise. — *ns.* **tit(t)ivā'-tion, tidivā'tion.** [Poss. coined from **tidy.**]

titlark *tit'lärk, n.* a pipit, esp. the meadow-pipit. [**tit³** and **lark¹.**]

title *tī'tl, n.* an inscription or descriptive placard: a chapter-heading: a section of a law-book: the name of a book, poem, tale, picture, etc.: a title-page: a book or publication, as an item in a catalogue (*publishers' jargon*): a credit title (*cinema*): a subtitle (*cinema*): an appellation of rank or distinction: a right to possession: a ground of claim: evidence of right: a title-deed: a fixed sphere of work, source of maintenance, or a certificate thereof, required as a condition for ordination: a cardinal-priest's parish in Rome: a championship (*sport*). — *v.t.* to designate: to give or attach a title to. — *adjs.* **ti'tled** having a title; **ti'tleless** nameless (*Shak.*): untitled. — *ns.* **ti'tler** a writer of titles: a claimant (*obs.*); **ti'tling** the giving or attaching of a title. — **ti'tle-deed** a document that proves right to possession; **ti'tle-holder** a person holding a title, esp. a championship in some sport; **ti'tle-leaf** the leaf on which is the title of a book; **ti'tle-page** the page of a book containing its title; **ti'tle-poem** that which gives its title to a book; **ti'tle-role** the part in a play which gives its name to it; **ti'tle-sheet** the first sheet of a book as printed, containing title, bastard-title, etc. [O.E. *tītul* or *titul* and O.Fr. *title* (Fr. *titre*) — L. *titulus*.]

titling *tit'ling, n.* a small stockfish: the meadow-pipit (esp. *Scot.*): also the hedge-sparrow. [Norw. dial. *titling*, small stockfish; O.N. *titlingr*, sparrow; cf. **tit³**.]

titmouse *tit'mows* (*Spens.* **titmose** -*mōs*), *n.* a tit, any of various kinds of little active acrobatic bird of *Parus* or kindred genus: — *pl.* **titmice** (*tit'mīs*). [**tit³**, and M.E. *mose*, titmouse — O.E. *māse*; Ger. *Meise*; confused with **mouse**.]

Titoism *tē'tō-izm, n.* the communism of Marshal *Tito* (1892–1980) of Yugoslavia, adhering to international communism but not at the sacrifice of national independence. — *n.* and *adj.* **Ti'toist.**

titoki *ti-tok'i, tē', n.* a New Zealand tree with reddish paniculate flowers. [Maori.]

titrate *tī'trāt, tī-trāt', v.t.* to subject to titration. — *ns.* **titrā'tion** measurement of the strength of a solution by finding how much of another solution of known strength is required to complete a chemical reaction; **titre** (*U.S.* **titer;** *tī'tər, tē'*) the concentration of a substance in a solution as determined by titration. [Fr. *titre*, standard.]

ti-tree. Same as **ti².**

titter¹ *tit'ər, v.i.* to giggle, snicker, or laugh restrainedly. — *n.* a stifled laugh. — *n.* **titt'erer.** — *n.* and *adj.* **titt'ering.** [Cf. Sw. dial. *tittra*.]

titter² *tit'ər, v.i.* to totter, sway. [O.N. *titra*, to shake.]

tittivate. See **titivate.**

tittle¹ *tit'l, n.* a dot, stroke, accent, vowel-point, contraction or punctuation mark: the smallest part. [O.Fr. *title* — L. *titulus*, a title.]

tittle² *tit'l,* (*dial.*) *v.t.* and *v.i.* to whisper: to tattle. — **titt'le-tatt'le** idle, empty talk. — *v.i.* to prate idly. — **titt'le-tatt'ler; titt'le-tatt'ling.**

tittlebat *tit'l-bat, n.* a childish form of **stickleback.**

tittup, titup *tit'əp, v.i.* to prance, skip about gaily. — *n.* a light springy step, a canter. — *adj.* **titt'upy, tit'upy** gay, lively: unsteady. [Imit.]

titty¹ *tit'i, n.* a teat: the breast. [Dim. of **tit¹,** teat.]

titty² *tit'i,* (*Scot.*) *n.* sister.

titubate *tit'ū-bāt, v.i.* to stagger, stumble. — *n.* **tit'ūbancy** staggering. — *adj.* **tit'ūbant.** — *n.* **titūbā'tion** staggering: unsteadiness: a tremor (esp. of the head), often a symptom of a cerebral or spinal disease. [L. *titubāre*, -*ātum*, to stagger.]

titule *tit'ūl, n.* and *v.t.* Same as **title.** — *adj.* **tit'ūlar** pertaining to title: in name or title only: nominal: having the title without the duties of an office: supplying a title to a cardinal-priest (as a titular church). — *n.* a titled person: one who enjoys the bare title of an office, without actual possession: a person invested with a title in virtue of which he holds a benefice, whether he performs its duties or not: that from which a church takes its name (*patron* if a saint or angel; *R.C.*). — *n.* **titularity** (-*ar'i-ti*). — *adv.* **tit'ularly.** — *adj.* **tit'ulary** titular. — *n.* one holding a title. — **titular bishop** (*R.C.*) a bishop without a diocese, taking his title from a place where there is no longer a bishop's see — before 1882 bishop in partibus infidelium. — **titular of the teinds** or **tithes** a layman invested with church lands after the Reformation in Scotland. [L. *titulus*.]

titup. See **tittup.**

tityre-tu *tit-, tīt-i-ri-tōō', -tū', n.* a member of a 17th-century fraternity of aristocratic hooligans. [Opening words of Virgil's first eclogue, *Tītyre tū*, Tityrus, thou (lying under the spreading beech), conjectured to indicate the class that had beech trees and leisure to lie under them.]

Tiw *tē'w,* **Tiu,** *tē'ōō, ns.* the old English war-god. [O.E. *Tīw*; cf. **Tuesday, Tyr.**]

tizwas. See **tiswas.**

tizzy *tiz'i, n.* a sixpence (*old slang*): a state of agitation, nervousness, confusion, or dither over little (*slang*; also **tizz**).

tmesis *tmē'sis,* (*gram.*) *n.* the separation or splitting up of a word into parts by one or more other words: — *pl.* **tmē'sēs.** [Gr. *tmēsis* — *temnein,* to cut.]

T N T Abbrev. for **trinitrotoluene,** see **trinitro-.**

to *tōō, tŏŏ, tə, prep.* serving as sign of the infinitive (which is sometimes understood) and forming a substitute for the dative case: in the direction of: as far as: all the way in the direction of: until: into the condition of: towards: beside: near: at: in contact with, close against: before: for: of: with the object or result of: against: in accordance, comparison, or relation with: in honour of, or expressing good wishes for: along with in addition. — *adv.* in one direction, forward: in or into position, contact, closed or harnessed condition. — **to and fro** alternately this way and that; **toing and froing** going backwards and forwards in an agitated way, or without achieving anything: also *fig.* [O.E. *tō*; Ger. *zu*, Goth. *du*; Gr. suffix -*de*.]

toad *tōd, n.* a toothless tailless amphibian that walks or crawls instead of jumping like the frog, esp. one of *Bufo* or kindred genus: a hateful or contemptible person or animal: bufo (*alchemy*). — *n.* **toad'y** a toad-eater, sycophant. — *v.t.* to fawn as a sycophant: — *pr.p.* **toad'ying;** *pa.t.* and *pa.p.* **toad'ied.** — *adj.* **toad'yish.** — *n.* **toad'yism.** — **toad'-eater** a fawning sycophant — originally a mountebank's assistant, whose duty was to swallow, or pretend to swallow, toads; **toad'-eating** sycophancy. — *adj.* sycophantic. — **toad'fish** a toadlike fish of many kinds; **toad'flax** any species of Linaria, a genus closely allied to snapdragon with flax-like leaves; **toad'-in-the-hole** a dish originally of beef, now usu. sausage-meat, cooked in batter; **toad'rush, -grass** a low rush (*Juncus bufonius*) with mostly solitary flowers; **toad'-spit** cuckoo-spit. — *adj.* **toad'-spott'ed** thickly stained or spotted like a toad. — **toad'-stone** a stone or concretion formerly believed to be found in a toad's head, and valued as an amulet: a basalt lava or tuff (Derbyshire; supposed to be from its markings; but poss. — Ger. *totes Gestein,* dead stone, from the lead- miner's point of view); **toad'stool** any mushroom-like fungus, often excluding the edible mushroom. [O.E. *tāde, tādige, tādie*.]

toast *tōst, v.t.* to dry and parch: to brown (as bread): to half-melt (as cheese): to warm or heat by rays: to drink to. — *v.i.* to drink toasts: to undergo, or be suitable for, toasting. — *n.* bread toasted: a piece of toasted bread, usu. one put in liquor: the person or thing drunk to, esp. the lady most admired for the moment: a proposal of health. — *adj.* **toast'ed.** — *ns.* **toast'er** one who toasts: a toasting-fork: an electric apparatus for making toast: that which can be toasted; **toast'ie** (*coll.*) a toasted sandwich (also **toast'y**); **toast'ing.** — *adj.* (*coll.*) hot. — **toast'ing-fork, -iron** a long-handled fork for toasting bread: a sword (*facet.*); **toast'master** the announcer of toasts, introducer of speakers, at a dinner; **toast'mistress; toast'-rack** a stand with partitions for slices of toast. — **on toast** served on a slice of toast: swindled: at one's mercy. [O.Fr. *toster* — L. *tostus,* roasted, pa.p. of *torrēre*.]

toaze *tōz* (*Shak.*). See **toze.**

tobacco *tə-bak'ō, n.* an American solanaceous plant, *Nicotiana tabacum,* or other species of the genus: its prepared leaves used for smoking, chewing, or snuffing: — *pl.* **tobacc'o(e)s.** — *ns.* **tobaccanā'lian** a smoker (*facet.*; after **bacchanalian**); **tobacc'onist** a smoker (*obs.*): a seller or manufacturer of tobacco. — **tobacc'o-heart** a functional disorder of the heart due to excessive use of tobacco; **tobacc'o-pipe** a pipe for smoking tobacco; **tobacc'o-plant; tobacc'o-pouch** a pouch for holding tobacco; **tobacc'o-stopper** an instrument for pressing down the tobacco in a pipe. [Sp. *tabaco,* from Haitian.]

Tobagonian *tə-bā-gō'ni-ən, adj.* of or pertaining to the island of *Tobago* in the South West Indies. — *n.* a native of Tobago.

to-be *tŏŏ-, tə-bē', n.* the future. — *adj.* (now usu. following and attached to the word it modifies) future.

Tobit *tō'bit, n.* an apocryphal Old Testament book, containing the story of *Tobit.*

toboggan *tə-bog'ən, n.* a flat sledge turned up in front. — *v.i.* to slide, coast, travel, on, or as if on, a toboggan. — Earlier also **tobogg'in, tobogg'an, tarbogg'in.** — *ns.* **tobogg'aner; tobogg'aning; tobogg'anist.** [Micmac *tobākun.*]

to-break *tŏŏ-, tə-brāk', (obs.) v.t.* to break in pieces: — *pa.t.* (B., Bunyan) **to'-brake'** (usu. printed *to brake*); *pa.p.* **to-bro'ken.** [O.E. *tōbrecan* — *pfx. tō-,* asunder, and *brecan,* to break.]

to-bruise *tə-brŏŏz', (obs.) v.t.* to bruise severely: to break up: — *pa.p.* (*Spens.*) **to-brusd'.** [O.E. *tō-brȳsan.*]

Toby *tō'bi, n.* a beer-mug or similar object shaped like a man with a three-cornered hat (also **To'by-jug;** also without *cap.*): Punch's dog.

toby *tō'bi, n.* the road (*thieves' slang*): robbery on the road: a stop-cock in a gas- or water-main under the road (*Scot.*): the cover protecting it (*Scot.*): — **high toby** highway robbery on horseback; **low toby** footpad robbery. [Shelta *tōbar.*]

toccata *to-kä'tə, (mus.) n.* primarily a work intended to display the performer's touch, or in which he seems to try the touch of an instrument in a series of runs and chords before breaking into a fugue: loosely, a sort of fantasia or overture. — *ns.* **toccatel'la, toccatina** (*-tē'nə*) a short toccata. [It., — *toccare,* to touch.]

toc emma *tok em'ə, (mil. slang)* a trench mortar. — **Toc H** (*äch*) a society for handing on the spirit of comradeship of the 1st World War, from its first meetings at Talbot House, at Poperinghe in Belgium. [Formerly signallers' names of the initial letters **T, M** and **T, H.**]

Tocharian, Tokharian *to-kä'ri-ən,* or *-kā',* **Tocha'rish, Tokha'rish** *-rish, ns.* an extinct Indo-European language, akin to Latin and Celtic, preserved in MSS discovered in the 20th century in Chinese Turkestan. [Gr. *Tocharoi,* a people guessed to be its speakers on the strength of the Uigur (language of Chinese Turkestan) name *Tochri.*]

tocher *tohh'ər, (Scot.) n.* a dowry. — *v.t.* to dower. — *adj.* **toch'erless.** — **toch'er-good** property given as tocher. [Ir. *tochar,* Gael. *tochradh.*]

toco *tō'kō, (slang) n.* punishment: — *pl.* **to'cos.** — Also **tō'kō:** — *pl.* **tō'kos.** [Origin uncertain; Gr. *tokos,* interest, and Hindi *thōkō — thoknā,* to thrash, have been suggested.]

tocology, tokology *tok-ol'ə-ji, n.* obstetrics. — *n.* **tocoph'-erol** vitamin E, whose deficiency causes sterility in some species. [Gr. *tokos,* birth, offspring, *logos,* discourse, *pherein,* to bring.]

tocsin *tok'sin, n.* an alarm-bell, or the ringing of it. [Fr. *tocsin* — Prov. *tocasenh — tocar,* to touch, strike, *senh* — L. *signum,* sign (L.L. bell).]

tod[1] *tod, (Scot.) n.* a fox: a sly person. — **Tod-low'rie** (i.e. Laurence) Reynard. [Origin unknown.]

tod[2] (*Spens.* **todde**) *tod, n.* a bush, esp. of ivy: an old wool weight, about 28 lb.: a load. — *v.i.* to yield a tod. — *v.t.* to yield a tod for.

tod[3] *tod,* in phrase **on one's tod,** alone. [Rhyming slang *on one's Tod Sloan.*]

today, to-day *tŏŏ-, tə-dā', n.* this or the present day. — *adv.* on the present day: nowadays. [O.E. *tōdæg(e).*]

todde. See **tod[2].**

toddle *tod'l, v.i.* to walk with short feeble steps, as a child: to saunter: to go, depart (*facet.*). — *n.* a toddling gait: an aimless stroll: a toddling child. — *n.* **todd'ler** one who toddles, esp. a child. — *adj.* **todd'ling.** [Orig. Northern dial.]

toddy *tod'i, n.* fermented palm juice: a mixture of spirits, sugar, and hot water. — **todd'y-cat** the palm-civet; **todd'y-ladle** a small ladle for mixing or serving toddy; **todd'y-palm** coconut, palmyra or other palm yielding toddy; **todd'y-stick** a stick used in mixing toddy. [Hindi *tāṛī — tāṛ,* a palm-tree, prob. of Dravidian origin.]

to-do *tə-, tŏŏ-dŏŏ', n.* a bustle: a stir: a commotion: — *pl.* **to-dos'.**

tody *tō'di, n.* a small West Indian insectivorous bird — the *green sparrow, green humming-bird,* etc., akin to the kingfishers. [L. *todus,* a small bird of some kind.]

toe *tō, n.* one of the five small members at the point of the foot: the front of a hoof: the corresponding part of a shoe, sock, golf-club head, etc.: the lowest part of the front of anything, esp. if it projects. — *v.t.* stand with the toes against: to kick: to strike with the toe of a club: to nail obliquely through the foot: to perform with the toe: to furnish with a toe, as a stocking. — *v.i.* to place the toes: — *pr.p.* **toe'ing;** *pa.t.* and *pa.p.* **toed.** — *adj.* **toed** (*tōd*) having toes: nailed obliquely. — **toe'cap** a cap covering the toe of a shoe; **toe'clip** an attachment to a bicycle pedal that receives the toe; **toe'-dance** one performed on tiptoes. — Also *v.i.* — **toe'-hold** a place to fix the toes in: a small established position: a hold in which the toes are held and the foot is bent back or twisted (*wrestling*); **toe'-jump** (*ice-skating*) a jump executed by pushing off with the toe of one's free foot; **toe'-loop** (*ice-skating*) a toe-jump and a loop in combination; **toe'nail** a nail on a human or animal toe: an obliquely driven nail; **toe'-piece.** — **big** or **great toe** largest of the toes; **little toe** smallest of the toes; **on one's toes** poised for a quick start, alert, eager; **take to one's toes** to run away; **toe the line** to stand with toes against a marked line, as in starting a race: to conform; **toe to toe** (*fig.*) in close, direct confrontation (*adj.* **toe'-to-toe'**); **tread on the toes of (someone)** to offend (someone). [O.E. *tā* (*pl. tān*); O.N. *tā,* Ger. *Zehe.*]

toe-rag *tō'rag, (slang) n.* a beggar, tramp: generally, a ruffian or rascal: a despicable person. — Also **toe= ragg'er.** [Prob. from the strips of rag used by tramps to wrap around their toes in place of socks.]

to-fall *tŏŏ'föl, (arch.) n.* a beginning, incidence. [**to, fall.**]

toff *tof, (slang) n.* a person of the upper classes: a swell: a good sort. — *adj.* **toff'ish.** — *n.* **toff'ishness.** — *adj.* **toff'y.** [Perh. **tuft.**]

toffee, toffy *tof'i, n.* a hard-baked sweetmeat, made of sugar and butter. — Earlier and *U.S.* **taff'y.** — **toff'ee= app'le** a toffee-coated apple on a stick. — *adj.* **toff'ee= nose(d)** (*slang*) supercilious, conceited. — **for toffee** (*coll.*) at all, as in *he can't dance for toffee,* etc. [Ety. unknown.]

tofore *tŏŏ-, tə-fōr', -för', adv.* (*Shak.*), *prep., conj.* (*obs.*) before. [O.E. *tōforan* (prep.).]

toft *toft, n.* a homestead (*hist.*): a hillock (*dial.*). [Late O.E. *toft* — O.N. *topt, tupt, toft.*]

tofu *tō'fŏŏ, n.* unfermented soy bean curd, having a pale, creamy colour and a bland flavour. [Jap. — Chin. *toufu — tou,* beans, *fu,* rotten.]

tog[1] *tog, (slang) n.* a garment — generally in *pl.* — *v.t.* to dress: — *pr.p.* **togg'ing;** *pa.t.* and *pa.p.* **togged.** — *n.* **togg'ery** clothes. — **long'-togs** (*naut.*) shore clothes; **tog up** to dress esp. in one's best clothes. [Prob. ultimately L. *tŏga,* a robe.]

tog[2] *tog, n.* a unit of measurement of thermal insulation as a property of textile fabrics. — **tog rating, value** the amount of thermal insulation provided by a fabric, measured in togs. [App. an invention — perh. conn. with **tog[1].**]

toga *tō'gə, n.* the mantle or outer garment of a Roman citizen, a long piece of cloth wound round and draped over the body. — Also **toge** (*tōg; Shak.* conjectured). — *adjs.* **tō'ga'd, tō'gaed, tō'gate, -d, toged** (*tōgd; Shak.*). — **toga praetexta** (*prē-, prī-teks'tə, -ta*) a toga with a deep border of purple, worn by children, magistrates, etc.; **toga virilis** (*vir-ī'lis, wir-ē'lis*) the garb of manhood. [L. *tŏga;* cf. *tegĕre,* to cover; **thatch.**]

together *tə-, tŏŏ-gedh'ər, adv.* in or to the same place: at the same time: in or into connection, company, or concert. — *adj.* (*slang,* chiefly *U.S.*) well-organised, mentally composed, emotionally stable, etc. — *n.* **togeth'erness** unity: closeness: a sense of unity or community with other people. — **get, put it (all) together** (*slang*, chiefly *U.S.*) to perform something successfully, get something right: to become well-organised, stable, etc.: to establish a good relationship (with). [O.E. *tōgædere* — *tō*, to, *geador*, together.]

toggle *tog'l*, *n.* a cross-piece on a rope, chain, rod, etc., to prevent slipping through a hole, or to allow twisting: a short bar acting as a button, passed through a loop for fastening: an appliance for transmitting force at right angles to its direction. — *v.t.* to hold or furnish with a toggle: to fix fast. — **togg'le-iron** a harpoon with a toggle instead of barbs; **togg'le-joint** an elbow or knee joint: a mechanism consisting of two levers hinged together, force applied to straighten the hinge producing a considerable force along the levers; **togg'le-switch** in telecommunications and electronics, a switch which, in a circuit having two stable or quasi-stable states, produces a transition from one to the other. [App. conn. with **tug** and **tow**[1].]

togue *tōg*, *n.* the Great Lake char (or trout), a gigantic salmonid of North America. [From Indian name.]

toheroa *tō-ə-rō'ə*, *n.* an edible shellfish found at low tide buried in sandy beaches. [Maori.]

toho *tō-hō'*, *interj.* a call to pointers to stop: — *pl.* **tohos'**.

tohu bohu *tō'hōō bō'hōō*, chaos. [Heb. *thōhū wa-bhōhū*, emptiness and desolation (Gen. i. 2).]

toil[1] *toil*, *v.i.* to struggle hard: to labour hard: to make one's way by strong effort. — *v.t.* to effect or work out with toil: to subject to toil (*arch.* or *dial.*). — *n.* contention (*obs.*): a struggle: hard labour. — *adj.* **toiled.** — *n.* **toil'er.** — *adj.* **toil'ful.** — *n.* and *adj.* **toil'ing.** — *adjs.* **toil'less; toil'some** involving toil: toiling: owing to toil (*Spens.* **toyl'som, toyle'some**). — *adv.* **toil'somely.** — *n.* **toil'someness.** — *adj.* **toil'-worn** worn with toil. [A.Fr. *toiler* (Fr. *touillier*) said to be — L. *tudiculāre*, to stir.]

toil[2] *toil*, (usu. in *pl.*, often *fig.*) *n.* a net: a snare. — *ns.* **toile** (*twäl*) a thin dress material; **toilet** (*toil'it*) a cloth for the shoulder during hair-dressing (*arch.*): a toilet-cover: a toilet-table: a dressing-table with a mirror: the articles used in dressing: the mode or process of dressing: a reception of visitors during dressing (*arch.*): the whole dress and appearance of a person, any particular costume: a dressing-room, bathroom, or lavatory: the cleansing and dressing of a wound. — *v.t.* to take to the toilet or otherwise assist with toilet procedures. — *adj.* **toil'eted** dressed. — *ns.* **toil'etry** any article or preparation used in washing and dressing oneself: — *pl.* **toil'etries; toilette** (*twä-let'*) a toilet; **toilinet'** (*toi-*), **toilinette** (*twäl-i-net'*) a kind of woollen cloth used for waistcoats, silk and cotton warp with woollen weft. — **toil'et-cloth, -cover** a dressing-table cover; **toil'et-glass** a mirror set on the dressing-table; **toil'et-paper** paper for the lavatory; **toil'et-roll** a roll of toilet-paper; **toil'et-service, -set** the utensils collectively used in dressing; **toil'et-soap** soap for personal use; **toil'et-table** a dressing-table; **toilet tissue** soft, absorbent toilet-paper; **toilet training** the training of children to control bladder and bowels and to use the lavatory; **toilet water** a lightly perfumed liquid similar to Cologne. [Fr. *toile*, dim. *toilette* — L. *tēla*, web.]

toing and froing. See to.

toise *toiz*, *n.* an old French lineal measure = 6·395 feet (very nearly 2 metres). [Fr., — L. *tendĕre*, *tēnsum*, to stretch.]

toiseach, toisech *tō'shəhh* (*hist.*) *n.* an ancient Celtic noble below a mormaor. [Gael.]

toison *twa-zɔ̃*, (Fr.) *n.* a fleece. — **toison d'or** (*dor*) the golden fleece.

to kalon *to ka'lon*, (Gr.) the beautiful.

tokamak *tō'kə-mak*, *n.* a tyre-shaped device for producing thermonuclear power in which plasma is held in place by a complex magnetic field generated by internal electric currents. — Also *adj.* [Russ., acronym from *toroidalnaya kamera s magnitnym polem*, toroidal chamber with a magnetic field.]

Tokay *tō-kā'*, *n.* a sweetish and heavy wine with an aromatic flavour, produced at *Tokay* (*Hung.* Tokaj, *tō'koi*) in Hungary: the grape that yields it.

toke *tōk*, (*U.S. slang*) *n.* a puff on a cigarette (esp. one containing marijuana). — Also *v.i.* [Poss. short for **token.**]

token *tō'kn*, *n.* a sign: a symbol: a portent: an indication: an evidence: a plague-spot (*obs.*): an authenticating sign, word, or object: a keepsake: a coin or voucher, issued privately, redeemable in current money or goods (as *gift, record, token*): in Presbyterian churches a metal voucher admitting to communion (superseded by the communion card): a measure of hand-press work, usu. 250 pulls: a unit of computer code representing a word or character used in a program. — *adj.* serving as a symbol: hence, being a mere show or semblance, as *token force, token resistance*. — *v.t.* to betoken. — *adj.* **tō'ken'd** (*Shak.*) indicated by plague-spots. — *n.* **tō'kenism** the practice of doing something once to give an impression of doing it regularly, e.g. employing one coloured person to avoid a charge of racialism. — **to'ken-money** money current for more than its intrinsic value as metal: private tokens. — **by the same token** further in corroboration, or merely by the way; **more by token** see **more**[1]; **the Lord's tokens** (*Shak.*) plague-spots. [O.E. *tācen*; Ger. *Zeichen*, a mark.]

Tokharian, Tokharish. See **Tocharian.**

toko; tokology. See **toco; tocology.**

tokoloshe *tok-o-losh'i*, *n.* in Bantu folklore, a hairy malevolent dwarf-like creature with supernatural powers. [Zulu *tikoloshe*.]

Tok Pisin *tok piz'in*, *n.* Melanesian pidgin, as spoken in Papua New Guinea. [**talk pidgin.**]

tola *tō'lə*, *n.* an Indian unit of weight = 180 grains troy (11·66 grammes). [Hind., — Sans. *tulā*, weight.]

tolbooth. See **toll**[1].

tolbutamide *tol-būt'əm-īd*, *n.* a drug taken by mouth in the treatment of diabetes.

told *tōld*, *pa.t.* and *pa.p.* of **tell.**

tole[1], **toll** *tōl*, *v.t.* (now *U.S.* and *dial.*) to lure, decoy. — *ns.* **tol'ing, toll'ing** (*U.S.*) the use of toll-bait: a method of decoying ducks, etc., by exciting curiosity. — **toll'-bait** (*U.S.*) chopped bait thrown to attract fish. [M.E. *tollen* — root of O.E. (*for*)*tyllan*; see **till**[1].]

tole[2] *tōl*, *n.* painted or japanned tinware, popular in the 18th and 19th cents. [Fr. *tôle*, sheet metal, from a dial. word for table.]

Toledo *tō-lē'dō*, *n.* a sword-blade made at *Toledo* (*-lā'*) in Spain: — *pl.* **Tolē'dos.**

tolerate *tol'ə-rāt*, *v.t.* to endure: to endure with patience or impunity: to allow, allow to exist. — *n.* **tolerabil'ity.** — *adj.* **tol'erable** endurable: passable: fair. — *adv.* **tol'erably.** — *n.* **tol'erance** the ability to endure: the disposition or willingness to tolerate or allow: the permissible range of variation. — *adj.* **tol'erant** tolerating: enduring: capable of enduring (e.g. unfavourable conditions, a parasite, a drug) without showing serious effects (*biol.* and *med.*): indulgent: favouring toleration. — *adv.* **tol'erantly.** — *ns.* **tolerā'tion** the act of tolerating: the allowance of what is not approved: the liberty given to a minority to hold and express their own political or religious opinions; **tolerā'tionist; tol'erātor.** — **tolerance dose** the maximum dose which can be permitted to a specific tissue during radiotherapy involving irradiation of any other adjacent tissue. [L. *tolerāre*, *-ātum* — *tollĕre*, to lift up.]

toll[1] *tōl*, *n.* a tax for the liberty of using a bridge or road, selling goods in a market, etc.: a portion of grain kept by a miller in payment for grinding: a place where there is or was or might have been a toll-bar, a road junction (*Scot.*): the cost in damage, injury, or lives (as *toll of the road*): a toll-call. — *v.i.* to take or pay toll. — *v.t.* to take toll of: to take as toll. — *adj.* **toll'able** subject to toll. — *ns.* **toll'age** payment of toll: the amount paid as toll; **toll'er** a toll-gatherer. — **tolbooth, tollbooth** (*tōl'* or *tol'bōōth, -bōōdh*; *Scot.* *-bəth*) an office where tolls are collected: a town-hall: a prison: often a combination of these; **toll'-bar** a movable bar across a road, etc., to stop passengers liable to toll; **toll'bridge, -gate** a bridge, gate, where toll is taken; **toll'-call** a short-distance telephone trunk-call: a trunk call (*U.S.*, etc.); **toll'dish** a dish for measuring the toll in mills; **toll'-gath'erer**. — *adj.* and *adv.* **toll'-free'**. — **toll'-house; toll'man** the man who collects toll: a toll-gatherer; **tolsel** (*tōl'sel*), **tolzey** (-*zi*), **tolsey** (*tol'si*) local names (app. — O.E. *seld*, seat, or *sæl*, hall) for a tolbooth or exchange. — **take toll of** to inflict loss, hardship, pain, etc., on. [O.E. *toll*; cf. Du. *tol*, Ger. *Zoll*; supposed to be from L.L. *tolōneum* — Gr. *telōnion*, customs — *telos*, fulfilment, tax, etc.; by some connected with **tell, tale**.]

toll² *tōl*, *v.i.* to sound, as a large bell, esp. with a measured sound. — *v.t.* to cause to sound, as a bell: to sound, strike, signal, announce, summon, send, by tolling: to toll for the death of. — *n.* the sound of a bell tolling. — *n.* **toll'er**. [Prob. **tole¹**.]

toll³ *tōl*, (*law*) *v.t.* to bar: to take away the right of. [A.Fr. *toller* — L. *tollĕre*, to take away.]

toll⁴. Same as **tole¹**.

tol-lol *tol-lol'*, (*old slang*) *adj.* pretty good. — *adj.* **tol= lol'ish** tolerable.   [tolerable.]

tolsel, tolsey. See **toll¹**.

tolt *tōlt*, *n.* an old English writ removing a court-baron cause to a county court.   [A.Fr. *tolte* — L.L. *tolta* — L. *tollĕre*, to take away.]

tolter *tol'tər*, (*dial.*) *v.i.* to flounder about.

Tolu *tō-lōō'*, *n.* (in full **balsam of Tolu** a balsam yielded by the South American papilionaceous tree *Myroxylon toluifera* (also without *cap.*). — *ns.* **tol'uate** any salt or ester of toluic acid; **toluene** (*tol'ū-ēn*), **tol'uol** methyl benzene, a colourless flammable liquid ($C_6H_5 \cdot CH_3$) used as a solvent and in the manufacture of other organic chemicals. — *adj.* **tolū'ic**. — *n.* **tolū'idine** (-*i-dēn*) an amine ($C_6H_4 \cdot CH_3NH_2$) derived from toluene, used in making dyes. [From Santiago de *Tolú* in Colombia.]

tolzey. See **toll¹**.

Tom *tom*, *n.* short for *Thomas*: (without *cap.*) a male, esp. a cat: (without *cap.*) a name for a big bell. — **Tom'-and-Jerr'y** hot rum and eggs, spiced and sweetened; **tom'-cat; Tom Collins** a cocktail of gin, lime-juice, soda, etc.; **Tom'-nodd'y** the puffin: a fool; **Tom= trot** a kind of toffee. — **Long Tom** a long gun, esp. one carried amidships on a swivelling carriage; **Old Tom** gin; **Tom and Tib, Tom, Dick, and Harry** anybody: people in general; **Tom o' Bedlam** formerly, a madman let out with a licence to beg; **Tom Thumb** a famous dwarf in English folklore, hence any very small person; **Tom Tidd'ler's ground** a place where wealth is to be had for the picking up: debatable land: no man's land (from a children's game so called).

tomahawk *tom'ə-hök*, *n.* a North American Indian war-axe. — *v.t.* to assail or kill with a tomahawk: to hack, cut up, or slate. [Virginian Indian *tämähäk*.]

tomalley *to-mal'i*, *n.* American lobster fat ('liver'), eaten as a delicacy: extended to tamal. [Said to be Carib.]

toman *tō-män'*, *n.* a myriad, or ten thousand: a former Persian gold coin worth 10 000 dinars. [Pers. *tumän*.]

tomato *tə-mä'tō* (*U.S.* -*mā'*), *n.* the love-apple (*Lycopersicum esculentum* or *Solanum lycopersicum*), a South American plant close akin to the potato: its red or yellow pulpy edible fruit: — *pl.* **toma'toes**. — **gooseberry tomato, strawberry tomato** the Cape gooseberry.   [Sp. *tomate* — Mex. *tomatl*.]

tomb *tōōm*, *n.* a grave: a vault for the disposal of dead bodies: a sepulchral monument. — *v.t.* to entomb: to bury. — *adjs.* **tombic** (*tōōm'ik*, -*bik*); **tomb'less**. — **tomb'stone** a memorial stone over a tomb.   [O.Fr. (Fr.) *tombe* — L. *tumba* — Gr. *tymbos*.]

tombac, tombak *tom'bak*, *n.* an alloy of copper with a little zinc: an alloy of copper and arsenic. [Fr. *tombac* — Malay *tambaga*, copper.]

tomboc *tom'bok*, *n.* a Javanese long-handled weapon.

tombola *tom-bō'lə*, *tom'*, *n.* a kind of lottery (at a fête,

etc.): a type of bingo, played esp. in the Services.   [It., — *tombolare*, to tumble.]

tombolo *tom'bə-lō*, *n.* a bar of sand or gravel connecting an island with another or with the mainland: — *pl.* **tom'bolos**. [It.]

tomboy *tom'boi*, *n.* a high-spirited romping girl: a girl with boyish looks, dress, habits, etc.: formerly, a hoyden: an immodest woman (*Shak.*). — *adj.* **tom'-boyish**. [**Tom** and **boy**.]

tome *tōm*, *n.* a big book or volume.   [Fr., — L. *tomus* — Gr. *tomos* — *temnein*, to cut.]

tomentum *tō-men'təm*, *n.* a matted cottony pubescence. — *adjs.* **tomentose** (*tō-mən-tōs'*, *tō-men'tōs*), **tomen'-tous**. [L.]

tomfool *tom'fōōl'*, *n.* a great fool: a buffoon: a trifling fellow. — *adj.* extremely foolish. — *v.i.* to play the fool. — *n.* **tomfool'ery** foolish trifling or jesting: buffoonery: trifles, ornaments: jewellery (*rhyming slang*). — *adj.* **tom'foolish**. — *adj.* **tomboy'ish**.   [**Tom**.]

tomium *tō'mi-əm*, *n.* the cutting edge of a bird's bill. — *adj.* **tō'mial**. [Latinised from Gr. *tomeion*, a knife-edge — *temnein*, to cut.]

tommy *tom'i*, *n.* a penny roll, bread: food: a tommy-shop: the truck system: (sometimes with *cap.*) a private in the British army. — *v.t.* to oppress by the truck system. — **Tommy Atkins** a generic name for the private in the British army; **tomm'y-bar** a rod for turning a tubular spanner or the like; **tomm'y-gun** a light machine-gun (after its American inventor, General J. T. *Thompson*); **tomm'y-rot** absolute nonsense; **tomm'y-shop** a truck-shop. — **soft tommy** soft bread, as opposed to hardtack or sea-biscuit.   [From the name **Thomas**.]

tomography *tō-mog'rə-fi*, *n.* radiography of a layer in the body by moving the X-ray tube and photoplate in such a way that only the chosen plane appears in clear detail. — *ns.* **tom'ogram** a radiogram produced by tomography; **tom'ograph** a machine for making tomograms. — *adj.* **tomograph'ic**. [Gr. *tomos*, slice, *graphein*, to draw.]

tomorrow, to-morrow *tə-*, *tōō-mor'ō*, *n.* the day after today: the future. — *adv.* on the day after today: in the future. [O.E. *tō morgen*.]

tompion¹, tompon. Same as **tampion** (see **tamp**).

tompion² *tom'pi-ən*, (*obs.*) *n.* a watch of the kind made by Thomas *Tompion* (1639–1713).

tomtit *tom'tit'*, *n.* the blue or other tit.   [**Tom, tit³**.]

tom-tom *tom'-tom*, *n.* an Indian drum: any primitive drum or substitute: (esp. formerly) a Chinese gong, tam-tam. — *v.i.* to beat thereon. — Also (esp. formerly) **tam'-tam, tum'-tum.**

-tomy -*tə-mi*, in composition used to denote surgical incision into an organ. [Gr. -*tomia*, the operation of cutting — *tomē*, a cut — *temnein*, to cut.]

ton¹ *tun*, *n.* a measure of capacity, varying with the substance measured — timber, wheat, etc. (see **ton-nage**): a weight = 20 cwt = 2240 lb = 1016 kg (2400 lb was formerly a *long ton*): in U.S. usually = 2000 lb = 907·2 kg (*short*) or 2240 lb (*long*): 100 units of various kinds, e.g. 100 cu. ft in measuring the internal capacity of a ship: £100 (*coll.*): a score, total, etc. of 100 (*coll.*): 100 runs (*cricket*; *coll.*): 100 m.p.h. (preceded by *a* or *the*; *slang*): a great weight (*coll.*): (in *pl.*) many, a great amount (*coll.*). — **-tonn'er** in composition, a vehicle, vessel, etc. weighing a specified number of tons or having a specified amount of tonnage: a load of a specified number of tons. — *adj.* **ton'-up'** orig. of a motor-cyclist, having done a ton: noisy and reckless: travelling at 100 m.p.h. — **metric ton** see **tonne**.   [O.E. *tunne*, a vat, tub; see **tun**.]

ton² *tɔ̃*, *n.* fashion: people of fashion. — *adj.* **ton(n)ish** (*ton'ish*) modish, having ton. — *adv.* **ton(n)'ishly**. — *n.* **ton(n)'ishness**. [Fr.]

tonal, tonality. See **tone¹**.

tonalite *tō'nə-līt*, *n.* a quartz-biotite diorite, found at Monte *Tonale*, Tirol.

to-name *tōō'-nām*, *n.* a byname, nickname: an additional name used to distinguish persons whose names are alike. [O.E. *tōnama* — pfx. *tō-*, meaning in addition to, *nama*, name.]

tonant *tōn'ənt, adj.* thundering. [L. *tonāns, -antis*, pr.p. of *tonāre*, to thunder.]

tondo *ton'dō, n.* a circular painting or circular carving in relief: — *pl.* **ton'di** (*-dē*), **ton'dos**. — *n.* **tondi'no** (*-dē'nō*) a circular or semicircular moulding (*archit.*): a small tondo: — *pl.* **tondi'ni** (*-nē*), **tondi'nos**. [It., short for *rotondo*, round, — L. *rotundus*.]

tone[1] *tōn, n.* the character of a sound: quality of sound: accent: intonation: vocal inflexion, rise or fall in pitch: a sound of definite pitch: a major second, one of the larger intervals between successive notes in the scale, as C and D: a Gregorian psalm-tune: vocal expression: bodily firmness, elasticity, or tension, esp. in muscles: the prevailing character or spirit: mood: temper: harmony or general effect of colours: depth or brilliance of colour: a tint or shade. — *v.t.* to intone: to give tone or the desired tone to. — *v.i.* to take a tone: to harmonise (with *in*). — *adjs.* **tōn'al** of tone: according to key; **tōnal'itive** of tonality. — *n.* **tōnal'ity** a relation in key: a key: a rendering of colour relations. — *adjs.* **toned** having a tone (in compounds). braced up: treated to give tone: slightly tinted; **tone'less** soundless: expressionless: dull: relaxed: listless. — *adv.* **tone'lessly**. — *ns.* **tone'lessness; toneme** (*tō'nēm*) in a tone language, a phoneme consisting of a particular intonation. — *adjs.* **tonēm'ic; tonetic** (*-et'*) of or relating to linguistic tones, tone languages or intonation. — *adv.* **tonet'ically**. — *adj.* **tonic** (*ton'ik*) relating to tones: producing tension: giving tone and vigour to the system (*med.*): giving or increasing strength. — *n.* a tonic medicine: a keynote (*mus.*): tonic water: any person or thing that enlivens, invigorates, etc. — *ns.* **tonicity** (*ton-is'i-ti*) the property or condition of having tone: mode of reaction to stimulus: the healthy state of muscular fibres when at rest; **tōn'us** tone: a tonic spasm. — *adj.* **tōn'(e)y** (*slang*) high-toned: fashionable. — **tonal fugue** one in which the answer conforms to the tonality of the scale; **tone'-arm** orig. that part of a gramophone connecting sound-box to horn: the arm that carries an electric pick-up; **tone control** a manual control in a radio set which adjusts the relative amplitude of high, medium, and low frequencies. — *adj.* **tone'-deaf** unable to appreciate or distinguish differences in musical pitch. — **tone language** a language (e.g. Chinese) in which difference of intonation distinguishes words of different meaning that would otherwise sound the same; **tone picture** a piece of descriptive music; **tone poem** a piece of programme music, not divided into movements, conveying or translating a poetic idea or literary theme; **tone row** in serial music, the basic set of notes in the chosen order; **tonic sol-fa** (*mus.*) a system of notation and teaching devised by Sarah Glover (1785–1867) and developed by John Curwen, using sol-fa syllables (modified) and their initial letters for the notes of the scale with *doh* (*do*) for the tonic, and dividing the bar by colons, dots, and inverted commas; **tonic spasm** a prolonged uniform muscular spasm (opp. to *clonic spasm* or **clonus**); **tonic water** aerated quinine water. — **tone down** to give a lower tone to: to moderate: to soften, to harmonise the colours of as to light and shade, as a painting; **tone up** to heighten: to intensify: to make healthier, more vigorous. [Gr. *tonos*, pitch, tension, partly through Fr. *ton* and L. *tonus*.]

tone[2] *tōn,* (*obs.* or *dial.*) *pron.* and *adj.* the one. — *Scot.* **tane** (*pron.*), **tae** (*adj.*). [that one; cf. **tother**.]

toneme, toney. See **tone**[1].

tong *tong, n.* a Chinese guild, association, or secret society. [Chin. *t'ang*.]

tonga[1] *tong'gə, n.* a light two-wheeled Indian vehicle. [Hindi *tāngā*.]

tonga[2] *tong'gə, n.* a Fijian toothache remedy made from an aroid root (*Epipremnum*). [Arbitrary invention.]

tonga-bean. See **tonka-bean**.

tongs *tongz, n.pl.* a gripping and lifting instrument,

consisting of two legs joined by a pivot, hinge, or spring. [O.E. *tang, tange*; O.N. *töng*, Ger. *Zange*.]

tongue *tung, n.* the fleshy organ in the mouth, used in tasting, swallowing, and speech: the tongue of an ox, etc., as food: the rasping organ in molluscs: the power of speech: the manner of speaking: speech: discourse: voice: utterance: a vote (*Shak.*): a language: anything like a tongue in shape: the catch of a buckle: the pointer of a balance: a point of land: a bell clapper: the reed of a musical instrument: a flap in the opening of a shoe or boot: any narrow projection: a langue or language (q.v.) of a religious or military order. — *v.t.* to utter: to pronounce (*dial.*): to articulate: to assail with words (*Shak.*): to lick: to touch with the tongue: to furnish with a tongue: to talk, prate (with *it*): to produce or play by tonguing (*mus.*). — *v.i.* to give tongue: to stick out: to practise tonguing (*mus.*). — *adjs.* **tongued** having a tongue; **tongue'less** having no tongue: unspoken of (*Shak.*). — *ns.* **tongue'let** a little tongue; **tongue'ster** a babbler; **tongu'ing** articulation to separate the notes in playing wind instruments (see also **flutter-tonguing** under **flutter**). — *adj.* **tongue-doubt'ie** (i.e. **doughty**; *Milt.*) bragging. — *adj. and adv.* **tongue'-in-cheek'** ironical(ly) or whimsical(ly), not sincere(ly) or serious(ly). — **tongue'-lashing** a severe verbal reprimand. — *adjs.* **tongue'-tacked, -tied** impeded by a short fraenum: unable to speak out. — **tongue'-twister** a formula or sequence of words difficult to pronounce without blundering; **tongue'-work** babble, chatter. — **give tongue** to give utterance: to give voice as hounds on a scent; **hold one's tongue** see **hold**[1]; **lose one's tongue** to become speechless from emotion; **on the tip of one's tongue** see **tip**[1]; **speaking in tongues, gift of tongues** glossolalia; **with (one's) tongue in (one's) cheek** tongue-in-cheek (*adv.*). [O.E. *tunge*; O.N. *tunga*, Ger. *Zunge*, the tongue; L. *lingua* (from *dingua*).]

tonic, tonicity. See **tone**[1].

tonight, to-night *tə-, tōo-nīt', n.* this night: the night of the present day. — *adv.* on this night or the night of today: last night (*obs.*; *Shak.*). [O.E. *tō niht*.]

tonish. See **ton**[2].

tonite *tō'nīt, n.* a blasting explosive made from guncotton and barium nitrate. [L. *tonāre*, to thunder.]

tonk[1] *tonk,* (*coll.*) *v.t.* to strike: to defeat: to hit (a cricket ball) into the air: to hit (a ball) with a flat, wooden sound, or with an unenergetic or casual stroke. — *n.* **tonk'er**. [Imit.]

tonk[2] *tonk,* (*Austr. slang*) a penis: a homosexual: an effeminate, weak or ineffectual person. [Ety. unknown.]

tonka-bean *tong'kə-bēn', n.* the coumarin-scented seed of a large papilionaceous tree (*Dipteryx*) of Guiana, used for flavouring snuff, etc. — Also **tonga-** (*tong'gə-*), **tonquin-** (*tong'kēn-*) **bean**. [Said to be the Guiana Negroes' name.]

tonker. See **tonk**[1].

tonlet *tun'lət, n.* one of a set of overlapping strips that make up the skirt on a suit of armour: a skirt of armour. [M.Fr. *tonnel*, a short skirt; also Fr. *tonnelet*, dim. of *tonneau*, a cask, barrel (similarly made up of strips).]

tonnag *tō'nag, n.* a shawl with a shaped neck and side fastening. [Gael.]

tonnage *tun'ij, n.* a tax of so much a *tun* on imported wines (sometimes **tunnage**; *hist.*): a charge or payment by the *ton*: the carrying capacity of a ship in *tons* (orig. in *tuns* of wine); *register ton* =100 cu. feet, *freight ton* =40 cu. feet, of space for cargo: the total amount of shipping so measured: a duty on ships, estimated in tons. — **gross tonnage** the total space capable of carrying cargo in a ship, measured in register tons; **net register tonnage** gross tonnage less deducted spaces (those spaces required in running the ship). [See **ton, tun**.]

tonne *tun,* (Fr. pron. *ton*), *n.* the preferred name for a **metric ton**, equal to 1000 kilograms (0·984 ton). [Fr.]

tonneau *ton'ō*, *n*. the rear part of a motor-car body, orig. opening at the back: a tonne. [Fr., cask, tun.]

tonnell. Obs. form of **tunnel.**

-tonner. See **ton**[1].

tonnish. See **ton**[2].

tonometer *tōn-om'ə-tər*, *n*. a device for determining the frequencies of tones (*mus.*): an instrument for measuring fluid pressure within the eyeball, or blood pressure: an instrument for measuring vapour pressure. — *n.* **tonom'etry.** [Gr. *tonos*, pitch, tension, *metron*, measure.]

tonquin-bean. See **tonka-bean.**

tonsil *ton'sl*, *-sil*, *n*. either of two glands at the root of the tongue. — *adj.* **ton'sillar.** — *n.* **tonsillec'tomy** surgical removal of a tonsil. — *adj.* **tonsillit'ic.** — *ns.* **tonsilli'tis** inflammation of the tonsils; **tonsillot'omy** complete or partial removal of a tonsil. — Also **tonsilitis,** etc. [L. *tōnsillae* (pl.).]

tonsor *ton'sər*, *n*. a barber. — *adj.* **tonso'rial.** — *n.* **ton'sure** (*-shər*) the act or mode of clipping the hair, or of shaving the head: in the R.C. and Eastern Churches, the shaving or cutting of part of the hair of the head on entering the priesthood or a monastic order: the shaven part. — *adj.* **ton'sured** having the crown of the head shaven, as a priest: shaven: bald: clipped. [L. *tōnsor*, barber, *tōnsūra*, a shearing — *tondēre*, *tōnsum*, to clip.]

tontine *ton'tēn*, *ton-tēn'*, *n*. a scheme of life annuity, increasing as the subscribers die. — Also *adj.* — *n.* **tontin'er.** [From Lorenzo *Tonti*, a Neapolitan, its inventor (1653).]

tonus, tony. See **tone**[1].

Tony *tō'ni*, *n*. in U.S., an award for meritorious work in the theatre. [After U.S. actress *Antoinette* Perry.]

tony *tō'ni*, (*obs. slang*) *n*. a simpleton. [**Antony.**]

too *tōō*, *adv*. as well, in addition, also, likewise (never at the beginning of a sentence in English usage): undesirably in excess: so much as to be incompatible with a condition: in affectation, extremely. — *adjs.* **too'-too, too too** exquisite: extravagantly and affectedly sentimental, gushing. — *adv.* all too: quite too. — **too much** more than is reasonable, tolerable, etc.: also used as an interjection expressing approval, amazement, etc. (*slang*, chiefly *U.S.*). [Stressed form of **to.**]

tooart. Same as **tuart.**

toodle-oo, toodle-pip *tōō'dəl-ōō'*, *-pip'*, (*old coll.*) *interjs.* good-bye. [App. imit. of a motor-car horn.]

took *tŏŏk*, *pa.t.* and obsolete *pa.p.* of **take.**

tool *tōōl*, *n*. a working instrument, esp. one used by hand: the cutting part of a machine-tool: a weapon, esp. a gun (*slang*): a penis (*vulg.*): one who is used as the mere instrument of another: (esp. in *pl.*) anything necessary to the pursuit of a particular activity. — *v.t.* to shape or finish with a tool: to mark with a tool, esp. to ornament or imprint designs upon (a book cover), or to chisel the face of (stone): to supply with tools, esp. with machine tools for a particular purpose (also **tool up**): to drive (a coach or other vehicle; *slang*): to carry or draw in a vehicle. — *v.i.* to work with a tool: to provide tools (also **tool up**): to travel (along) in a vehicle, esp. smoothly and skilfully, and usu. at moderate speed: of a vehicle, draught animal, to travel (along, etc.). — *ns.* **tool'er; tool'ing** workmanship done with a tool. — **tool'bag, tool'box** a bag, box for carrying and storing tools; **tool'house** a shed or outhouse for keeping tools in; **tool'kit** a set of tools; **tool'maker** a worker who makes or repairs tools, esp. machine-tools; **tool'man** a man who works with tools or in a toolroom; **tool'pusher** the supervisor of drilling operations at an oil-well; **tool'room** that part of a factory occupied by toolmakers; **tool'-shed.** — **tooled up** (*slang*) carrying a weapon, esp. a gun. [O.E. *tōl*.]

toom *tōōm*, *tüm*, *tim* (now only Scots), *adj*. empty. — *n.* a rubbish tip. — *v.t.* to empty. [O.E. *tōm*, clear.]

toon[1] *tōōn*, *n*. an Indian tree of the mahogany family, with red wood and astringent bark. [Hind. *tūn*.]

toon[2], **toun** *tōōn*, (*Scot.*) *n*. same as **town.**

toorie *tōōr'i*, (*Scot.*) *n*. a small heap: a knob of hair: a tuft or bobble on a bonnet, or the bonnet itself. [Dim. of *toor*, Scots for **tower.**]

toot[1] *tōōt*, *v.i.* to pry, peer, peep about (*Spens.*): to be prominent (*obs.*). — *n.* a lookout place (*obs.*): a hill on which a lookout is posted (*S.W. England*). — *n.* **toot'er.** [O.E. *tōtian*, to stick out, peep out.]

toot[2], **tout** *tōōt*, *v.i.* to make short sounds, as on a flute or horn. — *v.t.* to blow, as a horn, etc: to inhale (a drug, usu. cocaine) (*U.S. slang*). — *n.* a blast as of a horn: a drinking binge (*U.S. and Can., coll.*): a snort (*q.v.*) of cocaine, or any drug (esp. cocaine) for snorting (*U.S. slang*): a toilet (*Austr. slang*). — *n.* **toot'er** one who toots, or his instrument. [Prob. imit.]

toot[3]. See **tut**[1].

tooth *tōōth*, *n*. one of the hard bone-like bodies set in the jaws, used for biting and chewing: a hard projection of similar use in invertebrates: taste or relish: a tooth-like projection, prong, cog, jag, as on a leaf-margin, comb, saw, or wheel: — *pl.* **teeth** (*tēth*) q.v. — *v.t.* to furnish with teeth: to cut into teeth. — *v.i.* of cog-wheels, to interlock. — *adjs.* **toothed** (*tōōtht*, also *tōōdhd*) having teeth: dentate; **tooth'ful** full of teeth: toothsome. — *n.* a small drink of spirits, etc. — *adjs.* **tooth'less** lacking teeth: powerless or ineffective; **tooth'some** palatable, tasty: attractive, pleasant, agreeable. — *n.* **tooth'someness.** — *adj.* **tooth'y** with prominent teeth: toothsome: biting (*Scot.*). — **tooth'ache** an ache or pain in a tooth; **tooth'ache-tree** the prickly ash (*Xanthoxylum*); **tooth'brush** a brush for cleaning the teeth; **toothbrush moustache** a small stiff moustache; **tooth'comb** a fine-tooth(ed) comb (q.v. under **fine**[1]); **tooth'-drawer** (*Shak.*) an extractor of teeth. — *n.* and *adj.* **tooth'-drawing.** — **tooth'-or'nament** dogtooth; **tooth'-paste, -pow'der** a paste, powder, used with a toothbrush; **tooth'pick** an instrument for picking shreds of food from between the teeth: a Bowie knife (*U.S. slang*); **tooth'-picker** (*Shak.*) a toothpick: one who picks teeth, as the bird trochilus; **tooth'shell** Dentalium; **tooth'wash** a liquid preparation for cleansing the teeth; **tooth'wort** a pale fleshy plant (*Lathraea squamaria*) of the broomrape family, parasitic on tree-roots, with tooth-like scale-leaves: the cruciferous coral-root (*Cardamine*, or *Dentaria*, *bulbifera*). — **a colt's tooth** an addiction to youthful pleasures; **armed to the teeth** armed as completely as possible, from top to toe; **a sweet tooth** a taste for sweet things; **by the skin of one's teeth** see **skin**; **cast, throw, in someone's teeth** to fling at someone as a taunt or reproach; **get one's teeth into** to tackle, deal with, vigorously, eagerly, etc.; **in, to, someone's teeth** to someone's face: in direct affront; **in spite of someone's teeth, in the teeth of** in direct opposition to; **long in the tooth** elderly, like a horse whose gums are receding; **set one's teeth on edge** see **edge**; **take the teeth out of** to render harmless or powerless; **tooth and nail** with all possible vigour and fury. [O.E. *tōth* (pl. *tēth*); Goth. *tunthus*, L. *dēns*, *dentis*, Gr. *odous*, *odontos*, Sans. *danta*.]

tootle *tōōt'l*, *v.i.* to make feeble sounds, as on the flute: to go casually along, esp. by car. — *n.* a soft sound on the flute, etc.: a casual trip, a drive. [Freq. of **toot**[2].]

toots. See **tut**[1].

tootsie, tootsy (-wootsy) *tōōt'si* (*-wŏŏt'si*), *ns.* jocular or childish words for a foot or toe. [Perh. a childish pron. of **foot.**]

top[1] *top*, *n*. the highest or uppermost part or place: the upper end or surface: a lid or cover: a topsail: a top-boot (esp. in *pl.*): a trench parapet: a small platform at the head of the lower mast: a crest or tuft (*naut.*): a handful or bundle of flax, wool, etc., for spinning: topspin: the earliest part (as *top of the morning* — a conventional Irishman's greeting): a circus tent (*slang*; **the big top** the main tent): (esp. in *pl.*) the part of a root vegetable that is above the ground: (in *pl.*) in oil-refining, the first part of a volatile mixture to come off in the distillation process: the highest position (e.g. in a profession, company, salary scale, scale of authority or privilege, etc.). — *adj.* highest: best: most important, able, etc. — *v.t.* to cover on the top: to tip: to rise above: to surpass: to rise to the top of: to surmount: to be on or at the top of: to cover, as a male animal (*Shak.*): to take off the top of: to hit (the ball) on the upper half (*golf*): to kill (*slang*). — *v.i.* to finish up, round off (with *off* or *up*): — *pr.p.* **topp'ing;** *pa.t.* and *pa.p.* **topped.** — *adjs.* **top'full** (*Shak.*) full to the top or brim; **top'less** without a top: without superior (*Shak.*): (of female garb) leaving the breasts uncovered: (of a place, entertainment, etc.) that features women with their breasts uncovered. — *n.* **top'-lessness.** — *adjs.* **top'most** (*-mōst, -məst*) uppermost: highest; **topped.** — *ns.* **topp'er** one who, or that which, tops in any sense: one who excels (*coll.*): a top hat (*coll.*); **topp'ing** the act of one who tops: (the action of) that which tops: (*pl.*) pieces cut from the top: a sauce or dressing to go over food. — *adj.* surpassing, pre-eminent: arrogant (*U.S.*). — *adv.* **topp'ingly.** — **top'-boot** a long-legged boot with a showy band of leather round the top. — *adj.* **top'-booted** wearing top-boots. — — **top brass** see **brass; top'coat** an overcoat; **top dog** the winner, leader or dominant person; **top drawer** the highest level, esp. of society (**out of the top drawer,** belonging to this social rank). — *adj.* **top'-draw'er.** — *v.t.* **top'-dress.** — **top'-dress'ing** surface dressing of manure: the application of it: any superficial covering or treatment (*fig.*). — *adjs.* **top'-flight** excellent, superior, of the highest class; **top-gallant** (*tə-, top-gal'ənt*) above the topmast and topsail and below the royal mast (also *n.*). — **top'-hamp'er** unnecessary weight on a ship's upper-deck; **top'-hat'** a tall cylindrical hat of silk plush. — *adj.* upper class: designed to benefit high executives, or the rich, as *top-hat budget, top-hat* (*insurance*) *policy.* — *adjs.* **top'-heav'y** having the upper part too heavy or large for the lower (often *fig.*, e.g. of an organisation with too many administrative staff): tipsy; **top'-hole'** (*slang*) tiptop (also *interj.*). — **top'knot** a crest, tuft of hair, often a piece of added hair, or knot of ribbons, etc., on the top of the head: the head (*slang*): a small fish (of several species) akin to the turbot. — *adjs.* **top'knotted; top'-level** at the highest level; **top'-line** important enough to be mentioned in a headline. — *v.i.* to feature in a headline: to star. — **top-lin'er** one who is top-line: a principal performer, star. — *adjs.* **top'loftical, top'lofty** (*facet.*) high and mighty: stuck-up. — **top'loftiness; top'man** a man stationed in one of the tops: a top-sawyer; **top'mast** (*-məst, -mäst*) the second mast, or that immediately above the lower mast; **top'minnow** a small, surface-feeding, soft-rayed fish belonging to any of various species, either viviparous (of the family *Cyprinodontidae*) or egg-laying (of the family *Poeciliidae*) (also **mosquito-fish**). — *adj.* **top'-notch** (*slang*) topping. — **topped crude** crude oil after some of its lighter constituents have been removed by distillation; **topping lift** (*naut.*) tackle running from the masthead for raising booms; **topp'ing-out** see **top up** below. — *adjs.* **top'-priority** very urgent; **top'-proud** (*Shak.*) proud in the highest degree. — **top'sail** (*-sl, -sāl*) a sail across the topmast; **top'-saw'yer** the upper sawyer in a sawpit: a superior, a person of importance (*coll.*); **top secret** profoundly secret and of the highest importance; **top'side** the upper part: the outer part of a round of beef: (also in *pl.*) the part of the outer surface of a vessel above the water-line. — Also *adv.* — **tops'man** a head drover, a foreman (*Scot.*): a hangman (*slang*); **top'-soil** the upper part or surface of the soil; **top'-soil'ing** removal of the top-soil; **top'spin** spin imparted to a ball by hitting it sharply on the upper half with a forward and upward stroke to make it travel higher, further, or more quickly; **top'-stone** a stone placed on the top, or forming the top; **top table** the place assigned for those rated of chief importance at a meeting or banquet; **top-up, topping-up** see **top up** below. — **at the top of one's voice** at one's loudest; **go over the top** to

go over the front of a trench and attack the enemy: to take sudden action after hesitation: to exceed the bounds of reason, decorum, etc.; **(in the) top flight** in the highest class; **off the top of one's head** without previous thought or preparation; **on top of the world** near the North Pole: on a high mountain: revelling in existence; **over the top** (*coll.*) too far, extreme, to an excess, to, at or of an unreasonable or unnecessary degree; **(the) tops** (*slang*) the very best; **top one's part** to surpass oneself in playing it; **top out** to finish (a building) by putting on the top or highest course (*n.* **topp'ing-out**); **top the bill** to be the most important attraction in a programme of entertainment, etc.; **top up** to fill up, e.g. with fuel oil, alcoholic beverage: to bring (e.g. a wage) up to a generally accepted or satisfactory level (*ns.* **top'-up, topp'ing-up**). [O.E. *top*; Ger. *Zopf.*]

top² *top, n.* a toy that can be set spinning on its pointed base (also **spinning top**): a grooved cone held back between the strands in rope-making: a marine gasteropod of the genus Trochus, with a pearly flattish-based conical shell (also **top'-shell**). — *ns.* **top'maker; top'-making.** — **sleep like a top** to sleep very soundly. [App. late O.E. *top* (but the meaning is doubtful).]

toparch *top'ärk, n.* the ruler of a district. — *n.* **top'archy** a toparch's territory. [Gr. *toparchēs* — *topos*, a place, *archein*, to rule.]

topaz *tō'paz, n.* a precious stone, silicate of aluminium and fluorine, yellowish, bluish or colourless: a variety of orange and tangerine hybrid: (*loosely*) a shade of dark yellow. — *adj.* **tō'pazine.** — *n.* **topaz'olite** a yellow garnet. — **oriental topaz** a yellow corundum. [Gr. *topazos*, a green gem.]

tope¹ *tōp, v.i.* to drink hard. — *interj.* (*obs.*) used in pledging a health. — *n.* **tō'per** a drunkard. [Poss. Fr. *toper*, to accept a wager.]

tope² *tōp, n.* a Buddhist stupa or dome for relics. [Hindi *tōp* — Sans. *stūpa*, a heap.]

tope³ *tōp, n.* a species of small shark. [Said to be Cornish.]

tope⁴ *tōp, n.* in (East) India, a grove (e.g. of mangoes), a plantation. [Tamil *tōppu* — Telugu *topu.*]

topectomy *top-ek'tə-mi, n.* the excision of a part of the cerebral cortex as treatment for certain mental illnesses. [Gr. *topos*, place, *ek*, from, and **-tomy.**]

topee. See **topi.**

topek. Same as **tupik.**

Tophet *tō'fet, n.* an ancient place of human sacrifice near Jerusalem, the valley of Hinnom or part of it, later a place of refuse disposal: hence Hell. [Heb. *tōpheth.*]

tophus *tō'fəs, n.* a gouty deposit: — *pl.* **tō'phi** (*-fī*). — *adj.* **topha'ceous.** [L. *tōphus, tōfus*, porous stone, tufa.]

topi¹, topee *tō-pē', tō'pē, n.* a hat, esp. a sola hat, pith-helmet, worn esp. in India. — **to'pi-wall'ah** a European in India. [Hindi *ṭopī*, hat (perh. from Port. *topo*, top).]

topi² *tō'pi, n.* a large African antelope with curved horns and long muzzle. [App. from a native word.]

topiary *tō'pi-ə-ri, n.* mural decoration in fanciful landscape: a branch of gardening, the clipping of trees into imitative and fantastic shapes. — Also *adj.* — *adj.* **topiā'rian.** — *n.* **tō'piarist.** [L. *topiārius* — *topia* (pl.), landscape, landscape gardening — Gr. *topos*, a place.]

topic *top'ik, n.* a head under which a rhetorician might look up matter for discourse: a general consideration suitable for argument: a subject of discourse or argument: a matter. — *adj.* **top'ical** local: relating to a topic or subject: relating to matters of interest of the day. — *n.* **topical'ity** the quality of being topical: an item or matter possessing that quality. — *adv.* **top'ically.** [Gr. *topikos*, pertaining to place or to commonplaces, *ta topika*, the general principles of argument — *topos*, a place.]

to-pinch a false emendation of some Shakespeare editors (*Merry Wives* IV, iv. 59), for *to pinch*, the second of two infinitives having *to* where the first is without *to*.

topography *top-og'rə-fi, n.* the detailed study, description, or features of a limited area. — *n.* **topog′rapher.** — *adjs.* **topographic** (*top-ə-graf′ik*), **-al.** — *adv.* **topograph′ically.** [Gr. *topographiā* — *topos*, a place, *graphein*, to describe.]

topology *top-ol′ə-ji, n.* the topographical study of a particular place: topographical anatomy: a branch of geometry concerned with those properties of a figure which remain unchanged even when the figure is bent, stretched, etc.: the study of those properties of sets of points (e.g. geometrical figures) that are invariant under one-to-one continuous transformations (*math.*): the interconnection, organisation, etc. of computers within a network. — *adjs.* **topolog′ic(al).** — *adv.* **topolog′ically.** — *n.* **topol′ogist.** [Gr. *topos*, a place, *logos*, a discourse.]

toponymy *top-on′i-mi, n.* the study of place names (also *n.sing.* **toponym′ics**): the nomenclature of regions of the body. — *n.* **toponym** (*top′ə-nim*) a place name: something named after, or with a name derived from that of, its place of origin. — *adjs.* **topon′ymal, toponymic** (-*ə-nim′ik*), **-al.** [Gr. *topos*, place, *onyma* (*onoma*), name.]

topos *top′os, n.* a stock theme, topic or expression in literature or rhetoric: — *pl.* **top′oi** (-*oi, -ē*). [Gr., lit., a place.]

topped, topping, etc. See **top**¹.

topple *top′l, v.i.* to overbalance and fall headlong: to threaten to fall from top-heaviness. — *v.t.* to cause to topple. [**top**¹.]

to prepon *to pre′pon*, (Gr.) the fitting: the becoming or seemly.

topsyturvy *top′si-tûr′vi,* also **top′side-tur′v(e)y,** (*Scot.* **tap′salteer′ie,** as *adj., adv., n.*) *advs.* bottom upwards. — *adj.* turned upside down. — *n.* confusion. — *v.t.* to turn upside down. — *n.* **topsyturvifica′tion** a turning upside down. — *adv.* **topsytur′vily.** — *ns.* **topsytur′viness; topsytur′vydom.** [**top**, and the obs. *terve*, to turn (cf. O.E. *tearflian*, to roll); **so, set,** and **side** are only conjectures.]

toque *tōk, n.* a 16th-century form of cap or turban: a hair-pad (*obs.*): a woman's close-fitting brimless or nearly brimless hat: a macaque (*Macacus pileatus*) of Ceylon. [Fr.]

tor, torr *tör, n* a hill, a rocky height. [O.E. *torr*, tor — L. *turris*, tower, or perh. from Celtic.]

Torah, Thorah *tō′, tö′rə, n.* the Mosaic Law: the book of the law, the Pentateuch. [Heb. *Tōrāh*.]

toran(a) *tör′, tör′əm*(-ə), *ns.* in India, a type of arched gateway: also a garland of flowers or leaves hung between two points. [Hind.]

torbanite *tör′bən-īt, n.* a shale, almost a coal, once mined for oil at *Torbane* Hill, Bathgate, Scotland.

torbernite *tör′bərn-īt, n.* a bright green radioactive hydrous phosphate of copper and uranium. [After *Torbern Bergmann* (1735–84), Sw. chemist.]

torc. See **torque**.

torch *törch, n.* a stick of inflammable material carried or stuck up to give light: a large candle: a portable electric lamp: an appliance producing a hot flame for welding, burning, etc.: a glowing flower or inflorescence, as of mullein: a tall cactaceous plant: a source of enlightenment (*fig.*). — *v.t.* to light with torches: to sing (a torch-song) (*rare; U.S.*). — *ns.* **torch′er** (*Shak.*) a light-giver; **torchère** (*tor-sher′;* from Fr.) a tall ornamental candlestick or lampstand. — **torch′-bear′er** one who carries a torch: a leading, prominent figure in a cause, etc. (*fig.*); **torch′-dance; torch′light; torch′-lily** the red-hot poker (Kniphofia or Tritoma); **torch′-race** a race in which the runners carried torches and passed them to others; **torch′-singer; torch′-song** a popular song of the 1930s giving lugubrious expression to the pangs of unrequited love: a sentimental or melancholy love song; **torch′-staff** (*pl.* **torch′-staves;** *Shak.*) a staff for carrying a torch; **torch′-thistle** a Cereus. — **carry the torch (for)** to suffer unrequited love (for). [Fr. *torche* — L. *torquēre, tortum*, to twist.]

torchon *tör-shõ, n.* (Fr.) a duster or dish-cloth: (in full

torchon lace) peasants' bobbin lace of loose texture and geometrical design, or a machine-made imitation: (**torchon paper**) a rough paper for water-colour drawing. [Fr., — *torcher*, to wipe.]

torcular *tör′kū-lər, n.* a tourniquet. [L. *torcular, -āris,* a wine-press, oil-press.]

tordion *tor-di-ōn′, tor′di-ən, n.* a dance similar to, but less spirited than, a galliard, esp. common in the 15th and 16th centuries. [Fr. — O.Fr. *tourdion* — Fr. *tordre,* to twist.],

tore¹ *tōr, tör, pa.t.* and obs. *pa.p.* of **tear**².

tore². See **torus**.

toreador *tor′i-ə-dör, n.* (before the days of professional bullfighting) a name used for a bullfighter, esp. on horseback. — *n.* **torero** (*tor-ā′rō*) a bullfighter on foot: — *pl.* **tore′ros.** — **toreador pants** tight-fitting calf-length trousers for women (resembling those worn by toreadors). [Sp.]

to-rend *tə-, tōō-rend′,* (*obs.*) *v.t.* to rend in pieces: — *pa.p.* (*Spens.*) **to-rent′.**

toreutic *tör-ū′tik, -ōō′, adj.* of chased or embossed metal-work. — *n.sing.* **toreu′tics** artistic work in metal. [Gr. *toreutikos, -ē, -on* — *toreuein,* to bore.]

torgoch *tör′gohh, n.* the red-bellied char. [W.]

tori, toric. See **torus**.

torii *tör′ē-ē, n.* a Japanese Shinto temple gateway. [Jap.]

torment *tör′ment, n.* torture: anguish: a source of distress. — *v.t.* **torment** (-*ment′*) to torture: to put to extreme pain: to distress: to afflict: to pester: to harass: to agitate, stir violently: to distort, force violently. — *adj.* **tormen′ted.** — *adv.* **torment′edly.** — *n.* **tor′mentil** a four-petalled Potentilla with an astringent woody root, growing on heaths. — *n.* and *adj.* **torment′ing.** — *adv.* **tormen′tingly.** — *ns.* **tormen′tor** one who, or that which, torments: a torturer, an executioner (*B.*): a long meat-fork: a wing in the first groove of a stage; **tormen′tum** a Roman machine for hurling missiles. [L. *tormentum* — *torquēre,* to twist.]

tormina *tör′mi-nə, n.pl.* gripes. — *adjs.* **tor′minal, tor′-minous.** [L., — *torquēre,* to twist.]

torn *törn, tōrn, adj.* and *pa.p.* of **tear**². — *adj.* **torn′-down** (*U.S.*) unruly. — **that's torn it!** (*coll.*) an expression of annoyance indicating that something has spoilt one's plans, etc.

tornado *tör-nā′dō, n.* orig. a violent tropical Atlantic thunderstorm: a very violent whirling wind-storm affecting a narrow strip of country: (*loosely*) a hurricane: — *pl.* **torna′does.** — *n.* (*poet.*) **tornade′.** — *adj.* **tornadic** (-*nad′ik*). [Prob. Sp. *tronada,* thunderstorm, altered as if from Sp. *tornada,* turning.]

toroid, -al. See under **torus**.

torpedo *tör-pē′dō, n.* a member of the genus **Torpedo** of cartilaginous fishes with organs on the head that give an electric shock, giving name to the family **Torpedinidae** (-*pə-din′i-dē*), related to the skates and rays: a self-propelled submarine weapon of offence (usually cigar-shaped), carrying an explosive charge which goes off when it hits a ship or other object: a bomb, cartridge, case of explosives, or detonator of various kinds, used in warfare, in boring, as a fog-signal, firework, etc.: — *pl.* **torpē′does, -dos.** — *v.t.* to attack, strike, destroy, by torpedo: to wreck (e.g. a plan). — *adj.* **torpē′dinous** benumbing. — *ns.* **torpē′doer; torpē′doist.** — **torpe′do-boat** a small swift warship discharging torpedoes; **torpe′do-boom** a spar for carrying a torpedo, projecting from a boat or anchored in a channel; **torpe′do-net** a net hung round a ship to intercept torpedoes; **torpe′do-tube** a kind of gun from which torpedoes are discharged. — **torpe′do-boat destroyer** a swifter, more powerful, type of torpedo-boat (orig. to destroy ordinary torpedo-boats; also called **destroyer**). [L. *torpēdō, -inis,* numbness, the torpedo (fish) — *torpēre,* to be stiff.]

torpid *tör′pid, adj.* numb: lethargic: having lost the power of motion and feeling: sluggish: dormant. — *n.* (*Oxford*) orig. a second boat of a college, or its crew: (in *pl.*) the Lent term races of eight-oared clinker-built

boats. — *v.t.* **tor′pefy** to benumb, paralyse. — *n.*
torpesc′ence. — *adj.* **torpesc′ent** becoming torpid. —
n. **torpid′ity.** — *adv.* **tor′pidly.** — *ns.* **tor′pidness; tor′-**
pitude; tor′por numbness: inactivity: dullness: stupidity. [L. *torpidus, torpefacĕre, torpēscere, torpor* —
torpēre, to be numb.]
torque *törk, n.* the measure of the turning effect of a
tangential force: a force or system of forces causing
or tending to cause rotation or torsion: a necklace in
the form of a twisted band (also **torc**). — *adjs.* **torquate,**
-d (*tör′kwāt, -id*) collared; **torqued** (*törkt*) twisted. —
torque′-converter (*mech.*) a device which acts as an
infinitely variable gear; **torque′-meter.** [L. *torquēre,*
to twist; *torquēs, -is,* a necklace; *torquātus,* wearing a
torquēs.]
torr¹. See **tor.**
torr² *tör, n.* a unit used in expressing very low pressures,
¹/₇₆₀ of a standard atmosphere. [E. *Torricelli;* see
Torricellian.]
torrefy *tor′i-fī, v.t.* to scorch: to parch: — *pr.p.* **torr′efying;**
pa.t. and *pa.p.* **torr′efied.** — *n.* **torrefac′tion.** [L.
torrēre, to parch, roast, *facĕre,* to make.]
torrent *tor′ənt, n.* a rushing stream: a variable mountain
stream: an abounding, strong or turbulent flow. —
adj. rushing in a stream. — *adj.* **torrential** (*-en′shl*). —
n. **torrentiality** (*-en-shi-al′i-ti*). — *adv.* **torren′tially.** —
adj. **torrent′uous.** — **torr′ent-bow** a bow of prismatic
colours formed by the spray of a torrent. [L. *torrēns,*
-entis, boiling, pr.p. of *torrēre,* to dry.]
torret *tor′it.* See **terret.**
Torricellian *tor-i-chel′i-ən, adj.* pertaining to the Italian
mathematician Evangelista *Torricelli* (1608–47) who
discovered in 1643 the principle of the barometer. —
Torricellian tube the barometer; **Torricellian vacuum**
the vacuum in the barometer.
torrid *tor′id, adj.* scorching or parching: violently hot:
dried with heat: intensely passionate, emotional, etc.
— *ns.* **torrid′ity, torr′idness.** — **torrid zone** the belt
round the earth between the tropics. [L. *torridus* —
torrēre, to parch, roast.]
Torridonian *tor-i-dō′ni-ən,* (*geol.*) *n.* and *adj.* Pre-Cambrian of the N.W. Highlands of Scotland, as around
Loch *Torridon.*
torse¹ *törs, n.* a heraldic wreath. — *n.* **torsade** (*-sād′*) an
ornament like a twisted cord. [Fr., — L. *torquēre,*
to twist.]
torse². See **torso.**
torsel *tör′sl, n.* a plate in a brick wall to support the end
of a beam. — Also **tassel.** [L. *taxillus,* a die, It.
tassello, Fr. *tasseau.*]
torsion *tör′shən, n.* twisting: a twist: the strain produced
by twisting: the force with which a thread or wire tends
to return when twisted: the checking of a haemorrhage
by twisting the cut end of the artery (*surg.*). — *ns.*
torsibility (*-si-bil′i-ti*); **tor′siograph** an instrument for
measuring and recording the frequency and amplitude
of torsional vibrations in a shaft. — *adjs.* **tor′sional;**
tor′sive twisted spirally. — **tor′sion-bal′ance** an instrument for measuring very minute forces by a horizontal
needle suspended by a very fine filament; **torsion bar**
a metal bar which absorbs force by twisting, used esp.
in vehicle suspension. [L. *torsiō, -ōnis* — *torquēre,*
tortum, to twist.]
torsk *törsk, n.* a North Atlantic fish (*Brosmius brosme*)
of the cod family, with long single dorsal fin. [Sw.,
Norw., Dan. *torsk* — O.N. *thorskr;* cf. Ger. *Dorsch,*
haddock.]
torso *tör′sō, n.* the trunk of a statue or body, without
head or limbs: — *pl.* **tor′sos.** — Also **torse** (Fr.). [It.,
stalk, core, torso — L. *thyrsus* — Gr. *thyrsos.*]
tort *tört, n.* wrong, injury (*Spens.*): any wrong, not arising
out of contract, for which there is a remedy by
compensation or damages (*Eng. law*). — *adj.* **tortious**
(*tör′shəs*) wrongful: of the nature of a tort. — **tort′-**
feasor (*-fē-zər*) one guilty of tort. [Fr., — L.L. *tortum*
— L. *torquēre, tortum,* to twist.]
torte *tör′tə, tört, n.* a rich sweet cake or pastry, Austrian

in origin, often garnished or filled with fruit, nuts,
cream, chocolate, etc.: — *pl.* **tor′ten, tor′tes** or **tortes.**
[Ger., perh. — L.L. *torta,* a round loaf.]
tortellini *tör-tə-lē′ni, n.pl.* small round pasta cases filled
with meat and seasoning and boiled in water. [It.,
ult. — L.L. *torta,* a round loaf of bread.]
torticollis *tör-ti-kol′is,* (*path.*) *n.* wry-neck. [L.L., — L.
tortus, twisted, *collum,* neck.]
tortile *tör′tīl, adj.* twisted: wreathed: coiled. — *n.* **tortility**
(*-til′*). — *adj.* **tor′tive** (*Shak.*) turned awry. [L. *tor-*
tilis, tortīvus — *torquēre,* to twist.]
tortilla *tör-tē(l)′ya, -yə, n.* a Mexican round flat maize
cake cooked on a griddle, usu. eaten hot with a filling:
a thick Spanish omelet made mainly of potato and
egg. [Sp., dim. of *torta,* cake.]
tortious. See **tort.**
tortive. See **tortile.**
tortoise *tör′təs, n.* any land or freshwater (rarely marine)
chelonian (now, in Britain, usu. restricted to land
forms): a testudo (*mil.*). — **tortoise beetle** any of
various beetles (*Cassidinae*) of the family *Chrysomel-*
idae which resemble the tortoise, having broad, often
brightly-coloured or metallic wing-covers: (*specif.*) a
green leaf-beetle (*Cassida viridis*); **tor′toise-plant**
elephant's-foot; **tortoise-shell** (*tör′tə-shel*) the shell of
a tortoise: a translucent mottled material, the horny
plates (esp. of the back) of the hawksbill turtle: a
similar synthetic material: a tortoise-shell butterfly or
cat. — *adj.* made of, or mottled like, tortoise-shell. —
tortoise-shell butterfly a butterfly with orange or reddish wings marked with black and yellow, edged with
blue, etc. — *Aglais urticae* (small), *Nymphalis poly-*
chlorus (large tortoise-shell); **tortoise-shell cat** a
domestic cat (nearly always female) mottled in yellow
and black. [L.L. *tortuca.*]
Tortrix *tör′triks, n.* the typical genus of **Tortricidae**
(*-tris′i-dē*), a large family of small moths whose caterpillars commonly live in rolled-up leaves: (without
cap.) any moth of this genus: — *pl.* **tortrices** (*-trī′sēz*).
— *n.* **tortrī′cid** any moth of the family. — Also *adj.*
[Invented L., twister.]
tortuous *tör′tū-əs, adj.* full of windings: far from straightforward (*fig.*). — *n.* **tortuos′ity.** — *adv.* **tor′tuously.** —
n. **tor′tuousness.** [L. *tortuōsus* — *torquēre, tortum,* to
twist.]
torture *tör′chər, n.* a putting to the rack or severe pain
to extort a confession, or as a punishment: extreme
pain: anguish. — *v.t.* to put to torture: to subject to
extreme pain: to exact by torture: to distort violently.
— *adj.* **tor′tured** suffering or entailing torture or
anguish: fraught with worries or difficulties, painful
(*coll.*): violently distorted. — *n.* **tor′turer.** — *n.* and *adj.*
tor′turing. — *adv.* **tor′turingly.** — *adj.* **tor′turous** causing torture or violent distortion. [Fr., — L. *tortūra,*
torment — *torquēre.*]
toruffled *tə-, too-ruf′ld,* (*arch.*) *adj.* (*Milt.* **to ruffl'd**)
ruffled up. [Pfx. *to-,* intens., **ruffle¹.**]
torus *tō′, tö′rəs, n.* a large moulding, semicircular or
nearly so in section, common at the base of a column: a
figure generated by the revolution of a circle or other
conic section about a straight line in its own plane:
the receptacle of a flower: a ridge (*zool.*): a ring-shaped
discharge-tube: — *pl.* **to′rī.** — *n.* **tore** (*tör; törit.* *archit.*
and *geom.*) a torus. — *adjs.* **toric** (*tor′, tör′, tör′*) of,
or having the form of, a torus or a part of a torus;
toroid (*tor′, tör′, tör′*) shaped like an anchor-ring. —
n. a coil or transformer of that shape. — *adj.* **toroid′al.**
— *ns.* **torula** (*tör′ū-lə*) a yeast-like micro-organism;
tor′ulin a vitamin in yeast. — *adj.* **tor′ulose** (*bot.*) with
small swellings at intervals. — *ns.* **torulō′sis** infection
with a torula affecting the nervous system; **tor′ulus** the
socket of an insect's antenna. [L. *tŏrus,* a bulge,
swelling, bed, torus moulding; dim. *tŏrŭlus.*]
Tory *tō′, tö′ri, n.* a Conservative in politics: a bigoted or
extreme Conservative: one who sided with the British
in the Revolution (*U.S. hist.*). — Also *adj.* — *v.t.*
Tō′rify, Tō′ryfy to infect with Tory principles. — *n.*

Tō′ryism the principles of the Tories. [Ir. *toiridhe*, a pursuer; first applied to the Irish bog-trotters and robbers; next, about 1680, to the most hot-headed asserters of the royal prerogative.]

tose. See **toze.**

tosh¹ *tosh*, (*Scot.*) *adj.* neat, trim: comfortable, friendly, intimate. — Also *adv.* — *v.t.* to trim.

tosh² *tosh*, (*slang*) *n.* bosh, twaddle. — *adj.* **tosh′y.**

toshach *tō′shəhh, tosh′əhh, n.* a phonetic rendering of **toiseach.**

tosher *tosh′ər*, (*university slang*) *n.* a non-collegiate student. [From **unattached.**]

toss *tos*, *v.t.* to fling, jerk: to fling up, or about, or to and fro: to agitate: to turn the leaves of (*obs.*): to tilt in drinking: to drink. — *v.i.* to be tossed: to be in violent commotion: to tumble about: to fling: to toss up a coin. — *infin.* (*Spens.*) **toss′en;** *pa.t.* and *pa.p.* **tossed** (*tost*), rarely **tost.** — *n.* an act of throwing upward: a throwing up or back of the head: confusion, commotion: a toss-up. — *n.* **toss′er.** — *adv.* **toss′ily** pertly. — *n.* and *adj.* **toss′ing.** — *adj.* **toss′y** pert, contemptuous. — **toss′pot** a toper, a drunkard; **toss′-up′** the throwing up of a coin to decide anything: an even chance or hazard. — **argue the toss** to dispute a decision; **toss off** to perform, produce quickly, cursorily: to drink off: to remark casually: to masturbate (*slang*); **toss out** to dress smartly, fancily; **toss up** to throw a coin in order to decide: to cook and serve up hastily. [Origin unknown.]

tosticated *tos′ti-kā-tid*, (*slang*), *adj.* fuddled: perplexed — also **toss′icāted.** — *n.* **tosticā′tion** perplexity. [A mispronunciation of **intoxicated,** associated with **toss.**]

tot¹ *tot*, *n.* anything little, esp. a child, a drinking-cup, or a dram. — *n.* **tott′ie, tott′y** (*dim.*). — *adj.* (*dial.*) very small. [Cf. Icel. *tottr*, a dwarf.]

tot² *tot*, *v.t.* and *v.i.* to add up or total (also **tot up**): — *pr.p.* **tott′ing;** *pa.t.* and *pa.p.* **tott′ed.** — *n.* an addition of a long column. — *n.* **tott′ing-up′.** [total.]

tot³ *tot*, (*slang*) *n.* a bone: anything retrieved from a dust-bin or the like. — *ns.* **tott′er** a raker of dust-bins and heaps; a rag-and-bone-man, scrap dealer; **tott′ing** retrieval of objects from refuse. [Orig. uncertain.]

total *tō′tl*, *adj.* whole: complete: including all: co-ordinating everything towards one end. — *n.* the whole: the entire amount. — *v.t.* to bring to a total, add up: to amount to: — *pr.p.* **tō′talling;** *pa.t.* and *pa.p.* **tō′talled.** — *ns.* **totalisā′tion, -z-; tō′talisātor, -z-, tō′talīser, -z-,** (familiarly shortened to **tote** *tōt*), a system of betting in which the total amount staked (minus tax, etc.) is divided among the winners in proportion to the size of their stake: an automatic betting-machine, the *pari mutuel.* — *v.t.* **tō′talise, -ize** to find the sum of: to bring to a total. — *v.i.* to use a totalisator. — *adj.* **totalitarian** (*tō-tal-i-tā′ri-ən*) belonging to a form of government that includes control of everything under one authority, and allows no opposition. — Also *n.* — *ns.* **totalitā′rianism; totality** (*tō-tal′i-ti*) condition or fact of being total: an entirety: completeness: the whole. — *adv.* **tō′tally.** — **total abstainer** one who abstains altogether from all forms of alcohol; **total depravity** the theological doctrine that man is totally corrupt and completely dependent on God for spiritual regeneration; **total internal reflection** (*phys.*) the complete reflection of a light ray at the boundary of a medium with a lower refractive index; **total recall** see **recall; total theatre** dramatic entertainment comprising in one performance all or most of the following — acting, dancing, gymnastic feats, singing and instrumental music of various kinds, elaborate costumes and other visual effects, sometimes poetry; **total war** see **war¹.** — **total allergy syndrome** a condition in which a person suffers from a collection of symptoms attributable to accumulated allergies to substances encountered in the modern environment. [L.L. *tōtālis* — L. *tōtus*, whole.]

Totanus *tot′ə-nəs*, *n.* the redshank genus, giving name to the **Totaninae** (*-nī′nē*), the tattler subfamily of sand-pipers, with toes webbed at the base. [It. *totano.*]

totara *tō′tə-rə, n.* a large New Zealand tree, a variety of Podocarpus, valued for its hard reddish timber. [Maori.]

tote¹ *tōt*, (*orig. U.S.*) *v.t.* to carry. — **tote bag** a large bag for shopping, etc. [Origin unknown.]

tote² *tōt*, (*slang*) *v.t.* to add (with *up*). [total.]

tote³. See **total.**

to-tear *tə-, tōō-tār′*, *v.t.* to tear in pieces: — *pa.p.* (*Spens.*) **to-torne′.** [Pfx. *to-*, asunder, and **tear².**]

totem *tō′təm*, *n.* any species of living or inanimate thing regarded by a class or kin within a local tribe with superstitious respect as an outward symbol of an existing intimate unseen relation: any outward symbol given undue respect. — *adj.* **totemic** (*-tem′ik*). — *ns.* **tō′temism** the use of totems as the foundation of a social system of obligation and restriction; **tō′temist** one designated by a totem. — *adj.* **totemist′ic.** — **totem pole** a pole carved and painted with totemic symbols, set up by Indians in the north-west of North America. [From Algonquin.]

tother, t′other *tudh′ər*, *pron.* and *adj.* the other. [**that other;** cf. **tone²** and Scots **tae, tane.**]

totidem verbis *tōt-ī′dəm vûr′bis, tot-i′dem ver′-, wer′bēs,* (L.) in just so many words.

totient *tō′shənt*, *n.* the number of totitives of a number. [L. *totiēs*, so many.]

toties quoties *tō′shi-ēz kwō′shi-ēz, tot′i-ās kwot′i-ās,* (L.) as often as.

totipotent *tō-tip′ə-tənt*, (*zool.*) *adj.* capable of development into a complete organ or embryo: capable of differentiation. [L. *totus*, entire, and **potent.**]

totitive *tot′i-tiv*, *n.* a number less than another and prime to it. [L. *tot*, so many.]

toto caelo *tō′tō sē′, kī′lō,* (L.) by the whole heavens: diametrically opposite.

to-torne. See **to-tear.**

totter¹ *tot′ər*, *v.i.* to sway: to waver: to rock: to threaten to fall: to reel: to stagger: to be on the verge of ruin. — *n.* a tottering movement. — *n.* **tott′erer.** — *n.* and *adj.* **tott′ering.** — *adv.* **tott′eringly.** — *adj.* **tott′ery** shaky. [Cf. Norw. dial. *tutra, totra*, to quiver, Sw. dial. *tuttra.*]

totter². See **tot³.**

tottered *tot′ərd*, *adj.* a variant of **tattered** (*Shak.*): later (from association with **totter**) ruinous. — *adj.* **tott′ring** (*Shak.*) hanging in rags.

tottie, totty. See **tot¹.**

totting. See **tot².³**

totty *tot′i*, *adj.* unsteady: dazed: tipsy. [Cf. **totter.**]

toucan *tōō′kən, -kan, -kän′, n.* any member of the *Rhamphastidae,* large South American fruit-eating birds, with an immense beak. — *n.* **tou′canet** a smaller kind of toucan. [Fr., — Tupí *tucana.*]

touch *tuch*, *v.t.* to come or be in contact with: to cause to be in contact: to meet without cutting, or meet tangentially (*geom.*): to get at: to reach as far as: to attain: to equal, rival, or compare with: to make a light application to: to begin to eat, eat a little of: to affect, esp. injuriously: to impress: to affect with emotion, esp. pity: to have to do with: to concern: to hit, wound, or injure: to strike home to: to play (*mus.*): to call at (as a port): to mark or modify by light strokes: to tinge: to cause to touch the ground behind the goal-line (commonly with *down; Rugby football*): to test as with a touchstone: to receive, draw, pocket: to extract money from (*for* so much): to make some reference to, say something about: to bribe (*obs.*): to cheat (*slang*). — *v.i.* to be or come in contact: to make a passing call at a port: to verge: to make some mention or reference (with *on, upon*): to have reference. — *n.* the act, condition, impression, sense, or mode of touching: a feeling: a slight application, modification, stroke: a small quantity: a slight affection of illness: a tinge: a trace: a smack: ability, skill: a trait: a little: a slight hit, wound, blemish, reproach: the manner or nicety of producing tone on (now esp.) a keyed instrument: the instrument's response: a characteristic manner: a stroke of art: the relation of communication, sympathy, harmony: communication, contact: a game in which one has to pursue and touch others: a test, as of touchstone: a touchstone: a black marble or similar monumental stone (*obs.*): an official stamp of fineness on gold, etc.: fineness: stamp (*fig.*): either side of the field outside the bounds (*football*, etc.): theft (*slang*): a sum got by theft or by touching (*slang*): that which will find buyers at such and such a price (*slang*). — *adj.* **touch′able** capable of being touched: fit to be touched. — *n.* **touch′ableness.** — *adj.* **touched** having been touched: slightly unsound mentally. — *n.* **touch′er.** — *adv.* **touch′ily.** — *n.* **touch′iness.** — *n.* **touch′ing.** — *adj.* affecting: moving: pathetic. — *prep.* concerning. — *adv.* **touch′ingly.** — *n.* **touch′ingness.** — *adjs.* **touch′less** without a sense of touch: intangible; **touch′y** over-sensitive: irascible. — **touch′-and-go′** a narrow escape: a critical or precariously balanced situation. — *adj.* precarious: off-hand. — **touch′-box** a tinder-box for a matchlock; **touch′-down** in Rugby and American football, touching of the ball to the ground by a player behind the goal-line (if his own goal, also called a **touch′-back**): of aircraft, the act of alighting; **touch′-hole** the small hole of a cannon through which the fire is communicated to the charge; **touch′-in-goal** (*Rugby football*) the areas at each end of the pitch behind the goal-lines and outside the touch-lines; **touch′-judge** an official who marks when and where the ball goes into touch (*Rugby football*); **touch′-line** the side boundary in football, etc.; **touch′=mark** the maker's official stamp on pewter; **touch′-me=not** the plant balsam (from its explosive fruit): lupus: a forbidden topic. — *adj.* stand-offish. — **touch-me=not′ishness; touch′-paper** paper steeped in saltpetre for firing a train; **touch′-piece** a coin or medal formerly given by a king to those he touched for king's-evil; **touch′-plate** one bearing the pewterers' official stamp; **touch′-screen** (*comput.*) a screen of a visual display unit that doubles as an input device, and is operated by being touched. — Also *adj.* — **touch′stone** Lydian stone, a highly siliceous, usually black stone, or other stone for testing gold or silver by streak, as black marble: any criterion. — *adj.* **touch′-tone** of telephones, having push buttons (rather than a dial) that cause distinct tones to sound at the exchange. — *v.t.* and *v.i.* **touch′-type** to type without looking at the keys of the typewriter. — **touch′-typist; touch′wood** decayed wood that can be used as tinder. — **an easy, a soft touch** (*coll.*) a person or institution easily persuaded, esp. to lend money; **in, out of, touch**, in, out of, communication or direct relations; **near touch** a close shave; **touch down** of aircraft, to alight; **touch off** to trigger (also *fig.*); **touch up** to improve by a series of small touches: to lash lightly, stimulate; **touch wood,** (*U.S.*) **knock (on) wood** to touch something wooden as a superstitious guard against ill-fortune (also used as interjections, to accompany the gesture or independently). [O.Fr. *tuchier* (Fr. *toucher*); origin doubtful.]

touché *too̅′shā, too̅-shā′, interj.* claiming or acknowledging, hit in fencing, or a point scored in argument, etc. [Fr., touched, scored against.]

tough *tuf, adj.* stiff and dense: tenacious: hard to cut, chew, break up or penetrate: resistant: viscous, sticky: capable of, or requiring, strenuous effort and endurance: unyielding: robust: laborious: refractory: criminal, ruffianly: unlucky (*coll.*). — *n.* a rough: a criminal, hooligan (also **tough guy**). — *interj.* (*coll.*) tough luck. — *v.t.* or *v.i.* **tough′en** to make or become tough. — *n.* **tough′ener.** — *n.* and *adj.* **tough′ening.** — *n.* **tough′ie** (*coll.*) a tough person, problem, etc. — *adj.* **tough′ish** rather tough. — *adv.* **tough′ly.** — *n.* **tough′-ness.** — **tough luck** see **luck.** — *adj.* **tough′-mind′ed** hard-headed, unsentimental, determined. — **get tough with** (*coll.*) to deal with (more) severely, sternly. [O.E. *tōh.*]

touk. See **tuck².**

toun *too̅n, n.* a Scots spelling of **town.**

toupee *too̅-pē′, -pā′,* or *too̅′, n.* a tuft, lock, fringe, or patch, esp. of false hair: a wig with a top-knot. — Also **toupet** (*too̅-pā′, too̅′pā*). [Fr. *toupet.*]

tour *too̅r, n.* a round: a prolonged journey from place to place, e.g. for pleasure, or to give entertainment as a performer, or to give lectures, play matches, etc.: a pleasure trip or outing: a shift or turn of work: a period of military service in a particular place (also **tour of duty**): a border of false hair (*hist.*). — *v.i.* to make a tour, go on tour. — *v.t.* to make a tour through or of: to tour with (a play). — *n.* **tour′er** a touring-car: a tourist. — *n.* and *adj.* **tour′ing.** — *ns.* **tour′ism** the activities of tourists and those who cater for them; **tour′ist** one who makes a tour, esp. a sight-seeing traveller or a sportsman. — *adjs.* **touris′tic; tour′isty** (*derog.*) designed for, or full of, tourists. — **tour′ing-car** a long motor-car, suitable for touring; **tourist class** the cheapest class of accommodation on a boat or aeroplane; **tour operator** a person or firm organising (esp. package-tour) holidays. — **Grand Tour** a journey through Western Europe, once fashionable as completing a youth's education. [Fr.; see **turn.**]

touraco *too̅′rə-kō,* or *-kō′, n.* an African bird (*Turacus*) of the plantain-eater family, with a horny shield on the forehead and remarkable pigments in its feathers: — *pl.* **touracos.** [Supposed to be a W. African name.]

tourbillion *too̅r-bil′yən,* **tourbillon** *too̅r-bē′yɔ̃, ns.* a swirl: a vortex: a whirlwind: a whirling firework: a whirling or revolving mechanism or system. [Fr. *tourbillon,* whirlwind — L. *turbō, -inis.*]

tour de force *too̅r də fors,* (Fr.) a feat of strength or skill.

tour d'horizon *too̅r dor-ē-zɔ̃,* (Fr.) a general survey, review.

tourmaline *too̅r′mə-lēn, n.* a beautiful mineral of complex and varying composition, usually black (schorl) or blackish, strongly pyro-electric and pleochroic. [Fr., — Sinh. *tòramalli,* carnelian.]

tournament *too̅r′nə-mənt, n.* a military sport of the Middle Ages in which combatants engaged in single combat or in troops, mainly on horseback, with spear and sword: a military and athletic display: a series of games to determine a winner or winning team by elimination. — *n.* **tourney** (*too̅r′, tûr′, tör′ni*) a tournament. — *v.i.* to ride in a tournament. — *n.* **tour′neyer.** [O.Fr. *tournoiement, tornoi — torner —* L. *tornāre,* to turn.]

tournedos *too̅r′nə-dō, n.* a small beef fillet served with some kind of garnish: — *pl.* **tour′nedos** (*-dōz*). [Fr.]

tourney, tourneyer. See **tournament.**

tourniquet *too̅r′ni-ket, -kā, n.* any appliance for compressing an artery: a turnstile (*rare*). [Fr., — L. *tornāre,* to turn.]

tournure *too̅r-nür′, n.* contour, the characteristic turn of line: a bustle or pad worn at the waist. [Fr.]

touse, touze, towse, towze *towz, v.t.* to haul, to pull about: to dishevel, rumple, tumble: to worry: to rack (*obs.*): to tease out (*obs.*). — *v.i.* to touse each other: to be toused: to tussle: to rummage. — *n.* a tousing. — *n.* **tous′er, tows′er** one who touses (*cap.*) a common name for a big dog. — *n.* and *adj.* **tous′ing.** — *v.t.* **tousle, touzle** (*towz′l, Scot. too̅z′l*) to disarrange, to tumble: to dishevel. — *v.i.* to tussle: to touse things. — *n.* a tousled mass. — *adj.* **tousy, towsy** (*towz′i, Scot. too̅z′i*) shaggy, unkempt, tousled: rough. — **tousy tea** (*Scot.*) high tea. [Prob. from a lost O.E. word answering to Ger. *zausen.*]

tous-les-mois *too̅-lā-mwä′, n.* a West Indian Canna with bright red flowers, or the edible starch of its rhizome. [Fr., every month, but perh. really from a native name.]

toustie *too̅s′ti,* (Scott) *adj.* irascible. [Perh. a mixture of **testy** and **tout².**]

tout¹ *towt, v.i.* to look out for custom in an obtrusive, aggressive or brazen way. — *v.t.* to watch or spy on: to advertise, praise or recommend strongly. — *n.* one who touts: a low fellow who hangs about racing-stables, etc., to pick up profitable information. — *n.* **tout′er.** [App. related to **toot¹.**]

tout², **towt** *towt*, (*Scot.*) *v.i.* to pout. — *n.* a pet, a fit of the sulks: a sudden illness. — *adj.* **tout'ie** petulant.

tout³ *tōō,* (Fr.) *adj.* all: every: whole. — *adv.* quite: entirely. — **tout à fait** (*tōō ta fe*) entirely; **tout au contraire** (*tōō tō kɔ̄-trer*) quite the contrary; **tout à vous** (*tōō ta vōō*) wholly yours; **tout court** (*kōōr*) quite brief(ly), without preface, simply; **tout de même** (*də mem*) all the same; **tout de suite** (*tōōt swēt, tōōd*) at once, immediately; **tout ensemble** see **ensemble; tout le monde** (*lə mɔ̄d*) all the world, everybody.

tout⁴. See **toot².**

touze, touzle. See **touse.**

tovarish *to-vä'rish, n.* comrade. [Russ. *tovarishch.*]

tow¹ *tō* (*Scot.* tow), *v.t.* to pull with a rope, primarily by water: to pull along. — *v.i.* to proceed by being towed. — *n.* the condition of being towed: an act of towing: a tow-rope: that which is towed: a rope, esp. a bell-rope or a hangman's rope (*Scot.*). — *ns.* **tow'age** an act of towing: a fee for towing; **tow'er.** — *n.* and *adj.* **tow'ing.** — **tow'bar** a metal bar or frame used for towing trailers, etc.; **tow'ing-bitts** upright timbers projecting above the deck for fastening tow-lines to; **tow'-iron** a toggle-iron used in whaling; **tow'line, -rope** a line used in towing; **tow'-net, tow'ing-net** a dragnet for collecting objects of natural history, etc.; **tow'path, tow'ing-path** a path for horses towing barges; **tow'-plane** an aeroplane which tows gliders. — **have, take, in tow** to tow (another vehicle, vessel, etc.): to take along with one, be accompanied by: to have, assume, charge of; **on tow** (of vehicles), **under tow** (of vessels) being towed. [O.E. *togian,* to drag.]

tow² *tō, n.* prepared fibres of flax, hemp, or jute: esp. separated shorter fibres. — *adj.* of or like tow. — *adj.* **tow'y.** — **tow'-head** a person with light-coloured or tousled hair. — *adj.* **tow'-headed.** [O.E. *tow-* (in compounds).]

toward *tō'ərd, tōrd, adj.* (*arch.*) or (*dial.*) approaching: at hand: impending: getting on: on hand: favourable: well-disposed: apt: ready to do or learn: on the left or near side. — *adv.* in the direction facing one, inward. — *prep.* (now more commonly **towards**) (*tə-, tōō-wörd'(z), twörd(z), tōrd(z), törd(z)*) in the direction of: with a tendency to: for, as a help to: near, a little short of. — *n.* **tow'ardliness.** — *adj.* **tow'ardly** (*arch.*) favourable: promising: well-disposed: tractable. — Also *adv.* — *n.* **tow'ardness.** — *prep.* **towards** (*tə-wordz'*) toward. [O.E. *tōweard,* adj., adv., prep. — *tō,* to, suff. *-weard, -ward.*]

towel *tow'əl, n.* a cloth for drying: formerly a cloth for various purposes, as a table-napkin, an altar-cloth. — *v.t.* to rub with a towel: to cudgel: to thrash: — *pr.p.* **tow'elling;** *pa.t.* and *pa.p.* **tow'elled.** — *n.* **tow'elling** a rubbing with a towel: an absorbent cloth for towels, sometimes used for dressing-gowns, curtains, etc.: a thrashing. — **tow'el-gourd** the loofah; **tow'el-horse, -rack** a frame for hanging towels on; **tow'el-rail** a rod for hanging towels on. — **a lead towel** a bullet: **an oaken towel** a cudgel; **throw in the towel** see **throw¹.** [O.Fr. *toaille,* from Germanic; cf. O.H.G. *dwahila — dwahan, twahan,* O.E. *thwēan,* to wash.]

tower *towr, tow'ər, n.* a lofty building, standing alone or forming part of another: a fortress: (esp. 17th cent.) a woman's high head-dress: a lofty or vertical flight. — *v.i.* to rise into the air: to be lofty: to stand on high. — *v.t.* (*Milt.*) to rise aloft into. — *adjs.* **tow'ered; tow'ering** very high, elevated: very violent; **tow'erless; tow'ery** having towers: lofty. — **tower block** a tall residential or office building; **tow'er-mill** see **smock-mill** under **smock; tow'er-shell** a gasteropod (Turritella) with elongated many-whorled spiral shell, or its shell. — **tower of strength** a stable, reliable person; **tower over** to be considerably taller than: to be markedly superior to. [O.Fr. *tur* — L. *turris,* a tower.]

towhee *tow'hē, tō'hē, n.* an American finch, the chewink, ground-robin, or marsh-robin. [Imit.]

towmont, towmond, towmon *tow'mən(t),-mən(d),* (*Scot.* and *N. of England*) *ns.* forms of **twelvemonth.**

town *town, n.* orig. an enclosure (*obs.*): in Scotland (*Scot.* **tōōn**) a farmstead or similar group of houses: a populous place bigger or less rural than a village: a municipal or political division (which may include villages and towns in the ordinary sense) of a county (*U.S.*): the principal town of a district: an urban community: the people of a town, esp. fashionable society, tradesmen (distinguished from academic inhabitants), or immoral classes: the business or shopping centre: urban communities generically. — *adj.* of a town: urban. — *n.* **townee', tow'nie** a townsman, not a member of the university or a country dweller. — *adj.* **town'ish** characteristic of town as opposed to country. — *n.* **town'ling** a town-dweller. — *adj.* **town'ly** townish. — *ns.* **town'ship** a village, a community or local division: a parish (*hist.*): a farm in joint tenancy (*Scot.*): a thirty-six square mile block of public land (*U.S.*): a site for a town (*Austr.*): a small settlement (*Austr.*): the territory or district of a town: the corporation of a town: a subdivision of a county or province (*U.S.*): an administrative district (*U.S.*): an urban settlement of black and coloured Africans (*S.Afr.*); **town'y** a townsman: a fellow-townsman. — *adj.* townish. — **town clerk** a secretary and legal adviser of a town; **town council** the governing body in a town; **town councillor; town'-crī'er** one who makes public proclamations in a town; **town'-dweller; town'-end'** the end of the main street; **town (towns) gas** usu. a mixture of coal-gas and carburetted water-gas, made and supplied for domestic or trade use; **town hall** a public hall for the official business of a town: a townhouse; **town'house** a house or building for transacting the public business of a town; **town house** a house in town belonging to the owner of another in the country: a fashionable, esp. terraced, house in a town, etc.; **town'land** (chiefly *hist.*) the land forming a manor: in Ireland, a sub-parochial land division, or a township: in Scotland, the enclosure round a farm; **town'-meet'ing** in New England, a meeting of the voters of a town; **town'-plann'ing** deliberate designing in the building and extension of towns to avoid the evils of fortuitous and speculative building; **town's'-bairn** (*Scot.*) a native of a town, esp. one's own; **town'scape** a portion of a town which the eye can view at once: a picture of it: the design or building of (part of) a town. — Also *v.t., v.i.* — **town'scaping; towns'folk** the people of a town; **town'skip** (*Dickens*) a city urchin; **towns'man** an inhabitant or fellow-inhabitant of a town: — *fem.* **towns'-woman; towns'people** townsfolk; **town'-talk'** the general talk of a town: the subject of common conversation. — **go to town** (*coll.*) to act, behave, perform enthusiastically, with thoroughness, without restraint; **on the town** out to amuse oneself in town; **take to town** (*slang*) to mystify, bewilder; **town and gown** the general community and the members of the university. [O.E. *tūn,* an enclosure, town; O.N. *tūn,* enclosure, Ger. *Zaun,* hedge.]

to-worne *tə-wörn', -wörn', adj.* (*Spens.*) worn-out. [Pfx. *to-,* intens., **worn.**]

tow-rag. A mistaken spelling of **toe-rag.**

towse, towsy. See **touse.**

towt. See **tout².**

towy. See **tow².**

towze. See **touse.**

toxic *toks'ik, adj.* of poison: poisonous: poisoned: due to poison. — *adj.* **tox'ical.** — *adv.* **tox'ically.** — *adj.* **tox'icant** poisonous. — *n.* a poisonous substance. — *ns.* **toxica'tion, toxicity** (*-is'*) toxic quality; **tox'in** a ptomaine: a specific poison of organic origin; **tox'oid** a toxin that has been treated to remove its toxic properties without destroying its ability to stimulate formation of antibodies. — *n.* **toxaemia** (*-ē'mi-ə;* Gr. *haima,* blood) blood poisoning. — *adj.* **toxaem'ic.** — *n.* **tox'aphene** (*-ə-fēn*) chlorinated camphene used as an insecticide. — *adj.* **toxicolog'ical.** — *ns.* **toxicol'ogist; toxicol'ogy** the science of poisons; **toxicomā'nia** a morbid craving for poisons. — *adjs.* **toxicoph'agous,**

toxiph'agous (Gr. *phagein*, to eat) poison-eating. — *ns.*
toxicophō'bia, toxiphō'bia (Gr. *phobeein*, to fear) morbid fear of poisoning. — *n.* and *adj.* toxiphō'biac. — *ns.* toxocara (*tok-sə-kär'ə*) a parasitic worm found in the intestines of dogs and known to cause disease (toxocarī'asis) and eye damage in humans; toxoplasmō'sis infection of animals and man by micro-organisms, prob. protozoa, of the genus *Toxoplasma*. — toxic shock syndrome a group of symptoms, including high fever, vomiting, and diarrhoea, sometimes occurring in menstruating women using tampons, and attributed to a toxin apparently associated with staphylococcal infection. [Gr. *toxon*, a bow, *toxikos,* for the bow, *toxikon*, arrow-poison.]

toxophilite toks-of'i-līt, *n.* a lover of archery: an archer. — *adj.* toxophilit'ic. — *n.* toxoph'ily love of archery: archery. [Gr. *toxon*, a bow, *phileein*, to love.]

toy *toi, n.* a plaything: a trifle: a thing only for amusement or look: a matter of no importance: a jest, idle tale (*arch.*): a trivial dance-tune, or the like (*arch.*): a whim, crotchet: an old woman's cap with side flaps (*Scot.*): a dwarf breed: amorous sport (*arch.*). — *adj.* made in imitation as a plaything. — *v.i* to trifle: to sport: to dally amorously. — *n.* toy'er. — *n.* and *adj.* toy'ing. — *adj.* toy'ish given to toying or trifling: playful: wanton (*obs.*). — *adv.* toy'ishly. — *n.* toy'ishness. — *adj.* toy'some sportive: playful: whimsical: disposed to toy: wanton (*obs.*). — toy'-boy (*slang*) a young gigolo, the pet of older, richer women; toy dog a very small pet dog; toy'man, -woman a seller of toys; toy'shop a shop where toys are sold. [Poss. Du. *tuig*, tools; Ger. *Zeug*, stuff.]

toylsom, toylesome. See toil[1].

toze, tose (*Shak.* toaze), *tōz, v.t.* to tease out, card, comb: to draw out, elicit. [M.E. *tosen*, akin to tease.]

tozie *tōz'i,* (*Scott*) *n.* a shawl made from a goat's inner coat.

tra-. See trans-.

trabeate, -d *trab', trāb'i-āt, -id, adjs.* built of horizontal beams, not arches and vaults. — *ns.* trabeā'tion an entablature: a combination of beams in a structure; trabecula (*trə-bek'ū-lə*) a cell, row of cells, band, or rodlike structure running across a cavity or forming an internal support to an organ: — *pl.* trabec'ūlae (*-lē*). — *adjs.* trabec'ūlar; trabec'ūlate, -d having trabeculae: transversely barred. [L. *trabs, trabis*, beam; dim. *trabecula*.]

tracasserie *tra-kas-(ə)-rē,* (Fr.) *n.* turmoil.

trace[1] *trās, n.* a way, course (*Spens.*): a beaten path (*U.S.*): a track: a footprint: a vestige: an indication, mark of what is or has been: a mental or neural change caused by learning: a small quantity that can just be detected: a tracing: a line marked by a recording instrument: an intersection with or projection on a surface: the ground-plan of a work (*fort.*). — *v.i.* to proceed (*arch.*): to walk (*arch.*): to move (*arch.*): to tread a measure (*obs.*): to be traceable, date back. — *v.t.* to traverse: to track: to follow step by step: to detect: to discover the whereabouts of: to follow or mark the outline of, esp. mechanically or on a translucent paper: to outline, delineate, or write: to produce as tracery: to cover with tracery. — *n.* traceabil'ity. — *adj.* trace'able that may be traced. — *n.* trace'ableness. — *adv.* trace'ably. — *adj.* trace'less. — *adv.* trace'lessly. — *ns.* trā'cer one who traces: an instrument for tracing: a probe for tracing a nerve, etc.: a device by which a projectile leaves a smoke-trail: a projectile equipped with it: a chemical substance used to mark the course followed by a process. — *adj.* trā'ceried. — *ns.* trā'cery ornamentation in flowing outline: ornamental open-work in Gothic architecture; trā'cing the act of one who traces: a drawing copied mechanically or on translucent paper laid over the original: an instrumental record. — trace element a micro-nutrient, a substance (as zinc, copper, molybdenum, etc.) whose presence in the soil in minute quantities is necessary for plant and animal growth; tracer bullet; tracer element (*physiol.,*

etc.) an isotope, often a radio-isotope, used for experiments in which its particular properties enable its position to be kept under observation; tracer shell; tra'cing-paper translucent paper for tracing on. [Fr. *trace* — L. *tractus*, pa.p. of *trahēre*, to draw.]

trace[2] *trās, n.* (usu. in *pl.*) a rope, chain, or strap attached to an animal's collar, for drawing a vehicle: a bar for transmitting motion: the vascular tissue branching from the cylinder to pass into a leaf or branch (*bot.*): a short piece of wire, gut or nylon connecting the hook to the fishing line. — *v.t.* to harness in traces. — *n.* trā'cer a trace-horse: a boy who attends a trace-horse. — trace'-horse a horse that draws in traces. — kick over the traces see kick. [O.Fr. *trays, trais,* pl. of *trait*, draught; cf. trait.]

trachea *tra-kē'ə, U.S. trā', n.* the windpipe: the air-tube in air-breathing arthropods: a conducting tube in xylem (*bot.*): — *pl.* trachē'ae (*-ē*). — *adj.* trachē'al. — *n.pl.* Trachēā'ria arachnids with tracheae, but no lung-books. — *ns.* and *adjs.* trachēā'rian; trā'cheary. — *n.pl.* Trachēā'ta arthropods with tracheae. — *adjs.* trā'cheate, -d having a trachea. — *ns.* tracheid(e) (*trə-kē'īd, -id*, or *trak'i-*) a long tubelike but closed cell in xylem; tracheitis (*trak-i-ī'tis*) inflammation of the trachea; tracheos'copy inspection of the trachea; tracheos'tomy surgical formation of an opening into the trachea; tracheot'omy cutting into the trachea; trachī'tis a wrong form of tracheitis. [Mediaeval L. *trāchēa* for L. *trāchīa* — Gr. *trācheia* (*artēriā*), rough (artery).]

trachelate *trak'ə-lāt, adj.* having a neck. [Gr. *trachēlos*, neck.]

Trachinus *tra-kī'nəs, n.* the weever genus of fishes, giving name to the family Trachinidae (*-kin'i-dē*). [L.L. *trachina*, said to be a local name of a fish.]

trachitis. See under trachea.

trachoma *tra-kō'mə, n.* a disease of the eye, with hard pustules on the inner surface of the eyelids. [Gr. *trāchōma*.]

Trachypterus *trak-ip'tə-rəs, n.* the dealfish genus, giving name to the ribbon-fish family Trachypteridae (*-ter'i-dē*). [Gr. *trāchys*, rough, *pteron*, fin.]

trachyte *trak'īt, n.* a fine-grained intermediate igneous rock answering to the coarse-grained syenite, commonly porphyritic with sanidine. — *adjs.* trachytic (*trə-kit'ik*); trach'ytoid. [Gr. *trāchys*, rough.]

tracing. See under trace[1].

track[1] *trak, n.* a mark left: a beaten path: a made path: a sequence, path of thoughts or actions: the predetermined line of travel of an aircraft: a course, usu. oval-shaped, on which races are run: a railway line, the rails and the space between: the groove cut in a gramophone record by the recording instrument: one out of several items recorded on a disc or tape: one of several areas or paths on magnetic recording equipment receiving information from a single input channel: in motion-pictures, etc., the sound-track: any of several or more or less demanding courses of study designed to meet the respective needs of students divided into groups according to ability. (*U.S.*): the endless band on which the wheels of a caterpillar vehicle run (*adj.* tracked equipped with such metal bands): in a factory, etc., a conveyor carrying goods in process of manufacture: the distance between a pair of wheels measured as the distance between their respective points of contact with the ground. — *v.t.* to follow the track of: to find by so doing: to traverse: to beat, tread (a path, etc.): to follow the progress of: to follow the movement of (satellite, spacecraft, etc.) by radar, etc., and record its positions. — *v.i.* to follow a trail: to make one's way (*coll.*): to run in alignment, esp. (of gramophone needles) to follow the grooves: to move a dolly camera in a defined path while taking a shot (tracking shot). — *ns.* track'age provision of railway tracks; track'er; track'ing the action of the verb: the division of study courses or students into tracks (q.v. above) (*U.S.*). — *adj.* track'less without a path: untrodden: leaving no trace: running without rails. — *adv.* **track'lessly.** — *n.* **track'lessness.** — **track event** in a sports competition, a race of any kind. — *adj.* **track'-laying** of a vehicle, having caterpillar tracks. — **track'man** (*U.S.*) a plate-layer; **track record** a record of past performance orig. that of an athlete, now generally that of any individual, company, etc.; **track shoe** a lightweight spiked running shoe worn by athletes; **track suit** a warm one worn by athletes before and after, e.g. a race, or when in training; **track'-walker** one who has charge of a railway track; **track'way** a beaten track: an ancient road. — **across the tracks, the wrong side of the tracks** a slum or other socially disadvantageous area; **in one's tracks** just where one stands; **keep track of** keep oneself informed about; **make tracks** to make off: to go quickly; **off the beaten track** away from frequented roads: out of the usual (*fig.*); **off the track** off course, in the wrong direction; **on the right, wrong track** pursuing a correct, mistaken course; **the beaten track** (*fig.*) the normal, conventional, routine; **track down** to find after intensive search; **tracker dog** one used for tracking, especially in police searches. [Fr. *trac*; prob. Gmc.; cf. next word.]

track[2] *trak*, *v.t.* to tow. — *v.i.* to travel by towing. — *ns.* **track'age** towing; **track'er** one who tows: a tug: a pulling part in the action of any organ. — **track'-boat** a towed boat; **track'road** a towpath; **track'-scout** a trekschuit. [See **trek**.]

tracklement *trak'l-mənt*, (*dial.*) *n.* a condiment, accompaniment, etc. [Ety. uncertain.]

tract *trakt*, *n.* a stretch or extent of space or time: a region, area: a trace, track (*Shak.*, *Spens.*): a tractate: a pamphlet or leaflet, esp. political or (now) religious: a psalm sung instead of the Alleluia in Lent (*R.C.*); also **tract'us** (perh. as drawn out, perh. as sung at a stretch without answers): a region of the body occupied by a particular system (e.g. *the digestive tract*). — *v.t.* (*Spens.*) to trace, track. — *n.* **tractabil'ity.** — *adj.* **tract'able** easily drawn, managed or taught: docile. — *ns.* **tract'ableness; tractā'rian** a writer of tracts, esp. (*cap.*) of the *Tracts for the Times* (Oxford, 1833–41 — Pusey, Newman, Keble, Hurrell Froude, etc.). — Also *adj.* — *ns.* **Tractār'ianism** the system of religious opinion promulgated in these, its main aim to assert the authority and dignity of the Anglican Church — the Oxford movement; **tract'ate** a treatise, a tract; **tractā'tor** a tractarian. — *adj.* **tract'ile** (*-īl*) ductile, capable of being drawn out. — *ns.* **tractility** (*-il'*); **traction** (*trak'shən*) the act of drawing or state of being drawn: the pulling on a muscle, organ, etc., by means, e.g. of weights, to correct an abnormal condition (*med.*): the propulsion of vehicles. — *adjs.* **trac'tional; tract'ive** pulling. — *ns.* **tract'or** an aeroplane with a screw-propeller in front: a traction-engine: a vehicle that propels itself or hauls other vehicles or agricultural implements: the short front section of an articulated lorry, containing the engine and driver's cab: a motorised plough: (in *pl.*) bars of different metals which, drawn over diseased parts, were supposed to give relief; **tractorā'tion** the use of these bars; **tract'rix** a curve such that the intercept of a tangent by a fixed straight line is constant. — **trac'tion-engine** a locomotive for hauling on roads, fields, etc. [L. *tractus*, *-ūs*, a dragging, draught, tract, *tractus*, *tractātus*, pa.ps. of *trahĕre*, *tractāre*, to draw.]

trad *trad*, *adj.* a shortened form of *traditional*, esp. in *traditional jazz*, a rhythmically monotonous style of jazz which originated in New Orleans round about the beginning of the 20th century. — Also *n.*

trade *trād*, *n.* a track, trail, treading (*Spens.*): a way of traffic: resort (*Shak.*): a way, a course (*obs.*): a practice: an occupation, way of livelihood, esp. skilled but not learned: shopkeeping: commerce: buying and selling: a craft: men engaged in the same occupation, esp. the liquor trade or the book trade: customers: commodities, esp. for barter: a deal: rubbish (*dial.*): medicine: (in *pl.*) the trade-winds. — *v.i.* to tread, go (*obs.*): to

resort, esp. for commerce: to ply: to occupy oneself (*obs.*): to have dealings or intercourse: to engage in commerce: to deal: to traffic: to buy and sell: to reckon, count, presume (with *on*), esp. unscrupulously. — *v.t.* to tread (*obs.*): to exchange (esp. commercially), to barter: to buy and sell. — *adjs.* **trade'able, trad'able; trād'ed** (*Shak.*) versed, practised; **trade'ful** (*Spens.*) busy in traffic; **trade'less.** — *n.* **trād'er** one who trades: a trading ship. — *n.* and *adj.* **trād'ing.** — **trade board** a council representing employers and employees in a trade; **trade cycle** the recurring series of conditions in trade from prosperity to depression and back to prosperity; **trade discount** a discount offered to others in the same trade; **traded option** (*Stock exchange*) an option that can itself be bought and sold. — *adj.* **trade'-fallen** (**trade'-falne;** *Shak.*) unsuccessful in trade, bankrupt. — **trade gap** the amount by which a country's visible imports exceed its visible exports in value; **trade'-in** that which is given in part payment; **trade journal** a periodical containing information and comment on a particular trade; **trade'mark, trade mark** any name or distinctive device warranting goods for sale as the production of any individual or firm; **trade'name** a name serving as a trademark: a name in use in the trade; **trade'-off** the giving up of one thing in return for another, usu. as an act of compromise (also *v.* **trade off**); **trade plate** a temporary number plate attached to a vehicle by dealers, etc. prior to its being registered; **trade price** the price at which goods are sold to members of the same trade, or by wholesale to retail dealers; **trade route** a route followed by caravans or trading ships; **trade sale** an auction sale of goods by producers, etc., to persons in the trade; **trade secret** a secret and successful formula, process, technique, etc. known only to one manufacturer; **trades'-folk, -people** shopkeepers: mechanics: craftsmen: people employed in trade; **trades'man** a shopkeeper: a craftsman: a mechanic: — *fem.* **trades'woman.** — *adj.* **trades'manlike.** — **trade union** an organised association of workers of an industry for the protection of their common interests; **trade unionism; trade unionist; trades union** an association of trade unions, as the **Trades Union Congress (T.U.C.).** — *adj.* **trade'-weighted** (*econ.*) of exchange-rates, weighted according to the significance of the trade carried on with the various countries listed. — **trade wind** a wind blowing toward the thermal equator and deflected westward by the eastward rotation of the earth; **trading estate** an industrial estate; **trading post** a store, etc. established in an esp. remote, thinly-populated or hostile area; **trading stamp** a stamp given to a purchaser of goods who, when he has accumulated a specified number, may exchange them without payment for articles provided by the trading stamp firm. — **Board of Trade** a department of government for matters of industry and commerce; **trade down (up)** to deal in lower grade, cheaper (higher grade, dearer) goods; **trade in** to give in part payment; **trade off** see **trade-off** above. [Prob. L.G. *trade*; akin to **tread**.]

Tradescantia *trad-is-kan'shi-ə*, *n.* the spider-wort genus: (without *cap.*) any plant of this genus. [After the English gardener, naturalist, and traveller John *Tradescant* (*c.* 1567–1637).]

tradition *trə-dish'ən*, *n.* a handing over (*law*): oral transmission from generation to generation, esp. (often with *cap.*) of certain Christian, Judaic and Islamic doctrines and customs: a tale, belief or practice thus handed down: a long-established belief or custom: anything bound up with or continuing in the life of a family, community, etc.: the continuous development of a body of, e.g. literature, music. — *adjs.* **tradi'tional, tradi'tionary.** — *ns.* **tradi'tionalism; tradi'tionalist; traditional'ity.** — *advs.* **tradi'tionally, tradi'tionarily.** — *ns.* **tradi'tioner, tradi'tionist** one who adheres to tradition. — *adj.* **traditive** (*trad'i-tiv*) traditional. — *n.* **trad'itor** a traitor, betrayer (*obs.*): one who under persecution gave up sacred books or objects or the names of his fellows (*hist.*). — **traditional jazz** see **trad.** [L. *trāditiō, -ōnis, trāditor, -ōris* — *trādĕre*, to give up — *trāns*, over, *dăre*, to give.]

traduce *trə-dūs'*, in U.S. *-dōōs'*, *v.t.* to translate (*obs.*): to propagate or transmit (*obs.*): to calumniate: to defame. — *ns.* **traduce'ment; tradū'cer; Tradū'cian** (*-shi-ən*) one who believes that children receive soul as well as body from their parents through natural generation. — Also *adj.* — *ns.* **Tradū'cianism; Tradū'cianist.** — *n.* and *adj.* **tradū'cing.** — *adv.* **tradū'cingly.** — *n.* **traduction** (*-duk'-shən*). — *adj.* **traduc'tive** transmitted. [L. *trāducĕre, trāductum* — *trāns*, across, *dūcĕre*, to bring.]

traffic *traf'ik*, *n.* commerce, trade: immoral or illegal trading: dealing: a trading voyage (*obs.*): commodities (*obs.*): transportation of goods and persons on a railway, on an air route, etc.: vehicles, pedestrians, etc. (collectively), using a thoroughfare: a passing to and fro. — *v.i.* to trade: to trade immorally or illegally: to intrigue. — *v.t.* to trade in, or barter: to use, pass to and fro on (a highway, etc.): — *pr.p.* **traff'icking;** *pa.t.* and *pa.p.* **traff'icked.** — *ns.* **traff'icātor** formerly, a movable pointer by means of which the driver of a vehicle gave warning of a change of direction; **traff'-icker.** *n.* and *adj.* **traff'icking.** — *adj.* **traff'icless.** — **traffic circle** a road intersection where traffic circulates in one direction only, a roundabout (*U.S.* and *Can.*); **traffic island** a raised section in the centre of a road to separate lanes, guide traffic, etc.; **traffic jam** congestion, and resultant stoppage, of traffic, e.g. at a busy junction; **traff'ic-lights, -sig'nals** coloured lights to regulate street traffic at crossings; **traff'ic-man'ager** the manager of the traffic on a railway, etc.; **traff'ic-returns'** statistics of passengers and goods carried and money received in return; **traffic warden** an official controlling road traffic, esp. the parking of vehicles. [From a Romance language; cf. Fr. *trafic*, It. *traffico*, Sp. *tráfico*; origin obscure.]

tragacanth *trag'ə-kanth*, *n.* a gum (also **gum tragacanth**) got from several spiny shrubs of the genus Astragalus: the plant yielding it. [Gr. *tragakantha* — *tragos*, goat, *akantha*, thorn.]

tragedy *traj'i-di*, *n.* a species of drama in which the action and language are elevated, and the ending usually sad, esp. involving the fall of a great man: the art of such drama: any sad story or turn of events: anything with death or killing in it (*journalism*). — *ns.* **tragedian** (*trə-jē'di-ən*) a writer or (usually) an actor of tragedy; **tragedienne** (*trə-jē-di-en'*; Fr. **tragédienne** *trä-zhā-di-en'*) an actress of tragic rôles. — *adjs.* **tragic** (*traj'ik*), **-al** pertaining to, of the nature of, tragedy. — *adv.* **trag'ically.** — *n.* **trag'icalness.** — **trag'i-com'edy** a play (or story) in which grave and comic scenes or themes are blended: a comedy that threatens to be a tragedy. — *adjs.* **trag'i-com'ic, -al.** — *adv.* **trag'i-com'ically.** [L. *tragoedia* — Gr. *tragōidiā*, tragedy, app. lit. goat-song — *tragos*, a he-goat, *ōidē*, song (variously explained).]

tragelaph *trag'*, *traj'i-laf*, *n.* a fabulous animal, part goat, part stag: a harnessed antelope (**Tragelaphus** *-el'ə-fəs*). — *adj.* **tragel'aphine.** [Gr. *tragelaphos* — *tragos*, a goat, *elaphos*, a deer.]

tragi. See **tragus.**

tragic, etc. See **tragedy.**

tragopan *trag'ō-pan*, *n.* a brilliant Asiatic horned pheasant. [Gr. *tragopān*, hornbill — *tragos*, goat, *Pān*, the god Pan.]

tragus *trā'gəs*, *n.* a small prominence at the entrance of the external ear: any of the hairs growing in the outer ear, esp. from this part: — *pl.* **trā'gi** (*-jī*). — *n.* **tragule** (*trag'ūl*) a chevrotain. — *adj.* **trag'uline** (*-īn*). [Gr. *tragos*, goat, tragus.]

trahison *tra-ē-zɔ̄*, (Fr.) *n.* treason: treachery. — **trahison des clercs** (*dā kler*) the treason of intellectuals, the entry of academics into politics.

traik *trāk*, (*Scot.*) *v.i.* to go wearily or toilsomely: to stray: to get lost: to gad: to decline in health. — *n.* a loss, esp. of sheep: the mutton of sheep that have died of disease or accident. — *adj.* **traik'it** worn out. — **traik after** to dangle after. [**trek.**]

trail¹ *trāl*, *v.t.* to draw along or near the surface: to drag wearily: to drag along: to carry (as a weapon) with butt near the ground, or horizontally: to lead on: to quiz (*coll.*): to cover with a trailing ornament: to track, follow: to lag behind: to advertise (a forthcoming programme, etc.) by trailer: — *v.i.* to be drawn out in length: to hang, float, or drag loosely behind: to sprawl over the ground or a support: to straggle: to lag: to be losing in a game or competition: to move with slow sweeping motion or with dragging drapery: to drag oneself along. — *n.* anything drawn out in length or trailed: a train, tail: the track of a star on a stationary photographic plate: a track, as of game: a beaten path in the wilds: a path, route: part of a gun-carriage resting on the ground behind: an act or manner of trailing. — *n.* **trail'er** one who trails: a tracker: a creeping plant: an esp. two-wheeled conveyance, towed or dragged by a car, bicycle, or tractor: a house on wheels, a caravan (*U.S.*): a short film advertising a forthcoming entertainment on television or in the cinema: the blank piece of film at the end of a reel. — *v.t.* to advertise (a programme, etc.) by trailer. — **trail'-blazer** a pioneer: a person or thing that leads the way in anything. — *adj.* and *n.* **trail'-blazing.** — **trailing edge** the rear edge; **trail'-net** a drag-net. — **trail a pike** (*obs.*) to serve as a soldier; **trail away, off** esp. of a sound, to become fainter; **trail one's coat** (*Ir.*) to invite a quarrel. [Ety. doubtful; O.E. *træglian*, to pluck, pull, and O.Fr. *trailler*, to tow, perh. — L. *tragula*, sledge, drag-net, are possibilities.]

trail² *trāl*, *n.* an aphetic form of **entrail.**

train¹ *trān*, *v.t.* to draw along (*arch.*): to allure (*obs.*): to draw on (*obs.*): to instruct and discipline: to cause to grow in the desired manner: to prepare for performance by instruction, practice, diet, exercise, or otherwise: to bring up: to direct, aim (as a gun or telescope). — *v.i.* (*Spens.* **trayne**) to trail, drag (*rare*): to prepare oneself by instruction, exercise, diet, or otherwise: to be under drill: to travel by rail. — *n.* that which is dragged along or follows: a tail: tail-feathers or trailing back-feathers: the part of a dress that trails: a retinue: a series: a sequence: a number of things in a string, as animals, railway carriages or wagons: a process: a line of combustible material to fire a charge: a set of wheels acting on each other, for transmitting motion: artillery and other equipment for a siege or battle: a lure: a thing dragged on the ground to make a scent: a sledge (*Canada*). — *adj.* **train'able.** — *adj.* **trained** having received training: having a train. — *ns.* **trainee'** one who is under training; **trainee'ship** the period of being a trainee: the position of, or maintenance provided for, a trainee; **train'er** one who prepares men for athletic feats, horses for a race, or the like: any machine or device used in training, esp. an aeroplane with duplicated controls for training pilots: a canvas, etc. shoe, usu. laced, with a thick rubber, etc. sole, for for exercising in; **train'ing** practical education in any profession, art, or handicraft: a course of diet and exercise for developing physical strength, endurance, or dexterity. — **train'-band** (*hist.*) a band of citizens trained to bear arms; **train'-bearer** one who holds up a train, as of a robe, or gown; **train ferry** a ferry that conveys railway trains; **train'ing-college** former name for a college of education; **train'ing-ship** a ship in which boys are trained for the sea; **train mile** a unit of railway traffic, a run of one mile by one train; **train'-spotter** one who collects locomotive numbers as a hobby; **train'-spotting.** — **in train** in progress; **in training** undergoing training: physically fit; **train fine** to bring body or mind to a high pitch of efficiency. [Mainly O.Fr. *traïner, trahiner* (Fr. *traîner*), to drag (nouns *train, traïne*); partly with overlap of meanings, from O.Fr. *traïne*, guile.]

train² *trān*, *n.* (usu. **train'-oil'**) whale-oil extracted from the blubber by boiling. [Du. *traen* (now *traan*), tear, exudation.]

traipse, trapes *trāps, v.i.* to trail: to trudge: to gad: to go in a slatternly way. — *n.* a slattern: a trudge. — *n.* and *adj.* **traips'ing, trapes'ing.** — *v.i.* **trape** to traipse. [Origin unknown.]

trait *trā,* or *trāt, n.* a stroke, touch: a characteristic. [Fr., — L. *trahĕre, tractum,* to draw.]

traitor *trā'tər, n.* a betrayer: one who commits treason (*fem.* **trait'ress**). — Also *adj.* — *ns.* **trai'torhood, trait'-orism, trai'torship.** — *adjs.* **trait'orly** (*Shak.*); **trait'-orous.** — *adv.* **trait'orously.** — *n.* **trait'orousness.** [Fr. *traître* — L. *trāditor* — *trādĕre,* to give up.]

traject *trə-jekt', v.t.* to take across (*obs.*): to transmit. — *n.* (*traj'ikt*) a crossing: a ferry: a transference, transmission (*rare*). — *ns.* **trajec'tion** (*-shən*) a passage (*obs.*): a crossing: a transmission: a transposition; **trajectory** (*traj'ik-tər-i,* or *trə-jekt'ər-i*) the curve described by a body under the action of given forces. [L. *trājicĕre, -jectum* — *trāns,* across, *jacĕre,* to throw.]

tralaticious, tralatitious *tral-ə-tish'əs, adj.* transmitted: traditional: handed on, second-hand. [L. *trālātīcius* — *trānslātum,* serving as supine to *trānsferre;* see **transfer.**]

tram[1] *tram, n.* a barrow or car shaft: a vehicle for minerals in mines: a tramway: a tramway-car. — Also *adj.* — **tram'-car** a tramway-car; **tram'-conductor; tram'-line** a line of tramway: (in *pl.*) the lines marking the sides of a tennis or badminton court and the lines parallel to them inside the court; **tram'-road** a track with sunken rails (legally one not running along a road); **tram'-stop** a stopping-place for tram-cars; **tram'way** a track or system of tracks with sunken rails along a road; **tram'way-car** a carriage for conveying passengers on a tramway. [Cf. L.G. *traam,* beam, shaft, etc.]

tram[2] *tram, n.* silk yarn for weft, of two or more strands. [Fr. *trame* — L. *trāma,* weft.]

tram[3] *tram.* See **trammel.**

trammel *tram'l, n.* a net whose inner fine-meshed layer is carried through by the fish through the coarse-meshed outer layer, and encloses it in a pocket: a fowling net: a hobble: shackles for making a horse amble: anything that confines: an instrument for describing an ellipse (also **tram**): a contrivance for adjusting a hook in a fireplace: (in *pl.*) a tress. — *v.t.* to confine: to impede: to entangle: — *pr.p.* **tramm'elling;** *pa.t.* and *pa.p.* **tramm'elled.** — *n.* **tramm'eller.** — **tramm'el-net'** a trammel. [O.Fr. *tramail,* a net — L.L. *tramacula,* from L. *trēs,* three, *macula,* a mesh.]

tramontane *tra-mon'tān, adj.* beyond the mountains (the Alps from Rome): foreign: uncivilised. — *n.* a dweller beyond the mountains: a foreigner: a barbarian. — *n.* **tramontana** (*trä-mon-tä'na*) in Italy, a north wind. [It. *tramontana* — L. *trāns,* beyond, *mōns, montis,* a mountain.]

tramp *tramp, v.i.* to tread, esp. heavily or noisily: to walk: to go on a walking tour or long walk: to go about as a vagrant: to go in a tramp steamer. — *v.t.* to traverse on foot: to trample: to tread in a tub in washing clothes (*Scot.*). — *n.* a foot-journey: the sound of heavy footsteps: a vagrant: a plate of iron worn on the sole for pressing a spade or for giving a foothold on ice: the footrest of a spade: a cargo-boat with no fixed route (also **tramp steamer**): a prostitute, an immoral woman (*slang*). — *adv.* with tramping noise. — *n.* **tramp'er.** [M.E. *trampen;* cf. Ger. *trampen.*]

trampet, trampette *tram-pet', n.* a small trampoline used for springing off, in gymnastic vaulting. [Dim. of **trampoline.**]

trample *tramp'l, v.t.* to tread roughly under foot: to treat with pride, to insult. — *v.i.* to tread roughly or in contempt: to tread forcibly and rapidly. — *n.* a trampling. — *ns.* **tramp'ler; tramp'ling.** — Also *adj.* [Freq. of **tramp.**]

trampolin(e) *tram'pə-lin, -lēn, ns.* a framework holding a piece of canvas, stretched and attached by springs, for

acrobats, gymnasts, diving learners, etc., to jump, somersault, etc. on. — *n.* **tram'polinist.** [It. *trampolino,* springboard.]

tran-. See **trans-.**

trance[1] *träns, n.* a dazed, abstracted, ecstatic or exalted state: a deep sleeplike state, profound and prolonged: catalepsy. — *v.t.* to throw into a trance: to entrance. — *adv.* **tranced** (*tränst, trän'sid*) in a trance. — *adv.* **tranc'edly.** [Fr. *transe* — *transir* — L. *trānsīre,* to go across, in L.L. to die.]

trance[2], transe *träns, (Scot.) n.* a through passage.

tranche *träsh, n.* a slice: a block, portion, esp. of an issue of shares. [Fr., slice — *trancher,* to cut]

tranchet *trā'shä, n.* a shoemaker's paring knife: a neolithic or mesolithic flint with a chisel-shaped end (*archaeol.*). [Fr., — *trancher,* to cut.]

tranect *tran'ekt, (Shak.) n.* a ferry. [As if L. *trāns,* across, *nectĕre,* to join; but supposed to be a misprint for **traject.**]

trangam *trang'gəm, n.* a trumpery gimcrack. [Origin unknown.]

trangle *trang'gl, (her.) n.* a diminutive of the fesse. [Obs. Fr.]

trankum *trang'kəm, (Scott) n.* a trinket. [**trinket.**]

trannie, tranny. See **transistor.**

tranquil *trangk'wil, adj.* calm: peaceful. — *n.* **tranquillīsā'-tion, -z-.** — *v.t.* **tranq'uillise, -ize** to make tranquil. — *n.* **tranquilli'ser, -z-** that which tranquillises: a sedative drug. — *adv.* **tranquilli'singly, -z-.** — *n.* **tranquill'ity.** — *adv.* **tran'quilly.** [L. *tranquillus.*]

trans- *tranz-, tränz-, trənz-, trans-, träns-, trəns-, pfx.* across, beyond, through. — Also **tran-, tra-.** [L. *trāns,* across, beyond.]

transact *tranz-akt', tränz-, trənz-, -s-, v.t.* to conduct, negotiate: to perform: to deal with (*arch.*). — *v.i.* to negotiate: to have to do. — *ns.* **transac'tion** the act of transacting: an agreement: a piece of business performed: (*pl.*) the reports or publications of certain learned societies; **transac'tor.** — **transactional analysis** (*psych.*) a form of psychotherapy based on the concept of three 'ego-states' — child, adult and parent — in any one personality, and aimed at adjusting the balance between them, esp. so as to improve the patient's interpersonal relations. [L. *trānsactum,* pa.p. of *trānsigĕre* — *agĕre,* to carry on.]

transalpine *tranz-al'pīn, tränz-, adj.* beyond the *Alps* (orig. from Rome): crossing the Alps. [L. *trānsalpīnus* — *Alpae,* Alps.]

transandine *tranz-an'dīn, tränz-, trənz-, adj.* beyond, or crossing, the *Andes.* — Also **transandē'an** (or *-an'di-ən*). [Pfx. **trans-.**]

transatlantic *tranz-ət-lan'tik, tränz-, adj.* beyond the *Atlantic* Ocean: crossing the Atlantic. [Pfx. **trans-.**]

transaxle *tranz'ak-səl, (engineering) n.* in a motor vehicle, a driving axle and differential gear-box forming an integral unit. [*transmission axle.*]

transcalent *tranz-kā'lənt, tränz-, adj.* pervious to, allowing the passage of, heat. [Pfx. **trans-,** L. *calēns, -entis* — *calēre,* to be hot.]

transcaucasian *tranz-kö-kā'zhən, tränz-, adj.* across or beyond the *Caucasus* mountains in south-west U.S.S.R.: (with *cap.;* also *n.*) of or relating to the region or the people of *Transcaucasia,* south of the Caucasus mountains. [Pfx. **trans-.**]

transceiver *tran-sē'vər, trän-, n.* a piece of radio equipment (e.g. a walkie-talkie) whose circuitry permits both transmission and reception. [*trans*mitter and re*ceiver.*]

transcend *tran-send', trän-, v.t.* to rise above: to surmount: to surpass: to exceed: to pass or lie beyond the limit of. — *ns.* **transcend'ence, transcend'ency.** — *adjs.* **transcend'ent** transcending: superior or supreme in excellence: surpassing others: as applicable to *being,* relating to the absolute, transcending all limitation — as applicable to *knowledge,* pertaining to what transcends experience, being given *a priori:* beyond human knowledge: abstrusely speculative, fantastic; **transcen-**

den'tal transcending: supereminent, surpassing others: concerned with what is independent of experience: vague: of a function, not capable of being produced or expressed algebraically. — *v.t.* **transcenden'talise, -ize.** — *ns.* **transcenden'talism** the investigation of what is *a priori* in human knowledge, or independent of experience: that which is vague and illusive in philosophy: the American reaction against Puritan prejudices, humdrum orthodoxy, old-fashioned metaphysics, materialistic philistinism, and materialism — best associated with the name of R. W. Emerson (1803–82); **transcenden'talist.** — *advs.* **transcenden'tally; transcend'ently.** — *n.* **transcend'entness.** — **transcendental meditation** a system of meditation designed to promote spiritual well-being and a relaxed state of consciousness through silent repetition of a mantra. [L. *trānscendĕre* — *scandĕre*, to climb.]

transcontinental *tranz-kont-i-nent'l, tränz-, adj.* extending or passing across, or belonging to the farther side of, a *continent.* [Pfx. **trans-.**]

transcribe *tran-skrīb', trän-, v.t.* to write over from one book into another: to copy: to transliterate: to arrange (a composition) for an instrument, voice, or combination other than that for which it was composed (*mus.*): to record for future broadcasting or the like: to broadcast a transcription of: to transfer (information) from one type of storage system to another (*comput.*): to cause to undergo transcription (q.v.) (*genetics*). — *ns.* **transcrīb'er; transcript** (*tran'skript, trän'*) a written or printed copy, esp. a legal or official copy of (sometimes secret) proceedings, testimony, etc.: a length of RNA transcribed from a DNA template, or of DNA transcribed from a RNA template (*genetics, biochemistry*); **transcrip'tion** the act or result of transcribing: the natural process by which a molecule of RNA is synthesised on the model of a DNA template carrying the necessary genetic information (*genetics*). — *adjs.* **transcrip'tional; transcrip'tive.** — *adv.* **transcrip'tively.** [L. *trānscrībĕre, -scrīptum.*]

transcriptase *tran-skrip'tāz, trän-,* (*genetics*) *n.* the enzyme that brings about transcription (q.v.) (see also **reverse transcriptase** under **reverse**). [*transcription* and *-ase.*]

transducer *trans-dū'sər, träns-, -z-,* in U.S. *-dōōs', n.* a device that transfers power from one system to another in the same or in different form. — *ns.* **transduc'tion** transfer, esp. transfer of genetic material from one bacterial cell to another by bacteriophage; **transduc'tor** an arrangement of windings on a laminated core or cores, part of a device for amplifying current. [L. *trānsdūcĕre, -ductum,* to lead across.]

transe. Same as **trance²**.

transect *tran'sekt, trän', n.* a sample belt of vegetation marked off for study. — Also *v.t.* [**tran(s)-, sect²**.]

transenna *tran-sen'ə, n.* a screen enclosing a shrine. [L. *trānsenna.*]

transept *tran'sept, trän-, n.* part of a church at right angles to the nave, or of another building to the body: either wing of such a part where it runs right across. — *adjs.* **transept'al** of a transept; **transept'ate** divided by transverse septa. [L. *saeptum* (used in pl.) fence, enclosure.]

transfard *trans-färd', (Spens.)* transferred (*pa.t.*).

transfection *trans-fek'shən, träns-, (microbiol.) n.* the introduction of DNA isolated from a cell or virus into another cell. — *v.t.* **transfect'** to cause transfection in (a cell). [*transfer* and in*fection*.]

transfer *trans-fûr', träns-, v.t.* to carry or bring over: to convey from one place, person, ownership, object, group, football club, etc., to another: to change over: to convey (as a design) to another surface. — *v.i.* to change over, esp. (*U.S.*) from one railway, train, or station, to another: — *pr.p.* **transferr'ing;** *pa.t.* and *pa.p.* **transferred'.** — *ns.* **trans'fer** the act of transferring: conveyance from one person, place, etc., to another: that which is transferred or is to be transferred (as a picture): a transfer-ticket; **transferabil'ity** (also

transferrabil'ity, transferribil'ity). — *adj.* **trans'ferable** (also **transfer'able, transferr'able, transferr'ible** (*-fûr'*)). — *ns.* **transferee'** the person to whom a thing is transferred: one who is transferred; **trans'ference** the act of transferring or conveying: passage from place to place: unconscious transferring of one's hopes, desires, fears, etc., from one person or object to another (*psych.*); **trans'feror** (*law*), **transferr'er** (*general*), one who transfers. — **transferable vote** a vote which, if the candidate voted for should be out of the running, is to be transferred to another as second (third, etc.) choice; **trans'fer-book** a register of the transfer of property, shares, etc.; **trans'fer-day** a day for registering transfer of bank-stock and government funds at the Bank of England; **transfer list** a list of footballers available for transfer to another club; **trans'fer-paper** a prepared paper used for transferring impressions with copying-presses, etc.; **trans'fer-ticket** a ticket for a journey to be resumed on another route. [L. *trānsferre* — *ferre*, to carry.]

transferrin *trans-fer'in, träns-,* (*biochemistry*) *n.* a protein in the blood that transports iron. [Pfx. **trans-** and L. *ferrum,* iron.]

transfigure *trans-fig'ər, träns-, v.t.* to change the appearance of: to glorify. — *ns.* **transfiguration** (*-ə-* or *-ū-rā'-shən*) a transformation or glorification in appearance: (with *cap.*) the Christian festival of the transfiguration of Christ (Matt. xvii. 2), celebrated on the 6th of August; **transfig'urement.** [L. *trānsfigūrāre — figūra,* form.]

transfinite *trans-fī'nīt, träns-, adj.* surpassing what is finite: (of a cardinal or ordinal number) surpassing all finite numbers (*math.*). [Pfx. **trans-.**]

transfix *trans-fiks', träns-, v.t.* to pierce through: to paralyse with sudden emotion. — *n.* **transfixion** (*-fik'-shən*). [L. *trānsfigĕre, -fīxum — fīgĕre,* to fix.]

transform *trans-förm', träns-, v.t.* to change the shape of: to change to another form, appearance, substance, character: to change the form of (an algebraic expression or geometrical figure). — *v.i.* to be changed in form or substance.— *n.* (*träns'*) an expression or figure derived from another (*math.*): any of a group of linguistic constructions related in some way through the application of transformational rules: in digital computers, a process that alters the form of information without changing its meaning. — *adj.* **transform'able.** — *ns.* **transformā'tion** change of form, constitution, or substance: metamorphosis: transmutation: a transformed person (*Shak.*): false hair: (in full **transformation scene**) a scene on the stage that changes in presence of the audience or in which the characters of the pantomime were transformed into those of the harlequinade: change from one linguistic transform to another of the group: (also **transformational rule**) any of a number of grammatical rules converting the deep structure of a sentence into its surface structure (*linguistics*): reflection, rotation, translation, or dilatation (*geom.*). — *adjs.* **transformā'tional; transform'ative; transformed'.** — *n.* **transform'er** one who, that which, transforms: an apparatus for obtaining an electric current from another of a different voltage. — *n.* and *adj.* **transform'ing.** — *ns.* **transform'ism** the theory of mutability of species; **transform'ist.** — *adj.* **transformis'tic.** — **transformational grammar** a method of studying or describing a language by stating which elements or structures can be derived from or related to others by transformation: a grammatical description which includes transformational rules. — **conformal transformation** a change of shape which still preserves a one-to-one matching of points in the original surface with points in the new surface, as in map making. [L. *trānsförmāre — förma,* form.]

transfuse *trans-fūz', träns-, v.t.* to pour out into another vessel: to transfer to another's veins: to treat by transfusion: to cause to pass, enter, or diffuse through: to imbue: to instil: to cause to be imbibed. — *n.* **transfū'ser.** — *adj.* **transfū'sible.** — *ns.* **transfū'sion**

(-*zhən*) transfusing, esp. of blood; **transfū'sionist.** — *adj.* **transfū'sive** (-*siv*) tending or having power to transfuse. — *adv.* **transfū'sively.** [L. *trānsfundĕre* — *fundĕre, fūsum*, to pour.]

transgress *trans-gres'*, *träns-*, *-z-*, *v.t.* to pass beyond the limit of or set by: to overstep, exceed: to infringe. — *v.i.* to offend by violating a law: to sin. — *n.* **transgression** (-*gresh'ən*) an overstepping: an infringement: sin. — *adjs.* **transgress'ional; transgressive** (-*grəs'iv*). — *adv.* **transgress'ively.** — *n.* **transgress'or.** [L. *trānsgredī, -gressum — gradī, gressum*, to step.]

tranship, transship *tran(s)-ship'*, *trän(s)-*, *trən-* *v.t.* to transfer from one ship or other conveyance to another. — *v.i.* to change ship, etc. — *ns.* **tran(s)ship'ment; tran(s)shipp'er; tran(s)shipp'ing.** [Pfx. **tran(s)-.**]

transhume *trans-(h)ūm'*, *träns-*, *-z-*, *v.t.* and *v.i.* to transfer or pass from summer to winter or from winter to summer pastures. — *n.* **transhu'mance.** — *adj.* **transhu'-mant.** [Sp. *trashumar* — L. *trāns, humus*, ground.]

transience, transiency. See **transient.**

transient *tran'zi-ənt*, *trän'*, *-si-*, *adj.* passing: of short duration: making, or for persons making, only a short stay: passing (*mus.*). — *n.* a temporary resident, worker, etc.: a brief alteration in a wave-form, etc., as a sudden surge of voltage or current (*phys.*). — *ns.* **tran'sience, tran'siency.** — *adv.* **tran'siently.** — *n.* **tran'-sientness.** [L. *trānsiēns, -euntis* — pr.p. of *trānsīre*, to cross — *īre, itum*, to go.]

transilient *tran-sil'i-ənt*, *trän-*, *trən-*, *adj.* leaping or passing across. — *n.* **transil'iency.** [L. *trānsilīre — salīre*, to leap.]

transilluminate *tranz-i-lū'mi-nāt*, *tränz-*, *-s-*, *-loo'*, *v.t.* to throw a strong light through. — *n.* **transilluminā'tion.** [Pfx. **trans-.**]

transire *tranz-ī'ri*, *tränz-*, *-s-*, (L. *träns-ē're*), *n.* customs warrant for clearing. [L. *trānsīre*; cf. **transient.**]

transisthmian *tranz-is(th)'mi-ən*, *tränz-*, *-s-*, *adj.* across an isthmus. [Pfx. **trans-.**]

transistor *tranz-ist'ər*, *tränz-*, *-s-*, *n.* an amplifier with crystal and two cat's whiskers: a later development of this, a three-electrode semiconductor device, able to perform many functions of multi-electrode valves. — *n.* **transistorisā'tion, -z-.** — *v.t.* **transistorise, -ize** to fit with a transistor. — **transistor (radio)** a small portable radio (*slang* shortenings **trann'ie, trann'y**). [*transfer* and re*sistor*.]

transit *tran'zit*, *trän'*, *-sit*, *n.* the conveyance or passage of things or people over, across, or through: passenger transport (esp. *U.S.*): the passage of a heavenly body over the meridian: the passage of a smaller body over the disc of a greater: a transit-circle, -instrument, or -theodolite. — *v.i.* to pass across. — *v.t.* to pass across: to reverse. — *n.* **transition** (-*sizh'ən*, *-zish'ən*, *sish'ən*) passage from one place, state, stage, style or subject to another: a change of key, esp. an abrupt one not using modulation (*mus.*): in archit, esp. the passage from Romanesque or Norman to Gothic. — *adj.* transitional. — *adjs.* **transi'tional, transi'tionary.** — *adv.* **transi'tionally.** — *adj.* **trans'itive** passing over: having the power of passing: taking a direct object (*gram.*). — *adv.* **trans'itively.** — *n.* **trans'itiveness.** — *adv.* **trans'itorily.** — *n.* **trans'itoriness.** — *adj.* **trans'-itory** going or passing away: lasting or appearing for a short time: speedily vanishing. — **transit camp** a camp where e.g. refugees, immigrants, soldiers, etc. are temporarily accommodated before travelling on to a further destination; **tran'sit-circle** a transit-instrument with a graduated circle for declinations; **tran'sit-duty** a duty chargeable on goods passing through a country; **tran'sit-instrument** a telescope mounted in the meridian and turned on a fixed east and west axis; **transit lounge** a lounge for transit passengers at an airport; **transit passenger** a passenger stopping briefly at an airport between flights; **tran'sit-theodolite** one whose telescope can be reversed; **tran'sit-trade** the trade of carrying foreign goods through a country. — **in transit** of goods, etc., in the process of being transported from

one place to another. [L. *trānsitus, -ūs, trānsitiō, -ōnis — īre, itum*, to go.]

translate *trans-lāt'*, *träns-*, *trəns-*, *-z-*, *v.t.* to remove to another place: to remove to heaven, especially without death: to enrapture: to render into another language: to express in another artistic medium: to interpret, put in plainer terms, explain: to transfer from one office (esp. ecclesiastical) to another: to transform: to renovate, make new from old: to perform a translation on (*mech., math.*): to interpret genetic information stored in (RNA) in the synthesis of a protein or polypeptide (*biol.*). — *v.i.* to practise translation: to admit of translation. — *adj.* **translā'table.** — *n.* **translā'tion** the act of translating: removal to another place, see, etc.: rendering into another language: a version: the working up of new things from old materials: motion, change of place, such that every point moves in the same direction at the same speed: similar change of place of a geometrical figure: an algebraic function obtained by adding the same constant to each value of the variable in a given function, thus moving the graph of this function (or moving the rectangular axes parallel to themselves) while preserving its shape: the automatic retransmission of a telegraphic message: the process by which genetic information stored in RNA causes a protein or polypeptide to be synthesised to a particular pattern (*biol.*). — *adjs.* **translā'tional; translā'tive** (*gram.*) denoting, as in Finnish, 'turning into'. — *n.* the translative case. — *n.* **translā'tor.** — *adj.* **trans'latory** (also *-lā'*) of, relating to, direct onward motion without rotation. [L. *trānslātum*, used as supine of *trānsferre*; see **transfer.**]

transleithan *tranz-lī't(h)ən*, *tränz-*, *-s-*, *adj.* beyond the river *Leitha*, once in part the boundary between Austria and Hungary: Hungarian. [Pfx. **trans-.**]

transliterate *tranz-lit'ə-rāt*, *tränz-*, *-s-*, *v.t.* to write in letters of another alphabet, etc. — *ns.* **transliterā'tion; translit'erātor.** [L. *littera*, letter.]

translocation *tranz-lō-kā'shən*, *tränz-*, *-s-*, *n.* transference from place to place, esp. of materials within the body of a plant: the transfer of a portion of a chromosome to another part of the same chromosome or to a different chromosome (*genetics*). — *v.t.* **translocate'.** [L. *locus*, place.]

translucent *tranz-loo'sənt*, *tränz-*, *-s-*, *-lū'*, *adj.* shining through: imperfectly transparent: clear. — *ns.* **translu'cence, translu'cency.** — *adv.* **translu'cently.** — *adj.* **translu'cid** translucent. — *n.* **translucid'ity.** [L. *tränslūcēns, -entis — lūcēre*, to shine — *lūx, lūcis*, light.]

translunar *tranz-loo'nər*, *tränz-*, *-s-*, *adj.* pertaining to the region beyond the moon's orbit round the earth. — *adj.* **translun'ary** (or *tranz'*) beyond the moon: visionary. [Pfx. **trans-.**]

transmarine *tranz-mə-rēn'*, *tränz-*, *-s-*, *adj.* across or beyond the sea. [L. *trānsmarīnus — mare*, sea.]

transmew *tranz-mū'*, *tränz-*, *-s-*, (*Spens.*) *v.t.* to transmute. [O.Fr. *transmuer* — L. *transmūtāre*; see **transmute.**]

transmigrate *tranz'mī-grāt*, *tränz'*, *-s-*, *-grāt'*, *v.i.* to remove to another place of abode: of the soul, to pass into another body. — *v.t.* to cause to transmigrate. — *n.* **trans'migrant** (or *-mī'*) one who transmigrates: an alien entering a country on his way to another in which he means to settle. — *adj.* transmigrating. — *ns.* **transmigrā'tion; transmigrā'tionism** belief in the transmigration of souls; **transmigrā'tionist.** — *adj.* **trans'migrātive** (or *-mī'grə-tiv*). — *n.* **trans'migrātor.** — *adj.* **transmī'gratory** (-*grə-tər-i*). [L. *trānsmigrāre, -ātum — migrāre*, to migrate.]

transmissible, transmission, etc. See **transmit.**

transmit *tranz-mit'*, *tränz-*, *-s-*, *v.t.* to send on: to pass on: to hand on: to communicate: to give to posterity: to send out or broadcast (radio signals, programmes, etc.): to transfer (e.g. power from one part of a machine to another): to allow the passage of, act as a medium for (heat, energy, light, sound, etc.) — *v.i.* to send out a radio signal, etc.: — *pr.p.* **transmitt'ing;** *pa.t.* and *pa.p.* **transmitt'ed.** — *n.* **transmissibil'ity.** — *adj.* **trans-**

miss'ible (also **transmitt'able**, less correctly **-ible.**). — *n.* **transmission** (-*mish'ən*) the process of transmitting or being transmitted: that which is transmitted: a programme, message, etc. sent out by radio, etc.: the system of interdependent parts in a motor vehicle, by which power is transferred from the engine to the wheels. — *adjs.* **transmiss'ional; transmiss'ive** having the quality of transmitting or of being transmitted. — *ns.* **transmissiv'ity; transmitt'al; transmitt'er** one who or that which transmits: apparatus for sending forth anything, as signals, messages, etc. [L. *trānsmittĕre, -missum* — *mittĕre, missum,* to send.]

transmogrify *tranz-mog'ri-fī, tränz-, -s-, (coll., facet.) v.t.* to transform, transmute: — *pr.p.* **transmog'rifying;** *pa.t.* and *pa.p.* **transmog'rified.** — *n.* **transmogrificā'- tion.** [A grotesque concoction.]

transmontane *tranz-mon'tān, tränz-, -s-, adj.* another form of **tramontane.**

transmove *tranz-mōōv', tränz-, -s-, (Spens.) v.t.* to transmute. [App. for **transmew,** remodelled on **move.**]

transmundane *tranz-mun'dān, tränz-, adj.* not belonging to this world, out of, beyond, this world. [L.L. *transmundanus* – *mundus,* world.]

transmute *tranz-mūt', tränz-, -s-, v.t.* to change to another form or substance. — *n.* **transmūtabil'ity.** — *adj.* **transmū'table.** — *n.* **transmū'tableness.** — *adv.* **transmū'tably.** — *ns.* **transmūtā'tion** a changing into a different form, nature, or substance, esp. that of one chemical element into another; **transmūtā'tionist.** — *adj.* **transmū'tative** serving or tending to transmute. — *n.* **transmū'ter.** [L. *trānsmūtāre*—*mūtāre,* to change.]

transnational *tranz-nash'nəl, tränz-, -s-, adj.* transcending national boundaries, concerning more than one nation. [Pfx. **trans-.**]

transoceanic *tranz-ō-shi-an'ik, tränz-, -s-, adj.* across or crossing the ocean. [Pfx. **trans-.**]

transom *tran'səm, n.* a cross-piece: a cross-beam: a structure dividing a window horizontally: a lintel: a small window over the lintel of a door or window. [O.Fr. *traversin,* — *traverse,* cross-piece.]

transonic(s). Common spelling of **trans-sonic(s).**

transpacific *trans-pə-sif'ik, tränz-, adj.* crossing the Pacific: beyond the Pacific. [Pfx. **trans-.**]

transpadane *trans'pə-dān, träns'-, -z-, -pā'dān, adj.* beyond the Po (from Rome). [L. *Padus,* the Po.]

transparent *trans-pār'ənt, träns-, trəns-, -z-, -par', adj.* able to be seen through: pellucid: pervious to rays: shining through (*Shak.*): easily detected, understood: obvious, evident: ingenuous. — *ns.* **transpar'ence** (*rare*), **transpar'ency** the quality of being transparent: that which is transparent: a picture, photograph, design, device visible, or to be viewed, by transmitted light: Thackeray's humorous translation of the German title *Durchlaucht.* — *adv.* **transpar'ently.** — *n.* **transpar'entness.** [L.L. *trānspārēns, -entis* — L. *pārēre,* to appear.]

transpersonal *trans-pûr'sə-nəl, träns- adj.* going beyond, transcending, the individual personality: denoting a form of psychology or psychotherapy that utilises mystical, psychical or spiritual experience as a means of increasing human potential. [Pfx. **trans-.**]

transpicuous *tran-spik'ū-əs, trän-, trən-, (Milt.) adj.* transparent. [L. *trānspicĕre,* to see through — *specĕre,* to look.]

transpierce *trans-pērs', träns-, v.t.* to pierce through: to permeate. [Pfx. **trans-.**]

transpire *tran-spīr', trän-, v.t.* to give off as vapour: to exhale: to emit through the skin. — *v.i.* to exhale: to give off water-vapour (as plants) or waste material through the skin (as animals): to become known, come to light: (*loosely*) to happen. — *adj.* **transpir'able.** — *n.* **transpiration** (*tran-spi-rā'shən*) the act or process of transpiring: exhalation through the skin: emission of water vapour through the stomata, etc. — *adj.* **transpīr'atory.** [L. *spīrāre,* to breathe.]

transplant *trans-plänt', träns-, -z-, v.t.* to remove (a plant) from the ground where it grows and plant in another place: to graft upon another animal or another part of the same: to remove and establish elsewhere. — *v.i.* to bear transplanting. — *n.* **trans'plant** a part or organ removed from its normal position and grafted into another position in the same individual or into another individual: the act of transplanting. — *adj.* **trans'plan'table.** — *ns.* **transplantā'tion; transplan'ter; transplan'ting.** [L. *trānsplantāre* — *plantāre,* to plant.]

transponder *tranz-pon'dər, tränz-, -s-, n.* a radio or radar device which, on receiving a signal, transmits a signal of its own. [*transmitter responder.*]

transpontine *trans-pon'tīn, träns-, -z-, adj.* across a bridge: on the Surrey side of the Thames, hence, from the type of theatrical productions there in the 19th century, melodramatic (*old*). [L. *pōns, pontis,* a bridge.]

transport *trans-pōrt', -pört', träns-, -z-, v.t.* to carry, convey, remove: to send overseas, as a convict: to translate (as a minister): to put to death (*Shak.*): perh., to carry off (as by the fairies) (*Shak.*): to carry away by strong emotion: to throw into an ecstasy. — *ns.* **trans'port** carriage, conveyance, of goods or people from one place to another: the management of, arrangements for, such conveyance: means of conveyance for getting from place to place: the conveyance of troops and their necessaries: a ship, wagon, etc., for this purpose: ecstasy: one who has been transported or sentenced to transportation; **transportabil'ity.** — *adj.* **transport'able** that may be transported: liable, or rendering liable, to transportation. — *ns.* **transport'al; transport'ance** (*Shak.*) conveyance, transport; **transportā'tion** removal: removal of offenders beyond seas: conveyance of goods or people: means of transport: tickets or passes for transport. — *adj.* **transport'ed.** — *adv.* **transport'edly.** — *ns.* **transport'edness; transport'er** someone or something that transports, esp. a large vehicle for carrying heavy goods. — *n.* and *adj.* **transport'ing.** — *adv.* **transport'ingly.** — *adj.* **transport'ive** tending or having power to transport. — **transport café** a roadside café catering mainly for long-distance lorry drivers; **transporter bridge** a bridge with a travelling carriage suspended from a girder; **trans'port= rider** (*S.Afr.*) a carrier by wagon; **trans'port-ship** a ship used for carrying troops, stores, etc. [L. *trānsportāre* — *portāre,* to carry.]

transpose *trans-pōz', träns-, -z-, v.t.* to transform (*Shak.*): to transfer: to turn, alter: to change the order of, interchange: to write, perform, or render in another key (*mus.*). — *adj.* **transpōs'able.** — *ns.* **transpōs'al** a change of place or order; **transpōs'er.** — *n.* and *adj.* **transpōs'ing.** — *n.* **transposition** (-*pō-, -pə-zish'ən*). — *adjs.* **transposi'tional; transpositive** (-*poz'*). — **transposing instrument** an instrument that by a mechanical device transposes music into another key: one for which music is written in a different key from the actual sounds. [Fr. *transposer;* see **pose.**]

transputer *trans-pū'tər, träns-, (comput.) n.* a chip capable of all the functions of a microprocessor, including memory, and able to process in parallel rather than sequentially. [*transistor* and *computer.*]

transsexual, trans-sexual *trans-seks'ū-əl, träns-, n.* a person anatomically of one sex and apparently normal physically, but having an abnormally strong desire to belong to the opposite sex: one who has had medical and surgical treatment to alter the external sexual features so that they resemble those of the opposite sex. — Also *adj.* — *n.* **transsex'ualism.** [Pfx. **trans-.**]

trans-shape *trans-shāp', träns-, (Shak.) v.t.* to transform.

trans-ship, transship. Same as **tranship.**

trans-sonic *trans-son'ik, träns-, adj.* relating to the range of speeds close to, or equalling, that of sound. — Often **transonic** (*tran-, trän-son'ik*). — *n.sing.* **trans(-s)on'ics** the study of such speeds. [L. *sonus,* sound.]

transubstantiate *tran-səb-stan'shi-āt, trän-, -zəb-, v.t.* to change to another substance. — *ns.* **transubstantiā'tion** a change into another substance: the doctrine that, in the consecration of the elements of the eucharist, the whole substance of the bread and wine is converted into Christ's body and blood, only the appearances of bread and wine remaining (cf. **consubstantiation**); **transubstantiā′tion(al)ist, transubstan′tiātor** one who believes in transubstantiation. [L. *substantia*, substance.]

transude *tran-sūd′, trän-, -zūd′, v.i.* and *v.t.* to ooze out. — *ns.* **tran′sūdate** a substance that transudes, e.g. a fluid that passes through a membrane or the walls of a blood-vessel; **transūdā′tion.** — *adj.* **transū′datory.** [L. *sūdāre*, to sweat.]

transume *tran-sūm′, trän-, -zūm′, v.t.* (*obs.*) to transcribe officially. — *ns.* **transumpt** (*-sumt′*) a copy of a legal writing; **transumption** (*-sum′shən*) transcription: metaphor: transference. — *adj.* **transumptive** (*-sump′-tiv*). [L. *trān(s)sūmĕre*, to transcribe — *sūmĕre*, to take.]

transuranic *trans-ū-ran′ik, träns-, -z-, adj.* of greater atomic number than *uranium.* — Also **transurā′nian, transurā′nium.** [Pfx. **trans-**.]

transvalue *trans-val′ū, träns-, -z-, v.t.* to evaluate anew. — *n.* **transvaluā′tion.** [Pfx. **trans-**.]

transverse[1] *tranz′vûrs, tränz′, -vûrs′, adj.* set, sent, lying, etc. crosswise. — *adj.* **crosswise.** — *n.* anything set crosswise. — *v.t.* (*-vûrs′*) to cross: to thwart: to reverse: to transform. — *adj.* **transvers′al** transverse. — *n.* a line cutting a set of lines. — *n.* **transversal′ity.** — *advs.* **transvers′ally; transverse′ly.** — *n.* **transver′sion.** — **transverse flute** see **flute; transverse wave** (*phys.*) a wave motion in which the disturbance of the medium occurs at right angles to the direction of wave propagation. — **by transverse** (*Spens.*) awry. [L. *trānsversus* — *vertĕre, versum,* to turn.]

transverse[2] *tranz-vûrs′, tränz-, v.t.* to turn from prose into verse. — *n.* **transver′sion** (*-shən*). [A pun in Buckingham's *Rehearsal.*]

transvest *tranz-vest′, tränz-, v.t.* and *v.i.* to dress oneself in the clothes of another, esp. of the opposite sex. — *adj.* **transvest′ic.** — *n.* and *adj.* **transvestite** (*-vest′īt*) (one) given to this. — *ns.* **transvest′ism; transvest′itism.** [Pfx. **trans-**, and L. *vestis — vestīre, vestītum,* to dress; cf. **travesty**.]

tranter *trant′ər,* (*dial.*) *n.* a hawker: a carrier. — *v.t.* and *v.i.* **trant** (back-formation) to hawk. [Cf. L.L. *trāvetārius.*]

trap[1] *trap, n.* a snare, gin: a device for catching: a hidden danger: one who catches offenders (*slang*): trickery (*slang*): a pitfall: a trap-door: a ventilating door in a mine: a lock: a bend in a pipe to stop foul gases: a light carriage: a contrivance for throwing up or releasing a ball or clay pigeons: the mouth (*slang*): a bunker or other hazard (*golf*): (in *pl.*) drums or other percussion instruments (*jazz*). — *v.t.* to catch in a trap: to provide with traps: to control (a ball) so that it stops dead (*football*). — *v.i.* to act as a trapper: — *pr.p.* **trapp′ing;** *pa.t.* and *pa.p.* **trapped.** — *ns.* **trapp′er** one who traps animals for their fur: a boy who minds a mine trap: a horse for a trap; **trapp′iness.** — *n.* and *adj.* **trapp′ing.** — *adj.* **trapp′y** full of traps, treacherous. — **trap′-ball** an old game played with a ball, bat, and trap; **trap′-door** a door set in a floor, stage or ceiling, esp. flush with its surface; **trap-door spider** one that makes a lair in the ground and covers it with a hinged door composed of earth and silk; **trap′-fall** a trap-door that gives way beneath the feet: a pitfall; **trap′-shooting** clay pigeon shooting; **trap′-stick** a bat for trap-ball. [O.E. *trappe — træppe, treppe.*]

trap[2] *trap,* (*geol.; old-fashioned*) *n.* vaguely, a dark fine-grained igneous rock (lying often in steps or terraces). — *adj.* **trapp′ean** (or *-ē′*). — **trap′-rock.** [Sw. *trapp — trappa,* a stair.]

trap[3] *trap, n.* a fault (*mining*): a ladder leading to a loft (*Scot.*): a flight of steps (*Scot.*). — *adj.* **trap′-cut** of gems, cut in steps, step-cut. — **trap′-ladder, -stair.** [Cf. Du. *trap,* step; cf. foregoing word.]

trap[4] *trap, n.* a horse-cloth (*obs.*): (in *pl.*) personal luggage. — *v.t.* to caparison, deck with trappings. — *adj.* **trapped.** — *n.* **trapp′er** (*hist.*) a covering, protective for use in battle, or decorative, worn by a horse. — *n.pl.* **trapp′ings** gay, colourful clothes: ornaments, esp. those put on horses: characteristic accompaniments, adornments, paraphernalia (of office, etc.). [App. conn. with Fr. *drap,* Sp. and Port. *trapo,* L.L. *drappus* (*trapus*), cloth.]

trapan. A variant spelling of **trepan**[1].

trape, trapes. See **traipse.**

trapezium *trə-pē′zi-əm, n.* orig., any quadrilateral that is not a parallelogram: one with no sides parallel (*U.S.*): one with one (and only one) pair of parallel sides (*Brit.*): a wrist-bone articulating with the thumb metacarpal: — *pl.* **trapē′zia, -ziums.** — *n.* **trapēze** (*trə-pēz′*) a swing-like apparatus used by acrobats, consisting of one or more cross-bars suspended between two ropes. — *v.i.* to perform or go on a trapeze. — *adjs.* **trapē′zial** pertaining to a trapezium; **trapē′ziform** having the form of a trapezium. — *ns.* **trapē′zius** (also **trapezius muscle**) (either of two triangular halves of) a large, flat, quadrilateral-shaped muscle extending up to the thoracic spine to the neck, and across the back of the shoulders, that draws the head and shoulders back; **trapēzohē′dron** a solid figure whose faces are trapezia or trapezoids; **trapezoid** (*trap′i-zoid,* also *trə-pē′zoid*) a quadrilateral with no sides parallel: one with two sides parallel (*U.S.*): a wrist-bone next to the trapezium. — Also *adjs.* — *adj.* **trapezoid′al.** [Latinised from Gr. *trapezion,* dim. of *trapeza,* a table; lit. four-legged — *tetra-,* four, *peza,* a foot.]

trappean. See **trap**[2].

Trappist *trap′ist, n.* a Cistercian of the reformed rule established by De Rancé (1626–1700), abbot of La Trappe in Normandy — austere and silent. — Also *adj.* — *n.* **Trapp′istine** (*-tēn, -tin*) a nun of an affiliated order.

trapunto *trə-pun′tō, -pōon′, n.* an Italian type of quilting done by stitching the design through two layers of fabric, and inserting wadding between the threads of the back layer. [It., quilting.]

trash[1] *trash, v.t.* (*Shak.*) to check. — *n.* (*dial.*) a leash or other restraint. [Origin obscure.]

trash[2] *trash, n.* broken twigs, hedge-cuttings, splinters: sugar-cane refuse: scraps: anything worthless: rubbish: paltry stuff: nonsense: a worthless person (*Shak.*): worthless people: poor whites (*U.S.*). — *v.t.* to free from trash: to lop the tops from: to discard, reject, or expose, as worthless: to wreck, vandalise (esp. *U.S.*). — — *n.* **trash′ery** trash, rubbish. — *adv.* **trash′ily.** — *ns.* **trash′iness; trash′trie** (*Scot.*) trash. — *adj.* **trash′y** like trash: worthless. — **trash′-can** (*U.S.*) a receptacle for refuse. [Prob. Scand.; cf. Norw. dial. *trask,* trash, O.N. *tros,* fallen twigs.]

trash[3] *trash, v.t.* to wear out, to harass. — *v.i.* to trudge. [Cf. Sw. *traska,* Norw. *traske.*]

trashtrie. See **trash**[2].

trass *tras, n.* an earthy volcanic tuff used as a hydraulic cement. — Also **tarras′, terras′.** [Du. *tras.*]

trattoria *trät-tō-rē′ə, n.* an Italian restaurant: — *pl.* **trattō′rias, trattō′rie** (*-rē-ā*). [It.]

trauchle *tröhh′l,* (*Scot.*) *v.t.* to bedraggle: to weary with drudgery or plodding. — *v.i.* to drudge: to trail along. — *n.* a troublesome task: drudgery. [Cf. Flem. *tragelen,* to go heavily.]

trauma *trö′mə, trow′mə, n.* a wound: an injury: an emotional shock that may be the origin of a neurosis (*psych.*): the state or condition caused by a physical or emotional shock: — *pl.* **trau′mas, trau′mata.** — *adj.* **traumatic** (*-mat′ik*) relating to, resulting from, or causing, wounds: of, causing, a lasting emotional shock: (*loosely*) frightening, unpleasant. — *adv.* **traumat′ically.** — *v.t.* **trau′matise, -ize** to inflict a mental or physical trauma on. — *ns.* **trau′matism** (*-mə-tizm*) a condition due to a wound; **traumatol′ogy** the study of wounds and of the effects of injuries. — *adj.* **traumatolog′ical.** — *n.* **traumatonas′ty** a nastic movement after wounding. [Gr. *trauma, -atos,* a wound.]

travail[1] *trav′al, -əl, n.* excessive labour: toil: labour in childbirth: *obs.* for **travel.** — *v.i.* to labour: to suffer the pains of childbirth: *obs.* for **travel.** — *adj.* **trav′ailed** toilworn: wearied: experienced: having been in travail. — **trav′ail-pain, -pang.** [O.Fr. (Fr.) *travail.*] **travail².** See **travois.**

trave *trāv,* (*obs.*) *n.* a beam or shaft (e.g. of a cart): a frame in which to shoe a fractious horse. [O.Fr. *trave,* beam — L. *trabs.*]

travel *trav′l, v.i.* to journey: to be capable of withstanding a journey: to go: to walk (*dial.*): to go round soliciting orders: to go on circuit: to move along a course: to go with impetus: to pass: to move: *obs.* for **travail.** — *v.t.* to journey over or through: to conduct or send on a journey (*arch.*): — *pr.p.* **trav′elling;** *pa.t.* and *pa.p.* **trav′elled.** — *n.* journeying: impetus: power of going: range of movement: passage: *obs.* for **travail:** (in *pl.*) an account of journeys. — *adj.* **trav′elled** having made journeys: transported: not in its original place: experienced: beaten, frequented. — *n.* **trav′eller** one who travels or has travelled: a wayfarer: one of the travelling people: one who travels for a mercantile house: a ring that slides along a rope or spar: a piece of mechanism that moves on a gantry, etc. — *n.* and *adj.* **trav′elling.** — *n.* **travelogue** (*trav′ə-log*) a talk, lecture, article, or film on travel. — **travel agency** an agency which provides information, brochures, tickets, etc., relating to travel; **travel agent; traveller's cheque** a cheque which can be cashed at any foreign branch or specified agent of the bank issuing it; **trav′eller's-joy** the virgin's-bower, *Clematis vitalba,* sometimes called old man's beard; **traveller's tale** an amazing account, esp. an untrue one, about what one professes to have seen abroad; **trav′eller's-tree** a Madagascan tree (*Ravenala*) of the banana family with great leaves on two sides only, accumulating water in the leaf-bases; **travelling folk, people** the name by which itinerant people often call themselves, in preference to the derogatory names gipsies or tinkers. — *adj.* **trav′el-sick** suffering from travel sickness. — **travel sickness** nausea experienced, as a result of motion, by a passenger in a car, ship, aircraft, etc. — *adjs.* **trav′el-soiled, -stained, trav′el-taint′ed** (*Shak.*) showing the marks of travel. — **travelling-wave tube** a device used in communications for increasing signal power, amplification being produced by interaction between a wave of radio frequency travelling on a wire helix and an electron beam travelling at roughly the same velocity inside the helix. [**travail.**]

travelator. Another spelling of **travolator.**

traverse *trav′ûrs, adj.* cross: oblique. — *n.* a crossing or passage across: a straight length in a zigzag course: a passage across the face of a rock in mountaineering: a survey by measuring straight lines from point to point and the angles between: anything set or lying across: an obstruction: adversity: a curtain, screen, partition: a barrier: a parapet: a cross-piece: a gallery from one side of a large building to another: a screened-off compartment: a denial or contradiction: an opposing, counteracting movement (*fencing*). — *v.t.* (or -*vûrs′*) to cross: to pass through, across, or over: to move about over: to pass over by traverse: to survey by traverse: to oppose: to thwart: to dispute: to deny, contradict: to turn sideways. — *v.i.* to make a traverse: to move to the side: to direct a gun to the right or left. — *adj.* **trav′ersable.** — *n.* **travers′al** the action of traversing. — *adj.* **trav′ersed** crossed, passed over: set crosswise (*Shak.*). — *n.* **trav′erser** one who traverses: a platform for shifting wagons and carriages sideways. — *n.* and *adj.* **trav′ersing.** — **traversing bridge** one that can be withdrawn horizontally. [Fr. *travers, traverse, traverser* — L. *trāns, vertĕre, versum,* to turn.]

travertine *trav′ər-tīn, -tēn, -tin, n.* a pale limestone deposited from solution, e.g. from springs. — Also **travertin.** [It. *travertino* — L. *tīburtīnus (lapis),* stone of Tibur.]

travesty *trav′is-ti, n.* disguise, esp. of a man as a woman or vice versa: burlesque: ridiculously inadequate representation (of). — *v.t.* to disguise: to burlesque. — **travesty role** (*theatr.*) a role intended to be taken by a performer of the opposite sex to that of the character. [Fr. *travesti,* pa.p. of *travestir,* to disguise — L. *trāns, vestīre,* to clothe; cf. **transvest.**]

travis *trav′is,* obs. or dial. for **traverse.** — See also **treviss.**

travois *trä-voi′ (pl. travois trä-voiz′),* **travail** *trä-vā′i, ns.* a North American Indian drag, a pair of trailing poles attached to each side of the saddle, joined by a board or net. [Canadian Fr. pron. of Fr. *travail.*]

travolator *trav′ō-lā-tər, n.* a moving way for the conveyance of foot-passengers. [From stem of **travel,** in imitation of **escalator.**]

trawl *tröl, n.* an open-mouthed bag-net for dragging along the sea-bed: a trawl-line (q.v.): an act of trawling. — *v.t.* and *v.i.* to catch or fish with a trawl or (*Scot.* and *U.S.*) a seine-net. — *v.t.* to search over, comb, investigate thoroughly, in order to gather information. — *v.i.* to look for something (e.g. a suitable person for a post, etc.) by gathering suggestions from various sources (with *for;* strictly, a meaning developed from **troll²**). — *ns.* **traw′ler** one who trawls: a trawling vessel; **traw′ling.** — **trawl′erman** one manning a trawler; **trawl′-fish** fish caught with a trawl; **trawl′-line** a buoyed line with baited hooks at intervals; **trawl′-net.** [Cf. **trail¹** and M.Du. *traghel,* drag-net.]

tray¹ *trā, n.* a flat low-rimmed vessel used for carrying articles (as crockery, etc.). — *n.* **tray′ful:** — *pl.* **tray′fuls.** — **tray′-cloth** a cloth for covering a tray; **tray′mobile** (*Austr.*) a household trolley, for serving tea, etc. [O.E. *trīg, trēg,* board.]

tray² *trā.* See **trey.** — **tray′-trip** (*Shak.*) a game played with dice.

trayne. See **train¹.**

treacher, treachour *trech′ər, n.* (*obs.*) a deceiver by trickery: a betrayer: a traitor. — Also **treach′erer.** — *adj.* **treach′erous** ready to betray: not to be trusted: misleadingly inviting in appearance. — *adv.* **treach′erously.** — *ns.* **treach′erousness; treach′ery** betrayal: readiness to betray: falseness: treason; **treach′etour** (*Spens.*) a deceiver: a traitor. [O.Fr. *trecheor,* deceiver — *trechier,* to trick; cf. **trick.**]

treacle *trē′kl, n.* orig. an antidote or prophylactic against bites, hence against poisons, etc.: the dark, viscous uncrystallisable syrup obtained in refining sugar (also called **black treacle**): also molasses, the drainings of crude sugar: blandishments, esp. when suggestive of the cloying and nauseating taste and thickness of treacle: intolerable sentimentality. — *v.t.* to dose or smear with treacle. — *v.i.* to treacle trees in order to collect moths. — *n.* **trea′cliness.** — *adj.* **trea′cly** of, or like, treacle: thick and sweet: unctuously blandishing: intolerably sentimental. — **trea′cle-mustard** the cruciferous plant *Erysimum cheiranthoides.* [O.Fr. *triacle* — Gr. *thēriakē (antidotos,* an antidote to the bites) of beasts — *thērion,* a wild beast.]

tread *tred, v.i.* to set the foot down: to step: to walk: to trample: to copulate, as a cock: same as **trade** (*Scot.*). — *v.t.* to walk on: to press with the foot, as in threshing, pressing grapes, tramping clothes, packing: to trample: to render by treading: to perform by treading, dance: to copulate with as a cock-bird: to oppress (*fig.*): — *pa.t.* **trod;** *pa.p.* **trodd′en, trod.** — *n.* a footprint: a track: the act or manner of treading: a step or tramp: a thing or part trodden on, as of a step: the part that touches the ground, as of a shoe, a wheel: distance between wheels or pedals: the cicatricula, or the chalaza, of an egg: same as **trade** (*Scot.*). — *ns.* **tread′er; tread′ing; tread′le, tredd′le** a foot-lever for working a machine: a pedal: the chalaza of an egg (once thought to be derived from the cock) (*dial.*). — *v.i.* to work a treadle. — *ns.* **tread′ler; tread′ling.** — **tread′mill** a cylinder turned by treading on boards on its outside, as formerly by prisoners: a mill so worked: routine drudgery (*fig.*); **tread′-wheel** a wheel or cylinder turned by treading outside or inside: a treadmill. — **tread water** to float upright by an action as if of climbing a ladder.

[O.E. *tredan*; Ger. *treten*; O.N. *trotha*; cf. **trade**.]

treague *trēg*, (*Spens.*) *n.* a truce. [L.L. *tregua*, *treuga* — Goth. *triggwa*, treaty.]

treason *trē'zn*, *n.* betraying of the government or an attempt to overthrow it: treachery: disloyalty. — *adj.* **trea'sonable** pertaining to, consisting of, or involving treason. — *n.* **trea'sonableness.** — *adv.* **trea'sonably.** — *adj.* **trea'sonous.** — **treason felony** the crime of desiring to depose the sovereign, intimidate parliament, stir up a foreign invasion, etc. — declared by statute in 1848. — **constructive treason** anything that may be interpreted as equivalent to actual treason by leading naturally to it; **high treason** offences against the state; **misprision of treason** knowledge of the principal crime and concealment thereof; **petty treason** the murder of a husband by a wife, a master by a servant, etc. [A.Fr. *tresun*, O.Fr. *traïson* (Fr. *trahison*) — *traïr* (*trahir*) — L. *tradĕre*, to betray.]

treasure *trezh'ər*, *n.* wealth stored up: riches: anything much valued: a valued, indispensable servant, helper, etc. — *v.t.* to hoard up: to collect for future use: to value greatly: to store, enrich. — *ns.* **treas'urer** one who has the care of a treasure or treasury: one who has charge of collected funds; **treas'urership**; **treas'ury** place where treasure is deposited: (often with *cap.*) a department of a government which has charge of the finances: mistakenly applied to a beehive tomb in prehistoric Greece. — **treas'ure-chest** a box for keeping articles of value; **treas'ure-city** a city for stores, magazines, etc.; **treas'ure-house** a house for holding treasures: a treasury: a store of valuable things; **treasure hunt** a hunt for treasure: a game in which competitors attempt to win a prize by being first to complete a course indicated by clues which have to be solved; **treas'ure-trove'** (*trové*, pa.p. of A.Fr. *trover*, to find) ownerless objects of intrinsic or historical value found hidden (in England gold and silver only), property of the crown; **Treasury bench** the first row of seats on the Speaker's right hand in the House of Commons, occupied by the members of the government; **Treasury bill** a security entitling the holder to a stated amount to be paid from the Consolidated Fund at a specified date; **Treasury note** a currency note issued by the Treasury; **treasury tag** a short piece of cord with a metal tag at each end, for holding papers together. [O.Fr. *tresor* (Fr. *trésor*) — L. *thēsaurus* — Gr. *thēsauros*.]

treat *trēt*, *v.t.* to deal with: to handle: to discuss: to behave towards: to act upon: to deal with the case of: to deal with (disease) by applying remedies: to subject to a process: to stand a drink or other gratification to. — *v.i.* to negotiate: to deal (with *of*): to stand treat. — *n.* a free entertainment, pleasure excursion, or feast: a turn or act of providing and paying: a source of great gratification: negotiation, parley (*Spens.*). — *adj.* **treat'able** able to be treated: tractable, moderate (*obs.*). — *ns.* **treat'er**; **treat'ing**; **treat'ise** (*-iz, -is*) a written composition, esp. one treating a subject formally or systematically; **treat'ment** the act or manner of treating: management: behaviour to anyone: way of applying remedies; **treat'y** negotiation: a formal agreement, esp. between states: entreaty (*Shak.*). — **treaty port** a port opened by treaty to foreign trade. — **Dutch treat** see **Dutch**; **stand treat** see **stand**; **the (full) treatment** (*coll.*) the appropriate method (in every detail) of dealing, whether ceremoniously or punitively, with a particular type of person, case, etc. [O.Fr. *traitier* — L. *tractāre*, to manage — *trahĕre*, *tractum*, to draw.]

treble *treb'l*, *adj.* triple: threefold: in the treble (*mus.*): high-pitched. — *n.* that which is triple or threefold: three times as much: the highest part, soprano (*mus.*): a treble singer, voice, instrument, string, sound, etc.: the narrow inner ring on a dartboard, or a hit on this: a bet involving three horse-races, the stake and winnings from the first being bet on the second, and those from the second on the third. — *v.t.* to make three times as much. — *v.i.* to become threefold. — *n.*

treb'leness. — *adv.* **treb'ly.** — **treble chance** a mode of competing in football pools in which, in a selection of matches made from a list, the aim is to pick all draws, they counting most, the away win and home win chances less; **treble clef** the G clef on the second line. — *adj.* **treb'le-dated** living three ages. [O.Fr., — L. *triplus*; see **triple**.]

trebuchet *treb'ū-shet*, *trā-bü-shā'*, *n.* a mediaeval military engine for launching stones, etc. [O.Fr.]

trecento *trā-chen'tō*, *n.* and *adj.* 14th-century (in Italian art, etc.). — *n.* **trecen'tist.** [It., three (for thirteen) hundred.]

treck. Same as **trek** (*v.i.* and *n.*).

tre corde *trā kor'dā*, (It.) three strings: a direction to piano players to release the soft pedal.

treddle. Same as **treadle.** See **tread.**

tredrille, tredille *tra-d(r)il'*, *n.* a card game for three. [After **quadrille** — L. *trēs*, three.]

tree *trē*, *n.* a large plant with a single branched woody trunk (sometimes loosely applied): timber: a wooden structure or part of various kinds: a saddle-tree: a boot- or shoe-tree: a gallows: a cross for crucifixion: a branching figure or structure, as an arborescent aggregate of crystals (e.g. *lead tree*), a pedigree, a branching stand for rings, etc. (*ring-tree, mug-tree*). — *v.t.* to drive into a tree, to corner (also *fig.*): to form on a tree. — *v.i.* to take refuge in a tree. — *adj.* wooden: in composition, inhabiting, frequenting, growing on trees: taking the form of a tree: dendritic. — *adjs.* **tree'less**; **treen** (*trē'ən*) of a tree (*Spens.*): wooden. — *n.* small articles of wood, esp. eating and drinking vessels of past times. — *n.* **tree'ship** existence as a tree. — **tree bicycle** a mechanical device used for climbing trees; **tree'-bur'ial** disposal of the dead in the branches of trees; **tree'-calf** a light-brown calf bookbinding, in conventional imitation of a branching tree; **tree'-creeper** a little bird (*Certhia*) that runs up tree-trunks in search of insects; **tree'-fern** a fern with a tall woody trunk; **tree'-frog** an arboreal amphibian, esp. one of the family *Hylidae*, nearer to toads than to frogs; **tree'-hopper** any of the homopterous leaping insects of the family *Membracidae*; **tree'-kangaroo'** a tree-climbing kangaroo (*Dendrolagus*); **tree'-lil'y** a xerophytic tree-like plant of the Brazilian campos (*Vellozia*); **tree'-line** same as **timber-line.** — *adj.* **tree'-lined** (of roads, etc.) having trees along either side. — **tree'-mall'ow** *Lavatera arborea*, a tree-like plant of the Malvaceae family, having reddish-purple flowers; **tree'-moss'** moss or lichen growing on a tree: a moss like a tiny tree in shape; **treenail, trenail** (*trē'nāl, tren'l*) a long wooden pin or nail to fasten the planks of a ship to the timbers; **tree'-on'ion** a variety of onion with bulbs in the place of flowers; **tree'-peony** a shrub (*Paeonia suffruticosa*, also called **Moutan**) of the family Ranunculaceae, native to China and Tibet, with pale pink flowers, from which many garden varieties have been developed; **tree rings** annual rings; **tree'-shrew** a squirrel-shrew, any insectivore of the East Indian family Tupaiidae, squirrel-like animals akin to shrews; **tree'-snake** a tree-dwelling snake; **tree'-sur'geon** one who preserves diseased trees by filling cavities, amputating damaged branches, etc.; **tree'-sur'gery**; **tree'-toma'to** a South American solanaceous shrub (*Cyphomandra*) or its tomato-like fruit; **tree'top** the top of a tree; **tree'-trunk**; **tree'-wor'ship**; **tree'-wor'shipper.** — **at the top of the tree** in the highest position in e.g. a profession; **family tree** pedigree, **tree of heaven** ailanto; **tree of lead** Saturn's tree; **tree of life** arbor vitae: a tree in the Garden of Eden (Gen. ii. 9); **tree of silver, Diana's tree** an arborescent deposit of silver; **up a tree** in difficulties. [O.E. *trēow, trēo*; cf. Gr. *drȳs*, oak, *dory*, spear; Sans. *dru*, tree.]

treen. See under **tree.**

tref *trāf*, **trefa** *trā'fə*, *adjs.* in the Jewish religion, forbidden as food, not kosher. [Heb. *terēphāh*, torn flesh — *taraph*, to tear.]

trefoil *trē'foil, tre'foil*, *n.* a three-lobed form, ornament, or aperture, as in tracery or heraldry: a leaf of three leaflets: a trifoliate plant, esp. of the clover genus (*Trifolium*). — *adj.* **tre′foiled.** — **bird's-foot trefoil** see **bird.** [A.Fr. *trifoil* — L. *trifolium* — *tres*, three, *folium*, a leaf.]

tregetour *trej′ə-tər, n.* a juggler (*obs.*): a trickster: a deceiver. [O.Fr. *tresgetour* — *tresgeter* — L. *trans*, *jactāre*, to throw.]

trehala *tri-hä′lə, n.* Turkish manna, a sweet substance got from the cocoons of a type of beetle. [Turk. *tīqālah*.]

treille *trāl, n.* a trellis. — *n.* **treill′age** trelliswork: a trellis. — *adj.* **treill′aged.** [Fr., — L. *trichila*, a bower.]

trek *trek, v.t.* to drag. — *v.i.* to journey by ox-wagon: to migrate: to tramp and camp, dragging one's equipment: to make a long hard journey, usu. on foot: — *pr.p.* **trekk′ing;** *pa.t.* and *pa.p.* **trekked.** — *n.* a journey or stage: a migration. — *n.* **trekk′er.** — **trek′-ox; trek′schuit** (*-s′hhoit, -skoit*) a towed canal-boat. [Du. *trekken*, to draw.]

trellis *trel′is, n.* a structure of cross-barred or lattice-work. — *v.t.* to provide with a trellis: to train on a trellis. — *adj.* **trell′ised.** — **trell′is-win′dow** same as **lattice-window; trell′is-work** lattice-work. [O.Fr. *treliz* — L. *trīlix, -īcis*, woven with triple thread, modified by association with **treille,** q.v.]

trema *trē′mə, n.* an orifice: a diaeresis, two dots placed as a mark of separate pronunciation over a vowel-letter. — *adj.* **trematic** (*tri-mat′ik*) of the gill-slits. — *n.* **trematode** (*trem′ə-tōd*) any member of the **Tremato′da,** a class of parasitic, unsegmented flat-worms with adhesive suckers. — *n.* and *adj.* **trem′atoid.** [Gr. *trēma, -atos*, a hole.]

tremble *trem′bl, v.i.* to shake, as from fear, cold, or weakness: to quiver: to vibrate: to pass tremulously. — *v.t.* to set trembling. — *n.* the act of trembling: tremulousness: a tremulous state: (in *pl.*) a morbid trembling: (in *pl.; specif.*) a condition of muscular weakness and trembling in cattle and sheep caused by eating certain plants esp. white snakeroot (*Eupatorium rugosum*), also a name for milk sickness (q.v.) in humans. — *adj.* **tremblant** (*trem′blənt*) (of jewellery) having the stones set on springs, so as to give a trembling effect. — *ns.* **trem′blement; trem′bler** one who or that which trembles: any of a number of West Indian birds of the family *Mimidae*: a vibrating device that makes and breaks a circuit (*elect.*). — *adj.* (of jewellery) tremblant. — *n.* and *adj.* **trem′bling.** — *adv.* **trem′blingly.** — *adj.* **trem′bly** tremulous. — **trembling poplar** the aspen. [O.Fr. (Fr.) *trembler* — L. *tremulus*, trembling — *tremēre*, to shake.]

Tremella *tri-mel′ə, n.* a genus of gelatinous fungi, such as witches' meat, found on decaying wood, etc. [L. *tremulus*, quivering.]

tremendous *tri-men′dəs, adj.* awe-inspiring: huge (*hyperb. coll.*): prodigious, extraordinary, very good (*slang*). — *adv.* **tremen′dously.** — *n.* **tremen′dousness.** [L. *tremendus*, to be trembled at.]

trémie, tremie *trā-mē, trem′i, n.* a hopper-like device for laying concrete under water. [Fr., hopper — L. *trimodia*, a three-peck measure.]

tremolando, tremolant. See **tremolo.**

tremolite *trem′ə-līt, n.* a calcium-magnesium amphibole, usually in long prisms, or fibres, pale or colourless. — *adj.* **tremolitic** (*-lit′ik*). [From the Val *Tremola* in the Alps, where the mineral found is not true tremolite.]

tremolo *trem′ō-lō,* (*mus.*) *n.* a tremulous effect as by a rapid succession of interruptions or of up and down bows: a device in an organ or electronic instrument for producing this: — *pl.* **trem′olos.** — Also *adj.* — *n., adj.,* and *adv.* **tremolan′do:** — *pl.* **tremolandi, tremolan′dos.** — *n.* and *adj.* **trem′olant** tremolo. [It. *tremolo, tremolando, tremolante*.]

tremor *trem′ər, n.* a quiver: a quavering: a thrill: an involuntary agitation: a vibration. — *adj.* **trem′orless.** [L. *tremor, -ōris*.]

tremulous *trem′ū-ləs, adj.* trembling: quivering. — *adj.* **trem′ūlant** tremulous. — *n.* tremolant. — *v.i.* and *v.t.*

trem′ūlate. — *adv.* **trem′ūlously.** — *n.* **trem′ūlousness.** [L. *tremulus*, trembling, and L.L. *tremulāre, -ātum*, to tremble.]

trenail. See under **tree.**

trench *trench, trensh, n.* a long narrow cut in the earth, often used in warfare as a cover for troops: a deep furrow or wrinkle in the skin. — *v.i.* to make trenches: to dig deep with spade or plough: to encroach: to border, verge. — *v.t.* to cut: to make trenches in: to put in a trench: to furnish with a trench: to entrench: to divert by a trench (*Shak.*). — *n.* **trench′ancy** causticity. — *adj.* **trench′ant** (*Spens.* **trench′and**) cutting: incisive, forthright. — *adv.* **trench′antly.** — *n.* **trench′er** one who trenches. — **trench′-coat** a short waterproof coat with belt as used in trench warfare: a coat based on this, for man or woman; **trench′-feet′, -foot′** a diseased condition of the feet owing to exposure to cold and wet, esp. affecting soldiers in trench warfare; **trench′-fe′ver** a disease causing pain in joints and muscles, prevalent among soldiers living in trenches, caused by a Rickettsia and transmitted by lice; **trench′-mor′tar** a small smooth-bore gun, throwing large shells short distances, useful in trench warfare; **trench′-plough** a plough for ploughing more deeply than usual. — *v.t.* to plough with a trench-plough. — **trench warfare** warfare in which each side entrenches itself in lines facing the enemy. [O.Fr. *trenche*, cut (Fr. *tranche*, slice), *trencher* (Fr. *trancher*, to cut, to slice) to cut, prob. — L. *truncāre* (see **truncate**).]

trenchard. See **trencher.**

trencher *tren′chər, -shər, n.* a plate or platter: a board. — *n.* **trenchard** (*tren′shərd*) the word used at St. Andrews University for a trencher-cap. — **tren′cher-cap** a college-cap, mortar-board. — *adj.* **tren′cher-fed** (of fox-hounds) kept each by his owner, not in a pack. — **tren′cher-friend, -knight** (both *Shak.*) one who frequents the table of another, a parasite; **tren′cher-man** a hearty eater. [A.Fr. *trenchour* (Fr. *tranchoir*) — *trencher*, to cut.]

trend *trend, v.i.* to turn, wind: to have a tendency or prevailing direction. — *n.* a bend (*dial.*): general tendency. — *adj.* **tren′dy** (*coll.*) in the forefront of fashion in any sphere. — *n.* (*derog.*) a trendy person. — *n.* **trend′setter** one who helps to give a new direction to fashion. — *adj.* **trend′setting.** [O.E. *trendan*.]

trendle-tail. See **trundle.**

trenise *trə-nēz′, n.* the fourth movement of a quadrille. — Also **la trenise.**

trental *tren′tl, n.* a series of thirty requiem masses. [L.L. *trentāle* — L. *trigintā*, thirty.]

trente-et-quarante *trãt-ā-ka-rãt, n.* the card-game rouge-et-noir. [Fr., thirty and forty.]

trepan¹ *tri-pan′, n.* a decoy: a snare: an entrapping. — *v.t.* to ensnare: to lure: — *pr.p.* **trepann′ing;** *pa.t.* and *pa.p.* **trepanned′.** — *n.* **trepann′er.** — *n.* and *adj.* **trepann′ing.** [Earlier *trapan*; prob. conn. with **trap.**]

trepan² *tri-pan′, n.* an obsolete cylindrical saw for perforating the skull: a tool for boring shafts. — *v.t.* to remove a piece of the skull from: to cut a cylindrical disc from: to cut an annular groove in. — *ns.* **trepanation** (*trep-ə-nā′shən*); **trepann′er.** — *n.* and *adj.* **trepann′ing.** [Fr. *trépan* — L.L. *trepanum* — Gr. *trypanon* — *trypaein*, to bore.]

trepang *tri-pang′, n.* sea-slug, a holothurian eaten by the Chinese. [Malay *trīpang*.]

trephine *tri-fēn′, -fīn′, n.* an improved trepan. — *v.t.* to perforate with the trephine. [Earlier *trafine* — L. *tres fīnes*, three ends, with a suggestion of **trepan².**]

trepidation *trep-i-dā′shən, n.* trembling: alarmed agitation: a libration of the celestial sphere assumed to explain a supposed oscillation of the ecliptic (*old astron.; Milt.*). — *adjs.* **trep′id** quaking; **trep′idatory.** [L. *trepidāre, -ātum*, to hurry with alarm — *trepidus*, restless.]

Treponema *trep-ə-nē′mə, n.* a genus of spirochaetes, one of which, *Treponema pallidum*, causes syphilis: (without *cap.*) a bacterium of this genus: — *pl.* **treponē′mata,**

trepone̊'mas. [Gr. *trepein*, to turn, *nēma*, thread.]

trespass *tres'pəs, v.i.* to interfere with another's person or property: to enter unlawfully upon another's land: to encroach (on): to intrude (with *on*): to sin. — *n.* act of trespassing: any injury to another's person or property: a sin. — *n.* **tres'passer.** [O.Fr. *trespasser* — L. *trāns, passus,* a step.]

tress¹ *tres, n.* a plait or braid of the hair of the head: a long lock, braided or not. — *v.t.* to form into tresses. — *adjs.* **tressed** braided: in tresses: having tresses; **tress'y** having or like tresses. [Fr. *tresse* — L.L. *tricia,* perh. Gr. *tricha,* threefold *treis,* three.]

tress², tressel. See **trestle.**

tressure *tresh'ər, (her.) n.* a subordinary, half the breadth of the orle, and usually borne double, and flowered and counter-flowered with fleurs-de-lis. — *adj.* **tress'-ured** having a tressure. [Fr., from *tresser,* to plait.]

trestle *tres'l, n.* a support composed of a horizontal beam on sloping legs: a braced framework. — Also **tress'el.** — *n.* **tress** a trestle. — **trest'le-bridge** one resting on trestlework; **trest'le-table** one of boards laid on trestles; **trest'lework** a braced framework. [O.Fr. *trestel* (Fr. *tréteau*) and *treste, trestre* — L. *trānstrum,* cross-beam.]

tret *tret, n.* an allowance to purchasers of 4 lb. on every 104 lb. for waste. [Poss. A.Fr. *tret,* pull, turn of the scale or Fr. *traite,* transport, both — *traire,* to draw — L. *trahĕre, tractum.*]

trevally *tri-val'i, n.* an Australian horse-mackerel (Caranx) of various species. [Prob. a modification of **cavally.**]

treviss, trevis *trev'is,* **travis** *trav'is, trāv'is, ns.* forms of **traverse:** a stall partition: a stall.

trew. An old spelling of **true.**

trews *trōōz, n.pl.* (orig. *sing.*) trousers, esp. of tartan cloth. — **trews'man** a wearer of trews. [Ir. *trius,* Gael. *triubhas;* cf. **trouse, trousers.**]

trey *trā, n.* the three in cards and dice: a set of three: the third tine of a deer's horn (in full **trey-ant'ler, -tine;** also **tray, trez** *trā, trāz*): a threepenny bit (also **trey'bit, tray, tray'bit;** *slang*). [O.Fr. *treis, trei* — L. *trēs,* three.]

trez. See **trey.**

tri- *trī-, tri-* in composition, three, threefold. [L. *trēs, tria,* and Gr. *treis, tria.*]

triable. See **try.**

triacid *trī-as'id, adj.* having three replaceable hydrogen atoms: capable of replacing three hydrogen atoms of an acid. **[tri-.]**

triaconter *trī-ə-kon'tər, n.* an ancient ship, perhaps with thirty men to each group of oars. [Gr. *triākontērēs* — *triākonta,* thirty.]

triact *trī'akt, adj.* three-rayed. — *adjs.* **trīact'inal** (*-i-nəl* or *-ī'nəl*), **trīact'ine** (*-in*). [tri- and Gr. *aktīs, -īnos,* ray.]

triad *trī'ad, -əd, n.* a group, set, or union of three: in Welsh literature, a group of three sayings, stories, etc., about related subjects: a group of three lines or stanzas in different metres: a chord of three notes, esp. the common chord (*mus.*): an atom, element, or radical with a combining power of three (*chem.*): any of many Chinese secret societies (orig. so named from their use of the triangle in their rituals), some founded in the 17th century to resist the Manchu regime, some now associated with criminal activities, esp. heroin trading. — *adjs.* **trī'ad, trīad'ic.** — *n.* **trī'adist** a composer of triads. [L. *trias* — Gr. *trias, triados* — *treis,* three.]

triadelphous *trī-ə-del'fəs, (bot.) adj.* with three bundles of stamens. **[tri-,** and Gr. *adelphos,* a brother.]

triage. See **try.**

triakisoctahedron *trī-ə-kis-ok-tə-hē'drən, n.* a solid figure like an octahedron with a three-faced pyramid on each face. [Gr. *triakis,* three times.]

trial¹ *trī'əl, n.* a trying: examination by a test: examination by a court to determine a question of law or fact, esp. the guilt or innocence of a prisoner: (often in *pl.*) examination, sometimes merely formal, of a candi-

date: a testing journey, as of motor-cars, motor-cycles: a trial match: suffering: temptation: attempt: a piece used as a test: a troublesome thing, a nuisance. — *adj.* done, taken, etc., for the sake of trial. — *n.* **trial'(l)ist** a person taking part in a trial or test: a player under consideration for a place in a major team (*sport*). — **trial balance** (*book-k*) in the double-entry system, a statement drawn up of the credit and debit totals to demonstrate that they are equal; **trial balloon** same as **ballon d'essai; tri'al-day** (*Shak.*) day of trial; **tri'al-fire** (*Shak.*) a fire for trying or proving; **trial marriage** for a couple intending matrimony, a period of living together with a view to testing their compatibility; **trial run** a test drive in a motor vehicle to ascertain its efficiency: any introductory test, rehearsal, etc.; **trial trip** an experimental trip of a new vessel, to test her sailing-powers, etc. — **by trial and error** by trying out several methods and discarding those which prove unsuccessful; **on trial** undergoing proceedings in a court of law: on probation, as an experiment; **stand trial** to undergo trial in a court of law; **trial of strength** a contest to find out who is the stronger (or strongest): a struggle between two irreconcilable parties, prolonged until one of them weakens. [A.Fr. *trial* — *trier,* to try.]

trial² *trī'əl, adj.* threefold, trinal. — *ns.* **tri'alism** the doctrine of the existence of body, soul and spirit in man: a scheme for turning the Dual Monarchy into a triple (Austria, Hungary, and a South Slav state; *hist.*); **tri'alist; trīality** (*-al'i-ti*). [L. *trēs, tria,* three, after **dual.**]

Trial *tri-al, (Fr.) n.* a tenor with special aptitude for comedy parts, often noted more for his acting than for his vocalism. [After the French tenor, Antoine *Trial* (1736-1795), renowned for his comedy rôles at the Opéra-Comique in Paris.]

trialogue *trī'ə-log, n.* a dialogue between three persons. [On false analogy of **dialogue,** as if *dia-* meant two.]

triandrous *trī-an'drəs, (bot.) adj.* with three stamens. — *n.pl.* **Trian'dria** in Linnaeus's classification a class of plants with three stamens. — *adj.* **trian'drian.** [tri- and Gr. *anēr, andros,* a man (male).]

triangle *trī'ang-gl* (also *-ang'*), *n.* a plane figure with three angles and three sides (*math.*): part of the surface of a sphere bounded by three arcs of great circles (*spherical triangle*): any mark or thing of that shape: a musical instrument of percussion, formed of a steel rod bent in triangle-form, open at one angle: a tripod, esp. for a pulley for raising weights, or formerly (usu. in *pl.*) for binding soldiers to for flogging. — *adjs.* **tri'angled; triang'ular** having three angles: of a number, capable of being represented by dots in a triangle, as 1, 3, 6, 10, etc.: involving three persons or parties. — *n.* **triangular'ity.** — *adv.* **triang'ularly.** — *v.t.* **triang'ulate** to survey by means of a series of triangles. — *adj.* marked with, made up of, triangles: triangular. — *adv.* **triang'ulātely.** — *n.* **triangulā'tion** the act or process of triangulating, e.g. for map-making: the series of triangles so used. — **the eternal triangle** an emotional situation involving two men and a woman or two women and a man. [L. *triangulum* — *angulus,* an angle.]

triapsidal *trī-aps'i-dəl, adj.* with three apses. — Also **triaps'al. [tri-.]**

triarch¹ *trī'ärk, (bot.) adj.* having three xylem strands in the stele. [tri- and Gr. *archē,* origin.]

triarch². See **triarchy.**

triarchy *trī'är-ki, n.* government by three persons: a state governed by a triumvirate: a state divided into three parts each having its own ruler: one of three such parts. — *n.* **trī'arch** a ruler of a triarchy: a member of a triumvirate. [Gr. *triarchiā* — *archē,* rule.]

Trias *trī'əs, (geol.) n.* the oldest Mesozoic or Secondary system. — *adj.* **Triassic** (*trī-as'ik*). [Gr. *trias,* triad, from its threefold division in Germany — Bunter, Muschelkalk, Keuper.]

triathlon *trī-ath'lon, n.* a sporting contest consisting of three events, usually swimming, running and cycling. [tri- and Gr. *athlon*, a contest.]

triatic (stay) *trī-at'ik* (*stā*), *n.* a rope joining adjacent mastheads to which tackle is attached: each of a pair of stays joining the tops of direction-finding masts diagonally and supporting from their points of intersection a vertical aerial. [Origin obscure.]

triatomic *trī-ə-tom'ik, adj.* consisting of three atoms: having three replaceable atoms or groups: trivalent. — *adv.* **triatom'ically.** [tri-.]

triaxial *trī-ak'si-əl, adj.* having three axes. — *n.* a triaxial sponge spicule. — Also **triax'on.** [tri-, Gr. *axōn*, and L. *axis*, axle.]

tribade *trib'ad, n.* a woman homosexual. — *adj.* **tribad'ic.** — *ns.* **trib'adism, trib'ady** lesbian masturbation simulating heterosexual intercourse in the missionary position. [Fr. through L. *tribas, -adis* — Gr. *tribas, -ados* — *tribein,* to rub.]

tribal, etc. See **tribe.**

tribasic *trī-bā'sik, adj.* capable of reacting with three equivalents of an acid: (of acids) having three replaceable hydrogen atoms. [tri-, **base.**]

tribble *trib'l, n.* a horizontal frame with wires stretched across it for drying paper.

tribe *trīb, n.* a division of a nation or people for political purposes: a set of people theoretically of common descent: an aggregate of families, forming a community: a race: a breed: a class or set of people: (*loosely*) a classificatory division. — *adj.* **trī'bal.** — *ns.* **trī'balism** the existence of tribes as a social phenomenon: (loyalty to) the conventions, etc., of one's tribe; **trī'balist.** — *adj.* **trī'balistic.** — *adv.* **trī'bally.** — *adj.* **tribe'less.** — *ns.* **tribes'man, tribes'woman.** — *n.pl.* **tribes'people.** [L. *tribus, -ūs,* one of the divisions of the ancient Roman people: that these were originally three is only a conjecture.]

triblet *trib'lit, n.* a tapering mandrel on which rings, nuts, etc., are forged. [Fr. *triboulet.*]

tribo- *trī'bo-, trib', -ō-,* in composition, rubbing, friction. — *ns.* **tribo-electric'ity** generation of electric charges by friction; **tribol'ogy** the study of friction, wear, lubrication, etc., between surfaces moving in contact with one another; **tribol'ogist; triboluminescence** (*-es'əns*) emission of light caused by friction. — *adj.* **tribolumines'cent.** — *n.* **tribom'eter** a sled-like apparatus for measuring sliding friction. [Gr. *tribein,* to rub.]

tribrach *trī'brak, n.* a foot of three short syllables. — *adj.* **tribrach'ic.** [Gr. *tribrachys — brachys,* short.]

tribrom(o)- *trī-brōm'(ō)-,* in composition, having three atoms of bromine, esp. replacing hydrogen.

tribulation *trib-ū-lā'shən, n.* severe affliction: the state of being in pawn (*obs. slang*): a rowdy gang (*Shak.*). [L. *tribulāre, -ātum,* to afflict — *tribulum,* a sledge for separating grain from chaff by rubbing — *terēre,* to rub.]

tribune *trib'ūn, n.* a magistrate elected by the Roman plebeians to defend their rights: a champion of popular rights: in this and the following sense, sometimes used as the title of a newspaper: a platform for speaking from: a raised area or stand: bishop's stall or throne. — *n.* **tribunal** (*trib-, trīb-ū'nl; Spens. trib'*) a judgment-seat: a court of justice or arbitration: a body appointed to adjudicate in some matter or to enquire into some disputed question: a confessional. — *adj.* of, of the nature of, or authorised by, a tribunal. — *ns.* **trib'-unāte, trib'uneship** the office of tribune; **Trib'unite** a member of the Tribune Group. — *adjs.* **tribunitial, -icial** (*-ish'l*), **tribunitian, -ician** (*-ish'ən*). — **Tribune Group** a left-wing group within the British parliamentary Labour party. [L. *tribūnus,* tribune, *tribūnal,* tribunal — *tribus,* a tribe.]

tribute *trib'ūt, n.* a payment in acknowledgment of subjection: an act, gift, words, or other expression of approbation: (*loosely*) a testimony, a credit (to): a percentage of ore or its value received by a miner. — *adv.* **trib'utarily.** — *n.* **trib'utariness.** — *adj.* **trib'utary**

paying tribute: contributing: paid in tribute. — *n.* a payer of tribute: a stream that runs into another. — *n.* **trib'uter** a miner paid by tribute. — **trib'ute-mon'ey** money paid as tribute. [L. *tribūtum — tribuĕre,* to assign.]

tricameral *trī'kam-ə-rəl, -kam'-, adj.* having three chambers. [tri-, L. *camera,* chamber.]

tricar *trī'kär, n.* a motor-tricycle with a passenger's seat in front: a three-wheeled motor-car. [tri-.]

tricarpellary *trī-kär'pəl-ər-i,* or *-pel'ər-i,* (*bot.*) *adj.* of or with three carpels. [tri-.]

trice *trīs, v.t.* (*naut.*) to haul: to haul and make fast. — *n.* a pulley (*obs.*): a moment (as if the time of a single tug). [M.Du. *trisen* (Du. *trijsen*), to hoist.]

tricephalous *trī-sef'ə-ləs, adj.* three-headed. [Gr. *trikephalos — kephalē,* a head.]

triceps *trī'seps, adj.* three-headed. — *n.* a muscle with three separately arising heads, esp. the muscle at the back of the upper arm that straightens the elbow. [L. *trīceps, -cipitis — caput,* head.]

triceratops *trī-ser'ə-tops, n.* an ornithischian, quadrupedal, herbivorous dinosaur of the Cretaceous period, having a horn over each eye and one on its nose. [tri- and Gr. *keras, -atos,* horn, *ōps,* face.]

tricerion *trī-sē'ri-on,* (*Greek Church*) *n.* a three-branched candlestick. [Late Gr., — Gr. *kēros,* wax.]

trich- *trik-,* **tricho-** *-ō-, -o'-,* in composition, hair. [Gr. *thrix,* gen. *trichos.*]

trichiasis *trik-ī'ə-sis, n.* turning in of hairs around an orifice, esp. of eyelashes so that they rub against the eye: the presence of hair-like filaments in the urine. [L.L. — Gr. *thrix, trichos,* hair.]

Trichina *trik'i-nə, tri-kī'nə,* **Trichinella** *trik-i-nel'ə, ns.* a genus of nematode worms parasitic in rat, pig, and man, the adult in the small intestine, the larva encysted in muscle: (without *cap.*) a worm of the genus: — *pl.* **-ae** (*-ē*), **-as.** — *ns.* **trichiniasis** (*trik-i-nī'ə-sis*), **trichinō'sis** a disease caused by trichinae; **trichinīsā'tion, -ization** infestation with trichinae. — *adjs.* **trich'inised, -z-, trich'inosed** (*-nōst*) infested with trichinae; **trichinot'ic, trich'inous** pertaining to trichinosis. [Gr. *trichinos,* of hair — *thrix, trichos,* hair.]

trichite *trik'īt, n.* a hairlike crystallite. — *adj.* **trichitic** (*-it'ik*). [Gr. *thrix, trichos,* hair.]

Trichiurus *trik-i-ū'rəs,* or *-ōō'rəs, n.* a genus of hair-tails, giving name to the family **Trichiu'ridae,** akin to mackerels and tunnies. [trich- and Gr. *ourā,* tail.]

trichlor(o)- *trī-klōr'(ō)-, -klör',* in composition, having three atoms of chlorine, esp. replacing hydrogen. — *n.* **trichlor(o)ethylene** (*trī-klōr(-ō)-eth'i-lēn, -klör*) an acetylene derivative, used as a solvent, in paint manufacture, and as an analgesic and anaesthetic (*coll.* shortening **trike** *trīk*).

tricho-. See **trich-.**

trichobacteria *trik-ō-bak-tē'ri-ə, n.pl.* filamentous bacteria. [tricho-.]

trichogyne *trik'ō-jīn, -jin, n.* in red seaweeds, and some fungi, a threadlike prolongation of the female organ. [tricho- and Gr. *gynē,* woman, female.]

trichoid *trik'oid, adj.* hairlike. [Gr. *trichoeidēs.*]

trichology *trik-ol'ə-ji, n.* the scientific study of hair and its disorders. — *adj.* **tricholog'ical.** — *n.* **trichol'ogist** one versed in trichology: a name affected by hairdressers. [Gr. *thrix, trichos,* a hair.]

trichome *trik'ōm, trīk'ōm, n.* a plant hair or outgrowth from the epidermis. [Gr. *trichōma,* a growth of hair.]

trichomonad *trik-ə-mon'ad, n.* a parasitic protozoon of the genus **Trichomonas** (*tri-kom'* or *-kə-mon'*). — *n.* **trichomoni'asis** (*-mon-ī'*) a sexually-transmitted disease caused by trichomonads, found in human beings and in animals. [tricho- and *monas, -ados,* a unit.]

Trichophyton *trik-of'i-tən, n.* a genus of fungi causing ringworm: (without *cap.*) any fungus of this genus. — *n.* **trichophytō'sis** ringworm caused by Trichophyton. [tricho- and Gr. *phyton,* plant.]

Trichoptera *trik-op'tər-ə, n.pl.* an order of insects with hairy wings, the caddis-flies. — *n.* **trichop'terist** a student of the caddis-flies. — *adj.* **trichop'terous.** [tricho- and Gr. *pteron*, wing.]

trichord *trī'körd, adj.* three-stringed: with three strings to one note. — *n.* a three-stringed instrument: a triad. [Gr. *trichordos* — *chordē*, a string.]

trichosis *trik-ō'sis, n.* arrangement, distribution, or morbid condition of hair. [Gr. *trichōsis*, hairiness.]

trichotillomania *trik-ō-til-ō-mā'ni-ə, n.* a neurosis in which the patient pulls out tufts of his own hair. [tricho-, Gr. *tillein*, to pull, and **mania**.]

trichotomous *trī-kot'ə-məs, adj.* divided into three: forking in threes. — *v.t.* and *v.i.* **trichot'omise, -ize** to divide in three or threes. — *adv.* **trichot'omously.** — *n.* **trichot'omy** trichotomous division or forking. [Gr. *tricha*, threefold — *treis*, three, *tomē*, a cutting — *temnein*, to cut.]

trichroic *trī-krō'ik, adj.* having or exhibiting three colours, esp. when viewed in different directions. — *n.* **trī'chroism.** [Gr. *trichroos*, three-coloured.]

trichromatic *trī-krō-mat'ik, adj.* characterised by three colours: having three fundamental colour-sensations. — *n.* **trichro'mat** one who has normal colour vision. — *adjs.* **tri'chrome** trichromatic; **trichrō'mic** trichromatic. — *n.* one who has three fundamental colour-sensations. — *n.* **trichrō'matism.** [Gr. *trichrōmatos* — *chrōma*, colour.]

trichronous *trī'kro-nəs, adj.* trisemic. [Gr. *trichronos* — *chronos*, time.]

trick *trik, n.* an artifice: a deceitful device: a deception: a prank: a performance aimed at astonishing, puzzling, or amusing: an expedient: a knack: a characteristic habit, mannerism, trait: a spell or turn, esp. at the helm: a round of play at cards: the cards so played and taken by the winner, forming a unit in scoring: a trinket, toy, or gimcrack: a watch (*slang*): an outline sketch (*her.*): the customer of a prostitute (*slang*). — *v.t.* to deceive, to cheat: to beguile: to dress or decorate fancily (with *out*): to trim: to sketch in outline. — *adj.* of the nature of, for the purpose or performance of, a trick: adroit and trim (*obs.*). — *ns.* **trick'er; trick'ery** the act or practice of playing tricks: artifice: stratagem: imposition. — *adv.* **trick'ily.** — *n.* **trick'iness.** — *n.* and *adj.* **trick'ing.** — *adj.* **trick'ish** tricky. — *adv.* **trick'ishly.** — *n.* **trick'ishness.** — *adj.* **trick'less.** — *n.* **trick'siness.** — *adj.* **trick'some.** — *ns.* **trick'ster** a cheat: one who practises trickery; **trick'stering** playing the trickster. — *adjs.* **tricks'y** pranked up: capricious: sportive: mischievous: tricky: ticklish; **trick'y** addicted to trickery: clever in tricks: ticklish: difficult to handle: complicated. — **trick cyclist** an acrobat who performs tricks on a unicycle or cycle: a psychiatrist (*mil. slang*). — **do the trick** to bring something about; **how's tricks?** (*slang*) how are you?; **trick or treat** the (children's) practice of dressing up to visit neighbouring houses on Hallowe'en, threatening to play a trick unless a treat is produced; **turn a trick** (*slang*, esp. *U.S.*) to have casual sexual relations with someone, esp. for money; **up to (one's) tricks** misbehaving. [O.Fr. *trique*, Northern form of *triche*, deceit; perh. in part of other origin.]

trickle[1] *trik'l, v.i.* to run in drops or in a small irregular stream. — *v.t.* to emit in a trickle. — *n.* a drop (*obs.*): a succession of drops: a trickling rill. — *n.* **trick'let** a little rill. — *n.* and *adj.* **trick'ling.** — *adj.* **trick'ly** trickling. — *n.* **trick'le-down** (orig. and esp. *U.S.*) filtration of benefits, esp. money, downwards through the social community. — *adj.* of or pertaining to the idea that economic benefits received by advantaged sectors, e.g. large companies, ultimately filter down to benefit the less well off. [M.E. *triklen*, prob. for *striklen*, freq. of **strike**.]

trickle[2] *trik'l,* (*Spens.*) *adj.* ticklish, precarious (another reading **tickle**). [Prob. **trick**.]

trick-track *trik'-trak, n.* a form of backgammon in which pegs as well as pieces are used. — Also **tric'-trac, tick'-tack.** [Fr. *tric trac*; imit.]

triclinic *trī-klin'ik,* (*min.*) *adj.* referred to three unequal

axes obliquely inclined to each other. [Gr. *treis*, three, *klīnein*, to bend.]

triclinium *trī-klin'i-əm,* (*Rom. ant.*) *n.* a couch running round three sides of a table for reclining on at meals: a dining-room. [L. *triclīnium* — Gr. *triklīnion* — Gr. *treis*, three, *klīnē*, a couch.]

tricolour, tricolor *trī'kul-ər, adj.* three-coloured. — *n.* (*trī'*) a three-coloured flag, esp. that of France (*trē-kol-or*). — *adj.* **trī'coloured.** [L. *tricolor* and Fr. *tricolore*.]

triconsonantal *trī-kon-sə-nant'l, adj.* having three consonants. — Also **triconsonan'tic.** [tri-.]

tricorn, tricorne *trī'körn, adj.* three-horned: three-cornered. — *n.* a three-cornered hat. [L. *tricornis*, three-horned — *cornū*, a horn.]

tricorporate *trī-kör'pə-rāt, -rit,* **-d** *-id, adjs.* three-bodied (with one head). [tri- and L. *corpus, -oris*, body.]

tricostate *trī-kos'tāt, adj.* three-ribbed. [tri- and L. *costa*, rib.]

tricot *trē'kō, n.* a hand-knitted woollen fabric, or imitation: a soft, slightly-ribbed cloth for women's garments. — *n.* **tricoteuse** (*trē-kot-əz*) (lit. a woman who knits) in the French Revolution, one of the women who enthusiastically attended public meetings and executions, knitting as they sat: a 19th-century two-tiered work-table for knitters. [Fr. *tricot*, knitting.]

tricrotic *trī-krot'ik, adj.* (in measuring an arterial pulse) having three waves to one beat of the pulse: triple-beating. — *n.* **tri'crotism.** — *adj.* **tri'crotous.** [Gr. *trikrotos*, rowed with triple stroke — *krotos*, a beat.]

tric-trac. See **trick-track.**

tricuspid, -ate *trī-kus'pid, -āt, adjs.* with three cusps or points. [L. *tricuspis, -idis* — *cuspis*, a point.]

tricycle *trī'si-kl, n.* a three-wheeled cycle: a light three-wheeled car for the use of a disabled person. — Coll. shortening **trike** (*trīk*). — *vs.i.* to ride a tricycle. — *n.* **tri'cycler.** — *adj.* **tricyclic** (*trī-sī'klik*) having three whorls or rings: of a chemical compound, having three rings in its molecular structure, some compounds of this type being used as antidepressant drugs. — *ns.* **tri'cycling** (-*si-*); **trī'cyclist.** — **tricycle undercarriage, landing-gear** an aircraft's undercarriage, landing-gear, having three wheels. [tri- and Gr. *kyklos*, circle, wheel.]

Tridacna *trī-dak'nə, n.* a genus of giant clams of the Indian Ocean, the greatest known bivalves (more than 200 kg): (without *cap.*) any clam of this genus. [Gr. *tridaknos*, eaten at three bites (applied to a big oyster) — *duknein*, to bite.]

tridactyl, -ous *trī-dak'til, -əs, adjs.* three-toed: three-fingered. [tri- and Gr. *daktylos*, finger, toe.]

tridarn *trē'därn, n.* a Welsh dresser having three tiers or stages. [Welsh.]

tride. An obs. spelling (*Spens.; Shak.*) of **tried** (see **try**).

trident *trī'dənt, n.* a three-pronged spear, esp. that of the sea-god Poseidon or Neptune: anything of like shape. — *adjs.* **tri'dent, tridental** (-*dent'*), **trident'āte** three-pronged; **tridented** (*trī-dent'id*) three-pronged: (*trī'-dənt-id*) having a trident. [L. *tridēns, -dentis* — *dēns*, tooth.]

Tridentine *trī-, trī-dent'īn, adj.* of Trent in Southern Tirol, or the Council (1545–63) held there. — *n.* a native of Trent: one who accepts the degrees of the Council, an orthodox Roman Catholic. [L. *Tridentum*, Trent.]

tridimensional *trī-dī-men'shən-əl, adj.* having three dimensions. [tri-.]

tridominium *trī-dō-min'i-əm, n.* threefold rule. [tri- and L. *dominium*, lordship.]

triduan. See **triduum.**

triduum *trid'ū-əm,* or *trīd', n.* a space of three days: a three days' service. — *adj.* **trid'ūan** lasting three days. [L. *trīduum* — *diēs*, day.]

tridymite *trid'i-mīt, n.* an orthorhombic form of silica, in hexagonal scales, often combined in threes. [Gr. *tridymos*, threefold.]

trie. An obs. spelling of **try.** — **tried, tries, trier** see **try.**

triecious. See **trioecious.**

triennial *trī-en'yəl, adj.* continuing three years: happening every third year. — *adv.* **trienn'ially.** [L. *triennis* — *annus,* a year.]

trierarch *trī'ər-ärk, (Gr. hist.) n.* the commander of a trireme: one required (alone or with others) to fit out a trireme. — *adj.* **tri'erarchal.** — *n.* **tri'erarchy** the office of trierarch: the obligation of fitting out ships. [Gr. *triērarchos* — *triērēs,* a trireme, *archein,* to rule.]

trieteric *trī-i-ter'ik, adj.* biennial. [Gr. *trietērikos* — *trietēris,* a biennial festival — *treis,* three, *etos,* a year (both years being counted).]

triethyl *trī-eth'il, adj.* having three ethyl groups. — *n.* **triethylamine** (*-mēn'*) an oily liquid answering to ammonia with ethyl replacing all the hydrogen. [**tri-.**]

trifacial *trī-fā'shl, adj.* threefold and pertaining to the face. — **trifacial nerve** the trigeminal nerve. [**tri-** and L. *faciēs,* face.]

trifarious *trī-fā'ri-əs, adj.* arranged in three rows: facing three ways. [L. *trifārius.*]

trifecta *trī-fek'tə, (Austr.; horse-racing) n.* same as **triple.** [**tri-,** *perfecta.*]

triffid *trif'id, n.* in John Wyndham's science-fiction novel *The Day of the Triffids* (1951), a monstrous stinging plant, mobile and rapidly multiplying, of invasive habit and malign intent. — *adjs.* **triffid'ian, triff'idy** in the nature of or reminiscent of a triffid or triffids.

trifid *trif'id, trī'fid, adj.* cleft into three parts (*bot.,* etc.): (of a spoon) having a three-pointed decorative top to its handle. [L. *trifidus,* cleft into three parts — *findere,* to split.]

trifle *trī'fl, n.* anything of little importance or value: a small amount: a light confection of whipped cream or white of egg, sponge-cake, wine, etc.: a kind of pewter or articles made from it. — *v.i.* (often with *with*) to busy oneself idly: to play, toy: to behave without seriousness or respect: to meddle irresponsibly: to sport: to dally. — *v.t.* to spend or pass idly: to play with: to render trivial in comparison (*Shak.*). — *n.* **tri'fler.** — *adj.* **tri'fling** of small value, importance, or amount: trivial. — *adv.* **tri'flingly.** — *n.* **tri'flingness.** — **a trifle** slightly. [O.Fr. *trufle,* mockery, deception.]

trifocal *trī-fō'kəl, adj.* of a spectacle lens, giving separately near, intermediate, and far vision. — *n.pl.* **trifo'cals** spectacles with such lenses. [**tri-.**]

trifoliate *trī-fō'li-āt, adj.* with three leaves or leaflets. — *ns.* **Trifō'lium** the clover or trefoil genus: (without *cap.*) any plant of this genus; **trifoly** (*trif'ə-li; Browning*) trefoil. [L. *trifolium* — *folium,* leaf.]

triforium *trī-fō'ri-əm, -fō', (archit.) n.* a gallery, storey, or arcade over an aisle: — *pl.* **trifo'ria.** [L.L.; connection with *trēs,* three, and *foris,* door, does not appear.]

triform *trī'förm, adj.* having a triple form — also **tri'-formed.** [L. *trifōrmis* — *fōrma,* form.]

trifurcate *trī'fər-kāt,* or *-fûr', adj.* three-forked. — *v.i.* to divide into three branches. — *adj.* **tri'furcated** (or *-fûr'*). — *n.* **trifurcā'tion.** [L. *trifurcus* — *furca,* a fork.]

trig[1] *trig, adj.* trim, neat (chiefly *Scot.*): tight, sound. — *v.t.* to make trig: to stuff: to block, hold back with a wedge. — *n.* a block or wedge to stop a wheel. — *adv.* **trig'ly.** — *n.* **trig'ness.** [O.N. *tryggr,* faithful, secure; cf. **true.**]

trig[2] *trig, n.* an abbreviation of **trigonometry, trigonometric(al).**

trigamy *trig'ə-mi, n.* the having of three legal or supposed husbands or wives at once: a third marriage (*eccles. law*). — *n.* **trig'amist** one who has committed trigamy. — *adj.* **trig'amous** of the nature of, involving, living in, trigamy. [Gr. *trigamos,* thrice married — *gamos,* marriage.]

trigeminal *trī-jem'i-nl, adj.* threefold: three-branched. — **trigeminal nerve** a facial nerve having three branches, supplying the eye, nose, skin, scalp and muscles of mastication (also called **trifacial nerve**). — **trigeminal neuralgia** another term for **tic-douloureux.** [L.

trigeminus, born three at a birth — *geminus,* born at the same birth.]

trigger *trig'ər, n.* a lever that releases a catch so as to fire a gun or set a mechanism going: anything that starts a train of actions. — *v.t.* (often with *off*) to set in action. — *adj.* of something activated by or acting as a trigger. — **trigger finger** the finger used to pull the trigger on a gun, i.e. the forefinger of the dominant hand: a condition in which a finger is subject to involuntary muscular spasm, esp. where it cannot be straightened when unclenching the fist (*path.*). — *adj.* **trigg'er-happy** over-ready to shoot (*lit.* and *fig.*): irresponsibly willing to take the risk of beginning a fight or a war. — **trigg'er-happiness; trigg'erman** a gangster's bodyguard: the man who actually fired the shot. [Du. *trekker* — *trekken,* to pull.]

triglot *trī'glot, adj.* in, using, three languages, trilingual. — *n.* a book which is written in three languages. [**tri-** and Gr. *glōtta,* tongue.]

triglyceride *trī-glis'ər-īd, n.* any of a group of commonly occurring fats, those fatty acid esters of glycerol in which all three hydroxyl groups have had their hydrogen atoms replaced by acid radicals. [**tri-.**]

triglyph *trī'glif, n.* a three-grooved tablet in the Doric frieze. — *adj.* **triglyph'ic.** [Gr. *triglyphos* — *glyphein,* to carve.]

trigon *trī'gon, n.* a triangle: a set of three signs 120° apart, the zodiac being divided into four trigons — the first or *watery* trigon, Cancer, Scorpio, Pisces; the *earthly,* Taurus, Virgo, Capricorn; the *airy,* Gemini, Libra, Aquarius; the *fiery,* Aries, Leo, Sagittarius (*astrol.*). — *adjs.* **trigonal** (*trig'ə-nl*) of a trigon: triangular: trigonous: bounded by three planes: three-faced, forming half a hexagon in section: of symmetry about an axis, such that a rotation through 120° gives the same figure; **trigonic** (*trī-gon'ik*) of a trigon: triangular; **trigonous** (*trig'ə-nəs*) triangular in section, or nearly so — as with convex (or concave) faces, or rounded angles. [Gr. *trigōnon* — *gōniā,* an angle.]

trigonometry *trig-ə-nom'i-tri, n.* the branch of mathematics that treats of the relations between the sides and angles of triangles. — *n.* **trigonom'eter** one versed in or occupied with trigonometry: an instrument for solving triangles. — *adjs.* **trigonometric** (*-nə-met'rik*), **-al.** — *adv.* **trigonomet'rically.** — **trigonometrical point** (*geog.,* etc.) in triangulation, a fixed point whose position as vertex of a triangle is calculated astronomically (often shortened to **trig point**). [Gr. *trigōnon,* a triangle, *metron,* a measure.]

trigram *trī'gram, n.* an inscription of three letters: a figure of three lines. — *adjs.* **trigrammat'ic, trigramm'ic.** [**tri-** and Gr. *gramma,* a letter.]

trigraph *trī'gräf, n.* a combination of three letters for one sound. [**tri-** and Gr. *graphē,* a writing.]

Trigynia *trī-jin'i-ə, n.pl.* in the Linnaean system an order of plants (in various classes) with three pistils. — *adjs.* **trigyn'ian, trigynous** (*trij'i-nəs*). [**tri-** and Gr. *gynē,* a woman, female.]

trihedral *trī-hed'rəl, -hēd', (geom.,* etc.) *adj.* having three faces. — *n.* a trihedral figure, formed by three planes meeting at a point. — Also **trihed'ron** (or *-hēd'*). [**tri-** and Gr. *hedrā,* a seat.]

trihybrid *trī-hī'brid, n.* a cross between parents differing in three independently heritable characters. — Also *adj.* [**tri-.**]

trihydric *trī-hī'drik, adj.* having three hydroxyl groups. [**tri-.**]

trike. See **trichloroethylene** and **tricycle.**

trilateral *trī-lat'ər-əl, adj.* three-sided: of, having, three parties or participants. — *n.* a triangle. — *ns.* **trilat'eralism; trilat'eralist; trilatera'tion** a technique involving the measurement of selected sides of a triangulation (q.v.) network, for map-making, surveying, etc. [**tri-** and L. *latus, lateris,* side.]

trilby *tril'bi, n.* a soft felt hat (also **trilby hat**): (in *pl.*) feet (*slang*): — *pl.* **tril'bies** or **tril'bys.** [From George du Maurier's novel, *Trilby* (1894).]

trild *trild*, (*Spens*.). See **trill**[2].

trilemma *tri-*, *trī-lem'ə*, *n.* a form of argument or a situation differing from a dilemma in that there is a choice of three instead of two. [After **dilemma.**]

Trilene® *trī'lēn*, *n.* trichlorethylene.

trilinear *trī-lin'i-ər*, *adj.* consisting of, having, or referred to three lines. — *adj.* **trilin'eate** marked with three lines. [**tri-** and L. *līnea*, line.]

trilingual *trī-ling'gwəl*, *adj.* in or using three languages, esp. native or habitual languages. [**tri-** and L. *lingua*, tongue.]

triliteral *trī-lit'ər-əl*, *adj.* consisting of three letters. — *n.* **trilit'eralism** the characteristic (as of Semitic languages) of having roots of three consonants. [**tri-** and L. *littera*, a letter.]

trilith *trī'lith*, *n.* a form of megalithic monument consisting of two upright stones supporting another lying crosswise. — Also **trilithon** (*trī'*, *trī'*). — *adj.* **trilith'ic.** [**tri-** and Gr. *lithos*, stone.]

trill[1] *tril*, *n.* a trillo: a tremulous sound: a run or roulade of bird-song: a consonant-sound produced by vibration. — *v.t.* and *v.i.* to play, sing, pronounce, sound, with a trill. — *n.* **trill'o** (*mus.*) a shake: — *pl.* **trill'oes.** [It. *trillo*; imit.]

trill[2] *tril*, *v.t.* and *v.i.* to twirl: to roll: to trundle: to pour in a fine stream: — *pa.t.* **trilled** (*Spens.* **trild**). [Cf. Norw. and Sw. *trilla*, to roll.]

trilling *tril'ing*, *n.* a threefold compound of crystals: one child of triplets. [**tri-** and **-ling**; cf. Dan. and Sw. *trilling*; Ger. *Drilling*.]

trillion *tril'yən*, *n.* the cube of a million: the cube of ten thousand (orig. *U.S.*, and before 1948 in France): (*loosely*; esp. in *pl.*) an enormous number (*coll.*). — *n.* and *adj.* **trill'ionth.** [Fr., — **tri-**, after **million.**]

Trillium *tril'i-əm*, *n.* a three-leaved trimerous genus of the lily family: (*without cap.*) any plant of this genus. [L. *trēs*, three.]

trillo. See **trill**[1].

trilobe *trī'lōb*, *n.* something that has three lobes. — Also *adj.* — *adjs.* **trilobate(d)** (*trī'* or *-lō'*), **trī'lobed** having three lobes. — *n.* **trilobite** (*trī'lō-bīt* or *tril'ə-bīt*) any fossil arthropod of a Palaeozoic order (**Trilobi'ta**), with broad head-shield and body longitudinally furrowed into three lobes. — *adj.* **trilobitic** (*-bit'ik*) [**tri-** and Gr. *lobos*, lobe.]

trilocular *trī-lok'ū-lər*, *adj.* three-celled. [**tri-** and L. *loculus.*]

trilogy *tril'ə-ji*, *n.* a group of three tragedies: any similar group, as of novels: a triad. [Gr. *trilogiā* — *logos*, discourse.]

trim *trim*, *v.t.* to put in due condition: to fit out: to make ready for sailing: to adjust the balance of (a boat or aircraft): to dress, arrange: to set in order: to decorate (clothes, etc.) as with ribbons, lace, contrasting edging, etc.: to make tidy or neat: to clip into shape: to make compact: to reduce the size of, by removing what could be regarded as excess: to smooth: to take or put by trimming: to rebuke sharply: to thrash: to cheat (*slang*): to adjust the inclination of a plane to the horizontal. — *v.i.* to balance: to balance or fluctuate between parties, be a trimmer: to adjust one's behaviour as expediency dictates: — *pr.p.* **trimm'ing**; *pa.t.* and *pa.p.* **trimmed.** — *adj.* in good order: neat: tidy: well-kept: clean-cut: slim. — *adv.* trimly. — *n.* condition for sailing or flight: balance: condition, order: a fit, trim condition: humour, disposition, temper, way: array: fittings: the colour-scheme and chrome parts on the outside of a motor-vehicle, or the upholstery, door-handles, etc. inside it: decorative additions to clothes, e.g. contrasting edging, etc.: an act of trimming: window-dressing (*U.S.*): parts trimmed off: adjustment of an aircraft's controls to achieve stability in a desired condition of flight. — *adv.* **trim'ly.** — *ns.* **trimm'er** one who or that which trims: one who fluctuates between parties, attaching himself wherever he sees advantage and adjusting his opinions, etc. to match his changing loyalties: a time-server: a scold:

anything trouncing or redoubtable: a small horizontal beam on a floor into which the ends of joists are framed: a float bearing a baited hook and line, used in fishing for pike: a trimming tab: something fine, excellent, approved of (*Austr.* and *N.Z.*, *coll.*); **trimm'ing** making trim: balancing: clipping: (usu. in *pl.*) ornamental additions: (in *pl.*) accessories: (in *pl.*) sauces and other accompaniments for a dish: (in *pl.*) fittings: (in *pl.*) parts trimmed off. — *adj.* that trims. — *adv.* **trimm'ingly.** — *n.* **trim'ness.** — **trimming tab, trim'tab** a tab or aerofoil on an aircraft or boat, that can be adjusted in mid-passage to trim the craft. — **trim one's sails** to rule one's conduct, principles, etc., to accord with prevailing circumstances. [O.E. *trymman*, *trymian*, to strengthen, set in order — *trum*, firm.]

trimaran *trī'mə-ran*, *n.* a boat with three hulls. [**tri-** and cata*maran*.]

trimer *trī'mər*, (*chem.*) *n.* a substance in which molecules are formed from three molecules of a monomer. — *adjs.* **trimer'ic** (*chem.*) having the same empirical formula but a relative molecular mass three times as great; **trim'erous** (*bot.*) having three parts, or parts in three. [**tri-** and Gr. *meros*, part.]

trimester *tri-mes'tər*, *n.* three months: an academic term. — *adj.* **trimes'trial.** [L. *trimēstris*, of three months — *mēnsis*, a month.]

trimeter *trim'i-tər*, *n.* a verse of three measures (dipodies or feet). — *adjs.* **trim'eter, trimetric, -al** (*trī-met'rik, -l*) consisting of three measures, esp. iambic. [Gr. *trimetros* — *metron*, measure.]

trimethyl *trī-meth'il*, *adj.* containing three methyl radicals in combination. — *ns.* **trimethylamine** (*-ə-mēn'*) a gas, $(CH_3)_3N$, which can be got from herring-brine, corresponding to ammonia with methyl replacing all the hydrogen; **trimeth'ylene** (*-ēn*) cyclopropane. [**tri-**.]

trimetric. See **trimeter.**

trimonthly *trī-munth'li*, *adj.* every three months. [**tri-**.]

trimorphism *trī-mör'fizm*, *n.* occurrence of three forms in the same species (*biol.*): the property of crystallising in three forms (*chem.*). — *adjs.* **trimor'phic, trimor'phous.** [**tri-** and Gr. *morphē*, form.]

trimtab. See **trim.**

Trimurti *tri-mōōr'ti*, *n.* the Hindu trinity, Brahma, Vishnu, and Siva. [Sans. *tri*, three, *mūrti*, shape.]

trin. See **trine**[1].

Trinacrian *tri-*, *trī-nā'kri-ən*, *adj.* Sicilian: (*without cap.*) three-pointed: with three extremities. — *adj.* **trinacriform** (*trin-ak'ri-förm*) three-pronged. [Gr. *Trīnakriā*, Sicily, *trīnax, -akos*, a three-pronged mattock, *thrīnax*, a trident.]

trinal, trinary. See **trine**[1].

trindle *trin'dl*, *n.* a piece of wood, etc., laid between the cords and boards of a book to flatten before cutting: a wheel, esp. of a barrow. — *v.t.* and *v.i.* to roll, to trundle. — **trin'dle-tail** a trundle-tail. [**trundle.**]

trine[1] *trīn*, *adj.* threefold: 120° apart (*astrol.*): hence, benign (*astrol.*). — *n.* a triad: the aspect of two planets, as seen from the earth, distant from each other one-third of the zodiac or 120°: a triplet. — *v.t.* to join in trine aspect. — *n.* **trin** (*trin*) a triplet (by birth): a trilling. — *adjs.* **trinal** (*trī'nl*), **trī'nary.** [L. *trīnus* — *trēs, tria*, three.]

trine[2] *trīn*, *v.i.* to go. — **trine to the (nubbing-) cheat** (*cant*) to go the gallows.

tringle *tring'gl*, *n.* a curtain-rod. [Fr.]

Trinidadian *trin-i-dad'i-ən, -dād'i-ən*, *adj.* of or pertaining to the island of *Trinidad* in the West Indies. — *n.* a native of Trinidad.

triniscope *trin'i-skōp*, *n.* a cathode-ray tube for colour television. [L. *trīnus*, triple, Gr. *skopeein*, to view.]

trinitro- *trī-nī'trō-*, in composition, having three nitro-groups (NO_2), esp. replacing hydrogen. — *ns.* **trini'trin** glyceryl trinitrate or nitroglycerine, used to treat angina pectoris; **trini'trate** a nitrate with three nitrate groups in the molecule; **trinitroben'zene** $C_6H_3(NO_2)_3$, answering to benzene C_6H_6; **trinitrophe'nol** a similar derivative of phenol, esp. picric acid; **trinitrotol'uene**

or **-tol′uol** a high explosive (familiarly **TNT**), a trinitro-derivative of toluene. **[tri-.]**

trinity *trin′i-ti, n.* threefoldness: three in one: a triad: esp. (with *cap.*) the triune God of orthodox Christians (Father, Son, Holy Ghost): (with *cap.*) any symbolical representation of the persons of the Trinity: (with *cap.*) Trinity Sunday: (with *cap.*) Trinity term. — *adj.* **Trinitā′rian** of, in relation to, believing in, the Trinity: of the Trinitarians. — *n.* one who holds the doctrine of the Trinity: a member of a religious order founded at Rome in 1198 to redeem Christian captives from the Muslims — also *Mathurins* and *Redemptionists*: a member of Trinity College. — *n.* **Trinitā′rianism.** — **Trinity House** a lighthouse and pilot authority for England, and in part Scotland and Northern Ireland, chartered at Deptford in 1514; **Trinity Sunday** the Sunday after Whitsunday; **Trinity term** one of the terms of the English law-courts beginning after Trinity Sunday (now **Trinity law sittings**): the university term beginning after Trinity Sunday. [L. *trīnitās, -ātis* — *trīnus,* threefold.]

trinket *tring′kit, n.* a small ornament or piece of jewellery: any paltry or trumpery object or observance: a delicacy (*obs.*). — *v.i.* (*obs.*) to have traffickings or underhand dealings. — *ns.* **trink′eter** (*obs.*) an intriguer; **trink′-eting; trink′etry** trinkets collectively. [Poss. O.Fr. *trenquet,* small knife.]

trinkum *tring′kəm.* Same as **trankum.** — Also **trink′um= trank′um.**

trinomial *trī-nō′mi-əl, adj.* consisting of three words: of three terms connected by the sign plus or minus. — *n.* a trinomial name or expression. — *ns.* **trino′mialism** the system of naming by three words (for genus, species, and subspecies); **trino′mialist.** [After **binomial.**]

trio *trē′ō, n.* a set of three: a composition for, or combination of, three performers (*mus.*): the second division of a minuet, scherzo, or march (said to have been originally for three instruments), followed by a repetition of the first (*mus.*): — *pl.* **tri′os.** [It.]

triode *trī′ōd, adj.* with three electrodes. — *n.* a three-electrode valve. **[tri-** and Gr. *hodos,* a path, way.]

Triodion *trī-ō′di-on,* (*Greek church*) *n.* a service-book for the ten weeks before Easter. [Mod. Gr. *triōdion* — *ōdē,* hymn.]

trioecious, triecious *trī-ē′shəs, adj.* having male, female, and hermaphrodite flowers on different plants. **[tri-** and Gr. *oikos,* house.]

triolet *trī′ō-lit, trē′ō-lā, -let, n.* an eight-lined poem rhymed *ab aa abab,* lines 4 and 7 repeating 1, and 8 repeating 2. [Fr.]

triones *trī-ō′nēz, n.pl.* the seven stars of the Plough. [L. *triōnēs,* plough-oxen.]

trionym *trī′ə-nim, n.* a trinomial. — *adj.* **trionymal** (*-on′i-məl*). [Gr. *triōnymous* — *onyma* (*onoma*), name.]

trior. See **try.**

trioxide *trī-oks′īd, n.* a compound with three atoms of oxygen. **[tri-.]**

trip[1] *trip, v.i.* to move with short, light steps or skips: to stumble: to catch one's foot: to make a slip in chastity, accuracy, etc.: to tip up: to make an excursion: to experience the hallucinatory effects of LSD or similar drug (also **trip out;** *slang*). — *v.t.* to cause to stumble or fall by catching the foot (often with *up*): to catch in a fault: to dance trippingly: to trip or dance upon: to loose, as an anchor, from the bottom, by a long rope: to release by striking: to tilt up: — *pr.p.* **tripp′ing;** *pa.t.* and *pa.p.* **tripped.** — *n.* a light, short step or skip: a catching of the foot: a stumble: a point in coursing, when the hare is thrown off its legs: a slip, lapse: a single journey or run, one way or to and fro: a pleasure excursion, jaunt: a specially arranged run at a cheap fare: a company of excursionists: a striking part that releases a catch: a hallucinatory experience under the influence of a drug such as LSD, or (*loosely*) a quantity of a drug that will produce such an experience (*slang*): any stimulating experience (good or bad) (*slang*). —

adj. **tripp′ant** (*her.*) tripping, with right foot raised. — *n.* **tripp′er** one who trips: an excursionist, esp. of the disturbing kind: a device that when struck, passed over, etc., operates a switch. — *adjs.* **tripp′erish, tripp′-ery** of, like, savouring of, the vulgar or noisy tripper. — *n.* and *adj.* **tripp′ing.** — **tripp′ingly.** — **trip′= hammer** a tilt-hammer; **trip′-hook** (*Browning*) some kind of instrument of torture; **trip′-wire** a wire which releases some mechanism when pulled, e.g. by being tripped over. [O.Fr. *triper;* of Gmc. origin; cf. O.E. *treppan,* to tread, Ger. *trappe(l)n,* Du. *trippen, trappen, trippelen,* Sw. *trippa.*]

trip[2] *trip, n.* a small flock of sheep, wildfowl, etc. [Perh. akin to **troop.**]

tripartite *trī-pär′tīt, adj.* in three parts: cleft in three nearly to the base (*bot.*): relating to three parties. — *ns.* **tripar′tism** division into three parts, esp. political parties (*rare*): an established system of dialogue between three related groups, specif. government, employers, and unions, for mutually acceptable planning and follow-up; **tripartition** (*-tish′ən*). [L. *trīpartītus* — *partīrī,* to divide — *pars,* part.]

tripe *trīp, n.* entrails (*arch.*): parts of the compound stomach of a ruminant, prepared as food — the paunch or rumen (*plain tripe*), and the smaller reticulum (*honeycomb tripe*): rubbish, poor stuff (*coll.*): claptrap (*coll.*). — *n.* **trīp′ery** a place for the preparation or sale of tripe. — **tripe′hound** (*slang*) a newspaper reporter: a dog (*Austr.*); **tripe′man, -wife, -woman** a dresser or seller of tripe; **tripe′-shop.** — *adj.* **tripe′= visag′d** (*Shak.*) with a face like tripe. — **tripe de roche** (*trēp də rosh;* Fr.) rock-tripe. [O.Fr. (Fr.) *tripe;* origin obscure.]

tripedal *trip′-, trīp′i-dl, trī-pē′dl, adj.* three-footed. [tri- and L. *pēs, pedis,* foot.]

tripersonal *trī-pûr′sən-əl, adj.* consisting of three persons. — *ns.* **triper′sonalism; triper′sonalist** a believer in the Trinity; **tripersonal′ity.** **[tri-.]**

tripetalous *trī-pet′əl-əs, adj.* three-petalled. **[tri-** and Gr. *petalon,* leaf.]

triphenyl- *trī-fē′nil-,* in composition, containing three phenyl radicals in combination. — *ns.* **triphenylamine** (*-ə-mēn*) a crystalline compound answering to ammonia with all the hydrogen replaced by phenyl; **tri-phenylmē′thane** a crystalline solid used in the preparation of dyes. **[tri-.]**

triphibious *trī-fib′i-əs, adj.* using or taking place in the three elements, land, water, air. **[tri-,** and grotesquely, **-phibious,** after **amphibious.**]

triphone *trī′fōn, n.* a shorthand sign representing a triphthongal sound. **[tri-** and Gr. *phōnē,* sound.]

triphthong *trif′thong, n.* a combination of three vowel sounds in one syllable: (*loosely*) a trigraph. — *adj.* **triphthongal** (*-thong′gl*). **[tri-** and Gr. *phthongos,* sound.]

triphyllous *trī-fil′əs, adj.* three-leaved. **[tri-** and Gr. *phyllon,* a leaf.]

Triphysite *trif′i-zīt, -sīt, n.* a believer in the existence of three natures in Christ — human, divine, and a third resulting from the union of these. **[tri-** and Gr. *physis,* nature.]

tripinnate *trī-pin′āt, -it, adj.* pinnate with the pinnae themselves pinnate, and their pinnae again pinnate. **[tri-.]**

Tripitaka *trip-i-tä′kə, -pit′ə-kə, n.* (also without *cap.*) the whole body of the northern Buddhist canonical writings, comprising the three divisions of *sutras,* or discourses of the Buddha for the laity; *Vinaya,* or discipline for the order; and *Abhidharma,* or metaphysics. [Pali, lit. three baskets.]

triplane *trī′plān, n.* an aeroplane with three sets of main planes, one above another. **[tri-.]**

triple *trip′l, adj.* threefold: consisting of three: three times as much: third (*Shak.*). — *n.* a quantity three times as much: a thing (e.g. a star) that is triple: a peal of bells interchanging in three sets: a betting system requiring that the horses which finish first, second and third in a race are selected in correct order. — *v.t.* and *v.i.* to treble. — *ns.* **trip′leness; trip′let** three of a kind, or three united: three lines rhyming together: a group of three notes occupying the time of two, indicated by a slur and the figure 3 (*mus.*): one of three born at a birth: a state in which there are two unpaired electrons (*chem.*): a cycle for three riders. — *adj.* **trip′lex** triple. — *n.* (*Shak.*) triple time. — *adj.* **trip′licate** threefold: made thrice as much: as the cubes of the quantities. — *n.* a third copy or thing corresponding to two others of the same kind: the triplicate ratio. — *v.t.* to make threefold. — *ns.* **triplica′tion** the act of triplicating: a reply to a duplication; **triplicity** (*trip-lis′i-ti*) tripleness: a triad: a trigon (*astrol.*); **trip′ling** a making triple: a triplet, trilling or trin. — *adv.* **triply** (*trip′li*). — *n.* (*tri-plī′*; *Scots law*) a pursuer's reply to a defender's duply. — *v.t.* and *v.i.* to reply to a duply. — **Triple Alliance** the league of England, Sweden, and the Netherlands formed against France in 1668: the alliance of Britain, France, and Holland against Spain in 1717: the alliance between Germany, Austria, and Italy, 1883–1915, counterbalanced by the **Triple Entente**, a friendly understanding (developing into an alliance) between Britain, France, and Russia; **triple crown** the pope's tiara: the distinction won by coming out best in a series of matches between England, Scotland, Wales, and Ireland, in which each country plays the other three (*Rugby*, etc.). — *adj.* **trip′le-crowned** having three crowns or a triple crown, as the pope. — **triple event** Two Thousand Guineas, St Leger, and Derby. — *adj.* **trip′le-head′ed** three-headed. — **triple jump** an athletic event, based on a hop, skip and jump, in which a competitor tries to cover the longest possible distance; **triple point** the temperature and pressure at which solid, liquid, and gaseous phases of a substance can co-exist, esp. triple point of water, 273·16K; **triple time** time or rhythm of three beats, or of three times three beats, in a bar. — *adj.* **trip′le-turned** (*Shak.*) three times faithless. — **Triplex® glass** a combination of glass and mica in three layers. — *adj.* **triplicate-ternate** see **triternate**. [Fr., — L. *triplus* — Gr. *triploos* (*triplous*); and L. *triplex*.]

triploid *trip′loid*, *adj.* having three times the haploid number of chromosomes. — *n.* **trip′loidy**. [Gr. *triploos*, triple.]

triply. See **triple.**

tripod *trī′pod*, *trip′od*, *n.* anything on three feet or legs, esp. a stand for an instrument: the stool on which the priestess sat at Delphi to deliver an oracle. — *adj.* **three-legged.** *adj.* **tripodal** (*trip′əd-əl*) — *n.* **tripody** (*trip′ə-di*) a verse or group of three feet. [Gr. *tripous*, *tripodos* — *pous*, *podos*, foot.]

tripoli *trip′ə-li*, *n.* diatomite. [Orig. brought from *Tripoli* in Africa.]

tripos *trī′pos*, *n.* a Cambridge honours examination: the list of successful candidates in it: a tripod (*obs.*). [Prob. traceable to the custom by which a B.A., known as Mr *Tripos*, sat on a three-legged stool and disputed in the Philosophy School at Cambridge on Ash Wednesday, his speech being called the Tripos speech.]

trippant, tripper, tripping, etc. See **trip**[1].

trippet *trip′it*, *n.* a trivet: in a machine, a piece which projects in order to strike another part of the mechanism regularly. [Cf. **trivet** and O.Fr. *trepied*.]

tripple *trip′l*, (*S.Afr.*) *n.* a horse's ambling canter, between a fast walk and a slow trot. — Also *v.i.* — *n.* **tripp′ler.** [Du. *trippelen*.]

tripsis *trip′sis*, *n.* pulverisation: shampooing: massage. [Gr. *tripsis* — *tribein*, to rub.]

triptane *trip′tān*, *n.* trimethyl butane, a powerful aviation fuel. [*tri*methyl *butane*, with *b* altered to *p*.]

tripterous *trip′tər-əs*, *adj.* three-winged. [Gr. *tripteros* — *pteron*, wing.]

triptote *trip′tōt*, *adj.* used in three cases only. — *n.* a triptote word. [Gr. *triptōtos* — *ptōsis*, a case, falling.]

triptych *trip′tik*, *n.* a set of three tablets, painted panels, etc., hinged together. — *n.* **triptyque** (*trēp-tēk*; Fr.) an international pass for a motor-car. [Gr. *triptychos*, threefold — *ptyx*, *ptychos*, a fold — *ptyssein*, to fold.]

tripudium *trī-pū′di-əm*, *tri-pōōd′i-ōōm*, *n.* an ancient Roman religious dance in triple time, or dance generally: divination from the hopping of birds feeding, or from the dropping of scraps from their bills. — *adj.* **tripu′diary.** — *v.i.* **tripu′diate** to dance for joy: to exult: to stamp. — *n.* **tripudiā′tion.** [L. *trīpudium*, prob. from *trēs*, three, *pēs*, *pedis*, foot.]

triquetra *trī-kwet′rə*, *n.* an ornament consisting of three interlaced arcs, common in early art in northern Europe. — *adjs.* **triquet′ral, triquet′rous** triangular: three-edged with concave faces (*bot.*). — *adv.* **triquet′rously.** — *n.* **triquet′rum** a Wormian bone: — *pl.* **triquet′ra.** [L. *triquetrus, -a, -um,* triangular — *trēs,* three.]

triradiate *trī-rā′di-āt, adj.* three-rayed. — Also **trirā′dial.** [tri-.]

trireme *trī′rēm, n.* an ancient galley — esp. a war-galley — with three sets of rowers. [L. *trirēmis* — *rēmus,* an oar.]

trisaccharide *trī-sak′ə-rīd, n.* a sugar that hydrolyses into three molecules of simple sugars. [tri-.]

trisagion *tris-ag′i-on, n.* an ancient hymn consisting of the words 'O Holy God, holy and mighty, holy and immortal, have mercy on us': loosely, the Tersanctus. [Gr. *tris,* thrice, *hagios,* holy.]

trisect *trī-sekt′, v.t.* to cut or divide into three (usu. equal) parts. — *ns.* **trisec′tion** (-*shən*); **trisect′or** one who trisects: esp. one who thinks he can trisect an angle by Euclidean methods (i.e. using straight-edge and compasses) which has been proved to be impossible: a line that trisects; **trisect′rix** a curve of polar equation $r = 1 + 2\cos\theta$, by which an angle can be trisected. [tri- and L. *secāre, sectum,* to cut.]

triseme *trī′sēm, adj.* equal to three short syllables. — *n.* a trisemic foot, the tribrach, iamb, trochee. — *adj.* **trisē′mic.** [Gr. *trisēmos* — *sēma,* a sign.]

trishaw *trī′shō, n.* a three-wheeled light vehicle pedalled by a driver behind the passenger seat. [**tri-,** rick*shaw.*]

triskaidekaphobia, also **-deca-,** *tris-kī-dek-ə-fōb′i-ə, n.* fear of the number thirteen. — *n.* **triskaidek′aphobe** one who suffers from triskaidekaphobia. [Gr. *tr(e)iskaideka,* thirteen, *phobos,* fear.]

triskele *tris′kēl, n.* a figure consisting of three radiating curves or legs, as in the arms of the Isle of Man. — Also **triskelion** (*tris kel′i-on*): — *pl.* **triskel′ia.** [tri- and Gr. *skelos,* a leg.]

Trismegistus *tris-mi-gis′təs, adj.* thrice greatest, an epithet of Thoth, the Egyptian Hermes. [Latinised from Gr. *trismegistos.*]

trismus *triz′məs, n.* tetanic spasm of the muscles of mastication, causing difficulty in opening the mouth. [Latinised from Gr. *trismos,* a creaking, grating — *trizein,* to grate, gnash.]

trisoctahedron *tris-ok-tə-hē′dron, n.* a solid with twenty-four faces, three for every face of an octahedron: — *pl.* **trisoctahē′drons, trisoctahē′dra.** [Gr. *tris,* thrice, and **octahedron.**]

trisomic *trī-sōm′ik, adj.* of an otherwise normal diploid organism in which one chromosome type is represented thrice instead of twice. — *ns.* **tri′sōme** a chromosome that occurs three times in a cell instead of twice: a trisomic individual; **tri′sōmy** a trisomic condition. [tri-.]

trist, triste *trist,* (*arch.*) *adj.* sorrowful: dismal. — Also **trist′ful** (*Shak.*). [Fr. *triste* — L. *tristis,* sad.]

tristich *tris′tik, n.* a group of three lines of verse: — *pl.* **tris′tichs** (-*tiks*). — *adjs.* **tristich′ic; tris′tichous** (*biol.*) in or having three rows. [Gr. *tristichiā,* a triple row, tristich — *stichos,* a row.]

tristimulus values *trī-stim′ū-ləs val′ūz,* amounts of each of three colour primaries that must be combined to form an objective colour match with a sample. [tri-.]

trisula *tri-sōō′lə, n.* the trident of Siva. — Also **trisul′.** [Sans. *triśūla.*]

trisulcate *trī-sul′kāt, adj.* having three forks or furrows.

[L. *trisulcus* — *sulcus*, a furrow.]
trisulphide *trī-sul'fīd, n.* a sulphide with three atoms of sulphur to the molecule. [**tri-.**]
trisyllable *tri-sil'ə-bl*, also *trī-, n.* a word of three syllables. — *adjs.* **trisyllabic** (-*ab'ik*), **-al.** — *adv.* **trisyllab'ically.** [**tri-.**]
tritagonist *tri-tag'ən-ist, n.* the third actor in the Greek drama. [Gr. *tritagōnistēs* — *tritos*, third, *agōnistēs*, an actor.]
tritanopia *trī-tən-ō'pi-ə, n.* inability to distinguish the colour blue. — *adj.* **trītanōp'ic.** [Gr. *tritos*, a third, Mod. L. *anopia*, blindness, i.e. blindness to a third of the spectrum.]
trite¹ *trīt, adj.* worn: worn-out: well-trodden: used till novelty and interest are lost: hackneyed. — *adv.* **trite'ly.** — *n.* **trite'ness.** [L. *trītus*, rubbed, pa.p. of *terēre*, to rub.]
trite² *trī'tē*, (Gr. *mus.*) *n.* the third string of the lyre or tone of the tetrachord, reckoned downwards. [Gr. *tritē* (fem.), third.]
triternate *trī-tûr'nāt, adj.* thrice ternate — ternate with each division ternate, and each again ternate. — Also **trip'licate-ter'nate.** [**tri-.**]
tritheism *trī'thē-izm, n.* belief in three Gods: belief that the Father, Son, and Holy Ghost are actually different beings. — *n.* **tri'theist.** — *adjs.* **tritheis'tic, -al.** [**tri-** and Gr. *theos*, a god.]
trithionic *trī-thī-on'ik, adj.* containing three sulphur atoms (**trithionic acid**, $H_2S_3O_6$). — *n.* **trithionate** (*trīthī'-ən-āt*) a salt of trithionic acid. [**tri-** and *theion*, sulphur.]
tritiate. See **tritium.**
tritical *trit'i-kl, adj.* trite, common. — *adv.* **trit'ically.** — *ns.* **trit'icalness, trit'icism** triteness. [Formed from **trite¹** in imitation of **critical**, etc.]
Triticum *trit'i-kəm, n.* the wheat genus of grasses. — *n.* **trit'icale** a hybrid cereal grass, a cross between wheat and rye, grown as a food crop. — *adj.* **triticeous** (-*ish'əs*) wheatlike. [L. *trīticum*, wheat — *terēre*, *trītum*, to rub.]
tritium *trish'i-əm, trit', n.* an isotope of hydrogen of triple mass. — *v.t.* **tritiate** (*trish'i-āt, trit'i-āt*) to replace normal hydrogen atoms in (a compound) by tritium. — *ns.* **tritiā'tion; trit'ide** a compound of tritium with another element or radical; **triton** (*trī'tən*) the nucleus of tritium, composed of one proton and two neutrons. [Gr. *tritos*, third.]
Tritoma *trit'ō-mə*, wrongly *trī-tō'mə, n.* a synonym of Kniphofia. [Gr. *trĭtŏmos*, thrice cut — *tomē*, a cut (from the splitting capsule).]
Triton *trī'tən, n.* a minor Greek sea-god, son of Poseidon and Amphitrite, represented with a dolphin's tail, sometimes horse's forelegs, blowing a conch: sometimes in *pl.* for the attendants of Poseidon: applied to a seaman or a ship: a genus of large gasteropods with shells that can be used like conchs: a disused generic name for newts: the larger of the two satellites of the planet Neptune, the other being Nereid. [Gr. *Trītōn, -ōnos.*]
triton. See **tritium.**
tritone *trī'tōn*, (*mus.*) *n.* an augmented fourth, an interval of three whole tones. [Gr. *trĭtŏnos* — *tonos*, tone.]
Tritonia *trī-tō'ni-ə, n.* a genus of iridaceous S. African plants: (without *cap.*) a plant of this genus, sometimes called montbretia.
tritubercular *trī-tū-bûr'kū-lər, adj.* having three tubercles or cusps — also **trituber'culate.** — *ns.* **trituber'culism, trituber'culy.** [**tri-.**]
triturate *trit'ū-rāt, v.t.* to rub or grind to a fine powder. — *n.* the fine powder thus obtained. — *ns.* **triturā'tion; trit'urātor.** [L.L. *trītūrāre, -ātum* — L. *terēre*, to rub.]
triumph *trī'əmf, n.* in ancient Rome, a solemn procession in honour of a victorious general: a pageant: festivity (*obs.*): pomp, observance (*obs.*): a captive led in triumph (*Milt.*): exultation for success: complete or signal victory or achievement: trump (*obs.*). — *v.i.* to celebrate a victory with pomp: to rejoice for victory:

to obtain victory, prevail (often with *over*): to exult, insult (often with *over*): to show in glory (*Shak.*). — *v.t.* (*Milt.*) to triumph over. — *adj.* **triumphal** (*trī-umf'l*) pertaining to triumph: used in celebrating victory. — *n.* (*Milt.*) a token of victory. — *n.* **triumph'alism** an attitude of righteous pride and self-congratulation in the defeat of perceived evil. — *adj.* **triumph'ant** celebrating or having achieved a triumph: exultant: transcendent in glory (*Shak.*): triumphal (*Shak.*). — *adv.* **triumph'antly.** — *ns.* **tri'umpher; triumph'ery** (*Shak.*) see **triumvir.** — *n.* and *adj.* **tri'umphing.** — **triumphal arch** an arch erected in connection with the triumph of a Roman general: any decorative arch in public rejoicings, etc. — **church triumphant** see **church.** [L. *triumphus*; akin to Gr. *thriambos*, a hymn to Bacchus.]
triumvir *trī-um'vər, trē-ōōm'vir, n.* one of three men in the same office or government: one of three sharing supreme power: — *pl.* **trium'virī, trium'virs.** — *adj.* **trium'viral.** — *n.* **trium'virate** (*obs.* **trium'viry;** *Shak.* **trium'phery**) an association of three men in office or government, or for any political ends — esp. that of Pompey, Crassus, and Caesar (60 B.C.), and that of Octavian (Augustus), Mark Antony, and Lepidus (43 B.C.): any trio or triad. [L. *triumvir*, from the gen. pl. *trĭum virōrum*, of three men.]
triune *trī'ūn, adj.* three in one. — *n.* a trinity in unity. — *n.* **triū'nity.** [L. *trēs, tria*, three, *ūnus*, one.]
trivalent *trī-vā'lənt, triv'ə-lənt, adj.* having a valency of three. — *ns.* **trivā'lence** (or *triv'əl-*), **trivā'lency** (or *triv'əl-*). [**tri-** and **-valent.**]
trivalve *trī'valv, adj.* three-valved. — *n.* that which is three-valved. — *adjs.* **tri'valved, trival'vūlar.** [**tri-** and L. *valva*, a door-leaf.]
trivet *triv'it, n.* a tripod, esp. one for a pot or kettle: a bracket with three projections for fixing on the top bar of a grate: a three-legged pot: a usu. metal plate placed in a pressure cooker to raise the food to be cooked off the bottom of the vessel. — **right as a trivet** perfectly right (from its stability). [O.E. *trefet*, app. — L. *tripēs, tripedis* — *pēs*, a foot.]
trivia *tri'vi-ə, n.pl.* trifles, trivialities, unimportant details. — *adj.* **trivial** (*triv'i-əl*) of the trivium: to be found anywhere: of little importance: trifling: vernacular (*biol.*): specific, opp. to generic (of a name; *biol.*): with value zero (*math.*). — *n.* **trivialisā'tion, -z-.** — *v.i.* **triv'ialise, -ize** to make trivial, unimportant. — *ns.* **triv'ialism** a trivial matter or remark; **triviality** (*-al'i-ti*) the state or quality of being trivial: that which is trivial, a trifle. — *adv.* **triv'ially.** — *ns.* **triv'ialness; triv'ium** in mediaeval schools the group of liberal arts first studied — grammar, rhetoric, and logic: the three anterior radii of an echinoderm. [L. *trivium*, a place where three ways meet — *trēs*, three, *via*, a way.]
tri-weekly *trī-wēk'li, adj.* occurring or appearing once in three weeks or three times a week. — *adv.* once in three weeks: three times a week. — *n.* a periodical appearing three times a week. [**tri-.**]
-trix *-triks, suff.* denoting a feminine agent: — *pl.* **-trixes, -trices** (*-trī-sēz, -tri-siz*). [L.]
trizone *trī'zōn, n.* a unit or country formed of three zones, e.g. the area of West Germany comprised in the British, French, and American zones of occupation after World War II also called **Trizōn'ia.** — *adj.* **trizō'nal.** [**tri-** and **zone.**]
troad, troade (*Spens.*). See **trod¹.**
troat *trōt, v.i.* to bellow, as a buck. — Also *n.* [O.Fr. *trout, trut*, interj. used to urge on animals.]
trocar *trō'kär, n.* a surgical perforator used with a cannula: sometimes a cannula. [Fr. *trocart* — *trois*, three, *carre*, side.]
trochaic. See **trochee.**
trochal. See **trochus.**
trochanter *trō-kan'tər, n.* a rough eminence on the thighbone for insertion of muscles: the second segment of an insect's leg. — *adj.* **trochanteric** (*-ter'ik*). [Gr. *trochantēr* — *trechein*, to run.]
troche, trocheameter. See **trochus.**

trochee _trō'kē_, (_pros._) _n._ a foot of two syllables, a long followed by a short: in English, etc., a stressed followed by an unstressed. — _adj._ **trochaic** (-kā'ik). — _n._ a trochaic verse. [Gr. _trochaios_ (_pous_, foot), running, tripping — _trochos_, a running — _trechein_, to run.]

Trochelminthes, Trochidae. See **trochus.**

trochilus _trok'i-ləs_, _n._ a concave moulding: the crocodile bird: (with _cap._) a genus of humming-birds, formerly including all of them, giving name to the humming-bird family **Trochil'idae.** — _adj._ **trochil'ic** pertaining to rotatory motion. [Gr. _trochilos_, a crocodile bird, a wren, a pulley sheaf — _trechein_, to run.]

trochiscus, trochisk, trochite. See **trochus.**

trochlea _trok'li-ə_, (_zool._) _n._ any pulley-like structure, esp. a foramen through which a tendon passes. — _adj._ **troch'lear.** — **trochlear nerve** the fourth cranial nerve. [L. _trochlea_ — Gr. _trochiliā_, a pulley.]

trochoid, etc. See **trochus.**

trochus _trō'kəs_, _n._ a wheel or hoop (_Gr._ ant.): the inner ring of cilia in a rotifer: (with _cap._) the top genus of molluscs. — _adj._ **tro'chal** wheel-like. — _n._ **troche** (_trōk, trōsh, trōch; trō'kē_ is frowned upon) a round medicinal tablet. — _ns.pl._ **Trochelminthes** (_trōk-el-min'thēz_; Gr. _helmins, helminthos,_ worm) the rotifer phylum of animals; **Troch'idae** the top family of molluscs. — _ns._ **trochisc'us, troch'isk** a troche; **troch'ite** an encrinite joint; **troch'oid** the curve traced by a fixed point, not on the circumference, in the plane of a rolling circle. — _adj._ wheel-like: like a Trochus: trochoidal. — _adj._ **trochoid'al** of the nature of a trochoid. — _ns._ **trochom'-eter** or (_ill-formed_) **trocheam'eter** a hodometer; **troch'-ophore, troch'osphere** a free-swimming, pelagic larval form of many invertebrates; **troch'otron** _trocho_idal magne_tron_, a high-frequency counting tube which deflects a beam on to radially disposed electrodes. [Gr. _trochos_, a wheel — _trechein_, to run.]

trock (_Scot._). See **truck**[1].

troctolite _trok'tə-līt_, _n._ troutstone, a coarse-grained basic igneous rock composed of feldspar spotted with olivine. [Gr. _trōktēs_, a kind of sea-fish — _trōgein_, to gnaw, nibble, _lithos_, stone.]

trod[1] _trod_ (_Spens._) **troad, troade, trode,** _trōd_), (_obs._) _n._ a track: path: footing. — **hot trod** (_Scott_) the pursuit of moss-troopers. [O.E. _trod, trodu,_ track, trace; cf. **tread.**]

trod[2], **trodden.** See **tread.**

trode. See **trod**[1].

troelie, troely. See **troolie.**

trog _trog_, (_coll._) _v.i._ to walk, usu. heavily and wearily: — _pr.p._ **trogg'ing;** _pa.t._ and _pa.p._ **trogged.** [Poss. from **trudge** and **slog.**]

troggs _trogz_, (_Scot._) _n._ and _interj._ troth.

troglodyte _trog'lə-dīt_, _n._ a cave-dweller: an anthropoid ape (_obs._ and _misapplied_). — Also _adj._ — _n._ **Troglodytes** (-_lod'i-tēz_) the wren genus. — _adjs._ **troglodytic** (-_dit'ik_), **-al** cave-dwelling. — _n._ **trog'lodytism** (-_dīt-izm_). [Gr. _trōglodytēs_ — _trōglē_, a hole, _dyein,_ to get into.]

trogon _trō'gon_, _n._ any member of a family (**Trogon'idae**) of tropical and esp. South American birds with brilliant plumage, the first and second toes turned back, including the quetzal. [App. Gr. _trōgōn_, nibbling.]

Troic _trō'ik_, _adj._ Trojan. [Gr. _Trōikos._]

troika _troi'kə_, _n._ a Russian vehicle for three horses abreast: a team of three horses abreast: a team of three men, etc., acting equally as leaders. [Russ., — _troe_, a set of three.]

troilism _troi'lizm_, _n._ sexual activity between three people (of two sexes). — _n._ **troi'list.** [Origin uncertain; perhaps Fr. _trois_, three, influenced by **dualism.**]

troilite _trō'il-īt_, _n._ native ferrous sulphide, found in meteorites. [After Dominico _Troili_, who observed it in the 18th cent.]

Trojan _trō'jən_, _adj._ of Troy. — _n._ a citizen or inhabitant of Troy: a boon companion: a doughty, trusty, or hard-working person: a good fellow. — **Trojan horse** the gigantic wooden horse inside which the Greeks entered Troy: a person, organisation, placed within a country, group, etc., with the purpose of destroying it: a concealed insertion of coded material within a program (_comput. jargon_). [L. _Trōjānus_ — _Trōja,_ Troy.]

troke (_Scot._). See **truck**[1].

troll[1] _trōl_, _n._ in Scandinavian mythology, a goblin or supernatural dwarf (earlier giant). [O.N.]

troll[2] _trōl_, _v.t._ to roll (_obs._): to trundle (_arch._): to spin (_arch._): to circulate, pass about the table (_arch._): (_Milt._ **troule**) to move nimbly, wag (the tongue): to utter fluently, set rolling off the tongue (_obs._): to sing the parts of in succession, as of a catch or round (_arch._): to fish for, or in, with a spinning or otherwise moving bait: to allure (_obs._): to convey by trolley. — _v.i._ to roll (_obs._): to move or run about (_obs._): to sing a catch: to stroll, ramble (_obs._): to fish with revolving or trailing lure (see also **trawl**): to travel by trolley. — _n._ a moving round, repetition: a round song: trolling: a lure for trolling. — _ns._ **troll'er; trolley** (_trol'i_; rarely **troll'y**): — _pl._ **troll'ies**) a costermonger's cart: a low wheelbarrow: a small truck: a bogie: a pulley, receptacle, or car travelling on an overhead wire or rail: a trolley-wheel: a tram-car (_U.S._): — _pl._ **troll'eys.** — _n._ and _adj._ **troll'ing** (_trōl'_). — **troll'ey-bus** a bus that receives power by a trolley-wheel from a pair of overhead wires; **troll'ey-car'** (_U.S._) a tram-car so driven; **troll'ey-man** a man who works a trolley or on a trolley; **troll'ey-ta'ble** a tiered trolley for a dining-room; **troll'ey-wheel** a grooved wheel by which a bus, tram-car, etc., obtains current from an overhead wire; **troll'ing-bait, -spoon** a metallic revolving lure used in trolling. — **off one's trolley** daft, crazy. [Cf. O.Fr. _troller_ (Fr. _trôler_), to quest, Ger. _trollen,_ to roll.]

trolley[1], **trolly** _trol'i_, _n._ lace with pattern outlined with thicker thread or a flat border: — _pl._ **troll'eys, troll'ies.** [Cf. Flem. _tralje,_ trellis.]

trolley[2], **trolly.** See **troll**[2].

troll-my-dame(s) _trōl-mi-dām_(z)_', (_Shak._) _ns._ an old game like bagatelle, in which bullets were trolled into a little arcade. — Also **trou-madame** (_trōō-mä-däm_). [Fr. _trou-madame_ — _trou,_ hole, associated with **troll**[2].]

trollop _trol'əp_, _n._ a slatternly woman: a draggle-tail: a strumpet. — _v.i._ (_Scot._) to draggle: to go, dress, or work in a slovenly way. — _n._ **trollopee'** (18th cent.) a woman's loose dress. — _adjs._ **troll'oping, troll'opish, troll'opy.** [Perh. **troll**[2].]

Trollopean, -pian _tro-lə-pē'ən_, _adj._ of, in the style of, the novels of Anthony _Trollope_ (1815–82). — _n._ an admirer of his novels.

trolly. See **trolley**[1], **troll**[2].

tromba marina _trom'bə mə-rē'nə_, an obsolete viol, generally one-stringed, with an irregular bridge, played in harmonics, giving a trumpet-like tone. [It., marine (speaking) trumpet.]

trombiculid _trom-bik'ū-lid_, _adj._ of or pertaining to any of the mite family (_Trombiculidae_). — _n._ a trombiculid mite or harvest-bug (q.v.).

trombone _trom-bōn'_, _n._ a brass musical wind instrument, consisting of a tube bent twice on itself, with a slide. — _n._ **trombōn'ist.** [It.; augm. of _tromba,_ trumpet.]

tromino _trom'in-ō_, _n._ a flat, three-sided shape made up of a number of identical squares placed edge to edge: — _pl._ **-nos, -noes.** [_tri_-and (on a false analogy) **domino.**]

trommel _trom'əl_, _n._ a revolving cylindrical sieve for cleaning or sizing minerals. [Ger. _Trommel,_ drum.]

tromometer _trom-om'i-tər_, _n._ an instrument for measuring slight earthquake shocks. — _adj._ **tromomet'ric.** [Gr. _tromos_, a trembling, _metron,_ a measure.]

trompe, tromp _tromp_, _n._ an apparatus for producing a blast of air in a furnace by falling water. [Fr.]

trompe l'œil _trɔp lœ-y'_, (Fr.) lit. 'something that deceives the eye': appearance of reality achieved by use of minute, often trivial, details or of other effects in painting, architecture, etc.

tron _tron_, **trone** _trōn_, (chiefly _Scot._) _ns._ a public weighing machine, used also as a place of punishment as by nailing the ear: the market-place: a system of weights used at the tron. [O.Fr. *trone* — L. *trŭtina* — Gr. *trȳtanē*, a pair of scales.]

-tron *-tron, suff.* signifying agent, instrument, particularly (1) thermionic valve, e.g. *klystron*, (2) elementary particle, e.g. *positron*, (3) particle accelerator, e.g. *cyclotron*. [Gr.]

trona *trō'nǝ, n.* a native combination of acid and normal sodium carbonate. [Sw., — Ar. *trōn* for *natrūn*; see **natron**.]

tronc *trongk*, Fr. *trɔ̃, n.* a collection of tips to be divided out later, e.g. among waiters: the system by which this is done. [Fr., collecting box.]

trone. See tron.

troolie, troelie, troely *trōō'li, n.* the bussu palm: its leaf. [Tupi *tururi*.]

troop *trōōp, n.* a body of soldiers: (in *pl.*) military forces: a band of people: a flock, herd, swarm of animals: (esp. in *pl.*) a great number: a division of a cavalry squadron: a group of (Boy) Scout patrols: a troupe: the command of a troop of horse: a drum signal for assembling. — *v.i.* to assemble (*arch.*): to consort (*arch.*): to pass in a body or in rapid succession: to be off, pack. — *v.t.* to cause to troop: to receive and carry ceremonially along the ranks (as *troop the colour* or *colours*). — *n.* **troop'er** a private cavalry soldier (proverbially a swearer): a private soldier in armoured (tank) units: a mounted policeman (*U.S.* and *Austr.*): a cavalry horse: a troop-ship. — **troop'-carrier** a motor vehicle, ship or aeroplane for carrying troops; **troop's horse** a cavalry horse; **troop'-ship** a ship for transporting troops. [Fr. *troupe* — L.L. *troppus*; poss. Gmc.]

troopial. Same as troupial.

tropaeolum *trop-ē'ǝ-lǝm, n.* the Indian cress and canary-creeper genus, South American trailing or climbing plants constituting a family **Tropaeolā'ceae**, akin to the geraniums — misnamed nasturtium. — *n.* **tropae'-olin** any of a group of dyes of complex structure. [Gr. *tropaion*, a trophy (from the shield-shaped leaves and helmet-like flowers).]

troparion *trop-ār'i-on*, or *-ar'*, (*Greek church*) *n.* a stanza or short hymn: — *pl.* **tropar'ia**. [Dim. of Gr. *tropos*, trope.]

trope *trōp, n.* a figure of speech, properly one in which a word or expression is used in other than its literal sense — metaphor, metonymy, synecdoche, irony (*rhet.*): a short cadence peculiar to Gregorian melodies: a phrase formerly interpolated in different parts of the mass. — *v.t.* to furnish with tropes. — *adj.* **trop'ical**, *n.* **trop'ist** see under **tropic**. [Gr. *tropos*, a turn — *trepein*, to turn.]

-trope *-trōp*, in composition, a tendency towards or affinity for, as in *heliotrope*. — **-tropic** adjective combining form. [Gr. *tropos*, a turn.]

troph-, tropho- *trof-, -ō-, -o'-, trǝf-*, **-troph-, -trophy**, *-trǝf*(*-i*) in composition, nutrition. — *ns.* **trophallax'is** (Gr. *allaxis*, exchange), **trophobiō'sis** (Gr. *biōsis*, way of life) mutual exchange of nutriment in symbiosis. — *adjs.* **trophallac'tic, trophobiot'ic; trophesial** (*-ē'zi-ǝl, -shl*) relating to trophesy. — *n.* **troph'esy, tropho-neurō'sis** a state of deranged nutrition owing to disorder of the trophic action of the nerves. — *n.pl.* **trophi** (*trō'fī*) the mouth-parts of an insect: teeth of the pharynx of a rotifer. — *adj.* **troph'ic** relating to nutrition. — *n.* **troph'oblast** the differentiated outer layer of epiblast in a segmenting mammalian ovum. — *adj.* **trophoblast'ic.** — *ns.* **trophol'ogy** the study of nutrition; **troph'oplasm** protoplasm which is mainly concerned with nutrition; **trophotax'is, trophot'ropism** chemotaxis, chemotropism, where the stimulating substance is food. — *adjs.* **trophotact'ic, trophotrop'ic.** — *n.* **trophozō'ite** in Protozoa, the trophic phase of the adult, which generally reproduces by schizogony. — **trophic level** a division of an ecosystem consisting of all organisms whose food is obtained from plants by the same number of intermediate steps; **trophic structure** a feature of an ecosystem, measured and described

in terms of standing crop per unit area or energy fixed per unit area per unit time. [Gr. *trophē*, food, *trophos*, a feeder; *trephein*, to feed.]

Trophonian *trō-fō'ni-ǝ n, adj.* of the deified *Trophōnius* (Gr. *Trophōnios*) or the cave in Boeotia where he delivered oracles and conferred solemnising mystic experiences.

trophy *trō'fi, n.* a memorial of victory, orig. arms or other spoils set up on the spot: displayed spoils, as skulls and antlers: a piece of plate or suchlike awarded as a prize: a memorial of success, glory, etc.: an ornamental group of weapons, flags, etc., or a representation of it. — *v.t.* to set with trophies: to bestow trophies on. — *adj.* **trō'phied.** [Fr. *trophée* — L. *trophaeum* (classical *tropaeum*) — Gr. *tropaion* — *tropē*, a turning — *trepein*, to turn.]

tropic *trop'ik, n.* an imaginary circle on the celestial sphere about 23° 28′ N. (*tropic of Cancer*) or S. (*of Capricorn*) of the equator, where the sun turns on reaching its greatest declination north or south: a corresponding circle on the terrestrial globe: (*pl.*) the part of the earth between the tropics of Cancer and Capricorn: a turning-point or limit. — *adj.* of, relating to, the sun's turning: of the tropics: of, of the nature of, a tropism. — *adj.* **trop'ical** of, relating to, a tropic or the tropics: found in, characteristic of, the tropics: fervidly hot: luxuriant: of a trope, figurative. — *adv.* **trop'ically.** — *ns.* **trop'ism** (*biol.*) orientation in response to stimulus: a general term for heliotropism, geotropism, etc.; **tropist** (*trōp'*) a user of tropes: one who understands the Bible as figurative. — *adjs.* **tropistic** (*trop-ist'ik*) of tropism; **tropolog'ic, -al.** — *adv.* **tropolog'ically.** — *ns.* **tropol'ogy** figurative language: a moral interpretation of the Bible; **trop'opause** (Gr. *pausis*, a ceasing) the boundary between troposphere and stratosphere; **trop'ophyte** (*-fīt*; Gr. *phyton*, plant) a plant adapted to alterations of moisture and drought. — *adjs.* **tropophytic** (*-fit'ik*), **tropōph'ilous.** — *ns.* **trop'oscatter** the propagation of radio waves by using irregularities in the troposphere to scatter the signals beamed up by means of high-powered UHF transmitters and parabolic antennas; **trop'osphere** the lowest layer of the atmosphere in which temperature falls as height increases. — *adj.* **troposphĕr'ic.** — **tropical month, year** see **month, year; trop'ic-bird** a tropical sea-bird (Phaethon) with long tail-feathers. [Gr. *tropos*, a turning.]

troppo *trop'ō*, (It.) *adj.* and *adv.* in music, too much: excessively.

trossers *tros'ǝrz, n.* an obs. form of **trousers.**

trot *trot, n.* a pace between walking and running (in a horse with legs moving together diagonally): an act or spell of trotting: continual activity in moving about: a toddling child: in angling, a trotline: one of the single lines attached to a trotline: a crib, literal translation (*U.S.*). — *v.i.* to go, ride, or drive at a trot: to jog: to bustle about: to fish using a baited hook which travels downstream just above the bottom. — *v.t.* to cause to trot: to conduct around: to bring out for exhibition: to draw out so as to make a butt of: to jog on one's knee: to trot upon: to execute at a trot: — *pr.p.* **trott'ing;** *pa.t.* and *pa.p.* **trott'ed.** — *ns.* **trott'er** one that trots: a horse trained to trot in harness racing: a foot, esp. of a sheep or pig; **trott'ing** the action of the verb: harness racing; **trottoir** (*trot-wär;* Fr.) a paved footway at the side of a street. — **trot'line** in angling, a long line across a waterway to which shorter lines with baited hooks are attached. — **on the trot** (*coll.*) in succession, without a break: busy, bustling about; **the trots** (*slang*) diarrhoea; **trot out** to exhibit the paces of: to bring forward, adduce, produce for show: to walk out with. [O.Fr. *trot* (n.) *troter* (vb.); perh. Gmc.; cf. O.H.G. *trottōn*, Eng. **tread.**]

trot² *trot*, (*Shak.*) *n.* a beldame, crone. [A.Fr. *trote*.]

Trot *trot*, (*derog.*) *n.* and *adj.* coll. for **Trotskyist, Trotskyite.**

trot-cozy, -cosey *trot'-kō'zi*, (*Scott*) *n.* a riding-hood.

[App. **trot**[1] (Jamieson says **throat**) and **cosy**.]

troth *trōth, troth, (arch.) n.* a variant of **truth**: faith, fidelity. — *v.t. (Shak.)* to betroth. — *interj.* in truth. — *adjs.* **troth'ful; troth'less**. — **troth'-plight** a plighting of troth, betrothal. — *v.t. (arch.)* to betroth. — *adj. (Shak.)* betrothed. — Also **troth'-plighted**. — **troth'= ring** a betrothal ring.

Trotskyism *trot'ski-izm, n.* the form of Communism associated with Leon *Trotsky* (pseudonym of Lev Davidovich Bronstein, 1879–1940), who advocated world-wide revolution. — *ns.* **Trot'skyist, Trot'skyite**. — Also *adjs.*

trottoir. See **trot**[1].

trotyl *trō'til, n.* trinitrotoluene. [trini*trot*oluene, and -**yl**.]

troubadour *trōō'bə-dōōr, -dōr, -dör, n.* one of a class of lyric poets of chivalric love, who first appeared in Provence, and flourished from the 11th to the 13th century. [Fr., — Prov. *trobador* — *trobar* (Fr. *trouver*) to find.]

trouble *trub'l, v.t.* to agitate: to disturb: to muddy: to make turbid: to molest: to afflict: to annoy: to busy or engage overmuch: to put to inconvenience. — *v.i.* to take pains: to put oneself to inconvenience: to be troublesome. — *n.* disturbance: affliction: distress: a scrape: travail: anything amiss: disease: uneasiness: exertion: the taking of pains: a cause of trouble. — *adj.* **troub'led** (-ld). — *adv.* **troub'ledly**. — *n.* **troub'ler**. — *adj.* **troub'lesome** causing or giving trouble or inconvenience: vexatious: importunate. — *adv.* **troub'- lesomely**. — *n.* **troub'lesomeness**. — *n.* and *adj.* **troub'- ling**. — *adj.* **troub'lous** *(arch. or poet.)* full of trouble or disorder: agitated: tumultuous: disturbing. — *adv.* **troub'lously**. — *n.* **troub'lousness**. — *adj.* **troub'lefree** easy, not beset with problems. — **troub'le-house -state, -town, -world** one who disturbs the peace of a house, state, etc.; **troub'lemaker** one who disturbs the peace and (usu.) incites others to do so; **troub'le-mirth** a kill-joy; **troub'leshooter** an expert detector and mender of any trouble, mechanical or other; **troub'leshooting**. — Also *adj.* — **trouble spot** a place where trouble, esp. social or political unrest, often occurs. — **ask, look, for trouble** to behave in such a way as to bring trouble on oneself; **I'll trouble you to** please; **in trouble** *(euph.)* pregnant (when unmarried); **trouble someone for** to ask someone to provide, pass, etc. [O.Fr. *trubler* (Fr. *troubler*) from a L.L. freq. of L. *turbāre*, to disturb *turba*, a crowd.]

trou-de-loup *trōō-də-lōō', n.* a pit with a vertical stake in the middle — a defence against cavalry: — *pl.* **trous= de-loup** (*trōō-*). [Fr., wolf-hole.]

trough *trof, n.* a long, narrow vessel for watering or feeding animals: a vessel for kneading, brewing, wash- ing, tanning, or various domestic and industrial pur- poses: a vessel for liquid over which gases are collected (*pneumatic trough*): a channel, gutter, or conduit: a long narrow depression: a hollow between wave-crests: a low point (*fig.*): an elongated area of low atmos- pheric pressure, usu. extending from a depression and marking a change of air-mass (*meteor.*). — **trough'= fault** (*geol.*) a pair of parallel faults with downthrow between them; **trough'-shell** a lamellibranch with a somewhat triangular shell fancied to resemble a knead- ing-trough (*Mactra*). — **troughing and peaking** ranging between low and high points or levels. [O.E. *trog*; Ger. *Trog*.]

troule (*Milt.*). See **troll**[2].

trou-madame. Same as **troll-my-dame(s)**.

trounce[1] *trowns, v.t.* to harass (*obs.*): to indict (*dial.*): to punish, beat, rebuke or censure severely. — *ns.* **trounc'er; trounc'ing**. [Origin obscure.]

trounce[2] *trowns, (dial. or arch.) v.i.* to skip, prance, move briskly. — *v.t.* to whisk off, make to skip. [Origin obscure.]

troupe *trōōp, n.* a company, esp. of performers. — *v.i.* to travel about as a member of a theatrical troupe. — *n.* **troup'er** a member of a theatrical troupe: an experi-

enced actor: an experienced person (*fig.*). [Fr. See **troop**.]

troupial, troopial *trōō'pi-əl, n.* a bird (*Icterus icterus*) famous for its song: any bird of the Icteridae. [Fr. *troupiale* — *troupe*, troop.]

trouse *trōōz, trowz, (hist.) n.* Irish close-fitting breeches: trews. — Also in *pl.* (now vulg.) trousers. [See **trews**.]

trousers *trow'zərz, obs. trossers tros'ərz, (Shak.) strossers stros', ns.pl.* long breeches: a garment worn on the lower part of the body with a loose tubular branch for each leg: any other garment of similar form, as pan- talettes. The sing. is used to form compounds, as **trous'er-butt'on, -clip, -leg', -pock'et, -stretch'er**, etc. — *adj.* **trou'sered** wearing trousers. — *n.* **trou'sering** (usu. in *pl.*) material for trousers. — **trouser suit** a women's suit, consisting of a jacket and trousers. — **(caught) with one's trousers down** (taken) unawares; **wear the trousers** of a wife, to be the dominant partner in a marriage. [See preceding.]

trousseau *trōō'sō, n.* a bride's outfit: a bundle (*arch.* and *rare*): — *pl.* **trou'sseaux, trou'sseaus** (*-sōz*). [Fr., dim. of *trousse*, bundle.]

trout *trowt, n.* a freshwater fish (*Salmo fario*) of the salmon genus, much sought after by anglers: extended to various fishes related or superficially like: an un- pleasant, interfering old person, usu. a woman: — *pl.* **trout** (rarely **trouts**). — *n.* **trout'er** one who fishes for trout. — *adj.* **trout'ful** abounding in trout. — *n.* and *adj.* **trout'ing** trout-fishing. — *adj.* **trout'less**. — *ns.* **trout'let, trout'ling** a little trout. — *adj.* **trout'y**. — **trout'-bas'ket** an osier or willow creel for carrying trout. — *adj.* **trout'-coloured** speckled like a trout: white, with spots of black, bay, or sorrel. — **trout'-farm** a place where trout are reared artificially; **trout'-rod** a fishing-rod for trout; **trout'-spoon** a small revolving spoon used as a lure for trout; **trout'stone** troctolite; **trout'-stream** a stream in which trout are caught. [O.E. *truht* — L. *tructa, tructus* — Gr. *trōktēs*, a sea-fish with sharp teeth — *trōgein*, to gnaw, nibble.]

trouvaille *trōō-vä'ē, n.* a happy find. [Fr.]

trouvère *trōō-ver', **trouveur** trōō-vər', ns.* one of the mediaeval narrative or epic poets of northern France. [Fr.]

trove. See **treasure**.

trover *trō'vər, n.* orig., finding and keeping: hence, for- merly, a legal action brought to recover goods from a person to whom they do not belong. [O.Fr. *trover* (Fr. *trouver*), to find.]

trow[1] *trō, (arch.) v.t.* to trust: to believe (often elliptically for *I trow* or *trow you?*). [O.E. *trēowan* (*trēowian, trūwian*); O.N. *trūa*, Ger. *trauen*.]

trow[2] *trow, (Shetland and Orkney) n.* a form of **troll**[1].

trow[3] *trow, (dial.) n.* any of various small boats or barges, usu. flat-bottomed. [**trough**.]

trowel *trow'əl, n.* a flat or scoop-shaped tool with a short handle, for plastering, gardening, etc. — *v.t.* to dress, apply, move, with or as if with a trowel: — *pr.p.* **trow'elling**; *pa.t.* and *pa.p.* **trow'elled**. — *n.* **trow'eller**. — **lay it on with a trowel** to spread something thickly: to say grossly flattering things. [O.Fr. *truelle* — L.L. *truella* (L. *trulla*, dim. of *trua*, a ladle).]

trowsers *trow'zərz, (arch.) n.* A variant spelling of **trousers**.

troy *troi, n.* a system of weights used for precious stones and metals, the pound (no longer in legal use) of 5760 grains being divided into 12 ounces of 20 pennyweight (also *adj.*). — Also called **troy weight**. [*Troyes*, in France.]

Troyan *troi'ən, (Shak., Spens.) adj.* Trojan.

truant *trōō'ənt, n.* a vagrant (*obs.*): a vague term of reproach (*obs.*): an idler (*arch.*): one who, idly or without excuse, absents himself from school (also *fig.*). — Also *adj.* — *v.i.* to play truant. — *ns.* **tru'ancy, tru'antry, tru'antship**. — **play truant** to stay from school without leave or good reason. [O.Fr. *truant* (Fr. *truand*), prob. from Celtic.]

Trubenise, -ize® *trōō'bən-īz, v.t.* to stiffen (a fabric) by binding together two layers by an intermediate layer of cellulose acetate.

trucage, truquage *trü-käzh,* (Fr.) *n.* faking of works of art. — *n.* **truqueur** (*trü-kœr*) a faker of works of art.

truce *trōōs, n.* a suspension of hostilities: a respite. — *adjs.* **truce′less; trucial** (*trōō′shl, -syəl, -shi-əl*) bound by a truce. — **truce′-break′er.** — **Trucial States** a group of Arab sheikhdoms, on the S. coast of the Persian Gulf, in treaty with Britain. — **Truce of God** a cessation of war, decreed by the Church, more or less observed, esp. in the 11th and 12th centuries, in France, Italy, England, etc., from Saturday (afterwards from Wednesday) evening to Monday morning, also during Advent and Lent and on certain holy days. [M.E. *trewes, treowes,* pl. of *trewe* — O.E. *trēow,* truth, pledge, treaty; cf. **true.**]

truchman *truch′mən,* (*obs.*) *n.* an interpreter: — *pl.* **truch′men** or **truchmans.** [Ar. *turjamān*; cf. **dragoman.**]

truck[1] *truk, v.t.* to exchange: to barter: to pay in goods. — *v.i.* to traffic: to have dealings or intercourse: to barter: to bargain: to potter about: to do nothing (*slang*): to move along, make progress generally (*slang*). — *Scot.* **trock** (*trok*), **troke** (*trōk*). — *n.* exchange of goods: barter: payment in goods: (*Scot.* **trock, troke**) dealings, intercourse: a small job, chore: small goods (*coll.*): rubbish (*coll.*): fresh vegetables, market-garden produce (*U.S.*). — *ns.* **truck′age** barter; **truck′er** one who trucks: a market-gardener (*U.S.*); **truck′ing.** — **truck′-farm** (*U.S.*) a market-garden; **truck′-farmer; truck′-farming; truck′-shop** (*hist.*) a shop operated by employers in which their workmen are obliged to buy goods; **truck system** the practice of paying workmen in goods instead of money, forbidden by the Truck Acts, 1831, etc. — **have no truck with** to have nothing to do with. [O.Fr. *troquer,* to truck; Sp. *trocar,* to barter, It. *truccare,* to truck.]

truck[2] *truk, n.* a small or solid wheel: an open railway wagon for goods: a trolley: a bogie: a low flat barrow: a small two-wheeled barrow with a turned-up front: a motor vehicle of heavier construction than a car, designed for the transportation of commodities, or freq. a specific commodity: a lorry (esp. *U.S.*): a cap at the top of a mast or flagstaff. — *v.i.* to drive a truck (chiefly *U.S.*). — *v.t.* to convey by truck: to put on a truck. — *ns.* **truck′age** carriage by truck: charge for carriage by truck: supply of trucks; **truck′er, truck′man** (chiefly *U.S.*) a lorry driver; **truck′ing.** — **truck′-load.** [L. *trochus,* a wheel — Gr. *trochos* — *trechein,* to run.]

truckle *truk′l, n.* a pulley-wheel: a castor (*obs.*): a truckle-bed: a barrel-shaped cheese (*dial.*). — *v.t.* to move on rollers. — *v.i.* to sleep in a truckle-bed: to behave with servility (usu. with *to*). — *n.* **truck′ler.** — *n.* and *adj.* **truck′ling.** — **truck′le-bed** a low bed that may be wheeled under another. [Gr. *trochileia, -iā,* etc., a pulley — *trochos,* a wheel.]

truculent *truk′-, trōōk′ū-lənt, adj.* very fierce (*arch.*): cruel (*arch.*): aggressive and discourteous. — *ns.* **truc′ulence, truc′ulency.** — *adv.* **truc′ulently.** [L. *truculentus* — *trux,* wild, fierce.]

trudge *truj, v.i.* to walk with labour or effort: to plod doggedly. — *v.t.* to plod wearily or doggedly along, over, etc. — *n.* a heavy or weary walk: a trudger. — *n.* **trudg′er.** — *n.* and *adj.* **trudg′ing.** [Origin obscure.]

trudgen (incorrectly **trudgeon**) *truj′ən, n.* a swimming stroke in which each hand alternately is raised above the surface, thrust forward, and pulled back through the water. — Also *adj.* [John *Trudgen,* who popularised the stroke in England.]

true *trōō, adj.* faithful: constant: trusty: genuine: properly so called: typical: conformable: accurately adjusted or in tune: straight or flat: agreeing with fact: actual: absolute: corrected: accurate: exact: right: rightful: honest: sincere: truthful. — *adv.* **truly:** faithfully: honestly: in accurate adjustment: dead in tune: after the ancestral type. — *v.t.* to adjust accurately. — *n.* that which is true, truth: accurate adjustment. — *n.* **true′ness.** — *adv.* **tru′ly.** — **true bill** a bill of indictment endorsed, after investigation, by a grand jury, as containing a case for the court. — *n.* **true blue,** *adj.* **true′-blue′** see **blue**[1]. — *adjs.* **true′-born** of genuine birth: pure-bred: true to the qualities of the breed: legitimate; **true′-bred** pure-bred: typical: of good breeding; **true′-devot′ed** (*Shak.*) full of honest zeal; **true′-dispos′ing** (*Shak.*) just; **true′-heart′ed** sincere: faithful. — **true′-heart′edness; true′-love** one truly or really beloved: a sweetheart: a faithful lover: a true-love-knot: a quatrefoil: a four-leaved clover (**true′-love grass**) (*obs.*): herb-Paris. — Also *adj.* — **true′-love-knot, true′-lov′er′s-knot** an ornamental or symbolic knot or interlaced design, as a two-looped bow or a knot with two interlaced loops; **true′man** (*arch.*) an honest man; **true′penny** (*Shak.*) an honest fellow. — *adj.* **true-seem′ing** (*Spens.*) seeming (falsely or truly) to be true. — **true time** the time according to the position of the sun, as opposed to mean time. — **out of true** not straight, not properly balanced, adjusted, or calibrated. [O.E. *trēowe*; O.N. *tryggr,* Ger. *treu.*]

truffle *truf′l, trōōf′l, n.* any fungus of the genus Tuber or the family Tuberaceae: its underground edible fructification: a rich confection, made with chocolate, butter, etc., usu. shaped into balls. — *adj.* **truff′led** cooked, stuffed, dressed, with truffles. — **truff′le-dog, -pig** one trained to find truffles. [O.Fr. *truffle* (Fr. *truffe*); poss. — L. *tūber,* lump, swelling.]

trug *trug,* (*dial.*) *n.* a flat wooden fruit-basket. [Prob. **trough.**]

truism *trōō′izm, n.* a self-evident truth: a commonplace or trite statement. — *adj.* **truist′ic.** [**true.**]

trull *trul,* (*arch.*) *n.* a prostitute. [Cf. Ger. *Trolle.*]

Trullan *trul′ən, adj.* held in the domed hall of the palace at Constantinople — applied to the Sixth Ecumenical Council (680-1) and esp. to the Council of 692, not accepted by the Western Church. [L.L. *trullus,* a dome — L. *trulla,* a ladle.]

truly. See **true.**

trumeau *trōō-mō′, n.* a piece of wall or pillar between two openings: — *pl.* **trumeaux** (*-mōz′*). [Fr.]

trump[1] *trump,* (*obs.*) *v.t.* to deceive. — *n.* **trump′ery** showy and worthless stuff: rubbish: ritual foolery. — Also *adj.* [Fr. *tromper,* to deceive.]

trump[2] *trump,* (*arch.* or *poet.*) *n.* a trumpet: a blast: a Jew's-harp (now *Scot.*). — *v.t.* and *v.i.* to trumpet. — **trump marine** the tromba marina. [O.Fr. *trompe.*]

trump[3] *trump, n.* a card of a suit that takes any card of any other suit: ruff, an old card-game like whist: a good, trusty fellow (*coll.*). — Also *adj.* — *v.t.* to play a trump card upon instead of following suit: to take in this way (also *fig.*): of an Oxford University college, to gain (a student) by trumping. — *v.i.* to play trumps on another suit. — *n.* **trump′ing** at Oxford University, the system whereby colleges may offer an award and a place (which must be accepted) to other colleges' gifted applicants, so ensuring a more even spread of talented students among the colleges. — **trump′-card** the card turned up to determine the trump suit: any card of that suit: a means of triumph (*fig.*): a victorious expedient (*fig.*). — **no′-trumps** a declaration in bridge whereby no suit is more powerful than the rest. — *adj.* **no′-trump.** — **no′-trump′er** a hand suitable for no-trumps; **turn up trumps** (*fig.*) to behave in a very helpful or generous way, esp. unexpectedly. [**triumph.**]

trump[4] *trump, n.* (*obs.*) an obstruction cast in one's way. — *v.t.* to cast as an obstruction (*obs.*): to allege (*obs.*): to concoct and put forward unscrupulously (with *up*). — *adj.* **trumped′-up.** [**trump**[3], affected by, or partly from, **trump**[1].]

trumpet *trum′pit, n.* an orchestral, military, and signalling wind instrument of powerful and brilliant tone, in its present form a narrow tube bent twice upon itself, with cupped mouthpiece and flaring bell, giving, by action of the lips and breath-pressure, harmonics of its fundamental, the scale filled up by use of crooks, slides, or valves: applied to other instruments more or less like: a speaking-trumpet: an ear-trumpet: a trumpet-shaped object, as a flared bell or horn, a corolla or corona: a sound of, or as if of, a trumpet: a trumpeter: an organ reed-stop of trumpet-like tone. — *v.t.* to sound or play on a trumpet or with trumpet-like sound: to proclaim, celebrate, summon, denounce, expel, etc., by trumpet. — *v.i.* to sound a trumpet: to make a sound like a trumpet: — *pr.p.* **trum'peting**; *pa.t.* and *pa.p.* **trum'peted**. — *adj.* **trum'peted** sounded on a trumpet: loudly extolled: having a trumpet: funnel-shaped. — *n.* **trum'peter** one who plays or sounds the trumpet: one who proclaims, praises, or denounces: a loud-voiced crane-like South American bird (*Psophia*): a trumpeter swan: a kind of domestic pigeon: a large Australian and New Zealand food-fish (*Latris*) or other fish that trumpets when caught. — *n.* and *adj.* **trum'peting**. — **trum'pet-call** a conventional phrase or passage played on the trumpet as a signal: any call to action; **trumpeter swan** an American swan, the largest of the world's swans; **trum'pet-fish** the snipe-fish or bellows-fish (*Macrorhamphosus* or *Centriscus*), a long-snouted fish akin to the pipefish: a flute-mouth, a sea-fish with a tubular muzzle; **trum'pet-flower** a name for various bignoniaceous, solanaceous, and other plants with large trumpet-shaped flowers; **trum'pet=ma'jor** a head-trumpeter in a regiment; **trumpet marine** the tromba marina. — *adj.* **trum'pet-shaped** like the bell of a trumpet. — **trum'pet-shell** Triton; **trum'pet=tone** the sound of a trumpet: a loud voice. — *adj.* **trum'pet-tongued** proclaiming loud as a trumpet. — **trum'pet-tree, -wood** a South American Cecropia whose hollow branches the Indians use as trumpets. — **blow one's own trumpet** to sound one's own praises; **feast of trumpets** a Jewish feast in which trumpets played an important part. [Fr. *trompette*, dim. of *trompe*, trump.]

truncal. See **trunk.**

truncate *trungk-āt'*, *v.t.* to cut short: to lop: to delete those digits of a number which are not considered to be significant (*math.*): to maim: to replace (an edge or corner where similar faces meet) by a symmetrically placed face (*crystal.*, *geom.*). — *adjs.* **trunc'ate, -d** appearing as if squared off at the tip: ending in a transverse line or plane, esp. one parallel to the base. — *adv.* **trunc'ately.** — *n.* **truncā'tion.** — **truncation error** (*math.*) one caused by operating with a truncated number or numbers. [L. *truncāre, -ātum* — *truncus*; cf. **trunk.**]

truncheon *trun'shən, -chən, n.* a broken or cut piece: a length for grafting or planting: a broken spear: a spear-shaft: a short staff: a cudgel (*arch.*, except that of a policeman): a staff of authority. — *v.t.* to carve (an eel): to beat with a truncheon. — *adj.* **trun'cheoned** furnished with a truncheon: armed with a lance. — *n.* **trun'cheoner** (*Shak.*) one armed with a truncheon. [O.Fr. *tronchon* (Fr. *tronçon*) — *tronc*; see **trunk.**]

trundle *trun'dl, n.* a little wheel, castor: a roller: a hoop: a truck (*obs.*): a trundle-bed: a spool of golden thread (*her.*). — *v.t.* and *v.i.* to wheel, esp. heavily or clumsily: to roll: to twirl: to spin (*arch.*): to bowl along. — **trun'dle-bed** a truckle-bed; **trun'dle-tail, tren'dle-tail, trin'dle-tail** a curly-tailed dog. [O.E. *trendel.*]

trunk *trungk, n.* the stem of a tree: the body of an animal apart from head and limbs: the body generally: a main line of road, railway, telephone, etc.: a junction circuit between telephone exchanges (*U.S.*): the main body of anything: the shaft of a column: the body of a pedestal: a chest or box, esp. for travelling: a box for fish: a box-like channel, trough, shaft, conduit, or chute: a tube: a speaking-tube: a telescope (*obs.*): a pea-shooter (*obs.*): a large hollow piston: a proboscis: same as **bus** (*comput.*): (in *pl.*) the game of trou-madame: (in *pl.*) trunk-hose, also breeches, esp. those worn on the stage over tights, or pants worn for sports, swimming, etc.: the boot, luggage compartment of an automobile (*U.S.*). — *adj.* **trunc'al** pertaining to the trunk: principal; **trunked** having a trunk: truncated,

beheaded (*Spens.*): pertaining to radio trunking. — *ns.* **trunk'ful** as much as will fill a trunk: — *pl.* **trunk'fuls; trunk'ing** casing: a system of sharing a number of radio channels among a number of users of mobile (e.g. car) radio communication systems, the users being able to use any channel which is free at any given time. — **trunk'-call'** the former name for a long-distance telephone call, involving connection between two centres, a **national call; trunk dialling** the dialling of trunk telephone calls directly, connections not being made by an operator; **trunk'fish** the coffer-fish; **trunk'-hose', -breech'es** full breeches reaching from waist to mid-thigh, worn in the 16th and early 17th centuries; **trunk'-line** the main line of a railway, canal, gas or oil pipeline, etc.; **trunk'-mail** a travelling trunk; **trunk'=maker** a maker of travelling trunks; **trunk'-road** a main road, esp. one administered by central authority; **trunk'sleeve** (*Shak.*) a puffed sleeve; **trunk'-work** (*Shak.*) clandestine visiting in a trunk. [Fr. *tronc* and L. *truncus*, a stock, a torso — *truncus*, maimed; with associations of Fr. *trompe*, a trump, a proboscis.]

trunnion *trun'yən, n.* either of a pair of side projections on which anything (as formerly a big gun) is pivoted to move in a vertical plane: a stick, club (*Scott*). — *adj.* **trunn'ioned** provided with trunnions. [Fr. *trognon*, stump.]

truquage, truqueur. See **trucage.**

truss *trus, n.* a bundle, esp. of hay or straw, or a block cut from a stack (esp. 56 lb of old hay, 60 lb of new, 36 of straw): a framed structure for supporting a weight: an attachment for holding a yard to the mast: a tuft of flowers or fruit at the top of the main stalk or stem: a corbel (*archit.*): a surgical appliance for retaining a reduced hernia: a close-fitting coat or (in *pl.*) breeches (*hist.*). — *v.t.* to bundle up: to muffle up: to tuck up: to lace up, tie the points of (*hist.*): to string up, hang (*obs.*): to fix for cooking, as with a skewer: to catch in the talons, esp. in the air, and carry off (*falconry*): to furnish with a truss. — *v.i.* to pack up: to make off. — *adj.* **trussed.** — *ns.* **truss'er; truss'ing.** — **truss'-beam** a wooden beam strengthened by a steel tie-rod: a steel framework acting as a beam. [Fr. *trousse* (n.), *trousser* (vb.).]

trust *trust, n.* worthiness of being relied on: fidelity: confidence in the truth of anything: confident expectation: a resting on the integrity, friendship, etc., of another: faith: hope: credit (esp. sale on credit or on promise to pay): ground of confidence: that which is given or received in confidence: charge: responsibility: anything felt to impose moral obligations: an arrangement by which property is handed to or vested in a person, to use and dispose of it for the benefit of another: an estate so managed for another: an arrangement for the control of several companies under one direction, to cheapen expenses, regulate production, beat down competition, and so obtain a maximum return. — *adj.* held in trust. — *v.t.* to place trust in: to believe: to expect confidently: to hope: to give credit to: to commit to trust. — *v.i.* to have trust: to rely (with *to*). — *ns.* **trustee'** one to whom anything is entrusted: one to whom the management of a property is committed in trust for the benefit of others; **trustee'-ship** the state of being or action of a trustee: a trust territory; **trust'er.** — *adj.* **trust'ful** trusting. — *adv.* **trust'fully.** — *n.* **trust'fulness.** — *adv.* **trust'ily.** — *n.* **trust'iness.** — *adj.* **trust'ing** confiding. — *adv.* **trust'ingly.** — *adj.* **trust'less** not to be trusted: distrustful. — *n.* **trust'lessness.** — *adv.* **trust'worthily.** — *n.* **trust'worthiness.** — *adjs.* **trust'worthy** worthy of trust or confidence: trusty; **trust'y** to be trusted: deserving confidence: faithful: honest: strong: firm: involving trust (*Shak.*): — *compar.* **trust'ier,** *superl.* **trust'iest.** — *n.* one who can be trusted: a well-behaved prisoner, often granted special privileges: a greatcoat (*Ir.*). — **trust, trustee, account** a savings account, the balance of which can be left to a beneficiary; **trust'-buster** (*U.S.* and *coll.*) one who works for or achieves the break-up of business trusts, e.g. by legislation; **trust company, corporation** a commercial enterprise formed to act as a trustee; **trust'-deed** a deed conveying property to a trustee; **trust'-estate'** an estate held by trustees; **trust fund** a fund of money, etc., held in trust; **trust'-house** hotel or tavern owned by a trust company, not privately or by liquor manufacturers; **trust, trustee, stock** that in which a trustee may legally invest trust funds without being personally liable if it should depreciate in value; **trust territory** a territory ruled by an administering country under supervision of the Trusteeship Council of the United Nations (also **trusteeship**). — **active,** or **special, trust** a trust in which the trustee's power of management depends upon his having the right of actual possession; **breach of trust** a violation of duty by a trustee, etc.; **in trust** as a charge, for safe-keeping, for management as a trustee; **investment trust** an organisation which invests its stockholders' money and distributes the net return among them; **Public Trustee** a government officer (and his department) empowered to act for the state as trustee, executor, etc.; **on trust** on credit: (accepted) without question; **split investment trust** a trust (which must be wound up at a specified date) offering two classes of shares, income and capital, the former earning dividend but to be repaid at par, the latter without dividend but increasing in capital value; **trustee savings bank** a savings bank statutorily controlled under trustees and having its general fund guaranteed by the state; **unit trust** type of investment trust in which given amounts of different securities form a unit, choice of a number of differently constituted units being available. [O.N. *traust,* trust; Ger. *Trost,* consolation.]

truth *trooth, n.* faithfulness: constancy: veracity: agreement with reality: fact of being true: actuality: accuracy of adjustment or conformity: in the fine arts, a faithful adherence to nature: that which is true or according to the facts of the case: the true state of things, or facts: a true statement: an established fact: true belief: known facts, knowledge. — *adj.* **truth'ful** habitually or actually telling what one believes to be true: put forward in good faith as what one believes to be true: conveying the truth. — *adv.* **truth'fully.** — *n.* **truth'fulness.** — *adj.* **truth'less.** — *n.* **truth'lessness.** — *adjs.* **truth'like; truth'y** (*rare*) true: truthful. — **truth drug, truth serum** any of various drugs, such as scopolamine or thiopentone sodium, which make subjects under questioning less wary in their replies; **truth'-teller.** — *adj.* **truth'-telling.** — **truth table** a Boolean logic table in which the binary digits 0 and 1 are assigned values either 'true' or 'false'; **truth'-value** in logic, the truth or falsity of a statement. — **God's truth** a thing or statement absolutely true; **in truth** truly, in fact; **moment of truth** see **moment;** **of a truth** (*B.*) truly; **tell the truth** to speak truthfully, not to lie. [O.E. *trēowth* — *trēowe, trīewe,* true.]

try *trī, v.t.* to separate out (*obs.*): to sift (*obs.*): to render: to extract (*obs.*): to refine (*obs.*): to purify (*obs.*): to test: to prove by testing (*Shak.*): to use, treat, resort to, experimentally: to put to the test: to strain: to annoy, irritate, afflict: to experience, undergo (*Milt.*): to examine critically: to examine and decide the truth, justice, guilt or innocence, of, as a judge: to conduct in court, as a lawyer (*U.S.*): to attempt, endeavour, essay (*usu.* with *to*). — *v.i.* to make an effort: (*Spens.* **trie**) to turn out, prove: to lie to, keep head to wind (*naut.; Shak.*): — *3rd pers. pr.t.* **tries;** *pr.p.* **try'ing;** *pa.t.* and *pa.p.* **tried** (*trīd*). — *n.* a trial: effort: in Rugby football, the score of three points (Rugby League) or four points (Rugby Union) gained by a player who succeeds in placing the ball with his hand over the goal line: in American football, an attempt to gain further points after scoring a touchdown. — *adj.* (*Spens.* **trye**) choice, purified. — *adj.* **trī'able** subject to legal trial: that can be tried. — *ns.* **trī'age** sorting out: in war, etc., the selection for treatment of those casualties most likely to survive: broken coffee-beans; **trī'al** see separate article. — *adj.* **tried** (*trīd*) proved good by test. — *ns.* **trī'er** one who tries in any sense: a test — also **trī'or,** in the sense of one appointed to decide on a challenge to a juror, or a peer who is a juror in the trial of a peer; and **try'er** (*cricket*) in the sense of one who is assiduous in trying to win; **try'ing.** — *adj.* making trial or proof: adapted to try: searching, severe: testing: distressing: causing strain. — *adv.* **try'ingly.** — **try'-house** a place in which oil is extracted from blubber, etc.; **try'-on** an act of trying on a garment: an attempt at imposition by audacity (*slang*); **try'-out'** a test performance; **trysail** (*trī'sl*) a reduced sail used by small craft, instead of the mainsail, in a storm: a small fore-and-aft sail set with a boom and gaff. — **try and** (*coll.*) try to; **try back** to revert, hark back; **try for** make an attempt to reach or gain; **try it on** to attempt to do something risky or audacious: to see how far one can go unscathed; **try on** to put on for trial, as a garment; **try out** to test. [O.Fr. *trier,* to pick out.]

Trygon *trī'gon, n.* the sting-ray genus. [Gr. *trȳgōn,* a sting-ray.]

tryp *trip, n.* short for **trypanosome.**

trypaflavine *trip-a-flā'vēn, n.* acriflavine.

trypanosome *trip'an-a-sōm, n.* a flagellate protozoon (**Trypanosō'ma** of various species, fam. **Trypanosomat'idae**) parasitic in the blood of vertebrates. — *adj.* **trypanocidal** (*-sī'dl*). — *ns.* **tryp'anocide** (*-sīd;* L. *caedĕre,* to kill) a drug that kills trypanosomes; **trypanosomiasis** (*-sō-mī'a-sis*) disease caused by a trypanosome, esp. sleeping-sickness. [Gr. *trȳpanon,* a borer — *trȳpaein,* to bore, *sōma,* body.]

trypsin *trip'sin, n.* a digestive ferment secreted by the pancreas. — *adj.* **tryp'tic.** — *n.* **tryptophan(e)** (*trip'tō-fan, -fān*) an amino-acid obtained e.g. by the cleavage of casein by pancreatic enzymes. [Gr. *trīpsis,* rubbing (as first got by rubbing down the pancreas with glycerine), or *trȳein,* to wear out, modelled on **pepsin.**]

trysail. See **try.**

tryst *trīst,* (chiefly *Scot.*) *n.* an appointment to meet: appointed place of meeting: a cattle-fair. — *v.t.* to make an appointment with. — *v.i.* to agree to meet. — *n.* **tryst'er.** — **trys'ting-day, -place, -stile, -tree.** — **bide tryst** to wait for a person at the appointed place and time. [O.Fr. *triste,* a hunter's station.]

Tsabian. See **Sabian.**

tsaddik, tsaddiq. See **zaddik.**

tsamba *tsam'ba, n.* a Tibetan barley dish. [Tibetan.]

tsar, also **czar,** rarely **tzar,** *zär, tsär,* (*hist.*) *n.* the title of the emperors of Russia and of the kings of Bulgaria: a great potentate or despot. — *ns.* **tsar'dom, czar'dom; tsar'evi(t)ch, czar'evi(t)ch** (Russ. *tsär-ye'vēch*) a son of a tsar; **tsarev'na, czarev'na** a daughter of a tsar: a wife of a tsarevitch; **tsarina, czarina** (*-ē'na;* not a Russian form), **czarit'za, tsarit'sa** a Russian empress; **tsar'ism, czar'ism** the government of the Russian tsars: absolutism; **tsar'ist, czar'ist** an upholder of tsarism; **tsesar'-evi(t)ch, cesar'evi(t)ch, -wi(t)ch** (Russ. *-ye'vēch*) the eldest son of a tsar: heir to the tsardom; **tsesarev'na, cesarev'na** the wife of a tsar's eldest son. [Russ. *tsar',* etc. — L. *Caesar,* Caesar.]

tsessebe *tses'a-bi,* (*S. Afr.*) *n.* the sassaby. [Tswana *tshêsêbê.*]

tsetse *tset'si, n. lossina morsitans,* or other species of the African genus Glossina, small flies that transmit trypanosome parasites and cause sleeping-sickness, nagana (**tsetse-fly disease**), etc. — Also **tset'se-fly.** [Tswana.]

Tshi *ch(w)ē, n.* Same as **Twi.**

T-shirt. See **tee[1].**

tsigane. See **tzigany.**

tsotsi *tsot'si, n.* a young coloured South African hooligan or thug. [Corr. of *zoot suit* (q.v.).]

tsuba *tsoō'ba, n.* a metal plate at the top of a Japanese scabbard, serving as a sword-guard, often highly ornamental. [Jap.]

Tsuga *tsoō'ga, n.* the hemlock spruce genus. [Jap. *tsuga,* larch.]

tsunami *tsoo̅-nä'mē, n.* a very swiftly travelling sea wave that attains great height. [Jap. *tsu*, harbour, *nami*, wave.]

tsutsugamushi disease *tsoo̅-tsoo̅-gə-moo̅'shi diz-ēz'*, scrub-typhus. [Jap. *tsutsuga*, illness, *mushi*, insect.]

Tswana *(t)swä'nə, n.* a Negro people of southern Africa: a member of this people: their language, of the Bantu family: — *pl.* **Tswan'a(s)**. — Also *adj.*

tuan[1] *too̅-än', n.* sir: lord: a title of respect. [Malay.]

tuan[2] *too̅'ən, n.* any of several small Australian marsupials of the genus *Phascogale*. [Australian native name.]

Tuareg *twä'reg, n.* a nomadic Berber of the Sahara: the language of the Tuaregs. [Ar. *tawāriq*.]

tuart, tooart *too̅'ərt*, **tewart** *tū'*, *ns.* a strong-timbered Eucalyptus (*E. gomphocephala*). [Australian Aboriginal.]

tuatara *too̅-a-tä'rə, n.* a New Zealand lizard-like reptile (Sphenodon or Hatteria), the sole survivor of the class Rhynchocephalia. [Maori, spine on the back.]

tuath *too̅'ə*, (*Ir. hist.*) *n.* a people: an ancient territorial division. [Ir. *tūath*.]

tub *tub, n.* an open wooden vessel made of staves and hoops: a small cask: anything like a tub: a tubful: a pulpit: a clumsy ship or boat: a bath: a pit-shaft casing: a bucket, box, or vehicle for bringing up coal from the mine: a tubfish. — *v.t.* to set, bathe, treat, in a tub: to line with a tub. — *v.i.* to take a bath. — *ns.* **tubb'er; tubb'iness; tubb'ing** the art of, or material for, making tubs: mine-shaft lining: rowing in clumsy boats: the taking of baths. — *adjs.* **tubb'ish** round and fat; **tubb'y** sounding like an empty tub: dull in sound: plump, round like a tub. — *n.* **tub'ful** as much as a tub will hold: — *pl.* **tub'fuls.** — **tub'fast** (*Shak.*) treatment of venereal disease by fasting and sweating in a hot tub; **tub'fish** the sapphirine (or other) gurnard. — *v.i.* **tub'-thump'.** — **tub'-thump'er** a declamatory or ranting preacher or public speaker; **tub'-thump'ing.** [Cf. L.G. *tubbe*.]

tuba *tū'bə, too̅'bə, n.* a straight trumpet (*Rom. ant.*): the bombardon (**bass tuba**) or (sometimes) other low-pitched brass instrument of the saxhorn class: a powerful organ reed-stop: a tube (*anat.*): — *pl.* **tu'bas;** L. **tu'bae** (*-bē, -bī*). [L. and It. *tuba*.]

tube *tūb, n.* a pipe: any long hollow body: a telescope or other optical instrument (**optic tube;** *arch.*): a collapsible cylinder from which material in the form of paste or viscous liquid can be squeezed out: a thermionic valve: underground railway in tube-shaped tunnel: the united part of calyx, corolla, etc.: any vessel in a plant or animal body: an aircraft (*slang*): a television set (*slang*): a can or bottle of beer (*Austr. slang*). — *v.t.* to furnish with, fit with, enclose in, a tube: to insert a tube in the neck of (a horse) to help breathing. — *v.i.* to travel by tube. — *n.* **tub'age** insertion of a tube. — *adjs.* **tub'al, tub'ar; tu'bate** tubular. — *n.* **tubec'tomy** surgical cutting or removal of the Fallopian tubes. — *adj.* **tubed** (*tūbd*). — *n.* **tube'ful.** — *adjs.* **tube'less; tubic'olar, tub'icole** (also *n.*), **tubic'olous** inhabiting a tube; **tubiflo'rous** having tubular flowers; **tub'iform** shaped like a tube. — *ns.* **tub'ing** the act of making or supplying tubes: tubes collectively: material for tubes; **tub'oplasty** (*med.*) surgical repair of a Fallopian tube. — *adj.* **tub'ular** having the form of a tube: made of or with tubes: having a sound like that made by the passage of air through a tube. — *n.* **Tubulā'ria** a genus of Hydrozoa. — *adj.* and *n.* **tubulā'rian.** — *n.* **tubular'ity.** — *v.t.* **tub'ulate** to form into a tube: to furnish with a tube. — *adj.* tubular. — *adj.* **tub'ulated.** — *ns.* **tubulā'tion; tub'ulature; tub'ule** a small tube. — *n.pl.* **Tubuliflo'rae** a section of the Compositae with tubular disc-flowers. — *adjs.* **tubuliflo'ral, tubuliflo'rous; tub'ulous** tubular. — **tubal ligation** the placing of a clip or ligature round a loop in each of the Fallopian tubes as a means of sterilisation; **tube'-foot** in echinoderms, a tube protruding through a pore, used in locomotion and respiration; **tubeless tyre, tire** see **tyre; tube'-skirt** a very tight skirt; **tube'-well** a pipe used to obtain water from beneath the ground, with perforations just above its sharp point; **tube'-worm** a worm that makes a tube to dwell in; **tubular bells** an orchestral musical instrument in the percussion section, consisting of a number of metal tubes suspended in a frame, giving the sound of bells when struck. [Fr., — L. *tubus*, a pipe.]

tuber *tū'bər, n.* a lump: a rounded swelling: a knob: a protuberance: a swelling, usually underground, in a plant where reserves are stored up — of stem nature (as in the potato, Jerusalem artichoke, etc.), or of root nature (as in the dahlia): (with *cap.*) the truffle genus of fungi, giving name to the **Tuberā'ceae,** saprophytic Ascomycetes, many with edible underground fructifications (truffles). — *adjs.* **tuberā'ceous; tuberif'erous; tu'beriform; tuberose** (*tū'bə-rōs, -rōz*) tuberous. — *n.* (*tū'bə-rōs, -rōz;* often, by false association with **tube** and **rose,** *tūb'rōz*) a Mexican amaryllid (*Polianthes tuberosa*) grown for its fragrant creamy-white flowers, propagated by tubers. — *n.* **tuberosity** (*-ros'i-ti*). — *adj.* **tub'erous** having tubers: of the nature of, or like, a tuber: knobbed. — **tuberous root** a fleshy root resembling a tuber but not having buds or eyes. [L. *tūber*, a swelling, from root of L. *tumēre*, to swell.]

tubercle *tū'bər-kl, n.* a small tuber, protuberance, or swelling: a nodule: a nodule or morbid growth in the lung or elsewhere, in cases of tuberculosis. — *adjs.* **tu'bercled** having tubercles; **tubercular** (*-bûr'*) nodular: having tubercles: affected by, suffering from, tuberculosis; **tuber'culate, -d** having, covered with, tubercles. — *ns.* **tuberculā'tion; tu'bercule** a tubercle; **tuber'culin** a preparation from a culture of tubercle bacillus used for testing for tuberculosis; **tuberculīsā'tion, -z-.** — *v.t.* **tuber'culise, -ize** to infect with tuberculosis. — *n.* **tuberculo'ma** a slow-growing, circumscribed tuberculous lesion. — *adjs.* **tuber'culose, -d** tuberculous: tuberculated. — *n.* **tuberculō'sis** consumption or phthisis, a disease caused by the **tubercle bacillus** (*Bacillus tuberculosis*), characterised by development of tubercles. — *adj.* **tuber'culous** of, affected by, tuberculosis: tuberculated (now *rare*). — *n.* **tuber'culum** a tubercle. — *adj.* **tuber'culin-test'ed** (of milk) from cows that have been tested for and certified free from tuberculous infection. [L. *tūberculum*, dim. of *tūber*.]

tuberose. See under **tuber.**

tubfast. See tub.

tubicolar, tubiform, tubing, tubular, etc. See tube.

tuchun *too̅-chün', doo̅-jün', n.* a Chinese military governor. [Chin.]

tuck[1] *tuk,* (*Shak.*) *n.* a rapier. [Fr. *estoc* — Ger. *Stock,* stick.]

tuck[2] *tuk, Scot.* **touk** *too̅k,* (*dial.*) *ns.* a stroke, tap, beat, esp. of a drum. — Also *v.i.* and *v.t.* [O.N.Fr. *toker, toquer* (Fr. *toucher*), to touch.]

tuck[3] *tuk, v.t.* to draw or thrust in or together: to stuff, cram: to fold under: to gather or gird up (often with *up*): to contract (with *up*): to enclose by pressing clothes closely around or under: to put tucks in: to put, stow, away: to dress, full, or put on tenters: to hamper: to eat (with *in; slang*): to hang (with *up; slang*). — *v.i.* to make an onslaught upon food (usu. with *in* or *into*). — *n.* an act of tucking: a pleat or fold, now one stitched down: the gathering of the bottom planks of a ship at the stern (*naut.*): eatables, esp. delicacies (*slang*). — *n.* **tuck'er** a piece of cloth tucked or drawn over the bosom: a fuller: food (*Austr. slang*). — *v.t.* (*U.S. slang*) to tire exceedingly (often with *out*). — **tuck'-box** a box of or for tuck, at a boarding school; **tuck'erbag, tuck'erbox** (*Austr.*) a bag, box, for carrying food in; **tuck'-in'** (*slang*) a hearty feed. — *adj.* contrived for tucking in an edge. — **tuck'(ing)-mill** a fulling-mill; **tuck'-out** (*slang*) a tuck-in; **tuck'-shop** (*orig. schoolboys', etc. slang*) a confectioner's or a pastrycook's shop: now esp. such a shop or anything similar on school premises. [O.E. *tūcian*, to disturb, afflict; cf. Ger. *zucken*, to twitch.]

tuckahoe *tuk'ə-hō, n.* an edible but tasteless underground fungus of the southern United States: the edible rootstock of several American aroids: an inhabitant of eastern Virginia. [From Algonquian.]

tucket *tuk′it*, (*arch.*) *n.* a flourish on a trumpet. [Cf. **tuck**[2], and It. *toccata*, a touch.]

tucutuco *tōō-kōō-tōō′kō*, **tucotuco** *tōō-kō-tōō′kō*, *n*s. a South American rodent of mole-like habits: — *pl.* **-cos.** [From its cry.]

Tudor *tū′dər*, *adj.* pertaining to the Welsh family of *Tudor*, the time when it held the English throne (1485–1603), or the style of architecture (Late Perpendicular) that prevailed then. — *adj.* **Tudoresque′.** — **Tudor flower** a trefoil ornament frequent in Tudor architecture; **Tudor rose** a red and white rose (combining Lancaster and York) adopted as a badge by Henry VII.

Tuesday *tūz′di*, *n.* the third day of the week. [O.E. *Tīwes dæg*, the day of *Tīw* (the God of war), translating L. *diēs Martis*, Mars's day; but etymologically, *Tīw*, O.N. *Tȳr*, answers to L. *Jūpiter* (for *Djew pater*), Gr. *Zeus*.]

tufa *tōō′fə*, *tū′fə*, *n.* calc-sinter (often *calcareous tufa*): tuff or other porous rock (*obs.*). — *adj.* **tufā′ceous.** [It. *tufa*, a variant of *tufo* — L. *tōfus*, a soft stone.]

tuff *tuf*, *tōōf*, *n.* a rock composed of fine volcanic fragments and dust: tufa or other porous rock (*obs.*). — *adj.* **tuffā′ceous.** [Fr. *tuf*, *tuffe* — It. *tufo*; see **tufa.**]

tuffe *tuf*, *n.* (*Shak.*) Same as **tuft.** — *n.* **tuff′et** a tuft: a tussock: a mound.

tuft *tuft*, *n.* a bunched cluster: a clump: a crest: a separate lock of hair: one of the cut or uncut loops of wool, etc., forming the pile of a carpet or rug: a goatee or imperial beard: a small tassel: a gold tassel formerly worn on a nobleman's cap in the English universities: hence a titled undergraduate: a person of social consequence. — *v.t.* to separate into tufts: to make or adorn with tufts: to beat (as a covert): to dislodge. — *adj.* **tuft′ed** having or made of tufts: having many short crowded branches all arising at or near the same level (*bot.*): (of birds) with a tuft or crest of feathers on the head. — *ns.* **tuft′er** a hound that drives deer out of cover; **tuft′ing.** — *adj.* **tuft′y.** — **tuft′-hunt′er** a toady; **tuft′-hunt′ing.** [Supposed to be — O.Fr. *tuffe* (Fr. *touffe*) — L. *tūfa*, crest — Gmc. (cf. O.L.G. *top*, top); but there are difficulties.]

tuftaffety, also **tuff-**, **tuft-**, *tuf-taf′ə-ti*, and **-taffeta** *-tə*, (*arch.*) *n*s. a taffeta with tufted pile. — *adj.* of or wearing tuftaffety: richly dressed.

tug *tug*, *v.t.* to pull forcibly: to haul: to tow: to drag. — *v.i.* to pull forcibly: to strive: to toil: — *pr.p.* **tugg′ing;** *pa.t.* and *pa.p.* **tugged.** — *n.* a forcible or jerking pull: a hard struggle: a rope or chain for pulling: a name for various parts of harness, as a trace, a loop to receive a shaft: a tug-boat: an aeroplane towing a glider. — *n.* **tugg′er** one who tugs. — *n.* and *adj.* **tugg′ing.** — *adv.* **tugg′ingly.** — **tug′-boat** a towing vessel; **tug-of-love′** a dispute over the guardianship of a child, e.g. between divorced parents, or natural and foster parents; **tug-of-war′** a laborious contest: a contest in which opposing teams tug at a rope and strive to pull one another over a line. [M.E. *toggen*, intens. from root of O.E. *tēon*; cf. **tow**[1].]

tugrik *tōō′grēk*, *n.* the standard unit of currency of Mongolia. [Mongolian.]

tui *tōō′ē*, *n.* a New Zealand honey-bird, *Prosthemadera novaeseelandiae*, of glossy blue-black plumage with tufts of white at the neck, the parson-bird. [Maori.]

tuille *twēl*, *n.* in plate armour, a steel plate hanging below the tasses. — *n.* **tuillette′** (*dim.*). [Fr., — L. *tēgula*, a tile.]

tuilyie, **tuilzie** *tūl′i*, *tūl′yi*, (*Scot.*; *obs.*) *n.* a fight, brawl, tussle. — *v.i.* to struggle. [O.Fr. *tooil*.]

tuism *tū′izm*, *n.* apostrophe: reference to, or regard for the interests of, a second person. [L. *tū*, thou.]

tuition *tū-ish′ən*, *n.* guardianship (*obs.*): teaching, instruction. — *adjs.* **tui′tional**, **tui′tionary.** [L. *tuitiō*, *-ōnis* — *tuērī*, *tuitus*, to watch over.]

tular(a)emia *tōō-lə-rē′mi-ə*, *n.* a disease of rodents caused by a bacterium (*Bacterium tularense*, or *Pasteurella tularensis*) transmitted to man either by insects or directly, causing fever, etc. — *adj.* **tular(a)e′mic.** [*Tulare* county, California, where it was first discovered, and Gr. *haima*, blood.]

tulban. See **turban.**

tulchan *tulhh′ən*, *n.* a calf's skin set beside a cow to make her give milk freely. — **tulchan bishop** (*Scot. hist.*) a titular bishop appointed to transmit most of the revenues of a diocese to the nobles (1572). [Gael. *tul*(*a*)*chan*, a hillock.]

tule *tōō′lā*, *n.* a large American bulrush (Scirpus). [Sp., — Nahuatl *tollin*.]

tulip *tū′lip*, *n.* any plant or flower of the bulbous liliaceous genus **Tu′lipa**, with showy, usually solitary, flowers: a showy person. — *ns.* **tulipant′** (*obs.*) a turban; **tulipomā′nia** a craze for tulip-growing. — *adj.* **tu′lip-eared** prick-eared, as a dog. — **tu′lip-pop′lar** the tulip tree; **tu′lip-root** a disease affecting the stem of oats; **tu′lip tree** a North American timber tree (Liriodendron), of the Magnolia family, with tulip-like flowers; **tu′lip-wood** its wood. — **African tulip tree** a tree of the genus *Spathodea*, of the Bignoniaceae. [O.Fr. *tulipe*, *tulippe*, *tulipan* — Turk. *tulbend*, turban.]

tulle *tōōl*, *tūl*, *tül*, *n.* a delicate thin silk network fabric. [Fr.; from *Tulle*, in the department of Corrèze.]

Tullian *tul′i-ən*, *adj.* of or like *Tully*, i.e. Marcus *Tullius* Cicero — Ciceronian.

tulwar *tul′wär*, *n.* an Indian sabre. [Hind. *talwār*.]

tum. See **tummy.**

tumble *tum′bl*, *v.i.* to roll, wallow, toss about: to perform as a dancer or acrobat: to turn over in flight or fall: to fall headlong, floundering, or revolving: to collapse, fall in a heap: to come confusedly and hastily: to come by chance (usu. with *on*): to comprehend (often with *to*; *slang*). — *v.t.* to send tumbling or headlong: to overthrow: to bundle from one place to another: to jumble: to throw about: to disorder, rumple. — *n.* act of tumbling: a fall: a somersault: a tumbled condition or mass. — *ns.* **tum′bler** one who tumbles: an acrobat: a large drinking-glass or tall cup, formerly one that could not stand: a tumblerful: a tumbrel: a toy weighted to rock and right itself: a pigeon that turns back-somersaults in the air: a dog that performed antics in catching rabbits (*obs.*): a revolving barrel or cage: part of a lock that holds the bolt in place, till it is moved by the key: part of a firearm lock that receives the thrust of the mainspring and forces the hammer forward: one of a gang of London ruffians who set women on their heads (*early 18th cent.*): a machine which dries (clothes, etc.) by tumbling them in a strong current of hot air (also **tum′ble-**, **tum′bler-drī′er**): a machine consisting of a revolving drum in which (gem)stones are polished (also **tum′bling-barrel, -box**); **tum′blerful** as much as will fill a tumbler: — *pl.* **tum′blerfuls.** — *n.* and *adj.* **tum′bling.** — **tum′ble-bug, -dung** (*U.S.*) a dung-beetle (from its activity of rolling pellets of dung); **tum′ble-car, -cart** a vehicle with wheels and axle in one piece. — *adj.* **tum′bledown** dilapidated, threatening to fall. — **tum′bler-switch** a switch that is turned over to put electric current off or on; **tum′ble-weed** a type of plant that snaps off above the root, curls into a ball, and rolls about in the wind; **tumbling-barrel, -box** see **tumbler** above. — **tumble in** or **home** to incline inward above the extreme breadth, of a ship's sides: to fit, as a piece of timber into other work: to go to bed; **tumble over** to toss about carelessly, to upset: to fall over; **tumble up** to get out of bed: to throw into confusion: to scurry up on deck. [Freq. from O.E. *tumbian*; cf. Ger. *tummeln*.]

tumbrel, tumbril *tum′brəl*, *-bril*, *n*s. an old instrument of punishment, pillory or cucking-stool (*obs.*): a tip-cart: a two-wheeled military cart (*arch.*): a dung-cart: the name given to the carts that conveyed victims to the guillotine during the French Revolution. [O.Fr. *tomberel* (Fr. *tombereau*) — *tomber*, to fall.]

tumefy *tū′mi-fī*, *v.t.* and *v.i.* to swell: — *pr.p.* **tu′mefying;**

pa.t. and *pa.p.* **tu'mefied.** — *adj.* **tumefacient** (*tū-mi-fā'shənt*). — *n.* **tumefac'tion.** — *v.i., v.t.* **tumesce'** (*coll.*) to (cause to) have an erection. — *n.* **tumescence** (*tū-mes'əns*) a tendency to swell: a swelling. — *adjs.* **tumesc'ent; tu'mid** swollen or enlarged: inflated: falsely sublime: bombastic. — *n.* **tumid'ity.** — *adv.* **tu'midly.** — *n.* **tu'midness.** — *n.* **tumorigen'esis** (Gr. *genesis*, creation) the causing or production of tumours. — *adjs.* **tumorigen'ic, tumorgen'ic** causing or producing tumours. — *ns.* **tumorigenic'ity, tumorgenic'ity.** — *adj.* **tu'morous.** — *n.* **tumour, tumor** (*tū'mər*) swelling: turgidity: a morbid swelling or enlargement, now esp. a new growth of cells in the body without inflammation. [L. *tumefacĕre, tumēscĕre, tumidus, tumor* — *tumēre,* to swell, *facĕre,* to make.]

tummy *tum'i, n.* a childish form of **stomach.** — Also **tum, tum'-tum.** — **tumm'y-button** a childish term for navel.

tumour, etc. See **tumefy.**

tump[1] *tump,* (*dial.*) *n.* a hillock, mound, or barrow: a clump. — *v.t.* to make a mound around. — *adj.* **tump'y** hummocky. [Origin unknown.]

tump[2] *tump,* (*U.S.*) *v.t.* to drag. — **tump'-line** a strap across the forehead or chest for carrying burdens or hauling. [Prob. from an Indian word.]

tumphy *tum'fi,* (*Scot.*) *n.* a blockhead: coaly fireclay.

tum-tum[1]. See **tom-tom.**

tum-tum[2]. See **tummy.**

tumular, tumulary, tumuli. See **tumulus.**

tumult *tū'mult, -məlt, n.* violent commotion, usu. with uproar: a riot: a state of violent and confused emotion. — *v.i.* (*Milt.*) to make a tumult. — *v.t.* (*arch.*) to put in tumult. — *adj.* **tumult'uary** (*-mult'*) acted or acting in tumult: haphazard: chaotic: tumultuous. — *v.i.* **tumult'uate** (*arch.*) to make a tumult. — *v.t.* (*arch.*) to disturb with tumult: to make a tumult in. — *n.* **tumultuā'tion** (*arch.*). — *adj.* **tumult'uous** full of tumult: disorderly: agitated: noisy. — *adv.* **tumult'uously.** — *n.* **tumult'uousness.** [L. *tumultus, -ūs* — *tumēre,* to swell.]

tumulus *tū'mū-ləs,* L. *tōō'mōō-lōōs, n.* a burial mound, a barrow: — *pl.* **tu'muli** (*-lī, -lē*). — *adjs.* **tu'mular, -ary.** [L., — *tumēre,* to swell.]

tun *tun, n.* a large cask: an obsolete liquid measure — 216 gallons of ale, 252 of wine: a ton (*obs.*). — *v.t.* to put in a tun. — *ns.* **tunn'age** see **tonnage; tunn'ing.** — *adj.* **tun'bellied.** — **tun'belly** a pot-belly; **tun'-dish** (*Shak.*) a wooden funnel. [O.E. *tunne*; cf. **ton**[1].]

tuna[1] *tōō'nə, tū'nə, n.* a prickly-pear, plant or fruit. [Haitian.]

tuna[2] *tōō'nə, tū'nə, n.* a kind of large sea-fish of the mackerel family: its flesh as food: — *pl.* **tu'na, tu'nas.** — Also **tuna-fish, tunn'y(-fish).** [Sp., — L. *tunnus* — Gr. *thynnos*.]

tuna[3] *tōō'nə, n.* a New Zealand eel. [Maori.]

tunable. See **tune.**

tund *tund,* (*arch.*) *v.t.* and *v.i.* to beat, thump. [L. *tundĕre*.]

tundra *tōōn'-, tun'drə, n.* an Arctic plain with permanently frozen subsoil, and lichens, mosses, and dwarfed vegetation. [Lapp.]

tundun. See **turndun.**

tune *tūn, n.* tone: a melody or air: melodiousness: accurate adjustment in pitch or frequency: harmonious adjustment (*fig.*): frame of mind, temper. — *v.t.* to adjust the tones of: to put in condition for producing tones in tune: to put in smooth working order: to synchronise: to adjust (a radio receiver) so as to produce the optimum response to an incoming signal: to put in accord, bring to a desired state: to begin to play or sing (*arch.*): to start the singing of (*arch.*): to utter, express, or celebrate in music (*arch.*). — *v.i.* to give forth musical sound. — *adj.* **tūn'able** tuneful: in tune. — Also **tune'able.** — *n.* **tun'ableness.** — *adv.* **tun'ably.** — *adjs.* **tuned** (*tūnd*); **tune'ful** full of tune: melodious: musical. — *adv.* **tune'fully.** — *n.* **tune'fulness.** — *adj.* **tune'less** without tune: not melodious or tuneful: unmusical: without sense of tune: silent (*poet.*). — *ns.*

tun'er one who tunes instruments, engines, etc.: one who makes music, or sings: an apparatus for receiving radio signals: a knob, dial, etc. by which a radio or television receiver is adjusted to different wavelengths: in organs, an adjustable flap for altering the pitch of the tone; **tun'ing.** — *adj.* **tun'y** tuneful, esp. in a superficial obvious way. — **tuner amplifier** a piece of hi-fi equipment incorporating a radio receiver and an amplifier which can also be used with a record-player or tape deck; **tune'smith** (*facet.*) a songwriter or composer of light music; **tun'ing-fork** a two-pronged instrument giving a sound of known pitch or vibration; **tun'ing-key, tun'ing-hammer** a key for turning wrest-pins; **tun'ing-peg, -pin** a peg about which the end of a string is wound and by which it is tuned. — **call the tune** see **pay the piper** at **pipe**[1]; **change one's tune, sing another tune** to alter one's attitude, or way of talking; **in tune** true in pitch: in accord (*fig.*); **out of tune** not true in pitch: not agreeing (*fig.*); **to the tune of** to the amount of; **tune in** to adjust a wireless receiver for reception (often with *to*); **tune one's pipes** see **pipe**[1]; **tune out** to adjust a wireless receiver so as to eliminate: to ignore; **tune up** to put instruments into tune for beginning: of engines, etc., to (be) put into smooth working order: to begin to perform, strike up. [A form of **tone**[1].]

tung-oil *tung'-oil, n.* wood-oil obtained from seeds of the **tung'-tree** or Chinese varnish tree (*Aleurites fordii* or other species). [Chin. *yu-t'ung,* tung-oil.]

tungsten *tung'stən, n.* an element (symbol W; at numb. 74), a rare metal also known as wolfram, chiefly got from wolframite, used for making lamp filaments and high-speed steel. — *n.* **tung'state** a salt of **tung'stic acid** (H_2WO_4). [Sw., lit. heavy stone — *tung,* heavy, *sten,* stone.]

Tungus *tōōng'gōōs, tōōng-gōōs', -gōōz', n.* a member of an Eastern Siberian people and race, of the type usually called Mongol: — *pl.* **Tungus, Tunguses:** their language. — Also *adj.* — *n.* **Tungus'ic** the family of Ural-Altaic languages that includes Tungus and Manchu. — *adj.* of or relating to (speakers of) these languages (also **Tungus'ian**). [Russ. *Tunguz;* Chin. *Tung-hu.*]

tunic *tū'nik, n.* a Roman shirt-like undergarment: applied also to the Greek chiton, and to various similar garments, usually a sort of belted coat and gown, or blouse: a close-fitting soldier's or policeman's jacket: a tunicle: an investing layer, membrane, or integument (*biol.*). — *n.pl.* **Tunicā'ta** the Urochorda, a class of sub-phylum of degenerate Chordata, including the ascidians. — *n.* **tu'nicate** a member of the Tunicata. — *adjs.* **tu'nicate, -d** (*bot.* and *zool.*) having a tunic: formed in concentric coats: of the Tunicata. — *n.* **tu'nicin** (*-ni-sin*) a gelatinous substance in the tests of tunicates. — *adj.* **tu'nicked.** — *n.* **tu'nicle** a little tunic: an ecclesiastical vestment like a dalmatic, worn by a sub-deacon or a bishop at mass. [L. *tunica.*]

Tunker *tungk'ər, n.* See **Dunker.**

Tunku *tōōng'kōō,* (Malay) *n.* prince.

tunnage. See **tun, ton**[1].

tunnel *tun'l, n.* a passage cut underground: any tubular passage: an animal's burrow, in earth, wood, etc.: a tunnel-net: a flue, chimney: see also **snake.** — *v.t.* to make a passage or passages through: to hollow out: to catch in a tunnel-net. — *v.i.* to make a tunnel: — *pr.p.* **tunn'elling;** *pa.t.* and *pa.p.* **tunn'elled.** — *n.* **tunn'eller.** — *n.* and *adj.* **tunn'elling.** — **tunn'el-net** a funnel-shaped net; **tunnel vault** same as **barrel vault; tunnel vision** a medical condition in which one is unable to see objects other than those straight ahead: single-minded concentration on one's own pursuits or viewpoints to the total exclusion of those of others. [O.Fr. *ton(n)el* (Fr. *tonneau*) cask, and *tonnelle,* vault, tunnel-net, dims. of *tonne,* cask.]

tunny *tun'i, n.* a tuna, esp. *Thunnus thynnus.* [L. *tunnus* — Gr. *thynnos.*]

tuny. See **tune.**

tup *tup*, *n.* a ram: a paving rammer: a pile-driving monkey: the striking-face of a steam-hammer. — *v.t.* to copulate with (a ewe): to put to the ram. — *v.i.* (of sheep) to copulate: — *pr.p.* **tupp'ing**; *pa.t.* and *pa.p.* **tupped.** [Origin unknown.]

Tupaia *tōō-pī'ə*, *n.* a genus of insectivores giving name to the tree-shrew family **Tupai'idae.** [Malay *tūpai* (*tānah*, ground), squirrel.]

tupek. See **tupik.**

tupelo *tōō'pə-lō*, *n.* an American gum-tree (*Nyssa*): — *pl.* **tu'pelos.** [From an Indian name.]

Tupi, Tupi *tōō-pē'*, *tōō'pē*, *n.* a S. American Indian of a group of peoples inhabiting the Atlantic coast and the Amazon basin: their language, serving as a lingua franca. — Also *adj.* — *adj.* **Tupi'an.**

tupik *tū'pik*, **tupek** *-pek*, *ns.* an Eskimo skin tent. [Eskimo.]

tuppence, tuppenny. Coll. for **twopence, -penny.**

tuptowing. See **typto.**

tuque *tūk*, *n.* a Canadian cap made by tucking in one tapered end of a long cylindrical bag, closed at both ends. [Fr. *toque*.]

tu quoque *tū kwō'kwē*, *tōō kwok'we*, (L.) you too, you're another.

turacin *tū'rə-sin*, *n.* the soluble red colouring matter of touraco feathers, containing copper. — *ns.* **tu'raco** same as **touraco; turacoverdin** (*-kō-vûr'din*) a pigment in touraco feathers, the only pure green pigment found in birds.

Turanian *tū-rā'ni-ən*, (*obs. philol.*) *adj.* of Asiatic languages, neither Iranian nor Semitic: latterly almost the same as Ural-Altaic. — *n.* a speaker of one of those languages. [Pers. *Turān*, not Iran, applied to those parts of the Sassanian Persian empire beyond the Oxus.]

turban *tûr'bən* (*obs.* **tulipant', tul'ban;** *Shak.* **tur'band, tur'bond;** *Spens.* **turribant';** *Milt.* **tur'bant**) *ns.* a head-covering worn by people of certain Eastern nations, consisting of a cap with a sash wound round it: a ladies' headdress of similar appearance. — *adj.* **tur'baned** wearing a turban. [Turk. *tulbend* — Pers. *dulband*; cf. **tulip.**]

turbary *tûr'bə-ri*, *n.* the right to take peat from another's ground: a place where peat is dug. [L.L. *turbāria* — *turba*, turf; of Gmc. origin; see **turf.**]

Turbellaria *tûr-bə-lā'ri-ə*, *n.pl.* a class of ciliated flatworms. — *n.* and *adj.* **turbellā'rian.** [L. *turbellae*, a disturbance.]

turbid *tûr'bid*, *adj.* disordered: muddy: thick. — *ns.* **turbidim'eter** a device for determining the surface area of a powder by measuring the light-scattering properties of a fluid suspension; **tur'bidite** the sediment deposited by a turbidity current; **turbid'ity.** — *adv.* **tur'bidly.** — *n.* **tur'bidness.** — **turbidity current** a volume of sediment-carrying water which flows violently down a slope under water. [L. *turbidus* — *turba*, tumult.]

turbinacious *tûr-bin-ā'shəs*, (*Scott*) *adj.* (of the smell of whisky) peaty. [A blundering form from L.L. *turba*, peat, under the influence of L. *turbō, -inis*, a spinning-top, a swirl.]

turbine *tûr'bin* (sometimes *-bīn*), *n.* a rotary motor in which a wheel or drum with curved vanes is driven by reaction or impact or both by a fluid (water in the **water-turbine,** steam in the **steam-turbine,** expanding hot air in the **gas-turbine**) admitted to it and allowed to escape. — *adj.* **tur'binal** turbinate. — *n.* a scroll-like bone of the nose. — *n.* **tur'binate** a turbinal: a turbinate shell. — *adj.* **tur'binate, -d** shaped like a top or inverted cone: spirally coiled: scroll-like: turbinal. — *adj.* **tur'bined** having, driven by, a turbine or turbines. — *n.* **Tur'bo** a tropical genus of turbinate wide-mouthed gasteropods, large specimens often used as ornaments: (without *cap.*) a member of this genus: — *pl.* **turbines** (*tûr'bi-nēz*): (without *cap.*) a turbocar: — *pl.* **tur'bos:** (without *cap.*) turbocharging. — **turbo-** in composition, having, connected to, driven by, a turbine. —

tur'bine-pump a contrivance for raising water by the inverted action of a turbine wheel; **tur'bine-steam'er** a ship driven by steam-turbine; **tur'bocar, turbo car** a car propelled by a turbocharged engine. — *adj.* **tur'bocharged.** — **tur'bocharger** a turbine operated by the exhaust gases of an engine, thereby boosting its power; **tur'bocharging.** — *adj.* **turbo-elec'tric** using a form of electric drive in which turbine-driven generators supply electric power to motors coupled to propeller, axle shafts, etc. — **tur'bofan** a gas-turbine aero-engine in which part of the power developed is used to drive a fan which blows air out with the exhaust and so increases thrust (also **turbofan engine**); **tur'bo-gen'-erator** a generator of electric power, driven by a steam-turbine; **tur'bo-jet'** (an aeroplane powered by) an internal-combustion aero-engine in which the gas energy produced by a turbine-driven compressor is directed through a nozzle to produce thrust; **tur'boprop** a jet-engine in which the turbine is coupled to a propeller; **tur'bo-ram'-jet** an engine consisting of a turbo-jet mounted within the duct of a ram-jet; **tur'bo=su'percharger** an aero-engine supercharger operated by a turbine driven by the exhaust gases of the engine. [L. *turbō, -inis*, a whirl, a spinning-top.]

turbit *tûr'bit*, *n.* a domestic pigeon having white body, coloured wings, and short beak. [Ety. dub.]

turbith. See **turpeth.**

Turbo, turbo-. See **turbine.**

turbond (*Shak.*). See **turban.**

turbot *tûr'bət*, *n.* a large, highly-esteemed flatfish (*Psetta maxima*) with bony tubercles: extended to various more or less similar fishes. [O.Fr. *turbot*.]

turbulent *tûr'bū-lənt*, *adj.* tumultuous, violently disturbed: in violent commotion: producing commotion: stormy: of fluid, showing turbulence: insubordinate, unruly: having an exciting, disturbing effect. — *ns.* **tur'bulātor** a device which creates turbulence, e.g. in order to mix or disperse fluids: a device fitted to a ship's funnel to assist the dispersal of smoke, fumes, etc.; **tur'bulence** disturbed state (also, esp. formerly, **tur'bulency**): unruly character or action: irregular eddying motion of particles in a fluid: irregular movement of large volumes of air (also **atmospheric turbulence**). — *adv.* **tur'bulently.** [L. *turbulentus* — *turba*, a turmoil.]

Turco *tûr'kō*, (*coll.*) *n.* an Algerian infantryman in the French service: — *pl.* **Tur'cos.** [It., Turk.]

Turcoman. Same as **Turkoman.**

Turcophil *tûr'kō-fil*, **Turcophile** (*-fīl*), *ns.* one who favours the Turks (Gr. *philein*, to love). — Also *adj.* — *ns.* **Turcophilism** (*-kof'il-izm*); **Tur'cophobe** (Gr. *phobein*, to fear) one who fears or dislikes the Turks. — Also *adj.* — *n.* **Turcopho'bia.** [Gr. *Tourkos*, Turk.]

turcopole *tûr'kō-pōl*, *n.* a light-armed soldier of the Knights of St John of Jerusalem. — *n.* **tur'copolier** (*-pō-lēr*) their commander — always an Englishman. [Mod. Gr. *Tourkopoulon*, a Turkish boy.]

turd *tûrd*, *n.* a lump of dung: a despicable person (*vulg.*). [O.E. *tord*.]

turdion *tûr-di-ōn'*, *tûr'-*. Same as **tordion.**

Turdus *tûr'dəs*, *n.* the thrush genus. — *adjs.* **tur'dine** (*tûr'-dīn, -din*) of, resembling, or belonging to a thrush or the thrushes; **tur'doid** thrush-like. [L.]

tureen *tə-rēn'*, *tū-rēn'*, *n.* a large dish for holding soup, vegetables, etc., at table. [Fr. *terrine* — L. *terra*, earth.]

turf *tûrf*, *n.* the surface of land matted with the roots of grass, etc.: a cake of turf cut off: a sod: peat: horse-racing, the race-course, the racing world: — *pl.* **turfs,** sometimes **turves.** — *v.t.* to cover with turf. — *adjs.* **turfed; tur'fen** (*arch.*). — *ns.* **tur'finess; tur'fing; tur'fite** (*slang*) one devoted to horse-racing (also **turf'man;** chiefly *U.S.*). — *adj.* **tur'fy** of, like, or abounding in, turf: pertaining to horse-racing. — **turf'-account'ant** a euphemism for bookmaker. — *adj.* **turf'-clad** covered with turf. — **turf'-drain** one covered with turf; **turf'ing-iron** an implement for cutting turf; **turf'-spade** a long narrow spade for digging turf. — **turf out** to throw out forcibly. [O.E. *turf*; O.N. *torf*.]

turgent *tûr′jənt, adj.* (*obs.*) turgid. — *adv.* (*obs.*) **tur′gently.** — *ns.* **turgescence** (*-jes′əns*) the act or process of swelling up: swollenness: distension of cells and tissues with water; **turgesc′ency.** — *adjs.* **turgesc′ent** swelling: growing big; **tur′gid** swollen: extended beyond the natural size: dilated: inflated: pompous: bombastic: firm and tense by distension with water (*bot.*). — *ns.* **turgid′ity, tur′gidness.** — *adv.* **tur′gidly.** — *n.* **turgor** (*tûr′gör*) the state of being full, the normal condition of the capillaries: balance of osmotic pressure and elasticity of cell-wall (*bot.*). [L. *turgēre*, to swell.]

Turing machine *tū′ring mə-shēn′,* a hypothetical computer, able to perform an infinite number of calculations. [First described by A. M. *Turing* (1912–54), British mathematician.]

turion *tū′ri-ən, n.* an underground bud, growing upward into a new stem. [L. *turiō, -ōnis*, a shoot.]

Turk *tûrk, n.* a native or citizen of *Turkey*: a Muslim of the former Ottoman empire: any speaker of a Turkic language: a Muslim (*obs.*): any one with qualities ascribed to Turks, esp. an unmanageable unruly person: a Turkish horse: a Turkish ship. — *adj.* Turkish. — *adj.* **Turki** (*tōōr′kē*) of the Turkish distinguished from the Tatar branch of Turko-Tatar languages. — *n.* a Turki speaker or language. — *n.* **Turkess** (*tûrk′es*; *rare*) a Turkish woman. — *adjs.* and *ns.* **Turk′ic, Turko-Ta′tar** (of) that branch of the Ural-Altaic languages to which Turkish belongs. — *adj.* **Turk′ish** of Turkey, the Turks, or their language: Turkic. — *n.* the language of the Turks. — *ns.* and *adjs.* **Turk′man, Turk′men** same as **Turkoman.** — **Turkey carpet** a soft thick kind of carpet; **Turkey hone** novaculite; **Turkey merchant** one trading with the Near East; **Turkey oak** a Levantine species of oak (*Quercus cerris*); **Turkey red** a fine durable red dye, obtained from madder, but now mostly chemically; **Turkey stone** Turkey hone: the turquoise (*rare*); **Turkish bath** a kind of hot-air bath, the patient being sweated, rubbed down, massaged, and gradually cooled; **Turkish delight** a gelatinous sweetmeat, orig. Turkish; **Turkish manna** trehala; **Turk's cap** (**lily**) the martagon lily (*Lilium martagon*), from the appearance of the rolled-back petals of the nodding flower; **Turk's head** a kind of knot: a long broom: a figure set up for practice in swordsmanship. — **Grand Turk** (*hist.*) the Ottoman Sultan; **turn Turk** to become Muslim: to be completely reversed.

turkey *tûrk′i, n.* formerly, a guinea-fowl (thought to have come from *Turkey*): now, an American genus (*Meleagris*) of the pheasant family: a domestic breed of that genus: its flesh as food (in *U.S.* also a substitute): extended to various big birds, as bustard, ibis, brush turkey: a play, film, etc. that is a complete failure (*slang*, chiefly *U.S.*). — **turkey buzzard, vulture** an American vulture; **turk′ey-cock** a male guinea-fowl (*obs.*): a male turkey: a strutting, pompous, vain or gobbling blusterer; **turk′ey-hen** a guinea-hen (*obs.*): a female turkey; **turk′ey-trot′** a kind of ragtime dance. — **cold turkey** see **cold; talk turkey** (*U.S.*) to talk bluntly: to talk business.

Turki. See **Turk.**

turkis, turkies. See **turquoise.**

Turkoman *tûr′kō-man, n.* a member of a branch of the Turkish family dwelling north from Persia. — *pl.* **Turk′omans.** — Also *adj.* — Also **Tur′coman, Turk′man, Turk′men.**

turlough *tûr′lohh,* (*Ir.*) *n.* a pond dry in summer. [Ir. *turloch.*]

turm (*Milt.* **turme**), *tûrm, n.* a troop. [L. *turma.*]

turmeric *tûr′mər-ik, n.* a plant (*Curcuma longa*) of the ginger family: its rootstock, or a powder made from it, used in making curry-powder and as a dye. — **turmeric paper** a chemical test-paper impregnated with turmeric, changed from yellow to brown by alkali. [Cf. Fr. *terre-mérite* — as if from L. *terra merita*, deserved earth; origin unknown.]

turmoil *tûr′moil* (*Shak. -moil′*), *n.* commotion: disquiet: tumult. — *v.t.* (formerly *-moil′; arch.*) to harass with commotion: to toss about. — *v.i.* (*dial.*) to toil. [Origin unknown.]

turn *tûrn, v.i.* to revolve: to rotate, to spin, whirl: to move round: to hinge: to depend: to issue: to change or reverse direction or tendency: to return: to deviate: to direct oneself, face (with *to, towards*): to shape one's course: to betake oneself: to direct one's attention: to change sides, religion, mode of life: to be fickle: to change: to be transformed, converted (often with *into*): to become: to result, prove or lead in the issue: to be shaped on the lathe: to sour: to change colour: to become giddy: to be nauseated: to bend back, become turned: to beat to windward. — *v.t.* to rotate: to move round: to change the direction of: to deflect: to bend: to bend back the edge of: to reverse: to pass round or beyond: to perform by turning: to wind: to set outside-in, or remake in that form: to set upside-down: to direct: to point: to apply: to send, drive, set: to pour or tumble out: to employ in circulation, pass through one's hands: to translate: to change: to make sour: to nauseate: to make giddy: to infatuate: to transfer, hand over: to convert, make: to make the subject of (with *to* or *into*): to render: to put by turning: to return, give back: to form in a lathe: to shape: to round off, fashion: to pass, become (a certain age, hour, etc.): to cause or persuade (an enemy agent) to work for one's own side. — *n.* act, occasion, or place of turning: new direction or tendency: a twist: a winding: a complete revolution: a bend: a single traversing of a beat or course: a short walk (or ride or drive): a fit of illness or emotion, esp. an emotional shock, jar, or feeling of faintness: an embellishment in which the principal note is preceded by that next above and followed by that next below (or vice versa in the **inverted turn**), the whole ending (and sometimes beginning) with the principal note (*mus.*): turning-point: a culmination: a time or moment of change: a crisis: a spell: a recurring opportunity or spell in rotation or alternation: rotation: a trick: a performer's act or the performer: a shift: a bout: fashion: manner: cast of mind: aptitude: bent: occasion, exigency: a vicissitude: a characteristic quality or effect: act of kindness or malice: an inverted type serving for a temporarily missing letter: a complete financial transaction, covering the buying and selling of a commodity, etc. — *adj.* **turned** fashioned: wrought in a lathe: beyond the age (now commonly without *of*): reversed: outside-in: upside-down (esp. of type): soured. — *ns.* **turn′er** one who, or that which, turns: one who uses a lathe: a member of a gymnastic club (*U.S.*, from *Ger.*); **turn′ery** the art of turning in a lathe: turner's work: a turner's shop; **turn′ing** rotation: reversal: a bend: the act of making a turn: a winding: deviation: a place where a road strikes off: a shaping, esp. the art of shaping wood, metal, etc., into forms having a curved (generally circular or oval) transverse section, and also of engraving figures composed of curved lines upon a smooth surface, by means of a turning-lathe: (in *pl.*) a shaving from the lathe: in pottery, the shaping of a vase: conversion, transformation. — **turn′about** a turning to face the opposite way (also *fig.*; also **turn′(a)round**); **turn′again** (*arch.*) a refrain; **turnaround** see **turnabout** and **turnround; turn′back** a folded-back part: one who abandons an enterprise. — *adj.* **turn′-back** (able to be) folded back. — **turn′broach** a turnspit; **turn′buckle** a coupling with screw-threads for adjusting tension; **turn′coat** a renegade to his principles or party; **turn′cock** valve which by turning regulates flow of water: an official who turns off and on the water for the mains, etc. — *adj.* **turn′-down** folded down. — *n.* a turn-down part: a turn-down collar: a turning down, rejection; **turning circle** the smallest possible circle in which a vehicle can turn round; **turn′ing-lathe; turn′ing-point** the point at which anything turns in its course: a maximum or minimum point on a graph: a critical point; **turn′ing-**

saw a sweep-saw, a thin-bladed saw held taut in a frame, used for cutting in curves; **turn′key** an under-jailer: a turncock: (a contract for) a job in which the contractor is to complete the entire operation, leaving the building, plant, etc., ready for use (also *adj.*); **turnkey system, package** (*comput.*) a computer system complete with hardware and software, usu. designed, installed, tested and maintained by the supplier and ready for immediate use by the purchaser; **turn′off, turn′-off** a smaller road leading from a main one: **(turn-off)** see **turn off** below; **turn-on** see **turn on** below; **turn′-out′** a getting out of bed: a coming on duty: a call to come on duty: a siding, passing-place, or turning-place (*arch.*): a movable tapered rail for changing to another track: a muster or assembly: a carriage and its horses, a team: output: get-up: a strike (*arch.*): a striker (*arch.*); **turn′over** a turning over: a transference: a part folded over: a newspaper article begun on the front page and continued overleaf: a small pie made by folding over the crust: a small shawl (*arch.*): an apprentice turned over to a new master to complete his apprenticeship (*dial.*): the total amount of money changing hands in a business: the number of employees starting or finishing employment at a particular place of work over a given period: the money value of total sales over a period. — *adj.* folded over, or made to fold over. — **turnover tax** a tax paid every time goods change hands during manufacture and marketing; **turn′-penny** (*arch.*) one who is eager for profit; **turn′-pike** a spiked barrier (*hist.*): a turnstile (*obs.*): a toll-gate: a turnpike-road: a motorway on which tolls are paid (*U.S.*): a winding stair (also **turnpike stair;** *Scot.*); **turn′pike-man** a toll-gate keeper; **turn′pike-road** a road on which there are or were tollgates: a main road; **turn′round, turn′around** a turning round: the whole process of docking, unloading, taking on cargo, passengers, or both, and setting sail again; generally, the whole process of dealing with something and passing it on to the next stage: a complete reversal of direction; **turn′-screw** (*arch.*) a screw-driver; **turn′skin** (*arch.*) a werewolf; **turn′spit** one who turns a spit: a long-bodied, short-legged dog employed to drive a wheel by which roasting-spits were turned: a spit, roasting-jack; **turn′-stile** a revolving frame that allows one person to pass at a time; **turn′stone** a bird (*Arenaria*), intermediate between the true plovers and sandpipers, that turns over pebbles on the beach in search of food; **turn′table** a rotating table, platform, or disc, or pair of rings, one rotating within another, as for turning a locomotive, carrying a gramophone record, cementing a micro-scope slide, turning a camera, etc.; **turn′-up** (or *tûrn-up′*) a disturbance: a thing or part that is turned up, esp. the cuff at the bottom of a trouser-leg: an unexpected or fortuitous result or occurrence: a piece of good luck. — *adj.* turned up. — **a good (bad) turn** a helpful service (disservice); **at every turn** everywhere: incessantly; **(take) a turn for the better, worse** (to make) an improvement, deterioration; **by turns** one after another: at intervals; **in turn** one after another, in succession; **in one's turn** when it is one's occasion, opportunity, duty, etc.; **not turn a hair** to be quite undisturbed or unaffected; **on the turn** at the turning-point, changing: on the point of turning sour; **serve its, one's, turn** to answer the purpose: to do well enough; **take a turn** to go for a stroll: to have a go (*coll.*); **take one's turn, take turns** to participate in rotation; **to a turn** exactly, perfectly (as if of the spit); **turn about** to face round to the opposite quarter: to spin, rotate; **turn about, turn and turn about** alternately: in rotation; **turn a deaf ear to** to ignore; **turn adrift** to unmoor and let float away: to cast off; **turn again** to turn back: to revert; **turn against** to use to the injury of: to render hostile to: to rebel against; **turn an enemy's flank, line** or **position** to manoeuvre so as to attack in the rear: to outwit; **turn an honest penny** see **penny; turn around one's (little) finger** to be able to persuade to anything; **turn aside** to avert: to deviate: to avert the

face; **turn away** to dismiss from service, to discharge: to avert, to turn or look in another direction: to deviate, to depart: to refuse admittance to; **turn back** to cause to retreat: to return: to fold back; **turn colour** to change colour; **turn down** to bend, double, or fold down: to invert: to lower, as a light, volume on a radio, etc.: to reject; **turn forth** to expel; **turn in** to bend inward: to enter: to register (a score): to surrender, hand over voluntarily: to go to bed (*coll.*); **turn in on oneself** to become introverted; **turn into** to become by a process of change; **turn it up, in** stop (saying) it (*imper., coll.*); **turn King's (Queen's) evidence** see **evident; turn loose** to set at liberty; **turn off** to deviate: to dismiss: to divert: to complete, achieve by labour: to shut or switch off: to make (someone) lose interest or enthusiasm, to bore, be disliked by or distasteful to (*n.* **turn′-off**) (*slang*): to give in marriage (*arch.*): to hang (*obs. slang*); **turn of speed** a burst of speed; **turn of the century, year** the period of the end of one century, year, and the beginning of the next; **turn on** to set running (as water): to set in operation by switching on (also *fig.*): to depend on: to turn towards and assail: to give (a person) a sense of heightened awareness and vitality as do psychedelic drugs (*slang*): to rouse the interest of, excite (*n.* **turn′-on**) (*slang*); **turn one's hand to** to apply oneself to; **turn someone's head** or **brain** to make someone giddy: to infatuate with success; **turn out** to bend outwards: to drive out, to expel: to remove the contents of: to dress, groom, take care of the appearance of: to put to pasture (as cattle): to produce and put forth: to prove in the result: to muster: to go on strike: to switch off (a light): to get out of bed (*coll.*): to go out of doors (*coll.*); **turn over** to roll over: to set the other way up: to change sides: to hand over, pass on: to handle or do business to the amount of: to examine by turning the pages: to ponder: to rob (*slang*); **turn round** of a ship, aircraft, etc., to arrive, unload, reload and leave again; **turn tail** see **tail¹; turn the other cheek** to accept harm, violence, etc., without defending oneself; **turn the scale** to decide, determine; **turn the stomach** to nauseate; **turn the tables** see **table; turn to** to have recourse to: to point to: to result in: to change or be changed into: to set to work; **turn turtle** see **turtle²; turn up** to point upwards: to fold upwards: to come, or bring, to light: to appear by chance: to set face up: to invert: to grub up: to disturb: to make brighter, as a light, radio volume, etc. (as if by turning a knob): to refer to, look up: to disgust (*coll.*); **turn-up for the book(s)** a totally unexpected occurrence; **turn upon** to cast back upon, retort: to hinge on. [O.E. *turnian, tyrnan,* and perh. partly O.Fr. *torner* (Fr. *tourner*); all from L. *tornāre,* to turn in a lathe — *tornus,* a turner's wheel — Gr. *tornos,* lathe, compasses.]

Turnbull's blue *tûrn′bəlz blo͞o,* ferrous ferricyanide (or possibly ferric ferrocyanide). [From *Turnbull,* a Glasgow manufacturing chemist (18th cent.), not the discoverer.]

turndun *tûrn′dun,* **tundun** *tun′,* *ns.* an Australian bull-roarer. [Aboriginal.]

turner¹ *tûr′nər, n.* a 17th-century Scots bodle. [Origin doubtful; cf. Fr. *tournois,* coined at *Tours.*]

turner². See **turn.**

Turneresque *tûr-nər-esk′, adj.* resembling the work of the painter J. M. W. *Turner* (1775–1851). — Also **Turne-rian** (*-nē′ri-ən*).

turnip *tûr′nip, n.* the swollen edible root of *Brassica rapa* or (*Swedish turnip*) of *B.* rutabaga, cruciferous bien-nials: the root as food: the plant producing it: extended to more or less similar roots and plants, as the American papilionaceous *prairie turnip* (*Psoralea es-culenta*): a big watch (*slang*): a dunderhead. — *v.t.* to plant with turnips: to feed on turnips. — **tur′nip-flea′** a leaping beetle that eats young turnip and cabbage plants; **tur′nip-fly′** a fly whose maggots burrow in turnip-roots: the turnip-flea; **tur′nip-lan′tern** a lantern made by scooping out the flesh of a turnip; **tur′nip-top′** the green sprout of a turnip in its second year, used as a vegetable. [See **neep;** the first part may be from **turn** or Fr. *tour,* implying roundness.]

turnover.... turnpike ... turnskin. See **turn.**

turnsole *tûr'sōl, n.* a plant whose flowers are supposed to face the sun, as heliotrope or the euphorbiaceous *Chrozophora tinctoria:* a deep-purple dye got from the latter: litmus. [Fr. *tournesol* — L. *tornāre* (see **turn)** *sōl,* the sun.]

turnspit ... turntable. See **turn.**

turpentine *tûr'pən-tīn, n.* a balsam, orig. that of the terebinth tree (*Chian turpentine*), now generally of conifers: popularly, oil of turpentine: a tree that yields turpentine, esp. the terebinth. — *v.t.* to treat or smear with turpentine. — *adj.* **tur'pentiny.** — **tur'pentine-tree** the terebinth-tree. — **oil** (or **spirit**) **of turpentine** (*coll.* **turps**) an oil distilled from turpentine. [O.Fr. *terbentine* — L. *terebinthina (rēsīna),* terebinth (resin); see **terebinth.**]

turpeth *tûr'pəth,* **turbith** *-bith, ns.* an Oriental Ipomoea or its cathartic root. — **turpeth mineral** basic mercuric sulphate. [L.L. *turpethum, turbithum* — Pers. and Ar. *turbed, turbid.*]

turpitude *tûr'pi-tūd, n.* baseness: depravity: vileness. [L. *turpitūdō* — *turpis,* base.]

turps. See **turpentine.**

turquoise *tûr'kwäz, -k(w)oiz, -kwöz,* formerly **turkis** (*Milt., Tenn.*), **turkies** (*Shak.*) *tûr'kiz, -kis, ns.* a massive opaque sky-blue to pale green mineral, a hydrous basic aluminium phosphate, found in Persia: blue colour of the stone. — *adj.* of turquoise: of the colour of turquoise. — *ns.* and *adjs.* **tur'quoise-blue'** turquoise; **tur'quoise-green** pale bluish green. — **bone** or **fossil turquoise** odontolite. [O.Fr. *turkeis,* and later Fr. *turquoise,* Turkish, as first brought through *Turkey* or from *Turkestan.*]

turret[1] *tur'it, n.* a small tower, usu. attached to a building, often containing a winding stair: a tower, often revolving, carrying a gun: part of a lathe that holds the cutting tool. — *adj.* **turr'eted** having turrets: formed like a tower or a long spiral. — **turr'et-clock** a clock for a tower: a large clock with movement quite separate from the dials; **turr'et-gun** one for use in a revolving turret; **turret lathe** a lathe having a number of tools carried on a turret mounted on a saddle which slides on the lathe bed; **turr'et-ship** a warship with gun-turrets. [O.Fr. *tourete,* dim. of *tur;* see **tower.**]

turret[2]**.** Same as **terret.**

turribant. See **turban.**

turriculate, -d *tur-ik'ū-lāt, -id adjs.* turreted: formed in a long spiral. — *n.* **Turritell'a** the tower-shell genus of gasteropods. [L. *turris,* a tower; dim. *turricula.*]

turtle[1] *tûr'tl, (arch.) n.* a turtle-dove: a constant or demonstrative lover. — **tur'tle-dove** any dove of the genus *Turtur* or *Streptopelia,* a favourite cage-bird, a type of conjugal affection and constancy: the mourning dove (*U.S.*). [O.E. *turtla, turtle* — L. *turtur;* cf. Ger. *Turtel,* Fr. *tourtereau, tourterelle.*]

turtle[2] *tûr'tl, n.* any marine chelonian: sometimes a freshwater chelonian: esp. in U.S. a terrestrial chelonian: the edible flesh of a turtle, esp. the green turtle: turtle-soup: a drawing device which converts information from a computer into pictures — orig. a device (*floor turtle*) with a pen or pens, which could be made to move across a flat surface with paper, etc. on it, now often simulated by graphics on a screen (a *screen turtle*) (*comput.*). — *v.i.* to hunt or catch turtles. — *ns.* **tur'tler** a hunter of turtles; **tur'tling** the hunting of turtles. — **tur'tleback** anything arched like a turtle's back, esp. a structure over a ship's bows or stern; **turtle graphics** (*comput.*) drawing by means of a turtle (q.v.); **tur'tle-neck** (a garment having) a high close-fitting neckline. — *adj.* **tur'tle-necked.** — **tur'tle-shell** the shell of the hawk's-bill turtle, commonly called tortoise-shell; **tur'tle-soup** a soup made from the flesh, fat, and gelatinous tissue of the female green turtle (*Chelone mydas*); **tur'tle-stone'** a septarium. — **mock turtle** a soup made of calf's head or other meat in lieu of turtle

meat; **turn turtle** to render a turtle helpless by turning it on its back: to turn bottom up. [Fr. *tortue,* Sp. *tortuga,* or Port. *tartaruga,* tortoise, assimilated to foregoing — all from L.L. *tortuca.*]

turves. See **turf.**

Tuscan *tus'kən, adj.* of Tuscany in Italy: Doric as modified by the Romans, with unfluted columns, and without triglyphs (*archit*). — *n.* classical Italian as spoken in Tuscany: a native of Tuscany: an ancient Etruscan. [L. *Tuscānus,* Etruscan.]

tusche *tōōsh, n.* a substance used in lithography for drawing the design which then does not take up the printing medium. [Ger. *tuschen,* to touch up (with paint, etc.).]

tush[1]*, tush, (Shak.) n.* a tusk: a small tusk: a horse's canine tooth. [O.E. *tūsc;* cf. **tusk**[2]**.**]

tush[2] *tush, (arch.) interj.* pshaw: pooh. — Also *v.i.* — *n.* **tush'ery** word coined by R. L. Stevenson meaning (a style of period novel, etc. using) would-be archaic language.

tusk[1]**.** Same as **torsk.**

tusk[2] *tusk, n.* a long, protruding tooth: a tush: a sharp projection. — *v.t.* to pierce with the tusks. — *adjs.* **tusked, tusk'y.** — *n.* **tusk'er** a boar, elephant, etc., with tusks. — *adj.* **tusk'less.** — **tusk'-shell** the mollusc Dentalium or its shell. [O.E. *tūx (tūsc);* cf. **tush**[1]**.**]

tuskar, tusker *tus'kər,* **twiscar** *twis'kər, (Orkney* and *Shetland) ns.* a peat-spade. [O.N. *torfskeri* — *torf,* turf, *skera,* to cut.]

tusky. See **tusk**[2]**.**

tussac-grass. See **tussock.**

tussah *tus'ə,* **tusseh** *-e, ns.* Faulty forms of **tusser.**

tusser, tussore, tasar *tus'ər, n.* a fawn-coloured silk from wild Indian silkworms: its colour: a dress made of it. — Also **tuss'er-silk.** [Hind. *tasar,* shuttle — Sans. *tasara,* silkworm.]

tussie mussie *tus'i mus'i.* Same as **tuzzi-muzzy.**

tussis *tus'is, (med.) n.,* a cough. — *adjs.* **tuss'al, tuss'ive.** [L.]

tussle *tus'l, n.* a sharp struggle. — *v.i.* to struggle. [Freq. of **touse;** cf. **tousle.**]

tussock *tus'ək, n.* a tuft: a bunchy clump of grass, rushes, etc.: tussock-grass: a tussock-moth. — *adj.* **tuss'ocky.** — **tuss'ock-, tuss'ac-grass** a large grass (*Poa flabellata*) of the Falkland Islands, forming great tufts; **tuss'ock=moth** any moth of the family Lymantriidae (akin to Lasiocampidae), from the tufts of hair on the caterpillars. [Origin obscure.]

tussore. Same as **tusser.**

tut[1] *tut, interj.* an exclamation of rebuke, mild disapprobation, impatience, etc. — *v.i.* to say 'tut': — *pr.p.* **tutt'ing;** *pa.t.* and *pa.p.* **tutt'ed.** — Also **tut'-tut',** *Scot.* **toot, toots, tuts.**

tut[2] *tut, n.* work paid by measurement or piece. — *v.i.* to do such work. — **tut'work; tut'worker; tut'(work)man.** [Origin unknown.]

tutania *tū-tā'ni-ə, n.* a kind of Britannia metal. [From W. *Tutin* (c. 1780), its maker or inventor.]

tutee. See **tutor.**

tutelage *tū'ti-lij, n.* guardianship: state of being under a guardian: tuition. — *adjs.* **tu'telar, tu'telary** protecting: having the charge of a person or place. — *ns.* a guardian spirit, god, or saint. [L. *tūtēla,* guard — *tūtārī,* to guard — *tuērī,* to look to.]

tutenag *tū'ti-nag, n.* an alloy of zinc, copper, etc.: (*loosely*) zinc. [Marathi *tuttināg.*]

tutiorism *tū'ti-ər-izm, n.* in R.C. moral theology, the doctrine that in a case of doubt between right and wrong one should take the safer course, i.e. the one in verbal accordance with the law. — *n.* and *adj.* **tū'tiorist.** [L. *tūtior, -ōris,* safer, comp. of *tūtus,* safe.]

tutor *tū'tər, n.* a guardian: a guardian of the person and estate of a boy under fourteen, or girl under twelve (*Scots law*): a private instructor: a coach: one who helps a boy or girl with lessons: a college officer who has supervision of an undergraduate: a college teacher who instructs by conference with a small group of students: an instruction-book. — *v.t.* to act as tutor to: to instruct: to coach: to control: to discipline. — *ns.* **tutee'** a person who is tutored; **tu'torage** tutorship: tutoring: charge for tutoring: tutelage (*obs.*); **tu'toress, tu'tress** (*obs.* **tu'trix**) a female tutor. — *adj.* **tutorial** (*tū-tō'ri-al, -tō*) of a tutor. — *n.* a conference or sitting with a college tutor. — *adv.* **tuto'rially.** — *n.* **tu'toring.** — *v.t.* and *v.i.* **tu'torise, -ize.** — *ns.* **tu'torism; tu'torship.** [L. *tūtor, -ōris*, a guardian — *tuērī*, to look to.]

tuts (*Scot.*). See **tut**[1].

tutsan *tut'san, n.* parkleaves, a species of St John's wort (*Hypericum androsaemum*) once regarded as a panacea. [O.Fr. *toutesaine, tout* — L. *tōtus*, all, *sain* — L. *sānus*, sound.]

tutti *tōōt'(t)ē,* (*mus.*) *pl. adj.* all (performers). — *n.* a passage for the whole orchestra or choir, or its rendering. [It., pl. of *tutto* — L. *tōtus*, all.]

tutti-frutti *tōōt'(t)ē- frōōt'(t)ē, n.* a confection, esp. ice-cream, flavoured with different kinds of fruit. [It., all fruits.]

tut-tut *tut'-tut.* Same as **tut**[1].

tutty *tut'i, n.* crude zinc oxide. [O.Fr. *tutie*—L.L. *tutia* — Ar. *tūtiyā*.]

tutu[1] *tōō'tōō, n.* any of several New Zealand shrubs of the genus *Coriaria*, having poisonous black berries. [Maori.]

tutu[2] *tōō'tōō, n.* a ballet dancer's short, stiff, spreading skirt. [Fr.]

tu-whit tu-whoo *tōō-(h)wit' tōō-(h)wōō', an owl's hoot. — *v.i.* **tu-whoo'** to hoot.

tuxedo *tuk-sē'dō,* (orig. *U.S.*) *n.* a dinner-jacket: — *pl.* **tuxe'dos, -does.** [From a fashionable club at *Tuxedo Park, N.Y.*]

tuyère. See **twyer.**

tuzz *tuz,* (*Dryden*) *n.* a tuft. — **tuzz'i-muzzy** (*obs.*) a posy.

twa *twā, twö, twä,* also **twae, tway** *twā, adjs.* and *ns.* Scots forms of **two.** — *adj.* and *adv.* **twa'fald** (*-föld*) twofold: bent double. — *n.* and *adj.* **twa'some** see **twosome.** — *adj.* **twa'-loft'ed** two-storied.

twaddle *twod'l, n.* senseless or prosy commonplace talk: a talker of twaddle (*obs.*). — *v.i.* to talk twaddle. — *n.* **twadd'ler.** — *n.* and *adj.* **twadd'ling.** — *adj.* **twadd'ly.** [Perh. **twattle**.]

twain *twān,* (*arch.*) *adj.* two. — *n.* a couple, pair. — **in twain** asunder. [O.E. *twēgen* (masc.), two.]

twaite *twāt, n.* one of the British species of shad. — Also **twaite shad.** [Origin unknown.]

twal *twöl, twäl, adj.* and *n.* a Scots form of **twelve.** — *ns.* **twal'hours** (*-ōōrz*) a noonday meal or refreshment; **twal'penny** a shilling in old Scots money, an old penny sterling. — Also **twal'pennies.**

twang[1] *twang,* (*dial.*) *n.* a sharp flavour: an aftertaste: a smack, suggestion. [**tang**[3], affected by next.]

twang[2] *twang, n.* the sound of a plucked string: a nasal tone: a twinge (*dial.*): a local intonation (*coll.*). — *v.t.* and *v.i.* to sound with a twang. — *n.* and *adj.* **twang'ing.** — *adv.* **twang'ingly.** — *n.* **twangle** (*twang'gl*) a slack or jangly twanging. — *v.t.* and *v.i.* to sound with a twangle. — *n.* and *adj.* **twang'ling** (*-gling*). — *adv.* **twang'lingly** (*-gling-li*). — *adj.* **twangy** (*twang'i*). — *n.* **twank** (*dial.*) a short twang: a slap. [Imit.]

twankay *twang'kā, n.* a kind of green tea: gin (*slang*). [*Tong-ke* or Tun-chi in China.]

'twas *twoz, twəz,* a contraction of **it was.**

twat *twot, twat, n.* (*vulgarly*) the vulva: (*blunderingly*) part of a nun's dress (*Browning*): a coarse general term of reproach (*slang*). [Origin obscure.]

twattle *twot'l, n.* chatter: babble: twaddle. — *v.t.* and *v.i.* to babble. — *n.* **twatt'ler.** — *n.* and *adj.* **twatt'ling.** [Perh. conn. with **tattle**.]

tway *twā, adj.* and *n.* a form of **twain** (*Spens.*): a form of **twain,** or of **two** (**twae**) (*Scot.*). — **tway'-blade** an orchid (*Listera*) with small green flowers and one pair of leaves: also an American orchid (*Liparis*).

tweak *twēk, v.t.* to twitch, to pull: to pull or twist with sudden jerks. — *n.* a sharp pinch or twitch: agitation, perplexity (*obs.*). [App. conn. with **twitch**[1].]

twee *twē,* (*coll.*) *adj.* small and sweet: sentimentally pretty. — *adv.* **twee'ly.** — *n.* **twee'ness.** [*tweet* for 'sweet', and later *riny* and *wee*.]

tweed *twēd, n.* a rough woollen cloth much used for men's suits: (in *pl.*) clothes of tweed. — *adj.* **tweed'y** of or resembling tweed: of a predominantly upper-class, hearty, outdoorsy type. [Said to be from a happy misreading of **tweel,** the cloth being made in the Tweed basin; or perhaps a shortening of *tweeled* (twilled).]

tweedle *twē'dl, v.i.* to play casually, strum, tootle: to pipe as a bird. — *v.t.* to pipe into acquiescence: to wheedle. — *ns.* **tweedledee', tweedledum'** a fiddler (in conjunction as types of the almost indistinguishable; orig. the proverbial names of two rival musicians). — *v.i.* **tweedledee'** to tweedle: to fiddle. [Prob. imit., influenced by **wheedle**.]

tweedy. See **tweed.**

tweel *twēl,* a Scots form of **twill**[1].

'tween. A contraction of **between.** — *adj.* **'tween'-deck** lodging between decks. — *n.* and *adv.* **'tween-decks.** — *n.* **tween'y** (*coll.*) a between-maid.

tweer[1]. See **twyer.**

tweer[2]. See **twire**[1].

tweet *twēt,* **tweet'-tweet'** *ns.* the note of a small bird. — *vs.t.* and *vs.i.* to pipe as a small bird. — *n.* **tweet'er** a loudspeaker used in high-fidelity sound reproduction for the higher frequencies (also (*coll.*) **top tweet**). [Imit.]

tweezers *twēz'ərz, n.pl.* small pincers for pulling out hairs, etc. — *v.t.* **tweeze** (esp. *U.S.*) to grasp or pluck with or as if with tweezers. — **tweez'er-case** an étui. [Obs. *tweeze,* a surgeon's case of instruments — Fr. *étui.*]

twelfth *twelfth, adj.* last of twelve: immediately following the eleventh in order, position, etc.: equal to one of twelve equal parts. — *n.* a twelfth part: a person or thing in twelfth position: a tone eleven (conventionally twelve) diatonic degrees above or below a given tone (*mus.*): an octave and a fifth. — *adv.* **twelfth'ly** in the twelfth place. — **Twelfth'-cake** an ornamental cake partaken of on Twelfth-night; **Twelfth'-day** the twelfth day after Christmas, Epiphany, 6 January; **twelfth man** (*cricket*) a player selected beyond the necessary eleven to play if required as a substitute; **Twelfth'-night** the evening of 6 January: also the evening of 5 January; **Twelfth'-tide** the season of Epiphany. — **the (glorious) Twelfth** 12 August, opening day of the grouse-shooting season. [O.E. *twelfta* — *twelf.*]

twelve *twelv, n.* the cardinal number next above eleven: a symbol representing that number: a set of that number of things or persons: an article of a size denoted by 12: a score of twelve points: the hour of midday or midnight: the age of twelve years: (in *pl.*) duodecimo. — *adj.* and *adv.* **twelve'fold.** — *ns.* **twelve'mo** (*pl. -mos*) duodecimo, written 12mo; **twelve'-month** a year. — *adj.* of the number twelve: twelve years old. — *adj.* **twelve'-penny** shilling. — **twelve score** two hundred and forty (yards); **Twelve Tables** the earliest code of Roman law, civil, criminal, and religious, made by the decemvirs in 451–449 B.C. — *adj.* **twelve'-tone** (or **-note**) pertaining to music based on a pattern formed from the twelve notes of the chromatic scale, esp. as developed by Arnold Schönberg (1874–1951) and his pupils (**twelve-tone, -note, row** the basic pattern of notes; see also **series, serial**). — **the Twelve** the twelve apostles. [O.E. *twelf* (Ger. *zwölf,* and Goth. *twa-lif*), that is, prob. two left; see **eleven.**]

twenty *twen'ti, adj.* twice ten: nineteen and one: an indefinite number. — *n.* the number next above nineteen: a score: an old English division of infantry. — *n.pl.* **twen'ties** the numbers twenty to twenty-nine: the years so numbered in life or any century: a range of temperatures from twenty to just less than twenty-nine degrees. — *adj.* **twen'tieth** next after the nineteenth: last of twenty: equal to one of twenty equal parts. — *n.* a twentieth part: a person or thing in twentieth position. — *n., adj.,* and *adv.* **twen'tyfold** twenty times as many or much. — *adj.* **twen'tyish** about twenty. —

twen′ty-five′ a line on a hockey pitch (and formerly on a rugby pitch) twenty-five yards from the goal-line; **twen′ty-four′** a sheet folded into twenty-four leaves (forty-eight pages): a form arranged for printing it. — *n.* **twenty-four′mo** (written 24mo, for L. *in vīcēsimō quārtō*) a book made up of sheets folded in twenty-four leaves (forty-eight pages). — Also *adj.* — **twenty-pence, -penny piece** in Britain, a coin worth 20 pence. — *adj.* **twen′ty-twen′ty** of human vision, normal. — **twen′ty-two′** a line on a rugby pitch twenty-two metres from the goal-line. — **and twenty** (*Shak.*) supposed to be a mere intensive (as *good even and twenty; sweet and twenty;* 3cc **sweet**). [O.E. *twēntig*, prob. — *twēgen*, twain, and suff. *-tig* (Goth. *tigjus*), ten; Ger. *zwanzig*.]

'twere. A contraction of **it were.**

twerp *twûrp*, (*slang*) *n.* a contemptible person, either stupid or a cad, or both. [Origin uncertain; a connection with one T.W. Earp, once president of the Oxford University union, has been suggested.]

twi-, twy- *twī*, *pfx*, two: double. — *adjs.* **twi′-, twy′fold** twofold; **twi′-, twy′forked** bifurcate; **twi′-, twy′formed** having two forms; **twi′-, twy′-natured** of double nature. [O.E. *pfx. twi-*.]

Twi *ch(w)ē*, *n.* a dialect, and also a literary language, of Ghana. — Also **Tshi.** — Also *adj.*

twibill *twī′bil*, *n.* a double-headed axe. [O.E. *twibill* — *pfx.* **twi-, bill**[1].]

twice *twīs*, *adv.* two times: doubly: for a second time. — *n.* **twi′cer** one who is both compositor and pressman: one who habitually goes to church twice on Sunday (*eccles. slang*). — *adjs.* **twice′-born** born twice, as Bacchus: of high Hindu caste: regenerate (*theol.*); **twice′-laid** made of old yarns twisted anew; **twice′-told** counted twice: told twice: hackneyed. — **at twice** in two stages or operations; **twice over** twice (emphatically). [Late O.E. *twiges* — *twiga, twiwa, tuwa,* twice, with adverbial gen. ending.]

twichild *twī′chīld*, *n.* one who has become a child again. [*Pfx.* **twi-.**]

twiddle *twid′l*, *v.t.* to twirl idly: to finger idly, play with: to rotate. — *v.i.* to twirl: to trifle with something. — *n.* a twirl: a curly mark, ornament. — *n.* **twidd′ler.** — *n., adj.* **twidd′ling.** — *adj.* **twidd′ly.** — **twidd′ling-line** formerly, a line for steadying the steering-wheel: a string for setting the compass-card to play freely. — **twiddle one′s thumbs** to rotate the thumbs around each other: to be idle (*fig.*). [Prob. suggested by **twirl, twist,** and **fiddle.**]

twier. See **twyer.**

twig[1] *twig*, *n.* a small shoot or branch: a divining-rod. — *adj.* made of twigs. — *v.t.* to birch, switch. — *adjs.* **twigg′en** (*Shak.*) covered with, made of, wickerwork; **twigg′y; twig′some.** [O.E. *twig*; cf. Ger. *Zweig*.]

twig[2] *twig*, (*coll.*) *v.t.* and *v.i.* to observe: to understand. [Poss. Ir. *tuigim*, discern; cf. Gael. *tuig*, understand.]

twig[3] *twig*, (*slang*) *n.* fettle: fashion: recognisable condition. — *v.i.* to act vigorously. — *n.* **twigg′er** (*obs.*) a vigorous breeder: a wanton. [Origin obscure.]

twight *twīt*, *v.t.* (*Spens.*) for **twit**[1].

twilight *twī′līt*, *n.* the faint light after sunset and before sunrise: dim light or partial darkness: a period of decay following a period of success, vigour, greatness, etc. (*fig.*). — *adj.* of twilight: faintly illuminated: obscure, indefinite: partial, transitional. — *v.t.* to illuminate faintly. — *adjs.* **twī′lighted, twī′lit.** — **twilight sleep** partial anaesthesia in childbirth by the use of drugs; **twilight zone** a dilapidated, decaying part of a city or town typically situated between the main business and commercial area and the suburbs: any area or state transitional or indefinite in character. — **twilight of the Gods** see the ety. at **Ragnarök.** [*Pfx.* **twi-, light.**]

'twill. A contraction of **it will.**

twill[1] *twil*, or (*Scot.*) **tweel, twēl,** *ns.* a woven fabric showing diagonal lines, the weft yarns having been worked over one and under two or more warp yarns: the appearance so produced. — *v.t.* to weave with a twill. — **cavalry twill** a strong woollen twill used esp.

for trousers. [O.E. *twilic.*]

twill[2] *twil*, **twilt** *twilt.* Dialect forms of **quill, quilt.**

twilled *twil′id*, *adj.* prob., protected against floods by plaited osiers (the word so used still at Stratford; *Shak.*): according to some, ridged like twilled cloth: or reedy, from an alleged obs. word *twill*, a reed.

twilly *twil′i*, *n.* a willowing-machine. [**willow.**]

twin[1] *twin*, **twine** *twīn*, (*obs.* and *Scot.*) *vs.t.* and *vs.i.* to separate: to part. — *vs.t.* to deprive. [**twin**[2].]

twin[2] *twin*, *n.* one of two born at a birth: one very like, or closely associated with, another: a counterpart: a pair of twins or pair generally (*obs.*): a combination of two crystals symmetrically united about a plane that is a possible face of each or an axis that is a possible edge of each, or of more than two by repetition. — *adj.* twofold, double: born two at a birth: forming one, or composed, of two like parts or counterparts: very like another. — *v.t.* to couple, or to produce, like a twin or twins. — *v.i.* to be born at the same birth: to bring forth two at once: to be paired or suited: — *pr.p.* **twinn′ing;** *pa.p.* **twinned.** — *ns.* **twin′er** (*Walter de la Mare*) a double limerick; **twin′ling** a twin. — *adj.* **twinned** produced at one birth: constituting a twin. — *ns.* **twinn′ing; twin′ship** the condition or relation of a twin or twins. — **twin′-ax′is** the axis of symmetry of a twin crystal; **twin bed** one of a matching pair of single beds; **twin′-birth** a birth of twins: a twin: a pair of twins. — *adj.* **twin′-born** born at the same birth. — **twin′-broth′er** a brother born at the same birth; **twin′flower** a N. American plant of the genus *Linnaea* having paired flowers; **twin′-plane′** the plane of symmetry of a twin crystal. — *adj.* **twin′-screw** with two propellers on separate shafts. — **twin′-set** a cardigan and jumper made more or less to match; **twin′-sist′er** a sister born at the same birth; **twin town** a town paired with another foreign town of similar size for the purpose of social, cultural and commercial exchanges; **twin′-tub** a type of washing-machine with separate drums for washing and spin-drying. — **the Twins** Gemini. [O.E. *getwinn* (n.), twin, *twinn* (adj.), double; cf. *pfx.* **twi-**]

twine[1] *twīn*, *n.* a twisted cord: string or strong thread: a coil: a twist: a twisted stem or the like: an act of twisting or clasping. — *v.t.* to wind: to coil: to wreathe: to twist: to twist together: to encircle: to make by twisting. — *v.i.* to wind: to coil: to twist: to make turns: to rise or grow in spirals: to wriggle. — *adj.* **twīned.** — *n.* **twī′ner** one who, or that which, twines: a twining plant. — *n. and adj.* **twī′ning.** — *adv.* **twī′ningly.** — *adj.* **twī′ny.** — **twining plant** one that climbs by twining its stem round a support. [O.E. *twīn*, double or twisted thread, linen thread; cf. Du. *twijn*.]

twine[2] *twīn*, *n.* a variant of **twin**[1].

twiner[1]. See **twin**[2].

twiner[2]. See **twine**[1].

twinge *twinj*, *v.t.* to tweak or pinch: to affect with a momentary pain. — *v.i.* to feel or give a momentary pain. — *n.* a tweak, a pinch: a sudden short shooting pain: a brief pang. [O.E. *twengan*, to pinch.]

twink *twingk*, *v.i.* to blink: to twinkle. — *n.* a twinkling, a moment. [Root of **twinkle.**]

twinkle *twing′kl*, *v.i.* to blink: to quiver the eyelid: to shine by flashes: to glitter: to sparkle: to flicker, vibrate. — *v.t.* to guide by twinkling. — *n.* a blink: a wink: a glitter: a quiver: a flicker: a sparkle: a twinkling: a dance step. — *ns.* **twink′ler; twink′ling** a quick motion of the eye: the time occupied by a wink: an instant: the scintillation of the fixed stars. — *adj.* scintillating: quivering: blinking (*obs.*). [O.E. *twinclian.*]

twinter *twin′tər*, (*Scot.*) *adj.* two years old. — *n.* a two-year-old sheep or other animal. [O.E. *twiwintre*, two-winter.]

twire[1] *twīr*, **tweer** *twēr*, (*Shak.*) *vs.i.* to peer. — *ns.* (*obs.*) a glance, leer. [Cf. M.H.G. *zwieren*, to peer.]

twire[2]. See **twyer.**

twirl *twûrl*, *v.t.* and *v.i.* to spin: to whirl: to twist: to coil. — *n.* a twist: a spin: a whirl: a whorl: a curly figure. — *n.* **twirl′er.** — *adj.* **twirl′y.** — **twirl one′s thumbs** to twiddle one's thumbs.   [Connection with O.E. *thwiril*, churn handle, whisk, doubtful.]

twirp. An alternative spelling of **twerp.**

twiscar. See **tuskar.**

twist *twist, v.t.* to twine: to unite or form by winding together: to form from several threads: to wind spirally: to form into a spiral: to wring: to wrest: to distort: to force, pull out of natural shape, position, etc.: to entangle: to impart a spin to: to force round: to eat heartily (often with *down; old slang*): to pervert, warp. — *v.i.* to twine: to coil: to move spirally or tortuously: to turn aside: to revolve: to writhe: in the card-game vingt-et-un (pontoon), to deal or receive a card face upwards. — *n.* that which is twisted or formed by twisting: a cord: a strand: thread: silk thread: warp yarn: a twisted part: torsion: an act or manner of twisting: a contortion: a wrench: a wresting: a turning aside: a spin, screw, or break: a distortion: a perverted bent or set: an unexpected event or change of direction (*lit.* and *fig.*): a tangle: a twisted roll of tobacco or bread: a small curled piece of lemon, etc. flavouring a drink: a spiral ornament in the stem of a glass: a twig (*obs.*): the fork of the body (*obs.*): a mixed drink (*slang*): a good appetite (*slang*).   *adjs.* **twist'able; twist'ed.** — *n.* one who, or that which, twists: a sophistical, slippery, shuffling, or dishonest person: a ball sent with a twist: a tornado (*U.S. coll.*). — *n.* and *adj.* **twist'ing.** — *adj.* **twist'y.** — **twist drill** a drill for metal having one or more deep helical grooves round the body. — **round the twist** (*coll.*) crazy, mad; **the twist** a dance which became popular in 1962, in which the dancer constantly twists the body; **twist someone's arm** to persuade someone, esp. forcefully. [O.E. *twist*, rope (found in the compound *mæst-twist*, a stay).]

twit[1] *twit, v.t.* to upbraid: to taunt: — *pr.p.* **twitt'ing;** *pa.t.* and *pa.p.* **twitt'ed.** — *n.* a reproach. — *v.t.* **twitt'er** (*Fielding*) to twit. — *n.* and *adj.* **twitt'ing.** — *adv.* **twitt'ingly.**   [O.E. *ætwītan*, to reproach — *æt*, against, *wītan*, to wite.]

twit[2] *twit,* (*slang*) *n.* a fool.   [Prob. **twit**[1].]

twitch[1] *twich, v.t.* to jerk: to pluck: to snatch: to steal: to pinch or twinge. — *v.i.* to jerk: to move spasmodically: to carp, sneer. — *n.* a sudden, quick pull: a spasmodic contraction of the muscles: a twinge: a noose: the sudden tapering of a vein of ore: the yips (q.v.) (*golf*). — *n.* **twitch'er** one who, or that which, twitches: a bird-watcher whose main interest is the spotting of as many rare species as possible (*coll.*). — *n.* and *adj.* **twitch'ing.** — *adj.* **twitch'y** which twitches: on edge, nervous (*coll.*).   [Related to O.E. *twiccian*, to pluck; Ger. *zwicken*.]

twitch[2] *twich,* **twitch grass.** Forms of **quitch, quitch grass** (see **couch grass**).

twite *twīt, n.* the mountain linnet, *Acanthis flavirostris,* a N. European finch with streaked brown plumage. [From its note.]

twitten *twit'n,* (*dial.*) *n.* a narrow lane between two walls or hedges. — Also **twitt'ing.**   [Perh. related to L.G. *twiete*, alley, lane.]

twitter[1] *twit'ər, n.* a tremulous feeble chirping: a flutter of the nerves. — *v.i.* to make a succession of small tremulous noises: to palpitate. — *v.t.* to chirp out: to twiddle. — *ns.* **twitt'erer.** — *n.* and *adj.* **twitt'ering.** — *adv.* **twitt'eringly.** — *adj.* **twitt'ery.**   [Imit.; cf. Ger. *zwitschern.*]

twitter[2] *twit'ər,* **twitt'er-bone** *-bōn, ns.* an excrescence on a horse's hoof. — *adj.* **twitt'er-boned.**   [A form of **quitter.**]

twitter[3], **twitting**[1]. See **twit**[1].

twitting[2]. See **twitten.**

'twixt. Abbreviation for **betwixt.**

twizzle *twiz'əl, v.t.* to twirl, spin.   [Prob. formed under influence of **twist** and **twirl.**]

two *tōō, n.* the sum of one and one: a symbol representing two: a pair: a deuce, card with two pips: a score of two points, strokes, etc.: an article of a size denoted

by two: the second hour after midnight or midday: the age of two years. — *adj.* of the number two: two years old. — *n.* **two'er** anything that counts as, or for, two, or scores two. — *adj.* and *adv.* **two'fold** in two divisions: twice as much: (esp. *Scot.* **twafald** *twä,* **twö-föld**) in a doubled-up position. — *ns.* **two'foldness; two'ness** the state of being two: duality; **two'some** (*Scot.* **twa'some**) a company of two: a tête-à-tête: a single (*golf*). — *adj.* consisting of two: performed by two. — **two bits** twenty-five cents. — *adjs.* **two'-bit** paltry; **two'-bottle** able to drink two bottles of wine at a sitting. — **two'-by-four'** (a piece of) timber measuring four inches by two inches in cross-section (somewhat less when dressed); **two'-deck'er** a ship with two decks or with guns on two decks: a bus or tram-car carrying passengers on a roofed top. — *adjs.* **two'-digit** in double figures; **two'-dimen'sional.** — **two'-dimensional'ity** the property of having length and breadth but no depth. — *adjs.* **two'-edged** having two cutting edges: capable of being turned against the user; **two'-eyed'** having two eyes (**two-eyed steak** (*slang*) a bloater); **two'-faced** having two faces: double-dealing, false; **two'-fisted** clumsy: capable of fighting with both fists: holding the racket with both hands (*tennis*); **two'-foot** measuring, or with, two feet; **two'-footed** having two feet: capable of kicking and controlling the ball equally well with either foot (*football,* etc.). — **two'-for-his-heels'** a knave (from the score for turning up a knave in cribbage). — *adjs.* **two'-forked** having two prongs or branches; **two'-four'** (*mus.*) with two crotchets to the bar; **two'-hand** (*Shak.*) for two hands; **two'-hand'ed** with or for two hands: for two persons: ambidextrous: strapping. — **two-hand'er** anything designed for, written for or requiring both hands or two people (e.g. actors). — *adj.* **two'-head'ed** having two heads: directed by two authorities; **two'-horse** for two horses (**two=horse race** any contest in which only two of the participants have a genuine chance of winning); **two'=inch** measuring two inches; **two'-leaved, -leafed** with two leaves or leaflets: with leaves in twos; **two'-legged** with two legs; **two'-line** (*print.*) having double depth of body; **two'-lipped** having two lips: bilabiate; **two'=mast'ed** having two masts. — **two'-mast'er** a two-masted ship. — *adj.* **two'-pair (-of-stairs)** on a second floor. — *n.* a room so situated. — *adjs.* **two'-part** composed of two parts or for two voices; **two'-part'ed** bipartite: divided into two nearly to the base. — **twopence** (*tup'əns*), or (decimalised currency) **two pence** (*too pens*), the sum of two pennies: a coin worth two pence. — *adj.* **twopence-coloured** see under **penny.** — **two-pence piece, -penny piece** in Britain, a coin worth 2 pence (also **two'penny-piece**). — *adj.* **twopenny** (*tup'-ni*) sold, offered at, or worth, twopence: cheap, worthless. — *n.* ale sold at twopence a quart: in leapfrog, the head. — *adjs.* **twopenny-halfpenny** (*tup'ni-hāp'ni*), **twopence-halfpenny** paltry, petty. — *ns.* **two-penn'y-worth, two-penn'orth** (*tōō-pen'ərth*), also (chiefly *Scot.*) **twopenceworth** (*tup'*); **two'-piece** anything consisting of two separate parts, pieces or members. — Also *adj.* — *adjs.* **two'-ply** having two layers, or consisting of two strands: woven double; **two'-roomed.** — *n.* and *adj.* **two'-score** forty. — **two'seater** a vehicle or aeroplane seated for two. — *adj.* **two'-sid'ed** having two surfaces, aspects, or parties: facing two ways: double-faced: having the two sides different. — **two-sid'edness; two'-step** a gliding dance in duple time: a tune for it. — *v.i.* to dance the two-step. — *adjs.* **two'-stor'eyed, -stor'ey;** **two'stroke** consisting of two piston strokes, as an engine cycle: relating to, or designed for, such an engine. — *v.t.* **two'-time** to deceive: to double-cross. — **two'-timer** one who deceives or double-crosses. — *adjs.* **two'-timing; two'-tone** having two colours or two shades of the same colour. — **two'-up** an Australian game in which two coins are tossed and bets made on both falling heads up or both tails up. — *adj.* **two'-way** permitting passage along either of two ways esp. in opposite directions: able to receive and send signals (*radio*): of communication between two persons, groups, etc., in which both participate equally: involving shared responsibility: able to be used in two ways: having a double mode of variation or two dimensions (*math*.). — *adj.* **two'-wheeled, two'-wheel'er** a vehicle with two wheels, esp. a motor-cycle, or formerly a hansom cab. — *adj.* **two'-year-old**. — *n.* a child, colt, etc., aged two. — **be two** to be at variance; **in two** asunder, so as to form two pieces; **in two twos, two ticks** (*slang*) in a moment; **put two and two together** see put[1]; **that makes two of us** (*coll.*) the same thing applies to me; **two or three** a few; **two-pot screamer** (*Austr. slang*) a person who gets drunk on a comparatively small amount of alcohol; **two-power standard** (*hist.*) the principle that the strength of the British navy must never be less than the combined strength of the navies of any two other powers; **two-speed gear** a gear-changing contrivance with two possibilities; **two-up, two-down** (a small, traditionally built terraced house) having two bedrooms upstairs and two reception rooms downstairs. [O.E. *twā*, fem. and neut., two (masc. *twēgen*); Ger. *zwei*, Goth, *twai*; Gr. *dyo*, L. *duo*, Sans. *dva*, Gael. *dà*.]

'twould *twŏŏd*. A contraction of **it would**.

twy- *pfx*. See **twi-**.

twyer, twyere, tweer, twier, twire, tuyère *twēr*, also *twīr*, *twē-yer'*, *ns*. a nozzle for a blast of air. [Fr. *tuyère*.]

Tyburn *tī'bərn*, *n.* the historic place of execution in London. — **Ty'burn-tick'et** a certificate of exemption from certain parochial offices formerly granted to the prosecutor of a felon to conviction; **Ty'burn-tipp'et** a halter; **Ty'burn-tree** the gallows.

Tyche *tī'kē*, (*Gr. myth.*) *n.* the goddess of fortune. — *n.* **ty'chism** a theory that accepts pure chance. [Gr. *tychē*, chance.]

Tychonic *tī-kon'ik*, *adj*. pertaining to the Danish astronomer, *Tycho* Brahe (1546–1601), or his system.

tycoon *tī-kōōn'*, *n.* the title by which the Shoguns of Japan were known to foreigners: a business magnate. — *ns.* **tycoon'ate** the shogunate; **tycoon'ery**. [Jap. *taikun*, great prince — Old Chin. *t'ai*, great, *kiun*, prince.]

tyde. A Spenserian spelling of **tied**, *pa.t.* and *pa.p.* of **tie**.

tye *tī*, *n.* an inclined trough for washing ore. — *v.t.* to wash in a tye. [O.E. *tēag*, case, chest.]

tyg. Same as **tig**[2].

tying *tī'ing*, *pr.p.* of **tie**.

tyke, tike *tīk*, (chiefly *Northern*) *n.* a dog: a cur: a rough-mannered fellow: a small child (*coll.*): a Yorkshireman. — *adj.* **tyk'ish**. [O.N. *tīk*, bitch.]

tylectomy *tī-lek'tə-mi*, *n.* the same as **lumpectomy**. [Gr. *tylē*, lump, *ektomē*, cutting out.]

tyler. See **tile**.

Tylopoda *tī-lop'ə-də*, *n.pl.* a section of the ungulates with padded toes — camels and llamas. — *n.* and *adj.* **ty'lopod**. [Gr. *tylos*, a knob, callus, *pous, podos*, a foot.]

tylosis *tī-lō'sis*, *n.* an ingrowth from a neighbouring cell through a pit into a vessel (also, perh. orig., **thylose** *thī'lōs*, **thylosis** *thī-lō'sis*; *pl.* **thylo'ses**; perh. — Gr. *thylakos*, a pocket; *bot.*): an inflammation of the eyelids: a callosity: — *pl.* **tylō'ses**. — *n.* **tylote** (*tī'lōt*) a cylindrical sponge spicule, knobbed at both ends. [Gr. *tylos*, a knob, callus.]

tymbal. Same as **timbal**.

tymp *timp*, *n.* the plate of a blast-furnace opening. [**tympan**.]

tympan *tim'pən*, *n.* any instrument of the drum kind (*arch.*): a tympanum: an ancient Irish stringed instrument played with a bow (Ir. *tiompan*): a frame covered with parchment or cloth, on which sheets are placed for printing (*print.*): material placed between the platen and the paper to give an even impression (*print.*). — *adj.* **tym'panal** (*anat., zool.*) of the tympanum. — *n.pl.* **tym'pani** see **tympano** below. — *adj.* **tympanic** (*-pan'ik*) of or like a drum or tympanum: tympanitic. — *n.* a bone of the ear, supporting the drum-membrane. — *adj.* **tym'paniform** (or *-pan'*) drum-shaped: drum-like.

— *ns.* **tym'panist** a drummer (**tim'panist** one who plays the timpani); **tympani'tēs** flatulent distension of the belly. — *adj.* **tympanitic** (*-it'ik*) of, affected with, tympanites. — *ns.* **tympani'tis** inflammation of the membrane of the ear; **tym'pano** (*pl.* **-i -ē**) a variant of **timpano**; **tym'panum** a drum: a drum-head: the middle ear: the membrane separating it from the outer ear — the drum (also **tympanic membrane**) in insects a vibratory membrane in various parts of the body, serving as an eardrum: in birds the resonating sac of the syrinx: an air-sac in the neck in grouse, etc.: the recessed face of a pediment (*archit.*): a space between a lintel and an arch over it (*archit.*): a wheel for scooping up water: — *pl.* **tym'pana**; **tym'pany** any swelling, esp. of the abdomen: tympanites: a blowing up as with pride: a drum (*rare*). [L. *tympanum* — Gr. *tympanon, typanon*, a kettledrum — *typtein*, to strike.]

tynd, tyn'd, tyned, tynde, tyne (also *Scot.*), (*Spens.*; *Shak.*). See **tind, tine**[2,5].

Tynwald *tin'wold*, *n.* the parliament of the Isle of Man. [O.N. *thing-völlr* — *thing*, assembly, *völlr*, field.]

type *tīp*, *n.* a mark or stamp: the device on a coin or medal: a distinguishing mark: insignia: a designation: an emblem: a foreshadowing: an anticipation: an exemplar: a model or pattern: a kind: the general character of a class: that which well exemplifies the characteristics of a group: a person of well-marked characteristics: (*loosely* and *derogatorily*) a person: a simple chemical compound representative of the structure of more complex compounds: the actual specimen on which the description of a new species or genus is based (**type specimen**): a rectangular piece of metal or of wood on one end of which is cast or engraved a character, sign, etc., used in printing: printing types collectively, letter: print: lettering. — *adj.* serving as a type. — *v.t.* to prefigure, foreshadow: to symbolise: to be the type of: to determine the type of (*med.*): to exemplify: to typewrite: to print (*rare*). — *v.i.* to typewrite. — *adjs.* **ty'pal**; **typic** (*tip'*) typical; **typ'ical** pertaining to, or constituting, a type: emblematic: figurative: characteristic: representative: typographical (*rare*). — *n.* **typical'ity**. — *adv.* **typ'ically**. — *ns.* **typ'icalness**; **typifica'tion**; **typ'ifier**. — *v.t.* **typify** (*tip'*) to make or be a type of: — *pr.p.* **typ'ifying**; *pa.t.* and *pa.p.* **typ'ified**. — *ns.* **typing** (*tīp'ing*); **typist** (*tīp'ist*) one who uses a typewriter: one whose occupation is typewriting; **typog'rapher** a compositor: a person engaged in or skilled in typography: a beetle that bores letter-like tunnels in the bark of pine and other trees. — *n.pl.* **typograph'ia** matter relating to printers and printing. — *adjs.* **typograph'ic, -al.** — *adv.* **typograph'ically**. — *ns.* **typog'raphist** one versed in the history or art of printing; **typog'raphy** the art or style of printing. — *adj.* **typolog'ical**. — *ns.* **typol'ogist**; **typol'ogy** the study of types and their succession in biology, archaeology, etc.: the doctrine that things in the New Testament are foreshadowed symbolically in the Old; **typomā'nia** a craze for printing one's lucubrations: a craze for finding types in the Old Testament. — **type'-bar** a line of type cast in one piece: in a typewriter, a lever with a type-face; **type'-body** a measurement of breadth of shank for a size of type; **type case** a tray with compartments for storing printing types. — *v.t.* **type'cast** to cast (someone) in a rôle that accords with what he is by nature: to cast continually for the same kind of part. — *p.adj.* **type'cast**. — **type'-cutter** one who engraves dies for printing types; **type'-cyl'inder** the cylinder of a rotary printing-machine on which plates are fastened for printing; **type'-face** the printing surface of a type: the manner in which it is cut: a complete range of type cut in a particular style; **type'-founder** one who founds or casts printers' type; **type'-founding**; **type'-foundry**; **type'-genus** the genus that gives name to its family. — *adj.* and *adv.* **type'-high** of or at the standard type height (*c.* 0·918 in; 23·317 mm) — measured in the direction of the shank: at the height required for printing — of a woodcut, etc. — **type'=**

holder a bookbinder's pallet or holder for use in hand-stamping; **type locality** area in which a genus or a geological formation occurs most typically or in which it was classified; **type'-met'al** metal used for making types: an alloy of lead with antimony and tin, and sometimes copper; **type'script** typewritten matter or copy: type in imitation of handwriting or of typewriting. — *adj.* typewritten. — **type'setter** a compositor: a machine for setting type; **type'setting**; **type'= species** a species taken as the one to which the generic name is primarily attached; **type specimen** a holotype. — *v.t.* and *v.i.* **type'write** to print or copy with a typewriter. — **type'writer** a machine, usu. with a keyboard, for printing as a substitute for handwriting: a typist (*rare*); **type'writing.** — *adj.* **type'written.** [L. *typus* — Gr. *typos*, blow, mark, stamp, model; *typtein*, to strike.]

-type -*tīp, suff.* of the same type as: resembling. [**type.**]

Typha *tī'fə, n.* the reed-mace genus, tall erect herbs growing esp. in marshy areas, giving name to a family of monocotyledons, **Typhā'ceae.** — *adj.* **typhā'ceous.** [Gr. *typhē*, reed-mace.]

typhlitis *tif-lī'tis, n.* inflammation of the blind-gut. *adj.* **typhlitic** (-*lit'ik*). — *n.* **typhlol'ogy** the study of blindness and the blind. [Gr. *typhlos*, blind.]

Typhoeus *tī-fō'ūs, tī-fē'əs, n.* a monster of Greek mythology buried under Etna. — *adj.* **Typhoean** (*tī-fō'i-ən, tī-fē'ən*). [Gr. *Typhōeus.*]

typhoid *tī'foid, adj.* like typhus. — *n.* (for **typhoid fever**) enteric fever caused by the bacillus *Salmonella typhosa*, long confounded with typhus, on account of the characteristic rash of rose-coloured spots. — *adj.* **typhoid'al.** [Gr. *typhōdēs*, delirious — *typhos*, a fever, *eidos*, likeness; cf. **typhus.**]

Typhon *tī'fon, -fən, n.* son of Typhoeus, later identified with him, father of dangerous winds: (without *cap.*) a whirlwind (*obs.*). — *adjs.* **Typhonian** (-*fō'ni-ən*), **Typhonic** (-*fon'ik*; also without *caps.*). — *n.* **typhoon** (-*fōon'*) a violent cyclonic storm of the China seas and West Pacific area. [Gr. *Typhōn*, Typhon, *typhōn*, a whirlwind; but partly also from Port. *tufão* — Ar., Pers., Hind. *tūfān*, a hurricane (perh. itself from Gr.), and partly from Chin. *t'ai fung*, a great wind.]

typhus *tī'fəs, n.* a dangerous fever transmitted by lice harbouring a Rickettsia and marked by the eruption of red spots. — *adjs.* **ty'phoid** (q.v.); **ty'phous.** [Latinised from Gr. *typhos*, fever, stupor, delusion; cf. *typhein*, to smoke.]

typical, typify, typist, typography, etc. See under **type.**

typo *tī'po, (coll.)* short for **typographer:** a typographical error, a literal: — *pl.* **ty'pos.**

typto *tip'tō, v.i.* to conjugate the Greek verb *typtō*, I strike: to work at Greek grammar: — *pr.p. (Scott)* **tup'towing.**

Tyr *tir, tür, n.* the old Norse war-god. [O.N. *Tȳr*; O.E. *Tīw*; cf. **Tuesday.**]

tyramine *tī'rə-mēn, n.* a colourless crystalline amine found in cheese, ergot, mistletoe and decayed animal tissue or derived from phenol, similar in action to adrenaline. [*tyr*osine, *amine.*]

tyrant *tī'rənt, obs.* **tyran** *tī'rən, ns.* in the orig. Greek sense, an absolute ruler, or one whose power has not been constitutionally arrived at: now usu. a ruler who uses his power arbitrarily and oppressively: an oppressor: a bully: a tyrant-bird. — *vs.t.* and *vs.i. (obs.)* **ty'ran(ne),**

ty'rant. — *n.* **tyr'anness** a female tyrant. — *adjs.* **tyrannic** (*ti-ran'ik*; sometimes *tī-*), **-al.** — *adv.* **tyrann'-ically.** — *n.* **tyrann'icalness.** — *adj.* **tyrannicī'dal.** — *n.* **tyrann'icide** the killing or the killer of a tyrant. — *n.pl.* **Tyrann'idae** the tyrant-bird family. — *n.* **tyrannis** (*ti-ran'is*; Gr.) a régime illegally set up. — *v.i.* **tyrannise, -ize** (*tir'*) to act as a tyrant: esp. to rule with oppressive severity. — *v.t.* to act the tyrant to. — *n.* **tyrannosaur(us)** (-*ran'ə-sör, -sör'əs*) a large bipedal carnivorous lizard-hipped dinosaur of the carnosaur group of theropods, common during the Cretaceous period. — *adj.* **tyrannous** (*tir'*) despotic: domineering: overpowering: oppressive. — *adv.* **tyr'annously.** — *n.* **tyranny** (*tir'*) absolute or illegally established power: the government or authority of a tyrant: absolute power cruelly administered: oppression: cruelty: harshness. — **ty'rant-bird, ty'rant-fly'catcher** any member of an American family of birds akin to the pittas and cotingas. [Gr. *tyrannos*, partly through O.Fr. *tirant* (Fr. *tyran*) and L. *tyrannus*.]

tyre *tīr, n.* a variant spelling of **tire**[2]: a rubber band, cushion, or tube round a wheel-rim. — *adjs.* **tyred**; **tyre'less.** — **tyre chain** see **chain; tyre gauge** a device for measuring the air pressure in a pneumatic tyre. — **tubeless tyre** a pneumatic tyre that has no inner tube, and, being self-sealing, deflates only slowly when punctured. [See **tire**[2].]

Tyrian *tir'i-ən, adj.* of *Tyre*: red or purple, like the dye formerly prepared at the ancient Mediterranean port of Tyre. — *n.* a native of Tyre. — **Tyrian cynosure** the north star, a guide to Tyrian mariners.

tyro. See **tiro.**

tyroglyphid *ti-rog'li-fid, n.* a mite of the genus **Tyrog'lyphus,** including the cheese-mite and the flour-mite. [Gr. *tyros*, cheese, *glyphein*, to carve.]

Tyrolese *tir-ə-lēz', adj.* relating to the mountainous west Austrian province of *Tyrol* (Tirol), or to its people. — *n.* a native of Tyrol. — *n.* and *adj.* **Tyrolē'an** (or *tir-ō'li-ən*). — *n.* **Tyrolienne** (*ti-rō-li-en'*) a Tyrolese peasants' dance, song, or tune with yodelling.

Tyronensian. See **Tironensian.**

tyrones. See **tiro.**

tyrosine *tī'rō-sēn, n.* an amino-acid formed by decomposition of proteins, first got from cheese. — *n.* **ty'rosinase** an enzyme found in plants and animals that assists in converting tyrosine to melanin. [Gr. *tyros*, cheese.]

Tyrrhenian *ti-rē'ni-ən, n.* and *adj.* Etruscan. — Also **Tyrrhēne'.** — **Tyrrhenian Sea** that part of the Mediterranean between Tuscany and Sardinia and Corsica. [Gr. *Tyrrhēnia*, Etruria.]

Tyrtaean *tər-tē'ən, adj.* of or pertaining to *Tyrtaeus* (Gr. *Tyrtaios*), a Greek martial poet of the 7th century B.C.

tystie *tī'sti, (dial.) n.* the black guillemot. [Scand.; cf. O.N. *theist.*]

tyte. See **tite.**

tythe. See **tithe.**

tqaddik, tzaddiq. See **zaddik.**

tzar. See **tsar.**

tzigany *tsig'ä-ni, -ə-ni, -ny', n.* a Hungarian gypsy. — Also *adj.* — Also **tsigane** (*tsi-gän'*). [Hung. *cigány*, gypsy; cf. It. *zingano, zingaro,* Ger. *Zigeuner.*]

tzimmes *tsi'mis, n.* a sweetened stew or casserole of vegetables, fruit and sometimes meat: — *pl.* **tzimm'es.** [Yiddish.]

---

fāte; fär; hûr; mīne; mōte; för; mūte; mōon; fŏot; dhen (then); *el'ə-mənt* (element)

U

U¹, u $\bar{u}$, *n*. the twenty-first letter in our alphabet, derived from V, a form of Y which the Romans borrowed from the Greeks. From V, the lapidary and capital form, the uncial and cursive forms U and *u* were developed, gradually V (used until modern times initially) becoming appropriated as the symbol for the consonant sound (see **V**) and the medial form *u* as the symbol for the vowel. In mod. English the vowel has the sounds exemplified in *rule*, *put*, *but*, and the diphthongal sound that serves as the name of the letter. — *adj*. (*cap*.; of words, phrases, customs, etc.) ordinarily used by, found in, the upper classes. — *adj*. **non'-U** not so used or found (U for *u*pper class). — **U'-bend** an air-trap in the form of a U-shaped bend in a pipe; **U'-boat** a German submarine (Ger. *Unterseeboot*); **U'-bolt, U'-trap, U'-tube** a bolt, drain-trap, tube, bent like the letter U. — *adj*. **U'-shaped**. — **U'-turn** a turn made by a vehicle which reverses its direction of travel, crossing into the oncoming traffic on the other side of the road: any reversal of direction (*fig*.).

U² $\overline{oo}$, *n*. A Burmese title of respect, prefaced to a man's name. [Burmese.]

uakari *wa-ka'ri*, *n*. any of various short-tailed, long-haired South American monkeys of the genus *Cacajao* (fam. *Cebidae*), related to the saki. — Also **ouakari**. [Tupí.]

Übermensch *ü'bər-mensh*, (Ger.) *n*. a superman.

uberous *ū'bə-rəs*, *adj*. yielding abundance of milk: abounding. — *n*. **u'berty** fruitfulness: abundant productiveness. [L. *über*, udder, fruitfulness.]

uberrima fides *ū-ber'ə-mə fī'dēz*, $\overline{oo}$-*be-r ē'ma fī'dās*, (L.) complete faith.

uberty. See **uberous**.

ubiety *ū-bī'i-ti*, *n*. the state of being in a definite place, whereness: location. [L. *ubi*, where.]

ubique *ū-bī'kwē*, $\overline{oo}$-*bē'kwe*, (L.) *adv*. everywhere.

ubiquinone *ū-bik'wi-nōn*, (*biochem*.) *n*. a quinone involved in the transfer of electrons during cell respiration. [L. *ubíque*, everywhere, and **quinone**.]

ubiquity *ū-bik'wi-ti*, *n*. existence everywhere at the same time: omnipresence. — *adj*. **ubiquā'rian** found everywhere: ubiquitous. — *n*. **ubiquitā'rian** one who believes that Christ's body is everywhere, in the Eucharist as elsewhere. — Also *adj*. — *adjs*. **ubiq'uitary** being everywhere at once; **ubiq'uitous** to be found everywhere. — *adv*. **ubiq'uitously**. [L. *ubíque*, everywhere — *ubi*, where.]

ubi supra *ū'bī sōō'prə*, $\overline{oo}$'*bē sōō'prä*, (L.) where mentioned above.

udal *ū'dl*, (*Orkney* and *Shetland*) *adj*. allodial: without feudal superior. — *n*. an estate so held. — *n*. **u'daller** a holder of such an estate. [O.N. *ōthal*.]

udder *ud'ər*, *n*. the organ containing the mammary glands of the cow, mare, etc.: a dug or teat. — *adjs*. **udd'ered; udd'erful** with full udder; **udd'erless** unsuckled. [O.E. *ūder*; Ger. *Euter*, L. *über*, Gr. *outhar*.]

udo $\overline{oo}$'*dō*, *n*. a Japanese species of Aralia with edible shoots: — *pl*. **u'dos**. [Jap.]

udometer *ū-dom'i-tər*, *n*. a name for a rain-gauge, never included in the official glossary of British meteorological terms. — *adj*. **udomet'ric**. [Through Fr. — L. *ūdus*, wet, Gr. *metron*, a measure.]

uds *udz*, in oaths, for **God's**, or for **God save** (as in *uds my life*).

uey *ū'i*, (*Austr. coll*.) *n*. a U-turn (*usu. fig*.), as in *do a uey*.

UFO *ū'ef-ō'*, *ū'fō*, (*coll*.) *n*. an *u*nidentified *f*lying *o*bject, such as a flying saucer: — *pl*. **UFOs, ufos**. — *ns*. **ufology** (*ū-fol'ə-ji*) the study of UFOs; **ufol'ogist**.

ug. See **ugly**.

ugh *uhh, ug, ōoh, ûh, interj*. an exclamation of repugnance. — *n*. used as a representation of a cough or grunt.

ugli® *ug'li*, *n*. a cross between the grapefruit, the seville orange and the tangerine, or its fruit. [**ugly**; from the fruit's unprepossessing appearance.]

ugly *ug'li*, *adj*. frightful, horrible (*obs*.): offensive to the sight or other sense, or to refined taste or moral feeling: ill-natured: threatening: disquieting: suggesting suspicion of evil. — *n*. an ugly person (*coll*.): a shade attached to a lady's hat (mid-19th-cent.). — *v.t*. (*rare*) to make ugly. — *v.t*. **ug** (*obs*. or *dial*. in all meanings), to excite loathing in: to loathe. — *v.i*. to feel loathing. — *n*. **uglificā'tion**. — *v.t*. **ug'lify** to make ugly. — *adv*. **ug'lily**. — *n*. **ug'liness**. — *adj*. **ug'some** disgusting: hideous. — *n*. **ug'someness**. — **ugly customer** a dangerous antagonist; **ugly duckling** a despised member of a family or group who later proves the most successful; **ugly man** (*obs*.) an actual garrotter, distinguished from his confederates. [O.N. *uggligr*, frightful, *uggr*, fear.]

Ugrian *ū'gri-ən*, $\overline{oo}$', *adj*. of that division of the Finno-Ugrian languages and peoples that includes the Magyars, Ostyaks, and Voguls. — Also *n*. — *adjs*. **U'gric; U'gro-Finn'ic** Finno-Ugrian. [Russ. *Ugri*, the Ugrian peoples.]

uh-huh *u'hu, m'hm, interj*. a sound used in place of 'yes'.

uhlan $\overline{oo}$'*län, ū'*, *n*. a light cavalryman in semi-oriental uniform: a Prussian lancer. [Ger. *Uhlan* — Polish *ulan*, orig. a light Tatar horseman — Turk. *oḡlān*, a young man.]

uhuru $\overline{oo}$-*hōō'rōō*, *n*. freedom (e.g. from slavery): national independence. [Swahili — *huru*, free.]

uillean(n) pipes $\overline{oo}$'*li-ən pīps*, Irish bagpipes, worked by squeezing bellows under the arm. — Also **union pipes**. [Ir. *piob uilleann; piob*, pipe, *uilleann*, gen. sing. of *uille*, elbow.]

uinta(h)ite *ū-int'ä-īt*, *n*. a natural tarlike asphalt found in the *Uinta* valley, Utah. — *n*. **uint'athēre** any animal of the genus **Uintathē'rium**, gigantic Eocene fossil ungulates from *Uinta* County, Wyoming.

uitlander *æ'it-, āt', ā'it-land-ər*, (chiefly *hist*.) *n*. a foreigner (orig. a British person in the Transvaal or Orange Free State). [Du. equivalent of **outlander**.]

ukase *ū-kāz'*, *-kās'*, *n*. an edict with force of law in Tsarist Russia: an edict with bearing on existing legislation issued by the Presidium of the Supreme Soviet and subject to later ratification by the Supreme Soviet: any arbitrary decree from any source. [Russ. *ukaz*.]

uke *ūk*, *n*. coll. abbrev. of **ukulele**.

ukelele. A common spelling of **ukulele**.

ukiyo-e $\overline{oo}$-*kē'yō-(y)ā*, *n*. a Japanese style of painting and print-making flourishing between the 17th and 19th centuries, typically depicting scenes from everyday life. [Jap., world, life picture.]

Ukrainian *ū-krān'i-ən*, $\overline{oo}$-*krīn'i-ən*, *n*. a native or citizen of (the) *Ukraine*, a republic of the U.S.S.R., a rich agricultural region in S.W. Russia: its language, Ruthenian. — Also *adj*.

ukulele *ū-kə-lā'li*, $\overline{oo}$-*kōo-lā'lä*, *n*. a small, usually four-stringed, guitar. [Hawaiian, jumping flea.]

ulcer *ul'sər*, *n*. an open sore, on the skin or a mucous membane, often discharging pus: a continuing source of evil, pain or corruption, an unsound element (*fig*.). — *v.t*. and *v.i*. to ulcerate. — *v.i*. **ul'cerate** to form an ulcer. — *v.t*. to cause an ulcer in: to affect with insidious corruption. — *n*. **ulcerā'tion**. — *adjs*. **ul'cerātive;**

For other sounds see detailed chart of pronunciation.

ul'cered; ul'cerous. — *adv.* **ul'cerously.** — *n.* **ul'cerousness.** — **ulcerative dermal necrosis** a fungus disease of salmon. [L. *ulcus, ulcĕris*; cf. Gr. *helkos.*]

ule, hule *ōō'lā, n.* a Central American rubber tree (*Castilloa*): its crude rubber. [Sp. *hule* — Nahuatl *ulli.*]

ulema *ōō'li-mə, n.* the body of professional theologians, expounders of the law, in a Muslim country: a member of such a body. [Ar. *'ulema*, pl. of *'ālim*, learned.]

Ulex *ū'leks, n.* the gorse genus: (without *cap.*) any plant of this genus. [L. *ūlex, -icis*, a kind of rosemary or the like.]

ulicon, ulichon, ulikon *ōō'li-kən.* Same as **eulachon**.

uliginous *ū-lij'i-nəs, adj.* slimy: oozy: swampy: growing in swampy places. [L. *ūlīginōsus* — *ūlīgō, -inis*, moisture.]

ulitis *ū-lī'tis, n.* inflammation of the gums. [Gr. *oula*, gums, *-itis.*]

ullage *ul'ij, n.* the quantity a vessel lacks of being full, or sometimes the amount left in the vessel: loss by evaporation or leakage: dregs (*slang*). — *v.t.* to reckon the ullage of: to affect with ullage: to fill up: to draw off a little from. — *n.* **ull'ing** the making good of ullage. [A.Fr. *ulliage*, O.Fr. *eullage* — *œiller*, to fill up.]

Ulmus *ul'məs, n.* the elm genus, giving name to the family **Ulmā'ceae**, akin to the nettles. — *adj.* **ulmā'ceous** of or like an elm: of its family. — *n.* **ul'min** a gummy exudation from elms and other trees. [L. *ulmus*, elm.]

ulna *ul'nə, n.* the inner and larger of the two bones of the forearm: — *pl.* **ul'nae** (*-nē*). — *adj.* **ul'nar.** — *n.* **ulnā'rē** the bone of the carpus opposite the ulna: — *pl.* **ulnā'ria.** [L. *ulna*, elbow, arm; cf. **ell**, and Gr. *ōlenē*, forearm.]

ulosis *ū-lō'sis, n.* the formation of a scar. [Gr. *oulōsis* — *oulē*, a scar.]

Ulothrix *ū'lō-thriks, n.* a genus of filamentous algae, giving name to the **Ulotrichales** (*ū-lot-ri-kā'lēz*), an order of multicellular uninucleate green algae, marine and freshwater. — *adj.* **ulotrichous** (*ū-lot'ri-kəs*) woolly-haired. — *n.* **ulot'richy** (*-ki*) woolly-hairedness. [Gr. *oulos*, woolly, *thrix, trichos*, hair.]

ulster *ul'stər, n.* a long loose overcoat, first made in *Ulster*, N. Ireland. — *adj.* **ul'stered** wearing an ulster. — *ns.* **ulsterette'** a light ulster. — **Ul'sterman, Ul'sterwoman** a native or inhabitant of Ulster.

ult. See **ultimate**.

ulterior *ul-tē'ri-ər, adj.* on the further side: beyond: in the future: remoter: (of e.g. a motive) beyond what is avowed or apparent. — *adv.* **ultē'riorly.** [L. *ulterior* — *ultrā* (adv. and prep.), *uls* (prep.), beyond.]

ultima *ul'tə-mə, n.* the last syllable of a word. — **ultima ratio** (*ul'tə-mə rā'shē-ō, ōol'ti-ma rä'ti-ō*; L.) the last argument; **ultima ratio regum** (*rē'gəm, rā'gōom*; L. the last argument of kings (i.e. war; once inscribed on French cannon). [L., fem. of *ultimus*, last.]

ultimate *ul'ti-māt, -mit, adj.* furthest: last: final: fundamental: maximum: most important: limiting. — *n.* a final point: a fundamental. — *n.* **ul'timacy** (*-mə-si*) — *adv.* **ul'timately.** — *n.* **ultimā'tum** final terms: a last offer or demand: a last word: a final point: something fundamental: — *pl.* **ultimā'ta.** — *adj.* **ul'timate** (*abbrev.* **ult.**) in the last (month). — *n.* **ultimogeniture** (*-jen'*) succession of the youngest, as in borough-English (q.v.) — opp. to *primogeniture.* — **the ultimate deterrent** the hydrogen bomb. [L. *ultimus*, last.]

ultima (or **Ultima**) **Thule.** See **Thule**.

ultimus haeres *ul'ti-məs hē'rēz, ōol'ti-məos hī'rās*, (L.) in law, the crown or the state, which succeeds to the property of those who die intestate, or without next of kin; **ultimus Romanorum** (*rō-mən-ōr'əm, -ōr', -ōom*) last of the Romans.

ultion *ul'shən, n.* revenge: avengement. [L. *ultiō, -ōnis.*]

Ultonian *ul-tō'ni-ən, adj.* of Ulster. — *n.* an Ulsterman or -woman. [L.L. *Ultōnia*, Ulster; O.Ir. *Ult-*, stem of *Ulaid*, Ulster.]

ultra- *ul'trə-, pfx.* (1) beyond in place, position (as **ultra-Neptunian** beyond the planet Neptune): (2) beyond the limit, range, etc., of (as **ultra-microscopic**): (3) beyond the ordinary, or excessive(ly) (as **ul'tra-**

Conserv'ative, ul'tra-Conserv'atism, ul'tra-fash'ionable, ul'tra-mod'ern, ul'tra-Prot'estant). — *adj.* **ul'tra** extreme, esp. in royalism, fashion, or religious or political opinion. — *n.* an extremist. — *ns.* **ultraism** (*ul'trə-izm*) (an) extreme principle(s), opinion(s), or measure(s): an attempt to pass beyond the limits of the known; **ul'traist.** [L. *ultrā*, beyond.]

ultrabasic *ul-trə-bā'sik, (petr.) adj.* extremely basic, very poor in silica. [Pfx. **ultra-** (3).]

ultracentrifuge *ul-trə-sen'tri-fūj, n.* a very fast-running type of centrifuge. — *v.t.* to subject to the action of an ultracentrifuge. — *adj.* **ultracentrif'ugal** (or *-fū'gəl*). [Pfx. **ultra-** (2).]

ultracrepidate *ul-trə-krep'i-dāt, v.i.* to criticise beyond the sphere of one's knowledge. — *n.* and *adj.* **ultracrepidā'rian.** [From Apelles's answer to the cobbler who went on from criticising the sandals in a picture to finding fault with the leg, *nē sūtor ultrā crepidam*, the cobbler must not go beyond the sandal.]

ultrafiche *ul'trə-fēsh, n.* a sheet of microfilm the same size as a microfiche but with a greater number of microcopied records on it. [Pfx. **ultra-** (3).]

ultrafilter *ul'trə-fil-tər, (biol.) n.* an extremely fine filter which retains particles as fine as large molecules. — *v.t.* to pass through an ultrafilter. — *ns.* **ultrafil'trate** a substance that has passed through an ultrafilter; **ultrafiltrā'tion.** [Pfx. **ultra-** (2).]

ultra-high *ul-trə-hī', adj.* very high. — **ultra-high frequency** see **frequency**. [Pfx. **ultra-** (3).]

ultraism, ultraist. See **ultra-**.

ultramarine *ul-trə-mə-rēn', adj.* overseas: from overseas: deep blue. — *n.* a deep blue pigment, orig. made from lapis-lazuli brought from beyond the sea: its colour. [L. *ultrā*, beyond, *marīnus*, marine.]

ultramicro- *ul-trə-mī-krō -, pfx.* smaller than, dealing with smaller quantities than, **micro-**, e.g. *n.* **ultramicrochem'istry** chemistry dealing with minute quantities, sometimes no greater than one-millionth of a gram.

ultramicroscope *ul-trə-mī'krə-skōp, n.* a microscope with strong illumination from the side, whereby the presence of ultramicroscopic objects can be observed through the scattering of light from them. — *adj.* **ultramicroscopic** (*-skop'ik*) too small to be visible under the ordinary microscope: pertaining to ultramicroscopy. — *n.* **ultramicroscopy** (*-kros'kə-pi*). [Pfx. **ultra-** (2).]

ultramicrotome *ul'trə-mī'krə-tōm, n.* a microtome for cutting ultra-thin sections for examination with the electron microscope. — *n.* **ultramicrotomy** (*-ot'ə-mi*). [Pfx. **ultra-** (2).]

ultramontane *ul-trə-mon'tān, adj.* beyond the mountains (i.e. the Alps): orig. used in Italy of the French, Germans, etc.: afterwards applied by the northern nations to the Italians: hence, extreme in favouring the Pope's supremacy. — *ns.* **ultramon'tanism** (*-tən-izm*); **ultramon'tanist.** [L. *ultra*, beyond, *montānus* — *mōns, montis*, a mountain.]

ultramundane *ul-trə-mun'dān, adj.* beyond the world, or beyond the limits of our system. [Pfx. **ultra-** (1).]

ultra-rapid *ul-trə-rap'id, adj.* of a motion-picture film, exposed at much greater speed than that at which it is to be exhibited, giving a slow-motion picture. [Pfx. **ultra-** (3).]

ultrared *ul'trə-red', adj.* infra-red. [Pfx. **ultra-** (1).]

ultrasensual *ul'trə-sen'sū-əl, -shōo-əl, adj.* beyond the reach of the senses. [Pfx. **ultra-** (2).]

ultrashort *ul'trə-shört', adj.* (of electromagnetic waves) of less than ten metres' wavelength. [Pfx. **ultra-** (3).]

ultrasonic *ul-trə-son'ik, adj.* pertaining to, or (of an instrument or process) using, vibrations of the same nature as audible sound waves but of greater frequency. — *adv.* **ultrason'ically.** — *n.sing.* **ultrason'ics** the study of such vibrations, used medically for diagnostic and therapeutic purposes. — *n.* **ultrasonography** (*-sən-og'rə-fi*) the directing of ultrasonic waves through body tissues to detect abnormalities. — **ultrasonic communication** underwater communication using ultrasonic waves. [Pfx. **ultra-** (2).]

ultrasound *ul-trə-sownd'*, *n.* sound vibrations too rapid to be audible, useful esp. in medical diagnosis. [Pfx. **ultra-** (2).]

ultrastructure *ul'trə-struk'chər*, *n.* the ultimate structure of protoplasm at a lower level than can be examined microscopically. [Pfx. **ultra-** (2).]

ultra-tropical *ul'trə-trop'ik-əl*, *adj.* beyond the tropics: hotter than the tropics. [Pfx. **ultra-** (1), (3).]

ultraviolet *ul-trə-vī'ə-lit*, *adj.* beyond the violet end of the visible spectrum: pertaining to, or using, radiations of wavelengths less than those of visible light. — **ultra-violet star** one of a class of invisible stars giving out intense ultraviolet radiation. [Pfx. **ultra-** (1).]

ultra vires *ul'trə vī'rēz*, *ool'trä wē'räs*, (L.) beyond one's powers or authority.

ultra-virtuous *ul'trə-vûr'tū-əs*, *adj.* prudish. [Pfx. **ultra-** (3).]

ultroneous *ul-trō'ni-əs*, *adj.* spontaneous, voluntary. — *adv.* **ultrō'neously**. — *n.* **ultrō'neousness**. [L. *ultrōneus* — *ultrō*, spontaneously.]

ululate *ül'ū-lāt*, also *ul'*, *v.i.* to hoot or screech. — *adj.* **ul'ulant**. — *n.* **ulula'tion** howling, wailing. [L. *ülülāre*, *-ātum*, to hoot.]

ulyie, ulzie *ül'(y)i*, obs. Scots forms of **oil**.

um *əm*, *um*, *interj.* expressing hesitation in speech.

umbel *um'bəl*, *n.* a flat-topped inflorescence in which the flower stalks all spring from about the same point in an axis (which in a **compound umbel** is grouped in the same way with other axes). — *adjs.* **um'bellar** (or *-bel'*); **um'bellate, -d** constituting an umbel: having umbels. — *adv.* **um'bellately**. — *n.* **umbellifer** (*um-bel'i-fər*) any plant of the Umbelliferae. — *n.pl.* **Umbellif'erae** the carrot and hemlock family of plants with (usu. compound) umbels, schizocarpic fruit, leaves with sheathing bases. — *adj.* **umbellif'erous**. — *n.* **um'bellule** a partial umbel. [L. *umbella*, a sunshade, dim. of *umbra*, a shade.]

umber[1] *um'bər*, *n.* a brown earthy mineral (hydrated oxides of iron and manganese) used as a pigment. — *v.t.* to colour with umber. — *adj.* brown like umber. — *adjs.* **um'bered, um'bery**. — **um'ber-bird** the umbrette. — **burnt umber** umber heated to give a dark reddish-brown colour; **raw umber** untreated umber, a yellowish-brown colour. [It. *terra d'ombra*, shadow earth, or poss. Umbrian earth.]

umber[2] *um'bər*, *n.* the grayling. [L. *umbra*.]

umbilicus *um-bil'i-kəs*, *um-bi-lī'kəs*, *n.* the navel: a depression at the axial base of a spiral shell: a small depression. — *adjs.* **umbilical** (*-bil'*; sometimes *-bi-lī'*) relating to the umbilicus or the umbilical cord; **umbil'icate** navel-like: having a depression like a navel. — *n.* **umbilica'tion**. — **umbilical cord** the navel-string, a long flexible tube connecting the foetus to the placenta: an electrical cable or other servicing line attached to a rocket vehicle or spacecraft during preparations for launch: the lifeline of an astronaut outside his vehicle in space by which he receives air and communicates with the vehicle: any similar connection of fundamental importance. [L. *umbilīcus*, the navel; Gr. *omphalos*.]

umbles *um'blz*, *n.pl.* entrails (liver, heart, etc.), esp. of a deer. — Also **hum'bles, num'bles**. — **um'ble-pie** also **hum'ble-pie', num'ble-pie'** a pie made from the umbles of a deer. [O.Fr. *nombles*, from *lomble*, loin — L. *lumbulus*, dim. of *lumbus*, loin.]

umbo *um'bō*, *n.* the boss of a shield: a knob: the protuberant oldest part of a bivalve shell: a knob on a toadstool cap: a projection on the inner surface of the eardrum where the malleus is attached: — *pl.* **umbō'nēs, um'bos**. — *adjs.* **um'bonal** (*-bən-əl*); **um'bonate** (*bot.*) having a central boss. — *n.* **umbonā'tion**. [L. *umbō, -ōnis*.]

umbra *um'brə*, *n.* a shadow: the darker part of the shadow or dark inner cone projected in an eclipse (*astron.*): the darker part of a spot: a shade or ghost: an uninvited guest who comes with an invited one: — *pl.* **um'brae**

(*-brē*), **um'bras**. — *adjs.* **umbraculate** (*um-brak'ū-lāt*) overshadowed by an umbraculum; **umbrac'uliform** umbrella-shaped. — *n.* **umbrac'ulum** an umbrella-shaped structure. — *adjs.* **um'bral** of an umbra; **um'brated** (*her.*) faintly traced; **umbratic** (*-brat'*; *rare*), **-al, umbratile** (*um'brə-tīl, -til*), **umbratilous** (*-brat'i-ləs*) shadowy: shaded: shade-giving: indoor: secluded; **um-brif'erous** shade-giving; **umbrose** (*-brōs'*) shade-giving: dusky; **um'brous** shaded. [L. *umbra*, shade, shadow, dim. *umbrāculum*, adj. *umbrātilis*.]

umbrage *um'brij*, *n.* shade, shadow: that which casts a shade: a shelter: a shadowy appearance: a pretext, colour: an inkling: suspicion of injury: offence. — *v.t.* to shade: to offend. — *adj.* **umbrā'geous** shady or forming a shade. — *adv.* **umbrā'geously**. — *n.* **umbrā'-geousness**. [Fr. *ombrage* — L. *umbrāticum* (neut. adj.) — *umbra*, a shadow.]

umbrated . . . umbratilous. See **umbra**.

umbre *um'bər*. See **umbrette**.

umbrel. See **umbriere**.

umbrella *um-brel'ə*, *n.* a portable shelter against sun, rain, etc., now usu. a canopy with a sliding framework of ribs on a stick: anything of similar form, as a jellyfish disc: a protection (*fig.*): a general cover (*fig.*): a cover of fighter aircraft for ground forces (*mil.*). — Also (*obs.*) **ombrell'a, umbrell'o** (*pl.* **umbrellos, -oes**). — *adjs.* **umbrella** covering many or a variety of things; **um-brell'aed, umbrell'a'd** with an umbrella. — **umbrell'a-ant** the sauba ant; **umbrell'a-bird** any of a number of birds of the *Cotinga* genus with umbrella-like crest and a lappet attached to the throat or breast; **umbrell'a-fir** a Japanese conifer with radiating tufts of needles; **umbrella group, organisation** a group of representatives of small parties, clubs, etc., which acts for all of them where they have common interests; **umbrell'a-stand** a rack or receptacle for closed umbrellas and walking-sticks; **umbrell'a-tree** a tree of any kind with leaves or branches arranged umbrella-wise, esp. a small magnolia. [It. *ombrella, ombrello* — *ombra*, a shade — L. *umbra*.]

umbrere. See **umbriere**.

umbrette *um-bret'*, *n.* the hammerhead (*Scopus umbretta*), a brown African bird akin to the storks, remarkable for its huge nest. — Also **um'bre** (*-bər*), **umber-bird**. [Fr. *ombrette* — *ombre*, umber.]

Umbrian *um'bri-ən*, *adj.* of *Umbria*, in central Italy. — *n.* a native thereof: an Indo-European language akin to Oscan.

umbriere *um'bri-ēr*, (*Spens.*) *n.* a visor. — Also **um'brere, um'bril, um'brel**. [O.Fr. *ombriere, ombrel*, shade.]

umbriferous, umbrose, umbrous. See **umbra**.

umiak, oomia(c)k, oomiac *ōō'mi-ak, ōōm'yak*, *n.* an open skin boat, manned by women. [Eskimo.]

umlaut *ōōm'lowt*, *n.* a vowel-change brought about by a vowel or semivowel (esp. *i, j*) in the following syllable: (*loosely*) the two dots placed over a letter representing an umlauted vowel in German. — *v.t.* to bring about umlaut in. [Ger., *um*, around, *Laut*, sound.]

umph *hm(h)*, *mf*. Same as **humph**[1].

umpire *um'pīr*, *n.* a third person called in to decide a dispute or a deadlock: an arbitrator: an impartial person chosen to supervise the game, enforce the rules, and decide disputes (*cricket*, etc.). — Also *v.i.* and *v.t.* — *ns.* **um'pirage, um'pireship**. [M.E. *noumpere*, *oumper* — O.Fr. *nomper* — *non-*, not, *per*, *pair*, peer, equal.]

umpteen *um(p)'tēn'ti*, (*slang*) *adjs.* an indefinitely large number. — *adjs.* **ump'teenth, ump'tieth** latest or last of many. [*Umpty* in Morse, a dash, from its sound on a telegraph key.]

umquhile *um'hwīl*, *adv.* and *adj.* A Scots form of **um'while**, formerly, late, whilom. [O.E. *ymb(e) hwīle*, about or at a time.]

un, 'un *un*, *ən*, (*dial.*) *pron.* and *n.* for **one**: also for **him**. [O.E. accus. *hine*.]

There is hardly a limit to words with prefix **un-**, *and only* *a selection is given below. Words from* **unabashed** *to* **unzoned** *are listed continuously, either in the text or at the foot of the page, and words beginning with un- in which un- is not a prefix follow after these.*

un- *un-, pfx.* (1) meaning 'not' (in many cases, the resultant word is more than a mere negation; it has a positive force; e.g. **unkind** usu. means 'cruel' rather than just 'not kind'): (2) indicating a reversal of process, removal, or deprivation: (3) merely emphasising reversal or deprivation already expressed by the simple word, as in **unbare, unloose;** sometimes (in *Shakespeare* and *Milton*) added to a present participle with a passive meaning. The meaning is often ambiguous, esp. in participial adjs. (Partly O.E. *un-*, neg.; cf. Ger. *un-*, L. *in-*, Gr. *an-*, *a-*; partly O.E. *on-* (or *un-*), the unstressed form of *and-*; cf. Ger. *ent-*, Gr. *anti*, against). — *adjs.* **unaba'ted** not made less in degree; **una'ble** not able: not having sufficient strength, power, or skill (to do): weak, incompetent (*arch.*): ineffectual (*arch.*); **unaccent'ed** without accent or stress in pronunciation: not marked with an accent; **unaccomm'odated** unprovided; **unaccomm'odating** not compliant; **unaccom'panied** not accompanied, escorted, or attended: having no instrumental accompaniment (*mus.*); **unaccom'plished** not achieved:lacking accomplishments. — *ns.* **unaccom'plishment** the fact of not being achieved; **unaccountabil'ity.** — *adj.* **unaccount'able** difficult or impossible to explain: not answerable (to a higher authority): (of a person) puzzling in character. — *n.* **unaccount'ableness.** — *adv.* **unaccount'ably** inexplicably. — *adjs.* **unaccount'ed-for** unexplained: not included in an account; **unaccus'tomed** not customary: not habituated. — *n.* **unaccus'tomedness.** — *adj.* **unacknowl'edged** not acknowledged, recognised, confessed, or noticed. — *n.* **unacquaint'ance** want of acquaintance (often with *with*). — *adj.* **unacquaint'ed** (*Scot.* **unacquaint'**) not on a footing of acquaintance: ignorant of (with *with*, or, *Swift*, *in*): uninformed: unknown (*obs.*): unusual (*Spens.*). — *n.* **unacquaint'edness.** — *adjs.* **unact'able** unfit for the stage; **unact'ed** not performed; **unac'tive** inactive; **unadop'ted** not adopted (**unadopted road** a road for the repairing, maintenance, etc., of which the Local Authority is not responsible); **unadul'terate, -d** unmixed, pure, genuine; **unadvis'able** inadvisable: not prepared to accept advice. — *n.* **unadvis'ableness.** — *adv.* **unadvis'ably.** — *adj.* **unadvised'** not advised: without advice: not prudent or discreet: ill-judged: inadvertent (*Spens.*). — *adv.* **unadvis'edly.** — *n.* **unadvis'edness.** — *adj.* **unaffect'ed** not affected or influenced: untouched by emotion: without affection: not assumed: plain: real: sincere. — *adv.* **unaffect'edly.** — *n.* **unaffect'edness.** — *adjs.* **unaffect'ing; unagree'able** disagreeable: inconsistent (with): discordant; **unāk'ing** (*Shak.*) unaching; **unā'lienable** inalienable. — *adv.* **unā'lienably.** — *adjs.* **unaligned'** non-aligned; **unalive'** not fully aware of (with *to*): lacking in vitality; **unallayed'** unmixed, unqualified: not diminished, unquenched; **unallied'** not akin: without allies; **unalloyed'** not alloyed or mixed, pure (*lit.* and *fig.*); **un-Amer'ican** not in accordance with American character, ideas, feeling, or traditions: disloyal, against American interests. — *vs.t.* **un-Amer'icanise, -ize** to make un-American; **unanch'or** to loose from anchorage. — *v.i.* to become loose or unattached: to weigh anchor. — *adjs.* **unaneled, unanneld** (*Shak.* (*un-ə-nēld'*) without extreme unction; **unan'imated** not animated or lively: not actuated (by); **unannealed'** not annealed (but see also **unaneld**); **unan'swerable** impossible to answer: not to be refuted, conclusive. — *n.* **unan'swerableness.** — *adv.* **unan'swerably.** — *adjs.* **unan'swered** not answered: unrequited; **unappeal'able** not admitting of an appeal to a higher court, conclusive, final; **unapplaus'ive** not applauding; **unappoint'ed** not appointed: not equipped; **unapprehend'ed; unapprehen'sible; unapprehen'sive** without understanding: without fear. — *n.* **unapprehen'siveness.** — *adjs.* **unapprised'** not informed; **unapproach'able** out of reach, inaccessible: standoffish: inaccessible to advances or intimacy: beyond rivalry. — *n.* **unapproach'ableness.** — *adv.* **unapproach'ably.** — *adjs.* **unapproached'; unappro'priate** unappropriated: inappropriate; **unappro'priated** not taken possession of: not applied to some purpose: not granted to any person, corporation, etc.; **unapproved'** untested (*obs.*): unproved: unsanctioned: not approved of; **unapprov'ing.** — *adv.* **unapprov'ingly.** — *adj.* **unapt'** unfitted: unsuitable: not readily inclined or accustomed (to): lacking in aptitude, slow. — *adv.* **unapt'ly.** — *n.* **unapt'ness.** — *adj.* **unar'guable** that cannot be argued: irrefutable. — *adv.* **unar'guably.** — *adjs.* **unar'gued** (*Milt.*) undisputed: not debated. — *v.t.* **unarm'** to help to put off armour: to deprive of arms, to disarm: to make harmless. — *v.i.* to take off one's armour. — *adjs.* **unarmed'** without weapons: defenceless: unprotected: unaided or without accessory apparatus: without arms or similar limbs or appendages; **unar'moured** without armour, armour-plating; **unart'ful** artless, genuine: inartistic: unskilful. — *adv.* **unart'fully.** — *adjs.* **unartic'ulate** not articulate; **unartic'ulated** not jointed: not in distinct syllables; **unartist'ic** not coming within the sphere of art: not concerned with art: inartistic; **unasked'** not asked: not asked for: uninvited; **unassayed'** not attempted: untested; **unassumed'; unassum'ing** making no assumption: unpretentious, modest. — *adv.* **unassum'ingly.** — *n.* **unassum'ingness.** — *adjs.* **unassured'** uncertain (of): doubtfully recognised (*Spens.*): insecure: lacking in self-assurance, diffident: not insured against loss; **unatōn'able** irreconcilable (*arch.*): that cannot be atoned for; **unattached'** not attached: detached: not arrested: not belonging to a club, party, college, diocese, department, regiment, etc.: not married or about to be; **unattaint'ed** not legally attainted: unstained: not blemished by partiality (*Shak.*); **unattempt'ed** not attempted: not made the subject of an attempt or attack; **unattend'ed** not accompanied or attended: not attended to (*arch.*); **unatten'tive** inattentive (the latter being the preferred form); **unaugment'ed** not augmented: without the augment (*gram.*); **unauspi'cious** inauspicious (*Shak.*); **unavail'able** not available: of no avail (*arch.*). — *n.* **unavail'ableness.** — *adv.* **unavail'ably.** — *adj.* **unavail'ing** of no avail or effect, useless. — *n.* **unavoidabil'ity.** — *adj.* **unavoid'able** not to be avoided: inevitable: not voidable (*law*). — *n.* **unavoid'ableness.** — *adv.* **unavoid'ably.** — *adjs.* **unavoid'ed** not avoided: unavoidable, inevitable (*Shak.*); **unaware'** not aware: unwary (*Shelley*). — *adv.* unawares. — *n.* **unaware'ness.** — *adv.* **unawares'** without being, or making, aware: without being perceived: unexpectedly. — *n.* in the phrase **at unawares**, unexpectedly, at a sudden disadvantage.

Words with prefix un- (*continued*).

adjs. **unbacked'** without a back: without backing or backers: unaided: not moved back: riderless: never yet ridden. — *v.t.* **unbag'** to let out of a bag. — *adj.* **unbaked'** not baked: immature. — *n.* **unbal'ance** want of balance. — *v.t.* to throw off balance: to derange. — *adjs.* **unbal'anced** not in a state of equipoise: without a counterpoise or compensation: without mental balance, erratic or deranged: (of e.g. a view, judgment) not giving due weight to all features of the situation: not adjusted so as to show balance of debtor and creditor (*book-k.*); **unball'asted** without ballast: un-

steady, unstable, flighty; **unbanked'** not deposited in, provided with, or having, a bank. — *v.t.* **unbar'** to remove a bar to remove a bar from or of: to unfasten. — *v.i.* to become unbarred. — *adj.* **unbarbed'** without barb: without bard, caparison, or armour (so prob. in *Coriolanus*): uncropped, untrimmed. — *vs.t.* **unbare'** to bare, lay bare; **unbark'** to strip of bark. — *adjs.* **unbarked'** not deprived of bark: deprived of bark; **unbash'ful** free from bashfulness: shameless (*Shak.*); **unba'ted** unblunted (*Shak.*): undiminished. — *v.t.* (*obs.*) **unbe'** to cause not to be. — *v.i.* to cease to be, or be non-existent (*Hardy*). — *v.t.* **unbear'** to free from the bearing-rein. — *adj.* **unbear'able** intolerable. — *n.* **unbear'ableness.** — *adv.* **unbear'ably.** — *adjs.* **unbear'ing** barren; **unbea'vered** without a beaver or hat: having the beaver of the helmet open; **unbecom'ing** unsuitable: not suited to the wearer, or not showing her, him to advantage: (of behaviour, etc.) not befitting, unseemly (with *to*, *in*; *arch.*, without prep. or with *of*). — *n.* the transition from existence to non-existence. — *adv.* **unbecom'ingly.** — *n.* **unbecom'ingness.** — *v.t.* **unbed'** to rouse, remove, dislodge from a bed. — *adjs.* **unbedd'ed** unstratified: not put to bed; **unbedimmed'** (*Wordsworth*); **unbedinned'** (*Leigh Hunt*) not made noisy. — *v.t.* **unbeget'** to undo the begetting of. — *adjs.* **unbegged'** (of a person) not entreated: not begged for; **unbeginn'ing** without beginning; **unbegot'; unbegott'en** not yet begotten: existing independent of any generating cause. — *v.t.* **unbeguile'** to undeceive. — *adjs.* **unbeguiled'** not deceived; **unbegun'** not yet begun: without beginning; **unbehōl'den** unseen: under no obligation of gratitude; **unbe'ing** non-existent. — *n.* non-existence. — *adjs.* **unbeknown', unbeknownst'** (*coll.*) unknown. — *advs.* unobserved, without being known. — *n.* **un'belief** (or *-lēf'*) disbelief, or withholding of belief, esp. in accepted religion. — *adj.* **unbeliev'able** incredible: (*loosely*) astonishing, remarkable. — *adv.* **unbeliev'ably.** — *v.t.* and *v.i.* **unbelieve'** to disbelieve: to refrain from believing: to cease to believe. — *adj.* **unbelieved'.** — *n.* **unbeliev'er** one who does not believe, esp. in the prevailing religion: a habitually incredulous person. — *adj.* **unbeliev'ing.** — *adv.* **unbeliev'ingly.** — *v.t.* **unbelt'** to ungird. — *adj.* **unbelt'ed** without a belt: freed from a belt. — *v.t.* **unbend'** to relax from a bending tension, as a bow: to straighten: to undo, unfasten (*naut.*): to relax (the mind): to allow a frown, etc., to disappear from (the brow, etc.). — *v.i.* to become relaxed: to behave with freedom from stiff-

---

ness, to be affable. — *adjs.* **unbend'able; unbend'ed; unbend'ing** not bending: unyielding: resolute. — *n.* a relaxing. — *adv.* **unbend'ingly.** — *n.* **unbend'ingness.** — *adj.* **unbent'** not bent: relaxed: not overcome. — *v.t.* **unbeseem'** to misbecome: to fail to fulfil (*Byron*). — *adj.* **unbeseem'ing.** — *adv.* **unbeseem'ingly.** — *vs.t.* **unbespeak'** to cancel an order for; **unbi'as** to free from bias. — *adj.* **unbi'ased** (sometimes **unbi'assed**). — *adv.* **unbi'as(s)edly.** — *n.* **unbi'as(s)edness.** — *adjs.* **unbib'lical** contrary to, unwarranted by, the Bible; **unbid'** not prayed for (*Spens.*): unbidden: not bid; **unbidd'en** not bid or commanded: uninvited: spontaneous. — *v.t.* **unbīnd'** to remove a band from: to loose: to set free. — *n.* **unbīnd'ing** the removal of a band or bond: a loosing: a setting free. — *adj.* loosening: not binding. — *n.* and *adj.* **unbirth'day** (*Lewis Carroll*) (pertaining to) a day other than one's birthday. — *vs.t.* **unbish'op** to deprive of the status of bishop; **unbitt'** (*naut.*) to take off from the bitts. — *adj.* **unbitt'ed** without a bit: unbridled. — *adj., n., adv.* **unblame'able, unblame'-ableness, unblame'ably,** older spellings of **unblāmable,** etc. — *adjs.* **unblenched'** (or, *Milt.*, **un'**) unflinching: unstained; **unblench'ing** unflinching. — *v.t.* **unbless'** to withhold happiness from: to deprive of blessing. — *adjs.* **unblessed', unblest'.** — *n.* **unbless'edness.** — *adj.* **unblind'** not blind. — *v.t.* to free from blindness or from blindfolding. — *adj.* **unblind'ed.** — *v.t.* **unblind'-fold** (*pa.p. Spens.* **unblind'fold**). — *adj.* **unblink'ing** without blinking: not wavering: not showing emotion, esp. fear. — *adv.* **unblink'ingly.** — *adjs.* **unblowed'** (*Shak.*), **unblown'** (or *un'*) not blown: yet in the bud, not yet having bloomed; **unblush'ing** not blushing: without shame: impudent. — *adv.* **unblush'ingly.** — *adjs.* **unbod'ied** disembodied: not having a body or a form; **unbō'ding** not expecting. — *v.t.* **unbolt'** to draw back a bolt from. — *v.i.* to become unbolted: to explain, expound (*Shak.*). — *adj.* **unbolt'ed** unfastened by withdrawing a bolt: not fastened by bolts: not separated by bolting or sifting: coarse. — *v.t.* **unbonn'et** to remove the bonnet from. — *v.i.* to uncover the head. — *adjs.* **unbonn'eted** bare-headed: in Shak. *Othello,* according to some, without taking off the cap, on equal terms; **unbooked'** not entered in a book: unreserved: not literary; **unbook'ish** unlearned: not given to or depending on reading: not savouring of books. — *adjs.* **unborn'** not yet born: non-existent: without beginning; **unborr'owed** not borrowed: original. — *v.t.* **unbo'som** to pour out, tell freely (what is in the mind): to reveal

to the eye: (*refl.*) to confide freely (also *v.i.*). — *n.* **unbo'somer.** — *adjs.* **unbott'omed** bottomless: having no foundation or support: not founded (in, on); **unbought'** obtained without buying: not bribed; **unbound'** not bound: loose: without binding (also *pa.t.* and *pa.p.* of **unbind,** freed from bonds); **unbound'ed** not limited: boundless: having no check or control. — *adv.* **unbound'edly.** — *n.* **unbound'edness.** — *adj.* **unbowed'** not bowed or bent: not vanquished or overcome, free. — *vs.t.* **unbox'** to remove from a box or crate; **unbrace'** to undo the braces, points, or bands of: to loose or relax. — *adjs.* **unbraced'** (*Spens.* **unbrāste**) not braced: with clothing unfastened: (of drum) with tension released: relaxed (*lit.* and *fig.*); **unbraid'ed** not plaited: untarnished, unfaded (*Shak.*); **unbreath'able** not respirable; **unbreathed'** not exercised or practised (*Shak.*): out of breath: not out of breath: not breathed: not even whispered; **unbreathed'-on** untouched by breath, esp. the breath of detraction; **unbreath'ing** not breathing; **unbred'** ill-bred: untrained: not yet born (*Shak.*). — *v.t.* **unbreech'** to remove the breeches, breech, or breeching from. — *adj.* **unbreeched'** wearing no breeches. — *v.t.* **unbrī'dle** to free from the bridle: to free from (usu. politic) restraint. — *adj.* **unbrī'dled** not bridled: unrestrained. — *n.* **unbrī'dledness.** — *adjs.* **un-Brit'ish** not in accordance with British character or traditions; **unbrizzed** see **unbruised; unbroke'** (*arch.*) unbroken; **unbrō'ken** not broken: (of a record) not surpassed: uninterrupted: not thrown into disorder: not variegated: not infringed. — *adv.* **unbrō'kenly.** — *n.* **unbrō'kenness.** — *adj.* **unbruised'** (*Shak.* **un'brused;** *Scott* **unbrizzed'**) not bruised or crushed. — *v.t.* **unbuck'le** to unfasten the buckle(s) of: to unfasten. — *v.i.* to undo the buckle(s) of a garment, etc.: to unbend (*fig.*). — *adj.* **unbudd'ed** not yet in bud: not yet having emerged from the bud. — *v.t.* **unbuild'** to demolish, pull down. — *adjs.* **unbuilt'** (or *un'*) not built: not built upon; **unbuilt'-on.** — *v.i.* and *v.t.* **unbun'dle** to price and sell separately the constituents of a larger package of products or services. — *n.* **unbun'dling.** — *v.t.* **unbur'-den,** (*arch.*) **unbur'then** to free from a burden: to discharge, cast off, as a burden: (*refl.*) to tell one's secrets or anxieties freely. — *adjs.* **unbur'dened,** (*arch.*) **unbur'thened** not burdened: relieved of a burden. — *v.t.* and *v.i.* **unburr'ow** to bring or come out of a burrow. — *v.t.* **unbur'y** to disinter. — *v.t.* **unbutt'on** to loose the buttons of. — *v.i.* to loose one's buttons: to unbend and tell one's thoughts. — *adj.* **unbutt'oned** without a

---

---

button: with buttons loosed: in a relaxed confidential state.

Words with prefix **un-** (*continued*).

adjs. **uncalled'** not called or summoned: not invited: not called up for payment; **uncalled'-for** (or **uncalled for**) not required, unnecessary: unprovoked: offensively or aggressively gratuitous. — *adv.* **uncann'ily.** — *n.* **uncann'iness.** — *adj.* **uncann'y** weird, supernatural: (of e.g. skill) much greater than one would expect from an ordinary human being: unsafe to associate with: unpleasantly severe (*Scot.*): unsafe (*Scot.*). — *v.t.* **uncap'** to remove a cap from. — *v.i.* to take off one's cap. — *adj.* **uncā'pable** (*Shak.*) incapable. — *v.i.* **uncape'** (*Shak.*) prob. a misprint for **uncope:** some have explained as to uncouple hounds, to unkennel a fox, etc. — *adjs.* **uncared'-for (uncared for)** neglected: showing signs of neglect; **uncare'ful** careless: care-free; **uncar'ing** without anxiety, concern, or caution: not caring about (*Burns*). — *v.t.* **uncase'** to take out of a case: to flay (*obs.*): to undress (*Shak.*): to lay bare. — *v.i.* to strip (*Shak.*). — *adjs.* **uncaused'** without any precedent cause, self-existent; **unceas'ing** ceaseless: never-ending. — *adv.* **unceas'ingly.** — *adjs.* **unceremō'-nious** informal: off-hand. — *adv.* **unceremō'niously.** — *n.* **unceremō'niousness.** — *adj.* **uncer'tain** not certain (of, about): not definitely known or decided: subject to doubt or question (**in no uncertain terms** unambiguously): not to be depended upon: subject to vicissitude: hesitant, lacking confidence. — *adv.* **uncer'tainly.** — *ns.* **uncer'tainness; uncer'tainty (uncertainty principle** the principle that it is not possible to measure accurately at the same time both position and velocity). — *adjs.* **uncer'tified** not assured, attested, or guaranteed; **uncess'ant** (*Milt.*) incessant. — *v.t.* **unchain'** to release from a chain: to remove a chain from: to let loose. — *adjs.* **unchained'; unchan'cy** (*Scot.*) unlucky: ill-omened: dangerous: ticklish. — *v.t.* **uncharge'** to unload: to acquit (*Shak.*). — *adj.* **uncharged'** not charged: not attacked (*Shak.*). — *n.* **unchar'ity** want of charity. — *v.t.* **uncharm'** to free from a spell: to destroy the magical power of. — *adjs.* **uncharmed'** not affected by a spell: not charmed; **unchar'ming** not charming or attractive. — *v.t.* **unchar'nel** to take from a charnel. — *adjs.* **unchart'ed** (*lit.* and *fig.*) not mapped in detail: not shown in a chart; **unchart'ered** not holding a charter: unauthorised. — *n.* **unchas'tity** lack, or breach, of chastity. — *v.t.* **uncheck'** (*Shak.*) to fail to check. —

adjs. **uncheck'able; unchecked'** not checked or verified: not restrained: not contradicted (*Shak.*). — *v.t.* **unchild'** (*Shak.*) to make childless: to change from being a child. — *adjs.* **unchild'like; unchris'om** (*Lamb*) unchristened. — *v.t.* **unchrist'en** to annul the christening of: to deprive of a name: to unchristianise (*Milt.*). — *adjs.* **unchrist'ened** unbaptised: without a name; **unchris'tian** non-christian (*rare*): against the spirit of Christianity: uncharitable: unreasonable, outrageous (*coll.*). — *v.t.* to unchristianise (*obs.*). — *v.t.* **unchris'-tianise, -ize** to cause to change from the Christian faith or character. — *adj.* **unchris'tianlike.** — *adv.* **unchris'-tianly.** — *adj.* unchristianlike. — *vs.t.* **unchurch'** to deprive of church membership, or of the possession of a church: to take the status of a church from; **unci'pher** (*obs.*) to decipher. — *adj.* **uncir'cumcised** not circumcised: gentile: unpurified (*fig.*). — *n.* **uncircumcis'ion** uncircumcised condition: the uncircumcised, the gentiles (*B.*). — *adjs.* **unciv'il** not civilised (*Spens.*): discourteous: unseemly: against civic good; **unciv'ilised, -z-** not civilised: away from civilised communities. — *adv.* **unciv'illy.** — *v.t.* **unclasp'** to loose from a clasp: to relax from clasping: to open. — *v.i.* to close in a clasp. — *adjs.* **unclassed'** without class divisions: unclassified: not placed in a class; **unclass'ifiable** (or *-fī'-*) that cannot be classified; **unclass'ified** not classified: of a road, minor, not classified as a motorway, A-road or B-road: not on the security list; **unclean** (*-klēn'*) not clean: foul: ceremonially impure: lewd; **uncleaned'** not cleaned. — *n.* **uncleanliness** (*-klen'*). — *adj.* **uncleanly** (*-klen'*). — *adv.* (*-klēn'*). — *n.* **uncleanness** (*-klēn'nis*). — *adjs.* **uncleansed** (*-klenzd'*); **uncler'ical** not characteristic of, or befitting, a clergyman. — *v.t.* **unclew** (*arch.*) to unwind, unfold, undo. — *v.t.* **uncloak'** to divest of a cloak: to show up. — *v.i.* to take one's cloak off. — *v.t.* **unclog'** to free from a clog or obstruction. — *adj.* **unclogged'** not clogged. — *v.t.* **unclois'ter** to free or remove from the cloister. — *adj.* **unclois'tered** not cloistered: without a cloister: freed or taken from a cloister. — *v.t.* and *v.i.* **unclose** (*un-klōz'*) to open. — *adjs.* **unclose** (*un-klōs'*) not close; **unclosed** (*un-klōzd'*) not closed: unenclosed: opened. — *v.t.* **unclothe'** to take the clothes off: to divest of covering. — *adj.* **unclothed'.** — *v.t.* and *v.i.* **uncloud'** to clear of clouds or obscurity. — *adj.* **uncloud'ed** free from clouds, obscurity or gloom: calm. — *n.* **uncloud'edness.** — *adj.* **uncloud'y.** — *vs.t.* **unclutch'** to release from a clutch; **uncock'** to let down the hammer of: to spread

---

uncheered' *adj.* un- (1).
uncheer'ful *adj.* un- (1).
uncheer'fully *adv.* un- (1).
uncheer'fulness *n.* un- (1).
unchewed' *adj.* un- (1).
unchiv'alrous *adj.* un- (1).
unchō'sen *adj.* un- (1).
unchron'icled *adj.* un- (1).
uncir'cumscribed *adj.* un- (1).
unclad' *adj.* un- (1).
unclaimed' *adj.* un- (1).
unclass'ical *adj.* un- (1).
unclass'y *adj.* un-(1).
unclear' *adj.* un- (1).
uncleared' *adj.* un- (1).
unclear'ly *adv.* un- (1).
unclear'ness *n.* un- (1).
unclench' *v.t.* and *v.i.* un- (2).
unclipped', unclipt' *adjs.* un- (1).
unclō'ven *adj.* un- (1).
unclub(b)'able *adj.* un- (1).
unclutt'ered *adj.* un- (1).
uncollect'ed *adj.* un- (1).
uncol'oured *adj.* un- (1).
uncombed' *adj.* un- (1).
uncommend'able *adj.* un- (1).
uncommend'ably *adv.* un- (1).
uncommend'ed *adj.* un- (1).

uncommer'cial *adj.* un- (1).
uncommū'nicable *adj.* un- (1).
uncommū'nicated *adj.* un- (1).
uncommū'nicative *adj.* un- (1).
uncommū'nicativeness *n.* un- (1).
uncommū'ted *adj.* un- (1).
uncompact'ed *adj.* un- (1).
uncompass'ionate *adj.* un- (1).
uncompelled' *adj.* un- (1).
uncom'pensated *adj.* un- (1).
uncompet'itive *adj.* un- (1).
uncomplain'ing *adj.* un- (1).
uncomplain'ingly *adv.* un- (1).
uncomplais'ant (or *-kom'*) *adj.* un- (1).
uncomplais'antly (or *-kom'*) *adv.* un- (1).
uncomplē'ted *adj.* un- (1).
uncomplī'ant *adj.* un- (1).
uncomply'ing *adj.* un- (1).
uncomprehend'ed *adj.* un- (1).
uncomprehend'ing *adj.* un- (1).
unconceal'able *adj.* un- (1).
unconcealed' *adj.* un- (1).
unconceal'ing *adj.* un- (1).
unconcert'ed *adj.* un- (1).
unconcil'iatory *adj.* un- (1).
unconfed'erated *adj.* un- (1).

unconfessed' *adj.* un- (1).
unconfused' *adj.* un- (1).
unconfus'edly *adv.* un- (1).
uncongē'nial *adj.* un- (1).
uncongenial'ity *n.* un- (1).
unconject'ured *adj.* un- (1).
unconnect'ed *adj.* un- (1).
unconq'uerable *adj.* un- (1).
unconq'uerableness *n.* un- (1).
unconq'uerably *adv.* un- (1).
unconq'uered *adj.* un- (1).
unconscien'tious *adj.* un- (1).
unconscien'tiously *adv.* un- (1).
unconscien'tiousness *n.* un- (1).
unconsent'ing *adj.* un- (1).
unconsoled' *adj.* un- (1).
unconsol'idated *adj.* un- (1).
unconstitū'tional *adj.* un- (1).
unconstitū'tional'ity *n.* un- (1).
unconstitū'tionally *adv.* un- (1).
unconsumed' *adj.* un- (1).
uncon'summated *adj.* un- (1).
uncontain'able *adj.* un- (1).
uncontam'inated *adj.* un- (1).
uncon'templated *adj.* un- (1).
unconten'tious *adj.* un- (1).
uncontradict'ed *adj.* un- (1).
uncontrived' *adj.* un- (1).

out from a haycock. — *adj.* **uncoff'ined** not put into a coffin: removed from a coffin. — *v.t.* and *v.i.* **uncoil'** to unwind. — *adjs.* **uncoined'** not coined: (*Shak.* **uncoyned**) variously explained, but prob. meaning 'natural', 'not artificial or counterfeit'. — *v.t.* **uncolt'** (*Shak.*, punningly; Falstaff has used *colt*, to cheat) to deprive of a horse. — *v.t.* and *v.i.* **uncombine'** to separate (*Dickens*). — *adj.* **uncom(e)atable** (*un-kum-at'ə-bl*) inaccessible: out of reach. — *n.* **uncome'liness.** — *adjs.* **uncome'ly** not comely: indecent: unseemly; **uncom'fortable** feeling, involving, or causing discomfort or disquiet. — *n.* **uncom'fortableness.** — *adv.* **uncom'fortably.** — *adjs.* **uncom'forted; uncommitt'ed** not pledged to support any party, policy or action: impartial: not committed (**uncommitted logic array** (often abbrev. **ULA, ula;** *comput.*) a microchip whose logic circuits are left unconnected during manufacture and completed later to the customer's specification); **uncomm'on** not common: unusual: remarkably great: strange. — *adv.* (*old slang*) remarkably, very. — *adv.* **uncomm'only** rarely (esp. *not uncommonly*, frequently): in an unusually great degree. — *n.* **uncomm'onness.** — *adjs.* **uncom'panied** unaccompanied; **uncompan'ionable** unsociable; **uncompan'ioned** without a companion or an equal; **uncom'plicated** straightforward, not made difficult by the variety of factors involved: (of a person) simple in character and outlook; **uncompliment'ary** not at all complimentary, derogatory; **uncompō'sable** incapable of being composed or reconciled; **uncompound'ed** not compounded, unmixed; **uncomprehen'sive** not comprehensive: incomprehensible (*Shak.*); **uncom'promising** refusing to compromise: unyielding: out-and-out. — *adv.* **uncom'promisingly.** — *n.* **uncom'promisingness.** — *adj.* **unconceiv'able** inconceivable. — *n.* **unconceiv'ableness.** — *adv.* **unconceiv'ably.** — *adj.* **unconceived'.** — *n.* **unconcern'** want of concern or anxiety: indifference. — *adj.* **unconcerned'** not concerned, not involved (in): impartial: uninterested: indifferent: untroubled, carelessly secure: sober, unaffected by liquor (*obs.*). — *adv.* **unconcern'edly.** — *n.* **unconcern'edness.** — *adj.* **unconcern'ing.** — *n.* **unconcern'ment.** — *adjs.* **unconclu'sive** inconclusive; **unconcoct'ed** not digested: crude: not elaborated or finished (*fig.*); **uncondi'tional** not conditional: absolute, unlimited. — *n.* **unconditional'ity.** — *adv.* **uncondi'tionally.** — *n.* **uncondi'tionalness.** — *adjs.* **uncondi'tioned** not subject to condition or limitation: infinite, absolute, unknowable: (of a person, response) not conditioned

by learning or experience (**unconditioned stimulus** one provoking an unconditioned response): not put into the required state; **unconfi'nable** not to be confined: unbounded (*Shak.*). — *v.t.* **unconfine'** to release from restraint: to divulge (*Keats*). — *adj.* **unconfined'** not confined: not restricted: unlimited: set free. — *adv.* **unconfi'nedly.** — *adjs.* **unconfirmed'** not confirmed: not yet having received confirmation: uncorroborated: not yet firm or strong: ignorant (*Shak.*); **unconform'** (*Milt.*) unlike. — *n.* **unconformabil'ity** the state or the quality of being unconformable: an unconformity in stratification (*geol.*). — *adj.* **unconform'able** not conforming (to e.g., *hist.*, the practices of the Church of England): unwilling to conform: showing an unconformability (*geol.*). — *n.* **unconform'ableness.** — *adv.* **unconform'ably.** — *adj.* **unconform'ing** not conforming. — *n.* **unconform'ity** want of conformity (*arch.*): nonconformity (*obs.*): a breach of continuity in direction, etc. of rock strata (*geol.*). — *v.t.* and *v.i.* **uncongeal'** to thaw, melt. — *adjs.* **uncon'jugal** (*Milt.*) not suited to, or fitting in, marriage; **unconjunc'tive** (*Milt.*) impossible to be joined; **unconnī'ving** refusing indulgence (*Milt.*); **uncon'scionable** (of a person) unscrupulous: not conformable to conscience: outrageous, inordinate. — *n.* **uncon'scionableness.** — *adv.* **uncon'scionably.** — *adj.* **uncon'scious** without consciousness: unaware (of): not self-conscious. — *n.* (with **the**) the deepest, inaccessible level of the psyche in which are present in dynamic state repressed impulses and memories. — *adv.* **uncon'sciously.** — *n.* **uncon'sciousness.** — *v.t.* **uncon'secrate** to deprive of consecrated character. — *adj.* **unconsecrated.** — *adjs.* **uncon'secrated** not consecrated; **unconsentā'neous** (*Peacock*) not in agreement; **unconsid'ered** not esteemed: done without considering; **unconsid'ering; uncon'stant** (*Shak.*) inconstant; **unconstrain'able** unconstrained'. — *adv.* **unconstrain'edly.** — *n.* **unconstraint'** absence of constraint. — *adjs.* **uncontemned'** (*Shak.*) not despised; **uncontest'able** incontestable; **uncontest'ed; uncontrōll'able** not capable of being controlled: absolute, not controlled (*arch.*): indisputable (*obs.*). — *n.* **uncontrōll'ableness.** — *adv.* **uncontrōll'ably.** — *adj.* **uncontrolled'** not controlled: not disputed (*obs.*). — *adv.* **uncontrōll'edly.** — *adjs.* **uncontrovert'ed** not disputed; **uncontrovert'ible; unconven'tional** not conventional: free in one's ways. — *n.* **unconventional'ity.** — *adjs.* **unconvers'able** not able or not disposed to converse freely; **uncool'** (*coll., derog.*) not sophisticated or smart, old-fashioned; **unco-or'dinated** not co-ordi-

---

uncontrover'sial *adj.* un- (1).
unconvers'ant *adj.* un- (1).
unconvert'ed *adj.* un- (1).
unconvert'ible *adj.* un- (1).
unconvict'ed *adj.* un- (1).
unconvinced' *adj.* un- (1).
unconvinc'ing *adj.* un- (1).
uncooked' *adj.* un- (1).
unco-op'erative *adj.*
  (also without *hyphen*) un- (1).
unco(-)op'eratively *adv.* un- (1).
uncoquett'ish *adj.* un- (1).
uncor'dial *adj.* un- (1).
uncork' *v.t.* un- (2).
uncorrect'ed *adj.* un- (1).
uncorrob'orated *adj.* un- (1).
uncor'seted *adj.* un- (1).
uncount'able *adj.* un- (1).
uncount'ed *adj.* un- (1).
uncourt'liness *n.* un- (1).
uncourt'ly *adj.* un- (1).
uncrate *v.t.* un- (2).
uncropped *adj.* un- (1).
uncrow'ded *adj.* un- (1).
uncrump'le *v.t.* un- (2).
uncrush'able *adj.* un- (1).
uncrystallis'able, -z- *adj.* un- (1).
uncrys'tallised, -z- *adj.* un- (1).

uncuck'olded *adj.* un- (1).
unculled *adj.* un- (1).
uncult'ivable *adj.* un- (1).
uncult'ivated *adj.* un- (1).
uncum'bered *adj.* un- (1).
uncurb'able *adj.* un- (1).
uncurbed' *adj.* un- (1).
uncurd'led *adj.* un- (1).
uncured' *adj.* un- (1).
uncurr'ent *adj.* un- (1).
uncurtailed' *adj.* un- (1).
undam' *v.t.* un- (2).
undam'aged *adj.* un- (1).
undammed' *adj.* un- (1, 2).
undamned' *adj.* un- (1).
undamped' *adj.* un- (1).
undaunt'able *adj.* un- (1).
undealt' *adj.* un- (1).
undear' *adj.* un- (1).
undebarred' *adj.* un- (1).
undebased' *adj.* un- (1).
undebauched' *adj.* un- (1).
undecayed' *adj.* un- (1).
undecīd'able *adj.* un- (1).
undeclared' *adj.* un- (1).
undecompōs'able *adj.* un- (1).
undecomposed' *adj.* un- (1).
undefaced' *adj.* un- (1).

undefeat'ed *adj.* un- (1).
undefend'ed *adj.* un- (1).
undefiled' *adj.* un- (1).
undelayed' *adj.* un- (1).
undelay'ing *adj.* un- (1).
undelect'able *adj.* un- (1).
undel'egated *adj.* un- (1).
undelib'erate *adj.* un- (1).
undeliv'ered *adj.* un- (1).
undelud'ed *adj.* un- (1).
undemand'ing *adj.* un- (1).
undemocrat'ic *adj.* un- (1).
undemon'strable *adj.* un- (1).
undemon'strative *adj.* un- (1).
undemon'strativeness *n.* un- (1).
undeplored' *adj.* un- (1).
undepraved' *adj.* un- (1).
undeprē'ciated *adj.* un- (1).
undepressed' *adj.* un- (1).
undeprived' *adj.* un- (1).
undescend'ible, -able *adjs.* un- (1).
undescried' *adj.* un- (1).
undespair'ing *adj.* un- (1).
undespair'ingly *adv.* un- (1).
undespoiled' *adj.* un- (1).
undestroyed' *adj.* un- (1).
undetect'able *adj.* un- (1).
undetect'ed *adj.* un- (1).

nated: having clumsy movements, as if muscles were not co-ordinated. — *vs.t.* **uncope′** to unmuzzle, or unsew the mouth of (a ferret; cf. **uncape**); **uncord′** to free (e.g. a trunk) from cords. — *adjs.* **uncorrupt′** incorrupt; **uncorrupt′ed; uncost′ly** inexpensive; **un-coun′selled** not given advice: not advised. — *v.t.* **uncou′ple** to loose from being coupled: to disjoin. — *v.i.* to become detached: to uncouple hounds. — *adjs.* **uncoup′led** not married: detached; **uncour′teous** discourteous; **uncouth** (*un-kōōth′*; O.E. *uncūth*, unknown, strange — *un-*, *cūth*, known) unknown (*obs.*): unfamiliar (*arch.*): strange and wild or unattractive: awkward, ungraceful, uncultured, esp. in manners or language (see also **unco** below). — *adv.* **uncouth′ly.** — *n.* **uncouth′ness.** — *adj.* **uncov′enanted** not promised or bound by covenant: not included in a covenant: not having subscribed to the Solemn League and Covenant of 1643. — *v.t.* **uncov′er** to remove the cover of: to lay open: to expose: to drive out of cover. — *v.i.* to take off the hat. — *adj.* **uncov′ered.** — *v.t.* **uncowl′** to withdraw the cowl from. — *adjs.* **uncowled′; uncoyned** see **uncoined.** — *v.t.* **uncreate′** to deprive of existence. — *adj.* **uncrea′ted** not (yet) created: not produced by creation (*Milt.*). — *n.* **uncreat′edness.** — *adjs.* **uncrea′ting; uncred′ible** (*obs.*) incredible; **uncred′itable** (*obs.*) discreditable; **uncrit′ical** not critical, without discrimination: not in accordance with the principles of criticism. — *adv.* **uncrit′ically.** — *v.t.* **uncross′** to change, move, from a crossed position. — *adj.* **uncrossed′** not crossed — not passed over, marked with a cross, thwarted, etc.: not marked off as paid (*Shak.*). — *v.t.* **uncrown′** to dethrone: to take the crown off. — *adjs.* **uncrowned′** not crowned: not yet formally crowned: possessing kingly power without the actual title (**uncrowned king, queen** (*facet.*) a man, woman having supreme influence, or commanding the highest respect, within a particular group): unfulfilled; **uncrudd′ed** (*Spens.*) uncurdled; **uncul′tured** not cultured: not cultivated; **uncūr′able** (*Shak.*) incurable; **uncū′rious** incurious: not strange. — *v.t. and v.i.* **uncurl′** to take or come out of curl, twist, roll. — *adjs.* **uncurled′** not curled: unrolled, uncoiled; **uncurl′ing.** — *vs.t.* **uncurse′** to free from a curse, unsay a curse upon; **uncur′tain** to remove a curtain from. — *adjs.* **uncur′tained** curtainless; **uncus′tomed** (of goods) on which customs duty is unpaid, or not payable: unaccustomed (*arch.*): not customary (*arch.*); **uncut′** not cut: not shaped by cutting: not abridged: of a book, (*biblio-*

graphically) with margins not cut down by the binder (even though opened with a paper-cutter), (*popularly*) unopened: of illegal drugs, not adulterated.

Words with prefix un- (continued).

adjs. **undashed′** undismayed; **undāt′ed** with no date marked or assigned: unending; **undaunt′ed** not daunted: bold, intrepid. — *adv.* **undaunt′edly.** — *n.* **undaunt′edness.** — *adj.* **undawn′ing** not yet dawning or showing light. — *v.i.* **undazz′le** to recover from a dazed state (*Tennyson*). — *adjs.* **undazz′led** not dazzled; **undead′** dead but not at rest, of a ghost, vampire, etc. — *n.pl.* such spirits. — *v.t.* **undeaf′** (*Shak.*) to free from deafness. — *adj.* **undeceiv′able** incapable of deceiving (*obs.*) or of being deceived. — *v.t.* **undeceive′** to free from a mistaken belief, reveal the truth to. — *adjs.* **undeceived′** not deceived: set free from a delusion; **undē′cent** indecent (*dial.*): unfitting (*arch.*): unhandsome (*obs.*); **undecīd′ed** not decided or settled: uncertain, irresolute. — *adv.* **undecīd′edly.** — *adjs.* **undecī′pherable** indecipherable; **undecī′sive** indecisive. — *v.t.* **undeck′** to divest of ornaments. — *adjs.* **undecked′** not adorned: having no deck; **undeclīn′ing** unbowed, unsubmissive; **undeed′ed** (*Shak.*) unused in any action, undefied′ (*Spens.* **undefide′**) not defied or challenged; **undefīn′able; undefined′** not defined: indefinite. — *v.t.* **undē′ify** to deprive of the nature or honour of a god. — *n.* **undelight′** lack of delight. — *adjs.* **undelight′ed; undelight′ful;undenī′able** not to be denied, indisputable: not to be refused: obviously true or excellent. — *n.* **undenī′ableness.** — *adv.* **undenī′ably** assuredly, one cannot deny it. — *adj.* **undenominā′tional** not confined to or favouring any particular sect. — *n.* **undenominā′tionalism.** — *adj.* **undepend′able** (a word formed irregularly, neither from a noun nor from a transitive verb) not to be depended upon. — *n.* **undepen′dableness.** — *adjs.* **undepen′ding** (*obs.*) independent; **undescen′ded** (of the testes) remaining in the abdominal cavity, failing to move down into the scrotum; **undescrī′bable** indescribable; **undescribed′; undescried′.** — *n.* **un′desert** want of desert, unworthiness. — *v.t.* **undeserve′** to fail or cease to deserve. — *adj.* **undeserved′** not deserved. — *adv.* **undeser′vedly.** — *ns.* **undeser′vedness; undeser′ver** (*Shak.*) one who is not deserving or worthy. — *adj.* **undeser′ving.** — *adv.* **undeser′vingly.** — *adj.* **undesigned′.** — *adv.* **undesign′edly.** — *n.* **undesign′edness.** — *adj.* **undesign′ing** not designing: artless: straightforward: sincere. — *n.* **un-**

undē′viating *adj.* un- (1).	**undispūt′edly** *adv.* un- (1).	**undriv′en** *adj.* un- (1).
undē′viatingly *adv.* un- (1).	**undissō′ciated** *adj.* un- (1).	**undroop′ing** *adj.* un- (1).
undevout′ *adj.* un- (1).	**undissolved′** *adj.* un- (1).	**undrowned′** *adj.* un- (1).
undiagnosed′ *adj.* un- (1).	**undissol′ving** *adj.* un- (1).	**undrunk′** *adj.* un- (1).
undigest′ed *adj.* un- (1).	**undistilled′** *adj.* un- (1).	**undubbed′** *adj.* un- (1).
undilut′ed *adj.* un- (1).	**undistort′ed** *adj.* un- (1).	**undug′** *adj.* un- (1).
undimin′ishable *adj.* un- (1).	**undistract′ed** *adj.* un- (1).	**undulled′** *adj.* un- (1).
undimin′ished *adj.* un- (1).	**undistract′edly** *adv.* un- (1).	**uneat′able** *adj.* un- (1).
undimmed′ *adj.* un- (1).	**undistract′edness** *n.* un- (1).	**uneat′ableness** *n.* un- (1).
undint′ed *adj.* un- (1).	**undistract′ing** *adj.* un- (1).	**uneat′en** *adj.* un- (1).
undiplomat′ic *adj.* un- (1).	**undisturbed′** *adj.* un- (1).	**uneclipsed′** *adj.* un- (1).
undirect′ed *adj.* un- (1).	**undistur′bedly** *adv.* un- (1).	**uned′ucable** *adj.* un- (1).
undisappoint′ing *adj.* un- (1).	**undisturb′ing** *adj.* un- (1).	**uned′ucated** *adj.* un- (1).
undisclosed′ *adj.* un- (1).	**undivers′ified** *adj.* un- (1).	**uneffaced′** *adj.* un- (1).
undiscom′fited *adj.* un- (1).	**undivine′** *adj.* un- (1).	**uneffect′ed** *adj.* un- (1).
undiscord′ant *adj.* un- (1).	**undivorced′** *adj.* un- (1).	**unelab′orate** *adj.* un- (1).
undiscour′aged *adj.* un- (1).	**undivulged′** *adj.* un- (1).	**unclab′orated** *adj.* un- (1).
undiscov′erable *adj.* un- (1).	**undoc′umented** *adj.* un- (1).	**unelat′ed** *adj.* un- (1).
undiscov′erably *adv.* un- (1).	**undoomed′** *adj.* un- (1).	**unelect′ed** *adj.* un- (1).
undiscov′ered *adj.* un- (1).	**undrain′able** *adj.* un- (1).	**unelect′rified** *adj.* un- (1).
undiscuss′able, -ible *adjs.* un- (1).	**undrained′** *adj.* un- (1).	**unembarr′assed** *adj.* un- (1).
undishon′oured *adj.* un- (1).	**undramat′ic** *adj.* un- (1).	**unembell′ished** *adj.* un- (1).
undismant′led *adj.* un- (1).	**undread′ed** *adj.* un- (1).	**unembitt′ered** *adj.* un- (1).
undismayed′ *adj.* un- (1).	**undread′ing** *adj.* un- (1).	**unembod′ied** *adj.* un- (1).
undisor′dered *adj.* un- (1).	**undream′ing** *adj.* un- (1).	**unemphat′ic** *adj.* un- (1).
undispatched′ *adj.* un- (1).	**undried′** *adj.* un- (1).	**unemp′tied** *adj.* un- (1).
undispensed′ *adj.* un- (1).	**undrilled′** *adj.* un- (1).	**unenclosed′** *adj.* un- (1).
undispūt′ed *adj.* un- (1).	**undrink′able** *adj.* un- (1).	**unencumb′ered** *adj.* un- (1).

desirabil'ity. — *adj.* **undesīr'able** not to be wished for. — *n.* an undesirable or objectionable person or thing. — *n.* **undesīr'ableness.** — *adv.* **undesīr'ably.** — *adjs.* **undesired'; undesīr'ing; undesīr'ous; undeter'minable** indeterminable; **undeter'minate** indeterminate. — *ns.* **undeter'minateness; undeterminā'tion.** — *adjs.* **undeter'-mined** not settled, not fixed: not ascertained: not limited; **undeterred'** not discouraged or prevented (from); **undevel'oped** not developed or built, not built on or used for public works. — *v.t.* **undid'** *pa.t.* of undo. — *adjs.* **undiff'erenced** (*her.*) without a modification to distinguish a cadet from the main line; **undifferen'tiated** not differentiated. — *v.t.* **undight** (*un-dīt'; Spens.*) to undo, take off, doff (*pa.t.* and *pa.p.* **undight').** — *adj.* unadorned: not dressed, (of hair) loose (*Spens.*, etc.). — *adj.* **undig'nified.** — *v.t.* **undig'nify** to deprive of dignity. — *adjs.* **undipped'** not dipped: unbaptised; **undiscerned'** unobserved, unperceived. — *adv.* **undis-cern'edly.** — *adj.* **undiscern'ible.** — *adv.* **undiscern'ibly.** — *adj.* **undiscern'ing** showing lack of discernment or discrimination. — *n.* want of discernment. — *adjs.* **undischarged'** not paid or settled: (of e.g. obligation) not carried out: not released from debt or other liability: (of gun) not fired; **undisc'iplinable.** — *n.* **undisc'ipline** lack of discipline. — *adjs.* **undisc'iplined** untrained: unruly; **undiscord'ing** (*Milt.*) not discordant; **undiscrim'inating** not making distinctions: not showing critical taste or ability; **undiscussed'** unsettled (*obs.*): not discussed; **undisguīs'able; undisguised'** not disguised: frank, open. — *adv.* **undisguīs'edly.** — *adjs.* **undisposed'** not disposed (usu. with **-of**): disinclined (*Shak.*): disinclined (to); **undissem'bled** unfeigned: undisguised, unconcealed; **undistemp'ered** not deranged, disturbed, ruffled, or in unhealthy condition; **undistinc'tive** not distinctive: undistinguishing; **undisting'uishable** indistinguishable. — *n.* **undisting'uish-ableness.** — *adv.* **undisting'uishably.** — *adjs.* **undisting'-uished** not distinguished or observed: not marked out by conspicuous qualities, not famous: not having an air of distinction; **undisting'uishing** not discriminating; **undistrib'uted** not distributed (**undistributed middle** the fallacy of reasoning without distributing the middle term, i.e. without making it universal, in at least one premise); **undivert'ed** not turned away: not amused; **undivert'ing; undivest'ed** (*Richardson*) detached. — *adv.* **undivest'edly.** — *adjs.* **undivid'able** indivisible; **undivī'ded** not divided: (of one's attention to something) wholly concentrated, not distracted. — *adv.* **undivī'dedly.** — *n.* **undivī'dedness.** — *v.t.* **undo** (*un-dōō'*) to

reverse the doing of: to cancel, annul: to bring to nothing: to unfasten by unbolting, etc.: to open: to unbutton, untie, etc.: to unravel: to solve (a problem, riddle) (*arch.*): to bring ruin on: to seduce (*arch.*): to prevent the happening or being of (*Shak.*). — *v.i.* to come undone: to reverse what has been done: — *pa.t.* **undid'**; *pa.p.* **undone** (*un-dun'*). — *v.t.* **undock'** to take (a ship) out of dock: to release (a space-craft) from its coupling with another space-craft, station, etc. in space. — Also *v.i.* — *adjs.* **undocked'** not docked or cut short; **undoc'tored** without a doctor's degree: not patched up, tampered with, or sophisticated. — *ns.* **undoer** (*un-dōō'ər*) one who undoes: one who ruins: a seducer; **undo'ing** the reversal of what has been done: unfastening: opening: ruin or cause of ruin. — *adj.* **undomes'tic** not domestic: not content with, adapted to, or relating to, home life: unhomelike (*Coleridge*). — *v.t.* **undomes'ticate** to make undomestic: to untame. — *adjs.* **undomes'ticated** not domesticated: not tamed: emancipated from mere domestic interests; **undone** (*un-dun'*) not done: annulled: brought to naught: unfastened (**come undone** to become unfastened, detached; also (*fig.*) to go wrong: opened: ruined: seduced. — *v.t.* and *v.i.* **undoub'le** to unfold, open out. — *adjs.* **undoubt'able** indubitable; **undoubt'ed** not doubted: unquestioned: certainly genuine or such as is represented: indubitable. — *adv.* **undoubt'edly** without doubt, certainly. — *adjs.* **undoubt'ful; undoubt'ing.** — *adv.* **undoubt'ingly.** — *adj.* **undraped'** without drapery: nude. — *v.t.* and *v.i.* **undraw'** to draw back. — *adjs.* **undreamed', undreamt'** (also with **-of**) not imagined even in a dream. — *v.t.* **undress'** to remove the clothes or dressing from. — *v.i.* to take off one's clothes. — *n.* (*un'*) scanty or incomplete dress: ordinary, informal dress: uniform for ordinary occasions. — Also *adj.* — *adj.* **undressed'** not dressed — not set in order, or made trim, or treated or prepared for use, etc.: divested of clothes (**get undressed** to take one's clothes off). — *n.* **undress'ing.** — *adjs.* **undross'y** (*Pope*) pure; **undue'** not due or owing: unjustifiable: inappropriate: excessive (**undue influence** (*law*) a strong influence over another person which might prevent the exercise of that person's freewill). — *adv.* **undū'ly** unjustifiably: more than is right or reasonable, excessively: wrongfully (*arch.*). — *adjs.* **undū'teous** undutiful (*poet.*); **undū'tiful.** — *adv.* **undū'tifully.** — *n.* **undū'ti-fulness.** — *adjs.* **undyed'** not dyed; **undy'ing** not dying, immortal: unceasing. — *adv.* **undy'ingly.** — *n.* **undy'-ingness.**

---

unendang'ered *adj.* un- (1).
unendowed' *adj.* un- (1).
unendūr'able *adj.* un- (1).
unendūr'ably *adv.* un- (1).
unengaged' *adj.* un- (1).
unenjoy'able *adj.* un- (1).
unenlight'ened *adj.* un- (1).
unenquīr'ing *adj.* un- (1).
unenriched' *adj.* un- (1).
unenslaved' *adj.* un- (1).
unentailed' *adj.* un- (1).
unen'tered *adj.* un- (1).
unen'terprising *adj.* un- (1).
unentertained' *adj.* un- (1).
unentertain'ing *adj.* un- (1).
unenthralled' *adj.* un- (1).
unenthusiast'ic *adj.* un- (1).
unentīt'led *adj.* un- (1).
uneq'uable *adj.* un- (1).
unerā'sable *adj.* un- (1).
unescāp'able *adj.* un- (1).
unescort'ed *adj.* un- (1).
unespied' *adj.* un- (1).
unessayed' *adj.* un- (1).
uneth'ical *adj.* un- (1).
unevangel'ical *adj.* un- (1).
unē'ven *adj.* un- (1).

unē'venly *adv.* un- (1).
unē'venness *n.* un- (1).
unevent'ful *adj.* un- (1).
unevent'fully *adv.* un- (1).
unev'idenced *adj.* un- (1).
unexact'ing *adj.* un- (1).
unexagg'erated *adj.* un- (1).
unexalt'ed *adj.* un- (1).
unexam'ined *adj.* un- (1).
unex'cavated *adj.* un- (1).
unexcelled' *adj.* un- (1).
unexcī'table *adj.* un- (1).
unexcī'ted *adj.* un- (1).
unexcī'ting *adj.* un- (1).
unexclu'ded *adj.* un- (1).
unexclu'sive *adj.* un- (1).
unexclu'sively *adv.* un- (1).
unexem'plified *adj.* un- (1).
unex'ercised *adj.* un- (1).
unexhaus'ted *adj.* un- (1).
unexpan'ded *adj.* un- (1).
unexpec'tant *adj.* un- (1).
unexpec'ted *adj.* un- (1).
unexpec'tedly *adv.* un- (1).
unexpec'tedness *n.* un- (1).
unexpen'sive *adj.* un- (1).
unexpen'sively *adv.* un- (1).

unexpē'rienced *adj.* un- (1).
unex'piated *adj.* un- (1).
unexpired' *adj.* un- (1).
unexplain'able *adj.* un- (1).
unexplained' *adj.* un- (1).
unexploit'ed *adj.* un- (1).
unexplored' *adj.* un- (1).
unexposed' *adj.* un- (1).
unexpressed' *adj.* un- (1).
unexpress'ible *adj.* un- (1).
unex'purgated *adj.* un- (1).
unexten'ded *adj.* un- (1).
unexten'uated *adj.* un- (1).
unexting'uishable *adj.* un- (1).
unexting'uishably *adv.* un- (1).
unexting'uished *adj.* un- (1).
unextreme' *adj.* un-(1).
unfā'dable *adj.* un- (1).
unfā'ded *adj.* un- (1).
unfā'ding *adj.* un- (1).
unfā'dingly *adv.* un- (1).
unfā'dingness *n.* un- (1).
unfall'en *adj.* un- (1).
unfal'tering *adj.* un- (1).
unfal'teringly *adv.* un- (1).
unfamed' *adj.* un- (1).
unfamil'iar *adj.* un- (1).

Words with prefix **un-** (*continued*).

adjs. **uneared'** not eared: untilled (*Shak.*); **unearned'** not earned by work: (**unearned income** income, e.g. dividends, that is not remuneration for work done; **unearned increment** increase in value of land independent of owner's labour or expenditure): (of something pleasant or unpleasant) unmerited. — *v.t.* **unearth'** to dig up, disinter: to bring out of obscurity, bring to light: to expel from a burrow. — *adj.* **unearthed'** not connected to earth electrically: dug up, brought to light, etc.   *n.* **unearth'liness.** — *adj.* **unearth'ly** celestial: weird, ghostly: unconscionable, absurd (esp of an early hour). — *n.* **unease'** lack of ease: discomfort: apprehension. — *adv.* **uneas'ily.** — *n.* **uneas'iness.** — *adjs.* **uneas'y** not at ease: disquieted: apprehensive: showing troubled restlessness (*lit.* and *fig.*): uncomfortable: (now *rare*) not easy to be done: difficult because of physical obstacles (*obs.*); **uneath** (*un-ēth'*; O.E. *unēathe*; see **eath;** *arch.*) difficult: distressing. — *adv.* with difficulty: in hardship: hardly, scarcely: almost (*Spens.*). — Also (*adv.*) **uneth',** **uneathes',** **un- nethes'.** — *adjs* **uneconom'ic** not in accordance with sound economics; **uneconom'ical** not economical. — *v.t.* **unedge'** to blunt. — *adjs.* **uned'ifying** not instructing or uplifting morally or aesthetically: morally degrading or degraded; **uned'ited** never edited, never before published; **unemo'tional.** — *adv.* **unemo'tionally.** — *adjs.* **unemo'tioned** impassive; **unemploy'able; unem- ployed'** out of work: not put to use or profit: for or pertaining to those who are out of work. — *n.* the number of people out of work in a given period. — *n.* **unemploy'ment (unemployment benefit** a weekly payment supplied under the national insurance scheme to a person who is unemployed). — *adjs.* **unenchant'ed** (*Milt.* **uninchant'ed); unendeared'** (*Milt.* **unindeared')** not made precious; **unend'ing** endless: everlasting: never ceasing, incessant: thorough-going (*Carlyle*). — *adv.* **unend'ingly.** — *n.* **unend'ingness.** — *adjs.* **unen- force'able** that cannot be (esp. legally) enforced; **unen- forced'; un-Eng'lish** not English in character; **un-Eng'- lished** not translated into English; **unen'viable** not to be envied. — *adv.* **unen'viably.** — *adjs.* **unen'vied; unen'vious; unen'vying; unē'qual** not equal: not equal (to): inadequate (*obs.*): unjust (*obs.*): excessive (*obs.*): varying, not uniform: (of an agreement, etc.) not evenly balanced, e.g. with regard to concessions made or advantages gained. — Also *adv.* (*Shak.*). — *n.* one who is not equal in rank, ability, etc. — *adj.* **unē'qualled** without an equal. — *adv.* **unē'qually.** — *adjs.* **uneq'-**

uitable inequitable; **unequiv'ocal** unambiguous: explicit: clear and emphatic. — *adv.* **unequiv'ocally.** — *adj.* **unerr'ing** making no error, infallible: not, or never, missing the mark (*lit.* and *fig.*). — *adv.* **unerr'ingly.** — *n.* **unerr'ingness.** — *v.t.* **uness'ence** to deprive of essence or being (*Lamb*). — *adjs.* **unessen'tial** without being, immaterial (*Milt.,* etc.): not of the essence: inessential, not necessary, not important; **unestab'lished** not established: not on the establishment or permanent staff; **uneth** see **uneath** above; **unexam'pled** unprecedented, without like or parallel; **unexcep'tionable** not liable to objection or criticism, exactly right, excellent: without exception (*Ruskin*). — *n.* **unexcep'tionableness.** — *adv.* **unexcep'tionably.** — *adj.* **unexcep'tional** not admitting, or forming, an exception: unexceptionable. — *adv.* **unexcep'tionally.** — *adjs.* **unex'ecuted** not executed: not brought into action (*Shak.*); **unexpē'rient** (*Shak.*) inexperienced; **unexpress'ive** not expressive: inexpressible, beyond the power of description (*Shak., Milt.*); **unexpug'nable** inexpugnable; **unextinct'** not extinguished or dead (*fig.*); **uncyed'** unseen, unobserved.

Words with prefix **un-** (*continued*).

adj. **unfa'bled** not fabled, real. — *n.* **un'fact** a fact that must not be acknowledged, or a falsehood that must pass as fact, esp. in international politics. — *adj.* **unfail'ing** never failing or giving out: infallible: constant: inexhaustible. — *adv.* **unfail'ingly.** — *adj.* **unfair'** not fair, ugly: inequitable, unjust: involving deception or fraud and leading to undue advantage over business rival(s). — *v.t.* (*Shak.*) to deprive of beauty. — *adv.* **unfair'ly.** — *ns.* **unfair'ness; unfaith'** want of faith or trust. — *adj.* **unfaith'ful** not of the approved religion: not faithful, violating trust: breaking faith with one's husband, wife or lover, usu. by having sexual intercourse with someone else: not true to the original. — *adv.* **unfaith'fully.** — *n.* **unfaith'fulness.** — *adjs.* **unfail'- ible** (*Shak.*) infallible; **unfash'ionable** not fashionable: incapable of being fashioned (*obs.*): shapeless (*Shak.*). — *n.* **unfash'ionableness.** — *adv.* **unfash'ionably.** — *adj.* **unfash'ioned** not formed: not shaped: not made polished, elegant, etc. (*obs.*). — *v.t.* **unfasten** (*un-fäs'n*) to release from a fastening: to unfix (*Shak.*). — *v.i.* to become loose or open. — *adjs.* **unfas'tened** released from fastening: not fastened; **unfa'thered** without a father or acknowledged father: deprived of a father; **unfa'therly** unbefitting a father; **unfath'omable** not able to be fathomed (*lit.* and *fig.*). — *n.* **unfath'omableness.** — *adv.* **unfath'omably.** — *adjs.* **unfath'omed** not

---

unfamiliar'ity *n.* un- (1).	**unflagg'ing** *adj.* un- (1).	**unforgiv'ingness** *n.* un- (1).
unfamil'iarly *adv.* un- (1).	**unflagg'ingly** *adv.* un- (1).	**unfor'midable** *adj.* un- (1).
unfanned' *adj.* un- (1).	**unflatt'ering** *adj.* un- (1).	**unfor'matted** *adj.* un- (1).
unfastid'ious *adj.* un- (1).	**unflatt'eringly** *adv.* un- (1).	**unform'ulated** *adj.* un- (1).
unfault'y *adj.* un- (1).	**unflā'voured** *adj.* un- (1).	**unforsā'ken** *adj.* un- (1).
unfā'vourable *adj.* un- (1).	**unflawed'** *adj.* un- (1).	**unforthcom'ing** *adj.* un- (1).
unfā'vourableness *n.* un- (1).	**unflinch'ing** *adj.* un- (1).	**unfor'tified** *adj.* un- (1).
unfā'vourably *adv.* un- (1).	**unflinch'ingly** *adv.* un- (1).	**unfossilif'erous** *adj.* un- (1).
unfeas'ible *adj.* un- (1).	**unfloored'** *adj.* un- (1).	**unfoss'ilised, -z-** *adj.* un- (1).
unfeath'ered *adj.* un- (1).	**unflus'tered** *adj.* un- (1).	**unfos'tered** *adj.* un- (1).
unfed' *adj.* un- (1).	**unfō'cus(s)ed** *adj.* un- (1).	**unfran'chised** *adj.* un- (1).
unfelled' *adj.* un- (1).	**unford'able** *adj.* un- (1).	**unfranked'** *adj.* un- (1).
unfem'inine *adj.* un- (1).	**unforeknow'able** *adj.* un- (1).	**unfrē'quent** *adj.* un- (1).
unfenced' *adj.* un- (1).	**unforeknown'** *adj.* un- (1).	**unfrequen'ted** *adj.* un- (1).
unferment'ed *adj.* un- (1).	**unforesee'able** *adj.* un- (1).	**unfrequent'edness** *n.* un- (1).
unfer'tilised, -z- *adj.* un- (1).	**unforesee'ing** *adj.* un- (1).	**unfrē'quently** *adv.* un- (1).
unfeued' *adj.* un- (1).	**unforeseen'** *adj.* un- (1).	**unfright'ened** *adj.* un- (1).
unfig'ured *adj.* un- (1).	**unforetold'** *adj.* un- (1).	**unfrō'zen** *adj.* un- (1).
unfil'ial *adj.* un- (1).	**unforewarned'** *adj.* un- (1).	**unfruc'tuous** *adj.* un- (1).
unfil'ially *adv.* un- (1).	**unfor'feited** *adj.* un- (1).	**unfruit'ful** *adj.* un- (1).
unfill'able *adj.* un- (1).	**unforged'** *adj.* un- (1).	**unfruit'fully** *adv.* un- (1).
unfilled' *adj.* un- (1).	**unforgett'able** *adj.* un- (1).	**unfruit'fulness** *n.* un- (1).
unfilmed' *adj.* un- (1).	**unforgett'ably** *adv.* un- (1).	**unfū'elled** *adj.* un- (1).
unfil'tered *adj.* un- (1).	**unforgiv'able** *adj.* un- (1).	**unfulfilled'** *adj.* un- (1).
unfired' *adj.* un- (1).	**unforgiv'en** *adj.* un- (1).	**unfunn'y** *adj.* un- (1).
unfirm' *adj.* un- (1).	**unforgive'ness** *n.* un- (1).	**unfurred'** *adj.* un- (1).
unfished' *adj.* un- (1).	**unforgiv'ing** *adj.* un- (1).	**unfurr'owed** *adj.* un- (1).

sounded, of unknown depth: of unascertained meaning (*fig.*); **unfazed'** not perturbed; **unfeared'** not feared: unafraid (*obs.*); **unfear'ful** not afraid. — *adv.* **unfear'-fully.** — *adjs.* **unfear'ing; unfeat'ured** without marked or well-formed features (*lit.* and *fig.*); **unfeed'** not retained by a fee: unpaid; **unfeel'ing** without feeling: without kind or sympathetic feelings: hard-hearted. — *adv.* **unfeel'ingly.** — *n.* **unfeel'ingness.** — *adj.* **unfeigned'** not feigned, real: not feigning, sincere. — *adv.* **unfeign'-edly.** — *n.* **unfeign'edness.** — *adjs.* **unfeign'ing; unfell'-owed** unmatched; **unfelt'** not felt: intangible (*Shak.*). — *v.t.* **unfett'er** to free from fetters. — *adjs.* **unfett'ered** unrestrained; **unfeu'dal** not marked by social attitudes and assumptions like those under the feudal system. — *v.t.* **unfeud'alise, -ize** to defeudalise. — *adjs.* **unfiled'** (*Spens.* **unfilde'**) not rubbed with a file (**file²**), unpolished; **unfiled'** (now *dial.*) undefiled (cf. **file³**); **unfiled'** not placed on a file (**file¹**); **unfill'eted** not bound with a fillet: not boned; **unfil'terable, unfil'trable** unable to pass through a filter (or an ordinary filter); **unfine'** not fine; **unfin'ished** — *n.* **unfin'ishing** (*Milt.*) the leaving unfinished. — *adjs.* **unfit'** not fit: not fitting or suitable: not in fit condition: not meeting required standards. — *n.* an unfit person. — *v.t.* to make unfit: to make unsuitable (for): to disqualify. — *adv.* **unfit'ly** unsuitably, inappropriately. — *n.* **unfit'ness.** — *adj.* **unfitt'ed** not provided (with): without fittings: not made to fit, or tested for fit: not adapted, qualified, or able. — *n.* **unfitt'edness.** — *adj.* **unfitt'ing** unsuitable. — *adv.* **unfitt'ingly.** — *v.t.* **unfix'** to unfasten, detach: to unsettle (*fig.*). — *v.i.* to become loose. — *adj.* **unfixed'.** — *ns.* **unfix'edness, unfix'ity.** — *adj.* **unflapp'able** (*coll.*) imperturbable, never agitated or alarmed. — *n.* **unflappabil'ity.** — *adv.* **unflapp'ably.** *adj.* **unfledged'** not yet fledged: undeveloped: of early youth. — *v.t.* **unflesh'** to remove the flesh from. — *adjs.* **unfleshed'** deprived of flesh, reduced to a skeleton: not fleshed, not having tasted blood, uninitiated; **unflesh'ly** spiritual: incorporeal: not carnal. — *v.i.* **unflush'** to lose a flush of colour (*Arnold*). — *v.t.* **unfold'** (cf. **fold¹**) to open the folds of: to spread out: to tell: to disclose, make known: to reveal, display. — *v.i.* to open out, spread open to the view (*lit.* and *fig.*). — *v.t.* **unfold'** (cf. **fold²**) to let out from a sheep-fold. — *adjs.* **unfold'ed** not folded: opened out from folds; **unfold'ed** not enclosed in a sheep-fold. — *n.* **unfold'er.** — *n.* and *adj.* **unfold'ing** opening out from folds: disclosing. — *n.* and *adj.* **unfold'ing** letting out from a sheep-fold. — *adj.* (of a star; *Shak.*) showing the time for unfolding sheep.

— *v.t.* **unfool'** to undo the fooling of. — *adjs.* **unfoot'ed** untrodden; **unforbid'** (*Milt.*), **unforbidd'en; unforced'.** — *adv.* **unfor'cedly.** — *adjs.* **unfor'cible** without strength (*obs.*): incapable of being forced or (*Milt.*) enforced; **unforebōd'ing** not giving or feeling foreboding; **unfore'skinned** (*Milt.*) circumcised; **unfor'ested** not wooded: not reckoned as deer-forest: deforested; **unforgott'en** (*arch.* **unforgot'**). — *v.t.* **unform'** to unmake. — *adjs.* **unfor'mal** informal; **unfor'malised, -z-** not made formal; **unformed'** unmade, uncreated: formless, unshaped: immature, undeveloped; **unfor'tunate** unlucky: regrettable: of ill omen: (esp. formerly) living by prostitution. — *n.* an unfortunate person. — *adv.* **unfor'tunately** in an unlucky way: by bad luck: I'm sorry to say. — *ns.* **unfor'tunateness; unfor'tune** (*arch.*). — *adjs.* **unfor'tuned; unfought'** (*arch.* **unfought'en**); **unfound'** not found; **unfound'ed** not founded: without foundation, baseless: without bottom, bottomless (*Milt.*). — *adv.* **unfound'edly.** — *adjs.* **unframed'** not formed or fashioned (*lit.* and *fig.*): not set in a frame; **unfraught'** not fraught or charged. — *v.t.* to unload, discharge. — *adj.* **unfree'** not free. in servitude: not free of a corporation. — *n.* **unfree'man** one who is not free of a corporation. — *v.t.* and *v.i.* **unfreeze'** to thaw: to (allow to) progress, move, etc. after a temporary restriction or stoppage: to free (prices, wages, funds) from the control imposed by a standstill order. — *adj.* **unfrett'ed** not eaten away or rubbed: not annoyed or worried. — *n.* **unfriend'** one who is not a friend. — *adj.* **unfriend'ed** not provided with or supported by friends. — *ns.* **unfriend'edness; unfriend'liness.** — *adj.* **unfriend'ly** ill-disposed: somewhat hostile. — *adv.* **unfriend'kindly.** — *n.* **unfriend'ship** (*arch.*) unfriendliness. — *adj.* **unfright'ed** (*arch.*) not frightened. — *v.t.* **unfrock'** to strip of a frock or gown: to depose from priesthood: to remove from a comparable position in another sphere of activity. — *adjs.* **unfrocked'; unfumed'** not fumigated: undistilled (*Milt.*); **unfund'ed** not funded, floating, as a public debt, in the form of exchequer bills and bonds, to be paid up at certain dates. — *v.t.* **unfurl'** to release from being furled: to unfold, display. — *v.i.* to spread open. — *v.t.* **unfur'nish** to deprive (*Shak.*): to deprive of men, defences, furniture. — *adj.* **unfur'nished** not furnished: unsupplied.

Words with prefix **un-** (*continued*)

adjs. **ungain'** (*obs.*, *arch.*, or *dial.*; from **gain²**) indirect: inconvenient: unpleasant: ungainly, awkward: unskilled; **ungain'ful.** — *n.* **ungain'liness.** — *adj.* **ungain'ly**

ungainsaid' *adj.* **un-** (1).	**ungraced'** *adj.* **un-** (1).	**unhand'seled** *adj.* **un-** (1).
ungainsay'able *adj.* **un-** (1).	**ungrace'ful** *adj.* **un-** (1).	**unhang'** *v.t.* **un-** (2).
ungall'ant *adj.* **un-** (1).	**ungrace'fully** *adv.* **un-** (1).	**unhanged'** *adj.* **un-** (1).
ungall'antly *adv.* **un-** (1).	**ungrace'fulness** *n.* **un-** (1).	**unhar'dened** *adj.* **un-** (1).
ungar'bled *adj.* **un-** (1).	**ungrammat'ic, -al** *adjs.* **un-** (1).	**unhar'dy** *adj.* **un-** (1).
ungar'mented *adj.* **un-** (1).	**ungrammat'ically** *adv.* **un-** (1).	**unharmed'** *adj.* **un-** (1).
ungar'nered *adj.* **un-** (1).	**ungrat'ified** *adj.* **un-** (1).	**unharm'ful** *adj.* **un-** (1).
ungar'nished *adj.* **un-** (1).	**ungrave'ly** (*Shak.*) *adv.* **un-** (1).	**unharm'fully** *adv.* **un-** (1).
ungar'tered *adj.* **un-** (1).	**ungroomed'** *adj.* **un-** (1).	**unharm'ing** *adj.* **un-** (1).
ungath'ered *adj.* **un-** (1).	**ungrown'** *adj.* **un-** (1).	**unharmo'nious** *adj.* **un-** (1).
ungauged' *adj.* **un-** (1).	**ungrudged'** *adj.* **un-** (1).	**unhar'vested** *adj.* **un-** (1).
ungen'erous *adj.* **un-** (1).	**ungrudg'ing** *adj.* **un-** (1).	**unhast'ing** *adj.* **un-** (1).
ungen'erously *adv.* **un-** (1).	**ungrudg'ingly** *adv.* **un-** (1).	**unhast'y** *adj.* **un-** (1).
ungenteel' *adj.* **un-** (1).	**unguer'doned** *adj.* **un-** (1).	**unhaunt'ed** *adj.* **un-** (1).
ungenteel'ly *adv.* **un-** (1).	**unguessed'** *adj.* **un-** (1).	**unhaz'arded** *adj.* **un-** (1).
ungen'uine *adj.* **un-** (1).	**unguid'ed** *adj.* **un-** (1).	**unhaz'ardous** *adj.* **un-** (1).
ungen'uineness *n.* **un-** (1).	**unguilt'y** *adj.* **un-** (1).	**unheat'ed** *adj.* **un-** (1).
ungift'ed *adj.* **un-** (1).	**ungyve'** *v.t.* **un-** (2).	**unhedged'** *adj.* **un-** (1).
ungild' *v.t.* **un-** (2).	**ungyved'** *adj.* **un-** (1).	**unheed'ed** *adj.* **un-** (1).
ungild'ed *adj.* **un-** (1).	**unhab'itable** *adj.* **un-** (1).	**unheed'edly** *adv.* **un-** (1).
ungilt' *adj.* **un-** (1).	**unhabit'uated** *adj.* **un-** (1).	**unheed'ful** *adj.* **un-** (1).
ungiv'ing *adj.* **un-** (1).	**unhacked'** *adj.* **un-** (1).	**unheed'fully** *adv.* **un-** (1).
unglad' *adj.* **un-** (1).	**unhack'neyed** *adj.* **un-** (1).	**unheed'ing** *adj.* **un-** (1).
unglazed' *adj.* **un-** (1).	**unhailed'** *adj.* **un-** (1).	**unheed'ingly** *adv.* **un-** (1).
unglossed' *adj.* **un-** (1).	**unhall'ow** *v.t.* **un-** (2).	**unheed'y** *adj.* **un-** (1).
unglove' *v.t.* **un-** (2).	**unhall'owed** *adj.* **un-** (1).	**unhelped'** *adj.* **un-** (1).
ungloved' *adj.* **un-** (1).	**unhamp'ered** *adj.* **un-** (1).	**unhelp'ful** *adj.* **un-** (1).

awkward, clumsy, uncouth. — *adv.* awkwardly. — *adjs.* **ungalled'** not made painful by rubbing: not irritated or inflamed (*fig.*); **ungazed'** not gazed (at; also **ungazed'-upon**). — *v.t.* **ungear'** to unharness (*arch.*): to disconnect a part of a system of moving parts (also *fig.*). — *adjs.* **ungeared'** (*econ.*; of a business, etc.) having its capital in the form of ordinary shares rather than loans requiring fixed interest; **ungē'nial** not sympathetically cheerful: not comfortably warm, raw: not congenial: not favourable to natural growth; **ungen'-itured** (*Shak.*) without means of generation, or not produced by ordinary generation. — *n.* **ungentil'ity**. — *adjs.* **ungen'tle** not gentle: not of gentle birth: not of or befitting the gentle; **ungen'tlemanlike** not like or befitting a gentleman. — Also *adv.* — *n.* **ungen'-tlemanliness**. — *adj.* **ungen'tlemanly** unbecoming a gentleman: not gentlemanlike. — Also *adv.* — *n.* **ungen'tleness**. — *adv.* **ungent'ly**. — *adj.* **ungermane** (*-jər-mān'*) irrelevant. — *v.t.* **unget'** to deny the begetting of: to disown. — *adjs.* **ungetat'able, unget-at'-able** (*coll.*) inaccessible; **unghost'ly** not pertaining to or like a ghost: not spiritual. — *v.t.* **ungird'** to free from a girdle or band: to undo the fastening of and take off. — *adj.* **ungirt'** (or **ungird'ed**) not girt: freed from the girdle: not tightened up, not strengthened for action (*fig.*). — *v.t.* **ungirth'** to remove a girth from: to free from a girth. — *adj.* **ungirthed'**. — *v.t.* **unglue'** to loosen or detach (something glued). — Also (*rare*) *v.i.* — *adj.* **unglued'** no longer held or fixed together by glue (**become, come unglued** to go awry, become confused, come apart; *fig.*). — *v.t.* **ungod'** to divest of divinity: to make godless. — *adj.* **ungod'like**. — *adv.* **ungod'lily** in an ungodly manner. — *n.* **ungod'liness**. — *adjs.* **ungod'ly** not godly: outrageous, unconscionable (*coll.*); **ungored'** (*Shak.* **ungord'**; another reading **ungorg'd'**) unwounded; **ungorged'** not gorged or sated; **ungot'**, **ungott'en** not got or acquired: unbegotten; **ungov'-ernable** uncontrollable: unruly. — *n.* **ungov'ernable-ness**. — *adv.* **ungov'ernably**. — *adj.* **ungov'erned**. — *v.t.* **ungown'** to deprive or divest of a gown: to unfrock. — *adjs.* **ungowned'** not wearing a gown: deprived of one's gown; **ungrā'cious** without grace: graceless: ungraceful: wanting in courtesy, affability or urbanity: behaving with a bad grace: unmannerly: rendering offensive or disagreeable. — *adv.* **ungrā'ciously**. — *n.* **ungrā'ciousness**. — *adjs.* **ungrād'ed** not classified in grades: not adjusted to easy gradients; **ungrassed'** not grown with grass; **ungrate'ful** not feeling gratitude: disagreeable, irksome: not repaying one's labour,

thankless. — *adv.* **ungrate'fully**. — *n.* **ungrate'fulness**. — *adjs.* **ungrazed'** not grazed: (of land) not grazed by livestock; **unground'** not ground; **unground'ed** not based (with *in*): without basis, unreal, false: without sound fundamental instruction. — *adv.* **unground'edly**. — *n.* **unground'edness**. — *v.t.* **unguard'** to render, or leave, unguarded. — *adj.* **unguard'ed** without guard: unprotected: unscreened: incautious: inadvertent. — *adv.* **unguard'edly**. — *n.* **unguard'edness**. — *v.t.* **ungum'** to free from gum or gummed condition. — *adj.* **ungummed'** not gummed: freed from gum or gumming (**come ungummed** of a plan, to go amiss; *slang*).

Words with prefix **un-** (*continued*).

adj. **unhā'ble** an *obs.* form of **unable**. — *v.t.* **unhair'** to deprive of hair. — *v.i.* to become free from hair. — *adjs.* **unhaired'** freed from hair; **unhalsed** (*un-höst'*; *Scott*) unsaluted. — *v.t.* **unhand'** to take the hands off: to let go. — *adv.* **unhand'ily** awkwardly. — *n.* **unhand'-iness**. — *adjs.* **unhan'dled** not handled or managed: not broken in; **unhand'some** not handsome: unskilful in action (*obs.*): unseemly: ungenerous: ungracious: clumsy, inconvenient (*obs.*). — Also *adv.* (*Spens.*). — *adv.* **unhand'somely**. — *n.* **unhand'someness**. — *adj.* **unhand'y** not skilful, awkward: not convenient. — *adv.* **unhapp'ily** in an unhappy manner: unfortunately, regrettably, I'm sorry to say: unsuccessfully: maliciously (*obs.*): unfavourably (*Shak.*): shrewdly (*Shak.*). — *n.* **unhapp'iness**. — *adj.* **unhapp'y** bringing misfortune: not fortunate: miserable: infelicitous, inapt: mischievous (*obs.*). — *v.t.* (*Shak.*) to make unhappy or unfortunate. — *v.t.* **unhar'bour** to dislodge from shelter. — *adj.* **unhar'boured** without a shelter: dislodged from shelter. — *v.t.* **unhar'ness** to take the armour or the harness off. — *adj.* **unhar'nessed** not in, or freed from, armour or harness. — *v.t.* **unhasp'** to unfasten by undoing a hasp. — *v.i.* **unhat'** to take off the hat from respect. — *adjs.* **unhatched'** (**unhatch'd**; *Shak.*) not out of the egg: not developed: not shaded: unhacked; **unhatt'ed** hatless. — *n.* **unhatt'ing** lifting of the hat. — *vs.t.* **unhead'** to take the head from; **unheal'** see **unhele**. — *adjs.* **unheal'able; unhealed'**. — *n.* **unhealth'** ill-health. — *adj.* **unhealth'ful**. — *adv.* **unhealth'fully**. — *n.* **unhealth'fulness**. — *adv.* **unheal'thily**. — *n.* **unheal'thiness**. — *adjs.* **unheal'thy** not healthy: morbid: unfavourable to health: dangerous (*slang*); **unheard'** not heard: not granted a hearing: not heard of, unknown to fame: unprecedented (in Shak., *K. John* V, ii. 133, understood by some as unhaired, beardless); **unheard'-of**. —

<table>
<tr><td>

unher'alded *adj.* un- (1).
unherō'ic, -al *adjs.* un- (1).
unherō'ically *adv.* un- (1).
unhewn' *adj.* un- (1).
unhidd'en *adj.* un- (1).
unhind'ered *adj.* un- (1).
unhired' *adj.* un- (1).
unhitch' *v.t.* un- (2).
unhome'like *adj.* un- (1).
unhome'ly *adj.* un- (1).
unhon'oured *adj.* un- (1).
unhood' *v.t.* un- (2).
unhood'ed *adj.* un- (1, 2).
unhook' *v.t.* un- (2).
unhū'man *adj.* un- (1).
unhū'manise, -ize *v.t.* un- (2).
unhum'bled *adj.* un- (1).
unhunt'ed *adj.* un- (1).
unhurr'ied *adj.* un- (1).
unhurr'iedly *adv.* un- (1).
unhurr'ying *adj.* un- (1).
unhurt' *adj.* un- (1).
unhurt'ful *adj.* un- (1).
unhurt'fully *adv.* un- (1).
unhurt'fulness *n.* un- (1).
unhygien'ic *adj.* un- (1).
unhy'phenated *adj.* un- (1).

</td><td>

unīdentifi'able *adj.* un- (1).
unīdent'ified *adj.* un- (1).
unidiomat'ic *adj.* un- (1).
unidiomat'ically *adv.* un- (1).
unillumed' *adj.* un- (1).
unillu'minated *adj.* un- (1).
unillu'minating *adj.* un- (1).
unillu'mined *adj.* un- (1).
unill'ustrated *adj.* un- (1).
unimbued' *adj.* un- (1).
unimmor'tal (*Milt.*) *adj.* un- (1).
unimpaired' *adj.* un- (1).
unimpart'ed *adj.* un- (1).
unimpēd'ed *adj.* un- (1).
unimpēd'edly *adv.* un- (1).
unimplored' *adj.* un- (1).
unimport'ance *n.* un- (1).
unimport'ant *adj.* un- (1).
unimpreg'nāted (or *-im'*) *adj.* un- (1).
unimpressed' *adj.* un- (1).
unimpress'ible *adj.* un- (1).
unimpress'ionable *adj.* un- (1).
unimpress'ive *adj.* un- (1).
unimpris'oned *adj.* un- (1, 2).
unimpugnable (*-pūn'*) *adj.* un- (1).
uninaug'urated *adj.* un- (1).
unincit'ed *adj.* un- (1).

</td><td>

uninclosed' *adj.* un- (1).
unincor'porated *adj.* un- (1).
unin'dexed *adj.* un- (1).
uninfect'ed *adj.* un- (1).
uninflamed' *adj.* un- (1).
uninflamm'able *adj.* un- (1).
uninflāt'ed *adj.* un- (1).
uninflect'ed *adj.* un- (1).
unin'fluenced *adj.* un- (1).
uninfluen'tial *adj.* un- (1).
uninhab'itable *adj.* un- (1).
uninhab'ited *adj.* un- (1).
uninhib'ited *adj.* un- (1).
unini'tiated *adj.* un- (1).
unin'jured *adj.* un- (1).
uninquīr'ing *adj.* un- (1).
uninquis'itive *adj.* un- (1).
uninscribed' *adj.* un- (1).
uninspired' *adj.* un- (1).
uninspīr'ing *adj.* un- (1).
uninstruct'ed *adj.* un- (1).
uninstruct'ive *adj.* un- (1).
uninsured' *adj.* un- (1).
unin'tegrated *adj.* un- (1).
unintellect'ual *adj.* un- (1).
unintell'igent *adj.* un- (1).
unintelligibil'ity *n.* un- (1).

</td></tr>
</table>

v.t. **unhearse'** (used by Spens. in the *pa.t.***unherst'**) app. to remove from a hearse or a stand for candles at a funeral. — *adj.* **unhearsed'** without a hearse. — *vs.t.* **unheart'** (*Shak.*) to dishearten. — *adv.* **unheed'ily** unheedfully. — *v.t.* **unhele'**, **unheal'** (*Spens.*) to uncover, disclose; **unhelm'** to divest of helmet. — *adjs.* **unhelmed'**, **unhel'meted** without, or divested of, helm or helmet; **unhelp'able** incapable of receiving help; **unheppen** (*un-ep'n*; *Yorks., Linc., Tennyson*; O.N. *heppinn*, dexterous) clumsy. — *v.t.* (*pa.t.*) **unherst** see **unhearse**. — *adj.* **unhes'itating** not hesitating or doubting: prompt: ready. — *adv.* **unhes'itatingly**. — *adj.* **unhide'-bound** not having a skin confining the body (*Milt.*). — *v.t.* **unhinge'** to take from the hinges: to derange. — *adj.* **unhinged'**. — *n.* **unhinge'ment**. — *adjs.* **unhip'** square, not trendy (*slang*); **unhistor'ic, -al** not mentioned in history: not in accordance with history: not having actually existed or happened. — *vs.t.* **unhive'** to drive from a hive; **unhoard'** to take from a hoard. — *adv.* **unhō'lily**. — *n.* **unhō'liness**. — *adjs.* **unhōl'pen** not helped (*arch.*); **unhō'ly** not holy: very wicked: unconscionable, outrageous, unearthly (*coll.*); **unhon'est** (*obs.*) unseemly, indecent, dishonourable: immoral: dishonest. — *v.t.* **unhoop'** to remove hoops from. — *adjs.* **unhoped'** unexpected (*obs.*): beyond what was expected with hope (*arch.*; now **unhoped'-for**); **unhope'ful**. — *adv.* **unhope'fully**. — *v.t.* **unhorse'** to dislodge or throw from a horse: to take a horse or horses from. — *adj.* **unhos'pitable** (now usu. **inhospitable**). — *v.t.* **unhouse'** to deprive of or drive from a house or shelter. — *adjs.* **unhoused'** houseless: deprived of a house; **unhous'eled** (*Shak.* **unhouzz'led**) not having received the sacrament; **unhung'** not hung: without hangings: unhanged; **unhus'banded** uncultivated: without a husband. — *v.t.* **unhusk'** to strip the husk from. — *adj.* **unhyph'enated** without a hyphen or hyphens.

Words with prefix **un-** (*continued*).

adjs. **unīdē'a'd** without ideas: with unfurnished mind; **unīdē'al** not ideal: not idealistic: conveying no idea (*obs.*): without ideas (*obs.*): without ideals. — *n.* **unīdē'alism**. — *adjs.* **unīdēalist'ic**; **unimag'inable**. — *n.* **unimag'inableness**. — *adv.* **unimag'inably**. — *adj.* **unimag'inative** not imaginative, prosaic. — *adv.* **unimag'inatively**. — *n.* **unimag'inativeness**. — *adjs.* **unimag'ined**; **unimpass'ioned** not impassioned, calm, tranquil; **unimpeach'able** not to be impeached: not liable to be accused: free from fault: blameless; **unimpeached'**; **unim'portuned** (or *-tünd', -chōōnd'*; often

-pör') not persistently begged (to do something); **unimposed'**; **unimpōs'ing** unimpressive: not burdensome (*Thomson*); **unimproved'** not made better: not cultivated, cleared, or built upon: not put to use; **uninchanted** see **unenchanted**; **unincum'bered** unencumbered; **unindeared** see **unendeared**; **unin'dexed** not index-linked; **uninforce'able, uninforced** same as **unenforceable, unenforced**; **uniform'ative; uninformed'** not having received information: untaught: not imbued with life or activity; **uninform'ing; unin'terested** not personally concerned: not taking an interest; **unin'teresting**. — *adv.* **unin'terestingly**.

Words with prefix **un-** (*continued*).

v.t. **unjoint'** to disjoint. — *adjs.* **unjoint'ed** disjointed, incoherent: without joints; **unked, unket, unkid** (*ōōngk'id, ungk'id, -it*; *N. and W. England*; forms of **uncouth**) strange, uncomfortable, lonely, eerie; **unkempt'** (see **kemb**) uncombed: unpolished, rough; **unkenned', unkent'** unknown. — *v.t.* **unkenn'el** to dislodge (a fox) from a hole: to let out from a kennel. — *adjs.* **unkept'** not kept: untended; **unket, unkid** see **unked**; **unkīnd'** unnaturally wicked (*obs.*): wanting in kindness: cruel; **unkin'dled** not kindled. — *n.* **unkīnd'liness** want of kindliness. — *adj.* **unkīnd'ly** unnatural: not kind. — *adv.* unnaturally (*Milt.*): against right feeling (*Shak.*): in an unkindly manner: cruelly. — *n.* **unkīnd'ness** want of kindness or affection: cruelty: ill-feeling: a flock of ravens (*obs.*). — *v.t.* **unking'** to deprive of kingship or of a king. — *adjs.* **unking'like; unking'ly** unbecoming a king: unlike a king. — *v.t.* **unkiss'** (*Shak.*) to annul by means of a kiss. — *adjs.* **unkissed'** not kissed; **unknelled** (*un-neld'*) without tolling. — *v.t.* **unknight** (*un-nīt'*) to divest of knighthood. — *adj.* **unknight'ed** not knighted. — *n.* **unknight'liness**. — *adj.* **unknightly** (*un-nīt'li*) unlike, or unbecoming to, a knight. — *adv.* in an unknightly manner. — *v.t.* **unknit** (*un-nit'*) to undo the knitting of: to untie: to smooth out from a frown: to relax. — *v.i.* to become unknit. — *adj.* loose, unfirmed. — *v.t.* **unknot** (*un-not'*) to free from knots: to untie. — *adj.* **unknowable** (*un-nō'a-bl*) incapable of being known. — *n.* an unknowable thing: the first or original cause: that which is cognisable only in its relations. — *n.* **unknow'ableness**. — *adj.* **unknow'ing** ignorant, unaware: ignorant (of) (*arch.*): not knowing (*arch.* or *poet.*): unwitting: unknown (to) (*dial.*). — *adv.* **unknow'ingly**. — *n.* **unknow'ingness**. — *adj.* **unknown** (*un-nōn'*) not known. — *n.* an unknown

---

unintell'igible *adj.* **un-** (1).	**unjoy'ful** *adj.* **un-** (1).	**unliv(e)'able** *adj.* **un-** (1).
unintell'igibly *adv.* **un-** (1).	**unjoy'ous** *adj.* **un-** (1).	**unlive'liness** *n.* **un-** (1).
unintend'ed *adj.* **un-** (1).	**unjust'** *adj.* **un-** (1).	**unlive'ly** *adj.* **un-** (1).
uninten'tional *adj.* **un-** (1).	**unjus'tifiable** (or *-fī'*) *adj.* **un-** (1).	**unlopped'** *adj.* **un-** (1).
unintentional'ity *n.* **un-** (1).	**unjus'tifiably** (or *-fī'*) *adv.* **un-** (1).	**unlos'able** *adj.* **un-** (1).
uninten'tionally *adv.* **un-** (1).	**unjus'tified** *adj.* **un-** (1).	**unlost'** *adj.* **un-** (1).
unintermitt'ed *adj.* **un-** (1).	**unjust'ly** *adv.* **un-** (1).	**unlove'liness** *n.* **un-** (1).
unintermitt'edly *adv.* **un-** (1).	**unjust'ness** *n.* **un-** (1).	**unlove'ly** *adj.* **un-** (1).
unintermitt'ing *adj.* **un-** (1).	**unlā'belled** *adj.* **un-** (1).	**unluxur'iant** *adj.* **un-** (1).
unintermitt'ingly *adv.* **un-** (1).	**unlabō'rious** *adj.* **un-** (1).	**unluxur'ious** *adj.* **un-** (1).
uninter'pretable *adj.* **un-** (1).	**unlā'dylike** *adj.* **un-** (1).	**unmacad'amised, -z-** *adj.* **un-** (1).
uninterrup'ted *adj.* **un-** (1).	**unlament'ed** *adj.* **un-** (1).	**unmaimed'** *adj.* **un-** (1).
uninterrup'tedly *adv.* **un-** (1).	**unleased'** *adj.* **un-** (1).	**unmaintain'able** *adj.* **un-** (1).
unintox'icating *adj.* **un-** (1).	**unleav'ened** *adj.* **un-** (1).	**unmaintained'** *adj.* **un-** (1).
unintroduced' *adj.* **un-** (1).	**unleis'ured** *adj.* **un-** (1).	**unmali'cious** *adj.* **un-** (1).
uninured' *adj.* **un-** (1).	**unleis'urely** *adj.* **un-** (1).	**unmalleabil'ity** *n.* **un-** (1).
uninven'tive *adj.* **un-** (1).	**unlet'** *adj.* **un-** (1).	**unmall'eable** *adj.* **un-** (1).
uninvest'ed *adj.* **un-** (1).	**unlibid'inous** (*Milt.*) *adj.* **un-** (1).	**unman'acle** *v.t.* **un-** (2).
uninvid'ious *adj.* **un-** (1).	**unlife'like** *adj.* **un-** (1).	**unman'acled** *adj.* **un-** (1, 2).
uninvī'ted *adj.* **un-** (1).	**unlim'ited** *adj.* **un-** (1).	**unman'ageable** *adj.* **un-** (1).
uninvī'ting *adj.* **un-** (1).	**unlim'itedly** *adv.* **un-** (1).	**unman'ageableness** *n.* **un-** (1).
uninvolved' *adj.* **un-** (1).	**unlim'itedness** *n.* **un-** (1).	**unman'ageably** *adv.* **un-** (1).
unī'onised, -z- *adj.* **un-** (1).	**unlin'eal** *adj.* **un-** (1).	**unman'aged** *adj.* **un-** (1).
unī'roned *adj.* **un-** (1).	**unliq'uefied** *adj.* **un-** (1).	**unmas'culine** *adj.* **un-** (1).
unjā'ded *adj.* **un-** (1).	**unliq'uidated** *adj.* **un-** (1).	**unmā'ted** *adj.* **un-** (1).
unjaun'diced *adj.* **un-** (1).	**unlit'** *adj.* **un-** (1).	**unmater'nal** *adj.* **un-** (1).
unjeal'ous *adj.* **un-** (1).	**unlit'erary** *adj.* **un-** (1).	**unmathemat'ical** *adj.* **un-** (1).

fāte; fär; hûr; mīne; mōte; för; mūte; mōōn; fŏŏt; dhen (then); *el'ə-mənt* (element)

person or quantity: (with *the*) that which is unknown. — *n.* **unknown'ness.**

Words with prefix **un-** (*continued*).

adjs. **unlā'boured** showing no traces of labour: unworked: unrestrained, easy; **unlā'bouring.** — *vs.t.* **unlace'** to free from being laced: to undo the lacing of: to carve (esp. a rabbit) (*obs.*): to undo, destroy (*Shak.*); **unlade'**to unload. — *adj.* **unlā'den** not laden. — *n.* **unlā'ding.** — *adj.* **unlaid'** not laid. — *vs.t.* **unlash'** (*naut.*) to loose the lashings of; **unlast, unlaste** (*un-läst', -läst'*) Spenserian *pa.t.* and *pa.p.* of **unlace; unlatch'** to lift the latch of. — *n.* **un'law** breach of law (*arch.*): a fine, penalty (*Scots law; obs.*). — *v.t.* **unlaw'** to annul, repeal: to fine (*obs.*). — *adj.* **unlaw'ful** forbidden by law: illegitimate: illicit: acting illegally. — *adv.* **unlaw'fully.** — *n.* **unlaw'fulness.** — *vs.t.* **unlay'** (*naut.*) to untwist; **unlead** (*un-led'; print.*) to take the lead or leads from. — *adjs.* **unlead'ed** (esp. of petrol) having no lead added: (of type) without leading (*print.*); **unleal'** unfaithful. — *v.t.* **unlearn'** to undo the process of learning: to rid one's mind of, eliminate habit(s) of. — *adj.* **unlearned** (*-lûr'nid*; also *poet. -lûrnd'*) having no learning: (*-lûrnd'*) not learnt, got up, acquired: eliminated by unlearning. — *adv.* **unlear'nedly.** — *n.* **unlear'nedness.** — *adj.* and *pa.p.* **unlearnt** (*-lûrnt'*) not learnt: eliminated by unlearning. — *v.t.* **unleash'** to free from a leash, let go. — *adjs.* **unled'** not led, without guidance; **unless'oned** not instructed; **unlett'able** (of a building) that cannot be let, usu. because it is in unfit condition; **unlett'ered** unlearned: illiterate: without lettering; **unlī'censed** without a licence: unauthorised; **unlich** (*un-lich'*; *Spens.*) unlike; **unlicked'** not licked: not licked into shape. — *v.t.* **unlid'** to uncover, open. — *adjs.* **unlidd'ed** lidless; **unlight'ed; unlight'ened; unlight'some** (*Milt.*) without light. — *adj.* and *adv.* (tending to become a *prep.*) **unlike'** not like: unlikely (*Spens., Shak.*). — *n.* one who or that which is unlike. — *adj.* **unlik(e)'able** not likeable. — *ns.* **unlike'lihood, unlike'liness** improbability. — *adj.* **unlike'ly** not likely: improbable: unpromising (*obs.*): unprepossessing (*obs.* or *dial.*): unsuitable (*obs.*). — *adv.* in an unlikely manner, improbably. — *n.* **unlike'ness** want of resemblance. — *vs.t.* **unlim'ber** to remove (a gun) from its limber ready for use; **unlime'** to free from lime. — *adj.* **unlimed'** not limed. — *v.t.* **unline'** to remove the lining from. — *adj.* **unlined'** without lines or lining. — *v.t.* **unlink'** to undo the linking or links of. — *v.i.* to become unlinked. — *adjs.* **unlinked'** not linked; **unliq'uored** (*Milt.*) not in liquor, sober; **unlist'ed** not entered in a list: (of a telephone number) not listed in a directory, ex-directory (*U.S.*): (of companies and securities) not quoted on the Stock Exchange's official list; **unlis'tened** not listened to (*poet.*; also **unlis'tened-to**); **unlis'tening.** — *v.t.* **unlive** (*un-liv'*) to undo the living of: to live in the contrary manner to: to live down: (*un-līv'*) to deprive of life (*Shak.*). — *adjs.* **unlived'-in** not lived in; **unliv'ing.** — *v.t.* **unload'** to take the load or charge from: to discharge: to disburden: to remove as a load: to get rid of: to dump. — *v.i.* to discharge freight. — *adj.* **unload'ed** not loaded: discharged. — *ns.* **unload'er; unload'ing.** — *adj.* **unlocā'ted** not located: not surveyed or marked off (*U.S.*). — *v.t.* **unlock'** to undo the locking of: to free from being locked up: to let loose: to open, make accessible, or disclose. — *v.i.* to become unlocked. — *adjs.* **unlock'able; unlocked'; unlog'ical** not logical: illogical; **unlooked'** not looked (at, into); **unlooked'-for** unexpected. — *vs.t.* **unloose'** to loosen, unfasten, detach (also, more usu., **unloos'en**): to set free: to discharge (a debt, etc.) (*Scot.*); **unlord'** to strip of the dignity of a lord. — *adjs.* **unlord'ded** deprived of, or not raised to, the rank of lord: not lorded over, without a lord; **unlord'ly; unlov'able** (also **unlove'able**). — *v.t.* **unlove'** to cease to love: not to love. — *n.* (*un'*) absence of love. — *adjs.* **unloved'; unlov'erlike; unlov'ing.** — *adv.* **unlov'ingly.** — *n.* **unlov'ingness.** — *adv.* **unluck'ily** in an unlucky way: by bad luck: I'm sorry to say, unfortunately. — *n.* **unluck'iness.** — *adj.* **unluck'y** unfortunate: ill-omened: bringing ill-luck: not praiseworthy (*arch.*).

Words with prefix **un-** (*continued*).

adjs. **unmade'** not made: self-existent: subjected to unmaking; **unmaid'enly** unbecoming a maiden: not like a maiden; **unmade-up'** not made up: (of a road) not made (q.v.): (of a person) not wearing make-up; **unmail'able** (*U.S.*) incapable of being transmitted or delivered by post; **unmailed'** not clad in mail (**mail¹**): not sent by post (**mail²**); **unmā'kable.** — *v.t.* **unmake'** to undo the making of: to undo, ruin. — *n.* **unmā'king.** — *v.t.* **unman'** to deprive of the nature, attributes or powers of humanity, manhood, or maleness: to deprive of fortitude: to deprive of men. — *adv.* **unman'fully.** — *adj.* **unman'like.** — *n.* **unman'liness.** — *adjs.* **unman'ly** not becoming a man: unworthy of a noble mind: base: cowardly; **unmanned'** without a crew: without a garrison: without inhabitants: untamed (esp. of a hawk): deprived of fortitude; **unmann'ered** unman-

unmatric'ulated *adj.* un- (1).	**unmix'edly** *adv.* un- (1).	**unnour'ishing** *adj.* un- (1).
unmatured' *adj.* un- (1).	**unmod'ernised, -z-** *adj.* un- (1).	**unobjec'tionable** *adj.* un- (1).
unmeek' *adj.* un- (1).	**unmod'ifiable** *adj.* un- (1).	**unobjec'tionably** *adv.* un- (1).
unmell'owed *adj.* un- (1).	**unmod'ifiableness** *n.* un- (1).	**unobnox'ious** *adj.* un- (1).
unmelo'dious *adj.* un- (1).	**unmod'ified** *adj.* un- (1).	**unobscured'** *adj.* un- (1).
unmelt'ed *adj.* un- (1).	**unmod'ulated** *adj.* un- (1).	**unobstruc'ted** *adj.* un- (1).
unmem'orable *adj.* un- (1).	**unmois'tened** *adj.* un- (1).	**unobstruc'tive** *adj.* un- (1).
unmer'cenary *adj.* un- (1).	**unmolest'ed** *adj.* un- (1).	**unobtain'able** *adj.* un- (1).
unmer'chantable *adj.* un- (1).	**unmort'gaged** *adj.* un- (1).	**unobtained'** *adj.* un- (1).
unmet'alled *adj.* un- (1).	**unmort'ified** *adj.* un- (1).	**unobtru'sive** *adj.* un- (1).
unmetaphor'ical *adj.* un- (1).	**unmoth'erly** *adj.* un- (1).	**unobtru'sively** *adv.* un- (1).
unmetaphys'ical *adj.* un- (1).	**unmourned'** *adj.* un- (1).	**unobtru'siveness** *n.* un- (1).
unmethod'ical *adj.* un- (1).	**unmown'** *adj.* un- (1).	**unob'vious** *adj.* un- (1).
unmeth'odised, -z-*adj.* un- (1).	**unmuni'tioned** *adj.* un- (1).	**unocc'upied** *adj.* un- (1).
unmet'rical *adj.* un- (1).	**unmur'muring** *adj.* un- (1).	**unoff'ered** *adj.* un- (1).
unmil'itary *adj.* un- (1).	**unmur'muringly** *adv.* un- (1).	**unoiled'** *adj.* un- (1).
unmilked' *adj.* un- (1).	**unmūs'ical** *adj.* un- (1).	**unopposed'** *adj.* un- (1).
unmilled' *adj.* un- (1).	**unmūs'ically** *adv.* un- (1).	**unoppress'ive** *adj.* un- (1).
unming'led *adj.* un- (1).	**unmū'tilated** *adj.* un- (1).	**unordained'** *adj.* un- (1).
unministē'rial *adj.* un- (1).	**unneed'ed** *adj.* un- (1).	**unor'ganised, -z-** *adj.* un- (1).
unmirac'ulous *adj.* un- (1).	**unneed'ful** *adj.* un- (1).	**unornamen'tal** *adj.* un- (1).
unmī'ry *adj.* un- (1).	**unneed'fully** *adv.* un- (1).	**unor'namented** (or **-ment'**) *adj.*
unmissed' *adj.* un- (1).	**unnō'ted** *adj.* un- (1).	un- (1).
unmistāk'able *adj.* un- (1).	**unnō'ticeable** *adj.* un- (1).	**unor'thodox** *adj.* un- (1).
unmistāk'ably *adv.* un- (1).	**unnō'ticed** *adj.* un- (1).	**unor'thodoxly** *adv.* un- (1).
unmistrust'ful *adj.* un- (1).	**unnō'ticing** *adj.* un- (1).	**unor'thodoxy** *n.* un- (1).
unmixed' *adj.* un- (1).	**unnour'ished** *adj.* un- (1).	**unoss'ified** *adj.* un- (1).

For other sounds see detailed chart of pronunciation.

nerly: free from mannerism. — *n.* **unmann′erliness.** — *adj.* **unmann′erly** not mannerly: ill-bred. — *adv.* in an unmannerly manner. — *v.t.* **unman′tle** to divest of a mantle: to dismantle (*rare*). — *v.i.* to take off one's mantle. — *adjs.* **unmanufac′tured** in a raw state; **unmanured′** not manured: untilled (*obs.*); **unmarked′** bearing no mark: not noticed; **unmar′ketable** not suitable for the market, not saleable; **unmarred′** (*Spens.* **unmard′**) not marred; **unmarr′iable** (*obs.*), **unmarr′iageable.** — *n.* **unmarr′iageableness.** — *adj.* **unmarr′ied** not married, usu. never having been married: freed from marriage. — *v.t.* **unmarr′y** to dissolve the marriage of. — *v.i.* to dissolve one's marriage. — *v.t.* **unmask′** to take a mask or a disguise from: to discover the identity of (e.g. a thief) (*fig.*): to reveal the place of (a gun, battery) by firing: to expose, show up. — *v.i.* to put off a mask. — *adj.* **unmasked′** not wearing a mask: undisguised: divested of mask or disguise: revealed (of e.g. identity). — *ns.* **unmask′er; unmask′ing.** — *adjs.* **unmas′tered** uncontrolled: not overcome: without a master; **unmatch′able; unmatched′** matchless: not accompanied by a match or like; **unmatē′rial** not composed of matter; **unmatē′rialised, -z-; unmean′ing** meaningless: purposeless: expressionless. — *adv.* **unmean′ingly.** — *n.* **unmean′ingness.** — *adjs.* **unmeant** (*un-ment′*); **unmeas′urable** immeasurable: too great to measure: inordinate: not susceptible of measurement. — *adv.* **unmeas′urably.** — *adjs.* **unmeas′ured; unmechan′ic, -al.** — *v.t.* **unmech′anise, -ize** to disorganise (*Sterne*). — *adjs.* **unmech′anised, -z-** disorganised: not mechanised; **unmedicinable** (*un-med′sin-ə-bl*) incurable: unable to cure; **unmed′itated** not meditated, unpremeditated; **unmeet′** not meet, unfit. — *adv.* **unmeet′ly.** — *n.* **unmeet′ness.** — *adj.* **unmen′tionable** not fit to be mentioned. — *n.* **unmen′tionableness.** — *n.pl.* **unmen′tionables** otherwise *inexpressibles*, a 19th-cent. would-be humorous name for trousers: now usu. used for articles of underclothing. — *adj.* **unmer′ciful** merciless: excessively and unpleasantly great. — *adv.* **unmer′cifully.** — *n.* **unmer′cifulness.** — *adjs.* **unmer′itable** (*Shak.*) undeserving; **unmer′ited.** — *adv.* **unmer′itedly.** — *adjs.* **unmer′iting; unmet′** not met: (of a payment, need, etc.) not satisfied; **unmē′ted** not meted or measured. — *v.t.* **unmew′** to free, release as if from a mew or cage. — *adjs.* **unmind′ed** unheeded; **unmind′ful** not keeping in mind, regardless (of). — *adv.* **unmind′fully.** — *n.* **unmind′fulness.** — *adj.* **unmit′igable** that cannot be mitigated. — *adv.* **unmit′igably.** — *adj.* **unmit′igated** not mitigated: unqualified, out-and-out.

— *adv.* **unmit′igatedly.** — *adjs.* **unmoaned′** not lamented; **unmō′dish** unfashionable; **unmon′eyed** (**unmon′ied**) without money: not rich. — *v.t.* **unmoor′** to loose from moorings. — *v.i.* to cast off moorings. — *adjs.* **unmor′al** having no relation to morality: amoral; **unmor′alised, -z-** not moralised upon: having no moral attached: without morality; **unmor′alising, -z-.** — *n.* **unmoral′ity** detachment from questions of morality. — *adjs.* **unmor′tised** disjoined from a mortise (*lit.* and *fig.*); **un-Mosā′ic** not of or according to *Moses* or the Mosaic law; **unmō′tivated** having no motive: lacking incentive; **unmō′tived** without motive: without an artistic motive. — *v.t.* **unmould′** to change or destroy the form of. — *adj.* **unmould′ed** not moulded. — *v.t.* **unmount′** to remove from mountings or mount: to dismount. — *v.i.* to dismount. — *adjs.* **unmount′ed** not mounted; **unmov′able** (also **unmove′able**) immovable: not movable. — *adv.* **unmov(e)′ably.** — *adj.* **unmoved′** not moved, firm: not touched by emotion, calm. — *adv.* **unmov′edly.** — *adj.* **unmov′ing.** — *v.t.* **unmuff′le** to take a muffle, muffling, or covering from. — *v.i.* to throw off mufflings. — *v.t* **unmuzz′le** to take a muzzle off. — *adj.* **unmuzz′led.** — *n.* **unmuzz′ling.**

Words with prefix **un-** (*continued*).

v.t. **unnail′** (*un-nāl′*) to free from nails or from being nailed. — *adjs.* **unnam(e)able** (*un-nā′mə-bl*) impossible to name: not to be named; **unnamed** (*un-nāmd′*); **unnaneld** Shakespearian spelling of **unaneled; unnative** (*un-nā′tiv*) not native; **unnatural** (*un-nat′ū-rəl*) not according to nature: without natural affection: monstrous, heinous: (of a sexual act, vice, etc.) considered not only immoral but also unacceptably indecent or abnormal (e.g. buggery, sodomy). — *v.t.* **unnat′uralise, -ize** to make unnatural: to divest of nationality. — *adj.* **unnat′uralised, -z-** not naturalised. — *adv.* **unnat′urally** in an unnatural way (esp. *not unnaturally* of course, naturally). — *n.* **unnat′uralness.** — *adjs.* **unnavigable** (*un-nav′*) not navigable; **unnav′igated.** — *adv.* **unnecessarily** (*un-nes′*). — *n.* **unnec′essariness.** — *adjs.* **unnec′essary** not necessary; **unneighboured** (*un-nā′bərd*) without neighbours. — *n.* **unneigh′bourliness.** — *adj.* **unneigh′bourly** not neighbourly, friendly, or social. — *adv.* in an unneighbourly manner. — *v.t.* **unnerve** (*un-nûrv′*) to deprive of nerve, strength, or vigour: to weaken: to disconcert. — *adjs.* **unnerved′; unnerv′ing.** — *v.t.* **unnest** (*un-nest′*) to turn out of a nest (*lit.* and *fig.*). — *adv.* **unnethes** see **uneath.** — *adjs.* **unnett′ed** not enclosed in a net; **unnō′ble** not noble: ignoble (*Spens.*,

---

unostentā′tious *adj.* **un-** (1).
unostentā′tiously *adv.* **un-** (1).
unostentā′tiousness *n.* **un-** (1).
unovercome′ *adj.* **un-** (1).
unoverthrown′ *adj.* **un-** (1).
unox′idised, -z- *adj.* **un-** (1).
unpac′ified *adj.* **un-** (1).
unpaid′ *adj.* **un-** (1).
unpained′ *adj.* **un-** (1).
unpain′ful *adj.* **un-** (1).
unpal′sied *adj.* **un-** (1).
unpam′pered *adj.* **un-** (1).
unpar′donable *adj.* **un-** (1).
unpar′donableness *n.* **un-** (1).
unpar′donably *adv.* **un-** (1).
unpar′doned *adj.* **un-** (1).
unpar′doning *adj.* **un-** (1).
unpar′tial *adj.* **un-** (1).
unpas′teurised, -z- *adj.* **un-** (1).
unpas′toral *adj.* **un-** (1).
unpas′tured *adj.* **un-** (1).
unpā′tented *adj.* **un-** (1).
unpathed (*-pädhd′*) *adj.* **un-** (1).
unpathet′ic *adj.* **un-** (1).
unpath′wayed *adj.* **un-** (1).
unpatriot′ic *adj.* **un-** (1).
unpatriot′ically *adv.* **un-** (1).

unpat′ronised, -z- *adj.* **un-** (1).
unpeace′able *adj.* **un-** (1).
unpeace′ableness *n.* **un-** (1).
unpeace′ful *adj.* **un-** (1).
unpeace′fully *adv.* **un-** (1).
unped′igreed *adj.* **un-** (1).
unpeg′ *v.t.* **un-** (2).
unpen′sioned *adj.* **un-** (1).
unpepp′ered *adj.* **un-** (1).
unperceiv′able *adj.* **un-** (1).
unperceiv′ably *adv.* **un-** (1).
unperceived′ *adj.* **un-** (1).
unperceiv′edly *adv.* **un-** (1).
unpercep′tive *adj.* **un-** (1).
unper′forated *adj.* **un-** (1).
unperformed′ *adj.* **un-** (1).
unperform′ing *adj.* **un-** (1).
unperfumed′ (or *-pûr′*) *adj.* **un-** (1).
unper′ilous *adj.* **un-** (1).
unper′ishable *adj.* **un-** (1).
unper′ished *adj.* **un-** (1).
unper′ishing *adj.* **un-** (1).
unper′jured *adj.* **un-** (1).
unper′petrated *adj.* **un-** (1).
unperplex′ *v.t.* **un-** (2).
unperplexed′ *adj.* **un-** (1).
unper′secuted *adj.* **un-** (1).

unpersuād′able *adj.* **un-** (1).
unpersuād′ableness *n.* **un-** (1).
unpersuād′ed *adj.* **un-** (1).
unpersuās′ive *adj.* **un-** (1).
unperturbed′ *adj.* **un-** (1).
unphilosoph′ic, -al *adjs.* **un-** (1).
unphilosoph′ically *adv.* **un-** (1).
unphonet′ic *adj.* **un-** (1).
unpierced′ *adj.* **un-** (1).
unpill′owed *adj.* **un-** (1).
unpī′loted *adj.* **un-** (1).
unpinned′ *adj.* **un-** (1, 2).
unpit′ied *adj.* **un-** (1).
unpit′iful *adj.* **un-** (1).
unpit′ifully *adv.* **un-** (1).
unpit′ifulness *n.* **un-** (1).
unpit′ying *adj.* **un-** (1).
unpit′yingly *adv.* **un-** (1).
unplagued′ *adj.* **un-** (1).
unplait′ *v.t.* **un-** (2).
unplait′ed *adj.* **un-** (1, 2).
unplanked′ *adj.* **un-** (1).
unplanned′ *adj.* **un-** (1).
unplant′ed *adj.* **un-** (1).
unplast′ered *adj.* **un-** (1).
unplay′able *adj.* **un-** (1).
unpleat′ed *adj.* **un-** (1).

---

fāte; fär; hûr; mīne; mōte; för; mūte; mōōn; fōōt; dhen (then); *el′ə-mənt* (element)

Shak.). — *v.t.* to deprive of nobility. — *adjs.* **unnumbered** (*un-num'bərd*) not counted, too many to be numbered: not marked or provided with a number; **unnurtured** (*un-nûr'chərd*) not nurtured or educated: ill-bred.

Words with prefix **un-** (*continued*).

adjs. **unobē'dient** disobedient; **unobeyed'** (*Milt.*); **unobserv'able.** — *n.* **unobser'vance** failure to observe (rules, etc.): failure to notice: lack of observing power: inattention. — *adjs.* **unobser'vant; unobserved'.** — *adv.* **unobserv'edly.** — *adjs.* **unobser'ving; unoffend'ed; unoffend'ing; unoffen'sive** inoffensive; **unoff'icered; unoffi'cial** not official. — *adv.* **unoffi'cially.** — *adj.* **unoffi'cious** not officious. — *adv.* **unoften** (*un-of'n; rare*) seldom (usu. as *not unoften*). — *adjs.* **unō'pened** not opened: of a book, not having the leaves cut apart; **unop'erative** inoperative. — *v.t.* **unor'der** to countermand. — *adjs.* **unor'dered** disordered: unarranged, not ordered or commanded; **unor'derly** not orderly; **unor'dinary** not ordinary; **unorig'inal** not original: without origin or birth (*Milt*). — *n.* **unoriginality** (-*al'*). — *adjs.* **unorig'inate, -d** not originated; **unowed'** not owed or due: unowned (*Shak.*); **unowned'** unavowed, unacknowledged: ownerless: (*un-ō'nid*) lost (*Milt.*).

Words with prefix **un-** (*continued*).

v.t. **unpack'** to undo the packing of: to take out of a pack: to open: to remove a pack from (a pack animal). — *v.i.* to do unpacking. — *adj.* **unpacked'** subjected to unpacking: (*un'pakt'*) not packed. — *ns.* **unpack'er; unpack'ing.** — *adj.* **unpaged'** without numbering of pages. — *v.t.* **unpaint'** to free from paint: to paint out, obliterate by painting over. — *adjs.* **unpaint'able; unpaint'ed** not painted; **unpaired'** not paired: not forming one of a pair; **unpal'atable** unpleasant to taste, distasteful, disagreeable (*lit.* and *fig.*). — *adv.* **unpal'atably.** — *v.t.* **unpan'el** (*obs.*; also **unpann'el**; from *panel n.*, a saddle) to unsaddle. — *adjs.* **unpan'elled** not panelled; **unpanged'** without pangs. — *v.t.* **unpā'per** to remove paper from. — *adj.* **unpā'pered** not papered. — *v.t.* **unpar'adise** to turn out of Paradise: to make no longer a paradise. — *adjs.* **unpar'agoned** unmatched; **unpar'allel** not parallel; **unpar'alleled** without parallel or equal; **unpared'** (of fruit) not having the skin removed: (of nails) not cut; **unparent'al** not befitting a parent; **unpā'rented** without parent or acknowledged parent, or parental care; **unparliament'ary** contrary to the usages of Parliament: not such as may be spoken, or (of language) used, in Parliament; **unpass'able** impassable: (of money) not current. — *n.* **unpass'ableness.** — *adjs.* **unpass'ionate, unpass'ioned** without passions: calm: dispassionate; **unpatt'erned** unexampled, unequalled: without a pattern; **unpaved'** without pavement: gelded (*Shak.*); **unpavil'ioned** without a canopy. — *v.t.* **unpay'** to make good, undo, do away by payment. — *adjs.* **unpay'able; unpeeled'** not peeled: (Shak., *Love's Lab. Lost* II, i. 88) according to some, stripped, desolate (others think it a misprint for **unpeopled**, without servants, the folio reading); **unpeer'able** not to be matched; **unpeered'** unequalled. — *v.t.* **unpen'** to let out from a pen. — *adjs.* **unpenned'** unwritten: unconfined: let loose; **unpenn'ied** without pennies; **unpent'** not penned in. — *v.t.* **unpeo'ple** to empty of people. — *adj.* **unpeo'pled** uninhabited: without servants: depopulated. — *v.t.* **unperch'** to drive from a perch. — *adj.* **unper'fect** (now *rare*) imperfect: unskilled. — *n.* **unperfec'tion** (*obs.*). — *adv.* **unper'fectly** (*obs.*). — *ns.* **unper'fectness** (*rare*); **un'per'son** an individual whose existence is officially denied, ignored, or deleted from record, e.g. one who has been politically superseded. — *v.t.* to make (someone) into an unperson. — *v.t.* **unpervert'** to reconvert. — *adj.* **unpervert'ed** not perverted. — *v.t.* **unpick'** to pick loose, undo by picking. — *adjs.* **unpick'able** impossible to pick: able to be unpicked; **unpicked'** not gathered: not selected: not having had unwanted material removed by picking: picked loose; **unpill'ared** stripped of pillars: without pillars. — *v.t.* **unpin'** to free from pins or pinning: to unfasten the dress of by removing pins. — *adj.* **unpinked', unpinkt'** (*Shak.*) not pinked, not adorned with punched holes. — *v.t.* **unplace'** to displace. — *adj.* **unplaced'** not assigned to or set in a place: not inducted to a church: not appointed to an office: not among the first three in a race; **unplained'** (*Spens.*) not lamented; **unplau'sible** implausible. — *adv.* **unplau'sibly.** — *adjs.* **unplau'sive** not approving; **unpleas'ant** not pleasant: disagreeable. — *adv.* **unpleas'antly.** — *ns.* **unpleas'antness** the state or quality of being unpleasant, disagreeableness: a disagreeable incident: disagreement involving open hostility; **unpleas'antry** want of pleasantness: any unpleasant occurrence, any discomfort. — *adjs.* **unpleased'; unpleas'ing** not pleasing: displeasing. — *adv.* **unpleas'ingly.** — *adj.* **unpleas'urable.** — *adv.* **unpleas'urably.** — *v.t.* **unplumb'** to remove the lead from. — *adj.* **unplumbed'** unsounded: unfathomed. — *v.t.* **unplume'** to strip of feathers or plumes (often *fig.*). — *adj.* **unpoint'ed** not pointed:

---

without point or points: with joints uncemented. — *v.t.* **unpoi′son** to rid of poison, cure of poisoning. — *adjs.* **unpoi′soned** not poisoned; **unpol′icied** without organised political organisation: impolitic; **unpolite′** unpolished (*obs.*): impolite: inelegant (*obs.*). — *adv.* **unpolite′ly.** — *n.* **unpolite′ness.** — *adj.* **unpolled′** not polled: not having voted. — *v.t.* **unpope′** to divest of popedom. — *adjs.* **unpor′tioned** without a portion; **unpossessed′** not possessed: unprejudiced (*obs.*): not in possession; **unpossess′ing** (*Shak.*) without possessions; **unposs′ible** (*Shak.*; *dial.*) impossible; **unpost′ed** not posted, in any sense: not posted up: without a post; **unpō′table** undrinkable, unfit to drink; **unprac′ticable** (formerly common) impracticable; **unprac′tised** having little or no practice or experience, inexpert: not carried out in practice: not yet familiar through practice (*obs.*). — *n.* **unprac′tisedness.** — *v.t.* **unpraise′** to dispraise: to deprive of praise. — *adjs.* **unpraised′** not praised; **unpraise′worthy.** — *vs.t.* **unpray′** to revoke the praying of; **unpreach′** to recant in preaching: to undo the preaching of. — *adjs.* **unpreach′ing** not preaching; **unprec′edented** (*-pres′,* or *-prēs′*) not warranted by judicial, etc., precedent: of which there has been no previous instance. — *adv.* **unprec′edentedly.** — *v.i.* **unpredict′** (*Milt.*) to revoke what has been predicted. — *n.* **unpredictabil′ity.** — *adj.* **unpredict′able** that cannot be foretold: (of a person, thing) liable to behave in a way that cannot be predicted. — *adv.* **unpredict′ably.** — *adjs.* **unpreferred′** without preferment or advancement; **unpreg′nant** (*Shak.*) slow-witted, unready, ineffective: not quickened by a lively sense (of); **unprelat′ical** unbecoming in or to a prelate: not episcopal; **unpremed′itable** not to be foreseen; **unpremed′itated** not studied or purposed beforehand. — *adv.* **unpremed′itatedly.** — *ns.* **unpremed′itatedness; unpremedită′tion.** — *v.t.* **unprepare′** to make unprepared. — *adj.* **unprepared′** not prepared or ready: not prepared for death: without preparation. — *adv.* **unprepā′redly.** — *n.* **unprepā′redness.** — *adjs.* **unprepossessed′** not prepossessed or prejudiced; **unprepossess′ing** not predisposing others in one's favour, unpleasing; **unpresent′able** not fit to be seen; **unpretend′ing** not pretending or making pretence: modest. — *adv.* **unpreten′dingly.** — *adjs.* **unprevail′ing** unavailing; **unpreven′table.** — *n.* **unpreven′tableness.** — *adjs.* **unpreven′ted** not anticipated or preceded (*obs.*): not prevented or obviated; **unpriced′** having no fixed or stated price: beyond price, priceless. — *v.t.* **unpriest′** to divest of priesthood. — *adjs.* **unpriest′ly** unbecoming, unlike, not of the nature

of, a priest; **unprin′cipled** uninstructed (*Milt.*): without good principles: not based on or in accordance with principles: not restrained by conscience: profligate; **unprint′able** not fit to be printed; **unprint′ed; unprīz′able** (*Shak.*) worthless: beyond price; **unprized′** not prized; **unprocē′dūral** not in accordance with established or accepted procedures; **unprofessed′; unprofess′ional** not of a profession or the profession in question: beyond the limits of one's profession: unbecoming to a member of a particular profession. — *adv.* **unprofess′ionally.** — *adjs.* **unprof′ited** without profit or advantage; **unprop′er** improper: common, not one's own (*Shak.*). — *adv.* **unprop′erly.** — *adj.* **unpropor′tionable** out of due proportion. — *adv.* **unpropor′tionably.** — *adj.* **unpropor′tionate** out of due proportion. — *adv.* **unpropor′tionately.** — *adj.* **unpropor′tioned** not proportioned. — *v.t.* **unprot′estantise, -ize** to transform from Protestantism: to strip of Protestant character. — *adj.* **unprotest′ed** not objected to or protested against. — *v.t.* **unprovide′** (*Shak.*) to unfurnish, to deprive of what is necessary. — *adj.* **unprovī′ded** not furnished, provided, or provided for (also **unprovī′ded-for**). — *adv.* **unprovī′dedly.** — *adj.* **unprov′ident** (*Shak.*) improvident. — *v.t.* **un′provoke** (*Shak.*) to counteract provocation of. — *adj.* **unprovoked′** not provoked: uncalled for. — *adv.* **unprovō′kedly.** — *adj.* **unprovō′king.** — *v.t.* **unpurse′** to relax (the lips) from pursing: to disburse. — *adjs.* **unpurveyed′** (*Spens.* **unpurvaide′**) unprovided or unprepared (*obs.*): not provided with (with *of*; *Spens.*): not purveyed; **unputdown′able** (*coll.*) of a book, too absorbing to be set aside, compelling one to read to the end without interruption.

Words with prefix **un-** (*continued*).
adj. **unqual′it(i)ed** (*Shak.*) bereft of qualities. — *v.t.* **unqueen′** to deprive of a queen: in bee-keeping, to deprive (a beehive) of a queen bee. — *adj.* **unques′tionable** not to be questioned, certain, beyond doubt: averse to conversation, or perh. impatient of question (*Shak.*). — *adv.* **unques′tionably** in such a way as to be unquestionable: certainly, without doubt. — *adjs.* **unques′tioned** not called in question: not subjected to questioning: not examined; **unques′tioning; unquī′et** disturbed: restless: uneasy. — *n.* disquiet, inquietude. — *v.t.* to disquiet. — *adv.* **unquī′etly.** — *n.* **unquī′etness.** — *adj.* **unquōt′able** unsuitable or unfit for quotation. — *v.i.* **unquote′** to close a quotation: to mark the end of a quoted passage with superscript comma(s). — used as *interj.* to indicate that a quotation is finished.

unpros′perous *adj.* un- (1).	**unqual′ifiable** *adj.* un- (1).	**unrebuked′** *adj.* un- (1).
unpros′perously *adv.* un- (1).	**unqual′ified** *adj.* un- (1).	**unrecap′turable** *adj.* un- (1).
unpros′perousness *n.* un- (1).	**unqual′ifiedly** *adv.* un- (1).	**unreceipt′ed** *adj.* un- (1).
unprotec′ted *adj.* un- (1).	**unqual′ifiedness** *n.* un- (1).	**unreceived′** *adj.* un- (1).
unprotec′tedness *n.* un- (1).	**unqual′ify** *v.t.* un- (2).	**unrecep′tive** *adj.* un- (1).
unprotest′ing *adj.* un- (1).	**unquanti′fied** *adj.* un- (1).	**unrecip′rocated** *adj.* un- (1).
unprov′able *adj.* un- (1).	**unquant′ised, -z-** *adj.* un- (1).	**unreck′onable** *adj.* un- (1).
unproved′ *adj.* un- (1).	**unquarr′ied** *adj.* un- (1).	**unreck′oned** *adj.* un- (1).
unprō′ven *adj.* un- (1).	**unqueen′** (*Shak.*) *v.t.* un- (2).	**unreclaim′able** *adj.* un- (1).
unprovis′ioned *adj.* un- (1).	**unqueened′** *adj.* un- (2).	**unreclaim′ably** *adv.* un- (1).
unprovoc′ative *adj.* un- (1).	**unqueen′like** *adj.* un- (1).	**unreclaimed′** *adj.* un- (1).
unpruned′ *adj.* un- (1).	**unqueen′ly** *adj.* un- (1).	**unrec′ognīsable, -z-** (or -*nīz′*) *adj.* un- (1).
unpub′lished *adj.* un- (1).	**unquelled′** *adj.* un- (1).	
unpuck′ered *adj.* un- (1).	**unquench′able** *adj.* un- (1).	**unrec′ognīsably, -z-** (or -*nīz′*) *adv.* un- (1).
unpulled′ *adj.* un- (1).	**unquench′ably** *adv.* un- (1).	
unpunct′ual *adj.* un- (1).	**unquenched′** *adj.* un- (1).	**unrec′ognised, -z-** *adj.* un- (1).
unpunctual′ity *n.* un- (1).	**unquick′ened** *adj.* un- (1).	**unrec′ognising, -z-** *adj.* un- (1).
unpunct′uated *adj.* un- (1).	**unraced′** *adj.* un- (1).	**unrecollect′ed** *adj.* un- (1).
unpun′ishable *adj.* un- (1).	**unraised′** *adj.* un- (1).	**unrecommend′able** *adj.* un- (1).
unpun′ishably *adv.* un- (1).	**unran′somed** *adj.* un- (1).	**unrecommend′ed** *adj.* un- (1).
unpun′ished *adj.* un- (1).	**unrat′ed** *adj.* un- (1).	**unrec′ompensed** *adj.* un- (1).
unpur′chas(e)able *adj.* un- (1).	**unrat′ified** *adj.* un- (1).	**unrec′oncīlable** (or -*sīl′*) *adj.* un- (1).
unpur′chased *adj.* un- (1).	**unrav′ished** *adj.* un- (1).	**unreconcīl′ableness** *n.* un- (1).
unpurged′ *adj.* un- (1).	**unreach′able** *adj.* un- (1).	**unrec′oncīlably** (or -*sīl′*) *adv.* un- (1).
unpū′rified *adj.* un- (1).	**unreached′** *adj.* un- (1).	**unrec′onciled** (or -*sīld′*) *adj.* un- (1).
unpur′posed *adj.* un- (1).	**unreac′tive** *adj.* un- (1).	**unrecord′ed** *adj.* un- (1).
unpursued′ *adj.* un- (1).	**unreaped′** *adj.* un- (1).	**unrecount′ed** *adj.* un- (1).

— *adjs.* **unquot'ed** (of a company) not quoted on the Stock Exchange list; **unracked'** not drawn off from the lees: not stretched on the rack: not strained. — *v.t.* **unrake'** to uncover by raking. — *adj.* **unraked'** not raked: uncovering by raking: not banked up, as a fire. — *v.t.* **unrav'el** to disentangle: to unknit. — *v.i.* to become disentangled. — *adj.* **unrav'elled.** — *ns.* **unrav'eller; unrav'elling; unrav'elment.** — *adjs.* **unrā'zored** unshaven; **unread** (*un-red'*) not informed by reading: not perused; **unreadable** (*un-rēd'ə-bl*) indecipherable: too dull or ill-written to be read. — *n.* **unread'ableness.** — *adv.* **unreadily** (*-red'*). — *n.* **unread'iness.** — *adjs.* **unread'y** not ready, prepared, or prompt: hesitating, holding back: (*Shak.*, etc.) undressed or not dressed (**make unready** *obs.* to undress): in *Shak.*, etc., redeless; **unrē'al** not real or like reality: incredible, amazing (*coll.*): a general expression of appreciation or admiration (*slang*; orig. *U.S.*). — *v.t.* **unrē'alise, -ize** to divest of reality. — *adj.* **unrē'alised, -z-.** — *n.* **unrē'alism.** — *adj.* **unrealist'ic.** — *n.* **unreal'ity** want of reality or existence: an unreal thing. — *adv.* **unrē'ally.** — *n.* **unrea'son** lack of reason or reasonableness: nonsense: injustice (*obs.*): (**abbot of unreason** see **abbot**). — *adj.* **unrea'sonable** not agreeable to reason: exceeding the bounds of reason, immoderate: not influenced by reason. — *n.* **unrea'sonableness.** — *adv.* **unrea'sonably.** — *adjs.* **unrea'soned** not argued out; **unrea'soning** not reasoning: showing lack of reason, irrational. — *adv.* **unrea'soningly.** — *v.t.* **unreave'** (from *dial. reeve, reave,* to wind or unwind) to unweave (*Spens.*): to unwind (*dial.*). — *adjs.* **unrebā'ted** unblunted: undulled: without rebate; **unrecall'able; unrecalled'; unrecall'ing** (*Shak.; Milt.*) impossible to undo, not to be recalled; **unrecked'** not regarded or cared about; **unreconcil'iable** (*Shak.*) unreconcilable; **unreconstruct'ed** not reconstructed: not adjusted or reconciled to reconstruction (*U.S. hist.*); **unrecūr'ing** (*Shak.*) incurable; **unred'** (*Spens.*) for unread (unrecounted, untold); **unredeem'able; unredeemed'** not redeemed, esp. spiritually or from pawn: without compensatory quality or circumstance, hence unmitigated, unrelieved; **unredressed', unredrest'** not redressed: without redress or possibility of escape (*Spens.*). — *v.t.* **unreeve'** to withdraw from being reeved. — *n.* **unregen'eracy.** — *adjs.* **unregen'erate** not regenerate: unrepentant, refusing to be reformed; **unregen'erated.** — *v.t.* **unrein'** to relax the rein of, give rein to. — *adjs.* **unreined'** unchecked; **unrelen'ting.** — *adv.* **unrelen'tingly.** — *ns.* **unrelen'tingness; unrelen'tor** (*Keats*) one who does not relent; **unreliabil'-**

ity (see note at **rely**). — *adj.* **unreli'able** not to be relied upon. — *n.* **unreli'ableness.** — *adjs.* **unrelig'ious** not connected with religion: not religious without being necessarily contrary or hostile to religion: irreligious; **unremitt'ed.** — *adv.* **unremitt'edly.** — *adj.* **unremitt'ent.** — *adv.* **unremitt'ently.** — *adj.* **unremitt'ing** not remitting or relaxing: continued: incessant. — *adv.* **unremitt'ingly.** — *n.* **unremitt'ingness.** — *adj.* **unremorse'ful** feeling no remorse. — *adv.* **unremorse'fully.** — *adjs.* **unremorse'less** (*obs.*) remorseless; **unremov'able** not removable: immovable, fixed, constant (*obs.*); **unremoved'** not removed: fixed, unshaken (*obs.*); **unrepeat'able** not repeatable: indecent, gross: that cannot be done, etc. again; **unrepeat'ed; unreprov'able; unreproved'** (or *-prōō'vid*) not reproved: not liable to reproof, blameless (*Spens., Milt.*); **unreprov'ing; unrequired'** unasked: unasked-for: unnecessary. — *n.* **unreserve'** absence of reserve. — *adj.* **unreserved'** not reserved: without reserve or reservation: unrestricted, unqualified. — *adv.* **unreser'vedly.** — *n.* **unreser'vedness.** — *adjs.* **unresist'ed; unresist'ible** (*rare*) irresistible; **unresist'ing.** — *adv.* **unresis'tingly.** — *adjs.* **unresolv'able; unresolved'** not resolved, determined, settled, or solved: irresolute: undecided: not separated into its constituent parts. — *n.* **unresol'vedness** irresolution. — *adjs.* **unrespect'ed; unrespect'ive** inattentive, unthinking (*Shak.*): undiscriminating (*Shak.*): indiscriminate; **unres'pited** (*Milt.*) without respite or pause. — *n.* **unrest'** want of rest: disquiet: disturbance: discontent verging on insurrection. — *adj.* **unrest'ful** not restful: uneasy: full of unrest. — *n.* **unrest'fulness.** — *adj.* **unrest'ing.** — *adv.* **unrest'ingly.** — *n.* **unrest'ingness.** — *adjs.* **unrev'erend** not reverend: not reverent, irreverent, unreverent (*Shak.*); **unrev'erent** not reverent; **unrevert'ed** not turned back; **unrid'** unridden (*arch.*). — *v.t.* **unridd'le** to read the riddle of: to solve. — *adj.* **unridd'leable.** — *n.* **unridd'ler.** — *v.t.* **unrig'** to strip of rigging, or of clothes, etc. — *adj.* **unrigged'** without rigging: stripped of rigging. — *n.* **unright'** (*arch.*) wrong: unfairness, injustice. — *adj.* (*arch.*) wrong. — *adj.* **unrigh'teous.** — *adv.* **unrigh'teously.** — *n.* **unrigh'teousness.** — *adj.* **unright'ful.** — *adv.* **unright'fully.** — *n.* **unright'fulness.** — *v.t.* **unrip'** to rip up or open: to strip, lay bare: to disclose. — *adj.* **unripped'** not ripped: ripped up or open. — *n.* **unripp'ing.** — *vs.t.* **unriv'et** to loose from being riveted: to detach (*fig.*); **unrobe'** to strip of a robe, to undress. — *v.i.* to take off a robe, esp. of state. — *v.t.* **unroll'** to open out from a rolled state: to strike off the roll (*Shak.*). — *v.i.* to become unrolled.

---

unrecov'erable *adj.* **un-** (1).	**unrel'ative** *adj.* **un-** (1).	**unrepen'ted** *adj.* **un-** (1).
unrecov'erably *adv.* **un-** (1).	**unrelaxed'** *adj.* **un-** (1).	**unrepen'ting** *adj.* **un-** (1).
unrecov'ered *adj.* **un-** (1).	**unreliev'able** *adj.* **un-** (1).	**unrepen'tingly** *adv.* **un-** (1).
unrect'ified *adj.* **un-** (1).	**unrelieved'** *adj.* **un-** (1).	**unrepī'ning** *adj.* **un-** (1).
unreduced' *adj.* **un-** (1).	**unreliev'edly** *adv.* **un-** (1).	**unrepī'ningly** *adv.* **un-** (1).
unredūc'ible *adj.* **un-** (1).	**unrel'ished** *adj.* **un-** (1).	**unreplace'able** *adj.* **un-** (1).
unreel' *v.t.* and *v.i.* **un-** (2).	**unreluc'tant** *adj.* **un-** (1).	**unreplen'ished** *adj.* **un-** (1).
unrefined' *adj.* **un-** (1).	**unremain'ing** *adj.* **un-** (1).	**unreport'able** *adj.* **un-** (1).
unreflect'ed *adj.* **un-** (1).	**unremark'able** *adj.* **un-** (1).	**unreport'ed** *adj.* **un-** (1).
unreflect'ing *adj.* **un-** (1).	**unremarked'** *adj.* **un-** (1).	**unrepose'ful** *adj.* **un-** (1).
unreflect'ingly *adv.* **un-** (1).	**unrem'edied** *adj.* **un-** (1).	**unrepōs'ing** *adj.* **un-** (1).
unreflect'ive *adj.* **un-** (1).	**unremem'bered** *adj.* **un-** (1).	**unrepresent'ative** *adj.* **un-** (1).
unreform'able *adj.* **un-** (1).	**unremem'bering** *adj.* **un-** (1).	**unrepresent'ed** *adj.* **un-** (1).
unreformed' *adj.* **un-** (1).	**unremūn'erative** *adj.* **un-** (1).	**unsepriev'able** *adj.* **un-** (1).
unrefract'ed *adj.* **un-** (1).	**unren'dered** *adj.* **un-** (1).	**unreprieved'** *adj.* **un-** (1).
unrefreshed' *adj.* **un-** (1).	**unrenewed'** *adj.* **un-** (1).	**unrep'rimanded** *adj.* **un-** (1).
unrefresh'ing *adj.* **un-** (1).	**unrenowned'** *adj.* **un-** (1).	**unreproached'** *adj.* **un-** (1).
unrefū'ted *adj.* **un-** (1).	**unrent'** *adj.* **un-** (1).	**unreproach'ful** *adj.* **un-** (1).
unregard'ed *adj.* **un-** (1).	**unrepaid'** *adj.* **un-** (1).	**unreproach'ing** *adj.* **un-** (1).
unregard'ing *adj.* **un-** (1).	**unrepair'** *n.* **un-** (1).	**unreprodūc'ible** *adj.* **un-** (1).
unreg'imented *adj.* **un-** (1).	**unrepair'able** *adj.* **un-** (1).	**unrepug'nant** *adj.* **un-** (1).
unreg'istered *adj.* **un-** (1).	**unrepaired'** *adj.* **un-** (1).	**unrepuls'able** *adj.* **un-** (1).
unreg'ulated *adj.* **un-** (1).	**unrepeal'able** *adj.* **un-** (1).	**unreq'uisite** *adj.* **un-** (1).
unrehearsed' *adj.* **un-** (1).	**unrepealed'** *adj.* **un-** (1).	**unrequīt'ed** *adj.* **un-** (1).
unrejoiced' *adj.* **un-** (1).	**unrepelled'** *adj.* **un-** (1).	**unrequīt'edly** *adv.* **un-** (1).
unrejoic'ing *adj.* **un-** (1).	**unrepen'tance** *n.* **un-** (1).	**unrescind'ed** *adj.* **un-** (1).
unrelāt'ed *adj.* **un-** (1).	**unrepen'tant** *adj.* **un-** (1).	**unresent'ed** *adj.* **un-** (1).

— *v.t.* **unroof'** to strip the roof from. — *adj.* **unroofed'** not roofed: stripped of its roof. — *vs.t.* **unroost'** (*Shak.*) to drive out of a roost; **unroot'** to tear up by the roots. — *adj.* **unroot'ed** without root: not rooted (out): rooted out. — *v.t.* **unrope'** to loose from a rope. — *adjs.* **unrough'** not rough: (*Shak.* **unruffe'**) beardless; **unrude'** not rude: also (*obs.,* prob. by confusion from obs. *unride* — O.E. *ungerȳde,* rough — *gerȳde,* smooth, easy) rude, uncouth; **unruff'able** (*Dickens*) imperturbable. — *v.t.* **unruff'le** to restore or recover from ruffling. — *adj.* **unruff'led** smooth: calm: not disturbed or flustered. — *n.* **unrule'** anarchy. — *adj.* **unruled'.** — *ns.* **unrul'iment** (*Spens.*), **unrul'iness.** — *adj.* **unrul'y** ungovernable: unmanageable: turbulent: stormy.

Words with prefix **un-** (*continued*).
v.t. **unsadd'le** to take the saddle from: to dislodge from the saddle. — *adjs.* **unsadd'led; unsaid'** not said (see also **unsay**); **unsailed'** unnavigated; **unsail'orlike;** **unsained'** unblessed. — *v.t.* **unsaint'** to divest of saintliness or of the title of saint. — *n.* **unsaint'liness.** — *adjs.* **unsaint'ly; unsanc'tified.** — *v.t.* **unsanc'tify** to undo the sanctification of: to desecrate. — *adjs.* **unsan'itary** without (regard to) sanitation, unhealthy; **unsā'table** (*Browning*), **unsā'tiable** (now *rare*) insatiable. — *adv.* **unsā'vourily.** — *n.* **unsā'vouriness.** — *adj.* **unsā'voury** not savoury, tasteless: of ill savour: offensive. — *v.t.* **unsay'** to retract: —*pa.t.* and *pa.p.* **unsaid'.** — *adj.* **unsay'able** that cannot be said. — *v.t.* **unscabb'ard** to unsheathe. — *adj.* **unscāl'able** that cannot be climbed. — *v.t.* **unscale'** to remove scales from. — *adjs.* **unscaled'** unclimbed: cleared of scales: scaleless; **unscanned'** not scanned as verse: not scrutinised: (*Shak.* **un'skan'd**) unconsidered; **unscathed'** not harmed, not injured; **unscav'engered** (*Dickens*) not cleared of rubbish; **unscep'tred** without a sceptre: deposed; **unsciss'ored** not cut with scissors; **unscott'ified** deprived of Scottish qualities or characteristics. — *v.t.* **unscram'ble** to decode from a scrambled state, or to restore to natural sound: to restore (something in which categories have been deliberately jumbled) to a system of classification and separation. — *adj.* **unscreened'** not screened: unsifted. — *v.t.* **unscrew'** to loose from a state of being screwed: to open, loose, or detach by screwing. — *v.i.* to admit of unscrewing: to come unscrewed. — *adjs.* **unscrip'ted** not using a script: unrehearsed: of comments, moves, etc., not planned, not in the script (*radio, TV*); **unscrip'tural** not in accordance with, or not warranted by, the Bible. — *adv.* **unscrip'turally.** — *adj.* **unscru'pled** un-

scrupulous: not scrupled at. — *v.t.* **unseal'** to remove or break the seal of: to free from sealing or closure: to open (sometimes prob. for **unseel**). — *adj.* **unsealed'** not sealed: freed from a seal: opened. — *v.t.* **unseam'** to undo a seam of: to rip open (*Shak.*). — *adjs.* **unseamed'** without seams; **unsearch'able** inscrutable, not possible to be searched into: mysterious. — *n.* **unsearch'ableness.** — *adv.* **unsearch'ably.** — *adj.* **unsearched'.** — *v.t.* **unsea'son** (*Spens.*) to affect disagreeably. — *adj.* **unsea'sonable** not in season: ill-timed. — *n.* **unsea'sonableness.** — *adv.* **unsea'sonably.** — *adj.* **unsea'soned** not seasoned: unseasonable (*Shak.*). — *v.t.* **unseat'** to oust, remove, or throw from a seat, esp. on horseback or in Parliament. — *adjs.* **unseat'ed** not seated: ousted, thrown, removed from a seat; **unse'cret** (*Shak.*) failing to preserve secrecy; **unsee'able** invisible; **unseed'ed** not seeded: in lawn-tennis tournaments, etc., not placed in the draw of top players; **unsee'ing** not seeing: unobservant: without insight or understanding. — *v.t.* **unseel'** to unsew the eyes of, undo the seeling of. — *n.* **unseem'ing** (*Shak.*) not seeming. — *adj.* (*obs.*) unbecoming, unseemly. — *n.* **unseem'liness.** — *adj.* **unseem'ly** not seemly, becoming, or decent: ill-looking. — *adv.* in an unseemly manner. — *adj.* **unseen'** not seen: invisible: inexperienced, not well up (*obs.*). — *n.* an unprepared passage for translation. — *adjs.* **unseiz'able; unseized'** not seized: not taken or put in possession. — *adv.* **unsel'dom** not seldom (*lit.* and *rarely*): misused to mean seldom (as in *not unseldom,* frequently). — *n.* **un'self** altruism: impersonality. — *v.t.* **unself'** to divest of personality, individuality, selfhood, or selfishness. — *adj.* **unselfcon'scious.** — *adv.* **unselfcon'sciously.** — *n.* **unselfcon'sciousness.** — *adj.* **unself'ish.** — *adv.* **unself'ishly.** — *n.* **unself'ishness.** — *adjs.* **unsem'inar'd, unsem'inaried** (*Shak.*) without means of generation. — *v.t.* **unsense'** to deprive of sense or consciousness. — *adjs.* **unsensed'** meaningless; **unsens'ible** (*obs.* or *dial.*) insensible. — *adv.* **unsens'ibly** (*obs.*) insensibly, imperceptibly: without sense. — *vs.t.* **unsens'ualise, -ize** to free from the dominion of the senses; **unset'** to undo the setting of. — *adj.* not set: unplanted. — *v.t.* **unsett'le** to change from being settled: to make uncertain, unstable, or restless: to unfix. — *v.i.* to become unsettled. — *adj.* **unsett'led** not settled, fixed, or determined: changeable: not having the dregs deposited: not yet inhabited and cultivated: turbulent, lawless. — *adv.* **unsett'ledly.** — *ns.* **unsett'ledness; unsett'lement.** — *n.* and *adj.* **unsett'ling.** — *v.t.* **unsew'** to undo the stitching of (a garment, etc.). — *adj.* **unsewn'**

---

unresent'ful *adj.* **un-** (1).	**unrewar'ded** *adj.* **un-** (1).	**unroused'** *adj.* **un-** (1).
unresent'ing *adj.* **un-** (1).	**unrewar'dedly** *adv.* **un-** (1).	**unroy'al** *adj.* **un-** (1).
unrespon'sive *adj.* **un-** (1).	**unrewar'ding** *adj.* **un-** (1).	**unroy'ally** *adv.* **un-** (1).
unrespon'sively *adv.* **un-** (1).	**unrhymed', unrimed'** *adj.* **un-** (1).	**unrubbed'** *adj.* **un-** (1).
unrespon'siveness *n.* **un-** (1).	**unrhyth'mical** *adj.* **un-** (1).	**unrum'pled** *adj.* **un-** (1).
unrestored' *adj.* **un-** (1).	**unrhyth'mically** *adv.* **un-** (1).	**unsafe'** *adj.* **un-** (1).
unrestrain'able *adj.* **un-** (1).	**unribbed'** *adj.* **un-** (1).	**unsafe'ly** *adv.* **un-** (1).
unrestrained' *adj.* **un-** (1).	**unridd'en** *adj.* **un-** (1).	**unsafe'ness** *n.* **un-** (1).
unrestrain'edly *adv.* **un-** (1).	**unrid(e)'able** *adj.* **un-** (1).	**unsafe'ty** *n.* **un-** (1).
unrestraint' *n.* **un-** (1).	**unrī'fled** *adj.* **un-** (1).	**unsal(e)abil'ity** *n.* **un-** (1).
unrestric'ted *adj.* **un-** (1).	**unringed'** *adj.* **un-** (1).	**unsal(e)'able** *adj.* **un-** (1).
unrestric'tedly *adv.* **un-** (1).	**unripe'** *adj.* **un-** (1).	**unsal'aried** *adj.* **un-** (1).
unretard'ed *adj.* **un-** (1).	**unrī'pened** *adj.* **un-** (1).	**unsalt'ed** *adj.* **un-** (1).
unretent'ive *adj.* **un-** (1).	**unripe'ness** *n.* **un-** (1).	**unsalu'ted** *adj.* **un-** (1).
unretouched' *adj.* **un-** (1).	**unris'en** *adj.* **un-** (1).	**unsanc'tioned** *adj.* **un-** (1).
unreturn'able *adj.* **un-** (1).	**unrī'valled** *adj.* **un-** (1).	**unsan'dalled** *adj.* **un-** (1).
unreturned' *adj.* **un-** (1).	**unriv'en** *adj.* **un-** (1).	**unsapped'** *adj.* **un-** (1).
unreturn'ing *adj.* **un-** (1).	**unrō'manised, -z-** *adj.* **un-** (1).	**unsashed'** *adj.* **un-** (1).
unreturn'ingly *adv.* **un-** (1).	**unroman'tic, -al** *adjs.* **un-** (1).	**unsāt'ed** *adj.* **un-** (1).
unreveal'able *adj.* **un-** (1).	**unroman'tically** *adv.* **un-** (1).	**unsā'tiate, -d** *adjs.* **un-** (1).
unrevealed' *adj.* **un-** (1).	**unros'ined** *adj.* **un-** (1).	**unsā'tiating** *adj.* **un-** (1).
unreveal'ing *adj.* **un-** (1).	**unrott'ed** *adj.* **un-** (1).	**unsāt'ing** *adj.* **un-** (1).
unrevenged' *adj.* **un-** (1).	**unrott'en** *adj.* **un-** (1).	**unsatir'ical** *adj.* **un-** (1).
unrevenge'ful *adj.* **un-** (1).	**unrouged** (-rōōzhd') *adj.* **un-** (1).	**unsatisfac'tion** *n.* **un-** (1).
unreversed' *adj.* **un-** (1).	**unround'** *adj.* **un-** (1).	**unsatisfac'torily** *adv.* **un-** (1).
unrevised' *adj.* **un-** (1).	**unround'** *v.t.* **un-** (2).	**unsatisfac'toriness** *n.* **un-** (1).
unrevoked' *adj.* **un-** (1).	**unround'ed** *adj.* **un-** (1).	**unsatisfac'tory** *adj.* **un-** (1).

(also **unsewed'**) not sewn (**unsewn binding** a bookbinding in which the gathered sections are held in place by a process other than sewing, esp. perfect binding or burst binding (q.v.)). — *v.t.* **unsex'** to divest of sex: to divest of the characteristics or of the qualities expected of one's own sex. — *adjs.* **unsexed'; unsex'ist; unsex'ual.** — *v.t.* **unshack'le** to loose from shackles: to remove a shackle from. — *adj.* **unshack'led.** — *v.t.* **unshad'ow** to clear of shadow: to reveal. — *adjs.* **unshad'owable** impossible to shadow forth; **unshad'owed** not darkened. — *v.t.* **unshale'** to shale or shell, strip the husk from: to reveal. — *adj.* **unshamed'** not ashamed: not put to shame. — *v.t.* **unshape'** to deprive of shape: to undo, destroy, to confound. — *adjs.* **unshaped'; unshape'ly; unshāp'en.** — *v.t.* **unsheathe'** to draw from the sheath: to uncover. — *adjs.* **unsheathed'** drawn from the sheath: not sheathed; **unshed'** not shed: unparted (*Spens.*). — *v.t.* **unshell'** to shell, remove the shell from. — *adjs.* **unshent'** uninjured: not disgraced. — *v.t.* **unship'** to take or put out of a ship or boat, etc.: to remove from a fixed or allotted place (as oars from the rowlocks). — *v.i.* to admit of or undergo unshipping. — *adj.* **unshod'** shoeless: with shoe or shoes removed. — *vs.t.* **unshoe'** to strip of a shoe or shoes; **unshout'** (*Shak.* **unshoot'**) to revoke the shouting of by a contrary shout. — *adj.* **unshowered** (*unshowrd'*, *-show'ərd*) not watered by showers. — *v.t.* **unshroud'** to uncover. — *adjs.* **unshrubbed'** (**unshrubd'** *Shak.*) without shrubs; **unshunn'able; unshunned'** (**unshun'd'** *Shak.*) inevitable. — *v.t.*, *v.i.*, and *adj.* **unshut'** open. — *v.t.* **unshutt'er** to open or remove the shutters of. — *adjs.* **unsift'ed** not sifted: not critically examined: inexperienced; **unsight'** (*obs.*), **unsight'ed** not seen: (of gun, etc.) having no sights: fired without use of sights. — *n.* **unsight'liness.** — *adj.* **unsight'ly** displeasing to the eye: ugly. — *v.t.* **unsin'ew** to take the strength from. — *adjs.* **unsin'ewed** (*Shak.* **unsinn'owed**); **unsis'tered** without a sister. — *n.* **unsis'terliness.** — *adjs.* **unsis'terly; unsist'ing** (*Shak., Meas.*) variously explained as unassisting, unresisting, insisting, unresting; **unsiz(e)'able** (*obs.*) inordinately big: too little, immature; **unsized'** not fitted, adjusted, or sorted in respect of size: not treated with size; **unskinned'** skinned: not skinned. — *vs.t.* **unsling'** to free from slings or from being slung: — *pa.t.* and *pa.p* **unslung'; unsluice'** to let flow: to open the sluice of. — *adj.* **unsmooth'.** — *v.t.* **unsmoothe'** to roughen: to wrinkle. — *adjs.* **unsmoothed'; unsmote'** unsmitten. — *v.t.* **unsnarl'** to disentangle. — *adj.* **unsoaped'** not soaped: unwashed. — *n.* **unsociabil'ity.** — *adj.* **unsō'-** **ciable** disinclined to associate with others. — *n.* **unsō'ciableness.** — *adv.* **unsō'ciably.** — *adjs.* **unsō'cial** not social: not regarding or conducing to the good of society: not sociable: (of hours of work) not falling within the normal working day; **unsō'cialised, -z-** not socialised, not aware of one's function in, or lacking attributes for living in, society. — *ns.* **unsō'cialism, unsocial'ity.** — *adv.* **unsō'cially.** — *v.t.* **unsock'et** to take out of the socket. — *adjs.* **unsod', unsodd'en** unboiled: not soaked or saturated. — *adv.* **unsoft'** (*Spens.*) not softly. — *v.t.* **unsolder** (*un-sod'ər*, or *-sol'*, *-sö'*, *-sō'*, *-sōl'*) to separate from being soldered. — *adjs.* **unsol'emn** not solemn: informal; **unsolv'able** impossible to solve; **unsolved'** not solved; **unsoote'** (*Spens.*) unsweet; **unsophis'ticate** (now *rare*), **unsophis'ticated** genuine, unadulterated: unfalsified: free from artificiality: ingenuous: inexperienced in evil. — *ns.* **unsophis'ticatedness; unsophisticā'tion.** — *adjs.* **unsort'ed** not sorted or arranged: ill-chosen: unfitting, unsuitable; **unsought'** not sought or solicited. — *v.t.* **unsoul'** to deprive of soul or spirit. — *adjs.* **unsouled'** deprived of, or not endowed with, soul; **unsound'** not sound; **unsound'able** unfathomable; **unsound'ed** not sounded, pronounced, or made to sound: unfathomed, unplumbed. — *adv.* **unsound'ly.** — *n.* **unsound'ness.** — *adj.* **unsourced'** having no source, or no established or authenticated source. — *v.t.* **unspar'** to withdraw a spar from. — *adjs.* **unspared'** not spared: unstinted; **unspār'ing** not sparing, liberal, profuse: unmerciful. — *adv.* **unspār'ingly.** — *n.* **unspār'ingness.** — *v.t.* **unspeak'** to retract. — *adj.* **unspeak'able** unutterable: inexpressible, esp. in badness. — *n.* **unspeak'ableness.** — *adv.* **unspeak'ably.** — *adjs.* **unspeak'ing; unsped'** without achievement or success: unaccomplished. — *v.t.* **unspell'** to free from a spell. — *adj.* **unspent'** not spent. — *v.t.* **unsphere'** to draw or remove from its sphere. — *adjs.* **unspied'** (*Spens.* **unspide'**, *Milt.* **unspi'd'**) unobserved; **unspir'ited.** — *v.t.* **unspir'itualise, -ize** to deprive of spirituality. — *adv.* **unspir'itually.** — *adj.* **unsprung'** not sprung: without springs. — *v.t.* **unstack'** to remove from a stack. — *adjs.* **unstanch'able, unstaunch'able; unstanched', unstaunched'** (or *un'*) not stanched: unsated (*Shak.*): leaky, hence incontinent (*Shak.*). — *v.t.* **unstarch'** to free from starch. — *adj.* **unstarched'** not starched. — *v.t.* **unstate'** (*Shak.*) to deprive of state or dignity. — *adjs.* **unstat'ed** not stated; **unstat'ūtable** contrary to statute. — *adv.* **unstat'ūtably.** — *adjs.* **unstayed'** not stayed or restrained: unsupported: unstable (*Spens.*): without stays; **unstay'ing** without stop.

— *adv.* **unstead′ily.** — *n.* **unstead′iness.** — *adj.* **unstead′y.** — *v.t.* to make unsteady. — *vs.t.* **unsteel′** to soften, to disarm; **unstep′** to remove, as a mast, from its place. — *adj.* **unsterc′orated** not manured. — *v.t.* **unstick′** to free from sticking. — *v.i.* to come off from the surface: — *pa.t.* and *pa.p.* **unstuck′.** — *adj.* detached, loosened from sticking: (**come unstuck** of a plan, to go amiss; *slang*). — *vs.t.* **unstitch′** to take out the stitches of; **unstock′** to deplete of stock: to remove the stock from: to launch (*obs.*). — *adjs.* **unstocked′** not stocked: without stock: not wearing a stock; **unstock′inged** not wearing a stocking or stockings. — *v.t.* **unstop′** to free from being stopped: to draw out the stop of. — *adj.* **unstopp′able** not able to be stopped. — *adv.* **unstopp′ably.** — *adj.* **unstopped′** not stopped: of a consonant, open: without a pause at the end of the line. — *vs.t.* **unstopp′er** to take the stopper from; **unstow′** to empty of contents: to take out of stowage. — *adj.* **unstrained′** not strained or purified by straining: not subjected to strain: not forced, natural. — *v.t.* **unstrap′** to undo the straps of. — *adjs.* **unstreamed′** (of schoolchildren) not divided into classes according to ability; **unstrī′ated** not striped. — *v.t.* **unstring′** to take the strings from: to loose the strings of: to take from a string: to put out of tone: to disorganise. — *v.i.* to loose the strings of one's purse. — *adj.* **unstringed′** not stringed, not provided with strings. — *v.t.* **unstrip′** (now *dial.*) to strip. — *adjs.* **unstripped′** not stripped; **unstrung′** with strings removed or slacked: not strung: relaxed: disorganised: unnerved; **unstuck** see **unstick;** **unstud′ied** not studied: not having studied: without premeditation: unlaboured: spontaneous: natural, easy; **un′stuffy** (*fig.*) not stodgy or strait-laced; **unsub′stan′tial** not substantial, real, corporeal, solid, or strong. — *v.t.* **unsubstan′tialise, -ize.** — *ns.* **unsubstan′tial′ity; unsubstantiā′tion.** — *adj.* **unsucceed′ed** without a successor. — *n.* **unsuccess′** want of success: failure. — *adj.* **unsuccess′ful.** — *adv.* **unsuccess′fully.** — *n.* **unsuccess′fulness.** — *adjs.* **unsuccess′ive** not successive: not in, or passing by, succession; **unsuff′erable** (*obs.*) insufferable; **unsuffi′cient** (*obs.*) insufficient. — *v.t.* **unsuit′** to make unsuitable. — *n.* **unsuitabil′ity.** — *adj.* **unsuit′able.** — *n.* **unsuit′ableness.** — *adv.* **unsuit′ably.** — *adjs.* **unsuit′ed** not suited or adapted; **unsuit′ing; unsummed′** uncounted; **unsumm′ered** not possessing the characteristics of summer; **unsung′** not sung: not celebrated in song; **unsunned′** not exposed to the sun: not lighted, warmed, affected by the sun: not exposed to view; **unsunn′y; unsupport′able** insupportable: inde-

fensible; **unsupport′ed.** — *adv.* **unsupport′edly.** — *adjs.* **unsure** (*un-shoor′*) insecure: precarious: uncertain: doubtful: not assured: untrustworthy; **unsured′** not made sure; **unsurmount′able** insurmountable; **unsuspect′** (*Milt.*) not subject to suspicion; **unsuspec′ted** not suspected: not known or supposed to exist. — *adv.* **unsuspec′tedly.** — *n.* **unsuspec′tedness.** — *adj.* **unsuspec′ting.** — *adv.* **unsuspec′tingly.** — *ns.* **unsuspec′tingness; unsuspi′cion** absence of suspicion. — *adj.* **unsuspi′cious.** — *adv.* **unsuspi′ciously.** — *n.* **unsuspi′ciousness.** — *vs.t.* **unswadd′le** to unswathe; **unswathe′** to take swathings or bandages from. — *adjs.* **unsway′able** (*Shak.*); **unswayed′** (*Shak.* **unswai′d′**) not wielded: not controlled: uninfluenced: not swung. — *v.t.* **unswear′** to retract the swearing of. — *v.i.* to recall an oath. — *n.* **unswear′ing.** — *adjs.* **unsworn′** not confirmed, or not bound, by oath; **unsyll′abled** not syllabled, not articulated; **unsymmet′rical.** — *adv.* **unsymmet′rically.** — *adj.* **unsymm′etrised, -z-.** — *n.* **unsymm′etry** asymmetry.

*Words with prefix **un-*** (*continued*).

vs.t. **untack′** to detach from tacking; **untack′le** to strip of tackle: to free from tackle: to unharness. — *adj.* **untaint′ed** not tainted: unblemished: not attainted. — *adv.* **untaint′edly.** — *adjs.* **untaint′edness.** — *adj.* **untaint′ing; untām′able** (also **untame′able**). — *n.* **untam(e)′ableness.** — *adv.* **untam(e)′ably.** — *adj.* **untame′** not tame. — *v.t.* to make untame, undo the taming of. — *adj.* **untamed′.** — *n.* **untamed′ness.** — *v.t.* **untang′le** to disentangle. — *adjs.* **untang′led; untaught′** uninstructed: not taught or communicated by teaching: spontaneous, native, inborn. — *v.t.* **untax′** to remit a tax on. — *adj.* **untaxed′** not taxed: not charged with any fault. — *v.t.* **unteach′** to undo the teaching of. — *adj.* **unteach′able** not teachable. — *n.* **unteach′ableness.** — *vs.t.* **unteam′** to unyoke; **untem′per** to destroy the temper of, deprive of suitable temper. — *adjs.* **untem′pered** not tempered: not regulated; **untem′pering** (*Shak.*) unconciliating; **unten′able** (or *-tē′*) not tenable, not defensible. — *n.* **unten′ableness.** — *v.t.* **unten′ant** to deprive of a tenant: to dislodge. — *adjs.* **unten′antable; unten′anted** not occupied. — *v.t.* **untent′** to remove from a tent. — *adjs.* **untent′ed** having no tents: of a wound, unprobed, undressed, or impossible to treat with a tent: unheeded (*Scot.*); **untent′y** careless (*Scot.*). — *v.t.* **unteth′er** to release from a tether. — *adj.* **unteth′ered** not tethered. — *v.t.* **unthatch′** to strip of thatch. — *adj.* **unthatched′** not thatched. — *v.t.* and

unskil′fulness *n.* **un-** (1).	**unsol′dierly** *adj.* **un-** (1).	**unspun′** *adj.* **un-** (1).
unskilled′ *adj.* **un-** (1).	**unsolic′ited** *adj.* **un-** (1).	**unsquared′** *adj.* **un-** (1).
unskimmed′ *adj.* **un-** (1).	**unsolic′itous** *adj.* **un-** (1).	**unstā′ble** *adj.* **un-** (1).
unslain′ *adj.* **un-** (1).	**unsol′id** *adj.* **un-** (1).	**unstā′bleness** *n.* **un-** (1).
unslaked′ *adj.* **un-** (1).	**unsolid′ity** *n.* **un-** (1).	**unstaid′** *adj.* **un-** (1).
unsleep′ing *adj.* **un-** (1).	**unsol′idly** *adv.* **un-** (1).	**unstaid′ness** *n.* **un-** (1).
unslept′-in *adj.* **un-** (1).	**unson′sy** (*Scot.*) *adj.* **un-** (1).	**unstain′able** *adj.* **un-** (1).
unslipp′ing *adj.* **un-** (1).	**unsoured′** *adj.* **un-** (1).	**unstained′** *adj.* **un-** (1).
unslum′bering *adj.* **un-** (1).	**unsown′** *adj.* **un-** (1).	**unstamped′** *adj.* **un-** (1).
unslum′brous *adj.* **un-** (1).	**unspe′cialised, -z-** *adj.* **un-** (1).	**unstates′manlike** *adj.* **un-** (1).
unslung′ *adj.* **un-** (1).	**unspecif′ic** *adj.* **un-** (1).	**unstead′fast** *adj.* **un-** (1).
unsmart′ *adj.* **un-** (1).	**unspec′ified** *adj.* **un-** (1).	**unstead′fastly** *adv.* **un-** (1).
unsmiled′-on *adj.* **un-** (1).	**unspec′tacled** *adj.* **un-** (1).	**unstead′fastness** *n.* **un-** (1).
unsmil′ing *adj.* **un-** (1).	**unspectac′ular** *adj.* **un-** (1).	**unster′ile** *adj.* **un-** (1).
unsmil′ingly *adv.* **un-** (1).	**unspec′ulative** *adj.* **un-** (1).	**unster′ilised, -z-** *adj.* **un-** (1).
unsmirched′ *adj.* **un-** (1).	**unspilled′** *adj.* **un-** (1).	**unstī′fled** *adj.* **un-** (1).
unsmitt′en *adj.* **un-** (1).	**unspilt′** *adj.* **un-** (1).	**unstig′matised, -z-** *adj.* **un-** (1).
unsmoth′erable *adj.* **un-** (1).	**unsplint′erable** *adj.* **un-** (1).	**unstilled′** *adj.* **un-** (1).
unsnap′ *v.t.* **un-** (2).	**unspoiled′** *adj.* **un-** (1).	**unstim′ulated** *adj.* **un-** (1).
unsneck′ *v.t.* **un-** (2).	**unspoilt′** *adj.* **un-** (1).	**unstint′ed** *adj.* **un-** (1).
unsnuffed′ *adj.* **un-** (1).	**unspoke′** (*Shak.*) *adj.* **un-** (1).	**unstint′ing** *adj.* **un-** (1).
unsoftened (*-sof′*(ə)*nd*) *adj.* **un-** (1).	**unspō′ken** *adj.* **un-** (1).	**unstoop′ing** *adj.* **un-** (1).
unsoftening (*-sof′*(ə)*ning*) *adj.* **un-** (1).	**unsport′ing** *adj.* **un-** (1).	**unstrapped′** *adj.* **un-** (1).
unsoiled′ *adj.* **un-** (1).	**unsports′manlike** *adj.* **un-** (1).	**unstrat′ified** *adj.* **un-** (1).
unsol′aced *adj.* **un-** (1).	**unspott′ed** *adj.* **un-** (1).	**unstrength′ened** *adj.* **un-** (1).
unsōld′ *adj.* **un-** (1).	**unspott′edness** *n.* **un-** (1).	**unstressed′** *adj.* **un-** (1).
unsōl′dierlike *adj.* **un-** (1).	**unsprink′led** *adj.* **un-** (1).	**unstriped′** *adj.* **un-** (1).

v.i. **unthaw'** to thaw. — *adj.* **unthawed'** not thawed. — *v.t.* and *v.i.* **unthink'** to think to the contrary, reverse in thought. — *n.* **unthinkabil'ity.** — *adjs.* **unthink'able** that cannot be thought: outside the realm of thought: beyond the power of thought: inconceivable: unimaginable: utterly impossible (often of things impending but too painful to think about); **unthink'ing** not thinking: thoughtless. — *adv.* **unthink'ingly.** — *n.* **unthink'-ingness.** — *adj.* **unthought'ful.** — *adv.* **unthought'fully.** — *n.* **unthought'fulness.** — *adj.* **unthought'-of.** — *v.t.* **unthread'** to take a thread from: to unweave: to loosen: to find one's way through. — *adj.* **unthread'ed** not threaded. — *n.* **un'thrift** a prodigal: a spendthrift: unthriftiness. — *adj.* prodigal. — *adv.* **unthrift'ily.** — *n.* **unthrift'iness.** — *adj.* **unthrift'y** not thrifty: wasteful: prodigal: not thriving: unprofitable. — *n.* **unthrift'y-he(a)d** (*Spens.*) unthriftiness. — *vs.t.* **unthrone'** to dethrone; **untie'** to loose from being tied: to unbind: to solve, resolve. — *v.i.* to come loose. — *adj.* **untied'** not tied: loosed: not loosed, still tied (Shak., *Pericles*). — *v.t.* **untile'** to strip of tiles. — *adjs.* **untiled'** not tiled: stripped of tiles; **untim'bered** not strongly timbered (*Shak.*): unwooded. — *n.* **untime'liness.** — *adj.* **untime'ly** not timely: before the time, premature: immature: unseasonable, ill-timed: inopportune. — *adv.* at an unsuitable time: too early, prematurely: unseasonably: inopportunely. — *adj.* **untime'ous** (*untī'məs*) untimely. — *adv.* **untime'ously.** — *v.t.* **untin'** to take the tin from. — *adjs.* **untinned'** not tinned; **untī'tled** having no title: deprived of title; **untoch'ered** (*Scot.*) without tocher; **untold'** (or *un'*) not counted: innumerable: not narrated: not communicated: not informed. — *v.t.* **untomb'** to disentomb. — *adjs.* **untombed'** not entombed; **untoned'** not toned: without tones; **untouch'-able** impossible to touch: not to be equalled or touched. — *n.* one whose excellence in some respect cannot be rivalled: (esp. formerly) a Hindu of very low caste, a member of one of the scheduled castes. — *adjs.* **untouched'** not touched: intact: unrivalled; **untoward** (*un-tō'ərd, -tə-wörd'*) not easily guided: froward: awkward: inconvenient: unlucky: unfavourable: unfitting. — *n.* **unto'wardliness, untoward'liness.** — *adv.* **unto'-wardly, untoward'ly.** — *adj.* untoward. — *n.* **unto'-wardness, untoward'ness.** — *v.t.* **untrace'** to loose from traces. — *adjs.* **untrace'able** impossible to trace; **un-traced'; untrā'ded** unfrequented, as for trade (*obs.*): unhackneyed (*Shak.*). — *vs.t.* **untread'** (*Shak.*) to tread back, to retrace; **untreas'ure** to despoil (of treasure). — *adjs.* **untreat'able** intractable (*obs.*): that cannot be

treated; **untreat'ed; untressed'** not dressed in tresses; **untried'** not tried, tested, attempted, experienced, subjected to trial in court: (Shak., *Pericles*, **untride'**) prob. not ventured upon, hence not noticed or dealt with. — *v.t.* **untrim'** to deprive of trimming or trimness. — *adjs.* **untrimmed'** not trimmed; **untrod', untrodd'en** not trodden upon: unfrequented; **untroub'led** not troubled or disturbed: not turbid. — *adv.* **untroub'ledly.** — *adj.* **untrue'** not true: false: not faithful: dishonest: inexact: not in accordance with a standard. — *adv.* (*Shak.*) untruly, untruthfully. — *ns.* **untrue'ness; untru'ism** an untrue platitude. — *adv.* **untru'ly** falsely. — *v.t.* **untruss'** to unpack: to unfasten: to untie (esp. points of clothes): to untie the points of. — *adj.* **untrussed', untrust'** not trussed: untied: with points untied. — *ns.* **untruss'er; untruss'ing; untrust'** distrust. — *adj.* **untrust'ful** not trusting: not trustworthy: not to be trusted. — *n.* **untrust'iness** (*obs.*). — *adv.* **untrust'worthily.** — *n.* **untrust'worthiness.** — *adjs.* **untrust'worthy** not worthy of trust; **untrust'y** not trusty, not deserving trust. — *n.* **untruth'** unfaithfulness: falseness: falsity: that which is untrue: a lie. — *adj.* **untruth'ful** not truthful. — *adv.* **untruth'fully.** — *n.* **untruth'fulness.** — *v.t.* **untuck'** to unfold or undo from being tucked up or in: to take out tucks from. — *adjs.* **untucked'** not tucked; **untuck'-ered** not having a tucker on; **untūn'able** (also **untune'-able**) harsh. — *n.* **untūn'ableness.** — *adv.* **untūn'ably.** — *v.t.* **untune'** to put out of tune. — *adjs.* **untuned'** not tuned: put out of tune; **untune'ful.** — *adv.* **untune'fully.** — *n.* **untune'fulness.** — *vs.t.* **unturf'** to strip of turf; **unturn'** to turn backwards. — *adjs.* **unturn'able; un-turned'** not turned; **unturn'ing; untū'tored** untaught: uninstructed. — *vs.t.* and *vs.i.* **untwine'** to untwist: to separate by untwisting; **untwist'** to twist backwards so as to open out: to straighten out from a twist. — *adj.* **untwist'ed** not twisted: subjected to untwisting. — *ns.* **untwist'ing.** — *adj.* **unty'pable** that cannot be defined as a particular type.

Words with prefix un- (continued).
adjs. **unused** (*un-ūzd'*) not used: (also *un-ūst'*) unaccustomed: unusual (*arch.*); **unuseful** (*-ūs'*). — *adv.* **unuse'-fully.** — *n.* **unuse'fulness.** — *adj.* **unūs'ual.** — *adv.* **unūs'ually** more than usually: in an unusual way. — *n.* **unūs'ualness.** — *adj.* **unutt'erable** beyond utterance, inexpressible: not to be uttered. — *n.* an unutterable thing: (in *pl.*) trousers (*old slang*). — *adv.* **unutt'erably.** — *adjs.* **unutt'ered; unval'uable** not valuable, of little worth: invaluable, priceless (*obs.*); **unval'ued** not prized

unstruck' *adj.* **un-** (1).	**unsuppōs'able** *adj.* **un-** (1).	**untailed'** *adj.* **un-** (1).
unstruc'tured *pa.p., adj.* **un-** (1).	**unsuppressed'** *adj.* **un-** (1).	**untā'ken** *adj.* **un-** (1).
unstuffed' (*Shak.* **un'stuft**) *adj.* **un-** (1).	**unsur'faced** *adj.* **un-** (1).	**untal'ented** *adj.* **un-** (1).
unsubdū'able *adj.* **un-** (1).	**unsurmised', -z-** *adj.* **un-** (1).	**untalked'-of** *adj.* **un-** (1).
unsubdued' *adj.* **un-** (1).	**unsurpass'able** *adj.* **un-** (1).	**untan'gible** *adj.* **un-** (1).
unsub'ject *adj.* **un-** (1).	**unsurpass'ably** *adv.* **un-** (1).	**untanned'** *adj.* **un-** (1).
unsubject'ed *adj.* **un-** (1).	**unsurpassed'** *adj.* **un-** (1).	**untapped'** *adj.* **un-** (1).
unsub'limated *adj.* **un-** (1).	**unsurprised'** *adj.* **un-** (1).	**untar'nished** *adj.* **un-** (1).
unsublimed' *adj.* **un-** (1).	**unsurveyed'** *adj.* **un-** (1).	**untarred'** *adj.* **un-** (1).
unsubmerged' *adj.* **un-** (1).	**unsuscept'ible** *adj.* **un-** (1).	**untast'ed** *adj.* **un-** (1).
unsubmiss'ive *adj.* **un-** (1).	**unsuspend'ed** *adj.* **un-** (1).	**untaste'ful** *adj.* **un-** (1).
unsubmitt'ing *adj.* **un-** (1).	**unsustain'able** *adj.* **un-** (1).	**untear'able** *adj.* **un-** (1).
unsubscribed' *adj.* **un-** (1).	**unsustained'** *adj.* **un-** (1).	**untech'nical** *adj.* **un-** (1).
unsub'sidised, -z- *adj.* **un-** (1).	**unsustain'ing** *adj.* **un-** (1).	**untell'able** *adj.* **un-** (1).
unsubstan'tiated *adj.* **un-** (1).	**unswall'owed** *adj.* **un-** (1).	**untemp'ted** *adj.* **un-** (1).
unsubt'le *adj.* **un-** (1).	**unsweet'** *adj.* **un-** (1).	**untenabil'ity** *n.* **un-** (1).
unsucc'oured *adj.* **un-** (1).	**unsweet'ened** *adj.* **un-** (1).	**untend'ed** *adj.* **un-** (1).
unsucked' *adj.* **un-** (1).	**unswept'** *adj.* **un-** (1).	**untend'er** *adj.* **un-** (1).
unsued'-for, -to *adjs.* **un-** (1).	**unswer'ving** *adj.* **un-** (1).	**unten'dered** *adj.* **un-** (1).
unsull'ied *adj.* **un-** (1).	**unswer'vingly** *adv.* **un-** (1).	**unten'derly** *adv.* **un-** (1).
unsumm'oned *adj.* **un-** (1).	**unsympathet'ic** *adj.* **un-** (1).	**unter'minated** *adj.* **un-** (1).
unsuper'fluous (*Milt.*) *adj.* **un-** (1).	**unsympathet'ically** *adv.* **un-** (1).	**unterres'trial** *adj.* **un-** (1).
unsu'pervised *adj.* **un-** (1).	**unsym'pathising, -z-** *adj.* **un-** (1).	**unterr'ified** *adj.* **un-** (1).
unsupp'le *adj.* **un-** (1).	**unsym'pathy** *n.* **un-** (1).	**unterr'ifying** *adj.* **un-** (1).
unsupp'leness *n.* **un-** (1).	**unsystemat'ic, -al** *adjs.* **un-** (1).	**untest'ed** *adj.* **un-** (1).
unsupplied' *adj.* **un-** (1).	**unsystemat'ically** *adv.* **un-** (1).	**unthanked'** *adj.* **un-** (1).
	unsys'tematised, -z- *adj.* **un-** (1).	**unthank'ful** *adj.* **un-** (1).

or highly esteemed: without having a value assigned: invaluable, priceless (now *rare*); **unvar′nished** not varnished: not artfully embellished or sophisticated. — *v.t.* **unveil′** (*obs.* **unvail′, unvaile′**) to remove or set aside a veil from: to open to public view by ceremonial removal of a covering: to disclose, reveal. — *v.i.* to remove one's veil: to become unveiled, to reveal oneself. — *adj.* **unveiled′** without a veil: with veil set aside or removed: unconcealed and undisguised. — *ns.* **unveil′er; unveil′ing** the ceremonial removal of a covering. — *adjs.* **unvent′ed** not vented: without a vent; **unverā′cious** not truthful. — *n.* **unverac′ity.** — *adj.* **unversed′** not experienced or skilled: not put in verse. — *n.* **unvir′tue** lack of virtue. — *adj.* **unvir′tuous.** — *adv.* **unvir′tuously.** — *adjs.* **unvis′itable** unable to visit (*obs.*): unfit to be visited: unsuitable for visiting; **unvis′ited.** — *vs.t.* **unvīs′or, unviz′ard** to remove or open the visor of. — *vs.i.* to unvisor oneself: to unmask. — *v.t.* **unvoice′** to change to, or utter with, a voiceless sound. — *adj.* **unvoiced′** not given voice to: without voice. — *n.* **unvoic′ing** change to a voiceless sound. — *adjs.* **unvoy′ageable** not navigable, impassable; **unvul′-gar.** — *v.t.* **unvul′garise, -ize** to free from vulgarity.

Words with prefix **un-** (*continued*).

adjs. **unwaged′** not remunerated by wages: unpaid: unemployed; **unware′** (O.E. *unwær*) unwary (*obs.*): unaware, without knowing (*Spens., Milt.*): unexpected (*obs.*). — *adv.* unknowingly: unexpectedly. — *adv.* **unware′ly** unwarily (*obs.*): suddenly, unexpectedly (*Spens.*). — *n.* **unware′ness** (*arch.*) unwariness. — *advs.* **unwares′** unawares (*arch.*): unexpectedly, suddenly: unknowingly (*Shak.*); **unwā′rily.** — *n.* **unwā′riness.** — *adjs.* **unwā′ry** not wary: (*Spens.* **unwarie**) unexpected; **unwashed′, (***B.***)** **unwash′en (the great unwashed** see **great**). — *v.t.* **unwa′ter** to drain (esp. a mine). — *adjs.* **unwa′tered** freed from water: not watered; **unwa′tery; unwayed′** not accustomed to roads: (hence) intractable. — *n.* **unweal′** affliction, ill. — *v.t.* **unweap′on** to disarm. — *adjs.* **unweap′oned** unarmed: disarmed; **unweath′-ered** not worn by the weather or atmospheric agencies. — *v.t.* **unweave′** to undo from being woven. — *adjs.* **unwedge′able (unwedg′able;** *Shak.*) unable to be split with wedges; **unweened′** unexpected; **unweet′ing** unwitting. — *adv.* **unweet′ingly** unwittingly. — *adjs.* **unweighed′** not weighed: not pondered: unguarded; **unweigh′ing** (*Shak.*) thoughtless, inconsiderate; **unwept′** not wept for; **unwhole′some** not wholesome:unsound: tainted in health, taste or morals. — *adv.* **unwhole′-**

somely. — *n.* **unwhole′someness.** — *adv.* **unwiel′dily.** — *n.* **unwiel′diness.** — *adjs.* **unwiel′dy (***Spens.***, etc., un-wel′dy)** difficult to wield or move, from bulk or weakness: heavily awkward: unmanageable. — *v.t.* **unwill′** to will the contrary of: to deprive of will. — *adjs.* **unwilled′** not willed: involuntary; **unwill′ing** reluctant: done reluctantly: not willed, unintentional (*Shak.*). — *adv.* **unwill′ingly.** — *n.* **unwill′ingness.** — *v.t.* **unwind** (un-wīnd′) to undo the winding of: to free from being wound: to wind down or off: to slacken: to relax (*coll.*). — *v.i.* to become unwound: to relax (*coll.*): — *pa.t.* and *pa.p.* **unwound** (un-wownd′). — *adj.* not wound: released from being wound. — *n.* and *adj.* **unwind′ing** uncoiling. — *adj.* not winding. — *v.t.* **unwire′** to take the wire from. — *n.* **unwis′dom** lack of wisdom: foolishness: injudiciousness. — *adj.* **unwise′** not wise: injudicious: foolish. — *adv.* **unwise′ly.** — *n.* **unwise′ness.** — *v.t.* **unwish′** (*Shak.*) to wish to be away, not to be, to be unfulfilled, or to be undone. — *adjs.* **unwished′-for** not wished for; **unwish′ful; unwish′ing; unwist′** not known (*arch.; Spens.*, etc.): unknowing (*Spens*). — *vs.t.* **unwlt′** (*Shak.*) to deprive of wits; **unwitch′** to free from witchcraft. — *adj.* **unwithdraw′ing** liberal, lavish; **unwithhold′en** (*Coleridge*) not held back, not restrained; **unwithhold′ing** not holding back. — *adv.* **unwitt′ily.** — *adj.* **unwitt′ing** without knowing: unaware: not cognisant: unintentional. — *adv.* **unwitt′-ingly.** — *n.* **unwitt′ingness.** — *adj.* **unwitt′y** foolish: unskilled: without wit. — *v.t.* **unwive′** to deprive of a wife. — *adj.* **unwived′** without a wife. — *v.t.* **unwo′man** to make unwomanly. — *n.* **unwo′manliness.** — *adj.* **unwo′manly** not befitting or becoming a woman: not such as a woman is expected to be. — *adv.* in an unwomanly manner. — *adjs.* **unwont′** (now *rare*; *Spens.*, etc.), **unwont′ed** unaccustomed: unusual. — *adv.* **unwont′edly.** — *n.* **unwont′edness.** — *adj.* **un-word′ed** speechless: not expressed in words. — *v.t.* **unwork′** to undo. — *adjs.* **unwork′able** not workable: impracticable; **unworked′** not worked; **unwork′ing; un-work′manlike** not like or worthy of a good workman. — *n.* **unworld′liness.** — *adjs.* **unworld′ly** not of this world: spiritual: above worldly or self-interested motives; **unwormed′** not worm-eaten: (of a dog) not having had the worm or lytta cut out. — *n.* **unworth′** lack of worth. — *adj.* unworthy. — *adv.* **unwor′thily.** — *n.* **unwor′thiness.** — *adjs.* **unwor′thy** not worthy: worthless: unbecoming: discreditable: undeserved; **unwound** see **unwind.** — *v.t.* **unwrap** (un-rap′) to remove wrappings from: to unroll, unwind. — *v.i.* to become

---

unwrapped. *adj.* **unwreaked** (*un-rēkt'*) unrevenged. —
v.t. **unwreathe** (*un-rēdh'*) to take out of a wreathed
condition. — *v.t.* and *v.i.* **unwrink'le** to smooth out
from a wrinkled state. —*adj.* **unwrink'led** not wrinkled,
smooth. — *v.t.* **unwrite'** to undo the writing of. — *adjs.*
unwrīt'ing not writing; **unwritt'en** not written or reduced to writing, oral: (of a rule, law, etc.) traditional,
generally accepted: containing no writing; **unwrought**
(*un-röt'*) not done or worked: not fashioned, formed,
composed, or worked up: not mined: not tilled: undone, brought back to an original state; **unyeaned'**
unborn; **unyiel'ding** not yielding: stiff. obstinate. —
adv. **unyiel'dingly.** — *n.* **unyiel'dingness.** — *v.t.* **unyoke'**
to loose from a yoke or harness: to disjoin. — *v.i.* to
unyoke an animal: to cease work. — *adjs.* **unyoked'**
not yoked or harnessed: freed from yoke or harness:
unrestrained (*Shak.*); **unzoned'** not in zones: ungirt.

una corda ūn'ạ kör'dạ, ōōn'ä kör'dä, (It.; *mus.*) one string
(soft pedal).

unalist *ū'nạl-ist, n.* a holder of one benefice. [L. *ūnus*, one.]

unanimous *ū-nan'i-mạs, adj.* of one mind: without a
dissentient. — *n.* **unanimity** (*ū-nạn-im'i-ti*) agreement
without a dissentient. — *adj.* **unan'imously.** [L. *ūn-
animus — ūnus*, one, *animus*, mind.]

unau *ū'nö, ōō'now, n.* the two-toed sloth. [Fr., from
Tupí.]

una voce *ūn'ạ vō'sē, ōōn'ä wō'ke*, (L.) with one voice.

unberufen *ōōn-bạ-rōōf'ạn*, (Ger.) *adj.* not called for —
used as an exclamation to avert the ill-luck that may
possibly follow an over-confident or boastful statement.

uncate. See **uncus.**

unce *uns, n.* Scots form of **ounce.**

uncial *un'shạl, -si-ạl, adj.* pertaining to an inch or an
ounce: of a form of writing in (usu. large) somewhat
rounded characters used in ancient manuscripts. — *n.*
an uncial letter: uncial writing: MS written in uncials.
[L. *unciālis — uncia*, a twelfth.]

unciform, uncinate, etc. See **uncus.**

uncle *ung'kl, n.* the brother of one's father or mother, or
an aunt's husband, or a great-uncle (used with *cap.* as
a title either before a man's first name, or independently): an elderly man, esp. a Negro (*U.S.*): a pawnbroker (*slang*): (with *cap.*) a title sometimes used by
children for male friends of their parents. — *v.t.* to
address as uncle. — *n.* **un'cleship** the state of being an
uncle. — **Uncle Sam** the United States or its people;
Uncle Tom (*U.S. derog.*) an American Negro whose
co-operative attitude to white people is thought to

show disloyalty to the Negro cause (based on the hero
of Harriet Beecher-Stowe's *Uncle Tom's Cabin.*).
[O.Fr. *uncle* (Fr. *oncle*) — L. *avunculus*, a maternal
uncle.]

unco *ung'kọ, -kō, (Scot.) adj.* strange, unusual: fearsome:
remarkable: great. — *n.* a stranger: a piece of news: a
remarkable thing: — *pl.* **un'cos.** — *adv.* remarkably,
very. — **unco guid** (*gid*) the obtrusively rigorous in
morals. [**uncouth.**]

uncouth. See **un-.**

unction *ungk'shạn, n.* an anointing: that which is used for
anointing: ointment: that quality in language which
raises emotion or devotion: warmth of address: religious glibness: divine or santifying grace: gusto. — *n.*
unctūos'ity unctuousness. —*adj.* **unc'tūous** oily: greasy:
full of unction: offensively suave and smug. — *adv.*
unc'tūously. — *n.* **unc'tūousness.** — **extreme unction**
(*R.C. Church*) the sacrament of anointing a person
with consecrated oil in his last hours. [L. *unctiō,
-ōnis*, unction, besmearing, *ūnctum*, fat.]

uncus *ung'kạs, n.* a hook or hook-like process: — *pl.* **unci**
(*un'sī*). — *adjs.* **unc'ate** hooked; **unciform** (*un'si-förm*)
hook-shaped; **un'cinate, -d** unciform: hooked at the
end. — *n.* **uncī'nus** a hooklet: a marginal tooth of a
mollusc's radula: a hooked chaeta in annelids: — *pl.*
uncī'nī. [L. *uncus* and *uncinus*, hook.]

undate *un'dāt, un'dāted (-id), adjs.* wavy. [L. *unda*, a
wave.]

undated. See **un-.**

undé, unde. See **undee.**

undecimal *un-des'i-mạl, adj.* based on the number eleven.
— *n.* **undec'imole** (*mus.*) a group of eleven notes in time
of eight. [L. *undecim*, eleven — *ūnus*, one, *decem,*
ten.]

undee, undée, undé, unde *un'dā, (her.) adj.* wavy. [Fr.
ondé; cf. **oundy, undate.**]

under *un'dạr, prep.* beneath: below: in or to a position
lower than that of, especially vertically lower: at the
foot of: within, on the covered side of: short of: in or
into subjection, subordination, obligation, liability,
etc., to: in course of: in the state of: (of cultivated land)
supporting a specified crop: by the authority or
attestation of: in accordance with: in the aspect of:
referred to the class, heading, name, etc., of: in the
reign or administration of: within the influence of (a
particular sign of the zodiac). — *adv.* in or to a lower
(esp. vertically lower) position: in or into a lower
degree or condition: in or into subjection: in or into a
covered, submerged, or hidden state: below: under par

---

unvī'tal *adj.* un- (1).
unvi'tiated *adj.* un- (1).
unvit'rifiable *adj.* un- (1).
unvit'rified *adj.* un- (1).
unvō'cal *adj.* un- (1).
unvō'calised, -z- *adj.* un- (1).
unvul'nerable (*Shak.*) *adj.* un- (1).
unwaked' *adj.* un- (1).
unwāk'ened *adj.* un- (1).
unwalled' *adj.* un- (1).
unwand'ering *adj.* un- (1).
unwant'ed *adj.* un- (1).
unward'ed *adj.* un- (1).
unwar'like *adj.* un- (1).
unwarmed' *adj.* un- (1).
unwarned' *adj.* un- (1).
unwarped' *adj.* un- (1).
unwarr'antable *adj.* un- (1).
unwarr'antably *adv.* un- (1).
unwarr'anted *adj.* un- (1).
unwarr'antedly *adv.* un- (1).
unwāst'ed *adj.* un- (1).
unwāst'ing *adj.* un- (1).
unwatched' *adj.* un- (1).
unwatch'ful *adj.* un- (1).
unwatch'fully *adv.* un- (1).
unwatch'fulness *n.* un- (1).

unwā'vering *adj.* un- (1).
unwā'veringly *adv.* un- (1).
unweakened (*-wēk'*) *adj.* un- (1).
unweaned' *adj.* un- (1).
unwearable (*-wār'*) *adj.* un- (1).
unweariable (*-wē'*) *adj.* un- (1).
unwea'riably *adv.* un- (1).
unwea'ried *adj.* un- (1).
unwea'riedly *adv.* un- (1).
unwea'ry *adj.* un- (1).
unwea'rying *adj.* un- (1).
unwea'ryingly *adv.* un- (1).
unwebbed' *adj.* un- (1).
unwed' *adj.* un- (1).
unwedd'ed *adj.* un- (1).
unweed'ed *adj.* un- (1).
unwel'come *adj.* un- (1).
unwel'comed *adj.* un- (1).
unwel'comely *adv.* un- (1).
unwel'comeness *n.* un- (1).
unwell' *adj.* un- (1).
unwell'ness *n.* un- (1).
unwet' *adj.* un- (1).
unwett'ed *adj.* un- (1).
unwhipped' (unwhipt') *adj.*
  un- (1).
unwhis'tleable *adj.* un- (1).

unwife'like *adj.* un- (1).
unwife'ly *adj.* un- (1).
unwigged' *adj.* un- (1).
unwil'ful *adj.* un- (1).
unwinged' *adj.* un- (1).
unwink'ing *adj.* un- (1).
unwink'ingly *adv.* un- (1).
unwiped' *adj.* un- (1).
unwinn'owed *adj.* un- (1).
unwith'ered *adj.* un- (1).
unwith'ering *adj.* un- (1).
unwithheld' *adj.* un- (1).
unwithstood' *adj.* un- (1).
unwit'nessed *adj.* un- (1).
unwon' *adj.* un- (1).
unwood'ed *adj.* un- (1).
unwooed' *adj.* un- (1).
unworn' *adj.* un- (1).
unworr'ied *adj.* un- (1).
unwor'shipful *adj.* un- (1).
unwor'shipped *adj.* un- (1).
unwoundable (*-wōōnd'*) *adj.* un- (1).
unwound'ed *adj.* un- (1).
unwō'ven *adj.* un- (1).
unwrung' *adj.* un- (1).
unzeal'ous *adj.* un- (1).
unzip' *v.t.* un- (2).

(*golf*). — *adj.* lower: subordinate: falling short. — *n.* **un′derling** a contemptuous word for a subordinate: a weakling. — *adj.* **un′dermost** lowest: inmost. — *adv.* -in or to the undermost place. — **under-and-over** see **over-and-under** under **over**. — **go, knock, snow under** see these words; **under age, arms,** etc. see these words; **under the counter** see **count**²; **under the lee** to the leeward. [O.E. *under*; Goth. *undar*, O.N. *undir*, Ger. *unter*, L. *infrā*.]

under- *un-dər-*, in composition, (1) below, beneath; (2) lower in position (*lit.*); (3) lower in rank, or subordinate; (4a) too little in quantity, too small, insufficient; (4b) in too small a degree, insufficiently; (5) not coming, or not allowed to come, to the surface or into the open. — *v.i.* **underachieve′** to achieve less than one's potential or less than expected, esp. academically. — *ns.* **underachiev′er; underachieve′ment.** — *v.t.* and *v.i.* **underact′** to make too little of in acting: to play, for the sake of effect, with little emphasis. — *ns.* **underac′tion** subordinate action: less than normal or adequate action; **underact′or.** — *adj.* **un′der-age** (when) not of full, or the required, age: immature. — *n.* **underā′gent** a subordinate agent. — *adj.* and *adv.* **un′derarm** placed or held under the arm: with the arm below the shoulder. — *v.t.* **underbear′** (*Shak.*) to sustain: (*pa.p.* **underborne′** *Shak.*) perh. to trim (on the lower part), perh. to line or support by a foundation, perh. to have sewn underneath or on strips of tinsel. — *ns.* **un′derbearer** (*dial.*) one who helps to carry a coffin; **underbear′ing.** — *adj.* unassuming. — *n.* **un′derbelly** the under surface of a body or of something suggesting a body: soft underbelly (q.v.). — *v.t.* **underbid′** to offer at a price lower than that of: to outbid: to bid less than the value of (*bridge*). — *v.i.* to bid unduly low. — *n.* (*bridge*) a bid too low to be valid, or less than the hand is worth. — *n.* **underbidd′er** one who underbids: the next below the highest bidder. — *v.t.* **underbite′** to bite insufficiently with acid, as in etching. — *adj.* **underbitt′en.** — **un′derblanket** a blanket of a warm material placed under, rather than over, a person in bed. — *adv.* **un′der-board** (*obs.*) secretly — opp. to *above-board.* — *adjs.* **un′der-bonnet** relating to the engine of a motor vehicle, generally to be found under the bonnet; **underborne** see **underbear.** — *ns.* **un′derbough** a lower branch; **un′der-boy** a boy in the lower school; **un′derbreath** a subdued voice: rumour. — *adj.* **underbred′** of inferior breeding or manners: not pure-bred. — *ns.* **un′derbridge** a bridge carrying a road or railway distinguished from one over it; **un′derbrush** undergrowth or brushwood or shrubs. — *v.t.* to clear of underbrush. — *v.t.* **underbuild′** to build under in support, underpin: to build too little upon or in. — *n.* **un′derbuilder** a subordinate or assistant builder. — *n.* and *v.t.* **un′derbush** underbrush. — *v.t.* **underbuy′** to buy at less than the price paid by, or the value of. — *ns.* **un′dercard** (*boxing*) a programme of matches supporting the main event; **un′dercarriage** the supporting framework under the body of a carriage or wagon: the landing-gear of an aircraft, or its main part; **un′dercart** (*coll.*) an aircraft's landing-gear, the undercarriage; **un′dercast** an air-passage crossing under a road in a mine; **un′dercharge** too small a charge. — *v.t.* **undercharge′** to charge too little, or too little for. — *adj.* **underclad′** not wearing clothes enough. — *ns.* **un′derclay** a bed of clay underlying a coal-seam representing the soil in which the plants grew; **un′derclass** (*U.S.*) a low, or the lowest, social class; **underclass′man** (*U.S.*) a sophomore or freshman; **un′der-clerk** a subordinate clerk; **un′der-clerk′ship; un′dercliff** a terrace of material that has fallen from a cliff. — *v.t.* **un′derclothe** to

provide with underclothing. — *adj.* **un′derclothed** provided with underclothing: (*-klōdhd′*) underclad. — *n.pl.* **un′derclothes** and *n.sing.* **un′derclothing** clothes worn under others, esp. those next to the skin. — *v.t.* **underclub′** (*golf*) to hit with a club which has too great loft to achieve the desired distance. — Also *v.i.* — *ns.* **un′dercoat** a coat worn under another: an underskirt (*obs.*): an underlayer of fur or hair, or of paint. — *v.t.* **un′dercool** to supercool: to cool insufficiently. — *n.* **un′der-coun′tenance** (*Wordsworth*) that which underlies the superficial aspect of the face. — *adj.* **un′dercover** working, done, in secret: (**under cover of** hidden by, using as concealment). — *ns.* **un′dercovert** a covert of undergrowth; **un′der-craft** (*Sterne*) a sly trick. — *v.t.* **undercrest′** (*Shak.*) to bear like a crest. — *ns.* **un′dercroft** (cf. Du. *krocht*, crypt), a crypt, vault; **un′dercurrent** a current under the surface (*lit.* and *fig.*). — *adj.* running below or unseen. — *v.t.* **undercut′** to cut under: to cut away under the surface, so as to leave part overhanging: to undermine: to strike with a heavy blow upward: to underbid: to go beyond in lowering prices. — *adj.* made so as to cut from the underside: effected by undercutting: having the parts in relief cut under. — *n.* (**un′**) the act or effect of cutting under: a blow dealt upward: the tender-loin, or fillet, or underside of a sirloin. — *n.* **un′derdamper** (*mus.*) in a type of upright piano, a damper positioned below the hammers. — *v.t.* **underdevel′op.** — *adj.* **underdevel′oped** insufficiently developed: of a country, with resources inadequately used, having a low standard of living, and backward in education. — *n.* **underdevel′opment.** — *v.t.* **underdo′** to do, perform, act, or esp. cook, insufficiently or inadequately: — *pa.t.* **underdid′;** *pa.p.* **underdone′.** — *ns.* **underdo′er; un′derdog** the dog that gets the worst of it in a fight: anyone in adversity: a person dominated, or being or likely to be beaten, by another. — *adj.* **underdone′** done less than is requisite: insufficiently or slightly cooked. — *vs.t.* **underdrain′** to drain by deep underground ditches; **un′derdraw** to draw or describe with moderation or reticence or short of the truth: to cover the underside of with boards or lath and plaster. — *ns.* **un′derdrawing** an outline drawing on a canvas, etc., done before paint is applied; **un′derdress** underclothing: a dress or part of a dress worn or showing under another. — *v.t.* and *v.i.* **underdress′** to dress too plainly or simply. — *adj.* **underdressed′.** — *n.* **un′derdrive** a gear which transmits to the driving shaft a speed less than engine speed. — *adjs.* **under-driv′en** driven from beneath; **un′derearth** underground. — *ns.* **underemploy′ment** making too little use (of): the condition of having too large a part of the labour force employed: partial employment, or employment on work requiring less skill than the worker has; **un′der-espi′al** a subordinate spy (*Scott*). — *v.t.* **underes′timate** to estimate or value too low. — *n.* an estimate that falls short of the truth or true quantity. — *n.* **underestimā′tion.** — *v.t.* **underexpose′** to expose too little, esp. (*phot.*) to light. — *ns.* **underexpōs′ure; un′derfelt** an older term for underlay, usu. of felt. — *adj.* **underfin′ished** (of cattle and sheep) having too little finish (q.v.). — *v.t.* **un′derfire′** to fire or bake insufficiently. — *n.* **un′derflow** undercurrent. — *adv.* **underfoot′** beneath one's feet. — *v.t.* to underpin. — *adj.* (**un′**) downtrodden. — *n.* **un′derfur** short fur hidden by longer hairs; **un′dergarment** any article of clothing worn under another, esp. that worn next to the skin, underclothing. — *v.t.* **undergird′** to brace with ropes under the bottom: to support (*fig.*). — *adj.* **un′derglaze** applied or done before glazing (as *underglaze painting* in a vitrifiable pigment before the glaze

---

undercapitalisā′tion, -z- *n.* **under-** (4a).
undercap′italised, -z- *adj.* **under-** (4a).
undercon′sciousness *n.* **under-** (5).
un′der-constable *n.* **under-** (3).
un′dercook *n.* **under-** (3).

un′derdeck *n.* **under-** (2).
underfed′ *adj.* **under-** (4b).
un′derfeed′ *v.t., v.i.* **under-** (4b).
underfulfil′ *v.t.* **under-** (4b).
underfund′ing *n.* **under-** (4b).
un′derfloor *adj.* **under-** (1).

un′dergown *n.* **under-** (1).
undergrown′ *adj.* **under-** (4b).
un′der-hangman *n.* **under-** (3).
un′derkeeper *n.* **under-** (3).
un′derking *n.* **under-** (3).
un′derkingdom *n.* **under-** (3).

is applied). — *n.* **undergrad′uate** a student who has not taken any degree (*coll.* contraction **un′dergrad**). — *adj.* pertaining to such. — *ns.* **undergrad′uateship**; **undergraduette′** a slang feminine of *undergraduate.* — *adj.* **un′derground** under the surface of the ground: of a railway, running through underground tunnels: secret: characterised by avant-gardism and experimentation, rejection of current trends or norms, appeal to a minority, anti-establishment tendencies, etc. — *n.* the underworld: an underground place: an underground railway: underlying ground: low ground: a secret resistance movement, or body of people: a group whose activities are partly concerned with resisting things they disapprove of in social, artistic, and political life. — *adv.* **underground′** beneath the surface of the earth: secretly. — *ns.* **un′dergrove** a grove of low trees under taller trees; **un′dergrowth** low plants growing under taller, esp. shrubs under trees: stunted growth. — *adv.* **underhand′** surreptitiously: with the hand below the elbow or shoulder. — *adj.* **un′derhand** surreptitious, secret: unobtrusive (*Shak.*): not straightforward: delivered underhand. — *n.* an underhand ball: (with *the*) a subordinate position. — *adj.* and *adv.* **underhan′ded** underhand: short of hands. — *adv.* **underhan′dedly.** — *n.* **underhan′dedness.** — *adjs.* **underhon′est** (*Shak.*) not quite honest; **underhung′** (or *un′*) (of a lower jaw) protruding: having a protruding lower jaw: running on rollers on a rail below. — *n.* **under-jaw′** the lower jaw. — *adj.* **un′derjawed** with a heavy or underhung under-jaw. — *v.t.* **underkeep′** (*Spens.*) to keep under or in subjection. — *adjs.* **underlaid** see **underlay**; **underlain** see **underlie.** — *vs.t.* **underlap′** to extend beneath and some way beyond the edge of; **underlay′** to support or furnish with something laid under: to lay under: to put down, surpass (*Spens.*): often erroneously for **underlie** — of which it is the *pa.t.* — *v.i.* (*mining*) to hade: — *pa.t.* and *pa.p.* **underlaid′.** — *n.* (*un′*) something laid under, e.g. felt or rubber to help preserve carpet, or (*printing*) piece of paper, etc., pasted under to bring to type-height. — *ns.* **underlay′er** one who underlays: (*un′*) a lower layer, substratum; **un′derlease** a sublease. — *v.t.* and *v.i.* (*-lēs′*) to sublease. — *v.t.* **underlet′** to let below the full value: to sublet. — *ns.* **underlett′er**; **underlett′ing.** — *v.t.* **underlie′** to lie beneath (*lit.* and *fig.*): to undergo: to be subject or liable to: — *pr.p.* **underly′ing**; *pa.t.* **underlay′**; *pa.p.* **underlain′.** — *n.* (*mining*) a hade. — *v.t.* **underline′** to draw a line under: to stress. — *n.* (*un′*) a caption, legend. — *ns.* **un′derlinen** underclothing, properly of linen; **un′derling** see **under**; **un′derlip** a lower lip; **un′derlooker** a mine manager's assistant. — *adj.* **underly′ing** lying beneath (*lit.* and *fig.*): fundamental: present though not immediately obvious. — *n.* **un′derman** an inferior: a subordinate: a man subjected to adverse conditions. — *v.t.* (*-man*) to man with too few. — *adjs.* **undermanned′**; **undermast′ed** with masts too small; **undermen′tioned** mentioned underneath or hereafter. — *v.t.* **undermine′** (*Spens.* **underminde′**) to dig beneath (e.g. a wall) in order that it may fall: to wash away, remove by burrowing, etc., the ground from under: to weaken gradually or insidiously (*fig.*): to intrigue against: to tamper with the fidelity of. — *ns.* **undermī′ner**; **undermī′ning**; **un′dernice′ness** want of niceness or delicacy; **un′dernote** a subdued note: an undertone: a note added below. — *v.t.* to note below. — *adj.* **undernour′ished** living on less food than is necessary for satisfactory health and growth (also *fig.*). — *n.* **undernour′ishment.** — *n.pl.* **un′derpants** an undergarment worn by men and boys, covering the buttocks and sometimes the legs. — **un′derpass** a road passing under another road, a railway, etc.; **un′derpassion** an underlying or subconscious passion. — *v.t.* **underpeep′** (*Shak.*) to peep under. — *v.i.* **underperform′** to do less well than expected, possible, etc. — *v.t.* **underpin′** to support by building underneath, or to prop up (also *fig.*): to corroborate. — *n.* **underpinn′ing.** — *v.t.* **underplant′** to plant smaller plants in between (trees of taller plants). — *v.i.* **underplay′** to play a low card while holding up a higher. — *v.t.* to play down, understate. — *v.t.* and *v.i.* to underact. — *n.* (*un′*) the act of so doing. — *ns.* **un′derplot** a subordinate plot in a play or tale: a secret scheme, a trick; **un′der-power** (*Wordsworth*) an auxiliary power. — *v.t.* **underpraise′** to praise below desert. — *adj.* **underpriced′** having too low a price. — *v.t.* **underprize′** (*obs.* **underprise′**) to underpraise (*Shak.*): to value too little. — *adj.* **underpriv′ileged** not enjoying normal social and economic rights. — Also *n.* — *v.t.* and *v.i.* **under-produce′.** — *n.* **under-produc′tion** too little production: production short of demand. — *adj.* **underproof′** (of alcohol) lower or weaker than proof. — *vs.t.* **underquote′** to offer at a price lower than; **underrate′** to rate too low. — *n.* (*un′*) a price less than the worth. — *adj.* inferior (*Swift*). — *n.* **under-representā′tion** too little representation: less representation than one is entitled to. — *adjs.* **under-represent′ed**; **un′der-ripe′** not quite ripe. — *n.* **un′der-roof** a roof under another (*Tennyson*). — *v.t.* **underrun′** to run or pass beneath: to take aboard on one side (as a cable, line, net, for examination, clearing, baiting) and put overboard on the other. — *v.i.* to move under: to run on the underside. — *ns.* **underrunn′ing**; **un′der-saw′yer** a bottom-sawyer: an inferior, an unimportant person. — *v.t.* **undersay′** (*Spens.* **undersaye′**) to say in answer or contradiction (*obs.*). — *n.* **un′der-school** the lower or junior school (*obs.*). — *v.t.* **underscore′** to underline. — *n.* **un′derscrub** brushwood. — *v.t.* **underseal′** to coat exposed parts of underside of (a motor vehicle) with corrosion-resisting substance. — Also *n.* (*un′*). — *ns.* **underseal′ing**; **un′dersec′retary** a secretary immediately under the principal secretary; **under-sec′retaryship**; **un′derself** the subconscious self. — *v.t.* **undersell′** to sell below the price charged by: to sell too cheap. — *ns.* **undersell′er**; **un′dersense** a deeper sense: a secondary sense: a subconscious awareness; **un′derset** an undercurrent: a lower vein of ore: a set of underclothing. — *v.t.* (*-set′*) to set under: to prop: to sublet (*obs.*). — *adjs.* **undersexed′** having less than normal interest in sexual relations or activity; **un′dershapen** (*Tennyson*) imperfectly formed. — *n.* **un′dershirt** a man's collarless undergarment usu. of woven cotton, which may or may not have sleeves. — *v.t.* **undershoot′** to fail to reach by falling short (also *fig.*). — *n.* (*aero.*) a falling short of the mark in landing. — *n.pl.* **un′dershorts** (*U.S.*) short underpants. — *adj.* **un′dershot** driven by water passing under: underhung. — *ns.* **un′dershrub** a shrubby plant, or a low shrub; **un′derside** the lower surface. — *v.t.* **undersign′** to sign below. — *adjs.* **un′dersigned** (or *-sīnd′*) whose signature is appended; **un′dersized** below the usual or desired size. — *ns.* **un′derskinker** (*Shak.*) an assistant tapster; **un′derskirt** a petticoat: a foundation for a dress or skirt; **un′dersky** a lower sky (*poet.*). — *adj.* **underslung′** suspended, or supported, from above, or hung so as to extend below a part which, in another arrangement, it might be wholly above. — *n.* **un′dersong** a burden, refrain, etc., of song or of sound: an undertone less pleasant in quality (*fig.*). — *v.i.* and *v.t.* **underspend′** to spend less than one could or should (of e.g. a budget). — *n.* the amount left unspent from an allocated budget, etc. —

---

un′dermeaning *n.* **under-** (5).
un′dernamed *adj.* **under-** (1).
underpaid′ *adj.* **under-** (4b).
underpay′ *v.t.* and *v.i.* **under-** (4b).
underpay′ment *n.* **under-** (4a).
underpeo′pled *adj.* **under-** (4b).

underpop′ulated *adj.* **under-** (4b).
underpow′ered *adj.* **under-** (4b).
underprepara′tion *n.* **under-** (4b).
underprepared′ *adj.* **under-** (4b).
underprop′ *v.t.* **under-** (1).
un′dersea *adj.* **under-** (1).

undersea′ *adv.* **under-** (1).
un′der-shepherd *n.* **under-** (3).
un′dersheriff *n.* **under-** (3).
un′dersleeve *n.* **under-** (1).
un′dersoil *n.* **under-** (2).
un′derten′ancy *n.* **under-** (3).

adj. **understaffed'** having too few members of staff. — *v.t.* **understate'** to state more moderately than truth would allow or require: to state or describe, or to use artistically, without emphasis. — *adj.* **understät'ed** effective through simplicity, without embellishment or dramatic emphasis. — *ns.* **understate'ment** (or *un'*); **un'dersteer** a tendency in a motor-car to follow a wider curve than the turning applied by the steering wheel should cause it to follow. — Also *v.i.* — *n.* **un'derstock'** (*arch.*) a stocking. — *vs.t.* **understock'** to supply with an insufficient amount of stock; **understood** see **understand.** — *ns.* **un'derstor(e)y** the smaller trees and bushes forming a lower level of cover beneath the tallest trees in a forest, etc.; **un'derstrapper** an inferior agent, an underling. — *adj.* **un'derstrapping** subordinate. — *n.* **un'derstratum** an underlayer: — *pl.* **un'derstrata.** — *v.t.* **un'derstudy** to study (a part), or to study the part of (an actor or other person) in order to take over in an emergency, or in due course. — Also *v.i.* — *n.* one who understudies. — *ns.* **un'derthirst** (*Wordsworth*) an underlying or subconscious thirst; **un'derthrust** (*geol.*) a fault in which one mass of rock is moved under another relatively static layer. — *adj.* **undertimed'** (of a photograph) underexposed. — *ns.* **un'dertint** a subdued tint: a tint showing through; **un'dertone** a subdued tone of voice, sound, colour, etc.: a tone felt as if pervading, underlying, or perceptible through others, including (*fig.*) an emotional tone: a difference tone (q.v.): a low state of body. — *adj.* **un'dertoned** in an undertone: (*-tond'*) wanting in tone. — *ns.* **un'dertow** (*-tō*) an undercurrent opposed to the surface current: the recoil or back-draught of a wave; **un'der-trick** a trick short of the number declared; **under-turn'key** an assistant jailer; **undervaluā'tion.** — *v.t.* **underval'ue** to value below the real worth: to rate as inferior (with *to*) (*Shak.*): to reduce the value of: to esteem too lightly. — *n.* (*un'*) a value or price under the real worth. — *ns.* **underval'uer; un'dervest** an undershirt, or a similar garment for a woman; **un'derviewer** an underlooker; **un'dervoice** a subdued voice; **un'derwater** underground water: undertow. — *adj.* existing, acting, carried out, etc., below the surface of the water: below the waterline. — Also *adv.* — *ns.* **un'derwear** underclothing; **un'derweight** shortness of weight: short weight. — *adj.* short in weight. — *v.t.* **underwhelm'** (*facet.*) to fail to impress. — *n.* **un'derwing** a wing covered by another, as an insect's hind-wing: a moth (*Catocala*, etc.) with conspicuous hind-wings. — *adj.* and *adv.* under the wing. — *ns.* **un'derwit** inferior wit: a half-wit; **un'derwood** undergrowth: a coppice. — *v.t.* **underwork'** to undermine: to work secretly against (*obs.*; *Shak.* *pa.t.* **underwrought'**): to employ too little in work: to work for less than the wage of. — *v.i.* to do less work than is desirable. — *n.* (*un'*) a substructure: underhand, inferior, or subordinate work. — *ns.* **un'derworker; un'der-work'man; un'derworld** the world beneath the heavens: the world or a region, beneath the earth: the place of departed souls: the part of the world below the horizon: the antipodes: a submerged, hidden, or secret region or sphere of life, esp. one given to crime, profligacy, or intrigue. — *v.t.* **un'derwrite** to write (something) beneath: to sign one's name beneath (*obs.*): to subscribe (one's name) (*obs.*): to subscribe to (a statement, etc.): to agree to (*Shak.*): to accept the risk of insuring: to guarantee to take, or find others to take (certain shares, under certain conditions): to write too little about: (*refl.*) to write below the level of which one is capable. — *v.i.* to practise as an underwriter. — *ns.* **un'derwriter** one who practises insurance business, esp. in ships; **un'derwriting.** — *v.t.* **underwrought** see **underwork.**
underachieve ... to ... **underfire.** See **under-.**
underfong *un-dər-fong'*, (*Spens.*) *v.t.* to overcome, entrap:

to undertake. [O.E. *underfangen*, pa.p. of *underfōn*, to receive, take, steal.]
underfoot ... to ... **underglaze.** See **under-.**
undergo *un-dər-gō'*, *v.t.* to be subjected to: to endure or suffer: to pass through, experience: to enjoy, partake of (*Shak.*): to take in hand (*Shak.*). — *adj.* **undergō'ing** (*Shak.*) enduring. [Late O.E. *undergān* — *gān*, to go.]
undergraduate ... to ... **undermining.** See **under-.**
undern *un'dərn*, (*obs.*) *n.* the third hour, about nine in the morning: terce: the forenoon: the afternoon or early evening: a light meal. — *n.* **un'derntime** (*Spens.* **un'dertime**) the time of the midday meal. [O.E. *undern*.]
underneath *un-dər-nēth'*, *adv.* and *prep.* beneath, below in position (*lit.* and *fig.*): under the control of (*arch.*). — *n.* the under part or side. [O.E. *underneothan*.]
underniceness ... to ... **understaffed.** See **under-.**
understand *un-dər-stand'*, *v.t.* to comprehend: to grasp with the mind: to be able to follow the working, logic, meaning, etc., of: to take the meaning of (a sign, person): to realise: to have a sympathetic, usu. tacit, perception of the character, aims, etc., of (a person): to know the meaning of: to be expert in: to have knowledge or information (that), to have been informed: to assume, take to be true: to interpret (as), take to mean: to imply: (*refl.*) to know how to behave (*Shak.*): to stand under (*Shak.*): hence, to support. — *v.i.* to have understanding: to comprehend: — *pa.t.* and *pa.p.* **understood'**, *arch. pa.p.* **understand'ed.** — *adj.* **understand'able.** — *ns.* **understand'er** one who understands: a supporter (*Browning*): one who stands in the pit of a theatre (*obs.*); **understand'ing** the act of comprehending: the power to understand: intellect: an informal agreement: an understood condition (e.g. *on the understanding that*): sympathetic or amicable agreement of minds: (in *pl.*) feet, legs, shoes, boots (*slang*). — *adj.* intelligent: discerning: sympathetic. — *adv.* **understand'ingly.** — *adj.* **understood'** (often *gram.*) implied but not expressed. — **understand each other** or **one another** to have reached an agreement, sometimes collusive. [O.E. *understandan* — *under*, *standan*, to stand.]
understate ... to ... **understudy.** See **under-.**
undertake *un-dər-tāk'*, *v.t.* to receive (*obs.*): to perceive (*Spens.*): to assume (*Shak.*): to be surety for (*Shak.*): to pledge oneself (that): to take upon oneself: to take upon oneself to deal with, manage, or look after): to set about, engage in: to engage in contest with. — *v.i.* to promise (*arch.*; sometimes with *for*): to become a surety (for): to conduct funerals (*coll.*): — *pa.t.* **undertook';** *pa.p.* **undertā'ken**, (*Shak.*, etc.) **undertā'en'**, (*Spens.*) **undertane'.** — *adj.* **undertā'kable.** — *ns.* **un'dertaker** one who takes in hand an enterprise, task, or encounter: one who manages funerals: a projector, entrepreneur: a contractor: a publisher (*obs.*): a stage producer (*obs.*): a compiler or editor (*obs.*): a sponsor or surety (*obs.*): a tax farmer (see **farmer**) (*obs.*): one of the Fife adventurers who tried to colonise the island of Lewis (*c.* 1600): one of those who undertook to manage the House of Commons for the Stewart kings: one of the English and Scottish settlers on forfeited lands in Ireland; **un'dertaking** that which is undertaken: any business or project engaged in: a task one sets oneself: the business of conducting funerals. — Also *adj.* [12th cent. *undertaken*, to entrap — O.E. *under*, late O.E. *tacan*; see **take.**]
underthirst, underthrust. See **under-.**
undertime. See **underntime** at **undern.**
undertimed ... to ... **underwater.** See **under-.**
underway. See under **way²** and **weigh².**
underwear ... to ... **underwrought.** See **under-.**
undies *un'diz*, (*coll.*) *n.pl.* women's underclothing. [**under.**]

---

un'dertenant *n.* **under-** (3).
un'der-tū'nic *n.* **under-** (1).

underuse (*-ūz'*) *v.t.* **under-** (4b).
underuse (*-ūs'*) *n.* **under-** (4a).

underutilisā'tion, -z- *n.* **under-** (4a).
underū'tilise, -ize *n.* **under-** (4b).

undine *un'dēn, un-dēn'* (Ger. *ōon-dē'nə*), *n.* according to Paracelsus, a water-spirit that can obtain a human soul by bearing a child to a human husband. — **un'dinism** (*psych.*) a preoccupation with water, specif. with urine and the act of urination. [L. *unda*, a wave.]

undulate *un'dū-lāt, v.t.* and *v.i.* to move like or in waves: to make or be wavy: to vibrate. — *adj.* wavy: with wavy margin, surface, or markings. — Also **un'dulated.** — *n.* **un'dulancy.** — *adj.* **un'dulant** undulating: rising and falling. — *adv.* **un'dulately.** — *adj.* **un'dulating.** — *adv.* **un'dulatingly.** — *ns.* **undula'tion** an undulating, a wavelike motion or form: waviness: a wave; **undula'tionist** one who holds the undulatory theory of light. — *adjs.* **un'dulatory** of the nature of undulation: undulating: wavy: referring light to waves in a medium; **un'dulose, un'dulous** (*both rare*) undulating. — **undulant fever** Malta, Mediterranean, Neapolitan, or Rock fever, a remittent fever with swelling of the joints and enlarged spleen, caused by a bacterium (Brucella) transmitted by goat's (or cow's) milk. [L. *undulātus*, undulated — *unda*, a wave.]

unguent *ung'gwənt, n.* ointment. — *n.* **unguentā'rium** a vessel for holding unguents. — *adj.* **ung'uentary** of or for unguents. — *n.* an unguentarium: a perfumer, maker of or dealer in unguents. [L. *unguentum* — *unguĕre*, to anoint.]

unguis *ung'gwis, n.* a claw or nail: the claw of an insect's foot: the claw of a petal: — *pl.* **ung'ues** (*-gwēz*). — *adjs.* **ung'ual** (*-gwəl*) of or bearing a claw; **unguiculate** (*unggwik'ū-lāt*), **-d** clawed; **unguiform** (*ung'gwi-förm*). [L. *unguis*, a nail.]

ungula *ung'gū-lə, n.* a hoof (*zool.*): a section of a cylinder, cone, etc., cut off by a plane oblique to the base (*geom.*): — *pl.* **ung'ulae** (*-lē*). — *adj.* **ung'ulate** hoofed. — *n.* a hoofed animal, a member of the order **Ungulā'ta,** hoofed digitigrade mammals, as artiodactyls and perissodactyls. — *adjs.* **unguled** (*ung'gūld*; *her.*) with claws or hoofs tinctured specially; **ung'uligrade** walking on hoofs. [L. *ungula*, claw, hoof — *unguis*, nail.]

uni *ū'ni, n.* a coll. shortening of **university.**

uni- *ū-ni-*, in composition, one. — *adj.* **uniax'ial** having one axis, esp. (*crystal.*) one optic axis or (*biol.*) one main line of growth or unbranched axis. — *adv.* **uniax'ially.** — *adj.* **unicam'eral** (L. *camera*, vault; see **chamber**) having or consisting of but one chamber. — *ns.* **unicam'eralism** the system or principle of having one legislative chamber; **unicam'eralist.** — *adjs.* **unicell'ular** of or having but one cell; **unicen'tral** having a single centre; **ū'nicolor** (or *-kul'*), **ū'nicolour, -ed, unicol'orate, unicol'orous** of one uniform colour. — *n.* **ū'nicorn** (L. *cornū*, a horn) a fabulous animal mentioned by ancient Greek and Roman authors as a native of India, with a body like a horse and one straight horn: an unfortunate translation of the Hebrew *re'ēm* (Assyr. *rīmu*) anticipated by the *monokerōs* of the Septuagint — variously understood as the rhinoceros, wild ox, ox-antelope (*B.*): applied to various animals with the appearance of a single horn, as the narwhal (also **un'icorn-whale**), a moth (**un'icorn-moth**) whose caterpillar has a long process, an American Pacific gasteropod (*Latirus*, etc.) with a spine on the lip of the shell (**un'icorn-shell**): a team of two abreast and one in front, or a carriage drawn by it: an old Scottish gold coin bearing a unicorn, worth 18s. Scots: (*cap.*) one of the Scottish pursuivants. — *adj.* one-horned. — *adv.* with two abreast and one in front. — *adj.* **unicos'tāte** (L. *costa*, rib.) one-ribbed. — *n.* **ū'nicycle** an acrobat's one-wheeled cycle. — *adjs.* **unidirec'tional** mainly or wholly in one direction; **unifil'ar** (L. *filum*, thread) with one thread; **uniflō'rous** (L. *flōs, flōris*, a flower) one-flowered; **unifo'liate** (L. *folium*, leaf; *bot.*) with only one leaf: unifoliolate; **unifo'liolāte** (L. *foliolum*, dim. of *folium*, leaf; *bot.*) having a single leaflet, but compound in structure; **unilā'biate** (L. *labium*, lip) one-lipped; **unilat'eral** (L. *latus, lateris*, side) one-sided: on one side: affecting, involving, etc. only one person, group, etc. out of

several: produced with one side of the tongue only, as a Welsh *ll* (*phon.*). — *ns.* **unilat'eralism; unilat'eralist** one who favours unilateral action, esp. in abandoning or reducing production of nuclear weapons; **unilateral'ity.** — *adv.* **unilat'erally.** — *adjs.* **unilingual** (L. *lingua*, tongue) of, in, using, one tongue, language; **unilit'eral** (L. *littera* (*lītera*), letter) of, or involving, one letter or script; **unilō'bar, unilōbed'** having one lobe; **unilob'ular** having one lobule; **uniloc'ular** having but one loculus or cavity; **uninū'clear** with a single nucleus; **uninū'cleate; unip'arous** (L. *parĕre*, to bring forth) producing one at a birth: monochasial (*bot.*); **unipar'tīte** not divided into parts; **u'niped** (L. *pēs, pedis*, foot) one-footed. — *n.* a one-footed person, animal, or object. — *adjs.* **uniper'sonal** existing as only one person; **uniplā'nar** lying in one plane. — *n.* **ū'nipod** (Gr. *pous, podos*, foot) a one-legged support, e.g. for a camera. — *adj.* **unipō'lar** of, from, or using one pole: of a nerve cell, having one process only. — *n.* **unipolar'ity.** — *adj.* **unisē'rial** in one series or row. — *adv.* **unisē'rially.** — *adj.* **unisē'riate** uniserial. — *adv.* **unisē'riately.** — *adjs.* **ū'nisex** of a style, esp. in clothes, adopted by both sexes: applicable to, usable by, etc. persons of either sex; **unisex'ual** of one sex only. — *n.* **unisexual'ity.** — *adv.* **unisex'ually.** — *n.* **ū'nison** (or *-zən*; L. *sonus*, sound, *sonāre*, to sound) identity of pitch: loosely, pitch differing by one or more octaves: a sound of the same pitch: complete agreement. — *adj.* in unison. — *adj.* **unis'onal.** — *adv.* **unis'onally.** — *n.* **unis'onance.** — *adjs.* **unis'onant; unis'onous.** — *ns.* **univa'lence** (or *-iv'əl-*), **univa'lency** (or *-iv'əl-*). — *adj.* **univa'lent** (*chem.*) having a valency of one, capable of combining with one atom of hydrogen or its equivalent. — *adj.* and *n.* (pertaining to) one of the single chromosomes which separate in the first meiotic division. — *adj.* **ū'nivalve** having one valve or shell only. — *n.* a shell of one valve only: a mollusc whose shell is composed of a single piece. — *adjs.* **unival'vular; univā'riant** having one degree of freedom; **univā'riate** (of a distribution) having one variate only; **univol'tine** (It. *volta*, a turn, winding) of silkworms, having one brood a year. [L. *ūnus*, one; Gr. *oinē*, ace (on dice); O.E. *ān*, one.]

Uniat *ū'ni-ət, n.* a member of any community of Christians, esp. in eastern Europe and Asia, that acknowledges the papal supremacy but which is allowed to retain its own customs and practices with regard to all else — clerical matrimony, communion in both kinds, church discipline, rites and liturgy. — Also **U'niate** (*-āt, -ət*). [Russ. *uniyat* — *uniya*, union — L.L. *uniō, -ōnis* — L. *ūnus*, one.]

uniaxial ... to ... unicentral. See uni-.

unicity *ū-nis'i-ti, n.* oneness: uniqueness. [L. *ūnicus*, unique.]

unicolor ... to ... unifoliolate. See uni-.

uniform *ū'ni-förm, adj.* alike: alike all over, throughout, or at all times: unvarying: of a military or other uniform. — *n.* a distinctive garb for members of a body: a suit of it. — *v.t.* to make uniform: to clothe in uniform. — *adj.* **ū'niformed** wearing uniform. — *n.* and *adj.* **uniformitā'rian.** — *ns.* **uniformitā'rianism** the doctrine that geological changes were brought about not in the main by great convulsions but by such action as may be seen going on now; **uniformitā'rianist; uniform'ity** the state or fact of being uniform: agreement with a pattern or rule: sameness: likeness between parts. — *adv.* **ū'niformly.** — *n.* **ū'niformness.** [L. *ūniformis* — *ūnus*, one, *fōrma*, form.]

unify *ū'ni-fī, v.t.* to make into one: to consolidate. — *adjs.* **ū'nifiable; unif'ic** making one. — *n.* **unificā'tion.** — *adj.* **ū'nified.** — *n.* **ū'nifier.** — *n.* and *adj.* **ū'nifying.** — **unified field** an ultimate basis on which the physicist seeks to bring within a single theory the workings of all natural phenomena; **unified scale** the scale of atomic and molecular weights based on the mass of the carbon-12 isotope of carbon being taken as 12 exactly. — **Unification Church** see **Moonies.** [L.L. *unificāre* — L.

ūnus, one, *facĕre*, to make.]

unigeniture *ū-ni-jen'i-chər, n.* the state or fact of being the only begotten. — *n.* **Unigen'itus** (from its first word) a bull of Clement XI (1713) condemning 101 propositions of the Jansenist Quesnel. [L.L. *ūnigenitus*, only-begotten.]

unilabiate ... to ... **uninucleate.** See **uni-**.

Unio *ū'ni-ō, n.* the pearl-mussel genus of freshwater molluscs, giving name to the family **Unionidae** (*ū-ni-on'i-dē*). — *n.* **union** (*ūn'yən; Shak.*) a fine large pearl, a unique or single pearl. [L. *ūniō, -ōnis*, prob. — *ūnus*, one (cf. **solitaire** as applied to a diamond set by itself).]

union[1] *ūn'yən, n.* a uniting: the state of being united: the state of wedlock: a united whole: combination: a growing together in healing: general concord: the incorporation of states in a federation or in a single state: a single state (or sometimes a federation) thus formed: an association or league, esp. a trade union: a student's club: (*formerly*) a combination of parishes for poor law purposes: its workhouse or poorhouse: a connecting part for pipes, etc.: a device emblematic of union borne in the canton of a flag: the same device used separately as a flag, as the Union Jack: a textile fabric of more than one kind of fibre: the set formed from all the elements present in two (or more) sets. — *n.* **ūnionīsā'tion, -z-.** — *v.t.* **ūn'ionise, -ize** to recruit into a trade union: to organise the workforce of into a trade union. — *ns.* **ūn'ionism** (also *cap.*); **ūn'ionist** an advocate or supporter of or believer in union or trade unions: a member of a trade union: (*cap.*) an opponent of Irish Home Rule, esp. a Liberal Unionist (see **Liberal**) — hence a Conservative: (*cap.*) a supporter of the federal union of the United States, esp. at the time of the Civil War. — Also *adj.* — **union catalogue** a library catalogue combining, usu. alphabetically, the contents of a number of catalogues or listing the contents of a number of libraries; **union flag** a flag symbolising union, esp. the national flag of the United Kingdom, consisting of a union of the crosses of St George, St. Andrew, and St Patrick, commonly called the **Union Jack; union language** an artifical language formed from related dialects; **union list** a list of materials available on a specific subject, in each case naming the library, and locating the material precisely in it; **union pipes** see **uillean(n) pipes; Union Shona** see **Shona; union suit** combinations for man or boy. — **art union** an association aiming at promotion of an interest in the fine arts, esp. by raffling pictures; **the Union** the legislative incorporation of England and Scotland in 1707, or of Ireland with both in 1801: the American Union or United States: the Union of South Africa (1910). [Fr. *union* — L.L. *ūniō, -ōnis* — L. *ūnus*, one.]

union[2]. See **Unio**.

unionised[1]. See **un-**.

unionised[2]. *Pa.t.* and *pa.p.* of **unionise** (see under **union**[1]).

uniparous ... to ... **unipolarity.** See **uni-**.

unique *ū-nēk', adj.* sole: without a like: often used loosely for unusual, pre-eminent: found solely in, belonging solely to, etc. (with *to*). — *n.* anything that is unique. — *adv.* **unique'ly.** — *n.* **unique'ness.** [Fr., — L. *ūnicus* — *ūnus.*]

uniserial ... to ... **unisonous.** See **uni-**.

unit *ū'nit, n.* one: a single thing or person: a single element, section, or item, regarded as the lowest subdivision of a whole: a group of persons forming a subdivision of a larger body: a distinct part within a piece of electrically powered equipment which has its own specific function: a single complete domestic fixture combining what are sometimes separate parts: a usu. independently owned dwelling apartment, one of several into which a building is divided, a home-unit (*Austr.*): the least whole number: anything taken as one: a quantity by reference to which others are measured. — *adj.* of the character or value of a unit: individual. — *adj.* **ū'nital.** — *n.* **Unitā'rian** one who asserts the unity of the Godhead as opposed to the Trinity, ascribes divinity to God the father only, and who believes that each congregation should have independent authority: one who believes in the unity of God, in freedom of, and tolerance of the differences in, religious beliefs, etc.: a member of a particular body holding such doctrines: a monotheist generally: (without *cap.*) a holder of some belief based on unity or union. — Also *adj.* — *n.* **Unitā'rianism** (also without *cap.*). — *adj.* **ū'nitary** pertaining to unity or to a unit: of the nature of a unit: integral: based on unity. — *n.* **unitīsā'tion, -z-.** — *v.t.* **ū'nitise, -ize** to convert into unit trusts (*commerce*): to make into, or treat as, a unit. — **unitary taxation** (*U.S.*) the system of taxing multinational companies on their worldwide income rather than merely that received within the area under the taxation authority's jurisdiction; **unit furniture** furniture which may be bought as single items rather than as sets or suites; **u'nitholder** one holding a unit of securities in a unit trust; **unit-pack'aging** a method of packaging (pills, etc.) in which the items are individually encased; **unit price; unit-pri'cing** a method of pricing foodstuffs, etc. by showing the cost per agreed unit, e.g. kilogram, pound, as well as, or instead of, the overall price of the item; **unit trust** see **trust.** — **unit of account** a monetary unit not necessarily corresponding to any actual denomination of currency and in certain cases of variable value, used as a basis of exchange or comparison or as a unit in accounting. [For **unity.**]

unite *ū-nīt', v.t.* to make one: to join into one: to join: to combine: to clasp: to marry: to have in combination: to make to agree or adhere. — *v.i.* to become one: to combine: to join: to grow or act together. — *n.* (also *ū'*) an English gold coin of James I, worth 20s., later 22s. — *adj.* **unī'ted.** — *adv.* **unī'tedly.** — *ns.* **unī'tedness; unī'ter.** — *n.* and *adj.* **unī'ting.** — *n.* **union** (*ū-nish'ən*) conjunction. — *adj.* **unitive** (*ū'ni-tiv*) harmonising, uniting. — *adv.* **u'nitively.** — **United Brethren** see **Moravian; United Free Church** see under **free; United Irishmen** a radical political organisation which, agitating for absolute emancipation, parliamentary reform and universal suffrage, caused the 1798 rising; **United Kingdom (of Great Britain and Ireland;** from 1922 **Northern Ireland)** the official title adopted in 1801 for the kingdom consisting of England and Wales, Scotland, and Ireland; **United Nations** an association of states that in 1945 undertook many of the functions of the dissolved League of Nations; **United Presbyterian Church** see under **presbyter; United Provinces** Holland, Zealand (Zeeland), Utrecht, Gelderland, Groningen, Friesland, and Overyssel, united in 1579 under the Union of Utrecht; **United Reformed Church** a church formed by the union in 1972 of the Presbyterian Church in England and the Congregational Church in England and Wales; **United States** a federal union of states, esp. that of (north) America. [L. *ūnītus*, pa.p. of *ūnīre*, to unite — *ūnus*, one.]

unity *ū'ni-ti, n.* oneness: the number one: the state or fact of being one or at one: that which has oneness: a single whole: the arrangement of all the parts to one purpose or effect: a unite (*Dickens*). — **unity element** (*math.*) an identity element for multiplication. — **the unities** (of *place, time*, and *action*) the three canons of the classical drama — that the scenes should be at the same place, that all the events should be such as might happen within a single day, and that nothing should be admitted not directly relevant to the development of the plot. [L. *ūnitās, -ātis* — *ūnus*, one.]

univalence ... to ... **univariate.** See **uni-**.

universe *ū'ni-vûrs, n.* all that is: the whole system of things: the cosmos: a system of stars such as the galactic system: the world. — *adj.* **univers'al** of the universe: comprehending, affecting, or for use by, the whole world or all people: without exception: comprising all the particulars: all-round: unlimited: capable of being applied to a great variety of uses. — *n.* that which is universal: a universal proposition: a general term: a universal concept. — *n.* **universalīsā'tion, -z-.** — *v.t.*

univer'salise, -ize-. — *ns.* Univer'salism the doctrine or belief of universal salvation, or the ultimate salvation of all mankind, and even of the fallen angels; Univer'salist a believer in Universalism. — Also *adj.* — *adj.* universalis'tic. — *n.* universality (-*sal'*) the state or quality of being universal. — *adv.* univer'sally. — *n.* univer'salness. — universal beam a beam made in a standard size; universal donor one whose blood can be transfused into persons of the other blood groups without causing destruction of their red blood cells; universal joint one capable of turning all ways; universal second see universal time; universal time mean solar time, Greenwich time, in which the value of the second is subject to irregularities which are due to characteristics of the earth's rotation. [L. *ūniversum*, neut. sing. of *ūniversus*, whole, *ūnus*, one, *vertĕre*, *versus*, to turn.]

university *ū-ni-vûr'si-ti*, *n.* a corporate body (*obs.*): an institution of higher learning with power to grant degrees, its body of teachers, students, graduates, etc., its college or colleges, or its buildings. — *adj.* universitā'rian. — university of the air an earlier name for the Open University (q.v.). [L. *ūniversitās -ātis*, a whole, in L.L. a corporation; see foregoing.]

univocal *ū-niv'ə-kl* or *ū-ni-vō'kl*, *adj.* of one voice: having one meaning only: unmistakable: unambiguous: of things of the same species (*obs.*). — *n.* a word with but one meaning. — *adv.* univocally. [L. *ūnivocus* — *ūnus*, one, *vōx*, *vōcis*, a voice.]

univoltine. See uni-.

unked, unkempt, unket, unkid. See un-.

unless *un-les'*, *ən-les'*, *conj.* (tending to pass into a *prep.*) if not. [Earlier followed by *than* or *that*: *on lesse than*, on a less condition than.]

unneath *ə-nēth'*, (*dial.*) *prep.* underneath. [Cf. aneath, underneath.]

uno animo *ū'nō*, *ōō'nō*, *an'i-mō*, *adv.* with one mind. [L.]

until *un-til'*, *ən-til'*, *prep.* and *conj.* till. [Pfx. *und-*, as far as; till.]

unto *un'tōō*, *-tōō*, (*arch.* or *formal*) *prep.* to. — *conj.* (*obs.*) until. [Pfx. *und-*, as far as; to.]

up *up*, *adv.* in, to, toward a higher place, level, or state: aloft: on high: towards a centre (as a capital, great town, university): in residence, at school or college: northward: to windward: in or to a more erect position or more advanced stage of erection: out of bed: on horseback: in an excited state: in revolt: with (increased) vigour, intensity, or loudness: afoot: amiss: into prominence, notice, consideration: forward for sale: in or into court: into custody, keeping, possession: away in a receptacle, place of storage or lodging (as a sheath, purse, stable): ahead in scoring: into closed or compact state, together: to a total: in, near, towards arrival, overtaking, or being abreast: as far as: all the way: to a standstill: at an end: to a finish: thoroughly, completely, fully: well informed, versed. — Also elliptically passing into a verb or interjection by omission of *go*, *come*, *put*, etc., often followed by *with*. — *adj.* placed, going, or directed up: risen: (of time) ended: having gained (so many) more holes than an opponent (*golf*): — *compar.* upp'er; *superls.* up'most, upp'ermost see below. — *prep.* in an ascent along, through, or by: to or in a higher position on: to or in an inner or more remote part of: along against the current: along: up into (*U.S.*). — *n.* a rise: a high place: a success, spell of prosperity: one who is in prosperity. — *v.t.* to drive upstream (as swans for owner marking): to lift or haul up: to raise, increase. — *v.i.* (*coll.*) to set up: to move up: to intervene boldly, start into activity or speech: — *pr.p.* upp'ing; *pa.t.* and *pa.p.* upped (*upt*). — *adjs.* up'most uppermost; upp'er (see above) higher: superior: higher in rank. — *n.* the part of a boot or shoe above the sole and welt: an upper tooth: a drug producing a stimulant or euphoric effect, or a pep pill containing such a drug (*slang*). — *adj.* upp'ermost (see above) highest: first to come into the mind. — *adv.* in the highest place, first. — *n.* upp'ing

the action of up *v.t.* (q.v.). — *adj.* upp'ish assuming, pretentious, snobbish. — *adv.* upp'ishly. — *n.* upp'ishness. — *adj.* upp'ity uppish: difficult to control, resistant to persuasion. — *advs.* up'ward (-*wərd*), upwards from lower to higher: from outlet towards source: from modern to more ancient: in the upper part (upward, upwards, of more than; and upwards and higher, and more). — *prep.* up'ward upwards along. — *adj.* up'ward directed upward: ascending: placed high. — *n.* (*Shak.*) top. — *adv.* up'wardly. — up'wardness a rising tendency: a state of being high. — *adjs.* up'-and-com'ing alert and pushful: likely to succeed (in a career, etc.); up'-and-down' (see also up and down below) undulating: going or working both, or alternately, up and down: downright (*U.S.*); up'-and-o'ver (of a door, etc.) raised to a horizontal position when opened. — Also up'-o'ver. — up'-and-un'der (*Rugby*) a movement in which the ball is kicked high and forwards, and the players rush to try to catch it; up'-beat an unaccented beat, at which the conductor raises his baton: an optimistic note or mood: a promising development. — *adj.* (up'beat) (*coll.*) cheerful: optimistic. — up'-bow a movement of the bow from point towards nut over the strings; up'-current, -draught a rising current of air. — *adj.* upfront see up front below. — up'land inland, hilly, or high-lying country: upper or high land, as opp. to meadows, riversides, etc. (*U.S.*). — *adj.* high-lying: remote: inland: rural: of the uplands. — up'lander. — *adj.* upland'ish (*obs.*) rustic: rural: outlandish. — up'-line a railway line for upgoing trains (i.e. those going to, not from, e.g. a city); upper atmosphere the region of the atmosphere above about 20 miles from the earth. — *adjs.* upp'er-brack'et in an upper grouping in a list, etc.; upp'er-case' (*print.*) lit. kept in an upper case, capital as opposed to small (of letters). — upper class(es) the people of the highest social rank (*adj.* upp'er-class'); upper crust the top of a loaf: the head: a hat: the aristocracy, or the upper class(es) in any society (*adj.* upp'er-crust'); upp'ercut an upward short-arm blow; upper hand mastery, advantage; upper house in a bicameral legislature, the house that is the more restricted in membership, e.g. House of Lords, Senate of U.S. and other countries; Upper Roger corruption of Hindi *Yuva-rājā*, young prince; upper-stock see stock[1]; upper storey (story) any storey above the first floor: the brain (*slang*); upper ten (thousand) the richest or most influential class; upp'erworks the upper part of a structure (of a ship above the load-line): the head (*slang*); upp'ing-block, -stock, -stone a horse block; up'side the upper side. — *adv.* on the upper side. — *adv.* up'side-down', upside down (earlier up so down; *Spens.* up'sideowne') with the upper part undermost: in, or into, complete confusion. — *adj.* turned upside down. — *adv.* up'sides (with) on a par (with): beside. — up'-train a railway train proceeding towards the chief terminus; upward mobility the (desired) state of the upwardly mobile, those people moving (or attempting to move) to a higher social rank or position of greater status. — be up in to have a knowledge of; it is all up (with) there is no hope (for); not up (*tennis*) called when the ball bounces twice before the player manages to hit it; on one's uppers with soles worn off one's shoes: very short of money; on the up (*cricket*) of a stroke, played or the ball rises from its bounce; (on) the up and up (in) a state of continuous progress towards ever greater success: honest, on the level; something is up something is amiss, something unusual or unexpected is happening or has happened; up against face to face with, confronted with (up against it in almost desperate straits); up and doing bestirring oneself; up and down to and fro: here and there through or about: throughout: vertically: out-and-out; up for available for or undergoing (some process): standing as a candidate for; up front (also as *adj.*, up-front', upfront') at the front: to the forefront: foremost: of money, paid in advance: candidly, openly; ups and

downs undulations: vicissitudes; **up to** as far up as: into the immediate neighbourhood or presence of: immersed or embedded as far as: about, meditating or engaged in doing (*coll.*): capable of and ready for (*coll.*): incumbent upon (orig. *U.S.*); **up to date** to the present time or time in question: containing all recent facts, statistics, etc.: knowing the latest developments of fashion, usage, etc. (*adj.* **up′-to-date′**); **up top** (*coll.*) in the head, in respect of intelligence; **up to the minute, moment** right up to the present time (*adjs.* **up-to-the= minute, -moment** very up-to-date); **up town** into town: in or to the residential part of a town (*U.S.*); **up with** abreast of: even with: to take off, swallow: put, get, etc. up (see under **up**), often as an exclamation of approbation and partisanship; **up yours** (*vulg. slang*) an expression of strong refusal, defiance, contempt, etc.; **what's up (with you**, etc.)? what's the matter, trouble?   [O.E. *ūp*, *upp*, up, *uppe*, above, *uppian*, to rise; Ger. *auf.*]

up- in composition, has meanings of *adv.*, *prep.* (and *adj.*; see previous article) **up.** Many of the compounds are *arch.* or *poet.* — *adv.* **up′-along** (*dial.*) up the road: homeward. — *v.i.* **up-anch′or** to weigh anchor. — *vs.t.* **upbear′** to raise aloft: to hold up: to sustain; **upbind′** to bind up: — *pa.p.* **upbound′,** (*Spens.*) also **upbound′en.** — *v.t.* and *v.i.* **upblow′** to blow up or upward: (of the wind) to spring up. — *adj.* **upblown′** (or *up′*) inflated. — *vs.t.* **upbraid′** see separate article; **upbrast′** (*Spens.*) *pa.t.* of **upburst**; **upbray′** (*Spens.*) see separate article. — *n.* **up′break** a break-up: an outbreak. — *v.t.* (-**brāk′**) to break up or open. — *v.i.* to break out. — *n.* **up′bringing** bringing up. — *vs.t.* **upbrought′** (*Spens.*) *pa.p.* of *obs.* **upbring′** to bring up; **upbuild′** to build up. — *n.* **upbuild′ing** (or *up′*) building up: development: edification. — *adj.* **upburn′ing** flaming upwards. — *ns.* **upbuoy′ance** (*rare*) buoying up; **up′burst** a bursting upwards. — *v.t.* and *v.i.* (-*bûrst′*). — *adj.* **upburst′ing.** — *adv.* **upby′, upbye′** (*Scot.*) up the way, a little farther on or up: up there: at the big house. — *n.* **up′cast** an upward throw: an upthrow: material thrown up: an upward current of air from a mine: a shaft carrying it (**up′cast-shaft**): a chance, accident, fluke, or acc. to some, throw or final throw at bowls (*Shak.*): a reproach (*Scot.*): an upset (*Scot.*). — *adj.* thrown or turned upward. — *vs.t.* (-*käst′*) to cast up; **upcatch′** to catch up: — *pa.t.* and *pa.p.* **upcaught′.** — *adv.* **up′-Chann′el** along the English Channel from west to(-wards) east (also *adj.*). — *v.t.* **upcheer′** to encourage: — *pa.t.* **upcheered′,** (*Spens.*) **upcheard′.** — *adj.* **up′coast** up the coast. — *adv.* (-*kōst′*). — *v.i.* **upcoil′** to coil upwards: to coil up. — *ns.* **up′come** produce, outcome: outward appearance of promise (*Scot.*; *obs.*): decisive movement (*Scot.*); **up′-country** the interior, inland part. — *adj.* (-*kun′*) of or in the interior. — *adv.* in or to the interior. — *v.t.* **update′** to bring up to date. — *n.* (*up′*) the act of bringing up to date: that which is brought up to date. — *v.t.* **up-end′** to set on end: to affect or alter greatly, turn upside down. — *v.i.* to rise on end. — *n.* **up′flow** an upward flowing. — *v.i.* (-*flō′*) to stream up. — *adj.* **up′flung** (or -*flung′*). — *v.t.* **upfoll′ow** to follow (*Keats*). — *n.* **up′gang** (*Scot.*) ascent. — *v.t.* **upgath′er** to gather up or together. — *ns.* **upgradā′tion**; **up′grade** an upward slope or course. — *adj.* and *adv.* uphill. — *v.t.* (-*grād′*) to raise in status, quality, value, etc. — *v.i.* **upgrow′** to grow up: — *pr.p.* **upgrow′ing**; *pa.t.* **upgrew′**; *pa.p.* **upgrown′.** — *n.* and *adj.* **up′growing.** — *adj.* **up′grown.** — *n.* **up′growth** the process of growing up, development: that which grows up: a structure that has grown upward. — *adj.* **up′hand**

lifted by hand. — *v.t.* **uphaud′** Scots form of **uphold.** — *n.* **upheav′al** a heaving up: the bodily elevation of tracts of country: a profound, thorough, or revolutionary change or movement. — *vs.t.* **upheave′; upheld, uphild** see **uphold.** — *adj.* **up′hill** ascending: difficult. — Also *n.* — Also *adv.* (-*hil′*). — *adv.* **uphill′ward** (*Milt.*). — *vs.t.* **uphoard′** (*Spens.*, *Shak.* **uphoord′**) to hoard or heap up; **uphold′** to hold up: to sustain: to countenance: to defend: to keep in repair or good condition: (chiefly *Scot.*, **uphaud′**) to maintain, warrant: — *pa.t.* **upheld′**; *pa.p.* **upheld′,** (*Spens.*) **uphild′.** — *n.* **uphold′er** a support or supporter: a dealer in second-hand clothes, furniture, etc. (*obs.*): a funeral undertaker (*obs.*): an upholsterer (*obs.*). — *n.* and *adj.* **uphold′ing.** — *v.i.* **upjet′** to spout up. — *n.* **up′keep** maintenance. — *vs.t.* **upknit′** to knit up: to bring together, reconcile, or perhaps conclude, explain or sum up (*Spens.*); **uplay′** to lay up, to hoard; **uplead′** to lead up: — *pa.t.* and *pa.p.* **upled′.** — *v.i.* **uplean′** (*Spens.*) to rest one's weight. — *v.t.* **uplift′** to lift up, raise: to elevate: to raise to a higher moral or spiritual level: to elate: to collect (e.g. a parcel), draw (money) (*Scot.*): to increase (e.g. an interim dividend) (*commerce*): — *pa.ps.* and *adjs.* **uplift′** (*arch.*), **uplift′ed.** — *n.* **up′lift** a lifting up, raising: upheaval: elevation, esp. moral or spiritual, or the feeling thereof: an increase (*commerce*). — *adj.* (*up′*) designed to raise higher, usu. of a brassière holding up the breasts. — *n.* **uplift′er.** — *n.* and *adj.* **uplift′ing.** — *adv.* **uplift′ingly.** — *adj.* **uplight′ed** lighted up. — *n.* **up′lighter** a light-fitting that sits e.g. on the floor or a low table and throws light upwards, e.g. on to a picture. — *v.t.* **uplock′** to lock up. — *adj.* **uplock′ed** (*Shak.*). — *v.i.* **uplook′** to look up. — *n.* **up′look** an upward look. — *adj.* **up′lying** upland, elevated. — *ns.* **up′make** the action or mode of making up: constitution (especially mental or moral): slip-proofs arranged in page form; **up′maker**; **up′making** filling-up, esp. between bilge-ways and ship's bottom before launching: arrangement of lines into columns or pages (*print.*). — *adj.* **up-mar′ket** of (buying, selling, or using) commodities relatively high in price, quality or prestige. — Also *adv.* — *v.t.* to make (more) up-market. — *preps.* **upo′** (*ə-pō′*; from *up of*; *arch.* or *dial.*) upon; **upon** (*ə-pon′*, *ə-pən*) on. — *adv.* thereon, on the surface (*Shak.*): on the person (*arch.*): thereafter (*Shak.*): close in approach (*Shak.*). — *adjs.* **up-perch′ed** (*Keats*) perched aloft; **uppiled′** piled up; **up-pricked′** pricked up, erected. — *n.* **up′-putting** (*Scot.*) lodging and entertainment. — *v.t.* **upraise′** to raise or lift up: to exalt: to excite, arouse (*Milt.*). — *adj.* **upraised′.** — *vs.t.* **uprate′** to upgrade: to increase the rate or size of; **uprear′** to raise up: to rear up. — *adj.* **upreared′.** — *n.* **uprest** see **uprist.** — *adj.* **up′right** (also *up′rīt′*, *up-rīt′*) right or straight up: in an erect position (**upright piano** one with the strings in a vertical plane): of habitual rectitude: honest: just: supine (e.g. *lying upright*; *obs.*). — *n.* **up′right** an upright post, stone, stroke, or the like: a vertical member of a structure: an upright piano: an elevation (*obs.*): verticality: a basket-maker's tool. — *v.t.* to set erect or right side up. — *adv.* (*up′rīt*, *up′rīt′*, *up-rīt′*) vertically: honestly. — *advs.* **upright′eously** (*Shak.*) with moral right; **up′rightly** in an upright manner: honestly: vertically. — *ns.* **up′right-man** (*obs. cant*) a sturdy beggar, leader of a gang; **up′rightness**; **uprīs′al**; **uprise′** (or *up′*) rising. — *v.i.* (-*rīz′*) to rise up, arise: — *pa.t.* **uprose′**; *pa.p.* **upris′en.** — *n.* **upris′ing** (or *up′*) a rising up: a violent revolt against a ruling power. — *adj.* which rises up or is rising up. — *n.* **uprist′** (*Shelley* **uprest′**) rising. —

---

upboil′ *v.i.*	**updrawn′** *adj.*	**up′going** *adj.*
upclimb′ *v.t.* and *v.i.*	**upfill′** *v.t.*	**upgoing** (-*gō′* or *up′*) *n.*
upclose′ *v.t.* and *v.i.*	**up′filling** *n.*	**upgrade′able** *adj.*
upcurl′ *v.t.* and *v.i.*	**upflash′ing** *adj.*	**up′gush** *n.*
upcurved′ *adj.*	**upfurl′** *v.t.*	**upgush′** *v.i.*
updrag′ *v.t.*	**upgaze′** *v.i.*	**up′gushing** *adj.*
updraw′ *v.t.*	**upgo′** *v.i.*	**uphang′** *v.t.*

v.i. **uprist′** (*Coleridge*), **upryst′** (*Spens.*) an old form of *upriseth*, mistakenly used for a *pa.t.* or *pa.p.* (or perh. from a misunderstanding of the noun). — *n.* **up′roar** see separate entry. — *v.t.* and *v.i.* **uproll′** to roll up or close: to roll upward. — *v.t.* **uproot′** to pull up by the roots: to destroy (*fig.*): to remove forcibly and completely (from e.g. native land). — *ns.* **uproot′al** uprooting; **uproot′er; uproot′ing.** — *v.i.* **uprose′** *pa.t.* of **uprise.** — *v.i.* **upryst** see **uprist.** — *v.t.* **upset′** to overturn, capsize: to spill or tip out: to interfere with, defeat (a plan): to disconcert: to distress: to disorder (a bodily process or organ): to affect temporarily the health of (a person). — *v.i.* to be upset: — *pa.t.* and *pa.p.* **upset′.** — *n.* (*up′set′*) an overturn or derangement. — *adj.* (*up′set*) of a price, the lowest that will be accepted, at which bidding is started: (*upset′*) disturbed, anxious, unhappy. — *n.* **upsett′er.** — *adj.* **upsett′ing** causing upset: conceited, assuming (*Scot.*). — *n.* overturning: overthrow (*up′*) presumption, overweening assumption (*Scot.*). — *v.t.* and *v.i.* **upshoot′** to shoot upward. — *ns.* (*up′*) an upshooting: that which shoots up: upshot (*Shak.*); **up′shot** the final shot (*archery*): the outcome, final result: the conclusion of an argument: the substance, general effect: aim (*Spens.*): end (*obs.*). — *adj.* (*up′shot′*) shot upward. — Also *pa.t.* and *pa.p.* of **upshoot.** — *n.* **up′sitting** sitting up, esp. after illness or childbirth (*arch.*): a reception of company on the occasion (*obs.*): sitting up at night as part of courtship (*S.Afr.*): listlessness (*obs. Scot.*). — *adj.* (*obs. Scot.*) listless. — *vs.i.* **upspeak′** to begin to speak: — *pa.t.* **upspoke′,** (*arch.*) **upspake′; upspear′** (of grass) to shoot up straight like a spear (*Cowper*); **upspring′** to spring up: to come into being: — *pa.t.* **upsprang′;** *pa.p.* **upsprung′.** — *n.* **up′spring** (*Shak.*) a lively dance (acc. to others, *adj.*, newly introduced). — *adv.* **up′stage** towards the back of the stage. — *adj.* towards the back of the stage: stand-offish, superior (*slang*). — *v.t.* (*up-stāj′*) to treat in a supercilious manner: to move upstage so that (another actor) has to turn his back to the audience, and thus to put him at a disadvantage: to divert interest or attention away from (someone or something). — *adv.* **upstairs′** in or toward a higher storey, or (*fig.*) position. — *adj.* **up′stair(s)** of or in an upper storey or flat. — *n.* **upstairs′** the part of a building above the ground floor: (the occupants (usu. the householder and his family) of) the upper part of a house, as opposed to the servants′ quarters in the basement. — *v.i.* **upstand′** (*Milt.*) to stand up: — *pa.t.* **upstood′.** — *n.* (*building*) a turned-up edge on a horizontal or sloping plane where it adjoins a vertical plane. — *adj.* **upstand′ing** erect: on one′s feet (*Scot.*): straight and well-built: honest and downright. — *v.i.* **upstare′** to stare upward: (of hair) to stand up (*Spens.*). — *adj.* **upstar′ing.** — *n.* **up′start** one who has suddenly risen to wealth, importance, or power, a parvenu. — *adj.* newly or suddenly come into being: characteristic of a parvenu: pretentious and vulgar: new-fangled: standing on end (*Spens.*). — *v.i.* **upstart′** to start up. — *adj.* **up′state** (*U.S.*) pertaining to a part of a state away from, and usu. to the north of, the principal city of the state. — Also *adv.* — *v.t.* **upstay′** to sustain. — *adv.* **up′stream′** against the current. — *adj.* (*up′*) further up the stream: going against the current. — *v.i.* (*-strēm′*) to stream up. — *n.* **up′stroke** an upward stroke: an upward line in writing. — *v.i.* **upsurge′** to surge up. — *n.* (*up′*) a surging up. — *n.* **upsur′gence.** — *vs.t.* **upswarm′** (*Shak.*) to send up in a swarm; **upsway′** to swing up. — *n.* **up′swing** an upward swing: an economic recovery. — *n.* **up′take** the act of lifting

up: a pipe or flue with upward current: the act of taking up: mental apprehension (orig. *Scot.;* in *Scot.* usu. **up′tak; gleg in, at, the uptak** quick to understand). — *v.t.* (*-tāk′*) to take up. — *v.t.* **uptear′** to pull up or out by the roots, from the base, etc. — *adj.* **up′-tem′po** played or sung at a fast tempo. — *v.t.* **upthrow′** to throw up. — *n.* (*up′*) an upheaval, uplift: the amount of vertical displacement of the relatively raised strata at a fault. — *v.t.* **upthrust′** to thrust upward. — *n.* (*up′*). — *v.i.* **upthun′der** to send up a noise like thunder (*Coleridge*). — *v.t.* **uptie′** to tie up: to conclude, wind up (*fig.*). — *adj.* **uptight′** (*coll.*) tense, in a nervy state: angry, irritated: conventional, strait-laced. — *prep.* **up-till′** (*obs.* and *Scot.*) up to. — *adj.* **up′torn** (also **uptorn′,** *pa.p.* of **uptear**). — *adj., adv.* and *n.* **up′town′** (in or toward) the upper part or (*U.S.*) the residential quarters of a town. — *v.t.* and *v.i.* **uptrain′** to train up, educate (*obs.*). — *n.* **up′trend** upward tendency. — *adj.* **up′trilled** trilled high (*Coleridge*). — *n.* **up′turn** an upheaval: a disturbance: a movement upward, a rise: an upturned part. — *adj.* **up′turned.** — *n.* and *adj.* **upturn′ing.** — *n.* **upvaluā′tion.** — *v.t.* **upval′ue** to increase the value of. — *n.* **upwell′ing** a welling up: the rising to the surface of nutriment-bearing water from the depths of the ocean. — *v.t.* and *v.i.* **upwind** (*up-wīnd′*) to wind up: — *pa.t.* and *pa.p.* **upwound′.** — *adv.* **upwind** (*up-wind′*), **up-wind′** against the wind. — *v.t.* (*pa.p.*) **upwrought′** wrought up.

upadaisy. Same as **ups-a-daisy.**

upaithric *ū-pī′thrik, adj.* from the same root as, and identical in meaning with, **hypaethral** (q.v.).

Upanis(h)ad *ōō-pan′i-shad, ōō-pä′ni-shäd, n.* any of a number of Sanskrit theosophic or philosophical treatises. [Sans. *upa,* near, *ni-ṣad,* a sitting down.]

upas *ū′pɔs, n.* (in full **u′pas-tree′**) a fabulous Javanese tree that poisoned everything for miles around: Javanese tree (*Antiaris toxicaria,* of the mulberry family): the poison of its latex. [Malay, poison.]

upbraid *up-brād′, v.t.* to reproach or chide: to adduce in reproach (against, to, a person; *obs.*). — *v.i.* to utter reproaches. — *n.* (*obs.*) reproach, reproof. — *n.* **upbraid′er.** — *n.* and *adj.* **upbraid′ing.** [O.E. *ūpbregdan.*]

upbray *up-brā′,* (*Spens.*) *v.t.* to upbraid: to bring reproach on. — *n.* an upbraiding. [From *upbrayd,* obs. pa.t. of **upbraid.**]

Up-Helly-Aa *up-hel′i-ä, n.* a mid-winter festival, representing an older Celtic fire festival, held on the last Tuesday of January in Lerwick, Shetland, and now including guisers (q.v.) and the ceremonial burning of a Viking ship. [**up,** at an end, finished, and *Scot. haliday,* holiday, i.e. the end of the Yule holiday.]

upholster *up-hōl′stɔr, v.t.* to furnish with stuffing, springs, covers, etc.: to cushion, be a cover to: to provide with curtains, carpets, etc. — *v.i.* to do upholstery. — *n.* (*obs.*) an upholsterer. — *ns.* **uphōl′sterer** one who makes or deals in furniture, beds, curtains, etc.: *fem.* **uphōl′stress; uphōl′stery** upholsterer′s work or goods. [Back formation from *upholsterer* — **upholder** in obs. sense (q.v.).]

uphroe *ū′frō.* Same as **euphroe.**

upmost. See **up.**

upo′, upon. See **up-.**

upper, uppermost. See **up.**

uproar *up′rōr, -rör, n.* insurrection, commotion and tumult (now *rare*): loud outcry, clamour. — *v.t.* **uproar′** (*Shak.*) to throw into uproar or confusion. — *v.i.* to make an uproar. — *adj.* **uproar′ious.** — *adv.* **uproar′iously.** — *n.* **uproar′iousness.** [Du. *oproer* — *op,* up,

---

roeren (Ger. *rühren*, O.E. *hrēran*) to stir; modified by association with **roar**.]

ups-a-daisy *ups'ə-dā'zi, interj.* of encouragement in lifting a child or helping to climb.

upsey, upsee, upsy *up'si,* (*obs.*) *prep.* in the manner of (e.g. *upsey whore*). — *adv.* (in full **upsey Dutch, English, Friese,** in the German, English, Frisian manner, of drinking) deeply, heavily, heartily. — *n.* a carousal. — *interj.* a Bacchanalian exclamation. [Du. *op zijn,* in his (i.e. the; 'manner' understood).]

upsilon. See **ypsilon.**

upsy. Same as **upsey.**

upsy-daisy. Same as **ups-a-daisy.**

uptrain. See **up-; up-train.** See **up.**

ur *ûr, interj.* filling a gap in speech, when hesitant.

ur- *ōōr-, pfx.* primitive, original. [Ger.]

urachus *ū'rə-kəs, n.* a ligament connecting the bladder with the umbilicus. [Gr. *ourachos,* the fetal structure from which it is formed.]

uracil. See **urea.**

uraemia *ū-rē'mi-ə, n.* retention of waste materials in the blood. — *adj.* **urae'mic.** — Also **urē'mia, urē'mic.** [Gr. *ouron,* urine, *haima,* blood.]

uraeus *ū-rē'əs, n.* the snake symbol on the head-dress of Egyptian gods and kings. [Gr. *ouraios,* a kind of snake; prob. Egyptian.]

Ural *ū'rəl, n.* a river and mountain range of Russia. — *adjs.* **Uralian** (*ū-rā'li-ən*) of the Ural Mountains (**Uralian emerald** a semi-precious green garnet): pertaining to Uralic (also *n.*). — *n.* **Uralic** (*ū-ral'ik*) a language group comprising Finno-Ugric and the Samoyed languages. — *adj.* **Uralian.** — *n.* **ū'ralite** an alteration product, hornblende after augite. — *adj.* **uralitic** (*-lit'ik*). — *n.* **uralītīsā'tion, -z-.** — *v.t.* **ū'ralitise, -ize** to turn into uralite. — *adj.* **Ural-Altaic** (*-al-tā'ik*) of the Ural and Altai Mountains: applied to a family of languages — Finno-Ugrian, Turko-Tatar, Mongolian, Manchu, Tungus, etc., and their speakers.

urali. Same as **wourali.**

uranalysis. See under **urine.**

Urania *ū-rā'ni-ə, n.* the Muse of astronomy: a name for Aphrodite. — *adjs.* **Uranian** (also without *cap.*; *ū-rā'ni-ən*) heavenly: of the heavens: astronomical: of Urania or of Uranus, god or planet; **uranic** (*ū-ran'ik*) of uranium in higher valency: celestial: of the palate. — *ns.* **uranide** (*ū'rən-īd*) a transuranium element; **uranin** (*ū'rən-in*) a sodium or potassium salt of fluorescein (from its fluorescence, like that of uranium glass); **uraninite** (*ū-ran'i-nīt*) pitchblende; **uraniscus** (*ū-rən-isk'əs*) the roof of the mouth; **ū'ranism** a type of male homosexuality; **ū'ranite** autunite: torbernite. — *adj.* **uranit'ic.** — *ns.* **uranium** (*ū-rā'ni-əm*) a radioactive metal (U; at. numb. 92) named by Klaproth, 1789, after the recently discovered planet (**uranium glass** a yellow fluorescent glass containing uranium compounds); **uranog'rapher.** — *adjs.* **uranograph'ic, -al.** — *ns.* **uranog'raphist; uranog'raphy** descriptive astronomy, esp. of the constellations; **uranol'ogy** astronomy; **uranom'etry** astronomical measurement; **ū'ranoplasty** plastic surgery of the palate; **Uranos'copus** the stargazer genus of fishes. — *adj.* **ū'ranous** of uranium in lower valency. — *ns.* **Uranus** (*ū'rə-nəs* or *ū-rā'*) an old Greek god, father of Kronos (Saturn) and the Titans: a planet discovered in 1781 by Herschel; **ū'ranyl** (*chem.*) the group UO₂. [Gr. *ouranos,* heaven.]

urao *ōō-rä'ō, n.* natron. [Sp. *urao,* from Carib.]

urari. Same as **wourali.**

urate *ū'rāt.* See **uric.**

urban *ûr'bən, adj.* of or belonging to a city. — *adj.* **urbane** (*ûr-bān'*) pertaining to, or influenced by, a city: civilised: refined: courteous: smooth-mannered. — *adv.* **urbane'ly.** — *n.* **urbanisā'tion, -z-.** — *v.t.* **ur'banise, -ize** to make (a district) town-like, as opposed to rural, in character. — *adj.* **urbanist'ic** pertaining to the planning and development of towns. — *ns.* **ur'banite** (chiefly *U.S.*) one who lives in a town or city; **urbanity** (*-ban'i-ti*) the quality of being urbane: also townish-ness, town-life; **urbanol'ogist** one who studies urban conditions; **urbanol'ogy.** — **urban district** a thickly-populated district, a subdivision of a country, administered by an **Urban District Council; urban guerrilla** one who is engaged in terrorist activities in towns and cities; **urban renewal** (esp. *U.S.*) the clearing and/or redevelopment of slums or the like. [L. *urbānus* — *urbs,* a city.]

urceolus *ûr-sē'ō-ləs, n.* a pitcher-shaped structure, with contracted mouth, as the sheath of some rotifers. — *adj.* **ur'ceolate** having the form of an urceolus. [L. *urceolus,* dim. of *urceus,* a pitcher.]

urchin *ûr'chin, n.* a hedgehog: a sea-urchin: a deformed person, hunchback (*obs.* or *dial.*): an elf or imp (*obs.*): a mischievous child, esp. a boy: a child. — *adj.* like, of the nature of, due to, an urchin. — *n.pl.* **ur'chin-shows** appearances of elves or goblins. — *adj.* **ur'chin-snout'ed** with a snout like a hedgehog. [O.Fr. *herichon, hericon* (Fr. *hérisson*) — L. *ēricius,* a hedgehog.]

urd *ûrd, n.* an Indian plant of the bean family (*Phaseolus mungo*), or its edible blackish seed. — Also **urd bean, black gram.** [Hindi.]

urdé, urdée, urdee, urdy *ûr'dā, -dē, -di,* (*her.*) *adjs.* pointed: having points. [Origin obscure.]

Urdu *ōōr'dōō, ōōr-dōō', n.* and *adj.* a form of Hindustani incorporating many Persian and Arabic words, the official literary language of Pakistan. [Hind. *urdū,* camp (language); cf. **horde.**]

ure¹ *ūr,* (*obs.*) *n.* use, practice, operation. [O.Fr. *uevre* (Fr. *œuvre*) — L. *opera,* work, service.]

ure² *ūr,* (*obs.*) *n.* the urus. [L. *ūrus.*]

ure³ *ûr,* (*hist.; Orkney and Shetland*) *n.* an eighth of a mark, or land paying so much in feu-duty. [Cf. Norw., Sw., Dan. *öre* — L. *aureus,* a gold solidus.]

urea *ū-rē'ə,* by some *ū', n.* carbamide, CO(NH₂)₂, a substance found in mammalian urine, the chief form in which nitrogenous waste is carried off. — *n.* **ū'racil** a base in ribonucleic acid. — *adj.* **urē'al** (or *ū'ri-əl*). — *ns.* **ureide** (*ū'rē-īd*) an acyl derivative of urea, such as urethan; **ū'ridine** a pyrimidine nuleoside based on uracil and ribose. **urea resins** thermosetting resins made by heating urea and aldehyde, usu. formaldehyde. [Gr. *ouron,* urine.]

uredo *ū-rē'dō, n.* rust in plants: a rust-fungus in its summer stage (also **urē'do-stage**): — *pl.* **uredines** (*ū-rē'-di-nēz*). — *n.pl.* **Uredinā'lēs** the Uredineae. — *adj.* **uredine** (*ū'ri-dīn*). — *n.pl.* **Uredineae** (*ū-ri-din'i-ē*) the rust-fungi, an order of parasitic Basidiomycetes. — *adj.* **uredin'ial** (*U.S.*). — *ns.* **uredin'iospore, urē'diospore** (*U.S.*) a uredospore; **uredin'ium, urē'dium** (*U.S.*) a uredosorus — both *pl.* **-ia.** — *adj.* **urē'dinous.** — *ns.* **urēdoso'rus** (*-sō', -sō'*) a pustule containing uredospores; **urē'dospore** a spore produced by rust-fungi in the uredo-stage. [L. *ūrēdō, -inis,* blight — *ūrĕre,* to burn.]

ureide. See **urea.**

uremia, uremic. Same as **uraemia, uraemic.**

Urena *ū-rē'nə, n.* a tropical genus of the mallow family, yielding a jute substitute: (without *cap.*) any plant of the genus. [Malayalam *uren.*]

urent *ū'rənt, adj.* burning, stinging. [L. *ūrēns, -entis,* pr.p. of *ūrĕre,* to burn.]

uresis *ū-rē'sis, n.* urination. [Gr. *ourēsis.*]

ureter *ū-rē'tər, n.* a duct that conveys urine from the kidneys to the bladder or cloaca. — *adjs.* **urē'teral, ureteric** (*ū-ri-ter'ik*). — *n.* **urēterī'tis** inflammation of a ureter. [Gr. *ourētēr, -ēros — ouron,* urine.]

urethan(e) *ū'ri-than, -thān,* or *-than', -thān', ns.* an anaesthetic, NH₂·COOC₂H₅, prepared from urea and ethyl alcohol.

urethra *ū-rē'thrə, n.* the canal by which the urine is discharged from the bladder: — *pl.* **-as, -ae** (*-ē*). — *adjs.* **urē'thral; urethrit'ic.** — *n.* **urēthrī'tis** inflammation of the urethra. — **non-specific urethritis** a disease resembling gonorrhoea, not associated with any identifiable virus. [Gr. *ourēthrā — ouron,* urine.]

uretic *ū-ret'ik, adj.* pertaining to, or occurring in, urine.

[Gr. *ourētikos — ouron*, urine.]

urge *ûrj, v.t.* to press forward, esp. with earnestness, or insistence (success, an enterprise, etc.; *arch.*): to put forward (an argument, etc.; or in argument, with *that*): to stimulate, excite (*arch.*): to hasten (*arch.*): to incite: to allege earnestly: to advise strongly: to drive, impel. — *v.i.* to press: to be urgent or insistent: to push on. — *n.* an impulse: a prompting. — *ns.* **ur'gence** (*rare*), **ur'gency.** — *adj.* **ur'gent** urging: pressing: calling for immediate attention. — *adv.* **ur'gently.** — *n.* **ur'ger.** — *n.* and *adj.* **ur'ging.** [L. *urgēre*.]

urial, oorial *ōō'ri-əl, n.* a Himalayan wild sheep. [Punjabi *hureāl*.]

uric *ū'rik, adj.* of, or got from, or present in, urine. — *ns.* **ū'rate** a salt of uric acid; **ū'ricase** an enzyme occurring in the liver and kidneys, which catalyses the oxidation of uric acid. — **uric acid** an acid, $C_5H_4O_3N_4$, present in urine and blood. [Gr. *ouron*, urine.]

Uriconian *ū-ri-kō'ni-ən, adj.* of the Roman station *Uriconium* (*Viroconium*) on the site of Wroxeter in Shropshire: applied to the apparently Pre-Cambrian igneous rocks forming the Wrekin, etc.

uridine. See urea.

Urim *ū'rim*, **Thummim** *thum'im, ns.pl.* first mentioned in Exod. xxviii. 30, apparently a pair of objects used as a kind of traditional oracle. [Heb. *ūrīm, t*(*h*)*ummīm*.]

urinant *ū'rin-ənt,* (*her.*) *adj.* diving, head downward. — *n.* **ū'rinātor** a diver. [L. *ūrīnārī*, to plunge.]

urine *ū'rin, n.* the excretory product, usually amber liquid, of the kidneys, chief means of voiding nitrogenous waste. — *v.i.* (*obs.*) to urinate. — *ns.* **ū'rinal** (or *-rī'*) a chamber-pot (*arch.*): a vessel for urine, esp. for an incontinent or bed-ridden person: a room or building having fixed receptacle(s) for use in urination; **urinal'ysis** analysis of urine, e.g. to detect disease. — Also **uranal'ysis.** — *adj.* **ū'rinary** pertaining to, or like, urine. — *n.* a reservoir for urine. — *v.i.* **ū'rinate** to discharge urine. — *n.* **urinā'tion.** — *adjs.* **ū'rinātive; urinif'erous** conveying urine; **urinip'arous** producing urine; **urinogen'ital** pertaining jointly to urinary and genital functions or organs. — *ns.* **urinol'ogy, urinos'copy,** etc., barbarous forms for **urology,** etc.; **urinom'eter** (ill-formed) a hydrometer for urine. — *adj.* **ū'rinous** like, of the nature of, urine. [L. *ūrīna*; cf. Gr. *ouron*.]

urite *ū'rīt, n.* an abdominal segment. [Gr. *ourā*, a tail.]

urman *ōōr-män', n.* (swampy) pine forest. [Russ., — Tatar *ŭrmăn*.]

urn *ûrn, n.* a vase with rounded body, usually a narrowed mouth and often a foot: esp. such a vase for ashes of the dead: hence any respository for the dead: a monumental imitation of a burial-urn: a river-source (*poet.*): a vessel for water: a container into which to put voting-tablets, etc. (*Rom. hist.*, etc.): a ballot-box: a closed vessel with a tap and now usu. with heating device inside, for making tea or coffee in quantity: a moss-capsule: an urn-shaped body. — *v.t.* to enclose in an urn. — *adjs.* **urn'al; urned.** — *n.* **urn'ful** as much as an urn will hold: — *pl.* **urn'fuls. — urn'field** a late Bronze Age cemetery of cinerary urns. — *adj.* **urn'-shaped** rounded with narrowed mouth. [L. *urna*.]

urning *ûr'ning, n.* a (esp. male) homosexual. [Ger., irreg. — *Urania* (Aphrodite), q.v.]

uro-¹ *ū-rō-, -ro-,* in composition, urine. — *n.* **ū'rochrome** the yellow pigment in urine. — *adjs.* **urogen'ital** urinogenital; **urograph'ic.** — *ns.* **urog'raphy** radiological examination of the urinary tract; **urokī'nase** (or *-kin'-*) an enzyme, found in human urine, which dissolves blood clots, used in the treatment of pulmonary embolisms; **urolag'nia** sexual arousal caused by, or associated with, urination or urine; **ū'rolith** a calculus in the urine or the urinary tract; **urolithī'asis** the formation of uroliths: the condition caused by uroliths. — *adjs.* **urolog'ic(al). — *ns.* **urol'ogist; urol'ogy** the scientific study of urine (*obs.*): the branch of medicine dealing with diseases and abnormalities of the urinary tract and their treatment; **uropoië'sis** formation of urine; **uros'copy** diagnostic examination of urine; **urō'-**

sis disease of the urinary organs. [Gr. *ouron*, urine; cf. L. *ūrīna*.]

uro-² *ū-rō-, -ro-,* in composition, tail: posterior part. — *n.* **ū'rochord** (*-körd*) a notochord confined to the caudal region, as in larval ascidians: any member of the **Urochord'a,** a subphylum of Chordata having a urochord in the larva — ascidians and kindred forms. — *adjs.* **urochor'dal, urochor'date.** — *n.pl.* **Urodē'la** (Gr. *dēlos*, clear, plain) the (permanently) tailed Amphibia. — *ns.* and *adjs.* **urodē'lan, ū'rodele.** — *adj.* **urodē'lous.** — *ns.* **ū'romere** (Gr. *meros*, part) an abdominal segment of an arthropod; **ū'ropod** an abdominal appendage of an arthropod; esp. just before the telson. — *adj.* **uropygial** (*-pij'i-əl*). — *ns.* **uropyg'ium** (Gr. *ouropȳgion* or *orropȳgion — orros*, the end of the sacrum, *pȳgē*, buttocks) the rump in birds; **ū'rosome** (Gr. *sōma*, body) the tail region; **urostege** (*ū'rō-stēj*), **urostegite** (*ū-ros'ti-jīt*; Gr. *stegē*, roof, deck) a snake's ventral tail-plate. — *adj.* **urosthen'ic** (Gr. *sthenos*, strength) having a tail developed for propulsion. — *n.* **ū'rostyle** (Gr. *stȳlos*, column) a prolongation of the last vertebra. [Gr. *ourā*, tail.]

Ursa *ûr'sə, n.* the Latin name of two constellations, *Ursa Major* and *Ursa Minor*, the Great and the Little Bear. — *adj.* **ur'sine** of a bear: bear-like. — *n.* **Ur'sus** the bear genus. [L. *ursus, ursa*, bear.]

urson *ûr'sən, n.* the Canadian porcupine. [Fr. *ourson*, dim. of *ours* — L. *ursus*, bear.]

Ursuline *ûr'sū-lin, -līn, adj.* of or pertaining to St *Ursula*, esp. of the female teaching order founded by St Angela Merici of Brescia in 1537. — Also *n.*

Ursus. See Ursa.

Urtica *ûr-tī'kə*, commonly *ûr'ti-kə, n.* the nettle genus, giving name to the family **Urticaceae** (*ûr-ti-kā'si-ē*) akin to (or including) elms and mulberries (without *cap.*) a plant of the nettle genus. — *adjs.* **urticā'ceous** like or of the nature of a nettle: of the nettle family; **ur'ticant** stinging: irritating. — *n.* **urticā'ria** nettle-rash. — *adjs.* **urticā'rial, urticā'rious.** — *v.t.* **ur'ticate** to sting: to flog with nettles. — *n.* **urticā'tion.** [L. *urtīca*, a nettle — *ūrĕre*, to burn.]

urubu *ōō-rōō-bōō', n.* a S. American vulture. [Tupí *urubú*.]

urus *ū'rəs, n.* the aurochs.

urva *ûr'və, n.* the crab-eating mongoose of south-eastern Asia [Nepali.]

us *us, pron.* the objective (dative and accusative) case of **we.** — Also in editorial and royal use as a singular. — *adv.* **us'ward** toward us. — Also *n.* as in *to usward.* [O.E. *ūs*.]

usage *ū'zij, -sij, n.* use: act or mode of using: treatment: practice: custom: interest on money (*obs.*): (in *pl.*, with *the*) four ceremonies in the celebration of the eucharist, dispute about which caused a separation of the Nonjurors into two groups: the normal or acceptable speech patterns, vocabulary, etc. of a language or dialect. — *ns.* **ū'sager** one of the Nonjurors who maintained 'the usages'; **ū'sance** usage: interest, or lending at interest (*Shak.*): time allowed for payment of foreign bills of exchange. [O.Fr., — L. *ūsus*, use.]

use¹ *ūz, v.t.* to put to some purpose: to avail oneself of: to observe, practise, follow (*arch.*): to resort to (a place) (*arch.*): to behave, comport (oneself) (*arch.*): to habituate (*Scot.*): to treat or behave towards: to make use of (a person; see following article): to take or consume (drugs or alcohol) regularly (*slang*; also as *v.i.*). — *v.i.* to be accustomed (to; used chiefly in the past tense, pronounced in this sense *ūst*; **use(d)n't** *ūs'nt*, for *used not*): to be in the habit of so doing (*arch.*): to accustom oneself (to) (*Scot.*): to resort (*arch.*). — *adjs.* **ū'sable; used** (*ūzd*) already made use of: second-hand: accustomed, customary (*obs.*): experienced, expert (*Scot.*). — *n.* **ū'ser** one who uses: continual enjoyment of a right (cf. **non-user;** Fr. *user*): a right established by long use (*law*). — *adjs.* **used'-up'** exhausted; **user= friend'ly** (of a computer or software item) designed to be easily understood and operable by non-specialists, guiding the user by means of clear instructions, menus, etc.: generally, of any product, etc. designed with the ease of the user in mind, deliberately not off-putting. — **be able to use** (usu. as **can, could use**) to feel better for, want, need (*coll.*); **use up** to consume: to exhaust: to tire out.   [Fr. *user* — L.L. *ūsāre* — L. *ūtī, ūsus,* to use.]

use² *ūs, n.* the act of using: the state or fact of being used: an advantageous purpose to which a thing can be applied: the fact of serving a purpose: usefulness: employment causing wear: a need to use (with *for*): the manner of using: the power of using (e.g. tongue, limb): the habit of using: custom: ordinary experience (*Shak.*): a distinctive form of public worship or service peculiar to a church, diocese, etc.: the profit derived from property: interest for money (*arch.*; also *fig.* in *Shak.*): (in *pl.*) a form of equitable ownership peculiar to English law by which one person enjoys the profit of lands, etc., the legal title to which is vested in another in trust. — *adj.* **use'ful** advantageous, serviceable (**useful,** or **applied, arts** those arts with a utilitarian purpose, e.g. weaving, pottery, as opposed to the fine arts (see **art**)). — *adv.* **use'fully.** — *n.* **use'fulness.** — *adj.* **use'less** having no use: not answering any good purpose or the end proposed. — *adv.* **use'lessly.** — *n.* **use'lessness.** — **have no use for** to have no liking for: **in use** in employment or practice: **make use of** to use, employ: to take the help, etc., of (a person) in obtaining an end with no intention of repaying him: **of no use** useless: **of use** useful: **out of use** not used or employed: **use and wont** the customary practice.   [L. *ūsus* — *ūtī,* to use.]

usher *ush'ər, n.* a door-keeper: one who escorts persons to seats in a hall, etc.: an officer who introduces strangers or walks before a person of rank: an under-teacher or assistant (*hist.*): — *fem.* **ush'eress, usherette'** (esp. in a theatre or cinema). — *v.t.* to conduct: to show (in, out): to introduce, lead up to (now usu. with *in*). — *ns.* **ush'ering; ush'ership.**   [A.Fr. *usser,* O.Fr. *ussier* (Fr. *huissier*) — L. *ostiārius,* a door-keeper — *ostium,* a door.]

Usnea *us'ni-ə, n.* a genus of lichens, tree-moss: (without *cap.*) a lichen of this genus.   [Pers. *ushnah,* moss.]

usque ad nauseam *us'kwi ad nö'zi-am, ōōs'kwe ad now'-se-am,* (L.) to the point of disgust.

usquebaugh *us'kwi-bö, n.* whisky.   [Ir. and Gael. *uisge-beatha* — *uisge,* water, *beatha,* life.]

Ustilago *us-ti-lā'gō, n.* a genus of basidiomycetous fungi, of the family **Ustilaginaceae** (*-laj-i-nā'si-ē*) and order **Ustilaginales** (*-laj-i-nā'lēz*) or **Ustilagin'eae,** the smut-fungi. — *adjs.* **ustilagin'eous, ustilag'inous.**   [L. *ustilāgō, -inis,* a kind of thistle.]

ustion *us'chən,* (*obs.*) *n.* burning: cauterisation by burning. — *n.* **ustulation** (*us-tū-lā'shən*) burning: roasting.   [L. *ūstiō, ōnis.*]

usual *ū'zhōō-əl, adj.* occurring in ordinary use: common: customary. — *n.* (*coll.*) normal health: one's habitual drink, etc. — *adv.* **ū'sually.** — *n.* **ū'sualness.** — **as usual** as is or was usual; **the usual** (*coll.*) menstruation.   [L. *ūsuālis* — *ūsus,* use.]

usucapion *ū-zū-kā'pi-ən,* **usucaption** *-kap'shən,* (*Rom. law*) *ns.* the acquisition of property by long possession and enjoyment. — *n.* **usucā'pient** one who claims or holds by usucapion. — *v.t.* **ū'sucapt** (*-kapt*) to acquire so. — *adj.* **usucapt'ible.**   [L. *ūsūcapĕre* — *ūsus,* use, *capĕre, captum,* to take.]

usufruct *ū'zū-frukt, n.* the use and profit, but not the property, of a thing: life-rent. — *v.t.* to hold in usufruct. — *adj.* **usufruc'tuary.** — *n.* one who has usufruct.   [L.L. *ūsūfrūctus* — L. *ūsus* (*et*) *frūctus,* use and fruit.]

usure, usurer, etc. See **usury.**

usurp *ū-zûrp', v.t.* to take possession of by force, without right, or unjustly: to assume (the authority, place, etc., of someone, or something, else): to take possession of (the mind): to take or borrow (a name or a word): to supplant (*arch.*). — *v.i.* to practise usurpation: to encroach (on). — *n.* **usurpā'tion.** — *adj.* **usur'patory.**

— *n.* **usurpā'ture** (*poet.*) usurpation. — *adj.* **usurped'.** — *adv.* **usur'pedly.** — *n.* **usur'per.** — *n.* and *adj.* **usur'ping.** — *adv.* **usur'pingly.**   [Fr. *usurper* and L. *ūsūrpāre,* perh. from *ūsus,* use, *rapĕre,* to seize.]

usury *ū'zhə-ri, n.* the taking of (now only iniquitous or illegal) interest on a loan: interest (*arch.*). — *n.* **ū'sure** (*obs.*) interest: usury. — *v.i.* (*obs.*) to practise usury. — *n.* **ū'surer** a money-lender (now for excessive interest): — *fem.* **ū'suress.** — *adjs.* **ū'suring** (*Shak.*) taking or expecting usury; **usū'rious.** — *adv.* **usū'riously.** — *n.* **usū'riousness.** — *adj.* **ū'surous** (*obs.*).   [L.L. *ūsūria,* L. *ūsūra* — *ūtī, ūsus,* to use.]

usus loquendi *ūz'əs lo-kwen'dī, ōōs'ōōs lo-kwen'dē,* (L.) current usage of speech.

usward. See **us.**

ut¹ *ōōt, ut, n.* a syllable representing the first note of the scale, now generally superseded by *do.*   [See **Aretinian, gamut.**]

ut² *ut, ōōt,* (L.) *adv., conj.* as. — **ut infra** (*in'frə, ēn'frä*) as below; **ut supra** (*sū'prə, sōō'prä, sōō'*) as above.

utas *ū'tas,* (*obs.*) *n.* the octave of a festival.   [M.Fr. *huituves* — O.Fr. *outaves* (pl.) — L. *octāva,* eight.]

ute. See **utilise.**

Ute *ūt, ū'ti, n.* (a member of) a N. American Indian people of Utah, Colorado and New Mexico; the Uto-Aztecan language of this people: — *pl.* **Ute, Ū'te** or **Utes, Ū'tes.** — *adj.* of this people or language.   [Shortening of *Utah.*]

utensil *ū-ten'sil,* formerly *ū', n.* any useful or ceremonial tool or vessel.   [O.Fr. *utensile* — L. *ūtēnsilis,* fit for use — *ūtī,* to use.]

uterus *ū'tər-əs, n.* the womb: — *pl.* **ū'terī.** — *n.* **uterec'tomy** hysterectomy. — *adj.* **ū'terine** (*-īn*) of, in, or for the uterus: of the same mother by a different father. — *ns.* **uterī'tis** inflammation of the womb; **ū'terogestā'tion** gestation in the womb; **uterot'omy** hysterotomy.   [L.]

Utgard *ōōt'gärd,* (*Scand. myth*) *n.* the abode of the giants.   [O.N. *ūt,* out, *garthr,* garth, yard.]

utile *ū'tīl, adj.* (with *to*) useful, profitable.   [M.E. — O.Fr. — L. *ūtilis,* useful — *ūtī,* to use.]

utilise, -ize *ū'ti-līz, v.t.* to make use of, turn to use. — *adj.* **ū'tilīsable, -z-.** — *ns.* **utilisā'tion, -z-; ū'tilīser, -z-; util'ity** usefulness: the power to satisfy the wants of people in general (*philos.*): profit (*obs.*): a useful thing: a public utility, public service, or a company providing such (esp. *U.S.*): (usu. in *pl.*) stock or bond of public utility: a small truck, pick-up or van (short form **ute**; *Austr.*). — *adj.* produced or supplied primarily for usefulness: provided in order that the public may be supplied in spite of rise of prices: (of a breed of dog) originally bred to be useful, to serve a practical purpose. — **utility man** an actor of the least important parts: a person who can be used to fill any gap: (also **utility player**) a player who can play in any of various positions as required (*sport*); **utility pole** (*U.S.*) a pole supporting power cables, telegraph wires, etc.; **utility room** a room, esp. in a private house, where things required for the work of running the house are kept.   [Fr. *utiliser, utilité* — L. *ūtilis,* useful — *ūtī,* to use.]

utilitarian *ū-til-i-tā'ri-ən, adj.* consisting in, based upon, or pertaining to, utility or to utilitarianism: concerned with, looking to, usefulness alone, without regard to, or without caring about, beauty, pleasantness, etc. — *n.* one who holds utilitarianism: one who looks to usefulness alone. — *v.t.* **utilitā'rianise, -ize** to make to serve a utilitarian purpose. — *n.* **utilitā'rianism** the ethical theory which finds the basis of moral distinctions in the utility of actions, i.e. their fitness to produce happiness.   [Jeremy Bentham's coinage from **utility.**]

utility. See **utilise.**

uti possidetis *ū'tī pos-i-dē'tis,* L. *ōō'tē pos-i-dā'tis,* in international law, the principle under which belligerents keep the territory or property they possess at the close of hostilities unless otherwise agreed.   [L., as you possess.]

utis *ū'tis,* (*Shak.*) *n.* clamour, din.   [M.E. *ūthēs,* hue and cry, app. — O.E. *ūt*, out, *hæs*, hest.]

utmost *ut'mōst*, -*məst*, *adj.* outmost: last: in the greatest degree, extreme. — *n.* the limit: the extreme: the most or greatest possible: the end (*Shak.*). [O.E. *ūtemest*, with double superlative suffix -*m-est* from *ūte*, out.]

Uto-Aztecan *ū'tō* -*az'tek-ən*, *n.* a large linguistic and geographic group of North American Indians, of central and western North America, incl. Shoshone, Hopi, Ute, Comanche, Nahuatl (Aztec): an individual belonging to this group. — *adj.* of or pertaining to any of these languages or peoples. [**Ute, Aztec.**]

Utopia *ū-tō'pi-ə*, *n.* an imaginary state described in Sir Thomas More's Latin political romance or satire *Utopia* (1516): (often without *cap.*) any imaginary state of ideal perfection. — *adj.* **Utō'pian** (also without *cap.*). — *n.* an inhabitant of Utopia: one who imagines or believes in a Utopia: (often without *cap.*) one who advocates impracticable reforms or who expects an impossible state of perfection in society. — *v.t.* and *v.i.* **utō'pianise, -ize.** — *ns.* **utō'pianiser, -z-; utō'pianism; utō'piast; ū'topism** (-*təp-izm*); **ū'topist.** [lit. 'no place', from Gr. *ou*, not, *topos*, a place; *Eutopia* (Gr. *eu*, well), 'ideal place' coined, poss. by More himself, in a punning reference to *Utopia*.]

Utraquist *ū'trə-kwist*, *n.* a Calixtine, or asserter of the right of the laity to communicate in both kinds (i.e. to take the wine as well as the bread). — Also *adj.* — *n.* **U'traquism.** [L. *utrāque* — *sub utrāque specie*, under each kind.]

utricle *ū'tri-kl*, *n.* a little bag, bladder, or cell: a bladder-like envelope of some fruits: a chamber in the inner ear. — *adj.* **utric'ular** like or having a utricle. — *ns.* **Utriculā'ria** the bladderwort genus of Lentibulariaceae: (without *cap.*) any plant of this genus; **utric'ulus** a utricle: — *pl.* -**lī.** [L. *ūtriculus*, a small bag, dim. of *ūter*, *ūtris*, a bag, a bottle.]

utter¹ *ut'ər*, *adj.* outer (*arch.*): extreme: total: out-and-out: — *superl.* **utt'erest.** — *adv.* **utt'erly.** — *adj.* and *n.* **utt'ermost** utmost. — *n.* **utt'erness.** — **utter barrister** formerly a barrister of rank next below a bencher: one who pleads without the bar, an ordinary barrister, not a king's or queen's counsel or a serjeant-at-law. [O.E. *ūtor*, outer — *ūt*, out.]

utter² *ut'ər*, *v.t.* to put (money) in circulation: to (try to) pass off (a forged document, etc.) as genuine or put (counterfeit money) into circulation: to offer for sale (*obs.*): to put out, emit, esp. with force (*lit.* and *fig.*; *arch.*): to speak, pronounce, give voice to. — *v.i.* (*coll.*) to make a remark or express an opinion. — *adj.* **utt'erable.** — *ns.* **utt'erableness; utt'erance** an act of uttering: a manner of speaking: the expression in speech, or in other sound, of a thought or emotion (e.g. **give utterance to**): a stretch of speech in some way isolated from, or independent of, what precedes and follows it (*linguistics*); **utt'erer; utt'ering** circulation. — *adj.* **utt'erless** that cannot be uttered in words. [M.E. *uttren*—O.E. *ūt*, out; and M.Du. *uteren*, to announce.]

utterance¹ *ut'ər-əns*, *n.* extremity, the bitter end (*Shak.*): the utmost degree (*obs.*): the utmost effort or force (*arch.*). [Fr. *outrance* — *outre* — L. *ultrā*, beyond.]

utterance². See utter².

utu *ōō'tōō*, (*Maori*) *n.* settlement (whether monetary or in kind) of a debt: retribution, vengence.

uva *ū'və*, *n.* a grape: a grape-like berry, one formed from a superior ovary. — *n.* **uvea** (*ū'vi-ə*) the posterior pigment-bearing layer of the iris of the eye: the iris, ciliary body, and choroid. — *adj.* **ū'veal** of the uvea. — *n.* **uveitis** (*ū-vi-ī'tis*) inflammation of the iris, ciliary body, and choroid. — **u'va-ursi** (*ûr'sī*; L. *ursī*, bear's) bear-berry: an infusion of its leaves. [L. *ūva.*]

uvarovite *ōō-vä'rō-vīt*, *n.* a green lime-chrome garnet. [After Count S. S. *Uvarov*, Russian minister of education.]

uvula *ū'vū-lə*, *n.* the fleshy conical body suspended from the palate over the back part of the tongue: — *pl.* **ū'vulas, -lae** (*lē*). — *adj.* **ū'vular** of, produced by vibration of, the uvula. — *adv.* **ū'vularly.** — *n.* **uvulī'tis** inflammation of the uvula. [Dim. from L. *ūva*, grape.]

uxorial *uk-sō'ri-əl*, -*sö'*, -*zō'*, -*zö'*, *adj.* of a wife. — *n.* **uxo'ricide** (-*sīd*) a wife-killer: wife-killing. — *adjs.* **uxorilo'cal** matrilocal; **uxo'rious** excessively or submissively fond of a wife. — *adv.* **uxo'riously.** — *n.* **uxo'riousness.** [L. *uxor*, -*ōris*, a wife.]

Uzbeg *uz'beg*, **Uzbek** -*bek*, *ns.* a member of a Turkic people of Turkestan: their language. — Also *adjs.*

For other sounds see detailed chart of pronunciation.

V

V, v *vē, n.* the twenty-second letter of our alphabet, a differentiated form of U (q.v.), representing a voiced labiodental sound: an object or mark shaped like the letter: as a Roman numeral V = 5; V̄ = 5000. — **V'-agents** poisonous gases, less volatile than G-agents; **V'-bomb** (Ger. *Vergeltungswaffe*, retaliation weapon) a self-propelled long-range projectile, as a rocket or a flying bomb, made by the Germans in World War II; **V'-day** Victory day — *specif.* 8 May 1945, when Germany surrendered unconditionally; **V'-neck** the neck of a garment cut to a point below. — *adjs.* **V'-necked**; **V'-shaped.** — **V'-sign** a sign made with the index and middle fingers in the form of a V, with palm turned outwards in token of victory, with palm inwards as a sign of contempt or derision.

vac *vak, n.* a colloquial shortening of **vacation,** and of **vacuum-cleaner.** — *v.t.* and *v.i.* to clean with a vacuum-cleaner: — *pr.p.* **vack'ing**; *pa.t.* and *pa.p.* **vacked.**

vacant *vā'kənt, adj.* empty: unoccupied: of or at leisure: thoughtless: inane. — *ns.* **vacance** (*və-kans', -käns',* or *va'; Scot.*) vacation; **vā'cancy** emptiness: leisure: idleness: inanity: empty space: a gap: a situation unoccupied: a room available (in a motel, boarding-house, etc.). — *adv.* **vā'cantly.** — *v.t.* **vacate** (*və-kāt', U.S. vā'kāt*) to make or leave empty: to quit: to annul, to make useless (*obs.*). — *n.* **vacā'tion** a vacating: a voiding: holidays, esp. of schools, colleges, law-courts: leisure: an intermission. — *v.i.* (esp. *U.S.*) to take a holiday. — *n.* **vacā'tionist** a holiday-maker. — *adj.* **vacā'tionless.** — *n.* **vacā'tur** the act of annulling in law. — **vacant possession** (of property) (the state of being ready for) occupation immediately after purchase, the previous owner or occupier already having left. [L. *vacāre, -ātum,* to be empty; pr.p. *vacāns, -antis*; 3rd pers. pr. indic. pass. *vacātur*.]

vaccine *vak'sēn, -sin, adj.* of, derived from, the cow: of vaccinia: of vaccination. — *n.* cowpox virus or lymph containing it: any preparation used to confer immunity to a disease by inoculation. — *adj.* **vac'cinal** (*-sin-*) of or due to vaccine or vaccination. — *v.t.* **vac'cinate** to inoculate with vaccine. — *ns.* **vaccinā'tion**; **vac'cinātor.** — *adj.* **vac'cinatory.** — *n.* **vaccin'ia** cowpox: in humans, a mild or localised reaction to inoculation with the vaccinia virus against small pox. — *adj.* **vaccin'ial.** [L. *vaccīnus — vacca,* a cow.]

Vaccinium *vak-sin'i-əm, n.* a genus including cranberry, whortleberry, and cowberry, giving name to a family **Vacciniā'ceae,** or a division **Vaccinioid'eae** of Ericaceae: (without *cap.*) a plant of this genus. [L. *vaccīnium,* whortleberry.]

vacherin *vash-rɛ,* (Fr.) *n.* (*cook.*) a dessert made with meringue and whipped cream, usu. with ice-cream, fruit, nuts, etc.

vacillate *vas'i-lāt, v.i.* to sway to and fro: to waver: to be unsteady. — *adjs.* **vac'illant** vacillating; **vac'illāting.** — *adv.* **vac'illātingly.** — *n.* **vacillā'tion.** — *adj.* **vac'illatory** wavering. [L. *vacillāre, -ātum.*]

vacked, vacking. See **vac.**

vacuum *vak'ū-əm, n.* theoretically, an entirely (in practice, a very nearly completely) empty space (also *fig.*; *pl.* **vac'ūums, vac'ūa**): a vacuum-cleaner (*coll.*; *pl.* **vac'-ūums**). — *v.t.* and *v.i.* to clean with a vacuum-cleaner. — *adj.* pertaining to a vacuum: containing a vacuum: in which a vacuum is used to carry out a specific operation. — *v.t.* **vac'ūate** (*obs.*) to empty: to evacuate: to annul. — *ns.* **vacūā'tion**; **vac'ūist** one who thinks there are empty spaces in nature; **vacū'ity** emptiness: space unoccupied: idleness, listlessness: vacancy of mind. — *adjs.* **vac'ūolar** of a vacuole; **vac'ūolate, -d**

having vacuoles. — *ns.* **vacūolā'tion**; **vac'ūole** a very small cavity, esp. in protoplasm; **vacūolīsā'tion, -z-** formation of vacuoles. — *adj.* **vac'ūous** empty: exhausted of air, etc.: mentally vacant. — *adv.* **vac'ūously.** — *n.* **vac'ūousness.** — **vacuum brake** a brake in the working of which suction by vacuum(s) supplements the pressure applied by the operator, esp. a braking system of this type applied simultaneously throughout a train. — *v.t.* and *v.i.* **vac'ūum-clean'.** — **vacuum cleaner** an apparatus for removing dust by suction; **vacuum concrete** concrete enclosed in special shuttering which enables suction to be applied to remove excess water; **vacuum flask** a flask for keeping liquids hot or cold by aid of a vacuum lining. — *adj.* **vac'uum=packed'** sealed in a container from which most of the air has been removed. — **vacuum pump** a general term for apparatus which displaces gas against a pressure; **vacuum tube** a sealed glass tube in which a vacuum has been made, e.g. a thermionic valve. — **ultra-high vacuum** a very close approach to complete vacuum, important for certain work of scientists and technologists. [L. *vacuus,* neut. *vacuum,* empty.]

vade *vād, v.i.* to fade (*Shak.*): to pass away (*Spens.*): to depart (*obs.*). [Partly a form of **fade,** partly from, or associated with, L. *vādēre,* to go.]

vade-mecum *vā'di-mē'kəm, vä'-, -mā'kōōm, n.* a handbook, pocket-companion. [L. *vāde,* go (imper. of *vādēre), mēcum,* with me.]

vae *vā.* Same as **voe.**

vae victis *vē vik'tēs, vī, wī wik',* (L.) woe to the conquered.

vagabond *vag'ə-bond, adj.* roving: without settled home: unsettled. — *n.* one who wanders without settled habitation: an idle wanderer: a vagrant: (often playfully or vaguely) a scamp, a rascal. — *v.i.* to play the vagabond. — *n.* **vag'abondage.** — *v.i.* **vag'abondise, -ize** to wander like a vagabond. — *adj.* **vag'abondish.** — *n.* **vag'abondism.** [Fr. *vagabond* and L. *vagābundus — vagāri,* to wander.]

vagal. See **vagus.**

vagary *vā'gə-ri, və-gā'ri, n.* a devious excursion: a digression or rambling: a freakish prank: a caprice: — *pl.* **vagaries.** — *adjs.* **vagā'rious**; **vagā'rish.** [App. L. *vagārī,* to wander.]

vagi. See **vagus.**

vagile *va'jīl, -jil, adj.* having the ability to move about. — *n.* **vagility** (*-jil'*) the quality of being vagile: hence the ability to succeed in the struggle for existence. [L. *vagus,* wandering.]

vagina *və-jī'nə, n.* a sheath: a sheathing leaf-base: a female genital passage: — *pl.* **vagī'nae** (*-nē*), **-nas.** — *adj.* **vagī'nal** (or *vaj'i-nəl*). — *adv.* **vagīn'ally.** — *adjs.* **vag'-inant** sheathing; **vag'inate, -d** sheathed: having a sheath; **vaginic'oline, -olous** living in a sheath. — *ns.* **vaginis'mus** spasmodic contraction of the vagina; **vaginī'tis** inflammation of the vagina; **vagin'ula** (or *-jīn'*; *pl.* **-lae** *-lē*), **vag'inule** a little sheath, esp. one surrounding the base of a moss seta. [L. *vāgīna,* sheath.]

vagitus *vaj-ī'təs, n.* a cry or wail, esp. of a baby. [L. *vagīre,* to cry.]

vagrant *vā'grənt, adj.* wandering: without settled dwelling: unsettled: uncertain, erratic. — *n.* one who has no settled home: a tramp. — *n.* **vā'grancy.** [Perh. A.Fr. *wakerant* of Gmc. origin (cf. **walk**), assimilated to L. *vagārī,* to wander.]

vagrom *vā'grəm, adj.* (*Shak.*) Dogberry's perversion of **vagrant** (*Much Ado* III, iii, 26).

vague *vāg, adj.* lacking precision or sharpness of definition: indistinct: blurred: lacking in character and purpose, or addicted to haziness of thought. — *n.* a vague state: an indefinite expanse. — *v.i.* to be vague: to wander (*Scot.*; now *rare*). — *adv.* **vague'ly.** — *n.* **vague'ness.** [L. *vagus*, wandering — *vagārī*, to wander.]

vagus *vā'gus*, *n.* the tenth cranial nerve, concerned in regulating heart beat, rhythm of breathing, etc.: — *pl.* **vā'gi** (*-jī*). — *adj.* **vā'gal** (*-gəl*). [L., wandering.]

vahine *vä-hē'nä*, *n.* in Polynesia, a woman or wife. [Tahitian.]

vail[1]. An obs. spelling of **veil.**

vail[2] *vāl*, (*arch.*) *v.t.* to lower, let down: to doff in salutation or submission. — *v.i.* to lower a sail: to lift one's hat: to yield: to do homage (*Shak.*): to go down: to abate. — *n.* (*Shak.*) setting. [O.Fr. *valer*, or aphetic for *avale*.]

vail[3] *vāl*, (*arch.*) *v.i.* and *v.t.* to profit, avail. — *n.* (usu. in *pl.*; also **vales**) a tip, perquisite, dole, or bribe. [O.Fr. *valoir*, vail, to be worth.]

vain *vān*, *adj.* empty, devoid (*obs.*): without real worth: futile: unavailing: thoughtless: empty-minded: pettily self-complacent: valuing oneself inordinately on some trivial personal distinction: conceited. — *n.* **vain'esse** (*Spens.*) vanity, futility. — *adv.* **vain'ly.** — *n.* **vain'ness** vanity. — *adj.* **vainglorious** (*-glö'*, *-glō'*) given to, or proceeding from, vainglory. — *adv.* **vainglo'riously.** — **vainglo'riousness; vain'glo'ry** vain or empty glory in one's own performances: idle boastfulness. — *v.i.* to boast vainly. — **for vain** (*Shak.*) in vain, vainly; **in vain** fruitlessly: to no end; **take in vain** to utter with levity. [Fr. *vain* — L. *vānus*, empty.]

vair *vār*, *n.* a kind of squirrel fur, bluish-grey and white, represented heraldically by rows of blue and white shields or bells. — *adjs.* **vairé**, **vairy** (*vā'ri*) charged or variegated with vair. [O.Fr., — L. *varius*, variegated.]

Vaishnava *vīsh'nä-vä*, *-nə-və*, *n.* a worshipper of Vishnu. — Also *adj.* [Sans.]

Vaisya *vīs'yä*, *vīsh'*, **Vaishya** *vīsh'yä*, *ns.* a member of the third caste among the Hindus. [Sans. *vaiçya* — *viç*, settler.]

vaivode. Same as **voivode.**

vakass *vä'käs*, *n.* an Armenian ephod.

vakil, vakeel *vä-kēl'*, *n.* an Indian agent, representative, or pleader. [Hind., — Ar. *vakīl*.]

valance *val'əns*, *n.* a hanging border of drapery: a hinged panel on the side of a vehicle allowing access to the engine: a side panel on a vehicle or locomotive which partially covers a wheel or wheels and is designed to reduce drag or catch splashes. — Also **val'ence.** — *adj.* **val'anced** furnished with a valance. [Poss. A.Fr. *valer*, to descend.]

Valdenses. Same as **Waldenses.**

vale[1] *vāl*, *n.* a valley (chiefly *poet.*): the world (*fig.*, as in *vale of tears*, *earthly vale*). — **vale of years** old age. [Fr. *val* — L. *vallis*, a vale.]

vale[2] *vā'lē*, L. *vä'lä*, or *wä'*, *n.* and *interj.* farewell (addressed to one person). — *n.* and *interj.* **valete** (L. *-lā'tā*) (addressed to more than one person). [L. *vale*, imper. of *valēre*, to be well.]

valediction *val-i-dik'shən*, *n.* a bidding farewell: a farewell. — *n.* **valedicto'rian** (*U.S.*) the speaker of a college valedictory address. — *adj.* **valedic'tory** saying farewell: farewell: taking leave. — *n.* (*U.S.*) a farewell oration spoken by a graduand. [L. *valē*, farewell, *dīcēre*, *dictum*, to say.]

valence[1] *vā'ləns*, *n.* valency (*chem.*): chemical bond (*chem.*). — *n.* **vā'lency** combining power: its degree as measured by the number of hydrogen (or equivalent) atoms with which an atom can combine, or by the charge on an ion: the numerical arrangement of chromosomes (as single, paired, etc.; *biol.*): the capacity (expressed numerically) of a verb to combine dependent elements within a sentence (*linguistics*). *biol.*). — **-valent** (or *-və-lənt*) in composition, having a stated valency, as in *trivalent.* — **valency electrons** those of the outermost shell of the atom, largely responsible

for its chemical and physical properties. [L. *valēre*, to be strong.]

valence[2]. See **valance.**

Valenciennes *val-ən-sēnz'*, *-si-en'*, *vä-lä-syen'*, *n.* a kind of lace made at *Valenciennes* in France, the design being made at the same time as the ground and with the same thread.

-valent. See **valence**[1].

Valentine *val'ən-tīn*, *n.* the name of several saints on whose day, 14th February, the birds were fabled to choose their mates: (without *cap.*) a person chosen freely or selected by lot, or the first of the other sex seen that day, assigned in mock betrothal for a year (the person now normally being freely chosen, and the relationship between chooser and chosen usu. being rather more tenuous): (without *cap.*) an amatory or grotesque missive or a gift sent that day: a bird's love-song (*Tenn.*). — **Saint Val'entide** (*Spens.*) the season of St Valentine's Day.

Valentinian *val-ən-tin'i-ən*, *n.* a follower of the Gnostic *Valentinus* (died *c.* A.D. 160). — Also *adj.*

valerian *və-lē'ri-ən*, *n.* the plant all-heal (*Valeriana officinalis*) or other plant of the genus, which gives name to the family **Valeriana'ceae**, akin to the teasels: its rhizome and roots which have medicinal properties. — *adj.* **valeriana'ceous** of this family. — **valerianic** (*-an'ik*) or **valeric** (*-er'ik*) **acid** a fatty acid $C_5H_{10}O_2$ (in several isomers). — **Greek valerian** Jacob's ladder; **red** or **spur valerian** a plant (*Centranthus*) akin to valerian. [Perh. from someone called *Valerius*, or from L. *valēre*, to be strong.]

vales. See **vail**[3].

valet *val'it* (or *val'ā*), *n.* a man-servant who attends to clothes and toilet. — *v.t.* (*val'it*) to serve or attend to as valet. — *n.* **val'eting.** — **valet de chambre** (*val'ā də shäbr'*) an attendant: a footman; **valet de place** (*val'ā də plas*) one who serves as a guide, messenger, etc., esp. for strangers. [Fr.]

valeta. Same as **veleta.**

valetudinarian *val-i-tū-di-nā'ri-ən*, *adj.* pertaining to ill-health: sickly: weak: anxious and fanciful about one's own health. — *n.* a valetudinarian person. — *n.* **valetūdinā'rianism.** — *adj.* and *n.* **valetūd'inary** (*-ə-ri*) valetudinarian. [L. *valētūdinārius* — *valētūdō*, state of health — *valēre*, to be strong.]

valgus *val'gəs*, *adj.* bow-legged: of a deviation from the longitudinal alignment of the body in which the distal part of the deformity turns away from the midline (*med.*). — Also **val'gous** (*rare*). — *n.* the condition of being bow-legged: (for *tālipēs valgus*) out-turned club-foot. [L., bow-legged.]

Valhalla *val-hal'ə*, *n.* the palace of bliss for the souls of slain heroes (*Scand. myth.*): a general burial-place or monument for a nation's great men. [O.N. *Valhöll* — *valr*, the slain, *höll*, hall.]

vali *vä-lē'*, *n.* a governor, esp. of a vilayet. [Turk.]

valiant *val'yənt*, *adj.* strong (*obs.*): brave: actively courageous: heroic. — *n.* (obs.) a valiant person. — *ns.* **val'iance, val'iancy** valour: a deed of valour. — *adv.* **val'iantly.** [Fr. *vaillant* — L. *valēre*, to be strong.]

valid *val'id*, *adj.* strong (*arch.*): sound: legally adequate, or efficacious: fulfilling all the necessary conditions: in logic, well based, applicable. — *v.t.* **val'idate** to make valid: to ratify: to confirm, substantiate. — *ns.* **valida'tion** the act of validating: the checking of the correctness of input data (*comput.*); **valid'ity.** — *adv.* **val'idly.** — *n.* **val'idness.** [L. *validus* — *valēre*, to be strong.]

valine *vä'lēn*, *val'*, *n.* an amino-acid, $C_5H_{11}NO_2$, essential to health and growth in humans and vertebrate animals. [From *valeric* acid.]

valise *və-lēz'* (or *-ēs'*; now *rare* except *U.S.*) *n.* a travelling bag for hand and saddle: a kit-bag. [Fr.; cf. It. *valigia*, Sp. *valija*.]

Valium® *val'i-əm*, *n.* a proprietary name for diazepam, a tranquilliser.

Valkyrie *val'kir-i*, *val-kīr'i*, *-kir'i*, *-kēr'i*, (*Scand. myth.*) *n.* any one of the minor goddesses who conducted the

slain from the battlefield to Valhalla: — *pl.* **Valkyries,
Valkyr′iur.** [O.N. *Valkyrja* — *valr*, the slain, and the
root of *kjōsa*, to choose; cf. O.E. *Wælcyrige*, Ger.
Walküre.]

vallar, vallary. See **vallum.**

vallecula *va-lek′ū-la, n.* a groove or furrow: — *pl.* **vallec′-
ulae** (*-lē*). — *adjs.* **vallec′ular, vallec′ulate.** [L.L. dim.
of L. *vallis*, valley.]

valley *val′i, n.* an elongated hollow between hills: a stretch
of country watered by a river: a trough between ridges:
the hollow of an M-shaped roof: — *pl.* **vall′eys.**
[O.Fr. *valee* (Fr. *vallée*) — *val* — L. *vallis*, a valley.]

Vallisneria *val-is-nē′ri-a, n.* a tropical and subtropical
genus of submerged water-plants of the frogbit family.
[After Antonio *Vallisnieri* (1661–1730), Italian naturalist.]

vallum *val′am, n.* a rampart: a wall of sods, earth, or other
material, esp. of that thrown up from a ditch. — *adjs.*
vall′ar, -y applied to a crown bestowed in ancient
Rome on the first to mount an enemy's rampart. [L.]

valonia, vallonia, valonea *va-lō′ni-a, n.* a tanning material,
acorns of a Levantine oak (valonia oak, *Quercus
aegilops*) or similar species [It. *vallonea* — Gr.
bulanos, an acorn.]

Valonia *va-lō′ni-a, n.* a genus of marine green algae,
forming the family **Valoniā′ceae.**

valour, U.S. **valor** *val′ar, n.* intrepidity: courage: bravery:
value, worth (*obs.*). — *n.* **valorīsā′tion, -z-** fixing of
price. — *v.t.* **val′orise, -ize** to fix or stabilise the price
of (esp. by a policy imposed by a government or
controlling body). — *adj.* **val′orous** intrepid: courageous. — *adv.* **val′orously.** [O.Fr. *valour* — L.L.
valor, -ōris — L. *valēre*, to be strong.]

valse *väls, n., v.i.* and *v.t.* waltz. [Fr.]

value *val′ū, n.* worth: a fair equivalent: intrinsic worth or
goodness: recognition of such worth: that which renders anything useful or estimable: the degree of this
quality: relative worth: high worth: esteem: efficacy:
excellence: price: precise meaning: relative duration
(*mus.*): relation with reference to light and shade
(*paint.*): the special determination of a quantity
(*math.*): the exact amount of a variable quantity in a
particular case: the sound represented by a written
symbol (*phon.*): (in *pl.*) moral principles, standards,
etc. — *v.t.* to estimate the worth of: to rate at a price:
to esteem: to prize. — *v.t.* or *v.i.* (*Shak.*) to be worth.
— *adj.* **val′uable** having value or worth: of high value.
— *n.* a thing of value, a choice article — often in *pl.*
— *n.* **val′uableness.** — *adv.* **val′uably.** — *v.t.* **val′uate**
to appraise. — *n.* **valuā′tion** estimation of value. —
adj. **valuā′tional.** — *n.* **val′uātor** an appraiser. — *adjs.*
val′ued that has a value assigned: priced: highly esteemed: prized; **val′ueless.** — *n.* **val′uer** one who estimates values, a valuator: one who sets a high value.
— **valuable consideration** (*law*) a consideration (q.v.)
having material or monetary value; **valuation roll** a list
of properties and their assessed values for local taxation purposes; **value added** the difference between the
overall cost of a manufacturing or marketing process
and the final value of the goods; **value judgment** a
personal estimate of merit in a particular respect; **value
received** a phrase indicating that a bill of exchange,
etc., has been accepted for a valuable consideration.
— **good value** full worth in exchange; **value-added tax**
a tax on the rise in value of a product due to the
manufacturing and marketing processes (abbrev.
VAT); **value in exchange** exchange value: the amount
of other commodities for which a thing can be exchanged in the open market (*econ.*). [O.Fr. *value*,
fem. pa.p. of *valoir*, to be worth — L. *valēre*.]

valuta *vä-lū′ta, -lōō′, n.* the comparative value of a
currency: a standard of money. [It.]

valvassor. See **vavasour.**

valve *valv, n.* a leaf of a folding-door: a single piece
forming part or the whole of a shell: one of the parts
of a dry fruit separating in dehiscence: a structure or
device that regulates flow or passage or allows it in

one direction only: a rectifier (*elect.*): loosely, a
thermionic valve used in wireless apparatus as rectifier,
amplifier, oscillator or otherwise. — *v.t.* (*rare*) to fit
with a valve or valves. — *v.t.* and (*rare*) *v.i.* (often with
off) to release gas through a valve (from, e.g. a vacuum
system, hot-air balloon, etc.). — *adjs.* **val′val; val′var;
val′vate** with or having a valve or valves: meeting at
the edges without overlapping (*bot.*); **valved; valve′less.**
— *ns.* **valve′let, val′vula** (*pl.* **-lae** *-lē*; in composition,
valvūlo-), **val′vule** a little valve. — *adj.* **val′vūlar** of or
having a valvule or valve. — *n.* **valvūlī′tis** inflammation
of a valve of the heart. [L. *valva*, a folding-door.]

vambrace *vam′brās, n.* armour for the forearm. — Also
vant′brace, (*Milt.*) **vant′-brass.** — *adj.* **vam′braced.**
[A.Fr. *vantbras* for *avant-bras*, forearm.]

vamoose *va-mōōs′,* **vamose** *-mōs′,* (*slang*) *vs.i.* to make off.
— *vs.t.* to leave. [Sp. *vamos*, let us go.]

vamp[1] *vamp, n.* the part of a boot or shoe covering the
front of the foot: anything patched up: a simple and
uninspired improvised accompaniment. — *v.t.* to provide with a vamp: to repair with a new vamp· to patch
up: to give a new face to: to improvise inartistically
(*mus.*). — *v.i.* to improvise crude accompaniments: to
trudge (now *dial.*). — *n.* **vam′per.** — *n.* and *adj.*
vamp′ing. [O.Fr. *avanpié* — *avan* (Fr. *avant*), before,
pié (Fr. *pied*) — L. *pēs, pedis,* foot.]

vamp[2]. See **vampire.**

vampire *vam′pīr, n.* in eastern European folklore, a dead
person that leaves the grave to prey upon the living:
a blood-sucker, a relentless extortionate parasite or
blackmailer: an adventuress who allures and exploits
men (short form **vamp**): a vampire-bat: a stage trap.
— *v.t.* to prey upon. — *n.* **vamp** see above. — *v.t.* to
allure. — *adj.* **vampir′ic.** — *v.i.* **vam′pirise, -ize** to play
the vampire. — *v.t.* (*lit.* and *fig.*) to suck the blood of.
— *n.* **vam′pirism** belief in human vampires: the actions
of a vampire. — *adj.* **vamp′ish.** — **vam′pire-bat′** a
blood-sucking Central and South American bat (as
Desmodus, Diphylla): applied to various bats wrongly
supposed to be blood-suckers (as Vampyrus). [Some
Slav. languages have *vampir*.]

vamplate *vam′plāt, n.* a guard for the hand on a lance.
[A.Fr. *van-* for *avant*, before, *plate*, plate.]

van[1] *van, n.* a shortened form of **vanguard** (*lit.*, or *fig.* as
in *in the van of modern fashion*). — Also (*Shak.*) **vant,
vaunt.** — *adj.* and *adv.* **van′ward** towards the van or
front.

van[2] *van,* (*lawn tennis*) *n.* short for **(ad)vantage.**

van[3] *van, n.* a winnowing basket or shovel: a shovel for
testing ore: a test of ore by washing on a shovel: a
wing: a windmill sail. — *v.t.* to winnow or test with a
van. — *n.* **vann′er** one who vans: an ore-separator. —
n. and *adj.* **vann′ing.** [Southern form of **fan;** perh. in
part directly from L. *vannus* or O.Fr. *van*.]

van[4] *van, n.* a large covered wagon: a light vehicle,
whether covered or not, used in transporting goods:
a railway carriage or compartment for luggage, the
guard, etc. — *v.t.* and *v.i.* to send, convey, confine,
travel, or tour in a van: — *pr.p.* **vann′ing;** *pa.t.* and
pa.p. **vanned.** — *n.* **vann′er** a horse suitable for a van.
[An abbreviated form of **caravan.**]

vanadium *va-nā′di-am, n.* a silvery metallic element (V;
at. numb. 23). — *ns.* **vanadate** (*van′a-dāt*) a salt of
vanadic acid. — *adj.* **vanadic** (*va-nad′ik*) of vanadium
in higher valency. — *n.* **van′adinite** (or *-nad′-*) a mineral,
lead vanadate and chloride. — *adj.* **van′adous** of
vanadium in lower valency. [Named by a Swedish
chemist Sefström from O.N. *Vana-dīs*, the goddess
Freyja.]

Van Allen radiation belts *van al′an rā-di-ā′shan belts,* zones
of intense particle radiation surrounding the earth at
a distance of above 1200 miles (1930 km) from it. [J.
A. *Van Allen,* American physicist, b. 1914.]

Vandal *van′dal, n.* one of a fierce people from north-
eastern Germany who overran Gaul, Spain, and North
Africa, sacked Rome in 455, destroyed churches, etc.:
(usu. without *cap.*) one who destroys what is beautiful:

(without *cap.*) one who wantonly damages property. — *adjs.* **Van′dal; Vandal′ic.** — *v.t.* **van′dalise, -ize** to inflict wilful and senseless damage on (property, etc.). — *n.* **Van′dalism** (or *van′-*).

Vandyke *van-dīk′*, or *van′-*, *n.* a painting by the great Flemish artist Anthony *Van Dyck* (1599–1641): (in the following, usu. without *cap.*) a deeply cut collar similar to those seen in his portraits (also called **Vandyke collar**): a point of a deep-cut edging: a short pointed beard (also called **Vandyke beard**). — *v.t.* and *v.i.* to notch or zig-zag. — *adj.* **vandyked′.** — **van′dyke brown** a deep brown used by Van Dyck: a mixture of lampblack or other material and ochre.

vane *vān*, *n.* a flag: a weathercock or revolving plate, or a streamer, serving to show how the wind blows: a heraldic or ornamental plate fixed on a pinnacle: a blade of a windmill, propeller, revolving fan, or the like: a fin on a bomb or a paravane: a sight on an observing or surveying instrument: the web of a feather. — *adjs.* **vaned** having a vane or vanes; **vane′less.** [Southern form of **fane.**]

Vanessa *və-nes′ə*, *n.* the red admiral genus of butterflies: (without *cap.*) a butterfly of this genus. [Perh. for *Phanessa* — Gr. *Phānēs*, a mystic divinity.]

vang *vang*, *n.* a guy-rope to steady a gaff. [A form of **fang.**]

vanguard *van′gärd*, *n.* the foremost of an army, etc.: the forefront: those who lead the way or anticipate progress. — *n.* **van′guardism** the condition of being or practice of positioning oneself as or within the vanguard of a movement (esp. political). [Fr. *avant-garde* — *avant*, before, *garde*, guard.]

vanilla *və-nil′ə*, *n.* a flavouring substance got from the pods of *Vanilla planifolia*, a Mexican climbing orchid, and other species: the plant yielding it. — *n.* **vanill′in** its aromatic principle (C₈H₈O₃). [Sp. *vainilla* — *vaina* — L. *vāgīna*, a sheath.]

vanish *van′ish*, *v.i.* to disappear: to fade out: to cease to exist: to become zero: to exhale, emanate (*Shak.*). — *v.t.* to cause to disappear. — *n.* a vanishing: a glide with which a sound ends. — *n.* **van′isher.** — *n.* and *adj.* **van′ishing.** — *adv.* **van′ishingly.** — *n.* **van′ishment.** — **vanishing cream** cosmetic cream that, when rubbed over the skin, virtually disappears; **vanishing point** the point at which parallel lines seen in perspective converge: the verge of disappearance of anything. [Aphetic for **evanish.**]

vanitas *van′it-as*, *n.* a 17th–century Dutch still-life painting in which motifs such as the hour-glass, skull or candle feature as reminders of the transience and vanity of human life and aspirations: any painting of this genre. [L., vanity.]

Vanitory® *van′i-tər-i*, *n.* (often without *cap.*) a unit consisting of a wash-hand basin and a dressing-table. — Also **Vanitory unit.** — Also *adj.* (usu. without *cap.*).

vanity *van′i-ti*, *n.* the quality of being vain: that which is vain. — **van′ity-bag, -box, -case** one containing a mirror and cosmetic appliances. — **Vanity Fair** the world, or any place or society in it where people are wholly devoted to vanity, triviality, and empty ostentation (from the fair at the town of Vanity, in Bunyan's *Pilgrim's Progress*); **vanity unit** a Vanitory unit or the like. [Fr. *vanité* — L. *vānitās, -ātis*; see **vain.**]

vanner, vanning, etc. See **van³, van⁴.**

vanquish *vangk′wish*, *v.t.* to conquer: to overcome. — *v.i.* to be victor. — *adj.* **vanq′uishable.** — *ns.* **vanq′uisher; vanq′uishment.** [A.Fr. *venquir, venquiss-* (Fr. *vaincre*) — L. *vincĕre*, to conquer.]

Vansittartism *van-sit′ərt-izm*, *n.* extreme anti-Germanism. [From the British diplomat Lord *Vansittart* (1881–1957).]

vant *vant*, (*Shak.*) *n.* Same as **van¹.**

vantage *van′tij*, *n.* advantage: a now less usual form of advantage (*lawn tennis*): opportunity (*Shak.*): excess, addition (*Shak.*). — *v.i.* (*Spens.*) to benefit, profit. — *adj.* **van′tageless.** — **van′tage-ground, -point** a

favourable or commanding position.   [A.Fr. *vantage*; cf. **advantage.**]

vantbrace, vant-brass. Same as **vambrace.**

vanward. See **van¹.**

vapid *vap′id*, *adj.* insipid: dull: flat. — *n.* **vapid′ity.** — *adv.* **vap′idly.** — *n.* **vap′idness.** [L. *vapidus.*]

vaporetto *vä-pə-ret′ō*, It. *va-po-ret′tō*, *n.* a small steamship that plies the canals in Venice: — *pl.* **vaporett′os, -i** (*-ē*). [It., — *vapore*, a steamboat.]

vapour, or (esp. *U.S.*) **vapor,** *vā′pər*, *n.* a substance in the form of a mist, fume, or smoke, esp. one coming off from a solid or liquid: a gas below its critical temperature, liquefiable by pressure: water in the atmosphere: (in *pl.*) exhalations supposed to arise in the stomach or elsewhere in the body, affecting the health (*old med.*): (in *pl.*, usu. with *the*) low spirits, boredom, nervous disorder: anything insubstantial, vain, or transitory: a fanciful notion: bluster. — *v.i.* to pass off in vapour: to evaporate: to brag: to emit vapour: to bluster. — *v.t.* to make to pass into vapour: to steam: to affect with the vapours: to boast: to drive by bluster: to destroy by disintegration into a vapour: to obliterate (*coll.*). — *adjs.* **vā′porable** capable of being turned to vapour; **vāporif′ic** vaporising; **vā′poriform** existing in the form of vapour. — *n.* **vāporim′eter** an instrument for measuring vapour pressure or vapour. — *adj.* **vāporīs′able, -z-.** — *n.* **vāporīsā′tion, -z-.** — *v.t.* **vā′porise, -ize** to convert into vapour: to spray. — *v.i.* to become vapour. — *ns.* **vāporīs′er, -z-** an apparatus for discharging liquid in a fine spray; **vāporos′ity.** — *adj.* **vā′porous** of, in the form of, like, or full of vapour: vain: affected with the vapours: insubstantial: flimsy: vainly fanciful. — *adv.* **vā′porously.** — *n.* **vā′porousness.** — *adj.* **vā′poured** full of vapours: affected with the vapours. — *n.* **vā′pourer** one who vapours: a moth (*Orgyia*) of the tussock family. — *n.* and *adj.* **vā′pouring.** — *adv.* **vā′pouringly.** — *adj.* **vā′pourish** vapoury. — *n.* **vā′pourishness.** — *adj.* **vā′poury** full of vapour: affected with the vapours. — **va′pour-bath** a bath in vapour: a place or apparatus for the purpose; **vapour density** the density of a gas or vapour relative to that of hydrogen at the same temperature and pressure; **vapour trail** a white trail of condensed vapour left in the sky from the exhaust of an aircraft.   [L. *vapor, -ōris.*]

vapulate *vap′ū-lāt*, *v.t.* to flog. — *v.i.* to be flogged. — *n.* **vapulā′tion** a flogging.   [L. *vāpulāre, -ātum*, to be flogged.]

vaquero *vä-kā′rō*, *n.* a herdsman: — *pl.* **vaque′ros.** [Sp., — L. *vacca*, a cow.]

vara *vä′rä*, *n.* a Spanish-American linear measure, varying from 33 to 43 inches (*c.* 84–110 cm). [See **vare.**]

varactor *var-ak′tər*, *n.* a two-electrode semi-conductor device in which capacitance varies with voltage.

varan *var′ən*, *n.* a monitor lizard. — *n.* **Var′anus** the monitor genus, constituting the family **Varanidae** (*-an′*). [Ar. *waran.*]

Varangian *va-ran′ji-ən*, *n.* a Scandinavian settler in what became Russia: a member of the bodyguard of the Eastern emperors (chiefly Scandinavian): their Scandinavian language (*Scott*). — Also *adj.* [L.L. *Varangus* — Late Gr. *Barangos* — O.N. *Væringi*.]

vardy *vär′di*, *n.* a once fashionable form of **verdict.**

vare *vār*, *n.* a vara: a wand of authority. [Sp. *vara*, a rod — L. *vāra*, a trestle, forked stick — *vārus*, crooked.]

varec, varech *var′ek*, *n.* kelp: wrack. [Fr.; of Scand. origin: cf. **wrack, wreck.**]

vareuse *vä-rœz′*, (*southern U.S.*) *n.* a kind of loose jacket. [Fr.]

vargueño *vär-gān′yō*, *n.* a cabinet or desk of a kind made at *Vargas* (Bargas) near Toledo: — *pl.* **vargue′ños.**

variable *vā′ri-ə-bl*, *adj.* that may be varied: changeable: tending or liable to change or vary: showing variations: unsteady: quantitatively indeterminate (*math.*): changing in brightness (*astron.*). — *n.* a quantity subject to continual increase or decrease (*math.*): a quantity which may have an infinite number of values in the same expression (*math.*): a shifting wind: a variable star. — *ns.* **variabil′ity; vā′riableness.** — *adv.* **vā′riably.** — *ns.* **vā′riance** variation: deviation: alteration: discrepancy: disagreement: dispute: the average of the squares of the deviations of a number of observations from the mean; **vā′riant** a different form of the same thing (esp. a word): a different reading: a specimen slightly differing from the type. — *adj.* changeful: varying: diversified: different: diverging from type. — *n.* **vā′riate** any one of the observed values of a quantity: a variant: the variable quantity which is being studied (*statistics*). — *v.t.* and *v.i.* to change, vary. — *n.* **variā′tion** a varying: a change: continuous change: difference in structure or character among offspring of the same parents or among members of a related group: departure from the mean or usual character: the extent to which a thing varies: a variant: declination of the compass: an inequality in the moon's motion discovered by Tycho Brahe: a change in the elements of an orbit by the disturbing force of another body: transformation of a theme by means of new figures in counterpoint, florid treatment, changes in tempo, key, and the like (*mus.*): a solo dance (*ballet*). — *adj.* **variā′tional** pertaining to variation. — *n.* **variā′tionist** a composer of variations: one who attaches importance to variation. — *adj.* **vā′riative** variational. — **variable costs** costs which, unlike fixed costs (q.v.) vary with the level of production; **variable gear** see **gear;** **variable-geometry aeroplane** an aeroplane of varying wing, swept-back for flight, but at right angles for take-off and landing, so removing the need for long runways and high landing-speeds. — *adj.* **va′riable= sweep′** (of an aircraft wing) of which the sweep-back may be varied, as on a variable-geometry aeroplane. — **at variance** in disagreement or dissension. [Partly through O.Fr., from L. *variāre, -ātum,* to vary — *varius;* see **vary.**]

variae lectiones vā′ri-ē lek-shi-ōn′ēz, va′, wa′ri-ī lek-ti-ōn′ās, (L.) various readings.

varicella var-i-sel′ə, *n.* chickenpox. — *adjs.* **varicell′ar; varicell′oid** resembling varicella; **varicell′ous** pertaining to varicella. [Irreg. dim. of **variola.**]

varices, varicocele, varicose. See under **varix.**

varicoloured vā′ri-kul′ərd, *adj.* diversified in colour. [L. *varius,* various, *color,* colour.]

Varidase® vär′i-dāz, *n.* the proprietary name of a drug used to liquefy, for draining away, clotted blood, thick pus, and dead tissue in deep infections.

varied. See **vary.**

variegate vā′ri-(ə-)gāt, *v.t.* to diversify, esp. with colours in patches. — *adj.* **vā′riegated.** — *ns.* **variega′tion; vā′riegātor.** [L. *variegātus* — *varius;* see **vary.**]

variety və-rī′ə-ti, *n.* the quality of being various: diversity: difference: many-sidedness, versatility: a varied set: a kind differing in minor characters: a race not sufficiently distinct to be counted a species: music-hall entertainment, a succession of varied turns: — *pl.* **varī′eties.** — *adj.* of, for, performing in, music-hall entertainment. — *adj.* **varī′etal** (*biol.*) of or having the character of a variety. — *adv.* **varī′etally.** — **variety meat** offal (*U.S.*): processed meat, sausage, etc. (orig. *U.S.*). [L. *varietās, -ātis* — *varius,* various.]

variform. See **various.**

variola və-rī′ə-lə, *n.* smallpox: sheep-pox. — *adj.* **varī′olar.** — *v.t.* **variolate** (vā′ri-ə-lāt) to inoculate with smallpox virus. — *ns.* **vāriolā′tion** inoculation with smallpox virus; **vā′riolātor** one who practices variolation; **variole** (vā′ri-ōl) a pock-like marking: a spherule in variolite; **vā′riolite** (Gr. *lithos,* stone) a fine-grained basic igneous rock with spherules of radiating feldspar resembling pock-marks. — *adjs.* **vāriolit′ic** of or like variolite; **vā′rioloid** resembling smallpox. — *n.* modified smallpox occurring in the vaccinated. — *adj.* **variolous** (və-rī′ə-ləs) of, pertaining to, suffering from, smallpox: covered with varioles. [L.L. *variola,* pustule, pox — L. *varius,* various, spotted.]

variometer, variorum. See **various.**

various vā′ri-əs, *adj.* varied, different: several: unlike each other: changeable: uncertain: variegated. — *adj.* **vā′riform** of various forms. — *n.* **vāriom′eter** (Gr. *metron,* measure) an instrument for comparing magnetic forces: a variable inductance of two connected coils, one rotating within the other: an instrument that indicates by a needle the rate of climb and descent (*aero.*). — *adj.* **vārio′rum** with the notes of various commentators or editors (L. *cum notīs variōrum*): with the readings of various manuscripts or editions. — *n.* a variorum edition: a succession of changes (*jocular*). — *adv.* **vā′riously.** — *n.* **vā′riousness.** [L. *varius;* see **vary.**]

variscite var′i-sīt, *n.* a greenish mineral, hydrated aluminium phosphate. [L. *Variscia,* Vogtland, in Saxony.]

varistor və-ris′tər, *n.* a two-electrode semi-conductor used to short-circuit transient high voltages in delicate electronic devices. [*vari*able resis*tor.*]

Varityper® vā′ri-tī-pər, *n.* a typewriter-like machine which has changeable type. — *n.* **vā′ritypist.**

varix vā′riks (L. va′, wa′riks), *n.* an abnormally dilated, lengthened, and tortuous vein, artery, or lymphatic vessel: dilatation: a ridge marking a former position of the mouth of a shell: — *pl.* **varices** (va′, vā′ri-sēz; L. va′rikās, wa′). — *n.* **varicocele** (var′i-kō-sēl; Gr. *kēlē,* tumour) an enlargement of the veins of the spermatic cord or those of the scrotum. — *adj.* **var′icose** of the nature of, like, pertaining to, affected by, a varix or varices: abnormally dilated or enlarged permanently, as a vein: dilated. — *ns.* **varicosity** (var-i-kos′i-ti) the state of being varicose: a distended place; **varicot′omy** the surgical removal of a varix or a varicose vein. [L. *varix, -icis,* a varicose vein.]

varlet vär′lit, *n.* an attendant (*arch.*): a municipal officer (*obs.*): a knave (*arch.*): — *fem.* (*rare*) **var′letess.** — *ns.* **var′letry** (*Shak.*) the rabble, the crowd; **varlett′o** (*Shak.,* sham It.) a varlet. [O.Fr. *varlet;* cf. **valet.**]

varmint, varment vär′mint, *n.* old variants (now *dial.* or *slang*) of **vermin:** a noxious or troublesome animal or person: (perh. another word) a skilled amateur sportsman (*obs.*). — *adj.* natty, dashing: sharp, cunning.

varna vûr′nə, vär′nə, *n.* any of the four great Hindu castes. [Sans., class.]

varnish vär′nish, *n.* a resinous solution that dries to give a glossy coat to a surface: a gloss or glaze: a specious show: an application of varnish. — *v.t.* to coat with varnish: to give a fair show to. — *ns.* **var′nisher; var′nishing.** — **var′nishing-day** a day before the opening of a picture exhibition when exhibitors may varnish or retouch their pictures after they have been hung; **var′nish-tree** the tung-tree or other tree whose resinous juice is used for varnishing or for lacquering. [Fr. *vernis;* prob. — Mediaeval L. *veronix,* sandarac.]

Varroa var′ō-ə, (also without *cap.*) *n.* an Asiatic mite (*Varroa jacobsoni*)which parasitises and kills the honey-bee: infection by this mite. [L.L.]

varsal vär′səl, (*coll.*) *adj.* universal.

varsity vär′si-ti, (*coll.*) *n.* and *adj.* university.

varsovienne vär-sō-vi-en′, *n.* a dance imitated from the Polish mazurka: a tune for it. [Fr., fem. of *Varsovien* — *Varsovie,* Warsaw.]

vartabed vär′tə-bed, *n.* a member of an Armenian order of clergy. [Armenian *vartabet.*]

Varuna vu′rōō-nä, var′, vär′, *n.* an ancient Indian Vedic god of the heavens, later of the waters. [Sans.; cf. Gr. *Ouranos.*]

varus vā′rəs, *adj.* (*med.*) of a deviation from the longitudinal alignment of the body in which the distal part of the deformity turns towards the midline. — *n.* (for *tālipēs vārus*) in-turned club-foot. [L. *vārus,* bent, knock-kneed.]

varve värv, (*geol.*) *n.* a seasonal layer of clay deposited in still water, of service in fixing Ice Age chronology. — *adjs.* **varve(d)** stratified in distinct layers of annual deposit. [Sw. *varv,* layer.]

varvel(led). Same as **vervel(led).**

vary *vā'ri, v.t.* to make different: to diversify, modify: to alter or embellish (a melody) preserving its identity (*mus.*): to express variously (*Shak.*): to change to something else: to make of different kinds. — *v.i.* to alter or be altered: to be or become different: to change in succession: to deviate: to disagree: to be subject to continuous increase or decrease (*math.*): — *pr.p.* **vā'rying;** *pa.t.* and *pa.p.* **vā'ried.** — *n.* a change. — *adj.* **vā'ried.** — *adv.* **vā'riedly.** — *n.* **vā'rier** one who varies. — *n.* and *adj.* **vā'rying.** For **variance, variation,** etc., see **variable.** [M.E. — (O.) Fr. *varier* or L. *variāre* — L. *varius,* various.]

vas (L. *väs, wäs*), *n.* a vessel, tube, duct, carrying liquid: — *pl.* **vasa** (*vā'sə*; L. *vä'sa, wä'.* — **vas(o)-** (*vas* (-*ō*)) in composition, vas: **vas deferens.** — *adj.* **vā'sal.** — *n.* **vasec'tomy** (Gr. *ek,* out, *tomē,* a cut) excision of the vas deferens, or part of it, esp. in order to produce sterility. — *adj.* **vas'iform** tubular: vase-shaped. — *ns.* **vasoconstric'tion** narrowing of a blood-vessel; **vasoconstric'tor** a nerve or drug that causes vasoconstriction. — *adj.* **vasoconstric'tory.** — *ns.* **vasodilatā'tion** expansion of a blood-vessel; **vasodilā'tor** a nerve or drug that causes vasodilatation. — *adjs.* **vasodil(at)ā'tory; vasomō'tor** causing constriction or expansion of blood-vessels. — *ns.* **vasopress'in** a pituitary hormone that raises blood pressure, regulates kidney secretion, etc. — also prepared synthetically; **vasopress'or** a substance that causes a rise of blood pressure. — **vas def'erens** a spermatic duct: — *pl.* **vā'sa deferen'tia** (-*shyə*). [L. *vās, vāsis,* vessel.]

vasculum *vas'kū-ləm, n.* a botanist's collecting case: — *pl.* **vas'culums, vas'cula.** — *adj.* **vas'cular** of, relating to, composed of, or provided with conducting vessels. — *n.* **vascularisā'tion, -z-** the formation of blood-vessels in an organ or tissue. — *v.t.* **vas'cularise, -ize** to render vascular. — *n.* **vascular'ity.** — *adv.* **vas'cularly.** — *n.* **vas'culature** a vascular system. — *adj.* **vas'culiform** vase-shaped. — **vascular bundle** a strand of conducting tissue in the higher plants, composed of xylem, phloem, and cambium; **vascular cryptogams** the pteridophytes, or ferns and their allies; **vascular plants** seed-plants and pteridophytes. [L. *vāsculum,* dim. of *vās,* a vessel.]

vase *väz,* old-fashioned *vöz,* or (as still *U.S.*) *väs, väz, n.* a vessel, usually tall, round in section, and ornamental, anciently used for domestic purposes: the body of the Corinthian capital (*archit.*). - **vase'-paint'ing** the decoration of vases with pigments, esp. the decoration of the pottery of the ancient Greeks. [Fr., — L. *vās.*]

vasectomy. See **vas.**

Vaseline® *vaz'* or *vas'i-lēn, n.* a name applied to products of a certain firm, consisting in large part, but not solely, of petroleum jelly (*paraffinum molle*) and preparations thereof. — Also *v.t.* [Ger. *Wasser,* water, and Gr. *elaion,* oil.]

vasiform, vasomotor, vasopressin, etc. See **vas.**

vassail. See **vessel.**

vassal *vas'əl, n.* one who holds land from, and renders homage to, a superior: one who holds land from a superior in return for the payment of feu-duty (*Scots law*): a dependant, retainer: a bondman, slave: a low wretch (*Shak.*). — *adj.* in the relation or state of a vassal: subordinate: servile: of a vassal. — *v.t.* to subject. — *ns.* **vass'alage** prowess, or deeds of prowess (*obs.*): the state of being a vassal: dependence: subjection: a fee, fief: vassals collectively; **vass'aless** a female vassal; **vass'alry** vassals collectively. [Fr., — L.L. *vassallus,* servant — Celtic; cf. Bret. *goaz,* man, W. *gwas,* boy, servant.]

vast *väst, adj.* waste, desert (*obs.*): boundless: huge: exceedingly great: great (18th cent. in hyperbole; e.g. *vast surprise*). — *n.* immensity, an immense tract, boundless or empty expanse of space or time: a waste: a huge quantity, vast amount (*dial.* or *coll.*). — *ns.* **vastid'ity, vast'itude, vast'ity** vastness: a vast extent. — *adv.* **vast'ly.** — *n.* **vast'ness.** — *adj.* **vast'y** vast. — **a vast**

many (*obs.*) a great many. [L. *vastus,* waste, desolate, huge; cf. **waste.**]

vat *vat, n.* a large vessel or tank, esp. for fermentation, dyeing, or tanning: dyeing liquor. — *v.t.* to put in a vat. — *n.* **vat'ful** as much as a vat will hold: — *pl.* **vat'fuls.** [Southern form of **fat²** — O.E. *fæt;* cf. Du. *vat,* O.N. *fat,* Ger. *Fass.*]

Vat, VAT *vat, n.* (sometimes without *cap*(*s*).) a colloquial acronym for *value-added tax.* — *n.* **Vatman, VATman** (sometimes without *cap*(*s*).) an employee of the Customs and Excise Board responsible for administering, assessing, collecting, etc. value-added tax.

vatic *vat'ik, adj.* prophetic: oracular: inspired. — *n.* **vat'icide** (-*sīd;* L. *caedēre,* to kill) the killer or killing of a prophet. — *adj.* **vaticinal** (-*is'i-nl*). — *v.t.* and *v.i.* **vati'cinate** (chiefly ironical) to prophesy. — *ns.* **vaticinā'tion** prophecy; **vati'cinator** a prophet. [L. *vātēs,* a prophet, *vāticinārī,* to prophesy.]

Vatican *vat'i-kən, n.* an assemblage of buildings on the Vatican Hill in Rome, including one of the pope's palaces: the papal authority. — *ns.* **Vat'icanism** the system of theology and ecclesiastical government based on absolute papal authority, ultramontanism; **Vat'icanist** one who upholds such a system; **Vaticanol'ogist** (*coll.*) one who studies Vatican affairs, history, etc. — **Vatican City** a small area on the Vatican Hill set up as an independent papal state in 1929; **Vatican Council** the council that met in St Peter's (1869) and proclaimed papal infallibility (1870), or the similar council (**Vatican II**) held between 1962 and 1965. [L. *Mōns Vāticānus,* the Vatican Hill.]

vaticide, vaticinate, etc. See **vatic.**

vau *wow, n.* the digamma (see **episemon**). [L., — Gr. *wau* — Semitic *wāw.*]

vaudeville *vō'də-vil, vōd'vil, n.* originally a popular song with topical allusions: a play interspersed with dances and songs incidentally introduced and usually comic: variety entertainment. — Also *adj.* — *n.* **vaudevill'ian** one who performs in or writes material for vaudeville. — Also *adj.* — *n.* **vau'devillist** a composer of vaudevilles. [From *vau* (*val*) *de Vire,* the valley of the Vire, in Normandy, where they were composed in the 15th century.]

Vaudois¹ *vō-dwä, n.* a native of the Swiss Canton *Vaud* (*pl.* **Vaudois**): its French. — Also *adj.* [Fr.]

Vaudois² *vō-dwä, n.* and *adj.* Waldensian. [Fr.; same root as **Waldenses.**]

vaudoo, vaudoux. See **voodoo.**

vault¹ *völt,* earlier *vöt, n.* an arched roof or ceiling: a chamber with an arched roof or ceiling, esp. underground: a cellar: a wine-cellar: hence (in *pl.*) a public-house: a burial-chamber: a cavern: anything vault-like. — *v.t.* to shape as a vault: to roof with an arch: to form vaults in. — *v.i.* to curve in a vault. — *n.* **vaul'tage** an arched cellar (*Shak.*): a cavern: a range of vaults: vaulted work. — *adj.* **vaul'ted** arched: concave overhead: covered with an arch or vault. — *n.* **vaul'ting** vaulted work. — *adj.* **vaul'ty** (*Shak.*) vault-like. [O.Fr. *vaute, vaulte, voute, volte* (Fr. *voûte*) — L. *volvĕre, volūtum,* to roll.]

vault² *völt,* earlier *vöt, v.i.* to leap, esp. by resting on the hand or a pole. — *v.t.* to vault over or upon. — *n.* an act of vaulting. — *n.* **vaul'ter.** — *n.* and *adj.* **vault'ing.** — **vault'ing-horse** a wooden horse for gymnastic exercise; **vault'ing-house** (*obs.*) a brothel. [App. O.Fr. *volter,* to leap.]

vaunce *vöns, v.t.* and *v.i.* obs. aphetic form of **advance:** — *pr.p.* (*Spens.*) **vaunc'ing.**

vaunt¹ *vönt* (also *U.S.* vänt), *v.i.* to boast: to behave boastfully or exultingly. — *v.t.* to boast: to boast of: to make known by display (*Spens.*). — *n.* a boast: boastful demeanour. — *adj.* **vaunt'ed.** — *ns.* **vaunt'er; vaunt'ery** vaunting. — *adj.* **vaunt'ful.** — *n.* and *adj.* **vaunt'ing.** — *adv.* **vaunt'ingly.** [O.Fr. *vanter* — L.L. *vānitāre* — L. *vānitās,* vanity — *vānus,* vain; partly aphetic for **avaunt².**]

vaunt² *vönt,* (*Shak.*) *n.* the first part. [Cf. **van¹.**]

vauntage vönt'ij, (Spens.) n. Same as **(ad)vantage**.
vaunt-courier vönt-kōō'ri-ər, n. one sent in advance: a forerunner. [Fr. avant-courier.]
vaurien vō-ryẽ, (Fr.) n. a good-for-nothing.
vaut, vaute. Old forms of **vault**[1,2].
vavasour vav'ə-sōōr, **valvassor** val'və-sör, ns. one who held his lands of a tenant in chief. — n. **vav'asory** the tenure or the lands of a vavasour. [O.Fr., app. — L.L. vassus vassōrum, vassal of vassals — vassus, vassal.]
vaward vö'ərd, (Shak.) n. a form of **vanguard**: forefront. — adj. front.
vawte. Same as **vaut(e)**.
've v. A shortened form of **have**.
Veadar vē'ə-där, n. an intercalary month in the Jewish calendar, following Adar in embolismic years. [Heb. ve, and.]
veal vēl, n. calf's flesh as food: a calf (obs.). — adj. of veal. — adj. **veal'y** like veal or like a calf: immature. [O.Fr. veël (Prov. vedel) — L. vitellus, dim. of vitulus; cf. Gr. italos, a calf.]
veale vēl (Spens.). Same as **veil**.
Vectian vek'tiən, (geol.) adj. of or pertaining to the Isle of Wight or the specific geological formation of which it is a part. [L. Vectis, the Isle of Wight.]
vector vek'tər, n. a directed quantity, as a straight line in space, involving both its direction and magnitude (math.): a carrier of disease or infection: the course of an aircraft, missile, etc.: a one-dimensional sequence of elements within a matrix (comput.): such a sequence having a single identifying code or symbol, esp. one acting as an intermediate address (q.v.) (comput.). — v.t. to direct, esp. from the ground, (an aircraft in flight) to the required destination. — adj. **vecto'rial**. — ns. **vec'tograph** a picture giving a three-dimensional effect when looked at through special spectacles; **vec'toring** (comput.) the process of transferring control (in a program) to an intermediate vector; **vec'torscope** an instrument that displays the phase and amplitude of an applied signal, e.g. of the chrominance signal in colour television. [L. vector, -ōris, bearer, carrier — vehĕre, vectum, to convey.]
Veda vā'də, or vē', n. any one of, or all of, four ancient holy books of the Hindus: — pl. **Vedas**. — n. **Vedan'ta** a system of Hindu philosophy based on the Vedas. — adjs. **Vedan'tic, Ve'dic**. — ns. **Ve'dism; Ve'dist** one learned in the Vedas. [Sans. veda, knowledge; cf. **wit**, L. vidēre, to see, Gr. oida, I know; Sans. Vedānta — anta, end.]
vedalia vi-dā'li-ə, n. an orig. Australian ladybird, Rodolia cardinalis, introduced elsewhere to control insect pests.
Vedda ved'ə, n. (a member of) an aboriginal people of Sri Lanka. — adj. **Vedd'oid** of, pertaining to, or resembling, the Veddas: of a S. Asian race, dark-skinned and curly-haired, to which the Veddas belong. — Also n.
vedette vi-det', n. a mounted sentry stationed to watch an enemy: a small vessel **(vedette'-boat)** for like purpose: (və-det; Fr.) a stage or film star. [Fr., — It. vedetta — vedere — L. vidēre, to see.]
Vedic, Vedism, Vedist. See **Veda**.
veduta ve-dōō'tə, It. -tä, n. a panoramic view of a town, etc.: — pl. **-te** (-tā). — n. **vedutis'ta** a painter of vedute: — pl. **-ti** (-tē). [It., a view.]
vee vē, n. the twenty-second letter of the alphabet (V, v): a mark or object of that shape. — in composition (also **V-** (q.v.)), shaped like the letter V, as in **vee-gutter, vee-joint**, etc.
veena. Same as **vina**.
veer[1] vēr, v.i. to change direction, esp. (of the wind) clockwise: to change course, esp. away from the wind: to turn, wind: to come round or shift round in mental attitude. — v.t. to turn, shift: to turn away from the wind. — n. a shifting round. — n. and adj. **veer'ing**. — adv. **veer'ingly**. [Fr. virer.]
veer[2] vēr, (naut.) v.t. to pay out: to slack. [M.Du. vieren.]
veery vēr'i, n. the tawny thrush of North America. [Prob. imit.]

veg vej, n. a coll. contraction of **vegetable(s)**. — Also **vegg'ie, veg'ie** (esp. in pl.).
Vega vē'gə, n. the first-magnitude star α Lyrae. [Ar. al wāqi' (al nasr), the falling (vulture).]
vega vā'gə, n. a low fertile plain: a tobacco-field (Cuba). [Sp.]
Vegan vē'gən, n. (often without cap.) one of a sect of vegetarians using no animal produce at all. — Also adj. — adj. **vegan'ic** pertaining to manuring with material which is purely vegetable organic. — n. **Vē'ganism** (also without cap.).
vegetable vej'i-tə-bl, n. an organism belonging to the great division distinguished from animals by being unable to deal with solid food, commonly but not necessarily fixed in position — a plant: a plant or part of one used for food, other than those reckoned fruits: a person whose capabilities are so low, esp. because of damage to the brain, that he is scarcely human: a dull, uninteresting person. — adj. of, for, derived from, composed of, of the nature of, vegetables. — adv. **veg'etably** in the manner of a vegetable. - adj. **veg'etal** vegetable: vegetative: of a level of life below the sensitive. — n. (rare) a plant, vegetable. — adj. **veg'etant** vegetating. — n. **vegetarian** (-tā'ri-ən) one who lives wholly on vegetable food, with or without dairy products, honey, and eggs. — Also adj. — n. **vegetā'rianism** the theory or practice of a vegetarian. — v.i. **veg'etate** to grow or live as, or like, a vegetable: to increase vegetatively: to live an inactive, almost purely physical, or dull life. — adj. **veg'etāted** covered with vegetation. — n. and adj. **veg'etāting**. — n. **vegetā'tion** the process of vegetating: vegetable growth: a plant (obs.): a plantlike growth: growing plants in mass. — adj. **veg'etātive** growing, as plants: producing growth in plants: concerned with the life of the individual rather than of the race (biol.): by means of vegetative organs, not special reproductive structures (biol.): pertaining to unconscious or involuntary bodily functions as resembling the process of vegetable growth (biol.): without intellectual activity, unprogressive. — adv. **veg'etātively**. — n. **veg'etātiveness**. — adj. **vegete** (vi-jēt') vigorous. — n. **veg'etive** (Shak.) a vegetable. — adj. vegetative. — n. and adj. **vegg'ie** (coll.) vegetarian: vegetable (also **veg**, **veg'ie**). — **vegetable ivory** corozo-nut; **vegetable kingdom** that division of natural objects which consists of vegetables or plants; **vegetable marrow** a variety of pumpkin cooked as a vegetable: the akee fruit; **vegetable mould** mould consisting mostly of humus; **vegetable parchment** paper treated with sulphuric acid; **vegetable sheep** in New Zealand, a dense cushion of composite plants (Raoulia, Haastia) at a distance resembling a sheep; **vegetative nervous system** the nervous system regulating involuntary bodily activity, as the secretion of the glands, the beating of the heart, etc.; **vegetative organs** leaves, stems, roots; **vegetative reproduction** reproduction by detachment of part of the plant-body: budding. [L. vegetābilis, animating, vegetāre, to quicken, vegetus, lively; cf. **vigour**.]
veggie, vegie vej'i. See under **veg, vegetable**.
vehement vē'(h)ə-mənt, adj. forcible: impetuous: very strong or urgent. — ns. **vē'hemence, vē'hemency**. — adv. **vē'hemently**. [L. vehemēns, -entis.]
vehicle vē'i-kl, n. a means of conveyance or transmission: a medium: a substance with which a medicine, a pigment, etc., is mixed for administration or application: a structure in or on which persons or things are transported, esp. by land: **(space vehicle)** a structure for carrying burdens through air or space or (also **launch vehicle**) a rocket used to launch a spacecraft. — adj. **vehicular** (vi-hik'ū-lər). — **vehicle-actuated signals** see **pad**[2]. [L. vehiculum — vehĕre, to carry.]
Vehm, Fehm fām, **Vehmgericht, Fehmgericht** -gə-rihht, ns. a mediaeval German, esp. Westphalian, court in which initiated persons held of the emperor power to try capital cases in public or in secret, their lower officers executing the guilty on the spot or where they could find them: — pls. **Vehm'e, Fehm'e, Vehm-**,

Fehmgerichte (-ə). — *adj.* **Vehm'ic, Vehm'ique, Fehm'ic.** — Forms without **-gericht** also without *cap.* [Ger. *Vehm, Fehm,* now *Feme,* criminal court, *Gericht,* court, judgment.]

veil *vāl, n.* a curtain: a covering: a covering for the head, face, or both, for protection, concealment, or ceremonial reason: a nun's or novice's head-covering: a piece of gauzy drapery worn on the head by a bride: a gauzy face-covering worn by ladies: a humeral: a disguise or concealment: an obstruction of tone in singing: a velum. — *v.t.* to cover with a veil: to cover: to conceal, disguise, or obscure. — *v.i.* to wear a veil. — *adj.* **veiled.** — *n.* **veil'ing** the act of concealing with a veil: a veil: material for making veils. — Also *adj.* — *adjs.* **veil'less** wanting a veil: uncovered; **veil'y** like a veil, diaphanous. — **eucharistic** or **sacramental veils** linen or silk covers for eucharistic vessels and elements; **draw a veil over** to conceal discreetly: to refrain from mentioning; **take the veil** to become a nun. [O.Fr. *veile* (Fr. *voile*) — L. *vēlum,* a curtain, veil, sail.]

veilleuse *vā-yœz', n.* a shaded night-lamp. [Fr., *veiller,* to watch.]

vein *vān, n.* one of the vessels or tubes that convey the blood back to the heart: loosely, any blood vessel: one of the horny tubes forming the framework of an insect's wing: a vascular bundle forming a rib, esp. a small rib, in a leaf: a small intrusion, or a seam of a different mineral running through a rock: a fissure or cavity: a streak in wood, stone, etc.: a streak running through one's nature, a strain of character or ability: (a recurrent characteristic streak in) manner, style: a mood or humour. — *v.t.* to form veins or the appearance of veins in. — *adj.* **veined** having veins: streaked, variegated. — *ns.* **vein'ing** formation or disposition of veins: streaking; **vein'let.** — *adjs.* **vein'ous** full of veins; **vein'y** veined: veinous. — **vein'stone, vein'stuff** gangue. [Fr. *veine* — L. *vēna.* See **vena.**]

Vela *vē'lə, n.* the Sail, a southern constellation: one of the divisions of Argo. [L., pl. of *vēlum,* sail.]

vela, velamen, velar, velarium, velate, etc. See **velum.**

velatura *vel-ə-tōō'rə, n.* a method of glazing a painting by rubbing with the hand. [It.]

Velcro® *vel'krō, n.* a type of fastening for clothes, etc. consisting of two strips of specially treated nylon fabric which when pressed together form a secure fastening.

veld, also (outside S. Africa) **veldt,** *felt, velt, n.* in South Africa, open, unforested, or thinly-forested grass-country. [Du. *veld* (formerly *veldt*), field.]

veld(-)schoen (older form of **veld'skoen**). Same as **velskoen.**

vele *vēl,* (*Spens.*) *n.* Same as **veil.**

veleta *və-lē'tə, n.* a dance or dance-tune in slow waltz time. — Also **valē'ta.** [Sp., weather-cock.]

veliger. See **velum.**

velitation *vel-i-tā'shən, n.* a skirmish. [L. *vēlitātiō, -ōnis* — *vēles, -itis,* a light-armed soldier.]

vell *vel, n.* the fourth stomach of a calf, used in making rennet. [Origin unknown.]

velleity *ve-lē'i-ti, n.* volition in its lowest from: mere inclination. [L.L. *velleitās,* irregularly formed from L. *velle,* to wish.]

vellenage *vel'ən-āj* (*Spens.*). Same as **villeinage.**

vellet *vel'it* (*Spens.*). Same as **velvet.**

vellicate *vel'i-kāt, v.t.* and *v.i.* to twitch. — *n.* **vellicā'tion.** [L. *vellicāre, -ātum,* to pluck.]

vellon *ve-lyōn', n.* billon: old Spanish copper money. [Sp. *vellon* — Fr. *billon.*]

Vellozia *ve-lō'zi-ə, n.* the Brazilian tree-lily genus, giving name to an African and S. American family **Vellozia'ceae,** akin to the amaryllids. [José *Vellozo* (1742–1811), Brazilian botanist.]

vellum *vel'əm, n.* a finer kind of parchment prepared by lime-baths and burnishing from the skins of calves, kids, or lambs: a manuscript, etc. printed on vellum. — *adj.* made of, printed on, etc. vellum. [O.Fr. *velin* — *vel,* calf.]

veloce *vā-lō'chā,* (*mus.*) *adj.* and *adv.* with great rapidity. [It.]

velocipede *vi-los'i-pēd, n.* a dandy-horse, bone-shaker, or other early form of bicycle: a swift-footed person. — *adj.* swift of foot. — *v.i.* to ride a velocipede. — *n.* and *adj.* **velocipē'dean, -ian.** — *n.* **veloc'ipēder** (or *-pēd'*). — *n.* and *adj.* **velocipedestrian** (*-pi-des'tri-ən*). — *n.* **veloc'i-pēdist** (or *-pēd'*). [Fr. *vélocipède* — L. *vēlōx, -ōcis,* swift, *pēs, pedis,* foot.]

velocity *vi-los'i-ti, n.* rate of motion (distance per unit of time) in stated direction: loosely, speed. — **velocity=distance law** (*astron.*) the law that the more distant a nebula the greater is its speed of recession. [L. *vēlōcitās, -ātis* — *vēlōx,* swift.]

velodrome *vel'ə-drōm, n.* a building containing a cycle-racing track. [Fr. *vélodrome.*]

velour(s) *və-lōōr', n.* a polishing pad for silk hats: a woollen stuff with velvet-like pile. — Also *adj.* — *ns.* **veloutine** (*vel-ōō-tēn'*) a velvety corded wool fabric; **velure** (*və-lōōr', -lūr'; Shak.*) velvet: a velours. — *v.t.* to dress with a velours. — *adj.* **velutinous** (*-lōō', -lū'*) velvety. [Fr. *velours.*]

velouté (sauce) *və-lōō-tā'* (*sös*), *n.* a smooth white sauce made with stock. [Fr., velvety.]

velskoen *fel'skōōn,* (*S.Afr.*) *n.* a shoe made of rawhide. [Du. *vel,* skin, *schoen,* shoe.]

velt-mareschal (*Scott*) *n.* Ger. *Feldmarschall,* field marshal.

velum *vē'ləm* (L. *vā', wā'lōōm*), *n.* a veil, integument, or membrane: the membrane joining the rim of a young toadstool with the stalk: the pendulous soft palate: a ciliated disc, a locomotor organ in some molluscan larvae: an in-turned rim in jellyfishes: — *pl.* **vē'la.** — *n.* **velamen** (*vi-lā'men,* L. *vā-lā'men*) a multi-layered sheath of dead cells on some aerial roots: — *pl.* **velā'mina** (L. *vā-lā'mi-na*). — *adj.* **vē'lar** of the velum: produced by the back of the tongue brought close to, or in contact with, the soft palate (*phon.*). — *n.* a velar consonant, back consonant. — *adj.* **velar'ic** pertaining to a velar. — *n.* **velarīsā'tion, -z-.** — *v.t.* **ve'larise, -ize** to pronounce (a non-velar sound) with the back of the tongue brought close to the soft palate, esp. through the influences of a vowel sound. — *adj.* **ve'larised, -z-.** — *n.* **velā'rium** (L. *vā-lā'ri-ōōm*) an awning over an auditorium: in Scyphozoa, the thin marginal region of the umbrella: — *pl.* **velā'ria.** — *adjs.* **vē'late, -d** having a velum. — *n.* **vē'liger** (*-jər*) a mollusc larva with a velum. [L. *vēlum,* veil, sail, *vēlāmen, -inis,* covering, *vēlārium,* awning.]

velure, velutinous. See **velour(s).**

velvet *vel'vit, n.* a silk fabric with soft close short pile: an imitation with silk pile: any of various other velvety fabrics: the velvet-like covering of a growing antler: a velvety surface or skin: gains, winnings (*slang*). — *adj.* made of velvet: soft like velvet. — *n.* **vel'veret** a cotton with a silk pile. — *adj.* **vel'veted** clad in velvet. — *n.* **velveteen'** a cotton, or mixed cotton and silk, imitation of velvet; **vel'vetiness; vel'veting** velvet material. — *adj.* **vel'vety** soft and smooth like velvet: deep and soft in colouring. — **vel'vet-crab, vel'vet-fidd'ler** a swimming crab with velvety pile; **vel'vet-duck, vel'vet-sco'ter** a black duck with a white mark on the wing; **vel'vet=guards** (*Shak.*) velvet trimmings, applied metaphorically to the citizens who wore them; **vel'vet-leaf** false pareira: tree-mallow; **vel'vet-pa'per** flock paper; **vel'vet-pile** material with a soft nap. — **on velvet** in a safe or advantageous position: secure against losing, whatever happens; **the velvet glove** gentleness, concealing strength (see **iron hand** at **iron**). [L.L. *velvettum,* conn. with L. *villus,* a tuft.]

vena *vē'nə,* (L. *vā', wā'na*), *n.* vein: — *pl.* **ve'nae.** — *adj.* **vē'nal** venous. — *ns.* **venation** (*vi-nā'shən*) arrangement of veins or nervures: the veins themselves considered together; **venepunc'ture, veni-** the puncturing of a vein, esp. with a hypodermic needle; **venesec'tion** the opening of a vein so as to let blood as a remedial measure. — *adj.* **venose** (*vē'nōs, -nōs'*) veiny: veined: with noticeable veins. — *n.* **venosity** (*vē-nos'i-ti*) the state or quality of being venous, or of having or being like venous blood. — *adj.* **vē'nous** pertaining to, or contained in, veins: of blood, deprived of oxygen and, in man, dark red in colour: veined. — *n.* **venule** (*ven'ūl*) a branch of a vein in an insect's wing: any of the small-calibre blood vessels into which the capillaries empty and which unite to form veins. — **vē'na cā'va** (L. *căva*, hollow) either of two large veins entering the right auricle: — *pl.* **vē'nae cā'vae** (-*ē*); **vē'na contrac'ta** the point of minimum cross-sectional area in a jet of fluid discharged from an orifice. [L. *vēna*; see **vein**.]

venal[1] *vē'nl, adj.* for sale: to be bought or bought over: corruptly mercenary. — *n.* **venality** (*-nal'i-ti*). — *adv.* **vē'nally.** [L. *vēnālis* — *vēnum*, goods for sale; Gr. *ōnē*, purchase.]

venal[2]. See **vena**.

venatic, -al *vi-nat'ik, -əl, adjs.* pertaining to hunting. — *adv.* **venat'ically.** — *ns.* **venation** (*vi-nā'shən*; *rare*) hunting: a hunt; **venā'tor** a huntsman, hunter. — *adj.* **venatorial** (*ven-ə-tō'ri-əl, -tö'*). [L. *vēnāri*, to hunt, *vēnātiō*, hunting, *vēnātor*, a hunter.]

venation. See **vena, venatic.**

vend *vend, v.t.* to sell or offer for sale, deal in, esp. in a small way: to utter (perh. for **vent**). — *n.* a sale: the amount sold. — *ns.* **vendee'** a buyer; **ven'der, -dor** a seller; **vendibil'ity.** — *adj.* **vend'ible** that may be sold, offered for sale, or readily sold. — *n.* a thing for sale: a possible object of trade. — *n.* **ven'dibleness.** — *adv.* **ven'dibly.** — *ns.* **venditā'tion** offering for sale; **vendi'tion** sale. — **vending machine** a slot-machine dispensing goods. [Fr. *vendre* or L. *vendĕre*, to sell — *vēnum dăre*, to offer for sale.]

vendace *ven'dəs, n.* a whitefish (*Coregonus vandesius*) found in the Castle Loch and Mill Loch at Lochmaben: another species (*C. gracilior*) in Derwentwater and Bassenthwaite Lake. — Also **ven'dis, ven'diss.** [Possibly O.Fr. *vendese, vendoise* (Fr. *vandoise*), dace.]

vendange *van'danj, n.* the harvest of grapes: vintage. — Also **vendage** (*ven'dij*). [M.E. — (O.)Fr. *vendange*; see **vintage**.]

Vendean *ven-dē'ən, n.* an inhabitant of La *Vendée*, in France: one of those who there resisted the Revolution. — Also *adj.*

vendee. See **vend.**

Vendémiaire *vä-dā-myer', n.* the first month in the French Revolutionary calendar, about 22 September to 21 October. [Fr., — L. *vīndēmia*, vintage — *vīnum*, wine, *dēmĕre*, to take away — *dē*, from, *emĕre*, to take.]

vendetta *ven-det'ə, n.* a blood-feud: any similarly prolonged, violent, etc. feud or quarrel. [It., — L. *vindicta*, revenge — *vindicāre*, to claim.]

vendeuse *vä-dœz', n.* a saleswoman. [Fr.]

vendible, venditation, vendition, etc. See **vend.**

vendis(s). See **vendace.**

vendor. See **vend.**

vendue *ven-dū', (U.S.) n.* a public auction sale. [Du. *vendu* — Fr. *vendue*.]

veneer *və-nēr', v.t.* to overlay or face with a thin sheet of fine wood or other substance: to disguise with superficial refinement. — *n.* a thin slice for veneering: a specious superficial show: a grass-moth (**veneer'-moth** from its markings). — *ns.* **veneer'er; veneer'ing.** [Formerly **fineer** — Ger. *furniren* — O.Fr. *fornir* (Fr. *fournir*), It. *fornire*, to furnish.]

venefic, -al *vi-nef'ik, -əl, veneficious ven-i-fish'əs, veneficous* *vi-nef'i-kəs, adjs.* acting by poison or potions or by sorcery. — *advs.* **venef'ically, venefic'(i)ously.** [L. *venēficus* — *venēnum*, poison, *facĕre*, to do.]

venepuncture. See **vena.**

venerate *ven'ə-rāt, v.t.* to revere. — *adj.* **ven'erable** worthy of reverence: hallowed by associations or age: agedlooking: an honorific prefix to the name of an archdeacon, or one in process of canonisation. — *n.* **ven'erableness.** — *adv.* **ven'erably.** — *ns.* **venerā'tion** the act of venerating: the state of being venerated: awed

respect; **ven'erātor.** [L. *venerārī, -ātus.*]

venerer. See **venery**[2].

venery[1] *ven'ə-ri, n.* sexual indulgence. — *adjs.* **venereal** (*vi-nē'ri-əl*) pertaining to sexual desire or intercourse: transmitted by sexual intercourse: pertaining to or affected by venereal disease; **venē'rean** pertaining to Venus or her service, or to sexual desire or intercourse. — *n.* one addicted to venery. — *ns.* **venereol'ogist; venereology** (*vi-nē-ri-ol'ə-ji*) the study of venereal diseases. — *adj.* **venē'reous** lustful: venereal: aphrodisiac. — **venereal disease** any of various contagious diseases characteristically transmitted by sexual intercourse. [L. *venereus* — *Venus, Venĕris*, the goddess of love; conn. with L. *venerārī*, to worship.]

venery[2] *ven'ər-i, n.* hunting: game. — *n.* **ven'erer** a gamekeeper: a hunter. [O.Fr. *venerie* — *vener* — L. *vēnārī*, to hunt.]

venesection. See **vena.**

Venetian *vi-nē'sh(y)ən, adj.* of Venice. — *n.* a native or inhabitant of Venice: a Venetian blind. — *adj.* **Vene'tianed** having Venetian blinds or shutters. — **Venetian blind** a window-blind of horizontal slats adjustable to let in or keep out light; **Venetian mast** a spirally banded pole for street decoration; **Venetian mosaic** see **terrazzo**; **Venetian red** ferric oxide as a pigment.

venewe *ven'ū,* **veney** *ven'i.* Shakespearian forms of **venue**.

venge *venj, v.t.* (*Shak.*) to avenge. — *adj.* **venge'able** revengeful (*Spens.*): destructive (*dial.*): extraordinarily great (*obs.*). — *adv.* **venge'ably.** — *n.* **venge'ance** the infliction of injury in punishment or revenge: retribution: harm, mischief (*Shak.*): a curse (*Shak.*). — *adv.* (*Shak.*) extremely, exceedingly. — *adj.* **venge'ful** vindictive, revengeful: retributive. — *adv.* **venge'fully.** — *ns.* **venge'fulness; venge'ment** (*Spens.*) vengeance, penal retribution; **ven'ger** (*Spens.*) an avenger. — **what a** (or **the**) **vengeance** used to intensify questions; **with a vengeance** orig., with a curse: violently, thoroughly, exceedingly (*coll.*). [O.Fr. *venger* — L. *vindicāre*.]

venial *vē'ni-əl, adj.* pardonable: excusable: permissible (*Milt.*). — *n.* **veniality** (*-al'i-ti*). — *adv.* **vē'nially.** — **venial sin** sin other than mortal. [L. *veniālis*, pardonable — *venia*, pardon.]

Venice *ven'is, n.* a city and former republic of Italy. — *adj.* **Venetian.** — **Venice glass** a fine glass made near Venice, formerly believed to shiver if poison were poured into it; **Venice gold** (*Shak.*) gold-thread made in Venice; **Venice talc** steatite; **Venice treacle** a supposed antidote for all poisons, of many ingredients; **Venice turpentine** larch turpentine, formerly shipped from Venice. [Fr. *Venise* — L. *Venetia*.]

venin. See **venom.**

venipuncture. See **vena.**

venire *ve-nī'rē, ve-, we-nē're* (in full **venire facias** *fā'shi-as, fa'ki-as; hist.* and *U.S.*) *n.* a writ issued to the sheriff requiring him to cause a certain number of qualified persons to appear in court at a specified time so that jurors may be chosen from them: the persons so caused to appear. — **veni'reman** (*U.S.*) a juror.

venison *ven'(i-)zn,* or (esp. in Scotland) *-i-sən, n.* a beast of the chase, esp. a deer (*Shak.*): its flesh as food: now deer's flesh. [A.Fr. *venison* (Fr. *venaison*) — L. *vēnātiō, -ōnis,* hunting — *vēnārī,* to hunt.]

venite *vi-nī'ti* (L. *ve-, we-nē'te*), *n.* the 95th Psalm, beginning *Venīte exultēmus.*

Venn diagram *ven dī'ə-gram, (math.)* a diagram in which sets and their relationships are represented, by circles or other figures. [John *Venn* (1834–1923), mathematician.]

vennel *ven'l, (Scot.) n.* a lane. [Fr. *venelle* — L. *vēna,* a vein.]

venom *ven'əm, n.* poison, esp. snake-poison: spite (*fig.*). — *adj.* (*Shak.*) poisonous. — *v.i.* (*obs.*) to poison: to envenom. — *n.* **ven'in** any of various toxic substances in venom. — *adjs.* **ven'omed** venomous: charged with poison, envenomed; **ven'omous** poisonous: having power to poison, esp. by bite or sting: malignant, full of spite. — *adv.* **ven′omously.** — *n.* **ven′omousness.** — *adj.* **ven′om′d-mouth′d** (*Shak.*) having a venomous mouth, slanderous. [O.Fr. *venim* (Fr. *venin*) — L. *venēnum*, poison.]

venose, venosity, venous. See under **vena.**

ven'son. Same as **venison.**

vent[1] *vent, n.* a slit in a garment, now in the back of a coat: a crenel (*obs.*). [Fr. *fente* — L. *findĕre*, to split; cf. **fent.**]

vent[2] *vent, n.* an opening: an aperture: an air-hole or passage: a touch-hole: an outlet: a volcanic orifice: an animal's or bird's anus: a chimney (*Scot.*): issue: emission: discharge: escape: passage into notice: publication: utterance: expression: an otter's rise to the surface for breath: the opening in a parachute canopy through which air escapes at a controlled rate. — *v.t.* to give a vent or opening to: to let out, as at a vent: to allow to escape: to publish: to utter: to discharge: to emit: to pour forth: to scent: to sniff at: to lift or open so as to admit air (*Spens.*). — *v.i.* to have or find an outlet: to discharge smoke, to function as a chimney, draw (*Scot.*): to sniff or snuff: to take breath or rise for breath. — *ns.* **vent′age, vent′ige** (*Shak.*) a finger-hole, as in a flute: a small hole. — *adj.* **vent′ed.** — *ns.* **vent′er** one who utters or publishes; **vent′iduct** (L. *dūcĕre, ductum,* to lead) a ventilating pipe or passage. — *n.* and *adj.* **vent′ing.** — **vent′-hole** a hole for admission or escape of air, fumes, etc., or to admit light; **vent′-peg, -plug** a plug for stopping the vent of a barrel; **vent′-pipe** an escape-pipe, as for steam or foul gases. — **give vent to** to allow to escape or break out: to give, usu. violent, expression to (an emotion). [Fr., — L. *ventus,* wind; partly Fr. *éventer,* to expose to air; associated with foregoing and following words.]

vent[3] *vent, (obs.) n.* a sale: a market. — *v.t. (obs.* or *dial.)* to sell. [O.Fr. *vente* — L. *vendĕre, -ītum,* to sell.]

ventail, (*Spens.*) **ventayle, ventaile,** *ven′tāl, n.* in mediaeval armour, the part of a helmet protecting the lower part of the face. [Fr. *ventail,* O.Fr. *ventaille*; ety. confused; ultimately from L. *ventus,* wind.]

ventana *ven-tä′nä, n.* a window. [Sp.]

ventayle. See **ventail.**

venter[1] *ven′tər, n.* the belly, abdomen: a womb or mother (*law*): a swelling or protuberance: a medial swelling: the dilated basal part of an archegonium: a shallow concave surface of a bone: the upper side or surface of a leaf, etc. — *adj.* **ven′tral** of the belly: on the upper side or towards the axis (*bot.*): on the side normally turned towards the ground — opp. to *dorsal* (*zool.*). — *n.* a ventral fin. — *adv.* **ven′trally.** — *n.* **ven′tricle** a cavity in the body: esp. a cavity in the brain, or a contractile chamber of the heart: the womb (*Shak.*). — *adjs.* **ven′tricose, ven′tricous** bellying: swollen in the middle or at one side, or all round at the base: big-bellied; **ventric′ular** of, of the nature of, a ventricle: abdominal. — *ns.* **ven′tricule, ventric′ulus** a ventricle; **ventriculog′raphy** radiography of the brain after the cerebrospinal fluid in the lateral ventricles has been replaced by air or positive contrast medium. — **ventral fins** the posterior paired fins. [L. *venter, -tris,* dim. *ventriculus.*]

venter[2] *ven′tər.* An old form (*Milt.*) of **venture.**

ventiduct. See **vent**[2].

ventifact *ven′ti-fakt, n.* a stone shaped and/or polished by wind-blown sand. [L. *ventus,* wind, art*ifact.*]

ventige. See **vent**[2].

ventil *ven′til, n.* a valve for giving sounds intermediate between the open harmonics in wind instruments: a valve in an organ for controlling the wind supply to various stops. [Ger., — L.L. *ventīle,* shutter, sluice — *ventus,* wind.]

ventilate *ven′ti-lāt, v.t.* to fan, winnow, blow upon: to open or expose to the free passage of air: to provide with duct(s) for circulating air or for escape of air: to cause (blood) to take up oxygen, by supply of air: to supply air to (lungs): to expose to examination and discussion, to make public. — *adj.* **ven′tilable.** — *n.*

ventilā′tion. — *adj.* **ven′tilātive.** — *n.* **ven′tilātor** one who ventilates: a contrivance for introducing fresh air: a machine which ventilates the lungs of a person whose respiratory system is not functioning adequately (also **ventilator machine**). [L. *ventilāre, -ātum,* to fan, wave, agitate — *ventus,* wind.]

venting. See **vent**[2].

ventose *ven-tōs′,* or *ven′, adj.* windy: flatulent: puffed up with conceit. — *n.* **Ventôse** (*vã-tōz*) the sixth month of the French Revolutionary calendar, about 19 February to 20 March. — *n.* **ventosity** (*ven-tos′i-ti*) windiness. [L. *ventōsus — ventus,* wind.]

ventral. See under **venter**[1].

ventre *ven′tər.* An old form of **venture.**

ventre à terre *vã-tra-ter,* (Fr.) belly to the ground: at high speed.

ventricle, etc. See under **venter**[1].

ventriloquism *ven-tril′ə-kwizm, n.* the art of speaking so as to give the illusion that the sound comes from some other source. — *adj.* **ventriloquial** (*-lō′kwi-əl*). — *adv.* **ventrilō′quially.** — *v.i.* **ventril′oquise, -ize** to practise ventriloquism. — *n.* **ventril′oquist.** — *adjs.* **ventriloquis′tic, ventril′oquous.** — *n.* **ventril′oquy** ventriloquism. [L. *ventriloquus,* one who speaks by a spirit in the belly — *venter,* the belly, *loquī,* to speak.]

ventripotent *ven-trip′ə-tənt, (facet.) adj.* with great capacity or appetite for food. [After Rabelais — L. *venter,* belly, *potēns,* powerful — *posse,* to be able.]

venture *ven′chər, n.* chance, luck, hazard (*arch.*): that which is put to hazard (esp. goods sent by sea at the sender's risk): an undertaking whose issue is uncertain or dangerous: an attempt: a thing put forward as an attempt: a prostitute (*Shak.*). — *v.t.* to send on a venture: to expose to hazard: to risk: to take the risk of: to dare to put forward. — *v.i.* to make a venture: to run a risk: to dare. — *n.* **ven′turer.** — *adj.* **ven′turesome** inclined to take risks: involving the taking of risk: risky. — *adv.* **ven′turesomely.** — *n.* **ven′turesomeness.** — *n.* and *adj.* **ven′turing** (*Milt.* **ven′tring**). — *adv.* **ven′turingly.** — *adj.* **ven′turous** (*Spens., Milt.,* etc., **ven′trous, ven′t′rous**) adventurous: daring. — *adv.* **ven′turously.** — *n.* **ven′turousness.** — **Venture Scout** a member of senior branch of the Scout organisation, formerly called Rover (Scout); **Venture Air, Sea, Scout; venture capital** money supplied by individual investors or business organisations for a new, esp. speculative, business enterprise, also called **risk capital.** — **at a venture** at hazard, random. [For **a(d)venture.**]

Venturi (tube), also without *cap.,* *ven-tōōr′ē* (*tūb*), a tube or duct, wasp-waisted and expanding at the ends, used in measuring flow rate of fluids, as a means of acclerating air flow, or to provide suction. [G.B. *Venturi* (1746–1822), Italian physicist.]

venue *ven′ū, n.* (*Shak.* **venewe, veney**) a hit in fencing: a bout or match: a lunge, attack: the place where an action is laid (*law*): the district from which a jury comes to try a question of fact: in England, usually the county where a crime is alleged to have been committed: a scene of action: a meeting-place, esp. for a sport. — **change of venue** change of place of trial; **lay the venue** to specify the place where the trial is to be held. [O.Fr. *venue,* arrival — *venir* — L. *venīre,* to come.]

venule. See **vena.**

Venus *vē′nəs, n.* the goddess of love, orig. of spring, patron of flower-gardens, later identified with the Greek Aphrodite (*Roman myth.*): an alluring grace (*obs.*): venery (*obs.*): the most brilliant of the planets, second in order from the sun: copper (*alchemy*): a genus of lamellibranch molluscs, including the quahog: (without *cap.*) a mollusc of this genus, or related genera (**ve′nus-shell′** a shell, or animal, of the genus.). — *ns.* and *adjs.* **Venusian** (*ven-ōō′si-ən, -shi-ən, -shən, ven-ū′*), less commonly **Venutian** (*ven-ōō′shi-ən, -shən, ven-ū′*) (an inhabitant) of the planet Venus. — **Venus's comb** an umbelliferous plant (*Scandix pecten-Veneris*) with long-beaked fruits set like comb teeth; **Venus's flower-basket** a beautiful glass sponge; **Venus's fly=**

trap, **Venus Fly Trap** see **Dionaea**; **Venus's girdle** a ribbon-like ctenophoran (*Cestus*); **Venus's looking= glass** a campanulaceous garden plant (*Specularia*) with small bright flowers. — **girdle of Venus** (*palmistry*) a line on the palm forming a semicircle from between the first and second to between the third and fourth fingers, apparently indicative of a hysterical and de- sponding temperament; **mount of Venus** the elevation at the base of the thumb: (*mons Veneris*) a fatty elevation on the human female pubic symphysis. [L., orig. personified from *venus, -eris*, desire; akin to *venerāri*, to worship.]

venville *ven'vil, n.* a form of tenure in parishes around Dartmoor that gives tenants certain rights to the use of land on Dartmoor. [Origin obscure.]

Vera *vē'rᵊ, n.* a machine that records television pictures and sound on magnetic tape for almost immediate reproduction. [*vision electronic recording appara- tus*.]

veracious *vᵊ-rā'shᵊs, adj.* truthful. — *adv.* **verā'ciously**. — *n.* **veracity** (*-ras'i-ti*) truthfulness. [L. *vērāx, -ācis* — *vērus*, true.]

veranda, verandah *vᵊ-ran'dᵊ, n.* a roofed gallery, terrace, or open portico along the front or side of a building. — *adj.* **veran'da'd, veran'dahed** having a veranda. [Hindi *varaṇḍā*, app. — Port. *varanda*, a balcony.]

Veratrum *vᵊ-rā'trᵊm, n.* the white hellebore genus: (with- out *cap.*) a plant of this genus. — *ns.* **veratrin(e)** (*ver'ᵊ-trin, -trēn*) an alkaloid or mixture of alkaloids got from white hellebore rhizomes, sabadilla, etc. [L. *vērātrum*, hellebore.]

verb *vûrb, n.* (*gram.*) the part of speech which asserts or predicates something. — *adj.* **ver'bal** of, pertaining to, derived from, a verb or verbs: of, in, of the nature of, in the matter of, or concerned with, words, or words rather than things: word for word: verbose (*Shak.*): oral. — *n.* a word, esp. a noun, derived from a verb: an oral statement, esp. an arrested suspect's confession of guilt, made to the police, or claimed by them to have been made (*slang*): (an) insult, (piece of) abuse or invective (*slang*). — *v.t.* (*slang*) of the police, to attribute to, or extract from (a suspect, etc.) such a statement or admission: — *pr.p.* **verb'alling**; *pa.t.* and *pa.p.* **verb'alled**. — *n.* **verbalīsā'tion, -z-**. — *v.t.* **ver'- balise, -ize** to turn into a verb: to put in words. — *v.i.* to use many words. — *ns.* **ver'balism** an expression: wording: undue attention to words alone: literalism; **ver'balist** one skilled in words: a literalist: one who looks to words alone; **verbal'ity** the quality of being verbal or merely verbal: mere words. — *adv.* **ver'bally**. — *n.* **verbā'rian** a coiner of words. — *n.* **ver'biage** superfluity of words: wording (*rare*). — *n.* and *adj.* **verb'icide** (*-sīd*) (the quality of) destroying the meaning of a word. — *v.i.* **verbigerate** (*-ij'ᵊ-rāt*). — *n.* **verbigerā'- tion** the morbid and purposeless repetition of certain words and phrases at short intervals, e.g. as occurs in schizophrenia. — *adjs.* **verb'less; verbose'** using· or containing more words than are desirable: wordy. — *adv.* **verbose'ly**. — *ns.* **verbose'ness, verbosity** (*-bos'*). — **verbal inspiration** dictation of every word of a book (usu. the Bible) by God; **verbal note** in diplomacy, an unsigned reminder of a neglected, though perhaps not urgent, matter; **verbal noun** a form of a verb, e.g. infinitive or gerund, functioning as a noun. [L. *verbum*, word.]

Verbascum *vᵊr-bas'kᵊm, n.* the mullein (q.v.) genus. [L.]

verbatim *vᵊr-bā'tim, -ba'tim, adv.* word for word (also *adj.*): by word of mouth (*Shak.*). — **verbatim et litter- atim** (*-ā'tim, -a'tim*) word for word and letter for letter. [L.]

Verbena *vûr-bē'nᵊ, n.* the vervain genus, giving name to the family **Verbenaceae** (*vûr-bi-nā'si-ē*), closely related to the labiates: (without *cap.*) a plant of this genus, or one of similar appearance. — *adj.* **verbenā'ceous**. — **verbe'na-oil'** an oil got from the kindred plant *Lippia citriodora* (called **lemon-scented verbena**) or from lemon-grass. [L. *verbēna*, a leafy twig, sacred bough.]

verberate *vûr'bᵊr-āt,* (*arch.*) *v.t.* to beat. — *n.* **verberā'tion.** [L. *verberāre, -ātum*, to scourge.]

verbiage, verbicide, verbose, etc. See **verb.**

verdant *vûr'dᵊnt, adj.* green: fresh green or grass-green: green, unsophisticated, raw and gullible. — *n.* **ver'- dancy.** — *adv.* **ver'dantly.** — *ns.* **ver'derer, -or** (*hist.*) a forest officer who had charge of the vert and venison; **ver'det** copper acetate; **ver'dure** fresh greenness: green- ery: fresh savour (*obs.*). — *adjs.* **ver'dured** clad with verdure; **ver'dureless; ver'durous.** [O.Fr. *verd* (Fr. *vert*) — L. *viridis*, green.]

verd-antique *vûrd-an-tēk'* (*obs.* Fr.), or **verde-antico** *ver'- dā-än-tē'kō* (It.). *ns.* a breccia of serpentine containing calcite, etc. — **oriental verd-antique** a green porphyry. [Antique green; Fr. now *vert*.]

verdelho *vᵊr-del'yōō, n.* (a white Madeira made from) a white grape grown orig. in Madeira, now also in Portugal, Sicily, Australia and S. Africa. [Port.]

verderer, verderor, verdet. See **verdant.**

verdict *vûr'dikt,* formerly (*Spens., Milt.*) **verdit** *-dit, n.* the finding of a jury on a trial: judicial decision or decision generally. — **open verdict** see **open; special verdict** a verdict in which specific facts are found and put on the record. [O.Fr. *verdit* and L.L. *vērēdictum* — L. *vērē*, truly, *dictum*, said.]

verdigris *vûr'di-grēs, n.* basic cupric acetate: popularly, the green coating of basic cupric carbonate that forms in the atmosphere on copper, brass, or bronze. — *v.t.* to coat with verdigris. [O.Fr. *verd de Grèce*, green of Greece.]

verdit. See **verdict.**

verditer *vûr'di-tᵊr,* (*arch.*) *n.* a blue or green pigment, hydrated cupric carbonate. [O.Fr. *verd-de-terre*, earth green.]

verdoy *vûr'doi,* (*her.*) *adj.* charged with flowers, leaves, or vegetable charges, as a bordure. [Fr. *verdoyé*, *pa.p.* of *verdoyer*, to become green.]

verdure, etc. See **verdant.**

verecund *ver'i-kund, adj.* modest. [L. *verēcundus.*]

Verein *fᵊr-īn',* (Ger.) *n.* union, association.

Verey light. See **Very light.**

verge[1] *vûrj, n.* a rod: a rodlike part: the axis of a clock pallet: a watch with a verge: an intromittent organ: a wand or staff of office: extent of jurisdiction (esp. of the lord-steward of the royal household): a precinct: a pale: a range: scope: jurisdiction: a limit, boundary: a rim: the brink, extreme edge: the horizon: the edge of a roof projecting beyond the gable: a grass edging. — *v.t.* to edge. — *v.i.* to border, be on the edge (with *on*; also *fig.*): to act as verger. — *ns.* **ver'ger** (see **virger** at **virge**) one who looks after the interior of a church building, etc.: attendant in a church: a pew-opener (*obs.*); **ver'gership.** — **verge'-board** a barge board. — **on the verge of** (*fig.*) on the point of: on the brink of. [L. *virga*, a rod; the area of jurisdiction of the holder of the office symbolised by the rod, hence, limit, boundary.]

verge[2] *vûrj, v.i.* to incline: to tend downward: to slope: to tend: to pass gradually, merge. — *n.* **ver'gency.** [L. *vergĕre*, to bend.]

Vergilian. Same as **Virgilian.**

verglas *ver'glä, n.* a film of ice on rock. [Fr., (*verre*, glass, *glace*, ice) from O.Fr.]

veridical *vi-rid'i-kl, adj.* truth-telling: coinciding with fact: (of a dream or vision) corresponding exactly with what has happened or with what happens later: seemingly true to fact. — *n.* **veridicality** (*-kal'i-ti*). — *adv.* **verid'- ically.** — *adj.* **verid'icous** truthful. [L. *vēridicus* — *vērus*, true, *dīcĕre*, to say.]

verier, veriest. See **very.**

verify *ver'i-fī, v.t.* to testify: to assert or prove to be true: to ascertain, confirm, or test the truth or accuracy of: to back up (*Shak.*): — *pr.p.* **ver'ifying**; *pa.t.* and *pa.p.* **ver'ified.** — *n.* **verifiabil'ity.** — *adj.* **ver'ifiable.** — *n.* **verificā'tion.** — *adj.* **ver'ificatory.** — *n.* **ver'ifier.** [L. *vērus*, true, *facĕre*, to make.]

verily. See **very.**

verisimilar *ver-i-sim'i-lər, adj.* truth-like. — *adv.* **verisim'-ilarly.** — *ns.* **verisimil'itude; verisimil'ity** (*obs.*). — *adj.* **verisim'ilous.** [L. *vērisimilis* — *vērus*, true, *similis*, like.]

verism *ver', vēr'izm, n.* use of everyday contemporary material, including what is ugly or sordid, in the arts, esp. in early 20th-cent. Italian opera (It. **verismo** *vā-rēs'mō*): the theory supporting this. — *adj.* and *n.* **ver'ist.** — *adj.* **verist'ic.** [L. *vērus*, true.].

vérité. See **cinéma vérité** under **cinema.**

verity *ver'i-ti, n.* truth: a truth: truthfulness: sincerity: faithfulness: — *pl.* **ver'ities.** — *adj.* **ver'itable** true: genuine: real, actual: truly so to be called. — *adv.* **ver'itably.** — **of a verity** (*arch.*) assuredly. [L. *vēritās, -ātis* — *vērus*, true.]

verjuice *vûr'jōōs, n.* juice of unripe fruit. — *adj.* sour. — *adj.* **ver'juiced** soured. [Fr. *verjus* — *vert* (L. *viridis*), green, and *jus*, juice (L. *jūs*, broth).]

verkramp *fər-kramp', adj.* (used predicatively) in S. Africa, narrow-minded, illiberal and rigidly conservative in attitude, esp. towards black and coloured people. — *adj.* (used attributively) and *n.* **verkrampte** (*-kram(p)'tə*) (a person) of such rigidly conservative political attitudes. [Afrik., restricted.]

verlig *fər-lihh', adj.* (used predicatively) in S. Africa, liberal, politically enlightened, esp. towards black and coloured people. — *adj.* (used attributively) and *n.* **verligte** (*-lihh'tə,*) (a person) of such enlightened and liberal political attitudes. [Afrik., enlightened.]

vermeil *vûr'mil, -māl, n.* and *adj.* bright red, scarlet, vermilion: silver-gilt or gilt bronze. — *v.t.* to colour with vermeil. — Also **ver'mil, ver'meille** (*Spens.* **ver'-mell, ver'mily**). [O.Fr. and Fr., — L. *vermiculus*, a little worm, kermes, dim. of *vermis*, worm; cf. **vermil-ion.**]

vermes *vûr'mēz, n.pl.* worms: (*cap.*) in old classifications a subkingdom of animals, according to Linnaeus including all invertebrates except arthropods, later mainly flat-worms, thread-worms, annelids, now abandoned. — *adjs.* **ver'mian; ver'micīdal** (L. *caedĕre*, to kill). — *n.* **ver'micide** a worm-killing agent. — *adjs.* **vermic'ular** of, like, of the nature of, caused by, a worm: vermiculated: peristaltic; **vermic'ūlate, -d** worm-eaten: marked, inlaid, rusticated, with curving lines in the appearance of worm-tracks or worms. — *ns.* **vermicūlā'tion** any wormlike appearance or action, esp. the movement of the intestines: vermicular decoration or rustication; **ver'micule** a little worm; **vermic'-ūlite** an altered mica that curls before the blowpipe flame and expands greatly at high-temperature, forming a water-absorbent substance used in seed-planting, and also used as insulating material. — *adjs.* **vermic'-ūlous** wormy; **ver'miform** having the form of a worm; **vermifugal** (*-mif'ū-gl*) expelling worms. — *n.* **ver'-mifuge** (*-mi-fūj*) a drug that expels worms. — *adj.* **vermiv'orous** worm-eating. — **vermiform appendix** see **appendix** at **append.** [L. *vermis*, a worm.]

vermicelli *vûr-mi-sel'i,* or *-chel'i, n.* a very slender macaroni: (more usu. **chocolate vermicelli**) short thin pieces of chocolate used for decoration of cakes, sweets, etc. — Also *adj.* [It., pl. of *vermicello*, dim. of *verme*, worm, L. *vermis*.]

vermicidal, etc., **vermiculite,** etc, **vermiform, vermifugal,** etc. See **vermes.**

vermil, etc. See **vermeil.**

vermilion *vər-mil'yən, n.* a bright-red pigment, mercuric sulphide: its bright scarlet colour. — *adj.* bright scarlet. — *v.t.* to colour vermilion. [O.Fr. *vermillon* — *vermeil*; see **vermeil.**]

vermin *vûr'min, n.* a collective name for obnoxious insects such as bugs, fleas, and lice, troublesome animals such as mice, rats, animals destructive to game such as weasels, polecats, also hawks and owls: odious, despicable people: any one species or individual of these. — *v.i.* **ver'minate** to breed vermin. — *n.* **verminā'tion.** — *adjs.* **ver'mined** infested with vermin; **ver'minous, ver'-miny** infested with vermin: like vermin. — **ver'min-**

kill'er. [Fr. *vermin* — L. *vermis*, a worm.]

vermis *vûr'mis, n.* in lower vertebrates, the main portion of the cerebellum: in mammals, the central lobe of the cerebellum. [L., worm.]

vermivorous. See **vermes.**

vermouth *vûr'məth, vār'-, vûr'mōōt, n.* a drink with white wine base, flavoured with wormwood or other aromatic herbs. [Fr. — Ger. *Wermut(h)*, wormwood (O.E. *wermōd*).]

vernacular *vər-nak'ū-lər, adj.* (of language) indigenous, native, spoken by the people of the country or of one's own country: of, in, or using the vernacular language: of the jargon or idiom of a particular group: (of other things) native, local, endemic, esp. of architecture or general style of building. — *n.* a native language or dialect: a class jargon: profane language (*facet.*). — *n.* **vernacularisā'tion, -z-.** — *v.t.* **vernac'ularise, -ize** to make vernacular. — *ns.* **vernac'ularism** a vernacular expression or idiom: the use of the vernacular; **vernac'-ularist** a user of the vernacular; **vernacularity** (*-lar'i-ti*). — *adv.* **vernac'ularly.** [L. *vernāculus* — *verna*, a home-born slave.]

vernal *vûr'nəl, adj.* of, happening or appearing in spring: springlike: fresh and youthful (*poet.*). — *n.* **vernalīsā'-tion, -z-.** — *v.t.* **ver'nalise, -ize** to make springlike: to freshen: to hasten the development of (seeds or seedlings) by treating them in various ways before planting, e.g. by subjecting them to a low temperature. — *n.* **vernality** (*-nal'i-ti*) springlike quality: freshness. — *adv.* **ver'nally.** — *adj.* **ver'nant** (*Milt.*) flowering or sprouting in spring. — *n.* **vernā'tion** arrangement of leaves in the vegetative bud (rarely that of the individual leaf). — **vernal grass** an early-sprouting meadow grass (*Anthoxanthum odoratum*) that gives its scent of coumarin to hay. [L. *vernālis*, vernal, *vernāre*, to sprout — *vēr*, spring.]

Verner's law. See **law**[1].

vernicle *vûr'ni-kl, n.* a sudarium with the face of Christ, held to have been miraculously impressed on it when St *Veronica* wiped his face: any representation of this: a medal or badge bearing it, worn by pilgrims who had been at Rome.

vernier *vûr'ni-ər, n.* a short scale sliding on a graduated scale to give fractional readings, invented by the Burgundian P. *Vernier* (*c.* 1580–1637): a small auxiliary device that enables a piece of apparatus to be adjusted very accurately (e.g. a **vernier condenser** a condenser of small capacitance connected in parallel with one of larger capacitance): a small rocket engine used to make the movement of a booster rocket, or of a ballistic missile, more precisely as required. — Also *adj.*

vernissage *ver-nēs-äzh', n.* varnishing-day. [Fr., varnishing.]

Veronal®, veronal, *ver'ə-nal, -nəl, n.* barbitone.

veronica *və-ron'i-kə, n.* (with *cap.*) the speedwell genus: any plant of this genus: a vernicle: (Sp. *vā-rō'nē-kä*) in bullfighting, the action of a torero when, without moving feet or legs, he swings his open cape to divert the charging bull. [St *Veronica*.]

véronique *vā-ro-nēk', (Fr.) adj.* (used after the noun) served with white grapes, e.g. *sole véronique*. [Origin uncertain.]

verquere *vər-k(w)ēr', n.* an obsolete form of backgammon. — (*Scott*) **verquire'.** [Du. *verkeeren*, to turn round, to play at backgammon.]

verrel *ver'l, n.* old (now *dial.*) form of **ferrule.**

verrey, verry *ver'i.* Same as **vairé.**

verruca *ve-rōō'kə, n.* a wart: a wartlike outgrowth: — *pl.* **verru'cae** (*-sē*; L. *-kī*), **verru'cas.** — *adjs.* **verru'ciform** (*-si-förm*) wartlike; **verrucose'** (or *ver'*, or *-rōō'*), **verru'-cous** (or *ver'*) warty. — *n.* **verru'ga** (Sp.; also *pl.* **verru'gas**) a fever with warty tumours, endemic in Peru. [L. *verrūca*, a wart.]

vers *ver, (Fr.) n.* verse. — **vers de société** (*də so-syā-tā*) light verse on topics of society; **vers d'occasion** (*dok-az-yɔ̃*) occasional verse, produced for a particular event; **vers libre** (*lē'br*) free verse, hence **verslibrist** (*ver-lē'brist*), (Fr.) **verslibriste** (*ver-lē'brēst'*), *ns.*, a writer of free verse. [Fr.]

versability *vûr-sə-bil'i-ti*, (*obs.*) *n.* aptness to be turned round. [L. *versābilis — versāre*, to turn about.]

versal[1] *vûr'səl*, *vär'səl*, (*obs. coll.*) *adj.* whole: single, individual. [For **universal.**]

versal[2] *vûr'səl*, *n.* an ornamental letter at the beginning of a section, e.g. in an illuminated manuscript. [**verse, -al.**]

versant[1] *vûr'sənt*, *adj.* versed, conversant: busied, concerned. [L. *versāns, -antis*, pr.p. of *versāre*, to turn over, consider.]

versant[2] *vûr'sənt*, *n.* the general slope of surface of a country. [Fr. *versant — verser*, to turn over — L. *versāre.*]

versatile *vûr'sə-tīl*, *adj.* turning freely: dangling as an anther attached by the middle of the back (*bot.*): capable of free movement, reversible, as a toe (*zool.*): changeable: unsteady: turning easily from one thing to another: of many-sided ability: capable of many uses. — *adv.* **ver'satilely.** — *ns.* **ver'satileness, versatility** (*-til'i-ti*). [L. *versātilis — versāre*, freq. of *vertĕre*, to turn.]

verse *vûrs*, *n.* a line of metre: metrical composition, form, or work: versification: a stanza: a short division of a chapter, esp. of the Bible: a portion of an anthem to be performed by a single voice to each part: a versicle. — *v.t.* and *v.i.* to versify. — *ns.* **verse'let** a little verse: a short poem; **ver'ser** a writer of verse; **ver'set** a very short organ interlude or prelude: a versicle: a little scrap of verse; **ver'sicle** a little verse: in liturgy, the verse said by the officiant. — *adj.* **versic'ular** of or in verse. — *ns.* **versifica'tion** the making of verse: manner of construction of verse: a turning into verse or its product; **ver'sificātor, ver'sifier** a maker of verses. — *v.i.* **ver'sify** to make verses. — *v.t.* to tell in verse: to turn into verse — *pr.p.* **ver'sifying;** *pa.t.* and *pa.p.* **ver'sified.** — *n.* **ver'sing** the composing of verse. — **verse'-maker; verse'-making; verse'-man** a writer of verses; **verse'-monger** a scribbler of verses; **verse'= mongering; verse'-smith** an artificer of verse. — **free verse** see **free.** [O.E. *fers*, reinforced by Fr. *vers*, both — L. *versus, vorsus, -ūs*, a line, row, verse — *vertĕre*, to turn.]

versed[1] *vûrst*, *adj.* thoroughly acquainted, skilled (with *in*). — *v.t.* **verse** to make conversant (with *in*). [L. *versātus*, pa.p. of *versārī*, to busy oneself.]

versed[2] *vûrst*, (*math.*) *adj.* lit. turned, reversed. — *n.* **versine** (*vûr'sīn*), contr. **versin**, the **versed sine**, one minus the cosine. [L. *versus*, pa.p. of *vertĕre*, to turn.]

verselet, verset, versicle, etc. See **verse.**

versicoloured *vûr'si-kul-ərd*, *adj.* diversely or changeably coloured. [L. *versicolor, -ōris — vertĕre, versum*, to change, *color*, colour.]

versicular, versification, etc. See **verse.**

versiform *vûr'si-förm*, *adj.* varying in form. [L. *versus*, turned, **-form.**]

versin(e). See **versed**[2].

version *vûr'shən*, *n.* a turning: translation: a Latin prose (*Scot. obs.*): a particular form in which something is embodied, as a particular way of telling a story: a variant. — *adj.* **ver'sional.** — *ns.* **ver'sioner, ver'sionist** producer of a version. [L. *versiō, -ōnis — vertĕre, versum*, to turn.]

verslibrist. See **vers.**

verso *vûr'sō*, *n.* a left-hand page of an open book: the reverse of a coin or medal: — *pl.* **ver'sos.** [L. *versō* (*foliō*), turned leaf (abl.).]

verst *vûrst*, *n.* a Russian measure, almost two-thirds of an English mile (approx. 1 km). [Russ. *versta.*]

versus *vûr'səs*, (*law, games*) *prep.* against — abbreviated **v** and **vs.** [L.]

versute *vər-sūt'*, *adj.* crafty, wily. [L. *versūtus.*]

vert[1] *vûrt*, *n.* in forest law, every green leaf or plant having green leaves that may serve as cover for deer: the right or power to cut green trees or wood (*arch.*): a green

colour, represented by parallel lines sloping diagonally from the dexter chief to the sinister base (*her.*). [Fr. *vert* — L. *viridis*, green.]

vert[2] *vûrt*, *n.* a familiar shortening of **convert** or **pervert** (esp. to Roman Catholicism). — *v.i.* to become a vert.

vertebra *vûr'ti-brə*, *n.* a joint of the backbone: — *pl.* **ver'tebrae** (*-brē, -brī*). — *adj.* **ver'tebral.** — *adv.* **ver'- tebrally.** — *n.pl.* **Vertebrā'ta** the backboned animals. — *adj.* **ver'tebrate** backboned: of the Vertebrata: articulated: firm of character. — *n.* a backboned animal. — *adj.* **ver'tebrated** having a backbone: articulated like a backbone. — *n.* **vertebrā'tion** vertebral structure: division into vertebrae or vertebra-like segments: backbone (*fig.*). — **vertebral column** spinal column. [L., — *vertĕre*, to turn.]

vertex *vûr'teks*, *n.* the top or summit: the zenith (*astron.*): the crown of the head (*anat.*): the point opposite the base (*geom.*): the meeting-point of the lines bounding an angle: the intersection of a curve with its axis: — *pl.* **ver'tices** (*-ti-sēz*). — *adj.* **ver'tical** (*-ti-kl*) of or at the vertex: perpendicular to the plane of the horizon: in the direction of the axis (*bot.*): comprising the various stages in the production of the same goods: in strata: (of mechanism) in which one part is above another. — *n.* a vertical line or position. — *n.* **verticality** (*-kal'i-ti*). — *adv.* **ver'tically.** — *ns.* **ver'ticalness; verticity** (*-tis'i-ti*) power of turning; **ver'tiport** an airport designed for vertical take-off and landing. — **vertical angles** opposite angles formed by intersecting lines; **vertical circle** a great circle of the heavens passing through the zenith and the nadir; **vertical grouping** in primary schools, the teaching of groups of children of various ages together — also called **family grouping; vertical scanning** (*TV*) scanning in which the lines are vertical, not, as normally, horizontal; **vertical take-off** (*aero.*) immediate take-off without preliminary run. — Also as *adj.* [L. *vertex, -icis*, eddy, summit — *vertĕre*, to turn.]

verticil *vûr'ti-sil*, (*bot.*) *n.* a whorl. — *n.* **verticillas'ter** an inflorescence so condensed as to look like a whorl. — *adjs.* **verti'cillate, -d** whorled. [L. *verticillus*, dim. of *vertex.*]

vertigo *vər-tī'gō*, often *vûr'ti-gō*, L. *ver-tē', wer-, n.* giddiness: dizziness: a whirling: — *pl.* **vertigos, vertigoes** or **vertigines** (*-tij'i-nēz*). — *adj.* **vertiginous** (*-tij'*) dizzy: giddy: whirling: dizzying. — *adv.* **vertig'inously.** — *n.* **vertig'inousness.** [L. *vertīgō, -inis — vertĕre*, to turn.]

vertiport. See **vertex.**

Vertoscope® *vûrt'ō-skōp*, *n.* a device in which any photographic negative can be viewed immediately as a positive. [L. *vertĕre*, to turn, Gr. *skopeein*, to view.]

vertu *vər-tōō'*, *n.* an erroneous form of **virtu.** — *ns.* **vertu, vertue** (*vûr'tū*) old forms of **virtue.** — *adj.* **ver'tuous** (*Spens.*) possessing virtue or power.

Verulamian *ver-ōō-lā'mi-ən, ver-ū-, adj.* of or pertaining to St Albans, or Francis Bacon, Baron *Verulam*, Viscount St Albans (1561–1626). [L. *Verulāmium*, an ancient British city near the site of St Albans.]

verumontanum *ver-ōō-mon'tā'nəm*, (*anat.*) a ridge on the male urethra where the duct conveying prostatic fluid, sperm and other fluids enter it. [L. *veru*, spit, *montanus*, hilly.]

vervain *vûr'vān*, *n.* a wild verbena, long believed to have great magical and medicinal powers. [O.Fr. *verveine* — L. *verbēna.*]

verve *vûrv*, *n.* enthusiasm that animates a poet or artist: gusto: spirit: animation: energy. [Fr.]

vervel *vûr'vl*, **varvel** *vär'*, *ns.* a ring for a hawk's jess. — *adjs.* **ver'velled, var'velled.** [Fr. *vervelle.*]

verven *vûr'vən*, (*Spens.*) *n.* vervain.

vervet *vûr'vit*, *n.* an African guenon monkey. [Fr.]

very *ver'i*, *adj.* true: so called in the true or full sense of the word — that and nothing less, even or exactly that: veritable: actual: mere: precise: extreme: — used, chiefly formerly, in *compar.* **ver'ier**, and also (oftener) in *superl.* **ver'iest**, most truly so called, merest. — *adv.* in high degree: utterly: quite: truly: precisely. — *adv.*

ver'ily truly: of a certainty: really. — **in very deed** of a truth, certainly; **the very thing** precisely what is wanted or needed; **very high frequency** see under **frequent**. [Older *verray, veray* — A.Fr. *ver(r)ai* (Fr. *vrai*), from a derivative of L. *vērus*, true; cf. Ger. *wahr*.]

Very light *ver'i līt*, a signalling or illuminating coloured flare fired from a pistol. — Also **Verey light**. [Edward W. *Very*, inventor, 1877.]

vesica *vi-sī'kə, ves'i-*, (*anat.*) *n.* a bladder, sac, esp. the urinary bladder: — *pl.* **vesicae** (*vi-sī'sē, ves'i-*). — *adjs.* **vesical** (*ves'i-kl*) of or pertaining to a vesica; **ves'icant** blistering. — *n.* anything that causes blisters, including any war 'gas' that blisters and destroys tissues. — *v.t.* and *v.i.* **ves'icate** to blister. — *n.* **vesicā'tion**. — *n.* and *adj.* **ves'icatory** (or *-ik'*) vesicant. — *ns.* **ves'icle** a small globule, bladder, sac, blister, cavity, or swelling: a primary cavity of the vertebrate brain; **vesic'ula** a vesicle: — *pl.* **vesic'ulae** (*-lē*). — *adjs.* **vesic'ular; vesic'ulate, -d**. — *n.* **vesiculā'tion** formation of vesicles. — *adj.* **vesic'ulose**. — **vesica piscis** (*pis'is*; L. *wā-, vā-sē'ka pis'kis*; fish's bladder) a halo in the form of two circular arcs each (properly) passing through the other's centre, enclosing the whole figure. [L. *vēsica*, bladder, blister.]

Vespa *ves'pə, n.* the common wasp genus, giving name to the family **Ves'pidae** (without *cap.*) any insect of this genus. — *n.* **ves'piary** (modelled on *apiary*) a wasps' nest. — *adjs.* **ves'pine** of wasps: wasplike; **ves'poid** wasplike. [L. *vespa*, wasp.]

vesper *ves'pər, n.* evening: (usu. *pl.*) the last but one of the seven canonical hours: (usu. *pl.*) evensong, evening service generally: a vesper-bell: (*cap.*) Venus as the evening star, Hesperus. — *adjs.* **ves'peral; vespertī'nal, ves'pertine** of or pertaining to the evening: happening, opening, appearing, active, or setting, in the evening. — **ves'per-bell** the bell that summons to vespers. [L. *vesper*; cf. Gr. *hesperos*.]

vespiary, vespine, vespoid. See **Vespa**.

vessel *ves'l, n.* a utensil for holding something: a craft or structure (usually bigger than a boat) for transport by water: a conducting tube for body-fluids in animals, for water in plants: a person regarded as a receptacle, recipient, or embodiment (*B.*): vessels collectively, plate (*Scott* **vessail, vassail**). — **the weaker vessel** a woman (1 Pet. iii. 7). [O.Fr. *vessel* (Fr. *vaisseau*) — L. *vāscellum*, dim. of *vās, vāsis*, a vessel.]

vest *vest, n.* garb, dress (*obs.*): a garment (*obs.*): a robe (*obs.*): a vestment (*obs.*): a waistcoat (chiefly *U.S.*): an undershirt: an additional facing to the front of a bodice. — *v.t.* to clothe: to robe: to drape: to put vestments on: to invest: to settle, secure, or put in fixed right of possession (*law*): to endow (*law*). — *v.i.* to descend, devolve, or to take effect, as a right. — *adj.* **vest'ed** clad: robed: wearing vestments: not contingent or suspended, hence (*law*) already acquired. — *n.* **vest'ing** the act or fact of clothing, investing, securing legally, etc.: material for waistcoats. — **vested interest** a particular interest in the continuance of an existing system, institution, etc., for personal reasons, often financial: (in *pl.*) interests already established: (in *pl.*) the class of persons who have acquired rights or powers in any sphere of a country's activities; **vest'-pocket** a waistcoat-pocket. — *adj.* small enough to go into one (also *fig.*). [L. *vestis*.]

Vesta *ves'tə, n.* the Roman goddess of the hearth and household: a minor planet discovered in 1807: (without *cap.*) a wax-stemmed match: a short match with wooden stem: — *pl.* **ves'tas**. — *adj.* **ves'tal** (often with *cap.*) pertaining or consecrated to Vesta: of or like the Vestal virgins: virgin: chaste. — *n.* one of the Roman patrician virgins consecrated to Vesta: a woman dedicated to celibacy: a nun: a virgin: a woman of spotless chastity. [L.]

vestiary *vest'i-ər-i, n.* a vestry, robing-room, or cloakroom. — *adj.* pertaining to clothes. [L. *vestiārium*; see **vestry**.]

vestibule *ves'ti-būl, n.* a forecourt (*ant.*): an entrance-hall:

part of a railway carriage connecting with and giving access to the next (*U.S.*): a cavity serving as entrance to another, esp. that of the inner ear (*anat.*). — *v.t.* to furnish with a vestibule. — *adj.* **vestib'ular**. — *n.* **vestib'ulum** a vestibule. [L. *vestibulum*.]

vestige *ves'tij, n.* a footprint: a trace: a surviving trace of what has almost disappeared: a reduced and functionless structure, organ, etc., representing what was once useful and developed (*biol.*); also **vestig'ium**: — *pl.* **vestig'ia**. — *adj.* **vestig'ial**. [L. *vestīgium*, footprint.]

vestiment *ves'ti-mənt*, (*obs.*; *Spens.*) *n.* vestment, garb, garment. — *adjs.* **vestimental** (*-men'tl*), **vestiment'ary**. [L. *vestīmentum*.]

vestiture *ves'ti-chər*, (*rare*) *n.* investiture: clothes: covering, as hair, feathers, scales. [L.L. *vestītūra* — L. *vestis*.]

vestment *vest'mənt, n.* a garment: a ceremonial garment, esp. one worn in religious ceremonies: a covering. — *adj.* **vest'mented**. [L. *vestīmentum* — *vestīre*, to clothe, *vestis*, a garment.]

vestry *ves'tri, n.* a room in which vestments are kept and parochial meetings held: a small room attached to a church: in Anglican and Episcopalian parishes, a meeting of church members or their elected representatives: the committee who meet thus for parish business: a robing-room: a cloakroom: apparel. — *adj.* **ves'tral**. — **ves'try-clerk** an officer chosen by the vestry to keep the parish accounts and books; **ves'tryman** a member of a vestry; **ves'try-room** a vestry: meeting-place of a vestry. — **common vestry** an assembly of all the ratepayers; **select vestry** a board of representatives of the ratepayers. [Prob. through O.Fr. — L. *vestiārium* — *vestis*, a garment.]

vesture *ves'chər, n.* garb (*arch.*): a garment (*arch.*): vegetation clothing the soil. — *v.t.* to cover, clothe. — *adjs.* **vest'ural; vest'ured**. — *n.* **vest'urer** a keeper of vestments. [O.Fr., — L.L. *vestītūra* — *vestis*, garment.]

Vesuvian *vi-sōō'vi-ən*, or *-sū', -zōō', adj.* of, of the type of, the volcano *Vesuvius*. — *ns.* **vesu'vian** a smoker's slow-burning match (*arch.*): vesuvianite; **vesu'vianite** the mineral idocrase, silicate of aluminium and calcium, found in blocks ejected by Vesuvius.

vet[1] *vet, n.* (*coll.*) a veterinary surgeon. — *v.t.* to treat, or examine, medically (animal; also, *facet.*, person): to examine (e.g. a writing) thoroughly and critically (and pass as sound or correct): — *pr.p.* **vett'ing**; *pa.t.* and *pa.p.* **vett'ed**.

vet[2]. See **veteran**.

vetch *vech, n.* the tare or other species of the papilionaceous genus *Vicia*: extended to some kindred plants. — *n.* **vetch'ling** any plant of the sweet-pea genus (Lathyrus). — *adj.* **vetch'y** abounding with or consisting of vetches. — **bitter vetch** various species of *Vicia* and Lathyrus; **kidney vetch** see **kidney**; **milk vetch** Astragalus. [O.N.Fr. *veche* (Fr. *vesce*) — L. *vicia*.]

veteran *vet'ə-rən, n.* one who has seen long service: an old and experienced soldier: one old or long experienced in any activity: an ex-serviceman or re-enlisted soldier (*U.S.*; *coll.* **vet**). — *adj.* old, experienced: long exercised, esp. in military life. — **veteran car** an old motor-car, specif. one made before 1905. [L. *veterānus* — *vetus, veteris*, old.]

veterinary *vet'ə-rin-ər-i, adj.* concerned with diseases of animals. — *n.* one skilled in the diseases of domestic animals. — Also **veterinā'rian, veterinary surgeon**. [L. *veterīnārius* — *veterīnae*, cattle, beasts of burden.]

vetiver *vet'i-vər, n.* cuscus roots.

vetkoek *fet'kook*, (*S. Afr.*) *n.* a deep-fried cake, usu. unsweetened, but otherwise similar to a doughnut. [Afrik., — Du. *vet*, fat, *koek*, cake.]

veto *vē'tō, n.* any authoritative prohibition: the power of rejecting or forbidding: the right to reject or forbid a proposed measure, esp. the right of any one of the five permanent members of the Security Council of the United Nations to prevent the Council taking action on any matter other than purely procedural: — *pl.* **vetoes** (*vē'tōz*). — *v.t.* to reject by a veto: to withhold assent to: to forbid. — **local veto** power of a district to prohibit the liquor trade within its bounds. [L. *vetō*, I forbid.]

vettura *vet-tōō'ra, n.* a carriage, cab, or car. — *n.* **vetturino** (*-rē'nō*) its driver or proprietor: — *pl.* **vetturi'ni** (*-nē*). [It., — L. *vectūra*, a carrying — *vehĕre*, to convey.]

vex *veks, v.t.* to harass: to distress: to annoy: to tease: to trouble, agitate, disturb: to discuss to excess. — *v.i.* (now *rare*) to grieve, fret. — *n.* (*Scot.*) a grief. — *n.* **vexā'tion** a vexing: state or feeling of being vexed: a source of grief or annoyance. — *adj.* **vexā'tious** vexing: wantonly troublesome: (of a law action) brought on insufficient grounds, with the intention merely of annoying the defendant. — *adv.* **vexā'tiously.** — *n.* **vexātiousness.** — *adjs.* **vex'atory; vexed** (*vekst*). — *adv.* **vex'edly.** — *ns.* **vex'edness; vex'er.** — *n. and adj.* **vex'ing.** — *adv.* **vex'ingly.** — *n.* **vex'ingness.** — **vexed question** a matter greatly debated. [Fr. *vexer* — L. *vexāre*, to shake, annoy.]

vexata quaestio *vek-sä'ta kwēs'ti-ō, vek-, wek-sä'ta kwīs'-ti-ō,* (L.) a disputed question.

vexillum *vek-sil'əm, n.* a Roman standard: a vexillation: a scarf on a pastoral staff: a standard (*bot.*): the series of barbs on the sides of the shaft of a feather: — *pl.* **vexill'a.** — *n.* **vex'illary** a standard-bearer: one of a company of Roman veterans serving under a special standard. — *adj.* of, pertaining to, under, a vexillum. — *ns.* **vexillā'tion** a company under one vexillum; **vexillol'ogist; vexillol'ogy** the study of flags. [L. *vehĕre*, to carry.]

vezir. See **vizier.**

via¹, viâ *vī'a, vē'* (L. *vē'a, wē'*), *prep.* by way of. [L. *viā*, abl. of *via*, way.]

via² *vī'a, vē'a, vē'a, wē'*, (L.) *n.* a way, road. — **via crucis** (*krōō'sis, -kis*) way of the Cross (succession of stations of the Cross — see **station**); **via dolorosa** (*dol-ə-rō'sə, do-lō-rō'sa*) the way to Calvary (lit. mournful way); **Via Lactea** (*lak'ti-ə, -te-a*) Milky Way; **via media** (*mē'di-ə, me'di-a*) a middle course: **via trita, via tuta** (*trī'tə, trē'ta, tūt'ə, tōō'ta*) beaten path, safe path.

via³ *vē'a,* (*obs.*) *interj.* of dismissal or incitement — come: be off: enough of that. [It., — L. *via*, way.]

viable *vī'ə-bl, adj.* capable of living, surviving, germinating, or hatching: (of plan, project) of such a kind that it has a prospect of success. — *n.* **viabil'ity.** [Fr., — *vie* — L. *vīta*, life.]

viaduct *vī'ə-dukt, n.* a structure carrying a road or railway over a valley, etc. [After **aqueduct** — L. *via*, a way.]

vial *vī'əl, n.* same as **phial:** a spirit-level. — *n.* **vī'alful.** — *adj.* **vī'alled** put or contained in a vial. — **pour out vials of wrath** to inflict judgment (Rev. xvi. 1): to storm, rage.

viameter *vī-am'i-tər,* (*arch.*) *n.* a hodometer: a cyclometer. [L. *via*, road, Gr. *metron*, measure.]

viand *vī'ənd, n.* an article of food: (usu. in *pl.*) food. [Fr. *viande* — L. *vīvenda*, food necessary for life — *vīvĕre*, to live.]

viaticum *vī-at'ik-əm* (L. *vē-*, *wē-ä'ti-kŏōm*), *n.* money, provisions, etc., for a journey: the eucharist given to persons in danger of death (*R.C. Church*). — *n.pl.* **viat'icals** baggage. [L. *viāticum* — *via*, way.]

viator *vī-ā'tər* (L. *vē-*, *wē-ä'tōr*), *n.* traveller, wayfarer. — *adj.* **viatorial** (*vī-ə-tō'ri-əl, -tō'*). [L. *viātor, -ōris* — *via*, a way.]

vibes *vībz,* (*coll.*) *n.pl.* feelings, sensations, etc., experienced or communicated (shortening of **vibrations**). — *n.sing.* or *pl.*, also *n.* **vibe** (*vīb*), coll. shortenings of **vibraphone.** — *n.* **vī'bist** (*coll.*).

vibex *vī'beks, n.* a streak due to extravasation of blood: — *pl.* **vibices** (*vī-, vi-bī'sēz*). [L. *vībīces*, weals.]

vibraculum *vī-brak'ū-ləm, n.* a long bristle, a modified zooid, in some Polyzoa: — *pl.* **vibrac'ula.** — Also **vibraculā'rium:** — *pl.* **-a.** [Coined from L. *vibrāre*, to shake.]

vibra-. Variant of **vibro-.**

vibraharp. Same as **vibraphone.**

Vibram® *vē'brəm, n.* tough, heavily-patterned, rubber used, without nails, for the soles of shoes for rock-climbing. — *n.pl.* **vibs** (*vibz; coll.*) shoes with Vibram soles. [*Vitale Bram*ini, inventor.]

vibrancy, vibrant. See **vibrate.**

vibraphone *vī'brə-fōn, n.* an instrument having metal bars under which are electrically-operated resonators, played by striking the bars with small hammers. — Also **vī'braharp** (*U.S.*). — *n.* **vī'braphōnist.** [L. *vibrāre*, to shake, Gr. *phōnē*, voice.]

vibrate *vī'brāt, -brāt', v.i.* to shake: to tremble: to oscillate: to swing: to change to and fro, esp. rapidly: to resound, ring: to tingle, thrill. — *v.t.* to brandish (*obs.*): to cause to vibrate: to measure by single vibrations: to give off in vibrations. — *n.* **vibrancy** (*vī'brən-si*). — *adjs.* **vī'brant** vibrating: thrilling: resonant; **vī'bratile** (*-brə-tīl,* in U.S. *-til, -təl*) vibratory: having or capable of vibratory motion. — *ns.* **vibratility** (*-til'i-ti*); **vibrā'tion** a vibrating: state of being vibrated: tremulousness: quivering motion: a whole period or movement to and fro of anything vibrating: sometimes a half period or movement one way: (in *pl.*) feelings communicated from person to person (*coll.*): (in *pl.*) feelings aroused in one by a person, place, etc. (*coll.*). — *adjs.* **vibrā'tional; vibrā'tionless.** — *n.* **vibratiuncle** (*vī-brā-shi-ung'kl*) a small vibration. — *adj.* **vī'brative** (*-brə-tiv*) vibrating: consisting in vibrations: causing vibrations. — *n.* **vī'brātor** that which vibrates: a vibrating part in many appliances: a vibrating tool: a type of dildo that can be made to vibrate mechanically. — *adj.* **vibratory** (*vī'brə-tər-i*) of, of the nature of, causing, or capable of, vibration. [L. *vibrāre, -ātum,* to tremble.]

vibrato *vē-brä'tō,* or *vi-, n.* a throbbing effect, without perceptible change of pitch, in singing and in stringed and wind instrument playing, obtained by varying breath pressure or by the shaking movement of the finger on a string: — *pl.* **vibra'tos.** [It.]

vibrio *vib'ri-ō,* or *vīb', n.* a bacterium of the genus **Vibrio,** with a slight spiral curve and usually one flagellum, as that of cholera: — *pl.* **vib'rios.** — *n.* **vibriō'sis** infection with these bacteria. [L. *vibrāre*, to shake.]

vibrissa *vī-bris'ə, n.* a tactile bristle, as a cat's whisker: a vaneless rictal feather: a bristle, hair, as in the nostril: — *pl.* **vibriss'ae** (*-ē*). [L., a hair in the nostril.]

vibro- *vī-brō-, -bro-,* in composition, vibration. — *ns.* **vī'broflotation** a process for compacting sand; **vī'brograph, vibrom'eter** an instrument for recording vibrations. [L. *vibrāre, -ātum,* to tremble, to shake.]

vibronic *vī-bron'ik,* (*phys.*) *adj.* of, relating to, caused by, etc., electronic vibration. [*vibration, electronic.*]

vibs. See **Vibram.**

Viburnum *vī-bûr'nəm, n.* the guelder-rose and wayfaring-tree genus of Caprifoliaceae: (without *cap.*) any plant of the genus. [L. *vīburnum,* the wayfaring tree.]

vicar *vik'ər, n.* one who holds authority as the delegate or substitute of another: a deputy or substitute: a parson of a parish who receives only the smaller tithes or a salary (*Ch. of Eng.*): a bishop's deputy (*R.C.*). — *ns.* **vic'arage** the benefice or residence of a vicar; **vic'aress** vicariate; **vic'aress** an abbess's deputy: a vicar's wife. — *adjs.* **vicarial** (*vī-, vi-kā'ri-əl*) delegated: of a vicar or vicars; **vicā'riate** delegated. — *n.* office, authority, time of office, or sphere of a vicar, in any sense. — *adj.* **vicā'rious** filling the place of another: exercised, performed or suffered by one person or thing instead of another: (*loosely*) not experienced personally but imagined through the experience of others. — *adv.* **vicā'riously.** — *ns.* **vicā'riousness; vic'arship** the (time of) office of a vicar; **vic'ary** (*obs.*) a vicarship. — **vic'ar-apostol'ic** formerly one to whom the pope delegated some remote portion of his jurisdiction: now usu. a titular bishop appointed to a country where there are no sees: one exercising authority in a vacant see or during the bishop's incapacity; **vic'ar-cho'ral** a cleric or layman who sings in an English cathedral choir; **vic'ar-forane** (*for-ān',* a form of **foreign**) a rural dean; **vic'ar-gen'eral** an official performing the work of an archdeacon under the bishop (*R.C.*): a lay official representing the bishop, the chancellor of the diocese; **vicarious sacrifice** the suffering and death of Christ held by orthodox Christians to be accepted by God in lieu of the punishment to which guilty man is liable. — **Vicar of Bray** one who turns his coat without difficulty to suit the times — from Simon Aleyn, vicar of *Bray*, Berkshire, from 1540 to 1588; **Vicar of Christ** (*R.C.*) the pope, as representative of Christ on earth. [L. *vicārius*, substituted; see **vice-**.]

vice[1] (in U.S. **vise**) *vīs*, *n.* a screw (*obs.*): a winding stair or its newel: a tool for gripping an object that is being worked on: a grip (*Shak.*). — *v.t.* to grip, force, jam, strain, as with a vice. [Fr. *vis*, screw — L. *vītis*, a vine.]

vice[2] *vīs*, *n.* a blemish or fault: immorality: depravity: an immoral habit: a bad trick or habit as in a horse: (*cap.*) the personification of a vice in a morality play, usually a farcical part: hence, a buffoon. — *adj.* **vicious** (*vish'əs*) addicted to vice or bad habits: immoral: depraved: bad: faulty: malignant, spiteful: ill-tempered: foul, impure, morbid: impaired, nullified by a flaw: mistaken (*Shak.*). — *adv.* **vic'iously**. — *n.* **vic'iousness**. — **vice squad** a police squad whose task is to see that the laws dealing with gambling, prostitution, etc., are observed; **vicious circle** reasoning in a circle, seeking to prove a proposition by means of a conclusion drawn from it: a process in which an evil is aggravated by its own consequences; **vicious intromission** see under **intromit**. [Fr., — L. *vitium*, a blemish; L.L. *viciōsus* for L. *vitiōsus*, faulty, vicious.]

vice[3] *vī'si*, *vī'sē*, *vīs*, *prep.* in place of: in succession to. — **vice versa** (*vûr'sə*) the other way round. [L. *vice*, abl. (nom. not used), turn, place, alteration.]

vice- *vīs-*, in composition, in place of. — *n.* **vice** place, stead (*rare*): short for **vice-president, vice-chancellor** or the like. — **vice'-ad'miral** a navy officer ranking next under an admiral; **vice'-ad'miralty** the office or jurisdiction of a vice-admiral; **vice'-chair'** a vice-chairman; **vice'-chair'man** a deputy chairman: a croupier; **vice'=chair'manship**; **vice'-cham'berlain** the Lord Chamberlain's deputy and assistant; **vice'-chan'cellor** one acting for a chancellor: in certain British universities, the head of administration, the chancellor being titular head only; **vice'-chan'cellorship**; **vice'-con'sul** a consul's deputy: one who acts as consul in a less important district; **vice'-con'sulate; vice'-con'sulship; vice'-count'y** part of a county divided for floristic purposes; **vice'=dean** a canon chosen to represent an absent dean; **vicegerency** (*-jer'* or *-jēr'ən-si*). — *adj.* **vicegerent** (*-jer'*, *-jēr'*; L. *vicem gerēns, -entis*, wielding office) acting in place of another, having delegated authority. — *n.* one ruling or acting in place of a superior. — **vice'=gov'ernor** deputy governor; **vice'-king** one who acts in place of a king; **vice'-mar'shal** same as **air-marshal; vice'-pres'idency; vice'-pres'ident** a president's deputy or assistant: an officer next below the president. — *adj.* **vice'-presiden'tial**. — **vice'-princ'ipal** assistant principal; **vice'-queen** a woman representing a queen: a viceroy's wife, vicereine. — *adj.* **vice-re'gal** of a viceroy. — **vicere'gent** properly, a substitute for a regent: often blunderingly for vicegerent; **vicereine** (*vīs'ren'*, *-rān'*) a viceroy's wife: a vice-queen (*rare*); **vice'roy** a governor acting in the name of the sovereign; **vice'roy'alty, vice'royship**. [**vice**[3].]

vicenary *vis'i-nər-i*, *adj.* based on the number twenty. [L. *vicēnārius* — *vīcēnī*, twenty each — *vīgintī*, twenty.]

vicennial *vī-sen'yəl*, *adj.* lasting, or coming at the end of, twenty years. [L. *vīcennium* — *vīciēs*, twenty times, *annus*, a year.]

vicesimal, etc. See **vigesimal**.

Vichyite *vē'shē-īt, vish'i-īt*, *n.* an adherent of the French Government (1940–42) ruling the unoccupied part of France from *Vichy*, and collaborating with the Germans. — Also *adj.* — *adj.* **vichyssois** (*vē-shē-swä'*) of the Vichyite government: — *fem.* **vichyssoise** (*-swäz'*). — *n.* **vichyssoise'** a cream soup usu. served chilled, with

ingredients such as potatoes and leeks. — **Vichy (water)** mineral water from Vichy springs, containing sodium bicarbonate, etc., or a natural or artificial water resembling it. [*Vichy*, city in central France.]

viciate. See **vitiate**.

vicinage *vis'i-nij*, *n.* neighbourhood. — *adj.* **vic'inal** (or *-īn'əl*) neighbouring: local: having substituted groups on adjacent carbon atoms (*org. chem.*): of crystal faces, very nearly in the plane of a normal face. — *n.* **vicin'ity** neighbourhood: nearness. [L. *vīcīnus*, neighbour — *vīcus*, street, village, district.]

viciosity. See **vitiosity** under **vitiate**.

vicious. See under **vice**[2].

vicissitude *vi-sis'i-tūd*, *n.* change: alternation: mutation: change of fortune. — *adj.* **vicissitū'dinous**. [L. *vicissitūdō, -inis*; see **vice**[3].]

vicomte *vē-kɔ̃*, (Fr.) *n.* in France, a noble equal in rank to a viscount: — *fem.* **vicomtesse** (*-es*).

victim *vik'tim*, *n.* a living being offered as a sacrifice: one subjected to death, suffering, or ill-treatment: a prey: a sufferer. — *n.* **victimīsā'tion, -z-**. — *v.t.* **vic'timise, -ize** to make a victim of: to treat oppressively in revenge: to cheat. — *n.* **vic'timiser, -z-**. — *adj.* **vic'timless** (of crimes) involving no injured party, as loitering, drunkenness, etc. — *n.* **victimol'ogist; victimol'ogy** the behavioural study of victims of crime, to establish their role in its commission. [L. *victima*, a beast for sacrifice.]

victor *vik'tər*, *n.* a winner in contest: — *fem.* **vic'toress, vic'tress, vic'trix**. — *adjs.* **vic'tor, victo'rious** (*-tō'*, *-tö'*) having gained a victory: winning in contest: of, with, marking victory. — *adv.* **victo'riously** — *ns.* **victo'riousness; victory** (*vik'tər-i*) a contest gained: success against an opponent: (*cap.*) the Greek goddess Nikē. — *adj.* **vic'toryless** — **victory ship** a successor to the liberty ship. [L. *victor, -ōris* — *vincĕre, victum*, to conquer.]

victoria *vik-tō'ri-ə, -tö'*, *n.* a gigantic water-lily of the Brazilian genus **Victoria**: a low, light, four-wheeled carriage with a folding hood: (also with *cap.*) a large red plum (also **victoria plum**). — *adj.* **Victo'rian** of, contemporary with, typical of, the reign (1837–1901) of Queen Victoria: strict but somewhat conventional in morals, inclining to prudery and solemnity: of the state (colony 1851–1901) of Victoria in Australia. — *n.* a contemporary of Queen Victoria: a person of Victorian morality or outlook: a native or inhabitant of Victoria. — *n.pl.* **Victoriana** (*vik-tō-ri-ä'nə, -tö-*, or *-ā'nə*; also without *cap.*) bric-à-brac and other characteristic possessions or creations of the Victorian age. — *n.* **Victo'rianism**. — **Victoria Cross** a bronze Maltese cross, a decoration for conspicuous bravery in the field, founded by Queen Victoria (1856); **Victoria Day** Empire Day, a holiday on or near Queen Victoria's birthday (24 May).

victorine *vik-tə-rēn'*, *n.* a fur tippet with long ends: a variety of peach. [Woman's name.]

victor ludorum *vik'tər lōō-dō'rəm, vik'tör lōō-dō'rōōm*, (L.) in school sports, etc., the most outstanding athlete.

victress, victrix. See **victor**.

victual *vit'l*, *n.* (commonly in *pl.*) food, esp. human food: grain crops, cut or ready for cutting (*Scot.*, in *sing.*). — *v.t.* to supply or store with provision. — *v.i.* to lay in victuals: to feed (*rare*): — *pr.p.* **victualling** (*vit'l-ing*); *pa.t.* and *pa.p.* **victualled** (*vit'ld*). — *ns.* **vict'uallage** provisions; **victualler** (*vit'l-ər*) a purveyor of provisions: a victualling-ship. — *adj.* **vict'ualless**. — **vict'ualling-bill'** a customs document warranting the captain of an outward-bound vessel to ship bonded stores for the voyage; **vict'ualling-off'ice, -ship** an office supplying, or a ship conveying, provisions to the navy; **vict'ualling-yard'** a public establishment for the collection and supply of provisions to the navy. — **licensed victualler** see **licence**. [O.F. *vitaille* — L.L. *victuālia* — L. *victuālis*, relating to living — *vivĕre, victum*, to live.]

vicuña *vi-kōō'nyə*, *n.* a wild species of the llama genus:

cloth of its wool, or an imitation. [Sp., from Quechua.]

vidame *vē-däm'*, *n*. in French feudal jurisprudence, the deputy of a bishop in temporal affairs: a minor noble. [Fr., — L.L. *vicedominus*.]

vide *vī'dē*, *vē'*, *wē'dä*, (L.) see. — **vide infra** (*in'frə*, *ēn'frä*) see below; **vide supra** (*sū'prə*, *sōō'prä*) see above.

videlicet *vi-del'i-sit*, *vi-*, *wi-dā'li-ket*, L. to wit, namely; usu. abbrev. **viz.**

videndum *vī-den'dəm*, *vi-*, *wi-den'dōōm* (*pl*. **videnda** *-də*, *-da*) L. thing(s) to be seen.

video *vid'i-ō*, *n*. television: a video recorder: video recording: — *pl*. **vid'eos**. — *adj*. pertaining to the bandwidth and spectrum position of the signal arising from TV scanning, or to the signal, or to the resultant image, or to television: using, used for, relating to, etc., the system of video recording. — *v.t*. and *v.i*. to make a video recording (of): — *pr.p*. **vid'eoing**, *pa.p*. **vid'eoed**. — **vid'eotex** a system used to display pages of information on a television screen, as teletext or viewdata (q.v.). — **video camera** a camera which records its (moving) film on to videotape; **vid'eocassette'** a cassette containing videotape; **videocassette recorder** a videotape recorder in which videocassettes are used; **videocon'ference; videocon'ferencing** live discussion between people in different places using electronically linked telephones and video screens; **vid'eodisc** a disc on which visual images and sound can be recorded for playing back on a television set or similar apparatus; **vid'eofit** a type of identikit picture put together on television; **video frequency** that in the range required for a video signal; **video game** an electronically-operated game played by means of a visual display unit; **vid'eogram** a commercial video film: a prerecorded videocassette or videodisc; **video nasty** a pornographic or horror video film; **vid'eophone**, also **vid'eotel'ephone**, a telephone with accompanying means of transmitting a picture of each speaker; **video recorder** a machine for recording and playing back television broadcasts or films made on videotape, using videotape or videodiscs; **video signal** that part of a TV signal which conveys all the information required for establishing the visual image; **videotape** magnetic tape for recording visual images, esp. television programmes or films; **videotape recorder** a tape recorder that records visual images on magnetic tape and replays them; **vid'eotext** any of the systems used for displaying user-selected pages of information on the television screen, videotex; **video tube** a television tube. [L. *vidēre*, to see.]

vidette. A faulty form of **vedette**.

Vidicon® *vid'i-kon*, *n*. a camera tube operating on the photoconducting principle. [*Video icon*(oscope).]

vidimus *vī'di-məs* (L. *vē'*, *wē'di-mōōs*), *n*. an attested copy: an inspection, as of accounts, etc. [L. *vidimus*, we have seen — *vidēre*, to see.]

viduous *vid'ū-əs*, *adj*. widowed: empty. — *n*. **vid'ūage** widowhood: widows collectively. — *adj*. **vid'ūal**. — *n*. **vidū'ity** widowhood. [L. *vidua*, a widow, *viduus*, deprived, bereaved.]

vie *vī*, *v.i*. to make a vie (*obs*.): to contend in rivalry. — *v.t*. to stake (*obs*.): to declare, bid (*obs*.; *cards*): to put forward in competition or emulation, or (*Shak*.) repeatedly: — *pr.p*. **vy'ing;** *pa.t*. and *pa.p*. **vied** (*vīd*). — *n*. (*obs*.) a bid, challenge, stake. — *n*. **vī'er**. — *adv*. **vy'ingly**. [Fr. *envier* — L. *invitāre*, to challenge, invite.]

vielle *vē-el'*, *n*. a hurdy-gurdy, a lute played by a wheel: a mediaeval stringed and bowed instrument resembling a viol. [Fr.]

Viennese *vē-e-nēz'*, *adj*. of *Vienna*, the capital of Austria. — *n. sing*. and *pl*. an inhabitant, the inhabitants of Vienna. — **vienna** (or **Vienna) loaf** a long, round-ended loaf of white bread; **vienna steak** a meat rissole.

vi et armis *vī et är'mis*, *vē*, *wē et är'mēs*, L. by force of (lit. and) arms.

Vietnamese *vē-et-nəm-ēz'*, *n*. a native or inhabitant, or the language, of *Vietnam*: — *pl*. same as *sing*. — Also *adj*.

vieux jeu *vyø zhø*, (Fr., lit. old game or joke), a subject that has lost all novelty.

view *vū*, *n*. an act, possibility or opportunity of looking: range or field of sight: whole extent seen: a prospect, wide or distant extent seen: that which is seen: inspection: appearance: aspect: the picture of a scene: general survey of a subject: mode of thinking of something: opinion: intention, purpose: expectation. — *v.t*. to see: to look at: to look at on television: to observe: to consider: to examine intellectually. — *v.i*. to watch television. — *adj*. **view'able** able to be seen: sufficiently interesting to be looked at or watched. — *ns*. **view'er** one who views: an inspector: one appointed to examine and report: a colliery superintendent: a television watcher: an apparatus used to project film for purposes of editing and cutting: device with magnifying lens, etc., for viewing transparencies; **view'ership** the estimated number of viewers of a television programme; **view'iness** character of being viewy; **view'ing**. — *adj*. **view'less** (*poet*.) invisible. — *adv*. **view'lessly**. — *adjs*. **view'ly** (*dial*.) pleasing to look at; **view'y** (*coll*.) holding or expressing opinions vague or purely speculative: inclined to attach undue importance to certain aspects or views: one-sided: cranky. — **view'data** a communications system by which information can be received and requested via a telephone line and presented through a television or video display; **view'finder** a camera attachment or part for determining the field of view; **view'-halloo'** the huntsman's cry when the fox breaks cover; **view'phone** another name for **videophone; view'point** point of view: standpoint: a selected position for admiring scenery. — **dissolving views** pictures thrown on a screen and made to pass one into another; **in view** in sight: in mind: as an aim or prospect; **in view of** in a position to see or to be seen by: having regard to; **on view** open to general inspection; **take a dim view of** to regard unfavourably; **view away** to see breaking cover; **with a view to** having in mind: with a design of. [Fr. *vue* — *vu*, pa.p. of *voir* — L. *vidēre*, to see.]

vifda *vif'dä*, *n*. See **vivda**.

vigesimal *vī-jes'i-məl*, *adj*. based on the number twenty (more rarely **vicesimal** *vī-ses'i-məl*). — *adj*. **viges'imo-** (or **vices'imo-**) **quar'to** twenty-four-mo. [L. *vigēsimus* (*vīcēsimus*), twentieth — *vigintī*, twenty.]

vigia *vi-jē'ə* (Sp. *vi-hhē'ä*), *n*. a danger warning on a chart. [Sp. *vigía*, look-out — L. *vigilia*.]

vigil *vij'il*, *n*. watching, esp. by night, esp. for religious exercises: the eve of a holy day: a religious service by night: a keeping awake, wakefulness: — *n*. **vig'ilance** watchfulness: wakefulness: a guard, watch (*Milt*.): a planned effort to uncover and punish corruption and bribery (*India*). — *adj*. **vig'ilant** watchful. — *ns*. **vigilante** (*-an'ti*; originally, *U.S*. from Sp.) a member of an organisation to look after the interests, threatened in some way, of a group: a member of a vigilance committee; **vigilan'tism**. — *adv*. **vig'ilantly**. — **vigilance committee** (*U.S*.) an unauthorised body which, in the absence or inefficiency of regular government, exercises powers of arrest, punishment, etc.: any self-appointed association for the compulsory improvement of local morals according to its own standards. [L. *vigilia* — *vigil*, awake, watchful; cf. *vigēre*, to be lively.]

vigneron *vēn-yə-rɔ̄*, *n*. a vine-grower. [Fr.]

vignette *vēn-yet'*, *n*. orig. a design of vine-leaves and tendrils: a small embellishment without a border, in what would have been a blank space, esp. on a title-page or as a headpiece or tailpiece: a photographic portrait shading off around the head: the illustration on a bank-note: a character sketch, a word-picture. — *v.t*. to make a vignette of. — *ns*. **vignett'er; vignett'ist**. [Fr., — *vigne* — L. *vīnea*, a vine, a vineyard.]

vigorish *vig'ə-rish*, (*U.S. slang*) *n*. a percentage of a gambler's winnings taken by the bookmaker, organisers of a game, etc.: excessive interest charged on a loan. [Prob. Yiddish, — Russ.. *vӯigrӯsh*, profit, winnings.]

vigoro *vig′ə-rō*, (*Austr.*) *n.* a 12-a-side game having similarities to cricket and baseball. [Poss. from **vigour.**]

vigour, *U.S.* **vigor**, *vig′ər*, *n.* active strength: vital power: forcefulness: activity: energy. — *adj.* **vig′orous.** — *adv.* **vig′orously.** — *n.* **vig′orousness.** [A.Fr. *vigour* (Fr. *vigueur*), and L. *vigor*, *-ōris* — *vigēre*, to be strong.]

vihara *vē-hä′rə*, *n.* a Buddhist or Jain precinct, temple, or monastery. [Sans. *vihāra.*]

vihuela *vi-wā′lə*, *n.* an old Spanish musical instrument, akin to the guitar. [Sp.]

viking *vī′king*, *n.* (also with *cap.*) any of the Scandinavian adventurers who raided, traded with, and settled in, many parts of Europe between the eighth and eleventh centuries: any aggressive sea-raider, a pirate. — *n.* **vī′kingism.** [O.N. *vīkingr*, prob. — O.E. *wīcing*, pirate.]

vilayet *vil-ä′yet*, *n.* a Turkish province. [Turk. *vilāyet* — Ar. *welāyeh*.]

vild, vilde *vīld*, *adj.* an old variant (*Spens.*, *Shak.*) of **vile.** — *adv.* **vild′ly.** — *n.* **vild′ness.**

vile *vīl*, *adj.* worthless: mean: paltry: base: detestable: loathsome: foul: depraved: very bad. — *adv.* (*Shak.*, *Spens.*) vilely. — *adv.* **vile′ly.** — *ns.* **vile′ness; vilificā′tion** (*vil-*) act of vilifying: defamatory speech: abuse; **vilifier** (*vil′*). — *v.t.* **vilify** (*vil′*) to make vile: to disparage: to defame: — *pr.p.* **vil′ifying;** *pa.t.* and *pa.p.* **vil′ified.** — *v.t.* **vilipend** (*vil′*; L. *vīlipendĕre* — *pendĕre*, to weigh) to despise, make light of: to disparage: to slander, vilify. — *v.i.* to use vilification. [O.Fr. *vil* and L. *vīlis*, worthless.]

viliaco *vil-yä′kō*, **viliago,** (*Shak.*) **villiago** *-gō*, (*obs.*) *ns.* a coward. — Also (*Scott*, prob. *erron.*) **villagio:** — *pls.* **-oes, -os.** [It. *vigliacco* — L. *vīlis*, worthless.]

vilification, etc. See **vile.**

vill *vil*, *n.* a township, or feudal territorial unit (*hist.*): a manor (*hist.*): a village (*poet.*). — *ns.* **vill′a** orig., a country house or farmhouse with subsidiary buildings: a country seat, in Italy often a castle: a detached house of some size: a superior middle-class dwelling-house; **vill′adom** villas collectively: the villa-dwelling world. — *adjs.* **vill′ar** of a vill; **villatic** (*-at′ik*; *Milt.*) farmyard: village. — **villa home, unit** (*Austr.*) a terraced, esp. single-storey house, typically joined to the next house by a garage. [L. *villa*, a country house, partly through O.Fr. *ville*, farm, village, etc. (Fr., town), and It. *villa*, country house.]

villa. See **vill.**

village *vil′ij*, *n.* a manor, a parish, or an outlying part of a parish: an assemblage of houses smaller than a town: a small municipality (*U.S.*): a residential complex temporarily housing participants at a particular event, esp. the athletes and officials taking part in international games: the people of a village. — *adj.* of, dwelling in, a village. — *ns.* **vill′ager** an inhabitant of a village; **villagery** (*vil′ij-ri*; *Shak.* **villagree**) villages collectively or perh. village people; **villagisā′tion, -z-** the organisation of land, esp. in Africa and Asia, so that it is under the control of villages (as opposed to nationalisation): the removal of scattered groups of population into large new villages, esp. in Africa and Asia. — **village cart** see **cart; village college** an adult educational and recreational centre serving a rural area (also **community college**). [Fr. *village*, L. *villāticus.*]

villagio. See **viliaco.**

villagree (*Shak.*). See **village.**

villain *vil′ən*, *n.* a villein (*orig.*): a violent, malevolent or unscrupulous evil-doer: playfully, a wretch: the wicked enemy of the hero or heroine in a story or play: a criminal (*slang*). — *adj.* low-born: base: villainous. — *ns.* **vill′ainage, vill′anage** villeinage; **vill′ainess** a she-villain. — *adj.* **vill′ainous** (or **vill′anous**) of the nature of, like, or suited to a villain: detestable, vile. — *adv.*

(*Shak.*) villainously. — *adv.* **vill′ainously (vill′anously).** — *ns.* **vill′ainy (vill′any)** the act (*obs.* the words) of a villain: extreme wickedness: an atrocious crime: disgrace (*obs.*); **vill′an** a villein. [O.Fr. *villain* — L.L. *villānus* — L. *villa*, a country house.]

villanelle *vil-ə-nel′*, *n.* a poem, on two rhymes, in five tercets and a quatrain, the first line repeated as sixth, twelfth, and eighteenth, the third as ninth, fifteenth, and last. [Fr., — It. *villanella* — *villano*, rustic.]

villanous(ly). See under **villain.**

Villanovan *vil-ə-nō′vən*, *adj.* of an early Iron Age culture of which remains occur at *Villanova*, near Bologna.

villany. See under **villain.**

villar, villatic. See **vill.**

-ville *-vil*, (*slang*) in composition, a supposed world, milieu, etc., frequented by a specified type of person, characterised by a specified quality, etc., as in *squaresville, dullsville*. [The suffix *-ville* in names of towns, esp. in U.S. — Fr. *ville*, town.]

villeggiatura *vi-lej-ə-tōō′rə*, *n.* country retirement or holiday. [It.]

villein *vil′ən*, *-in*, (*hist.*) *n.* orig. app. a free villager: later (13th cent.) a serf, free in relation to all but his lord, and not absolutely a slave: developing later into a copyholder. — *n.* **vill′e(i)nage** a villein's tenure or status. [A.Fr.; cf. **villain.**]

villenage. See under **villein.**

villi, villiform. See **villus.**

villiago. See **viliaco.**

villication *vil-i-kā′shən*, (*Smollett*) *n.* app. intended as a Scots pronunciation of **vellication.**

villus *vil′əs*, *n.* a long soft hair: a hair-like process: — *pl.* **vill′i** (*-ī*). — *adjs.* **vill′iform** having the form of villi; **vill′ose, vill′ous** covered with or formed of villi: like the pile of velvet. — *n.* **villos′ity.** [L. *villus*, wool.]

vim *vim*, (*slang*) *n.* energy, vigour. [App. L. *vim*, accus. of *vīs*, force.]

vimana *vi-män′ə*, *n.* the central shrine of an Indian temple with pyramidal roof: a temple gate: a heavenly chariot, chariot of the gods. [Sans. *vimāna*, lit. a marking out.]

vimineous *vim-in′i-əs*, *adj.* with long flexible shoots. [L. *vīmineus* — *vīmen*, *-inis*, osier, switch.]

Vimule® *vim′ūl*, *adj., n.* (denoting) a type of contraceptive cap for the cervix with a two-tiered dome.

vin *vẽ*, (Fr.) *n.* wine. — **vin blanc** (*blä*) white wine; **vin ordinaire** (*ör-di-när′*) inexpensive table wine for ordinary use; **vin rosé** rosé (q.v.). — **les grands vins** wines from famous vineyards.

vina *vē′nə*, *n.* an Indian stringed instrument with fretted finger-board over two gourds. [Sans. *vīnā*.]

vinaceous. See under **vine.**

vinaigrette *vin-ā-gret′*, *n.* a box or bottle for aromatic vinegar or smelling-salts: a mixture of oil, vinegar and seasoning and herbs, used as a salad dressing. — *adj.* (esp. past positive) of a dish, served with this dressing. [Fr., — *vinaigre*, vinegar.]

vinal, Vinalia. See under **vine.**

vinasse *vi-nas′*, *n.* residue in alcoholic distillation, esp. in beet-sugar-making, a source of potash salts. [Fr.]

vinblastine *vin-blas′tēn*, *n.* a drug derived from the Madagascar or rosy periwinkle (*Vinca rosea*), used in the treatment of cancer, esp. leucaemias and lymphomas. [Contr. of *vinca*leuco*blastine* — **Vinca** and **leucoblast.**]

Vinca *ving′kə*, *n.* the periwinkle genus: (without *cap.*) any plant of this genus. [L. *vinca-pervinca.*]

Vincentian *vin-sen′shən*, *-shyən*, *adj.* pertaining to St Vincent de Paul (1576–1660) or to the charitable associations founded by him, or to St Vincent of Lérins (d. 450), or other Vincent.

vincible *vin′si-bl*, *adj.* that may be overcome. — *n.* **vincibil′ity.** [L. *vincibilis* — *vincĕre*, *victum*, to conquer.]

vincristine *vin-kris′tēn*, *n.* an alkaloid substance derived from the madagascar or rosy periwinkle, *Vinca rosea*, used in the treatment of certain types of blood cancer. [L. *vinca*, and *crista*, fold.]

vinculum *ving′kū-ləm*, *n.* a bond: a horizontal line placed above, equivalent to brackets (*math.*): a tendinous band (*anat.*): — *pl.* **vinc′ula.** [L., — *vincīre*, to bind.]

vindaloo *vin′də-loo̅, n.* a type of very hot Indian curry.

vindemial *vin-dē′mi-əl, (arch.) adj.* pertaining to the vintage. — *v.i.* (*arch.*) **vindē′miate** to gather grapes, or other fruit. [L. *vīndēmia*, vintage; see **vintage.**]

vindicate *vin′di-kāt, v.t.* to justify: to clear from criticism, etc.: to defend with success: to make good a claim to: to lay claim to: to maintain: to avenge (*obs.*): to free (*obs.*). — *n.* **vindicability** (-*kə-bil′i-ti*). — *adj.* **vin′dicable.** — *n.* **vindicā′tion** act of vindicating: defence: justification: support. — *adj.* **vin′dicative** (or *vin-dik′ə-tiv*) vindicating: tending to vindicate: revengeful, vindictive (*Shak.*). — *ns.* **vindic′ativeness** vindictiveness; **vin′dicātor** one who vindicates: — *fem.* **vin′dicātress.** — *adv.* **vin′dicatorily.** — *adj.* **vin′dicatory** (-*ə-tər-i*, or -*ā-tər-i*) serving or tending to vindicate: punitive: retributive: avenging. [L. *vindicāre*, -*ātum*.]

vindictive *vin-dik′tiv, adj.* revengeful: pursuing revenge: punitive (as in *vindictive damages*): retributive (as in *vindictive justice*). — *adv.* **vindic′tively.** — *n.* **vindic′tiveness.** [L. *vindicta*, revenge; see **vindicate.**]

vine *vīn, n.* a woody climbing plant (*Vitis vinifera* or other of the genus) that produces grapes: a climbing or trailing stem or (*U.S.*) plant (*hort.*). — *v.t.* to remove vines from, e.g. vines and pods from (peas). — *adjs.* **vinā′ceous** wine-coloured; **vī′nal** of, due to, wine. — *n.pl.* **Vinā′lia** (L. *vē-nä′li-a*) a Roman wine festival celebrated on 23 April, when last year's vintage was tasted and offered to Jupiter: also a vintage festival, 19 August. — *ns.* **vī′ner** a vine-grower; **vinery** (*vī′nə-ri*) a hot-house for rearing vines. — *adj.* **vinicul′tural** (*vīn-*, *vin-*). — *ns.* **vin′iculture** cultivation of the vine for wine-making, and often also the making of the wine; **vinicul′turist; vinificā′tion** (*vin-*) the process of converting grape-juice, etc., into wine; **vinificā′tor** a condensing device that collects the alcoholic vapour produced by the fermentation. — *adj.* **vī′nolent** addicted to wine. — *ns.* **vinol′ogist** (*vīn-*, *vin-*); **vinol′ogy** scientific study of vines, esp. grapevine; **vīnos′ity** vinous character: characteristic qualities of a particular wine: addiction to wine. — *adjs.* **vī′nous** pertaining to wine: like wine: wine-coloured: caused by or indicative of wine; **vī′ny** pertaining to, like, consisting of, or bearing vines: entwining. — **vine′-branch** a branch of a vine: a centurion's badge. — *adj.* **vine′-clad** covered with vines. — **vine′-disease** a disease affecting the vine; **vine′-dresser** one who trims and cultivates vines; **vine′-fretter** a small insect that infests vines, esp. Phylloxera or other greenfly; **vine fruit** the fruit of the vine in any form, i.e. as grape or raisin, etc.; **vine′-gall** a gall on a vine, esp. one made by a weevil; **vine′-leaf** the leaf of a vine; **vine′-mildew** a disease of vines due to the oidium stage of a mildew fungus, *Uncinula*; **vine′-prop** a support for a vine; **vine′-rod** a Roman centurion's badge; **vine′-stock** the stock on which a vine of another kind is grafted; **vineyard** (*vin′yərd*, -*yärd*) a plantation of vines: a particular sphere of labour, esp. of an intellectual, academic or spiritual kind. — **dwell under one's vine and fig-tree** to live at peace on one's own land. [O.Fr. *vine, vigne* — L. *vīnea*, a vineyard, a vine — *vīnum*, wine; Gr. *oinos*, wine.]

vinegar *vin′i-gər, n.* a condiment and pickling medium, a dilute impure acetic acid, made from beer, weak wine, etc. — *v.t.* to apply vinegar to. — *n.* **vinegarrette′** a vinaigrette. — *adjs.* **vin′egarish** sourish; **vin′egary** like or flavoured with vinegar: sour (also *fig.*). — **vin′egar-eel′** a minute threadworm that breeds in vinegar; **vin′egar-fly′** a fruit-fly; **vin′egar-plant′** a bacterium causing acetic fermentation. [Fr. *vinaigre* — *vin* (L. *vīnum*), wine, *aigre*, sour (L. *ācer*, keen, sharp, pungent).]

vinew *vin′ū, v.t.* and *v.i.* to make or become mouldy. — *n.* mouldiness. — *adj.* **vin′ewed** mouldy: musty. [O.E. *fynegian*, to mould — *fynig*, mouldy — *fyne*, mould.]

vingt-et-un *vē-tā-ä̃, n.* a card game, its object to have a total of pips in one's hand nearest to, but not exceed-

ing, twenty-one. — Also **vingt-un** (*vē̃-tǟ*). [Fr. *vingt-et-un*, twenty-one.]

vinho verde *vēn′yō ver′de*, a light, sharp, immature (lit 'green') Portuguese wine. [Port., lit. green wine.]

viniculture. See **vine.**

vino *vē′nō, (slang) n.* wine. — *pl.* **vi′nos.** [It. and Sp.]

vinolent, vinology, vinous, etc. See **vine.**

vint[1] *vint, n.* a card game like contract bridge. [Russ.]

vint[2]. See **vintage.**

vintage *vint′ij, n.* the gathering of grapes and preparation for wine-making: a season's yield of grapes or wine: the time of gathering grapes: wine, esp. of a good year: the product of a particular period: a period of origin. — *adj.* pertaining to the grape vintage: of wine, of a specified year and of good quality: generally, e.g. of a play by an author or of a period, among the (best and) most characteristic: out of date and no longer admired. — *v.t.* to strip of grapes: to gather (grapes): to make (wine), esp. of a good year. — *n.* and *v.t.* **vint** (back-formation from **vintage**). — *ns.* **vint′ager** a worker at the vintage; **vint′aging.** — **vintage car** an old-fashioned car (specif. built between 1919 and 1930; **post-vintage thoroughbred** see under **thorough**); **vintage year** one in which a particular product (usu. wine) reaches an exceptionally high standard. [A.Fr. *vintage*, O.Fr. (Fr.) *vendange* — L. *vīndēmia* — *vīnum*, wine, grapes, *dēmere*, to remove — *dē*, out of or away, *emēre*, to take; modified by influence of **vintner.**]

vintner *vint′nər, n.* a wine-seller. — *n.* **vint′ry** a wine-store: a wine-shop. [O.Fr. *vinetier* — L.L. *vīnetārius* — L. *vīnum*, wine.]

viny. See **vine.**

vinyl *vīn′il, n.* an organic radical $CH_2 = CH$ — , the equivalent of a molecule of ethylene with a hydrogen atom removed: any vinyl polymer, plastic or resin. — Also *adj.* — *ns.* **vinylidene** (*vīn-il′i-dēn*) the bivalent radical $CH_2:C=$; **Vinylite** (*vīn′il-īt*) proprietary name for a series of vinyl resins. — **vinyl resins, plastics** thermoplastic resins, polymers or co-polymers of vinyl compounds, e.g. polymers of **vinyl chloride** CH_2CHCl, and **vinyl acetate** $CH_3COOCH:CH_2$.

viol *vī′əl, n.* any member of a class of instruments, forerunners of the violin class, represented now by the double-bass. — *ns.* **viola** (*vi-ō′lə*) a tenor fiddle, slightly bigger than the violin, tuned a fifth lower; **violer** (*vī′ə-lər*) a viol player: a fiddler; **violin** (*vī-ə-lin′*, or *vī′*) a musical instrument with four strings (E, A, D, G) played with a bow: a violinist; **vī′olinist** (or -*lin′*) a player on the violin. — *adj.* **violinist′ic.** — *adv.* **violinist′ically.** — *n.* **violist** (*vī′əl-ist*) a player on the viol: (*vē-ō′list*) a player on the viola; **violoncellist** (*vē-*, *vī-ə-lən-chel′ist*) a cello-player; **violoncell′o** a bass instrument of the violin class, commonly called **cello:** — *pl.* **violoncell′os; violone** (*vē-ō-lō′nā*, *vī′ə-lōn*) a bass viol, bigger than the viola da gamba — an earlier version of the present double-bass. — **vī′ol-de-gam′boys** (*Shak.*) the viola da gamba; **violin′-bow; violin spider** a very small brown and orange spotted spider of S.America, whose bite can be fatal to humans; **violin′-string.** — **viola da braccio** (*dä brät′chō*; It., viol for the arm) a tenor viol, held along the arm; **viola da gamba** (*gäm′ba*; It., viol for the leg) a bass viol, resembling the cello; **viola d'amore** (*dä-mō′rā*; It., of love) a tenor viol with sympathetic strings under the finger-board; **viola da spalla** (*späl′la*; It., for the shoulder) a bigger form of tenor viol. [Partly **vielle;** partly Fr. *viole* and It. *viola*, dim. *violino*, augmentative *violone*, and its dim. *violoncello*; origin doubtful; cf. L.L. *vitula*, and **fiddle.**]

viola. See **viol.**

Viola *vī′ə-lə, n.* the violet and pansy genus of plants, giving name to the family **Violā′ceae,** with spurred zygomorphic flowers: (without *cap.*) any plant of this genus. — *adj.* **violā′ceous** of the Violaceae: violet-coloured. [L. *vĭŏla*.]

violate *vī′ə-lāt, v.t.* to do violence to (*obs.*): to fail to observe duly: to abuse: to ravish: to profane. — *adj.*

violated: defiled. — *adj.* **vī′olable** that may be violated. — *adv.* **vī′olably.** — *n.* **violā′tion.** — *adj.* **vī′olātive** causing, tending to, or involving violation. — *n.* **vī′olātor.** [L. *violāre, -ātum* — *vīs*, strength.]

viold (*Milt.*). Same as **vialled.**

violent *vī′ə-lənt, adj.* intensely forcible: impetuous and unrestrained in action: overmasteringly vehement: due to violence: wrested: expressing violence. — *v.t.* (*obs.*) to force. — *v.i.* (*Shak.*) to rage. — *n.* **vi′olence** the state or quality of being violent: excessive, unrestrained, or unjustifiable force: outrage: profanation: injury: rape. — *adv.* **vi′olently.** [L. *violentus* or *violēns, -entis* — *vīs*.]

violer. See **viol.**

violet *vī′ə-lit, n.* any plant or flower of the genus Viola: extended to unrelated plants, as **dame's-violet, water=violet** (see **dame**[1], **water**): a bluish purple. — *adj.* bluish purple. — **shrinking violet** (*facet.*) a shy, hesitant person. [Fr. *violette* — L. *viola*.]

violin, violist, violoncello, etc. See **viol.**

V.I.P. Abbrev. for **very important person.**

viper *vī′pər, n.* the adder: any member of its genus (**Vī′pera**) or family (**Viperidae** *vī-per′i-dē*): extended to some other snakes, as the pit-vipers, horned vipers: an ungrateful or treacherous, malignant person (*fig.*). — *adjs.* **viperiform** (*-per′*); **vī′perine** (*-pər-īn*) related to or resembling the viper; **vī′perish** venomous: spiteful: like a viper; **vī′perous** having the qualities of a viper: venomous: malignant. — *adv.* **vī′perously.** — **viper's bugloss** a stiff bristly boraginaceous plant (*Echium*) of dry places with intensely blue flowers, once thought a remedy or prophylactic for snake-bite; **viper's grass** black salsify. [L. *vīpera* — *vīvus*, living, *parēre*, to bring forth.]

viraemia. See under **virus.**

virago *vi-rä′gō, vi-rā′gō, n.* a heroic or manlike woman: an amazon: a scold: a termagant: — *pl.* **vira′goes, -gos.** — *adjs.* **viraginian** (*vi-rə-jin′i-ən*), **viraginous** (*vi-raj′*), **vira′goish.** [L. *virāgō, -inis* — *vir*, a man.]

viral. See **virus.**

viranda, virando (*pl.* **viran′dos**). Obs. forms of **veranda(h).**

virelay *vir′ə-lā, n.* an old French lyric form in two-rhymed stanzas of short lines, linked by recurrent lines. [Fr. *virelai*, app. from meaningless refrain *vireli*, but associated with *virer*, turn, *lai*, a song.]

virement *vē-rə-mā, vīr′mənt, n.* authorised transference of a surplus to balance a deficit under another head: authorised redirection of funds for one purpose to a more urgent occasion. [Fr.]

virent *vīr′ənt, adj.* verdant (*arch.*): fresh (*obs.*): green (*arch.*). — *n.* **virescence** (*vir-, vīr-es′əns*). — *adj.* **viresc′ent** turning green: inclining to green: fresh: green: abnormally green. [L. *virēns, -entis*, pr.p. of *virēre*, to be green; *virēscēns*, pr.p. of *virēscēre*, to become green.]

Vireo *vir′i-ō, n.* a genus of American singing birds, the greenlets, giving name to the family **Vireonidae** (*-on′i-dē*): (without *cap.*) a bird of this family: — *pl.* **vir′eos.** [L. *vireō, -ōnis*, perh. greenfinch.]

virescence, virescent. See **virent.**

viretot *vir′i-tot*, (*Scott* after *Chaucer*) *n.* rush, dash, gad. [Origin obscure.]

virga *vûr′gə, n.* (also *n.pl.*) trails of water, drops, or ice particles coming from a cloud but not reaching the ground as precipitation. [L., a twig, streak in the sky.]

virgate *vûr′gāt, adj.* rodlike: twiggy. — *n.* an old land measure, commonly 30 acres. [L. *virga*, rod.]

virge *vûrj, n.* obs. Latinised spelling of **verge**[1]. — *n.* **virg′er** (*obs.* except in certain cathedrals, esp. St Paul's) verger.

Virgilian, Vergilian *vər-jil′i-ən, adj.* of, in the manner of, *Virgil* (*Vergilius*), the Roman poet (70–19 B.C.).

virgin *vûr′jin, n.* a maiden: one (esp. a woman) who has had no sexual intercourse: a madonna, a figure of the Virgin: Virgo, a sign, and a constellation, of the zodiac. — *adj.* in a state of virginity: of a virgin: maidenly: pure: chaste: undefiled: in the original condition —

unattained, untouched, unexploited, never scaled, felled, captured, wrought, used, etc.: never having previously undergone or been affected by the thing mentioned. — *v.t.* (with *it*; *Shak.*) to continue chaste. — *adj.* **vir′ginal** of or appropriate to a virgin or virginity: in a state of virginity: like a virgin: parthenogenetic. — *adv.* **vir′ginally.** — *ns.* **vir′ginhood, virgin′ity** state or fact of being a virgin. — *adj.* **vir′ginly** pure. — *adv.* chastely. — **virgin birth, generation** parthenogenesis: (**Virgin Birth**) (the doctrine of) the birth of Christ, His mother being a virgin. — *adj.* **virg′in-born** born of a virgin. — **virgin gold** gold in the condition in which it is found; **virgin knot** the fastening of a Greek or Roman woman's girdle, loosed at marriage; **vir′gin's-bow′er** traveller's-joy (*Clematis vitalba*); **virgin soil** soil never previously tilled or cultivated: material as yet untried or unaffected. — **the (Blessed) Virgin** Mary the mother of Christ; **the Virgin Queen** Elizabeth I of England. [Partly through Fr., — L. *virgō, -inis*.]

virginal[1] *vûr′jin-əl, n.* (often in *pl.*, also *pair of virginals*) an old keyboard instrument, a spinet, esp. a box-shaped spinet. — *v.i.* (*Shak.*) to finger, as on a virginal. [Perh. as played by young ladies; see above.]

virginal[2], **virginhood,** etc. See **virgin.**

Virginia *vər-jin′yə, n.* a tobacco grown and manufactured in *Virginia*. — *adj.* **Virgin′ian.** — *n.* a native or citizen of Virginia. — *n.* **virgin′ium** (*chem.*) a name proposed for the element of atomic number 87 (see **francium**). — **Virginia creeper** an American climbing-plant near akin to the vine, bright red in autumn; **Virginia stock** see **stock**[1]. [After Elizabeth, the *virgin* queen.]

virginity, etc. See **virgin.**

Virgo *vûr′gō, vir′gō, wir′gō, n.* the Virgin in the Zodiac: a person born between 23 August and 22 September, under the sign of the Virgin. — *n.* **Virgō′an** a person born under the sign of the Virgin. — Also *adj.* — **virgo intacta** (*in-tak′tə, -ta*; L., untouched) a woman who has not had sexual intercourse. [L.]

virgule *vûr′gūl, n.* a slanting line, an old form of comma. — *adj.* **vir′gulate** shaped like a rod. [Fr., — L. *virgula*, dim. of *virga*, a twig, rod.]

viricide. See **virus.**

virid *vir′id, adj.* green. — *n.* **viridesc′ence.** — *adj.* **viridesc′ent** greenish. — *ns.* **virid′ian** a green pigment, hydrated chromium sesquioxide; **vir′idite** an indeterminate green decomposition product in rocks; **virid′ity** verdure: greenness. [L. *viridis*, green — *virēre*, to be green.]

virile *vir′īl*, sometimes *vīr′*, also *-il, adj.* having qualities of a mature male human being: robustly masculine: manly: of a man, sexually potent. — *n.* **virilescence** (*vir-il-es′əns*) development of male character in the female. — *adj.* **virilesc′ent.** — *n.* **virilisā′tion, -z-** the development of male sexual characteristics in the female. — *adjs.* **vir′ilised, -ized; vir′ilising, -z-.** — *ns.* **vir′ilism** presence of male sexual characteristics in the female; **viril′ity** the state or quality of being a man: the power of a mature male: the power of procreation: manhood: masculinity: vigour, energy. [L. *virīlis* — *vir*, a man; cf. O.E. *wer*, man, and **werewolf**.]

virion. See **virus.**

virl *virl*, (now *Scot.*) *n.* Same as **ferrule.**

virogene, virology, virose, etc. See under **virus.**

virtu *vûr-tōō′, n.* a love of the fine arts: taste for curiosities: objects of art or antiquity. — *adjs.* **virtuose** (*-tū-ōs′*), **virtuō′sic** exhibiting the qualities of a virtuoso. — *ns.* **virtuosity** (*-os′*) the character of a virtuoso: exceptional technical skill in music or other fine art: interest in or knowledge of articles of virtu; **virtuoso** (*vir-tū-ō-ō′sō, vûr-tū-ō′sō, -zō*) one skilled or interested in works of art, antiquities, curiosities, and the like: a musician (or other artist) of the highest technical skill: — *pl.* **virtuō′sos, virtuō′si** (*-sē*): — *fem.* **virtuō′sa, pl.* **virtuō′se** (*-sā*); **virtuō′sōship.** — **article, object of virtue** an object of artistic or antiquarian interest, a curio. [It. *virtù* — L. *virtūs, -ūtis*; see **virtue**.]

virtual, etc. See **virtue.**

virtue *vûr′tū, n.* excellence: worth: moral excellence: the practice of duty: a good quality, esp. moral: an accomplishment (*rare*): valour (now *rare*): sexual purity: (*loosely*) virginity: inherent power: efficacy: one of the orders of the celestial hierarchy. — *adj.* **vir′tual** virtuous (*obs.*): having virtue or efficacy (*arch.*): in effect, though not in fact: not such in fact but capable of being considered as such for some purposes. — *ns.* **vir′tualism** the doctrine of Christ's virtual presence in the eucharist; **vir′tualist; virtual′ity** essential nature: potentiality. — *adv.* **vir′tually** in effect, though not in fact: (*loosely*) almost, nearly. — *adjs.* **vir′tueless; vir′tuous** having virtue: morally good: blameless: righteous: practising duty: according to the moral law: chaste. — *adv.* **vir′tuously.** — *n.* **vir′tuousness.** — **virtual image** see **image.** — *adj.* **vir′tue-proof** (*Milt.* **vertue-**) impregnable in virtue. — **by, in, virtue of** through the power, force, or efficacy of: because of: on account of; **make a virtue of necessity** to do as if from sense of duty (or with a sense of duty called in for the occasion) something one must needs do; **seven principal virtues** faith, hope, charity, justice, prudence, temperance, and fortitude — the first three the *theological*, the last four the *moral* virtues; **the cardinal virtues** see **cardinal.** [O.Fr. *vertu* and L. *virtus*, bravery, moral excellence — *vir*, a man; cf. Gr. *hērōs*, Sans. *vīra*, a hero, O.E. *wer*, man.]

virtuose, -osic, etc. See **virtu.**

virtute officii *vûr-tū′ti of-is′i-ī, vir-, wir-tōō-te of-ik′i-ē,* (L.) by virtue of office.

virucidal, etc. See under **virus.**

virulent *vir′ū-lənt,* or *-ōō-, adj.* highly poisonous or malignant: venomous: acrimonious. — *ns.* **vir′ulence, vir′ulency.** — *adv.* **vir′ulently.** [L. *vīrulentus* — *vīrus,* see **virus.**]

virus *vī′rəs, n.* venom: contagious or poisonous matter (as of ulcers, etc.): the transmitted cause of infection: a pathogenic agent, usu. a protein-coated particle of RNA or DNA, capable of increasing rapidly inside a living cell: any corrupting influence. — *n.* **viraemia** (*vī-rē′mi-ə*) the presence of viruses in the bloodstream. — *adjs.* **vīrae′mic; vī′ral** pertaining to or caused by a virus; **vī′ricidal** (or *vir′*). — *ns.* **vī′ricide** (or *vir′*) a substance that destroys or eliminates a virus; **vī′rion** (or *vir′*) a virus particle in its mature, infectious state; **vī′rogene** a virus-forming gene; **vī′roid** a particle of RNA, uncoated by protein, that can cause some diseases in plants; *adj.* **virolog′ical.** — *ns.* **virol′ogy** the study of virus, viruses and virus diseases; **virol′ogist.** — *adj.* **vī′rose** poisonous: foul. — *n.* **virō′sis** a disease caused by a virus. — *adjs.* **vī′rous** virose; **vī′rucidal.** — *n.* **vī′rucide** same as **viricide.** — **virus disease** a disease caused by a virus. [L. *vīrus,* venom; Gr. *īos,* Sans. *viṣa,* poison.]

vis *vis, vēs, wēs,* (L.) *n.* force, power. — **vis comica** (*kom′ik-ə, kōm′ik-a*) comic power; **vis inertiae** (*in-ûr′shi-ē, in-ert′i-ī*) the power of inertia: passive resistance; **vis major** (*mā′jər, mä′yor*) superior force; **vis mortua** (*mör′tū-ə, mor′tōō-a*) force of pressure, dead force; **vis viva** (*vī′və, vē′va, wē′wa*) living force, equal to the mass of a moving body multiplied by the square of its velocity. — **vis a tergo** (*ā tûr′gō, ä ter′gō*) compulsion from behind.

visa *vē′zə,* **visé** *vē′zä, ns.* an authenticating endorsement on a passport, etc. — *vs.t.* to put a visa on — *pa.ts.* and *pa.ps.* **vi′saed, vi′séed.** [L. *vīsa,* pa.p. fem. of *vidēre,* to see, and Fr. *visé,* pa.p. masc. of *viser,* to examine.]

visage *viz′ij, n.* the face. — *adj.* **vis′aged.** — *n.* **visagiste** (*vē-zazh-ēst*) an expert in facial make-up. — Also **vis′agist** (*viz′ə-jist*). [Fr. *visage* — L. *vīsus,* look.]

vis-à-vis *vē-za-vē, adv.* face-to-face. — *prep.* face-to-face with: in relation to, with regard to. — *n.* one who faces, or is opposite to, another: a light carriage with seats facing each other: an S-shaped couch: an opposite number. [Fr. *vis,* face (— L. *vīsus,* look), *à,* to.]

viscacha *vis-kä′chə, n.* a S. American burrowing rodent of heavy build. — Also **vizca′cha, bisca′cha, bizca′cha.**

— *n.* **viscachera** (*-chä′rə*) a settlement of viscachas. [Sp., — Quechua *huiscacha.*]

viscera, visceral, viscerate, visceri-, viscero-, etc. See **viscus.**

viscid *vis′id, adj.* semi-fluid, sticky, glutinous, viscous: of a surface, clammy and covered with a sticky secretion (*bot.*). — *ns.* **viscid′ity; viscin** (*vis′in*) the sticky substance present in the fruits of mistletoe. [L.L. *viscidus* — L. *viscum;* see **viscous.**]

visco-, visco(si)meter, etc. See **viscous.**

viscose *vis′kōs, n.* the sodium salt of cellulose xanthate, used in the manufacture of **viscose rayon.** [See **viscous.**]

viscount *vī′kownt, n.* an officer who acted as administrative deputy to an earl, a sheriff (*hist.*): (esp. with *cap.*) a similar official in Jersey: a title of nobility next below an earl (first granted in 1440): the son or young brother of a count: — *fem.* **viscountess** (*vī′kownt-es*) the wife of a viscount: a woman holding a viscounty in her own right: a size of roofing slate, 18 × 10 inches (457 × 254 mm). — *ns.* **vi′scountcy, vi′scountship** a viscounty; **vi′scounty** a viscount (*obs.*): the jurisdiction of, or territory under, a viscount (*hist.*): the rank or dignity of a viscount. [O.Fr. *visconte* (Fr. *vicomte*) — *vis-* (L. *vice,* in place of), *conte,* count, after L.L. *vicecomes* — L. *comes,* a companion.]

viscous *vis′kəs, adj.* resistant, or highly resistant, to flow owing to forces acting between the molecules: tenacious: sticky: viscid. — *n.* **vis′cousness.** — **vis′cō-** in composition, viscous, viscosity. — *adj.* **viscōelas′tic** having both viscous and elastic properties. — *n.* **viscom′eter** an instrument for measuring viscosity. — *adjs.* **viscōmet′ric, -al.** — *n.* **viscom′etry.** — Also **viscōsim′eter, viscōsimet′ric, -al, viscōsim′etry.** — *n.* **viscos′ity.** — **viscous flow** a type of fluid flow in which there is a continuous steady motion of the particles, the motion at a fixed point always remaining constant; **viscous water** water thickened by addition of chemicals, used in fighting forest fires. [L.L. *viscōsus,* sticky — L. *viscum,* bird-lime, mistletoe; cog. with Gr. *ixos,* mistletoe.]

Viscum *vis′kəm, n.* a genus of parasitic plants including the common mistletoe: (without *cap.*) bird-lime. [L.]

viscus *vis′kəs,* (*med., zool.*) *n.* any one of the organs situated within the chest and the abdomen — heart, lungs, liver, etc.: — *pl.* **viscera** (*vis′ər-ə;* in common use, esp. the abdominal organs). — *adj.* **visc′eral** of, relating to, the viscera: instinctive or intuitive, not cerebral or rational (*coll.*): having to do with the more earthy feelings and emotions (*coll.*). — *v.t.* **visc′erate** to disembowel. — **visc′erō-** in composition, of or pertaining to the viscera or to a viscus. — Also **visc′eri-.** — *ns.* **viscerōptō′sis** (Gr. *ptōsis,* a falling) abnormally low position of the intestines in the abdominal cavity; **viscerōtonia** (*-tōn′*) a pattern of temperament associated with the endomorphic body type — extravert, sociable, fond of bodily comforts. — *adj.* **viscerōton′ic.** [L. *vīscus,* pl. *vīscera.*]

vise¹ *vīz* (*obs.*), *v.t.* to advise: to look at. — *v.i.* to look (with *on*): to consider (with *on*). [Partly **advise;** partly Fr. *viser* — L. *vidēre, vīsum,* to see.]

vise². U.S. spelling of **vice¹.**

visé, viséed. See **visa.**

Vishnu *vish′nōō, n.* the second god of the Hindu triad; he became specially the benefactor of man in his many *avatars* or incarnations. [Sans.]

visible *viz′i-bl, adj.* that may be seen: in sight: obvious: (of supplies of a commodity) actually in store, known to be available: relating to goods rather than services (*econ.*): ready or willing to receive a visitor or visitors. — *n.* a visible thing (often in *pl.*). — *ns.* **visibil′ity** the state or quality of being visible, or perceivable by the eye: the clearness of the atmosphere: clarity and range of vision in the atmospheric conditions, seeing: a visible thing (usu. in *pl.*): a sight, show place (*obs.*): an appearance (*obs.*): the power of seeing, sight (*obs.*); **vis′ibleness.** — *adv.* **vis′ibly.** — **Visible Church** the body of professing Christians, as opp. to the *Invisible Church*, which consists of those spiritually minded persons who live up to the ideals of the Church, together with the departed saints in heaven; **visible exports, imports** see **exports, imports; visible horizon** see **horizon; visible means** means or resources which are apparent to or ascertainable by others; **visible radiation** electromagnetic radiation which can be detected by the eye, light; **visible speech** a system of phonetic characters each of which suggests the configuration of the organs in producing the sound. [Through O.Fr. or direct from L. *vīsībilis* — *vidēre*; see **vision**.]

visie; visier. See **vision; vizier.**

Visigoth *viz'i-goth, n.* one of the Western Goths, as distinguished from the Ostrogoths or Eastern Goths; they formed settlements in the south of France and in Spain, and their kingdom in the latter lasted into the 8th century. — *adj.* **Visigoth'ic.** [L.L. *Visigothī* — Gmc. word meaning perh. noble Goths, perh. west Goths.]

visile *viz'īl, -il, adj.* of or pertaining to sight: learning by means of visual images and recalling such images readily. — *n.* one whose imagery naturally takes a visual form. [On the analogy of **audile**, from L. *vidēre, vīsum*, to see.]

visiogenic *viz-i-ō-jen'ik, adj.* suitable artistically for television transmission. [L. *vidēre, vīsum*, to see, and root of Gr. *gignesthai*, to be produced.]

vision *vizh'ən, n.* the act of seeing: the faculty of sight: anything seen: television, esp. as opposed to sound radio: a look, glance: a vivid concept or mental picture: hence, a person or scene of great beauty (sometimes ironically): a pleasing imaginative plan for, or anticipation of, future events: an apparition: a revelation, esp. divine, in sleep or a trance (sometimes without article): the act or power of perceiving imaginative mental images: imaginative perception: foresight: mystical awareness of the supernatural. — *v.t.* to see as a vision, to imagine: to present, or to call up, as in a vision. — *n.* **visie** (*Scot.*; *viz'ī*) a close or careful look: aim: a sight on the muzzle of a gun. — Also **viz'y, vizz'ie.** — *v.t.* and *v.i.* (*Scot.*) to look at, or look, closely: to aim. — Also **vizz'ie.** — *adj.* **vis'ional** of, pertaining to, a vision: derived from a vision. visionary, not real: pertaining to sight. — *adv.* **vis'ionally.** — *n.* **vis'ionariness.** — *adj.* **vis'ionary** capable of seeing visions: apt to see visions: given to reverie or fantasy: out of touch with reality, unpractical: of the nature of, or seen in, a vision, visional: fanciful, not real: impracticable: characterised by visions or fantasy: pertaining to physical or mental vision. — *n.* one who sees visions: one who forms impracticable schemes. — *adj.* **vis'ioned** inspired so as to see visions: seen in a vision: produced by, or associated with, a vision. — *ns.* **vis'ioner** a visionary; **vis'ioning** seeing visions; **vis'ionist** one who professes to be a visionary: one who believes that the Biblical details of creation were revealed in vision. — *adj.* **vis'ionless** destitute of vision. — **vision mix; vision mixer** one who blends or combines different camera shots in television or films. — **beatific vision** see **beatify**. [Fr., — L. *visiō, visiōnis* — *vidēre, vīsum*, to see; cf. Gr. *idein*, Eng. *wit*.]

visiophone *viz'i-ə-fōn, n.* a videophone (q.v. under **video**.) [*vision* and tele*phone*.]

visit *viz'it, v.t.* (of God or a human being) to come to, or to go to see, in order to succour: to go to with intention of injuring: to go to see professionally: to pay a call upon, or to be in the habit of doing so: to go to stay with: to make a stay in, as migratory birds: to go to for sight-seeing, pleasure, or religious purposes: to examine, inspect, esp. officially: to punish (a person) (with *with; arch.*): to punish, as wrong-doing (*arch.*): to inflict (punishment, etc.) (with *on*): (of an idea) to take temporary hold on the mind of: to afflict, trouble, as with disease (*arch.*). — *v.i.* to be in the habit of seeing or meeting each other at home: to make a

visit or visits: to chat (*U.S.*). — *n.* an act of visiting: a short stay: a sight-seeing excursion: an official or a professional call: a place one visits (*Cowper*): a chat (*U.S.*). — *adjs.* **vis'itable** subject to official visitation: attractive to visitors; **vis'itant** paying visits, visiting. — *n.* one who visits: one who is a guest in the house of another: a supernatural visitor: a migratory bird: (with *cap.*) one of an order of nuns founded by St Francis de Sales in 1610, also called *Salesians, Order* (or *Nuns*) *of the Visitation.* — *n.* **visitā'tion** the act of visiting: a long and wearisome visit: a formal visit by a superior, esp. ecclesiastical: an examination by authority: the act of a naval commander in boarding the vessel of another state to ascertain her character and object: a visit of a herald to a district for the examination of its arms, pedigrees, etc. (*hist.*): a visit of God, or of a good (or evil) supernatural being: a dispensation of divine favour or displeasure: a sore affliction: the operation of a destructive power, or an instance of it: an influence acting on the mind: the object of a visit (*rare*): an unusual and extensive irruption of a species of animals into a region: (with *cap.*) a festival to commemorate the visit of the Virgin Mary to Elizabeth, observed by the Roman and Greek Churches on 2 July. — *adjs.* **visitā'tional, vis'itātive.** — *n.* **vis'itātor** an official visitor. — *adj.* **visitatō'rial.** — *ns.* **visitee'** the person to whom a visit is paid; **vis'iting** the act, or an instance, of paying a visit: a visitation, in the senses of divine dispensation, heavy affliction, or influence operating on the mind. — *adj.* that visits: often opp. to *resident*: pertaining to visiting. — *n.* **vis'itor** (now rarely **vis'iter**) one who visits, calls on, or makes a stay with a person: a person authorised to visit for purposes of inspection or supervision: — *fem.* **vis'itress.** — *adj.* **visitō'rial.** — **vis'iting-book** a book recording the names of persons who have called or are to be called on: a visitors' book (*Thackeray*); **vis'iting-card** a small card bearing the name and address, or title, left in paying visits, and sometimes sent as an act of courtesy or in token of sympathy; **vis'iting-day** a day on which one is at home and ready to receive callers; **visitor general** (*hist.*) a personal representative of the King of Spain appointed to investigate affairs, esp. in Spanish America; **visitors' book** a book in which visitors write their names and sometimes comments; **visitors' passport** (also **British Visitors' Passport**) a simplified form of passport, valid for one year for visits not exceeding three months to certain countries, obtainable at post offices. — **visitation of the sick** an office in the Anglican Church for use by clergy visiting the sick; **visit with** (*U.S.*) to visit: to be a guest with: to chat with. [Fr. *vīsiter* — L. *vīsitāre*, freq. of *vīsěre*, to go to see, visit — *vidēre*, to see.]

visite *vi-zēt', n.* a woman's light short cloak worn in the mid 19th century. [Fr.]

visive *viz'iv,* (*rare*) *adj.* of or pertaining to sight, visual: able to see: able to be seen. [L.L. *vīsīvus* — L. *vīsus*, sight.]

visne *vē'ni,* (*law*) *n.* a venue. [O.Fr. *visné*, neighbourhood — L. *vīcīnus*, neighbour.]

visnomy *viz'nə-mi,* (*arch.* and *dial.*) *n.* physiognomy. — Also **vis'nomie.** [Variant of **physiognomy**.]

vison *vī'sən, n.* the American mink. [Fr.; origin unknown.]

visor, also **vizor,** *vīz'ər, n.* a part of a helmet covering the face, or the upper part of the face, movable, and perforated to allow of seeing and breathing: a mask: a disguise, feigning appearance: face, aspect (*obs.*): (*lit.* and *fig.*): a hood placed over a signal light: the peak of a cap: a movable flap on a motor-car windscreen, used as a shade against the sun. — *v.t.* to disguise, or cover with, a visor. — *adj.* **vis'ored, viz'ored** having a visor: wearing a visor: masked. — **vis'or-mask** a vizard-mask. [A.Fr. *viser* (Fr. *visière*) — *vis*, countenance.]

vista *vis'tə, n.* a view or prospect, esp. through, or as through, an avenue: an avenue or other long narrow opening or passage: the trees, etc., that form the avenue: a mental view or vision extending far into the past or future, or into any subject engaging the thoughts. — Also **vis'to** (*pl.* **vis'tos**). — *v.t.* (*rare*) to make into, or see in, vistas. — *adjs.* **vista'd, vis'taed** (*-təd*) having, or forming, a vista or vistas (*lit.* and *fig.*); **vis'tal; vis'taless** (*-tə-les*). [It. *vista*, sight, view — L. *vidēre, vīsum,* to see.]

visual *vizh'ū-əl, viz'ū-əl, adj.* of, pertaining to, sight: concerned with seeing, or (*fig.*) with mental vision: attained by, or received through, sight: of the nature of, or conveying, a mental vision: visible, having visibility: optic, as in **visual axis** (see **optic axis** under **optic**): of the eye (*poet.*): of beams, coming from the eye (*obs.*). — *n.* a visible: a rough sketch of the layout of an advertisement: (often in *pl.*) a drawing, piece of film, etc., as distinct from the words or sound accompanying it. — *n.* **visualīsā'tion, -z-.** — *v.t.* **vis'ualise, -ize** to make visible, externalise to the eye: to call up a clear visual image of. — *v.i.* to call up a clear visual image: to become visible (*med.*). — *ns.* **vis'ualīser, -z-; vis'ualist** a visualiser: a visile; **visual'ity** (*Carlyle*) the quality or state of being visible to the mind: a mental picture. — *adv.* **vis'ually.** — **visual aid** a picture, photograph, film, diagram, etc., used as an aid to teaching; **visual arts** painting, sculpture, films, etc. as opposed to literature, music, etc.; **visual purple** see **purple.** — **visual display unit** (*comput.; abbrev.* **VDU**) a cathode ray tube which displays data, entered by keyboard or light pen, from a computer's memory.   [L.L. *vīsuālis* — L. *vīsus,* sight.]

visuo- in composition, sight.   [L. *vīsus.*]

vita *vī'tə, vē', wē'ta,* (L.) *n.* life. — **vita patris** (*-tä pat'ris*) in the father's lifetime.

Vitaceae. See **Vitis.**

Vita glass® *vī'tə gläs,* a type of glass that transmits ultraviolet rays.

vital *vī'tl, adj.* being a manifestation of organic life: supporting, or necessary to, life: life-giving, invigorating: characteristic of life, or of living things: animate, living: full of life: lively, energetic: capable of living (*obs.*): pertaining to life, birth, and death: due to a living agency: fatal to life: essential, or (loosely) highly important. — *n.* **vitalisā'tion, -z-.** — *v.t.* **vi'talise, -ize** to give life to: to stimulate activity in: to give vigour to: to make lifelike. — *n.* **vi'taliser, -z-.** — *adj.* **vi'talising, -z-.** — *ns.* **vi'talism** the doctrine that there is a vital principle (q.v.); **vi'talist** one who holds this doctrine. — *adj.* **vitalis'tic.** — *adv.* **vitalis'tically.** — *n.* **vitality** (*-tal'*) the state or quality of being vital: the principle of life, power of living: the state of being alive: the quality of being fully or intensely alive: the capacity to endure and flourish: animation, liveliness: a living or vital thing or quality: — *pl.* **vital'ities.** — *adv.* **vi'tally.** — *n.pl.* **vi'tals** (rarely in *sing.*) the interior organs essential for life: the part of any whole necessary for its existence. — *n.* **vi'tascope** a form of motion-picture projector. — *adj.* **vi'tative** concerned with the preservation of life. — *n.* **vi'tativeness** love of life, assigned by the phrenologists to a protuberance under the ear. — **vital air** (*obs.*) oxygen; **vital force** the force on which the phenomena of life in animals and plants depend — distinct from chemical and mechanical forces operating in them; **vital functions** the bodily functions that are essential to life, as the circulation of the blood; **vital principle** that principle — the *anima mundi* — which, according to the doctrine of vitalism, gives life to all nature: a principle that directs all the actions and functions of living bodies; **vital signs** (the level or rate of) breathing, heartbeat, etc.; **vital spark, flame** the principle of life in man: hence, life or a trace of life; **vital stain** (*bot., zool.*) a stain that can be used on living cells without killing them; **vital statistics** statistics dealing with the facts of population — births, deaths, etc.: a woman's bust, waist and hip measurements (*facet.*).   [L. *vītālis* — *vīta,* life — *vīvĕre,* to live; cog. with Gr. *bios,* life.]

vitamin *vit'ə-min, vīt'* (orig. **vitamine** *-mēn*), *ns.* any of

numerous organic substances, 'accessory food factors', present in minute quantities in nutritive foods and essential for the health of the animal organism, designated provisionally vitamin A, B_1, B_2, etc., C, D, D_2, D_3, E, (F), G (now B_2), H, K, K_1, etc., L, M (also B_c), (P), PP (a vitamin effective against pellagra, as nicotinic acid), X (later P), but later analysed and given names indicating something of their nature; see **retinol; aneurin (thiamine), riboflavin, pantothenic acid, nicotinic acid (niacin), pyridoxine (adermin), cyanocobalamin, folic acid, pteroic acid; ascorbic acid; calciferol; tocopherol; linoleic, linolenic, acid; biotin; phylloquinone (phytonadione), menadione; citrin (bioflavonoid).** — *v.t.* **vi'taminise, -ize** to add vitamins to (a food). — **vitamin B complex** a group of vitamins formerly regarded as being a single vitamin.   [Coined in 1906 from L. *vīta,* life, and (inappropriately) **amine.**]

vitascope, vitative. See **vital.**

vite *vēt,* (*mus.*) *adv.* quickly.   [Fr.]

vitellus *vi-, vī-tel'əs, n.* the yolk of an egg: — *pl.* **vitell'ī.** — *adj.* **vit'ellary** pertaining to the vitellus: yellow like the yolk of an egg. — *n.* **vitell'icle** a yolk-sac. — *adj.* **vitelligenous** (*-ij'*) producing yolk. — *ns.* **vitell'in** a phosphoprotein present in yolks of eggs; **vitell'ine** a vitellus. — *adj.* **vitellary.**   [L., a yolk; a transferred use of *vitellus* — *vitulus,* a calf.]

Vitex *vī'teks, n.* a genus of trees or shrubs, chiefly tropical, of the family Verbenaceae, having a drupe with a four-celled stone; some species yield valuable timber: (without *cap.*) any plant of this genus.   [L.]

vitiate *vish'i-āt, v.t.* to render faulty or defective: to spoil: to make impure: to deprave, corrupt, pervert, debase: to make ineffectual or invalid or inconclusive: to violate, ravish (*obs.*): to adulterate (*obs.*). — Earlier **vi'ciate.** — *adj.* (*arch.*) **vitiated.** — *adj.* **vi'tiable.** — *ns.* **vitiā'tion; vi'tiātor; vitios'ity** (also **vicios'ity**) the state or quality of being vicious, or (*Scots law*) faulty.   [L. *vitiāre, -ātum* — *vitium;* see **vice**[2].]

viticetum, viticide, viticulture, etc. See **Vitis.**

vitiligo *vit-i-lī'gō, -ə-lē'gō, n.* a skin abnormality in which irregular patches of the skin lose colour and turn white.   [L. *vitilīgo,* a skin eruption.]

vitilitigation *vit-i-lit-i-gā'shən,* (*rare*) *n.* vexatious wrangling. — *v.i.* (*rare*) **vitilit'igate.**   [Formed from L. *vitilītigāre, -ātum,* to quarrel disgracefully — *vitium,* a blemish, *lītigāre,* to quarrel.]

vitiosity. See **vitiate.**

Vitis *vī'tis, n.* the grapevine genus of woody climbing plants of the family **Vitaceae** (*vī-tā'sē-ē*) or *Ampelidaceae.* — *ns.* **viticetum** (*vīt-* or *vit-i-sē'təm;* would-be Latin) a plantation of vines; **vit'icide** a vine pest. — *adj.* **vitic'olous** living on vines. — *ns.* **vit'iculture** cultivation of the vine; **viticul'turist.** — *adj.* **vitif'erous** bearing vines.   [L. *vītis,* a vine — *viēre,* to twist.]

vitrage *vē-träzh, vit'rij, n.* (used also adjectivally) a kind of thin curtain for windows or glazed doors.   [Fr., glass window.]

vitrail *vit'rāl, vē-trä'ē, n.* stained glass: — *pl.* **vitraux** (*vē-trō', vit'*). — *adj.* **vitrailled** (*vit'rāld*). — *n.* **vit'raillist** a maker of glass, esp. stained glass.   [Fr.]

vitrain *vit'rān, n.* a separable constituent of bright coal, of vitreous appearance.   [L. *vitrum,* glass, and suff. *-ain.*]

vitraux. See under **vitrail.**

Vitreosil®. See under **vitreous.**

vitreous *vit'ri-əs, adj.* glassy: pertaining to, consisting of, or like glass: glass green in colour: resembling glass in absence of crystalline structure, in lustre, etc. (*geol.*). — *ns.* **Vit'reosil**® vitreous silica used for apparatus which is subject to large temperature variations; **vitreos'ity, vit'reousness; vitresc'ence.** — *adjs.* **vitresc'ent** tending to become glass, capable of being turned into glass; **vitresc'ible.** — *ns.* **vitrescibil'ity; vit'reum** the vitreous humour of the eye. — *adj.* **vit'ric.** — *n.pl.* **vit'rics** glassy materials: glassware. — *n.sing.* the study of glass and its manufacture. — *ns.* **vitrifac'tion, vitrificā'tion** the act, process, or operation of vitrifying, or converting into glass: the state of being vitrified: a vitrified substance; **vitrifac'ture** the manufacture of glass. — *adjs.* **vit'rifiable; vit'rified; vit'riform** having the form or appearance of glass. — *v.t.* and *v.i.* **vit'rify** to make into, or to become, glass or a glassy substance. — *ns.* **Vitrī'na** a genus of thin-shelled land molluscs, between slugs and true snails — the glass-snails; **vit'rine** (*-rēn, -rin*) a glass display case used to protect delicate articles, exhibit specimens, etc. — **vitreous electricity** an old name for positive electricity, because glass becomes positively charged when rubbed with silk; **vitreous humour** the jelly-like substance filling the posterior chamber of the eye of a vertebrate, between the lens and the retina; **vitrified forts, walls** certain ancient Scottish, French, etc., forts or walls in which the silicious stone has been vitrified by fire, whether by intention or accident is uncertain. [L. *vitrum*, glass.]

vitriol *vit'ri-əl, n.* oil of vitriol (q.v.): a hydrous sulphate of a metal, as *blue, green,* and *white vitriol,* respectively that of copper (cupric), iron (ferrous), and zinc: rancorous, caustic criticism, etc. (*fig.*). — *v.t.* **vit'riolāte** to convert into, or to treat with, vitriol. — *n.* **vitriolā'tion.** — *adj.* **vitriolic** (*-ol'*) pertaining to, or having the qualities of, vitriol: biting, scathing, expressing intense ill-will. — *n.* **vitriolisā'tion, -z-.** — *v.t.* **vit'riolise, -ize** to vitriolate: to injure with vitriol. — **elixir of vitriol** aromatic sulphuric acid (i.e. sulphuric acid mixed with certain other substances for use in medicine); **oil of vitriol** concentrated sulphuric acid — because formerly prepared from green vitriol. [Fr., — L.L. *vitriolum* — L. *vitreus,* of glass.]

vitro- *vit'rō-,* in composition, glass. — *n.* **Vit'rolite**® (*-līt*) a kind of opaque glass with a fire-finished surface. [L. *vitrum,* glass.]

vitro-di-trina *vit'rō-di-trē'nä, n.* a Venetian white glass in which fine threads of cane form a lace-like pattern. [It., glass of lace.]

Vitruvian *vi-trōō'vi-ən, adj.* of, or in the style of, *Vitruvius* Pollio, a Roman architect under Augustus: denoting a kind of convoluted scrollwork.

vitta *vit'ə, n.* a fillet or band for the head: a strap or sash: a stripe of colour (*bot.* and *zool.*): a thin, elongated cavity containing oil, found in the pericarps of some fruits (*bot.*): — *pl.* **vitt'ae** (*-ē*). — *adj.* **vitt'ate** having vittae: striped lengthwise. [L.]

vittle(s) *vit'l(z)*. A variant (esp. *dial.*) form of **victual(s).**

vitular *vit'ū-lər, adj.* pertaining to a calf or to calving. — *adj.* **vituline** (*vit'ū-līn*) pertaining to a calf or to veal. [L. *vitulus,* a calf.]

vituperate *vi-tū'pə-rāt,* or *vī-, v.t.* to assail with abusive reproaches, revile. — *v.i.* to use abusive language. — *adj.* **vitū'perable** deserving vituperation. — *n.* **vitūperā'-tion** the act of vituperating: censure: railing: abuse. — *adj.* **vitū'perative** (*-rət-* or *-rāt-*) containing vituperation: uttering, or prone to utter, abuse. — *adv.* **vitū'peratively.** — *n.* **vitū'perātor.** — *adj.* **vitū'peratory** vituperative. [L. *vituperāre, -ātum* — *vitium,* a fault, *parāre,* to set in order, prepare.]

Vitus. — **St Vitus's dance.** See **chorea.**

viva¹ *vē'vä,* (It.; Sp.) *interj.* long live.

viva². See **viva voce.**

vivace *vē-vä'che,* (*mus.*) *adj.* lively: — *superl.* **vivacis'simo.** [It.]

vivacious *vi-vā'shəs,* or *vī-, adj.* long-lived, or tenacious of life (*arch.*): lively, full of vitality: sprightly, sportive. — *adv.* **vivā'ciously.** — *ns.* **vivā'ciousness, vivāc'ity** the state of being vivacious: vitality (*obs.*): tenacity of life, or longevity (*arch.*): vigour: animation: liveliness or sprightliness of temper or behaviour: a vivacious act or saying (*rare*). [L. *vīvāx, vīvācis* — *vīvěre,* to live.]

vivamente. See **vivo.**

vivandière *vē-vä-dyer,* (*hist.*) *n.* in the French and some other Continental armies, a female attendant in a regiment, who sold spirits and provisions: — *masc.* **vivandier** (*-dyā*). [Fr., fem. of *vivandier* — It. *vivandiere,* a sutler — assumed L.L. *vivanda,* food.]

vivarium *vī-vā'ri-əm, n.* an artificial enclosure for keeping or raising living animals, as a park, a fish-pond: a glass-sided box, etc.: — *pl.* **vīvā'ria, -iums.** — Also **vī'vary.** [L. *vīvārium* — *vīvus,* alive — *vīvěre,* to live.]

vivat *vī'vat, vē'vat, wē'wat,* (L.) *interj.* long live.

viva voce *vī'və vō'sē, vē'vä, wē'wä vō', wō'ke, adv. phrase* by the living voice: by oral testimony. — *n.* (usu. *viva* alone) an oral examination. — *v.t.* (usu. **viva**) to examine orally. [L.]

vivda *viv'dä, vev'dä, n.* in Shetland, meat hung and dried without salt. — Also **vif'da.** [Perh. O.N. *vöthvi,* muscle.]

vive¹ *vīv,* (*Scot.* and *obs.*) *adj.* lively, forcible: vivid. — *adv.* **vive'ly.** — *n.* **vīv'ency** (*rare*) vitality. [Fr., or L. *vīvus,* alive.]

vive² *vēv,* (Fr.) *interj.* long live.

viver¹ *vē'vər,* (*obs.* and *dial.*) *n.* a fish-pond. [A.Fr., — L. *vīvārium;* see **vivarium.**]

viver² *vī'vər,* (*dial.*) *n.* a fibre, rootlet. [Variant of **fibre.**]

Viverra *vi-, vī-ver'ə, n.* the civet genus, giving name to the family **Viverr'idae** (*-i-dē*), and the subfamily **Viver-rinae** (*-ī'nē*). — *n.* any of the Viverridae, esp. one of the Viverrinae. — *adj.* **viverr'ine** of or like the ferret or the civet family. [L. *viverra,* a ferret.]

vivers *vē'vərz,* (*Scot.*) *n.pl.* food, eatables. [Fr. *vivres* — L. *vīvěre,* to live.]

vives *vīvz, n.sing.* a disease of horses, swelling of the submaxillary glands. [O.Fr. *avives, vives* — Sp. *avivas* — Ar. *addhība* — *al,* the, *dhība,* she-wolf.]

vivi- *vi'vi-,* in composition, alive, living. — *adj.* **viviparous** (*vī-vip'ə-rəs,* or *vi-;* L. *parěre,* to produce) producing living young that have reached an advanced stage of development — opp. to *oviparous:* germinating from a seed still on the parent plant (*bot.*): producing bulbils or young plants in the flower clusters, etc. (*bot.*). — *ns.* **vivip'arism** viviparous reproduction; **viviparity** (*vivi-par'i-ti*), **vivip'arousness** the quality of being viviparous. — *adv.* **vivip'arously.** — *ns.* **vivip'ary** viviparity in plants; **vivisection** (*-sek'shən;* L. *sectiō* — *secāre,* to cut) the act or practice, or an instance, of making surgical operations on living animals for the purposes of physiological research or demonstration: merciless and minute examination or criticism (*fig.*). — *v.t.* **vivisect'** to practise vivisection on. — Also *v.i.* — *adj.* **vivisec'tional.** — *n.* **vivisec'tionist** one who practises or defends vivisection. — *adj.* **vivisec'tive** practising vivisection. — *ns.* **vivisec'tor** one who practises vivisection; **vivisectō'rium** a place for vivisection; **vivisepulture** (*-sep'l-chər*) burial alive. [L. *vīvus.*]

vivianite *viv'yə-nīt, n.* ferrous phosphate, blue by oxidation, often found coating fossil fishes and bones. [After J. G. *Vivian,* who first found it crystallised.]

vivid *viv'id, adj.* full of life, vigorous: lively, intense: very bright: presenting a clear and striking picture: forming brilliant mental images. — *adv.* **viv'idly.** — *ns.* **viv'idness, vivid'ity.** — *adj.* **vivif'ic** vivifying. — *ns.* **vivificā'tion; viv'ifier.** — *v.t.* **viv'ify** to endue with life: to make vivid: to assimilate, convert into living tissue. [L. *vīvidus* — *vīvěre,* to live.]

viviparous, vivisection, etc. See **vivi-.**

vivo *vē'vō,* (*mus.*) *adj.* lively. — *adv.* **vivamente** (*vē-vä-men'tä*) in a lively manner. [It.]

vivres. Same as **vivers.**

vixen *vik'sn, n.* a she-fox: an ill-tempered woman. — *adjs.* **vix'en, vix'enish, vix'enly** ill-tempered, snarling. [South. dial. form of *fixen* — O.E. *fyxen,* fem. of *fox.*]

viz. See **videlicet.**

vizament *viz'ə-mənt,* (*Shak.*) *n.* for **advisement.**

vizard *viz'ərd, n.* a mask (*lit.* and *fig.*). — *v.t.* (*obs.*) to mask: to disguise, conceal. — *adj.* **viz'arded** masked: pretended. — **viz'ard-mask** a mask: a masked woman: a prostitute. [Variant of **visor.**]

vizcacha. See **viscacha.**

vizier, vizir *vi-zēr', viz'yər, viz'i-ər, n.* a minister or councillor of state in various Muslim states. — Also **visier', vezir', wizier'.** — *ns.* **vizier'ate, vizir'ate, vizier'ship, vizir'ship** the office of a vizier. — *adj.* **vizier'ial, vizir'ial.**

— **Grand Vizier** in pre-Republican Turkey, the prime minister, and at one time also commander of the army. [Ar. *wazīr*, a porter — *wazara*, to bear a burden.]

vizor. Same as **visor.**

vizsla *viz′lə, vizh′lə, n.* a Hungarian breed of hunting dog with smooth red or rust-coloured coat. [*Vizsla,* a town in Hungary.]

vizy, vizzie. See **visie** under **vision**.

Vlach *vlak, n.* one of a non-Slav people of south-eastern Europe, found chiefly in Rumania, a Walachian. [O.Slav. *Vlachŭ* — O.H.G. *walh,* a foreigner, esp. a Slav or a Latin.]

vlei *flā, n.* low-lying ground where a shallow lake forms in the wet season (*Afrik.*): a swamp (local *U.S.*). — Also **vly.** [Dial. Du., — Du. *wallei,* valley.]

voar *vōr, vör, n.* in Orkney and Shetland, spring, seed-time. [O.N. *vár,* spring; cf. **ware²**.]

vocable *vō′kə-bl, n.* that which is sounded with the voice — a word, or a single sound of a word: a term, name (*obs.*). — *adj.* capable of being uttered. — *adjs.* **vocab′-ular** (*vō-, və-kab′*) of or concerning words; **vocabular′-ian** of or pertaining to vocabulary. — *n.* a person much, or too much, concerned with words. — *adj.* **vocab′-ularied.** — *ns.* **vocab′ulary** a list of words explained in alphabetical order: a dictionary: any list of words: the words of a language: the words known to and used by, e.g. a particular person: the words used in a (particular) science or art: the signs or symbols used in any non-verbal type of communication, e.g. in computer technology: a collection of forms used in an art or by a particular practitioner of an art; **vocab′ulist** the maker of a vocabulary: a lexicographer. — *adj.* **vō′cal** having a voice: uttered by the voice: oral: sung, or for singing — opp. to *instrumental*: giving forth sound: resounding: talkative: eloquent: concerned in the production of speech: of or pertaining to a vowel: having a vowel function: voiced. — *n.* (often in *pl.*) singing, or that which is sung, esp. in a piece of popular music. — *adj.* **vō′calic** containing (esp. many) vowels: of, pertaining to, or of the nature of, a vowel or vowels. — *n.* **vōcalisā′tion, -z-.** — *v.t.* **vō′calise, -ize** to form into voice, to articulate: to sing: to give expression to: to make vocal, endow with power of expression: to convert into a vowel: to utter with voice (*phon.*): to insert the vowel points, as in Hebrew. — *v.i.* to sing: to sing on a vowel or vowels. — *ns.* **vocalise** (*vō-kə-lēz′*; *mus.*) a wordless composition or exercise for solo voice; **vō′caliser, -z-; vō′calism** exercise of the vocal organs: the art of using the voice in singing: a vocal sound: system of vowels; **vō′calist** a singer — esp. opp. to *instrumentalist*; **vōcal′ity; vō′calness.** — *adv.* **vō′cally.** — *adjs.* **vocicul′tūral** (*vō-si-*) pertaining to voice-training; **vocūlar** (*vok′; rare*) vocal. — *n.* **vocule** (*vok′ūl*) a slight vowel sound completing the articulation of certain consonants. — **vocal c(h)ords** in air-breathing vertebrates, folds of the lining membrane of the larynx, by the vibration of the edges of which, under the influence of the breath, the voice is produced; **vocal music** music produced by the human voice alone, as opp. to *instrumental music*; **vocal score** a musical score showing the singing parts in full. [L. *vocabulum* and *vōcālis* — *vōx, vōcis,* voice.]

vocal, etc. See under **vocable.**

vocalion *vō-kā′li-ən, n.* a musical instrument resembling a harmonium, with broad reeds. [**vocal,** and suff. *-ion,* as in **accordion**.]

vocation *vō-kā′shən, n.* a calling, summons (*rare*): a calling by God to his service in special work or in a special position, or to a state of salvation: a fitness for God's or other specified work: a way of living or sphere of activity to which one has been called by God, or for which one has a special fitness: one's occupation, business, or profession. — *adj.* **vocā′tional** pertaining to, concerned with, or in preparation for, a trade or occupation. — *n.* **vocā′tionalism** the giving of an important place in education to vocational training. — *adv.* **vocā′tionally.** — *adj.* **vocative** (*vok′ə-tiv*) per-taining to the act of calling: applied to the grammatical case used in direct personal address. — *n.* the case of a word when a person or thing is addressed: a word in that case. [L. *vocātiō, -ōnis,* and *vocātīvus* — *vocāre,* to call.]

voces. See **vox.**

vocicultural. See under **vocable.**

vociferate *vō-sif′ə-rāt, v.i.* to cry with a loud voice, to bawl. — *v.t.* to utter in a loud voice. — *n.* **vocif′erance** clamour. — *adj.* **vocif′erant** clamorous. — *ns.* **vociferā′-tion** the act of vociferating: a violent or loud outcry; **vocif′erātor; vociferos′ity** (*rare*). — *adj.* **vocif′erous** making a loud outcry: noisy. — *adv.* **vocif′erously.** — *n.* **vocif′erousness.** [L., — *vōx, vōcis,* voice, *ferre,* to carry.]

vocoder *vō-kō′dər, n.* an electronic device, similar to a synthesiser, for imposing human speech patterns on to the sound of musical instruments. [*vocal codifier.*]

vocular, vocule. See under **vocable.**

vodka *vod′kə, n.* a Russian spirit, properly distilled from rye, but sometimes from potatoes, etc. [Russ., dim. of *voda,* water.]

voe *vō, n.* in Orkney and Shetland, a bay, creek. [O.N. *vágr,* a creek.]

voetganger *fōōt′hhäng-ər, fōōt′gäng-ər,* (*S.Afr.*) *n.* a locust before its wings grow: a pedestrian: an infantryman. [Du. *voet,* foot, *gang,* walk.]

voetstoots *fōōt′stōō(ə)ts,* (*S. Afr.*) *adj.* (of something sold) as it stands, with any defects it has, visible or not. — Also *adv.* [Afrik.]

vogie *vō′gi,* (*Scot.*) *adj.* vain: merry. [Origin obscure.]

vogue *vōg, n.* the chief place in popular esteem (*obs.*): popularity: a place in popular favour, or the period of it: the mode or fashion at any particular time. — *adj.* in vogue, fashionable. — *v.t.* (*arch.* or *obs.*) to give vogue to, or to repute, reckon. — *adjs.* **vog′uey, vog′uish.** — **vogue word** a word much used at a particular time. [Fr. *vogue* (orig. the course of a rowing vessel) — *voguer,* to row — It. *vogare*; ety. uncertain.]

voice *vois, n.* sound produced by the vocal organs of living beings, esp. of human beings in speech or song: sound given out by anything: the faculty or power of speech or song: the ability to sing, esp. well: a mode of utterance: the quality and range of musical sounds produced by a singer: a singer: a part for a singer, or one of the parts in an instrumental composition: utterance, expression: what one says (*obs.*): an ex-pressed wish or opinion: a vote, approval: a medium of expression: one who speaks: rumour, report, repu-tation (*obs.*): sound uttered with resonance of the vocal cords (*phon.*): a mode of inflecting verbs to indicate whether that represented by the subject acts or is acted upon, or acts so as to affect itself (*gram.*; see **active, passive, middle**). — *v.t.* to utter (*rare*): to give utterance or expression to: to act as mouthpiece of (*rare*): to endow with voice: to rumour or esp. (in impers. construction) to be rumoured or commonly stated (*obs.*): to speak of (*obs.*): to acclaim (*obs.*): to nominate, appoint, elect (*obs.*): to regulate the tone of (*mus.*): to write the voice parts of: to utter with vibration of the vocal cords (*phon.*). — *adjs.* **voiced** endowed with voice: having a voice of a specified kind: uttered with voice (*phon.*); **voice′ful** having a voice: vocal (with *with*): full of sound. — *n.* **voice′fulness.** — *adj.* **voice′less** having no voice: speechless, silent: unspoken: failing to, or unable to, express one's opinion or desire, or to make this felt: having no vote: not voiced (*phon.*). — *ns.* **voice′lessness; voic′er; voic′ing** the regulation of the tone of organ pipes, ensuring proper power, pitch, and quality. — **voice′-box** the larynx; **voice′-over** the back-ground voice of an unseen narrator in a film, etc.; **voice′-print** an electronically recorded visual represen-tation of speech indicating frequency, amplitude and duration; **voice vote** a vote judged on the relative strengths of the shouted 'ayes' and 'noes'. — **give voice to** to express; **in my voice** (*Shak.*) in my name; **in voice**

in good condition for singing or speaking; **with one voice** unanimously. [A.Fr. *voiz, voice* (Fr. *voix*) — L. *vōx, vōcis*; akin to Gr. *epos*, a word.]

void *void, adj.* containing nothing, empty, deserted: unoccupied, unutilised: having no holder, vacant: devoid, destitute, free (with *of*): worthless (*obs.*): ineffectual, useless: not binding in law, null, invalid. — *n.* an empty space: (with *the*) the expanse of space: emptiness: a lack (*rare*): an emotional lack strongly felt (*fig.*): an unfilled space (*archit.*): the total absence of cards of a particular suit (*bridge*, etc.). — *v.t.* to make vacant, to empty, clear: to send out, discharge, emit: to send away, dismiss (*obs.*): to remove, clear away (*obs.*): to go away from, withdraw from, quit (*obs.*): to avoid (*obs.*): to lay aside, divest oneself of (*obs.*): to make of no effect, to nullify. — *adj.* **void'able** that may be voided: that may be either voided or confirmed (*law*). — *n.* **void'ance** the act of voiding or emptying: the state of being void: of a benefice, the fact or state of being vacant. — *adj.* **void'ed** (*her.*) having the inner part cut away and showing the tincture of the field — said of a charge. — *ns.* **void'ee** (*hist.*) wine and light food taken before going to bed, or before the departure of guests; **void'er** (*lit.* and *fig.*) one who empties, or (*hist.*) one who clears a table: a tray for carrying away dirty dishes, crumbs, etc., or a tray, etc., for carrying sweetmeats (*obs.*): a contrivance in armour for covering an unprotected part of the body; **void'ing** the act of voiding: that which is voided (often in *pl.*); **void'ness.** — **void'ing-lobby** (*obs.*) an anteroom. [O.Fr. *voide*, empty — popular L. *vocitus* — *vocitāre*, to empty — *vocuus*, for L. *vacuus.*]

voilà *vwä-lä*, (Fr.) *interj.* behold: there is, or there are. — **voilà tout** (*tōō*) that is all.

voile *voil, n.* any of several kinds of thin semi-transparent material. [Fr., veil.]

voir dire *vwär dēr* (*law*), an oath administered to a witness. [O.Fr. *voir*, true, truth, *dire*, to say.]

voisinage *voi'si-nij,* (*obs.*) *n.* neighbourhood, or the neighbourhood. [Fr.]

voiture *vwä-tür, n.* a carriage. — *n.* **voiturier** (*vwä-tür-yā*) the driver of a carriage or coach. [Fr.]

voivode *voi'vōd*, **vaivode** *vä'vōd, ns.* orig., the leader of an army: later, in south-east Europe, the title of the head of an administrative division: in Moldavia and Walachia, the former title of the princes: in Turkey, an inferior administrative official. — *ns.* **voi'vodeship**, **vai'vodeship.** [Russ. *voevoda* (Serb. *vojvoda*, Pol. *wojewoda*), a general.]

voix céleste *vwä sä-lest,* in an organ, a labial stop with a soft, tremulous sound. [Fr., heavenly voice.]

vol *vol,* (*her.*) *n.* two wings displayed and conjoined in base. [Fr.]

vola *vō'lə, n.* the hollow of the hand or foot: — *pl.* **volae** (*vō'lē*) — *adj.* **vo'lar** pertaining to the palm or to the sole. [L.]

volable *vol'ə-bl,* (*Shak.*) *adj.* nimble-witted. [L. *volāre*, to fly.]

volage *vō'läzh, adj.* giddy, flighty: fickle. — Also **volageous** (*vō-lā'jəs*). [Fr.]

Volans *vō'lanz, n.* the Flying Fish, a southern constellation. [L. *pr.p.* of *volāre*, to fly.]

volant *vō'lənt, adj.* flying: passing lightly through the air: flying or pertaining to flight (*zool.*): of armed forces, etc., organised for rapid movement (*obs.*): nimble: represented as flying (*her.*). — *adj.* **volante** (*vō-län'tā*; *mus.*) moving lightly and rapidly. — *n.* **vo'lary** an aviary. — *adjs.* **volat'ic** (now *rare*) flying about; **volatile** (*vol'ə-tīl*, in U.S. *-til, -təl*) capable of flying: moving lightly and rapidly about: evaporating very quickly: flighty, apt to change: explosive: not retaining information after the power supply is cut off (*comput.*). — *n.* a creature capable of flying: a volatile substance. — *ns.* **vol'atileness, volatility** (*-til'-*). — *adj.* **vol'atilīsable, -z-** (or *-at'-*). — *n.* **volatilīsā'tion, -z-**. — *v.t.* and *v.i.* **vol'atilise, -ize** (or *-at'-*) to make or become volatile. — *v.t.* to cause to evaporate: to make light, unsub-

stantial, delicate (*fig.*). — *n.* **vol'ery** a volary: a place for repair, etc., of aircraft. — *adj.* **vol'itant** flying: flitting: fluttering: moving about: able to fly. — *v.i.* **vol'itate** to flutter, fly. — *n.* **volitā'tion** flight: power of flying. — *adjs.* **volitā'tional**; **volitō'rial** having the power of flight. — **volatile alkali** (*obs.*) ammonia; **volatile oils** see **essential oils.** [L. *volāre*, to fly, *volitāre*, to flit, flutter.]

volante[1] *vō-lan'tä, n.* a two-wheeled covered vehicle with long shafts, with a chaise-body hung before the axle — the horse, or one of the horses, being ridden by a postillion. [Sp.]

volante[2]. See **volant.**

Volapük *vol', vōl'ə-pük,* or *-puk,* or *-pük', n.* an early international language invented about 1879 by Johann Schleyer of Constance, Baden. — *n.* **Volapük'ist** one versed in Volapük: one who advocates the adoption of Volapük. [Lit. world-speech — *vol*, for Eng. *world, pük,* for Eng. *speak.*]

volar. See **vola.**

volary, volatile, etc. See **volant.**

vol-au-vent *vol-ō-vä, n.* a kind of pie of light puff pastry filled with meat, or fish, etc. [Fr., lit. flight in the wind.]

volcano *vol-kā'nō, n.* a centre of eruption of subterranean matter, typically a more or less conical hill or mountain, built of ash and lava, with a central crater and pipe: a state of affairs, emotional condition, etc., suggestive of a volcano because an upheaval or outburst seems imminent (*fig.*): a form of firework: — *pl.* **volcan'oes.** — *adjs.* **volca'nian** (*Keats*); **volcanic** (*vol-kan'ik*) pertaining to, of the nature of, produced or caused by, a volcano: characterised by the presence of volcanoes. — *adv.* **volcan'ically.** — *ns.* **volcanicity** (*-kə-nis'i-ti*) vulcanicity; **volcanisā'tion, -z-**. — *v.t.* **vol'canise, -ize** to subject to the action of volcanic heat. — *adj.* **vol'canised, -z-**. — *ns.* **volcanism, volcanist** (also with *cap.*) **vulcanism, vulcanist.** — *adj.* **volcanolog'ical.** — *ns.* **volcanol'ogist** a vulcanologist, one who studies volcanoes and volcanic phenomena; **volcanol'ogy** vulcanology. — **volcanic ash(es), bomb** see **ash, bomb; volcanic dust** fine particles of powdered rock blown out from a volcano; **volcanic glass** rock without a crystalline structure, as obsidian, pumice, etc., produced by rapid cooling of molten lava; **volcanic mud, sand** volcanic ash which has been deposited under water and sorted and stratified; **volcanic rocks** those formed by volcanic agency. [It. *volcano* — L. *Volcānus, Vulcānus,* god of fire.]

vole[1] *vōl, n.* in certain card games, (the winning of) all the tricks in one deal. — *v.i.* to win all the tricks in one deal. — **go the vole** to risk all for great gain: to try everything. [Fr., — L. *volāre* to fly.]

vole[2] *vōl, n.* any of numerous blunt-nosed, short-eared, mouselike or ratlike rodents, including the so-called water-rat and some field-mice. [For *vole-mouse*, i.e. field-mouse, of Scand. origin.]

volens *vō'lenz,* (*law*) *adj.* consenting to a course of action which involves a risk of some sort (therefore unable to sue if injury occurs). — Also *n.* [Pr.p. of L. *velle,* to be willing.]

volente Deo *və-len'tē dē'ō, vō-, wō-len'tā dā'ō,* or *de'ō,* (L.) God willing.

volery. See under **volant.**

volet *vol'ā, n.* a short veil worn at the back of the head (*hist.*): one of the wings of a triptych picture. [O.Fr. (mod. Fr., a shutter) — L. *volāre,* to fly.]

Volga-Baltaic *vol'gä-böl-tā'ik, adj.* of, pertaining to, the group of languages to which Estonian, Finnish, and Lapp belong. [*Volga* river, *Baltic* Sea.]

volitant, volitation, volite. See **volant.**

volition *vō-lish'ən, n.* the act of willing or choosing: the exercise of the will, or the result of this: the power of determining. — *adjs.* **voli'tient** (*rare*) willing; **voli'tional, voli'tionary.** — *adv.* **voli'tionally.** — *adjs.* **voli'tionless; vŏl'itive** of, pertaining to, the will: originating in the will: willed, deliberate: expressing a wish (*gram.*).

— *n.* a desiderative verb, etc. [Fr., — L.L. *volitiō* — L. *volō*, pres. indic. of *velle*, to will, be willing.]

Völkerwanderung *fælk-ər-vän'dər-ŏŏng*, (Ger.) *n.* the migration of Germanic and other peoples, chiefly in the 4th to 6th centuries.

Volkskammer *folks'käm-ər, n.* the parliament of the German Democratic Republic. [Ger. *Volk*, people, *Kammer*, chamber.]

Volkslied *folks'lēt, n.* a folk-song. [Ger.]

volksraad *folks'rät, n.* a legislative assembly, esp. (with *cap.*) that of the Transvaal or the Orange Free State before 1900. [Du. *volk*, people, *raad*, council.]

volley *vol'i, n.* a flight of missiles: the discharge of many missile-throwing weapons (e.g. small arms) at once: a round fired by every gun in a battery: an outburst of many, e.g. words, at once (*fig.*): in tennis, cricket, etc., a return of the ball before it reaches the ground — a **half-volley** is a return by striking the ball immediately after it bounces: a ball so returned: — *pl.* **voll'eys.** — *v.t.* to discharge in a volley: to return (a ball) before it bounces: to fire a volley or volleys at. — *v.i.* to fly, be discharged, in a volley: to sound, produce sounds, like a volley: to roll, move, be emitted, like a volley: to make a volley at tennis, etc. — *adj.* **voll'eyed.** — **voll'ey-ball** a game in which a large ball is volleyed by the hand over a high net. [Fr. *volée*, a flight — L. *volāre*, to fly.]

volost *vō'lost, n.* a division for local government in Russia (*hist.*): a soviet of a rural district. [Russ. *volost.*]

volpino *vol-pē'nō, n.* a small Italian dog with long, straight hair and fox-like appearance: — *pl.* **volpin'os.** [It., — *volpe* — L. *vulpēs*, fox.]

volplane *vol'plän, v.i.* to glide down to earth in an aeroplane with the engine shut off: to glide to earth. — *n.* a descent of this kind. [Fr. *vol plané* — *vol*, flight, *plané*, pa.p. of *planer*, to glide.]

Volscian *vol'shən, n.* one of the *Volscī*, an ancient Italian people incessantly at war with the Romans for 200 years previous to 338 B.C.: their Italic language. — *adj.* of, pertaining to, the Volsci.

Volsungs *vol'sŏŏngz, n.pl.* a famous heroic race in old German legend, its founder *Volsung* being the grandson of Woden or Odin.

volt[1], **volte** *volt, n.* a sudden movement or leap to avoid a thrust (*fencing*): a gait of a horse going sideways round a centre: a track made by a horse executing this movement. — *n.* **vol'tage.** [Fr. *volte* — It. *volta* — L. *volvēre, volūtum*, to turn.]

volt[2] *vōlt, n.* the MKSA and SI unit of electromotive force, electric potential, or potential difference, the difference of potential between two points in a conductor carrying a current of one ampere when the power dissipated between them is one watt. — **volta-** (*vol'tə-*) used in composition for *voltaic*, as in **vol'ta-electric'ity, vol'ta-elec'tric.** — *n.* **voltage** (*volt', vōlt'*) electromotive force in volts: power, intensity (*fig.*). — *adj.* **voltaic** (*vol-tā'ik*) pertaining to Alessandro *Volta*, who constructed the first electrical battery, a **voltaic pile**, and established the science of current electricity: of electricity, generated by chemical action: used in producing such electricity: of, pertaining to, caused by, voltaic electricity. — *ns.* **vol'taism** the branch of electricity that treats of the production of an electric current from the chemical interaction of two immersed dissimilar metals; **voltameter** (*vol-tam'i-tər*) an instrument for measuring an electric current by means of the amount of metal deposited, or gas liberated, from an electrolyte in a given time by the passage of the current; **vōlt'meter** an instrument for measuring electromotive force directly, calibrated in volts. — **voltaic cell** a primary cell. [Alessandro *Volta*, Italian scientist (1745–1827).]

volta *vol'tə, n.* an old dance, the lavolta: turn, time (*mus.*): — *pl.* **vol'te** (*-tā*). [It.]

voltage[1,2]; **voltaic.** See **volt**[1,2]; **volt**[2].

Voltairian, Voltairean *vol-tār'i-ən, adj.* pertaining to *Voltaire*, French poet, dramatist, historian, and sceptic

(1694–1778). — *n.* one who advocates the views and principles of Voltaire. — *ns.* **Voltair'ianism, Voltair'eanism, Voltair'ism** the spirit of Voltaire — i.e. a sceptical and sarcastic attitude, especially towards Christianity — or a manifestation of it, or adherence to his doctrines.

voltameter; volte. See **volt**[2]; **volt**[1].

volte-face *volt-fäs, n.* a turning round: a sudden and complete change in opinion or in views expressed (*fig.*). [Fr.]

voltigeur *vol-ti-zhœr', n.* a vaulter or tumbler: in the French army, one of a light-armed company of picked men for skirmishing (*hist.*). [Fr., — *voltiger*, to flutter, vault.]

voltinism *vol'tin-izm, n.* breeding rhythm, brood frequency. [It. *volta*; see **volta.**]

voluble *vol'ū-bl, adj.* easy to roll or revolving readily or smoothly (*rare; Milt.* **volubil**): flowing smoothly: fluent in speech: too fluent or glib: (*loosely*) talkative, verbose: changeable (*rare*): twining (*bot.*). — *ns.* **volubil'ity, vol'ubleness.** — *adv.* **vol'ubly.** [L. *volūbilis* — *volvēre, volūtum*, to roll.]

volucrine *vol'ū krin, -krīn, adj.* pertaining to birds, bird-like. [L. *volucris*, a bird — *volāre*, to fly.]

volume *vol'ūm, n.* a roll or scroll, which was the form of ancient books: a book, whether complete in itself or part of a larger work: anything (esp. in the natural world) that may be studied as a book: (often in *pl.*) a rounded mass: a quantity: bulk: cubical content: dimensions: fullness of tone: loudness, or the control for adjusting it on a radio, etc. — *v.i.* to swell, rise, roll. — *v.t.* to send out in volumes, or great quantity: to make into, bind into, a volume. — *adj.* of, concerned with, large volumes or amounts. — *adj.* **vol'umed** having the form of a volume or roll: bulky: consisting of (so-many) volumes. — *ns.* **volumenom'eter, volumom'eter** an instrument for measuring the volume of a solid body by the quantity of fluid it displaces; **volu'meter** an instrument for measuring the volumes of gases. — *adjs.* **volumet'ric, -al.** — *adv.* **volumet'rically.** — *adjs.* **volu'minal** pertaining to cubical content; **volu'minous** consisting of many coils, windings, folds: bulky, filling much space: in many volumes: capable of filling many volumes: having written much, as an author. — *adv.* **volu'minously.** — *ns.* **volu'minousness, volumino'sity; vol'umist** (*rare*) an author. — **volumetric analysis** the estimation of the amount of a particular constituent present in a compound by determining the quantity of a standard solution required to satisfy a reaction in a known quantity of the compound. — **speak, express, volumes** to mean much, to be very significant. [Fr., — L. *volūmen, -inis*, a roll — *volvēre, volūtum*, to roll.]

voluntary *vol'ən-tər-i, adj.* acting by choice, able to will: proceeding from the will: spontaneous, free: done or made without compulsion or legal obligation: designed, intentional: freely given, or supported by contributions freely given: free from state control: subject to the will: of or pertaining to voluntaryism. — *n.* one who does anything of his own free-will: a volunteer (*obs.*): a piece of music played at will: a voluntary or extempore composition of any kind: a piece of music played before, during, or after a church service: an unwarranted fall from a horse: an upholder of voluntaryism. — *adv.* **vol'untarily.** — *ns.* **vol'untariness; vol'untarism** the philosophical doctrine that the will dominates the intellect: voluntaryism; **vol'untarist.** — *adj.* **voluntaris'tic.** — *ns.* **vol'untaryism** the principle or practice of reliance on voluntary action, not coercion: the principle or system of maintaining the church by voluntary offerings, instead of by the aid of the state: the principle or system of maintaining voluntary schools; **vol'untaryist.** — *adj.* **vol'untātive** voluntary. — **voluntary muscle** a muscle, or muscular tissue, that is controlled by the will; **voluntary school** in England, a school supported by voluntary subscriptions, in many cases controlled by a religious body. [L.

voluntārius — *voluntās*, choice — *volō*, pres. indic. of *velle*, to will.]

volunteer *vol-ən-tēr'*, *n.* one who enters any service, esp. military, of his own free choice: a soldier belonging to any body other than the regular army: one who acts of his own free will, esp. (*law*) in a transaction, without either legal obligation to do so or promise of remuneration: one to whom property is transferred without his giving valuable consideration. — *adj.* consisting of, or pertaining to, volunteers: giving voluntary service: given voluntarily: of a plant or plants, growing spontaneously. — *v.t.* to offer voluntarily to give, supply, perform: to give (information) unasked. — *v.i.* to enter into any service of one's own free-will or without being asked. [Fr. *volontaire* — L. *voluntārius.*]

voluptuary *və-lup'tū-ər-i*, *n.* one excessively given to bodily enjoyments or luxury, a sensualist. — *adj.* promoting, or characterised by, sensual pleasure. — *adj.* **voluptuous** (*və-lup'tū-əs*) full of, or suggestive of, pleasure, esp. sensuous: pertaining to, consisting of, derived from, or ministering to, sensual pleasure: shapely and sexually attractive: given to excess of pleasure, esp. sensual. — *adv.* **volup'tuously.** — *ns.* **volup'tuousness, voluptuos'ity.** [L. *voluptuārius* — *voluptās*, pleasure.]

Völuspa *vol-us-pa'*, *væl'ōōs-pa*, *n.* one of the poems of the Elder Edda: (without *cap.*) a sibyl or prophetess — a wrong use, found in Scott's *Pirate.* [O.N. *Völuspā*, the song of the sibyl — *völva*, a wise woman.]

volutation *vol-ū-tā'shən*, (*rare* or *obs.*) *n.* the action of rolling, turning, wallowing (*lit.* and *fig.*). [L. *volūtātiō, -ōnis* — *volūtāre* — *volvĕre, volūtum*, to roll.]

volute *və-*, *vo-lūt'*, *-lōōt'*, *n.* a spiral scroll used esp. in Ionic capitals: a spiral form: a thing or part having such a shape: any marine shell of the genus *Voluta* or kindred genera, allied to the whelks, or the animal itself: a whorl of a spiral shell. — *adj.* rolled up in any direction, having a spiral form. — *adj.* **volū'ted** in spiral form: having a volute or volutes. — *ns.* **vol'ūtin** a substance found in granular form (**volutin granules**) in the cytoplasm of various cells, believed to contribute to the formation of chromatin; **volū'tion** a revolving movement: a convolution: a whorl. — *adj.* **vol'ūtoid** like a volute. [L. *volvĕre, volūtum*, to roll.]

volva *vol'və*, *n.* a sheath enclosing the whole of the fruit body of some agarics. — *adj.* **vol'vate** possessing a volva. [L.; see **vulva.**]

volve *volv*, *v.t.* and *v.i.* to turn over (*obs.*): to ponder (*fig.*). [L. *volvĕre.*]

Volvox *vol'voks*, *n.* a genus of simple organisms found in ponds, canals, etc., commonly regarded as algae, consisting of green flagellate cells united by protoplasmic bridges in a hollow spherical colony. [Formed from L. *volvĕre.*]

volvulus *vol'vū-ləs*, *n.* twisting of an abdominal viscus causing internal obstruction. [Formed from L. *volvĕre.*]

vomer *vō'mər*, *n.* a bone of the skull in most vertebrates — in man, a thin flat bone, shaped like a wedge or ploughshare, forming part of the middle partition of the nose. — *adj.* **vomerine** (*vō'* or *vo'*). — **vo'mero-** used in composition, as **vomeronas'al**, pertaining to the vomer and the nasal cavity. [L. *vōmer*, a ploughshare.]

vomica. See under vomit.

vomit *vom'it*, *v.i.* to throw up the contents of the stomach by the mouth, to spew: of an emetic, to cause vomiting: to issue with violence. — *v.t.* to spew: to throw out with violence: to cause to vomit: — *pr.p.* **vom'iting;** *pa.t.* and *pa.p.* **vom'ited.** — *n.* the act of vomiting: matter ejected from the stomach: vile persons or things (*fig.*): something that excites vomiting, an emetic. — *ns.* **vom'ica** a cavity in the lung containing pus; **vom'iting.** — *adj.* **vom'itive** causing to vomit. — *n.* an emetic. — *ns.* **vom'ito** the worst form of yellow fever, usually attended with the black vomit; **vom'itory** a door of a

large building by which the crowd is let out (also, *Roman hist.*, **vomitō'rium**): a vent (*lit.* and *fig.*): an emetic (*arch.*). — *adj.* emetic. — *n.* **vomituri'tion** violent retching. [L. *vomĕre, -itum*, to throw up; Gr. *emeein.*]

voodoo, voudou *vōō'dōō*, or *-dōō'*, *n.* superstitious beliefs and practices of African origin found among Negroes of the West Indies and southern United States, formerly including serpent-worship, human sacrifice and cannibalism, but now confined to sorcery: any form of magic-working: a Negro sorcerer or witch. — *adj.* of, pertaining to, carrying out, voodoo practices. — *v.t.* to bewitch by voodoo charms. — Also **vaudoo', vaudoux** (*vō-dōō'*). — *ns.* **voo'dooism** (or *-dōō'*) voodoo superstitions; **voo'dooist** (or *-dōō'*). — *adj.* **voodooist'ic.** [West African *vodu*, a spirit.]

voortrekker *fōr-trek'ər*, *fōōr'*, or *vōr-*, *n.* (usu. with *cap.*) one of the Dutch farmers from Cape Colony who took part in the Great Trek into the Transvaal in 1836 and following years: (without *cap.*) a pioneer. [Cape Du., Du. *voor-*, before, and **trek.**]

vor *vōr*, (*Shak.*, King Lear IV, vi. 247, in dialect passage) *v.t.* perh. means to warn.

Vor *vōr*, *n.* an American aid to aircraft navigation. [**V**ery-**H**igh-**F**requency **O**mni-**D**irectional-**R**ange.]

voracious *və-rā'shəs*, *vö-*, *vō-*, *adj.* eating greedily or in large quantities: taking in, engulfing, much (*fig.*): very eager, or insatiable (*fig.*): characterised by greediness (*lit.* and *fig.*). — *adv.* **vorā'ciously.** — *ns.* **voracity** (*-ras'*), **vorā'ciousness.** [L. *vorāx, vorācis* — *vorāre*, to devour.]

voraginous *vō-raj'i-nəs*, *vö-*, (*obs.* or *rare*) *adj.* pertaining to a whirlpool: voracious. — *n.* **vorā'go** (*-gō*) a gulf: — *pl.* **vorā'goes.** [L. *vorāgo* — *vorāre.*]

vorant *vō'rənt*, *vō'*, (*her.*) *adj.* devouring. [L. *vorāns, -antis*, pr.p. of *vorāre*, to devour.]

vorpal *vōr'pəl*, *adj.* a nonsense word coined by Lewis Carroll to describe a sword, now used to mean sharp-edged.

vortex *vōr'teks*, *n.* a whirling motion of a fluid forming a cavity in the centre, a whirlpool, an eddy, a whirlwind: according to a hypothesis of Descartes, etc., a rotary movement of atoms or particles of subtle matter round an axis, or the matter itself in rotation, such phenomena accounting for the formation of the universe and the relative motion of its parts: a pursuit, way of life, situation, etc., that engulfs one irresistibly or remorselessly, taking up all one's attention or energies (*fig.*): — *pl.* **vor'tices** (*-ti-sēz*), **vor'texes.** — *adj.* **vor'tical** of or pertaining to a vortex: whirling. — *adv.* **vor'tically.** — *ns.* **vor'ticism** (*-tis-izm*) a British movement in painting, a development from futurism, blending cubism and expressionism, and emphasising the complications of machinery that characterise modern life; **vor'ticist** one who holds the theory of vortices, or who supports vorticism; **vortic'ity** the amount of vortical motion in a fluid. — *adjs.* **vor'ticose, vortic'-ūlar, vortiginous** (*-ij'*) vortical. — **vortex theory** a theory that the material atom consists of a vortically moving frictionless fluid — a conception of Lord Kelvin's. [L. *vortex, vertex, -icis* — *vortĕre, vertĕre*, to turn.]

Vorticella *vōr-ti-sel'ə*, *n.* a genus of ciliated infusorians belonging to the order *Peritricha*, in which the cilia are restricted to a fringe round the mouth: (without *cap.*) any organism of this genus: — *pl.* **-ae** (*-ē*). [Dim., from L. *vortex.*]

Vosgian *vōzh'i-ən*, *adj.* of or pertaining to the *Vosges* Mts. — Also **Vosg'ean.**

votary *vō'tə-ri*, *n.* one devoted as by a vow to some service, worship, or way of life: one enthusiastically addicted to a pursuit, study, etc.: a devoted worshipper or adherent: — *fem.* **vō'taress.** — *adj.* (*obs.*) consecrated by, or of the nature of, vows: of the nature of a vow. — *n.* **vō'tarist** a votary. — *adj.* **vōt'ive** given, erected, etc., by vow: undertaken or observed in fulfilment of a vow: consisting of, or expressing, a vow or a wish. — **votive offering, picture, tablet** one dedicated in fulfilment of a vow.   [L.L. *vōtārius* — L. *vovēre*, *vōtum*, to vow.]

vote *vōt, n.* an earnest desire (*obs.*): an expression of a wish or opinion in an authorised formal way: collective opinion, decision by a majority: votes or voters of a certain class collectively: a voter: the right to vote: that by which a choice is expressed, as a ballot: the total number of votes cast. — *v.i.* to express choice, esp. at an election, by vote: to declare oneself in favour of, or against (with *for, against*), esp. by vote. — *v.t.* to determine by vote: to grant by vote: to bring about (a specified result or change) by vote: to declare by general consent (*coll.*): to pronounce, adjudge to be (*coll.*): to propose, suggest (*coll.*): to present for voting: to record the votes of. — *adj.* **vote′less.** — *n.* **vō′ter.** — **voting machine** a machine on which to register votes. — **split one's vote(s)** to divide one's votes among two or more candidates; **split the vote** to injure a cause by influencing a body of possible supporters to vote in some other way (*n.* **vote′-splitt′ing**); **vote Conservative, Labour,** etc., to give one's vote, on a particular occasion or habitually, to the Conservative, Labour, etc., candidate or party; **vote down** to defeat or suppress by vote, or otherwise; **vote in** to elect; **vote of no confidence** the legal method of forcing the resignation of a government or governing body; **vote straight** to give one's vote honestly; **vote with one's feet** to indicate one's dissatisfaction with a situation or conditions by leaving.   [L. *vōtum*, a wish — *vovēre, vōtum,* to vow.]
voteen *vō-tēn′,* (Ir.) *n.* a devotee.   [Perh. **devote.**]
votive. See **votary.**
vouch *vowch, v.t.* to call upon to witness, esp. to a title to real estate (*arch.*; also **vouch to warrant, vouch to warranty**) to cite as authority: to assert, declare (*obs.*): to assert or guarantee to be true: to support by evidence: to testify (that): to be sponsor for (*rare*): to guarantee legal possession of (*Shak.*): to vouchsafe, condescend to grant (*arch.*): to second, support (*Milt.*). — *v.i.* to bear witness, or be surety (with *for*). — *n.* an assertion: an attestation. — *ns.* **vouchee′** the person summoned to witness to a title to real estate: a person quoted as authority or appealed to as witness; **vouch′er** (partly A.Fr. *voucher,* infin.; partly suff. *-er*) the act of vouching to warrant: a piece of evidence, or a written document serving as proof: a paper which confirms the truth of anything, as a receipt, a certificate of correctness: a ticket, etc., substituting, or exchangeable, for cash or goods: one who vouches or gives witness: a mechanical contrivance used in shops for automatically registering the amount of money drawn.   [O.Fr. *voucher, vocher,* to call to defend — L. *vocāre,* to call.]
vouchsafe *vowch-sāf′,* formerly also (*Milt.*) **voutsafe** *vowt′-sāf, vs.t.* to warrant safe, guarantee (*obs.*): to condescend to grant (*arch.*): to condescend to allow, to accept, or to engage in (*obs.*): to condescend, be graciously willing to tell, etc. — *v.i.* to condescend: — *pr.p.* **vouchsāf′ing;** *pa.t.* and *pa.p.* **vouchsafed′.** — *n.* **vouchsafe′ment.**   [Orig. two words, **vouch, safe.**]
voudou. See **voodoo.**
vou(l)ge *vōōzh, n.* a weapon carried by foot-soldiers in the 14th century, having a blade fixed on a long staff. [Fr.]
voulu *vōō-lü,* (Fr.) *adj.* deliberate, studied.
voussoir *vōō-swär′, n.* one of the wedge-like stones that form part of an arch. — *v.t.* to form with voussoirs. [Fr., through L.L., from L. *volūtus* — *volvēre,* to roll.]
voutsafe. See **vouchsafe.**
vow *vow, n.* a voluntary promise made to God, or to a saint, or to a god or gods: a binding undertaking or resolve: a solemn or formal promise of fidelity or affection: a firm assertion: an earnest wish or prayer. — *v.t.* to give, dedicate, by solemn promise: to promise or threaten solemnly: to maintain solemnly. — *v.i.* to make vows. — *adj.* **vowed** bound by religious vows (*obs.*): devoted, confirmed, undertaken, etc., by vow, or as by vow. — *n.* **vow′ess** (*hist.*) a woman who has

taken a vow: a nun. — **vow′-fellow** (*Shak.*) one bound by the same vow. — **baptismal vows** the promises made at baptism by the person baptised, or by the sponsors or parents in his name; **simple vow** a more limited, less permanent vow than a solemn vow; **solemn vow** such a vow as the Church takes under her special charge, solemnly accepts, as those of poverty, obedience, and chastity, involving complete and irrevocable surrender.   [O.Fr. *vou* (Fr. *vœu*) — L. *vōtum* — *vovēre,* to vow.]
vowel *vow′əl, n.* a speech-sound produced by the unimpeded passage of the breath (modified by the vocal cords into voice) through the mouth, different vowel sounds being made by altering the form and position of the tongue and the lips: a letter (as *a, e, i, o, u*) used alone or in combination to represent a vowel sound: (in *pl.*) an IOU (*old slang*). — *adj.* vocal: of, representing, of the nature of, a vowel. — *vs.t.* **vow′el, vow′elise, -ize** to insert vowel signs in (words written primarily with consonants only): to use as a vowel: to modify by vowel sounds′ (**vowel**) to promise to pay, offer an IOU (*old slang*). — *adjs.* **vow′elled** having vowels, esp. in a marked degree: having a vowel or vowels of a specified kind; **vow′elless** without vowels; **vow′elly** full of vowels. — **vowel gradation** ablaut; **vowel mutation** umlaut; **vowel point** a mark inserted, e.g. in Hebrew, to indicate a vowel; **vowel′-rhyme** assonance.   [Fr. *voyelle* — L. *vōcālis* — *vōx, vōcis,* voice.]
vox *voks,* (L. *vōks, wōks), n.* voice: — *pl.* **voces** (*vō′sēz, -kēs, wō′*). — **vox angelica** (*an-jel′i-kə, an-gel′i-ka*), **vox caelestis** (*sē-les′tis, kī-*) voix céleste; **vox humana** (*hū-mä′nə, hōō-mä′na*) in organ-building, a reed-stop producing tones resembling those of the human voice; **vox populi, vox Dei** (*pop′ū-lī, dē′ī, po′pōō-lē, de′ē* or *dā′ē*) the voice of the people is the voice of God, hence **vox populi** (often shortened to **vox pop**) public or popular opinion.   [L. *vōx.*]
voyage *voi′ij, n.* a journey of any kind (*arch.*): travel (*obs.*): a military expedition (*obs.*): an enterprise (*obs.*): a passage by water or by air to some place at a considerable distance: a round trip: a cruise: an account of such a journey. — *v.i.* to make a voyage, cruise, journey. — *v.t.* to traverse, pass over. — *adj.* **voy′ageable** navigable. — *ns.* **voy′ager; voyageur** (*vwä-yä-zhœr′*) in Canada one who kept up communication by canoe between trading-posts: a boatman: a trapper. [O.Fr. *veage, voiage,* etc. — L. *viāticum;* see **viaticum.**]
voyeur *vwä-yœr′, n.* one who derives gratification from surreptitiously watching sexual acts or objects: a peeping Tom: one who takes a morbid interest in sordid sights. — *n.* **voy′eurism.** — *adj.* **voyeuris′tic.**   [Fr., one who sees.]
vraic *vräk, n.* a Channel Islands name for seaweed, used for fuel and manure. — *ns.* **vraick′er** a gatherer of vraic; **vraick′ing** the gathering of vraic.   [Dial. Fr.; see **varec.**]
vraisemblance *vrä-, vre-sä-bläs′, n.* verisimilitude: a picture.   [Fr. *vrai,* true, *semblance,* appearance.]
vril *vril, n.* electric fluid represented as the common origin of the forces in matter, in E. G. L. Bulwer-Lytton's *The Coming Race,* 1871.
vroom *vrōōm, vrŏŏm,* (*coll.*) *n.* power, drive, energy, etc. — *v.i.* to travel speedily.   [Imit.]
vrouw *vrow, frow, n.* a woman, goodwife, housewife. [Du.]
VTOL *vē′tol, n.* a system enabling aircraft to land and take off vertically: an aircraft operating by this system. [Vertical take-off and landing.]
vug *vug, n.* a Cornish miner's name for a cavity in a rock, usu. lined with crystals. — *adj.* **vugg′y.**
Vulcan *vul′kən, n.* the god of fire and metal-working (*Roman myth.*): a planet (*intramercurial planet*) once postulated between the sun and Mercury: (without *cap.*) a blacksmith or an iron-worker. — *n.* **Vulcanā′lia** an ancient Roman festival in honour of Vulcan, held on 23 August. — *adjs.* **Vulcā′nian** of, pertaining to, like, related to, sprung from, made by, Vulcan: (with-

out *cap.*) volcanic: without *cap.*) of a volcanic eruption, discharging gases and ash but little or no lava; **vulcanic** (*-kan'ik*) volcanic: (with *cap.*) of Vulcan. — *n.* **vulcanicity** (*-is'i-ti*) volcanic action or phenomena. — *adj.* **vulcanī'sable, -z-**. — *n.* **vulcanīsā'tion, -z-**. — *v.t.* **vul'canise, -ize** to treat (rubber, etc.) with sulphur or sulphur compounds, etc. to improve its strength or otherwise modify its properties. — *v.i.* to admit such treatment. — *ns.* **vul'canism** volcanic activity (also **vol'canism**): (with *cap.*) the teaching of the Vulcanists; **Vul'canist, Vol'canist** (*hist.* of *geol.*) a Plutonist, a follower of James Hutton (1726–97), who asserted the geological importance of subterranean heat and the igneous origin of such rocks as basalt — opp. to *Neptunist*: (without *cap.*) a vulcanologist; **vul'canite** the harder of the two kinds of vulcanised rubber, the softer kind being called *soft rubber*: a general name for any igneous rock of fine grain-size. — *adj.* **vulcanolog'ical.** — *ns.* **vulcanol'ogist; vulcanol'ogy** the scientific study of volcanoes and volcanic phenomena. — **vulcanised fibre** a fibre obtained by treating paper pulp with zinc chloride solution, used for low-voltage insulation; **Vulcan's badge** a cuckold's horns. [L. *Vulcānus*.]

vulgar *vul'gər, adj.* pertaining to the common people: plebeian: vernacular: public: common, usual, customary: common to all: prevalent: commonplace: low: unrefined: coarse: lacking in taste, manners, delicacy, etc.: spiritually paltry, ignoble, debased, or pretentious. — *n.* the common people: one of the unrefined, of the uneducated, or of those not in good society: a class of inferior persons (*obs.*): the common language of a country. — *n.* **vulgā'rian** a vulgar person: a rich unrefined person. — Also *adj.* — *n.* **vulgarisā'tion, -z-**. — *v.t.* **vul'garise, -ize** to make common or ordinary: to make unrefined or coarse. — *ns.* **vul'garism** a vulgar phrase: coarseness: an instance of this; **vulgarity** (*-gar'*). — *adv.* **vul'garly.** — **Vulgar era** the Christian era; **vulgar fraction** a fraction written in the common way (one number above another, separated by a line), as opposed to a *decimal fraction*; **vulgar tongue** the vernacular. [L. *vulgāris* — *vulgus*, the people.]

Vulgate *vul'gāt,* or *-git, n.* an ancient Latin version of the Scriptures, made by St Jerome and others in the 4th century, and later twice revised — so called from its common use in the R.C. church: (without *cap.*) a comparable accepted text of any other book or author. — *adj.* of or pertaining to the Vulgate: (without *cap.*;

of speech, etc.) commonly used or accepted. [L. *vulgāta* (*editio*), popular edition (of the Bible); see **vulgar.**]

vulgo *vul'gō, vōōl', wōōl'gō,* (L.) *adv.* commonly.

vulgus *vul'gəs, n.* the common people: in some public schools, a short verse task in Latin. [L.; see **vulgar.**]

vulnerable *vul'nər-ə-bl, adj.* capable of being wounded: liable to injury, or hurt to feelings: open to successful attack: capable of being persuaded or tempted: in contract bridge, of a side that has won a game towards the rubber, liable to increased penalties (or premiums) accordingly. — *v.t.* **vuln** (*vuln; her.*) to wound. — *adj.* **vulned** (*her.*). — *ns.* **vulnerabil'ity, vul'nerableness.** — *adj.* **vul'nerary** pertaining to wounds: useful in healing wounds. — *n.* anything useful in curing wounds. — *v.t.* **vul'nerate** (*obs.*) to wound. — *n.* **vulnerā'tion** (*obs.*). [L. *vulnerāre,* to wound — *vulnus, vulneris,* a wound.]

Vulpes *vul'pēz, n.* the genus including the common fox. — *adj.* **vulpine** (*vul'pin, -pīn*) of, pertaining to, or like a fox: cunning. — *ns.* **vul'picīde** the killing of a fox, except in hunting: a fox-killer; **vul'pinism** craftiness. — **vulpine opossum, phalanger** the common Australian opossum (*Trichosurus vulpecula*). [L. *vulpēs,* a fox.]

vulpinite *vul'pin-īt, n.* a granular scaly form of the mineral anhydrite. [*Vulpino* in Lombardy.]

vulsella *vul-sel'ə, n.* a forceps with toothed or clawed blades: — *pl.* **vulsell'ae** (*-ē*). — Also **vulsell'um:** — *pl.* **-a.** [L.]

vulture *vul'chər, n.* any of a number of large rapacious birds of prey, feeding largely on carrion, regarded as belonging to two families: one who or that which resembles a vulture. — Also *adj.* — *adjs.* **vul'turīne, vul'turish, vul'turous** of, pertaining to, or like a vulture: rapacious. — *ns.* **vul'turism** (*Carlyle*) rapacity; **vul'turn** (*-tûrn; obs.*) the Australian brush turkey. [O.Fr. *voutour, voltour,* etc. (Fr. *vautour*) — L. *vulturius* — *vultur.*]

vulva *vul'və, n.* the external organ of generation of the female mammal, or the orifice of it. — *adjs.* **vul'val, vul'var, vul'vate; vul'viform** oval: like a cleft with projecting edges. — *n.* **vulvī'tis** inflammation of the vulva. — **vul'vo-** used in composition, as **vul'vo-ū'terine,** pertaining to the vulva and the uterus. [L. *vulva, volva,* wrapping, womb.]

vum *vum,* (*U.S. dial.*) *v.t.* and *v.i.* a corruption of **vow,** in the phrase *I vum.*

vying *vī'ing, pr.p.* of **vie.**

W

W, w *dub'l-ū, n.* the twenty-third letter of our alphabet, a 5th-century addition to the Roman alphabet, being a doubled u or v used to express the voiced consonantal sound heard e.g. in Eng. *way, weak, warrant*; from the 13th century it was regularly used in writing English, superseding the letter wen (q.v.). In mod. Eng. *w* is found as a consonant and also as the second component in certain vowel and diphthong digraphs, i.e. those in *law, few, now*. The unvoiced form of the consonant is written *wh* (corresponding to O.E. *hw*), as in *what, when*, but many English people substitute the voiced sound in pronouncing words spelt *wh*, and Northern speakers insist upon sounding *hw*. *W* is no longer pronounced in *write, two*, etc., or in *whole* (which represents a dialectal variation of O.E. *hāl*). O.E. *cw* has become *qu*, as in *queen*, from O.E. *cwēn*.

wa' *wö*, Scots form of **wall**.

Waac *wak, n.* the Women's Army Auxiliary Corps (founded 1917), or a member of it, now **WRAC**. — *n.* **Waaf** (*waf*) the Women's Auxiliary Air Force (1939), or a member, now **WRAF**. [From the initial letters.]

wabain. See **ouabain**.

wabble(r). See **wobble**.

waboom. See **wagenboom**.

wabster. See **webster**.

wacke *wak'ə, n.* an old name for a decomposed basalt. [Ger., — O.H.G. *wagge*, a pebble; cf. **greywacke**.]

wacky *wak'i*, (*slang*) *adj.* crazy. — *n.* **wack'iness**. [Perh. conn. with *whack*, or with dial. *whacky*, left-handed, a fool.]

wad[1] *wod, n.* a pad of loose material as hay, tow, etc., thrust in to aid packing, etc.: formerly a little mass of paper, tow, or the like, now a disc of felt or paper, to keep the charge in a gun: a bundle as of hay: a roll or bundle, as of bank notes: a compact mass, often small: a lump of a soft substance (*rare*). — *v.t.* to form into a mass: to pad, stuff out: to stuff a wad into: — *pr.p.* **wadd'ing**; *pa.t.* and *pa.p.* **wadd'ed**. — *n.* **wadd'ing** a wad, or the materials for wads: sheets of carded cotton for stuffing garments, etc.: cotton-wool. [Origin uncertain; cf. Sw. *vadd*, wadding; Ger. *Watte*, Fr. *ouate*.]

wad[2], **wadd** *wod, n.* an earthy ore of manganese, mainly hydrated oxide of manganese. [Ety. dub.]

wad[3]. See **wed**.

waddle *wod'l, v.i.* to take short steps and sway from side to side in walking, as a duck does: of an inanimate thing, to move in a way suggestive of this: to become a defaulter (*Stock Exchange slang*). — *n.* the act of waddling: a clumsy, rocking gait. — *adj.* **wadd'ling**. [Freq. of **wade**.]

waddy *wod'i, n.* a native Australian wooden club used in warfare: a cowboy: a walking-stick. — Also **wadd'ie**. — *v.t.* to strike with a waddy. [Perh. from Eng. **wood**[1].]

wade *wād, v.i.* to go (*obs.*; *lit.* and *fig.*): to walk through a substance that yields with difficulty to the feet, as water: to go (through) with difficulty or labour (*fig.*). — *v.t.* to cross by wading: to cause to cross thus. — *n.* the act of wading: a ford (*coll.*). — *n.* **wā'der** one who wades: a bird that wades in search of food, e.g. the snipe, sandpiper, etc., and sometimes larger birds such as the heron, etc.: a high waterproof boot. — *n.* and *adj.* **wā'ding**. — **wade in** to make a very vigorous attack; **wade into** to tackle, as a job, energetically: to make a vigorous attack on (*lit.* and *fig.*). [O.E. *wadan*, to go; Ger. *waten*.]

wadi, wady *wod'i, n.* the dry bed of a torrent: a river-valley. [Ar. *wādī*.]

wadmal *wäd'* or *wud'məl*, (*hist.*) *n.* a thick or coarse woollen cloth, woven esp. in Orkney and Shetland. — Also **wad'maal, wad'mol(l)**. [O.N. *vathmāl — vāth*, cloth, *māl*, measure.]

wadset *wod'set,* (*Scot.*) *n.* a mortgage: something pledged or pawned. — Also **wadsett**. — *v.t.* to mortgage: to pawn. — *n.* **wad'setter** mortgagee. [**wad**, which see under **wed**, and **set**.]

wady. See **wadi**.

wae *wā, n.* (*Spens.*) woe. — *adj.* (*Scot.*) sorrowful. — *adjs.* **wae'ful (wae'fu'), wae'some** (*Scot.*) woeful, pitiful. — *n.* **wae'ness** sadness. — *interj.* **waesucks'** alas! [Dial. form of **woe**.]

Wafd *woft, n.* a Nationalist party in Egypt founded in 1918, dissolved in 1953.

wafer *wā'fər, n.* a very thin crisp cake or biscuit baked in **wafer-irons** or **-tongs**, formerly eaten with wine: a similar biscuit eaten with ice-cream, etc.: a thin round cake of unleavened bread, usu. stamped with a cross, an Agnus Dei, the letters I.H.S., etc., used in the Eucharist: a thin leaf of coloured paste for sealing letters, etc.: a thin cake of paste used to form a cachet or wrapping for powders (*med.*): a thin slice of silicon from which chips are cut: a thin slice of anything. — *v.i.* to close, fasten, stick (as on a wall), with a wafer. — *adj.* **wā'fery** like a wafer. — **waf'er-cake** a wafer. [O.N.Fr. *waufre* (O.Fr. and Fr. *gaufre*) — M.L.G. *wafel*, cake of wax.]

waff[1] *waf, wöf,* (*Scot.*) *adj.* wandering, stray: worthless, paltry: listless. — *n.* a worthless person. [Variant of **waif**[1].]

waff[2] *waf, n.* (*Scot.*) a waving, or a slight, hasty motion: a signal: a quick light blow: a puff, or a blast: a sudden ailment: a faint, usu. disagreeable, odour: a glimpse: a ghost. — *v.t.* and *v.i.* (*dial.* or *obs.*) to wave, flap, flutter, wave away. [Noun from verb, which is a variant of **wave**.]

waff[3] *waf,* (*dial.*) *v.i.* to bark. — Also **waugh**. [Imit.]

waffle[1] *wof'l, n.* a kind of cake made from batter, baked in an iron utensil of hinged halves called a **waff'le-ī'ron**. [Du. *wafel*, wafer.]

waffle[2] *wof'l,* (*dial.*) *v.i.* to wave. [Freq. of **waff**[2].]

waffle[3] *wof'l,* (*slang*) *v.i.* to talk incessantly or nonsensically: to waver, vacillate. — Also *n.* [Freq. of **waff**[3].]

waft *wäft, woft, waft, v.t.* to bear, convey, transport, propel, safely or lightly, on the surface of or through a fluid medium, as air or water (*poet.*; also *fig.*): to signal to, beckon (perh. for **waff**[2]): to turn (Shak., *Wint. Tale* I, ii. 372). — *v.i.* to float, sail, pass through the air: — *pa.t.* **waft'ed**; *Spens.* **weft**; *pa.p.* **waft'ed**; *Spens.* **weft**. — *n.* a scent, or sound, or puff or smoke or vapour carried by the air: a rush of air (also *fig.*): a slight taste, esp. an unpleasant one: an act of wafting, or of waving: a waving movement: a passage across the sea or other water (*obs.*): a flag or substitute hoisted as a signal, esp. an ensign, stopped together at the head and middle portions, slightly rolled up lengthwise, and hoisted at different positions at the after-part of a ship (also **weft, wheft**): the act of displaying such a signal. — *ns.* **waft'age** the act of wafting: transportation through air or across water; **waft'er; waft'ing; waft'ure** (*Shak.* — Rowe's emendation, *Jul. Caes.* II, i. 246) the act of wafting or of waving: a waving motion: a beckoning: something wafted. [From obs. *wafter*, a convoying vessel, prob. — L.G. or Du. *wachter*, guard.]

wag *wag, v.i.* to move, or be moved, from side to side, or to shake to and fro: to oscillate: to move, or to move one's limbs: to move on, be off (*arch.*): to play truant (*slang*): of tongue, chin, beard, etc., to move in light, gossiping or indiscreet talk: of the world, etc. (in the sense of human affairs), to go (in respect of good fortune and bad). — *v.t.* to move, shake, wave, to and fro or up and down: to brandish (*obs.*): to move, stir a limb, etc.: to move in chatter or indiscreet talk: to move so as to express reproof or derision, etc.: — *pr.p.* **wagg′ing;** *pa.t.* and *pa.p.* **wagged.** — *n.* a shake: an act of wagging: ability to wag: truant (in **to play the wag**): a droll, mischievous fellow, a habitual joker, a wit (perh. from obs. **wag′halter,** one who deserves hanging): a fellow (*obs.*). — *n.* **wagg′ery** mischievous merriment or jesting: an instance of such. — *adj.* **wagg′ish** droll, mischievous, etc. — *adv.* **wagg′ishly.** — *n.* **wagg′-ishness.** — **wag′-at-the-wa′′, wag′-at** (or **-by)-the-wall′** (*Scot.* and *Northern*) a hanging clock with exposed pendulum and weights. [M.E. *waggen,* from same root as O.E. *wagian,* to shake.]

wage *wāj, v.t.* to pledge, offer as a pledge (*obs.*): to wager (*obs.*): to hazard (*obs.*): to engage in, to carry on, esp. war: to hire for pay, to pay wages to, or to bribe (*obs.*): to let out for pay (*Spens.*). — *v.i.* (*Shak.*) to be equal in value: to contend, battle. — *n.* a gage or pledge (*obs.*): payment for services, esp. not professional, or (*fig.*) reward (both often **wages,** *pl.* in form, but sometimes construed as *sing.*). — *adj.* and *n.pl.* **wage′-less.** — *n.* **wā′ger** a pledge (*obs.*): the act of giving a pledge (*obs.*): something staked on an issue: a bet: that on which bets are laid: a hazard (*rare*): a contest for a prize (*rare*): an offer to make oath (*law*). — *v.t.* to hazard on the issue of anything. — *v.i.* to lay a wager. — *n.* **wā′gerer.** — **wage′-earn′er** one who works for wages: one who earns the money that sports, or money that helps to support, the household; **wage′-earn′ing; wage′-freeze** a fixing of wages at a certain level for some time ahead; **wage′-packet** a small envelope in which a worker's wages are issued: (*loosely*) wages; **wa′ger-boat** a light boat for a race between single scullers; **wa′ge(s)-fund** or **wa′ges-fund theory** the theory (now abandoned) that there is at any given time in a country a determinate amount of capital available for the payment of labour, therefore the average wage depends on the proportion of this fund to the number of persons who have to share in it; **wage slave** one who has to earn wages to live, esp. if the wages are considered poor; **wage(s) slip** a pay slip; **wage′-work** work done for wages. — **living wage** see **living; wage-push inflation** inflation caused by wage increases; **wager of battle** (*hist.*) trial by combat, a usage which permitted the accused and accuser, in defect of sufficient direct evidence, to challenge each other to mortal combat. [M.E. *wagen* — O.N.Fr. *wagier* (O.Fr. *gagier*), to pledge (through popular L. from a Gmc. word).]

wagenboom *vä′gən-bōm,* **-bōōm,** **waboom** (*Afrik.*) *vä′bōōm, ns.* a S. African tree (*Protea grandiflora*) whose wood is used in making wagon wheels. [Du., wagon-tree.]

wagger-pagger(-bagger) *wag′ər-pag′ər(-bag′ər),* (*coll.,* esp. *facet.*) *n.* a wastepaper-basket.

waggle *wag′l, v.i.* and *v.t.* to wag, esp. in an unsteady manner. — Also *n.* — *adj.* **wagg′ly.** [Freq. of **wag.**]

waggon, etc. See **wagon.**

wagmoire *wag′moir,* (*Spens.*) *n.* a quagmire.

wag-'n-bietjie. See under **wait**[1].

Wagnerian *väg-nē′ri-ən, adj.* pertaining to or characterised by the ideas or style of Richard *Wagner* (1813–83), German composer of music-dramas: pertaining to Rudolf *Wagner* (1805–1864), physiologist. — *n.* a follower or admirer of Richard Wagner. — *adj.* **Wagneresque′.** — *ns.* **Wag′nerism, Wagne′rianism** the art theory of Richard Wagner, its main object being the freeing of opera from traditional and conventional forms, and its one canon, dramatic fitness; **Wag′nerist, Wag′nerite** an adherent of Wagner's musical methods.

wagon, waggon *wag′ən, n.* a four-wheeled vehicle, esp. one for carrying heavy goods: an open railway truck or a closed railway van: a movable piece of furniture

with shelves (see **dinner-wagon**): a chariot (*obs.*). — *v.t.* to transport by wagon. — *v.i.* to travel in a wagon. — *ns.* **wag′onage** conveyance by wagon, or money paid for it: a collection of wagons (*Carlyle*); **wag′oner, wagg′oner** one who drives a wagon: a charioteer (*obs.*); **wagonette′** a kind of carriage with one or two seats crosswise in front, and two back seats arranged lengthwise and facing inwards; **wag′onful.** — **wa′gon-box, -bed** the carrying part of a wagon; **wag′on-load** the load carried by a wagon: a great amount; **wag′on-lock** a kind of iron shoe or other device placed on the rear-wheel of a wagon to retard motion in going downhill; **wag′on-roof, -vault** a barrel vault; **wag′on-train** a collection or service of army vehicles for the conveyance of ammunition, provisions, the sick, etc.: a train of usu. horse-drawn wagons used by pioneer settlers to travel into new territory; **wag′onwright** a maker of wagons — **on (off) the wagon** (*slang*) abstaining (no longer abstaining) from alcohol; **the Wagon** Ursa Major; **the Wag(g)oner** the constellation Auriga. [Du. *wagen;* cf. O.E. *wægn,* Eng. **wain.**]

wagon-lit *vä-gɔ̄-lē′, n.* a sleeping-carriage on a continental train: — *pl.* **wagons-lit** (pron. as *sing.*; sometimes **wagon-lits**). [Fr. *wagon* (— Eng. **wagon**) *lit,* bed.]

wagtail *wag′tāl, n.* any bird of the *Motacilla* and *Dendronanthus* genera, forming with the pipits the family *Motacillidae* — so named from their constant wagging of the tail: applied also to other birds, as an American water-thrush and an Australian fly-catcher: (*contemptuously*) a pert or obsequious person (*obs.*): a harlot (*obs.*).

Wahabi, Wahabee *wä-hä′bē, n.* one of a sect of Muslims founded in Central Arabia about 1760 by Abd-el-*Wahhab* (1691–1787), whose aim was to restore primitive Islam. — Also **Waha′b(i)ite.** — *n.* **Waha′bi(i)sm** the doctrine and practices of the Wahabis.

wahine *wä-hē′ne, n.* a Maori woman. [Maori.]

wahoo[1] *wa-hōō′, n.* the burning bush (genus Euonymus or *Evonymus*), an ornamental shrub with scarlet-coated seeds. [Dakota Indian *wanhu.*]

wahoo[2] *wa-hōō′, n.* a Californian buckthorn (*Rhamnus purshiana*) which yields cascara sagrada: the winged elm, with hard-grained wood: also the rock-elm. [Creek Indian *ûhawhu.*]

wahoo[3] *wa-hōō′, n.* a large fast-moving marine food and game fish, *Acanthocybium solandri,* akin to the mackerel. [Origin unknown.]

waid, waide. Old spellings of **weighed,** *pa.t.* and *pa.p.* of **weigh:** in Shak., *Tam. Shrew* III, ii. 56 or 57 prob. for **swayed** (see **sway**).

waif[1] *wāf, n.* a piece of property found ownerless, as a strayed animal, or goods cast up by the tide (*Spens.*). **waift, weft;** also *fig.*): stolen goods abandoned by the thief (*obs.*): a homeless wanderer: a neglected ownerless child. — *adj.* (*Scot.*) vagabond, neglected. — *v.t.* (*rare;* in *pa.p.*) to cast up as a waif. — **waif and stray** strayed property — same as **waif** alone: (in *pl.*) homeless, destitute persons. [O.Fr. *waif;* prob. — Scand.; cf. O.N. *veif,* any flapping or waving thing.]

waif[2] *wāf, n.* a streak, puff — same as **waff**[2].

waift. See **waif**[1].

wail *wāl, v.i.* to lament or sorrow audibly, esp. with prolonged high-pitched mournful cries: of eyes, to weep (*Shak.*). — *v.t.* to bemoan: to grieve over. — *n.* the action of wailing: a cry of woe: an animal cry or mechanical sound suggesting this. — *n.* **wail′er.** — *adj.* **wail′ful** sorrowful: expressing woe. — *n.* and *adj.* **wail′ing.** — *adv.* **wail′ingly.** — **Wailing Wall** a wall in Jerusalem, fifty-nine feet high, a remnant of the western wall of the temple dating back to before the destruction of the city in 66 A.D., where Jews traditionally pray and from which they were excluded for a time. [M.E. *weilen, wailen;* cf. O.N. *væla.*]

wain *wān, n.* a wagon, esp. for hay or other agricultural produce (now usu. *poet.*): a chariot (*obs.*). — *v.t.* (*rare*) to carry. — *n.* **wain′age** the team and implements necessary for the cultivation of land: land under cultivation. — **wain′wright** one who makes wagons. — **the Lesser Wain** the constellation Ursa Minor, or the seven stars in it; **the Wain** Charles's Wain or the Lesser Wain. [O.E. *wægen, wæn* — *wegen,* to carry; cf. Du. *wagen,* Ger. *Wagen,* Eng. **wagon.**]

wainscot *wān′skot, -skət,* or *wen′, n.* fine oak for panelling, etc.: woodwork, esp. panelled, on an interior wall: similar lining of other material: the lower part of an interior wall when lined with material different from that on the upper part: a collector's name for certain noctuid moths. — *v.t.* to line with, or as if with, boards or panels: to grain in imitation of oak: — *pr.p.* **wain′scoting, wain′scotting;** *pa.t.* and *pa.p.* **wain′scoted, wain′scotted.** — *n.* **wain′scoting, wain′scotting** the act of lining with boards or panels: materials for making a wainscot: wainscots collectively. — **wainscot chair** a heavy oak chair with a panelled back, seat, etc. [Orig. perh. wood used for a partition in a wagon — Du. *wagen-schot,* oak-wood — *wagen,* wagon, or M.Du. *waeghe,* wave (from the appearance of the grain of the wood), *schot,* partition.]

waist *wāst, n.* the smallest part of the human trunk, between the ribs and the hips: a narrow middle part of an insect: the part of a garment that lies round the waist of the body: a woman's blouse or bodice (*U.S.*): the narrow middle part, as of a musical instrument: the middle part of a ship: the middle (of the day or night) (*obs.*): something that surrounds, a girdle (*obs.*). — *adj.* **waist′ed** having a waist, often of specified type. — *n.* **waist′er** a seaman stationed in the waist, performing menial duties, esp. a greenhand on a whaler. — **waist′-anch′or** an anchor stowed in the waist of a ship; **waist apron** an apron covering the body only from the waist down; **waist′band** part of a garment that fits the waist: a belt or sash; **waist′belt** a belt for the waist: **waist′boat** a boat carried in the waist of a vessel; **waist′cloth** a loin cloth: (in *pl.*) coloured cloths hung about a ship's waist as ceremonial decoration or to conceal the men in a naval action (*obs.*); **waist′coat** (*wās′, wāst′kōt; arch.,* now *dial., wes′kət*) a garment, plain or ornamental, reaching to or below the waist, and now sleeveless, intended to show partly, worn by men at different periods under doublet, coat, jacket, etc.: a woman's similar garment or front; **waistcoateer′** (*obs.*) a strumpet; **waist′coating** material for men's waistcoats, esp. of a fancy pattern. — *adjs.* **waist′-deep, -high** as deep, high, as to reach up to the waist. — **waist′line** a line thought of as marking the waist, but not fixed by anatomy in women's fashions: the measurement of a waist. [M.E. *wast,* from presumed O.E. *wæst,* growth, size; cf. Icel. *vöxtr,* O.E. *wæstm,* growth, Eng. **wax².**]

wait¹ *wāt, v.i.* to keep watch, be on guard (*Spens.* **waite;** *obs.*): to be on the watch for someone, lie in ambush (*obs.*): to be, remain, in expectation or readiness (with *for*): to be, remain, in a place in readiness (also **wait about, around):** to delay action: to be delayed: to be in attendance, or in readiness to carry out orders: to bring food to the table and clear away used dishes. — *v.t.* to watch, watch for, or lie in ambush for (*obs.*): to be, remain, in expectation of, await (*obs.*): to postpone, as a meal, for some purpose (*coll.*): to attend on, attend, escort (*obs.*). — *n.* an ambush — now used only in such phrases as *to lie in wait, to lay wait:* a watchman, sentinel, or spy (*obs.*): the act of waiting or of expecting: a delay: the period of attendance of a lord- or lady-in-waiting: (in *pl.*) musicians employed by a town to play on ceremonial occasions (*hist.*): (in *pl.*) persons who welcome in Christmas by playing or singing out of doors at night: a member of the town, or of a Christmas, band of waits. — *ns.* **wait′er** a watchman (*obs.*): a customs officer (*obs.*): one who waits, esp. at table in a hotel dining-room, etc.: an attending servant (*obs.*): a salver or tray: a dumb-waiter: a uniformed attendant at the London Stock Exchange; **wait′erage** (*rare*) service; **wait′erhood** (*rare*), **wait′ering** (*rare*) the employment of a waiter; **wait′ing**

the act of waiting: attendance. — Also *adj.* — *adv.* (*rare*) **wait′ingly.** — *n.* **wait′ress** a female waiter. — **wait′-a-bit** (also often *adj.*) a name given to various plants, esp. S. African (*Afrik.* **wag-'n-bietjie** *vuhh′ə(n)-bē-kē*) with thorns that catch the clothing of the passer-by; **wait′-a-while** a wait-a-bit: an Australian wattle growing in dense thickets; **wait′ing-list, wait′-list** a list of people waiting, as candidates awaiting a vacancy, etc.; **wait′ing-maid, -wom′an** a female attendant; **wait′ing-room** a room for the use of persons waiting; **wait′ing-vass′al** (*obs.*) an attendant; **wait′-list** see **waiting-list.** — *v.t.* to add someone's name to a waiting-list, esp. for a seat on an aircraft. — **wait′-on** see **wait on** below. — **lie in wait** to be in hiding ready to attack or surprise (*lit.* and *fig.*); **lords,** and **grooms, in waiting** certain officers in the Lord Chamberlain's department of the royal household; **minority waiter** meaning uncertain — perh. a waiter, or a tide-waiter, out of employment; **play a waiting game** (*lit.* and *fig.*) to avoid action as far as possible in the hope of having an opportunity later to use one's energies with maximum effect; **wait attendance** (*Shak.*) to remain in attendance; **wait off** (*racing*) to allow oneself to be temporarily outdistanced by other competitors, reserving one's energies for the final stretch; **wait on** to wait for (*dial.*): to continue to wait (*Scot.*): to wait upon: of a hawk, in falconry, to circle or hover in the air above the falconer's head (*n.* **wait′-on**); **wait table** to wait at table during a meal; **wait up** to stay out of bed waiting (with *for*); **wait upon, on** to call upon, visit formally: to accompany: to attend and serve: to be connected with or follow as a consequence: to carry out the duties of (an office; *B.*): to gaze at, keep under observation (*obs.*). [O.N.Fr. *waitier* (O.Fr. *guaitier,* Fr. *guetter*), to watch, attend; of Gmc. origin; cf. O.H.G. *wahta* (Ger. *Wacht*), a watchman; cog. with O.E. *wacan,* to watch.]

wait². See **wit¹.**

waive *wāv, v.t.* to put away, reject, to abandon, forsake, to vacate, to resign (*obs.*): to outlaw (a woman — her status in the eyes of the law being such that the usual term was not applicable to her) (*hist.*): to abandon (stolen goods) (*obs.*): to give up voluntarily, as a claim or a contention (*law*): to refrain from claiming, demanding, taking, or enforcing: to forgo: to evade, avoid (*arch.*): to defer, postpone: to leave out of consideration, disregard (*obs.*). — *n.* **wai′ver** the act, or an act, of waiving, or a written statement formally indicating this. [A.Fr. *weyver* — O.Fr. *guesver,* to abandon; from same root as **waif¹.**]

waivode, waiwode(ship). Same as **voivode,** etc.

wake¹ *wāk, v.i.* to be, or to remain, awake, or active or vigilant: to keep watch or vigil, or to pass the night in prayer: to hold a wake: to awake, be roused from, or as from, sleep, from indifference, etc. (often with *up*): to become animated or lively: to be stirred up, aroused: to hold a late revel (*obs.*). — *v.t.* to rouse from sleep: to keep vigil over: to excite, stir up: to disturb with noise: to animate: to reanimate, revive: — *pa.t.* **waked** (*wākt*) and **woke** (*wōk*); *pa.p.* **waked, wo′ken,** (*rare*) **woke.** — *n.* the act or state of waking (*obs.*, except in **sleep and/or wake, wake and/or dream**): a serenade (*James Hogg*): the feast of the dedication of a church, formerly kept by watching all night: a festival: (usu. in *pl.*) an annual holiday (*dial.*): a watch or vigil beside a corpse, sometimes with revelry. — *adj.* **wake′ful** not asleep: unable, or indisposed, to sleep: vigilant: waking: awakening or rousing (*Milt.*). — *adv.* **wake′fully.** — *n.* **wake′fulness.** — *adj.* **wake′less** sound, undisturbed. — *v.i.* **wā′ken** to be, or become, awake: to become active or lively: to remain awake, keep watch (*obs.*). — *v.t.* to rouse from sleep, unconsciousness, inaction: to excite, stir up, evoke. — *adj.* (*Scot.*) **waking,** awake. — *adj.* **wā′kened.** — *n.* **wā′kener** one who or that which wakens. — *adj.* **wā′kening.** — *n.* the act of one who wakens: the revival of an action (*Scots law*). — *ns.* **wā′ker** one who wakes; **wā′king.** — *adj.* that wakes, keeps watch, or is vigilant: that rouses or becomes awake: passed, or experienced, in the waking state. — **wake′man** (*arch.*) a watchman. — *adj.* **wake′rife** (*-rif, -rīf*; *Scot.*) useful: vigilant. — **wake′-robin** the cuckoo-pint, *Arum maculatum*: the spotted orchis, *Orchis maculata*: applied to various other flowers, esp. in U.S., to any of the genus Trillium; **waking hours** the period of the day during which one is normally awake. — **wake a night, the night** to remain awake, or be up and about, all night; **wake(n) to, wake up to** to become conscious of, alive to. [A combination of an O.E. strong verb *wacan*, to be born, to awake, and an O.E. weak verb *wacian*, to be awake, to watch; cf. **watch**.]

wake² *wāk, n.* the streak of smooth-looking or foamy water left in the track of a ship: disturbed air behind a flying body: a track on land (*rare*): a trail of light behind a moving body: the rear of, area passed through by, someone or something. — **in the wake of** (*fig.*) close behind: immediately after (usu. implying consequence). [Of Scand. origin; cf. O.N. *vök*, an ice hole, *vökr*, moist.]

wakiki *wä′kē-kē, n.* shell money. [Melanesian.]

Walachian. See **Wallachian**.

wald. See **weld¹**.

Waldenses *wol-den′sēz, n.pl.* a Christian community of austere morality and devotion to the simplicity of the Gospel, orig. followers of Peter *Waldo*, a merchant of Lyons and preacher in the second half of the 12th century; their chief centre was, and is, the Alps in S.E. France and Piedmont (also **Valdenses** (*val-*)). — *adj.* and *n.* **Walden′sian**.

waldflute *wöld′flōōt, n.* an organ flute stop usu. of 4-foot pitch. [Formed after Ger. *Waldflöte*, lit. forest flute.]

waldgrave *wöld′grāv, n.* in mediaeval Germany, a head forest-ranger: an old German title of nobility. — *n.* **waldgravine** (*wöld′grä-vēn*) the wife of a waldgrave. [Ger. *Waldgraf* — *Wald*, forest, *Graf*, count.]

waldhorn *wöld′hörn, n.* a hunting-horn, a French horn without valves: an organ reed-stop. [Ger.]

wale¹ *wāl, n.* same as **weal²**: a ridge on the surface of cloth: texture: a vertical ridge in knitted fabrics: a horizontal timber used to bind together piles driven in a row: (in *pl.*) planks all along the outer timbers on a ship's side, bends. — *v.t.* to mark with wales: to make or furnish with, or secure with, wales. [O.E. *walu*; cf. O.N. *völr*, a rod.]

wale² *wāl,* (*Scot.* and *North.*) *n.* the act of choosing: choice: the scope of choice: the pick or best. — *v.t.* and *v.i.* to choose, pick. [O.N. *val*, choice; Ger. *Wahl*, choice; from the root of **will¹**.]

waler *wā′lər,* n. in India, a horse imported from New South *Wales*, or from Australia generally.

Walhalla *val-hal′ə, n.* Same as **Valhalla**.

wali *wä′lē, n.* Same as **vali**.

Walian *wā′li-ən, adj.* of or pertaining to (North or South) *Wales* (as *North Walian* or *South Walian*). — *n.* a native or inhabitant of (North or South) Wales.

walise. Scottish form of **valise**.

walk *wök, v.i.* to roll, or to toss about (*obs.*): of a biped, to move along leisurely on foot with alternate steps, the walker always having at least one foot on the ground: of a quadruped, to move along in such a way that there are always at least two feet on the ground: to pace: to journey on foot: to ramble, go on foot for pleasure, etc.: of an inanimate object, to be in motion (*obs.*): to make progress (*naut.*): of the tongue, to wag (*obs.*): to make slow progress: to circulate, spread, be rife (*obs.*): to go restlessly about (as a ghost): to move: to behave in a certain way, follow a certain course: to move off, depart, withdraw: to conduct oneself, behave: to be associated and in concord (*obs.*): to go to first base after receiving four pitches (*baseball*): of an object, to disappear (*coll.*). — *v.t.* to pass through or upon, perambulate, traverse: to follow, trace out, on foot: to measure, wear out, etc. by walking: to go through (a dance) at a slow pace: to circulate (*obs.*): to full, as cloth or yarn (*dial.*): to cause to walk, or to

move as if walking: to lead or accompany by walking. — *n.* the action, or an act, of walking: a spell of walking, especially for pleasure: a perambulation in procession: a walking-race: a gait: that in or through which one walks: a possible or suitable route or course for walking: a path or place for walking: a tree-bordered avenue: a place for animals, as young hounds, to train or to exercise: a run for fowl: a place where a game-cock is kept: high pasture-ground (*obs.*): a division of a forest: a distance walked, or a distance as measured by the time taken to walk it: conduct: a course of life, sphere of action: a hawker's district or round: a hunting-ground (*obs.*): (in *pl.*) grounds, park (*obs.*): a flock of snipe or of wagtails. — *adj.* **walk′able**. — *n.* **walk′er** one who walks or takes part in walking-races: a colporteur or (*dial.*) a vagrant: a forester (*hist.*): one who trains and walks young hounds: any bird that walks, not hops: a stick-insect: any device which helps esp. babies and elderly people to walk: a man of good social standing who accompanies a female V.I.P. on official engagements in the absence of her husband (*U.S. slang*). — *interj.* (with *cap.*; also **Hook′ey Walk′er**; *arch. slang*) an exclamation of incredulity (also, as *n.*, humbug). — *n.* **walk′ing** the verbal noun of walk: pedestrianism: the sport of walking-races: the condition of a surface from the point of view of one who walks on it: the act or process of fulling cloth. — *adj.* that walks, or that moves as if walking: that oscillates: used in or for walking: performed by walking: worked by a person or animal who walks. — *adv.* **walk′about** on the move, as in *go walkabout*, esp. temporarily back into the bush (of Australian aborigines), or meeting the public on foot (of royalty, politicians, etc.). — *n.* a wandering, a journey: a walk by royalty, etc. in order to meet the public. — **walk′-around′** a dancing performance by Negroes in which a large circle is described: a march in procession about the stage (*theat.*): the music for either of these; **walk′-away** (*coll.*) an effortless victory; **walk′er-on′** one who plays parts in which he has nothing to say; **walk′ie-talk′ie, walk′y-talk′y** a portable radiotelephone transmitting and receiving set. — *adj.* **walk′-in** of a cupboard, etc., big enough to walk into and move around in. — **walk′ing-beam** a beam or oscillating lever for transmitting power, as that actuating the cable in cable-drilling for oil; **walking case** a patient not confined to bed; **walking fern** an American fern of the genus *Camptosorus*, whose frond tips take root when touching the ground; **walk′ing-fish** any of various fishes, mainly Asiatic, which are able to move about on land; **walk′ing-gentleman, -lady** an actor or actress playing very small non-speaking parts for which a good appearance is required; **walk′ing-leaf** a leaf-insect; **walk′ing-orders, -papers, -ticket** (*slang*) dismissal; **walk′ing-part** one in which the actor has nothing to say; **walk′ing-race** a race in which competitors must walk rather than run; **walk′ing-stick, -cane, -staff** a stick, cane, or staff used in walking; **walk′ing-stick, -straw, -twig** a stick-insect; **walk′ing-toad** a natterjack; **walk′-mill** a fulling-mill: a machine operated by the walking of a horse; **walk′-on** a walking-part. — *adj.* **walk′-on** of an air-service or aeroplane, for which one does not have to purchase a ticket in advance, the seats being non-bookable: pertaining to a walking-part. — **walk′-out** the act of walking out, usually to indicate disapproval: a sudden industrial strike; **walk′-over** a race where only one competitor appears, and has merely to cover the course to win: an easy or unopposed victory, usu. in sport; **walk′way** a road, path, etc., constructed for pedestrians only; **walky-talky** see **walkie-talkie** above. — **charity walk, sponsored walk** an organised walk in aid of charity, each participant having obtained from a sponsor or sponsors an agreement to contribute according to distance covered; **walk a tight-rope** to follow a narrow and difficult route beset with dangers, as if on a tight-rope; **walk away from** to outdistance or outdo easily: to have nothing more to do with; **walk away with** to win with ease; **walking wounded** casualties not requiring stretchers or not confined to bed (also *fig.*); **walk into** (*coll.*) to beat: to storm at: to eat heartily of: to collide or meet with unexpectedly; **walk it** (*coll.*) to succeed, win easily; **walk off** to leave: to depart: to get rid of by walking, as disagreeable feelings or effects; **walk off with** to take surreptitiously or feloniously: to win easily; **walk on** to walk ahead: to continue to walk: to have a walking-part; **walk on air** to be exultant or light-hearted; **walk one's chalks** to quit, go away without ceremony; **walk out** to leave, esp. as a gesture of disapproval: to strike; **walk out on** (*coll.*) to desert, leave in the lurch; **walk out with** to go for walks with as a stage of courtship (also **walk with**); **walk over** to cross, or traverse: to win an uncontested race: to have an easy victory or easy success (*coll.*): to disregard the rights or feelings of (*coll.*); **walk tall** (*coll.*) to be proud, have self-respect; **walk the chalk, chalkmark** to walk along a chalked line as a test of sobriety: to keep a correct course in manners or morals; **walk the hospitals** to be a student under clinical instruction at a general hospital or infirmary; **walk the plank** see **plank**; **walk the streets** to wander about in search of work, or simply aimlessly: to be a prostitute. [M.E. *walken, walkien*, to walk, to full — O.E. *wealcan*, to roll, revolve, *wealcian*, to roll up, curl; cog. with Ger. *walken*, to full cloth.]

Walkman® *wök'mən, n.* a small, portable cassette-recorder/radio with headphones, designed for personal use whilst walking, travelling, etc.: — *pl.* **Walkmans, -men.**

Walkyrie *vol'kir-i, -kir'*, also *wol-, val-, wal-*. Same as **Valkyrie.** [O.E. *wælcyri(g)e.*]

wall *wöl, n.* an erection of brick, stone, etc., for security or to enclose a space such as a piece of land: the side of a building or of a room: a very steep smooth rock face (*mountaineering*): (in *pl.*) fortifications: any bounding surface suggestive of a wall, e.g. the membranous covering or lining of an organ of the body or of a plant or animal cell: the side next to the wall: a defence, means of security (*fig.*): a barrier, e.g. that experienced physically and psychologically by long-distance runners (*fig.*): in mah-jongg, the arrangement of the tiles before the hands are drawn: in mining, one of the surfaces of rock enclosing the lode. — *v.t.* to enclose with, or as with, a wall: to fortify with, or as with, walls: to divide as by a wall. — **wall-** in composition, growing on, living in, for hanging on, or otherwise associated with, a wall. — *adj.* **walled** enclosed with a wall: fortified. — *ns.* **wall'er** one who builds walls; **wall'ing** walls collectively: materials for walls. — *adj.* **wall'-less.** — **wall bars** horizontal bars fixed to a wall, used by gymnasts; **wall'-board** building-board; **wall'covering** wallpaper, or anything used in the same way; **wall'-cress** rockcress, or any species of Arabis; **wall-eye** see separate entry; **wall'-facing** a facing for a wall; **wall'fish** a snail; **wall'flower** one of the Cruciferae, with fragrant flowers, yellow when wild, found on old walls: any other plant of the same genus (*Cheiranthus* or *Cheirinia*): a person who remains a spectator at a dance, usu. a woman who cannot obtain partners (*coll.*): a yellowish-red colour (also **wallflower brown); wall'-fruit** a fruit-tree growing against a wall: its fruit; **wall'-game** a variety of football played at Eton against a wall — 'at the wall' instead of 'in the field'; **wall'-gill'yflower** a wallflower; **wall'-knot** a nautical method of tying the strands at the end of a rope; **wall'-liz'ard, -newt** a common lizard living in the chinks of walls; **wall'-moss** a yellow lichen: the common stone-crop; **wall'-mustard, -rocket** a yellow-flowered cruciferous plant (*Diplotaxis*) of walls, quarries, etc.; **wall'-paint'ing** the decoration of walls with ornamental painted designs: a work of art painted on a wall; **wall'paper** paper, usually coloured or decorated, for pasting on the walls of a room: something of a bland or background nature, lacking originality or noteworthiness, etc. (*fig., coll.*); **wall pass** (*football*) a

one-two; **wall'-pepp'er** the common stonecrop; **wall'-plate** a horizontal piece of timber or of rolled steel on a wall, etc., to bear the ends of joists, etc.; **wall'-rue** a small fern growing on walls, etc., one of the spleen-worts; **wall'-space** space on a wall, e.g. on which to hang a picture; **Wall Street** a street in New York, the chief financial centre in the United States: hence, American financial interests; **Wall Streeter** a financier based in Wall Street. — *adj.* **wall'-to-wall** of carpets, etc., covering the entire floor: covering, crowding the entire room, space, etc., of an uninterrupted or monotonous nature (*fig.; coll.*). — **wall'-tree** a tree trained against a wall; **wall unit** a piece of furniture attached to or standing against a wall; **wall'-wort** a name applied to various plants growing on walls, as pellitory (*Parietaria officinalis*), wall-pepper, etc.: see also separate article. — **drive to the wall** to push to extremities; **go to the wall** (*obs.* **walls**) to be hard pressed: to be forced to give way: to fail, go under: to give precedence to something else; **hang by the wall** to remain unused; **push,** or **thrust, to the wall** to force to give place; **the wall** the right of taking the side of the road near the wall when encountering another person, as in the phrase to **give,** or **take, the wall; turn one's face to the wall** to resign oneself to death or despair; **up the wall** (*coll.*) mad, distracted; **wall a rope** to make a wall-knot on the end of a rope; **walls have ears** see **ear; wall up** to block with a wall: to entomb in a wall; **with one's back to the wall** in desperate straits: at bay. [O.E. *wall* (W.S. *weall*) — L. *vallum*, a rampart.]

walla. See **wallah.**

wallaba *wol'ə-bə, n.* a valuable caesalpiniaceous tree of the Guianas and Brazil, with durable streaked reddish wood. [Native name.]

wallaby *wol'əb-i, n.* any of a number of small marsupials of the family *Macropodidae.* — **on the wallaby, on the wallaby track** (*coll.; Austr.*) travelling through the bush with one's swag, esp. looking for work; **the Wallabies** the Australian national Rugby Union football team. [Native Austr. *wolabā.*]

Wallace's line *wol'is-iz līn*, a line passing through the East Indian group of islands between Bali and Lombok, roughly separating the very different faunas of the Oriental region and the Australian region, or rather a transitional region. [Alfred Russel *Wallace* (1823–1913), naturalist.]

Wallachian, Walachian *wol-ā'ki-ən, n.* a Vlach. — *adj.* of or pertaining to the region of Rumania which was formerly the principality of *Wal(l)achia*, or to the Vlach people.

wallah *wol'ə, -ə, n.* (often in combination) one employed in, or concerned with, a specific type of work: one who occupies an eminent position in an organisation, etc. — Also **wall'a.** — **competition wallah** a member of the Indian Civil Service who obtained appointment by the competitive system instituted in 1856. [Hindi -*wālā*, properly an adjectival suffix, in one sense comparable to L. *-ārius* or Eng. *-ar, -er, -or.*]

wallaroo *wol-ə-rōō', n.* a large kangaroo (*Macropus robustus*). — Also known as **euro.** [Aboriginal *wolarū.*]

wallet *wol'it, n.* a bag for carrying necessaries on a journey: a bag with the opening at the middle and a pouch at each end: a pocket-book, a small case for holding money, papers, etc.: a bag for tools: anything protuberant and hanging loosely (*Shak.*). [M.E. *walet*, poss. — *watel*, a bag of woven material; cf. **wattle**[1].]

wall-eye *wöl'ī, n.* an eye in which the iris is pale, or the white part is very large or noticeable (e.g. as the result of a squint): the disease of the eye called glaucoma: any of various fishes (*U.S.*). — *adj.* **wall'-eyed** very light grey in the eyes, or in one eye: having a divergent squint: having a staring or a blank expression or (*fig.*) appearance: glaring, fierce (*Shak.*). [The adj. is the earlier; O.N. *vagleygr*, perh. conn. with mod. Icel. *vagl*, a film over the eye.]

wallies. See **wally.**

Walloon wol-ōōn', adj. of or pertaining to a people living chiefly in southern Belgium and adjacent parts of eastern France, or to their language. — n. a man or woman of this people: their language, a dialect of French. [Fr. Wallon; of Gmc. origin, cog. with **Welsh, Walachian.**]

wallop wol'əp, v.i. to gallop (obs.): to move quickly but clumsily, noisily, and with effort: to flounder: to bubble and boil (perh. a different word): to flap about (Scot.). — v.t. (coll.) to beat soundly, thrash: to strike with force. — n. a gallop (obs.): a plunging movement (coll.): a heavy blow (coll.): physical or financial power (coll.): a flapping rag (Scot.): beer (slang). — adv. with a wallop: heavily or noisily. — ns. **wall'oper** one who or that which wallops: something extremely large or big (coll.); **wall'oping.** — adj. that wallops: extremely large or big, bouncing, whopping (coll.). — **wallop in a tow, tether** (Scot.) to be hanged. [O.N.Fr. waloper (Fr. galoper); cf. **gallop.**]

wallow¹ wol'ō, v.i. to roll about in mud, etc., as an animal does (implying enjoyment): to immerse or indulge oneself (in emotion, etc.): to flounder: in a bad sense, to live in filth or gross vice: to surge, heave, blow, well up, etc. — v.t. (obs.) to cause to wallow in lit. senses. — n. the act of wallowing: the place, or the filth, an animal wallows in: a hollow or depression suggestive of a wallowing-place: a rolling gait (obs.): the swell of the sea (poet.). — ns. **wall'ower; wall'owing.** — adj. that wallows: very rich (slang). [O.E. wealwian — L. volvĕre.]

wallow² wol'ō, (dial.) v.i. to fade away. — adj. **wall'owed** withered, faded. [O.E. wealwian.]

wallsend wölz'end, n. orig. coal dug at Wallsend (at the end of the Roman Wall) in Northumberland: later, coal of a certain quality and size.

wallwort wöl'wərt, n. dwarf elder (also called Danewort, Dane's blood, etc.), a plant with an offensive smell and taste: see also under **wall.** [O.E. wealhwyrt, wǽlwyrt — wealh, a foreigner, or (prob. orig.), from the belief that it grew on battlefields) wǽl, slaughter, and wyrt, a root, a plant.]

wally¹ wö'li, wa'li, (Scot.) adj. excellent, fine-looking, ample (a general term of commendation): made of china, glazed earthenware, etc.: tiled. — adv. (obs.) finely, well. — n, an ornament: (in pl.) finery: a showy trifle: china, glazed earthenware, etc. — also (in pl.) fragments of such used as children's playthings: (in pl.) dentures (slang). — pl. **wall'ies.** — Also **wa'ly.** [Ety. uncertain; perh. **wale²**.]

wally² wö'li, (also with cap.; slang) n. a hopelessly inept or foolish-looking person: generally, a fool. [Ety. uncertain; cf. **wallydrag**; perh. conn. with short form of the name Walter.]

wallydrag wol'i-drag, **wallydraigle** wol'i-drā-gl, (Scot.) ns. a person or animal that is feeble, worthless, or slovenly: the youngest of a family. [Poss. **waly²**, and **drag**, **draigle** (Scots form of **draggle**).]

walnut wöl'nut, n. a genus (Juglans) of beautiful trees, some yielding valuable furniture wood: their wood: the nut of the Common or English Walnut: walnut-juice. — adj. made from walnutwood: light brown in colour. — **wal'nut-juice** juice from the husk of walnuts, used to stain the skin; **wal'nutwood.** — **black walnut** a North American walnut, the timber of which is more valuable than that of common walnut, though the fruit is inferior. [O.E. walhhnutu — w(e)alh, foreigner, hnutu, a nut.]

Walpurgis night val-pûr'gis nīt, or -pōōr', the eve of the first of May, when witches, according to German popular superstition, rode on broomsticks and he-goats to hold revel with their master the devil, esp. on the Brocken in the Harz Mountains. [So called because 1 May is the day of St Walpurga, abbess of Heidenheim, who died about 778.]

walrus wöl'rəs, wol'rəs, n. an aquatic, web-footed, carnivorous animal, also called the morse or seahorse, allied to the seals, having the upper canine teeth developed into enormous tusks: a walrus moustache (coll.). — **walrus moustache** one with long drooping ends. [Du. walrus, walros, lit. whale horse; of Scand. origin.]

Walter Mitty. See **Mitty.**

Waltonian wol-tō'ni-ən, adj. of or pertaining to Izaak Walton (1593–1683), who wrote The Compleat Angler. — n. a disciple of Walton: an angler.

walty wol'ti, (naut.) adj. inclined to lean or roll over. [Obs. adj. walt, unsteady (— O.E. wealt, found only in unwealt, steady), and suff. -y.]

waltz wölts, wöls, n. orig. a German dance performed by couples with a rapid whirling motion: a slower circling dance, also in triple time: the music for such: a piece of instrumental music in 3–4 time (**concert waltz**). — v.i. to dance a waltz: to move trippingly, to whirl (slang; also v.t.): to walk quickly and arrogantly or determinedly (coll.; also v.t.). — ns. **waltz'er** one who waltzes: a waltzing mouse: a type of fairground roundabout in which the customers are spun while they are revolving; **waltz'ing.** — **waltzing mouse** a mouse of a breed that moves forward in small circles, not in a straight line. — **waltz into** to storm at; **waltz Matilda** see **Matilda.** [Ger. Walzer — walzen, to roll, dance.]

waly¹. See **wally¹.**

waly² wā'li, (Scot.) interj. alas! [**wellaway.**]

wamble wom'bl, (dial.) v.i. of intestines, stomach, to give the feeling of working or rolling: to quake: to twist or wriggle: to move unsteadily. — v.t. to turn round, or upside down, or over and over. — n. a rolling in the stomach: a feeling of nausea: an unsteady, rolling or staggering movement. — ns. **wam'bliness; wam'bling.** — Also adj. — adv. **wam'blingly.** — adj. **wam'bly** affected with, or causing, sickness: unsteady. — adj. **wam'ble-cropped** sick at stomach. [Perh. two or more verbs; cf. Dan. vamle, to feel sick, conn. with L. vomĕre, to vomit; also Norw. vamla, vamra, to stagger.]

wame wām, (dial.) n. the womb or (more frequently) the belly: a protuberant part or a hollow enclosed part. — Also (in 17th-cent. literature) wem(b), weamb. — adj. **wamed** having a wame (usu. of a specified kind). — n. **wame'ful** a bellyful. [Variant of **womb.**]

wammus. See **wamus.**

wampee wom-pē', n. an edible Asiatic fruit (Clausena; family Rutaceae) about the size of a large grape, with a hard yellow rind. [Chin. hwang-pī, lit. yellow skin.]

wampish wom'pish, (Scott) v.t. to brandish, flourish, wave about. — Also v.i. [Origin uncertain.]

wampum wom'pəm, wöm'pəm, n. a shortened form of the N. American Indian (Algonquian) name for beads made from shells, used as money, etc. — **wam'pumpeag** (-pēg) the word of which wampum is a shortened form — lit. white string of beads. — **wam'pum-belt** a belt consisting of shell beads so arranged as to convey a message, record a treaty, etc.

wampus. See **wamus.**

wamus wöm'əs, wom'əs, (U.S.) n. a kind of cardigan, or a strong jacket, buttoned at neck and wrists. — Also **wamm'us, wamp'us.** [Du. wammes — O.Fr. wambais, a military tunic orig. worn under armour.]

wan¹ won, adj. dark, gloomy (obs.): wanting colour: pale and sickly: faint. — n. (rare) wanness. — v.t. and v.i. to make or to become wan. — **wan'd** (Shak., Ant. and Cleo., II, i. 21) perh. for pa.p. **wanned.** — adv. **wan'ly.** — n. **wan'ness.** — adj. **wann'ish** somewhat wan. [O.E. wann, dark, lurid; not found in other Gmc. languages.]

wan² wan, old pa.t. of **win¹**: gained, or took (Spens.).

wanchancy, wanchancie won-chan'si, (Scot.) adj. unlucky, dangerous, or uncanny. [O.E. privative or negative pfx. wan- (of Gmc. origin; seen in mod. Du. and in Eng. **wanton**), **chance,** and suff. -y.]

wand wond, n. orig. something slender and supple, as a twig, or a thin stem or branch, or a young shoot of a willow used in basketmaking (now poet. and dial.): something slender and rigid as a light walking-cane (obs.), a rod of authority, a caduceus, a rod used by a fairy, a magician, a conjurer, a conductor, or a diviner: a measuring rod: a mark in archery.   [O.N. *vöndr*, a shoot of a tree; Dan. *vaand*.]

wander *won'dər*, *v.i.* to ramble or move with no definite object, or with no fixed course, or by a round-about way (*lit.* and *fig.*): to go astray, deviate from the right path or course, the subject of discussion, the object of attention, etc. (*lit.* and *fig.*): to lose one's way (*coll.*): to be incoherent in talk, disordered in mind, or delirious. — *v.t.* to traverse: to lead astray, or to bewilder (*coll.*). — *n.* a ramble, stroll. — *adj.* **wan'dered** astray: incoherent: bewildered. — *n.* **wan'derer** one who or that which wanders, esp. habitually or from inclination: (with *cap.*) a Covenanter who left his home to follow a dispossessed minister (*hist.*). — *adj.* and *n.* **wan'dering**. — *adv.* **wan'deringly**. — **Wandering Jew** a legendary Jew in folklore esp. of north-western Europe who cannot die but must wander till the Day of Judgment, for an insult offered to Christ on the way to the Crucifixion — names given him are *Cartaphilus*, *Ahasuerus*, *Buttadeus*, etc.; **wandering Jew** any of several trailing or creeping plants; **wandering sailor** a name given to various other similar plants; **wandering nerve** the vagus; **Wanderjahre** (*van'dər-yā-rə*; Ger.) years of journeymanship or of wandering; **wanderlust** (*won'dər-lust*; *van'dər-lŏŏst*) an urge to travel or to move from place to place; **wander plug** an electrical plug on a flexible wire capable of being inserted in any appropriate socket; **wan'der-year** a year spent in travel to complete training before settling down to a trade or profession.   [O.E. *wandrian*; Ger. *wandern*; allied to **wend**, and to **wind**[2].]

wanderoo *won-də-rŏŏ'*, *n.* usu. applied to the lion-tailed macaque, a native of the Malabar coast of India: properly, a langur of Sri Lanka.   [Sinhalese *wanderu*, monkey.]

wandle *won'dl*, (*dial.*) *adj.* supple, pliant, nimble. — Also **wanle, wannel**.   [Ety. uncertain.]

wandoo *won'dŏŏ*, *n.* a W. Australian eucalyptus (*Eucalyptus redunca*) having white bark and durable brown wood.   [Aboriginal.]

wane *wān*, *v.i.* to decrease in size, esp. of the moon — opp. to *wax* — or (*obs.*) to decrease in volume: to decline in power, prosperity, intensity, brightness, etc.: to draw to a close. — *n.* gradual decrease or decline (esp. in phrases, as **on the wane, in wane, in the, her, its wane),** or the time when this is taking place: a defective edge or corner on a plank of wood. — *adjs.* **waned** diminished: dying or dead; **wan'ey, wan'y**. — *adj.* and *n.* **wan'ing**.   [O.E. *wanian, wonian*, to lessen (O.N. *vana*) — *wana, wona* (also *wan, won*) deficient, lacking.]

wang[1] *wang*, (*obs.*) *n.* the cheek: a wang-tooth. — **wang'=tooth** a molar.   [O.E. *wange*.]

wang[2]. See **whang**[1].

wangan, wangun. See **wanigan**.

wangle *wang'gl*, (*coll.*) *v.t.* to obtain or accomplish by craft: to manipulate. — *v.i.* to use tricky methods to attain one's ends. — *n.* an exercise of such methods. — *ns.* **wang'ler; wang'ling**.   [Origin uncertain.]

wanhope *won'hōp*, (*obs.*) *n.* despair.   [Pfx. *wan-* (see **wanchancy**), **hope**.]

wanigan *won'i-gən*, *n.* in a lumber camp, a chest for supplies, or a kind of houseboat for loggers and their supplies: also the pay-office. — Also **wan'gan, wan'gun**.   [Algonquian.]

wanion *won'yən*, (Shak., Scott) *n.* found only in phrases — e.g. **with a (wild) wanion** with a vengeance, vehemently; **with a (wild) wanion to him** bad luck to him, a curse on him!   [Earlier (*in the*) *waniand*, (in the) waning (of the moon), i.e. in an unlucky time.]

wank *wangk*, (*vulg. slang*) *v.i.* (of men) to masturbate. — *n.* an act or instance of masturbation. — *n.* **wank'er** one who masturbates: a worthless, contemptible person.   [Origin unknown.]

Wankel engine *wang'kəl en'jin*, a rotary automobile engine having an approximately triangular central rotor turning in a close-fitting oval-shaped chamber rather than conventional pistons and cylinders.   [F. *Wankel* (b. 1902), the German engineer who invented it.]

wankle *wong'kl*, (*dial.*) *adj.* unstable, unsteady: changeable: not to be depended on.   [O.E. *wancol*; of Gmc. origin.]

wanle, wannel. See **wandle**.

wanness. See **wan**[1].

wannion. Same as **wanion**.

wannish. See **wan**[1].

wanrestful *won-rest'fŏŏl, -fl*, (*Scot.*) *adj.* restless.   [Pfx. *wan-* (see **wanchancy**), and **restful**.]

want[1] *wont, n.* the state or fact of being without or of having an insufficient quantity: absence or deficiency of necessities: poverty: (in *pl.*) difficult or straitened circumstances (*obs.*): a lack, deficiency: a blemish (*obs.*): a defect, feebleness, in intelligence (**have a want**; Scot.): (in *pl.*) requirements or desires. — *v.t.* to be destitute of or deficient in: to lack, be without (Shak., *Macbeth* III, vi. 8, *who cannot want*, for *who can want, the thought?*): to feel need of, desire: to require, need: to fall short (of something) by (a specified amount): to dispense with, do without (now *dial.*). — *v.i.* to be deficient, entirely lacking (*arch.*): to be in need or destitution: to lack (with *for*). — *n.* **want'age** (*U.S.*) deficiency, shortage. — *adj.* **want'ed** lacking: needed: desired: searched for, esp. by the police. — *n.* **want'er** one who wants. — *adj.* **want'ing** absent, missing, lacking: deficient (with *in*, or, *obs.*, with *of*): failing to help, do justice to, come up to (with *to*): slow to (with *infin.*; *obs.*): below the desired or expected standard (in the phrase **found wanting**): defective mentally (*dial.*): poor, needy (*obs.*). — Also *n.* — *prep.* without, lacking, less. — **want ad** (chiefly *U.S.*) a small advertisement, esp. in a newspaper, specifying goods, property, employment, etc. required by the advertiser; **want'-wit** a fool, one without sense. — Also *adj.* — **want in, out, up, down**, etc. (*Scot.*) to want to get in, out, etc.   [O.N. *vant*, neut. of *vanr*, lacking, and O.N. *vanta*, to lack.]

want[2] *wont*, (*dial.*) *n.* a mole. — **want'-catcher; want'hill**.   [O.E. *wand*; cf. Norw. *vand*; prob. same root as **wind**[2] and **wend**.]

wanthriven *won-thriv'n*, (*Scot.*) *adj.* stunted: ill-grown: emaciated.   [Pfx. *wan-*, wanting, **thriven**.]

wanton *won'tən*, *adj.* undisciplined, unruly, unmanageable (*obs.*): thoughtlessly cruel: self-indulgent, luxurious (*obs.*): lascivious, or (*obs.*) amorous: immoral, licentious, lewd: insolent, arrogant, merciless in power or prosperity (*obs.*): unprovoked, unjust, merciless: capricious (*arch.*): of persons, jovial (*obs.*): of animals and inanimate things, frisky, gay, moving freely or capriciously (*poet.*): growing luxuriantly (*poet.*): unrestrained, prodigal. — *n.* a spoilt child or pampered, effeminate person (*obs.*): a roguish, sportive child, animal, etc. (*obs.*): a lewd person, esp. female: a trifler. — *v.i.* to frolic: to play lasciviously, or amorously: to idle, go idly: to trifle: to indulge oneself, run into excesses: to grow luxuriantly, ramble unchecked. — *v.t.* to use wastefully, dissipate (also **wanton away).** — *v.i.* **wan'tonise, -ize** (*arch.*) to play the wanton. — *adv.* **wan'tonly**. — *n.* **wan'tonness**. — **play the wanton** to trifle, or (*obs.*) to behave lewdly.   [M.E. *wantowen* — pfx. *wan-* (prob. akin to **wane**), O.E. *togen*, pa.p. of *tēon*, to draw, lead, educate; cf. Ger. *ungezogen*, ill-bred, rude.]

wanty *won'ti*, *n.* a belt used to secure a load on a pack-horse's back (*obs.*): the belly-band of a shafthorse (*dial.*): a short rope, esp. one used for binding hay on a cart (*dial.*).   [**wame**, and **tie**.]

wanworth *won'wûrth*, (*Scot.*) *n.* a very low price: a bargain. — *adj.* **wanword'y** worthless: unworthy.   [Pfx. *wan-*, wanting, **worth**[1].]

wanze *wonz*, (*obs.*) *v.i.* to decrease, waste away.   [O.E. *wansian*.]

wap[1] *wop*, *v.t.* to throw, pull, quickly or roughly (*dial.*): to strike, drub (*coll.*): to flap (*Scot.*): — *pr.p.* **wapp'ing**; *pa.t.* and *pa.p.* **wapped**. — *n.* a smart blow: a shake, flap (*Scot.*): a blast, storm (*Scot.*): a fight, quarrel (*Scot.*). [Cf. **whop.**]

wap² *wop, v.t.* (*obs.*) to wrap, bind. — *n.* (*dial.*) a turn of a string with which anything is tied: a bundle of hay. [Ety. uncertain.]

wapens(c)haw. See **wappens(c)haw.**

wapentake *wop'n-tāk,* (esp. *hist.*) *n.* a name given in Yorkshire and certain other shires to a territorial division of the county similar to the *hundred* of southern counties. [Late O.E. *wǣpen(ge)tæc,* O.N. *vāpnatak,* lit. weapon-taking, assent at a meeting being signified by brandishing a weapon.]

wapins(c)haw. See **wappens(c)haw.**

wapiti *wop'i-ti, n.* a species (*Cervus canadensis*) of deer of large size, native to N. America. [Algonquian.]

wappend *wop'nd, adj.* (Shak., *Timon,* IV, ii. 38) perh. for *wappered* (now *dial.*), fatigued, tired; perh. meaning incontinent, unchaste, and conn. with *obs.* sense of **wap¹** , to copulate.

wappens(c)haw *wop'n-shö, wap', n.* in Scottish usage, a periodical gathering of the people within an area for the purpose of seeing that each man was armed in accordance with his rank, and ready to take the field when required (*hist.*): a rifle-shooting competition (in *S.Afr.* equivalent to Du. *wapenschouwing*). — Also **wap'ens(c)haw, wap'ins(c)haw, weap'on-s(c)haw.** — *ns.* **wapp'ens(c)hawing** (app. an older form than wappenshaw), **weap'on-s(c)hawing.** [See **weapon, show.**]

wapper *wop'ər,* (*dial.*) *v.i.* to blink: to move tremulously. — *adj.* **wapp'er-eyed** blinking. — *n.* **wapp'er-jaw** a projecting under-jaw. — *adj.* **wapp'er-jawed.** [Cf. Du. *wapperen,* to oscillate.]

war¹ *wör, n.* a state of conflict: a contest between states, or between parties within a state (**civil war**) carried on by arms: any long-continued struggle, often against or between impersonal forces (*fig.*): fighting (*poet.*): open hostility: the profession of arms: an army, or war equipment (*rare; poet.*): a contest, conflict. — *v.i.* to make war: to carry on war: to contend: — *pr.p.* **warr'ing;** *pa.t.* and *pa.p.* **warred.** — *adj.* of, characteristic of, resulting from, or relating to war. — *adj.* **war'like** of or pertaining to war: martial, military: equipped for fighting (*obs.*): intended for use in war (*obs.*): fond of war: bellicose. — *ns.* **war'likeness; warr'ior** a skilled fighting man (*poet.*, except when used of one at an early stage of civilisation): a redoubtable person: — *fem.* **warr'ioress** (*rare*). — **war baby** a baby born during a war, esp. a serviceman's illegitimate child: any discreditable or troublesome result of war; **war bonnet** a head-dress, often with long trailing chains of feathers, worn by members of certain N. American Indian tribes; **war bride** a soldier's bride, met as a result of wartime movements or postings; **war chest** funds set aside to pay for a war, political campaign, etc.; **war cloud** a cloud of smoke and dust over a battlefield: a sign that war is threatening or impending (*fig.*); **war correspondent** a journalist or other person assigned to a seat of war so as to give first-hand reports of events; **war crime** one connected with war, esp. one that violates the code of war; **war'-cry** a cry used in battle for encouragement or as a signal: a slogan (*fig.*); **war dance** a dance engaged in by some savage tribes before going to war: a dance imitating the actions of a battle; **War Department** the name borne from 1784–1857 by what became the War Office — still used in speaking of property, as stores or land; **war'dog** a dog used in war: an old warrior: a war hawk; **war'-drum** a drum beaten as a summons to war, or during a battle: a sign of impending war (*fig.*); **war'fare** (from **fare,** *n.*) an engaging in, waging, or carrying on of war: an armed contest: conflict or struggle of any kind (*fig.*). — *v.i.* (*obs.; lit.* and *fig.*) to wage war. — *n.* **war'farer.** — *adj.* and *n.* **war'faring.** — **war'-game** a mock or imaginary battle or military exercise used to train personnel in tactics, a kriegspiel: a game, esp. with detailed rules and using models, in which players enact historical or imaginary battles, etc.; **war'-god, -godd'ess** a deity who

presides over war, assigning victory or defeat, etc.; **war hawk** one who is eager for war; **war'head, war'-head** the section of a torpedo or other missile containing the explosive material; **war'-horse** a charger, a horse used in battle: an old warrior in any field of conflict, or any standard, familiar, rather hackneyed piece of music, etc. (*fig.*); **war kettle** among Red Indians, a kettle set on the fire as part of the ceremony of going to war; **war loan** a loan raised to pay for a war; **war'lord** a commander or commander-in-chief, esp. where and when the military power is great — now usu. derogatory; **war machine** a machine used in warfare: the combined technical and administrative military resources mobilised by a country, alliance, etc. in order to engage in war; **war'man** (*rare*) a warrior; **war memorial** a monument erected to the memory of those (esp. from a particular locality) who died in a war; **war'monger** a mercenary soldier (*Spens.*): one who encourages war, esp. for personal gain; **war'mongering; war neurosis** a better term for shellshock; **war note** (*poet.*) a summons to war; **War Office** a department of the civil government, formerly headed by the Secretary of State for War, since 1964 absorbed in the Ministry of Defence: premises of the department in Whitehall; **war paint** paint applied to the face and person by savages, indicating that they are going to war: full-dress, or finery, esp. a woman's make-up (*coll.*); **war'path** among the Red Indians, the path followed on a military expedition: the expedition itself: **in on the warpath** (*fig.*) engaged in conflict, in a mood for battle; **war'plane** any aircraft designed or intended for use in warfare; **war'-proof** (*rare*) a valour proved in war. — *adj.* able to withstand attack. — **war'ship** an armed vessel for use in war; **war'-song** a song sung by men about to fight: a song celebrating brave deeds in war; **war'time** a period during which a war is being fought. — *adj.* of or pertaining to, characteristic of, a time of war. — **war trial** the trial of a person accused of war crimes. — *adjs.* **war'-wast'ed** ravaged by war; **war'-wea'ried, -wea'ry** wearied with, or tired of, war. — **war'-whoop** a cry uttered on going into battle; **war widow** a woman whose husband has been killed in war; **war'-wolf** a mediaeval siege engine: a fierce warrior (*Scott*; but see also **werewolf**). — *adj.* **war'-worn** worn, wasted, ravaged, marked, wearied, by war. — **carry the war into the enemy's camp, country** to take the offensive boldly (*lit.* and *fig.*); **civil war** see **civil; cold war** an intense, remorseless struggle for the upper hand by all means short of actual fighting; **declare war (on, against)** to announce formally that one is about to begin hostilities: to set oneself to get rid of (*fig.*); **go to war** to resort to armed conflict; **go to the wars** (*arch.*) to go to fight in a foreign country; **have been in the wars** (*fig.*) to show signs of having been knocked about; **holy war** see **holy; make, wage, war** to carry on hostilities; **private war** warfare between persons in their individual capacity, as by duelling, family feuds, etc.; **total war** war with every weapon at the combatant's disposal, sticking at nothing and sparing no-one; **war of nerves** systematic attempts to undermine morale by means of threats, rumours and counter-rumours, etc. [Late O.E. *werre* — O.N.Fr. *werre* (O.Fr. and Fr. *guerre*) — O.H.G. *werra,* quarrel.]

war² *wär, wör,* **warre** (*Spens.*; now *Scot.* and *North.* **waur** *wör*) *adj.* and *adv.* worse: — *superl.* **warst, waurst.** — *v.t.* (*Scot.*) to defeat, worst: to excel. [O.N. *verre.*]

waratah *wor'ə-ta, n.* any of a genus of Australian proteaceous shrubs with very showy flowers (*Telopea*). [Aboriginal.]

warble¹ *wör'bl, v.i.* to sing in a quavering way, or with variations (sometimes used disparagingly): to sing sweetly as birds do: to make, or to be produced as, a sweet quavering sound: to yodel (*U.S.*). — *v.t.* to sing in a vibratory manner, or sweetly: to express, or to extol, in poetry or song: to cause to vibrate or sound musically. — *n.* the action, or an act, of warbling: a quavering modulation of the voice: a song. — *n.*

war′bler one that warbles: a songster: a singing-bird: any bird of the family *Sylviidae* — willow-wren, reed-warbler, whitethroat, blackcap, etc.: any of numerous small, brightly-coloured American birds of a different family, *Parulidae*: a whistle used in infant classes, etc.: in bagpipe music, an ornamental group of grace-notes. — *n.* and *adj.* **war′bling.** — *adv.* **war′blingly.** [O.N.Fr. *werbler* (O.Fr. *guerbler*); of Gmc. origin.]

warble[2] *wör′bl, n.* a small hard swelling on a horse's back, caused by the galling of the saddle, etc.: a swelling caused by a warble fly or a botfly. — **warble fly** any of several flies of the same family as botflies whose larvae cause painful swellings that spoil the hides of horses, cattle, etc. [Ety. uncertain.]

warby *wör′bi*, (*Austr. coll.*) *adj.* worn-out, decrepit, unattractive: unwell, unsteady. [Poss. from Eng. dial. *warbie*, a maggot.]

ward *wörd*, *v.t.* to watch over, guard (*arch.*): to protect (with *from*) (*arch.*): to parry or keep away (now usually **ward off**): to enclose, as machinery, in order to prevent accidents (*rare*): to place in a ward. — *v.i.* to act on the defensive. — *n.* an act of watching or guarding: the state of being guarded: a look-out, watch: care, protection: guardianship: custody: in feudal times, control of the lands of a minor: a person, as a minor, under a guardian: a body of guards: a guarded place, as a court of a castle (**inner** and **outer ward**): a means of guarding, as a bolt, bar: a part of a lock of special configuration to prevent its being turned by any except a particular key, or the part of the key of corresponding configuration: a defensive motion or position (*fencing*; also *fig.*): a division of a county (*Scot.* and *North.*): an administrative, electoral, etc. division of a town, etc.: a division of an army (*obs.*; *van(t)ward* (vanguard), *middle ward, rearward* (rear-guard)): a division or department of a prison: a room with several beds in a hospital, etc.: the patients in a ward collectively. — *adj.* **ward′ed** (of a lock, key) having a ward or wards. — *n.* **ward′en** one who guards or keeps people, animals or things (esp. buildings): a gatekeeper or sentinel (*rare*): a regent (*hist.*): the governor of a town, district, etc. (*hist.*): a title of certain officers of the crown: a member of certain governing bodies: a superintendent: the head of certain institutions, as schools, colleges, hostels, etc.: one appointed for duties among the civil population in cases of fire or air-raids or to control traffic circulation and parking of motor vehicles. — *v.t.* (*rare*) to guard as a warden. — *ns.* **ward′enry** (*rare*) the office of, or district in the charge of, a warden: guardianship (*Thomas Hardy*); **ward′enship** the office of warden; **ward′er** one who guards or keeps: one in charge of prisoners in a jail (*fem.* **ward′ress**) — now officially a 'prison officer': a staff, baton, of authority (*hist.*). — *v.t.* to guard as a warder. — *n.* and *adj.* **ward′ing.** — *n.* **ward′ship** the office of, or the state of being under, a guardian: protection, custody (*fig.*): the state of being in guardianship (*fig.*): in English feudal law, the guardianship which the feudal lord had of the land of his vassal while the latter was a minor. — **ward′-corn** (*hist.*) a payment in corn in lieu of military service: misunderstood as the duty of keeping watch in order to give the alarm by blowing a horn; **ward′= mote** a meeting of ward, or of a court of a ward; **ward′robe** a room or a piece of furniture for containing clothes or theatrical costumes: one's stock of wearing apparel: raiment — of colours, flowers, etc. (*fig.*; *Milt.*); **ward′rop**: a department of a royal or noble household having charge of robes, wearing apparel, jewels, etc.; **wardrobe mistress** one who looks after the theatrical costumes of a company or of an individual actor or actress; **ward′rober** (*hist.*) one in charge of a royal or noble wardrobe; **wardrobe trunk** a trunk in which clothing may be hung as in a wardrobe; **ward′-room** the mess-room of the officers of a warship: the officers collectively. — **ward in Chancery** a minor under the protection of the Court of Chancery; **Warden of the**

Cinque Ports, or **Lord Warden (of the Cinque Ports),** the governor of the Cinque Ports, having the authority of an admiral and the power to hold a court of admiralty; **Wardens of the Marches** officers formerly appointed to keep order in the marches or border districts of England and Scotland. [O.E. *weardian*; cf. Ger. *warten*, to wait, attend, take care of.]

-ward(s) *-wərd(z), -wörd(z), suffs.* forming adjs. and advs. with the sense of motion towards. [O.E. *-weard* (gen. *-weardes*), cog. with Ger. *-wärts*; conn. with O.E. *weorthan*, to become, L. *vertĕre*, to turn.]

warden[1] *wör′dn, n.* a kind of pear used esp. in cooking. — **warden pie** a pie made of warden pears. [Origin uncertain; perh. — A.Fr. *warder* (Fr. *garder*), to keep.]

warden[2]. See **ward**.

Wardian *wör′di-ən, adj.* denoting a kind of glass case for transporting delicate ferns and other such plants, or for keeping them indoors. [Nathaniel Bagshaw *Ward* (1791–1868), the inventor.]

Wardour Street English *wör′dər strēt ing′glish*, sham-antique diction, as in some historical novels — from *Wardour Street*, London, once noted for antique and imitation-antique furniture; now given over to the business side of entertainment, esp. of films.

wardrobe, wardrop. See **ward**.

ware[1] *wār, n.* (now usu. in *pl.*) articles of merchandise or (*dial.*) produce collectively: an article of merchandise (*rare*): pottery, as **Delftware, Wedgwood ware** (see **delf, Wedgwood**): articles of fine workmanship, as **Benares ware,** ornamental metal-work from India: in composition, with defining word, articles of the same type or material, as *hardware, earthenware.* — *n.* **ware′house** a building or room for storing goods: a shop. — *v.t.* (*-howz*) to deposit in a warehouse, esp. a bonded warehouse: to store up (*fig.*). — *n.* **ware′housing** act of depositing goods in a warehouse: the practice of covertly building up a block of company shares, using one or more front companies, etc. to obtain shares on behalf of the true purchaser (*Stock exchange slang*). — **ware′houseman** a man who keeps, or is employed in, a warehouse or a wholesale store; **ware′housing system** the plan of allowing importers of dutiable goods to store them in a government warehouse without payment of duties until ready to bring the goods into market; **ware potatoes** large potatoes sold to the public for consumption, as opposed to seed-potatoes (q.v.). [O.E. *waru*; cf. Ger. *Ware*.]

ware[2] *wār*, (*Scot.* and *dial.*) *n.* springtime. [O.N. *vár.*]

ware[3] *wār, adj.* aware (*arch.*): wary, cautious (*arch.*; sometimes with *of*): prudent (*arch.*; esp. in phrase **ware and wise**). — *v.i.* and *v.t.* (*arch.*; usu. in *imper.*) to beware, beware of: in hunting, to avoid, refrain from riding over, etc. (sometimes *wör*). — *adj.* **ware′less** (*arch.*) incautious: unaware (with *of*). — *adv.* **wār′ily.** — *ns.* **wār′iment** (*Spens.*) wariness; **wār′iness.** — *adj.* **wār′y** guarding against deception or danger: cautious: circumspect: thrifty (*obs.*). — **be wary of** to show caution in regard to. [O.E. *wær*; cf. O.N. *varr*; see **aware.**]

ware[4] *wār*, (*Scot.* and *dial.*) *n.* seaware, seaweed. [O.E. *wār*; cf. **ore**[2].]

ware[5] *wār*, arch. *pa.t.* of **wear.**

ware[6] *wār*, (*Scot.*) *v.t.* to spend. [O.N. *verja*, to clothe, hence to invest; cf. **wear**[1].]

warehouse, etc. See **ware**[1].

wareless. See **ware**[3].

warfare. See **war**[1].

warfarin *wör′fə-rin, n.* a crystalline insoluble substance ($C_{19}H_{16}O_4$) used as a rodenticide and (in the form of its sodium salt) as a medical anticoagulant. [*Wis*consin *A*lumni *R*esearch *F*oundation (the patent owners) and coum*arin.*]

warhable *wör-hā′bl*, (*Spens.*) *adj.* fit for war. [**war**, and **able.**]

warily, wariment, wariness, etc. See **ware**[3].

warison, warrison *wor′, war′i-sən*, (*obs.*) *n.* wealth: reward or punishment: used by Scott erroneously for a note of assault. [O.N.Fr. (O.Fr. *guarison*) — *warir*, to guard; cf. **garrison.**]

wark *wörk*, Scots form of **work** (*n.*).

warling *wör'ling*, (*obs.*) *n.* one who is disliked — in the proverb 'It is better to be an old man's darling than a young man's warling'. [Prob. formed to rhyme with 'darling'.]

warlock *wör'lok, n.* a wizard: a magician (*Scot.*): a demon: a warrior who cannot be wounded with metals (*Dryden*, erroneously). — *n.* **war'lockry** sorcery. [O.E. *wǣrloga*, a breaker of an agreement — *wǣr*, a compact, *lēogan*, to lie; the ending -(*c*)*k* appears earliest in Scots.]

warlord. See **war**[1].

warm *wörm, adj.* having moderate heat: hot: imparting heat or a sensation of heat: retaining heat: affecting one, pleasantly or unpleasantly, as heat does (*fig.*): strenuous: harassing: characterised by danger or difficulty: passionate: angry: excited: ardent, enthusiastic: lively, glowing: affectionate: amorous: indelicate (*coll.*): comfortable, well-to-do (*coll.*): of a colour, containing red or, sometimes, yellow: esp. in a game, close to discovery or attainment: of a scent or trail, fresh. — *v.t.* to make warmer: to interest: to excite: to impart brightness or suggestion of life to: to beat (*coll.*). — *v.i.* to become warm or ardent: (with *to*) to begin to enjoy, approve of, feel enthusiastic about or fond of. — *n.* a beating (*coll.*): an officer's thick overcoat (also **British warm**): a warm area, environment (*coll.*): an act or instance of warming up or being warmed up (*coll.*). — *adv.* **warmly.** — *adj.* **warmed.** — *ns.* **warm'er; warm'ing** the action of making or becoming warm: a beating (*slang*). — *adv.* **warm'ly.** — *ns.* **warm'ness; warmth.** — *adj.* **Warm'blood** a race of horse developed from pedigree bloodlines from native European mares for competition jumping and dressage: (also without *cap.*) a horse of this type. — Also *adj.* — *adjs.* **warm'-blood'ed** homothermous, idiothermous, having bodily temperature constantly maintained at a point usu. above the environmental temperature: ardent, passionate; **warmed'-o'ver** (*U.S.*), **-up'** heated anew. — **warm front** (*meteor.*) the advancing front of a mass of warm air. — *adj.* **warm'-heart'ed** affectionate: hearty: sympathetic: generous. — **warm'-heart'edness; warm'ing-pan** a covered pan, with a long handle, for holding live coals to warm a bed: a person put into a situation to hold it till another is able to take it; **warm'-up** a practice exercise before an event: a preliminary entertainment, etc. intended to increase the excitement or enthusiasm of the audience. — **a warm reception** (*fig.*) display of hostility: a vigorous resistance or attack; **keep a place warm** to occupy or hold it for someone until he is ready to fill it himself; **warm up** to make or become warm: to heat, as cooked food: to become animated, interested, or eager: to limber up prior to any athletic event, contest, etc. [O.E. *wearm*; cf. Ger. *warm*.]

warn[1] *wörn, v.t.* to give notice of danger or evil to: to notify in advance: to caution (with *against*): to instruct, command: to summon: to bid, instruct, to go or to keep away (with *off, away,* etc.; *lit.* and *fig.*): to admonish: to forbid (*obs.*). — *v.i.* to give warning — specif., of a clock about to strike. — *ns.* **warn'er; warn'ing** a caution against danger, etc.: something that gives this: previous notice: notice to quit, of the termination of an engagement, etc.: a summons: call: an admonition: the sound accompanying the partial unlocking of the striking train, just before a clock strikes. — Also *adj.* — *adv.* **warn'ingly.** — **warning coloration** conspicuous coloration on an animal to deter potential attackers, such as the gaudy colours of some stinging insects. [O.E. *warnian, warenian, wearnian,* to caution (cf. Ger. *warnen*), and perh. in part *wiernan,* to refuse, forbid.]

warn[2] *wörn,* (*Shak.* and *dial.*) *v.t.* to warrant.

warp *wörp, v.t.* to cast, throw (*obs.*): to lay (eggs), or to bring forth (young), esp. prematurely (*dial.*): to twist out of shape: to turn from the right course: to distort:

to cause to contract or wrinkle (*Shak.*): to pervert, as the mind or character: to misinterpret, give a deliberately false meaning to: to arrange, as threads, so as to form a warp: to entwine (*obs.*): to move, as a vessel, by hauling on ropes attached to posts on a wharf, etc.: to improve (land) by flooding so that it is covered by a deposit of alluvial mud: to choke, as a channel, with alluvial mud: in rope-making, to stretch into lengths for tarring. — *v.i.* to be twisted out of shape: to become perverted or distorted (*fig.*): to swerve: to move with effort, or on a zigzag course: of cattle, sheep, etc., to miscarry. — *n.* the state or fact of being warped: the permanent distortion of a timber, etc.: a mental twist or bias (*fig.*): the threads stretched out lengthwise in a loom to be crossed by a woof (also *fig.*): a twist, shift or displacement to a different or parallel position within a (usu. conceptual) framework, scale, etc. (as *time-warp*): a rope used in towing, one end being fastened to a fixed object: alluvial sediment: a reckoning of four (herrings, oysters, etc.), thirty-three warps making a long hundred, and five long hundreds a mease or maze. — *adj.* **warped** twisted by shrinking: distorted: perverted: covered or filled with a deposit of alluvial sediment. — *ns.* **war'per; war'ping.** [O.E. *weorpan, werpan*; cf. Ger. *werfen*, O.N. *verpa*.]

warragal, warragle, warragul. See **warrigal**.

warran(d). Obs. forms of **warrant**[1].

warrant[1] *wor'ənt, v.t.* to protect, defend, keep (*obs.*): to give assurance against danger, etc. (*rare*; with *against, from*): to secure, guarantee the possession of, to: to guarantee to be as specified or alleged: to attest, guarantee, the truth of — (*coll.*) equivalent to 'to be sure, be convinced', 'to be bound' (also in phrases **I (I'll) warrant you, I warrant me**): to predict or to presage (*obs.*): to authorise: to justify, be adequate grounds for. — *n.* a defender (*obs.*): a defence (*obs.*): one who or that which vouches, a guaranty: a pledge, assurance: a proof: that which authorises: a writ for arresting a person or for carrying a judgment into execution, or for seizing or searching property: in the services, an official certificate inferior to a commission, i.e. appointing a non-commissioned officer: authorisation: justification: a writing authorising the payment of money or certifying payment due, etc.: a form of warehouse receipt for goods: a voucher (*obs.*): a document issued to a stockholder entitling him to buy further stock at a stated price. — *n.* **warr'andice** (-*dis*; *Scot.; arch.*) a guarantee: a clause in a deed by which the grantor binds himself to make good to the grantee the right conveyed. — *adj.* **warr'antable** that may be permitted: justifiable: of good warrant, estimable (*obs.*): of sufficient age to be hunted. — *n.* **warr'-antableness.** — *adv.* **warr'antably.** — *adj.* **warr'anted.** — *ns.* **warrantee'** one to whom a warranty is given; **warr'anter** one who authorises or guarantees: a warrantor; **warr'anting; warr'antise** (-*tīz*; *obs.* or *arch.*) an act of guaranteeing: a guarantee: assurance: authorisation; **warr'antor** (*law*) one who gives warranty: a warranter; **warr'anty** (*law*) an act of warranting, esp. in feudal times the covenant by which the grantor of land warranted the security of the title to the recipient (**general warranty** against the claims of all and every person; **special warranty** against the claims of the grantor, or others claiming through or by him): an undertaking or assurance expressed or implied in certain contracts: a guarantee: authorisation: justification: evidence. — **warr'ant-off'icer** in the services, an officer holding a warrant (see also **branch-officer**): a police officer whose duty it is to serve warrants. — **distress warrant** a warrant authorising distraining of goods; **general warrant** a warrant for the arrest of suspected persons, no specific individual being named or described in it; **of (good) warrant** (*obs.*) esteemed, important; **of warrant** (*obs.*) allowed, warranted; **out of warrant** (*obs.*) not allowed; **take warrant on oneself** (*arch.*) to make oneself responsible; **warrant of attachment** a writ authorising the seizure of property; **warrant**

of attorney see **attorney**. [O.Fr. *warantir* (*guarantir*); of Gmc. origin.]

warrant[2] *wor'ənt, n.* in coal-mining, underclay. [Perh. the same as **warrant**[1].]

warray *wör-ā', (obs.) v.t.* to make war upon. — *v.i.* to make war. — Also **warrey'**. [O.Fr. *werreier* (*guerreier*).]

warre. See **war**[2].

warren *wor'ən, n.* a piece of ground kept for breeding game, esp. hares, rabbits, partridges, etc. (**beasts, fowls, of warren;** *hist.*): the right of keeping or of hunting this (*hist.*): a series of interconnected rabbit burrows: the rabbits living there: a densely-populated slum dwelling or district: a maze of narrow passages. — *n.* **warr'ener** the keeper of a warren (*hist.*): one who lives in a warren. [A.Fr. *warenne* (O.Fr. *garenne*), of Gmc. origin.]

warrey. See **warray**.

warrigal *wor'i-gal, wor'ə-gl, n.* the Australian wild dog, the dingo: a wild Australian horse. — *adj.* wild, savage. — Also **warr'agal, warr'agle, warr'agul**. [Aboriginal.]

warrior, warship. See under **war**[1].

warrison. See **warison**.

warsle *wörs'l.* Scots form of **wrestle**.

warst. See **war**[2].

wart *wört, n.* a small, hard excrescence on the skin: a small protuberance. — *adjs.* **wart'ed; wart'less; wart'y** like a wart: overgrown with warts. — **wart'-cress** swine's-cress; **wart'-hog** any of a genus of wild hogs found in Africa, with large wart-like excrescences on their cheeks; **wart'weed** a kind of spurge (its caustic juice thought to cure warts); **wart'wort** any of a family of lichens having a warty thallus: a wartweed. — **warts and all** with blemishes or shortcomings known and accepted. [O.E. *wearte*; Ger. *Warze*; prob. allied to L. *verrūca*.]

wartime. See **war**[1].

warwolf. See **werewolf**.

war-wolf. See **war**[1].

wary. See **ware**[3].

was *woz,* used as the *1st* and *3rd pers. sing.* of the *pa.t.* of the verb **to be**. [O.E. *wæs — wesan*, to be; see **wast, were, wert**.]

wase *wāz, (dial.) n.* a wisp of hay, straw, etc.: a pad on the head to ease the pressure of a burden. [Gmc. word; perh. Scand.]

wase-goose. See **wayzgoose**.

wash *wosh, v.t.* to cleanse, or to free from impurities, etc., with water or other liquid: to wet, moisten: to have the property of cleansing: (of an animal) to clean by licking: to flow over, past, against: to sweep along, down, etc.: to form or erode by flowing over: to cover with a thin coat of metal or paint: in mining, to separate from earth by means of water: to launder (money, goods, etc.) (*coll.*). — *v.i.* to clean oneself, clothes, etc., with water: to wash clothes, etc., as one's employment: to stand cleaning (with *well, badly,* etc.): to be swept or carried by water: to stand the test, bear investigation (*coll.*): — *pa.p.* **washed,** *arch.* **wash'en.** — *n.* a washing: the process of washing: a collection of articles for washing: that with which anything is washed: a lotion: the break of waves on the shore: the sound of water breaking, lapping, etc.: the rough water left behind by a boat, etc., or the disturbed air behind an aerofoil, etc. (also *fig.*): the shallow part of a river or arm of the sea: a marsh or fen: erosion by flowing water: alluvial matter: a liquor of fermented malt prior to distillation: waste liquor, refuse of food, etc.: a watery mixture: a thin, tasteless drink: insipid discourse, in speech or writing: a broad but thin layer of colour put on with a long sweep of the brush: a thin coat of paint, metal, etc.: the blade of an oar: in mining, the material from which valuable minerals may be extracted by washing. — *adj.* **wash'able.** — *n.* **wash'er** one who washes: a washing-machine: a ring, usu. flat, of metal, rubber, etc., to keep joints or nuts secure, etc. (perh. a different word). — *v.t.* to fit with a washer or washers. — *ns.* **wash'ery** a wash-house (*arch.*): a place in which an industrial washing process takes place (e.g. of coal, ore or wool); **wash'iness** the state of being watery: feebleness; **wash'ing** the act of cleansing, wetting, or coating, with liquid: clothes, or other articles, washed, or to be washed: a thin coating: the action of breaking, lapping, etc.: (usu. in *pl.*) liquid that has been used to wash something, or matter separated or carried away by water or other liquid. — *adj.* that washes: used for washing: washable. — *adj.* **wash'y** watery, moist: thin, feeble. — *adj.* **wash'-and= wear'** of garments, easily washed, quick-drying, and requiring no ironing. — **wash'-away** the destruction of part of a road, railway, etc., by flooding: the breach so caused; **wash'-ball** a ball of toilet-soap; **wash'-basin, -bowl, wash'hand basin** a bowl to wash face, hands, etc., in; **wash'-board** a corrugated board for rubbing clothes on in washing (also **wash'ing-board**), also used as a percussion instrument in certain types of music: a thin plank on a boat's gunwale to prevent the sea from breaking over: a skirting-board (*dial.*); **wash'= bott'le, wash'ing-bott'le** a bottle containing liquid used for purifying gases: a bottle with tubes through the stopper, enabling a stream of cleansing liquid to be directed on a chemical or a piece of apparatus; **wash'= cloth** a piece of cloth used in washing; **wash'-day** a day (or the regular day) when one washes one's clothes and linen (also **wash'ing-day**); **wash'-dirt** earth to be washed for gold; **wash'-drawing** one made with washes. — *adjs.* **washed'-out** deprived of colour, as by washing: deprived of energy or animation (*coll.*); **washed'-up'** deprived of energy or animation (*coll.*): done for, at the end of one's resources (*slang*): finished (with *with*; *slang*). — **wash'erman** a man who washes clothes, esp. for a living: — *fem.* **wash'erwoman; wash'-gild'ing** a gilding made with an amalgam of gold from which the mercury is driven off by heat, leaving a coating of gold; **wash'-house, wash'ing-house** a house or room for washing clothes in; **wash'-in, -out** an increase, or decrease, in the angle of incidence, i.e. the angle between the chord of a wing and the wind relative to the aeroplane, in approaching the wing-tip along the camber; **wash'= ing-blue** see **blue; wash'ing-line** a clothes-line; **wash'ing= machine** a machine for washing clothes; **wash'ing= powder** a powdered preparation used in washing clothes; **wash'ing-soda** see **soda; wash'ing-up'** cleaning up, esp. of dishes and cutlery after a meal: collectively, the items of crockery, etc. to be washed after use (**washing-up machine** a dish-washer); **wash'land** an area of land periodically flooded by overflow water from a river, stream, or from the sea; **wash'-leather** split sheep-skin prepared with oil in imitation of chamois: buff leather for regimental belts; **wash'-out** an erosion of earth by the action of water: the hole or channel made by such: a complete failure (*coll.*): a useless person (*coll.*): see **wash-in; wash'-pot** a vessel for washing one's hands, etc. in; **wash'room** a room containing lavatories and facilities for washing: a lavatory (chiefly *U.S.*); **wash'-stand, wash'hand-stand** a piece of furniture for holding ewer, basin, and other requisites for washing the person; **wash'-tub** a tub for washing clothes; **wash'-up** a washing-up: a washing-up place: anything cast up by the sea, etc.: the washing of ore: a quantity of gold obtained by washing. — **come out in the wash** (of a stain, etc.) to disappear on washing: to become intelligible, work out satisfactorily (*coll.*); **wash away** to obliterate; **wash down** (of liquid) to carry downward: to wash from top to bottom: to help the swallowing or digestion of (a solid food); **wash its face** (*slang*) of an undertaking, just to pay its way; **wash one's brain** (*obs. slang*) to drink copiously: (for **brain-wash** see under **brain**); **wash one's hands of** see **hand**; **wash out** to remove by washing: to wash free from dirt, soap, etc.: to disappear or become fainter as a result of washing: to cancel (*coll.*): to exhaust (*coll.*; esp. in *pass.*): to bring the blade of an oar not cleanly out of the water (*rowing*); **wash up** to wash one's hands and face (esp. *U.S.*): to wash the dishes and cutlery after a meal: to sweep up on to the shore: to spoil, finish (*coll.*; esp. in *pass.*). [O.E. *wæscan, wascan*; found in other Gmc. languages as O.H.G. *wascan* (Ger. *waschen*); same root as **water**.]

washing *wosh'ing,* (Shak., *Rom.* I, i. 69) *adj.* for **swashing**.

Washingtonia *wosh-ing-tō'ni-ə, n.* a genus of ornamental fan palms of California and Mexico: (also without *cap.*) a synonym of sequoia. [Named after George *Washington* (1732–99).]

wasp *wosp, n.* any of a large number of insects belonging to the order Hymenoptera and constituting many families, including the *Vespidae*, to which the common wasp (*Vespa vulgaris*) and the European hornet (*Vespa crabro*) belong: a petulant and spiteful person. — *n.* **was'pie** a ladies' corset which is laced or fitted tightly to draw the waist in: a similarly cinched belt. — *adj.* **was'pish** like a wasp: having a slender waist, like a wasp: quick to resent an injury: spiteful, virulent. — *adv.* **was'pishly.** — *n.* **was'pishness.** — *adj.* **was'py** waspish. — *adj.* **was'pish-head'ed** (*Shak.*) hot-headed, passionate. — **wasp('s) nest** the nest of a wasp: a place very full of enemies or of angry people, or circumstances in which one is assailed indignantly from all sides (*fig.*). — *adjs.* **wasp'-tongu'd** (Shak., 1 *Hen. IV*, I, iii. 236; 1st quarto **wasp-stung**, others **wasp-tongue**) biting in tongue, shrewish; **wasp'-waist'ed** very slender-waisted: laced tightly. [O.E. *wæsp, wæps*; cf. Ger. *Wespe*, L. *vespa*.]

wassail *wos'(ā)l, was'l, n.* the salutation uttered in drinking a person's health (*hist.*): a liquor in which such healths were drunk, esp. ale with roasted apples, sugar, nutmeg, and toast (*hist.*): a festive occasion: revelry: a drinking-bout: a drinking or festive song. — *v.i.* to hold a wassail or merry drinking-meeting: to sing good wishes, carols, etc., from house to house at Christmas. — *v.t.* to drink to or pour libations for (as fruit-trees). — *ns.* **wass'ailer** one who wassails: a reveller; **wass'-ailing; wass'ailry.** — **wass'ail-bout** a carouse; **wass'ail=bowl, -cup** a cup from which healths were drunk. [O.N. *ves heill*, 'be in health'.]

wasserman *wos'ər-mən,* (*obs.*) *n.* a sea-monster, shaped like a man. [Ger. *Wassermann — Wasser*, water, *Mann*, man.]

Wassermann('s) reaction, test *väs'ər-man(z) rē-ak'shən, test,* a test of the blood serum, or of the cerebrospinal fluid, to determine whether the person from whom it is drawn is suffering from syphilis. [A. von *Wassermann* (1866–1925), German bacteriologist.]

wast¹ *wost,* used (*arch.* or *dial.*) as *2nd pers. sing. pa.t.* of the verb **be.** [See **was.**]

wast², **wastfull, wastness.** Obs. spellings of **waste, wasteful, wasteness.**

wast³. An obs. spelling of **waist.**

waste *wāst, adj.* uncultivated, and at most sparsely inhabited: desolate: lying unused: unproductive: devastated, ruinous (*obs.*): in a devastated condition (as in **lay waste**): empty, unoccupied: refuse, rejected, superfluous: useless, vain (*obs.*). — *v.t.* to devastate: to consume, wear out, impair gradually: to cause to decline, shrink physically, to enfeeble: to put an end to, kill (*obs.* or *slang*): to impoverish (*obs.*): to expend, spend, consume or pass (*obs.*): to spend, use, occupy, unprofitably: to use, bestow, where due appreciation is lacking (often in passive): to fail to take advantage of: to turn to waste material: to injure (an estate or property) (*law*). — *v.i.* to be diminished, used up, or impaired by degrees: to lose strength or flesh or weight (often **waste away**): of time, to be spent (*obs.*): to be used to no, or little, purpose or affect: to use, consume, spend too lavishly. — *n.* an uncultivated, unproductive, or devastated region: a vast expanse, as of ocean or air: vast (*n.*; Shak., *Ham.* I, ii. 198, quartos 2, 3, 4): a disused working: an act or process of wasting: consumption or expenditure (*obs.*): too lavish, or useless, expenditure, or an example of it: squandering: a profusion (*arch.*): superfluous, refuse, or rejected,

material: a waste-pipe: gradual decay: destruction: loss: (in *pl.*) ravages (*obs.*): that which is laid waste (*obs.*): injury done to an estate or property by the tenant (*law*). — *n.* **wāst'age** loss by use or natural decay, etc.: (esp. in the phrase **natural wastage**) loss of employees through retirement, voluntary resignation, etc. rather than forced dismissal: useless or unprofitable spending: loss, or amount of loss, through this: a devastated or ruined place (*Scot.*): waste ground (*Scot.*). — *adjs.* **wāst'ed** unexploited or squandered: exhausted, worn out: shrunken, emaciated: extremely drunk or high on drugs (*slang*; esp. *U.S.*); **waste'ful** causing devastation, consuming, destructive (*obs.* or *rare*): causing wasting of the body (*rare*): lavish (*obs.*): characterised by, or addicted to, over-lavishness: uninhabited, unfrequented, desolate (*poet.*): vain, profitless (*obs.*). — *adv.* **waste'fully.** — *ns.* **waste'fulness; waste'ness** the state of being waste: devastation (*B.*). — *v.t.* **wāst'er** (*Scot.*) to use, spend thriftlessly (whence *adj.* **wāst'erful,** *adv.* **wāst'erfully,** *n.* **wāst'erfulness**). — *n.* one who or that which wastes: a spendthrift: a good-for-nothing (*coll.*): a class of thief (*hist.*): an inferior article, esp. one spoilt in the making: an animal that is not thriving, or that is not suitable for breeding purposes. — *adj.* **waste'rife** (*-rif, -rīf*; *Scot.*) wasteful. — *n.* wastefulness. — *ns.* **wastery** see **wastry** below; **wāst'ing.** — *adj.* that is undergoing waste: destroying, devastating: enfeebling. — *n.* **wāst'-rel** refuse: a waster, esp. a profligate: a neglected child. — *adj.* waste, refuse: of an animal, feeble: going to waste: spendthrift. — *ns.* **wāst'ry, wāst'ery** (*Scot.*) prodigality. — *adj.* improvident. — **waste'-bas'ket, waste'paper-bas'ket** a basket for holding useless scraps of paper, etc.; **waste'-book** a day-book or journal, or a rougher record preliminary to it; **waste'-gate** a gate for discharging surplus water from a dam, etc.; **waste'-land** a desolate, barren area (*lit.* and *fig.*); **waste paper** used paper no longer required for its original purpose: paper rejected as spoiled; **waste'-pipe** a pipe for carrying off waste or surplus water; **waste product** material produced in a process that is discarded on the completion of that process; **wasting asset** any asset (esp. a natural resource, such as a mine) whose value decreases with its depletion and which cannot be replaced or renewed. — **go to waste** to be wasted; **grow to waste** (*obs.*) of a time, to come near an end; **in waste** (*obs.*) to no effect, in vain; **lay waste** see **lay**³; **run to waste** orig. of liquids, to be wasted or lost. [O.Fr. *wast* (*guast*) — L. *vāstus*, waste.]

wastel *wos'tl,* **was'tel-bread** (*-bred*), (*obs.*) *ns.* bread made from the finest of the flour. [O.Fr. *wastel*, a variant of *guastel, gastel* (Fr. *gâteau*, cake); of Gmc. origin.]

waster¹ *wās'tər,* (*obs.*) *n.* a wooden sword for practising fencing with: a cudgel: practice or play with a waster. — **play at waster(s)** to practise fencing. [Ety. uncertain.]

waster², **wasterful.** See **waste.**

waster³ *wās'tər,* (*Scot.*) *n.* a four-pronged or five-pronged salmon-spear. [Earlier *wa(w)sper* — **spear**, modified after **leister**; ety. otherwise obscure.]

wat¹ *wot,* (*obs.*) *n.* a hare. [Prob. *Wat*, for Walter.]

wat² *wät,* (*Scot.*) *adj.* wet: drunken. [Variant of **wet.**]

wat³ *wät.* Scots form of **wot**¹.

wat⁴ *wät, n.* a Thai Buddhist temple or monastery. [Sans. *vātā*, enclosed ground.]

watch *woch, n.* the state of being awake (*obs.*): a religious vigil (*obs.*; survives in **watch-night**, q.v.): a wake: a flock (of nightingales) (*obs.*): a division of the night, of fixed length (*hist.*): (in *pl.*) the period (of the night) (*poet.*): the act or state of remaining on the alert or of observing vigilantly: the lookout: close observation: the act of guarding: surveillance: the office or duty of keeping guard or of being a sentinel (*obs.*) **(stand upon one's watch** (*B.*) to fulfil the duty of watchman): a lying in ambush (*obs.*): one who watches: a watchman, or a body of watchmen, esp. (*hist.*) the body of men who, before the institution of a police force, patrolled the streets at night: a sentinel, or the military guard of a place (obs.): in early 18th century, a name applied to certain companies of irregular troops in the Highlands: a period, usu. of four hours (but see **dog-watch)** of duty on deck: the part, usu. a half (the port — formerly larboard — and the starboard watch), of the ship's officers and crew who are on duty at the same time: a sailor's or fireman's turn or period of duty: something that measures or marks time or the passage of time, as a marked candle, the cry of a watchman, a clock (obs.): the dial of a clock (obs.): a small timepiece for carrying in the pocket, on the wrist, etc. — v.i. to remain awake: to keep vigil: to attend the sick by night: to be on the alert: to look out (with for): to look with attention: to keep guard: to keep guard over (with over). — v.t. to keep in view, to follow the motions of with the eyes (lit. and fig.): to look at, observe, attentively: of a barrister, to attend the trial of (a case) on behalf of a client not directly involved in it: to catch in an act (Shak.): to have in keeping: to guard: to tend: to beware of danger to or from, to be on the alert to guard or guard against (coll.): to be on the alert to take advantage of, as an opportunity: to wait for (obs.): to keep (a hawk) from sleep, in order to tame it (Shak.). — adj. **watch'able** that may be watched: (of an entertainment, esp. a TV programme) having enjoyment or interest value (coll.). — n. **watch'er** one who watches: one of a class of angels. — adj. **watch'ful** wakeful (arch.): spent in watching (arch.): habitually on the alert or cautious: watching or observing carefully: characterised by vigilance: requiring vigilance, or in which one must be on the alert. — adv. **watch'fully.** — n. **watch'fulness.** — **watch'-bill** a list of the officers and crew of a ship, as divided into watches, with their several stations; **watch'-box** a sentry-box; **watch cap** a close-fitting navy blue cap worn by sailors in cold weather; **watch'case** the outer case of a watch: a sentry-box (Shak.); **watch'-chain** a chain for securing a watch to one's clothing; **watch'-clock** a watchman's clock; **watch'-committ'ee** a committee of a local governing body exercising supervision over police services, etc.; **watch'-crystal** see watch-glass below; **watch'-dog** a dog kept to guard premises and property: any person or organisation closely monitoring governmental or commercial operations, etc. to guard against inefficiency and illegality (fig.; also adj.); **watch'-fire** a fire lit at night as a signal: a fire for the use of a watching party, sentinels, scouts, etc.; **watch'-glass** a sand-glass: a glass covering for the face of a watch (also **watch'-crystal):** a small curved glass dish used in laboratories to hold small quantities of a solution, etc.; **watch'-guard** a chain, strap, etc., used to attach a watch to the clothing; **watch'-house** a house in which a guard is placed: a lock-up, police station; **watching brief** instructions to a counsel to watch a legal case: (loosely) responsibility for observing developments, etc. in a specific area (fig.); **watch'-key** a key for winding a watch; **watch'-light** a light used for watching or sitting up in the night; **watch'maker** one who makes or repairs watches; **watch'making; watch'man** a man who watches or guards, now usu. a building, formerly the streets of a city, at night; **watch'man's clock** a clock recording the times of a watchman's visits; **watch'-night** orig. a late service (up to and including midnight) held once a month by Wesleyan Methodists: later a service lasting until midnight held by various denominations on Christmas Eve or New Year's Eve: the last night of the year. — Also adj. — **watch'-officer** the officer in charge of the ship during a watch, also called **officer of the watch; watch'-out** a lookout; **watch'-paper** a round piece of paper, often decorated, formerly put inside the outer case of a watch to prevent rubbing; **watch'-pocket** a small pocket for holding a watch; **watch'-spring** the mainspring of a watch; **watch'-strap** a strap for fastening a watch round the wrist; **watch'-tower** a tower on which a sentinel is placed to look out for the approach of danger; **watch'word** the password

to be given to a watch or sentry (obs.): any signal: a maxim, rallying-cry. — **Black Watch** the 42nd and 73rd Regiments, now the 1st and 2nd Battalions of the Black Watch or Royal Highland Regiment; **on the watch** vigilant, looking out (for danger, etc.); **watch after** (Thackeray) to follow the movements of (with one's eyes); **watch and ward** the old custom of watching by night and by day in towns and cities: uninterrupted vigilance; **watch in** to keep awake to welcome (the New Year); **watch one's step** to step with care: to act warily, be careful not to arouse opposition, give offence, etc. (fig.; coll.); **watch out** (coll.; orig. U.S.) to look out, be careful; **watch over** to guard, take care of; **watch up** (Thackeray) to sit up at night. [O.E. wæcce (n.), wæccan, wacian (vb.); cog. with wacan, to wake.]

watchet woch'it, (arch.) n. a pale blue: a material of this colour: an angling fly. — adj. pale blue. [O.Fr. wachet; perh. orig. a material.]

wate. See wit[1].

water wö'tər, n. in a state of purity, at ordinary temperatures, a clear transparent colourless liquid, perfectly neutral in its reaction, and devoid of taste or smell. extended to the same substance (H_2O) in solid or gaseous state (ice, steam): any body of this (in varying degrees of impurity), as the ocean, a lake, river, etc.: the surface of a body of water: a river valley (Scot.): one of the four elements recognised by early natural philosophers: a quantity of the liquid used in any one stage of a washing operation: a liquid resembling or containing water: mineral water: tears: saliva: (usu. in pl.) the amniotic fluid, filling the space between the embryo and the amnion: urine: sweat: rain: transparency, lustre, as of a diamond: class, quality, excellence (esp. in the phrase **of the first, purest, water):** (in pl.) waves, moving water, a body of water. — v.t. to wet, overflow, irrigate, supply, dilute with water: to soften by soaking (obs.): of a river, etc., to surround, as a city (obs.; also **water about):** to wet and press so as to give a wavy appearance to: to increase (the nominal capital of a company) by the issue of new shares without a corresponding increase of actual capital. — v.i. to fill with, or shed, water: of the mouth (also, obs. and Scot., the teeth), to secrete saliva at the sight or thought of food, or (fig.) in anticipation of anything delightful: of an animal, to drink: to take in water. — adj. pertaining to, or used in, the storage or distribution of water: worked by water: used, living, or operating, on or in water: by way of or across water: made with, or formed by, water. — n. **wa'terage** conveyance (e.g. of cargo or passengers) by water: money paid for this. — adj. **wa'tered** soaked in or with, sprinkled, supplied with, water: having a supply of water in the form of a river, rivers, etc.: periodically flooded: diluted: weakened (fig.): marked with a wavy pattern by watering: of capital or stock, increased in nominal value without any corresponding increase in the assets. — ns. **wa'terer** a vessel for watering with; **wa'teriness; wa'tering** the act of one who, or that which, waters: the act of drinking (obs.): dilution with water: the art or process of giving a wavy, ornamental appearance: such an appearance. — adj. **wa'terish** resembling, or abounding in, or charged with, water: dilute, thin, poor. — n. **wa'terishness.** — adjs. **wa'terless; wa'tery** of or pertaining to water: full of water: moist: consisting of, or containing, water: like water: thin or transparent: tasteless: weak, vapid: associated with, or controlling, the sea, the tides, rain, etc.: watering, eager (Shak., Troil. III, ii. 20). — **wa'ter-bag** a bag for holding water: a camel's reticulum; **wa'ter-bail'iff** a custom-house officer who inspects ships on reaching or leaving port (obs.): an official whose duty it is to enforce byelaws relating to fishing, or to prevent poaching in protected waters (also — now Scot. — **wa'ter-bail'ie); wa'ter-ball'ast** water carried by a ship to balance or redress the change of draught due to consumption of fuel or provisions or discharge of cargo: water carried for purposes of stability: **wa'ter-**

barom'eter a barometer in which water is substituted for mercury; wa'ter-barr'el, -cask a barrel, cask, for holding water; wa'ter-bath a bath composed of water: a vessel of water in which other vessels can be immersed in chemical work; wa'ter-batt'ery a voltaic battery in which the electrolyte is water: a battery nearly on a level with the water (*fort.*); Wa'ter-bearer Aquarius; wa'ter-bed a bed whose mattress is a large water-filled plastic bag: a rubber mattress filled with water, sometimes used to prevent bed-sores; wa'ter-beetle any of a large number of beetles living on or in water, having fringed legs by means of which they swim easily; wa'ter-bell'ows a form of blower, worked, e.g. by a column of water falling through a vertical tube, formerly used to supply a blast for furnaces; wa'ter-bird a bird that frequents the water: wa'ter-bis'cuit a thin plain biscuit made with water; wa'ter-blink in Arctic regions, a patch of sky reflecting the colour, and hence indicating the presence, of open water: (in *pl.*) the plant blinks (q.v.); wa'ter-blis'ter one containing watery fluid, not blood or pus; wa'ter-bloom, -flow'ers large masses of algae, chiefly blue-green, which sometimes develop very suddenly in bodies of fresh water; wa'ter-bo'a the anaconda (*Eunectes murinus*); wa'ter-boat'man any of a number of aquatic hemipterous insects having one pair of legs suggestive of sculls. — *adj.* wa'ter-borne floating on water: conveyed by water, esp. in a boat: transmitted by means of water, as a disease. — wa'ter-bott'le a skin or leather bag, or a glass, rubber, etc., bottle for containing water; wa'ter-bouget (-*boo̅-jət*; *hist.*) a skin or leather bottle used to carry water, usu. one of a pair hung on opposite ends of a yoke. — *adj.* wa'ter-bound detained by floods: of a macadam road, or road surfacing, formed of broken stone, rolled, and covered with a thin layer of hoggin(g), which is watered in and binds the stones together. — wa'ter-box a water-jacket; wa'ter-brain gid; wa'ter-brash pyrosis, a sudden gush into the mouth of acid fluids from the stomach, accompanied by a burning sensation (heartburn) in the gullet; wa'ter-break a piece of broken water wa'ter-breather any animal that breathes by means of gills. — *adj.* wa'ter-breathing. — wa'ter-brose (*Scot.*) brose made of meal and water alone; wa'ter-buck any of several antelopes, esp. *Cobus ellipsiprymnus*; wa'ter-buffalo the common domestic buffalo (Bubalus) of India, etc.; wa'ter-bug any of a large variety of hemipterous insects, including water-boatmen, etc., found in or beside ponds, etc.; wa'ter-bull a mythical amphibious animal like a bull; wa'ter-bus a small boat used to transport passengers on a regular route on an inland waterway; wa'ter-butt a large barrel for rain-water, usu. kept out of doors; wa'ter-cannon a high-pressure hose pipe, used to disperse crowds; wa'ter-carriage conveyance by water: facilities for it; Wa'ter-carrier Aquarius; wa'ter-cart a cart for conveying water, esp. for the purpose of watering streets or roads; wa'ter-cell one of several cells in a camel's stomach used for storing water; wa'ter-cement hydraulic cement; wa'ter-chestnut a water-plant (*Trapa natans*, or other species) of or akin to the Onagraceae: its edible seed: a Chinese sedge, *Eleocharis tuberosa*, or its edible tuber; wa'ter-chute (-*shoo̅t*, -*shoo̅t*) an artificial cascade or slope leading to water, down which people (sometimes in boats or toboggans) slide for sport; wa'ter-clock a clock which is made to go by the fall of water: a clepsydra; wa'ter-closet (abbrev. W.C.) a closet used as a lavatory, the discharges being carried off by water; wa'ter-cock the kora, a large E. Indian gallinule; wa'ter-colour a pigment diluted with water and gum (or other substance), instead of oil: a painting in such a colour or colours; wa'ter-colourist a painter in water-colours. — *v.i.* wa'ter-cool to cool by means of water, esp. circulating water. — *adj.* wa'ter-cooled. — wa'ter-cooler a machine for cooling by means of water or for keeping water cool. — *adj.* and *n.* wa'ter-cooling. — wa'ter-core in an apple or other fruit, an abnormality

consisting of water-soaked tissue, esp. close to the core: in founding, a hollow core through which water may be passed; wa'tercourse a channel through which water flows or has flowed: an artificial water-channel: a stream, river; wa'ter-cow a female water-buffalo or water-bull; wa'ter-craft a boat: boats collectively: skill in swimming, etc., or in managing boats; wa'ter-crane an apparatus for supplying water from an elevated tank, esp. to a locomotive tender: a hydraulic crane; wa'tercress (often, esp. formerly, in *pl.*) a perennial cress (*Nasturtium officinale*) growing in watery places, used as a salad; wa'ter-culture a method of cultivation, often an experimental means of determining the mineral requirements of a plant, the plant being grown with its roots dipping into solutions of known composition; wa'ter-cure medical treatment by means of water; water cycle the cycle in which water from the sea evaporates into the atmosphere, later condenses and falls to earth as rain or snow, then evaporates directly back into the atmosphere or returns to sea by rivers; wa'ter-deck a decorated canvas cover for a dragoon's saddle; wa'ter-deer a small Chinese musk-deer of aquatic habits: in Africa, one of the chevrotains; wa'ter-diviner one who, usu. with the help of a divining-rod, detects, or tries to detect, the presence of underground water; wa'ter-doctor a hydropathist: (*formerly*) one who divined diseases from the urine; wa'ter-dog any variety of the dog (formerly a specific variety, a small poodle) valuable to sportsmen in hunting water-fowl on account of its aquatic habits: a water-vole: an otter (*obs.*): also various other animals: an experienced sailor (*coll.*): a good swimmer: a small irregular floating cloud supposed to indicate rain; wa'ter-drinker a drinker of water: a teetotaller; wa'terdrive the use of water pressure, either occurring naturally or by waterflood (q.v.), to drive oil or gas, etc. from a reservoir; wa'ter-drop a drop of water: a tear; wa'ter-drop'wort a genus (*Oenanthe*) of umbelliferous plants, including the common water-dropwort (*O. fistulosa*) and hemlock water-dropwort, or water-hemlock (*O. crocata*). — *adj.* wa'tered-down much diluted (*lit.* and *fig.*). — wa'ter-elder the guelder-rose; wa'ter-engine an engine for raising water: an engine worked by water: an engine for extinguishing fires (*obs.*); wa'ter-equiv'alent thermal capacity, the product of the specific heat of a body and its mass; wa'terfall a fall or perpendicular descent of a body of water, a cataract or cascade: a neck-tie (*obs.*): a chignon (*obs.*); wa'ter-fern any of the the Hydropterideae or rhizocarps, water or marsh plants differing from ferns in the narrower sense in being heterosporous, classified in two families, Marsileaceae and Salviniaceae; wa'ter-finder a water-diviner; wa'ter-flag the yellow iris; wa'ter-flea the common name for any of numerous minute aquatic crustaceans; wa'ter-flood an inundation; wa'terflood (also with *hyphen*) the process or an instance of waterflooding; wa'terflooding in oil, gas or petroleum production, a method of injecting water to maintain pressure in a reservoir and to drive the oil, etc. towards the production wells; wa'ter-flow a current of water. — *adj.* wa'ter-flowing streaming. — wa'ter-fly an aquatic insect: an insignificant, troublesome person (*Shak.*); wa'ter-fowl a fowl that frequents water: swimming game-birds collectively; wa'ter-frame Arkwright's spinning-machine, which was driven by water; wa'terfront the buildings or part of a town along the edge of and facing the sea, a river etc.; wa'ter-gall (*obs.* and *dial.*) a watery appearance in the sky accompanying the rainbow: also a secondary rainbow; wa'ter-gap a gap in a mountain range containing a stream; wa'ter-gas a mixed gas obtained by passing steam (blue water-gas) or steam and air (semi-water-gas) over incandescent coke, or other source of carbon; wa'ter-gate a floodgate: a gate admitting to a river or other body of water: a street leading to the water (*Scot.*); Wa'tergate a U.S. political scandal involving the attempted break-in at the Democratic Party headquarters (the *Watergate* building, Washington D.C.) in 1972 by agents employed by President Richard Nixon's re-election organisation, and the subsequent attempted cover-up by senior White House officials who had approved the break-in; the term has since been extended to describe any similar misuse of power by politicians or other public figures, or any widespread public scandal (see also -**gate**); **wa'ter-gauge, -gage** an instrument for measuring the quantity or height of water: water pressure expressed in inches: an instrument for measuring differences in pressure; **wa'ter-gilding** wash-gilding; **wa'ter-glass** a water-clock: an instrument for making observations beneath the surface of water: a glass vessel for containing water, as one for keeping plants: a finger-bowl (*obs.*): a tumbler: a concentrated and viscous solution of sodium or potassium silicate in water, used as adhesive, protective covering, etc., and, esp. formerly, for preserving eggs; **wa'ter-god** a deity presiding over a tract of water; **water gong** (*mus.*) the effect of dipping a vibrating gong into and raising it out of water to produce upward and downward glissandos; **water gruel** gruel made with water: anything insipid; **wa'ter-guard** river, harbour, or coast police; **wa'ter-hammer** a wave of increased pressure travelling through water in a pipe caused by a sudden stoppage or change in the water flow: the concussion and noise so caused: **wa'ter-head** the source, as of a stream: the region where this is found: a dammed-up body of water, or its quantity, height, or pressure; **wa'ter-hemlock** a poisonous plant, *Cicuta virosa*: any other plant of the same genus: water-dropwort (q.v.); **wa'ter-hen** any of a number of ralline birds, esp. *Gallinula chloropus* — also called the moorhen; **wa'ter-hole** a pool in which water has collected, as a spring in a desert or a pool in the dried-up course of a river; **wa'ter-horse** a water-spirit like a horse: a kelpie; **wa'ter-hyacinth** a tropical floating aquatic plant (*Eichhornia crassipes*); **wa'ter-ice** sweetened fruit juice or a substitute diluted with water, frozen and served with meals as a kind of ice cream; **wa'tering-call** a cavalry trumpet-signal to water horses; **wa'tering-can, -pot** a vessel used for watering plants; **wa'tering-cap** (*obs.*) a cavalryman's fatigue cap; **wa'tering-hole** a water-hole, where animals go to drink: a place where humans seek (esp. alcoholic) refreshment (*coll.*); **wa'tering-house** (*obs.*) an inn or other place where horses are watered; **wa'tering-place** a place where water may be obtained: a place to which people resort to drink mineral water, or for bathing, etc.; **wa'tering-trough** a trough in which horses and cattle drink: a trough between the rails containing water to be scooped up by locomotives; **wa'ter-jacket** a casing containing water placed round, e.g. the cylinder-block of an internal-combustion engine, to keep it cool — also **wa'ter-box; wa'ter-jet.** — *adj.* operated by a jet of water. — **wa'ter-joint** a joint in a pavement that is raised to prevent water lying in it: a joint in sheet-metal roofing forming a channel for rain-water; **wa'ter-jump** a place where a jump across a stream, pool, ditch, etc., has to be made, as in a steeplechase; **water key** (*mus.*) in brass instruments, a sprung lever that allows drainage of accumulated moisture; **wa'ter-leaf** any plant of the genus *Hydrophyllum* or the family *Hydrophyllaceae*, N. American herbs with sharply toothed leaves and cymose flowers: an ornament used in the capitals of columns, probably representing the leaf of some water plant (*archit.*); **wa'ter-lemon** a species of passion-flower, or its edible fruit; **wa'ter-lens** a simple lens formed by placing a few drops of water in a vessel, e.g. a small brass cell with blackened sides and a glass bottom; **wa'ter-level** the level formed by the surface of still water: an instrument in which water is used for establishing a horizontal line of sight: a water-table (*geol.*): a slightly inclined road to carry off water (*mining*); **wa'terlily** a name commonly given to the different species of Nymphaea and Nuphar, and also to other members of the family Nymphaeaceae

— the three British species are the white waterlily (*Nymphaea alba*), and the yellow waterlilies (*Nuphar luteum* and *Nuphar minimum* — the latter being rare); **wa'ter-line** any of several lines on a ship to which it is submerged under different conditions of loading, e.g. the *light water-line* marking the depth when it is without cargo: in shipbuilding, any of certain lines on a vessel parallel with the water showing the contour of the hull at various heights: the water-level: the outline of a coast: in paper, a chain-line, one of the wider-spaced lines visible by transmitted light (up and down the page in folio, octavo, etc., crosswise in quarto). — *v.t.* **wa'terlog** to make unmanageable by flooding with water, as a boat: to saturate with water so as to make heavy or inert, or unfit for use, or to impede life or growth (also *fig.*). — *adj.* **wa'terlogged.** — **wa'ter-lot** a lot of ground which is under water; **wa'ter-main** a large subterranean pipe supplying water; **wa'terman** a man who plies a boat for hire, a boatman, a ferryman: a good oarsman: one whose employment is supplying water, e.g. (*hist.*) to cab- or coach-horses: an imaginary being living in water; **wa'termanship** oarsmanship; **wa'termark** the line of the greatest height to which water has risen: a tidemark: a ship's water-line: a distinguishing mark in paper, a design visible by transmitted light, made by the mould or the dandy-roll. — *v.t.* to mark with a watermark: to impress as a watermark. — **wa'ter-meadow** a meadow kept fertile by flooding from a stream; **wa'ter-measure** a measurement formerly used in dealing with goods, as coal, salt, etc., sold on board ship — the bushel, etc., being larger than the standard bushel, etc.; **wa'ter-melon** a plant (*Citrullus vulgaris*) of the cucumber family, of African origin, having a pulpy, pleasantly flavoured fruit: the fruit itself; **wa'ter-me'ter** an instrument for measuring the quantity of water passing through a particular outlet; **wa'ter-mil'foil** see **milfoil; wa'ter-mill** a mill driven by water; **wa'ter-moc'assin** a poisonous snake of the southern United States; **wa'ter-mole** the desman: the duckbill; **wa'ter-monkey** a porous earthenware jar for keeping drinking-water in hot climates, round, with narrow neck — also *monkey-jar*; **wa'ter-motor** any water-wheel or turbine, esp. any small motor driven by water under pressure; **wa'ter-mouse** the water-vole: any mouse of the genus Hydromys (*Austr.*); **wa'ter-music** (*hist.*) music performed, or composed for performance, during an excursion by water; **wa'ter-nix'ie** a nixie; **wa'ter-nymph** a naiad; **wa'ter-opossum** the yapok; **water-ouzel** see **ouzel; wa'ter-parsnip** any plant of the aquatic umbelliferous genus Sium, esp. the skirret; **wa'ter-parting** a watershed, divide; **wa'ter-pepper** a very acrid persicaria (*Polygonum hydropiper*) of wet places; **wa'ter-pipe** a pipe for conveying water: a hookah; **wa'ter-pistol** a weapon or toy for throwing a jet of water or other liquid; **wa'ter-plane** a plane passing through any water-line of a ship: the plane of the surface of water: a canal on the level without locks (*hist.*): a seaplane; **wa'ter-plant** a plant that grows in water; **wa'ter-plantain** a plant (*Alisma plantago*) having plantain-like leaves: any other plant of the same genus; **wa'ter-plate** a plate having a double bottom and a space for hot water, used to keep food warm; **wa'ter-poet** a writer of doggerel verse (John Taylor, 1580–1653, a writer of jingling verses, etc., for a time a Thames waterman, called himself 'the Water-poet'); **wa'ter-po'lo** an aquatic ball-game played by swimmers, seven a side: also, a similar game played by contestants in canoes; **wa'ter-pore** a hydathode: a madreporite; **wa'ter-pot** a pot or vessel for holding water; **wa'ter-power** the power of water, employed to move machinery, etc.: a flow or fall of water which may be so used; **wa'ter-pox** varicella; **wa'ter-privilege** the right to the use of water, esp. for driving machinery: a place where this right may be exercised. — *adj.* **wa'terproof** coated, e.g. with rubber, so as to be impervious to water: so constructed that water cannot enter. — *n.* a material or an outer garment made impervious to water. — *v.t.*

and *v.i.* to make, become, or be, impervious to water, esp. by coating with a solution. — **wa'terproofing** the act of making any substance impervious to water: the material with which this is done; **wa'ter-pump** a pump for raising water: used humorously of the eyes; **water=purpie** see **purpie; wa'terquake** a seismic disturbance affecting the sea; **wa'ter-rail** the common rail (*Rallus aquaticus*) of Europe; **wa'ter-ram** a hydraulic ram; **wa'ter-rat** the popular name of the water-vole: the American musk-rat: a pirate: a sailor or boatman; **wa'ter-rate** a rate or tax for the supply of water; **wa'ter-reactor** a water-cooled nuclear reactor. — *adjs.* **wa'ter-repell'ent, wa'ter-resis'tant** resistant to penetration by water: treated with a substance which is resistant to water. — **water rice** Zizania; **wa'ter-rug** a kind of water dog — perh. from **rug**[1] (Shak., *Macb.* III, i. 94); **wa'ter-sapphire** (trans. of Fr. *saphir d'eau*) an intense blue variety of cordierite used as a gemstone; **wa'ter-seal** a seal formed by water in a trap; **wa'tershed** the line separating two river-basins: a drainage or a catchment area (*erron.*): a slope or structure down which water flows: a crucial point or dividing line between two phases, conditions etc.; **wa'ter-shoot** a channel for the overflow of water: a water-chute. — *adjs.* **wa'ter-shot** (*rare*) crossed by streams; **wa'terside** on the brink of water, shore of a sea, lake, etc. — *n.* the edge of a sea, lake, etc., a shore. — *v.i.* **wa'ter-ski.** — *n.* a type of ski used in water-skiing. — **wa'ter-skiing** the sport of being towed at speed on skis behind a motor-boat; **wa'tersmeet** a meeting-place of two streams; **wa'ter-smoke** water evaporating as visible mist; **wa'ter-snake** a snake frequenting the water; **wa'ter-softener** a device or substance for removing the causes of hardness in water; **wa'ter-soldier** an aquatic plant (*Stratiotes aloides*) common in lakes and ditches in the east of England; **wa'ter-souchy** (*-sōō'chi, -sōō'shi*) fish served in the water in which it is boiled (Du. *waterzootje — zootje*, boiling); **water spaniel** see **spaniel; wa'ter-spider** an aquatic spider, esp. *Argyroneta aquatica*, which has a sub-aquatic bell-shaped web inflated with air carried down in bubbles; **wa'ter-spirit** a water-sprite; **wa'ter-splash** a shallow stream running across a road; **wa'ter-spout** a pipe, etc., from which water spouts: the spout of water: torrential rain: a disturbance like a very small tornado, a revolving column of cloud, mist, spray; **wa'ter-spring** (*B.*) a spring; **wa'ter-sprin'kle** (*Spens.*) a spray of water: a sprinkle; **wa'ter-sprite** a spirit inhabiting the water. — *adj.* **wa'ter-standing** (*Shak.*) brimming with tears. — **water=starwort** see **starwort** under **star; wa'ter-strider** any long-legged aquatic insect of the family *Hydrobatidae*; **wa'ter-supply** the obtaining and distribution of water, as to a community: amount of water thus distributed; **wa'ter-table** a moulding or other projection in the wall of a building to throw off the water: the level below which fissures and pores in the strata are saturated with water (*geol.*); **wa'ter-tap** a tap or cock used for letting out water; **wa'ter-thermom'eter** a thermometer filled with water instead of mercury, and used for showing the point at which water has its greatest density; **wa'ter-thief'** (*Shak.*) a pirate; **wa'ter-thrush** *Seiurus motacilla* or *S. noveboracensis*, N. American warblers with brownish backs and striped underparts, living near water; **water thyme** anacharis. — *adj.* **wa'tertight** so tight as not to admit water or let it escape: such that no flaw, weakness, or source of misinterpretation, can be found in it (*fig.*). — **water-tight compartment** a division of a ship's hull or other underwater structure so formed that water cannot enter it from any other part: a part, esp. of one's thoughts or beliefs, shut off from the influence of other parts (*fig.*); **wa'tertightness; water torture** torture using water, esp. dripping it slowly on to the victim's forehead; **wa'ter-tower** a tower containing tanks in which water is stored so that it may be delivered at sufficient pressure for distribution to an area: a vertical pipe supplied with water under high pressure, used in

fire-fighting; **wa'ter-tunnel** (*aero.*) a tunnel in which water is circulated instead of air to obtain a visual representation of flow; **wa'ter-twist** a kind of cotton-yarn, first made by the water-frame: in spinning, more than the usual amount of twist; **water vapour** water in gaseous form, esp. when evaporation has occurred at a temperature below boiling-point. — *adj.* **wa'ter=vas'cular** of or pertaining to vessels in certain invertebrates which contain a mixture of water and a nutritive fluid: in echinoderms, of the system of coelomic canals (**water-vascular system**) associated with the tube-feet and supplying fluid for their movement. — **wa'ter-vine** a name for various plants yielding a refreshing watery sap; **wa'ter-violet** a plant of the genus *Hottonia* of aquatic herbs with racemose flowers and crowded submerged leaves; **wa'ter-vole** *Arvicola amphibius*, a large British vole commonly known as the water-rat; **wa'ter-wag'on** a wagon used to convey water; **wa'ter=wag'tail** a wagtail, esp. the pied wagtail; **wa'ter-wave** a wave of water: a wave in the hair made by setting it when wet. — *v.t.* to make such a wave in (hair). — **wa'terway** a series of pieces of timber, extending round a ship at the junction of the decks with the sides, having a groove connecting with the scuppers to carry off water: any channel for water: a stretch of navigable water: a route over, or by, water; **wa'ter-weed** any plant with very small flowers and leaves growing in ponds, etc., esp. anacharis (q.v.); **wa'ter-wheel** a wheel moved by water: an engine for raising water; **wa'ter-wings** a wing-like inflated device for keeping one afloat in water; **wa'ter-witch** a dowser; **wa'terwork** (usu. in *pl.*) any apparatus or plant by which water is supplied, as to a town, etc.: an ornamental fountain, cascade, etc. (*obs.*): a textile fabric, used like tapestry (*obs.*): used humorously of shedding tears, euphemistically of the human urinary system. — *adj.* **wa'ter-worn** worn by the action of water. — **wa'ter-yam** a plant with farinaceous rootstock, the lattice-leaf. — **above water** out of difficulties, esp. financial; **be, go, on the water-wagon** (*slang*) to abstain from alcoholic liquors; **cast one's water** to examine one's urine to aid in the diagnosis of disease; **deep water** or **waters** water too deep for safety: difficulty or distress (*fig.*); **high water, high'=wa'termark** see **high; hold water** to be correct or well-grounded, to bear examination; **keep one's head above water** (*fig.*) to keep solvent; **like water** copiously: extravagantly, recklessly; **low water, low'-wa'termark** see **low; make a hole in the water** (*slang*) to drown oneself; **make the mouth water** to arouse a delightful feeling of anticipation or desire; **make water** (of a boat) to leak, take in water; **make, pass, water** to micturate; **oil on troubled waters** anything that allays or assuages, from the effect of pouring oil on rough water; **pour, throw cold water on, over** to discourage by one's unwillingness or indifference; **still waters run deep** a quiet exterior often conceals strong emotions, resolution, cunning, etc.; **under water** below the surface; **water down** (*lit.* and *fig.*) to make less strong; **water of crystallisation, hydration** the water present in hydrated compounds, which, when crystallised from solution in water, retain a definite amount of water; **water of life** spiritual refreshment: whisky, brandy, etc.; **water on the brain** hydrocephalus; **water on the knee** an accumulation of serous fluid in the knee-joint. [O.E. *wæter*; cf. Du. *water*, Ger. *Wasser*; cog. with Gr. *hydōr*, L. *ūdus*, wet, *unda*, a wave, Sans. *udan*, water.]

Waterloo *wö-tər-lōō'*, or *wö'*, *n.* a final defeat. — **Waterloo cracker** (*obs.*) a kind of firework. [*Waterloo*, near Brussels, where Napoleon was finally defeated in 1815.]

watertight, waterway, watery. See **water.**

Watling Street *wot'ling strēt*, one of the great Roman highways of Britain, running from near London through St Albans to Wroxeter: often extended at either end to include the roads to Dover and Chester: loosely applied to other Roman roads: the Milky Way (*obs.*). [O.E. *Wæclinga stræt*, the street of Wæcel' people — of whom nothing is known; the O.E. name of St Albans was *Wæclinga ceaster*.]

watt *wot, n.* the practical and M.K.S. unit of power, equal to a rate of working of one joule per second. — *n.* **watt′age** an amount of power expressed in watts. — **watt′-hour′** a common unit of electrical energy, being the work done by one watt acting for one hour; **watt′meter** an instrument containing a series (*current*) and a shunt (*voltage*) coil whose combined torque produces a deflection of the needle that is a direct measure of the circuit power in watts.   [James *Watt* (1736–1819).]

Watteau *wot′ō, adj.* applied to articles or features of women's dress resembling the costumes in the paintings of Antoine *Watteau* (1684–1721) — as **Watteau bodice,** one with a square opening at the neck and short sleeves. — *adj.* **Watt′eauish.**

wattle[1] *wot′l, n.* a twig or flexible rod (*dial.*): (collective *sing.* or in *pl.*) material for fences, roofs, etc., in the form of rods, branches, etc., either interwoven to form a network or loose: a hurdle (*dial.*): any of various Australian acacias: (perh. a different word) the coloured fleshy excrescence under the throat of some birds, or a similar excrescence or process on any part of the head of a bird, fish, etc. — *v.t.* to bind with wattle or twigs: to form by plaiting twigs. — *adj.* **watt′led.** — *n.* **watt′ling** the act of making wattles by interweaving twigs, etc.: wattle-work, or the material for it. — **watt′lebark** the bark of various wattles, used for tanning; **watt′le-bird** any of a number of honey-eaters of Australia that have ear-wattles; **watt′le-work** wickerwork. — **wattle and daub, dab** wattle-work plastered with mud and used as a building material. [O.E. *watul, watel*; origin uncertain.]

wattle[2] *wot′l, (hist.; Orkney* and *Shetland) n.* the obligation to entertain the foud on his annual journey, or a tax for which it was later commuted.   [Perh. Norw. dial. *veitla* — O.N. *veizla,* entertainment.]

waucht. See **waught.**

wauff. Variant of **waff**[1,2].

waugh[1] *wö, interj.* expressing sorrow, anger, etc. — usu. attributed to North American Indians.

waugh[2]. See **waff**[3].

waught, waucht *wöht, (Scot.) n.* a large draught. — *v.t.* and *v.i.* to drink in large draughts.   [Perh. conn. with **quaff.**]

wauk, wauk-mill. Same as **waulk, waulk-mill.**

waukrife. Same as **wakerife** (see under **wake**[1]).

waul[1]**, wawl** *wöl, v.t.* to cry as a cat or a newly-born baby. — Also *n.* — *n.* and *adj.* **waul′ing, wawl′ing.**   [Imit.]

waul[2]**, wawl** *wöl, (Scot.; obs.) v.i.* to roll the eyes.   [O.E. *wealwian,* to roll, wallow.]

waulk *wök, v.t.* to walk, full (cloth). — **waulk′-mill** a fulling-mill.   [See **walk.**]

waur, waurst. See **war**[2].

wave *wāv, n.* a ridge on the surface of a liquid, esp. of the sea: a surge, consisting of vibrating particles of liquid, moving across the surface of a body of liquid such as the sea (*transverse wave*) — the vibrations of the individual particles being at right angles to the line of advance: a unit disturbance in any travelling system of vibrating particles as a light-wave (*transverse wave*) or a sound-wave (*longitudinal wave* — the vibrations of the particles being in the direction of advance): an undulating or vibratory motion (e.g. as a signal): or sound: the sea, or other body of water (*poet.*): curved inequality of surface: a line or streak like a wave: an undulation: an undulating succession of curves in hair, or one of these: a movement of the raised hand expressing greeting, farewell etc.: a swelling up or increase, normally followed by a subsidence or decline (*fig.*). — *v.i.* to move like a wave: to move backwards and forwards: to float or to hover (*obs.*): to flutter, as a signal: to make a signal in this way: to move the raised hand in greeting, farewell, etc.: to undulate: to waver, vacillate (*obs.*). — *v.t.* to move backwards and forwards: to brandish: to waft or beckon: to express

by a wave: to direct, signal an instruction to, by a wave: to raise into inequalities of surface: to give an undulating appearance to. — *adjs.* **waved** showing a wave-like form or outline: undulating: of hair, artificially made to undulate: indented (*her.*): having on the margin a succession of curved segments or incisions: moved to and fro; **wave′less.** — *n.* **wave′let** a little wave. — *adj.* **wave′like.** — *v.i.* **wāv′er** to move to and fro: to shake, be unsteady, be in danger of falling: to falter, show signs of giving way: to vacillate: to vary, change. — *n.* **wāv′erer.** — *n.* and *adj.* **wāv′ering.** — *adv.* **wāv′eringly** in a wavering or irresolute manner. — *n.* **wāv′eringness.** — *adjs.* **wāv′erous, wāv′ery** unsteady. — *ns.* **wave′son** goods floating on the sea after a shipwreck; **wāv′iness** the state or quality of being wavy. — *n.* and *adj.* **wāv′ing.** — *adj.* **wāv′y** full of, or rising in, waves: playing to and fro: undulating. — **wave′band** a range of wavelengths occupied by transmission of a particular type; **wave energy, wave power** energy or power derived, by means of some device, from the movement of sea waves; **wave′form, wave′shape** a graph showing variation of amplitude of electrical signal, or other wave, against time; **wave′front** in a propagating vibratory disturbance, the continuous locus of points which are in the same phase of vibration; **wave′guide** (*electronics*) a hollow metal conductor, usu. rectangular, within which very high-frequency energy can be transmitted efficiently; **wave′-length** the distance between two successive similar points on an alternating wave, e.g. between successive maxima or between successive minima: the distance, measured radially from the source, between two successive points in free space at which an electromagnetic wave has the same phase; **wave mechanics** the part of quantum mechanics dealing with the wave aspect of the behaviour of radiations; **wave′meter** an instrument for measuring wavelengths, directly or indirectly; **wave′-mo′tion** undulatory movement: motion in waves, or according to the same laws; **wave number** in an electromagnetic wave, the reciprocal of the wavelength, i.e. the number of waves in unit distance; **wave′-offering** an ancient Jewish custom of moving the hands in succession towards the four points of the compass in presenting certain offerings — opp. to the *heave-offering,* in which the hands were only lifted up and lowered; **wave power** see **wave energy; waveshape** see **waveform; wave train** a group of similar waves, of limited duration, produced by a single disturbance; **Wavy Navy** the Royal Naval Volunteer Reserve, so called from the undulating gold braid on officers' sleeves. — **make waves** to create a disturbance, make trouble; **on the same wavelength as** in tune with, having the same attitude of mind, background knowledge, etc.; **wave aside** to dismiss (a suggestion, etc.) as irrelevant or unimportant; **wave down** to signal to stop by waving.   [O.E. *wafian,* to wave; cf. O.N. *vafra,* to waver.]

wavelet. See **wave.**

wavellite *wā′vəl-īt, n.* hydrated phosphate of aluminium, occurring commonly in flattened globular aggregates, showing a strongly developed internal radiating structure.   [Named after Dr *Wavel* or *Wavell,* who discovered the mineral near Barnstaple.]

waver, waverous, waveson, etc. See **wave.**

wavey, wavy *wā′vi, n.* the snow-goose.   [Cree.]

wavy. See **wave.**

waw *wö, (Scott) n.* a wave — *Spens.* **wawe.**   [Prob. from a lost O.E. form akin to *wæg,* wave.]

wawl. See **waul**[1,2].

wax[1] *waks, n.* any of a class of substances of plant or animal origin, usu. consisting of esters of monohydric alcohols, e.g. beeswax, $C_{30}H_{61}O \cdot CO \cdot C_{15}H_{31}$: any of certain hydrocarbons of mineral origin, as ozokerite: any substance like a wax in some respect, as that in the ear: a substance used to seal letters: that used by shoemakers to rub their thread: in mining, puddled clay: a thick sugary substance made by boiling down the sap of the sugar-maple, and cooling by exposure to the air: a person easily influenced (*fig.*): in Shak., *Timon*, I, i. 48, explanation uncertain — according to some, wax tablets, others have thought expansive growth (see **wax²**). — *v.t.* to smear, rub, or (*obs.*) join with wax. — *adj.* **wax′en** made of wax: like wax: easily impressed, penetrated, effaced. — *ns.* **wax′er** one who or that which waxes; **wax′iness; wax′ing.** — *adj.* **wax′y** resembling wax in texture or appearance: soft: impressible: impressionable (*fig.*): pallid, pasty. — **wax′-berry** (the fruit of) the wax-myrtle; **wax′bill** any of various small seed-eating birds of the weaver-finch family with coloured bills like sealing-wax; **wax′=chandler** a maker of, or dealer in, wax candles; **wax′=cloth** cloth covered with a coating of wax, used for table-covers, etc.: a popular name for all oil floor-cloths; **wax′-doll** a child's doll having the head and bust made of hardened beeswax; **waxed leather** leather finished with a high wax polish on the flesh side; **wax′-end,** better **waxed end,** a strong thread having its end stiffened by shoemakers' wax, so as to go easily through the hole made by the awl; **wax′-flower** an artificial flower made of wax: any of several plants, as a white-flowered climbing plant of Madagascar, an epiphyte of British Guiana, and plants of the genus *Eriostemon* of Australia; **wax′-insect** an insect that secretes wax, as any of several of the Coccidae, etc.; **wax′-light** a candle or taper made of wax; **wax′-moth** a bee-moth; **wax′-myrtle** the U.S. candle-berry tree; **wax′-painting** encaustic painting; **wax′-palm** either of two S. American palms yielding wax; **wax′-paper** paper spread with a thin coating of white wax and other materials; **wax plant** any of several plants of the genus Hoya, esp. *Hoya carnosa* of Australia and E. Asia, an asclepiadaceous climbing plant, with clusters of waxy white or pink star-shaped flowers, and succulent leaves; **wax pocket** in bees, a ventral abdominal pouch which secretes wax. — *adj.* **wax′-red** (*Shak.*) bright-red like sealing-wax. — **wax′-tree** a tree from which wax is obtained, as a Japanese sumac (*Rhus succedanea*), the wax-myrtle, a privet (*Ligustrum lucidum*), etc.; **wax′wing** a member of a a genus of passerine birds (Bombycilla) with small red horny appendages, resembling red sealing-wax, on their wings; **wax′work** work made of wax, esp. figures or models formed of wax; **wax′worker.** — *n.pl.* or *n.sing.* **wax′works** an exhibition of wax figures. — **waxy degeneration** a morbid process in which the healthy tissue of various organs is transformed into a peculiar waxy albuminous substance. — **lost wax** see **cire perdue.** [O.E. *weax*; O.N. *vax*, Du. *was*, Ger. *Wachs*.]

wax² *waks, v.i.* to grow or increase, esp. of the moon, as opp. to *wane*: to pass into another state, become, as *wax lyrical* (*fig.*): — *pa.p.* (*arch.*) **wax′en** grown — also (*obs.*) *pa.t. pl.* (as Shak., *Mids. N. Dr.*, II, i. 56) and *infin.* [O.E. *weaxan*; O.N. *vaxa*, Ger. *wachsen*, allied to L. *augēre*, to increase, Gr. *auxanein*.]

wax³ *waks,* (*coll.*) *n.* a passion, fit of anger. — *adj.* **wax′y** (*coll.*) irate, incensed. [Origin uncertain.]

way¹ *wā,* (*Spens.*) *v.t.* to weigh, esteem. [Variant of **weigh.**]

way² *wā, n.* passage: a road, street, track: direction of motion: the correct or desired route or path: length of space, distance (also in *pl.* (*coll.*, esp. *U.S.*)): district: room or opportunity to advance: freedom of action, scope: manner (of life): condition, state: advance in life: normal, habitual, course or conduct: (in *pl.*) characteristic conduct, idiosyncrasies: manner, style: method: means: course: respect: will: progress or motion through the water, headway (*naut.*): the direction of the weave, grain, etc.: (in *pl.*) the machined surfaces of the top of a lathe bed on which the carriage slides, shears: (in *pl.*) the framework of timbers on which a ship slides when being launched. — *v.i.* (*Spens.*) to journey. — *adj.* **way′less** without a path. — **way=bagg′age** (*U.S.*) baggage to be laid down at a way-station; **way′-bill** a list of passengers and goods carried by a public vehicle: a list of places to be visited on a journey: a document giving details regarding goods sent by rail; **way′-board, weigh′-board** a thin stratum or seam separating thicker strata; **way′bread** (*dial.*; O.E. *wegbræde* — *brād*, broad) the common plantain. — *v.i.* **way′fare** (*arch.*) to travel, esp. on foot. — *n.* (*arch.*) travel, esp. on foot. — **way′farer** a traveller, esp. on foot. — *n.* and *adj.* **way′faring.** — **way′faring=tree** the *Viburnum lantana*, a large shrub common in hedges; **way′-freight** freight for a way-station. — *adjs.* **way′-going** (*Scot.*) departing; **way′gone** exhausted by travelling. — *v.t.* **waylay′** to lie in ambush for: to attack or seize in the way: to lie in wait for in order to converse with (*fig.*): to obstruct or intercept (*obs.*). — **waylay′er; way′-leave** permission to pass over another's ground or property; **way′-maker** a pioneer: a precursor; **way′-mark** a guide-post: something which serves as a guide to a traveller. — *v.t.* to mark out (a path, etc.) with guide-posts, signs, etc. — **way′-passenger** one taken up or set down at a way-station or an intermediate point on a coach or bus route; **way point** a point for stopping, changing course, etc., on a journey; **way′-post** a guide-post; **way′side** the border of a way, path, or highway. — *adj.* growing or lying near the wayside. — **way′=station** (*U.S.*) an intermediate station between principal stations; **way′-traffic** (*U.S.*) local traffic, as distinguished from through or express traffic; **way′-train** (*U.S.*) a train stopping at most of the stations on a line; **way′-warden** one elected to supervise the upkeep of roads in a district; **way′wiser** an instrument for measuring distance travelled. — *adj.* **way′worn** worn-out by travel. — **be by way of** to be supposed, alleged (inaccurately) to be, do; **by, with, one's way of it** (*Scot.*) according to one's belief or assertion; **by the way** incidentally: while travelling: beside one's path; **by way of** travelling through, via: as if for the purpose of: in character of, as a substitute for; **come one's way** to come in the same direction: to come within one's experience or reach, to become attainable (*fig.*); **committee of ways and means** the House of Commons when it sits to consider methods of raising supplies; **from way back** from or since a long time ago (*coll.*); **get one's (own) way** to get what one wants; **give way (to)** see **give; go one's way, go one's own way** see **go; go out of the, one's, way** to give oneself trouble: to make a special point (of doing something); **go the way of all the earth, of all flesh** to die; **have a way with** to be good at dealing with or managing (people, etc.); **have a way with one** to have a fascinating personality or persuasive manner; **have it both ways** (usu. with a *neg.*) to benefit from two actions, situations, arguments, etc., each of which excludes the possibility, validity, etc. of the other; **have it one's (own) way** to do, think, etc. as one pleases, with no regard for others' advice or opinions; **have one's way** to carry one's point, get what one wants; **have way** (*naut.*) to be in motion, as a vessel; **in a bad way** in a serious condition: very upset; **in a fair way to** likely to succeed in; **in a small, big** (or **large**) **way** on a petty, or a large or grandiose, scale; **in a way** in a state of agitation or distress: to some extent: from one point of view; **in his,** etc., **(own) way** as far as his, etc., individual merits go, leaving aside the disadvantageous aspects; **in no way** not at all; **in the family way** see **family; in the way** on the way: in the path (*lit.* and *fig.*): impending, obstructing; **in the way of** in a good position for effecting or attaining: in the habit of (*coll.*): in respect of; **lead the way** to act as a guide in any movement; **look the other way** to look away, sometimes deliberately in order not to see someone or something (also *fig.*); **lose the, one's, way** to become lost; **make one's way** to push oneself forward (*lit.* and *fig.*); **make way** to give place: to advance; **no way** see **no²; one way and another** considering various aspects; **on the, one's, way** moving towards a destination or event: in progress; **on the way out** becoming unpopular, unfashionable, etc.; **out of the way** so as not to hinder or obstruct: lost, hidden (*Shak.*) (**out-of-the-way** see **out**);

put oneself out of the way same as go out of one's way; take one's way to set out, proceed: to follow one's own inclination or plan; the Way the Christian Religion (Acts ix. 2, etc.); under way in motion, as a vessel (also underway); Way of the Cross a series of pictorial representations of the stages of Christ's progress to Calvary: devotions used in connection with these stages; ways and means resources: methods e.g. of raising money for the carrying on of government. [O.E. *weg*; Ger. *Weg*; akin to Sans. *vahati*, he carries, akin to L. *vehĕre*, to carry, draw.]

way³, 'way *wā*, *adv.*, a shortened form of **away**, far: at a considerable distance or interval of time. — *adj.* **way-out'** (*slang*) lost in what one is doing (as, orig., playing avant-garde jazz): excellent, unusual, very satisfying, far-out, eccentric.

waygoose. See **wayzgoose.**

wayment *wā-ment'*, (*Spens.*) *v.t.* and *v.i.* to lament, grieve. — *n.* lamentation, grief. [O.Fr. *waimenter* — *wai*, alas!]

way-out. See **way³.**

wayward *wā'wərd*, *adj.* wilful: capricious: irregular. — *adv.* **way'wardly.** — *n.* **way'wardness.** [For **awayward** — **away**, and suff. **-ward**.]

wayzgoose, wase-goose *wāz'gōos*, *n.* a printers' annual dinner or picnic. — Earlier **way'goose.** [Origin obscure.]

wazir *wä-zēr'*, *n.* a vizier. [Ar. *wazīr*.]

we *wē*, *pron. pl.* of I: I and others: used for I by monarchs: also used by editors, etc.: used when speaking patronisingly, esp. to children, to mean 'you'. [O.E. *wē*; cog. with Goth. *weis*, Ger. *wir*.]

weak *wēk*, *adj.* soft (*obs.*): wanting strength: not able to sustain a great weight: easily overcome: frail: wanting health: feeble of mind: wanting moral or mental force: impressible, easily led: lacking artistic force: unconvincing: inconclusive: inconsiderable (*Shak.*): having little of the important ingredient: of a verb, inflected by regular syllabic addition instead of by change of main vowel: of a Germanic noun or adj., having inflexions in *-n*: of a sound or accent, having little force: of a verse line, having the accent on a normally unstressed syllable: tending downward in price: of an interaction between nuclear particles, having a decay time of approx. 10^{-10} seconds. — *v.t.* **weak'en** to make weaker: to reduce in strength or spirit. — *v.i.* to grow weak or weaker: to become less resolute or determined, show signs of giving in. — *ns.* **weak'ener; weak'liness; weak'ling** a weak or feeble creature. — *adv.* **weak'ly.** — *adj.* sickly: not robust: feeble. — *n.* **weak'ness** the state of being weak: a liking or fondness for. — **weaker sex** women; **weaker vessel** see **vessel.** — *adj.* **weak'-eyed** having weak eyes or sight. — **weak'fish** any of a group of weak-mouthed food-fish of the genus *Cynoscion* (fam. Sciaenidae), esp. *Cynoscion regalis*; **weak force, interaction**, a force involved in radioactive decay, supposed to be one of four forces governing the universe. — *adjs.* **weak'-hand'ed** powerless; **weak'-head'ed** having a feeble intellect: easily affected by alcoholic liquor; **weak'-heart'ed** of weak spirit: softhearted; **weak'-hinged** ill-balanced; **weak'-kneed** having weak knees: weak in will; **weak'-mind'ed** having feeble intelligence: having, or showing, lack of resolution: too easily convinced or persuaded. — **weak'-mind'edness; weak moment** a moment of weakness; **weak side, point** that side or point in which a person is most easily influenced or most liable to temptation. — *adj.* **weak'-sight'ed.** — **weak sister** (*coll.*; esp. *U.S.*) a weak, unreliable member of a group. — *adjs.* **weak'-spir'ited** bearing wrong tamely, cowardly; **weak'-will'ed** lacking a strong will, irresolute. [O.N. *veikr*; allied to O.E. *wāc*, pliant — *wīcan*, to yield; Du. *week*, Ger. *weich*.]

weal¹ *wēl*, *n.* the state of being well (*arch.*): a sound or prosperous state: welfare: commonwealth (*obs.*). — *adj.* **weal'-balanced** (Shak., *Meas.*, IV, iii. 108) perh. kept in a state of just proportion by reasons of state,

perh. for well-balanced. — **weals'man** (*Shak.*) a statesman. — **the public, general,** or **common, weal** the well-being, interest, and prosperity of the country. [O.E. *wela, weola*, wealth, bliss; allied to **well²**.]

weal² *wēl*, *n.* a raised streak left by a blow with a lash, etc. [See **wale¹**.]

weal³. Same as **weel¹.**

weald *wēld*, (*poet.*) *n.* open country or wooded country. — *adj.* **Weald'en** pertaining to the Weald: of a series of freshwater beds at the base of the Cretaceous, seen in the Weald. — Also *n.* — **the Weald** a district, once forested, between the North and South Downs. [O.E. (W.S.) *weald*, a forest, wold; cf. **wold**.]

wealk'd. See **welkt.**

wealth *welth*, *n.* prosperity, well-being (*arch.*): valuable possessions of any kind: riches: an abundance (*fig.*). — *adv.* **wealth'ily.** — *n.* **wealth'iness.** — *adj.* **wealth'y** rich: prosperous. — **wealth tax** a tax on personal property and riches. [M.E. *welthe* — *wele* — O.E. *wela*; see **weal¹**.]

weamb. See **wame.**

wean¹ *wān*, (*Scot.*) *n.* a child. [**wee ane.**]

wean² *wēn*, *v.t.* to accustom to nourishment other than the mother's milk: to reconcile to the want of anything (with *from*): to estrange the affections of from any object or habit. — *ns.* **wean'el** (*Spens.*) a weanling; **wean'er** a young animal, esp. a pig, that has recently been weaned. — *adj.* **wean'ling** newly weaned (also *fig.*). — *n.* a child or animal newly weaned. — **wean'ing-brash** a severe form of diarrhoea that supervenes, at times, on weaning. [O.E. *wenian*, to accustom; O.N. *venja*, Ger. *gewöhnen*, to accustom, *entwöhnen*, to disuse, wean.]

weapon *wep'n*, *n.* any instrument of offence or defence. — *adjs.* **weap'oned; weap'onless** having no weapons. — *n.* **weap'onry** weapons collectively: armament. — **weap'on-salve** a salve supposed to cure a wound by being applied to the weapon that made it. [O.E. *wǣpen*; Goth. *wēpna*, arms, Ger. *Waffe*.]

weapon-s(c)haw. See **wappens(c)haw.**

wear¹ *wār*, *v.t.* to be dressed in: to carry on the body: to arrange, as clothes, in a specified way: to display, show: of a ship, to fly (a flag): to consume, waste, damage, by use, time, exposure: to make by friction: to exhaust, to weary: to bring gradually into: to enable to last, endure (*Scot.*; *wēr*): to spend, as a period of time (*poet.*): to traverse (*Spens.*): to edge, guide, conduct, as sheep into a fold (*Scot.*): to tolerate, accept, or believe. — *v.i.* to be wasted by use or time: to consume slowly: of time, to be spent, pass, esp. tediously (*poet.*; usu. in *pa.p.*): to last under use: to resist the ravages of age: to stand the test of time: to be in fashion (*Shak.*): to pass into: to become (*obs.*): to go, move, slowly (*Scot.*). — *pa.t.* **wore** (*wōr, wör*), arch. **ware;** *pa.p.* **worn** (*wōrn, wörn*). — *n.* the act of wearing: lessening or injury by use or friction: durability: fitness for wearing: articles worn (usu. in composition, as *menswear*): fashion. — *n.* **wearabil'ity.** — *adj.* **wear'able** fit to be worn: good for wearing. — *n.* **wear'er.** — *adj.* **wear'ing** made or designed for wear: consuming: exhausting. — *n.* the process of wasting by attrition or time: the action of carrying on the body, or displaying, or flying: durability: passing: that which is worn, clothes (*obs.*). — **wear'ing-apparel** dress; **wear'-iron** an iron plate to take the wear due to friction. — **the worse for wear** worn, showing signs of wear: showing signs of exhaustion, intoxication, etc.; **wear and tear, tear and wear** damage by wear or use; **wear away** to impair, consume, by wear: to decay or fade out: to pass off; **wear down** (*fig.*) to diminish, or overcome, gradually by persistence; **wear off** to rub off by friction: to diminish by decay: to pass away by degrees; **wear out** to impair by use: to render, become, useless by decay: to consume tediously: to harass; **wear thin** to become thin, threadbare, through use; **(win and) wear** to (win and) enjoy possession of. [O.E. *werian*, to wear; O.N. *verja*, to clothe, Goth. *wasian*.]

wear² wār, (naut.) v.t. and v.i. to bring, or be brought, to another course by turning the helm to windward: — pa.t. and pa.p. **wore.** [Prob. **veer¹**.]

wear³ wēr, n. another spelling of **weir¹**.

wear⁴, weir wēr, (Scot.) v.t. to guard: to ward off. [O.E. werian.]

wearish wēr′ish, adj. tasteless, savourless (lit. and fig.; obs.): feeble, withered, shrunk (dial.). [Late M.E. werische; cf. **wersh**.]

weary¹ wē′ri, adj. having the strength or patience exhausted: very tired: causing weariness: tiresome, tedious: puny (dial.). — v.t. to make weary: to reduce the strength or patience of: to harass. — v.i. to become weary or impatient: to long (with for; Scot.). — adjs. **wea′ried** tired; **wea′riful** wearisome. — adv. **wea′rifully.** — adj. **wea′riless** incessant. — adv. **wea′rily.** — n. **wea′riness.** — adj. **wea′risome** causing weariness: tedious. — adv. **wea′risomely.** — n. **wea′risomeness.** — **Weary Willie** (slang) a tramp: a person habitually lackadaisical or deficient in energy. — **weary out** to exhaust. [O.E. wērig, weary.]

weary² wē′ri, (Scot.) n. a curse, as in **weary on you, weary fall you.** [**weary¹**, prob. with some association with obs. **wary** (O.E. wiergan), to curse.]

weasand wē′zənd, n. the gullet: the windpipe: the throat. — **wea′sand-pipe** (Spens.). [O.E. wǣsand; O.S. wāsend, O.H.G. weisant.]

weasel wē′zl, n. a small carnivore (Mustela nivalis) with long slender body, active, furtive, and bloodthirsty, eating frogs, birds, mice, etc.: any of various related species: a person resembling a weasel, esp. in bad qualities: a small amphibious military vehicle for carrying personnel or supplies. — v.i. to equivocate: to extricate oneself from, circumvent (an obligation, etc.), esp. indefensibly (with out of, round, etc.). — n. **wea′sel(l)er.** — adj. **wea′selly.** — **wea′sel-cat** linsang; **wea′sel-coot** the female or young male of the smew. — adj. **wea′sel-faced** with a lean sharp face. — **weasel word** a word that makes a statement evasive or misleading. — **weasel out** to evade obligation. [O.E. wesle.]

weather wedh′ər, n. atmospheric conditions as to heat or cold, wetness, cloudiness, etc.: type or vicissitude of atmospheric conditions or of fortune: formerly, (specif.) a storm or adverse weather: the direction in which the wind is blowing (naut.): the angle the sail of a windmill makes with the perpendicular to its axis. — v.t. to affect by exposing to the air: to sail to the windward of: to gain or pass, as a cape: to come safely through (lit. and fig.): to shelter from (obs.): to set, as the sails of a windmill: to slope, as a roof. — v.i. to become discoloured, disintegrated, etc., by exposure. — adj. (naut.) toward the wind, windward. — adj. **weath′ered** having the surface altered in colour, form, texture, or composition by the action of the elements (geol.): seasoned by exposure to weather: made slightly sloping so as to throw off water (archit.). — n. **weath′ering** weather conditions (obs.): the action of the elements in altering the form, colour, texture, or composition of rocks (geol.): seasoning by weather: a slight inclination given to the top of a cornice or moulding, to prevent water from lodging on it (archit.): the act of passing to windward of (naut.). — v.t. **weath′erise, -ize** to make (a fabric) weather-proof. — adjs. **weath′erly** (naut.) making little leeway when close-hauled; **weath′ermost** (naut.) furthest to windward. — n. **weatherom′eter** an instrument used to determine the weather-resisting properties of paints. — **weath′er-anchor** the anchor lying to windward. — adjs. **weath′er-beaten** damaged or worn away by, or seasoned by, the weather; **weath′er-bitten** worn or defaced by exposure to the winds. — **weath′er-board** the windward side of a ship: a plank in a porthole, etc., of a vessel placed so as to keep off rain, without preventing air from circulating: a board shaped so as to shed water from a building. — v.t. to fit with such planks or boards. — **weath′er-boarding** thin boards

placed overlapping to keep out rain: exterior covering of a wall or roof. — adj. **weath′er-bound** detained by bad weather. — **weath′er-bow** the windward side of the bow; **weath′er-box, -house** a toy constructed on the principle of a barometer, consisting of a house with the figures of a man and wife who come out alternately as the weather is respectively bad or good; **weath′er-chart** a weather-map; **weath′er-cloth** a protecting tarpaulin on deck; **weath′ercock** a vane (often in the form of a cock) to show the direction of the wind: one who changes his opinions, allegiance, etc., easily and often. — v.t. to act as a weathercock for: to supply with a weathercock: (with it) to behave like a weathercock. — adj. **weath′er-driven** driven by winds or storms. — **weath′er-eye** the eye considered as the means by which one forecasts the weather (also fig.). — v.t. **weath′er-fend** (Shak.) to defend from the weather, to shelter. — **weather forecast** a forecast of the weather based on meteorological observations; **weath′er-ga(u)ge** the position of a ship to the windward of another: advantage of position; **weath′er-gall** (Scot. -gaw) an imperfect rainbow, or other supposed sign of coming weather; **weath′er-glass** a glass or instrument that indicates the changes of the weather: a barometer; **weath′er-gleam** (dial.) a bright aspect of the sky at the horizon. — adj. **weath′er-headed** (Scott) flighty. — **weath′er-helm** a keeping of the helm somewhat to the weather side when a vessel shows a tendency to come into the wind; **weather-house** see **weather-box; weath′erman** one who prepares weather forecasts or who delivers such forecasts on radio or television; **weath′er-map** a map indicating meteorological conditions over a large tract of country; **weath′er-notation** a system of abbreviation for meteorological phenomena. — adj. **weath′er-proof** proof against rough weather. — n. weather-proof material. — v.t. to make weather-proof. — **weath′er-prophet** one who foretells weather: a device for foretelling the weather; **weath′er-roll** the lurch of a vessel to windward when in the trough of the sea; **weather report** loosely, a weather forecast; **weath′er-satellite** a satellite used for the study of cloud formations and other meteorological conditions; **weath′er-ship** a ship engaged on meteorological work; **weath′er-side** the windward side; **weath′er-sign** a phenomenon indicating change of weather: any prognostic; **weath′er-stain** discoloration produced by exposure; **weath′er-station** a station where phenomena of weather are observed; **weath′er-strip** a thin piece of some material used to keep out wind and cold; **weath′er-symbol** a conventional sign indicating a meteorological phenomenon; **weath′er-vane** a weathercock; **weather window** a period of time in which the weather is suitable for a particular purpose, e.g. oil-drilling (also fig.). — adj. **weath′er-wise** skilful in foreseeing the changes of the weather (lit. and fig.). — adv. with regard to weather conditions. — adj. **weath′er-worn** worn away or damaged by wind, storms, etc. — **above the weather** too high in the air to experience the weather conditions on the ground: not, or no longer, under the weather; **keep one's weather eye open** to be alert: to keep a sharp lookout; **keep, have, the weather of** to be to the windward of: to have the advantage of; **make fair weather** (Shak.) to be conciliatory, to flatter; **make good, bad**, etc., **weather of it** to behave well or badly in a storm (lit. and fig.); **make heavy weather of** to find excessive difficulty in; **stress of weather** violent and unfavourable winds; **under the weather** indisposed, seedy: drunk; **weather along** to make headway against adverse weather; **weather a point** (fig.) to gain an advantage or accomplish a purpose against opposition; **weather on** to gain on in a windward direction (lit. and fig.); **weather out** to hold out against till the end; **weather the storm** to come safely through a period of difficulty, etc. [O.E. weder; O.N. vedhr, Ger. Wetter.]

weave¹ wēv, v.t. to make by crossing threads, strands, strips, etc., above and below one another: to interlace, as in a loom to form cloth: to work into a fabric, story, etc.: to depict by weaving: to unite, work into a whole: to construct, contrive. — *v.i.* to practise weaving: — *pa.t.* **wōve**, rarely **weaved**; *pa.p.* **wōv'en**; cf. **wove**. — *n.* the texture of a woven fabric. — *ns.* **weav'er** one who weaves: any bird of a passerine family (*Ploceidae*) resembling the finches, so called from their remarkable woven nests; **weav'ing** the act or art of forming a web or cloth by the intersecting of two distinct sets of fibres, threads, or yarns — those passing longitudinally from end to end of the web forming the *warp*, those crossing and intersecting the warp at right angles forming the *weft*. — **weav'er-bird** a weaver or, less commonly, a weaver-finch; **weav'er-finch** any member of a family of small finch-like birds (*Estrildidae*) which includes the waxbills; **weaver's knot, hitch** the sheet-bend. [O.E. *wefan*; O.N. *vefa*, Ger. *weben*; cog. with Gr. *hyphē*, a web, *hyphainein*, to weave.]

weave² *wēv*, *v.i.* to move to and fro: to wind in and out: to move back or forward with sinuous movements of the body (*boxing*): to fly with a weaving motion (*aero.*). — *v.t.* to move to and fro or up and down: to make a signal to by waving something. — *n.* and *adj.* **weav'ing**. — **get weaving** (*slang*) to get busy, get on the move. [M.E. *weve*; of uncertain origin.]

weazand *wē'zənd*, *n.* Same as **weasand**.

weazen *wē'zn*, Variant of **wizen**.

web *web*, *n.* that which is woven: a whole piece of cloth as woven in the loom: a kind of cloth or weave: a thin metal plate or sheet: in paper-making, an endless wire-cloth working on rollers: a large sheet or roll of paper: in birds, the vexillum of a feather: any connective tissue (*anat.*): the fine texture spun by the spider, etc., as a snare: the skin between the toes of water-fowl, etc.: a film over the eye (*obs.*): anything like a cloth web in complication or a spider's web in flimsiness or in power to entangle: a plot, snare. — *v.t.* to envelop, or to connect, with a web. — *adj.* **webbed** having a web: having the toes or fingers united by a web of skin. — *n.* **webb'ing** a narrow woven fabric of hemp, used for belts, etc., for various purposes in upholstery, and as tapes conducting webs of paper in a printing-machine: the state of being palmate (*zool.*): the webs of webbed hands or feet. — *adj.* **webb'y**. — *adj.* **web'-fing'ered**. — **web'-foot** a foot the toes of which are united with a web or membrane. — *adj.* **web'=foot'ed**. — **web offset** a method of offset printing using a reel of paper. — *adj.* **web'-toed**. — **web'wheel** a wheel in which the rim, spokes and centre are formed from one single piece of material: a wheel with a web or plate instead of spokes; **web'worm** (*U.S.*) any of a number of caterpillars spinning webs in which they feed or rest. — **web and pin** or **pin and web** (*Shak.*) see **pin**. [O.E. *webb*; O.N. *vefr*, Ger. *Gewebe*; from root of **weave¹**.]

weber *vā'bər*, *wē'bər*, *n.* the M.K.S. unit of magnetic flux. [Wilhelm *Weber*, German physicist (1804–91).]

webster *web'stər*, (*obs.*) *n.* a weaver. — Also (*Scot.*) **wab'ster**. [O.E. *webbestre*, a female weaver — *web-ban*, to weave.]

wecht *wehht*, (*Scot.*) *n.* an instrument for winnowing or for measuring grain. [Perh. conn. with **weigh**.]

wed *wed* (*Scot.* **wad** *wöd*) *v.t.* to marry: to join in marriage: to unite closely: to wager (*obs.*). — *v.i.* to marry: — *pr.p.* **wedd'ing**; *pa.t.* **wedd'ed** or, *dial.*, **wed**; *pa.p.* **wed-d'ed** or, *dial.* and *poet.*, **wed**. — *n.* (*obs.*; Scot. **wad**) a pledge, security. — *adj.* **wedd'ed** married: of or pertaining to marriage: closely joined: persistently devoted. — *n.* **wedd'ing** marriage: marriage ceremony. — **wedd'ing-bed** the bridal bed; **wedd'ing-breakfast** a meal served after a wedding; **wedd'ing-cake** a highly decorated cake served at a wedding, and also divided among absent friends; **wedd'ing-cards** cards announcing a wedding, sent to friends; **wedd'ing-day** the day of marriage: its anniversary; **wedd'ing-dower** the marriage portion; **wedd'ing-dress** a bride's dress; **wedd'ing=favour** a white rosette worn by men at a wedding;

wedd'ing-finger the ring-finger; **wedd'ing-garment** a garment worn at a wedding; **wedd'ing-march** music in march time played as the bride's party enters the church and at the close of a marriage ceremony; **wedd'ing-ring** a plain, usu. gold, ring given by the groom to the bride at a wedding: any more or less similar ring given by the bride to the groom. — **penny wedding** a wedding where the guests paid for the entertainment, and sometimes contributed to the outfit; **silver, ruby, golden, diamond wedding (anniversary)** the celebrations of the 25th, 40th, 50th, and 60th anniversaries of a wedding. [O.E. *weddian*, to promise, to marry (Ger. *wetten*, to wager) — *wedd*, a pledge; Goth. *wadi*, Ger. *Wette*, a bet.]

we'd *wēd*, a contraction of **we had** or **we would**.

wedeln *vā'dəln*, (also with *cap.*) *n.* a style of downhill skiing in which the skis, kept parallel and close together, are swivelled rapidly from side to side. — *n.pl.* such swivelling movements. — *v.i.* (also with *cap.*) to execute wedeln on a downhill run. [Ger., orig. to wag one's tail.]

wedge *wej*, *n.* a piece of wood or metal, thick at one end and sloping to a thin edge at the other, used in splitting, fixing tightly, etc.: anything shaped more or less like a wedge, as an ingot of gold or silver (*obs.*), a formation of troops, the flying formation of geese and other wildfowl, a large piece, e.g. of cake, a stroke in cuneiform characters: an iron-headed golf-club with much loft used for approaching: a stroke with such a club: a shoe in which the heel and sole together form a wedge and there is no gap under the instep (also **wedge-heeled shoe**). — *v.t.* to cleave with a wedge: to force or drive with a wedge: to thrust in tightly: to crowd closely: to fasten or fix with a wedge or wedges: to make into a wedge. — *v.i.* to force one's way like a wedge: to become fixed or jammed by, or as if by, a wedge: to make a stroke with a wedge (*golf*). — *adj.* **wedged**. — *adv.* **wedge'wise** in the manner of a wedge. — *ns.* **wedg'ie** (*coll.*) a wedge-heeled shoe; **wedg'ing** a method of joining timbers. — *adjs.* **wedge'-shaped** shaped like a wedge; **wedge'-tailed** having a tail in which the rectrices form the shape of a wedge, the central pair being longest, the outer pair shortest. — **the thin,** or **small, end of the wedge** a small beginning that is bound to be followed by a large or significant (and usu. unwelcome) development; **the (wooden) wedge** at Cambridge, the student lowest on the classical tripos list (on the analogy of wooden spoon (q.v.), from *Wedg*wood, a student at Christ's College, whose name was last on the first list, of 1824). [O.E. *wecg*; O.N. *veggr*, Ger. dial. *weck*, a wedge.]

Wedgwood® *wej'wŏŏd*, *n.* superior pottery, including that lightly glazed with cameo reliefs in white, made by Josiah *Wedgwood* (1730–95) and his successors. — Also **Wedgwood ware**. — **Wedgwood blue** a greyish-blue colour typical of Wedgwood pottery.

wedlock *wed'lok*, *n.* matrimony: the married state, esp. in the phrase **born in**, or **out of, wedlock**, i.e. legitimate or illegitimate. — **break wedlock** to commit adultery. [O.E. *wedlāc* — *wedd*, a pledge, and suff. *-lāc* implying action of some kind.]

Wednesday *wenz'di*, *wed'nz-di*, *n.* the fourth day of the week. [O.E. *Wōdnes dæg*, Woden's day.]

wee¹ *wē*, (*Scot.*) *n.* a short distance, a short time. — *adj.* tiny. — **Wee Free** a member of the minority of the Free Church that refused to join with the United Presbyterian Church in 1900. [M.E. *we, wei*, a bit, time, or space, as in phrase *a little wei*.]

wee² *wē*, *interj.* imitating the squeal of a young pig. — Also *v.i.* and *n.*

wee³ *wē*. Same as **wee-wee**.

weed¹ *wēd*, *n.* any useless plant of small growth: any plant growing where it is not wanted by man: any wild herb: a thick growth of wild herbs: anything useless, troublesome, or obnoxious: a worthless animal: a weak, ineffectual and/or unmanly man: (often with *the*) tobacco, or a cigar or cigarette (*coll.*): marijuana (*slang*). — *v.t.* to free from weeds: to remove, uproot (weeds, etc.) (often with *out*): to identify and remove (something or someone inferior, unwanted, *etc.*) from a group or collection (*usu.* with *out*). — *v.i.* to remove weeds. — *adj.* **weed′ed.** — *ns.* **weed′er; weed′ery** a place full of weeds; **weedicide** (*wēd′i-sīd*; L. *-cīda* — *caedĕre*, to kill) a chemical weedkiller; **weed′iness; weed′ing** the action of the verb to weed: what is weeded out. — *adjs.* **weed′less; weed′y** weed-like: full of weeds: lanky, ungainly: of worthless, insipid, etc. character. — *adj.* **weed′-grown** overgrown with weeds. — **weed′ing-chisel, -forceps, -fork, -hook, -tongs** (*pl.*) garden implements of varying forms for destroying weeds; **weed′killer** anything, esp. a chemical preparation, for killing weeds. [O.E. *wēod*, a herb.]

weed² *wēd*, *n.* a garment, or (as collective *sing.*) clothing (*arch.*): armour (*arch.*): (in *pl.*) a widow's mourning apparel. — *adj.* **weed′y** clad in widow's mourning. [O.E. *wæd*, *wēde*, clothing; O.H.G. *wāt*, cloth.]

weed³ *wēd*, (*Scot.*) *n.* any sudden illness, cold, or relapse with febrile symptoms, esp. in women after confinement or nursing: a fever in horses, etc. — Also **weid.** [From *wedenonfa* — O.E. *wēden-* (in composition), mad, and Scot. *onfa′*, **onfall.**]

week *wēk*, *n.* the space of seven days, esp. from Sunday to Saturday (inclusive): the working days of the week: (in *pl.*) an indefinite period. — *adj.* **week′ly** coming, happening, or done, once a week. — *adv.* once a week: every week. — *n.* a publication appearing once a week. — **week′day** any day of the week except Sunday, and now usu. also excluding Saturday; **week′-end, week′end** (or *-end′*) the non-working period from Friday evening to Sunday evening (a **long week-end** usu. incorporating Friday and Monday or yet more liberally extended). — *v.i.* to spend a week-end holiday. — **week-end′er; week-end′ing; week′night** the evening or night of a weekday. — **a prophetic week** (*B.*) seven years; **a week of Sundays** (*coll.*) seven weeks: a long time; **a week, two weeks,** etc. **today** one week, two weeks, etc. from today; **Feast of Weeks** a Jewish festival 7 weeks after the Passover (also **Shabuoth, Shavuot** or **Pentecost**); **Great Week, Holy Week, Passion Week** the week preceding Easter Sunday; **in by the week** (*obs.*) trapped, caught; **this day week** a week from today; **week about** in alternate periods of seven days; **week in, week out** continuously without a break. [O.E. *wice*; Du. *week*, Ger. *Woche*.]

weeke *wēk*, (*Spens.*) *n.* Same as **wick³.**

weel¹ *wēl*, *n.* a whirlpool. [O.E. *wǣl.*]

weel² *wēl*, *n.* a trap or snare for fish (*dial.*): a bearing resembling such (*her.*). [O.E. *wile-* (in composition) — *wilige*; cf. **willy¹.**]

weel³ *wēl*, *adv.* Scots form of **well².** — *adj.* **weel-faur'd, -far'd,** etc. See **well-favoured** under **well².**

weeldlesse. See under **wield.**

weem *wēm*, (*Scot.*) *n.* a subterranean dwelling. [Early Gael. *uaim*, cavern.]

ween *wēn*, (*arch.* or *obs.*) *v.t.* to think or fancy: to believe: to expect. — *v.i.* (*Shak.*) to imagine expectantly. [O.E. *wēnan*; cog. with *wēn*, expectation, hope.]

weeny *wē′ni*, (*coll.* esp. *childish*) *adj.* very small, tiny. [*wee* and *tiny* or *teeny.*]

weep *wēp*, *v.i.* to express grief by shedding tears: to wail or lament: to drip, rain: to ooze in drops: to leak: to exude: to be pendent, as a weeping-willow. — *v.t.* to lament: to pour forth: to express while, or by, weeping: to exude: — *pa.t.* and *pa.p.* **wept.** — *ns.* **weep′er** one who weeps: a white border round the sleeve of a mourning dress: a crape hat-band: a widow's crape-veil: anything pendent: a weephole; **weep′ie, weep′y** (*slang*) a highly emotional film, play or book. — *n.* and *adj.* **weep′ing.** — *adv.* **weep′ingly.** — *adj.* **weep′y** tearful (*coll.*): oozy (*dial.*). — **weep′hole** a hole in a wall, etc. to allow water to escape from behind it; **weep′ing-ash** a variety of the common European ash, with drooping branches; **weep′ing-birch** a variety of the white birch, with drooping branches; **Weeping**

Cross, weep′ing-cross (*hist.*) a wayside cross where penitents might pray: in phrases as **come home by weeping-cross,** to experience bitter regret, disappointment or failure; **weep′ing-elm** a variety of wych-elm, with drooping branches. — *adj.* **weep′ing-ripe** (*Shak.*) ripe or ready for tears. — **weep′ing-rock** a rock through which water percolates slowly; **weep′ing-spring** a spring from which water escapes slowly; **weep′ing-tree** a tree with long pendulous branches; **weep′ing-willow** an ornamental Chinese willow (*Salix babylonica*), with pendent branches. [O.E. *wēpan*; allied to *wēp*, clamour; Goth. *wōpjan.*]

weet. Dial. form of **wet.** — Also *Spens.*

weet(e), weeten, weeting, see **wit¹; weetingly, weetless,** obs. forms of **wittingly, witless.**

weever *wē′vər*, *n.* a genus of fishes (Trachinus), of which two species are British, with sharp dorsal and opercular spines capable of inflicting serious wounds. [Prob. O.Fr. *wivre*, serpent, weever — L. *vīpera*; cf. **wivern, viper.**]

weevil *wēv′l*, *n.* a popular name for a large number of beetles (the group Rhynchophora, esp. the family Curculionidae) with the anterior part of the head prolonged into a beak or proboscis, which, either in the larval or the adult form, damage fruit, nuts, grain, or trees: any insect injurious to stored grain. — *adjs.* **weev′illed, weev′iled, weev′illy, weev′ily** infested by weevils. [O.E. *wifel.*]

wee-wee *wē′wē*, (*coll.*, esp. *childish*) *n.* the act of urinating: urine. — Also *v.i.* [Ety. unknown.]

weft *weft*, *n.* the threads woven into and crossing the warp: the thread carried by the shuttle (also **woof):** a web: a film, cloud. — *v.i.* (*rare*) to form a weft. — *n.* **weft′age** texture. [O.E. *weft, wefta*; allied to *wefan*; see **weave¹.**]

weft(e)¹ *weft*, (*Spens.*) *n.* a waif, a castaway. [Variant of **waif¹.**]

weft(e)² *weft*. See **waft;** (*Spens.*) *pa.p.* of **waive.**

Wehrmacht *vār′mähht*, *n.* the German armed forces (1935–45). [Ger., — *Wehr*, defence, *Macht*, force.]

weid. See **weed³.**

Weigela *wī′gi-lə, -gel′, n.* a genus of deciduous shrubs with large, showy pink, purplish or white flowers: (without *cap.*) a plant of this genus. [C. E. von *Weigel* (1748–1831), German botanist.]

weigh¹ *wā, v.t.* to compare with by, or as if by, the balance (with *against*): to find the heaviness of: to be equal to in heaviness: to counterbalance: to raise, as a ship's anchor: to apportion: to hold in the hand(s) in order to, or as if to, estimate the weight: to estimate the value of: to ponder in the mind, consider carefully: to consider worthy of notice: to keep evenly outspread (*Milt.*). — *v.i.* to have weight: to be considered of importance: to balance evenly (*Shak.*): to have value (*Shak.*): to press heavily: to weigh anchor. — *adj.* **weigh′able** capable of being weighed. — *n.* **weigh′age** the rate paid for the weighing of goods. — *adj.* **weighed** experienced: considered, balanced. — *ns.* **weigh′er** an officer who weighs articles or tests weights; **weigh′ing; weight** the heaviness of a thing, esp. as determined by weighing: quantity as determined in this way: the force with which a body is attracted to the earth, measured by the product of the mass and the acceleration: a mass of metal adjusted to a standard and used for finding weight: a method of estimating, or a unit of, weight: the amount something ought to weigh: a standard amount that a boxer, etc., should weigh: scales (*Spens.*): a heavy object: anything heavy or oppressive: a ponderous mass: pressure: importance: power: impressiveness: the frequency of an item in a frequency distribution or a number indicating this. — *v.t.* to make heavier (*lit.* and *fig.*): to attach weights to: to hold down in this way: to increase the weight of, as fabrics, by adding chemicals: to assign a handicap weight to (a horse; also *fig.*): to oppress, burden: to assign greater value, importance, etc. to one factor than to another: to attach numbers indicating their relative frequency to (items in a frequency distribution). — *adv.* **weigh′tily.** — *ns.* **weigh′tiness; weight′ing** a weighting allowance. — *adj.* **weight′less.** — *n.* **weight′lessness** the condition of a freely falling body at the beginning of the fall when its inertia exactly balances the gravitational force, or that of a space traveller and his unpowered space craft in orbit beyond the earth's atmosphere. — *adj.* **weigh′ty** heavy: important: having much influence: being the fruit of judicious consideration and hence worthy of attention: severe (Shak., *Timon*, III, v. 104). — **weigh′-bank** (*Scot.*) the beam of a balance: (in *pl.*) a pair of scales; **weigh′-board** see **way-board; weigh′bridge** a machine for weighing vehicles with their loads; **weigh′-house** a public building for weighing goods, ascertaining the tonnage of boats, etc.; **weigh-in** see **weigh in; weigh′ing-machine′** a machine or apparatus for weighing; **weigh-out** see **weigh out; weighting allowance** a salary differential to balance the higher cost of living in a particular area; **weight′-lifter; weight′-lifting** a sport in which competitors lift and hold above their heads (or attempt to) a barbell made increasingly heavy as the competition progresses; **weight′-watcher** a person, esp. female, who is attempting to reduce weight by careful dieting, esp. one who attends meetings of an association of like people. — **by, in, with, weight** (*Shak.*) fully; **throw one's weight about** to over-exercise one's authority: to domineer; **weigh down** to force down: to depress (*fig.*): to preponderate over, outweigh; **weigh in** to ascertain one's weight before a boxing match or other sports competition, or after a horse-race (*n.* **weigh′-in**): to join in a project (*slang*); **weigh in with** (*fig.*) to produce (a new argument, etc.) in a discussion; **weigh out** to weigh and dispense in portions accordingly: to ascertain one's weight before a horse-race (*n.* **weigh′-out**); **weight of metal** (now *rare*) the total weight of the projectiles thrown at one discharge from a ship's guns; **weigh to the beam** (*Shak.*) to outweigh completely; **weigh up** to force up (*lit.* and *fig.*): to consider carefully and assess the quality of, as a person (*coll.*); **weigh with** (*fig.*) to appear important to, to influence. [O.E. *wegan*, to carry; Ger. *wiegen*; L. *vehĕre*, to carry.]

weigh² *wā*, *n.* a variant of **way** in the phrase 'under way', through confusion with the phrase 'to weigh anchor'.

weight¹. See **weigh¹.**

weight². Same as **wecht.**

weil. Same as **weel¹.**

Weil's disease *vīlz diz-ēz′*, a type of severe jaundice caused by a spirochaete carried by the urine of rats. [H.A. *Weil* (1848–1916), German physician.]

Weimar Republic *vī′mär ri-pub′lik*, the federal republic in Germany that was founded in 1919 and lasted until 1933, its constitution having been established at *Weimar*. — *n.* **Weimaraner** (*vī-mə-rän′ər, wī-, vī′, wī′*) (any one of) a breed of grey short-haired gun dogs with docked tails, orig. developed at *Weimar*.

weir¹, wear *wēr*, *n.* a dam across a river: a fence of stakes set in a stream for catching fish. [O.E. *wer*, an enclosure, allied to *werian*, to protect; cf. Ger. *Wehr*, a dam, *wehren*, to ward.]

weir². Another spelling of **wear⁴.**

weird *wērd*, (*arch.* and *Scot.*), *n.* fate: (*cap.*; in *pl.*) the Fates: a witch: one's lot, esp. if evil: a happening, esp. uncanny: a tale of fate: a spell or charm. — *adj.* concerned with, controlling, fate: unearthly, uncanny: peculiar, odd (*coll.*). — *v.t.* (*Scot.*) to destine, doom: to hand over to as one's fate: to forewarn. — *ns.* **weird′ie, weird′o** (*pl.* **weird′os**) an eccentric: someone unconventional in dress, etc. — *adv.* **weird′ly.** — *n.* **weird′ness.** — **dree one's weird** see **dree; the Weird Sisters** the Fates: applied by some also to the Norns, the Fates of Scandinavian mythology: the witches in *Macbeth.* [O.E. *wyrd*, fate; allied to *weorthan*, to become; Ger. *werden*.]

weise. See **wise².**

Weismannism *vīs′man-izm*, *n.* the doctrine in biology of August *Weismann* (1834–1914), whose central teach-

ing is that acquired characters are not transmitted.

weize. See **wise².**

weka *we′kə*, *n.* any of the flightless rails (*Ocydromus*) of New Zealand. [Maori, imit.]

welaway. See **welladay.**

welch *welsh*, an old form of **Welsh** and **welsh.**

welcome *wel′kəm*, *adj.* received with gladness: admitted willingly: causing gladness: free (to): free to take or enjoy. — *n.* the act of welcoming: a kindly reception: a reception. — *v.t.* to greet: to receive with kindness or pleasure: to accept or undergo gladly. — *interj.* expressing pleasure, as to a guest on his arrival. — *ns.* **wel′comeness; wel′comer.** — *adj.* **wel′coming.** — **bid a welcome** to receive with professions of kindness; **he's, you're,** etc. **welcome** it is (or was) no trouble, no thanks are needed; **make someone welcome** to welcome someone, make him feel welcome; **outstay one's welcome** to stay too long; **wear out one's welcome** to stay too long or visit too often. [O.E. *wilcuma* — *wil-* (*willa*, will, pleasure), and *cuma*, guest, with later alteration suggesting a connection with **well²** and **come**, prob. under the influence of e.g. O.Fr. *bien venuz*; cf. O.N. *velkominn.*]

weld¹ *weld*, *n.* a scentless species of mignonette, also known as dyer's rocket, yielding a yellow dye: the dye itself. — Also (*Scot.*) **wald.** [Cf. Ger. *Wau.*]

weld² *weld*, *v.t.* to join (two pieces of metal) by raising the temperature at the joint by means of external heat or (**resistance welding**) of a heavy electric current or (**arc welding**) of an electric arc and often by then applying pressure, or (**cold welding**) by pressure alone: to join closely. — *v.i.* to undergo welding: to be capable of being welded. — *n.* a welded joint. — *n.* **weldabil′ity.** — *adj.* **weld′able.** — *n.* **weld′er, weld′or.** — *n.* and *adj.* **weld′ing.** — *adj.* **weld′less** having no welds. — *n.* **weld′ment** the action or process of welding: a welded assembly. — **Weld′mesh®** (also without *cap.*) a type of fencing formed of two sets of parallel lengths of wire welded together at right angles to each other. [Same as obs. or dial. verb *well*, meaning melt, weld; prob. from pa.p.]

weld³ *weld*, (*obs.* and *dial.*) *v.t.* a variant of **wield.**

welfare *wel′fār*, *n.* the state of faring or doing well: freedom from calamity, etc.: enjoyment of health, etc.: prosperity: welfare work. — *ns.* **wel′farism** the social policies characteristic of a welfare state; **wel′farist.** — **welfare state** a social system or state in which socialist principles have been put into effect with the purpose of ensuring the welfare of all who live in it, e.g. by paying unemployment benefit, old-age pensions, etc. and by providing other social services; **welfare work** efforts to improve conditions of living for a class, as the very poor, or a group, as employees or workers; hence **welfare worker.** [**well²**, **fare.**]

welk¹ *welk*, (*obs.*) *v.i.* to wither, shrivel: to wane, decline (*Spens.* **welke**). — Also *v.t.* [M.E. *welken*; cf. Ger. *welk*, withered.]

welk². See **welkt.**

welkin *wel′kin*, *n.* the sky or region of clouds. — *adj.* (*Shak.*) sky-blue. [O.E. *wolcnu*, pl. of *wolcen*, cloud, air, sky; Ger. *Wolke*, cloud.]

welkt, wealk'd *welkt*, *adj.* (*Shak.*) twisted — in some mod. editions **whelk'd.** — *v.i.* **welk** (*Scott*, founding on *Shak.*) apparently, to twist about. [**whelk¹**.]

well¹ *wel*, *n.* a spring: a mineral spring: a source (*fig.*): a lined shaft sunk in the earth whence a supply of water, oil, etc., is obtained: an enclosure in a ship's hold round the pumps: the vertical opening enclosed between the outer ends of the flights in a winding stair: a lift-shaft: the open space in the middle of a court-room: a cavity: an eddy. — *v.i.* to issue forth, as water from the earth (*lit.* and *fig.*). — *v.t.* to pour forth. — *n.* **well′ing** an outpouring. — **well′-boat, -smack** a fishing-boat having a well for holding live fish; **well′-borer** a person engaged, or a machine employed, in well-boring; **well′-boring** sinking wells by drilling through rock; **well′-curb** the stone ring built round the mouth of a well; **well′-deck** an enclosed space on the deck of a ship; **well′-drain** a pit drawing the water from wet land; **well′-dressing** the festal decoration of wells and springs, as in Derbyshire on Ascension-day, etc.; **well′-head** the source of a spring: a fountain-head (*fig.*): a spring in a marsh (*Scot.*): the top of a well, or a structure built over it; **well′-hole** a hole for a well of any kind: the shaft of a well: a shaft for machinery; **well′-house, well′-room** a room built over a well; **well′-sinker** one who digs wells; **well′-sinking**; **well′-spring** a fountain. — **the wells** any place where mineral wells are situated; **well over** to overflow. [O.E. *wella*; cf. *weallan*, to boil, O.N. *vella*, to boil.]

well² *wel* (*compar.* **bett′er**; *superl.* **best**), *adj.* (usu. predicative) good in condition: in health: fortunate: comfortable: satisfactory. — *n.* (*Spens.*) good health or fortune. — *adv.* rightly: skilfully: thoroughly: intimately: favourably, successfully: abundantly: with some degree of luxury: with reason or propriety: conveniently: to a considerable extent: clearly: easily: very possibly: very, esp. in combination, as (*Shak.*) **well′-accom′plisht**: so be it (as a sign of assent). — *interj.* expressing surprise, hesitation, resignation, etc., or introducing resumed narrative. — *adjs.* **well′-acquaint′ed** having intimate personal knowledge; **well′-advised′** prudent: in one's right mind (*Shak.*); **well′-aimed′**. — *interj.* **well′anear′** (*Shak.*) welladay. — *adj.* **well′-appoint′ed** well-equipped. — **well′-appoint′edness.** — *adjs.* **well′-bal′anced** having the parts properly adjusted for smooth working: sane and sensible; **well′-becom′ing** befitting well: proper or suitable; **well′-behaved′** behaving or acting in accordance with propriety or with requirements. — **well′-be′ing** welfare. — *adjs.* **well′-beloved′** (-*luvd′* or -*luv′id*) very dear; **well′-beseem′ing** well-becoming; **well′-beseen′** (*obs.*) showy in appearance; **well′-born′** born of a good family, not of mean birth; **well′-breathed′** (-*brēdhd′* or -*bretht′*) strong of lung: exercised: not out of breath; **well′-bred′** educated to polished manners: of good stock; **well′-built′** (of a building, buildings, a person, a garment, etc.) of strong or well-proportioned make or form; **well′-chos′en** (now esp. of words in a speech) carefully chosen; **well′-condi′tioned** in a desirable condition; **well′-conduct′ed** properly managed: acting properly; **well′-connec′ted** having friends or relatives in positions of importance or in the upper social strata; **well′-defined′** clearly and precisely determined; **well′-derived′** (*Shak.*) of good stock or antecedents; **well′-desired′** (*Shak.*) much sought after; **well′-devel′oped** having developed to an advanced, elaborate, good, desirable, etc. state; **well′-direct′ed** skilfully aimed (*lit.* and *fig.*); **well′-disposed′** healthy (*obs.*): well-placed or well-arranged: inclined to be friendly: favourable. — **well′-doer** one who lives uprightly or does good: one who thrives and is prosperous (*dial.*). — *n.* and *adj.* **well′-doing.** — *adjs.* **well′-dressed′** wearing stylish clothes; **well′-earned′** thoroughly deserved; **well′-ed′ucated** having a good education; **well′-endowed′** (*coll. facet.*) of a man, having a large penis: of a woman, having large breasts; **well′-en′tered** (*Shak.*) instructed, initiated; **well′-famed′** (*Shak.*) very famous; **well′-fa′voured** (*Scots* forms **weel′-faird′, -faur′d′, -far′d′, -far′t′, -faurt′**) good-looking; **well′-fed′** plump: given nutritious food; **well′-formed′** shapely, well-proportioned: correct according to the established rules of grammar (*linguistics*); **well′-found′** commendable (*obs.*): adequately provided, fully equipped; **well′-found′ed** built on secure foundations: based on solid evidence or sound reasoning; **well′-giv′en** (*obs.*) well-disposed; **well′-got′ten** obtained honestly; **well′-graced′** (*Shak.*) popular; **well′-groomed′** well-dressed; **well′-ground′ed** firmly founded; **well′-heeled′** prosperous, rich; **well′-hung′** hung skilfully: of meat, hung long enough to mature; **well′-informed′** having sound and sufficient information on a particular subject: full of varied information; **well′-inten′tioned** having, or arising from, good intentions or purpose; **well′-judged′** correctly

calculated, judicious; **well′-judg′ing; well′-knit′** (of a person) strongly built: closely and firmly connected; **well′-known′** fully known: celebrated: notorious; **well′-lik′ing** (*arch.*) in good condition, plump. — *n.* (*obs.*) approbation, fondness. — *adjs.* **well′-lined′** with a good lining: full of money; **well′-look′ing** good-looking; **well′-made′; well′-mann′ered** polite; **well′-marked′** obvious, decided; **well′-mean′ing** well-intentioned; **well′-meant′** rightly, kindly, intended; **well′-mind′ed** favourably inclined: well-disposed. — *adv.* **well′-nigh′** nearly, almost. — *adjs.* **well′-off′** in good circumstances; **well′-oiled′** (*slang*) drunk; **well′-ord′ered** correctly governed: properly arranged; **well′-placed′** in a good position (for some purpose): in a position senior enough or intimate enough to gain information, etc.; **well′-pleas′ing** acceptable; **well′-plight′ed** well-folded (see **plight²**); **well′-preserved′** in good condition, not decayed: looking youthful or younger than one's age; **well′-propor′tioned** having correct or pleasing proportions; **well′-read′** (-*red′*) of wide reading; **well′-reg′ulated** well-ordered; **well′-respect′ed** highly esteemed: given due consideration (Shak., 1 *Hen. IV*, IV, iii. 10); **well′-round′ed** suitably curved: symmetrical: well constructed and complete; **well′-seen′** (*arch.*) experienced, skilful; **well′-set′** properly arranged, or well placed: fitly put together: firmly fixed: strongly built; **well′-set-up′** (*coll.*) well-built, shapely; **well′-spent′** spent usefully or profitably; **well′-spo′ken** spoken well or fittingly: ready, graceful, or courteous in speech; **well′-stacked** see **stack; well′-tem′pered** having a good bodily or mental constitution (*obs.*): good-tempered: of steel, mortar, etc., tempered satisfactorily: tuned in equal temperament (*mus.*); **well′-thewed′** (*obs.*) well-mannered, of good disposition: abounding in moral wisdom; **well′-thought′-of** esteemed; **well′-thought-out′** reasoned soundly and arranged with skill; **well′-thumbed′** showing marks of much handling; **well′-tim′bered** strongly built of wood: well-built: furnished with much growing timber; **well′-timed′** opportune: keeping accurate time; **well′-to-do′,** (*Scot.*) **well′-to-live′** (*Shak.* **well to live**) prosperous, well-off; **well′-trodd′en** frequently followed or walked along (usu. *fig.*); **well′-turned′** accurately rounded: shapely: felicitously expressed; **well′-uphol′stered** (*facet.*; of a person) plump, fat; **well′-warr′anted** having good credit. — **well′-willer** a well-wisher; **well′-wish** (*rare*) act of wishing well. — *adj.* **well′-wished** (*Shak.*) being the object of good wishes. — **well′-wisher.** — *adj.* and *n.* **well′-wishing.** — *adjs.* **well′-won′** gained honestly or by hard endeavour; **well′-worked-out′** thoroughly or logically planned or developed; **well′-worn′** much worn: trite: becomingly worn (*rare*). — **all very well** an ironic phrase used to introduce an objection to what has gone before; **as well** see **as; as well as** in addition to: no less than; **do well** see **do; very well** a phrase signifying assent, sometimes ironic; **well and good** a phrase signifying acceptance of facts or a situation; **well and truly** completely, thoroughly; **well away** progressing rapidly: far away: drunk (*slang*); **well done** an expression of praise: (of meat) well, thoroughly, cooked; **well enough** in a moderate but sufficient degree; **well in** (*coll.*) having a good relationship: prosperous (*Austr.*); **well met** see **meet; well now, well then** phrases used to preface questions, conclusions, comments, or requests for such, or other remarks; **well up in** (*coll.*) well versed in, well acquainted with; **well, well** an expression of surprise; **wish someone well** to wish someone success or good fortune. [O.E. *wel*; cog. with Goth. *waila*, Ger. *wohl*; from the root of **will¹**.]

we′ll *wēl*, a contraction of **we will** or **we shall.**

welladay *wel′ə-dā*, **wellaway, welaway** *wel′ə-wā*, *interjs.* alas. [O.E. *wei lā wei*, woe lo! woe, with *wei* (O.N. *vei*) substituted for the orig. O.E. form *wā*.]

wellie. See **welly².**

Wellingtonia *wel-ing-tō′ni-ə*, *n.* a synonym of Sequoia. [Named after the Duke of *Wellington* (1769–1852).]

wellingtons *wel′ing-tənz*, *n.pl.* a kind of riding-boots covering the knee in front, but cut away behind: shorter closely-fitting boots, worn under the trousers (**half´-well´ingtons**): rubber boots loosely covering the calves: (in *sing.*) one of a pair of wellingtons. — Also **wellington boot.** [As previous word.]

Wellsian *wel´zi-ən, adj.* of, pertaining to, or characteristic of, H. G. *Wells* (1866–1946), historian and writer of stories and novels with scientific or social interest.

welly[1] *wel´i, (dial.) adv.* corr. of **well-nigh.**

welly[2], **wellie** *wel´i, (coll.) n.* a wellington of the loose rubber kind. — Also **well´y-, well´ie-boot´.**

Welsh, (*obs.*) **Welch** *welsh, adj.* pertaining to *Wales* or its inhabitants. — *n.pl.* the inhabitants of Wales. — *n.sing.* their language. — **Welsh dresser** a dresser usu. with open shelves above cupboards and drawers; **Welsh harp** a large harp with three rows of strings, two tuned in unison and in the diatonic scale, the third in the sharps and flats of the chromatic; **Welsh hook** an old weapon; **Welsh´man** a native of Wales; **Welsh onion** the cibol; **Welsh rabbit, Welsh rarebit** see **rabbit; Welsh´woman.** [O.E. (Angl. and Kentish) *welisc* — *wealh,* foreigner; Anglo-Saxons' name for Britons, etc.; related to the name of an ancient Celtic tribe, the *Volcae.*]

welsh *welsh, v.i.* to run off from a race-course without settling or paying one's bets: to dodge fulfilling an obligation. — *v.t.* to cheat in such a way. — Also **welch.** — *n.* **welsh´er, welch´er.** [Of uncertain origin.]

Welsummer *wel´sum-ər n.* a breed of large poultry with golden plumage, prolific egg-layers. [After the Dutch village of *Welsum,* where it was first bred.]

welt[1] *welt, n.* a band or strip fastened to an edge to give strength or for ornament: a narrow strip of leather used in one method of sewing the upper to the sole of a shoe: a weal: a lash, blow. — *v.t.* to furnish with a welt: to lash, beat. [Origin obscure.]

welt[2] *welt, v.t.* and *v.i.* to wither, dry. [Perh. **welk**[1].]

Welt *velt, (Ger.) n.* world. — *ns.* **Weltanschauung** (*velt´an-show-ŏŏng*) outlook upon the world, world-philosophy; **Weltgeist** (*velt´gīst*) the world-spirit; **Weltpolitik** (*velt´pol-i-tēk*) world politics: the policy of taking a forceful part in international affairs; **Weltschmerz** (*velt´shmerts*) world-sorrow: sympathy with universal misery: thoroughgoing pessimism.

welter *wel´tər, v.i.* to roll or tumble about (*rare* or *dial.*): to wallow about in dirt or moral degradation, etc. (*rare*): to be, or lie, soaked, as in blood (*poet.*): to be sunk (in) (*lit.* and *fig.*): to roll, toss, about in the waves: to roll, surge, as the sea (*poet.*). — *v.t.* (*rare*) to make (one's way) in a weltering manner. — *n.* a state of turmoil or confusion: confusion, agitation: a surging mass. — *adj.* **wel´tering.** [M.Du. *welteren*; cf. O.E. *gewæltan,* to roll.]

welter-weight *wel´tər-wāt, n.* a boxer over 61 kg (9 st 9 lb), amateur 63·5 kg (10 st), and not over 66.7 kg (10 st 7 lb), amateur 67 kg (10 st 8 lb): a wrestler over 68 kg (10 st 10 lb) and not over 74 kg (11 st 8 lb): an unusually heavy weight, carried mostly in steeplechases and hurdle-races. — **wel´ter-race** a race in which such weights are carried; **wel´ter-stakes** the stakes in a welter-race. — **light welter-weight** a boxer, amateur only, whose weight is between 60 kg (9 st 6 lb) and 63·5 kg (10 st). [Origin obscure.]

Welwitschia *wel-wich´i-ə, n.* a South-west African genus of one species, belonging to the Gnetaceae, with one pair of leaves that grow indefinitely: (without *cap.*) a plant of this genus. [After F. *Welwitsch* (1806–72), Austrian traveller.]

wem(b). See **wame.**

wen[1] *wen, n.* a sebaceous cyst. — *adjs.* **wenn´ish, wenn´y** wen-like. [O.E. *wen(n),* a swelling, a wart; Du. *wen*; origin obscure.]

wen[2] *wen, n.* a rune (Þ), having the value of modern English *w,* adopted (as Þ þ) into the O.E. alphabet. — Now more usually **wyn** or **wynn** (*win*). [O.E., orig. *wynn,* joy (of which *w* is the initial letter).]

wench *wench, -sh, n.* a child (*obs.*): a damsel, girl: a

working-girl, a maid-servant: a mistress (*obs.* or *arch.*): a whore (*obs.* or *arch.*). — *v.i.* to frequent the company of whores: to associate innocently with women (*Scot. winch*): to go courting (*dial.*). — *n.* **wench´er** one who indulges in lewdness. [O.E. *wencel,* a child.]

wend *wend, v.t.* to turn (*obs.*): to turn to the opposite tack (*naut.*): to turn, direct one's course (*obs.*; *refl.*): to change (*obs.*). — *v.i.* to turn (*obs.*): to change (*obs.*): to depart (*arch.*): to make one's way (*arch.*; also *fig.*): — *pa.t.* and *pa.p.* **wend´ed,** (*obs.*) **went** (now used as *pa.t.* of **go**). — **wend one's way** to make one's way, follow the road, esp. in a leisurely fashion. [O.E. *wendan,* a common Gmc. verb.]

Wend *wend, n.* one of a branch of the Slavs which once occupied the north and east of Germany: one of the Slavic population of Lusatia (part of Brandenburg, Saxony and Silesia) who still speak the Wendish tongue. — *adjs.* **Wend´ic, Wend´ish.** — *ns.* the Wendish language. [Ger. *Wende*; origin obscure.]

wendigo. See **windigo.**

Wendy House® *wen´di hows,* a structure of cloth or the like, decorated to simulate a little house, stretched over a rigid frame, usu. erected indoors for children to play in. [From the house built for *Wendy* in J. M. Barrie's *Peter Pan.*]

Wenlock *wen´lok, (geol.) adj.* denoting a group or series of rocks of the Upper Silurian period, consisting of limestone and shale, and largely developed in the neighbourhood of *Wenlock* in Shropshire.

wennish, wenny. See **wen**[1].

Wensleydale *wenz´li-dāl, n.* a breed of long-woolled sheep: a variety of cheese. [*Wensleydale* in North Riding of Yorks.]

went *went,* properly *pa.t.* of **wend,** but now used as *pa.t.* of **go.** — *n.* (*Spens.*) a path: a journey: a way: a course.

wentletrap *wen´tl-trap, n.* any member of a genus (Scalaria) of gasteropod molluscs, having a spiral shell with many deep whorls, crossed by elevated ribs. [Du. *wenteltrap* (Ger. *Wendeltreppe*) a winding staircase, a spiral shell.]

wept *wept, pa.t.* and *pa.p.* of **weep.**

were *wür, v.i.* the *pl.* of **was,** used as *pa.t.* (*pl.*) and *pa.subj.* (*sing.* and *pl.*) of **be.** [O.E. *wæron,* subj. *wære*; Ger. *waren, wäre.*]

we're *wēr,* a contraction of **we are.**

werewolf *wēr´wŏŏlf,* **werwolf** *wûr´wŏŏlf, ns.* a person supposed to be able to change himself for a time into a wolf (*Scot.* **war´wolf**): a member of an underground Nazi organisation (also *adj.*). — *adjs.* **were´wolfish, wer´wolfish.** — *n.* **were´wolfism** lycanthropy. [O.E. *werwulf* — *wer,* man, *wulf,* a wolf.]

wergild *wür´gild,* **weregild** *wēr´gild, ns.* among Teutonic peoples, a fine by which homicide and other heinous crimes against the person were expiated. [O.E. *wergield,* from *wer,* man, *gield* — *gieldan,* to pay.]

Wernerian *vûr-nē´ri-ən, adj.* pertaining or according to the opinions or system of A. G. *Werner* (1750–1817), who attributed all geological phenomena to the action of water: Neptunian. — *n.* an upholder of Werner's theories. — *n.* **wer´nerite** scapolite.

wersh *wersh, (Scot.) adj.* tasteless, unsalted: sickly, feeble: of weather, raw. [**wearish.**]

wert *wûrt,* used (*arch.* or *dial.*) as the *2nd pers. sing.* of the past indicative (for **wast**) and subjunctive of **be.** [**were,** and suff. *-t.*]

Wertherian *vûr-tē´ri-ən, adj.* pertaining to or resembling the character of *Werther* in Goethe's romance, 'The Sorrows of Young Werther' — morbidly sentimental. — *n.* **Wer´therism.**

werwolf. See **werewolf.**

wesand *wē´zənd, n.* (*Spens.*). Same as **weasand.**

Wesleyan *wez´, wes´li-ən, adj.* pertaining to Wesleyanism. — *n.* an adherent of Wesleyanism. — *n.* **Wes´leyanism** the system of doctrine and church polity of the Wesleyan Methodists — Arminian Methodism. [Named after John *Wesley* (1703–91).]

west *west, n.* the quarter where the sun sets: one of the four chief points of the compass: the direction faced when one stands with one's back to the high altar of a church: the regions in the west of any country, esp. (*Amer.*) those beyond the Appalachian Mts. (see **Middle West**, under **middle**) or beyond the Mississippi or the Rocky Mountains (see **Far West** under **far**). — *adj.* situated towards, or (of wind) coming from, the west: opposite the high altar of a church. — *adv.* towards the west. — *v.i.* to move towards the west. — *v.i.* **west′er** to turn westward: to change into the west. — *n.* and *adj.* **west′ering.** — *adj.* **west′erly** lying or moving towards the west: from the west. — *adv.* towards the west: from the west. — *n.* a westerly wind. — *adj.* **west′ern** situated in the west: belonging to the west: moving towards, or (of wind) coming from, the west. — *n.* an inhabitant of a western region or country: a film or novel whose scene is the western United States, esp. the former Wild West. — *n.* **west′erner** a person belonging to the west. — *v.t.* and *v.i.* **west′ernise, -ize** to make or become like the people of Europe and America in customs, or like their institutions, practices, ideas. — *ns.* **westernisā′tion, -z-;** **west′ernism** idiom or other characteristic of a western people. — *adj.* **west′ernmost** furthest to the west. — *ns.* **West′ie** a West Highland terrier; **west′ing** space or distance westward: departure westward: direction or course towards the west. — *adjs.* **west′lin** (*Scot.*) western; **west′most** most westerly. — *adj.* and *adv.* **west′ward** towards the west. — *advs.* **west′wardly, west′wards** towards the west. — *adv.* **west′-about** towards the west. — **West Bank** the Jordanian territory to the west of the river Jordan and the Dead Sea, annexed by Israel in 1967; **West Banker** an inhabitant of the West Bank. — *adj.* **west′bound.** — **west′-by-north′ (-south′)** 11¼ degrees north (south) from due west; **West Country** the south-western part of England; **West End** the fashionable quarter in the west of London: a similar district in other large towns; **Western Church** the Latin Church, as distinguished from the Eastern or Greek Church; **Western Empire** the western division of the later Roman Empire; **Western Wall** same as **Wailing Wall; West Highland (white) terrier** a breed of small white terrier with a short, stiff coat and small, pointed ears; **West Indian, West Indies** see **Indian; west′-north** (or **south**)**-west′** 22½ degrees north (south) from the west; **West Saxon** a southern dialect of Old English, the chief literary dialect before the Norman Conquest. — **go west** to go to America: to go to the western states or western frontier: to die (with reference to the setting sun, the Islands of the Blest, or Tyburn), or to be destroyed or completely dissipated; **the West Europe** or Europe and America; **westward ho!** to the west! an old cry of London watermen plying westwards; **Wild West** the western United States in the days of the first settlers, chiefly cattlemen and goldminers, before the establishment of law and order; **Wild West show** a performance of roping or riding of steers, shooting, etc. by (people dressed as) cowboys. [O.E.; a common Gmc. word; cf. L. *vesper*.]

Westminster *west′min-stər, n.* used for Parliament — from the London borough where the Houses of Parliament are situated: Westminster Hall, a court of justice: Westminster School, or a past or present pupil of it.

Westphalian *west-fā′li-ən, adj.* pertaining to *Westphalia,* a duchy, a kingdom, a province of Prussia and, since 1946, part of the German land of Nordrhein-Westfalen. — *n.* a native of Westphalia.

wet *wet, adj.* containing, soaked with, covered with, water or other liquid: rainy: bringing or foreboding moisture: tearful: grown in damp soil: using liquid: given to drinking, or tipsy (*slang*): allowing the sale of intoxicating liquors: ineffectual, or crazy (*slang*): in politics, moderately conservative (*derog.*). — *n.* water, moisture, wetness: the rain: an act of wetting: a dram, a debauch: a weak, ineffectual, wavering person (*coll.*): in politics, a moderate conservative (*derog.*). — *v.t.* to

make wet: to soak with water: to make (tea) by pouring water on the leaves (*dial.*): to celebrate by drinking (*slang*): — *pr.p.* **wett′ing;** *pa.t.* and *pa.p.* **wet,** or **wett′ed.** — *adv.* **wet′ly.** — *n.* **wet′ness.** — *adj.* **wett′ish** somewhat wet. — **wet-and-dry paper** a stiff paper coated with powdered silicon carbide, like a fine sandpaper, used either wet or dry for smoothing surfaces; **wet assay** the use of the processes of solution, flotation, or other liquid means to determine a given constituent in ores, metallurgical residues, and alloys; **wet′back** (*U.S.*) one illegally entering the U.S.A. from Mexico by wading or swimming the Rio Grande; **wet blanket** see **blanket; wet bob** (*slang*) a schoolboy at Eton who goes in for rowing; **wet′-cell** a cell with a liquid electrolyte; **wet=dock** a dock maintaining a level nearly uniform with that of high water; **wet dream** an erotic dream with ejaculation of semen; **wet fish** fresh fish, as contrasted with frozen or dried fish. — *adj.* **wet′-fly** (of angling) with the fly underwater. — **wet′land** (also in *pl.*) marshy land. — *adj.* **wet′-look** made of a glossy material, usu. PVC, which gives the appearance of being wet. — **wet meter** a gas-meter in which the gas to be measured passes through water; **wet′-nurse** a nurse who suckles a child for its mother; **wet pack** (the wrapping of a person in) blankets or the like dampened with warm or cold water as a medical treatment; **wet plate** (*phot.*) a plate coated with collodion and sensitised with a salt of silver; **wet′-rot** a form of decay in timber, caused by certain fungi which develop in wood which is alternately wet and dry. — *adj.* **wet′-shod** having shoes or feet wet. — **wet suit** a suit for wearing in cold water, which allows water to pass through but retains body heat; **wetting (out) agent** a substance that promotes wetting, e.g. a substance, such as an acid, oil, or hydrocarbon, added to a heterogeneous mixture to facilitate the absorption or adhesion between the constitutents. — **wet behind the ears** very young, immature, gullible; **wet bulb thermometer** a psychrometer; **wet one's whistle** (*coll.*) see under **whistle; wet out** to wet thoroughly: to cleanse by so doing, as raw material in textile manufacture; **wet the bed** to urinate accidentally in bed. [O.E. *wǣt* (noun and adj.), *wǣtan* (verb): the short vowel is from the M.E. pa.t. and pa.p. of the verb.]

wether *wedh′ər, n.* a castrated ram. [O.E.; cf. Ger. *Widder.*]

we've *wēv,* a contraction of **we have.**

wex(e). Obs. form of **wax**[1,2,3].

wey *wā, n.* a measure or weight for dry-goods differing with different articles as 40 bushels of salt or corn, etc. [Variant of **weigh**.]

weyard, weyward. Obs. spellings of **weird,** found in older editions of *Macbeth.*

wezand. Obs. form of **weasand.**

whack (*h*)*wak,* (*coll.*) *v.t.* to strike hard and smartly: to put or take with violence: to beat decisively: to parcel out, share. — *v.i.* to strike: to settle accounts. — *n.* a blow: a share: an attempt. — *adj.* **whacked** (*coll.*) exhausted. — *n.* **whack′er** (*coll.*) something big of its kind: a blatant lie. — *adj.* **whack′ing** (*coll.*) very large, astounding. — *n.* a beating (*lit.* and *fig.*). — *interj.* **whack′ō** (*coll.*) an expression of pleasure or enthusiasm: — *pl.* **whack′o(e)s.** — **out of whack** (*coll.*) out of order, not straight. [From the sound made.]

whacky. Same as **wacky.**

whaisle, whaizle (*h*)*wā′zl,* (*Scot.*) *v.i.* to wheeze. [A form of **wheezle**; see **wheeze**.]

whale[1] (*h*)*wāl, n.* any of an order of cetaceous mammals, including the *toothed* whales, such as the sperm whales and the dolphins, and the *whalebone* whales, such as the right whales and the rorquals, in which the teeth are only embryonic: a person with a large appetite (*slang; lit.* and *fig.*): something very large of its kind (*slang*): (*cap.*) the constellation Cetus. — *v.i.* to catch whales. — *ns.* **whāl′er** a whale-boat: a whale-man: something very large of its kind (*slang*); **whāl′ery** whaling. — *adj.* **whāl′ing** connected with whale-catching: very large or impressive (also *adv.*). — *n.* the business of catching whales. — **whale′-back** a turtle-back: a kind of steamboat used on the Great Lakes, to carry grain, etc., having rounded upper deck, etc.: a mound shaped like the back of a whale; **whale′-boat** a long, narrow boat sharp at both ends once used in the pursuit of whales: a similar boat carried on a large vessel as a life-boat; **whale′bone** a light flexible substance consisting of the baleen plates of whales: an article made of this. — *adj.* made of whalebone. — **whale′-calf** a young whale. — also **calf whale; whale′=fisher; whale′-fishery; whale′-fishing; whale′-head** the shoebill (also **whale-headed stork**); **whale′-line** strong rope used for harpoon-lines in the whale-fishery; **whale′-louse** a genus (*Cyamus*) of amphipod Crustacea parasitic on the skin of cetaceans; **whale′-man** a person or ship employed in whale-fishing; **whale′-oil** oil got from the blubber of a whale; **whale's bone** (*obs.*) ivory, as from the walrus; **whale(s′) food** small animals eaten by whales, esp. the Clio genus; **whale′-shark** a huge but harmless shark of tropical seas; **whal′ing-gun** a contrivance for killing whales by means of a projectile; **whal′ing-master** the captain of a whaler; **whal′ing-port** a port where whalers are registered. — **bull, cow, whale** an adult male, female, whale; **a whale of a time** (*coll.*) a very enjoyable time. [O.E. *hwæl*; cf. O.N. *hvalr*, Ger. *Walfisch*.]

whale² (*h*)*wāl*, (*slang*) *v.t.* to thrash: to strike violently. — *n.* **whāl′ing** a thrashing. [Perh. **wale**¹; perh. from *whale*bone whip.]

whally (*h*)*wöl′i*, (*Spens.*) *adj.* wall-eyed: showing much white. [From **wall-eye**.]

wham (*h*)*wam*, *n.* a resounding noise caused by a hard blow. — *v.i.* to hit with a wham: — *pr.p.* **whamm′ing**; *pa.t.* and *pa.p.* **whammed.** — *v.t.* to (cause to) hit with a wham. — Also used as *adv.* and *interj.* [Imit.]

whample (*h*)*wöm′pl*, (*h*)*wam′pl*, (*Scot.*) *n.* a blow: a sudden blow.

whang¹ (*h*)*wang*, *n.* a leather thong: a thick slice: a penis (*vulg.*; also **wang**). — *v.t.* to flog: to throw, push, pull, violently: to cut in great slices. [*thwang*, obs. form of **thong**.]

whang² (*h*)*wang*, *n.* a resounding noise: a blow. — *v.i.* to make, or hit with, the sound of a blow, explosion, etc. — *v.t.* to (cause to) hit with a whang. — Also used as *adv.* and *interj.* [Imit.]

whangam (*h*)*wang′gam*, (*Goldsmith*) *n.* an imaginary animal.

whangee (*h*)*wang-ē′*, *n.* any of several grasses of a genus (Phyllostachys) allied to the bamboos, found in China and Japan: a cane made from the stem of one. [Prob. Chin. *huang*, yellow, *li*, bamboo.]

whap. Same as **whop.**

whare (*h*)*wor′i*, *hwär′ā*, *fär′ā*, (*New Zealand*) *n.* a house. [Maori.]

wharf (*h*)*wörf*, *n.* a landing-stage, built esp. along the shore, for loading or unloading vessels: the bank of a river (*Shak.*): — *pl.* **wharfs, wharves.** — *v.t.* to strengthen or secure by means of a wharf (*obs.*): to place on, or bring to, a wharf. — *ns.* **wharf′age** the dues paid for using a wharf: accommodation at a wharf; **wharf′-ing** material for making a wharf: wharfs; **wharfinger** ((*h*)*wörf′in-jər*) one who has the care of, or owns, a wharf. — **wharf′-rat** the common brown rat: a fellow who loafs continually about a wharf. [Late O.E. *hwearf*, bank, shore: allied to *hweorfan*, to turn.]

wharve. See **whorl** (*spinning*).

what (*h*)*wot*, *interrog. pron.* neuter of **who**: used to form a question regarding identity, selection from an indefinite number, nature, value, etc. — also used elliptically (as for *what did you say, do you think? what is it?*): who (*obs.*). — Also *interrog. adj.* — *rel. pron.* and *adj.* that which: such . . . as: which (*dial.*): any (thing) whatever: whoever (*Shak.*). — *indef. pron.* (or *n.*) something: a portion, bit (*Spens.*): fare (in phrase **such homely what**; Spens. *F.Q.* VI, ix. 7, 4). — *adv.* why? (*obs.*): in what way, how? to what degree?. — *conj.* as

much as (*dial.*): that (as in **but what**, that . . . not). — *interj.* used in summoning, calling attention, expressing surprise, disapprobation, or protest, etc. — *adjs.* **what′en, whatt′en** (*dial.*; from *whatkin*, what kind) what: what kind of; **what′na** (from *whatkin* a) same as **whaten.** — *n.* **what′ness** what a thing is: essence: quiddity. — *ns.* **what′abouts** the things one is occupied about; **what′-d'you** (or **ye**)**-call(-it, -'em**, etc.) a word substituted for the name of a thing (or person) in forgetfulness or contempt. — *prons.* **whatev′er, what-e′er′** anything which: no matter what: what? (*coll.*). — *adjs.* any or all that, no matter what. — *ns.* **what's′=his-(her-, its-)name, what′sit,** (*U.S.*) **what′sis** (*coll.*) that person, or thing, indicated or understood (often used when the name of the person, etc. has been forgotten). — *adj.* **what′-like** (*dial.*) of what kind, character, or appearance. — *n.* **what′not** see separate article. — *adj.* **what′so** (*arch.*) of whatever kind. — *pron.* whatever (*arch.*): whoever (*obs.*): whosoever (*obs.*). — *adjs.* and *prons.* **whatsoev′er, whatsoe′er′** whatever; **whatsomev′er** (*dial.*) whatsoever. — *n.* **what′-you-may-call-it** same as **what-d'you-call-it.** — **and what and all** and so on, and suchlike things; **know what it is** to know what is involved in an action or experience: to have experienced, suffered, it; **or whatever** or whatever else arises, etc.; **so what?** what of it?; **what about** an expression used to make a suggestion, ask for an opinion, etc.; **what an if** (*Shak.*) what if, or though; **what else?** could anything else be the case?; **what for** . . . for what reason, or intended for what purpose (*dial.*; in standard English **what** . . . **for**): punishment, esp. a whipping (*slang*); **what for a** (*obs.*) what kind of; **what have you** (*coll.*) what not: anything else of the kind; **what ho** a loud hail, summons; **what if** what would it matter if? (also **what matter if**): what would happen if?; **what** . . . **like?** a common form of request for a description or opinion of something or someone, as *what is she like?, what does this look, sound, like?*; **what next?** what is to be done next?: what will happen next? (often said in despair or trepidation); **what not** elliptical for 'what may I not say?' implying the presence or existence of many other things; **what of** what comes of, follows from?: what do you think of?; **what of it?** does it matter? (usu. implying that one thinks that it does not); **what then?** what would come of it?, what would be the consequence?; **what's what** the true position of affairs: the proper, conventional, or profitable way to behave or proceed; **what though** what matters it though: notwithstanding the fact that; **what time** (*arch.*) at the very time when; **what with** by reason of. [O.E. *hwæt*, neut. of *hwā*, who; Ger. *was*, L. *quod*.]

Whatman paper® (*h*)*wot′mən pā′pər*, fine quality paper used for drawings, engravings, filtering, etc. [Name of manufacturing firm.]

whatna. See **what.**

whatnot (*h*)*wot′not*, *n.* a light piece of furniture with shelves for bric-à-brac, etc.: anything, no matter what: a nondescript article. [**what, not.**]

whatsis, what(t)en, etc. See under **what.**

whaup (*h*)*wöp*, (*Scot.*) *n.* a curlew — sometimes **great whaup** as opp. to **little whaup,** the whimbrel. [Primarily imit.; history uncertain.]

whaur (*h*)*wör*, a Scots form of **where.**

wheal¹. Variant of **weal**².

wheal² (*h*)*wēl*, *n.* a Cornish name for a mine.

whear(e). Obs. spelling of **where.**

wheat (*h*)*wēt*, *n.* any cereal grass of the genus Triticum, or its grain, furnishing a white or brown flour for bread, etc. — known as *bearded*, or *beardless* or *bald*, according to the presence or the absence of the awns or beard; as *white, red,* or *amber,* according to colour; and as *winter* or *spring* (also *summer*) according to whether it is a type normally sown in autumn or spring. — *adj.* **wheat′en** made of wheat: wholemeal. — **wheat′=berry, wheat′-corn** the grain of wheat; **wheat′-bird** the chaffinch; **wheat′-crop; wheat′-ear** an ear of wheat; **wheat′-eel** (also **wheat′-worm**) a small nematode worm that makes its way up wheat stems to the ears: the disease it causes — also *ear-cockle*; **wheat'-field; wheat'= fly** the name of several flies that destroy wheat, e.g. the Hessian fly; **wheat'-germ** the vitamin-rich germ or embryo of wheat, part of a grain of wheat; **wheat'-meal** meal made of wheat, esp. wholemeal; **wheat'-midge** a dipterous insect that lays its eggs in the flowers of wheat-heads, and whose reddish larvae devour the kernels; **wheat'-mildew** either of two fungus diseases of wheat; **wheat'-moth** any of several small moths whose larvae devour stored wheat; **wheat'sheaf** a sheaf of wheat; **wheat-worm** see **wheat-eel**. — **wheat-ear stitch** a fancy stitch in embroidery. [O.E. *hwǣte*; Ger. *Weizen*; allied to **white**; named from its colour.]

wheatear (h)*wēt'ēr, n.* a bird akin to the chats, a common summer visitant of Britain. [Prob. corr. of **white arse**.]

Wheatstone('s) bridge (h)*wēt'stən(z) brij*, an apparatus for measuring electrical resistance, much used, but not invented, by Sir Charles *Wheatstone* (1802–75).

whee (h)*wē, interj.* an expression of delight, exuberance, etc.

wheech (h)*wēhh, (Scot.) v.i.* to move rapidly with a whizzing sound: to dart: to do, deal with, etc. rapidly (with *through*). — *v.t.* to carry, remove rapidly: to throw. — *n.* a rapid movement or throw: a whizzing sound. [Imit.]

wheedle (h)*wēd'l, v.t.* and *v.i.* to entice by soft words, flatter, cajole: to obtain by coaxing (with *out of*): to cheat by cajolery (with *out of*). — *n.* a piece of wheedling: a coaxing person (*obs.*). — *n.* **wheed'ler.** — *adj.* **wheed'lesome** coaxing. — *n.* **wheed'ling.** [Perh. from O.E. *wǣdlian*, (orig.) to be in want, to beg.]

wheel (h)*wēl, n.* a circular frame turning on an axle: an old instrument of torture: a steering-wheel: a potter's wheel: a spinning-wheel: a rotating firework: a bicycle or tricycle (*coll.*): the wheel by which a spit is turned (*Shak.*): the wheel attributed to Fortune personified, the emblem of mutability: hence, the course of events: a celestial sphere (*obs.*): a disc: a circular design: a circular motion: (in *pl.*) the parts of a machine, esp. fig.: one or more short lines following a bob at the end of a stanza: a refrain: a dollar (*slang*). — *v.t.* to cause to turn or revolve, esp. round an axis or pivot, as a body of troops: to cause to move in a circular course: to encircle (*Milt.*): to make wheel-shaped (*rare*): to put a wheel or wheels on: to form, or treat, on the wheel: to convey on wheels: to propel on wheels: (with *out, forward*, etc.) to bring out, forward, etc., to produce. — *v.i.* to turn round or on an axis: to change direction: to move in a circle: to reel, be giddy: to roll forward: to wander, roam (*Shak.*): to travel in a wheeled vehicle: to ride a bicycle or tricycle (*coll.*): to be provided with wheels on which to be propelled. — *adj.* **wheeled** having wheels: moving on wheels: formed into a wheel (*rare*). — *ns.* **wheel'er** one who wheels: a cyclist (*coll.*): a maker of wheels (*dial.*): in composition, that which wheels, or has such-and-such a kind of or so-many wheels: a wheel-horse; **wheel'ie** (*coll.*) a manoeuvre, esp. on a bicycle or motorbike, involving travelling for a short distance with the front wheel(s) off the ground; **wheel'- ing** the act of moving or conveying on wheels: a turning or circular movement: a rather coarse woollen yarn. — *adj.* **wheel'y** like a wheel. — **wheel'-animal, -animal- cule** a rotifer; **wheel'barrow** a barrow with one wheel in front and two handles and legs behind: loosely, any other hand-cart; **wheel'base** the distance between the front and rear axles of a vehicle: the area enclosed by lines joining the points at which the wheels of a locomotive, etc., touch the rails or the ground, or the length of this area; **wheel'-carriage** any kind of carriage moved on wheels; **wheel'-chair** a chair moving on wheels, esp. an invalid's chair; **wheel'-clamp** a device that immobilises an illegally parked car until it is removed after payment of a fine. — Also *v.t.* — *adj.* **wheel'-cut** of glass, cut, or ground and polished, on a wheel. — **wheel'-cutter** a machine for cutting teeth on

wheels; **wheel'er-deal'er; wheel'er-deal'ing** (*coll.*; *orig. U.S.*) shrewd dealing or bargaining in business, politics, etc. to one's maximum advantage and often with little regard for others; **wheel'-horse** one of the horses next to the wheels in a team; **wheel'-house** a shelter in which a ship's steering-wheel is placed: a paddle-box: a prehistoric wheel-shaped dwelling; **wheel'-lock** formerly, a lock for firing a gun by means of a small steel wheel; **wheel'man** a steersman: a cyclist; **wheel'-plough** a plough running on wheels, or the depth of whose furrow is regulated by a wheel; **wheel'-race** the part of a race in which the water-wheel is fixed; **wheel'-spin** rotation of the wheels without forward or backward movement of the vehicle; **wheel'-window** a circular window with radiating tracery; **wheel'work** a combination of wheels and their connection in machinery; **wheel'wright** a wright who makes wheels and wheel-carriages. — **at the wheel** driving a vehicle, or steering a boat (also *fig.*); **big wheel** a person of importance or self-importance; **break a butterfly (fly,** etc.**) on the wheel** to inflict a punishment out of all proportion to the offence: to employ great exertions for insignificant ends; **go on wheels** (*fig.*) to move swiftly, smoothly, and hence pleasantly; **left, right, wheel** (a command to perform) a swing to the left, or right; **potter's wheel** a horizontal revolving disc on which clay vessels are shaped; **put a spoke in someone's wheel** see **spoke; put one's shoulder to the wheel** see **shoulder; wheel and axle** one of the mechanical powers, in its primitive form a cylindrical axle, on which a wheel, concentric with the axle, is firmly fastened, the power being applied to the wheel, and the weight attached to the axle; **wheel and deal** (*coll.*; *orig. U.S.*) to engage in wheeler-dealing; **wheeling and dealing** (*coll.*; *orig. U.S.*) same as **wheeler= dealing; wheel of fortune** Fortune's wheel (see **wheel**): a gambling device; **wheel of life** see **zoetrope; wheels within wheels** said of a situation in which a complication of influences is at work. [O.E. *hwēol*; O.N. *hjōl*.]

wheen (h)*wēn, (Scot.) n.* a few. — *adj.* (*obs.*) few. — **a wheen** a few: a good many: (used adverbially) a little. [O.E. *hwǣne* — *hwōn*, adv., a little.]

wheenge. See whinge.

wheeple (h)*wē'pl, (Scot.) v.i.* to make a long drawn-out cry such as that of the curlew: to whistle feebly. — Also *v.t.* and *n.* [Imit.]

wheesht. See whisht.

Wheeson (*Shak., 2 Hen. IV*, II. i. 99), Whitsun.

wheeze (h)*wēz, v.i.* to breathe with a hissing sound: to breathe audibly or with difficulty. — *v.t.* to utter with such a sound. — *n.* the act, or sound, of wheezing: a gag (*theatrical slang*): a catch-phrase (*slang*): a standard joke (*slang*): a cunning plan (*coll.*). — *adv.* **wheez'ily.** — *ns.* **wheez'iness; wheez'ing.** — *v.i.* **wheez'le** (*Scot.*) to make wheezy sounds. — *adj.* **wheez'y.** [Prob. O.N. *hvǣsa*, to hiss.]

wheft. See waft.

whelk¹ *wilk, (h)welk, n.* a popular name for a number of marine gasteropods, esp. applied to species of the genus Buccinum common on the coasts of northern seas. — *adjs.* **whelked** ridged like a whelk; **whelk'y** knobby, rounded: formed in a shell (Spens., *Virgil's Gnat*, 105). [Wrong form of older *welk* — O.E. *wiloc, weoluc*; origin obscure.]

whelk² (h)*welk, n.* a pimple: by confusion with **wale¹**, the mark of a stripe on the body, a wrinkle, an inequality or protuberance. [Late O.E. (W.S.) *hwylca* — *hwelian*, to suppurate.]

whelk'd. See welkt.

whelm (h)*welm, (arch.) v.t.* to turn, as a hollow vessel, upside down, esp. so as to cover something else (now *dial.*): to cover completely, in this way (*obs.*), now with water, etc.: to overturn, overthrow: to plunge deep: to submerge: to overpower: to overburden: to ruin, destroy: to pass over in such a way as to submerge it. [M.E. *whelmen*, to turn over.]

whelp (h)*welp, n.* the young of the dog kind and of lions, etc. — a puppy, a cub, etc.: (*contemptuously*) a young man: a ridge running longitudinally on the barrel or drum of a capstan or windlass to control the cable: a sprocket on a wheel. — *v.i.* and *v.t.* to bring forth (young).   [O.E. *hwelp*; O.N. *hvelpr*.]

whemmle (*h*)*wem′l*, **whomble, whommle, whummle** (*h*)*wum′l*, (*dial.*) *ns.* an overthrow, overturn: confusion. — *vs.t.* to overturn: to turn upside down: to throw into a state of disorder or agitation: to cover as with an inverted dish. — *vs.i.* to capsize.   [By metathesis from **whelm**.]

when (*h*)*wen, adv.* (*interrog.* and *rel.*) and *conj.* at what time?: at which time: at or after the time that: upon or after which: while: although: at which (or *rel. pron.*). — *n.* the time: which time. — *interj.* (*Shak.*) an exclamation of impatience, like *what!* — *conjs.* **when′as′** (*arch.*) when: in as much as: whereas; **whenev′er, whene′er′** at every time when: as soon as (*Scot.*); **whensoev′er** at what time soever. — **or whenever** or at any comparable time; **say when** tell me when to stop; **seldom when** (*Shak.*) seldom that.   [O.E. *hwanne, hwonne* (Ger. *wann, wenn*); from the stem of interrog. pron. *hwā*, who.]

whence (*h*)*wens, adv.* and *conj.* (also **from whence**) from what place: from which place? from which things: wherefore. — *n.* a place of origin: a source. — *adv.* **whenceforth′** (*Spens.*) whence. — *conjs.* **whencesoev′er, whencev′er** from what place, cause, or source soever.   [M.E. *whennes, whannes*.]

whe′r. See **whether.**

where (*h*)*wār, adv.* (*interrog.* and *rel.*) and *conj.* at or to which place: at what place?: to what place?: from what source (*lit.* and *fig.*): to a, or the, place in which (*arch.*): in what circumstances or condition: at what point (*fig.*): whereas: wherever: in, at, or to which (or *rel. pron.*). — *n.* the, or a, place: which place. — *n.* **where′ness** the state of having place or position: position, situation. — *adv.* and *conj.* **whereabout′** about which, about where: near what?: on what errand (*Shak.*; *n.* what one is about) — also **where′abouts.** — *n.* **where′about,** now usu. *pl.* **where′abouts,** one's situation, esp. approx. — *conj.* **whereaf′ter** after which. — *advs.* and *conjs.* **whereagainst′** against which; **whereas′** when in fact: but on the contrary: taking into consideration, in view of, the fact that: where (*obs.*); **whereat′** at which: at what?; **whereby′** by which; **wherefor′** for which; **where′fore** (-*fǝr*) for which, or what, reason: why? — *n.* the cause. — *advs.* and *conjs.* **wherefrom′** whence; **wherein′** in which place or respect: in what?; **whereinsoev′er** in whatever place or respect; **wherein′to** (or -*in-tōō′*) into which: into what?; **whereof′** of which: wherewith (*Shak.*): of what?; **whereon′** on which: on what?; **whereout′** out of which; **where′so, wheresoe′er′, wheresoev′er** in or to what place soever: whencesoever (*arch.*); **wherethrough′** through which: through the agency of which; **whereto′** to which: to what?; **where-un′der** under which; **whereuntil′** (*Shak.*) to what: whereunto; **whereun′to** (or -*un-tōō′*; *arch.*) whereto: for what purpose?; **whereupon′** upon or in consequence of which: on what grounds (*Shak.*); **where′er′, wherev′er** at whatever place; **wherewith′, wherewithal′** with which?: with what. — *n.* (usu. **wherewithal′**) the means. — **from where** whence: from the, or a, place where; **or wherever** or in (or towards) any comparable place; **see, look,** etc., **where** behold; **tell someone where to get off** (*coll.*) to tell someone that his behaviour is unacceptable and will not be tolerated; **where away?** a query as to the direction of an object sighted by the lookout (*naut.*): where are you going? (*dial.*); **where it is** (*coll.*) the real situation, point, or explanation; **where it's at** (*slang*) (the scene of) whatever is considered to be the most important, exciting, with-it, etc.; **where you are** what you are saying or getting at.   [O.E. *hwær, hwār*; from stem of **who**; cf. **there**.]

wherret. See **whirret.**

wherry (*h*)*wer′i, n.* a shallow, light boat, sharp at both ends for speed: a kind of barge: — *pl.* **wherr′ies.** —

wherr′yman a man employed in a wherry, esp. one who rows a wherry.   [Ety. dub.]

whet (*h*)*wet, v.t.* to sharpen by rubbing: to make keen: to excite: to incite (*obs.*): to preen (*obs.; rare*): — *pr.p.* **whett′ing;** *pa.t.* and *pa.p.* **whett′ed.** — *n.* the act of sharpening: sharpness: a time, occasion (*dial.*): an incitement or stimulus: something that sharpens the appetite: an appetiser. — *n.* **whett′er.** — **whet′-slate** novaculite; **whet′stone** a stone for sharpening edged instruments: a stimulant. — **whet on** or **forward** (*Shak.*) to urge on.   [O.E. *hwettan*, cog. with *hwæt*, sharp; Ger. *wetzen*.]

whether (*h*)*wedh′ǝr* (*Shak.*, often scanned as one syllable; also spelt **whe′r**) *interrog.* and *rel. pron.* (*arch.*) which (of two). — *conj.* introducing the first of two alternative words, phrases, or clauses, the second being introduced by *or*, or (in the case of clauses) sometimes by *or whether*: introducing a single dependent question. — **whether or no** (sometimes **not**) whether so or not so: in any case, in any event.   [O.E. *hwæther*, from stem of *hwā*, who, with the old compar. suff. -*ther*; cog. with Goth. *hwathar*, Ger. *weder*; also with L. *uter*, Ionic Gr. *koteros*, Sans. *katara*.]

whew¹, wheugh *hū,* (*h*)*wū, interj.* expressing wonder or dismay. — *n.* a whistling sound, esp. one noting astonishment. — *v.i.* to utter such a sound.   [Imit.]

whew² (*h*)*wū,* (*dial.*) *v.i.* to bustle about.   [Perh. **whew¹**.]

whewellite *hū′ǝl-īt, n.* calcium oxalate.   [Named after William *Whewell* (1794–1866).]

whey (*h*)*wā, n.* the watery part of milk, separated from the curd, esp. in making cheese. — *adj.* of or containing whey: like whey: whey-coloured. — *adjs.* **whey′ey, whey′ish** of whey: like whey. — *n.* **whey′ishness.** — **whey′-face** a pale or white face. — *adj.* **whey′-faced** pale, esp. with terror. — **whey′-tub.**   [O.E. *hwæg*; L.G. *wey*.]

which (*h*)*wich, interrog. pron.* what one of a number?: what? (*obs.*): of what sort or kind? (*obs.*). — Also used adjectively. — *rel. pron.* who, whom (*obs.*): now used chiefly of things, ideas, etc., not persons: that: often having as antecedent a circumstance or statement, being equivalent to 'and that' or 'but that'. — *prons.* and *adjs.* **whichev′er, whichsoev′er** every one which: any one, no matter which. — **the which** (*obs.*) which; **which . . . he** (*obs.*) who; **which . . . his** (*obs.*) whose; **which is which?** which is the one, which is the other?   [O.E. *hwilc, hwelc*, from the stem of *hwā*, who, and *līc* (from a word meaning body, form), like; Goth. *hweileiks*, Ger. *welch, welcher*; L. *qualis*; cf. **such** and **each**.]

whicker (*h*)*wik′ǝr,* (*dial.*) *v.i.* to neigh: to bleat: to snigger, titter. — *n.* a neigh, bleat or titter.   [Imit.]

whid¹ (*h*)*wid,* (*Scot.*) *n.* a rapid noiseless movement. — *v.i.* to move quickly, to whisk. — *v.i.* **whidd′er** to whiz.   [Perh. conn. with O.N. *hvitha*, a squall, O.E. *hwitha*, a breeze.]

whid² (*h*)*wid, n.* a lie (*Scot.*): a word (*obs. slang*): a quarrel (*dial.*). — *v.i.* to lie. — **cut boon whids** to speak good words.   [Poss. O.E. *cwide*, a word — *cwethan*, to say.]

whidah(-bird). See **widow-bird.**

whidder. See **whid¹.**

whiff¹ (*h*)*wif, n.* a sudden puff of air or smoke from the mouth: a slight inhalation: a puff of smell: a slight blast: a small amount, esp. of something causing or associated with a transient sensation (*fig.*): a cigarette (*slang*): a small cigar: a jiffy (*coll.*): a light kind of outrigger boat: a glimpse (*dial.*). — *v.t.* to throw out in whiffs: to puff: to drive or convey by, or as if by, a whiff: to inhale, smell. — *v.i.* to go out or off in a whiff: to move with, or as with, a puff of air: to blow slightly: to smell. — *ns.* **whiff′er; whiff′et** a whippersnapper. — *v.i.* **whiff′le** to blow in puffs: to move as if blown by a puff: to talk idly: to make a slight whistling or puffing sound: to veer: to vacillate: to prevaricate. — Also *v.t.* — *adj.* **whiff′led** (*slang*) drunk. — *n.* **whiff′ler** one who whiffles: a swaggerer: a contemptible person. — *n.* **whiff′lery** levity: trifling. — *n.* and *adj.* **whiff′ling.** — *adj.* **whiff′y.** — *n.* **whift** (*dial.*) a breath, snatch. [Prob. partly M.E. *weffe*; imit.]

whiff[2] (*h*)*wif*, *n.* a fish akin to the turbot. [Ety. dub.]

whiff[3] (*h*)*wif*, *v.i.* to fish with a hand-line towed behind a boat. — *n.* **whiff′ing.** [Perh. **whiff**[1].]

whiffer, whiffet, whiffle, etc. See **whiff**[1].

whiffler[1] (*h*)*wif′lər*, (*hist.*) *n.* an official who clears the way for a procession. [Perh. *wifel*, obs. javelin, battle-axe; affected by **whiff**[1] and **whiffle**.]

whiffler[2]. See **whiff**[1].

whiffletree (*h*)*wif′l-trē*, *n.* Same as **whippletree.**

whiffy, whift. See **whiff**[1].

Whig (*h*)*wig*, *n.* a name applied to members of one of the great English political parties — applied in the late 17th century to those upholding popular rights and opposed to the King; after 1830 almost superseded by 'Liberal': a Scottish Presbyterian, first so called in the middle of the 17th century: one of those who in the colonial period were opposed to British rule (*U.S.*): one of the party formed from the survivors of the old National Republican party and other elements, first so called in 1834 — it fell to pieces in the 1850s (*U.S.*). — *adj.* of, pertaining to, or composed of, Whigs. — *n.* **Whigg′archy** government by Whigs. — *adj.* **Whigg′ish.** — *adv.* **Whigg′ishly.** — *ns.* **Whigg′ery, Whigg′ism, Whigg′ishness, Whig′ship** Whig principles. [Prob. short for **whiggamore**.]

whig[1] (*h*)*wig*, (*Scot.*) *v.i.* to jog along. — *v.t.* to urge forward: — *pr.p.* **whigg′ing**; *pa.t.* and *pa.p.* **whigged.** [Origin uncertain.]

whig[2] (*h*)*wig*, (*dial.*) *n.* sour milk: whey: buttermilk. — *v.t.* and *v.i.* to curdle. [Prob. allied to **whey**.]

whiggamore (*h*)*wig′ə-mōr, -mör*, *n.* one of the 7000 Western Covenanters who marched on Edinburgh in 1648, sealing the doom of Charles I: a Scottish Presbyterian, a Whig. [Origin disputed; most prob. *whig*, to urge forward, *mere*, mare.]

Whiggery, etc. See **Whig.**

whigmaleerie, whigmaleery (*Scot.*) (*h*)*wig-mə-lē′ri*, *n.* a trinket, knick-knack: a fantastic ornamentation: a whim. [Origin uncertain.]

while (*h*)*wīl*, *n.* a space of time: time and trouble spent. — *conj.* (also **whilst**) during the time that: at the same time that: as long as: although: notwithstanding the admitted fact that: until (*North. dial.*). — *prep.* (*Shak.*; *North. dial.*) until. — *v.t.* to pass without irksomeness (with *away*). — *conj.* **whiles** (*B.*) while, at the same time that: until (*Shak.*). — *adv.* (*Scot.*) at times (orig. gen. of O.E. *hwīl*). — *adv.* **whī′lom** (*arch.*) formerly, once. — *adj.* former (orig. dat. pl. of O.E. *hwīl*, time). — *adv.* **while-ere′** (*arch.*) a little while ago, formerly. — **all the while** during all the time (that); (**every**) **once in a while** now and then; **the while** (*Shak.*) at the present time, in the meantime; **the whilst** (*obs.*) while: in the meantime. [O.E. *hwīl*; Goth. *hweila*, Ger. *Weile*.]

whilk (*h*)*wilk*, *pron.*, *obs.* and *dial.* form of **which.**

whilly (*h*)*wil′i*, **whillywha(w)** (*h*)*wil′i-(h)wö, -(h)wä*, *vs.t.* to wheedle, cajole. — *ns.* cajolery: a coaxing, insinuating, person. — *adjs.* smooth-tongued, wheedling. [Origin obscure.]

whilom, whilst. See **while.**

whim (*h*)*wim*, *n.* a fantastic creation of brain or hand (*obs.*): a whimsical person (*obs.*): a caprice: a fancy: a vertical rope drum revolved by a horse, used for hoisting from shallow shafts. — *v.i.* (*obs.*) of the head, to turn round, swim: to be whimsical. — *v.t.* to desire as a caprice: to turn aside by a whim (*obs.*). — *adjs.* **whimm′y** full of whims; **whim′sical** (-*zi*-) full of whim: odd, fantastical: delicately fanciful: (*loosely*) expressing gently humorous tolerance. — *ns.* **whimsical′ity, whim′sicalness.** — *adv.* **whim′sically.** — *n.* **whim′sy, whim′sey** a whim, freak: whimsical behaviour: delicate, or affectedly delicate, fantasy. — *adj.* full of whims, changeable. — *adv.* **whim′sily.** — *n.* **whim′siness.** — **whim′-wham** a ridiculous notion: an odd device: a fanciful trifle. [**whim-wham** is recorded earlier than **whim**; cf. O.N. *hvima*, to have the eyes wandering.]

whimbrel (*h*)*wim′brəl*, *n.* a species of small curlew. — Also

wim′brel. [Prob. imit. of bird's cry; dim. suff. -*rel*.]

whimmy. See **whim.**

whimper (*h*)*wim′pər*, *v.i.* to cry feebly, brokenly, and querulously or whiningly: to make a plaintive sound. — *v.t.* to express or utter in a whimper. — *n.* a peevish cry. — *n.* **whim′perer.** — *n.* and *adj.* **whim′pering.** — *adv.* **whim′peringly.** [Imit.; cf. Ger. *wimmern*.]

whimple (*h*)*wim′pl*. Same as **wimple.**

whimsical, whimsy, whim-wham, etc. See **whim.**

whin[1] (*h*)*win*, *n.* gorse, furze. — *adj.* **whinn′y** abounding in whins. — **whin′chat** a bird that frequents whins, very similar in appearance, esp. when it assumes its duller autumn plumage, to the stonechat, to which it is allied. [Prob. Scand.]

whin[2]. See **whinstone.**

whine (*h*)*wīn*, *v.i.* to utter a plaintive cry: to complain in an unmanly way. — *v.t.* to express or utter in a whine: to cause to make a whining noise. — *n.* a plaintive cry: an affected nasal tone of utterance. — *ns.* **whī′ner; whī′niness; whī′ning.** — *adv.* **whī′ningly.** — *adj.* **whī′ny.** [O.E. *hwīnan*, to whine; O.N. *hvīna*, to whistle through the air.]

whinge (*h*)*wenj*, (*h*)*winj*, (orig. *dial.*) *v.i.* to whine: to cry fretfully: to complain peevishly (also *Austr.*). — *n.* a peevish complaint. — *adj.* and *n.* **whinge′ing.** — *n.* **whing′er.** — Also (*Scot.*) **wheenge.** [O.E. *hwinsian*, from root of *hwīnan*; see **whine.**]

whinger (*h*)*wing′ər*, *n.* a dirk. — Also **whin′iard** and **whin′yard.** [Origin obscure.]

whinid′st (*Shak.*, *Troil.* II, i. 15) folio reading for which Johnson conjectured *vinewd′st.*

whinny[1] (*h*)*win′i*, *v.i.* to neigh: — *pr.p.* **whinn′ying**; *pa.t.* and *pa.p.* **whinn′ied.** — *n.* a neigh. [Imit.]

whinny[2]. See **whin**[1].

whinstone (*h*)*win′stōn, -stən*, *n.* any hard and compact kind of rock, usually basalt or the like: a piece of this. — Also **whin.** — **Whin Sill** a sheet of intrusive quartz-dolerite or quartz-basalt exposed almost continuously for nearly 200 miles from the Farne Islands to Middleton-in-Teesdale. [*whin* (origin obscure), and **stone.**]

whiny. See **whine.**

whinyard. See **whinger.**

whip (*h*)*wip*, *n.* a lash with a handle for punishing or driving: a stroke administered as by a whip: a whipping motion: a driver, coachman: one who enforces the attendance and discipline of a political party: a call made on members of parliament to be in their places against an important division (called, according to number of times message is underlined as indication of urgency, **three-line whip,** etc.; **five-line whip** is no longer used): a whipper-in, the person who manages the hounds: a simple form of hoisting apparatus, a small tackle consisting of a single rope and block: a preparation of whipped cream, eggs, etc.: a whipping or overcasting: an appeal for contributions (usu. **whip′round**): an individual share in money collected in equal amounts: an instant (*Scot.*): an arm carrying a sail of a windmill: a long twig or slender branch: a fairground ride consisting of an arrangement of cars that move with sudden jerks. — *v.t.* to strike with a lash: to drive, or make to move, with lashes: to punish with lashes, or (*loosely*) by spanking: to strike in a manner suggesting a lash: to lash with sarcasm: to defeat, outdo (*coll.*): to stiffen (e.g. cream, white of egg) or make (eggs, etc.) frothy, by rapid agitation with a whisk or similar utensil: to keep together, as a party: to fish with fly: to overlay, as one cord with another: to bind round: to sew lightly: to overcast, as a seam: to move quickly, snatch (with *up, away, out,* etc.): to rouse (with *up*). — *v.i.* to move nimbly: to move in the manner of a whiplash: to make a cast in fishing with fly: — *pr.p.* **whipp′ing**; *pa.t.* and *pa.p.* **whipped, whipt.** — *adj.* **whip′like.** — *ns.* **whipp′er** one who or that which whips: an officer who inflicts the penalty of whipping; **whipp′iness; whipp′ing** the act of one who or that which whips: corporal punishment, esp. with the whip or lash: a defeat: a binding of twine, e.g. at the end of a rope: material for binding in this way: overcasting. — *adj.* **whipp'y** whip-like: pliant: supple. — *n.* **whip'ster** a term of contempt formerly with various meanings, chiefly remembered for Shak., *Oth.* V, ii. 242, a whippersnapper. — **whip'-and-derr'y** a hoisting apparatus consisting of a whip and a derrick; **whip'bird** the coachwhipbird; **whip'cat** a tailor; **whip'cord** cord for making whips: a fabric with a bold steep warp twill, used chiefly for dresses, suitings, and coatings: a whip-like seaweed, as *Chorda filum* or *Chordaria flagelliformis.* — *adjs.* **whip'cord; whip'cordy** like whipcord. — *v.t.* **whip'-graft** to graft by fitting a tongue cut on the scion to a slit cut slopingly in the stock. — Also *n.* — *ns.* **whip'-grafting; whip'-hand** the hand that holds the whip: the advantage; **whip'-handle** the handle or stock of a whip: an advantage; **whip'jack** a whining beggar who pretends to be a sailor; **whip'lash** the lash of a whip: something resembling the lash of a whip (also *fig.*): a whiplash injury. — *v.i.* to move like a whiplash. — **whipp'er-in** one who keeps the hounds from wandering: one who enforces the discipline of a political party, a whip (*obs.*): at any moment in a race, the horse in the last place (*slang*); **whipp'ersnapper** a little or young insignificant but pretentious or irritating person; **whipp'ing-boy** a boy formerly educated along with a prince and punished for the royal pupil's faults: one on whom falls the odium or punishments of the shortcomings of others; **whipp'ing-cheer** (*obs.*) flogging; **whipp'ing-cream** cream with enough butterfat in it to allow it to be beaten stiff; **whipp'ing-post** a post to which offenders are tied to be whipped: the punishment itself; **whipp'ing-top** (or **whip'-top**) a top kept spinning by means of a whip; **whip-round** see **whip**; **whip'-saw** a narrow saw for dividing timber lengthwise, usu. set in a frame and often worked by two persons. — *v.t.* to cut with a whip-saw: to have the advantage of at every point (*slang*). — **whip'-scorpion** any arachnid of the order Pedipalpida, slightly resembling true scorpions but being without sting and having usu. a whip-like appendage at the rear of the body; **whip'-snake** any of various snakes resembling a whiplash, as *Masticophis flagelliformis*, the coach-whip snake, and species of Philodryas, etc.; **whip'-socket** a socket to hold the butt of a whip; **whip'staff** a former steering device, a tailor: a vertical wooden lever controlling a ship's rudder; **whip'stall** (*aero.*) a stall as the result of which the nose of the aircraft whips forward and down. — *v.i.* and *v.t.* to go, or put, into such a stall. — **whip'-stitch** a small overcasting stitch: a hasty composition: a tailor: a kind of half-ploughing, raftering (*dial.*). — Also *v.t.* and *v.i.* — **whip'-stock** the rod or handle of a whip: in an oil-well, a tapered steel wedge used to deflect the drill bit from a straight line. — *adjs.* **whip'-tail, -tailed** having a long, slender tail. — **whip-top** see **whipping-top**; **whip'worm** a worm of the genus Trichocephalus, with posterior end thick and anterior long and thin, found parasitic in human intestines. — **fair crack of the whip** see **crack**; **whip and spur** with great haste; **whip in** to act as a whipper-in; **whip into shape** to get (esp. a person) into a desired state or condition, esp. by force or rigorous training; **whiplash injury** a neck injury caused by the sudden jerking backwards and then forwards of the head, common in motor-vehicle accidents in which the vehicle is hit from behind; **whip the cat** to practise small economies: to work by the day as a dressmaker, tailor, etc., going from house to house: to idle: to play a practical joke. [M.E. *whippen*; cf. Du. *wippen*, to shake.]

whippet (*h*)*wip'it, n.* a breed developed from a cross between a greyhound and spaniel or terrier: a racing-dog: a small speedy tank. — *n.* **whipp'eting** training, racing, of whippets. [Partly **whip**, and partly obs. *whippet*, to move briskly.]

whippletree (*h*)*wip'l-trē, n.* the cross-piece of a carriage, plough, etc., which is made so as to swing on a pivot and to which the traces of a harnessed animal are fixed

(often used in conjunction with a doubletree). [From **whip**.]

whip-poor-will (*h*)*wip-pōōr-wil', or -pər-, n.* a species of goatsucker, a native of N. America. [Imitative of its call.]

whippy, whipster, etc. See **whip**.

whir(r) (*h*)*wûr, n.* a sound from rapid whirling or vibratory motion. — Also *adv.* — *v.i.* to whirl round with a buzzing noise: to fly, move, with such a sound. — *v.t.* to hurry away with, or as if with, a whirring or whizzing sound: — *pr.p.* **whirr'ing;** *pa.t.* and *pa.p.* **whirred.** — *n.* **whirr'ing.** [Imit.; cf. Dan. *hvirre*, to whirl.]

whirl (*h*)*wûrl, n.* a turning with rapidity: anything that revolves, esp. rapidly: a great or confusing degree, as of activity or emotion: commotion, agitation: a whorl. — *v.i.* to revolve rapidly: to move rapidly, esp. in an agitated manner: to turn swiftly round or aside. — *v.t.* to turn round rapidly: to carry, or move, away rapidly, as on wheels: to throw violently. — *n.* **whirl'er.** — *n.* and *adj.* **whirl'ing.** — **whirl'-about** the act of whirling about: anything that turns round rapidly; **whirl'-** (**whorl'-, hurl'-**)**bat** (*obs.*) translating L. *caestus* (see **cestus**²); **whirl'blast** a whirling blast of wind; **whirl'-bone** the round bone of a bone turning in a socket: the knee-cap; **whirl'igig** (-*gig*) a toy that is spun or whirled rapidly round: a merry-go-round: anything that revolves rapidly (*lit.* and *fig.*): an ancient instrument of punishment, consisting of a pivoted wooden cage in which the prisoner was spun round: any water-beetle of the family Gyrinidae, esp. *Gyrinus natator* (also **whirligig beetle**); **whirl'ing-dervish** one of an order of Muslim devotees who dance or spin round, the dancing dervishes, founded in 1273; **whirl'ing-table** a machine exhibiting the effects of centripetal and centrifugal forces (also **whirl'ing-machine**): a potter's wheel; **whirl'-pool** a circular current in a river or sea, produced by opposing tides, winds, or currents: an eddy: a huge whale-like sea monster (*obs.*); **whirl'wind** a small rotating wind-storm, which may extend upwards to a height of many hundred feet — a miniature cyclone: something which moves in a similarly rapid and destructive way. — *adj.* referring to anything which develops very rapidly or violently. — **whir'lybird** (*slang*) a helicopter. — **give something a whirl** (*coll.*) to try something out; **whirlpool bath** see **Jacuzzi**®. [M.E. *whirlen* — O.N. *hvirfla*, freq. of *hverfa*, to turn round; Ger. *wirbeln*.]

whirr. See **whir(r)**.

whirret (*h*)*wir'it, (obs.) n.* a blow. — *v.t.* to give a sharp blow to. — Also **wherret.** [Poss. imit.]

whirry (*h*)*wûr'i, (Scot.) v.i.* and *v.t.* to move rapidly. [Prob. from **whirr**.]

whirtle. See **wortle**.

whish (*h*)*wish, v.i.* to move with the whizzing sound of rapid motion: to say 'whish'. — *interj.* asking for silence, hush! — Also **whisht.** — *n.* **whisht** silence: a whisper. — *adj.* silent. — *v.i.* to keep silent. — Also (*Scot.*) **wheesht.** — **haud, hold, one's wheesht, whisht** to keep silence.

whisk¹ (*h*)*wisk, v.t.* to move quickly and lightly: to sweep rapidly: to beat up with a quick, light movement. — *v.i.* to move nimbly and rapidly. — *n.* a rapid sweeping motion: a small bunch of anything used for a brush: a small instrument for beating or whisking, esp. eggs: a type of women's neckerchief or large collar worn in the later 17th century (*hist.*): a hairlike appendage, as on an insect: a tuft: a panicle esp. of millet: the common millet. — *ns.* **whis'ker** he who, or that which, whisks: formerly, hair on the upper lip, now usu. hair on the side of the face, side-whiskers (esp. in *pl.*): a long bristle on the face of a cat, etc.: a hair's breadth, a very small amount (*fig.*): a very thin, strong fibre or filament made by growing a crystal, e.g. of silicon carbide, silicon nitride or sapphire: either of two bars extending on each side of the bowsprit (*naut.*); **whiskeran'do** a whiskered person, in allusion to Don Ferolo *Whisker-*

andos in Sheridan's *Critic*: — *pl.* **whiskeran′dos.** — *adjs.* **whiskeran′doed, whis′kered, whis′kery** having whiskers; **whis′king** moving briskly. — *adj.* **whis′ky= fris′ky** flighty. [Scand., earliest uses Scot.]

whisk² (*h*)*wisk, n.* the earlier name for whist. [Said to be from **whisk¹**, from the rapid action of sweeping the cards off the table.]

whisket (*h*)*wis′kit, n.* Variant of **wisket.**

whisky¹ (*Ir.* and *U.S.* **whiskey**) (*h*)*wis′ki, n.* as legally defined, a spirit obtained by distillation from a mash of cereal grains saccharified by the diastase of malt: formerly applied also to a spirit obtained from potatoes, beetroot, or any starch-yielding material: a glass of any of such spirits. — *adj.* **whis′keyfied, whis′kified** intoxicated. — **whisk(e)y sour** a sour having whisky as its chief ingredient; **Whisky Insurrection** an outbreak against the excise regulations which occurred in Western Pennsylvania in 1794; **whis′ky-liver** cirrhosis of the liver, from too much whisky; **whisky mac** a drink made of whisky and ginger wine; **whisky toddy** toddy having whisky for its chief ingredient. [Gael. *uisgebeatha* — *uisge*, water, *beatha*, life; cf. L. *vita*, life.]

whisky², **whiskey** (*h*)*wis′ki, n.* a light gig. [**whisk¹**.]

whisky-john (*h*)*wis′ki-jon, n.* the grey or Canada jay — Also **whis′ky-jack.** [From Amer. Indian name of similar sound.]

whisper (*h*)*wis′par, v.i.* to speak with a low sound: to speak in a whisper: to speak covertly, spread rumours: to plot secretly: to make a sound like soft speech. — *v.t.* to utter in a low voice or under the breath, or covertly, or by way of gossip. — *n.* a low hissing voice or sound: a sound uttered with breath not voice: voiceless speech with narrowed glottis (*phon.*): a hissing or rustling sound: cautious or timorous speaking: a secret hint: a rumour. — *n.* **whis′perer** one who whispers: a secret informer. — *n.* and *adj.* **whis′pering.** — *advs.* **whis′- peringly** in a whisper or low voice; **whis′perously** in a whisper. — *adj.* **whis′pery.** — **whispering campaign** an attack by means of furtively spread rumours; **whis′- pering-gallery, -dome** a gallery or dome so constructed that a whisper or slight sound is carried to an unusual distance. [O.E. *hwisprian*; Ger. *wispern*, O.N. *hviskra*; allied to **whistle.**]

whiss (*h*)*wis, v.i.* to hiss, whistle, wheeze, etc. [Imit.]

whist¹ (*h*)*wist, interj.* hush. silence: be still. — *adj.* (*arch.*) hushed, silent: attentive. — *v.i.* to become silent. — *v.t.* (*Spens.*) to hush or silence. [Imit.]

whist² (*h*)*wist, n.* a card game played by two against two, in which the object is to take a majority of the thirteen tricks, each trick over six scoring one point. — **whist′= drive** a progressive whist party; **whist′-player.** — **dummy whist** whist played with a dummy hand; **long whist** a game of ten points; **short whist** a game of five points. [**whisk²**; said to be assimilated to **whist¹**, because of the silence during play.]

whistle (*h*)*wis′l, v.i.* to make a shrill sound by forcing the breath through the contracted lips or the teeth: to make such a sound in derision, etc.: of a bird, to pipe, sing: to make a like sound with an instrument: to sound shrill: to make a call or signal by whistling: to whizz through the air: to become an informer: to give a landlord information that leads to raising rent (*Scott*). — *v.t.* to perform or utter by whistling: to call or bring by a whistle (often with *up*): to send with a whistling sound. — *n.* an act of whistling: the sound made in whistling, or one like it: a small wind instrument giving a high-pitched sound by air impinging on a sharp edge: an instrument sounded by escaping steam, etc., as on steam locomotives: a summons: the throat (*slang*). — *adjs.* **whis′tleable; whis′tled** (*slang*) drunk. — *ns.* **whis′- tler** one who, or that which whistles: a large kind of marmot: a broken-winded horse: a fabulous bird whose whistle was fatal to the hearer (*Spens.*); **whis′- tling.** — *adv.* **whis′tlingly.** — **whis′tle-blower** (*slang*) one who blows the whistle on someone or something; **whis′tle-blowing** (*slang*). — Also *adj.* — *adj.* **whis′tle(d)= drunk** (*obs.*) too drunk to whistle. — **whis′tle-fish** a

rockling; **whis′tle-stop** (*coll.*) a small town or railway-station, where trains stop only by signal (**whistle-stop speech** an electioneering speech made on tour (orig. at railway stations); **whistle-stop tour** orig. such an electioneering tour, now any rapid tour involving brief stops at many places). — *v.i.* of a political candidate, to make an electioneering tour with many brief personal appearances. — **whis′tling-shop** (*slang*) a place, as a room in a prison, where liquor was sold without a licence; **whistling swan** an American swan with a musical whistling call. — **blow the whistle** (*slang*) to expose, give information (usu. to the authorities) about, illegal or underhand practices: to declare (something) illegal, underhand or otherwise unacceptable; **boatswain's whistle** (also **pipe, call**) a whistle of special shape used by a boatswain or boatswain's-mate to summon sailors to various duties; **go whistle** (*Shak.*) to go to the deuce; **pay for one's whistle** to pay highly for one's caprice (from Benjamin Franklin's story of a whistle he, as a boy, bought at an exorbitant price); **penny whistle,** or **tin whistle,** see **flageolet; pigs and whistles** see **pig²; wet one's whistle** (*coll.*) to take a drink of liquor; **whistle away** see **whistle off; whistle down the wind** from the practice of casting a hawk off down the wind when turning it loose, to abandon: to talk to no purpose; **whistle for** to summon by whistling: to ask for in vain (*coll.*); **whistle for a wind** a superstitious practice of old sailors during a calm; **whistle in the dark** to do something to quell one's fear; **whistle off, whistle away** to send off or dismiss by, or as if by, a whistle (*hawking*): to turn loose: to abandon; **worth the whistle** worth the trouble of calling for. [O.E. *hwistlian*.]

whit (*h*)*wit, n.* the smallest particle imaginable: a bit. [By-form of **wight**.]

white (*h*)*wīt, adj.* of the colour of pure snow: snowy: of the light complexion characteristic of Europeans: that absorbs the minimum and reflects the maximum of light rays: pale, pallid: bloodless: colourless: pure: unblemished: innocent: purified from sin: bright: burnished, as of steel: unburnished, of silver: light-coloured or golden, as wine: clothed in white: pertaining to the Carmelite monks: in continental Europe, anti-revolutionary (*politics*): auspicious, favourable: reliable, honest: (of a witch) not malevolent, using her power for good purposes: without bloodshed, as a war. — *n* the colour of snow: anything white, as a white man, a white butterfly, the centre of a target, the albuminous part of an egg, a pigment: a member of a white political party. — *v.t.* to make white. — *adj.* **white′ly** (*obs.* except *Scot.*) whitish, pale. — *v.t.* **whīt′en** to make white: to bleach: to free from guilt, or to make to appear guiltless. — *v.i.* to become or turn white. — *ns.* **whīt′ener** one who, or that which, whitens: artificial milk for coffee or tea; **white′ness; whīt′ening** act or process of making or becoming white: a substance used to make white, whiting. — *n. pl.* **whites** leucorrhoea: white attire. — *ns.* **Whīt′(e)y** (also without *cap.*; *coll.*, often *derog.*) a white man: white men as a race; **whīt′ing** a small sea-fish allied to the cod, so-called from its white colour: ground chalk free from stony matter and other impurities, extensively used as a size, colour, etc. (also **white′ning, Spanish white** and — the finest quality — **Paris white**). — *adj.* **whīt′ish** somewhat white. — *ns.* **whīt′ishness; whitster** ((*h*)*wit′star; Shak.*) a bleacher of cloth or clothes. — *adj.* **whīt′y** whitish. — *n.* (also with *cap.*) see **Whitey** above. — **white admiral** any of a genus of butterflies, of the same family as the red admiral, having white bands on the wings; **white′-ale** (*dial.*) ale brewed or mixed with ingredients, such as flour, eggs, etc., that give it a whitish colour; **white ant** a termite (Isoptera); **white′-arm** sword, bayonet or lance — a translation of Fr. *arme blanche*; **white arsenic** see **arsenic; white′bait** the fry of various species of herring, sprat, etc.; **white′bass** a silvery food fish of the American Great Lake region; **white′beam** a small tree (*Sorbus,* or *Pyrus, aria*) with leaves white and downy on the underside; **white′-bear** the polar bear; **white′=**

beard an old man. — *adjs.* **white′-bearded; white′- bellied; white′-billed.** — **white′-bonnet** one employed to bid at an auction to raise prices; **white′-bottle** bladder-campion; **White′boy** a member of an association of Irish peasants first formed in County Tipperary about 1761 for the purpose of redressing grievances, who, wearing white shirts, committed agrarian outrages by night; **white′boyism** the principles of the Whiteboys; **white′-brass** an inferior alloy of copper and zinc; **white bread** bread made from flour which has been refined by boulting. — *adj.* **white′-breasted.** — **white bryony** see **bryony; white′cap** the male redstart, or other bird with light-coloured head: a crested wave: a member of a self-constituted vigilance committee who, under the guise of purifying the morals of the community, deal violently with persons of whom they disapprove; **white cell, white blood cell** a white corpuscle; **white coal** water-power (Fr. *houille blanche*); **white coffee** see **coffee.** — *adj.* **white′-collar** pertaining to, or desig-nating, the class of workers, as clerks, etc., who are not engaged in manual labour (**white-collar crime** crimes entailing some intellectual effort and commit-ted without physical exertion or violence, as embez-zlement, etc.). — **white copper** a light-coloured alloy of copper; **white corpuscle** a leucocyte, one of the colourless amoeba-like cells occurring in suspension in the blood plasma of many animals, in lymph, etc. — *adjs.* **white′-crested, -crowned** of birds, having the crest or crown white. — **white crops** grain, as barley, rye, wheat; **white damp** carbon monoxide; **whited sepulchre** one professedly righteous but inwardly wicked, a hypocrite (Matt. xxiii. 27); **White Dwarf** (also without *caps.*) the name given to a small class of stars outside the normal spectral sequence, because their luminosities are extremely low for their spectral type; **white elephant** see **elephant; White Ensign** a flag with a white field and St George's cross, with the Union Jack in the canton, till 1864 the flag of the White Squadron, now flown by the Royal Navy and the Royal Yacht Squadron; **white′-eye** any bird of the genus *Zosterops* or of related genera of the fam. *Zosteropidae*, most species of which have a conspicu-ous ring of minute white feathers round the eye; **white′-face** white make-up, esp. as worn by a tradi-tional type of clown. — *adjs.* **white′-faced** having a face pale with fear or from illness: wearing white make-up, e.g. as a clown: of animals, having the face, or part of it, white: with white front (also **white′-fronted**); **white′- favoured** wearing white favours. — **white feather** see **show the white feather** under **feather; white′fish** a general name for such fish as the whiting, haddock, menhaden, etc.: any species of Coregonus; **white flag** an emblem of truce or surrender; **white flour** wheat flour with most of the bran and wheatgerm removed; **white′-fly** any of several insect pests belonging to the family *Aleurodidae*; **White Friar** (also without *caps.*) one of the Carmelite order of friars, so called from their white dress; **white frost** hoar-frost — *adj.* **white-fronted** see **white-faced.** — **white gold** gold alloyed with nickel or palladium to give it a white colour; **white goods** household linen: refrigerators, washing ma-chines, freezers and the like, usu. painted with white enamel. — *adj.* **white′-hand′ed** having white hands or paws: having hands unstained with guilt. — **white′- hass, -hawse** (*Scot.*) a white-pudding; **white′head** the blue-winged snow-goose: a breed of domestic pigeons. — *adj.* **white′-headed** of an animal, having the head wholly or partly white: having white hair: favourite, darling, as **white′-headed boy** (*Ir.*). — **white′-heart** a cultivated cherry, related to the gean, with soft, tender flesh and pale skin; **white heat** the degree of heat at which bodies become white: an intense state, as of emotion, activity, etc.; **white′-herring** a fresh or un-cured herring; **white hole** a suggested source of the matter and energy observed flowing into the universe (cf. **black hole); white′-honeysuckle** an azalea known also as the clammy or swamp azalea; **white hope** a

person on whom hopes for success, honour, etc. are grounded (*often* **great white hope); white horse** a white-topped wave: a figure of a horse on a hillside, formed by removing the turf from the underlying chalk, the most famous being in Oxfordshire, at Uffington. — *adj.* **white′-hot′.** — **White House** the official residence, in Washington, of the President of the U.S.A.; **white iron** pig-iron or cast-iron in which all the carbon is in chemical combination with the iron; **white knight** (*Stock exchange slang*) a company which comes to the aid of another facing an unwelcome takeover bid by making a more favourable offer; **white′-lady** a spectral figure said to be associated with the fortunes of a family, as in some German castles: a cocktail made of gin, orange liqueur and lemon juice: methylated spirits as a drink, sometimes mixed with similar substances (*Austr. slang*); **white lead** basic lead carbonate used in painting white; **white leather** see **leather; white′-leg** an ailment of women after parturition (also called **milk- leg); white lie** see **lie; white light** light containing all wavelengths in the visible range at the same intensity — the term is used, however, to cover a wide range of intensity distribution in the spectrum; **white′-lime** (*obs.*) white-wash; **white line** a longitudinal line, either con-tinuous or broken, on a highway to separate lanes of traffic. — *adjs.* **white′-listed** having white stripes on a darker ground; **white′-livered** having a pale look (once thought to be caused by a white liver): cowardly. — **white man** one of the white race: one assumed to deal fairly with others (*coll.*); **white matter** pale-coloured, fibrous nerve tissue in the brain and spinal cord; **white meat** food made of milk, butter, eggs, etc.: the flesh of poultry, rabbits, calves, etc.: the lighter parts of the cooked flesh of poultry (e.g. the breast), as opposed to the darker meat of the leg; **white metal** a tin-base alloy with over 50 per cent. of tin: sometimes, an alloy in which lead is the principal metal; **white night** a sleepless night: in northern latitudes, a summer night which never becomes completely dark; **white noise** a mixture of sound waves covering a wide frequency range; **white′-out** a phenomenon in snow regions in fog or overcast conditions in which earth and sky merge in a single whiteness; **white paper** a statement, printed on white paper, issued by government for the infor-mation of parliament; **white′-pot** a Devonshire dish of sliced rolls, milk, eggs, sugar, etc., baked; **white′- precipitate** a white mercurial preparation used exter-nally; **white′-pudding** an oatmeal and suet pudding in a sausage skin; **white pyrites** marcasite; **white race** one of the main divisions of mankind, distinguished gen-erally by light complexion and certain types of hair and skull — also known as Caucasian; **white rat** an albino strain of the brown rat, much used in laboratory experiments; **white′-rent** (*hist.*) the tinner's poll-tax of eightpence to the Duke of Cornwall: rent paid in silver; **white rhinoceros** an African two-horned rhinoceros, not much lighter than the black rhinoceros; **white rose** in the Wars of the Roses, the emblem of the House of York. — *adj.* **white′-rumped.** — **White Russian** Bel-orussian; — **white sale** a sale of linen goods at reduced prices; **white′-salt** salt dried and calcined; **white sauce** a sauce made with roux, liquid such as milk or a chicken or veal stock, and such flavouring as desired; **white′-seam** (*Scot.*) plain needlework. — *v.i.* to do plain needlework. — *adj.* **white′-shoe** (*slang;* orig. *U.S.*) namby-pamby. — **white slave** a girl procured for prostitution purposes (esp. when exported), whence **white slaver, white slavery** and **white slave traffic; white′smith** a worker in tinned or white iron: a tin-smith; **white spirit** a petroleum distillate used as a substitute for turpentine in mixing paints, and in paint and varnish manufacture; **White Squadron** one of three divisions of the British Navy in former times: white-painted vessels built in 1883 and following years as part of a strong U.S. Navy; **white squall** see **squall; white squire** (*Stock Exchange slang*) a friendly party to whom a company chooses to transfer the bulk of

fāte; fär; hûr; mīne; mōte; för; mūte; mōon; fŏot; dhen (then); *el′ə-mənt* (element)

its shares as a defence against a takeover move; **white stuff** (*slang*) heroin, morphine or cocaine; **white sugar** refined sugar; **white′thorn** the common hawthorn; **white′throat** either of two warblers of the same genus (*Sylvia*) as the blackcap, having white throat feathers: a species of American sparrow: any of several species of humming-bird; **white tie** a white bow tie, part of formal evening dress: hence, formal evening dress (also *adj.*); **white vitriol** zinc sulphate; **white voice** a singing voice of pure, neutral tone, expressing no emotion. — *adj.* **white′wall** of pneumatic tyres, having a broad white band around the side-walls. — Also *n.* **white′-ware** articles made of white porcelain, pottery, or other ceramic material; **white′wash** a liquid, as lime and water, or whiting, size and water, used for coating walls: a wash for the skin: false colouring: a glass of sherry after other wines: an act of whitewashing. — *v.t.* to cover with whitewash: to give a fair appearance to: to attempt to clear (a stained reputation), to attempt to cover up (a misdemeanour, esp. by one in an official position) so decisively in a game that he fails to score at all (*coll.*). — **white′washer** one who whitewashes; **white′-water** shoal water near the shore, breakers: the foaming water in rapids, etc.; **white′-wax** bleached beeswax: Chinese wax; **white whale** the beluga; **white wine** yellowish-coloured or uncoloured (as opp. to *red*) wine; **white′-wing** the velvet scoter, or an American scoter closely allied to it: the chaffinch. — *adj.* **white′-winged.** — **white′wood** a name applied to a large number of trees or their timber — the American tulip-tree, whitewood cedar (*Tecoma*, or *Tabebuia, leucoxylon*; Bignoniaceae), etc.; **whīt′ing-pout** see **pout**[2]; **whīt′ing-time** (*Shak.*) bleaching-time. — *adj.* **whīt′y-brown** white with a tinge of brown. — **bleed white** (*fig.*) to drain completely of resources; **China white** a very pure variety of white lead — also **silver white** and **French white; mark with a white stone** see **stone; white-eyed monkey** any of the mangabeys, monkeys with white upper eyelids; **white-footed mouse** the deer mouse; **white-headed boy** see **white-headed; white-headed eagle** the N. American bald eagle; **white man's burden** (*Kipling*) his alleged obligation to govern backward coloured peoples; **white of (an) egg** the albumen, the pellucid viscous fluid surrounding the yolk; **white of the eye** that part of the ball of the eye which surrounds the iris or coloured part; **white out** to erase (written or typed material) with correcting fluid before making a correction: to omit or cover up (secret or sensitive material in a report, transcript, etc.) so leaving areas of blank paper on the page(s); **whiter than white** extremely white: very pure, very law-abiding; **zinc white** see **zinc.** [O.E. *hwīt*; O.N. *hvítr*, Ger. *weiss*.]

Whitechapel (*h*)*wīt′chap-l*, *n.* a lead from a one-card suit, straightforward leading out of winning cards, or other type of unskilful play (*whist*): the intentional pocketing of an opponent's ball (*billiards*). — **Whitechapel cart** see **cart.** [*Whitechapel* in London.]

Whitehall (*h*)*wīt′höl*, *n.* a street with government offices, in London: the British government or its policy.

whither[1] (*h*)*widh′ər*, *adv.* and *conj.* to what place?: to which place: (used relatively) to which: to what: whithersoever. — *adv.* **whithersoev′er** to whatever place. — *adv.* **whith′erward(s)** in what direction, to what point. — **no whither** to no place. [O.E. *hwider*, allied to **who.**]

whither[2]. See **wuther.**

whiting. See **white.**

whitleather (*h*)*wit′ledh-ər*, *n.* leather dressed with alum, white leather: the paxwax of the ox. [**white leather.**]

Whitley Council (*h*)*wit′li kown′səl*, a joint standing industrial council (national or local), composed of representatives of employers and work-people in an organised trade, to consider and settle conditions of employment, etc. — Also called **industrial council.** [Recommended (1917) in the 'Whitley Report' — the report of a Reconstruction Sub-committee presided

over by Rt. Hon. J. H. *Whitley*.]

whitling (*h*)*wit′ling*, *n.* a kind of trout, probably a young bull-trout. [**white**, and suff. **-ling.**]

whitlow (*h*)*wit′lō*, *n.* a painful inflammation of a finger or toe, esp. near the nail, paronychia. — **whit′low-grass** any of several plants alleged to cure whitlows, as a small British saxifrage (*Saxifraga tridactylites*), or a small crucifer (*Draba verna*): whitlow-wort; **whit′low-wort** any of a number of plants of the genus Paronychia. [Perh. a corr. of *whick-flaw*, quick-flaw (cf. **quick** and **flaw**) or of *whitflaw*, — **white** and **flaw.**]

Whit-Monday (*h*)*wit′-mun′dā*, *n.* the Monday following Whitsunday.

whitret. See **whit(t)ret.**

whitster. See **white.**

Whitsun (*h*)*wit′sn*, *adj.* pertaining to, or observed at, Whitsuntide. — *n.* Whitsuntide. — **Whit′sun-ale** a festival formerly held at Whitsuntide; **Whit′sunday** the seventh Sunday after Easter, commemorating the day of Pentecost, when the converts in the primitive Church wore white robes: in Scotland, one of the term-days (May 15) on which rents, annuities, etc., are payable, the Whitsunday removal terms in towns being fixed as May 28; **Whit′suntide** the season of Pentecost, comprising **Whit′sun-week, Whit′-week**, the week beginning with Whitsunday. [**white, Sunday.**]

whittaw (*h*)*wit′ō*, (*dial.*) *n.* a saddler. — Also **whitt′awer.** [**white, tawer.**]

whitter. Same as **witter.**

whitterick. See **whit(t)ret.**

whittie-whattie (*h*)*wit′i-*(*h*)*wot′i*, (*Scot.*) *v.i.* to mutter, whisper: to shilly-shally. — *n.* vague language intended to deceive: a frivolous excuse. [Perh. formed from **what.**]

whittle[1] (*h*)*wit′l*, *v.t.* to pare or cut with a knife: to shape with a knife: to diminish gradually (often with *down*): to lessen the force or scope of (often with *down*). — *v.i.* to cut wood aimlessly: to peach, or to confess at the gallows (*obs. slang*): to fret (*dial.*). — *n.* a large knife, usu. clasp or sheath. — *ns.* **whitt′ler; whitt′ling. whittle away, whittle away at** to whittle, whittle down (usu. *fig.*). [M.E. *thwitel* — O.E. *thwītan*, to cut.]

whittle[2] (*h*)*wit′l*, (*dial.*) *n.* a woollen shawl: a blanket. [O.E. *hwītel*, a white mantle — *hwīt*, white.]

whit(t)ret (*h*)*wit′rət*, (*h*)*wut′rət*, **whitterick** (-ə) *rik*, (*Scot.*) *ns.* a weasel.

Whity, whity. See **white.**

whizz, whiz (*h*)*wiz*, *v.i.* to make a hissing sound, like an arrow or ball flying through the air: to move rapidly. — *v.t.* to cause to whizz: — *pr.p.* **whizz′ing;** *pa.t.* and *pa.p.* **whizzed.** — *n.* a hissing sound: a bargain, agreement (*slang*). — Also *adv.* — *ns.* **whizz′er; whizz′ing.** — *adv.* **whizz′ingly.** — **whizz′-bang** (*slang*) a light shell of high velocity which is heard arriving before the sound of a gun's report: a firework suggestive of this; **whiz(z)′-kid** (*slang*) one who achieves success rapidly and at a relatively early age, because of high intelligence, progressive ideas, pushfulness, etc. [Imit.; cf. **wheeze, hiss.**]

who *hōō*, *rel.* and *interrog. pron.* what person?: which person: he who, the person who: whoever: of what name, standing, etc. (objective case **whom** — O.E. *hwām*, which was orig. dat. of *hwā*, who, and replaced in the 12th and 13th centuries the older accus. *hwone*; possessive case **whose** — M.E. *hwas*, from O.E. *hwæs*, gen. of *hwā*). — *prons.* **whoev′er, whosoev′er** and **who′so** (*arch.*) every one who: whatever person (objective case **whom′ever, whomsoev′er;** possessive case **whosev′er, whosesoev′er).** — **who's who** a directory listing names and biographical details of prominent people. — **as who should say** as if one should say; **know who's who** to know the position and influence of everyone; **the who** (*Shak.*) who; **who but he** who else?, he only. [O.E. *hwā*; cog. with Goth. *hwas*, O.H.G. *hwer*, Ger. *wer*; also with Sans. *ka*, L. *quis*.]

whoa (*h*)*wō*, *interj.* stop. — *interj.* **whoa-ho-ho(a)′** (*obs.*) used to hail a person from a distance.

who-dun-it, whodunnit $h\overline{oo}$-dun'it, (coll.) n. a story concerned with the elucidation of a crime mystery. [**who, done** (vulg. pa.t. of **do), it.**]

whole hōl, adj. sound in health (arch.; B.): uninjured: restored to health: healed: not broken: undamaged: not broken up, or ground, or deprived of any part: containing the total amount, number, etc.: complete: of a sister or brother, full-blooded: in mining, as yet unworked: from which no constituents have been removed, as **whole blood, milk,** etc. — n. the entire thing: a system or combination of parts. — adv. wholly. — n. **whole'ness.** — adj. **whole'some** healthy in body, taste, morals or (Shak.) condition: indicating health: conducive to bodily or spiritual health: remedial (obs.): propitious (Shak.): reasonable, sensible (Shak.). — adv. **whole'somely.** — ns. **whole'someness; whōl'ism** same as **holism.** — adj. **whōlist'ic.** — adv. **wholly** (hōl'li, hō'li) completely, altogether. — adj. **whole'-coloured** all of one colour. — **whole'food** food, unprocessed or processed as little as possible, produced without any artificial fertilisers, pesticides, etc. — adjs. **whole'-foot'ed** (coll.) unreserved; **whole'grain** (of bread, flour, etc.) made from the complete grain, with no parts discarded during manufacture; **whole'-heart'ed** hearty, generous, zealous and sincere. — adv. **whole'-heart'edly.** — adj. **whole'-hog** (slang) out-and-out, complete. — **whole'-hogg'er** one who is inclined to go the whole hog. — adjs. **whole'-hoofed** having undivided hoof; **whole'-length** giving the whole figure: full-length. — n. a portrait, statue giving the whole figure. — **whole'-meal** meal made from entire grains of wheat (also adj.); **whole note** (U.S.) a semibreve; **whole number** a unit, or a number composed of units, an integral number; **whole'sale** sale of goods, usually by the whole piece or large quantity, to a retailer. — adj. buying and selling, or concerned with buying and selling, thus: extensive and indiscriminate. — adv. by wholesale: extensively and indiscriminately. — **whole'saler** one who sells by wholesale. — adjs. **whole'-skinned** unhurt: safe in reputation; **whole'-souled'** whole-hearted. — **whole step** (U.S.) a whole tone; **whole'-stitch** a lace-making stitch used to fill in a pattern; **whole tone** (mus.) an interval of two semitones. — adjs. **whole'-wheat** wholemeal; **wholl'y-owned** referring to a company all of whose shares are owned by another company. — **go the whole hog** to do a thing thoroughly or completely: to commit oneself to anything unreservedly; **out of whole cloth** with no regard for the truth, in a barefaced manner; **the whole** all the: the complete; **upon, on, the whole** generally speaking: all things considered; **whole life insurance** a life insurance policy on which premiums are payable up to the death of the insured person; **with whole skin** safe, unscathed. [O.E. hāl, healthy; O.N. heill, Ger. heil; see **hale¹**.]

whom, whomever, whomsoever. See **who.**

whommle, whomble (h)wom'l, (h)wum'l. Same as **whemmle.**

whoobub $h\overline{oo}$'bub, (obs.) n. Same as **hubbub.**

whoop (h)wōōp, hōōp, sometimes **hoop** hōōp, ns. a loud eager cry: a N. American Indian war-cry: a form of hide-and-seek: ((h)ōōp) the long noisy inspiration heard in whooping-cough. — v.i. to give a loud cry of triumph, eagerness, scorn, etc.: to hoot. — v.t. to cheer, or insult, with shouts: to summon, or to urge on, by whooping. — interj. (Shak.) ho! — ns. **whoop'er** one who whoops: a whooping swan or whooping crane (also **hoop'er**); **whoop'ing.** — **whoop'ing-cough, hoop'-ing-cough** pertussis, an infectious and epidemic disease, mostly attacking children, characterised by catarrh of the respiratory tract and by periodic spasms of the larynx that end in a long crowing inspiration; **whooping crane** an American crane (Grus americana), on the brink of extinction; **whooping swan** a swan (Cygnus cygnus cygnus) with a whooping call, common in N. Europe and Asia. — **whoop it up** (coll.) to indulge in noisy, boisterous entertainments or celebrations. [O.Fr. houper, to shout.]

whoopee (h)wōōp'ē, interj. an exclamation of delight. — Also n. — **make whoopee** (coll.) to indulge in hilarious amusements or dissipation. [**whoop.**]

whoops wōōps. Same as **oops.**

whoosh, woosh (h)wōōsh, n. the sound of, or like that made by, something large passing rapidly through the air. — v.i. to make such a sound: to do something with, or as if with, such a sound (also v.t.). — Also adv. [From the sound.]

whoot. Obs. variant of **hoot.**

whop, whap (h)wop, (coll. or dial.) v.t. to whip, thrash: to defeat or surpass: to throw or pull suddenly or violently. — v.i. to strike, or to move, quickly: to flop down: — pr.p. **whopp'ing, whapp'ing;** pa.t. and pa.p. **whopped, whapped.** — n. a blow: a bump: the noise made by either of these. — n. **whopp'er** one who whops: anything very large, esp. a monstrous lie. — adj. **whopp'ing** very large. — n. thrashing. [Variant of **wap¹**; origin obscure, prob. partly imitative.]

whore hōr, hōr, n. a prostitute: any unchaste woman: an allegedly corrupt religious community or practice. — v.i. to be, or to have to do with, a whore or whores. — v.t. to make a whore of, debauch: to spend in whoring. — n. **whore'dom** whoring: any illicit sexual intercourse: idolatry. — adj. **whō'rish.** — adv. **whō'-rishly.** — n. **whō'rishness.** — **whore'house** a brothel; **whore'master** (obs.) a whoremonger. — adj. **whore'-masterly** libidinous. — **whore'mistress** a woman who runs a brothel; **whore'monger** a lecher: a pander; **whore's'-bird** a whore's child: used as a vulgar term of abuse; **whore's'-egg** a sea-urchin; **whore'son** (-sən) son of a whore: a bastard: a term of coarse contempt or familiarity. — adj. mean, scurvy. — **whore after** to pursue (an unworthy, dishonest or selfish goal). [Late O.E. hōre, prob. — O.N. hōra, adulteress.]

whorl (h)wörl, (h)wûrl, n. a group of similar members arising from the same level on a stem, and forming a circle around it: a single turn in a spiral shell: a convolution, e.g. in the ear: a disc on the lower part of a spindle serving as a flywheel (also **wharve;** spinning): in a fingerprint, a ridge forming a complete circle: a type of fingerprint having such ridges. — adj. **whorled** having whorls: arranged in the form of a whorl or whorls. [Late M.E. wharwyl, etc., variants of **whirl.**]

whorl-bat. See **whirl-bat.**

whortleberry (h)wûr'tl-ber-i, -bər-i, n. a widely-spread heath plant with a dark blue edible berry, called also the bilberry, in Scotland, blaeberry, sometimes contracted to **whort:** extended to certain other plants of the same genus (Vaccinium). [Variant of **hurtle-berry.**]

whose hōōz, pron. the possessive case of **who** (q.v.) and also **which.** — **whosesoever, whoso, whosoever** see **who.**

whot (h)wot, adj. (Spens.). Obs. variant of **hot¹.**

whow (h)wow, (Scot.) interj. of deploration. — Often **eh whow** (or **aich** (āhh) **wow**).

whummle. See **whemmle.**

whunstane. Scots form of **whinstone.**

why (h)wī, adv. and conj. for what cause or reason, on which account?: therefore: (used relatively) on account of which. — interj. expressing sudden realisation, or protest, or marking resumption after a question or a slight pause, or (Shak.) to call a person. — adv. **whyev'er** (coll.) for whatever reason. — **why'-not** a challenge for reasons: a dilemma (obs.) (**at a why-not,** obs., at a disadvantage). — **for why** (arch. and dial.) for what reason: because; **the why and wherefore** the whole reason; **why, so!** (Shak.) so let it be! [O.E. hwī, hwȳ, instrumental case of hwā, who, and hwæt, what.]

whydah(-bird). See **widow-bird.**

-wich. See **wick².**

wick¹ wik, (dial.) n. a creek. [O.N. vīk, a bay.]

wick² wik, n. a village or town (dial.): a farm (dial.): as suffix (-ik, -wik, also -wich -ij, -ich, -wich) in Berwick, Greenwich, etc. [O.E. wīc, prob. an old Gmc. borrowing from L. vīcus, a village.]

wick[3] *wik, n.* the twisted threads of cotton or other substance in a candle, lamp, or lighter, which draw up the inflammable liquid to the flame. — **get on someone's wick** (*coll.*) to irritate someone. [O.E. *wēoce, wēoc*; allied to Du. *wick*, a roll of lint, Ger. *Wieche*.]

wick[4] *wik, v.t.* and *v.i.* in curling, to strike (a stone) in an oblique direction. [Perh. O.E. *wīcan*, to bend, yield, give way.]

wick[5] *wik*, (*obs.* or *dial.*) *adj.* wicked. [O.E. *wicca* wizard, *wicce*, witch.]

wicked *wik'id, adj.* evil in principle or practice: sinful: ungodly: (of an animal) vicious: cruel: mischievous, spiteful: very bad, harmful, or offensive: roguish (*coll.*): unlucky (*Shak.*): excellent, admirable (*slang*): — *n.* a wicked person (*B.*): (with *the*) wicked persons collectively. — *adv.* **wick'edly.** — *n.* **wick'edness.** — **the wicked one** the devil. [M.E. *wicked, wikked,* prob. — *wicke, wikke,* wicked — O.E. *wicca,* wizard.]

wicken, wicky. See **quicken**[1].

wicker *wik'ər, n.* a small pliant twig or osier: wickerwork. — *adj.* made of twigs or osiers: encased in wickerwork. — *adj.* **wick'ered** made of wicker: covered with wickerwork. — **wick'erwork** basketwork of any kind. [M.E. *wiker,* of Scand. origin; cf. O.E. *wīcan,* to bend.]

wicket *wik'it, n.* a small gate: a small door in or near a larger one: a grill or loop-hole (*obs.*): an opening or a window with a grille, as at a ticket-office, bank, etc. (*U.S.*): (the following meanings all *cricket*) the upright arrangements of three stumps with two bails on top which the batsman defends against the bowling: a stump: the pitch, esp. in respect of its condition: a batsman's stay at the wicket, or his joint stay there with another: a batsman's innings. — **wick'et-door, -gate** a wicket; **wick'et-keeper** in cricket, the fieldsman who stands immediately behind the striker's wicket. — **get, take,** etc., **a wicket** to bowl a batsman, or have him put out in any way as a result of one's bowling; **keep wicket** to be wicket-keeper; **over, round, the wicket** (of bowling) delivered with the hand nearer, farther away from, the wicket; **sticky wicket** see **stick**[1]; **throw down the wicket** to put down the wicket in fielding by throw of the ball; **win by so-many wickets** to win with so-many wickets still to fall. [O.N.Fr. *wiket* (Fr. *guichet*); of Gmc. origin.]

widdershins, widershins, etc. Variants of **withershins**.

widdle *wid'l,* (*hypocoristic*) *v.i.* to urinate. [Poss. — **wee**[3], **piddle**.]

widdy[1] *wid'i,* (*dial.*) *n.* a rope, esp. one made of osiers: a halter for hanging. [Variant of **withy**.]

widdy[2] *wid'i.* Dial. form of **widow**.

wide *wīd, adj.* extending far: having a considerable distance between the sides: broad: of a specified breadth: roomy: expanded: opened as far as possible: far apart: far from the point aimed at, or (*rare*) place mentioned: very different: of large scope, comprehending or considering much (*fig.*): astute, wily (*slang*): lax in morals (*slang*): lax, reverse of *narrow* (*phon.*). — *n.* wideness: in cricket, a ball bowled out of reach of the batsman: a penalty run allowed for this. — *adv.* (now usu. **far and wide**) to a great distance, over a large region: at a distance (*Spens.*): far from the point aimed at, the subject under discussion, the truth, etc.: far to one side (with *of*): so that there is a large space or distance between. — **-wide** in composition, extending throughout a specified area, etc. as *nationwide, countrywide.* — *adv.* **wide'ly.** — *v.t.* and *v.i.* **wī'den** to make or grow wide or wider: to throw open (*Shak.*). — *ns.* **wī'dener** one who, or that which, widens: a kind of tool; **wide'ness.** — *adj.* **wīd'ish.** — *n.* **width** (*width*) breadth. — *advs.* **width'ways, width'wise** in the direction of the width, across. — *adjs.* **wide'-angle** (*phot.*) pertaining to a lens having an angle of view of 60° or more and a short focal length; **wide'-awake'** fully awake: on the alert: keen and knowing (*coll.*). — *n.* (*wīd'ə-wāk*) a low wide-brimmed soft felt hat. — **wide'-awake'ness.** — *adjs.* **wide'-bod'y, -bod'ied** of aircraft, having a wide fuselage. — **wide'-boy** (*slang*) an astute or wily person,

esp. one prone to sharp practice. — *adj.* **wide'chapped** (*Shak.*) open-mouthed; **wide'-eyed** showing great surprise: naive, credulous. — **wide'-gab** the fish known also as the angler. — *adjs.* **wide'-open** opened wide: open to attack (*coll.*): lax in enforcing laws and regulations (*U.S.*); **wide'-rang'ing** covering a wide range of topics, interests, cases, etc. — **wide screen** a wide curved cinema screen designed to give the viewer a greater sense of actuality in the picture (*adj.* **wide'-screen**; also *fig.*). — *adjs.* **wide'-spec'trum** (of antibiotic, etc.) effective against a wide range of micro-organisms; **wide'spread** extended or extending widely: found, operative, etc., in many places; **wide'-stretched** (*Shak.*) large; **wide'-watered** bordered or covered by, or having, wide waters. — **to the wide** completely: utterly; **wide of** (*Shak.*) indifferent to, far from observing; **wide of the mark** far out, astray from the truth. [O.E. *wīd*; O.N. *vīthr,* Ger. *weit.*]

widgeon. See **wigeon**.

widget *wij'it, n.* a gadget: an unnamed small manufactured item or component. [Ety. obscure; perhaps an alteration of **gadget**.]

widow *wid'ō, n.* a woman who has lost her husband by death and has not married again: in the early Church, one of a special class of pious women: an extra hand in some card games: a short last line at the end of a paragraph which stands at the top of a page or column of print (*print.*). — *v.t.* to bereave of a husband (or wife): to strip of anything valued: to endow with a widow's right (*Shak.*): to be a widow to (*Shak.*). — *ns.* **wid'ower,** (*dial.*) **wid'ow-man** a man whose wife is dead; **wid'owerhood; wid'owhood** the state of being a widow, or (*rarely*) of being a widower: a widow's right (*Shak.*). — **wid'ow-bewitched** a grass-widow; **wid'ow-bird** any of a group of African birds (genus Vidua, sub-family Viduinae; L. *viduus,* widowed) belonging to, or related to, the weaver-finch family, having much black in the plumage, called also **whidah(-bird), whydah(-bird)** ((h)wī'də, (h)wi') in the belief that they were named from *Whydah* (Ouidah) in Dahomey: any of various birds of a related family (*Ploceidae*); **wid'ow's-bench** (*hist.*) a widow's share of her husband's estate besides her jointure; **wid'ow's-chamber** the apparel and bedroom furniture of the widow of a London freeman, to which she was entitled; **widow's cruse** a source of supply that never fails (1 Kings xvii. 10–16); **widow's man** (*naut.*) any of a number of fictitious persons formerly entered as a part of a ship's company in order that the pay allotted to them might be set aside for widows' pensions; **widow's mite** a small offering generously given (Mark xii. 42; see also **mite**); **widow's peak** a point of hair over the forehead, like the cusped front of a widow's cap in former days; **widow's weeds** the mourning dress formerly worn by all widows; **wid'ow-wail** a dwarf shrub (*Cneorum*) with pink, scented flowers, native to Spain and south France: daphne or mezereon (*Daphne mezereum*). — **golf,** etc. **widow** a woman whose husband frequently goes off to play golf (or whatever); **the Widow** Veuve (Fr., widow) Clicquot, a famous brand of champagne. [O.E. *widewe*; Ger. *Witwe,* L. *vidua,* bereft of a husband, Sans. *vidhavā.*]

width. See **wide**.

wiel. Same as **weel**[1].

wield *wēld, v.t.* to rule (*obs.*): to possess, enjoy, gain (*obs.*): to control, manage: to use with skill: to utter (*obs.*). — *adj.* **wield'able** capable of being wielded. — *ns.* **wield'er; wield'iness.** — *adjs.* **wield'less** (*Spens.* weeldlesse) unmanageable; **wield'y** easy to wield: manageable: dexterous, active (*obs.*). — **wield the sceptre** to have supreme command or control. [O.E. *weldan* (not recorded); W.S. *wealdan*); Goth. *waldan,* Ger. *walten.*]

Wiener schnitzel *vē'nər shnit'səl,* (Ger.) a veal cutlet dressed with bread-crumbs and eggs. [Ger., Viennese cutlet.]

wife *wīf, n.* a woman: a married woman: the woman to whom one is married: the mistress of a house, a hostess

(*obs.*), often in this sense *goodwife* (q.v.): — *pl.* **wīves.**
— *n.* **wife′hood** the state of being a wife. — *adjs.*
wife′less without a wife; **wife′-like; wife′ly.** — **wife′=
swapping** (*coll.*) a form of sexual activity in which
married couples exchange partners temporarily. —
take to wife see **take.** [O.E. *wīf*; O.N. *vīf*, Ger. *Weib*.]

wig[1] *wig, n.* an artificial covering of hair for the head
worn to conceal baldness, or for fashion's sake, as in
the full-dress **full-bottomed wig** of Queen Anne's time,
still worn by the Speaker and by judges, and the smaller
tie-wig, still represented by the judge's undress wig and
the barrister's or advocate's frizzed wig: a judge (*slang*).
— *adj.* **wigged** wearing a wig. — *n.* **wigg′ery** false hair:
excess of formality (*Carlyle*). — *adj.* **wig′less** without
a wig. — **wig′-block** a block or shaped piece of wood
for fitting a wig on; **wig′-maker** a maker of wigs. —
wigs on the green a fray. [Short for **periwig.**]

wig[2] *wig,* (*coll.*) *v.t.* to scold: — *pr.p.* **wigg′ing;** *pa.t.* and
pa.p. **wigged.** — *n.* **wigg′ing** (*coll.*) a scolding. [**wig**[1].]

wigan *wig′ən, n.* a stiff canvas-like fabric for stiffening
garments: a plain grey cloth for boot-linings, etc.
[*Wigan,* the town.]

wigeon, (*now rarely*) **widgeon,** *wij′ən, n.* any of various
ducks of the genus *Anas* which have the bill shorter
than the head, the legs short, feet rather small, wings
long and pointed, and the tail wedge-shaped: in the
U.K., specif. *A. penelope*: a fool (*obs.*). [Of uncertain
origin.]

wiggle *wig′l, v.i.* and *v.t.* to waggle, wriggle. — *n.* a
wiggling motion. — Also *v.i., v.t.,* and *n.* **wigg′le=
wagg′le.** — *n.* **wigg′ler** one who wriggles. — *adj.* **wigg′ly**
wriggly: much or irregularly waved. — **get a wiggle on**
(*slang*) to hurry. [Freq. of verb from which is derived
dial. *wig,* to wag; connected with M.L.G. *wiggelen*.]

wight[1] *wīt, n.* a creature or a person (*arch., dial.,* or
ironically): a supernatural being (*obs.*). [O.E. *wiht,*
a creature, thing; Ger. *Wicht;* cf. **whit.**]

wight[2] *wīt,* (*arch.* and *dial.*) *adj.* swift, nimble: courageous,
strong. — *adv.* **wight′ly.** [O.N. *vīgr,* warlike — *vīg,*
war (O.E. *wīg*).]

wight[3]. Same as **wite**[1].

wigwag *wig′wag, v.i.* to twist about: to signal by means
of flags. — *n.* the act of wigwagging: a level-crossing
signal which gives its indication, with or without a red
light, by swinging about a fixed axis. — *adj.* twisting.
— *adv.* to and fro. [Dial. *wig* (from same root as
wiggle) and **wag.**]

wigwam *wig′wom, -wam, n.* an American Indian dome-
shaped hut, made by laying bark, skins, etc. over a
framework of sticks: any similar construction, such as
a tepee. [Eng. corr. of Algonquian word.]

wilco *wil′kō, interj.* in signalling, telecommunications,
etc., an abbrev. of 'I *wil*l *co*mply' (with instructions).

wild[1] *wīld, adj.* being in a state of nature, not tamed or
cultivated: of an undomesticated or uncultivated kind:
uncivilised: uninhabited: desolate: tempestuous: violent: fierce: passionate: unrestrained: licentious: agitated: shy: distracted: very angry: very enthusiastic,
eager, keen (with *about*): strong and irrational: fantastic: crazy: disordered: unconsidered: wide of the
mark: fresh and natural: (*cap.*) applied to the extreme
Evangelical party in the Church of Scotland (*hist.*): (of
a playing-card) having any value desired. — Also *adv.*
— *n.* (also in *pl.*) an uncultivated region: a wilderness
or desert (also *fig.*): an empty region of air or water
(*poet.*). — *n.* **wīld′ing** that which grows wild or without
cultivation: a wild crab-apple: a garden plant self-
sown, an escape. — *adj.* uncultivated, or wild. — *adj.*
wild′ish somewhat wild. — *adv.* **wild′ly.** — *n.* **wild′ness.**
— **wild animals** undomesticated animals; **wild ass** any
of several Asiatic or African asses, as the onager, living
naturally in a wild state; **wild birds** birds not domesticated, esp. those protected at certain seasons under
the Acts of 1880 onwards; **wild boar** a wild swine, esp.
Sus scrofa, from which most domestic swine are
derived. — *adj.* **wild′-born** born in the wild. — **wild
card** a person allowed to compete in a sports event

despite his lacking the stipulated qualifications, etc.:
(the offering of) such a chance to compete: a character
which can stand for any other character or group of
characters in a file, etc. (*comput.*); **wild′cat** an undomesticated species of cat (*Felis sylvestris*) native to
Europe: any of various small wild animals of the cat
family: the skins of these: a quick-tempered, fierce
person: a speculative or unsound financial scheme
(*U.S.*): one who takes part in such a scheme (*U.S.*):
an exploratory well (*U.S.*). — *adj.* (of business, scheme,
etc.) haphazard, reckless, unsound financially: (of a
strike), unauthorised by union officials: (of an oil-well)
exploratory (*U.S.*). — *v.t.* and *v.i.* (*U.S.*) to drill an
experimental well in an area of unknown productivity
in search of oil, gas, ore, etc. — **wild′catter** (*U.S.*);
wild′-cherry any uncultivated tree bearing cherries, as
the gean (*Prunus avium*), or its fruit; **wild′-dog** any wild
species of the dog genus or family, as the dhole, the
dingo, etc.; **wild duck** any duck excepting the domesticated duck: specif., the mallard; **wild′fire** a sweeping, destructive fire: a need-fire: a composition of
inflammable materials: Greek fire (**like wildfire** extremely fast): lightning without thunder: a disease of
sheep: will-o'-the-wisp; **wild′-fowl** the birds of the duck
tribe: game-birds; **wild′-fowler; wild′-fowling** the pursuit of wild-fowl; **wild′-goose** a bird of the goose kind
that is wild or feral: a flighty or foolish person: (in *pl.,*
Wild-geese; *hist.*) Irish Jacobites who migrated to the
Continent after the abdication of James II, esp. those
who joined the French army; **wild′-grape** a grape-vine
(Vitis or Muscadinia) in the wild state, or its fruit:
Coccoloba (see **grape-tree**); **wild′-hon′ey** the honey of
wild bees; **Wild Hunt** in Germanic legend, a host of
phantoms rushing along, accompanied by the shouting
of huntsmen and the baying of dogs; **Wild Huntsman**
their leader; **wild′-indigo** any of several plants of
different genera belonging to the same family (Papilionaceae) as indigo, as an American tumble-weed
(*Baptisia tinctoria*); **wild′-land** land completely uncultivated; **wild′life** wild animals, birds, etc. regarded
collectively (**wildlife park** a safari park); **wild man** a
man of extreme or radical views in politics; **wild mare**
a seesaw: an instrument of punishment, the horse;
wild′(-)oat a tall perennial weed close akin to the
cultivated oat; **wild olive** see **oleaster; wild rice** Zizania;
wild service see **service**[2]; **wild silk** tusser; **wild thyme** see
thyme; wild track a sound-track recorded indepen-
dently of a photographic track, but used in editing;
wild′-water the foaming water in rapids, etc.; **wild′=
Will′iams** (*dial.*) ragged-Robin; **wild′-wood** wild uncultivated, or unfrequented, wood. — Also *adj.* — **run
wild** to take to loose living: to live or grow in freedom
from constraint or control: to revert to the wild or
uncultivated state; **sow one's wild oats** see **oat; wild and
woolly** unpolished: unrestrained; **wild-goose chase** see
chase. [O.E. *wilde;* common Gmc. word.]

wild[2] *wīld,* obs. variant of **weald, wield.**

wildebeest *vild′i-bāst, wild′i-bēst, vild′ə-bēst,* (*S.Afr.*) *n.* a
gnu. [Du. *wilde,* wild, *beest,* ox.]

wilderness *wil′dər-nəs, n.* a region uncultivated and uninhabited: a pathless or desolate tract of any kind, as
an extent of sea: a part of a garden or estate allowed
to run wild, or cultivated in imitation of natural
woodland: conditions of life, or a place, in which the
spirit feels desolate (*fig.*): the present world: a large
confused or confusing assemblage: wildness (*obs.*). —
v.t. **wil′der** (prob. formed from *wilderness; poet.*) to
cause to stray: to bewilder. — *v.i.* to wander wildly or
widely. — *adjs.* **wil′dered; wil′dering.** — *n.* **wil′derment.**
— **crying in the wilderness** see **cry; in the (political)
wilderness** not in office: not having any office, being
passed over or refused office. [M.E., — *wilderne,*
wild, wilderness — O.E. *wilddēoren* — *wild,* wild, *dēor,*
animal.]

wildgrave *wīld′grāv,* (*obs.*) *n.* a waldgrave. [Ger. *Wild-
graf* — *Wild* (Eng. adj. **wild**), game, *Graf,* count.]

wilding. See **wild**[1].

wile *wīl, n.* a trick: deceit: a pleasing artifice: (in *pl.*) cajolery. — *v.t.* to beguile, inveigle: to coax, cajole: to make to pass easily or pleasantly (with *away*; confused with **while**). — *adj.* **wile′ful** full of wiles. — *adv.* **wīl′ily.** — *n.* **wīl′iness.** — *adj.* **wīl′y** full of craft or cunning: using tricks or stratagem. [O.E. *wīl, wīle*; cf. **guile**.]

wilful. See under **will**[1].

Wilhelmstrasse *vil′helm-shträ-sǝ, n.* a street in Berlin: formerly, the German Foreign Office.

wili *vē′lē, n.* in the ballet *Giselle* (based on a legendary theme from Heinrich Heine) the spirit of a maiden who dies before her wedding-day.   [Of Slav origin; cf. Czech *víla*, fairy.]

wilily, wiliness. See **wile.**

will[1] *wil, n.* the power or faculty of choosing or determining: the act of using this power: volition: choice or determination: pleasure: inclination: lust: command: arbitrary disposal: feeling towards, as in **good-** or **ill-will** (see **good, ill**): the disposition of one's effects at death: the written document containing this. — *v.t.* to wish for, desire (*arch.*): to command, order, require (*obs.*): to decree: to seek to force, influence (oneself or another to perform a specified action) by silent exertion of the will: to dispose of by will, to bequeath: —in the foregoing senses, *pa.t.* and *pa.p.* **willed** *2nd pers. pres. indic.* **will′est**; *3rd pers.* **wills:** used with the infinitive of a verb to form (in sense) a future tense, expressing in the second and third person simple futurity (as **shall** in the first), or custom, or persistent habit, and in the first person promise or determination on the part of the speaker: with ellipsis of verb of motion, as 'I will unto the king' (*arch.*): also, in third person, can: to be likely to: —in these senses, *pa.t.* **would** (*wŏŏd*); *2nd pers. sing.* **wouldst**; no *pa.p.*; *2nd pers. sing. pres. indic.* **wilt**; *3rd pers.* **will.** — *v.i.* to exercise choice, choose, decree: to be willing. — *adj.* **wil′ful** governed only by one's will, obstinate: done intentionally: willing (*Shak.*). — *adv.* (*Shak.*) wilfully. — *adv.* **wil′fully.** — *n.* **wil′fulness.** — *adjs.* **will′able; willed** having a will: voluntary: given, or disposed of, by will: brought under another's will, as in hypnotism: in combination, having a will of a particular kind, as *weak-willed, strong-willed*, etc. — *n.* **will′er** one who wills. — *adj.* **will′ing** not reluctant: eager: ready and prompt to act: voluntary: chosen: intentional (*rare*): of or pertaining to the will. — *adv.* **will′ingly.** — *n.* **will′ingness.** — *adj.* **will′ing-heart′ed** heartily consenting. — **willing horse** a person or animal always prepared to work hard at any task; **will power** the ability to control one's actions, emotions, impulses, etc. — **at will** when or as one chooses; **a will of one's own** a strong, self-assertive will; **by my will** (*Shak.*) voluntarily: with my consent; **conjoint, joint, will** a testamentary act by two persons jointly in the same instrument; **have one's will** to obtain what one desires; **tenant at will** one who holds lands only so long as the owner pleases; **with a will** heartily and energetically; **work one's will** to do exactly what one chooses.   [O.E. *willa*, will, *willan, wyllan* (pa.t. *wolde, walde*), to wish; Goth. *wiljan*, Ger. *wollen*, L. *velle*.]

will[2], **wull** *wil, wul*, (*Scot.*) *adjs.* and *advs.* at a loss: astray: bewildered. — *adjs.* **will′yard, will′yart** wilful: shy. [O.N. *villr*, astray; cf. **wild**[1].]

willemite *wil′ǝm-īt, n.* orthosilicate of zinc, Zn₂SiO₄, white when pure but commonly red, brown, or green through the presence of manganese or iron — noteworthy as exhibiting an intense bright yellow fluorescence in ultraviolet light.   [*Willem* (or William) I of the Netherlands.]

Willesden paper *wilz′dǝn pā′pǝr*, a specially treated paper which keeps out wet and acts as a sound and heat insulator, placed under slates in roofing.   [*Willesden*, orig. place of manufacture.]

willet *wil′it, n.* a N. American bird of the snipe family, belonging to the tattler group — known locally as the stone-curlew.   [Imit.]

willey. See **willy**[1].

willie. See **willy**[2].

willies *wil′iz*, (*slang*) *n.pl.* the creeps.

williewaught *wil′i-wöhht*, (*Scot.*) *n.* a deep draught. [From misunderstanding of Burns, *Auld Lang Syne*, iv. 3, 'a right guid willie (or guid-willie) waught' (where 'guid willie' means 'good will'), a generous and friendly draught.]

williwaw *wil′i-wö, n.* a gust of cold wind blowing seawards from a mountainous coast, e.g. in the Straits of Magellan: a sudden squall (also *fig.*).   [Origin uncertain.]

will-o'-the-wisp *wil′-ō-dhǝ-wisp′, n.* the ignis fatuus: any elusive and deceptive person or thing: — *pl.* **wills-** or **-wisps.** [Orig. *Will-with-the-wisp* — *Will*, abbrev. of William, and **wisp** (q.v.).]

willow *wil′ō, n.* any tree or shrub of the genus Salix, having slender, pliant branches: any of several plants resembling it: the wood of the willow: a cricket-bat or baseball-bat: a willowing-machine. — *v.t.* to clean in a willowing-machine. — *adjs.* **will′owed** abounding with, or grown with, willows; **will′owish** like a willow: of the colour of willow leaves: slender and supple; **will′owy** abounding in willows: flexible: slender and graceful. — **will′ow-grouse** a species of grouse (*Lagopus albus*) found in northern regions of the world; **will′ow-herb** a perennial herb (*Epilobium* or *Chamaenerion*) of the evening primrose family (including rosebay, bay-willow, French or Persian willow) with willow-like leaves and seeds; **will′owing-machine** a machine in which a spiked revolving cylinder, usu. contained in a spiked box, loosens or cleans cotton, wool, rags for paper, etc.; **willow pattern** a blue design of Chinese character but English origin used on china from the late 18th cent. onwards; **will′ow-warbler, -wren** a small European sylviine bird (*Phylloscopus trochilus*); **will′ow-weed** one of various species of Polygonum or knot-weed: the purple loosestrife.   [O.E. *welig*; L.Ger. *wilge*, Du. *wilg*.]

will-worship *wil′-wûr′ship*, (*B.*) *n.* worship after one's own will or fancy, superstitious observance without divine authority.   [**will**[1], **worship**.]

willy[1], **willey** *wil′i*, (*dial.*) *n.* a willow basket: a willowing-machine. — *v.t.* to clean in a willowing-machine. [O.E. *wilige*; allied to **willow**.]

willy[2], **willie** *wil′i, n.* hypocoristic for the penis.

willyard, willyart. See **will**[2].

willy-nilly *wil′i-nil′i, adv.* willing or unwilling: compulsorily. — *adj.* having no choice: vacillating (*erron.*). [**will**[1] and **nill**.]

willy-willy *wil′i-i-wil′i*, (*Austr.*) *n.* a cyclone.   [Aboriginal.]

Wilson's disease *wil′sǝnz diz-ēz′*, a hereditary, degenerative disease of the nervous system and liver, in which there is an accumulation of copper in the tissues. [Samuel *Wilson*, 1878–1937, English neurologist.]

wilt[1] *wilt, v.i.* to droop, become limp: to lose energy: to lose self-confidence or courage (*fig.*). — *v.t.* to render limp, cause to droop: to cause to lose spirit, self-confidence, courage. — *n.* the act of wilting: any of various diseases that cause wilting of plants.   [Orig. dial.; perh. from **welk**[1].]

wilt[2] *wilt, 2nd pers. sing.* of **will**[1].

Wilton *wil′tǝn, n.* (in full **Wilton carpet**) a carpet differing from a Brussels carpet in having a cut pile, long made at *Wilton*, in Wilts.

wily. See **wile.**

wimble[1] *wim′bl, n.* an instrument for boring holes, turned by a handle: a gimlet: an auger: a kind of brace: an instrument for boring in soft ground. — *v.t.* to bore through with a wimble.   [Through O.Norm.Fr., from M.Du. *wimpel*.]

wimble[2] *wim′bl*, (*Spens.*) *adj.* active, nimble.   [A Northern word, now dial.; of Scand. origin.]

wimbrel. See **whimbrel.**

wimp *wimp*, (*slang*) *n.* an ineffectual person: a young girl (*old*). — *adjs.* **wimp′ish, wimp′y.**   [Origin obscure.]

wimple *wim′pl, n.* a veil folded round the head, neck and cheeks (still part of a nun's dress): a fold, wrinkle, ripple: a turn, wind: a crafty twist (*Scot.*). — *v.t.* to wrap in, or hide with, a wimple: to enwrap, enfold: to blindfold (*Shak.*; in *pa.p.*): to lay in folds. — *v.i.* to meander: to ripple: to lie in folds (*Spens.*). — Also **whimple**.   [O.E. *wimpel*, neck-covering; cf. O.H.G. *wimpal*, a light robe, Ger. *Wimpel*, a pennon, Fr. *guimpe*, a nun's veil, Eng. *gimp*, a thin cloth for trimming.]

Wimpy® *wim'pi*, *n.* a kind of hamburger.   [Orig. the name of a hamburger-loving character in a comic strip.]

win[1] *win*, *v.t.* to get by labour: to gain in contest: to secure: to achieve, effect: to reach: to be the victor in: to induce: to gain influence over: to obtain the favour of: to mine (an ore): to open up (a new portion of a coal-seam). — *v.i.* to gain the victory: to make one's way, betake oneself (*dial.*): to get oneself (into a desired place, state, etc.): — *pr.p.* **winn'ing**; *pa.t.* and *pa.p.* **won** (*wun*). — *n.* (*coll.*) a victory, success. — *adj.* **winn'able**. — *ns.* **winn'er** one who wins: something very good or successful (*slang*); **winn'ing** the act of one who wins: (usu. in *pl.*) that which is won: a shaft or pit to open a bed of coal. — *adj.* that wins: of or pertaining to the act of winning: attractive, prepossessing: persuasive. — *adv.* **winn'ingly**. — *n.* **winn'ingness**. — **winning gallery** in real tennis, the gallery furthest away from the net at either end of the court, any shot played into this winning a point; **winn'ing-post** the goal of a race-course. — **win by a (short) head** to win very narrowly; **win in a canter** to win easily; **win of** (*obs.*) to get the better of; **win on, upon** to gain on: to get the better of: to obtain favour with, influence over; **win, or gain, one's spurs** to earn one's knighthood by valour on the field, hence to gain recognition or reputation by merit of any kind; **win out** to get out: to be successful (*coll.*; also **win through**); **win over** to bring over to one's opinion or party.   [O.E. *winnan*, to struggle, to suffer; O.N. *vinna*, Ger. *gewinnen*, to win.]

win[2] *win*, (*Scot.*) *v.t.* to dry by exposure to the wind: — *pr.p.* **winning**; *pa.t.* and *pa.p.* **won**.   [**win**[1] influenced by **wind**[1].]

win[3], **winn** *win*, **wing** *wing*, (*slang*) *ns.* a penny.

wince[1] *wins*, *v.i.* to kick (obs. or *dial.*): to shrink or start back: to make an involuntary movement, e.g. in pain: to be affected acutely, as by a sarcasm: to be restive, as a horse uneasy at its rider. — *n.* a kick (*obs.*): an involuntary start back or shrinking. — *n.* **win'cer**. — *n.* and *adj.* **win'cing**.   [Cf. O.Fr. *guinchir*, *ganchir*, to wince — a Gmc. word; cf. O.H.G. *wenkan* (Ger. *wanken*), to wince.]

wince[2]. See **winch**[1].

wincey, winsey *win'si*, *n.* a cloth, plain or twilled, usu. with a linen or cotton warp and woollen filling. — *n.* **winceyette'** a plain cotton cloth of light weight, raised slightly on both sides.   [Orig. Scot. — **linsey-woolsey**.]

winch[1] *winch*, *winsh*, *n.* a reel or roller: the crank of a wheel or axle: a powerful type of hauling or hoisting machine. — *v.t.* to haul, hoist, etc. using such a machine (with *up*, *in*, etc.). — Also **wince**. — **winch'man** one who operates a winch or takes part in winching operations, e.g. aboard a helicopter.   [O.E. *wince*, from a Gmc. and Indo-European root.]

winch[2]. See **wench**.

Winchester *win'chəs-tər*, *adj.* formerly used of various measures (as 'Winchester bushel'), the standards of which were kept at *Winchester*. — *n.* a narrow-necked bottle for liquid chemicals, orig. so called as it contained a 'Winchester quart' (approx. 80 fluid ounces, or 2·25 litres).

Winchester disc (*comput.*). Same as **hard disc**.

Winchester (rifle)® *win'chəs-tər* (*rī'fl*), orig. a tradename for a repeating rifle made by Oliver F. *Winchester*, American manufacturer: now a tradename for firearms, etc., produced by the makers of the rifle.

wincopipe. Obs. form of **wink-a-peep**.

wind[1] *wind* (*poet.* *wīnd*), *n.* air in motion: a current of air, usually horizontal, either natural or produced by artificial means: any of the directions from which the wind may blow: breath: power of breathing: flatulence: conceit: empty, insignificant words: the wind instruments in an orchestra: their players: air impregnated with scent of game: a hint or suggestion, as of something secret: part of the body covering the stomach (*slang*): a disease of sheep in which the inflamed intestines are distended by gases. — *v.t.* (*wīnd*) to sound or signal by blowing: (following meanings *wind*) to perceive by the scent: to expose to wind: to drive, punch hard, so as to put out of breath: to allow to recover wind: to burp (a baby): — *pr.p.* **wīnd'ing**, **wind'ing**; *pa.t.* and *pa.p.* **wind'ed** and (as a horn) **wound** (*wownd*). — *ns.* **wind'age** the difference between the size of the bore of a gun and that of the ball or shell: the influence of the wind in deflecting a missile, the amount of deflection due to wind, or the allowance made for it: air friction on a moving, esp. revolving, part of a machine; **wind'er** one who sounds a horn; **wind'er** (*slang*) a blow that takes one's breath away. — *adv.* **wind'ily**. — *n.* **wind'iness**. — *adj.* **wind'less** without wind. — *adv.* and *adj.* **wind'ward** towards or on the side the wind blows from. — Also *n.* — *adv.* **wind'wards**. — *adj.* **wind'y** like, characterised by, exposed to, the wind: moved, played, produced, by wind (*poet.*): controlling the winds (*poet.*): suffering from, producing, or produced by, flatulence: suggestive of wind, as insubstantial, changeable, boastful, conceited, wordy (*fig.*): frightened, nervous (*coll.*). — **wind'-bag** the bellows of a bagpipe, or (*obs.*) organ: the lungs or chest (*facet.*): an inflated bag as a charm to procure a favourable wind: a person of mere words, an excessively talkative person (*slang*); **wind band** a musical ensemble made up of wind instruments; **wind'-blow** windthrow. — *adj.* **wind'-bound** hindered from sailing by contrary wind. — **wind'-break** a protection against the force of the wind, such as a fence or line of trees. — *adj.* **wind'-broken** of a horse, broken-winded. — **wind'burn** inflammation of the skin due to over-exposure to the wind. — *adj.* **wind'-changing** fickle. — **wind'-chart** a chart showing the direction of the wind; **wind'cheater** a close-knitted pullover: an anorak; **wind'-chest** the box or reservoir that supplies compressed air to the pipes or reeds of an organ; **wind'-cone** (*aero.*) a sleeve floating from the top of a mast, its angle with the ground giving a rough conception of the velocity of the wind, and its angle in a horizontal plane the wind direction; **wind'-drop'sy** tympanites; **wind'-egg** an addle egg: one soft-shelled or imperfectly formed; **wind'fall** fruit blown off a tree by the wind: any unexpected money or other advantage; **windfall tax** a tax levied on **windfall profits,** profits arising, esp. suddenly and unexpectedly, as a result of events not directly connected with the company, etc. concerned, such as changes in currency exchange rates. — *adj.* **wind'fallen** blown down by wind. — **wind'-flower** an anemone, esp. the wood-anemone; **wind'-furnace** any form of furnace using the natural draught of a chimney without aid of a bellows; **wind'-gall** a puffy swelling about the fetlock joints of a horse; **wind'-gauge** an instrument for measuring the velocity of the wind: a gauge for measuring pressure of wind in an organ: appliance fixed to a rifle by means of which the force of the wind is ascertained so that allowance may be made for it in sighting; **wind'-gun** an air-gun; **wind'-hover** (*hov'*, *huv'ər*) the kestrel; **wind'-instrument** a musical instrument sounded by means of wind, esp. by the breath; **wind'jammer** a large sailing vessel: a wind-resisting golf blouse (*coll.*); **wind machine** in the theatre, a machine which produces wind or the sound of wind; **wind'mill** a mill in which the motive-power is the wind acting on a set of vanes or sails: a wind-driven set of vanes used to pump water, generate electricity, etc.: any device which is caused to rotate by reason of its being carried through the air, and so develops power (*aero.*). — *v.t.* and *v.i.* (to cause) to move like the vanes of a windmill. — **wind′pipe** the passage for the breath between the mouth and lungs, the trachea; **wind power** wind considered as an energy source, e.g. for the generation of electricity by means of windmills, etc. — *adj.* **wind′-rode** (*naut.*) riding at anchor with head to the wind. — **wind′rose** a rosette-like diagram showing the relative frequency and strength of winds in a locality for given periods of the year; **wind′row** a row of hay, etc., raked together to be made into cocks: a row of peats, etc., set up for drying. — *v.t.* to arrange in windrows. — **wind′-sail** (*naut.*) a wide funnel of canvas used to convey a stream of air below deck: a vane of a windmill; **wind′screen** a shelter against wind, esp. a transparent screen on motor-cars, etc. — *adjs.* **wind′-shak′d, -shaken** agitated by the wind. — **wind shear** (*meteor.*) a sudden change in wind velocity or direction; **wind′shield** a windscreen (*U.S.*): a device to protect e.g. a microphone from the wind; **wind′ship** a wind-powered ship, a sailing-ship; **wind′-side** the side next the wind; **wind′-sleeve, -sock** a wind-cone; **wind′storm** a storm consisting of very strong winds; **wind′-sucker** (of a horse) a crib-biter; **wind′surfing** (also called **sailboarding**) the sport of sailing on a **sailboard**, (*q.v.*). — *v.i.* **wind′surf** to sail on a sailboard. — **wind′surfer.** — *adjs.* **wind′swept** exposed to, or swept by, the wind; **wind′-swift** swift as the wind. — **wind′throw** the blowing-down of trees by the wind. — *adj.* **wind′-tight** air-tight. — **wind′-tunnel** an experimental apparatus for producing a uniform steady air-stream past a model for aerodynamic investigation work. — **a capful of wind** a slight breeze; **before the wind** carried along by the wind; **between wind and water** that part of a ship's side which is now in, now out of, the water owing to the fluctuation of the waves: in a vulnerable or precarious place or position; **cast** or **lay an anchor to windward** to make prudent provision for the future; **cast, fling, throw, to the winds** to scatter, throw away, recklessly: to abandon (restraint, prudence, caution, discretion, etc.); **down the wind** moving with the wind: towards decay (*obs.*; *fig.*); **fight windmills** same as **tilt at windmills** below; **fling to the winds** see **cast**, etc. **to the winds** above; **get one's wind** to recover one's breath; **get the wind of** to get on the windward side of; **get to windward of** to secure an advantage over; **get the wind up** (*slang*) to become nervous, apprehensive, agitated; **get wind of** to get a hint or intimation of; **have the wind of** to be on the trail of; **how the wind blows** or **lies** the state of the wind: the position of affairs; **in the wind** astir, afoot; **in the wind's eye, in the teeth of the wind** right against the wind; **like the wind** rapidly; **on the windy side** (*Shak.*) on the windward side, from which one cannot be attacked, hence safe, at an advantage; **put the wind up someone** (*slang*) to make someone apprehensive or agitated; **raise the wind** see **raise**; **sail close to (or near) the wind** to keep the boat's head so near to the wind as to fill but not shake the sails: to be in danger of transgressing an approved limit; **second wind** power of respiration recovered after breathlessness: the energy necessary for a renewal of effort (*fig.*); **sow the wind and reap the whirlwind** to act wrongly and receive a crushing retribution; **take the wind out of someone's sails** (*fig.*) to deprive someone of an advantage, to frustrate, discomfit someone; **throw to the winds** see **cast**, etc. **to the winds** above; **tilt at windmills** to struggle with imaginary opposition, as Don Quixote, who charged at a windmill thinking it was an enemy; **wind chill factor** see **chill factor**; **wind(s) of change** a pervasive influence bringing change, immortalised as a phrase by Harold Macmillan, speaking as Prime Minister in 1960 of the inevitability of African independence, but previously used by the poet A. C. Swinburne in *Tiresias*. [O.E.; allied to O.N. *vindr*, Ger. *Wind*, L. *ventus*.]

wind² *wīnd, v.t.* to turn, to twist, to coil: to encircle: to screw the mechanism of, as a time-piece: to make, direct, as one's way, or to traverse, by turning and

twisting: to insinuate (*refl.*): to change the course of, deflect, control (*rare* or *obs.*): to turn to one's left, as a horse: to bring in, involve (*obs.*; also **wind up**), or to extricate, stealthily: to wind up (*arch.*; *fig.*; *q.v.*): to weave (*Spens.*): to wield (*obs.* and *dial.*): to haul or hoist, as by a winch. — *v.i.* to turn round something: to twist: to move, go, by turns and twists, or (*fig.*) deviously: to meander: to go (*obs.*): to writhe, wriggle (*obs.* and *dial.*): to extricate oneself (with *out*; *obs.*): to be twisted, warped (*dial.*): of a horse, to turn to the left: — *pr.p.* **wīnd′ing**; *pa.t.* and *pa.p.* **wound** (*wownd*); chiefly *naut.* **wīnd′ed**; Burns *pa.t.* **win′t.** — *n.* a turn, coil, or twist: a turning: a twisted condition. — *n.* **wīnd′er** one who winds: an instrument for winding: a clock or watch key: an electrically driven winding-engine for hoisting a cage or cages up a vertical mineshaft: a man who operates such an engine: a twisting plant: a triangular step at the turn of a stair or in a spiral staircase. — *adj.* and *n.* **wīnd′ing.** — *adv.* **wīnd′ingly.** — **wīnd′ing-engine** a machine for hoisting; **wīnd′ing-sheet** a sheet for enwrapping a corpse: the dripping grease that clings to the side of a candle (*dial.*); **wīnd′ing-stair** a stair constructed around a solid or hollow newel; **wīnd′ing-strips** two pieces of wood with parallel edges, used for testing the trueness of timber, etc.; **wīnd′-up** the close, finish: an instance of winding up. — **turn the wind** (now *rare*) to go, move, or cause to move, from side to side or on a winding course (*lit.* and *fig.*); **wind a ship** to turn her about end for end; **wind down** to relax, become quiet after a period of activity: to lose strength: to reduce the strength or scope of; **wind up** to bring, or come, to a conclusion: to adjust for final settlement: to terminate the activities of, liquidate (a commercial firm, etc.): to excite very much (esp. in *pa.p.* **wound up** excited; *fig.*): to coil completely: to wind the spring or the mechanism of tightly: to furl (*obs.*): to tighten: to hoist, as by a winch: to restore to harmony (*Shak.*): to tease: to irritate, annoy, anger (*slang*); **wind up and down** (*obs.*) to revolve in the mind. [O.E. *windan*; cf. Ger. *winden*, O.N. *vinda*, Goth. *windan*; cf. **wend, wander.**]

windac. See **windas.**

windage. See **wind¹.**

windas *wind′as,* (*obs.*) *n.* a windlass: (*R.L. Stevenson,* **wind′ac**) an instrument for bending a cross-bow. [A.Fr. *windas*; cf. O.N. *vindāss — vinda,* to wind, *āss,* pole.]

windigo *win′di-gō,* **wendigo** *wen′,* *ns.* a mythical monster among some N. Amer. Indian tribes, which eats human flesh. [Ojibwa *wintiko.*]

windlass¹ *wind′ləs, n.* any of various modifications of the wheel and axle employing a revolving cylinder, used for hauling or hoisting: a windas for a cross-bow (*obs.*). — *v.i.* to use a windlass. — *v.t.* to hoist by means of such. [Prob. from **windas.**]

windlass² *wind′ləs,* (*obs.*) *n.* a circuitous movement, esp. to intercept game: an indirect, crafty action. — *v.i.* to take a roundabout course. [Prob. from *wanlace,* an earlier A.Fr. form, of unknown origin.]

windle *win′dl, n.* an appliance for winding yarn. — Also (*Scot.*) **winn′le.** [**wind².**]

windlestraw *win′dl-strö, n.* a thin, dry stalk of grass: any of various long-stalked species of grass, as rye-grass: anything light or insubstantial: a lanky or feeble person. — Also (*Scot.*) **windlestrae** (*win′l-strā*). [O.E. *windelstrēaw — windel,* a woven basket, *strēaw,* straw.]

windock. See **winnock.**

windore *win′dör, -dōr,* (*Ben Jonson,* etc.; *obs.*) *n.* a form of **window.** [For *wind-door,* a popular derivation of **window.**]

window *win′dō, n.* an opening in the wall of a building, etc., for air and light: the frame in the opening: the space immediately behind the opening: a window-pane: any opening suggesting a window: (in *pl.*) the eyes, or (*Shak.*) the eyelids: (esp. with *cap.*) orig. the code-name for strips of metallic foil which when scattered from aircraft derange radar reception: a closed outcrop of strata lying beneath a thrust plane and exposed by denudation (*geol.*): a weather-window (*q v*). In various technical uses designating a part that is clear, free of a particular type of obstruction, etc.: a period of time when conditions are suitable for a particular activity, as a **launch window** (planetary positions, weather conditions, etc., for the launch of a spacecraft), **re-entry window** (for the re-entry of a spacecraft), etc.: a rectangular section of a screen which can be used independently of the rest of the screen (*comput.*). — *v.t.* to furnish with windows: to make rents in (*Shak.*). — *adj.* **win'dowed** having a window or windows, or openings or holes resembling these: placed in a window (Shak., *Ant. and Cleo.* IV, xii. 72). — *n.* **win'dowing** (*comput.*) the process of displaying an image or data from a file in a window. — *adj.* **win'dowless** having no windows. — **win'dow-bar** a wooden or iron bar between the panes of a window: a bar fitted into a window for security: (*Shak.* **window= barne** emended *bars, Timon* IV, iii. 116) lattice-work across a woman's stomacher; **win'dow-blind** a blind or screen for a window; **win'dow-bole** see **bole**³; **win'dow-box** a box for growing plants in on a window-sill; **win'dow-curtain** a curtain hung over a window, inside a room; **win'dow-dressing** the arranging of goods in a shop window: the art of doing so effectively: (the art of) presenting a cause, situation, etc., in a favourable light; **window envelope** an envelope with a transparent panel through which the address of the recipient on the enclosed letter can be read; **win'dow-frame** a frame that surrounds a window; **win'dow-gardening** the cultivation of plants indoors before a window, or in boxes fitted on the outside sill; **window-glass** glass suitable or used for windows; **win'dow-ledge** a window-sill; **win'dow-pane** a sheet of glass set in a window; **win'dow-sash** a frame in which panes of glass are set; **win'dow-screen** any ornamental device for filling the opening of a window; **win'dow-seat** a seat in the recess of a window: a seat beside a window in a bus, aeroplane, etc. — *v.i.* **win'dow-shop.** — **win'dow-shopping** gazing in shop windows rather than making actual purchases; **win'dow-sill** the sill of a window opening; **win'dow-tax** a tax levied on windows of houses (repealed 1851). [M.E. *windowe, windoge* — O.N. *vindauga* — *vindr*, wind, *auga*, eye.]

windring *wīnd'ring, adj.* (Shak., *Temp.* IV, i. 128) perh. for **winding** or **wandering**.

winds. See **winze**².

Windsor *win'zər, adj.* pertaining to *Windsor*, in Berkshire, as in **Windsor chair,** a chair with a solid wooden seat that has sockets into which the legs and the (usu. slender, spindle-shaped) uprights of the back are fitted; **Windsor knot** a type of wide, triangular knot used in tying a tie; **Wind'sor-soap** a kind of perfumed toilet-soap (usu. brown).

wine *wīn, n.* the fermented juice of grapes: a liquor made from other fruits: intoxication (*fig.*): a wine-drinking, a wine-party: a rich red colour. — Also *adj.* — *v.t.* to supply with wine: to treat with wine. — *v.i.* to take wine, especially at a wine-party. — *adj.* **wī'n(e)y** like wine: intoxicated. — *ns.* **wī'nery** (orig. *U.S.*) a place where wine is prepared; **wino** (*wī'nō; coll.*) an alcoholic addicted to wine: — *pl.* **wī'nos.** — **wine'-bag** a wine-skin: a tippler; **wine bar** a bar that specialises in serving wines and usually food; **wine'-berry** a grape (*obs.*): a redcurrant, a gooseberry, or a bilberry (*dial.*): a raspberry (*Rubus phoenicolasius*) of China and Japan: the tutu, or another New Zealand tree, the makomako; **wine'-bibber** a continual drinker of wine: a drunkard; **wine'-bibbing; wine'-biscuit** a biscuit orig. intended to be served with wine; **wine'-cask** a cask for holding wine; **wine'-cellar** a cellar for storing wine. — *adj.* **wine=coloured** of the colour of red wine. — **wine'-cooler** a receptacle for cooling wine in bottles about to be served at table; **wine funnel** a type of funnel, usu. made of silver or pewter, used for decanting wine from the bottle; **wine'-glass** a small glass used in drinking wine;

wine'-glassful; wine'-grower one who cultivates a vineyard and makes wine. — *n.* and *adj.* **wine'-growing.** — **wine lake** a surplus of wine bought up by an economic community to prevent a fall in prices; **wine'-list; wine'= meas'ure** an old English liquid measure, its gallon ⅚ of the gallon in beer-measure; **wine'-merchant** a dealer in wine, esp. wholesale; **wine'-palm** any palm yielding palm-wine (as *Borassus, Raphia*); **wine'-party** a drinking-party; **wine'-press** a machine in which grapes are pressed in the manufacture of wine; **wine'-sap** a variety of deep-red winter apple; **wine'-skin** a bag for holding wine, made out of a skin; **wine'-stone** crude argol; **wine'-taster** one whose business it is to sample wines; **wine'-tasting** (a gathering for) sampling wines; **wine'-vat, -fat** a vat in which grapes are pressed in winemaking; **wine'-vault(s)** a vaulted wine-cellar: a place where wine is tasted or drunk. — **Adam's wine** water; **red wine** see **red; Rhine, Rhenish, wine** wine produced on the banks of the *Rhine*, esp. hock; **spirit of wine** alcohol; **white wine** see **white.** [O.E. *wīn*; Goth. *wein*, Ger. *Wein*; all from L. *vīnum*; cog. with Gr. *oinos*.]

wing¹ *wing, n.* the organ of a bird, insect, or other creature, by which it flies: an animal organ resembling a wing: flight: means of flying: anything resembling a wing: a fan or vane: (usu. in *pl.*) a sail: any side-piece, on a building, etc.: the side of a stage: side scenery: a plane of an aeroplane: the mudguard of a motor vehicle: a similar part of a carriage: a side-piece on the back of an armchair: one of the longer sides of crown-works or horn-works in fortification: the flank corps or division of an army on either side: the ships on either extremity of a fleet ranged in line: a section of a political party: (a player on) either the extreme left or extreme right of the forward line in football, etc.: either edge of a football, etc. pitch, along which such a player moves: a group of three squadrons in the Royal Air Force: (in *pl.*) a qualified pilot's badge: formerly, the badge of any member of an air-crew other than the pilot: a flock (of plover): means or power of rapid movement (*fig.*): protection (*fig.*). — *v.t.* to furnish, or transport, with wings: to lend speed to: to supply with side-pieces: to bear in flight, to waft: to effect on wings: to traverse by flying: to wound in the wing: to wound in the arm or shoulder. — *v.i.* to soar on the wing: to go with speed. — *adj.* **winged** (*wingd* or *wing'id*) furnished with wings: (*wingd*) of a stem, bearing the thin flattened bases of decurrent leaves, of a fruit or seed, having a flattened appendage: (*wingd*) wounded in the wing, shoulder, or arm: swift: lofty, sublime: (in **winged words,** rendering Homer's *epea pteroenta*) spoken, uttered, flying from one person to another: full of flying birds (*Milt.*). — *adv.* **wing'edly** on or by wings. — *n.* **wing'er** one who plays in a position on the wing in football, etc. — *adj.* **wing'less** without wings. — *n.* **wing'let** a small wing: a bastard wing: a wing-like appendage: a small vertical wing attached to the tip of an aeroplane wing to improve lift. — *adj.* **wing'y** having, resembling, or soaring on, wings: lofty. — *adv.* **wing'-and-wing** in the condition of a ship sailing before the wind with the foresail at one side and the mainsail at the other. — **wing(back) chair** an armchair with wings (see **wing** above); **wing'beat** a beat or flap of a bird's or insect's wing; **wing'-case** the horny case or cover over the wings of some insects, as the beetles; **wing collar** a man's stiff collar, worn upright with the points turned down; **wing'-commander** a Royal Air Force officer corresponding in rank to a naval commander or to a lieutenant-colonel; **winged bean** a legume orig. from S.E. Asia (*Psophocarpus tetragonolobus*), of special value for its high protein content; **winged bull** a common form in Assyrian sculpture, symbolic of domination; **winged elm** an elm tree of N. America, its young branches having corky projections; **winged words** see **winged** above. — *adj.* **wing'-footed** having wings attached to the feet (*myth.*, etc.): fast-moving, swift (*poet.*): aliped (*zool.*). — **wing forward** one of the two outside men of the second row of the scrum, a flanker (*Rugby football*). — *adj.* **wing'-led** (Shak., *Cymb.* II, iv. 24, some editions) presumably, led in wings or divisions. — **wing'-loading** (*aero.*) the maximum flying weight of an aeroplane divided by the total area of the main planes, including the ailerons; **wing mirror** a rear-view mirror projecting from the wing, or more generally, the side of a vehicle; **wing nut** a butterfly-nut (q.v.); **wing'-sheath** a wing-case; **wing'-shell**: a mollusc of genus Malleus, or allied genus, or its shell: a wing-snail; **wing'-shoot'ing** the act or practice of shooting flying birds, **wing'-shot** a shot at a bird on the wing: one who shoots flying birds. — *adj.* shot in the wing, or while on the wing. — **wing'-snail** a pteropod; **wing'span, wing'-spread** the distance from tip to tip of a bird's extended wings, or of the wings of an aircraft; **wing walker** one who performs stunts on the wing of an airborne aeroplane; **wing walking.** — **birds of one wing** (*obs.*) birds of the same kind; **flying wing** see **fly**; **in the wings** (*coll.*) waiting in reserve; **lend wings** to to give speed to; **make, take, wing** to begin flight: to depart; **on, upon, the wing** flying: in motion: departing; **on the wings of the wind** with the highest speed; **under someone's wing** under someone's protection. [O.N. *vængr*, a wing.]

wing². See **win³**.

wingding *wing'ding*, (chiefly *Amer.*) *n.* a wild party: a lavish social function: a drug-addict's seizure: a pretended seizure. [Origin uncertain.]

winge *winj*, (*dial.*). Non-Scottish (esp. *Austr.*) variant of **whinge.**

wink¹ *wingk, v.i.* to move the eyelids, or an eyelid, quickly: to give a hint, or convey amused understanding, by a sign of this kind: to shut the eyes (*obs.*): to blink: to seem not to see: to connive (usu. with *at*): to flicker, twinkle. — *v.t.* to close and open quickly: to flicker: to express by flash-lights. — *n.* the act of winking: a hint, as by winking: a blink: a closing of the eyes for sleep: a short spell of sleep: a very small time or distance. — *ns.* **wink'er** one who winks: a horse's blinker (usu. in *pl.*): an eye (*dial.*): the nictitating membrane of a bird's eye: a small bellows in an organ, regulated by a spring, controlling variations of wind-pressure: (in *pl.*) direction indicators on a motor vehicle, consisting of flashing lights (*coll.*); **wink'ing** the act of giving a wink. — *adj.* (*Shak.*) closed, or with eyes shut, or blind. — *adv.* **wink'ingly.** — **wink'-a-peep** (*dial.*) the scarlet pimpernel. — **easy as winking** very easily indeed; **forty winks** (*coll.*) a short nap; **like winking** (*slang*) very rapidly; **tip someone the wink** see **tip.** [O.E. *wincian*; Ger. *winken*.]

wink² *wingk, n.* one of the small coloured discs used in the game of tiddlywinks. [Short for **tiddlywink**.]

winkle *wing'kl, n.* a periwinkle (see **periwinkle²**): the penis (*slang* or *hypocoristic*). — *n.* **wink'ler** that which or one who winkles out: a person who evicts tenants on behalf of the property owner. — **wink'le-pickers** shoes with long pointed toes, esp. popular in the early 1960s. — **winkle out** (*fig.*) to force out gradually and with difficulty (perh. derived from Ger. *Winkel*, corner).

winn. See **win³**.

winna *win'ə, wun'ə*. A Scots form of **will not**.

winnable, winner, winning, winningly. See **win¹,²**.

winnle. See **windle.**

winnock *win'ək*, **win'dock** *win'dək* (*Scot.*) *ns.* a window. [Scot. development of M.E. *windoge*; see **window**; cf. **warlock**.]

winnow *win'ō, v.t.* to separate the chaff from by wind: to fan: to sift: to separate: to blow upon: to waft: to diffuse: to set in motion (*Milt.*): to flap, flutter (*rare*). — *v.i.* to separate chaff from grain: to fly: to blow in gusts. — *n.* a fan for winnowing. — *adj.* **winn'owed** (Shak., *Hamlet* V, ii. 201) perh. wise. — *ns.* **winn'ower; winn'owing.** — **winn'owing-fan, -machine** a fan, machine, for winnowing. [O.E. *windwian*, to winnow — *wind*; see **wind¹**.]

wino. See **wine.**

winsey. Same as **wincey.**

winsome *win'səm, adj.* cheerful: pleasant: attractive. — *adv.* **win'somely.** — *n.* **win'someness.** [O.E. *wynsum*, pleasant — *wyn*, joy (Ger. *Wonne*) — and *-sum* (see suff. **-some**).]

win't (*Burns*). See **wind²**.

winter *win'tər, n.* the cold season of the year — in northern temperate regions, from November or December to January or February; astronomically, from the winter solstice to the vernal equinox: a year (usu. in *pl.*): any season of cheerlessness. — *adj.* wintry: suitable for wear or use in winter: sown in autumn, as **winter wheat, winter barley, winter crop,** etc. — *v.i.* to pass the winter. — *v.t.* to feed and keep through winter. — *adj.* **win'tered** having seen many winters, aged (*obs.*): exposed to winter: worn in winter (*Shak.*). — *v.t.* **win'terise, -ize** to make suitable for use under wintry conditions. — *adj.* **win'terly** cheerless. — *n.* **win'triness.** — *adj.* **win'try, win'tery** resembling, or suitable to, winter: stormy: cheerless. — **win'ter-aconite** see **aconite**; **win'ter-apple** an apple that keeps well in winter, or that does not ripen till winter. — *adj.* **win'ter-beaten** (*Spens.*) beaten or injured by the cold of winter. — **win'ter-berry** a name given to several shrubs of the genus Ilex, growing in the eastern parts of N. America; **win'ter-bloom** the witch-hazel: a species of azalea; **win'ter-bourne** an intermittent spring of water, as found in the chalk-districts; **win'ter-bud** a bud protected by scales in which next year's shoot passes the winter; **win'ter-cherry** any species of Physalis, esp. *Physalis alkekengi*: its edible fruit: the balloon-vine, or its fruit. — *adj.* **win'ter-clad** warmly clad. — **win'ter-clover** the partridge-berry; **win'ter-cress** a cruciferous plant (Barbarea) formerly cultivated for winter salad; **win'ter-garden** an ornamental garden of evergreens, etc., or a conservatory with flowers, for winter: (in *pl.*, with *cap.*) used sometimes as the name of a theatre, concert-hall, etc.; **win'tergreen** a plant of genus Pyrola, also of Chimaphila: a plant of genus Gaultheria, whose oil is an aromatic stimulant, used in flavouring confectionery and in medicine (**chick'weed-win'tergreen** either of two plants — *Trientalis europaea* or *Trientalis americana* — belonging to the Primulaceae, having white starlike flowers). — *v.t.* **win'ter-ground** (Shak., *Cymb.* IV, ii. 229) assumed by Steevens to mean 'to protect, as a plant, from the inclemency of winter'. — **winter quarters** the quarters of an army during winter: a winter residence; **winter sports** open-air sports practised on snow and ice, as skiing, etc.; **win'ter-sweet** a Japanese shrub (*Chimonanthus praecox*) of the family Calycanthaceae, whose fragrant yellow flowers appear before the leaves: another name for marjoram; **win'ter-tide** (*arch.*) winter. — *adj.* **win'ter-weight** of clothes, heavy enough or thick enough to be suitable for cold weather. [O.E.; cf. O.N. *vetr*, Ger. *Winter*; from Indo-European root seen in **wet, water**.]

winter's-bark *win'tərz-bärk, n.* a stimulant, aromatic, and tonic bark, named from Captain *Winter*, who first brought it from the Strait of Magellan in 1579.

wintle *win'tl*, (*Scot.*) *v.i.* to stagger. — *n.* a stagger. [Flem. *windtelen* — *winden*, to wind.]

wintry. See **winter.**

winy. See **wine.**

winze¹ *winz*, (*Scot.*) *n.* a curse. [Flem. *wensch*; from root of **wish¹**.]

winze² *winz, n.* in mining, a small ventilating shaft between two levels. — Also **winds.** [Perh. **wind²**.]

wipe *wīp, v.t.* to clean or dry by rubbing: to clear away (with *away, off, out, up*): to draw across something in order to, or as if to, clean it: to apply solder to (e.g. a joint between two lengths of lead piping) with a piece of cloth or leather: to strike (*coll.*): to clear (magnetic tape) of its content (also *fig.*). — *n.* the act of cleaning by rubbing: a blow: a brand, a scar (Shak., *Lucr.* 537): a handkerchief (*slang*): a style of film editing in which the picture on the screen appears to be pushed or wiped off the screen by the following one. — *ns.* **wipeout** (*wīp'owt; slang*) a fall from a surf- or skateboard, skis, etc., esp. a spectacular one: a complete failure or disaster; **wī'per** one who wipes, esp. one who is employed in cleaning in certain industrial jobs: that which wipes or is used for wiping: a mechanism attached to a rotating or oscillating part that causes forwards-and-backwards motion in another part (*weaving*): a moving arm or other conducting device for making a selected contact out of a number of possible connections (*elect.*): a moving arm, usu. electrically operated, for removing raindrops, etc., from the windscreen of a motor vehicle; **wī'ping** the act of one who wipes: a thrashing. — **wipe out** to obliterate, annihilate or abolish: to fall from a surfboard, skis, etc. (*slang*). [O.E. *wīpian*; O.H.G. *wīfan*, to wind round, *waif*, bandage, Goth. *weipan*, to crown.]

wire *wīr, n.* a thread or rope of metal: a piece of wire, or (in *pl.*) a group or network of wires, used for some purpose: the metal thread used in telegraphy, etc.: a metallic string of a musical instrument: a metal knitting-needle (*Scot.*): a telegram (*coll.*): a clever pickpocket (*slang*): a lash, made of wire (*Shak.*): a fence made of wire. the telephone system (*coll.*): a wire stretched over or across the starting and finishing line on a racetrack, hence esp. the finishing line itself (orig. *U.S.*; also *fig.*). — *adj.* formed of, pertaining to, or using, wire: running on wire: pertaining to wiredrawing. — *v.t.* to bind, support, protect, snare, or furnish, with wire: to supply, as a building, with wires necessary for carrying an electric current: to send, or to inform, by telegraph: to place (a croquet-ball) where a hoop hampers it. — *v.i.* to telegraph. — *adjs.* **wired; wire'less** without a wire or wires: of or pertaining to telegraphy or telephony without wires. — *n.* wireless telegraphy or telephony, radio: a receiving or transmitting set used for this purpose: a message or broadcast so transmitted: broadcast programmes: broadcasting generally. — *v.t.* and *v.i.* to communicate by radio. — *n.* **wī'rer** one who wires, or who uses wire, e.g. to snare animals. — *adv.* **wī'rily.** — *ns.* **wī'riness; wī'ring** the action of the verb: the complex of wires in an electrical system or installation. — *adj.* **wī'ry** made of, or like, wire: flexible and strong: of a person, strong and able to endure. — **wire bar** (*metallurgy*) copper of a high purity cast into a tapered ingot and used to produce copper wire; **wire'-bird** the St Helena plover, named from the wire-grass that is its habitat; **wire'-bridge** a suspension-bridge; **wire brush** a brush with wire bristles, for cleaning rust off metal, dirt off suede shoes, etc.; **wire'-dancer** a performer on a tight wire; **wire'-dancing; wired'-glass** glass in which a wire mesh has been incorporated during rolling as a resistance against fire and explosion blast. — *v.t.* **wire'draw** to draw into wire by pulling through successively smaller holes in a hard steel dieblock: to throttle a fluid by passing it through a small orifice, thus reducing the pressure: to draw or spin out to a great length: to strain the meaning of. — **wire'drawer; wire'drawing.** — *adj.* **wire'drawn** (*fig.*) spun out into needless fine distinctions. — **wired wireless** the transmission of signals by means of electromagnetic waves guided by conductors, the frequencies being of the same order as those used for radio communication; **wire gauge** any system for designating the diameter of wires by means of a set of numbers: the diameter of a particular piece of wire; **wire'-gauze** a kind of stiff close fabric made of fine wire; **wire'-grass** a kind of fine meadow-grass (*Poa compressa*): any of various other grasses with wiry stems; **wire'-guard** wire-netting placed in front of a fire; **wire'-hair** a wire-haired terrier. — *adj.* **wire'-haired** having a coat of rather rough, hard hair. — **wire'-heel** in horses and cattle, a defect or disease of the foot; **wireless station** a station for wireless transmission; **wireless telegraphy, telephony** signalling through space, without the use of conducting wires between transmitter and receiver, by means of electromagnetic waves generated by high-

frequency alternating currents; **wire'-line** one of the close-set white lines in laid paper, perpendicular to the water-lines; **wire'-man** one who puts up or who takes care of wires; **wire nail** a common type of nail, round or elliptical in cross-section, cut from steel wire; **wire'=nett'ing** a texture of galvanised wire woven in the form of a net; **wire'photo** a photograph sent over a wire circuit by electrical means; **wire'-puller** one who exercises an influence felt but not seen: an intriguer; **wire'-pulling; wire'-rope** a rope of twisted wire. — *adjs.* **wire'-sewed, -stitched** sewed with wire instead of thread; **wire'-stringed.** — *v.t.* **wire'tap** to tap (a telephone). — **wire'-walker** a wire-dancer; **wire'-way** transportation by means of wires; **wire wheel** a wheel, esp. on a sports car, etc., in which the rim is connected to the hub by wire spokes; **wire wool** a mass of very fine wire for scouring; **wire'work** the making of wire, or of objects of wire: articles, or fabric, made of wire; **wire'worker; wire'working; wire'-worm** a name given to the larvae of click-beetles, from their slenderness and uncommon hardness. — *adj.* **wire'wove** denoting a fine quality of writing-paper (see **wove**). — **give** (someone) **the wire** (chiefly *mil.*) to give advance information; **pull the wires** to be a wire-puller (q.v.); **wire away** or **in** to act or work with vigour; **wire-haired terrier** a type of wire-haired fox-terrier; **wire into** to eat vigorously and assiduously. [O.E. *wīr*; O.N. *vīrr* (in composition).]

wirricow. See **worricow.**

wis *wis*, also **wist** *wist, Shak.* **wish** *wish*, (all *sham arch.*), *v.t.* to know: to believe. [Partly from misunderstanding of the adv. **iwis** (q.v.) as *I wis*, partly a new present from the pa.t. **wist** (see **wit**[1]).]

wisard *wiz'ərd, n.* Same as **wizard.**

wisdom. See under **wise.**

wise[1] *wīz, adj.* having knowledge: learned: able to make good use of knowledge: judging rightly: discreet: skilful: dictated by wisdom: containing wisdom: pious, godly: skilled in magic (*dial.*): normal mentally (*dial.*). — *n.* **wisdom** (*wiz'dəm*) the quality of being wise: judgment: the ability to make right use of knowledge: a wise discourse, saying or teaching (*arch.*): learning (*hist.*): skilfulness, speculation, spiritual perception (*B.*): sanity (*Shak.*): (with *cap.*) the apocryphal Book of the Wisdom of Solomon: (with *cap.*) Jesus Christ. — *n.* **wise'ling** one who pretends to be wise. — *adv.* **wise'ly.** — *n.* **wise'ness.** — **Wisdom literature** writings of the ancient Middle East which consist of philosophical reflections on life or maxims and precepts about the right conduct of one's life: Jewish pre-Christian literature of this type as contained in the book of Job, Proverbs, Ecclesiastes, Wisdom of Solomon, Ecclesiasticus, and certain Psalms, to which list some add the N.T. Epistle of James; **wis'dom-tooth** any of four double back teeth cut after childhood, usually from the late teens; **wise'crack** a lively, pungent retort or comment. — *v.i.* to make such. — *adj.* **wise'cracking** making, or addicted to making, wisecracks. — **wise guy** a conceited, over-confident person: a smart alec. — *adjs.* **wise'-heart'ed** having wisdom: prudent; **wise'=like** (*Scot.; wīs'*) sensible, judicious: decent: fitting: looking as if capable of playing one's part well. — **wise woman** a witch: a midwife (*Scot.*). — **never, none, the wiser** still in ignorance; **put someone wise** (*slang*) to put someone in possession of information, make aware; **the Wise Men (of the East), Three Wise Men** the three Magi (in some traditions kings) who according to Matt. ii came to worship the baby Jesus at Bethlehem; **wise to** (*slang*) aware of; **wise up** (*slang*) to make or become aware, in possession of information. [O.E. *wīs*; Ger. *Weise*; from root of **wit**.]

wise[2], **weise, weize** *wīz,* (*Scot.*) *v.t.* to guide in a certain direction. [O.E. *wīsian* — *wīs*; **wise**[1].]

wise[3] *wīz,* (*arch.*) *n.* way, manner, now chiefly in the phrases **in any wise, in no wise** in any way, in no way, **on this wise** in this way, and as a *suff.*, meaning in the manner of, e.g. **likewise, otherwise** or (*coll.*) in the matter of, e.g. **money-wise, business-wise.** [O.E. *wīse*; Ger. *Weise*; akin to **wise**[1] and **wit**; doublet **guise.**]

wiseacre *wīz'ā-kər, n.* one who unduly assumes an air of superior wisdom: a wise guy: a simpleton quite unconscious of being such. [M.Du. *wijssegger* — O.H.G. *wīzago,* a prophet.]

wiseling. See **wise**[1].

wisent *wē'zənt, vē', n.* another name for the European bison. [Ger.]

wish[1] *wish, v.i.* to have a desire: to long: to be inclined: to express a desire, esp. as part of a superstitious ritual. — *v.t.* to desire or long for: to express a desire for: to ask: to invoke: to bid: to recommend (*obs.*): to foist, palm off (with *on, on to; coll.*): to bewitch (*dial.*): to greet, wish (someone) well (*S. Afr.*). — *n.* desire, longing: a thing desired: an expression of desire: (usu. in *pl.*) an expression of desire for good fortune for another: a malediction (*obs.*). — *n.* **wish'er.** — *adj.* **wish'ful** having a wish or desire: eager: desirable, desired (*obs.*). — *adv.* **wish'fully.** — *n.* **wish'fulness.** — *n.* and *adj.* **wish'ing.** — **wish fulfilment** (*psych.*) the satisfaction of a desire in dreams, day-dreams, etc.; **wishful thinking** (*psych.*) a type of thinking in which the individual substitutes the fantasy of the fulfilment of the wish for the actual achievement: a belief that a particular thing will happen, or is so, engendered by desire that it should happen, or be so: loosely, thinking about and wishing for an event or turn of fortune that may not take place; **wish'ing-bone, wish'bone** the V-shaped bone formed by the fused clavicles in a bird's breast, the merrythought, pulled apart in playful divination, the longer part indicating the first to be married or fulfilment of a wish; **wish'ing-cap** a cap by wearing which one obtains everything one wishes; **wish'ing-stone, -tree, -well,** etc., a stone, tree, well, etc., supposed to have the power of making a wish expressed at it come true. — **wish someone further** (*slang*) to wish someone was in some other place, not present; **wish someone joy of something** (usu. *iron.*) to hope that the possession of something will be of benefit to someone. [O.E. *wȳscan,* to wish; Ger. *wünschen,* Sw. *önska.*]

wish[2]. See **wis.**

wishtonwish *wish'tən-wish, n.* the N. American prairie-dog: the whip-poor-will (*Fenimore Cooper*). [Amer. Ind.]

wish-wash *wish'-wosh,* (*coll.*) *n.* anything wishy-washy. — *adj.* **wish'y-wash'y** thin and weak: diluted: feeble: of poor quality. [Formed from **wash.**]

wisket *wis'kit,* (*dial.*) *n.* a basket. [Scand., from same root as **whisk**[1].]

wisp *wisp, n.* a small bundle of straw or hay: a tuft, a shred: a thin strand or band: a small broom: a twisted bunch used as a torch: the will-o'-the-wisp: a flock (of snipe). — *v.t.* to make into a wisp or bundle: to rub down with a wisp. — *v.i.* to fall, drift, or otherwise move, in wisps or like a wisp. — *adj.* **wis'py** wisp-like, light and fine in texture: flimsy, insubstantial. [Origin uncertain.]

wist *wist,* (*sham arch.*) *v.t.* and *v.i.* to know. [See **wis, iwis, wit**[1].]

Wistaria *wis-tā'ri-ə, n.* a genus of papilionaceous plants, some of the species among the most magnificent ornamental climbers known in English gardens, named from the American anatomist Caspar *Wistar* (1761–1818) — also, wrongly, **Wistē'ria** (so spelt by Thomas Nuttall, who named it): (without *cap.*) any plant of this genus.

wistful *wist'fool, -fl, adj.* intent (*obs.*): earnest (*obs.*): longing: yearning with little hope: pensive. — *adv.* **wist'fully.** — *n.* **wist'fulness.** [Most prob. for **wistly.**]

wistiti *wis'ti-ti, n.* a marmoset. [Fr. *ouistiti*; from its cry.]

wistly *wist'li,* (*Shak.*) *adv.* longingly, earnestly. [Prob. for *whistly,* silently; see **whist**[1].]

wit[1] *wit, v.t.* and *v.i.* (*arch.* except in legal use) to know: to be aware (with *of*): to recognise, discern: to know

how: — *infin.* **wit,** *Spens., Shak.* and others **weet(e)** (*wēt*); *Spens.* **weet'en,** also **wot** (*wot*); *pr.t. 1st pers. sing.* **wot,** *Scot.* **wat** (*wöt*), **wite, wyte** (*wīt*); *2nd* **wost** (*wott'-est*); *3rd* **wot** (*wots, wott'eth*), *Scot.* **wate, wait, wats**; *pl.* 1st, 2nd, 3rd, **wot**; *pa.t.* **wist** (*wott'ed*); *pr.p.* **witt'ing, weet'ing** (*wott'ing*); *pa.p.* **wist.** — *n.* **witt'ing** (*obs.* and *dial.*) knowledge: information. — *adj.* cognisant: conscious: deliberate. — *adv.* **witt'ingly** knowingly: by design. — **do to wit** to cause to know; **to wit** that is to say, namely — the O.E. gerund *tō witanne.* [O.E. *witan,* to know (pres. tense *wāt, wāst, wāt,* pl. *witon; pa.t. wiste,* or *wisse,* pl. *wiston, pa.p. wist*); Goth. *witan,* to observe, Ger. *wissen*; cf. L. *vidēre,* to see; Gr. *idein.*]

wit[2] *wit, n.* the mind (*obs.*): the understanding (*arch.*): imagination or invention (*arch.*): ingenuity: intelligence, sense (in phrase **have the wit to**): a mental faculty (chiefly in *pl.*): the power of combining ideas with a pointed verbal effect: the product of this power: humour, wittiness: a person endowed with wit: information (*obs.*; in phrase **to get wit of**). — *adj.* **wit'less** lacking wit, wisdom, sense: without intellectual faculties (*obs.*): out of one's mind: stupid, unintelligent: unaware, unconscious. — *adv.* **wit'lessly.** — *ns.* **wit'lessness; wit'ling** one who has little wit: a pretender to wit. — *adj.* **witt'ed** having wit or understanding (usu. in composition, as *quick-witted*). — *n.* **witticism** (*wit'i-sizm*) a witty remark: a sentence or phrase affectedly witty: (*formerly*) a jibe. — *adv.* **witt'ily.** — *n.* **witt'iness.** — *adj.* **witt'y** possessed of wit: amusing, droll: sarcastic: ingenious (*B.*): wise, discreet, sensible (*obs.*). — **wit'-cracker** one who makes witty remarks in a crisp style; **wit'-monger** a poor would-be wit; **wit'-snapper** (*Shak.*) one who affects wit or repartee. — *v.t.* **wit'-wanton** (with *it; obs.*) to indulge in irreverent wit. — **at one's wits' end** utterly perplexed; **have one's wits about one** to be alert and resourceful; **live by one's wits** to gain a livelihood by ingenious expedients rather than by honest labour; **the five wits** the five senses. [O.E. (*ge*)*wit* — **wit**[1].]

witan *wit'an, n.pl.* members of the witenagemot: the witenagemot. — *n.* **witenagemot** (*wit'ən-ə-gə-mōt'*; popularly -*nag'*) the supreme council of England in Anglo-Saxon times, composed of the bishops, the ealdormen of shires, and a number of the king's friends and dependents. [Pl. of O.E. *wita,* a man of knowledge (*witena,* gen. pl.); *gemōt,* meeting; see preceding words.]

witch[1] *wich, n.* a woman regarded as having supernatural or magical power and knowledge usu. through compact with the devil or a minor evil spirit: a hag, crone: a fascinating woman (*coll.*): the craig-fluke: a curve whose equation is $x^2y = 4a^2(2a - y)$. — *v.t.* to bewitch: to effect, change, transport, etc., by means of witchcraft: to fascinate. — *v.i.* to practise witchcraft or fascination. — *ns.* **witch'ery** witchcraft: fascination; **witch'ing** sorcery: enchantment. — *adj.* suited to witchcraft: weird: fascinating. — *adv.* **witch'ingly.** — **witch'craft** the craft or practice of witches: the black art, sorcery: supernatural power; **witch'-doctor** in tribal societies, a magician who detects witches and counteracts evil magical influences: one who professes to heal by means of magic; **witches' brew** (*fig.*) a heady concoction of disparate elements, a confused or mysterious mixture; **witch'es'-broom** a dense tuft of poorly developed branches formed on a woody plant attacked by a parasite (chiefly fungi and mites); **witch'es'-butter** Nostoc and other gelatinous blue-green algae; **witch'es'-meat** Tremella; **witches' Sabbath** see **Sabbath**; **witch'es'-thimble** a name for various plants with thimble-like flowers, as the foxglove; **witch'-finder** one whose business was to detect witches: a witch-doctor; **witch hunt** (orig. *U.S.*) the searching out of political opponents for exposure on grounds of alleged disloyalty to the state, etc.: also applied to any similar non-political search or persecution of a group or an individual; **witch'knot** one, esp. in the hair, supposed to be tied by means of witchcraft; **witch'-meal** the inflammable pollen of the club-moss.

— *adj.* **witch'-ridden** ridden by witches. — **witch'-wife** (*Scot.*) a woman who practises witchcraft. [M.E. *wicche* (both masc. and fem.) — O.E. *wicca* (masc.), *wicce* (fem.), wizard, witch, and verb *wiccian*; ety. dub.]

witch² *wich, n.* any of several trees with pliant branches, as the wych-elm, the rowan, etc. — *n.* **witch'en** the mountain ash: the wych-elm. — **witch'-alder** any of a genus of N. American shrubs related to the witch-hazel — not an alder; **witch'-elm** the wych-elm; **witch'-hazel** any of a number of trees, as the wych-elm, the hornbeam, or a N. American shrub (*Hamamelis virginica*) from whose bark is made a supposed remedy for bruises, etc. — a distillate of the bark dissolved in alcohol. [O.E. *wice*; allied to *wīcan*, to give way.]

witchetty *wich'ə-tē, n.* any of the edible grubs of species of certain moths (*Cossus*) and of longicorn beetles. — Also **witchetty grub.** [Aboriginal.]

wite¹, wyte *wīt, v.t.* (*obs.* or *Scot.*) to blame: to lay the blame on. — *n.* (now *dial.*) blame, reproach. — *adj.* **wite'less** (now *dial.*) blameless. [O.E. *wītan*, to see, blame; allied to **wit**.]

wite². See **wit¹.**

witenagemot. See **witan.**

wltgat, witgatboom *vit'hhat* (*-bōōm*), *n.* a S. African evergreen tree (*Boscia albitrunca*) with pale bark, hard coarse-grained, white wood, and edible roots used esp. a coffee substitute when roasted: any of various species of the genus *Bosica.* [Afrik., — *wit*, white, *gat*, hole, *boom*, tree.]

with¹ *n.* Same as **withe.**

with² *widh, with, prep.* denoting nearness, agreement, or connection: by, beside: among: on the side of: in the company of: in the possession or care of: containing: supplemented by: possessing: characterised by: in the same direction as: at the time of: at the same time as: immediately after: in competition or contest against: in respect of, in the regard of: by, by means of, through: because of: in spite of: using: from (as in *to part with*). — *adv.* **withal** (*widh-öl'*) with all or the rest: besides: therewith: thereupon: nevertheless, for all that. — *prep.* an emphatic form of *with*, used after its object. — **be with someone** to understand someone; **feel, be,** or **think, with** to feel as, or be of the same opinion as, the other person specified; **in with** (*coll.*) friendly with; **with it** (*slang*) following current trends in popular taste; **with that** thereupon. [O.E. *with*, against; O.N. *vith*, Ger. *wider*. It ousted the O.E. *mid*, with (Ger. *mit*).]

withdraw *widh-drö'*, or *with-, v.t.* to draw back or away: to take back or away: to take from deposit or investment, as money: to remove (with *from*): to deflect, turn aside (*rare*): to recall, retract, unsay. — *v.i.* to retire: to go away: to take back what one has said, or to recall a motion one has proposed: — *pa.t.* **withdrew** (*-drōō'*); *pa.p.* **withdrawn'.** — *ns.* **withdraw'al** an act or gradual process of withdrawing: the stage in which, or process whereby, an addict is deprived of a drug in order to break his addiction: coitus interruptus; (*rare*) **withdraw'ment; withdraw'er.** — *adj.* **withdrawn'** (of place) secluded: remote: (of a person or his manner) detached: uncommunicative: introverted. — **withdrawal symptom** any of a number of symptoms, such as pain, nausea, sweating, caused by depriving a person of a drug to which he is addicted; **withdraw'ing-room** a room used to retire into: a drawing-room. [Pfx. *with-*, against, back, and **draw.**]

withe *widh, with,* or *wīdh, n.* a flexible twig, esp. of willow: a band of twisted twigs: a halter (*obs.*): an elastic handle to a tool to save the hand from the shock of blows: a boom-iron. — *v.t.* to bind with a withe or withes: to take with a noose of withes. — *adj.* **with'y** made of withes: like withes, flexible: wiry and agile. [O.E. *withthe*; O.N. *vīthir*, Ger. *Weide*, willow; cf. **withy.**]

wither *widh'ər, v.i.* to fade or become dry: to lose freshness: to languish, decline, to decay, waste. — *v.t.* to cause to dry up, fade, or decay: to blight (*fig.*): to cause to feel very unimportant or despicable: to dry, as tea. — *adj.* **with'ered.** — *ns.* **with'eredness; with'ering.** —

adj. fading, becoming dry, etc., or causing to do so: used for drying or curing: blasting, blighting, scorching (*fig.*): snubbing. — *adv.* **with'eringly.** — **with'ering= floor** the drying-floor of a malthouse. [M.E. *wederen*, to expose to weather.]

witherite *widh'ər-īt, n.* the chief source of barium compounds — barium carbonate, occurring as orthorhombic crystals in pseudohexagonal pyramids. [Dr W. *Withering*, who first discriminated it from barytes, 1784.]

withers *widh'ərz, n.pl.* the ridge between the shoulderbones of a horse. — *adj.* **with'er-wrung** injured in the withers. — **wring someone's withers** to wound someone by a snub, etc.: to cause someone anguish. [O.E. *wither*, against, an extension of *with*, against.]

withershins *widh', wid'ər-shinz,* (*Scot.*) *adv.* in the contrary direction, contrary to the course of the sun: in the wrong way — opp. to *deasil.* [L.G. *weddersins*; cf. O.E. *wither*, against, L.G. *sind*, direction, O.E. *sīth*, journey.]

withhault. Pseudo-archaic *pa.t.* of **withhold.**

withhold *widh-hōld'*, or *with-, v.t.* to hold back, restrain: to keep back: to refuse to give: to keep in bondage or custody (*obs.*). — *v.i.* to refrain (with *from* or infin.; *obs.*): to postpone (*Pope*): — *pa.t.* and *pa.p.* **withheld'** (*arch. pa.p.* **withhold'en**). — *ns.* **withhold'er; withhold'-ment.** — **withholding tax** (*U.S.*) income tax deducted at source, incl. tax levied by a country on dividends, etc. paid to a non-resident. [Pfx. *with-*, against, and **hold.**]

within *widh-in'*, or *with-, prep.* in or to the inner part of (*arch.*): inside: in the limits of: not going beyond: on the inner side of (*obs.*): entered from: into. — *adv.* in the inner part: inwardly: in the mind, soul, heart: behind the scenes: at home (*arch.*): indoors: in or to an inner room (*arch.*): herein. — **within land** (*obs.*) inland; **within reach** in a position from which it can be obtained, or attained, without much difficulty, effort, or loss of time. [O.E. *withinnan* — *with*, against, with, *innan*, in.]

without *widh-owt'*, or *with-, prep.* outside, or out of (*arch.*): outside the limits of (*arch.*): beyond (*arch.*): not with: in absence of: not having: not using: with no help from: free from. — *adv.* on the outside: outwardly: outside, not members of, a particular group or society: out of doors (*arch.*). — *conj.* (*arch.* or *dial.*) unless, except. — *adj.* **without'-door** (*Shak.*) outward. — *prep.* **without'en** (*arch.*) without. — **from without** from the outside; **without distinction** indiscriminately; **without doors** out of doors: outside the family, nation, etc.: outside Parliament. [O.E. *withūtan* — *with*, against, *ūtan*, outside.]

withstand *widh-stand'*, or *with-, v.t.* and *v.i.* to stand, maintain one's position (against): to oppose or resist: to hinder (*obs.*): — *pa.t.* and *pa.p.* **withstood'.** — *n.* **withstand'er.** [O.E. *withstandan* — *with*, against; see **stand.**]

withwind *with'wind,* **withywind** *widh'i-wīnd,* (*dial.*) *ns.* bindweed, or other climbing plant. [O.E. *withewinde*; cf. **withy** and **wind².**]

withy *widh'i, n.* the osier willow: any willow: a flexible twig or branch, esp. one used for binding. [O.E. *wīthig*, willow; cf. **widdy**, **withe.**]

witling. See **wit².**

witloof *wit'lōf, n.* a kind of chicory with large leaves. [Du., lit. white leaves.]

witness *wit'nis, n.* knowledge brought in proof: testimony of a fact: that which furnishes proof: one who sees or has personal knowledge of a thing: one who gives evidence: one who or that which attests. — *v.t.* to have direct knowledge of: (*loosely*) to see: to be the scene of: to give testimony to: to attest: to act as legal witness of: to sign: to show: to evince (*arch.*). — *v.i.* to give evidence. — *n.* **wit'nesser.** — **wit'ness-box** the enclosure in which a witness stands when giving evidence in a court of law. — **bear witness** to give, or be, evidence (esp. with *to*); **with a witness** (*Shak.*) with a vengeance;

witness (such and such) let (such and such) serve as evidence. [O.E. (*ge*)*witnes* — (*ge*)*wit*; see **wit**[2].]

witter *wit'ər*, (chiefly *Scot.*) *v.i.* to talk or mutter peevishly or ineffectually (esp. with *on*). [Ety. dub.]

witticism. See **wit**[2].

witting, witty, etc. See **wit**[1,2].

wittol *wit'əl, n.* one who knows his wife's faithlessness, and submits to it. — *adj.* **witt'olly** (*Shak.*) like a wittol or contented cuckold. [M.E. *wetewold*; associated with **cuckold** (q.v.), and perh. from **witwall**, or from **wit**[1].]

witwall *wit'wöl*, (*dial.*) *n.* the green woodpecker, or the greater spotted woodpecker. [Cf. Ger. *Wittewal*, *Wiedewall*; cf. also **woodwale**.]

witwanton. See **wit**[2].

wive *wīv, v.t.* to take for a wife: to provide with a wife: to become the wife of. — *v.i.* to marry a wife. — *n.* **wive'hood** (*Spens.*) wifehood. [O.E. *wīfian* — *wīf*, wife.]

wivern *wī'vərn*, (*her.*) *n.* a fictitious monster, winged and two-legged, allied to the dragon and the griffin. [O.N.Fr. *wivre*, a viper — L. *vīpera*.]

wives *wīvz, pl.* of **wife**.

wizard *wiz'ərd, n.* one, usu. a man, who practises witchcraft or magic: one who works wonders: a wise man (*obs.*). — *adj.* with magical powers: wonderful, delightful (*slang*). — *adv.* **wiz'ardly** like a wizard. — *n.* **wiz'ardry** sorcery. [M.E. *wysar(d)* — *wys*, wise, and noun suff. -*ard*.]

wizen *wiz'n, adj.* dried up, thin, shrivelled (now usu. **wiz'ened**). — *v.i.* and *v.t.* to become, or to make, dry and shrivelled. — *adj.* **wiz'en-faced** having a thin, shrivelled face. — Also **weazen,** etc. [O.E. *wisnian*, to wither; cog. with O.N. *visna*, to wither.]

wizier. Same as **vizier.**

wo. Same as **woe**, or as **whoa**. — Also **wo ha ho.**

woad *wōd, n.* a genus (Isatis) of cruciferous plants, mostly natives of countries round the Mediterranean — **dyer's woad** (*Isatis tinctoria*) yielding a good and very permanent dye, largely superseded by indigo: a blue dye. — *adj.* **woad'ed** dyed blue with woad. [O.E. *wād*; Ger. *Waid*.]

wobbegong *wob'i-gong, n.* a carpet shark. [Aboriginal.]

wobble *wob'l, v.i.* to move unsteadily or uncertainly from side to side: to move along thus: to quiver: to quaver (*coll.*): to vacillate. — Also *v.t.* — *n.* an unsteady, unequal motion or movement. — *ns.* **wobb'ler; wobb'-liness; wobb'ling.** — *adj.* **wobb'ly** shaky: inclined to wobble. — *n.* (*coll.*) a fit, tantrum. — Also **wabb'le, wabb'ler,** etc. — **wobb'le-board** a sheet of hardboard shaken to obtain certain sound-effects. [L.G. *wabbeln*.]

wock. See **wok.**

Woden *wō'dən, n.* the chief god of the ancient Germanic peoples. — Also **Wō'tan.** — *n.* **Wō'denism** the worship of Woden. [O.E. *Wōden*; O.H.G. *Wuotan*; cf. **Odin.**]

wodge *woj*, (*coll.*) *n.* a large or roughly-cut portion: a lump. [**wedge.**]

woe, wo *wō, n.* grief (*arch.*): misery: (often in *pl.*) a misfortune or calamity: a physical pain (*obs.*): a curse: (often **wō,** *pl.* **wōs**) an exclamation of grief. — *adj.* (*arch.* and *dial.*) sad, wretched, sorry. — *adjs.* **woe'ful, wō'ful, woe'some** (*Scot.* **wae'some**) sorrowful or afflicted: bringing misery or calamity: deplorable: wretched, paltry. — *adv.* **woe'fully, wō'fully.** — *n.* **woe'fulness, wō'fulness.** — *adjs.* **woe'begone, wō'begone** (see **bego**) beset with woe: dismal-looking, suggesting misery; **woe'-wea'ried, -worn** wearied, worn with woe. — **in weal and woe** in prosperity and adversity; **woe is me** (*arch.*) unhappy that I am! cursed am I; **woe unto** calamity will befall: may calamity befall; **woe worth the day** see **worth**[2]. [O.E. (interj.) *wā*; Ger. *Weh*; L. *vae*; cf. **wail.**]

wog *wog, n.* an offensive name for an Arab, an Egyptian, etc.: a foreigner generally, usu. coloured. [Perh. from **(golly)wog**; pop. thought to be an acronym, of which several expansions are propounded.]

woggle *wog'l, n.* the ring a Scout threads his neckerchief through.

woiwode. Same as **voivode.**

wok, wock *wok, n.* a hemispherical pan used in Chinese cookery. [Chin.]

woke, woken. See **wake**[1].

wold *wōld, n.* an open tract of country, now chiefly upland country. [O.E. (Angl.) *wald*, forest, applied orig. to wooded parts of the country; cf. **weald.**]

wolf *woŏlf, n.* the common name of certain gregarious and rapacious species of the genus Canis — including the common wolf (*Canis lupus*), the grey or timber wolf, and the coyote: anything very ravenous: a greedy and cunning person: a tuberculous excrescence, or cancerous growth (*obs.*): a dissonance heard in a keyed instrument tuned by unequal temperament (*mus.*): an extraneous non-harmonic note made by the bow on a string of a violin, etc. (*mus.*): a man who pursues women (*coll.*): — *pl.* **wolves** (*woŏlvz*). — *v.i.* to hunt for wolves (also **wolve** *woŏlv*). — *v.t.* (often with *down* or *up*; *coll.*) to devour ravenously. — *ns.* **wolf'er, wolv'er** one who hunts wolves; **wolf'ing, wolv'ing** the hunting of wolves for their skins. — *adjs.* **wolf'ish, wolv'ish** like a wolf: rapacious: ravenous. — *adv.* **wolf'ishly, wolv'-ishly.** — *ns.* **wolf'kin, wolf'ling** a young wolf. — **Wolf Cub** one who belongs to the Wolf Cubs, a junior division of the Boy Scouts organisation (now Cub Scouts); **wolf'-dog** a dog of large breed formerly used in hunting wolves: a cross between a wolf and a domestic dog; **wolf'-fish** any genus of fierce and voracious salt-water fishes — called also sea-wolf; **wolf'-hound** a wolf-dog, esp. of large size, as the Russian wolf-hound (see **borzoi**); **wolf'-note** (*mus.*) a wolf; **wolf'-pack** a pack of wolves: a flotilla of submarines surfacing together for attack; **wolf's'-bane, wolfs'bane** an aconite, esp. *Aconitum lycoctonum*; **wolf's'-foot, -claw** the club-moss (Lycopodium); **wolf'-skin** the skin or pelt of a wolf; **wolf's'-peach** the tomato; **wolf'-spī'der** any spider of the genus (Lycosa) to which the true tarantula belongs, or of the family Lycosidae; **wolf'-tooth** a small supernumerary premolar in a horse; **wolf'-whistle** a two-note whistle uttered in admiration, typically by a man at the sight of a woman. — **cry wolf** to give a false alarm — from the story of the boy who cried 'Wolf' when there was none, and was not believed when there was one; **have a wolf by the ears** to be in a very difficult situation; **have a wolf in the stomach** to be ravenously hungry; **keep the wolf from the door** to keep away poverty or hunger; **see a wolf** to be tongue-tied (in allusion to an old superstition); **throw, fling to the wolves** to abandon to certain destruction; **wolf in sheep's clothing** someone who behind a kindly and inoffensive exterior is dangerous and unscrupulous. [O.E. *wulf*; Ger. *Wolf*; L. *vulpēs*, fox, *lupus*, wolf; Gr. *lykos*.]

Wolffian *woŏl'fi-ən, vol'fi-ən, adj.* pertaining to, or associated with, the German embryologist K. F. *Wolff* (1733–94): designating the renal organs in the embryo of vertebrates.

Wolfian[1] *woŏl'fi-ən, vol'fi-ən, adj.* pertaining to the philosophy of Christian *Wolf* (1679–1754), who systematised and popularised the philosophy of Leibniz, and gave a strong impulse to that development of natural theology and rationalism. — Also **Wolff'ian.** — *n.* **Wolf'ianism.**

Wolfian[2] *woŏl'fi-ən, vol'fi-ən, adj.* pertaining to, or associated with, Friedrich August *Wolf* (1759–1824) — applied esp. to his theory that the *Odyssey* and *Iliad* are composed of numerous ballads, strung together by subsequent editors.

wolfram *woŏlf'rəm, n.* (also **wolf'ramite**) a native compound of tungstate of iron and manganese: tungsten. [Ger.; origin uncertain.]

wollastonite *woŏl'əs-tən-īt, or -əs', n.* a pyroxene of relatively simple composition, silicate of calcium, $CaSiO_3$ — also called **tabular spar.** [After the scientist W. H. *Wollaston* (1766–1828).]

wolly *wo'li*, (*slang*) a uniformed policeman, esp. a raw young constable. [Ety. uncertain; cf. **wally**².]

Wolof *wō'lof*, *n.* a tribe living near the Senegal River in western Africa: a member of the tribe: its language. — Also *adj.*

wolve, wolver. See **wolf.**

wolverene, wolverine *wōōl-və-rēn'*, *n.* the American glutton: its fur. [Extension of **wolf.**]

wolves, wolvish. See **wolf.**

woman *wōōm'ən*, *n.* an adult female of the human race: a wife (now *dial.*): a mistress: the female sex, women collectively: a female attendant: a charwoman or daily domestic help (*coll.*): the reverse or Britannia side of a coin: — *pl.* **women** (*wim'ən*). — Also *adj.* — *v.t.* to cause to act like a woman (*obs.*): (with *it*) to play the part of a woman: to provide or staff with a woman or women: to call a person 'woman' abusively. — *adj.* **wo'man'd** (*Shak.*) accompanied by a woman. — *adv.* **wom'anfully** like a woman of spirit. — *n.* **wom'anhood** the state, character, or qualities of a woman: womenkind. — *v.t., v.i.* **wom'anise, -ize** to make, become, effeminate: (*v.i., derog.*) of a man, to pursue women with a view to amorous adventures. — *n.* **wom'aniser, -z-.** — *adj.* **wom'anish** effeminate: feminine. — *adv.* **wom'anishly.** — *ns.* **wom'anishness; wom'ankind** a woman (*obs.*): (also **wom'enkind, wom'enfolk, -folks**) a group of women taken together, as the women of a family, or the female sex. — *adj. and adv.* **wom'an-like.** — *n.* **wom'anliness.** — *adj.* **wom'anly** like or becoming a woman: feminine. — *adv.* in the manner of a woman. — **wom'an-bod'y** (*Scot.*) a woman. — *adjs.* **wom'an-born** born of woman; **wom'an-built** built by women. — **wom'an-child** a female child: — *pl.* **wom'en-children.** — *adj.* **wom'an-grown** grown to womanhood. — **wom'an-hater** a man who hates women, a misogynist; **wom'an-post** (*Shak.*) a female messenger; **wom'an-quell'er** a killer of women; **wom'an-suffrage, women's suffrage** possession of the electoral franchise by women. — *adjs.* **wom'an-tired** (*Shak.*) hen-pecked (**tire**⁵); **wom'an-vested** wearing women's clothes. — **women's liberation** a movement of active feminists forming part of the women's movement (*coll.* contr. **women's lib); women's liberationist** (*coll.* contr. **women's libber); women's movement** the movement amongst women to try to achieve equality with men, with regard to e.g. job opportunities, pay, legal status, etc.; **women's rights** equal rights with men thus sought by women; **wom'enswear** clothes for women. — **kept woman** a mistress; **play the woman** to give way to weakness; **woman of the town** a whore; **woman of the world** a woman of fashion, or of worldly wisdom: a woman who knows and makes allowance for, or accepts, the ways of the world: a married woman (*obs.*); **Women's Royal Voluntary Service** (from its formation in 1938 until 1966 the **Women's Voluntary Service**) a nationwide service assisting government departments, local authorities and other voluntary bodies in organising and carrying out welfare and emergency work for the community. [O.E. *wimman* — *wīfman* — *wīf*, a woman, *man*, man, human being.]

womb *wōōm*, *n.* the uterus, the organ in which the young of mammals are developed and kept till birth: the abdomen, or the stomach, or the bowels (*obs.*): the place where anything is produced: any deep cavity. — *v.t.* (*Shak.*) to enclose. — *adj.* **womb'y** (*Shak.*) hollow, capacious. [O.E. *wamb, womb*; Ger. *Wamme*, paunch.]

wombat *wom'bat*, *n.* an animal belonging to any of several species of heavy, burrowing marsupials of the family *Vombatidae*. [Aboriginal.]

women. See **woman.**

womera. Same as **woomera.**

won¹ *wun, wŏn*, *v.i.* to dwell, abide (*arch.* and *dial.*): to be, or become, accustomed (*obs.*). — *n.* (*obs.*) a dwelling, an abode: habit, custom. — *n.* **won'ing** dwelling. — **did won** (*Spens.*) was accustomed. [O.E. *wunian*, Du. *wonen*, Ger. *wohnen*, to dwell.]

won² *wun, pa.t.* and *pa.p.* of **win**¹,².

won³ *wun, wōōn, wŏn*, *n.* the standard monetary unit of North and South Korea. [Korean.]

wonder *wun'dər*, *n.* the state of mind produced by something new, unexpected, or extraordinary: admiration (*obs.*): the quality of being strange or unexpected: a strange, astonishing, admirable, thing or happening: a prodigy: a miracle: a sweet friedcake, a cruller (*U.S.*). — *v.i.* to feel wonder: to be amazed (with *at*): to speculate: to feel doubt. — *v.t.* to speculate, to ask oneself (with noun clause or direct quotation). — *adj.* **won'dered, wond'red** (*obs.*) marvellous: having performed, or able to perform, wonders (*Shak.*). — *n.* **won'derer.** — *adj.* **won'derful** exciting wonder: strange: expressing vague commendation, admirable, extremely good (*coll.*). — *adv.* (*arch.* or *dial.*) wonderfully. — *adv.* **won'derfully.** — *n.* **won'derfulness.** — *n.* and *adj.* **won'dering.** — *adv.* **won'deringly.** — *n.* **won'derment** surprise: an expression of wonder: a wonderful thing: quality of being wonderful. — *adjs.* **won'derous, won'drous** such as may excite wonder. — Also *adv.* — *adv.* **won'drously.** — *n.* **won'drousness.** — **won'derland** a land of wonders; **won'der-monger** a wonder-worker: one who talks much of wonders, esp. incredible ones; **won'der-mongering.** — *adjs.* **won'der-struck, -strick'en** struck with wonder or astonishment. — **won'der-work** a prodigy, miracle: thaumaturgy; **won'der-worker; won'der-working.** — *adj.* **won'der-wounded** (*Shak.*) wonder-stricken. — **bird of wonder** the phoenix; **for a wonder** by way of an unexpected but pleasant change; **nine days' wonder** something that astonishes everybody for the moment; **no wonder, small wonder** it isn't surprising; **seven wonders of the world** see **seven; to a wonder** (*arch.*) marvellously: extremely well. [O.E. *wundor*; Ger. *Wunder*, O.N. *undr*.]

wondrous. See **wonder.**

wonga-wonga *wong'(g)ə-wong'(g)ə*, *n.* the large Australian white-faced pigeon (also **wong'a**): any of several varieties of hardy evergreen climbing vine of the family *Bignoniaceae*. [Aboriginal.]

wonky *wongk'i*, (*coll.*) *adj.* unsound: shaky: amiss: awry. [Cf. **wankle.**]

wont historically *wunt*, commonly *wŏnt*, *adj.* used or accustomed. — *n.* habit. — *v.i.* to be accustomed. — *adj.* **wont'ed** accustomed, habituated: usual. — *n.* **wont'edness.** — *adj.* **wont'less** (*arch.*) unaccustomed. [Orig. pa.p. of **won**¹.]

won't *wŏnt*, will not. [Contr. of M.E. *wol not*.]

woo *wōō*, *v.t.* to try to win the affection of: to court: to solicit eagerly: to seek to gain. — Also *v.i.*: — *pa.t.* and *pa.p.* **wooed** (*wōōd*). — *n.* **woo'er.** — *n.* and *adj.* **woo'ing.** — *adv.* **woo'ingly.** [O.E. *wōgian*, to woo; origin obscure.]

woobut. Same as **woubit.**

wood¹ *wōōd*, *n.* a tree (*obs.*): the Cross (*obs.*): a collection of growing trees (often in *pl.*): wooded country: the hard part of the substance of trees and shrubs, xylem: trees cut or sawed, timber: a kind of timber or wood: firewood: the cask or barrel, as distinguished from the bottle: a woodblock (*print.*): (commonly in *pl.*) the woodwinds of an orchestra: a wooden-headed golf-club: a bowl (*bowls*): an idol made of wood: the pulpit (*slang*). — *v.t.* to cover with trees: to supply or load with wood. — *v.i.* to take in a supply of wood. — *adjs.* **wood'ed** supplied with wood: covered with trees; **wood'en** made of, or like, wood: of a golf-club, with head made of wood: hard: dull, insensible: heavy, stupid: lacking animation or grace of manner or execution: clumsy. — *adv.* **wood'enly.** — *ns.* **wood'enness** wooden quality: want of spirit or expression; **wood'iness** the state or quality of being woody. — *adj.* **wood'less** without wood. — *n.* **wood'lessness.** — *adjs.* **wood'sy** (*-zi*; *U.S.*) pertaining to, or characteristic of, woods; **wood'y** abounding with woods: inhabiting woods (*Spens.*): situated in a wood: pertaining to wood: consisting wholly or largely of wood: ligneous: like wood in texture, or smell, or taste, etc. — **wood'-**

acid wood-vinegar; **wood'-alcohol** wood-spirit; **wood'= anemone** any anemone growing in woods, esp. *Anemone nemorosa*, which has a single whorl of leaves and a white flower; **wood'-ant** a large forest-dwelling ant: a termite infesting the wood of old buildings; **wood'-ash** (often in *pl.*) ash obtained by burning wood or plants — a source of potassium salts; **wood'bine, wood'bind** the honeysuckle: applied also to other climbers, such as some kinds of ivy, the Virginia-creeper, etc.: perh. bindweed (Shak., *Mids. N. Dr.* IV, i. 48); **wood'block** a die cut in relief on wood and ready to furnish ink impressions: a woodcut; **wood'-borer** any of a number of insect larvae, or of molluscs, or of Crustacea, that bore in wood. — *adjs.* **wood'-boring; wood'-born** born in the woods. — **wood'-carver; wood'= carving** the process of carving in wood: an object, or part of one, so ornamented or made; **wood'-chat** a species of shrike; **wood'chip** a chip of wood: woodchip board or paper (**woodchip board** chipboard; **woodchip paper** (wall)paper incorporating chips of wood for texture); **wood'-coal** coal like wood in texture, lignite or brown coal: charcoal; **wood'cock** a genus (Scolopax) of birds allied to the snipes, but of a more bulky body, and with shorter and stronger legs: a stupid person, a simpleton (*arch.*); **wood'cock's-head** (*obs.*) a tobacco-pipe; **wood'craft** skill in the chase and everything pertaining to life in the woods: forestry generally: skill in working or carving wood; **wood'cut** a design for printing incised into the surface of a block of wood cut plank-wise, i.e. along the grain: an impression taken from this; **wood'-cutter** one who cuts wood: one who makes woodcuts; **wood'-cutting; wood'-engraver** one who makes wood-engravings: any of certain beetles that make a pattern of furrows in the wood of trees; **wood'-engraving** a design for printing, incised into the surface of a block of hard wood cut across the grain: an impression taken from this: the art of cutting such designs; **wood'en-head** a blockhead, stupid person. — *adj.* **wood'en-head'ed** having a head of wood: stupid. — **wood'en-head'edness; wooden horse** the Trojan horse (q.v.): an instrument of punishment (see **horse**): a ship (*arch.*); **wooden kimono, overcoat** (*U.S. slang*) a coffin; **wooden leg** an artificial leg made of wood; **wooden overcoat** see **wooden kimono** above; **wooden pear** an Australian tree whose pear-shaped seed-vessels have a woody outside; **wooden spoon** a spoon of wood presented to the person standing lowest in the mathematical tripos list at Cambridge: a booby prize; **wood'en-tongue** woody-tongue; **wooden type** large type cut in wood; **wood'-evil** diarrhoea of herbivorous animals; **wood'-fibre** a thick-walled, elongated, dead element found in wood — developed by the elongation and lignification of the wall of a single cell, differing from a tracheide in inability to conduct water; **wood'-flour, wood'-meal** a fine powder, made from sawdust and wood waste, used as a filler in many industries, in the manufacture of guncotton and dynamite, and as an absorbent in surgical dressings; **wood'= fretter** a wood-borer; **wood'-germander** *Teucrium scorodonia*, which has racemes of yellow flowers; **wood'-grouse** the capercailzie; **wood'-hole** a place where wood is stored; **wood'-honey** wild honey; **wood'-horse** a saw-horse; **wood'-house** a house or shed in which wood for fuel is deposited: (without hyphen) a variant of **woodwose** (see below); **wood'-hyacinth** the wild hyacinth or English bluebell, a flower of the genus *Endymion* (or *Scilla*); **wood'-ī'bis** any bird of the genera *Mycteria* (or *Tantalus*) and *Ibis* of the subfamily *Mycteriinae* of storks; **wood'land** land covered with wood (also *adj.*); **wood'lander** an inhabitant of woodland; **wood'-lark** a species of lark that perches on trees but sings chiefly on the wing; **wood lot** a piece of land reserved entirely for the growing of timber; **wood'louse** (*pl.* **wood'lice**) any of numerous isopod crustaceans of family Oniscidae, found in damp places, under stones and bark, in woodwork, among moss, etc.: a booklouse: a termite (*U.S.*); **wood'man** a man who cuts down

trees: a forest officer: a huntsman; **wood-meal** see **wood-flour; wood'-mite** any of numerous small mites found in woods; **wood'mouse** a type of fieldmouse, *Apodemus sylvaticus*, with large ears and a long tail; **wood'-naphtha** methanol; **wood'-nightshade** *Solanum dulcamara*, bitter-sweet; **wood'-note** (*Milt.*) a wild musical note, like that of a songbird; **wood'-nymph** a nymph of the woods; **wood'-offering** (*B.*) wood burned on the altar; **wood'-oil** gurjun balsam: tung-oil: also various other oils obtained from trees; **wood'-opal** a form of common opal which has replaced pieces of wood entombed as fossils in sediments, in some cases retaining the original structure; **wood'-owl** the European brown owl, or other owl living in woods; **wood'= paper** paper made from wood-pulp; **wood'pecker** any of a family (*Picidae*) or birds in the order Picariae, remarkable for modification of the skull and bill enabling the latter to be used to drill holes, and for the long flexible tongue, used to extract insects from crevices; **wood'-pigeon** the ring-dove, a common species of pigeon (*Columba palumbus*) living in woods: in New Zealand, the kuku (q.v.); **wood'-pile** a pile of wood, esp. firewood; **wood'-pulp** wood mechanically or chemically pulped for paper-making; **wood'-reeve** overseer of a wood; **wood'ruff** (O.E. *wudurofe*; meaning of second element unknown) a plant of the genus Asperula of rubiaceous plants with whorled leaves and a funnel-shaped corolla, esp. *sweet woodruff* which has small white flowers and a pleasant scent — (*obs.*) **wood'-roof; wood'-rush** any plant of the genus Luzula, of the same family as the true rushes, growing in woods; **wood'-sage** wood-germander; **wood'-sandpiper** a common European tattler; **wood-sanicle** see **sanicle; wood'-screw** a screw for fastening pieces of wood or wood and metal; **wood'shed** a shed for storing firewood: an intensive, esp. private, practice or rehearsal (*mus. slang*; orig. *U.S.*). — *v.t.* and *v.i.* to practise (a piece of music), esp. intensively and alone (*mus. slang*; orig. *U.S.*). — **wood'-shock** the pekan; **wood'-skin** an Indian canoe made of bark, or the bark itself; **woods'-man** a woodman; **wood'-sorrel** any plant of the genus Oxalis, esp. *Oxalis acetosella*, with trifoliate leaves and white or rose-tinted flowers, which yields potassium binoxalate, $KHC_2O_4 \cdot H_2O$; **wood'-spirit** a spirit living among trees: methyl alcohol, methanol; **wood'-spite** the green woodpecker; **wood'-stamp** a stamp made of wood, as for stamping fabrics in colours; **wood'-stone** petrified wood; **wood'-sugar** xylose; **wood'-swallow** any of the fly-catching *Artamidae*, also called swallow-shrikes, the resemblance to shrikes being more fundamental than that to swallows; **wood'-tar** a product of destructive distillation of wood, containing paraffins, naphthalene, phenols; **wood'thrush** a singing-thrush common in the woods of the eastern United States, reddish-brown above, olive on the rump, white spotted with black on the breast: locally in Britain, the missel-thrush or the song-thrush; **wood'-tick** any tick of the family Ixodidae, the young of which are transferred to man and animals from bushes; **wood'-tin** a botryoidal or reniform variety of cassiterite showing a concentric structure of radiating brown, wood-like fibres; **wood'= vinegar** crude acetic acid obtained from wood, pyroligneous acid; **wood'wale** (meaning of second element uncertain; cf. **witwall**) a woodpecker, esp. the green woodpecker; **wood'-warbler** a yellowish-green European warbler, *Phylloscopus sibilatrix*: any bird of the genera *Dendroica, Vermivora*, etc. of the American family Parulidae; **wood'ward** an officer to guard the woods; **wood'-wasp** a large hymenopterous insect (*Sirex*) that bores wood with its ovipositor; **wood'-wax, -waxen** dyer's greenweed; **wood'wind** a wind-instrument, formerly usu. of wood, some now of metal (e.g. silver) or other material — flute, oboe, bassoon, clarinet, etc.: (used collectively) the section of an orchestra comprising these; **wood'-wool** fine wood shavings; **wood'work** a part of any structure made of wood: carpentry or joinery: goalposts, etc. (*football*, etc.; *coll.*); **wood'worker** a craftsman or worker in wood; **wood'worm** a larva that bores in wood; **wood'-wose, wood'house** (O.E. *wuduwāsa*: meaning of second element uncertain; *obs.* or *her.*) a wild man of the woods, a figure sometimes found as a supporter in heraldry: a satyr, faun; **wood'-wren** the willow-warbler or willow-wren (*Phylloscopus trochilus*): the wood-warbler or yellow willow-wren (*Phylloscopus sibilatrix*) — neither being properly a wren; **wood'yard** a yard in which wood is cut and stored; **wood'y-night'-shade** same as **wood-nightshade; wood'y-tongue** actinobacillosis, a chronic inflammation of cattle, rarely of sheep and swine, occasionally transmitted to man, due to infection, usu. of the tongue, by the fungus *Actinobacillus ligniersi*. — **Commissioners of Woods and Forests** a department (1810–1924) having charge of the Crown woods and forests; **knock (on) wood** see **touch wood** under **touch; not see the wood for the trees** to fail to grasp the whole because of the superabundance of, or one's over-concentration on, detail; **out of the wood(s)** out of difficulty or danger; **something nasty in the woodshed** (*facet.*) an unpleasant or shocking experience in one's past; **touch wood** see **touch; wood-wool slabs** slabs made from long wood shavings with a cementing material, used for linings, partitions, etc. [O.E. *wudu*; cog. with O.N. *vithr*, wood, O.Ir. *fid*, timber.]

wood² *wōod*, (*Shak.*; *Scot.* **wud** *wud*) *adj.* mad: fierce, furious. — *n.* **wood'ness.** [O.E. *wōd*; O.N. *ōthr*, Ger. *Wut*, madness.]

woodburytype *wōod'bər-i-tīp*, *n.* a photo-mechanical process in which an exposed and developed bichromated film is forced into a metal plate by great pressure, and so forms a matrix for subsequent printing. [Named from the inventor.]

woodchuck *wōod'chuk*, *n.* a N. American species of marmot (*Marmota* or *Arctomys monax*). [Corr. of an Amer. Indian name.]

woodie *wōod'i*, *-ē*, (*Scot.*) *n.* the gallows. [**widdy¹**.]

woodsy, woodwose, woody. See under **wood.**

wooer, wooing, etc. See **woo.**

woof¹ *wōof*, *n.* weft: thread for a weft: texture. — *adjs.* **woofed** (*wōoft*, *wōof'id*) woven; **woof'y** dense in texture. [M.E. *oof*, with *w* added by association with **warp**, etc. (*oof* being the normal development of O.E. *ōwef* — *on*, *wefan*, to weave).]

woof² *wōof*, (*N.Eng.*) *n.* a cat-fish. [Origin obscure.]

woofer *wōof'ər*, *n.* a large loudspeaker used to reproduce low-frequency sounds only. — Cf. **tweeter.** [Imit. of a dog's bark.]

wool *wōol*, *n.* a modification of hair in which the fibres are shorter, curled, and possess an imbricated surface — the covering of sheep, etc.: short, thick human hair: any light, fleecy substance like wool: any substance with a fibrous texture, resembling wool, e.g. steel-wool: thread or yarn made from animal wool: fabric woven or knitted from it. — *adjs.* **woolled** (*wōold*) bearing wool; **wooll'en** made of, or pertaining to, wool: clad in, or covered with, wool: rustic (*obs.*). — *n.* cloth made of wool. — *n.* **wooll'iness.** — *adj.* **wooll'y** consisting of, or like, wool: clothed with wool: lacking in clearness, firmness or definition (*fig.*): having the atmosphere or quality of the Wild West (*coll.*). — *n.* a garment of wool, esp. a knitted one: — *pl.* **wooll'ies.** — *n.* **wool'sey** (*-zi*) a fabric of cotton and wool. — *adv.* **wool'ward** (*obs.*) with wool next the skin, esp. as a penance. — **wool'-ball** a ball of wool, such as is sometimes found in a sheep's stomach. — *adj.* **wool'-bearing** bearing or yielding wool. — **wool'-card, wool'-comb** a machine for **wool'-carding, wool'-combing** separating the fibres of wool preparatory to spinning; **wool'-carder, wool'-comber; wool church** an English, esp. E. Anglian, church built or converted using funds accrued during the Tudor wool trade boom, freq. appearing of inappropriate size and grandeur for its setting; **wool'-clip** crop of wool; **wool'-driver** a buyer-up of wool. — *adj.* **wool'-dyed** dyed before spinning or

weaving. — **wool'fat** lanolin; **wool'fell** the skin with the wool still on it; **wool'-gath'ering** absent-minded dreaming. — *adj.* dreamy: absent-minded. — **wool'-grower** one who raises sheep for the production of wool; **wool'-growing.** — **wooll'en-drā'per** one who deals in woollen goods; **wooll'en-drā'pery; wooll'en-mill** a mill where wool is spun and woven into material; **woolly aphis** a type of plant-louse (*Eriosoma lanigerum*) covered with hair resembling cotton-wool, that infests esp. apple-trees; **wooll'y-bear** the hairy caterpillar of a number of moths, including the tiger-moths: the larva of the carpet beetle — *adjs.* **wooll'y-haired, -head'ed** having the hair like wool. — **wool'man** a dealer in wool; **wool'-mill** a woollen-mill; **wool'-oil** any oil obtained from wool-fat: an oil used to oil wool before spinning; **wool'-pack** the package in which wool was formerly done up for sale: a bundle weighing 240 lb: cirro-cumulus cloud: the woolsack (*obs.*); **wool'-packer; wool'-picker** a machine for cleaning wool; **wool'sack** the seat of the Lord Chancellor in the House of Lords, being a large square sack of wool covered with scarlet: the office of Lord Chancellor; **wool'-shears** shears used in shearing sheep; **wool'sorter** one who sorts wool according to quality, etc.; **wool'-staple** the fibre or pile of wool: a market where wool was sold; **wool'-stapler** a dealer in wool: a woolsorter; **wool'-winder** one who packs fleeces; **wool'work** needlework imitative of tapestry. — **against the wool** against the texture of the wool, the wrong way; **dye in the wool** see **dye; great, much, cry and little wool** much palaver and little result; **pull, draw, the wool over someone's eyes** to hoodwink, deceive, someone; **woolly-hand crab** the mitten-crab (q.v.); **woolsorter's disease** anthrax. [O.E. *wull*; Goth. *wulla*, Ger. *Wolle*, L. *vellus*.]

woold *wōold*, *v.t.* to wind a rope or chain round. — *adj.* **woold'ed.** — *ns.* **woold'er** a stick used in woolding a mast or yard: a pin in a ropemaker's top; **woold'ing.** [Du. *woelen*; Ger. (*be*)*wuhlen*.]

woollen, woolly, woolsey. See **wool.**

woomera *wōom'ər-ə*, **womera** *wom'*, **woomerang** *wōom'ər-ang*, *ns.* a throwing-stick. [Aboriginal.]

woon *wōon*, (*Spens.*) *v.i.* Same as **won¹.**

woorali, woorara. See **wourali.**

woosel(l). See **ouzel.**

woosh. See **whoosh.**

woot, woo't *wōot*, (*Shak.*) wilt (thou)? — Also **wot.**

wootz *wōots*, *n.* steel made in India, from ancient times, by fusing iron with carbonaceous matter. [For *wook* — Kanarese *ukku*, steel.]

woozy *wōo'zi*, *adj.* fuddled (with drink, drugs, etc.): dazed, dizzy: blurred, woolly, vague. — *adv.* **wooz'ily.** — *n.* **wooz'iness.** [Origin obscure.]

wop¹ *wop*, *n.* a derogatory term for an Italian, or other foreigner of olive complexion. [It. (dial.) *guappo* — Sp. *guapo*, bold, handsome.]

wop² *wop*, *v.t.* Same as **whop.**

worcester *wōos'tər*, (*hist.*) *n.* fine woollen material made at *Worcester*: **Worcester (china)** fine china made there from mid-18th cent. — **worces'terberry** a N. Amer. species of gooseberry (*Ribes divaricatum*), not a hybrid; **Worcester(shire) sauce** a pungent sauce orig. made in Worcestershire.

word *wûrd*, *n.* a unit of spoken language: a written sign representing such an utterance: (in *pl.*) language: a saying: a brief conversation: a rumour: a hint: a signal or sign: a message: a promise: a declaration: a password: a watch-word: a war-cry: a set of bits stored and transferred as a single unit of meaning (*comput.*): (in *pl.*) verbal contention. — *v.t.* to express in words: to speak to, or of, in words (*obs.*; *rare*): to flatter (*Shak.*). — *v.i.* to speak, talk. — *n.* **word'age** words generally, esp. text as opposed to pictures, etc.: verbiage, wordiness: quantity of words, length of text: choice of words, wording. — *adj.* **word'ed** expressed in words. — *adv.* **word'ily.** — *ns.* **word'iness; word'ing** speaking, utterance (*arch.*): the act of expressing in words: choice of words, phrasing. — *adj.* **word'ish**

(*obs.*) verbose. — *n.* **word'ishness.** — *adjs.* **word'less** unspoken: silent; **word'y** using, or containing, too many words: conducted in words. — *adj.* **word'-blind.** — **word'-blindness** the lack, or loss, of the ability to read, a non-technical name for both **alexia** and **dyslexia; word'book** a book with a collection of words: a dictionary, or vocabulary. — *adj.* **word'bound** unable to find expression in words: bound by a promise. — **word'-building** the formation of words from letters or from root words and affixes; **word finder** a book designed as a tool for finding a required word: a thesaurus; **word'-lore** information about the history, use, etc., of words; **word'-memory** the power of recalling words to the mind; **word'-painter; word'-painting** the act or art of describing vividly in words. — *adj.* **word'-per'fect** having memorised (words to be repeated, recited, etc.) exactly. — **word'-picture** a description in words that presents an object, scene, etc., to the mind as if in a picture; **word play** puns, etc.; **word processing; word processor** any of several types of machine that perform electronically the tasks of typing, data-recording, dictating, transcribing, etc., some incorporating screens for visual display; **word'-puzzler** a person who engages in puzzles or games involving words; **word salad** (*psych.*) a confused outpouring of speech, most often occurring in cases of schizophrenia; **word'smith** an accomplished user of words (sometimes *iron.*): a coiner of words; **word'-splitting** hair-splitting; **word'-square** a square grid composed of a set of words that read the same down as they do across. — **a good word** a recommendation, favourable mention, praise; **at a word** without more ado, at once: to be brief, in short (*obs.*); **a word in one's ear** a confidential conversation; **be as good as one's word** see **good; break one's word** to fail to fulfil a promise; **by word of mouth** orally, through the spoken word (*adj.* **word'-of-mouth'**); **eat one's words** to retract, apologise, usu. under compulsion; **fair words** (*arch.*) pleasant, conciliatory words — usu. implying flattery or deceit; **get a word in edgeways** see **edge in a word** under **edge; have a word with** to have some conversation with; **have words (with)** to quarrel, dispute (with); **in a word, in one word** in short, to sum up; **in so many words** explicitly: bluntly; **in word** in speech only, in profession only; **my word** mild interj. expressing surprise, annoyance, etc.; **not the word for it** not a strong enough word to express or describe it; **of few, or many, words** taciturn, or verbose; **pass one's word** to make a promise; **put words into someone's mouth** to attribute, or supply, to someone, words that he did not, or does not intend to, use; **take someone at his word** to accept statements as being literally true; **take the words out of someone's mouth** to say exactly what someone was about to say himself; **take (up) the word** to begin speaking, continue a discourse begun by someone else; **the last word** the closing remark in an argument, esp. if having an appearance of conclusiveness: the conclusive statement: the ultimate authority: (also **latest word**) the most up-to-date, or the most finished, example; **the Word** the Scriptures: the gospel message: the second person in the Trinity, the Logos; **word for word** literally, verbatim.   [O.E.; Goth. *waurd*, O.N. *orth*, Ger. *Wort*; L. *verbum*, word, Gr. *eirein*, to say, speak.]

Wordsworthian *wûrdz-wûr'thi-ən, adj.* pertaining to the poet William *Wordsworth* (1770–1850) or his style. — *n.* an admirer or imitator of Wordsworth.

wore *wōr, wör, pa.t. of* **wear**[1,2].

work *wûrk, n.* effort directed to an end: employment: that on which one works: the product of work, anything made or done: materials for work: needlework: a deed: doings: the result of action: any production of art, as a literary composition: a book: manner of working, workmanship: (in *pl.*) a factory, workshop (as *adj.*, of a racing-car, entered officially in a race by the manufacturer): the act of producing an effect by means of a force (F) whose point of application moves through

a distance (s) in its own line of action — measured by the product of the force and the distance (W = Fs; *phys.*): (in *pl.*) walls, trenches, etc. (*fort.*): (usu. in *pl.*) an action in its moral aspect, esp. as tending to justification (*theol.*): (in *pl.*) mechanism, e.g. of a watch: the spin given to a ball by a bowler to cause it to break on pitching (*cricket*): (by confusion with O.E. *wærc*), ache, trouble, fuss (*dial.*). — *v.i.* to make efforts to achieve or attain anything: to be occupied in business or labour: to move, make one's way, slowly and laboriously: to move, become, etc., in a manner not intended or desired: to be in action: to operate, function: to produce effects: to behave in the desired way when worked: to prove practicable: to ache, be painful (*dial.*): to ferment: to be agitated, move convulsively: to strain, labour: to sail in a course, esp. to beat to windward (*naut.*): to contrive, plan (*arch.*). — *v.t.* to make by labour: to bring into any state by action: to effect or strive to effect: to carry on operations in: to keep in operation: to keep employed: to put in motion: to purge (*dial.*): to influence: to affect powerfully: to provoke, excite: to prepare for use by manipulation: to cause to ferment: to fashion, make: to embroider: to make (as one's way) by effort: to solve: to make use of, make profit through (*coll.*): to influence, cajole, or trick (*coll.*): — *pa.t.* and *pa.p.* **worked** or **wrought** (see separate article). — *ns.* **workabil'ity, work'ableness.** — *adjs.* **work'able** that may be worked, esp. practicable; **workaholic** (-ə-hol'ik) addicted to work, coined facetiously in imitation of *alcoholic* (see **-aholic**). — Also *n.* — *adj.* **worked** that has been treated or fashioned in some way: embroidered: ornamented. — *ns.* **work'er** one who works: a toiler: one employed in manual work: in social insects, one of a caste of sterile individuals that do all the work of the colony; **work'erist** a supporter of proletarian rights and values, esp. (*derog.*) one of upper or middle class. — Also *adj.* — *adj.* **work'ful** industrious. — *n.* **work'ing** the act or process of shaping, making, effecting, solving, fermenting, etc.: an exposition of the process of calculation: manner of operating or functioning: endeavour (*obs.*): (in *pl.*) deeds (*obs.*): mental or emotional activity (*obs.*): contortion due to agitation: slow and laborious progress: (in *pl.*) the parts of a mine, etc., where work is, or has been, carried on. — *adj.* active: operational: labouring: having a job or employment: relating to labour, a job or employment: stirring the emotions (*obs.*). — *adj.* **work'less** having no job, unemployed. — Also *n.pl.* — *adj.* **work'some** (*Carlyle*) industrious. — *adj.* **work'aday** suitable for a work day: toiling: dull, prosaic. — Also *n.* — **work'-bag, -basket** a bag, basket, for holding materials for work, esp. needlework; **work bench** a bench, often purpose-built, at which a craftsman, mechanic, etc., works; **work'boat** one used for work such as fishing, harbour maintenance, carrying industrial supplies, etc. rather than for naval or passenger service; **work'book** a book of exercises, often with spaces for the answers, to accompany another book: a record book of jobs undertaken, in progress or completed; **work'-box** a box for holding instruments or materials for work; **work'-day** a day for work, a week-day. — *adj.* pertaining to a work-day. — **worker participation** scc **participate; worker priest** a priest in the Roman Catholic Church who also works full-time or part-time in a secular job in order to understand better the problems of lay people; **work ethic** the general working attitude of a group towards work, esp. one (**Protestant work ethic**) which places a high moral value on (hard) work; **work'-fellow** one who is engaged in the same work with another; **work'folk, work'folks** work-people; **work'force** the number of workers engaged in a particular industry, factory, etc.: the total number of workers potentially available; **work'-girl** a girl or young woman employed in manual labour; **work'horse** a horse used in a labouring capacity rather than for recreation, racing, etc.: a person or machine heavily depended on to do arduous work; **work'house** (*hist.*) a house where any work or manufacture is carried on: a house of shelter for the poor, who are given work to do; **work-in** see **work in** below; **work'ing-beam** a walking-beam; **working breakfast, lunch,** etc. one arranged as an alternative to a formal meeting, for the discussion of diplomatic or other business; **work'ing-class** that of manual workers (often in *pl.*; also *adj.*); **work'ing-day** a day on which work is done: the period of actual work each day. — *adj.* laborious: plodding: ordinary. — **work'ing-drawing** a drawing of the details of a building by which the builders are guided in their work; **work'ing-edge** an edge of a piece of wood trued square with the working-face to assist in truing the other surfaces square; **work'ing-face** that face of a piece of wood which is first trued and then used as a basis for truing the other surfaces; **working girl** (*coll*; orig. *U.S.*) a prostitute; **working hours** the period of the day during which work is normally done, and offices, shops, etc. are open; **work'ing-house** (*obs.*) workshop; **working lunch** see **working breakfast; working majority** a majority sufficient to enable the party in office to carry on without accidental defeats; **working man, woman** a worker, esp. a manual one; **work'ing-model** a model of a machine that can do, on a smaller scale, the same work as the machine; **working paper** one produced as a basis for discussion, to report on progress made, etc., rather than as a final statement; **work(ing) party** a group of persons who carry out a specially assigned task: a group appointed to investigate a subject, as methods of attaining maximum efficiency in an industry; **working week** that part of the week in which work is normally done — esp. Monday to Friday: any week in which such work is done, as opposed e.g. to holidays; **work'load** the amount of work assigned to an individual, machine, etc. for completion within a certain time; **work'man** a man who works, esp. manually: a skilful artificer. — *adjs.* **work'man-like** like a workman: becoming a skilful workman: well performed; **work'manly** becoming a skilful workman. — *adv.* in a manner becoming a skilful workman. — **work'manship** the skill of a workman: manner of making: that which is made or produced by one's hands (also *fig.*); **work'master** a master workman, overseer, or employer: — *fem.* **work'-mistress; work'-mate** work-fellow: a companion at work; **work'-out** see **work out** below; **work'-people** people engaged in manual labour, workers; **work'piece** a piece of work in progress, being manufactured: something on which a tool or machine works; **work'-place** the office, factory, etc. where one works; **work'-room** a room for working in; **works committee, council** a body on which both employer and employees meet to handle labour relations within a business; **work'shop** a room or shop where work is done: a group of people working on a creative or experimental project: such a project. — *adj.* **work'-shy** hating, avoiding work, lazy (also used as *n.*). — **work station** in a production line, a position at which a particular job is done: in an office or other work place, a computer terminal having a keyboard, screen and processor, or the location of this; **work study** a time and motion study; **work'-table** a table on which work is done, esp., formerly, a small table used by ladies at their needlework; **work'top** a surface designed to be used for working on, fitted e.g. along the top of kitchen units, etc.; **work'wear** overalls or other clothing for work, issued to factory-workers, etc.; **work'-woman** a woman who makes her living by manual labour. — *adj., n.* **work'y-day** (*obs.*) workaday. — **a work of time** a change, achievement, etc., requiring, or brought about by, time; **give someone the works** (*slang*) to give someone the full punitive, coercive, ceremonious, etc. treatment considered appropriate to his case; **have one's work cut out** to have one's work prescribed: to be faced with a difficult task; **make short work of** see **short; Ministry** (previously **Office) of Works** formerly, the body which has the management and control of public works and buildings, of which

the expenses are defrayed from public money; **out of work** without employment (*adj.* and *n.pl.* **out'-of-work'** unemployed (people)); **place of work** one's workplace (q.v.); **public works** building, etc., operations financed by the state; **set to work** to employ in, or to engage energetically in, a piece of work; **Seven Works of Corporal Mercy** to feed the hungry, give drink to the thirsty, clothe the naked, visit prisoners, visit the sick, harbour strangers, bury the dead; **Seven Works of Spiritual Mercy** to convert sinners, instruct the ignorant, counsel the doubtful, console the afflicted, bear wrongs patiently, forgive injuries, pray for the living and the dead; **shoot the works** see **shoot; the works** (*coll.*) the lot, everything; **work at** to apply oneself to; **work double tides** (*naut.*) to work night and day; **work for, against** to exert oneself in support of, in opposition to; **work in** to intermix: to introduce carefully and deliberately (*fig.*): to make to penetrate: of workers, to continue at work, esp. by occupying the premises and taking over the running of the business, as a protest against proposed factory closure, dismissal, etc. (*n.* **work'-in**); **work into** to make way gradually into: to insinuate: to change, alter, into; **work of art** a production in one of the fine arts (also *fig.*); **work off** to separate and throw off: to get rid of gradually: to print ready for circulation: to pass, palm, off (*coll.*): to dispose of by hanging (*slang*); **work on, upon** to act or operate upon: to influence, or try to do so; **work one's passage** to earn one's passage by services on board (also *fig.*); **work out** to effect by continued labour: to expiate: to make by cutting, digging, etc. (*obs.*): to exhaust: to solve or calculate: to study fully (*rare*): to develop in detail, elaborate: to come out by degrees: to turn out in the end: to reach a final (satisfactory) result: of an athlete, etc., to train, exercise (*n.* **work'-out); work over** to do, work at, thoroughly or elaborately: to examine in detail: to beat up, thrash (*n.* **work'(ing)-over**)(*slang*); **work the oracle** (*slang*) to achieve the desired result by manipulation, intrigue, wire-pulling, favour, etc.: to raise money; **work to rule** of workers, to observe all the regulations scrupulously for the express purpose of slowing down work, as a form of industrial action (*n.* **work'-to-rule'**); **work up** to excite, rouse: to create by slow degrees: to expand, elaborate: to use up, as material: to set at an irksome or needless task (*naut.*): to make one's, its, way gradually upwards: to reach, achieve, by effort and gradually; **work with** (*fig.*) to strive to influence by appeals, etc. [O.E. *weorc*; O.N. *verk*, Ger. *Werk*; further conn. with Gr. *ergon*.]

world *wûrld, n.* the earth: the earth and its inhabitants: the universe: the system of things: the present state of existence: any analogous state: any planet or heavenly body: public life or society: a sphere of interest or activity: environment: the public: the materialistically minded: mundane interests: a secular life: the course of life: one of the three kingdoms of nature: a class or division: a very large extent of country, as the 'New World': very much or a great deal, as 'a world of good': a large quantity: time, as in 'world without end': possibility, as in 'nothing in the world': the ungodly (*B.*). — *adj.* **world'ed** containing worlds. — *ns.* **world'-liness; world'ling** one who is devoted to worldly pursuits and temporal possessions: a mortal (*obs.*). — *adj.* **world'ly** pertaining to the world, esp. as distinguished from the world to come: devoted to this life and its enjoyments: bent on gain: mortal (*obs.*). — Also *adv.* — **World Bank** the popular name of the International Bank for Reconstruction and Development, an agency of the United Nations set up in 1945 to make loans to poorer countries; **world'-beater** (*coll.*) a person, product, enterprise, etc. that is supreme in its class. — *adj.* **world'-beating.** — **World Court** the popular name of the Permanent Court of International Justice at the Hague, set up under the League of Nations in 1921 to settle or advise on disputes between states; **world language** a language either widely used internationally or designed for international use. — *adj.* **world′ly=mind′ed** having the mind set on the present world. — *n.* **world′ly-mind′edness.** — *adjs.* **world′ly-wise′** having the wisdom of those experienced in, and affected by, the ways of the world; **world′-old** exceedingly ancient. — **world power** a state, group of states, etc., strong enough to make its influence felt in world politics; **world′scale** the scale of freight rates for oil-tankers; **World Series** (*baseball*) a set of championship matches played annually in the U.S.; **world′-view** outlook on or attitude to the world or life; **World War** a war of world-wide scope, esp. the Great War of 1914–1918 (First World War, World War I) and that of 1939–45 (Second World War, World War II). — *adjs.* **world′-wearied, -weary** tired of the world, bored with life. — *adj.* and *adv.* **world′wide** (extending) over, or (found) everywhere in, the world. — **all the world** everybody: everything; **all the world and his wife** (*coll.*) everybody: an ill-assorted assembly; **best, worst, of both worlds** the advantage, disadvantage, of both alternatives in a choice; **carry the world before one** to pass through every obstacle to success; **dead to the world** (*coll.*) deeply asleep: in a drunken stupor; **for all the world** precisely, entirely; **Fourth World** see **fourth**; **go to the world** (*Shak.*) to get married; **in the world** an intensive phrase, usu. following an interrogative pronoun or adverb; **next world** life after death; **on top of the world** (*coll.*) in a state of great elation or happiness; **out of this world** wonderful, delightful, good beyond all experience; **the New World** the western hemisphere, the Americas; **the Old World** the eastern hemisphere, comprising Europe, Africa, and Asia; **the other world** the nonmaterial sphere, the spiritual world; **the whole world** the sum of what is contained in the world; **the world is one's oyster** see **oyster**; **the world's end** the most distant point possible; **think the world of** to be very fond of; **Third World** see **third**; **world without end** eternally (*adj.* **world′-without-end′**). [O.E. *woruld, world, weorold,* orig. meaning age or life of man — *wer,* man, and the root of **old**; O.N. *veröld,* O.H.G. *weralt* (Ger. *Welt*).]

worm *wûrm, n.* a snake, a dragon (*arch.*): any creeping or crawling animal (*obs.*): loosely used for any elongate invertebrate lacking appendages, as an earthworm or marine worm (Chaetopoda), a flat-worm (Platyhelminthes), a round-worm (Nematoda): a grub: a maggot: anything spiral: the thread of a screw: the lytta or vermiform cartilage of the tongue of a dog or other carnivorous mammal: a spiral pipe for condensation in distilling: anything that corrupts, gnaws, or torments: remorse: a mean, grovelling creature: (in *pl.*) any intestinal disease arising from the presence of parasitic worms: any ailment supposed to be caused by a worm, as toothache (*obs.*): a tick or mite in the hand, etc., esp. one alleged humorously to infest the hands of idlers (*obs.*). — *v.i.* to seek for or catch worms: to move, make one's way, like a worm, to squirm: to work slowly or secretly. — *v.t.* to cause to be eaten by worms: to treat for, rid of, worms: to work (oneself) slowly or secretly (*refl.*): to elicit by slow and indirect means: to remove the lytta or vermiform cartilage from the tongue of. — *adj.* **wormed** bored, injured by worms. — *ns.* **worm′er; worm′ery** a place, apparatus, etc. in which worms are bred, e.g. as fishing-bait. — *adj.* **worm′y** like a worm: grovelling: containing a worm: abounding in worms: pertaining to worms: danksmelling: dismal, like the grave. — **worm′-cast** a little spiral heap of earth voided by an earthworm or lugworm as it burrows. — *adjs.* **worm′-eaten** eaten into by worms: old: worn-out; **worm′-eating** living habitually on worms. — **worm′-fence** a zigzag fence formed of stakes crossing at their ends; **worm′-fever** a feverish condition in children ascribed to intestinal worms; **worm′-gear** a gear connecting shafts whose axes are at right angles but do not intersect, consisting of a core carrying a single-or multi-start helical thread of special form (the *worm*), meshing in sliding contact with a concave face gear-wheel (the *worm-wheel*); **worm′=gearing; worm′-grass** pinkroot: a kind of stonecrop (*Sedum album*); **worm′-hole** the hole made by a woodworm, earthworm, etc. — *adj.* **worm′-holed** perforated by worm-holes. — **worm′-powder** a vermifuge; **worm′=seed** any of a number of plants acting, or reputed to act, as anthelmintics, as species of Artemisia (e.g. *Artemisia santonica*), *Erysimum cheiranthoides* (treacle worm-seed, treacle mustard), *Chenopodium anthelminticum,* etc.: the drug santonica; **worm′-tube** a twisted shell or tube produced by several marine worms; **worm′-wheel** see **worm′-gear.** [O.E. *wyrm,* dragon, snake, creeping animal; cog. with Goth. *waurms, a serpent,* O.N. *ormr,* Ger. *Wurm;* also with L. *vermis.*]

Wormian *wûrm′i-ən, adj.* associated with the name of the Danish anatomist Olaus Worm (1588–1654), applied esp. to the supernumerary bones developed in the sutures of the skull.

wormwood *wûrm′wŏŏd, n.* the bitter plant Artemisia *absinthium,* formerly used as a vermifuge, with which absinthe is flavoured: bitterness. — cf. **absinthe.** [O.E. *wermōd* (Ger. *Wermuth*), wormwood; of doubtful origin, but influenced by **worm** and **wood**[1].]

worn *wŏrn, wörn, pa.p.* of **wear**[1]. — *adj.* that has been worn: showing effects of wear, or (*fig.*) of work, worry, illness, age, etc.: of land, exhausted: hackneyed, trite. — *adj.* **worn′-out** much injured or rendered useless by wear: wearied: past, gone.

worral, worrel *wor′əl, n.* a monitor lizard. [Ar. *waral,* lizard.]

worricow, worrycow, wirricow *wur′i-kow,* (*Scot.*) *n.* a hobgoblin: the devil: anything frightful or even only grotesque. [**worry** (vb.), and *cow,* a hobgoblin.]

worrit *wur′it, v.t., v.i.,* and *n.* Dial. form of **worry.**

worry *wur′i, v.t.* to tear with the teeth: to devour ravenously (*Scot.*): to harass: to pester: to tease: to cause to be anxious: to make, get, etc., by persistent methods: to choke (*Scot.*). — *v.i.* to trouble oneself: to be unduly anxious: to fret: — *pa.t.* and *pa.p.* **worr′ied.** — *n.* the act of worrying: trouble, perplexity: over-anxiety: a cause of this: the act of injuring by biting and shaking. — *ns.* **worr′ier; worr′iment** (*coll.*) worry, anxiety. — *adj.* **worr′isome** inclined to worry: causing trouble. — *n.* and *adj.* **worr′ying.** — *adv.* **worr′yingly.** — **worry beads** a string of beads providing an object for the hands to play with, thus relieving mental tension — esp. popular in Greece; **worr′yguts** (*coll.*), **worr′ywart** (-*wört; coll.,* esp. *U.S.*) a person who worries unnecessarily or to excess. — **I should worry!** it is nothing for me to worry about; **worry down** to swallow with a strong effort; **worry out** to find a solution of by intense or anxious effort. [O.E. *wyrgan,* found in compound *āwyrgan,* to harm; cf. Du. *worgen,* Ger. *würgen,* to strangle.]

worry cow. See **worricow.**

worse *wûrs, adj.* (used as *compar.* of **bad, ill**) bad or evil in a greater degree: less well than before. — *adv.* badly in a higher degree: less well: with more severity. — *v.t.* (*obs.*) to worst. — *v.i.* and *v.t.* **wors′en** to grow, or make, worse. — *n.* **worse′ness.** — *adj.* and *adv.* **wors′er** a redundant comparative of *worse.* — **for better or for worse** whatever may befall of good fortune or bad; **for the worse** to a worse state; **go by, with, the worse** (*obs.*) to lose, be defeated; **have the worse** to be at a disadvantage: to be defeated; **none the worse for** not harmed by; **put to the worse** (*B.*) to defeat; **the worse for** harmed or impaired by; **worse off** poorer. [O.E. *wyrsa* (Goth. *wairsiza*), formed with compar. suffix from a Gmc. root *wers,* found in Ger. (*ver*)*wirren,* to confuse, entangle.]

worship *wûr′ship, n.* adoration paid, as to a god: religious service: profound admiration and affection: the act of revering or adoring: dignity, reputation, high standing (*arch.*): a position of honour (*obs.*): (with *cap.*; preceded by *Your, His,* etc.) a title of honour in addressing or referring to certain magistrates, etc. — *v.t.* to pay divine honours to: to adore or idolise: to honour, respect, treat with signs of honour (*obs.*). — *v.i.* to perform acts of adoration: to take part in religious service: — *pr.p.* **wor′shipping;** *pa.t.* and *pa.p.* **wor′-shipped.** — *adjs.* **wor′shipable** capable of being worshipped; **wor′shipful** worthy of worship or honour: used as a term of respect: worshipping, adoring. — *adv.* **wor′shipfully.** — *n.* **wor′shipfulness.** — *adj.* **wor′-shipless** without worship or worshippers. — *n.* **wor′-shipper.** — **house,** or **place, of worship** a church or chapel, synagogue, mosque, temple; **win one's worship** (*obs.*) to gain honour or fame. [O.E. *weorthscipe* — *weorth, wurth,* worth, suff. *-scipe, -ship.*]

worst *wûrst, adj.* (used as *superl.* of **bad, ill**) bad or evil in the highest degree. — *adv.* in the highest degree of badness. — *n.* the highest degree of badness: the most evil state or effect: the least good part. — *v.t.* to get the advantage over in a contest: to defeat: to damage or make worse (*obs.*). — *v.i.* (*obs.*) to grow worse. — **do one's worst** to do one's utmost in evil or mischief; **get the worst of it** to be defeated in a contest, be the loser in a given situation; **if the worst comes to the worst** if the worst, or least desirable, possibility occurs: if all else fails. [O.E. *wyrst, wyrrest, wyrresta,* from the same source as **worse**.]

worsted[1] *wŏŏst′id,* or *wŏŏrst′id, n.* orig., a fine wool fabric: twisted thread or yarn spun out of long, combed wool: smooth, closely-woven material made from this: woollen yarn for ornamental needlework. — *adj.* made of worsted yarn. — **worst′ed-work** needlework done with worsted. [*Worstead,* village near Norwich, England.]

worsted[2] *wûrst′id, pa.t.* and *pa.p.* of **worst**.

wort[1] *wûrt, n.* any herb or vegetable (now *rare* except in composition): specif. a plant of the cabbage kind (*obs.*). [O.E. *wyrt,* a root, herb; Ger. *Wurz, Wurzel,* a root.]

wort[2] *wûrt, n.* malt unfermented or in the act of fermentation (*sweetwort*): such liquor boiled with hops (*hopped-wort*): malt extract used as a medium for the culture of micro-organisms. [O.E. *wyrt;* allied to **wort**[1].]

worth[1] *wûrth, n.* value: price: that quality which renders a thing valuable: merit: moral excellence: merit: importance: possessions (*obs.*). — *adj.* equal in value to: having a certain value: worth while: having possessions to the value of: deserving of. — *adj.* **worth′ful** honourable: meritorious: valuable. — *adv.* **worth′ily** (*-dh-*). — *n.* **worth′iness** (*-dh-*). — *adj.* **worth′less** (*-th-*) having no value, virtue, excellence, etc.: useless: unworthy (*obs.*). — *adv.* **worth′lessly.** — *n.* **worth′lessness.** — *adj.* **worth′y** (*-dh-*) having worth: valuable: estimable (used patronisingly): deserving: deserving of: suited to, in keeping with: of sufficient merit: of high social position (*obs.*). — *n.* a man of eminent worth: a notability, esp. local (sometimes ironical): anything of value, an excellence (*Shak.*): — *pl.* **wor′thies.** — *v.t.* (*obs.*) to make worthy, to honour. — *adj.* **worthwhile′** such as to repay trouble and time spent on it (predicatively **worth while;** see **while**): good: estimable. — **for all one is worth** with all one's might or energy; **for what it is worth** a phrase implying that the speaker is doubtful of the truth of what he has reported or unwilling to be responsible for its accuracy; **nine worthies** usu. given as Hector, Alexander the Great, Julius Caesar; Joshua, David, Judas Maccabaeus; Arthur, Charlemagne, Godfrey of Bouillon; **worthiest of blood** in questions of succession, male as opposed to female; **worth it** worth while. [O.E. *weorth, wurth* (Ger. *Wert*), value.]

worth[2] *wûrth, v.i.* to be, become, happen, as in the phrase **woe worth** woe be (to; with the noun in the dative). [O.E. *weorthan,* to become; cf. Ger. *werden.*]

-worthy *-wûr′dhi, adj. suffix* fit, in good condition for, as in *roadworthy*: deserving of, as in *trustworthy, noteworthy.* [**worth**[1].]

wortle *wûr′tl, n.* a perforated plate through which wire,

tubing, is drawn to make it thinner. — Also **whirtle.** [Ety. uncertain.]

wosbird *wŏz′bûrd,* (*dial.*) *n.* form of **whore's-bird.**

wost. See **wit**[1].

wot[1]**, wotteth,** etc. See **wit**[1].

wot[2]**.** See **woot.**

wot[3]**.** A facetious spelling of **what.**

Wotan. See **Woden.**

wotcher *wot′chər,* (*slang*) *interj.* a greeting, developed from *arch.* **what cheer?** how are you?

woubit *wŏŏ′bit, n.* (usu. **hairy woubit**) a hairy caterpillar, esp. one of a tiger-moth: applied derogatorily to a person, often implying smallness and shabbiness. — Also **woo′but, ou′bit, oo′bit.** [M.E. *wolbode, wolbede;* prob. — *wol,* wool; meaning of second element unknown.]

would *wŏŏd* (formerly, e.g. in *Spens., wōld) pa.t.* of **will**[1]. — *n.* the desired or intended, opp. to *could,* or *should.* —*adj.* **would′-be** aspiring, or merely professing, to be: meant to be. — *n.* a vain pretender.

wouldst. See **will**[1].

Woulfe-bottle *wŏŏlf′-bot′l, n.* a form of usu. three-necked bottle used for purifying gases, or dissolving them in suitable solvents — from the London chemist Peter *Woulfe* (c. 1727–1803).

wound[1] *wownd, pa.t.* and *pa.p.* of **wind**[1,2].

wound[2] *wŏŏnd, n.* any division of soft parts produced by external mechanical force — whether incised, punctured, contused, lacerated, or poisoned: any cut, bruise, hurt, or injury (also *fig.*). — *v.t.* to make a wound in (*lit.* and *fig.*), to injure. — *adj.* **wound′able** capable of being wounded. — *n.* **wound′er.** — *adv.* **wound′ily** (*arch.*) excessively. — *n.* and *adj.* **wound′ing.** — *adj.* **wound′less** unwounded: invulnerable (*obs.*): harmless. — *adj.* and *adv.* **wound′y** (*arch.*) excessive(ly). — **wound′wort** any of several plants of popular repute as vulneraries, as the kidney-vetch, a number of plants of genus Stachys (marsh or clown's woundwort). [O.E. *wund* (Ger. *Wunde,* O.N. *und*); also O.E. *wund,* wounded.]

wourali, woorali *wŏŏ-rä′li,* **woora′ra** (*-rä′rə*), **oura′li, oura′ri** (*-rä′ri*), **ura′li** (*ōō-*), **ura′ri** *ns.* the plant yielding curare (q.v.). [Carib. variants of *kurari;* see **curare**.]

wou-wou. See **wow-wow.**

wove, woven *pa.t.* and *pa.p.* of **weave.** — **wove paper** paper that shows in its fabric the marks of a fine wire gauze sieve or mould.

wow[1] *wow,* (*Spens.*) *v.i.* to woo.

wow[2] *wow, interj.* an exclamation of wonder, tinged with other emotions as aversion, sorrow, or admiration, pleasure (see **whow**). — *v.i.* to howl. — *v.t.* (*slang*) to impress (an audience, etc.) considerably, to amaze, bowl over. — *n.* a bark: a howl: rhythmic or arrhythmic changes in reproduced sound, fundamentally arising from fluctuation in speed of either reproducer or recorder: anything thrillingly good, successful, or according to one's wishes (*slang*). — *interj.* **wowee′** an intensification of **wow.** — *n.* **wow′ser** (*-zər;* perh. not connected with **wow;** esp. *Austr. slang*) a puritanical person who tries to interfere with the pleasures of others, a spoil-sport. [Imit.]

wowf *wowf,* (*Scot.*) *adj.* crazy. [Origin unknown.]

wowser. See under **wow**[2].

wow-wow, wou-wou *wow′-wow, n.* the name for two types of gibbon found in Indonesia, the *silver gibbon* of Java and the *agile gibbon* of Sumatra. [Imit. of its cry.]

wox, woxen (*obs.*) *pa.t.* and *pa.p.* of **wax**[2].

wrack[1] *rak, n.* vengeance, punishment (*obs.*): destruction, devastation. — Cf. **rack**[2] . — *adj.* **wrack′ful** (*rare*) destructive. [O.E. *wræc* — *wrecan,* to drive; connected, and confused, with **wrack**[2].]

wrack[2] *rak, n.* a wreck (*dial.*): wreckage: seaweed cast ashore, or growing where it is exposed by the tide (*arch.*): any of the *Fucaceae,* the bladder-wrack family of seaweeds. [M.Du. or M.L.G. *wrak;* cf. **wrack**[1].]

wrack[3] *rak, v.t.* to torture, torment. [An erron. spelling of **rack**[1].]

wraith *rāth, n.* a spectre: an apparition, esp. of a living person: a thin, pale person (*fig.*). [Orig. Scot.; perh. O.N. *vörthr*, a guardian.]

wrangle *rang'gl, v.i.* to argue, debate, dispute (*arch.*): to dispute noisily or peevishly. — *v.t.* to obtain, persuade, spend, tire, in or by wrangling: to debate. — *n.* a noisy dispute: the action of disputing, esp. noisily. — *ns.* **wrang'ler** one who disputes, esp. angrily: a stubborn foe (*Shak.*): in the University of Cambridge, one of those who attained the first class in the examinations for mathematical honours (**senior wrangler** the student taking the first place; **second wrangler** the student next in order of merit, and so on; this method of classification has been abandoned, and since 1909 the first class has been arranged alphabetically): a herdsman, esp. of horses (*Western U.S.*); **wrang'lership.** — *adj.* **wrang'lesome** given to wrangling. — *n.* and *adj.* **wrang'ling.** [M.E. *wranglen*, a freq. verb allied to **wring**.]

wrap¹ *rap, v.t.* to roll or fold together: to fold, lap, round something: to enfold, envelop (*lit.* and *fig.*): to embrace: to hide, obscure: to cover by folding or winding something round (often with *up*). — *v.i.* to wind, twine: (with *up*) to put on wraps: to dress warmly: — *pr.p.* **wrapp'ing;** *pa.t.* and *pa.p.* **wrapped.** — *n.* a protective covering, for a person or thing, now esp. an outdoor garment: a single turn or fold round: (*in pl.*; *coll.*) secrecy, concealment. — *ns.* **wrapp'age** the act of wrapping: covering: wrapping materials; **wrapp'er** one who, or that which, wraps: formerly, a loose outer garment for a woman: a loose paper book cover: a paper band, as on a newspaper for the post. — *v.t.* to cover, or cover up, with a wrapper. — *n.* **wrapp'ing** (also **wrapp'ing-paper**) coarse paper for parcels, etc. — **wrap'around** a wraparound skirt, blouse, dress, etc. (also **wrap'round**): on a visual display unit, the automatic division of input into lines, whereby a new line is started as the last character position on the previous line is occupied: (also **wrap'round**) a plate of flexible material, as plastic, rubber or metal that wraps round a cylindrical plate (*printing*): (also **wrap'round**) a separately printed sheet that is wrapped round a gathering for binding (*printing*): (also **wrap'round**) a strip advertising a special offer, etc., wrapped round the dustcover of a book, etc. — *adj.* (of a blouse, skirt, dress, etc.) designed so as to be wrapped round the body with one edge overlapping the other, and tied, tucked in, etc. rather than fastened by a zip, row of buttons, etc. (also **wrap'over, wrap'round**): (of a windscreen, etc.) curving round from the front to the sides (also **wrap'round**). — **wrap'over** a wraparound skirt or other garment; **wrap'-ras'cal** a loose greatcoat worn in the eighteenth century (a humorous term). — **wraparound** see **wraparound** above. — **keep under wraps** (*coll.*) to keep secret, conceal; **take the wraps off** (*coll.*) to reveal, disclose; **wrapped up in** bound up in: comprised in: engrossed in, devoted to; **wrap up** (*slang*) to settle completely: to have completely in hand: (as *interj.*) be quiet! [M.E. *wrappen*, also *wlappen*.]

wrap², wrapt. Erroneous forms of **rap², rapt.**

wrasse *ras, n.* a genus (Labrus) of bony fishes representative of the large family Labridae, and including many species on European and N. African coasts. [Cornish *wrach*.]

wrast. Obs. Northern form of **wrest** directly from O.N.

wrate. Obs. and Scot. *pa.t.* of **write.**

wrath *röth, roth,* (*Scot.*) *räth, n.* violent anger: an instance, or fit, of this: holy indignation: violence or severity (*fig.*): ardour (*Shak.*). — *adj.* (*arch.*) violently angry. — *v.t.* and *v.i.* (*obs.*) to make, or to become, angry. — *adj.* **wrath'ful** very angry: springing from, or expressing, or characterised by, wrath. — *adv.* **wrath'fully.** — *n.* **wrath'fulness.** — *adv.* **wrath'ily.** — *n.* **wrath'iness.** — *adjs.* **wrath'less; wrath'y** (chiefly *U.S.*) inclined to wrath: like, expressing, or characterised by, wrath. [O.E. *wrǣththu* — *wrāth*, adj.; cf. **wroth.**]

wrawl *röl,* (*Spens.*) *v.i.* to cry as a cat, to caterwaul. [Imit.]

wraxle *rak'sl,* (*dial.*; *S.W. England*) *v.i.* to wrestle. — *n.* **wrax'ling.** [O.E. *wraxlian;* cf. **wrestle.**]

wreak *rēk, v.t.* to drive out (*obs.*): to give expression, vent, free play to: to find expression, outlet, for (*refl.*): to bestow: to punish (*obs.*): to harm (*obs.*): to avenge (*arch.*): to take vengeance on (*obs.*): to revenge (with *of*) (*obs.*): to inflict: to effect or bring about: — *pa.t.* **wreaked,** *arch.* **wrōke;** *pa.p.* **wreaked,** *arch.* **wrōk'en,** *Spens.* **wrōke, ywrōke.** — *n.* punishment, vengeance (*arch.*): damage (*Spens.*). — *n.* **wreak'er** (*arch.*). — *adjs.* **wreak'ful** revengeful: avenging; **wreak'less** unpunished. [O.E. *wrecan;* O.N. *reka,* to drive, pursue, avenge; Ger. *rächen,* conn. with L. *urgēre.*]

wreak(e) *rēk,* (*Spens., Shak.*) for **reak²,** variant of **reck.** — Also (*Milt.*) **wreck.**

wreath *rēth, n.* a circlet of interwoven materials, esp. flowers, etc.: a single twist or coil in a helical object: a drift or curl of vapour or smoke: a snowdrift: a defect in glass: — *pl.* **wreaths** (*rēdhz*). — *v.t.* **wreathe** (*rēdh*) to form by twisting: to twist together: to form into a wreath: to twine about or encircle: to twist: to cause to twist or contort: of snow, to cover by drifting (*Scot.*): to encircle, decorate, etc. with a wreath or wreaths. — *v.i.* to be interwoven: to twine: to twist: of snow, to form a drift or wreath (*Scot.*): to turn (*obs.*): to form coils. — *adjs.* **wreathed** (or *rēdh'id*); **wreath'en** (-*dh*-; *arch. pa.p.*) wreathed. — *n.* **wreath'er** (-*dh*-). — *adjs.* **wreath'less; wreath'y** (-*th*- or -*dh*-). — **wreath'-filament** the usual type of filament in large gas-filled electric lamps, the filament wire being festooned from a horizontal supporting spider. [O.E. *writha;* allied to *writhan,* to writhe.]

wreck¹ *rek, n.* destruction: the act of wrecking or destroying: the destruction of a ship: a badly damaged ship: shipwrecked property: anything found underwater and brought ashore: the death of a large number of oceanic birds, e.g. during a storm: the remains of anything ruined: a person ruined mentally or physically. — *v.t.* to destroy or disable: to involve in a wreck: to cast up, as on the shore: to ruin. — *v.i.* to suffer wreck or ruin. — *ns.* **wreck'age** the act of wrecking: wrecked material: a person, or persons, whose life is, or lives are, ruined; **wreck'er** a person who purposely causes a wreck or who plunders wreckage: one who criminally ruins anything: a person who (or machine which) demolishes or destroys: a person or ship employed in recovering disabled vessels or their cargo: a person, vehicle or train employed in removing wreckage: a vehicle equipped with a hoisting device, used to tow wrecked or disabled motor vehicles (*U.S.*): a person who is employed in demolishing buildings, etc. — *adj.* **wreck'ful** (*poet.*) causing ruin. — *n.* and *adj.* **wreck'ing.** — **wreck commissioners** a tribunal that inquires into shipping disasters; **wreck'fish** the stone bass, a large perch of the Atlantic, Mediterranean and Tasman Sea, *Polyprion americanus,* having the reputation of frequenting wrecked ships; **wreck'-master** a person taking charge of a disabled ship or train and its cargo or freight. — **receivers of wrecks** wreck-masters. [A.Fr. *wrec, wrek,* etc., of Scand. origin; allied to **weak.**]

wreck². See **wreak(e).**

wren *ren, n.* a member of a genus (Troglodytes) of small birds, having the wings very short and rounded, and the tail short and carried erect, or of any of several related genera, together forming the family *Troglodytidae:* specif. in the U.K., *T. troglodytes:* extended to various very small birds, as the **golden-crested wren** (goldcrest) the **willow wren** (willow warbler). — **wren'-tit** a Californian bird (*Chamaea fasciata*) resembling the wren and the titmouse. [O.E. *wrenna, wrænna.*]

Wren *ren, n.* a member of the W.R.N.S.

wrench *rench, rensh, v.t.* to wring or pull with a twist: to force by violence: to sprain: to distort. — *v.i.* to perform, or to undergo, a violent wrenching. — *n.* an act or instance of wrenching: a violent twist: a sprain: an instrument for turning nuts, etc.: emotional pain at parting or change: in coursing, bringing the hare round at less than a right angle. [O.E. *wrencan*, to deceive, twist, *wrenc*, deceit, twisting; cf. Ger. *renken*, to twist, *Rank*, trick, intrigue.]

wrenching *rensh'ing*, (Shak., *Hen. VIII*, I, i. 167; older editions) *n.* for *renching*, from dial. verb. *rench,* to rinse.

wrest *rest, v.t.* to turn, twist, or (*obs.*) screw: to twist, extract, or take away, by force or unlawfully: to get by toil: to twist from truth or from its natural meaning: to misinterpret: to pervert: to derive improperly (*Spens.*): to sprain (*Scot.*). — *v.i.* (*Spens.*) to force a way. — *n.* the act of wresting: violent pulling and twisting: distortion: an instrument, like a wrench, for tuning the piano, etc. — *n.* **wrest'er.** — **wrest'-pin'** a pin round which the end of a wire (as a piano wire) is wound, turned by the wrest. [OE. *wræstan*; Dan. *vriste.*]

wrestle *res'l, v.i.* to contend by grappling and trying to throw another down: to struggle: to strive: to apply oneself keenly: to pray earnestly: to writhe, wriggle: to proceed with great effort (*lit.* and *fig.*). — *v.t.* to contend with in wrestling: to push with a wriggling or wrestling motion: (with *out*) to go through, carry out, with a great struggle. — *n.* the act, or a bout, of wrestling: a struggle. — *ns.* **wrest'ler; wrest'ling** the action of the verb to wrestle: a sport or exercise in which two persons struggle to throw and pin each other to the ground, governed by certain fixed rules. [O.E. *wræstan*, to wrest.]

wretch *rech, n.* an exile, outcast (*obs.*): a most miserable, unfortunate or pitiable person: a worthless, or despicable, person: a being, creature (in pity, sometimes admiration). — *adj.* (*Spens.*) wretched. — *adj.* **wretch'ed** (*-id*) very miserable: unfortunate, pitiable: distressingly bad: despicable: worthless. — *adv.* **wretch'edly.** — *n.* **wretch'edness.** [O.E. *wrecca*, an outcast — *wrecan*; see **wreak.**]

wrethe *rēth,* (*Spens.*) *v.t.* and *v.i.* Same as **wreathe.**

wrick *rik, v.t.* to twist, sprain, strain. — *n.* a sprain, strain. [Allied to L.G. *wrikken*, to turn.]

wrier, wriest. See **wry.**

wriggle *rig'l, v.i.* and *v.t.* to twist to and fro: to move, advance, sinuously (*lit.* and *fig.*): to use evasive tricks. — *n.* the act or motion of wriggling: a sinuous marking, turn, or bend. — *ns.* **wrigg'ler; wrigg'ling.** — *adj.* **wrigg'ly.** [L.G. *wriggeln*; cf. Du. *wriggelen*, to wriggle.]

wright *rīt* (*Scot. rihht*), *n.* a maker or repairer (chiefly used in compounds, as **shipwright,** etc.): a carpenter or joiner (*Scot.*). [O.E. *wyrhta, wryhta,* allied to *wyrht*, a work — *wyrcan*, to work.]

wring *ring, v.t.* to twist: to expel moisture from by hand twisting or by roller pressure: to force out by twisting: to force out: to clasp and shake fervently: to clasp convulsively, as the hands (in grief or agitation): (of a shoe) to pinch: to pain: to distress, afflict: to extort: to subject to extortion: to bend out of its position: to wreathe, coil: to distort. — *v.i.* to writhe: to twist: to feel pain: — *pa.t.* and *pa.p.* **wrung,** *obs.* **wringed.** — *n.* an act or instance of wringing: a cider-, wine-, or cheese-press. — *ns.* **wring'er** one who wrings: a machine for forcing water from wet clothes (also **wring'-ing-machine); wring'ing.** — **wring'-bolt** a bolt with a ring or eye, used to secure a ship's planks against the frame till they are permanently fixed in place. — *adj.* **wring'ing-wet** so wet that water can be wrung out. — *n.pl.* **wring'-staves** (*sing.* **-staff**) strong pieces of wood used in applying wring-bolts. — **wring from** to extort from; **wring off** to force off by wringing; **wring out** to squeeze out by twisting: to remove from liquid and twist so as to expel the drops. [O.E. *wringan*, to twist; Du. *wringen,* Ger. *ringen.*]

wrinkle¹ *ring'kl,* (*coll.*) *n.* a tip, valuable hint: a handy dodge or trick: an idea, notion, suggestion. [Perh. from O.E. *wrenc*, a trick; perh. same as **wrinkle².**]

wrinkle² *ring'kl, n.* a small crease or furrow on a surface:

a crease or ridge in the skin (esp. as a result of ageing): an unevenness: a minor problem or difficulty to be smoothed out. — *v.t.* to contract into wrinkles or furrows: to make rough. — *v.i.* to shrink into ridges. — *adjs.* **wrink'led; wrink'ly** full of wrinkles: liable to be wrinkled. — *n.* (esp. in *pl.; derog.*) an elderly person. [History obscure; adj. **wrinkled** is prob. used earlier than noun and verb.]

wrist *rist, n.* the joint by which the hand is united to the arm, the carpus: the part of the body where that joint is, or the part of a garment covering it: a corresponding part of an animal: a wrist-pin. — *n.* **wrist'let** a band or strap for the wrist: a bracelet: a watch for wearing on the wrist (also **wrist'-watch,** or **wrist'let-watch**): a handcuff (*slang*). — *adj.* **wrist'y** making extensive use of the wrist(s), as in a golf shot, etc. — **wrist'band** a band or part of a sleeve covering the wrist; **wrist'-drop** inability to extend the hand, often caused by lead-poisoning; **wrist'-pin** a pin joining the end of a connecting rod to the end of a piston-rod; **wrist'-shot** in golf, a short stroke using power mainly from the wrist, usu. played with an iron club. — **a slap, smack on the wrist** (*coll.*) a small (and often, by implication, ineffectual) punishment. [O.E.; allied to *wrīthan*, to twist; Ger. *Rist.*]

writ¹ *rit, arch. pa.t.* and *pa.p.* of **write.** — **writ large** written in large letters, hence (*fig.*) on a large scale, or very obvious.

writ² *rit, n.* a writing (*rare*): a legal or formal document: a written document by which one is summoned or required to do, or refrain from doing, something (*law*). — **Holy Writ** the Scriptures; **serve a writ on** to deliver a summons to. [O.E. (*ge*)*writ*; O.N. *rit*, Goth. *writs*.]

write *rīt, v.t.* to form (letters or words) with a pen, pencil, or other implement on a (usu. paper) surface: to express in writing: to compose: to draw, engrave, etc.: to record: to decree or foretell: to indicate (a quality, condition, etc.) clearly: to communicate, or to communicate with, by letter. — *v.i.* to perform, or to practise, the act of writing: to be employed as a clerk: to compose, as articles, novels, etc.: to work as an author: to compose, or to send, a letter: to communicate with a person by letter: — *pr.p.* **wrīt'ing;** *pa.t.* **wrōte,** (*arch.*) **writ** (*rit*); *pa.p.* **written** (*rit'n*), (*arch.*) **writ.** — *adjs.* **wrīt'able** capable of being expressed or described in writing: suitable for writing with; **wrīt'ative** (*rare*) inclined, or characterised by inclination, to write. — *n.* **wrīt'er** one who writes: a professional scribe or clerk: an ordinary legal practitioner in a Scottish country town: an author: his works: one who paints lettering for signs: a seller (of options) (*Stock exchange*): — *fem.* **wrīt'eress** (*rare*). — *adj.* **writ'erly** having, showing an accomplished literary style. — *ns.* **wrīt'ership** the office of a writer; **wrīt'ing** the act of one who writes: that which is written: (often *pl.*) a literary production, or composition: handwriting, penmanship: the state of being written. — *adj.* **writt'en** reduced to, expressed in, writing — opp. to *oral.* — **write'-back** an amount restored to a company's accounts because the size of an earlier liability had been overestimated; **write-down** see **write down** below. — *adj.* **write'-in** (*U.S.*) of or relating to a candidate not listed in the ballot paper, but whose name is written in by the voter. — *n.* such a candidate or vote. — **write'-off** a crashed aircraft (*airmen's slang*): a car so badly damaged that the cost of repair would exceed the car's value: a total loss: see also **write off** below; **writer's cramp** see under **cramp; write-up** see under **write up** below; **writ'ing-book** a book of paper for practising penmanship; **writ'ing-case** a portable case containing materials for writing; **writ'ing-desk** a desk with a sloping top for writing on: a portable writing-case; **writ'ing-ink** ink suited for writing with; **writ'ing-master** a master who teaches the art of penmanship: the yellow-bunting; **writ'ing-paper** paper finished with a smooth surface, for writing on; **writ'ing-school** (*obs.*) a school for penmanship; **writ'-ing-table** a table fitted or used for writing on; **written**

law statute law as distinguished from common law. — *adj.* **writt'en-off** (of a person) killed (*airmen's slang*): (of an aircraft) wrecked (*airmen's slang*): (of a car) damaged beyond reasonable repair: completely ruined: see also **write off** below. — **nothing to write home about** see **home**; **write down** to put down in written characters: to write in disparagement of: to write so as to be intelligible or attractive to people of lower intelligence or inferior taste: to reduce the book value of an asset (*n.* **write'-down**); **write (in) for** to apply for: to send away for; **write off** to cancel, esp., in book-keeping, to take (e g a bad debt) off the books: to regard, accept, as an irredeemable loss: to destroy, damage irredeemably, (a car, etc.) (*n.* **write'-off**; *adj.* **writt'en-off**); **write oneself off** (*airmen's slang*) to get killed; **write out** to transcribe: to write in full: to exhaust one's mental resources by too much writing (*refl.*): to remove a character or scene from the script of a film, broadcast, etc.; **Writer to the Signet** a member of an ancient society of solicitors in Scotland who formerly had the exclusive right to prepare all summonses and other writs pertaining to the supreme court of justice, and still have the exclusive privilege of preparing crown writs; **write up** to put a full description of in writing: to write a report or review of: to write in praise of, esp. to praise above its merits: to bring the writing of up to date: to increase the book value of an asset (*n.* **write'-up**); **writing** (also, esp. *U.S.*, **handwriting**) **on the wall** a happening or sign foreshowing downfall and disaster (Dan. v. 5 ff.).   [O.E. *wrītan*, orig. meaning to scratch; O.N. *rīta.*]

writhe *rīdh, v.t.* to twist: to coil: to wreathe: to twist violently: to contort: to distort (*obs.*). — *v.i.* to twist, esp. in pain. — *n.* (*rare*) a twist or a contortion. — *adj.* **writhen, wrythen** (*ridh'ən; arch.*) twisted, convoluted, contorted. — *n.* and *adj.* **writh'ing.** — *adv.* **writh'ingly.**   [O.E. *wrīthan*, to twist; O.N. *rītha*; cf. **wreath, wrest, wrist.**]

writhled *rith'ld,* (*arch.*) *adj.* wrinkled, shrivelled.   [Perh. **writhe.**]

written. See **write.**

wrizled *riz'ld,* (*Spens.*) *adj.* wrinkled.   [Perh. **writhled.**]

wroath *rōth,* (*Shak.*) *n.* misfortune.   [Prob. from **ruth.**]

wroke, wroken. See **wreak.**

wrong *rong, adj.* crooked, curved, twisted, bent (*obs.*): not according to rule: incorrect: erroneous: not in accordance with moral law: wicked: not that (thing) which is required, intended, advisable, or suitable: amiss, unsatisfactory: not working properly, out of order: mistaken, misinformed: under, inner, reverse. — *n.* whatever is not right or just: any injury done to another: damage, harm (*rare*): wrong-doing: the state or position of being or doing wrong. — *adv.* not correctly: not in the right way: astray. — *v.t.* to do wrong to: to harm physically (*obs.* and *Scot.*): to impair, spoil (*obs.*): to seduce: to deprive of some right: to defraud: to impute fault to unjustly: to dishonour. — *n.* **wrong'er** one who wrongs. — *adj.* **wrong'ful** wrong: unjust: unlawful: not legitimate: unjustly held (*Spens.*). — *adv.* **wrong'fully.** — *n.* **wrong'fulness.** — *adv.* **wrong'ly.** — *n.* **wrong'ness.** — *adj.* **wrong'ous** (*-gəs, -əs*) unjust, illegal. — *adv.* **wrong'ously.** — **wrong'-do'er** an offender, transgressor; **wrong'-do'ing** evil or wicked action or conduct. — *v.t.* **wrong'-foot'** to cause to be (physically or mentally) off balance, or at a disadvantage. — *adj.* **wrong'-head'ed** obstinate and perverse, adhering stubbornly to wrong principles or policy. — *adv.* **wrong'-head'edly.** — **wrong'-head'edness.** — *adj.* **wrong'-mind'ed** having erroneous views. — **wrong side** see **side.** — *adj.* **wrong'-timed'** inopportune. — **wrong 'un** (*coll.*) a dishonest character, a rogue: in cricket, a googly. — **do oneself wrong** (*obs.*) to be mistaken; **get hold of the wrong end of the stick** see **end; get on the wrong side of someone** to arouse dislike or antagonism in someone; **get out of bed on the wrong side** to arise in the morning in an ill temper; **go wrong** to fail to work properly: to make a mistake or mistakes: to stray

from virtue; **have wrong** (*obs.*) to suffer injustice or injury; **in the wrong** holding an erroneous view or unjust position: guilty of error or injustice; **private wrong** a violation of the civil or personal rights of an individual; **public wrong** a crime which affects the community; **put in the wrong** to cause to appear in error, guilty of injustice, etc.; **the wrong foot,** etc. see **foot.**   [O.E. *wrang,* a wrong; most prob. O.N. *rangr,* unjust; allied to O.E. *wringan,* to wring, like Fr. *tort,* from L. *tortus,* twisted.]

wroot. Obs. form of **root²** and **wrote.**

wrote *rōt, pa.t.* of **write.**

wroth *rōth, roth, adj.* wrathful: in commotion, stormy.   [O.E. *wrāth,* angry; cf. O.N. *reithr.*]

wrought *röt, pa.t.* and *pa.p.* of **work,** now used chiefly in certain senses: — e.g. fashioned: ornamented: manufactured: beaten into shape, shaped by tools (as metal). — **wrought'-iron** malleable iron, iron containing only a very small amount of other elements, but containing slag in the form of particles elongated in one direction, more rust-resistant than steel and welding more easily. — *adj.* **wrought'-up** in an agitated condition, overexcited.   [O.E. *worhte, geworht, pa.t.* and *pa.p.* of *wyrcan, wircan,* to work.]

wrung *rung, pa.t.* and *pa.p.* of **wring.**

wry *rī, adj.* twisted or turned to one side: not in the right direction: expressing displeasure or irony (*fig.*): perverse, distorted (*fig.*): — *compar.* **wry'er** or **wri'er;** *superl.* **wry'est** or **wri'est.** — *n.* (*rare*) distortion. — *v.i.* to swerve, to go astray (*obs.*): to be deflected, undergo deflection (*obs.*): to writhe. — *v.t.* to give a twist to: to avert, as the face: to pervert. — *adv.* **wryly.** — *adv.* **wry'ly.** — *n.* **wry'ness.** — **wry'bill** a New Zealand bird allied to the plovers with bent sideways. — *adj.* **wry'-mouthed** having a crooked mouth: unflattering. — **wry'-neck** a twisted position of the head on the neck due to disease of the cervical vertebrae or to affections (esp. rheumatic) of the muscles of the neck; **wry'neck** a member of a genus of small birds (Jynx) allied to the woodpecker, which twist round their heads strangely when surprised. — *adj.* **wry'-necked** having a wry neck: played with the head on one side (Shak., *Merch. of Ven.,* II, v. 30). — **make a wry face** or **mouth** to pucker up the face, or mouth, as in tasting anything bitter or astringent, or in sign of disgust or pain.   [O.E. *wrīgian,* to strive, move, turn.]

wrythen. See **writhe.**

wud. Scots form of **wood¹,².**

wulfenite *wŏŏl'fən-īt, n.* a molybdate of lead, $PbMoO_4$, occurring commonly as yellow crystals in veins with other lead ores, named after F. X. von *Wulfen* (1728–1805), an Austrian mineralogist.

wull¹ *wul,* (*Spens.* and *dial.*) *v.i.* Same as **will¹.**

wull². See **will².**

wunderkind *vŏŏn'dər-kint, n.* a child prodigy: one who shows great talent, attains great success, etc. at an early (or comparatively early) age: — *pl.* **wun'derkinder** (*-kin-dər*).   [Ger., lit. wonder child.]

wunner. See **oner** under **one.**

wurley *wûr'lē,* (*Austr.*) *n.* an Aborigine's hut, traditionally made of branches, bark, leaves and plaited grass: a nest, esp. a rat's nest: — *pl.* **wur'leys** or **wur'lies.** [Aboriginal.]

Würm *vürm, n.* the fourth stage of glaciation in the Alps. — *adjs.* **Würm, Würm'ian.**   [From a river of Upper Bavaria.]

wurst *vŏŏrst, wûrst, n.* a large German sausage of several types.   [Ger., lit. something rolled; cf. L. *vertere,* to turn.]

wurtzite *wûrts'īt, n.* sulphide of zinc, ZnS, of the same composition as sphalerite, but crystallising in the hexagonal system, in black hemimorphic, pyramidal crystals.   [From French chemist C. A. *Wurtz.*]

wushu, Wushu, wu shu, Wu Shu *wŏŏ'shŏŏ, n.* the Chinese martial arts, kung fu.   [Chin., — *wu,* military, *shu,* art.]

wuther *wudh'ər,* (*dial.*) *v.i.* to move swiftly or with force:

to make a sullen roaring, as the wind: to throw or beat violently. — *n.* a blow or blast, or the sound of these: a tremble. — *adj.* **wuth'ering.** — Also **whither** ((*h*)*widh'-ər*).   [From O.N.]

wuzzle *wuz'l,* (*U.S.*) *v.t.* to jumble.

wyandotte *wī'an-dot, n.* a useful breed of the domestic fowl, of American origin.   [From the N. American tribe so called.]

wych-elm *wich'elm, n.* a common wild elm, also called Scotch elm or witch-hazel. — **wych'-hazel** same as **witch-hazel.**   [**witch**² and **elm**.]

Wyclifite, Wycliffite *wik'lif-īt, adj.* pertaining to the English reformer and translator of the Bible, John *Wyclif, Wycliffe* (*c.* 1329–84). — *n.* a follower of Wyclif; a Lollard.

wye *wī, n.* the letter Y (q.v.) or anything shaped like it. — **wye'-level** see **Y.**

Wykehamist *wik'əm-ist, n.* a pupil, or former pupil, of Winchester College, which was founded by William of *Wykeham,* Bishop of Winchester (1324–1404).

wylie-coat *wī'li-kōt,* (*Scot.*) *n.* a flannel undervest or petticoat: a nightdress.   [Unknown first element, and prob. **coat**.]

wynd *wīnd,* (*Scot.*) *n.* a lane, narrow alley in a town. [Same as **wind**².]

wysiwyg *wiz'i-wig,* (*comput.*) an acronym for *what you see* (i.e. on the screen) *is what you get* (on the print-out).

wyte. See **wit¹, wite¹.**

wyvern. Same as **wivern.**

fāte; fär; hûr; mīne; mōte; för; mūte; mōon; fŏot; dhen (then); *el'ə-mənt* (element)

X

X, x *eks, n.* the twenty-fourth letter in our alphabet, and twenty-first of the Roman alphabet, taken from the Chalcidian Greek, and of the same form, though perhaps not the same origin, as Ionic and classical Greek chi (Χ, χ; pron. *k-h,* and later *hh*); used in Old English medially and finally as a variant for *cs.* In modern English, medially and finally, it has the value of *ks,* as in *extinct, axe,* and, medially only, of *gz,* as in *exist,* or *ksh,* as usu. in *luxury,* or *gzh,* as in *luxurious*; at the beginning of a word it is usu. pronounced *z,* or, rarely, *gz.* As Roman numeral X stands for ten, ✕ for a thousand, X̄ for ten thousand; X (see also **chi**) as an abbreviation represents the word Christ — **Xian, Xmas**; *x* in algebra is the first of the unknown quantities; used to indicate various things, as a choice on a ballot paper, an error on an examination paper, or a kiss. — **X′-body** an inclusion in a plant-cell suffering from a virus disease; **X′-chromosome** a chromosome associated with sex-determination, usually occurring paired in the female zygote and cell, and alone in the male zygote and cell; **X′-factor** that part of a serviceman's pay intended as compensation for the particular disruptions and disadvantages of life in the armed forces; **X′-particle** a meson; **X′-rays** electromagnetic rays of very short wavelength which can penetrate matter opaque to light-rays, produced when cathode rays impinge on matter — discovered by Röntgen in 1895. — *adj.* **X′-ray.** — *n.* a photograph taken by X-rays. — *v.t.* to photograph or treat by, or otherwise expose to, X-rays. — **characteristic X′-rays** secondary X-rays emitted when X-rays fall on matter, which contain monochromatic radiations that vary in wavelength according to the atoms from which they are scattered; **X-ray astronomy** a branch of astronomy using satellites or rockets to detect and measure X-ray emissions from certain heavenly bodies; **X-ray crystallography** the study of crystal structures as shown by their diffraction of X-rays; **X-ray micrography** the preparation, and study through the microscope, of radiographs obtained by means of X-rays; **X-ray spectrum** a wavelength or frequency diagram in which a series of lines indicate by their positions the particular X-rays emitted by a body as the result of cathode-ray bombardment; **X-ray telescope** a telescope designed to investigate the emission of X-rays from stars; **X-ray therapy** the use of X-rays for medical treatment; **X-ray tube** an evacuated tube in which X-rays are emitted from a metal target placed obliquely opposite to an incandescent cathode whose rays impinge on the target.

xanth- *zanth-,* **xantho-** *zan′thō-, -thō′-,* in composition, yellow. — *ns.* **xan′thate** a salt of xanthic acid; **xanthein** (*zan′thē-in*) a soluble yellow colouring matter of flowers; **xanthene** (*zan′thēn*) a white crystalline compound of carbon, hydrogen, and oxygen, from which are derived **xanthene dyestuffs.** — *adj.* **xan′thic** of a yellow tint, esp. as a description of flowers: pertaining to xanthin or xanthine: designating **xanthic acid,** any of a series of addition compounds of an alcohol with carbon disulphide, esp. ethyl-xanthic acid. — *ns.* **xan′thin** a name given to the insoluble yellow colouring matter of various flowers: also to a principle in madder: (usu. **xan′thine**) a white substance, closely allied to uric acid, found in muscle tissue, the liver and other organs, urine, etc., leaving a lemon-yellow residue when evaporated with nitric acid; **Xan′thium** (Gr. *xanthion,* a plant used for dyeing the hair yellow) any of a small but widely distributed genus of composite plants whose fruits bear hooked prickles very troublesome to sheep and other animals. — *n.pl.* **Xanthochroi** (*zan-thok′rō-ī*; Gr. *chroā,* or *chroiā,* skin) one of the five groups of men, according to Huxley and other ethnologists, comprising the fair whites. — *n.* **xanthochroia** (*-thō-kroi′ə*) yellowness of the skin. — *adjs.* **xanthochrō′ic, xan′thochroid** (*-kroid*; also used as *n.*). — *n.* **xanthochroism** (*-thok′rō-izm*) a condition in which all pigments other than yellows disappear, as in goldfish, or normal colouring is replaced by yellow. — *adj.* **xanthochroous** (*-thok′rō-əs*) xanthochroic. — *ns.* **xanthochrō′mia** any yellowish discoloration, esp. of the cerebrospinal fluid; **xanthoma** (*zan-thō′mə*) a yellow tumour composed of fibrous tissue and of cells containing cholesterol ester, occurring on the skin (e.g. in diabetes) or on the sheaths of tendons, or in any tissue of the body. — *adjs.* **xanthom′atous; xanthomelanous** (*zan-thō-mel′ə-nəs*) applied to a type of men with black hair and yellow or olive skins. — *ns.* **xanthophyll** (*zan′thō-fil*) $C_{40}H_{56}O_2$, one of the two yellow pigments present in the normal chlorophyll mixture of green plants; **xanthop′sia** the condition in which objects appear yellow to the observer, as in jaundice or after taking santonin; **xanthop′terin(e)** (*-in*) a yellow pigment obtained from the wings of yellow butterflies and the urine of mammals. — *adj.* **xanthous** (*zan′thəs*) yellow. — *ns.* **Xanthoxylum** (*zan-thok′si-ləm*; Gr. *xylon,* wood) a genus of the Rutaceae, comprising over one hundred species, of which many are found in Brazil and the W. Indies, esp. either of two species known respectively as the prickly-ash and Hercules club, or their dried bark; **Xanthura, Xanthoura** (*-thū′, -thōō′rə*; Gr. *ourā,* tail) a genus of American jays, with yellow tail. [Gr. *xanthos,* yellow.]

Xanthian *zan′thi-ən, adj.* pertaining to *Xanthus,* capital of ancient Lycia in Asia Minor.

Xanthium. See under **xanth-.**

Xantippe *zan-tip′i, n.* a scold, shrew. — Also **Xanthippe** (*-thip′i*). — (*Shak.* older editions **Zan′tippe, Zen′tippe**). [Gr. *Xanthippē,* wife of Socrates.]

xcbcc *zē′bek, n.* a small three-masted vessel much used by the former corsairs of Algiers. [Fr. *chebec,* influenced by Sp. form; perh. from Turkish or Arabic.]

Xema *zē′mə, n.* the genus of fork-tailed gulls. [Arbitrarily invented 1819.]

xen- *zen-, zēn-,* **xeno-** *zen-ō-, zi-no′-,* in composition, strange, foreign, guest. — *n.* **Xenar′thra** (Gr. *arthron,* a joint) a group of American edentates — ant-eaters, sloths, and armadillos — having the dorsolumbar vertebrae jointed in an unusual manner. — *adj.* **xenar′thral** having additional facets for articulation on the dorsolumbar vertebrae. — *n.* **xē′nia** (*bot.*) the direct influence of pollen upon endosperm (explained by double fertilisation) or upon the mother-plant of the embryo. — *adj.* **xenial** (*zē′ni-əl*) of or belonging to hospitality, or relations with guests. — *ns.* **xenium** (*zē′ni-əm*) a present made to a guest or an ambassador: an offering, or a compulsory gift, to a ruler, the Church, etc.: — *pl.* **xē′nia; xen′ocryst** (*-krist*) a crystal or mineral grain which has been incorporated by magma during its uprise; **xenodochium** (*zen-ō-do-kī′-əm*; Gr. *docheion,* a receptacle) a building for the reception of strangers, as a guest-house in a monastery; **xenogamy** (*zen-og′ə-mi*; Gr. *gamos,* marriage; *bot.*) cross-fertilisation; **xenogenesis** (*zen-ō-jen′ə-sis*; Gr. *genesis,* birth) the (imagined) generation of something altogether and permanently unlike the parent. — *adjs.* **xenogenet′ic; xenogenous** (*zi-noj′-i-nəs*) due to outside cause. — *ns.* **xenogloss′ia** (Gr. *glōssa,* tongue) in psychical research, knowledge by a person of a language which he has never learned; **xen′ograft** a graft from a member of a different species; **xen′olith** a fragment of rock of extraneous origin which has been incorporated in magma; **xenomania** (*-mā′ni-ə*; Gr. *maniā*, madness) an inordinate attachment to things foreign; **xenomenia** (*-mē′ni-ə*; Gr. *mēniaia*, menses) vicarious menstruation, in which, in the absence of normal menstruation, bleeding occurs at regular monthly intervals from other parts of the body (e.g. the nose). — *adj.* **xenomorphic** (*-mȯr′fik*; Gr. *morphē*, form) allotriomorphic. — *ns.* **xenon** (*zen′*, *zēn′on*) a zero-valent element (Xe; at. numb. 54), a heavy gas present in the atmosphere in proportion of 1 : 13 × 10⁷ by volume, and also a fission product; **xen′ophile** one who likes foreigners or things foreign; **xen′ophobe** (*-fōb*; Gr. *phobos*, fear) one who fears or hates foreigners or things foreign; **xenophobia** (*-fō′bi-ə*), **xenoph′oby** fear or hatred of things foreign; **xenophya** (*zen-of′i-ə*; Gr. *xenophyēs*, strange in shape or nature) elements of a shell or skeleton not secreted by the organism itself. — *adj.* **xenoplas′tic** in experimental zoology, of transplantation in which transplant and host belong to the young germs of different species or genera. — *ns.* **Xen′opus** a genus of African aquatic frogs (see **platanna** (frog)); **xenotime** (*zen′ō-tīm*; Gr. *xenos*, strange, in error for *kenos*, empty, vain, and *timē*, honour, in reference to the fact that the mineral was at first supposed to contain a new metal) yttrium phosphate, often containing small quantities of cerium, erbium, and thorium, and an important source of these rare elements; **Xenurus** (*zē-nū′rəs*; Gr. *ourā*, tail) a genus of armadillos in which the tail is almost without plates. — *adj.* **xenū′rine.** — **xenon lamp** a high-pressure lamp, containing traces of xenon, used in film projectors, high-speed photography, etc. [Gr. *xenos*, (n.) guest, host, stranger, (adj.) strange, foreign.]

xer- *zēr-*, **xero-** *zē-rō-*, in composition, dry. — *ns.* **xeran′sis** a drying up; **Xeranthemum** (*-an′thi-məm*; Gr. *anthemon*, flower) a genus of plants of southern Europe, belonging to the thistle family: a species of these known as everlasting: (without *cap.*) any plant of this genus. — *adjs.* **xeran′tic** drying up; **xerarch** (*zē′rärk*; Gr. *archē*, beginning) of a plant succession, starting on land where conditions are very dry. — *n.* **xerasia** (*zi-rā′si-ə*) a morbid dryness of the hair. — *adj.* **xē′ric** dry, lacking in moisture: xerophytic. — *ns.* **xerochasy** (*zi-rok′ə-si*) dehiscence on drying; **xeroderma** (*zē-rō-dûr′mə*; Gr. *derma*, skin), **xeroder′mia** a disease characterised by abnormal dryness of the skin and by overgrowth of its horny layer. — *adjs.* **xerodermat′ic**, **xeroder′matous**, **xeroder′mic.** — *adj.* **xerograph′ic.** — *ns.* **xerog′raphy** a non-chemical photographic process in which the plate is sensitised electrically and developed by dusting with electrically-charged fine powder; **xeroma** (*-rō′*) xerophthalmia; **xē′romorph** (*-mȯrf*; Gr. *morphē*, form) a xerophyte. — *adjs.* **xeromor′phic**, **xeromor′phous** of parts of a plant, protected against excessive loss of water by thick cuticles, coatings of hairs, and similar structural characters. — *n.* **xerophagy** (*zi-rof′ə-ji*; Gr. *phagein*, to eat) the eating of dry food, or of bread, vegetables and water, as a form of fast. — *adj.* **xerophilous** (*-of′il-əs*; Gr. *philos*, loving) of a plant, tolerant of a droughty habitat. — *ns.* **xeroph′ily** adaptation to dry conditions; **xērophthalmia** (*-of-thal′mi-ə*; Gr. *ophthalmos*, eye) a dry lustreless condition of the conjunctiva due to deficiency of vitamin A in the diet; **xē′rophyte** (*-fīt*; Gr. *phyton*, plant) a plant able to inhabit places where the water supply is scanty, or where conditions, e.g. excess of salts, make it difficult to take in water. — *adj.* **xerophytic** (*-fit′*) able to withstand drought. — *ns.* **xeroradiog′raphy** X-ray photography by xerography; **xerō′sis** abnormal dryness, as of the skin, mouth, eyes, etc.; **xerostoma** (*-os′tom-ə*; Gr. *stoma*, mouth), **xerostō′mia** excessive dryness of the mouth due to insufficiency of the secretions; **xerotes** (*zē′rō-tēz*) a dry habit of body. — *adj.* **xerotic** (*-rot′*) of bodily tissues, abnormally dry.

— *ns.* **xerotripsis** (*-trip′sis*; Gr. *tripsis* — *tribein*, to rub) dry friction; **Xerox**® a registered trademark used inter alia in respect of copying machines operating a xerographic method of reproduction: a copy so produced. — *v.t.* to produce a copy by this method. [Gr. *xēros*, dry.]

xerafin, **xeraphim** *sher′ə-fēn*, *-fēm*, (Port.) *ns.* a silver coin of Goa.

Xeres *hher′es*, (Sp.) *n.* wine of Xeres (Jerez), sherry.

Xhosa *kō′sə*, *-zə*, *n.* a group of Bantu-speaking tribes from the Cape district of South Africa, formerly often known as Kaffirs: a member of one of these tribes: the language of these tribes. — Also **Xosa.** — *adj.* **Xho′san.**

xi *zī*, *ksī*, *ksē*, *n.* the fourteenth letter of the Greek alphabet (Ξ, ξ), answering to X: as a numeral ξ′ = 60, ͺξ = 60 000.

Xian. See under X.

xiph-, **xipho-** *zif-*, *zif-o-*, *-ō-*, in composition, sword. — *ns.* **xiphihumeralis** (*-i-hū-mər-ā′lis*) in vertebrates, a muscle leading from the xiphoid cartilage to the humerus; **xiphiplas′tron** in chelonians, one of the plates composing the plastron, lying posterior to the hypoplastron. — *adj. and n.* **xiphiplas′tral.** — *n.* **xiphister′num** a posterior element of the sternum. — *adjs.* **xiph′oid** sword-shaped: pertaining to, or designating, the **xiphoid process** or xiphisternum (also, when cartilaginous, known as **xiphoid cartilage**); **xiphoid′al.** — *n.* **xiphop′agus** (Gr. *pēgnynai*, to fix, fasten together) a monster consisting, as did the Siamese twins, of twins joined in the region of the xiphoid cartilage. — *adjs.* **xiphopagic** (*-paj′ik*), **xiphop′agous**; **xiphophyllus** (*-ə-fil′-əs*; Gr. *phyllon*, leaf) with sword-shaped leaves. — *n.* **Xiphosura** (*-ō-sū′rə*; formed irreg. from Gr. *ourā*, tail) an order of Arthropoda of which the only survivors are the king-crabs. — *adj. and n.* **xiphosu′ran.** [Gr. *xiphos*, a sword.]

Xiphias *zif′i-as*, *n.* the common swordfish genus, giving name to the family **Xiphī′idae.** [Gr. *xiphias*, swordfish — *xiphos*, sword.]

Xmas *eks′məs*, *kris′məs*, *n.* short for **Christmas** (see also **X**).

xoanon *zō′ə-non*, *n.* a primitive statue, said to be fallen from heaven, orig. of wood, later overlaid with ivory and gold. [Gr. *xoanon* — *xeein*, to carve.]

Xosa. See **Xhosa.**

X-rays. See under X.

xylem *zī′ləm*, *n.* woody tissue — usu. consisting of vessels, tracheides, and fibres, all with lignified walls, with some more or less lignified parenchyma — concerned in the conduction of aqueous solutions, and with mechanical support. — *ns.* **xy′lene** C₆H₄(CH₃)₂, any of three dimethyl-benzenes, occurring in coal-tar but not separable by fractional distillation; **xy′lenol** (CH₃)₂·C₆H₃·OH, any of six monohydric phenols derived from xylenes. — *adj.* **xy′lic** pertaining to xylem: designating any of six acids, derivatives of xylene: — *ns.* **xy′litol** a sweet crystalline alcohol got from xylose, that can be used as a sugar substitute; **xylobal′samum** (Gr. *balsamon*, the balsam tree) the dried twigs, or the wood, of the balm of Gilead tree; **xy′locarp** a hard and woody fruit, as a coconut. — *adj.* **xylocarp′ous.** — *ns.* **xy′lochrome** (Gr. *chrōma*, colour) a mixture of substances to which the colour of heartwood is due — including tannins, gums, and resins; **xy′logen** (*-jen*) xylem. — *adj.* **xylogenous** (*-loj′ən-əs*; *bot.*) growing on wood. — *ns.* **xylography** (*zī-log′rə-fi*) the art of engraving on wood; **xyl′ograph** an impression or print from a wood block: an impression of the grain of wood for surface decoration; **xylog′rapher.** — *adjs.* **xylograph′ic**, **-al**; **xy′loid** woody, ligneous. — *ns.* **xyloidin**, **xyloidine** (*zi-loi′din*; Gr. *eidos*, form, appearance) an explosive like gun-cotton, prepared by the action of strong nitric acid on starch or woody fibre — pyroxylin, or similar substance; **xy′lol** (L. *oleum*, oil) xylene; **xylol′ogy** the study of the structure of wood; **xylō′ma** in fungi, a sclerotium-like body which forms spores internally and does not put out branches which develop into sporophores; **xylom′eter** an instrument for determining the specific gravity of wood. — *adj.* **xylon′ic** designating an acid obtained by oxidising xylose. — *ns.* **xylonite, Xy′lonite®** a non-thermosetting plastic of the nitrocellulose type; **xylophagan** (-*lof′ə-gən*; Gr. *phagein*, to eat) one of the **Xyloph′aga,** a genus of boring bivalves; **xy′lophage** (-*fāj*) an insect-larva, mollusc, etc., that eats or bores in wood. — *adjs.* **xylophagous** (-*lof′ə-gəs*) wood-eating; **xyloph′ilous** fond of wood, living upon wood. — *n.* **xy′lophone** (Gr. *phōnē,* voice) a musical instrument consisting of a graduated series of wooden bars, which are rested on straw, etc., and are struck by wooden hammers: an instrument used to measure the elastic properties of wood. — *adj.* **xylophon′ic.** — *ns.* **xyloph′onist; Xylopia** (-*lō′pi-ə*; Gr. *pikros,* bitter) a genus of trees and shrubs of the custard-apple family, natives of the tropics, chiefly in America; **xylopyrog′raphy** designs on wood made with a hot poker; **xylorim′ba** an extended xylophone combining the ranges of the *xylo*phone and the ma*rimba*; **xy′lose** a pentose found in many plants, also known as wood-sugar ($C_5H_{10}O_5$). — *adjs.* **xylot′-omous** (Gr. *tomē,* a cut) of insects, wood-boring, wood-cutting; **xylotypograph′ic** pertaining to, or printed from, wooden type. — *ns.* **xylotypog′raphy; xy′lyl** (-*lil*) any of the univalent radicals, C_8H_9, of the xylenes or their derivatives. [Gr. *xylon,* wood.]

Xyris *zī′ris, n.* a genus of sedge-like plants, usu. with yellow flowers, of the family **Xyridaceae** (*zir-i-dā′si-ē*) and order **Xyridales** (-*dā′lēz*). — *adj.* **xyridā′ceous** (-*shəs*) of the Xyridaceae. [Gr. *xўris,* a kind of iris.]

xyst. See **xystus.**

xyster *zis′tər, n.* a surgeon's instrument for scraping bones. [Gr. *xystēr,* a graving tool.]

xystus *zis′təs,* (*ant.*) *n.* a covered portico used by athletes for their exercises: an open colonnade: a tree-planted walk. — Also **xyst, xys′tos.** [L., — Gr. *xystos* or -*on,* perh. orig. a cleared or raked place — *xyein,* to scrape; cf. **xyster.**]

For other sounds see detailed chart of pronunciation.

Y

Y, y *wī, n.* the twenty-fifth letter of our alphabet, twenty-third of the Roman alphabet, derived, as are also U and V, from Greek upsilon (Y, υ); it is used to represent a consonant sound as in *year* (*y* = O.E. ȝ; M.E. ȝ, yogh), and the vowel and diphthongal sounds, *i*, as in *hymn, folly*; *ī*, as in *my, pyre*; *ə*, as in *satyr*, *û*, as in *myrrh*; also in digraphs, as *oy* instead of *oi* when final, e.g. in *toy*. Early printers used y as a substitute for thorn (þ), which their founts lacked: hence it came to be so used in MSS. and inscriptions, as *yat* or *yᵗ* for *that*, *ye* for *the*; cf. **ye²**. As a mediaeval numeral, Y = 150; Ȳ = 150000. — **Y′-alloy** an aluminium-base alloy of duralumin type, containing copper 4%, magnesium 1·5%, silicon 0·7%, nickel 2%, iron 0·6%, and titanium 0·2%; **Y′-chromosome** one of a pair of chromosomes associated with sex-determination (the other being the **X-chromosome**); **Y′-level** a type of engineers' level whose essential characteristic is the support of the telescope, namely, Y-shaped rests in which it may be rotated, or reversed end-for-end. — Also **wye′-level**; **Y′-moth** any of a genus of destructive noctuid moths with a silvery Y-shaped mark on the forewings; **Y′-track** a short track laid at right angles to a railway-line, connected with it by two switches resembling a Y, used for reversing engines.

y- *i-, pfx.* derived from O.E. pfx. ge- (ȝe-), orig. a preposition meaning 'with, together', seen in O.E. nouns and adjectives, as *geféra*, companion, *getheaht*, counsel, *gelīc*, alike, etc., and in verbs, as *gethēodan*, to join together, *gerinnan*, to congeal, but even in O.E. times often used with no very definite meaning; in primitive Germanic *gi-* imparted a perfective meaning to past participles; in O.E. (as *ge-*) and in M.E. (as ȝe-, *y-, i-*, etc.) it was prefixed to past participles indiscriminately, and it was in this way used freely by Spenser and other archaisers.

-y¹ *-i, suff.* forming adjectives with the senses 'characterised by', 'full of', 'having the quality of', 'inclined to', as *icy, sandy, slangy, shiny*. [O.E. *-ig*.]

-y² *-i, suff.* forming nouns denoting (1) a diminutive, or a term of affection, as *doggy, daddy*; (2) a person or thing having a certain specified characteristic, as *fatty*. [Orig. Scot. **-ie** in names, etc.]

-y³ *-i, suff.* forming nouns denoting a quality, state, action or entity, as *fury, jealousy, subsidy, society*. [O.Fr. *-ie*, — L. *-ia*.]

yabber *yab′ər, (Austr.) n.* talk, conversation, jabber. — *v.i.* to talk, jabber. [Aboriginal word *yabba*, language — perh. modified by **jabber**.]

yabby, yabbie *yab′i, (Austr.) n.* a small freshwater crayfish, often used as bait. [Aboriginal.]

yacca *yak′ə, n.* either of two evergreens (Podocarpus) of the West Indies, or their wood. [Sp. *yaca*, from Taino.]

yacht *yot, n.* orig. a light fast-sailing vessel: a sailing, steam, etc., vessel elegantly fitted up for pleasure-trips or racing. — *v.i.* to sail or race in a yacht. — *n.* **yacht′er** one engaged in sailing a yacht. — *n.* and *adj.* **yacht′ing**. — *adj.* **yacht′-built** built on the model of a yacht. — **yacht′-club** a club of yachtsmen; **yachts′man, -woman** one who keeps or sails a yacht; **yachts′manship** the art of sailing a yacht. — **land′-, sand′-yacht** a wheeled boat with sails, for running on land, usu. sea-beaches; **land′-, sand′-yachting**. [Du. *jacht* (formerly *jagt*), from *jagen*, to chase; Ger. *jagen*, to hunt.]

yack, *or* **yak** *yak*, in full **yackety-yak** *yak′i-ti-yak′*, (*slang*) *ns.* persistent, often idle or stupid talk. — *vs.i.* to talk persistently, esp. in a foolish or gossiping manner. —

Also **ya(c)k′ety-ya(c)k′, yak′ity-yak′**. [Imit.]

yacker. Same as **yakka**.

yaff *yaf, (Scot.) v.i.* to bark like a snarling dog: to scold, nag. [Imit.]

yaffle (*dial.*) *yaf′l*, **yaffingale** (*Tennyson*) *yaf′ing-gāl, ns.* the green woodpecker. [From its sound; influenced by **nightingale**.]

yager *yā′gər, n.* Same as **jäger**.

yagger *yag′ər, (Scot.) n.* a pedlar. [Variant of **jagger** (see **jag²**).]

Yagi *yä′gi, yag′i, adj.* denoting a type of highly directional television or radio astronomy aerial, with several elements in a close parallel arrangement, fixed at right angles to a central support that points in the direction of strongest reception. [Hidetsugu *Yagi*, born in 1886, Japanese electrical engineer.]

yah¹ *yä*. Variant of **yea**.

yah² *yä, interj.* an exclamation of derision, contemptuous defiance (also **yah′-boo** and **yah-boo sucks**) or disgust.

Yahoo *yä-hōō′, n.* a name given by Swift in *Gulliver's Travels* to a class of animals with the forms of men but the understanding and passions of brutes: (without *cap.*) a brutal or boorish lout.

Yahwe(h) *yä′wä, n.* Jehovah (q.v.). — *n.* **Yah′wist** Jehovist. — Also **Yah′ve(h), Yah′vist**.

Yajurveda *yuj′ōōr-vā-də*, or *-ve-, n.* one of the four Vedas, the Veda of prayers. [Sans.]

yak¹ *yak, n.* a species of ox found in Tibet, and domesticated there, covered all over with a thick coat of long silky hair, that of the lower parts hanging down almost to the ground. [Tibetan.]

yak², yakety-yak, etc. See **yack**.

yakhdan *yak′dän, n.* a box used for carrying ice, strapped on to the back of an animal. [Pers. *yakh*, ice, *dän*, box.]

yakka *yak′ə, (Austr.) n.* hard toil. — Also **yacker, yakker**. [Aboriginal (Queensland) word.]

Yakut *yä-kōōt′, n.* a member of a mixed Turkish race in Siberia, in the Lena district: their Turkic language.

yakuza *yə-kōō′za, n.* a Japanese gangster, typically involved in drug-dealing, gambling, extortion, gunrunning or prostitution. — *pl.* **yaku′za**. [Jap., from *ya*, eight, *ku*, nine, *za* or *sa*, three, this being the worst hand of cards in gambling.]

yald. See **yauld**.

yale *yāl, n.* a fabulous beast, depicted in heraldry, resembling a horse with tusks, horns and an elephant's tail. [L. *eale*.]

Yale® **lock** *yāl lok*, a trademark for certain kinds of lock. [Linus *Yale* (1821–68), American locksmith.]

Y-alloy. See under **Y**.

yam *yam, n.* a large tuberous root like the potato, growing in tropical countries: any plant of the genus Dioscorea, some species of which yield these tubers: a variety of potato (*Scot.*): a sweet-potato (*Southern U.S.*). [Port. *inhame*.]

Yama *yum′ə, yam′ə, n.* in Hindu mythology, the first mortal. [Sans.]

yamen *yä′men, n.* the offices and residence of a mandarin. [Chin.]

yammer *yam′ər, (dial. and coll.) v.i.* to lament, wail: to whine: to make an outcry: to express yearning. — Also *n.* — *n.* and *adj.* **yamm′ering**. [O.E. *gēom(e)rian* — *gēomor*, sad; influenced in M.E. by Du. *jammeren*.]

yamulka. Same as **yarmulka**.

Yang. See **Yin**.

yang *yang, n.* any of various species of Dipterocarpus, all valuable timber trees. [Thai.]

yank *yangk, v.t.* (*coll.*) to carry, move, pull with a jerk.

fāte; fär; hûr; mīne; mōte; för; mūte; mōōn, fōōt; dhen (then); el′ə-mənt (element)

— *v.i.* to pull or jerk vigorously (*coll.*): to move actively (*fig.*). — *n.* a blow, buffet (*Scot.*): a strong jerk (*coll.*). — *n.* **yank'er** (*Scot.*) a rap: a big lie. — *adj.* **yank'ing** active (*Scot.*): pulling, jerking (*coll.*). — *n.* **yank'ie** (*Scot.*) a scold: an impudent woman. [Ety. dub.]

Yankee *yang'ki, n.* in America, a citizen of the New England States, or an inhabitant of the northern United States, or as opposed to the southern: in British usage, generally an inhabitant of the United States. — Also *adj.* — Also **Yank** (*coll.*). — *n.* **Yank'eedom** the land of Yankees: Yankees generally. — Also *adj.* — *adj.* **Yank'eefied.** — *n.* **Yank'eeism** Yankee characteristics. — **Yankee bet** a combined bet on several horses at once, consisting of doubles, trebles and accumulators (qq.v.); **Yank'ee-Doo'dle** a Yankee (from a popular song). [Prob. Du. *Jantje*, Johnnie, or *Jan Kees*, John Cornelius, both said to be used by the Dutch settlers as nicknames for British settlers.]

yaourt. See **yoghurt.**

yap *yap, v.i.* to bark sharply or constantly (as a small dog): to speak constantly, esp. in a noisy or foolish manner (*coll.*): to scold (*coll.*). — *n.* a yelp: a cur: incessant, foolish chatter (*coll.*): a fool, bumpkin (*U.S.*): the mouth (*slang*). — *ns.* **yapp'er, yap'ster** a dog. [Imit.]

yapok, yapock *yap'ak, n.* the S. American amphibious opossum (*Chironectes minimus*), which feeds on shrimps, etc. [From river *Oyapok*, in French Guiana.]

yapon. See **yaupon.**

yapp *yap, n.* a limp leather binding in which the cover overlaps the edges of the book. [*Yapp*, a bookseller.]

yapper, yapster. See **yap.**

Yarborough *yär'bar-a, n.* a hand containing no card above a nine. [From an Earl of *Yarborough*, said to have betted against its occurrence.]

yard[1] *yärd, n.* a straight thin branch, a wand of authority, a stick for beating as punishment, or a rod for measuring (*obs.*): in English speaking countries, a measure of 3 feet or 36 inches and equivalent to 0·9144 metre: a piece of material this length: a long beam on a mast for spreading square sails: the penis (*arch.*). — *n.* **yard'age** the aggregate number of yards: the length, area, or volume measured or estimated in linear, square, or cubic yards: the cutting of coal at so much a yard. — **yard'-arm** either half of a ship's yard (right or left) from the centre to the end; **yard'land** a virgate, a yard of land; **yard'stick** a stick 3 feet long: any standard of measurement (*fig.*). — Also **yard'wand.** — **by the yard** sold or measured in yard lengths: in large quantities (*fig.*); **yard of ale,** etc., a tall slender glass for ale, etc., or its contents; **yard of land** a measure of area of land, a virgate. [O.E. *gyrd, gierd,* a rod, measure; Du. *garde,* Ger. *Gerte*; conn. Goth. *gazds,* a prickle, sting; and prob. L. *hasta,* a spear.]

yard[2] *yärd, n.* an enclosed place, esp. near a building, often in composition, as 'backyard', 'courtyard', 'farmyard', 'prison-yard', or where any special work is carried on, as 'brickyard', 'wood-yard', 'dockyard': a garden. — *v.t.* to enclose in a yard. — *n.* **yard'age** the use of a yard, or the charge made for such. — **yard'man** the person having special charge of a farmyard: one employed in a railway-yard in making up trains, etc.; **yard'-master** one who has the special oversight of a railway-yard. — **the Yard** New Scotland Yard, the London Metropolitan Police headquarters. [O.E. *geard,* fence, dwelling, enclosure; Ger. *Garten*; conn. with L. *hortus,* Gr. *chortos*.]

yardang *yär'däng, n.* a ridge formed by wind erosion from sand, silt, etc., usually lying parallel to the prevailing wind direction. [Turk. abl. of *yar,* steep bank, precipice.]

yare *yär, adj.* (*arch.* and *dial.*) ready, prepared: quick, brisk: easily handled, manageable. — *interj.* (*Shak.*) quick! — *adv.* **yare'ly** (*arch.* and *dial.*) promptly: skilfully. [O.E. *gearu, gearo,* ready, prompt; Du.

gaar, done, cooked sufficiently, Ger. *gar,* wholly.]

yarfa. See **yarpha.**

yarmulka, yarmulke *yär'mal-ka, n.* the skullcap worn by Jewish males, esp. during prayers or ceremonial occasions. [Yiddish, — Pol. *yarmulka,* small cap.]

yarn *yärn, n.* spun thread: one of the threads of a rope, or these collectively: a sailor's story, spun out to some length, and often having incredible elements: a story generally (*coll.*). — *v.i.* to tell stories. [O.E. *gearn,* thread; O.N. *garn,* Ger. *Garn.*]

yarpha, yarfa *yär'fa, n.* peaty soil in Shetland: clayey, sandy, or fibrous peat: a peat-bog. [O.N. *jörfi,* gravel.]

yarr *yär, (dial.) n.* the corn spurrey, *Spergula arvensis.* [Cf. Fris. *jîr.*]

yarrow *yar'ō, n.* a strong-scented plant, *Achillea millefolium,* or similar species of milfoil. [O.E. *gearwe*; Ger. *Garbe.*]

yarta, yarto. See **jarta.**

yashmak *yash'mak,* or *-mak', n.* the double veil worn by Muslim women in public, the eyes only being uncovered. [Ar. *yashmaq.*]

yatag(h)an *yat'a-gan, n.* a long Turkish dagger, without guard, usu. curved. [Turk. *yātāghan.*]

yate *yāt, (Spens.) n.* a gate. [Variant of **gate.**]

yatter *yat'ar, (Scot.) n.* tiresome, importunate or persistent chatter. — *v.i.* to jabber indefatigably. — *n.* and *adj.* **yatt'ering.** — *adv.* **yatt'eringly.** [Imit.]

yaud *yöd, yäd, (Scot.) n.* a mare: an old mare: an old horse generally. [O.N. *jalda.* Cf. **jade**[1].]

yauld, yald *yöld, yäld, (Scot.) adjs.* active, nimble, strong. [Ety. unknown.]

yaup *yöp, (Scot.) adj.* hungry. [O.E. *gēap,* shrewd.]

yaupon *yö'pan, n.* a bushy evergreen shrub of the holly genus, native to the S.E. coasts of the U.S., its leaves yielding the medicinal 'black drink' of the Indians. — Also **yapon** (*yö'*), **yupon** (*yoo'*). [Amer. Indian.]

yaw *yö, v.i.* of a ship, to deviate temporarily from, to turn out of the line of, its course: to move unsteadily or zigzag (*fig.*): to deviate in a horizontal direction from the line of flight (*aero.*). — *v.t.* to cause to deviate from course, zigzag, etc. — *n.* a deviation from the course, zigzag, etc. — *n.* a deviation from the course: the angular motion of an aircraft in a horizontal plane about the normally vertical axis. [Origin uncertain; cf. O.N. *jaga,* to move to and fro, as a door on its hinges.]

yawey. See **yaws.**

yawl[1] *yöl, v.i.* to howl. — *n.* a howl. [Variant of **yowl.**]

yawl[2] *yöl, n.* a ship's small boat, generally with four or six oars: a small fishing-boat: a small sailing-boat with jigger and curtailed mainboom. [Du. *jol.*]

yawn *yön, v.i.* to take a deep involuntary breath from drowsiness, boredom, etc.: to gape: to gape with astonishment (*Shak.*): to be wide open, as a chasm. — *v.t.* to render, to make, or to effect, by yawning: to utter with a yawn. — *n.* an involuntary deep breath from weariness or boredom: a chasm, opening: dullness (*Shelley*): a boring event, person, etc. (*coll.*). — *adj.* **yawn'ing** gaping, opening wide: drowsy: causing drowsiness or sleep (Shak., *Macb.,* III, ii. 43). — *n.* the action of the verb to yawn. — *adv.* **yawn'ingly.** — *adj.* **yawn'y.** [O.E. *gānian,* to yawn, and *geonian, ginian* (in composition, *gīnan, gīnan,* pa.t. *gān*), to gape widely; O.N. *gīna,* to gape.]

yawp *yöp,* (chiefly *U.S.*) *v.i.* to utter or cry harshly or hoarsely and noisily: to yelp, bark. — *n.* such a harsh, etc. cry. — *n.* **yawp'er.** [Imit.; cf. **yap, yelp.**]

yaws *yöz, n.* a tropical epidemic and contagious disease of the skin — also known as framboesia, button scurvy, verruga Peruviana, buba or boba, etc. — *adj.* **yaw'(e)y** pertaining to yaws. [Origin uncertain; perh. Amer. Indian.]

ybet *i-bēt',* obs. *pa.p.* of **beat.**

yblent *i-blent',* obs. *pa.p.* of **blend, blind.**

ybore *i-bōr', -bör',* obs. *pa.p.* of **bear.**

ybound(en) *i-bownd'(an),* obs. *pa.ps.* of **bind.**

ybrent *i-brent',* obs. *pa.p.* of **burn.**

Y-chromosome. See under **Y.**

yclad *i-klad'*, **ycled** *i-kled'*, obs. forms of **clad**, *pa.p.* of **clothe.**

yclept *i-klept*, or **ycleped** (*Milt.* **ycleap'd**) *i-klēp'id*, *i-klēpt'*. See **clepe.** — *infin.* (*Spens.*) **ycleepe.**

ycond *i-kond'*, obs. *pa.p.* of **con.**

ydrad *i-drad'*, **ydred** *i-dred'*, obs. *pa.ps.* of **dread.**

ye[1] *yē*, *yi*, *pron.* the second person pl. (sometimes sing.) pronoun, now *arch.*, *B.*, *dial.*, *poet.*; cf. **you.** Formerly, as in the A.V. of the English Bible, *ye* was always used as a nominative, and *you* as a dative or accusative; later *ye* was sometimes used for all these cases. [M.E. *ye*, nom.; *your*, gen.; *you*, *yow*, dat. and accus. pl. — O.E. *gē*, nom. ye; *ēower*, gen.; *ēow*, dat. and accus.]

ye[2] *thē*, *thi*, *demons. adj.* archaic script for 'the', arising from the thorn letter, ᚦ. See **Y.**

yea *yā*, *adv.* yes: verily: indeed more than that. — *n.* an affirmative vote or voter. [O.E. *gēa*; Du. and Ger. *ja*, O.N. *jā*; cf. **yes.**]

yead, yede, yeed *yēd*, (*Spens.*) *v.i.* to go, proceed: — *pa.ts.* **yod** (*yod*), **yode** (*yōd*). [O.E. *ēode*, went, used as pa.t. of *gān*, to go.]

yeah *ye*, *yä*, *ye'ə* (*coll.*) *adv.* yes.

yealdon *yel'dən*, (*Scott*, as if Cumberland dialect) *n.* Same as **eldin.**

yealm. See **yelm.**

yean *yēn*, (*arch.* and *dial.*) *v.t.* and *v.i.* esp. of a sheep, to bring forth (young). — *n.* **yean'ling** a lamb or a kid. — Also *adj.* [O.E. *ge-*, *eanian*, to bring forth; *ēacen*, increased, pregnant.]

year *yēr*, *yûr*, *n.* a period of time determined by the revolution of the earth in its orbit: the time taken by any specified planet to revolve round the sun: the period beginning with 1st January and ending with 31st December, consisting of 365 days, except in a **leap year**, when one day is added to February, making the number 366 — the present **legal, civil** or **calendar year:** a space of twelve calendar months, or a period within each twelve-month space characterised by a particular activity, etc.: students etc. as a group at the same stage of their education: (in *pl.*) a period of life, esp. age or old age: (in *pl.*) a very long time: — *pl.* **years** (collective *pl.*, used adjectively with numeral prefixed, **year**, e.g. *a three year period*). — *n.* **year'ling** an animal a year old: a bond maturing after one year (*finance*). — *adj.* a year old: maturing after one year (*finance*). — *adj.* **year'ly** happening every year: lasting a year: for a year. — *adv.* once a year: from year to year. — *n.* a publication appearing, event occurring, etc., once a year. — **year'-book** a book published annually, reviewing the events of the past year; **year-end** the end of the (esp. financial) year. — Also *adj.* — *adjs.* **year'long** lasting a year; **year'-round** existing, lasting, open, etc; throughout the year; **year'-on-year'** (*econ.*) of figures, set against figures for the equivalent period in the previous year. — **anomalistic year** the earth's time of passage from perihelion to perihelion — 365 days, 6 hours, 13 minutes, 49 seconds; **astronomical year** the time of one complete mean apparent circuit of the ecliptic by the sun — 365 days, 5 hours, 48 minutes, 46 seconds — called also the **equinoctial, natural, solar,** or **tropical year; canicular year** the Sothic year (see **Sothic**); **ecclesiastical year** the year as arranged in the ecclesiastical calendar, with the saints' days, festivals, etc.; **embolismic year** a year of thirteen lunar months (384 days) occurring in a lunisolar calendar such as that of the Jews; **financial year, fiscal year** see **finance, fisc; Hebrew year** a lunisolar year, of 12, or 13, months of 29 or 30 days (in every cycle of nineteen years the 6th, 8th, 11th, 14th, 17th, and 19th having thirteen months instead of twelve); **Julian year** the year according to the Julian calendar (introduced by Julius Caesar, modified by Augustus; superseded by the Gregorian calendar), a period of 365½ days, longer than an astronomical year by about 11 minutes (see **style**); **leap-year** see above; **legal, civil,** or **calendar, year** the year by which dates are reckoned; it has begun on

different dates at different periods, and for six centuries before 1752 it began in England on 25th March; since then (earlier in Scotland) it has begun on 1st January; **lunar year** a period of twelve lunar months or 354 days; **Platonic year** a cycle of years at the end of which the heavenly bodies were supposed to be again in the same place as at the Creation — also **great,** or **perfect, year; sabbatical year** see **Sabbath; sidereal year** the period required by the sun to move from a given star to the same star again — having a mean value of 365 days, 6 hours, 9 minutes, 9·6 seconds; **the year dot** see **dot; year in, year out** (happening, done, etc.) every year: with monotonous regularity; **Year of Grace,** or **of our Lord** a formula used in stating any particular year since Christ's birth. [O.E. *gēar*; Ger. *Jahr*, O.N. *ār*, Gr. *hōrā*, season.]

yeard, yeard-hunger. See **yird.**

yearn[1] *yûrn*, *v.t.* to desire strongly, feel longing for (*obs.*; also **earn**): to express a desire for, ask for (*obs.*): to cause to mourn (*Shak.*). — *v.i.* to feel earnest desire: to feel compassion, tenderness, grief (also used impersonally, as 'it yearns me': *obs.*; also **earn**): to express longing, as in sound or appearance. — *n.* a yearning. — *n.* and *adj.* **yearn'ing.** — *adv.* **yearn'ingly.** [O.E. *geornan* (W.S. *giernan*), to desire: allied to *georn*, desirous, eager; cf. Ger. *gern*, willingly.]

yearn[2] *yûrn*, (*obs.* and *dial.*) *v.t.* to earn. [**earn**[1].]

yearn[3]. See **earn**[2].

yeast *yēst*, *n.* a substance used in brewing, baking, etc., consisting of minute fungi, which produce zymase, and hence induce the alcoholic fermentation of carbohydrates: the froth on beer (*obs.*): spume or foam of water (*Shak.*): leaven (*fig.*). — *v.i.* (*lit.* and *fig.*) to ferment, or be covered with froth. — *n.* **yeast'iness.** — *adj.* **yeast'y** like yeast: frothy, foamy: insubstantial. — **yeast'-plant** any of a group of tiny, one-celled fungi (Saccharomyces) that produce alcoholic fermentation in saccharine fluids; **yeast'-powder** dry powdered yeast used in baking: baking-powder. [O.E. *gist*, *gyst*; Ger. *Gäscht*, *Gischt*.]

yede, yeed. See **yead.**

yegg *yeg*, (*U.S.*) *n.* a burglar, esp. a burglar of safes. — Also **yegg'man.** [Poss. the name of an American safe-breaker.]

yeld *yeld*, **yell** *yel*, (*Scot.*) *adjs.* barren: not giving milk: unproductive. [Late O.E. *gelde*; cf. **geld.**]

yeldring *yeld'ring*, *n.* Same as **yoldring.** — Also **yeld'rock.**

yelk. Same as **yolk**[1].

yell[1] *yel*, *v.i.* to howl or cry out with a sharp noise: to scream from pain or terror. — *v.t.* to utter with a yell. — *n.* a sharp outcry: a particular cry affected by an American college: something or someone very funny (*slang*). — *n.* **yell'ing.** — *v.i.* **yell'och** (*-əhh*; *Scot.*) to yell. — *n.* a yell. [O.E. (Angl.) *gellan*; Ger. *gellen*; conn. with O.E. *galan*, to sing.]

yell[2]. See **yeld.**

yellow *yel'ō*, *adj.* of the colour of sulphur or of the primrose: of the colour of gold: of Mongolic race: of mixed black and white race: cowardly, base (*coll.*): sensational (*coll.*). — *n.* the colour of the rainbow between the orange and the green: any dye or pigment producing such a colour: a yolk: (in *pl.*) peach-yellows (see **peach**[2]), or other plant disease in which the foliage yellows: (in *pl.*) jaundice in horses, etc. — *v.t.* and *v.i.* to make, or become, yellow. — *adj.* **yell'owish** somewhat yellow. — *ns.* **yell'owishness; yell'owness** the quality or state of being yellow: jealousy (*obs.*; *fig.*). — *adj.* **yell'owy** yellowish. — *adjs.* **yell'ow-backed, -bellied, -billed, -breasted, -covered, -crowned, -eyed, -footed, -fronted, -headed, -horned, -legged, -necked, -ringed, -rumped, -shouldered, -spotted,** etc. — **yell'owback** a cheap, sensational novel, specif. one with yellow board or paper covers, common in the 19th cent.; **yell'ow-bell'y** (*slang*) a coward (*adj.* **yell'ow-bell'ied**); **yellow berries** Persian berries; **yell'ow-bird** any of various birds of a yellow colour — the golden oriole, etc.; **yell'ow-boy** (*slang*) a gold coin: a mulatto or dark quadroon (*fem.* **yell′ow-girl**); **yell′ow-bunting** the yellow-hammer; **yell′owcake** uranium oxide, got during the processing of uranium ore in the form of a yellow precipitate; **yellow card** an official warning to a football, etc. player (signalled by the showing of a yellow card), typically following an infringement (not used in English domestic football matches since 1981): any similar warning, or symbol of it (*fig.*); **yell′ow-dog** a mongrel: a cur: a base or cowardly person (also used adjectivally; esp. in U.S., meaning not a member of, or antagonistic to, a trade union); **yell′ow-earth** yellow ochre; **yellow fever** an acute disease occurring in tropical America and West Africa, caused by infection with a virus transmitted to man by the bite of a mosquito *Aëdes aegypti* (former name *Stegomyia fasciata*), characterised by high fever, acute nephritis, jaundice, and haemorrhages; **yellow flag** a flag of a yellow colour, displayed by a vessel in quarantine or over a military hospital or ambulance; **yell′ow-hammer, -ammer** a bunting (*Emberiza citrinella*), so named from its yellow colour — also called **yellow≈bunting; Yellow Jack** (*slang*) yellow fever; **yellow line** a yellow line on a road indicating parking restrictions; **yell′ow-metal** a brass consisting of sixty parts copper and forty parts zinc; **Yellow Pages®** a telephone directory, printed on yellow paper, which classifies participating subscribers alphabetically according to trades, professions, services, etc.; **yellow pepper** see **pepper; yellow peril** the danger that the yellow races may crush the white and overrun the world; **yellow poplar** the American tulip-tree, or its wood; **yellow press** newspapers abounding in exaggerated, sensational articles; **yell′ow-rattle** see **rattle; yellow ribbon** in the U.S., a symbol of welcome for those returning home after having undergone some danger, orig. a decoration on U.S. cavalrymen's tunics, given to sweethearts as favours; **yell′ow-root** golden-seal; **yell′ow-snow** snow sometimes observed in the Alps and in the Antarctic regions, coloured yellow by the growth on it of certain algae; **yell′ow-soap** common soap composed of tallow, resin, and soda; **yell′ow-spot** the macula lutea, the small area at the centre of the retina in vertebrates at which vision is most distinct; **yellow streak** a tendency to dastardly behaviour; **yell′ow-wash** a lotion consisting of a mixture of mercuric chloride and lime water; **yell′ow-weed** the common ragwort: goldenrod: the plant weld (*dial.*); **yell′ow-wood** any of various woods that are light in colour, as satinwood, or yield yellow dye, as that of *Cladrastis lutea* (Southern U.S.): any of the trees that yield these woods; a tree, as a sumach, that gives yellow dye from a part other than the wood; **yell′ow-wort** an annual of the gentian family — also **yell′ow-cen′taury; yell′ow-yite, -yoldring, -yorling,** or **-yowley** same as **yoldring.** — **yellow brick road** a path to fame, wealth, etc.; **yellow-eyed grass** any plant of the genus Xyris, growing abundantly in the pine-barrens of the Southern U.S.   [O.E. *geolu;* Ger. *gelb;* cog. with L. *helvus,* light bay.]

yelm, yealm *yelm,* (*dial.*) *n.* a bundle of straw laid straight, ready for thatching. — *v.t.* to straighten and order (straw) for thatching.   [O.E. *glim,* a handful of reaped corn, a bundle.]

yelp *yelp, v.i.* to boast (*obs.*): to utter a sharp cry or bark. — *n.* a sharp, quick cry or bark. — *n.* **yelp′er.** — *n.* and *adj.* **yelp′ing.**   [O.E. *gielpan,* to boast, exult; O.N. *gjalpa,* to yelp.]

yelt *yelt,* (*dial.*) *n.* a young sow.   [O.E. *gilte* — M.L.G. *gelte,* a spayed sow.]

yen[1] *yen, n.* formerly a Japanese gold or silver coin: the Japanese monetary unit since 1871: — *pl.* **yen.**   [Jap., — Chin. *yüan,* round, a dollar.]

yen[2] *yen,* (*coll.*) *n.* an intense desire, longing, urge. — *v.i.* to desire, yearn.   [Chin. *yeen,* craving, addiction.]

yenta *yen′tə,* (*U.S.*) *n.* a gossip: a shrewish woman.   [From the personal name.]

yeoman *yō′mən, n.* a gentleman serving in a royal or noble household, ranking between a sergeant and a groom (*hist.*): after the fifteenth century, one of a class of small farmers, commonly freeholders, the next grade below gentlemen (often serving as foot soldiers; *hist.*): a man of small estate, any small farmer or countryman above the grade of labourer: an assistant to an official: a member of the yeomanry cavalry or of the yeomen of the guard: a petty officer on a war vessel whose duties are clerical: — *pl.* **yeo′men.** — *adj.* **yeo′manly** of yeoman's rank: humble and honest: staunch: brave. — *adv.* staunchly, bravely. — *n.* **yeo′manry** the collective body of smaller freeholders: a cavalry volunteer force in Great Britain formed during the wars of the French Revolution, later mechanised as part of the Territorials. — **yeoman('s) service** powerful aid, such as came from the yeomen in the English armies of early times. — **Yeomen of the Guard** a veteran company of picked soldiers, employed in conjunction with the gentlemen-at-arms, on special occasions, as the sovereign's bodyguard — constituted a corps in 1485 by Henry VII, and still wearing the costume of that period.   [M.E. *yoman, yeman;* perh. for **young man.**]

yep *yep,* (esp. *U.S.*) dial. and coll. variant of **yes.**

yerba *yûr′bə, n.* a herb, esp. (also **yerba mate, yerba de maté**) Paraguay tea or maté (q.v.).   [Sp., — L. *herba.*]

yerd, yerd-hunger. See **yird.**

yerk *yûrk,* (all meanings now *dial.*) *v.t.* of a shoemaker, to draw (stitches) tight: to bind or tie with a jerk: to throw or thrust with a sudden, quick motion: to move with a jerk: to lash out with: to utter jerkily: to beat: to rouse, excite (*fig.*). — *v.i.* to draw tight, bind, strike, move, rise, with a jerk: to kick: to engage in with energy or eagerness: to gibe, carp.   [Origin obscure; earlier than **jerk.**]

Yersinia *yər-sin′i-ə, n.* a genus of bacteria spread by animals or birds, one of which, *Yersinia pestis,* causes plague and others **yersinio′sis,** an acute infection of the small intestine: (without *cap.*) a bacterium of this genus: — *pl.* **yersin′ias** or **yersin′iae** (*-i-ē*).   [A.E.J. *Yersin,* French bacteriologist, 1863–1943.]

yes *yes, adv.* ay: a word of affirmation or consent: used to indicate that the speaker is present, or (often said interrogatively) to signal someone to speak or act: formerly, on the contrary: yea. — *n.* a vote or answer of yes: one who votes or answers yes: — *pl.* **yes(s)′es, yes's.** — **yes′-man** (*coll.*) one who agrees with everything that is said to him: an obedient follower with no initiative.   [O.E. *gēse, gīse — gēa, gē,* yea, and *sī,* let it be.]

yeshiva, yeshivah *yə-shē′və, n.* a school for the study of the Jewish Scripture, the Talmud: a seminary for the training of rabbis: an orthodox Jewish elementary school: — *pl.* **yeshi′va(h), yeshi′va(h)s, yeshi′voth.**   [Heb. *yĕshībhāh,* a sitting.]

yesk. See **yex.**

yest, yesty. Obs. forms of **yeast, yeasty.**

yester *yes′tər* (*dial.* and *arch.* **yes′tern**), *adj.* relating to yesterday: last. — *adv.* **yestreen′** (contr. of **yestereven;** *Scot.* and *poet.*) yesterday evening. — *n.* **yes′terday** the day last past: (often in *pl.*) the (recent) past. — *adv.* on the day last past: formerly: in the (recent) past. — **yestereve′(n), yestereve′ning, yestermorn′, yestermorn′- ing** the evening, morning, of yesterday; **yesternight′** last night; **yes′teryear** (orig. *D. G. Rossetti*) last year, or the past in general.   [O.E. *geostran, giestran* (always followed by *dæg,* etc.); Ger. *gestern;* cf. L. *hesternus,* Gr. *chthes.*]

yet *yet, adv.* in addition, besides: up to the present time: still: hitherto: at the same time: even: before the affair is finished. — *conj.* nevertheless: however. — **as yet** up to the time under consideration.   [O.E. *gīet, gīeta;* Ger. *jetzt.*]

yeti *yet′i, n.* the abominable snowman.   [Native Tibetan name.]

yett *yet,* (*Scot.*) *n.* a gate, door.   [Variant of **gate.**]

yeuk. See **yuke.**

yeve *yēv,* (*obs.*) *v.t.* to give: — *pa.p.* (*Spens.*) **yeven** (*yev′ən*).   [O.E. *giefan;* cf. **give.**]

yew *ū, n.* any tree of genus Taxus — family Taxaceae, itself a division of the group Coniferae — widely diffused over the northern parts of the world, with narrow lanceolate or linear leaves, esp. *Taxus baccata* (in Europe long planted in graveyards) which yields an elastic wood good for bows: its wood: a bow made of its wood: yew twigs regarded as emblematic of grief. — *adj.* **yew'en** (*arch.*) made of yew. — **yew'-tree**. [O.E. *īw, ēow*; Ger. *Eibe*.]

yex *yeks,* (*dial.*) *v.i.* to hiccup, belch, spit. — *n.* a hiccup, etc. — Also **yesk**. [O.E. *geocsian*, to sob.]

Yezidi *ye'zi-di, n.* one of a sect in Armenia and the Caucasus believing in a Supreme God but paying respect also to the devil, believing him to have been reinstated as chief angel (called by them *Yazid*), and other minor gods. — Also **Yez'di, Yez'idee, Zez'idee**, etc.

yfere *i-fēr',* (*obs.*) *adv.* together, in company. [See **fere**[1], and **infere**.]

Yggdrasil(l) *ig'drə-sil,* (*Scand. myth.*) *n.* the ash-tree binding together heaven, earth, and hell, and extending its branches over the whole world and above the heavens. — Also **Ygdrasil**. [O.N.; perh. — *Yggr*, a surname of Odin, and *drusil*, horse.]

yglaunst *i-glönst',* (*Spens.*) *pa.p.* of **glance**.

ygo, ygoe *i-gō',* (*Spens.*) *pa.p.* of **go**: ago. [**go**.]

yibbles. See **able**.

yicker. See **yikker**.

Yiddish *yid'ish, n.* a language spoken by Jews, based on ancient or provincial German with Hebrew and Slavonic additions, usu. written in the Hebrew alphabet. — *ns.* **Yid** (*offensive*) a Jew. — *adj.* **Yidd'isher** in, pertaining to Yiddish: Jewish. — *n.* a Jew, a speaker of Yiddish. — *n.* **Yidd'ishism** an idiom or other speech characteristic derived from Yiddish. [Ger. *jüdisch*, Jewish.]

yield *yēld, v.t.* to pay or repay, or to reward (*obs.*): to render as due or fitting (*arch.*): to grant, accord: to admit, concede: to give out: to furnish, afford: to produce: to deliver, surrender, relinquish, resign. — *v.i.* to submit: to cease fighting or contesting: to give way under pressure: to give place. — *n.* an amount yielded: a product: the return of a financial investment, usually calculated with reference to the cost and dividend. — *adj.* **yield'able** that may be yielded: inclined to yield. — *ns.* **yield'ableness; yield'er**. — *adj.* **yield'ing** giving, or inclined to give, way: compliant. — *n.* a giving way: compliance. — *adv.* **yield'ingly**. — *n.* **yield'ingness**. — **yield point** in the case of iron and annealed steels, the stress at which a substantial amount of plastic deformation takes place suddenly. — **yield up the ghost** to give up the ghost (see **ghost**). [O.E. (W.S.) *gieldan*, to pay; O.H.G. *gelten*, O.N. *gjalda*.]

yikker *yik'ər, v.i.* (of an animal) to utter sharp little cries. — Also *n.* [Imit.]

yill *yil, n.* Scots form of **ale**.

yin, yince *yin, yins.* Scots forms of **one, once** generally written **ane, 'ance**.

Yin, Yang *yin, yang, ns.* the two opposing principles of Chinese philosophy and religion influencing destiny, the former negative, feminine and dark, the latter positive, masculine and light. [Chin. *yin*, dark, *yang*, bright.]

yince-errand. See **errand**.

Yinglish *ying'glish,* (*facet.* orig. *U.S.*) *n.* a mixture of Yiddish and English spoken by U.S. Jews: a dialect of English containing a large number of Yiddishisms. — Also **Yeng'lish**.

yip *yip, v.t.* to give a short, sudden cry — esp. of a dog. — Also *n.* — **the yips** (*golf*) an involuntary twitch or similar short, sudden nervous reaction causing a player to persistently miss (esp. short) putts. [Imit.]

yippee *yip-ē', interj.* expressing delight, exultation, etc.

yippy *yip'i, n.* one of a group of young people with ideals based on those of the hippies. [From the *Youth International Party* of 1968.]

yird *yûrd, n.* a Scots form of **earth**. — Also **eard** (*ûrd, erd*), **yeard, yerd**. — *vs.t.* to bury. — **eard'-house, yird'-house,** etc. an earth-house (see **earth**); **eard'-, yeard'-, yerd'-, yird'-hunger** earth-hunger: the hunger sometimes felt by persons approaching death: voracious hunger. — *adjs.* **eard'-hungry,** etc. [**earth**.]

yirk. Same as **yerk**.

yite *yīt,* (*dial.*) *n.* the yellow-hammer. [Origin obscure.]

-yl *-il, suff.* forming nouns denoting a radical, as carbonyl, carboxyl, etc. [Gr. *hȳlē*, matter.]

ylang-ylang *ē'lang-ē'lang, n.* a tree (*Canangium odoratum*) of the Malay Archipelago and Peninsula, the Philippines, etc., or an essence (also **ylang-ylang oil**) distilled from its flowers. [Tagálog.]

ylem *ī'ləm, n.* the prime substance whence according to some theories, the elements are sprung. [O.Fr. *ilem* — L. *hylem*, accus. of *hȳlē* — Gr. *hȳlē*, matter.]

Y-level, Y-moth. See **Y**.

ylike (*Spens.*). Same as **alike**.

ylke. Obs. spelling of **ilk**[1].

ymolt *i-mōlt'* (*Spens.*), **ymolten** *i-mōl'tən* (*obs.*), *v.t.* pa.ps. of **melt**.

ympe, ympt (*Spens.*). Same as **imp**[1], **imped**.

ynambu *ē-näm-boō', n.* a very large tinamou. [Port. *inambu*; of Tupí origin, related to **tinamou**.]

Ynd (*Spens.*). Same as **Ind**.

yo *yō, interj.* calling for, or accompanying, effort, etc.: — *pl.* **yos**. — *interjs.* **yo-(hō-)hō'** calling for attention: same as yo-heave-ho; **yo-heave'-hō'** formerly, a sailors' chant while hauling on ropes.

yob *yob,* (*slang*) *n.* a raw recruit: a teenage loafer: a lout. — *adj.* **yobb'ish**. — *adv.* **yobb'ishly**. — *n.* (*slang*) **yobb'o** a yob: — *pl.* **yobb'os** or **yobb'oes**. [Back-slang for **boy**.]

yock. See **yok**.

yod(e). See **yead**.

yodel, yodle *yō'dl, v.t.* and *v.i.* to sing or shout, changing frequently from the ordinary voice to falsetto and back again after the manner of the mountaineers of the Tirol. — *n.* a song or phrase sung, or a cry made, in this fashion. — Also **jodel** (*yō'dl*). — *n.* **yō'deller, yō'dler**. [Ger. dial. *jodeln*.]

yoga *yō'gə, n.* a system of Hindu philosophy showing the means of emancipation of the soul from further migrations and union with the supreme being: any of a number of systems of physical and mental disciplines by means of which such emancipation is attained: yogic exercises. — *ns.* **yō'gi** (*-gē*), **yō'gin** a Hindu ascetic who practises the yoga system, consisting in the withdrawal of the senses from external objects, long continuance in unnatural postures, etc.: — *fem.* **yōgi'ni**. — *adj.* **yō'gic**. — *n.* **yō'gism**. — **hatha yoga** (*hath'ə, hut'ə*; Sans. *haṭha*, force) a form of yoga (the most common in the Western Hemisphere) stressing the importance of physical exercises and positions and breathing-control in promoting physical and mental well-being. [Sans., union.]

yogh *yohh, n.* the M.E. letter ȝ, derived from O.E. ȝ, representing esp. *y* and *hh* sounds. [Origin uncertain, but appropriate as exemplifying the two chief sounds of the letter.]

yoghourt, yoghurt, yogurt *yog'ərt, yō'gərt, n.* a semi-liquid food made from fermented milk. — Also **yaourt** (*yä'oōrt*). [Turk. *yōghurt*.]

yogi(n), etc. See **yoga**.

yohimbine *yo-him'bēn, n.* an alkaloid obtained from the bark of *Corynanthe johimbe*. [Of Bantu origin.]

yoicks *yoiks, interj.* an old fox-hunting cry. — *vs.i.* or *vs.t.* **yoick(s)** to make, or urge on by, this cry.

yojan *yō'jan,* **yojana** *yō'ja-nə, ns.* an Indian measure of distance, usu. about five miles. [Hind. *yojan* — Sans. *yojana*, (distance covered in one) yoking.]

yok, yock *yok,* (*theatre slang*) *n.* a laugh. — Also *v.i.* [Imit.]

yoke *yōk, n.* that which joins together: the frame of wood joining draught oxen at the necks: any similar frame, as one for carrying pails: a part of a garment that fits the shoulders (or the hips): a stretch of work, e.g. from meal-time to meal-time (*dial.*): a mark of servitude: slavery: an oppressive burden: a bond of union: a pair or couple, as of oxen. — *v.t.* to put a yoke on: to join together: to attach a draught-animal to: to enslave: to set to work (*fig.*). — *v.i.* to be joined: to go together: to set to work (*Scot.*). — *n.* **yōk′ing** (*dial.*) as much work as is done at a stretch. — **yoke′-devil** (*Shak.*) a companion devil; **yoke′-fellow, -mate** an associate, partner, fellow-worker. — *adj.* **yoke′-toed** zygodactyl. [O.E. *geoc*; Ger. *Joch*; L. *jugum*, Gr. *zygon*.]

yokel *yō′kl*, *n.* a country bumpkin. — *adj.* **yō′kelish.** [Ety. dub.]

yokul. See **jokol.**

yold. Obs. *pa.t.* and *pa.p.* of **yield.**

yoldring *yōld′ring*, *n.* a yellow-hammer. [Variant of dial. *yowlring* — O.E. *geolu*; see **yellow.**]

yolk[1] *yōk*, (rare) **yelk** *yelk*, *ns.* the yellow part of the egg of a bird or reptile: the nutritive non-living material contained by an ovum. — *adjs.* **yolked, yolk′y** like yolk. — **yolk′-sac** (*zool.*) the yolk-containing sac which is attached to the embryo by the **yolk′-stalk**, a short stalk by means of which yolk substance may pass into the alimentary canal of the embryo. [O.E. *geolca, geoleca* — *geolu*, yellow.]

yolk[2] *yōk*, *n.* wool-oil. — *adj.* **yolk′y.** — Cf. **suint.** [O.E. *ēowocig*, yolky.]

Yom Kippur *yōm kip′ŏŏr*, the Day of Atonement, a Jewish fast day. — **Yom Tob** or **Tov** (*tōb, tōv*) any religious festival. [Heb. *yōm*, day, *kippūr*, atonement, *tōbh*, good.]

yomp *yomp*, (*esp. mil. coll.*) *v.i.* to carry heavy equipment on foot over difficult terrain. [Poss. imit.]

yon *yon*, (now *poet.* or *dial.*) *adj.* that: those: yonder. — Also *pron.* that: the thing you know of. — *adv.* yonder. — *prep.* **yond** (*Scot.* usu. **yont**) across, or through (*obs.*): to, or in, a position beyond. — *adj.* and *pron.* yon. — *adv.* yonder. — *adv.* **yon′der** to, or at, a distance within view. — *adj.* that, those, at a distance within view (or so conceived). — *pron.* that one, yon. — *adj.* (*dial.*) **yon′derly** mentally or emotionally distant, vague, absent-minded: mentally or physically weak or low (*arch.*). — **hither and yon(d)** (*dial.*) hither and thither; **hither, or here, and yonder** hither and thither; **the yonder** the farther, more distant. [O.E. *geon* (adj., pron.), *geond* (prep., adv.), and M.E. *yonder*.]

yond *yond*, (Spens., *F.Q.* II, viii. 40, 9) *adj.* furious, mad. [Said to be due to misunderstanding of a passage in an earlier writer: Chaucer's *Clerk's Tale* 1143 has been suggested, but 16th-cent. black-letter Chaucers do not have the word in this line.]

yonder. See **yon.**

yongthly. Same as **youngthly** (see **young**).

yoni *yō′nē*, *n.* a representation of the female genitals, the symbol under which the Hindu deity Sakti is worshipped. [Sans.]

yonker. Obs. form of **younker.**

yonks *yongks*, (*coll.*) *n.* ages, a long time. [Origin unknown.]

yont. See **yon.**

yoo-hoo *yŏŏ′-hŏŏ*, *interj.* a call to attract someone's attention.

yoop *yŏŏp*, *n.* and *interj.* a word imitative of a sobbing sound.

yopper *yop′ər*, *n.* one employed on the Government's Youth Opportunities Programme which ended in 1983.

yore *yōr, yör*, *adv.* (*obs.*) long ago. — *n.* time long ago or long past. — Also *adj.* — **(days) of yore** (in) times past. [O.E. *gēara*, formerly; app. connected with *gēar*, a year.]

yorker *yörk′ər*, (*cricket*) *n.* a ball pitched to a point directly under the bat — formerly called a tice. — *v.t.* **york** to bowl (or attempt to bowl) someone out with a yorker. [Prob. from *Yorkshire*, but history quite unknown.]

Yorkie *yö′r′ki*, (*coll.*) *n.* (also without *cap.*) a Yorkshire terrier.

Yorkish *york′ish*, *adj.* pertaining to the county or city of *York*: adhering to the House of York in the Wars of the Roses. — *n.* **York′ist** one of this party. — Also *adj.* — *adj.* **York′shire** of or from the county of Yorkshire: —abbrev. **Yorks.** — *n.* one of a breed of animal, esp. pigs, originating in Yorkshire. — **Yorkshire fog** a tall grass, *Holcus lanatus*; **Yorkshire grit** a grit from Yorkshire used for polishing; **Yorkshire pudding** a pudding made of unsweetened batter, and baked along with meat or in meat dripping — orig. under the spit so as to catch the drippings; **Yorkshire terrier** a small longhaired kind of terrier.

Yoruba *yo′rŏŏ-ba, yō′*, *n. sing.* and *pl.* a linguistic group of coastal West Africa: a member of the group: the language of the group. — *adjs.* **Yo′ruba, Yo′ruban.**

you *ū*, *pron.* the commonly used second person pronoun (all cases), orig. plural (cf. **thou**), now standard for both singular and plural: (indef. *pron.*) anyone: the personality (or something in tune with the personality) of the person addressed (*coll.*). — **you-all′** (*U.S.*) you (esp. in *pl.*); **you′-know-what′, you′-know-who** some unspecified but well-understood or well-known thing or person. [O.E. *ēow* (perh. through a later form *eōw*), orig. only dat. and accus.; cf. **ye**[1].]

you'd *yŏŏd, yōōd*, a contraction of **you had** or **you would.**

youk. See **yuke.**

you'll *yŏŏl, yōōl*, a contraction of **you will** or **you shall.**

young *yung*, *adj.* not long born: in early life: in the first part of growth: youthful: vigorous: relating to youth: junior, the younger of two persons having the same name: inexperienced: newly arrived: miniature (*coll.*). — *n.* the offspring of animals: (with *the*) those who are young. — *adj.* **youngish** (*yung′(g)ish*) somewhat young. — *n.* **young′ling** a young person or animal. — *adj.* youthful, young. — *adv.* **young′ly** (*rare*) in youth: in the manner of youth. — *ns.* **young′ness; young′ster** a young person, esp. a young man, or formerly, a vigorous young man: a child (*coll.*); **youngth** (*Spens.*) youth. — *adj.* **youngth′ly** (*Spens.*) youthful. — **young blood** fresh accession of strength, personnel, ideas, etc.; **Young England** during the corn-laws struggle (1842–45), a little band of young Tory politicians, who hated Free Trade and Radicalism, and professed a sentimental attachment to earlier forms of social life in England; **Young England, America**, etc., the rising generation in England, America, etc. — *adj.* **young′-eyed** (*Shak.*) with the bright eyes of youth. — **young fog(e)y** young(ish) person with (esp. vociferously proffered) conservative or reactionary opinions. — *adj.* **young fo′g(e)yish.** — **Young Ireland** a group of Irish politicians who broke away from O'Connell about 1844, because of his rooted aversion to physical force; **Young Italy** an association of Italian republican agitators, active about 1834, under the lead of Mazzini; **young lady, man** a girl- or boyfriend, sweetheart; **young offender** a law-breaker aged between 17 and 21 (**young-offender(s′) institution** an establishment, now replacing the borstal, for the detention of young offenders who are given custodial sentences); **young person** in Factory Acts, etc., a person who is under eighteen years of age but no longer a child: someone aged fourteen and over, but under seventeen (*law*); **Young Turk** one of a body of Turkish reformers who brought about the revolution of 1908: (also without *caps.*) a progressive, rebellious, impetuous, etc. member of an organisation. — **with young** pregnant. [O.E. *geong*; Ger. *jung*; also conn. with L. *juvenis*, Sans. *yuvan*, young.]

youngberry *yung′ber-i, -bər-i*, *n.* a large reddish-black fruit, a cross between a variety of blackberry and a variety of dew-berry. [B. M. *Young*, an American fruitgrower, and **berry.**]

Young('s) modulus *yung(z) mod′ū-ləs*, the coefficient of elasticity of stretching — for a stretched wire, it is the ratio of the stretching force per unit cross-sectional area to the elongation per unit length. [Thomas

Young (1773–1829), English physicist.]

younker *yung'kər, n.* a young person: a young gentleman or knight (*Spens.*).   [Old Du. *jonckher* (Du. *jonker*), from *jong heer*, young master or lord; Ger. *Junker*.]

your *yör, ūr, pron.* (*gen. pl.*) or *poss. adj.* of or belonging to you: used to denote a person of a class well known — the ordinary (implying some contempt; *coll.*): of or relating to an unspecified person or people in general. — *prons.* **yourn** (*dial.*) yours; **yours** (a double genitive) used predicatively or absolutely: short for 'your letter'. — **you and yours** you and your family or property; **yours faithfully, sincerely, truly,** etc., **yours to command,** etc., forms used conventionally in letters just before the signature: also sometimes used by a speaker to mean himself (*coll.*).   [O.E. *ēower, gen. of gē, ye.*]

you're *yör, ūr,* a contraction of **you are.**

yourself *ūr-self', yör-, pron.* the emphatic form of **you:** in your real character: having command of your faculties: sane: in good form: the reflexive form of **you** (objective): — *pl.* **yourselves'.**

yourt. See **yurt.**

youth *yōōth, n.* the state of being young: early life, the period immediately succeeding childhood: an early period of existence: a young person, esp. a young man (*pl.* **youths** *yōōdhz*): young persons collectively: recentness, freshness (*Shak.*). — *adj.* **youth'ful** pertaining to youth or early life: young: suitable to youth: fresh: buoyant, vigorous. — *adv.* **youth'fully.** — *ns.* **youth'fulness; youth'head, youth'hood** (*obs.*) youth. — *adjs.* **youth'ly** (*Spens.*) young, youthful (also *adv.*); **youth'some** youthful; **youth'y** (*Scot.*) young. — **youth club** a place or organisation providing leisure activities for young people; **youth custody** a custodial sentence of between four and eighteen months passed on a person aged between 15 and 21; **youth hostel** a hostel where hikers, etc., who are members of an organisation find inexpensive and simple accommodation. — *v.i.* to stay in youth hostels. — **youth hosteller; youth leader** a social worker who works with the youth of a particular community or area. — **Youth Training Scheme** (esp. abbreviated **YTS**) a Government-sponsored scheme launched in 1983 to give training and job experience to any unemployed school-leaver desiring it.   [O.E. *geoguth — geong,* young; Ger. *Jugend.*]

you've *yōōv, yŏŏv,* a contraction of **you have.**

yow(e) *yow,* (*dial.*) *n.* variant of **ewe.**

yowie[1] *yow'i,* (*Scot.*) *n.* a little ewe.

yowie[2] *yow'i,* (*Austr. folklore*) *n.* an ape-like man, about 2–2½ metres tall.   [Ety. unknown.]

yowl *yowl, v.i.* to cry mournfully, as a dog: to yell, bawl. — *n.* a distressed cry. — *n.* **yowl'ing** a howling.   [M.E. *youlen;* cf. O.N. *gaula,* to howl.]

yowley. Same as **yoldring.**

yo-yo *yō'-yō, n.* a toy consisting of a reel attached to, and manoeuvred by, a string which winds and unwinds round it — similar to the 18th-cent. bandalore or quiz: any person or thing resembling a yo-yo in movement or ease of manipulation. — Also *adj.* — *v.i.* to operate a yo-yo: to move rapidly up and down: to fluctuate rapidly, be very unsettled.   [Orig. a trademark.]

ypight *i-pīt',* obs. *pa.p.* of **pitch.**

yplast *i-plāst',* obs. *pa.p.* of **place.**

yplight *i-plīt',* obs. *pa.p.* of **plight.**

ypsilon *ip-sī'lon, -sē ',* or *ip'si-, n.* the twentieth letter of the Greek alphabet (Y, υ): as a numeral, υ' = 400; υ = 400000. — Also **upsilon** (*ŭp-sī'lon, ŭp'si-, up'si-*). — *adjs.* **ypsiliform** (*-sil'*), **ypsiloid** (*ip'sil-oid*) shaped like an ypsilon.   [Gr., simple u.]

yrapt *i-rapt'* (*Spens.*). Same as **rapt.**

yravished *i-rav'ish-id* (Malone's emendation of Shak. *iranyshed*) obs. *pa.t.* of **ravish.**

yrent *i-rent',* obs. *pa.p.* of **rend.**

yrivd *i-rīvd',* obs. *pa.p.* of **rive.**

ysame *i-sām,* (*Spens.*) *adv.* together.   [Perh. **in** and **same** (n.).]

yshend *i-shend',* (*Spens.*). Same as **shend.**

yslaked *i-slākt',* obs. *pa.p.* of **slake** (Shak., *Pericles* III,

line 1, quenched or relaxed the energies of).

ythundered *i-thun'də-rid,* (*Spens.*) *v.t., pa.p.* struck by a thunderbolt.

ytost *i-tost',* (*Spens.*) *pa.p.* of **toss.**

Y-track. See **Y.**

ytterbium *i-tûr'bi-əm, n.* a metallic element (Yb; at. numb. 70) a member of the rare-earth group: the name orig. given to a substance later shown to consist of a mixture of this and lutetium. — *n.* **ytter'bia** ytterbium oxide (Yb₂O₃).   [*Ytterby,* a Swedish quarry.]

yttrium *it'ri-əm, n.* a metallic element (Y; at. numb. 39) in the third group of the periodic system, usu. classed with the rare-earths. — *n.* **ytt'ria** its oxide, a yellowish-white powder. — *adjs.* **ytt'ric, ytt'rious; yttrif'erous.** — *ns.* **ytt'ro-cē'rite** a mineral, usu. violet in colour, found embedded in quartz, a fluoride of yttrium, cerium, etc.; **ytt'ro-col'umbite, -tan'talite** a brownish mineral found at Ytterby, a tantalate of yttrium, iron, calcium, etc.   [From *Ytterby;* see **ytterbium.**]

yu *yü, ū, n.* precious jade (nephrite or jadeite). — Also **yu'-stone.**   [Chin. *yü, yü-shih.*]

yuan *yü-än, n.* the monetary unit of the People's Republic of China: — *pl.* **yuan.**   [Chin. *yüan.*]

yuca (also **yucca**), *yuk'ə, n.* cassava. — *n.* **Yucc'a** (sometimes **Yuc'a**) a genus of plants of the family Liliaceae, natives of Mexico, New Mexico, etc., some (as *Yuca gloriosa,* the Spanish dagger) cultivated in gardens on account of the singularity and splendour of their appearance: (without *cap.*) any plant of this genus.   [Of Carib origin.]

yucker *yuk'ər, n.* the American flicker or golden-winged woodpecker.   [Imit. of its note.]

yuck(y). See **yuke.**

yucky, yukky *yuk'i,* (*slang*) *adj.* dirty, unpleasant. — *n.* **yuck, yuk** messiness, etc. — *interj.* expressing distaste, disgust.   [Imit.]

yuft *yuft, n.* Russia leather.   [Russ. *yuft.*]

yuga *yōō'gə, n.* one of the Hindu ages of the world. — Also **yug.**   [Sans.]

Yugo-Slav, Yugoslav *yōō'gō-släv,* or *-släv', n.* a native, citizen, or inhabitant of Yugoslavia, one of the southern group of Slavs consisting of Serbs, Croats, and Slovenes: the Slavonic language (Serbo-Croatian) dominant in Yugoslavia. — Also *adj.* — *adjs.* and *ns.* **Yugoslav'ian, Yugoslav'ic.** — Also **Jugo-Slav, Jugoslav,** etc.   [Serbo-Croatian *jugo- — jug,* the south, and **Slav.**]

yuk, yukky. See **yucky.**

yuke *yōōk,* **yuck** *yuk* (*dial.*) *vs.i.* to itch. — *ns.* itching: the itch. — Also **youk, yeuk, euk, ewk.** — *adjs.* **yuk'y, yuck'y** itchy.   [Same as **itch;** prob. influenced by the M.Du. form, *jeuken.*]

yulan *yōō'lan, n.* a Chinese magnolia, with large white flowers.   [Chin.]

Yule *yōōl, n.* the season or feast of Christmas. — **Yule log** the block of wood cut down in the forest, then dragged to the house, and set alight in celebration of Christmas; **Yule'tide** the time or season of Yule or Christmas. — Also **yule, yule'tide.**   [O.E. *gēol,* Yule, *se ǣrra gēola,* December; O.N. *jōl.* Not conn. either with O.N. *hjōl,* wheel, or M.E. *youlen, yollen,* to cry out or yawl.]

yum-yum *yum'-yum',* (*coll.*) *interj.* expressing delighted or pleasant anticipation, esp. of delicious food. — *interj.* **yumm'y** yum-yum. — *adj.* delicious, attractive, etc.   [Imit.]

yumpie, Yumpie, *yum'pi, n.* one of the young upwardly-mobile people, a dismissive designation for young rising or ambitious professionals. — Also **yump.** — See also **yuppie.**

yunx *yungks, n.* Variant of **Jynx.**

yup *yup, yəp.* Same as **yep.**

yupon. See **yaupon.**

yuppie, yuppy (both also with *cap.*), *yup'i, n.* a young urban professional, a dismissive designation for the young city careerist, the word now being commoner than **yumpie** (q.v.) and even explained by some as derived acronymically from *y*oung *u*pwardly-mobile *p*eople.

yurt, yourt *yōort, n.* a light tent of skins, etc., used by nomads in Siberia.   [From Russ.]

ywis. Same as **iwis.**

ywrake *i-rāk′,* **ywroke** *i-rōk′,* **ywroken** *i-rō′kən,* (*Spens.*) obs. *pa.ps.* of **wreak.**

For other sounds see detailed chart of pronunciation.

Z

Z, z zed, n. the twenty-sixth and last letter in our alphabet, is derived through the Greek *zeta* (Z, ζ), from *zayin*, the seventh Semitic letter. Its sound is a voiced sibilant, either voiced *s* as in 'zeal', or a voiced *sh* as in 'azure': used in Scots to represent M.E. ʒ (the letter yogh), as in *capercailzie*: used as a contraction-mark (=;) in *viz.*, *sciz.*, *oz.*, etc.: as a mediaeval Roman numeral, Z = 2000. See also under **cedilla, zed** and **zeta**[1].

zabaglione zä-bäl-yō'ni, n. a frothy custard made from egg yolks, marsala and sugar. — Also **zabaione** (-bə-yō'ni). [It.]

zabeta za-bē'ta, (Ar.) n. a stated tariff.

Zabian zā'bi-ən, adj. and n. Same as **Sabian**.

zabra zä'brä, (hist.) n. a small vessel on the Spanish coast. [Sp.]

zabtieh. Same as **zaptieh**.

zack zak, (Austr. slang) n. formerly a sixpenny, now a five-cent, piece.

zaddik, tsaddik, tsaddiq, tzaddik, tzaddiq, tsad'ik, n. in Judaism, a Hasidic leader, or person of extraordinary piety: — *pl.* **zaddikim,** etc. or **zadd'iks,** etc. [Heb. *saddīq*, righteous, just.]

Zadkiel zad'ki-əl, n. the name assumed by Richard James Morrison (1794–1874), compiler of a popular astrological almanac.

zag zag n. a new line, or sharp change, of direction on a zigzag course. — Also *v.i.*: — *pr.p.* **zagg'ing;** *pa.t.* and *pa.p.* **zagged.** [-zag extracted from **zigzag.**]

zaffre, zaffer zaf'ər, n. the impure oxide (used as a pigment) obtained by partially roasting cobalt ore previously mixed with two or three times its weight of fine sand. [Fr. *zafre*, of Ar. origin.]

zaire zä-ēr', n. the standard unit of currency of *Zaire*, a republic of central Africa: — *pl.* **zaire'.** — *adj.* **Zairean** (-ē'ri-ən), adj. of or relating to Zaire. — n. a native of Zaire.

zakuska zä-koos'ka, n. an hors-d'œuvre: a snack: — *pl.* **zakuski** (-kē). [Russ.]

zalambdodont za-lam'dō-dont, adj. having molar teeth with V-shaped ridges, as some Insectivora. — Also n. [Gr. *za-*, very, *lambda*, the letter Λ (= L), *odous*, *odontos*, a tooth.]

Zalophus zal'ō-fəs, n. a genus of eared seals. [Gr. *za-*, intens., *lophos*, a crest.]

zaman zə-män', **zamang** zə-mäng', ns. the saman, rain-tree. [Carib.]

zamarra, zamarro thä-mär'ä, -ō, (Sp.) ns. a shepherd's sheepskin coat: — *pls.* **-s.**

Zambian zam'bi-ən, adj. of or pertaining to the republic of *Zambia* (formerly Northern Rhodesia) in central Africa. — n. a native of Zambia.

zambo zam'bō, n. the offspring of a Negro man and an American Indian woman: anyone of mixed Negro and Indian blood: — *pl.* **zam'bos.** [Sp.]

zambomba thäm-bom'bä, n. a simple Spanish musical instrument, made by stretching a piece of parchment over a wide-mouthed jar and inserting a stick in it, sounded by rubbing the stick with the fingers. [Sp.]

zamboorak. Same as **zumboorak.**

Zamia zā'mi-ə, n. a genus of palm-like trees or low shrubs of the family *Cycadaceae* some species of which yield an edible starchy pith: (without *cap.*) a plant of this genus. [Named through misreading in Pliny *azaniae nuces*, pine cones that open on the tree — Gr. *azanein*, *azainein*, to dry.]

zamindar(i). Same as **zemindar(i).**

zamouse za-moos', n. the short-horned buffalo of West Africa. [Ar. *jāmūs.*]

zampogna tsam-pō'nyä, n. the Italian bagpipe. [It.]

zander zan'dər, n. Same as **sander.**

zanella zə-nel'ə, n. a mixed twilled fabric for covering umbrellas. [Origin uncertain.]

zanja thäng'hhä, n. an irrigating canal. — n. **zanjero** (-hhä'rō) one who superintends the distribution of water in irrigation canals: — *pl.* **zanje'ros.** [Sp.]

zante zan'tē, n. the same as **zan'te-wood,** the wood of the European smoke-tree, from *Zante*, one of the principal Ionian Islands: satinwood. — *ns.* **Zan'tiot** (-ot), **Zan'-tiote** (-ōt) a native of Zante. — **Zante currant** the small seedless fruit of a Zante grape.

Zantedeschia zan-ti-des'ki-ə, n. a genus of plants of the Araceae, including *Zantedeschia aethiopica*, known as calla lily. [Francesco *Zantedeschi*, Italian botanist.]

Zanthoxylum. Same as **Xanthoxylum.**

Zantiot(e). See **zante.**

Zantippe. See **Xantippe.**

zany zā'ni, n. an assistant clown or buffoon (hist.): a toady (arch.): a simpleton (dial.): one who plays the fool (coll.). — adj. of, or pertaining to, a zany: crazy, clownish (coll.). — v.t. to play the zany to. — n. **zā'nyism** the condition or habits of a buffoon. [Fr. *zani* — It. *zanni*, a corr. of *Giovanni*, John.]

zanze zän'ze, n. an African musical instrument. [Ar. *sanj*, castanets, cymbals.]

Zanzibari zan-zib-är'i, n. a native of Zanzibar.

zap zap, (coll.) v.t. to hit, strike, destroy, kill, etc. (lit. and fig.): to erase (comput.) to cause to move quickly. — v.i. to go speedily or suddenly: to keep changing television channels, using a remote-control device. — n. vitality, force. — interj. expressing suddenness. — adj. **zapp'y** (slang) showy, punchy, speedy, vigorous, or otherwise impressive. — **zap (it) up** to make (things) livelier. [Imit.]

zapata zə-pä'tə, adj. denoting a type of flowing moustache drooping down on each side of the mouth. [Emilio *Zapata*, Mexican revolutionary (1879–1919), who wore a moustache of this shape.]

zapateado thä-pä-te-ädh'ō, n. a lively Spanish dance, for a solo performer, with much clicking and stamping of the heels: — *pl.* **zapatead'os.** [Sp.]

Zapodidae za-pod'i-dē, n.pl. the jumping-mouse family. [Formed from Gr. *za-*, very, *pous*, *podos*, foot, and suff. *-idae*.]

Zaporogian zä-pō-rō'ji-ən, adj. pertaining to the Little Russian or Ukraine Cossacks dwelling near the Porogi or falls of the Dnieper. — n. one of these people. [Russ. *za*, beyond, and *porogi*, rapids.]

zapotilla zap-ō-til'ə, n. Same as **sapodilla.**

zaptieh zap'ti-e, n. a Turkish policeman. — Also **zap'tiah, zab'tieh.** [From Turk.]

zarape sä-rä'pe, n. Same as **serape.**

Zarathustrian zar-ə-thoos'tri-ən, adj. and n. Zoroastrian. — *ns.* **Zarathus'trianism, Zarathus'trism** Zoroastrianism. — adj. and n. **Zarathus'tric** Zoroastrian.

zaratite zä'rə-tīt, n. a hydrous carbonate of nickel, found usually as an incrustation on chromite. [From *Zárate*, a Spaniard.]

zareba zə-rē'bä, n. in the Sudan, a stockade, thorn-hedge, etc., against wild animals or enemies: a fortified camp generally. — Also **zaree'ba, zari'ba, zere'ba, zeri'ba.** [Ar. *zarībah*, pen or enclosure for cattle.]

zarf zärf, n. an ornamental holder for a hot coffee-cup. — Also **zurf.** [Ar. *zarf*, a vessel.]

zarnich zär'nik, n. a native sulphide of arsenic, as orpiment, realgar. — Also **zar'nec.** [Ar. *zarnīkh.*]

zarzuela thär-thoo-ä'lä, -thwä', n. a Spanish kind of operetta or vaudeville — named from the royal residence of La *Zarzuela*.

---

fāte; fär; hûr; mīne; mōte; fōr; mūte; moon; foot; dhen (then); el'ə-mənt (element)

zastruga *zas-trōō'gä*, *n.* one of a series of long parallel snow-ridges on open wind-swept regions of snow. — Also **sastru'ga:** — *pl.* **-gi** (*-gē*). [Russ.]

zati *zä'ti*, *n.* the bonnet-monkey.

zax. Variant of **sax**[1].

'zbud. See **'sblood.**

Zea *zē'ə*, *n.* a genus of cereals having monoecious flowers; the only species is *Zea mays*, maize or Indian corn: (without *cap.*) the fresh styles and stigmas of this plant, formerly used as a diuretic. [Gr. *zeā* or *zeia*, one-seeded wheat.]

zeal *zēl*, *n.* strong feeling, as love, anger, etc., or passionate ardour (*B.*): intense (sometimes fanatical) enthusiasm: activity arising from warm support or enthusiasm: a zealot (*obs.*). — *n.* **zeal'ant**, **zel'ant** (*Bacon*) a zealot. — *adjs.* **zeal'ful; zeal'less.** — *ns.* **zealot** (*zel'ət*) an enthusiast: a fanatic: (with *cap.*) one of a militant Jewish sect vigorously opposing the Roman domination of Palestine until the ruin of Jerusalem in 70 A.D; **zealotism** (*zel'*) the character of a zealot; **zealotry** (*zel'*). — *adj.* **zealous** (*zel'*) full of zeal: warmly engaged in, or ardent in support of, anything: devoted. — *adv.* **zealously** (*zel'*). — *n.* **zealousness** (*zel'*). [O.Fr. *zele* — L. *zēlus* — Gr. *zēlos* — *zeein*, to boil.]

zebec, zebeck. Variants of **xebec.**

zebra *zē'brə*, *zeʹbrə*, *n.* any of a group of striped animals of the genus *Equus* — all of which are peculiar to the African continent: any animal, fish, plant or mineral having stripes reminiscent of a zebra's. — *n.* **ze'brass** the offspring of a male zebra and a female ass. — *adjs.* **zē'brine**, **zē'broid.** — *ns.* **zebrinn'y** (cf. **hinny**) the offspring of a male horse and a female zebra; **ze'brule**, **ze'brula** the offspring of a male zebra and a female horse. — **zebra crossing** a stripe-marked street crossing where pedestrians have priority; **ze'bra-finch** an Australian weaver-bird with black and white striped markings; **ze'bra-par(r)'akeet** the budgerigar; **zebra spider** any of several striped spiders of the *Salticidae*; **ze'bra-wood** the hard and beautifully striped wood of a Guiana tree, *Connarus guianensis*: the tree itself: applied also to various other trees or their wood. [African.]

zebu *zē'bū*, *zē'bōō*, *n.* a humped domestic ox (*Bos indicus*) very nearly allied to the common ox, diffused over India, China, the east coast of Africa, etc. [Fr. *zébu*, the name taken by Buffon from the exhibitors of one at a French fair in 1752.]

zebub *zē'bub*, *n.* the zimb. [Ar. (dial.) *zubāb*, a fly.]

zecchino *tsek-kē'nō*, *n.* a gold coin, the sequin: — *pl.* **zecchi'nos** or **zecchi'ni** (*-ē*). — Also **zecchine** (*zek'ēn*). [See **sequin.**]

Zechstein *zek'stīn*, *n.* a deposit of calcareous rock, the higher of the two series into which the Permian System of Germany is divided. [Ger., — *Zeche*, mine, *Stein* stone.]

zed *zed*, in U.S. **zee** *zē*, *ns.* the twenty-sixth letter of the alphabet (Z, z): a bar of metal of form similar to the letter Z. [Fr. *zède* — L. and Gr. *zēta*.]

zedoary *zed'ō-ə-ri*, *n.* certain species of curcuma, natives of India, China, etc., whose rootstocks are aromatic, bitter, and pungent. [Through mediaeval L. — Ar. *zedwār*.]

zee *zē*. See **zed.**

Zeeman effect *zā'män if-ekt'*, the splitting of a spectral line into several symmetrically disposed components which occurs when the source of light is placed in a strong magnetic field. [Named from Dutch physicist Pieter *Zeeman* (1865–1943).]

zein *zē'in*, *n.* a protein found in Indian corn. [**Zea**.]

zeitgeist *tsīt'gīst*, *n.* the spirit of the age. [Ger.]

Zeitvertreib *tsīt'fər-trīp*, (Ger.) *n.* a pastime.

zek *zek*, *n.* an inmate of a U.S.S.R. prison or labour camp. [Russ. slang, poss. from abbrev. *zk* for *zaklyuchénnyi* prisoner.]

zel *zel*, *n.* a form of Oriental cymbal. [Turk. *zīl*.]

Zelanian *zə-lā'ni-ən*, *adj.* in zoogeography, pertaining to New Zealand.

zelant. See **zeal.**

zeloso *zel-ō'sō*, (*mus.*) *adv.* with fervour. [It.]

zelotypia *zel-ō-tip'i-ə*, *n.* jealousy: morbid zeal in the prosecution of any project or cause. [Gr. *zēlotypiā*, jealousy — *zēlos*, zeal, *typtein*, to strike.]

zemindar *zem-in-där'*, or *zem'*, *n.* under the Mogul emperors of India, the farmer of revenue from land held in common by the cultivators, as responsible for the revenue: later the actual native proprietor paying revenue direct, and not to any intermediate superior. — Also **zamindar.** — *n.* **zem'indary** the jurisdiction of a zemindar: the system of land-tenure and taxation under such. Also **zam'indari**, **zem'indari**, etc. [Hindi *zamīndār* — Pers. *zamīn*, land, and *-dar*, holder.]

zemstvo *zems'tvō*, *n.* in Russia, from 1864 until 1917, a district and provincial assembly to which the administration of certain of the affairs of the district and the province was committed: — *pl.* **zems'tvos.** [Russ.]

Zen *zen*, *n.* a Japanese Buddhist sect which holds that the truth is not in scriptures but in man's own heart if he will but strive to find it by meditation and self-mastery. — Also *adj.* — *adj.* **Zen'ic.** — *n.* **Zen'ist.** [Jap. — Chin. *ch'an* — Pali *jhāna*, Sans. *dhyāna*, religious contemplation.]

zenana *ze-nä'nə*, *n.* in India and Iran, apartments in which women are secluded, corresponding to the harem in Arabic-speaking Muslim lands. — **zenana mission** a mission to women of the zenanas, necessarily conducted by women. [Pers. *zanāna* — *zan*, a woman.]

Zend *zend*, *n.* the Avesta or Zend-Avesta: Avestan, the ancient East-Iranian Indo-European language in which the Zend-Avesta was long orally preserved and at last written — closely related to the Vedic Sanskrit. — **Zend-Aves'ta** (properly meaning the Avesta with the commentary on it), the ancient sacred writings of the Parsees, including works of widely differing character and age, collected into their present canon under Shah-puhar or Shah-pur II (309–338 A.D.). [Pers. *zend*, *zand*, commentary.]

zendik *zen'dik*, *n.* an unbeliever in revealed religion in the East: one who practises magic. [Ar. *zendīq*.]

Zener cards *zē'nər kärdz*, a set of 25 cards, consisting of five sets of five, each set having one symbol, used in parapsychological experimentation. [Invented by K.E. *Zener*, 1903–61, U.S. psychologist.]

Zener diode *zē'nər dī'ōd*, a type of semiconductor device, a diode whose sudden increase in reverse current makes it useful in voltage-limiting circuits. [C.M. *Zener*, U.S. physicist, born 1905.]

zenith *zen'ith*, U.S. *zēn'*, *n.* the point on the celestial sphere vertically above the observer's head, one of the two poles of the horizon, the other being the nadir: the greatest height (*lit.* and *fig.*). — *adj.* **zen'ithal.** — **zenithal projection** a type of projection in which the plane of projection is tangential to the sphere. — **zen'ith-dis'tance** the angular distance of a heavenly body from the zenith; **zen'ith-sec'tor** any of several instruments for measuring zenith-distances, used before the invention of the telescope. [O.Fr. *cenit(h)*, ultimately from Ar. *samt*, short for *samt-ar-ras*, lit. way, direction, of the head.]

Zentippe. See **Xantippe.**

zeolite *zē'ō-līt*, *n.* any of a large group of alumino-silicates of sodium, potassium, calcium, and barium, containing very loosely held water. — *adjs.* **zeolitic** (*-lit'*); **zeolit'iform.** — **zeolite process** a water-softening process using zeolites — formerly zeolites occurring naturally, now synthetic ones. [Gr. *zeein*, to boil (in allusion to the fact that many intumesce under the blowpipe), *lithos*, a stone.]

zephyr *zef'ər*, *n.* the west wind: a soft, gentle breeze: thin light worsted or woollen yarn: a shawl, jersey, or other garment made of such: any of various types of lightweight material, as a gingham, a flannel with a silk warp, a thin woollen cloth, etc.: anything very light and fine of its kind: (*cap.*) the god of the west wind. [Gr. *Zephyros*; akin to *zophos*, darkness, the west.]

zeppelin *zep′əl-in, n.* a dirigible, cigar-shaped airship of the type designed by Count *Zeppelin* (*c.* 1900).

zerda *zûr′də, n.* a fennec.   [Ar. *zardawa.*]

zereba, zeriba. Same as **zareba.**

Zernebock *zûr′nə-bok, n.* Czerni Bog, an evil god of the Slavs, wrongly described by Scott in *Ivanhoe* as a god 'of the ancient Saxons'.

zero *zē′rō, n.* a cipher: nothing: the point from which the reckoning begins on scales, such as those of the barometer, etc.: the lowest point (*fig.*): zero hour: — *pl.* **zē′ros.** — *v.t.* to set at, adjust to, zero. — *adj.* having no measurable size, amount, etc.: not any (*coll.*). — *adj.* **zē′rōth** denoting a term in a series regarded as preceding the 'first' term. — **ze′ro-coupon bond** a bond that carries no interest, but has a redemption price higher than its issue price; **ze′ro-grazing** a system of dairy farming in which the cattle are kept indoors and cut grass is brought to them, thus avoiding the wastage caused by conventional grazing; **zero hour** the exact time (hour, minute, and second) fixed for launching an attack or beginning an operation; **zero option** a proposal, originally made by President Reagan of the United States, to limit or abandon the deployment of (medium range) nuclear missiles if the opposing side does likewise. — *v.t.* **zē′ro-rate** to assess at a zero rate of value-added tax. — *adj.* **ze′ro-ra′ted** of goods on which the purchaser pays no value-added tax and on which the seller can claim back any value-added tax already paid by him. — **ze′ro-ra′ting.** — *adjs.* **ze′ro-sum** of a game, etc., in which the total cumulative gains equal the total cumulative losses; **ze′ro-valent** (*chem.*) incapable of combining with other atoms. — **absolute zero** see **absolute; zero-base(d) budgeting** a system in which the budget of an organisation, department, etc. is drawn up anew each year without reference to any previous budget; **zero in (on)** (*slang*) to direct oneself straight towards a target: to focus one's attention or energies on, as if on a target: to aim for, move towards. [Fr. *zéro* — Ar. *sifr*; cf. **cipher.**]

zerumbet *zə-rum′bet,* or *ze′, n.* an E. Indian drug, allied to cassumunar and zedoary.   [Pers. *zerunbād.*]

zest *zest, n.* orange or lemon peel, or the oil squeezed from it, used as a flavouring: anything that gives a relish: piquancy: relish: enthusiasm. — *adj.* **zest′ful.** — *adv.* **zest′fully.** — *n.* **zest′fulness.** — *adj.* **zest′y.** [Fr. *zeste*, orig. the woody thick skin quartering a walnut; origin obscure.]

zeta¹ *zē′tə, n.* the Greek z (Z, ζ): as a numeral ζ′ = 7; ζ = 7000.

zeta² *zē′tə,* (*hist.*) *n.* a small room or closet of some kind, as perh. the sexton's room over a church porch.   [Gr. *diaita,* a dwelling.]

Zeta *zē′tə, n.* British equipment for research into fusion reactions and aspects of plasma physics.   [*zero energy thermonuclear apparatus.*]

zetetic *zē-tet′ik, adj.* proceeding by inquiry. — *n.* a search, investigation: a seeker, the name taken by some of the Pyrrhonists.   [Gr. *zētētikos* — *zēteein,* to seek.]

Zeuglodon *zū′glō-don, n.* a genus of fossil whales, so named from the yoke-like double-rooted formation of their cheek teeth. — *adj.* and *n.* **zeug′lodont.** — *n.pl.* **Zeuglodon′tia** a suborder of Cetacea, represented by the zeuglodonts.   [Gr. *zeuglē,* the strap or loop of the yoke, *odous, -ontos,* a tooth.]

zeugma *zūg′mə, n.* a figure of speech by which an adjective or verb is applied to two nouns, though strictly appropriate to only one of them. — *adj.* **zeugmat′ic.** [Gr., — *zeugnynai,* to yoke.]

Zeus *zūs, n.* the greatest of the national deities of Greece, son of Kronos (Saturn) and Rhea. His consort was Hera; his supreme seat, Mount Olympus in Thessaly. [Gr.]

Zeuxian *zūk′si-ən, adj.* pertaining to Zeuxis, styled 'of 'Heraclea' and 'of Ephesus' (*fl. c.* 420–400 B.C.), a Greek painter who excelled in accuracy of imitation of natural objects and in rendering types of sensuous beauty.

zeuxite *zūk′sīt, n.* a ferriferous tourmaline.   [Gr. *zeuxis,* joining — *zeugnynai,* to join.]

zeze *zā′zā, n.* a stringed musical instrument played in countries of eastern and central Africa.   [Swahili.]

Zezidee. See **Yezidi.**

zho *zhō, n.* one, esp. the male, of a kind of hybrid domestic cattle in parts of the Himalayas — said to be a cross between the male yak and the common horned cow. — Also **zo, dso** and **dzo** (*dzō*). — *ns.* **zhomo** (*zhō′mō*) the female of this cross. — Also **dsō′mo, jō′mo; zō′bō** the male of this cross. — Also **zō′bu, dsō′bō.** — Pl. in all cases **-s.**   [Tibetan *mdzo.*]

zibel(l)ine *zib′ə-lin, -līn, adj.* pertaining to the sable. — *n.* the fur of the sable: (*zib′ə-lēn*) a soft woollen material with a lustrous pile.   [Fr., — It. *zibellino,* prob. from Slav.; cf. **sable.**]

zibet *zib′it, n.* an Asiatic civet.   [It. *zibetto* — Ar. *zabād*; cf. **civet.**]

ziff *zif,* (*Austr. slang*) *n.* a beard, goatee.   [Ety. unknown.]

ziffius *zif′i-əs,* (*Spens.*) *n.* a sea-monster, perh. a swordfish.   [Cf. **Xiphias, Ziphius.**]

zig *zig, n.* a new line, or sharp change, of direction on a zigzag course. — Also *v.i.:* — *pr.p.* **zigg′ing;** *pa.t.* and *pa.p.* **zigged.**   [**zig-** extracted from **zigzag.**]

zigan *zi-gan′, n.* Variant of **tzigany.**

ziganka *zi-gang′kə, n.* a Russian country-dance: the music for such, usu. quick, with a drone bass.   [Russ. *tsyganka,* a gypsy woman.]

Zigeuner *tsi-goi′nər,* (Ger.) *n.* a gypsy: — *pl.* **Zigeu′ner.**

ziggurat *zig′ŏŏ-rat, n.* a Babylonian temple-tower, pyramidal in general shape, consisting of a number of storeys each successive one of which was smaller than that below it. — Also **zikkurat** (*zik′*).   [Assyrian *ziqquratu,* a pinnacle, top of a mountain.]

zigzag *zig′zag, n.* a short, sharp turning: a line, road, fence, moulding, with sharp angles to right and left alternately. — *adj.* having short, sharp alternate turns: bent from side to side alternately. — *v.t.* to form with short, alternate turns. — *v.i.* to move forward making an alternation of short, sharp turns: — *pr.p.* **zig′-zagging;** *pa.t.* and *pa.p.* **zig′zagged.** — *adv.* with frequent sharp turns. — also **zig′zaggy.** — *n.* **zigzagg′ery** angular crookedness. — *adj.* **zig′zaggy** zigzag.   [Fr. *zigzag*; Ger. *Zickzack.*]

zikkurat. Same as **ziggurat.**

zilch *zilch,* (*slang*) *n.* zero, nothing.   [Origin unknown.]

zillah, zila *zil′a, n.* an administrative district in India.   [Ar. *dila* (in Hindi pronunciation, *zila*), a rib, thence a side, a district.]

zillion *zil′yən,* (*coll.*) *n.* an extremely large but unspecified number, many millions — analogous in formation and use to *million, billion.* — *n.* and *adj.* **zill′ionth.**

zimb *zimb, n.* an Ethiopian dipterous insect, like the tsetse, hurtful to cattle.   [Amharic, a fly.]

Zimbabwean *zim-bä′bwi-ən, adj.* of or pertaining to the Republic of Zimbabwe (formerly Rhodesia) in southern Africa. — *n.* a native of Zimbabwe.

zimbi *zim′bi, n.* a kind of cowrie used as money.   [Port. *zimbo*; of African origin.]

Zimmer® *zim′ər, n.* a metal frame held in front of one, used as an aid to walking. — Also without *cap.* [Name of original manufacturer.]

zimocca *zi-mok′ə, n.* a type of bath-sponge.   [Mod. L.]

zinc *zingk, n.* a bluish-white metallic element (Zn; at. numb. 30), resistant to atmospheric corrosion, it is a constituent of several alloys (e.g. brass) and is used in galvanising, battery electrodes, etc. — Also *adj.* — *v.t.* to coat with zinc: — *pr.p.* **zincing** (*zingk′ing*), **zinck′ing, zink′ing;** *pa.t.* and *pa.p.* **zinced** (*zingkt*), **zincked, zinked.** — *adj.* **zincif′erous** (*zingk-*), **zinkif′erous** containing or producing zinc. — *ns.* **zincite** (*zingk′īt*) a native oxide of zinc, brittle, translucent, deep red; **zinc(k)ifica′tion, zinkifica′tion** the process of coating or impregnating an object with zinc. — *v.t.* **zinc(k)′ify, zink′ify** to cover or impregnate with zinc. — *adj.* **zinc(k)′y, zink′y** pertaining to, containing, or looking like, zinc. — *ns.*

zinco (*zing'kō*) a line block executed in zinc, i.e. the normal line block: — *pl.* **zinc'os; zinc'ode** (*obs.*) an anode; **zinc'ograph** a plate or picture produced by zincography; **zincographer** (*-kog'rə-fər*). — *adjs.* **zincograph'ic, -al.** — *n.* **zincography** (*-kog'rə-fi*) an engraving process in which zinc is covered with wax and etched: any process in which designs for printing are made on zinc plates. — *adj.* **zinc'oid** like zinc. — *n.* **zincol'ysis** (*obs.*) electrolysis. — *adj.* **zinc'ous** pertaining to, or like, zinc. — **zinc'-blende** sphalerite, native sulphide of zinc; **zinc'-bloom** basic zinc carbonate, hydrozincite; **zinc'-colic** a colic caused by the slow poison of zinc oxide; **zinc ointment** a mixture of zinc oxide and suitable ointment base (wool fat, petroleum jelly, etc.); **zinc oxide** a whitish solid, much used as a paint pigment in the rubber and other industries, and also medicinally, as an antiseptic and astringent (also called **flowers of zinc**); **zinc white** zinc oxide used as a pigment; **zinc'-worker.** [Ger. *Zink*; origin unknown.]

Zincalo *zing'kə-lō, n.* a name in Spain for a gypsy: — *fem.* **Zin'cala,** *pl.* **Zin'cali.** [Sp. Romany name.]

zineb *zin'əb, n.* an organic fungicide and insecticide sprayed on cereal grasses, fruit trees, etc. [*Zinc* ethylene *b*isdithiocarbamate, its chemical name.]

Zinfandel, zinfandel *zin'fən-dəl, n.* a black wine-grape of California: the wine produced from it. [Origin obscure.]

zing *zing, n.* a short shrill humming sound, as made by a bullet or vibrating string: zest, spirit, vitality, etc. (*coll.*). — *v.i.* to move very swiftly, esp. with a high-pitched hum. — *adj.* **zing'y** (*coll.*) full of zest, etc. [Imit.]

Zingaro *zing'gə-rō, n.* a name in Italy for a gypsy: — *pl.* **Zing'ari;** *fem.* **Zing'ara,** *pl.* **Zing'are.** — Also **Zing'ano,** etc. [Cf. **Zincalo; Zigeuner.**]

zingel *tsing'əl, zing'əl, n.* a fish of the perch family, found in the Danube. [Ger.]

Zingiberaceae *zin-ji-bə-rā'sē-ē, n.pl.* any of a family of perennial tropical monocotyledonous herbs, with horizontal thickened rootstock and cone-like inflorescence. — *n.* **Zin'giber** the typical genus of this family, *Zingiber officinale* being the common ginger: (without *cap.*) any plant of this genus. — *adjs.* **zingibera'ceous, zinzibera'ceous.** [L. *zingiber* — Gr. *zingiberis,* ginger.]

zingy. See **zing.**

Zinjanthropus. See **nutcracker man** at **nut.**

zinke *tsing'kə, n.* an old wind instrument like the cornet. [Ger.]

zinked, zinkify, etc. See **zinc.**

zinkenite *zingk'ən-īt, n.* a steel-grey mineral, essentially sulphide of lead and antimony. [J. K. L. *Zincken,* a mine director.]

Zinnia *zin'i-ə, n.* a genus of American composite plants: (without *cap.*) any plant of this genus. [From J. G. *Zinn,* botanist (1727–59).]

zinziberaceous. See **Zingiberaceae.**

Zion *zī'ən, n.* Jerusalem: the Israelitish theocracy: the Christian Church: heaven. — *ns.* **Zī'onism** the movement which secured national privileges and territory in Palestine for the Jews and which now helps to maintain and develop the state of Israel; **Zī'onist** a supporter of Zionism. — *adv.* **Zī'onward** heavenward. [Heb. *tsīyōn,* orig. the name of a part of one of the hills of Jerusalem.]

zip *zip, n.* the ping or sound of a bullet striking an object or whizzing through the air: a whizzing sound: a zip-fastener: energy, vigour (*coll.*). — *v.i.* and *v.t.* to whizz: to fasten with a zip: to be full of, act with, proceed with, or (usu. **zip up**) infuse with, life and energy (*coll.*): — *pr.p.* **zipp'ing;** *pa.t.* and *pa.p.* **zipped.** *n.* **zipp'er** a zip-fastener. — *adjs.* **zipp'ered** provided with a zip-fastener; **zipp'y** (*coll.*) quick, energetic, lively. — **zip-fastener** (*zip-fäs'nər*) a fastening device for clothes, etc., on which two sets of teeth can be opened or interlocked by pulling a slide. — *adjs.* **zip'-front, zip'-neck, zip'top,** etc. having the front-,

neck- or top-opening, etc. fastened with a zip; **zip'-on, zip'-off, zip'-in,** etc. able to be added, removed, inserted, etc. by means of a zip. [Imit.]

zip code *zip cōd, (U.S.)* the postal code. [*z*one *i*mprovement *p*lan.]

Ziphius *zif'i-əs, n.* a genus of whales, giving name to the family **Ziphī'idae,** the beaked whales. [Gr. *xiphios,* sword-fish — *xiphos,* sword.]

zircon *zûr'kən, n.* a tetragonal mineral, zirconium silicate, of which jacinth and jargoon are varieties. — *ns.* **zircall'oy** an alloy of zirconium with tin, chromium and nickel, widely used (esp. in the nuclear power industry) for its heat- and corrosion-resistant properties; **zircō'nia** oxide of zirconium. — *adj.* **zirconic** (*-kon'*) of zirconium. — *n.* **zircō'nium** a metallic element (Zr; at. numb. 40), highly resistant to corrosion. — **cubic zirconia** a synthetic stone used as a diamond substitute, produced from zirconia heated with any of various stabilising metallic oxides. [Ar. *zarqūn* — Pers. *zargūn,* gold-coloured; cf. **jargoon.**]

zit *zit, (slang*; esp. *U.S.) n.* a spot, pimple. [Origin obscure.]

zither *zidh', zith'ər, n.* a stringed instrument having a wooden frame and flat sounding-board with from twenty-nine to forty-two metal strings, placed on a table or on the knees, the strings being played by a plectrum on the right thumb. — Also **zith'ern.** [Ger.]

ziz. See **zizz.**

Zizania *zi-* or *zī-zā'ni-ə, n.* a genus of tall aquatic grasses, known as **wild, water, Indian,** or **Canada rice** (ordinary cultivated rice is of genus *Oryza*). [Gr. *zizanion,* darnel.]

zizel *ziz'əl, n.* the ground-squirrel. [Ger. *Ziesel.*]

Zizyphus *ziz'i-fəs, n.* a genus of shrubs of the buckthorn family, the jujube trees. [L., jujube tree.]

zizz, ziz *ziz, (slang) n.* a nap, sleep. — Also *v.i.* [Representation of *z-z-z-z...,* the conventional phoneticisation of snoring used in strip cartoons, etc.]

zloty *zlot'i, zwot'ŭ, n.* the monetary unit of Poland. — *pl.* **zloty, zlotys.** [Pol. *zloty,* lit. golden.]

zo. See **zho.**

zoa. See **zoon** under **zoo-.**

Zoantharia *zō-an-thā'ri-ə, n.pl.* an order of Anthozoa the members of which may be either solitary or colonial and possess either six, or more than eight, simple tentacles including sea-anemones and many corals. — *adj.* and *n.* **zoanthā'rian.** [Mod. L., — Gr. *zōion,* animal, *anthos,* flower.]

zoanthropy *zō-an'thrə-pi, n.* a form of mental delusion in which a man believes himself to be a beast. — *adj.* **zōanthropic** (*-throp'*). [Gr. *zōion,* animal, *anthrōpos,* man.]

Zoanthus *zō-an'thəs, n.* the typical genus of **Zoan'thidae** (*-ē*), a family of Anthozoa permanently attached by their bases and having no solid skeleton. [Gr. *zōion,* an animal, *anthos,* a flower.]

zoarium *zō-ā'ri-əm, n.* the zooids of a polyzoan colony collectively. [Gr. *zōarion,* dim. of *zōion,* an animal.]

zobo, zobu. See **zho.**

zocco *zok'ō, n.* a socle. — Also **zocc'olo:** — *pls.* **zocc'os, zocc'olos.** [It. *zocco, zoccolo;* see **socle.**]

zodiac *zō'di-ak, n.* an imaginary belt in the heavens, about 18° wide, through which the ecliptic passes centrally, and which forms the background of the motions of the sun, moon, and planets; it is divided into twelve equal parts of 30° called **signs of the zodiac,** named from the constellations that once corresponded to them but do so no longer. The constellations, with the appropriate symbols of the corresponding signs, are as follows: Aries (*Ram*), ♈; Taurus (*Bull*), ♉; Gemini (*Twins*), ♊; Cancer (*Crab*), ♋; Leo (*Lion*), ♌; Virgo (*Virgin*), ♍; Libra (*Balance*), ♎; Scorpio (*Scorpion*), ♏; Sagittarius (*Archer*), ♐; Capricornus (*Goat*), ♑; Aquarius (*Water-bearer*), ♒; Pisces (*Fishes*), ♓: a year (*obs.*): a set of twelve, or a recurrent series or course (*fig.*). — *adj.* **zodī'acal.** — **zodiacal light** a faint illumination of the sky, lenticular in form and elongated in the direction of the ecliptic on either side of the sun, fading away at about 90° from it; best seen after sunset or before sunrise in the tropics. [Fr. *zodiaque* — L. *zōdiacus* — Gr. *zōidiakos*, of figures — *zōidion*, a small carved or painted figure — *zōion*, an animal.]

zoea *zō-ē'ə*, *n.* a larval stage of certain decapod crustaceans, e.g. of crabs. — Also **zooea** (*zō-ē'ə*). — *pl.* **zoē'ae** (also **zoē'as**). — *adjs.* **zoē'al, zooē'al; zō'eform.** [Gr. *zōē*, life.]

zoechrome. See **zoetrope.**

zoetic *zō-et'ik*, *adj.* pertaining to life, vital. [Gr. *zōē*, life.]

zoetrope *zō'i-trōp*, *n.* the 'wheel of life', an instrument in which figures on the inside of a rotating cylinder are made visible through slots and provide an illusion of animated motion: (also **zō'echrome**) any of several early processes for colour cinematography, using rapidly repeated images of the selected colours in sequence on a screen, the synthesis arising from persistence of vision in the eye. — *adj.* **zoetropic** (-*trop'ik*). [Gr. *zōē*, life, *tropos*, a turning — *trepein*, to turn, *chrōma*, colour.]

Zohar *zō'här*, *n.* one of the most important cabbalistic texts, being an allegorical interpretation of the Pentateuch. [Heb., brightness, splendour.]

zoiatria *zō-i-at'ri-ə*, *zō-i-ə-trī'ə*, *n.*, **zoiatrics** *zō-i-at'riks*, *n.sing.* veterinary surgery. [Gr. *zōion*, an animal, *iātreiā*, healing.]

zoic *zō'ik*, *adj.* pertaining to animals: of rocks, containing evidences of life, in the form of fossils. [Gr. *zōikos*, of animals — *zōion*, an animal.]

Zoilism *zō'i-lizm*, *n.* carping and unjust criticism. — *adj.* **Zoil'ean** characteristic of *Zoilus*, a Greek grammarian who flourished in the time of Philip of Macedon, and assailed Homer with such asperity that his name became proverbial for a captious and malignant critic. — *n.* **Zō'ilist** a carping critic.

zoisite *zois'īt*, *zō'is-īt*, *n.* an orthorhombic mineral closely allied to epidote. [Baron S. *Zois* von Edelstein (1747–1819), Slovenian nobleman.]

zoism *zō'izm*, *n.* the doctrine that life originates from a specific vital principle. — *n.* **zō'ist** one who maintains this theory. [Gr. *zōē*, life.]

Zolaism *zō'lä-izm*, *n.* the literary principles and practice of the French novelist Émile *Zola* (1840–1902), who aimed at what he called 'naturalism' (q.v.).

Zöllner's lines *tsæl'nərz līnz*, rows of parallel lines appearing to be not parallel through the optical effect of oblique intersecting lines. — Also **Zöllner's illusion, pattern.** [J. K. F. *Zöllner* (1834–82), German physicist.]

Zollverein *tsol'fər-īn*, *n.* a customs union: a union of the German states, under the leadership of Prussia, to enable them to act as one state in their commercial relations with other countries (*hist.*). [Ger., *Zoll*, duty, *Verein*, union.]

zombi, zombie *zom'bi*, *n.* orig. in Africa, the deity of the python: in American voodooism, the snake deity: a corpse reanimated by sorcery: the power supposed to enter such a body: a stupid or useless person: a very slow-moving, lethargic person. — *n.* **zom'biism** belief in a zombi, or practice of rites associated with it. [W. African *zumbi*, fetish.]

zomboruk. Same as **zumbooruk.**

zona(e), zonal, zonary, etc. See under **zone.**

zonda *son'də*, *n.* a dry, hot, and dusty wind blowing from the Andes across the Argentine pampas, during July and August. [Sp.; perh. from Amer. Indian.]

zone *zōn*, *n.* a girdle, a belt, an encircling stripe of different colour or substance: one of the five great belts into which the surface of the earth is divided by the tropics and arctic and antarctic circles: any continuous tract with particular characteristics: a region: a group of strata characterised by a distinctive fauna or flora, and bearing the name of one fossil, called the **zonal index** (*geol.*): a set of crystal faces all parallel to the same line (the **zonal, zone axis**): that part of the surface of

a sphere between two parallel planes, intersecting the sphere (*math.*). — *v.t.* to encircle, as with a zone: to mark with zones, divide into, or assign to, zones. — *n.* **zō'na** (*pl.* **zō'nae -ē**) a girdle: a zone: an area, patch, strip, or band (*zool.*): herpes zoster. — *adj.* **zō'nal,** **zō'nary** like a zone: arranged in zones: pertaining to a zone; **zō'nate(d)** marked with zones, belted. — *n.* **zonā'tion** (*bot.*) the formation of bands differentiated by colour or other characteristics, or the arrangement of such bands: the occurrence of vegetation in well-marked bands, each band having its characteristic dominant species. — *adjs.* **zoned** wearing a zone: having zones; **zone'less.** — *n.* **zō'ning** division into zones: assignment according to zones. — *adj.* **zō'noid** like a zone. — *ns.* **Zonotrichia** (*zō-nō-trik'i-ə*; Gr. *thrix, trichos*, hair) a genus of American sparrows, some with white or golden crowns; **zō'nula** a small zone. — *adj.* **zō'nular** like a zone or zonule. — *ns.* **zon'ule, zon'ulet** a little zone or girdle; **Zonurus** (*zō-nū'rəs*; Gr. *ourā*, tail) a tropical African genus of lizards with tail ringed with spiny scales, giving name to the family **Zonu'ridae.** — **zona pellucida** the transparent outer layer of an ovum; **zonal defence** (*football*, etc.) a method of defending in which a player patrols a particular area of the field rather than marking a specific opponent; **zone'-ticket** a railway ticket available for a time between any stations of a group. [L. *zōna* — Gr. *zōnē*, a girdle — *zōnnynai*, to gird.]

zonked *zongkt*, (*slang*) *adj.* utterly exhausted: intoxicated: under the influence of drugs. [Origin unknown.]

zoo- *zō-ō-*, *zō-o'-*, **zō-** *zō-*, in composition, esp. in zool. terms, etc., animal. — *n.* **zoo** (*zōō*) orig., the Zoological Gardens, London: now any similar collection of animals. — *adj.* **zoobiotic** (*zō-ō-bī-ot'ik*) parasitic on, or living in association with, an animal. — *n.* **zooblast** (*zō'ō-blast*; Gr. *blastos*, a germ) an animal cell. — *adj.* **zōochem'ical.** — *n.* **zōochem'istry** the chemistry of the animal body. — *adj.* **zoochorous** (*zō-ō-kōr'əs, -kōr'*; Gr. *chōreein*, to spread) of spores or seeds, dispersed by animals. — *ns.* **zō'ochore; zō'ochory** the condition of being dispersed by animals; **zō'oculture** (*U.S.*) the domestication and control of animals; **zōocytium** (*-sish'i-əm*; Gr. *kytos*, a hollow vessel) a zoothecium: — *pl.* **zōocyt'ia; zōoden'drium** (*zool.*) the branched stalk connecting the members of the colony in certain colonial Infusoria; **zooecium** (*zō-ē'shi-əm*; Gr. *oikiā*, a house) the body-wall or enclosing chamber of a polyzoan individual: — *pl.* **zooe'cia; zō'ogamete** a motile gamete. — *adj.* **zoogamous** (*zō-og'ə-məs*; Gr. *gamos*, marriage) pertaining to zoogamy. — *ns.* **zōog'amy** sexual reproduction of animals; **zoogeny** (*zō-oj'ə-ni*; Gr. -*geneia*, suff. denoting production) the doctrine, or the process, of the origination of living beings — also **zoogony** (-*og'*). — *adjs.* **zōogenic** (-*jen'*), **zōog'enous** produced from animals. — *n.* **zoog'rapher.** — *adjs.* **zōogeograph'ic, -al.** — *ns.* **zōogeog'raphy** the science of the distribution of animals on the surface of the globe; **zōogloea** (-*glē'ə*; Gr. *gloiā*, glue) a mucilaginous mass of bacteria embedded in slimy material derived from swollen cell walls. — *adjs.* **zōogloe'ic; zōogloe'oid.** — *n.* **zōogonid'ium** a swarm-spore: — *pl.* **zōogonid'ia.** — *adj.* **zoog'onous** (*zool.*) viviparous. — *ns.* **zōog'ony** zoogeny; **zō'ograft** (-*gräft*) a piece of tissue from the living body of an animal grafted on the human body; **zō'ografting; zōog'rapher, zōog'raphist** one who pursues **zoog'raphy,** the study or description of animals and their habits, or, the painting of animals. — *adjs.* **zōograph'ic, -al.** — *ns.* **zooid** (*zō'oid*; Gr. *eidos*, form) earlier, a free-moving cell, as a sperm-cell: in alternation of generations, an individual of an asexually-produced form: usu., an individual forming part of a colonial organism. — *adj.* **zōoid'al.** — *ns.* **zōol'ater** (Gr. *latreiā*, worship) one who worships animals; **zōolatr'īa, zōol'atry** worship of animals. — *adj.* **zōol'atrous.** — *n.* **zoolite** (*zō'ō-līt*; Gr. *lithos*, a stone) a fossil animal. — Also **zō'olith.** — *adjs.* **zōolith'ic, zōolit'ic; zoological** (*zō-ō-loj'i-kl*, or *zōō-ō-*;

zoological garden, park a garden or park where living wild animals are kept, studied and exhibited). — *adv.* **zōolog′ically.** — *ns.* **zool′ogist** (*zō-*, or *zōō-*) one versed in zoology (*zō-ol′ə-ji*, or *zōō-ol′*), the science of animal life included along with botany in the science of biology. — *adj.* **zōomagnet′ic.** — *ns.* **zōomag′netism** animal magnetism; **zoomancy** (*zō′ō-man-si*; Gr. *manteiā*, divination) divination by observation of animals. — *adjs.* **zōōman′tic; zōōmet′ric.** — *ns.* **zōometry** (*-om′ə-tri*; Gr. *metron*, a measure) comparative measurement of the parts of animals; **zō′omorph** (*-mörf*; Gr. *morphē*, form) in art, a representation of an animal form: an image or symbol of a god, etc., who is conceived as having an animal form. — *adj.* **zōomor′phic** pertaining to zoomorphism: representing animals in art. — *ns.* **zōomor′phism** the representation, or the conception, of a god or a man in an animal form. — Also **zōomor′phy; zō′on** a morphological individual, the total product of a fertilised ovum, or the group of zooids constituting a compound animal: — *pl.* **zō′a, zō′ons.** — *adjs.* **zō′onal** like a zoon; **zōon′ic** relating to animals. — *n.* **zō′onite** one of the segments of an articulated animal. — *adjs.* **zōonit′ic; zōonom′ic.** — *ns.* **zōon′omist; zoonomy** (*zō-on′ə-mi*; Gr. *nomos*, law) animal physiology. — Also **zōonō′mia; zoonosis** (*zō-on′ə-sis*; Gr. *nosos*, disease) a disease communicated to man from the lower animals, as hydrophobia, etc.: a disease due to animal parasites: — *pl.* **zōon′osēs.** — *adj.* **zōonot′ic.** — *ns.* **zōopathol′ogy** the study of disease in animals; **zoopathy** (*zō-op′ə-thi*; Gr. *pathos*, suffering) animal pathology. — *adj.* **zōop′eral.** — *ns.* **zōop′erist; zōop′ery** (Gr. *peirā*, experiment) experimentation on animals. — *n.pl.* **Zoophaga** (*zō-of′ə-gə*; Gr. *phagein*, to eat) the carnivorous animals collectively. — *n.* **zōoph′agan** a carnivorous animal. — *adj.* **zōoph′agous** or relating to the Zoophaga: feeding on animals. — *ns.* **zō′ophile** (*-fīl*; Gr. *philos*, loving) a zoophilist: a zoophilous plant; **zōophil′ia, zōoph′ilism, zōoph′ily** love of animals: erotic fondness for animals; **zoophilist** (*zō-of′il-ist*) a lover of animals: one who has zoophilia. — *adj.* **zōoph′ilous** loving animals: experiencing zoophilia: pollinated by animals other than insects (*bot.*): of insects, feeding on animals (*zool.*). — *n.* **zōophōb′ia** (Gr. *phobos*, fear) dread of animals, or of animal ghosts. — *adj.* **zōoph′obous.** — *n.* **zōophorus** (*-of′ə-rəs*; Gr. *pherein*, to bear) a continuous frieze sculptured in relief with figures of men and animals. — *adj.* **zōophoric** (*-för′*). — *n.pl.* **Zoophyta** (*zō-of′it-ə*; Gr. *phyton*, plant) in older classifications, a group of invertebrates having no power of locomotion, as sponges, corals, etc. — *n.* **zō′ophyte** (*-fīt*) any plant supposed to resemble an animal (*obs.*): (now old-fashioned) any of numerous invertebrates resembling plants, as sponges, corals, sea-anemones, etc., esp. hydroid colonies of a branched form. — *adjs.* **zōophytic** (*-fit′*), **-al; zōoph′ytoid; zōophytolog′ical** (*-fīt-*). — *ns.* **zōophytol′ogist; zōophytol′ogy; zōoplank′ton** floating and drifting animal life. — *adj.* **zōoplas′tic** (Gr. *plassein*, to form) pertaining to **zō′oplasty**, the operation of transplanting living tissue from one of the lower animals to man. — *n.* **zōopsychology** (*zō-ō-sī-kol′ə-ji*) the psychology of the lower animals. — *adj.* **zōoscop′ic.** — *ns.* **zōoscopy** (*-os′kop-i*; Gr. *skopeein*, to look at) a form of mental delusion in which one sees imaginary animals, esp. snakes; **zō′osperm** (Gr. *sperma*, seed) a spermatozoid: a zoospore. — Also **zōosper′mium.** — *adj.* **zōospermat′ic.** — *ns.* **zōosporan′gium** (*bot.*) a sporangium in which zoospores are formed; **zō′ospore** (Gr. *sporos*, a seed) a swarm-spore: an asexual reproductive cell that can swim by means of flagella. — *adjs.* **zōospor′ic; zōos′porous.** — *ns.* **zō′otaxy** (Gr. *taxis*, arrangement) the science of the classification of animals, systematic zoology; **zōotechnics** (*-tek′niks*; Gr. *technē*, art) **zō′otechny** the science of the breeding and domestication of animals; **zōothap′sis** (Gr. *thaptein*, to bury) premature burial: — *pl.* **zōothap′sēs** (*-sēz*). — *adj.* **zōothē′cial** (*-shi-*). — *ns.* **zōothecium** (*-thē′shi-əm*,

or *-si-*; Gr. *thēkion*, casket, dim. of *thēkē*, box) the tubular sheath of certain social infusorians: — *pl.* **zōothē′cia; zōothē′ism** the attribution of divine qualities to an animal. — *adj.* **zōotheis′tic.** — *ns.* **zōother′apy** (Gr. *therapeiā*, treatment) veterinary therapeutics; **zō′othome** (Gr. *thōmos*, heap) a group of zooids, as a mass of coral. — *adjs.* **zōotom′ic, -al.** — *adv.* **zōotom′ically.** — *ns.* **zōot′omist** (Gr. *tomē*, a cut) one who dissects the bodies of animals, an anatomist; **zōot′omy** the dissection of animals: comparative anatomy; **zōotox′in** a toxin produced by an animal, as a snake; **zō′otrope** a zoetrope. — *adj.* **zōotrophic** (*-trof′ik*; Gr. *trophos*, food) pertaining to the nourishment of animals. — *ns.* **zōot′rophy; zō′otype** an animal serving as a type. — *adj.* **zōotypic** (*-tip′ik*). [Gr. *zōion*, animal.]

zooea(l). See **zoea.**

zooks *zōōks,* *interj.* Same as **gadzooks.**

zoom *zōōm,* *v.i.* to make a loud, deep, persistent buzzing noise: to move with this sound: to move very quickly: to use the stored energy of the forward motion of an aircraft in order to gain height (*aero.*): to soar (*fig.*): to change focus rapidly, as with a zoom lens. — *v.t.* to cause to zoom. — *n.* the act of zooming: a zooming noise. — **zoom lens** a lens of variable focal length used, e.g., for bringing television, cinematograph, or cine-camera pictures from distance to close-up without moving the camera: a similar lens used in still cameras and in microscopes. [Imit.]

zoon politikon *zō′on po-lit′i-kon,* (Gr.) (said of a human being) a political animal.

zoot suit *zōōt sūt, sōōt,* a flashy type of man's suit with padded shoulders, fitted waist, knee-length coat, and trousers narrow at the ankles (introduced late 1940s). — *n.* **zoot′suiter** one who wears a zoot suit. [Origin unknown; prob. rhyming with **suit.**]

zoozoo *zōō′zōō,* (*dial.*) *n.* the wood-pigeon. [From the sound made by it.]

zopilote *sō-pi-lō′te,* *n.* one of the smaller American vultures — the turkey-buzzard, or the urubu. [Mex. Sp.]

zoppo *tsop′pō,* (*mus.*) *adj.* with syncopation. [It.]

zorgite *zör′gīt,* *n.* a metallic copper-lead selenide, found at Zorge, in the Harz Mountains, Germany.

zoril, zorille, zorillo, zorino. See **zorro.**

Zoroastrianism *zōr-,* *zor-ō-as′tri-ən-izm,* *n.* an ancient religion founded or reformed by *Zoroaster* — the Greek pronunciation of Zarathustra — set forth in the Zend-Avesta, and still adhered to by the Guebres in Iran and Parsees in India. — *n.* and *adj.* **Zoroas′trian.** [L. *Zōroastrēs* — Gr.]

zorro *sor′ō,* *n.* a S. American fox or fox-like wild dog: — *pl.* **zorr′os.** — *ns.* **zoril, zorille** (*zor′il, -il′*) an African skunk-like musteline animal (*Zorilla*); **zorillo** (*sor-ē′yō, zor-il′ō*) a S. American skunk: — *pl.* **zorill′os; zorino** (*zor-ēn′ō*) a euphemism for skunk fur used to make garments: — *pl.* **zorin′os.** [Sp. *zorro, zorra,* fox, *zorilla* (Fr. *zorille*) skunk.]

zoster *zos′tər,* *n.* an ancient Greek waist-belt for men: herpes zoster or shingles. [Gr. *zōstēr,* a girdle.]

Zostera *zos-tē′rə,* *n.* the eelgrass or grasswrack genus. [Gr. *zōstēr,* a kind of grasswrack.]

Zouave *zōō-äv′, zwäv,* *n.* one of a body of French infantry of great dash, orig. Algerians, wearing a quasi-Moorish dress: any of a number of volunteer regiments modelling themselves on the Zouaves who fought on the side of the North in the American Civil War: a woman's short embroidered jacket. [From the *Zouaoua,* an Algerian tribe.]

zounds *zowndz, zōōndz,* (*arch.*) *interj.* an exclamation of anger and astonishment. [A corr. of *God's wounds.*]

zowie *zow′i,* (*U.S.*) *interj.* expressing surprise and pleasure. — *n.* (with *cap.*) the slang in use among hippies.

zucchetto *tsōō-ket′ō,* *n.* the skullcap of an ecclesiastic, covering the tonsure: — *pl.* **zucchett′os.** — Also **zuchett′a, -o** (*pl. -os*). [It. dim. of *zucca,* a gourd.]

zucchini *zōō-kē′nē,* (*U.S.* and *Austr.*) *n.* a courgette: — *pl.* **zucchi′ni, zucchi′nis.** [It.]

zufolo tsŏ͞o'fō-lō, n. a small flute or flageolet used in training singing-birds. — Also **zuff'olo**: — pl. **zuf(f)'oli** (-ē). [It.]

zugzwang tsŏ͞ohh'tsväng, n. in chess, a blockade position in which any move is disadvantageous to the blockaded player. [Ger.]

Zulu zŏ͞o'lŏ͞o, n. a branch of the great Bantu family, belonging to S. Africa, conspicuous for physical development: a member thereof: the language of the Zulus. — adj. pertaining to the Zulus, their language, etc. [Native name.]

zulu zŏ͞o'lŏ͞o n. a type of two-masted fishing vessel formerly used in N.E. Scotland. [Said to have been introduced during the Zulu war 1878–79.]

zum Beispiel tsŏ͞om bī'shpēl, (Ger.) for example — often **z.B.**

zumbooruk zum'bŏ͞o-ruk or, -bŏ͞o', n. a small cannon mounted on a swivel, carried on the back of a camel. — Also **zum'booruck, zom'boruk, zam'boorak**. [Hind. zambūrak; from Pers.]

Zuñi zŏ͞o'nye, sŏ͞o'nye, n. one of a tribe of Pueblo Indians living in large communal houses near the Zuñi river in New Mexico. — adj. and n. **Zu'ñian**.

zupa zū'pə, n. a confederation of village communities governed by a **zū'pan**, in the early history of Serbia, etc. [Serbian.]

zurf. Same as **zarf**.

zuz zŏ͞oz, n. a silver coin of ancient Palestine. [Heb.]

Zwanziger tsvan'tsi-gər, n. an old Austrian silver coin, equivalent to twenty kreutzers. [Ger., — zwanzig, twenty.]

Zwieback tsvē'bäk, or tswē', n. biscuit rusk, or a sweet spiced bread toasted. [Ger.]

Zwinglian zwing'gli-ən, tsving'li-ən, adj. pertaining to the Swiss reformer Huldreich Zwingli (1484–1531), or his doctrines, esp. his divergence from Luther in the doctrine of the Eucharist — Zwingli rejected every form of local or corporeal presence, whether by transubstantiation, impanation, or consubstantiation. — n. a follower of Zwingli. — ns. **Zwing'lianism; Zwing'lianist**.

zwischenzug zvish'ən-zŏ͞og, tsvish'ən-tsŏ͞ok, (chess) n. an interim move, made to play for time. [Ger., — zwischen, between, Zug, move.]

zwitterion tsvit'ər-ī-ən, n. an ion carrying both a positive and a negative charge. [Ger. Zwitter, a hybrid, and ion.]

Zygaena zī-jē'nə, n. the burnet moth genus, typical of the family **Zygae'nidae**: the hammerhead genus of sharks, now called Sphyrna. — adjs. **zygae'nid, zygae'nine, zygae'noid**. [Gr. zygaina, a shark.]

zygo- zī'gō-, zig'ō, **zyg-** zīg-, zig-, in composition, yoke, union or presence of two similar things. — adj. **zy'gal** pertaining to a zygon: formed like a letter H. — n. **zygan'trum** (Gr. antron, a cave) in snakes and some lizards, an additional vertebral articulation, consisting of a fossa on the posterior surface of the neural arch, into which fits the zygosphene. — adj. **zygapophyseal, -ial** (-fīz'i-əl). — n. **zygapophysis** (-pof'i-sis; Gr. apophysis, process) one of the yoke-pieces or articulations of the vertebrae: — pl. **zygapoph'ysēs**. — adj. **zygobranchiate** (-brangk'i-āt; Gr. branchia, gills) having paired, symmetrically placed, gills: belonging to the **Zygobranchiā'ta**, a division of the Gastropoda. — ns. and adjs. **zy'gobranch, zygobranch'iate**. — n. **Zy'gocactus** a Brazilian genus of jointed, branching cactuses having zygomorphic flowers: (without cap.) a cactus of this genus. — adjs. **zygocardiac** (-kär'di-ak; Gr. kardiā, heart) a term used to describe certain paired lateral ossicles in the gastric mill of Crustacea; **zygodactyl** (-dak'til; Gr. daktylos, toe) having two toes before and behind, as parrots. — Also **zygodactyl'ic, zygodac'tylous**. — n. **zygodac'tylism**. — adj. **zy'godont** (Gr. odous, odontos, tooth) pertaining to molar teeth

whose cusps are paired: possessing such molars. — n. **zygoma** (-gō'mə) the arch formed by the malar bone and the zygomatic process of the temporal bone of the skull. — adj. **zygomat'ic** pertaining to the zygoma, or in the region of it (as **zygomatic arch**; **zygomatic fossa** the lower part of the fossa bridged over by the zygomatic arch; **zygomatic muscles** two muscles, major and minor, arising from the zygomatic arch). — adjs. **zygomor'phic, zygomorphous** (mör'fəs; Gr. morphē, form) yoke-shaped — of flowers symmetrical about one plane only. — ns. **zygomor'phism, zy'gomorphy**. — n.pl. **Zygomycetes** (-mī-sē'tēz; Gr. mykēs, mykētos, a mushroom) a group of fungi (moulds, etc.), a division of the Phycomycetes, marked by the production of zygospores. — n. **zygomycete'**. — Also adj. — adj. **zygomycē'tous**. — n. **zy'gon** a connecting bar: an H-shaped fissure of the brain. — n.pl. **Zygophyllaceae** (-fil-ā'sē-ē; Gr. phyllon, a leaf) the bean caper family, desert and steppe plants akin to Rutaceae, the typical genus being **Zygophyll'um**. — adj. **zygophyllā'ceous**. — n. **zy'gophyte** (-fīt; Gr. phyton, a plant) a plant in which reproduction takes place by means of zygospores. — adjs. **zygopleural** (-plŏ͞o'rəl; Gr. pleurā, side) bilaterally symmetrical; **zy'gose** pertaining to zygosis. — ns. **zygosis** (-gōsis; biol.) conjugation; **zy'gosphene** (-sfēn; Gr. sphēn, wedge) in snakes and some lizards, an additional vertebral articulation, consisting of a process on the anterior surface of the neural arch, which fits into the zygantrum: **zy'gospore** (Gr. sporā, a seed) a spore produced by the union of buds from two adjacent hyphae in the process of conjugation by which some fungi multiply. — Also **zy'gosperm**. — n. **zy'gote** (Gr. zygōtos, yoked; bot. and zool.) the product of the union of two gametes: by extension, the individual developing from that product. — adj. **zygotic** (-got'). — **zygotic number** (bot.) the diploid chromosome number. [Gr. zygon, yoke.]

zylonite. Erroneous spelling of **Xylonite**.

zyme zīm, n. a ferment: a disease-germ. — n. **zy'mase** any of a group of enzymes inducing the alcoholic fermentation of carbohydrates. — adj. **zy'mic** relating to fermentation. — n. **zy'mite** a priest using leavened bread in the Eucharist. — **zym(o)-** in composition, relating to fermentation. — n. **zy'mogen** a non-catalytic substance formed by plants and animals as a stage in the development of an enzyme. — adjs. **zymogen'ic; zy'moid** like a ferment; **zymolog'ic, -al** pertaining to zymology. — ns. **zymol'ogist** one skilled in zymology; **zymol'ogy** the science of fermentation; **zymol'ysis** the action of enzymes. — adj. **zymolit'ic**. — ns. **zymom'eter, zymosim'eter** an instrument for measuring the degree of fermentation; **zymō'sis** fermentation: the morbid process, thought to be analogous to fermentation, constituting a zymotic disease. — adjs. **zymotech'nic, -al** producing and utilising fermentation. — n.sing. **zymotech'nics** the art of managing fermentation. — adj. **zymot'ic** pertaining to fermentation: of the nature of, pertaining to, or causing, an infectious disease. — n. an infectious disease. — adv. **zymot'ically**. [Gr. zȳmē, leaven, zȳmōsis, fermentation.]

zym(o)-. See **zyme**.

zymome zī'mōm, n. an old name for the part of gluten insoluble in alcohol. [Gr. zȳmōma, a fermented mixture.]

zymurgy zī'mûr-ji, n. the department of technological chemistry that treats of wine-making, brewing, distilling, and similar processes involving fermentation. [Gr. zȳmē, leaven, ergon, work.]

Zyrian zir'i-ən, n. one of a people of north-western U.S.S.R.: their Finno-Ugric language. — Also adj.

zythum zī'thəm, n. a kind of beer made by the ancient Egyptians — much commended by Diodorus Siculus, a writer of the first century B.C. [Gr. zȳthos.]

Appendices

Phrases and quotations from Latin, Greek and modern foreign languages

Single foreign words, and certain phrases often used in an English context, are given in the main dictionary

abiit, excessit, evasit, erupit (L.) he is gone, he is off, he has escaped, he has broken away.—Cicero, *In Catilinam*, II. i. 1.

ab imo pectore (L.) from the bottom of the heart.

à bon chat, bon rat (Fr.) to a good cat, a good rat—well matched: set a thief to catch a thief.

ab ovo usque ad mala (L.) from the egg to the apples—of a Roman banquet: from the beginning to the end.

absens haeres non erit (L.) the absent one will not be the heir—out of sight, out of mind.

ab uno disce omnes (L.) from one (offence) learn all (the race).—Virgil, *Aen.*, I. 65-66: hence, from one example you may know the rest.

abusus non tollit usum (L.) abuse does not do away with use—i.e. an abuse is not a reason for giving up the legitimate use of a thing.

a capite ad calcem (L.) from head to heel.

à chacun son goût (Fr.) to everyone his own taste. See also **chacun (à) son goût.**

à chaque saint sa chandelle (Fr.) every saint his candle: to every patron his meed of service.

Acherontis pabulum (L.) food for Acheron—of a bad person.—Plautus, *Casina*, II. i. 12.

actum est de republica (L.) it is all up with the state.

actum ne agas (L.) do not do what is already done—quoted as a proverb by Terence, *Phormio.*, II. iii. 72 (or 1. 419).

ad Calendas Graecas (L.) at the Greek Calends—i.e. never, as the Greeks had no Calends.

adhuc sub judice lis est (L.) the dispute is still before the court.—Horace, *A.P.*, 78.

ad majorem Dei gloriam (L.) for the greater glory of God —the Jesuit motto.

adscriptus glebae (L.) bound to the soil—of serfs.

ad utrumque paratus (L.) prepared for either case.

ad vitam aut culpam (L.) for life or till fault: of appointments, for life unless misconduct necessitates dismissal.

advocatus diaboli (L.) devil's advocate. See Dict.

aequam memento rebus in arduis servare mentem (L.) remember to keep a calm mind in difficulties.—Horace, *Od.*, II. iii. 1.

aequitas sequitur legem (L.) equity follows law.

age quod agis (L.) do what you are doing—i.e. with all your powers.

aide-toi, le ciel t'aidera (Fr.) help yourself and heaven will help you.

aliquando bonus dormitat Homerus (L.). See **indignor.**

aliquid haeret (L.) something sticks.

Allah il Allah, a. corr. of Ar. *lā ilāha illā 'llāh* = there is no God but the God.

Allahu akbar (Ar.) God is great.

alter ipse amicus (L.) a friend is another self.

amabilis insania (L.) a pleasing madness or rapture.—Horace, *Od.*, III. 4. 5-6.

amantium irae amoris integratio est (L.) lovers' quarrels are a renewal of love.—Terence, *Andr.*, III. iii. 23.

amare et sapere vix deo conceditur (L.) to be in love and to be wise is scarce granted even to a god.—Laberius.

amari aliquid (L.) some touch of bitterness.—Lucretius, *De Rer. Nat.*, iv. 1130.

a mensa et toro (L.) from bed and board.

amicus Plato, amicus Socrates, sed magis amica veritas (L.) Plato is dear to me (or is my friend), Socrates is dear, but truth is dearer still.—L. version of saying attributed to Aristotle.

amicus usque ad aras (L.) a friend as far as the altars—i.e. as far as may be without offence to the gods.

amor sceleratus habendi (L.) the accursed love of possessing.—Ovid, *Met.*, I. 131.

amor vincit omnia (L.). See **omnia.**

anathema sit (L.) let him be accursed.—1 Cor. xvi. 22.

anch' io son pittore (It.) I, too, am a painter (said by Correggio on looking at Raphael's 'St Cecilia').

anērithmon gelasma. See **kymatōn anērithmon gelasma.**

anguis in herba (L.) a snake in the grass.—Virgil, *Ecl.*, III. 93.

anima naturaliter Christiana (L.) a soul naturally Christian, i.e. one who behaves like a Christian without the benefit of Christian revelation.—Tertullian, *Apologia*, xvii.

animula vagula (L.) little soul flitting away—beginning of a poem ascribed to the dying Hadrian, translated or paraphrased by Prior, Pope, Byron, and Dean Merivale.

à nos moutons. See **revenons.**

ante Agamemnona. See **vixere fortes.**

a parte ante (L.) on the side before, from past eternity—opp. to **a parte post**, in future eternity.

a posse ad esse (L.) from the possible to the actual.

après moi (nous) le déluge (Fr.) after me (us) the deluge: then the deluge may come when it likes—attributed to Mme. de Pompadour and to Louis XV. Cf. **emou thanontos.**

aquila non capit muscas (L.) an eagle does not catch flies.

arbiter elegantiae (L.) judge of good taste—said by Tacitus, *Annals*, XVI. 18, of Gaius Petronius, an exquisite at the court of Nero (prob. same as Petronius Arbiter).—Also quoted as **arbiter elegantiarum.**

Arcades ambo (L.) Arcadians both: two of the same stamp.—Virgil, *Ecl.*, VII. 4.—Rendered by Byron blackguards both, *Don Juan*, IV. xciii.

ariston men hydōr (Gr.) water is best.—Pindar, *Olympian Odes*, i. 1.

ars est celare artem (L.) true art is to conceal art.

ars longa, vita brevis (L.) art is long, life is short.—Seneca, *De Brevitate Vitae*, 1. Cf. **ho bios brachys.**

asbestos gelōs (Gr.) inextinguishable laughter.—Homer, *Iliad*, I. 599, etc.

asinus ad lyram (L.) an ass at the lyre, one ignorant of music or art: one unsuited to an occupation.—From a Greek proverbial expression *onos pros lyran.*

astra castra, numen lumen (L.) the stars my camp, God my lamp.

Athanasius contra mundum (L.) Athanasius against the world: one resolute man facing universal opposition.

atra cura (L.) black care. See **post equitem.**

at spes non fracta (L.) but hope is not yet crushed.

au bout de son latin (Fr.) at the end of his Latin, at the end of his knowledge, at his wits' end.

auctor quae pretiosa facit (L.) gifts that the giver adds value to.—Ovid, *Her.*, XVII. 71-2.

audentes fortuna juvat (L.) fortune favours the daring.—Virgil, *Aen.*, X. 284.

audi alteram partem (L.) hear the other side.—St Augustine, *De Duabus Animabus*, XIV. 2.

auditque vocatus Apollo (L.) and Apollo hears when invoked.—Virgil, *Georg.*, IV. 7.

aufgeschoben ist nicht aufgehoben (Ger.) put off is not given up.

aujourd'hui roi, demain rien (Fr.) king today, nothing tomorrow.

au plaisir de vous revoir (Fr.) till I have the pleasure of seeing you again.

auribus teneo lupum (L.) I am holding a wolf by the ears. —Terence, *Phormio*, III. ii. 21.

auri sacra fames (L.) accursed hunger for gold.—Virgil, *Aen.*, III. 57.

au royaume des aveugles les borgnes sont rois (Fr.) in the kingdom of the blind the one-eyed are kings.—As a Latin proverb, *beati monoculi in regione caecorum.*

aurum omnes, victa jam pietate, colunt (L.) all worship gold, piety being overthrown.—Propertius, III. xiii. 48.

auspicium melioris aevi (L.) augury of a better age.

aussitôt dit, aussitôt fait (Fr.) no sooner said than done.

Austriae est imperare orbi universo (L.) it is Austria's part to command the whole world—often **A.E.I.O.U.**

aut amat aut odit mulier, nihil est tertium (L.) a woman either loves or hates, there is no third course.—Syrus, 42.

autant d'hommes (or **de têtes**), **autant d'avis** (Fr.) so many men, so many minds. Cf. **quot homines.**

aut Caesar aut nullus, or **nihil** (L.) either Caesar or nobody (nothing): all or nothing.

aut insanit homo aut versus facit (L.) either the man is mad or he is making verses.—Horace, *Sat.*, II. vii. 117.

aut inveniam viam aut faciam (L.) I shall either find a way or make one.

aut non tentaris aut perfice (L.) either do not attempt or else achieve.—Ovid, *A.A.*, I. 389.

aut prodesse volunt aut delectare poetae (L.) poets seek either to profit or to please.—Horace, *A.P.*, 333.

aut regem aut fatuum nasci oportet (L.) one should be born either king or fool.—Proverb; quoted by Seneca.

autres temps, autres mœurs (Fr.) other times, other manners.

aut vincere aut mori (L.) to conquer or to die.

aut vitam aut culpam. An incorrect variant of **ad vitam aut culpam** (q.v.).

aux absents les os (Fr.) the bones to the absent.

aux grands maux les grands remèdes (Fr.) to desperate evils desperate remedies.

auxilium ab alto (L.) help from on high.

ave, Caesar (or **imperator**), **morituri te salutant** (L.) hail, Caesar, men doomed to die salute thee (said by gladiators).

a verbis ad verbera (L.) from words to blows.

à vieux comptes nouvelles disputes (Fr.) old accounts breed new disputes.

a vinculo matrimonii (L.) from the bond of matrimony.

avi numerantur avorum (L.) ancestors of ancestors are counted |to me|.

avis au lecteur (Fr.) notice to the reader.

avise la fin (Fr.) weigh well the end.

avito viret honore (L.) he is green with ancestral honours.

avoir la langue déliée (Fr.) to have the tongue unbound, to be glib of speech.

barba tenus sapientes (L.) sages as far as the beard—i.e. with an appearance of wisdom only.

battre la campagne (Fr.) to scour the country, to beat the bush.

bayer aux corneilles (Fr.) to gape at the crows, to stare vacantly.

beatus ille qui procul negotiis . . . paterna rura bobus exercet suis (L.) happy he who, far removed from business . . . tills with his own oxen the fields that were his father's.— Horace, *Epod.*, ii. 1.

bella gerant alii, tu, felix Austria, nube (L.) let others wage wars; do thou, lucky Austria, make marriages.— Matthias Corvinus of Hungary.

bella, horrida bella (L.) wars, horrid wars.—Virgil, *Aen.*, VI. 86.

bellaque matribus detestata (L.) and wars abhorred by mothers.—Horace, *Od.*, I. i. 24-5.

bellum nec timendum nec provocandum (L.) war is neither to be feared nor provoked (Pliny the Younger, *Panegyricus*, 16, **nec times bellum, nec provocas**).

belua multorum capitum (L.) monster with many heads the irrational mob.—Horace, *Epistolae*, I. i. 76.

beneficium accipere libertatem est vendere (L.) to accept a favour is to sell one's liberty.—Syrus, 49.

bene orasse est bene studuisse (L.) to have prayed well is to have endeavoured well.

bene qui latuit bene vixit (L.) he has lived well who has lived obscure.—Ovid, *Trist.*, III. iv. 25.

benigno numine (L.) with favouring godhead.—Horace, *Od.*, III. iv. 74.

bibere venenum in auro (L.) to drink poison from a cup of gold.

biblia abiblia (Gr.) books that are no books.

bis dat qui cito dat (L.) he gives twice who gives promptly. —Proverb; by Bacon.

bis peccare in bello non licet (L.) in war one may not blunder twice.

bis pueri senes (L.) old men are twice boys.

blandae mendacia linguae (L.) falsehoods of a smooth tongue.

bon avocat, mauvais voisin (Fr.) a good lawyer is a bad neighbour.

bon jour, bonne œuvre (Fr.) better day, better deed.

bonnes nouvelles adoucissent le sang (Fr.) good news sweetens the blood.

Borgen macht Sorgen (Ger.) borrowing makes sorrowing.

boutez en avant (Fr.) push forward.

brevis esse laboro, obscurus fio (L.) I labour to be brief, and I become obscure.—Horace, *A.P.*, 25-26.

briller par son absence (Fr.) to be conspicuous by its absence.

brûler la chandelle par les deux bouts (Fr.) to burn the candle at both ends.

buen principio, la mitad es hecha (Sp.) well begun is half-done.

cadit quaestio (L.) the question drops.

caeca invidia est (L.) envy is blind.—Livy, xxxviii. 49.

caelebs quid agam (L.) (you wonder) what I, a bachelor, am about.—Horace, *Od.*, III. viii. 1.

caelum non animum mutant qui trans mare currunt (L.) they change their sky, not their mind, who scour across the sea.—Horace, *Epist.*, I. xi. 27.

Caesar non supra grammaticos (L.) Caesar has no authority over the grammarians.

ça ira (Fr.) it will go—refrain of a famous song of the French Revolution.

callida junctura (L.) a skilful connection.—Horace, *A.P.*, 47-48.

candida Pax (L.) white-robed Peace.—Tibullus, I. x. 45.

cantabit vacuus coram latrone viator (L.) the empty-handed traveller will sing in presence of the robber.— Juvenal, X. 22.

carent quia vate sacro (L.) because they lack a sacred bard. —Horace, *Od.*, IV. ix. 28.

carpe diem, quam minimum credula postero (L.) enjoy the present day, trust the least possible to the future.— Horace, *Od.*, I. xi. 8.

causa sine qua non (L.) an indispensable cause.

cave quid dicis, quando, et cui (L.) beware what you say, when, and to whom.

cedant arma togae (L.) let arms yield to the gown: let military authority yield to civil.—Cicero, *De Officiis*, I. xxii. 77, *in Pisonem*, xxx. 73.

cela va sans dire (Fr.) that goes without saying: of course.

cela viendra (Fr.) that will come.

celui qui veut, peut (Fr.) who will, can.

ce monde est plein de fous (Fr.) this world is full of madmen.

c'en est fait de lui (Fr.) it is all up with him.

ce n'est que le premier pas qui coûte (Fr.). See **il n'y a.**

certum est quia impossibile est (L.) it is certain because it is impossible.—Tertullian.

c'est-à-dire (Fr.) that is to say.

c'est égal (Fr.) it's all one (to me): it makes no odds.

c'est le commencement de la fin (Fr.) it is the beginning of the end.—Attrib. to Talleyrand.

c'est magnifique, mais ce n'est pas la guerre (Fr.) it is magnificent, but it is not war (said at Balaklava by a

French general watching the charge of the Light Brigade).

c'est pire (or **plus**) **qu'un crime, c'est une faute** (Fr.) it is worse than a crime, it is a blunder (on the execution of the Duc d'Enghien; attributed to various persons, incl. Boulay de la Meurthe).

c'est selon (Fr.) that is according to the circumstances.

c'est (une) autre chose (Fr.) that is quite another thing.

ceterum censeo (L.) but I think (said of persistent obstruction like that of Cato).

chacun (à) son goût (Fr.) everyone to his taste. Also à **chacun son goût**.

chapeaux bas (Fr.) hats off.

cherchez la femme (Fr.) look for the woman: there's a woman at the bottom of it.—Dumas *père*.

che sarà sarà (It.) what will be will be.

chiesa libera in libero stato (It.) a free church in a free state (Cavour's ideal for Italy).

chi tace confessa (It.) who keeps silence, confesses.

circulus in probando (L.) arguing in a circle, using the conclusion as one of the arguments.

civis Romanus sum (L.) I am a Roman citizen.—Cicero, *In Verrem*, VI. 57.

clarior e tenebris (L.) the brighter from the darkness.

clarum et venerabile nomen (L.) an illustrious and venerable name.—Lucan, IX. 202.

cogito, ergo sum (L.) I think, therefore I am. (Descartes's fundamental basis of philosophy.)

comitas inter gentes, or **comitas gentium** (L.). See **comity** in Dict.

conditio sine qua non (L.) an indispensable condition.

conjunctis viribus (L.) with united powers.

conquiescat in pace (L.) may he |or she | rest in peace.

conscia mens recti (L.) a mind conscious of rectitude.—Ovid, *Fast.*, IV. 311. Cf. **mens sibi**.

consensus facit legem (L.) consent makes law or rule.

consuetudo pro lege servatur (L.) custom is held as a law.

consule Planco (L.) when Plancus was consul, when I was a young man.—Horace, *Od.*, III. xiv. 28.

contraria contrariis curantur (L.) opposites are cured by opposites.

corruptio optimi pessima (L.) the corruption of the best is the worst of all.

così fan tutte (It.) so do they all (of women): they are all like that.

coûte que coûte (Fr.) cost what it may.

crambe repetita (L.) cauld kale het again—cold cabbage warmed up.—Juvenal, VII. 154.

credat Judaeus Apella, non ego (L.) let the Jew Apella believe that, for I don't.—Horace, *Sat.*, I. v. 100.

credo quia absurdum (L.) I believe it because it is absurd; — **quia impossibile** because it is impossible (based on Tertullian; see **certum est quia impossibile est**).

crescit eundo (L.) it grows as it goes.—Lucretius VI. 341.

cucullus non facit monachum (L.) the cowl does not make the monk.

cuilibet (or **cuicunque**) **in arte sua (perito) credendum est** (L.) every (skilled) person is to be trusted in his own art.— Coke.

cujus regio, ejus religio (L.) whose the region, his the religion—the principle that the established religion should be that of the prince in each state.

curiosa felicitas (L.) studied felicity of expression—said by Petronius Arbiter, *Saturae (Satyricon)*, 118, 5 of Horace's style: (*loosely*) curious felicity.

da dextram misero (L.) give the right hand to the unhappy.

da locum melioribus (L.) give place to your betters.—Terence, *Phormio*, III, ii. 37.

damnosa haereditas (L.) an inheritance of debts (*Roman law*): any hurtful inheritance.—Gaius, *Institutes*, ii. 163.

damnum absque injuria (L.) loss without legal injury.

das Ding an sich (Ger.) the thing in itself.

das Ewig-Weibliche zieht uns hinan (Ger.) the eternal feminine draws us upward.—Goethe, *Faust*, at end.

data et accepta (L.) expenditures and receipts.

date obolum Belisario (L.) give a penny to Belisarius (ascribed to the great general when reduced to beggary).

Davus sum, non Oedipus (L.) I am Davus, not Oedipus— no good at riddles.—Terence, *Andria*., I. ii. 23.

decus et tutamen (L.) an ornament and a protection (inscription round the milled edge of the one-pound coin, earlier used on a coin of Charles II, at John Evelyn's suggestion).—Virgil, *Aen.*, V. 262 (in full *viro decus et tutamen in armis*, an ornament for a man and a protection in the field, in reference to a leather corslet).

de die in diem (L.) from day to day.

de gustibus non est disputandum (L.) there is no disputing about tastes.

de l'audace, encore de l'audace, et toujours de l'audace (Fr.) to dare, still to dare, and ever to dare (Danton's famous phrase).

delenda est Carthago (L.) Carthage must be wiped out (a saying constantly repeated by Cato).

de mal en pis (Fr.) from bad to worse.

de minimis non curat lex (L.) the law does not concern itself about very small matters.—Bacon, *Letter* cclxxxii.

de mortuis nil nisi bonum (L.) say nothing but good of the dead.

de nihilo nihilum. See gigni.

de omni re scibili et quibusdam aliis (L.) about all things knowable, and some others.

de pis en pis (Fr.) worse and worse.

der grosse Heide (Ger.) the great pagan (Heine's name for Goethe).

desipere in loco. See dulce.

desunt cetera (L.) the rest is wanting.

de te fabula narratur (L.) the story is about you.—Horace, *Sat.*, I. i. 69-70.

detur digniori (L.) let it be given to the more worthy; **detur pulchriori** let it be given to the fairer.

deus nobis haec otia fecit (L.) it is a god that hath given us this ease.—Virgil, *Ecl.*, I. 6.

dicamus bona verba (L.) let us speak words of good omen. —Tibullus, II, ii. 1.

Dichtung und Wahrheit (Ger.) poetry and truth.

dictum de dicto (L.) hearsay report.

dictum sapienti sat est (L.) a word to the wise is enough (usu. quoted as **verbum**).—Plautus, *Persa*, IV. vii. 19.

diem perdidi (L.) I have lost a day (said by the Emperor Titus).

Dieu défend le droit (Fr.) God defends the right; **Dieu vous garde** God keep you.

Die Wacht am Rhein (Ger.) the Watch on the Rhine (a famous German patriotic song).

digito monstrari (L.) to be pointed out with the finger: to be famous.—Persius, I. 28.

dignus vindice nodus (L.). See **nec deus intersit**.

di grado in grado (It.) by degrees.

dis aliter visum (L.) the gods have adjudged otherwise.—Virgil, *Aen.*, II. 428.

disjecta membra (L.) scattered limbs (after Ovid, *Met.*, III. 724); **disjecti membra poetae** limbs of the dismembered poet.—Horace, *Sat.*, I. iv. 62.

distinguo (L.) I distinguish.

divide et impera (L.) divide and rule.

docendo discimus (L.) we learn by teaching.

doctor utriusque legis (L.) doctor of both laws (civil and canon).

doli capax (L.) capable of committing a wrong—opp. to *doli incapax*.

Domine, dirige nos (L.) Lord, direct us (the motto of London).

Dominus illuminatio mea (L.) the Lord is my light.

domus et placens uxor (L.) a home and a pleasing wife.—Horace, *Od.*, II. xiv. 21-22.

dorer la pilule (Fr.) to gild the pill.

dormitat Homerus (L.). See **indignor**.

dos moi pou stō kai tēn gēn kinēsō (Gr.) give me where to stand, and I will move the earth (attributed to Archimedes).

do ut des (L.) I give that you may give.

dulce, 'Domum' (L.) sweet strain, 'Homeward'—from a Winchester school song sung before the holidays; dulce est desipere in loco it is pleasant to play the fool on occasion.—Horace, *Od.*, IV. xii. 28; dulce et decorum est pro patria mori it is sweet and glorious to die for one's country.—Horace, *Od.*, III. ii. 13.

dum casta (L.) while (she is) chaste.

dum spiro, spero (L.) while I breathe, I hope.

dum vivimus, vivamus (L.) let us live while we live.

dux femina facti (L.) a woman was leader in the deed.— Virgil, *Aen.*, I. 364.

écrasez l'infâme (Fr.) crush the vile thing. Voltaire against the Roman Catholic Church of his time.

edax rerum. See tempus.

ego et rex meus (L.) I and my king.—Cardinal Wolsey.

eheu fugaces . . . labuntur anni (L.) alas! the fleeting years slip away.—Horace, *Od.*, II, xiv. 1-2.

eile mit Weile (Ger.) make speed with leisure. Cf. festina lente.

ein Mal, kein Mal (Ger.) just once counts nothing.

ek parergou (Gr.) as a by-work.

Eli, Eli, lama sabachthani (Matt. xxvii. 46), Eloi, Eloi, lamma sabachthani (Mark xv. 34) (Gr. transliterations of Aramaic) my God, my God, why has thou forsaken me?

emou thanontos gaia michthētō pyri (Gr.) when I am dead let earth be mingled with fire. Cf. après moi le déluge.

entbehren sollst du, sollst entbehren (Ger.) thou must abstain, abstain thou must.—Goethe, *Faust*, Part I. (Studierzimmer, ii).

en toutōi nika (Gr.) conquer in this (sign). See in hoc (signo) vinces.

epea pteroenta (Gr.) winged words.—Homer (*Iliad*, I. 201, etc.). See also Dict. under wing[1].

ephphatha (Aramaic) be opened (Mark vii. 34).

e pluribus unum (L.) one out of many—before 1956 regarded as motto of the United States.

eppur si muove (It.) it does move all the same (attrib. to Galileo after he had recanted his doctrine that the earth moves round the sun).

erectos ad sidera tollere vultus (L.). See os homini.

ergo bibamus (L.) therefore let us drink.

Erin go bragh (Ir.) Erin forever.

errare est humanum (L.) to err is human.

es korakas (Gr.) to the ravens: go and be hanged.

esse quam videri (L.) to be, rather than to seem.

est modus in rebus (L.) there is a mean in (all) things.— Horace, *Sat.*, I. i. 106.

esto perpetua (L.) be lasting.

est quaedam flere voluptas (L.) there is in weeping a certain pleasure.—Ovid, *Trist.*, IV. iii. 37.

et hoc (or id) genus omne (L.) and all that sort of thing.

et in Arcadia ego (L.) I, too, lived in Arcadia. (Inscription from tomb, used in Poussin's picture 'The Arcadian Shepherds'.)

et tu, Brute (L.) you too, Brutus. (Caesar's alleged exclamation when he saw Brutus amongst his assassins.)

euphemeite (Gr.) hush! (shouted at the start of a Greek drama).

eventus stultorum magister (L.) the outcome is the school-master of fools.—Livy, XXII, 39.

ex abusu non arguitur ad usum (L.) from the abuse no argument is drawn against the use. Cf. abusus non.

exceptio confirmat (or probat) regulam (L.) the exception proves the rule. (See except in Dict.).

exegi monumentum aere perennius (L.) I have reared a monument more lasting than brass.—Horace, *Od.*, III. xxx. 1.

exempla sunt odiosa (L.) examples are hateful.

exitus acta probat (L.) the outcome justifies the deed.— Ovid, *Her.*, II. 85.

ex nihilo (or nilo) nihil (or nil) fit (L.) out of nothing nothing comes. See gigni.

ex pede Herculem (L.) (we recognise) Hercules from his foot.

experientia docet stultos (L.) experience teaches fools.

experto crede, or (Virgil, *Aen.*, XI. 283) credite (L.) trust one who has tried, or had experience.

expertus metuet, or metuit (L.) he who has experienced it will fear (or fears).—Horace, *Epist.*, I. xviii, 87.

exstinctus amabitur idem (L.) the same man (maligned living) when dead will be loved.—Horace, *Epist.*, II. i. 14.

ex ungue leonem (L.) (judge, or infer) the lion from his claws.

faber est quisque fortunae suae (L.) every man is the fashioner of his own fortunes.—Proverb quoted by Sallust, *De Republica*, I.

fable convenue (Fr.) fable agreed upon—Voltaire's name for history.

facile est inventis addere (L.) it is easy to add to things invented already.

facilis descensus Averno, or Averni (L.) descent to Avernus is easy.—Virgil, *Aen.*, VI. 126.

facinus majoris abollae (L.) the crime of a larger cloak, i.e. of a philosopher.—Juvenal, III. 115.

facit indignatio versum (L.) indignation makes verse.— Juvenal. I. 79.

facta non verba (L.) deeds, not words.

factum est (L.) it is done.

facundi. See fecundi.

faire bonne mine (Fr.) to put a good face on the matter.

falsus in uno, falsus in omnibus (L.) false in one thing, false in all.

fama nihil est celerius (L.) nothing is swifter than rumour. —Livy.

fama semper vivat (L.) may his (or her) fame live for ever.

far niente (It.) doing nothing.

farrago libelli. See quicquid.

fas est et ab hoste doceri (L.) it is right to learn even from an enemy.—Ovid, *Met.*, IV. 428.

Fata obstant (L.) the Fates oppose.—Virgil, *Aen.*, IV. 440.

Fata viam invenient (L.) the Fates will find out a way.— Virgil, *Aen.*, X. 113.

favete linguis (L.) favour me with your tongues—keep silent to avoid ill omen.—Horace, *Od.*, III. i. 2.

fecundi (or facundi) calices quem non fecere disertum? (L.) whom have not full cups made eloquent?—Horace, *Epist.*, I. v. 19.

felicitas multos habet amicos (L.) prosperity has many friends.

felix qui potuit rerum cognoscere causas (L.) happy is he who has been able to understand the causes of things.— Virgil, *Georg.*, II. 490.

fendre un cheveu en quatre (Fr.) to split a hair in four.

fenum (or foenum) habet in cornu (L.) he has hay on his horn (sign of a dangerous bull).—Horace, *Sat.*, I. iv. 34.

festina lente (L.) hasten gently.

fiat experimentum in corpore vili (L.) let experiment be made on a worthless body.

fiat justitia, ruat caelum (L.) let justice be done, though the heavens should fall.

fiat lux (L.) let there be light.

fide, sed cui vide (L.) trust, but take care in whom.

fidus Achates (L.) faithful Achates (friend of Aeneas): hence, a close friend.—Virgil.

finem respice (L.). See respice finem.

finis coronat opus (L.) the end crowns the work.

fin mot de l'affaire (Fr.) the bottom of the matter, the explanation.

flectere si nequeo superos, Acheronta movebo (L.) if I can't move the gods, I'll stir up hell.—Virgil, *Aen.*, VII. 312.

flecti non frangi (L.) to be bent, not broken.

foenum. See fenum.

forsan et haec olim meminisse juvabit (L.) perhaps some day we shall like to remember even these things.—Virgil, *Aen.*, I. 203.

Fors Clavigera (L.) Fortune the club-bearer (used as a title by Ruskin).

fortes Fortuna adjuvat (L.) Fortune helps the brave (Terence, *Phorm.*, I. iv. 26): **forti et fideli nihil difficile** to the brave and faithful nothing is difficult; **fortis cadere, cedere non potest** the brave man may fall, he cannot yield.

fortiter in re, suaviter in modo (L.). See **suaviter**.

Fortuna favet fatuis (L.) Fortune favours fools; **Fortuna favet fortibus** Fortune favours the bold.

frangas, non flectes (L.) you may break, you shall not bend.

fraus est celare fraudem (L.) it is a fraud to conceal a fraud.

frontis nulla fides (L.) no reliance on the face, no trusting appearances.—Juvenal, II. 8.

fruges consumere nati (L.) born to consume the fruits of the soil.—Horace, *Epist.*, I. ii. 27.

fugit hora (L.) the hour flies.—Persius, V. 153.

fuimus Troes; fuit Ilium (L.) we were Trojans; Troy was. — Virgil, *Aen.*, II. 325.

fulmen brutum (L.) a harmless thunderbolt.

furor arma ministrat (L.) rage supplies arms.—Virgil, *Aen.*, I. 150.

gaudet tentamine virtus (L.) virtue rejoices in trial.

geflügelte Worte (Ger.) winged words. See **epea.**

genus irritabile vatum (L.) the irritable tribe of poets.— Horace, *Epist.*, II. ii. 102.

gibier de potence (Fr.) gallows-bird.

gigni de nihilo nihilum, in nihilum nil posse reverti (L.) from nothing nothing can come, into nothing nothing can return.—Persius, III. 84.

giovine santo, diavolo vecchio (It.) young saint, old devil.

gli assenti hanno torto (It.) the absent are in the wrong.

gloria virtutis umbra (L.) glory (is) the shadow of virtue.

glückliche Reise (Ger.) prosperous journey to you.

gnōthi seauton (Gr.) know thyself.—Inscribed on the temple of Apollo at Delphi. See also **nosce teipsum.**

Gott mit uns (Ger.) God with us—Hohenzollern motto.

gradu diverso, via una (L.) with different step on the one way.

gradus ad Parnassum (L.) a step, or stairs, to Parnassus, a Latin or Greek poetical dictionary.

Graeculus esuriens (L.) the hungry Greekling.—Juvenal, III. 78.

Graecum est: non legitur (L.) this is Greek; it is not read (placed against a Greek word in mediaeval MSS, a permission to skip the hard words).

grande chère et beau feu (Fr.) ample cheer and a fine fire; **grande fortune, grande servitude** great wealth, great slavery.

gratia placendi (L.) the delight of pleasing.

graviora manent (L.) greater dangers remain (Virgil, *Aen.*, VI. 84); **graviora quaedam sunt remedia periculis** some remedies are more grievous than the perils (Syrus).

gravis ira regum est semper (L.) the anger of kings is always serious.

grosse Seelen dulden still (Ger.) great souls suffer in silence.—Schiller, *Don Carlos*, I. iv., end of scene.

grosse tête et peu de sens (Fr.) big head and little wit.

gutta cavat lapidem (L.) the drop wears away the stone. — Ovid, *Pont.*, IV. x. 5.

habendum et tenendum (L.) to have and to hold.

habent sua fata libelli (L.) books have their destinies.— Maurus, *De Litteris, Syllabis et Metris.*

hanc veniam petimusque damusque vicissim (L.) this liberty we ask and grant in turn.—Horace, *A.P.*, 11.

Hannibal ad portas (L.) Hannibal at the gates.—Cicero, *Philippica*, I. v. 11.

haud longis intervallis (L.) at no long intervals.

helluo librorum (L.) a glutton of books.

heu pietas! heu prisca fides! (L.) alas for piety! alas for the ancient faith!—Virgil, *Aen.*, VI. 879.

hiatus valde deflendus (L.) a gap deeply to be deplored.

hic finis fandi (L.) here (was, or let there be) an end of the speaking.

hinc illae lacrumae (L.) hence |came| those tears.— Terence, *Andria*, I. i. 99; also Horace, *Epist.*, I. xix. 41.

hinc lucem et pocula sacra (L.) from this source |we draw| light and draughts of sacred learning.

ho bios brachys, hē de technē makrē (Gr.) life is short and art is long.—Attributed to Hippocrates.

hoc age (L.) this do.

hoc erat in votis (L.) this was the very thing I prayed for. — Horace, *Sat.*, II. vi. 1.

hoc opus, hic labor est (L.) this is the toil, this the labour. —Virgil, *Aen.*, VI. 129.

hoc saxum posuit (L.) placed this stone.

hoc (or sic) **volo, sic jubeo, sit pro ratione voluntas** (L.) this (thus) I will, thus I command, be my will sufficient reason.—Juvenal, VI. 223.

hodie mihi, cras tibi (L.) me today, you tomorrow.

hominibus plenum, amicis vacuum (L.) full of men, empty of friends.

hominis est errare (L.) it belongs to man to err.

homo alieni juris (L.) one under control of another; **homo antiqua virtute ac fide** a man of the antique virtue and loyalty (Terence, *Adelphi*, III. iii. 88 or 1. 442); **homo homini lupus** man is a wolf to man; **homo multarum litterarum** a man of many literary accomplishments; **homo nullius coloris** a man of no colour, one who does not commit himself; **homo sui juris** one who is his own master; **homo sum: humani nihil a me alienum puto** I am a man: I count nothing human indifferent to me (Terence, *Heaut.*, I. i. 25); **homo trium litterarum** man of three letters—i.e. *fur* = thief; **homo unius libri** a man of one book.

hon hoi theoi philousi apothnēskei neos (Gr.) whom the gods love dies young.—Menander. Cf. **quem di diligunt . . .**

honi soit qui mal y pense (O.Fr.) the shame be his who thinks ill of it—the motto of the Order of the Garter.

honneur et patrie (Fr.) honour and native land.

honores mutant mores (L.) honours change manners.

honor virtutis praemium (L.) honour is the reward of virtue.

honos alit artes (L.) honour nourishes the arts (Cicero, *Tusculanae Disputationes*, I. ii. 4); **honos habet onus** honour has its burden.

hora fugit (L.) the hour flies.

horas non numero nisi serenas (L.) I number none but shining hours. |Common on sundials.|.

horresco referens (L.) I shudder in relating.—Virgil, *Aen.*, II, 204.

horribile dictu (L.) horrible to relate.

hostis honori invidia (L.) envy is an enemy to honour; **hostis humani generis** enemy of the human race.

humanum est errare (L.) to err is human.

hurtar para dar por Dios (Sp.) to steal in order to give to God.

hypage Satana (Gr.) away Satan.—Matt. iv. 10.

hypotheses non fingo (L.) I do not frame hypotheses (i.e. unverifiable speculations).—Newton.

ich dien (Ger.) I serve.

ici on parle français (Fr.) here French is spoken.

idem velle atque idem nolle ea demum firma amicitia est (L.) to like and dislike the same things is indeed true friendship.—Sallust, *Catalina*, 20.

Iesus Hominum Salvator (L.) Jesus, Saviour of men.

ignorantia juris neminem excusat (L.) ignorance of the law excuses nobody.

ignoti nulla cupido (L.) for a thing unknown there is no desire.—Ovid, *A.A.*, III. 397.

ignotum per ignotius (L.) the unknown by the still more unknown.

i gran dolori sono muti (It.) great griefs are mute.

il a inventé l'histoire (Fr.) he has invented history.

il a le diable au corps (Fr.) the devil is in him: he is full of devilment, or of vivacity, wit, enthusiasm, etc.: he can't sit still.

il a les défauts de ses qualités (Fr.) he has the defects that answer to his good qualities.

il faut de l'argent (Fr.) money is necessary.

il faut laver son linge sale en famille (Fr.) one should wash one's dirty linen in private.

il gran rifiuto (It.) the great refusal (the abdication of Pope Celestine V).—Dante, *Inferno*, III. 60.

Ilias malorum (L.) an Iliad of woes.

ille crucem sceleris pretium tulit, hic diadema (L.) that man got a cross, this man a crown, as the price of his crime.—Juvenal, XIII. 105.

ille terrarum mihi praeter omnes angulus ridet (L.) that corner of the earth to me smiles sweetest of all.—Horace, *Od*., II. vi. 13-14.

il meglio è l'inimico del bene (It.) the better is the enemy of the good.

il n'y a pas à dire (Fr.) there is nothing to be said.

il n'y a que le premier pas qui coûte (Fr.) it is only the first step that counts. (Mme du Deffand on St Denis walking after decapitation.)

ils n'ont rien appris ni rien oublié (Fr.) they have learned nothing and forgotten nothing |said of the French *Émigrés*, often of the Bourbons|.

impar congressus Achilli (L.) unequally matched against Achilles.—Virgil, *Aen*., I. 475.

incedis per ignis suppositos cineri doloso (L.) you walk on fires covered with treacherous ash.—Horace, *Od*., II. i. 7-8.

incidis in Scyllam cupiens vitare Charybdim (L.) you fall into Scylla trying to avoid Charybdis.—Philip Gaultier de Lille.

incredulus odi (L.) I hate and disbelieve.—Horace, *A.P.*, 188.

indignor quandoque bonus dormitat Homerus (L.) I am annoyed whenever good Homer slumbers.—Horace, *A.P.*, 359. Usually cited as **aliquando** (= sometimes) **bonus**, etc.

infandum, regina, jubes renovare dolorem (L.) thou bidst me, queen, renew unspeakable woes.—Virgil, *Aen*., II. 3.

in hoc (signo) vinces (L.) in this sign thou wilt conquer—i.e. in the Cross [the motto of Constantine the Great]. See **en toutōi nika.**

in magnis et voluisse sat est (L.) in great things even to have wished is enough.—Propertius, II. x. 6.

in meditatione fugae (L.) in contemplation of flight.

inopem me copia fecit (L.) plenty has made me poor.—Ovid, *M*., III. 466.

integer vitae scelerisque purus (L.) blameless in life and clear of offence.—Horace, *Od*., I. xxii. 1.

inter arma silent leges (L.) amid wars laws are silent (Cicero).

interdum stultus bene loquitur (L.) sometimes a fool speaks aright.

invita Minerva (L.) against the will of Minerva: uninspired.—Horace, *A.P.*, 385.

ira furor brevis est (L.) rage is a brief madness.—Horace, *Epist*., I. ii. 62.

Italia irredenta (It.) unredeemed Italy—the parts of Italy still under foreign domination after the war of 1866—South Tirol, etc.

jacta est alea (L.) the die is cast (quoted as said by Caesar at the crossing of the Rubicon).

je n'en vois pas la nécessité (Fr.) I don't see the necessity for that [said by the Comte d'Argental in reply to a man who pleaded, 'But one must live somehow'].

joci causa (L.) for the joke.

judex damnatur cum nocens absolvitur (L.) the judge is condemned when the guilty is acquitted.—Syrus, 247.

Jup(p)iter optimus maximus (L.) Jupiter best and greatest; **Jup(p)iter Pluvius** rain-bringing Jupiter; **Jup(p)iter Tonans** Jupiter the thunderer.

justum et tenacem propositi virum (L.) a man upright and tenacious of purpose.—Horace, *Od*., III. iii. 1.

j'y suis, j'y reste (Fr.) here I am, here I stay [said by Macmahon at the Malakoff].

kai ta leipomena, kai ta loipa (Gr.) and the rest: and so on.

kalos kagathos, kalokagathos (Gr.) good and honourable: a perfect gentleman.

kat' exochēn (Gr.) pre-eminently: *par excellence*.

keine Antwort is auch eine Antwort (Ger.) no answer is still an answer: silence gives consent.

Kirche, Küche, Kinder (Ger.) church, kitchen, children—said, e.g. during the Nazi period, to be the proper interests of a German woman.

ktēma es aei (Gr.) a possession for ever.

kymatōn anērithmon gelasma (Gr.) innumerable smiles of the waves.—Aeschylus, *Prom*., 89-90.

laborare est orare (L.) work is prayer.

labore et honore (L.) by labour and honour.

labuntur et imputantur (L.) [the moments] slip away and are laid to our account (inscription on sundials). Also **pereunt et imputantur** (q.v.).

la donna è mobile (It.) woman is changeable.

la garde meurt et ne se rend pas (Fr.) the guard dies, it does not surrender.

la grande nation (Fr.) the great nation—i.e. France.

lā ilāha illā 'llāh (Ar.) there is no god but God.

langage des halles (Fr.) language of the market-place.

l'appétit vient en mangeant (Fr.) appetite comes as you eat.

la propriété c'est le vol (Fr.) property is theft [from Proudhon].

la reyne le veult (s'avisera) (Norm. Fr.) See **le roy.**

lasciate ogni speranza, voi ch'entrate (It.) abandon all hope ye who enter.—Dante, *Inferno*, III. 9. From the inscription over the gate of hell.

latet anguis in herba (L.) there is a snake hidden in the grass.—Virgil, *Ecl*., III. 93.

laudator temporis acti (L.) one who praises past times.—Horace, *A.P.*, 173.

le génie n'est qu'une grande aptitude à la patience (Fr.) genius is merely a great aptitude for patience (attributed to Buffon).

le grand monarque (Fr.) the great king—i.e. Louis XIV.

le jeu ne vaut pas la chandelle (Fr.) the game is not worth the candle.

l'empire c'est la paix (Fr.) the empire means peace [said by Louis Napoleon in 1852].

le roy (or la reyne) le veult (Norm. Fr.) the king (or queen) wills it—form of royal assent.

le roy (la reyne) s'avisera (Norm. Fr.) the king (or queen) will deliberate—form of refusal.

le style est l'homme (même) (Fr.) the style is the man himself (from Buffon).

l'état, c'est moi (Fr.) I am the state [alleged to have been said by Louis XIV].

liberté, égalité, fraternité (Fr.) liberty, equality, fraternity—a slogan of the French Revolution.

limae labor (L.) the labour of the file, of polishing.—Horace, *A.P.*, 291.

littera scripta manet (L.) what is written down is permanent. See **vox audita.**

lucri causa (L.) for the sake of gain.

lucus a non lucendo (L.) the grove (*lucus*) (is so named) from its *not* shining (*lucendo*).

ludere cum sacris (L.) to trifle with sacred things.

l'union fait la force (Fr.) union makes strength.

lupus in fabula (L.) the wolf in the fable: talk of the devil.—Terence, *Adelphi*, IV. i. 21.

macte virtute (L.) be honoured in your valour, virtue—used by Cicero, Virgil, Livy (**macte virtute esto**—Cato to one coming out of a resort of vice, acc. to Horace, *Sat*., I. ii. 31-32).

magna est veritas et praevalebit (L.) truth is great and will prevail (Vulgate, **et prevalet**).

magni nominis umbra (L.) the mere shadow of a mighty name.—Lucan, I. 135..

man spricht Deutsch (Ger.) German spoken here.

matre pulchra filia pulchrior (L.) a daughter fairer than her fair mother.—Horace, *Od.*, I. xvi. 1.

maxima debetur puero reverentia (L.) the greatest reverence is due to the boy—i.e. to the innocence of his age.—Juvenal, XIV, 47.

mea virtute me involvo (L.) I wrap myself in my virtue.—Horace, *Od.*, III, xxix. 54-55.

mēden agan (Gr.) [let there be] nothing in excess.

medio tutissimus ibis (L.) thou wilt go safest in the middle.—Ovid, *Met.*, II. 137.

mega biblion, mega kakon (Gr.) big book, great evil.

mē kinei Kamarinan (Gr.) do not stir up Kamarina (a pestilent marsh in Sicily): let well alone.

mens sana in corpore sano (L.) a sound mind in a sound body.—Juvenal, X. 356.

mens sibi conscia recti (L.) a mind conscious of rectitude.—Virgil, *Aen.*, I. 604. Cf. **conscia mens recti**.

mirabile dictu (L.) wonderful to tell; **mirabile visu**, wonderful to see.

mole ruit sua (L.) falls by its own weight.—Horace, *Od.*, III. iv. 65.

monstrum horrendum, informe, ingens (L.) a frightful monster, ill-shapen, huge.—Virgil, *Aen.*, III. 658.

morituri te salutant. See **ave**.

muet comme un poisson (Fr.) dumb as a fish.

natura abhorret vacuum (L.) nature abhors a vacuum.

naturam expellas furca, tamen usque recurret (L.) though you drive out nature with a pitchfork, yet will she always return.—Horace, *Epist.*, I. x. 24.

natura non facit saltus (or **saltum**) (L.) nature does not make leaps (or a leap).

naviget Anticyram (L.) let him sail to Anticyra [where hellebore could be had, to cure madness].—Horace, *Sat.*, II. iii. 166.

nec cupias, nec metuas (L.) neither desire nor fear.

nec deus intersit nisi dignus vindice nodus inciderit (L.) let not a god intervene unless a knot occur worthy of the untier.—Horace, *A.P.*, 191-2.

ne cede malis (L.) yield not to misfortune.—Virgil, *Aen.*, VI. 95.

necessitas non habet legem (L.) necessity has no law.

nec pluribus impar (L.) no unequal match for several (suns).—Louis XIV's motto.

nec scire fas est omnia (L.) it is not permitted to know all things.—Horace, *Od.*, IV. iv. 22.

ne exeat (L.) let him not depart.

negatur (L.) it is denied.

nemo me impune lacessit (L.) no one provokes me with impunity—the motto of the kings of Scotland and of the Order of the Thistle; **nemo repente fuit turpissimus** no one ever became utterly bad all at once.—Juvenal, II. 83.

ne obliviscaris (L.) do not forget.

neque semper arcum tendit Apollo (L.) Apollo does not always bend his bow.—Horace, *Od.*, II. x. 19-20.

ne quid nimis (L.) [let there be] nothing in excess.

nescis, mi fili, quantilla prudentia mundus regatur (L.) you know not, my son, with what a small stock of wisdom the world is governed.—Attributed to Oxenstierna and others.

nescit vox missa reverti (L.) a word published cannot be recalled.—Horace, *A.P.*, 390.

n'est-ce pas? (Fr.) is it not so?

ne sutor ultra (or **supra**) **crepidam** (L.) a cobbler should not criticise (a work of art) beyond (or above) the sandal—let the cobbler stick to his last (quoted as *ne sutor supra crepidam judicaret* by Pliny, *N.H.*, 35.85, and as *ne sutor ultra crepidam* by Erasmus, *Adagia*, I. vi. xvi. See also **ultracrepidate** in Dict.).

ne temere (L.) not rashly—a papal decree of 1907 denying recognition to the marriage of a Catholic unless contracted before a priest.

nich wahr? (Ger.) is it not true? isn't that so?

nihil tetigit quod non ornavit. See **nullum**.

nil actum credens dum quid superesset agendum (L.) thinking nothing done while anything was yet to do.—Lucan, II. 657; **nil admirari** to wonder at nothing.—Horace, *Epist.*, I. vi. 1; **nil desperandum** nothing is to be despaired of.—Horace, *Od.*, I. vii. 27.

n'importe (Fr.) no matter.

nisi Dominus frustra (L.) except the Lord (keep the city, the watchman waketh but) in vain.—Ps. cxxvii—the motto of Edinburgh.

nitor in adversum (L.) I strive in opposition.—Ovid, *Met.*, II. 72.

non amo te, Sabidi, nec possum dicere quare (L.) I do not love thee, Sabidius, nor can I tell you why.—Martial, I. xxxiii.

non compos mentis (L.) not of sound mind.

non est inventus (L.) he has not been found (he has absconded).

non licet (L.) it is not allowed.

non liquet (L.) it is not clear.

non mi ricordo (It.) I don't remember.

non multa, sed multum (L.) not many, but much.

non nobis, Domine (L.) not unto us, O Lord.—Psalm cxv.

non olet pecunia (L.) the money does not stink.—Attributed to Vespasian, of revenue from an unsavoury source.

non omnia possumus omnes (L.) we cannot all do everything.—Virgil, *Ecl.*, viii. 63.

non omnis moriar (L.) I shall not wholly die.—Horace, *Od.*, III. xxx. 6.

non placet (L.) it does not please—a negative vote.

non possumus (L.) we cannot—a form of refusal.

non tali auxilio nec defensoribus istis tempus eget (L.) not for such aid nor for these defenders does the time call.—Virgil, *Aen.*, II. 521.

nonumque prematur in annum (L.) and let it be kept unpublished till the ninth year.—Horace, *A.P.*, 388.

non ut edam vivo sed ut vivam edo (L.) I do not live to eat, but eat to live.—Quintilian.

nosce teipsum (L.) know thyself—a translation of **gnōthi seauton** (q.v.).

nous avons changé tout cela (Fr.) we have changed all that.—Molière, *Le Médecin malgré lui*, II. iv.

nous verrons (ce que nous verrons) (Fr.) we shall see (what we shall see).

nulla dies sine linea (L.) no day without a line, without painting (or writing) a little.

nulla nuova, buona nuova (It.) no news is good news.

nullius addictus (or **adductus**) **jurare in verba magistri** (L.) bound to swear to the words of no master, to follow no one blindly or slavishly.—Horace, *Epist.*, I. i. 14.

nullum (scil. **scribendi genus**) **quod tetigit non ornavit** (L.) he touched no form of literature without adorning it.—From Johnson's epitaph on Goldsmith.

nunc est bibendum (L.) now is the time to drink.—Horace, *Od.*, I. xxxvii. 1.

obscurum per obscurius (L.) (explaining) the obscure by means of the more obscure.

oderint dum metuant (L.) let them hate so long as they fear.—Accius, *Atreus*, Fragment IV; quoted in Cicero, *Philippica*, I. xiv.

odi profanum vulgus et arceo (L.) I loathe and shun the profane rabble.—Horace, *Od.*, iii. i. 1.

O fortunatos nimium, sua si bona norint, agricolas (L.) Oh too happy farmers, if they but knew their luck.—Virgil, *Georg.*, II. 458.

ohe! jam satis (L.) hold! enough now (a common phrase).

ohne Hast, ohne Rast (Ger.) without haste, without rest.—Goethe's motto.

olim meminisse juvabit. See **forsan**.

omne ignotum pro magnifico (L.) everything unknown (is taken to be) magnificent.—Tacitus, *Agric.*, 30.

omnem crede diem tibi diluxisse supremum (L.) believe each day to have dawned as your last.—Horace, *Epist.*, I. iv. 13.

omne tulit punctum qui miscuit utile dulci (L.) he has carried every vote who has combined the useful with the pleasing.—Horace, *A.P.*, 343.

omne vivum ex ovo (L.) every living thing comes from an egg. —Attributed to Harvey.

omnia mea mecum porto (L.) all I have I carry with me.

omnia mutantur. See **tempora mutantur.**

omnia vincit amor, et nos cedamus amori (L.) love overcomes all things, let us too yield to love.—Virgil, *Ecl.*, X. 69.

ore rotundo (L.) with round, full voice (mouth).—Horace, *A.P.*, 323.

O sancta simplicitas! (L.) O holy simplicity!

os homini sublime dedit caelumque tueri jussit et erectos ad sidera tollere vultus (L.) he gave man an up-turned face and bade contemplate the heavens and raise looks to the stars.—Ovid, *Met.*, I. 85.

O si sic omnia! (L.) Oh that he had done all things thus, or Oh that all things were thus!

O tempora! O mores! (L.) O the times! O the manners! Occurs in Cicero's first speech against Catiline.

otia dant vitia (L.) idleness begets vice.

otium cum dignitate (L.) dignified leisure.

ouk esti? (Gr.) is it not so?

ovem lupo committere (L.) to entrust the sheep to the wolf.

pace tua (L.) by your leave.

pallida Mors aequo pulsat pede pauperum tabernas regumque turres (L.) pale Death knocks with impartial foot at poor men's huts and kings' castles.—Horace, *Od.*, I. iv. 13-14.

palmam qui meruit ferat (L.) let him who has won the palm wear it.—Dr Jortin, *Lusus Poetici*, viii. 20.

panem et circenses (L.) bread and (Roman) circus-games —food and amusements at public expense.—Juvenal, X. 81.

panta men kathara tois katharois (Gr.) all things are pure to the pure.—Titus, I. 15.

panta rhei (Gr.) all things are in a flux (a saying of Heraclitus).

parcere subjectis et debellare superbos (L.) to spare the vanquished and put down the proud.—Virgil, *Aen.*, VI. 854.

par nobile fratrum (L.) a noble pair of brothers.—Horace, *Sat.*, II. iii. 243.

parturiunt montes, nascetur ridiculus mus (L.) the mountains are in travail, an absurd mouse will be born.—Horace, *A.P.*, 139.

parva componere magnis. See **si parva.**

pas op (Afrik.) look out.

pathēmata mathēmata (Gr.) sufferings [are] lessons.

paulo majora canamus (L.) let us sing of rather greater things.—Virgil, *Ecl.*, IV. I.

pax vobiscum (L.) peace be with you.

peccavi (L.) I have sinned.

pecunia non olet. See **non olet pecunia.**

pereant qui ante nos nostra dixerunt (L.) perish those who have said our good things before us.—Attributed to Donatus and to Augustine.

pereunt et imputantur (L.) [the moments, hours] pass away and are reckoned to our account.

perfervida. See **praefervida.**

per varios casus, per tot discrimina rerum (L.) through various chances, through so many crises of fortune.—Virgil, *Aen.*, I. 204.

pleidiol wyf i'm gwlad (W.) loyal am I to my country (inscription round the edge of a Welsh one-pound coin).

pleon hēmisy pantos (Gr.) the half is more than the whole.—Hesiod, *Erga*, 40.

plus ça change, plus c'est la même chose (Fr.) the more that changes the more it is the same thing (no superficial or apparent change alters its essential nature).

poeta nascitur, non fit (L.) the poet is born, not made.

pollōn onomatōn mia morphē (Gr.) one shape of many names.—Aeschylus, *Prometheus*, 210.

polyphloisboio thalassēs (Gr.) of the much-sounding sea.—Homer, *Il.*, I. 34; also Hesiod, *Erga*, 648.

populus vult decipi, ergo decipiatur (L.) the public wishes to be fooled, therefore let it be fooled.—Ascribed to Cardinal Caraffa.

poscimur (L.) we are called on [to sing, etc.].

post equitem sedet atra cura (L.) behind the horseman sits black care.—Horace, *Odes*, III. i. 40.

post hoc, ergo propter hoc (L.) after this, therefore because of this (a fallacious reasoning).

pour encourager les autres (Fr.) to encourage the others (Voltaire, *Candide*, on the shooting of Admiral Byng); **pour épater les bourgeois** to startle the stick-in-the-muds; **pour faire rire,** to raise a laugh; **pour mieux sauter** see **reculer** below; **pour passer le temps** to pass away the time; **pour prendre congé,** or **PPC,** to take leave.

praefervida (misquoted as **perfervida**). See **Scotorum.**

principiis obsta (L.) resist the first beginnings.—Ovid, *R.A.*, 91. Cf. **venienti,** etc.

probatum est (L.) it has been proved.

probitas laudatur et alget (L.) honesty is commended and left out in the cold.—Juvenal, I. 74.

procul este, profani (L.) keep your distance, uninitiated ones.—Virgil, *Aen.*, VI. 258.

proh pudor! (L.) oh, for shame!

proxime accessit (*pl.* **accesserunt**) (L.) came next [to the prizeman].

pulvis et umbra sumus (L.) we are dust and a shadow. —Horace, *Od.*, IV. vii. 16.

purpureus pannus (L.) a purple patch.—From Horace, *A.P.*, 15-16.

quamdiu se bene gesserit (L.) during good behaviour.

quantum mutatus ab illo (L.) how changed from that (Hector who came back clad in Achilles's spoils).—Virgil, *Aen.*, II. 274.

que diable allait-il faire dans cette galère? (Fr.) what the devil was he doing in that galley?—Molière, *Les Fourberies de Scapin*, II. vii.

quem di diligunt adolescens moritur (L.) whom the gods love dies young.—Plautus's translation of **hon hoi theoi . . .**

quem Iupiter vult perdere dementat prius, or **quem deus perdere vult, prius dementat** (L.) whom Jupiter (a god) wishes to destroy, he first makes mad.

que sais-je (sçai-je)? (Fr.) what do I know?—Montaigne's motto.

que voulez-vous? (Fr.) what would you?

quicquid agunt homines . . . nostri est farrago libelli (L.) whatever men do is the medley of our little book. —Juvenal, I. 85-86.

quicquid delirant reges plectuntur Achivi (L.) whatever madness possesses the chiefs, it is (the common soldiers or people of) the Achaeans who suffer.—Horace, *Epist.*, I. ii. 14.

quicunque vult salvus esse (L.) whosoever will be saved (the beginning of the Athanasian creed).

quid hoc sibi vult? (L.) what does this mean?

quid rides? mutato nomine de te fabula narratur (L.) why do you laugh? with change of name the story is about you.—Horace, *Sat.*, I. i. 69-70.

quién sabe? (Sp.) who knows?

quieta non movere (L.) not to move things that are at rest—to let sleeping dogs lie.

qui facit per alium facit per se (L.) he who acts through another is himself responsible.

quis custodiet ipsos custodes? (L.) who will guard the guards themselves?—Juvenal, VI. 347-8.

quis desiderio sit pudor aut modus tam cari capitis? (L.) what shame or stint should there be in mourning for one so dear?—Horace, *Od.*, I. xxiv. 1.

qui s'excuse s'accuse (Fr.) he who excuses himself accuses himself.

quis separabit? (L.) who shall separate [us]?

qui tacet consentit (L.) who keeps silence consents.

qui va là? (Fr.) who goes there?

quod avertat Deus (L.) which may God avert.

quod bonum, felix, faustumque sit (L.) may it be right, happy, and of good omen.

quod erat demonstrandum (L.) or **Q.E.D.**, which was to be proved or demonstrated; **quod erat faciendum**, or **Q.E.F.**, which was to be done.

quod ubique, quod semper, quod ab omnibus (L.) what everywhere, what always, what by all (has been believed).—St Vincent of Lérin's definition of orthodoxy.

quorum pars magna fui (L.) in which I bore a great share. —Virgil, *Aen.*, II. 6.

quot homines, tot sententiae (L.) as many men, so many minds or opinions.—Terence, *Phormio*, II. iv. 14 (or 1. 454).

quousque tandem abutere, Catilina, patientia nostra? (L.) how far, O Catiline, will you abuse our patience?— Cicero, *In Catilinam*.

quo vadis? (L.) whither goest thou?

rara avis (L.) a rare bird, rare person or thing.—Juvenal, VI. 165.

rari nantes in gurgite vasto (L.) here and there some swimming in a vast whirlpool.—Virgil, *Aen.*, I. 118.

reculer pour mieux sauter (Fr.) to draw back to take a better leap.

redolet lucerna (L.) it smells of the lamp.

re galantuomo (It.) the honest king—king and gentleman [said of Victor Emmanuel II].

religio loci (L.) the religious spirit of the place.—Virgil, *Aen.*, VIII. 349.

rem acu tetigisti (L.) you have touched the thing with a needle, hit it exactly.—Proverbial expression used by Plautus.

remis velisque (L.) with oars and sails; also **remis ventisque** with oars and winds (Virgil, etc.): with all vigour.

res angusta domi (L.) straitened circumstances at home.—Juvenal, III. 165.

res ipsa loquitur (L.) the thing speaks for itself: the accident is in itself evidence of negligence.

respice finem (L.) look to the end.—Playfully perverted into **respice funem**, beware of the (hangman's) rope.

resurgam (L.) I shall rise again.

retro me, satana (L.) in Vulgate, **vade retro me, satana**, get thee behind me, Satan (Matt. xvi. 23, Mark viii. 33, Luke iv. 8): stop trying to tempt me.

revenons à nos moutons (Fr.) let us return to our sheep, i.e. our subject.—From the mediaeval farce, *L'Avocat Pathelin*.

rhododaktylos Eōs (Gr.) rosy-fingered Dawn.—Homer, *Odyssey*, II. 1.

rien ne va plus (Fr.) lit. nothing goes any more—used by croupiers to indicate that no more bets may be made.

risum teneatis, amici? (L.) could you keep from laughing, friends?—Horace, *A.P.*, 5.

Roma locuta, causa finita (L.) Rome has spoken, the cause is ended.

ruat caelum. See fiat justitia.

rudis indigestaque moles (L.) a rude and shapeless mass.—Ovid, *Met.*, I. 7.

ruit. See mole.

rus in urbe (L.) the country in town.—Martial, XII. 57, 21.

rusticus expectat dum defluat amnis (L.) waits like the yokel for the river to run by.—Horace, *Epist.*, I. ii. 42.

salaam aleikum (Ar.) peace be upon you.

salus populi suprema lex esto (L.) let the welfare of the people be the final law (Cicero, *De Legibus*, III. iii: **suprema est lex**).

sans peur et sans reproche (Fr.) without fear and without reproach.

sapere aude (L.) dare to be wise.—Horace, *Epist.*, I. ii. 40.

sartor resartus (L.) the tailor retailored.

sauter à pieds joints (Fr.) to take a standing jump.

sauve qui peut (Fr.) save himself who can: every man for himself.

Scotorum praefervida ingenia (L.) the ardent tempers of the Scots.—Buchanan, *Hist. Scot.*, XVI, 1i.

selon les règles (Fr.) according to the rules.

semel insanivimus omnes (L.) we have all played the fool once.—J. B. Mantuanus, *Ecl.*, i. 217.

se non è vero, è ben trovato (It.) if it is not true, it is cleverly invented.

sero venientibus ossa (L.) the bones to the late-comers.

sic itur ad astra (L.) such is the way to the stars.—Virgil, *Aen.*, IX. 641.

si componere magnis parva, etc. See **si parva**, etc.

sic transit gloria mundi (L.) so passes away earthly glory.

sic volo. See hoc volo.

sic vos non vobis (L.) thus do you, not for yourselves.— Ascribed to Virgil.

Sieg heil (Ger.) victory hail!

si jeunesse savait, si vieillesse pouvait (Fr.) if youth but knew, if age but could.

s'il vous plaît (Fr.) if you please.

similia similibus curantur (L.) likes are cured by likes—a hair of the dog that bit one.

si monumentum requiris, circumspice (L.) if you seek (his) monument, look round you (inscription for the architect Christopher Wren's tomb in St Paul's).

simplex munditiis (L.) elegant in simplicity.—Horace, *Od.*, I. v. 5.

sine Cerere et Libero friget Venus (L.) without Ceres and Bacchus (food and drink) Venus (love) is cold.— Terence, *Eun.*, IV. v. 6.

sine ira et studio (L.) without ill-will and without favour.

sint ut sunt aut non sint (L.) let them be as they are or not at all.

si parla Italiano (It.) Italian spoken.

si parva licet componere magnis (L.; Virgil, *Georg.*, IV. 176); **si componere magnis parva mihi fas est** (Ovid, *Met.*, V. 416-7) if it permissible to compare small things to great.

siste, viator (L.) stop, traveller.

si vis pacem, para bellum (L.) if you would have peace, be ready for war.

skias onar anthrōpos (Gr.) man is a dream of a shadow. — Pindar, *Pyth.*, VIII. 95.

solitudinem faciunt, pacem appellant (L.) they make a desert and call it peace.—Tacitus, *Agric.*, 30.

solventur risu tabulae: tu missus abibis (L.) the bills will be dismissed with laughter—you will be laughed out of court.—Horace, *Sat.*, II. i. 86.

solvitur ambulando (L.) (the problem of reality of motion) is solved by walking—by practical experiment, by actual performance.

spero meliora (L.) I hope for better things.

splendide mendax (L.) splendidly false, nobly lying.— Horace, *Od.*, III. xi. 35.

spretaeque injuria formae (L.) (and) the insult of beauty slighted.—Virgil, *Aen.*, I. 27.

stans pede in uno (L.) standing on one foot.—Horace, *Sat.*, I. iv. 10.

stat pro ratione voluntas (L.) See **hoc volo.**

stet fortuna domus (L.) may the fortune of the house last long.

Sturm und Drang (Ger.) storm and stress.

sua si bona. See O fortunatos, etc.

suaviter in modo, fortiter in re (L.) gentle in manner, resolute in deed.

suggestio falsi. See suppressio veri, etc.

sunt lacrimae rerum (L.) there are tears for things (unhappy).—Virgil, *Aen.*, I. 462.

suo motu (L.) on one's own initiative.

suppressio veri suggestio falsi (L.) suppression of truth is suggestion of the false. (In law, **suppressio veri** is passive, **suggestio falsi** active, misrepresentation.)

sursum corda (L.) lift up your hearts.

surtout, pas de zèle (Fr.) above all, no zeal.

sutor ne ultra (or supra) crepidam. See ne sutor . . .

tacent, satis laudant (L.) their silence is praise enough.— Terence, *Eun.*, III. ii. 23.

tantae molis erat Romanam condere gentem (L.) a task of such difficulty was it to found the Roman race.—Virgil, *Aen.*, I. 33.

tantaene animis caelestibus irae? (L.) are there such violent passions in celestial minds?—Virgil, *Aen.*, I. 11.

tempora (orig. **omnia**) **mutantur, nos et mutamur in illis** (L.) the times (all things) change, and we with them.

tempus edax rerum (L.) time, consumer of things.—Ovid, *Met.*, XV. 234.

tempus fugit (L.) time flies.

thalassa, thalassa! or **thalatta, thalatta!** (Gr.) the sea, the sea! (the exulting cry of Xenophon's men on beholding the sea).—Xenophon, *Anabasis*, IV. 7.

timeo Danaos et dona ferentes (L.) I fear the Greeks, even when bringing gifts.—Virgil, *Aen.*, II. 49.

tiré à quatre épingles (Fr.) as neat as can be.

ton d'apameibomenos prosephē (Gr.) addressed him in reply.—Homer (*passim*).

totus, teres, atque rotundus (L.) complete, smooth, and round.—Horace, *Satires*, II. vii. 86.

toujours perdrix (Fr.) partridge every day—too much of a good thing.

tout comprendre c'est tout pardonner (Fr.) to understand all is to pardon all; **tout est perdu fors l'honneur** all is lost but honour [attrib. to Francis I after Pavia]; **tout vient (à point) à qui sait attendre** all things come to him who can wait.

traduttore traditore (It.) a translator is a traitor or betrayer; *pl.* **traduttori traditori.**

tria juncta in uno (L.) three things in one.

ubi bene, ibi patria (L.) where it goes well with me, there is my fatherland.

ubi saeva indignatio ulterius cor lacerare nequit (L.) where fierce indignation can tear his heart no longer.—Part of Swift's epitaph.

und so weiter (Ger.), or **u.s.w.**, and so forth.

urbi et orbi (L.) to the city (Rome) and to the world, to everyone.

uti possidetis (L.) lit. as you possess—the principle of letting e.g. belligerents keep what they have acquired.

vade in pace (L.) go in peace.

vade retro me, satana. See **retro.**

varium et mutabile semper femina (L.) woman is ever a fickle and changeable thing.—Virgil, *Aen.*, IV. 569.

vedi Napoli, e poi muori (It.) see Naples, and die.

veni Creator Spiritus (L.) come, Creator Spirit—the beginning of an early Latin hymn.

venienti occurrite morbo (L.) run to meet disease as it comes.—Persius, III. 63.

veni, vidi, vici (L.) I came, I saw, I conquered.—Ascribed to Caesar on his victory over Pharnaces.

vera incessu patuit dea (L.) the true goddess was revealed by her gait.—Virgil, *Aen.*, I. 405.

verbum sapienti sat est (L.) a word to the wise is enough—often abbrev. *verb. sap.* and *verb. sat.* See **dictum.**

veritas odium parit (L.) truth begets hatred.—Terence, *Andria*, I. i. 41.

vestigia . . . nulla retrorsum (L.) no footprints backwards (at the lion's den): sometimes used to mean no going back.—Horace, *Epist.*, I. i. 74-75.

victrix causa deis placuit, sed victa Catoni (L.) the gods preferred the winning cause, but Cato the losing.—Lucan, I. 128.

video meliora proboque, deteriora sequor (L.) I see the better course and approve it, I follow the worse.—Ovid, *Met.*, VII. 20.

vigilate et orate (L.) watch and pray.

viresque acquirit eundo (L.) (Fama, hearsay personified) gains strength as she goes.—Virgil, *Aen.*, IV. 175.

Virgilium vidi tantum (L.) I just saw Virgil [and no more].—Ovid, *Trist.*, IV. x. 51.

virginibus puerisque canto (L.) I sing for maidens and boys—for the young person.—Horace, *Od.*, III. i. 4.

virtus post nummos (L.) virtue after money—i.e. money first.—Horace, *Epist.*, I. i. 54.

vita brevis, ars longa (L.) life is short, art is long (see **ho bios,** etc.); **vita sine litteris mors est** life without literature is death.

vive la bagatelle (quasi-Fr.) long live folly.

vive ut vivas (L.) live that you may live; **vive, valeque** life and health to you.

vivit post funera virtus (L.) virtue lives beyond the grave.

vixere fortes ante Agamemnona multi (L.) many brave men lived before Agamemnon.—Horace, *Od.*, IV. ix. 25-26.

vogue la galère! (Fr.) row the boat: row on: come what may!

volenti non fit injuria (L.) no wrong is done to one who consents.

volo, non valeo (L.) I am willing, but unable.

volto sciolto e pensieri stretti (It.) open face, close thoughts.

vous l'avez voulu, George Dandin (Fr.) you would have it so.—Molière, *George Dandin*, Act 1.

vox audita perit, littera scripta manet (L.) the heard word is lost, the written letter abides; **vox et praeterea nihil** a voice and nothing more (of a nightingale).

Wahrheit und Dichtung (Ger.) truth and poetry.

Wein, Weib, und Gesang (Ger.) wine, women and song.

wer da? (Ger.) who is there?

wie geht's? (Ger.) how are you?

zonam perdidit (L.) he has lost his money-belt: he is in needy circumstances; **zonam solvere** to loose the virgin zone, i.e. marry.

List of abbreviations, symbols, etc.

(1) *There is now a tendency to spell abbreviations, esp. of scientific terms and names of international organisations, without stops. In the list below, we have generally left stops out, but it should be understood that in most cases neither method of writing (with or without stops) is wrong.*

(2) *In order to save space, abbreviations for the names of societies and associations are given, but, except for some special reason, abbreviations for the designations of those belonging to any particular organisation—as Associate, Fellow, Associate Fellow, Member, or Associate Member—are not specifically included.*

(3) *The Greek alphabet is given on page 1786.*

A Associate . . . See note (2) above; Amateur; Academician; argon; ampere; angstrom; atomic (in **A-bomb**); denoting the first, or a high, class (as in **A-road**); advanced (in **A-level**); ace (*cards*); adult—formerly used to mark a motion picture at a showing of which any child under 14 should be accompanied by an adult, superseded by **PG**; Australian; Austria (IVR).

Å Ångström.

a are (metric measure); atto- (see p 1790); accepted; acre; active; afternoon; *annus* year; *ante* before.

ā, āā in prescriptions, *ana* (Gr.), i.e. of each a like quantity.

A1, A2, etc. See p 1792.

AA Automobile Association; Australian Army; Alcoholics Anonymous; anti-aircraft; formerly used to mark motion pictures to which no child under 14 may be admitted, superseded by the designation **15**.

āā. See **ā.**

AAA Amateur Athletic Association; American Automobile Association; Australian Automobile Association.

AAM air-to-air missile.

A and M (Hymns) Ancient and Modern.

A and R artists and repertoire (or recording).

AAQMG Assistant Adjutant and Quartermaster General.

AAS *Academiae Americanae Socius* Fellow of the American Academy.

AB able-bodied seaman; *Artium Baccalaureus* Bachelor of Arts; Alberta.

ABA Amateur Boxing Association; American Bar Association.

Abb. Abbess; Abbot; Abbey.

abbr., abbrev. abbreviated; abbreviation.

ABC Associated British Cinemas; American Broadcasting Company; Australian Broadcasting Commission; Audit Bureau of Circulations.

ABCC Association of British Chambers of Commerce.

abd abdicated; abridged.

ABFM American Board of Foreign Missions.

ab init. *ab initio* from the beginning.

abl. ablative.

ABM anti-ballistic missile.

Abp Archbishop.

ABPA Australian Book Publishers' Association.

abr. abridged; abridgement.

ABRC Advisory Board for Research Councils.

ABRO (*ab'rō*) Animal Breeding Research Organisation.

ABS Associate of the Building Societies Institute; Association of Broadcasting Staff.

abs., absol. absolute(ly).

abs., abstr. abstract.

abs. re. *absente reo* the accused being absent.

ABTA (*ab'tə*) Association of British Travel Agents.

AC aircraft(s)man; Aero Club; Alpine Club; Companion of the Order of Australia; appellation (d'origine) contrôlée (see Dict.); athletic club; *ante Christum* before Christ; (or **ac**) alternating current (*elect.*).

Ac actinium.

a/c account.

ACA Associate of the Institute of Chartered Accountants in England and Wales; Associate of the Institute of Chartered Accountants in Ireland.

ACARD Advisory Council for Applied Research and Development.

ACAS (*ā'kas*) Advisory, Conciliation and Arbitration Service.

acc. (or **acct.**, **a/c**) account; accountant; (or **accus.**) accusative; according.

ACC Association of County Councils.

ACCA Associate of the Chartered Association of Certified Accountants.

AC/DC alternating current/direct current; see also in Dict.

ACE Allied Command Europe; Advisory Centre for Education.

ACER (*ā'sər*) Australian Council for Educational Research.

ACGB Arts Council of Great Britain.

ACMA Associate of the Institute of Cost and Management Accountants.

ACP African, Caribbean and Pacific.

ACT Australian Capital Territory.

act. active; acting.

ACTH. See **adren(-o)-** in Dict.

ACTT Association of Cinematograph Television and Allied Technicians.

ACTU Australian Council of Trade Unions.

ACW aircraft(s)woman.

AD *anno Domini* in the year of the Lord; Dame of the Order of Australia; air defence.

ad advertisement; after date; *ante diem* before the day.

ADAS Agricultural Development and Advisory Service.

ADC aide-de-camp; (or **AD and C**) advise duration and charge; analog-to-digital converter.

ad fin. *ad finem* at, towards, or to, the end.

ADI approved driving instructor.

ad inf. *ad infinitum* to infinity.

ad init. *ad initium* at or to the beginning.

ad int. *ad interim* in the meantime.

adj. adjective; adjourned; adjustment.

Adjt. Adjutant.

Adjt.-Gen. Adjutant-General.

ad lib. *ad libitum* at pleasure.

ad loc. *ad locum* at the place.

Adm. Admiral.

admin. administration.

ADN People's Democratic Republic of Yemen (IVR).

ADP automatic data processing; adenosine diphosphate.

adv. advent; adverb; *adversus* against; advocate; advisory.

ad val. *ad valorem* according to value.

advt advertisement.

AE Air Efficiency Award.

ae., aet. *aetatis* of his age, aged (so many years).

AEA Atomic Energy Authority (UK); Air Efficiency Award.

AEB Associated Examining Board.

AEC Atomic Energy Commission (USA).

AEI Associated Electrical Industries.

AERE Atomic Energy Research Establishment.

aet after extra time. See also **ae**.

AEU Amalgamated Engineering Union.

AEW airborne early warning.

AF Associate Fellow . . . See note (2) above; Admiral of the Fleet; audio frequency.

AFA Amateur Football Association.

AFC Air Force Cross; Association Football Club.

AFG Afghanistan (IVR).

AFL-CIO American Federation of Labor and Congress of Industrial Organisations.

AFM Air Force Medal.

AFP Agence France Press.

AG Adjutant-General; (or **A-G**) Attorney-General; *Aktiengesellschaft* (Ger.) joint stock company.

Ag *argentum* silver.

agm annual general meeting.

AGR advanced gas-cooled reactor.

agr., agric. agriculture.

Agt Agent.

AH *anno Hegirae* in the year of Hegira—i.e. from the flight of Mohammed (AD 622, 13 Sept.).

Ah ampere hour.

AHA Area Health Authority.

ahl *ad hunc locum* at this place.

AHS *anno humanae salutis* in the year of human salvation.

ahv *ad hanc vocem* at this word.

AI artificial insemination; artificial intelligence.

AID artificial insemination by donor; Agency for International Development (USA).

AIDS. See **acquire** in Dict.

AIH artificial insemination by husband.

AK Knight of the Order of Australia; Alaska.

aka also known as.

AL Albania (IVR); Alabama.

Al aluminium.

Al(a) Alabama.

Alas. Alaska.

Alba. Alberta.

Alban. *Albanensis* of St Albans.

Alcan (*al'kan*) Aluminium Company of Canada.

Ald. Alderman.

ALF Animal Liberation Front.

alg. algebra.

ALGOL, Algol (*al'gol*) Algorithmic language.

ALP Australian Labor Party.

alt. alternate; altitude; alto.

Alta. Alberta.

ALU arithmetic and logic unit (*comput.*).

AM Associate Member . . . See note (2) above; *Artium Magister* Master of Arts; (or **am**) *ante meridiem* before noon; *Anno Mundi* in the year of the world; *Ave Maria* Hail Mary; amplitude modulation; Member of the Order of Australia; Albert Medal.

Am americium.

Am., Amer. America; American.

AMA American Medical Association; Australian Medical Association.

AMC American Motors Corporation.

AMDG *ad majorem Dei gloriam* to the greater glory of God.

AMMA Assistant Masters' and Mistresses' Association.

ammo (*am'ō*) ammunition.

AMP adenosine monophosphate.

amp. ampere.

amt amount; air mail transfer.

amu atomic mass unit.

an. *anno* in the year; anonymous; *ante* before.

anal. analysis; anology.

anat. anatomy.

ANC African National Congress.

anc. ancient(ly).

AND Andorra (IVR).

Ang. *Anglice* in English.

anme *anonyme* (Fr.) limited liability.

anon. anonymous.

ANS autonomic nervous system.

ans. answer.

antiq. antiquities; antiquarian.

ANU Australian National University.

ANZAAS (*an'zəs, -zas*) Australian and New Zealand Association for the Advancement of Science.

Anzac (*an'zak*) (a soldier serving with the) Australian-New Zealand Army Corps.

Anzus (*an'zəs*) (the alliance between) Australia, New Zealand and the United States.

AO Army Order; Officer of the Order of Australia.

AOB any other business.

AOC appellation d'origine contrôlée (see Dict.); Air Officer Commanding.

AOCB any other competent business.

AOC-in-C Air Officer Commanding-in-Chief.

AOF Ancient Order of Foresters.

aor. aorist.

AP Associated Press.

APEX (*ā'peks*) Association of Professional, Executive, Clerical and Computer Staff; advance purchase excursion.

apo. apogee.

Apoc. Apocalypse; Apocrypha(l).

app. appendix; apparent(ly); apprentice.

appro. approval; approbation.

approx. approximate(ly).

APR annual percentage rate.

Apr. April.

APRC *anno post Romam conditam* in the year after the founding of Rome (753 BC).

APT Advanced Passenger Train; Association of Polytechnic Teachers.

apt. apartment.

AQ achievement quotient.

aq. *aqua* water.

Ar argon.

Ar., Arab. Arabic.

ar *anno regni* in the year of the reign.

ar., arr. arrive(s); arrival.

AR Arkansas.

ARA Associate of the Royal Academy; Amateur Rowing Association.

ARAMCO (*a-ram'kō*) Arabian-American Oil Company.

ARC Agricultural Research Council.

arccos inverse cosine.

arch. archaic; architecture.

archaeol. archaeology.

Archd. Archdeacon; Archduke.

archit. architecture.

arcsin inverse sine.

arctan inverse tangent.

arg. *argentum* silver.

arith. arithmetic(al).

Ariz. Arizona.

Ark. Arkansas.

Arm. Armenian; Armoric.

ARP air raid precautions.

ARR *anno regni regis* or *reginae* in the year of the king's or the queen's reign.

arr. arranged; arrive(s); arrival.

art. article; artificial; (or **arty.**) artillery.

AS Anglo-Saxon; *anno salutis* in the year of salvation; Assistant Secretary.

As arsenic.

ASA Amateur Swimming Association; American Standards Association; Advertising Standards Authority.

asap as soon as possible.

Asaph of St Asaph.

ASC American Society of Cinematographers.

ASCII (*as'ki*) American Standard Code for Information Interchange (a computer code).

Asda (*az'də*) Associated Dairies.

Asdic (*az'dik*) an acronym from Allied (or Anti-) Submarine Detection and Investigation Committee, used for a particular device for locating submerged objects.

ASE Amalgamated Society of Engineers; Association for Science Education.

ASEAN, Asean (*a'si-an*) Association of South-East Asian Nations.

ASF Associate of the Institute of Shipping and Forwarding Agents.

ASH (*ash*) Action on Smoking and Health.

ASLEF (*az'lef*) Associated Society of Locomotive Engineers and Firemen.

ASLIB (*az'lib*) Association of Special Libraries and Information Bureaux (now Association for Information Management).

ASM air-to-surface missile.

Ass., Assoc. Association.

Asst Assistant.

AST Atlantic Standard Time.

ASTMS (often *as'təmz*) Association of Scientific, Technical and Managerial Staffs.

astr., astron. astronomy.

astrol. astrology.

ASW anti-submarine warfare.

AT alternative technology.

At astatine.

ATA Air Transport Auxiliary.

ATC Air Training Corps; air traffic control; automatic train control.

ATM automatic (or automated) teller machine.

atm. atmosphere.

at. no., at. numb. atomic number.

ATP adenosine triphosphate (see Dict.).

ATS Auxiliary Territorial Service (superseded by **WRAC**); anti-tetanus serum.

ats at suit of (*law*).

Att. Attic (Greek); Attorney.

Att.-Gen. Attorney-General.

attrib. attribute(d); attributive(ly).

Atty Attorney.

ATV Associated Television.

at. wt atomic weight.

AU (or **ÅU**) Ångström unit (now usu. Ångström; abbrev. Å); astronomical unit.

Au *aurum* gold.

AUC *anno urbis conditae* or *ab urbe condita* in the year from the building of the city—Rome (753 BC).

AUEW Amalgamated Union of Engineering Workers.

Aufl. *Auflage* (Ger.) edition.

Aug. August.

aug. augmentative.

AUS Australia, including Papua New Guinea (IVR).

AUT Association of University Teachers.

aut., auto. automatic.

Auth. Ver., AV Authorised Version.

AV audio-visual.

av *annos vixit* lived (so many) years.

av. (or **ave**) avenue; average.

AVM Air Vice-Marshal.

avoir., avdp. avoirdupois.

AVR Army Volunteer Reserve.

AWACS (*ā'waks*) airborne warning and control system (aircraft).

AWOL (*ā'wol*) absent, or absence, without official leave.

AWRE Atomic Weapons Research Establishment.

ax. axiom.

AZ Arizona.

az. azimuth.

AZT azidothymidine (a drug used in the treatment of AIDS).

B Baron; British; Bachelor; boron; bel; black (on lead pencils); Belgium (IVR).

B magnetic flux density.

b born; book; bowled; billion; barrel(s).

b breadth.

2B, 3B. Same as **BB, BBB** (on lead pencils).

B1, B2, etc. See page 1792.

BA *Baccalaureus Artium* Bachelor of Arts; British America; British Association (for the Advancement of Science); British Academy; Buenos Aires; British Airways; Booksellers' Association (of Great Britain and Ireland).

Ba barium.

BAA British Airports Authority.

BAAB British Amateur Athletic Board.

BABS beam, or blind, approach beacon system.

BAC British Aircraft Corporation.

Bach. Bachelor.

BACIE British Association for Commercial and Industrial Education.

BADA British Antique Dealers' Association.

BAe British Aerospace.

BAFTA (*baf'tə*) British Academy of Film and Television Arts.

BAgr(ic) Bachelor of Agriculture.

BAI *Baccalaureus in Arte Ingeniaria* Bachelor of Engineering.

bal. balance.

BALPA (*bal'pə*) British Airline Pilots' Association.

B and B bed and breakfast.

B and FBS British and Foreign Bible Society.

b and s brandy and soda.

BAOR British Army of the Rhine.

Bap., Bapt. Baptist.

bap., bapt. baptised.

Bar. Barrister.

bar. baritone.

BARB Broadcasters' Audience Research Board.

BArch Bachelor of Architecture.

Bart Baronet.

Bart's St Bartholomew's Hospital, London.

BAS Bachelor of Agricultural Science; British Antarctic Survey.

BASF *Badische Anilin und Soda-Fabrik* (German chemical company).

BASIC. See Dict.

BASW British Association of Social Workers.

BAT British-American Tobacco Company.

bat., batt. battalion; battery.

BB Boys' Brigade; double, or very, black (on lead pencils).

bb books.

BBB triple black, blacker than **BB** (on lead pencils).

BBBC British Boxing Board of Control.

BBC British Broadcasting Corporation (orig. Company).

BBFC British Board of Film Censors.

BC Before Christ; Board of Control; British Columbia; Battery Commander.

BCAL (*bē'kal'*) British Caledonian (Airways).

BCC British Council of Churches.

BCE Before the Common Era (= BC).

bcg bacillus of Calmette and Guérin, an attentuated strain of the tubercle bacillus, used for inoculation.

BCh *Baccalaureus Chirurgiae* Bachelor of Surgery.

BCL Bachelor of Civil Law.

BCom(m) Bachelor of Commerce.

BCS British Computer Society.

BD Bachelor of Divinity.

bd bound.

BDA British Dental Association.

Bde Brigade.

BDH British Drug Houses.

BDI *Bundesverband der Deutschen Industrie* (Ger.) Federation of German Industry.

BDS Bachelor of Dental Surgery; Barbados (IVR).

bds boards.

BE Bachelor of Engineering; Board of Education.

Be beryllium.

be bill of exchange.

BEA British European Airways (now incorporated in **BA**).

BEAB British Electrical Approvals Board.

BEAMA British Electrical and Allied Manufacturers' Association.
BEd Bachelor of Education.
Beds Bedfordshire.
BEF British Expeditionary Force.
bef. before.
Belg. Belgian; Belgium; Belgic.
BEM British Empire Medal.
Benelux (*ben'i-luks*) a name for Belgium, the Netherlands and Luxembourg.
BEng. Bachelor of Engineering.
Berks Berkshire.
B ès L *Bachelier ès Lettres* (Fr.) Bachelor of Letters.
B ès S *Bachelier ès Sciences* (Fr.) Bachelor of Sciences.
bet. between.
BeV billion electron-volt(s) (in USA, where billion means 1000 million, same as **GeV**).
bf brought forward; bloody fool.
BFI British Film Institute.
BFPO British Forces Post Office.
BG Bulgaria (IVR).
BH British Honduras (IVR).
BHC benzene hexachloride (see Dict.).
bhp brake horse-power.
BHS British Home Stores.
Bi bismuth.
Bib. Bible.
Bibl. Biblical.
bibl. bibliotheca (= a library, book-collection, or catalogue).
biblio, bibliog. bibliography.
BICC British Insulated Callender's Cables.
BIFU Banking Insurance and Finance Union.
BIM British Institute of Management.
biog. biography.
biol. biology.
BIPM *Bureau International des Poids et Mesures* (Fr.) International Bureau of Weights and Measures.
BIR British Institute of Radiology.
BIS Bank for International Settlements.
bis. bissextile (= having a day added, as a leap year).
Bk berkelium.
bk book; bank; bark.
bkg banking.
bkt basket.
BL Bachelor of Law; Bachelor of Letters; British Legion; British Leyland; British Library.
bl barrel; bale; bill of lading.
BLAISE British Library Automated Information Service.
bldg building.
BLESMA (*bles'mə*) British Limbless Ex-Servicemen's Association.
BLit(t) *Baccalaureus Lit(t)erarum* Bachelor of Literature or Letters.
BLLD British Library Lending Division.
BLMC British Leyland Motor Corporation.
BLRD British Library Reference Division.
Blvd Boulevard.
BM Bachelor of Medicine; British Museum; *Beatae Memoriae* of blessed memory; Brigade Major.
BMA British Medical Association.
BMEWS ballistic missile early warning system.
BMJ British Medical Journal.
BML British Museum Library.
BMus Bachelor of Music.
BMW *Bayerische Motoren Werke* (Ger.) Bavarian motor works.
BMX bicycle motocross.
Bn Baron.
bn battalion; billion.
BNB British National Bibliography.
BNEC British National Export Council.
BNFL British Nuclear Fuels Limited.
BNOC (sometimes *bē'nok*) British National Oil Corporation.
b.o. branch office; buyer's option; (or **B.O.**) body odour.

BOA British Optical Association.
BOAC British Overseas Airways Corporation (now incorporated in **BA**).
BOC British Oxygen Company.
BOCM British Oil and Cake Mills.
BOD biochemical oxygen demand.
Boh. Bohemia, Bohemian.
Bol. Bolivia.
bor. borough.
BOSS (*bos*) Bureau of State Security (S.Afr.).
BoT Board of Trade (since 1970 incorporated in **DTI**).
bot. botany; bought; bottle.
BOTB British Overseas Trade Board.
Boul. Boulevard.
BP British Pharmacopoeia; British Petroleum; Baden Powell; be prepared.
Bp Bishop.
bp boiling-point; bills of parcels; bills payable; (or **b.pl.**) birthplace; *bonum publicum* the public good.
BPC British Printing Corporation; British Pharmaceutical Codex.
BPharm Bachelor of Pharmacy.
BPhil *Baccalaureus Philosophiae* Bachelor of Philosophy.
bpi bits per inch.
BQ *Bene quiescat* may he (or she) rest well.
Bq becquerel.
bque barque.
BR British Rail; Brazil (IVR).
Br bromine.
Br. Brother; British.
br bank rate.
br. branch; brig; brown; bridge.
Braz. Brazil; Brazilian.
BRCS British Red Cross Society.
BRD *Bundesrepublik Deutschland* (Ger.) German Federal Republic.
BRE Building Research Establishment.
b.rec. bills receivable.
Bret. Breton.
Brig. Brigadier.
Brig.-Gen. Brigadier-General.
Brit. Britain; Britannia; British; Briton.
BRN Bahrain (IVR).
Bro. Brother.
Bros. Brothers.
BRS British Road Services.
BRU Brunei (IVR).
BS Bachelor of Science or of Surgery; Blessed Sacrament; Balance Sheet; (or **bs**) Bill of Sale; British Shipbuilders; Bahamas (IVR).
BSA Building Societies Association; Birmingham Small Arms.
BSAC British Sub Aqua Club.
BSC British Steel Corporation; British Sugar Corporation.
BSc Bachelor of Science.
BSI British Standards Institution; Building Societies Institute.
BSM British School of Motoring.
BS(S) British Standards (Specification).
BST British Summer Time; British Standard Time; Bachelor of Sacred Theology.
BT British Telecom.
Bt Baronet.
BTA British Tourist Authority.
BTG British Technology Group.
BTO British Trust for Ornithology.
B.T.U. See under **board** in Dict.
Btu British thermal unit.
bu. bushel(s).
Bucks Buckinghamshire.
Bulg. Bulgaria; Bulgarian.
BUNAC British Universities North America Club.
BUPA (*bōo'pə, bū'*) British United Provident Association.
BUR Burma (IVR).

bus., bush. bushel(s).

BV *Beata Virgo* Blessed Virgin; *Bene vale* farewell; *Besloten Vennootschap* (Dutch) limited company.

BVM The Blessed Virgin Mary.

BVM(&)S Bachelor of Veterinary Medicine and Surgery.

BWB British Waterways Board.

BWTA British Women's Temperance Association.

BWV *Bach Werke Verzeichnis* (Ger.) catalogue of Bach's works.

BYOB Bring your own booze/bottle/beer.

C carbon; coulomb; Conservative; Cuba (IVR); clubs (*cards*).

C symbol for electrical capacitance.

°C degree(s) Celsius, centigrade.

c centi- (see p 1790); *caput* chapter; cent; centime; *circa* about; caught; cold.

¢ cent(s); cedi(s).

© copyright.

CA Chartered Accountant (Scotland and Canada; in Scotland, a member of the Institute of Chartered Accountants of Scotland); County Alderman; California.

Ca calcium.

ca *circa* about; cases.

CAA Civil Aviation Authority.

CAB Civil Aeronautics Board (USA); Citizens' Advice Bureau.

CACM Central American Common Market.

CAD (often *kad*) computer-aided design.

cad cash against documents.

c.-à-d. *c'est-à-dire* (Fr.) that is to say.

CAE College of Advanced Education (Austr.); computer-aided engineering.

CAI computer-aided (or -assisted) instruction.

CAL (often *kal*) computer-assisted learning.

cal calorie.

Cal., Calif. California.

Caltech California Institute of Technology.

CAM (often *kam*) computer-aided manufacturing.

Cam., Camb. Cambridge.

Cambs Cambridgeshire.

CAMRA (*kam'rə*) Campaign for Real Ale.

CAN customs assigned number.

Can. Canon; Canto; (or **Can**) Canadian.

C and A Clemens and August (clothing stores).

c and b caught and bowled (by).

c and f cost and freight.

C and G City and Guilds (of London Institute).

C & W country and western (music).

Cant. Canterbury; Canticles.

Cantab. *Cantabrigiensis* of Cambridge.

Cantuar. *Cantuaria* Canterbury; *Cantuariensis* of Canterbury.

CAP Common Agricultural Policy.

cap. capital; *caput* chapter; *capitulum* head, chapter; *capiat* let him (or her) take.

caps capitals (in printing).

Capt. Captain.

CAR Central African Republic.

Car. *Carolus* Charles.

car. carat.

CARD Campaign Against Racial Discrimination.

Card. Cardinal.

Cards Cardiganshire.

CARE (*kār*) Co-operative for American Relief to Everywhere.

CARICOM (*kar'i-kom*) Caribbean Community.

carp. carpentry.

CAS Chief of Air Staff.

CASE Confederation for the Advancement of State Education; Co-operative Awards in Science and Engineering.

CAT College of Advanced Technology; computer-aided (or -assisted) typesetting; see also under **compute** in Dict.

cat. catechism; catalogue.

Cath. Catholic.

cath cathedral.

CB Companion of the Order of the Bath; confined (or confinement) to barracks; Cape Breton; Citizens' Band.

Cb columbium (now niobium).

CBC Canadian Broadcasting Corporation.

CBE Commander of the Order of the British Empire.

CBI Confederation of British Industry.

CBM Californian Business Machines.

CBS Confraternity of the Blessed Sacrament; Columbia Broadcasting System.

CC Companion of the Order of Canada; County Council; Cricket Club; closed circuit (transmission).

cc cubic-centimetre(s); *capita* chapters; (or **c.c.**) carbon copy/copies (now used also of photocopies).

CCA current cost accounting.

CCCP. See **USSR**.

CCF Combined Cadet Force.

C.Chem. chartered chemist.

CCPR Central Council of Physical Recreation.

CCS Corporation of Certified Secretaries.

CD *Corps Diplomatique* (Fr.) Diplomatic Corps; Civil Defence; contagious disease(s); Canadian Forces Decoration; compact disc.

Cd cadmium.

cd candela.

CDN Canada (IVR).

Cdr Commander.

CDSO Companion of the Distinguished Service Order.

CDT craft, design and technology.

CDV Civil Defence Volunteers.

cdv *carte de visite* (Fr.) visiting card.

CE Civil Engineer; Christian Endeavour; Council of Europe; Common Era (= AD).

Ce cerium.

CEDO Centre for Education Development Overseas (formerly **CREDO**).

CEF Canadian Expeditionary Force.

CEGB Central Electricity Generating Board.

CEI Council of Engineering Institutions.

cel. celebrated.

Celt. Celtic.

cen. central; century.

CEng Chartered Engineer.

cent. *centum* a hundred; century; central.

CENTO (*sen'tō*) Central Treaty Organisation.

CERN (*sûrn*) *Conseil Européen pour la Recherche Nucléaire* (Fr.) European Organisation for Nuclear Research.

cert. certainty; (or **certif.**) certificate; certificated; certify.

Cestr. *Cestrensis* of Chester.

CET Central European Time; Council for Educational Technology.

cet. par. *ceteris paribus* other things being equal.

CF Chaplain to the Forces.

Cf californium.

cf calf (book-binding).

cf. *confer* compare.

CFA *Communauté financière d'Afrique* (Fr.) African Financial Community.

cf (and) i cost, freight, and insurance.

CFC chlorofluorocarbon.

cg centigram(me)(s).

c.g. centre of gravity.

CG(L)I City and Guilds (of London) Institute.

CGM Conspicuous Gallantry Medal.

CGPM *Conférence Générale des Poids et Mesures* (Fr.) General Conference of Weights and Measures.

CGS (or **cgs**) centimetre-gramme-second (unit or system); Chief of the General Staff.

CGT capital gains tax; *Confédération Générale du Travail* (Fr.) General Confederation of Labour.

CH Companion of Honour; *Confederatio Helvetica* Switzerland (also IVR).

Ch. Chief; China; Church; Champion.

ch central heating.
ch. chaldron; chapter; child.
Chal., Chald. Chaldee; Chaldaic.
Chamb. Chamberlain.
Chanc. Chancellor; Chancery.
Chap. Chaplain; Chapter.
Chas Charles.
ChB *Chirurgiae Baccalaureus* Bachelor of Surgery.
CHE Campaign for Homosexual Equality.
chem. chemistry; chemical.
Ch. Hist. Church History
Chin. China; Chinese.
Ch.J. Chief-Justice.
ChM *Chirurgiae Magister* Master of Surgery.
choc. chocolate.
CHP combined heat and power.
Chr. Christ; Christian.
Chron. Chronicles.
chron. chronicle; chronology; chronological.
CI Channel Islands; Ivory Coast (IVR).
Ci curie.
CIA Central Intelligence Agency (USA).
Cia *Compagnia* (It.) Company.
Cic. Cicero.
Cicestr. *Cicestrensis* of Chichester.
CID Criminal Investigation Department; Council of Industrial Design.
CIE *Córas Iompair Éireann* (Ir.) Transport Organisation of Ireland; Companion of the Order of the Indian Empire.
Cie *Compagnie* (Fr.) Company.
cif cost, insurance, freight.
CIGS Chief of Imperial General Staff (now **CGS**).
CII Chartered Insurance Institute.
CIM Commission on Industry and Manpower; computer-integrated manufacture.
C-in-C Commander-in-Chief.
CIO. See **AFL-CIO**.
CIOB Chartered Institute of Building.
CIPA Chartered Institute of Patent Agents.
CIPFA Chartered Institute of Public Finance and Accountancy.
CIPM *Comité International des Poids et Mesures* (Fr.) International Committee of Weights and Measures.
CIR Commission on Industrial Relations.
cir., circ. *circa, circiter, circum* about.
circs. circumstances.
CIS Chartered Institute of Secretaries.
CIT Chartered Institute of Transport.
cit. citation; citizen.
CITES Convention on International Trade in Endangered Species (of Wild Fauna and Flora).
civ. civil; civilian.
CJ Chief-Justice.
CKD complete(ly) knock(ed) down (used of a vehicle assembled from imported sets of parts.
CL Sri Lanka (IVR).
Cl chlorine.
cl centilitre(s); *cum laude* with praise.
cl. class; clause.
class. classical; classification.
CLitt Companion of Literature.
CLP constituency Labour party.
CLR computer language recorder.
CLT computer language translator.
CM Certificated Master; Corresponding Member; Common Metre; *Chirurgiae Magister* Master of Surgery.
Cm curium.
cm centimetre(s); *carat métrique* (Fr.) metric carat; *causa mortis* by reason of death.
Cmd Command Paper (now **Cmnd**).
CMEA Council for Mutual Economic Assistance.
CMG Companion of the Order of St Michael and St George.
CMHR combustion modified highly resilient.
CMI computer-managed instruction.

Cmnd Command Paper.
CMRST Committee on Manpower Resources for Science and Technology.
CMS Church Missionary Society.
CN Denoting an irritant 'gas' used in the same manner as **CS** (see below).
CNAA Council for National Academic Awards.
CND Campaign for Nuclear Disarmament.
CNR Canadian National Railway.
CNRS *Centre National de la Recherche Scientifique* (Fr.) National Centre for Scientific Research.
CNS central nervous system.
CO conscientious objector; Colonial Office (before Aug. 1966); combined operations; Commonwealth Office (from Aug. 1966; see also **FCO**); Commanding Officer; Criminal Office; Crown Office; Colombia (IVR); Colorado.
Co cobalt.
Co. Company; County.
c/o care of.
coad coadjutor.
COBOL, Cobol (*kō'bol*) a computer language.
coch., cochl. *cochleare* a spoon, spoonful. **coch. amp.**—*amplum* a tablespoonful. **coch. mag.**—*magnum* a large spoonful. **coch. med.**—*medium* a dessertspoonful. **coch. parv.**—*parvum* a teaspoonful.
COCOM (*kō'kom*) Coordinating Committee for Multilateral Export Controls.
Cod. Codex.
c.o.d. cash (or collect) on delivery.
co-ed. co-educational.
C of A Certificate of Airworthiness.
C of E Church of England; Council of Europe.
C of I Church of Ireland.
C of S Church of Scotland; Chief of Staff.
cog. cognate.
c.o.g. centre of gravity.
COGB Certified Official Government Business.
COHSE (*kō'zi*) Confederation of Health Service Employees.
COI Central Office of Information.
COL computer-oriented language.
Col. Colonel; Colorado; Colossians.
col. column.
coll. college; colleague; collector; colloquial.
collat. collateral(ly).
colloq. colloquial(ly).
Colo. Colorado.
Coloss. Colossians.
COM computer output microfilm.
Com. Commander; Commodore; Committee; Commissioner; Commonwealth; Communist.
com. common; comedy; commerce; committee; commune.
Comdr Commander.
Comdt Commandant.
COMECON (*com'i-kon*) Council for Mutual Economic Aid, or Assistance (Communist Nations).
Cominform, Comintern. see Dict.
COMINT (*kom'int*) Communications Intelligence.
comm. commentary; commander; communication.
Commissr Commissioner.
commn commission.
Commy Commissary.
comp. comparative; composition; compositor; compare; compound; compounded.
compar. comparative; comparison.
COMSAT (*kom'sat*) Communications Satellite (USA).
Com. Ver. Common Version.
Con. Consul.
con. *contra* against; *conju(n)x* consort; conclusion; conversation; convenience.
conc. concentrated; concentration.
Cong. Congress; Congregation(al).
conj. conjunction; conjunctive.
Conn. Connecticut.
conn. connection; connected; connotation.

cons. consonant.
con. sec. conic section.
Consols. Consolidated Funds.
cont., contd continued.
contr. contracted; contraction.
contr. bon. mor. *contra bonos mores* contrary to good manners or morals.
conv. conventional.
co-op. co-operative.
Cop., Copt. Coptic.
Cor. Corinthians; Coroner.
CORE (*kōr, kŏr*) Congress of Racial Equality (USA).
Cor. Mem. Corresponding Member.
Corn. Cornish; Cornwall.
corol., coroll. corollary.
Corp. Corporation; Corporal.
corr. corrupted; corruption; correspond.
Cor. Sec. Corresponding Secretary.
CoS Chief of Staff.
cos cosine.
cosec cosecant.
cosech hyperbolic cosecant.
cosh hyperbolic cosine.
CoSIRA (*ko-sī'rə*) Council for Small Industries in Rural Areas.
COSLA (*koz'lə*) Convention of Scottish Local Authorities.
cosmog. cosmography.
Coss. *consules* Consuls.
cot cotangent.
coth hyperbolic cotangent.
CP Clerk of the Peace; Common Pleas; Carriage Paid; College of Preceptors; Communist Party; Cape Province (S. Afr.); Canadian Press.
cp candle-power.
cp. compare.
CPA Chartered Patent Agent.
CPAC Consumer Protection Advisory Committee.
CPAG Child Poverty Action Group.
CPC Clerk of the Privy Council.
CPI consumer price index.
Cpl Corporal.
cpp current purchasing power.
CPR Canadian Pacific Railway.
CPRE Council for the Protection of Rural England.
CPRS Central Policy Review Staff.
CPS *Custos Privati Sigilli* Keeper of the Privy Seal.
cps cycles per second; characters per second.
CPSA Civil and Public Services Association.
CPSU Communist Party of the Soviet Union.
CPU central processing unit.
CQSW Certificate of Qualification in Social Work.
CR *Carolus rex* King Charles; *civis romanus* a Roman citizen; *Custos Rotulorum* Keeper of the Rolls; Community of the Resurrection (Anglican); Costa Rica (IVR).
Cr chromium.
cr. credit; creditor; crown.
CRAC Careers Research and Advisory Centre.
CRE Commission for Racial Equality.
cres., cresc. crescendo; crescent.
crim. con. criminal conversation (i.e. adultery).
CRMP Corps of Royal Military Police.
CRO cathode-ray oscilloscope; Commonwealth Relations Office (until 1966); Criminal Records Office.
CRT cathode-ray tube.
CS Court of Session; Clerk to the Signet; Civil Service; Christian Science; Chemical Society; orthobenzylidene malononitrile, an irritant 'gas' synthesised (1928) by Corson and Stoughton and used in riot control; Czechoslovakia (IVR).
Cs caesium.
c/s cycles per second (hertz).
CSA Confederate States of America.
CSE Certificate of Secondary Education.
CSEU Confederation of Shipbuilding and Engineering Unions.

CSIRO Commonwealth Scientific and Industrial Research Organisation.
CSO community service order.
CSP Council for Scientific Policy; Chartered Society of Physiotherapists.
CST Central Standard Time.
CSU Civil Service Union.
CSV community service volunteer.
CSYS Certificate of Sixth Year Studies.
CT. Same as **CAT** (see under **compute** in Dict.); Connecticut.
Ct. Connecticut.
ct cent; carat.
CTC Cyclists' Touring Club; city technical college.
CTOL conventional take-off and landing.
CTT capital transfer tax.
Cu *cuprum* copper.
cu., cub. cubic.
CUP Cambridge University Press.
cur., curt current (this month).
cusec cubic feet per second.
CV Cross of Valour (Australia).
cv *curriculum vitae* (see Dict.), or *cursus vitae* course, progress, of life.
2CV *deux chevaux* (Fr.) two horsepower (car).
cva cerebrovascular accident (see Dict.).
CVO Commander of the (Royal) Victorian Order.
cwo cash with order.
cwr continuous welded rail.
CWS Co-operative Wholesale Society.
cwt hundred-weight(s)—**c** (*centum* a hundred), **wt** (weight).
CY Cyprus (IVR).
cyc., cyclo. cyclopaedia.
Cym. Cymric.

D deuterium; Deutsch (catalogue of Schubert's works); Federal Republic of Germany (IVR); diamonds (*cards*); dinar.
D electric flux (displacement).
3-D three-dimensional (see **dimension** in Dict.)
d day; diameter; deci- (see p 1790); *dele* delete; dead; died; deserted; degree; *denarius* or *denarii* a penny or pence (before 1971); duke.
DA District Attorney; Diploma of Art; Diploma in Anaesthetics; duck's arse (hairstyle); dinar (Algeria).
da deca- (see p 1790).
D(A)AG Deputy (Assistant) Adjutant-General.
daf (*daf*) Doorn Automobielfabriek (Netherlands motor factory).
DAFS Department of Agriculture and Fisheries for Scotland.
Dan. Daniel; Danish.
D and C. dilatation and curettage (an operation which cleans out a body-cavity, esp. the womb).
DAR Daughters of the American Revolution.
DAT digital audio tape.
DATEC data and telecommunications.
dau. daughter.
dB decibel.
DBE Dame Commander of the Order of the British Empire.
dbl double.
DBS direct broadcast(ing) by satellite; direct broadcast(ing) satellite.
DC *Da capo* (It.) return to the beginning (*mus.*); District of Columbia; (or **dc**) direct current (*elect.*); District Commissioner.
DCE domestic credit expansion.
DCh Doctor of Surgery.
DCL Doctor of Civil Law; Distillers Company Limited.
DCM Distinguished Conduct Medal.
DCMG Dame Commander of the Order of St Michael and St George.
DCS Deputy Clerk of Session.
DCVO Dame Commander of the (Royal) Victorian Order.

DD *Divinitatis Doctor* Doctor of Divinity; *Deo dedit* gave to God; *dono dedit* gave as a gift.

dd *dono dedit* gave as a gift; (or **D/D**) days after date; (or **D/D**) day's date.

D-day. See Dict.

DDD *dat, dicat, dedicat* gives, devotes, and dedicates; *dono dedit dedicavit* gave and dedicated as a gift.

DDR *Deutsche Demokratische Republik* (Ger.) German Democratic Republic (also IVR).

DDS Doctor of Dental Surgery.

DDT dichlorodiphenyltrichloroethane, an insecticide.

DE Department of Employment; Delaware.

DEA Department of Economic Affairs.

Dec. December.

dec. deceased.

dec., decl. declaration; declension.

DEd Doctor of Education.

def. definition; (or **deft**) defendant.

deg. degree(s).

Del. Delaware.

del. delegate; (or **delt**) *delineavit* drew it.

demon., demons. demonstrative.

DEng Doctor of Engineering.

dent. dental; dentist; dentistry.

DEP Department of Employment and Productivity.

Dep., Dept., dep., dept. department; deputy.

dep. deposed; depart(s); departure.

der., deriv. derivation; derived.

derv. See Dict.

DES Department of Education and Science.

DesRCA Designer of the Royal College of Art.

Deut. Deuteronomy.

DEW distant early warning.

DF Defender of the Faith; Dean of the Faculty.

DFC Distinguished Flying Cross.

DFM Distinguished Flying Medal.

dft defendant; draft.

DG *Dei gratia* by the grace of God.

dg decigram(me)(s).

DGB Deutscher Gewerkschaftsbund (the German trade union federation).

d.h. *das heisst* (Ger.) that is to say.

DHSS Department of Health and Social Services (formerly Security).

dial. dialect.

diam. diameter.

DIANE Direct Information Access Network for Europe.

DIC Diploma of the Imperial College.

dict. dictator; dictionary.

diff. different; difference.

DIG Disabled Income Group.

DIH Diploma in Industrial Health.

dil. dilute.

DIN (sometimes *din*) *Deutsche Industrie-Norm* (Ger.) German Industrial Standards.

DIng *Doctor Ingeniariae* Doctor of Engineering.

Dip. Diploma, as e.g. **Dip. Ed.,** Diploma in Education, **Dip. Tech.,** Diploma in Technology.

Dir. Director.

dis. discontinued.

disc. discount; discoverer.

diss. dissertation.

dist. distance; distinguish; district; distilled.

div. divide; division; divine; divorced.

DIY do-it-yourself.

DJ dee-jay, disc-jockey.

DK Denmark (IVR).

DL Deputy Lieutenant.

dl decilitre(s).

DLit(t) *Doctor litterarum* or *litteraturae* Doctor of Letters or Literature.

DLO direct labour organisation.

DM Deutsche Mark (Federal German currency).

dm decimetre(s).

DMus Doctor of Music.

DMZ demilitarised zone.

DNA deoxyribonucleic acids (see Dict.).

DNB Dictionary of National Biography.

Dnr dinar (Yugoslav currency).

do *ditto* (It.) the same (aforesaid).

DOA dead on arrival.

d.o.b. date of birth.

DOC District Officer Commanding; *Denominazione di Origine Controllata* (It.) the Italian equivalent of appellation contrôlée (see Dict.).

DOCG *Denominazione di Origine Controllata e Garantita* (It.) a label reserved for superior DOC wines.

DOE (or **DoE**) Department of the Environment; Department of Energy (USA).

DOG Directory of Opportunities for Graduates.

DOI, DoI Department of Industry.

dols dollars.

DOM *Deo optimo maximo* to God, best and greatest; *Dominus Omnium Magister* God the master of all; dirty old man; Dominican Republic (IVR).

Dom. *Dominus* Lord; Dominion.

dom. domestic.

DOMS Diploma in Ophthalmic Medicine and Surgery.

Dor. Doric.

doz. (sometimes *duz*) dozen.

DP Displaced Person; data processing; duly performed (the work of the class).

DPH Diploma in Public Health.

DPh, DPhil *Doctor Philosophiae* Doctor of Philosophy.

DPM Diploma in Psychological Medicine.

dpm distintegrations per minute.

DPP Director of Public Prosecutions.

dpt department.

DR dry riser.

Dr Doctor; debtor; Drummer; Driver; drachma (Greek currency).

dr dead reckoning.

dr. dram; drawer.

DS *Dal segno* (It.) from the sign (*mus.*); disseminated sclerosis.

Ds *dominus* (L.) dominee (S. Afr.).

ds, D/S days after sight.

DSC Distinguished Service Cross.

DSc *Doctor Scientiae* Doctor of Science.

DSM Distinguished Service Medal.

DSO Distinguished Service Order.

dsp *decessit sine prole* died without issue.

DT data transmission; (or **dt, DT's, dt's**) delirium tremens.

DTh *Doctor Theologiae* Doctor of Theology.

DTI Department of Trade and Industry.

DUKW. See **duck**[4] in Dict.

Dunelm. *Dunelmensis* of Durham.

DUP Democratic Unionist Party.

DV *Deo volente* God willing.

dvp *decessit vita patris* died in father's lifetime.

dwt pennyweight—**d** (*denarius* a penny), **wt** (weight); deadweight tonnage.

DY Dahomey (IVR).

Dy dysprosium.

dyn dyne; dynamo; dynamometer.

DZ Algeria (IVR).

E East; English; exa- (see p 1790); Spain (IVR); European—indicating a standardised EEC system of measure or food additives (see **E number** in Dict.).

E energy.

e See pp 1792, 1790.

EAK Kenya (IVR).

E and OE errors and omissions excepted.

eaon except as otherwise noted.

EAP English for academic purposes.

EAT Tanzania (IVR).

EAU Uganda (IVR).

Ebor. *Eboracum* York; *Eboracensis* of York.

EBU European Broadcasting Union.

EC East Central; Established Church; Ecuador (IVR).

ECA Economic Commission for Africa.
Eccl., Eccles. Ecclesiastes; **(eccl., eccles.)** ecclesiastical.
ecclesiol. ecclesiology.
Ecclus. Ecclesiasticus.
ECE Economic Commission for Europe.
ECG electrocardiogram (-graph).
ECG(D) Export Credits Guarantee (Department).
ECLAC Economic Commission for Latin America and the Caribbean.
ECO English Chamber Orchestra.
ECOSOC United Nations Economic and Social Council.
ECSC European Coal and Steel Community.
ECT electroconvulsive therapy.
ECU English Church Union; (usu. *ā'kū*) European currency unit.
ECWA Economic Commission for Western Africa.
Ed. Editor.
ed., edit. edited; edition.
EdB Bachelor of Education.
EDC European Defence Community.
Edenburgen. *Edenburgensis* of Edinburgh.
EDF European Development Fund.
Edin. Edinburgh.
edit. edited; edition.
EDP electronic data processing.
EDS English Dialect Society.
EDT eastern daylight time (USA).
EE errors excepted.
EEC European Economic Community.
EEG electroencephalogram (-graph).
EET Eastern European Time.
EETPU Electrical, Electronic, Telecommunication and Plumbing Union.
EETS Early English Text Society.
EEZ exclusive economic zone.
EFL English as a foreign language.
EFTA (*ef'tə*) European Free Trade Association.
EFTS electronic funds transfer system.
E.G. equivalent grade.
e.g., eg, ex. gr. *exempli gratia* for example.
EGU English Golf Union.
EI East Indies.
EIB European Investment Bank.
EIS Educational Institute of Scotland.
ejusd. *ejusdem* of the same.
EKCO (*ek'ō*) E. K. Cole (manufacturer of electrical goods).
El Al Israeli airline (lit. 'towards the sky').
ELDO (*el'dō*) European Launcher Development Organisation (now **ESA**).
elec., elect. electric; electricity.
ELF extremely (or extra) low frequency.
Elien. *Eliensos* of Ely.
ELINT (*el'int*) Electronic Intelligence.
ELT English language teaching.
EMA European Monetary Agreement.
EMF European Monetary Fund.
emf electromotive force.
EMI EMI Limited (formerly Electrical and Musical Industries Limited).
Emp. Emperor, Empress.
EMS European Monetary System.
emu electromagnetic unit.
ency., encyc. encyclopaedia.
ENE east-north-east.
ENG Electronic News Gathering.
Eng. England; English.
eng. engineer; engraver; engraving.
ENO English National Opera.
Ens. Ensign.
ENSA (*en'sə*) Entertainments National Services Association.
ENT Ear, Nose and Throat.
ent., entom. entomology.
Ent. Sta. Hall Entered at Stationers' Hall.
Env. Ext. Envoy Extraordinary.

EOC Equal Opportunities Commission.
eod every other day.
EOKA. See Dict.
EP extended play (record); electroplated.
Ep. Epistle.
EPA European Productivity Agency; Environmental Protection Agency (USA).
Eph. Ephesians.
Epiph. Epiphany.
Epis., Episc. Episcopal.
EPNS electroplated nickel silver; English Place-Name Society.
EPP European People's Party.
EPU European Payments Union.
ER *Elisabeth Regina* Elizabeth, Queen.
Er erbium.
ER(I) *Edwardus Rex* (*Imperator*) Edward, King (and Emperor).
ERA Equal Rights Amendment.
ERNIE (*ûr'ni*) electronic *r*andom *n*umber *i*ndicator *e*quipment (computer).
Es einsteinium.
ESA European Space Agency.
Esc. escudo (Portuguese currency).
ESCA electron spectroscopy for chemical analysis.
ESCAP Economic and Social Commission for Asia and the Pacific.
Esd. Esdras.
ESE east-south-east.
ESL English as a second language.
ESN educationally subnormal.
ESP extra-sensory perception; English for special (or specific) purposes.
esp., espec. especially.
Esq., Esqr. Esquire.
ESRC Economic and Social Research Council.
ESRO (*ez'rō*) European Space Research Organisation (now **ESA**).
ESSO (*es'ō*) Standard Oil.
EST Eastern Standard Time; electric shock treatment.
est. established; estimated.
Esth. Esther.
ESU English-Speaking Union.
ET eastern time; ephemeris time; Arab Republic of Egypt (IVR).
ETA estimated time of arrival; (*et'ə*) *Euzkadi ta Askatasuna* Basque separatist organisation.
et al. *et alii, aliae*, or *alia* and others; *et alibi* and elsewhere.
etc., &c. *et ceteri* or *cetera* and the others, and so forth.
ETD estimated time of departure.
et seq. or sq. (sing.) *et sequens,* **et sqq.** (pl.) *et sequentes* or *sequentia* and the following.
ETU Electrical Trades Union (now **EEPTU**).
ETUC European Trade Union Confederation
ety., etym. etymology; etymological.
EU Evangelical Union.
Eu europium.
Euratom (*ū-rat'əm*) *Eur*opean *Atom*ic *E*nergy Community.
eV electron-volt.
EVA extravehicular activity (*astronautics*).
Ex., Exod. Exodus.
ex. examined; example; exception; excursus; executive; export.
Exc. Excellency.
exc. except; exception.
ex. div. *extra dividendum* without dividend.
exec. executive.
ex. gr. *exempli gratia* for the sake of example.
ex lib. *ex libris* from the books (of)—as on bookplates.
Exod. Exodus.
Exon. *Exonia* Exeter; *Exoniensis* of Exeter.
exp. export; exponential.
exr executor.
exrx executrix.
ext. extension; externally; extinct; extra; extract.

Ez. Ezra.
Ezek. Ezekiel.

F Fellow . . . See note (2), p 1744, Fahrenheit; farad; fluorine; France (IVR); fine (on lead pencils).
F force.
f following; farthing; female; feminine; fathom; foot; forte; folio; femto- (see p 1790).
f frequency.
F₁, F₂. See Dict.
FA Football Association; Faculty of Actuaries.
Fa. Florida.
FAA Federal Aviation Administration (USA).
fam. familiar; family.
FANY (*fan'i*) First Aid Nursing Yeomanry.
FAO Food and Agriculture Organisation (of the United Nations).
FAS Fellow of the Society of Arts; Fellow of the Antiquarian Society; (also **fas**) free alongside ship.
FBA Fellow of the British Academy.
FBI Federal Bureau of Investigation.
FC football club.
FCA Fellow of the Institute of Chartered Accountants in England and Wales, or in Ireland.
FCCA Fellow of the Chartered Association of Certified Accountants.
FCMA Fellow of the Institute of Cost and Management Accountants.
FCO Foreign and Commonwealth Office (**FO** and **CO** combined in 1968).
fcp, fcap foolscap.
FD *Fidei Defensor* Defender of the Faith.
FDA Food and Drug Administration (USA).
FDR *Freie Demokratische Republik* (Ger.) Free Democratic Republic (West Germany).
Fe *ferrum* iron.
Feb. February.
fec. *fecit* did it, or made it (sing.).
Fed (*fed*) Federal Reserve Board; Federal Reserve System.
FEI *Fédération Équestre Internationale* (Fr.) International Equestrian Federation.
fem. feminine.
FET field-effect transistor.
feud. feudal.
ff *fecerunt* did it, or made it (pl.); folios; following (pl.).
f f fortissimo.
FH fire hydrant.
FIAT (*fē'ɔt*) *Fabbrica Italiana Automobile Torino* (It.) Italian Motor Works in Turin.
Fid. Def. *Fidei Defensor* Defender of the Faith.
FIDE *Fédération Internationale des Échecs* (Fr.) International Chess Federation.
FIDO Fog Investigation and Dispersal Operation; Fog Intensive Dispersal Operation; fog, intensive dispersal of; Film Industry Defence Organisation.
fi. fa. *fieri facias* (see Dict.).
FIFA (*fē'fə*) *Fédération Internationale de Football Association* (Fr.) International Association Football Federation.
FIFO (*fī'fō*) first in, first out.
fig. figure; figurative(ly).
FILO (*fī'lō*) first in, last out.
Fimbra Financial Intermediaries, Managers and Brokers Regulatory Association.
FINA *Fédération Internationale de Natation Amateur* (Fr.) International Amateur Swimming Federation.
FIS Family Income Supplement; *Fédération Internationale de Ski* (Fr.) International Ski Federation.
FISA *Fédération Internationale du Sport Automobile* (Fr.) International Automobile Sports Federation.
FJI Fellow of the Institute of Journalists; Fiji (IVR).
FL Liechtenstein (also IVR); Florida.
fl. *floruit* flourished; florin.
Flor., Fla. Florida.
fl. oz. fluid ounce(s).
FM frequency modulation; Field-Marshal.

Fm fermium.
fm fathom.
FO Foreign Office (see **FCO**); Field Officer; Flying Officer; Full Organ.
fo., fol. folio.
fob free on board.
FOC father of the chapel.
foc free of charge.
FOCA Formula One Constructors' Association.
FOE Friends of Europe; (or **FoE**) Friends of the Earth.
for free on rail.
FOREST (*for'ist*) Freedom Organisation for the Right to Enjoy Smoking Tobacco.
FORTRAN, Fortran. See Dict.
FP fireplug; former pupil; Free Presbyterian.
fp forte-piano; freezing-point.
FPA Family Planning Association.
FPS, fps foot-pound-second.
Fr francium; franc.
Fr. Father; France; French; Friar; Friday.
fr. fragment; franc; frequently.
frat. fraternise; fraternity.
FRCP Fellow of the Royal College of Physicians (**Edin.**, of Edinburgh; **Lond.**, of London; **Irel.**, of Ireland).
FRCPS Glasg. Fellow of the Royal College of Physicians and Surgeons of Glasgow.
FRCS Fellow of the Royal College of Surgeons (**Ed.**, of Edinburgh; **Eng.**, of England; **Irel.**, of Ireland).
F(R)FPSG (formerly) Fellow of the (Royal) Faculty of Physicians and Surgeons of Glasgow (now **FRCPS Glasg.**).
FRG Federal Republic of Germany.
Fri. Friday.
FRPS Fellow of the Royal Photographic Society.
FRS Fellow of the Royal Society (**E**, of Edinburgh).
FSF Fellow of the Institute of Shipping and Forwarding Agents.
FSA Fellow of the Society of Antiquaries (**Scot.**, of Scotland).
FSH follicle-stimulating hormone.
FT Financial Times.
ft foot, feet; fort.
fth, fthm fathom.
fur. furlong(s).
fut. future.
fwd forward.
f.w.d. four-wheel drive; front-wheel drive.
fz sforzando.
FZS Fellow of the Zoological Society.

G Gauss; giga- (see p 1790).
G constant of gravitation, the factor linking force with mass and distance.
g gram(me).
g acceleration of gravity (see **gravity** in Dict.).
GA General Assembly; Georgia.
Ga gallium.
Ga. Georgia.
Gael. Gaelic.
Gal. Galatians.
gal., gall. gallon(s).
G. and S. Gilbert and Sullivan.
g and t gin and tonic.
GAR Grand Army of the Republic (USA).
GATT (*gat*) General Agreement on Tariffs and Trade.
gaz. gazette; gazetteer.
GB Great Britain (also IVR).
Gb. gilbert.
GBA Alderney, Channel Islands (IVR).
GBE (Knight or Dame) Grand Cross of the British Empire.
GBG Guernsey, Channel Islands (IVR).
gbh grievous bodily harm.
GBJ Jersey, Channel Islands (IVR).
GBM Isle of Man (IVR).
GBS George Bernard Shaw.
GBZ Gibraltar (IVR).

GC George Cross.

GCA ground control(led) approach system or control apparatus; Guatemala (IVR).

GCB (Knight or Dame) Grand Cross of the Bath.

GCE General Certificate of Education.

GCH (Knight) Grand Cross of Hanover.

GCHQ Government Communications Headquarters.

GCM General Court-martial; (or **gcm**) greatest common measure.

GCMG (Knight or Dame) Grand Cross of the Order of St Michael and St George.

GCSE General Certificate of Secondary Education.

GCVO (Knight or Dame) Grand Cross of the (Royal) Victorian Order.

Gd gadolinium.

Gdns gardens.

GDP gross domestic product.

GDR German Democratic Republic (East Germany).

Ge germanium.

GEC General Electric Company.

Gen. Genesis; (or **Genl**) General.

gen. gender; genitive; genus.

gent. gentleman.

Geo. Georgia; George.

geog. geography.

geol. geology.

geom. geometry.

Ger. German.

ger. gerund.

GeV giga-electron-volt (the equivalent of a thousand million electron-volts, same value in Europe as **BeV** in USA).

GH Ghana (IVR).

GHQ General Headquarters.

GI government (or general) issue (US Army); hence, common soldier.

Gib. Gibraltar.

GIGO garbage in, garbage out.

Gk Greek.

GKN Guest, Keen and Nettlefold.

Gl glucinum (now beryllium).

Glam. Glamorganshire.

GLC Greater London Council.

Gld guilder (Dutch currency).

GLORIA Geological Long Range Asdic.

Glos. Gloucestershire.

GM George Medal; (or **G-M**) Geiger-Müller counter; General Motors.

gm gram(me).

GMAG Genetic Manipulation Advisory Group.

GMBATU General, Municipal, Boilermakers and Allied Trades Union.

GmbH *Gesellschaft mit beschränkter Haftung* (Ger.) limited liability company.

GMC General Medical Council.

GMT Greenwich Mean Time.

GMWU General and Municipal Workers Union.

GNP gross national product.

GOC General Officer Commanding.

GOM Grand Old Man (orig. W. E. Gladstone).

Gov. Governor; (or **Govt**) Government.

GP General Practitioner; Gallup Poll; *Gloria Patri* glory to the Father; grand prix.

GPDST Girls' Public Day School Trust.

GPI general paralysis of the insane.

GPO General Post Office.

GR Greece (IVR).

Gr. Greek.

gr. grain; grammar; gross; gunner.

GR(I) *Georgius Rex (Imperator)* George, King (and Emperor).

GS General Staff; General Service; Geological Society.

gs guineas.

GSM Guildhall School of Music and Drama; gram(me)s per square metre.

GSO General Staff Officer.

GSP Good Service Pension.

GT *gran turisimo* used of a fast motor-car built for touring in style.

GTC General Teaching Council (Scotland).

gu. guinea; gules.

guin. guinea.

GUM *Gosudarstvenni Universalni Magazin* (Russ.) State Universal Store.

GUS Great Universal Stores.

GUT grand unified theory.

GUY Guyana (IVR).

GW gigawatt.

GW(R) Great Western (Railway) (now incorporated in **BR**).

Gy gray.

H hydrogen; henry; hydrant; hospital; hard (on lead pencils); Hungary (IVR); hearts (*cards*).

2H. Same as **HH** (on lead pencils).

h hecto- (see p 1790); hour; hot.

h height; Planck('s) constant (see p 1790).

ℏ Dirac's constant (see p 1790).

HA Heavy Artillery.

Ha hahnium.

ha hectare; *hoc anno* this year.

Hab. Habakkuk.

HAC Honourable Artillery Company; high-alumina cement.

Hag. Haggai.

h and c hot and cold (water laid on).

Hants Hampshire (*Hantshaving*, orig. name of county).

HB hard black (on lead pencils).

hbar hectobar.

HBM His (or Her) Britannic Majesty.

HC Heralds' College; House of Commons; Holy Communion.

HCF (or **Hon CF**) Honorary Chaplain to the Forces; (or **hcf**) highest common factor.

HCM His (or Her) Catholic Majesty.

HDL high-density lipoprotein.

HE His Excellency; His Eminence; High Explosive; Horizontal Equivalent.

He helium.

Heb., Hebr. Hebrew; Hebrews.

HEH His (or Her) Exalted Highness.

her. heraldry; *heres* heir.

Herts Hertfordshire.

HEW Department of Health, Education and Welfare (USA).

HF high frequency.

Hf hafnium.

hf half; **hf-bd** half-bound; **hf-cf** half-calf; **hf-mor** half-morocco.

HG His (or Her) Grace.

Hg *hydrargyrum* mercury.

HGV heavy goods vehicle.

HGW heat-generating waste.

HH His (or Her) Highness; very hard (on lead pencils).

hh hands.

hhd hogshead.

HI Hawaiian Islands.

HIDB Highlands and Islands Development Board.

Hi-Fi, hi-fi (*hī'fī*) high fidelity.

HIH His (or Her) Imperial Highness.

HIM His (or Her) Imperial Majesty.

HIS *hic iacet sepultus* here lies buried.

hist. historian; history.

HIV human immunodeficiency virus.

HJ(S) *hic jacet (sepultus)* here lies buried.

HK House of Keys (Isle of Man); Hong Kong (also IVR).

HKJ Jordan (IVR).

hl hectolitres.

HLI Highland Light Infantry (incorporated in Royal Highland Fusiliers).

HLW high-level waste.

HM His (or Her) Majesty.

HMA Headmasters' Association.

HMAS His (or Her) Majesty's Australian Ship.
HMC His (or Her) Majesty's Customs; Headmasters' Conference.
HMCS His (or Her) Majesty's Canadian Ship.
HMG His (or Her) Majesty's Government.
HMI His (or Her) Majesty's Inspector, Inspectorate.
HMP *hoc monumentum posuit* erected this monument.
HMS His (or Her) Majesty's Ship or Service.
HMSO His (or Her) Majesty's Stationery Office.
HMV His Master's Voice (gramophone company).
HNC Higher National Certificate.
HND Higher National Diploma.
Ho holmium.
ho. house.
Hon. Honourable; Honorary.
Hons Honours.
Hon. Sec. Honorary Secretary.
hor. horizon; horology.
hort., hortic. horticulture; horticultural.
Hos. Hosea.
HOTOL (*hō'tol*) horizontal take-off and landing.
HP hire-purchase; High Priest; half-pay; (or **hp**) horsepower.
HQ headquarters.
HR House of Representatives; Home Rule; highly resilient.
Hr Herr.
hr hour.
HRE Holy Roman Emperor (or Empire).
HRH His (or Her) Royal Highness.
HRIP *hic requiescit in pace* here rests in peace.
HRT hormone replacement therapy.
HS *hic situs* here is laid.
HSE Health and Safety Executive; *hic sepultus* (or *situs*) *est* here is buried (or laid).
HSH His (or Her) Serene Highness.
HSS *Historiae Societatis Socius* Fellow of the Historical Society.
HST High Speed Train.
HT high tension.
HTLV human T(-cell) lymphotrophic virus.
HTV Harlech Television.
Hung. Hungary; Hungarian.
Hunts Huntingdonshire.
HV, hv high voltage; high velocity.
h.w. hit wicket.
HWM high water mark.
Hz hertz (cycles per second).

I iodine; Island, Isle; Italy (IVR).
I electric current.
3i Investors in Industry.
IA Institute of Actuaries; Iowa.
Ia. Iowa.
IAAF International Amateur Athletic Federation.
IAEA International Atomic Energy Agency.
IAM Institute of Advanced Motorists.
IARF International Association for Religious Freedom.
IAS Indian Administrative Service.
IATA (*ī-at'ə*) International Air Transport Association.
IB Institute of Bankers.
ib., ibid. *ibidem* in the same place.
IBA Independent Broadcasting Authority.
IBF International Badminton Federation.
IBM International Business Machines.
IBRD International Bank for Reconstruction and Development (World Bank).
IC integrated circuit.
i/c in charge.
ICA Institute of Contemporary Arts.
ICAEW Institute of Chartered Accountants in England and Wales.
ICAI Institute of Chartered Accountants in Ireland.
ICAO International Civil Aviation Organisation.
ICAS Institute of Chartered Accountants of Scotland.

ICBM intercontinental ballistic missile.
ICBP International Council for Bird Preservation.
ICC International Cricket Conference.
ICE Institution of Civil Engineers; internal combustion engine.
ICFC Industrial and Commercial Finance Corporation (now Investors in Industry (3i)).
ICFTU International Confederation of Free Trade Unions.
ich., ichth. ichthyology.
IChemE Institute of Chemical Engineers.
ICI Imperial Chemical Industries.
ICJ International Court of Justice; International Commission of Jurists.
ICL International Computers Ltd.
ICMA Institute of Cost and Management Accountants.
icon. iconography.
ICRC International Committee of the Red Cross.
ICRP International Commission on Radiological Protection.
ICS Indian Civil Service (in Republic of India, **IAS**).
ICWA Institute of Cost and Works Accountants.
ID Intelligence Department; identification; infectious diseases; Idaho.
id. *idem* the same.
Id(a). Idaho.
IDA International Development Association.
IDB Illicit Diamond Buying (in S. Africa).
IDD International Direct Dialling.
IDN *in Dei nomine* in the name of God.
IDV International Distillers and Vintners.
IE Indo-European.
i.e., ie *id est* that is
IEA Institute of Economic Affairs; International Energy Agency.
IEC International Electrotechnical Commission.
IEE Institution of Electrical Engineers.
IF intermediate frequency.
IFAD International Fund for Agricultural Development.
IFC International Finance Corporation.
IFS Irish Free State (1922-37).
IG Indo-Germanic; Inspector General.
IHC, IHS for the Greek capitals **IHC** (**H**, capital eta and **C**, a form of sigma—see the Greek alphabet on p 1786), first two and last letters of *Iesous* Jesus, often misread as *Jesus Hominum Salvator* Jesus Saviour of Men.
ihp indicated horse-power.
IL Institute of Linguists; Israel (IVR): Illinois.
ILC irreversible letter of credit.
ILEA (*il'i-ə*) Inner London Education Authority.
Ill. Illinois.
ill. illustration; illustrated.
ILN Illustrated London News.
ILO International Labour Organisation or (its secretariat) International Labour Office.
ILP Independent Labour Party.
ILW intermediate level waste.
IMechE Institution of Mechanical Engineers.
IMF International Monetary Fund.
imit. imitative.
IMM Institution of Mining and Metallurgy.
IMO International Maritime Organisation.
Imp. Imperial; *Imperator* Emperor.
imp. (or **imperf.**) imperfect; (or **imper.**) imperative; *imprimatur* let it be printed; (or **impers.**) impersonal.
IMunE Institution of Municipal Engineers.
IN Indiana.
In indium.
in inch(es).
inc. including; incorporated; inclusive.
incl. including; included; inclusive.
incog. *incognito* (It.) unknown, avoiding publicity.
incorp. incorporated.
IND. Same as **IDN**; India (IVR).
Ind. Indiana; Independent.
ind., indic. indicative.

indecl. indeclinable.
indef. indefinite.
indiv. individual.
Ind. Ter. Indian Territory.
INF intermediate-range nuclear forces.
inf. *infra* below; infantry; infinitive.
infra dig. *infra dignitatem* beneath one's dignity.
init. *initio* in the beginning.
INLA Irish National Liberation Army.
in lim. *in limine* on the threshold, at the outset.
in loc. *in loco* in its place.
in loc. cit. *in loco citato* in the place cited.
in pr. *in principio* in the beginning.
INRI *Jesus Nazarenus Rex Judaeorum* Jesus of Nazareth King of the Jews.
Inst. Institute.
inst. instant—the present month; institute.
Inst. P. Institute of Physics.
int. interest; interior; interpreter; international; integral.
Interpol. See Dict.
interrog. interrogation; interrogative(ly).
in trans. *in transitu* in transit.
intrans. intransitive.
intro., introd. introduction.
inv. *invenit* designed it; invented; invoice.
IOB Institute of Building.
IOC International Olympic Committee.
IoJ Institute of Journalists.
IOM Isle of Man.
IOU I owe you.
IOW Isle of Wight.
IPA Institute of Practitioners in Advertising; International Publishers' Association; International Phonetic Alphabet; International Phonetic Association.
IPC International Publishing Corporation.
IPCS Institution of Professional Civil Servants.
IPD *in praesentia Dominorum* in presence of the Lords (of Session).
IPS Inter Press Service.
IQ Intelligence Quotient.
iq *idem quod* the same as.
IQS Institute of Quantity Surveyors.
IR Inland Revenue; Irish; Iran (IVR).
Ir iridium.
Ir. Irish.
ir infra-red.
IRA Irish Republican Army.
IRB Irish Republican Brotherhood.
IRBM intermediate range ballistic missile.
Irel. Ireland.
IRL Ireland (IVR).
IRO Inland Revenue Office.
IRQ Iraq (IVR).
IS Iceland (IVR).
Is., Isa. Isaiah.
ISBN International Standard Book Number.
ISCh Incorporated Society of Chiropodists.
ISD international subscriber dialling.
ISIS (*ī'sis*) Independent Schools Information Service.
Is(l) island.
ISO Imperial Service Order; International Organisation for Standardisation.
ISS International Social Service.
ISSN International Standard Serial Number.
ISTC Iron and Steel Trades Confederation.
IT Information Technology.
It. Italian; Italian vermouth.
ITA Independent Television Authority (now **IBA**).
ita initial teaching alphabet.
ital. italic; Italian.
ITB Industrial Training Board.
ITF International Trade Federations.
ITMA Institute of Trade Mark Agents; (*it'mä*) it's that man again.
ITN Independent Television News.

ITO International Trade Organisation.
ITS International Trade Secretariats.
ITT International Telephone and Telegraph Corporation.
ITU International Telecommunication Union.
ITV Independent Television.
IU international unit.
IU(C)D intra-uterine (contraceptive) device.
IUCN International Union for the Conservation of Nature.
IUPAC International Union of Pure and Applied Chemistry.
IUPAP International Union of Pure and Applied Physics.
IVF in vitro fertilisation.
IVR International Vehicle Registration.
IW Isle of Wight.
IWC International Whaling Commission.

J joule; jack (*cards*); Japan (IVR).
J. Judge; Justice.
JA Jamaica (IVR).
JAL Japan Air Lines.
Jan. January.
Jas James
JC *Juris Consultus* Jurisconsult; Jesus Christ; Justice Clerk.
JCB (*J. C. Bamford*, manufacturer of) a type of mobile excavator.
JCD *Juris Civilis Doctor* Doctor of Civil Law.
JCR junior common room.
JCWI Joint Council for the Welfare of Immigrants.
Jer. Jeremiah.
JET Joint European Torus.
JFK John Fitzgerald Kennedy.
JHS. See **IHC**.
JMB Joint Matriculation Board.
Jno. John.
Jo. Joel.
Josh. Joshua.
JP Justice of the Peace.
Jr., Jun., Junr Junior.
JUD *Juris Utriusque Doctor* Doctor both of Canon and of Civil Law.
Jud., Judg. Judges.
Jul. July.
Jun. June; Junior.
junc. junction.
jurisp. jurisprudence.

K Kelvin (thermometer scale); kelvin; *kalium* potassium; king (*cards*); one thousand; (sometimes) 1024 (*comput.*); kwacha (Zambian currency); kina (Papua New Guinea currency); Köchel (catalogue of Mozart's works); Kirkpatrick (catalogue of Domenico Scarlatti's works); Kampuchea (IVR).
k kilo- (see p 1790); one thousand; 1024 (*comput.*).
Kans. Kansas.
KB Knight of the Bath; Knight Bachelor; King's Bench.
KBE Knight Commander of the Order of the British Empire.
KC King's Counsel; King's College; Kennel Club.
KCB Knight Commander of the Bath.
KCMG Knight Commander of the Order of St Michael and St George.
Kčs *koruna československá* (Czech) (Czechoslovakian) koruna.
KCVO Knight Commander of the (Royal) Victorian Order.
Ken. Kentucky.
KG Knight of the Order of the Garter.
kg kilogram(me)(s).
KGB *Komitet Gosudarstvennoi Bezopasnosti* (Russ.) Committee of State Security.
KGCB Knight of the Grand Cross of the Bath.
kilo kilogram(me); kilometre.
k.k. *kaiserlich-königlich* (Ger.) Imperial-Royal.

KKK Ku Klux Klan.
KL Kuala Lumpur.
KLH Knight of the Legion of Honour.
KLM *Koninklijke Luchtvaart Maatschappij* (Du.) Royal Dutch Airlines.
KM Knight of Malta.
km kilometre(s).
km/h kilometres per hour.
kn knot (nautical, etc., measure).
KO, ko knock out (see Dict.); kick off.
K of L Knight of Labour.
KP Knight of the Order of St Patrick.
kpg, kph kilometres per gallon, hour.
Kr krypton.
kr kreutzer; krone.
KS, Ks. Kansas.
KT Knight of the Thistle.
Kt Knight.
Kt Bach. Knight Bachelor.
ktl *kai ta leipomena* or *kai ta loipa* (Gr.) and the rest, and so forth.
kW kilowatt.
KWAC (*kwak*) keyword and context.
kWh kilowatt-hour.
KWIC (*kwik*) keyword in context.
KWOC (*kwok*) keyword out of context.
KWT Kuwait (IVR).
KY, Ky. Kentucky.

L Lake; Latin; Liberal; lumen; learner (driver); *libra* pound; litre; lecturer; elevated railroad (see Dict.); Luxembourg (IVR).
L symbol for inductance; luminance.
l litre; latitude; league; left; long; (or **lb**) *libra* pound; line.
l length.
LA Law Agent; Literate in Arts; Los Angeles; Louisiana; Library Association.
La lanthanum.
La. Louisiana.
Lab. Labour.
lab. laboratory.
LAC Licentiate of the Apothecaries' Company; leading aircraft(s)man.
LAIA Latin American Integration Association.
Lam. Lamentations.
LAMDA London Academy of Music and Dramatic Art.
LAN local area network.
Lancs Lancashire.
lang. language.
LAO Laos (IVR).
LAR Libya (IVR).
LASER (*lā'zər*) *l*ight *a*mplification by *s*timulated *e*mission of *r*adiation.
Lat. Latin.
lat. latitude.
LB Liberia (IVR).
lb *libra* pound; leg before (wicket).
lbf pound force.
lbw leg before wicket.
LBC London Broadcasting Company.
lc lower-case (in printing); *loco citato* in the place cited; left centre; letter of credit.
LCC London County Council (now **GLC**).
LCD liquid crystal display.
LCh, LChir *Licentiatus Chirurgiae* Licentiate in Surgery.
LCJ Lord Chief-Justice.
LCM, lcm least common multiple.
LCP Licentiate of the College of Preceptors.
LCST Licentiate of the College of Speech Therapists.
LD Lady Day; lethal dosage.
Ld Lord.
LDC less developed country.
LDL low-density lipoprotein.
Ldp, Lp Lordship.
LDS Licentiate in Dental Surgery; Latter-Day Saints.

LDV Local Defence Volunteers (later Home Guard).
LEA Local Education Authority.
LEAP Life Education for the Autistic Person.
lect. lecture.
LED light emitting diode.
leg. legal; legate; legislature.
Leics Leicestershire.
Leip Leipzig.
LEM lunar excursion module.
LEPRA (*lep'rə*) Leprosy Relief Association.
Lev., Levit. Leviticus.
lex. lexicon.
LF low frequency.
LGU Ladies Golf Union.
lh left hand.
LHD *Litterarum Humaniorum Doctor* Doctor of Letters; Doctor of Humanities.
LI Long Island; Light Infantry.
Li lithium.
Lib. Liberal.
lib. *liber* book.
lib. cat. library catalogue.
Lieut. Lieutenant.
LIFO (*lī'fō*) last in, first out.
LILO (*lī'lō*) last in, last out.
Lincs Lincolnshire.
Linn. Linnaean, Linnaeus.
liq. liquid.
lit. literal(ly); literature; literary.
lith., litho., lithog. lithograph; lithography.
Lit. Hum. *litterae humaniores* humane letters, the humanities.
Lit(t)D *Litterarum Doctor* Doctor of Letters.
LJ Lord Justice.
LL Lord Lieutenant.
ll lines.
LLB *Legum Baccalaureus* Bachelor of Laws.
LLCM Licenciate of the London College of Music.
LLD *Legum Doctor* Doctor of Laws.
LLM *Legum Magister* Master of Laws.
LLW low-level waste.
LM long metre.
lm lumen.
LMS London Missionary Society; London, Midland and Scottish (Railway) (now incorporated in **BR**).
ln natural logarithm.
LNE(R) London and North-Eastern (Railway) (now incorporated in **BR**).
LNG liquefied natural gas.
LOB Location of Offices Bureau.
loc. cit. *loco citato* at the place quoted.
L of C line of communication.
log logarithm.
lon., long. longitude.
Lond. London.
Londin. *Londiniensis* of London.
Lonrho *Lon*don *Rho*desian (industrial conglomerate).
loq. *loquitur* speaks.
LP long-playing (record); Lord Provost; low pressure; Labour Party.
LPG liquefied petroleum gas.
LPO London Philharmonic Orchestra.
Lr lawrencium; lira (Italian currency).
LRAM Licenciate of the Royal Academy of Music.
LRCP Licentiate of the Royal College of Physicians (**Edin.**, of Edinburgh; **Lond.**, of London; **Irel.**, of Ireland).
LRCS Licenciate of the Royal College of Surgeons (**Ed.**, of Edinburgh; **Eng.**, of England; **Irel.**, of Ireland).
LS Lesotho (IVR); Linnaean Society; *loco sigilli* in the place of the seal.
LSA Licentiate of the Society of Apothecaries.
LSD lysergic acid diethylamide (a hallucinatory drug).
L.S.D. *librae, solidi, denarii* pounds, shillings, pence.
LSE London School of Economics.
LSO London Symphony Orchestra.
LT low tension.

Lt. Lieutenant.
LTA Lawn Tennis Association.
Lt.-Col. Lieutenant-Colonel.
Ltd limited liability.
Lt.-Gen. Lieutenant-General.
LTh Licentiate in Theology.
Lu Lutetium.
LV luncheon voucher.
Lw (now **Lr**) lawrencium.
LWM low water mark.
LWT London Weekend Television.
lx lux.

M Member . . . See note (2) p 1744; mega- (see p 1790); money; *mille* a thousand; million(s); Malta (IVR).
M. *Monsieur* (Fr.) Mr (pl. **MM.**).
m milli- (see p 1790); metre; mile; married; male; masculine; *meridiem* noon; *mille* a thousand; million(s); maiden over: mark(s).
m mass.
3M Minnesota Mining and Manufacturing Company.
MA *Magister Artium* Master of Arts; Massachusetts; Morocco (IVR).
Mac., Macc. Maccabees.
mach. machinery.
mad, MAD (*mad*) mutual assured destruction.
MAFF Ministry of Agriculture, Fisheries and Food.
mag. magazine; magnetic.
Maj. Major.
MAL Malaysia (IVR).
Mal. Malachi.
Man., Manit. Manitoba.
Man. Dir. Managing Director.
M & B ® a trade mark of May and Baker Ltd. (used e.g. for sulphonamides prepared by this firm and, esp. formerly, others).
M & S Marks & Spencer.
Mar. March.
marg. margin; marginal; margarine.
Marq. Marquis.
mas., masc. masculine.
MASER (*mā'zər*) *m*icrowave *a*mplification by *s*timulated *e*mission of *r*adiation—see Dict.
MASH (*mash*) mobile army surgical hospital.
Mass. Massachusetts.
math., maths mathematics.
Matt. Matthew.
max. maximum.
mb millibar.
MB *Medicinae Baccalaureus* Bachelor of Medicine; mark of the Beast.
MBA Master of Business Administration.
MBE Member of the Order of the British Empire.
MBFR Mutual Balanced Force Reduction.
MC Member of Congress; Master of Ceremonies; Member of Council; Military Cross; Monaco (IVR).
MCA monetary compensatory amounts.
MCC Marylebone Cricket Club; Member of the County Council.
MCh *Magister Chirurgiae* Master of Surgery.
MCP male chauvinist pig.
Mc/s megacycles per second (megahertz).
MD *Medicinae Doctor* Doctor of Medicine; mentally deficient; Managing Director; Maryland.
Md mendelevium.
Md. Maryland.
Mdlle, Mlle *Mademoiselle* (Fr.) Miss.
Mdm Madam.
MDS Master of Dental Surgery.
ME Maine; Methodist Episcopal; Mining or Mechanical Engineer; Most Excellent; Middle English; Middle East; myalgic encephalomyelitis.
Me. Maine.
mech. mechanic; mechanical.
med. medical; medicine; mediaeval; *medius, -a, -um* middle.
Mem. Member.

mem. memorandum; *memento* remember.
memo. memorandum.
MEP Member of the European Parliament.
Messrs *Messieurs* (Fr.) Sirs, Gentlemen; used as pl. of **Mr.**
met., metaph. metaphysics; metaphor; metaphorical.
met., meteor. meteorology.
metal., metall. metallurgy.
meth(s). methylated spirits.
MeV mega-electron-volt(s).
MEX Mexico (IVR).
Mex. Mexico; Mexican.
MEZ *Mitteleuropäische Zeit* (Ger.) Central European Time.
mf mezzo-forte.
mfd manufactured.
MFH Master of Foxhounds.
mfrs manufacturers.
mft *mistura* (for classical L. *mixtura*) *fiat* let a mixture be made.
mfv motor fleet vessel.
MG machine gun; Morris Garage.
Mg magnesium.
mg milligram(me)(s).
Mgr Monseigneur, Monsignor.
MHA Member of the House of Assembly.
MHG Middle High German.
MHR Member of the House of Representatives.
MHz megahertz.
MI Michigan; Military Intelligence; **MI5** Security Services, **MI6** Secret Intelligence Service (initials based on wartime Military Intelligence departments).
Mic. Mica.
Mich. Michigan.
MICR magnetic ink character recognition.
MIDAS (*mī'das*) Missile Defence Alarm System.
Middx. Middlesex.
Mig *Mi*koyan and *G*urevich, aircraft designers.
mil., milit. military.
Min. Ministry.
min. mineralogy; minimum; minute.
MIND the name of the National Association of Mental Health.
Minn. Minnesota.
mips, MIPS million instructions per second.
MIRAS (*mī'ras*) mortgage income relief at source.
MIRV. See Dict.
misc. miscellaneous; miscellany.
Miss. Mississippi.
MIT Massachusetts Institute of Technology.
MJ megajoule(s).
MJI Member of the Institute of Journalists.
MK (on cars) mark.
Mkk markka (Finnish currency).
MKS metre-kilogram-second unit, or system.
MKSA metre-kilogram-second-ampere unit, or system.
ml millilitre(s).
MLA Member of Legislative Assembly; Modern Language Association.
MLC Member of Legislative Council; Meat and Livestock Commission.
MLitt *Magister Litterarum* Master of Letters or Literature.
Mlle *Mademoiselle* (Fr.) Miss;—pl. **Mlles** *Mesdemoiselles.*
MLR minimum lending rate.
MM (Their) Majesties; Martyrs; Military Medal.
MM. *Messieurs* (Fr.) Gentlemen, Sirs.
mm millimetre(s).
MMC Monopolies and Mergers Commission.
Mme *Madame* (Fr.) Mrs;—pl. **Mmes** *Mesdames.*
Mn manganese.
MN Merchant Navy; Minnesota.
MND motor neurone disease.
MO Medical Officer; modus operandi; Missouri.
Mo molybdenum.
Mo. Missouri.

mo. month.
MOD Ministry of Defence.
mod. modern; moderate.
mod. con. modern convenience.
Mods moderations.
MOH Medical Officer of Health.
mol mole (unit).
mol. wt molecular weight.
Mon. Monmouthshire; Monday.
Monsig. Monsignor.
Mont. Montana; Montgomeryshire.
MOR middle-of-the-road.
Mor. Morocco.
MORI (*mö'ri*) Market and Opinion Research Institute.
morn. morning.
mos months.
MOS(T) metal oxide silicon (transistors).
MOT Ministry of Transport (now Transport Industries).
MP Member of Parliament; Military Police; Metropolitan Police; Municipal Police (USA); mounted police.
mp mezzo-piano; melting-point.
mpg, mph miles per gallon, hour.
MPharm Master of Pharmacy.
MPS Member of the Pharmaceutical Society; Member of the Philological Society.
MR Master of the Rolls.
Mr Mister; Master.
MRA Moral Rearmament.
MRC Medical Research Council.
MRCA multirole combat aircraft.
MRCP Member of the Royal College of Physicians.
MRG Minority Rights Group.
mRNA messenger-RNA.
Mrs Mistress (fem. of **Mr,** Mister).
MS manuscript; Master of Surgery; *Memoriae Sacrum* Sacred to the Memory; milestone; Mississippi; multiple sclerosis; Mauritius (IVR).
Ms. See Dict.
ms millisecond(s); (or **M/S**) months (after) sight; manuscript.
MSC Manpower Services Commission.
MSc Master of Science.
MSF medium standard frequency.
MSG monosodium glutamate.
msl mean sea-level.
MSS, mss manuscripts.
MST mountain standard time.
MSW Medical Social Worker.
MT Mechanical Transport; mean time; Montana.
Mt, mt mount.
MTB motor torpedo-boat.
MTh Master of Theology.
mth month.
Mts, mts mountains.
MUFTI Minimum Use of Force Tactical Intervention.
mus. music; museum.
MusB(ac) Bachelor of Music.
MusD(oc) Doctor of Music.
MusM Master of Music.
Mv mendelevium (now **Md**).
mv merchant vessel; motor vessel; muzzle velocity.
MVO Member of the Royal Victorian Order.
MV medium wave; megawatt; Master of Wine; Malawi (IVR).
MWGM Most Worshipful (or Worthy) Grand Master (Freemasonry).
MX missile experimental.
Mx Middlesex.
myst. mysteries.
myth. mythology.

N nitrogen; newton; neper; North, Northern; naira (Nigerian currency); Norway (IVR).
n name; noun; *natus* born; neuter; noon; nano- (see p 1790); new.
NA North America; Netherlands Antilles (IVR).

Na *natrium* sodium.
NAACP National Association for the Advancement of Colored People (USA).
NAAFI (*naf'i*) Navy, Army and Air-Force Institute(s) (providing canteens for the armed forces).
NACODS (*nā'kodz*) National Association of Colliery Overmen, Deputies and Shotfirers.
NACRO (*nak'rō*) National Association for the Care and Resettlement of Offenders.
Nah. Nahum.
NAHT National Association of Head Teachers.
NAI non-accidental injury.
NALGO (*nal'gō*) National and Local Government Officers' Association.
N and Q Notes and Queries.
NAO National Audit Office.
Nap. Napoleon.
NAPO National Association of Probation Officers.
NAS National Academy of Sciences (USA); see **NAS/UWT.**
NASA (*nas'ə*) National Aeronautics and Space Administration (USA).
NAS/UWT National Association of Schoolmasters/Union of Women Teachers.
Nat. National.
nat. *natus* born.
NATFHE National Association of Teachers in Further and Higher Education.
nat. hist. natural history.
NATO (*nā'tō*) North Atlantic Treaty Organisation.
nat. ord. natural order.
Nat. Phil. natural philosophy.
Nat. Sci. Natural Science(s).
NATSOPA (*nat-sō'pə*) National Society of Operative Printers, Graphical and Media Personnel.
NATTKE National Association of Television, Theatrical, and Kinematographic Employees.
Nat. West., NatWest National Westminster Bank.
naut. nautical.
nav. naval; navigation.
NAVAR combined navigation and radar system.
Nazi *Nazionale Sozialisten* (Ger.) German National Socialist Party.
NB New Brunswick; North Britain; North British; North bag (in postal sorting); (or **nb**) *nota bene* note well, or take notice.
Nb niobium.
NBC National Broadcasting Company (USA); nuclear, biological and chemical.
nbg no bloody good.
NBL National Book League.
NBPI National Board for Prices and Incomes (usu. **PIB**).
NBS National Bureau of Standards (USA).
NC New Church; numerical control; North Carolina.
NCB National Coal Board (now British Coal Corporation).
NCC Nature Conservancy Council.
NCCL National Council for Civil Liberties.
NCO non-commissioned officer.
NCR National Cash Register Company.
NCT National Childbirth Trust.
ncv no commercial value.
Nd neodymium.
ND, N.Dak. North Dakota.
nd no date, not dated.
NDPS National Data Processing Service.
NDT non-destructive testing.
NE north-east; New England; Nebraska.
Ne neon.
NEB New English Bible; National Enterprise Board.
Neb., Nebr. Nebraska.
NEC National Executive Committee; National Exhibition Centre.
NED New English Dictionary (now **OED**).
NEDC National Economic Development Council (Neddy).

NEDO National Economic Development Office.
neg. negative.
Neh. Nehemiah.
NEI *non est inventus* has not been found.
nem. con. *nemine contradicente* no one contradicting.
nem. diss. *nemine dissentiente* no one dissenting.
Nep. Neptune.
NERC Natural Environmental Research Council.
Neth. Netherlands.
neut. neuter.
Nev. Nevada.
New M. New Mexico.
NF Norman French; Northern French; National Front.
N.F., Nfd Newfoundland.
NFER National Foundation for Educational Research.
NFS National Fire Service.
NFT National Film Theatre.
NFU National Farmers' Union.
NFWI National Federation of Women's Institutes.
NGA National Graphical Association.
NGO non-governmental organisation.
NH New Hampshire.
NHBRC National House-Builders' Registration Council (or Certificate).
NHI National Health Insurance.
NHS National Health Service.
NI Northern Ireland; national insurance.
Ni nickel.
NIBMAR (*nib'mär*) No Independence Before Majority Rule.
NIC National Incomes Commission (Nicky); Nicaragua (IVR).
NIG Niger (IVR).
NIMBY (*nim'bi*) not in my back yard.
NIRC National Industrial Relations Court.
NIREX (*nī'reks*) Nuclear Industry Radioactive Waste Executive.
NJ New Jersey.
NKVD *Narodny Komitet Vnutrennikh Del* (Russ.) People's Committee of Internal Affairs.
nl *non licet* it is not permitted; *non liquet* it is not clear; *non longe* not far.
NL Netherlands (IVR).
NLRB National Labour Relations Board (USA).
NM, N.Mex. New Mexico.
n mile international nautical mile.
NMR nuclear magnetic resonance.
NNE north-north-east.
NNI noise and number index.
NNW north-north-west.
N.O. New Orleans; natural order.
No nobelium.
no (or **No**) *numero* (in) number; not out.
nom., nomin. nominative.
Non-Coll. Non-Collegiate.
non-com. non-commissioned.
Noncon. Nonconformist.
non obst. *non obstante* notwithstanding.
non pros. *non prosequitur* does not prosecute.
non seq. *non sequitur* it does not follow (see Dict.).
non-U not upper class.
NOP National Opinion Poll.
nop not otherwise provided.
NORAD North American Air Defence Command.
Noraid (*nör'ād*) name of an US organisation giving support to N. Irish republicanism.
Northants. Northamptonshire.
Northumb. Northumberland.
Norvic. *Norvicensis* of Norwich.
Nos, nos numbers.
Notts Nottinghamshire.
Nov. November.
NP Notary Public; New Providence; (or **np**) new paragraph.
Np neptunium.
np no place (of publication).
NPFA National Playing Fields Association.

NPG National Portrait Gallery.
NPL National Physical Laboratory.
nr near.
NRA National Rifle Association.
NRDC National Research Development Corporation.
NRPB National Radiological Protection Board.
NS New Style; Nova Scotia.
ns nanosecond(s); not specified.
NSB National Savings Bank.
NSM New Smoking Material.
NSPCC National Society for Prevention of Cruelty to Children.
NSRA National Small-bore Rifle Association.
NSU non-specific urethritis.
NSW New South Wales.
NT New Testament; Northern Territory; National Trust; no trumps (*cards*).
ntp normal temperature and pressure.
NTS National Trust for Scotland.
NU name unknown.
NUAAW National Union of Agricultural and Allied Workers.
NUBE (*nū'bi*) National Union of Bank Employees.
NUGMW National Union of General and Municipal Workers.
NUI National University of Ireland.
NUJ National Union of Journalists.
NUM National Union of Mineworkers.
Num., Numb. Numbers.
NUPE (*nōō'pā, nū'pē*) National Union of Public Employees.
NUR National Union of Railwaymen.
NUS National Union of Students; National Union of Seamen.
NUT National Union of Teachers.
NV New Version; Nevada.
NV(A)LA National Viewers' and Listeners' Association.
nvd no value declared.
NVM Nativity of the Virgin Mary.
NW north-west.
NWT Northwest Territories (Canada).
NY New York (city or state).
NYC New York City.
NYO National Youth Orchestra.
NZ New Zealand (also IVR).
NZAP New Zealand Associated Press.
NZBC New Zealand Broadcasting Corporation.
NZPA New Zealand Press Association.

O oxygen.
O. Ohio.
o old.
o/a on account of.
O&C Oxford and Cambridge (Schools Examination Board).
O&M organisation and management.
OAP Old Age Pension (or Pensioner).
OAPEC (*ō-ā'pek*) Organisation of Arab Petroleum-Exporting Countries.
OAS on active service; Organisation of American States.
OAU Organisation of African Unity.
OB outside broadcast.
ob. *obiit* died.
Ob., Obad. Obadiah.
obdt obedient.
OBE Officer of the Order of the British Empire.
obj. object; objective.
obl. oblique; oblong.
obs. obsolete; observation.
o/c overcharge.
OC Officer of the Order of Canada; Officer Commanding.
OCCA (*ok'ə*) Oil and Colour Chemists' Association.
OCF Officiating Chaplain to the Forces.
OCR optical character recognition (or reader).

Oct. October.
oct. octavo.
OCTU Officer Cadet Training Unit.
OD Ordnance Datum or Data; overdose (see Dict.).
ODECA *Organisación de Estados Centro-americanos* Organisation of Central American States.
OE Old English.
OECD Organisation for Economic Co-operation and Development.
OED Oxford English Dictionary.
OEEC Organisation for European Economic Co-operation (now **OECD**).
OF Old French; Oddfellow.
off. official; officinal.
OFT Office of Fair Trading.
OH Ohio.
OHMS On His (or Her) Majesty's Service.
OIRT *Organisation Internationale de Radiodiffusion et Télévision* (Fr.) International Organisation of Radio and Television (in East Europe).
OK. See Dict.
OK, Okla. Oklahoma.
Old Test. Old Testament.
OM Order of Merit; Old Measurement.
ON Old Norse.
ONC ordinary national certificate.
OND ordinary national diploma.
ono or near(est) offer.
Ont. Ontario.
O/o offers over.
OP *Ordinis Praedicatorum* of the Order of Preachers (or Dominicans); opposite prompt (*theat.*).
Op. Opera; Opus.
op out of print.
op. opposite; operation.
op. cit. *opere citato* in the work cited.
OPEC (*ō'pek*) Organisation of Petroleum-Exporting Countries.
opp. opposed; opposite.
Ops Operations; Operations officer; Operations room.
OP's other people's.
opt. optative; *optime* very well indeed.
OR other ranks; operations research.
OR, Or., Ore., Oreg. Oregon.
ord. ordained; order; ordinary; ordnance.
orig. origin; original(ly).
ORTF *Organisation de Radio et Télévision Française* French Radio and Television Organisation (until 1975).
OS Old Style; Ordinary Seamen; outsize; Ordnance Survey.
Os Osmium.
OSA *Ordinis Sancti Augustini* of the Order of St Augustine.
OSB *Ordinis Sancti Benedicti* of the Order of St Benedict.
OSF *Ordinis Sancti Francisci* of the Order of St Francis.
OSHA Occupational Safety and Health Administration.
osp *obiit sine prole* died without issue.
OStJ Officer of Order of St John of Jerusalem.
OSS Office of Strategic Services (USA, formerly).
OT Old Testament, occupational therapy.
OTC Officers' Training Corps; over the counter.
OTT over the top.
OU Open University; Official Unionist.
OUDS Oxford University Dramatic Society.
OUP Oxford University Press.
Oxbridge Oxford and Cambridge.
Oxf. Oxford.
OXFAM (*oks'fam*) Oxford Committee for Famine Relief.
Oxon. *Oxonia* Oxford; *Oxoniensis* of Oxford.
oz ounce(s) (15th cent. It. *ōz*, abbreviation of *onza*).

P phosphorus; parking; President; Prince; pedal; peta- (see p 1790); Portugal (IVR).

P power.
p new penny; new pence; piano; pico- (see p 1790); page.
p. participle.
p- para- (*chem.*).
PA Press Association; Publishers Association; personal assistant; Public Address (system); Panama (IVR).
Pa protactinium; pascal.
PA, Pa., Penn., Penna Pennsylvania.
pa. past.
p.a. (or **pa**) per annum; participial adjective.
PA(B)X Private Automatic (Branch) Exchange.
paint. painting.
PAK Pakistan (IVR).
Pal. Palestine.
pam. pamphlet.
Pan. Panama.
Pan Am Pan-American (World Airways Incorporated).
P and O Peninsular and Oriental (Steamship Navigation Co.).
p & p postage and packaging.
pa.p. past participate.
par. paragraph; parallel; parish.
Pasok Panhellenic Socialist Movement.
pass. passive.
PAT Professional Association of Teachers.
pa.t. past tense.
Pat. Off. Patent Office.
PAYE Pay As You Earn (Income Tax).
PB Pharmacopoeia Britannica; Plymouth Brethren.
Pb *plumbum* lead.
PBB polybrominated biphenyl.
PBI poor bloody infantry.
PBX private branch exchange.
PC Police Constable; Privy Councillor; *Patres Conscripti* Conscript Fathers; personal computer.
PCB polychlorinated biphenyl.
pc postcard.
PCC parochial church council.
pce piece.
PCM pulse code modulation.
pcm per calendar month.
PCP phencyclidine.
PCS Principal Clerk of Session.
Pd palladium.
pd paid.
PDI pre-delivery inspection
PDQ pretty damn quick.
PDSA People's Dispensary for Sick Animals.
PE Protestant Episcopal; physical education; Peru (IVR).
p/e price-earnings ratio.
PEC photoelectric cell.
PEI Prince Edward Island.
PEN (*pen*) Poets, Playwrights, Editors, Essayists, and Novelists.
Pen. Peninsula.
Penn., Pa. Pennsylvania.
Pent. Pentecost.
PEP Political and Economic Planning; personal equity plan.
per. period; person.
per an. per annum.
per cent. See Dict.
perf. perfect.
perh. perhaps.
per mil(l) by the thousand; in each thousand.
per pro. *per procurationem* by the agency (of).
Pers. Persian.
pers. person; personal.
PERT programme evaluation and review technique.
Pes. peseta (Spanish currency).
Petriburg. *Petriburgensis* of Peterborough.
PF Procurator Fiscal; Patriotic Front.
Pf pfennig (German currency).
pf piano-forte.
PFLP Popular Front for the Liberation of Palestine.

PG paying guest; parental guidance (motion picture certificate denoting possible unsuitability for young children).

Pg. Portugal; Portuguese.

PGA Professional Golfers' Association.

PGM Past Grand Master.

pH pH value (see Dict.).

phar., pharm. pharmaceutical; pharmacopoeia; pharmacy.

PhB *Philosophiae Baccalaureus* Bachelor of Philosophy.

PhD *Philosophiae Doctor* Doctor of Philosophy.

Phil. Philippians; Philadelphia, philology; philological; philosophy; philosophical.

Philem. Philemon.

Phil. Trans. Philosophical Transactions.

phon., phonet. phonetics.

phonog. phonography.

phot. photography.

phr. phrase.

phys. physiology; physics; physician.

PI Philippines (IVR).

PIA Pakistan International Airlines.

PIB Prices and Incomes Board—National Board for Prices and Incomes.

PIN personal identification number.

pinx. *pinxit* painted it.

PL Primrose League; Poet Laureate; Public Library; Poland (IVR).

pl. plural.

PLA Port of London Authority.

PLC public limited company.

PLO Palestine Liberation Organisation.

PLP Parliamentary Labour Party.

PLR public lending right.

plu., plur. plural.

plup. pluperfect.

PLUTO (*plōo'tō*) Pipeline Under the Ocean (1944; later dismantled).

PM Past Master; (or **pm**) *post meridiem* after noon; Postmaster; (or **pm**) *post mortem* after death; Prime Minister; Provost-Marshal.

Pm promethium.

pm premium.

PMBX private manual branch exchange.

PMG Postmaster-General; Paymaster-General.

PMO Principal Medical Officer.

Pmr Paymaster.

PMRAFNS Princess Mary's Royal Air Force Nursing Service.

PMT premenstrual tension.

pn promissory note.

PNdB perceived noise decibel.

PNG Papua New Guinea.

PO Post Office; Petty Officer; Pilot Officer.

Po polonium.

po postal order.

po. pole.

POA Prison Officers' Association.

pod pay on delivery.

POEU Post Office Engineering Union.

Pol. Econ. Political Economy.

Poo post office order.

POP Post Office preferred.

pop. population; popular.

POS point of sale.

pos., posit. positive.

POUNC Post office Users' National Council.

POW prisoner of war.

PP parish priest; present pupil; past President.

pp pages; *per procurationem* by proxy (also *per pro* for and on behalf of); pianissimo.

pp. past participate.

PPA Pre-School Playgroups Association.

PPC *pour prendre congé* (Fr.) to take leave.

ppc picture post-card.

PPE Philosophy, Politics and Economics.

PPI Plan Position Indicator.

ppm parts per million.

PPP Private Patients' Plan.

PPS *post postscriptum* a later additional postcript; Parliamentary Private Secretary.

PQ Province of Quebec.

PR prize ring; Puerto Rico: Proportional representation; *Populus Romanus* the Roman people; public relations.

Pr praseodymium.

Pr. Prince; priest; Provençal.

pr. pair; per; present; price.

PRB Pre-Raphaelite Brotherhood.

Preb. Prebend; Prebendary.

pref. preface.

prep. preparations; preparatory; preposition.

Pres. President.

pret. preterite.

Prin. Principal.

PRN *pro re nata* for special occasion arising.

PRO Public Relations Officer; Public Record Office.

pro. professional; prostitute; probationary.

prob. probably.

Prof. Professor.

PROP (*prop*) Preservation of the Rights of Prisoners.

prop. proper(ly); proposition; property.

Prot. Protestant.

pro tem. *pro tempore* for the time being.

Prov. Proverbs; Provincial; Provost.

prox. *Proximo* (*mense*) next (month).

prox. acc. *proxime accessit* next (in order of merit) to the winner.

Pru. Prudential Assurance Company.

PS *postscriptum* written after (something), a postcript; Philological Society; Pharmaceutical Society.

Ps., Psa. Psalm(s).

PSA pleasant Sunday afternoon; Property Services Agency (now Crown Suppliers); Public Services Authority.

PSBR public sector borrowing requirement.

psc passed staff college.

pseud. pseudonym.

PSGB Pharmaceutical Society of Great Britain.

PSIS Permanent Secretaries Committee on the Intelligence Services.

PST Pacific Standard Time.

PSV public service vehicle.

PT physical training; pupil teacher; purchase tax.

Pt platinum.

pt part; pint(s); post-town.

PTA Parent/Teacher Association.

pta peseta.

PTE Passenger Transport Executive.

Pte private (military).

PTFE polytetrafluoroethylene.

PTO please turn over.

pty. proprietary.

PU pick-up.

Pu plutonium.

Pub. Doc. public document.

pulv. *pulvis* powder (*pharm.*).

PVA polyvinyl acetate.

PVC polyvinyl chloride (a type of plastic).

Pvt. Private (*mil.*).

PW Policewoman.

pw per week.

PWD Public Works Department.

PWR pressurised water reactor.

pwt pennyweight.

PX post exchange.

pxt *pinxit* painted.

PY Paraguay (IVR).

Q queen (*cards*).

Q symbol for electric charge; quality (-value).

Q., Qu. query, question; (or **Que.**) Quebec; (or **Qld.**) Queensland.

q *quadrans* farthing; query; quintal; quart; quarter.
QAB Queen Anne's Bounty.
QANTAS (*kwon'təs*) Queensland and Northern Territory Aerial Service.
QARANC Queen Alexandra's Royal Army Nursing Corps.
QARNNS Queen Alexandra's Royal Naval Nursing Service.
QB Queen's Bench.
QC Queen's Counsel; Queen's College.
qd *quasi dicat* as if he would say.
qe *quod est* which is.
QE2 Queen Elizabeth the Second (liner).
QED *quod erat demonstrandum* which was to be demonstrated.
QEF *quod erat faciendum* which was to be done.
QEH Queen Elizabeth Hall.
QEI *quod erat inveniendum* which was to be found.
qid *quater in die* four times a day.
ql *quantum libet* as much as you please.
Qld. See **Q., Qu.**
QM Quartermaster.
qm *quomodo* in what manner, how.
QMG Quartermaster-General.
QMS Quartermaster-Sergeant.
QPM Queen's Police Medal.
QPR Queen's Park Rangers (Football Club).
qq quartos.
qqv *quae vide* which (pl.) see (sing. **qv**).
qr quarter.
QS Quarter-Sessions.
qs, quant. suff. *quantum sufficit* a sufficient quantity.
QSM Queen's Service Medal (New Zealand).
QSO Queen's Service Order (New Zealand); quasi-stellar object (quasar).
qt quantity; quart(s).
q.t. quiet.
qto quarto.
qty quantity.
Qu. Queen; question.
qu., quar. quart; quarter(ly).
quango quasi-autonomous non-governmental organisation; quasi-autonomous national government organisation.
Que. See **Q, Qu.**
qv *quod vide* which (sing.) see (pl. **qqv**); *quantum vis* as much as you will.
qy query.

R *rex, regina* King, Queen; rand (S. African currency); Röntgen unit; (or **Réau**) Réaumur's thermometric scale; Romania (IVR); River.
R symbol for electric resistance.
® registered trade mark.
r right; radius; *recipe* take; run(s).
RA Royal Academy or Academician; Royal Artillery; Rear Admiral; Argentina (IVR).
Ra radium.
RAAF Royal Australian Air Force.
Rabb. Rabbinical.
RAC Royal Automobile Club; Royal Armoured Corps; Royal Arch Charter.
Rad. Radical.
rad. *radix* root; radian; radical; radius.
RADA (*rä'də*) Royal Academy of Dramatic Art.
RADAR Royal Association for Disability and Rehabilitation.
RADC Royal Army Dental Corps.
RAEC Royal Army Educational Corps.
RAeS Royal Aeronautical Society.
RAF (coll. *raf*) Royal Air Force.
RAM Royal Academy of Music; random access memory.
r.a.m. relative atomic mass.
RAMC Royal Army Medical Corps.
RAN Royal Australian Navy.

R and A Royal and Ancient (Golf Club) St Andrews.
R and B rhythm and blues (type of popular music).
R and D research and development.
R and R rest and recreation/recuperation.
RAOC Royal Army Ordnance Corps.
RAPC Royal Army Pay Corps.
RAS Royal Astronomical Society; Royal Asiatic Society.
RAuxAF Royal Auxiliary Air Force.
RAVC Royal Army Veterinary Corps.
RAX rural automatic exchange.
RB Rifle Brigade; Botswana (IVR).
Rb rubidium.
RBA Royal Society of British Artists.
RBS Royal Society of British Sculptors.
RC Roman Catholic; Red Cross; Royal College of Art; Taiwan (IVR).
RCA Royal Canadian Academy; Radio Corporation of America; Central African Republic (IVR).
RCAF Royal Canadian Air Force.
RCB Congo (IVR).
RCGP Royal College of General Practitioners.
RCH Chile (IVR).
RCM Royal College of Music; Regimental Court-martial.
RCMP Royal Canadian Mounted Police.
RCN Royal Canadian Navy.
RCO Royal College of Organists.
RCOG Royal College of Obstetricians and Gynaecologists.
RCP Royal College of Physicians; Royal College of Preceptors.
RCS Royal College of Surgeons; Royal Corps of Signals; Royal College of Science.
RCT Royal Corps of Transport.
RCVS Royal College of Veterinary Surgeons.
RD Rural Dean; Naval Reserve Decoration; refer to drawer.
Rd Road; rand (S. African currency).
RDC Rural District Council.
RDS Royal Dublin Society.
RE Royal Engineers; Royal Society of Etchers and Engravers; Royal Exchange; religious education.
Re rhenium.
Réau Réaumur's thermometric scale.
rec. *recipe* take.
recd received.
REconS Royal Economic Society.
recpt receipt.
Rect. Rector; Rectory.
ref. referee; reference.
Ref. Ch. Reformed Church.
Reg. Prof. Regius Professor.
regt. regiment.
rel. relating; relation; relative.
rel. d. relative density.
REME (*rē'mi*) Royal Electrical and Mechanical Engineers.
rep. representative; republic; report; reporter.
rept receipt; report.
retd retired; returned.
Rev. revise(d); revision; Revelations; (or **Revd**) Reverend.
rev revolution.
Rev. Ver. Revised Version.
RF *République française* (Fr.) French Republic; radio frequency.
Rf rutherfordium.
RFA Royal Fleet Auxiliary.
RFC Royal Flying Corps (now **RAF**); Rugby Football Club.
RFU Rugby Football Union.
RGG Royal Grenadier Guards.
RGN Registered General Nurse.
RGS Royal Geographical Society.
Rgt Regiment.
RH Royal Highness; Haiti (IVR).

Rh   rhodium; rhesus (see Dict.).
rh   right hand.
RHA   Royal Horse Artillery; Royal Hibernian Academy; Road Haulage Association; Regional Health Authority.
rhet.   rhetoric.
RHF   Royal Highland Fusiliers.
RHG   Royal Horse Guards.
RHistS   Royal Historical Society.
RHM   Rank Hovis McDougall.
RHS   Royal Humane Society; Royal Horticultural Society; Royal Historical Society; Royal Highland Show.
RI   Royal Institute of Painters in Water Colours; Rhode Island; religious instruction; Royal Institution; Indonesia (IVR).
RIA   Royal Irish Academy.
RIAM   Royal Irish Academy of Music.
RIAS   Royal Incorporation of Architects in Scotland.
RIBA   Royal Institute of British Architects.
RIC   Royal Irish Constabulary; Royal Institute of Chemistry.
RICS   Royal Institution of Chartered Surveyors.
RIGB   Royal Institution of Great Britain.
RIM   Mauritania (IVR).
RIP   *requiescat in pace* may he (or she) rest in peace.
RIPHH   Royal Institute of Public Health and Hygiene.
RJET   remote job entry terminal.
RL   Lebanon (IVR).
RLO   returned letter office.
RLS   Robert Louis Stevenson.
Rly, rly   railway.
RM   Royal Mail; Royal Marines; resident magistrate; riding master; Madagascar (IVR).
RMA   Royal Military Academy, Sandhurst.
RMetS   Royal Meteorological Society.
RMM   Mali (IVR).
RMN   Registered Mental Nurse.
RMO   Resident Medical Officer.
RMP   (Corps of) Royal Military Police.
RMS   Royal Mail Steamer; Royal Microscopical Society.
RN   Royal Navy.
Rn   radon.
RNA   ribonucleic acids (see Dict.).
RNAS   Royal Naval Air Service(s).
RNCM   Royal Northern College of Music.
RNIB   Royal National Institute for the Blind.
RNLI   Royal National Lifeboat Institution.
RNR   Royal Naval Reserve.
RNVR   Royal Naval Volunteer Reserve.
RNZAF   Royal New Zealand Air Force.
RNZN   Royal New Zealand Navy.
ro   *recto* on the right-hand page.
ROC   Royal Observer Corps.
Roffen.   *Roffensis* of Rochester.
ROI   Royal Institute of Oil Painters.
ROK   Korea (IVR).
ROM (*rom*)   read-only memory.
Rom.   Romans.
rom.   roman (in printing).
Rom. Cath.   Roman Catholic.
ro-ro   roll-on-roll-off.
ROSLA (*roz'lə*)   raising of school leaving age.
RoSPA (*ros'pə*), **RSPA**   Royal Society for the Prevention of Accidents.
RP   Reformed Presbyterian; Regius Professor; Received Pronunciation; Royal Society of Portrait Painters; retinitis pigmentosa.
RPA   radiation protection adviser.
RPB   recognised professional body.
RPI   retail price index.
RPM   retail price maintenance.
rpm, rps   revolutions per minute, second.
RPN   reverse Polish notation.
RPO   Royal Philharmonic Orchestra.
RPS   Royal Photographic Society.
RPV   remotely-piloted vehicle.

RR   Right Reverend.
RRE   Royal Radar Establishment.
RRP   recommended retail price.
RS   Royal Society.
Rs   Rupees.
RSA   Royal Society of Arts; Royal Scottish Academy or Academician; Republic of South Africa.
RSC   Royal Society of Chemistry; Royal Shakespeare Company.
RSE   Royal Society of Edinburgh.
RSFSR   Russian Soviet Federated Socialist Republic.
RSG   Regional Seats of Government; rate support grant.
RSGS   Royal Scottish Geographical Society.
RSL   Royal Society of Literature.
RSLA   raising of school leaving age.
RSM   Regimental Sergeant-Major; Royal Society of Medicine; Royal School of Music; San Marino (IVR).
RSO   railway sub-office; railway sorting office; rural sub-office; radiological safety officer; Resident Surgical Officer.
RSPA.   See **RoSPA.**
RSPB   Royal Society for the Protection of Birds.
RSPCA   Royal Society for the Prevention of Cruelty to Animals.
RSS (or **SRS**) *Regiae Societatis Socius* Fellow of the Royal Society; Royal Statistical Society.
RSSA   Royal Scottish Society of Arts.
RSSPCC   Royal Scottish Society for Prevention of Cruelty to Children.
RSV   Revised Standard Version.
RSVP   *répondez s'il vous plaît* (Fr.) reply, if you please.
RSW   Royal Scottish Water Colour Society.
RT   radiotelephone, -phony.
RTE   *Radio Telefis Éireann* (Ir.) Irish Television.
Rt Hon.   Right Honourable.
RTO   Railway Transportation (or Traffic) Officer.
Rt Rev.   Right Reverend.
RTZ   Rio Tinto Zinc Corporation Limited.
RU   Rugby Union; Burundi (IVR).
Ru   ruthenium.
RUC   Royal Ulster Constabulary.
RUKBA   Royal United Kingdom Beneficent Association.
R-unit   Röntgen unit—unit of measurement of X-ray radiation.
RV   Revised Version; recreational vehicle.
RW   Right Worthy.
RWA   Rwanda (IVR).
RWS   Royal Society of Painters in Water Colours.
Ry, ry   railway.
RYA   Royal Yachting Association.
RYS   Royal Yacht Squadron.
RZS   Royal Zoological Society (**E,** of Edinburgh).

S   sulphur; square; stokes; Schmieder (catalogue of Bach's works); siemens; South; Sabbath; Saint; society; sun; Sweden (IVR); spades (*cards*).
s   second(s).
SA   South Africa; South America; South Australia; Salvation Army; ; sex-appeal; *Société anonyme* (Fr.) limited liability company; Society of Arts; Society of Antiquaries (**Scot.,** of Scotland).
sa   *secundum artem* according to art; *sine anno* without date.
SAA   Small Arms Ammunition; South African Airways; Society of Incorporated Accountants (formerly, and Auditors).
SABC   South African Broadcasting Corporation.
SABENA   *Société anonyme belge d'exploitation de la navigation aérienne* (Fr.) Belgian national airline.
SAC   senior aircraftsman.
sae   stamped addressed envelope.
Salop.   See in Dict.
SALT (*sölt*)   Strategic Arms Limitation Talks (or Treaty).
SAM (*sam*)   surface-to-air missile.
Sam.   Samuel.
SARAH   Search and Rescue and Homing.

Sarum *Sarumensis* of Salisbury.
SAS *Societatis Antiquariorum Socius* Fellow of the Society of Antiquaries; Scandinavian Airlines System; Special Air Service.
Sask. Saskatchewan.
Sat. Saturday.
S.A.T.B. soprano, alto, tenor, bass.
SAYE save as you earn.
Sb *stibium* antimony.
SBN Standard Book Number.
SC *senatus consultum* a decree of the Roman senate; South Carolina; Special Constable; Supreme Court; Staff College; Staff Corps.
Sc scandium.
sc *scilicet* namely; *sculpsit* (he) sculptured (this); (or **s. caps, sm. caps**) small capitals (in printing).
s/c self-contained.
ScB *Scientiae Baccalaureus* Bachelor of Science.
SCCL Scottish Council for Civil Liberties.
ScD *Scientiae Doctor* Doctor of Science.
SCDA Scottish Community Drama Association.
SCE Scottish Certificate of Education.
SCF Save the Children Fund.
Sch. schilling (Austrian currency); school.
sci.fa. *scire facias* that you cause to know.
sci. fi. science fiction.
scil., sciz. *scilicet* namely (cf. **viz**).
SCL Student of Civil Law.
SCM Student Christian Movement; State Certified Midwife.
Scot. Scotland; Scottish.
SCPS Society of Civil and Public Servants.
SCR senior common room.
Script. Scripture.
SCUBA (*skoo'bə*) self-contained underwater breathing apparatus.
sculp., sculpt. *sculpsit* (he) sculptured (this); sculpture; sculptor.
SD Senior Deacon; *salutem dicit* sends greeting; standard deviation; Swaziland (IVR); South Dakota.
sd *sine die* without a day (fixed).
SDA Scottish Development Agency.
S.Dak. South Dakota.
SDC single data converter.
SDD Scottish Development Department.
SDI Strategic Defence Initiative.
SDLP Social and Democratic Labour Party.
SDP social, domestic and pleasure; Social Democratic Party.
SDR(s) special drawing rights.
SE south-east; Society of Engineers.
Se selenium.
SEAC South-East Asia Command.
SEAQ Stock Exchange Automated Quotation(s) (UK).
SEATO South-East Asia Treaty Organisation.
SEC Securities and Exchange Commission (USA).
Sec., Secy Secretary.
sec secant.
sec. *secundum* in accordance with; second; section.
sech hyperbolic secant.
sec. leg *secundum legem* according to law.
sec. reg. *secundum regulam* according to rule.
sect. section.
SED Scottish Education Department.
Sem. seminary; Semitic.
SEN State Enrolled Nurse.
Sen. Senator; senior.
Sep., Sept. September; Septuagint.
seq. *sequens* following (pl. **seqq.,** *sequentes* or *sequentia*).
ser. series; sermon.
SERC Science and Engineering Research Council.
Serg., Sergt Sergeant.
Serj., Serjt Sergeant.
Serps, SERPS (*sûrps*) state earnings-related pension scheme.
Sess. Session.

SET Selective Employment Tax.
SETI search for extra-terrestrial intelligence.
SF science fiction; Sinn Fein; signal frequency; Finland (IVR).
SFA Scottish Football Association; Sweet Fanny Adams (= nothing at all).
sfz sforzando.
SG Solicitor-General.
sg specific gravity.
SGF Scottish Grocers' Federation.
SGHWR steam-generating heavy water reactor.
SGP Singapore (IVR).
SHAEF Supreme Headquarters of the Allied Expeditionary Force.
SHAPE (*shāp*) Supreme Headquarters Allied Powers Europe.
shv *sub hoc verbo* or *sub hac voce* under this word.
SI Système International (d'Unités)—see p 1790.
Si silicon.
SIB Securities and Investments Board.
sig. signature.
SIGINT, Sigint (*sig'int*) signals intelligence.
sin sine.
sing. singular.
sinh hyperbolic sine.
SIPRI Stockholm International Peace Research Institute.
SIS Secret Intelligence Service.
sit. vac. situation vacant.
SJ Society of Jesus.
SL Solicitor at Law; Sergeant-at-Law; (or **S Lat.**) South latitude.
SLADE (*slād*) Society of Lithographic Artists, Designers, Engravers and Process Workers.
SLBM submarine-launched ballistic missile.
sld sailed.
SLP Scottish Labour Party; Scottish Liberal Party.
slp *sine legitima prole* without lawful issue.
SM Short Metre; Sergeant-Major; *Sa Majesté* (Fr.) His (or Her) Majesty.
Sm samarium.
SMC Scottish Mountaineering Club.
SME Surinam (IVR).
Smith. Inst. Smithsonian Institution.
SMLondSoc *Societatis Medicae Londiniensis Socius* Member of the London Medical Society.
SMM *Sancta Mater Maria* Holy Mother Mary.
SMMT Society of Motor Manufacturers and Traders.
SMO Senior Medical Officer.
SMP School Mathematics Project.
smp *sine mascula prole* without male issue.
SN Senegal (IVR).
Sn *stannum* tin.
sn *secundum naturam* according to nature.
SNCF *Société Nationale des Chemins de Fer français* (Fr.) French national railways.
SNO Scottish National Orchestra.
SNP Scottish National Party.
SO Staff Officer; Signal Officer; standing order; special order.
so seller's option.
s.o.b. son of a bitch.
Soc. Society.
SOE Special Operations Executive.
SOGAT (*sō'gat*) Society of Graphical and Allied Trades.
Sol., Solr Solicitor.
sol. solution.
Sol.-Gen. Solicitor-General.
sop. soprano.
SOR sale or return.
SOS. See Dict.
SP starting price.
sp *sine prole* without issue.
sp. spelling; species (pl. **spp.**).
SPCK Society for Promoting Christian Knowledge.
SPG Special Patrol Group.
sp.gr. specific gravity (now relative density).

sport. sporting.

SPQR *Senatus Populusque Romanus* (L.) the Senate and People of Rome.

SPR Society for Psychical Research.

sps *sine prole superstite* without surviving issue.

spt seaport.

SPUC Society for the Protection of the Unborn Child.

sp.vol. specific volume.

sq. (or **Sq.**) square; *sequens* following (in pl. **sqq.,** *sequentes* or *sequentia*).

sqn squadron.

SR Southern Region; Southern Railway (now incorporated in **BR**).

Sr senior; Sir; Señor; strontium.

sr steradian.

SRC Student Representative Council.

SRCh State Registered Chripodist.

SRI *Sacrum Romanum Imperium* Holy Roman Empire.

SRN State Registered Nurse.

SRO self-regulatory organisation.

SRS (or **RSS**) *Societatis Regiae Socius* Fellow of the Royal Society.

SRU Scottish Rugby Union.

SS Saints; *Schutzstaffel* (Ger.) Hitler's bodyguard.

ss steamship; screw steamer.

SSAFA Soldiers', Sailors' and Airmen's Families Association.

SSC Solicitor before the Supreme Court (Scotland); *Societas Sanctae Crucis* Society of the Holy Cross.

SSD *Sanctissimus Dominus* Most Holy Lord (the Pope).

SSE south-south-east.

SSM surface-to-surface missile.

SSN Standard Serial Number.

SSP statutory sick pay.

SSPCA Scottish Society for Prevention òf Cruelty to Animals.

SSRC Social Science Research Council.

SSSI site of special scientific interest.

SST supersonic transport.

SSW south-south-west.

St Saint; Strait; Street.

st. stone (weight).

Staffs Staffordshire.

START (*stärt*) Strategic Arms Reduction Talks.

STD subscriber trunk dialling; sexually transmitted disease.

std standard.

Ste *Sainte* (Fr.) fem. of Saint.

ster., stereo stereophonic; stereotype.

ster., stg sterling.

STOL (*stol*) short take-off and landing.

STOPP Society of Teachers Opposed to Physical Punishment.

STP *Sanctae Theologiae Professor* Professor of Theology.

stp standard temperature and pressure.

str steamer.

str. strong.

STS Scottish Text Society.

STUC Scottish Trades Union Congress.

STV Scottish Television; Single Transferable Vote.

SU strontium unit—unit of measurement of strontium radiation; Scripture Union; Soviet Union (also IVR).

sub. subject.

subj. subject; subjunctive.

subst. substitute; substantive.

suf., suff. suffix.

Sun. Sunday.

sup. superfine; superior; (or **superl.**) superlative; supreme; *supra* above; supine; supplement.

Sup. Ct Superior Court; Supreme Court.

superl. superlative.

supp., suppl. supplement.

Supr. Supreme.

Supt. Superintendent.

Surg. surgeon; surgery.

Surv.-Gen. Surveyor-General.

SV *Sancta Virgo* Holy Virgin; *Sanctitas Vestra* Your Holiness.

Sv sievert.

sv *sub voce* under that heading; *sub verbo* under the word.

SW south-west; small women('s); short wave.

SWA South West Africa (IVR).

SWALK (*swölk, swalk*) sealed with a loving kiss.

SWAPO (*swä'pō*) South-West Africa People's Organisation.

SWG standard wire gauge.

SWP Socialist Workers' Party.

SWRI Scottish Women's Rural Institute.

SY Seychelles (IVR).

SYHA Scottish Youth Hostels Association.

sym. symbol.

syn. synonym.

synop. synopsis.

SYR Syria (IVR).

syr. *syrupus* syrup.

syst. system.

T tritium; tesla; tera- (see p 1790); Thailand (IVR).

t tonne (cf. **l,** litre).

t time.

TA Territorial Army.

Ta tantalum.

TAFE (*tāf*) Technical and Further Education.

tal. qual. *talis qualis* just as they come, average quality.

Tam. Tamil.

tan tangent.

T and AVR Territorial and Army Volunteer Reserve (now **TA**).

tanh hyperbolic tangent.

Tas. Tasmania.

TASS (*tas*) *Telegrafnoye Agentsvo Sovietskovo Soyuza* (Russ.) telegraph agency of the Soviet Union; Technical, Administrative and Supervisory Section (of **AUEW**).

Tb terbium.

TB tuberculosis.

TBD torpedo-boat destroyer.

Tc technetium.

tc tierce.

TCCB Test and County Cricket Board.

TCD Trinity College Dublin; Twentieth Century Dictionary.

TCL Trinity College of Music, London.

TCP trichlorophenylmethyliodasalicyl (a proprietary germicide).

TD Territorial Decoration; *Teachta Dála* (Ir.) member of the Dáil.

Te tellurium.

tech. technical; technology.

TEFL (often *tef'əl*) teaching English as a foreign language.

tel. telephone.

tel., teleg. telegram; telegraph.

temp. temporal; *tempore* in the time of; temperature; temporary.

Ten., Tenn. Tennessee.

ten. tenor.

Ter., Terr. Territory; terrace.

term. termination.

TES Times Educational Supplement.

TESL (often *tes'əl*) teaching English as a second language.

Test. Testament.

Teut. Teutonic.

Tex. Texas.

Text. Rec. *textus receptus* the revised text.

TF Territorial Force.

tf till forbidden.

TFR Territorial Force Reserve.

TG transformational grammar; Togo (IVR).

TGWU Transport and General Workers' Union.
Th thorium.
Th. Thursday.
ThD Doctor of Theology.
theat. theatrical.
theol. theology; theologian.
theor. theorem.
THES Times Higher Educational Supplement.
Thess. Thessalonians.
THF Trust Houses Forte.
ThL Theological Licenciate.
Tho., Thos Thomas.
Thu., Thur. Thursday.
THWM Trinity High-water Mark.
TI Tube Investments.
Ti titanium.
tid *ter in die* thrice a day.
TIF *Transports Internationaux par Chemin de Fer* (Fr.) International Rail Transport.
Tim. Timothy.
TIR *Transports Internationaux Routiers* (Fr.) International Road Transport.
TIROS Television and Infrared Observation Satellite.
Tit. Titus.
Tl thallium.
TLC tender loving care.
TLS Times Literary Supplement.
TM transcendental meditation.
Tm thulium.
TN trade name; Tunisia (IVR); Tennessee.
TNT trinitrotoluene.
TO turn over; Telegraph-office; Transport Officer.
Toc H Talbot House.
TOEFL Test of English as a Foreign Language.
tom. *tomus* tome or volume.
tp township; troop.
TPI Town Planning Institute.
tpr teleprinter.
TR Turkey (IVR).
tr. transpose; transactions; translator; trustee.
trans. transitive; translated; translation.
transf. transferred.
treas. treasurer.
TRH Their Royal Highnesses.
trig. trigonometry.
Trin. Trinity.
TRRL Transport and Road Research Laboratory.
Truron. *Truronensis* of Truro.
TSB Trustee Savings Bank.
TSO town sub-office.
TSSA Transport Salaried Staffs' Association.
TT teetotal; Tourist Trophy; tuberculin tested; Trinidad and Tobago (IVR).
TTL to take leave.
Tu., Tues. Tuesday.
TUC Trades Union Congress.
TUI Trade Union Internationals.
TV television.
TVA Tennessee Valley Authority.
TVP texturised vegetable protein.
TWA Trans-World Airlines.
TWI Training within Industry.
TX Texas.
typ., typo. typographer, typography.

U uranium; universal (motion picture certificate indicating that persons of any age will be admitted); Unionist; upper-class (see Dict. under U); Uruguay (IVR).
UAE United Arab Emirates.
UAR United Arab Republic.
UCAR Union of Central African Republics.
UCATT (*uk'ət*) Union of Construction, Allied Trades and Technicians.
UCCA (*uk'ə*) Universities Central Council on Admissions.

UCI *Union Cycliste Internationale* (Fr.) International Cycling Union.
UDA Ulster Defence Association.
UDC Urban District Council; Universal Decimal Classification.
UDI Unilateral Declaration of Independence.
UDM Union of Democratic Mineworkers.
UDR Ulster Defence Regiment.
UDT United Dominions Trust.
UEFA (*ū-ā'fə*) Union of European Football Association.
UF United Free Church (of Scotland).
UFF Ulster Freedom Fighters.
UFO unidentified flying object.
UGC University Grants Committee.
UHF ultra high frequency.
UHT ultra high temperature.
UJD *Utriusque Juris Doctor* Doctor of both Laws (Canon and Civil).
UK United Kingdom.
UKADGE United Kingdom Air Defence Ground Environment.
UKAEA United Kingdom Atomic Energy Authority.
ULA uncommitted logic array.
ULCC ultra large crude carriers.
ULF ultra low frequency.
ult., ulto *ultimo* in the last (month); ultimate(ly).
UMIST (*ū'mist*) University of Manchester Institute of Science and Technology.
UN United Nations.
UNA United Nations Association.
UNCSTD United Nations Conference on Science and Technology for Development.
UNCTAD, Unctad (*ungk'tad*) United Nations Conference on Trade and Development.
UNDP United Nations Development Programme.
UNDRO (*un'drō*) United Nations Disaster Relief Organisation.
UNEF (*ū'nef*) United Nations Emergency Force.
UNEP United Nations Environment Programme.
UNESCO (*ū-nes'kō*) United Nations Educational, Scientific and Cultural Organisation.
UNFPA United Nations Fund for Population Activities.
UNHCR United Nations High Commission(er) for Refugees.
UNICEF (*ū'ni-sef*) United Nations International Children's Emergency Fund—now United Nations Children's Fund.
UNIDO (*ū-nē'dō*) United Nations Industrial Development Organisation.
Unifil United Nations Interim Force in Lebanon.
Unit. Unitarian.
UNITA (*ū-nē'tə*) *União Nacional por Independência Total de Angola* (Port.) National Union for the Total Liberation of Angola.
Univ. University; Universalist.
UNO United Nations Organisation.
UNRRA United Nations Relief and Rehabilitation Administration.
UNRWA (*un'rə*) United Nations Relief and Works Agency.
UP United Presbyterian; United Press.
UPI United Press International.
UPU Universal Postal Union.
UPW Union of Post Office Workers.
URC United Reformed Church.
Uru. Uruguay.
US United States; United Service(s); Under-secretary.
us *ut supra* as above.
USA United States of America (also IVR); United States Army.
USAF United States Air Force.
USCL United Society for Christian Literature.
USDAW (*uz'dō*) Union of Shop, Distributive and Allied Workers.
USIS United States Information Service.
USM Unlisted Securities Market.

USN   United States Navy.
USPG   United Society for the Propagation of the Gospel.
USS   United States Ship or Steamer.
USSR   (also **CCCP** (Russ.)) Union of Soviet Socialist Republics.
usu.   usually.
USW   ultrasonic waves; ultrashort waves.
usw   *und so weiter* (Ger.) and so forth.
UT   Universal Time; Utah.
Ut.   Utah.
ut dict.   *ut dictum* as said.
ut sup.   *ut supra* as above.
UU   Ulster Unionist.
uv   ultraviolet.
UVF   Ulster Volunteer Force.
UWIST (*ū'wist*)   University of Wales Institute of Science and Technology.
UWT.   See **NAS/UWT.**
ux.   *uxor* wife.

V   vanadium; volt; Vatican City (IVR).
V   symbol for electric potential difference.
v   velocity; *versus* against; *vide* see; verb; verse; volume.
V1   *Vergeltungswaffe 1* German flying bomb.
V2   German flying rocket.
VA   Royal Order of Victoria and Albert; Vicar Apostolic; volt-ampere(s).
VA, Va.   Virginia.
vac.   vacuum; vacation.
VAD   Voluntary Aid Detachment.
val.   value.
V and A   Victoria and Albert Museum.
var.   variant; variety; variable.
var. lect.   *varia lectio* variant reading.
VAT (often *vat*)   Value-added Tax.
Vat.   Vatican.
vb   verb.
VC   Victoria Cross; Vice-Chancellor (also **V-c**); Vice-Consul.
VCR   video cassette recorder.
VD   Venereal   Disease(s);   Volunteer   (Officers') Decoration.
vd   various dates; vapour density.
VDC   Volunteer Defence Corps.
VDM   *Verbi Dei Minister* Preacher of God's Word.
VDQS   *Vins délimités de qualité supérieure* (Fr.) wines of superior quality from approved vineyards.
VDT   visual display terminal.
VDU   visual display unit.
VE   Victory in Europe (1945).
veg.   vegetable(s).
vel.   velocity.
Ven.   Venerable.
Venet.   Venetian.
VERA   versatile reactor assembly; vision electronic recording apparatus.
verb. sap.   *verbum sapienti*, or **verb. sat.**, *verbum sat(is)* a word to the wise is enough.
Vert.   Vertebrata.
ves.   vessel.
Vet., Veter.   Veterinary.
Vet. Surg.   Veterinary Surgeon.
VF   voice frequency; video frequency.
VFL   Victorian Football League.
VG   Vicar-General; (or **vg**) very good.
vg   *verbi gratia* for example.
VHF   very high frequency.
v.i.   verb intransitive.
Vic.   Vicar; Vicarage.
Vict.   Victoria; Victoria University.
vid.   *vide* see.
vil(l).   village.
VIP   Very Important Person.
VIR   *Victoria Imperatrix Regina.* See **VRI.**
Vis., Visc.   Viscount.

viz   *videlicet* namely (z = mediaeval Latin symbol of contraction).
VJ   Victory over Japan (1945).
vl   *varia lectio* variant reading (pl. **vvll**).
VLCC   very large crude carrier.
VLF   very low frequency.
VLLW   very low level waste.
VLSI   very large scale integration (*comput.*).
VMH   Victoria Medal of honour (of the Royal Horticultural Society).
VN   Vietnam (IVR).
vo   *verso* on the left-hand page.
VOA   Voice of America.
voc.   vocative.
vocab.   vocabulary.
vol.   volunteer; volume.
VP   Vice-President.
VR   *Victoria Regina* Queen Victoria.
VRD   Volunteer Reserve Decoration.
VRI   *Victoria Regina et Imperatrix* Victoria, Queen and Empress.
VRQ   verbal reasoning quotient.
VS   Veterinary Surgeon; *volti subito* turn quickly.
vs   *versus* against.
VSO   Voluntary Service Overseas.
VSOP   very special old pale.
VT, Vt   Vermont.
v.t.   verb transitive.
VTO(L) (*vē'tol*)   vertical take-off (and landing).
VTR   video tape recorder.
Vul., Vulg.   Vulgate.
vul., vulg.   vulgar.
vvll.   See **vl**.
VW   *Volkswagen* (Ger.) people's car.
vy   various years.

W   *wolframium* tungsten;   watt;   West;   Welsh; women('s); winter.
w   weak.
WA   West Africa; Western Australia; Washington.
WAAC (*wak*)   Women's Army Auxiliary Corps (now **WRAC**).
WAAF (*waf*)   Women's Auxiliary Air Force (earlier and later **WRAF**).
WAG   Gambia (IVR).
WAGBI   Wildfowl Association of Great Britain and Ireland.
WAL   Sierra Leone (IVR).
Wal.   Walloon.
WAN   Nigeria (IVR).
Wash.   Washington.
WASP (*wosp*)   White Anglo-Saxon Protestant.
Wb   weber.
WBA   West Bromwich Albion (Football Club); World Boxing Association of America.
WBC   World Boxing Council.
WC   water-closet; Western Central; Wesleyan Chapel.
WCC   World Council of Churches.
W/Cdr   Wing Commander.
WCL   World Confederation of Labour.
WCT   World Championship Tennis.
WD   War Department; Dominica, Windward Islands (IVR).
4-w/d   four-wheel drive.
WEA   Workers' Educational Association.
Wed.   Wednesday.
wef   with effect from.
WEU   Western European Union.
wf   wrong fount (in printing).
WFA   White Fish Authority.
WFTU   World Federation of Trade Unions.
WG   Granada, Windward Islands (IVR).
wg   wire gauge.
WHO   World Health Organisation.
WI   West Indies; Wisconsin; Women's Institute.
Wigorn.   *Wigorniensis* of Worcester.
Wilts   Wiltshire.

Winton. *Wintoniensis* of Winchester.
WIPO World Intellectual Property Organisation.
Wis(c). Wisconsin.
wk week.
WL St Lucia, Windward Islands (IVR).
WLA Women's Land Army (disbanded 1950).
WLF Women's Liberal Federation.
Wm William.
WMO World Meteorological Organisation.
WNP Welsh National Party.
WNW west-north-west.
WO War Office (1964 absorbed in Ministry of Defence); Warrant Officer; walk-over.
Worcs Worcestershire.
Wp, Wpfl Worshipful.
WP Warsaw Pact.
wp weather permitting.
wpb wastepaper basket.
WPBSA World Professional Billiards and Snooker Association.
wpm words per minute.
WR Western Region.
WRAC (*rak*) Women's Royal Army Corps.
WRAF (*raf*) Women's Royal Air Force.
WRI Women's Rural Institute.
WRNS Women's Royal Naval Service.
WRP Worker's Revolutionary Party.
WRVS Women's Royal Voluntary Service (previously **WVS**).
WS Writer to the Signet; Western Samoa (IVR).
WSW west-south-west.
wt weight.
WTO Warsaw Treaty Organisation.
WV St Vincent, Windward Islands (IVR); West Virginia.
WVa West Virginia.
WVS Women's Voluntary Service (now **WRVS**).
WWF World Wildlife Fund.
wx women's extra.
WY, Wy., Wyo. Wyoming.
WYSIWYG (*wiz'i-wig*) what you see (on the screen) is what you get (in the print-out) (*comput.*).

X Formerly used to mark motion pictures to which persons under eighteen will not be admitted, superseded by the designation **18**.
X, Xt Christ. (*X* = Gr. *Ch*).
x *ex* (L. without), as in **xd**, ex dividend.
xd See **x** above.
Xe. xenon.
Xm., Xmas Christmas.
Xn, Xtian Christian.

Y yttrium; yen (Japanese currency).
y year; yard.
Yb ytterbium.
yd yard.
ye the (the **y** not being a **y** but representing the old letter thorn, **þ**).
Yeo. Yeomanry.
YHA Youth Hostels Association.

YMCA Young Men's Christian Association.
Yn yen (Japanese currency).
YOP (*yop*) Youth Opportunity Programme.
Yorks. Yorkshire.
yr your; younger; year.
YT Yukon Territory.
yt that (**y** as in **ye** above).
YTS Youth Training Scheme.
YTV Yorkshire Television.
YU Yugoslavia (IVR).
YV Venezuela (IVR).
YWCA Young Women's Christian Association.

Z Zambia (IVR).
z zero; zenith; zone.
ZA South Africa (IVR).
ZANU (*zä'nōo*) Zimbabwe African National Union.
ZAPU (*zä'pōo*) Zimbabwe African People's Union.
zb *zum Beispiel* (Ger.) for example.
Zech. Zechariah.
Zeph. Zephaniah.
ZETA zero energy thermonuclear apparatus.
Zl zloty (Polish currency).
Zn zinc.
ZPG zero population growth.
ZR Zaire (IVR).
Zr zirconium.
ZST Zone Standard Time.
ZW Zimbabwe (IVR).

@ at
& and
&c etc
© copyright.
¢ cent(s); cedi(s); colón(s).
° degree (as in 10°C).
ħ Dirac's constant (see p 1790).
£ pound(s).
number.
% per cent.
%₀ per thousand.
₦ naira (Nigerian currency).
® registered trade mark.
$ dollar(s).
¥ yen.
♂ male.
♀ female.
† died.
* born.
‚‚ ditto.
♠ spade.
♡ heart.
♢ diamond.
♣ club.
15 motion picture certificate indicating that persons under 15 years of age will not be admitted.
18 motion picture certificate indicating that persons under 18 years of age will not be admitted.

Musical terms, signs and abbreviations

Pitch

The **pitch** (high or low) of a musical sound depends on its frequency, i.e. the number of vibrations per second; it is denoted by the position of a note on the staff (see below).

The **staff** (or **stave**) consists of the five horizontal lines and four spaces on which the notes are written. To accommodate notes beyond its compass, short lines (**ledger lines**) may be added.

The **clef**, the sign placed at the beginning of each staff, defines the pitch of the note. There are three clefs in use today. The G (treble) clef and the F (bass) clef are always fixed in the same position on the staff and denote the position of G and F respectively.

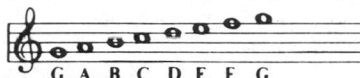

G or treble clef

F or bass clef

The third, or C clef, is movable and is named the soprano, alto, or tenor clef according as it is placed on the 1st, 3rd, or 4th line of the staff. Middle C is shown in each example:

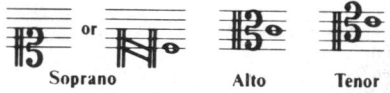

The **key signature** is the arrangement of sharps or flats at the beginning of a piece or section of a piece, and at the start of each subsequent line, showing in which key the music is to be performed.

Values of Notes and Rests

In the example below, each note is twice the length of that which follows. The sign to the right of each note is a rest of equal duration:

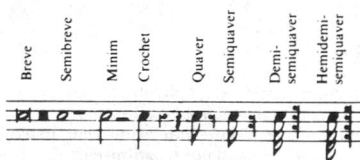

A **dot** added to a note or rest lengthens it by half its value:

A **double dot** added to a note or rest lengthens it by half as much again as one dot:

Notes of quaver denomination or less are usually joined together to form units of crotchet or minim value.

The staff is divided into **bars**, or measures, with an equal number of beats, by vertical lines (**bar lines**); the most strongly accented beat is usually the first note in each bar:

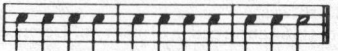

The main sections of a piece or movement are terminated by a **double bar**, as shown above.

Silence for a complete bar is usually indicated by a semibreve rest, whatever the time value of the bar. A number added above indicates silence for that number of bars.

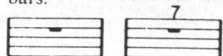

Repetition of Passages, Bars or Notes

Repeat the group of notes:

Repeat the bar:

Repeat the bar so many times:

Repeat the note as shown:

Time Signature

The sign, consisting of a lower and an upper figure, follows the key signature at the beginning of a piece or section of a piece; the lower figure shows the value of the note used as the basic beat (2 = minim, 4 = crotchet, etc.), the upper number of such beats in the bar:

Terms, Directions and Signs

acccl., accelerando. Gradually increasing in speed.

acciaccatura. An ornament played as quickly as possible before the principal note to which it is attached:

accidental. A sign (sharp ♯, flat ♭, or natural ♮) used to contradict temporarily a key signature by inflecting a note up or down a semitone. Its effect lasts only for the bar in which it appears (and only for that octave), unless the note is tied over into the next bar.

ad lib., ad libitum. The performer is at liberty to play the passage freely as regards rhythm or tempo, or to omit the passage, depending on the context.

alla breve. Two minims ($\frac{2}{2}$) to the bar, instead of four crotchets ($\frac{4}{4}$), i.e. an indication that the tempo should be doubled:

anim., animato. Animatedly.

appoggiatura. An ornament that 'leans' on the note to which is is attached. Unlike the acciaccatura, which is virtually timeless, it usually occupies half the time value of the succeeding note:

arco. With the bow (cf. **pizzicato**).

a tem., a tempo. In time, i.e. reverting to the original speed.

bind. See **tie**.

cal., calando. Gradually decreasing in speed and volume.

colla voce. An instruction to the accompanist to follow the singer closely (lit. 'with the voice').

col legno. Strike the strings with the stick of the bow (lit. 'with the wood').

common time. Four crotchet beats in the bar, usu. written as:

con sordino. Attach mute to instrument.

cresc., crescendo. Gradually increasing in volume. Also:

dash. When placed over or under a note, implies a very detached staccato style.

D.C., da capo (al fine, or al segno). The performer must return to the beginning of the movement (and play to the end, *or* to the sign 𝄋).

decresc., decrescendo. Gradually decreasing in volume. Also:

dim., diminuendo. Gradually becoming softer.

dot. When placed over or under a note, implies a detached, staccato style, but less so than the dash. The dot combined with a slur implies a style midway between the dot and legato, i.e. slightly detached.

dot, double dot. See *Values of Notes and Rests*.

double flat. ♭♭. Used before a note already flattened to lower it another semitone. It is cancelled by a natural and a flat (♮♭).

double sharp. 𝄪. Used before a note already sharpened to raise it another semitone. It is cancelled by a natural and a sharp (♮♯).

down bow. ⊓. Direction for bowing (a stringed instrument) by 'pulling' the bow.

D.S., dal segno. The performer must return to and play from the sign 𝄋 (lit. 'from the sign').

f, forte. Loud (lit. 'strong').

ff, fortissimo. Very loud.

fff, fortississimo. As loud as possible.

figured bass. A harmonic shorthand to enable keyboard players of the 17th and 18th centuries to accompany chamber and orchestral music without requiring written-out parts. It consists of the bass line with numerals to indicate the correct chords.

fine. End. See under **D.C.**

flat. ♭. Sign used in a key signature (see section on *Pitch*) to lower the note in the corresponding position on the staff, and in all octaves throughout the piece, by one semitone, cancelled by a natural sign. See also **accidental**.

fp, forte-piano. Loud, then immediately soft.

fz, forzato. Accented (lit. 'forced').

grace note. An ornament such as an acciaccatura or appoggiatura.

harmonic. In string music, a sign placed over a note to indicate that is to be played as a harmonic by lightly touching the string:

inverted turn. See **turn**.

leg., legato. Smoothly, without a break between the notes; opposite of staccato.

loco. Indicating a return to the pitch as printed, after having played an octave higher or lower.

marc., marcato. In a marked manner, each note emphasised.

mf, mezzo-forte. Moderately loud (lit. 'half-strong').

M.M. Maelzel's metronome. Sometimes used to precede the indication of a metronome setting:

M.M. = 70 means 70 crotchet beats a minute.

mordent. An ornament consisting of two auxiliary or grace notes, similar in performance to the acciaccatura in that it is played as quickly as possible before the principal note:

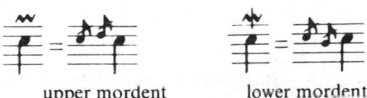

upper mordent   lower mordent

mp, mezzo-piano. Moderately soft (lit. 'half-soft').

natural. ♮. Restores to its original pitch a note that has been inflected by an accidental sharp or flat.

ornament. A melodic embellishment, specifically an auxiliary or grace note such as an acciaccatura, appoggiatura, turn, etc.

ossia. Used to propose a usually easier alternative (lit. 'or').

ottava, 8va or 8. Indicates that a note or passage is to be played an octave higher or lower depending whether it is written above or below the stave. **Col** or **con 8va** means that the printed notes are to be played along with the octave.

p, piano. Soft.

pp, pianissimo. Very soft.

ppp, pianississimo. As soft as possible.

pause. ⌢. Placed over a note or rest, to show that it is to be held longer than the indicated time value. Placed over the double bar it indicates the end of the piece.

ped. Depress 'loud' pedal on a piano. An asterisk indicates when it is to be released:

pizz., pizzicato. Pluck the string with finger instead of playing it with the bow; cancelled by arco.

presa. A symbol (⚹, ⦙ or ⦙:) used to indicate the points at which successive instrumental or voice parts enter a canon.

rall., rallentando. Becoming gradually slower.

repeat sign. Placed at the beginning and end of a passage to show that it is to be repeated. The repetition is implied even when the sign is omitted at the beginning.

rinf., rfz, rf, rinforzato. Reinforced, suddenly accented.

rit., ritardando. Gradually decreasing in speed.

rubato. Indicating a certain, limited freedom in performance as regards tempo, the limitation being that the beat should be returned to without an overall loss of time within the phrase so treated.

segno. 𝄋. See **D.C.** and **D.S.**

segue. Usually to warn that the next movement follows with scarcely a break (lit. 'follows').

sempre. Always; as in *sempre legato*, smooth throughout.

senza sordino. Remove mute from instrument (lit. 'without mute').

sf, sfz, sforzando, sforzato. Forced, strongly accented. Sometimes indicated by >.

sfp, sforzato-piano. A strong accent followed immediately by piano.

shake. See **trill.**

sharp. ♯. Sign used in a key signature (see section on *Pitch*) to raise the note in the corresponding position on the staff, and in all octaves throughout the piece, by one semitone; cancelled by a natural. See also **accidental.**

simile. Continue performing in like manner, i.e. as already marked (lit. 'like').

slur. Shows that the notes over which it is placed are to be (*a*) performed in a smooth (legato) manner; (*b*) played in one bow (see also **dot**); or (*c*) sung to one syllable. Also used to indicate phrasing.

smorz., smorzando. Gradually slower and softer.

sost., sostenuto. Sustained.

sotto voce. Barely audible (lit. 'under the breath').

spiritoso. Spirited, lively.

staccato. Detached, i.e. each note shortened; opposite of legato.

staff, stave. See section on *Pitch.*

sul ponticello. Play with the bow close up to the bridge (lit. 'on the bridge').

sul tasto. Play with the bow close up to, or on, the fingerboard (lit. 'on the key', i.e. fingerboard).

tempo primo, tempo 1mo. Take up the original tempo.

ten., tenuto. Strictly, hold for the full note value, but in practice draw out slightly beyond that.

tie or **bind.** Links a note and its repetition to show that the first note is sustained for the total time value of both notes and not replayed.

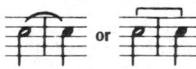

tre corde. Release soft pedal (lit. 'three strings'): see **una corda.**

tremolo. In string music, the rapid repetition of one note (for the time value of that note) by a quick movement at the point of the bow. In piano music a similar effect is achieved by alternating the note with its octave.

trill or **shake.** An alternation, variable in speed, of two notes a tone or a semitone apart, usually ending in a turn, and beginning on the principal note or, in early music, on the note above:

triplet. A group of three notes performed in the time of two:

T.S., tasto solo. In early music with a figured bass, implies that the bass line should be played without added harmonies (lit. 'one key alone').

turn. An ornament of four notes, played differently according to whether the sign is placed above or after the principal note:

The **inverted turn** is played similarly, but begins on the note below the principal note:

una corda, U.C. Depress 'soft' pedal, (lit. 'one string'; in a grand piano depressing the 'soft' pedal allows the hammers to strike only one of the three strings).

up bow. ∨ . Direction for bowing (a stringed instrument) by 'pushing' the bow.

V.S., volte subito. Turn over the page quickly.

Some first names

Masculine names are marked *m.*, feminine names *f.*

Aaron *ā'rən, m.* (Heb.) lofty, mountaineer.—Ar. *Harun, Haroun.*

Abel *ā'bl, m.* (Heb.) breath, vanity.

Abigail *ab'i-gāl, f.* (Heb.) father rejoiced, or father of exaltation.—Dims. **Abby, Nabby, Gail.**

Abner *ab'nər, m.* (Heb.) the (divine) father (is) light.

Abraham *ā'brə-həm,* **Abram** *ā'brəm, m.* (Heb.) perhaps father of a multitude, high father.—Dims. **Abe, Aby, Bram.**

Absalom *ab'sə-ləm, m.* (Heb.) father of peace.

Ada *ā'də, f.* prob. for **Adelaide** or other Gmc. name in ‚Adel-, Adal- (noble).

Adalbert. See **Albert.**

Adam *ad'əm, m.* (Heb.) man, earth, red earth.—Scottish dims. **Edie** (*ēd'i*), **Yiddie.**

Adela *ad'i-lə,* **Adèle** *-del',* **Adella** *-del'ə, f.* (Gmc.) noble.

Adelaide *ad'i-lād, f.* Fr. *Adélaïde* from Ger. *Adelheid* (from *Adelheidis*), noble kind (i.e. sort).—Dims. **Addie, Addy.**

Adeline, Adelina *ad'i-lin, -lēn, -līn, -ə, f.* (Gmc.) noble.—Dims. **Addie, Addy.**

Aden *ā'dən, m.* form of **Aidan.**—Also (from Heb. *Adin*) ornament.

Adina *ə-dē'nə, f.* (Heb.) desire.

Adolphus *ə-dol'fəs, m.* (Gmc.) noble wolf.—Fr. *Adolphe,* It. and Sp. *Adolfo,* Ger. *Adolf,* O.E. *Æthelwulf.*

Adrian, Hadrian *(h)ā'dri-ən, m.* (L.) of Adria (in Italy).—Fem. **Adrianne** (*-an'*), **Adrienne** (*-en'*), **Adriane** (*ad-ri-än'*), **Adriana** (*-ä'nə*).

Aeneas, Eneas *ē-nē'əs, m.* (Gr.) commended.—Fr. *Enée.*—Used for **Angus.**

Afra *af'rə, ā'frə, f.* (Heb.) dust. (Now rare.)

Agatha *ag'ə-thə, f.* (Gr.) good.—Dim. **Aggie.**

Agnes *ag'nis, f.* (Gr.) chaste.—Dims. **Aggie, Aggy, Annis, Annot, Nance, Nancy, Nessa, Nessie, Nesta.**—L. *Agneta,* It. *Agnese,* Fr. *Agnès,* Sp. *Inés.*—Confused with **Ann.**

Aidan, Aiden *ā'dən, m.* (Gael.) a dim. form from Gael. *aod(h)* fire.

Aileen *ā'lēn, ī'lēn, f.* Anglo-Irish form of **Eileen, Evelyn** and **Helen.**—Ir. *Aibhlin.*

Ailie *ā'li, f.* Scottish dim. of **Alison, Alice,** and **Helen.**

Ailsa *āl'sə, f.* from the Scottish island rock, Ailsa Craig.—Confused with **Elsa.**

Ai(th)ne. See **E(i)thne.**

Alan, Allan, Allen, Alyn *al'ən, m.* (prob. Celt.) harmony.—Fr. *Alain,* W. *Alun.*—Fem. **Alana** (*ə-lä'nə*), **Alanna** (*ə-lan'ə*).

Alaric *al'ə-rik, m.* (Gmc.) noble ruler.

Alasdair, Alastair. See **Alexander.**

Alban *öl', al'bən, m.* (L.) of Alba (near Rome).

Albert *al'bərt, m.* (Gmc.) nobly bright.—Dims. **Al, Bert, Bertie.**—Obs. Scot. **Halbert** (dims. **Hab, Habbie, Hob, Hobbie**).—L. *Albertus,* Fr. *Albert,* It. and Sp. *Alberto,* Ger. *Adalbert, Albert, Albrecht,* O.E. *Æthelbeorht.*—Fem. **Albertina** (*-ē'nə*), **Albertine** (*-ēn*).

Aldis, Aldous, Aldus *öl'dəs, m.* (Gmc.) old.

Aldred *öl-drid, m.* See **Eldred.**

Aldwin, Aldwyn *öl'dwin, m.* (Gmc.) old friend.

Aled *al'id, m.* from the name of the Welsh river.

Alethea *al-i-thē'ə, f.* (Gr.) truth.

Alexander *al-ig-zan'dər, -zän', m.* (Gr.) defender of men.—Also (from Gael.) **Alasdair, Alastair, Alistair, Alister** (*al'is-tər*).—Scot. **Elshender.**—Dims. **Alec(k), Alex, Alick, Eck, Ecky, Sanders, Sandy,** or (as an Englishman's nickname for a Scotsman) **Sawnie.**—Fr. *Alexandre,* It. *Alessandro,* Sp. *Alejandro.*—Fem. **Alexandra, Alexandrina** (*-drē'nə, -drī'nə*).—Dim. **Alexa, Sandra.**

Alewyn. See **Alvin.**

Alexis *ə-lek'sis, m.* and *f.* (Gr.) helper.—Fem. **Alexia.**

Alfonso. See **Alphonsus.**

Alfred *al'frid, m.* (Gmc.) elf counsel (good counsellor).—Dims. **Alf, Alfie, Alured** (*-ū-rəd*).—L. *Alfredus, Aluredus,* O.E. *Ælfred.*

Algernon *al'jər-nən, m.* (O.Fr.) moustached.—Dim. **Algy.**

Alice, Alys *al'is,* **Alicia** *ə-lish'i-ə, -lis'i-ə,* **Alissa, Alyssa** *-lis'ə, f.* (Gmc.) from O.Fr. *Aliz* for Gmc. *Adalheidis* (see **Adelaide**).—Dims. **Ailie, Ali, Allie, Ally, Ellie, Elsie.** See also **Alison.**

Aline *ə-lēn',* or *al'ēn, f.* for **Adeline.**

Alison, Allison *al'i-sən, f.* a form of **Alice,** mainly Scots, now considered a separate name.—Dims. **Ailie, Ali, Elsie.**

Alissa. See **Alice.**

Alistair. See **Alexander.**

Allan, Allen. Forms of **Alan.**

Alma *al'mə, f.* (L.) fostering, nourishing, loving.

Almeric *al'mə-rik, m.* See **Emery.**

Aloys, Aloysius. See **Lewis.**

Alphonsus *al-fon'səs, m.* (Gmc.) noble ready.—Ger. *Alfons,* Sp. *Alfonso, Alonso,* Port. *Afonso,* Fr. *Alphonse,* It. *Alfonso.*

Althea *al-thē'ə, al', f.* (Gr.) a healer, or wholesome.

Alun *al'ən, m.* from the name of a Welsh river.

Alured. See **Alfred.**

Alvin, Alvyn *al'vin,* **Alewyn, Aylwin** *āl'win,* **Alwin, Alwyn** *al'win, m.* (Gmc.) elf (good or noble) friend.—O.E. *Aelfwine, Aethelwine.*

Alvis. See **Elvis.**

Alyn. See **Alan.**

Alys, Alyssa. See **Alice.**

Amabel *am'ə-bel, f.* (L.) lovable.—Derivative **Mabel.**

Amadeus *am-ə-dē'əs, m.* (L.) love God.—Fr. *Amédée.*

Amalia *a-mä'li-ə, -mä'.* See **Amelia.**

Amanda *ə-man'də, f.* (L.) lovable.—Dim. **Mandy.**

Amber *am'bər, f.* (Eng.) from the precious material.

Ambrose *am'brōz, m.* (Gr.) of the immortals, divine.—L. *Ambrosius,* It. *Ambrogio,* W. *Emrys.*

Amelia *ə-mē'li-ə, -mēl'yə, f.* (Gmc.) struggling, labour.—Gr. *Amalia,* Fr. *Amélie,* It. *Amelia, Amalia.*—Dim. **Millie.**

Amos *ā'mos, m.* (Heb.) strong, bearing a burden.

Amy *ā'mi, f.* (Fr.) beloved.—L., It., Sp. *Amata,* Fr. *Aimée.*

Amyas *ām', am'i-as, m.* prob. for **Amadeus.**

Anastasia *an-ə-stā'zhə, -zi-ə, f.* (Gr.) resurrection.—Dim. **Stac(e)y** (*stā'si*).

Andrew *an'drōō, m.* (Gr.) manly.—Dims. **Andie, Andy, Dandy, Drew.**—Gr., L., Ger. *Andreas,* Fr. *André,* It. *Andrea,* Sp. *Andrés.*—Fem. **Andrea** (*-dri-ə*), **Andrina** (*-drē'nə*).

Aneurin, Aneirin *a-nā'rin, -nī', -noi', m.* (W.) meaning doubtful, perh. for L. *Honorius.*

Angela *an'ji-lə, f.,* **Angel** *ān'jəl, m.* and *f.,* (Gr.) angel, messenger.—Fem. deriv. **Angelica** (*-jel'ik-ə*).—Dims. **Angelina** (*an-ji-lē'nə, -lī'nə*), **Angie, Angy** (*an'ji*).

Angharad *an-gar'ad, -hhar'ad, f.* (W.) much loved.

Angus *ang'gəs, m.* (Celt.) perh. one choice.—Gael. *Aonghas.*—**Aeneas** is used as a substitute.

Ann, Anne *an,* **Anna** *an'ə,* **Hannah** *han'ə, f.* (Heb.) grace.—Dims. **Anita** (*ə-nē'tə,* Sp.), **Anneka, Annika** (*an'ək-ə,* Sw.), **Annette** (*a-net',* Fr.), **Annie, Nan, Nana, Nance, Nancy, Nanna, Nannie, Nanny, Nina** (*nē'nə, nī'nə*), **Ninette** (*nē-net',* Fr.), **Ninon** (*nē-nõ',* Fr.).

Annabel, Annabelle, Annabella *an'ə-bel, -bel'ə,* **Annaple,** *an'ə-pl.* prob. for **Amabel.**

Annis, Annot. Dims. of **Agnes.**

Anona *ə-nō'nə, f.* poss. from L. *annona,* produce, crops, personified as a goddess, but thought of as dim. of **Ann.**

Anselm *an'selm, m.* (Gmc.) god-helmet.

1773

Anthea *an-thē'ə, an', f.* (Gr.) flowery.

Anthony, Antony *an'tə-ni, m.* (L.) from a Roman family name, meaning unknown.—Dims. **Tony** (*tō'ni*), **Nanty**.—L. *Antonius*, Fr. *Antoine*, It. and Sp. *Antonio*, Russ. *Anton*, Ger. *Antonius, Anton*.—Fem. **Antonia**.—Dims. **Antoinette** (Fr.), **Net, Nettie, Netty**.

April *ā'pril, f.* (L.) from the name of the month.

Arabella *ar-ə-bel'ə, f.* origin and meaning doubtful; perh. for **Amabel**, or perh. (L. *orabilis*) easily entreated.—Dims. **Bel, Bell, Bella, Belle**.

Archibald *är'chi-bld, -böld, m.* (Gmc.) genuine and bold.—Dims. **Arch, Archie, Archy, Baldie**.—L. *Archibaldus*, Fr. *Archembault*, It. *Arcibaldo*, O.E. *Eorconbeald*.—See also **Gilleasbuig**.

Arleen, Arlene *är'lēn, f.* variants of **Aline**.

Arnold *är'nld, -nold, m.* (Gmc.) eagle strength.—Fr. *Arnaud, Arnaut*.

Arthur *är'thər, m.* (Celt.) perh. bear, or (Ir.) stone; or from a Roman family name *Artorius*.—L. *Arturus*, It. *Arturo*.

Asa *ā'sə, -zə, m.* (Heb.) healer.

Ashley, Ashleigh *ash'li, m.* and *f.* (Gmc.) from the surname derived from common place name, meaning ash wood.

Athanasius *ath-ə-nā's(h)i-əs, -z(h)-, m.* (Gr.) undying.

Athelstan, Athelstane *ath'l-stan, -stän, m.* (Gmc.) noble stone.—O.E. *Æthelstān*.

Aubrey *ö'bri, m.* (Gmc.) elf rule.—Ger. *Alberich*, O.E. *Ælfric*.

Audrey *ö'dri, f.* (Gmc.) noble power.—O.E. *Æthelthryth*, whence the forms **Etheldred** (*eth'əl-dred*), **Etheldreda** (*-drē'də*).

Augustine *ö'gəs-tēn, ö-gus'tin*, **Austin** *ös'tin, m.* (L.) belonging to Augustus.—L. *Augustinus*, Ger. and Fr. *Augustin*, It. *Agostino*, Sp. *Agustin*.

Augustus *ö-gus'təs, m.* (L.) venerable, exalted.—Dims. **Gus, Gussie, Gustus**.—Ger. *August*, Fr. *Auguste*.—Fem. **Augusta**.

Aurelius *ö-rē'li-əs, m.* (L.) golden (Roman family name).—Fem. **Aurelia**.—Dim. **Aurelian, m.**

Auriel, Auriol *ör'i-əl, f.* derivs. of L. *aurum*, gold.

Aurora *ö-rö'rə, -rö'rə*, **Aurore** *-rör', -rör', f.* (L.) dawn.

Austin. See **Augustine**.

Ava *ā'və, f.* origin and meaning uncertain.—Perh. Latin.

Averil *av'ə-ril, m.* and *f.* (Gmc.) perh. boar-favour.—Associated in people's minds with **Avril**.

Avice, Avis *ā'vis, av'is, f.* origin obscure.

Avril *av'ril, m.* and *f.* (Fr.) April.

Aylmer *āl'mər*, **Elmer** *el'mər, m.* (Gmc.) noble, famous.—O.E. *Æthelmær*. Or from the surname.

Aylwin. See **Alvin**.

Baldwin *böld'win, m.* (Gmc.) bold friend.—L. *Balduinus*, Fr. *Baudouin*, It. and Sp. *Baldovino*, Ger. *Balduin*.

Balthazar, Balthasar *bal't(h)ə-zär, bal-thä'zər, m.* (Babylonian *Bal-sarra-uzur*, whence *Belshazzar*) Bel defend the king.—Ger. *Balthasar*, Fr. *Balthazar*, It. *Baldassare*, Sp. *Baltasar*.

Baptist *bap'tist, m.* (Gr.) baptiser.—Ger. *Baptist*, Fr. *Baptiste, Batiste*, It. *Battista*, Sp. *Bautista*.—Fem. **Baptista**.

Barbara *bär'bə-rə, f.* (Gr.) foreign, stranger.—Dims. **Bab, Babs, Babbie**, (Scot. **Baubie**) **Barbie**.

Bardolph *bär'dolf, m.* (Gmc.) bright wolf.—Fr. *Bardolphe*, It. *Bardolfo*.

Barnabas *bär'nə-bəs*, **Barnaby** *-bi, m.* (Heb.) son of exhortation.—Dim. **Barney**.

Barney *bär'ni, m.* See **Bernard, Barnabas**.

Barry *bar'i, m.* (Ir.) spear.

Bartholomew *bär-, bər-thol'ə-mū*, **Bartlemy** *bärt'l-mi, m.* (Heb.) son of Talmi.—Dims. **Bart, Bat**.—L. *Bartholomaeus*, Fr. *Barthélemy, Bartholomé*, It. *Bartolomeo*, Sp. *Bártolo, Bártolomé, Bartolomeo*, Ger. *Bartholomäus, Barthel*.

Basil *baz'il, m.* (Gr.) kingly.—L. *Basilius*, Fr. *Basile*, It. and Sp. *Basilio*.

Beatrice, Beatrix *bē'ə-tris, -triks, bē-ā'triks, f.* (L.) making happy.—Obs. form **Bettrice** (*bet'ris*).—Dims. **Bee, Beatty, Trix, Trixie**.

Beck, Becky *bek('i), f.* See **Rebecca**.

Belinda *bə-lin'də, f.* (Gmc.) the second part meaning snake, the first unexplained.—O.H.G. *Betlindis*.

Bell, Belle *bel*, **Bella** *bel'ə, f.* See **Isabella**, also **Annabel, Arabella**.

Benedict, Benedick *ben'i-dikt, -dik*, **Bennet** *ben'it, m.* (L.) blessed.—L. *Benedictus*, Ger. *Benedikt*, Fr. *Benoît*, It. *Benedetto*, Sp. *Benedicto, Benito*.—Fem. *Benedicta*.

Benjamin *ben'jə-min, m.* (Heb.) son of the right hand (i.e. of good fortune).—Dims. **Ben, Benjie, Bennie**.—It. *Beniamino*, Sp. *Benjamin*.

Berenice *ber-i-nī'sē, ber-nē'sē, ber'i-nēs*, **Bernice** *bûr-nēs', f.* (Gr.), from the Macedonian form of *Pherenikē*, victory-bringer.—Dims. **Bunnie, Bunny**.—See also **Veronica**.

Bernard *bûr'nərd, m.* (Gmc.) bear-hard.—Dims. **Bernie, Barney**.—L. *Bernardus*, Fr. *Bernard, Bernardin*, It. *Bernardo, Bernardino*, Sp. *Bernardo, Bernal*, Ger. *Bernhard, Barend, Berend*.—Fem. **Bernadette**.

Bert *bûrt*, **Bertie** *bûr'ti, m.* for **Albert, Bertram** or **Herbert**.—Both are used for any name ending in -bert, and (*f.*) for **Bertha**.

Bertha *bûr'thə, f.* (Gmc.) bright.—Dims. **Bert, Bertie**.—Ger. *Berta, Bertha*, Fr. *Berthe*, It. and Sp. *Berta*, O.E. *Bercta*.

Bertram *bûr'trəm, m.* (Gmc.) bright raven.—Dims. **Bertie, Bert**.—Fr. *Bertrand*, It. *Bertrando*, Sp. *Beltrán*.

Beryl *ber'il, f.* (Gr.) from the precious stone.

Bess, Bessie, Beth, Betsy, Bettina, Betty. See **Elizabeth**.

Beverley *bev'ər-li, m.* and *f.* (Gmc.) from the surname and place name meaning beaver meadow or stream.

Bevis *bev'is, bēv'is, m.* from a French form of the Germanic name *Bobo* (Frankish), *Bobba* (O.E.).

Biddie, Biddy *bid'i, f.* See **Bridget**.

Bill. See **William**.

Blanche, Blanch *blänsh, f.* (Fr.—Gmc.) white.—It. *Bianca*, Sp. *Blanca*, Ger. *Blanka*, Fr. *Blanche*.

Blodwen *blod'win, f.* (W.) white flower.

Bob. See **Robert**.

Boris *bor'is, bö', m.* (Russ.) fight.

Bram. See **Abraham**.

Brandon *bran'dən, m.* from the surname, in Irish meaning descendant of Brendan.

Brandy, Brandi *bran'di, f.* from the drink brandy.

Brenda *bren'də, f.* perh. a fem. form of the Norse name *Brand*, brand, or sword, or a fem. form of **Brendan**; a Shetland name popularised by Scott's *Pirate*.

Brendan *bren'dən, m.* (Ir.) meaning uncertain—stinking hair has been suggested.

Brett *bret, m.* (Eng.) from L. *Brit(t)o*, Briton.

Brian, Bryan *brī'ən, m.* (Celt.) meaning doubtful.

Bridget, Brigid *brij'it*, **Bride** *brīd, f.* (Celt.) strength; name of a Celtic fire-goddess, an Irish saint; partly from the Swedish saint *Brigitto* (prob. a different name).—Fr. *Brigide, Brigitte*, Sp. *Brigida*, It. *Brigida, Brigita*, Scand. *Birgitta, Brigitta*.—Dims. **Biddie, Biddy, Bridie** (*brī'di*) (Scand. *Birgit, Britt, Britt(a)*).

Briony, Bryony *brī'ə-ni, f.* (Eng.) from the plant name.

Bronwen *bron'win, f.* (W.) white breast.

Bruce *broos, m.* from the surname, orig. from Normandy, and the place name *Brieuse*.

Bruno *broo'nō, m.* (Gmc.) brown.

Bryan. See **Brian**.

Brynmor *brin'mör, m.* (W.) from the place name formed from *bryn*, hill and *mawr*, great.—Dim. **Bryn**.

Bryony. See **Briony**.

Bunnie, Bunny *bun'i, m.* and *f.* (Eng.) a general pet-name, or (*f.*) a dim. of **Berenice**.

Bunty *bun'ti, f.* (Eng.) a pet-name.

Caleb *kā'lib, m.* (Heb.) dog, or bold.

Cameron *kam'ə-rən, m.* (Gael.) hooked or crooked nose; from the surname and clan name.

Camilla *kə-mil'ə, f.* (L.) a free-born attendant at a sacrifice; in Virgil, name of a queen of the Volsci.—Fr. *Camille.*

Candace, Candice *kan'dis, f.* meaning unknown; dynastic name of the queens of ancient Ethiopia.—Dim. **Candy.**

Candida *kan'di-də, f.* (L.) white.

Caradoc *kə-rad'ɔk, m.* (W.) beloved, dear.—L. *Caractacus* (from old Celt. form *Caratacus*), Ir. *Carthac(h).*—See also **Cedric.**

Carl, Karl *karl, m.* Germanic forms of **Charles.**

Carla, Carleen, Carlene, Carlotta. See **Charles.**

Carmen *kär'mən* (Sp.), **Carmel** *kär'məl* (Heb.), *f.* the garden.

Carol, Carola, Carole, Caroline, Carolyn. See under **Charles.**

Casimir, Kasimir *kas'i-mir, m.* (Pol.) proclamation of peace.

Caspar, Kaspar *kas'pər, m.* See **Jasper.**

Cassandra. See Dict.

Catherine, Catharine, Katherine, Katharine, Kathryn *kath'(ə-)rin,* **Catherina** *-ə-rē'nə,* **Katrine** *kat'rin,* **Katerina** *kat-ə-rē'nə,* **Katrina, Kathleen** *kath'lēn* (Ir. *Caitlin), f.* from Gr. *Aikaterinē,* of unknown origin, later assimilated to *katharos,* pure.—Fr. *Catherine,* It. *Caterina,* Sp. *Catalina,* Ger. *Katharina,* Dan., etc. *Karin, Karen,* Gael. *Catriona.*—Dims. **Casey, Cathie, Cathy, Kate, Katie, Katy, Kathie, Kathy, Kay, Kit, Kittie, Kitty.**

Catriona *kə-trē'ə-nə, kat-ri-ō'nə, f.* See **Catherine.**

Cecil *ses'il,* also *sēs', sis', m.* (L.) the Roman family name *Caecilius* (lit. blind).—Fem. **Cecilia** *(si-sil'yə, -sēl'yə),* **Cecily** *(ses'i-li),* **Cicely** *(sis'(i-)li),* **Sisley.**—Fr. *Cécile,* Ger. *Cäcilia,* Ir. *Sile* (see **Celia**).—Dims. **Sis, Cis, Sissy, Sissie, Cissy, Cissie.**

Cedric *sed'rik, m.* prob. a mistake of Scott's for *Cerdic* (name of the first king of the West Saxons, but apparently not really English—perh. a British name related to **Caradoc**).

Celeste *si-lest',* **Celestine** *si-les'tēn, -tīn, -tin, f.* (L.) heavenly.

Celia, Caelia *sē'li-ə, f.* fem. of the Roman family name *Caelius* (poss. heavenly).—Fr. *Célie;* Ir. *Sile* (anglicised *Sheila, Shelagh,* etc.).—Sometimes used for **Cecilia.**

Celina. See **Selina.**

Ceri *ker'i, m* and *f.* (W.) to love.

Chad *chad, m.* (Celt.) battle; name of the Northumbrian saint, Bishop of Mercia.—O.E. *Ceadd(a).*

Charis *kar'is, f.* (Gr.) grace.

Charity *char'i-ti, f.* (Eng.) charity.—Deriv. **Cherry.**

Charles *chärlz, m.* (Gmc.) manly.—Also **Carol** *kar'ol.*—L. *Carolus,* Fr. *Charles,* Ger. *Carl, Karl.,* It. *Carlo,* Sp. *Carlos,* Czech *Karol,* Ir. *Cathal,* Gael. *Tearlach.*—Dims. **Charlie, Charley, Chae, Chay** *(chā).*—Fem. **Carla, Karla** *(kär'lə),* **Carleen, Carlene** *(kär-lēn'),* **Carol, Carole** *(kar'əl),* **Carola** *(-lə),* **Caroline** *(kar'ə-līn, -lēn, -lin),* **Carolyn, Carlotta** *(kär-lot'ə),* **Charlene** *(shär'lēn, -lēn'),* **Charlotte** *(shär'lət).*—Ger. *Karla.*—Dims. **Caddie, Carly, Carrie, Lina** *(lē'nə),* **Lottie, Chat** *(shat),* **Chatty, Sharley.**

Charmaine, Sharmaine *shär-mān', f.* (L.) derived from *Carminea,* fem. of Roman clan name *Carmineus.*—Confused with **Charmian.**

Charmian *shär'mi-ən, kär', f.* (Gr.) joy.—Confused with **Charmaine.**

Cher, Chère *shär,* **Cherie, Sherry** *sher'i, f.* (Fr.) dear one.

Cherry *cher'i, f.* from the fruit, or see **Charity.**—Deriv. **Cheryl** *(cher'il, sher'il).*

Chloe *klō'i, f.* (Gr.) a green shoot, verdure.

Chloris *klō', klō'ris, f.* (Gr.) name of a flower-goddess, also greenfinch or a kind of grape.

Christabel *kris'tə-bel, f.* (L.—Gr.) anointed, or Christ, and (L.) fair.

Christian *kris'ti-ən, -chən, m.,* also *f.,* belonging to Christ.—L. *Christianus,* Fr. *Chrétien,* It. and Sp. *Cristiano.*—Dims. **Chris, Christie, Christy.**—Fem. **Christiana** *(-ti-ä'nə),* **Christina** *(-tē'nə),* **Christine** *(kris'tēn* or *-tēn'),* **Kirsteen** *(kûrs'tēn),* **Kirsten**

(kris'tən).—Dims. **Chris, Chrissie, Kirsty, Teenie, Tina** *(tē'nə).*

Christopher *kris'tə-fər, m.* (Gr.) carrying Christ.—L. *Christophorus,* Fr. *Christophe,* It. *Cristoforo,* Sp. *Cristóbal,* Ger. *Christoph.*—Dims. **Chris, Kester, Kit** (Scot. fem. **Crystal, Chrystal**).

Cicely. See **Cecilia.**

Cindy, Sindy *sin'di, f.* dims. of **Cynthia, Lucinda.**

Clara *klā'rə,* **Clare, Claire** *klär,* **Clarinda** *klə-rin'də, f.* (L.) bright.—Fr. *Claire,* Ger. *Klara,* It. *Chiara.*—Derivatives **Clarice** *(klar'is),* **Clarissa.**

Clarence *klar'əns, m.* from the dukedom.

Claribel *klar'i-bel, f.* (L.) brightly fair.

Claud, Claude *klöd,* **Claudius** *-i-əs, m.* (L.) lame.—Fem. **Claudia** (Fr. *Claude).*

Clement *klem'ənt, m.* (L.) mild, merciful.—Dim. **Clem.**—Fem. **Clemency, Clementina** *(-ē'nə),* **Clementine** *(-ēn, -īn).*

Clifford *klif'ərd, m.* from the surname.

Clive *klīv, m.* from the surname.

Clodagh *klō'də, f.* (Ir.) name of a river in Tipperary.

Clotilda, Clothilda *klō-til'də, f.* (Gmc.) famous fighting woman.—Fr. *Clot(h)ilde.*

Clovis *klō'vis, m.* See **Lewis.**

Cody *kō'di, m.* and *f.* from the Irish surname.

Colette *kol-et', f.* See **Nicholas.**

Colin *kol'in, m.* orig. a dim. of **Nicholas;** used also for **Columba;** now regarded as a separate name.

Colley *kol'i,* orig. dim. of **Nicholas.**

Con(n)or *kon'ər, m.* (Ir.) high desire.—Ir. *Conchob(h)ar,* or *Conchub(h)ar.*—Dims. **Corney, Corny.**—**Cornelius** is used as a substitute.

Conrad, Conrade, Konrad *kon'rad, m.* (Ger.) bold in counsel.—Ger. *Konrad,* It. *Corrado.*

Constance *kon'stəns, f.* (L.) constancy.—L. *Constantia,* Fr. *Constance,* It. *Costanza,* Ger. *Konstanze.*—Dims. **Con, Connie. Constant** *kon'stənt, m.* firm, faithful.—L. *Constans, Constantius,* It. *Constante, Costanzo,* Ger. *Konstanz.*—Deriv. **Constantine** *(kon'stən-tīn),* with *-ine.*

Cora *kō'rə, kö'rə, f.* (poss. from Gr. *korē,* girl) a name that first appears in J. Fenimore Cooper's *The Last of the Mohicans,* used also as a dim. e.g. of Sp. *Corazon,* heart.

Coralie *kor'ə-li, f.* (Fr.) perh. coral, a modern French invention.

Cordelia *kör-dē'li-ə, f.* perh. (L.) warm-hearted.

Corey *kō'ri, kö'ri, m.* from the Irish surname.

Corinne *ko-rin', -rēn',* **Corinna** *-rin'ə, f.* (Gr.) dim. of *korē,* maiden.

Cornelius *kör-nē'li-əs, m.* (L.) a Roman family name, prob. related to L. *cornu,* horn.—Used for **Connor.**—Dims. **Corney, Corny.**—Fem. **Cornelia.**

Cosmo *koz'mō, m.* (Gr.) order.—It. *Cosimo, Cosmo,* Fr. *Cosme, Côme,* Sp. *Cosme.*

Courtney *kört'ni, m.* and *f.* from the surname.

Craig *krāg, m.* from the surname.

Cressida *kres'i-də, f.* (Gr.) English form of *Chryseis,* accus. *Chryseida,* daughter of *Chryses.*

Crispin *kris'pin,* **Crispian** *-pi-ən,* **Crispinian** *-pin'i-ən,* **Crispus,** *-pəs, m.* (L.) curly.

Crystal. See **Christopher.**

Cuthbert *kudh', kuth'bərt, m.* (O.E.) well-known, bright.—Dim. **Cuddie.**

Cynthia *sin'thi-ə, f.* (Gr.) of Mount Cynthus in Delos, an epithet of Artemis (Diana), huntress and moon-goddess, who was born in Delos.—Dims. **Cindy, Sindy.**

Cyprian *sip'ri-ən, m.* (Gr.) of Cyprus.

Cyril *sir'il, m.* (Gr.) lordly.

Cyrus *sī'rəs, m.* (Pers.) throne.—Dim. **Cy.**

Daisy *dā'zi f.* (Eng.) a translation of Fr. *Marguerite.*—See **Margaret.**

Dale *dāl, m.* and *f.* from the surname.

Damian *dā'mi-ən,* **Damon** *-mən, m.* (Gr.) perh. connected with *damaein,* to tame.

Dane *dān, m.* from the surname.

Daniel *dan'yəl, m.* (Heb.) the Lord is judge.—Dims. **Dan, Danny.**—Fem. **Daniela** *(i-ā'lə),* **Daniella, Danielle** *(-el').*

Daphne *daf'nē, -ni, f.* (Gr.) laurel.

Darren *dar'ən, m.* from the Irish surname.

Dar(r)yl, *dar'il, m.* (O.E.) darling.

David *dā'vid, m.* (Heb.) beloved.—Dims. **Dave, Davie, Davy** (obs. **Daw, Dawkin**).—Fem. **Vida** *vē'də* (Scot. **Davina**, *də-vē'nə, -vī'nə*).

Dawn *dön, f.* (Eng.) dawn.

Dean *dēn, m.* from the surname.

Deanna. See **Diana**.

Deborah *deb'ə-rə, di-bō'rə, -bö', **Debra** deb'rə, f.* (Heb.) bee.—Dims. **Deb, Debbie, Debby.**

Declan *dek'lən, m.* (Ir.) an Irish saint's name.—Ir. *Deaglan.*

Dee *dē, m.* and *f.* of multiple origin, e.g. from the surname, the river name, or as a shortening of any name with the initial D.

Deirdre *dēr'dri, f.* (Ir.) meaning doubtful.

Delia *dē'li-ə, f.* (Gr.) of the island of Delos.

Delroy *del'roi, m.* a variant of **Elroy.**

Delyth *del'ith, f.* (W.) pretty.

Demetrius *di-mē'tri-əs, m.* belonging to Demeter.

Denis, Dennis, *m.,* **Denise**, *f.* See **Dionysius.**

Denzil *den'zil, m.* from the surname, from a Cornish place name.

Derek, Derrick *der'ik, m.* See **Theodoric.**

Dermot *dûr'mət, m.* (Celt.) free of envy.—Ir. *Diarmuid,* Gael. *Diarmaid.*

Desideratus *di-sid-ə-rā'təs,* **Desiderius** *dez-i-dē'ri-əs, m.* (L.), **Désiré** *dā-zē-rā', m.* (Fr.) longed for.—Fem. **Desiderata, Désirée.**

Desmond *dez'mənd, m.* (Ir.) from the surname or the district.

Diana *dī-an'ə,* **Dian(ne)** *dī-an', dē-,* **Diane** *dē-än', dī-an',* **Deanne** *dē-an',* **Deanna** *-an'ə, f.* (L.) the Roman goddess Diana, identified with Artemis.—Dims. **Di, Die** (*dī*).

Dick, Dickie, Dickon. See **Richard.**

Diggory *dig'ə-ri, m.* (Fr.) from *Degarre,* a hero of romance, an exposed child (prob. Fr. *égaré,* astray).

Dilys *dil'is, f.* (W.) sure, constant, genuine.

Dinah *dīnə, f.* (Heb.) judged, or dedicated.

Dionysius *dī-ə-nis'i-əs, -niz', m.* (Gr.), **Denis, Dennis** *den'is* (Fr.—Gr.), belonging to Dionysus or Bacchus.—Fr. *Denis, Denys,* It. *Dionigi,* Sp. *Dionisio.*—Fem. **Dionysia, Denise** (*di-nēz'*).—Dims. masc. **Dion** (*dī'ən, dē'ən*), fem. **Dionne** (*dē-on'*).

Divina *di-vē'nə, f.* a variant of **Davina** (see **David**) influenced by 'divine'.

Dod, Doddy. See **George.**

Dolores *də-lō'rēz, -lö', f.* (Sp.) sorrows.—Dim. **Lola.**

Dolly, Doll, Dol. See **Dorothy.**

Dominic(k) *dom'i-nik, m.* (L.) Sunday.—L. *Dominicus,* It. *Domenico,* Sp. *Domingo,* Fr. *Dominique.*

Donald *don'əld,* **Donal** *dō'nəl, don', m.* (Celt.) world chief.—Gael. *Domhnall.*—Dims. **Don, Donnie.**

Donna *don'ə, f.* (It.) mistress, lady.

Dora *dö'rə, dö'rə, f.* prob. a dim. of **Dorothy**; used also for **Theodora** and names of like ending.

Dorcas *dör'kəs, f.* (Gr.) gazelle.

Doreen *dō'rēn, dö', dō-rēn', dö-, f.* (Ir.) sullen; or for **Dorothy.**

Doris *dor'is, dō'ris, dö', f.* (Gr.) the name of a sea-nymph; meaning doubtful.

Dorothy *dor'ə-thi,* **Dorothea** *-thē'ə, f.* (Gr.) gift of God.—Fr. *Dorothée, Dorette,* Ger. *Dorothea.*—Dims. **Dol, Doll, Dolly, Dora, Do, Dot.**

Dougal, Dugald *dōō'gəl(d), m.* (Celt.) dark stranger.—Gael. *Dùghall.*

Douglas *dug'ləs, m.* (and *f.*) from the surname, or the river.

Drew. See **Andrew.**

Duane, Dwane *dwān, m.* (Ir.) from the surname *O Dubhain,* from *dubh,* black.

Dudley *dud'li, m.* from the surname.

Duke. See **Marmaduke.**

Dulcie *dul'si, f.* (L.) sweet—a modern invention.

Duncan *dung'kən, m.* (Celt.) brown, brown warrior.—Gael. *Donnchadh.*

Dwane. See **Duane.**

Dwight *dwīt, m.* from the surname.

Dylan *dil'ən, m.* (W.) wave, the name of a sea-god.

Eamon(n), Eamunn *ā'mən, em'ən, m.* Irish form of **Edmund.**

Earl, Earle *ûrl, m.* (U.S.) from the title.

Ebenezer *eb-i-nē'zər, m.* (Heb.) stone of help.—Dim. **Eben.**

Ebony *eb'ə-ni, f.* (Eng.) from the material.

Eck, Ecky. See **Alexander.**

Ed, Eddie, dims. of **Edgar, Edmund, Edward, Edwin.**

Edgar *ed'gər, m.* (O.E.) happy spear.—O.E. *Eadgar.*—Dims. **Ed, Eddie, Eddy, Ned, Neddie, Neddy.**

Edie. See **Adam, Edith.**

Edith *ē'dith, f.* (O.E.) happy or rich war.—O.E. *Eadgyth.*—Dims. **Edie, Edy.**

Edmund *ed'mənd, m.* (O.E.) happy protection.—Fr. *Edmond,* Ir. *Eamon.*—Dims. **Ed, Eddie, Eddy, Ned, Neddie, Neddy.**

Edna *ed'nə, f.* (Heb.) pleasure, delight.

Edward *ed'wərd, m.* (O.E.) rich guard.—Ger. *Eduard,* Fr. *Édouard,* It. *Eduardo, Edoardo, Odoardo.*—Dims. **Ed, Eddie, Eddy, Ned, Neddie, Neddy, Ted, Teddie, Teddy.**

Edwin *ed'win, m.* (O.E.) prosperity or riches, friend.—Dims. **Ed, Eddie, Eddy, Ned, Neddie, Neddy.**—Fem. **Edwina** (*-wē'nə*).

Effie *ef'i, f.* dim. of **Euphemia.**

Egbert *eg'bərt, m.* (O.E.) sword-bright.

Eileen *ī'lēn, ī-lēn', f.* (Ir.) an old name perh. meaning pleasant; used as a substitute for **Helen.**

E(i)luned *i-lin'əd, f.* (W.) idol, image.

Eirene. See **Irene.**

E(i)thne *eth'ni,* **E(i)thna** *-nə,* **Aine, Aithne** *ön'yi, f.* (Ir.) from *aodhnait,* dim. of *aodh,* fire. See also **Aidan.**

Elaine *i-lān', f.* an O.Fr. form of **Helen.**

Eldred *el'drid,* **Aldred** *öl'drid, m.* (O.E.) old counsel.—O.E. *Ealdred.*

Eleanor, Eleanore *el'i-nər,* **Elinor, Leonora** *lē-ə-nō'rə, -nö'rə, f.* same as **Helen.**—It. *Eleonora,* Ger. *Eleonore, Lenore,* Fr. *Éléonore, Aliénor.*—Dims. **Ella, Ellen, Nell, Nellie, Nelly, Nora.**

Eleazer *el-i-ā'zər, m.* (Heb.) God is help.

Elfleda *el-flē'də, f.* (O.E. *Æthelflœd*) noble-clean, and O.E. *Æflœd)* elf-clean.

Elfreda *el-frē'də, f.* (O.E.) elf-strength.—O.E. *Ælfthryth.*

Elgiva *el-jī'və, f.* (O.E.) elf-gift. O.E.—*Ælfgyfu,* or noble gift (O.E. *Æthelgyfu*).

Eli *ē'lī, m.* (Heb.) height.

Elias *i-lī'əs,* **Elijah** *i-lī'jə, m.* (Heb.) the Lord is Yah.

Elizabeth, Elisabeth *i-liz'ə-beth,* **Eliza** *i-lī'zə, f.* (Heb.) God is satisfaction.—Fr. *Elizabeth, Élise,* It. *Elisabetta, Elisa,* Ger. *Elisabeth, Elise,* Sp. *Isabel* (q.v.)—Dims. **Bess, Bessie, Bessy, Bet, Beth, Betsy, Bettina, Betty, Elsie, Libby, Lisa** (*lī'zə, lē', lē'sə*), **Liza** (*lī'zə* or *lē'*), **Lise** (*lēz*), **Lisbeth, Lizbeth, Liz** (*liz*), **Lizzie, Lisette** (*li-zet'*).

Ella *el'ə, f.* (Gmc.) all.—Also a dim. of **Eleanor** or of **Isabella** or other name in -ella.

Ellen *el'in, f.* a form of **Helen,** also used for **Eleanor.**

Elma *el'mə, f.* for **Wilhelmina,** or a combination of **Elizabeth Mary.**

Elmer. See **Aylmer.**

Eloisa. See **Heloise.**

Elroy *el'roi, m.* a variant of **Leroy.**

Elsa *el'sə,* **Elsie** *-si.* See **Elizabeth, Alison, Alice.**

Elshender. Scots form of **Alexander.**

Elspeth *el'spəth,* **Elspet** *el'spət,* Scots forms of **Elizabeth.**

Elton *el'tən, m.* from the surname.

Eluned. See **E(i)luned.**

Elvira *el-vē'rə,* or *-vī', f.* (Sp.) prob. of Gmc. origin, elf-counsel.

Elvis *el'vis,* **Alvis** *al', m.* (Ir.) from *Ailbhe,* the name of an Irish saint.

Elwyn *el'win, m.* (W.) perh. fair face.

Emery, Emory *em'ə-ri,* **Almeric** *al'mər-ik, m.* (Gmc.) work-rule, energetic rule.—L. *Amalricus,* Ger. *Emerich,* It. *Amerigo.*

Emily *em'(i-)li*, **Emilia** *i-mil'i-ə*, fem. of the Roman family name *Aemilius*.—L. *Aemilia*, Ger. *Emilie*, Fr. *Émilie*, It. *Emilia*.—Sometimes confused with **Amelia.**

Emlyn *em'lin*, *m.* (W.) meaning uncertain.—L. *Aemilianus*, pertaining to the family *Aemilius*, has been suggested.

Emma *em'ə*, *f.* (Gmc.) whole, universal.—Also a shortened form of various names beginning Ermin-, Irmin-.—Dims. **Emm, Emmie.**

Emmanuel, Immanuel *i-man'ū-il*, *m.* (Heb.) God with us.—Sp. *Manuel*, Port. *Manoel.*

Emmeline, Emeline *em'i-lēn*, *-līn*, *f.* prob. for **Amelia.**

Emrys *em'ris*, *m.* Welsh form of **Ambrose.**

Ena *ē'nə*, *f.* (Ir.) fire; or a shortened form of **Eugenia** or other name of similar sound.

Enid *ē'nid*, *f.* (W.) possibly wood-lark.

Enoch *ē-nək*, *m.* (Heb.) poss. consecrated, or teaching.

Ephraim *ēf'* or *ef'rā-im*, *m.* (Heb.) fruitful.

Erasmus *i-raz'məs*, *m.* (Gr.) lovely, deserving love.—Dim. **Rasmus.**

Erastus *i-ras'təs*, *m.* (Gr.) lovely.—Dim. **Rastus.**

Eric *er'ik*, *m.* (Gmc.; O.N. *Eirikr*) perh. sole ruler.—Ger. *Erich*, O.E. *Yric.*—Fem. **Erica** (*er'i-kə*) (associated with Gr. *ereikē*, heath).

Ermentrude, Irmentrude *ûr'min-trōōd*, *f.* (Gmc.) prob. Ermin (the god) and strength.

Ernest *ûr'nist*, *m.* (Gmc.) earnest.—Ger. *Ernst*, It. and Sp. *Ernesto.*—Dim. **Ernie.**—Fem. **Ernestine.**

Errol *er'əl*, *m.* of obscure origin, perh. from the Scottish place name, perh. a variant of **Eryl.**

Eryl *er'il*, *m.* and *f.* (W.) watcher.

Esau *ē'sö*, *m.* (Heb.) hairy.

Esme *ez'mi*, *m.*, *f.* (Fr.) beloved (a Scottish name).

Esmeralda *ez-mi-ral'də*, *f.* (Sp.) emerald.

Estella *es-tel'ə*, **Estelle** *es-tel'*, *f.* See **Stella.**—Perh. sometimes for **Esther.**

Esther *es'tər*, **Hester** *hes'tər*, *f.* poss. Pers., star; or Babylonian, *Ishtar*, the goddess Astarte.—Dims. **Essie, Hetty.**

Ethel *eth'l*, *f.* (O.E.) noble (not used uncompounded in O.E.).

Ethelbert *eth'l-bərt*, *m.* (O.E.) noble-bright.

Etheldred, -a. See **Audrey.**

Ethelind *eth'ə-lind*, **Ethelinda** *-lin'də*, *f.* (Gmc.) noble snake.

Ethelred *eth'l-red*, *m.* (O.E.) noble counsel.

Ethne, Ethna. See **Eithne.**

Etta *et'ə*, *f.* See **Henrietta.**

Eugene *ū'jēn*, *m.* (Gr.) well-born.—L. *Eugenius*, Fr. *Eugène*, Ger. *Eugen.*—Dim. **Gene.**—Fem. **Eugenia.**—Fr. *Eugénie.*—Dims. **Ena, Gene.**

Eulalia *ū-lā'li-ə*, *f.* (Gr.) fair speech.

Eunice *ū-nī'sē*, *ū'nis*, *f.* (Gr.) happy victory.

Euphemia *ū-fē'mi-ə*, *f.* (Gr.) of good report.—Dims. **Effie, Euphan, Euphie, Phemie** (*fə'mi*), **Phamie.**

Eusebius *ū-sē'bi-əs*, *m.* (Gr.) pious.

Eustace *ū'stis*, **Eustachius** *ū-stā'ki-əs*, *m.* (Gr.) rich in corn (Gr. *eustachys*, confounded with *eustathēs*, stable).—Ger. *Eustatius*, Fr. *Eustache*, It. *Eustachio*, Sp. *Eustaquio.*—Fem. **Eustacia.**

Eva *ē'və*, **Eve** *ēv*, *f.* (Heb.) life.—Fr. *Eve*, Ger., It., Sp. *Eva.*—Dims. **Evie, Evelina** (q.v.), **Eveleen** (Ir.).

Evan, Ewen *ū'ən*, *m.* Anglicised Welsh form of **John.**—W. *Ifan.*

Evangeline *i-van'ji-lēn*, *-lin*, *-līn*, *f.* (Gr.) bringer of good news.

Evelina *ev-i-lē'nə*, *-lī'nə*, *f.*, **Eveline** *ev'i-lēn*, *ēv'lin*, *f.*, **Evelyn** *ēv'lin*, *ev'i-lin*, *m.* and *f.*, partly dims. of **Eve**, partly from the surname Evelyn, partly from Gmc. *Avelina*, from *Avi*, a frequent element in names.

Everard *ev'ə-rärd*, *m.* (Gmc.) boar-hard.—Ger. *Eberhard*, *Ebert*, Fr. *Évraud.*

Ewan, Ewen *ū'ən*, *m.* See **Owen.**

Ezekiel *i-zē'ki-əl*, *m.* (Heb.) God will strengthen.—Ger. *Ezechiel*, *Hesechiel*, Fr. *Ézéchiel.*—Dim. **Zeke.**

Ezra *ez'rə*, *m.* (Heb.) help.—L. *Ezra*, *Esdras*, Fr. *Esdras*, Ger. *Esru.*

Fabian *fā'bi-ən*, *m.*—L. *Fabianus*, a derivative of the family name *Fabius*, perh. connected with *faba*, bean.

Faith *fāth*, *f.* (Eng. or Fr.) faith.

Fanny *fan'i*, *f.* See **Francis.**

Farquhar *fär'kər*, *fär'hhər*, *m.* (Gael.) manly.—Gael. *Fearchar.*

Faustina *fös-tī'nə*, **Faustine** *-tēn'*, *f.* (L.) fortunate.

Fay *fā*, *f.* (Fr.) perh. faith, perh. fairy.

Feargal *fûr'gəl*, *m.* (Ir.) said to be an Irish version of the saint's name *Virgilius.*

Felix *fē'liks*, *m.* (L.) happy.—Fem. **Felicia** (*fi-lish'i-ə*, *-lis'i-ə*), **Felice** (*fi-lēs'*, confused with **Phyllis**) happy, **Felicity**, happiness.

Fenella *fin-el'ə*, *f.* anglicisation of Gael. *Fionnghuala*, white shoulder.—Ir. **Finola** (*fi-nō'lə*).—Dims. **Nola** (*nō'lə*), **Nuala** (*nōō'lə*).

Ferdinand *fûr'di-nənd*, *m.* (Gmc.) journey-risk.—Ger. *Ferdinand*, Fr. *Ferdinand*, *Ferrand*, Sp. *Fernando*, *Hernando*, It. *Ferdinando*, *Ferrando.*

Fergus *fûr'gəs*, *m.* (Gael.) supremely choice.—Gael. *Fearghas.*

Fidelia *fi-dē'li-ə*, *f.* (L.) faithful.

Finlay, Findlay, Finley *fin'li*, *-lā*, *m.* (Gael.) a sunbeam.

Finn *fin*, **Fionn** *fyun*, *fūn*, *m.* (Ir. and Gael.) fair.—Dim. **Fintan** (*fin'tən*).—Deriv. **Finbarr** (*-bär*) fair-head.

Finola. See **Fenella.**

Fiona *fē-ō'nə*, *fē'ə-nə*, *f.* (Gael.) fair.

Flavia *flā'vi-ə*, *f.* (L.) yellow, fair.

Fleur *flûr*, *f.* (Fr.) flower.

Flora *flō'*, *flö'rə*, *f.* (L.) name of the Roman flower-goddess.—Dims. **Flo, Florrie** (*flor'i*).

Florence *flor'ins*, *f.* (L.) blooming; also, born in Florence.—L. *Florentia* (masc. *Florentius*).—Dims. **Flo, Florrie, Flossie, Floy.**

Floyd *floid*, *m.* prob. a variant of Welsh **Lloyd.**

Francis *frän'sis*, *m.* (Fr.) Frankish, French.—L. *Franciscus*, Fr. *François*, It. *Francesco*, Sp. *Francisco*, Ger. *Franz*, *Franziskus.*—Dims. **Frank, Francie, Frankie.**—Fem. **Frances** (*frän'sis*, *-səz*).—L. *Francisca*, Fr. *Françoise*, It. *Francesca* (dim. *Franceschina*), Sp. *Francisca*, Ger. *Franziska.*—Dims. **Fanny, Frank, Francie, Francine, Frankie.**

Freda *frē'də*, *f.* dim. of **Winifred**, or for **Frieda.**

Frederick, Frederic *fred'rik*, *m.* (Gmc.) peace-rule.—L. *Fredericus*, Ger. *Friedrich*, *Fritz*, Fr. *Frédéric*, It. *Federico*, *Federigo*, Sp. *Federico.*—Dims. (both genders) **Fred, Freddie, Freddy.**—Fem. **Frederica** (*fred-ə-rē'kə*).—Ger. *Friederike*, Fr. *Frédérique.*

Frieda *frē'də*, *f.* (Gmc.) peace. Used as a dim. for any feminine name with the element *fred* or *frid.*

Fulk, Fulke *fōōlk*, *m.* (Gmc.) people.

Gabriel *gā'bri-əl*, *m.* (Heb.) God is mighty, or man of God.—Dims. **Gabe, Gabby** (*gab'i*).—Fem. **Gabrielle.**

Gaenor. See **Gaynor.**

Gail *gāl*, *f.* dim. of **Abigail**—now regarded as a name in its own right.

Gareth *gar'ith*, *m.* O.Fr. *Gahariet*, prob. from some W. name.

Gary, Garry *gar'i*, *m.* perh. a dim. of **Gareth**; perh. for **Garvey** (Gmc.) spear-bearer.

Gaspar *gas'pər*, *m.* See **Jasper.**

Gavin, Gawain *gä'win*, *gö'in*, *m.* (W.) perh. white hawk.

Gay, Gaye *gā*, *m.* and *f.* (Eng.) gay, cheerful.

Gaynor, Gaenor *gā'nər*, *f.* (W.) a form of *Guinevere* (see **Jennifer**).

Gemma *jem'ə*, *f.* (It.) a gem.

Gene *jēn*, for **Eugene, Eugenia.**

Genevieve *jen'i-vēv*, *f.* (Fr.—Celt.) meaning obscure.—Fr. *Geneviève.*

Geoffrey, Jeffrey *jef'ri*, *m.* (Gmc.). Two names have run together—district-peace (O.H.G. *Gaufrid*) and traveller-peace (O.H.G. *Walahfrid*).—L. *Gaufridus*, *Galfridus*, Sp. *Geofredo*, Fr. *Geoffroi.*—Dims. **Geoff, Jeff.**—Confounded with **Godfrey.**

George *jörj, m.* (Gr.) husbandman.—L. *Georgius,* Fr. *Georges, George,* Ger. *Georg,* It. *Giorgio,* Sp. *Jorge,* Gael. *Seòras.*—Dims. **Geordie, Georgie, Georgy, Dod, Doddy.**—Fem. **Georgia, Georgiana** (-*i-ä'nə*), **Georgette, Georgina** (-*ē'nə*).—Dim. **Georgie.**

Geraint *ger-īnt', m.* (W.) from L. *Gerontius* (Gr. *geronteios*), old.

Gerald *jer'əld, m.* (Gmc.) spear-wielding.—L. *Geraldus, Giraldus,* Fr. *Géraud, Giraud, Girauld,* It. *Giraldo,* Ger. *Gerold, Gerald.*—Fem. **Geraldine** (-*ēn*).

Gerard *jer'ärd, -ərd, jər-ärd' m.* (Gmc.) spear-hard.—L. *Gerardus,* Fr. *Gérard,* It. *Gerardo,* Ger. *Gerhard.*

Gerda *gûr'də, f.* (O.N.) in Norse mythology, the name of the wife of the god Frey.

German *jûr'mən, m.* (L.) German.—Fem. **Germaine** (*jûr-mān'*; Fr., *zher-men'*).

Gerrie, Gerry *jer'i, m.* Dims. of **Gerald, Gerard.**

Gertrude *gûr'trōōd, f.* (Gmc.) spear-might.—Dims. **Gert, Gertie, Trudy.**

Gervase *jûr'vis, -vāz, m.* (Gmc.) spear-servant.—Also **Gervas, Jervis, Jarvis** (*jär'*).—Fem. **Gervaise** (*jûr-vāz',* Fr. *zher-vez'*).

Gideon *gid'i-ən, m.* (Heb.) hewer.

Gil. See **Gilbert, Giles.**

Gilbert *gil'bərt, m.* (Gmc.) bright hostage.—L. *Gilbertus,* Fr. *Guilbert, Gilbert,* It. and Sp. *Gilberto,* Ger. *Gilbert, Giselbert.*—Dims. **Gib, Gibbie, Gil.**

Giles *jīlz, m.* (Fr.—Gr.) kid.—L. *Aegidius,* Fr. *Gilles,* Ger. *Agidius,* It. *Egidio,* Sp. *Egidio, Gil.*

Gill, Gillian *jil, jil'i-ən, f.* See **Julian.**—Also **Jill, Jillian.**

Gilleasbuig *gi-les'pig,* **Gillespie** *-les'pi, m.* (Gael.) servant of the bishop.—Traditionally translated as **Archibald,** app. through a misunderstanding of the latter's derivation.

Gina *jē'nə, f.* dim. of **Georgina** or **Regina.**

Ginger, Ginny. See **Virginia.**

Gladys *glad'is, f.* Welsh *Gwladys* for **Claudia.**

Glen(n) *glen, m.* from the surname, related to **Glyn.**

Glenda *glen'də, f.* poss. valley (see **glen** in Dict.).

Gloria *glō'ri-ə, glö', f.* (L.) glory.

Glyn *glin, m.* (W.) valley.—Fem. **Glynis.**

Godfrey *god'fri, m.* (Gmc.) God's peace.—L. *Godofridus,* Fr. *Godefroi,* Ger. *Gottfried,* It. *Goffredo, Godofredo,* Sp. *Godofredo, Gofredo.*—Confused with **Geoffrey.**

Godwin *god'win, m.* (O.E.) God-friend.

Gordon *gör'dən, m.* from the surname.

Grace *grās, f.* (Fr.) grace.

Graham *grā'əm, m.* from the surname—also sometimes **Graeme.**

Granville *gran'vil, m.* from the surname.

Gregory *greg'ə-ri, m.* (Gr.) watcher.—L. *Gregorius,* Ger. *Gregor, Gregorius,* Fr. *Grégoire,* It. and Sp. *Gregorio.*—Dim. **Greg.**

Grenville *gren'vil, m.* from the surname.

Greta *grē'tə, gret'ə.* See **Margaret.**

Greville *grev'il, m.* from the surname.

Griffith *grif'ith, m.* (W.) ruddy, rufous.—W. *Gruffydd.*

Grizel, Grizzel, Grissel, Grisell *griz'l,* **Griselda, Grizelda** *gri-zel'də, f.* (Gmc.) perh. grey war, perh. Christ war.—Ger. *Griseldis,* It. *Griselda.*—Dim. **Zelda.**

Gudrun *gōōd'rən, f.* (Gmc.) war-counsel, in mythology the wife of Siegfried and sister of Gunther.

Guinevere *gwin'ə-vēr, f.* See **Jennifer.**

Gustavus *gus-tā'vəs, -tä'vəs, m.* (Gmc.) meditation (?) staff.—L. *Gustavus,* Swed. *Gustaf,* Ger. *Gustav,* Fr. *Gustave.*

Guy *gī, m.* (Gmc.) perh. wood, perh. wide.—O.H.G. *Wido, Wito,* L., Ger., It., and Sp. *Guido,* It. *Guy, Guyon.*

Gwendolen *gwen'də-lin, f.* (W.) white (second element obscure).—Dims. **Gwen, Gwenda, Gwennie.**

Gwillym, Gwilym. See **William.**

Gwyneth *gwin'ith, f.* (W.) blessed.

Hab, Habbie. See **Albert.**

Hadrian. See **Adrian.**

Hal *hal.* See **Henry.**

Halbert *hal'bərt, m.* an old Scots form of **Albert.**

Haley. See **Ha(y)ley.**

Hamish *hā'mish, m.* See **James.**

Hannah *han'ə, f.* See **Ann.**

Harold *har'əld, m.* (Gmc.) army rule.

Harriet, Harriot *har'i-ət,* fem. forms of **Henry.**—Dim. **Hatty.**

Hartley *härt'li, m.* from the surname.

Harvey, Hervey *här'vi, m.* from French **Hervé,** a form of *Haerveu,* name of a Breton saint, of uncertain meaning, perh. worthy in battle; also from the surname.

Hatty. See **Henry.**

Ha(y)ley *hā'li, f.* from the surname.

Hazel *hā'zəl,* **Heather** *hedh'ər, f.* from the plants.

Hector *hek'tər, m.* (Gr.) holding fast.—Dim. **Heck.**—Ger. *Hektor,* It. *Ettore,* Sp. *Héctor.*

Hedwig *hed'wig, f.* (Ger.) contention-fight.

Heidi *hī'di, f.* (Ger.) dim. of *Adelheid* (see **Adelaide**).

Helen *hel'ən, -in,* **Helena** *hel'i-nə,* **Ellen** *el'ən, f.* (Gr.) bright.—L. *Helena,* Fr. *Hélène,* Ger. *Helene,* It. and Sp. *Elena.*—Dims. **Lena** (*le'nə*), **Nell, Nellie, Nelly.**

Helga *hel'gə, f.* (Gmc., Norse) holy.

Heloise, Eloise *(h)el ō ēz',* **Eloisa** *el-ō-ē'zə, f.* (Gmc.) sound or whole, and wide, or perh. related to **Louisa.**—Fr. *Héloïse.*

Henry *hen'ri,* **Harry** *har'i, m.* (Gmc.) house ruler.—L. *Henricus, Enricus,* Fr. *Henri,* It. *Enrico,* Sp. *Enrique,* Ger. *Heinrich* (dims. *Heinz, Heinze, Hinz, Hinze*), Du. *Hendrik.*—Fem. **Henrietta, Harriet, Harriot.**—Fr. *Henriette,* It. *Enrichetta,* Sp. *Enriqueta.*—Dims. **Hatty, Hetty.**

Hephzibah *hef'zi-bä, f.* (Heb.) my delight is in her.

Herbert *hûr'bərt, m.* (Gmc.) army-bright.—Ger. *Herbert,* It. *Erberto,* Sp. *Heriberto.*—Dims. **Bert, Bertie.**

Hercules *hûr'kū-lēz, m.* L. name of the Greek hero Herakles, glory of Hera (Greek goddess).—It. *Ercole.*

Herman, Hermann *hûr'mən, m.* (Gmc.) army man, warrior.—Ger. *Hermann.*

Hermione *hər-mī'ə-nē, f.* (Gr.) a derivative of *Hermes* (Greek god).

Hervey. See **Harvey.**

Hester. See **Esther.**

Hetty *het'i, f.* dim. of **Hester** and **Henrietta.**

Hew, another spelling of **Hugh,** preferred by certain families.

Hezekiah *hez-i-kī'ə, m.* (Heb.) Yah is strength, or has strength.—Fr. *Ézéchias,* Ger. *Hiskia.*

Hilary *hil'ə-ri, m.* and *f.* (L.) cheerful.—L. and Ger. *Hilarius,* Fr. *Hilaire,* It. *Ilario,* Sp. *Hilario.*—Also fem. **Hilaria.**

Hilda *hil'də, f.* (Gmc.) battle.

Hildebrand *hil'di-brand, m.* (Gmc.) battle sword.

Hildegard *hil'di-gärd, f.* (Gmc.) know battle.

Hiram, Hyram *hī'rəm, m.* (Heb.) noble.

Hob, Hobbie *hob, -i, m.* for **Halbert, Robert.**

Hodge *hoj, m.* for **Roger.**

Holly *hol'i, f.* (Eng.) from the plant.

Homer *hō'mər, m.* (U.S.) from the name of the poet.

Honor *on'ər,* **Honora** *ho-nō'rə, -nö'rə,* **Honoria** *-ri-ə, f.* (L.) honour, honourable.—Dims. **Nora, Norah** (Ir. **Noreen**).—Masc. **Honorius.**

Hope *hōp, m.* and *f.* (Eng.) hope.

Horace *hor'is,* **Horatio** *ho-rā'shō, m.* (L.) the Roman family name *Horatius.*—Fem. **Horatia.**

Hortensia *hör-ten'syə, f.* (L.) fem. of a Roman family name—gardener.

Howel(l). See **Hywel.**

Hubert *hū'bərt, m.* (Gmc.) mind-bright.

Hugh, Hew *hū,* **Hugo** *hū'gō, m.* (Gmc.) mind.—L., Ger., Sp. *Hugo,* Fr. *Hugues,* It. *Ugo, Ugone,* W. *Huw.*—Dims. **Huggin, Hughie** (obs. **Huchon**).

Hulda *hul'də, f.* (Gmc.) name of a Germanic goddess—gracious. Also (Norse) covered.

Huldah *hul'də, f.* (Heb.) weasel.

Humbert *hum'bərt, m.* (Gmc.) prob. giant-bright.—It. *Umberto.*

Humphrey, Humphry *hum'fri, m.* (Gmc.) prob. giant-peace.—Ger. *Humfried,* Fr. *Onfroi,* It. *Onofrio,* Sp. *Hunfredo.*—Dims. **Humph, Numps, Dump, Dumphy.**

Huw *hū, m.* Welsh form of **Hugh.**

Hyacinth *hī'ə-sinth, m.* and *f.* (Gr.) the flower hyacinth (masc. in Greek).—See also **Jacinthe.**

Hyram. See **Hiram.**

Hywel, Howel(l) *how'əl, m.* (W.) eminent.

Iain, Ian *ē'ən, m.* Gaelic for **John.**

Ianthe *ī-an'thē, f.* (Gr.) violet flower (name of a sea-nymph).

Ida *ī'də, f.* (Gmc.) labour.

Ifan *ē'van, m.* Welsh form of **John.**

Ifor *ē'vor, m.* Welsh form of **Ivo, Ivor.**

Ignatius *ig-nā'shəs, m.* Latinised from a late Greek form of the Roman (perh. orig. Samnite) family name *Egnatius* (meaning unknown), assimilated to L. *ignis,* fire.—Fr. *Ignace,* Ger. *Ignaz,* It. *Ignazio,* Sp. *Ignacio.* See **Inigo.**

Igor *ē'gör, m.* Russian form of the Scandinavian name *Ingvarr,* watchfulness of Ing (the god Frey).

Ike. See **Isaac.**

Ilana *i-lä'nə,* **Ilona** *-lō', forms of* **Helen.**

Immanuel. See **Emmanuel.**

Imogen *im'ə-jən, f.* prob. a misprint for *Innogen* in Shakespeare's *Cymbeline,* poss. O. Ir., a daughter, girl.

Ina *ī'nə, ē'nə, f.* dim. of any of several names ending in **-ina.**

Ines, Inez *ī'nez, ē'nez,* Sp. *ē-nās', f.* See **Agnes.**

Ingeborg *ing'i-börg, f.* (Scand.) stronghold of Ing (the god Frey).—Dims. **Inge** (*ing'ə*), **Inga** (*ing'(g)ə*).

Ingram *ing'(g)rəm, m.* raven of Ing (Frey).

Ingrid *ing'(g)rid, f.* (Scand.) ride of Ing (Frey), or maiden of the Ingvaeones.

Inigo *in'-i-gō, m.* (Sp.) either a form of **Ignatius** or another name confused with it.—L. *Enecus, Ennecus,* Sp. *Íñigo.*

Iona *ī-ō'nə, f.* from the place name.

Ira *ī'rə, m.* (Heb.) watchful.

Irene, Eirene *ī-rē'nē,* also *ī-rēn', ī'rēn, f.* (Gr.) peace.

Iris *ī'ris, f.* (Gr.) rainbow, iris (plant)—name of the Greek goddess Hera's messenger.

Irmentrude. See **Ermentrude.**

Isa *ī'zə, f.* (Scot.) dim. of **Isabella.**

Isaac, Izaak *ī'zək, m.* (Heb.) laugh.—Dims. **Ik, Ike, Iky.**

Isabella *iz-ə-bel'ə,* **Isabel, Isobel** *iz'ə-bəl,* or (Gael.) **Iseaba(i)l, Ishbel,** *ish'bəl,* (Scot.) **Isbel** *iz'bəl, f.* (Sp.— Heb.) forms of **Elizabeth,** now regarded as an independent name.—Sp. *Isabel,* Fr. *Isabelle* (*Isabeau*), It. *Isabella.*—Dims. **Bel, Bell, Belle, Bella, Ella, Ib, Ibby, Isa** (*ī'zə*), **Tib, Tibbie, Tibby.**

Isaiah *ī-zī'ə,* or *-zā', m.* (Heb.) Yahwe helps.—L. *Isaias,* Ger. *Jesaias,* Fr. *Isaïe, Esaïe,* Sp. *Isaías,* It. *Isaia.*

Isodor, Isidore, Isadore *iz'i-dör, -dör, m.* (Gr.) perh. gift of Isis.—Sp. *Isidro, Isidoro.*—Fem. **Isidora, Isadora.**

Isla *ī'lə, f.* from the place name.

Isold, Isolde, Isolda *i-zold', -ə,* **Isolt** *i-zolt', f.* perh. (Gmc.) ice-rule; or a Welsh name.

Israel *iz'rā-əl, -el, m.* (Heb.) ruling with the Lord.

Ivan *ī'vən, ē-vän', m.* (Russ.). See **John.**

Ivo, Ivor *ī'vō, ī'vər,* or *ē', m.* prob. Celtic, but perh. from a Gmc. root meaning yew.—W. *Ifor,* Fr. *Ives, Yves, Ivon, Yvon;* fem. *Ivette, Yvette, Ivonne, Yvonne.*

Ivy *ī'vi, m.* and *f.* (Eng.) from the plant.

Jabez *jā'biz, m.* (Heb.) perh. sorrow, perh. height.

Jacinth(e) *ja-sinth', Jacintha -sin'thə,* **Jacinta** *-sin'tə, f.* forms of the flower-name hyacinth (Gr. *hyakinthos,* larkspur); also from the precious stone jacinth (O. Fr. *jacinte*).—Masc. **Jacinth.**

Jack *jak, m.* See **John.**

Jackeline. See **James.**

Jacob *jā'kəb, m.* (Heb.) follower, supplanter, or deceiver.—It. *Giacobbe,* Sp. *Jacob.*—Dim. **Jake.** See also **James.**

James *jāmz, m.* Same as **Jacob.**—L. *Jacobus* (later *Jacŏbus* (*-o-*), *Jacŏmus,* whence the forms with *m*), Fr.

Jacques, It. *Jacopo, Giacomo, Iachimo,* Sp. *Jacobo, Diego, Jaime, Jago,* Ger. *Jakob,* Gael. *Seamas, Seamus, Seumas* (anglicised vocative **Hamish**).—Dims. **Jim, Jimmie, Jimmy, Jem, Jemmie, Jamie,** (*jām'i,* Scot.), **Jeames** (*jēmz,* Scot. and burlesque).—Fems. **Jacoba** (*jə-kō'bə*), **Jacobina** (*-bē'nə*), **Jackeline** (*jak'ə-lēn, -lin*), **Jacqueline, Jaqueline** (*zhak'(ə)lin, -lēn*), **Jacquelyn** (*jak'*), **Jacquetta** (*-ket'ə*), **Jamesina** (*-sī'nə*).—**Jemima** has nothing to do with **James.**

Jan. See **John.**

Jane *jān,* **Jean** *jēn,* **Joan** *jōn,* **Jo(h)an(n)a** *jō-an'ə,* **Joann(e)** (*jō-an'*), fems. of **John.**—L. *Johanna,* Fr. *Jeanne* (dim. *Jeannette*), It. *Giovanna,* Sp. *Juana* (dim. *Juanita*), Ger. *Johanna,* Gael. *Seonag, Sine* (anglicised *Sheena*), W. *Sian,* Ir. *Siobhan.*—Dims. **Janet** (*jan'it*), **Janetta, Janey, Janie, Janice, Jeanette, Jeannie, Jen, Jenny, Jennie, Jess, Jessie, Jessy, Netta, Nettie, Nita** (*nē'tə*)—some of them regarded as separate names.

Janet *jan'it, f.* a dim. of **Jane,** regarded as an independent name.—Gael. *Seonaid,* Ir. *Sinead.*

Janice *jan'is, f.* orig. a dim. of **Jane,** now regarded as a separate name.

Jared *jar', jä'rid,* **Jarrad** *jar'əd, m.* (Heb.) descent.

Jarvis. See **Gervase.**

Jasmine *jas'min,* (Fr.), **Yasmin** *yaz'min* (Ar.) *f.* the flower jasmine.—Deriv. **Jessamine.**

Jason *jā'sən, m.* poss. Gr. rendering of Heb. Joshua or Jesus, or simply (Gr.) a healer.

Jasper *jas'pər,* **Gaspar** *gas'pər, m.* prob. Pers. treasurebringer.—Fr. *Gaspard,* Ger. *Kaspar.*

Jean *jēn, f.* See **Jane,** etc. For Fr. *m.* (*zhā*), see **John.**

Jedidiah, Jedediah *jed-i-dī'ə, m.* (Heb.) Yah is friend.

Jeffrey *jef'ri, m.* See **Geoffrey.**

Jem, Jemmie. Dims. of **James.**

Jemima *ji-mī'mə, f.* (Heb.) meaning unknown (day, dove, pure, fortunate have been suggested).—Not connected with **James.**—Dim. **Mima.**

Jennifer, Jenifer *jen'i-fər, f.* the orig. Cornish form of W. *Guinevere,* perh. white wave, or white phantom.—Dims. **Jen, Jennie, Jenny.**

Jenny, Jennie *jen'i, jin'i, f.* See **Jane, Jennifer.**

Jeremiah *jer-i-mī'ə,* **Jeremias** *-əs,* **Jeremy** *jer'i-mi, m.* (Heb.) Yah is high, or heals, or founds.—Dim. **Jerry** (*jer'i*).

Jerome *jer'ōm, ji-rōm', m.* (Gr.) holy name.—L. and Ger. *Hieronymus,* Fr. *Jérôme,* It. *Geronimo, Gerolamo, Girolamo,* Sp. *Jerónimo.*

Jerry *jer'i, m.* dim. of **Jeremy,** also of **Gerald, Gerard, Jerome.**

Jervis *jûr'vis, m.* See **Gervase.**

Jess *jes,* **Jessie** *f.* forms of **Janet,** chiefly Scots. See **Jane.**

Jessamine. See **Jasmine.**

Jesse *jes'i, m.* (Heb.) Yah is.

Jessica *jes'i-kə, f.* (app. Heb.) perh. Yah is looking.

Jethro *jeth'rō, m.* (Heb.) superiority.

Jill *jil,* **Jillian** *-yən, -i-ən, f.* See **Julian.**

Jim, Jimmie. See **James.**

Jinny. See **Virginia.**

Jo, for **Joanna, Joseph, Josepha, Josephine.**—Deriv. **Jolene** (*jō'lēn*).

Joachim *jō'ə-kim, m.* (Heb.) Yah has set up.—Sp. *Joaquin,* It. *Gioacchino.*

Joan, Jo(h)an(n)a, Joann, Joanne. See **Jane.**

Joannes. See **John.**

Job *jōb, m.* (Heb.) perh. pious, or persecuted, afflicted.— Ger. *Hiob,* It. *Giobbe.*

Jocelyn, Jocelin *jos'(ə-)lin, m.* and *f.* perh. (Gmc.) one of the Geats (a people of southern Sweden), or (L.) connected with *Justin, Justus.*—Also fem. **Joceline.**

Jock *jok, m.* See **John.**

Jodi(e), Jody *jō'di, f.* dims. of **Judith** or **Joanna.**

Joe, Joey, for **Joseph, Josepha, Josephine.**

Joel *jō'əl, m.* (Heb.) Yah is the Lord.

John, Jon *jon, m.* (Heb.) poss. Yah is gracious.—L. *Jo(h)annes,* Fr. *Jean,* It. *Giovanni* (*Gian, Gianni*), Sp. *Juan,* Port. *João,* Ger. *Johann, Johannes* (dim. *Hans*), Du. *Jan,* Russ. *Ivan,* Ir. *Seán* (anglicised *Shane,*

Shawn), *Eoin*, Gael. *Iain (Ian)*, W. *Ifan, Ieuan, Sîon.*—Dims. **Johnnie, Jack** (from **Jankin**), **Jackie**, (Scot. **Jock, Jockie**), **Jan**, obs. **Jankin**.—Fem. see under **Jane.**

Joleen, Jolene. See **Jo.**

Jonas *jō'nəs,* **Jonah** *-nə, m.* (Heb.) dove.

Jonathan *jon'ə-thən, m.* (Heb.) Yah has given.

Jonquil *jong'kwil, f.* from the flower.

Joseph *jō'zif, m.* (Heb.) Yah increases.—L. *Josephus,* Fr. *Joseph,* It. *Giuseppe* (dim. *Beppo*), Sp. *José* (dims. *Pepe, Pepillo, Pepito*), Ger. *Joseph, Josef.*—Dims. **Jo, Joe, Joey, Jos** (*jos*).—Fem. **Josepha** (*-sē'fə, -ze'fə*), **Josephine** (*jō'-zi-fēn*).—Dims. **Jo, Joe, Josie, Jozy.**

Joshua *josh'ū-ə, m.* (Heb.) Yah delivers.—L. and Ger. *Josua,* Fr. and Sp. *Josué,* It. *Giosuè.*—Dim. **Josh.**

Josiah *jōz-ī'ə,* **Josias** *-əs, m.* (Heb.) Yah supports.

Joy *joi, f.* (Eng.) joy.

Joyce *jois, f.* (Gmc.) a Geat (see **Jocelyn**).

Judith *jōō'dith, f.* (Heb.) Jewess.—Dims. **Judy, Judie.**

Julian *jōō'lyən, -li-ən, m., f.* (L.) derived from, belonging to Julius.—Dim. **Jule.**—Fem. **Juliana** (*-ä'nə*), **Jillian, Gillian** (*jil'yən, -i-ən*).—Dims. **Jill, Leanne, Lian(ne)** (*lē-an'*), **Lian(n)a** (*-an'ə*).

Julius *jōō'li-əs, m.* (L.) a Roman family name, perh. downy-bearded.—Dim. **Jule.**—Fr. *Jules,* It. *Giulio.*—Fem. **Julia.**—Dims. **Julie, Juliet.**

June *jōōn, f.* (L.) from the month.

Justus *jus'təs, m.* (L.) just.—Derivs. **Justin** (fem. **Justina,** *-tī'nə, tē',* **Justine** *-tēn*), **Justinian** (*-tin'yən, -i-ən*).

Karen, Karin *kä'rən,* **Kate, Katherine, Katharine, Kathryn, Kathleen, Katrine, Katerina, Katrina, Kay.** See **Catherine.**

Karl, Karla. See **Charles.**

Keiron. See **Kieran.**

Keith *kēth, m.* from the surname or place name.

Kelly *kel'i, m.* and *f.* (Ir.) from the surname.

Kenelm *ken'elm, m.* (O.E. *Cenhelm*) keen helmet.

Kenneth *ken'ith, m.* (Gael.) handsome.—Gael. *Coinneach.*—Dims. **Ken, Kennie, Kenny.**

Kerry *ker'i, m.* and *f.* (Ir.) from the name of the Irish county.

Kester *kes'tər, m.* See **Christopher.**

Kevin, Kevan *kev'in, m.* (Ir.) comely birth.

Keziah *ki-zī'ə, f.* (Heb.) cassia.

Kieran, Kieron, Keiron *kēr'ən, m.* (Ir.) an Irish saint's name, from *cíar,* dark. —Ir. *Ciaran.*

Kim *kim, m.* and *f.* shortening (as in Kipling's *Kim*) of Ir. **Kimball** (*kim'bəl*), orig. a surname, or of **Kimberl(e)y.**

Kimberl(e)y *kim'bər-li, f.,* orig. *m.,* from the S. African town.

King *king, m.* (U.S.) from the title.

Kirk *kûrk, m.* from the surname.

Kirsty *kûr'sti,* **Kirsteen** *-stēn, f.* See **Christian.**

Kit. See **Christopher, Catherine.**—**Kitty.** See **Catherine.**

Konrad. See **Conrad.**

Kurt *kûrt, m.* orig. a dim. of **Conrad.**

Kyle *kīl, m.* from the Irish and Scottish surname.

Lachlan *lahh'lən, m.* (Gael.) warlike.—Dims. **Lachie, Lachy.**

Lalage *lal'ə-jē, f.* (L.—Gr.) talkative, prattling.—Dim. **Lallie.**

Lambert *lam'bərt, m.* (Gmc.) land-bright.

Lance *läns, m.* (Gmc.) land.—Dims. **Lancelot, Launcelot.**

Lara *lä'rə, f.* (It.) explained as a form of *Larunda,* a nymph of Roman mythology, or as a dim. of *Larissa,* a Greek martyr.

Lar(r)aine. See **Lorraine.**

Larry. See **Lawrence.**

Laura *lö'rə, f.* (L.) laurel.—Also **Laurinda, Lora, Lorana, Lorinda.**—Dims. **Lauren** (thought of also as fem. of **Laurence**), **Lauretta, Lolly, Loretta.**

Laurence, Lawrence *lo', lö'rəns, m.* (L.) laurel.—L. *Laurentius.,* It. *Lorenzo,* Ger. *Lorenz.*—Dims. **Larry** (*lar'i*), **Laurie, Lawrie.**

Lavinia *lə-vin'i-ə, f.* (L.) origin unknown (second wife of Aeneas).

Lazarus *laz'ə-rəs, m.* (Gr. *Lazaros* from Heb.) a form of **Eleazar.**

Lea, Leah *lē'ə, f.* (Heb.) a cow.

Leander *li-an'dər, m.* (Gr.) lion man.

Leanne. See **Julian.**

Lee, Leigh *lē, m.* and *f.* from the surname.

Leila *lā', lē', lī'lə, f.* (Pers.) night.

Lemuel *lem'ū-əl, m.* (Heb.) consecrated to God.

Lena *lē'nə, f.* See **Helena, Magdalen.**

Leo *lē'ō, m.* (L.) lion.—Fem. **Leonie** (*lē'ə-ni*).

Leonard *len'ərd, m.* (Gmc.) lion-hard.

Leonora *lē-ə-nō'rə, -nö'rə,· f.* See **Eleanor.**

Leopold *lē'ō-pōld, m.* (Gmc.) people-bold.—Ger. *Luitpold, Leopold.*

Leroy *lə-roi', lē'roi, m.* (Fr.) from the surname, meaning (servant of) the king.

Leslie *m.,* **Lesley** *f., lez'li,* from the surname or place name.

Lester *les'ter, m.* from the surname, orig. a phonetic spelling of the place name Leicester.

Lettice *let'is,* **Letitia, Laetitia** *li-tish'yə, f.* (L.) gladness.—Dim. **Lettie, Letty.**

Lewis *lōō'is,* **Louis** *lōō'is, lōō'i,* **Ludovic(k)** *lū', lōō'dō-vik,* **Lodowick** *lō'dō-wik*—also **Aloys,** *-al'ō-is, -ois',* **Aloysius,** *-ish'əs, -ē'zi-əs, -is'i-əs, m.* (Gmc.) famous warrior.—L. *Ludovicus, Aloysius,* Fr. *Louis* (from *Chlodowig, Clovis*), Prov. *Aloys,* It. *Ludovico, Luigi, Aloysio,* Sp. *Luis, Aloisio,* Ger. *Ludwig.*—Dims. **Lewie, Louie, Lew.**—Fem. **Louisa** (*lōō-ē'zə*), **Louise** (*-ēz'*).—Dims. **Lou, Louie.**—Fr. *Louise,* It. *Luisa,* Ger. *Luise.*

Liam *lē'əm, m.* Irish form of **William.**

Lian, Liana, Lianne, etc. See **Julian.**

Libby. See **Elizabeth.**

Lily *lil'i,* **Lil(l)ian** *-ən,* **Lil(l)ias** *-əs, f.* prob. partly from the flower, partly for **Elizabeth.**

Linda, Lynda *lin'də,* (Gmc.) short for any feminine name ending in -lind (snake).—Now regarded as a name in its own right.—Dim. **Lindy.**

Lin(d)say, Lin(d)sey *lin(d)'zi, m.* and *f.* from the surname.

Lin(n)ette, Linnet, Lynette *li-net', f.* (Fr.) medieval French forms of Welsh **Eluned.**

Lionel *lī'ə-nəl, m.* (L.) young lion.

Liz, Lizzie, Lisa, Liza, Lisbeth, Lizbeth, Lise, Lisette. See **Elizabeth.**

Llewelyn *(h)lē-wel'in, lōō-el'in, m.* (W.) meaning doubtful.

Lloyd *loid, m.* (W.) grey.

Lodowick. See **Lewis.**

Lois *lō'is, f.* prob. (Gr.) good.

Lola *lō'lə, f.* for **Dolores,** or **Carlotta.**

Lora, Lorana. See **Laura.**

Lorcan *lör'kən, m.* (Ir.) poss. from Irish *lorc,* fierce.

Lord *lörd, m.* (U.S.) from the title.

Lorenzo *lō-ren'zō, lö-, m.* See **Laurence.**

Loretta. See **Laura.**

Lorinda *lō-rin'də, lö-, f.* See **Laura.**

Lorna *lör'nə, f.* invented by R. D. Blackmore for the heroine of his novel *Lorna Doone.*

Lorraine, Lar(r)aine *lə-rān', f.* (Fr.) from the region of France.

Lottie *lot'i, f.* See under **Charles.**

Lou. See **Lewis.**

Louis *m.,* **Louisa, Louise** *f.* See **Lewis.**

Lucas *lōō'kəs, m.* See **Luke.**

Lucinda. See **Lucius.**

Lucius *lōō'si-əs, -shəs, m.* (L.) a Roman name probably connected with L. *lux,* light.—Fem. **Luce, Lucia** (*-chē'ə;* It.), **Lucy, Lucinda, Lucilla, Lucil(l)e.**

Lucretius *lōō-krē'shəs, m.* (L.) a Roman name perh. meaning gain.—Fem. **Lucretia, Lucrece** (*-krēs*).

Ludovic(k). See **Lewis.**

Luke *lōōk,* **Lucas** *lōō'kəs, m.* (L.) of Lucania (in Italy).

Luther *lōō'thər, m.* (Gmc.) famous warrior.—L. *Lutherus,* Fr. *Lothaire,* It. *Lotario.*

Lydia *lid'i-ə, f.* (Gr.) Lydian woman.

Lynda. See **Linda.**

Lynette. See **Linette.**

Lynn(e) *lin, f.* dim. of **Linda** or **Linette.**

Mabel *mā'bl, f.* See **Amabel.**

Madel(e)ine. See **Magdalen(e).**

Madge *maj, f.* See **Margaret.**

Madoc *mad'ək, m.* (W.) fortunate.

Madonna *mə-don'ə, f.* (It.) my lady, a title of the Virgin Mary.

Maev(e). See **Meave.**

Magdalen(e) *mag'də-lin, -lēn,* **Madel(e)ine** *mad'(ə-)len, -lēn, -lin, f.* of Magdala on the Sea of Galilee.—Dims. **Lena** (*lē'nə*), **Maud, Maude** (*möd*), **Maudlin.**

Maggie, Mag. Dims. of **Margaret.**

Magnus *mag'nəs, m.* (L.) great.

Maida *mā'də, f.* origin obscure.

Màiri *mä'ri, f.* See **Mary.**

Maisie *mā'zi, f.* dim. of **Margaret,** now also sometimes regarded as a name in its own right.

Malachi *mal'ə-kī, m.* (Heb.) messenger of Yah.

Malcolm *mal'kəm, möl', m.* (Gael.) Columba's servant.

Malise *mal'is, m.* (Gael.) servant of Jesus.

Mamie *mā'mi, f.* a chiefly American dim. of **Mary,** used also for **Margaret.**

Mandy. See **Amanda.**

Manuel *man'ū-əl,* **Manoel.** See **Emmanuel.**

Marcia, Marcius. See **Mark.**

Marcus *mär'kəs.* See **Mark.**

Margaret *mär'gə-rit, f.* (Gr.) pearl.—Fr. *Marguerite* (dim. *Margot*), It. *Margherita,* Sp. *Margarita,* Ger. *Margarete* (dims. *Grete, Gretchen*).—Dims. **Madge, May, Maggie, Margie** (*mär'ji*), **Margery, Marjory, Meg, Megan** (*meg'ən,* W.), **Meggie, Meta** (*mē'tə*), **Maisie, Mysie, Peg, Peggie, Peggy, Greta, Rita.**

Maria, Marie. See **Mary.**

Marian, Marion *mar'i-ən, mā'ri-ən,* **Marianne** *mar-i-an', f.* (Fr.) orig. dims. of **Mary;** used also for the combination **Mary Ann.**—Dims. **Maynie, Mysie.**

Marigold *mar'i-gōld, f.* from the flower.

Marilyn *mar'i-lin.* See **Mary.**

Marina *mə-rē'nə, f.* (L.) of the sea.

Marjory, Margery *mär'jər-i, f.* orig. a dim. of **Margaret,** now regarded as a name in its own right.

Mark *märk,* **Marcus** *-əs, m.* (L.) a Roman name prob. derived from Mars (the god).—L. *Marcus,* It. *Marco,* Sp. *Marcos,* Ger. *Markus.*—Derivatives **Marcius** (*mär'shi-əs*; fem. **Marcia, Marsha**), strictly a Roman family name perh. of like origin, **Marcellus** (*-sel'əs*; fem. **Marcella**).

Marlene *mär'lēn, f.* (Gmc.) perh. a compound of **Mary** and **Helena.**

Marmaduke *mär'mə-dūk, m.* prob. (Celt.) servant of Madoc.—Dim. **Duke.**

Marsha. See **Mark.**

Martha *mär'thə, f.* (Aramaic) lady, mistress.—Dims. **Mat, Mattie, Matty, Pat, Pattie, Patty.**

Martin, Martyn *mär'tin, m.* (L.) prob. warlike, of Mars.—Fem. **Martina** (*-tē'nə*), **Martine** (*-tēn'*).

Mary *mā'ri,* **Maria** *mə-rī'ə, -rē'ə,* **Marie** *mä'ri, mə-rē', Miriam* *mir'i-əm, f.* (Heb.) prob. wished-for child; less probably rebellion.—Gr. *Mariam,* L., It., Ger. *Maria,* Sp. *María,* Fr. *Marie* (dim. *Marion*), Gael. *Màiri,* Ir. *Maire.*—Dims. **May, Moll, Molly, Mally, Mamie, Marietta** (*mar-i-et'ə*), **Marilyn, Maureen** (*mö-rēn',* or *mö'*), **Minnie, Poll, Polly.**

Mat, Matty. See **Martha, Matilda, Matthew.**

Mat(h)ilda *mə-til'də, f.* (Gmc.) battle-might.—Dims. **Mat, Matty, Maud, Maude, Patty, Tilly, Tilda.**

Matthew *math'ū,* **Matthias** *mə-thī'əs, m.* (Heb.) gift of Yah.—Gr. *Matthaios,* L. *Matthaeus,* Fr. *Matthieu,* It. *Matteo,* Sp. *Mateo,* Ger. *Matthäus.*—Dims. **Mat, Matty.**

Maud, Maude *möd, f.* See **Matilda, Magdalen.**

Maudlin. See **Magdalen(e).**

Maurice *mor'is, mö'ris,* **Morris** (L.) Moorish, dark-coloured.—L. *Mauritius,* Fr. *Maurice,* It. *Maurizio,* Sp. *Mauricio,* Ger. *Moritz.*

Mavis *mā'vis, f.* (Eng.) thrush.

Maximilian *maks-i-mil'yən, m.* (L.) a combination of *Maximus,* greatest, and *Aemilianus.*—Dim. **Max.**

Maxwell *maks'wel, m.* from the surname.—Dim. **Max.**

May *mā, f.* partly for **Mary,** partly from the month.—Dim. **Minnie.**

Meave, Maeve, Maev *māv, f.* (Ir.) the goddess, or legendary queen of Connaught, Medb, or Meadhbh.

Meg, Megan. See **Margaret.**

Melanie *mel'ə-ni, f.* (Gr.) black.

Melicent. See **Millicent.**

Melissa *mə-lis'ə, f.* (Gr.) bee.

Melody *mel'ə-di, f.* (Eng.) melody.

Melvin, Melvyn *mel'vin, m.* from the surname, or formed from *Malvina,* a name from James Macpherson's Ossianic poems.

Mercy *mûr'si, f.* (Eng.) mercy.—Sp. *Mercedes* (mercies).

Meredith *mer'i-dith, m.* and *f.* from the surname.

Meriel, Merriel *mer'i-əl, f.* a form of **Muriel.**

Merle *mûrl, f.* from Fr. *merle,* blackbird.

Merlin. See **Myrddin.**

Merrick, Meyrick *mer'ik, m.* (W.) forms of Welsh *Meurig,* a variant of **Maurice.**

Mervyn. See **Myrddin.**

Meryl *mer'il, f.* a form of **Muriel.**

Meta. See **Margaret.**

Meyrick. See **Merrick.**

Mhairi *vä'rē, mä'rē, f.* (Gael.) vocative case of **Mairi,** used erroneously as its equivalent. See **Mary.**

Micah *mī'kə, m.* (Heb.) contraction of *Micaiah*—who is like Jehovah?

Michael *mī'kl, m.* (Heb.) who is like the Lord?—Fr. *Michel,* It. *Michele,* Sp. and Port. *Miguel,* Ger. *Michael* (dim. *Michel*).—Dims. **Mick, Micky, Mike.**—Fem. **Michaela, Michelle.**

Mildred *mil'drid, f.* (Gmc.; O.E. *Mildthryth*) mild power.—Dim. **Millie.**

Miles *mīlz, m.* (Gmc.) meaning doubtful, perh. merciful.

Millicent *mil'i-sənt,* **Melicent** *mel', f.* (Gmc.) work-strong.—Fr. *Mélisande.*—Dim. **Millie.**

Millie *mil'i, f.* See **Mildred, Millicent, Emilia, Amelia.**

Milton *mil'tən, m.* from the surname, esp. honouring the poet John Milton.

Mima *mī'mə, f.* See **Jemima.**

Mina *mē', mī'nə,* **Minella,** *f.* See **Wilhelmina.**

Minna *min'ə, f.* (Gmc.) memory, or love.

Minnie *min'i,* for **Minna, Mary, May,** or **Wilhelmina.**

Mirabel *mir'ə-bel, f.* (L.) wonderful.

Miranda *mi-ran'də, f.* (L.) to be admired or wondered at.

Miriam *mir'i-əm.* See **Mary.**

Moira, Moyra *moi'rə, f.* (Ir.) phonetic spelling of *Maire,* Irish form of **Mary;** (Gr.) a fate.

Moll, Molly *mol'i, f.* See **Mary.**

Mona *mō'nə, f.* (Ir.) noble.

Monica *mon'i-kə, f.* the name, possibly African, of St Augustine's mother; sometimes understood as (Gr.) alone, solitary.—Fr. *Monique.*

Montagu(e) *mon'tə-gū, m.* from the surname.—Dim. **Monty.**

Morag *mō'rag, mö', f.* (Gael.) great.

Moray. See **Murray.**

Morgan *mör'gən, m.* (W.) sea, sea-shore.—Fem. **Morgan, Morgana** (*-gä'nə*).

Morna *mör'nə, f.* (Gael.) beloved.

Morris. See **Maurice.**

Mortimer *mör'ti-mər, m.* from the surname.

Morven *mör'vən,* **Morwen(n)a** *mör-wen'ə, f.* (Celt.) perh. a wave of the sea.

Moses *mō'ziz, m.* meaning obscure.—Gr. *Mōysēs,* Ger. *Moses,* Fr. *Moïse,* It. *Moisè, Mosè,* Sp. *Moisés.*

Moyna *moi'nə, f.* perh. the same as **Mona.**

Mungo *mung'gō, m.* (Gael.) amiable.

Murdo *mûr'dō,* **Murdoch** *mûr'dəhh, -dək, m.* (Gael.) seaman.

Muriel *mū'ri-əl, f.* (Celt.) perh. sea-bright.

Murray, Moray *mur'i, m.* from the surname.

Myfanwy *mi-van'wi, f.* (W.) perh. *mabanwy,* child of water, or *my-manwy,* my fine one.

Myra *mī'rə, f.* app. an arbitrary invention; sometimes used as an anagram of **Mary.**

Myrddin *mûr'dhin, m.* (W.) thought to be from the place name *Carmarthen* (*Caerfyrddin* in Welsh), King Arthur's court magician being *Myrddin Emrys*, or 'Emrys of Camarthen', Latinised as *Merlin Ambrosius*; hence **Merlin; Mervyn** is the anglicised form of **Myrddin.**

Myrtle *mûr'tl,* **Myrtilla** *-til'ə, f.* from the shrub.

Mysie *mī'zi, f.* for **Margaret, Marian.**

Nadine *nä'dēn, f.* Fr. form of Russ. *Nadezhda,* hope.

Nahum *nä', nä'(h)əm, m.* (Heb.) consoling.

Nan, Nana, Nanna, Nannie, Nanny *nan, -ə, -i, f.* See **Ann.**

Nance, Nancy *nans, -i, f.* See **Ann, Agnes.**

Naomi *nā-ō'mi, -mī,* or *nā', f.* (Heb.) pleasant.

Nat *nat,* for **Nathaniel, Nathan, Natalia.**

Natalia, Natalie, (L.). See **Noel.**

Nathan *nä'thən, m.* (Heb.) gift.—Dim. **Nat.**

Nathaniel *nə-than'yəl, m.* (Heb.) gift of God.—Also **Nathanael** (*-ā-əl*).—Dim. **Nat.**

Neal(e). See **Nigel.**

Ned, Neddie, Neddy *ned, -i,* dims. of **Edward**; also of **Edgar, Edmund, Edwin.**

Nehemiah *nē-hi-mī'ə, m.* (Hcb.) consolation of Yah.

Neil *nēl.* See **Nigel.**

Nell, Nellie, Nelly *nel, -i, f.* dims. of **Helen, Ellen, Eleanor.**

Nessa, Nessie, Nesta, dims. of **Agnes.**

Netta, Nettie, dims. of **Janet(ta), Henrietta, Antoinette.**

Neville *nev'il, m.* from the surname.

Niall *nēl.* See **Nigel.**

Nicholas, Nicolas *nik'ə-ləs, m.* (Gr.) victory of the people.—Dims. **Nick, Colin** (q.v.), **Colley, Nicol, Nichol.**—Fem. **Nicola** (*nik'ə-lə*), **Nicole** (*ni-kōl'*).—Dims. **Nicolette, Colette.**

Nicodemus *nik-ə-dē'məs, m.* (Gr.) victory of the people.—Dims. **Nick, Noddy.**

Nigel *nī'jl,* **Neal(e), Neil, Niall** *nēl, m.* perh. (Ir.) champion, but understood as dim. of L. *niger,* black.

Nina, Ninette, Ninon. See **Ann.**

Ninian *nin'yən, m.* (Celt.) meaning unknown.—Also (Scot.) **Ringan** (*ring'ən*).

Nita *nē'tə, f.* for **Juanita.** See **Jane.**

Noah *nō'ə, m.* (Heb.) rest.

Noel *nō'əl, m.* and *f.* (Fr.—L.) birthday, i.e. Christmas.—Fr. *Nöel,* It. *Natale.*—Fem. also **Noele, Noelle, Noeleen, Noeline** (*-lēn*), **Natalia** (*nə-tā'li-ə,* or *-tä'*), **Natalie** (*nat'ə-li*).

Nola. See **Fenella.**

Nolan *nō'lən, m.* (Ir.) from the surname.

Noll, Nolly, *m.* See **Olive.**

Nona *nō'nə, f.* (L.) ninth.

Nora, Norah *nō'rə, nō', f.* orig. for **Honora, Leonora, Eleanor.**—Dim. (Ir.) **Noreen** (*-rēn'*).

Norma *nör'mə, f.* (L.) a rule, precept.

Norman *nör'mən, m.* (Gmc.) Northman.

Norna *nör'nə, f.* (Gmc.) a Norn or Fate.

Nualla. See **Fenella.**

Obadiah *ō-bə-dī'ə, m.* (Heb.) servant, or worshipper, of the Lord.

Octavius, Octavus *ok-tā'vi-əs, -vəs, m.* (L.) eighth.—Dims. **Tavy** (*tā'vi*), **Tave.**—Fem. **Octavia.**

Odette *ō-det', f.* See **Ottilia.**

Odo *ō'dō, m.* See **Otto.**

Olaf *ō'laf, -ləf, m.* (Scand.) ancestor-relics.

Olga *ol'gə, f.* (Russ.—Gmc.) holy.

Olive *ol'iv,* **Olivia** *ō-* or *ə-liv'i-ə, f.* (L.) olive.—Dim. **Livy** (*liv'i*).—**Oliver** *ol'i-vər, m.* (Fr.) olive-tree (but poss. orig. another name assimilated).—Dims. **Noll, Nolly,** (*nol, -i*).

Olwen, Olwin, Olwyn(e) *ol'wən, f.* (W.) white track.

Olympia *ō-* or *o-lim'pi-ə, f.* (Gr.) Olympian.

Omar *ō'mär, m.* (Heb.) eloquent.

Oona(gh). See **Una.**

Ophelia *ō-* or *ə-fē'li-ə, f.* prob. (Gr.) help.

Orlando *ör-lan'dō.* See **Roland.**

Osbert *oz'bərt, m.* (Gmc.) god-bright.

Oscar *os'kər, m.* (Gmc.) god-spear or (Ir. and Gael.) hero, warrior, champion.

Osmund, Osmond *oz'mənd, m.* (Gmc.) god-protection.

Osric *oz'rik, m.* (Gmc.) god-rule.

Oswald *oz'wəld, m.* (Gmc.) god-power.

Oswin *oz'win, m.* (Gmc.) god-friend.

Ottilia *ot-il'i-ə,* **Otilie** *ot'i-li, f.* (Gmc.) heritage—Dim. **Odette** (*ō-det'*).

Otto *ot'ō,* **Odo** *ō'dō,* **Otho** *ō'thō, m.* (Gmc.) rich.—It. *Ottone.*

Oughtred. See **Ughtred.**

Owen *ō'ən, m.* (W.) said to mean youth.—Ir. and Gael. **Ewan, Ewen** (*Eoghan*).—Used as a substitute for **Eugene.**

Paddy *pad'i,* dim. of **Patrick, Patricia.**

Pamela *pam'i-lə, f.* prob. an invention (as *pam-ē'lə*) of Sir Philip Sidney's.

Pansy *pan'zi, f.* (Fr.) thought; or from the name of the flower.

Parnel *pär'nəl, -nel', f.* See **Petronella.**

Pascal *pas'kəl, m.* (Fr.) Easter-child, **Pascoe** (*-kō*) being a Cornish variant.—Fem. **Pascale** (*-käl'*).

Pat, dim. of **Patrick, Patricia, Martha.**

Patience *pā'shəns, f.* patience.

Patrick *pat'rik, m.* (L.) nobleman, patrician.—Ir. *Padraig,* Gael. *Pàdruig.*—Dims. **Pat, Paddy.**—Fem. **Patricia** (*pə-trish'(y)ə*).—Dims. **Pat, Paddy.**

Patty *pat'i, f.* dim. of **Martha, Patience.**

Paul, Paullus, Paulus *pöl, -əs, m.* (L.) little.—It. *Paolo,* Sp. *Pablo.*—Deriv. **Paulinus** (*-ī'nəs*).—Fem. **Paula, Paulina, Pauline** (*-ēn*).

Pearce *pērs, m.* from the surname, derived from **Piers.**

Pearl *pûrl, f.* pearl.

Peg, Peggy *peg, -i, f.* dims. of **Margaret.**

Penelope *pi-nel'o-pi, f.* (Gr.) perh. weaver.—Dims. **Pen, Penny.**

Pepe, Pepito. See **Joseph.**

Percival, Perceval *pûr'si-vl, m.* (Fr.) penetrate the valley.

Percy *pûr'si, m.* from the surname.

Perdita *pûr'di-tə, f.* (L.) lost.

Peregrine *per'i-grin, m.* (L.) wanderer, traveller, pilgrim.—Dim. **Perry.**

Perkin. See **Peter.**

Pernel *pûr'nəl.* See **Petronella.**

Persis *pûr'sis, f.* (Gr.) Persian.

Peter *pē'tər, m.* (Gr.) rock.—Also **Piers** *pērz.*—L. *Petrus,* Fr. *Pierre,* It. *Pietro,* Sp. and Port. *Pedro,* Ger. *Peter, Petrus,* Norw. *Peer,* Ir. *Peadar.*—Dims. **Pete** (*pēt*), **Peterkin, Perkin** (*pûr'kin*).

Petronella, Petronilla *pet-rə-nel'ə, -nil'ə, f.* (L.) from the Roman family name *Petrōnius.*—Contracted **Parnel** (*pär'nəl*), **Pernel** (*pûr'nəl*).

Phelim *fē'lim, m.* (Ir.) ever good.

Philemon *fīl-, fil-ē'mon, m.* (Gr.) affectionate.

Philip *fil'ip, m.* (Gr.) lover of horses.—L. *Philippus,* Fr. *Philippe,* It. *Filippo,* Sp. *Felipe,* Ger. *Philipp.*—Dims. **Phil, Pip.**—Fem. **Philippa.**—Dim. **Pippa.**

Phillis, Phyllis *fil'is,* **Phillida, Phyllida** *fil'i-də, f.* (Gr.) a leafy shoot.

Philomena *fil-ō-mēn'ə, f.* (Gr.) I am loved, or strong in friendship.

Phineas, Phinehas *fin'i-əs, m.* (Heb.) meaning obscure—explained as Negro, oracle, serpent's mouth, etc.

Phoebe *fē'hi, f.* (Gr.) shining, a name of Artemis as moon-goddess.

Phyllis, Phyllida. See **Phillis.**

Pierce *pērs, m.* from the surname, derived from **Piers.**

Piers *pērz, m.* See **Peter.**

Pip *m.,* **Pippa** *f.* See **Philip.**

Polly *pol'i, f.* See **Mary.**

Poppy *pop'i, f.* from the flower.

Primrose *prim'rōz, f.* from the flower.

Priscilla *pri-sil'ə, f.* (L.) dim. of the Roman name *Priscus* (former).

Prudence *prōō'dəns, f.* prudence.—Dim. **Prue.**

Queenie *kwēn'i, f.* from *queen.*

Quintin *kwin'tin,* **Quinton** *-tən,* **Quentin** *kwen', m.* (L.) fifth.—L. *Quintianus.*

Rab, Rabbie. See **Robert.**

Rachel, Rachael *rā'chl, f.* (Heb.) ewe.—Ger. *Rahel,* Fr. *Rachel,* It. *Rachele,* Sp. *Raquel.*—Dims. **Ray, Rae.**

Rae *rā, f.* dim. of **Rachel,** used (esp. Scot.) independently.—Deriv. **Raelene** (*-lēn*).

Ralph *rāf, ralf, m.* (Gmc.) counsel-wolf.—O.E. *Rædwūlf,* Fr. *Raoul.*

Ramon *ra-mōn', m.* Spanish form of **Raymond.**—Fem. **Ramona** (*-mō'nə*).

Ranald *ran'əld, m.* See **Reginald.**

Randal *ran'dl,* **Randolph** *ran'dolf, m.* (Gmc.) shield-wolf.

Raoul *rä-ōōl', m.* See **Ralph.**

Raphael *raf'ā-el, -əl, m.* (Heb.) God heals.—It. *Raffaele, Raffaello.*

Rasmus, Rastus. See **Erasmus, Erastus.**

Ray *rā.* See **Rachel, Raymond.**—Also an independent name, *f.* and *m.*

Raymond, Raymund *rā'mənd, m.* (Gmc.) counsel (or might) protector.—Ger. *Raimund,* Sp. *Ramón, Raimundo* (fem. *Raimunda*), It. *Raimondo.*—Dims. **Ray, Rae.**

Rayner *rā'nər, m.* (Gmc.) counsel (or might), army (or folk).

Rebecca, Rebekah *ri-bek'ə, f.* (Heb.) noose.—Dims. **Beck, Becky.**

Regina *rə-jī'nə, -jē', f.* (L.) queen.—Dim. **Gina** (*jē'nə*).

Reginald *rej'i-nəld,* **Reynold** *ren'əld,* **Ronald** *ron',* **Ranald** *ran', m.* (Gmc.) counsel (or power) rule.—Ger. *Reinwald, Reinhold, Reinalt,* Fr. *Regnault, Regnauld, Renaud,* It. *Rinaldo, Reinaldo.*—Dims. **Reg** (*rej*), **Reggie** (*rej'i*), **Rex, Ron, Ronnie.**

René *ren'i, rə-nā', m.* (Fr.), **Renatus** *ri-nā'təs, m.* (L.) born again.—Fem. **Renée, Renata** (*-ä'tə*).

Reuben *rōō'bən, m.* (Heb.) behold a son, or renewer.

Rex *reks, m.* (L.) king.—Also for **Reginald.**

Reynold *ren'əld, m.* See **Reginald.**

Rhian *rē-an', f.* (W.) maiden.

Rhiannon *rē-an'ən f.* (W.) goddess or nymph.

Rhoda *rō'də, f.* (Gr.) rose.

Rhona *rō'nə, f.* origin and meaning obscure, poss. conn. with **Rowena.**

Rhys *rēs, m.* (W.) perh. impetuous man.

Richard *rich'ərd, m.* (Gmc.) rule hard.—It. *Riccardo,* Sp. *Ricardo.*—Dims. **Dick, Dickie, Dicky, Dicken, Dickon, Rick, Richie** (obs. **Diccon, Hick**).—Fem. **Ricarda** (*ri-kär'də*).

Ringan *ring'ən, m.* See **Ninian.**

Rita *rē'tə, f.* See **Margaret.**

Robert *rob'ərt,* **Rupert** *rōō'pərt, m.* (Gmc.) fame-bright.—L. *Robertus,* Fr. *Robert,* It. and Sp. *Roberto,* Ger. *Robert, Ruprecht, Rupprecht.*—Dims. **Bert, Bertie, Bob, Bobbie, Bobby, Dob, Dobbin, Hob(bie), Rob, Robbie, Robin** (*rob'in*; also *f.,* esp. in spelling **Robyn**), Scot. **Rab, Rabbie.**—Fem. **Roberta, Robina** (*ro-bē'nə*).

Roderick *rod'(ə-)rik, m.* fame-rule.—Ger. *Roderich,* Fr. *Rodrigue,* It. *Rodrigo, Roderico,* Sp. *Rodrigo, Ruy.*—Dims. **Rod, Roddy.**

Rodney *rod'ni, m.* and *f.* from the surname or place name.—Dim. **Rod.**

Rodolph. See **Rudolph.**

Roger *roj'ər, m.* (Gmc.) fame-spear.—O.E. *Hrōthgār,* Ger. *Rüdiger,* Fr. *Roger,* It. *Ruggero, Ruggiero,* Sp. *Rogerio.*—Dims. **Hodge, Hodgkin** (*hoj'kin*).

Roisin. See **Rose.**

Roland, Rowland *rō'lənd, m.* (Gmc.) fame of the land.—Ger., Fr., *Roland,* It. *Orlando,* Sp. *Roldán, Rolando.*

Rolf *rolf, m.* See **Rudolf.**

Roma *rō'mə, f.* from the name of the city.

Romola *rom'ə-lə, f.* (It.) fem. of *Romolo,* It. form of *Romulus,* founder of Rome.

Rona *rō'nə, f.* from the island-name, derived from Gael. *ron,* seal.—Not conn. with **Rhona.**

Ronald *ron'əld, m.* See **Reginald.**

Rory *rō'ri, rō',* (Ir.) **Ruadhri,** (Gael.) **Ruairidh** *rōō'ə-ri, m.* (Ir. and Scot.) red.

Rosalind, Rosaline *roz'ə-lind, -līn, -lēn, -lin, f.* (Gmc.) horse-snake, but associated with **Rose** (fair rose).

Rosamund, Rosamond *roz'ə-mənd, f.* (Gmc.) horse protection.—Associated with **Rose** (L. *rosa munda,* fine or pure rose, *rosa mundi,* rose of the world).

Rose *rōz,* **Rosa** *rō'zə, f.* (L.) rose. It may also be sometimes Gmc., horse.—Derivatives **Rosabel** (*roz'ə-bel*), **Rosabella** (*rōz-ə-bel'ə*), **Rosalia** (*rō-zā'li-ə*), **Rosalie** (*roz'* or *rōz'ə-li*) (L. *rosalia,* the hanging of rose garlands on tombs).—Dims. **Rosetta, Rosie, Roisin** (*ro-shēn'*), **Rosheen** (Ir.).

Roseanna, Rosan(n)a, Roseanne *rō-zan'(ə),* **Rosemarie** *rōz-mə-rē', f.* compounds of **Rose** with **Anna, Anne, Marie.**

Rosemary *rōz'mə-ri, f.* from the plant; also for **Rose Mary.**

Rosheen. See **Rose.**

Rowena *rō-(w)ē'nə, f.* perh. Geoffrey of Monmouth's mistake for W. *Rhonwen,* white skirt.

Roy *roi, m.* (Gael.) red.

Ruadhri, Ruairidh. See **Rory.**

Ruby *rōō'bi, f.* from the stone.—Also **Rubina** (*-bē'nə*).

Rudolf, Rudolph *rōō'dolf,* **Rodolph** *rō',* **Rolf** *rolf, m.* (Gmc.) fame-wolf.

Rufus *rōō'fəs, m.* (L.) red.

Rupert, Rupprecht. See **Robert.**

Russell *rus'əl, m.* from the surname.

Ruth *rōōth, f.* (Heb.) meaning obscure; used sometimes with associations with English *ruth.*

Ryan *rī'ən, m.* from the Irish surname.

Sabina *sə-bē'nə,* **Sabine** *-bēn, f.* (L.) woman of the Sabines (neighbours of the newly founded Rome).

Sabrina *sə-brē'nə, f.* the Latin name for the River Severn.

Sacha *sash'ə, m.* and *f.* (orig. masc. only), Russ. dim. of **Alexander.**

Sadie *sā'di,* **Sal** *sal,* **Sally.** See **Sarah.**

Salome *sə-lō'mi, f.* (Heb.) perfect, or peace.

Samantha *sa-man'thə, f.* (Heb.) meaning obscure.

Samson, Sampson *sam'sən, m.* (Heb.) of the sun.—Gr. *Sampsōn,* Fr. *Samson,* Ger. *Simson,* It. *Sansone,* Sp. *Sansón.*

Samuel *sam'ū-əl, m.* (Heb.) heard by God, or name of God.—Dims. **Sam, Sammy.**

Sancho *sun'chō, m.* (Sp.) holy.

Sandra *san'drə, sän', f.* It. dim. of **Alessandra;** sometimes used as a diminutive of **Alexandra** but now regarded as a separate name.

Sandy *san'di, m.* See **Alexander.**

Sarah, Sara *sā'rə, sä'rə, f.* (Heb.) princess, queen.—Dims. **Sadie** (*sā'di*), **Sal** (*sal*), **Sally.**

Saul *söl, m.* (Heb.) asked for.

Scott *skot, m.* from the surname.

Seamas, Seamus *shā'məs, m.* See **James.**

Sean *shön, m.* the Irish form of **John.**

Sebastian *si-bas'ti-ən, m.* (Gr.) man of Sebasteia (in Pontus)—Gr. *sebastos,* august, venerable.

Secundus *si-kun'dəs, m.* (L.) second.

Selina, Celina *si-lē'nə, f.* poss. connected with **Celia,** but associated with Gr. *selēnē,* moon.

Selwyn *sel'win, m.* from the surname.

Senga *seng'gə, f.* backward spelling of Agnes.

Seonaid *shö'nij, f.* the Gaelic form of **Janet.**

Septimus *sep'ti-məs, m.* (L.) seventh.

Serena *si-rē'nə, f.* (L.) calm, serene.

Seth *seth, m.* (Heb.) substitute, or compensation.

Seumas *shā'məs, m.* the Irish and Gaelic form of **James.**

Sextus *seks'təs, m.* (L.) sixth.

Shamus *shā'məs, m.* (Ir.) anglicisation of **Seumas.**

Shane *shān,* **Shaun, Shawn** *shön, m.* (Ir.) anglicisations of **Sean.**

Sharmaine. See **Charmaine.**

Sharon *sha', shā'ron, f.* (Heb.) a Biblical place name.

Sheena *shē'nə, f.* an anglicisation of **Sine.**

Sheila, Sheelagh *shē'lə, f.* See **Celia** and **Cecilia.**

Shelley *shel'i, m.* from the surname, and *f.* a variant of **Shirley.**

Sherry. See **Cher.**

Shirley *shŭr'li, f.* from the surname or place name.

Sholto *shol'tō, m.* perh. (Gael.) sower, propagator.

Shona *shō'nə, f.* (Scot.) perh. ultimately a dim. of **Catriona,** but thought of as an anglicisation of **Seonaid.**

Sian *shan, f.* the Welsh form of **Jane.**

Sibyl, now **Sybil** *sib'il,* **Sibylla** *sib-il'ə, f.* (L.) a Sibyl.—Dim. **Sib.**

Sidney, Sydney *sid'ni, m.* and *f.,* from the surname.

Siegfried *sēg'frēd,* **Sigurd** *sē'gŏŏrd, m.* (Gmc.), victory-peace.

Sigismund *sij'* or *sig'is-mund, -mŏŏnd,* **Siegmund** *sēg'mŏŏnd, m.* (Gmc.) victory-protection.

Sigrid *sēg'rid, f.* (O.N.) prob. victorious (second element obscure).

Silas *sī'ləs,* **Silvanus** *sil-vā'nəs,* **Silvester, Sylvester,** *sil-ves'tər,* **Silvius, Sylvius** *sil'vi-əs, m.* (L.) living in the woods.—Fem. **Silvia, Sylvia.**

Simon *sī'mən,* **Simeon** *sim'i-ən, m.* (Heb.) perh. hearing; perh. also (Gr.) snub-nosed.—Dims. **Sim, Simmy, Simkin.**—Fem. **Simone** (*-mōn'*).

Sindy. See **Cindy.**

Sine *shē'nə, f.* Gaelic form of **Jane.**

Sinead *shi-nād', f.* the Irish form of **Janet.**

Siobhan *shə-vön', f.* the Irish form of **Joan.**

Sion *shon, m.* the Welsh form of **John.**

Solomon *sol'ə-mən, m.* (Heb.) peaceable.—Ger. **Salomo,** Fr. *Salomon,* It. *Salomone,* Sp. *Salomón,* Port. *Salamão.*—Dims. **Sol, Solly.**

Somhairle. See **Sorley.**

Sonia. See **Sophia.**

Sophia *sə-fī'ə,* **Sophie, Sophy** *sō'fi, f.* (Gr.) wisdom.—Russ. (dim.) **Sonia, Sonya** (*son'yə*).

Sophronia *sə-frō'ni-ə, f.* (Gr.) prudent, temperate, of sound mind.

Sorcha *sor'ə-hhə, f.* (Ir.) bright.

Sorley, Somhairle *sör'li, m.* (Gael.) a form of Scandinavian *Somerled,* viking, lit. summer wanderer.

Stac(e)y. See **Anastasia.**

Stanislas *stan'is-las,* **Stanislaus** *-la'əs, m.* (Pol.) camp-glory.

Stanley *stan'li, m.* from the surname or place name.

Stella *stel'ə, f.* (L.) star.—Also **Estella** (*es-tel'ə*), **Estelle** (*-tel'*).

Stephen, Steven *stē'vən, m.* (Gr.) crown.—L. *Stephanus,* Fr. *Etienne,* It. *Stefano,* Sp. *Esteban,* Ger. *Stephan.*—Dims. **Steenie, Steve, Stevie.**—Fem. **Stephana** (*stef'ə-nə*), **Stephanie** (*-ni*).

Stewart, Steuart, Stuart *stū'ərt, m.* from the surname.

Susan *sŏŏ'zən, sū'zən,* **Susanna, Susannah** *-zan'ə, f.* (Heb.) lily.—Fr. *Suzanne.*—Dims. **Sue, Suke, Suky, Susie, Susy.**

Sybil. See **Sibyl.**

Sydney. See **Sidney.**

Sylvius, Sylvester, Sylvia. See **Silas.**

Tabitha *tab'i-thə, f.* (Aramaic) gazelle.

Taffy *taf'i, m.* an anglicised form of *Dawfydd,* the Welsh form of **David.**

Talbot *töl'bət, m.* from the surname.

Tam, Tammie. See **Thomas.**

Tamara *tə-mär'ə, f.* (Russ.) a Caucasian name, poss. from Heb. *tamar,* date-palm.

Tamsin *tam'sin, f.* a dim. of **Thomasina,** orig. Cornish. Now regarded as a separate name.

Tania, Tanya *tan'yə,* **Tarnya** *tärn'yə, f.* a dim. of Russ. *Tatiana.*

Tara *tä'rə, f.* from the place name in County Meath, Ireland.

Ted, Teddie, Teddy. Dims. of **Edward.**

Terence, Terrance *ter'əns, m.* (L.) from the Roman family name *Terentius;* used with its dim. **Terry** as a substitute for Ir. *Turlough,* like Thor.

Teresa, Theresa *tə-rē'zə,* **Theresia** *-zi-ə, f.* (Gr.) origin unknown—more probably connected with the island of Therasia than with reaping (Gr. *therizein,* to reap).—It. and Sp. *Teresa,* Fr. *Thérèse,* Ger. *Theresia, Therese.*—Dims. **Terry, Tessa, Tracy.**

Terry *ter'i.* See **Terence, Teresa.**

Tessa *tes'ə.* See **Teresa.**

Thaddaeus, Thaddeus *thə-dē'əs, thad'i-əs, m.* (Heb.) meaning obscure.—Used with its dims. **Thaddy, Thady** as a substitute for the Irish name **Tadhgh** (*thēg*), poet, which formerly in the form **Teague** (*tēg*) served as a general nickname for an Irishman, as Pat, Paddy, now.

Thea *thē'ə, f.* (Gr.) goddess.

Thecla *thek'lə, f.* (Gr.) god-famed.

Thelma *thel'mə, f.* poss. (Gr.) will, popularised by Marie Corelli.

Theobald *thē'ō-böld, tib'əld,* **Tybalt** *tib'əlt, m.* (Gmc.) people-bold.—Fr. *Thibaut, Thibault,* It. *Tebaldo,* Sp. *Teobaldo.*

Theodore *thē'ō-dōr, -dör, m.* (Gr.) gift of God.—Fem. **Theodora** (*-dō'rə, -dö'rə*).

Theodoric, Theoderic *thē-od'ə-rik, m.* (Gmc.) people-rule—Ger. *Dietrich* (dim. *Dirk.*).—Dim. **Derrick, Derek.**

Theodosius *thē-ō-dō'si-əs, m.* (Gr.) gift of God.—Fem. **Theodosia.**

Theophilus *thē-of'i-ləs, m.* (Gr.) beloved of God (or the Gods).—Fem. **Theophila.**

Theresa, Theresia. See **Teresa.**

Thomas *tom'əs, m.* (Heb.) twin.—Fr., Ger. *Thomas,* It. *Tommaso,* Sp. *Tomás.*—Dims. **Tom, Tommy** (Scot. **Tam, Tammie**).—Fem. **Thomasa** (*tom'ə-sə*), **T(h)omasina** (*tom-ə-sē'nə*), **Tomina** (*tom-ē'nə*).

Thorold *thor', thur'əld, m.* (Gmc.) Thor-strength.

Tib, Tibbie *tib, -i, f.* dims. of **Isabella,** mainly Scottish.

Tiffany *tif'ə-ni, f.* (Gr.) from *theophania,* revelation of God.

Tilly *til'i, f.* See **Matilda.**

Timothy *tim'ə-thi, m.* (Gr.) honoured of God.—Dims. **Tim, Timmie.**

Tina. See **Christian.**

Titus *tī'təs, m.* (L.) a Roman praenomen—meaning unknown.

Toby *tō'bi,* **Tobias** *-bī'əs, m.* (Heb.) Yah is good.

Tom, Tommy, Tomina. See **Thomas.**

Tony *tō'ni, m.* Dim. of **Anthony.**

Torquil *tör'kwil, m.* (Gael.) from a Norse name of obscure origin, the first part representing the name of the god *Thor.*

Trac(e)y *trā'si, m.* and *f.* deriv. of **Teresa;** the masc. form perh. from the surname.

Trevor *trev'ər, m.* from the surname.

Tristram, Tristrem *tris'trəm,* **Tristan** *-tən, m.* (Celt.) perh. tumult.

Trix, Trixy. See **Beatrice.**

Trudy. See **Gertrude.**

Tryphena *tri-fē'nə, f.* deriv. of Gr. *tryphe,* delicacy.

Turlough *tûr'lö, m.* (Ir. *Toirdhealbhac*) like Thor.—Represented by **Terence, Terry, Charles.**

Tybalt *tib'əlt, m.* See **Theobald.**

Tyrone *ti-rōn', m.* (Ir.) from the name of the Irish county.

Uchtred, Ughtred, Oughtred *ū'trid, m.* perh. (O.E.) thought-counsel.

Ulick *ū'lik, m.* an Irish form of **Ulysses,** but perh. really for a native name.

Ulric *ul'rik, m.* (Gmc.) wolf-rule.—Ger. *Ulrich.*—Fem. **Ulrica.**—Ger. *Ulrike.*

Ultan *ul'tən, ŏŏl', m.* (Ir.) the name of several Irish saints.

Ulysses *ū-lis'ez, m.* (L. form of Gr.) angry, or hater.—Gr. *Odysseus,* L. *Ulysses, Ulixes.* See **Ulick.**

Una *ū'nə, f.* (L.) one, from Spenser's heroine, personification of truth, but perh. suggested by Ir. **Oona(gh)** (*ŏŏ'nə*) meaning obscure.

Unity *ū'ni-ti, f.* from the noun.

Urban *ûr'bən, m.* (L.) of the town, urbane.

Uriah *ū-rī'ə, m.* (Heb.) perh. Yah is light.

Ursula *ûr'sū-lə, f.* (L.) little she-bear.

Valentine *val'in-tīn, m.* and *f.* (L.) healthy.
Valeria *və-lē'ri-ə, f.* (L.) fem. of a Roman family name.—
Also **Valerie, Valery** (*val'ə-ri*).—Derivative **Valerian**, *m.*
Vanessa *və-nes'ə, f.* a name invented by Swift from *Es*ther
*Van*homrigh.
Vanora *və-nō'rə, -nö', f.* (Scot.) a form of **Guinevere.**
Venetia *vi-nē'shə, f.* (L.) Venetian; perh. also a
Latinisation of **Gwyneth.**
Vera *vē'rə, f.* (L.) true; also (Russ.) faith.
Vere *vēr, m.* and *f.* from the surname.
Verena *və-rē'nə, f.* the name of a Swiss martyr (*c.* 300
A.D.).
Verity *ver'i-ti, f.* (L.) truth.
Vernon *vûr'nən, m.* (Eng.) from the surname, itself from a
place name in Normandy.
Veronica *vi-ron'i-kə, f.* (L.) true image; or (Gr.) a form of
Berenice.
Vesta *ves'tə, f.* (L.) the Roman hearth-goddess.
Victor *vik'tər, m.* (L.) conqueror.—Dim. **Vic.**—Fem.
Victoria *vik-tō'ri-ə, -tö', f.* victory.—Dim. **Vicky.**
Vida *vē'də,* a fem. dim. of **David.**
Vincent *vin'sənt, m.* (L.) conquering.
Viola *vī'ō-lə,* **Violet** -*lit, f.* (L.) violet (flower).
Virgil *vûr'jil, m.* (L.) from the Roman family name; perh.
specif. for the poet Publius *Vergilius* Maro.
Virginia *vər-jin'i-ə,* (L.) fem. of Roman family name.—
Dims. **Ginger** (*jin'jər*), **Ginny, Jinny** (*jin'i*).
Vivian *viv'i-ən, m.* and (chiefly in the form **Vivien**) *f.* (L.)
lively.—Also **Vyvyen, Vyvian.**

Walter *wöl'tər, m.* (Gmc.) rule-people (or army).—L.
Gualterus, Ger. *Walter, Walther,* Fr. *Gautier, Gauthier,*
Sp. *Gualterio,* It. *Gualtieri.*—Dims. **Wat, Watty** (*wot, -i*),
Wally, Walt.
Wanda *won'də, f.* (Gmc.) stock or stem.
Warren *wor'ən, m.* (Gmc.) a folk-name—meaning
uncertain.

Wayne *wān, m.* from the surname.
Wendy *wen'di, f.* an invention of J. M. Barrie's.
Wilfrid, Wilfred *wil'frid, m.* (Gmc.) will-peace.
Wilhelmina *wil-(h)əl-mē'nə* (Ger. *Wilhelmine*), a fem.
formed from *Wilhelm* (see **William**).—Dims. **Elma,
Wilma, Wilmett, Wilmot, Mina, Minnie, Minella.**
William *wil'yəm, m.* (Gmc.) will-helmet.—L. *Gulielmus,
Guilielmus,* Ger. *Wilhelm,* Fr. *Guillaume,* It.
Guglielmo, Sp. *Guillermo, Guillelmo,* Ir. *Liam,* Gael.
Uilleam, W. *Gwillym, Gwilym.*
Winifred *win'i-frid, f.* prob. orig. W., the same as
Guinevere, but assimilated to the English masculine
name *Winfred, Winfrith* (friend of peace).—Dims.
Win, Winnie, Freda (*frē'də*).
Winston *win'stən, m.* (Eng.) from the place name.

Xavier *zav'i-ər, m.* (Sp.—Ar.) splendid.
Xenia *zen'i-ə, f.* (Gr.) hospitable.

Yasmin. See **Jasmine.**
Yoland *yō'lənd,* **Yolande** *-land',* **Yolanda** *-land'ə, f.* app. a
mediaeval form of *Violante,* a derivative of **Viola.**
Yve, Yves *ēv,* **Yvon** *ē-vɔ̄',* Fr. derivative of **Ivo.**—Fem.
Yvonne (*ē-von'*), **Yvette** (*ē-vet'*).

Zachariah, Zechariah *zak-, zek-ə-rī'ə,* **Zachary** *zak'ə-ri,
m.* (Heb.) Yah is renowned.—Dims. **Zach, Zack.**
Zara *zä'rə, f.* (Heb.) poss. bright as the dawn.
Zedekiah *zed-i-kī'ə, m.* (Heb.) Yah is might.
Zeke *zēk, m.,* dim. of **Ezekiel.**
Zelda. See **Grizel.**
Zena *zē'nə, f.* perh. Pers., a woman.
Zenobia *zi-nō'bi-ə, f.* (Gr.) life from Zeus (but perh. a
Semitic name in Greek guise).
Zillah *zil'ə, f.* (Heb.) shade.
Zoe, Zoë *zō'ē, f.* (Gr.) life.
Zola *zō'lə, f.* from the Italian surname.

The Greek alphabet

Α	α	alpha	=	a	Ν	ν	nū	=	n
Β	β	bēta	=	b	Ξ	ξ	xī	=	x (*ks*)
Γ	γ	gamma	=	g	Ο	ο	omicron	=	o
Δ	δ	delta	=	d	Π	π	pī	=	p
Ε	ε	epsīlon	=	e	Ρ	ρ	rhō	=	r
Ζ	ζ	zēta	=	z	Σ	σ ς	sigma	=	s
Η	η	ēta	=	ē	Τ	τ	tau	=	t
Θ	θ ϑ	thēta	=	th (*th*)	Υ	υ	upsīlon	=	u ($\breve{oo}$, *ü*)

(often transcribed *y*)

Ι	ι	iōta	=	i
Κ	κ	kappa	=	k

Φ	φ	phī	=	ph (*f*)
Χ	χ	chī	=	kh (*hh*)

(often transcribed *ch*, as in Latin)

Λ	λ	lambda	=	l	Ψ	ψ	psī	=	ps
Μ	μ	mū	=	m	Ω	ω	ōmega	=	ō

The Greek alphabet, apart from its use as the official script in Greek-speaking areas, is of worldwide importance as a source of symbols used in all branches of science and mathematics. The equivalents in our alphabet given above are intended as a guide to transliteration and as an indication of the anglicised pronounciation of ancient Greek. We have not attempted to describe modern Greek pronunciation. See also Dict. under **digamma, episemon, koppa, san.**

The Russian alphabet

А	а	=	a (*ä*)
Б	б	=	b
В	в	=	v
Г	г	=	g
Д	д	=	d
Е	е	=	e (*ye*)
Ё	ё	=	(*yö*)

(often printed as E, e)

Ж	ж	=	zh (*zh*)
З	з	=	z
И	и	=	i (*ē*)
Й	й		(consonantal *y* sound; only used as the second letter of a diphthong)
К	к	=	k
Л	л	=	l
М	м	=	m
Н	н	=	n
О	о	=	o (*ö*)
П	п	=	p
Р	р	=	r

С	с	=	s
Т	т	=	t
У	у	=	u ($\overline{oo}$)
Ф	ф	=	f
Х	х	=	kh (*hh*)
Ц	ц	=	ts
Ч	ч	=	ch (*ch*)
Ш	ш	=	sh
Щ	щ	=	shch

(often pronounced rather as *sh* followed by consonantal *y*)

ъ	=	hard sign

(sign used to separate in pronunciation a following palatalised vowel from a preceding consonant either palatalised or unpalatalised)

ы	=	i (a sound similar to *i*)

ь	=	soft sign

(sign used after a consonant to indicate palatalisation, a sound like consonantal *y*)

Э	э	=	e (*e*)
Ю	ю	=	u (*y$\overline{oo}$*)
Я	я	=	ya (*yä*)

Roman numerals

$$I = 1 \quad V = 5 \quad X = 10 \quad L = 50 \quad C = 100 \quad D = 500 \quad M = 1000$$

From the above symbols the numbers are made up as follows:—

I	=	1	L	=	50
II	=	2	LI	=	51
III	=	3	LII, etc.	=	52, etc.
IV (or IIII, e.g. on clocks)	=	4	LX	=	60
V	=	5	LXI	=	61
VI	=	6	LXII, etc.	=	62, etc.
VII	=	7	LXX	=	70
VIII	=	8	LXXI	=	71
IX	=	9	LXXII, etc.	=	72, etc.
X	=	10	LXXX	=	80
XI	=	11	LXXXI	=	81
XII	=	12	LXXXII, etc.	=	82, etc.
XIII	=	13	XC	=	90
XIV	=	14	XCI	=	91
XV	=	15	XCII, etc.	=	92, etc.
XVI	=	16			
XVII	=	17	C	=	100
XVIII	=	18	CC	=	200
XIX	=	19	CCC	=	300
XX	=	20	CCCC or CD	=	400
XXI	=	21	D (or IↃ)	=	500
XXII, etc.	=	22, etc.	DC (or IↃC)	=	600
XXX	=	30	DCC (or IↃCC)	=	700
XXXI	=	31	DCCC (or IↃCCC)	=	800
XXXII, etc.	=	32, etc.	CM (or DCCCC or IↃCCCC)	=	900
XL	=	40	M	=	1000
XLI	=	41	MM	=	2000
XLII, etc.	=	42, etc.	$\overline{V}$[3] (or IↃↃ)[1]	=	5000

Other letters also were used as numerals in mediaeval times (see Dictionary). For additional information about mediaeval methods of writing numerals, see below.

1. The symbol Ↄ, known as the *apostrophus*, might be repeated one or more times after IↃ, each Ↄ making the number ten times greater, as IↃↃ = 5000, IↃↃↃ = 500000. A number of this type might be multiplied by two by adding (in front) as many C's as there were Ↄ's in the number, e.g. CCIↃↃ = 10000, CCCCIↃↃↃↃ = 1000000.

2. The symbols I,V,X,L,C,D,M are still used today. In the Middle Ages, and also in much later times, methods of writing numerals were common which are found neither in the Roman period nor in the present century. Some are noted below.

3. In the Middle Ages and later, a line was placed above a symbol representing a number 1000 times greater, as $\overline{X}$ = 10000. $|\overline{X}|$ and $|X|$ were variant methods of expressing 1000000.

4. In the Middle Ages and later, and still in medical usage, numerals could be written lower case, and j was often substituted for final i.

5. In the Middle Ages and later, Ⅽ appears with the same meaning as D, and there is sometimes a small version of the apostrophus. To take at random an example of the latter, the third volume of John Ray's *Historia Plantarum*, is dated cIↄ Iↄ CCIV—that is 1704.

Useful conversion tables

The following tables may be used for conversion from British to metric (SI) units and vice versa.

in to cm		cm to in	ft to m		m to ft	miles to km		km to miles
2·54	1	0·3937	0·3048	1	3·28084	1·60934	1	0·62137
5·08	2	0·7874	0·6096	2	6·562	3·219	2	1·243
7·62	3	1·1811	0·9144	3	9·843	4·828	3	1·864
10·16	4	1·5748	1·2192	4	13·123	6·437	4	2·485
12·70	5	1·9685	1·5240	5	16·404	8·047	5	3·107
15·24	6	2·3622	1·8288	6	19·685	9·656	6	3·728
17·78	7	2·7559	2·1336	7	22·966	11·265	7	4·350
20·32	8	3·1496	2·4384	8	26·247	12·875	8	4·971
22·86	9	3·5433	2·7432	9	29·528	14·484	9	5·592

sq in to cm^2		cm^2 to sq in	sq ft to m^2		m^2 to sq ft	sq miles to km^2		km^2 to sq miles
6·4516	1	0·155	0·0929	1	10·764	2·58999	1	0·3861
12·903	2	0·310	0·1858	2	21·528	5·18	2	0·772
19·355	3	0·465	0·2787	3	32·292	7·77	3	1·158
25·806	4	0·620	0·3716	4	43·056	10·36	4	1·544
32·258	5	0·775	0·4645	5	53·820	12·95	5	1·931
38·710	6	0·930	0·5574	6	64·583	15·54	6	2·317
45·161	7	1·085	0·6503	7	75·347	18·13	7	2·703
51·613	8	1·240	0·7432	8	86·111	20·72	8	3·089
58·064	9	1·395	0·8361	9	96·875	23·31	9	3·475

fl oz to cm^3 (ml)		cm^3 (ml) to fl oz	imp gal to litre		litre to imp gal	oz to g		g to oz
28·4131	1	0·03520	4·54609	1	0·21997	28·3495	1	0·03527
56·826	2	0·0704	9·092	2	0·4399	56·6990	2	0·07054
85·239	3	0·1056	13·638	3	0·6599	85·0485	3	0·10581
113·652	4	0·1408	18·184	4	0·8799	113·3980	4	0·14108
142·065	5	0·1760	22·730	5	1·0998	141·7475	5	0·17635
170·478	6	0·2112	27·277	6	1·3198	170·0970	6	0·21162
198·891	7	0·2464	31·823	7	1·5398	198·4465	7	0·24689
227·305	8	0·2816	36·369	8	1·7598	226·7960	8	0·28216
255·718	9	0·3168	40·915	9	1·9797	255·1455	9	0·31743

lb to kg		kg to lb	ton to tonne		tonne to ton	lbf to newton		newton to lbf
0·45359	1	2·20462	1·0160	1	0·984205	4·4482	1	0·2248
0·907	2	4·409	2·032	2	1·9684	8·896	2	0·4496
1·361	3	6·614	3·048	3	2·9526	13·345	3	0·6744
1·814	4	8·818	4·064	4	3·9368	17·793	4	0·8992
2·268	5	11·023	5·080	5	4·9210	22·241	5	1·1240
2·722	6	13·228	6·096	6	5·9052	26·689	6	1·3489
3·175	7	15·432	7·112	7	6·8894	31·138	7	1·5737
3·629	8	17·637	8·128	8	7·8736	35·586	8	1·7985
4·082	9	19·842	9·144	9	8·8578	40·034	9	2·0233

Examples of use of tables

Reading from line 7 of the first table:

$$7 \text{ in} = 17\cdot78 \text{ cm and } 7 \text{ cm} = 2\cdot7559 \text{ in.}$$

Values above 9 may be obtained by decimal point adjustment and addition. Taking an example based on the third table:

$$
\begin{aligned}
\text{To convert 573 miles to km} \quad 500 \text{ miles} &= 804\cdot7 \text{ km} \\
70 \text{ miles} &= 112\cdot65 \text{ km} \\
3 \text{ miles} &= 4\cdot828 \text{ km} \\
\hline
573 \text{ miles} &= 922\cdot178 \text{ km}
\end{aligned}
$$

Such results should be treated as approximations. In the example given the conversion of 500 miles is correct only to the nearest 0·1 km, therefore the final sum can be correct only to the same degree; hence the conversion of 573 miles from the table is correctly stated as '922·2 km to the nearest 0·1 km'. The precise figure for 573 miles is 922·154 112 km.

Temperature conversion table

°F to °C		°C to °F
−17·78	0	32·0
−12·22	10	50·0
− 6·67	20	68·0
− 1·11	30	86·0
4·44	40	104·0
10·00	50	122·0
15·56	60	140·0
21·11	70	158·0
26·68	80	176·0
32·24	90	194·0
37·80	100	212·0

Physical constants

c speed of light in vacuo,
$2 \cdot 997\ 925 \times 10^8$ metres per second (m·s^{-1}).

e electron charge,
$1 \cdot 602\ 192 \times 10^{-19}$ coulomb.

g standard acceleration of gravity, $9 \cdot 806\ 65$ metres per second per second (m·s^{-2}). (At Greenwich, $g = 9 \cdot 811\ 83$ metres per second per second.)

G gravitational constant,
$6 \cdot 664 \times 10^{-11}$ N·m^2·kg^{-2}.

h Planck('s) constant, the constant in the expression for the quantum of energy, $6 \cdot 626\ 196 \times 10^{-34}$ J·s.

$\hbar$ h-bar, Dirac's constant, $\dfrac{h}{2\pi}$ (Planck's constant divided by 2π), the unit in which electron spin is measured.

m_e the mass of an electron at rest, $9 \cdot 109\ 558 \times 10^{-31}$ kg.

m_p the mass of a proton at rest,
$1 \cdot 672\ 614 \times 10^{-27}$ kg.

m_n the mass of a neutron at rest,
$1 \cdot 674\ 92 \times 10^{-27}$ kg.

N_A Avogadro('s) number, constant, number of molecules in a mole of any substance, $6 \cdot 022\ 52 \times 10^{23}$ per mole.

Speed of sound at sea level at $0°$C, $331 \cdot 7$ metres per second.

Standard temperature and pressure (stp), $0°$C and $101\ 325$ N·m^{-2}.

Standard volume of ideal gas, $2 \cdot 241\ 36 \times 10^{-2}$ m^3·mol^{-1} at stp.

Melting point of ice, $0°$C or $273 \cdot 15$ K.

SI metric units of measurement

The Système International d'Unités has been internationally adopted as a coherent system of units for the measurement of all physical quantities.

Base units
Seven independent quantities have been chosen which are measured in the *base units* of the system (Table 2).

Derived units
To measure any other quantity, a *derived unit* is formed by multiplying or dividing any two or more base units, or powers of them, together; e.g. speed is measured in metres per second, where the metre and the second are base units. The more frequently used derived units have been given names of their own for convenience; e.g. power is measured in watts, where one watt is derived from one kilogram multiplied by one metre squared divided by one second cubed.

Symbols
Each unit name has an agreed symbol (column 3 in Table 2). In a unit compounded from more than one unit name, the symbols of the constituent units are written with a dot or small space between them; e.g. a newton metre is written N·m, N.m, or N m. Where a unit is raised to a power, the conventional algebraic indices are used; e.g. a metre squared, or square metre, is written m^2.

Division of units
The word *per* indicates division by all succeeding units. To indicate units which are to be divided, negative indices are preferred, but a solidus (/) may be used; e.g. metre per second is written m/s^{-1} or m/s, kilogram per metre cubed is kg·m^{-3} or kg/m^3.

Multiples and Submultiples
To avoid the use of many zeroes in either very large or very small numbers, prefixes indicating multiplication or division by some power of a thousand (Table 1) can be added to a unit, e.g. mega-: multiply by a million, so a megawatt (1 MW) is a million watts; milli-: divide by a thousand, so a milliwatt (1 mW) is a thousandth of a watt.

TABLE 1

prefix	abbrev.	factor	prefix	abbrev.	factor
exa-	E	10^{18} = million million million	*deci-	d	10^{-1} = tenth
peta-	P	10^{15} = thousand million million	*centi-	c	10^{-2} = hundredth
tera-	T	10^{12} = million million	milli-	m	10^{-3} = thousandth
giga-	G	10^{9} = thousand million	micro-	μ	10^{-6} = millionth
mega-	M	10^{6} = million	nano-	n	10^{-9} = thousand millionth
kilo-	k	10^{3} = thousand	pico-	p	10^{-12} = million millionth
*hecto-	h	10^{2} = hundred	femto-	f	10^{-15} = thousand million millionth
*deca- ⎱	da	10 = ten	atto-	a	10^{-18} = million million millionth
*deka- ⎰					

* These prefixes are used only exceptionally where kilo- or milli- would be impractical; thus a centimetre ($\frac{1}{100}$ metre) is accepted as an everyday unit of convenient size, but it is not a preferred SI unit.

TABLE 2

Equivalents are given to four significant figures' accuracy, except where they are exact as indicated by bold figures.

Quantity	SI unit	abbreviation and derivation	equivalent in British units	SI equivalent of one British unit
Base units				
Length	**metre**	m	3·281 feet	**0·3048** m
Mass*	**kilogram**	kg	2·205 pounds	**0·453 592 37** kg
Time	**second**	s	—	—
Temperature interval	**kelvin**	K	$\frac{9}{5}$ °Fahrenheit	$\frac{5}{9}$ K
Current, electric	**ampere**	A	—	—
Amount of substance	**mole**	mol	—	—
Luminous intensity	**candela**	cd	0·9833 candle	1·017 cd
Some derived and additional units				
Length	kilometre	km	0·6214 mile	1·609 km
	centimetre	cm	0·3937 inch	**2·54** cm
*Mass	tonne, metric ton	$t = Mg$	0·9842 ton	1·016 t
Area	metre squared	m²	10·76 ft²	0·092 90 m²
	hectare	ha = 10 000 m²	2·471 acres	0·4047 ha
Volume	metre cubed	m³	1·308 yd³	0·7646 m³
	litre	l = dm³	0·2200 gal (UK)	4·546 litres
*Weight; Force	newton	$N = kg \cdot m \cdot s^{-2}$	0·2248 lbf	4·448 N
Energy; Work; Heat	joule	$J = m \cdot N$ $= kg \cdot m^2 \cdot s^{-2}$	$\begin{cases} 0 \cdot 2388 \text{ calorie} \\ 0 \cdot 7376 \text{ ft lbf} \\ 1 \text{ kJ} = 0 \cdot 9478 \text{ Btu} \end{cases}$	**4·1868** J 1·356 J 1·055 kJ
Power	watt	$W = J \cdot s^{-1}$ $= kg \cdot m^2 \cdot s^{-3}$	0·001 341 hp	745·7 W
Velocity; Speed	metre per second	$m \cdot s^{-1}$	3·281 ft/s	**0·3048** m·s⁻¹
	kilometre per hour	$km \cdot h^{-1}$	0·6214 mile/h	1·609 km·h⁻¹
Pressure; Stress	pascal	$Pa = N \cdot m^{-2}$	1 kPa = 0·1450 lbf/in²	6·895 kPa
	bar	bar = 10⁵ Pa	14·50 lbf/in²	0·068 95 bar
Frequency	hertz	$Hz = s^{-1}$	1 c/s	1 Hz
Angle	radian	rad	57° 18′	$\frac{\pi}{\mathbf{180}}$ rad
Solid angle	steradian	sr	—	—
Temperature, absolute	degree Celsius or Centigrade	°C	$(\frac{9}{5} t °C + 32) °F$	$\frac{5}{9}(t °F - 32) °C$
	kelvin	K	$\frac{9}{5}$ degree Rankine	$\frac{5}{9}$ K
Potential difference; Electromotive force	volt	$V = kg \cdot m^2 \cdot s^{-3} \cdot A^{-1} = W \cdot A^{-1}$		
Resistance Reactance }electrical Impedance	ohm	$\Omega = kg \cdot m^2 \cdot s^{-3} \cdot A^{-2} = V \cdot A^{-1}$		
Capacitance, electrical	farad	$F = kg^{-1} \cdot m^{-2} \cdot s^4 \cdot A^2 = A \cdot s \cdot V^{-1}$		
Inductance, magnetic	henry	$H = kg \cdot m^2 \cdot s^{-2} \cdot A^{-2} = V \cdot s \cdot A^{-1}$		

* The mass of a body is the quantity of matter in it; its weight is the force with which the earth attracts it, and is directly proportional to its mass. The use of the term 'weight', where 'mass' is strictly intended, is acceptable in non-technical usage when referring to objects within the earth's atmosphere.

Mathematical symbols

+	plus	
−	minus	
±	plus or minus	
×	multiply by	
.	multiply by	
÷	divide by	
=	is equal to	
≡	is identically equal to	

$$\left.\begin{array}{c}\approx\\\hat{=}\\\doteqdot\end{array}\right\}\text{is approximately equal to}$$

≠	is not equal to
>	is greater than
≫	is much greater than
≯	is not greater than
<	is less than
≪	is much less than
≮	is not less than
⩾	is greater than or equal to
⩽	is less than or equal to
∩	intersection
∪	union
∈	is member of set
⊂	is a subset of
∃	there exists
∀	for all values of
*	denotes an operation
⇔	is equivalent to; if and only if
⇒	implies

$$\left.\begin{array}{c}\{\}\\\varnothing\end{array}\right\}\text{empty set}$$

$\{x, y\}$ the set whose members are x and y

E	universal set
N	the set of natural numbers
W	the set of whole numbers
Z	the set of integers
Q	the set of rational numbers
R	the set of real numbers
C	the set of complex numbers
→	maps to
∴	therefore
∵	because
∠	angle
∥	parallel
⊥	perpendicular

x^n $x.x.x\ldots$ to n factors

x^{-n} $\dfrac{1}{x^n}$

$\sqrt{x}$ the square root of x

$x^{\frac{1}{n}}$, $\sqrt[n]{x}$, the nth root of x

x^0 $= 1$

$x \to a$ x approaches the limit a

$x!$, $\underline{x}$ factorial x

∝   varies directly as

∞   infinity

i or j imaginary square root of -1

$\left.\begin{array}{c}\omega, \omega^2\\h, h^2\end{array}\right\}$ the complex cube roots of 1, $\frac{1}{2}(-1\pm\sqrt{3i})$

π pi; the ratio of the circumference of a circle to its diameter, 3·14159 …

e, ε (1) the base of natural logarithms, 2·718 28…
(2) the eccentricity of a conic section

$\log_n x$ $\log x$ to the base n

$\left.\begin{array}{c}\log_{10} x\\\lg x\end{array}\right\}$ $\log x$ to the base 10, i.e. common logarithm

$\log_e x$, $\ln x$ $\log x$ to the base e, i.e. natural or Napierian (q.v.) logarithm

M   modulus of common logarithms
$\log_{10} e = 0\cdot4343\ldots$
$(\log_{10} x = \log_e x \times 0\cdot4343)$

$\sin\theta = y/r$
$\cos\theta = x/r$
$\tan\theta = y/x$
$\sec\theta = r/x$
$\operatorname{cosec}\theta = r/y$
$\cot\theta = x/y$

$\left.\begin{array}{c}\sin^{-1} x\\\arcsin x\end{array}\right\}$ the principal value of the angle whose sine is x

Similarly $\cos^{-1} x$, $\arccos x$, etc.

sh x, sinh x (hyperbolic sine of x) $\frac{1}{2}(e^x - e^{-x})$

ch x, cosh x $\frac{1}{2}(e^x + e^{-x})$

th x, tanh x sh x/ch x

sech x, cosech x, coth x 1/ch x, 1/sh x, 1/th x

Σ	the sum of the terms
Π	the product of the terms
$|x|$	the absolute value of x
$\bar{x}$	the mean value of x

$\begin{vmatrix} a_1 & b_1 & c_1 \\ a_2 & b_2 & c_2 \\ a_3 & b_3 & c_3 \end{vmatrix}$ a determinant representing $a_1b_2c_3 - a_1b_3c_2 + a_3b_1c_2 - a_2b_1c_3 + a_2b_3c_1 - a_3b_2c_1$

$f(x)$, $F(x)$, $\phi(x)$, etc. value of function f, F, or ϕ, etc. at point x

Δ finite difference or increment

Δx, δx the increment of x

$\dfrac{dy}{dx}$, $D_x y$ the derivative of y with respect to x

$F'(x)$ stands for $\dfrac{d(F(x))}{dx}$

$\dfrac{d^n y}{dx^n}$ the nth derivative of y with respect to x

$\dfrac{\partial y}{\partial u}$ the partial derivative of y with respect to u, where y is a function of u and another variable (or variables)

$\nabla\left(\dfrac{\partial}{\partial x}, \dfrac{\partial}{\partial y}, \dfrac{\partial}{\partial z}\right)$ vector derivative

∇^n nth vector derivative

$\int$ integral

ISO paper sizes

The A series is used for standard book printing and stationery, the B series for posters, wall-charts, etc. The dimensions given are of trimmed sizes.

A series	mm	inches
A0	841 × 1189	33·11 × 46·81
A1	594 × 841	23·39 × 33·11
A2	420 × 594	16·54 × 23·39
A3	297 × 420	11·69 × 16·54
A4	210 × 297	8·27 × 11·69
A5	148 × 210	5·83 × 8·27
A6	105 × 148	4·13 × 5·83
A7	74 × 105	2·91 × 4·13
A8	52 × 74	2·05 × 2·91
A9	37 × 52	1·46 × 2·05
A10	26 × 37	1·02 × 1·46

B series		
B0	1000 × 1414	39·37 × 55·67
B1	707 × 1000	27·83 × 39·37
B2	500 × 707	19·68 × 27·83
B3	353 × 500	13·90 × 19·68
B4	250 × 353	9·84 × 13·90
B5	176 × 250	6·93 × 9·84
B6	125 × 176	4·92 × 6·93
B7	88 × 125	3·46 × 4·92
B8	62 × 88	2·44 × 3·46
B9	44 × 62	1·73 × 2·44
B10	31 × 44	1·22 × 1·73

Model of dictionary layout

headword and pronunciation

cross-reference to main entry

information on capitalisation

label for foreign word not regarded as naturalised English

headword with variant spelling

pronunciation simple respelling system showing syllabification and stress (') pattern.

fauna *fö'nə, n.* the assemblage of animals of a region or period: a list or account thereof: — *pl.* **faun′as, faun′ae** (*-ē*). — *n.* **faun** a Roman rural deity, protector of shepherds. — *adj.* **faun′al.** — *n.* **faun′ist** one who studies faunas. — *adj.* **faunist′ic.** [L. *Fauna, Faunus,* tutelary deities of shepherds — *favēre, fautum,* to favour.]

faurd. See **fa'.**

Faustian *fow′sti-ən, adj.* in the manner of *Faust* who, in German legend, made a bargain with the devil to gain limitless knowledge in exchange for his soul. — Also without *cap.*

faute de mieux *fōt də myø,* (Fr.) for want of better.

fauteuil *fō-tœ-y', also fō′til, n.* an armchair, esp. a president's chair: the seat of one of the forty members of the French Academy: a theatre stall. [Fr.]

fautor *fö′tər, n.* a favourer: a patron: an abettor. [L. *fautor — favēre,* to favour.]

Fauve, Fauvist *fōv, fōv′ist, ns.* one of a group of painters at the beginning of the 20th century, including Matisse, who viewed a painting as essentially a two-dimensional decoration in colour, not necessarily imitative of nature. — *n.* **Fauv′ism.** [Fr. *fauve,* wild beast.]

fauvette *fō-vet', n.* a warbler. [Fr.]

faux *fō,* (Fr.) *adj.* false. — **faux ami** (*fōz a-mē*) a word in a foreign language that does not mean what it appears to, e.g. in Italian, *pretendere* does not mean 'to pretend'. — *n. and adj.* **faux-naïf** (*fō-na-ēf*) (a person) seeming or pretending to be simple and unsophisticated. — **faux pas** (*fō pä*) a false step: a mistake, blunder.

fauxbourdon *fō-bōōr-dɔ̄.* Same as **faburden.**

favela *fä-vā′lə, n.* in Brazil, a shanty town. [Port.]

favel, favell *fā′vəl,* (*obs.*) *adj.* light-brown: chestnut. — *n.* (with *cap.*) a name for a chestnut horse, esp. as proverbial for cunning, from the deceitful but much-courted horse *Fauvel* in the O. Fr. *Roman de Fauvel;* hence **curry favell** (see **curry²**), from O. Fr. *estriller, toucher Fauvel.*

faveolate *fə-vē′ō-lāt, adj.* honeycombed. [L. *favus,* honeycomb.]

favism *fā′vizm, n.* an acute type of anaemia in which haemolysis is precipitated by contact with broad beans (by ingestion or pollen-inhalation), the original lesion being an enzyme deficiency in the red blood cells. [L. *fava,* broad bean, and *-ism.*]

Favonian *fə-vō′ni-ən, adj.* pertaining to the west wind, favourable. [L. *Favōnius,* the west wind.]

information on plural forms

pronunciation of foreign sounds

clear definitions in historical order

derivative word with stress mark (') following stressed syllable

reference to related word

classification label (shown *before* grammatical labels and meanings where it applies to all)

etymology explaining word formation